absolute pitch

— Guide words showing the alphabetical range of entries on the page

ab·ro·ga·tion (æbrəgéiʃən) *n.* the act of abrogating (e.g. a law) [fr. L. *abrogatio (abrogationis)*]

ab·rupt (əbrʌ́pt) *adj.* sudden, unexpected, *an abrupt halt* ‖ steep, precipitous ‖ rough, brusque in manner ‖ disconnected, *an abrupt style* [fr. L. *abrumpere (abruptus)*, to break away]

— Pronunciation respelling See Part 2.

A·bruz·zi e Mo·li·se (ɑbrú:ttsi:emɔ́li:ze) a region (area 5,954 sq. miles, pop. 1,221,900) in central Italy, formed of the provinces of Aquila, Campobasso, Chieti, Pescara and Teramo, lying in the highest and wildest part of the Apennines (Gran Sasso d'Italia, 9,560 ft), and bounded on the east by the Adriatic: olives, vines, almonds, sheep, hydroelectric power, oil

— Foreign pronunciation See Part 2.

Ab·sa·lom (æbsələm) the third and best-loved son of David, king of Judah (11 Samuel xiii–xix)

ABSCAM (æbskæm) an investigation conducted by the Federal Bureau of Investigation in 1978–80. Seven U.S. Congressmen and various state and local officials were convicted of bribery, conspiracy, and related charges after FBI agents impersonating an Arab sheikh and his associates had videotaped government officials accepting bribes. Critics accused the FBI of entrapment, but the courts ruled that the FBI acted within legal limits

ab·scess (æbses) *n.* a localized collection of pus occurring anywhere in the body **áb·scessed** *adj.* [fr. L. *abscessus*, a going away]

— Etymology See Part 5.

ab·scis·sa (æbsísə) *n.* (*math.*) the horizontal or x-coordinate in a plane coordinate system [L. = (part) cut off]

— Field label See Part 4A.

ab·scis·sion (æbsíʒən) *n.* a cutting off [fr. L. *abscissio (abscissionis)*]

ab·scond (æbskónd) *v.i.* to flee secretly, esp. to escape the law [fr. L. *abscondere*, to hide]

ab·sence (æbsəns) *n.* a being away ‖ a failure to be present ‖ lack, *absence of proof* [F.]

absence of mind inattention, mental abstraction

ab·sent (æbsənt) *adj.* away, not present ‖ abstracted, *an absent air* [F.]

ab·sent (æbsént) *v. refl.* to keep (oneself) away, *to absent oneself from a meeting* **ab·sen·tee** (æbsənti:) *n.* a person who is absent **ab·sen·tée·ism** *n.* persistent absence from work, usually without good reason [F. *absenter*]

— Stress-marked derivative See Part 1D.

absentee landlord a proprietor who does not live on his estate and care for his tenants but merely exploits his property

— Unsyllabicated main entry See Part 1A.

ab·sent·ly (æbsəntli:) *adv.* in an absent way, inattentively

ab·sent·mind·ed (æbsəntmáindid) *adj.* preoccupied and for that reason not paying attention to what one is doing

ab·sinthe, ab·sinth (æbsinθ) *n.* the plant wormwood ‖ a strongly alcoholic liqueur made from high-proof brandy, wormwood and other aromatics [F.]

— Spelling variants See Part 1B.

ab·sis·sic acid (æbsísik) (*chem.*) [$C_{15}H_{20}O_4$] organic inhibitor of plant growth marketed as Dormin. *abbr* ABA

ab·so·lute (æbsəlu:t) 1. *adj.* whole, complete ‖ pure, *absolute alcohol* ‖ having unrestricted power, *an absolute ruler* ‖ not conditioned by, or dependent upon, anything else ‖ (*gram.*) of a case not determined by any other word in the sentence (*ABLATIVE) ‖ (*philos.*) existing independently of any cause outside itself and of our sense perceptions 2. *n.* something that is absolute **the Absolute** the self-existent, the First Cause, God [F. *absolut*]

— Multiple definitions in several parts of speech See Part 3A.

— Cross-reference to related term See Part 3C.

absolute address location of stored information in a digital computer

absolute alcohol ethyl alcohol containing not less than 99% pure ethyl alcohol by weight

absolute altimeter radio or similar apparatus designed to indicate the true vertical height of an aircraft above the terrain

absolute code (*computer*) code for an absolute address

absolute dud (*mil.*) a nuclear weapon that fails to explode when launched at, or emplaced on, a target

absolute expansion the true expansion of a liquid irrespective of the expansion of the containing vessel

absolute film *ABSTRACT FILM

— Defining cross-reference See Part 3C.

absolute humidity the humidity of the air measured by the number of grams of water vapor present in one cubic meter of the air

absolute music music which does not illustrate or depict (in contrast to program music)

absolute pitch the pitch of a note as determined by a simple frequency, not a combination

---

PRONUNCIATION KEY USED IN THIS DICTIONARY

(Continued)

ʃ	*fi*sh, a*c*tion, fi*ss*ion
t	*t*ime, we*t*, le*tt*er
θ	*th*ick, tru*th*
ð	mo*th*er, *th*ough
ʌ	d*u*ck, t*ou*gh, r*u*dder
ə:	b*ir*d, l*ear*n
u	b*u*ll, c*u*shion, b*oo*k
uə	p*oor*, s*ewer*
u:	f*oo*d, tr*u*e
ju:	*u*nite, conf*u*se
v	*v*erb, o*v*er, wa*v*e
w	*w*ell, *w*a*v*er
x	lo*ch*
j	*y*outh, *y*ellow
z	*z*oom, ro*s*e

Foreign Sounds

y	l*u*ne
ɔ̃	b*on*
ɑ̃	*an*
ɛ̃	v*in*
œ̃	br*un*

Stress

The symbol ′ marks the primary stress in pronouncing the word. The syllable in which the primary stress symbol appears is pronounced with greater emphasis than other syllables.

The symbol ˏ marks the secondary stress of a word. The syllable under which this symbol appears is pronounced with less emphasis than the syllable with primary stress.

THE NEW LEXICON
◇ WEBSTER'S ◇
DICTIONARY
OF THE
ENGLISH LANGUAGE

VOLUME

2

LEXICON PUBLICATIONS, INC.

NEW YORK

Contents

Dictionary Part II

Encyclopedic Supplements

or·a·cy (ɔ́rəsi:) *n.* ability to hear and speak, from "literacy." The term was coined by British surgeon Andrew Wilkinson

O·ra·dea Ma·re (ɔrɑ́djəmɑ́re) (*Hung.* Nagyrárad, *G.* Grosswardein) a city (pop. 178,407) of W. Rumania (Transylvania). Industries: cotton and silk textiles, metallurgy. Greek Orthodox and Roman Catholic cathedrals (18th c.)

o·ral (ɔ́rəl, óurəl) **1.** *adj.* using speech rather than writing, spoken, *an oral examination* ‖ of or relating to the mouth, *oral surgery* ‖ done or taken by the mouth, *an oral dose* ‖ (*phon.*) spoken through the mouth with the nasal passage closed **2.** *n.* an oral examination [fr. L. *os* (*oris*), mouth]

oral history a cohesive record of an individual life or of an event (usu. relevant as social history) assembled through systematic interviewing of the person or persons concerned

O·ran (ɔrɑn) a port (pop. 500,000) of W. Algeria, in a rich agricultural district. Industries: chemicals and plastics, metalwork, tobacco, wool, clothing

O·range (ɔrɑ̃ʒ) a market town (pop. 26,468) of Vaucluse, S. France, north of Avignon. Its Roman remains include an amphitheater, triumphal arch and aqueduct

or·ange (ɔ́rindʒ, ɒ́rindʒ) **1.** *n.* the reddish-yellow, globose or nearly globose fruit (a large berry) of any of certain trees of genus *Citrus*, fam. *Rutaceae*, which are native to China and Indochina but widely cultivated in tropical and subtropical climates ‖ any evergreen tree of genus *Citrus* which bears oranges, esp. *C. sinensis*, the common or sweet orange, *C. aurantium*, the Seville (or sour or bitter) orange, and *C. reticulata*, the mandarin orange ‖ the color of the fruit, a reddish yellow **2.** *adj.* having the color orange [M.E. *orenge, orange* fr. O. F. fr. Arab. *nāranj*]

or·ange·ade (ɔrindʒéid, ɒrindʒéid) *n.* a drink made from sweetened orange juice with water added ‖ a carbonated soft drink resembling this

orange blossom the white sweet-smelling flowers of the orange tree, traditionally carried in bridal bouquets

Orange Bowl the postseason college football game in Miami, Fla.

Orange, Cape a cape on the north coast of Brazil, near the French Guiana border

orange-flower water a solution of the essential oil (neroli) of the Seville orange, used in perfumery and in cooking

orange forces (*mil.*) those forces used in an enemy role during military maneuvers

Orange Free State a central province (area 49,866 sq. miles, pop. 1,932,000) of South Africa. Capital: Bloemfontein. It consists largely of high, undulating plains. Agriculture: stock raising (cattle and sheep), cereals. Resources: gold, coal, oil. Industries: fertilizer, agricultural machinery, clothing, cement. HISTORY. The region was occupied by Bushmen, Bechuanas and Zulus when the first Dutch settlements were made (early 19th c.). Boer settlers arrived (1836) as a result of the Great Trek, and established a republic (1837). It was annexed by Britain (1848) but became independent (1854) as the Orange Free State. Disagreements between the Boer government and the British led to the Boer War, in which Britain annexed the Orange Free State (1900). It was incorporated in the Union of South Africa (1910)

Or·ange·man (ɔ́rindʒmən, ɒ́rindʒmən) *pl.* **Or·ange·men** (ɔ́rindʒmən, ɒ́rindʒmən) *n.* a member of a Protestant political organization founded (1795) to maintain Protestant ascendancy in Ireland. Branches of the organization, now devoted to upholding Protestantism generally, have been formed in many English-speaking countries [after William III of England, prince of *Orange*]

orange pekoe a black tea from India or Sri Lanka made from the small top leaves only

Orange River the chief river (1,300 miles long) of South Africa, rising in the Drakensberg range in Lesotho and flowing westward through Orange Free State and Cape Province to the Atlantic. Chief tributary: the Vaal. A sandbar near its mouth prevents navigation. The Orange River Project (begun 1962) has harnessed the river for irrigation and hydroelectricity

or·ang·e·ry (ɔ́rindʒəri:, ɒ́rindʒəri:, ɔ́rindʒri:, ɒ́rindʒri:) *pl.* **or·ang·e·ries** *n.* a building specially designed for growing oranges in cool climates, and for protecting trees and shrubs against frost [F. *orangerie* fr. *oranger*, orange tree]

orange stick a small slender stick of orangewood designed for manicuring nails

or·ange·wood (ɔ́rindʒwud, ɒ́rindʒwud) *n.* the wood of the orange tree used esp. for carving

o·rang·u·tan (ɔrǽŋutæn, ouræ̃ŋutæn) *n.* *Pongo pygmaeus*, a large heavy reddish-brown anthropoid ape found in Borneo and Sumatra. It is well developed for arboreal life. having long, powerful arms, with hooking hands. Adult males may exceed 4 ft in height and 160 lbs in weight [fr. Malay *orang utan*, man of the forest]

Or·a·sul Sta·lin (ɔ́rəʃulstǽlin) *BRASOV

o·rate (ɔréit, ouréit) *pres. part.* **o·rat·ing** *past* and *past part.* **o·rat·ed** *v.i.* to hold forth in a bombastic style [fr. L. *orare* (*oratus*), to pray, and back-formation fr. ORATION]

o·ra·tion (əréiʃən, ouréiʃən) *n.* a formal speech or discourse, esp. one given on a ceremonial occasion [fr. L. *oratio* (*orationis*)]

or·a·tor (ɔ́rətər, ɒ́rətər) *n.* a person who speaks in public, esp. one distinguished by his eloquence [A.F. *oratour*]

Or·a·to·ri·an (ɔrətɔ́ri:ən, ɔrətóuri:ən, ɒrətɔ́ri:ən, ɒrətóuri:ən) *n.* a member of the Congregation of the Oratory

or·a·tor·i·cal (ɔrətɔ́rik'l, ɒrətɒ́rik'l) *adj.* of or relating to an orator or to oratory ‖ given to using oratory [fr. L. *orator*, orator]

or·a·to·ri·o (ɔrətɔ́ri:ou, ɔrətóuri:ou, ɒrətɔ́ri:ou, ɒrətóuri:ou) *n.* a dramatic musical composition, esp. on a religious theme, with arias, recitative and choruses and with orchestral accompaniment, performed as a concert, without action, costume or scenery [Ital., used originally of musical services at the Oratory of St Philip Neri in Rome]

or·a·to·ry (ɔ́rətɔri:, ɔ́rətouri:, ɒ́rətɔri:, ɒ́rətouri:) *pl.* **or·a·to·ries** *n.* a chapel or a private place of worship [fr. L. *oratorium*, place of prayer]

oratory *n.* the art of public speaking ‖ rhetorical speech or language [fr. L. *oratoria* (*ars*), (art) of speaking]

Oratory, Congregation of the the religious society founded in Rome by St Philip Neri in 1564. Its members are secular priests living in community without vows. They are devoted to preaching, confessing and catechizing

orb (ɔrb) **1.** *n.* a sphere ‖ a heavenly body, e.g. the sun, moon etc. ‖ a round ball surmounted by a cross, as part of judicial or royal regalia in Christian countries, symbolizing the domination by Christ of secular power **2.** *v.t.* to form into a circle or sphere ‖ *v.i.* to move in an orbit ‖ to form an orb. [fr. L. *orbis*, ring, circle]

or·bic·u·lar (ɔrbíkjulər) *adj.* spherical ‖ circular ‖ (*anat.*, e.g. of a muscle) surrounding, encircling ‖ (*bot.*, of a leaf) round or shield-shaped ‖ (of rocks) containing rounded bodies, e.g. minerals grouped concentrically [fr. F. *orbiculaire* or L. *orbicularis*]

or·bic·u·late (ɔrbíkjuleit, ɔrbíkjulit) *adj.* orbicular [fr. L. *orbiculatus*]

or·bit (ɔ́rbit) **1.** *n.* the closed path, usually elliptical, in which a planet moves around the sun, or a satellite around the parent body ‖ the path of a body (e.g. a particle) in a force field (cf. ORBITAL) ‖ a sphere of influence or region of activity, *such matters are outside my orbit* ‖ the bony socket of the eye ‖ (*zool.*) the border or ring around the eye of a bird **2.** *v.i.* to move in an orbit ‖ *v.t.* to revolve in an orbit around ‖ to cause to revolve in an orbit

or·bit·al (ɔ́rbit'l) **1.** *adj.* of, relating to or describing an orbit **2.** *n.* a subdivision of the energy levels of the electronic structure of an atom (or molecule) in which the motion of a single electron is represented in terms of quantized state of angular momentum, that is described mathematically by a wave function [fr. F. *orbite* or L. *orbita*, path, orbit]

orbital index (*craniometry*) the ratio of the length of the orbit of the eye to its greatest height, multiplied by 100

orbital injection (*aerospace*) the process of providing a space vehicle with sufficient velocity to establish an orbit

orbital steering (*biochem.*) process by which atoms within enzymes are guided at precise angles to permit them to form new molecular compounds in a biochemical reaction

or·bit·er (ɔ́rbitər) *n.* (*aerospace*) term applied generically to a spacecraft sent as a probe into orbit around a planet or other celestial body, as contrasted to a probe sent as a surface landing vehicle, or lander

orc (ɔrk) *n.* a cetacean of the genus *Orcinus* (or *Orca*), esp. the killer whale ‖ a grampus [fr. *orque* fr. L. *orca*, kind of whale]

Or·ca·gna (ɔrkɑ́njɑ), Andrea di Cione (c. 1308–c. 1368), Italian painter, architect and sculptor. The tabernacle in Orsanmichele, Florence, is his chief sculptural work. The altarpiece in the Strozzi chapel of S. Maria Novella, Florence, is the only painting certainly by him

or·ce·in (ɔ́rsi:in) *n.* a purple nitrogenous dye, the chief ingredient of archil and cudbear, formed by the action of ammonia and oxygen on orcinol [ORCIN]

or·chard (ɔ́rtʃərd) *n.* a stretch of land with cultivated fruit trees ‖ the trees collectively [O.E. *ortgeard* prob. fr. L. *hortus*, garden + O.E. *geard*, fence, enclosure]

or·ches·tra (ɔ́rkistrə, ɔ́rkestrə) *n.* a large body of instrumental musicians who perform symphonies etc., or a smaller group of musicians who play dinner music or dance music ‖ the instruments of either of such a group ‖ the orchestra pit in a theater ‖ (*Am.=Br.* orchestra stalls) the section of seats on the main floor of a theater, esp. the section nearest the stage ‖ the main floor of a theater **or·ches·tral** (ɔrkéstrəl) *adj.* [L. fr. Gk *orchēstra*, space where the chorus danced fr. *orcheesthai*, to dance]

orchestra pit the pit of a theater, where the orchestra sits

or·ches·trate (ɔ́rkistreit) *pres. part.* **or·ches·trat·ing** *past* and *past part.* **or·ches·trat·ed** *v.t.* to arrange, score or compose (music) for performance by an orchestra ‖ *v.i.* to arrange etc. music in this way **or·ches·trá·tion** *n.*

or·chid (ɔ́rkid) *n.* a member of *Orchidaceae*, order *Orchidales*, a family of perennial monocotyledonous terrestrial plants, epiphytes or saprophytes. They are cosmopolitan, and very abundant in the Tropics. The flowers differ from the normal monocotyledonous type, being more varied and complicated, with specialized pollinia and a twisted ovary. Many are cultivated for the brilliance of the flowers ‖ (*pl.*) compliments, praise **or·chi·da·ceous** (ɔrkidéiʃəs) *adj.* of, like or being a member of *Orchidaceae* [fr. Mod. L. *Orchidaceae* fr. L. *orchis* (assumed *orchidis*) fr. Gk *orchis*, testicle (from the shape of the roots)]

or·chil (ɔ́rtʃil, ɔ́rkil) *n.* archil [O.F. *orchel, orcheil*]

or·chis (ɔ́rkis) *n.* an orchid, esp. a member of genus *Orchis* [L. fr. Gk *orchis*, testicle (from the shape of the roots)]

or·cin (ɔ́rsin) *n.* orcinol

or·ci·nol (ɔ́rsinɔl, ɔ́rsinoul) *n.* a colorless crystalline phenol, $C_6H_3CH_3(OH)_2$, obtained from some lichens, aloes and derivatives of toluene, used to manufacture dyes [fr. Mod. L. *orcina* fr. Ital. *orcello*, archil]

or·dain (ɔrdéin) *v.t.* to consecrate (someone) a Christian deacon, priest etc. ‖ to qualify (a man) as a rabbi ‖ to appoint, decree, establish [A.F. *ordeiner, ordeigner* and O. F. *ordener* fr. L. *ordinare*, to put in order]

or·deal (ɔrdí:l, ɔ́rdi:l, ərdí:əl) *n.* a severe or exacting experience that tests character or powers of endurance, *24 hours of motor racing is a heavy ordeal* ‖ (*hist.*) an ancient method of establishing guilt or innocence, esp. in medieval Europe, by making an accused person undergo some painful or difficult physical test and seeing if God sustained him [O.E. *ordāl, ordēl*]

or·der (ɔ́rdər) *n.* a sequence, arrangement, the way one thing follows another, *alphabetical order* ‖ the condition in which everything is controlled as it should be, is in its right place, performing its correct function etc., *to put one's affairs in order* ‖ the proper working of the law, peaceful regularity of public life, *the police restored order after the riots* ‖ the rules, laws and structures which constitute a society, *the social order* ‖ (*philos.*) the natural, moral or spiritual system governing things in the universe ‖ the procedure by which a meeting or other assembly is governed, *a point of order* ‖ conformity with this, *to call a speaker to order* ‖ an authoritative instruction, command ‖ (*commerce*) an instruction to a tradesman or manufacturer to supply goods ‖ the goods supplied ‖ something ordered, e.g. in a restaurant, *has the girl brought your order?* ‖ a pass authorizing admission, *an order to view a house* ‖ (*archit.*) one of the orders of architecture ‖ a military or monastic brotherhood under discipline ‖ a secret fraternity united by common interest or for social purposes, *the Masonic order* ‖ (*pl.*) a social class, *the lower orders* ‖ a sort or kind, thought of as part of a hierarchy, *sentiments of a noble order* ‖ a group of people distinguished by special award made e.g. by the sovereign, or the award itself, *the order of the Garter* ‖ (*theol.*) one of the nine ranks of angels (*ANGEL) ‖ (*pl., eccles.*) the office of an ordained man in the Christian Church, *in deacon's orders* ‖ (*pl., eccles.*) ordination, *to take holy orders* ‖ (*eccles.*) a prescribed form of service ‖ (*eccles.*) one of the grades in the Christian ministry (*MAJOR ORDERS, *MINOR ORDERS) ‖ (*biol.*, in plant and animal classification) a category of closely allied organisms between family and class ‖ (*pl., mil.*) commands issued by an officer in command or by the competent authority, *standing orders* ‖ (*mil.*) equipment for a given purpose, *full marching order* ‖ (*mil.*) the position of a rifle after the command 'order arms' ‖ (*law*) a decision by a court or judge, usually not a final judgment ‖ (*finance*) a written direction to pay money or surrender goods ‖ (*math.*) degree of complexity, *an equation of the first order* **in order** in sequence ‖ in good condition ‖ according to the rules, e.g. of a meeting etc. ‖ suitable, *a toast would be in order* **in order that** with the intention that, *he worked hard in order that he might leave earlier* **in order to** (+infin.) for the purpose of (+pres. part.) **in short order** with no delay, *do it in short order* **of the order of** about as many as or as large as **on order** (of goods) requested but not yet delivered **on the order of** similar to, roughly like in style **out of order** out of proper sequence ‖ not according to the rules ‖ not in working condition ‖ inappropriate **to order** according to the specific requirements of the buyer, *a suit made to order* [fr. O.F. *ordre* fr. L. *ordo*]

order *v.t.* to put in order, *to order one's affairs* to give authoritative instruction to (someone) to do something or for (something) to be done ‖ (of fate) to ordain ‖ to request (goods etc.) to be supplied ‖ to prescribe as a remedy, *the doctor ordered complete rest* **to order arms** (*mil.*) to bring the rifle to an upright position with its butt against one's right foot, and remain at attention [M.E. *ordren* fr. *ordre*, order]

Or·der·ic Vi·ta·lis (ɔ́rdərikvaitéilis) (1075–c. 1143), Norman chronicler. His 'Historia ecclesiastica' is a valuable source for the history of his times

or·der-in-coun·cil (ɔ́rdərinkáunsəl) *pl.* **or·ders-in-coun·cil** *n.* an order issued by the British sovereign on the advice of the privy council, or by the governor general of a Commonwealth country with the advice of a similar council. Such orders are usually issued to deal with an emergency (e.g. those of 1807 and 1809 in answer to the Continental System) or with matters still subject to Crown prerogative (e.g. the government of a colony)

or·der·li·ness (ɔ́rdərli:nis) *n.* the quality or state of being orderly

or·der·ly (ɔ́rdərli:) **1.** *adj.* in good order, well arranged, *an orderly office* ‖ disciplined and peaceable, *an orderly crowd* ‖ (*mil.*) of, relating to or charged with the execution or sending out of orders **2.** *pl.* **or·der·lies** *n.* a soldier attendant on an officer to carry messages, orders, etc. ‖ an attendant in charge of cleaning etc. in a hospital, often in a military hospital

orderly market *DISORDERLY MARKET

Orderly Marketing Agreement formal trade agreement between the U.S.A. and a foreign country in which the latter voluntarily agrees to limit, for a specified period, its exports to the U.S.A. of a particular industrial commodity, as an alternative to the imposition of quotas or higher tariffs *abbr.* **OMA**

orderly officer (*Br., mil.*) the officer of the day

orderly room a room in a barracks used for administrative workers

orders of architecture the characteristic styles of classical architecture, esp. as applied to columns. The five orders are: Doric, Ionic, Corinthian, Tuscan and Composite. The variations occur principally in the capitals but also in the heights of the columns relative to their width

Or·di·nal (ɔ́rd'n'l) *n.* the service book used in Anglican ordinations ‖ a book of directions for Roman Catholic services for every day in the year [fr. M.L. *ordinale*]

or·di·nal (ɔ́rd'n'l) **1.** *adj.* (of a number) showing position or order in a series, e.g. second (cf. CARDINAL NUMBER) ‖ of or relating to an order of plants or animals **2.** *n.* an ordinal number [fr. L.L. *ordinalis*, denoting order in a series]

ordinal value (*statistics*) a numerical evaluation representing only rank in a comparison with others

or·di·nance (ɔ́rd'nəns) *n.* a decree or authoritative order, e.g. of a council or municipal government ‖ a religious ceremony or rite that is not a sacrament ‖ (*Br., hist.*) a piece of legislation issued by the sovereign by virtue of the royal prerogative without the approval of parliament [O. F. *ordenance, ordonance*]

or·di·nand (ɔ́rd'nænd) *n.* a candidate for ordination [fr. L. *ordinandus* fr. *ordinare*, to ordain]

or·di·nar·i·ly (ɔrd'nέərili:, ɔ́rd'nerili:) *adv.* generally, in the usual course of events

or·di·nar·i·ness (ɔ́rdineri:nis) *n.* the quality of state of being ordinary

or·di·nar·y (ɔ́rdineri:) *pl.* **or·di·nar·ies** *n.* (*eccles.*) a Church official (e.g. an archbishop, or a bishop or his deputy) having ecclesiastical jurisdiction over his territory ‖ (*eccles.*) an order of service, esp. the parts of the Mass that remain the same from day to day ‖ (in certain states of the U.S.A.) a judge of a court of probate ‖ (*heraldry*) a charge of the simplest, commonest kind ‖ (*Am.–Br.* penny farthing) an early type of bicycle, popular about the 1870s, with a very large front wheel and a much smaller back wheel **in ordinary** (in titles) in regular attendance or service, *physician in ordinary* **out of the ordinary** unusual, exceptional or remarkable, *the performance was nothing out of the ordinary* [fr. O.F. and A. F. *ordinarie* fr. M. L. *ordinarius* adj. and *ordinarium* n. and fr. ORDINARY adj.]

ordinary *adj.* usual, *the ordinary way of getting there is by ship* ‖ not exceptional or unusual, undistinguished, *he shows only an ordinary amount of skill* [fr. L. *ordinarius*, regular]

ordinary seaman a sailor in the American or British merchant marine or in the Royal Navy, ranking below an able-bodied seaman

ordinary shares (*Br.*) common stock

or·di·nate (ɔ́rdnit, ɔ́rd'nit, ɔ́rd'neit) *n.* (*math.*) the vertical or *y*-coordinate in a plane coordinate system [fr. L. *ordinatus*, ordered]

or·di·na·tion (ɔrd'néiʃən) *n.* an ordaining or being ordained, esp. into the Christian ministry [fr. L. *ordinatio* (*ordinationis*)]

ord·nance (ɔ́rdnəns) *n.* heavy guns, artillery ‖ military stores and materials (ammunition, small arms etc.) ‖ the branch of the U.S. army or the British War Office concerned with the supply of essential stores and the maintenance of arsenals and depots [var. of ORDINANCE]

ordnance datum (*Br.*) mean sea level as defined for the ordnance survey

ordnance survey the government survey of Great Britain and Northern Ireland, including the preparation of official maps

Or·do·vi·cian (ɔrdəvíʃən) *adj.* (*geol.*) of the period or system of the Paleozoic era between the Cambrian and the Silurian (*GEOLOGICAL TIME) **the Ordovician** the Ordovician period or system of rocks [fr. L. *Ordovices*, a Celtic tribe from Wales]

or·dure (ɔ́rdjuər, ɔ́rdʒər) *n.* excrement, dung [F.]

Or·dzho·ni·kid·ze (ɔrdʒɒnikí:dze) (formerly Dzaudzhikau) the capital (pop. 287,000) of the North Ossetian A.S.S.R., R.S.F.S.R., U.S.S.R. Industries: food processing, zinc metallurgy, chemicals

Ore. Oregon

ore (ɔr, our) *n.* a naturally occurring metallic compound from which the metal can be extracted [O.E. *ār*, brass and O.E. *ōra*, unwrought metal]

ö·re (ɔ́:rə) *pl.* **ö·re** *n.* either of two units of currency of Denmark and Norway equal to 1/100 of a krone ‖ a Swedish unit of currency equal to 1/100 of a krona ‖ a coin of the value of any of these [Dan. and Norw. *øre* and Swed. *öre* fr. L. *aureus*, a gold coin]

o·re·ad (ɔ́ri:æd, óuri:æd) *n.* (*Gk* and *Rom. mythol.*) a mountain nymph [fr. L. *Oreas* (*Oreadis*) fr. Gk fr. *oros*, mountain]

o·rec·tic (ouréktik, ɔréktik) *adj.* (*philos.*) relating to or characterized by desire or appetite [fr. Gk *orektikos* fr. *oregein*, to desire, grasp after]

ore dressing the separation of an ore from waste material and from other ores

Oreg. Oregon

o·reg·a·no (ɔrégənou, ərégənou) *n.* origanum [Span. *orégano*, wild marjoram]

Or·e·gon (ɔ́rigən, ɒ́rigən, ɔ́rigɒn, ɒ́rigɒn) (*abbr.* Oreg., Ore.) a state (area 96,981 sq. miles, pop. 2,649,000) on the N. Pacific coast of the U.S.A. Capital: Salem. Chief city: Portland. It is mountainous (wooded Cascade and coast ranges) in the west, with plateaus in the east. Agriculture: beef and dairy cattle, wheat, fruit (irrigation is needed in the east). Main resources: timber, nickel, fish, building materials. Industries: lumber and forest products, food processing, metallurgy. State university (1872) at Eugene. Oregon was jointly occupied (1818–46) by Britain and the U.S.A., and was ceded (1846) by Britain to the U.S.A., of which it became (1859) the 33rd state

Oregon Question (*Am. hist.*) a dispute (1840s) over the western part of the boundary, left undetermined by the Anglo-American boundary commission of 1818, between the U.S.A. and Canada. The dispute was settled (1846) by a treaty extending the boundary along the 49° parallel from the Rocky Mtns to the Pacific coast. This gave the present states of Oregon, Washington and Idaho to the U.S.A., while Britain obtained Vancouver Is.

Oregon Trail the 2,000-mile overland route from the Missouri to the Columbia which was followed by American pioneers (1840s) moving west to settle in the Oregon region

O·rel (ourél, ɔrél) an agricultural market (pop. 209,000) of the R.S.F.S.R., U.S.S.R., 200 miles south of Moscow: engineering industries

O·re·lla·na (ɔreljánɑ, ɔrejánɑ), Francisco de (c. 1470–1550), Spanish explorer who discovered (1542) the Amazon

O·ren·burg (ɔ́renburg, ɔ́rənbə:rg) (formerly Chkalov 1938–57) a city (pop. 482,000) of the central R.S.F.S.R., U.S.S.R., on the Ural River, center of a mining region: metallurgy, engineering, brewing, food processing

O·ren·se (ɔrénse) (*Rom.* Aurium) a province (area 2,694 sq. miles, pop. 411,339) of N.W. Spain (*GALICIA)

O·res·tes (ɔrésti:z, ourésti:z) son of Agamemnon and Clytemnestra. He killed his mother and her lover, Aegisthus, to avenge their murder of Agamemnon. He was pursued by the Erinyes but was acquitted by the Areopagus

Ö·re·sund (ɔ́:rəsʌnd) the strait (3½–17 miles wide) separating Zealand Is., Denmark, from Sweden

Orff (ɔrf), Carl (1895–1982), German composer. Among his compositions are 'Carmina Burana' (1937), a scenic oratorio based on medieval secular poems, and the dramatic works 'Antigone' (1949) and 'Trionfo di Afrodite' (1955)

Or·ford (ɔ́rfərd), 1st earl of *WALPOLE, SIR ROBERT

orfray *ORPHREY

or·gan (ɔ́rgən) *n.* a musical wind instrument, in its modern forms the largest, most versatile, and most powerful of instruments. It sounds when compressed air is passed through its pipes from bellows (usually electrically powered). It is played by manuals (keyboards) and foot pedals, and is controlled by stops which make possible a wide variety of tone qualities ‖ any of several similar keyboard instruments without pipes, e.g. the reed organ and the electric organ ‖ any of certain simple wind instruments of a specified kind, e.g. a barrel organ ‖ a structure of an animal (e.g. lung, stomach) or of a plant (e.g. pistil, leaf) adapted for some specific and usually essential function, *the organs of digestion* ‖ a means or instrument of action, *parliament is the chief organ of government in England* ‖ a medium of communication of opinion or information, esp. a publication attached to some group, party etc. [fr. L. *organum* fr. Gk *organon*, instrument]

or·gan·dy, or·gan·die (ɔ́rgəndi:) *n.* a fine, thin, stiff, semitransparent muslin used esp. for clothing and curtains [F. *organdi*]

or·gan-grind·er (ɔ́rgəngraindər) *n.* a street musician who plays a barrel organ

or·gan·ic (ɔrgǽnik) *adj.* of or relating to an organ of the body ‖ (*med.*) affecting the structure of the organism or an organ, *an organic disease* (*cf.* FUNCTIONAL) ‖ (*biol.*) having the physical structure characteristic of living organisms ‖ (*chem.*) of or relating to the compounds of carbon (other than some of its simpler compounds) ‖ inherent, structural, *the organic characteristics of this society* ‖ organized, systematic, esp. having parts that work together in a way that recalls the complex interactions of bodily organs, *the novel is an organic whole* ‖ (*law*) pertaining to the fundamental and constitutional laws by which countries or states are

CONCISE PRONUNCIATION KEY: **(a)** æ, *cat*; ɑ, *car*; ɔ *fawn*; ei, *snake*. **(e)** e, *hen*; i:, *sheep*; iə, *deer*; εə, *bear*. **(i)** i, *fish*; ai, *tiger*; ə:, *bird*. **(o)** o, *ox*; au, *cow*; ou, *goat*; u, *poor*; ɔi, *royal*. **(u)** ʌ, *duck*; u, *bull*; u:, *goose*; ə, *bacillus*; ju:, *cube*. x, *loch*; θ, *think*; ð, *bother*; z, *Zen*; ʒ, *corsage*; dʒ, *savage*; ŋ, *orangutang*; j, *yak*; ʃ, *fish*; tʃ, *fetch*; 'l, *rabble*; 'n, *redden*. Complete pronunciation key appears inside front cover.

governed **or·gán·i·cal·ly** *adv.* [fr. L. *organicus* fr. Gk *organon*, instrument]

Organic Act of 1902 a U.S. Congressional act of the Theodore Roosevelt administration, which provided a constitution, a judicial code, and a system of laws for the Philippines

organic chemistry the branch of chemistry concerned with the compounds of carbon but excluding its simpler compounds (e.g. carbon dioxide, hydrogen cyanide) (cf. INORGANIC CHEMISTRY)

or·gan·ism (ɔ́rgənizəm) *n.* (*biol.*) a living being or entity adapted for living by means of organs separate in function but dependent on one another ‖ any living being or its material structure, the *organism of the herring is being studied* ‖ any complete whole which by the integration, interaction and mutual dependence of its parts is comparable to a living being [fr. ORGANIZE]

or·gan·ist (ɔ́rgənist) *n.* a person who plays the organ

or·gan·iz·a·ble (ɔ́rgənaizəb'l) *adj.* capable of being organized

Or·ga·ni·za·ción de los Es·ta·dos Cen·tro·a·me·ri·ca·nos (ɔrgɑni:sɑsjɔ́ndelɔsestɑ́ðɔssentrɔɑmeri:kɑ́nɔs) (*abbr.* ODECA) an organization of Central American states created in 1951 to advance economic, cultural and social cooperation among its members, which include all the republics of Central America except Panama

or·gan·i·za·tion (ɔrgənizéiʃən) *n.* an organizing or being organized ‖ the way in which something is organized ‖ an association or society of people working together to some end, e.g. a business firm or a political party **or·gan·i·zá·tion·al** *adj.* [fr. M.L. *organizatio* (*organizationis*)]

organization chart (*management*) graphic table of duties and responsibilities of officers and departments of an organization

Organization for Economic Cooperation and Development (*abbr.* O.E.C.D.) the organization which replaced (1961) the Organization for European Economic Cooperation. It encourages the economic growth of member countries, works for the expansion of world trade, and helps underdeveloped countries. Its 24 members are: Australia, Austria, Belgium, Canada, Denmark, Finland, France, Great Britain, Greece, Iceland, Irish Republic, Italy, Japan, Luxembourg, the Netherlands, New Zealand, Norway, Portugal, Spain, Sweden, Switzerland, Turkey, the U.S.A. and West Germany. Headquarters: Paris

Organization for European Economic Cooperation (*abbr.* O.E.E.C.) an organization set up (1948) by 16 European nations to coordinate their economic activities and to assist the administration of the Marshall Plan. It was replaced by the Organization for Economic Cooperation and Development (1961)

organization man managerial employee of a large enterprise who is dominated by corporate ideology, ethics, aspirations and social expectations. The term was coined by William H. Whyte, *The Organization Man* (1956)

Organization of African Unity (*abbr.* O.A.U.) a Pan-African movement founded 1963 and now comprising nearly all independent African states

Organization of American States (*abbr.* O.A.S.) a body set up (1948) to promote social, economic and technical cooperation among American states and to act as a regional agency of the U.N. It has 32 member states. Headquarters: Washington, D.C.

Organization of Central American States an economic, cultural and social union of Costa Rica, Guatemala, Honduras, Nicaragua and El Salvador, formed in 1951

Organization of Petroleum Exporting Countries (*abbr.* O.P.E.C.) cartel formed (1960) by Iran, Iraq, Kuwait, Saudi Arabia and Venezuela to counter price cuts by American and European oil companies. It was later joined by Qatar (1961), Indonesia and Libya (1962), Abu Dhabi (now part of the United Arab Emirates) (1967), Algeria (1969), Nigeria (1971), and Ecuador and Gabon (1973). Originally limited to preventing further cuts in oil prices, by 1970 it began to press for price increases; in the period 1974–8 prices quadrupled, and in 1979 there was a 100 percent increase. By 1981, however, conservation measures by consuming countries coupled with high production by Saudi Arabia led to an oil surplus in consuming countries and by 1983 there was a worldwide glut, leading to a precipitous reduction in price. O.P.E.C. members officially reduced the production ceiling and cut the benchmark price per barrel, but disagreement among participating countries on both production quotas and price weakened O.P.E.C.'s position during the late 1980s

or·gan·ize (ɔ́rgənaiz) *pres. part.* **or·gan·iz·ing** *past* and *past part.* **or·gan·ized** *v.t.* to give an orderly or organic structure to, arrange the parts of (something) so that it works as a whole, *to organize an army* ‖ to make arrangements for, prepare, *to organize an expedition* ‖ to unionize (workers or an industry) ‖ *v.i.* to become organic or systematized **ór·gan·iz·er** *n.* someone who or something that organizes ‖ (*biol.*) a substance that acts as an inductor in embryonic development [fr. M. L. *organizare*]

or·gan·iz·er (ɔ́rgənaizər) *n.* (*physiol.*) a region in the primitive nervous system of all animals that imposes a pattern of responses during early stages of development

or·ga·no·gen·e·sis (ɔrgənoudʒénisis, ɔrgænədʒénisis) *n.* (*biol.*) morphogenesis [fr. Gk *organon*, organ+GENESIS]

or·ga·nog·ra·phy (ɔrgənɔ́grəfi:) *n.* (*biol.*) the describing of the organs of animals or plants [fr. Gk *organon*, organ+*graphos*, written]

or·ga·no·ther·a·py (ɔrgənouθérəpi:, ɔrgænəθérəpi:) *n.* the treatment of disease by the administration of extracts from animal organs [fr. Gk *organon*, organ+THERAPY]

or·ga·num (ɔ́rgənəm) *pl.* **or·ga·na** (ɔ́rgənə), **or·ga·nums** *n.* (*mus.*) a medieval form of part writing in which the cantus firmus is paralleled exactly at a fourth, fifth or octave above or below ‖ (*mus.*) one of the parts accompanying the cantus firmus in this way [L. fr. Gk *organon*, instrument, organ]

or·gan·za (ɔrgǽnzə) *n.* a fine dress fabric of silk, rayon etc. like organdy, but stiffer [prob. fr. *Lorganza*, a trademark]

or·gan·zine (ɔ́rgənzi:n) *n.* a fine, strong silk thread in which the twist runs opposite to the strand, used for the warp in silk weaving [F. *organsin* fr. Ital.]

or·gasm (ɔ́rgæzəm) *n.* the climax of excitement in sexual intercourse ‖ an instance of this **or·gás·tic** *adj.* [fr. Mod. L. *orgasmus* fr. Gk *orgaein*, to swell]

or·gi·as·tic (ɔrdʒi:ǽstik) *adj.* of, like or having the nature of an orgy [fr. Gk *orgiastikos* fr. *orgiazein*, to celebrate orgies]

or·gy (ɔ́rdʒi:) *pl.* **or·gies** *n.* a bout of debauchery ‖ a display of excessive indulgence, *an orgy of self-pity* ‖ (*pl., Gk and Rom. hist.*) secret ceremonial rites in honor of any of certain gods [earlier *orgies* pl. fr. F. *orgies* fr. L. fr. Gk *orgia*, secret rites]

O·ri·be (ɔrí:be), Manuel (1792–1857), Uruguyan general. He founded the Blanco (or nationalist) party in opposition to Riviera. He was president (1835–8)

or·i·el (ɔ́ri:əl, óuri:əl) *n.* a windowed part of a room projecting from a face of a building and often supported by a corbel or bracket ‖ the window of such a projection ‖ any projecting upper-story window [O.F. *oriol*, porch, passage]

or·i·ent (ɔ́ri:ənt, óuri:ənt) **1.** *n.* a highquality pearl, or its special luster **the Or·i·ent** the countries lying east of Europe, esp. the Far East (opp. OCCIDENT) **2.** *adj.* (*rhet.*) lustrous, bright (used orig. of the finest kinds of precious stones and pearls, from the East) [F. fr. L. *oriens* (*orientis*), the east, rising sun]

or·i·ent (ɔ́ri:ent, óuri:ent) *v.t.* to determine the position of (someone or something) with reference to the points of the compass ‖ to place with regard to points of the compass ‖ to adjust (someone or something) to the surroundings or a situation ‖ to turn or guide in a specified direction ‖ to cause to face eastward, esp. to build (a church) with its altar at the eastern end, or bury (a body) with the feet pointing east [F. *orienter*, to place facing east]

Or·i·en·tal (ɔri:ént'l, ouri:ént'l) **1.** *adj.* of, relating to, characteristic of or coming from the Orient **2.** *n.* a native or inhabitant of the Orient, esp. of the Far East [F.]

Oriental beetle the Asiatic beetle

Or·i·en·tal·ism (ɔri:ént'lizəm, ouri:ént'lizəm) *n.* a characteristically Oriental trait, practice etc. ‖ the study of Oriental civilization, languages etc. **Or·i·én·tal·ist** *n.* a specialist in Oriental civilization, languages etc.

Or·i·en·tal·ize (ɔri:ént'laiz, ouri:ént'laiz) *pres. part.* **Or·i·en·tal·iz·ing** *past* and *past part.* **Or·i·en·tal·ized** *v.t.* to make Oriental in character or tastes ‖ *v.i.* to become Oriental in character or tastes

or·i·en·tate (ɔ́ri:enteit, óuri:enteit) *pres. part.* **or·i·en·tat·ing** *past* and *past part.* **or·i·en·tat·ed** *v.t.* to orient [fr. F. *orienter*]

or·i·en·ta·tion (ɔri:entéiʃən, ouri:entéiʃən) *n.* an orienting or being oriented ‖ position with relation to the points of the compass‖ situation of a church on an east-west axis so that the altar is at the east end ‖ (*chem.*) the relative position of atoms or groups about a nucleus or existing configuration ‖ the ordering of chemical groups, molecules or crystals in a particular or desired sense [fr. ORIENT v. or ORIENTATE]

O·rien·te (ɔrjénte) the easternmost and largest province (area 14,128 sq. miles, pop. 2,600,000) of Cuba. Capital: Santiago. Agriculture: chiefly sugarcane. Mining. manganese, chromite, nickel, iron ore

or·i·en·teer·ing (ɔri:entíəriŋ) *n.* outdoor sport developed in Scandinavia in which competing participants find their way from checkpoint to checkpoint in an unfamiliar area using a map and a compass

or·i·fice (ɔ́rifis, ɒ́rifis) *n.* a mouthlike opening, *nasal orifice* [F.]

or·i·flamme (ɔ́riflæm, ɒ́riflæm) *n.* (*hist.*) the ancient royal standard of France, a red silk banderole dedicated to St Denis, carried into battle by French kings (11th-15th cc.) ‖ a symbol or rallying point in a struggle, campaign etc. [fr. O.F. *oriflambe* fr. L. *aurum*, gold+*flamma*, flame]

o·ri·ga·mi (ɔrəgɑ́mi:) *n.* the art or process of folding paper into representational or decorative forms [Jap.]

o·rig·a·num (ɔrígənəm, ərígənəm) *n.* *Origanum vulgare*, wild marjoram, and any of several other fragrant aromatic plants of fam. *Labiatae* and fam. *Verbenaceae*, used in cooking for seasoning

Or·i·gen (ɔ́ridʒen, ɒ́ridʒen) (c. 185–c. 254), Christian theologian. He was head of the Catechetical school of Alexandria (203–31). He was a biblical critic and exegete and expounded the allegorical meanings of the Scriptures (e.g. in 'Hexapla'). His 'De principiis' set forth a comprehensive Christian philosophy, but it survives only in fragments. His 'Contra Celsum' is an outstanding apologetic

Or·i·gen·ism (ɔ́ridʒənizəm, ɒ́ridʒənizəm) *n.* the doctrines attributed to Origen, condemned by the Council of Constantinople (553) **Ór·i·gen·ist** *n.*

or·i·gin (ɔ́ridʒin, ɒ́ridʒin) *n.* the point in time or space at which a thing first exists ‖ the first existence of something ‖ a source or cause, *the origin of a dispute* ‖ (esp. *pl.*) a person's parentage or ancestry, *of humble origins* ‖ (*anat.*) the point of attachment of a muscle that is most firmly fixed [F. *origine* fr. L. *origo* (*originis*), beginning, source]

o·rig·i·nal (ərídʒin'l) **1.** *adj.* of, relating to or belonging to an origin or beginning, *the original plans were changed* ‖ firsthand, not copied or derivative, *an original work by Cézanne* ‖ inventive, creative, *an original mind* ‖ designating something from which a copy, translation, summary etc. has been made, *let us look at the original passage* **2.** *n.* a model or archetype that has been copied, translated etc., *the original of this copy is in the Louvre* ‖ (*old-fash.*) a person who is eccentric in behavior or character [F.]

o·rig·i·nal·i·ty (ərídʒinǽliti:) *n.* the quality or state of being original, esp. creative or novel [fr. F. *originalité*]

ori·gi·nal sin (*Christian theol.*) the sin into which all men are said to be born as a result of the Fall

o·rig·i·nate (ərídʒineit) *pres. part.* **o·rig·i·nat·ing** *past* and *past part.* **o·rig·i·nat·ed** *v.i.* (with 'in', 'from', 'with') to have its source or beginning, *their friendship originated in a chance meeting* ‖ *v.t.* to cause to begin, be the source of, *to originate a new dance step* **o·rig·i·ná·tion** *n.* origin , an originating or being originated [etym. doubtful]

or·i·na·sal (ɔri:néiz'l, ouri:iéiz'l) **1.** *adj.* sounded through both nose and mouth, e.g. of the French nasalized vowels in 'cinq', 'pain' etc. **2.** *n.* an orinasal sound [fr. L. *os* (*oris*), mouth+NASAL]

Or·i·no·co (ɔrinóukou, ourinóukou) the chief river of Venezuela. From its source in the Sierra Parima (on the Brazilian frontier) to the Atlantic Ocean it is about 1,500 miles long. An arm, the Casiquiare, links it with the Río Negro and the Amazon. It has the third largest river basin in South America, draining almost 380,000 sq. miles

o·ri·ole (ɔ́ri:oul, óuri:oul) *n.* a member of *Oriolidae,* an Old World family of passerine birds of warm and tropical regions, esp. *Oriolus oriolus,* the golden oriole, the male of which is bright yellow with black wings and tail ‖ a member of *Icteridae,* a New World family of birds including the Baltimore Oriole [fr. M.L. and Mod. L. *oriolus* fr. L. *aureolus* adj., golden]

O·ri·on (ɔráiən, ouráiən) a constellation in the southern part of the zodiac, represented in charts as a hunter with belt and sword [L. fr. *Oriōn,* a giant and hunter of Gk mythol.]

O·ri·on (ɔráiən) (*mil.*) four-engine, turboprop, all weather, long-range, land-based antisubmarine aircarft (P-3 and EP-3), capable of carrying a varied assortment of search radar, nuclear depth charges and homing torpedoes

or·i·son (ɔ́riz'n,ɒ́riz'n) *n.* (*rhet.*) a prayer [O.F. *oreisun, orison*]

O·ris·sa (ɔrísə, ourísə) a state (area 60,136 sq. miles, pop. 26,370,271) of India on the Bay of Bengal. Capital: Bhubaneswar. Products: rice, tobacco, jute, turmeric, sugarcane, iron, manganese, fish, lumber, textiles

O·ri·ya (ɔrí:jə) *n.* one of the main Indic languages of India, spoken in Orissa, and closely related to Bengali

Or·i·za·ba (ɔri:sú bə) *CITLALTEPETL

Ork·ney Islands (ɔ́rkni:) an archipelago (90 islands and islets, a third of them inhabited) forming a county (land area 376 sq. miles, pop. 18,900) of Scotland, off the northeast coast. Main islands: Pomona (or Mainland), Hoy. County town: Kirkwall, on Pomona. Products: oats, root vegetables, lobster, cod. herring. Livestock: sheep, cattle

Orlando (ourlǽndou) a city (pop. 128,291) in the U.S.A. in east central Florida about 100 mi (160km) northeast of Tampa; seat of Orange County. Industries: citrus groves, aerospace industries, tourism. Walt Disney World is 15 mi (24km) southwest

orle (ɔrl) *n.* (*heraldry*) a band, half the width of the bordure, following the outline of the shield but not touching the edge of it [F. fr. O.F. *urle, ourle*]

Or·lé·a·nais (ɔrleiænei) a former province of France around the middle Loire, in the Paris basin, comprising Loiret, Loir-et-Cher and Eure-et-Loire departments. It is an agricultural region: cereals (*BEAUCE), sugar beet, vegetables, fruit. It contains large forests. Main towns: Orléans (the historical capital), Chartres, Blois. There are light industries. Part of the royal domain from the 10th c., it was created a duchy-apanage (1344) and was united to the French crown (1498)

Or·le·an·ist (ɔrlí:ənist, ɔ́rli:ənist) *n.* a supporter of the Orléans family which claims the French throne by descent from Louis XIV's younger brother Philippe, duc d'Orléans (1640-1701)

Or·lé·ans (ɔrleiɑ̃) the name of four princely houses of France, younger branches of the houses of Valois and Bourbon

Orléans, Charles, duc d' (1391–1465), son of Louis, duc d'Orléans. He was captured at Agincourt (1415) and held prisoner in England until 1440. He was a poet and a patron of letters

Orléans, Louis, duc d' (1372–1402), brother of Charles VI of France. His struggle for the throne after 1392 weakened France in the Hundred Years' War and led to his murder. He was the founder of the house of Valois-Orléans

Orléans, Louis-Philippe-Joseph, duc d' (1747–93), 'Philippe Egalité', French revolutionist. He helped the Jacobins to power and voted for the execution of Louis XVI. He was himself guillotined

Orléans, Phillippe, duc d' (1640–1701), brother of Louis XIV. He was the founder of the house of Bourbon-Orléans

Orléans, Phillippe, duc d' (1674–1723), son of Philippe, duc d'Orléans. As regent of France (1715–23) during the minority of Louis XV, he reversed the policy of Louis XIV. His attempt to reform the finances on the advice of John Law ended in disaster

Orléans a city (pop. 106,246) of Loiret, France, on the Loire, historic capital of Orléanais. It is a rail center. Industries: engineering, textiles, food processing. Cathedral (13th–17th cc.). Joan of Arc forced the English to raise the siege of Orléans (1429)

Or·ley (ɔrlí:), Bernard van (c. 1492–1542), Flemish painter, strongly influenced by the Italians, esp. by Raphael. He also executed cartoons for tapestries

Or·lon (ɔ́rlɒn) *n.* a synthetic fiber somewhat like nylon, used in clothing etc. fabric made of this [trademark]

or·lop (ɔ́rlɒp) *n.* the lowest deck of a ship, esp. of a warship [Du. *overloop,* a covering]

Or·lov (ʌrlɔ́f), Count Grigori Grigoriyevich (1734–83), Russian nobleman. A lover of Catherine II, he was a leader of the plot which brought her to the throne

Or·mazd, Or·muzd (ɔ́rməzd) in the Zoroastrian religion, the supreme deity and creator of the world, patron of good, opposed to Ahriman, patron of evil

or·mer (ɔ́rmər) *n.* a haliotis [dial. F. fr. F. *ormier,* contr. of *oreille-de-mer* or fr. L. *auris maris,* sea ear (fr. its shape)]

or·mo·lu (ɔ́rməlu:) *n.* an alloy of copper, zinc and tin, made to resemble gold, used esp. for furniture decoration [F. *or moulu,* ground gold]

Or·monde (ɔ́rmənd), James Butler, 12th earl and 1st duke of (1610–88), Irish statesman. As lord lieutenant of Ireland (1644–7, 1648–50, 1661–9 and 1677–84), he upheld the policies of Strafford and the Stuart monarchy

Ormuzd *ORMAZD

or·na·ment 1. (ɔ́rnəmənt) *n.* an object, detail etc. meant to add beauty to something to which it is attached or applied or of which it is a part ‖ such objects, details etc. collectively, *a stone window rich in ornament* ‖ (*mus.*) a grace note or group of them, e.g. a turn or trill ‖ (*rhet.*) a person who enhances or does credit to his society, milieu, profession etc. ‖ (*eccles.*) an accessory used in worship or church furnishing **2.** (ɔ́rnəment) *v.t.* to add ornament or ornaments to **or·na·men·tal** (ɔrnəmént'l) *adj.* **or·na·men·ta·tion** (ɔrnəmentéiʃən) *n.* an ornamenting or being ornamented ‖ ornaments collectively [O. F. *ournement, ornement*]

or·nate (ɔrnéit) *adj.* elaborately adorned, *an ornate ceiling* ‖ (of literary style) making use of elaborate rhetorical devices [fr. L. *ornare* (*ornatus*), to adorn]

Orne (ɔrn) a department (area 2,371 sq. miles, pop. 293,500) of N.W. France (*NORMANDY). Chief town: Alençon

or·ner·y (ɔ́rnəri:) *adj.* (*pop.*) inclined to be stubborn and not cooperative [altered fr. ORDINARY]

or·ni·tho·log·i·cal (ɔrnəθəlɒ́dʒik'l) *adj.* of or pertaining to ornithology

or·ni·thol·o·gist (ɔrnəθɒ́lədʒist) *n.* a specialist in ornithology

or·ni·thol·o·gy (ɔrnəθɒ́lədʒi:) *n.* the branch of zoology which deals with birds [fr. Mod. L. *ornithologia* fr. Gk *ornithologos,* dealing with birds fr. *ornis* (*ornithos*), bird+*logos,* discourse]

or·ni·tho·rhyn·chus (ɔrnəθərɪ́ŋkəs) *n.* the platypus [Mod. L. *Ornithorhynchus,* name of genus fr. Gk *ornis* (*ornithos*), bird+*rhunchos,* bill]

or·o·gen·e·sis (ɔroudʒénisis) *pl.* **or·o·gen·e·ses** (ɔroudʒénisi:z) *n.* orogeny ‖ an orogeny **o·rog·e·ny** (ɔrɒ́dʒəni:, ourɒ́dʒəni:) *pl.* **o·rog·e·nies** *n.* the process by which mountains are made, esp. by folding of the earth's crust ‖ a series of mountain-making movements allied in area and period [fr. Gk *oros,* mountain+GENESIS]

or·o·graph·ic (ɔrəgrǽfik, ɒrəgrǽfik) *adj.* of or pertaining to mountains or to orography **or·o·gráph·i·cal** *adj.*

o·rog·ra·phy (ɔrɒ́grəfi:, ourɒ́grəfi:) *n.* the physical geography of mountains [fr. Gk *oros,* mountain+*graphos,* written]

o·ro·ide (ɔ́rouaid, óurouaid) *n.* a gold-colored alloy, chiefly of copper and zinc or tin, used for making cheap jewelry [F. *or,* gold+Gk *eidos,* form]

O·ron·tes (ɔrɒ́nti:z, ourɒ́nti:z) (*Arab.* Nahr el 'Asi) an unnavigable river (246 miles long) rising near Baalbek in central Lebanon and flowing north through W. Syria (where it is dammed for irrigation) and into Turkey, then southwest, passing Antioch, to the Mediterranean

O·ro·si·us (ɔróuʃi:əs), Paulus (early 5th c. A.D.), Spanish Christian theologian and historian, disciple of St Augustine. His history of the world, 'Adversus paganos historiarum libri VII', was translated into Anglo-Saxon by Alfred the Great and was popular in medieval Europe

o·ro·tund (ɔ́rətʌnd, óurətʌnd) *adj.* (of voice, utterance) full and ringing clear ‖ (of style, delivery etc.) bombastic, pompous [fr. L. *ore rotundo,* with a round mouth]

O·roz·co (ɔrɔ́skɔ), José Clemente (1883–1949), Mexican painter, well known for his murals painted in the U.S.A. (1927–32) and in Mexico City

O·roz·co y Ber·ra (ɔrɔ́skɔi:bérrɑ), Manuel (1816–81), Mexican archaeologist and historian, whose 'Historia del México antiguo' made him the world's foremost authority on the civilization of Anáhuac

or·phan (ɔ́rfən) **1.** *n.* a child whose parents are dead ‖ a child one of whose parents is dead **2.** *adj.* designating an orphan, *an orphan child* **3.** *v.t.* to bereave (a child) of his parents by death, *children orphaned by the war* **ór·phan·age** *n.* an institution for the care and education of orphans [fr. L.L. *orphanus* fr. Gk *orphanos,* bereaved, without parents]

Or·phe·us (ɔ́rfi:əs, ɔ́rfju:s) (*Gk mythol.*) Thracian hero and musician regarded as the founder of Orphism. He was able to charm trees and wild beasts with the music of his lyre. When his wife Eurydice died, Orpheus went to Hades and persuaded Pluto to let him bring her back, but he lost her when he broke the condition not to look at her during the return journey. He was killed and dismembered by the bacchantes

Or·phic (ɔ́rfik) *adj.* of Orpheus, esp. of the secret rites and mysteries associated with Orphism ‖ mysterious, esoteric in language **Ór·phism** *n.* an ascetic cult of ancient Greece, stressing the transmigration of souls, moral and ritual purity and individual responsibility for guilt, and having mystical rites of initiation and purification [fr. Gk *Orphikos*]

or·phrey, or·fray (ɔ́rfri:) *pl.* **or·phreys, or·frays** *n.* a band, usually of rich embroidery, attached to an ecclesiastical vestment [M.E. *orfreis,* embroidery fr. O.F.]

or·pi·ment (ɔ́rpəmənt) *n.* arsenic trisulfide, As_2S_3, existing as a crystalline mineral or an amorphous yellow powder, used for dyeing [O.F. fr. L. *auripigmentum,* gold pigment]

or·pine, or·pin (ɔ́rpin) *n. Sedum telephium,* fam. *Crafsulaceae,* a plant native to Europe and N. Asia, now found in cool climates. It has succulent leaves and pinkish purple blossoms, formerly used as a healing agent [F. *orpin,* prob. fr. *orpiment,* orpiment (fr. the color of the flowers of a related plant)]

Or·ping·ton (ɔ́rpiŋtən) *n.* a member of a breed of large, deep-chested, shortlegged poultry, commonly buff-colored [fr. *Orpington,* town in Kent, England]

Orr (ɔr), John Boyd *BOYD ORR

or·rer·y (ɔ́rəri:) *pl.* **or·rer·ies** *n.* a clockwork model to illustrate relative positions and movements of the planets in the solar system, invented c. 1700 by George Graham (1675-1751), and popular in the 18th c. [after Charles Boyle, 4th earl of *Orrery* (1676-1731), for whom one was made]

or·ris (ɔ́ris,ɒ́ris) *n.* a plant of the genus *Iris,* esp. *I florentina* ‖ orrisroot [prob. alteration of IRIS]

or·ris·root (ɔ́risru:t, ɔ́risrut, ɒ́risru:t, ɒ́risrut) *n.* the fragrant rootstock of any of several European irises, esp. *Iris florentina,* smelling of violets and used in perfumery and medicine

Or·si·ni (ɔrsí:ni:), Felice (1819–58), Italian revolutionary. His unsuccessful attempt (1858) to assassinate Napoleon III as a traitor to the Italian revolutionary cause was instrumental in obtaining French intervention in Italy

Or·te·ga y Gas·set (ɔrtéigəi:gɑsét), José (1883–1955), Spanish essayist and philosopher. His best known book in translation is 'The Revolt of the Masses' (1932), a critique of modern social and cultural developments

ortho- (ɔ́rθou) *prefix* straight or vertical ‖ correct or proper ‖ regular [fr. Gk *orthos,* straight]

or·tho·ce·phal·ic (ɔrθousəfǽlik) *adj.* having a skull with a height from 70 to 75% of the length **or·tho·ceph·a·lous** (ɔrθəséfələs) *adj.* [fr. ORTHO-+Gk *kephalē,* head]

or·tho·chro·mat·ic (ɔrθoukrəmǽtik) *adj.* (*photog.*) of a film which is sensitive to green as well as to blue and violet wavelengths and thus gives a more accurate tone representation than ordinary film ‖ (*photog.,* of a plate etc.) sensitive to all colors except red [fr. ORTHO-+Gk *chrōmatikos,* chromatic]

or·tho·clase (ɔ́rθəkleiz, ɔ́rθəkleis) *n.* potassium feldspar, $KAlSi_3O_8$, a monoclinic mineral found in granite and other rocks and having cleavage at right angles (cf. PLAGIOCLASE) **or·tho·clas·tic** (ɔrθəklǽstik) *adj.* (of crystals) cleaving in directions at right angles to each other ‖ of or pertaining to orthoclase [fr. ORTHO-+Gk *klasis,* breaking, cleavage]

or·tho·don·tia (ɔ̞rθədɒ́nʃiːə, ɔ̞rθədɒ́nʃə) *n.* orthodontics **or·tho·dón·tic** *adj.* of or pertaining to orthodontics **or·tho·dón·tics** *n.* the branch of dentistry concerned with the prevention and correction of displacement or overcrowding of the teeth **or·tho·dón·tist** *n.* [Mod. L. fr. Gk *orthos,* straight, correct+*odous (odontos),* tooth]

or·tho·dox (ɔ́rθədɒks) *adj.* of, conforming to or holding the official, accepted or standard opinions, not heretical or independent, *orthodox Marxism* (cf. HETERODOX) ‖ standardized, conventional, *is there an orthodox way of cooking an omelet?* **Or·tho·dox** of or belonging to the Orthodox Eastern Church [fr. Gk *orthodoxos,* right in opinion]

Orthodox Eastern Church that part of the Christian Church centered on the patriarchate of Constantinople, which became separate from western Christendom in 1054, when it refused to accept the supremacy of the pope and was excommunicated by Pope Leo IX. This excommunication was annulled in 1965. The Orthodox Church comprises 16 autocephalous patriarchates. Four of them date from Apostolic times but they diminished in influence with the rise of Islam. They are Constantinople (310,000, created 381), Alexandria (90,000, created 537), Antioch (287,000, created 519) and Jerusalem (45,000, created 451). The largest Churches are the Russian (end of 10th c., autocephalous in 1448, and dominant since, though its numerical strength, perhaps 100 million, is uncertain), the Greek (7 million, autocephalous in 1833), the Rumanian (4th c., 14 million, autocephalous 1925), the Serbian (9th c., 7½ million, autonomous 1219 and fully autocephalous 1879) and the Bulgarian (9th c., 6 million, autocephalous 917). The others are the Georgian, Albanian, Finnish, Polish, Cypriot, Czechoslovak and Mt Sinai. Orthodox communities in W. Europe, Australia and North and South America belong to the patriarchate of Antioch or that of Jerusalem. There are over 150 million Orthodox in the world. Before its break with Rome the Orthodox Church suffered several schisms as a result of Nestorian and Monophysite heresies. These produced the Ethiopian Church (mid-4th c., 5 million), the Armenian Church (end of 5th c., 4 million), the Coptic Church (mid-5th c., 3,000,000) and several smaller schismatic bodies. The leading Orthodox patriarchates are represented on the World Council of Churches. Doctrinally the orthodox differ little from Rome, but they accept only the first seven ecumenical councils (until 787), and deny purgatory and the Immaculate Conception. Emphasis is placed on ritual, monasticism and mysticism, and the priesthood is not always celibate. Historically they are closely associated with eastern European nationalism.

orthodox sleep (*physiol.*) the portion of sleep without dreams or rapid eye movement, important for body-function renewal *Cf* PARADOXICAL SLEEP

or·tho·dox·y (ɔ́rθədɒksiː) *pl.* **or·tho·dox·ies** *n.* the quality or state of being orthodox (cf. HETERODOXY) ‖ an orthodox opinion or practice [fr. Gk *orthodoxia*]

or·tho·ep·ic (ɔrθouépik) *adj.* of or pertaining to orthoepy **or·thó·e·pist** *n.* a specialist in orthoepy

or·tho·e·py (ɔ́rθouepiː, ɔrθóuəpiː) *n.* the correct pronunciation of the words of a language ‖ the study of this [fr. Gk *orthoepeia,* correctness of diction]

or·tho·fer·rite (ɔ̞rθəféraɪt) *n.* (*computer*) a wafer of rare earth and iron magnetized to have the capability to store and transmit information

or·tho·gen·e·sis (ɔ̞rθədʒénisis) *n.* (*biol.*) evolution in a definite direction through variations which, irrespective of natural selection or external forces, gradually produce a new and distinct type **or·tho·ge·net·ic** (ɔ̞rθoudʒənétik) *adj.* [Mod. L. fr. Gk *orthos,* straight+*genesis,* origin]

or·thog·nath·ic (ɔ̞rθəgnǽθik) *adj.* orthognathous

or·thog·na·thism (ɔrθɒ́gnəθizəm) *n.* the quality or state of being orthognathous

or·thog·na·thous (ɔrθɒ́gnəθəs) *adj.* having straight jaws which do not project (cf. PROGNATHOUS) [fr. ORTHO-+Gk *gnathos,* jaw]

or·thog·o·nal (ɔrθɒ́gən'l) *adj.* right angled, rectangular [F. fr. L. fr. Gk *orthos,* right+*gōnia,* angle]

or·tho·graph·ic (ɔ̞rθəgrǽfik) *adj.* of or relating to orthography ‖ correct in spelling ‖ (*geom.*) of or containing perpendicular lines or right angles ‖ of a kind of projection used in mapmaking and architecture, in which all the rays are parallel, the viewer being assumed to be at an infinite distance **or·tho·gráph·i·cal** *adj.* [fr. ORTHOGRAPHY and fr. ORTHO-+Gk *graphos,* written]

or·thog·ra·phy (ɔrθɒ́grəfiː) *pl.* **or·thog·ra·phies** *n.* correct spelling ‖ spelling rules ‖ spelling of any style or kind, *he uses an old-fashioned orthography* ‖ an orthographic projection [O.F. *ortografie* fr. L. *orthographia* fr. Gk]

or·tho·ker·a·tol·o·gy (ɔ̞rθəkeratɒ́lədʒiː) *n.* (*med.*) technique for correcting astigmatism by gradually altering cornea shape utilizing periodic changes of contact lenses

or·tho·mo·lec·u·lar medicine (ɔ̞rθəməlékjulərmédisin) a philosophy of medicine that holds that disease, esp. mental illness, is curable by restoring normal body chemistry

or·tho·mor·phic projection (ɔ̞rθəmɔ́rfikprədʒékʃən) (*cartography*) map projection in which the scale, although varying throughout the map, is the same in all directions at any point, so that very small areas are represented by correct shape and bearings

or·tho·pe·dic, or·tho·pae·dic (ɔ̞rθəpíːdik) *adj.* of, relating to or used in orthopedics

or·tho·pe·dics, or·tho·pae·dics (ɔ̞rθəpíːdiks) *n.* the prevention or curing of deformities of bones, joints, ligaments, muscles and tendons, esp. in children **or·tho·pé·dist, or·tho·páe·dist** *n.* [fr. F. *orthopédie* and Mod. L. *orthopaedia* fr. Gk *orthos,* correct+*paidion,* child and *paideia,* rearing of children]

or·tho·phos·phor·ic acid (ɔ̞rθoufɒsfɔ́rik, ɔ̞rθoufɒsfórik) phosphoric acid

or·tho·psy·chi·a·try (ɔ̞rθəsikáiətriː) *n.* prevention and treatment of abnormal behavior integrating psychiatry, psychology, pediatrics, social services and the schools to stimulate healthy emotional development

or·thop·ter·an (ɔrθɒ́ptərən) **1.** *n.* an orthopteron **2.** *adj.* belonging to the order *Orthoptera* [Mod. L. *Orthoptera*]

or·thop·ter·on (ɔrθɒ́ptərən, ɔrθɒ́ptərɒn) *n.* a member of *Orthoptera,* an order of insects including grasshoppers, crickets, mantises etc., usually having leathery fore wings and pleated hind wings. They have chewing mouthparts, and are mostly vegetarian. They are largely terrestrial, and undergo incomplete metamorphosis **or·thóp·ter·ous** *adj.* [Mod. L. sing. of *Orthoptera* fr. Gk *orthos,* straight+*pteron,* wing]

or·thop·tic (ɔrθɒ́ptik) *adj.* of or relating to orthoptics **or·thóp·tics** *n.* the treatment of defective vision by exercises of the eye muscles etc. [fr. ORTHO-+Gk *optikos,* of or relating to sight]

orthoptics (*med.*) technique of eye exercises designed to correct the visual axes of eyes not properly coordinated for binocular vision — **orthoptist** *n.*

or·tho·rhom·bic (ɔ̞rθərɒ́mbik) *adj.* (of crystals) having three unequal axes of symmetry at right angles to each other

or·tho·scope (ɔ́rθəskoup) *n.* an instrument for viewing the retina of the eye, the refraction due to the cornea being compensated by a layer of water **or·tho·scop·ic** (ɔ̞rθəskɒ́pik) *adj.* giving an image of correct proportions [fr. ORTHO-+Gk *skopein,* to examine]

or·thos·ti·chous (ərθɒ́stikəs) *adj.* (e.g. of leaves) arranged in vertical ranks [ORTHOSTICHY]

or·thos·ti·chy (ɔrθɒ́stikiː) *pl.* **or·thos·ti·chies** *n.* (*bot.*) a hypothetical line along a stem axis connecting a pair or row of leaves or flowers growing in a direct line ‖ an arrangement of leaves etc. along such a line [fr. ORTHO-+Gk *stichos,* row]

or·thot·ics (ɔrθɒ́tiks) *n.* **1.** (*med.*) branch of medicine dealing with the mechanical support of weak joints and muscles —**or·thot·ic** *adj.* —**or·thot·ist** *n.* **2.** (*podiatry*) insert worn in shoe to support the foot, esp. for sports

or·tho·trop·ic (ɔ̞rθətrɒ́pik) *adj.* (*bot.,* of a root or stem) growing more or less vertically **or·thot·ro·pism** (ɔrθɒ́trəpizəm) *n.* (*bot.*) the tendency to grow vertically ‖ (*bot.*) vertical growth **or·thot·ro·pous** (ɔrθɒ́trəpəs) *adj.* (*bot.,* of an ovule) having the chalaza, hilum and micropyle in a straight line [fr. Mod. L. *orthotropus* fr. Gk fr. *ortho-,* straight+*tropos,* turning, turned]

Or·tiz Ru·bio (ɔrtíːsrúːbjɔ), Pascual (1877–1963), Mexican engineer, statesman and president of the Republic (1930–2)

or·to·lan (ɔ́rt'lən) *n. Emberiza hortulana,* a European bunting, formerly often caught and fattened for eating ‖ the sora ‖ the bobolink [F. fr. Prov. *ortolan* or Ital. *ortolano,* gardener]

O·ru·ro (ɔrúːrɔ) a city (pop. 124,091) of W. Bolivia, at 12,160 ft, the center of a mining district: gold, silver, copper, tin

Or·vi·e·to (ɔrvjétɔ) an ancient town (pop. 23,220) of Umbria, Italy. Cathedral (1290–1319), with frescos by Fra Angelico and Signorelli

Or·well (ɔ́rwəl, ɔ́rwel), George (Eric Arthur Blair, 1903–50), English novelist and satirist. His best-known works include 'Animal Farm' (1945) and '1984' (1949), expressing his fears for the destruction of the liberty of the individual

Or·well·i·an (ɔrwéliːən) *adj.* of the world described in *1984,* a novel by George Orwell, of totalitarian superstates where citizens are under constant surveillance and language and thoughts are controlled

-ory *suffix* having the function or effect of, as in 'vomitory' [A.F. *-ori, -orie,* O.F. *-oir, -oire* fr. L. *-orius, -oria, -orium*]

-ory *suffix* denoting place or instrument, as in 'oratory' [O.N.F. and A.F. *-orie* fr. L. *-oria,* -orium]

or·yx (ɔ́riks, óuriks) *pl.* **or·yx·es, or·yx** *n.* a member of *Oryx,* a genus of large antelopes with long, straight horns, found in the desert regions of Africa and Arabia [L. fr. Gk *orux,* pickaxe, antelope]

or·zo (ɔ́rzou) *n.* pasta in the shape of rice

os (ous) *pl.* **o·sar** (óusɑr) *n.* an esker [Swed. *ås,* a ridge]

O·sa·ka (ousɑ́kə) the second largest city (pop. 2,623,124) in Japan, a port laced by canals, on Osaka Bay, W. central Honshu, and center of the industrial belt: textiles, shipbuilding, iron and steel, chemicals. University (1931)

o·sar *pl.* of os ‖ taken as *sing. n.* (*pl.* **o·sars**) an esker [Swed. *åsar,* pl. of *ås,* a ridge]

Os·born (ɒ́zbərn), Henry Fairfield (1857–1935), U.S. paleontologist. As president (from 1908) of the American Museum of Natural History, he developed it into an outstanding research center with the world's largest and most important collection of fossil vertebrates

Os·borne (ɒ́zbərn), Dorothy (1627–95), English letter writer. Her fame rests on the series of letters she wrote to her future husband, Sir William Temple

Os·can (ɒ́skən) *n.* a member of a people anciently inhabiting central Italy ‖ their Italic language

Os·car (ɒ́skər) *n.* one of the annual Academy Awards presented since 1927 by the U.S. Academy of Motion Picture Arts and Sciences, founded (1927) in Hollywood, Calif. Awards are made in about 25 categories, notably for the best film production and best acting

Oscar (*mil.*) NATO term for U.S.S.R. class of subcruiser carrying missiles with 60-mi range

Os·car I (ɒ́skər) (1799–1859), king of Sweden and Norway (1844–59), son of Bernadotte

Oscar II (1829–1907), king of Sweden (1872–1907) and of Norway (1872–1905), son of Oscar I. He rejected Norwegian demands for greater autonomy, and the two kingdoms divided (1905)

Osceola (asiːóulə) (1803–38) American Seminole Indian, a leader of the Florida Seminoles during the Seminole Wars. Lured under a flag of truce to St. Augustine, Fla., he and other chiefs were seized and imprisoned by the U.S. government (1837). He died in a cell at Ft. Moultrie in Charleston harbor, S.C.

os·cil·late (ɒ́səleit) *pres. part.* **os·cil·lat·ing** *past* and *past part.* **os·cil·lat·ed** *v.i.* (of a rigid body pivoted on an axle) to swing to and fro ‖ to vibrate ‖ to waver, vacillate, *his ideas oscillate a good deal* ‖ to vary in condition or degree, fluctuate, *the temperature oscillated wildly during that month* ‖ *v.t.* to cause to oscillate [fr. L. *oscillare (oscillatus),* to swing]

oscillating mine (*mil.*) a hydrostatically controlled mine that maintains a preset depth below the surface independently of the rise and fall of the tide

os·cil·la·tion (ɒsəléiʃən) *n.* an oscillating ‖ fluctuation ‖ (*elec.*) a current fluctuation in a circuit from positive to negative or from maxima to minima ‖ (*phys.*) a single swing of an oscillating body, e.g. of a pendulum from one extreme to another ‖ (*math.*) the variation between highest and lowest values of a function **ós·cil·la·tor** *n.* something which oscillates ‖ (*elec.*) a device for the production of oscillations ‖ a device for measuring rigidity by means of the vibrations of a loaded wire [fr. L. *oscillatio (oscillationis)*]

os·cil·la·to·ry (ɒ́sələtɔri:, ɒ́sələtouri:) *adj.* characterized or marked by oscillation [fr. L. *oscillare (oscillatus),* to swing]

os·cil·lo·gram (əsíləgræm) *n.* a record made by an oscillograph or by an oscilloscope

os·cil·lo·graph (əsíləgræf, əsíləgrɑf) *n.* an instrument recording rapidly changing electrical quantities (e.g. voltage) usually indirectly by means of some sensitive element, e.g. a beam of cathode rays (cf. OSCILLOSCOPE) [fr. OSCILLATE+Gk *graphos,* written]

os·cil·lo·scope (əsíləskoup) *n.* (*phys.*) an instrument in which a beam of electrons is directed through horizontal and vertical deflecting plates to which an electrical potential is applied, causing deflection of the electron beam. The electrons fall on a fluorescent screen and produce a temporary trace. The instrument is used to analyze rapidly changing electrical quantities (e.g. voltage) [fr. OSCILLATE+Gk *skopein,* to look at]

os·cine (ɒ́sain) *adj.* of or relating to *Oscines,* a suborder of passerine birds with a highly specialized vocal apparatus [fr. Mod. L. *Oscines,* L. pl. of *oscen (oscinis),* songbird]

os·cu·lant (ɒ́skjulənt) *adj.* (*biol.*) forming a link connecting two species, groups etc. [fr. L. *osculans (osculantis)* fr. *osculari,* to kiss]

os·cu·lar (ɒ́skjulər) *adj.* (*rhet.*) of the mouth ‖ (*rhet.*) of kissing ‖ (*biol.*) of an osculum [fr. L. *oscularis* fr. *osculum,* little mouth, kiss]

os·cu·late (ɒ́skjuleit) *pres. part.* **os·cu·lat·ing** *past* and *past part.* **os·cu·lat·ed** *v.t.* (*math.,* of a curve, surface etc.) to coincide in three or more points with ‖ *v.i.* (*biol.*) to have characters intermediate between two groups, genera, species etc. [fr. L. *osculari (osculatus),* to kiss]

os·cu·la·tion (ɒskjuléiʃən) *n.* (*rhet.*) the act of kissing ‖ (*math.,* of a curve, surface etc.) the fact of coinciding in three or more points [fr. L. *osculatio (osculationis)* fr. *osculari,* to kiss]

os·cu·lum (ɒ́skjələm) *pl.* **os·cu·la** (ɒ́skjələ) *n.* one of the orifices or openings of a sponge through which water leaves the body [L.=a little mouth]

OSHA (*acronym*) U.S. **O**ccupational **S**afety and **H**ealth **A**dministration *Cf* NIOSH

O·shog·bo (ouʃɒ́gbou) a town (pop. 282,000) of W. Nigeria, about 50 miles northeast of Ibadan: cacao processing

O·si·an·der (ɔuzi:ǽndər), Andreas (Andreas Hosemann, 1498–1552), German Lutheran theologian. He put forward a mystical interpretation of the doctrine of justification by faith which led to a breach with other Lutherans

o·sier (óuʒər) **1.** *n.* any of several varieties of willow, esp. *Salix viminalis,* with pliable twigs used for basketry etc. ‖ a willow rod so used **2.** *adj.* of or made of osier [F.]

O·si·ris (ousáiris) the ancient Egyptian god of the underworld and judge of the dead, brother and husband of Isis and father of Horus. He was also often associated with fertility and its sources, the Nile and the sun: he was revived by Isis after being killed by his brother Seth, symbolizing the yearly renewal of the natural world

Os·lo (ɒ́zlou, ɒ́slou) (called Kristiania, 1624–1924) the capital (pop. 454,872), chief port and industrial center of Norway, at the head of Oslo fiord, in the southeast. Industries: food processing, mechanical engineering, shipbuilding, textiles, paper. Fortress (1300), royal palace (19th c.), town hall (1931–50), university (1811), national theater, museums. Oslo was founded c. 1050, destroyed by fire (1624) and rebuilt

Os·man I (ɒsmɑ́n) (1259–1326), Turkish leader. A vassal of the Seljuks, he proclaimed his independence and founded the Ottoman Empire (c. 1288)

Os·man·li (ɒzmǽnli:) **1.** *adj.* Ottoman **2.** *n.* an Ottoman ‖ the Turkic language of Turkey [fr. Turk. *osmiānli,* of or belonging to OSMAN]

Os·me·ña (ɔsménjɑ), Sergio (1878–1961), Filipino statesman, president (1944–6). Leader of the government in exile after the death of Quezon, he returned to the Philippines with the U.S. invasion forces

os·mic (ɒ́zmik) *adj.* (*chem.*) of compounds of osmium esp. when quadrivalent

os·mi·um (ɒ́zmi:əm) *n.* (*chem.*) a hard grayish metallic polyvalent element (symbol Os, at. no. 76, at. mass 190.2) of the platinum group, used finely divided as a catalyst for gas reactions and in alloys with platinum and iridium [Mod. L. fr. Gk *osmē,* smell (from its pungent smell)]

os·mole (ɒ́zmoul) *n.* (*chem.*) unit of osmotic pressure equal to that of an ideal solution, with a concentration of 1 mole of solute per liter

os·mo·sis (ɒzmóusis, ɒsmóusis) *n.* the passage of a solvent, but not its solute, through a semipermeable membrane into a more concentrated solution, tending to equalize the concentrations on either side of the membrane **os·mot·ic** (ɒzmɒ́tik, ɒsmɒ́tik) *adj.* [fr. obs. *osmose,* osmosis]

osmotic shock (*biol.*) effect on a living system of a sudden change in osmotic pressure

os·mous (ɒ́zmous) *adj.* (*chem.*) of compounds of osmium, esp. when bivalent

os·mund (ɒ́zmənd, ɒ́smənd) *n.* a member of *Osmunda,* fam. *Osmundaceae,* a genus of tall rhizomic ferns, esp. *O. regalis* [origin unknown]

Os·na·brück (ɒ́znəbryk) an old city (pop. 160,200) in Lower Saxony, West Germany: iron and steel, mechanical engineering, textiles, paper. The cathedral was begun under Charlemagne

OSO (*abbr.*) **O**rbiting **S**olar **O**bservatory, a NASA solar research satellite

os·prey (ɒ́spri:) *n. Pandion haliaetus,* fam. *Pandionidae,* a hawk of cosmopolitan distribution with a white underside and head, a brown body, long pointed wings and long deeply curved opposed pairs of claws on its talons. It feeds entirely on fish ‖ a feather trimming for hats made from egret plumes [prob. fr L. *ossifraga,* lit. bonebreaker]

Os·sa (ɒ́sə) a mountain (6,490 ft) of Thessaly, Greece, overlooking the Gulf of Salonika

os·se·in (ɒ́si:in) *n.* the organic basis of bone tissue, believed identical with collagen and left when the mineral content is eliminated [fr. L. *osseus,* bony]

os·se·ous (ɒ́si:əs) *adj.* composed of or resembling bone, *osseous structure* ‖ having a bony skeleton, *osseous and cartilaginous fibers* ‖ rich in fossilized bones, *osseous layers* [fr. L. *osseus,* bony]

Os·set (ɒ́sit) *n.* a member of an Aryan people, possibly of Persian origin, living in the central Caucasus, U.S.S.R. (North Ossetian A.S.S.R. and N. Georgia, U.S.S.R.) since the 10th c., and speaking Ossetic

Os·se·tian (ɒsí:ʃən) **1.** *adj.* Ossetic **2.** *n.* an Osset

Os·set·ic (ɒsétik) **1.** *adj.* of the Ossets **2.** *n.* the Iranian language of the Ossets

Os·si·an (ɒ́si:ən, ɒ́ʃən) legendary Gaelic bard of the 3rd c. (*MACPHERSON)

os·si·cle (ɒ́sik'l) *n.* (*anat., zool.*) any of several small bones, esp. one of those in the middle ear, or in the sclerotic of some birds and reptiles ‖ any of several calcareous bodies, esp. one in the gastric mill of crustaceans, or in an echinoderm's test [fr. L. *ossiculum,* little bone]

os·si·fic (ɒsífik) *adj.* bone-forming [fr. L. *os (ossis),* bone]

os·si·fi·ca·tion (ɒsifikéiʃən) *n.* the process of becoming bone or an instance of this process ‖ the changing of body tissue into an osseous substance [OSSIFY]

os·si·fy (ɒ́sifai) *pres. part.* **os·si·fy·ing** *past* and *past part.* **os·si·fied** *v.i.* to change into bone ‖ (of ideas, behavior etc.) to make or become hardened, set or rigid ‖ *v.t.* to cause to change into bone ‖ to cause (ideas, behavior etc.) to become hardened, set or rigid [fr. L. *os (ossis),* bone]

os·so buc·co (ɒ́sou bú:kou) *n.* dish of veal shanks braised with chopped parsley, tomatoes, carrots, celery, onion, lemon peel, olive oil, dry white wine and seasonings

os·su·ar·y (ɒ́ʃu:eri:) *pl.* **os·su·ar·ies** *n.* a container, chamber etc. for the bones of the dead [fr. L.L. *ossuarium*]

Ostade *VAN OSTADE, Adriaen

Ostade *VAN OSTADE, Isaac

os·te·al (ɒ́sti:əl) *adj.* of, relating to, or like bone ‖ sounding like a bone when struck [fr. Gk *osteon,* bone]

Ost·end (ɒsténd) (*Flem.* Oostende) a port and resort (pop. 71,400) of W. Flanders, Belgium, on the North Sea: fisheries, oyster beds. The port handles goods and passenger traffic with England (coal imports, food products, exports)

Ostend Manifesto a secret dispatch sent (1854) to William L. Marcy, U.S. secretary of state under President Pierce, by the U.S. ministers to Great Britain, France and Spain, recommending that the U.S.A. acquire Cuba from Spain. If Spain would not sell Cuba, ran the dispatch, 'then by every law, human and divine, (the U.S.A. should) be justified in wresting it from Spain if (it possessed) the power'. Public reaction when the report leaked out led Marcy to reject the proposal

os·ten·si·ble (ɔsténsəb'l) *adj.* apparent, pretended, avowed, *ostensible motives* **os·tén·si·bly** *adv.* [F.]

os·ten·sive (ɒsténsiv) *adj.* (*logic*) directly demonstrative ‖ ostensible [L.L. *ostensivus* fr. L. *ostendere (ostensus),* to show]

os·ten·so·ry (ɒsténsəri:) *pl.* **os·ten·so·ries** *n.* (*Roman Catholicism*) a monstrance [fr. M.L. *ostensorium*]

os·ten·ta·tion (ɒstentéiʃən) *n.* unnecessary show or display of wealth, luxury, skill, learning etc. **os·ten·tá·tious** *adj.* fond of display, showy ‖ intended to attract attention, *an ostentatious manner* [F.]

os·te·o·ar·thri·tis (ɒsti:ouɑrθráitis) *n.* a degenerative condition in older people, chiefly of the knee and hip joints [fr. Gk *osteon,* bone+*arthritis,* gout]

os·te·o·blast (ɒ́sti:əblæst) *n.* a bone-forming cell [fr. Gk *osteon,* bone+*blastos,* bud]

os·te·oc·la·sis (ɒsti:ɒ́kləsis) *n.* (*surgery*) the operation of breaking a bone in order to correct a deformity etc. [Gk *osteon,* bone+*klasis,* fracture]

os·te·o·clast (ɒ́sti:əklæst) *n.* (*anat.*) a cell in developing bone concerned esp. with the breaking down of unnecessary bone parts ‖ (*surgery*) an instrument for breaking bones in osteoclasis [G. *osteoklast* fr. Gk *osteon,* bone+*klastos,* broken]

os·te·o·log·ic (ɒsti:əlɒ́dʒik) *adj.* of or relating to osteology **os·te·o·lóg·i·cal** *adj.*

os·te·ol·o·gist (ɒsti:ɒ́lədʒist) *n.* someone who specializes in osteology

os·te·ol·o·gy (ɒsti:ɒ́lədʒi:) *n.* the scientific study of bones and bony structure ‖ the bony structure of an organism or part of an organism [fr. Gk *osteon,* bone+*logos,* discourse]

os·te·o·ma (ɒsti:óumə) *pl.* **os·te·o·mas, os·te·o·ma·ta** (ɒsti:óumətə) *n.* (*med.*) a benign bony tumor **os·te·ó·ma·tous** *adj.* [fr. Gk *osteon,* bone]

os·te·o·my·e·li·tis (ɒsti:oumaiəláitis) *n.* inflammation of bone marrow [fr. Gk *osteon,* bone+*muelos,* marrow]

os·te·o·path (ɒ́sti:əpæθ) *n.* someone who specializes in osteopathy

os·te·o·path·ic (ɒsti:əpǽθik) *adj.* of or relating to osteopathy

os·te·op·a·thist (ɒsti:ɒ́pəθist) *n.* an osteopath

os·te·op·a·thy (ɒsti:ɒ́pəθi:) *n.* a form of medical treatment purporting to cure a wide variety of diseases primarily by manipulation of the joints of the body. This is based on the assumption that disease is due chiefly to skeletal deformation and its effects on nerves, blood vessels etc. [fr. Gk *osteon,* bone+*pathos,* feeling]

os·te·o·phyte (ɒ́sti:əfait) *n.* (*med.*) a small bony outgrowth **os·te·o·phyt·ic** (ɒsti:əfítik) *adj.* [fr. Gk *osteon,* bone+*phuton,* growth]

os·te·o·plas·tic (ɒsti:əplǽstik) *adj.* of or relating to osteoplasty

os·te·o·plas·ty (ɒ́sti:əplæsti:) *n.* (*surgery*) bone repair, esp. reconstruction of damaged or missing parts [fr. Gk *osteon,* bone+*plastos,* molded]

osteoporosis (ɑsti:oupoúrousis) condition characterized by decrease in bone mass with decreased density and enlargement of bone spaces producing porosity and fragility. Senile and postmenopausal, or primary, osteoporosis, the most common type, occurs only in elderly persons and postmenopausal women. Disuse, or secondary, osteoporosis involves bones immobilized by paralytic disease or traumatic fractures or that have been subjected to prolonged weightlessness during space flight. Exercise programs, calcium-enriched diet, and sometimes estrogen replacement, are used in prevention and treatment

os·te·ot·o·my (ɒsti:ɒ́təmi:) *pl.* **os·te·ot·o·mies** *n.* (*surgery*) an operation of cutting bone or removing pieces of bone [fr. Gk *osteon,* bone+*-tomia,* cutting]

Os·ti·a (ɒ́sti:ə) the port of ancient Rome, at the old mouth of the Tiber, now 3 miles from the sea and the modern bathing resort of Ostia Marina (or Lido di Roma). The Roman town (4th c. B.C.–3rd c. A.D.) has been extensively excavated

os·ti·ole (ɒsti:oul) *n.* a small aperture or pore, e.g. the opening of a perithecium or of a stoma ‖ an inhalant aperture of a sponge [fr. L. *ostiolum,* dim. of *ostium,* door]

ost·ler (ɒslər) *n.* (*hist.*) a hostler

ost·mark (ɒstmɑrk) *n.* unit of currency of East Germany, equal to 100 pfennig

Ost·pol·i·tik (ɒstpɒlitik) *n.* West Germany's policy toward Eastern Europe, esp. during 1969–74, that was a forerunner of détente

os·tra·cism (ɒstrəsizəm) *n.* an ostracizing or being ostracized

os·tra·cize (ɒstrəsaiz) *pres. part.* **os·tra·ciz·ing** *past* and *past part.* **os·tra·cized** *v.t.* to refrain deliberately and ostentatiously from having any sociable dealings at all with, esp. in order to punish by humiliating, *he was ostracized by the village after the inquest* ‖ (*Gk hist.*) to banish (someone considered dangerous to the state) for 5 or 10 years by popular vote. The votes were registered on potsherds [fr. Gk *ostrakizein* fr. *ostrakon,* a potsherd]

Os·tra·va (ɔ́strɑvɑ) (formerly Moravská-Ostrava) the chief town (pop. 323,459, of N. Moravia, on the Oder, center of Czechoslovakia's main coal-mining district: iron and steel, heavy engineering, machinery, chemicals

os·trich (ɔ́stritʃ, ɒstritʃ) *n. Struthio camelus,* fam. *Struthionidae,* a cursorial flightless bird inhabiting the sandy plains of Africa and formerly Arabia. It is the largest living bird, attaining a height of 6-8 ft and a weight of 300 lbs., and capable of running at 40 miles an hour. The males are black and white, the females and young have a brown head and neck. The legs are bare, but the bodies are well feathered. The wing and tail feathers are used for ornamental trimming, e.g. of hats. The adults are gregarious and polygamous [O.F. *ostruce, ostruche* fr. pop. L. *avistruthio* fr. *avis,* bird+L.L. *struthio* fr. Gk *strouthiōn,* ostrich]

Os·tro·goth (ɒstrəgɒθ) *n.* a member of the eastern division of the Goths. They invaded Italy (488) under their king, Theodoric, and founded a kingdom which was destroyed (552-5) by Justinian 1

Os·trov·sky (ʌstrɔ́fski), Alexander Nikolayevich (1823–86), Russian dramatist. His plays, e.g. 'The Storm' (1860), were remarkable for their liberal tendencies

Ost·wald (ɔ́stvɑlt), Wilhelm (1853–1932), German chemist. He was a pioneer in electrochemistry and catalysis, and formulated Ostwald's law stating that the dissociation of an electrolyte tends to completion with infinite dilution

Os·ty·ak (ɒsti:æk) *n.* a member of a Ugrian people living in W. Siberia ‖ their Ugric language

Os·wald (ɒzwɔld), St (c. 604–42), king of Northumbria (633–42). He received St Aidan from Iona, and gave him Holy Island as the center for the conversion of Northumbria. Feast: Aug. 5

Oswald St (c. 925–92), English prelate, bishop of Worcester (962–92) and archbishop of York (972–92). With St Dunstan, he was one of the leaders of the 10th-c. monastic revival in England. Feast: Feb. 28

Oswald, Lee Harvey (1939–63), the alleged assassin of President John F. Kennedy. Oswald was in turn shot and killed by Jack Ruby. The Warren Commission Report found that Oswald 'acting alone and without advice or assistance' was the assassin of President Kennedy. An avowed Marxist, Oswald had lived in the U.S.S.R. for a short time. He had a childhood background of emotional disturbance

Oś·wię·cim (ɔʃvjɛ̃tsim) *AUSCHWITZ

Os·wy (ɒzwi:) (*d.* 671), king of Northumbria (642–71). He summoned the Synod of Whitby (664)

O·ta·go (outɑ́gou) the southernmost province (area 25,530 sq. miles, pop. 279,000) of South Island, New Zealand: fruit, sheep, dairy produce, some gold. University at Dunedin (1869)

O·ta·ru (outɑ́ru:) a port (pop. 189,000) of W. central Hokkaido, Japan: fisheries

o·ta·ry (óutəri:) *n.* a member of *Otariidae,* a family of chiefly Antarctic seals having small, well-developed ears [fr. Mod. L. *otaria*]

OTB (*abbr.*) off-track betting, esp. in New York

OTC drug over-the-counter drug (which see)

OTEC (*acronym*) ocean thermal energy conversion, plants for conversion to tap tropical seas for electric power

oth·er (ʌ́ðər) **1.** *adj.* different, not the same, *your other hand, some other time* ‖ alternative, *he has no other place to go* ‖ further or additional, *give some other examples* ‖ remaining, *where are your other sons?* ‖ of very different kind, *his tastes are quite other than mine* ‖ former, *the youth of other days* **every other** alternate, *skip every other line* **on the other hand** used to introduce an argument or fact in contrast with a previous one **other things being equal** if the conditions were the same in everything but the point under discussion, *other things being equal I should prefer to live here: but it is damp* **the other day** recently, a few days ago **the other world** life after death **2.** *n.* or *pron.* other person or thing, *show me some others, keep this eye closed and open the other, others can do as they please* **among others** with others, *my life was there among others* **one after the other** in succession, *difficulties arose one after the other* **one from the other** apart, *it is hard to tell the twins one from the other* **someone or other** some unknown person, *someone or other has broken my pen* **some time or other** someday, *he hopes to go to Italy some time or other* **3.** *adv.* **other than** in any other way, *he did not examine it other than casually* ‖ besides, *is anyone other than yourself coming?* [O.E. *ōther*]

oth·er·wise (ʌ́ðərwaiz) **1.** *adv.* in another or different way, *you could hardly think otherwise* ‖ or else, *do it now, otherwise you will forget* ‖ in other respects, apart from that, *he was careless, but not otherwise to be blamed* ‖ under other circumstances, *he can't stay for two years, otherwise we would appoint him* **2.** *adj.* in a different state, *he does not wish it otherwise* ‖ different, *if circumstances were otherwise* [O.E *onōthre wīsan*]

oth·er·world·li·ness (ʌðərwə́:rldli:nis) *n.* the quality or state of being otherworldly

oth·er·world·ly (ʌðərwə́:rldli:) *adj.* concerned with spiritual matters, often to the exclusion of the affairs of this world ‖ hopelessly unpractical often because absorbed in speculation etc.

Oth·man (ɔθmɑ́n) (c. 578–656), 3rd Moslem caliph (644–56), father-in-law of Mohammed

O·tho (óuθou) (Holy Roman Emperors, and king of Greece) *OTTO

Otho, Marcus Salvius (32–69), Roman emperor (69). He was defeated by Vitellius shortly after his proclamation by the Praetorians, and committed suicide

o·tic (ɒtik, óutik) *adj.* of or relating to the ear [fr. Gk *otikos* fr. *ous (ōtos),* ear]

o·ti·ose (óuʃi:ous, óuti:ous) *adj.* (*rhet.*) idle, lazy, *otiose delights* ‖ superfluous, *otiose remarks* [fr. L. *otiosus,* at leisure]

O·tis (óutis), Elisha Graves (1811–61), American inventor. His invention of an elevator with a safety device (1852) made the building of skyscrapers a practical possibility

Otis, James (1725–83), American revolutionary leader. He was an eloquent critic of British colonial policy before the Revolutionary War

o·ti·tis (outáitis) *n.* inflammation of the ear [Mod. L. fr. Gk *ous (ōtos),* ear]

o·to·cyst (óutəsist) *n.* an organ of balance in invertebrates consisting of a sac containing a fluid and otoliths ‖ an embryonic auditory vesicle in vertebrates [fr. Gk *ous (ōtos),* ear+*kustis,* bladder]

o·to·lar·yn·gol·o·gy (outoulæriŋgɒlədʒi:) *n.* otorhinolaryngology [fr. Gk *ous, (ōtos),* ear+*larunx (larungos),* larynx+*logos,* discourse]

o·to·lith (óut'liθ) *n.* a granule of calcium carbonate in the inner ear of a vertebrate. Several are attached to nerve cells, and through gravity register the equilibrium of the animal. They are also present in the otocysts of invertebrates and in some fishes [fr. Gk *ous (ōtos),* ear+*lithos,* stone]

O·to·mí (outəmí:) *pl.* **O·to·mí, O·to·mís** *n.* one of the original peoples of Mexico, now living in the states of Querétaro and Guanajuato ‖ a member of this people ‖ their language, probably the first spoken in Mexico, now used by about 450,000

o·to·rhi·no·lar·yn·gol·o·gy (outourainoulæriŋgɒlədʒi:) *n.* the medical science treating of ear, nose and throat disorders [fr. Gk *ous (ōtos), ear+rhis (rhinos),* nose+*larunx (larungos),* larynx+*logos,* discourse]

o·to·tox·ic (outoutɒksik) *adj.* (*med.*) adversity affecting the ears, esp. the nerves —**o·to·tox·ic·i·ty** *n.*

O·tran·to, Strait of (outrǽntou) a channel (about 47 miles wide) between Albania and the heel of Italy, joining the Adriatic and Ionian Seas

ot·ta·va ri·ma (outɑ́vəri:mə) *pl.* **ot·ta·va ri·mas** *n.* a verse stanza of eight ten-syllabled lines (eleven-syllabled in Italian) rhyming abababcc [Ital.=octave rhyme]

Ot·ta·wa (ɒtəwə) the capital (pop. 291,000, with agglom. 717,978) of Canada, on hills along the Ottawa River in W. Ontario. Industries: lumber, pulp and paper, publishing, light manufacturing. Neo-Gothic parliament buildings (1916), national museums, University of Ottawa (1866). The town was founded in 1827 and was made the capital in 1867

Ottawa River the chief tributary (696 miles long) of the St Lawrence, separating Ontario, Canada, from Quebec

ot·ter (ɒtər) *n.* a member of *Lutra,* fam. *Mustelidae,* a genus of carnivorous aquatic mammals (cf. SEA OTTER). The otter has a flattish head, short ears, webbed toes, elongated tail and is approximately 2-4 ft in length. It feeds chiefly on fish and is of virtually cosmopolitan distribution ‖ its dark brown fur [O.E. *otr, ottor, oter*]

ot·ter·hound (ɒtərhaund) *n.* a dog of a rare British breed used for hunting otters. It derives partly from the bloodhound

otter trawl (*mil.*) in mine warfare, a device that, when towed, displaces sideway by use of kites to a predetermined distance, thus clearing a wide path *Cf* OROPESA SWEEP

Otto cycle the sequence of actions in a four-stroke internal-combustion engine: suction, compression, expansion, exhaust. The cycle results in two revolutions of the crankshaft [after Nikolaus August *Otto* (1832-91), German pioneer of the internal-combustion engine]

Ot·to I (ɔ́tou) 'the Great' (912–73), Holy Roman Emperor (962–73) and German king (936–73), son of Henry I. The greatest military and political power of his time in Europe, he repelled invasions of Magyars (955) and Slavs, and united the crowns of Germany and Italy

Otto II (953–83), Holy Roman Emperor jointly (967–73) with his father Otto I, and then alone (973–83), German king (961–83). He tried unsuccessfully to drive the Greeks from S. Italy (982)

Otto III (980–1002), Holy Roman Emperor (996–1002), German king (983–1002), but under the regency of his mother (983–91) and his grandmother (991–5). He was the son of Otto II

Otto IV (c. 1182–1218), Holy Roman Emperor (1209–15), German king (1208–15), son of Henry 'the Lion'. Excommunicated (1210) by Innocent III, he was deposed by Frederick II

Otto I (1815–67), king of Greece (1832–62), son of Louis I of Bavaria. He was chosen by a conference of European powers at London (1832) to rule the new kingdom of Greece. He proved extremely unpopular, and was deposed (1862) by a military revolt

Ot·to·car II (ɒtəkɑr) (c. 1230–78), king of Bohemia (1253–78). He expanded his territories to include Carinthia, Styria and part of Slovenia as well as Austria, Bohemia and Moravia, but was defeated (1276–8) by Rudolf I of Germany

Ot·to·man (ɒtəmən) **1.** *adj.* of or pertaining to the Turks or the Ottoman Empire **2.** *n.* a Turk [F. fr. Arab. *Othman*]

ot·to·man (ɒtəmən) *n.* an upholstered or cushioned seat, stool or sofa without a back

Ottoman Empire a Moslem state founded (c. 1288) in Asia Minor by Osman I. It expanded throughout Asia Minor and into Thrace (1345). The Ottomans captured Adrianople (1361), won a great victory at Kosovo Polje (1389), and took Serbia and Bulgaria. They captured Constantinople (1453). The Ottoman Empire reached its height during the reign (1520–66) of Suleiman II, when its power extended through the Balkans and S. Russia, throughout Asia Minor and down the valleys of the Tigris and Euphrates to the Persian Gulf, and through N. Africa as far west as Algeria. Its rulers assumed the caliphate (1517). The Ottomans were defeated at Lepanto (1571) and failed in their attempts to capture Vienna (1529 and 1683). Russia's desire to take advantage of the weakness of the Ottoman Empire (17th–19th cc.) gave rise to the Russo-Turkish Wars and the Eastern Question. The empire was severely weakened (19th c.) by its tyrannical and corrupt system of government and its disastrous financial position. It was overthrown (1922) by Atatürk, and in 1924 the Ottoman caliphate was abolished (*TURKEY)

Ot·way (ɒ́twei), Thomas (1652–85), English playwright and poet. His plays include two tragedies in blank verse, 'The Orphan' (1680) and 'Venice Preserv'd' (1682)

Oua·ga·dou·gou (wægədú:gu:) the capital (pop. 247,877) of Burkina Faso, a trading center and terminus of the railroad to Abidjan

Ou·ban·gui (u:bɑ̃gi:) *UBANGI

Oubangui-Chari *CENTRAL AFRICAN REPUBLIC

ou·bli·ette (u̧:bli:ét) *n.* an underground dungeon opening only at the top [F. fr. *oublier,* to forget]

ouch (autʃ) *interj.* used on feeling a twinge of pain or in response to a cutting remark

Oud (aut), Jacobus Johannes Pieter (1890–1963), Dutch architect. A participant in the De Stijl movement, he was among the first to design in the international style (*STIJL, DE)

Ou·de·narde, Battle of (ú:dənɑrd) a victory (1708) of an allied army under Marlborough and Eugène over the French during the War of the Spanish Succession

Oudjda *OUJDA

ought (ɔt) (*infin.* and *parts.* lacking, used only as present) *auxiliary v.* expressing duty or obligation, *we ought to tell them, it ought not to be allowed, he ought to have known better* ‖ expressing necessity or expedience, *the grass ought to be cut* ‖ expressing desirability, *you ought to have been with us yesterday* ‖ expressing strong likelihood, *he ought to win the race easily* [O.E. *āhte* past of *āgan,* owe]

ought *AUGHT

oughtn't (ɔ́t'nt) *contr.* of OUGHT NOT

ou·gi·ya (u:gíjə) *n.* unit of currency in Mauritania, equal to 5 koum

oui·ja (wí:dʒə, wí:dʒi:) *n.* a board marked with the alphabet and various signs, fitted with a planchette, and used to obtain messages in spiritualist practice [F. *oui,* yes and G. *ja,* yes]

Ouj·da, Oudj·da (u:dʒdɑ́) an industrial city (pop. 155,800) of N. Morocco near the Algerian frontier: lead and coal-mining center

Ou·lu (áulu:) (*Swed.* Uleåborg) a port (pop. 93,806) of Finland near the head of the Gulf of Bothnia processing and exporting lumber

ounce (auns) *n.* (*abbr.* oz.) a unit of weight equal to 1/16 of a pound avoirdupois (28.35 gms) or 1/12 of a pound troy (31.1 gms) ‖ a very little, *not an ounce of sympathy* [O.F. *unce*]

ounce *n. Felis uncia,* fam. *Felidae,* a large feline carnivore inhabiting the mountains of Asia [fr. O.F. *once, lonce*]

our (auər) *possessive adj.* of, pertaining to or belonging to us ‖ experienced, done or made by us ‖ (used formally, esp. by a sovereign, author or judge) my, *this is a mistake in our opinion* [O.E. *ūre* orig. genitive pl. of first pers. pron., 'of us', later inflected as adj.]

Our Lady a title of the Virgin Mary

ours (auərz) *possessive pron.* that or those belonging to us, *ours is an ancient race, this land of ours* [fr. O.E. possessive pron. *ur, ure,* our]

our·self (a̧uərsélf, ɑrsélf) *pl.* **our·selves** (a̧uərsélvz, ɑrsélvz) *pron.* refl. form of WE, *we blame ourselves for the accident* ‖ emphatic form of WE, *we did it ourselves* ‖ (*sing.,* used formally esp. by a sovereign, an author or a judge) myself

-ous *suffix* full of, as in 'gracious' ‖ possessing the qualities of, as in 'bulbous' ‖ (*chem.,* in contrast to *-ic* suffix) indicating the lower of two possible valencies, as in 'ferrous oxide'

oust (aust) *v.t.* (*law*) to dispossess of property or an inheritance ‖ (*law*) to take away (a privilege, right etc.) ‖ to force or drive out, eject [A. F. *ouster,* to take away]

oust·er (áustər) *n.* (*law*) an illegal or wrongful dispossession from property or an inheritance [A.F.=to oust]

out (aut) **1.** *adv.* away from a place, situation etc., *he flew out to Australia* ‖ on the outside, *to lock someone out* ‖ away from home, place of work etc., *he has just gone out* ‖ (*naut.*) away from land, *fishing 5 miles out* ‖ on strike, *the workers have walked out* ‖ not in office, *his party is out* ‖ outside, out-of-doors, *come out for a walk* ‖ into violent or sudden activity, *a fire broke out, war broke out* ‖ expressing disappearance, elimination or omission, *the stains will wash out, cross a word out, leave a word out* ‖ so as to be no longer functioning, burning etc., *put out the light* ‖ expressing finality, *my shirt is worn out, tired out* ‖ expressing projection, *his chin jutted out* ‖ into sight, *the sun came out* ‖ into or in circulation, *his book has just come out* ‖ in or into public knowledge, *the secret came out* ‖ openly, without reticence, *tell him right out* ‖ expressing distribution, *hand out the money* ‖ expressing extension or prolongation, *stretch out your arm* ‖ away from the center, interior etc., *spread out* ‖ into or in bloom, leaf etc., *crocuses come out early* ‖ having a determined purpose, *out to make money, out for success* ‖ expressing discord, *they fell out* ‖ into or in disuse, *long skirts have gone out* ‖ expressing selection, *pick out the winners* ‖ in error, *my guess was out by 200 points* ‖ (*Am.*=*Br.* down) in the condition of having lost money on a transaction ‖ (*pop.*) into or in a state of unconsciousness, *he passed out* ‖ (*baseball*) in a manner producing an out, *to strike out* ‖ (*baseball, cricket etc.*) with the turn at bat finished, *how was he put out?* **all out** with one's whole effort, *he has gone all out to win the election* **out and away** by far **out from under** (*pop.*) away from difficulty or danger **2.** *adj.* (*of* sizes of clothing) irregular, esp. very large ‖ (*baseball,* of a player) failing to get on a base or complete a successful play ‖ (*cricket,* of a batsman, after an appeal to the umpire) dismissed ‖ outward or giving access outward, *the out door* **3.** *prep.* forth from, *jump out the window* ‖ on the outside of, *hang it out the window* **4.** *n.* (*pop.*) a way out, an excuse ‖ (*baseball*) a failure to get on a base or complete a successful play ‖ (*printing*) a word or words inadvertently omitted from copy **5.** *interj.* get out! go away! **6.** *v.i.* (*rhet.*) to be revealed, *the truth will out* [O.E. *ūt*]

out- *prefix* beyond ‖ in excess of ‖ excelling

out·a·chieve (áutətʃi̧:v) *v.* to accomplish more than another person or persons

out·age (aútidʒ) *n.* **1.** monies not accounted for **2.** failure of electric power

out-and-out (áut'náut) **1.** *adj.* complete, thorough, *an out-and-out liar* **2.** *adv.* completely, thoroughly, *an out-and-out crazy plan*

out·back (áutbæk) *n.* (*Austral.,* with 'the') a district remote from the main population centers

out·bal·ance (autbǽləns) *pres. part.* **out·bal·anc·ing** *past* and *past part.* **out·bal·anced** *v.t.* to outweigh

out·bid (autbíd) *pres. part.* **out·bid·ding** *past* and *past part.* **out·bid** *v.t.* to offer a higher price than, esp. at an auction sale ‖ (*cards*) to bid more than

out·board (áutbɔrd, áutbo̧urd) **1.** *adj.* on or towards the outside of a ship, boat, aircraft etc. ‖ (of a boat) having an outboard motor **2.** *adv.* to or towards the outside of a boat, ship or aircraft

outboard motor a small internal-combustion engine that can be attached to the stern of a small boat

out·bound (áutbáund) *adj.* (*of* a ship) traveling away from her home port or country

out·brave (autbréiv) *pres. part.* **out·brav·ing** *past* and *past part.* **out·braved** *v.t.* to face up to and overcome by endurance, *to outbrave hostile criticism*

out·break (áutbrȩik) *n.* a sudden, violent bursting out, *the outbreak of war* ‖ an epidemic or near epidemic, *an outbreak of smallpox* ‖ a revolt, an insurrection

out·breed (autbrí:d) *pres. part.* **out·breed·ing** *past* and *past part.* **out·bred** (autbréd) *v.t.* to mate (animals not closely related, selected for their qualities) so as to improve stock ‖ to get rid of (an undesirable characteristic) by selective breeding **out·bréed·ing** *n.* voluntary marriage outside the tribe, clan or social group (cf. EXOGAMY) ‖ the policy or practice of outbreeding animals

out·build·ing (áutbi̧ldiŋ) *n.* a building separate from, but near to and serving, an adjacent house or building

out·burst (áutbə̧:rst) *n.* a violent emotional fit, *an outburst of laughter* ‖ an eruption, *sudden outbursts of flame*

out·cast (áutkæst, áutkɑ̧st) **1.** *adj.* cast out from home, friends etc. or by society, *an outcast waif* **2.** *n.* someone who has been so treated

out·caste (áutkæst, áutkɑ̧st) **1.** *n.* a person without caste or one driven from his caste **2.** *adj.* without caste

out·class (autklǽs, autklɑ́s) *v.t.* to surpass by so much as to seem to belong to a higher class

out·come (áutkʌ̧m) *n.* a result or consequence

out·crop (áutkrɒ̧p) **1.** *n.* (*geol.*) an exposure of a rock stratum at ground level ‖ the rocks so exposed **2.** *v.i. pres. part.* **out·crop·ping** *past* and *past part.* **out·cropped** to be exposed on the surface of the ground

out·cry (áutkra̧i) *pl.* **out·cries** *n.* a public expression of anger or disapproval

out·date (autdéit) *pres. part.* **out·dat·ing** *past* and *past part.* **out·dat·ed** *v.t.* to make out of date or obsolete

out·dis·tance (autdístəns) *pres. part.* **out·dis·tanc·ing** *past* and *past part.* **out·dis·tanced** *v.t.* to leave far behind in a race, competition etc.

out·do (autdú:) *pres. part.* **out·do·ing** *past* **out·did** (autdíd) *past part.* **out·done** (autdʌ́n) *v.t.* to do better than, surpass, *he outdoes everyone in athletics* **not to be outdone** refusing defeat or loss of advantage **to outdo oneself** to excell oneself

out·door (áutdɔ̧r, áutdo̧ur) *adj.* done or used outside the house ‖ of, in or characteristic of the open air

out·doors (autdɔ́rz, autdóurz) **1.** *adv.* out of the house, *please clean your boots outdoors* ‖ in the open air, *he prefers to be outdoors* **2.** *n.* the out-of-doors

out·er (áutər) **1.** *adj.* farther out or outside, *outer space* ‖ away from the center, *outer edges* ‖ of or pertaining to the outside, *outer clothing* ‖ objective, external, *outer relativity* (cf. INNER) **2.** *n.* the outside ring of a target ‖ a shot striking in this ring

outer city the suburbs

Outer Mongolia *MONGOLIAN PEOPLE'S REPUBLIC

out·er·most (áutərmo̧ust) *adj.* furthest out from the inside or the center, *outermost layers*

Outer Space Treaty of 1960 international agreement for universal protection of all astronauts

out·face (autféis) *pres. part.* **out·fac·ing** *past* and *past part.* **out·faced** *v.t.* to stare down ‖ to resist by bravery, *to outface an enemy* or by effrontery, *to outface one's judges*

out·fall (áutfɔ̧l) *n.* the vent of a drain ‖ the outlet of a river etc.

out·field (áutfi̧:ld) *n.* (*baseball, cricket*) the part of the field farthest from the batter or batsman or the players stationed there ‖ a field at some distance from its holder's farmhouse

out·field·er (áutfi̧:ldər) *n.* (*cricket* and *baseball*) someone who plays in the outfield

out·fit (áutfi̧t) **1.** *n.* articles or instruments required to equip or fit out, *a plumber's outfit* ‖ the act of equipping ‖ clothing etc. for a special purpose, *a tropical outfit* ‖ a collection of components, *a model glider outfit* ‖ (*pop.*) persons making up an organization, institution, regiment etc., *the whole outfit was against him* **2.** *v.t. pres. part.* **out·fit·ting** *past* and *past part.* **out·fi·ted** to supply with an outfit, *to outfit a child for school* ‖ to furnish, supply **óut·fit·ter** *n.* (*commerce*) a retail dealer in readymade clothing, sports material etc.

out·flank (autflǽŋk) *v.t.* (*mil.*) to extend one's own flank beyond the flank of (the enemy) ‖ to circumvent the plans of (an opponent) and retain the advantage

out·flow (áutflo̧u) *n.* a flowing out, *the outflow of science graduates* ‖ the amount of such a flowing out

out·gen·er·al (autdʒénərəl) *pres. part.* **out·gen·er·al·ing,** esp. *Br.* **out·gen·er·al·ling** *past* and *past part.* **out·gen·er·aled,** esp. *Br.* **out·gen·er·alled** *v.t.* to surpass in generalship, outmaneuver

out·go **1.** (áutgo̧u) *pl.* **out·goes** *n.* outflow ‖ expenditure (opp. INCOME) **2.** (autgóu) *pres. part.* **out·go·ing** *past* **out·went** (autwént) *past part.* **out·gone** (autgɔ́n, autgón) *v.t.* to go one better than, with an advantage over

out·go·ing (áutgo̧uiŋ) **1.** *adj.* going out, *the outgoing tide* ‖ leaving, *outgoing ships* ‖ retiring, *the outgoing government* ‖ willing to be sociable **2.** *n.* (*pl.*) outlay, expenditure, *he has heavy outgoings on his new house*

out·grow (autgróu) *pres. part.* **out·grow·ing** *past* **out·grew** (autgrú:) *past part.* **out·grown** (autgróun) *v.t.* to grow too big for, *to outgrow one's shirts* ‖ to grow away from, become too old for, to *outgrow childish habits* ‖ to grow faster than, *he has outgrown his elder brother*

out·growth (áutgro̧uθ) *n.* that which grows out from something, *a woody outgrowth on a tree trunk* ‖ a result, product or by-product

out·gun (autgʌ́n) *v.* (*slang*) to be or do better than someone else

out·haul (áuthɔ̧l) *n.* (*naut.*) a line used for hauling out a sail along a spar

out·house (áutha̧us) *pl.* **out·hous·es** (áutha̧uziz) *n.* a small outbuilding (shed, outdoor toilet etc.)

out·ing (áutiŋ) *n.* a pleasure trip or excursion, sometimes organized for a large number of people, *a family outing* || a walk outdoors || an athletic contest, *a successful first outing* [OUT v.]

out·land·ish (autlǽndiʃ) *adj.* bizarre-looking, *outlandish clothing* || uncouth, *outlandish manners* || very remote and without amenities, *an outlandish place* [O.E. *ūtlendisc* fr. *ūtland*, a foreign land]

out·last (autlǽst, autlɑ́st) *v.t.* to last longer than, outlive

out·law (áutlɔ) *n.* (*hist.*) a person deprived of the protection of the law [O.E. *ūtlaga*]

outlaw *v.t.* to place beyond or deprive of the benefit of the law || to cause, esp. by the force of public opinion, to be no longer tolerated || (*law*) to void the legal force of (an act, contract, claim etc.) [O.E. *ūtlagian, geūtlagian* fr. *ūtlaga*, an outlaw]

out·law·ry (áutlɔri:) *n.* (*hist.*) the process of outlawing || the state of being outlawed [A. F. *utlagerie, utlarie*]

out·lay 1. (áutlei) *n.* expenditure, *crippling outlay on armaments* || an instance of this, *an outlay of two months' wages* **2.** (autléi) *v.t. pres. part.* **out·lay·ing** *past* and *past part.* **out·laid** to expend (money)

out·let (áutlet, áutlit) *n.* an opening which provides a way to the outside, *the outlet of a water pipe, Poland's outlet to the sea* || a means of channeling, *an outlet for one's energies* || a stream flowing from a lake or larger stream etc. || (*commerce*) a market for goods || (*Am.*=*Br.* point) a pair of terminals in an electric wiring system at which current may be taken for use

out·li·er (áutlaiər) *n.* (*geol.*) a separate part of a rock formation detached from the principal part by erosion

out·line (áutlain) **1.** *n.* a line or lines bounding the outer limits of a figure, *the outline of a triangle* or a solid object seen as a plane figure, *the outline of a tree* || the shape defined by such bounding lines, *fill in the outline in red* || a sketch showing only the outer bounding lines || a rough draft of a plan, scheme of work etc. || a short summary, often in note form and omitting detail, *an outline of a syllabus* || a compendious presentation of general features, *an outline of history* || (*pl.*) general principles or chief elements of a subject, *the outlines of English common law* **in outline** drawn etc. so as to show only the outer bounding lines || indicating only the most significant matters **2.** *v.t. pres. part.* **out·lin·ing** *past* and *past part.* **out·lined** to draw or mark the outline of || to give the main points of, *to outline a plan*

out·live (autlív) *pres. part.* **out·liv·ing** *past* and *past part.* **out·lived** *v.t.* to live longer than, survive || to live down, *to outlive a disgrace*

out·look (áutluk) *n.* a prospect or view, *the house has a pleasant outlook* || a prospect for the future, *a bad outlook for employment* || a way of looking at things, *a narrow outlook on life*

out·ly·ing (áutlaiiŋ) *adj.* lying away from the center, *outlying troops* || remote, *outlying villages*

out·ma·neu·ver, out·ma·nœu·vre (autmənú:vər) *pres. part.* **out·ma·neu·ver·ing, out·ma·nœu·vring** *past* and *past part.* **out·ma·neu·vered, out·ma·nœu·vred** *v.t.* to win strategic advantage over by a tactical maneuver || to put oneself by cleverness or smartness in a stronger position than

out·match (autmǽtʃ) *v.t.* to be more than a match for, outdo

out·mod·ed (autmóudid) *adj.* left behind by changes or developments, *outmoded practices* || no longer widely accepted, *outmoded doctrines* || not fashionable, *outmoded dress* [trans. of F. *démodé*]

out·most (áutmoust) *adj.* outermost [var. of older *utmest*, utmost]

out·num·ber (autnʌ́mbər) *v.t.* to be greater than in number

out of *prep.* from the inside of, *out of the house* || from the total of, *10 out of 15* || away from, *out of town* || beyond the reach of, *out of sight* || outside the state or condition of, *out of wedlock* || from (a material etc.), *built out of stone, can you get a skirt out of it?* || due to, *out of hatred* || not having any more of, *out of breath* || (of a foal) born of (a specified dam)

out-of-bounds (áutəvbáundz) *adj.* and *adv.* (*sports*) beyond the limits of the area within which play is legal || beyond the limits of what is acceptable, e.g. as regards behavior

out-of-date (áutəvdéit) *adj.* old-fashioned, *out-of-date clothes* || not current, defective in regard to the present situation, *an out-of-date guidebook*

out-of-door (áutəvdɔ́r, áutəvdóur) *adj.* outdoor

out-of-doors (áutəvdɔ́rz, áutəvdóurz) **1.** *adj.* out-of-door **2.** *n.* everywhere outside the house || the countryside

out of doors *adv.* outdoors

out-of-pock·et (áutəvpɔ́kit) *adj.* (*Br.*, of expenses) for which one will be reimbursed

out-of-the-way (áutəvðəwéi) *adj.* distant, isolated || unusual || (*Br., pop.*, of price, esp. neg.) excessively high

out·pa·tient (áutpeiʃənt) *n.* a person who is treated, but not lodged and fed, in a hospital (opp. INPATIENT)

out·play (autpléi) *v.t.* to play a game better than (an opponent)

out·point (autpɔ́int) *v.t.* to make more points in a game etc. than (an opponent) || (*naut.*) to sail closer to the wind than (an opponent in a race etc.)

out·port (áutpɔrt, áutpourt) *n.* a port outside a town or other port

out·post (áutpoust) *n.* (*mil.*) a position held by a detachment in front of the main body of troops to prevent surprise action || (*mil.*) the soldiers holding this position || a military base established by agreement in another country || a settlement on a frontier or in a remote area

out·pour·ing (áutpɔriŋ, áutpouriŋ) *n.* the act of pouring out || something poured out

out·put (áutput) *n.* the total product of a factory, mill etc. || the amount produced of a specified product || the amount produced by an individual or by one machine || the amount of energy delivered by a machine || the creative work of an artist, *a large output of film music*

output system the portion of a computer or other device that provides data, e.g., paper, tape, cathode ray tube

out·rage (áutreidʒ) **1.** *n.* a violent attack, esp. on people's rights or feelings or property || a flagrant offense against order or dignity or against principles || a feeling of angry resentment provoked by great injustice or offense to one's dignity **to do outrage to** to outrage **2.** *v.t. pres. part.* **out·rag·ing** *past* and *past part.* **out·raged** to subject to an outrage || to make furious or angrily resentful [O.F. *ultrage, oultrage, outrage*]

out·ra·geous (autréidʒəs) *adj.* constituting an outrage || (*pop.*) extravagant, outré, *an outrageous fashion* [O.F. *outrageus, oultrageus*]

out·range (autréindʒ) *pres. part.* **out·rang·ing** *past* and *past part.* **out·ranged** *v.t.* to go beyond in range

out·rank (autrǽŋk) *v.t.* to have a higher rank or greater importance than

ou·tré (u:tréi) *adj.* (*of* dress, opinions etc.) exaggerated to the point of eccentricity || (of behavior) mildly shocking [F.]

out·reach (áutri:tʃ) *n.* **1.** the area of activities beyond the normal **2.** the distant uninhabited areas, e.g., in Australia **3.** (*social service*) provision of services to those unable to seek them

out·ride (autráid) *pres. part.* **out·rid·ing** *past* **out·rode** (autróud) *past part.* **out·rid·den** (autrídn) *v.t.* to ride faster or better than || to ride out (e.g. a storm)

out·rid·er (áutraidər) *n.* a person riding alongside or ahead of someone as protection or to clear the way

out·rig·ger (áutrigər) *n.* a projecting structure of wood etc., e.g. from a mast to extend a sail or from a building to support a hoisting tackle || a projecting metal bracket bearing the oarlock of a sculling boat to give greater leverage || a projecting floating device at one or both sides of some canoes, to prevent upsetting

out·right 1. (autráit, áutrait) *adv.* not by installments or degrees, once for all, *to destroy outright* || openly, straightforwardly, *tell him outright* **2.** *adj.* (áutrait) thorough, downright, *outright denial* || complete, *outright fraud*

out·ri·val (autráivəl) *pres. part.* **out·ri·val·ing,** esp. *Br.* **out·ri·val·ling** *past* and *past part.* **out·ri·valed,** esp. *Br.* **out·ri·valled** *v.t.* to do better than (a rival)

out·run (autrʌ́n) *pres. part.* **out·run·ning** *past* **out·ran** (autrǽn) *past part.* **out·run** *v.t.* to run faster than || (*fig.*) to go beyond the limits of, *his ambition outran his talents*

out·sell (autsél) *pres. part.* **out·sell·ing** *past* and *past part.* **out·sold** (autsóuld) *v.t.* to sell more than || (of a product) to exceed (another) in sales

out·set (áutset) *n.* the first stage, the beginning

out·shine (autʃáin) *pres. part.* **out·shin·ing** *past* and *past part.* **out·shone** (autʃóun), **out·shined** *v.t.* to shine brighter than || to surpass, *she outshone all rivals*

out·shoot (autʃú:t) *pres. part.* **out·shoot·ing** *past* and *past part.* **out·shot** (autʃɔ́t) *v.t.* to surpass in shooting

out·side (áutsáid, áutsaid) **1.** *n.* the surface, exterior, outer parts || the space or region situated beyond a boundary, or other limit || external appearance || superficial aspect **at the outside** (or **very outside**) at the most, *there were 20 people there at the outside* **2.** *adj.* on, of or nearer the outside || of, pertaining to or being the outer side of a curve, circle etc., *the outside wheel* || carried on out-of-doors, *outside activities* || (*Br., radio* or *television*) originating away from the studio || from a source other than some specified or understood group, *an outside opinion* || involving an extreme limit, *an outside estimate* || not connected with one's main work or preoccupation, *outside interests* || (of a chance) just within the limit of possibility **3.** *adv.* on or to the outside || out-of-doors **4.** *prep.* on or to the outer side of, *wait outside the office* || beyond the limits of, *outside the town* || apart from, other than, *no one knows outside the family*

out·sid·er (autsáidər) *n.* a person not included in some particular group, party, clique etc. || (*Br.*) a person held unfit to mix in good society || a competitor (horse, athlete etc.) believed to have only an outside chance in a race

out·size (áutsaiz) **1.** *n.* an unusually large size of clothing || an article of clothing of such a size **2.** *adj.* uncommonly large

out·skirts (áutskə:rts) *pl. n.* outlying parts remote from the center

out·smart (autsmɑ́rt) *v.t.* to outwit

out·spo·ken (autspóukən) *adj.* said without fear of the consequences, *outspoken criticism* || not conventionally or prudently reticent, *an outspoken book*

out·spread (áutspréd) **1.** *pres. part.* **out·spread·ing** *past* and *past part.* **out·spread** *v.t.* and (*rhet.*) to spread out **2.** *adj.* (*rhet.*) stretched or spread out

out·stand·ing (autstǽndiŋ) *adj.* conspicuous, standing out, *an outstanding feature of the landscape* || remarkable, *an outstanding achievement* || not yet settled or completed, *outstanding debts*

out·sta·tion (áutsteiʃən) *n.* an outlying station or settlement

out·stay (autstéi) *v.t.* to stay longer than || to surpass in staying power **to outstay one's welcome** to stay longer than one's hosts wish

out·stretched (áutstretʃt) *adj.* stretched out, *to lie outstretched*

out·strip (autstríp) *pres. part.* **out·strip·ping** *past* and *past part.* **out·stripped** *v.t.* to go at a quicker rate than and leave behind [OUT+obs. *strip*, to outstrip]

out·vote (autvóut) *pres. part.* **out·vot·ing** *past* and *past part.* **out·vot·ed** *v.t.* to defeat by a majority of votes

out·ward (áutwərd) **1.** *adj.* moving or directed toward the outside || exterior, *the outward appearance of the house* || superficial, *an outward appearance of calm* **2.** *adv.* towards the outside and away from the inside [O.E. *ūtweard*]

out·ward-bound (áutwərdbáund) *adj.* (of a ship) traveling away from the home port

out·ward·ly (áutwərdli:) *adv.* externally, *outwardly visible* || on the surface, *outwardly calm*

out·wards (áutwərdz) *adv.* outward [O.E. *ūtweardes*]

Outward WATS a Bell System long-distance telephone service that provides for bulk-rated outgoing station-to-station calls within geographical service areas

out·wear (autwέər) *pres. part.* **out·wear·ing** *past* **out·wore** (autwɔ́r, autwóur) *past part.* **out·worn** (autwɔ́rn, autwóurn) *v.t.* to last longer in use than, *this shirt will outwear three ordinary ones*

out·weigh (autwéi) *v.t.* to exceed in weight or importance

out·wit (autwít) *pres. part.* **out·wit·ting** *past* and *past part.* **out·wit·ted** *v.t.* to defeat by cleverness or cunning

out·work (áutwə:rk) *n.* a part of a defense system outside the principal fortifications || work subcontracted by a business and done off the premises

out·worn (áutwɔ́rn, áutwóurn) *past part.* of OUTWEAR ‖ *adj.* worn out, deprived of force by excessive use, *outworn quotations* ‖ outlived, *outworn conventions*

OV (*acronym*) orbiter vehicle, a space vehicle designed to orbit a celestial body

ova *pl.* of OVUM

o·val (óuvəl) **1.** *adj.* having the form of an ellipse ‖ egg-shaped **2.** *n.* an oval figure or shape [Mod. L. *ovalis* fr. *ovum* egg]

O·van·do Can·dia (ɔvɑ́ndɔkɑ́ndjɑ), Alfredo (1918–), Bolivian general, leader of the junta which deposed (1969) Siles Salinas shortly after the death of Gen. Rene Barrientos, and president (1969–70)

o·var·i·an (ouvέəri:ən) *adj.* of or pertaining to an ovary or the ovaries [fr. Mod. L. *ovarium*, ovary]

o·var·i·ec·to·my (ouvεəri:éktəmi:) *pl.* **o·var·i·ec·to·mies** *n.* (*surgery*) the removal of one or both ovaries [fr. Mod. L. *ovarium*, ovary+Gk *tomē*, a cutting]

o·var·i·ot·o·my (ouvεəri:ɒ́təmi:) *pl.* **o·var·i·ot·o·mies** *n.* (*surgery*) the incision of the ovary ‖ an ovariectomy [fr. Mod. L. *ovarium*, ovary+Gk *tomē*, cutting]

o·va·ry (óuvəri:) *pl.* **o·va·ries** *n.* one of a pair of female reproductive organs that produce eggs and (in vertebrates) female sex hormones (*ESTROGEN). These hormones are responsible for the production of female sexual characteristics (e.g. growth of breasts, shape of hips, tone of voice) and for the maintenance of the process of periodic fertility which in primates is known as the menstrual cycle (*ENDOCRINE GLAND) ‖ (*bot.*) the hollow chamber in which ovules are borne in angiospermous plants [fr. Mod. L. *ovarium* fr. *ovum* egg]

o·vate (óuveit) *adj.* (*biol.*) egg-shaped ‖ (*bot.*, of leaves) shaped like the outline of an egg, with the broad end at the base [fr. L. *ovatus*]

o·va·tion (ouvéiʃən) *n.* an enthusiastic public welcome, esp. a spontaneous outburst of applause expressing this [fr. L. *ovatio* (*ovarionis*) fr. *ovare*, to rejoice]

ov·en (ʌ́vən) *n.* an enclosed cavity of stone, brick, metal etc. for baking, roasting, heating or drying [O.E. *ofn, ofen*]

ov·en·bird (ʌ́vənbə:rd) *n.* a member of *Furnarius*, fam. *Furnariidae*, a genus of passerine birds native to South America. Their globular, oven-shaped nests, largely of clay and mud, have a winding entrance and inner partition ‖ *Seiurus aurocapillus*, an American warbler

o·ver (óuvər) **1.** *prep.* above, *the umbrella over his head* ‖ spread on the surface of, *paper littered over the desk* ‖ so as to cover, *ink spilled over the book* ‖ so as to close, *stretched over the neck of the bottle*‖ in excess of, *over a thousand books* ‖ while occupied with, *let's talk about it over a glass of beer* ‖ near, *he dozed over the fire* ‖ so as to dominate, influence, change the opinion of etc., *a mood has come over him* ‖ in authority with respect to, *he rules over two million people* ‖ in a relationship of superiority to, *he increased his lead over them* ‖ across or above and to the other side of, *it flew over the field* ‖ on the other side of, *he lives over the hill* ‖ along, *drive over the new route* ‖ by means of, *over the telephone* ‖ throughout, in every part of, *she traveled over the whole Commonwealth* ‖ during, *over several days* ‖ more than, *over 100 pounds* ‖ covered or submerged up to, *over his knees in water* ‖ up to and including, *you must stay over Tom's birthday* ‖ about, concerned, in regard to, *we quarreled over the color* ‖ in preference to, *he chose the cheaper model over the more expensive one* ‖ across and down from, *he fell over the edge* ‖ against and across the top of, *she stumbled over the mat* **2.** *adv.* across, *throw it over to me* ‖ across and down from an edge, height etc. ‖ expressing upward and outward motion from a container, *the milk boiled over*‖ so as to turn the upper surface forward and down, *fold it over* ‖ from one side to the other, *to turn over, he has gone over to the other party* ‖ expressing movement away from the perpendicular, *to knock a chair over, to fall over* ‖ so as to cover or change the whole surface, *whitewash it over* ‖ across a space or distance, *over in Ireland* ‖ away from a specified place, *in the next house over* ‖ (*pop.*) to one's or someone's house, *come over tonight* ‖ more, *it weighs two pounds and over* ‖ until a later time, *hold the work over* ‖ at the end or finish, *holidays are over* ‖ from beginning to end, *read it over* ‖ with thorough, precise and concentrated effort or attention, *talk the case over* ‖ in repetition, *count it three times over* ‖ afresh, *do it over again* ‖ from one person to another, *hand over the keys* **3.** *adj.* in excess, *the total was five dollars over* ‖ (*Br.*) remaining, left, *is there any soup over?* **4.** *n.* (*mil.*) a shot that falls beyond the target ‖ (*Br.*, esp. *pl.*) something in excess ‖ (*cricket*) the number of balls (usually six or eight) allowed between two calls of 'over!' from the umpire and bowled from each wicket alternately ‖ (*cricket*) the play during this period [O.E. *ofer*]

over- *prefix* over (adj., prep., adv.)

o·ver·act (ouvərǽkt) *v.t.* to act (a part) in an exaggerated way ‖ *v.i.* to perform or act in an exaggerated way

over again once more

over against as opposed to, in contradistinction to

o·ver·age (óuvəridʒ) *n.* (*commerce*) a surplus of goods

o·ver·age (óuvəréidʒ) *adj.* beyond a specified or usual age

o·ver·all (óuvərɔl) *n.* (*pl.*) loose trousers of durable material, with apron and shoulder straps, worn when doing heavy or dirty jobs ‖ (*Br.*) a coverall

overall *adj.* including everything, total, *the overall cost* ‖ from end to end, *overall length*

over and above in addition to, besides, *a sum over and above the original estimate*

over and over again and again, repeatedly

over and over again repeatedly

o·ver·arch (ouvərɑ́rtʃ) *v.t.* to form an arch over ‖ *v.i.* to form an arch

o·ver·arm (óuvərɑrm) *adj.* (esp. *Br.*) done with the arm raised above the shoulder ‖ of a swimming stroke in which the arm is lifted out of the water over the shoulder

o·ver·awe (ouvərɔ́) *pres. part.* **o·ver·aw·ing** *past* and *past part.* **o·ver·awed** *v.t.* to bring under submission or cause to feel humble by the effect of one's presence or manner or by majesty, beauty etc.

o·ver·bal·ance (ouvərbǽləns) *pres. part.* **o·ver·bal·anc·ing** *past* and *past part.* **o·ver·bal·anced** *v.t.* to cause to lose balance ‖ *v.i.* to lose one's or its balance

o·ver·bear (ouvərbέər) *pres. part.* **o·ver·bear·ing** *past* **o·ver·bore** (ouvərbɔ́r, ouvərbóur) *past part.* **o·ver·borne** (ouvərbɔ́rn, ouvərbóurn) *v.t.* to bear down by greater force, weight, determination etc. *v.i.* to bear excessively (e.g. of a fruit tree) **o·ver·béar·ing** *adj.* aggressively masterful

o·ver·bid **1.** (ouvərbíd) *v. pres. part.* **o·ver·bid·ding** *past* and *past part.* **o·ver·bid** *v.t.* to bid more than (someone) ‖ to bid more than the value of (something) ‖ (*Am.*=*Br.* overcall) to bid more than the value of (a hand of cards) ‖ (*Br.*, *cards*) to overcall (a preceding bid or player) ‖ **2.** (óuvərbid) *n.* an instance of bidding more than someone or more then the value of something

o·ver·blown (ouvərblóun) *adj.* (*of* flowers) just past full bloom [fr. OVER-+obs. *blow*, to blossom]

overblown *adj.* blowzy ‖ (of style) pretentious, windy [fr. older *overblow*, to blow excessively]

o·ver·board (óuvərbɔrd, óuvərbourd) *adv.* over the side of a ship etc., *to fall overboard* **to go overboard** to go to extremes

o·ver·bold (óuvərbóuld) *adj.* excessively bold

o·ver·book (ouvərbúk) *v.* to accept reservations beyond capacity, esp. for hotel and transportation facilities

o·ver·build (ouvərbíld) *pres. part.* **o·ver·build·ing** *past* and *past part.* **o·ver·built** (ouvərbílt) *v.i.* to build in excess of needs, market capacity etc. ‖ *v.t.* to build more buildings than are needed in (an area)

o·ver·bur·den (ouvərbə́:rd'n) *v.t.* to load or burden to excess

o·ver·buy (ouvərbái) *pres. part.* **o·ver·buy·ing** *past* and *past part.* **o·ver·bought** (ouvərbɔ́t) *v.t.* to buy in quantities greater than the demand ‖ *v.i.* to buy to excess, esp. beyond one's means or needs

o·ver·call **1.** (ouvərkɔ́l) *v.t.* (*cards*) to bid more than (the preceding bid or player) ‖ (*Br.*) to overbid (a hand of cards) **2.** (óuvərkɔl) *n.* (*Br., cards*) a bid which is more than one's partner's bid ‖ (*cards*) a bid which is more than the preceding bid ‖ an overbid

o·ver·cap·i·tal·ize (ouvərkǽpit'laiz) *pres. part.* **o·ver·cap·i·tal·iz·ing** *past* and *past part.* **o·ver·cap·i·tal·ized** *v.t.* to fix or estimate the capital of (a company etc.) higher than the actual cost or market value ‖ *v.i.* to put an unnecessarily large amount of capital in a business enterprise

o·ver·cast **1.** (ouvərkǽst, ouvərkɑ́st) *v.t. pres. part.* **o·ver·cast·ing** *past* and *past part.* **o·ver·cast** (*sewing*) to stitch (raw edges) to prevent unraveling **2.** (óuvərkæst, óuvərkɑst) *adj.* cloudy, covered with clouds

o·ver·cen·tral·i·za·tion (ouvərsentrəlizéiʃən) *n.* excessive concentration of power or control at one point, usu. at headquarters

o·ver·charge **1.** (ouvərtʃɑ́rdʒ) *v. pres. part.* **o·ver·charg·ing** *past* and *past part.* **o·ver·charged** *v.t.* to charge (someone) too high a price ‖ to charge (an amount) in excess of a specified price ‖ to load too highly with electricity, explosive etc., or as if with these, *to overcharge a story with emotion* ‖ *v.i.* to charge excessively **2.** (óuvərtʃɑrdʒ) *n.* an excessive charge

o·ver·choice (óuvərtʃɔis) *n.* availability of too many choices

o·ver·cloud (ouvərkláud) *v.t.* to cover over with clouds or shadows ‖ to be a worrying or saddening presence in, *fear of madness overclouded her last years*

o·ver·coat (óuvərkout) *n.* a warm coat worn over ordinary clothes in cold weather

o·ver·come (ouvərkʌ́m) *pres. part.* **o·ver·com·ing** *past* **o·ver·came** (ouvərkéim) *past part.* **o·ver·come** *v.t.* (*rhet.*) to conquer, *to overcome one's enemies* ‖ to get the better of, *sleep overcame him* ‖ to overpower or overwhelm (a person) physically, *he was overcome by the gas fumes* or emotionally, *she was overcome by fear* [O. E. *ofercuman*]

o·ver·con·fi·dent (ouvərkɒ́nfidənt) *adj.* more confident than is warranted

o·ver·con·tain (ouvərkəntéin) *v.* excessive restraint, e.g., of emotions

o·ver·crop (ouvərkrɒ́p) *pres. part.* **o·ver·crop·ping** *past* and *past part.* **o·ver·cropped** *v.t.* to exhaust the fertility of (a piece of land) by taking too many crops from it

o·ver·crowd (ouvərkráud) *v.t.* to crowd more people or things in (a given space) than there is room for or than is desirable or permitted

o·ver·cul·ture (óuvərkʌltʃər) *n.* the underlying culture of a society

o·ver·de·vel·op (ouvərdivéləp) *v.t.* to develop too much ‖ (*photog.*) to develop (a plate or film) for too long or at too high a temperature etc.

o·ver·do (ouvərdú:) *pres. part.* **over·do·ing** *past* **o·ver·did** (ouvərdíd) *past. part.* **o·ver·done** (ouvərdʌ́n) *v.t.* to exaggerate, carry too far, *he rather overdid his gratitude* ‖ (esp. *past part.*) to cook too long **to overdo it** to overtax one's strength ‖ to make too great a display

o·ver·dose **1.** (ouvərdóus) *v.t. pres. part.* **o·ver·dos·ing** *past* and *past part.* **o·ver·dosed** to give an excessive dose to **2.** (óuvərdous) *n.* an excessive dose

o·ver·draft (óuvərdræft, óuvərdrɑft) *n.* the overdrawing of a bank account ‖ the sum overdrawn ‖ (*Br.* esp. **o·ver·draught**) a draft passing over a fire in a furnace

overdraft checking account (*banking*) a checking account that permits drawing of checks in excess of credit balance up to a preset amount

o·ver·draw (ouvərdrɔ́) *pres. part.* **o·ver·draw·ing** *past* **o·ver·drew** (ouvərdrú:) *past part.* **o·ver·drawn** (ouvərdrɔ́n) *v.t.* to write a bank check for more money than is in (one's account) ‖ to exaggerate, *the characters in the novel were heavily overdrawn* ‖ *v.i.* to overdraw a bank account

o·ver·dress (ouvərdrés) *v.t.* to dress (someone) too showily or too smartly ‖ *v.i.* to dress in this way

o·ver·drive **1.** (óuvərdraiv) *n.* a system of very high gearing to save waste of a car's engine power at high speeds. An automatic transmission gear passes a higher speed to the propeller shaft than the speed maintained by the engine **2.** *v.t.* (ouvərdráiv) *pres. part.* **o·ver·driv·ing** *past* **o·ver·drove** (ouvərdróuv) *past part.* **o·ver·dri·ven** (ouvərdrivən) to overwork

o·ver·dub (óuvərdʌb) *v.* (*acoustics*) to add instrumental portions or voices to a finished recording

o·ver·due (ouvərdú:, ouvərdjú:) *adj.* not paid by the time it was due, *an overdue bill* ‖ behind the scheduled time of arrival, *the plane is overdue* ‖ more than ready, *overdue for independence*

o·ver·eat (ouvərí:t) *pres. part.* **o·ver·eat·ing** *past* **o·ver·ate** (ouvəréit, *Br.* also ouvərét) *past part.* **o·ver·eat·en** (ouvərí:t'n) *v.i.* to eat to the point of satiety and then eat more

o·ver·ed·u·cate (ouvərédʒukeit) *v.* to train to an unneeded capacity

CONCISE PRONUNCIATION KEY: **(a)** æ, *cat*; ɑ, *car*; ɔ *fawn*; ei, *snake*. **(e)** e, *hen*; i:, *sheep*; iə, *deer*; εə, *bear*. **(i)** i, *fish*; ai, *tiger*; ə:, *bird*. **(o)** o, *ox*; au, *cow*; ou, *goat*; u, *poor*; ɔi, *royal*. **(u)** ʌ, *duck*; u, *bull*; u:, *goose*; ə, *bacillus*; ju:, *cube*. x, *loch*; θ, *think*; ð, *bother*; z, *Zen*; ʒ, *corsage*; dʒ, *savage*; ŋ, *orangutang*; j, *yak*; ʃ, *fish*; tʃ, *fetch*; 'l, *rabble*; 'n, *redden*. Complete pronunciation key appears inside front cover.

o·ver·em·pha·size (ouvərémfəsaiz) *pres. part.* **o·ver·em·pha·siz·ing** *past* and *past part.* **o·ver·em·pha·sized** *v.t.* to put undue emphasis on

o·ver·em·ploy·ment (ouvərimplɔ́imənt) *n.* (*econ.*) the condition of having more jobs available than there is labor to fill them

o·ver·es·ti·mate 1. (ouvəréstəmeit) *v. pres. part.* **o·ver·es·ti·mat·ing** *past* and *past part.* **o·ver·es·ti·mat·ed** *v.t.* to put the value, amount etc. of (something) too high ‖ *v.i.* to make too high an estimate **2.** (óuvəréstəmit) *n.* an estimate that is too high

o·ver·ex·ploi·ta·tion (ouvəriksplɔitéiʃən) *n.* (*envir.*) to remove more of a natural resource than can be replaced

o·ver·ex·pose (ouvərikspóuz) *pres. part.* **o·ver·ex·pos·ing** *past* and *past part.* **o·ver·ex·posed** *v.t.* to expose excessively ‖ (*photog.*) to expose (a film etc.) for longer than is desirable

o·ver·fire air (óuvərfaiərέər) air forced into the top of an incinerator to fan the flame

o·ver·flow (ouvərflóu) *v.t.* (of liquids) to flow over the brim of, *the river overflowed its banks* ‖ to flood, *the river overflowed the surrounding countryside* ‖ *v.i.* to flood, spill over ‖ to be abundant, *their generosity overflows* [O.E. *oferflōwan*]

o·ver·flow (óuvərflou) *n.* a flowing over ‖ something which flows over ‖ an outlet or receptacle for excess fluids

o·ver·glaze 1. (ouvərgléiz, óuvərgleiz) *v.t. pres. part.* **o·ver·glaz·ing** *past* and *past part.* **o·ver·glazed** to glaze over, e.g. in painting, pottery etc. **2.** (óuvərgleiz) n. a glaze applied over another glaze **3.** *adj.* (óuvərgleiz) done on glaze, *overglaze painting*

o·ver·grown (óuvərgróun) *adj.* grown over with rank weeds etc., *an overgrown garden* ‖ grown to an excessive size [past part. of older *overgrow*]

o·ver·growth (óuvərgrouθ) *n.* excessive growth ‖ dense vegetation, esp. of weeds, *a rank overgrowth of nettles*

o·ver·hand (óuvərhænd) **1.** *adj.* thrown or executed with the hand above shoulder level ‖ sewn with stitches over two edges forming a seam **2.** *adv.* in an overhand way **3.** *n.* an overhand stroke or delivery an overhand seam **4.** *v.t.* to sew with overhand stitches **ó·ver·hand·ed** *adj.* and *adv.* overhand

o·ver·hang 1. (ouvərhǽŋ) *v. pres. part.* **o·ver·hang·ing** *past* and *past part.* **o·ver·hung** (ouvərhʌ́ŋ) *v.t.* to jut out over, *medieval houses overhung the street* ‖ *v.i.* to project **2.** (óuvərhæŋ) *n.* the part or amount that hangs over

o·ver·haul 1. (ouvərhɔ́l) *v.t.* to examine thoroughly and repair or correct defects in ‖ (esp. *naut.*) to overtake ‖ (*naut.*) to loosen (a rope) by hauling it through the block in the opposite direction to that in which it was hoisted ‖ (*naut.*) to release the blocks of (a tackle) **2.** (óuvərhɔl) *n.* a thorough examination followed by the necessary repairs, renovations etc.

o·ver·head (óuvərhed) **1.** *adj.* located. working etc. above one's head ‖ (of expenses) due to charges necessary to the carrying on of a business **2.** *n.* (*collect.*) expenses which are a general charge to a business and cannot be allotted to a particular job or process (e.g. rent, light, depreciation, administration, insurance, as opposed to materials, wages etc.) ‖ (*Br.*) an item of such expenditure **3.** *adv.* (óuvərhéd) above one's head

o·ver·hear (ouvərhíər) *pres. part.* **o·ver·hear·ing** *past* and *past part.* **o·ver·heard** (ouvərhə́:rd) *v.t.* to hear (conversation etc.) accidentally or by eavesdropping

o·ver·heat (ouvərhí:t) *v.i.* to become too hot ‖ *v.t.* to cause to become too hot ‖ to cause to become cross and excited

o·ver·hit (ouvərhít) *v.* (*sports*) to strike harder than necessary, e.g., a tennis ball

o·ver·housed (ouvərháuzd) *adj.* having excess or excessive housing accommodations

O·ver·ijs·sel (ouvəráis'l) a province (area 1,254 sq. miles, pop. 1,027,836) of the E. Netherlands. Capital: Zwolle

o·ver·in·dulge (ouvərindʌ́ldʒ) *pres. part.* **o·ver·in·dulg·ing** *past* and *past part.* **o·ver·in·dulged** *v.t.* to treat with inordinate indulgence ‖ *v.i.* to indulge in something (esp. food and drink) to excess

o·ver·in·flat·ed (ouvərinfléitid) *adj.* excessively overstated

o·ver·in·ter·pre·ta·tion (ouvərintə:rpritéiʃən) *n.* interpreting beyond the meanings intended

o·ver·is·sue (ouvəríʃu:, *Br.* ouvərísju:) **1.** *n.* an issue of notes, shares, bonds etc. in excess of the authorized amount or available capital **2.** *v.t. pres. part.* **o·ver·is·su·ing** *past* and *past part.* **o·ver·is·sued** to issue in excess

o·ver·joyed (ouvərdʒɔ́id) *adj.* exceedingly delighted [past part. of older *overjoy*]

o·ver·kill (óuvərkil) **1.** *n.* national capacity in nuclear armament over and above what would be needed to destroy an enemy ‖ an instance of destruction using this capacity **2.** *v.* to exert more force than necessary, e.g., having the effect of extirpating several times over

o·ver·lad·en (ouvərléid'n) *adj.* loaded or burdened too heavily

o·ver·land (óuvərlænd, óuvərlənd) **1.** *adv.* by land rather than sea **2.** *adj.* going or made entirely or partly by land

o·ver·lap 1. (ouvərlǽp) *v. pres. part.* **o·ver·lap·ping** *past* and *past part.* **o·ver·lapped** *v.t.* to cover partly ‖ to cover and extend beyond ‖ *v.i.* to coincide partly **2.** *n.* (óuvərlæp) an instance or place of overlapping ‖ the extent of overlapping ‖ the part that overlaps

o·ver·lay 1. (ouvərléi) *v.t. pres. part.* **o·ver·lay·ing** *past* and *past part.* **o·ver·laid** (ouvərléid) to cover the surface of ‖ (*printing*) to put an overlay on or get the overlay ready for **2.** *n.* (óuvərlei) a covering ‖ an ornamental covering of veneer etc. ‖ (*printing*) a layer of material used to secure a sharp, even impression by correcting for difference of metal height etc. ‖ a sheet of tracing paper laid over e.g. a cartographer's rough map, for corrections to be indicated, or one bearing matter to be taken in conjunction with other matter, e.g. a grid to be placed over an air photograph

o·ver·lie (ouvərlái) *pres. part.* **o·ver·ly·ing** *past* **o·ver·lay** (ouvərléi) *past part.* **o·ver·lain** (ouvərléin) *v.t.* to lie over or on [early M.E. *oferliggen*]

o·ver·load 1. (ouvərlóud) *v.t.* to load too heavily **2.** (óuvərloud) *n.* a load, charge etc. which is excessive

o·ver·look (ouvərlúk) *v.t.* to look over from above, *our house overlooks the valley* ‖ to decide not to punish, *to overlook someone's carelessness* ‖ to fail to notice, *he overlooked several errors* **o·ver·lóok·er** *n.* an overseer

o·ver·lord (oúvərlɔrd) *n.* (*hist.*) a feudal superior from whom lords held land and to whom they owed service ‖ an absolute ruler

o·ver·ly (óuvərli:) *adv.* excessively

o·ver·man (ouvərmǽn) *pres. part.* **o·ver·man·ning** *past* and *past part.* **o·ver·manned** *v.t.* to have or supply too many men for (a given purpose or place)

o·ver·man·tel (óuvərmænt'l) *n.* an ornamental structure, often with a mirror, over a mantel

o·ver·mark (ouvərmárk) *v.* to give higher grades than are warranted

o·ver·mas·ter·ing (ouvərmǽstəriŋ, ouvərmástəriŋ) *adj.* dominating, uncontrollable

o·ver·much (óuvərmʌtʃ) **1.** *adv.* to any great degree, *he doesn't enjoy such occasions overmuch* **2.** *adj.* too much, *there was overmuch drinking at the dinner*

o·ver·nice (óuvərnáis) *adj.* too scrupulous or particular

o·ver·night 1. (óuvərnáit) *adv.* during or for the night ‖ during the night just past **2.** (óuvərnait) *adj.* during the evening or night, *an overnight journey* ‖ lasting or staying one night, *overnight guests* ‖ used for a single night, *an overnight case* ‖ happening etc. in the space of one night, *overnight success*

o·ver·nu·tri·tion (ouvərnu:tríʃən) *n.* overeating, overfeeding

o·ver·oc·cu·pied (ouvərɔ́kju:paid) *adj.* crowded

o·ver·pass 1. (óuvərpæs, óuvərpɑs) *n.* (*Am.=Br.* flyover) a raised crossing, e.g. of a road over a railroad **2.** (ouvərpǽs, ouvərpás) *pres. part.* **o·ver·pass·ing** *past* **o·ver·passed** *past part.* **o·ver·passed, o·ver·past** *v.t.* to pass over, travel over, go beyond (e.g. an area) ‖ to get through, surmount (e.g. a difficulty) ‖ to go beyond, surpass in amount, value etc. ‖ to overlook, omit

o·ver·per·form (ouvərpərfɔ́rm) *v.* exceeding the intention of directions

o·ver·per·suade (ouvərpərswéid) *pres. part.* **o·ver·per·suad·ing** *past* and *past part.* **o·ver·per·suad·ed** *v.t.* to persuade (someone) to come to one's own point of view even against his own inclinations or better judgment

o·ver·play (ouvərpléi) *v.t.* to overact (a part) ‖ to make too much of, overstress ‖ (*cards*) to play (a hand) too optimistically ‖ (*golf*) to strike a ball beyond (the green)

o·ver·plus (óuvərplʌs) *n.* a surplus

o·ver·pow·er (ouvərpáuər) *v.t.* to overcome physically, *he overpowered the thief, the heat overpowered him* to supply with more power than is desirable or necessary

o·ver·pre·scribe (ouvərpriskráib) *v.* (*med.*) to prescribe more drugs than are required —**o·ver·pre·scrip·tion** *n.* the practice

o·ver·pres·sure (óuvərpreʃər) *n.* (*mil.*) **1.** the pressure resulting from the blast wave of an explosion, positive when it exceeds atmospheric pressure and negative during the passage of the wave when resulting pressures are less than atmospheric pressure **2.** the atmospheric pressure above normal expressed in lbs per sq in, creating a blast wave in a nuclear explosion

o·ver·print 1. (ouvərprínt) *v.t.* (*printing*) to print (matter) on top of something already printed ‖ (*printing*) to print matter on top of (something already printed) ‖ (*photog.*) to print too long or with excess of light ‖ to print too many copies of ‖ (*philately*) to make an overprint on (a stamp) **2.** (óuvərprint) n. (*philately*) a word, device, figure etc. printed across the surface of a stamp to alter its value or use ‖ a stamp bearing such a print ‖ something printed over other printed matter

o·ver·prize (ouvərpráiz) *pres. part.* **o·ver·priz·ing** *past* and *past part.* **o·ver·prized** *v.t.* to value excessively

o·ver·pro·duce (ouvərprədú:s, ouvərprədjú:s) *pres. part.* **o·ver·pro·duc·ing** *past* and *past part.* **o·ver·pro·duced** *v.t.* to produce in excess of demand or predetermined goals **o·ver·pro·duc·tion** (ouvərprədʌ́kʃən) *n.*

o·ver·proof (óuvərprú:f) *adj.* having higher alcoholic content than proof spirit

o·ver·qual·i·fied (ouvərkwɒ́lifaid) *adj.* having background and/or abilities beyond those required for a situation, e.g., a job

o·ver·quan·ti·fi·ca·tion (ouvərkwɒntifikéiʃən) *n.* placing too much emphasis on the quantity involved in a process

o·ver·rate (ouvərréit) *pres. part.* **o·ver·rat·ing** *past* and *past part.* **o·ver·rat·ed** *v.t.* to value or prize too highly ‖ (*Br.*) to rate (property) too highly

o·ver·reach (ouvərrí:tʃ) *v.t.* to defeat (oneself or one's purposes) by being too ambitious, too clever, too grasping etc. ‖ *v.i.* (of a horse) to strike the forefoot with the hind hoof

o·ver·ride (ouvərráid) *pres. part.* **o·ver·rid·ing** *past* **o·ver·rode** (ouvərróud) *past part.* **o·ver·rid·den** (ouvərríd'n) *v.t.* to decide to disregard or go against ‖ to dominate, *fear overrode all other emotions* ‖ to ride (a horse) beyond its strength ‖ of a broken bone) to overlap (another) [O.E. *oferrīdan*, to ride across]

o·ver·ripe (óuvərráip) *adj.* too ripe

o·ver·rule (ouvərrú:l) *pres. part.* **o·ver·rul·ing** *past* and *past part.* **o·ver·ruled** *v.t.* to give a legal decision or ruling about something which goes against (the decision or ruling of a lower authority)

o·ver·run 1. (ouvərrʌ́n) *v.t. pres. part.* **o·ver·run·ning** *past* **o·ver·ran** (ouvərrǽn) *past part.* **o·ver·run** (esp. *mil.*) to attack and obtain complete mastery over by weight of numbers, *they overran the enemy positions* ‖ to infest, *rats overran the house* ‖ to extend or go beyond (in space or time) ‖ (*printing*) to move (letters or words) from one line to another or (a line or lines) from one page to another, because of an addition or delection **2.** (óuvərrʌn) *n.* an overrunning ‖ the amount of this ‖ a clear area beyond a runway used in case of emergency in landing an aircraft

o·ver·sea 1. (óuvərsi:) *adv.* (*Br.*) overseas **2.** (óuvərsi:) *adj.* (*Br.*) overseas

o·ver·seas 1. (óuvərsí:z) *adv.* beyond the sea **2.** (óuvərsi:z) *adj.* of or pertaining to countries or people or things beyond the sea

o·ver·see (ouvərsí:) *pres. part.* **o·ver·see·ing** *past* **o·ver·saw** (ouvərsɔ́) *past part.* **o·ver·seen** (ouvərsí:n) *v.t.* to supervise, direct, *he oversees the export department* **ó·ver·se·er** *n.* a person in charge of work, a foreman or supervisor [O.E. *oferséon*]

o·ver·sell (ouvərsél) *pres. part.* **o·ver·sell·ing** *past* and *past part.* **o·ver·sold** (ouvərsóuld) *v.t.* (*commerce*) to sell more of (a commodity, stock etc.) than one can deliver or that can be bought with advantage ‖ (*pop.*) to praise too highly, make excessive claims for ‖ (*pop.*) to cause (someone) to expect something better than the reality

o·ver·sew (óuvərsou) *pres. part.* **o·ver·sew·ing** *past* **o·ver·sewed** *past part.* **o·ver·sewed,**

CONCISE PRONUNCIATION KEY: **(a)** æ, *cat*; ɑ, *car*; ɔ *fawn*; ei, *snake*. **(e)** e, *hen*; i:, *sheep*; iə, *deer*; εə, *bear*. **(i)** i, *fish*; ai, *tiger*; ə:, *bird*. **(o)** o, *ox*; au, *cow*; ou, *goat*; u, *poor*; ɔi, *royal*. **(u)** ʌ, *duck*; u, *bull*; u:, *goose*; ə, *bacillus*; ju:, *cube*. x, *loch*; θ, *think*; ð, *bother*; z, *Zen*; ʒ, *corsage*; dʒ, *savage*; ŋ, *orangutang*; j, *yak*; ʃ, *fish*; tʃ, *fetch*; 'l, *rabble*; 'n, *redden*. Complete pronunciation key appears inside front cover.

o·ver·sewn (óuvərsoun) *v.t.* to sew (a seam) or sew (two pieces of material) together with vertical stitches passing over the outside edge or edges ‖ to overcast

o·ver·sha·dow (ouvərʃǽdou) *v.t.* to cast a shade over ‖ to cause to seem to have less than full merit, because of detrimental comparisons, *he is overshadowed by his brilliant brother* [O.E. *ofersceadwian*]

o·ver·shoe (óuvərʃu:) *n.* a shoe or boot worn over a shoe for warmth or protection against wet

o·ver·shoot (ouvərʃú:t) *pres. part.* **o·ver·shoot·ing** *past* and *past part.* **o·ver·shot** (ouvərʃɒ́t) *v.t.* to shoot over or beyond (a mark), *the bullet overshot its target* ‖ to miss an objective because of aiming too far or for too much ‖ to pass beyond in error, *the plane overshot the airfield* **to overshoot the mark** to overdo something, go too far **to overshoot oneself** to attempt more than one can accomplish

o·ver·shot (óuvərʃɒt) *adj.* having the upper jaw or lip projecting over the lower one, e.g. in certain breeds of dog ‖ (of a wheel) turned by water flowing from above

o·ver·side 1. (óuvrsaid) *adv.* (of loading or unloading ships) over the side, i.e. into or from lighters, not directly onto a quay **2.** (óuvərsaid) *adj.* done over the side of a ship

o·ver·sight (óuvərsait) *n.* failure to notice something or an instance of this ‖ supervision, *he has general oversight of the works*

o·ver·sing (ouvərsíŋ) *v.* to sing with more effort than required

o·ver·size 1. (óuvərsáiz) *adj.* of a size larger than normal **2.** (óuvərsaiz) *n.* a size that is larger than normal

o·ver·skirt (óuvərskə:rt) *n.* an outer skirt worn over and often only partly concealing the skirt or trousers under it

o·ver·sleep (ouvərslí:p) *pres. part.* **o·ver·sleep·ing** *past* and *past part.* **o·ver·slept** (ouvərslépt) *v.i.* to sleep beyond the time for getting up ‖ *v.t.* (esp. *Br.*) to find (oneself) in the situation of having done this

o·ver·spend (ouvərspénd) *pres. part.* **o·ver·spend·ing** *past* and *past part.* **o·ver·spent** (ouvərspént) *v.t.* to spend more (money, energy) than is prudent ‖ *v.i.* to spend too freely

o·ver·spill (óuvərspil) *n.* a spilling over ‖ something that is spilled over, e.g. surplus population, *the new towns are meant to take the overspill from the capital*

o·ver·spread (ouvərspréd) *pres. part.* **o·ver·spread·ing** *past* and *past part.* **o·ver·spread** *v.t.* to spread over, cover the surface of [O.E. *ofersprǣdan*]

o·ver·sta·bil·i·ty (ouvərstəbíliti:) *n.* resistance to change

o·ver·state (ouvərstéit) *pres. part.* **o·ver·stat·ing** *past* and *past part.* **o·ver·stat·ed** *v.t.* to express in stronger terms than the truth warrants **ó·ver·státe·ment** *n.*

o·ver·stay (ouvərstéi) *v.t.* to stay beyond (a specified period), *to overstay one's leave* ‖ to continue a transaction in (a market) past the point of maximum profitability

o·ver·steer·ing (ouvərstíəriŋ) *n.* the necessity of steering more sharply in order to keep a course

o·ver·step (óuvərstép) *pres. part.* **o·ver·step·ping** *past* and *past part.* **o·ver·stepped** v.t. to go beyond (what is prudent or acceptable), *to overstep the limits of good taste*

o·ver·stock 1. (ouvərstɒ́k) *v.t.* to lay in or carry too large a stock of **2.** (óuvərstɒk) *n.* too large a stock

o·ver·struc·tured (ouvərstrʌ́ktʃərd) *adj.* having too much planned detail

o·ver·strung (ouvərstrʌ́ŋ) *adj.* (*of* nerves) intensely strained ‖ (of a person) excessively sensitive ‖ (*Br., mus.,* of a piano) having the strings arranged at different levels crossing obliquely, giving greater length of string

o·ver·sub·scribe (ouvərsəbskráib) *pres. part.* **o·ver·sub·scrib·ing** *past* and *past part.* **o·ver·sub·scribed** *v.t.* to subscribe more than is offered for sale (e.g. bonds), or than the amount required (e.g. a loan)

o·ver·sup·ply (ouvərsəplái) **1.** *n.* an excess supply **2.** *v.t. pres. part.* **o·ver·sup·ply·ing** *past* and *past part.* **o·ver·sup·plied** to supply in excess

o·ver·swing (óuvərswiŋ) *n.* (*golf*) a swing with excessive force resulting in too much follow-through and loss of balance

o·vert (óuvə:rt, ouvə́:rt) *adj.* unconcealed, public, *an overt attack on authority* [O.F. *overt* fr. *ovrir*, to open]

o·ver·take (ouvərtéik) *pres. part.* **o·ver·tak·ing** *past* **o·ver·took** (ouvərtúk) *past part.* **o·ver·tak·en** (ouvərtéikən) *v.t.* (*Br.*) to pass (another vehicle etc. going in the same direction as oneself) ‖ to catch up with, *he overtook me and we had a long talk* ‖ to happen to or come upon suddenly and usually disagreeably, *a storm overtook them two hours later* ‖ to catch up with and do better than (in competition), *exports have already overtaken last year's figure* ‖ *v.i.* (*Br.*) to pass a vehicle traveling in the same direction as oneself

o·ver·talk (óuvərtɔk) *n.* (*colloq.*) excessive talk

o·ver·tax (ouvərtǽks) *v.t.* to strain by making excessive demands on, *to overtax one's strength* ‖ to tax excessively

o·ver·tech·nol·o·gize (ouvərteknɒ́lədʒi:z) *v.* to rely excessively on technology (vs. human factors)

o·ver-the-coun·ter drug (ouvərðəkáuntərdrʌ́g) a drug sold directly to the public without prescription e.g., aspirin *also* OTC drug

o·ver-the-falls (ouvərðəfɔ́lz) *n.* (*surfing*) maneuver over the crest of a wave

over-the-ho·ri·zon radar (ouvərðəhəráiz'n réidər) (*mil.*) a radar device in which beams are reflected from ionosphere layers; used to detect ballistic missiles

o·ver·throw 1. (ouvərθróu) *v.t. pres. part.* **o·ver·throw·ing** *past* **o·ver·threw** (ouvərθrú:) *past part.* **o·ver·thrown** (óuvərθroun) to cause to fall from power, *to overthrow a government* ‖ (*games*) to throw (a ball) beyond the point intended ‖ (*rhet.*) to upset, overturn, *he overthrew the idols in the temple* **2.** (óuvərθrou) *n.* an overthrowing or being overthrown ‖ (*cricket*) a fielder's return throw not stopped at the wicket, thus allowing further runs ‖ (*baseball*) a throw which misses its intended receiver, resulting in an error

o·ver·time (óuvərtaim) **1.** *n.* extra time worked, beyond regular hours ‖ money paid for such work ‖ (*sports*) extra playing time beyond the usual fixed limits of the game when the score is a tie **2.** *adv.* beyond the usual hours‖ (*sports*) beyond the usual playing time **3.** *adj.* for overtime, *overtime pay* **4.** (óuvərtáim) *v.t. pres. part.* **o·ver·tim·ing** *past* and *past part.* **o·ver·timed** to give more than the proper time to, *to overtime a photographic exposure*

o·ver·tone (óuvərtoun) *n.* (*mus.*) one of the tones above the fundamental tone in a harmonic series ‖ the color of light reflected, e.g. by a paint film ‖ an implication or suggestion evoked by language

o·ver·top (ouvərtɒ́p) *pres. part.* **o·ver·top·ping** *past* and *past part.* **o·ver·topped** *v.t.* to rise above the top of ‖ to prevail over, go beyond in importance, quality of performance etc.

o·ver·train (ouvərtréin) *v.t.* to cause to lose condition by excessive training

o·ver·trick (óuvərtrik) *n.* (*cards*) a trick over the number of tricks bid or needed

o·ver·trump (ouvərtrʌ́mp) *v.t.* (*cards*) to play a higher trump than that of (another player) ‖ *v.i.* (*cards*) to play a higher trump than one already exposed

o·ver·ture (óuvərtʃuər, óuvərtʃər) *n.* a preliminary proposal or a formal offer intended to assess the state of mind of the person or group addressed ‖ (*mus.*) an orchestral piece preceding the rise of the curtain in an opera, musical comedy etc. [O.F.=opening]

o·ver·turn 1. (ouvərtə́:rn) *v.t.* to turn over, upset ‖ to overthrow (e.g. a government) ‖ *v.i.* to turn over, upset **2.** (ouvərtə:rn) *n.* an overturning or being overturned ‖ (*environ.*) the complete circulation or mixing of upper and lower waters of a lake when temperatures and densities are similar ‖ the period of the mixing

o·ver·val·ue (ouvərvǽlju:) *pres. part.* **o·ver·val·u·ing** *past* and *past part.* **o·ver·val·ued** *v.t.* to value too highly

o·ver·view (óuvərvju:) *n.* a general survey

o·ver·ween·ing (ouvərwí:niŋ) *adj.* arrogant, presumptuous, *overweening pride* [pres. part. of older *overween*, to be conceited]

o·ver·weight 1. (óuvərweit) *n.* weight over that usual or required, *the shopkeeper gave me overweight* ‖ bodily weight that is higher than is compatible with good health, *he suffers from overweight* **2.** (óuvərwéit) *adj.* beyond the allowed weights, *overweight luggage* ‖ suffering from bodily overweight **3.** (ouvərwéit) *v.t.* to emphasize to excess, *philosophers sometimes overweight their negativism* ‖ to overburden, *his prose was overweighted with metaphors*

o·ver·whelm (ouvərhwélm, ouvərwélm) *v.t.* to submerge suddenly by irresistible force, *the village was overwhelmed by a tidal wave* ‖ to overpower, the *defense was overwhelmed by superior numbers* ‖ to leave emotionally too moved for speech or expression, *his generosity overwhelmed us* [OVER+older *whelm*, to roll]

o·ver·wind (ouvərwáind) *pres. part.* **o·ver·wind·ing** *past* and *past part.* **o·ver·wound** (ouvərwáund) *v.t.* to wind (e.g. a watch spring) too much or too tightly ‖ (*elec.*) to wind (a magnet) so that magnetic saturation demands less current than usual

o·ver·work (ouvərwə́:rk) **1.** *v.t.* to work excessively ‖ to use too often, to *overwork an expression* ‖ to weary or exhaust with too much work ‖ *v.i.* to work too hard **2.** *n.* work in such quantity that mental or physical health is endangered or affected

o·ver·wrought (ouvərrɔ́t) *adj.* worked up, under great nervous tension, *an overwrought child* ‖ much too elaborate, *an overwrought style* [older past part. of OVERWORK]

O·vid (ɒvid) (Publius Ovidius Naso, 43 B.C.–c. 17 A.D.), Latin poet. His polished, witty poetry, written chiefly in elegiac couplets, treats mainly of three subjects: passion and desire ('Amores', 'Ars amatoria'), mythology ('Metamorphoses', 'Fasti') and the sorrows of exile ('Tristia')

o·vi·duct (óuvidʌkt) *n.* (*anat., zool.*) a tube carrying eggs (ova) from the ovary to the exterior and often possessing modified regions, e.g. the uterus or a region where shell is produced by specialized secretions [fr. M.L. or Mod. L. *oviductus*]

O·vie·do (ɔvi:éidou, *Span.* ɔvjéðɔ) a province (area 4,205 sq. miles, pop. 1,127,007) of N. Spain ‖ its capital (pop. 175,400), center of the region's coal and iron ore mining, with iron and steel, chemical, textile and food-processing industries. University (1604). It was the capital (9th–11th cc.) of Asturias

o·vi·form (óuvifɔrm) *adj.* ovoid [fr. L. *ovum*, egg+*forma*, form]

o·vine (óuvain) *adj.* of or related to sheep [fr. L. *ovinus*]

o·vip·a·rous (ouvípərəs) *adj.* (*zool.*) producing eggs which hatch outside the maternal body (cf. OVOVIVIPAROUS, cf. VIVIPAROUS) ‖ describing reproduction by such eggs **o·vi·par·i·ty** (ouvipǽriti:) *n.* [fr. L. *oviparus* fr. *ovum*, egg+*parere*, to bring forth]

o·vi·pos·it (óuvəpɒzit, ouvəpɒ́zit) *v.i.* (*zool.*, esp. of insects) to lay eggs [fr. L. *ovum*, egg+*ponere* (*positus*), to place]

o·vi·pos·i·tor (óuvəpɒzitər, ouvəpɒ́zitər) *n.* a specialized organ of female insects for depositing eggs, often capable of piercing animals or plants to deposit eggs inside them ‖ a tubular extension of the genital orifice in fish [fr. L. *ovum*, egg+*positor*, a placer fr. *ponere*, to place]

ov·i·sac (óuvisæk) *n.* (*zool.*) an egg capsule or receptacle, e.g. a Graafian follicle [fr. L. *ovum*, egg+SAC]

o·void (óuvɔid) **1.** *adj.* egg-shaped **2.** *n.* an egg-shaped body or surface [fr. Mod. L. *ovoides* fr. *ovum* egg]

o·vo·lo (óuvəlou) *pl.* **o·vo·li** (óuvəlai) *n.* (*archit.*) a convex, rounded molding, a quarter circle (Roman) or quarter ellipse (Greek) in section [fr. older Ital. *ovolo*, dim. of *ovo*, *uovo*, egg]

o·vo·tes·tis (óuvoutéstis) *pl.* **o·vo·tes·tes** (ouvoutésti:z) *n.* a hermaphrodite reproductive and endocrine gland produced in some animals, e.g. frogs, and in certain gastropods (*OVARY, *TESTICLE) [Mod. L. fr. L. *ovum*, egg+*testis*, testicle]

o·vo·vi·vip·a·rous (ouvouvaivípərəs) *adj.* (*zool.*, of many insects, some snails, a few reptiles etc.) producing eggs with definite shells, which hatch within the maternal body (cf. OVIPAROUS cf. VIVIPAROUS) [fr. L. *ovum*, egg+VIVIPAROUS]

o·vu·lar(óuvjulər) *adj.* relating to an ovule [fr. Mod. L. *ovularis* fr. *ovulum*, ovule]

o·vu·late (óuvjuleit) *pres. part.* **o·vu·lat·ing** *past* and *past part.* **o·vu·lat·ed** *v.i.* to produce an egg or eggs, or to discharge them from the ovary [fr. Mod. L. *ovulum*, ovule]

o·vule (óuvju:l) *n.* the structure within the ovary in seed plants containing the embryo sac and egg. It develops into the seed after fertilization [F.]

o·vum (óuvəm) *pl.* **o·va** (óuvə) *n.* (*biol.*) the usually nonmotile female haploid gamete ‖ a mature egg or egg cell, esp. of mammals, fish or insects [L.=egg]

owe (ou) *pres. part.* **ow·ing** *past* and *past part.* **owed** *v.t.* to have an obligation to pay or repay (money etc.) in return for money etc. that one has received ‖ to have or bear (a specified feeling) toward someone, *to owe someone gratitude* ‖ to be or feel obliged to render (something), *to owe allegiance to one's country* ‖ to have, enjoy etc. (something) as a result of the action, existence etc. of a specified person, cause etc., *she owes her life to the doctors* ‖ *v.i.* to be in debt, *he still owes for his piano* [O.E. *āgan,* to own]

O·wen (óuən), Robert (1771–1858), British social reformer and socialist. A successful cotton manufacturer, he acquired mills at New Lanark in Scotland (1799), which he ran on model lines, limiting working hours, providing good housing and education, and establishing one of the first cooperative stores. He campaigned for social legislation and was partly responsible for the Factory Act of 1819. He formed the Grand National Consolidated Trades Union (1843). In 'New View of Society' (1813) he expounded the view that character is formed by social environment, and he advocated the cooperative system

Owen Falls a waterfall near the exit of the Nile from Lake Victoria, Uganda. A large dam here converts the lake into a reservoir for Egypt and the Sudan, and produces hydroelectric power for Uganda and Kenya

Owens (óuənz), Jesse (1913–80), U.S. track star, best known for his outstanding performance in the 1936 Olympic Games in which he won four gold medals, placing first in the 100-m sprint, the 200-m sprint and the broad jump. He was also a member of the winning U.S. 400-m relay team. He also achieved the finest one-day performance in track history (May 25, 1935), when he equaled the 100-yd dash world record at 9.4 sec. and set a new world long-jump record of 26ft 8.25in (8.13m) that stood for 25 years. He also set records in the 220-yd dash (20.3 sec.) and the 220-yd low hurdles (22.6 sec.)

ow·ing (óuiŋ) *adj.* due to be paid, *a small sum is still owing* **owing to** as a result of, caused by, *delay owing to traffic jams* [OWE]

owl (aul) *n.* a member of *Strigidae,* a large cosmopolitan family of nocturnal birds of prey. They have flattened faces and forward-facing eyes, hooked bills and powerful claws, and their soft, fluffy plumage allows them to fly noiselessly ‖ a solemn-appearing person, usually stupid [O.E. *ūle*]

owl·et (áulit) *n. Athene noctua,* a small European owl ‖ a young owl

owl·ish (áuliʃ) *adj.* (*of* a person, or his appearance) having characteristics suggestive of those of an owl

own (oun) **1.** *adj.* (usually following a possessive adj.) belonging to oneself or itself (often used to denote exclusive or particular possession or agency), *he brought his own lunch, he did it by his own effort* **to be one's own man** to be independent of the control or influence of others **2.** *n.* that which belongs to one of one's own belonging to one, *to have no money of one's own* **on one's own** independent ‖ independently or without the help etc. of others, *can you finish on you own?* **to come into one's own** to get what rightly belongs to one (esp. recognition or prosperity) **to get one's own back** to get one's revenge, get even **to hold one's own** to maintain one's position or strength [O.E. *āgen,* past part. of *āgan,* to own]

own *v.t.* to have, possess, be the proprietor of, *he owns the house and land* ‖ to acknowledge, *would he own his authorship of it?* ‖ *v.i.* (with 'to') to make an admission, *he owned to a sense of shame* **to own up** (*pop.*) to confess, admit guilt ‖ (*pop.,* with 'to') to confess frankly that one has committed a crime etc. **ówn·er, ówn·er·ship** *ns* [O.E. *āgnian,* to seize, gain, win fr. *āgen,* own]

own-brand (óunbrǽnd) *adj.* of a product carrying a private brand name, esp. that of a retailer, in contrast with an advertised brand

own·er-oc·cu·pied (ounərɒ́kju:paid) *adj.* lived-in by the owner instead of by a rental tenant — **own·er-oc·cu·pa·tion** *n.* —**own·er-oc·cu·pee** *n.*

ox (ɒks) *pl.* **ox·en** (ɒ́ksən) *n.* a member of genus *Bos,* fam. *Bovidae,* esp. the adult castrated male of *B. taurus* kept as a draft animal or raised as food ‖ any of several animals of *Bos* and related genera, e.g. the bison, buffalo, yak [O.E. *oxa*]

ox·a·cill·in sodium [C_3H_3NO] (ɒksəsílin) *n.* (*pharm.*) semisynthetic substitute for penicillin effective against penicillin-resistant staphylococic infections; marketed as Prostaphin and Resistopen

ox·a·late (ɒ́ksəleit) *n.* a salt or ester of oxalic acid [F.]

ox·al·ic acid (ɒksǽlik) a poisonous acid, $(COOH)_2$, found in plants of genus *Oxalis* and other plants and also produced synthetically. It is used in dyeing, fabric printing, bleaching, in metal polishes etc. [fr. F. *oxalique* fr. L. *oxalis,* oxalis]

ox·a·lis (ɒ́ksəlis, ɒksǽlis) *n.* a member of *Oxalis,* fam. *Oxalidaceae,* a genus of plants of warm and tropical regions including wood sorrel etc., having purple, pink or white flowers and leaves with an acid taste [L. fr. Gk fr. *oxus,* sour]

ox·az·e·pam [$C_{15}H_{11}ClN_2O_2$] (ɒkséizəpæm) *n.* (*pharm.*) tranquilizing drug; marketed as Serax

ox·bow (ɒ́ksbou) *n.* a collar for an ox, consisting of a U-shaped wooden frame, the upper ends of which pass through the bar of the yoke ‖ a crescent-shaped bend in a river, or the land within this bend

Ox·bridge·an, -ian (ɒksbrídʒən) *adj.* showing the qualities of a graduate of Oxford or Cambridge universities

ox·cart (ɒ́kskɑrt) *n.* a cart drawn by an ox or oxen

oxen *pl.* of ox

Ox·en·stier·na (ɒ́ksənʃɛrnɑ), Count Axel Gustaffson (1583–1654), Swedish statesman. An extremely able diplomat, he wielded great influence in the Thirty Years' War as minister to Gustavus II and Christina

ox·eye daisy (ɒ́ksai) *Chrysanthemum leucanthemum,* a perennial composite with a woody stock, long white ray florets and yellow disk florets. It is a common grassland plant in temperate regions ‖ the black-eyed Susan any member of *Heliopsis,* a genus of yellow-flowered perennial plants of North America

Ox·fam (*acronym*) **Ox**ford Committee for **Fam**ine Relief

Ox·ford (ɒ́ksfərd) the county town (pop. 117,400) of Oxfordshire, England, a county borough, on the Thames (here called the Isis), seat of Oxford University. Industries: printing, automobile engineering, steel works. Christ Church cathedral (12th c.)

ox·ford (ɒ́ksfərd) a walking shoe laced above the instep ‖ a kind of cloth, usually cotton, used for shirts etc. [OXFORD, England]

Oxford and Asquith, 1st earl of *ASQUITH

Oxford Group Movement *MORAL RE-ARMAMENT

Oxford movement a 19th-c. reforming movement, also known as Tractarianism or Puseyism, within the Church of England. Led by Keble, Newman and Pusey, it began (1833) at Oxford University. It aimed at reaffirming the unbroken connection of the Church of England with the early Church, and at restoring the High Church ideals of the 17th c. Its views were publicized in 'Tracts for the Times' (1833–41), culminating in Newman's 'Tract 90' (1841) which attempted to interpret the Thirty-nine Articles in keeping with Roman Catholic doctrine. Through Anglo-Catholicism the movement has had a continuing effect on Anglican teaching, worship and ceremonial

Oxford, Provisions of (*Eng. hist.*) a scheme of government drawn up (1258) by the great council under the leadership of Simon de Montfort. It aimed at reforming central and local government and the king's household by appointing a baronial council to govern the country. Henry III's repudiation of the scheme precipitated the Barons' War (1264–6)

Ox·ford·shire (ɒ́ksfərdʃiər) (*abbr.* Oxon.) a county (area 749 sq. miles, pop. 541,800) in the S. Midlands of England. County town: Oxford

Oxford University a university in Oxford, England, consisting of 30 colleges. It was established as a center of learning c. 1167. University College was founded in 1249, Balliol in 1263 and Merton in 1264

ox·hide (ɒ́kshaid) *n.* leather made from the skin of an ox

ox·i·dase (ɒ́ksideiz,ɒ́ksideis) *n.* an enzyme causing oxidation of substrates by removal of hydrogen, which combines with oxygen [OXIDATION+DIASTASE]

ox·i·da·tion (ɒksidéiʃən) *n.* an oxidizing or being oxidized (cf. REDUCTION, *OXIDATION-REDUCTION) [fr. *oxidate,* to oxidize]

oxidation-reduction a chemical reaction (also called a redox reaction) in which one or more electrons are transferred from one ion, atom or molecule to another. All such reactions involve an oxidizing agent, which is reduced during the course of the reaction, and a reducing agent, which is oxidized

oxidation-reduction potential the potential (also called the redox potential) at which oxidation occurs at the anode and reduction at the cathode in an electrochemical cell. This potential is referred to that of a standard hydrogen electrode (taken as zero)

oxidation state the degree of oxidation of an atom or ion, usually expressed by a positive or negative number representing the formal ionic charge on each atom in a compound or complex ion, 0 representing the elemental state (*VALENCE)

ox·ide (ɒ́ksaid) *n.* a compound of oxygen with another element or with an organic radical **ox·i·dize** (ɒ́ksidaiz) *pres. part.* **ox·i·diz·ing** *past* and *past part.* **ox·i·dized** *v.t.* to combine with oxygen ‖ to remove one or more electrons from (a compound, ion or radical), thus changing the oxidation state to a larger positive or smaller negative number ‖ to cover (metal etc.) with an oxide coating ‖ *v.i.* to undergo oxidation [F.]

oxide of iridium metal that changes color in response to an electrical impulse and retains change, used in creating digital displays in watches, etc., developed by Bell Laboratories

ox·im·e·ter (ɒksímitər) *n.* (*med.*) device for measuring the oxygen content of blood in a person by passing a beam of light through the ear-lobe

ox·lip (ɒ́kslip) *n. Primula elatior,* a primula found in Europe and W. Asia ‖ a hybrid between the primrose and cowslip [O.E. *oxanslyppe,* ox's dropping, oxlip]

Ox·on. (ɒ́kson) *adj.* of Oxford University, *M.A.* (*Oxon.*) [fr. L. *Oxoniensis*]

Ox·o·ni·an (ɒksóuni:ən) **1.** *adj.* of the university or city of Oxford **2.** *n.* a student or graduate of Oxford University ‖ a native or resident of Oxford [fr. *Oxoflia,* Latinized name of Oxford]

ox·o·trem·or·ine [$C_{12}H_{18}N_2O$] (ɒksətrémɔrine) *n.* (*pharm.*) tremor-producing drug used in testing antitremor drugs

ox·tail (ɒ́ksteil) *n.* the skinned tail of an ox, used to make a soup or stew

Ox·us (ɒ́ksəs) *AMU-DARYA

ox·y·a·cet·y·lene (ɒksi:əsét'li:n) *adj.* of, consisting of or using a mixture of oxygen and acetylene, esp. as burned in a blowtorch to provide a sufficiently high temperature for welding or cutting metals [OXYGEN+ACETYLENE]

ox·y·ac·id (ɒksi:ǽsid) *n.* (*chem.*) an oxygen-containing acid

ox·y·gen (ɒ́ksidʒən) *n.* a colorless, tasteless, normally gaseous element (symbol O, at. no. 8, at. mass 15.9994) [F. *oxygène*]

—Oxygen forms about 1/5 of the earth's atmosphere, 8/9 by weight of water, and a considerable proportion by weight of organic matter and of many minerals. It is the most abundant element of the earth's atmosphere and crust, and is essential to animal and plant life. It combines readily with many other elements to form oxides, combustion and respiration both involving such combination. Pure oxygen is extracted from liquefied air. It is used in oxygen blowpipes and oxyhydrogen and oxyacetylene flames for cutting and welding. The use of large amounts of oxygen in steelmaking furnaces speeds the decarbonizing reaction and makes it possible to treat lower grades of ore. Chemical applications of oxygen include the manufacture of concentrated nitric acid from ammonia and the oxidation of hydrocarbons obtained from petroleum

ox·y·ge·nase (ɒ́ksidʒəneis) *n.* (*biochem.*) enzyme that makes possible the use of oxygen from the atmosphere by an organic cell

ox·y·gen·ate (ɒ́ksidʒəneit) *pres. part.* **ox·y·gen·at·ing** *past* and *past part.* **ox·y·gen·at·ed** *v.t.* to impregnate or treat with oxygen to fill (blood etc.) with oxygen by breathing **ox·y·gen·á·tion** *n.* [F. *oxygéner*]

oxygen-hydrogen welding a process of gas welding by burning a mixture of oxygen and hydrogen, producing very high temperatures

ox·y·gen·ize (ɒ́ksidʒənaiz) *pres. part.* **ox·y·gen·iz·ing** *past* and *past part.* **ox·y·gen·ized** *v.t.* to oxygenate

oxygen tent a tentlike canopy, placed over a patient's bed, in which a steady flow of oxygen is supplied to the patient

ox·y·he·mo·glo·bin, ox·y·hae·mo·glo·bin (ɒksi-hi:məglóubin, ɒksihí:məgloubin, ɒksiheməglóubin, ɒksihémǝglɒubin) *n.* an unstable compound of hemoglobin and oxygen, formed in the blood when oxygen is breathed (as air) into the lungs [OXYGEN+HEMOGLOBIN]

oxyhemoglobin *n.* (*chem.*) hemoglobin with oxygen

ox·y·hy·dro·gen (ɒksiháidrǝdʒǝn) *adj.* of, relating to, or consisting of a mixture of hydrogen and oxygen [OXYGEN+HYDROGEN]

ox·y·mo·ron (ɒksimóron, ɒksimóurɒn) *n.* a figure of speech in which apparently contradictory terms are combined to produce an epigrammatic effect, e.g. 'cruel only to be kind' [Gk *oxumōron* fr. *oxus*, sharp+*mōros*, foolish]

Ox·y·rhyn·chus (ɒksiríŋkǝs) (*Arab.* Behnesa) the site of an ancient Egyptian town about 100 miles south of Cairo, a rich source of Greek, Latin, demotic Egyptian, Coptic and Hebrew papyri

ox·y·to·cic (ɒksitóusik) **1.** *adj.* (*med.*) serving to hasten the process of birth by stimulating contraction of uterine smooth muscle **2.** *n.* (*med.*) an oxytocic substance **ox·y·tó·cin** *n.* a hormone from the posterior pituitary gland, stimulating contraction of the uterine smooth muscle [fr. Gk *oxutokion* fr. *oxus*, acute+*tokos*, childbirth]

ox·y·tone (ɒksitɒun) **1.** *adj.* (esp. in Greek) having an acute accent on the last syllable **2.** *n.* an oxytone word [fr. Gk *oxutunos* fr. *oxus*, acute+*tonos*, accent]

O·ya·pock (ɔjæpɔk) (or Oyapak) a river (300 miles long) rising in the Tumac-Humac Mtns of French Guiana, flowing northeast to form the Brazil–French Guiana boundary, and emptying into the Atlantic

o·yer and ter·mi·ner (óiǝrǝntǝ:rminǝr) *n.* (*Br. law*) a royal commission conferring power to hear and determine criminal cases (*Am. law*) any of certain superior courts with similar powers [A.F.-to hear and determine]

o·yez, o·yes (oujés, oujéz) *interj.* listen! (uttered usually three times by a public crier or court officer to command attention and silence before a proclamation is read) [O.F. *oiez, oyez,* imper. of *oir,* to hear]

O·yo (ɔ́jou) a trading center (pop. 75,000) of W. Nigeria, manufacturing cotton textiles

oys·ter (óistǝr) *n.* an edible marine bivalve lamellibranch mollusk of fam. *Ostreidae,* having a rough irregular shell and living free on the sea floor or attached to submerged rocks, usually in temperate or tropical coastal waters or estuaries ‖ any of several mollusks resembling this, e.g. a pearl oyster ‖ a choice morsel of meat contained in a hollow of the pelvic bone on each side of the back of a chicken ‖ a color between light gray and white [O.F. *oistre, uistre, huistre* fr. obs. Ital. *ostrea* fr. L. fr. Gk]

oyster bed a place on the ocean floor where oysters breed or are cultivated

oyster catcher a member of *Haematopus,* fam. *Haematopodidae,* a widely distributed genus of rather large wading shorebirds which feed on small mollusks and worms. They usually have black and white plumage, stout pink legs and a strong bill

oyster crab *Pinnotheres ostreum,* a crab the female of which lives as a commensal in the gill cavity of an oyster

oyster farm a tract of sea bottom where oysters are bred

O·zark Mountains (óuzark) a plateau (area about 50,000 sq. miles, elevation 1,500–2,500 ft), broken by hills, in parts of Missouri, Arkansas, Oklahoma, Kansas and Illinois: farming, livestock raising, lead and zinc mines

o·zo·ce·rite (ɒuzǝsíǝrait) *n.* a waxlike mineral fossil resin consisting of a mixture of hydrocarbons. It is used in making candles etc. [G. *ozokerit* fr. Gk *ozein,* to smell+*kēros,* wax]

o·zo·ke·rite (ɒuzǝkíǝrait) *n.* ozocerite

o·zone (óuzoun, ouzóun) *n.* an allotropic form of oxygen in which three atoms form one molecule (O_3). It has a pungent smell, is produced by a silent discharge of electricity, and is present in the air after a thunderstorm. It is used commercially for sterilizing water, bleaching, purifying air etc. **o·zon·ic** (ouzɒnik, ouzóunik) *adj.* **o·zo·nif·er·ous** (ouzounífǝrǝs) *adj.* **o·zon·ize** (óuzounaiz) *pres. part.* **o·zon·iz·ing** *past* and *past part.* **o·zon·ized** *v.t.* to convert into ozone ‖ to treat or combine with ozone **o·zon·iz·er** (óuzounǝizǝr) *n.* an apparatus that converts oyxen into ozone by passing a silent electrical discharge through it [Fr. fr. Gk *ozein,* to smell]

CONCISE PRONUNCIATION KEY: **(a)** æ, c*a*t; ɑ, c*ar*; ɔ f*aw*n; ei, sn*a*ke. **(e)** e, h*e*n; i:, sh*ee*p; iǝ, d*ee*r; ɛǝ, b*ear*. **(i)** i, f*i*sh; ai, t*i*ger; ǝ:, b*i*rd. **(o)** o, *o*x; au, c*ow*; ou, g*oa*t; u, p*oo*r; ɔi, r*oy*al. **(u)** ʌ, d*u*ck; u, b*u*ll; u:, g*oo*se; ǝ, b*a*cillus; ju:, c*u*be. x, lo*ch*; θ, *th*ink; ð, bo*th*er; z, *Z*en; ʒ, cor*s*age; dʒ, sava*g*e; ŋ, ora*ng*utang; j, *y*ak; ʃ, *f*ish; tʃ, fe*tch*; ˈl, rabb*le*; ˈn, red*den.* Complete pronunciation key appears inside front cover.

A. C. SYLVESTER, CAMBRIDGE, ENGLAND

Development of the letter P, beginning with the early North Semitic letter. Evolution of both the majuscule, or capital, letter P and the minuscule, or lowercase, letter p are shown.

P, p (pi:) the 16th letter of the English alphabet **to mind one's P's and Q's** to be careful to avoid language or behavior that could offend

Pa. Pennsylvania

pa (*phys. abbr.*) pascal, SI unit of pressure equal to the force of 1 newton acting over 1 sq. meter area

pab·u·lum (pǽbjuləm) (*rhet.*) nourishment [L.]

pa·ca (páːkə, pǽkə) *n.* a member of *Cuniculus*, fam. *Dasyproctidae*, a genus of Central and South American rodents about 2 ft long, esp. *C. paca*, which is valued as food [Port. and Span. fr. Tupi]

Pa·ca·rai·ma (pækəráimə) a mountain range extending west to east along a part of the Brazil-Venezuela boundary. Highest peak: Mt Roraima (9,210 ft)

pace (peis) **1.** *n.* rate of traveling or progressing ‖ manner of walking or running ‖ a step made in walking ‖ the distance covered by a single step in walking, often taken as 30 ins ‖ (*Rom. hist.*) a unit of measurement, the distance between successive impacts of the same heel (about 60 ins) ‖ any of the gaits of a horse ‖ a fast horse's gait in which just the feet on one side are lifted and set down, then the feet on the other **to go the pace** (*Br.*) to go very fast ‖ (*Br.*) to lead a gay, dissipated life **to keep pace with** to move or develop at the same speed as, *keep pace with the times* **to put (someone or an animal) through his** (or **its**) **paces** to test or rehearse the abilities of (someone or an animal) **2.** *v. pres. part.* **pac·ing** *past* and *past part.* **paced** *v.i.* to walk with regular steps ‖ *v.t.* (often with 'off', 'out') to measure by counting the paces needed to walk the length of, *he paced out the length of the garden* ‖ to establish or regulate the pace or speed of, *he paced the runner on his bicycle* [O.F. *pas*]

pa·ce (péisi:) *prep.* subject to the consent of, with due respect to the opinion of, *my view, pace the last speaker, is that we should adjourn* [L., ablative of *pax*, peace]

pace car (*auto racing*) a lead car that paces the field for one lap

pace lap (*auto racing*) warm-up run before a race

pace·mak·er (péismeikər) *n.* a person who sets the pace, e.g. for a race ‖ (*med.*) a part of the body serving to establish and maintain a rhythmic activity ‖ (*med.*) a device for stimulating the heart to resume a steady beat, or to restore the rhythm of an arrested heart

pac·er (péisər) *n.* a horse with a pacing gait, used esp. in harness racing

Pa·che·co A·re·co (pɑtʃékɔɑrékɔ), Jorge (1921–), Uruguayan journalist, politician and president (1967–72)

Pa·cho·mi·us (pəkóumi:əs), St (c. 292–c. 346), Egyptian ascetic. He founded the first Christian monastic community living a communal life under a rule (c. 318). Feast: May 14

pach·y·derm (pǽkidə:rm) *n.* (*zool.*) any of certain thick-skinned, hoofed mammals, esp. the rhinoceros and elephant **pach·y·der·ma·tous** *adj.* [F. *pachyderme* fr. Gk *pachus*, thick + *derma*, skin]

pach·y·o·ste·o·morph (pæki:ósti:oumɔrf) *n.* (*paleontology*) a level on the evolutionary scale where bone structure is heavy

pach·y·tene (pǽkiti:n) *adj.* of that part of the prophase stage in meiosis during which homologous chromosomes are associated as bivalents [fr. F. *pachytène* fr. Gk *pachus*, thick + *tainia*, band]

pa·ci·far·in (pɑsifǽrin) *n.* (*biochem.*) a substance produced by bacteria that prevents certain diseases *also* enterobactin

pa·cif·ic (pəsífik) *adj.* peaceful, seeking, making or tending toward peace, *pacific policies* ‖ unaggressive in disposition **Pa·cif·ic** of the Pacific Ocean or the regions bordering it **pa·cíf·i·cal·ly** *adv.* [fr. L. *pacificus*]

pac·i·fi·ca·tion (pæsifikéiʃən) *n.* a pacifying or being pacified ‖ (*mil.*) countering guerrilla activity [F.]

pa·cif·i·ca·to·ry (pəsífikətɔri:, pəsífikətɔuri:) *adj.* tending to promote peace [fr. *pacificator*, someone who pacifies, fr. L.]

Pacific Doctrine statement of U.S. policy by President Gerald Ford, December 7, 1976, of the normalization of relations with China, strategic partnership with Japan, assertion of U.S. interest in Southeast Asia and the acknowledged existence of political conflicts

Pacific Ocean the largest ocean (area incl. seas, gulfs and Antarctic waters: 63,800,000 sq. miles, over a third of the earth's surface), separating America from Asia and Australia. Length (Bering Strait–Antarctica): 9,000 miles. Width from Panama to Malaya: 11,000 miles. Submarine plateaus project hundreds of archipelagoes and single islands in the W. Pacific, with smaller ridges in mid-ocean. Average valley depth: 2,800 fathoms. Characteristic deeps along the continents and archipelagoes go down to 6 miles (6,300 fathoms in the Marianas trench). With its coasts it constitutes a great volcanic zone

Pacific standard time (*abbr.* P.S.T.) Pacific time

Pacific time (*abbr.* P.T.) one of the four standard time divisions of the U.S.A. and Canada, eight hours behind Greenwich time and three hours behind Eastern standard time

Pacific, War of the a war (1879–84) between Chile and the alliance of Bolivia and Peru, fought over possession of nitrate deposits in the Atacama region. It ended in the Treaty of Ancón (Ecuador) and the truce at Valparaíso (1884). A definitive treaty was signed in 1904

pac·i·fi·er (pǽsifaiər) *n.* someone who pacifies ‖ (*Am.*=*Br.* dummy) a rubber nipple for babies to suck

pac·i·fism (pǽsifizəm) *n.* the belief that war is morally wrong and, in the long run, ineffective, and that disputes should be settled by negotiation **pác·i·fist** *n.* a person who subscribes to this [PACIFIC]

pac·i·fy (pǽsifai) *pres. part.* **pac·i·fy·ing** *past* and *past part.* **pac·i·fied** *v.t.* to cause (someone) to be calm, satisfied or no longer angry ‖ to establish peace in (a country etc.) [F. *pacifier*]

pack (pæk) **1.** *n.* a bundle or parcel of things, esp. one carried on the shoulders or back ‖ a company of animals, esp. of wolves or hounds ‖ a company or gang of people ‖ a great quantity, *a pack of lies* ‖ a packet or container, *a pack of cigarettes* ‖ a complete set of playing cards ‖ (*industry*) the amount of food packed in one season ‖ (*rugby*) the forwards, esp. when together in a scrum ‖ an area of sea full of pack ice ‖ a piece of wet or dry cloth, applied hot or cold as a medical or cosmetic treatment ‖ a treatment in which such a cloth is applied **2.** *v.t.* (often with 'up') to put in a container with other things, esp. for carrying on a trip, *pack your toothbrush* ‖ (often with 'up') to fill (a container) with things, *to pack a suitcase* ‖ to fill tightly, cram, *a train packed with people* ‖ to make into a wrapped parcel, *to pack a lunch* ‖ to put into protective containers for marketing or shipping ‖ (with 'off') to send (someone) away, esp. summarily ‖ (*Br., pop.,* with 'up') to cease (an activity) ‖ *v.i.* to put things together for a trip ‖ to settle into a solid or compact mass ‖ to assemble, crowd together ‖ to be capable of being put in a container with other things, *this suit will pack without wrinkling* ‖ (*Br., pop.,* with 'up') to cease operating ‖ (with 'off') to leave hastily and unceremoniously **to send (someone) packing** to dismiss (someone) unceremoniously [M.E. *packe, pakke* prob. fr. M. Flem. *pac* or Du. or L.G. *pak*]

pack *v.t.* to select members of (a committee etc.) so as to secure an unfair advantage [origin unknown]

pack·age (pǽkidʒ) **1.** *n.* a parcel or wrapped bundle ‖ a box or wrapper in which something is packed **2.** *v.t. pres. part.* **pack·ag·ing** *past* and *past part.* **pack·aged** to make into a parcel, *packaged foods* [PACK, to put in a container]

package deal an all-or-nothing arrangement in which a related group of items or services is sold for a lump sum ‖ an agreement in which the approval and acceptance of one proposal is contingent upon the approval and acceptance of another

package store a shop licenced to sell in sealed containers liquor which may not be drunk on the premises

pack animal an animal, e.g. a mule, used for carrying loads

Pack·ard (pǽkərd), James Ward (1863–1928), U.S. engineer and inventor. He and his brother founded (1890) the Packard Electric Company, for which he invented many methods and instruments to improve incandescent lighting. He built (1899) the first Packard automobile and founded (1899) what became the Packard Motor Car Company

pack drill (*mil.*) punishment of a soldier by making him drill while carrying all his gear

packed tower (*envir.*) a pollution-control device that forces dirty air through a tower packed with crushed rock or wood chips while liquid is sprayed over the packing material, causing pollutants to dissolve or chemically react with the liquid

pack·er (pǽkər) *n.* someone who packs, esp. who packs goods professionally for transport or storage ‖ a firm that packs goods for transport or storage

pack·et (pǽkit) *n.* a small package or parcel ‖ a packet boat [dim. of PACK n.]

packet boat a boat sailing a regular route, carrying passengers, mail and packages

pack·horse (pǽkhɔrs) *n.* a horse used for carrying loads

pack ice blocks of sea ice crushed up together in a nearly solid mass

pack·ing (pǽkiŋ) *n.* the process of assembling things in a container, or of filling a container with things ‖ material (sawdust etc.) used to stuff the spaces between wrapped goods to prevent damage ‖ material used to fill cracks and joints etc. ‖ (*med.*) material used to fill an open wound or cavity to allow drainage and prevent closing

packing case a wooden crate in which goods are shipped or stored

packing fraction the difference between the mass of a group of nucleons in an atomic nucleus and the sum of their individual masses divided by the number of nucleons

packing house an establishment where food, esp. meat, is processed and packed to be sold at wholesale

packing ring a piston ring

pack·man (pǽkmən) *pl.* **pack·men** (pǽkmən) *n.* (*old-fash.*) a peddler

pack rat *Neotoma cinerea,* fam. *Cricetidae,* a rodent of the western U.S., about 6 ins long, with a bushy tail. It has plump cheek pouches in which it carries food and things to be hoarded

pack·sad·dle (pǽksæd'l) *n.* a saddle for carrying a load instead of a rider

pack·thread (pǽkθred) *n.* strong thick thread used for sewing or for tying up packages

pack·train (pǽktrein) *n.* a procession of pack animals, esp. of mules

pact (pækt) *n.* an agreement between two persons, or a treaty between states [O.F. *pact, pacte*]

pad (pæd) **1.** *n.* something soft, e.g. a flat cushion or thick mat, used as a shock absorber ‖ a piece of soft material used to fill or distend, *a shoulder pad* ‖ (*sports*) a protective guard worn on the front of the legs etc. ‖ a number of sheets of paper fastened together along one edge ‖ (*colloq.*) person's apartment or residence ‖ graft for a group ‖ a small absorbent cushion soaked in ink, for inking a rubber stamp ‖ the fleshy cushion forming the sole of the paw of a dog, cat etc. ‖ the paw of a fox, hare etc. ‖ an insect's pulvillus ‖ the floating leaf of certain water plants, esp. a lily pad ‖ the socket of a brace ‖ a tool handle into which different tools may be inserted **2.** *v.t. pres. part.* **pad·ding** *past* and *past part.* **pad·ded** to fill or line with soft material ‖ to lengthen (a piece of writing, speech etc.) by adding superfluous material [origin unknown]

pad 1. *v.i. pres. part.* **pad·ding** *past* and *past part.* **pad·ded** to walk steadily and unhurriedly ‖ to walk with muffled steps **2.** *n.* the dull sound of a footfall [rel. to PAD, cushion, and imit.]

Pa·dang (pádaŋ) a trading center (pop. 196,339) of W. Sumatra, Indonesia. Its port, Telukbayur, lies 4 miles south. University (1956)

padded cell a room in a mental hospital or prison having padded walls to prevent a violent occupant from injuring himself

pad·ding (pǽdiŋ) *n.* the act of someone who pads ‖ the material used to pad something ‖ (*mil.*) extraneous text added to a message for the purpose of concealing its beginning, ending, or length

pad·dle (pǽd'l) **1.** *v.i. pres. part.* **pad·dling** *past* and *past part.* **pad·dled** to wade or play in shallow water ‖ to toddle **2.** *n.* the act or a period of paddling [origin unknown]

paddle 1. *n.* a wooden pole with a broad blade at one end, used singly without an oarlock to propel and guide a canoe or other small craft ‖ the act or period of using this or of using an oar in this way ‖ any of several implements resembling a canoe paddle, for stirring, mixing, beating etc. ‖ one of the projecting boards of a paddle wheel ‖ a seal's flipper ‖ a table-tennis racket **2.** *v. pres. part.* **pad·dling** *past* and *past part.* **pad·dled** *v.t.* to propel (a canoe etc.) by using a paddle ‖ to convey (someone) in a canoe etc. propelled by a paddle ‖ (*pop.*) to spank ‖ *v.i.* to propel a canoe etc. by a paddle ‖ to row gently ‖ (of a bird) to move in water as if by means of paddles **to paddle one's own canoe** to get along without depending on others [origin unknown]

paddle box a structure covering the upper portion of a paddle wheel

paddle steamer a steam vessel propelled by a paddle wheel on each side

paddle tennis *PLATFORM TENNIS

paddle wheel a wheel with long boards projecting at right angles from its circumference, used to propel a boat

pad·dock (pǽdək) *n.* a small grassy enclosed area in which a horse can graze and exercise ‖ a racecourse enclosure in which the horses are walked for inspection and are saddled and unsaddled [var. of *parrock,* small field fr. O.E. *pearroc, pearruc*]

pad·dy (pǽdi:) *pl.* **pad·dies** *n.* rice before harvesting or before husking ‖ a wet field in which rice is grown [Malay *padi*]

paddy *n.* (*Br., pop.*) a fit of bad temper [Irish *Padraig,* Patrick (proper name)]

paddy wagon (*pop.*) a patrol wagon [prob. fr. *Paddy,* Irishman]

Paderewski (padərέfski:), Ignace Jan (1860–1941), Polish statesman, pianist and composer. After his U.S. debut as a pianist (1891) he became the most beloved pianist since Franz Liszt. He donated all of his concert receipts from 1914–8 to Polish war victims. He became Polish representative to Washington (1918–9) and prime minister of Poland (1919–20). He led the exiled Polish government during the German occupation of World War II (1940–1). Of his many musical compositions only the Minuet in G and Piano Concerto, op. 17 are still performed

pad·lock (pǽdlɒk) **1.** *n.* a small, portable lock, with a curved bar hinged to it at one end. The bar can be slipped through a hasp and staple, chain links etc., the free end then being fastened in the lock **2.** *v.t.* to fasten with a padlock [origin unknown]

pa·dre (pádrei, pádri:) *n.* (*armed services, pop.*) a chaplain [Span., Ital. and Port.=priest, father]

Pad·u·a (pǽdʒu:ə, pǽdju:ə) (*Ital.* Padova) a walled city (pop. 242,000) of Veneto, Italy, 22 miles west of Venice, an agricultural market. Industries: chemical and agricultural engineering and food processing. Principal monuments: Palazzo della Ragione (12th c.), Basilica of St Anthony (13th c.), cathedral (16th c.). University (1222)

pae·an (pí:ən) *n.* a choral song of praise, triumph or rejoicing ‖ (*rhet.*) any extravagant expression of praise, triumph etc. [L. fr. Gk *paian* a hymn to Apollo fr. *Paian, Paiōn,* a name for Apollo]

paederast * PEDERAST

paederasty *PEDERASTY

paediatric *PEDIATRIC

pae·do·gen·e·sis, pe·do·gen·e·sis (pi:doudʒénisis) *n.* (*zool.*) reproduction by animals sexually mature but in all other respects in a pre-adult or larval stage (e.g. in the axolotl and certain dipteran insects) [fr. Gk *pais* (*paidos*), child+*genesis,* origin]

pae·on (pí:ən) *n.* (*prosody*) a metrical foot of four syllables, one long (or stressed) and three short (or unstressed) in any order **pae·on·ic** (pi:ɒ́nik) *adj.* [L. fr. Gk *paiōn*]

Paes·tum (péstəm) (*Gk* Posidonia) an ancient city (now ruins) in S. Campania, Italy, near Salerno, founded by Greeks (c. 600 B.C.), with well preserved ruins of Doric preclassical temples

Pá·ez (páes), José Antonio (1790–1873), Venezuelan soldier and comrade-in-arms of Bolívar. He was in command of the llanero cavalry. On the separation of Venezuela from Gran Colombia he served (1831–5) as first president of the Republic, resuming office from 1839 to 1843. After exile (1850–8), he returned as dictator (1861–3)

pa·gan (péigən) **1.** *n.* a heathen, esp. one who worshipped the gods of ancient Greece and Rome **2.** *adj.* pertaining to or characteristic of a pagan [fr. L. *paganus,* civilian, in contrast to the Christian *miles,* soldier (of Christ)]

Pa·ga·ni·ni (pægəní:ni:), Niccolò (1782–1840), Italian violinist. His almost legendary virtuosity is reflected in the difficulty of many of his compositions

pa·gan·ism (péigənizəm) *n.* the state of being pagan ‖ pagan beliefs and practices [fr. eccles. L. *paganismus*]

pa·gan·ize (péigənaiz) *v.t. pres. part.* **pa·gan·iz·ing** *past* and *past part.* **pa·gan·ized** to make pagan [F. *paganiser*]

Page (peidʒ), Walter Hines (1855–1918), U.S. journalist and diplomat. As editor of several U.S. journals, incl. (1896–9) the 'Atlantic Monthly', he campaigned for reforms in southern agriculture, education and industry. Appointed (1913) U.S. ambassador to Great Britain, he strongly supported the Allied cause at the onset of the 1st world war. This alienated President Woodrow Wilson, who was then anxious to maintain American neutrality

page (peidʒ) **1.** *n.* one side of a piece of paper or leaf of a book ‖ (*loosely*) a leaf of a book ‖ (*computer*) a single sheet of data ‖ a fixed block or number of blocks of data or instructions **2.** *v.t. pres. part.* **pag·ing** *past* and *past part.* **paged** to make up (printed matter) into pages ‖ to number the pages of (a manuscript or printed text) [F.]

page 1. *n.* a boy or young man employed as a personal attendant in a royal or noble household ‖ a boy employed in a hotel to carry messages or otherwise be of personal service to guests ‖ a boy attendant upon the bride at a wedding ‖ (*hist.*) a young man in attendance upon a knight while himself in training for knighthood ‖ a boy attendant in a legislative body, esp. Congress **2.** *v.t. pres. part.* **pag·ing** *past* and *past part.* **paged** to attend as a page ‖ to summon (a person, e.g. in a hotel) by calling his name repeatedly [O.F.]

pag·eant (pǽdʒənt) *n.* a colorful spectacle, either on a fixed stage or site or taking the form of a procession of tableaux representing esp. historical events ‖ a sequence of things or events resembling such a spectacle ‖ pageantry **pág·eant·ry** *n.* pageants collectively ‖ spectacular, colorful display [M.E. *pagyn, padgin* etc., a movable stage, prob. fr. L.]

page proof (*printing*) a proof printed from type that has been made up into pages

pag·i·nal (pǽdʒin'l) *adj.* of or relating to a page of a book etc. [fr. L.L. *paginalis*]

pag·i·nate (pǽdʒineit) *pres. part.* **pag·i·nat·ing** *past* and *past part.* **pag·i·nat·ed** *v.t.* to divide (a printed text) into pages ‖ to number the pages of (a manuscript or printed text) **pag·i·ná·tion** *n.* a paginating or being paginated ‖ the numbers etc. distinguishing the pages of a book etc. [fr. L. *pagina,* page]

paging system an organized service that contacts via radio signal the carrier of a portable battery-operated receiver, e.g., a sales representative or physician, alerting him or her to make a telephone call in order to receive a message

pa·go·da (pəgoudə) *n.* an elaborately decorated Far Eastern sacred building, usually a tower with many stories that taper toward the top, with an upwardcurling, projecting roof over each story [fr. Port. and Ital. *pagode,* prob. fr. Pers.]

Pa·go Pa·go (pάŋgoupáŋgou) *SAMOA, AMERICAN

Pa·hang (pəhʌ́ŋ) the longest river (288 miles, navigable for 250) of Malaysia, flowing south and east from the central mountains to the South China Sea ‖ the state (area 13,820 sq. miles, pop. 419,000) through which it flows. Capital: Kuantan (a port). It came under British control in 1888 and joined the Federation of Malaya (now Malaysia) in 1948

Pah·la·vi, Peh·la·vi (pάləvi:), Mohammed Reza (1919–80), shah of Iran (1941–79). After dismissing Mossadegh (1953), he exercised more direct control of the government, and promoted social and economic reforms, social and economic reforms, launching the so-called White Revolution (1963). He sought to control social unrest through Savak, the secret police. From 1978 opposition to him centered around the Ayatollah Khomeini, and in 1979 the Shah was deposed. His admission to the U.S.A. for medical treatment caused Iranian militants to seize hostages at the U.S. embassy in Teheran. The Shah went to Panama, then to Egypt, where he died

Pahlavi, Pehlevi, Reza Shah (1877–1944), shah of Iran (1925–41). An army officer, he gained power by a coup d'état (1921) which overthrew the Kajar dynasty, and was proclaimed shah (1925). He did much to modernize Iran but, because of his pro-Axis tendencies, was forced by Britain and the U.S.S.R. to abdicate (1941) in favor of his son, Mohammed Reza Pahlavi

Pah·la·vi, Peh·le·vi (pɑ́ləvi:) *n.* the Persian language (3rd-7th cc.)

pahlavi, pehlevi *n.* a Persian gold coin containing 7.32 gms of gold, not constituting part of monetary circulation

Pah·sien (bɑ́ʃjén) *CHUNGKING

paid (peid) *past* and *past part.* of PAY ‖ *adj.* receiving wages or salary ‖ involving no stoppage of regular wages or salary, *paid holidays* **to put paid to** (*Br.*) to put an end to, esp. to thwart (some plan)

pail (peil) *n.* an open container, esp. of metal, usually almost cylindrical and wider at the top than at the bottom, having an arched handle at the top and used esp. for carrying liquids ‖ a pailful [etym. doubtful]

pail·ful (péilful) *pl.* **pail·fuls** *n.* the amount a pail will hold

paillasse *PALLIASSE

pail·lette (pæljét) *n.* a small piece of metal or foil used in enamel painting ‖ a spangle for ornamenting dresses [F., dim. of *paille*, straw]

pain (pein) **1.** *n.* an unpleasant sensation caused by the stimulation of certain nerves, esp. as a result of injury or sickness ‖ a distressing emotion, *his refusal caused her pain* ‖ (*pl.*) specially concentrated effort, *take pains to be accurate* ‖ (*pl.*) the labor of childbirth **on** (or **upon** or **under) pain of** with the certainty of incurring (some punishment) unless a specified command or condition is fulfilled, *you must sign the confession on pain of death* **to take pains** to make a special, concentrated effort **2.** *v.t.* to inflict esp. mental pain upon [O.F. *peine*]

Paine (pein), Thomas (1737–1809), British political writer and radical pamphleteer. He emigrated to Pennsylvania (1774) and supported the American colonies against Britain in his pamphlet 'Common Sense' (1776) and in his series 'The Crisis' (1776–83). Returning to Britain (1787), he wrote 'The Rights of Man' (1791–2) in answer to Burke's criticism of the French Revolution. He fled to France (1792), became a French citizen, and took a prominent part in French politics. His defense of deism in 'The Age of Reason' (1794–5) roused a storm of protest. He returned to the U.S.A. in 1802

pain·ful (péinfəl) *adj.* causing or characterized by pain ‖ requiring or showing laborious care or effort

pain·less (péinlis) *adj.* not causing pain ‖ not requiring trouble or hard work

pains·tak·ing (péinzteikiŋ) *adj.* showing or using great care and effort

paint (peint) **1.** *v.t.* to apply paint to (a surface) ‖ to create (a picture, design etc.) on a surface, using paint ‖ to represent in paint, *to paint a landscape* ‖ to make a vivid written or spoken description of ‖ to apply cosmetics to ‖ to apply medicine etc. to (a throat etc.) as if applying paint ‖ (with 'out') to efface by covering with paint ‖ *v.i.* to practice the art of creating pictures with paint **to paint the town red** to go out and celebrate on a grand scale **2.** *n.* a liquid or paste consisting of a suspension of a pigment in oil or water etc. When spread over a surface, it dries to form a hard, thin covering colored by the pigment ‖ a pigment mixed with a water-soluble gum so as to form a cake ‖ the hardened skin on a painted surface, *the paint on the door is scratched* ‖ (*pop.*) cosmetics [O.F. *peindre*]

paint·brush (péintbrʌʃ) *n.* a brush of bristle, hair or fiber for applying paint

painted lady *Vanessa cardui*, a common orange butterfly with black and white spots

painted printed circuit (*electr.*) an integrated circuit painted or printed with conductive paint

paint·er (péintər) *n.* a rope attached to the bow of a boat and used to tie it up to a stake or ring on shore or to a towing vessel [origin unknown]

painter *n.* an artist who paints pictures ‖ an artisan who applies paint to walls etc. as a profession [A.F. *peintour*]

paint·er·ly (péintərli:) *adj.* of a style of painting that emphasizes color, tone and texture rather than line

paint-in (péintin) *n.* a cooperative volunteer venture to paint what requires painting

paint·ing (péintiŋ) *n.* a picture produced by applying paint to a surface ‖ the act or art of making such pictures

pair (pɛər) **1.** *pl.* **pairs, pair** *n.* a set of two things of the same kind, *a pair of laces* ‖ a single unit made up of two corresponding parts, *a pair of pliers* ‖ a thing consisting of two complementary parts, *a pair of pajamas* ‖ two persons associated together, e.g. a husband and wife, two friends, partners or dancers ‖ two persons of opposing views in a legislative body etc. who agree mutually not to record their votes on some issue ‖ either of these persons, or their agreement ‖ two playing cards of the same denomination ‖ two horses in harness **2.** *v.t.* to join (two people or things) in a pair ‖ to divide or arrange into groups of two ‖ *v.i.* to form a pair ‖ (with 'with') to agree with (a member of opposite views) that neither will vote **to pair off** to divide (members of a group) into pairs ‖ to join (two people or things) in a pair ‖ (of two people or things in a larger group) to form a pair [F. *paire*]

pair bond (*anthropology*) a monogamous union —**pair-bonding** *n.*

paired-as·so·ci·ate learning (pɛ́ərdəsóuʃi:itlə́rniŋ) a system of learning of analogous units in pairs to speed recall, esp. in the study of languages

pair of binoculars binoculars

pair of scales a simple beam balance

pair of virginals a virginal

pair production the total and simultaneous transformation of a photon into an electron and a positron by interaction with the electric field of a nucleus

pai·sa (páisə) *pl.* **pai·se** (páisei) *n.* a monetary unit of India, one hundredth of a rupee ‖ a monetary unit of Pakistan, one hundredth of a rupee ‖ a coin worth 1 paisa [Hindi]

Pais·ley (péizli:) a town (pop. 94,025) in Renfrew, Scotland, adjoining Glasgow, a thread-spinning center since the early 18th–c. Abbey (15th c.)

pais·ley (péizli:) *adj.* of a soft woolen material printed usually in rich colors with an elaborate abstract pattern having a characteristic tear-drop-shaped motif ‖ of this pattern ‖ designating a garment, esp. a shawl, of this material [PAISLEY, Scotland]

pa·ja·mas, *Br.* **py·jam·as** (pədʒɑ́məz) *pl. n.* a loose-fitting sleeping garment consisting of jacket and trousers, the latter suspended by a cord or elastic around the waist ‖ loose silk or cotton trousers worn by men and women Moslems in Eastern countries [Hind. *pajama, paijama* fr. Pers. *pae*, foot, leg+*jamah*, clothing]

Pak·i·stan (pǽkistæn, pɑ́kistɑn) a republic in S. Asia, (area 310,404 sq. miles, pop. 84,580,000) Capital: Islamabad. Pakistan controls the northern and eastern portions (Azad Kashmir) of Kashmir. People: *INDIA (subcontinent). Languages: English, Urdu. Religion: Moslem (official). Pakistan is 19% cultivated and 3% forest. The Hindu Kush, Pamirs and E. Himalayas cross the far north. Highest peak: Tirich Mir (26,263 ft) in the Hindu Kush. The west (former Baluchistan and Northwest Frontier Province) is a partly desert plateau, mainly 1,500–6,000 ft, joining that of Afghanistan with mountain ranges running mainly north-south (*SALT RANGE, *SULAIMAN RANGE). River valleys lead to the great passes: the Khyber, Bolan and Gumal. The east (former Punjab and Sind) is a fertile alluvial plain (Indus, Jhelum, Chenab and Sutlej Rivers, *INDUS) with waste areas along the Indian frontier (*THAR). Average summer and winter temperatures (F.): Quetta (plateau) 78° and 40°, plains 87° and 62°. Rainfall: Quetta 10 ins, plains 20 ins, mountains 40 ins. Livestock: cattle, water buffaloes, poultry, sheep, goats, camels. Crops: cereals, cotton, sugarcane, rape, mustard, fruit, tobacco. Minerals and other resources: coal, chromite, gypsum, oil, natural gas, bauxite, sulfur, limestone, iron ore, salt. Manufactures and industries: textiles, cotton, jute, chemicals, steel, oil refining, carpets, newsprint, paper, cigarettes, tanning, embroidery, pottery, glass, aluminum, cement, jute milling, hydroelectricity. Exports: raw jute, jute manufactures, raw cotton, raw wool, fish, hides and skins, cotton textiles, wheat, rice. Imports: machinery, iron and steel, wheat, oil and fuels, rice, chemicals, metals, vehicles. Chief port: Karachi. There are three universities. Monetary unit: Pakistani rupee (divided into 100 paisa). HISTORY. Pakistan was formed (1947) from the predominantly Moslem parts of India, as a result of the campaign led by Jinnah and the Moslem League. The partition was followed by riots in which thousands were killed. Several million Hindu refugees fled to India, and as many Moslems migrated from India to Pakistan. The newly formed dominion was at war with India over the status of Kashmir (1947–9) until the U.N. imposed a cease-fire. Pakistan struggled against economic difficulties and food shortages. It joined the South East Asia Treaty Organization (1954) and the Central Treaty Organization (1955). It became a republic within the Commonwealth (1956) but its constitution was suspended (1958) after a military coup and Ayub Khan assumed the presidency. A new constitution (1962) provided for a presidential form of government. The longstanding dispute with India over Kashmir broke briefly into open war (1965). Anarchy spread (Mar. 1969) through wide areas esp. of E. Pakistan. Ayub Khan resigned as president in favor of Gen. Yahya Khan. In 1971 the army put down an insurrection by partisans claiming independence for the eastern region. The influx into India of millions of refugees contributed to the outbreak (Dec. 1971) of a new conflict between India and Pakistan. The defeat of the Pakistani army led to the proclamation of a republic under the name Bangladesh (Free Bengal) in the territory comprising E. Pakistan. Yahya Khan resigned and was succeeded by Ali Bhutto. Under a third constitution (1973) Bhutto became prime minister of Pakistan until the army seized control again (1977). Gen. Zia ul-Haq became president (1978), and Bhutto was arrested and hanged. In an Islamic revival, a new series of laws was passed (1979) based on Islamic tenets, and the Islamization was endorsed by referendum (1984). The constitution was amended (1985) to strengthen Zia's powers and allow him to appoint the prime minister. An influx of over 3,000,000 Afghan refugees burdened Pakistan's economy and strained its relations with the U.S.S.R.

Pak·i·stan·i (pækistǽni:, pɑkistɑ́ni:) **1.** *n.* a native or inhabitant of Pakistan **2.** *adj.* of or from Pakistan

pal (pæl) **1.** *n.* (*pop.*) a close friend, buddy **2.** *v.i. pres. part.* **pal·ling** *past* and *past part.* **palled** (*pop.*, with 'up') to become a pal or pals ‖ (*pop.*, with 'around') to be together as pals [Romany (Eng. use)=brother, buddy]

pal·ace (pǽlis) *n.* a large, often ornate residence of an emperor, king, pope etc. ‖ (esp. *Br.*) an archbishop's or bishop's residence ‖ a large mansion ‖ a large, often ornate place of public entertainment [O.F. *palais, paleis*]

pal·a·din (pǽlədin) *n.* (*hist.*) one of the 12 peers of Charlemagne's court ‖ (*rhet.*) a hero or champion [F. fr. Ital.]

palaeobotany *PALEOBOTANY

Palaeocene *PALEOCENE

palaeographer *PALEOGRAPHER

palaeographic *PALEOGRAPHIC

palaeography *PALEOGRAPHY

palaeolith *PALEOLITH

Pa·lae·ol·o·gus (peili:ɒ́ləgəs) a dynasty which ruled the Byzantine Empire (1261–1453). It was founded by Michael VIII, and ended with Constantine XI

palaeontologic *PALEONTOLOGIC

palaeontologist *PALEONTOLOGIST

palaeontology *PALEONTOLOGY

Palaeozoic *PALEOZOIC

Pa·la·mas (pɑlɑmɑ́s), Kostas (1859–1943), Greek nationalist poet. His chief works include 'Hymn to Athena' (1889), 'Twelve Books of the Gipsy' (1907), 'The King's Flute' (1910)

pal·an·quin, pal·an·keen (pælənkí:n) *n.* a covered litter or couch carried on poles by four or six bearers and used in parts of the Far East [Port. *palanquim* fr. E. Ind.]

CONCISE PRONUNCIATION KEY: **(a)** æ, *cat*; ɑ, *car*; ɔ *fawn*; ei, *snake*. **(e)** e, *hen*; i:, *sheep*; iə, *deer*; ɛə, *bear*. **(i)** i, *fish*; ai, *tiger*; ə:, *bird*. **(o)** ɒ, *ox*; au, *cow*; ou, *goat*; u, *poor*; ɔi, *royal*. **(u)** ʌ, *duck*; u, *bull*; u:, *goose*; ə, *bacillus*; ju:, *cube*. x, *loch*; θ, *think*; ð, *bother*; z, *Zen*; ʒ, *corsage*; dʒ, *savage*; ŋ, *orangutang*; j, *yak*; ʃ, *fish*; tʃ, *fetch*; 'l, *rabble*; 'n, *redden*. Complete pronunciation key appears inside front cover.

pal·at·a·bil·i·ty (pælətəbíliti:) *n.* the quality or state of being palatable

pal·at·a·ble (pǽlətəb'l) *adj.* pleasant to taste ‖ pleasant or acceptable to the mind, *even friendly criticism can be far from palatable* **pál·at·a·bly** *adv.* [PALATE]

pal·a·tal (pǽlət'l) **1.** *adj.* pertaining to the palate ‖ (*phon.*) of a sound made with the front of the tongue raised against the hard palate **2.** *n.* (*phon.*) a sound so made

pal·a·tal·i·za·tion (pælət'lizéiʃən) *n.* the quality or state of being palatalized ‖ an instance of this **pál·a·tal·ize** *pres. part.* **pal·a·tal·iz·ing** *past and past part.* **pal·a·tal·ized** *v.t.* (*phon.*) to produce (a sound) with the front of the tongue against or near the hard palate [F.]

pal·ate (pǽlit) *n.* the roof of the mouth, separating the mouth cavity from the nasal cavity ‖ the sense of taste, *pleasing to the palate* [fr. L. *palatum*]

pa·la·tial (pəléiʃəl) *adj.* having the size, magnificence etc. of a palace [fr. L. *palatium*, palace]

pa·lat·i·nate (pəlǽt'neit, pəlǽt'nit) *n.* (*hist.*) the land ruled by a count palatine **the Palatinate** (*hist.*) either of two regions of Germany which together composed (1356) an electorate of the Holy Roman Empire. Both were attached to Bavaria (late 18th c.). The Rhine Palatinate (on the middle Rhine) is now in Rhineland-Palatinate, the Upper Palatinate on the Czechoslovakian border, in Bavaria [PALATINE]

pal·a·tine (pǽlətain) **1.** *n.* (*hist.*) a medieval overlord having sovereign privileges within his domain **the Palatine** the Palatinate ‖ one of the seven hills of Rome **2.** *adj.* (used postpositively) having royal privileges, e.g. (*Br.*) the counties of Chester, Durham and Lancaster ‖ (used postpositively) having the privileges of a palatine ‖ of or pertaining to a palatinate [F. *palatin, palatine* fr. L. *palatinus*, belonging to the imperial palace]

pa·lat·ine *adj.* (*anat.*) palatal ‖ designating either of two bones that form the hard palate [F. *palatin, palatine* fr. L. *palatum*, palate]

pa·lav·er (pəlǽvər, pəlάvər) **1.** *n.* a long-drawn-out conferring or bargaining, esp. in tribal custom ‖ (*pop.*) any wordy discussion ‖ flowery, ingratiating language **2.** *v.i.* to engage in palaver or a palaver [Port. *palavra*, a word]

Pa·la·wan (pɑlάwɑn) the western-most island (area 4,550 sq. miles, pop. 236,635) of the Philippines, with a central mountain range rising to 6,839 ft: manganese mines

pa·laz·zo pants (pɑlάtsou) *n.* women's pants with very wide legs, esp. for pajamas

pale (peil) *n.* a length of wood driven into the ground, with a pointed upper end, used with others in a fence ‖ an enclosed district or territory ‖ (*heraldry*) a vertical stripe dividing the shield into two halves **the Pale** (*hist.*) an area of varying extent around Dublin, Ireland, under English rule (14th–16th cc.) ‖ (*hist.*) an area around Calais, France, under English control (1346–1558) **beyond the pale** socially unacceptable [F. *pal*]

pale *adj.* lacking intensity of color or of illumination, *pale moonlight* ‖ (of complexion) of a whitish color [O.F. *palle, pale*]

pale *pres. part.* **pal·ing** *past and past part.* **paled** *v.i.* to become pale ‖ to lose importance or quality, esp. by contrast, *her beauty pales, next to yours* ‖ *v.t.* to make pale [fr. O.F. *palir*, F. *pâlir*]

pa·le·a (péili:ə) *pl.* **pa·le·ae** (péili:i:) *n.* a small bract on the base of a floret of a composite flower ‖ the inner chaffy bract in the flower of a grass ‖ the scaly growth of the epidermis in a fern [L.=chaff]

pale·face (péilfeis) *n.* a white-skinned person (supposed American Indian name for a non-Indian)

Pa·lem·bang (pɑlembάŋ) the chief city (pop. 582,961) and trade center of S. Sumatra, Indonesia, a river port 56 miles from the South China Sea: metallurgy, shipbuilding. University (1960)

Pa·len·ci·a (pəlénsi:ə) a province (area 3,256 sq. miles, pop. 186,512) of N. Spain (*OLD CASTILE, *LEÓN)

Pa·len·que (pɑléŋke) a town in Chiapas, Mexico. It was an important center of Mayan civilization, discovered in 1773

pa·le·o·bot·a·ny, pa·lae·o·bot·a·ny (peili:oubɒ́t'ni:, pæli:oubɒ́t'ni:) *n.* the botany of fossil plants and plant impressions [fr. Gk *palaios*, ancient+BOTANY]

Pa·le·o·cene, Pa·lae·o·cene (péili:əsi:n, pæli:əsi:n) *adj.* (*geol.*) of the earliest epoch or series of the Tertiary (*GEOLOGICAL TIME) **the Paleocene, the Palaeocene** the Paleocene epoch or series of rocks [fr. Gk *palaios*, ancient+*kainos*, new]

pa·le·o·e·col·o·gy (peili:ouikɒ́lədʒi:) *n.* study of the ecology of past geological eras based on the analysis of fossils

pa·le·og·ra·pher, pa·lae·og·ra·pher (peili:ɒ́grəfər, pæli:ɒ́grəfər) *n.* a specialist in paleography

pa·le·o·graph·ic, pa·lae·o·graph·ic (peili:əgrǽfik, pæli:əgrǽfik) *adj.* pertaining to paleography

pa·le·og·ra·phy, pa·lae·og·ra·phy (peili:ɒ́grəfi:, pæli:ɒ́grəfi:) *n.* the science of deciphering ancient manuscripts or inscriptions [fr. Mod. L. *palaeographia* fr. Gk *palaios*, ancient+*graphos*, written]

pa·le·o·lith, pa·lae·o·lith (péili:əliθ, pǽli:əliθ) *n.* an unpolished chipped stone implement of the second period of the Stone Age. **Pa·le·o·lith·ic, Pa·lae·o·lith·ic** *adj.* of the second period of the Stone Age, characterized by the use of paleoliths. The Paleolithic period, which succeeded the Eolithic and preceded the Mesolithic, began with man's first certain attempts to shape tools and ended (in Europe) c. 8000 B.C. It is divided into epochs of cultural development: Abbevillian, Acheulean, Mousterian, Aurignacian and Magdalenian [fr. Gk *palaios*, ancient+*lithos*, stone]

pa·le·on·to·log·ic, pa·lae·on·to·log·ic (péili:ɒntəlɒ́dʒik, pǽli:ɒntəlɒ́dʒik) *adj.* pertaining to paleontology **pá·le·on·to·lóg·i·cal, pá·lae·on·to·lóg·i·cal** *adj.*

pa·le·on·tol·o·gist, pa·lae·on·tol·o·gist (peili:ɒntɒ́lədʒist, pæli:ɒntɒ́lədʒist) *n.* a specialist in paleontology

pa·le·on·tol·o·gy, pa·lae·on·tol·o·gy peili:ɒntɒ́lədʒi:, pæli:ɒntɒ́lədʒi:) *n.* the branch of geology concerned with the study of the fossil remains of animal and plant life of past geological periods [fr. Gk *palaios*, ancient+*onta* pl. of *on*, being+*logos*, word]

Pa·le·o·si·ber·i·an (peili:ousaibíəri:ən) *n.* a Siberian aborigine of an indeterminable racial classification

Pa·le·o·zo·ic, Pa·lae·o·zo·ic (peili:əzóuik, pæli:əzóuik) *adj.* of the era of geological history between the Mesozoic and the Precambrian, characterized by the development of invertebrates and the appearance of reptiles, amphibians and seed-bearing plants (*GEOLOGICAL TIME) **the Paleozoic, the Palaeozoic** this era [fr. Gk *palaios*, ancient+*zōē*, life]

Pa·ler·mo (pəléərmou, pələ́:rmou) the capital (pop. 673,200) and chief port of Sicily, Italy, in the northwest. Industries: shipbuilding, metallurgy, chemicals, food processing, wine, cork, tourism. Norman palace, Byzantine mosaics, churches and cathedral (11th–12th cc.), Renaissance and 18th-c. monuments. University (1779)

Pal·es·tine (pǽlistain) a region on the eastern shore of the Mediterranean, now included in Israel. It is the Holy Land for Jews (as the land promised them by God) and for Christians (as the birthplace and home of Jesus Christ), and is a place of pilgrimage for Moslems. Originally referred to in the Old Testament as Canaan, it developed a pastoral economy (4th millennium B.C.), and was conquered (c. 1468 B.C.) by Egypt. After several other invasions, Egypt regained control (c. 1300 B.C.), but Philistines settled on the coast, Aramaeans in N. Syria and Israelites in the hill country (c. 1300–1000 B.C.). In the face of the Philistine menace, the Israelite tribes united under Saul, David and Solomon (c. 1040–c. 932 B.C.), but split (c. 932 B.C.) into two kingdoms, Israel in the north and Judah in the south. The former fell (c. 722 B.C.) to the Assyrians under Sargon II, and the latter was conquered (586 B.C.) by the Babylonians under Nebuchadnezzar II. The whole area was conquered by Cyrus II of Persia (539 B.C.) and by Alexander the Great (333 B.C.). Attempts to impose Hellenism provoked the revolt of the Maccabees (c. 168–142 B.C.), after which the Jews obtained political independence (142–63 B.C.) until occupied by the Romans under Pompey. During the reign (37–4 B.C.) of the Roman puppet Herod, Christ was born in Bethlehem. Increasing Roman control provoked a Jewish revolt (66 A.D.), the destruction of the Temple (70 A.D.) and the expulsion of the Jews from Judaea. Palestine became a Roman province and, after 330, part of the Byzantine Empire. It fell to the Arabs (638), and despite the Crusades (1096–1270) remained under Moslem influence, being conquered (1516) by the Ottoman Turks. It continued under their rule until 1918, despite a brief invasion (1799) by Napoleon and Egyptian occupation (1831–40) under Ibrahim Pasha. The growth of Zionism (1890s) led to Jewish colonization from Europe. Turkish rule was ended by the British invasion (1917–18) under Allenby, aided by Lawrence. The Balfour Declaration (1917) established Palestine as the site of a national home for the Jews, and aroused bitter Arab opposition. Palestine became a British mandate (1920), but hostilities soon broke out between the Jews and Arabs. Jewish immigration increased (1930s) as a result of persecution in Europe and, despite a British attempt to limit it (1939), continued to grow during the 2nd world war. The U.N. recommended partition between the Arabs and Jews, but both sides refused (1947). The British mandate ended (May 14, 1948), and the State of Israel was proclaimed. After war (1948–9) between Israel and some states of the Arab League, Israel greatly increased her territory, Jerusalem was divided, Jordan acquired part of Palestine west of the Jordan and the Gaza Strip was occupied by Egypt. After the lightning third Israeli-Arab war (June 1967) Israel occupied Jordanian Palestine west of the Jordan as well as the Gaza Strip, while Jerusalem was reunited. The UN General Assembly reaffirmed the Palestinians' right to self-determination and national sovereignty (1974), and Jordan renounced its claims by signing the Rabat resolution proclaiming the Palestine Liberation Organization (PLO) the sole legitimate representative of the Palestinian people. None of the programs or strategies offered or advocated has provided a solution to the problem of a homeland for the Palestinians and many still live in refugee camps

Palestine Liberation Organization (pǽlistainlibəréiʃənɔrgənizéiʃən) (*abbr.* PLO) an organization composed of several Palestinian groups attempting to 'liberate' Palestine from what the view as an illegitimate Israeli state. Formed (1964) to represent Palestinian Arabs, it considers itself their political and military arm. Its charter vests supreme policy-making authority in the Palestine National Council. It was proclaimed sole legitimate representative of the Palestinian people by the Arab states (1974) and was recognized by the U.N. General Assembly as the 'representative of the Palestinian people.' Yasir Arafat became PLO chairman in 1969, but since 1983 the organization has been divided into pro- and anti-Arafat factions, the latter largely backed by Syria. Expelled from Jordan (1971), PLO forces established themselves in Lebanon, whence they launched attacks on Israel. Driven from Beirut (1982) by the Israeli army, they scattered throughout the Arab world. In 1985, Arafat and Jordan's King Hussein announced that the PLO would accept a negotiated settlement of the Arab-Israeli dispute, but Israel continued to refuse to negotiate with the PLO and the violence escalated. The PLO continued to be linked to and take credit for numerous terrorist activities worldwide

Pa·le·stri·na (pælistrí:nə), Giovanni Pierluigi da (c. 1525–94), Italian composer. He is best known for his noble polyphonic sacred choral works, including the 'Missa Papae Marcelli' (Mass dedicated to Pope Marcellus), many motets, a 'Stabat Mater' etc.

pal·ette (pǽlit) *n.* a small board on which a painter mixes his colors ‖ the range of colors used by a particular artist or for a particular picture ‖ (*armor*) one of the rounded iron plates at the armpit [F. dim. of *pale*, thin board]

palette knife an artist's thin, flexible knife used for mixing colors, cleaning the palette, and often for applying the paint

Pa·ley (péili:), William (1743–1805), English theologian whose 'Principles of Moral and Political Philosophy' (1785) and 'View of the Evidences of Christianity' (1794) had great popular success. His latitudinarianism was also expressed in 'Natural Theology' (1802)

pal·frey (pɔ́lfri:) *pl.* **pal·freys** *n.* (*hist.*) a small saddle horse, esp. for a lady [O.F. *palefrei*]

Pa·li (pάli:) *n.* the old Indic canonical language, in which the early Buddhist literature was written. Pali has died out in India but survives in Burma and Thailand as a religious and literary language [fr. Skr. *pāli-bhāsā*, language of the canonical texts]

pal·i·mo·ny (pǽləmounì:) *n.* settlement payment awarded to a separated partner of an unmarried couple that has lived together in division of assets or for maintenance; from the Lee Marvin-Michele Triola case

pal·imp·sest (pǽlimpsest) *n.* a parchment or tablet which has been reused after previous writing has been erased ‖ a manuscript on such a parchment or tablet [fr. L. *palimpsestus* fr. Gk *palin,* again+*psēstos* fr. *psēn,* to rub smooth]

pal·in·drome (pǽlindroum) *n.* a word, sentence etc. which reads the same backward and forward (e.g. 'Madam I'm Adam') [fr. Gk *palindromos,* running back again]

pal·ing (péiliŋ) *n.* a fence made of pales ‖ pales collectively

pal·in·gen·e·sis (pælindʒénisis) *n.* (*biol.*) recapitulation ‖ metempsychosis ‖ regeneration ‖ (*geol.*) re-formation of granitic magma by melting and recrystallization [fr. Gk *palin,* again+*genesis,* origin]

pal·i·node (pǽlinoud) *n.* a poem in which a previous poem, usually satirical, is retracted ‖ a recantation [fr. L. *palinodia* fr. Gk *palin,* again+*ōdē,* song]

pal·i·sade (pæliséid) **1.** *n.* a fence of wooden or iron pales ‖ (*mil. hist.*) a strong, sharply pointed wooden stake set with many others in a row, upright or oblique, as a defense work ‖ a fence made of such stakes **2.** *v.t. pres. part.* **pal·i·sad·ing** *past* and *past part.* **pal·i·sad·ed** to enclose or fortify with palisades [F. *palissade*]

palisade parenchyma a tissue of the mesophyll usually on the upper side of the leaf blade consisting of a regular array of thin-walled cylindrical cells with abundant chloroplasts (cf. SPONGY PARENCHYMA)

Pa·lis·sy (pæli:si:), Bernard (1510–c. 1589), French potter. His most striking achievement was with wares ornamented with colored subjects in high relief

pall (pɔl) *v.i.* to cease to be interesting or attractive [perh. fr. APPALL]

pall *n.* a large piece of cloth, draped over a coffin or tomb ‖ something that casts gloom over an area by covering it, *a pall of smoke* ‖ (*eccles.*) a linen-covered piece of cardboard used to cover the chalice ‖ (*eccles.*) a pallium ‖ (*heraldry*) a bearing representing the front half of a Church dignitary's pallium [O.E. *pæll,* a cloth fr. L.]

Pal·la·di·an (pəléidi:ən) *adj.* (*archit.*) in or of the style of Andrea Palladio

pal·lad·ic (pəlǽdik, pəléidik) *adj.* of compounds of tetravalent palladium

Pal·la·dio (pallɑ́djɔ), Andrea (Andrea di Pietro, 1508–80), Italian Renaissance architect. He was largely responsible for the revival of classical architecture, first in Italy, and then throughout Europe. His principal achievement was his series of great mansions which set the style for later building in Europe and the U.S.A. His 'I quattro libri dell'architettura' (1570) has been reprinted many times

pal·la·di·um (pəléidi:əm) *n.* a metallic element (symbol Pd, at. no. 46, at. mass 106.4) resembling and occurring with platinum, used as a catalyst and in some alloys **pal·la·dous** (pəléidəs) *adj.* of compounds of divalent palladium [Mod. L. after *Pallas,* name of an asteroid]

Pal·las (pǽləs) one of the names of the Greek goddess Athena

pall·bear·er (pɔ́lbɛərər) *n.* one of the little group of men who carry the coffin at a funeral or who are its closest attendants

pal·let (pǽlit) *n.* (*heraldry*) an ordinary resembling a pale but having half its width [dim. of PALE n.]

pallet *n.* a narrow, hard bed ‖ a mattress stuffed with straw [M.E. *pailet* fr. F. *paille,* straw]

pallet *n.* a potter's flat-bladed wooden tool used in shaping clay ‖ a small flat-bladed knife used to transfer gold leaf to the object being gilded ‖ (*mach.*) a click or pawl which engages with the teeth of a ratchet wheel to convert one kind of motion into another, esp. in a clock or watch ‖ a portable platform used to haul materials to be stored, transported etc. ‖ a valve regulating the airflow to an organ pipe [F. *palette,* dim. of *pale,* spade, blade]

pallet truck a mechanical hoist for transporting a pallet (platform)

pal·liasse, pail·lasse (pǽljæs) *n.* a thin hard mattress stuffed with straw [F. *paillasse*]

pal·li·ate (pǽli:eit) *pres. part.* **pal·li·at·ing** *past* and *past part.* **pal·li·at·ed** *v.t.* to cause (an evil) to seem less than it is, or disguise the gravity of (a fault) with excuses etc. ‖ to relieve (pain or disease) but not cure it [fr. L. *palliatus,* cloaked]

pal·li·a·tion (pæli:éiʃən) *n.* a palliating or being palliated ‖ something that palliates [F.]

pal·li·a·tive (pǽli:eitiv, pǽli:ətiv) **1.** *adj.* serving to palliate **2.** *n.* something that palliates [F. fem. of *palliatif,* serving to conceal or cloak]

pal·lid (pǽlid) *adj.* (e.g. of complexion) abnormally pale ‖ lacking brightness or warmth of color [fr. L. *pallidus*]

pal·li·um (pǽli:əm) *pl.* **pal·li·a** (pǽli:ə), **pal·li·ums** *n.* (*eccles.*) a circular white woolen band with pendants of white wool at front and back, worn by high Church dignitaries ‖ (*zool.*) the mantle of a mollusk or of a bird ‖ (*anat.*) the cortex of the brain [L.]

pal·lor (pǽlər) *n.* unusual paleness of the skin [L.]

palm (pɑm) **1.** *n.* the inner part of the hand, between wrist and fingers ‖ the corresponding part of a glove ‖ a flat extension of an implement, e.g. the blade of a paddle ‖ (*naut.*) the fluke of an anchor ‖ the broad flat part of an antler **to have an itching palm** to have a greedy desire for money **to hold** (or **have**) **someone in the palm of one's hand** to have someone at one's mercy **2.** *v.t.* to conceal in the palm, esp. for the purpose of cheating, *to palm a card* **to palm something off** (often with 'on') to get rid of something by inducing someone to take it [M.E. *paume* fr. F.]

palm *n.* a member of *Palmae* (or *Palmaceae*), order *Palmales,* a family of monocotyledonous, largely tropical trees and shrubs, generally having a tall trunk with no branches and a crown of large leaves ‖ the leaf of one of these trees ‖ one of these leaves or a substitute carried on Palm Sunday ‖ (*rhet.*) victory or success, or a token symbolizing this [O.E. *palm, palma, palme* fr. L. *palma*]

Pal·ma (pɑ́lmɑ), Ricardo (1833–1919), Peruvian writer, the author of 'Tradiciones peruanas' (1872–1910), a leading account of the colonial era. He is known as the creator of a new genre, the tradición (historical anecdote)

Pal·ma (pɑ́lmə) (*Span.* Palma de Mallorca) the capital (pop. 319,620) of the Balearic Is, Spain, a port and resort on S.W. Majorca. Catalan Gothic cathedral (13th–14th cc.)

pal·mar (pǽlmər, pɑ́lmər) *adj.* (*anat.*) of or in the palm

palm·a·ro·ta·tion (pɑmɑroutéiʃən) *n.* massage technique pressing whole hand firmly on flesh and moving circularly

pal·ma·ry (pǽlməri:, pɑ́lməri:) *adj.* (*rhet.*) worthy of the palm of victory [fr. L. *palmarius*]

Palmas *LAS PALMAS

pal·mate (pǽlmit, pǽlmeit, pɑ́lmit, pɑ́lmeit) *adj.* shaped like a hand spread open, esp. (*bot.,* of a leaf) divided into lobes arising from a common center ‖ (*zool.*) having the toes webbed, as in most aquatic birds **pál·mat·ed** *adj.* [fr. L. *palmatus*]

Pal·ma Vec·chio (pɑ́lmɑvékkjɔ) (Jacopo Negretti, c. 1480–1528), Venetian painter. He excelled as a colorist and is chiefly known for his religious paintings and landscape backgrounds

Pal·mer (pɑ́mər), Alexander Mitchell (1872–1936), U.S. Attorney General (1919–21) under President Wilson. Palmer ordered the mass arrests of alleged subversives that are known as the 'Palmer raids'

Palmer, Samuel (1805–81), English painter and engraver. He is best known for his visionary landscapes, which show the influence of William Blake

palm·er (pɑ́mər) *n.* (*hist.*) a pilgrim carrying a palm leaf in token of having visited the Holy Land ‖ (*hist.*) an itinerant begging monk [A.F. *palmer, paumer*]

Palmer Archipelago (formerly Antarctic Archipelago) an island group, part of the Falkland Islands Dependencies, between South America and the Antarctic

Palmer Peninsula the southern part of the Antarctic Peninsula

Palm·er·ston (pɑ́mərstən), Henry John Temple, 3rd Viscount (1784–1865), British statesman. He entered parliament as a Tory (1807), joined the Whigs (1829), and was foreign secretary (1830–41 and 1846–51) and prime minister (1855–8 and 1859–65). A conservative in domestic policy, he supported liberal movements abroad, notably in Belgium (1830–1), Spain, Portugal (1832–4) and Italy (1858–61), and opposed French and Russian expansion in the Eastern Question. He brought the Crimean War to a close, and maintained British neutrality in the American Civil War. His impulsive and high-handed approach to diplomacy brought him into conflict with his colleagues and Queen Victoria, as well as with foreign powers

Palmerston North an agricultural center (pop. 46,000) of S. North Island, New Zealand. University (1963)

palm·er·worm (pɑ́mərwə:rm) *n.* any of several caterpillars, esp. the larva of the moth *Dichomeris ligulellas,* which is very destructive to fruit trees

pal·met·to (pælmétou) *pl.* **pal·met·tos, pal·met·toes** *n.* any of several fan palms, esp. the cabbage palmetto and *Chamerops humilis,* the Mediterranean dwarf fan palm [Span. *palmito,* dim. of *palma,* palm]

palm·ist (pɑ́mist) *n.* a person who practices palmistry

palm·is·try (pɑ́mistri:) *n.* the practice or profession of foretelling a person's future or reading his character by interpreting the crease lines in the palm and other aspects of his hand [M.E. fr. *paume, palme,* palm]

pal·mit·ic acid (pælmítik, pɑlmítik) a waxy crystalline solid acid, $C_{15}H_{31}COOH$, contained in palm oil and in most vegetable and animal fats [fr. F. *palmitique*]

pal·mi·tin (pǽlmitin) *n.* a glyceride of palmitic acid occurring in palm oil and other fats [F. *palmitine*]

palm kernel the seed of a palm yielding palm oil

palm oil a very sticky fat extracted from the fruit or seed of certain palms. The oil is a source of vitamin A, and is used in making soaps and for margarine, cosmetics, lubricants etc.

palm reader security device requiring personal identification with an encoded plastic card and the placement of the palm of the hand in a reader that scans its shape and size

palm sugar a coarse brown sugar made from palm sap

Palm Sunday the Sunday before Easter. It commemorates Christ's triumphal entry into Jerusalem, when the crowd strewed palm leaves in his path

palm wine the fermented sap of various palms, a very popular drink, esp. in parts of Africa

palm·y (pɑ́mi:) *comp.* **palm·i·er** *superl.* **palm·i·est** *adj.* of or like a palm (tree), or having many palms ‖ flourishing, prosperous, *palmy days*

Pal·my·ra (pælmáirə) an ancient city of Syria which flourished (1st c. B.C.–3rd c. A.D.) as an oasis on the trade routes across the Syrian desert and as the center of an empire stretching from Asia Minor to Egypt. It was conquered (273) by the Romans under Aurelian. The ruins include the great temple of Baal

pal·my·ra (pælmáirə) *n.* *Borassus flabellifer,* a fan palm much cultivated in India and Ceylon. It is used for thatch, matting, umbrellas, hats etc. and for lumber. Its sap is rich in sugar [older *palmeira* fr. Port.]

Pal·o·mar, Mount (pǽləmɑr) the site, in S.W. California, of an observatory containing a 200-inch reflecting telescope (1948)

pal·o·mi·no (pæləmí:nou) *pl.* **pal·o·mi·nos** *n.* a horse of a light tan or golden color with a whitish mane and tail [Span. adj.=of or like a dove]

palp (pælp) *n.* a palpus [F. *palpe* fr. L.]

pal·pa·bil·i·ty (pælpəbíliti:) *n.* the quality or state of being palpable ‖ something palpable

pal·pa·ble (pǽlpəb'l) *adj.* tangible, perceptible to the touch ‖ easily perceptible to the mind, obvious, *a palpable falsehood* **pál·pa·bly** *adv.* [fr. L.L. *palpabilis* fr. *palpare,* to touch gently]

pal·pal (pǽlpəl) *adj.* of the nature of or serving as a palpus

pal·pate (pǽlpeit) *adj.* (*zool.*) having a palpus [fr. PALPUS]

palpate *pres. part.* **pal·pat·ing** *past* and *past part.* **pal·pat·ed** *v.t.* to examine by feeling, esp. in medical examination **pal·pá·tion** *n.* [fr. L. *palpare* (*palpatus*), to touch gently]

pal·pe·bral (pǽlpəbrəl) *adj.* of, pertaining to or located on or near the eyelid [fr. L. *palpebra,* eyelid]

pal·pi·tate (pǽlpiteit) *pres. part.* **pal·pi·tat·ing** *past* and *past part.* **pal·pi·tat·ed** *v.i.* to tremble ‖ (of the heart) to throb rapidly and strongly [fr. L. *palpitare* (*palpitatus*)]

pal·pi·ta·tion (pælpitéiʃən) *n.* an irregular and violent heartbeat resulting from malfunction or from physical or emotional stress ‖ a trembling [fr. L. *palpitatio* (*palpitationis*)]

pal·pus (pǽlpəs) *pl.* **pal·pi** (pǽlpai) *n.* the maxillary or labial feeler of an insect, usually occurring in pairs ‖ a sensory appendage of a crustacean, worm etc. [L.=a feeler]

pal·sied (pɔ́lzi:d) *adj.* affected with palsy

pal·sy (pɔ́lzi:) *pl.* **pal·sies** *n.* (not used technically) paralysis, sometimes with shaking tremors [M.E *palesie, parlesie* fr. O.F. *paralisie* fr. L. fr. Gk]

pal·tri·ness (pɔ́ltri:nis) *n.* the quality of being paltry

pal·try (pɔ́ltri:) *comp.* **pal·tri·er** *superl.* **pal·tri·est** *adj.* trivial, petty, *a paltry sum* ‖ mean, despicable, *a paltry trick* [origin unknown]

pa·lu·dal (pəlú:d'l, pǽljəd'l) *adj.* of or pertaining to marshes ‖ (*med.*) malarial **pal·u·dism** (pǽljədizəm) *n.* malaria [fr. L. *palus (paludis)*, marsh]

pal·y (péili:) *adj.* (*heraldry*) (of a shield) divided into four or more vertical strips differing alternately in tint [fr. F. *palé*]

Pa·mirs, the (pəmíərz) a plateau, largely at 12,000–13,000 ft, with several peaks over 20,000 ft (*COMMUNISM, MT) covering most of Tadzhikistan, U.S.S.R. and the borders of China, Kashmir, Pakistan and Afghanistan. It is the center from which the Himalayas, Karakoram, Kunlun, Tien Shan and Hindu Kush extend

Pam·li·co Sound (pǽmlikou) an inlet (80 miles long, 8–30 miles wide) between the E. North Carolina mainland and island strips off the coast. It joins Albemarle Sound on the north

pam·pas (pǽmpəs) *pl. n.* treeless plains in South America, south of the Amazon, esp. the cattle-raising grasslands of E. central Argentina [Span. *pampa* fr. Quechua=plain]

pampas grass *Cortaderia selloana*, a South American grass with whitish silky panicles carried on stalks up to 12 ft high

pam·per (pǽmpər) *v.t.* to overindulge (someone), coddle [prob. fr. L.G.]

pam·phlet (pǽmflit) *n.* a small printed publication sewn or stitched as a paper-covered booklet, comprising an essay or treatise of a controversial, topical nature ‖ a small printed publication, often just a folder, containing informative literature **pam·phlet·éer 1.** *n.* a person who writes controversial pamphlets **2.** *v.i.* to write such pamphlets [M.E. *Pamphilet, Panflet* fr. *Pamphilus*, title of a 12th-c. L. amatory poem]

Pam·plo·na (pæmplóunə) the capital (pop. 167,762) of Navarre, Spain, and historical capital of Navarre. Industries: textiles, paper, mechanical engineering. Gothic cathedral (14th–15th cc.), citadel (16th c.). Famous bullfight festival (July)

Pan (pæn) (*Gk mythol.*) the god of flocks and herds, represented as a man having the legs of a goat and often a goat's horns and ears

pan (pæn) **1.** *n.* any of a number of metal containers of different shapes, used in cooking and baking ‖ any shallow, open receptacle of metal, earthenware or plastic, used for any of a variety of domestic purposes ‖ any container like this in shape, e.g. a vessel in which gold etc. is separated from gravel by washing ‖ a vessel for heating or evaporating ‖ one of the receptacles in a beam balance etc. ‖ a salt pan ‖ a layer of hardpan ‖ a flat expanse of ice floating in the sea, smaller than an ice floe ‖ (*mil.*) in air intercept, a code meaning the calling station has an urgent message to transmit concerning the safety of a ship, aircraft, or other vehicle, or of a person on board or within sight **2.** *v. pres. part.* **pan·ning** *past* and *past part.* **panned** *v.t.* to wash (gravel or sand bearing gold etc.) in a pan to separate the valuable particles from the rest ‖ to separate (gold etc.) from gravel or sand in this way ‖ (*pop.*) to criticize harshly (a play, concert etc.) ‖ *v.i.* to search for gold etc. by washing gravel or sand in a pan ‖ (esp. with 'out') to yield gold etc. when washed in this way ‖ (with 'out') to turn out (in some specified way), *it panned out poorly for him* ‖ (with 'out') to turn out well, *the project didn't pan out* [O.E. *panne, ponne*]

pan *pres. part.* **pan·ning** *past* and *past part.* **panned** *v.i.* to move a cinema or television camera to get a panoramic effect or to follow a moving object ‖ (of the camera) to be moved in this way ‖ *v.t.* to move (the camera) in this way [PANORAMA]

pan *n.* the leaf of the betel palm ‖ a preparation of betel nut, chewed as a masticatory in the East Indies [Hind. *pān*, betel leaf]

pan- *prefix* all ‖ completely [Gk *pan*, neut. of *pas*, all]

PAN *n.* peroxyacetyl nitrate, a pollutant ingredient of smog created by the action of sunlight on hydrocarbons and nitrogen oxides in the air

pan·a·ce·a (pænəsí:ə) *n.* a cure for all ills, a universal remedy [L. fr. Gk *panakeia*]

pa·nache (pənǽʃ) *n.* a tuft of feathers, esp. on the headdress or helmet ‖ bravura, swagger [F. fr. Ital. *pennacchio* fr. *penna*, feather]

Pan-Af·ri·can·ism (pænǽfrikənizəm) *n.* any of several 20th-c. movements among African states (esp. the Organization of African Unity) to promote African cooperation and unity, and to eliminate colonialism and white supremacy from Africa

Pan·a·ma (pǽnəmɑ) a republic (area incl. former Canal Zone 29,754 sq. miles, pop. 1,921,700) occupying the Isthmus of Panama (the narrowest part of Central America) with many offshore islands. Capital: Panama City. People: Mestizo (72%), with African (West Indian), white and Indian minorities (incl. 62,000 tribal Indians). Languages: Spanish, Indian languages, English. Religion: 95% Roman Catholic, 5% Protestant. The land is 3% cultivated and 7% pasture. The Central American cordillera runs the length of the country, sloping from 11,410 ft (Chiquirí) near Costa Rica and 7,000 ft on the Colombian border to low hills (500–1,500 ft) in the center, where the Panama Canal crosses. The Caribbean slope and coastal plains are jungle-covered. Agriculture and population are concentrated on the drier Pacific side (forest and savanna). Average temperatures (F.): coasts 87°, interior 66°. Rainfall: Colón 128 ins, N. Pacific coast 6 ins, Panama City 69 ins. Livestock: cattle, hogs, poultry, horses. Agricultural products: bananas, rice, sugarcane, corn, cocoa, hemp, abaca, coffee, coconuts. Forest products: mahogany, dyewoods. Mineral resources: gold, salt. Manufactures and industries: sugar, beer and spirits, cement, clothing, oil refining. Exports: bananas, shrimps, sugar, cocoa, coffee. Imports: manufactures, machinery, vehicles, food, chemicals, petroleum products. Panama's large merchant fleet is mainly foreign-owned. Ports: Panama City, Colón. University: Panama City (1935). Monetary unit: balboa (100 cents). HISTORY. The region was inhabited by Indian tribes when it was visited (1501) by a Spanish expedition. The isthmus was crossed (1513) by Balboa and became a vital link in the treasure route from Peru to Spain. It became part of the viceroyalty of Peru (1542) and of New Granada (1740), and shared the history of Colombia until Nov.3, 1903 when, with the encouragement of the U.S.A., it seized its independence from Spain. Panama immediately gave the U.S.A. permission to construct, use and control the Panama Canal. The canal was completed (1914) and provides a main source of revenue for Panama. A series of revolts and coups d'état have characterized Panama since 1940. Arnulfo Arias was three times (1941, 1949, 1968) deposed by the National Guard. José Remón, elected in 1952, was assassinated in 1955. Ernesto della Guardia (president 1956–60), Robert F. Chiari (president 1960–4), and Marco Robles (president 1964–8) governed constitutionally. Friction grew with the U.S.A. over the status of the Canal Zone. There were riots and agitation (1958, 1959) to fly the Panama flag alongside the U.S. flag in the Zone and to obtain jurisdiction of the canal from the U.S.A. A U.S. Congressional resolution (1960) opposed Panama's demand to fly its flag, but President Eisenhower allowed it to be displayed at one place in the Zone. Presidents John F. Kennedy and Roberto Chiari agreed (1962) that the flag could be flown throughout the Zone. Further anti-American riots in 1964 led Panama to suspend diplomatic relations with the U.S.A. Relations with the U.S. were resumed that same year and conferences were held to revise the Treaty of 1903. After the third dismissal of Arias, Panama was governed by a military junta, initially headed by Col. José M. Pinilla and then by Gen. Omar Torrijos, who remained Panama's most powerful political figure until his death (1981). He directed the promulgation of a new constitution (1972), which was amended (1978) to provide for the election of a president by the National Assembly. In 1983 major reforms provided for the popular election of the president. Aristides Royo (president 1978–82) was succeeded by Nicolás Ardito Berletta (1984–5), who resigned and was succeeded by Vice-President Eric Arturo Delvalle

pan·a·ma (pǽnəmɑ) *n.* a hat of fine material plaited from the dried young leaves of the jipijapa ‖ a machine-made imitation of this

Panama, Bay of *PANAMA, GULF OF

Panama Canal a ship canal (51 miles long) crossing central Panama, connecting the Atlantic and the Pacific. Transit time: 7–8 hours (through 6 pairs of locks). A French attempt under de Lesseps to build a canal (1881–9) had collapsed in bankruptcy. The U.S.A. negotiated a treaty (1903) with Panama, under which the U.S.A. obtained the right to build a canal and to occupy and control the Panama Canal Zone (5 miles on either side of the canal) in return for a payment of $100 million and an annuity of $250,000, raised by 1955 to $1,930,000. The canal was opened to shipping (1914). The U.S.A. and Panama agreed (1965) that a new treaty should recognize Panama's sovereignty over the Canal Zone, to be integrated in Panama, but negotiations were not completed until 1978, when two treaties were ratified by the U.S. Senate guaranteeing the canal's neutrality after the year 2000 and stipulating U.S. supervision of the canal, with increasing Panamanian participation, until 2000. At that time Panama assumes legal control. A new 36-mile sea-level canal, ten miles west of the present one, able to handle double the amount of shipping and to take ships of 150,000 tons, is in preparation

Panama City (*Span.* Panamá) the capital (pop. 467,000) of Panama, near the Pacific terminus of the Panama Canal. It was founded by Spaniards (1519). Industries: food processing, brewing, light manufactures. Cathedral (1760), university (1935)

Panama, Congress of a meeting called (1826) by Simón Bolívar in the hope of achieving solidarity among the nations of America. The congress was attended only by Colombia, Peru, Mexico, and Central America. It was the first and last of its kind

Panama disease a fungus disease of the banana characterized by withering of the leaves and the dying-off of the shoots

Panama, Gulf of a large inlet of the Pacific on the south coast of Panama. Its inner part is called the Bay of Panama and is the site of Panama City

Panama, Isthmus of the link (420 miles long) between North and South America, separating the Atlantic and Pacific Oceans

Pan-A·mer·i·can (pænəmérikən) *adj.* of, involving or relating to all the nations of North, Central and South America or their people

Pan-American Conference, Second a conference held (1901) in Mexico City, at which nine delegations, incl. the U.S.A., agreed that all future disputes would be settled peacefully

Pan-American Conference, Third a conference held (1906) in Rio de Janeiro. It was marked by a serious lack of harmony and by Latin American resentment of President Theodore Roosevelt's 'big stick' Corollary

Pan-American Congress *INTERNATIONAL CONFERENCE OF AMERICAN STATES, FIRST

Pan-American Highway an international road system running from Fairbanks, Alaska to Buenos Aires, Argentina, with branches to all Central and South American countries

Pan-A·mer·i·can·ism (pænəmérikənizəm) *n.* the movement to promote social, economic and political cooperation among all the states of the Americas (*PAN-AMERICAN UNION)

Pan-American Union an international agency established (1890) by the first Pan-American Conference (1889–90) to promote inter-American cooperation. It offers technical and information services to all the American republics, serves as the repository for inter-American documents, and promotes economic, social, judicial, and cultural relations. It became (1948) the general secretariat for the Organization of American States. Pan-American Day (Apr. 14) celebrates the anniversary of its founding

Pan-Ar·a·bism (pænǽrəbizəm) *n.* a movement to promote the political unity of the Arab peoples. It arose (early 20th c.) as a reaction to the Turkish-sponsored Pan-Turanism movement, and developed also as a reaction to British Zionist policy in Palestine. It gave rise to the formation of the Arab League (1945) and to attempts to form a United Arab Republic

Pa·nay (pɑnái) an island (area 4,446 sq. miles,

CONCISE PRONUNCIATION KEY: **(a)** æ, *cat*; ɑ, *car*; ɔ *fawn*; ei, *snake*. **(e)** e, *hen*; i:, *sheep*; iə, *deer*; ɛə, *bear*. **(i)** i, *fish*; ai, *tiger*; ə:, *bird*. **(o)** o, *ox*; au, *cow*; ou, *goat*; u, *poor*; ɔi, *royal*. **(u)** ʌ, *duck*; u, *bull*; u:, *goose*; ə, *bacillus*; ju:, *cube*. x, *loch*; θ, *think*; ð, *bother*; z, *Zen*; ʒ, *corsage*; dʒ, *savage*; ŋ, *orangutang*; j, *yak*; ʃ, *fish*; tʃ, *fetch*; 'l, *rabble*; 'n, *redden*. Complete pronunciation key appears inside front cover.

pop. 2,144,544) of the central Philippines (Visayas), producing esp. rice. Chief town: Iloilo

pan·cake (pǽnkeik) **1.** *n.* a thin, flat cake made of batter cooked on a griddle, or in a pan ‖ (*wrestling*) maneuver in which an arm lock is placed over one of the opponent's arms and an attempt is made to grasp forearm or waist to pull opponent and twist for a backward fall **2.** *v. pres. part.* **pan·cak·ing** *past* and *past part.* **pan·caked** *v.i.* (*aviation*) to drop or land almost vertically though with the aircraft horizontal ‖ *v.t.* to cause (an aircraft) to do this

Pancake Day (*Br.*) Shrove Tuesday, when traditionally pancakes are eaten

Pan·cha·tan·tra (pʌ́ntʃətʌ́ntrə) a collection of didactic fables in Sanskrit of the 3rd or 4th c., still popular in India

Pan·chen Lama (pǽntʃən) *LAMA

pan·chro·mat·ic (pæŋkroumǽtik) *adj.* (of a photographic film) sensitive to all the wavelengths of the visible spectrum ‖ (of a lens) transmitting the whole of the visible spectrum

Pan·cras (pǽŋkrəs), St (*d.* 304), Roman martyr. According to legend, he was a boy of 14 when he was martyred. Feast: May 12

pan·cre·as (pǽŋkri:əs) *n.* a large gland that in man lies behind the stomach. It consists of two portions, one secreting digestive juices which pass into the duodenum, the other secreting insulin which passes into the bloodstream (*ISLET OF LANGERHANS) **pan·cre·at·ic** (pæŋkri:ǽtik) *adj.* [Mod. L. fr. Gk *pankreas*, sweetbread]

pan·cre·a·tin (pǽŋkri:ətin) *n.* any of several enzymes found in pancreatic juices, or a mixture of these ‖ a preparation containing such a mixture obtained from an animal's pancreas, for aiding digestion [fr. Gk *pankreas* (*pankreatos*), sweetbread]

pan·da (pǽndə) *n.* either of two mammals of fam. *Procyonidae*, related to the raccoon. *Ailuropoda melanoleuca*, the giant panda, is a black and white bearlike animal of Tibet and S. China. *Ailurus fulgens*, of the Himalayas, has long, reddish-brown fur marked with black and white, and closely resembles the raccoon [perh. Nepalese]

pan·dect (pǽndekt) *n.* a complete code of laws **the Pandects** a summary of Roman civil law (530–3), forming part of Justinian I's 'Corpus juris civilis' [F. *pandecte* fr. L. fr. Gk *pan*, all+*dechesthai*, to receive]

pan·dem·ic (pændémik) *adj.* (of a disease) affecting a whole country, or the whole world (cf. ENDEMIC) [fr. Gk *pandēmos*, universal]

pan·de·mo·ni·um (pændəmóuni:əm) *n.* a state of utter confusion and uproar [fr. *Pandaemonium*, name for the capital of Hell, coined by Milton fr. Gk *pan*, all+*daimōn*, demon]

pan·der (pǽndər) **1.** *v.i.* (with 'to') to give active encouragement (to someone or something that should not be encouraged) or provide gratification (for someone or something that should not be gratified) **2.** *n.* a procurer for prostitutes ‖ someone who encourages the vices or weaknesses of another [M.E. *Pandare* fr. L. *Pandarus* fr. Gk *Pandaros*, one of the leaders in the Trojan War. In medieval romances he is the go-between for Troilus and Cressida]

pan·dit (pʌ́ndit) *n.* a Hindu learned in religion, laws and science [Hindi]

Pan·do·ra (pændɔ́rə, pændóurə) (*Gk mythol.*) the first woman, sent to earth as a punishment for Prometheus's crime of stealing fire from the gods. Zeus gave her a box which, when opened, let loose all human misfortunes, but hope remained in the bottom to comfort mankind

pane (pein) *n.* a single sheet of glass in a window, greenhouse etc. ‖ a division of a window etc. containing such a sheet of glass in a frame ‖ a flat side or edge of a many-sided object [F. *pan*, a piece of cloth]

pan·e·gyr·ic (pænidʒírik) **1.** *n.* a speech or writing eulogizing someone or something **2.** *adj.* having the nature of a panegyric **pan·e·gýr·i·cal** *adj.* **pan·e·gýr·ist** *n.* [F. *panégyrique* fr. L. fr. Gk *panēgurikos*, fit for a public assembly]

pan·el (pǽn'l) **1.** *n.* a flat, rectangular piece of wood etc. forming part of a wall, door etc. but distinguished from the rest by being recessed, framed etc. ‖ a vertical strip of material let into or partially attached to a dress, skirt etc. as a structural or decorative element ‖ a thin board sometimes used instead of a canvas in oil painting ‖ a picture or photograph of much greater height than width ‖ a board etc. in which the controls or instruments of a machine etc. are set ‖ the padded lining of a saddle ‖ a pad used as a saddle ‖ a group of persons, usually experts, required to judge or give an answer, *a panel of jurors* **2.** *v.t. pres. part.* **pan·el·ing,** esp. *Br.* **pan·el·ling** *past* and *past part.* **pan·eled,** esp. *Br.* **pan·elled** to furnish with panels ‖ (*law*) to empanel **pán·el·ing,** esp. *Br.* **pán·el·ling** *n.* panels of wood applied to a wall or ceiling **pán·el·ist** *n.* a member of a panel (group of persons) [O.F.+piece of cloth]

panel code (*mil.*) prearranged code designed for visual communications, usu. between friendly units by making use of marking panels *also* marking panel

pang (pæŋ) *n.* a brief, keen spasm of pain ‖ a sudden mental or emotional pain, *pangs of conscience* [etym. doubtful]

Pan·gae·a (pændʒí:ə) *n.* (*geol.*) a hypothetical single continent of the Triassic period (200 million yrs. ago); coined by Alfred Wegener

pan·gen·e·sis (pændʒénisis) *n.* a theory of heredity proposed by Darwin, that each cell of the body throws off particles (gemmules) into the blood, which circulate, subdivide, and collect in the reproductive cells

Pan-Ger·man·ism (pǽndʒə́:rmənizəm) *n.* a movement (late 19th–20th cc.) to promote the union of all German-speaking people under German rule. It gave rise to German expansionist policy before the 1st world war, and its aims were later taken up by the National Socialist German Workers party

pan·go·lin (pǽŋgoulin) *n.* any of several members of genus *Manis*, order *Pholidota*, or related genera of scaly mammals of Asia and Africa, which feed on ants and roll themselves into a ball when attacked [Malay *peng-gōling*, roller]

pan·gram (pǽngræm) *n.* a sentence that involves all the letters of the alphabet preferably with little duplication, *the quick brown fox jumps over the lazy dog* —**pan·gram·mat·ic** *adj.*

pan·han·dle (pǽnhænd'l) **1.** *n.* a narrow, protruding strip of land or political territory, esp. the northern part of Texas between Oklahoma and New Mexico **2.** *v. pres. part.* **pan·han·dling** *past* and *past part.* **pan·han·dled** *v.i.* (*pop.*) to beg, esp. on the street

Pan·hel·len·ic (pænhəlénik) *adj.* relating to or including all Greece or all Greeks

pan·ic (pǽnik) **1.** *n.* intense, contagious fear affecting a body of people ‖ an instance of this fear, e.g. a widespread hysterical anxiety over the prevailing financial situation, resulting in hasty sale or protection of securities etc. ‖ intense, irrational fear felt by an individual **2.** *v. pres. part.* **pan·ick·ing** *past* and *past part.* **pan·icked** *v.i.* to lose rational control of one's behavior out of sudden intense fear ‖ *v.t.* to affect with panic **3.** *adj.* of, relating to or showing panic, *panic haste* [F. *panique* adj. fr. Gk *panikos*, of the god Pan, who was believed to cause unreasoning terror]

panic grass a member of *Panicum* or related genera of grasses incl. millet [fr. L. *panicum*, a kind of millet]

pan·ick·y (pǽniki:) *adj.* liable to panic ‖ beginning to feel panic

pan·ic-strick·en (pǽnikstrikən) *adj.* madly frightened, filled with panic

pan·i·cle (pǽnik'l) *n.* (*bot.*) a compound raceme ‖ a loose, irregular flower cluster [fr. L. *panicula* dim. of *panus*, tuft]

pan·ic-struck (pǽnikstrʌk) *adj.* panic-stricken

pan·ic·u·late (pəníkjulit) *adj.* arranged in panicles **pa·nic·u·lat·ed** (pəníkjuleitid) *adj.* [fr. Mod. L. *paniculatus* fr. *panicula*, panicle]

Pan-Is·lam (pǽnízlɑm) *n.* a movement (late 19th–early 20th cc.) to promote political unity among Moslem nations, led by Turkey before the 1st world war **Pán-Is·lám·ic** *adj.* **Pán-Ís·lam·ism** *n.*

Panjabi *PUNJABI

pan·jan·drum (pændʒǽndrəm) *n.* a mock title for a person of great self-importance [coined in 1755 by Samuel Foote (1720–77), Eng. playwright and actor]

Panj·nad (pʌndʒnʌ́d) *SUTLEJ

Pank·hurst (pǽŋkhə:rst), Emmeline (1858–1928), British suffragette. With her daughters Christabel (1880–1958) and Sylvia (1882–1960), she founded a militant suffragette movement (1903)

Pan·kow (pʌ́nkau) a suburb of East Berlin, seat of the government of the German Democratic Republic

panne (pæn) *n.* a soft fabric with a long pile, similar to velvet [F.]

pan·nier (pǽnjər) *n.* a large basket, esp. one of a pair slung over the back of a beast of burden ‖ a large basket with a lid ‖ one of two bags of canvas, plastic, leather etc. slung over the back wheel of a bicycle or motorcycle ‖ (*hist.*) a frame of whalebone or wire used to distend a skirt at the hips or a puffed arrangement of cloth over a skirt around the hips [F. *panier*]

pan·ni·kin (pǽnikin) *n.* (*Br.*) a small metal drinking cup ‖ (*Br.*) the amount it contains [PAN, container]

Pa·no·an (pʌ́nouən) *n.* a major family of South American Indian languages. The best known of the Panoan-speaking peoples live in E. Peru, with related tribes extending into W. Brazil

pan·o·plied (pǽnəpli:d) *adj.* (*hist.*) wearing a complete suit of armor ‖ (*rhet.*) magnificently clothed or decked [PANOPLY]

pan·o·ply (pǽnəpli:) *pl.* **pan·o·plies** *n.* (*hist.*) a complete suit of armor ‖ rich ceremonial dress ‖ (*rhet.*) splendid display [fr. Gk *panoplia*, the full armor of a hoplite]

pan·o·ram·a (pænərǽmə, pænərʌ́mə) *n.* a wide uninterrupted view over a scene ‖ a picture, unrolled so as to give the impression of such a wide, continuous view ‖ a comprehensive survey of a series of events, *a panorama of Elizabethan history* **pan·o·rám·ic** *adj.* **pan·o·rám·i·cal·ly** *adv.* [fr. PAN-+Gk *horama*, view]

pan·pipe (pǽnpaip) *n.* (often *pl.*) a primitive musical instrument consisting of several small reed pipes of graduated length fixed side by side, played by blowing into the mouthpieces [PAN, Gk deity]

Pan-Slav·ism (pænslʌ́vizəm) *n.* a movement (19th and early 20th cc.) to promote the independence of Slav peoples, and their cultural and political unity. It began with a congress in Prague (1848) and was strongly supported by Russia to further her expansion in the Balkans. This gave rise to the Russo-Turkish War of 1877–8, but the alliance of Slav states collapsed in the 2nd Balkan War (1913). Pan-Slavism also represented a threat to Austria-Hungary, whose determination to crush Serbia in 1914 occasioned the 1st world war

pan·sy (pǽnzi:) *pl.* **pan·sies** *n. Viola tricolor*, fam. *Violaceae*, a wild or cultivated plant with richly and variously colored flowers ‖ (*pop.*) an effeminate or homosexual man [older *pensee*, *pensy* fr. F. *pensée*, thought]

pant (pænt) **1.** *v.i.* to breathe quickly and in spasms, esp. after exertion, exposure to heat etc. ‖ (*rhet.* with 'for', 'after') to yearn ‖ (of the heart) to throb rapidly ‖ *v.t.* to utter gaspingly **2.** *n.* one of a series of spasms in labored breathing ‖ one of a series of throbs or gasps made by escaping steam [perh. shortened fr. O.F. *pantoisier, pantiser*]

pan·ta·lets, pan·ta·lettes (pænt'léts) *pl. n.* (*hist.*) long loose drawers, frilled at the bottom, worn by women and girls 1830–50 [dim. of PANTALOON]

pan·ta·loon (pænt'lú:n) *n.* (*pl., hist.*) tight trousers fastened with buttons below the calf or with straps under the shoe [after *Pantaloon*, a Venetian character in commedia dell' arte, usually depicted as a thin old man, wearing tight breeches continued below the knees as stockings, and who survives today as the butt of a clown in pantomime]

pant·dress (pǽntdres) *n.* woman's garment with a divided skirt resembling slacks

pan·tech·ni·con (pæntéknikən) *n.* (*Br.*) a very large moving van [fr. PAN-+Gk *technikon* adj., belonging to the arts]

Pan·tel·le·ri·a (pʌntelerí:ɑ) a volcanic Italian island (area 32 sq. miles, pop. 8,327) in the Mediterranean, halfway between Tunisia and Sicily (with which it is administered). Chief town: Pantelleria. Products: wine, sponges, fish

pan·the·ism (pǽnθi:izəm) *n.* the belief or theory that God and the universe are identical. Among its best-known proponents are the Roman Stoics and Spinoza **pán·the·ist** *n.* **pan·the·ís·tic** *adj.* [fr. PAN-+Gk *theos*, God]

pan·the·on (pǽnθi:ɒn, pǽnθi:ən) *n.* all the gods of a people, *the Hindu pantheon* ‖ a building where the famous dead of a nation are buried or memorialized ‖ a temple dedicated to all the gods **the Pantheon** a temple of this type built in Rome (c. 27 B.C.) and reconstructed in its present round, domed form c. 125 A.D. [L. fr. Gk fr. *pan*, all+*theios*, of or sacred to a god]

pan·ther (pǽnθər) *n.* a leopard, esp. a large

CONCISE PRONUNCIATION KEY: **(a)** æ, *cat*; ɑ, *car*; ɔ *fawn*; ei, *snake*. **(e)** e, *hen*; i:, *sheep*; iə, *deer*; ɛə, *bear*. **(i)** i, *fish*; ai, *tiger*; ə:, *bird*. **(o)** o, *ox*; au, *cow*; ou, *goat*; u, *poor*; ɔi, *royal*. **(u)** ʌ, *duck*; u, *bull*; u:, *goose*; ə, *bacillus*; ju:, *cube*. x, *loch*; θ, *think*; ð, *bother*; z, *Zen*; ʒ, *corsage*; dʒ, *savage*; ŋ, *orangutang*; j, *yak*; ʃ, *fish*; tʃ, *fetch*; 'l, *rabble*; 'n, *redden*. Complete pronunciation key appears inside front cover.

fierce one or a black one ‖ a cougar ‖ a jaguar [M.E. *pantere* fr. O.F. fr. L. fr. Gk]

pant·ie, pant·y (pǽnti:) *pl.* **pant·ies** *n.* (esp. *pl.*) underpants for a woman or a child

pan·tile (pǽntail) *n.* a roofing tile having a cross section shaped like an S with one curve larger than the other, designed to overlap the next tile [PAN, container+TILE]

pan·ti·soc·ra·cy (pæntisɔ́krəsi:) *n.* (*hist.*) a classless, utopian society in which all are equal and all rule [coined by Coleridge (1794) fr. Gk *pant-*, all+*isokratia,* equal rule]

pan·to·graph (pǽntəgræf, pǽntəgrɑf) *n.* an instrument for copying a drawing on any chosen scale, consisting of an assembly of hinged rods arranged as a parallelogram, the whole being able to rotate around a fixed point ‖ (*elec.*) a device at the end of a trolley pole used to collect current [fr. Gk *pant-*, all+*-graphos,* written]

pan·to·mime (pǽntəmaim) **1.** *n.* a form of entertainment in which story and emotion are conveyed by gesture only, without words, but often with music and decor ‖ an English theatrical entertainment, usually at Christmastime, based on a traditional fairy tale but including topical comedy, clowns, and song and dance ‖ dumb show **2.** *v. pres. part.* **pan·to·mim·ing** *past* and *past part.* **pan·to·mimed** *v.t.* to represent by pantomime ‖ *v.i.* to express oneself by pantomime [fr. L. *pantomimus,* an actor in dumb show fr. Gk fr. *pant-*, all+*mimos,* mimic]

pan·to·mim·ic (pæntəmímik) *adj.* of, relating to or having the nature of pantomime [fr. L. *pantomimicus*]

pan·try (pǽntri:) *pl.* **pan·tries** *n.* a larder ‖ a room where the silver, glass etc. under the care of a butler are kept [A.F. *panetrie,* O.F. *paneterie,* bread room]

pants (pænts) *pl. n.* trousers ‖ (esp. *Br.*) short underpants [abbr. of PANTALOONS]

pant·suit (pǽntsu:t) *n.* a woman's garment of pants and blouse and/or jacket of same fabric *Cf* PANTDRESS

pan·tu·ran·i·an·ism (pæntu:rǽni:ænizəm) *n.* extremist political ideology in Greece with a restored Ottoman Empire as its ultimate goal

Pan-Tu·ran·ism (pǽntúrənizəm, pǽnjúrənizəm) *n.* an early 20th-c. movement aimed at uniting all peoples sharing a common Turkish heritage [PAN-+*Turān,* ancient region of central Asia beyond the Oxus, north of Iran]

panty *PANTIE

pan·ty·hose or **pan·ti·hose** (pǽnti:houz) *n.* woman's garment consisting of panties and stockings as a single unit, originally conceived for women wearing miniskirts

Pa·o·li (pɑoli:), Pasquale (1725–1807), Corsican patriot. He was elected president (1755) by the Corsicans in their struggle against Genoese rule, but was forced to submit after Genoa sold the island to France (1768). He went into exile in Britain (1769–90) and persuaded the British government to intervene in Corsica (1794–6)

Pao·ting (báudíŋ) (or Tsingyuan) an agricultural trading center (pop. 265,000) of central Hopei, China

Pao·tow (búdóu) a steelmaking center (pop. 650,000) of Inner Mongolia, China, on the Hwang-ho

pap (pæp) *n.* soft, mashed or semi-liquid food for babies or invalids ‖ political patronage ‖ vapid literature etc. with no intellectual content [perh. fr. L.G. and G. *pappe,* Du. *pap*]

pa·pa (pɑ́pə, pəpɑ́) *n.* (a child's word for) father [F. fr. Ital. fr. L.]

pa·pa·cy (péipəsi:) *pl.* **pa·pa·cies** *n.* the office of the pope ‖ a pope's term of office ‖ the organization of the Roman Catholic Church [fr. M.L. *papatia* fr. *papa,* pope]

Pa·pa·go (pɑ́pəgou) *pl.* **Pa·pa·go, Pa·pa·gos** *n.* a Uto-Aztecan American Indian people, whose development was strongly influenced (1687–1767) by Jesuit missionaries and (after 1767) by Franciscan missionaries. They supported (19th c.) the U.S. government against the Apache Indians. They number about 11,000, settled on three reservations in S. Arizona and scattered throughout N.W. Sonora, Mexico

pa·pa·in (pəpéiin, pəpáiin) *n.* a protein-hydrolyzing enzyme occurring in the milky juice of the green papaya, used to aid digestion and for tenderizing meat [PAPAYA]

pa·pal (péipəl) *adj.* of the pope, his office, jurisdiction, acts etc. [F. or fr. eccles. L. *papalis*]

papal cross a cross with three cross-bars of graduated length, the longest and lowest being at or near the middle of the vertical shaft

papal infallibility (*Roman Catholicism*) the doctrine (defined in 1870) that the pope when speaking ex cathedra on questions of faith and morals will be incapable of error

Papal States (*hist.*) a region of central Italy ruled (754–1870) by the popes. Originally given (754) to the papacy by Pépin III, the states were not under effective papal rule until the 16th c. They were invaded (1796–1814) by the French, but restored (1815) to the papacy. The liberal reforms of Pius IX were withdrawn after the revolution of 1848. Most of the region was joined (1861) to the new kingdom of Italy, but Rome was defended by the French until 1870, when it, too, was seized. The papacy refused to recognize its loss of temporal power until the Lateran Treaty (1929) gave it sovereignty over the Vatican

pa·pa·raz·zo, *pl.* **-i** (pɑpɑrɑ́tsou) *n.* an aggressive free-lance, celebrity-chasing photographer

pa·pav·er·in (pəpǽvərin, pəpéivərin) *n.* papaverine

pa·pav·er·ine (pəpǽvəri:n, pəpéivəri:n) *n.* an alkaloid, $C_{20}H_{21}O_4N$, a constituent of opium, also made synthetically from vanillin. It is used to control spasms and for local anesthesia [fr. L. *papaver,* poppy]

pa·paw, paw·paw (pɔ́pɔ, pəpɔ́) *n.* the papaya ‖ any of several trees and shrubs of genus *Asimina,* fam. *Annonaceae,* esp. *A. triloba* of North America, which has an oblong yellow edible fruit ‖ this fruit [older *papaya, papay* fr. Span. and Port. fr. Carib.]

pa·pa·ya (pəpɑ́jə) *n. Carica papaya,* fam. *Caricaceae,* a Malaysian tree with a large yellow fruit like a honeydew melon, eaten fresh, cooked or preserved. It also grows in India and the West Indies, and is found well into central Africa [Span. fr. Carib.]

Pa·pe·e·te (pɑpi:éitei) the capital (pop. 25,342) of French Polynesia, a port and airport of W. Tahiti

Pa·pen (pɑ́pən), Franz von (1879–1969), German politician, chancellor of Germany (1932). He did much to bring Hitler to power, and helped to prepare the Nazi annexation of Austria (1938)

pa·per (péipər) **1.** *n.* a substance consisting of a felted thin sheet of compactly interlaced fibers of cellulose etc. obtained from wood, rags, straw etc. and used for writing, printing or drawing on, wrapping parcels, covering the walls of a room etc. ‖ a piece of this substance ‖ an essay, esp. on a scholarly subject ‖ an official document ‖ a set of examination questions or a student's written answers ‖ an essay which a student is required to write ‖ a newspaper ‖ (*pl.*) documents carried to prove identity, nationality etc. ‖ money (banknotes, bills etc.) in the form of written promises to pay ‖ a card, folder etc. containing or holding some item, *a paper of pins* ‖ (*pl.*) the collective letters, writings, documents etc. belonging or pertaining to a person **on paper** in writing ‖ hypothetically, in theory **2.** *adj.* made of paper ‖ hypothetical, not having any real substance, *paper promises* **3.** *v.t.* to cover (a wall etc.) with paper ‖ to distribute complimentary tickets to insure a substantial audience for a performance [A.F. and fr. O.F. *papier* fr. L. *papyrus* fr. Gk]

—Paper is prepared in a mill by reducing wood fiber, straw, grasses, rags etc. to a pulp by an alkali, extracting lignin and other noncellulose matter, bleaching (usually with chlorine or a hypochlorite), washing, adding a filler to give a smooth surface, rolling and drying. This process of manufacture originated in China 2,000 years ago. The qualities of the product range widely as to thickness (measured by the weight per area), surface etc.

pa·per·back (péipərbæk) *n.* a book bound in paper

paper chase the game of hare and hounds

paper factor (*chem.*) a natural terpene in the balsam fir tree, first discovered in newsprint, that is an effective insecticide affecting insect metamorphosis

paper gold (*economics*) special drawing rights for settlement of international accounts, through the International Monetary Fund *also* SDR

pa·per·hang·er (péipərhæŋər) *n.* a person who decorates rooms with wallpaper as a profession

paper knife a dull-bladed knife of wood, ivory etc. for opening letters, slitting the pages of untrimmed books etc.

paper money printed documents (e.g. dollar bills) issued by a government through banks and serving as currency

paper mulberry *Broussonetia papyrifera,* fam. *Moraceae,* an Asiatic tree used in making tapa, and grown as a shade tree in Europe and America

paper nautilus *Argonauta argos,* a dibranchiate cephalopod, the female of which produces a thin, non-chambered fragile shell in which the eggs are carried

paper tape (*computer*) a strip or roll of paper of varying widths from ¾ to 1 inch, on which punched holes carry data for computer input

pa·per-train (péipərtrein) *v.* to train a dog to defecate indoors on paper

pa·per·weight (péipərweit) *n.* a small, heavy object used to prevent papers from being scattered or blown away

paper work work such as filling in forms, keeping records, making out accounts etc.

pa·per·y (péipəri:) *adj.* having a consistency, or the flimsiness or thinness, of paper

Pa·phos (péifɒs) the ancient Greek center, in S.W. Cyprus, of the cult of Aphrodite, said to be where she set foot after emerging from the waves. Modern Paphos (pop. 7,000) is 10 miles distant

pa·pi·er col·lé (pɑpi:éər cɒléi) *n.* (*Fr.*) art technique utilizing glue, paper, paint, crayon and other media *syn* collage

pa·pier-mâ·ché, pa·per-mâ·ché (peipərməʃéi) *n.* a light, tough material made of paper pulp mixed with a liquid adhesive, shaped or molded, and allowed to dry [F.=chewed paper]

pa·pil·i·o·na·ceous (pəpili:ənéiʃəs) *adj.* (*bot.,* of certain flowers, e.g. the sweet pea) shaped like a butterfly ‖ of, relating or belonging to *Papilionaceae,* order *Rosales,* a large family of plants whose fruits are legumes [fr. L. *papilionaceus* fr. *papilio* (*papilionis*), butterfly]

pa·pil·la (pəpílə) *pl.* **pa·pil·lae** (pəpíli:) *n.* a small protuberance on a part of the body, e.g. the nipple, or on a plant ‖ a process extending into and nourishing the root of a growing tooth, hair or feather **pa·pil·lar·y, pa·pil·late** (pəpílit) *adjs* [L.=nipple]

pap·il·lo·ma (pæpəlóumə) *pl.* **pap·il·lo·ma·ta** (pæpəlóumətə), **pap·il·lo·mas** *n.* (*med.*) a benign tumor (e.g. a wart) of skin or mucous membrane [Mod. L. fr. *papilla,* nipple]

pap·il·lon (pǽpəlɒn) *n.* a dog of a toy spaniel breed with large, open, erect ears and a fine silky coat (red, ruby, chestnut, puce, black-and-white, dark yellow or white with markings of these colors) with long fringes [F.=butterfly]

pap·il·lose (pǽpilous) *adj.* papillate

Pa·pin (pæpɛ̃), Denis (1647–c. 1712), French physicist and pioneer in the development of the steam engine. He invented the autoclave, in which, under pressure, the boiling point of water was raised

Pa·pi·neau (pæpi:nou), Louis Joseph (1786–1871), Canadian politician and leader of the French-Canadian cause prior to the Rebellion of 1837. As speaker (1815–37) of the Legislative Assembly of Lower Canada, he inspired the Ninety-Two Resolutions, expressing French-Canadian grievances, passed (1834) by the Assembly

pa·pist (péipist) *n.* an advocate of papal supremacy ‖ (used in a hostile sense) a Roman Catholic **pa·pis·tic** (pəpístik), **pa·pís·ti·cal** *adjs* **pa·pist·ry** (péipistri:) *n.* [F. *papiste* or fr. 16th-c. L. *papista*]

pa·poose (pæpú:s, pəpú:s) *n.* a North American Indian baby [Algonquian]

pap·o·va·vi·rus (pǽpóuvəvairəs) *n.* (*med.*) deoxyribonucleic acid viral group believed to cause warts and neoplasms, esp. in animals

pap·pus (pǽpəs) *pl.* **pap·pi** (pǽpai) *n.* (*bot.*) a downy or feathery tuft in place of a calyx, used in the fruit dispersal of e.g. composite plants (e.g. the thistle, dandelion) [Mod. L. fr. Gk *pappos,* old man]

pap·py (pǽpi:) *comp.* **pap·pi·er** *superl.* **pap·pi·est** *adj.* soft and mushy like pap ‖ consisting of pap

pap·ri·ka (pæprí:kə, pǽprikə) *n.* a mildly pungent, red spice ground from the dried ripe fruit of sweet pepper ‖ the fruit itself [Hung.]

Pap smear or **Papanicolaou smear** diagnostic test to detect uterine or cervical cancer, named for U.S. scientist George N. Papanicolaou

Pap·u·a (pǽpju:ə) a former territory of Australia consisting of S.E. New Guinea with the

CONCISE PRONUNCIATION KEY: **(a)** æ, *cat*; ɑ, *car*; ɔ *fawn*; ei, *snake*. **(e)** e, *hen*; i:, *sheep*; iə, *deer*; ɛə, *bear*. **(i)** i, *fish*; ai, *tiger*; ə:, *bird*. **(o)** o, *ox*; au, *cow*; ou, *goat*; u, *poor*; ɔi, *royal*. **(u)** ʌ, *duck*; u, *bull*; u:, *goose*; ə, *bacillus*; ju:, *cube*. x, *loch*; θ, *think*; ð, *bother*; z, *Zen*; ʒ, *corsage*; dʒ, *savage*; ŋ, *orangutang*; j, *yak*; ʃ, *fish*; tʃ, *fetch*; 'l, *rabble*; 'n, *redden*. Complete pronunciation key appears inside front cover.

adjacent islands, now part of Papua New Guinea

Pap·u·an (pǽpju:ən) **1.** *adj.* pertaining to the former territory of Papua or to its native peoples, or to a group of unclassified languages spoken in Papua and New Guinea, New Britain and the Solomon Is, not belonging to the Austronesian family **2.** *n.* a member of any of the native races of Papua and New Guinea ‖ a language of the group spoken in Papua and New Guinea [fr. PAPUA fr. Malay *papuah,* frizzled, from the hair of Papuans]

Papua New Guinea a country (total area 178,260 sq. miles, pop. 3,400,000) occupying the eastern half of New Guinea and outlying islands (Bismarck Archipelago, N. Solomon Is, Trobriand Is, D'Entrecasteaux Is, Louisiade Archipelago, Woodlark Is) and islets. Capital and chief port: Port Moresby. Official languages: English, Pidgin English, Motu. Livestock: cattle (in the north). Exports: copra and shell, rubber, coconut oil, coffee, cocoa, tropical hardwoods, small quantities of gold and other minerals. Imports: food, chemicals, manufactured goods. HISTORY. The territory of Papua was annexed (1883) by Queensland, became a British protectorate (1884), and has been ruled by Australia since 1905. The northeast of New Guinea was occupied (1914) by Australia, was mandated (1920) to Australia by the League of Nations, and was placed under Australian trusteeship (1946) by the United Nations. The two territories were given a common administration (1949). The country became self-governing in 1973 and gained full independence in 1975, as a member of the British Commonwealth. Michael Somare became prime minister (1972–80, 1982–)

pap·ule (pǽpju:l) *n.* a pimple [fr. L. *papula*]

pap·y·ra·ceous (pæpiréiʃəs) *adj.* (*bot.*) of papery texture [fr. L. *papyrus,* paper fr. Gk]

pa·py·rus (pəpáirəs) *pl.* **pa·py·ri** (pəpáirai), **pa·py·rus·es** *n. Cyperus papyrus,* fam. *Cyperaceae,* an aquatic plant indigenous to the Nile Valley. The pith, shredded and pressed into sheets, was used to write on, chiefly by the ancient Egyptians, Greeks and Romans ‖ this material ‖ a document written on papyrus [L. fr. Gk *papuros*]

par (pɑr) **1.** *n.* equality of value, status or condition, *on a par with* ‖ average or normal state, quality, physical condition etc., *to feel below par* ‖ (*commerce*) nominal value, *to sell at par* ‖ (*golf*) the ideal number of strokes in which a hole, or the course, should be played by a scratch golfer **2.** *adj.* (*commerce*) at par ‖ average, normal [L.=equal, equality]

par *PARR

PAR or **par** (*mil. acronym*) perimeter acquisition radar, outermost radar antiballistic missile system *Cf* MSR

pa·ra (pɑ́rə) *n.* a Turkish coin equal to about 1/40 of a piaster ‖ a Yugoslav unit of currency equal to 1/100 of a dinar ‖ a coin of this value [Turk. *pārah,* piece]

para- (pǽrə) *prefix* beside, beyond ‖ amiss, faulty, irregular ‖ somewhat resembling ‖ chemically related to or derived from [fr. Gk *para* prep., beside]

par·a·bi·o·sis (pærəbaióusis) *n.* the anatomical and physiological conjunction of two organisms, e.g. in Siamese twins **par·a·bi·ot·ic** (pærəbaiótik) *adj.* [Mod. L. fr. *para-,* beside+ *-biosis,* mode of life]

par·a·blast (pǽrəblæst) *n.* the yolk of a meroblastic ovum **par·a·blás·tic** *adj.* [PARA-+Gk *blastos,* sprout, germ]

par·a·ble (pǽrəb'l) *n.* a story designed to teach a moral or religious principle by suggesting a parallel [F. *parabole* fr. L. fr. Gk]

pa·rab·o·la (pərǽbələ) *n.* (*geom.*) a plane curve derived from the section of a cone by a plane parallel to its side, and obeying the law that any point on the curve is equidistant from a fixed point (the focus) and from a fixed straight line (the directrix) [Mod. L. fr. Gk *parabolē,* juxtaposition]

par·a·bol·ic (pærəbɒ́lik) *adj.* having the nature of a parabola ‖ (*geom.*) relating to or having the form of a parabola **par·a·ból·i·cal** *adj.* [fr. L.L. *parabolicus*]

pa·rab·o·loid (pərǽbəlɔid) *n.* (*math.*) a quadric surface of which sections parallel to two coordinate planes are parabolas and sections parallel to the third plane are circles, ellipses or hyperbolas ‖ the equation of such a surface **pa·rab·o·lói·dal** *adj.* [PARABOLA]

par·a·ca·sein (pærəkéisi:n) *n.* casein (insoluble protein)

Par·a·cel·sus (pærəsélsəs), Philippus Aureolus (Theophrastus Bombastus von Hohenheim, 1493–1541), Swiss physician, alchemist and natural philosopher. Prominent in the Renaissance reaction against the medical doctrines of Galen and Avicenna, he combined the beginnings of a modern scientific spirit with a Neoplatonic pantheistic mysticism

par·a·chlor·o·phen·y·lal (pærəklɔroufénilal) *n.* (*pharm.*) drug that reduces the brain's serotonin level, used experimentally in treating schizophrenia and tremors *abbr.* **PCPA**

pa·rach·ro·nism (pərǽkrənizəm) *n.* an error in dating, esp. the dating of an event later than is correct [fr. Gk *para,* beside+*chromos,* time]

par·a·chute (pǽrəʃu:t) **1.** *n.* a collapsible umbrella-shaped contrivance of nylon or silk fabric used esp. in aeronautics. A person or thing suspended from it by cords can drop safely through the air because the fall is slowed by the resistance of the air gathered in the top ‖ (*zool.*) a patagium **2.** *v. pres. part.* **par·a·chut·ing** *past* and *past part.* **par·a·chut·ed** *v.t.* to land (a person or thing) by parachute ‖ *v.i.* to descend by parachute [F.]

parachute spinnaker a very large spinnaker used by racing yachts

par·a·chut·ist (pǽrəʃu:tist) *n.* a person, esp. a soldier, who makes descents from aircraft by parachute

Par·a·clete (pǽrəkli:t) *n.* (*theol.*) the Holy Ghost as comforter or advocate [F. *paraclet* fr. L. fr. Gk fr. *para,* beside+*kalein,* to call]

pa·rade (pəréid) **1.** *n.* an assembly of troops in strict order for inspection or drill ‖ a ceremonial procession, esp. of troops ‖ an area where troops assemble for inspection or drill ‖ a passing in review for appraisal, *a fashion parade* ‖ a pompous display, *to make a parade of one's learning* ‖ a place where people stroll for amusement, a promenade **on parade** exhibited for inspection **2.** *v. pres. part.* **pa·rad·ing** *past* and *past part.* **pa·rad·ed** *v.t.* to make a display of, *to parade one's talents* ‖ to cause (soldiers) to be drawn up for inspection or drill ‖ *v.i.* to assemble for the purpose of, and take part in, a parade ‖ to stroll, promenade, in order to attract attention [F. fr. Ital. *parata,* Span. *parada*]

par·a·di·chlor·o·ben·zene (pærədaiklɔroubénzi:n, pærədaiklouroubénzi:n) *n.* a white crystalline compound, $C_6H_4Cl_2$, used mainly as a moth repellent [PARA-+DI-+*chloro-,* containing chlorine+BENZENE]

par·a·digm (pǽrədim, pǽrədaim) *n.* an example serving as a pattern, *a paradigm of virtue* ‖ (*gram.*) a conjugation or declension serving to demonstrate the inflections of a word **par·a·dig·mat·ic** (pærədigmǽtik) *adj.* **par·a·dig·mát·i·cal·ly** *adv.* [F. *paradigme* fr. L. fr. Gk fr. *paradeiknunai,* to show side by side]

paradigmatic *adj.* (*linguistics*) of one of the two relationships operating between an element at a given level between elements of a sentence; of a syntactically interchangeable element, *we* (or *they*) *are going Cf* SYNTAGMATIC

par·a·di·sa·ic (pærədiséiik) *adj.* paradisiacal **par·a·di·sá·i·cal** *adj.* [fr. PARADISE or fr. L. *paradisus,* paradise]

par·a·di·sal (pærədáis'l) *adj.* paradisiacal [fr. L. *paradisus,* paradise]

par·a·dise (pǽrədais) *n.* a place or state in which spiritual bliss is enjoyed after death, the Christian or Moslem heaven ‖ (*Bible*) an intermediate place or state in which, after death, the souls of the righteous await judgment ‖ any place of or offering perfect happiness, *a swimmer's paradise* **Par·a·dise** the garden of Eden [F. *paradise* fr. L. fr. Gk fr. O. Pers.]

par·a·dis·i·ac (pærədísi:æk) *adj.* paradisiacal

par·a·di·si·a·cal (pærədisáiək'l) *adj.* of, relating to or like paradise [fr. L. *paradisiacus* fr. Gk]

par·a·dos (pǽrədɒs) *pl.* **par·a·dos, par·a·dos·es** *n.* (*mil.*) an earthwork erected to protect a position from rear attack [F.]

par·a·dox (pǽrədɒks) *n.* a statement which, though true, seems false and selfcontradictory ‖ a statement which is selfcontradictory and false, though it may seem true or clever ‖ a person or thing displaying contradictory qualities **par·a·dóx·i·cal** *adj.* [fr. L. *paradoxum* fr. Gk *paradoxos* adj., contrary to accepted opinion]

paradoxical sleep (*physiol.*) period in sleep when dreams occur *also* rem sleep

par·a·drop (pǽrədrɒp) *n.* delivery by parachute of personnel or cargo from an aircraft in flight

par·af·fin (pǽrəfin) **1.** *n.* an alkane ‖ a waxy, crystalline, white, odorless substance obtained by distilling wood, coal and esp. petroleum. It is a complex mixture of hydrocarbons, esp. alkanes, and is used as a stable and water-resistant coating or seal, and in candles etc. It is sometimes called paraffin wax ‖ kerosene (*Br.* paraffin oil) **2.** *v.t.* to coat or saturate with paraffin [fr. L. *parum,* too little+*affinis,* skin (from the chemical saturation of these hydrocarbons)]

paraffin hydrocarbon an alkane

paraffin oil (*Br.*) kerosene

paraffin series the homologous series of alkanes

paraffin wax *PARAFFIN

par·a·foil (pǽrəfɔil) *n.* airfoil parachute capable of aiding a guided, gliding descent

par·a·glide (pǽrəglaid) *n.* kitelike device used for directing the landing of a reentering space vehicle. *also* parawing

par·a·go·ge (pærəgóudʒi:) *n.* (*gram.*) the addition of a final letter or syllable to a word either so as to modify the meaning (e.g. 'ly' in 'worldly' fr. 'world'), or adventitiously (e.g. 'b' in 'limb' fr. O.E. 'lim') **par·a·gog·ic** (pærəgɒ́dʒik) *adj.* [L. fr. Gk *paragōgē,* a leading past]

par·a·gon (pǽrəgɒn, pǽrəgən) *n.* a model or pattern of something good, *a paragon of virtue* ‖ a perfect diamond of at least 100 carats ‖ (*printing, hist.*) a large size of type (about 20 point) [O.F. fr. Ital.]

par·a·gon·ite (pǽrəgənait) *n.* a form of mica with sodium replacing the potassium of the commoner type [fr. Gk *paragōn,* pres. part. of *paragein,* to mislead]

par·a·graph (pǽrəgræf, pǽrəgrɑf) **1.** *n.* a distinct unit of writing (generally containing more than one sentence, but shorter than a chapter), usually a subsection dealing with a particular point. It is always begun on a new line and usually indented (symbol ¶) ‖ a brief article or item in a newspaper or magazine **2.** *v.t.* to divide or arrange into paragraphs ‖ (*journalism*) to write a paragraph about ‖ *v.i.* to write paragraphs in a newspaper or magazine **pár·a·graph·er** *n.* a journalist who writes paragraphs **par·a·graph·ic** (pærəgrǽfik), **par·a·gráph·i·cal** *adjs* **par·a·graph·ist** (pǽrəgræfist, pǽrəgrɑfist) *n.* [F. *paragraphe* fr. L.L. fr. Gk]

paragraph loop (*figure skating*) a specified series of turns

Pa·ra·gua·ná (pɑrɑgwɑnɑ́) a peninsula on the northwest coast of Venezuela, enclosing the Gulf of Venezuela on the east

Par·a·guay (pǽrəgwei, pǽrəgwai) the chief tributary (1,500 miles long) of the Paraná, flowing from the central Mato Grosso, Brazil, across Paraguay (forming the northeastern and southwestern borders) to the Paraná estuary. It is navigable by large vessels past Asunción and by small steamers in the rainy season into the Mato Grosso (900 miles)

Paraguay a republic (area 157,000 sq. miles, pop. 3,270,000) of central South America. Capital: Asunción. People: Spanish-Guaraní Indian mestizos (93%), with minorities of tribal Indians, Italians, Japanese and Germans. Religion: predominantly Roman Catholic. Languages: Spanish, Guaraní. The land is 54% forest, 4% arable, and 40% suitable for pasture. The River Paraguay divides the country. The west is flat and largely semidesert (the Gran Chaco), with some forest. The east (containing 95% of the population) is a rolling plain, cultivated in the south, with hills (rising to 2,800 ft) separating the Paraguay and Paraná basins, and great rain forests (the Selva) in the north. In the center, on both sides of the Paraguay, is the Campo: marshland and savanna (cattle raising). Average temperatures (F.): Asunción 62° (Jul.) and 80° (Jan.), the Chaco 70° (Jul.) and 100° (Jan.). Rainfall: 80 ins near Brazil, 50 ins east of Asunción, 44 ins in Asunción, 32 ins in the Chaco. Livestock: cattle, horses. Agricultural products (eastern region): manioc, corn, cotton, sugarcane, peanuts, sweet potatoes, beans, onions, yerba maté, rice, tobacco, coffee, fruit. Forest products: cedar, hardwoods, quebracho extract, petitgrain oil, tung oil. Mineral resources (largely unexploited): iron, manganese, copper, mica. Industries: rum, meat, textiles, lace, consumer goods. Exports: cotton, quebracho extract, lumber, hides, tobacco, meat, yerba maté, vegetable oils. Imports: food, textiles, vehicles, machinery, chemicals, fuels and oil, paper. Port: Asunción (on River Paraguay, over 900 miles from the sea). University:

CONCISE PRONUNCIATION KEY: **(a)** æ, *cat;* ɑ, *car;* ɔ *fawn;* ei, *snake.* **(e)** e, *hen;* i:, *sheep;* iə, *deer;* ɛə, *bear.* **(i)** i, *fish;* ai, *tiger;* ə:, *bird.* **(o)** o, *ox;* au, *cow;* ou, *goat;* u, *poor;* ɔi, *royal.* **(u)** ʌ, *duck;* u, *bull;* u:, *goose;* ə, *bacillus;* ju:, *cube.* x, *loch;* θ, *think;* ð, *bother;* z, *Zen;* ʒ, *corsage;* dʒ, *savage;* ŋ, *orangutang;* j, *yak;* ʃ, *fish;* tʃ, *fetch;* 'l, *rabble;* 'n, *redden.* Complete pronunciation key appears inside front cover.

Asunción (1889). Monetary unit: guaraní (100 centimos). HISTORY. Paraguay, inhabited by Guaraní Indians, was ruled by Spain (16th c.–1811), which made it part of the viceroyalty of Río de la Plata (1776). It revolted, and declared its independence (May 14, 1811). Paraguay prospered under a series of dictatorships, but in the War of the Triple Alliance (1864–70) against Argentina, Brazil, and Uruguay it lost 305,000 out of a population of 525,000, and of the survivors only 28,000 were men. Its economy was shattered. Again in the Chaco War (1932–5) with Bolivia, it sustained 20,000 dead for the 20,000 sq. miles of borderland it gained in the wilderness of the Gran Chaco. The country remained neutral for most of the 2nd world war, and joined the U.N. (1945). Civil War (1947) and political instability were followed in 1954 by the election of Gen. Alfredo Stroessner. Ruling dictatorially, he introduced certain improvements, esp. in communications, and reforms, esp. women's suffrage (1963). He continued in power, being reelected to succeeding five-year terms

Paraguay tea maté

Pa·ra·í·ba (pɑraí:bə) *JOÃO PESSOA

par·a·jour·nal·ism (pærədʒə́:rn'lizəm) *n.* tendentious reporting

parakeet *PARRAKEET

par·a·kite (pǽrəkait) *n.* (*sports*) a slitted parachute with a sportsman harnessed in, launched from the ground or water by a motor vehicle —**parakite** *v.* —**parakiting** *n.*

par·a·lan·guage (pærəlǽŋgwidʒ) *n.* the inflections and other vocal and gestural nuances added to language to convey meaning, e.g., in sarcasm —**par·a·lin·guis·tic** *adj.* —**par·a·lin·guis·tics** *n.* the study

par·al·de·hyde (pərǽldəhaid) *n.* a polymer, $(CH_3CHO)_3$, of acetaldehyde, used in medicine as a hypnotic and sedative

par·a·le·gal (pæerəlí:g'l) *n.* a paraprofessional legal assistant; one trained to assist an attorney —**par·a·le·gal** *adj.*

par·a·lep·sis (pærəlépsis) *n.* paralipsis

par·a·lip·sis (pærəlípsis) *n.* a rhetorical device in which a speaker emphasizes something by professing not to speak of it (usually introduced by 'not to mention' or 'to say nothing of') [Gk *paraleipsis*]

par·al·lac·tic (pærəlǽktik) *adj.* of, relating to or caused by parallax

par·al·lax (pǽrəlæks) *n.* the apparent change of position or the difference in apparent direction of an object when viewed from two or more positions not on a line with the object. In astronomical calculations, parallax is expressed by the angle subtended at a celestial body by some suitably chosen standard base line (e.g. the equatorial radius of the earth, or the mean radius of the earth's orbit) [F. *parallaxe* fr. Gk *parallaxis*, alternation]

parallax-second *PARSEC

par·al·lel (pǽrəlel) **1.** *adj.* (of lines, curves or planes) equidistant from each other at all points and having the same direction or curvature ‖ (of a line, curved or plane) equidistant from another at all points, and having the same direction or curvature, *draw line AB parallel to CD* ‖ similar or analogous in tendency, purpose, time etc., *parallel situations* ‖ (*mus.*, of simultaneous melodic lines) maintaining a constant pitch difference ‖ (*mus.*, of intervals) moving consecutively, *parallel fifths* **2.** *n.* a line, curve or plane which is parallel to another ‖ a situation, event, narrative etc. which is similar to another ‖ similarity between situations etc., *strange parallels exist in their histories* ‖ a comparison, *to draw a parallel between two circumstances* ‖ the arrangement of electrical devices in a parallel circuit ‖ (*geog.*) a parallel of latitude ‖ (*printing*) a reference mark consisting of two vertical parallel lines (‖) ‖ (*mil.*) a long trench constructed parallel to a fortification etc. **3.** *v.t. pres. part.* **par·al·lel·ing,** esp. *Br.* **par·al·lel·ling** *past* and *past part.* **par·al·leled,** esp. *Br.* **par·al·lelled** to be parallel to ‖ to find or quote a fact, event, thing or circumstance that is similar to (another) [F. *parallèle* fr. L. fr. Gk *parallēlos*, beside one another]

parallel bars a gymnastic apparatus, consisting of two parallel horizontal bars of wood or tubular metal well above floor level, used for vaulting, balancing etc.

parallel circuit (*elec.*) a circuit arranged so that the positive poles or terminals are connected to one conductor and the negative poles or terminals to another

Parallel Development Doctrine British policy of racial separation urged for Rhodesia and South Africa prior to 1978

par·al·lel·e·pi·ped (pærəlelәpáipid) *n.* (*geom.*) a solid all of whose sides are parallelograms, opposite sides being parallel to one another [fr. Gk *parallēlepipedon* fr. *parellēlos*, parallel+*epipedon*, a plane surface]

par·al·lel·ism (pǽrəlelizəm) *n.* the quality or state or being parallel

parallel of latitude (*geog.*) any imaginary circle on the globe which forms the locus of points equidistant from the equator

par·al·lel·o·gram (pærəléləgræm) *n.* (*geom.*) a four-sided plane figure, the opposite sides of which are equal and parallel to one another [F. *parallélogramme* fr. L. fr. Gk]

parallel processing, concurrent processing (*computer*) an operation simultaneously storing or executing more than one program *also* concurrent processing *Cf* MULTIPROCESSING, MULTIPROGRAMMING

parallel ruler an instrument for drawing parallel lines. It consists of two rulers hinged together in such a way that they always remain parallel

pa·ral·o·gism (pərǽlədʒizəm) *n.* fallacious reasoning ‖ an instance of this **pa·ral·o·gís·tic** *adj.* [F. *paralogisme* fr. L.L. fr. Gk]

paralyse *PARALYZE

pa·ral·y·sis (pərǽlisiz) *pl.* **pa·ral·y·ses** (pərǽlisi:z) *n.* inability to move a muscle or group of muscles, often coupled with lack of sensation in the affected area. It is usually caused by diseases of the nervous system, brain damage, apoplexy or poliomyelitis, but it may be caused by certain poisons or by hysteria ‖ inability to act or move [L. fr. Gk *paralusis*]

paralysis ag·i·tans (ǽdʒitænz) *n.* Parkinson's disease

par·a·lyt·ic (pærəlítik) **1.** *adj.* of, characterized by or affected with paralysis **2.** *n.* a person affected with paralysis **par·a·lýt·i·cal·ly** *adv.* [F. *paralytique*]

par·a·lyze, par·a·lyse (pǽrəlaiz) *pres. part.* **par·a·lyz·ing, par·a·lys·ing** *past* and *past. part.* **par·a·lyzed, par·a·lysed** *v.t.* to effect with paralysis [F. *paralyser*]

par·a·mag·net·ic (pærəmægnétik) *adj.* of or designating a substance that exhibits paramagnetism **par·a·mag·net·ism** (pærəmǽgnitizəm) *n.* the property (possessed by many substances having a magnetic permeability close to but greater than unity) of being weakly attracted by an external field. The degree of magnetization is proportional to the strength of the applied field

Par·a·mar·i·bo (pærəmǽribou) the capital (pop. 67,718), chief port, and communications center of Suriname on the Suriname River estuary 15 miles from the coast, founded (1540) by the French

par·a·mat·ta (pærəmǽtə) *n.* a lightweight fabric of wool and cotton or silk [after *Paramatta*, town in New South Wales, Australia]

par·a·me·ci·um, par·a·moe·ci·um (pærəmí:si:əm) *n.* (*zool.*) any of several ciliate protozoans of genus *Paramoecium*, fam. *Holotricha*, found freeswimming in stagnant pools [Mod. L. fr. Gk. *parammēkēs*, oval]

par·a·med·ic (pærəmédik) *n.* **1.** trained medical worker (usu. with 2 yrs of training) capable of performing basic emergency medical functions **2.** (*mil.*) parachuting member of the medical corps —**paramedical** *adj.*

par·a·men·stru·um (pærəménstru:əm) *n.* (*med.*) period of four days before, and first four days during menstruation when women are most vulnerable to infection —**paramenstrual** *adj.*

pa·ram·e·ter (pərǽmitər) *n.* (*math.*) a variable which is kept constant while others are being investigated ‖ (*math.*) a variable of which other variables are taken to be functions **par·a·met·ric** (pærəmétrik) *adj.* [Mod. L. fr. Gk *para*, beside+*metron*, measure]

par·a·met·ric (pærəmétrik) *adj.* (*math.*) of an equation in which there is a symbol representing an arbitrary constant—the symbol can be given any numerical value desired

par·am·ne·sia (pæræmní:ʒə) *n.* the illusion of remembering something which in fact one is experiencing for the first time [Mod. L.]

par·a·mo (pǽrəmou) *pl.* **par·a·mos** *n.* a high, treeless plateau, esp. in the northern Andes [Span.]

paramoecium *PARAMECIUM

par·a·morph (pǽrəmɔrf) *n.* (*mineral.*) a pseudo morph formed by physical but not chemical changes **par·a·mór·phic** *adj.* **par·a·mór·phism** *n.* [PARA-+Gk *morphē*, form]

par·a·mount (pǽrəmaunt) *adj.* supreme in rank, importance etc. [A.F. *paramont*, above fr. O.F.]

par·a·mour (pǽrəmuər) *n.* (*old-fash., rhet.*) a married man's mistress or married woman's lover [M.E. fr. O.F. *par amour*, by or because of love]

par·a·myx·o·vi·rus (pærəmiksouvάirəs) *n.* (*med.*) a group of ribonucleic-acid-containing myxoviruses that cause mumps, measles, parainfluenza, etc.

Pa·ra·ná (pɑrɑnά, pərənά) a city (pop. 223,665) in E. Argentina, on the Paraná River 80 miles north of Rosario. It has a large river (oceangoing steamers) and railroad trade. Urquiza made it his capital, thus dividing Argentina between Buenos Aires and the rest

Pa·ra·ná (pɑrɑnά) a river (2,040 miles long) flowing from S. central Brazil, around lower Paraguay (as the southeastern-southern border) and through N.W. Argentina to a delta on the Río de la Plata. It is navigable by river steamer to the Paraguay and by boat, between waterfalls, nearly to the Río Grande. With the Paraguay and the Pilcomayo it drains most of S. Brazil and N. Argentina, all of Paraguay and part of Bolivia. Headstreams: Paranaíba, Río Grande.

Pa·ra·na·í·ba (pærənəí:bə) a headstream (530 miles long) of the Paraná, rising in the central highlands of S.E. Brazil

pa·rang (pάrɑŋ) *n.* a short sword used in Malaysia and Indonesia as a weapon or tool [Malay]

par·a·noi·a (pærənɔ́iə) *n.* a mental disorder in which the sufferer believes that other people suspect, despise or persecute him or, less commonly, in which the sufferer has delusions of grandeur **par·a·noi·ac** (pærənɔ́iæk) *n.* and *adj.* **pár·a·noid** *n.* and *adj.* [Mod. L. fr. Gk fr. *paranoos*, distracted]

par·a·pet (pǽrəpit, pǽrəpet) *n.* a low wall at the edge of a bridge, flat roof, balcony etc. to prevent people from falling off ‖ (*mil.*) a defensive work of earth or stone in front of a trench or along the top of a rampart [F. or fr. Ital. *parapetto* fr. *parare*, to protect+*petto*, chest]

par·aph (pǽrəf) *n.* a flourish at the end of a signature, formerly used to make forgery more difficult [F. *paraphe, parafe*]

par·a·pha·sia (pærəféiʒə) *n.* (*med.*) a pathological condition in which the person affected uses words other than those intended [Mod. L. fr. *para*, beside+*-phasia*, speech]

par·a·pher·nal·ia (pærəfərnéiljə, pærəfənéiljə) *pl. n.* (sometimes construed as singular) miscellaneous personal belongings or equipment ‖ (*law*) a wife's personal possessions as distinct from her dowry [M.L. fr. *paraphernalia (bona)*, wife's own (goods) fr. Gk]

par·a·phrase (pǽrəfreiz) *n.* a restatement in different words or free rendering of a text, passage etc. [F. fr. L. fr. Gk fr. *para-*, beside+*phrazein*, to tell]

paraphrase *pres. part.* **par·a·phras·ing** *past* and *past part.* **par·a·phrased** *v.t.* to make a paraphrase of ‖ *v.i.* to make a paraphrase [fr. F. *paraphraser*]

par·a·phras·tic (pærəfrǽstik) *adj.* having the nature of a paraphrase **par·a·phrás·ti·cal·ly** *adv.* [fr. M.L. *paraphrasticus* fr. Gk]

pa·raph·y·sis (pərǽfisis) *pl.* **pa·raph·y·ses** (pərǽfəsi:z) *n.* a sterile filament possessed by many cryptogamic plants [Mod. L. fr. *para*, beside+*phusis*, nature]

par·a·ple·gi·a (pærəplí:dʒi:ə) *n.* paralysis of both legs due to disease of or injury to the spinal cord **par·a·plé·gic** *adj.* and *n.* [Mod. L. fr. Gk *paraplēgia*, a stroke at the side]

par·a·po·di·um (pærəpóudi:əm) *pl.* **par·a·po·di·a** (pærəpóudi:ə) *n.* one of the unsegmented lateral locomotive processes on the body segments of certain annelid worms [PARA-+Gk *pous* (*podos*), foot]

par·a·po·lit·i·cal (pærəpəlítik'l) *adj.* semipolitical

par·a·pro·fes·sion·al (pærəprəféʃən'l) *n.* one trained to assist a professional, esp. in teaching, nursing, etc; e.g., paramedical, paralegal —**par·a·pro·fes·sion·al** *adj.*

par·a·pro·tein (pærəpróuti:n) *n.* (*biochem.*) plasma protein with some qualities unlike normal protein, esp. some globulins —**par·a·pro·tein·e·mi·a** *n.* having abnormal amount of paraproteins

CONCISE PRONUNCIATION KEY: **(a)** æ, *c*a*t*; ɑ, *c*a*r*; ɔ *f*aw*n*; ei, *sn*a*ke*. **(e)** e, *h*e*n*; i:, *sh*ee*p*; iə, *d*ee*r*; ɛə, *b*ea*r*. **(i)** i, *f*i*sh*; ai, *t*i*ger*; ə:, *b*i*rd*. **(o)** o, *o*x; au, *c*ow; ou, *g*oa*t*; u, *p*oo*r*; ɔi, *r*oy*al*. **(u)** ʌ, *d*u*ck*; u, *b*u*ll*; u:, *g*oo*se*; ə, *b*a*cill*u*s*; ju:, *c*u*be*. x, *lo*ch; θ, *th*ink; ð, *bo*th*er*; z, *Z*en; ʒ, *corsa*g*e*; dʒ, *sava*g*e*; ŋ, *orangut*an*g*; j, *y*ak; ʃ, *f*i*sh*; tʃ, *fe*tch; 'l, *rabb*le; 'n, *redd*en. Complete pronunciation key appears inside front cover.

par·a·psy·chol·o·gy (pærəsaikɔ́lədʒi:) *n.* the experimental study of psychic phenomena such as telepathy, clairvoyance etc.

par·a·quat [$C_{12}H_{14}N_2$] (pǽrəkwɒt) *n.* (*chem.*) herbicide used to spray marijuana fields; a weed killer

Pa·rá rubber (pɑrɑ́) rubber obtained from South American trees, esp. from *Hevea braziliensis*, fam. *Euphorbiaceae* [after *Pará*, a state and city of Brazil]

par·a·sail (pǽrəseil) *n.* (*sports*) a maneuverable type of parachute

par·a·se·le·ne (pærəsilí:ni:) *pl.* **par·a·se·le·nae** (pærəsilí:ni:) *n.* a bright patch on a lunar halo [Mod. L. fr. Gk *para*, beside+*selēne*, moon]

par·a·sex·u·al·i·ty (pærəsekʃu:ǽliti:) *n.* (*biol.*) capacity to reproduce with genes of different vegetative or somatic cells involving mitotic crossing over and loss of chromosomes, esp. among fungi —**par·a·sex·u·al** *adj.*

Pa·ra·shah (pɑ́rəʃɑ) *pl.* **Pa·ra·shoth** (pɑ́rəʃɑut) *n.* a reading from the Pentateuch in a synagogue, esp. on the sabbath and on feast days [Heb.=explanation]

par·a·site (pǽrəsait) *n.* an organism living in or on another living organism and deriving its nutriment partly or wholly from it, usually exhibiting some special adaptation, and often causing death or damage to its host (cf. SAPROPHYTE, cf. SYMBIONT) ‖ someone who associates with a person or organization for the purpose of living at the expense of that person or group, without contributing anything to their or its well-being [fr. L. *parasitus* fr. Gk]

par·a·sit·ic (pærəsítik) *adj.* of, relating to, having the nature of or characteristic of a parasite **par·a·sít·i·cal** *adj.* [fr. L. *parasiticus*]

par·a·sit·i·side (pærəsítisaid) *n.* a substance that destroys parasites [fr. L. *parasitus*, parasite+*caedere*, to kill]

par·a·sit·ism (pǽrəsaitizəm) *n.* the association of parasite and host ‖ (*med.*) a diseased state caused by parasites

par·a·sol (pǽrəsɔl, pǽrəsɒl) *n.* an umbrella to give shade from the sun [F. fr. Ital.]

par·a·sta·tal (pærəstéit'l) *adj.* of one serving government in an auxiliary capacity, of an organization sponsored by the state, e.g., an authority

par·a·sym·pa·thet·ic (pærəsimpəθétik) *adj.* of or relating to the parasympathetic nervous system

parasympathetic nervous system (*physiol.*) the portion of the autonomic nervous system which has motor nerve fibers originating in the head and sacral regions of the spinal cord and generally maintains muscle tone, induces secretion and dilates blood vessels (cf. SYMPATHETIC NERVOUS SYSTEM)

par·a·syn·the·sis (pærəsínθisis) *n.* (*linguistics*) the formation of derivatives from compound words and their use to build up new words [Gk *parasunthesis* fr. *para*, beside+*sunthesis*, composition]

par·a·syn·thet·ic (pærəsinθétik) *adj.* (*linguistics*) relating to or formed by parasynthesis [fr. Gk *parasunthetos*]

par·a·tac·tic (pærətǽktik) *adj.* (*gram.*) of, relating to or characterized by parataxis **par·a·tác·ti·cal·ly** *adv.*

par·a·tax·is (pærətǽksis) *n.* (*gram.*) coordination of clauses etc. in succession without connectives, e.g. 'he went, she stayed' (cf. HYPOTAXIS) [Gk=a placing beside]

par·a·thy·roid (pærəθáirɔid) **1.** *n.* one of (usually) four small endocrine glands, situated close to the thyroid gland or occasionally embedded in the gland, which produce a hormone regulating the metabolism of calcium and phosphorus **2.** *adj.* concerning or produced by these glands

par·a·troop (pǽrətru:p) *adj.* of, relating to or involving paratroops [PARATROOPS]

par·a·troop·er (pǽrətru:pər) *n.* a member of a body of paratroops

par·a·troops (pǽrətru:ps) *pl. n.* troops transported by air and dropped, with their arms and equipment, by parachute [PARACHUTE TROOPS]

par·a·ty·phoid (pærətáifɔid) **1.** *n.* an infectious enteric fever, resembling typhoid but milder **2.** *adj.* of, involving or designating this fever

par·a·vane (pǽrəvein) *n.* a device with sharp teeth, fitted with vanes which control its depth, towed by warships to cut the moorings of floating mines

par·a·wing (pǽrəwiŋ) *n.* a sail shaped glider parachute that unfurls during descent *Cf* PARAFOIL

par·a·zo·an (pærəzóuən) **1.** *n.* a member of the order *Parazoa*, the simplest animals of the subkingdom *Metazoa*. It denotes the grade of organization represented by sponges. Parazoans are a group of invertebrates of worldwide distribution, living and growing exclusively under water of any depth between several miles and a few inches and either salt or fresh **2.** *adj.* pertaining to the order *Parazoa* or to a parazoan **par·a·zó·ic** *adj.* [Mod. L. fr. Gk fr. *para*, akin+*zoon*, animal]

par·boil (pɑ́rbɔil) *v.t.* to boil until partially cooked, usually as a preparation for roasting etc. [O.F. *parboillir, parbouillir*]

par·buck·le (pɑ́rbʌk'l) **1.** *n.* a doubled rope, made fast above at its midpoint, each half forming a sling, used for lowering or hoisting a barrel, heavy gun etc. **2.** *v.t. pres. part.* **par·buck·ling** *past* and *past part.* **par·buck·led to** hoist or lower with this device [older *parbunkle, parbuncle*, origin unknown]

Par·cae (pɑ́rsi:) (*mythol.*) the Roman name for the three Fates

par·cel (pɑ́rs'l) **1.** *n.* one or more things secured by a string or wrapping to make a single object for handling and transport ‖ a number of things dealt with as a single unit, *a parcel of diamonds for sale* ‖ a portion, esp. of land forming part of a property **2.** *v.t. pres. part.* **par·cel·ing,** esp. *Br.* **par·cel·ling** *past* and *past part.* **par·celed,** esp. *Br.* **par·celled** (with 'out') to distribute in portions ‖ (esp. with 'up') to make a parcel of ‖ (*naut.*) to wrap or cover with parceling **pár·cel·ing,** esp. *Br.* **pár·cel·ling** *n.* the act of making a parcel ‖ (*naut.*) a strip of canvas, usually covered with pitch, used to cover a caulked seam or to bind around a rope so as to keep moisture out [F. *parcelle*]

parcel post the branch of the postal system which deals with parcels as distinct from letters

par·ce·nar·y (pɑ́rsəneri:) *n.* (*law*) coparcenary [A.F. *parcenarie*, O.F. *parçonerie*]

par·ce·ner (pɑ́rsənər) *n.* (*law*) a coparcener [A.F. fr. O.F. *parçonier*]

parch (pɑrtʃ) *v.t.* to make dry by heating, esp. to excess ‖ to make very thirsty ‖ to dry (beans, grain etc.) by exposure to steady, intensive heat ‖ *v.i.* to become hot and dry [origin unknown]

parch·ment (pɑ́rtʃmənt) *n.* (esp. *hist.*) the skin of a calf, kid or sheep prepared for writing on ‖ a sheet of such prepared skin ‖ paper made to resemble this ‖ a document written or printed on this material [M.E. *perchemin* fr. F. *parchemin*]

par·don (pɑ́rd'n) *n.* a pardoning or being pardoned ‖ (*law*) an official release from a penalty, or the document granting this ‖ (*pl.*, *Roman Catholicism*) indulgences **to beg someone's pardon** to ask someone to excuse one, e.g. for some minor breach of manners [M.E. fr. O.F. *perdun, pardun* fr. *pardonner*, to pardon]

pardon *v.t.* to choose to let (a person) be unpunished or no longer punished for wrongful acts they have committed ‖ to require no punishment for (a fault) ‖ to excuse or forgive [O.F. *pardoner* and F. *pardonner* fr. L.L. *perdonare* fr. *per-*, through, fully+*donare*, to give]

par·don·a·ble (pɑ́rd'nəb'l) *adj.* (of a crime, fault etc.) capable of being pardoned [F. *pardonnable*]

par·don·er (pɑ́rd'nər) *n.* (*hist.*) a priest licenced to sell papal indulgences

pare (pɛər) *pres. part.* **par·ing** *past* and *past part.* **pared** *v.t.* to cut off the outer surface, skin or edge of, *to pare an apple* ‖ to cut off (the outer surface, skin or edge) from something ‖ to reduce the bulk of (something) by removing successive thicknesses or portions, *his profits were pared down by taxes* [F. *parer*, to prepare, trim]

par·e·gor·ic (pærəgɔ́rik, pærəgɒ́rik) *n.* camphorated tincture of opium, used to relieve pain, e.g. of diarrhea [fr. L.L. *paregoricus* adj., soothing pain]

pa·ren·chy·ma (pəréŋkəmə) *n.* (*bot.*) a simple plant tissue that consists typically of unspecialized thin-walled cells of simple form and structure (cf. PROSENCHYMA). It may serve for photosynthesis (*PALISADE PARENCHYMA), storage or conduction, and occurs throughout the plant body (e.g. fleshy parts of fruit, softer parts of leaves and other storage organs). Parenchyma cells with specialized secretory functions may occur in various tissues and parts of the plant (*COLLENCHYMA, *SCLERENCHYMA) ‖ the characteristic or distinctive tissue of an organ, or an abnormal growth as distinguished from its supporting portion **par·en·chym·a·tous** (pæreŋkímətəs) *adj.* [Gk *parenchuma* fr. *para*, beside+*enchuma*, infusion]

par·ent (pέərənt, pǽrənt) *n.* someone who begets or gives birth to offspring ‖ an organism, thing or organization which is the source of a new one [O.F.]

par·ent·age (pέərəntidʒ, pǽrəntidʒ) *n.* immediate or remoter ancestry [F.]

pa·ren·tal (pərént'l) *adj.* pertaining to, characteristic of, or like a parent [fr. L. *parentalis*]

parental generation (*biol.*) a generation of individuals who are crossbred to produce hybrids

pa·ren·the·sis (pərénθisis) *pl.* **pa·ren·the·ses** (pərénθisi:z) *n.* a word, phrase or sentence, usually having its own complete meaning, inserted into a sentence which is grammatically complete without this insertion, and marked off from it by punctuation, e.g. 'it was surprisingly effective', or 'it was, to our surprise, effective' ‖ either of the punctuation marks (or) used to contain such a word, phrase etc., or to mark off several qualities or elements in a formula, equation etc. as units to be treated as a whole **pa·rén·the·size** *pres. part.* **pa·ren·the·siz·ing** *past* and *past part.* **pa·ren·the·sized** *v.t.* to insert parentheses in (a speech etc.) ‖ to insert (a word etc.) in a sentence as a parenthesis ‖ to place parentheses around (a written word etc.) [M.L. fr. Gk fr. *para*, beside+*en*, in+*thesis*, a placing]

par·en·thet·ic (pærənθétik) *adj.* constituting a parenthesis ‖ containing a parenthesis **par·en·thét·i·cal** *adj.* [fr. M.L. *parentheticus* fr. Gk]

par·ent·hood (pέərənthud, pǽrənthud) *n.* the state of being a parent

pa·rer·gon (pərə́:rgɒn) *pl.* **pa·rer·ga** (pərə́:rgə) *n.* a piece of work subsidiary to, or a by-product of, some main work [L. fr. Gk]

pa·re·sis (pərí:sis, pǽrisis) *n.* partial paralysis ‖ general paresis **pa·ret·ic** (pərétik) *n.* and *adj.* [Mod. L. fr. Gk=paralysis]

par ex·cel·lence (pɑréksəlɑ̃ns) *adv.* preeminently [F.=by excellence]

par·fait (pɑrféi) *n.* a dessert of ice cream, fruits and fruit syrups arranged in layers in a tall glass and topped with whipped cream

par·get (pɑ́rdʒit) **1.** *v.t. pres. part.* **par·get·ing, par·get·ting** *past* and *past part.* **par·get·ed, par·get·ted** to cover or coat with parget (plaster) **2.** *n.* pargeting ‖ the plaster used in pargeting **pár·get·ing, pár·get·ting,** *n.* ornamentation of plaster on a wall, esp. with incised patterns [prob. fr. O.F. *pargeter, parjeter*, to throw or cast over a surface]

par·gy·line [$C_{11}H_{13}N$] (pɑ́rgili:n) *n.* (*pharm.*) drug for relief of high blood pressure; marketed as Eutonyl

par·he·li·a·cal (pɑrhiláiəkəl) *adj.* of or like a parhelion

par·he·lic (pɑrhí:lik, pɑrhélik) *adj.* parheliacal [PARHELION]

parhelic circle a luminous ring sometimes seen around the sun, caused by scattering of ice crystals in the earth's atmosphere

par·he·li·on (pɑrhí:li:ən) *pl.* **par·he·li·a** (pɑrhí:li:ə) *n.* a bright patch sometimes visible on a parhelic circle [fr. L. *parelion* fr. Gk *para*, beside+*helios*, the sun]

Pa·ria, Gulf of (pɑ́rjɑ) an inlet (c. 100 miles long, 40 miles wide) between Trinidad and Venezuela, enclosed on the north by Paria peninsula, and connected with the Atlantic by two hazardous straits. Port of Spain. Trinidad, lies on this gulf

pa·ri·ah (pəráiə, pǽri:ə) *n.* a social outcast ‖ a member of a low caste in parts of S. India and Burma, usually employed as a servant or common laborer [fr. Tamil *paraiyar*, pl. of *paraiyan*]

pariah dog a mongrel dog of parts of N. Africa and Asia which lives by scavenging

Par·i·an (pέəri:ən) **1.** *adj.* of or pertaining to the island Paros, famous for fine white marble ‖ of or designating this marble **2.** *n.* a native or inhabitant of Paros ‖ a white porcelain used for statuettes etc. [fr. L. *Parius*]

par·i·es (pέəri:i:z) *pl.* **pa·ri·e·tes** (pəráiiti:z) *n.* (*biol.*, esp. *pl.*) a wall of a hollow organ, plant cell etc. [L.=wall]

pa·ri·e·tal (pəráiit'l) *adj.* of or relating to a wall of a body cavity etc. [F. *pariétal* fr. L.]

parietal bone either of two bones forming the upper part of the skull

pa·ri·e·tals (pəráiit'ls) *n.* rules regarding visitors of the opposite sex in a men's or women's dormitory

Pa·ri·ma, Serra (pɑríːmɑ) a mountain range rising to 8,000 ft extending north and south along part of the Venezuela-Brazil boundary. It is the source of the Orinoco River

par·i·mu·tu·el (pæriːmjúːtʃuːəl) *n.* a betting system by which all bets are recorded, the sums wagered on each eventuality are totaled, and the total sum wagered (minus a percentage for running costs and tax) is divided, in proportion to the stake, among those who placed bets on the winner ‖ the machine that totalizes the bets [F.=mutual wager]

par·ing (pέəriŋ) *n.* a strip of rind etc. that has been pared off something

Pa·ri·ni (pɑríːniː), Giuseppe (1729–99), Italian lyric poet. His 'Odi' and 'Il Giorno' are among the classics of Italian poetry

Par·is (pǽris) the son of King Priam of Troy. His abduction of Helen led to the Trojan War

Paris, Matthew (c. 1200–59), English chronicler and monk of St Albans. His 'Chronica majora' is a continuation of Roger of Wendover's chronicle, and is a valuable source for the period 1235–59

Paris the capital (pop. 2,183,000, with agglom. 8,510,000), and economic and cultural center of France, on the Seine in the central Paris basin. It is the country's chief river port and communications center, and concentrates a quarter of France's industry: luxury goods (esp. fine furniture, leather goods, haute couture and ready-made clothing, jewelry) in the city, heavy industry (mechanical, electrical and aeronautical engineering, motorcars, metallurgy, chemicals, food processing) in the suburbs. The city's geometric center and original site is the Île de la Cité in the Seine, containing the law courts, Sainte Chapelle (the Gothic chapel of St Louis, 1242–8) and Notre Dame. The left bank contains the university (or Latin) quarter, most of the remaining medieval buildings and, far west, the Eiffel Tower. The right bank, behind the Louvre and the Tuileries gardens, which stretch along the river, contains the financial and commercial section laced by the system of squares and boulevards laid out by Haussmann (19th c.): notably, the Place de l'Étoile (1836, surrounding the Arc de Triomphe) and the Place de la Concorde, with the Avenue des Champs-Élysées connecting them. Government buildings are spread throughout the center. Cultural institutions: university (1215), five national theaters, Louvre, Museum of Modern Art (1947), National Library, numerous other museums, academic and scientific institutes, and national schools. HISTORY. Paris developed as a Roman town (1st c. B.C.), and according to tradition, was saved from the Huns by St Geneviève (5th c.). It was temporarily the Merovingian capital under Clovis I and was besieged (885–7) by the Vikings. Its importance increased when Hugh Capet became king of France (987). The Sorbonne made it a center of theological learning (13th and 14th cc.). Louis XIV and Louis XV gave Paris some of its finest public buildings. Paris was the center of the French Revolution. It was besieged (1870–1) during the Franco-Prussian War, was shelled in the 1st world war, and was occupied by the Germans (1940–4) during the 2nd world war. It was the scene of the treaties (1947) between the Allies and Italy, Rumania, Bulgaría, Hungary and Finland after the 2nd world war. Massive urban renewal projects, such as the one at Beaubourg, have changed its face during the postwar period and plans are underway for major construction in Paris and the Paris Basin all the way to the mouth of the Seine River

Paris Commune *COMMUNE, THE

Pa·ris, é·cole de (eikɔldəpæriː) a name (invented c. 1925) for the painters and sculptors (e.g. Soutine, Chagall, Modigliani and Brancusi) who came to Paris from different countries and associated with the modern 20th-c. French school [F. = school of Paris]

Paris green a double salt of copper arsenite and copper acetate, used as a light green pigment and insecticide

par·ish (pǽriʃ) *n.* an administrative district of some churches, esp. a part of a diocese in the charge of a priest or minister ‖ (often construed as pl.) the residents of such a district ‖ the members of the congregation of a Protestant church ‖ a civil division in Louisiana, corresponding to a county [M.E. *parissche, parosche* fr. O.F. fr. L. fr. Gk *paroikia*, neighborhood, diocese]

parish clerk an official of a parish church appointed by the clergyman to perform certain duties

pa·rish·ion·er (pəríʃənər) *n.* someone who belongs to a parish [fr. M.E. *parishion* fr. O.F.+ -ER]

parish register a record of baptisms, marriages, burials etc. kept at a parish church

Pa·ri·sian (pəríːʒən, pəríʒən) **1.** *adj.* of, pertaining to or characteristic of Paris, France **2.** *n.* a native or resident of Paris [F. *parisien*]

Paris, Treaty of a treaty (1763) ending the Seven Years' War. Britain gained Canada and Cape Breton Is. and all French territory east of the Mississippi, and Florida from Spain. Control of India passed from France to Britain ‖ a treaty (1783) ending the Revolutionary War. The independence of the U.S.A. was recognized by Britain and the boundaries of the U.S.A. were fixed ‖ a treaty (1841) during the Napoleonic Wars after Napoleon's first abdication. It limited France to its boundaries of 1792 ‖ a treaty (1815) at the end of the Napoleonic Wars. It limited France to its boundaries of 1790 and imposed heavy reparations ‖ a treaty (1856) ending the Crimean War. The neutrality of the Black Sea was guaranteed ‖ a treaty (1898) ending the Spanish-American War. Spain 'relinquished' Cuba to the U.S.A. in trust for its inhabitants. Its provisions stressed the temporary character of U.S. occupation ‖ a treaty (1947) between the Allies and Italy, Finland, Rumania, Hungary and Bulgaria

par·i·ty (pǽritiː) *n.* equality in status, values etc. ‖ equality of purchasing power at a legally fixed ratio, between two convertible currencies at par ‖ equivalence (maintained by government price supports) between the current ratio of agricultural prices to the prevailing price structure and this ratio during a selected base period ‖ (*computer*) a redundant bit added to others to detect a bit inaccuracy ‖ (*math.*) odd or even function; oddness or evenness ‖ (*nuclear phys.*) the property that indicates whether an elementary particle has a mirror image in accordance with space reflection symmetry that holds that there is no fundamental difference between left and right ‖ (*football*) principle that all teams in a league exist in the same competitive class [fr. L. *paritas* fr. *par*, equal]

Park (pɑrk) Mungo (1771–1806), Scottish explorer. He made two expeditions to discover the course and mouth of the Niger (1795–7 and 1805–6). The first is described in his 'Travels in the Interior of Africa' (1799). In the second he died with all his party

Park, Robert Ezra (1864–1944), U.S. sociologist, secretary to Booker T. Washington. He studied the blacks and became an authority on race relations. His 'Introduction to the Science of Sociology' (1921, in collaboration with E. W. Burgess) promoted empirical research

park (pɑrk) **1.** *n.* a very large area of land belonging to the government preserved in its natural state and accessible to the public ‖ (*mil.*) space allotted to artillery, stores etc. in an encampment, or the artillery, stores etc. themselves ‖ an enclosed area that is used for games or sports, *a baseball park* ‖ a tract of grassland, with widely spaced trees, paths, small lakes, beds of shrubs and flowers etc., adjoining or surrounding a mansion ‖ a similar tract laid out (e.g. in a city) for the general public ‖ an area set aside for oyster breeding, covered by the sea at high tide **2.** *v.t.* to put or leave (a vehicle) temporarily by the roadside or in a space set aside for this purpose ‖ (*pop.*) to deposit for the time being in a certain place, *park your baggage in the hall* ‖ *v.i.* to put or leave a vehicle temporarily by the roadside or in a specially allotted space [O.F. *parc* fr. Gmc]

par·ka (pɑ́rkə) *n.* a long fur jacket with an attached hood, worn by Eskimos ‖ a similar garment of windproof fabric worn by campers, mountaineers etc. [Aleutian]

Par·ker (pɑ́rkər), Dorothy (1893–1967), U.S. writer and critic. Her often sardonic verse includes 'Enough Rope' (1926) and 'Not So Deep as a Well' (1936) and her short stories of social satire include 'Laments for the Living' (1930) and 'Here Lies' (1939)

Parker, Sir (Horatio) Gilbert (1860–1932), Canadian politician and writer, best known for his 'Pierre and His People' (1892) and other adventure stories of the Canadian northwest and of French Canada

Parker, Matthew (1504–75), English prelate, the first archbishop of Canterbury (1559–75) under the Elizabethan settlement. He guided the Church of England on a moderate course between Catholicism and extreme Protestantism, defending episcopal organization, and checking the rise of Puritanism. He revised the Thirty-nine Articles (1562), supervised the preparation of the Bishops' Bible (1568) and wrote 'De antiquitate ecclesiae' (1572)

Parker, Theodore (1810–60), U.S. theologian. He set forth his liberal and transcendentalist views in his 'Discourse of Matters Pertaining to Religion' (1842). He was a leader of antislavery and other reform movements

parking lot (*Am.*=*Br.* car park) a space provided for the temporary parking of motor vehicles

parking orbit (*aerospace*) the orbit of a space vehicle while it is serving as a launching and/or recovery station for another space vehicle

Park·in·son's disease (pɑ́rkinsnz) paralysis agitans, a chronic nervous disease characterized by a progressive tremor and weakening of muscular tone [after James *Parkinson* (1755–1824), Eng. neurologist, who first diagnosed it]

Parkinson's Law in an organization, 'Work expands to fill the time available for completion,' and 'Staff increases at a fixed rate regardless of the amount of work produced'; by C. Northcote Parkinson, English historian and satirist

Park·man (pɑ́rkmən), Francis (1823–93), U.S. historian, best known for his multivolume series 'France and England in North America' (1865–92)

park·way (pɑ́rkwei) *n.* a broad highway lined with trees and grass, sometimes landscaped in the middle and usually closed to heavy vehicles, usually having an imposed speed limit

par·lance (pɑ́rləns) *n.* way of speaking, esp. in regard to vocabulary and idiom [A.F. and O.F.]

par·lay (pɑ́rlei, pɑ́rliː) **1.** *n.* a bet or series of bets made by parlaying **2.** *v.t.* to lay (a former bet and its winnings) on a later race, contest etc. ‖ to make use of (some asset) to gain some greater advantage, *to parlay a small income into a fortune* [F. fr. Ital. *paroli* fr. *paro*, equal]

parle·ment (pærləmɑ̃) *n.* (*F. hist.*) any of the supreme judicial courts of the ancien régime, abolished in 1790 [F.]

par·ley (pɑ́rliː) **1.** *v.i.* to confer, esp. to talk peace terms with an enemy **2.** *pl.* **par·leys** *n.* an official conference, esp. for settling a dispute, e.g. one held under truce arrangements with an enemy [perh. fr. F. *parler*, to speak]

par·lia·ment (pɑ́rləmənt) *n.* the supreme legislative body of certain countries. The parliament of the United Kingdom comprises the sovereign, the lords spiritual and temporal assembled in the House of Lords, and the representatives of the counties, boroughs etc. meeting in the House of Commons [M.E. fr. O.F. *parlement*, a speaking]

—The English parliament developed out of the king's council of the 13th c., a feudal assembly of leading barons summoned at the king's will. Knights from each county were summoned to assemblies in 1213, 1227 and 1254, and Simon de Montfort's parliament (1265) also included representatives from the boroughs. Organization remained vague, however, even after Edward I's Model Parliament (1295). Parliament assumed the right to make laws (14th c.) and to control taxation (1340), and the division into Lords and Commons became permanent in the reign (1327–77) of Edward III. By 1377, parliament was claiming the right to examine public accounts and to impeach the king's officers, and by the end of the 15th c. its members claimed freedom of speech and freedom from arrest. The Commons increased their demands for privilege during the reign (1558–1603) of Elizabeth I, and serious constitutional conflicts marked the reigns of James I and Charles I. The Long Parliament (1640–53) opposed Charles in the Civil War (1642–52) and England was ruled (1653–60) under a written republican constitution. The Restoration (1660) renewed the problem of the relationship between king and parliament, and out of the opposition to the succession of James II arose the beginnings of the party division into Whigs and Tories. After the Glorious Revolution (1688), parliament was able to assert its supremacy in the Bill of Rights (1689) and the Act of Settlement (1701), though the administration and the executive remained in the hands of the sovereign. Parliament was enlarged by the Act of Union (1707) to represent Great Britain, and the 18th c. saw the development of political parties and of the cabinet. The office of prime minister also emerged at this time, though the prime minister was dependent on royal patronage to manage parliament. The Reform Act of 1832 slightly increased the electorate and began to redistribute seats, that of 1867 enfranchised urban workers, and that of 1884 virtually completed manhood suffrage. The ballot was introduced (1872) and the suffrage was extended (1918) to women of 30 and over, and (1928) to women of 21 and over. The Liberals (formerly the Whigs), the Conservatives (formerly the Tories) and, in the early 20th c., the Labour party developed nationwide organization. The Parliament Act (1911) limited the power of the House of Lords, giving legislative supremacy to the Commons and reduced the length of a parliament from seven years to five. The House of Lords admitted life peers and women (1958). Modern executive government is exercised, in the sovereign's name, by a cabinet and ministry represented in both Houses, and ultimately responsible to the Commons. The royal right to veto legislation has not been exercised since the 18th c.

par·lia·men·tar·i·an (pɑrləmentéəri:ən) *n.* a person well versed in parliamentary procedure ‖ (*hist.*) a supporter of parliament in the English Civil War, 1642–52 (cf. ROYALIST) **par·lia·men·tár·i·an·ism** *n.* the doctrine of government by a parliament

par·lia·men·ta·ry (pɑrləméntəri:) *adj.* of or relating to parliament ‖ in accordance with the uses and practices of parliament ‖ (of language) permitted to be used in parliament ‖ (*Br. hist.*) of or belonging to or supporting parliament in the English Civil War (1642–52)

parliamentary privilege the rights and immunities enjoyed by a member of parliament, e.g. freedom from charges of libel and slander while in pursuit of his parliamentary duties

par·lor, *Br.* **par·lour** (pɑ́rlər) *n.* (*old-fash.*) the best reception room of a house, not usually used as a living room ‖ a shop or business establishment specially equipped to perform some specified service, *a funeral parlor* ‖ (*Br.*) a room in an inn with chairs and tables, where customers can talk in comfort over their drinks [M.E. fr. A.F. *parlur,* O.F. *parleor*]

parlor car a railroad passenger car fitted out like a living room

par·lor·maid, *Br.* **par·lour·maid** (pɑ́rlərmeid) *n.* (*old-fash.*) a woman employed in a home to wait on the table, answer the door, and do light housework

parlour *PARLOR

parlourmaid *PARLORMAID

par·lous (pɑ́rləs) *adj.* (*rhet.*) involving danger or risk [M.E. *perlous* fr. *perilous*]

Par·ma (pɑ́rmə) a market city (pop. 178,000) of Etruscan origin in Emilia-Romagna, Italy. Industries: food processing, mechanical engineering, textiles. Romanesque-Gothic cathedral (12th c.) and baptistry (1196–1260), palace (16th–17th cc.), theater, museums. University (1502). It was the capital of the duchy of Parma and Piacenza (1545–1860)

Par·men·i·des (pɑrménidi:z) (c. 504–450 B.C.), Greek Eleatic philosopher. He regarded movement and change as illusions, and the universe as single, continuous and motionless. He discovered the law of contradiction and the possibility of logical proof. His work has come down to us in some 25 fragments of a poem in hexameters

Par·me·san (pɑ́rmizæn, pɑ́rmizɑn) **1.** *adj.* of or relating to Parma **2.** *n.* a hard, dry, sharp Italian cheese often used grated over spaghetti etc. [F. *parmesan* and Ital. *parmigiano*]

Par·mi·gia·ni·no (pɑrmi:dʒɑní:nou) (Francesco Maria Mazzola, 1503–40), Italian mannerist painter. His frescos are chiefly in Rome and Parma. The long necks and long hands of his figures help to express spiritual intensity

Par·na·í·ba (pɑrnəí:bə) a river (c. 900 miles long) in N.E. Brazil, flowing into the Atlantic

Par·nas·si·an (pɑrnǽsi:ən) **1.** *adj.* of, designating or characteristic of a 19th-c. school of French poets (incl. Leconte de Lisle, Gautier, Banville, Heredia, Sully Prudhomme and Coppée) who, in reaction against Romanticism, stressed perfection of poetic form and defended the notion of 'art for art's sake' (1866–76) ‖ of or relating to poetry as an art, esp. with regard to form alone **2.** *n.* a poet of the Parnassian school [fr. L. *Parnassius, Parnasius,* of Mt Parnassus]

Par·nas·sus (pɑrnǽsəs) a mountain (summit 8,062 ft) between Phocis and Boeotia, Greece, overlooking the Gulf of Corinth. It was sacred in antiquity to Apollo and the Muses

Par·nell (pɑrnél), Charles Stewart (1846–91), Irish nationalist politician. He organized an agrarian boycott and obstructed business in the House of Commons until Gladstone passed the Irish Land Act (1881). His influence as leader of the Home Rule movement waned when he was unjustly accused of political murders (1887) and when he was named as correspondent in a divorce suit (1889)

pa·ro·chi·al (pəróuki:əl) *adj.* relating to a parish ‖ (of opinions, ideas) narrowly limited in scope, provincial **pa·ró·chi·al·ism** *n.* narrowness of opinions or ideas [O.F.]

parochial school a school supported by a Church, esp. by the Roman Catholic Church

par·o·dy (pǽrədi:) **1.** *pl.* **par·o·dies** *n.* an imitation of the characteristic style of a writer, composer etc. or of a literary, artistic or musical work, designed to ridicule ‖ a poor imitation, travesty **2.** *v.t. pres. part.* **par·o·dy·ing** *past* and *past part.* **par·o·died** to make (someone or something) the subject of parody [fr. Gk *parōdia,* a burlesque poem or song]

par of exchange the recognized value of one nation's money in terms of that of another, esp. when both use the same metal as a standard of value

pa·role (pəróul) **1.** *n.* a promise given by a prisoner of war that in return for liberty or a degree of liberty he will respect certain conditions ‖ the conditional release of a civil prisoner ‖ liberation gained by parole ‖ (*mil.*) a password used by officers only **2.** *v.t. pres. part.* **pa·rol·ing** *past* and *past part.* **pa·roled** to release on parole [F.=formal promise]

par·o·mo·my·cin (pǽrəmoumɑisin) *n.* (*pharm.*) broad-spectrum antibiotic used in the treatment of amebiasis and bacillary dysenteries; marketed as Humatin

par·o·nym (pǽrənim) *n.* a paronymous word [fr. Gk *parōnumon* neut. adj., paronymous]

pa·ron·y·mous (pərónimәs) *adj.* (of words) having the same root ‖ (of words) pronounced alike but having different meanings [fr. Gk *parōnumos* fr. *para,* beside+*onoma,* name]

Par·os (péərɒs) an island (area 81 sq. miles, pop. 7,314) of the Cyclades, Greece, Famous for its white marble. Capital: Paros. Exports: wine, figs, wool

pa·ro·tic (pərótik) *adj.* (*anat.*) beside the ear [fr. Mod. L. *paroticus* fr. PARA-+Gk *ous* (*ōtos*), ear]

pa·rot·id (pərótid) **1.** *adj.* of or designating a salivary gland in front of and below each ear **2.** *n.* this gland [F. *parotide* or fr. L. *parotis* (*parotidis*) fr. Gk *para,* beside+*ous* (*ōtos*), the ear]

par·o·ti·tis (pærətáitis) *n.* inflammation of the parotid glands, e.g. in mumps ‖ mumps [fr. L. *parotis* (*parotidis*), the parotid gland]

par·ox·ysm (pǽrəksizəm) *n.* a sudden and violent muscular contraction and relaxation ‖ periodic intensification of an illness ‖ a sudden explosive burst of laughter, rage etc. **pár·ox·ys·mal** *adj.* [F. *paroxysme* fr. M.L. fr. Gk]

par·pen (pɑ́rpən) *n.* a perpend [O.F. *parpain*]

par·quet (pɑrkéi, pɑrkét) **1.** *n.* flooring consisting of pieces of wood arranged in a pattern, e.g. of parquetry ‖ the lower floor of some theaters, or the front section of this, i.e. excluding the part beneath the balcony **2.** *v.t.* to provide (a room) with parquet flooring ‖ to make (a floor) of parquet [F.]

par·quet·ry (pɑ́rkitri:) *n.* woodwork of small, thin inlaid pieces arranged in esp. geometric patterns, used for flooring etc. [F. *parqueterie*]

Parr *CATHERINE PARR

parr, *Br.* also **par** (pɑr) *n.* a young salmon before it becomes a smolt ‖ a young individual of any of several other fishes [origin unknown]

par·ra·keet, par·a·keet (pǽrəki:t) *n.* any of various small, slender, long-tailed parrots [O.E. *paroquet,* Ital. *parrochetto*]

par·ri·cid·al (pærisáid'l) *adj.* of, relating to or guilty of parricide [fr. L. *parricidalis*]

par·ri·cide (pǽrisaid) *n.* someone who murders his father ‖ (*rhet.*) someone who murders his mother or another close relative ‖ any of these crimes [F. fr. L.]

par·rot (pǽrət) **1.** *n.* any of a great number of tropical birds of the order *Psittaciformes,* with a strong, curved, hooked bill, and usually brilliant plumage. Many can be trained to imitate human speech and other sounds ‖ someone who repeats words or actions mechanically without using the intelligence **2.** *v.t.* to repeat mechanically, without using the intelligence [origin unknown]

parrot *n.* (*mil.*) transponder equipment used to identify friend or foe

parrot disease psittacosis

parrot fever psittacosis

parrot fish any of several brilliantly colored tropical marine fish, esp. of fam. *Scaridae,* having a beaklike projection of the jaw

Par·ry (pǽri:), Sir Charles Hubert Hastings (1848–1918), English composer. He is best known for his choral works, e.g. the cantata 'Blest Pair of Sirens'

par·ry (pǽri:) **1.** *v. pres. part.* **par·ry·ing** *past* and *past part.* **par·ried** *v.t.* to stop (a blow, weapon etc.) from striking by putting something in its path to change its direction ‖ to avert by interposing something, *to parry a question by asking another* ‖ *v.i.* to ward off a blow, weapon, unwelcome question etc. in that way **2.** *pl.* **par·ries** *n.* the act of parrying esp. in boxing, fencing etc. ‖ an instance of this [prob. fr. F. *parer,* to ward off]

parse (pɑrs, pɑrz) *pres. part.* **pars·ing** *past* and *past part.* **parsed** *v.t.* to define the grammatical function of (a word) by giving it the name of a part of speech ‖ to dissect (a sentence) according to the grammatical functions of its parts [fr. L. *pars* (*orationis*), part (of speech)]

par·sec (pɑ́rsek) *n.* (*astron.*) a unit of measurement equal to the distance giving rise to a heliocentric parallax of one second of arc (3.26 light-years) [PARALLAX+SECOND]

Par·see, Par·si (pɑ́rsi:) *n.* a member of a Zoroastrian sect descended from the Persians who fled to India (8th c.) to escape Moslem persecution. Today over 100,000 of them live in India, concentrated in Bombay, where the community has great influence in business. There are about 15,000 in Iran **Pár·see·ism, Pár·si·ism** *n.* [Pers. *Pārsī,* Persian]

par·si·mo·ni·ous (pɑrsəmóuni:əs) *adj.* too careful and sparing with money or assets ‖ scanty, meager, *a parsimonious contribution* [fr. L. *parsimonia,* parsimony]

par·si·mo·ny (pɑ́rsəmouni:) *n.* the quality of being parsimonious [fr. L. *parsimonia*]

pars·ley (pɑ́rsli:) *n. Petroselinum crispum,* fam. *Umbelliferae,* a European aromatic herb with divided, curly or smooth leaves, native to the Mediterranean. It is widely cultivated for use as a garnish and for flavoring ‖ any of certain other plants of fam. *Umbelliferae* [O.E. *petersilie* fr. L. fr. Gk fr. *petros,* stone+*selinon,* parsley]

pars·nip (pɑ́rsnip) *n. Pastinaca sativa,* fam. *Umbelliferae,* a European biennial plant. Its long whitish taproot, consisting mainly of phloem cells filled with starch, in cultivated varieties develops a sweet flavor after exposure to cold, and is used as a vegetable ‖ the root itself ‖ any of several similar or related plants [M.E. *passenep, pasnepe* perh. fr. O.F]

par·son (pɑ́rs'n) *n.* a Protestant clergyman, esp. one holding a benefice [M.E. *persone* fr. O.F.]

par·son·age (pɑ́rs'nidʒ) *n.* the house of a parish parson ‖ the house of any minister of religion [M.E. *personnage* fr. O.F.]

Par·son·i·an Resembling Theories (parsóuni:ən) (*social science*) theories hypothesizing (1) personalities and cultures can be analyzed as action systems; (2) each action system involves elements of maintenance of patterns, integration, goal attainment and adaptation; (3) societies evolve toward functional specialization; (4) social structures may be analyzed in terms of values, norms, collectivities and roles. These theories were developed by sociologist Talcott Parsons

par·son·ic (pɑrsónik) *adj.* of, like or characteristic of a parson **par·són·i·cal** *adj.*

Par·sons (pɑ́rs'nz), Sir Charles Algernon (1854–1931), British engineer. He invented the steam turbine (1884), which revolutionized marine engineering

Parsons, Per·sons (pɑ́rs'nz), Robert (1546–1610), English Jesuit. He worked with Campion for the reconversion of England to Catholicism (1580–1) and founded several seminaries abroad for training English priests

Parsons, Talcott (1902–79) U.S. sociologist. Considered the major theorist in American sociology through the 1950s and 1960s, he also

CONCISE PRONUNCIATION KEY: **(a)** æ, *cat;* ɑ, *car;* ɔ *fawn;* ei, *snake.* **(e)** e, *hen;* i:, *sheep;* iə, *deer;* εə, *bear.* **(i)** i, *fish;* ai, *tiger;* ə:, *bird.* **(o)** o, *ox;* au, *cow;* ou, *goat;* u, *poor;* ɔi, *royal.* **(u)** ʌ, *duck;* u, *bull;* u:, *goose;* ə, *bacillus;* ju:, *cube.* x, *loch;* θ, *think;* ð, *bother;* z, *Zen;* ʒ, *corsage;* dʒ, *savage;* ŋ, *orangutang;* j, *yak;* ʃ, *fish;* tʃ, *fetch;* 'l, *rabble;* 'n, *redden.* Complete pronunciation key appears inside front cover.

strongly influenced anthropology, psychology and, to a lesser degree, history. His functional approach to the study of society explained any society as a total system of inter-related institutions each fulfilling functions necessary for the continuing operation of the society. He founded (1946) and taught at Harvard University's department of social relations. His works include 'The Structure of Social Action' (1937) and 'The Social System' (1951)

part (pɑrt) **1.** *n.* that which is less than all, *to walk part of the way home* || one of several equal amounts, numbers, quantities etc. which, when combined, constitute a whole, *fifteen minutes is a fourth part of an hour* || one of several amounts, numbers, quantities etc. which are not necessarily equal, and which, when combined, constitute a whole || any activity, function, duty etc. allotted to or performed by an individual and regarded as contributing to some enterprise, event etc., *he wants no part in this affair* || the lines and actions assigned to a performer in a play, opera etc. || the function or task of performing these lines and actions, *to audition for a part in a play* || the printed or written lines of an actor || one of the parties in a transaction, contest, dispute etc. || an individual thing, organ, member etc. that constitutes an essential element in something, *the parts of a machine* || one of the units of a serial publication || (*mus.*) a series of notes, allotted to a particular type of voice or instrument in a composition, *sing the bass part* || (*mus.*) an individual score on which this is written or printed || (*Am.*=*Br.* parting) a dividing line formed where the hair is combed in opposite directions || (*pl.*) regions, *foreign parts* || (*pl., rhet.*) abilities, *a man of parts* **for my part** as far as I am concerned **in part** partly, *the house is furnished in part* **on my (his,** etc.) **part** for which I am (he is etc.) responsible, *it was a lapse on my part* **part and parcel** an essential element, *receptions are part and parcel of the mayor's job* **to play a part in** to contribute something towards the total effect or result or activity of, *saving plays a part in a sound economy* **to take in good part** to take no offense at, *he took the joke in good part* **to take part in** to participate in **to take someone's part** to side with (someone) in a dispute etc. **2.** *adv.* partly, *he is part Italian* [O.E. and F. fr. L. *pars (partis)*]

part *v.t.* to divide into parts, *the police parted the crowd* || to separate, *he parted the fighting dogs* || to comb (the hair) so as to make a part || *v.i.* (with 'from', 'with') to go away, take one's leave, *he parted with her on bad terms* || to leave one another, *we parted at midnight* || (with 'with') to let go of the possession of something, *he hated parting with his piano* || to draw apart, *the curtains parted* || to separate into two or more pieces, *the rope parted in the middle* **to part company** to cease to associate [F. *partir*]

par·take (pɑrtéik) *pres. part.* **par·tak·ing** *past* **par·took** (pɑrtúk) *past part.* **par·tak·en** (pɑrtéik'n) *v.i.* (with 'in' or 'of') to take or receive a share in, *to partake of someone's dinner* || (*rhet.*, with 'of') to eat (a meal), *he partook of his dinner alone* || (with 'of') to have some of the qualities of something [fr. older *partaker*, participator, trans. of L. *particeps*]

part·ed (pártid) *adj.* (*bot.*, of a cleft leaf) having divisions extending almost to the base || divided || separated

par·terre (pɑrtéər) *n.* an ornamental part of a garden consisting of formal flower beds and walks || the part of the ground floor of a theater which is behind the orchestra || the rear part of this, beneath the balcony [F.]

par·the·no·gen·e·sis (pɒrθənoudʒénisis) *n.* reproduction from an egg unfertilized by a spermatozoon, esp. in some insects, worms, algae and fungi **par·the·no·ge·net·ic** (pɒrθinoudʒənétik) *adj.* [fr. Gk *parthenos*, virgin+*genesis*, origin]

Par·the·non (párθənɒn, párθənən) a Doric temple on the Acropolis in Athens, dedicated to Athena, erected (447–432 B.C.) under Pericles by Ictinus and Callicrates and decorated with sculptures by Phidias. It represents the culmination of Greek classical architecture

Par·thi·a (párθi:ə) an ancient country of N.E. Iran. It was successively part of the empire of Assyria, Persia, Macedon and Syria before rebelling, under the Arsacid dynasty (c. 250 B.C.–c.226 A.D.), to form the Parthian Empire, which extended (1st c. B.C.) from Bactria and the Caspian Sea to the Euphrates and India. The empire (centered on Ctesiphon) and the dynasty were overthrown (c. 226) by the Sassanids

Par·thi·an shot (párθi:ən) a retort, hostile gesture etc., made in retreat [*Parthian*, of Parthia, whose cavalrymen turned to shoot their arrows while in real or feigned retreat]

par·tial (párʃəl) **1.** *adj.* of, affecting or involving only a part, *a partial explanation* || having or showing a bias in favor of one of several disputants, contestants etc., *a partial judgment* || (*pop.*, with 'to') fond of, *he is very partial to claret* **2.** *n.* (*mus.*) any note in the harmonic series [O.F. *parcial* fr. L.L.]

partial derivative (*math.*) the derivative of a function of more than one variable taken with respect to one variable while the others are considered as constants

partial fraction one of the fractions into which a given fraction may be separated, *1/6 and 3/12 are the partial fractions of 5/12*

par·ti·al·i·ty (pɒrʃi:ǽliti:, pɑrʃǽliti:) *n.* bias, *his judgment showed partiality* || (*pop.*) liking, fondness, *a partiality for sweets* [O.F. *parcialité, partialité*]

partial product (*math.*) the result of the multiplication of the unit figure of a multiplier of more than one digit

part·i·ble (pártəb'l) *adj.* (of property or an inheritance) able to be divided into parts [fr. L.L. *partibilis*]

par·tic·i·pant (pɑrtísəpənt) **1.** *n.* someone who participates **2.** *adj.* participating [fr. L. *participans (participantis)* fr. *participare*, to take part]

par·tic·i·pate (pɑrtísəpeit) *v.i. pres. part.* **par·tic·i·pat·ing** *past* and *past part.* **par·tic·i·pat·ed** (often with 'in') to be active or have a share in some activity, enterprise etc. [fr. L. *participare* (*participatus*)]

par·tic·i·pa·tion (pɑrtìsəpéiʃən) *n.* the act of participating [F. fr. L.]

participatory theater theatrical presentations in which the audience takes part

par·ti·cip·i·al (pɒrtisípi:əl) *adj.* of or having the nature and function of a participle [fr. L. *participialis*]

par·ti·ci·ple (pártisip'l, pártisəpəl) *n.* (*gram.*) a derivative of a verb which shows tense and voice and which functions in various verb forms (e.g. to form the English present progressive 'I am writing') or as an adjective (e.g. 'a written text') or in absolute constructions (e.g. 'all things being equal'). A participle may take an object (e.g. 'they like singing songs'), and may be modified by an adverb (e.g. 'the loudly swearing boys'). The present participle may also function as an adverb (e.g. 'steaming hot') [O.F.]

par·ti·cle (pártik'l) *n.* a small portion, *particles of dust, not a particle of evidence* || (*phys.*) an idealization in physics whereby a body is considered as having finite mass but infinitesimal size || (*phys.*) a fundamental particle || (*gram.*) a word used only in combination, or one that is not inflected || (*eccles.*) one of the Hosts distributed to communicants [fr. L. *particula*]

particle accelerator any of several devices used to accelerate charged particles (e.g. electrons, protons, deuterons, or other light nuclei) to extremely high speeds and energies in order to study their interaction with matter or with other particles (*CYCLOTRON, *BETATRON, *SYNCHROTRON, *VAN DE GRAAFF GENERATOR, *SYNCHROCYCLOTRON, *LINEAR ACCELERATOR)

particle board board made of resin-bonded bits of material

particle physics the branch of physics that deals with breakdown of the atom *Cf* ATOMIC PHYSICS, NUCLEAR PHYSICS, QUANTUM CHEMISTRY

par·ti-col·ored, *Br.* **par·ti-col·oured** (párti:kʌlərd) *adj.* partly of one color, partly of another [*parti* var. of PARTY adj.]

par·tic·u·lar (pərtíkjulər) **1.** *adj.* of, relating to or designating one thing singled out among many, *I wanted that particular book* || unusual, special, *take particular care not to offend him* || (*old-fash.*) concerned with details, minute, *a particular account of what occurred* || fussy, fastidious, *she is very particular about what she eats* || (*logic*, of a proposition) applicable to only some members of a class **2.** *n.* (*pl.*) details of information || (*logic*) a particular proposition **in particular** specifically, specially, by contrast with others, *I remember one day in particular* [O.F. *particuler*]

particular average (*maritime insurance*) a partial loss which must be borne only by the owner of the property in question, without the assistance of other interests (cf. GENERAL AVERAGE)

par·tic·u·lar·ism (pərtíkjulərizəm) *n.* (*theol.*) the doctrine that particular individuals are chosen by God for redemption || narrow allegiance to a particular party, sect, interest etc. || the political principle advocating individual rights and freedom for each state in a federation without regard to the interest of the whole

par·tic·u·lar·i·ty (pərtìkjulǽriti:) *pl.* **par·tic·u·lar·i·ties** *n.* the quality or state of being particular || a particular feature or detail [F. *particularité*]

par·tic·u·lar·ize (pərtíkjuləraiz) *pres. part.* **par·tic·u·lar·iz·ing** *past* and *past part.* **par·tic·u·lar·ized** *v.t.* to state (details or items) separately || *v.i.* to go into details [F. *particulariser*]

par·tic·u·lar·ly (pərtíkjulərli:) *adv.* in a particular manner || in particular

Par·ti·do Re·vo·lu·cio·na·ri·o Feb·re·ris·ta (pɑrtí:ðɔrevɔlu:sjɔnári:ɔfebrerí:stɑ) *FEBRERISTAS

Par·ti·do Re·vo·lu·cio·na·rio In·sti·tu·cio·nal (pɑrtí:ðɔrevɔlu:sjɔnárjɔi:nsti:tu:sjɔnál) (Institutional Revolutionary Party), the governing party of Mexico since 1929 (then called the Partido Nacional Revolucionario). It is regularly returned with 90% of the popular vote. Though basically democratic, it regulates the opposition and permits presidents to pick their own sucessors ('el tapadismo') and, in effect, their legislators

part·ing (pártiŋ) *n.* separation or division || a place where separation or division occurs || (*Br.*) a part (line of division of the hair) [PART v.]

Par·ti Que·be·cois (pɑrtí: keibəkwá) *n.* in Quebec, Canada, the political party of French-speaking population desiring national independence for Quebec

par·ti·san, par·ti·zan (pártiz'n) **1.** *n.* someone who actively supports (a party, cause or principle) || someone not in a regular army who engages in guerrilla warfare **2.** *adj.* of, relating to or characteristic of a partisan || one-sided, biased **pár·ti·san·ship, pár·ti·zan·ship** *n.* [F. fr. Ital.]

par·tite (pártait) *adj.* (*bot.*, of a cleft leaf) divided nearly to the base || (in compounds) divided into a specified number of parts, as in 'bipartite' [fr. L. *partitus*, divided]

par·ti·tion (pɑrtíʃən) **1.** *n.* a dividing into parts || something that divides a room etc. into parts, esp. a thin wall || one of the parts so separated || (*law*) the sale of jointly owned property and distribution of the proceeds among the co-owners || (*math.*) in set theory, the division of the members of the set into subsets such that each member belongs to one and only one of the subsets **2.** *v.t.* to divide into parts || (esp. with 'off') to separate (one area from another) by erecting a partition [F.]

par·ti·tive (pártitiv) **1.** *adj.* serving or tending to divide into parts || (*gram.*, of an adjective, article etc.) denoting only a part of a whole, e.g. 'some', 'any' **2.** *n.* a partitive word [fr. L. *partitivus*]

partizan *PARTISAN

part·ly (pártli:) *adv.* in part, not completely

part·ner (pártnər) **1.** *n.* someone associated with another in a common undertaking || one of two or more persons who are associated in a business or other joint venture and share risks and profits || (*naut., pl.*) a stout wooden frame surrounding a mast, pump etc., taking strain off the deck timbers **2.** *v.t.* to be the partner of [older *partener*, prob. var. of PARCENER]

part·ner·ship (pártnərʃip) *n.* the state of being a partner or partners || the relationship between partners || an association of persons who share risks and profits in a business or other joint venture || the legal contract binding such persons

part of speech one of the traditional classes of the words of a language according to their function (adjective, adverb, conjunction etc.) || a word regarded as belonging to one of these classes

par·ton (pártɒn) *n.* (*particle phys.*) hypothetical constituents of a proton and neutron that scatter high-energy electrons

partook *past* of PARTAKE

par·tridge (pártridʒ) *n.* any of certain plump gallinaceous game birds of *Perdix, Alectoris* and related genera, fam. *Phasianidae*, native to Europe, Asia and N. Africa, having short wings

CONCISE PRONUNCIATION KEY: **(a)** æ, *cat*; ɑ, *car*; ɔ *fawn*; ei, *snake*. **(e)** e, *hen*; i:, *sheep*; iə, *deer*; ɛə, *bear*. **(i)** i, *fish*; ai, *tiger*; ə:, *bird*. **(o)** o, *ox*; au, *cow*; ou, *goat*; u, *poor*; ɔi, *royal*. **(u)** ʌ, *duck*; u, *bull*; u:, *goose*; ə, *bacillus*; ju:, *cube*. x, *loch*; θ, *think*; ð, *bother*; z, *Zen*; ʒ, *corsage*; dʒ, *savage*; ŋ, *orangutang*; j, *yak*; ʃ, *fish*; tʃ, *fetch*; 'l, *rabble*; 'n, *redden*. Complete pronunciation key appears inside front cover.

and tail, variegated grayish-brown plumage and unfeathered legs || any of several somewhat similar gallinaceous game birds of North America, e.g. the bobwhite, the ruffed grouse || the tinamou [M.F. *pertrich, partrich* fr. O.F. *perdriz* fr. L. fr. Gk]

part-song (pártsɒŋ, pártsɒŋ) *n.* (*mus.*) a usually homophonic choral composition for several different voice parts, esp. unaccompanied

part-time (párttaim) *adj.* entailing less than the full number of hours of work, attendance etc., *a part-time job* || working, operating etc. for less than a full number of hours, *a part-time typist*

par·tu·ri·ent (partúəri:ənt, partjúəri:ənt) *adj.* giving birth or about to give birth || of or relating to parturition [fr. L. *parturiens* (*parturientis*) fr. *parturire*, to be in labor]

par·tu·ri·tion (parturíʃən, partjuríʃən, partʃuríʃən) *n.* the act of giving birth [fr. L. *parturitio* (*parturitionis*)]

part work one of a set of books published one part at a time

par·ty (párti:) *adj.* (*heraldry*, of a shield) divided into parts of different tinctures [F. *parti*, divided, separate]

party *pl.* **par·ties** *n.* a group of people united by some common interest or for some common purpose, *a party of tourists, a search party* || a group of people united in support of a common cause, esp. a national political organization || a gathering to which guests are invited in order to enjoy one another's company, *a cocktail party* || one of the persons or groups of persons engaged in a dispute or legal action || a person who knowingly assists, shares in or condones an action, *he refused to be a party to the deception* || (*pop.*) a person [M.E. *partie, partye* fr. F. *partie*]

party line the official policy of a political party || a single telephone line shared by two or more subscribers

party pooper one who fails to participate in an event designed for enjoyment

party wall a jointly owned wall dividing two properties

par·ve·nu (párvənu:, párvənju:) **1.** *n.* a person who has suddenly risen from comparative poverty or obscurity to wealth, power etc., esp. one who makes a vulgar, ostentatious display **2.** *adj.* like or characteristic of such a person [F. fr. past part. of *parvenir*, to arrive]

par·vis (párvis) *n.* an enclosed court in front of a building, esp. a church [F. *parvis*, O.F. *parecvis*]

par·y·lene (párəli:n) *n.* (*chem.*) plastic derived from paraxylene by polymerization; used as a thin, transparent insulator and protective covering

Pas·a·de·na (pæsədí:nə) a suburban residential city and winter resort (pop. 119,374) of S.W. California, 8 miles northeast of Los Angeles. California Institute of Technology (1891), Pasadena College (1902)

Pa·sar·ga·dae (pəsárgədi:) an ancient Persian city, founded (c. 550 B.C.) by Cyrus II. Ruins include his tomb

Pas·cal (pæskæl), Blaise (1623–62), French scientist, mathematician, philosopher and writer. He wrote mathematical and scientific treatises of great importance making contributions to hydraulics, pure geometry etc., and laid the foundation of the theory of probability (upon which Leibniz was to build his theory of the calculus). But his chief work was in Christian apologetics. He came into contact with the Jansenists in 1646. On Nov. 23, 1654 he had a mystical experience: he withdrew to Port Royal, lived ascetically, and wrote the brilliant 'Provincial Letters' (1656–7) in defense of the Jansenists, with Jesuit casuistry as the special target for attack. His most famous work, the so-called 'Pensées' (1670), is a series of fragments of a work in which Pascal set himself to persuade free thinkers of the truth of Christianity, broadly by exploring the limits of reason and the function of the imagination and affirming that at a certain point a leap into faith has to be made (the 'wager', as he put it: if you win you win all, if you lose you lose all, but have nothing to lose). On the literary level the 'Pensées' are unsurpassed examples of French classical prose: lucid, subtle and powerful. They can be said to have contributed to that science of the human heart from which the greatest works of French classical literature sprang

pas·cal (pæskál) *n.* a SI unit of pressure equal to a force of 1 newton per sq m; for Blaise Pascal *also* Pa

PASCAL *n.* (*computer*) a high-level program language around which a microcomputer was developed, requiring an intermediate P-code, a structure similar to ALGOL

pas·chal (pǽskəl) *adj.* of or relating to the Jewish Passover or the Christian Easter [F. *pascal*]

Pas·chal II (pǽskəl) (*d.* 1118), pope (1099–1118). He was involved in the Investiture Controversy with Emperors Henry IV and Henry V. He was captured (1110) and forced to recognize lay investiture, but later renounced this

paschal lamb a lamb eaten at the Passover festival || Christ

Pas·co·li (páskɔli:), Giovanni (1885–1912), Italian lyric poet, author of romantic verse expressing a mystical love of his native countryside. His works include 'Myricae' (1891), 'Primi Poemetti' (1903) and 'Poemi del Risorgimento' (1913)

Pas-de-Ca·lais (pædəkælei) a department (area 2,606 sq. miles, pop. 1,403,000) in N. France (*ARTOIS). Chief town: Arras

pa·se·o (pɑséiou) *n.* (*bullfighting*) procession preceding the fighting

pas·gang (pɑsgáŋ) *n.* (*skiing*) striding with a forward kick and pole push on the same side

pa·sha (páʃə, pəʃá, pǽʃə) *n.* a former courtesy title denoting high rank or office, used after the holder's name, in some Near Eastern, Middle Eastern or N. African countries [Turk. *pāshā*]

pasque-flow·er (pǽskflauər) *n.* *Anemone pulsatilla*, fam. *Ranunculaceae*, a low perennial European plant which puts out purple flowers at about Eastertime || any of several other plants of genus *Anemone* [earlier *passe-flower* fr. F. *passefleur* fr. *passer*, to surpass+*fleur*, flower]

pass (pæs, pɑs) *v.i.* to move along, proceed || to go by something in the course of moving, *keep to the left as you pass* || to go from one place, quality, state etc. to another, *to pass into a liquid state* || to cease, *wait till the danger passes* || (*rhet.*) to occur || (of time) to be spent, elapse, *days passed before news arrived* || to circulate or be transferred among people or places, *the rumor passed through the crowd within minutes* || to be interchanged, *angry letters passed between them* || to be just barely acceptable, *his suit is shabby, but it will pass* || to be judged satisfactory in an examination, inspection, course of study etc. || (of a proposed bill etc.) to be approved by a legislative body || (with 'for' or 'as') to be accepted (as something else), *a synthetic fiber that passes for wool, farthings no longer pass as legal tender in Britain* || (*law*, of a jury, the court etc., with 'on', 'upon') to pronounce the verdict or judgment || (*law*, of a judgment etc., with 'for' or 'against') to be pronounced, *judgment passed for the defendant* || (*ball games*) to throw, kick etc. the ball to a teammate || (*cards*) to decline one's turn to play, bid, take cards etc. || *v.t.* to go by, beyond, over, through etc. and leave behind, *they passed my house on the way* || to meet successfully the requirements of (an examination etc.) || to judge as satisfactory (someone being examined, their performance etc.) || to spend (time etc.), *we passed one night in Rome* || (of a committee, legislative body etc.) to approve (a motion, bill etc.) || to convey, esp. by handing, *please pass the butter* || to cause to go or move in a particular way or direction, *pass the rope over the pulley* || to cause to move past, *the general passed the troops in review* || to pronounce (a sentence or judgment), *to pass the death sentence on a prisoner* || to use (counterfeit money, invalid checks etc.) as if valid || to expel (feces, urine etc.) from the body || (*ball games*) to convey (the ball) to a teammate || (*baseball*, of the pitcher) to walk (a batter) || (*magic*) to transfer or manipulate (objects) by sleight of hand **to let** (or **allow to**) **pass** to permit (a statement, remark etc.) to be made without correcting or challenging it, in spite of one's reservations etc. **to pass away** to come to an end, cease || to die **to pass off** to come to an end, disappear, *the headache soon passed off* || to take place and be completed, *the demonstration passed off without violence* || to palm off, induce a person to accept (something that is not what it is said to be), *he passed the story off as his own* || to treat as unimportant, dismiss in an offhand way, *she passed off the accusation with a laugh* **to pass out** (*pop.*) to faint || (*pop.*) to lose consciousness through drinking too much alcohol || (*Br.*) to complete a course of instruction (esp. military) **to pass over** to consider and reject, *they passed him over for promotion* **to pass through** to undergo, experience, *to pass through a crisis* **to pass up** (*pop.*) to decline (an offer) or decide not to take advantage of (an opportunity) [F. *passer*]

pass *n.* a mark sufficient for passing an examination or test || a document which gives the holder permission to do what would otherwise be forbidden, or to enjoy a special privilege || a free ticket || (*ball games*) the passing of the ball to a teammate || (*baseball*) a walk || (*cards*) a declining of one's turn to play, bid etc. || a quick movement of the hands, made by a conjurer to confuse or mystify his audience || (*fencing*) a thrust with the weapon || (*bullfighting*) the movement executed by a matador with his cape in order to cause the bull to charge **a pretty pass** a difficult or critical state of affairs **to make a pass at** to try to attract sexually || to attempt to strike [F. *passe* and PASS v.]

pass *n.* a narrow way by which one can cross over or between mountains [M.E. *pas, paas*, pace fr. F. *pas*]

pass·a·ble (pǽsəb'l, pásəb'l) *adj.* moderately good, adequate || (of a river, stream etc.) capable of being crossed || (of a road) capable of being traveled along **páss·a·bly** *adv.* [F.]

pas·sa·ca·glia (pæsəkáljə) *n.* (*mus.*) an instrumental composition, originally a dance tune, in which a theme is constantly repeated (usually as a ground bass) in slow and stately triple time || (*hist.*) a Spanish or Italian dance which was the origin of this [Ital. fr. Span. *pasacalle*]

pas·sade (pəséid) *n.* (*manège*) a backward and forward movement of a horse over the same ground [F.]

pas·sage (pǽsidʒ) *n.* a corridor in a building || an alley, lane, channel, path or other way providing communication, *an underground passage* || a passage from one place, state or thing to another || a moving along, progressing, *the passage of time* || the passing of a measure by a legislative body || the right or opportunity to pass || a journey by sea or air, *a smooth passage* || a passenger's accommodation on board ship, *to book a passage* || the charge made for this || an esp. brief extract from a literary or musical work || (*rhet.*) a conversation, dispute etc. between two persons || a bowel movement || (*manège*) a horse's controlled slow sideways walk or trot [F.]

passage *pres. part.* **pas·sag·ing** *past* and *past part.* **pas·saged** *v.i.* (*manège*, of a horse) to move sideways || (*manège*, of a rider) to cause a horse to move sideways || v.t. (*manège*) to cause (a horse) to move sideways [F. *passager* fr. Ital. *passegiare*, to walk]

pas·sage·way (pǽsidʒwei) *n.* a way between two points, affording passage

pass·a·long (pǽsəlɔŋ) *n.* (*business*) price increase due to increase in costs

pas·sant (pǽsənt) *adj.* (*heraldry*, of an animal) walking and looking towards the dexter side with the dexter forepaw upraised [F.]

Pas·sau, Treaty of (pǽsau) a treaty (1552) between Maurice, elector of Saxony, and the future Emperor Ferdinand I. It granted full religious liberty to Lutherans and led on to the Peace of Augsburg (1555)

pass·book (pǽsbuk, pásbuk) *n.* a small book supplied by a bank to the holder of an account, in which the bank enters his credits and debits || a customer's book in which a storekeeper or merchant records the purchases not yet paid for

Pass·chen·daele, Battle of (pǽʃəndeil, pɑ́ʃəndɑlə) *YPRES, BATTLE OF

pass degree (*Br.*) a university academic degree gained by passing an examination at a lower level than the honors degree

pas·sé (pæséi, pǽsei) adj. no longer in style, out-of-date [F.=past]

passed ball (*baseball*) a pitch which the catcher fails to catch when he could be expected to do so, thus allowing a base runner to reach another base

passe·men·terie (pæsméntri:) *n.* decorative trimming or braid of gold thread, beads, silken cord, gimp etc. [F.]

pas·sen·ger (pǽsindʒər) *n.* a person who travels in a vehicle, ship, boat, aircraft etc. but is not the driver, nor one of the crew [M.E. *passager* fr. F.]

passenger pigeon *Ectopistes migratorius*, an extinct North American pigeon, once abundant in the Mississippi Valley

passe-par·tout (pæspartú:) **1.** *n.* a type of picture frame in which the glass is attached to the backing by an edging of adhesive tape || the tape used ‖ a mount surrounding a picture in a frame ‖ a master key **2.** *v.t.* to frame with a passe-partout [F. fr. *passer,* to pass+*partout,* all around]

pass·er·by (pǽsərbái, pɑ́sərbái) *pl.* **pass·ers·by** *n.* someone who passes by, esp. by chance

pas·ser·ine (pǽsərain, pǽsərin) **1.** *adj.* belonging to *Passeriformes,* an order of birds which perch, comprising more than half of all living birds **2.** *n.* a passerine bird [fr. L. *passerinus* fr. *passer,* sparrow]

pass-fail (pǽsféil) *n.* (*education*) a system of grading with only the two grades, vs. letter or number grading, esp. for academic work — **pass-fail** *adj.*

Pass·field (pǽsfiːld), 1st Baron *WEBB

pas·si·bil·i·ty (pæsəbíliti:) *n.* the quality of being passible

pas·si·ble (pǽsəb'l) *adj.* capable of suffering or of feeling emotion [O.F.]

pas·sim (pɑ́sim, pǽsim) *adv.* (of references to a cited work) scattered throughout, *see chapter V passim* [L.]

pass·ing (pǽsiŋ, pɑ́siŋ) **1.** *adj.* going past, *a passing taxi* ‖ transitory, *a passing whim* ‖ incidental, *a passing reference* ‖ (of a mark) indicating that one has passed an examination, course of study etc. **2.** *n.* the act of someone who or something that passes ‖ (*rhet.*) death **in passing** by the way, incidentally [PASS v.]

passing bell a church bell tolled to mark a person's death

passing note (*mus.*) a note in a melody which forms a discord with the harmony but which serves as a transition between two others which are not discordant

passing tone (*mus.*) a passing note

pas·sion (pǽʃən) *n.* intense or violent emotion, esp. sexual desire or love ‖ intense anger ‖ a great liking or enthusiasm, *a passion for swimming* ‖ a violent emotional outburst, *a passion of tears* ‖ the martyrdom of an early Christian **Pas·sion** the sufferings and death of Jesus Christ ‖ one of the Gospel accounts of this ‖ a musical work based on such an account

pas·sion·al (pǽʃən'l) *n.* a book containing accounts of the sufferings and martyrdom of Christian saints [fr. M.L. *passionale,* neut. of *passionalis* adj., relating to passion]

pas·sion·ate (pǽʃənit) *adj.* easily moved to strong emotion ‖ showing or inspired by strong emotion, *a passionate love letter* ‖ (of emotion) intense ‖ (*old-fash.*) easily angered [fr. M.L. *passionatus*]

pas·sion·flow·er (pǽʃənflauər) *n.* a member of *Passiflora,* fam. *Passifloraceae,* a genus of tropical American woody climbing plants. The parts of the flowers suggest the instruments of Christ's Passion (the stigmas suggesting the nails, the corona the crown of thorns, the anthers the five wounds). Some species produce edible fruit ‖ the flower of such a plant

passion fruit the edible fruit of a passionflower

Pas·sion·ist (pǽʃənist) *n.* a member of an austere Roman Catholic order founded (1720) in Italy by St Paul of the Cross. The Passionists take a special vow to keep the memory of the Passion alive in the hearts of the faithful. There is an order of nuns, founded 1771

pas·sion·less (pǽʃənlis) *adj.* without passion, not moved by or showing emotion

Passion play a play based on Christ's Passion, e.g. a medieval mystery (*OBERAMMERGAU)

pas·sive (pǽsiv) **1.** *adj.* acted upon by someone or something else ‖ not reacting to an external influence, inert ‖ offering no resistance ‖ (of a person) lacking initiative or drive ‖ (*gram.*) designating or expressed in a voice which denotes that the subject is also the object of the verb ‖ (*phys.*) of an instrument designed to reflect, but not record or amplify, energy impulses, e.g., transducer, filter **2.** *n.* (*gram.*) the passive voice [fr. L. *passivus*]

passive homing (*mil.*) the capability of homing requiring only the natural emanations from the target, e.g., heat, light, sound, magnetism, exhaust

passive jamming (*mil.*) creating confusion in enemy signals or radar by use of reflectors

passive resistance resistance to civil law, military occupation etc. by nonviolent means

passive satellite a satellite that reflects only signals sent to it

pas·siv·i·ty (pæsíviti:) *n.* the quality or state of being passive [fr. L. *passivus*]

pass·key (pǽskiː, pɑ́skiː) *pl.* **pass·keys** *n.* a master key ‖ any private key

Pass·o·ver (pǽsouvər, pɑ́souvər) *n.* a Jewish feast commemorating the release of the Israelites from slavery in Egypt, celebrated on the 14th day of Nisan and continuing for seven or (in modern Israel) eight days (*JEWISH CALENDAR) [PASS v.+OVER prep., fr. the passing over of the Jews, i.e. their exemption from the curse bringing death on the firstborn in all Egyptian homes (Exodus xii)]

pass·port (pǽspɔrt, pǽspourt, pɑ́spɔrt, pɑ́spourt) *n.* a document certifying nationality, issued by the government of a country, to a citizen intending to travel abroad ‖ something that enables a person to achieve a desired end, *a passport to success* [F. *passeport*]

pass·word (pǽswəːrd, pɑ́swəːrd) *n.* a word or phrase used to show that one is authorized to enter, pass a barrier etc. ‖ a word used by members of a secret society etc. in recognition of one another

past (pæst, past) **1.** *adj.* (of a period of time) just ended, *the past week has been very eventful* ‖ relating to an earlier time, *one's past life* ‖ (of a period of time, used post-positively) gone by, elapsed, *the time for talking is past* ‖ (of the holder of an office, position etc.) former, no longer in office, *a past president* ‖ (*gram.*) of or designating a tense that expresses an action or state in time that has gone by **2.** *n.* time that has gone by ‖ the earlier part of a person's life or the earlier history of a community, country, institution etc. ‖ (*pop.*) a wild or discreditable earlier life, *a woman with a past* ‖ (*gram.*) the past tense **3.** *prep.* beyond or further than (in time or place), *past his prime, just past the post office* ‖ (in time expressions) used to indicate the period after the hour, *10 past 8* ‖ going beyond or by, *he pushed past me, bullets whistled past our ears* ‖ beyond the scope, capacities or limit of, *those pants are past mending* **4.** *adv.* in such a way as to pass by, *the car drove past* [alt. past part. of PASS]

pas·ta (pɑ́stə) *n.* an alimentary paste of wheat flour used in processed form (noodles, macaroni, spaghetti etc.) or as fresh dough (ravioli) [Ital.]

paste (peist) **1.** *n.* a moist, fairly stiff mixture of liquid and a powdery substance ‖ a mixture of flour and butter, lard etc. used for pastry crust etc. ‖ a soft, creamy foodstuff made by pounding, grinding etc., *anchovy paste, almond paste* ‖ a hard, brilliant lead and glass substance used to make imitation jewels ‖ dampened clay used in making earthenware or porcelain ‖ an adhesive made typically from flour and water **2.** *v.t. pres. part.* **past·ing** *past* and *past part.* **past·ed** to make (something) stick, using paste, *to paste a photograph onto a mount* ‖ to cover with paste ‖ (*pop.*) to deal a hard blow or blows to, *he pasted him in the eighth round* [O.F. *paste*]

paste·board (péistbɔrd, péistbourd) **1.** *n.* a stiff material made by pasting together two or more sheets of paper **2.** *adj.* made of pasteboard ‖ (*fig.*) unsubstantial, being merely a facade, *he can only create pasteboard characters*

paste job a literary work made up of patches of other works

pas·tel (pæstél, pǽstel) *n.* a powdered pigment mixed with very little gum, compressed into small, colored sticks for drawing ‖ a stick of this material ‖ the art of drawing with such sticks ‖ a drawing made with these ‖ (of color) light in tone **pas·tél·ist,** esp. *Br.* **pas·tél·list** *n.* [F. fr. Ital. *Pastello,* woad]

pas·tern (pǽstərn) *n.* the part of the foot of a horse or other equine animal between the fetlock and the hoof (corresponding to the human ankle) ‖ (*loosely*) a corresponding part in other animals [M.E. *pastron* fr. O.F. *pasturon,* a hobble]

Pas·ter·nak (pǽstərnæk), Boris Leonidovich (1890–1960), Russian writer. His poetry includes 'Above Barriers', (1917) and 'Second Birth' (1932). He is best known in the West for his novel about the Russian Revolution, 'Dr. Zhivago' (1958). He won the Nobel prize for literature (1958)

paste-up (péistʌp) *n.* a mock-up of printed matter, esp. of a magazine, made by pasting sample matter on sheets of paper or card, to show what the finished product is to look like

Pas·teur (pæstəːr), Louis (1822–95), French chemist and biologist. His researches showing that the fermentation of milk and wine was due to the multiplication of bacteria and other microorganisms led to the discovery of the role of microorganisms in human and animal disease. From these findings, he developed immunization by inoculation of attenuated microbes, and the process of pasteurization. His work on asepsis greatly facilitated medical advances and he also established stereochemistry. The French government took up his work and created the Institut Pasteur (1888)

pas·teur·i·za·tion (pæstʃərizéiʃən, pæstərizéiʃən) *n.* a process which renders milk free of disease-producing bacteria and helps to prevent it from spoiling without destroying the vitamins or changing the taste. It involves heating the milk to 145°–150°F. for 30 minutes, or to 164°–168° for 15 seconds. It is also used in the production of other dairy products, wine and beer

pas·teur·ize (pǽstʃəraiz, pǽstəraiz) *pres. part.* **pas·teur·iz·ing** *past* and *past part.* **pas·teur·ized** *v.t.* to sterilize by by pasteurization [after PASTEUR]

pas·tiche (pæstíːʃ) *n.* a musical, literary or artistic work with elements borrowed from several sources ‖ a work which imitates or caricatures the work of someone else [F. fr. Ital. *pasticcio*]

past·ies (péistiːz) *n.* small adhesive covering for a woman's nipples, esp. to avoid laws against indecent exposure

pas·til (pǽstəl) *n.* a pastille

pas·tille (pæstíːl) *n.* a flavored or medicated lozenge ‖ a small cone made of an aromatic paste, used to perfume or disinfect the air [F.]

pas·time (pǽstaim, pɑ́staim) *n.* anything that serves as agreeable recreation [PASS+TIME]

pas·tis (pastíː) *n.* a licorice-flavored liqueur produced in France

past master someone who excels in an activity ‖ someone who has held the office of master in a guild, lodge etc.

Pas·to (pɑ́stɔ) a city (pop. 140,700) on a high plateau (8,400 ft) in S.W. Colombia: gold mines

pas·tor (pǽstər, pɑ́stər) *n.* a priest or minister in charge of a parish or congregation [M.E. and A.F. *pastour* fr. O.F. *pastor, pastur,* shepherd]

pas·to·ral (pǽstərəl, pɑ́stərəl) **1.** *adj.* of, relating to or characterized by the care of grazing animals, esp. sheep and goats, *a pastoral economy* ‖ (of land) used for grazing ‖ dealing with idealized country life, *pastoral poetry* ‖ relating to the office and work of a minister of religion **2.** *n.* a pastoral poem, play, opera etc. ‖ a circular letter sent by a bishop to his clergy, often to be read in all churches [fr. L. *pastoralis* fr. *pastor,* shepherd]

pas·to·rale (pæstərɑ́l, pæstərǽl) *n.* a musical composition with themes suggestive of pastoral life [Ital.]

Pastoral Epistles *TIMOTHY AND TITUS

pas·tor·ate (pǽstərit, pɑ́stərit) *n.* the office or period of office of a pastor ‖ the clergy in general, or a particular body of ministers [fr. M.L. *pastoratus*]

pas·tor·ship (pǽstərʃip, pɑ́stərʃip) *n.* the office or period of office of a pastor

past participle (*gram.*) a participle which expresses an action that is completed, usually with the auxiliary verbs 'have' or 'be'

past perfect (*gram.*) the pluperfect tense

pas·tra·mi (pəstrɑ́miː) *n.* highly spiced smoked shoulder of beef sliced thin and served hot in sandwiches or as a meat course [Yiddish fr. Rum. pastramă fr. pastră, to preserve]

pas·try (péistriː) *pl.* **pas·tries** *n.* dough consisting of flour, water or milk and a high proportion of butter etc., used baked as piecrust etc. ‖ baked goods consisting of this ‖ an individual tart, pie etc. made with this [prob. fr. PASTE]

pas·try·cook (péistriːkuk) *n.* a person hired by a restaurant etc. to make pastry ‖ a person who makes and sells pastries

pas·tur·a·ble (pǽstʃərəb'l, pɑ́stʃərəb'l) *adj.* (of land) suitable for pasture

pas·tur·age (pǽstʃəridʒ, pɑ́stʃəridʒ) *n.* grazing land, or grass for grazing ‖ the pasturing of cattle e.g. on common land [O.F. *pasturage,* Mod. F. *pâturage*]

pas·ture (pǽstʃər, pɑ́stʃər) *n.* grass or other vegetation that provides food for cattle, sheep, horses, goats etc. or for wild animals ‖ land which produces such vegetation ‖ a particular piece of such land [O.F. *pasture,* Mod. F. *pâture* fr. L.L. *pastura,* a grazing]

pasture *pres. part.* **pas·tur·ing** *past* and *past part.* **pas·tured** *v.t.* to cause (an animal) to feed on pasture ‖ *v.i.* (of an animal) to feed on pasture [O.F. *pasturer,* Mod. F. *pâturer*]

pas·ty (pǽstiː, péistiː) *pl.* **pas·ties** *n.* (esp. *Br.*) a small pie, consisting either of meat and vegetables or of fruit [M.E. *pastee* fr. O.F. *pastée*]

past·y (péisti:) *comp.* **past·i·er** *superl.* **past·i·est** *adj.* like paste in color or consistency ‖ pale, flabby, or unhealthy in appearance, *a pasty complexion* [PASTE]

pat (pæt) **1.** *n.* a gentle stroke or blow made with something flat (esp. with the hand) ‖ the sound of a gentle blow ‖ a small, neat piece of some soft substance, esp. butter **to give someone a pat on the back** to praise or congratulate someone **2.** *v.t. pres. part.* **pat·ting** *past* and *past part.* **pat·ted** to give a pat to, often as a sign of affection or sympathy, *to pat a dog* ‖ to shape with blows of the hands or of some flat implement, *pat the butter into half-pounds* **to pat on the back** to praise or congratulate [M.E. *pat, patte,* prob. imit.]

pat 1. *adv.* in exactly the right way or at exactly the right time, *his answer came pat* **2.** *adj.* glib, *a pat remark* **to stand pat** (*poker*) to play the hand as dealt without drawing further cards ‖ to stand firmly by what one has said, or the position one has taken [perh. fr. PAT v.]

pa·ta·gi·um (pətéidʒi:əm) *pl.* **pa·ta·gi·a** (pətéidʒi:ə) *n.* a membranous expansion between the fore and hind limbs of a bat, flying squirrel etc. ‖ the membranous skin in the angle of a bird's wing [M.L. fr. L. *patagium,* gold border on a tunic]

Pat·a·go·ni·a (pætəgóuni:ə) a region of S. Argentina, southernmost Chile and Tierra del Fuego, consisting of the E. Andes (ice-capped at this latitude and with several peaks over 10,000 ft) and arid tablelands stretching to the Atlantic. Temperatures and precipitation are low. Products: wool, petroleum. The native Indians are almost extinct

Pat·a·go·ni·an (pætəgóuni:ən) **1.** *adj.* of or relating to Patagonia or its inhabitants **2.** *n.* a native or inhabitant of Patagonia

Pa·tan (pɑ́tən) a Buddhist and Hindu pilgrimage place (pop. 135,000) and former capital (17th–18th cc.) of Nepal, near Katmandu: funeral mounds (3rd c. B.C.), temples

patch (pætʃ) **1.** *n.* a piece of material sewed on, let into, or otherwise attached to something in order to mend it ‖ any of the bits of cloth which, when sewn together, form patchwork ‖ a part of a surface, generally irregular in shape, which is in some way different from the rest, *the bald patch on his head* ‖ a small piece of adhesive tape used to cover a scratch, wound etc. ‖ (*computer*) insertion of an instruction in a program to correct, change, or add new material without destroying the routine, esp. an improvised patch ‖ a small piece of ground, esp. under a specified crop, *a potato patch* ‖ a passage in a literary or musical work ‖ (*mil.*) an emblem sewn on the sleeve of a soldier's uniform to indicate the unit to which he belongs ‖ (*Br.*) a period, stage, *going through a bad patch* ‖ a piece of cloth worn over an injured eye ‖ (*hist.*) a beauty spot worn on the face or neck **not a patch on** (esp. *Br.*) not nearly so good as **2.** *v.t.* to mend by putting a patch on or over, *to patch a hole* ‖ to make by sewing bits of cloth together, *to patch a quilt* **to patch up** to put together or mend in a makeshift way ‖ to put together out of odds and ends, *a book patched up out of old magazine articles* ‖ to become reconciled after (a quarrel etc.) [M.E. *pacche, patche,* origin unknown]

patch·board (pætʃbɔrd) *n.* (*electr.*) removable circuitry panel with multiple terminals adaptable to various electronic operations *also* patch panel

patch cord (*computer*) removable wire with connectors at both ends that can be inserted into proper sockets to create new circuits for input or output, esp. for punch-card operations —**patch plug** *n.* a cordless metal instrument capable of performing the function of a patch cord

Patch·en (pætʃən), Kenneth (1911–72), U.S. poet and novelist. His verse, concerned in the 1930s with social protest, includes 'Before the Brave' (1936) and 'First Will & Testament' (1939). His prose works include 'The Journal of Albion Moonlight' (1941) and the satirical 'Memoirs of a Shy Pornographer' (1945)

patch·i·ly (pætʃili:) *adv.* in a patchy way

patch·i·ness (pætʃi:nis) *n.* the quality or state of being patchy

patch·ou·li (pætʃuli:) *n.* *Pogostemon cablin,* fam. *Labiatae,* a heavy-scented plant cultivated in the Far East ‖ the essential oil distilled from its leaves, used as a fixative for many heavy perfumes and as an insect repellent in the Far East [Tamil]

patch panel (*computer*) perforated panel, often portable, capable of receiving patch cords to create new circuit connections *also* patch board, plugboard

patch pocket a pocket made by sewing cloth to the outside of a garment

patch test a test for an allergy made by applying to the skin a small piece of cloth soaked in the substance believed to cause the allergy, and observing the skin for irritation

patch·work (pætʃwə:rk) *n.* needlework made of assorted small pieces of material sewn together at the edges to form regular or free patterns ‖ something made up of miscellaneous, jumbled elements

patch·y (pætʃi:) *comp.* **patch·i·er** *superl.* **patch·i·est** *adj.* consisting of or containing patches ‖ uneven in quality, *a patchy performance*

pate (peit) *n.* (*pop., old-fash.*) the head, *his bald pate was glinting in the sun* **pát·ed** *adj.* (*pop.,* in combinations) having a specified kind of head or mind, *bald-pated, addlepated* [origin unknown]

pâ·té (pɑtei) *n.* an edible paste of finely minced meat or fish ‖ a small meat pie or patty [F.]

pâ·té de foie gras (pɑteidəfwɑgrɑ) *n.* a rich paste of the fat livers of geese [F.]

paté *PATTÉE

pa·tel·la (pətélə) *pl.* **pa·tel·lae** (pətéli:), **pa·tel·las** *n.* (*anat.*) the kneecap ‖ (*anat., bot.*) any pan-shaped formation **pa·tél·lar, pa·tél·late** *adjs* [L.=little dish]

pat·en (pæt'n) *n.* (*eccles.*) a plate used to cover the chalice and receive the host in the Eucharist ‖ any thin, circular metal disk [O.F. *patène*]

pa·ten·cy (péit'nsi:) *n.* the quality or state of being evident ‖ (*med.*) the quality or state of being unobstructed [PATENT]

pat·ent 1. (pæt'nt, *Br.* also péit'nt) *n.* an official paper conferring a right, privilege etc., esp. one issued by a government, guaranteeing an inventor and his heirs exclusive rights over an invention, process etc. for a given length of time ‖ this invention or process ‖ a document issued by the government authorizing the sale or grant of public lands ‖ the land so sold or granted **2.** (pæt'nt, péit'nt) *adj.* (of an invention) protected by a patent, *a patent lock* ‖ made or sold under a registered trademark or trade name ‖ of or relating to the granting of patents, *patent attorney* ‖ original and individual as if protected by a patent, *a patent way of pickling onions* ‖ evident, obvious ‖ (*med.,* of a body passage) unobstructed ‖ (*hist.,* of a document) open to public view ‖ (*biol.*) patulous **3.** (pæt'nt, *Br.* also péit'nt) *v.t.* to obtain a patent for (an invention) **pat·ent·ée** *n.* the person to whom a patent has been granted [F. *patent* adj., open and fr. L. *patens* (*patentis*) adj., open]

patent leather leather sprayed with varnish to give a hard, very shiny surface. It is used for shoes, handbags etc.

pat·ent·ly (pæt'ntli:, péit'ntli:) *adv.* obviously, evidently

patent office the government office which examines inventors' claims and grants patents

patent rolls (*Br.*) the annual roll of patents issued. The rolls are preserved in the Public Record Office in London

Pa·ter (péitər), Walter Horatio (1839–94), English essayist and critic. His elegant prose heralds the aestheticism of the 1890s. He wrote 'Studies in the History of the Renaissance' (1873), 'Marius the Epicurean' (1885), and 'Imaginary Portraits' (1887)

pa·ter·fa·mil·i·as (péitərfəmíli:əs) *n.* the father of a family, regarded as head of the household [L.]

pa·ter·nal (pətə́:rn'l) *adj.* of or relating to a father ‖ having or showing fatherly qualities, e.g. benevolence, *to take a paternal interest in someone's welfare* ‖ related through the father, *one's paternal grandmother* **pa·tér·nal·ism** *n.* the principle or practice of governing a country or running an organization etc. in a way that suggests a father's authoritative deciding of what is in the best interest of his children **pa·ter·nal·ís·tic** *adj.* **pa·ter·nal·ís·ti·cal·ly** *adv.* [fr. L.L. *paternalis* fr. L. *paternus* fr. *pater,* father]

pa·ter·ni·ty (pətə́:rniti:) *n.* the state of being a father ‖ descent from a father, male parentage, *of unknown paternity* ‖ authorship or origin, *he didn't deny his paternity of the scheme* [F. *paternité*]

pa·ter·nos·ter (péitərnɒ́stər) *n.* the Lord's Prayer, esp. as recited in Latin ‖ one of the large beads of a rosary on which the Lord's Prayer is said [L.=our father]

Pat·er·son (pætərs'n) a manufacturing city (pop. 137,970) in N. New Jersey. It is famous for its silk industry ('Silk City'). Manufactures: cotton goods, revolvers, airplane motors, textile machinery, foundry products

path (pæθ, pɑθ) *pl.* **paths** (pæðz, pɑðz, pæθs, pɑθs) *n.* a narrow way or trail, esp. one formed by the frequent passage of people or animals ‖ (*computer*) the proper sequence for executing a routine ‖ a narrow way specially constructed, *garden paths* ‖ any way or space by which people may pass, *the police cleared a path through the crowd for him* ‖ the course of a moving person or thing, *the path of a planet* ‖ line of progress, *his path through life was hard* [O.E. *pæth*]

Pa·than (pətɑ́n) *n.* a member of the chief people inhabiting Afghanistan and N.W. Pakistan, famous as soldiers [Hind. *pathān*]

pa·thet·ic (pəθétik) *adj.* arousing pity or sympathetic sorrow ‖ arousing pitying contempt, *his incompetence is pathetic* **pa·thét·i·cal·ly** *adv.* [fr. L.L. *patheticus* fr. Gk fr. *paschein,* to suffer]

pathetic fallacy (in literature) the attribution of human emotions or characteristics to natural phenomena, e.g. 'the frowning cliffs'

Pa·thet Lao (pɑθet lɑ́ou) North Vietnamese Communist-led forces in Laos

path·find·er (pæθfaindər, pɑ́θfaindər) *n.* someone who explores unknown regions ‖ someone who pioneers a new process or procedure etc. which has general applications ‖ (*mil.*) an aircraft sent ahead of a bombing force to find and mark the target by flares etc. ‖ the pilot of such an aircraft

path·less (pæθlis, pɑ́θlis) *adj.* having no paths ‖ unexplored

path·o·gen (pæθədʒen) *n.* an agent that produces disease, e.g. a bacterium or virus [fr. Gk *pathos,* suffering, disease+*genēs,* born of]

path·o·gene (pæθədʒi:n) *n.* a pathogen

path·o·gen·e·sis (pæθədʒénisis) *n.* the origin or development of a disease **path·o·ge·net·ic** (pæθədʒənétik), **path·o·gen·ic** (pæθədʒénik) *adjs* relating to pathogenesis ‖ causing or capable of causing a disease **pa·thog·e·ny** (pəθɒ́dʒəni:) *n.* pathogenesis [fr. Gk *pathos,* disease+*genesis,* origin]

pa·thog·no·mon·ic (pəθɒgnəmɒ́nik) *adj.* characteristic of or indicating with certainty the presence of a specific disease [fr. Gk *pathognōmonikos,* skilled in judging symptoms]

path·o·log·ic (pæθəlɒ́dʒik) *adj.* pertaining to pathology **path·o·lóg·i·cal** *adj.* pathologic ‖ involving or resulting from disease ‖ morbid, *his writings show a pathological vision of humanity* [fr. Gk *pathologikos* fr. *pathos,* disease+*logos,* word]

pa·thol·o·gist (pəθɒ́lədʒist) *n.* a specialist in pathology

pa·thol·o·gy (pəθɒ́lədʒi:) *n.* the study of disease and all its manifestations, esp. of the functional and structural changes caused by it ‖ all the manifestations of a disease, *the pathology of tuberculosis* [fr. Mod. L. or M.L. *pathologia* fr. Gk *pathos,* disease+*logos,* word]

pa·tho·mor·phol·o·gy (pæθəmɔrfɒ́lədʒi:) *n.* the science of abnormal diseases of the form and structure, e.g., histology, anatomy —**pa·tho·mor·phol·o·gic** *adj.* —**pa·tho·mor·pho·log·i·cal** *adj.*

pa·thos (péiθɒs) *n.* a quality in an experience, narrative, literary work etc. which arouses profound feelings of compassion or sorrow [Gk=suffering]

pa·tho·type (pæθətaip) *n.* an organism capable of causing disease

path·way (pæθwei, pɑ́θwei) *n.* a narrow way or footpath

Pa·ti·a·la (pʌti:ɑ́lə) a former princely capital (pop. 125,000) now in the Punjab, India, producing cotton thread, textiles and metalwork

pa·tience (péiʃəns) *n.* the capacity to put up with pain, troubles, difficulties, hardship etc. without complaint or ill temper ‖ the ability to wait or persevere without losing heart or becoming bored ‖ (*Br.*) solitaire (card game) **out of patience with** unable to put up with any longer **to have no patience with** to feel nothing but irritation with or contempt for, be unable to

CONCISE PRONUNCIATION KEY: **(a)** æ, *cat*; ɑ, *car*; ɔ *fawn*; ei, *snake*. **(e)** e, *hen*; i:, *sheep*; iə, *deer*; ɛə, *bear*. **(i)** i, *fish*; ai, *tiger*; ə:, *bird*. **(o)** ɒ, *ox*; au, *cow*; ou, *goat*; u, *poor*; ɔi, *royal*. **(u)** ʌ, *duck*; u, *bull*; u:, *goose*; ə, *bacillus*; ju:, *cube*. x, *loch*; θ, *think*; ð, *bother*; z, *Zen*; ʒ, *corsage*; dʒ, *savage*; ŋ, *orangutang*; j, *yak*; ʃ, *fish*; tʃ, *fetch*; 'l, *rabble*; 'n, *redden*. Complete pronunciation key appears inside front cover.

put up with [M.E. fr. O.F. *patience, pacience* fr. L.]

pa·tient (péiʃənt) 1. *adj.* showing or having patience 2. *n.* a person receiving medical attention ‖ a client of a doctor, dentist etc., whether sick or not [O.F. *pacient, passient* fr. L. *patiens* (*patientis*)]

pat·i·na (pǽt'nə) *n.* a surface formed on metal (esp. bronze) by long exposure to the air, or produced artificially by an acid ‖ a surface formed on wood by age or constant care and handling [L. *patina, patena,* a shallow bronze bowl]

Pa·ti·ño (putí:njɔ), Simón (1861–1947), Bolivian Indian who made himself a multi-millionaire from his tin-mining monopoly, although he was almost illiterate

pa·ti·o (pǽti:ou) *pl.* **pa·ti·os** *n.* an open courtyard enclosed by the walls of a house, characteristic of Spanish and Spanish-American houses ‖ an area, usually paved, adjoining a house, used esp. for outdoor cooking or dining [Span.]

Pat·more (pǽtmɔr, pǽtmour), Coventry Kersey Dighton (1823–96), English mystical poet. His subject in 'The Angel in the House' (1858–62) and 'The Unknown Eros' (1877) is human love as an image of divine love

Pat·mos (pǽtmɒs) a Greek island (area 13 sq. miles, pop. 2,486) of the Dodecanese. There is a tradition that St John wrote Revelation here in exile. Monastery (1088)

Pat·na (pǽtnə) the capital (pop. 473,001) of Bihar, India, on the Ganges, center of a famous rice-growing district. Handicrafts: metalwork, glass, carpets, pottery, leatherwork. Mosques (15th, 16th and 17th cc.), Sikh temple. It was the capital of the Maurya Empire (325–184 B.C.)

pat·ois (pǽtwɑ) *n.* the speech or dialect peculiar to one part of a country, differing from the standard written or spoken language [F., origin unknown]

Paton (péit'n), Alan (1903–) South African writer and political figure. He gained international fame with his novels 'Cry, the Beloved Country' (1948) and 'Too Late the Phalarope' (1953), which explored racial conflict in South Africa long before it became an international issue. His later works include nonfiction ('The Land and the People of South Africa,' 1955), short-story collections ('Tales from a Troubled Land,' 1961; 'Knocking on the Door,' 1975), and the novel 'Ah, But Your Land Is Beautiful' (1982). He helped found the Liberal party of South Africa, an anti-apartheid political organization

Pa·tos, La·go·a dos (ləgóəðuʃpátus) a lake (150 miles long, 37 miles wide) in S. Brazil, separated from the Atlantic by a sandy peninsula

Pa·tras (pətrǽs) (*Gk* Patrai) a port (pop. 111,607) of the N.W. Peloponnesus, Greece

pa·tri·al (péitri:'l) *n.* a citizen by reason of birth or adoption —**pa·tri·al·i·ty** *n.* the condition

pa·tri·arch (péitri:ɑrk) *n.* the father or head of a family or tribe, esp. one of the founders of the Jewish people in the Old Testament (Abraham, Isaac, Jacob, ten of Jacob's sons and Joseph's two sons) ‖ (*rhet.*) any venerable head of a large family or tribe ‖ (*rhet.*) any very old and dignified man ‖ (*Roman Catholic and Uniate Churches*) a bishop who ranks in jurisdiction immediately below the pope ‖ a bishop of the Orthodox Eastern sees of Constantinople, Alexandria, Antioch and Jerusalem ‖ the spiritual head of any of certain Eastern Churches (e.g. the Syrian, Coptic or Russian Orthodox Churches) ‖ (*Mormon Church*) a high dignitary who has the power to invoke and pronounce blessings [O.F. *patriarche* fr. L. fr. Gk fr. *patria,* clan+*archēs,* ruler]

pa·tri·ar·chal (pe̩itri:ɑ́rk'l) *adj.* relating to, like or ruled by a patriarch [fr. L.L. *patriarchalis*]

pa·tri·ar·chate (péitri:ɑ̩rkit) *n.* the district ruled by an ecclesiastical patriarch or his residence, office or term of office ‖ a patriarchal system [fr. M.L. *patriarchatus*]

pa·tri·ar·chy (péitri:ɑrki:) *pl.* **pa·tri·ar·chies** *n.* a social system in which the chief authority is the father or eldest male member of the family or clan ‖ a community characterized by this system [fr. Gk *patriarchia,* office of a patriarch]

pa·tri·cian (pətríʃən) 1. *n.* (*hist.*) a member of one of the privileged families of ancient Rome, who alone until the 4th c. B.C. had the right to hold office (cf. PLEBEIAN) ‖ a noble, esp. (*hist.*) in the Byzantine Empire and the medieval Italian city-states 2. *adj.* noble, aristocratic ‖ having or exemplifying qualities and standards associated with the aristocracy, i.e. sense of style, refinement without weakness, noble sentiment etc. ‖ (*Rom. hist.*) of or relating to the patricians [fr. L. *patricius,* belonging to the rank of *patres,* senators of Rome]

pa·tri·ci·ate (pətríʃi:it, pətríʃi:e̩it) *n.* (*Rom. hist.*) the body or class of patricians ‖ the rank or dignity of a patrician [fr. M.L. *patriciatus*]

pat·ri·ci·dal (pætrisáid'l) *adj.* of, relating to or guilty of patricide

pat·ri·cide (pǽtrisaid) *n.* the murder of a father by his child ‖ someone who murders his father [fr. L. *pater,* father+*caedere,* to kill]

Pat·rick (pǽtrik), St (c. 385–461), the patron saint of Ireland. He brought Christianity to Ireland (432 onwards) and founded the see of Armagh (c. 444). He wrote 'The Letter to Coroticus' and 'Confessions', a moving account of his work. Feast: Mar. 17

pat·ri·lin·e·al (pætrilíni:əl) *adj.* tracing kinship through the father rather than the mother [fr. L. *pater,* father+LINEAL]

pat·ri·lo·cal (pætrilóuk'l) *adj.* at or taking place at the habitation of the husband's family or tribe [fr. L. *pater,* father+LOCAL]

pat·ri·mo·ni·al (pætrimóuni:əl) *adj.* pertaining to or constituting a patrimony

pat·ri·mo·ny (pǽtrimo̩uni:) *pl.* **pat·ri·mo·nies** *n.* property, money etc. inherited from one's father or an ancestor ‖ anything valuable handed down by earlier generations and looked on as a trust, *our Roman patrimony* ‖ an endowment of an institution, e.g. a church or college [F. *patrimoine, patremoine* fr. L.]

pa·tri·ot (péitri:ət, péitri:ɒt, *Br.* also pǽtri:ət) *n.* a person who loves his native country and will do all he can for it [F. *patriote* fr. L.L. fr. Gk]

Patriot *n.* (*mil.*) U.S. air-defense, solid-fuel missile with command direction, under development

pa·tri·ot·ic (pe̩itri:ɒ́tik, *Br.* also pæ̩triɒ́tik) *adj.* inspired by, showing or aimed at arousing love of one's country, a *patriotic speech* **pa·tri·ót·i·cal·ly** *adv.* [fr. L.L. *patrioticus* fr. Gk]

pa·tri·ot·ism (péitri:əti̩zəm, *Br.* also pǽtriəti̩zəm) *n.* zealous love of one's country [PATRIOT]

pa·tris·tic (pətrístik) *adj.* of or relating to the Fathers of the Christian Church or to their writings **pa·trís·tics** *n.* the study of these writings [fr. L. *patres* pl. of *pater,* father]

Pa·tro·clus (pətróukləs) Greek warrior and friend of Achilles at the siege of Troy. When Achilles, slighted by Agamemnon, refused to fight, Patroclus took his arms and, mistaken for Achilles, was killed by Hector. Achilles fought again to avenge his friend

pa·trol (pətróul) *pres. part.* **pa·trol·ling** *past* and *past part.* **pa·trolled** *v.t.* to go the rounds of (an army camp, town etc.) for the purpose of guarding, inspecting etc. ‖ *v.i.* to go the rounds of a place in order to guard it etc. [F. *patrouiller* fr. *patouiller,* to tramp in mud]

patrol *n.* a patrolling ‖ an instance of this, *his patrol lasted until dark* ‖ the men, aircraft, ships etc. engaged in patrolling, *the patrol captured two prisoners* ‖ a subdivision of a troop of boy scouts or girl scouts, usually having six to eight members [F. *patrouille*]

patrol car a squad car

pa·trol·man (pətróulmən) *pl.* **pa·trol·men** (pətróulmən) *n.* a policeman who patrols an assigned area

patrol wagon an enclosed motor vehicle used by the police to transport people under arrest

pa·tron (péitrən) *n.* a person or institution that gives practical (e.g. financial) support to a cause, individual or group regarded as deserving it ‖ a person who lends his name to a deserving institution or cause as an indication of his approval and support ‖ a patron saint of a specified person, place, group etc., *St Christopher is the patron of travelers* ‖ a customer, esp. a regular one, in a shop, restaurant etc. ‖ (*Church of England*) a person who has the right of presentation to a benefice [M.E. *patroun* fr. O.F. *patrun, patron* fr. L.]

pa·tron·age (péitrənidʒ, pǽtrənidʒ) *n.* the material help and encouragement given by a patron ‖ the special protection of a patron saint ‖ the power of putting people into advantageous positions, bestowing privileges etc., *he owed the job to political patronage* ‖ (*commerce*) the support or orders of a customer, *your patronage is solicited* ‖ the granting of favors in a condescending way ‖ (*Church of England*) the right of presentation to a benefice [F.]

pa·tron·al (péitrən'l) *adj.* of, relating to or characteristic of a patron or a patron saint

pa·tron·ess (péitrənis, pǽtrənis) *n.* a female patron [fr. M.L. *patronissa*]

pa·tron·ize (péitrənaiz, pǽtrənaiz) *pres. part.* **pa·tron·iz·ing** *past* and *past part.* **pa·tron·ized** *v.t.* (of a patron) to give material support or encouragement to ‖ to be a regular customer at (a shop etc.) ‖ to treat in an offensively superior, condescending manner **pá·tron·iz·ing** *adj.* offensively condescending

patron saint a saint in the relationship of spiritual guardian to a person, group, place etc.

pat·ro·nym·ic (pætrənímik) 1. *n.* a name derived from that of the father or paternal ancestor, esp. by the addition of a suffix or prefix ‖ a family name 2. *adj.* of or relating to a patronymic [fr. L. *patronymicus* adj. fr. Gk fr. *patēr,* father+*onoma, onuma,* name]

pa·troon (pətrú:n) *n.* (*Am. hist.*) a landowner with manorial rights in New York or New Jersey dating from a Dutch grant of 1629 [Du.=patron]

pat·tée, pa·tée (pətéi) *adj.* (*heraldry*) of a cross whose four arms become much wider as they extend from the center [F. *patté, pattée,* pawed fr. *patte,* paw]

pat·ten (pǽt'n) *n.* (*hist.*) a clog or overshoe having a metal device under the sole to raise the wearer out of the mud [F. *patin*]

pat·ter (pǽtər) 1. *n.* the quick talk or chatter of a comedian or entertainer, salesman etc. ‖ the slang or private language used by a particular group or class, *thieves' patter* ‖ mechanically repeated words, *his prayers were a meaningless patter* 2. *v.t.* to repeat (words, prayers, a formula etc.) mechanically without considering the meaning ‖ *v.i.* to talk volubly but without much sense [fr. L. *paternoster,* our father, fr. the mechanical recitation of the Lord's Prayer in the rosary etc.]

patter 1. *v.t.* to make a series of short, light, rapid taps, *the rain was pattering on the roof* ‖ to run or move making a series of light tapping sounds, *she pattered up the aisle* 2. *n.* the noise made by pattering [PAT v.]

pat·tern (pǽtərn) 1. *n.* an orderly sequence consisting of a number of repeated or complementary elements, decorative motifs etc. ‖ a style of design or applied decoration, *these jugs come in several patterns* ‖ a model from which a copy can be made ‖ a sample of cloth, paper etc. showing the design or color, *take some from the seam as a pattern* ‖ a model to be followed as an example of excellence ‖ the model from which the mold is made for casting metal ‖ the way in which the shot or bullets are distributed on a target 2. *v.t.* to make or form in imitation of another person or thing, *pattern yourself on him* ‖ to decorate with a pattern [M.E. *patron* fr. F.]

pat·tern·ing (pǽtərniŋ) *n.* 1. (*med.*) technique of physical therapy utilizing biofeedback to control and modify nervous responses 2. (*zool.*) behavior developed in imitation or response to education

Pat·ter·son (pǽtərsən), Joseph Medill (1879–1946), U.S. journalist. He became (1914) co-editor (with Robert McCormick) of the 'Chicago Tribune' and founded with McCormick (1919) the 'New York Daily News', the first successful tabloid newspaper in the U.S.A.

Pat·ton (pǽt'n), George Smith (1885–1945), American general. In the 2nd world war he was a commander in the Allied invasion of N. Africa (1942), led the U.S. invasion of Sicily (1943) and commanded the U.S. 3rd Army in the Normandy invasion (1944), advancing rapidly into Germany (1945)

pat·ty (pǽti:) *pl.* **pat·ties** *n.* a little pie, generally with a savory filling ‖ a small, flat, esp. fried cake of minced meat etc. [fr. F. *pâté,* O.F. *pasté,* a pasty]

pat·u·lous (pǽtʃuləs) *adj.* (*bot.,* e.g. of tree branches) spreading outward from a center ‖ distended [fr. L. *patulus* fr. *patere,* to be open]

pau·ci·ty (pɔ́siti:) *n.* smallness, esp. insufficiency, in number or amount, *a paucity of trained operators* [F. *paucité* or fr. L. *paucitas* fr. *paucus,* few, little]

Paul (pɔl), St (*d.* c. 64 or c. 67 A.D.), the first Christian missionary and apostle to the gentiles. Born a Jew of Tarsus in Cilicia, he inherited his father's Roman citizenship. He studied Mosaic law in Jerusalem, and was zealous in persecuting Christians, being present at the martyrdom of Stephen. He was converted to Christianity by a vision while on the road to Damascus (c. 35) and changed his name from

Saul to Paul. His missionary journeys, recounted by Luke in the Acts of the Apostles, took him first to Cyprus and Asia Minor (c. 45–9). His preaching to the gentiles aroused controversy among Jewish Christians, and the first apostolic council took a compromise decision on the issue of gentile converts' submission to Jewish law (c. 50). His second journey (c. 50–3) was to Asia Minor, Macedonia, Athens and Corinth, and his third (c. 53–7) was to Ephesus, Macedonia and Corinth. Back in Jerusalem, he was arrested by the Roman authorities after a riot, was imprisoned for two years and was then sent to Rome, after appealing, as a Roman citizen, to Caesar. He was either martyred at this time (c. 64), or else was released, went to Spain, returned to Rome and was martyred c. 67. His letters to the early Churches include the Epistles to the Thessalonians, Corinthians, Galatians, Colossians, Philippians and Romans, and possibly the Epistle to the Ephesians. He did much to make Christianity a universal religion and was the first to enunciate the doctrine of justification by faith. Feast: June 29

Pau·li·cian (pɔlíʃən) *n.* a member of a dualistic heretical Christian sect (c. 7th c.–c. 11th c.) of Armenia

Pauli exclusion principle (*phys.*) a statement in quantum mechanics that since an electron is a fermion it cannot exist in a system containing other fermions that possess identical quantum numbers. The periodic system of the elements follows directly from this principle

Paul III (Alessandro Farnese, 1468–1549), pope (1543–49). Devoted to the cause of Catholic reform, he approved (1540) the founding of the Society of Jesus, and summoned (1545) the Council of Trent. He was a patron of the arts, and employed Michelangelo as architect, painter and sculptor at the Vatican. His pontificate marks the transition from the Renaissance to the Counter-Reformation

Paul·ine (pɔ́lain) *adj.* of St Paul, his writings or teaching [fr. L. *Paulinus*]

Paul·ist (pɔ́list) *n.* a member of an American community of Roman Catholic priests, founded (1858) for missionary work within the U.S.A.

Paul IV (Gian Pietro Carafa, 1476–1559), pope (1555–9). An extremist leader of the Counter-Reformation, he established (1559) the Index Librorum Prohibitorum and attempted to reform the clergy

Pau·low·ni·a (pɔlóuni:ə) *n.* a member of *Paulownia*, fam. *Scrophulariaceae*, a genus of ornamental trees with white or purple flowers, native to China and Japan, now widely cultivated in parks [after Anna *Paulovna*, daughter of Czar Paul I]

Paul V (Camillo Borghese, 1552–1621), pope (1605–21). He was a noted canon lawyer, and put Venice under interdict (1606) in an attempt to assert ecclesiastical supremacy over secular power

Paul VI (Giovanni Battista Montini, 1897–1978), pope (1963–78). He continued the 2nd Vatican Council convened by John XXIII. He made a pilgrimage to the Holy Land (1964), and he had discussions there with Patriarch Athenagoras I. He addressed the U.N. (1965) in New York and was the first pope to go to Latin America, when he visited (1968) a eucharistic congress at Bogotá. His encyclical 'Humanae Vitae' on married life (1968), reiterating the Roman Catholic Church's teaching against contraception, was called in question by many

Paul (1901–64), king of Greece (1947–64), brother of George II

Paul I (1754–1801), czar of Russia (1769–1801), son of Catherine II. He was mentally unstable. He reversed his mother's policy, revoking the privileges given to the nobility, improving the lot of the serfs and cutting off contacts with foreign countries. He took Russia into the French Revolutionary Wars against France (1798–9), but allied with France in 1801

Paul Bun·yan (bʌ́njən) (*Am. folklore*) a giant lumberjack, the hero of many tales in which he performs feats of strength and daring

Paul·ding (pɔ́ldiŋ), James Kirke (1778–1860), U.S. public official and writer who was one of the first to employ native American themes in literature. His 'The Lay of the Scottish Fiddle' (1813) satirized England's policy toward the U.S.A. during the War of 1812. In his play 'The Lion of the West' (1831) he introduced frontier humor to the stage, and the character of Davy Crockett

Pau·li (páuli:), Wolfgang (1901–58), Austrian physicist. He was awarded the Nobel prize (1945) for his work on atomic structure, esp. for his discovery of the exclusion principle. He also predicted (1931) the existence of the neutrino from his study of nuclear decay by beta-particle emission. This was confirmed in 1956

Pau·ling (pɔ́liŋ), Linus Carl (1901–), U.S. chemist and winner of the 1954 Nobel prize in chemistry for discovering the basic principles determining the structure of molecules, and their application to the explanation of the properties of matter. He was awarded the 1962 Nobel prize for peace

Pau·li·nus of No·la (pɔláinəsəvnóulə), St (353–431), bishop of Nola (409–31) and poet. His writings include poems to St Felix, metrical paraphrasings of the Psalms, and correspondence with Sts Augustine and Jerome. Feast: June 22

Paulinus of York, St (*d.* 644), 1st archbishop of York (632). He worked with St Augustine of Canterbury and temporarily converted Northumbria (625–32), but fled when Penda defeated King Edwin (632). Feast: Oct. 10

Paul of the Cross, St (Paolo Francesco Danei, 1694–1775), Italian priest, founder of the Passionists. Feast: Apr. 28

Paul the Deacon (c. 720–c. 799), Lombard historian. He wrote 'Historia Langobardorum', covering the history of the Lombards from the late 6th c. to the early 8th c.

paunch (pɔntʃ) *n.* a fat, protruding belly, esp. a man's ‖ (*zool.*) the rumen [M.E. fr. O.N.F. *panche*]

pau·per (pɔ́pər) *n.* a completely destitute person, esp. one entirely dependent on public charity **páu·per·ism, pau·per·i·zá·tion** *ns* **páu·per·ize** *pres. part.* **pau·per·iz·ing** *past* and *past part.* **pau·per·i·zed** *v.t.* to reduce to the condition of a pauper [L. adj.=poor]

Pau·sa·ni·as (pɔséini:əs) (*d.* c. 470 B.C.), Spartan general. He commanded the Greek force which defeated the Persians at Plataea (479 B.C.)

Pausanias (2nd c. A.D.), Greek geographer. His 'Description of Greece' is an important source for the history and topography of ancient Greece

pause (pɔz) *n.* a short period of time when sound, motion or activity stops before starting again, *a pause in a conversation* ‖ (*mus.*) the lengthening of a note, or the mark ⌢ or ⌢ indicating this **to give (someone) pause** to cause (someone) to hesitate or think again before taking action [F. fr. L. fr. Gk]

pause *pres. part.* **paus·ing** *past* and *past part.* **paused** *v.i.* to make a pause ‖ to hesitate, stop to reflect [fr. PAUSE or fr. L. *pausare* or F. *pauser*, to cease]

pav·an (pǽvən) *n.* (*hist.*) a slow stately dance for couples, originating in Italy and popular in Tudor England ‖ a musical composition in slow duple time, originally to accompany this dance [F. *pavane* fr. Span. or Ital.]

pa·vane (pəván) *n.* a pavan

Pavarotti (pɑvaróuti:), Luciano (1935–), Italian tenor, one of the principal singers with the Metropolitan Opera, La Scala and other leading companies. He made his debut (1961) as Rodolfo in Puccini's 'La Bohème' in Reggio Emilia and performed the same role in a film and in his Metropolitan Opera debut (1968). He has also achieved fame in such operas as 'Lucia di Lammermoor,' 'L'Elisir d'Amore,' and 'Rigoletto'

pave (peiv) *pres. part.* **pav·ing** *past* and *past part.* **paved** *v.t.* to cover (a road, path etc.) with a surface to walk or travel on **to pave the way for (or to)** to provide an easy road for (or to), *influential contacts paved the way to his success* [O.F. *paver*]

pa·vé (pɔvéi) *n.* a paved road or sidewalk ‖ a setting of jewels close together so that the metal is completely covered [F. past part. of *paver*, to pave]

pave·ment (péivmənt) *n.* a paved street or road ‖ any paved surface ‖ the material used in paving ‖ (esp. *Br.*) a sidewalk [O.F.]

pavement artist an artist who exhibits and sells his work on the pavement ‖ (*Br.*) a sidewalk artist

pave·way (péivwei) *n.* (*mil.*) family of laser-guided bombs targeted by air or ground; produced by Rockwell International and developed in 1965

Pa·vi·a (pəví:ə) an agricultural center (pop. 84,000) of Lombardy, Italy, 20 miles south of Milan. Red brick Romanesque churches, town hall (12th and 13th cc.), Gothic churches and castle (14th and 15th cc.). Cathedral (1488–1898). University (1361)

Pavia, Battle of a battle (1525) in which François I was defeated and captured by Emperor Charles V during the Italian Wars

pa·vil·ion (pəvíljən) *n.* a large tent, often open on one side ‖ a light, elegant building or shelter in a garden, park etc. ‖ one of several buildings into which a large institution, esp. a hospital is sometimes divided ‖ (*Br.*=*Am.* field house) a building attached to a playing field, in which players change, equipment is stored, and where spectators may sometimes be accommodated ‖ (*jewelry*) the lower part of a cut brilliant, below the girdle ‖ (*anat.*) the auricle of the ear [M.E. fr. F. *pavillon*, tent]

pav·ing (péiviŋ) *n.* a sidewalk or other paved surface ‖ material for a pavement [PAVE]

pav·ior, pav·iour (péivjər) *n.* a worker who lays paving ‖ a ramming machine for setting paving stones ‖ a specially hardened brick used for paving [older *pavier, pavyer* fr. PAVE]

Pav·lov (pǽvlɒv), Ivan Petrovitch (1849–1936), Russian physiologist. He worked on the simple reflex, showing by experiment with dogs how an original stimulus can be replaced by a secondary stimulus producing a 'conditioned reflex', and he showed the importance of such reflexes in the behavior patterns of animal and man. He also demonstrated the importance of the vagus nerve in controlling gastric and pancreatic secretion. Nobel prize (1904)

Pav·lo·va (pævlóuvə, pɑ́vlʌvɑ), Anna (1885–1931), Russian ballerina, the greatest solo dancer of her time

paw (pɔ) **1.** *n.* the foot of a four-footed animal having claws ‖ (*pop.*) a hand, esp. a clumsy or dirty one **2.** *v.t.* (of an animal) to strike, scrape or scratch with the hoof or paw ‖ (of a person) to feel, touch or handle with the hands in a rude or clumsy way [M.E. fr. O.F. *powe, poue*]

pawl (pɔl) **1.** *n.* a hinged catch engaging with the teeth of a wheel to prevent reverse motion ‖ a similar device on a capstan or windlass **2.** *v.t.* to hold firm with a pawl [etym. doubtful]

pawn (pɔn) **1.** *n.* the state of being pawned, *his suit is in pawn* ‖ something pawned **2.** *v.t.* to hand over as a pledge or security for a loan of money [O.F. *pan, pant*]

pawn *n.* (*chess*) one of the men of least size and value, each player having eight. A pawn can move forward only one square at a time (two on the initial move if the player chooses), but captures only a piece that is one square diagonally in front of it ‖ a person whom others use for their own ends [M.E. *poune* fr. A.F. and O.F.]

pawn·bro·ker (pɔ́nbroukər) *n.* a person licensed to lend money on articles pawned

Paw·nee (pɔní:) *pl.* **Paw·nee, Paw·nees** *n.* a member of a confederacy of North American Indians living in Nebraska, Oklahoma and Kansas ‖ their language

pawn·shop (pɔ́nʃɒp) *n.* a shop or office at which articles may be pawned

pawn ticket a pawnbroker's receipt, held by the client until he redeems the goods pawned

pawpaw *PAPAW

pax (pæks) *n.* (*eccles.*) a kiss given by the priest at High Mass to the deacon, and passed on to the subdeacon and others in the chancel and choir ‖ (*hist.*) a tablet with a representation of Christ or the Virgin Mary, passed among the priests and to the congregation, being kissed by all in turn [L.=peace]

Pax·ton (pǽkstən), Sir Joseph (1801–65), English architect. His Crystal Palace was one of the sources of modern architecture based on rigid frames and glazing. He designed many private houses

pay (pei) **1.** *v. pres. part.* **pay·ing** *past* and *past part.* **paid** (peid) *v.t.* to give (someone) money in return for goods, work or services ‖ to give (someone) money owed or due ‖ to discharge (a debt), *to pay one's bills* ‖ to give (a sum) in return for goods or services ‖ to yield as a recompense, *the investment paid 5% last year* ‖ to be rewarding to, *it will pay you to take that trip* ‖ to make return for, repay, *she paid his sarcasm in kind* ‖ to suffer (a penalty, consequences etc.) ‖ to give or render (a service, visit, compliment etc.), *please pay attention* ‖ *v.i.* to give money in return for goods, work or services ‖ to be profitable, *it pays to buy good quality* **to pay for** to meet the cost of, *how can you pay for a new car?* ‖ to suffer the consequences of, *make him pay for his rudeness* **to pay in** to deposit (money etc.) in an account **to pay off** to finish paying, *to pay off* *a mortgage* || to give (someone) his wages and dismiss him || (*naut.*) to cause or allow (a ship) to fall off to leeward || to recompense for good or evil || to turn out profitably, *it was a risk but it paid off* **to pay one's way** to pay one's share of costs or expenses || to remain solvent **to pay out** to distribute (money etc.), *they paid out hundreds of dollars in prizes* || (*past* and *past part.* **payed**) to pass along the slack of (a rope) **to pay up** to pay in full or on time **2.** *adj.* (of earth) yielding oil or valuable metals || made available for use by the insertion of a coin or coins in a slot, *a pay toilet* [M.E. fr. F. *payer*]

pay *pres. part.* **pay·ing** *past* and *past part.* **payed, paid** *v.t.* (*naut.*) to coat with pitch etc. so as to make waterproof [O.N.F. *peier* fr. L. fr. *pix*, pitch]

pay *n.* money received as wages or salary for work or services (always used instead of 'wage' or 'salary' in the armed services) **in the pay of** receiving money from, in return for work or services (often with the suggestion of being bribed) [O.F. *paie*]

pay·a·ble (péiəb'l) *adj.* that must, can, should, or may be paid, *the rent is payable in advance* || (of a mine etc.) profitable to work

pay-as-you-earn (péiəzju:ə́:rn) *n.* (*Br.*, *abbr.* P.A.Y.E.) the system of deducting income tax from wages before they are paid to the worker

pay·book (péibuk) *n.* (*Br.*) a serviceman's record of his pay and allowances

pay-ca·ble (péikéib'l) *n.* cable television programs for which a surcharge is made

pay·day (péidei) *n.* the day of the week or month on which wages or salary are regularly paid || the day on which stock transfers are paid for in the London Stock Exchange

pay dirt earth containing enough ore to be profitably worked by a miner || something that turns out to be a valuable source of information etc.

P.A.Y.E. *PAY-AS-YOU-EARN

pay·ee (peií:) *n.* a person to whom money is or should be paid, esp. a person to whom a check, money order etc. is made out

paying guest (abbr. P.G.) a boarder in a boardinghouse or in a private home

pay·load (péiloud) *n.* (*rocketry*) the warhead of a guided missile, or whatever is projected by it

pay·load (péiloud) *n.* the size and weight of cargo, instrumentation, and passenger capacity, but not including the fuel, of a plane or space vehicle

pay·mas·ter (péimæstər, péimɑstər) *n.* an official who pays troops, government employees etc.

paymaster general *pl.* **paymasters general, paymaster generals** (*Br.*) a government officer, nominally the head of the department responsible for arranging payments to most other government departments, but effectively free to assume any special responsibilities the prime minister may entrust to him

pay·ment (péimənt) *n.* a paying for work, services, goods bought, charges incurred, debts etc. || the money etc. paid for work or services || something given in return, or as a reward, punishment or revenge [F. *paiement*]

pay·off (péiɔf, péiɒf) *n.* a paying of wages, winnings etc. || (*pop.*) a final reckoning, *the payoff came when Interpol closed in* || (*pop.*) the climax of a dramatic situation or story

pay·o·la (peióulə) *n.* illegal or unethical payments for favors

pay·out ratio (péiautréiʃi:ou) (*securities*) the ratio of corporate dividends to earnings

pay·roll (péiroul) *n.* a list of employees and their wages or salaries || the whole body of people employed by a person or firm or institution || the total amount regularly paid in wages and salaries

Pay·san·dú (paisandú:) an industrial city and port (pop. 61,000) of W. Uruguay, on the east bank of the Uruguay River: meat-packing and frozen meats

pay station a telephone booth

pay telephone a telephone operated by a coin-in-the-slot device

Paz (pas), Octavio (1914–), Mexican poet, writer and diplomat, author of 'Raíz del hombre', 'Libertad bajo palabra', and 'Luna silvestre'

PBB (*chem. acronym*) **p**oly**b**rominated **b**iphenyl, a persistent toxic chemical used in a fire retardant

PCB (*chem. acronym*) **p**oly**c**hlorinated **b**iphenyls, a group of clear, slightly viscous nearly indestructible and highly toxic industrial compounds used in transformers and capacitors

PCM (*computer*) **1.** (*acronym*) **p**lug **c**ompatible **m**anufacturer, equipment producers who manufacture equipment compatible with IBM software. **2.** (*abbr.*) **p**unched **c**ard **m**achine. **3.** (*abbr.*) **p**ulse **c**ode **m**odulation

PCP (*med. abbr.*) phencyclidine hydrochloride [$C_{17}H_{25}N$], a depressant

P-day (pí:dei) *n.* (*mil.*) the time when the rate of production of an item available for military consumption equals the rate at which the item is required by the armed forces

pea (pi:) *n.* *Pisum sativum*, fam. *Papilionaceae*, a climbing or bushy annual plant with large green pods whose fresh or dried seeds are valued as a vegetable. The pods and vines are used as green manure and forage || one of the seeds of this plant || any of several leguminous plants, e.g. the chick pea [older *pease* sing. and pl., taken as a pl., fr. O.E. *pise* fr. L. fr. Gk *pison*]

Pea·bod·y (pí:bɒdi:, pí:bədi:), George (1795–1869), U.S. merchant, financier, and philanthropist. He established (1829) a banking and mercantile firm in London and amassed a fortune. He donated about $8.5 million to educational institutions and the poor

Peace (pi:s) a river (1,065 miles long) of British Columbia and Alberta, Canada rising in the Rocky Mtns, the main headstream of the Mackenzie

peace *n.* the condition that exists when nations or other groups are not fighting || the ending of a state of war || the treaty that marks the end of war || friendly relations between individuals, untroubled by disputes || freedom from noise, worries, troubles, fears etc., *peace of mind* **at peace** in a state of peace, friendliness or calm **the peace** or (*Br.*) **the king's** (or **queen's**) **peace** public order and security **to hold** (or **keep**) **one's peace** (*rhet.*) to be silent **to keep the peace** to prevent or avoid strife **to make (one's) peace** to put an end to a quarrel, become friendly again [M.E. *pais* fr. O.F. *pais*, Mod. F. *paix* fr. L. *pax* (*pacis*)]

peace·a·ble (pí:səb'l) *adj.* not given to fighting or quarreling || in a state of peace, **péace·a·bly** *adv.* [M.E. *peisible* fr. O.F.]

Peace Corps a U.S. government agency established (1961) by President John Kennedy to 'help foreign countries meet their urgent needs for skilled manpower'. A volunteer, who must be a U.S. citizen and at least 18 years old, undergoes intensive training in the language, history, culture and customs of the country to which he is to be sent, normally for a two-year term. Once overseas, he works directly with the people of the host country, speaking their language and sharing their lives

peace·ful (pí:sfəl) *adj.* calm, quiet, untroubled, undisturbed by noise, worries, fears etc., *peaceful summer evenings* || not warlike or violent, *to use peaceful means* || not given to fighting or quarreling

peace-keep·ing force (pí:ski:piŋfɔ̃rs) *n.* a United Nations combat-ready force of member nations combined into military body to maintain peace in an area involved in dispute

peace·mak·er (pí:smeikər) *n.* a person who restores peace or friendly relations

peace·nik (pí:snik) *n.* antiwar activist

peace offering something given to show that one wishes to end a quarrel

Peace of God (*hist.*) a truce in feudal warfare enjoined by the Church periodically from the 9th c. until 1095, when, at the Synod of Clermont-Ferrand, it became an official institution of the Church

peace pipe the calumet as a symbol of peace

peace·time (pí:staim) *n.* the time when a country is not at war

peach (pi:tʃ) **1.** *n.* *Prunus persica*, fam. *Rosaceae*, a small tree of the temperate zone, native to China, having lanceolate leaves. The fruit is a sweet, juicy, yellow or white drupe occurring in clingstone and freestone varieties and having a thin, downy skin || the fruit of this tree || (*pop.*) any particularly excellent person or thing, *a peach of a house* || a color resembling that of the fruit, a soft, pale, yellowish red **2.** *adj.* of the color peach [M.E. *peche* fr. F. *pêche*, O.F. *pesche, peche*]

peach *v.i.* (*pop.*) to turn informer [M.E. *apeche*, to impede, impeach]

Pea·cock (pí:kɒk), Thomas Love (1785–1866), English novelist and poet. 'Headlong Hall' (1816), 'Nightmare Abbey' (1818), and 'Crotchet Castle' (1831) are conversation pieces rather than novels. In a playful but effective way he wittily attacked both Romanticism and the myth of inevitable social progress. His 'Four Ages of Poetry' (1820) provoked Shelley into writing his 'Defense of Poetry'

pea·cock (pí:kɒk) *n.* a male member of *Pavo*, fam. *Phasianidae*, a genus of large gallinaceous birds, native to India and Asia but widely kept for their ornamental value. They occur in predominantly blue or white species. Their long, brilliantly colored tail coverts are marked with iridescent ocellate spots ('eyes'), and they display them in a vertical position fanned out magnificently || (*loosely*) the male or female of any of these birds [M.E. fr. O.E. *pēa* fr. L.+COCK]

peacock blue a bright iridescent blue, as seen on the neck plumage of a peacock

peacock butterfly *Nymphalis io*, a European butterfly with markings on its wings like the eyes on the peacock's tail

pea·fowl (pí:faul) *pl.* **pea·fowls, pea·fowl** *n.* a peacock or peahen

pea green a light, yellowish-green color

pea·hen (pí:hen) *n.* the female of the peacock [M.E. *pehen, pehenne* fr. O.E. *pēa henne*]

pea jacket a short, double-breasted black or navy blue overcoat worn esp. by seamen [prob. fr. M.Du. *pīe*, coarse woolen coat+JACKET]

peak (pi:k) *n.* a pointed top or projection || the pointed top of a mountain || a high mountain, esp. one that stands alone || the projecting brim at the front of a cap || the highest point, maximum, *tourism is at its peak in August* || (*elec.*) the maximum value of a varying quantity during a specified period || (*naut.*) the forepeak or the afterpeak || (*naut.*) the upper after corner of a fore-and-aft sail held by a gaff [var. of PIKE, sharp point]

peak *v.i.* (*old-fash.*) to be sickly and listless, become increasingly low in health and spirits [etym. doubtful]

peak *v.t.* (*naut.*) to raise (a yard, a gaff, oars) to or towards the vertical [fr. APEAK]

Peak District a plateau region of wild moors and crags in N. Derbyshire, England, a famous tourist area

peaked (pí:kt) *adj.* having a peak or point || (pí:kid) looking sickly and thin

peak·y (pí:ki:) *comp.* **peak·i·er** *superl.* **peak·i·est** *adj.* peaked (sickly looking) [PEAK n.]

peal (pi:l) **1.** *n.* a loud ringing of a bell or bells || a set of bells tuned to the notes of the major scale for ringing changes || a complete set or part of a set of changes, ringing on these || a sudden burst of noise, a *peal of thunder* **2.** *v.i.* (of bells, thunder, laughter etc.) to ring out, burst into sudden noise || *v.t.* (often with 'out') to sound vigorously in a peal, *the organ pealed out the wedding march* [M.E. *pele* fr. *apele*, appeal]

Peale (pi:l), Charles Willson (1741–1827), U.S. painter, best known for his portraits of leading figures of the Revolutionary period, incl. seven life portraits of George Washington. He founded (1784) Peale's Museum in Philadelphia, which held (1801) the first U.S. scientific exhibition, displaying the first complete skeleton of the American mastodon

Peale, Rembrandt (1778–1860), U.S. painter, who served (1808–10) as portrait painter at the court of Napoleon. He is best known for his portrait of Thomas Jefferson and his huge 'Court of Death' (1819)

pean *PAEAN

pea·nut (pí:nʌt) *n.* *Arachis hypogaea*, fam. *Papilionaceae*, a branched, trailing annual plant, probably indigenous to Brazil, but cultivated widely in warm regions for its oily, nutritious seeds || its nutlike seed

peanut butter an edible paste made from ground roasted peanuts

peanut oil an oil expressed from peanuts and used as a salad oil, in soaps, and as a vehicle in medicines

pear (pɛər) *n.* *Pyrus communis*, fam. *Rosaceae*, a tree native to W. Asia and E. Europe. Many strains and hybrids are cultivated in all temperate regions || its fruit, a fleshy, juicy, sweet pome, varying in color between yellow-green and russet, and usually tapering at the stem from a bulbous base [O.E. *pere* fr. L.]

Pearce (piərs), Charles Sprague (1851–1914), U.S. historical painter, best known for his 'The Beheading of John the Baptist' and 'The Arab

CONCISE PRONUNCIATION KEY: **(a)** æ, *cat*; ɑ, *car*; ɔ *fawn*; ei, *snake*. **(e)** e, *hen*; i:, *sheep*; iə, *deer*; ɛə, *bear*. **(i)** i, *fish*; ai, *tiger*; ə:, *bird*. **(o)** o, *ox*; au, *cow*; ou, *goat*; u, *poor*; ɔi, *royal*. **(u)** ʌ, *duck*; u, *bull*; u:, *goose*; ə, *bacillus*; ju:, *cube*. x, *loch*; θ, *think*; ð, *bother*; z, *Zen*; ʒ, *corsage*; dʒ, *savage*; ŋ, *orangutang*; j, *yak*; ʃ, *fish*; tʃ, *fetch*; 'l, *rabble*; 'n, *redden*. Complete pronunciation key appears inside front cover.

Jeweler', and for his mural decorations in the Library of Congress

pearl (pəːrl) **1.** *n.* a secretion, chiefly of calcium carbonate, produced by some mollusks ‖ a hard, lustrous, usually white, almost spherical deposit of this around a small solid irritant (e.g. a grain of sand) which finds its way into the mollusk's shell, or is put into it by man (*CULTURED PEARL), and is greatly prized for its luster, form and color ‖ something rare and precious, *his words are pearls of wisdom* ‖ (*printing*) a type roughly 5-point in size ‖ a very pale gray color with bluish overtones **to cast pearls before swine** to say wise or witty things to people unable to appreciate them **2.** *adj.* made of or resembling pearl [M.E. fr. F. *perle*]

pearl *v.t.* to ornament with pearls or with pearl-like drops ‖ to reduce (barley etc.) to hard, round grains by rubbing or grinding ‖ *v.i.* to seek for pearls by diving or fishing for pearl-bearing mollusks ‖ to form drops like pearls, *the perspiration pearled down his forehead* [F. *perler* or fr. PEARL n.]

pearl ash potassium carbonate, K_2CO_3, extracted from the ash of burned wood

pearl barley barley reduced to small, round grains by rubbing

pearl diver a person who dives for oysters or other mollusks in search of pearls

pearl fisher a pearl diver

Pearl Harbor a U.S. naval base in Hawaii. The Japanese attacked it treacherously and without warning (Dec. 7, 1941), destroying a large part of the U.S. Pacific fleet. As a result the U.S.A. entered the 2nd world war

pearl·ies (pə́ːrliːz) *pl. n.* (*Br.*) the traditional holiday dress of the London costermongers, decorated with hundreds of pearl buttons

pearl·ing *n.* (*surfing*) riding down a wave to a fall; from pearl diving

Pearl Islands a group of islands (area 450 sq. miles), belonging to Panama in the Gulf of Panama: pearl fisheries

pearl·ite (pə́ːrlait) *n.* a lamellar mixture of ferrite and cementite, a principal constituent of steel and cast iron ‖ perlite [PEARL]

pearl oyster any of several mollusks of genera *Aviculidae* and *Pinctada,* fam. *Pteriidae,* which often produce pearls. They are found chiefly in the Indian Ocean, the Persian Gulf, the S. Pacific, the Gulf of California and the Caribbean

pearl white bismuth oxychloride, used in cosmetics and as a white pigment ‖ any of several other white or pearly substances used in cosmetics etc.

pearl·y (pə́ːrliː) *comp.* **pearl·i·er** *superl.* **pearl·i·est** *adj.* of or like a pearl or mother-of-pearl ‖ decorated with mother-of-pearl or pearls ‖ abounding in pearls

pearly nautilus a nautilus of the genus *Nautilus*

Pear·son (píərs'n), Lester Bowles (1897–1972), Canadian statesman. He was secretary of state for external affairs (1948–57) and president of the U.N. General Assembly (1952–3). He was instrumental in settling the Suez Canal crisis (1956), and was awarded the Nobel peace prize (1957). He became leader of the Canadian Liberal party (1958) and was prime minister (1963–8)

Pea·ry (píəriː), Robert Edwin (1856–1920), American Arctic explorer. He made an expedition to Greenland (1886), crossed to the east coast of Greenland (1891–2), and was the first man to reach the North Pole (1909)

peas·ant (péz'nt) *n.* a hired farm laborer or the owner or tenant of a small farm or holding, in a country where the mass of farm workers and small farmers are very poor **péas·ant·ry** *n.* a body of peasants ‖ peasants collectively [A.F. *paisant,* O.F. *païsent, païsant*]

Peasants' Revolt a rebellion (1381) in East Anglia and S.E. England against the poll tax and the labor legislation following the Black Death. A mob led by Wat Tyler pillaged London and extracted promises of redress from Richard II, but the revolt was put down with great severity and Tyler was beheaded

Peasants' War a social, economic and religious revolt (1524–6) in Germany and Austria. The peasants demanded abolition of serfdom, freedom in selecting pastors, justice in the courts and restriction of labor dues. The revolt was brutally crushed with the approval of Luther, who had earlier been sympathetic toward the rebels

pea·shoot·er (píːʃuːtər) *n.* a toy blowpipe for shooting dried peas

pea soup thick soup made from dried peas ‖ (*Am. pop.*=*Br.* pea-souper) thick yellow fog or smog

pea-soup·er (píːsuːpər) *n.* (esp. *Br.*) pea soup (fog)

peat (piːt) *n.* a dense accumulation of water-saturated, partially decayed vegetable tissue. The first stage in the formation of coal, it is itself, after drying, used as a fuel, esp. in Ireland and Russia. Peat is also dug into soil to increase its capacity to retain moisture and is a source of plant food [M.E. *pete,* origin unknown]

peat bog a marsh containing peat

peat moss sphagnum

peat·y (píːtiː) *comp.* **peat·i·er** *superl.* **peat·i·est** *adj.* of, like, or consisting of peat

peau·de·soie (póudəswɑ́) *n.* a smooth, satiny, silk or rayon fabric used esp. for dresses [F.=skin of silk]

pea·vey (píːviː) *n.* a stout pole with a sharp spike and a hinged metal hook, for handling logs [after Joseph *Peavey,* its inventor]

peb·ble (péb'l) **1.** *n.* a small stone, naturally rounded and worn smooth by the action of water ‖ transparent rock crystal, used instead of glass in spectacles ‖ a lens of this ‖ pebbled leather or its surface **2.** *v.t. pres. part.* **peb·bling** *past* and *past part.* **peb·bled** to pave or cover with pebbles set in cement, plaster etc. ‖ to give a roughly indented surface to (leather etc.) **péb·bly** *adj.* [O.E. *papolstān, popelstān,* pebble stone]

pe·can (pikǽn, pikɑ́n, píːkæn) *n.* an edible, smooth-shelled, olive-shaped nut, the fruit of *Carya illinoensis,* a species of hickory often of great size, with rough bark and hard wood, found wild and cultivated in the southern U.S.A. and N. Mexico ‖ this tree ‖ the wood of this tree [older *paccan* fr. Algonquian]

pec·ca·dil·lo (pekədílou) *pl.* **pec·ca·dil·los, pec·ca·dil·loes** *n.* a trifling fault or transgression [Span.]

pec·cant (pékənt) *adj.* (*rhet.*) sinful ‖ (*rhet.*) offending against accepted rules or conventions ‖ (*med.*) diseased or causing disease [fr. L. *peccans* (*peccantis*) fr. *peccare,* to sin]

pec·ca·ry (pékəri:) *pl.* **pec·ca·ries** *n.* either of two members of *Tayassu,* fam. *Tayassuidae,* a genus of wild, gregarious, ungulate mammals of tropical America. They look like small, tusked pigs. Their tanned skins are used for gloves etc. [fr. Carib. *pakira, paquira*]

Pe·chen·ga (pətʃéŋgə) (*Finn.* Petsamo) an ice-free port (pop. 5,000) and naval base of the R.S.F.S.R., U.S.S.R. ‖ the territory (3,860 sq. miles) including it, ceded to the U.S.S.R. by Finland (1920)

Pe·cho·ra (pətʃɔ́rə) a river (1,125 miles long) of the northwest R.S.F.S.R., U.S.S.R., rising in the Urals and flowing through the Komi A.S.S.R. to the Barents Sea

peck (pek) *n.* a little-used dry measure, one quarter of a bushel, for measuring grain, equal to (*Am.*) 537.605 cu. ins or (*Br.*) 554.84 cu. ins ‖ a vessel holding this measure [M.E. *pek,* etym. doubtful]

peck 1. *v.t.* (of a bird) to strike or make holes in with the beak ‖ to make (a hole) by striking with a rapid movement ‖ to kiss perfunctorily ‖ *v.i.* (esp. with 'at') to make striking movements or holes in something with the beak or as if with the beak ‖ (with 'at') to nibble food without appetite **2.** *n.* an instance of pecking, *the bird gave him a nasty peck* ‖ a quick perfunctory kiss ‖ a little mark or hole made by or as if by pecking [prob. var. of PICK v.]

pecking order the natural hierarchy that exists in a flock of poultry, in which each bird is free to peck at another, less aggressive one without being pecked at by it, while having to submit to the pecking of another, more aggressive bird

peck·ish (pékiʃ) *adj.* irritable ‖ (esp. *Br., pop.*) pleasantly hungry

Pe·cock (píːkɒk), Reginald (c. 1395–c. 1460), English bishop. He is noted for his attempt to popularize theology and logic by writing in English. In his 'Repressor of Overmuch Blaming of the Clergy' (c. 1455) he tried to hold the Lollard movement in check by argument. He was himself accused of heresy (1457), for denying the doctrines of the Apostles' Creed. He recanted, and saw his books burned

Pe·cos (péikəs) a river (735 miles long) flowing through E. New Mexico across the Texas border and emptying into the Rio Grande River in S.W. Texas

Pécs (péitʃ) (*G.* Fünfkirchen) the center (pop. 173,396) of a coal-mining district in S.W. Hungary: metallurgy. Romanesque cathedral (11th c.). University (1367–1526, 1912)

pec·ten (péktən) *pl.* **pec·tens, pec·ti·nes** (péktəniːz) *n.* (*zool.*) any structure that suggests the teeth of a comb [L. *pecten* (*pectinis*), comb]

pec·tic (péktik) *adj.* relating to or derived from pectin [fr. Gk *pēktikos* fr. *pēktos,* congealed]

pec·tin (péktin) *n.* any of a group of polysaccharides occurring in plant tissues esp. in fruits, solutions of which readily form a gel. Added to jams or fruit juices, they induce setting into a jelly [PECTIC]

pec·ti·nate (péktineit) *adj.* divided into many lobes etc. like the teeth of a comb **péc·ti·nat·ed** *adj.* [fr. L. *pectinatus* fr. *pecten,* comb]

pec·to·ral (péktərəl) **1.** *adj.* of or relating to the chest or breast ‖ used in treating diseases of the chest or lungs ‖ worn on the chest or breast **2.** *n.* a pectoral muscle or fin ‖ a pectoral cross ‖ the decorated breastplate worn by the Jewish high priest ‖ a pectoral medicine [fr. L. *pectoralis* fr. *pectus* (*pectoris*), breast]

pectoral cross a cross worn on the chest by certain high Church dignitaries

pec·tose (péktous) *n.* any of several substances found with cellulose in plant tissue and converted into pectin by ripening [PECTIC]

pec·u·late (pékjuleit) *pres. part.* **pec·u·lat·ing** *past* and *past part.* **pec·u·lat·ed** *v.t.* to embezzle ‖ *v.i.* to embezzle money **pec·u·lá·tion, péc·u·la·tor** *ns* [fr. L. *peculari* (*peculatus*) fr. *peculium,* private property]

pe·cu·liar (pikjúːljər) **1.** *adj.* odd, unusual, strange ‖ (often with 'to') belonging to or associated with a particular person, place, time, thing etc., *this word is peculiar to Scottish dialect* ‖ (*canon law*) independent of the authority of the bishop of the diocese, *a peculiar church* **2.** *n.* (*printing*) an unusual and little-used character, e.g. an unusual accent ‖ (*canon law*) a church or parish under peculiar jurisdiction **pe·cu·li·ar·i·ty** (pikjuːliːǽriti:) *pl.* **pe·cu·li·ar·i·ties** *n.* a distinctive characteristic, a feature peculiar to a particular person, place, thing etc. ‖ oddness, unusualness ‖ an odd, unusual characteristic [obs. F. *peculier* or fr. L. *peculiaris,* relating to private property fr. *peculium,* private property]

pe·cu·ni·ar·i·ly (pikjúːniːerili:) *adv.* as regards money

pe·cu·ni·ar·y (pikjúːniːeri:) *adj.* consisting of money, *pecuniary reward* ‖ of or relating to money ‖ (of an offense) having a fine as penalty [fr. L. *pecuniarius* fr. *pecunia,* money]

pedagog *PEDAGOGUE

ped·a·gog·ic (pedəgɒ́dʒik, pedəgoudʒik) *adj.* of, characteristic of or like a pedagogue ‖ having to do with teaching **ped·a·góg·i·cal** *adj.* **ped·a·góg·ics** *n.* the science of teaching [fr. L. *paedagogicus* fr. Gk]

ped·a·gogue, ped·a·gog (pédəgɔg, pédəgɒg) *n.* a teacher, esp. a narrowminded pedant [O.F. *pedagoge, pedagogue* fr. L. fr. Gk fr. *pais* (*paidos*), child+*agein,* to lead]

ped·a·go·gy (pédəgoudʒi:, pédəgɒdʒi:) *n.* the science or profession of teaching [F. *pédagogie* fr. Gk]

ped·al (péd'l) **1.** *n.* a lever operated by the foot, e.g. to sound, sustain or dampen notes on a piano etc., work the brake etc. of a car, propel a bicycle etc. ‖ (*mus.*) a pedal point **2.** *v. pres. part.* **ped·al·ing,** esp. *Br.* **ped·al·ling** *past* and *past part.* **ped·aled,** esp. *Br.* **ped·alled** *v.t.* to operate by a pedal or pedals ‖ *v.i.* to operate a pedal or pedals [F. *pédale*]

ped·al (píːd'l) *adj.* (*zool.*) of or relating to a foot, esp. of a mollusk ‖ (péd'l) of, relating to or involving the use of a pedal or pedals [fr. L. *pedalis* fr. *pes* (*pedis*), foot]

pe·dal·fer (pədǽlfər) *n.* soil lacking a layer of calcium and magnesium carbonates (cf. PEDOCAL) [fr. Gk *pedon,* ground+L. *alumen,* alum+L. *ferrum,* iron]

ped·al·o (pédəlou) *n.* raft with pedalmotivated paddle wheel

pedal point (*mus.*) a single note, esp. in the bass, sustained while harmonies change in the other voices

ped·ant (péd'nt) *n.* a person who makes a tedious show of dull learning ‖ an overprecise person who is unimaginative about using rules or knowledge **pe·dan·tic** (pədǽntik) *adj.* **pe·dán·ti·cal·ly** *adv.* [F. *pédant* or Ital. *pedante,* teacher]

ped·ant·ry (péd'ntri:) *pl.* **ped·ant·ries** *n.* the pedantic show or use of learning or knowledge ‖

CONCISE PRONUNCIATION KEY: **(a)** æ, *cat;* ɑ, *car;* ɔ *fawn;* ei, *snake.* **(e)** e, *hen;* iː, *sheep;* iə, *deer;* ɛə, *bear.* **(i)** i, *fish;* ai, *tiger;* əː, *bird.* **(o)** o, *ox;* au, *cow;* ou, *goat;* u, *poor;* ɔi, *royal.* **(u)** ʌ, *duck;* u, *bull;* uː, *goose;* ə, *bacillus;* juː, *cube.* x, *loch;* θ, *think;* ð, *bother;* z, *Zen;* ʒ, *corsage;* dʒ, *savage;* ŋ, *orangutang;* j, *yak;* ʃ, *fish;* tʃ, *fetch;* 'l, *rabble;* 'n, *redden.* Complete pronunciation key appears inside front cover.

an instance of this || the quality or state of being pedantic [fr. Ital. *pedanteria*]

ped·ate (pédeit) *adj.* (*zool.*) having feet or foot-like extremities || (*bot.*, of leaves) palmate, with divided lobes [fr. L. *pedatus* fr. *pes* (*pedis*), foot]

ped·dle (péd'l) *pres. part.* **ped·dling** *past* and *past part.* **ped·dled** *v.t.* to sell (goods) as one travels from place to place || *v.i.* to travel around with goods to sell [perh. fr. PEDLAR]

ped·dler, *Br.* **ped·lar** (pédlər) *n.* someone who travels about peddling goods [possibly synonymous with earlier *pedder*, etym. doubtful]

ped·er·ast, paed·er·ast (pédəræst, pí:dəræst) *n.* a man who habitually practices pederasty

ped·er·as·ty, paed·er·as·ty (pédəræsti:, pí:dəræsti:) *n.* sodomy [fr. Mod. L. *paederastia* fr. Gk fr. *pais* (*paidos*), boy+*erastes*, lover]

ped·es·tal (pédistəl) *n.* a separate base supporting a column, statue, large vase etc. **to place (someone) on a pedestal** to attribute ideal qualities to (someone) [F. *piédestal* fr. Ital.]

pe·des·tri·an (pidéstri:ən) **1.** *n.* a person going about on foot **2.** *adj.* of, for or relating to pedestrians || dull, commonplace, lacking imagination, *a pedestrian performance* [fr. L. *pedester* (*pedestris*) adj., on foot]

pe·des·tri·an·i·za·tion (pidestri:ənizéiʃən) *n.* creating the condition of pedestrian dominance —**pe·des·tri·an·ize** *v.*

pe·di·at·ric, pae·di·at·ric (pi:diǽtrik) *adj.* of or relating to the medical care of children **pe·di·a·tri·cian, pae·di·a·tri·cian** (pi:di:ətríʃən) *n.* a specialist in pediatrics **pe·di·at·rics, pae·di·at·rics** (pi:diǽtriks) *n.* the branch of medicine concerned with the health and illnesses of children [fr. Gk *pais* (*paidos*), child+*iatrikos* fr. *iatros*, physician]

ped·i·cel (pédisəl) *n.* (*bot.*) a short, slender stalk holding a flower or fruit || (*zool.*) a stalk or stem-like structure [fr. Mod. L. *pedicellus*, dim. of *pediculus*, little foot]

ped·i·cel·lar·i·a (pedisəléəri:ə) *pl.* **ped·i·cel·lar·i·ae** (pedisəléəri:i:) *n.* (*zool.*) one of various minute pincerlike structures studding the surface of certain echinoderms. They keep the body free from debris and parasites [Mod. L. fr. *pedicellus*, pedicel]

ped·i·cel·late (pedisélit, pediséleit) *adj.* (*biol.*) having a pedicel or attached by a pedicel [fr. Mod. L. *pedicellus*, pedicel]

ped·i·cle (pédik'l) *n.* a pedicel [fr. L. *pediculus*, little foot]

pe·dic·u·lar (pədíkjulər) *adj.* of, pertaining to or infested with lice [fr. L. *pedicularis* fr. *pediculus*, louse]

pe·dic·u·late (pədíkjulit, pədíkjuleit) **1.** *adj.* belonging to *Pediculati*, an order of teleost fishes with elongated pectoral fins **2.** *n.* a pediculate fish [fr. L. *pediculus*, footstalk]

pe·dic·u·lo·sis (pədikjulóusis) *n.* infestation of the body with lice [fr. L. *pediculus*, louse]

pe·dic·u·lous (pedíkjuləs) *adj.* infested with lice [fr. L. *pediculosus*]

ped·i·cure (pédikjuər) *n.* chiropody || a chiropodist || (*loosely*) a cleaning, cutting and polishing of the toenails [F. *pédicure*]

ped·i·gree (pédigri:) *n.* a chart or table showing how and from whom a person or family is descended, a genealogical or family tree || a table of descent of purebred animals || ancestry **péd·i·greed** *adj.* (of domestic animals) having a recorded pedigree [older *pedegru* fr. F. *pié de grue*, crane's foot, a three-lined symbol used in genealogical tables]

ped·i·ment (pédimənt) *n.* (*archit.*) the gable over the front of a building with a two-pitched roof, triangular in classical architecture, later (e.g. in baroque) arched or broken at the peak **ped·i·men·tal** (pediméntʼl) *adj.* relating to, designating or like a pediment **péd·i·ment·ed** *adj.* having a pediment [older *peremint*, *periment*, perh. corrup. of PYRAMID]

pedlar *PEDDLER

ped·o·cal (pédəkæl) *n.* soil that has a hard layer of calcium and magnesium carbonates (cf. PEDALFER) [fr. Gk *pedon*, ground+L. *calx* (*calcis*), lime]

pedogenesis *PAEDOGENESIS

pe·dol·o·gy (pidɒ́lədʒi:) *n.* the scientific study of soils [fr. Russ. *pedologiya* fr. Gk *pedon*, ground+*logos*, word]

pe·dom·e·ter (pidɒ́mitər) *n.* an instrument which counts the number of steps taken by a person walking and measures the approximate distance covered [F. *pédomètre*]

Pe·dra·rias (peðrárjɑs) (Pedro Arias Dávila, c. 1440–1531), Spanish conquistador. As governor of Darien (from 1514) he ordered (1517) the execution of Núñez de Balboa. He founded (1519) Panama City and directed important expeditions

Pe·dro I (péidrou) 'the Cruel' (1334–69), king of Castile and León (1350–69). His reign was a period of unbroken civil war, in which he was supported by the Black Prince

Pedro II (1174–1213), king of Aragon (1196–1213). He helped Alfonso VIII of Castile to defeat the Moors (1212) and was killed fighting in alliance with the Albigenses

Pedro III 'the Great' (c. 1236–85), king of Aragon (1276–85) and of Sicily (1282–5), son of James I. His seizure of Sicily after the Sicilian Vespers (1282) provoked a French invasion of Aragon

Pedro IV 'the Ceremonious' (1319–87), king of Aragon (1336–87). He supported Castile against the Moors, and regained Majorca (1343–4)

Pedro I (1320–67), king of Portugal (1357–67)

Pedro II (1648–1706), king of Portugal (1683–1706), son of John IV. He concluded the Methuen Treaty (1703) with England

Pedro III (1717–86), king of Portugal (1777–86), son of John V. He ruled jointly with his niece and wife, Maria I

Pedro IV king of Portugal *PEDRO I, emperor of Brazil

Pedro I (1798–1834), emperor of Brazil (1822–31) and, as Pedro IV, king of Portugal (1826), son of John VI of Portugal. He remained in Brazil after the Portuguese royal family's exile there, and became its first emperor. He abdicated the Portuguese throne in favor of his daughter, Maria II

Pedro II (1825–91), emperor of Brazil (1831–89), son of Pedro I. An enlightened liberal, he opened the Amazon to trade (1867) but his abolition of slavery (1888) was unpopular with landowners. He was deposed (1889) and a federal republic was established

pe·dun·cle (pidʌ́ŋk'l) *n.* (*biol.*) a pedicel || (*anat.*) a stalklike band of white fibers joining different parts of the brain **pe·dun·cu·lar** (pidʌ́ŋkjulər) *adj.* [fr. Mod. L. *pedunculus*, footstalk, dim. of *pes* (*pedis*), a foot]

pe·dun·cu·late (pidʌ́ŋkjuleit, pidʌ́ŋkjulit) *adj.* having or growing on a peduncle **pe·dun·cu·lat·ed** (pidʌ́ŋkjəleitid) *adj.* [fr. Mod. L. *pedunculatus*]

pee (pi:) **1.** *v.i.* (*pop.*) to urinate **2.** *n.* (*pop.*) the act of urinating || (*pop.*) urine

Pee·bles (pí:b'lz) a former county in S.E. Scotland, site of Iron Age remains and Roman ruins

peek (pi:k) **1.** *v.i.* to peep, look, esp. in such a way as not to be seen **2.** *n.* a quick or furtive look [M.E. *pike*, *pyke*, origin unknown]

peek·a·boo (pí:kəbu:) *n.* a game played with in infant by someone who alternately hides and reveals himself or his face, crying 'peekaboo'

peek-a-boo *adj.* **1.** of a revealing woman's decolletage, esp. with eyelet holes. **2.** (*computer*) of a document retrieval system in which selection is made through cards with punched holes

Peel (pi:l), Sir Robert (1788–1850), British Tory statesman. He was secretary for Ireland (1812–18), and as home secretary (1822–7 and 1828–30) secured the passage of the Catholic Emancipation Act (1829). His legal reforms included the establishment (1829) of the London police. As prime minister (1834–5) he rallied the Tories in support of recent Whig reforms, and so laid the foundations of the Conservative party. In his second ministry (1841–6), he imposed an income tax (1842), lowered many tariffs and reorganized the banking system (1844). His repeal of the Corn Laws (1846) split the Conservative party into the Peelites, who supported the measure, and the followers of Disraeli, who opposed it

peel (pi:l) **1.** *v.t.* to remove the outer covering, skin, rind etc. from || (with 'off') to remove (an outer covering, skin, rind etc.), *he peeled off his raincoat* || *v.i.* (of an outer covering, skin etc.) to come off, flake off || to shed an outer covering or skin **to peel off** (of aircraft flying in formation) to break away from the formation in orderly succession, turning sharply and losing height || (of a warship or aircraft) to break away from a formation, e.g. to attack or investigate **to keep one's eyes peeled** to keep a sharp lookout, *keep your eyes peeled for a parking place* **2.** *n.* the rind or outer skin of a fruit or of some vegetables [older *pill*, prob. fr. O.E.]

peel *n.* a long-handled flat shovel for putting loaves into a bread oven and for taking them out [M.E. fr. O.F. *pele*]

peel *n.* (*hist.*) a 16th-c. fortified structure common on the Scottish border, housing the cattle on the ground floor and the family on the floor above [M.E. *pel*, *pele*, stake fr. A.F. and O.F.]

Peele (pi:l), George (c. 1558–c. 1596), English dramatist. 'The Old Wives' Tale' (1595) is his best-known work

peel·er (pí:lər) *n.* (*Br. hist.*) a policeman || (*Br. hist.*) a member of the Irish constabulary [after Sir Robert *Peel* who founded the Irish constabulary (1818) and the London police (1829)]

peel·ings (pí:liŋz) *pl. n.* the peel of a fruit or vegetable when stripped off

Peel·ite (pí:lait) *n.* (*Br. hist.*) a member of a political group which supported Peel in repealing the Corn Laws (1846), thereby seceding from the Conservative party. Led by Gladstone, the Peelites allied themselves by 1868 with the Liberal party

peen (pi:n) **1.** *n.* the thin end of the head of a hammer **2.** *v.t.* to strike or work with a peen [older *pen*, etym. doubtful]

peep (pi:p) **1.** *v.i.* to take a look through a small hole, around a corner, over a wall etc., esp. in such a way as not to be seen || to take a quick look || (with 'out') to be visible briefly, incompletely or from a distance, *his toes peeped out through the holes in his socks* || to come into view, as if from hiding, *the sun peeped through the clouds* || *v.t.* (with 'out') to cause to protrude a bit, *to peep one's head out* **2.** *n.* the act of peeping || a surreptitious, furtive glance || (*rhet.*) the first sign, *at peep of dawn* [etym. doubtful]

peep 1. *n.* the high, weak noise made by very young birds **2.** *v.i.* to utter a peep || *v.t.* to utter in a high, weak voice [M.E. *pepen*, imit.]

peep·er (pí:pər) *n.* a person who looks furtively

peeper *n.* any of several frogs, esp. of fam. *Hylidae*, that make a peeping sound

peep·hole (pí:phoul) *n.* a small hole which one can look through without being seen

peeping Tom an erotic pervert who hides himself and watches loving couples or women undressing [after *Peeping Tom*, the legendary tailor of Coventry who peeped at Lady Godiva]

peep show a miniature exhibition inside a box, consisting of entertaining pictures or objects looked at through a small hole fitted with a lens

peep sight the aperture sight of a rifle

peepul *PIPAL

peer (piər) *v.i.* to look closely, attentively, or as if one had difficulty in seeing || to come partly into view, peep out, *the moon peered out through the clouds* [etym. doubtful]

peer *n.* a member of one of the British degrees of nobility: a duke, marquis, earl, viscount, or baron || a nobleman of any country || someone having the same status in rank, age, ability etc. as another, *to be judged by one's peers* **péer·age** *n.* the peers of a country, esp. of Great Britain, as a body || the rank of a peer || a book containing the names of all the peers, with historical and genealogical details etc. **péer·ess** *n.* the wife or widow of a peer || a woman who holds the rank of a peer in her own right **péer·less** *adj.* so excellent as to have no equal [M.E. *per*, *peere* fr. O.F.]

peer group a group who regard themselves of equal standing in the milieu in which they exist

peer of the realm a British peer, entitled to sit in the House of Lords after his majority

peer pressure influence of one's friends on morals

peet·weet (pí:twi:t) *n.* the spotted sandpiper [imit.]

peeve (pi:v) **1.** *v.t. pres. part.* **peev·ing** *past* and *past part.* **peeved** to make peevish **2.** *n.* (*pop.*) a peevish mood, *he got up in a peeve* **a pet peeve** some trivial, frequent source of annoyance [backformation fr. PEEVISH]

peev·ish (pí:viʃ) *adj.* irritable, apt to complain, grumble and be ill-tempered || showing such crossness, *peevish gesture* [origin unknown]

pee·wee (pí:wi:) *n.* (*pop.*) an unusually small person, animal or thing || *PEWEE [imit., after the bird's cry]

peewit *PEWIT

peg (peg) **1.** *n.* a small piece of wood, metal, plastic etc., generally cylindrical and slightly tapered, used to hold together two parts of a construction, to secure a joint, bung a hole, hang things on, mark the score in cribbage or darts, fasten ropes to etc. ‖ a small screw for holding and adjusting the tension of the strings of a stringed instrument ‖ (*Br.*) a short drink of liquor ‖ a step or degree, *to move up a peg in an organization* ‖ something used as a pretext, *a peg to hang a claim on* ‖ (*Br.*) a clothes-peg ‖ one or the two end markers in croquet **a square peg in a round hole** (or **a round peg in a square hole**) a person who is out of place in the circumstances in which he finds himself **to take (someone) down a peg** to make (someone) less bumptious or self-satisfied **2.** *v. pres. part.* **peg·ging** *past* and *past part.* **pegged** *v.t.* to fasten, secure or attach with a peg or pegs ‖ to mark (a score) in cribbage etc. with pegs ‖ to mark (a distance) with pegs ‖ to fix or maintain (prices, wages etc.) at a certain level ‖ *v.i.* (with 'away', 'at' etc.) to work hard and steadily, *to peg away at one's thesis* ‖ (cribbage etc.) to keep score with pegs **to peg out** to mark out with pegs, *to peg out the site for a house* ‖ (*croquet*) to finish the game by hitting the peg with the ball [prob. fr. L.G.]

Peg·a·sus (pégəsəs) (*Gk mythol.*) a winged horse that sprang from the blood of Medusa. He caused the Hippocrene to spring forth on Mount Helicon ‖ a constellation of the northern hemisphere

peg·a·sus (pégəsəs) *n.* a member of *Pegasus* fam. *Pegasidae,* a genus of tropical marine fishes with a long snout, a small, toothless mouth and large, winglike fins

peg·board (pégbɔrd, pégbourd) *n.* a small board with holes in it into which pegs are stuck. It is used for scoring, esp. at cribbage

peg·leg (pégleg) *n.* an artificial leg, esp. a wooden one, fitted to the knee

peg·ma·tite (pégmətait) *n.* an exceptionally coarse-grained variety of granite **peg·ma·tit·ic** (pegmətítik) *adj.* [fr. Gk *pēgma* (*pēgmatos*), a thing joined together]

peg top a child's spinning top, wide at the top and narrowing to the point on which it spins

Pe·gu (pegú:) a river port and rail center (pop. 123,600) of S. Burma, a Buddhist pilgrimage place

Pé·guy (peigi:), Charles (1873–1914), French poet and essayist. He professed a mystical, patriotic socialism which opposed both anticlerical socialism and right-wing Catholicism. Most of his writings appeared in his 'Cahiers de la Quinzaine' from 1900. His poetry includes 'le Mystère de la charité de Jeanne d'Arc' (1910)

Pe·gu Yo·ma (pegú:jóumə) a mountain range in S. central Burma between the Irrawaddy and Sittang Rivers: Mt Popa, 4,981 ft

Pehlevi *PAHLAVI

Pei (pei), I(eoh) M(ina) (1917–), Chinese-American architect. Born in Canton, China, he came to the U.S.A. (1935) to study architecture and became a U.S. citizen in 1954. After practicing architecture in Boston, he founded his own firm in New York City (1955). One of the most prolific contemporary architects, he has designed such buildings as Denver's Mile High Center (1956), Washington, D.C.'s L'Enfant Plaza (1967), Boston's John Hancock Tower (1973), and the Fragrant Hill (Xiangshan) Hotel in Peking, China (1983)

peign·oir (penwάr, pénwɑr) *n.* a negligee [F. fr. *peigner,* to comb]

Pei·ping (péipíŋ) *PEKING

Pei·pus (pí:pəs) (*Estonian* Peipsi, *Russ.* Chudskoe Ozero) a lake (area 1,356 sq. miles) of the U.S.S.R., on the boundary between Estonia and the R.S.F.S.R. It drains into the Gulf of Finland. In 1242 Alexander Nevski defeated the Teutonic Knights on the frozen lake

Peirce (piərs), Charles Sanders (1839–1914), U.S. philosopher, mathematician and physicist, best known as the founder of the pragmatic movement in American philosophy, in which he developed a criterion of meaning in terms of conceivable effects or consequences in experience and a view of beliefs as 'habits of action.' He also wrote in numerous other fields, as well as working as an astronomer at the Harvard Observatory and as a physicist for the U.S. Coast and Geodetic Survey

Peirce (píərs) *PRAGMATISM

Peisistratus *PISISTRATUS

Pei·xo·to (peiʃótu), Floriano (1842–95), Brazilian soldier and president (1891–4) after leading (with da Fonseca) the Revolution of 1889 which overthrew the Empire and established the Republic

pe·jo·ra·tive (pidʒɔ́rətiv, pidʒórətiv, pédʒərei-tiv) **1.** *adj.* (of words or phrases) expressing disparagement **2.** *n.* a word or expression used in a pejorative sense [fr. L. *pejorare* (*pejoratus*), to make worse]

pek·an (pékən) *n.* the fisher (animal) [F., of Algonquian origin]

peke (pi:k) *n.* a pekingese

pe·kin (pi:kín) *n.* a usually striped, silk material, originally from China [after PEKING]

Pe·kin·ese (pi:kiní:z) *pl.* **Pe·kin·ese** *n.* a Pekingese

Pe·king (pi:kíŋ) (Beijing) the capital (pop. 9,230,687) of China, in N. Hopei (but administered directly by the government), 35 miles south of the Great Wall of China. It is an ancient communications center and traditionally China's center of learning. Industries: cotton milling, iron and steel, mechanical engineering, food processing, chemicals. It consists of the Inner, or Tatar, City (walls from 1437) and the Outer, or Chinese, City beside the south wall, enclosed in 1544. There are 16 gates. Within the Inner City, walls enclose the Imperial City, the former official district: Peking University, 1898, National Library, parks and monuments. Within this, purple walls enclose the Forbidden City, the former imperial precinct, a formal ensemble of palaces, temples, halls, gardens etc., now the seat of government. The Outer City, partly truck farms, contains the main commercial quarter and the old principal temples: the Altar of Heaven and the Temple of Agriculture (both 15th c.). Outside the Inner City are the Temples of the Earth (north), Moon (west) and Sun (east). A modern university (People's University, 1912) and residential quarter are outside the walls on the west, and the industrial district lies on the east. A city of great antiquity, Peking was destroyed (1215) by Genghis Khan and rebuilt, as a capital (1264), by Kublai Khan. It was the northern capital of China (1421–1928) and became the capital of the whole country in 1949 (*NANKING)

Pe·king·ese (pi:kiní:z, pi:kiŋí:s, pi:kiní:z, pi:kiní:s) **1.** *pl.* **Pe·king·ese** *n.* a native or inhabitant of Peking ‖ the Chinese dialect spoken in the Peking district ‖ a dog of an ancient, small breed, originally from China, popular as a pet. They have short legs, long silky hair, a flat nose, curled bushy tail, protruding eyes and a high-pitched yap **2.** *adj.* of or relating to Peking, its inhabitants, dialect etc.

Peking man an extinct man whose remains have been found near Peking, often regarded as a variety of pithecanthropus

Pe·kin·ol·o·gist or **Pe·king·ol·o·gist** (pi:kinɔ́lədʒi:st) *n.* expert in studies of the hierarchy of China —**Pe·kin·ol·o·gy** or **Pe·king·ol·o·gy** *n.*

pe·koe (pí:kou, *Br.* also pékou) *n.* a black tea of good quality made from selected young leaves picked with the down still upon them [Chinese *pek-ho* fr. *pek,* white+*ho,* down, hair]

pe·lage (pélidʒ) *n.* the fur or other coat of a mammal [F.]

Pe·la·gi·an (pəléidʒi:ən) **1.** *adj.* pertaining to Pelagius or Pelagianism **2.** *n.* a follower of Pelagius or upholder of Pelagianism [fr. L. *Pelagianus*]

Pe·la·gi·an·ism (pəléidʒi:ənizəm) *n.* the heresy originated by Pelagius. It denied original sin and the need for baptism, and held that grace was not necessary for salvation. It asserted that free will and the law are sufficient for man to live without sin. It arose is a reaction to gnosticism and Manichaeism, in the interests of a higher morality which Pelagius found lacking in Rome. Originally an attempt to heighten human responsibility, it fell into the extreme of diminishing divine grace. Opposed by St Augustine of Hippo, the heresy and Pelagius were condemned at several synods (411–18). A form of the heresy, with emphasis on free will, arose briefly (late 5th c.) in France but was condemned (528–9). Pelagianism long continued as a trend in Christian philosophy

pe·lag·ic (pəlǽdʒik) *adj.* of or occurring on the open sea. *pelagic navigation* ‖ (*zool.*) ocean-inhabiting (cf. DEMERSAL) [fr. L. *pelagicus* fr. Gk fr. *pelagos,* sea]

Pe·la·gi·us (pəléidʒi:əs) (c. 360–c. 422), English monk who settled in Rome (400). He was accused of heresy at several synods (411–18) and was banished from Rome (418) (*PELAGIANISM)

pel·ar·go·ni·um (pelɑrgóuni:əm) *n.* a member of *Pelargonium,* fam. *Geraniaceae,* a genus of flowering plants native to S. Africa. Many varieties and hybrids are cultivated for their ornamental flowers and foliage (*GERANIUM) [Mod. L. fr. Gk *pelargos,* stork]

Pe·las·gi·an (pəlǽzdʒi:ən) **1.** *n.* one of the aboriginal non-Greek inhabitants of Greece, Asia Minor and the Aegean Islands before the Achaean invasion (c. 2000 B.C.) **2.** *adj.* of or characteristic of the Pelasgians or their language [fr. L. *Pelasgius* fr. Gk]

Pe·las·gic (pəlǽzdʒik) *adj.* Pelasgian [fr. L. *Pelasgicus*]

Pe·lé (pelé), Edson Arantes do Nascimento (1940–), Brazilian soccer star and national hero

pe·lec·y·pod (pəlésipɒd) *n.* (*zool.*) a lamellibranch [fr. Gk *pelekus,* hatchet+*pous* (*podos*), foot]

Pe·lée (pəléi) a volcanic mountain (4,428 ft) in N. Martinique. Its eruption (1902) destroyed St Pierre with the loss of 40,000 lives

Pel·e·liu Island (péləlju:, pelalí:u:) one of the W. Caroline Is in the W. Pacific, site of a battle (1944) in the 2nd world war in which U.S. marines defeated Japanese forces and captured the island

pelf (pelf) *n.* (*rhet.*) money or riches referred to contemptuously, esp. to suggest they were dishonestly acquired

pel·i·can (pélikən) *n.* a member of *Pelecanus,* fam. *Pelecanidae,* a genus of large, web-footed, gregarious birds with a large wingspread. They are widely distributed in temperate and tropical zones. They are characterized by a very long bill, and a pouch in the upper throat in which they store the fish they catch before eating them [fr. L.L. *pelicanus, pelecanus* fr. Gk]

Pe·li·on (pí:li:ən) a mountain of Thessaly, Greece. In Greek mythology, the giants in revolt against Zeus placed it on top of Mt Ossa in order to attack Mt Olympus

pe·lisse (pelí:s) *n.* (*hist.*) a man's or woman's long, fur-lined cloak ‖ (*hist.*) a woman's long, loose cloak or coat [F. fr. Ital. *pelliccia,* furred garment]

pe·lite (pí:lait) *n.* rock composed of minute bits of clay or mud [fr. Gk *pelos,* earth, clay]

pel·la·gra (pəléigrə, pəlǽgrə) *n.* a disease, commonest in the Tropics, manifested by skin inflammation, diarrhea and nervous disorders. It is caused by a deficiency of niacin and protein [Ital. and Mod. L., perh. fr. Ital. *pelle,* skin+*agra,* tough]

pel·let (pélit) *n.* a little ball, e.g. of rolled-up paper ‖ a small piece of shot, fired singly from an air gun, or in groups packed into the cartridge of a shotgun [F. *pelote*]

Pell grants (pélgrǽnts) *n.* U.S. government student scholarships, varying in amount based on income, assets and expenses; named for Senator Claiborne Pell

pel·li·cle (pélik'l) *n.* (*biol.*) any thin skin or filmy protective covering ‖ the scum on a liquid ‖ any thin film or membrane **pel·lic·u·lar, pel·lic·u·late** *adjs* [fr. L. *pellicula,* dim. of *pellis,* skin]

pel·li·to·ry (pélitɔri:, pélitouri:) *pl.* **pel·li·to·ries** *n. Anacyclus pyrethrum,* a composite plant of S. Europe ‖ its roots, formerly used as an irritant, a salivant and a toothache remedy ‖ any of several plants resembling this plant, esp. feverfew and yarrow ‖ a member of *Parietaria,* fam. *Urticaceae,* a genus of plants allied to nettles [M.E. *peletre* fr. M.F. *piretre* fr. L. *pyrethrum*]

pell-mell (pélmél) **1.** *adv.* in great haste and confusion **2.** *adj.* confused, disorderly, *pell-mell haste* **3.** *n.* hurry and confusion, *the pell-mell of city life* [F. *pêle-mêle*]

pel·lu·cid (pelú:sid) *adj.* crystal clear, *pellucid waters* ‖ (of literary style, wording etc.) extremely clear **pel·lu·cid·i·ty** *n.* [fr. L. *pellucidus*]

pel·met (pélmit) *n.* a valance or fitting at the top of a window to hide the curtain rod [origin unknown]

Pe·lop·i·das (pəlɒ́pidəs) (*d.* 364 B.C.), Greek general, friend of Epaminondas. He drove the Spartans out of Thebes (378 B.C.) but was killed at Cynoscephalae

Pel·o·pon·nese (peləpəní:s) the Peloponnesus

Pel·o·pon·ne·sian (peləpəní:ʒən, peləpəní:ʃən) **1.** *adj.* of or relating to the Peloponnesus, its people etc. **2.** *n.* a native or inhabitant of the Peloponnesus

Peloponnesian War a decisive war (431– 404 B.C.) between Sparta and Athens caused by Spartan fear of the growing power of Athens and her maritime empire. After an indecisive start, Athens wasted her financial and naval

CONCISE PRONUNCIATION KEY: **(a)** æ, *cat*; ɑ, *car*; ɔ *fawn*; ei, *snake*. **(e)** e, *hen*; i:, *sheep*; iə, *deer*; εə, *bear*. **(i)** i, *fish*; ai, *tiger*; ə:, *bird*. **(o)** ɒ, *ox*; au, *cow*; ou, *goat*; u, *poor*; ɔi, *royal*. **(u)** ʌ, *duck*; u, *bull*; u:, *goose*; ə, *bacillus*; ju:, *cube*. x, *loch*; θ, *think*; ð, *bother*; z, *Zen*; ʒ, *corsage*; dʒ, *savage*; ŋ, *orangutang*; j, *yak*; ʃ, *fish*; tʃ, *fetch*; 'l, *rabble*; 'n, *redden*. Complete pronunciation key appears inside front cover.

superiority in a disastrous expedition to Sicily (415–413 B.C.). Sparta built a fleet with Persian aid, destroyed the remainder of the Athenian fleet at Aegospotami (405 B.C.) and Athens surrendered (404 B.C.). The war ruined Athens

Pel·o·pon·ne·sus (peləpəní:səs) (*Gk* Morea) a mountainous peninsula forming S. Greece, connected to the continent by the isthmus of Corinth. The region comprises eight historical regions of Greece: Achaea, Arcadia, Argolis, Corinth, Elis, Laconia, Messenia and Sicyonia. It was the site of Sparta and Corinth

Pe·lops (pí:lɒps) (*Gk mythol.*) the son of Tantalus, who served Pelops's limbs to the gods as food. Pelops was revived by the gods and, grown to manhood, he murdered a friend, thus perpetuating the strain of evil which was to be more marked in his sons, Atreus and Thyestes

pe·lo·ta (pəlóutə) *n.* any of several similar Basque, Spanish or Latin American games, esp. jai alai ‖ the ball used in these games [Span.=ball]

pel·o·ton (pélətən) *n.* ornamental glassware decorated with overlaid colored strands made in Italy. *also* Peloton glass

pelt (pelt) **1.** *v.t.* to strike by throwing things at continuously and in great quantity, *they pelted us with snowballs* ‖ to throw (objects) continuously, *to pelt snowballs at someone* ‖ *v.i.* (e.g. of rain) to pour or beat down continually with force ‖ (*pop.*) to run as fast as possible, *he came pelting around the corner* **2.** *n.* a hard blow ‖ a pelting **at full pelt** at full speed [origin unknown]

pelt *n.* the skin of an animal with the hair or wool on ‖ a raw hide after the hair or wool has been removed [perh. fr. PELTRY]

pel·tate (pélteit) *adj.* (*bot.*, of leaves) attached to the plant not at the edge or base but at the middle of the lower surface, e.g. in the nasturtium ‖ (*biol.*) shaped like a shield [fr. L. *peltatus* fr. *pelta*, shield]

Pel·tier effect (peltjéi) (*elec.*) the evolution or absorption of heat at a junction of two different metals in an electric circuit [after Jean *Peltier* (1785–1845), F. physicist]

pelt·ry (péltri:) *n.* pelts (skins) collectively [A.F. *pelterie*, O.F. *peleterie*]

pel·vic (pélvik) *adj.* related to or situated at or near the pelvis [fr. L. *pelvis*, basin]

pelvic arch the pelvic girdle

pelvic fin one of the posterior pair of fins attached to the pelvic girdle of a fish

pelvic girdle an arch of bones or cartilage to which the hind limbs of vertebrates are attached, and which forms part of the pelvis

pel·vis (pélvis) *pl.* **pel·vis·es, pel·ves** (pélvi:s) *n.* (*anat., zool.*) a bony cavity in vertebrates, formed in man by the pelvic girdle together with the coccyx and sacrum ‖ the bones that form this cavity, collectively ‖ the expansion of the ureter at its junction with the kidney [L.=basin]

Pem·ba (pémbə) a coral island (area 380 sq. miles, pop. 164,300) in the Indian Ocean, 34 miles north of Zanzibar, forming part of Tanzania. Chief town: Chake Chake. Pemba produces five-sixths of the country's cloves

Pem·broke (pémbruk), Richard de Clare, 2nd earl of (c. 1130–76), also known as Richard Strongbow. He subdued (1170) and ruled much of Ireland in the name of Henry II of England

Pembroke, William Marshal, 1st earl of (c. 1146–1219), English nobleman. He was adviser to Henry II, regent (1190–4) for Richard I, adviser to King John, and regent (1216–19) for Henry III

Pembrokeshire *DYFED

pem·mi·can, pem·i·can (pémikən) *n.* dried meat, pounded and compressed with fat, as prepared by North American Indians ‖ a similar preparation of concentrated food, carried by explorers, mountaineers etc. [Cree *pimecan*, *pimekan* fr. *pime*, fat]

pem·o·line [$C_9H_8N_2O_2$] (péməli:n) *n.* (*pharm.*) a central nervous system stimulant drug used for children; marketed as Cylert

pen (pen) *n.* a small enclosure, often outdoors, for farm animals ‖ the animals kept in this ‖ any small enclosure, e.g. a fortified dock for submarines [O.E. *penn*]

pen *n.* a female swan (cf. COB) [origin unknown]

pen 1. *n.* an instrument for writing in ink ‖ the nib of such a writing instrument ‖ a bird's feather, sharpened at the broad end and split to form a nib, formerly used for writing ‖ (*rhet.*) style or manner of writing, *he has a lively pen* ‖ professional writing, *a journalist lives by his pen* ‖ (*zool.*) the internal, feather-shaped shell of a squid **2.** *v.t. pres. part.* **pen·ning** *past* and *past part.* **penned** (*rhet.*) to write, *he penned a furious answer* [M.E. fr. O.F. *penne*, pen, feather]

pen *pres. part.* **pen·ning** *past* and *past part.* **penned** (with 'in', 'up') *v.t.* to shut up in a pen or other confined space [M.E. *pennen* fr. O.E.]

pe·nal (pí:n'l) *adj.* concerned with esp. legal punishment of crime, *penal code* ‖ constituting an esp. legal punishment for crime ‖ (of an offense) legally punishable **pé·nal·ize** *pres. part.* **pe·nal·iz·ing** *past* and *past part.* **pe·nal·ized** *v.t.* to inflict a penalty upon ‖ to subject to a disadvantage, *a tax on tobacco penalizes the smoker* **pe·nal·i·zá·tion** *n.* a penalizing or being penalized [F. *pénal* fr. L. fr. Gk]

Penal Laws (*Eng. hist.*) the laws (1559–1829) banning Roman Catholics from civil office and imposing penalties on them for failing to conform with the Church of England. The discrimination ended (1829) with the passing of Catholic Emancipation

penal servitude a legal punishment consisting of imprisonment with hard labor

penal times (*Eng. hist.*) the period (1559–1829) during which the Penal Laws were in force

pen·al·ty (pén'lti:) *pl.* **pen·al·ties** *n.* a punishment for breaking a law or otherwise committing an offense against established authority ‖ a disagreeable consequence suffered as a result of one's own folly or wrongdoing, *his hangover was a penalty for drinking too much* ‖ a fine, forfeit etc. incurred when some condition is not observed, some undertaking not fulfilled etc. ‖ (*games*) a disadvantage imposed as punishment for breaking the rules ‖ (*bridge*) the points added to the opponent's score when the declarer fails to make his contract **on** (or **upon** or **under**) **penalty of** with the certainty of incurring (some penalty) if a specified command or condition is not fulfilled, *no smoking under penalty of instant dismissal* [fr. M.L. *poenalitas* fr. *poenalis*, penal]

penalty area (*soccer* and *field hockey*) an area around the goal in which an offense by the defending side entitles the other side to a kick or hit at the goal defended only by the goalkeeper

pen·ance (pénəns) *n.* punishment or suffering undergone voluntarily to atone for sin or wrongdoing ‖ (*Roman Catholic and Orthodox Churches*) the sacrament by which the sins of those who sincerely repent, confess and perform the acts required by the priest are absolved ‖ the acts which a priest requires of a penitent **to do penance** (*Roman Catholic and Orthodox Churches*) to perform the acts required for absolution after confession ‖ to perform some act as atonement for sin or wrongdoing [O.F. *peneance, pennance* fr. L.]

Pe·nang (pi:nǽŋ, pi:nɑ́ŋ) a state (pop. 706,000) of Malaysia in W. Malaya, consisting of Penang Is. (Prince of Wales Is., 108 sq. miles) and a strip of territory on the peninsula, Province Wellesley (area 280 sq. miles). Capital: Penang (pop. 250,578), Penang Is. The British settled (1786) on Penang Is. It was ceded (1791) to Britain by the Sultan of Kedah. Province Wellesley was ceded (1800). Penang formed (1826), together with Malacca and Singapore, the Straits Settlements. It joined (1946) the Union, later (1948) the Federation, of Malaya

Pe·ñas, Gulf of (pénjɑs) an inlet of the Pacific on the southwest coast of Chile south of the Taitao Peninsula

pe·nat·es (pənéiti:z) *pl. n.* (*Rom. mythol.*) the household gods revered as the guardians of the home, worshipped in conjunction with Vesta (*LARES) [L.]

pence *PENNY

pen·chant (péntʃənt, pɑ̃ʃɑ̃) *n.* an inclination towards, a liking for, *a penchant for ice cream* [F. fr. pres. part. of *pencher*, to slope]

pen·cil (pénsəl) **1.** *n.* an instrument for writing or drawing, consisting of a slim cylinder esp. of wood, with a core of graphite or black lead which can be sharpened to a point and which is sometimes mechanically retractable ‖ a drawing instrument with a colored core of chalk, wax etc. ‖ anything like such an instrument in shape or function, *a styptic pencil* ‖ a long, converging, narrow beam of light ‖ (*geom.*) a number of lines passing through the same point and lying on a plane **2.** v.t. *pres. part.* **pen·cil·ing**, esp. *Br.* **pen·cil·ling** *past* and *past part.* **pen·ciled**, esp. *Br.* **pen·cilled** to write, draw or mark in pencil [M.E. fr. O.F. *pincel*, brush]

pencil beam a searchlight beam reduced to, or set at its minimum width. *also* focused beam

Pen·da (péndə) (c. 577–655), king of Mercia (632–55). He extended his kingdom by conquest to include the whole of England's Midlands

pen·dant (péndənt) **1.** *n.* something suspended, *chandelier pendants* ‖ a piece of jewelry hanging from a brooch, necklace, chain etc. ‖ a hanging electric-light fitting ‖ a companion piece, e.g. a picture meant to be seen in conjunction with another ‖ (*naut.*) a short line hanging from a masthead, with an eye for attaching gear or tackle ‖ (*Br., naut.*, pénənt) a narrow tapering flag ‖ (*archit.*) a decorative finial or spiked ornament projecting downward from a ceiling or roof **2.** *adj.* pendent [F. fr. pres. part. of *pendre*, to hang]

pen·dent (péndənt) *adj.* (*rhet.*) hanging, *pendent branches* ‖ (*rhet.*) overhanging, *pendent cliffs* ‖ undetermined, pending [fr. L. *pendens* (*pendentis*) fr. *pendere*, to hang]

pen·den·tive (pendéntiv) *n.* (*archit.*) one of the spherical triangular pieces of vaulting forming the support for a dome resting on a square ‖ (*archit.*) that part of a groined vault rising from a pier or corbel [fr. F. *pendentif, pendentive* fr. L.]

pend·ing (péndiŋ) **1.** *adj.* in process of being decided, settled, arranged etc., *the court case is still pending* ‖ about to happen, *hold this over for the pending meeting* **2.** *prep.* during the wait for, until, *a temporary arrangement pending a final settlement* ‖ until the completion of, *pending the armistice discussions there are to be no troop movements* [formed after F. *pendant*, L. *pendens*, hanging]

Pendragon, Uther *UTHER PENDRAGON

pen·drag·on (pendrǽgən) *n.* an ancient title of a British or Welsh supreme leader or chief [Welsh *pen*, head+*dragon*, dragon, the standard of a band of warriors]

pen·du·lous (péndʒuləs, péndjuləs, péndələs) *adj.* hanging down, *a pendulous dewlap* ‖ (*bot.*, of ovules, branches, flowers etc.) bending down from the point of origin, overhanging ‖ swinging to and fro [fr. L. *pendulus*]

pen·du·lum (péndʒuləm, péndjuləm, péndələm) *n.* a body suspended from a pivot and able to swing to and fro as a result of gravitational force, when displaced from its position of rest. It is used to regulate clockwork movement etc. [Mod. L. fr. L. *pendulus*, hanging down]

Pe·nel·o·pe (pinéləpi:) the wife of Odysseus. She faithfully waited 20 years for his return from Troy. She put off her many suitors by saying she must first finish a certain piece of weaving, each night unraveling her day's work

pe·ne·plain, pe·ne·plane (pí:ni:plein) *n.* (*geol.*) an area of land worn almost flat by erosion [fr. L. *paene*, almost+PLAIN (PLANE)]

pen·e·tra·bil·i·ty (penitrəbíliti:) *n.* the quality or state of being penetrable

pen·e·tra·ble (pénitrəb'l) *adj.* capable of being penetrated **pén·e·tra·bly** *adv.* [fr. L. *penetrabilis*]

pen·e·tra·li·a (penitréili:ə) *pl. n.* (*rhet.*) the innermost or most sacred parts, esp. of a temple [L. pl. of *penetrale*]

penetralium *n.* the innermost part

pen·e·trance (pénitrəns) *n.* (*genetics*) frequency in which a dominant gene or a recessive gene in a homozygote appears in a phenotype

pen·e·trate (pénitreit) *pres. part.* **pen·e·trat·ing** *past* and *past part.* **pen·e·trat·ed** *v.t.* to go into by piercing, *a splinter penetrated his eye* ‖ to make or force a way through, *damp is penetrating the brickwork* ‖ to spread through, *the smell penetrated the whole house* ‖ to see through or into, *he tried to penetrate the darkness* ‖ to discern, *to penetrate the meaning of someone's words* ‖ *v.i.* to go into something by piercing it, *the nail penetrated all the way through the wood* ‖ to make or force a way, *the army penetrated into the interior* ‖ to have an effect on the mind or feelings, *nothing she says penetrates enough to make him ashamed* ‖ (with 'into', 'through' or 'to') to discern the truth or meaning of something obscure **pén·e·trat·ing** *adj.* [fr. L. *penetrare* (*penetratus*)]

pen·e·tra·tion (penitréiʃən) *n.* the act of penetrating ‖ keenness of mind, insight ‖ (*mil.*) the depth to which a projectile penetrates into a target [fr. L.L. *penetratio* (*penetrationis*)]

pen·e·tra·tive (pénitreitiv) *adj.* penetrating [fr. M.L. *penetrativus*]

Peng·hu (pʌ́ŋgú:) *PESCADORES ISLANDS

Peng·pu (pʌ́ŋpú:) *FENGYANG

pen·guin (péŋgwin, péngwin) *n.* a member of *Spheniscidae,* order *Sphenisciformes,* a family of aquatic, flightless birds of Antarctic and subantarctic regions. They are characteristically whitebreasted with dark backs, scalelike fur and wings modified to flippers. They are gregarious and feed on fish and crustaceans [etym. doubtful]

pen·hold·er (pénhouldər) *n.* the part of a pen to which the nib is attached ‖ a device for holding a pen or pens

pen·i·cil·late (penisílit, penisíleit) *adj.* (*biol.*) of, designating or having a small tuft of hairs [fr. L. *penicillus,* painter's brush]

pen·i·cil·lin (penisílin) *n.* a mixture of antibiotic substances produced by molds of the genus *Penicillium,* preparations of which are widely used for their potent bacteriostatic action against a variety of pathogenic bacteria [fr. Mod. L. *Penicillium* fr. L. *penicillus,* painter's brush]

pen·i·cil·li·nase (penisílineis) *n.* (*biochem.*) an enzyme that opposes the action of penicillin on bacteria, found in penicillin resistant bacteria

pen·i·cil·li·um (penisíli:əm) *pl.* **pen·i·cil·li·a** (penisíli:ə) *n.* a member of *Penicillium,* fam. *Moniliaceae,* a genus of fungi comprising the familiar blue mold on cheese, jam etc. [Mod. L. fr. *penicillus,* painter's brush]

pen·in·su·la (pənínsulə, pənínsjulə) *n.* a piece of land that is almost an island, either connected to the mainland by a narrow neck or projecting into the sea, with the sea on three sides **pen·ín·su·lar** *adj.* [L. *paeninsula* fr. *paene,* almost+*insula,* island]

Peninsular War a war (1808–14) fought in the Iberian peninsula by Britain, Portugal and Spain against France, forming part of the Napoleonic Wars. To encourage Portuguese and Spanish resistance to Napoleonic rule, Britain sent an army, which was evacuated (1809) from Corunna by Sir John Moore, but which returned to Lisbon under Wellington. After two years of defensive warfare based on the lines of Torres Vedras, Wellington led an offensive (1812–14) which drove the French from Iberia. The war was notable for the guerrilla tactics of the Portuguese and Spanish and, by keeping over 200,000 French troops occupied in Spain, it contributed to Napoleon's downfall

pe·nis (pí:nis) *pl.* **pe·nes** (pí:ni:z), **pe·nis·es** *n.* the male organ of copulation in mammals [L.]

pen·i·tence (pénitəns) *n.* the quality or state of being penitent [O.F. *pénitence*]

pen·i·tent (pénitənt) **1.** adj. feeling or showing sorrow for having sinned or done wrong **2.** *n.* a penitent person ‖ (*Roman Catholic and Orthodox Churches*) a person receiving the sacrament of penance [O.F. *pénitent* fr. L. fr. *paenitere,* to repent]

pen·i·ten·tial (peniténʃəl) *adj.* relating to, expressing or having the nature of penitence or penance [fr. M.L. *poenitentialis*]

penitential psalms Psalms vi, xxxii, xxxviii, li, cii, cxxx and cxliii, or vi, xxxi, xxxvii, l, ci, cxxix and cxlii in the Douai version

pen·i·ten·tia·ry (peniténʃəri:) **1.** *pl.* **pen·i·ten·tia·ries** *n.* a prison for criminals ‖ such a prison, esp. a state or federal prison, in which the inmates are required to do labor ‖ (*Roman Catholicism*) a papal tribunal which deals with cases of conscience, dispensations, absolution of sins and indulgences **2.** *adj.* rendering liable to a prison sentence, *a penitentiary offense* ‖ relating to civil prisons ‖ of or relating to penance [fr. M.L. *poenitentiarius*]

Pen·ki (bʌ́ntʃí:) a town (pop. 449,000) of S. Liaoning, China, on the S. Manchurian railroad: iron and steel, coal, machinery, building materials

pen·knife (pénnaif) *pl.* **pen·knives** (pénnaivz) *n.* a pocketknife, originally one used for making and repairing quill pens

pen·man (pénmən) *pl.* **pen·men** (pénmən) *n.* a professional copyist or scribe ‖ a person with regard to the quality of his penmanship ‖ someone who excels in penmanship

pen·man·ship (pénmənʃip) *n.* style, manner or skill in handwriting or calligraphy

Penn (pen), William (1644–1718), English Quaker and founder of Pennsylvania. His lifelong aim was to secure toleration for the Society of Friends. Receiving a gift of land from Charles II in payment of a debt, he established a colony at Philadelphia (1682). He formulated a progressive and idealistic constitution with legislation by an assembly elected by popular vote, and granted full religious toleration

pen name a writer's pseudonym

pen·nant (pénənt) *n.* a long, narrow, triangular or tapering flag used esp. on ships for signaling etc. ‖ a similar flag as a symbol of sports championship [fr. PENNON, influenced by PENDANT]

pen·nate (pénit) *adj.* (*bot.*) pinnate [fr. L. *pennatus,* winged fr. *penna,* feather]

pen·ni (péni:) *pl.* **pen·ni·a** (péni:ə), **pen·nis** *n.* one-hundredth of a markka ‖ a coin of this value [Fin.]

pen·ni·less (péni:lis) *adj.* having no money or virtually none

pen·nis (pénis) *n.* unit of currency in Finland, equal to 1/100th mark

pen·non (pénən) *n.* a long flag, usually triangular or swallow-tailed, esp. (*hist.*) one borne on the lance of a knight ‖ (naut.) a pennant ‖ a bird's pinion [M.E. fr. O.F. *penon, pennon*]

Penn., Penna. Pennsylvania

Pen·nine Alps (pénain) *ALPS

Pen·nines (pénainz) a range of hills in N. central England, extending south from the Cheviot Hills (Scottish border) to Derbyshire and N. Staffordshire (Cross Fell, 2,892 ft)

Penn·syl·va·ni·a (pensəlvéini:ə, pensəlvéinjə) (*abbr.* Pa., Penn., Penna.) a state (area 45,333 sq. miles, pop. 11,865,000) of the eastern U.S.A., just north of the Mason-Dixon line. Capital: Harrisburg. Chief cities: Philadelphia, Pittsburgh. Except for the southeastern plain it is in the Appalachians (Allegheny and smaller ranges). Agriculture: cereals (esp. buckwheat), dairy and beef cattle, poultry, cigar tobacco, mushrooms. Resources: anthracite coal (sole American producer), bituminous coal, oil, natural gas, building materials. Industries: iron and steel (leading American state producer), metal products, textiles, plastics, machinery, food processing. Chief universities: University of Pennsylvania (1791) at Philadelphia, Pennsylvania State (1885) at University Park, Carnegie Institute of Technology (1900) at Pittsburgh. Pennsylvania was founded (1682) as a Quaker colony by William Penn, was one of the Thirteen Colonies, and became (1787) the 2nd state of the U.S.A.

Pennsylvania Dutch (*pl.*) the descendants of Germans who migrated to E. Pennsylvania in the 18th c. ‖ a dialect of High German spoken by these people ‖ a style of decoration and architecture peculiar to them

Penn·syl·va·ni·an (pensəlvéini:ən, pensəlvéinjən) **1.** *adj.* relating to the state of Pennsylvania ‖ of the period or system corresponding to the later or upper Carboniferous (*GEOLOGICAL TIME) **the Pennsylvanian** the Pennsylvanian period or system of rocks **2.** *n.* an inhabitant of Pennsylvania

Pennsylvania, University of a U.S. private educational institution in Philadelphia, Pa. Originally planned (1740) as a charity school, it was transformed (1755), chiefly by Benjamin Franklin, into an academy (the College and Academy of Philadelphia), with Franklin as its first president. The present name dates from 1791. It established (1765) the first medical school in North America and (1881) the first business school and (1892) the first anatomical institute in all America

pen·ny (péni:) *pl.* **pen·nies,** *Br.* also **pence** (pens) (except when referring to a number of separate coins) *n.* (symbol [¢]) a U.S. or Canadian coin worth one cent ‖ (symbol d) a British bronze coin, 100 of which make up one pound **a penny for your thoughts** what are you thinking about so abstractedly? **a pretty penny** a large sum of money spent or gained, *advertising costs them a pretty penny* **to turn an honest penny** (*Br.*) to earn some money by real work [O.E. *penig*]

penny arcade (*Am.=Br.* amusement arcade) a covered passageway or hall with slot machines etc.

penny black one of the first British adhesive postage stamps (1840)

penny dreadful (esp. *Br.*) a cheap book with stories about crime, horror, ghosts etc.

pen·ny-far·thing (péni:fárðiŋ) *n.* (*Br.*) an ordinary (early type of bicycle) [from the proportions of the two wheels]

pen·ny-pinch·ing (péni:pintʃiŋ) *adj.* (*pop.*) stingy

pen·ny·roy·al (péni:rɔ́iəl) *n.* *Mentha pulegium,* fam. *Labiatae,* a plant native to Europe used in cooking ‖ *Hedeoma pulegioides,* fam. *Labiatae,* an American plant from which an insect repellent is extracted [prob. fr. older *pulyole, ryale* fr. A.F. *puliol,* thyme+*real,* royal]

pen·ny·weight (péni:weit) *n.* (*abbr.* dwt) a unit of troy weight equal to 24 grains or 1/20 of a troy ounce

pen·ny-wise (péni:waiz) *adj.* (usually in the phrase) **penny-wise and pound-foolish** sensible in dealing with small sums of money, but reckless or extravagant with larger ones

pen·ny·wort (péni:wə:rt) *n.* *Cotyledon umbilicus,* fam. *Crassulaceae,* a European plant with round, peltate leaves, often found growing in crevices of walls ‖ a member of either *Hydrocotyle* or *Centella,* fam. *Umbelliferae,* genera of round-leaved marsh plants

pen·ny·worth (péni:wə:rθ) *pl.* **pen·ny·worth, pen·ny·worths** *n.* (esp. *Br.*) the amount one can buy for a penny, *a pennyworth of chewing gum*

Pe·nob·scot (penóbskɒt) *n.* a member of a tribe of Algonquian Indians living around the Penobscot River and Bay in Maine

pe·nol·o·gist (pi:nóləd3ist) *n.* a specialist in penology

pe·nol·o·gy (pi:nóləd3i:) *n.* the study of how to treat criminals and of how prisons or other establishments for their reform should be organized [fr. Gk *poinē,* punishment+*logos,* word]

pen·sile (pénsil) *adj.* (e.g. of nests) hanging ‖ (of birds) making a hanging nest [fr. L. *pensilis*]

pen·sion (pénʃən) **1.** *n.* a sum of money paid regularly to a person who no longer works because of age, disablement etc., or to his widow or dependent children, by the state, by his former employers, or from funds to which he and his employers have both contributed ‖ a similar sum paid, either by the state or by a firm or a private individual, to enable e.g. a research scientist or poet to live and carry on his work ‖ (pɑ̃sjɔ̃) a boardinghouse or boarding school in European countries outside Great Britain ‖ (pɑ̃sjɔ̃) the amount paid regularly for living in such an institution ‖ (pɑ̃sjɔ̃) accommodation at such an institution, *full pension is 10 francs a day* **2.** *v.t.* to pay a pension to ‖ (with 'off') to dismiss and pay a pension to, *it's time the old man was pensioned off* **pén·sion·a·ble** *adj.* entitled to a pension ‖ entitling to a pension, *the job is not pensionable* [F.]

pen·sion·ar·y (pénʃəneri:) **1.** *pl.* **pen·sion·ar·ies** *n.* a person who receives a pension ‖ a hireling **2.** *adj.* of, consisting of, relating to or receiving a pension [fr. M.L. *pensionarius*]

pen·sion·er (pénʃənər) *n.* a person who receives a pension ‖ (*Cambridge Univ.*) a student who pays for his room, board etc. [A.F. *pensionner*]

pen·sive (pénsiv) *adj.* deep in serious thought ‖ showing this state, *a pensive look* [F. *pensif, pensive*]

pen·stock (pénstɒk) *n.* a sluice gate for controlling the flow of water ‖ a conduit or channel by which water is led to a mill wheel etc. to make it work

pent (pent) *adj.* (usually with 'up' or 'in') shut in, confined, *pent up in school* [past part. of *pend,* obs. var. of PEN, to shut up]

penta- (péntə) *prefix* five [fr. Gk *pente,* five]

pen·ta·cle (péntək'l) *n.* (*hist.*) an ancient, five-pointed, star-shaped magical symbol [M.L. *pentaculum*]

pen·tad (péntæd) *n.* a group of five ‖ a period of five days or years ‖ a pentavalent element, atom or radical [fr. Gk *pentas* (*pentados*) fr. *pente,* five]

pen·ta·dac·tyl (pentədǽktil) *adj.* having five digits on the hand or foot ‖ having five parts like fingers [fr. PENTA-+Gk *dactulos,* finger]

pen·ta·gas·trin (pentəgǽstrin) *n.* (*pharm.*) gastric-secretion stimulant often used to measure secretory capacity

pen·ta·gon (péntəgon) *n.* a plane figure with five angles and five sides **the Pentagon** a pentagonal building in Arlington, Virginia, headquarters of the U.S. Department of Defense **pen·tag·o·nal** (pentǽgən'l) *adj.* [fr. L. *pentagonum* fr. Gk]

Pentagon Papers the mainly top-secret findings of an official U.S. survey ordered by President Lyndon B. Johnson's secretary of defense, Robert McNamara. The survey covered the decision-making process in the Vietnam War up until 1968. Publication (1971) of a purloined copy by the 'New York Times' and the 'Washington Post' provoked the Richard Nixon administration to attempt to impose prior restraint

pen·ta·gram (péntəgræm) *n.* a pentacle [fr. Gk *pentagrammon, pentegrammon* fr. *pente,* five+*gramma,* letter]

pen·ta·he·dral (pentəhí:drəl) *adj.* (of a solid figure) having five plane surfaces **pen·ta·hé·dron** *n.* such a solid figure [fr. PENTA-+Gk *hedra,* base, seat]

pen·tam·er·ous (pentǽmərəs) *adj.* (*biol.*) composed of five parts, esp. having whorls of five or a multiple of five parts [fr. PENTA-+Gk *meros,* part]

pen·tam·e·ter (pentǽmitər) *n.* a line of English verse, consisting of ten syllables forming five iambic feet ‖ a line of Latin or Greek verse, consisting of five feet [L. fr. Gk fr. *pente,* five+*metron,* measure]

pen·tane (péntein) *n.* one of three isomeric, low-boiling hydrocarbons, C_5H_{12}, found in petroleum. Two are liquid, one is a gas [fr. Gk *pente,* five]

pen·ta·pep·tide (pentəpéptaid) *n.* (*biochem.*) compound containing five amino acids linked by -CONH- (carbon, oxygen, nitrogen and hydrogen)

pen·ta·stich (péntəstik) *n.* a stanza or poem consisting of five lines [fr. Mod. L. *pentastichus* fr. Gk fr. *pente,* five+*stichos,* line of verse]

Pen·ta·teuch (péntətu:k, péntətju:k) *n.* the first five books of the Old Testament: Genesis, Exodus, Leviticus, Numbers and Deuteronomy. They are commonly attributed to Moses, but held by scholars to be a composite work of documents dating from the 9th c. B.C. to the 4th c. B.C. **Pén·ta·teuch·al** *adj.* [fr. L. *pentateuchus* fr. Gk fr. *pente,* five+*teuchos,* implement, book]

pen·tath·lon (pentǽθlɒn) *n.* an athletic competition in which each competitor has to take part in five events. In the present Olympic Games these are horseback riding, swimming, fencing, shooting and running [Gk fr. *pente,* five+*athlon,* competition]

pen·ta·va·lent (péntəveilənt, pentǽvələnt) *adj.* (*chem.*) having a valence of five (cf. QUINQUEVALENT) [fr. PENTA-+L. *valens* (*valentis*) fr. *valere,* to be strong]

pen·ta·zo·are [$C_{19}H_{27}NO$] (pentəzóuɑr) *n.* (*pharm.*) minimally addictive pain reliever used as a morphine substitute; marketed as Talwin

Pen·te·cost (péntikɔst, péntikɒst) *n.* the Jewish festival of Shabuoth ‖ the Christian festival celebrated on Whitsunday seven weeks after Easter in commemoration of the coming of the Holy Ghost (Acts ii) **Pen·te·cós·tal** *adj.* of Pentecost ‖ of or pertaining to the Holy Ghost [fr. L. *pentecoste* fr. Gk *pentēcostē* (*hēmera*), the fiftieth (day)]

Pen·thes·i·le·a (penθesilí:ə) queen of the Amazons, killed by Achilles in the siege of Troy

pent·house (pénthaus) *pl.* **pent·hous·es** (pénthauziz) *n.* a shed or other structure built against a main building with its roof sloping away from the larger building's wall ‖ a sloping roof projecting from the wall of a building to form a shelter ‖ a rooftop apartment or other structure [fr. older *pentice* fr. M.E., prob. fr. O.F. *apentis,* small sacred building dependent on a larger church]

pen·tode (péntoud) *adj.* (*phys.*) of a thermionic valve which has five electrodes (anode, cathode, control grid, screen grid and suppressor grid) [fr. PENTA-+Gk *hodos,* way]

pen·to·mi·no (pentəmí:nou) *n.* a many-sided, shaped figure designed to cover five squares on a game board

pen·tose (péntous) *n.* any of a group of monosaccharides having five carbon atoms in the molecule

pe·nult (pí:nʌlt, pinʌ́lt) *n.* the last syllable but one of a word or verse [shortened fr. PENULTIMATE and fr. older *penultima*]

pe·nul·ti·mate (pinʌ́ltəmit) **1.** *adj.* last but one **2.** *n.* the last syllable but one [fr. L. *paene,* almost+ULTIMATE]

pe·num·bra (pinʌ́mbrə) *pl.* **pe·num·bras, pe·num·brae** (pinʌ́mbri:) *n.* the partial shadow cast by a body where light from a given source is not wholly excluded, e.g. in an eclipse ‖ the outer shaded part of a sunspot **pe·núm·bral** *adj.* [Mod. L. fr. L. *paene,* almost+*umbra,* shade]

pe·nu·ri·ous (pənúəri:əs, pənjúəri:əs) *adj.* poor or showing extreme poverty [fr. M.L. *penuriosus* fr. L. *penuria,* poverty]

pen·u·ry (pénjəri:) *n.* poverty ‖ lack, scarcity, *penury of ideas* [fr. L. *penuria, paenuria*]

Pe·nu·ti·an (pənú:ti:ən, pənú:ʃən) *n.* a North American Indian linguistic stock including several linguistic families and extending from British Columbia to Mexico. There are about 5,000 Penutian-speaking Indians

Pen·za (pénzə) a rail center and river port (pop. 500,000) of the central R.S.F.S.R., U.S.S.R., 350 miles southeast of Moscow: lumber, pulp and paper, food processing, textiles, mechanical engineering

pe·on (pí:ən, pí:ɒn) *n.* (in Latin America) a laborer, esp. formerly one compelled to work for a master in order to work on a debt ‖ (in India, pju:n) an Indian foot soldier, policeman or servant ‖ any laborer **pe·on·age** (pí:ənidʒ) *n.* the condition of a peon ‖ (*loosely*) servitude of any kind [Span. *peon* and fr. Port. *peao,* pedestrian, F. *pion,* foot soldier fr. L. *pes,* foot]

pe·o·ny (pí:əni:) *pl.* **pe·o·nies** *n.* a member of *Paeonia,* fam. *Ranunculaceae,* a genus of usually herbaceous plants native to Europe and Asia, widely cultivated for their large, showy single or double red, pink, yellow or white flowers [O.E. *peonie* fr. L.L. fr. Gk]

peo·ple (pí:p'l) **1.** *pl. n.* human beings, *you can't treat people like cattle* ‖ other persons in general, *what will people say?* ‖ a collective group of persons, *village people* ‖ one's family or parents **a people** the members of a particular race or nation **the people** the working classes as contrasted with the privileged ‖ the electorate **2.** *v.t. pres. part.* **peo·pling** *past* and *past part.* **peo·pled** to populate ‖ to fill as if with people, *his memoirs are peopled with imaginary creatures* [A.F. *poeple, people* fr. L. *populus,* the populace]

people movers horizontal escalators; moving sidewalks

people sniffer chemical-electronic device for detecting persons

people's republic a Communist republic modeled on the U.S.S.R., such as was formed after the 2nd world war in many countries, e.g. in Albania, Bulgaria, Poland, China, North Korea

Pe·o·ri·a (pi:ɔ́ri:ə, pi:óuri:ə) an agricultural market city (pop. 124,160) of central Illinois: farm machinery, corn liquor

pep (pep) **1.** *n.* (*pop.*) energy, liveliness **2.** *v.t. pres. part.* **pep·ping** *past* and *past part.* **pepped** to put new life into, *to pep up a dull party* [shortened fr. PEPPER]

PEP (*acronym*) **P**ositron **E**lectron **P**roject, 1½-mi. ring accelerator at Stanford University, established in 1980

Pé·pin I (pépin, peipɛ̃) 'the Elder' (c. 580–c. 639), mayor of the palace of Austrasia (c. 615–c. 639), and ancestor of the Carolingian dynasty

Pépin II 'of Héristal' (c. 640–c. 714), mayor of the palace of Austrasia (c. 680–c. 714), grandson of Pépin I. His victory (687) over Neustria gave him effective rule over all the Frankish kingdoms of the Merovingians

Pépin III 'the Short' (c. 714–68), first Carolingian king of the Franks (751–68), son of Charles Martel. In return for the pope's support in obtaining the throne, he defended Rome (754) against the Lombards, and ceded to the pope the nucleus of the Papal States

pep·lum (pépləm) *n.* a short flounce joined to a waist or jacket and covering the hips [L. fr. Gk *peplos,* a large scarf worn around the body by women]

pe·po (pí:pou) *pl.* **pe·pos** *n.* the fleshy many-seeded fruit with firm rind of any plant of fam. *Cucurbitaceae,* order *Campanulales,* e.g. a pumpkin, melon or cucumber [L.=pumpkin]

pep·per (pépər) **1.** *n.* a product consisting of the dried, usually ground fruit of *Piper nigrum,* fam. *Piperaceae,* a plant native to the East Indies and cultivated in the Tropics. It is used universally as a culinary seasoning (*BLACK PEPPER, *WHITE PEPPER) ‖ this plant ‖ any of several similar condiments, e.g. cayenne pepper ‖ any of several plants of genus *Capsicum,* fam. *Solanaceae,* esp. *C. frutescens,* universally found in warm climates ‖ the fruit of any of these, e.g. the sweet pepper and the red pepper **2.** *v.t.* to season with the ground fruit of *Piper nigrum* ‖ to sprinkle or pelt as if with this [O.E. *pipor* fr. L. *piper* fr. Gk fr. an Oriental source]

pepper-and-salt *adj.* (of cloth or hair) having light and dark threads or hairs so closely mixed that they produce a speckled effect

pep·per·corn (pépərkɔrn) *n.* the dried berry of *Piper nigrum,* the pepper plant

peppercorn rent a purely nominal rent imposed to safeguard the rights of the owner

pepper gas riot-control gas that causes irritation of nose and throat. *also* pepper fog

pep·per·mint (pépərmint) *n.* *Mentha piperita,* fam. *Labiatae,* a small, perennial, aromatic plant with toothed leaves and pale purple flowers, native to Europe, but now found wild and cultivated in most temperate zones ‖ an oil with an aromatic taste, distilled from its leaves, stems and flowers, used in confectionery etc. ‖ a candy flavored with this ‖ any of several related plants, e.g. *M. arvensis*

pepper pot a West Indian dish of stewed meat or fish and vegetables incl. red peppers ‖ a highly seasoned soup

pepper shaker a small container with holes in the top, for sprinkling pepper on food

pepper tree *Schinus molle,* fam. *Anacardiaceae,* a tropical American evergreen tree which bears pungent red berries

pep·per·y (pépəri:) *adj.* containing or tasting of pepper ‖ irascible ‖ (of language, words etc.) fiery, biting

pep·py (pépi:) *comp.* **pep·pi·er** *superl.* **pep·pi·est** *adj.* full of pep

pep·sin (pépsin) *n.* an enzyme secreted in the stomach of higher vertebrates which, together with diluted hydrochloric acid, aids digestion by converting proteins into peptones ‖ a preparation containing this enzyme extracted from the stomach of a hog, calf etc. and used as a digestive aid etc. [fr. Gk *pepsis,* digestion]

pep·tic (péptik) *adj.* helping digestion, esp. by the action of pepsin ‖ of, like or involving pepsin ‖ relating to digestion or to gastric juice [fr. Gk *peptikos,* able to digest]

peptic gland one of the glands secreting gastric juice

peptic ulcer an ulcer of the stomach or duodenum resulting from the abnormal action of pepsin and other gastric juices on the mucous membrane of these areas. The term includes gastric and duodenal ulcers

pep·tide (péptaid, péptid) *n.* an amide formed by the condensation of certain amino acids [PEPTONE]

pep·tone (péptoun) *n.* any of several substances, produced by the action of pepsin on proteins, which are soluble and can be absorbed by the bloodstream **pep·to·nize** *pres. part.* **pep·to·niz·ing** *past* and *past part.* **pep·to·nized** *v.t.* to convert into a peptone [fr. G. *pepton* fr. Gk neuter of *peptos* adj., cooked, digested]

Pepys (pi:ps), Samuel (1633–1703), English diarist and naval administrator. As secretary to the admiralty (1673–9 and 1684–9), he expanded and reformed the administration of the English navy, and played an important part in the political life of the Restoration. His 'Diary' provides a vivid account of events in the period 1660–9 and is an intimate record of the daily life of the time. He was president of the Royal Society (1684–6) and wrote 'Memoirs Relating to the Royal Navy' (1690)

Pe·quot War of 1637 (pí:kwɒt) a war between the settlers of the American colony of Connecticut and the Pequot Indians, precipitated by the murder of John Oldham (c. 1600–1636), an English trader, by the Pequots. The Indians where virtually exterminated, while those taken captive were enslaved

per- *prefix* through, throughout ‖ thoroughly, completely ‖ (*chem.*) containing a large or the largest possible proportion of a specified element or radical [L.]

per (pə:r, pər) *prep.* for each, *three dollars per person* ‖ by means of, *send it per diplomatic agent* [L.]

per·ad·ven·ture (pə:rədvéntʃər) *adv.* (*old-fash., rhet.*) perhaps, possibly [M.E. *perauenture, parauenture* fr. O.F.]

Pe·rae·a (perí:ə) (*hist.*) the Roman name for Gilead

Pe·rak (péirɑk, pérə) a state (area 7,980 sq. miles, pop. 1,762,288) of Malaysia in N. Malaya, the chief tin-producing region. Capital: Ipoh. It became a British protectorate (1874) and joined the Federation of Malaya (1948)

per·am·bu·late (pərǽmbjuleit) *pres. part.* **per·am·bu·lat·ing** *past* and *past part.* **per·am·bu·lat·ed** *v.t.* (*rhet.*) to walk through, *to preambulate the countryside* ‖ *v.i.* (*rhet.*) to walk about, stroll [fr. L. *perambulare* (*perambulatus*)]

per·am·bu·la·tion (pərǽmbjuléiʃən) *n.* (*rhet.*) the act of perambulating ‖ (*rhet.*) a walk or stroll [A.F. and fr. M.L. *perambulatio* (*perambulationis*)]

per·am·bu·la·tor (pərǽmbjuleitər) *n.* (*Br.*) a baby carriage ‖ a wheeled odometer used by surveyors [fr. L. *perambulare* (*perambulatus*), to walk about]

per an·num (pərǽnəm) *adv.* (*abbr.* per an.) yearly, *he is paid $15,000 per annum* [L.]
per·brom·ic acid [$HBrO_{24}$] (pərbróumikǽsid) *n.* (*chem.*) bromine in its highest oxidation state; synthesized in 1968
per·cale (pərkéil) *n.* a smooth, closely woven cotton material [F. fr. Pers. *pargāl*]
per cap·i·ta (pərkǽpitə) *adv.* and *adj.* (*abbr.* per cap.) per head of population for each person [L.=by heads]
per·ceiv·a·ble (pərsí:vəb'l) *adj.* capable of being perceived or discerned **per·céiv·a·bly** *adv.*
per·ceive (pərsí:v) *pres. part.* **per·ceiv·ing** *past* and *past part.* **per·ceived** *v.t.* to become aware of through the senses, e.g. by hearing or seeing ‖ to become aware of by understanding, discern [fr. O.F. *perçoivre* fr. L.]
per·cent (pərsént) (*abbr.* p.c., pct, per ct. *symbol %*) **1.** *adv.* in a hundred, for each hundred, *prices have risen 6 percent in the past year* **2.** *pl.* **per·cent, per·cents** *n.* a hundredth part, *12 is 1 percent of 1,200* ‖ percentage, the amount or rate per hundred **per·cént·age** *n.* rate or proportion per hundred ‖ (*loosely*) a proportion, *a good percentage of the output goes to waste* **per·cen·tile** (pərséntail, pərséntil) *n.* (*statistics*) one of a hundred parts, each containing an equal number of members, into which a series of individual things, persons etc. has been divided **per·cents** *pl. n.* securities yielding a specified rate of interest, *to invest in 5 percents* [fr. L. *per centum*]
per cen·tum (pərséntəm) percent [L.]
per·cept (pɔ́:rsept) *n.* (*philos.*) a product of perception, a recognizable mental impression of something perceived [fr. L. *perceptum*]
per·cep·ti·bil·i·ty (pərsȩptəbíliti:) *n.* the quality of being perceptible
per·cep·ti·ble (pərséptəb'l) *adj.* capable of being perceived **per·cép·ti·bly** *adv.* [fr. L.L. *perceptibilis* fr. *percipere* (*perceptus*), to perceive]
per·cep·tion (pərsépʃən) *n.* the act of perceiving, *visual perception* ‖ the ability to perceive, esp. to understand ‖ (*philos.*) the action of the mind in referring sensations to the object which caused them (cf. SENSATION) ‖ (*psychol.*) awareness through the senses of an external object ‖ (*psychol.*) a percept ‖ (*law*) the collection of rents etc. **per·cép·tion·al** *adj.* of or having the nature of perception [O.F. and perh. fr. L. *perceptio* (*perceptionis*)]
per·cep·tive (pərséptiv) *adj.* capable of perceiving ‖ having or showing keen understanding or insight **per·cep·tiv·i·ty** (pərsȩptíviti:) *n.* [fr. L. *percipere* (*perceptus*)]
per·cep·tu·al (pərséptʃu:əl) *adj.* relating to or involving esp. sensory perception [fr. L. *percipere* (*perceptus*)]
Per·ce·val (pɔ́:rsivəl), Spencer (1762–1812), British statesman, Tory prime minister of Britain (1809–12). He was assassinated
perch (pə:rtʃ) *n. Perca fluviatilis,* fam. *Percidae,* a small, edible European freshwater fish with a broad, laterally flattened body and spiny fins ‖ *Perca flavescens,* a related North American food fish ‖ any of several related freshwater and marine fishes [F. *perche* fr. L. fr. Gk]
perch *n.* anything on which a bird alights or rests, e.g. a horizontal bar in a cage ‖ any resting place, esp. an elevated or temporary one, *he had a good view from his perch on the rooftop* ‖ (esp. *Br.*) a rod (measure of length) ‖ (esp. *Br.*) a square rod (measure of area) ‖ any of several cubic measures for stone, used in building ‖ a central pole joining the front and rear axles of a carriage [F. *perche*]
perch *v.i.* (of a bird) to alight or sit ‖ to sit or settle on or as if on a perch, *the child perched on his knee* ‖ *v.t.* to place on or as if on a perch [F. *percher*]
per·chance (pərtʃǽns, pərtʃɑ́ns) *adv.* (*rhet.*) perhaps, maybe [M.E. fr. A.F. *par chance,* by chance]
Perche (perʃ) an old French county west-southwest of Paris, finally united to the crown in 1525
perched water (*envir.*) ground water separated from underlying water table by a zone of impervious material. —**perched water table** *n.*
perch·er (pɔ́:rtʃər) *n.* a passerine bird
Per·che·ron (pɔ́:rtʃərɒn, pɔ́:rʃərɒn) *n.* a strong, fast-trotting cart horse of a breed that originated in Perche, France [F.]
per·chlo·rate (pə:rklɔ́reit, pə:rklóureit) *n.* a salt of perchloric acid
per·chlo·ric acid (pə:rklɔ́rik, pə:rklóurik) a strong, fuming, colorless acid, $HClO_4$, used in chemical analysis, in electroplating and as a catalyst
per·chlo·ride (pə:rklɔ́raid, pə:rklóuraid) *n.* a chloride having a relatively high proportion of chlorine
per·cip·i·ence (pərsípi:əns) *n.* power of perception **per·cíp·i·en·cy** *n.*
per·cip·i·ent (pərsípi:ənt) **1.** *adj.* readily capable of perceiving **2.** *n.* someone who perceives [fr. L. *percipiens* (*percipientis*) fr. *percipere,* to perceive]
per·co·late (pɔ́:rkəleit) *pres. part.* **per·co·lat·ing** *past* and *past part.* **per·co·lat·ed** *v.i.* to seep through a porous substance ‖ to become diffused, *to allow a rumor to percolate* ‖ (of coffee) to be brewed in a percolator ‖ *v.t.* to cause to filter gradually through a porous substance ‖ (of a liquid) to permeate (a substance) in this way ‖ to prepare (coffee) in a percolator [fr. L. *percolare* (*percolatus*), to strain]
per·co·la·tion (pə̧:rkəléiʃən) *n.* a percolating or being percolated [fr. L. *percolatio* (*percolationis*)]
per·co·la·tor (pɔ́:rkəlȩitər) *n.* a machine for percolating, esp. one for preparing coffee as a drink by passing boiling water repeatedly through the ground beans [fr. L. *percolare* (*percolatus*)]
per·cuss (pərkʌ́s) *v.t.* (*med.*) to tap (a part of the body) in order to make a diagnosis [fr. L. *percutere* (*percussus*), to strike]
per·cus·sion (pərkʌ́ʃən) *n.* the act of causing one body to make a sudden impact on another ‖ such an impact ‖ the sound produced by this ‖ (*med.*) the percussing of a body part ‖ (*mus.*) percussion instruments collectively, esp. as a section of an orchestra or band [fr. L. *percussio* (*percussionis*)]
percussion cap a small vessel containing a substance which initiates the explosion of the main body of explosive in the cartridge, shell, mine etc. to which it is fitted
percussion instrument a musical instrument in which the sound is produced by striking, e.g. a cymbal or drum
per·cus·sive (pərkʌ́siv) *adj.* of or characterized by percussion [fr. L. *percutere* (*percussus*), to strike]
Per·cy (pɔ́:rsi:), Sir Henry (1364–1403), called 'Harry Hotspur', English nobleman. He fought against the Scots, the French and the Welsh and was killed while leading a rebellion against Henry IV
Percy, Thomas (1729–1811), Bishop of Dromore and antiquarian. His 'Reliques of Ancient English Poetry' (1765) opened up the realm of ballads and folk literature to writers of the Romantic movement
Percy, Walker (1916–) U.S. novelist. He trained as a physician and practiced medicine for a year before contracting tuberculosis. During his convalescence he read existentialist philosophers, which influenced his writing in such novels as 'The Moviegoer' (1961; National Book Award, 1962), 'The Last Gentleman' (1966) and 'Love in the Ruins' (1971). Other novels include 'Lancelot' (1977), examining religious faith, and 'The Second Coming' (1980), dealing with mental breakdown
per di·em (pərdí:əm, pərdáiəm) **1.** *adv.* daily, by the day **2.** *adj.* daily, *a per diem allowance* **3.** *n.* the money allotted to someone, e.g. a salesman, for expenses incurred in connection with work [L.]
per·di·tion (pərdíʃən) *n.* damnation, eternal death [M.E. fr. O.F. *perdiciun*]
per·dur·a·bil·i·ty (pərdu̧ərəbíliti:, pərdju̧ərəbíliti:) *n.* the quality or state of being perdurable
per·dur·a·ble (pərdúərəb'l, pərdjúərəb'l) *adj.* (*theol.*) eternal ‖ (*rhet.*) extremely durable **per·dúr·a·bly** *adv.* [O.F. *perdurable, pardurable* fr. L.L.]
per·e·gri·nate (périgrineit) *pres. part.* **per·e·gri·nat·ing** *past* and *past part.* **per·e·gri·nat·ed** *v.i.* (*rhet.*) to travel about on foot ‖ *v.t.* (*rhet.*) to travel through [fr. L. *peregrinari* (*pergrinatus*), to travel abroad]
per·e·gri·na·tion (pȩrigrinéiʃən) *n.* (*rhet.*) a wandering about [F. *pérégrination* or fr. L. *peregrinatio* (*peregrinationis*)]
per·e·grine (périgrin, périgri:n) *n. Falco peregrinus,* fam. *Falconidae,* a bird of prey used in falconry. It is dark with a whitish breast, and has long pointed wings and tail. It is very swift in flight [fr. L. *peregrinus,* foreign (because peregrines were caught during migration)]
pe·rei·ra (pəréirə) *n. Geissospermum vellosii,* fam. *Apocynaceae,* a Brazilian tree yielding a bark used as a tonic etc. ‖ the bark itself [after Jonathan *Pereira* (1804–53), Eng. professor]
Perelman (pə́rlmən), S(idney) J(oseph) (1904–79) U.S. humorist, playwright and screenwriter, who used parody, hyperbole, puns and an extensive vocabulary in his satirical works. He wrote regularly for 'The New Yorker' from 1931 and his books include 'The Road to Miltown; or, Under the Spreading Atrophy' (1957) and 'Eastwood Ha!' (1977). His most successful Broadway play was 'One Touch of Venus' (1943), written with Ogden Nash and Kurt Weill
per·emp·to·ri·ly (pərémptərili:) *adv.* in a peremptory manner
per·emp·to·ri·ness (pərémptəri:nis) *n.* the quality of being peremptory
per·emp·to·ry (pərémptəri:, pérəmptə̧ri:, pérəmptou̧ri:) *adj.* imperious, curtly authoritative ‖ that cannot be denied or refused, *a peremptory command* ‖ (*law,* pérəmptəri:) final, absolute [fr. L. *peremptorius,* destructive, decisive]
per·en·ni·al (pəréni:əl) **1.** *adj.* perpetual, long-lasting, *a perennial source of amusement* ‖ (*bot.*) living more than two years ‖ (of a stream etc.) remaining active or lasting throughout the year **2.** *n.* perennial plant (cf. ANNUAL, cf. BIENNIAL) [fr. L. *perennis,* lasting through the year or years]
Peres (pérez), Shimon (1933–) Israeli political figure, a founder of the Labor party (1968) and prime minister (1984–). A protégé of David Ben-Gurion, he was elected to the Knesset (parliament) (1959) and held cabinet posts including that of defense minister (1974–7). He was leader of the opposition (1977–84)
Pé·rez Gal·dós (péreθgɑldɔ́s), Benito (1843–1920), Spanish novelist and dramatist. His 'Episodios Nacionales' (1873–1912) is a series of 46 novels based on Spanish history. His other works include the novels 'Doña Perfecta' (1876) and 'Fortunata y Jacinta' (1886–7). His objectivity and realism, together with his subtle observation and powers of characterization, make him a major figure in Spanish literature
Pé·rez Ji·mé·nez (péreshi:ménes), Marcos (1914–), Venezuelan soldier and dictator (1952–8) until his overthrow
per·fect (pɔ́:rfikt) **1.** *adj.* complete or correct in every way, conforming to a standard or ideal with no omissions, errors, flaws or extraneous elements ‖ utter, absolute, *a perfect idiot* ‖ (*gram.,* of a tense) expressing the completion of an action at the time of speaking or at the time indicated ‖ (*bot.,* of a plant or its flowers) hermaphrodite ‖ (*bot.,* of fungi) producing sexual spores ‖ (*mus.,* of the intervals of fourth, fifth or octave) neither major nor minor in character, remaining unaltered in character when inverted **2.** *n.* (*gram.*) the perfect tense **3.** (pərfékt) *v.t.* to put the finishing touches to, make as good as possible, *to perfect one's piano technique* [M.E. *parfit* fr. O.F.]
per·fect·a (pə:rféktɑ) *n.* (*horse racing*) method of betting on horse racing, placing combined bet on both first and second places in a horse race. *Cf* EXACTA
perfect binding book-binding technique using glue to replace sewing. —**perfect bound** *adj.*
perfect cadence (*mus.*) a cadence consisting of a dominant chord leading to the tonic chord in root position
per·fect·i·bil·i·ty (pərfȩktəbíliti:) *n.* the quality of being perfectible
per·fect·i·ble (pərféktəb'l) *adj.* capable of being perfected
perfecting machine (*Br.*) a perfecting press
perfecting press (*Am.*=*Br.* perfecting machine) a printing machine that prints both sides of the paper before the paper leaves the machine
per·fec·tion (pərfékʃən) *n.* the quality or state of being perfect ‖ an instance of this, *she is tired of hearing about her mother-in-law's perfections* ‖ a perfecting or being perfected **to perfection** perfectly, *he mimics her to perfection* **per·féc·tion·ism** *n.* the theory of the moral perfectibility of man **per·féc·tion·ist** *n.* a person who is not content with anything less than the very best [O.F.]
per·fec·tive (pərféktiv) **1.** *adj.* (*gram.,* e.g. in Russian) of a verbal aspect which expresses a completed action or state **2.** *n.* the perfective aspect ‖ a verb in this aspect
per·fec·to (pərféktou) *pl.* **per·fec·tos** *n.* a thick cigar that tapers at both ends [Span.=perfect]

CONCISE PRONUNCIATION KEY: **(a)** æ, *cat;* ɑ, *car;* ɔ *fawn;* ei, *snake.* **(e)** e, *hen;* i:, *sheep;* iə, *deer;* εə, *bear.* **(i)** i, *fish;* ai, *tiger;* ə:, *bird.* **(o)** o, *ox;* au, *cow;* ou, *goat;* u, *poor;* ɔi, *royal.* **(u)** ʌ, *duck;* u, *bull;* u:, *goose;* ə, *bacillus;* ju:, *cube.* x, *loch;* θ, *think;* ð, *bother;* z, *Zen;* ʒ, *corsage;* dʒ, *savage;* ŋ, *orangutang;* j, *yak;* ʃ, *fish;* tʃ, *fetch;* 'l, *rabble;* 'n, *redden.* Complete pronunciation key appears inside front cover.

per·fec·tor (pərféktər) *n.* a perfecting press [L.=someone who or something that perfects]
perfect participle (*gram.*) past participle
perfect pitch absolute pitch (ability to identify a note)
per·fer·vid (pərfə́:rvid) *adj.* (*rhet.*) very or excessively fervent [fr. Mod. L. *perfervidus* fr. L. *per,* very+*fervidus,* fervid]
per·fid·i·ous (pərfídi:əs) *adj.* characterized by, involving or guilty of perfidy [fr. L. *perfidiosus*]
per·fi·dy (pə́:rfidi:) *pl.* **per·fi·dies** *n.* treachery, faithlessness ‖ an instance of this [F. *perfidie*]
per·fo·li·ate (pərfóuli:it, pərfóuli:eit) *adj.* (*bot.*, of a leaf) having the basal lobes united around the stem so that the stem appears to pierce through the leaf [fr. PER-+L. *folium,* leaf]
per·fo·rate (pə́:rfəreit) *pres. part.* **per·fo·rat·ing** *past* and *past part.* **per·fo·rat·ed** *v.t.* to make a hole through, pierce, *a perforated eardrum* ‖ to make a row of holes through (paper etc.) so that it can easily be pulled into parts ‖ *v.i.* to make a perforation [fr. L. *perforare* (*perforatus*)]
per·fo·ra·tion (pə:rfəréiʃən) *n.* a perforating or being perforated ‖ a small hole cut or punched into something ‖ a series of holes made in paper etc. to facilitate division ‖ (*philately*) one of such a series of holes on a sheet of postage stamps ‖ (*philately*) one of the teeth left on a stamp after it has been torn off the sheet ‖ (*philately*) a classification according to the number of such teeth per 20 mm. [fr. L.L. *perforatio* (*perforationis*)]
per·fo·ra·tor (pə́:rfəreitər) *n.* a machine for making perforations [fr. L. *perforare,* to perforate]
per·force (pərfɔ́rs, pərfóurs) *adv.* (*rhet.*) through necessity [M.E. fr. O.F. *parforce,* by force]
per·form (pərfɔ́rm) *v.t.* to do, fulfill, carry out, accomplish (an action, obligation etc.) ‖ to render, execute (a stage role, play, piece of music, dance etc.), esp. before an audience ‖ *v.i.* to execute a stage role, play, piece of music etc., esp. in public, *the soloist performed poorly* ‖ to carry out, accomplish an action, function etc., *the engine performs well in cold weather* **per·fór·mance** *n.* the act of performing ‖ an instance of this, *there will be no performance of the play tonight* ‖ the quality or manner of performing, *to judge a car's performance* ‖ something performed, a deed, feat etc. [M.E. fr. O.F. *parfourmer, perfourmer*]
performance what is accomplished, contrasted with capability
per·form·a·tive (pərfɔ́rmətiv) *adj.* (*linguistics*) of a statement of performance; e.g., *I go. Cf* CONSTATIVE
per·fume (pə́:rfju:m, pərfjú:m) *n.* a sweet smell ‖ a sweet-smelling liquid for personal use prepared from essential oils from flowers or aromatic chemicals and fixed, e.g. with musk [F. *parfum*]
per·fume (pərfjú:m) *pres. part.* **per·fum·ing** *past* and *past part.* **per·fumed** *v.t.* to give a sweet smell to ‖ to apply perfume to **per·fúm·er** *n.* a person who or firm that makes or sells perfumes **per·fúm·er·y** *pl.* **per·fum·er·ies** *n.* a place where perfumes are manufactured ‖ the technique or business of making perfume ‖ perfumes collectively [F. *parfumer*]
per·func·to·ri·ly (pərfʌ́ŋktərili:) *adj.* in a perfunctory manner
per·func·to·ri·ness (pərfʌ́ŋktəri:nis) *n.* the quality of being perfunctory
per·func·to·ry (pərfʌ́ŋktəri:) *adj.* behaving or performing in an offhand manner without any show of interest or concern ‖ done, given etc. in this way, *a perfunctory kiss* [fr. L.L. *perfunctorius,* done carelessly or superficially]
per·fuse (pərfjú:z) *v.t. pres. part.* **per·fus·ing** *past* and *past part.* **per·fused** to cover or suffuse with a liquid ‖ to cause (a liquid) to flow over or through something [fr. L. *perfundere* (*perfusus*)]
per·fu·sion (pərfjú:ʒən) *n.* the act or an instance of perfusing, esp. a pouring over of water in baptism [fr. L. *perfundere* (*perfusus*)]
Per·ga·mum (pə́:rgəməm) an ancient city of N.W. Asia Minor (modern Bergama, Turkey, pop. 20,000). It was a powerful Hellenistic city (3rd–2nd cc. B.C.), famous for its library. Remains include the acropolis, amphitheater and temples
per·go·la (pə́:rgələ) *n.* a bower or covered walk made by training climbing plants over a trellis or similar support [Ital.]
Per·go·le·si (pergɔlézi:), Giovanni Battista (1701–36), Italian composer. His known works include the comic intermezzo 'La Serva Padrona' (1733), other operas, instrumental music and the 'Stabat Mater' (1736) for women's voices
per·haps (pərhǽps) *adv.* possibly, maybe [fr. PER+M.E. *hap,* chance, accident]
pe·ri (píəri:) *pl.* **pe·ris** *n.* (*Pers. mythol.*) a good fairy (originally an evil one) descended from fallen angels and excluded from Paradise ‖ a fairylike creature [fr. Pers. *pārī* or *perī*]
peri- (péri) *prefix* around, surrounding ‖ near [Gk prep. and adv.]
Per·i·an·der (péri:ændər) (*d.* 585 B.C.), Greek statesman, tyrant of Corinth (625–585 B.C.), one of the Seven Sages of Greece. Corinth reached a peak of prosperity and culture under his rule
per·i·anth (péri:ænθ) *n.* (*bot.*) the envelope of external floral whorls including calyx and corolla, esp. when these are not easily distinguished ‖ a cover or ring of cells surrounding the archegonium of certain bryophytes [fr. Mod. L. *perianthum* fr. Gk *peri,* around+*anthos,* flower]
per·i·ap·sis, pl **-ses, -sides** (peri:ǽpsis) *n.* (*astron.*) point in a celestial orbit nearest the center of the attraction. *Cf* HIGHER APSIS, LOWER APSIS
per·i·apt (péri:æpt) *n.* something worn as a charm [F. *périapte* fr. Gk]
per·i·car·di·ac (perikɑ́rdi:æk) *adj.* pericardial
per·i·car·di·al (perikɑ́rdi:əl) *adj.* of or pertaining to the pericardium
per·i·car·di·um (perikɑ́rdi:əm) *pl.* **per·i·car·di·a** (perikɑ́rdi:ə) *n.* the conical membranous sac enveloping the heart in vertebrates ‖ the cavity surrounding the heart in invertebrates [fr. Gk *perikardion* fr. *peri,* around+*kardia,* the heart]
per·i·carp (périkɑrp) *n.* (*bot.*) the ripened walls of a plant ovary (*FRUIT) that may be more or less homogeneous or consist of up to three layers (*ENDOCARP, *MESOCARP, *EPICARP) [fr. Mod. L. *pericarpium,* fr. Gk *perikarpion,* pod, husk fr. *peri,* around+*karpos,* fruit]
per·i·chon·dri·um (perikɔ́ndri:əm) *pl.* **per·i·chon·dri·a** (perikɔ́ndri:ə) *n.* the layer of fibrous connective tissue covering the surface of cartilage except at joints [fr. PERI-+Gk *chondros,* cartilage]
per·i·clase (périkleis) *n.* oxide of magnesium, MgO, found commonly in metamorphosed magnesian limestones [fr. Mod. L. *periclasia* fr. Gk *peri,* very+*klasis,* breaking (from its perfect cleavage)]
Per·i·cle·an (perikli:ən) *adj.* of or concerning Pericles or his time
Per·i·cles (périkli:z) (c. 495–429 B.C.), Athenian statesman, leader of the democratic party and ruler of Athens (c. 460–429 B.C.). He was noted for his oratory, his strong, reserved character and his successful policies. He strengthened the Athenian maritime empire, lavishly patronized the arts, notably music and the drama, adorned the Acropolis and democratized the regime. He foresaw and provoked the Peloponnesian War, having previously fortified Piraeus and reconstructed the navy. His name is given to the most brilliant age of Greek history, 'Periclean Athens' standing for one of the highest achievements of civilization
per·i·cra·ni·um (perikréini:əm) *pl.* **per·i·cra·ni·a** (perikréini:ə) *n.* the membrane externally surrounding the bony or cartilaginous cranium of a vertebrate [M.L. or Mod. L. fr. Gk fr. *peri,* around+*kranion,* cranium]
per·i·cy·cle (périsaik'l) *n.* (*bot.*) a thin layer of nonconducting parenchyma cells separating the endodermis from the stele in stems and roots of higher plants and associated with the development of cambium [fr. Gk *perikuklos* fr. *peri,* around+*kuklos,* circle]
per·i·cyn·thi·on (perisínθi:ən) *n.* point in a lunar orbit nearest the moon. *also* perilune. *Cf* APOCYNTHION, APOLUNE
per·i·derm (péridə:rm) *n.* (*bot.*) a protective layer developing in the epidermis of many roots, stems and other plant organs that in maturity consists of an initiating layer (phellogen), an inner parenchyma (phelloderm) and an external cork layer (phellem) ‖ (*anat.*) the outer layer of the epidermis, esp. of an embryo ‖ (*zool.*) the external culticular layer of a hydroid [Mod. L. *peridermis* fr. Gk *peri,* around+*derma,* skin]
pe·rid·i·um (pərídi:əm) *pl.* **pe·rid·i·a** (pərídi:ə), **pe·rid·i·ums** *n.* the exterior wall which envelopes the sporophore of many fungi [Gk. *pēridion,* small wallet]
per·i·dot (péridɒt) *n.* olivine [F. *péridot*]
per·i·ge·al (peridʒí:əl) *adj.* perigean
per·i·ge·an (peridʒí:ən) *adj.* of or pertaining to the perigee
per·i·gee (péridʒi:) *n.* (*astron.*) the point in the orbit of the moon or another satellite of the earth when it is nearest to the earth (cf. APOGEE) [F. *périgée* fr. L.L. fr. Gk *peri,* around+*gē,* the earth]
pe·rig·y·nous (pərídʒinəs) *adj.* (*bot.*, of flowers) having the sepals, petals and stamens on the rim of the receptacle containing the pistil ‖ (*bot.*, of sepals, petals or stamens) borne on this rim [fr. Mod. L. *perigynus* fr. Gk. *peri,* around+*gunē,* woman (used for the pistil)]
per·i·he·li·on (perihí:li:ən, perihí:ljən) *pl.* **per·i·he·li·a** (perihí:li:ə, perihí:ljə) *n.* (*astron.*) the point of a comet's or planet's orbit when it is nearest to the sun (cf. APHELION) [fr. Mod. L. *perihelium* fr. Gk *peri,* around+*hēlios,* sun]
per·il (pérəl) *n.* risk of serious injury, destruction, disaster, etc. ‖ the state of being exposed to such risk **at** (or **to**) **one's peril** taking the risk and assuming the responsibility for the ill effects that are likely to result from it **in peril of** (*rhet.*) in danger of losing, *in peril of one's life* [F. *péril*]
per·il·ous (pérələs) *adj.* involving or exposing one to peril [A.E. *perillous*]
perilure *PERICYNTHION
Per·im (périm) an island (area 5 sq. miles, pop. 300) in the Strait of Bab El Mandeb. It is a dependency of the People's Democratic Republic of Yemen
pe·rim·e·ter (pərímitər) *n.* the line bounding a closed plane figure or an area on the ground ‖ the length of this line ‖ an optical instrument for testing a person's field of vision **per·i·met·ric** (perimétrik) *adj.* [fr. L. *perimetros* fr. Gk fr. *peri,* around+*metron,* a measure]
per·i·ne·al (periní:əl) *adj.* pertaining to or situated in the perineum
per·i·ne·um (periní:əm) *n.* the region around the opening of the rectum and bladder [L.L. fr. Gk]
per·i·nu·clear (perinú:kli:ər) *adj.* (*biol.*) around a cell nucleus
pe·ri·od (píəri:əd) **1.** *n.* a portion of time forming a division in a development, life, chronology, timetable, etc., *the Elizabethan period of English history, Picasso's blue period, the school day is divided into 7 periods* ‖ (*phys.*) the interval of time required for the completion of a single complete cycle of some periodic or cyclical phenomenon (e.g. the period of a planetary orbit or the period of a simple harmonic vibration), being equal to the reciprocal of the frequency (cf. WAVELENGTH, cf. WAVE NUMBER) ‖ (*chem.*) one of the divisions of the periodic table consisting of a sequence of elements of increasing atomic number beginning with an alkali metal and ending with an inert gas ‖ (*gram.*) a complete, esp. a complex, sentence ‖ a pause marking the completion of a sentence ‖ the symbol (.) denoting this pause, or following an abbreviation, or marking a decimal ‖ a single menstruation ‖ (*mus.*) a group of (usually) eight or 16 measures divided into two phrases and ending with a cadence, generally forming a statement within a larger composition ‖ (*geol.*) a division of geological time, part of an era ‖ (*pl.*) rhetorical language **2.** *adj.* having the characteristics of a particular historical period, *period furniture* [F. *période* fr. L. fr. Gk fr. *peri,* around+*hodos,* way]
pe·ri·od·ic (piəri:ɔ́dik) *adj.* occurring again and again, at constant intervals ‖ recurring intermittently ‖ characterized by regularly recurring stages or processes, *the periodic motion of the planets* ‖ (*gram.*, of a sentence) in which the grammatical form and the meaning are not complete until the end is reached **pe·ri·ód·i·cal** **1.** *adj.* periodic ‖ (of a magazine etc.) published at regular intervals ‖ characteristic of or pertaining to such publications **2.** *n.* a periodical publication [F. *périodique* fr. L. fr. Gk]
pe·ri·o·dic·i·ty (piəri:ədísiti:) *pl.* **pe·ri·o·dic·i·ties** *n.* the quality or fact of recurring at constant intervals ‖ (*elec.*) frequency ‖ (*chem.*) the position of an element in the periodic table [F. *périodicité*]
periodic law a statement in chemistry: the chemical and physical properties of elements depend upon the structure of the atom and vary

with the atomic number in a systematic and roughly periodic way (*PERIODIC TABLE)

periodic table (*chem.*) a tabular arrangement of the elements based upon atomic number and emphasizing the periodic recurrence of properties. The modern periodic table in long-period form contains horizontally a very short period of two elements, two short periods of eight elements each, two long periods of 18 elements each, a very long period of 32 elements, and an incomplete period. Vertically there are 16 columns (excluding the lanthanide series and incomplete actinide series) comprising eight groups divided into two subgroups each. Elements to the left and in the center are metals, those to the right nonmetals. Metallic properties are most pronounced for elements in the lower left-hand corner, and nonmetallic properties most pronounced for elements in the upper right-hand corner. Transition from metallic to nonmetallic properties is usually gradual and continuous from left to right. The structure of the periodic table and the periodic law follow directly from the quantized structure of the atom

per·i·os·te·al (pęri:ɒ́sti:əl) *adj.* of the periosteum ‖ situated around a bone

per·i·os·te·um (pęri:ɒ́sti:əm) *pl.* **per·i·os·te·a** (pęri:ɒ́sti:ə) *n.* a fibrous membrane of connective tissue which closely surrounds all bones except at the joints [Mod. L. fr. Gk *peri,* around+*osteon,* bone]

per·i·o·tic (pęri:óutik) **1.** *adj.* of or designating the inner ear or the bony structure that surrounds it **2.** *n.* this bony structure [fr. PERI-+Gk *otikos* fr. *ous* (*ōtos*), ear]

per·i·pa·tet·ic (pęrəpətétik) *adj.* moving about from place to place **Per·i·pa·tet·ic 1.** *adj.* Aristotelian **2.** *n.* a follower of Aristotle, an Aristotelian (from Aristotle's habit of conversing with pupils while they walked in the Lyceum) **per·i·pa·tét·i·cal·ly** *adv.* [F. *péripatétique* fr. L. fr. Gk fr. *peri,* around+*patein,* to walk]

per·i·pe·tei·a, per·i·pe·ti·a (pęrəpitáiə) *n.* a sudden change or reversal of fortune in tragedy or real life [Gk *peripeteia* fr. *peri,* around+*piptein,* to fall]

pe·riph·er·al (pərífərəl) *adj.* of, concerning or constituting a periphery ‖ lying on a periphery ‖ (*computer*) of electronic or mechanical devices not part of the basic processor, e.g., card readers, printers, terminals, etc. ‖ (*anat.*) of those nerves which run outward from the brain and spinal cord to the tissues [fr. Gk *periphēres,* moving around]

pe·riph·er·y (pərífəri:) *pl.* **pe·riph·er·ies** *n.* the line bounding a figure, esp. a rounded one ‖ the outermost part of something thought of as ringed or circled, *the periphery of consciousness* ‖ the boundary or outer surface of a space or body ‖ (*anat.*) the areas in which the nerves terminate [fr. L.L. *peripheria* fr. Gk fr. *peri,* around+*pherein,* to carry]

per·i·phor·ic (pęrifɒ́nik) *adj.* (*acoustics*) of a speaker system with several speakers placed facing various directions

pe·riph·ra·sis (pərífrəsis) *pl.* **pe·riph·ra·ses** (pərífrəsi:z) *n.* circumlocution or an instance of this [L. fr. Gk fr. *peri,* around+*phrazein,* to declare]

per·i·phras·tic (pęrifrǽstik) *adj.* expressed in a roundabout fashion ‖ (*gram.*) formed by the use of auxiliary verbs etc. instead of by inflection, e.g. 'it does do' for 'it does' **per·i·phrás·ti·cal·ly** *adv.* [fr. Gk *periphrastikos*]

per·i·scope (périskoup) *n.* a tubular optical device used in submarines etc. and in scientific observation, by which light received by an oblique mirror or prism at one end of the tube is reflected by another at the other end. An observer can thus see without being exposed, or see around an obstacle **per·i·scop·ic** (periskɒ́pik) *adj.* [fr. Gk *peri,* around+*skopos,* observer]

per·ish (périʃ) *v.i.* to suffer utter ruin or destruction, or die a violent death, *the whole family perished in the fire* ‖ to suffer spiritual death **perish the thought!** don't even consider the possibility of such a thing! **pér·ish·a·ble** *adj.* liable to decay or deterioration, *perishable foods* **pér·ish·a·bles** *pl. n.* perishable goods **pér·ish·ing** *adj.* (of cold, pain etc.) extreme ‖ (*pop.*) damned, blasted, *a perishing nuisance* [M.E. fr. O.F. *perir* (*periss*)]

pe·ris·so·dac·tyl (pərisoudǽktəl) **1.** *adj.* having an odd number of toes, or toes placed evenly in relation to the axis of the foot ‖ of or belonging to *Perissodactyla,* an order of ungulate mammals having such toes, e.g. the horse, rhinoceros **2.** *n.* a mammal of this order [fr. Mod. L. *perissodactylus* fr. Gk *perissos,* uneven+*daktulos,* finger, digit]

per·i·stal·sis (pęristɔ́lsis, pęristǽlsis) *pl.* **per·i·stal·ses** (pęristǽlsi:z) *n.* a series of muscular contractions of a hollow structure, esp. of the alimentary canal, which force the contents along ‖ one of these contractions [Mod. L. fr. Gk]

per·i·stal·tic (pęristɔ́ltik, pęristǽltik) *adj.* of, relating to or characterized by peristalsis [fr. Gk *peristaltikos* fr. *peristellein,* to send around]

per·i·stome (péristoum) *n.* (*bot.*) the fringe of teeth surrounding the opening of a moss capsule ‖ (*zool.*) the area around the mouth in certain invertebrates [fr. Mod. L. *peristomas* fr. Gk *peri,* around+*stoma,* mouth]

per·i·style (péristail) *n.* a row of columns enclosing a courtyard or building, esp. supporting the roof ‖ the space so surrounded [F. *péristyle* fr. L. fr. Gk fr. *peri,* around+*stulos,* pillar]

per·i·the·ci·um (pęriθí:si:əm) *pl.* **per·i·the·ci·a** (pęriθí:si:ə) *n.* (*bot.*) a flask-shaped case enclosing the fruiting body in certain fungi [Mod. L. fr. Gk *peri,* around+*thēkē,* box]

per·i·to·ne·al, per·i·to·nae·al (pęritəní:əl) *adj.* of the peritoneum

per·i·to·ne·um, per·i·to·nae·um (pęritəní:əm) *pl.* **per·i·to·ne·a, per·i·to·nae·a** (pęritəní:ə) *n.* (*anat.*) the membrane lining the abdominal viscera and the interior of the abdominal wall [L. fr. Gk fr. *peri,* around+*teinein,* to stretch]

per·i·to·ni·tis (pęritənáitis) *n.* inflammation of the peritoneum caused by the spreading of infection from a diseased or ruptured visceral body [Mod. L. fr. Gk fr. *peritonos,* stretched over]

pe·ri·tus, pl **-ti** (péritəs) *n.* **1.** Vatican Council adviser. **2.** a theological adviser

per·i·wig (périwig) *n.* (esp. *hist.*) a wig [earlier *perwyke* fr. F. *perruque*]

per·i·win·kle (périwiŋk'l) *n.* any member of *Littorina,* fam *Littorinidae,* a genus of edible sea snails found on shore or in shallow water [O.E. *pinewinclan* pl.]

periwinkle *n.* a member of *Vinca,* fam. *Apocynaceae,* a genus of European, North American and W. Asian often creeping, perennial, evergreen plants with glossy leaves and blue or white flowers, esp. *V. major* and *V. minor* [O.E. *peruince* fr. L.]

per·jure (pə́:rdʒər) *pres. part.* **per·jur·ing** *past* and *past part.* **per·jured** *v. refl.* to make (oneself) guilty of perjury [O.F. *parjurer*]

per·jur·er (pə́:rdʒərər) *n.* a person guilty of perjury [A.F. *parjurour, perjurour*]

per·ju·ry (pə́:rdʒəri:) *pl.* **per·ju·ries** *n.* (*law*) the crime of swearing on oath that something is true which one knows is false, or of telling a lie when under oath to tell the truth ‖ failure to do what one has sworn on oath to do [A.F. *perjurie*]

perk (pə:rk) *v.t.* (with 'up') to restore good spirits or courage to, *a drink will perk him up* ‖ (with 'up') to make bright or gay in appearance, *to perk up a coat with a red scarf* ‖ *v.i.* (with 'up') to recover one's health, energy or good spirits after sickness, depression etc. [etym. doubtful]

perk *v.i.* (*pop.,* of coffee) to percolate

Perkins (pə́:rkənz), Frances (1882–1965) U.S. secretary of labor, the first woman cabinet member. Serving (1933–45) in the administration of Franklin D. Roosevelt, she greatly strengthened the Labor Department, esp. in the bureaus of Labor Statistics, Women and Children as well as championing such reforms as social security, federal public works and relief and legislation for minimum wages and maximum hours and abolition of child labor

perk·man (pə́:rkmæn) *n.* an official or businessman who receives substantial income in the form of perquisites of his job; coined by President Jimmy Carter in 1977

perk·y (pə́:rki:) *comp.* **perk·i·er** *superl.* **perk·i·est** *adj.* lively and cheerful ‖ cocky [PERK]

perks (pə:rks) *pl. n* (*Br., pop.*) perquisites

Perl·is (pə́:rlis) a state (area 316 sq. miles, pop. 147,726) of Malaysia in N.W. Malaya. Capital: Kangar. Part of Kedah until 1842, it was ruled by Siam (1842–1909), after which it was ceded to Britain. It joined the Federation of Malaya (1948)

per·lite (pə́:rlait) *n.* an acid, glassy, volcanic rock marked with concentric cracks separating small globular portions formed by tension during cooling **per·lit·ic** (pərlítik) *adj.* [F. fr. *perle,* pearl]

Perm (pə:rm) (called Molotov 1940–57) a river port and industrial center (pop. 1,028,000) of the western R.S.F.S.R., U.S.S.R., on the Kama: metallurgy, mechanical engineering, oil refining. University (1916)

perm (pə:rm) *n.* (esp. *Br., pop.*) a permanent wave

perm·al·loy (pə:rmǽlɔi, pə́:rməlɔi) *n.* an iron-nickel alloy of high magnetic permeability, giving little loss of energy by hysteresis [trademark *Permalloy* fr. PERMEABLE+ALLOY]

per·ma·nence (pə́:rmənəns) *n.* the quality or state of being permanent **pér·ma·nen·cy** *pl.* **per·ma·nen·cies** *n.* permanence ‖ someone or something that is permanent ‖ a permanent position [fr. M. L. *permanentia*]

per·ma·nent (pə́:rmənənt) **1.** *adj.* continuing and enduring without change **2.** *n.* (*pop.*) a permanent wave [fr. L. *permanens* (*permanentis*) fr. *permanere,* to remain to the end]

permanent magnet a magnet, usually of cobalt steel or nickel steel, which retains its magnetism for a long time

permanent magnetism magnetism retained by a substance in the absence of any external magnetic field

permanent memory (*computer*) data that are retained when power is cut off

permanent press durable press chemical and steaming process for treating fabric to retain creases. *also* durable press

permanent wave a wave set in hair by chemicals and sometimes heat, and lasting a long time

permanent way (*Br.*) a railroad track designed to carry a train service for many years

per·man·ga·nate (pərmǽŋgəneit) *n.* a salt of permanganic acid, esp. potassium permanganate

per·man·gan·ic acid (pə:rmæŋgǽnik) $HMnO_4$, a strong acid known only in solution and by its salts (permanganates)

per·me·a·bil·i·ty (pə:rmi:əbíliti:) *n.* the quality or state of being permeable (*MAGNETIC PERMEABILITY)

per·me·a·ble (pə́:rmi:əb'l) *adj.* able to be permeated [fr. L. *permeabilis*]

per·me·ance (pə́:rmi:əns) *n.* a permeating or being permeated ‖ the quality of being permeable

per·me·ase (pə́:rmi:eis) *n.* (*biochem.*) **1.** bacterial system that facilitates transportation of soluble substances in the cell. **2.** an enzyme in a cell membrane that concentrates lactose

per·me·ate (pə́:rmi:eit) *pres. part.* **per·me·at·ing** *past* and *past part.* **per·me·at·ed** *v.t.* to penetrate wholly, pervade, soak through, *a smell of baking permeated the house* ‖ *v.i.* to diffuse or spread through something **per·me·á·tion** *n.* [fr. L. *permeare* (*permeatus*), to pass through]

per men·sem (pə:rménsəm) *adv.* by the month [L.]

Per·mi·an (pə́:rmi:ən) *adj.* of the latest period or system of the Paleozoic era, characterized by the decline of amphibians and development of reptiles, by extensive glaciation, and by red sandstone and shales (*GEOLOGICAL TIME) **the Permian** the Permian period or system or rocks [after *Perm,* former Russian province in the Urals]

per·mis·si·bil·i·ty (pərmisəbíliti:) *n.* the quality or state of being permissible

per·mis·si·ble (pərmísəb'l) *adj.* that may be permitted **per·mís·si·bly** *adv.* [O.F.]

per·mis·sion (pərmíʃən) *n.* freedom, power, privilege etc. which one person or authority grants to another, *he has her permission to park in the drive* ‖ a permitting, or being permitted [fr. L. *permissio* (*permissionis*)]

per·mis·sive (pərmísiv) *adj.* permitting, tolerating ‖ morally tolerant in a high degree [O.F. *permissif, permissive*]

per·mis·siv·ist or **per·mis·sion·ist** (pərmísivist) *n.* one who believes in policy of indulgence of behavior not generally acceptable

per·mit 1. (pərmít) *v. pres. part.* **per·mit·ting** *past* and *past part.* **per·mit·ted** *v.t.* to give voluntarily or officially to (someone or something) some right, opportunity, power etc., *he permitted them to stay away from school* ‖ to accept or agree to (something), *how can you permit such insolence?* ‖ to make possible, *the addition of a window permits better air circulation* ‖ *v.i.* to provide opportunity, *drop in when time permits* ‖ (with 'of') to admit of, *there were too many present to permit of any intimacy* **2.** (pə́:rmit, pərmít) *n.* a written license issued by an au-

CONCISE PRONUNCIATION KEY: **(a)** æ, *cat;* ɑ, *car;* ɔ *fawn;* ei, *snake.* **(e)** e, *hen;* i:, *sheep;* iə, *deer;* εə, *bear.* **(i)** i, *fish;* ai, *tiger;* ə:, *bird.* **(o)** o, *ox;* au, *cow;* ou, *goat;* u, *poor;* ɔi, *royal.* **(u)** ʌ, *duck;* u, *bull;* u:, *goose;* ə, *bacillus;* ju:, *cube.* x, *loch;* θ, *think;* ð, *bother;* z, *Zen;* ʒ, *corsage;* dʒ, *savage;* ŋ, *orangutang;* j, *yak;* ʃ, *fish;* tʃ, *fetch;* 'l, *rabble;* 'n, *redden.* Complete pronunciation key appears inside front cover.

thority [fr. L. *permittere,* to let go, surrender, permit]

per·mit·tiv·i·ty (pə:rmitíviti:) *n.* dielectric constant ‖ the ratio of the induced polarity in a dielectric substance to the electric force producing it

per·mu·ta·tion (pə:rmju:téiʃən) *n.* (*math.*) any of the different arrangements in linear order that can be made of a given set of objects (*COMBINATION) ‖ (*math.*) the act or process of making such variations ‖ a change or the process of changing [O.F. *permutacion*]

per·mute (pərmjú:t) *pres. part.* **per·mut·ing** *past* and *past part.* **per·mut·ed** *v.t.* to change the order of (esp. things in a series) [fr. L. *permutare,* to exchange, interchange]

pern (pə:rn) *n.* the honey buzzard [fr. Mod. L. *pernis* fr. Gk *pternis,* a kind of hawk]

Per·nam·bu·co (pə:rnəmbú:kou) *RECIFE

per·ni·cious (pərníʃəs) *adj.* destructive, extremely injurious, or deadly, *a pernicious pest* [fr. F. *pernicieux* fr. L.]

pernicious anemia, *Br.* **pernicious anaemia** a severe type of anemia characterized by the presence of large red blood cells. It is treated by the administration of vitamin B_{12} and liver extract

per·nick·et·y (pərníkiti:) *adj.* (esp. *Br.*) persnickety [origin unknown]

Perón, Isabel (1931–) president of Argentina (1974–6). A dancer, she became the secretary, then the wife (1961) of the exiled Juan Peron. When Perón returned to Argentina and became president (1973) Isabel served as his vice-president and on his death she succeeded to the presidency. Unable to cope with severe economic problems and rising political violence, she was deposed in a military coup and placed under house arrest. Upon her release (1981) she went into exile in Spain

Pe·rón (perɔ́n, pəróun), Juan Domingo (1895–1974), Argentine general and statesman, nationalist dictator of Argentina (1946–55). With his wife Eva (1919–52), he did much to modernize Argentina and won the support of the trade unions, but instituted a police state. He was exiled by the army (1955) and settled in Spain, returning to Argentina (1973) for a short second tenure as president. He died after 9 months of a term marked by factionalism and violence and was succeeded by his third wife, Isabel, who was deposed by a military junta in 1976

per·o·ne·al (perəní:əl) *adj.* of or relating to the fibula [fr. Mod. L. *peronaeus* n., muscle connected with the fibula, fr. Gk *peronē,* fibula]

per·o·rate (pérəreit) *pres. part.* **per·o·rat·ing** *past* and *past part.* **per·o·rat·ed** *v.i.* to make or deliver a peroration [fr. L. *perorare* (*peroratus*)]

per·o·ra·tion (perəréiʃən) *n.* a protracted tedious speech, often pompously delivered ‖ the concluding portion of a speech, rhetorical composition etc. [fr. L. *peroratio* (*perorationis*), a summing up]

per·ox·ide (pərɒ́ksaid) **1.** *n.* an oxide which yields hydrogen peroxide when combined with an acid ‖ an oxide containing a high proportion of oxygen ‖ hydrogen peroxide **2.** *v.t. pres. part.* **per·ox·id·ing** *past* and *past part.* **per·ox·id·ed** to bleach (the hair) with hydrogen peroxide

per·ox·y·a·cet·yl nitrate (pərɒksiəsí:təl) (*envir.*) toxic element in smog, created by action of sunlight on hydrocarbon exhausts from automobiles

per·pend (pərpénd) *v.t.* and *i.* (*rhet.*) to ponder [fr. L. *perpendere*]

per·pend (pérpənd) *n.* a large stone extending through a wall from one side to another, to bind it

per·pen·dic·u·lar (pə:rpəndíkjulər) **1.** *adj.* (of a line, plane or surface) forming an angle of 90° with another line, plane or surface ‖ (of two lines, planes or surfaces) forming a 90° angle ‖ at right angles to the horizontal at any point on the earth's surface **Per·pen·dic·u·lar** (*archit.*) of an English Gothic style (14th–16th cc.) which succeeded the Decorated and is characterized by vertical lines, esp. in its window tracery **2.** *n.* a direction which is perpendicular, esp. as represented by a straight line, *draw a perpendicular to each side of the triangle* ‖ an instrument, e.g. a plumb line, for determining the perpendicular line from any point **per·pen·dic·u·lar·i·ty** (pərpəndikjulǽriti:) *n.* [O.F. *perpendiculer, perpendiculier* fr. L.]

per·pe·trate (pə́:rpitreit) *pres. part.* **per·pe·trat·ing** *past* and *past part.* **per·pe·trat·ed** *v.t.* to commit, perform (something bad), *to perpetrate a crime* **per·pe·trá·tion, pér·pe·tra·tor** *ns* [fr. L. *perpetrare* (*perpetratus*)]

per·pet·u·al (pərpétʃu:əl) **1.** *adj.* eternal, everlasting, *perpetual damnation* ‖ constant, continual, *he's in a perpetual bad temper* ‖ (*bot.*) flowering throughout the season **2.** *n.* a hybrid perpetual rose [F. *perpétuel*]

perpetual annuity an annuity under which payments cease only when the principal is repaid

perpetual calendar a table of calendar dates by which one can determine the day of the week of a given date within a wide range of years ‖ a mechanical calendar which can be set for any date within a period of several years

perpetual motion the motion of a hypothetical (but impossible) machine which would go on working forever without receiving energy from an outside source

per·pet·u·ate (pərpétʃu:eit) *pres. part.* **per·pet·u·at·ing** *past* and *past part.* **per·pet·u·at·ed** *v.t.* to make perpetual ‖ to cause to continue ‖ to save from oblivion, *a bronze plaque perpetuates his memory* **per·pet·u·á·tion, per·pét·u·a·tor** *ns* [fr. L. *perpetuare* (*perpetuatus*)]

per·pe·tu·i·ty (pə:rpitjú:iti:, pə:rpitú:iti:) *pl.* **per·pe·tu·i·ties** *n.* eternity ‖ the quality or state of being inalienable forever or for a period beyond certain limits ‖ (*law*) such an estate ‖ a perpetual annuity **in perpetuity** forever [M.E. *perpetuite* fr. F.]

per·ph·en·a·zine [$C_{21}H_{26}ClN_3OS$] (pə:rfénəzi:n) *n.* (*pharm.*) tranquilizer, antinauseant, and antiemetic; marketed as Trilafon

Per·pi·gnan (perpi:njã) the chief town (pop. 106,426) of Pyrénées-Orientales, France, and historic capital of Roussillon, 15 miles from Spain, an agricultural market. Cathedral (14th–15th cc.), fortress, and castle (14th–15th cc.)

per·plex (pərpléks) *v.t.* to make (someone) uncertain about the nature of, or the reason for or answer to, something difficult to understand ‖ to complicate (a situation etc.) [fr. obs. *perplex* adj. fr. L. *perplexus,* involved]

per·plex·i·ty (pərpléksiti:) *pl.* **per·plex·i·ties** *n.* the quality or state of being perplexed ‖ something which perplexes [fr. L.L. *perplexitas*]

per·qui·site (pə́:rkwizit) *n.* an extra profit or item received over and above one's agreed wage ‖ a tip, gratuity [fr. L. *perquisitum* fr. *perquirere* (*perquisitus*), to seek carefully for]

Per·rault (perou), Charles (1628–1703), French author. His 'Contes de ma mère l'oye' (1697) included some of the most famous of all fairy tales (Tom Thumb, Cinderella, Little Red Ridinghood)

Per·ret (perei), Auguste (1874–1954), French architect born in Belgium. He innovated the architectural use of reinforced concrete (1902–3), and successfully coordinated its use in a neoclassical style

Per·ry (péri:), Matthew Calbraith (1794–1858), American naval officer. He led a naval expedition which forced the opening of Japan to Western trade (1854)

Perry, Oliver Hazard (1785–1819), U.S. naval officer. As commander of the flagship 'Niagara' during the War of 1812, he defeated the British at the Battle of Lake Erie

per·ry (péri:) *pl.* **per·ries** *n.* (esp. *Br.*) a drink made from fermented pear juice [M.E. *pereye* fr. O.F.]

Perse, Saint-John *SAINT-JOHN PERSE

per se (pərséi) *adv.* intrinsically, considered independently of other things [L.=by itself]

per·se·cute (pə́:rsikju:t) *pres. part.* **per·se·cut·ing** *past* and *past part.* **per·se·cut·ed** *v.t.* to cause to suffer, esp. for religious or political reasons ‖ to vex, harass [F. *persécuter* fr. L. *persequi* (*persecutus*), to pursue]

per·se·cu·tion (pə:rsikjú:ʃən) *n.* a persecuting or being persecuted [M.E. *persecucion* fr. O.F. fr. L.]

persecution complex persecution mania

persecution mania a delusion that one is being persecuted

per·se·cu·tor (pə́:rsikju:tər) *n.* someone who persecutes [A.F. *persecutour* fr. L.]

Per·seph·o·ne (pərséfəni:) (*Gk mythol.*) the daughter of Zeus and Demeter. She was kidnapped by Pluto and made queen of the underworld, but was allowed to return to the earth every spring and summer

Per·sep·o·lis (pərsépəlis) the ancient residential capital (40 miles east of modern Shiraz) of the Achaemenid kings of Persia, sacked (331 B.C.) by Alexander III. Fine bas-reliefs cover the remaining palace walls

Per·se·us (pə́:rsi:əs, pə́:rsju:s) (*Gk mythol.*) son of Zeus and Danae. He cut off the head of Medusa, rescued and married Andromeda and founded Mycenae ‖ (*astron.*) a constellation of the northern hemisphere between Taurus and Cassiopeia

Perseus (c. 212–166 B.C.), last king of Macedon (179–168 B.C.), son of Philip V. He was attacked by the Romans (171 B.C.), overthrown (168 B.C.) and died a prisoner in Rome

per·se·ver·ance (pə:rsivíərəns) *n.* the quality of being persistent and persevering ‖ the act of persevering ‖ (*theol.*) a continuing in a state of grace leading to a state of glory [F.]

per·se·vere (pə:rsivíər) *pres. part.* **per·se·ver·ing** *past* and *past part.* **per·se·vered** *v.i.* to try hard and continuously in spite of obstacles and difficulties [F. *persévérer* fr. L.]

Per·shing (pə́:rʃiŋ), John Joseph (1860–1948), American general. He was commander in chief (1917–18) of the U.S. forces in France in the 1st world war, and was U.S. chief of staff (1921–4)

Per·shing (pə́:rʃiŋ) *n.* army surface-to-surface guided missile (XMGM-31A) utilizing a solid propellant, with a range of 400 nautical miles, and nuclear capability; developed in 1967 and manufactured by Martin Marietta

Per·sia (pə́:rʒə, pə́:rʃə) the ancient, and (since 1949) the official alternative name of Iran. (For geography *IRAN). HISTORY. The Iranian plateau saw the growth of an early civilization at Elam (c. 4000 B.C.). The Persians, an Aryan people, settled in S. Persia (2nd millennium B.C.), while the Medes, also an Aryan people, settled N.W. Persia (1st millennium B.C.), coming into conflict with the Assyrians (9th c. B.C.). The Medes established a strong kingdom (7th c. B.C.) and conquered Assyria (c. 616–606 B.C.), but were themselves conquered by the Persians (mid- 6th c. B.C.) under Cyrus II. His successors, the Achaemenids, built up a vast empire extending from Egypt to the Punjab and from the Dardanelles to Samarkand. The empire, founded on Zoroastrianism, was remarkable for its efficient organization, based on that of the Assyrians, and for its art, influenced by Egypt and Babylonia. The empire was weakened by the dynastic disputes of Cambyses II and Darius I, and by the Greek victories over Darius I and Xerxes I during the Persian Wars (499–449 B.C.). It fell (331 B.C.) to Alexander the Great at Arbela, and power passed to the Seleucids. Parthia broke away (mid-3rd c. B.C.) and formed an empire which rivaled Rome and which in turn was replaced by the Sassanids (c. 226–c. 641 A.D.), under whom the arts again developed. The Arabs took Ctesiphon, the capital (c. 641), and brought Islam to the whole country. Persia prospered under the Umayyad and Abbasid caliphates. Under the latter, the Seljuk Turks gained control, and poetry, philosophy, mathematics and astronomy flourished (10th–13th cc.). Genghis Khan incorporated Persia in the Mongol domains (1220), and a period of anarchy and destruction ensued until the Safavids gained power (1502–1736). This dynasty was at its height under Abbas I, in whose reign (1587–1629) Persian territory was extended and the Portuguese driven from the bases they had established on the Persian Gulf. Ottoman, Russian and Afghan raids were put down (early 18th c.) by Nadir Shah, who ruled despotically (1736–47). A period of civil war was ended (1794) by the Kajar dynasty (1794–1925), under whom Persia was drawn into European power politics, forming treaties with France (1807) and Britain (1814), and ceding most of her territory in the Caucasus to Russia (1828). Britain and Russia guaranteed Persian independence (1834), but Britain forced Persia to withdraw from Afghanistan (1857). The discovery of oil (1901) increased Western financial interest in Persia. A liberal constitution was introduced (1905) and Russia and Britain agreed to divide Persia into two zones of influence (1907). An army officer, Reza Khan, staged a coup detat (1921), established a dictatorship, and assumed the title of Reza Shah Pahlavi (1925). Under his rule, Persia was rapidly modernized. The name of the country was changed (1935) to Iran

Per·sian (pə́:rʒən, pə́:rʃən) **1.** *adj.* of ancient Persia or modern Iran, its people, language etc. **2.** *n.* a native or inhabitant of Persia or Iran ‖

CONCISE PRONUNCIATION KEY: **(a)** æ, *cat;* ɑ, *car;* ɔ *fawn;* ei, *snake.* **(e)** e, *hen;* i:, *sheep;* iə, *deer;* εə, *bear.* **(i)** i, *fish;* ai, *tiger;* ə:, *bird.* **(o)** ɒ, *ox;* au, *cow;* ou, *goat;* u, *poor;* ɔi, *royal.* **(u)** ʌ, *duck;* u, *bull;* u:, *goose;* ə, *bacillus;* ju:, *cube.* x, *loch;* θ, *think;* ð, *bother;* z, *Zen;* ʒ, *corsage;* dʒ, *savage;* ŋ, *orangutang;* j, *yak;* ʃ, *fish;* tʃ, *fetch;* 'l, *rabble;* 'n, *redden.* Complete pronunciation key appears inside front cover.

the Iranian language of Iran [M.E. *Persien* fr. F.]

Persian blinds persiennes

Persian cat a domestic cat of a breed having long, silky fur, stocky build and a round head

Persian Gulf an arm (area 77,000 sq. miles) of the Arabian Sea between Iran and Arabia: tideland oil wells, pearl fisheries

Persian lamb the skin of a Karakul lamb, with tight curly hair, used for coats etc. (cf. BROADTAIL, cf. ASTRAKHAN)

Persian Wars the struggle (499–449 B.C.) between the Greeks and the Persian Empire. Following the revolt of the Greeks of Ionia (499–494 B.C.), Darius I invaded Greece and was defeated at Marathon (490 B.C.). Xerxes I continued the campaigns, was victorious at Thermopylae (480 B.C.) and took Athens. But the Persian fleet was destroyed at Salamis (480 B.C.) and the army defeated at Plataea (479 B.C.), driving the Persians from the Aegean

per·si·ennes (pə̧:rzi:énz) *pl. n.* outside window blinds with adjustable slats, similar to Venetian blinds [F. fr. *persien* adj., Persian]

per·si·flage (pə́:rsiflaʒ) *n.* light-hearted and bantering speech, writing etc. [F.]

per·sim·mon (pərsímən) *n.* a member of *Diospyros,* fam. *Ebenaceae,* a genus of trees growing in hardwood forests and also cultivated, esp. *D. virginiana* of the southern and eastern U.S.A. and *D. kaki,* the Japanese persimmon. The ripe fruit, a large berry, is reddish orange and succulent ‖ the fruit of one of these trees [fr. Algonquian]

per·sist (pərsist) *v.i.* to continue, esp. in spite of opposition or difficulties, *he persists in doing what he shouldn't* ‖ to continue to exist, *the tradition has persisted to this day* [fr. L. *persistere,* to remain]

per·sist·ence (pərsístəns) *n.* the quality or state of being persistent ‖ the act of persisting [F. *persistance*]

per·sist·en·cy (pərsístənsi:) *n.* persistence [fr. L. *persistens*]

per·sist·ent (pərsístənt) *adj.* continuing in spite of opposition ‖ enduring, lasting or recurrent, *a persistent cough* ‖ (*bot.,* of a leaf) not falling although withered ‖ (*zool.,* of horns, hair etc.) permanent, not disappearing or falling off ‖ (*chem.,* of toxic chemicals) nondegradable or slowly degradable ‖ (*med.,* of a disorder) not readily cured [fr. L. *persistens* (*persistentis*)]

per·sis·tron (pə:rsístrən) *n.* (*electr.*) display panel utilizing solid-state electroluminescent amplification

Per·si·us (pə́:rsi:əs), Aulus Persius Flaccus (34–62), Roman poet and author of six satires extolling Stoic morality in private life

per·snick·et·y (pərsníkiti:) *adj.* fastidious, finicky, fussy ‖ complex, requiring careful, precise handling [alt. of PERNICKETY]

per·son (pí:rs'n) *n.* a man, woman or child, regarded as having a distinct individuality or personality, or as distinguished from an animal or thing ‖ someone regarded patronizingly, *there's a strange person to see you* ‖ the body of a human being, *attacks on the person of the president* ‖ an individual's self or being ‖ (*gram.*) one of the three referents for pronouns and the corresponding verb forms in many languages (*FIRST PERSON, *SECOND PERSON, *THIRD PERSON) ‖ (*theol.*) one of the modes of being of the trinitarian Godhead ‖ (*law*) a human being or a collection of human beings considered as having rights and duties ‖ (*zool.*) a single zooid in a colony **in person** being physically present, *apply in person* [O.F. *persone,* Mod. F. *personne,* a part in a drama]

per·so·na (pərsóunə) *n.* (*in Jung's psychology*) the personality assumed by an individual in adaptation to the outside world [L.=actor's mask, character acted]

per·son·a·ble (pə́:rs'nəb'l) *adj.* (*old-fash.,* of people) good-looking

per·son·age (pə́:rs'nidʒ) *n.* a person of eminence or importance ‖ a character in a play or novel [O.F.]

per·son·al (pə́:rs'n'l) **1.** *adj.* belonging or particular to one person, private, *a personal opinion, personal belongings* ‖ done by oneself, in person, *a personal intervention* ‖ of or concerning the body, *personal cleanliness* ‖ referring to a person without proper respect for his privacy, *personal remarks* ‖ considered as a person with human faculties of reason etc., *a personal God* ‖ (*gram.,* of a verb ending or pronoun) denoting the first, second or third person **2.** *n.* (esp. *pl.*) newspaper paragraphs about individual persons, or containing paid personal messages to individuals [O.F.]

personal distance the minimum distance from a person or animal subconsciously considered too close for comfort

personal equation the correction to be made in a reading, e.g. of a scientific instrument, in order to compensate for the tendency of an individual to err habitually in a particular direction

personal estate (*law*) personal property

per·son·al·ism (pə́:rs'n'lizəm) *n.* any philosophical system based on the assumption that the human person is the fundamental value

per·son·al·i·ty (pə̧:rs'nǽliti:) *pl.* **per·son·al·i·ties** *n.* the total of the psychological, intellectual, emotional and physical characteristics that make up the individual, esp. as others see him ‖ a person with regard to this total of characteristics, *he is a powerful personality* ‖ an eminent or famous person, *many personalities were at the banquet* ‖ the quality, state or fact of being a person ‖ pronounced individuality, *he lacks personality* ‖ (*pl.*) reference, esp. critical, to a person or people, *let us avoid personalities in this discussion* [O.F. *personalité*]

personality cult (in Marxist terminology) a deliberate, organized process of persuading a community that its leader has a supreme excellence in his personal qualities which entitles him to unquestioning loyalty

personality inventory (*psych.*) a psychological profile comparing certain personality traits and interests with the average. *Cf* MMPI

per·son·al·i·za·tion (pə̧:rs'n'lizéiʃən) *n.* the quality or state of being personalized ‖ the act of personalizing or an instance of this

per·son·al·ize (pə́:rs'n'laiz) *pres. part.* **per·son·al·iz·ing** *past* and *past part.* **per·son·al·ized** *v.t.* to personify ‖ to make personal, e.g. by labeling with one's name, *personalized writing paper*

per·son·al·ly (pə́:rs'n'li:) *adv.* in a personal way ‖ in person, not using an agent, *the manager personally conducted us* ‖ for one's part, so far as one is oneself concerned, *personally, I like him*

personal property (*law*) estate or property that consists of temporary or movable things, as opposed e.g. to land

personal tax a tax whose incidence falls directly on individuals, e.g., sales tax

per·son·al·ty (pə́:rs'n'lti:) *n.* personal property [fr. A.F. *personaltie*]

persona non gra·ta (pərsóunənoungrútə) *pl.* **per·so·nae non gra·tae** (pərsóuni:noungrúti:) a diplomat who is not acceptable to the government of the country he is accredited to ‖ any person who is not welcome in a particular group [L.]

per·son·ate (pə́:rs'nit, pə́:rs'neit) *adj.* (*bot.,* of a corolla) consisting of two lips with a projection of the lower lip closing the throat ‖ (*bot.,* of a flower, e.g. a snapdragon) having such a corolla [fr. L. *personatus,* masked]

personate (pə́:rs'neit) *pres. part.* **per·son·at·ing** *past* and *past part.* **per·son·at·ed** *v.t.* (*law*) to pretend to be (someone, or some kind of person, that one is not) for illegal purposes **per·son·á·tion, pér·son·a·tor** *ns* [fr. L. *personare* (*personatus*) fr. *persona,* mask]

per·son-day (pə́:rs'ndéi) *n.* unit of activity measurement of one person for one day

per·son·hood (pə́:rs'nhud) *n.* the distinctive qualities that make up an individual

per·son·i·fi·ca·tion (pərsɒnifikéiʃən) *n.* the treating of an abstract quality or thing as if it had human qualities ‖ an instance of this ‖ a person regarded as the embodiment of a quality, *she is the personification of generosity*

per·son·i·fy (pərsɒ́nifai) *pres. part.* **per·son·i·fy·ing** *past* and *past part.* **per·son·i·fied** *v.t.* to treat (an abstraction, thing or inanimate object) as a person, *the Greeks personified the forces of nature as gods* ‖ to be the embodiment of, *he is urbanity personified* [F. *personnifier*]

per·son·nel (pə̧:rs'nél) *n.* the body of employees in a service, business, factory etc., *military personnel* [F.]

Persons, Robert *PARSONS

per·spec·tive (pərspéktiv) *n.* the art of representing solid objects on a flat surface so that they seem to be in relation to one another in space just as the eye would see them ‖ a picture made using this technique ‖ the appearance of objects with reference to distance, relative position etc. ‖ relative importance, *to see problems in their true perspective* ‖ evaluation of events according to a particular way of looking at them, *historical perspective* ‖ a view or prospect [fr. M.L. *perspectiva* (*ars*), (the science of) optics]

perspective *adj.* of, pertaining to or depicted according to perspective [fr. L.L. *perspectivus* fr. *perspicere,* to look through, view]

per·spex (pə́:rspeks) *n.* a transparent acrylic resin, produced in England, essentially polymerized methyl methacrylate, used e.g. in aircraft (cf. LUCITE) [fr. *Perspex,* trademark]

per·spi·ca·cious (pə̧:rspikéiʃəs) *adj.* having clear insight, *a perspicacious judge of people* [fr. L. *perspicax* (*perspicacis*) fr. *perspicere,* to look through]

per·spi·cac·i·ty (pə̧:rspikǽsiti:) *n.* the quality of being perspicacious [fr. L. *perspicacitas*]

per·spi·cu·i·ty (pə̧:rspikjú:iti:) *n.* clearness of expression, lucidity [fr. L. *perspicuitas*]

per·spic·u·ous (pərspíkju:əs) *adj.* clearly expressed so as to be easily understood, *a perspicuous explanation* ‖ (of a person) clearly intelligible in speech or writing [fr. L. *perspicuus,* clear, transparent]

per·spi·ra·tion (pə̧:rspəréiʃən) *n.* sweat ‖ the act of sweating [F.=a breathing out]

per·spir·a·to·ry (pərspáirətɔ̧ri:, pərspáirətou̧ri:) *adj.* of, having the nature of or inducing perspiration [fr. L. *perspirare* (*perspiratus*), to perspire]

per·spire (pərspáiər) *pres. part.* **per·spir·ing** *past* and *past part.* **per·spired** *v.i.* and *t.* to sweat [fr. L. *perspirare,* to breathe through]

per·suad·a·ble (pərswéidəb'l) *adj.* able to be persuaded

per·suade (pərswéid) *pres. part.* **per·suad·ing** *past* and *past part.* **per·suad·ed** *v.t.* to cause (someone) to do something by reasoning, coaxing, urging etc., *to persuade a sick man to stay in bed* ‖ to cause (someone) to believe something by reasoning etc., *she persuaded him that she was telling the truth* [fr. L. *persuadere*]

per·sua·si·bil·i·ty (pərswȩizəbíliti:) *n.* the quality of being open to persuasion

per·sua·si·ble (pərswéizəb'l) *adj.* persuadable [fr. L. *persuasibilis*]

per·sua·sion (pərswéiʒən) *n.* a persuading or being persuaded ‖ capacity or power to persuade, *he spoke with great persuasion* ‖ a strongly held conviction, esp. a sectarian belief ‖ a religious sect, *the Methodist persuasion* [fr. L. *persuasio* (*persuasionis*)]

per·sua·sive (pərswéisiv) *adj.* able or tending to persuade or convince [fr. M.L. *persuasivus*]

pert (pə:rt) *adj.* forward and self-confident, and not entirely respectful, *a pert answer* ‖ jaunty, *a pert little spring outfit* ‖ in good spirits, lively, *feeling quite pert again* [M.E. *apert,* open, fr. O.F.]

PERT (*management acronym*) program evaluation and review technique, a management and decision-making system defining objectives, steps for achieving them, and procedures for evaluating progress toward them

per·tain (pə:rtéin) *v.i.* (with 'to') to be a natural part, *the illnesses pertaining to childhood* ‖ (with 'to') to be suitable, *the politeness pertaining to a guest* ‖ (with 'to') to have reference, *criticisms pertaining to their smartness and discipline* [O.F. *partenir,* to belong]

Perth (pə:rθ) the capital and commercial center (pop. 89,700), with agglom., incl. the port of Fremantle, 558,000) of Western Australia. Industries: automobiles, food processing, building materials, light manufactures. University (1912)

Perth a county (area 2,493 sq. miles, pop. 128,600) of central Scotland ‖ its county town (pop. 44,100), an agricultural market on the Tay, formerly the capital of Scotland (9th–15th cc.)

per·ti·na·cious (pə̧:rt'néiʃəs) *adj.* persistent and determined, often to the point of stubbornness [fr. L. *pertinax* (*pertinacis*)]

per·ti·nac·i·ty (pə̧:rt'nǽsiti:) *n.* the quality or state of being pertinacious [F. *pertinacité*]

per·ti·nence (pə́:rt'nəns) *n.* the quality or state of being pertinent [PERTINENT]

per·ti·nen·cy (pə́:rt'nənsi:) *n.* pertinence [fr. L. *pertinens*]

per·ti·nent (pə́:rt'nənt) *adj.* (often with 'to') referring centrally to the matter being discussed or considered, *pertinent details, information pertinent to this problem* [fr. L. *pertinens* (*pertinentis*) fr. *pertinere,* to belong]

per·turb (pərtə́:rb) *v.t.* to cause to be anxious [O.F. *perturber* fr. L. *perturbare,* to disturb physically]

per·tur·ba·tion (pə̧:rtərbéiʃən) *n.* a perturbing

or being perturbed || an irregular variation or a deviation from the predicted or usual course, e.g. of a celestial body under the influence of a weak but significant force from a source that is unaccounted for [O.F.]

per·turb·a·tive (pərtɜ́rbətiv) *adj.* (*meteor.*) disturbances in the regular motions of celestial bodies

per·tus·sis (pərtʌ́sis) *n.* (*med.*) whooping cough [Mod. L. fr. L. *per,* thoroughly+*tussis,* cough]

Pe·ru (pərú:) a republic (area 496,093 sq. miles, pop. 17,031,200) of W. South America. Capital: Lima. People: 53% mestizo or white, 46% Indian (mainly Quechua and Aymará, with little-known smaller groups in the east), 1% Asian and African. Languages: Spanish (official), Indian languages. Religion: mainly Roman Catholic (75%), with Protestant (1%) and Animist minorities. The land is 55% forest, 1% cultivated (mainly irrigated). West of the Andes, which run the length of W. Peru, is a narrow coastal belt (the *costa*) rising to 5,000 ft, mainly desert (oil fields), but with irrigated valleys, containing 25% of the population. The eastern foothills and jungle-covered Ucayali (upper Amazon) basin comprise the *montaña* and contain 13% of the population. The *sierra* (the Andes) is highest (above 18,000 ft except in the north) along the western crest, with smaller ranges, high plateaus and steep valleys in the east, and contains 62% of the population and most of the mines. Highest peak: Huascarán (22,180 ft). The climate ranges from tropical to polar. Average temperatures (F.): Lima (costa) 65°, Iquitos (montaña) 76°, Cuzco (sierra) 53°. Rainfall: Lima 1.7 ins, montaña 20–130 ins, Cuzco 23 ins. Agriculture employs 62% of the people. Main crops: (costa) cotton, sugar, rice, fruit, market vegetables, olives, (*montaña,* largely undeveloped) coffee, rubber (gathered wild), cacao, lumber, other tropical products, (*sierra*) root vegetables, cereals, coca plants. Livestock (mainly *sierra*): sheep, cattle, goats, llamas, alpacas, horses, mules, hogs. Exports: fish (2nd world producer) and fishmeal, copper, iron ore, silver, lead, zinc, petroleum, hides and skins, wool, cotton, sugar, coffee, cocaine. Other products: textiles, building materials, consumer goods, chemicals, guano, vanadium, antimony, tungsten, bismuth, gypsum, coal, barite, gold. Imports: machinery, vehicles, metals, chemicals, food, fuels, textiles. Chief port: Callao. There are 8 universities, the oldest being Lima (1551) and Arequipa (1821). Monetary unit: sol (100 centavos). HISTORY. The center of the Inca Empire, Peru was invaded (1532) and conquered (1533) by a Spanish expedition under Pizarro. It was organized during the colonial period under a viceroy and comprised the Audiencias of Panama, Bogotá, Quito, Charcas, Chile, and Buenos Aires. Its importance declined in the 18th c. with the creation of Nueva Granada (1739) and the River Plate (1776). San Martín led a liberation movement and proclaimed the independence of Peru (July 28, 1821). Final Spanish resistance was defeated (1824) by Bolívar. Independence was followed by a succession of dictatorships and revolts, and by war (1863–71) with Spain. Peru was involved in war with Chile (1879–84) over the mining of nitrates in Bolivia, and lost much territory. Some economic progress was made (late 19th c.). A popular uprising which overthrew (1930) the dictatorship of Augusto B. Leguía y Salcedo introduced a radical reform party, the Alianza Popular Revolucionaria Americana (APRA), under the leadership of Víctor Raúl Haya de la Torre. Subsequently the Apristas were largely kept from power by the ruling conservative groups. Peru declared war (1945) on the Axis and joined (1945) the U.N. In 1948 a military junta installed Gen. Manuel A. Odría as president. The constitutional presidency of Manuel Prado y Ugarteche (1956–62) was followed (1962) by another military coup in order to prevent Haya de la Torre from assuming the presidency. After new elections in 1963 in which the Popular Action and Christian Democrat parties and the army's approval won the presidency for Fernando Belaúnde Terry, a new social reform program was introduced. This concentrated on building and communications, incl. a new highway cutting into the trans-Andean forests (it opened up 3,500 acres of land with each completed mile), on a vigorous (25% of the budget) attempt to reduce Peru's 45% illiteracy rate, and on an agrarian reform plan (1964) which drew about 2 million Peruvians, mostly Indians, into Cooperación Popular projects for village improvement. Such a program, beyond Peru's fiscal capacity, was further hurt by scandal and corruption. Belaúnde's failure to make good his promise to expropriate the U.S.-owned International Petroleum Co. (IPC, a subsidiary of Standard Oil Company, New Jersey), which had been drilling in Peru since 1924, and pressure from the rich landowners, brought about his overthrow (1968) by a junta headed by Gen. Juan Velasco Alvarado. Velasco introduced a vigorous agrarian reform program. His seizure of U.S. tuna clippers (1969) for violating Peru's territorial waters (extended unilaterally to 200 miles) angered the U.S.A. His confiscation, within six days of his inauguration, of most of IPC's property posed for the U.S. government the dilemma of having either to apply the Hickenlooper amendment or risk the alienation of all Latin America by waging 'economic aggression'. A compromise with the U.S.A. was worked out, and his reform program thus lost some of its impact. A violent earthquake ravaged (May 31, 1970) 300 miles of the Pacific coast region and killed 50,000 people. In 1975, with Peru facing spiraling inflation and massive foreign debt Velasco Alvarado's government was replaced by a military junta led by Gen. Francisco Morales Bermúdez. The constitution was suspended and the parliament dissolved. A new constitution was prepared by an assembly elected (1978) for the purpose and elections were held (1980) to return Peru to civilian government. Belaúnde Terry was returned to office, succeeded by Alan García Pérez (1985–), who moved to alleviate continuing economic problems and to fight cocaine trafficking

Peru–Bolivian Federation a federal state created (1836) by Gen. Santa Cruz, president of Bolivia, who declared himself its Protector (1836–9). The union was opposed by Chile, which defeated (1839) Santa Cruz in the Battle of Yungay, after which the federation was dissolved

Peru Current the Humboldt Current

Pe·ru·gia (pərú:dʒə) a city (pop. 143,089) of N. Umbria, Italy. Industries: textiles, mechanical engineering, pharmaceuticals, tourism. Etruscan and Roman city walls, palace and churches (12th and 13th cc.), Gothic cathedral (14th–15th cc.)

Pe·ru·gi·no (peru:dʒí:nɔ) (Pietro di Vannucci, c. 1445–1523), Umbrian painter of religious subjects. His symmetrical compositions generally consist of well drawn, graceful figures contained in a landscape articulated with architectural elements. His work includes the Sistine Chapel fresco 'Christ Giving the Keys to St Peter' (1481) and the fresco 'Crucifixion with Saints' (1496, Sta Maria Maddalena de' Pazzi, Florence). He taught Raphael

pe·ruke (pərú:k) *n.* a wig, esp. one of those worn in the 17th to early 19th cc. [F. *perruque*]

pe·rus·al (pərú:z'l) *n.* the act or an instance of perusing

pe·ruse (pərú:z) *pres. part.* **pe·rus·ing** *past* and *past part.* **pe·rused** *v.t.* to read through carefully or critically [etym. doubtful]

Pe·ru·vi·an (pərú:vi:ən) **1.** *adj.* of Peru, its people, culture etc. **2.** *n.* a native or inhabitant of Peru [fr. Mod. L. *Peruvia,* Peru]

Peruvian bark cinchona

per·vade (pərvéid) *pres. part.* **per·vad·ing** *past* and *past part.* **per·vad·ed** *v.t.* to spread throughout and into every part of, *new ideas pervaded the nation* **per·va·sion** (pərvéiʒən) *n.* **per·va·sive** (pərvéisiv) *adj.* pervading or tending to pervade [fr. L. *pervadere* (*pervasus*), to pass through]

per·verse (pərvɜ́:rs) *adj.* willfully doing what is wrong or unreasonable || indicating such willfulness, *a perverse refusal* || obstinate, intractable || (*law,* of a verdict) contrary to the evidence or to judicial direction [F.]

per·ver·sion (pərvɜ́:rʒən) *n.* a perverting or being perverted || a deviation from usual behavior, esp. from normal sexual behavior [fr. L. *perversio* (*perversionis*)]

per·ver·si·ty (pərvɜ́:rsiti:) *pl.* **per·ver·si·ties** *n.* the quality or state of being perverse || an instance of this [F. *perversité* fr. L.]

per·ver·sive (pərvɜ́:rsiv) *adj.* perverting or tending to pervert [fr. L. *pervertere* (*perversus*), to pervert]

per·vert 1. (pərvɜ́:rt) *v.t.* to damage the mind or will of (a person) so that he thinks or acts in an immoral way || to cause to be misused, falsified, wrongly understood etc., *to pervert the course of justice* **2.** (pɜ́:rvərt) *n.* a person who is perverted, esp. someone given to homosexuality or other abnormal sexual practices [fr. F. *pervertir* fr. L. *pervertere,* to turn upside down]

per·vi·ous (pɜ́:rvi:əs) *adj.* capable of being permeated or passed through, e.g. by heat || (with 'to') willing to be influenced (by something stipulated, e.g. reason) [fr. L. *pervius,* having a way through]

Pe·sach (péisɑx) *n.* the Passover [Heb.]

Pe·sa·ro (pézɑrɔ) an Adriatic port (pop. 84,373) in the Marches, Italy: celebrated ducal palace (15th–16th cc.)

pe·sa·wa (pəsúwɑ) *n.* one hundredth of a cedi || a coin of this value [native word in Ghana]

Pes·ca·do·res Islands (peskədɔ́riz, peskədɔ́ri:z) (or Penghu) a group of 64 islands (area 50 sq. miles, pop. 115,600) that are a dependency of Formosa and lie between Formosa and Fukien, China

pe·se·ta (pəséitə) *n.* the basic Spanish monetary unit || a coin of this value [Span.]

Pe·sha·war (pəʃɔ́wər) a strategic communications center (pop. 268,366) of Pakistan in the valley leading to the Khyber Pass (11 miles west), a market for produce and handicrafts. Greek, Buddhist and Mogul remains

Pe·shi·to (pəʃí:tou) *n.* the Peshitta

Pe·shit·ta (pəʃí:tə) *n.* the principal Syriac version of the Bible [Syriac *p'shītâ p'shītô,* plain, simple]

pes·ky (péski:) *comp.* **pes·ki·er** *superl.* **pes·ki·est** *adj.* (*pop.*) annoyingly troublesome [perh. var. of *pesty* fr. PEST]

pe·so (péisou) *pl.* **pe·sos** *n.* the monetary unit of many South American republics and of the Philippines || a coin of this value [Span.=a weight]

pes·sa·ry (pésəri:) *pl.* **pes·sa·ries** *n.* an instrument worn in the vagina to prevent displacement of the uterus or as a contraceptive || a vaginal suppository [fr. M.L. *pessarium* fr. L. *pessum* fr. Gk *pessos,* an oval stone]

pes·si·mism (pésəmizəm) *n.* the tendency to expect the worst or to stress the worst aspect of things (opp. OPTIMISM) || the belief that the world is fundamentally evil **pés·si·mist** *n.* someone who persistently takes the worst view of things || someone who holds the metaphysical doctrine of pessimism **pes·si·mís·tic** *adj.* **pes·si·mís·ti·cal·ly** *adv.* [fr. L *pessimus,* worst]

Pest (pest) *BUDAPEST

pest (pest) *n.* an animal (e.g. an insect or rodent) which is destructive to crops, stored food etc. || a tiresome, annoying person || (*hist.*) the plague [F. *peste,* plague fr. L.]

Pes·ta·loz·zi (pestɑlɔ́tsi:), Johann Heinrich (1746–1827), Swiss educational reformer, influential in the development of modern primary education

pes·ter (péstər) *v.t.* to annoy with persistent requests, questions etc. [perh. fr. O.F. *empestrer,* to shackle]

pest·house (pésthaus) *pl.* **pest·hous·es** (pésthauziz) *n.* (*hist.*) a hospital or other establishment for people with deadly epidemic diseases, e.g. plague

pest·i·cide (péstisaid) *n.* a substance, e.g. an insecticide, used for destroying pests [fr. PEST+L. *caedere,* to kill]

pes·tif·er·ous (pestífərəs) *adj.* carrying infection || socially or morally harmful [fr. L. *pestiferus,* pest-bearing]

pes·ti·lence (péstələns) *n.* a deadly epidemic disease, esp. (*hist.*) the bubonic plague || something morally or socially pernicious [F. fr. L. *pestilentia*]

pes·ti·lent (péstələnt) *adj.* pestilential || harmful to society, esp. in a moral sense || tiresomely annoying [fr. L. *pestilens* (*pestilentis*) fr. *pestis,* plague]

pes·ti·len·tial (pestəlénʃəl) *adj.* of, causing or having the nature of pestilence [fr. M.L. *pestilentialis*]

pes·tle (pés'l, péstəl) *n.* a blunt-ended implement for reducing hard substances to powder by pounding them in a mortar || any of several instruments used for pounding or stamping [M.E. fr. O.F. *pestel, pesteil*]

pestle *pres. part.* **pes·tling** *past* and *past part.* **pes·tled** *v.t.* to pound or crush with a pestle || *v.i.* to use a pestle [O.F. *pesteler*]

pes·tol·o·gy (pestɔ́lədʒi:) *n.* the scientific study of pests, esp. insect pests, and of their control [fr. PEST+Gk *logos,* word]

CONCISE PRONUNCIATION KEY: (a) æ, *cat;* ɑ, *car;* ɔ *fawn;* ei, *snake.* (e) e, *hen;* i:, *sheep;* iə, *deer;* ɛə, *bear.* (i) i, *fish;* ai, *tiger;* ə:, *bird.* (o) o, *ox;* au, *cow;* ou, *goat;* u, *poor;* ɔi, *royal.* (u) ʌ, *duck;* u, *bull;* u:, *goose;* ə, *bacillus;* ju:, *cube.* x, *loch;* θ, *think;* ð, *bother;* z, *Zen;* ʒ, *corsage;* dʒ, *savage;* ŋ, *orangutang;* j, *yak;* ʃ, *fish;* tʃ, *fetch;* 'l, *rabble;* 'n, *redden.* Complete pronunciation key appears inside front cover.

pet (pet) **1.** *n.* a tame animal kept as a companion or for fun, and affectionately cared for ‖ someone who is treated as a favorite **2.** *adj.* kept as a pet ‖ favorite, *he's off on his pet topic again* **3.** *v. pres. part.* **pet·ting** *past* and *past part.* **pet·ted** *v.t.* to pat or caress (e.g. a pet animal) ‖ to pamper ‖ *v.i.* (*pop.*) to caress someone of the opposite sex in sexual play [origin unknown]

pet *n.* a fit of resentful or peevish ill humor, *to be in a pet* [etym. doubtful]

peta- (petə) standard international combining prefix for 10^{15}

Pé·tain (peitɛ̃), Henri Philippe (1856–1951), French soldier and statesman, marshal of France (1918–45). He defended Verdun (1916) and was the French commander in chief (1917–18). He became prime minister of France (1940), signed the armistice with Germany and was appointed head of state of the Vichy government (1940–4). He was tried for treason (1945) and condemned to death, but the sentence was commuted to life imprisonment

pet·al (pét'l) *n.* one of the colored, modified leaves forming part of the corolla of a flower **pét·aled, pét·alled** *adj.* [fr. Mod. L. *petalum* fr. Gk *petalon,* thin plate]

pet·al·oid (pét'lɔid) *adj.* (*bot.*) looking like or having the form of a petal ‖ (*biol.*) composed of petallike parts [fr. Mod. L. *petaloideus* fr. L. *petalum,* petal]

pe·tard (pitɑ́rd) *n.* (*hist.*) a kind of bomb once used to break down obstructions [F. *pétard*]

pet·cock (pétkɒk) *n.* a small cock or valve used to release air from a water pump or pipe, or to drain a steam cylinder, radiator etc.

Pe·tén, El (petén) a region of Central America, between N. Guatemala and S. Yucatán. It was one of the earliest centers of Mayan civilization and is known today for its archaeological ruins

Pe·ter (pí:tər), St (*d.* 64 or 67), chief of the 12 Apostles, brother of St Andrew. He was originally called Simon but Jesus gave him the Aramaic name 'Kepha', meaning rock, translated into Greek as 'Petros'. A fisherman on the Sea of Galilee, he was summoned by Jesus to be a disciple. Jesus's declarations to him recorded in Matthew xvi, 18–19 are the basis of the papal claim to supremacy in succession to Peter. Peter was present at Gethsemane, but afterwards he denied three times being a follower of Jesus. He was the first of the Apostles to whom Jesus appeared after the Resurrection, and became their acknowledged leader. He was imprisoned in Jerusalem and miraculously released. Peter preached in Asia Minor, and, according to tradition, went to Rome (c. 55) and was martyred under Nero. It is generally thought that he influenced the writing of the Gospel according to St Mark. Feast: June 29

pe·ter (pí:tər) *v.i.* (usually with 'out') to become gradually smaller in size or amount and finally cease to be, *her enthusiasm petered out* [origin unknown]

Peter I 'the Great' (1672–1725), czar of Russia (1682–1725). Assuming personal power (1689), he gave Russia an outlet to the Black Sea by capturing Azov from the Turks (1695–6). After extensive travels in Europe (1697–8), he began to Westernize Russian institutions. His victory over the Swedes (1709) in the Northern War gave Russia access to the Baltic. He moved the capital from Moscow to St Petersburg (1713). His other reforms included the reorganization of the army, the founding of a navy, the establishment of several hundred factories, the construction of canals and technical schools and the planning of the Russian Academy of Sciences. He established a new tax system and made the Church subject to the State. By often ruthless methods he made Russia an important European power

Peter III (1728–62), czar of Russia (1762). He was forced to abdicate in favor of his wife, Catherine II

Peter I (1844–1921), king of Serbia (1903–18) and of the country later called Yugoslavia (1918–21), grandson of Karageorge. On account of ill health, he made his son, Alexander I, regent (1914)

Peter II (1923–70), king of Yugoslavia (1934–45), son of Alexander I. After a regency under his cousin had formed an alliance with the Axis provoking a revolution, he seized personal power (1941) but went into exile when the Germans invaded (1941). The monarchy was abolished (1945)

Peter kings of Castile, León, Aragon and Portugal, and emperors of Brazil *PEDRO

Peter Ca·ni·sius (kənífəs), St (1521–97), Dutch Jesuit theologian who converted many Lutheran regions of W. and S. Germany to Catholicism. Feast: April 27

Peter Cla·ver (kléivər), St (Pedro Claver, c. 1581–1654), Spanish Jesuit missionary, known as the 'apostle of the blacks' for his ministering to W. African slaves in Colombia. Feast: Sept. 9

Peter Da·mi·an (déimi:ən), St (Pietro Damiani, 1007–72), Italian monk and reformer. He was associated with Pope Gregory VII in promoting clerical reform, and scathingly attacked clerical abuses in his 'Liber Gomorrhianus' (c. 1050). Feast: Feb. 23

Peter, Epistles of the 21st and 22nd books of the New Testament, of uncertain authorship (late 1st and early 2nd cc.), the first of which deals with Christian duties and encourages the Christians of Asia Minor under persecution

Peter Lombard *LOMBARD

Pe·ter·loo (pí:tərlú:) (*Br. hist.*) the name derisively given to a public disturbance in Manchester (1819), in which the magistrates ordered the cavalry to charge a large crowd peaceably assembled to petition for the repeal of the Corn Laws. There were several hundred casualties. The government's action in congratulating the magistrates greatly increased the growth of radicalism and of the reform movement [after St *Peter's* Fields, where the meeting was held +WATERLOO]

Peter Principle tenet that employees advance to the level of their incompetence; satirically conceived by Lawrence Peter, Canadian educator

Pe·ters·burg (pí:tərzbə:rg) a city (pop. 41,055) and port of entry in S.E. Virginia. During the American Revolution it was captured (1781) by British troops. In the Civil War it was finally taken, after a long Union siege (1865), by a force under Gen. Ulysses S. Grant. The victory was followed within a week by Gen. Robert E. Lee's surrender at Appomattox

pe·ter·sham (pí:tərʃəm) *n.* corded ribbon for stiffening waistbands, hatbands etc. ‖ a rough woolen cloth used mainly for men's coats [after Viscount *Petersham,* 19th-c. English nobleman]

pe·ter·son·ics (pi:tərsɒ́niks) *n.* (*acoustics*) the study of acoustic waves at microwave frequencies on solid substances (e.g., a railroad station, a house). *also* acoustoelectronics

Peter's pence a voluntary contribution paid annually by Roman Catholics for the expenses of papal administration ‖ (*hist.*) an annual tax of one penny formerly payable by every household in many European countries to the papal see

Peter the Hermit (c. 1050–1115), French preacher. After preaching the 1st Crusade (1096–9), he led a band of peasant followers through E. Europe, but had already left them before their defeat by the Turks. He reached the Holy Land in the company of other Crusaders

Peter Zeng·er Trial a landmark in British jurisprudence during the colonial period in America. Peter Zenger (1697–1746), a New York printer, was charged (1734) with seditious libel against the colonial government. His defense, Andrew Hamilton, denied that the alleged libels were false and set a precedent by upholding the right of publication of matters 'supported by truth.' Zenger was acquitted

pet·i·o·lar (péti:ələr) *adj.* (*biol.*) of, designating, like or attached to a petiole

pet·i·o·late (péti:əleit) *adj.* having a petiole **pét·i·o·lat·ed** *adj.*

pet·i·ole (péti:oul) *n.* (*bot.*) a stalk holding a leaf ‖ (*zool.*) something resembling this, esp. the slender stalk connecting thorax and abdomen in some insects, e.g. ants [fr. L. *petiolus,* little foot, stalk]

Pé·tion (peitjɔ̃) (Alexandre Sabès, 1700–1818), Haitian soldier and statesman. He founded (1807) a republic in S. Haiti, and served (1807–18) as its first president. He is known for his aid to Simón Bolívar's wars for independence

Pe·ti·pa (peti:pɑ), Marius (1822–1910), French dancer and choreographer. He was one of the chief creators of the Russian ballet and helped to make Diaghilev's achievements possible

pe·tite (pətí:t) *adj.* (of a person) small and neat in figure [F.]

pet·it·grain oil (péti:grein) a fragrant essential oil extracted from the leaves and branches of the Seville orange and other trees of genus *Citrus,* used in the production of soap and perfume [F. *petitgrain,* unripe bitter orange]

pe·ti·tion (pətíʃən) **1.** *n.* a formal request, esp. to a sovereign, a governing body etc., often a written one signed by a large number of people ‖ a solemn prayer to God, *the petitions of the litany* ‖ a formal written request to a court of law ‖ that which is requested, *your petition is granted* **2.** *v.t.* to make a petition to (someone) for something to be done ‖ to make a request for (something) ‖ *v.i.* to make a petition [F. *pétition* fr. L. fr. *petere,* to seek, request]

pe·ti·tion·a·ry (pətíʃəneri:) *adj.* of, relating to or involving a petition [fr. M.L. *petitionarius*]

Petition of Rights (*Eng. hist.*) a declaration (1628) by parliament that unparliamentary taxation, arbitrary imprisonment, billeting of soldiers on citizens and declaration of martial law in peacetime were illegal practices. Charles I accepted the petition, but his subsequent violation of it led to the Civil War (1642–52)

pet·it ju·ry (péti:dʒúəri:) a petty jury [F. *petit,* small]

pe·tit mal (pəti:mǽl) *n.* mild epilepsy characterized by momentary loss of consciousness (cf. GRAND MAL) [F.=small evil or illness]

pet name a name other than a person's true name or nickname, used affectionately

pet·nap·ping (pétnæpiŋ) *n.* theft of pet animals for ransom or other reason. —**pet·nap·per** *n.*

Pe·tra (pí:trə) an ancient citadel and former center of the caravan trade, in the E. Great Rift Valley in S. Jordan. It was the capital of the Edomites and Nabataeans: Nabataean, Hellenistic and Roman tombs and temples carved in the cliffs, and Frankish fortifications

Pe·trarch (pí:trɑrk, pétrɑrk) (Francesco de Petrarca, 1304–74), Italian poet and scholar, famous for his sonnets, which quickly influenced poets writing in other European languages, and esp. for his 'Rime in Vita e Morte di Madonna Laura'. They were written in the main tradition of courtly love, but they embody a celebration of love freed from allegory and mysticism. He used the Tuscan dialect. He also wrote in Latin, esp. the epic poem 'Africa' (1341). In many ways he is one of the first men of the Renaissance: he translated and collected classical manuscripts, visited Rome for the ruins of antiquity rather than the splendors of the Church, and in his extensive letters and essays on religious, philosophical and political subjects frequently expressed a humanistic point of view

pet·rel (pétrəl) *n.* any of several rather small, web-footed sea birds of fam. *Procellariidae* and fam. *Hydrobatidae,* having mainly dark or dark and white plumage. They are nocturnal, feeding far out at sea on creatures swimming near the surface. They breed in crevices and holes in rocks, a single egg being laid [older *pitteral,* perh. fr. a L. dim. of *Petrus,* St Peter (because he walked on the waves)]

Pe·trie (pí:tri:), Sir William Matthew Flinders (1853–1942), British archaeologist, He carried out many excavations in Egypt (1881–1924), notably at Abydos (1899), and was a pioneer of modern archaeological method, esp. in the use of pottery for establishing dates and periods

pet·ri·fac·tion (pɛtrifǽkʃən) *n.* (of organic matter) a converting or being converted into stone ‖ a petrified mass [fr. PETRIFY]

pet·ri·fi·ca·tion (pɛtrifikéiʃən) *n.* petrifaction [F. *pétrification*]

pe·tri·fy (pétrifai) *pres. part.* **pet·ri·fy·ing** *past* and *past part.* **pet·ri·fied** *v.t.* to turn (an organic structure) into stone, or a substance hard as stone, through the replacement of organic tissues by deposited silica, agate or calcium carbonate in solution ‖ to render (a person) rigid or numb with fear or horror ‖ *v.i.* to be turned into stone or a stony substance [F. *pétrifier* fr. L. fr. *petra,* rock]

Pe·trine (pí:train, pí:trin) *adj.* of or like St Peter or the doctrines connected with him [fr. L. *Petrus,* Peter]

pet·ro·chem·i·cal (pɛtroukémik'l) *n.* a chemical derived from petroleum or natural gas or from one of their derivatives, e.g. ethyl alcohol [fr. Gk *petros,* stone and *petra,* rock+CHEMICAL]

pet·ro·dol·lars (pétroudɒlərz) *n.* oil earnings of petroleum-exporting countries in excess of their domestic needs, usu. deposited in dollars in Western European banks

pet·ro·glyph (pétrəglif) *n.* a rock carving esp. a prehistoric one **pet·ro·glýph·ic** *adj.* [fr. F.

pétroglyphe fr. Gk *petra*, rock+*gluphē*, carving]

Pet·ro·grad (pétrəgræd) *LENINGRAD

pet·ro·graph·ic (petrəgræfik) *adj.* of or relating to petrography **pet·ro·gráph·i·cal** *adj.*

pe·trog·ra·phy (pətrógrəfi:) *n.* the scientific description and classification of rocks [fr. Gk *petra*, rock+*-graphos*, written]

pet·rol (pétrəl) *n.* (*Br.*) gasoline [F. *pétrole*]

pet·ro·la·tum (petrəléitəm) *n.* a yellowish and white gelatinous, tasteless hydrocarbon mixture derived from petroleum, used as a base for ointments, as a lubricant etc. [Mod. L. fr. M.L. *petroleum*, petroleum]

petrol bomb (*Br.*) Molotov cocktail

pe·tro·le·um (pətróuli:əm) *n.* an oily liquid mixture of complex hydrocarbons occurring naturally in the pores and fissures of sedimentary rock, usually in association with its gaseous form, natural gas [M.L. fr. L. *petra*, rock+*oleum*, oil]

—In the refining process, the crude oil is distilled, yielding fractions which constitute gasoline, kerosene, diesel fuel, fuel oil, lubricating oils and heavy fuel oils. The residue yields paraffin wax and asphalt. To increase the yield of motor fuel, the hydrocarbons in the heavier fractions are broken down by thermal or catalytic cracking. Petroleum is the source of petrochemicals used widely in manufacturing (plastics, synthetic fibers, drugs, detergents, fertilizers, insecticides and rust preventives). The chief petroleum producing areas of the world are the U.S.A., Venezuela, Russia and the areas bordering the Persian Gulf

petroleum jelly petrolatum

petroleum spirit (esp. *pl.*) white spirits

pet·ro·log·ic (pɛtrəlódʒik) *adj.* of or pertaining to petrology **pet·ro·lóg·i·cal** *adj.*

pe·trol·o·gist (pətrólədʒist) *n.* a specialist in petrology

pe·trol·o·gy (pətrólədʒi:) *n.* the branch of geology dealing with the origin, occurrence, structure and composition of rocks, based on field and laboratory tests [fr. Gk *petra*, stone+*logos*, word]

Pe·tro·ni·us (pitróuni:əs) (*d.* 66), Roman satirist, author of the novel the 'Satyricon', and probably the same Petronius as the Arbiter Elegantiae (arbiter of taste) at Nero's court, who committed suicide for political reasons

Pe·tro·pav·lovsk (pɛtroupávlɔfsk) an agricultural market and rail center (pop. 212,000) of N. Kazakhstan, U.S.S.R.: farm machinery, food processing, military equipment

Pe·tro·pav·lovsk-Kam·chat·ski (pɛtrʌpávlʌfskkɑmtʃátski) a port and naval base on the S.E. Kamchatka peninsula, U.S.S.R. Fish and shellfish canning factories

pet·ro·pol·i·tics (pɛtroupólitiks) *n.* the backstage manipulations among oil-producing countries, companies and related political figures

pe·tro·sal (pətróus'l) **1.** *adj.* hard, rocklike ‖ belonging or near to the hard portion of the temporal bone or the capsule of the internal ear, e.g. of the otic bone of fish **2.** *n.* a petrosal bone [fr. L. *petrosus*, rocky]

pet·rous (pétrəs) *adj.* of or like rock ‖ of the pyramidal part of the temporal bone between the sphenoid and the occipital bones [fr. L. *petrosus*, rocky]

Pe·tro·za·vodsk (pɛtrʌzɑvɔ́tsk) the capital (pop. 241,000) of the Karelian A.S.S.R., U.S.S.R., a port and rail center on Lake Onega: wood and machine industries

Pet·sa·mo (pétsɑmɔ) *PECHENGA

pet·ti·coat (péti:kɔut) *n.* an undergarment hanging from the waist, esp. one bedecked with lace, ruffles etc. to be worn under a skirt ‖ (*Br.*) a slip (dress-length undergarment) [earlier *petty coat*, little coat]

petticoat government domination by women in the home or in politics

petticoat insulator an insulator for high insulation, shaped like a number of superimposed inverted cups

pet·ti·fog·ger (péti:fɔgər) *n.* (*old-fash.*) a disreputable lawyer who handles petty cases ‖ someone given to pettifogging **pet·ti·fóg·ger·y** *n.* [fr. PETTY+(*obs.*) *fogger*, pettifogger, prob. fr. the FUGGER family]

pet·ti·fog·ging (péti:fɔgiŋ) **1.** *adj.* (of a person) quibbling over trivial details ‖ (of behavior) characteristic of such a person ‖ (of details) tiresomely trivial **2.** *n.* a quibbling over unimportant details [fr. PETTIFOGGER]

pet·ti·ly (pétili:) *adv.* in a petty manner

pet·ti·ness (péti:nis) *n.* the quality of being petty ‖ an instance of this

pet·tish (pétiʃ) *adj.* sulking or apt to sulk and be peevish [PET, fit of bad humor]

pet·ti·toes (péti:touz) *pl. n.* pig's feet as food [etym. doubtful]

Pet·ty (péti:), Sir William (1623–87), English statistician and economist. He put forward the view that land and labor were the basis of value in his 'Treatise of Taxes and Contributions' (1662). He wrote many works on trade, industry and population from a statistical point of view

pet·ty (péti:) *comp.* **pet·ti·er** *superl.* **pet·ti·est** *adj.* minor, trivial, *petty grievances* ‖ (of a person) giving minor matters, esp. minor faults or grievances, unwarranted importance ‖ characteristic of such a person [M.E. *pety* fr. F. *petit*, small]

petty cash small amounts of money for incidental expenses ‖ a fund drawn on for these expenses

petty jury a jury of 12 people that hears evidence and gives a verdict in a criminal or civil case on trial (cf. GRAND JURY)

petty larceny theft of property valued at less than a stated sum (which varies between $10 and $200 according to jurisdiction) ‖ (*Br. hist.*) theft of property valued at less than 12d.

petty officer (*Am. navy*) a member of one of three classes of noncommissioned naval officer of lowest rating: petty officer first class, petty officer second class and petty officer third class ‖ (*Br. navy*) an officer of a rank corresponding to that of non-commissioned officer in the army

petty sessions the meeting of two or more justices of the peace or magistrates to try certain minor offenses summarily, without a jury

pet·u·lance (pétʃuləns) *n.* the quality or state of being petulant [F. *pétulance*]

pet·u·lant (pétʃulənt) *adj.* discontented and irritable over trifles [F. fr. L. *petulans* (*petulantis*), forward, insolent]

pe·tu·ni·a (pitú:njə, pitjú:njə) *n.* a member of *Petunia*, fam. *Solanaceae*, a genus of herbaceous plants native to South America and widely cultivated for their variously colored, funnel-shaped flowers [Mod. L. fr. obs. F. *petun*, tobacco fr. Guaraní]

pe·tun·tse (petúntsə) *n.* china stone [Mandarin *pai-tun-tze*, white stone]

Peul (pju:l) *n.* a member of the Fulani people ‖ the Fulani language

Pevs·ner (péfsnər), Antoine (1886–1962), French sculptor, born in Russia, an originator of constructivism

pew (pju:) *n.* a long bench with a back used as church furniture [M.E. *puwe, pywe, pewe* fr. O.F. *puye, poye*, balcony, parapet]

pe·wee, pee·wee (pí:wi:) *n.* any of several North American olive-green flycatchers, esp. *Contopus virens*, the wood pewee [imit.]

pe·wit, pee·wit (pí:wit) *n.* the pewee ‖ the lapwing [imit.]

pew·ter (pjú:tər) **1.** *n.* any of several gray alloys of tin, usually with lead in the proportion roughly 4 to 1, or sometimes with a small amount of antimony or copper to harden it, used (esp. formerly) for plates, mugs etc. Pewter is malleable and does not tarnish ‖ utensils made of this alloy **2.** *adj.* made of this alloy [M.E. fr. O.F. *peutre, peautre, peaultre*, origin unknown]

pe·yo·te (peióuti:) *n.* any of several cacti growing in the southwest U.S.A. and Mexico, esp. mescal ‖ a stimulant from mescal buttons used in some esp. Mexican Indian religious rituals [Span. fr. Nahuatl *peyotl*, caterpillar]

pfen·nig (fénig)n. one hundredth of a deutsche mark ‖ a coin of this value [G.]

PG 1. (*pharm. abbr.*) **prostaglandin. 2.** a motion-picture rating indicating that parental guidance is suggested. *Cf* G, R, X

pH (*chem.*) a symbol signifying the negative logarithm (base 10) of the hydrogen ion concentration of a solution or pure liquid expressed in gram equivalents per liter. The range of values of pH extends from 0 to 14, 7 being the negative logarithm of the hydrogen-ion concentration in pure water at 25°C (1 x 10^{-7} gram liter) or neutrality. Smaller numbers signify increasing acidity, greater ones increasing basicity

Phae·dra (fí:drə, fédrɑ) (*Gk mythol.*) daughter of Minos, and wife of Theseus. She was seized by an unrequited passion for her stepson (*HIPPOLYTUS) and killed herself after causing his death

Phae·drus (fí:drəs) (c. 15 B.C.–c. 50 A.D.), Roman author of verse fables, largely based on Aesop, but told with originality and charm

Phaes·tus (féstəs) an ancient town of Crete with remains of a Minoan palace (c. 2200 B.C.)

Pha·ë·thon (féiəθən) (*Gk mythol.*) son of Helios. One day he drove the sun's chariot, and nearly set fire to the world when the horses bolted. Zeus struck him dead with a thunderbolt to save the world

pha·ë·ton (féiitən) *n.* a light, fourwheeled, open carriage drawn by one horse or two [after PHAETHON]

phag·o·cyte (fǽgəsait) *n.* any cell, esp. a leucocyte, able to ingest and destroy foreign particles harmful to the body **phag·o·cyt·ic** (fægəsítik) *adj.* **phag·o·cy·to·sis** (fægəsaitóusis) *n.* the ingestion and destruction of harmful microorganisms, foreign matter and tissue debris, that in vertebrates is accomplished by leucocytes, and that serves as an important defense and waste-disposal mechanism [fr. Gk *phagein*, to eat+*kutos*, cell]

phag·o·some (fǽgəsoum) *n.* (*cytol.*) a vesicle in a cell holding material captured by ameboid cells

phal·ange (fǽləndʒ, fəlǽndʒ) *pl.* **pha·lan·ges** (fəlǽndʒi:z) *n.* (*anat.*) a phalanx [F. *phalange* fr. L.]

pha·lan·ge·al (fəlǽndʒi:əl) *adj.* (*anat.*) of the bones of the fingers and toes [fr. Mod. L. *phalangeus* fr. L. *phalanx*, phalanx]

pha·lan·ger (fəlǽndʒər) *n.* a member of *Phalangeridae*, suborder *Diplotodontia*, a family of arboreal marsupials of Australia and New Guinea. They are mostly nocturnal, feeding on insects and fruit, and usually have a prehensile tail [Mod. L. fr. Gk *phalangion*, spider's web, from the structure of the hind feet]

phal·an·ster·y (fǽlənstɛri:) *pl.* **phal·an·ster·ies** *n.* a community living together and sharing property after the plan of Charles Fourier [fr. F. *phalanstère* fr. *phalange*, phalanx]

pha·lanx (féilæŋks, fǽlæŋks) *pl.* **pha·lanx·es, pha·lan·ges** (fəlǽndʒi:z) *n.* (*Gk hist.*) a body of Greek infantry formed in close ranks with shields joined ‖ any body of people solidly grouped for defensive or offensive action ‖ (*anat.*) *pl.* **phalanges** each of the bones composing the segments of finger and toe ‖ a phalanstery [L. fr. Gk *phalanx* (*phalangos*)]

Phalanx *n.* (*mil.*) a close-in weapons system providing automatic, autonomous terminal defense against antiship cruise missiles, including self-contained search-and-track radars, weapons control and 20-mm M61 gun firing subcaliber penetrators

phal·a·rope (fǽləroup) *n.* a member of *Phalaropodidae*, a family of small, lobate-toed wading birds of Europe and North America, breeding in the Arctic and wintering in warm climates. The female is more brightly colored than the male and conducts the courtship. The male incubates the egg [F. fr. Mod. L. *Phalaropus* fr. Gk *phalaris*, coot+*pous* (*podos*), foot]

phal·lic (fǽlik) *adj.* of or relating to a phallus or phallicism ‖ like a phallus **phal·li·cism** (fǽlisizəm) *n.* worship of the phallus as symbol of the generating force in nature [fr. Gk *phallikos* fr. *phallos*, phallus]

phal·lus (fǽləs) *pl.* **phal·li** (fǽlai) *n.* a symbol of the penis, used in Dionysian cults and other religions to represent the generative force [L. fr. Gk *phallos*, penis]

phan·er·o·gam (fǽnərəgæm) *n.* a seed plant or flowering plant (cf. CRYPTOGAM) [F. *phanérogame* fr. Gk *phaneros*, visible+*gamos*, sexual union]

phan·er·o·gam·ic (fænərəgǽmik) *adj.* of or designating a phanerogam [fr. Mod. L. *phanerogamia*, former bot. division, fr. *phanerogamus*, phanerogamic]

phan·er·og·a·mous (fænərógəməs) *adj.* phanerogamic [PHANEROGAM]

phan·o·tron (fǽnətrɒn) *n.* (*electr.*) a rectifier made of a hot cathode gas diode

phan·tasm (fǽntæzəm) *n.* an illusion ‖ a ghostly apparition, esp. of a person, dead or alive ‖ (*philos.*) the mental image of a person or an object [F. *fantasme* fr. L. fr. Gk *phantasma*]

phan·tas·ma·go·ri·a (fæntæzməgɔ́ri:ə, fæntæzməgóuri:ə) *n.* a constantly moving succession of real or imagined scenes, people or things, esp. characteristic of a dream or a fevered state **phan·tas·ma·gor·ic** (fæntæzməgɔ́rik, fæntæzməgórik) *adj.* [fr. Gk *phantasma*, phantasm+(perh.) *agora*, assembly]

CONCISE PRONUNCIATION KEY: **(a)** æ, *cat*; ɑ, *car*; ɔ *fawn*; ei, *snake*. **(e)** e, *hen*; i:, *sheep*; iə, *deer*; ɛə, *bear*. **(i)** i, *fish*; ai, *tiger*; ə:, *bird*. **(o)** o, *ox*; au, *cow*; ou, *goat*; u, *poor*; ɔi, *royal*. **(u)** ʌ, *duck*; u, *bull*; u:, *goose*; ə, *bacillus*; ju:, *cube*. x, *loch*; θ, *think*; ð, *bother*; z, *Zen*; ʒ, *corsage*; dʒ, *savage*; ŋ, *orangutang*; j, *yak*; ʃ, *fish*; tʃ, *fetch*; 'l, *rabble*; 'n, *redden*. Complete pronunciation key appears inside front cover.

phan·tas·mal (fæntǽzməl) *adj.* of, involving or having the nature of a phantasm

phan·tas·mic (fæntǽzmik) *adj.* phantasmal

phantasy *FANTASY

phan·tom (fǽntəm) **1.** *n.* something, esp. a ghost, that appears to be seen but that has no real physical existence ‖ someone who or something which is only apparently what they or it purports to be **2.** *adj.* illusory [M.E. *fantosme, fantome* fr. O.F.]

phantom order a draft contract with an industrial establishment for wartime production of a specific product. It provides for necessary preplanning in peacetime and for immediate execution of the contract when proper authority is received

Phantom II (*mil.*) U.S. twin-engine, supersonic multipurpose jet fighter/bomber (F-4 and RF-4), operative from land and aircraft carriers and employing both air-to-air and air-to-surface weapons; made by McDonnell Douglas

phar·aoh (fɛ́ərou, fǽrou) *n.* the title of ancient Egyptian kings **phar·a·on·ic** (fɛəreiɒ́nik) *adj.* [O.E. *pharaon* fr. L. fr. Gk fr. Heb. fr. Egypt.]

phar·i·sa·ic (færiséiik) *adj.* self-righteous and hypocritical **Phar·i·sa·ic** of, relating to or like the Pharisees **phar·i·sá·i·cal** *adj.* [fr. L. fr. Gk *pharisaïkos*]

phar·i·see (fǽrisi:) *n.* a hypocrite ‖ a self-righteous person **Phar·i·see** a member of a Jewish religious sect (2nd c. B.C.–2nd c. A.D.) which upheld strict obedience to the Torah, combined with traditional interpretations of it. The Pharisees were the opponents of the Sadducees [M.E. *pharise, farise* fr. O.F. fr. L. fr. Gk fr. Aram.]

phar·ma·ceu·tic (fɑrməsú:tik) *adj.* of or relating to pharmacy **phar·ma·céu·ti·cal** *adj.* **phar·ma·céu·tics** *n.* the science of the preparation and use of medicines **phar·ma·céu·tist** *n.* a pharmacist [fr. L. fr. Gk *pharmakeutikos* fr. *pharmakon,* poison, medicine]

pharmaceutical chemist a chemist engaged in research in or the production of medical chemicals ‖ (*Br.*) a druggist

phar·ma·cist (fɑ́rməsist) *n.* a person skilled or engaged in pharmacy

phar·ma·co·ge·net·ics (fɑrməkoudʒənétiks) *n.* study of interaction of drugs and genetic reactions. —**phar·ma·co·ge·net·ic** *adj.* —**phar·ma·co·ge·net·i·cist** *n.*

phar·ma·co·log·i·cal (fɑrməkəlɒ́dʒik'l) *adj.* of or relating to pharmacology

phar·ma·col·o·gist (fɑrməkɒ́lədʒist) *n.* a person trained or engaged in pharmacology

phar·ma·col·o·gy (fɑrməkɒ́lədʒi:) *n.* the study of the preparation, properties, uses and effects of drugs [fr. Mod. L. *pharmacologia* fr. Gk *pharmakon,* poison, medicine+*logos,* word]

phar·ma·co·poe·ia (fɑrməkəpí:ə) *n.* a book, esp. an official reference book, listing the properties, effects, recommended dosages and ways of administration of chemicals, medicinal preparations and esp. drugs. It usually gives standards and tests for drugs ‖ a stock of drugs **pharma·co·póe·ial** *adj.* [Mod. L. fr. Gk *pharmakon.* poison, medicine+*poiein,* to make]

phar·ma·cy (fɑ́rməsi:) *pl.* **phar·ma·cies** *n.* the art or profession of preparing and dispensing medicinal drugs ‖ a pharmacist's shop ‖ a drugstore [O.F. *farmacie, pharmacie* fr. L.L. fr. Gk fr. *pharmakon* poison, medicine]

Pha·ros, the (fɛ́ərɒs) a lighthouse on an island near Alexandria, completed (c. 280 B.C.) by Ptolemy II and destroyed by an earthquake (14th c.). It was one of the Seven Wonders of the World ‖ this island

Phar·sa·lus (fɑrséiləs) an ancient city of Thessaly, near which Julius Caesar defeated Pompey (48 B.C.)

pha·ryn·gal (fəríŋg'l) *adj.* pharyngeal [fr. Mod. L. *pharynx,* pharynx]

pha·ryn·ge·al (fəríndʒi:əl, fəríndʒəl, færindʒí:əl) *adj.* of, pertaining to or near the pharynx [fr. Mod. L. *pharyngeus*]

pharynges alt. *pl.* of PHARYNX

phar·yn·gi·tis (færindʒáitis) *n.* inflammation of the pharynx [Mod. L. fr. Gk *pharunx* (*pharungos*), throat]

phar·ynx (fǽriŋks) *pl.* **phar·yn·ges** (fəríndʒi:z), **phar·ynx·es** *n.* in vertebrates, the cavity of the alimentary canal between the mouth and the esophagus, communicating with the nasal passages and ears ‖ the corresponding part in invertebrates [Mod. L. fr. Gk *pharunx* (*pharungos*), throat]

phase (feiz) **1.** *n.* each of the successive aspects or stages in any course of change or development ‖ (*astron.*) an aspect in the cycle of changing form or quantity of illumination of the moon or of a planet ‖ (*chem., phys.*) a uniform, bounded portion of matter that is mechanically separable from a heterogeneous physico-chemical system (cf. STATE) ‖ (*phys.*) the progress of a cyclic harmonic motion in relation to some standard point of reference (in time or space), usually expressed in angular measure, 360 degrees representing a full period or cycle **in phase** in or of the same phase ‖ in a synchronized manner **out of phase** in or of different phases ‖ not in a synchronized manner **2.** *v.t. pres. part.* **phas·ing** *past* and *past part.* **phased** to cause to be in phase **to phase in** to bring in in phases or as a phase **to phase out** to stop using or cause to cease by phases ‖ to cease by phases **phá·sic** *adj.* [fr. F. *phase* and fr. Mod. L. *phases* pl. of *phasis,* phase fr. Gk *phainein,* to show, appear]

phased array antenna antenna with dipoles with varied signals so arranged so that beams can be formed and scanned rapidly

phase-down (féizdaun) *v.* to reduce in stages —**phase-down** *n.* —**phase out** *v.*

phase rule (*phys., chem.*) a law of heterogeneous systems in equilibrium: P+F=C+2, where P is the number of phases, C the number of components and F is the number of degrees of freedom

pheas·ant (féz'nt) *n.* a member of *Phasianus,* fam. *Phasianidae,* a genus of large, long-tailed gallinaceous game birds. The male has highly colored, varied plumage. They feed on insects, seeds and berries. They are native to Asia, but many species are now found in Europe and North America, esp. *P. colchicus* ‖ any of several related birds of fam. *Phasianidae,* e.g. the peacock, or any of several unrelated birds thought to resemble this, found in various parts of the world [M.E. fr. A.F. *fesant,* O.F. *fesan* fr. L. fr. Gk *phasianos* (*ornis*), Phasian bird, fr. R. *Phasis*].

phel·lem (féləm) *n.* (*bot.*) cork [fr. Gk *phellos,* cork]

phel·lo·derm (félədə:rm) *n.* (*bot.*) a secondary parenchymatous suberized cortex of trees, developed from the inner side of the phellogen (*PERIDERM) **phel·lo·dér·mal** *adj.* [fr. Gk *phellos,* cork+*derma,* skin]

phel·lo·gen (félədʒən) *n.* (*bot.*) a meristem (cork cambium) developing externally in dicotyledonous stems and giving rise to cork tissue and phelloderm **phel·lo·ge·nét·ic, phel·lo·gén·ic** *adjs* [fr. Gk *phellos,* cork+*genēs,* born of]

phen- (fi:n) *prefix* (*chem.*) relating to or derived from benzene [fr. Gk *phainein,* to show and *phainesthai,* to appear (from its originally denoting substances obtained in the manufacture of gas for lighting)]

phe·nac·e·tin, phe·nac·e·tine (finǽsitin) *n.* a white crystalline compound, $C_{10}H_{13}NO_2$, used medicinally to reduce pain or fever [PHEN-+*acetin,* acetic glycerin]

phen·cy·cli·dine [$C_{17}H_{25}N$] (fensáiklidi:n) *n.* (*pharm.*) a central-nervous-system depressant used by veterinarians

phe·net·ic (fenétik) *adj.* (*genetics*) of an organism classification method based on similarity of characteristics. —**phe·net·i·cist** *n.* —**phe·net·i·cal·ly** *adv.* —**phe·net·ics** *n. Cf* CLADISTIC

phen·for·min [$C_{10}H_{15}N_5$] (fenfɔ́rmin) *n.* (*pharm.*) an oral antidiabetic; marketed as DBI

Phenicia *PHOENICIA

Phenician *PHOENICIAN

phenix *PHOENIX

phe·no·bar·bi·tal (fi:noubɑ́rbitɑl, fi:noubɑ́rbitəl) *n.* a white crystalline powder, phenylethyl-barbituric acid, $C_{12}H_{12}N_2O_3$, used medicinally as a hypnotic and sedative

phe·nol (fí:noul, fí:nɒl) *n.* a white crystalline solid, organic hydroxy acid, C_6H_5OH, with a characteristic smell, poisonous and corrosive, distilled from coal tar and used as a disinfectant and in the manufacture of dyes and plastics ‖ any of the hydroxy derivatives of benzene **phe·nó·lic** *adj.* [fr. Gk *phaino-,* shining fr. *phainein,* to show and *phainesthai,* to appear]

phe·nol·o·gy (finɒ́lədʒi:) *n.* (*biol.*) a study of periodic biotic events, e.g. flowering, breeding, migration, in relation to climatic and other factors [PHENOMENON+Gk *logos,* word]

phe·nol·phthal·e·in (fi:noulθǽli:in) *n.* a white or yellowish compound, $C_{20}H_{14}O_4$, used as a laxative and as a chemical indicator. It turns red in basic solutions and loses its color in acid ones

phe·nom·e·nal (finɒ́mən'l) *adj.* (*philos.*) recognized by or experienced by the senses rather than through thought or intuition ‖ concerned with or constituting a phenomenon or phenomena ‖ extraordinary, unusual, *a phenomenal number of voters*

phe·nom·e·nal·ism (finɒ́mən'lizəm) *n.* (*philos.*) the theory that phenomena are the only things we can know and that everything else is either nonexistent or inaccessible to the human mind **phe·nóm·e·nal·ist** *n.* and *adj.* **phe·nom·e·nal·ís·tic** *adj.*

phe·nom·e·no·log·i·cal (finɒmən'lɒ́dʒik'l) *adj.* of, relating to or characterized by phenomenology ‖ (*philos.*) of, relating to or professing phenomenology

phe·nom·e·nol·o·gy (finɒmənɒ́lədʒi:) *n.* the observation and description of phenomena ‖ (*philos.*) a method of arriving at absolute essences through the analysis of living experience in disregard of scientific knowledge (*HUSSERL) [fr. PHENOMENON+Gk *logos,* word]

phe·nom·e·non (finɒ́mənɒn) *pl.* **phe·nom·e·na** (finɒ́mənə) *n.* (*philos.*) something known by sense perception rather than by thought or intuition ‖ any fact or event which can be described and explained in scientific terms ‖ an extraordinary or remarkable event, thing, person etc. [L.L. *phaenomenon* fr. Gk *phainomenon,* appearing, apparent fr. *phainesthai,* to appear]

phen·o·thi·a·zine [$C_{12}H_9NS$] (fenəθáiəzi:n) *n.* (*pharm.*) a deworming drug used by veterinarians

phe·no·type (fí:nətaip) *n.* the appearance of an organism due to the response of genotypic (inherited) characters to the environment ‖ all the individuals belonging to such a type (opp. GENOTYPE) **phe·no·typ·ic** (fi:nətípik), **phe·no·týp·i·cal** *adjs* [G. *phänotypus* fr. L. fr. Gk]

phen·tol·a·mine [$C_{17}H_{19}N_3O$] (fentɒ́ləmi:n) *n.* (*pharm.*) drug used to block action of the adrenal medulla used in diagnosis of tumors; marketed as Regitine

phen·yl (fén'l, fí:n'l) *n.* the monovalent radical, C_6H_5, of which benzene is the hydride. It is the basis of many aromatic derivatives [fr. Gk *phaino-,* shining fr. *phainein,* to show and *phainesthai,* to appear]

phen·yl·ke·to·nu·ri·a (fenilki:tounjú:ri:ə) *n.* (*med.*) genetic mental retardation due to inability of the body to metabolize the amino acid phenylalanine. *abbr.* **PKU**

pher·o·mone (fɛ́rəmoun) *n.* (*biochem.*) chemical substance secreted to produce a response by others of the same species, particularly by insects, esp. in relation to sexual attraction. —**pher·o·mon·al** *adj. Cf* ECTOHORMONE

phi (fai) *n.* the twenty-first letter (Φ, ϕ = ph) of the Greek alphabet

phi·al (fáiəl) *n.* a small glass bottle, esp. for medicines [M.E. fr. O.F. *fiole, phiole* fr. L. fr. Gk *phialē,* a flat shallow bowl]

Phi Be·ta Kap·pa (fáibeitəkǽpə) *n.* a national academic honorary society of the U.S.A., founded in 1776. College and university students may be elected to membership, usually in their senior year [fr. initial letters of Gk *philosophia biou kubernētēs,* philosophy the guide of life, the society's motto]

Phid·i·as (fídi:əs) (c. 500–c. 431 B.C.), Greek sculptor who was appointed by Pericles to beautify Athens. His works include the sculptural decoration of the Parthenon and the monumental statue of Athene which it housed, as well as the statue of Zeus at Olympia which was one of the Seven Wonders of the World

Phil·a·del·phi·a (filədélfi:ə) the fourth largest city (pop. 1,688,210) of the U.S.A., an international port, commercial and industrial center on the Delaware River, E. Pennsylvania. Industries: food processing, mechanical engineering, chemicals, metallurgy, shipbuilding, publishing, textiles, petroleum. Colonial monuments include the courthouse (1732), State House, or Independence Hall (1732–53), numerous private houses. University of Pennsylvania (1791). The city was founded as a Quaker settlement (1682) by Penn, was the scene of the Continental Congresses (1774–83) and the signing of the Declaration of Independence (1776), and was the capital of the U.S.A. (1790–1800)

phi·lan·der (filǽndər) *v.i.* (of a man) to flirt ‖ (of a man) to have many but casual love affairs **phi·lan·der·er** *n.* [fr. Gk *philandros* adj., (of a woman) loving men]

phil·an·throp·ic (filənθrópik) *adj.* doing good works, actively benevolent ‖ showing philanthropy **phil·an·thróp·i·cal** *adj.* [fr. F. *philanthropique* fr. Gk]

phi·lan·thro·pist (filǽnθrəpist) *n.* a humanitarian, esp. one who disinterestedly gives large gifts of money for particular causes

phi·lan·thro·py (filǽnθrəpi:) *pl.* **phi·lan·thro·pies** *n.* generous help or benevolence toward one's fellow men ‖ an instance of this [fr. L.L. *philanthropia* fr. Gk fr. *philos,* loving+*anthrōpos,* man]

phil·a·tel·ic (filətélik) *adj.* relating to philately

phi·lat·el·ist (filǽt'list) *n.* an expert in philately ‖ a stamp collector

phi·lat·e·ly (filǽt'li:) *n.* the collection and study of postage stamps, envelopes bearing postmarks etc., usually as a hobby [fr. F. *philatélie* fr. Gk *philos,* loving+*ateleia,* tax exemption (taken as=postage stamp)]

Phi·le·mon and Bau·cis (filí:mən, failí:mən, bɔ́sis) (*Gk mythol.*) a peasant and his wife who gave hospitality to Zeus and Hermes traveling incognito on the earth. They became priest and priestess of Zeus and, when they had grown very old together, they were turned into intertwined trees. Their names are a symbol of conjugal love

Philemon, Epistle to (filí:mən) the 18th book of the New Testament. It is a personal letter written by St Paul to Philemon, a Colossian, asking him to forgive his runaway slave

phil·har·mon·ic (filharmónik, filərmónik) *adj.* loving music (only used in titles of orchestras, musical societies etc.) [F. *philharmonique* fr. Gk *philos,* loving+*harmonikos,* harmonic]

phil·hel·lene (filhéli:n) *n.* a person who admires Greece, its people, culture etc. ‖ (*hist.*) a supporter of the cause of Greek independence **phil·hel·len·ic** (filhəlénik) *adj.* **phil·hel·len·ism** (filhélinizəm) **phil·hél·len·ist** *ns* [fr. Gk *philellēn* adj. fr. *philos,* loving+*Hellēn,* Hellene]

Phil·ip (fílip), St (*d.* c. 80), one of the 12 Apostles. Feast: May 1

Philip (Marcus Julius Philippus, 204–49), Roman emperor (244–9). The millennium of Rome's foundation was celebrated (248) during his reign

Philip II (382–336 B.C.), king of Macedon (359–336 B.C.). A great statesman and general, he unified his kingdom, favored Greek culture and created a highly skilled army. His defeat of Athens and Thebes (338) made Macedon the leading power in Greece. He was assassinated while preparing an expedition against the Persians, and was succeeded by his son Alexander the Great

Phi·lip·pic (filípik) *n.* any of a number of speeches in which Demosthenes warned his fellow-countrymen of the danger to which Greece was exposed by the expansion of Philip II of Macedon **phi·lip·pic** (*rhet.*) an angry tirade filled with invective

Phil·ip·pine (fílipi:n) *adj.* of or relating to the Philippine Is or the Republic of the Philippines

Philip V (238–179 B.C.), king of Macedon (221–179 B.C.), son of Demetrius II. He fought two wars against the Romans (215–205 B.C. and 200–197). He was defeated by Flamininus at Cynoscephalae (197)

Philip I (*Span.* Felipe) 'the Handsome' (1478–1506), king of Castile (1506), son of Emperor Maximilian I

Philip II (1527–98), king of Spain and the Two Sicilies (1556–98), of the Netherlands (1555–98) and, as Philip I, of Portugal (1580–98), son of Emperor Charles V. His reign was devoted to increasing the power of Spain and the Church. He married (1554) Mary I of England, but the English alliance ended with her death (1558). The Treaty of Cateau-Cambrésis (1559) left Spain as the dominant European colonial power, and Spain became still more powerful with the defeat of the Turks at Lepanto (1571). Philip governed repressively through the Inquisition. The northern provinces of the Netherlands rose (1567) against Alba, whom he had appointed governor, and were declared independent (1581). He unsuccessfully supported the Holy League against Henri IV, and failed in his attempt to invade England by the Armada (1588). He conquered Portugal (1580)

Philip III (1578–1621), king of Spain and the Two Sicilies (1598–1621) and, as Philip II, king of Portugal (1598–1621), son of Philip II of Spain. His reign marked the decline of the Spanish Empire, but was a golden age in Spanish culture (Cervantes, Lope de Vega, El Greco)

Philip IV (1605–65), king of Spain and the Two Sicilies (1621–65) and, as Philip III, king of Portugal (1621–40), son of Philip III of Spain. He was forced to reaffirm the independence of the Netherlands in the Treaties of Westphalia (1648) and to cede Roussillon and Artois to France in the Treaty of the Pyrenees (1659)

Philip V (1683–1746), first Bourbon king of Spain (1700–46), grandson of Louis XIV. His designation by Charles II as successor to the Spanish throne precipitated the War of the Spanish Succession. The attempts of his minister, Alberoni, to regain the territory lost by the Treaty of Utrecht (1713) resulted in his defeat by the Quadruple Alliance (1720). He concluded the Family Compact with France (1733) and regained the Two Sicilies (1734)

Philip kings of France and dukes of Burgundy *PHILIPPE

Philip 'the Magnanimous' (1504–67), landgrave of Hesse (1509–67) and a leader of the Reformation in Germany. He was a prominent member of the Schmalkaldic League, established the first Protestant university (Marburg, 1527) and tried to reconcile Luther and Zwingli (1529)

Philip (*d.* 1676), American Indian leader in King Philip's War

Philip, Prince, duke of Edinburgh (1921–), consort of Elizabeth II

Philip Ne·ri (níəri:), St (Filippo Romolo de' Neri, 1515–95), Italian priest. He founded the Congregation of the Oratory (1564). Feast: May 26

Phi·lippe I (filí:p) (1052–1108), king of France (1060–1108), son of Henri I. He enlarged his kingdom and supported Robert II of Normandy in his revolt against William I of England

Philippe III 'the Bold' (1245–85), king of France (1270–85), son of Louis IX. He gained possession of Toulouse, Auvergne and part of Poitou (1271), but died after an unsuccessful attempt to gain Aragon

Philippe IV 'the Fair' (1268–1314), king of France (1285–1314), son of Philippe III. He greatly increased royal authority, reduced feudal power and came into conflict with Pope Boniface VIII over clerical taxation. His stand against the papacy was approved by the States General, which he summoned for the first time (1302). He triumphed with the election to the papacy (1305) of the French Clement V, and the establishment (1309) of the papacy at Avignon. He acquired Navarre, Champagne, part of Flanders and Lyon for the French crown

Philippe V 'the Tall' (1294–1322), king of France (1316–22), son of Philippe IV. Appointed regent on the death (1316) of his brother Louis X, he proclaimed himself king on the death of Louis's posthumous son, Jean I, claiming that the succession was governed by Salic law. He frequently summoned the States General

Philippe VI (1293–1350), king of France (1328–50), the first of the Valois. His claim to the throne, based on Salic law, was disputed by Edward III of England, thus starting (1337) the Hundred Years' War. He was defeated at Crécy (1346) and lost Calais to the English. He acquired the Dauphiné (1343) and Montpellier (1349)

Philippe 'the Bold' (1342–1404), duke of Burgundy (1363–1404), son of Jean II. He distinguished himself in battle at Poitiers (1356). He was regent (1380–8) for Charles V, and was the effective ruler during much of Charles's reign

Philippe 'the Good' (1396–1467), duke of Burgundy (1419–67), son of Jean the Fearless. He supported the claims of Henry V of England to the French throne prior to making peace with Charles VII (1435). He extended his territories into the Netherlands, and founded (1429) the Order of the Golden Fleece

Philippe II Augustus (1165–1223), king of France (1180–1223), son of Louis VII. He allied himself (1189) with the future Richard I of England against Henry II, accompanied Richard on the 3rd Crusade (1190–1), and resumed the war against England. His victory over King John at Bouvines (1214) gained him Normandy, Anjou, Poitou, Maine and Touraine. His administrative reforms included the establishment of royal courts of justice. He fostered the growth of towns and trade, and was a founder of the University of Paris

Philippe E·ga·li·té (eigæli:tei) *ORLÉANS, Louis-Philippe Joseph, duc d'

Phi·lippe·ville (fi:li:pvi:l, fílipvil) *SKIKDA

Phi·lip·pi (filípai) an ancient town of Macedonia, near which Antony and the future Emperor Augustus decisively defeated Brutus and Cassius (42 B.C.)

Phi·lip·pi·ans, Epistle to the (filípi:ənz) the eleventh book of the New Testament, a letter of gratitude and advice written by St Paul during imprisonment either in Ephesus (c.53) or in Rome (c.60)

Philippine Islands the group of islands constituting the Republic of the Philippines

Philippine Sea, Battle of the a naval engagement (1944) during the 2nd world war in which a U.S. naval aviation force defeated the Japanese, paving the way for Gen. MacArthur's return to the islands

Phil·ip·pines, Republic of the (fílipi:nz) a republic (area 115,708 sq. miles, pop. 54,500,000) of S.E. Asia, comprising 7,107 islands, the northernmost part of the Malay Archipelago. Capital and chief town: Manila. Principal islands: Luzon, Mindanao, Mindoro, Palawan, and the Visayas. People: Filipino (Malay), 1% Chinese, small aborigine (pygmy) and Indonesian minorities. Language: Tagalog (official), 75 other Malayo-Polynesian languages. 35% also speak English, 2% Spanish. Religion: 75% Roman Catholic, with Protestant, Moslem, independent Catholic, Animist, Buddhist and other minorities. The islands are mountainous (few peaks over 5,000 ft) and largely volcanic, with fertile valleys. The land is 44% forest, 27% cultivated. Highest point: Mt Apo (9,540 ft), on Mindanao. Except for primitive tribes, the population is concentrated on the coasts. Average summer and winter temperatures (F.): coast 82° and 77°, interior mountains 70° and 60°. Rainfall: 40–120 ins. Rainy seasons: summer and autumn in W. Luzon and W. Visayas, winter in E. Luzon, E. Visayas, and N.E. Mindanao. Typhoons are frequent north of Samar. Livestock: water buffaloes (carabao), hogs, cattle, goats, poultry, horses. Crops: rice, abaca, copra, sugarcane, corn, coconuts, tobacco, coffee, sweet potatoes, fruit (esp. pineapples), vegetables. Forestry products: lumber, gums, resins, dyes, vegetable oils, rattan. Fisheries. Mineral resources: gold, copper, chromite, silver, lead, zinc, manganese, iron ore, mercury, coal, salt, nickel, uranium. Industries: textiles, tobacco, hydroelectricity, footwear, cement, wood products, plastics. coconut oil refining, rubber goods, embroidery, hats, mats, pottery. Exports: sugar, lumber, copra, minerals and metals, abaca, coconut oil. Imports: machinery, fuels and oil, textiles, cereals, vehicles, foodstuffs. Ports: Manila, Cebu, Iloilo, Davao, Zamboanga. There are 26 universities. Monetary unit: peso (100 centavos). HISTORY. Inhabited by Negritos, the islands were invaded by Indonesians (3rd millennium B.C.). They were visited by Japanese and Chinese traders (8th c. A.D.) and by Moslem Arab missionaries (14th–15th cc.). A Spanish expedition led by Magellan reached the Philippines (1521) and a Spanish settlement was founded (1565). Revolts against Spanish rule were unsuccessful until the Spanish-American War (1898), after which the Philippines were transferred to the U.S.A., which put down a Filipino rebellion (1899–1901). As trade with the U.S.A. developed, economic progress was made, and communications and education were improved. Quezon became (Sept. 1935) first president of the Philippines. The islands were occupied (1942–4) by the Japanese. The Philippines joined the U.N. (1945) and became a Republic (July 4, 1946), but continued to receive large amounts of U.S. aid to repair war damage and strengthen the economy. The Philippines joined the South East Asia Treaty Organization (1954). President Ramón Magsaysay (1953–7) ended the Communist-dominated Huk guerrilla movement. President Diosdado Macapagal (1961–5) tried unsuccessfully to confederate the Philippines with Malaya and Indonesia. President Ferdinand Marcos (1965–86) imposed martial law (1972–81) and changed the constitution (1981) to maintain his power after martial law was lifted. The assassination of the political opposition leader Benigno Aquino (1983) caused a political crisis. The opposition made substantial gains in the 1984 elections. After a court acquitted armed forces chief of staff Gen. Fabian Ver of complicity in the Aquino slaying,

CONCISE PRONUNCIATION KEY: **(a)** æ, *cat*; ɑ, *car*; ɔ *fawn*; ei, *snake*. **(e)** e, *hen*; i:, *sheep*; iə, *deer*; ɛə, *bear*. **(i)** i, *fish*; ai, *tiger*; ə:, *bird*. **(o)** o, *ox*; au, *cow*; ou, *goat*; u, *poor*; ɔi, *royal*. **(u)** ʌ, *duck*; u, *bull*; u:, *goose*; ə, *bacillus*; ju:, *cube*. x, *loch*; θ, *think*; ð, *bother*; z, *Zen*; ʒ, *corsage*; dʒ, *savage*; ŋ, *orangutang*; j, *yak*; ʃ, *fish*; tʃ, *fetch*; 'l, *rabble*; 'n, *redden*. Complete pronunciation key appears inside front cover.

criticism of Marcos and his government increased. A 1986 presidential election between Marcos and Aquino's widow, Corazon, led to widespread allegations of fraud and voter intimidation by the Marcos faction and ultimately led to Marcos's being deposed and forced to leave the country. Mrs. Aquino became president and attempted conciliation among all political groups in the country

Phil·ips (fílips), Ambrose (1674–1749), English poet, pioneer of sentimental landscape poetry in 'A Winter Piece' (1709) and 'Pastorals' (1710)

Phi·lis·ti·a (filísti:ə) the ancient region of Palestine inhabited by the Philistines

Phil·is·tine (fílisti:n, fílistain) *n.* a member of an ancient people who settled (c. 13th c. B.C.) in the coastal region of Palestine. They are thought to have spoken a Semitic language and to have originated in Crete. They were subdued by the Hebrews under Saul and David (10th c. B.C.) **phil·is·tine 1.** *adj.* lacking culture or having contempt for it **2.** *n.* a person with uncultivated tastes **phíl·is·tin·ism** *n.*

Phil·lips (fíləps), Wendell (1811–84), leading U.S. abolitionist, orator and reformer. He advocated Union separation from the slave states, and, after emancipation, headed the American Antislavery Society until its dissolution. He also campaigned for temperance and women's rights

Phil·lips curve (fílips) (*economics*) a graphic presentation of correlation between inflation and unemployment, conceived by A. W. H. Phillips, British economist

phil·lu·men·ist (filú:menist) *n.* a collector of matchbooks and/or matchbox labels —**phil·lu·men·y** *n.* the hobby

Phi·lo (fáilou) Jewish-Hellenistic philosopher (c. 20 B.C.–c. 54 A.D.). He believed in the divinity of the Jewish law but elaborated an allegorical interpretation of the Bible, purporting to show that it embodies the ideas of Greek philosophy, esp. Plato. His main work is his massive exegesis of the Pentateuch

phil·o·den·dron (filədéndrən) *pl.* **phil·o·den·drons, phil·o·den·dra** (filədéndrə) *n.* any of various members of genus *Philodendron,* tropical American climbing plants. Many are cultivated as house plants [Mod. L. fr. Gk, neuter of *philodendros* adj., treeloving]

phil·o·log·ic (filəlɒ́dʒik) *adj.* philological

phil·o·log·i·cal (filəlɒ́dʒik'l) *adj.* of or relating to philology

phi·lol·o·gist (filɒ́lədʒist) *n.* a specialist in philology

phi·lol·o·gy (filɒ́lədʒi:) *n.* the study of language from the written texts by which it is known ‖ the study of texts and their transmission [fr. L. *philologia,* love of talk fr. Gk]

Phil·o·me·la (filəmí:lə) (*Gk mythol.*) daughter of the king of Athens. She was raped and had her tongue torn out by Tereus, king of Thrace, the husband of her sister Procne. The gods turned Philomela into a nightingale and her sister into a swallow

phil·o·pro·gen·i·tive (filouproudʒénitiv) *adj.* (*rhet.*) tending to produce many offspring (*rhet.*) loving one's offspring [fr. Gk *philos,* loving+L. *progignere* (*progenitus*), to beget]

phi·los·o·pher (filɒ́səfər) *n.* a person who engages in the study of philosophy ‖ (*pop.*) a person who accepts misfortune with stoic calm [M.E. *philosophre* fr. O.E. fr. L. fr. Gk fr. *philos,* loving+*sophos,* wise]

philosopher's stone, philosophers' stone a mythical stone or substance much sought after by alchemists, who believed it had the power to change base metals into gold and to grant eternal youth

phil·o·soph·ic (filəsɒ́fik) *adj.* of or relating to philosophy ‖ (*pop.*) resigned in the face of troubles, wisely unemotional about what cannot be altered **phil·o·sóph·i·cal** *adj.* [fr. L.L. *philosophicus*]

phi·los·o·phize (filɒ́səfaiz) *pres. part.* **phi·los·o·phiz·ing** *past* and *past part.* **phi·los·o·phized** *v.i.* to theorize ‖ (*pop.*) to moralize [fr. Gk *philosophos,* philosopher]

phi·los·o·phy (filɒ́səfi:) *pl.* **phi·los·o·phies** *n.* the love or pursuit of wisdom, i.e. the search for basic principles. Traditionally, Western philosophy comprises five branches of study: metaphysics, ethics, aesthetics, epistemology and logic ‖ systematized principles of any subject or branch of knowledge, *the philosophy of history* ‖ an attitude towards life ‖ (*pop.*) calm resignation, *he faced the situation with philosophy* [M.E. fr. O.F. *philosophie* fr. L. *philosophia* fr. Gk fr. *philos,* loving+*sophos,* wise, a wise man]

phil·ter, phil·tre (fíltər) *n.* a potion supposed to make a person fall in love ‖ any magic potion [F. *philtre* fr. L. *philtrum* fr. Gk fr. *philein,* to love]

phi me·son (faí mí:sʌn) *n.* (*particle phys.*) an unstable elementary meson particle with negative charge parity and a large mass (1019 MEV). *also* phi

Phips, Phipps (fips), Sir William (1651–95), the first royal governor (1692–5) of Massachusetts. He appointed a commission to try those accused of witchcraft

phle·bit·ic (fləbítik) *adj.* relating to or having phlebitis

phle·bi·tis (fləbáitis) *n.* inflammation of the veins, usually in the legs [Mod. L. fr. Gk *phleps* (*phlebos*), vein]

phle·bol·o·gy (flebɒ́lədʒi:) *n.* (*med.*) medical study of the veins

phle·bot·o·my (fləbɒ́təmi:) *pl.* **phle·bot·o·mies** *n.* (*hist.*) the act or practice of opening a vein for the purpose of bloodletting as a cure for various ailments ‖ an instance of this [O.F. *flebothomie* fr. L. *phlebotomia* fr. Gk fr. *phleps* (*phlebos*), vein+*tomos,* a cutting]

phlegm (flem) *n.* mucus esp. when it occurs in excessive quantity in the respiratory passages ‖ (*hist.*) one of the four humors ‖ stoic self-possession, imperturbability **phleg·mat·ic** (flegmǽtik) *adj.* having or showing stoic self-possession, imperturbable **phleg·mát·i·cal** *adj.* [M.E. *fleen, fleume, fleme* fr. O.F. fr. L.L. fr. Gk *phlegma,* inflammation, phlegm]

phlo·em (flóuem) *n.* a complex tissue in the vascular system of higher plants, consisting of sieve tubes and companion cells and usually also parenchyma and sclerenchyma. It serves esp. in conduction. but also in support and storage [G. fr. Gk *phloos,* bark]

phlo·gis·tic (floudʒístik) *adj.* (*med.*) of or relating to inflammations ‖ (*hist.*) of or relating to phlogiston [fr. Gk *phlogistos,* inflammable and fr. PHLOGISTON]

phlo·gis·ton (floudʒístɒn, floudʒístən) *n.* (*hist.*) a hypothetical substance formerly assumed to be present in all substances which burn, and to escape during combustion, leaving an ash (calx) behind [Mod. L. fr. Gk fr. *phlogizein,* to set on fire]

phlox (flɒks) *n.* a member of *Phlox,* fam. *Polemoniaceae,* a genus of herbaceous plants native to North America and widely cultivated, having clusters of white, pink or purple, salver-shaped flowers [L.=a kind of flower, flame, fr. Gk]

Phnom Penh (p'nóumpén) the capital (pop. 70,000) and chief river port of Cambodia, on the Mekong River, an agricultural market and communications (rail and air) center. Industries: food processing, brewing, distilling, textiles, wood manufactures. Handicrafts: jewelry, goldwork

pho·bia (fóubi:ə) *n.* morbid and often irrational dread of some specific thing [Mod. L. fr. Gk *phobos,* fear]

Pho·cis (óusis) a region of central Greece on the N.E. Gulf of Corinth. It formed a league of 20 city-states (7th c. B.C.) to guard the oracle at Delphi and was involved in a series of wars to defend it (c. 590 B.C., c. 448 B.C. and 355–346 B.C.), in the last of which Phocis was conquered by Macedon

Phoe·be (fí:bi:) (*Gk mythol.*) Artemis as goddess of the moon

phoe·be (fí:bi:) *n.* a member of *Sayornis,* a genus of North American flycatchers, esp. *S. phoebe* [imit.]

Phoe·bus (fí:bəs) (*Gk mythol.*) Apollo as god of the sun

Phoe·ni·cian, Phe·ni·cian (finíʃən, finí:ʃən) **1.** *adj.* of Phoenicia, its colonies, people or language **2.** *n.* a native of Phoenicia

—The Phoenicians, a Semitic people, settled in Phoenicia (c. 3000 B.C.). Centered on Byblos, Tyre and Sidon, they were at the height of their power c. 1200–c. 800 B.C., trading throughout the Mediterranean. They exported cedar wood, purple dye, textiles, glass, metalwork, spices and perfumes, and founded trading stations and colonies, notably at Carthage (c. 814 B.C.). Phoenician seamen sailed into the Atlantic, and are thought to have reached Britain and to have explored the west coast of Africa. The Phoenicians were the first to devise an alphabet. Phoenicia was conquered (6th c. B.C.) by Persia, and Phoenicians made an important contribution to Persian sea power and craftsmanship

Phoe·ni·cia, Phe·ni·cia (finíʃə, finí:ʃə) an ancient country now forming the coastal region of Lebanon and part of Syria

Phoe·nix (fí:niks) the capital (pop. 764,911) and largest city of Arizona, center of an irrigated agricultural district: electrical and electronic engineering, farm machinery, aircraft, food processing, metallurgy, tourism

phoe·nix, phe·nix (fí:niks) *n.* (*Egypt. mythol.*) a bird of gorgeous plumage, sacred to the sun, reborn from the ashes of the funeral pyre which it made for itself when each life span of 500 or 600 years was over ‖ something or someone seen as resembling this bird, esp. with respect to its power of self-regeneration [O.E. and O.F. *fenix* fr. M.L. *phenix,* and L. *phoenix* fr. Gk *phoinix*]

Phoenix Islands eight coral islands (area 11 sq. miles, pop. 1,200), of which Canton and Enderbury have been jointly controlled by the U.S.A. and Great Britain since 1939, the rest being part of Kiribati

phon (fɒn) *n.* (*phys.*) a unit of loudness, equivalent to a sound intensity of 1 decibel [fr. Gk *phōnē,* sound, voice]

pho·nate (fóuneit) *pres. part.* **pho·nat·ing** *past* and *past part.* **pho·nat·ed** *v.i.* (*physiol.*) to produce a vocal sound **pho·ná·tion** *n.* [fr. Gk *phōnē,* voice]

phone (foun) **1.** *n.* a telephone **2.** *v.i.* and *t. pres. part.* **phon·ing** *past* and *past part.* **phoned** to telephone [TELEPHONE]

phone *n.* (*phon.*) a simple speech sound [fr. Gk *phōnē,* voice]

phone-in (fóunin) *n.* a broadcast program inviting audience telephone participation with questions or comments

pho·neme (fóuni:m) *n.* a class of closely related speech sounds in a given language considered as forming a unit **pho·né·mic** *adj.* **pho·né·mi·cal·ly** *adv.* **pho·né·mics** *n.* the branch of linguistics dealing with the phonemes of a particular language [fr. F. *phonème* fr. Gk]

pho·net·ic (fənétik, founétik) *adj.* of or relating to vocal sounds and speech ‖ consistently representing sounds by the same symbols, *phonetic spelling* ‖ relating to phonetics **pho·nét·i·cal·ly** *adv.* **pho·ne·ti·cian** (founitíʃən) *n.* a specialist in phonetics **pho·nét·i·cist** *n.* a phonetist **pho·nét·ics** *n.* the branch of language study concerned with the production of speech sounds, alone or in combination, and their representation in writing ‖ the phonetic system of a given language [fr. Mod. L. *phoneticus* fr. Gk *phōnētikos* fr. *phōnein,* to utter sound]

pho·ne·tist (fóunitist) *n.* a phonetician ‖ someone who advocates phonetic spelling [fr. Gk *phōnētos,* to be spoken]

phoney *PHONY

phon·ic (fɒ́nik, fóunik) *adj.* of or relating to sound, esp. speech sounds [fr. Gk *phōnē,* voice]

phon·ics (fɒ́niks) *n.* the use of sound-symbol (phoneme-grapheme) relationships in the teaching of reading

pho·no·an·gi·og·ra·phy (fóunouændʒi:ɒgrəfi:) *n.* (*med.*) analysis of blood flow by sound

pho·no·car·di·og·ra·phy (fóunoukɑrdi:ɒgrəfi:) *n.* (*med.*) the recording of heart sounds. —**pho·no·car·di·o·gram** *n.* the record —**pho·no·car·di·o·graph** *n.* the instrument used

pho·no·gram (fóunəgræm) *n.* a symbol representing a spoken word, sound or syllable, e.g. in shorthand [fr. Gk *phōnē,* sound, voice +*gramma,* letter, writing]

pho·no·graph (fóunəgræf, fóunəgrɑf) *n.* (*Am.*=*Br.* Gramophone) a machine for reproducing sounds recorded on a disk or cylinder **pho·no·graph·ic** (founəgrǽfik) *adj.* **pho·no·gráph·i·cal·ly** *adv.* [fr. Gk *phōnē,* sound+-*graphos,* written]

pho·nog·ra·phy (founɒ́grəfi:) *n.* phonetic spelling or writing ‖ a phonetic shorthand system [fr. Gk *phōnē,* sound+*graphia,* writing]

pho·no·lite (fóun'lait) *n.* a gray or green volcanic rock giving a ringing sound when struck **pho·no·lit·ic** (foun'lítik) *adj.* [fr. Gk *phōnē,* sound+*lithos,* stone]

pho·no·log·ic (foun'lɒ́dʒik) *adj.* relating to or according to the principles of phonology **pho·no·lóg·i·cal** *adj.*

pho·nol·o·gist (founɒ́lədʒist, fənɒ́lədʒist) *n.* a specialist in phonology

pho·nol·o·gy (founɒ́lədʒi:, fənɒ́lədʒi:) *n.* the study of speech sounds, esp. of the theory and

CONCISE PRONUNCIATION KEY: **(a)** æ, *cat;* ɑ, *car;* ɔ *fawn;* ei, *snake.* **(e)** e, *hen;* i:, *sheep;* iə, *deer;* ɛə, *bear.* **(i)** i, *fish;* ai, *tiger;* ə:, *bird.* **(o)** o, *ox;* au, *cow;* ou, *goat;* u, *poor;* ɔi, *royal.* **(u)** ʌ, *duck;* u, *bull;* u:, *goose;* ə, *bacillus;* ju:, *cube.* x, *loch;* θ, *think;* ð, *bother;* z, *Zen;* ʒ, *corsage;* dʒ, *savage;* ŋ, *orangutang;* j, *yak;* ʃ, *fish;* tʃ, *fetch;* 'l, *rabble;* 'n, *redden.* Complete pronunciation key appears inside front cover.

development of sound changes within a given language ‖ the system of phonetics of a language ‖ the study of phonetics or of phonemics [fr. Gk *phōnē*, voice, sound+*logos*, word]

pho·nons (fóunɒns) *n.* (*phys.*) a quantum of heat energy in the acoustic vibration of a crystal lattice

pho·no·pho·tog·ra·phy (fóunofətɒgrəfi:) *n.* photographic recording of vibrations created by speech. *Cf* VOICEPRINT

pho·nop·si·a (founópsi:ə) *n.* (*physiol.*) the visual perceptions of color resulting from sound

pho·no·tac·tics (fóunoutæktiks) *n.* (*linguistics*) analysis of sound structure and function in language. —**pho·no·tac·tice** *adj.*

pho·ny, pho·ney (fóuni:) *comp.* **pho·ni·er** *superl.* **pho·ni·est 1.** *adj.* (*pop.*) not genuine, counterfeit **2.** *pl.* **pho·nies** *n.* (*pop.*) a person who is not what he pretends to be [origin unknown]

pho·ny mine (fóuni:) (*mil.*) an object of any available material, used to simulate a mine in a phony minefield (which see)

phony minefield (*mil.*) an area of ground used to simulate a minefield with the object of deceiving the enemy

pho·rate [$C_7H_{17}O_2PS_3$] (fóurɑit) *n.* (*chem.*) toxic biodegradable insecticide used esp. to protect seeds

phos·gene (fɒ́zdʒi:n) *n.* carbonyl chloride, $COCl_2$, a colorless, poisonous gas with a smell like musty hay, used in the dyestuff industry and in chemical warfare in the 1st world war

phos·ge·nite (fɒ́zdʒinait) *n.* a mineral, $Pb_2Cl_2CO_3$, consisting of lead chloride and lead carbonate, occurring as tetragonal crystals [fr. Gk *phōs*, light+*genēs*, born, produced]

phos·pham·i·don [$C_{10}H_{19}ClNO_5P$] (fɒsfǽmidɒn) *n.* (*chem.*) organophosophorus insecticide and miticide

phos·pha·tase (fɒ́sfəteis) *n.* any of many enzymes in body tissues, which break down compounds of carbohydrates and phosphates [PHOSPHATE+DIASTASE]

phos·phate (fɒ́sfeit) *n.* any salt or ester of phosphoric acid ‖ (*pl.*) any of several substances containing these (e.g. phosphate of calcium), used as fertilizer to supply phosphorus **phos·phat·ic** (fɒsfǽtik) *adj.* of or containing phosphates or phosphoric acid **phos·pha·tide** (fɒ́sfətaid) *n.* (*biochem.*) one of a class of complex esters of phosphoric acid and an alcohol containing more than one hydroxyl group (e.g. glycerol) and containing usually fatty acids and a nitrogen base. They are found in all living cells in association with fats **phós·pha·tize** *pres. part.* **phos·pha·tiz·ing** *past* and *past part.* **phos·pha·tized** *v.t.* to treat with a phosphate or phosphates ‖ to change into a phosphate [F.]

phos·phene (fɒ́sfi:n) *n.* the bright image formed as a result of mechanical stimulation of the retina in the absence (usually) of light, e.g. when pressure is put on the eyeball with the eyelid shut [fr. Gk *phōs*, light+*phainein*, to show]

phos·phide (fɒ́sfaid, fɒ́sfid) *n.* (*chem.*) a binary compound consisting of phosphorus with another element or a radical [PHOSPHORUS]

phos·phine (fɒ́sfi:n, fɒ́sfin) *n.* a colorless, poisonous gas, PH_3, with a smell like garlic ‖ a basic orange dye [PHOSPHORUS]

phos·phite (fɒ́sfait) *n.* any salt or ester of phosphorous acid [F.]

phos·pho·e·nol·py·ru·vic acid (fɒsfoui:nɒlpairú:vik) (*biochem.*) high-energy phosphate that releases energy for muscular activity

phos·pho·fruc·to·ki·nase (fɒ́sfoufrʌktóukineis) *n.* (*biochem.*) an enzyme that catalyzes conversion of fructose in carbohydrate metabolism. —**phosphofructokinase disease** *med*

phos·pho·gly·cer·al·de·hyde [$OHCCHOHCH_2$-OPO_3H_2] (fɒsfouglisərǽldehaid) *n.* (*biochem.*) an intermediate product in the metabolism process of carbohydrates

phos·pho·lip·id (fɒsfoulípid, fɒsfouláipid) *n.* a phosphatide [PHOSPHORUS+LIPID]

phos·pho·lip·id (fɒsfoulípid) *n.* (*biochem.*) a lipid made up of an ester of phosphoric acid with an alcohol, a fatty acid and a nitrogen base, e.g., lecithin, sphingomyelin

phos·pho·pro·tein (fɒsfouprόuti:n, fɒsfouprόuti:in) *n.* a protein in which the protein molecule is combined with a phosphorus compound other than a nucleic acid or lecithin (e.g. caseinogen)

phos·phor (fɒ́sfər) *n.* any of a large number of naturally occurring or synthetic materials that are phosphorescent or fluorescent and that consist of sulfides, silicates, phosphates etc., often activated with a metallic impurity (e.g. copper, silver, lead). Phosphors are used for luminescent coatings in cathode-ray tubes, fluorescent lamps, luminous dials etc. [fr. L. *phosphorus*, phosphorus]

phosphor bronze a very hard, tough bronze containing a small amount of phosphorus. It is used in bearings, ships' propellers etc.

phos·pho·resce (fɒsfərés) *pres. part.* **phos·pho·resc·ing** *past* and *past part.* **phos·pho·resced** *v.i.* to exhibit phosphorescence [PHOSPHORUS]

phos·pho·res·cence (fɒsfərés'ns) *n.* a luminescence characterized by a temperature-dependent time rate of decay after the stimulation has been removed (cf. FLUORESCENCE), e.g. in many forms of bioluminescence [PHOSPHORESCENT]

phos·pho·res·cent (fɒsfərés'nt) *adj.* exhibiting phosphorescence [PHOSPHORUS]

phos·pho·ret·ed, phos·pho·ret·ted (fɒ́sfəretid) *adj.* combined with phosphorus

phos·phor·ic (fɒsfɔ́rik, fɒsfɒ́rik) *adj.* pertaining to phosphorus, esp. in compounds where this has a high valence [fr. F. *phosphorique*]

phosphoric acid a colorless, crystalline bitter acid, H_3PO_4, used in the manufacture of fertilizers, in sugar refining etc.

phos·pho·rism (fɒ́sfərizəm) *n.* phosphorus poisoning

phos·pho·rous (fɒ́sfərəs) *adj.* pertaining to phosphorus, esp. in compounds where this has a low valence [fr. F. *phosphoreux*]

phosphorous acid a crystalline acid, H_3PO_4, which absorbs oxygen easily, used as a reducing agent

phos·pho·rus (fɒ́sfərəs) *pl.* **phos·pho·ri** (fɒ́sfərai) *n.* a nonmetallic element (symbol P, at. no. 15, at. mass 30.9738) which can exist in several allotropic forms. White or yellow phosphorus is an unstable, poisonous, waxy substance which is highly inflammable, oxidizing with a faint glow in air at room temperature. Red phosphorus is a stable, less inflammable, nonpoisonous powder obtained by heating white phosphorus. Organic compounds of phosphorus are present in all living cells. Inorganic compounds are important constituents of minerals, soil, bones and teeth, and are used in the manufacture of matches [L. fr. Gk *phōsphoros* adj. fr. *phōs*, light+*phoros*, bringing]

phos·phu·ret·ed, phos·phu·ret·ted (fɒ́sferetid) *adj.* phosphoreted [fr. obs. *phosphuret*, phosphide fr. Mod. L. *phosphoretum*]

phot (fot, fout) *n.* a unit of illumination, being the illumination when 1 lumen is incident on 1 square centimeter of a surface [fr. Gk *phōs* (*phōtos*), light]

pho·tic zone (fóutik) (*envir.*) the region of aquatic environment in which the intensity of natural light is sufficient for photosynthesis

Pho·ti·us (fóuʃi:əs) (c. 820–c. 891), patriarch of Constantinople. A partisan of the Iconoclasts, he replaced St Ignatius as patriarch (858–67), but was not recognized by the papacy. He was again patriarch (877–86)

photo- (fóutou) *prefix* having to do with light ‖ having to do with photography or photographs [fr. Gk *phōs* (*phōtos*), light]

pho·to *pl.* **pho·tos** *n.* a photograph, esp. a snapshot

pho·to·au·to·troph (fóutouɔtoutrouf) *n.* (*biol.*) self-nourishing organism that utilizes light as an energy source, e.g., blue-green algae

pho·to·bi·ol·o·gy (fóutoubaiɒlədʒi:) *n.* study of effect of light on life. —**pho·to·bi·ot·ic** *adj.* —**pho·to·bi·ol·o·gist** *n.*

pho·to·bot·a·ny (fóutoubɒtəni:) *n.* branch of botany that deals with effect of light on plants

pho·to·cell (fóutousel) *n.* a photoelectric cell

pho·to·chem·i·cal (foutoukémik'l) *adj.* of or relating to photochemistry ‖ of or relating to the action of light on chemical properties or reactions

pho·to·chem·is·try (foutoukémistri:) *n.* the branch of chemistry dealing with the effects of electromagnetic radiation (esp. in the visible region of the spectrum) on chemical reactivity (e.g. in photography or photosynthesis)

pho·to·chro·mat·ic (fóutoukroumætik) *adj.* **1.** of color photography. **2.** of colored light.

pho·to·chrom·ism (fóutoukroumizəm) *n.* property of changing color under light or lack of light. —**pho·to·chrom·ic** *adj.*

pho·to·chron·o·graph (foutəkrónəgræf, foutəkrónəgrɑf) *n.* a camera taking exposures at timed intervals, used to record biological changes etc. ‖ a photograph taken by such a camera ‖ (*astron.*) a camera attached to a telescope and used to photograph a heavenly body at timed intervals ‖ (*phys.*) a device for recording small intervals of time

pho·to·co·ag·u·la·tion (fóutoucouægju:leiʃən) *n.* (*med.*) technique of causing tissue to coagulate under intense controlled light, e.g., in ophthalmological surgery. —**pho·to·co·ag·u·la·tive** *adj.* **pho·to·co·ag·u·la·tor** *n.* the instrument

pho·to·con·duc·tive (foutoukəndʌ́ktiv) *adj.* of, relating to or having the property of photoconductivity

pho·to·con·duc·tiv·i·ty (foutoukɒndʌktíviti:) *n.* the property of certain substances (e.g. selenium) of having an electrical conductivity that depends upon the nature and intensity of the electromagnetic radiation impinging upon them (*PHOTOELECTRIC CELL)

photoconductivity cell a type of photoelectric cell

pho·to·cop·i·er (fóutoukɒpi:ər) *n.* a machine for making photocopies

pho·to·cop·y (fóutoukɒpi:) **1.** *pl.* **pho·to·cop·ies** *n.* a photographic reproduction of a document, illustration, etc. **2.** *v.t. pres. part.* **pho·to·cop·y·ing** *past* and *past part.* **pho·to·cop·ied** to make a photocopy of

pho·to·cube (fóutoukju:be) *n.* a plastic cube that holds a photograph to inside surface for display

pho·to·cur·rent (fóutoukə:rənt, fóutoukʌrənt) *n.* a photoelectric current, i.e. one produced by the action of electromagnetic radiation in a photoelectric effect

pho·to·de·tect·or (fóutouditektər) *n.* (*electr.*) device sensitive to light, e.g., photodiodes, phototransistors, photoswitches. *also* photosensor

pho·to·do·sim·e·try (fóutoudousimetri:) *n.* the measurement of total radiation exposure through exposure of a photographic film

pho·to·dy·nam·ic (foutoudainǽmik) *adj.* of or relating to the toxic effect of light, esp. sunlight, on living organisms

pho·to·e·las·tic (foutouilǽstik) *adj.* relating to or having the property of photoelasticity

pho·to·e·las·tic·i·ty (foutoui:læstísiti:) *n.* the property in certain transparent isotropic solids of becoming birefringent when submitted to stress

—Stresses in engineering components may be investigated by modeling them in glass or a transparent plastic and examining the stressed model by polarized light. The stressed regions in the model rotate the plane of polarization of the light and produce a visible pattern from which the direction and size of the stresses may be deduced

pho·to·e·lec·tric (foutouiléktrik) *adj.* of any of the factors involved in the effect of electromagnetic radiation on the electrical behavior of matter

photoelectric cell one of three types of device utilizing a photoelectric effect: (a) a photoconductivity cell, consisting essentially of a photoconductive substance in a current-measuring circuit. It is used most often to measure the intensity or quantity of illumination falling on it. A change in conductivity caused by incident light results in a change in the current carried by the circuit, which is registered by an ammeter (*EXPOSURE METER) (b) a phototube, consisting of an evacuated glass bulb containing a photoemissive cathode and an anode held at a positive potential, which attracts the photoelectron produced in the cathode by incident light. The current so produced may be used to actuate other electrical devices (*ELECTRIC EYE, *PHOTOMULTIPLIER) (c) a photovoltaic cell, used to convert electromagnetic radiation to an electric current, e.g. in a solar battery

photoelectric effect any of several phenomena caused by the interaction of electromagnetic radiation with (usually metallic) substances (*PHOTOEMISSION, *PHOTOCONDUCTIVITY, *PHOTOVOLTAGE)

pho·to·e·lec·tric·i·ty (foutouilektrísiti:, foutoui:lektrísiti:) *n.* electricity produced by the action of electromagnetic radiation ‖ a branch of physics that deals with the physical effects of the interaction of light and matter

pho·to·e·lec·tron (foutouiléktrɒn) *n.* an electron released by photoemission

pho·to·e·mis·sion (foutouimíʃən) *n.* the process in which electromagnetic radiation incident upon a substance (usually a metal) causes the release of electrons. The process occurs only when the frequency of the radiation is greater than a threshold value characteristic of the substance. The kinetic energy of the photoelectrons is independent of the intensity of radiation, depending only on its frequency

pho·to·e·mis·sive (foutouimísiv) *adj.* emitting electrons when exposed to radiation of certain wavelengths, or capable of doing so

pho·to·en·grave (foutouingréiv) *pres. part.* **pho·to·en·grav·ing** *past* and *past part.* **pho·to·en·graved** *v.t.* to make a photoengraving of **pho·to·en·gráv·er** *n.* [backformation fr. PHOTOENGRAVING]

pho·to·en·grav·ing (foutouingréiviŋ) *n.* (*printing*) a process by which a printing block is made from a photograph: the photograph is photographed onto metal and the parts not to be printed are then mechanically etched away (cf. PHOTOGRAVURE) ‖ a print taken from such a block

pho·to·es·say (foutouései) *n.* a study of a subject presented principally through photographs

pho·to·fab·ri·ca·tion (foutoufæbrikéiʃən) *n.* (*electr.*) **1.** use of photographic process creating integrated circuits on silicon wafers. **2.** (*computer*) manufacture of miniaturized semiconductor circuits by photographic reduction before chemical etching

photo finish the finish of a race so close that a photograph at the finish line is required to identify the winner ‖ the end of any very close contest

pho·to·fis·sion (foutoufíʃən) *n.* (*nuclear phys.*) photo-induced nuclear fission

pho·to·flash bomb (foutoufĺæʃ) (*mil.*) bomb designed to produce a brief and intense illumination for medium-altitude night photography

pho·to·flood (fóutouflʌd) *n.* (*photog.*) an electric lamp to which excess voltage is supplied so that it emits especially bright light

pho·to·gen·ic (foutədʒénik) *adj.* photographing to advantage ‖ causing or producing light [fr. PHOTO-+Gk *genēs*, born, produced]

pho·to·gram·me·try (foutəgrǽmitri:) *n.* the art or process of making a survey or a map with the help of photographs taken esp. from the air [fr. *photogram*, var. of PHOTOGRAPH+Gk *-metria*, a measuring]

pho·to·graph (fóutəgræf, fóutəgrɑf) **1.** *n.* a reproduction usually on photographic paper, made by photography **2.** *v.t.* to take a picture of by photography ‖ *v.i.* to practice photography ‖ to appear (in a specified way) in a photograph, *she photographs badly* **pho·tog·ra·pher** (fətɒ́grəfər) *n.* a person who practices photography, esp. as a profession [fr. PHOTO-+Gk *graphos*, written]

pho·to·graph·ic (foutəgrǽfik) *adj.* pertaining to photography ‖ resembling the process of photography, *a photographic memory* **pho·to·gráph·i·cal·ly** *adv.*

photographic paper a piece of paper that has been coated with an emulsion containing silver salts. When exposed to the light passed through a negative and developed (*PHOTOGRAPHY) it gives a (positive) photograph (cf. FILM)

pho·tog·ra·phy (fətɒ́grəfi:) *n.* the art, process or occupation of producing photographs [fr. Gk *phōs* (*phōtos*), light+*graphia*, writing]

—A photographic film is exposed to an image formed by the optical system of a camera, producing a latent image on the film. This image consists of regions exposed to variable quantities of light which render an amount of silver salts susceptible to reduction according to the degree to which they were exposed. Development of the film consists of chemical reduction of the exposed portions without affecting the unexposed ones. By means of the reduction, black, colloidal particles of metallic silver are deposited with a density corresponding to the amount of incident light. The film is then fixed, i.e. all unaffected silver salts are removed by chemical extraction. (To this point in the process all steps are carried out in the absence of light.) Fixing is accomplished by the action of hypo, which forms a water-soluble complex with silver salts, and the film is then washed with water. Finally the film is dried, giving a negative. A photograph may be produced at any time from the negative by allowing light that has passed through the negative to fall upon a piece of photographic paper which is then treated in the same way as the negative was, giving a photograph or print (*ENLARGER). Color photography depends upon a method of confining the incident wavelengths to three ranges of the spectrum, usually by using filters. The reduction due to each range is specific to that range, subsequent transmission through the negative being therefore also specific and giving the corresponding color sensations

pho·to·gra·vure (foutəgrəvjúər) *n.* the process of printing from an etched copper plate (cf. PHOTOENGRAVING). A wiper removes all ink except that in the etched recesses, and these print in a tone related to their depth ‖ a print made by this process [F.]

pho·to·ki·ne·sis (foutoukiní:sis, foutoukainí:sis) *n.* movement in response to light **pho·to·ki·net·ic** (foutoukinétik, foutoukainétik) *adj.*

pho·to·lith·o (foutəlíθou) *pl.* **pho·to·lith·os** **1.** *n.* a photolithograph **2.** *v.t.* to photolithograph

pho·to·lith·o·graph (foutəlíθəgræf, foutəlíθəgrɑf) **1.** *v.t.* to print by photolithography **2.** *n.* a print made by protolithography [PHOTOLITHOGRAPHY]

pho·to·lith·o·graph·ic (foutəliθəgrǽfik) *adj.* of or produced by photolithography [PHOTOLITHOGRAPHY]

pho·to·li·thog·ra·phy (foutouliθɒ́grəfi:) *n.* a process of printing from a plate coated with a photographic film which has been exposed in a camera, developed, and made receptive to ink

pho·tol·y·sis (foutɒ́lisis) *n.* chemical decomposition effected by electromagnetic radiation [Mod. L. fr. Gk *phōs* (*phōtos*), light+*lusis*, a loosening]

pho·to·map (fóutoumæp) *n.* mosaic of aerial photographs with identification markings

pho·to·me·chan·i·cal (foutouməkǽnik'l) *adj.* of any mechanical printing process using a plate prepared photographically **pho·to·me·chán·i·cal·ly** *adv.*

pho·tom·e·ter (foutɒ́mitər) *n.* (*phys.*) an instrument used to measure illuminating power by comparing two sources of light **pho·to·met·ric** (foutəmétrik) *adj.* **pho·tom·e·try** (foutɒ́mitri:) *n.* (*phys.*) the comparison of illuminating powers, esp. of one source of light with a standard source ‖ the science which deals with this [fr. Gk *phōs* (*phōtos*), light+METER]

pho·to·mi·cro·graph (foutoumáikrəgræf, foutoumáikrəgrɑf) *n.* a photograph made by photomicrography **pho·to·mi·crog·ra·phy** (foutoumaikrɒ́grəfi:) *n.* the process of making photographs of the enlarged images, formed by a microscope, of very small objects [fr. PHOTO-+MICRO-+Gk *graphos*, written]

pho·to·mi·cros·co·py (foutoumaikrɒ́skəpi:) *n.* photomicrography

pho·to·mul·ti·pli·er (foutoumʌ́ltiplaiər) *n.* an electron multiplier having a photoelectric emission as its first stage

pho·ton (fóutɒn) *n.* (*phys.*) a fundamental particle of rest mass 0 that is regarded as the quantum of radiant energy. The photon has spin quantum number 1 (*ELECTROMAGNETIC WAVE) [fr. Gk *phōs* (*phōtos*), light]

pho·to·off·set (fóutouɔ́fset, fóutouɒ́fset) *n.* (*printing*) a process whereby a photolithographic plate transmits an image to a roller which transfers the impression to paper

pho·to·pe·ri·od (foutəpíəri:əd) *n.* (*biol.*) the relative duration of periods of light and dark as these affect the growth or behavior of plants and animals (e.g. budding or bird migration) **pho·to·pe·ri·od·ic** (foutəpiəri:ɒ́dik) *adj.* **pho·to·pe·ri·ód·i·cal·ly** *adv.* **pho·to·pe·ri·o·dic·i·ty** (foutəpiəri:ədísiti:) **pho·to·pé·ri·od·ism** *n.* (*biol.*) the response of an organism to the photoperiod

pho·to·phile (fóutəfail) *adj.* photophilic

pho·to·phil·ic (foutəfílik) *adj.* (*biol.*) flourishing in strong light **pho·toph·i·lous** (fətɒ́fələs) *adj.* **pho·tóph·i·ly** *n.* the quality or state of being photophilic [PHOTO-+Gk *philos*, loving]

pho·to·pho·bi·a (foutəfóubi:ə) *n.* (*med.*) abnormal dislike of or sensitivity to strong light [Mod. L. fr. Gk *phos* (*phōtos*), light+*phobia*, fear]

pho·to·pig·ment (foutoupígmənt) *n.* coloring material that changes under light

pho·to·po·la·rim·e·ter (foutoupoulərímitər) *n.* (*astron.*) device for examining features of planets utilizing telescopy, photography and polarized light

pho·to·pol·y·mer (foutoupɒ́limər) *n.* (*chem.*) a photosensitive plastic

pho·to·print (fóutəprint) *n.* (*printing*) a reproduction made by any photomechanical process

pho·to·real·ism (foutourí:əlizəm) *n.* form of realistic painting life situations (esp. the worst) with photographic detail. —**pho·to·real·ist** *n.*

pho·to·re·sist (foutouri:zíst) *n.* plastic that softens under light, used as coating on integrated circuits

pho·to·scan (foutouskǽn) *n.* a photographic record of radioactivity in various parts of a body. —**pho·to·scan** *v.* —**pho·to·scan·ner** *n.* the X-ray camera

pho·to·sen·si·tive (foutousénsitiv) *adj.* affected by the incidence of radiant energy, esp. light **pho·to·sen·si·tív·i·ty** *n.*

photosensor *PHOTODETECTOR

pho·to·sphere (fóutəsfiər) *n.* (*astron.*) the surface layer of the sun, consisting of a layer of gases of extremely low density at a very low pressure and high temperature (c. 6,000°C) in which heat-transfer processes produce many convective cells. They give this layer a granular appearance when photographed through a telescope (*CHROMOSPHERE, *CORONA) [fr. PHOTO-+Gk *sphaira*, sphere]

pho·to·stage (foutoustéidʒ) (*botany*) life stage of a seedling during which light is essential

pho·to·stat (fóutəstæt) **1.** *n.* a machine used to make photographs of documents etc. to any desired scale ‖ a photograph thus made **2.** *v.t. pres. part.* **pho·to·stat·ing**, esp. *Br.* **pho·to·stat·ting** *past* and *past part.* **pho·to·stat·ed**, esp. *Br.* **pho·to·stat·ted** to make a photostatic copy of **pho·to·stát·ic** *adj.* [fr. *Photostat*, a trademark]

pho·to·syn·the·sis (foutəsínθisis) *n.* the synthesis of chemical substances with the aid of light, esp. the formation of carbohydrates (e.g. in green plants) from carbon dioxide and water with the liberation of oxygen, in the presence of chlorophyll

pho·to·tax·is (foutətǽksis) *pl.* **pho·to·tax·es** (foutətǽksi:z) *n.* a taxis in response to light **pho·to·táx·y** *pl.* **pho·to·tax·ies** *n.* a phototaxis

pho·to·tel·e·graph (foutoutéləgræf, foutoutéləgrɑf) *n.* a picture or signal which has been transmitted by phototelegraphy **pho·to·tel·e·graph·ic** (foutoutələgrǽfik) *adj.*

pho·to·te·leg·ra·phy (foutoutəlégrəfi:) *n.* the transmission of photographs by telegraphy ‖ transmission of signals by light, e.g. by a heliograph

pho·tot·o·nus (foutɒ́t'nəs) *n.* a tonic condition (e.g. in phototropic plants) induced by the proper light conditions [Mod. L, fr. Gk *phōs* (*phōtos*), light+*tonos*, tone, tension]

pho·to·tran·sis·tor (foutoutrænzístər) *n.* (*electr.*) semiconductor with three electrodes that induce and amplify a current induced by light

pho·to·troph (foutoutróuf) *n.* an organism that uses light to turn carbon dioxide into oxygen and carbon dioxide

pho·to·troph·ic (foutətrɒ́fik) *adj.* able to use carbon dioxide, in the presence of light, for metabolism (*PHOTOSYNTHESIS) [fr. PHOTO-+Gk *trophē*, food]

pho·to·trop·ic (foutətrɒ́pik) *adj.* of, by, or capable of undergoing phototropism [fr. PHOTO-+Gk *tropos*, turning]

pho·tot·ro·pism (fətɒ́trəpizəm) *n.* a tropism in which light acts as a stimulus ‖ the reversible color change exhibited by certain substances when exposed to radiant energy

pho·to·tube (fóutətu:b, fóutətju:b) *n.* a type of photoelectric cell

pho·to·ty·po·graph·ic (foutoutaipəgrǽfik) *adj.* referring to or done by phototypography **pho·to·ty·po·gráph·i·cal** *adj.*

pho·to·ty·pog·ra·phy (foutoutaipɒ́grəfi:) *n.* a printing process using photomechanical means at the composing stage as well as later

pho·to·vol·tage (foutouvóultidʒ) *n.* the electromotive force developed in a conducting circuit when the boundary between certain dissimilar substances within the circuit is bathed in electromagnetic radiation ‖ any voltage produced in a photosensitive substance by electromagnetic radiation

pho·to·vol·ta·ic (foutouvɒltéiik) *adj.* photoelectric, *a photovoltaic cell*

phras·al (fréiz'l) *adj.* of or consisting of a phrase or phrases

phrase (freiz) **1.** *n.* a sequence of words expressing a single idea, esp. (*gram.*) a group of words without a subject and predicate, functioning together within a sentence ‖ an expression that is pithy or idiomatic ‖ (*mus.*) a small group of notes forming a unit of melody, often forming half of a period ‖ (*dance*) a sequence of movements forming a choreographic pattern **2.** *v.t. pres. part.* **phras·ing** *past* and *past part.* **phrased** to express in words, *this passage is badly phrased* ‖ (*mus.*) to divide or mark off into

phrases, esp. in performance [fr. L.L. *phrasis,* diction fr. Gk fr. *phrazein,* to point out, tell]
phrase marker (freiz) (*linguistics*) a signal of the end of a phrase
phra·se·o·gram (fréizi:əgræm) *n.* a single written character representing a whole phrase, esp. in shorthand [fr. Gk *phrasis,* diction+*gramma,* letter, writing]
phra·se·o·graph (fréizi:əgræf, fréizi:əgrɑf) *n.* a phrase for which a phraseogram is used [fr. Gk *phrasis,* diction+*graphos,* written]
phra·se·o·log·i·cal (freizi:əlɑ́dʒik'l) *adj.* of, relating to or involving phraseology
phra·se·ol·o·gy (freizi:ɒlədʒi:) *n.* manner of using and arranging words [fr. Mod. L. *phraseologia* fr. Gk fr. *phrasis,* diction+*logos,* word]
phras·ing (fréiziŋ) *n.* mode of expressing in words, *the phrasing of a request* ‖ (*mus.*) musical phrases with respect to composition or performance
phra·try (fréitri:) *pl.* **phra·trics** *n.* (*Gk hist.*) a subdivision of a phyle in the Athenian state ‖ a tribal or clan subdivision in primitive society [fr. Gk *phratria* fr. *phratēr,* member of the same clan]
phrenetic *FRENETIC
phren·ic (frénik) *adj.* (*anat.*) pertaining to the diaphragm [fr. Gk *phrēn* (*phrenos*), diaphragm]
phren·o·log·i·cal (fren'lɒ́dʒik'l) *adj.* of or relating to phrenology
phre·nol·o·gist (frinɒ́lədʒist) *n.* a person who practices phrenology
phre·nol·o·gy (frinɒlədʒi:) *n.* a study based on the outdated theory that mental faculties and dispositions can be judged by observing the shape of the skull as a whole and the different parts of its surface [fr. Gk *phrēn* (*phrenos*), mind+*logos,* discourse]
Phryg·i·a (frídʒi:ə) an ancient country of central Asia Minor, peopled by Indo-Europeans (c. 12th c. B.C.). It fell to Lydia (c. 7th c. B.C.)
Phryg·i·an (frídʒi:ən. *n.* a native of Phrygia ‖ the Indo-European language of the ancient Phrygians **2.** *adj.* of or pertaining to Phrygia
Phrygian mode (*mus.*) a medieval authentic mode represented by the white piano keys ascending from E ‖ (*mus.*) an ancient Greek mode represented by the white piano keys descending from D
phthal·ein (θǽli:n, fθǽli:n) *n.* any of a group of organic dyes derived from a phenol and phthalic anhydride, e.g. phenolphthalein [PHTHALIC]
phthal·ic (θǽlik, fθǽlik) *adj.* of any of three isomeric acids, $C_4H_4(COOH)_2$, formed by oxidizing benzene derivatives ‖ of an anhydride, $C_6H_4(CO)_2O$, produced by oxidation of naphthalene, used in making certain resins, solvents, dyes etc. [NAPHTHALENE]
phthis·ic (tízik) *adj.* of, relating to, or affected by phthisis **phthís·i·cal** *adj.* [M.E. *tisik, tisike* n., a wasting lung disease, fr. O.F. fr. Gk]
phthi·sis (θáisis, fθáisis) *n.* tuberculosis of the lungs ‖ any wasting disease [L. fr. Gk fr. *phthinein,* to decay]
phut (fʌt) *adv.* (*Br.,* only in) **to go phut** to burst, collapse, cease suddenly to be in working order [fr. Hind. *phatna,* to burst]
phy·col·o·gy (faikɒ́lədʒi:) *n.* algology [fr. Gk *phukos,* seaweed+*logos,* discourse]
phy·co·my·cete (faikoumáisi:t) *n.* a member of *Phycomycetes,* a large class of fungi, both saprophytic and parasitic, whose thallus ranges from a simple protoplasmic mass to a complex mycelium usually consisting of tubular septae, and whose reproduction is frequently asexual (often by the formation of conidia or sporangia), but which may take a variety of sexual forms. Phycomycetes include a number of plant or animal parasites (e.g. the mildew responsible for the Irish potato famine, 1845-9) **phy·co·my·cé·tous** *adj.* [fr. Mod. L. *Phycomycetes* fr. Gk *phukos,* seaweed+*mukēs,* mushroom]
Phyfe (faif), Duncan (c. 1768–1854), American cabinetmaker and interpreter of fashionable European styles
phy·lac·ter·y (filǽktəri:) *pl.* **phy·lac·ter·ies** *n.* either of two small, square leather boxes containing slips of vellum, on which are written portions of the Mosaic Law, worn one on the head, another on the left arm, by orthodox and conservative Jewish men at prayer, in token of the duty to obey the Law ‖ an amulet [M.E. *philaterie* fr. L. fr. Gk *phulaktērion,* a fort]
phy·le (fáili:) *pl.* **phy·lae** (fáili:) *n.* (*Gk hist.*) an ancient Hellenic tribe ‖ a political subdivision in the Athenian state ‖ (*Gk hist.*) a division in the Athenian army [Gk *phulē*]
phy·let·ic (failétik) *adj.* (*biol.*) of or relating to a phylum or to a line of descent [fr. Gk *phuletikos* fr. *phuletēs,* a tribesman]
phyl·lo·clad (fíləklæd) *n.* a phylloclade
phyl·lo·clade (fíləkleid) *n.* (*bot.*) a flattened or rounded stem which functions as a leaf, e.g. in cactus [fr. Mod. L. *phyllocladium* fr. Gk *phullon,* leaf+*klados,* branch]
phyl·lode (fíloud) *n.* (*bot.*) a flattened and expanded petiole functioning as a leaf, e.g. in the acacia [F. fr. Mod. L. fr. Gk *phullōdēs,* leaflike]
phyl·lo·tax·is (filətǽksis) *pl.* **phyl·lo·tax·es** (filətǽksi:z) *n.* (*bot.*) the arrangement of leaves on a stem ‖ the study of the principles governing this arrangement **phyl·lo·táx·y** *pl.* **phyl·lo·tax·ies** *n.* phyllotaxis [Mod. L. fr. Gk *phullon,* leaf+*taxis,* arrangement]
phyl·lox·e·ra (filɒ́ksərə) *pl.* **phyl·lox·e·rae** (filɒ́ksəri:), **phyl·lox·e·ras** *n.* a member of *Phylloxera,* fam. *Phylloxeridae,* a genus of plant lice very destructive esp. to grape vines, which spread from the U.S.A. to European countries [Mod. L. fr. Gk *phullon,* leaf+*xēros,* dry]
phy·lo·gen·e·sis (failədʒénisis) *n.* phylogeny [fr. Gk *phulon, phūlē,* tribe+*genesis,* origin]
phy·log·e·ny (failɒ́dʒəni:) *n.* the history of the development of a species or group of related organisms (cf. ONTOGENY) [G. *phylogenie* fr. Gk *phulon,* race+*-geneia,* birth, origin]
phy·lon (fáilɒn) *pl.* **phy·la** (fáilə) *n.* (*biol.*) a phylum [Mod. L. fr. Gk *phulon,* race]
phy·lum (fáiləm) *pl.* **phy·la** (fáilə) *n.* (*biol.*) the primary division of classification in the plant or animal kingdom, based on common characteristics and assumed common ancestry [Mod L. fr. Gk *phulon,* race]
phys·ic (fízik) **1.** *n.* a laxative **2.** v.t. *pres. part.* **phys·ick·ing** *past* and *past part.* **phys·icked** to purge [M.E. *fisike* fr. O.F. *fisique* fr. L. *physica*]
phys·i·cal (fízik'l) *adj.* of or pertaining to matter or nature ‖ pertaining to the body (in contrast to the mind) ‖ of or pertaining to the science of physics [fr. M.L. *physicalis*]
physical anthropology the branch of anthropology concerned with the evolution and biological classification of human races, based on comparative anatomy and physiology (*SOCIAL ANTHROPOLOGY)
physical chemistry the branch of chemistry in which physical methods and theory are applied to chemical systems
physical culture exercises and treatment to develop and tone up the body
physical education education in the development and care of the body through sports and exercise
physical geography *GEOGRAPHY
physical optics the branch of optics that describes and explains optical phenomena by means of the wave theory or quantum mechanics (cf. GEOMETRICAL OPTICS)
physical science any of the sciences dealing with inanimate matter or energy, including physics, chemistry, geology, astronomy etc.
physical therapy physiotherapy
phy·si·cian (fizíʃən) *n.* a doctor of medicine, licensed to diagnose and treat diseases ‖ such a doctor as distinguished from a surgeon [M.E. *fisicien* fr. O.F. fr. L.]
physician's assistant one trained (2 yrs. of special study) to aid a physician under his direction. *acronym* **PA**
phys·i·cist (fízisist) *n.* a specialist in physics
phys·i·co·chem·i·cal (fizikoukémik'l) *adj.* physical and chemical ‖ relating to physical chemistry [fr. Gk *phusikos,* natural, physical+CHEMICAL]
phys·ics (fíziks) *n.* the science of matter and energy, and their interactions. It is essentially based on measurement and mathematical processes ‖ physical properties or processes, *the physics of gravitation* [fr. L. *physica,* neut. pl., trans. of Gk *ta phusika,* natural things]
phys·i·o·crat (fízi:əkræt) *n.* (*hist.*) an adherent of the economic theory put forward by the Frenchman François Quesnay (1694-1774) that land is the source of all wealth and that it alone should be taxed. The physiocrats held that economic law is immutable, and advocated total freedom of trade. Their views influenced Turgot and Adam Smith [F. *physiocrate* fr. Gk *phusis,* nature+*kratos,* rule]
phys·i·og·nom·ic (fizi:ɒgnɒ́mik, fizi:ənɒ́mik) *adj.* of or relating to physiognomy or a physiognomy [fr. L.L. *physiognomicus* fr. Gk]
phys·i·og·no·my (fízi:ɒ́gnəmi, fizi:ɒ́nəmi:) *pl.* **phys·i·og·no·mies** *n.* the facial features as indicative of character ‖ the art of assessing character by studying the features of the face ‖ the general appearance of a landscape, situation etc. [M.E. *fisnomie* fr. O.F. fr. M.L. fr. Gk fr. *phusis,* nature+*gnōmōn,* judge]
phys·i·og·ra·pher (fizi:ɒ́grəfər) *n.* a specialist in physiography
phys·i·o·graph·ic (fizi:əgrǽfik) *adj.* of, pertaining to or involving physiography **phys·i·o·gráph·i·cal** *adj.*
phys·i·og·ra·phy (fizi:ɒ́grəfi:) *n.* a scientific description of natural phenomena ‖ physical geography [fr. Gk *phusis,* nature+*graphia,* writing]
phys·i·o·log·ic (fizi:əlɒ́dʒik) *adj.* physiological **phys·i·o·lóg·i·cal** *adj.* of physiology ‖ characteristic of normal, healthy functioning (cf. PATHOLOGICAL) [PHYSIOLOGY]
phys·i·ol·o·gist (fizi:ɒ́lədʒist) *n.* a specialist in physiology
phys·i·ol·o·gy (fizi:ɒ́lədʒi:) *n.* the branch of biology concerned with the functions of living organisms ‖ the functions, collectively, of an organism or its parts, *the physiology of the starfish* [fr. L. *physiologia,* natural science fr. Gk fr. *phusis,* nature+*logos,* discourse]
phys·i·o·ther·a·pist (fizi:ouθérəpist) *n.* a specialist in physiotherapy
phys·i·o·ther·a·py (fizi:ouθérəpi:) *n.* treatment of bodily disease or injury by applying heat or massage, giving muscle training etc. [fr. Gk *phusis,* nature+THERAPY]
phy·sique (fizí:k) *n.* the form, structure, organization or constitution of a person's body, *a stocky physique* [F.]
phy·so·stig·mine (faisəstígmi:n) *n.* a poisonous alkaloid, $C_{15}H_{21}N_3O_2$, used medically for contracting the pupil of the eye. It is obtained from the calabar bean [fr. Mod. L. *Physostigma* fr. Gk *phusa,* bladder+*stigma,* mark]
phy·so·sto·mous (faisəstóuməs) *adj.* (of fish) having a swim bladder connected with the intestinal canal by a pneumatic duct [fr. Gk *phusa,* bladder+*stoma,* mouth]
phy·tane $[C_{20}H_{42}]$ (fáitein) *n.* (*chem.*) hydrocarbon resulting from breakdown of chlorophyll, found as constituent of fossils 3 billion yrs. old
phy·to·gen·e·sis (faitədʒénisis) *n.* the origin, evolution or development of plants **phy·to·ge·net·ic** (faitədʒinétik) *adj.* [fr. Gk *phuton,* plant+GENESIS]
phy·to·gen·ic (faitədʒénik) *adj.* of or derived from plants [fr. Gk *phuton,* plant+*genēs,* born, produced]
phy·tog·e·ny (faitɒ́dʒini:) *n.* phytogenesis
phy·to·ge·og·ra·phy (faitoudʒi:ɒ́grəfi:) *n.* the study of the geographical distribution of plants [fr. Gk *phuton,* plant+GEOGRAPHY]
phy·tog·ra·phy (faitɒ́grəfi:) *n.* the description and (sometimes) systematic classification of plants [fr. Mod. L. *phytographia* fr. Gk *phuton,* plant+*graphia,* writing]
phy·to·pa·thol·o·gy (faitoupəθɒ́lədʒi:) *n.* the study of plant diseases, esp. parasitic diseases [fr. Gk *phuton,* plant+PATHOLOGY]
phy·toph·a·gous (faitɒ́fəgəs) *adj.* (esp. of insects) feeding on plants [fr. Gk *phuton,* plant+*phagos,* eating]
phy·tos·ter·ol (faitɒ́stərəl) *n.* any of several sterols derived from plants, e.g. ergosterol [fr. Gk *phuton,* plant+STEROL]
phy·to·tron (fáitoutrɒn) *n.* (*botany*) an apparatus or laboratory for growing plants under controlled conditions
pi (pai) *n.* the sixteenth letter (Π, π=p) of the Greek alphabet ‖ the symbol (π) used to denote the ratio of the circumference of a circle to the diameter. π=3.14159 ‖ this ratio
pi, pie 1. *n.* (*printing*) type metal jumbled together instead of being sorted into the case **2.** *v. pres. part.* **pi·ing, pie·ing** *past* and *past part.* **pied** *v.t.* (*printing*) to jumble up (type) ‖ *v.i.* (*printing,* of type) to become jumbled [perh. fr. PIE, baked dish]
pi·ac·u·lar (paiǽkjulər) *adj.* (of a fault) requiring atonement ‖ expiatory [fr. L. *piacularis,* expiatory fr. *piaculum,* atonement]
piaffe (pjæf) **1.** *v.i. pres. part.* **piaff·ing** *past* and *past part.* **piaffed** (*manège,* of a horse) to perform a slow trot without advancing or retreating **2.** *n.* the movement so executed **piáff·er** *n.* a piaffe [F. *piaffer*]

Piaget (pjazei), Jean (1896–1980) Swiss psychologist, the most influential theorist in the history of developmental psychology and the study of human development. He wrote more than fifty books as well as articles and lectures on psychology, epistemology, philosophy, logic, biology, sociology and pedagogy

pi·a ma·ter (páiəméitər) *n.* the highly vascular, delicate, innermost membrane of three which surround the brain and spinal cord (*MENINGES) [M.L.=tender mother]

pi·a·nis·si·mo (pi:ənísəmou, pjɑní:ssi:mɔ) (*mus., abbr.* pp.) **1.** *adj.* very soft **2.** *adv.* very softly **3.** *pl.* **pi·a·nis·si·mos** *n.* a pianissimo passage [Ital. superl. of *piano,* soft, softly]

pi·an·ist (pi:ǽnist, pjǽnist, pí:ənist) *n.* a person who plays the piano, esp. professionally **pi·a·nis·tic** (pi:ənístik) *adj.* relating to or suitable for performance on the piano **pi·a·nís·ti·cal·ly** *adv.* [fr. F. *pianiste*]

pi·a·no (pi:ɑ́nou) (*abbr. p.*) **1.** *adv.* (*mus.*) softly **2.** *adj.* (*mus.*) soft **3.** *pl.* **pi·a·ni** (pi:ɑ́ni:), **pi·a·nos** *n.* (*mus.*) a passage rendered softly [Ital.]

pi·an·o (pi:ǽnou, pjǽnou) *pl.* **pi·an·os** *n.* a musical stringed percussion instrument before which the player sits (as if at a table), playing on a horizontal keyboard. This usually has 88 keys, with corresponding wires (tuned by equal temperament) which are stretched over a sounding board inside the instrument. When a key is pressed down, its corresponding wires (usually 3 per key) are struck by a felt-covered wooden hammer to produce the note, which may be dampened or sustained by pedals. The keyboard consists of flat, white keys which correspond to the C major scale, with shorter, thinner, raised black ones which sound the other notes of the chromatic scale (*GRAND PIANO, *UPRIGHT PIANO) [Ital., shortened fr. *pianoforte*]

pi·an·o·for·te (pi:ænoufɔ́rti:, pi:ænoufɔ́rtei) *n.* a piano [Ital. fr. *piano,* soft+*forte,* loud (from its capacity for producing wide variations in volume)]

pi·a·no·la (pi:ənóulə) *n.* a player piano ‖ a mechanical attachment operating this [fr. *Pianola,* a trademark]

pi·as·sa·ba, pi·a·sa·ba (pi:əsɑ́bə) *n.* piassava

pi·as·sa·va, pi·a·sa·va (pi:əsɑ́və) *n.* either of two South American palms, *Attalea funefera* and *Leopoldinia piassaba,* which yield a woody brown fiber ‖ the fiber of either of these, used in the manufacture of brooms, brushes etc. [Port. *piassaba* fr. Tupi]

pi·as·ter, pi·as·tre (pi:ǽstər) *n.* a monetary unit of varying value used in many countries, e.g. Turkey, Egypt, Lebanon, Libya, the Sudan ‖ a coin of the value of any of these [F. *piastre* fr. Ital.]

Pia·ve (pjɑ́ve) a river in N.E. Italy, flowing 137 miles from the E. Alps to the Adriatic above Venice

pi·az·za (pi:ǽzə, pi:ɑ́zə, pi:ǽtsə, pi:ɑ́tsə) *n.* an open square in a town, closely surrounded by buildings, esp. in Italy ‖ (*archit.*) a portico or covered walk supported by arches ‖ a veranda [Ital.]

pi·broch (pí:brɒx) *n.* (*mus.*) a theme with a set of variations, usually martial but including dirges, played on the bagpipe [fr. Gael. *piobaireachd,* the art of playing the bagpipe]

pic (pik) *pl.* **pics, pix** (piks) *n.* a photograph ‖ (*pop.*) a movie [PICTURE]

pi·ca (páikə) *n.* (*printing*) a size of type equal to 12 point ‖ a typewriter face of 10 characters to the inch, 6 lines to the vertical inch [M.L.=directory]

pica *n.* (*med.*) a morbid craving to eat things not normally eaten, e.g. coal, chalk [Mod. L. or M.L.=magpie]

Pi·ca·bia (pi:kæbjæ), Francis (1879–1953), French painter, an originator of dada and surrealism

pi·ca·dor (pí:kədɔr) (*bullfighting*) a horseman who prods the bull in the neck and shoulders with a lance to weaken it [Span. fr. *picar,* to prick]

Pi·card (pi:kær), Jean (1620–82), French astronomer. He was the first to measure precisely a degree of the earth's meridian, thus calculating the earth's radius. His values were used by Newton

Pic·ar·dy (píkərdi:) (*F.* Picardie) a former province of N. France on the English Channel, comprising Somme, most of Aisne, the coast of Pas-de-Calais and part of Oise. It is a fertile chalk plateau, cut by the Somme. Crops: wheat, sugar beets, market produce. Industries: textiles, fishing. Main towns: Amiens (the old capital), Boulogne, Abbeville. Feudal Picardy, composed of free cities and petty fiefs, included large parts of Flanders. Annexed by the Crown (12th–14th cc.), it was disputed with England (14th–15th cc.) and Spain (16th–17th cc.) before being secured (1659)

pic·a·resque (pikərésk) *adj.* of or written in a genre of episodic, usually satiric fiction originating in 16th-c. Spain, in which a rogue is the hero [fr. Span. *picaresco* fr. *picaro,* rogue]

pic·a·roon (pikərú:n) *n.* a rogue, esp. a pirate ‖ a pirate ship [Span. *picarón* fr. *picaro,* rogue]

Pi·cas·so (pikɑ́sou, pi:kɑssɔ) (Pablo Ruiz y Picasso, 1881–1973), Spanish painter, sculptor and ceramist. He migrated to Paris just at the time when the gains of the Postimpressionists in rendering space and solid form were being consolidated. His 'blue period' (1901–4) and 'rose period' (1905–7), in which these colors dominate his work, preceded the analytical and geometrical investigation (1908–14) with Braque leading to the development of cubism. 'Les demoiselles d'Avignon' (1907) is one of his first major works in this style (*CUBISM). To this period also belong experiments with collage, and pictures which show the influence of the 'simplifications' of Negro art. His period of 'classicism' (1920–6) was characterized by monumental human figures, and full-on or profile treatment of races and bodies. He then turned to surrealism and abstraction (1926–36). His 'Guernica' (1937) is a powerful symbolic illustration of the horrors of war. Throughout his career Picasso moved from style to style with ease, or from painting to etching, sculpture, pottery, theater décor for ballet or poster-design. From all this activity some themes stand out: the gypsies, acrobats and absinthe-drinkers of the melancholy blue period, the sober abstractions of the early cubist paintings (guitars, fruit, household objects, but also pierrots), the newspaper and wood-grain of the collages, and from the later periods the obsessive bulls, goats and shepherds of Mediterranean life, the minotaurs of Mediterranean mythology, the succession of women companions lovingly analyzed and re-created, the images of grief and violence from 1937–45, his children, the gay variations, in rather flat bright hard colors, of later years, and at all times a celebration of the natural creation

pic·a·yune (piki:jú:n) **1.** *n.* anything of little value **2.** *adj.* of very small value ‖ picayunish **pic·a·yún·ish** *adj.* trivial ‖ too concerned with petty detail [F. *picaillon,* farthing fr. Prov. fr. *picalho,* money]

pic·ca·lil·li (píkəlili:) *pl.* **pic·ca·lil·lis** *n.* a relish of chopped vegetables and pungent spices [origin unknown]

Pic·card (pi:kɑr), Auguste (1884–1962), Swiss physicist. He made balloon ascents into the stratosphere and underwater explorations to great depths in a bathyscaphe

pic·co·lo (píkəlou) *pl.* **pic·co·los** *n.* a small flute pitched an octave higher than the standard flute [Ital.=small]

pice (pais) *pl.* **pice** *n.* a former monetary unit and coin in India and Pakistan, equal to 1/4 anna ‖ a monetary unit and coin in Nepal equal to one hundredth of a rupee [fr. Hindi *paisā*]

pich·i·ci·a·go (pitʃisi:ɑ́gou) *pl.* **pich·i·ci·a·gos** *n.* *Chlamydophorus truncatus,* a small South American burrowing armadillo that lives entirely underground. It has protective plates attached only at the spine, and truncated hind parts [fr. Span. *pichiciega,* prob. fr. Guaraní *pichey* little armadillo+Span. *ciego,* blind]

Pi·chin·cha (pitʃí:ntʃɑ) a volcano (15,918 ft) in Ecuador, northwest of Quito. In a battle (1822) fought nearby, Sucre defeated the royalist Spanish troops. The victory of the patriots led to the immediate proclamation of independence of the Audiencia of Quito, which became part of the Republic of Gran Colombia

pick (pik) **1.** *v.t.* to gather (a flower, fruit etc.) by severing it from the rest of the plant or tree ‖ to choose or select carefully ‖ to probe or scratch with an instrument or with one's fingers in order to remove extraneous matter from ‖ to steal from (the pockets of the clothes which someone is wearing) ‖ to pluck (a chicken etc.) ‖ to pierce or dig up (soil, rock etc.) by striking with a pick ‖ to pluck (the strings of a banjo, guitar etc.) ‖ to open (a lock) with a wire etc. instead of with a key, esp. for purposes of robbery ‖ to find an opportunity or pretext for, and begin (a quarrel, fight etc.) ‖ *v.i.* to work with a pick ‖ to eat sparingly or with small bites ‖ (of a bird, esp. a chicken) to tap at the ground or take bits of food up with the bill ‖ (of fruit etc.) to be or admit of being picked, *these berries pick easily* **to pick and choose** to be fastidious about making a choice, *there's no time to pick and choose* **to pick apart** to separate or rip into parts ‖ to find defects in (an argument etc.) **to pick at** to eat (one's food) in small bites and without appetite **to pick on** to choose, select ‖ to single out in order to attack, criticize or tease **to pick out** to select ‖ to distinguish from others, *he hoped no one would pick him out in the crowd* ‖ to cause to stand out, accentuate, *important passages are picked out in red* ‖ to play (a tune etc.) by searching hesitantly for the notes on a keyboard etc. **to pick up** to lift or take up ‖ to get or acquire, esp. by chance or casually, *to pick up some useful information* ‖ to meet casually and get to know (someone, esp. of the opposite sex) ‖ to increase (speed) ‖ to accelerate, *the train picked up after the slope* ‖ to improve in health, spirits or performance **2.** *n.* the act of selecting ‖ the right or privilege of selecting, *to have one's pick of the items* ‖ the person or thing selected ‖ someone or something selected as the best, *the pick of the lot* ‖ the amount of a crop that is picked at one time [rel. to O.E. *picung,* a pricking]

pick *n.* a pickaxe ‖ any of several tools used for picking, e.g. an ice pick ‖ a plectrum [prob. var. of PIKE]

pick **1.** *v.t.* (*weaving*) to throw (a shuttle) **2.** *n.* (*weaving*) one of the weft threads ‖ (*weaving*) the blow that impels the shuttle [var. of PITCH v.]

pick·a·back (píkəbæk) **1.** *adv.* piggyback **2.** *n.* a piggyback [origin unknown]

pick and roll (*basketball*) maneuver of defending a member of the team, then moving toward the goal to receive a pass

pick·ax, pick·axe (píkæks) *pl.* **pick·ax·es** *n.* a tool for breaking hard ground etc., consisting of a heavy iron or steel curved bar, having either two pointed ends or one end pointed and the other flattened to an edge, and having a long wooden handle that fits into its center [M.E. *pikois, picois* fr. O.F. *picois*]

pick·er (píkər) *n.* someone who picks, *a fruit picker* ‖ a tool or machine that picks, esp. a machine that separates and cleans fibers

picker *n.* (*weaving*) the instrument that impels the shuttle

pick·er·el (píkərəl) *pl.* **pick·er·el, pick·er·els** *n.* any of several rather small fierce pikes of North America ‖ (*Br.*) a young pike, *Esox lucius* [dim. of PIKE]

Pick·er·ing (píkəriŋ), Timothy (1745–1829), American Revolutionary general and statesman. As secretary of state (1795–1800), he was dismissed when President John Adams learned of his scheme with the Hamiltonian Federalists to steer the U.S.A. into war with France. He wrote 'Political Essays' (1812)

Pickering, William Henry (1858–1938), U.S. astronomer. He led (1878–1901) five solar eclipse expeditions and established several observatories and astronomical stations. He discovered (1899) the ninth satellite of Saturn, which he called Phoebe, and predicted (1919) the existence of a ninth planet, later named Pluto

pick·et (píkit) **1.** *n.* a small group of soldiers posted against surprise attack or sent out to counter enemy reconnoitering parties ‖ a group of workers posted to dissuade other workers or clients from entering their place of work during a strike ‖ a member of such a group ‖ a group of demonstrators, or a member of such a group, carrying placards to advocate a cause or register a protest ‖ a pointed stake used e.g. as part of a fence or to mark positions in surveying **2.** *v.t.* to protect by means of a picket fence ‖ to tether (an animal) to a stake driven into the ground ‖ to act as a picket at (a place of business etc.) ‖ to post (men) as a picket ‖ to guard (a military camp etc.) with a picket ‖ *v.i.* to act as a picket ‖ to set or place a picket [F. *piquet,* pointed stake]

picket fence (*bowling*) standing pins 1, 2, 4 and 7 or 1, 3, 6 and 10

picket ship (*mil.*) relay ship to extend range of radar signals in early-warning systems

Pick·ett (píkit), George Edward (1825–75), Confederate general, best known for 'Pickett's charge' in the Gettysburg Campaign, which resulted in the virtual annihilation of his division

pick·ings (píkiŋz) *pl. n.* scraps of good food left over, e.g. on a chicken after the meat has been carved ‖ (*fig.*) gleanings ‖ (*pop.*) goods or booty acquired dishonestly

pick·le (pík'l) **1.** *n.* a liquid (brine, vinegar etc.) in which food is preserved ‖ food or a piece of food (e.g. a cucumber) so preserved ‖ an acid solution for cleaning metal articles ‖ (*pop.*) an awkward situation, sorry plight ‖ (*Br., pop.*) a mischievous child **2.** *v.t. pres. part.* **pick·ling** *past* and *past part.* **pick·led to** preserve in, or treat with, a pickle, *to pickle walnuts* ‖ to give a bleached finish to (woodwork) [M.E. prob. fr. M. Du. *pekel, pekele*]

pick·lock (píklɒk) *n.* a device for picking locks ‖ a burglar

pick-me-up (píkmi:ʌp) *n.* (*pop.*) a drink, esp. an alcoholic one, taken to restore zest or energy

pick·pock·et (píkpɒkit) *n.* a person who picks people's pockets

pick·up (píkʌp) *n.* a picking up, e.g. of a ball from the ground, esp. just after its impact ‖ (*pop.*) recovery, *the stock market registered a good pickup* ‖ a device in a phonograph which converts the vibration of the needle into electrical impulses ‖ (*radio, television*) the reception of sound (or light) by the transmitter ‖ the apparatus used for this ‖ (*radio, television*) a place outside a studio where a broadcast originates ‖ the electrical system connecting the program from this place to the broadcasting station ‖ (*television*) the changing of light into electrical energy by the transmitter ‖ (*pop.*) a person whose acquaintance one makes casually, esp. for purposes of love-making ‖ acceleration, esp. of a car ‖ a light truck used esp. for deliveries

pick·y (píki:) *comp.* **pick·i·er** *superl.* **pick·i·est** *adj.* (*pop.*) choosy, finical, *a picky eater*

pi·clo·ram [$C_6H_3Cl_3N_2O_2$] (píklɔrɒm) *n.* (*chem.*) persistent defoliation herbicide used in Vietnam

pic·nic (píknik) **1.** *n.* an outing in which the people involved eat a meal outdoors, brought along for the occasion ‖ the food prepared for this ‖ (*pop.*) something easy or pleasant to do or experience, *the climb was no picnic* **2.** *v.i. pres. part.* **pic·nick·ing** *past* and *past part.* **pic·nicked** to have or participate in a picnic **pic·nick·er** *n.* [fr. F. *pique-nique*]

Pi·co Bo·lí·var (pí:kɔbɔlí:vɑr) the highest point (16,000 ft) in Venezuela in the Cordillera Mérida, a spur of the Andes east of Lake Maracaibo

Pi·co del·la Mi·ran·do·la (pí:kɔdellɑmi:rúndɔlɑ), Giovanni (1463–94), Italian philosopher and humanist. His encyclopedic learning, esp. in philosophy and languages, made him a typical man of the Renaissance. After meeting Ficino (1484) he joined the Neoplatonist school. His 'Conclusiones' (1486) are a compendium of contemporary philosophy and theology, and the first of these, 'Oratio de hominis dignitate', is a manifesto of the Renaissance humanist spirit. He was condemned for heresy by the pope (1487), but was saved by Lorenzo de' Medici

pic·o·line (píkəli:n) *n.* any of three isomeric bases, C_6H_7N, derived from pyridine and occurring in bones and coal tar. They are colorless liquids with a strong smell and are used as a sedative [fr. L. *pix* (*picis*), pitch+*oleum*, oil]

pic·o·line [$C_5H_4N\ (CH_3)$] (píkoli:n) *n.* (*chem.*) solvent for chemical synthesis, used to make nicotinic acid and for fabric waterproofing

pi·cor·na·vi·rus (píkɔrnævɑirəs) *n.* a group of small ether-resistant RNA viruses that include those causing poliomyelitis, Coxsackie foot-and-mouth disease and encephalomyocarditis

pi·cot (pí:kou) **1.** *n.* a small loop of thread forming a part of an ornamental edging to ribbon, lace etc. **2.** *v.t.* to give such edging to [F. dim. of *pic*, point]

pic·o·tee (pikətí:) *n.* a cultivated variety of carnation, sweet pea etc. with a dark-colored or spotted edge to the petals [F. *picoté, picotée*, spotted, pricked]

pic·rate (píkreit) *n.* a salt or ester of picric acid

pic·ric acid (píkrik) a bitter yellow crystalline acid, $C_6H_2(NO_2)_3OH$, used as a dye, in explosives etc. [fr. Gk *pikros*, bitter]

pic·rite (píkrait) *n.* a blackish-green igneous rock, largely composed of augite and olivine [fr. Gk *pikros*, bitter]

Pict (pikt) *n.* a member of a warlike people centered in N. and E. Scotland at the time of the Roman occupation of Britain **Píct·ish 1.** *adj.* of, relating to or like the Picts **2.** *n.* the language of the Picts [fr. L.L. *Picti*, perh. fr. L. *pictus*, painted]

pic·to·graph (píktəgræf, píktəgrɑf) *n.* a picture used to represent a thing, idea etc., e.g. in hieroglyphic writings ‖ a record consisting of such pictures **pic·to·graph·ic** (piktəgræ̍fik) *adj.* **pic·tog·ra·phy** (piktɒ́grəfi:) *n.* [fr. L. *pictus*, painted+Gk *graphos*, written]

pic·to·ri·al (piktɔ́ri:əl, piktóuri:əl) **1.** *adj.* of, containing, expressing or illustrating by pictures ‖ suggesting a mental image, *a pictorial style of writing* **2.** *n.* an illustrated periodical or newspaper [fr. L. L. *pictorius*]

pic·ture (píktʃər) **1.** *n.* a representation or image on a surface, e.g. a painting, drawing, print or photograph, esp. as a work of art ‖ a perfect likeness, *he is the picture of his father* ‖ a type, symbol, *he is the picture of health* ‖ a mental image, idea, *his book gives an accurate picture of monastic life* ‖ a film, movie ‖ a situation as a combination of circumstances, *have you understood the picture?* ‖ a picturesque sight, *the roses were a picture this year* **in the picture** (of actions, events or persons) forming part of the circumstances under consideration, *his candidacy remains very much in the picture* ‖ (*Br.*) informed as to what is going on **the pictures** (*Br., pop.*) the movies **to take a picture** to record on film the image of an object by means of a camera **2.** *v.t. pres. part.* **pic·tur·ing** *past* and *past part.* **pic·tured to** imagine, *picture yourself in his situation!* ‖ to depict, esp. in writing [M.E. fr. L. *pictura* fr. *pingere* (*pictus*), to paint]

picture hat a woman's large, wide-brimmed hat, worn esp. on dressy occasions

picture molding, *Br.* **picture moulding** a rod, wooden rail or molding running around the walls of a room, parallel to the ceiling and typically 2-3 feet below it, to take supports from which pictures hang

picturephone *VIDEOPHONE

picture postcard a postcard with a picture on one side of it

picture rail a picture molding

pic·tur·esque (piktʃərésk) *adj.* (of scenery, landscapes etc.) full of charm, esp. through having an irregular prettiness or quaintness or antique quality, rather than classical beauty, *a picturesque old village* ‖ (of language etc.) strikingly vivid **the picturesque** picturesqueness as an aesthetic concept [fr. F. *pittoresque* fr. Ital. *pittoresco*, in the style of a painter]

picture window a large window having a single pane of glass, which frames the scene outside

picture writing a form of record using pictorial symbols for things, ideas etc. ‖ pictures made in this kind of writing

pid·dle (píd'l) *pres. part.* **pid·dling** *past* and *past part.* **pid·dled** *v.i.* to trifle, waste time ‖ to urinate ‖ *v.t.* (with 'away') to pass (time etc.) wastefully **píd·dling** *adj.* trivial [etym. doubtful]

pid·dock (pídək) *n.* a member of *Pholas*, fam. *Pholadidae*, a genus of bivalve mollusks which characteristically bore holes in wood, clay, rocks etc. ‖ any mollusk of fam. *Pholadidae* [origin unknown]

pidg·in (pídʒin) *n.* any mixed language, spoken usually in trade, which uses the vocabulary of two or more languages and a simplified form of the grammar of one of them. Pidgin is used esp. in trading ports etc. ‖ pidgin English ‖ (*Br., pop.*, also **pigeon**) a strictly personal problem or concern, *that's his pidgin, not yours* [Chin. pronunciation of BUSINESS]

pidgin English a variety of pidgin used in the Far East between Chinese and English-speaking people ‖ a variety of pidgin used in Melanesia and N. Australia

pi-dog *PYE-DOG

pie (pai) *n.* a magpie [O.F.]

pie *PI

pie *n.* a dish of fruit, meat etc., baked with a pastry crust [etym. doubtful]

pie *n.* a former monetary unit and coin of India and Pakistan equal to 1/12 anna [Hindi *pāī*]

pie·bald (páibɔld) **1.** *adj.* marked in patches of two different colors, esp. black and white **2.** *n.* a piebald animal, esp. a horse [PIE, magpie+BALD]

piece (pi:s) **1.** *n.* a distinct part, separated or broken off from a whole, *a piece of cake, a piece of broken china* ‖ a single example or unit of a class of things, *a piece of furniture* ‖ a single unit belonging to a set, *a dinner service of 48 pieces* ‖ a coin of a specified kind, *a 50-cent piece* ‖ a musical or literary composition, esp. a short one, *play that piece again* ‖ a short recitation, esp. one rendered by a child ‖ (*checkers, chess* etc.) any of the men used in playing, esp. (*chess*) any man other than a pawn ‖ a cannon, field gun etc. ‖ a firearm ‖ a unit of manufactured goods, e.g. cloth or wallpaper, of a standard size **in one piece** integral, not being in nor consisting of separate pieces ‖ not broken **in pieces** broken in pieces or otherwise destroyed, *his plans are now in pieces* **of a piece** consistent, *his actions and principles are all of a piece* **to come to pieces** to be able to be disassembled into its component parts **to give (someone) a piece of one's mind** to rebuke (someone) severely and bluntly **to go to pieces** to lose control of oneself or suffer a nervous or emotional collapse **to take to pieces** to disassemble (something) into its component parts ‖ to come to pieces **2.** *v.t. pres. part.* **piec·ing** *past* and *past part.* **pieced** to mend or patch by adding a piece ‖ (with 'together') to join (things) so that they make a whole ‖ (often with 'out' or 'together') to make by joining parts or pieces, *to piece a quilt, he pieced out the story from their statements* [M.E. *pece* fr. O.F.]

pièce de ré·sis·tance (pjɛsdəreizi:stɑ̃s) *n.* the choice item in a collection or series, esp. the chief dish in a meal [F.]

piece goods textiles made and sold in standard lengths ‖ textiles sold by the retailer to the length a customer orders, cut from the bolt

piece·meal (pí:smi:l) **1.** *adv.* by degrees, one part after another, *he conquered the territory piecemeal* **2.** *adj.* done bit by bit, *the piecemeal conquest of the territory* [M.E. *pecemel* fr. *pece*, piece+*-mele*, by a (specified) measure]

piece of eight a former Spanish coin worth eight reals

piece of the action participation in a project, esp. the profits

piece·work (pí:swə:rk) *n.* work paid for by the amount done, not by the time taken (cf. TIMEWORK)

pie·crust (páikrʌst) *n.* the baked pastry of a pie

pied (paid) *adj.* parti-colored [PIE n., magpie]

Pied·mont (pí:dmɒnt) (*Ital.* Piemonte) a region (area 11,334 sq. miles, pop. 4,540,700) of N.W. Italy. Its center is the fertile basin (fodder crops, cereals, silk, wine) of the upper Po, open on the east toward the Lombardy plain, and surrounded north, west and south by the Graian, Cottian (forestry, cattle raising, hydroelectricity) and Ligurian Alps. Industry is centered in the chief city, Turin. By the 15th c. Piedmont was dominated by the dukes of Savoy, under whom it was joined (1748) to Sardinia. It was annexed (1798–1814) to France, was restored (1815) to Sardinia, and formed (1861) the nucleus of the new kingdom of Italy

Piedmont a plateau of the eastern U.S.A., extending from the coastal plain to the Appalachians and Blue Ridge Mtns, and from Alabama to New Jersey

Pien·chieng (bjéndʒíŋ) *KAIFENG

pie·pow·der, pie·pou·dre, court of (páipaudər) (*Eng. hist.*) a summary court held at medieval markets and fairs to enforce law merchant among itinerant traders [M. E.=M. L. *pede-pulverosus*, dusty-footed]

pier (piər) *n.* a breakwater of masonry ‖ a wooden-decked structure, supported on piles and built to extend for some distance into the sea or other body of water, used to give passengers access to vessels, now often containing places of entertainment, variety theaters etc. ‖ (*archit.*) a pillar or other structure supporting an arch or lintel or the span of ridge ‖ a buttress of masonry or brick ‖ a section of wall between two doors or other openings **píer·age** *n.* a toll paid for use of a pier or breakwater [M.E. *per* fr. M.L. *pera*, origin unknown]

Pierce (piərs), Franklin (1804–69), 14th president (1853–7) of the U.S.A., a Democrat. A dark-horse candidate for the presidency, he won the election by virtue of his moderate policies and his advocacy of the Compromise of 1850. His administration sponsored the Ostend Manifesto and ordered the bombardment of San Juan del Norte in Nicaragua. The West was further developed by the Gadsden Purchase. His efforts to reconcile the North and the South, notably the Kansas-Nebraska Bill (1854), were counter-productive

CONCISE PRONUNCIATION KEY: **(a)** æ, *c*a*t*; ɑ, *car*; ɔ *fawn*; ei, *snake*. **(e)** e, *hen*; i:, *sheep*; iə, *deer*; ɛə, *bear*. **(i)** i, *fish*; ai, *tiger*; ə:, *bird*. **(o)** o, *ox*; au, *cow*; ou, *goat*; u, *poor*; ɔi, *royal*. **(u)** ʌ, *duck*; u, *bull*; u:, *goose*; ə, *bacillus*; ju:, *cube*. x, *loch*; θ, *think*; ð, *bother*; z, *Zen*; ʒ, *corsage*; dʒ, *savage*; ŋ, *orangutang*; j, *yak*; ʃ, *fish*; tʃ, *fetch*; 'l, *rabble*; 'n, *redden*. Complete pronunciation key appears inside front cover.

pierce (piərs) *pres. part.* **pierc·ing** *past and past part.* **pierced** *v.t.* to make a hole in or through (something) using a sharp implement ‖ to affect (the senses, esp. the sense of hearing, or the emotions) intensely, *the whistle pierced his ears* ‖ to make a way into or through, *the cold pierced his clothes* ‖ to understand or see through, *to pierce a mystery* **pierc·ing** *adj.* penetrating sharply or deeply, *a piercing wind* [O.F. *percer*]

pier glass a large mirror, esp. one intended to go on the wall between two windows

Pi·e·ri·an (paiíəri:ən) *adj.* (*Gk mythol.*) of Pieria, a region of Thessaly where the Muses were worshiped ‖ of the Muses

Pie·ro del·la Fran·ce·sca (pjérɔdéllafrɑntʃéskɑ) (c. 1415–1492), Italian painter. His profound knowledge of perspective and use of its rules, his precise forms, grave faces and soft colors and his mastery of light and atmosphere combine spiritual majesty and a noble vision of Renaissance man. His most notable frescos include 'The Legend of the True Cross' (1452–9), 'The Resurrection' and 'The Flagellation'. Paintings include 'The Baptism', 'The Nativity', 'The Madonna della Misericordia' and 'The Brera Madonna' (c. 1472)

Pie·ro di Co·si·mo (pjérɔdikózi:mɔ) (1462–1521), Italian painter. His characteristic works have mythological or religious subjects with beautifully executed landscape backgrounds, esp. 'Death of Procris'

Pierre (piər) the capital (pop. 11,973) of South Dakota, on the Missouri

pi·er·rot (pi:əróu, pjérou) *n.* a comic character adopted from old French pantomime, with a floppy white costume and whitened face [F. dim. of *Pierre*, Peter (propername)]

pier table a low table placed between two windows

Pie·tà (pi:eitá, pjeitá) *n.* a painting or sculpture of the Virgin Mary mourning over the dead Christ. Very often Christ is lying across her knees [Ital.]

Pie·ter·mar·itz·burg (pi:tərmǽritsbə:rg) the capital (pop. 178,972) of Natal, South Africa, an agricultural market 40 miles inland from Durban: metallurgy, rubber, leather, footwear. Natal University (1909)

pi·e·tism (páiitizəm) *n.* the stressing in religious devotion of personal feeling rather than dogma and intellectual truth, sometimes involving exaggerated or ostentatious piety **Pi·e·tism** the practice and principles of a Lutheran movement, originating in Germany and led by Philipp Jakob Spener, stressing the importance of personal experience of God and of Bible study rather than the forms and dogma of religion [fr. G. *pietismus* fr. *pietist*, pietist]

pi·e·tist (páiitist) *n.* a person whose religious observances are marked by pietism **Pi·e·tist** an adherent of Pietism **pi·e·tís·tic** *adj.* [G. fr. L. *pietas*, piety]

pi·e·ty (páiiti:) *pl.* **pi·e·ties** *n.* devotion and reverence for God ‖ an act which shows this quality [O.F. *piete* fr. L.]

pi·e·zo·e·lec·tric (paii:zouiléktrik) *adj.* of, relating to, or characterized by piezoelectricity [fr. Gk *piezein*, to press+ELECTRIC]

pi·e·zo·e·lec·tric·i·ty (paii:zouilektrísiti:) *n.* the property of some asymmetric crystals (e.g. quartz) of acquiring opposite electrical charges on opposing faces when they are subjected to pressure (conversely, an applied electric potential results in a change of volume). Thus quartz oscillators are used as frequency stabilizers and ultrasonic generators [fr. Gk *piezein*, to press+ELECTRICITY]

pi·e·zom·e·ter (paiizómitər) *n.* an instrument for measuring pressure by its effect in the volume of a liquid or solid **pi·e·zo·met·ric** (paii:zəmétrik) *adj.* **pi·e·zom·e·try** (paiizómitri:) *n.* the measurement of the effect of hydrostatic pressure on the behavior of ground water [fr. Gk *piezein*, to press+METER]

pif·fle (pífəl) *n.* (*pop.*) twaddle, silly nonsense, *don't talk piffle!* **píf·fling** *adj.* (*pop.*) utterly trivial [perh. imit.]

pig (pig) **1.** a young hog less than 120 lbs in weight ‖ (*Br.*) any domestic hog ‖ a greedy, dirty or selfish person ‖ an oblong mass of iron, lead etc. obtained when the molten metal from a furnace cools in a trough ‖ a container for holding radioactive materials ‖ one of the molds in which this metal is cast ‖ pig iron **a pig in a poke** something which one buys or accepts without seeing it first, taking a chance on its being satisfactory **to make a pig of oneself** to eat too much **2.** *v.i. pres. part.* **pig·ging** *past and past part.* **pigged** (of a sow) to bring forth young ‖ (with "out") to gorge oneself [M.E. *pigge*, origin unknown]

pig bed a trough of sand into which molten metal from a furnace is run for cooling

pi·geon (pídʒən) *n.* a member of *Columbidae*, order *Columbiformes*, a large family of words of worldwide distribution having stout bodies, short legs, smooth plumage and small heads and beaks, esp. a member of a variety descended from *Columba livia*, the rock pigeon. Pigeons eat berries and seeds, and are often raised to eat. They utter a characteristic cooing sound. The fancy, specially bred varieties include carrier, fantail, tumbler and pouter pigeons ‖ one of the larger, domesticated birds of fam. *Columbidae* as distinguished from smaller, wild doves ‖ a clay pigeon [M.E. *pyjon*, *pejon* fr. O.F. *pijon*, *pyjoun*, young bird, young dove, and Mod. F. *pigeon*]

pigeon *PIDGIN (personal problem or concern)

pigeon breast a deformity consisting of a projecting sternum, often due to rickets **pí·geon-breast·ed** *adj.*

pigeon hawk *Falco columbarius*, an American falcon related to the merlin

pi·geon·hole (pídʒənhoul) **1.** *n.* a recess in a desk, cabinet etc. for keeping letters, papers etc. **2.** *v.t. pres. part* **pi·geon·hol·ing** *past and past part.* **pi·geon·holed** to put away for future attention or indefinitely ‖ to classify mentally ‖ to put away (papers) in the pigeonholes of a desk

pi·geon-toed (pídʒəntoud) *adj.* having the toes turned inwards

pig·fish (pígfiʃ) *pl.* **pig·fish·es, pig·fish** *n.* any of several fish that make a grunting sound when taken out of the water (*GRUNT)

pig·ger·y (pígəri:) *pl.* **pig·ger·ies** *n.* (*Br.*) a pig farm ‖ (*Br.*) a pigsty ‖ (*Br.*) a filthy place ‖ (*Br.*) filthiness

pig·gish (pígiʃ) *adj.* selfishly greedy

pig·gy (pígi:) *adj.* like a pig ‖ piggish

pig·gy·back (pígi:bæk) **1.** *adj.* of a transport system by which road-haulage loads in their vehicles are carried by rail ‖ of something carried along with another more important package **2.** *adv.* carried in this way ‖ on the back and shoulders, *to carry a child piggyback* **3.** *n.* a ride made piggyback ‖ a piggyback transport system

piggybacking funding of an organization already funded for a federal program, with an additional, related program

piggy bank a money box shaped like a pig, with a slot in the for the coins ‖ any small money box

pig·head·ed (píghedid) *adj.* stupidly obstinate

pig iron the impure iron, with a large content of combined carbon, obtained directly from a blast furnace

pig Latin a jargon in which each word begins with its first vowel, any consonants at the beginning being placed at the end and followed by 'ay', e.g. 'igpay atinLay' for 'pig Latin'

pig·let (píglit) *n.* a young pig [dim. of PIG]

pig·ment (pígmənt) *n.* a coloring matter, esp. in dry powdered form, used in paints etc. ‖ the coloring matter in the cells and tissues of an animal or plant [fr. L. *pigmentum* fr. *pingere*, to paint]

pig·men·tar·y (pígmənteri:) *adj.* of, relating to or containing pigment [fr. L. *pigmentarius*]

pig·men·ta·tion (pigmәntéiʃən) *n.* (esp. *biol.*) coloring or discoloring, esp. in tissues, as a result of pigment [fr. L. *pigmentatus*, painted]

pigmy *PYGMY

pig·nut (pígnʌt) *n.* an earthnut, esp. tuber of *Conopodium denudatum*, fam. *Umbelliferae*, of S. Europe ‖ any of several hickory nuts ‖ a tree bearing such a nut, esp. *Carya glabra*

pig·pen (pígpen) *n.* a pigsty

pig·skin (pígskin) *n.* leather made from a hog's skin ‖ (*pop.*) a football

pig·sty (pígstai) *pl.* **pig·sties** *n.* a partly covered enclosure in which pigs are kept ‖ a filthy place

pig·tail (pígteil) *n.* a braid of hair

pi·ka (páikə) *n.* a member of *Ochotona*, fam. *Ochotonidae*, a genus of small, short-eared, tailless rodents of Asia and W. North America, closely related to the rabbit [Tungus *peeka*]

Pike (paik), Zebulon Montgomery (1779–1813), U.S. explorer and army officer. On an expedition (1806–7) in the Southwest he discovered the peak which now bears his name

pike (paik) *n.* (*hist.*) a pointed projection or sharp tip, e.g. on the center of a shield or the head of an arrow [O.E. *piic*, *pīc*, pickax]

pike *pl.* **pike, pikes** *n.* a member of *Esox*, fam. *Esocidae*, a genus of voracious freshwater fishes of the northern hemisphere, with narrow, elongated snout and sharp teeth, esp. *E. lucius*. They are prized as game fish and as food ‖ any of several fishes resembling these, e.g. the barracuda and walleye pike [shortened fr. *pikefish* fr. PIKE, pointed projection (because of its pointed snout)]

pike *n.* (*hist.*) a weapon carried by a foot soldier, consisting of a long wooden shaft with a pointed metal head, superseded in the 18th c. by the bayonet [F. *pique*]

pike *n.* a gate or bar across a road where a toll is paid ‖ a road, esp. one on which a toll is levied ‖ a toll [short for TURNPIKE]

pike·let (páiklit) *n.* (*Br.*) a crumpet [shortened fr. older *barapicklet* fr. Welsh *bara pyglyd*]

pike·man (páikmən) *pl.* **pike·men** (páikmən) *n.* (*hist.*) a soldier armed with a pike

pike perch any of several fish of fam. *Percidae* resembling the pikes, e.g. the walleye pike and the sauger

pik·er (páikər) *n.* (*pop.*) someone who is mean with his money, and generally lacking in largeness of spirit [etym. doubtful]

Pikes Peak (paiks) a peak (14,110 ft) of the Rocky Mtns, in E. central Colorado, on the edge of the Great Plains

pike·staff (páikstæf, páikstɑf) *pl.* **pike·staffs, pike·staves** (páiksteivz) *n.* the wooden shaft of a pike ‖ a staff with a sharp metal tip at the lower end, used as a walking stick

pi·laf, pi·laff, pi·lau (pí:lɑf, pilɑ́f) *n.* an Oriental dish of rice boiled with fish, meat or chicken and spices [Pers. *pilāw*]

pi·las·ter (pilǽstər) *n.* (*archit.*) a rectangular column engaged in a wall and serving as a pier or as decoration [F. *pilastre* fr. Ital.]

Pi·late (páilət), Pontius, Roman procurator of Judea and Samaria (c. 26–c. 36 A.D.). He gave Christ up to the Jews to be crucified, in order to conciliate the Sanhedrin, though possibly against his own desire

pi·lau *PILAF

pil·chard (píltʃərd) *n.* *Sardinia pilchardus* (or *Sardinella pilchardus*), fam. *Clupeidae*, a small marine food fish like the related herring but smaller, found in great numbers along the coasts of Britain, and of Europe as far south as Portugal. The young are sardines [etym. doubtful]

Pil·co·ma·yo (pi:lkɔmɑ́jɔ) a river (1,000 miles long) flowing southeast from the Bolivian Andes above Potosí across the Gran Chaco (where it forms the Argentina-Paraguay border) to the River Paraguay just north of Asunción

pile (pail) **1.** *n.* a stout beam of wood or steel driven vertically into unfirm ground or the bed of a lake, river or sea, as a support for a superstructure, e.g. a house or causeway ‖ (*heraldry*) a wedge-shaped charge issuing point downwards from the top of an escutcheon **2.** *v.t. pres. part.* **pil·ing** *past and past part.* **piled** to support with or furnish with piles ‖ to drive piles into [O.E. *pīl* fr. L. *pilum*, a heavy javelin, pestle]

pile 1. *n.* a number of things lying one upon another, or a quantity of material placed in or as if in layers forming an elevated mass, *a pile of books, a pile of gravel* ‖ (*pop.*) a large amount of, *a pile of things to do* ‖ a funeral pyre ‖ (*elec.*) a battery of dry cells ‖ a nuclear reactor ‖ (*rhet.*) a large building or group of buildings **to make one's pile** to make a fortune **2.** *v. pres. part.* **pil·ing** *past and past part.* **piled** *v.t.* to place in a pile, *he piled the books on top of each other* ‖ (esp. with 'together' or 'up') to gather, accumulate ‖ to cover with a pile or piles, *a table piled with books* ‖ *v.i.* to crowd together, *they piled into his car* ‖ (esp. with 'up') to come together in or as if in a pile, *his debts are piling up* **to pile arms** (*mil.*) to stand rifles together, with their butts on the ground, so that they support one another in a pyramid [F.]

pile *n.* a soft, furry or velvety raised surface consisting of threads standing out from the surface of a fabric or carpet, either singly or as loops ‖ soft down, fur, hair or wool [fr. L. *pilus*, hair]

pile driver a machine used to drive piles into the ground with a drop hammer ‖ a person who operates this machine

pile·driv·er (páildraivər) *n.* (*slang*) one who hits with great force

piles (pailz) *pl. n.* hemorrhoids [origin unknown]

pi·le·um (páili:əm) *pl.* **pi·le·a** (páili:ə) *n.* the top

CONCISE PRONUNCIATION KEY: **(a)** æ, *cat*; ɑ, *car*; ɔ *fawn*; ei, *snake*. **(e)** e, *hen*; i:, *sheep*; iə, *deer*; ɛə, *bear*. **(i)** i, *fish*; ai, *tiger*; ə:, *bird*. **(o)** o, *ox*; au, *cow*; ou, *goat*; u, *poor*; ɔi, *royal*. **(u)** ʌ, *duck*; u, *bull*; u:, *goose*; ə, *bacillus*; ju:, *cube*. x, *loch*; θ, *think*; ð, *bother*; z, *Zen*; ʒ, *corsage*; dʒ, *savage*; ŋ, *orangutang*; j, *yak*; ʃ, *fish*; tʃ, *fetch*; 'l, *rabble*; 'n, *redden*. Complete pronunciation key appears inside front cover.

of a bird's head, from the nape to the bill [Mod. L. fr. L. *pileus*, felt cap]

pi·le·us (páili:əs) *pl.* **pi·le·i** (páili:ai) *n.* (*biol.*) the umbrella-shaped structure in a mushroom or a jellyfish [L.=a felt hat]

pile·wort (páilwə:rt) *n.* the lesser celandine (*CELANDINE) [fr. its use in treating piles]

pil·fer (pílfər) *v.t.* to steal in small quantities ‖ *v.i.* to commit petty thefts [prob. fr. A.F. and O.F. *pelfrer*, to pillage]

pil·grim (pílgrim) *n.* a person who makes a journey to some sacred place as an act of religious devotion **Pil·grim** (*Am. hist.*) any of the Puritan refugees, mostly Brownists, who sailed from England in the 'Mayflower' (1620) and founded Plymouth Colony in New England [M.E. *pelegrim, pilegrim* fr. O.F.]

pil·grim·age (pílgrəmidʒ) *n.* a journey made by a pilgrim ‖ a journey made for sentimental reasons, e.g. to a poet's birthplace [M.E. *pelrimage* fr. O.F.]

Pilgrimage of Grace (*Eng. hist.*) a rising in Lincolnshire and Yorkshire (1536) against Henry VIII's religious innovations, notably the suppression of the monasteries, as implemented by Thomas Cromwell. The leaders were executed (1537)

Pilgrim Father (*Am. hist.*) one of the Pilgrims

pi·li (pí:li:) *n.* *Canarium ovatum*, fam. *Burseraceae*, a Philippine tree bearing edible nuts ‖ the nut of this tree [Tagalog]

pi·lif·er·ous (pailífərəs) *adj.* (esp. *bot.*) having or producing hairs a covering of hair [fr. L. *pilus*, hair+*-fer*, bearing]

pil·ing (páiliŋ) *n.* the act of driving in piles ‖ (*collect.*) piles used in construction

Pi·li·pi·no (piləpí:nou) *n.* official language in the Republic of the Philippines, similar to Tagalog

pill (pil) **1.** *n.* a small ball or pellet of medicine usually coated with sugar, which is swallowed whole ‖ (with 'the') an oral contraceptive ‖ something unpleasant that must be accepted ‖ (*pop., old-fash.*) a disagreeable person **2.** *v.i.* (of a woolen sweater etc.) to form little balls of fiber on its surface [prob. fr. M. Du. and M.L.G. *pille* fr. L. *pilula*, little ball]

pill (preceded by 'the') an oral contraceptive pill

pil·lage (pílidʒ) **1.** *n.* the act of taking goods by force, esp. by armed force in war **2.** *v. pres. part.* **pil·lag·ing** *past* and *past part.* **pil·laged** *v.t.* to plunder (persons or places), esp. in wartime ‖ *v.i.* to make plundering raids [F. *pillage* n. fr. *piller* v.]

pil·lar (pílər) **1.** *n.* (*archit.*) a vertical structure of masonry, metal etc., of much greater height than thickness, used as a support for a superstructure or as an ornament ‖ anything like this in shape or function, *a pillar of smoke, idealism is a pillar of his philosophy* ‖ a chief supporter of a cause or institution, *a pillar of the Church* **from pillar to post** from one place of refuge, resource etc. to another **2.** *v.t.* to support or ornament with pillars [O.F. *piler*]

pillar box (*Br.*) a short, hollow metal pillar in a public place, for mailing letters etc.

Pillars of Hercules the two rocky promontories (Gibraltar in Europe and Gebel Musa in N. Africa) on either side of the Strait of Gibraltar. For the ancients they marked the finish of the civilized world at the western end of the Mediterranean. According to legend, they were parted by Hercules

pill·box (pílbɒks) *n.* a small round box used as a container for pills ‖ a small, round shallow hat, with no brim ‖ (*mil.*) a small gun shelter of reinforced concrete

pill·head (pílhed) *n.* one who is addicted to pills or hard drugs, esp. when not medically necessary

pil·lion (píljən) *n.* a saddle or spring seat for a second person at the back of a motorcycle or scooter ‖ a light saddle, esp. for a woman ‖ a pad placed behind a man's saddle for a woman to sit on **to ride pillion** (*Br.*) to ride on a pillion [prob. fr. Celt. fr. L. *pellis*, skin, pelt, felt]

Pill·nitz, Declaration of (pílnits) a statement issued (1791) by the Emperor Leopold II and Frederick William II of Prussia, calling on the European powers to restore Louis XVI's authority in France

pil·lo·ry (píləri:) **1.** *pl.* **pil·lo·ries** *n.* (*hist.*) a wooden framework with three holes into which the head and hands of an offender were locked, exposing him to public abuse and ridicule **2.** *v.t. pres. part.* **pil·lo·ry·ing** *past* and *past part.* **pil·lo·ried** (*hist.*) to set in a pillory ‖ to expose to public scorn [M.E. fr. O.F.]

pil·low (pílou) **1.** *n.* a rest and support for the neck or head of a recumbent person (in Western countries a cushion stuffed with down, feathers or other soft material) ‖ (*engin.*) a block, e.g. of wood, used as a cushioning support ‖ a small cushion supporting the design in the making of pillow lace **2.** *v.t.* to lay (the head etc.) on a pillow or on something serving as a pillow [O.E. *pylu, pyle*]

pil·low·case (píloukeis) *n.* a loose, removable cover of cotton or linen for a pillow

pillow lace handmade lace worked over bobbins on a pillow on which the pattern is marked out

pil·low·slip (píllouslip) *n.* pillowcase

pillow talk (*colloq.*) conversations about sex between partners, esp. in bed

pi·lo·car·pine (pailəkárpi:n, pailəkɔ́rpin) *n.* an alkaloid derived from jaborandi. It is used to contract the pupil of the eye, e.g. in counteracting effects of atropine [fr. Mod. L. *Pilocarpus* (genus) fr. Gk *pilos*, felt+*karpos*, fruit]

pi·lose (páilous) *adj.* covered with hair, esp. soft hair **pi·los·i·ty** (pailɒ́siti:) *n.* [fr. L. *pilosus* fr. *pilus*, hair]

pi·lot (páilət) **1.** *n.* a person qualified to direct a vessel on its course into or out of a port, river mouth, canal etc., or along a coast, and taking over navigational control from the master of the vessel while so employed ‖ a person qualified to operate the flying controls of an aircraft ‖ someone who acts as a guide ‖ (*engin.*) a machine part which guides another part in its movement ‖ a pilot light **2.** *adj.* serving as an experimental model for others to follow, *a pilot factory plant* ‖ (*engin.*) serving as a device to direct the operation of a larger device‖ serving as a guide, *a pilot dog* [older F. *pilotte, pilot* and Mod. F. *pilote* fr. Ital.]

pilot *v.t.* to act as the pilot of (a ship, aircraft etc.) ‖to guide (someone) [fr. PILOT n. or F. *piluter*]

pi·lot·age (páilətidʒ) *n.* the work of piloting ‖ the fee paid to a pilot [F.]

pilot balloon a small, unmanned balloon filled with hydrogen used to indicate the speed and direction of the wind

pilot boat a boat used to transport a pilot between a port and the vessel he is to pilot

pilot engine a locomotive sent ahead of a train to see if the track is clear

pilot fish either of two fishes of fam. *Carangidae*, *Seriola zonata* and *Naucrates ductor*, which follow sharks and ships for food, and were formerly thought to guide mariners. They are about 12 ins long and are found in warm waters

pi·lot·house (páiləthaus) *pl.* **pi·lot·hous·es** (páiləthauziz) *n.* the structure on a ship containing the wheel and navigating equipment

pilot lamp a small electric lamp in an electrical circuit, which shows by its light when the circuit is closed ‖ an electric lamp indicating the position of a switch or circuit breaker

pilot light a small burner kept alight to kindle a large burner when this is supplied with fuel, e.g. in a gas heater

pilot officer (*Br.*) an officer in the Royal Air Force ranking immediately below a flying officer

pi·lous (páiləs) *adj.* pilose [fr. L. *pilosus*, hairy]

Pil·sen (pílzen) (*Czech.* Plzen) an industrial center (pop. 165,400) of Bohemia, Czechoslovakia: metallurgy, heavy machinery, armaments, automobiles, beer

Pil·sud·ski (pilsú:dski:), Józef (1867–1935), Polish statesman and general. He commanded the Polish army in the service of Austria (1914–16). He declared Poland an independent republic (1918), with himself as head of state (1918–22). After a coup d'état, he ruled autocratically as premier (1926–8, 1930–5)

pil·u·lar (píljulər) *adj.* of or like a pill [fr. L. *pilula*, pill]

pil·ule (pílju:l) *n.* a small pill [F.]

Pi·ma (pí:mə) *pl.* **Pi·ma, Pi·mas** *n.* a member of a people of S. Arizona and N. Mexico ‖ their Uto-Aztecan language

Pi·man (pí:mən) *adj.* of, relating to or designating a family of Uto-Aztecan languages incl. Pima

pi·men·to (piméntou) *pl.* **pi·men·tos** *n.* allspice ‖ the pimiento [fr. Span. *pimienta*, Port. *pimenta*, pepper]

pi meson *PION

pi·mien·to (pimjéntou) *pl.* **pi·mien·tos** *n.* any of certain red sweet peppers used for stuffing olives, as a source of paprika etc. [Span. fr. *pimienta*, pepper]

pimp (pimp) **1.** *n.* a male procurer of clients for a prostitute **2.** *v.i.* to act as a pimp [etym. doubtful]

pim·per·nel (pímpərnel) *n.* a member of *Anagallis*, fam. *Primulaceae*, a genus of creeping plants with red, blue or white flowers, growing on cultivated land, by roadsides and on dunes. esp. *A. arvensis*, the scarlet pimpernel. The flowers close in bad weather [O.F. *pimprenele, pimpernelle* and F. *pimprenelle*]

pim·ple (pímp'l) *n.* a small, solid, rounded, raised area on the skin, caused by inflammation etc. **pím·pled, pím·ply** *adjs* [origin unknown]

pin (pin) **1.** *n.* a short, very thin, sharp-pointed length of metal, with a small, flat or round head at one end, used to fasten textiles, paper etc., or one without a head, mounted on a badge or brooch to fasten it to clothing ‖ any of several other fastening devices, e.g. a hairpin or safety pin, or a wooden peg used in carpentry ‖ a peg for fastening things to, e.g. one that holds and maintains the tension of a string of a piano, harp etc. ‖ a brooch ‖ (*carpentry*) the tenon of a dovetail ‖ a bottle-shaped piece of wood bowled at in ninepins or tenpins ‖ a linchpin ‖ something of very small value, *not worth a pin* ‖ (golf) the flagpole marking a hole ‖ a small cask holding 1/2 firkin ‖ (*pl., pop.*) the legs, to *knock someone off his pins* **2.** *v.t. pres. part.* **pin·ning** *past* and *past part.* **pinned** to fasten with or as if with a pin **to pin (someone) down** to hold (someone) down by force ‖ to cause (someone) to commit himself or to be specific, *you must pin him down to a particular day* **to pin (something) on someone** to put the blame for (something) on someone [O.E. *pinn*]

pi·ña co·la·da (pí:njəkoulάdə) *n.* drink with a pineapple juice base to which rum, coconut cream and ice are added

pin·a·fore (pínəfɔr, pínəfour) *n.* a sleeveless, apronlike garment fastened at the back and worn over good clothing, esp. by little girls

Pi·nar del Río (pinάrðelrí:ɔ) the westernmost province (area 5,211 sq. miles, pop. 588,000) of Cuba. Capital: Pinar del Río (pop. 27,000). Chief occupations: agriculture (tobacco, coffee, sugarcane, pineapples), cattle raising, lumbering, mining. It includes Cuba's largest copper mine, and huge asphalt deposits

pin·ball (pínbɔl) *n.* a game played on a pinball machine

pinball machine (*Am.*=*Br.* pin table) a glass-covered slot machine used for amusement or gambling. Steel balls are projected up a slope, and when they roll back down they make electric contact with pins projecting in a pattern, causing bulbs to flash and a score to be indicated

pince-nez (pǽnsnei, pínsnei) *pl.* **pince-nez** *n.* a pair of glasses, usually rimless, not hooked over the ears but simply held in place by a spring which grips the bridge of the nose [F.=pinch-nose]

pin·cer·like (pínsərlaik) *adj.* like pincers in function or action

pin·cers (pínsərz) *pl. n.* (sometimes construed as *sing.*) a tool consisting of two arms, hinged together not far from their curved gripping ends and serving as a pair of levers, used to crush, extract nails, grip etc. ‖ (*zool.*) an appendage for grasping, e.g. the chela of certain crustaceans [M.E. *pinsours* fr. A.F.]

pincers movement (*mil.*) a converging attack by two forces from opposed directions on a position

pinch (pintʃ) **1.** *v.t.* to grip between the forefinger and thumb with a sudden, strong pressure, *to pinch someone's arm* ‖ to grip a portion of the flesh of (someone) in this way ‖ to squeeze, *he pinched his finger in the door* ‖ to cause pain to by pressing tightly, *do the new shoes pinch you?* ‖ to cause to become thin, worn, haggard etc., *pinched by poverty* ‖ (often passive and with 'for') to restrict to a narrow space or range of activity, spending etc., *pinched for cash* ‖ (*naut.*) to sail (a boat) with the sails close-hauled ‖ (*pop.*) to steal ‖ (*pop.*) to arrest ‖ *v.i.* to exert painful pressure by squeezing ‖ to overeconomize, be stingy, *the more he pinched, the hungrier we became* **2.** *n.* the act or an instance of pinching between forefinger and thumb ‖ an amount which can be taken up between the forefinger and thumb, *a pinch of salt* || suffering caused by the pressure of poverty etc. **in a pinch** (*Am.*=*Br.* **at a pinch**) if absolutely necessary, *can you manage it in a pinch?* [O.N.F., origin unknown]

pinch·beck (píntʃbek) **1.** *n.* an alloy of copper and zinc used in cheap jewelry to imitate gold **2.** *adj.* made of pinchbeck || false, sham [after Christopher *Pinchbeck,* Eng. jeweler who invented it]

pinch effect (*electr.*) the constricting effect that occurs in a fluid conductor, e.g., liquid metal, subject to a large electric current with magnetism tending to push electrons toward the axis of the current

pinch·ers (píntʃərz) *pl. n.* pincers

pinch-hit (píntʃhit) *pres. part.* **pinchhit·ting** *past* and *past part.* **pinch-hit** *v.i.* (*baseball*) to bat for the regular player || (pop.) to act as substitute in an emergency [back-formation fr. PINCH HITTER]

pinch hitter (*baseball*) a player who pinch-hits for another || (*pop.*) someone who acts as a substitute for another person

Pin·chot (píntʃou), Gifford (1865–1946), U.S. forester and public official. He headed (1898–1910) what became the federal forest service, and co-founded (1912) Theodore Roosevelt's Progressive party

Pinck·ney (píŋkni:), Charles (1757–1824), U.S. statesman and governor of South Carolina (1789–92, 1796–8, 1806–8). His outline for the federal constitution, submitted to the Constitutional Convention of 1787, strongly influenced the constitution's final form

Pinckney, Charles Cotesworth (1746–1825), U.S. minister to France during John Adams' administration, in the mission which led to the X-Y-Z Affair

Pinckney, Thomas (1750–1828), U.S. statesman. While minister to England (1792–6), he served (1794–5) as envoy extraordinary to Spain, where he negotiated the Pinckney Treaty

Pinckney Treaty a U.S.-Spanish treaty negotiated (1795) by Thomas Pinckney, in which Spain granted the U.S.A. the use of the Mississippi River and the right to deposit merchandise at New Orleans, and which defined the boundaries of E. and W. Florida and Louisiana

pin·cush·ion (pínkuʃən) *n.* a small cushion in which pins and needles are stuck so as to be handy for use

Pin·dar (píndər) (c. 518–c. 438 B.C.), Greek lyric poet. He is best known for his choral odes celebrating the victors at the great Greek games and praising the gods

Pin·dar·ic (pindǽrik) **1.** *adj.* in the complex style of Pindar **2.** *n.* a Pindaric ode

Pin·dus (píndəs) a wooded mountain range (highest point 8,635 ft) running through N. Greece (between Epirus and Thessaly) and S.E. Albania

pine (pain) *n.* a member of *Pinus,* fam. *Pinaceae,* a genus of chiefly north temperate, coniferous, resinous trees with needlelike evergreen leaves, usually in clusters. There are over 90 species, widely cultivated for their easily worked lumber and for resinous products || the wood of any of these trees [O.E. *pīn* fr. L. *pinus*]

pine *pres. part.* **pin·ing** *past* and *past part.* **pined** *v.i.* (often with 'away') to lose vitality gradually through hunger, unhappiness etc. || (with 'for') to long for, often so intensely as to suffer [O.E. *pīnian,* to torment]

pin·e·al body (píni:əl) a small body lying behind the third ventricle of the brain in vertebrates. It is thought to be either a vestigial optical organ or an endocrine gland [F. *pinéal,* conical, shaped like a pinecone]

pineal eye an eyelike structure in some lizards, the tuatara etc., with a distinguishable retina and lens. It is an outgrowth of the roof of the forebrain

pineal gland the pineal body

pine·ap·ple (páinæp'l) *n. Ananas comosus,* fam. *Bromeliaceae,* a perennial tropical plant with spiny, recurved leaves and a short, thick stem, native to South America and widely cultivated for its fruit || the edible fruit of this plant, which has juicy, yellowish flesh and a covering of floral bracts topped with short, stiff leaves || (*archit.*) an ornament in the shape of this fruit

pine·cone (páinkoun) *n.* the cone of a pine tree

Pi·nel (pi:nel), Philippe (1745–1826), French physician. He pioneered in the humane treatment of the insane, esp. in his 'Traité médico-philosophique sur l'aliénation mentale' (1801)

pi·nene (páini:n) *n.* either of two oily unsaturated terpenes containing two rings, $C_{10}H_{16}$, obtained from oil of turpentine and occurring in many essential oils [PINE (tree)]

pine needle one of the aromatic, needlelike leaves of a pine

Pi·ne·ro (piníərou), Sir Arthur Wing (1855–1934), English playwright. His success between 1890 and 1900, notably in 'The Second Mrs Tanqueray' (1893), marked the break between the sentimentality and melodrama of the Victorian theater and the new realistic drama

Pi·ñe·ro (pi:njérɔ), Jesús Toribio (1897–1952), Puerto Rican farmer and public official, the first Puerto Rican to be appointed (1946) governor of Puerto Rico

pin·er·y (páinəri:) *pl.* **pin·er·ies** *n.* a field or hothouse where pineapples are cultivated || a pine grove or forest

Pines, Isle of (Painz) *CUBA

pine tar tar residue from the distillation of pine wood, used in roofing materials, paint etc., and in treating skin diseases

pine·tum (paini:təm) *pl.* **pi·ne·ta** (paini:tə) *n.* a plantation of pines of various species for scientific study or ornament [L.=pine grove]

pin·eyed (pínaid) *adj.* (*bot.*) having minute markings resembling eyes, esp. having concealed stamens, with the stigma visible within the corolla (cf. THRUM-EYED)

pin·feath·er (pínfeðər) *n.* a young feather, esp. one just emerging from the skin

pin·fire (pínfáiər) *v.* (*veterinary*) treatment of a horse for a leg ailment by use of electric needles applied to an anesthesized part affected

pin·fold (pínfould) **1.** *n.* a pound for confining stray animals **2.** *v.t.* to confine in a pinfold [O.E. *pundfald*]

ping (piŋ) **1.** *n.* a sharp ringing sound, e.g. of a pebble hitting a rock, a bullet flying through the air etc. **2.** *v.t.* to make this sound [imit.]

ping *v.i.* (*Am.*=*Br.* pink, of an internal combustion engine) to knock [imit.]

Ping-Pong (píŋpɒŋ) *n.* table tennis [Trademark]

Ping Pong 1. camera missile that takes pictures at predetermined heights and returns by parachute to the launching pad. **2.** requiring a patient, esp. insured or Medicaid-subsidized, to see various specialists or to bring in family members, ostensibly for diagnosis and treatment, but primarily for increasing the service charges

pin·guid (píŋgwid) *adj.* (*rhet.*) fatty or greasy || (*rhet.,* of soil) rich, fertile [fr. L.]

pin·head (pínhed) *n.* the head of a pin || a very small object || (*pop.*) a person of very low intelligence

pin·hole (pínhoul) *n.* a hole in paper etc., made by or as if by a pin || a hole into which a pin or peg fits

pin·ion (pínjən) *n.* the smallest and smallest-toothed of two or more gear wheels forming a train or set of gear wheels [fr. F. *pignon*]

pinion 1. *n.* a flight feather of a bird's wing || the end joint of a bird's wing **2.** *v.t.* to cut off or bind the pinions or wings of (a bird) to prevent flight || to bind (the arms) of a person so as to make him powerless || to make (someone) powerless by binding his arms [O.F. *pignon*]

pi·nite (páinait) *n.* an amorphous mineral consisting of aluminum potassium silicate [fr. G. *pinit* after the *Pini* mine in Saxony]

pink (piŋk) *n.* (*hist.*) a sailing vessel with a particularly narrow stern [prob. fr. M. Du. *pincke, pinke,* small seagoing ship]

pink *n.* (*Br.*) a salmon or grayling at the parr stage

pink 1. *n.* a member of *Dianthus,* fam. *Caryophyllaceae,* a genus of plants native to E. Europe, widely cultivated in temperate zones for their fragrant, white, pale red or crimson flowers || a pale, bluish-red color || a pigment, fabric etc. of this color || the scarlet coat of a fox hunter || the scarlet color of this coat **in the pink of health** (or **condition**) in perfect health (or condition) **2.** *adj.* having the color pink, *pink cheeks* || (*pop.*) tending towards communism [etym. doubtful]

pink *v.t.* to ornament (a fabric etc.) by making patterns of holes in it || to make small scallops with indented edges or zigzags in the border of (cloth or paper) || to thrust a sword lightly into, or wound superficially with a bullet, causing a small amount of surface bleeding || (often with 'out') to adorn, decorate gaily [etym. doubtful]

pink *v.i.* (*Br.,* of an internal combustion engine) to ping [imit.]

pink collar *adj.* **1.** of women workers in cosmetology. **2.** by extension, of jobs predominantly held by women

Pin·ker·ton (píŋkərtən), Allan (1819–84), U.S. detective and founder of the Pinkerton National Detective Agency. He headed (1861), under the name of E. J. Allen, an organization for obtaining military information on the southern states

Pinkerton National Detective Agency an organization founded (1850) in Chicago, Ill., by Allan Pinkerton, which specialized in railway theft cases. It thwarted (1861) an assassination plot against President-elect Lincoln in Baltimore, Md., and captured (1866) the ringleaders in a $700,000 Adams Express company theft. A Pinkerton man, James McParlan, broke up (1876) the Molly Maguires

pink·eye (píŋkai) *n.* a highly contagious form of conjunctivitis

Pin·kiang (bingyáŋ) *HARBIN

pink·ie, pink·y (píŋki:) *n.* (*pop.*) the little finger [prob. fr. Du. *pinkje,* dim. of *pink,* the little finger]

pinking shears a dressmaker's toothed shears for pinking the edges of fabric

Pink·ney (píŋkni:), William (1764–1822), U.S. diplomat. As U.S. commissioner to England under the Jay Treaty, he secured (1796) a claim of $800,000 for Maryland against the Bank of New England for losses and damages to American merchants caused by the British government

pin·na (pínə) *pl.* **pin·nae** (píni:), **pin·nas** *n.* (*bot.*) a leaflet of a pinnate leaf || (*zool.*) any of certain appendages, e.g. a wing, feather, fin or flipper || (*anat.*) the broad upper part of the auricle of the ear or the whole auricle [Mod. L. fr. L.=feather, wing]

pin·nace (pínis) *n.* (*hist.*) a six-oared or eight-oared boat of a man-of-war || a ship's boat for conveying the crew ashore etc. [F. *pinasse, pinace* prob. fr. L. *pinus,* pine tree]

pin·na·cle (pínək'l) **1.** *n.* a slender, usually pointed, turret ornamenting a gable, tower etc. || a slender peak of rock || (*fig.*) the highest point, climax, *the pinnacle of fame* **2.** *v.t. pres. part.* **pin·na·cling** *past* and *past part.* **pin·na·cled** to ornament with a pinnacle or pinnacles || to place on or as if on a pinnacle || to be the pinnacle of [M.E. *pinacle* fr. O.F. and F.]

pin·nate (píneit, pínit) *adj.* (*bot.,* of a compound leaf) having leaflets on each side of the rachis || (*zool.*) divided in a feathery manner with lateral processes [fr. L. *pinnatus* fr. *pinna,* feather, wing]

pin·nat·i·fid (pinǽtifid) *adj.* (*bot.*) having pinnately cleft leaves, the clefts reaching approximately halfway to the midrib [fr. L. *pinnatus,* pinnate]

pin·na·tion (pinéiʃən) *n.* the state or fact of being pinnate

pin·ni·ped (pínəped) **1.** *adj.* (*zool.*) of or belonging to *Pinnipedia,* a suborder of marine carnivores with flippers, including seals, sea lions and walruses **2.** *n.* an animal of this suborder [fr. Mod. L. *pinnipedia* fr. L. fr. *pinna,* fin+*pes* (*pedis*), foot]

pin·nu·late (pínjəleit) *adj.* having pinnules **pín·nu·lat·ed** *adj.*

pin·nule (pínju:l) *n.* (*bot.*) one of the secondary divisions of a bipinnate leaf || (*zool.*) a winglike or finlike part or organ [fr. L. *pinnula,* little plume or wing]

Pinochet Ugarte (pi:nouʃ eiu:gártei), Augusto (1915–) Chilean general and president (1974–). He became commander of the army (1973) and led the right-wing military coup that deposed Salvador Allende that same year. His efforts to suppress dissent led to massive civil rights violations

pi·noch·le, pi·noc·le (pí:nʌk'l, pí:nɒk'l) *n.* a card game, similar to bezique, which uses 48 cards taken from two packs, all cards below the eight being discarded and aces being kept in || the pairing and declaration of the queen of spades and the knave of diamonds in this game [origin unknown]

pi·no·cy·to·sis (pinəsaitóusis) *n.* a method by which some cells absorb outside material by forming a membrane around themselves retaining the material in a separate sac. **—pi·no·cy·tot·ic** *adj.* **—pi·no·cy·tot·i·cal·ly** *adv.*

pi·no·le (pinóuli:) *n.* flour made from ground

corn, mesquite beans etc. in the southwestern U.S.A. and Mexico [Span. fr. Nahuatl]

pi·ñon (pínjən, pí:njɔn) *n.* any of several low-growing pines of W. and S.W. North America, which bear edible nutlike seeds, e.g. *Pinus parryana, Pinus edulis* ‖ the seed of any of these trees [Span.]

Pi·no Suá·rez (pí:nɔswάres), José María (1869–1913), Mexican lawyer, writer, politician, and vice-president under Francisco Madero. He was assassinated with Madero by agents of Victoriano Huerta

pin·point (pínpɔint) **1.** *n.* the pointed end of a pin **2.** *v.t.* to locate (e.g. a target) precisely ‖ to direct (an attack, bomb etc.) on a small objective with great accuracy **3.** *adj.* (of a bombing target) requiring extreme accuracy of aim ‖ extremely precise, *pinpoint accuracy*

pin·prick (pínprik) *n.* a very small puncture made by or as if by a pin ‖ a small vexation or irritation, esp. a malicious remark meant to hurt a person's self-esteem

pins and needles a pricking sensation in a limb caused by a partial stoppage of the circulation **on pins and needles** in a state of nervous anxiety

pint (paint) *n.* any of various liquid or dry units of capacity equal to 1/8 gallon, esp., (*Am.*) a unit equal to 28.875cu. ins, (*Br.*) a unit equal to 34.678 cu. ins ‖ a dry measure equal 33.600 cu. ins ‖ (*Br.*) a pint pot of beer, ale or cider [M.E. *pynte* fr. F. *pinte*]

pin·ta (píntə, pí:ntə) *n.* a contagious tropical American disease marked by blotches and loss of pigment in patches [Span.=spot]

pin table (*Br.*) a pinball machine

pin·tail (pínteil) *n. Anas acuta,* fam. *Anatidae,* a freshwater duck of North America, Europe and Asia. The male has long, pointed central tail feathers ‖ *Pedioecetes phasianellus,* fam. *Tetraonidae,* a large grouse of the western U.S.A. and Canada with long middle tail feathers ‖ *Pterocles alchata,* fam. *Pteroclididae,* a long-winged, long-tailed bird somewhat like a pigeon in build, native to Europe, Africa and Asia

pin·tle (pínt'l) *n.* a thick pin or bolt, esp. when used as a pivot, e.g. that on which a rudder turns [O.E. *pintel,* penis]

pin·to (píntou) *pl.* **pin·tos** *n.* a pony or horse that is mottled, esp. with blotches of two or more colors ‖ a pinto bean [Span. fr. *pinto* adj., spotted, mottled]

pinto bean a variety of mottled kidney bean of the southwest U.S.A.

Pin·tu·ric·chi·o, Pin·to·ric·chi·o (pi:ntu:rí:kkjɔ, pi:ntɔrí:kkjɔ) (Bernardino di Betto, c. 1454–1513), Italian painter. His themes are religious, and their treatment notable for lively composition and brilliance of color. His chief works are fresco series, including 'The Dispute of St Catherine' (1492–5) in the Vatican, and 'Life of Pius II' (1503–8) in Siena

pin·up (pínʌp) *n.* (*pop.*) a picture of a pinup girl ‖ (*pop.*) a pinup girl

pinup girl (*pop.*) a sexually attractive young woman

pin·wheel (pínhwi:l, pínwi:l) *n.* (*Am.=Br.* whirligig) a child's toy consisting of a stick with miniature windmill sails which spin in the wind ‖ (*Am.=Br.* Catherine wheel) a rapidly rotating firework

pin·worm (pínwə:rm) *n.* any of several tiny, unsegmented worms of fam. *Oxyuridae* that infest the intestine and rectum, esp. of children

Pin·zón (pi:nθɔ́n), Vicente Yáñez (*d.* 1523), Spanish explorer, captain of 'La Niña' during Columbus' voyage of discovery. With Juan Díaz de Solís he explored (1508–9) Yucatán and Venezuela and discovered (1500) the mouth of the Amazon River

pi·on (pí:ɒn) *n.* (*particle phys.*) the group of three mesons with charges of +1.0 and −1 times the proton charge, no spin, a mass of about 138 MEV, used to bombard cancer cells. *also* pi meson **—pi·on·ic** *adj.*

pi·o·neer (paiəníər) **1.** *n.* a person who experiments and originates, or plays a leading part in the early development of something, *a pioneer of flying* ‖ an early settler, *pioneers of the American West* ‖ a member of a military unit which clears the way in advance of the main body of troops, building bridges, roads, trenches etc. **2.** *v.t.* to prepare, initiate and champion, *to pioneer flew methods of engineering* ‖ to explore and be among the first to develop (a region etc.) ‖ *v.i.* to be a pioneer [F. *pionnier,* O.F. *paonier,* foot soldier, pioneer]

Pioneer Venus Orbiter NASA's spacecraft circling Venus beginning December 1978

pi·ous (páiəs) *adj.* devout or showing religious devotion ‖ designating or making a hypocritical show or pretense of virtue, propriety etc. [fr. L. *pius,* dutiful]

pip (pip) *n.* a disease of poultry and other birds consisting of the accumulation of thick mucus in the mouth and throat **the pip** (*Br., pop.*) a feeling of crossness or depression [prob. fr. M. Du. *pippe,* Du. *pip*]

pip *n.* one of the marks on dice or dominoes ‖ (*Br.*) a star on the shoulder of an army officer's uniform, rank being indicated by the number of stars present ‖ one of the segments on the rind of a pineapple ‖ the root or rootstock of certain plants, e.g. lily of the valley, peony etc. ‖ a single flower in a clustered inflorescence [older-peep, origin unknown]

pip *n.* the seed of an apple, orange, pear, grape etc. [prob. shortened fr. PIPPIN]

pip *pres. part.* **pip·ping** *past* and *past part.* **pipped** *v.t.* (of a bird) to break (the shell of its egg) when hatching ‖ *v.i.* (of a bird) to break through the eggshell when hatching ‖ (of a shell) to break as a bird hatches out [prob. var. of PEEP]

pip *pres. part.* **pip·ping** *past* and *past part.* **pipped** *v.t.* (*Br., pop.*) to defeat, e.g. in an athletic contest ‖ (*Br., pop.*) to spoil completely, ruin, *that's pipped it!* ‖ (*Br., pop.*) to hit (a target) with a shot ‖ (*Br., pop.*) to fail (someone) in an examination ‖ (*Br., pop.*) to fail (an examination) ‖ (*Br., pop.*) to blackball [etym. doubtful]

pip *n.* a short high-pitched sound, used, e.g. on the radio, as a signal [imit.]

pip·age (páipidʒ) *n.* transportation of oil, natural gas, water etc. by pipes ‖ the charge for such transportation ‖ the pipes used, collectively

pi·pal, pee·pul (pí:pəl) *n.* the bo tree [Hindi *pīpal*]

pipe (paip) *pres. part.* **pip·ing** *past* and *past part.* **piped** *v.t.* to convey through pipes, *to pipe oil* ‖ to utter in a squeaky or shrill voice, *to pipe an answer* ‖ (*naut.*) to summon (a crew) by sounding a boatswain's whistle ‖ to play (a tune) on a pipe ‖ to furnish with pipes ‖ to ornament with piping ‖ *v.i.* to play a pipe, esp. the bagpipes ‖ to make squeaky or shrill sounds ‖ (*metall.,* e.g. of steel castings) to develop longitudinal cavities ‖ (*naut.*) to summon a ship's crew by sounding a boatswain's whistle **to pipe down** (*pop.*) to stop talking, or become quiet and subdued **to pipe up** to begin to sing or speak, *several children piped up with the answer* [O.E. *pīpian,* to blow a pipe, and M.E. *pipen,* to peep, chirp, fr. L.]

pipe *n.* a large cask, usually one containing 105 imperial gallons ‖ the amount held by this [O.F. and F.]

pipe *n.* a long hollow cylinder, used chiefly to convey fluids, gas etc. ‖ a musical wind instrument consisting of a hollow cylinder in which the air is made to vibrate, producing a note ‖ one of the hollow tubes in an organ, in which the note is produced in this way ‖ a tubular organ, vessel etc. in the body ‖ a device for smoking tobacco, opium etc. ‖ a quantity of tobacco etc. contained in the bowl of this device ‖ a session of smoking such a device ‖ (*naut.*) a boatswain's whistle or the sounding of it ‖ (*mining*) a cylindrical vein of ore ‖ the shrill sound of a bird ‖ (*pl.*) bagpipes [O.E. *pipe,* a musical tube fr. L.L.]

pipe bomb explosive device made of a pipe filled with explosives and a fuse

pipe clay fine, white plastic clay used to clean and whiten uniform belts etc., also to make clay tobacco pipes **pípe-cláy** *v.t.* to clean and whiten with pipe clay

pipe dream a hope or fantastic plan far removed from reality

pipe·fish (páipfiʃ) *pl.* **pipe·fish, pipe·fishes** *n.* a member of *Syngnathus,* fam. *Syngnathidae,* and related genera of lophobranch fishes covered with bony plates, having long tapering bodies, and jaws united to form a tube

pipe·line (páiplain) *n.* a long line of pipes jointed together, with pumping stations at intervals, used to convey liquids or gases, esp. to convey the crude product from an oil field to a port or refinery ‖ a channel of communication or transport

pipe major the chief player in a band of bagpipes

pipe of peace the calumet as a symbol of peace

pipe organ an organ in which the sound is produced by air vibrating in pipes (*ORGAN, cf. REED ORGAN)

pip·er (páipər) *n.* someone who plays a pipe, esp. the bagpipes

pi·per·a·zine (pi:pérəzi:n, pi:pérəzin) *n.* a basic compound, $C_4H_{10}N_2$, which forms crystalline salts in the presence of organic and inorganic acids [PIPERINE+AZOTE]

pi·per·i·dine (pipéridi:n, pipéridin) *n.* a basic liquid, $C_5H_{11}N$, with the odor of pepper, derived from piperine [fr. L. *piper,* pepper]

pip·er·ine (pípəri:n, pípərin) *n.* a crystalline alkaloid, $C_{17}H_{19}NO_3$,obtained from black pepper, and the active constituent of it [fr. L. *piper,* pepper]

pipe roll (*Br. hist.*) any of the annual accounts of royal revenue and expenditure kept by the Exchequer

pi·per·o·nal (paipérənæl) *n.* a crystalline aldehyde, $(CH_2O_2)C_6H_3CHO$, with the odor of heliotrope, used in perfumery [G.]

pipe·stone (páipstoun) *n.* a pink, hard, clayey stone used by American Indians to make tobacco pipes

pi·pette, pi·pet (paipét, pipét) *n.* a slender glass tube, open at both ends or with a rubber bulb at one end, used esp. in laboratories to take up liquids by suction [F. dim. of *pipe,* pipe]

pip·ing (páipiŋ) **1.** *n.* the music of pipes ‖ a high-pitched, pipelike sound made by or as if by a bird ‖ a system of pipes ‖ material of which pipes can be made ‖ an ornamental fold of cloth sewn along an edge e.g. of a loose cover and often threaded with cord ‖ an ornamental ridge of icing on a cake **2.** *adj.* playing on a pipe ‖ high-pitched, shrill treble, *a child's piping voice* **3.** *adv.* (in the phrase) **piping hot** (of food or liquid) very hot

pip·it (pípit) *n.* a member of *Anthus,* fam. *Motacillidae,* a genus of small birds resembling the lark in coloring and behavior, esp. *A. pratensis,* the meadow pipit of Europe and Asia ‖ any bird of fam. *Motacillidae* [prob. imit.]

pip·kin (pípkin) *n.* a small earthenware pan or pot for cooking [etym. doubtful]

Pip·pin (pípin) Frankish rulers *PÉPIN

pip·pin (pípin) *n.* any of several varieties of dessert apple [M.E. fr. O.F. pepin, seed]

pip·sis·se·wa (pipsísəwə) *n. Chimaphila umbellata,* fam. *Pyrolaceae,* an evergreen plant with astringent leaves sometimes used medicinally as a tonic and diuretic [fr. Algonquian]

pip-squeak (pípskwi:k) *n.* (*pop.*) a person one regards as of no consequence [prob. imit., originally used of a small. high-speed German shell in the lst world war]

pi·quan·cy (pí:kənsi:) *n.* a piquant flavor or quality

pi·quant (pí:kənt) *adj.* sharply stimulating the sense of taste, *a piquant sauce* ‖ stimulating the curiosity or interest [F.]

pique (pi:k) *pres. part.* **piqu·ing** *past* and *past part.* **piqued** *v.t.* to cause resentment in, esp. by wounding the pride of, *he was piqued by her remark* ‖ to stimulate, arouse, *to pique someone's curiosity* [fr. F. *piquer,* to prick]

pique *n.* resentment caused by injured self-esteem [F.]

pique 1. *n.* a score of 30 in piquet made before one's opponent begins to count **2.** *v. pres. part.* **piqu·ing** *past* and *past part.* **piqued** *v.t.* to make this score against (one's opponent) ‖ *v.i.* to make this score [F. *pic*]

pi·qué (pikéi, pi:kéi) *n.* a rather stiff fabric of esp. cotton with a ribbed surface [F. fr. *piquer,* to prick]

pi·quet (pikét, pikéi) *n.* an elaborate 17th-c. card game for two players, using only the 32 cards above the six, incl. the aces [F.]

pi·ra·cy (páirəsi:) *pl.* **pi·ra·cies** *n.* robbery of ships at sea ‖ robbery on land by a descent from the sea by persons not acting under the authority of a state ‖ unauthorized use of a patented or copyrighted work ‖ an instance of any of these [fr. M.L *piratia* fr. Gk]

Pi·rae·us (pairí:əs, piréiəs) (*Gk* Peiraieus) the chief port and industrial center (pop. 500,000) of Greece, adjoining Athens; chemicals, shipbuilding, textiles, mechanical engineering, building materials, light manufacturing

pi·ra·gua (pirάgwə, pirǽgwə) *n.* a pirogue [Span. fr. Carib]

Pi·ran·del·lo (pirəndélou, pi:rɑndéllɔ), Luigi (1867–1936), Italian playwright, short-story writer and novelist. His novels include 'The Late Mattia Pascal' (1904). His short stories

CONCISE PRONUNCIATION KEY: **(a)** æ, *cat*; ɑ, *car*; ɔ *fawn*; ei, *snake*. **(e)** e, *hen*; i:, *sheep*; iə, *deer*; εə, *bear*. **(i)** i, *fish*; ai, *tiger*; ə:, *bird*. **(o)** ɒ, *ox*; au, *cow*; ou, *goat*; u, *poor*; ɔi, *royal*. **(u)** ʌ, *duck*; u, *bull*; u:, *goose*; ə, *bacillus*; ju:, *cube*. x, *loch*; θ, *think*; ð, *bother*; z, *Zen*; ʒ, *corsage*; dʒ, *savage*; ŋ, *orangutang*; j, *yak*; ʃ, *fish*; tʃ, *fetch*; 'l, *rabble*; 'n, *redden*. Complete pronunciation key appears inside front cover.

were collected as 'Novelle per un anno' (1922). His best plays are grotesque and scintillating tragedies, notably 'Six Characters in Search of an Author' (1921) and 'Henry IV' (1922), in which the leading ideas of multiple personality and the relativity of reality are convincingly exploited, and in which he consistently plays with the ambiguity of dramatic illusions

Pi·ra·ne·si (pi:rɑnézi:), Giambattista (1720–78), Italian architect and etcher. His etchings include the 'Vedute' (views of ancient Rome) and 'Carceri d'Invenzione' (imaginary prisons). The dramatic power of these, with their expressive use of light and shade, influenced neoclassical architecture

pi·ra·nha (pirɑ́njə) *n.* a member of *Serrasalmus,* fam. *Characidae,* a genus of small, voracious fishes found in lakes and rivers of South America. They attack men and animals in the water [Port. fr. Tupi]

pi·rate (páirət) **1.** *n.* someone who commits piracy **2.** *v. pres. part.* **pi·rat·ing** *past* and *past part.* **pi·rat·ed** *v.t.* to use (another's copyright material) for one's own profit without permission or without paying fees ‖ *v.i.* to practice piracy **pi·rat·ic** (pairǽtik), **pi·rát·i·cal** *adjs* [fr. L. *pirata* fr. Gk fr. *peiran,* to attack]

Pi·renne (pi:ren), Henri (1862–1935), Belgian historian. He wrote a 'History of Belgium' (1899–1932) and was a specialist in medieval economic history, esp. the growth of towns

pi·rogue (piróug) *n.* a dugout canoe [F. fr. Carib]

pir·ou·ette (piru:ét) **1.** *n.* a rapid spin or whirl of the body on the point of the toe or ball of the foot, esp. in ballet **2.** *v.i. pres. part.* **pir·ou·et·ting** *past* and *past part.* **pir·ou·et·ted** to execute a pirouette [F.=spinning top]

Pi·sa (pí:zə) a city (pop. 103,500) of Tuscany, Italy, on the Arno. Its chief monuments, in the Piazza del Duomo, are the cathedral (11th–13th cc.), baptistry (12th c.), 12th-c. campanile or 'leaning tower' (179 ft high, 14 ft off the perpendicular) and Campo Santo (1203). University (1338)

pis al·ler (pí:zælei) *n.* an expedient resorted to only because there is no better alternative [F.=to go worse]

Pi·sa·nel·lo (pi:zɑnéllɔ) (Antonio Pisano, c. 1395–c. 1450), Italian painter and medalist, influenced by Gentile da Fabriano and the international Gothic style. His extant works include 'The Annunciation' (c. 1424) and 'St George and the Princess' (c. 1437). Few of his frescos survive, but his portrait medals and his drawings, esp. his studies of animals, are masterly

Pi·sa·no (pi:zɑ́nɔ), Andrea (c. 1270–1348), Italian sculptor. He carried on the work of Giotto on the campanile of Florence's cathedral, after working on the bronze doors of the baptistry (1330–6)

Pisano, Giovanni (c. 1245–after 1314), Italian sculptor and architect, son of Nicola Pisano. He worked toward a fusion of Gothic and classical elements, notably in his two pulpits, in St Andrea, Pistoia (c. 1297–1301) and in Pisa cathedral (1302–10)

Pisano, Nicola (c. 1220–c. 1287), Italian architect and sculptor. He initiated classical styles, making his influence felt throughout Italy. His best work includes pulpits in the baptistry at Pisa (1260) and in Siena cathedral (1265–8) and the fountains at Perugia (1278)

pis·ca·to·ri·al (piskətɔ́ri:əl, piskətóuri:əl) *adj.* piscatory

pis·ca·to·ry (pískətɔri:, pískətouri:) *adj.* of or relating to fishing or fishermen [fr. L. *piscatorius* fr. *piscator,* fisherman]

Pis·ces (páisi:z, písi:z) a southern constellation ‖ the twelfth sign of the zodiac, represented as a fish [L. pl. of *piscis,* fish]

pis·ci·cide (písisaid) *n.* **1.** extermination of fish life. **2.** the product used for the purpose **—pis·ci·cid·al** *adj.*

pis·ci·cul·ture (písikʌltʃər) *n.* the breeding and rearing of fish [fr. L. *piscis,* fish+*cultura,* culture]

pis·ci·na (pisí:nə, pisáinə *pl.* **pis·ci·nas, pis·ci·nae** (pisí:ni:, pisáini:) *n.* a stone basin with a drain, near the altar of a church, for carrying away water from liturgical ablutions [L.=tank, fishpond]

pis·cine (písain, písi:n) *adj.* of, relating to, like or characteristic of fish [fr. L. *piscis,* fish]

pis·civ·o·rous (pisívərəs) *adj.* (*zool.*) fish-eating [fr. L. *piscis,* fish+*-vorous,* devouring]

pi·si·form (páisifɔrm) *adj.* having the size and shape of a pea [fr. Mod. L. *pisiformis* fr. *pisum,* pea]

pisiform bone a small, rounded bone on the upper, outer side of the wrist

Pi·sis·tra·tus, Pei·sis·tra·tus (paisístrətəs) (c. 600–c. 527 B.C.), tyrant of Athens (c. 560–c. 527 B.C.). He gained power by a coup d'état and was twice exiled, but returned with increased power. He adorned Athens and encouraged art, commerce and farming

pis·mire (písmaiər) *n.* (*rhet.*) an ant [M.E. fr. PISS+*mire,* an ant (from the odor of anthills, caused by the formic acid discharged by ants)]

pi·so·lite (pízəlait, páisəlait) *n.* limestone formed of pea-shaped concretions **pis·o·lit·ic** (pizəlítik, paisəlítik) *adj.* [fr. Mod. L. *pisolithus* fr. Gk *pisos,* pea+*lithos,* stone]

piss (pis) **1.** *v.i.* (*pop.*) to urinate **2.** *n.* (*pop.*) urine [O.F. *pissier,* F. *pisser*]

Pis·sar·ro (pi:særou), Camille (1831–1903), French painter who specialized in landscapes in a wide range of media. One of the original Impressionists, he was represented in all eight Impressionist exhibitions

pis·ta·chi·o (pistǽʃi:ou, pistɑ́ʃi:ou) *pl.* **pis·ta·chi·os** *n. Pistacia vera,* fam. *Anacardiaceae,* a small dioecious tree native to W. Asia. Its fruit, a drupe, contains an edible seed, the pistachio nut, used as a flavoring in ice cream, confectionery etc. ‖ this nut ‖ the yellowish green color of the nut [fr. L. *pistacium* fr. Gk]

pis·til (pístil) *n.* (*bot.*) the female seedbearing organ of a flower, including the ovary, stigma and style **pis·til·late** (pístilit, pístileit) *adj.* having or bearing a pistil, esp. without a stamen [F. *pistil* and L. *pistillum*]

Pis·to·ia (pi:stɔ́jɑ) a city (pop. 84,700) in Tuscany, Italy: Romanesque cathedral (12th c.), baptistry (1337), medieval and Renaissance palaces and churches

pis·tol (pístəl) *n.* a small firearm held and fired with one hand [obs. F. *pistole*]

pis·tole (pistóul) *n.* any of several obsolete European gold coins, esp. a Spanish one [F.]

Pis·ton (pístən), Walter (1894–1976), American composer. His work includes symphonies, chamber music and a ballet, 'The Incredible Flutist' (1938)

pis·ton (pístən) *n.* a disk or short cylinder attached centrally to a rod and fitted closely inside a hollow cylinder, within which it can be driven up and down by fluid pressure (in engines) or create a partial vacuum on one side of it as the piston rod is moved up and down (in pumps or compressors) ‖ (*mus.*) a sliding valve in a brass wind instrument. When pressed, it causes an additional length of tubing to be opened, thus lowering the pitch [F. fr. Ital.]

piston ring an elastic, split metal ring surrounding a piston, giving a tighter fit inside the cylinder

piston rod a rod which moves or is moved by the piston to which it is attached

piston valve (*mus.*) a piston in a brass instrument

pit (pit) **1.** *n.* a deep hole in the ground, either natural or made by digging for minerals ‖ a deep hole for refuse ‖ a covered hole in the ground used as a trap for animals ‖ a deep hole for carrying out some operation, e.g. a sawpit ‖ a coal mine, including the shaft and all the workings ‖ a small depression in a surface, e.g. one left in the skin by the pustules of smallpox ‖ a hole made in the floor of a garage or workshop enabling a car or machine to be examined or repaired from below ‖ an enclosed, often sunken area for fights between animals, esp. cocks ‖ (*bot.*) a specialized depressed region of the secondary wall of plant cells that plays a role in the intercellular transport of fluids ‖ (*Am.=Br.* orchestra pit) the space, often depressed, in front of the stage in a theater, where the orchestra sits ‖ (*Br.*) the ground floor of a theater auditorium, esp. the back part, under the gallery ‖ (*Br.*) the audience in this part of the theater ‖ (*commerce*) an area of an exchange devoted to a particular commodity, *wheat pit* **2.** *v. pres. part.* **pit·ting** *past* and *past part.* **pit·ted** *v.t.* (with 'against') to match (one's strength, courage, willpower) against another's or against some natural force ‖ to make a pit in (the skin etc.), *a face pitted by smallpox* ‖ to set (one animal) to fight against another ‖ to put into a pit, usually for storage ‖ *v.i.* to become marked with pits [O.E. *pytt*]

pit 1. *n.* the stone of a peach, cherry, plum etc. **2.** *v.t. pres. part.* **pit·ting** *past* and *past part.* **pit·ted** to remove the pit from [Du.]

pi·ta (pí:tə) *n.* any of various plants yielding fiber, esp. the century plant ‖ the tough fiber obtained from such a plant, used for cordage ‖ flat, round bread used in the Middle East [Span.]

pit-a-pat (pítəpæt) **1.** *n.* movement and sound suggested by the fast beating of the heart or by light, rapid footsteps **2.** *adv.* in such a way as to make this sound, *her heart went pit-a-pat* **3.** *v.i. pres. part.* **pit-a-pat·ting** *past* and *past part.* **pit-a-pat·ted** to move pit-a-pat ‖ (esp. of the heart) to go pit-a-pat [imit.]

Pit·cairn Islands Group (pítkɛərn), a British colony in the central S. Pacific, consisting of Pitcairn Is. (area 1.75 sq. miles, pop. 70) and three adjacent uninhabited islands. The inhabitants are descended from the 'Bounty' mutineers and Tahitians and speak their own idiom of English. Religion: Seventh-Day Adventist. Products: fruit, vegetables, curios. Pitcairn became a British colony (1838) and has been administered since 1970 from New Zealand

pitch (pitʃ) **1.** *n.* a dark-colored, sticky, resinous substance, liquid when heated, hard when cold, which is a residue from distillation of tars, turpentine or fatty oils etc. and occurs naturally as asphalt. It is used for proofing wood or fabric, e.g. the hulls of boats or roofs, in the manufacture of soaps and plastics, and for road surfacing ‖ this substance as a criterion of blackness or obscurity ‖ a resin derived from certain conifers, sometimes considered to have medicinal properties **2.** *v.t.* to coat or smear with pitch [O.E. *pic* fr. L.]

pitch 1. *v.t.* to fix and set up, *to pitch a tent* ‖ to set or place in a definite position ‖ to throw, toss, *to pitch hay* ‖ (*baseball, cricket*) to throw or deliver (the ball) to the batter or batsman ‖ (*mus.*) to set (a part, note etc.) in a scale or key or at a particular pitch ‖ to set in a particular style, degree, manner, mood, feeling etc. ‖ *v.i.* to encamp ‖ (of a ship) to plunge or toss with bow and stern alternately rising and falling (cf. ROLL) ‖ to plunge headlong ‖ (*cricket,* of the ball) to fall in a specified way or place, *it pitched on the leg stump* ‖ to dip, slope, *the roof pitches steeply* ‖ (*baseball*) to throw the ball to the batter or be the player who throws the ball to the batter **to pitch in** to get down to work vigorously **to pitch into** (*pop.*) to attack violently **to pitch on** (or **upon**) (*Br., pop.*) to select arbitrarily, *when he needs a volunteer he always pitches on me* **2.** *n.* the act of pitching or an instance of this ‖ a place claimed for doing business in an open market, for street performance or for camping, (*Br.*) playing a game etc. ‖ (*baseball*) the act of pitching or manner in which the ball is pitched ‖ (*baseball*) a turn at pitching, *it's your pitch now* ‖ (*cricket*) the part of the ground between and immediately around the two wickets (cf. INFIELD, cf. OUTFIELD) ‖ (*cricket*) the way a ball falls with respect to the batsman ‖ the quality of a sound with respect to the frequency of vibration of the sound waves ‖ degree of intensity, *feelings raised to a high pitch* ‖ the degree of slope something, e.g. of a roof ‖ (*geol., mining*) the dip of a vein or bed ‖ (*mech.*) the distance between a point on a gear tooth and the corresponding point on the next one, or between a point on a screw thread and the corresponding point on the adjacent thread in a line parallel with the axis ‖ the pitching motion of a ship ‖ the highest point of a falcon's soaring before diving on to its prey ‖ (*pop.*) a line of talk, e.g. of a salesman [etym. doubtful]

pitch and toss a game in which coins are thrown at a mark by various players. The one who throws nearest has the first turn at tossing all the coins and keeping all those that fall with the head uppermost, the other players following in turn

pitch-black (pítʃblǽk) *adj.* (esp. of darkness, night) as black as pitch

pitch·blende (pítʃblend) *n.* (*mineral.*) a massive form of uraninite from which uranium and radium are extracted [fr. G. *pechblende*]

pitch circle a hypothetical circle around teeth of a gear wheel at the place where they come in contact with the teeth of another gear wheel

pitch-dark (pítʃdɑ́rk) *adj.* pitch-black

pitched battle a battle in which the opposing troops have fixed, clearly defined positions, studied and arranged in advance

pitch·er (pítʃər) *n.* a jug for holding liquids, esp. one with a wide lip and a handle or ears ‖ the amount of liquid that this holds || (*bot.*) a modified leaf of a pitcher plant, in which the petiole becomes tubular, with the blade forming a lid [M.E. *picher, pecher* fr. O.F.]

pitcher *n.* a person who pitches, esp. (*baseball*) the player who pitches the ball to the batter || (*golf*) an iron with a blade lofted more than a mashie niblick but less than a niblick, used for short approach shots to the green || (*Br.*) a brick-shaped granite paving stone

pitcher plant any of several insectivorous plants, e.g. a member of the American genus *Sarracenia,* fam. *Sarraceniaceae* or of the Malaysian genus *Nepenthes,* fam. *Nepenthaceae,* with leaves modified into tubular pitchers holding secretions for trapping and digesting their prey

pitch·fork (pítʃfɔrk) **1.** *n.* a longhandled fork with sharp, curved prongs for lifting and turning hay, straw etc. **2.** *v.t.* to shift with a pitchfork || to thrust (someone) suddenly or forcibly or without preparation (into some job or position) [older *pickfork,* prob. fr. PICK (sharp tool)+FORK]

pitch·ing (pítʃiŋ) *n.* a stone paving or walled facing on a slope || a foundation of coarse stone for a macadamized road

pitch pine any of several resinous pines which produce pitch, esp. *Pinus rigida* of E. North America || the wood of such a pine

pitch pipe a small tuning pipe used for setting the pitch for unaccompanied singers or for tuning an instrument

pitch·y (pítʃi:) *comp.* **pitch·i·er** *superl.* **pitch·i·est** *adj.* of the quality or nature of pitch || covered or smeared with pitch || dark or black

pit·e·ous (píti:əs) *adj.* arousing pity, *piteous cries* [M.E. *pytos, pitous* fr. O.F. and A.F.]

pit·fall (pitfɔl) *n.* a hidden danger or difficulty

pith (piθ) **1.** *n.* the medulla or central region of parenchymatous cells in the stem of a vascular plant || the soft white lining of e.g. orange peel || any spongy tissue resembling the pith of a vascular plant, e.g. the spongy core of a feather || the substance or gist of a matter || forceful relevance, *comments full of pith* **2.** *v.t.* to kill (an animal) by piercing or severing the spinal cord || to destroy the central nervous system by passing a wire up the vertebral canal of (e.g. a frog) || to remove pith from (a plant) [O.E. *pitha*]

pith·e·can·thrope (piθikǽnθroup) *n.* pithecanthropus

pith·e·can·thro·pus (piθikǽnθrəpəs, piθikənθróupəs) *pl.* **pith·e·can·thro·pi** (piθikǽnθrəpai, piθikənθróupai) *n.* a member of the extinct genus *Pithecanthropus* of primitive men characterized by their small cranial capacity and apelike facial profile. Examples have been found in Java and, with slight variations, at Peking (*PEKING MAN) [fr. Gk *pithēkos,* ape+*anthrōpos,* man]

pith·i·ly (píθili:) *adv.* in a pithy manner

pith·i·ness (píθi:nis) *n.* the quality of being pithy

pith·y (píθi:) *comp.* **pith·i·er** *superl.* **pith·i·est** *adj.* forcefully concise, tersely cogent || of, like or containing pith

pit·i·a·ble (píti:əb'l) *adj.* arousing or deserving pity || arousing or deserving pitying contempt **pít·i·a·bly** *adv.* [M.E. fr. O.F.]

pit·i·ful (pítifəl) *adj.* calling forth pity or compassion || contemptible

pit·i·less (píti:lis, pítilis) *adj.* showing or feeling no pity

Pit·man (pítmən), Sir Isaac (1813–97), English inventer (1837) of a shorthand system based on phonetic principles rather than orthographic principles

pit·man (pítmən) *pl.* **pit·men** (pítmən) *n.* someone who works in a pit, esp. a coal miner || (*mach., pl.* **pit·mans**) a connecting rod

pi·ton (pí:tɒn) *n.* (*mountaineering*) an iron peg or spike driven into rock, used as a step or support, or as a belay for the rope [F.]

pi·tot tube (pí:tou, pi:tóu) a device to measure the pressure of a fluid flow, and so its velocity, that is essentially a tube (with an opening turned upstream) connected to a manometer [after H. *Pitot,* F. engineer]

pit·prop (pítrɒp) *n.* a piece of wood used as a temporary support for the roof of a mine

pit saw a long saw handled by two men, one above and one below the log being sawn into planks. The man below is usually in a pit (cf. TOP SAWYER)

Pitt (pit), William, 1st earl of Chatham (1708–78), known as the 'Elder Pitt' and as the 'Great Commoner', British statesman. He led the opposition to Walpole and to George II's preoccupation with Hanover. As effective head of the administration (1756–61), he successfully directed British policy in the Seven Years' War (1756–63). He again formed an administration (1766–8) as lord privy seal, but suffered increasingly from mental and physical illness. His last years were devoted to urging the conciliation of the American colonies

Pitt, William (1759–1806), known as the 'Younger Pitt', British statesman, son of the Elder Pitt. He entered parliament (1781), was chancellor of the Exchequer (1782–3) and was appointed prime minister (1783–1801 and 1804–6) by George III. He refused to resign despite repeated Commons defeats during his first year in office, and gained a majority in the 1784 elections. A liberal Tory, he reduced the national debt and many tariffs, negotiated a commercial treaty with France (1786), placed India under government control (1784) and reorganized the government of Canada (1791). His free-trade policies were upset by the outbreak of the French Revolutionary Wars (1792–1802), in which he took the lead in organizing coalitions against the French (1793, 1798). He passed the Act of Union with Ireland (1800), but resigned when George III refused to approve Catholic Emancipation (1801). Recalled to office (1804), he organized another coalition against the French in the Napoleonic Wars, but died soon after the news of Napoleon's crushing victory at Austerlitz (1805)

pit·tance (pít'ns) *n.* a very small income wage or allowance [M.E. *pitance, pitaunce* fr. O.F. *pitance,* pity]

pit·ter-pat·ter (pítərpætər) **1.** *n.* a quick succession of light tapping sounds **2.** *adv.* with a quick succession of light taps **3.** *v.i.* to go pitter-patter [reduplication of PATTER]

Pitts·burgh (pítsbə:rg) a port (pop. 423,938, with agglom. 2,263,894) and industrial center in the coalfield of Pennsylvania, at the head of the Ohio River: iron and steel, chemical industries (esp. coal by-products), aluminum, glass, oil refining, food processing. Carnegie Institute of Technology (1900)

pi·tu·i·tar·y (pitú:iteri:, pitjú:ieri:) **1.** *adj.* of or relating to the pituitary gland **2.** *pl.* **pi·tu·i·tar·ies** *n.* the pituitary gland [fr. L. *pituitarius* fr. *pituita,* phlegm]

pituitary body the pituitary gland

pituitary gland a small vascular endocrine gland located at the base of the brain and found in most vertebrates. It consists of an anterior and posterior lobe. The posterior lobe secretes hormones affecting renal functions, contraction of smooth muscle and reproduction. The anterior lobe secretes hormones which control and regulate most of the other endocrine glands. Thus this gland directly or indirectly controls and regulates most basic body functions

pi·tu·i·trin (pitú:itrin, pitjú:itrin) *n.* an aqueous preparation of the pituitary glands of cattle, used as a source of pituitary hormones in the treatment of certain conditions in man [*Pituitrin,* a trademark]

pit viper any of several poisonous snakes esp. of the New World, belonging to fam. *Crotalidae,* incl. the rattlesnake, copperhead, water moccasin etc.

pit·y (píti:) **1.** *pl.* **pit·ies** *n.* a feeling of sympathy for the sufferings or privations of others || a cause of sorrow or regret, *it's a pity that it's raining* **to have** (or **take**) **pity on** to act with compassion toward **2.** *v.t. pres. part.* **pit·y·ing** *past* and *past part.* **pit·ied** to feel pity for [M.E. *pite* fr. O.F. and Mod. F. fr. L.]

pit·y·ri·a·sis (pitəráiəsis) *n.* any of several superficial skin diseases in man, characterized by the formation and shedding of thin scales || a similar disease of domestic animals [Mod. L. fr. Gk fr. *pituron,* bran, dandruff]

Pi·us II (páiəs) (Enea Silvio de' Piccolomini, 1405–64), pope (1458–64). He was a distinguished humanist poet and author. He failed in his ambition to drive the Turks from Europe

Pius IV (Giovan Angelo de' Medici, 1499–1565), pope (1559–65). He convened the last part (1562–3) of the Council of Trent, and supported the Counter-Reformation

Pius V, St (Michele Ghisliere, 1504–72), pope (1566–72). He enforced the decisions of the Council of Trent and launched a ruthless attack on Protestantism, excommunicating Elizabeth I of England (1570). He helped to organize the coalition which defeated the Turks at Lepanto (1571). Feast: May 5

Pius VI (Giovanni Angelo Braschi, 1717–99), pope (1775–99). He opposed the ecclesiastical measures of the French Revolution, but was forced to recognize the French republic and to cede territory after Napoleon invaded the Papal States (1796). He was deported to France (1798) and died in exile

Pius VII (Barnaba Chiaramonti, 1740–1823), pope (1800–23). He negotiated with Napoleon the Concordat of 1801, reestablishing Catholicism in France, and anointed Napoleon as emperor (1804). He was a prisoner of the French (1809–14). He restored the Society of Jesus (1814)

Pius IX (Giovanni Mastai-Ferretti, 1792–1878), pope (1846–78). His early liberal reforms were welcomed by Italian patriots, but were abandoned after revolution drove him to Gaeta (1848). He was restored to Rome (1850) and maintained there by a French armed force until 1870, when the French withdrew and Italy seized the remainder of the Papal States except Vatican City, to which the pope was thereafter confined. He promulgated the dogma of the Immaculate Conception (1854), and convened the 1st Vatican Council, which proclaimed papal infallibility (1870)

Pius X, St (Giuseppe Sarto, 1835–1914), pope (1903–14). He ordered the Church in France to surrender its property to the French government rather than submit to State control (1906). He condemned Modernism (1907). He encouraged frequent Communion (1905), reorganized the Curia (1908), revised the missal and breviary (1911), began a new codification of canon law, and encouraged the use of plainsong

Pius XI (Achille Ratti, 1857–1939), pope (1922–39). He established papal relations with Italy by the Lateran Treaty (1929). He condemned Fascism (1931), Nazism (1937) and Communism (1937). He was eloquent in his criticism of laissez-faire capitalism and urging of social reform, notably in the encyclical 'Quadragesimo Anno' (1931). He encouraged the laity to participate more in the work of the Church, and set up a radio station in the Vatican

Pius XII (Eugenio Pacelli, 1876–1958), pope (1939–58). He attempted to alleviate the suffering caused by the 2nd world war, and denounced Communist persecution of Christianity. He defined the dogma of the Assumption (1950)

piv·ot (pívət) *n.* a fixed shaft or pin having a pointed end which acts as the point of balance upon which a plate or bar can turn or oscillate || the pointed end of such a shaft or pin || the turning or oscillating movement of something mounted on such a shaft or pin || a person, thing or fact on which a set of circumstances etc. depends, *this point is the pivot of the argument* [F.]

pivot *v.t.* to supply with or balance on a pivot || *v.i.* to turn or oscillate on or as if on a pivot, *the whole movement pivots on him* [F. *pivoter*]

pivot *n.* (*sports*) the key participant in an action. **—pivotman** (*basketball*) the center

piv·ot·al (pívət'l) *adj.* of, relating to or having the nature of a pivot || having vital importance for some activity or for what will develop from a set of circumstances etc.

pix *PIC

pix *PYX

pix·el (píksel) *n.* the picture element in a television image

pix·ie, pix·y (píksi:) *pl.* **pix·ies** *n.* a small, mischievous elf or fairy [etym. doubtful]

pix·i·lat·ed, pix·il·lat·ed (píksəleitid) (*pop.*) slightly crazy || (*pop.*) rather drunk [PIXIE]

pix·y *PIXIE

Pi·zar·ro (pizárou), Francisco (c. 1475–1541), Spanish conquistador. After two unsuccessful attempts to explore Peru (1524–5, 1526–8), he landed there (1532), captured Cuzco (1533) and executed Atahualpa, the Inca king. He faced rebellions both from the Incas and from his own followers, in the course of which he was murdered

pi·zazz (pizǽz) *n.* (*slang*) a provocative vitality

piz·za (pí:tsə) *n.* a large, round, flat, breadlike crust spread with tomatoes, cheese and sometimes other ingredients, e.g. shreds of meat, anchovies and herbs, and baked [Ital.]

piz·ze·ri·a (pi:tsərí:ə) *n.* a place where pizzas are made and sold [Ital.]

piz·zi·ca·to (pitsikάtou) **1.** *adj.* (*mus.*, of a note) played on a stringed instrument by plucking the strings with the finger instead of using the bow **2.** *adv.* (*mus.*) in a pizzicato manner **3.** *pl.* **piz·zi·ca·ti** (pitsikάti:), **piz·zi·ca·tos** *n.* (*mus.*) a note or passage played pizzicato [Ital.]

PKU (*med. abbr.*) **phenylketonuria** (which see)

plac·a·bil·i·ty (plækəbíliti:, pleikəbíliti:) *n.* the quality of being placable

plac·a·ble (plǽkəb'l, pléikəb'l) *adj.* capable of being placated, or easily placated ‖ showing tolerance or forgiveness, *in a placable mood* [M.E. fr. O.F. fr. L. *placabilis*]

plac·ard (plǽkərd, plǽkərd) **1.** *n.* a notice for advertising or display purposes **2.** *v.t.* to set up placards in or on ‖ to advertise by such means ‖ to display as a placard [O. F. *plackart, placard* and Mod. F. *placard* fr. O.F. *plaquier*, to lay flat, plaster]

pla·cate (pléikeit, plǽkeit) *pres. part.* **pla·cat·ing** *past* and *past part.* **pla·cat·ed** *v.t.* to pacify, esp. by making concessions **pla·ca·tion** (pleikéiʃən) *n.* **pla·ca·to·ry** (pléikətɔri:, plǽkətɔri:, pléikətouri:, plǽkətouri:) *adj.* [fr. L. *placare* (*placatus*)]

place (pleis) **1.** *n.* a particular part of space, *this is the place where they first met* ‖ a particular spot or area on a surface, *a worn place on the carpet* ‖ a particular city, town, village, district etc., *it is one of the places he visited* ‖ position in space, or in some hierarchy, scale, orderly arrangement etc., *to lose one's place in a line* ‖ proper function that goes with status, *it's not your place to criticize* ‖ a building or area appointed for a specified purpose, *a place of worship* ‖ (in names) a square in a city ‖ (in street names) a short street ‖ (in names) a country mansion ‖ home, dwelling, *we ate supper at his place* ‖ a space, seat or other accommodation, in a theater, train etc. ‖ a particular passage in a book etc., *she always cries at the sad places* ‖ the point that one has reached in reading a book, etc. ‖ (*racing*) a position among the winners, esp. second or third ‖ an official position, *a place on the board* ‖ a stage or step in an argument or sequence, *in the first place we must define our terms* ‖ (*math.*) the position of a figure in relation to others in a series, esp. of decimals, *calculate to four decimal places* **in place** in the usual or correct place ‖ proper, appropriate **in place of** as a substitute for, rather than **out of place** inappropriate, unsuitable ‖ not in keeping with the surroundings etc., *he felt out of place in their company* **to give place to** to be succeeded by ‖ to yield one's position to **to go places** (*pop.*) to achieve worldly success or distinction **to know one's place** (*old-fash.*) to act humbly and respectfully in accordance with one's relatively low rank or standing **to take place** to occur, happen **to take the place of** to be a substitute for **2.** *v. pres. part.* **plac·ing** *past* and *past part.* **placed** *v.t.* to put in a particular place, position, rank, office, condition etc. ‖ to identify by recalling the context or circumstances connected, *she knew his face but couldn't place him* ‖ to invest (money) ‖ to give (an order for goods etc.) ‖ (followed by 'in', 'on' or 'upon') to bestow (confidence, trust etc.) upon something or someone‖ to pitch (the voice) in singing or speech ‖ *v.i.* (*racing*) to be among the first three contestants to finish, esp. to finish second in a horse or dog race **to be placed** (*Br., racing*) to be among the first three to finish [M.E. fr. F. fr. L. fr. Gk *plateia* (*hodos*), broad (street)]

pla·ce·bo (pləsí:bou) *pl.* **pla·ce·bos, pla·ce·boes** *n.* an inactive but harmless preparation given to humor a patient ‖ (*Roman Catholicism*) the first antiphon of vespers for the dead [L.=I shall be pleasing (first word of Psalm cxiv, 9 in the Vulgate)]

place-kick (pléiskik) **1.** *n.* (*football, rugby*) the act of kicking the ball after it has been placed on the ground for this purpose (in rugby, after a try has been scored or a free kick awarded) **2.** *v.t.* to kick (the ball) in this way ‖ *v.i.* to perform such a kick

place·man (pléismən) *pl.* **place·men** (pléismən) *n.* (esp. *Br.*, used pejoratively) a person who holds or seeks some political office out of self-interest rather than to do public service

place mat a mat placed under the dishes and eating utensils of a person at a dining table on which no cloth is laid

place·ment (pléismənt) *n.* a placing or being placed ‖ the manner of placing or being placed ‖ the finding of employment for a worker ‖ (*football*) the placing or position of the ball on the ground for a place-kick

pla·cen·ta (pləséntə) *pl.* **pla·cen·tas, pla·cen·tae** (pləsénti:) *n.* the vascular organ in most mammals which joins the fetus to the maternal uterus and acts as the site of metabolic exchange between them. The placenta arises from differentiated regions of the chorion and allantois brought into intimate relation with a specialized region of the uterine wall where fetal and maternal vascular systems are permitted to exchange nutriment and oxygen by diffusion without direct mixing of blood, the fetus being able to get rid of waste products ‖ any of various functionally similar organs in other animals ‖ (*bot.*) the part of the carpel bearing ovules [L.=cake fr. Gk]

pla·cen·tal (pləsént'l) *adj.* of, relating to or having a placenta [fr. Mod. L. *placentalis* fr. L. *placenta*]

plac·en·ta·tion (plæs'ntéiʃən) *n.* the development of the placenta ‖ the way the placenta is attached to the uterus ‖ (*bot.*) the way in which the placenta is attached to the pericarp [F.]

plac·er (pléisər) *n.* a deposit of sand or gravel e.g. in the bed of a stream, where gold or other valuable minerals can be obtained in particles [Span. *placer*, deposit]

placer mining the mining of placers by washing, dredging etc.

place value (*math*) the value of a digit due to its place as a numeral, e.g., units, tens, hundreds

plac·id (plǽsid) *adj.* (of temperament) not easily roused ‖ (of a person) having such a temperament **pla·cid·i·ty** (pləsíditi:) *n.* [fr. L. *placidus* fr. *placere*, to please]

plack·et (plǽkit) *n.* a slit or opening, e.g. one in the top of a skirt for convenience in putting on and fastening, or for getting at a pocket [perh. var. of PLACARD, (obs.) plate of armor]

plac·oid (plǽkɔid) **1.** *adj.* (*zool.*, of the hard scales or dermal teeth of an elasmobranch fish) plate-shaped **2.** *n.* (*zool.*) a fish having placoid scales [fr. *plax* (*plakos*), plate]

pla·gal (pléig'l) *adj.* (*mus.*, of certain medieval modes) having the fourth note of the range as keynote (cf. AUTHENTIC MODE) [fr. M. L. *plagalis* fr. *plaga*, plagal mode fr. Gk *plagios*, plagal, oblique]

plagal cadence (*mus.*) a cadence in which the subdominant chord resolves to the tonic chord

pla·gia·rism (pléidʒərizəm, pléidʒi:ərizəm) *n.* the act of plagiarizing or an instance of this ‖ a plagiarized idea etc. **plá·gia·rist** *n.* someone who plagiarizes [fr. L. *plagiarius*, a kidnapper]

pla·gia·rize (pléidʒəraiz, pléidʒi:əraiz) *pres. part.* **pla·gia·riz·ing** *past* and *past part.* **pla·gia·rized** *v.t.* to use and pass off (someone else's ideas, inventions, writings etc.) as one's own ‖ *v.i.* to take another's writings etc. and pass them off as one's own [PLAGIARY]

pla·gia·ry (pléidʒəri:, pléidʒi:əri:) *pl.* **pla·gia·ries** *n.* plagiarism ‖ a plagiarist [fr. L. *plagiarius*, a kidnapper]

pla·gi·o·clase (pléidʒi:əkleis) *n.* (*mineral.*) a triclinic feldspar with an oblique cleavage, esp. one containing sodium and calcium **pla·gi·o·clas·tic** (pleidʒi:əklǽstik) *adj.* [G. *plagioklas* fr. Gk *plagios*, oblique+*klasis*, cleavage]

pla·gi·o·trop·ic (pleidʒi:ətrópik) *adj.* (*bot.*, e.g. of most roots and lateral branches) having the longer axis inclined from the vertical **pla·gi·ot·ro·pism** (pleidʒi:ótrəpizəm) *n.* [fr. Gk *plagios*, oblique+*tropos*, a turning]

plague (pleig) **1.** *n.* an epidemic, often fatal disease caused by the bacterium *Pasteurella pestis*, occurring in various forms, e.g. as bubonic plague. After the Black Death, the plague broke out sporadically in Europe (14th-18th cc.), notably decimating London in 1665. It remains endemic in parts of Asia ‖ a social scourge, *a plague of petty thieving* ‖ a nuisance, annoyance **2.** *v.t. pres. part.* **pla·guing** *past* and *past part.* **plagued** to pester or harass, *plagued by insects* **plá·guey, plá·guy 1.** *adj.* (*pop.*) annoying, bothersome **2.** *adv.* (*pop.*) plaguily **plá·gui·ly** *adv.* [M.E. *plage* fr. O.F.]

plaice (pleis) *pl.* **plaice** *n. Pleuronectes platessa*, fam. *Pleuronectidae*, a European edible marine flatfish, laterally compressed. Both eyes are on the upper side of the body. It lies on the sea bed, and swims on one side. It has no air bladder ‖ any of several American flatfishes [M.E. *plais*, *plaice* fr. O.F. fr. L. *plotessa*]

plaid (plæd) **1.** *n.* a long piece of woolen cloth of tartan pattern worn esp. over the shoulder and breast by Scottish Highlanders ‖ cloth having a tartan pattern **2.** *adj.* made of cloth with a tartan pattern, *a plaid skirt* ‖ having a tartan pattern, *a plaid tablecloth* **pláid·ed** *adj.* wearing a plaid ‖ made of or wearing plaid [Gael. *plaide*]

plain (plein) **1.** *adj.* easy to see or understand ‖ simple, not embellished or complicated ‖ absolute, complete, *plain madness* ‖ (of food) unelaborate, not having unusual or spicy ingredients ‖ bluntly frank ‖ unsophisticated ‖ lacking physical beauty, but not ugly **2.** *n.* a large expanse of level, open country **3.** *adv.* manifestly, *it's just plain wrong* ‖ clearly, candidly, *she told him plain* [O.F. fr. L.]

plain·chant (pléintʃænt, pléintʃɑnt) *n.* plainsong

plain·clothes·man (pléinklóuzmən, pléinklóuðzmən) *pl.* **plain·clothes·men** (pléinklóuzmən, pléinklóuðzmən) *n.* a police officer, esp. a detective who does not wear a uniform when on duty

plain dealing straightforwardness, honesty in business or social relations

plain-laid (pléinléid) *adj.* (of a rope) made by laying three strands together with a right hand twist

plain sailing progress unimpeded by difficulties or obstacles, *once that is solved the rest will be plain sailing*

Plains Indian a member of any of the tribes of American Indians formerly inhabiting the prairies of the U.S.A., notably the Cheyennes, the Apaches, the Sioux, the Comanches, the Navahos, the Kiowas, the Arapahos and the Utes. As a result of the land grabs and the worst of the Indian Wars (1860-90), they lost the bison-hunting grounds on which they chiefly depended. Those who survived the conflict with the whites were concentrated on unfertile, game-poor reservations

plains·man (pléinzmən) *pl.* **plains·men** (pléinzmən) *n.* someone who lives in an area characterized by great plains

Plains of Abraham the Heights of Abraham

plain·song (pléinsɔŋ, pléinsɒŋ) *n.* an ancient nonmetrical modal type of chant without accompaniment for singing the Christian services, still used in the form of the Gregorian chant [trans. M.L. *cantus planus*]

plain·spo·ken (pléinspóukən) *adj.* frank and forceful in speech

plaint (pleint) *n.* (*law*, esp. *Br.*) a statement of grievance ‖ (*rhet.*) a complaint or lamentation [M.E. *plaint, plainte* fr. O.F.]

plain·tiff (pléintif) *n.* (*law*) a person who brings a lawsuit against another (cf. DEFENDANT) [O. F. *plaintif*]

plain·tive (pléintiv) *adj.* quietly mournful ‖ weakly complaining [M.E. fr. O.F. *plaintif*, *plaintive*]

plait (pleit, plæt) **1.** *n.* a length of hair, straw, ribbon etc. consisting of at least three interlaced strands **2.** *v.t.* to interlace at least three strands of (hair, ribbon etc.) to form a plait ‖ to make (a basket, mat etc.) by interlacing strands together [M.E. *pleyt, playt* fr. O.F. *pleit, ploit*, fold, crease]

plan (plæn) **1.** *n.* a design for a construction, layout, system etc. ‖ a drawing representing a horizontal section of a solid object (cf. ELEVATION) ‖ a detailed diagram, *a plan of Paris* ‖ a formulated scheme setting out stages of procedure, *a plan for the production of a book* ‖ (often *pl.*) a proposed or intended course of action, *what are your plans for this weekend?* ‖ (*art*, in perspective) any of the imaginary perpendicular planes interposed between the represented object and the eye **2.** *v. pres. part.* **plan·ning** *past* and *past part.* **planned** *v.t.* to make a design for (a building, garden, city etc.) ‖ to devise a program of action for, *a planned tour* ‖ to intend, *we plan to go there next summer* ‖ *v.i.* to make plans ‖ *PLANNED ECONOMY [F. fr. *plan* adj., flat fr. L.]

planch (plæntʃ) *n.* a flat slab, especially one of baked fireclay used in the kiln in enameling [F. *planche*, plank, slab]

planche (plæntʃ) *n.* (*gymnastics*) horizontal position supported on the hands

planch·et (plǽntʃit) *n.* a plain disk of metal from which a coin is made [dim. of PLANCH]

plan·chette (plæntʃét) *n.* a small, usually heart-shaped board used in some spiritualistic seances. It is mounted on two castors and a pencil. It moves when lightly touched by a person's fingers, and is supposed to trace out significant words [F. dim. of *planche*, plank]

Planck (plɑŋk), Max Karl Ernst Ludwig (1858–1947), German physicist. He propounded the quantum theory (1900). Nobel prize (1918)

Planck constant (*phys.*) the constant factor ($6.624 + 10^{-27}$ erg sec., symbol *h*) in the Planck radiation law and many other equations of quantum theory

Planck radiation law a law in physics relating the radiation associated with atomic processes to the energy changes involved (*SPECTROSCOPY). It may be expressed: Energy change=*h* (frequency of radiation) where *h* is the Planck constant ‖ a law in physics giving the distribution of energy over the range of wavelengths within a blackbody as a function of temperature (*QUANTUM THEORY)

plane (plein) *n.* a member of *Platanus,* fam. *Platanaceae,* a genus of tall, spreading trees of northern temperate regions, with large, simple, palmately lobed leaves and brittle bark which tends to flake away [F. fr. L. *platanus* fr. Gk]

plane 1. *n.* a carpenter's tool used for producing a smooth surface on wood by paring away irregularities. It consists of an adjustable blade fixed at an angle in a wooden or metal stock. Variations exist for cutting grooves, routing etc. **2.** *v. pres. part.* **plan·ing** *past* and *past part.* **planed** *v.t.* to work (wood) with this tool ‖ *v.i.* to work with this tool [F.]

plane 1. *adj.* flat, level ‖ (*math.*) lying on a surface which is a plane ‖ of such surfaces **2.** *n.* a level surface such that if any two points on it are joined by a straight line, every part of that line will lie in that surface ‖ an imaginary plane surface in which points or lines are regarded as lying, e.g., in perspective ‖ a level of development, existence, accomplishment, thought, value etc., *to consider a problem on the metaphysical plane* ‖ an aircraft ‖ one of the main supporting surfaces of an aircraft or hydroplane, for controlling balance and elevation in flight ‖ one of the natural faces of a crystal ‖ a main road in a mine [fr. L. *planus*]

plane *pres. part.* **plan·ing** *past* and *past part.* **planed** *v.t.* to glide ‖ to travel in an aircraft ‖ (of a boat or seaplane) to skim the surface of the water [F. *planer*]

plane chart a chart of a small area on which meridians and parallels of latitude are shown by equidistant straight lines on a flat surface

plane geometry that branch of geometry which deals with the properties and relations of plane figures

plane-po·lar·ized (pléinpóulәraizd) *adj.* (of a wave of light etc.) vibrating in a single plane (*POLARIZATION)

plane sailing a method of navigation which ignores the earth's curvature, treating its surface as a plane

plan·et (plǽnit) *n.* one of the bodies in space, other than a comet, meteor or satellite, which revolve around the sun of the earth's solar system, shining by reflected light from the sun ‖ any similar body revolving about a star (*ASTEROID, *MAJOR PLANET) [M.E. fr. O.F. *planete* fr. L. L. fr. Gk *planētēs,* wanderer]

plane table a drawing board with a ruler attached to its center, mounted on a tripod, used in making maps or surveys in the field by direct observation along the ruler

plan·e·tar·i·um (plænitέəri:əm) *pl.* **plan·e·tar·i·ums, plan·e·tar·i·a** (plænitέəri:ə) *n.* a complex system of optical projectors by means of which the positions and relative motions of the planets and visible stars are displayed on the inner surface of a large dome within which observers are situated ‖ the building containing this ‖ an orrery [Mod. L. fr. L.L. *planetarius,* planetary]

plan·e·tar·y (plǽniteri:) *adj.* of or pertaining to a planet or the planets ‖ of or pertaining to the earth ‖ of or designating an epicyclic train of gear wheels, esp. the transmission gear of a car ‖ (*phys.*) moving like a planet, *planetary electrons* [fr. L.L. *planetarius*]

plan·e·tes·i·mal (plænitésəməl) **1.** *adj.* of or designating a small solid heavenly body thought to have existed in the early stages of the solar system's evolution **2.** *n.* such a body [PLANET+INFINITESIMAL]

planetesimal hypothesis the theory that the planets were formed by accretion of planetesimals

plan·et·oid (plǽnitɔid) *n.* an asteroid

Plan·et·o·khod (planétoukɒd) *n.* (*aerospace*) U.S.S.R. vehicle for planetary exploration

plan·e·tol·o·gy (plænitɒ́lədʒi:) *n.* the study of the natural solar sytem, its orbiting bodies, planets and meteorites. —**plan·e·to·log·i·cal** *adv.* —**plan·e·tol·o·gist** *n.*

planet wheel a gear wheel revolving around another with which it engages in an epicyclic train

plan·gen·cy (plǽndʒənsi:) *n.* the quality of being plangent

plan·gent (plǽndʒənt) *adj.* making a loud reverberating sound, or a loud plaintive, drawn-out sound [fr. L. *plangens* (*plangentis*) fr. *plangere,* to beat]

planigraphy *TOMOGRAPHY

pla·nim·e·ter (plənímitər) *n.* an instrument which measures the area of a plane figure when a tracer is moved along the perimeter **pla·ním·e·try** *n.* measurement of the area of a plane figure [fr. F. *planimétre*]

plan·ish (plǽniʃ) *v.t.* to flatten, smooth, polish or toughen (metal) by hammering or rolling [fr. obs. F. *planir* (*planiss-*), to make smooth]

plan·i·sphere (plǽnisfiər) *n.* (*geom.*) a projection of a sphere upon a plane surface, esp. one of a part of the heavens to show the relative positions and movements of the heavenly bodies [M.E. *planisperie* fr. M.L. *planisphaerium* fr. L. *planus,* plane+*sphaera* fr. Gk *sphaira,* sphere]

plank (plæŋk) **1.** *n.* a long, heavy board, usually at least 2 ins thick and at least 8 or 9 ins wide ‖ a main idea, principle etc. in an argument, political program etc. ‖ planking **to walk the plank** (*hist.*) to be made to walk blindfold along and off a plank projecting from a ship over the sea (a method of killing used by pirates) **2.** *v.t.* to cover or provide with planks ‖ to cook and serve on a wooden board, *a planked steak* ‖ (*pop.,* esp. with 'down') to put (something) on a counter, table etc. with force ‖ to put down (money) in payment on the spot **plánk·ing** *n.* planks collectively [M.E. *planke* fr. O.N.F.]

plank·ton (plǽŋktən) *n.* minute plants (chiefly algae) and animals which float in great quantities near the surface of fresh or salt water. They provide the only source of food for many kinds of fish **plank·ton·ic** (plæŋktɒ́nik) *adj.* (*DIATOM, cf. NEKTON) [G. fr. Gk fr. *planktos* adj., drifting]

planned economy an economy in which government regulates labor, capital etc. in order to secure the success of an overall production plan, instead of leaving the forces of supply and demand to operate freely

planned obsolescence (*business*) quality in the design of a product that provides deterioration or outstyling before the end of the expected period of usefulness

planned parenthood * FAMILY PLANNING

planned shrinkage deliberate reduction in a population, esp. for the purpose of reducing necessary services

pla·no-con·cave (pléinoukɒnkéiv) *adj.* (esp. of a lens) flat on one side and concave on the other [fr. L. *planus,* flat+CONCAVE]

pla·no-con·vex (pléinoukɒnvéks) *adj.* (esp. of a lens) flat on one side and convex on the other [fr. L. *planus,* flat+CONVEX]

plant (plænt, plɑnt) *v.t.* to put the roots of (a plant) in the ground to enable it to grow, or to sow (seed) ‖ to stock with plants, *to plant a garden* ‖ to introduce (living things) in the hope that they will settle and multiply, *to plant settlers in a colony* ‖ to instill (ideas, principles etc.) in the mind ‖ to put firmly in position, *he planted himself in front of the door* ‖ (*pop.*) to place as a trap, *they planted marked bills to prove the man's guilt* ‖ (*pop.*) to deliver (a blow) ‖ (with 'out') to transplant (young plants) to the ground where they are to mature [O.E. *plantian* and O.F. *planter* fr. L.]

plant *n.* any organism belonging to the kingdom *Plantae* (cf. ANIMAL), characterized usually by lack of independent locomotion, absence of a central nervous system, cell walls composed of cellulose, and a nutritive system based on photosynthesis. Many plants exhibit a strong tendency to alternation of generations ‖ such an organism large enough to be handled, esp. one smaller than a shrub, bush or tree ‖ the assemblage of buildings, tools etc. used to manufacture some kind of goods or power ‖ mechanical equipment for a particular operation, *the power plant of a submarine* ‖ (*pop.*) a carefully planned swindle ‖ (*pop.*) a carefully planned trap laid to catch a wrongdoer [O.E. *plante* fr. L. *planta*]

Plan·tag·e·net (plæntǽdʒənit) an English royal dynasty founded by Geoffrey, count of Anjou (1113–51), father of Henry II. The Plantagenets ruled England (1154–1399, Henry II–Richard II), and most of W. France (1154–1205). Their succession was disputed (1399–1485) by the claimants of York and Lancaster, the dispute culminating in the Wars of the Roses (1455–85)

plan·tain (plǽntin, plǽntein) *n.* a member of *Plantago,* fam. *Plantaginaceae,*genus of plants with a radical, ribbed rosette of leaves. They are cosmopolitan weeds. The inflorescence is a spike or head [M.E. fr. O.F.]

plantain *n. Musa paradisiaca,* fam. *Musaceae,* a species of banana plant native to India ‖ its fruit, starchy and green-skinned, a basic food in the Tropics, commonly baked, boiled or fried [older *platan, plantane* fr. Span. *plátano, plántano*]

plan·tar (plǽntər) *adj.* pertaining to the sole of the foot, *a plantar wart* [fr. L. *plantaris* fr. *planta,* sole]

plan·ta·tion (plæntéiʃən) *n.* a group of growing plants or trees, *a fir plantation* ‖ an estate, esp. in a tropical or warm region, on which a crop such as sugarcane, cotton, tea etc. is cultivated ‖ (*hist.*) the settling of a colony or new country ‖ (*hist.*) a colony or settlement [fr. L. *plantatio* (*plantationis*), a planting]

Plantation System a U.S. socioeconomic form of production unique to the South, esp. between c. 1800 and 1860 (though less than one-fifth of southern farms were plantations). It was characterized by huge farms which were worked by slave labor and which cultivated single crops for profit, notably cash crops, i.e. cotton, rice, sugar and tobacco. The plantations did much of their own manufuturing. The planter-aristocrat lived a life of ease, but he lived in isolation from urban life and even from his fellow planters

plant·er (plǽntər, plɑ́ntər) *n.* a person who plants ‖ a machine used to plant ‖ a person who manages a plantation ‖ a container for potted or unpotted house plants ‖ (*hist.*) a colonist

plant·i·grade (plǽntigreid) **1.** *adj.* (*zool.*) walking on the soles of the feet, with the heel touching the ground (cf. DIGITIGRADE) **2.** *n.* (*zool.*) a plantigrade animal (e.g. man, bear etc.) [F. fr. L. *planta,* sole+*-gradus,* going, walking]

Plan·tin (plãtɛ̃, *Eng.* plǽntin), Christophe (c. 1520–89), French printer. He established his printing press in Antwerp (1555). His masterpiece is the eight-volume 'Biblia Polyglotta' (c. 1568–c. 1572). Typefaces based on Plantin's are still very commonly used

plant louse an insect, esp. an aphid, which infests plants

plan·u·la (plǽnjulə) *pl.* **plan·u·lae** (plǽnjuli:) *n.* the usually flattened, ovoid, young free-swimming larva of a coelenterate [Mod. L., dim. of L. *planus,* flat]

plaque (plæk) *n.* a flat piece of metal, ivory etc. attached to a wall or inset in wood, either as an ornament or to record a fact of historical interest ‖ (*virology*) in a culture, an area destroyed by a virus ‖ (*med.*) an area of psoriasis ‖ a localized area of atherosclerosis ‖ any abnormal flat area in or on the body [F. fr. Du. *plakke,* a kind of coin]

plash (plæʃ) **1.** *v.t.* to agitate (water) so that it makes a gentle splashing sound ‖ to sprinkle or splash so as to speckle ‖ *v.i.* to make a gentle splashing noise **2.** *n.* the sound of water plashing ‖ a plashing movement [etym. doubtful]

plash *v.t.* (esp. *Br.*) to break partially, bend down and interweave (stems, branches and twigs) so as to form a hedge ‖ to make or mend (a hedge) in this way [O.F. *plaisser, plaissier*]

plash *n.* a muddy pond or pool ‖ a puddle **plásh·y** *adj.* marshy, boggy [O.E. *plæsc*]

Plas·kett (plǽskit), John Stanley (1865–1941), Canadian astronomer, best known for his discovery (1922) of the dual star subsequently named 'Plaskett's twins'

plasm (plǽzəm) *n.* plasma

plas·ma (plǽzmə) *n.* (*biol.*) the viscous living matter of a cell surrounding the nucleus, the protoplasm ‖ the blood plasma ‖ (*mineral.*) a bright green variety of quartz allied to chalcedony, used as a semi-precious gem ‖ (*phys.*) an ionized gas produced at very high temperatures (e.g. in the stars) containing about equal numbers of positive and negative charges, which is a good conductor of electricity, and is affected by a magnetic field **plas·mat·ic** (plæzmǽtik), **plás·mic** *adjs* [L.L.=something shaped or molded, fr. Gk fr. *plassein,* to shape]

plasma engine a rocket engine utilizing thrust from magnetically accelerated ionized gases

plas·ma·gene (plǽzmədʒi:n) *n.* (*genetics*) one or a group of genes not in a chromosome. These can sometimes reproduce

plasma jet a stream of hot, ionized gas used in welding and in satellite propulsion

plas·ma·pause (plǽzməpɔz) *n.* the upper parameter of the plasmasphere

plasma physics branch of physics dealing with the ionzied gas in thermonuclear activity and cosmic reactions **—plasma physicist** *n.*

plas·ma·sphere (plǽzməsfiər) *n.* (*astron.*) the layer of ionized gas surrounding a planet

plasma torch a device for producng ionized gas

plas·mid (plǽzmid) *n.* **1.** (*genetics*) a self-reproducing particle of protoplasm, without a nucleus that determines hereditary characteristics. **2.** (*biol.*) cell cytoplasm capable of self-reproduction. **3.** (*phys.*) a section of plasma that has a distinct shape

plas·mo·di·um (plæzmóudi:əm) *pl.* **plas·mo·di·a** (plæzmóudi:ə) *n.* the vegetative stage in the life cycle of a slime mold, consisting of a motile mass of protoplasm containing several nuclei ‖ a member of *Plasmodium*, fam. *Plasmodiidae*, a genus of parasitic sporozoans including those causing malaria in man [Mod. L. fr. PLASMA+Gk *-ōdēs*, like]

plas·mol·y·sis (plæzmɒ́lisis) *n.* (*bot.*) contraction of the plant cell wall and loss of protoplasm from the cell wall, caused by the withdrawal of water from plant cells by osmosis [fr. Gk *plasma*, form+*lusis*, loosing]

plas·mon (plǽzmʌn) *n.* (*genetics*) the hereditary factors in cytoplasm

Plas·sey, Battle of (plǽsi:, plɑ́si:) a battle (1757) in which Clive decisively defeated the nawab of Bengal and prepared the way for British rule in India

plas·ter (plǽstər, plɑ́stər) *n.* a mixture of slaked lime, sand and water, sometimes with hair or fibers added as binding material, applied wet to an interior wall or ceiling and hardening to a smooth surface when dry ‖ plaster of paris ‖ a medicinal preparation spread on a cloth and applied to the body, *a mustard plaster* [O.E. *plaster* and O.F. *plastre* fr. L. fr. Gk]

plaster *v.t.* to cover (a wall etc.) with wet plaster ‖ to put (something adhesive) on a surface, esp. in great quantity or with force ‖ to apply a medicinal plaster to ‖ to treat (wine) with plaster of paris to neutralize acidity ‖ to bomb or shell heavily [fr. PLASTER *n.* or older F. *plaster*]

plas·ter·board (plǽstərbɔrd, plɑ́stərbɔrd, plǽstərbourd, plɑ́stərbourd) *n.* a board made by compressing sheets of fiber separated by a layer of partly set plaster of paris and used esp. as a surface to be plastered

plaster cast a sculpture cast in plaster of paris ‖ a firm covering made of gauze and plaster of paris used e.g. for holding a fractured bone in place

plas·ter·er's putty (plǽstərərz, plɑ́stərərz) a white paste of slaked lime,used for finishing

plaster of paris a white or pinkish powder, essentially the hemihydrate of calcium sulfate, $2CaSO_4 \cdot H_2O$, obtained by calcining gypsum. With water it forms a quick-setting paste, drying to form a tough, hard solid. It is used for casts and molds and building materials

plas·tic (plǽstik) **1.** *adj.* of material which changes shape when pressure is applied and retains its new shape when the pressure is removed (cf. ELASTIC) ‖ of the processes involved in using such materials to fashion things, *the plastic arts* ‖ of an object fashioned from such a material ‖ (*art*) of, relating to or characterized by three-dimensional movement, form and space ‖ pliable, easily influenced ‖ (*biol.*) capable of undergoing variation, growth, repair etc. ‖ (*colloq.*) unnatural, synthetic ‖ so changeable as to be phony **2.** *n.* a plastic material **plás·ti·cal·ly** *adv.* [fr. L. *plasticus*, able to be molded, fr. Gk fr. *plassein*, to shape, form]

—A plastic material is a substance which, though stable in normal use, was plastic under pressure or heat (or both) at some stage during manufacture. Plastics are usually polymers. If they soften again when reheated, they are said to be thermoplastic. If, after fashioning, they resist further applications of heat, they are thermosetting. The raw materials of the plastics industry are by-products of oil refining, coal distillation etc. The plastics industry has great importance in industrialized countries (*BAKELITE, CELLULOID, *POLYSTYRENE, *POLYETYHLENE)

Plas·ti·cine (plǽstisi:n) *n.* a plastic substance used as a substitute for modeling clay, drying very slowly and not adhering to the fingers. It cannot be fired in a kiln [Trademark]

plas·tic·i·ty (plæstísiti:) *n.* the quality or state of being plastic ‖ (*chem.*) the quality of being displaced within a molecular sphere of action

plas·ti·cize (plǽstisaiz) *pres. part.* **plas·ti·ciz·ing** *past* and *past part.* **plas·ti·cized** *v.t.* to make plastic ‖ *v.i.* to become plastic **plás·ti·ciz·er** *n.* any of a number of substances added to a plastic to improve its physical properties, e.g. its flexibility

plastic memory tendency of some plastics to return to a former shape

plastic surgery the branch of surgery concerned with correcting disfigurements due to injury, age or congenital deformities, usually by transference of skin or bone

plastic zone *RUPTURE ZONE

plas·tid (plǽstid) *n.* a small body of specialized protoplasm within the cell of some organisms (e.g. a chloroplast) [G. fr. Gk fr. *plassein*, to form]

plas·tral (plǽstrəl) *adj.* (*zool.*) of or pertaining to a plastron

plas·tron (plǽstrɒn, plǽstrən) *n.* a padded breast shield worn by a fencer ‖ (*hist.*) a steel breastplate ‖ (*zool.*) the ventral part of the shell of a tortoise or turtle ‖ a similar part in other animals ‖ a dicky (for a shirt or blouse) [F. fr. Ital.]

plat (plæt) **1.** *n.* a small piece of land ‖ a detailed plan or map **2.** *v.t. pres. part.* **plat·ting** *past* and *past part.* **plat·ted** to make a plan or map of [fr. PLOT]

Plata, Río de la *RÍO DE LA PLATA

Pla·tae·a, Battle of (plətí:ə) a battle fought (479 B.C.) during the Persian Wars. The Greeks, under Pausanias, destroyed a superior Persian army and forced the Persians to withdraw from Greece

plate (pleit) **1.** *n.* a flat, shallow dish (usually circular, and typically of porcelain or earthenware) from which food is eaten ‖ the food served on such a dish ‖ the main course of a meal (meat, vegetables, salad etc.) all served on one plate ‖ a thin flat piece of metal for engraving on or bearing an inscription ‖ a full-page illustration (usually on coated paper or some paper other than what is used for the text) bound in a book ‖ (*collect.*) domestic utensils (esp. tableware) made of gold, silver etc., or plated ‖ a thin coating of precious metal put on base metal by electrolysis, *the plate is wearing off these forks* ‖ (*photog.*) a rectangular piece of metal or glass, coated with a sensitized emulsion, on which a photograph is taken ‖ a thin flat piece of metal etc. of uniform thickness, varying in size and serving various purposes, e.g. to join a fractured bone or forming part of a ship's armor ‖ (*dentistry*) that part of a denture which fits against the mouth and holds the artificial teeth in position ‖ (*pop.*) a set of false teeth ‖ a metal or wooden dish used for taking up the collection in church ‖ (*printing*) a sheet of metal, cast from type or engraved, from which impressions are taken ‖ a printed impression from this, e.g. of an engraving ‖ (*archit.*) a horizontal beam supporting or supported by vertical ones ‖ a horse race carrying a gold or silver cup etc. as prize for the winner, or the trophy awarded ‖ (*hist.*) sheets or one sheet of armor metal ‖ (*baseball*) home plate ‖ (*baseball*) a piece of rubber upon which the pitcher stands when delivering the ball to the batter ‖ a thin cut of beef from the forequarter, below the short ribs ‖ (*anat., zool.*) a thin layer or scale, e.g. of bone, horny tissue etc. ‖ (*elec.*) the anode or positive element of an electron tube toward which the stream of electrons flows **2.** *v.t. pres. part.* **plat·ing** *past* and *past part.* **plat·ed** to cover with metal plates ‖ to cover with a thin layer (e.g. of metal) mechanically, chemically or electrically ‖ to make a solid plate of (type) for printing [M.E. fr. O.F. *plate*, a thin plate]

plate armor, *Br.* **plate armour** (*hist.*) armor consisting of steel plates riveted side by side with welded joints (cf. MAIL)

pla·teau (plætóu, *Br.* plǽtou) *pl.* **pla·teaus, pla·teaux** (plætóuz, *Br.* plǽtouz) *n.* a level, horizontal region at a considerable height above sea level or surrounding regions ‖ a roughly level section in a graph (e.g. of progress in production, showing little or no advance) [F.]

plate·ful (pléitful) *pl.* **plate·fuls** *n.* the amount of food etc. that fills a plate

plate glass thick polished glass made in large sheets and used for shop windows, mirrors etc.

plate·lay·er (pléitlei̯ər) *n.* (*Br.*) a tracklayer

plate·let (pléitlit) *n.* a microscopic, noncellular disk found in large numbers in vertebrate blood, that is involved in the activation of prothrombin. The rupture of blood vessels serves to initiate this process

plate mark a hallmark ‖ the rectangular depression surrounding an engraving where the metal plate has sunk into the paper

plat·en, *Br.* also **plat·ten** (plǽt'n) *n.* (*printing*) an iron plate in a hand press or platen press which presses the paper against the inked type ‖ the roller in a typewriter [M.E. *plateyne*, a flat plate of metal, fr. O.F. *platine*]

platen press a small printing press in which the type is secured in a vertical flat bed, and a platen brings the paper up into contact with it

plat·er (pléitər) *n.* someone who makes plates or applies them to ships etc. ‖ someone who plates with metals ‖ (*racing*) a horse only good enough to be entered for a selling race

plat·er·esque (plætərésk) *adj.* of a style of architecture of the early Spanish Renaissance characterized by rich ornamentation [fr. Span. *plateresco* fr. *plata*, silver]

Plate, River *RÍO DE LA PLATA

plate tracery (*archit.*) tracery consisting of flat surfaces of stone in which ornamental patterns have been traced, e.g. in early Gothic windows

plat·form (plǽtfɔrm) **1.** *n.* a raised structure of planks on which a speaker or performer stands, acts etc. so that he can be seen by an audience ‖ a raised structure next to the track, by which passengers enter or leave a train in a station ‖ the open area at the end of a railroad passenger car, trolley car etc. ‖ a ledge, e.g. on a cliff face ‖ a flat structure on which a gun is mounted ‖ a flat, esp. raised, piece of ground ‖ a statement of aims and policies in the program of a person or party seeking electoral support **2.** *adj.* of or designating a shoe sole from ½ in. to 3 ins. thick ‖ of or designating a shoe with such a sole [F. *plateforme*, flat form]

platform car (*rail.*) a flatcar

platform tennis paddleball game utilizing four walls of wire netting on an outdoor platform, similar to a small covered tennis court; usu. played in winter; developed in 1928 from paddle tennis

Plath (plɑeθ), Sylvia (1932–63) U.S. poet. Her first volume of verse 'Colossus,' was published in 1960. But it was only upon the posthumous publication of 'Ariel' (1965) that she became the most celebrated poet of her generation, based on her intense descriptions of extreme states of mind. Two other collections of verse were published following her suicide, 'Crossing the Water' (1971) and 'Winter Trees' (1971). She also wrote a semiautobiographical novel, 'The Bell Jar' (1963), an account of a young woman's struggle with mental breakdown

plat·ing (pléitiŋ) *n.* the process or result of covering with a plate or plates, esp. with a thin layer of metal ‖ the plates of a vessel, tank or other armored vehicle

pla·tin·ic (plətínik) *adj.* of or pertaining to platinum, esp. of compounds in which platinum is tetravalent (cf. PLATINOUS)

plat·i·nize (plǽt'naiz) *pres. part.* **plat·i·niz·ing** *past* and *past part.* **plat·i·nized** *v.t.* to coat with platinum black or combine or treat with platinum

plat·i·noid (plǽt'nɔid) **1.** *n.* an alloy of copper (60%), zinc (24%), nickel (14%) and wolfram (2%), used as a substitute for platinum in resistances and thermocouples ‖ a metal related to platinum **2.** *adj.* like platinum

pla·ti·no·tran (plǽt'noutræn) *n.* (*electr.*) device consisting of a microwave tube with a permanent magnet, used as a high-power saturated oscillator or amplifier in radar apparatus

plat·i·no·type (plǽt'noutai̯p) *n.* a photographic print of great lasting quality, in which platinum is used instead of silver ‖ the process of making such a print [PLATINUM+TYPE]

plat·i·nous (plǽt'nəs) *adj.* of or pertaining to platinum, esp. of compounds in which platinum is divalent (cf. PLATINIC)

plat·i·num (plǽt'nəm, plǽtnəm) *n.* a very heavy, ductile, malleable, silvery white metallic element (symbol Pt, at. no. 78, at. mass 195.09), very resistant to acids, heat and corrosion, and therefore used as a precious metal in jewelry and in some forms of chemical apparatus. An excellent conductor of electricity, the metal is used for electrical contacts and in the platinum resistance thermometer etc. The U.S.S.R. is the main producer [Mod. L. fr. Span. *platina*, platinum]

platinum black a black powder of finely divided platinum obtained by the reduction of platinum salts and used as a catalyst, esp. in hydrogenation or oxygenation

platinum blonde a woman with hair bleached silvery blond, or with hair naturally of this color

platinum metal any of six metallic elements including platinum and metals resembling or occurring with it: iridium, osmium, palladium, rhodium and ruthenium

plat·i·tude (plǽtitu:d, plǽtitju:d) *n.* a flat, stale or commonplace remark or statement uttered as if it were informative and important ‖ (in speech, writing, thinking) the quality of being dull or commonplace **plat·i·tú·di·nize** *pres. part.* **plat·i·tu·di·niz·ing** *past* and *past part.* **plat·i·tu·di·nized** *v.i.* to utter platitudes **plat·i·tú·di·nous** *adj.* [F. fr. *plat*, flat]

Pla·to (pléitou) (c. 428–c. 348 B.C.), Greek philosopher. At 20 he became a follower of Socrates. Their association continued until the death of Socrates, and thereafter Plato devoted his life to philosophy. In 388 he founded the Academy. Socrates was the crucial influence in his development as a philosopher, but Plato achieved a synthesis of all Greek thought that had preceded him. Plato's writings, mainly in dialogue form, deal with mathematics, politics, beauty, the laws of thought, education, love, friendship etc. But he never treated any specialized subject for its own sake: all are subordinated to his central interest, the Good, or virtue. Though he regarded mathematics as a valuable discipline to thought, he took little interest in science. His use of dialogue reflects his belief that man cannot find the truth alone, that he approaches it through discussion, through the clash of ideas and personalities. He often sets forth his ideas with the help of myths, some solemn, some playful, but always poetic. Socrates is the central character in all but the last dialogues. 'Apology' and 'Crito' deal with the trial and death of Socrates. Those that follow present the Socratic method of argument (*SOCRATIC IRONY). False ideas are exposed, but the main questions are left open. The personality of Socrates is most fully developed in 'Phaedo' and 'Symposium'. At the same time Plato begins to move away from the historical Socrates. His characteristic method of rising toward higher truth by a synthesis of antagonisms makes its appearance. He introduces his theory of ideas (*IDEA), and in the 'Republic' he formulates his conception of a perfect state. The late work ('Parmenides', 'Critias', 'Timaeus', 'Statesman,' 'Laws') becomes increasingly expository, and the Socratic element disappears. The Platonic doctrine that has most influenced philosophy is the theory of ideas. But his enormous influence springs equally from his elaboration and clarification of the laws of reasoning, and perhaps most of all from his own person as an embodiment of the search for truth

Pla·ton·ic (plətɔ́nik) *adj.* of, pertaining to or characteristic of Plato or Platonism ‖ of or designating love as Plato described it, a desire for union with the beautiful, ascending in a scale of perfection from human passion to ecstasy in the contemplation of the ideal **pla·ton·ic** of or designating love for a person, usually of the opposite sex, that is free of carnal desire **Pla·tón·i·cal·ly, pla·tón·i·cal·ly** *adv.* [fr. L. *Platonicus* fr. Gk]

Pla·to·nism (pléit'nizəm) *n.* the Platonic philosophy in its philosophical developments and transformations since Plato. The earliest Platonism was that taught in the Academy. With Plotinus it underwent fundamental changes, and for the next thousand years Platonism was known as Neoplatonism. Through Augustine it became the dominant current in Christian philosophy and remained so until the 13th c., when it was superseded by Scholasticism, stressing Aristotle. In Renaissance Italy it regained its original character with the rediscovery of Plato by Ficino and Pico della Mirandola. It had another significant revival in 17th-c. England (*CAMBRIDGE PLATONISTS). It played an important part in the development of the German idealist philosophers (Leibniz, Kant, Fichte and Hegel)

Pla·to·nist (pléit'nist) *n.* a follower of Plato or adherent of a Platonic philosophy [fr. M.L. *platonista*]

Pla·to·nize (pléit'naiz) *pres. part.* **Pla·to·niz·ing** *past* and *past part.* **Pla·to·nized** *v.t.* to interpret in a Platonic manner ‖ to make Platonic ‖ *v.i.* to philosophize in the manner of Plato, or be a Platonist [fr. Gk *platōnizein*]

pla·toon (plətú:n) *n.* (*mil.*) a tactical infantry unit, smaller than a company and under the command of a lieutenant [fr. F. *peloton*, little ball, platoon]

Platt (plæt), Orville Hitchcock (1827–1905), American legislator. He drew up the Platt Amendment (1905), which provided for U.S. intervention in Cuba

Platt Amendment a series of amendments to the Army Appropriations Bill of 1901, sponsored by U.S. Sen. Orville H. Platt, that defined U.S.-Cuba relations during the period 1901–34. The Platt Amendment essentially made Cuba a U.S. protectorate, limiting the island's treaty-making capacity, restricting its ability to contract public debt and giving the U.S.A. the right to maintain naval bases in Cuba and to intervene in Cuban affairs as necessary to preserve order or Cuba's independence. These provisions were appended to Cuba's constitution (1901), U.S. troops were withdrawn (1902) and the provisions were formalized by treaty (1903). Considered a symbol of 'Yankee imperialism,' the treaty was repealed by the U.S. (1934); however, the lease on the U.S. naval base at Guantánamo Bay was continued

Platt·deutsch (plɑ́tdɔitʃ) *n.* the vernacular Low German language spoken in N. Germany [G. *platt*, flat, low+*deutsch*, German]

Platte (plæt) a river (total length c. 930 miles) formed by the union of the North and South Platte Rivers in central Nebraska. The North Platte (618 miles long) rises in N. Colorado, flows across the Wyoming border into central Wyoming and turns east across the Nebraska border through central Nebraska, to unite with the South Platte River. The newly formed Platte (310 miles long) flows east and empties into the Missouri River

platten *PLATEN

plat·ter (plǽtər) *n.* a shallow, usually oval serving dish ‖ (*Br., old-fash.*) a plate or dish [M.E. *plater* fr. A.F. fr. *plat*, dish]

plat·y·hel·minth (plætihélminθ) *n.* a flatworm [fr. Mod. L. *Platyhelminthes*, name of the phylum fr. Gk *platus*, flat+*helmins* (*helminthos*), worm]

plat·y·pus (plǽtipəs) *n.* *Ornithorhynchus anatinus*, order *Monotremata*, a small, primitive aquatic Australian mammal, about 18 ins long. It has thick blackish-brown fur, a flat, leathery bill like that of a duck, no lips, a long, flat tail and webbed feet. It lays eggs, but nurses its young [Mod. L. fr. Gk *platupous* fr. *platus*, flat+*pous*, foot]

plat·yr·rhine (plǽtirain) *adj.* having a broad, esp. flat-bridged nose ‖ of or belonging to *Platyrrhina*, a division of *Anthropoidea* including all the New World monkeys [fr. Mod. L. *platyrrhinus* fr. Gk *platus*, flat+*rhis* (*rhinos*), nose]

plau·dits (plɔ́dits) *pl. n.* (rhet.) praise or approval [fr. L. *plaudite* (said by a Roman cast at the end of a performance), 2nd person pl. imper. of *plaudere*, to applaud]

plau·si·bil·i·ty (plɔzəbíliti:) *n.* the quality of being plausible [fr. L. *plausibilis*, praiseworthy]

plau·si·ble (plɔ́zəb'l) *adj.* (of a statement, argument etc.) apparently true or reasonable, winning assent, *a plausible explanation* ‖ (of a person) genuine, trustworthy etc. in appearance, but probably not to be trusted **pláu·si·bly** *adv.* [fr. L. *plausibilis*, praiseworthy]

Plau·tus (plɔ́təs), Titus Maccius (or Maccus) (c. 254–184 B.C.), Roman playwright. He adapted Greek comedies for the Roman stage. His 21 extant plays, incl. 'Miles Gloriosus', 'Menaechmi', 'Amphitruo' etc., contain boisterous, low-comedy portrayals of middle-class and lower-class life

play (plei) *n.* movement or activity, esp. quick or unconstrained, *the play of light and shade on the water* ‖ activity or exercise performed for amusement (cf. WORK) ‖ freedom of movement, scope, *to give full play to one's imagination* ‖ (*games*) manner of playing, *defensive play* ‖ a maneuver in a game etc. ‖ a turn to play, in a game ‖ a dramatic stage performance ‖ the written or printed text for this ‖ gambling, *he lost a fortune in an hour's play* **in play** as a joke, in fun, *he meant it in play* ‖ (*games*, of the ball) available for kicking etc. in accordance with the rules **out of play** (*games*, of the ball) not available for kicking etc. **to make a play for** to use various wiles in an effort to win the love, admiration, interest etc. of (someone) [O.E. *plega*]

play *v.t.* to take part in games or a game of, *to play tennis* ‖ to make music on (a musical instrument), *to play the piano* ‖ to perform (a piece of music) ‖ to perform the music of (a composer), *to play Beethoven* ‖ to act (a part) in a theatrical performance ‖ to perform the role of (a character) in such a performance ‖ to give a theatrical performance of, *they played 'Hamlet' to a full house* ‖ to perform in (a city etc.), *they played Brighton for a month* ‖ to accompany with music, *a band played the procession into the arena* ‖ to perform (a trick, joke etc.) ‖ (*ball games*) to strike or deliver, *he played the ball into the net* ‖ to direct (a jet of water, searchlight etc.), *the fireman played his hose into the flames* ‖ to take part in a game against, *England is playing Australia* ‖ to move, use, place etc. (a card, piece etc.) in a game, *he played his ace* ‖ to hazard, stake, *he played his last dollar* ‖ to place a bet on (something), *to play the horses* ‖ to include in a team, *England is playing three fast bowlers* ‖ to fill (a position) in a game, *he played center forward* ‖ to imitate or pretend to be, for fun, *to play pirates* ‖ to give (a fish) scope to exhaust itself by pulling against the line ‖ *v.i.* to engage in activity for amusement ‖ to trifle, toy, *stop playing with your food* ‖ to flutter, flit, in a light, erratic manner, *shadows played on the ceiling* ‖ to perform music on an instrument, *he played as only a virtuoso can* ‖ to give a (usually dramatic) performance, *they played to a full house* ‖ (of a fountain, jet of water etc.) to be in operation ‖ to take part in a game, *to play half-heartedly* ‖ (*games*, of ground) to be in a specified condition, *the court plays slowly after rain* ‖ to frolic, gambol ‖ to gamble ‖ to be serious in appearance but not in fact, *they're only playing* ‖ (of a play, film etc.) to be performed or be showing, *what's playing tonight?* ‖ (of a musical instrument) to respond to the performer, *the piano plays better now* ‖ (*mach.*) to show loose movement, *the steering plays badly* **to be played out** to be exhausted ‖ to be no longer effective ‖ to hold no more interest **to play around,** *Br.* also **to play about** to be active without doing anything useful ‖ (*pop.*) to engage in flirtation or illicit or promiscuous lovemaking **to play at** to take part in (some activity) in the spirit of make-believe or without being in earnest **to play back** to play and listen to (a recording which one has just made) **to play ball** to be cooperative **to play both ends against the middle** to set rivals or opposing interests against each other, to one's own advantage **to play by ear** to play a musical instrument without being able to read music or without reading the music ‖ to act in (a situation) as seems best while it is developing, rather than in accordance with some plan **to play down** to make (something) appear less important, worthy etc. than it really is **to play fair** to obey the rules ‖ to behave toward another person without cheating or deception **to play (someone) false** (*rhet.*) to deceive (someone) **to play for time** (*games*) to play out a game defensively, without risking real attack ‖ to seek to postpone an undesired event by dodges and delaying tactics **to play into someone's hands** to do something that gives one's opponent a sudden and overwhelming advantage **to play off** to play (one's allotted game or a particular stage) in a tournament etc. ‖ (*games*) to take part in a play-off to settle (a tie) **to play off one person against another** to set one person against another for one's own advantage **to play on** to take advantage of, exploit, *she won by playing on his weak points* ‖ (*cricket*) to put oneself 'out' by playing the ball on to the wicket **to play out** to play to its finish, *play out the game* ‖ to pay out, *to play out a line* **to play the field** to have dates or romantic involvements with many people, not confining one's interests to one person ‖ to operate over a broad area or range **to play the fool** to behave or act as if one were a fool **to play to the gallery** to seek to win admiration in a way that is beneath one, by appealing to those who will respond most easily **to play up** (*Br.*) to put all one's energy into a game ‖ to emphasize unduly, *the newspaper played up the issue* ‖ (*Br.*.*pop.*) to be a nuisance to **to play up to** to insinuate oneself into the favor of by flattery [O.E. *plegan*]

play·a·ble (pléiəb'l) *adj.* able to be played or played on

play·act (pléiækt) *v.i.* to make a pretense, be false or insincere in conduct **pláy·act·ing** *n.*

play-ac·tion pass (pléiækʃən) (*football*) play involving a feinted hand-off by the quarterback before passing to someone else

play·back (pléibæk) *n.* a playing back of a recording ‖ the part of a tape recorder etc. which serves to play back transcriptions

play·bill (pléibil) *n.* a poster or handbill advertising a theatrical performance ‖ a theater program

play·book (pléibuk) *n.* (*football*) set of diagrams of team's plays

play·boy (pléibɔi) *n.* a rich young man who cares chiefly about having a good time

play-by-play (pléibaipléi) *adj.* describing each development of a game etc. as it occurs, *a play-by-play account*

play·er (pléiər) *n.* a person who plays in a game ‖ a person who performs on a specified musical instrument ‖ a device for operating a piano mechanically ‖ (*old-fash.*) an actor

player piano a piano equipped with a mechanical attachment which depresses the keys by air pressure, reproducing notes that are represented by perforations on a paper roll

play·fel·low (pléifelou) *n.* (*old-fash.*) a playmate

play·ful (pléifəl) *adj.* tending or liking to play, *as playful as a kitten* ‖ lighthearted and humorous, *a playful mood*

play·go·er (pléigouər) *n.* a person who often goes to the theater

play·ground (pléigraund) *n.* a piece of ground set apart for children to play on, often attached to a school ‖ a favorite district for recreation, esp. as giving scope for some particular activity, *a climber's playground*

play·group (pléigru:p) *n.* an improvised neighborhood nursery school for child care

play·house (pléihaus) *pl.* **play·hous·es** (pléihauziz) *n.* (usually in titles) a theater ‖ a little house for children to play in

playing card one of the cards in a pack of 52 used in playing games. They are small rectangular pieces of pasteboard, grouped into four suits (hearts, diamonds, clubs, spades), each having 13 cards which comprise the ace (marked A), cards numbered 2 to 10, and three cards bearing pictures of figures called king, queen and jack (or knave). Such cards are also used by fortune-tellers and conjurers

playing field a field (esp. one attached to a school) for games and recreation

play·list (pléilist) *n.* schedule of recordings to be played on a radio broadcast

play·mate (pléimeit) *n.* a child's friend with whom he plays

play-off (pléiɔf, pléiɒf) *n.* (*games*) a match played to decide a tie or where a previous game has given an inconclusive result

play on words a pun

play·pen (pléipen) *n.* a portable enclosure in which very young children can play safely. It usually consists of a small square base enclosed by a wooden or metal railing with vertical bars or netting

play·room (pléiru:m, pléirum) *n.* a room children use to play in, or a recreation room

play·thing (pléiθiŋ) *n.* something designed to be played with ‖ (*rhet.*) a person treated as a toy by another or by fate etc.

play·time (pléitaim) *n.* a period set apart for play

play·wright (pléirait) *n.* a writer of theatrical plays

pla·za (plάzə, plǽzə) *n.* a public square in a town or city [Span. fr. (assumed) pop. L. *plattia* fr. L. *platea*, courtyard]

plea (pli:) *n.* (*rhet.*) an appeal ‖ (*rhet.*) a request ‖ an argument used to excuse ‖ (*law*) a statement made in court by either party in argument of his case [M.E. *plaid, plai* fr. O.F.]

plea bargaining negotiation between defense attorney in a criminal action and the prosecutor for a reduced charge in exchange for a plea of guilty

pleach (pli:tʃ) *v.t.* to plash (interweave stems, branches etc.) [M.E. *pleche* fr. O.F.]

plead (pli:d) *pres. part.* **plead·ing** *past* and *past part.* **plead·ed, pled** (pled) *v.i.* to beg with emotion and at length, implore, *to plead for mercy* ‖ (*law*) to state a plea ‖ (*law*) to argue in court ‖ *v.t.* (*law*) to cite (something) in legal defense, *he pleaded ignorance* ‖ (*law*) to argue (a case) in court **to plead (not) guilty** (*law*) to admit (deny) guilt, as a method of procedure [O. F. *plaidier*]

plead·ing (plí:diŋ) *n.* the act of making a plea ‖ an instance of this ‖ (*law*) the written statements setting forth the cause of the plaintiff and the response of the defendant

pleas·ant (pléz'nt) *adj.* agreeable, pleasing [O.F. *plaisant, pleisant*]

pleas·ant·ry (pléz'ntri:) *pl.* **pleas·ant·ries** *n.* (in conversation) pleasant, goodhumored joking back and forth ‖ an instance of this

please (pli:z) *pres. part.* **pleas·ing** *past* and *past part.* **pleased** *v.t.* to gratify, satisfy, give pleasure to ‖ *v.i.* to desire and intend, *do as you please* ‖ to make oneself pleasant, agreeable etc., *the desire to please* ‖ to win favor, *dogs obey in order to please* ‖ (in requests or commands) be good enough to, *please come along* **if you please** if you wish ‖ expressing surprise (ironic), *then she turned on her heel, if you please* **please God** if it is God's wish ‖ may it be God's wish **to please oneself** to do as one wishes **pléased, pléas·ing** *adjs* [M.E. *plaise, pleise, plese* fr. O.F.]

pleas·ur·a·ble (pléʒərəb'l) *adj.* giving or capable of giving pleasure **pléas·ur·a·bly** *adv.* [PLEASURE]

pleas·ure (pléʒər) *n.* a general feeling of satisfaction, enjoyment ‖ something which causes this feeling, *your visit will be a pleasure* ‖ self-gratification, *he lives for pleasure* [M.E. *plesir, plaisir* fr. O.F.]

pleat (pli:t) **1.** *n.* a fold, esp. one made by doubling cloth etc. upon itself and pressing or stitching it in place or allowing it to hang free **2.** *v.t.* to make a pleat or pleats in [var. of PLAIT]

ple·bei·an, ple·bi·an (pləbí:ən) **1.** *n.* a member of the common people ‖ (*Rom. hist.*) a member of the lowest class in ancient Rome, without privileges until the 4th c. B.C. (cf. PATRICIAN) **2.** *adj.* of or characteristic of the common people, uncultured, vulgar [fr. L. *plebeius*, of the plebeians]

pleb·i·scite (plébisait, plébisit) *n.* a vote of the entire electorate on a national issue (e.g. constitutional change) ‖ a vote of the people to decide whether a contested region should be attached to one country or another or, in some cases, become autonomous [F. *plébiscite*]

plec·tog·nath (pléktɒgnæθ) **1.** *adj.* (*zool.*) of *Plectognathi*, an order of fishes covered with bony plates, spines etc. and having small mouths with powerful jaws **2.** *n.* a member of this order, e.g. the globefish [fr. Gk *plektos*, plaited+*gnathos*, jaw]

plec·tron (pléktrɒn) *n.* a plectrum

plec·trum (pléktrəm) *pl.* **plec·tra** (pléktrə), **plec·trums** *n.* a small implement of ivory, wood, metal etc., used for plucking the strings of a mandolin, banjo etc. [L. fr. Gk *plēktron*, something to strike with]

pledge (pledʒ) **1.** *n.* something of value left as security for a loan or as a guarantee that an obligation will be met ‖ a solemn promise ‖ the state of being pledged, *in pledge* ‖ (*old-fash.*) a toast ‖ a person who has agreed to become a member of a club, fraternity etc. but who has not yet been initiated **to take the pledge** to make a solemn promise to abstain from alcoholic drink **2.** *v.t. pres. part.* **pledg·ing** *past* and *past part* **pledged** to hand over as security for a loan ‖ to commit (oneself, one's reputation etc.) ‖ to promise, to pledge allegiance to the flag ‖ (*old-fash.*) to drink a toast to ‖ to agree to become a member of (a club, fraternity etc.) ‖ to cause to be a pledge in a club, fraternity etc. [O.F. *plege*, hostage, security]

Plé·iade (pléiəd, pléijæd) a group of French poets who under Henri II set out to freshen French poetry with new forms (esp. the sonnet), and to clear the language of useless rhetoric. They were: Ronsard, Du Bellay, Rémy Belleau (1528–77), Jodelle, Jean Dorat (1508–88), Baïf and Pontus de Tyard (1521–1605)

Ple·ia·des (pláiədi:z) the seven brightest stars in the constellation Taurus ‖ (*Gk mythol.*) the seven daughters (Alcyone, Celaeno, Electra, Maia, Merope, Asterope, Taygete) of Atlas who were changed into stars by Zeus [L. fr. Gk *Pleias (Pleiados)*]

Pleiocene *PLIOCENE

plei·ot·ro·py (plaiɒ́trəpi:) *n.* (*genetics*) ability of a gene to produce various characteristics

Pleis·to·cene (pláistəsi:n) *adj.* of the earlier epoch or series of the Quaternary era, characterized by the formation of glaciers (*GEOLOGICAL TIME) **the Pleistocene** the Pleistocene epoch or series of rocks [fr. Gk *pleistos*, most+*kainos*, recent]

Plek·ha·nov (pljəkhάnʌf), Georgi Valentinovich (1857–1918), Russian Marxist political philosopher. He was one of the founders of the Russian Social Democratic party (1898) and became the leader of the Mensheviks. He took refuge in Finland after the Bolshevik revolution (1917). His works include 'Anarchism and Socialism' (1896)

ple·na·ri·ly (plí:nərili:, plénərili:) *adv.* in a plenary manner

ple·na·ry (plí:nəri:, plénəri:) *adj.* complete, absolute, *plenary powers* ‖ (of a legislative body) attended by all members, *a plenary session* [fr. L.L. *plenarius*]

plenary indulgence (*Roman Catholicism*) an indulgence which remits in full the temporal punishment incurred by a sinner

plench (plentʃ) *n.* tool combining pliers and wrench operable from the handle; originally used on space vehicles

plen·i·po·ten·ti·ar·y (plenipəténʃi:eri:, plenipəténʃəri:) **1.** *adj.* invested with unlimited power ‖ of or relating to a plenipotentiary **2.** *pl.* **plen·i·po·ten·ti·ar·ies** *n.* an ambassador or envoy with full powers of decision [fr. M.L. *plenipotentiarius* fr. *plenus*, full+*potens*, powerful]

plen·i·tude (plénitu:d, plénitju:d) *n.* completeness ‖ (*rhet.*) abundance, *a plenitude of natural gifts* [O. F.]

plen·te·ous (plénti:əs) *adj.* (*rhet.*) plentiful [M.E. *plentifous, plentivous* fr. O.F.]

plen·ti·ful (pléntifəl) *adj.* abundant, *plentiful supplies* ‖ producing or yielding abundantly, *a plentiful harvest*

plen·ty (plénti:) **1.** *n.* prosperity, abundance, *years of plenty* ‖ more than enough, *plenty of money* ‖ a great quantity, *he lost plenty of money in the business* ‖ (esp. with 'in') the quality or state of being plentiful, *compliments in plenty* **2.** *adj.* abundant, *money was plenty but goods were scarce* **3.** *adv.* (*pop.*) more than adequately, *it is plenty large enough* [M.E. *plente, plenteth* fr. O.F.]

ple·num (plí:nəm) *pl.* **ple·nums, ple·na** (plí:nə) *n.* the entirety of a space regarded as being filled with matter (opp. VACUUM) ‖ (esp. of a legislative body) a full assembly [L. neuter of *plenus* adj., full]

ple·o·mor·phic (pli:oumɔ́rfik) *adj.*, characterized by pleomorphism

ple·o·mor·phism (pli:oumɔ́rfizem) *n.* (*biol.*) the occurrence of two or more distinct forms at different stages in one life cycle [fr. Gk *pleon*, more+*morphē*, form]

ple·o·nasm (plí:ənæzəm) *n.* the using of more words than necessary in expressing an idea, with redundancy ‖ an instance of this or a redundant word or expression, e.g. 'falsely fraudulent' **ple·o·nás·tic** *adj.* **ple·o·nás·ti·cal·ly** *adv.* [fr. L. *pleonasmus* fr. Gk *pleon*, more]

ple·o·pod (plí:əpɒd) *n.* (*zool.*) one of the swimming appendages attached to the abdomen of a crustacean [fr. Gk *plein*, to swim+*pous (podos)*, foot]

ple·si·o·saur (plí:si:əsɔr) *n.* a Mesozoic marine reptile of the suborder *Plesiosauria*, order *Sauropterygia*, 40 ft or more in length, having four large paddlelike limbs [fr. Mod. L. *plesiosaurus* fr. *plesios*, near+*saurus*, lizard]

ples·sor (plésər) *n.* a plexor

Ples·sy v. Fer·gu·son (plési:, fə́:rgəsən) a decision (1896) of the U.S. Supreme Court led by Melville W. Fuller, which enunciated the 'separate but equal' doctrine of racial segregation. It ruled that segregation was legal if equal facilities were offered for both races

pleth·o·ra (pléθərə) *n.* a great quantity, esp. more than desirable, *a plethora of examples* ‖ an unhealthy physical condition caused by an excess of blood and characterized by a highly flushed complexion **pleth·or·ic** (pleθɔ́rik, pleθɒ́rik) *adj.* (esp. of speech, writing etc.) pretentious ‖ having an excess of blood [M.L. fr. Gk *plēthorē* fr. *plēthein*, to become full]

pleu·ra (plúərə) *pl.* **pleu·rae** (plúəri:), **pleu·ras** *n.* a thin serous membrane lining the chest cavity and surrounding each lung in most air-breathing mammals [M.L. fr. Gk *pleura*, rib, side]

pleu·ri·sy (plúərisi:) *n.* inflammation of the pleura, resulting in fever and sharp pain in the chest or side [O.F. *pleurisie*]

pleu·rit·ic (pluritik) *adj.* of or having pleurisy [fr. F. *pleurétique* or fr. L. *pleuriticus*]

pleu·ro·dont (plúərədɒnt) **1.** *adj.* (of some lizards) having the teeth consolidated with the inner edge of the jaw **2.** *n.* a lizard having pleurodont teeth [fr. Gk *pleura*, rib, side+*odous* (*odontos*), tooth]

pleu·ro·pneu·mo·ni·a (plúərounu:móunjə, plúərounju:móunjə) *n.* a combination of pleurisy and pneumonia ‖ a severe, often fatal inflammation of the lungs of farm animals, esp. cattle [Mod. L. fr. Gk *pleura*, rib+PNEUMONIA]

Plev·en (plévən) an agricultural market (pop. 122,916) of N. central Bulgaria

Plex·i·glass, Plex·i·glas (pléksiglæs, pléksiglɑs) *n.* a clear transparent thermoplastic synthetic resin used for cast and molded transparent parts and for coatings [Trademark]

plex·im·e·ter (pleksímitər) *n.* a thin plate of ivory, hard rubber etc. which is placed on some part of the body to receive the blow of the plexor in medical percussion. Gk *plēxis*, stroke+*metron*, measure]

plex·or (pléksɔr) *n.* a small rubber-headed hammer used in medical percussion [fr. Gk *plēxis*, stroke]

plex·us (pléksəs) *n.* (*anat.*) a network of intertwining nerves or blood vessels, *the solar plexus* ‖ an exceedingly complex organization or network [L.=a twining, braid]

pli·a·bil·i·ty (plaiəbíliti:) *n.* the quality of being pliable

pli·a·ble (pláiəb'l) *adj.* readily bent, pliant ‖ readily influenced **plí·a·bly** *adv.* [F.]

pli·an·cy (pláiənsi:) *n.* the quality of being pliant

pli·ant (pláiənt) *adj.* (of materials) pliable ‖ (of people) readily yielding to influence [F.]

pli·ca (pláikə) *pl.* **pli·cae** (pláisi:) *n.* (*biol.*) a fold of skin, membrane etc. ‖ a crusty, matted condition of the hair caused by disease or vermin [M.L.=a fold]

pli·cate (pláikeit) *adj.* (*zool.*) folded ‖ (*bot.*) pleated, *a plicate leaf* **plí·cat·ed** *adj.* [fr. L. *plicare* (*plicatus*), to fold]

pli·ca·tion (plaikéiʃən) *n.* a folding or being folded ‖ a fold, esp. (*geol.*) a fold in a stratum [O.F.]

pli·ers (pláiərz) *pl. n.* small pincers with long jaws, used for handling small objects, for bending or cutting wire etc. [fr. older *ply* v., to fold]

plight (plait) *n.* a state of distress, predicament [M.E. *plit*, *plyt* fr. A. F.]

plight *v.t.* (*rhet.*) to pledge (esp. in) **to plight one's troth** to make a promise of marriage [O.E. *plihtan*, fr. *pliht*, danger]

Plim·soll line (plímsəl, plímsɔl, plímsɒl) (*naut.*) a diagram of lines on the hull of a cargo boat indicating the depth to which the vessel may be safely loaded (varying according to the season and the salinity of the water) in conformity with a British Merchant Shipping Act of 1876 [after Samuel *Plimsoll* (1824-98), Br. reformer who campaigned for this in the interest of crews]

Plimsoll mark a Plimsoll line

plim·solls (plímsəlz, plímsɔlz, plimsɒlz) *pl. n.* (*Br., old-fash.*) sneakers, tennis shoes [origin unknown]

plinth (plinθ) *n.* (*archit.*) the rectangular base of a column ‖ (*Br.*) the base of a wall which projects just above ground level ‖ a similar base on which a statue, vase etc. is placed [fr. L. *plinthus* fr. Gk]

Plin·y (plíni:) 'the Younger' (Gaius Plinius Caecilius Secundus, c. 62–c. 114), Roman author and administrator, nephew of Pliny the Elder. He served in several public offices and was consul (100). His one extant oration is a 'Panegyric on Trajan' (100). His 'Letters' (c. 97–c. 111) give a valuable account of contemporary upper-class life

Pliny 'the Elder' (Gaius Plinius Secundus, 23–79), Roman writer and administrator. Only his encyclopedic 37-volume 'Natural History' (77) survives. He died in the eruption of Vesuvius

Pli·o·cene (pláiəsi:n) *adj.* of the latest epoch or series of the Tertiary (*GEOLOGICAL TIME) **the Pliocene** the Pliocene epoch or series of rocks [fr. Gk *pleon*, more+*kainos*, new]

PLO (*acronym*) **P**alestine **L**iberation **O**rganization (which see)

PL/I (*computer abbr.*) **P**rogramming **L**anguage **One,** used for simple general purposes

plod (plɒd) **1.** *v.i. pres. part.* **plod·ding** *past* and *past part.* **plod·ded** to walk heavily and slowly ‖ to make slow, laborious progress when working, *to plod through a lesson* **2.** *n.* a laborious tread or the sound of this **plód·der** *n.* someone who works diligently and learns by hard work rather than by natural aptitude [prob. imit.]

Plo·es·ti (ploujéʃt) the chief petroleum-refining center (pop. 199,300) of Rumania, in Walachia, 34 miles north of Bucharest

Plom·bières Agreement (plɔ̃bjɛər) a secret pact (1858) between Napoleon III and Cavour at Plombières in the Vosges, providing for French support for Piedmont in a war against Austria

plonk (plɒŋk) **1.** *n.* a plunk **2.** *v.t.* and *i.* to plunk

plop (plɒp) **1.** *n.* the sound made when an object or body drops into a liquid **2.** *v.i. pres. part.* **plop·ping** *past* and *past part.* **plopped** to make this sound ‖ to fall with a plop ‖ to let one's body fall wearily, *to plop into a chair* [imit.]

plot (plɒt) **1.** *n.* a small piece of ground, esp. one used or to be used for a particular purpose, *a building plot* ‖ a ground plan ‖ a secret, usually evil, plan or conspiracy ‖ the plan of events in a novel, play etc. ‖ a chart showing the progress of a ship, submarine or aircraft, or any comparable chart, *a plot of the month's sales* ‖ a point of intersection marked on a chart **2.** *v. pres. part.* **plotting** *past and past part.* **plot·ted** *v.t.* to plan secretly (esp. something evil) ‖ to make a plan or map of ‖ to mark (a position, course etc.) on a chart ‖ to construct the plan of (events in a novel, play etc.) ‖ to determine and mark (a point) e.g. on a graph, by working from coordinates ‖ to draw (a curve) by means of points so marked ‖ (*math.*) to represent (an equation) by means of such a curve ‖ *v.i.* to conspire [origin unknown]

Plo·ti·nus (ploutáinəs) (205-70), Roman philosopher of Egyptian birth. After studying in Alexandria, he established his Neoplatonic school in Rome (244). From 253 he wrote the 'Enneads' (published posthumously by his pupil Porphyry). He used the metaphysical myths of Plato (esp. the dialectic of love) to create a mystic religion of union with the One through contemplation and ecstatic vision. Through St Augustine his theory of the human spirit entered into the mainstream of Western philosophy

plot·ter (plɒ́tər) *n.* someone who makes a plot, conspirator ‖ someone who marks plots on a chart ‖ a device for marking plots ‖ (*computer*) a peripheral output device for data analysis

plough (plau) **1.** *n.* *PLOW ‖ (*Br.*) land which has been plowed ‖ **2.** *v.t.* *PLOW ‖ (*Br., old-fash.*) to fail (someone) in an examination ‖ (*Br., old-fash.*) to fail (an examination) ‖ *v.i.* (*Br., old-fash.*) to fail in an examination [O.E. *plōh*]

plough·boy *PLOWBOY

plough·man *PLOWMAN

plough·share *PLOWSHARE

Plov·div (plóudif) the second largest city (pop. 309,242) of Bulgaria, on the Maritsa, the market for a rich farm area: tobacco (national center), food processing, silk weaving. As Philippopolis, it prospered (4th c. B.C.) under Philip II of Macedon

plov·er (plʌ́vər, plóuvər) *n.* any of several small wading birds of fam. *Charadriidae*. They are cosmopolitan and gregarious and nest on the ground. Some species are edible and the eggs are considered a delicacy [O.F. *plovier*, plover, rain bird]

plow, esp. *Br.* **plough** (plau) **1.** *n.* an agricultural implement drawn by a tractor, oxen, horses etc., used for cutting through and turning over soil, esp. in a field to be planted ‖ any implement or device resembling this ‖ (*bookbinding*) a device for cutting the edges of books ‖ (*carpentry*) a plane for making a groove etc. **2.** *v.t.* to turn over, break up etc. (soil) with a plow ‖ to furrow as if with a plow, *to plow one's way through a crowd* ‖ (of ships) to cut through the surface of (water) ‖ (*carpentry*) to cut a groove etc. in with a plow ‖ (*bookbinding*) to cut the edges of (a book) with a plow ‖ *v.i.* to work with a plow ‖ (of a field etc.) to admit of plowing ‖ (with 'through', 'along' etc.) to cut a way as a plow does, *to plow through the snow* ‖ to proceed slowly and laboriously, *to plow through a dull book* ‖ to operate a bookbinder's or carpenter's plow **to plow back** to bury (a growing crop) by plowing through it so as to enrich the soil ‖ to use (profits) to develop the enterprise which yielded them **to plow into** to begin (work) with vigor and enthusiasm [O.E. *plōh*]

plow·boy, esp. *Br.* **plough·boy** (pláubɔi) *n.* a boy who leads the horse or horses of a horse-drawn plow

plow·man, esp. *Br.* **plough·man** (pláumən) *pl.* **plow·men,** esp. *Br.* **plough·men** (pláumən) *n.* someone who plows

plow·share, esp. *Br.* **plough·share** (pláuʃɛər) *n.* the cutting and turning blade of a plow [M.E.]

ploy (plɔi) *n.* a cunning tactic or gambit, e.g. in a game [origin unknown]

PLSS (*acronym*) **p**ortable **l**ife **s**upport **s**ystem

pluck (plʌk) **1.** *v.t.* to pull off or out with sudden sharp force, *to pluck feathers from a chicken* ‖ to pull the feathers from, *to pluck a chicken* ‖ to pull quickly at, *to pluck a harp string* ‖ to pick, *to pluck a flower* ‖ (*pop.*) to swindle ‖ *v.i.* (with 'at') to give a quick little pull, *to pluck at someone's sleeve* **to pluck up** to revive one's flagging spirits and courage **to pluck up one's courage** to overcome nervousness or timidity **2.** *n.* an act of plucking ‖ the heart, lungs and liver of a slaughtered animal used for food ‖ courage **plúck·i·ly** *adv.* **plúck·y** *comp.* **pluck·i·er** *superl.* **pluck·i·est** *adj.* courageous [O.E. *pluccian*]

plug (plʌg) **1.** *n* a piece of wood etc. used to fill a gap or hole ‖ (*Br.*) the release mechanism in the flushing system of a toilet ‖ smoking or chewing tobacco compressed into a solid cake ‖ a fireplug ‖ any electrical connection, esp. the male part ‖ a spark plug ‖ (*pop.*) the favorable mention of a product etc., esp. on a radio or television program ‖ the mass of igneous rock filling in the channel leading to a volcanic vent ‖ (*pop.*) an old, worn-out horse ‖ (*angling*) a lure that darts and dives, usu. used for catching pike **2.** *v. pres. part.* **plug·ging** *past* and *past part.* **plugged** *v.t.* to insert a plug in ‖ (*pop.*) to publicize (something) frequently, esp. on a radio or television program ‖ *v.i.* (with 'up') to become obstructed, *drains that won't plug up* ‖ (*pop.*, with 'away') to persevere laboriously, *plugging away at geometry* **to plug in** to connect (an electrical device) to an outlet [M. Du. *plugge*, bung]

plug·o·la (plʌgóulɑ) *n.* special promotion for a product, e.g., a song, in exchange for a payment or favor

plug-ug·ly (plʌ́gʌ́gli:) *pl.* **plug-ug·lies** *n.* (*old-fash.*) a tough guy, esp. a member of a gang using intimidation for political ends

plum (plʌm) *n.* *Prunus domestica*, fam. *Rosaceae*, a small tree widely cultivated in temperate regions ‖ the edible fleshy fruit of the tree, or of other trees of the same genus ‖ the bluish-red color of many varieties of this fruit ‖ (*pop.*) an opportunity, appointment etc. offering exceptional advantages [O.E. *plūme* fr. L. fr. Gk]

plum·age (plú:midʒ) *n.* the feathers of a bird [O.F.]

plu·mate (plú:meit, plú:mit) *adj.* (of bodily hairs, antennae etc.) having a main shaft that bears tiny hairs or threadlike parts [Mod. L. *plumatus*, covered with feathers fr. *pluma*, feather]

plumb (plʌm) **1.** *n.* a small, heavy piece of metal, usually lead, attached to a line and used to indicate the vertical ‖ a similar contrivance for ascertaining the depth of water in a well etc. **out of plumb** not vertical **2.** *adj.* vertical ‖ (*cricket*, of a wicket) perfectly level **3.** *adv.* vertically **4.** *v.t.* to ascertain the depth of (water etc.) by sounding ‖ to come to understand completely, *to plumb someone's mind* ‖ to test for verticality, *to plumb a wall* ‖ to do the work of a plumber on (something), *to plumb a joint* [fr. F. *plomb*, lead]

plum·ba·go (plʌmbéigou) *n.* graphite ‖ (*bot.*) a member of *Plumbago*, fam. *Plumbaginaceae*, a genus of perennial tropical woody plants, bearing spikes of blue and white flowers and having alternate leaves [L.]

plumb bob the metal weight on the end of a plumb line

plum·be·ous (plʌ́mbi:əs) *adj.* of or resembling lead ‖ lead-colored ‖ (*ceramics*) lead-glazed [fr. L. *plumbeus*]

plumb·er (plʌ́mər) *n.* a skilled worker who fits, repairs and maintains pipes, bathroom fixtures, cisterns, drains etc. [O.F. *plummier*, *plommier*]

plum·bic (plʌ́mbik) *adj.* containing or pertaining to lead ‖ (*chem.*) of compounds in which lead exerts a valence of 4 [fr. L. *plumbum*, lead]

plumb·ing (plʌ́miŋ) *n.* the craft of a plumber ‖ the entire water-supply and drainage system of a building ‖ the act of using a plumb [PLUMB]

plum·bism (plʌ́mbizəm) *n.* (*med.*) lead poisoning, esp. when chronic [fr. L. *plumbum*, lead]

CONCISE PRONUNCIATION KEY: **(a)** æ, *cat*; ɑ, *car*; ɔ *fawn*; ei, *snake*. **(e)** e, *hen*; i:, *sheep*; iə, *deer*; ɛə, *bear*. **(i)** i, *fish*; ai, *tiger*; ə:, *bird*. **(o)** o, *ox*; au, *cow*; ou, *goat*; ɔi, *royal*. **(u)** ʌ, *duck*; u, *bull*; u:, *goose*; ə, *bacillus*; ju:, *cube*. x, *loch*; θ, *think*; ð, *bother*; z, *Zen*; ʒ, *corsage*; dʒ, *savage*; ŋ, *orangutang*; j, *yak*; ʃ, *fish*; tʃ, *fetch*; 'l, *rabble*; 'n, *redden*. Complete pronunciation key appears inside front cover.

plumb line a cord suspending a lead weight used in sounding ‖ a similar device for determining verticality

plum·bous (plʌ́mbəs) *adj.* containing or pertaining to lead ‖ (*chem.*) of compounds in which lead exerts a valence of 2 [fr. L. *plumbosus,* full of lead]

plumb rule a strip of wood fitted with a plumb line and bob, used esp. by carpenters

plum·bum (plʌ́mbəm) *n.* lead (the metal) [L.]

plum duff a flour pudding with raisins or currants, boiled or steamed

plume (plu:m) *n.* a feather, esp. a large feather ‖ a cluster or tuft of feathers worn as an ornament or as a symbol of office, rank etc. ‖ (*envir.*) visible emission from a chimney flue or volcano ‖ (*geol.*) in plate tectonics, a hypothetical force of molten material from the earth's center that drives plates ‖ anything having the lightness and form of a feather, *a plume of smoke* ‖ (*biol.*) a featherlike appendage or part [O.F.]

plume *pres. part.* **plum·ing** *past* and *past part.* **plumed** *v.t.* to adorn with plumes ‖ (of a bird) to dress the feathers of (itself) ‖ (of a bird) to preen (its feathers) ‖ (*rhet.,* of a person) to feel pride in (oneself), *he plumed himself on the way they had listened to him* [O.F. *plumer,* to pluck (a bird)]

plum·met (plʌ́mit) **1.** *n.* the weight attached to a plumb line, a sounding line or a fishing line ‖ the line and bob together ‖ a clock weight **2.** *v.i.* to drop vertically downwards [O.F. *plommet, plombet, plummet,* a ball of lead]

plu·mose (plú:mous) *adj.* (*zool.*) having feathers ‖ (*biol.*) plumate **plumos·i·ty** (plu:mɒ́siti:) *n.* [fr. L. *plumosus*]

plump (plʌmp) **1.** *v.i.* to fall heavily, *to plump into a chair* ‖ (with 'for') to decide on (one of several courses of action, choices etc.) ‖ to come or go suddenly with determination or in a huff, *to plump out of a room* ‖ (*Br.*) to vote for one candidate only, even though entitled to vote for two or more ‖ *v.t.* to drop. place, put down etc. heavily, *she plumped the package on the table,* or with abrupt unconcern, *she plumped the baby in his cot* **2.** *adv.* suddenly and heavily downwards, *it fell plump into the water* **3.** *n.* the act of falling heavily or the sound of this [M. Du. *plompen*]

plump 1. *adj.* (of people) pleasantly rounded, without being fat ‖ (of animals) fleshy, *a plump chicken* **2.** *v.t.* (with 'up') to knead (a pillow, cushion etc.) so as to shake up the feathers etc. in it ‖ *v.i.* (with 'out', e.g. of sails) to become rounded or distended [M. Du. *plomp,* bulky]

plum pudding a rich suet pudding containing raisins, currants, candied citrus peel, eggs, nuts and spices, boiled or steamed, and eaten esp. at Christmas

plu·mule (plú:mju:l) *n.* (*bot.*) the primary bud of an embryo normally located on the apex of the hypocotyl (which develops into the primary shoot of a seedling) ‖ a small or downy feather [fr. L. *plumula,* small feather]

plum·y (plú:mi:) *comp.* **plum·i·er** *superl.* **plum·i·est** *adv.* plumelike, feathery ‖ covered with plumes

plun·der (plʌ́ndər) **1.** *v.t.* to strip (a person or place) of goods by force, esp. in wartime ‖ *v.i.* to commit robbery **2.** *n.* the act of plundering ‖ the goods obtained by plundering [G. *plündern*]

plun·der·age (plʌ́ndəridʒ) *n.* (*maritime law*) the embezzlement of goods on shipboard ‖ the goods embezzled

plunge (plʌndʒ) **1.** *v. pres. part.* **plung·ing** *past* and *past part* **plunged** *v.t.* to thrust (something) forcefully into something else, *to plunge a knife into someone's heart* ‖ to force (something or someone) into a new set of circumstances, *attitudes liable to plunge us into war* ‖ *v.i.* to throw oneself into water, esp. headfirst ‖ to go headlong, make one's way swiftly and resolutely, *to plunge into a thicket* ‖ (esp. of a ship) to pitch **2.** *n.* the act of plunging ‖ a leap into or as if into water ‖ (*old-fash.*) an act or instance of engaging in heavy gambling, reckless speculation etc. **to take the plunge** to decide to take a risk despite the possible consequences **plúng·er** *n.* (*mech.*) a moving machine part serving as a ram in a hydraulic press, a piston in a force pump etc. ‖ a pistonlike part in a tire valve unit ‖ a rubber suction cup attached to the end of a wooden rod and used to clear a blockage in a water pipe, drain etc. [O.F. *plungier*]

plunk (plʌŋk) **1.** *n.* the dull, short sound made by the forceful impact of inelastic bodies ‖ a twang ‖ (*pop.*) a forceful blow **2.** *v.t.* to put (something) down suddenly and heavily, *he plunked his books on the table* ‖ to pluck the strings of (e.g. a banjo) ‖ *v.i.* to make a twanging sound ‖ to fall or sink heavily **3.** *adv.* with the sound of a plunk [imit.]

plu·per·fect (plu:pə́:rfikt) **1.** *adj.* (*gram.*) expressing an action completed before a past time either spoken of or implied **2.** *n.* (*gram.*) a pluperfect tense or form [shortened fr. L. *plus quam perfectum,* more than perfect]

plu·ral (plúərəl) **1.** *adj.* of or including more than one ‖ (*gram.*) of or designating more than one of the things referred to ‖ (*gram.,* in languages having dual number) involving more than two **2.** *n.* (*gram.*) the plural number ‖ the plural form of a word ‖ a word in the plural form [O.F. *plurel*]

—The most common pattern for the formation of the written plural of English nouns is the addition of -s or -es. A final -es is added to words ending in -ss, -sh, -ch, -s, -x (e.g. masses, rashes, marches, gases, foxes), or to words ending in -y preceded by a consonant or by -qu, the -y being changed to -i- (e.g. navy- navies, soliloquy-soliloquies) or to some words ending in -o preceded by a consonant (e.g. tomato -tomatoes). -s alone is added to most words ending in -o preceded by a consonant, and to all words ending in -o preceded by a vowel (e.g. pianos, radios). The minor formations of plurals of English nouns include -s for many words ending in -f, the -f changing to -ve- (e.g. calf-calves). -en is added in some cases (e.g. ox-oxen), or -ren is added (e.g. child-children). Change of vowel is another formation (e.g. man-men, goose - geese). Sometimes the plural is the same as the singular (e.g. Chinese, sheep, moose). In some cases the plural may be different or may remain the same (e.g. fish-fishes or fish-fish). Some words have only one form, which may be singular or plural (e.g. scissors). Some Latin and Greek plurals are carried over into English (e.g. alumnus-alumni, analysis-analyses). Some other foreign plurals are also carried over (e.g. Hebrew seraph -seraphim). The plurals of letters, symbols etc. add -'s (e.g. two p's, a row of+'s)

plu·ral·ism (plúərəlizəm) *n.* the holding of more than one office, esp. of more than one ecclesiastical benefice, by the same person ‖ (*philos.*) the doctrine that there is more than one universal principle (cf. MONISM, cf. DUALISM) **plú·ral·ist** *n.* **plu·ral·ís·tic** *adj.*

plu·ral·i·ty (pluərǽliti:) *pl.* **plu·ral·i·ties** *n.* the state of being plural ‖ a great number ‖ the holding of more than one office by one person ‖ (*eccles.*) the holding of two or more benefices by one person ‖ (in a political election involving three or more candidates) a number of votes obtained by one candidate exceeding that of any other candidate but not constituting an absolute majority [O.F. *pluralité*]

plural vote the casting of more than one vote or the right to cast more than one vote ‖ the right to vote in more than one constituency

plus (plʌs) **1.** *prep.* added to, 4 plus 2 is 6 ‖ (*pop.*) in addition to, *he arrived with a trunk plus a large suitcase* **2.** *adj.* indicating addition, *the plus sign* ‖ positive, *a plus quantity* ‖ (used postpositively) somewhat more than, *a C plus mark* ‖ (*pop.,* used predicately) having as an addition, *he was plus $10 on the sale* ‖ (*bookkeeping*) credit, *the plus side of an account* ‖ (*elec.*) positive **3.** *pl.* **plus·es, plus·ses** *n.* a plus sign ‖ a plus quantity ‖ an additional quantity [L.=more]

plus fours men's loose, baggy trousers that overlap about 4 ins below the knees, worn esp. for golf

plush (plʌʃ) **1.** *n.* a fabric resembling velvet, but having a longer, softer pile **2.** *adj.* luxurious and expensive, *a plush hotel* [F. *pluche*]

plus sign (*math.*) the symbol (+) used to indicate addition

Plu·tarch (plú:tɑrk) (c. 46–c. 125), Greek essayist and biographer. He wrote 'Moralia', a group of dialogues and essays, but is most famous for his 'Parallel Lives of Illustrious Greeks and Romans', a book of great historical value. He portrayed character and its moral implications in a racy, anecdotal style

plu·tar·chy (plú:tɑrki:) *pl.* **plu·tar·chies** *n.* a plutocracy

Plu·to (plú:tou) (*Gk mythol.*) the god of departed spirits and of the underworld (*HADES) ‖ the ninth planet of the solar system in order of distance from the sun. It is the second smallest planet of the system (diameter=3,600 miles, mass=1.76 x 10^{20} tons). It has the greatest inclination and eccentricity in orbit of all the planets (sidereal period=248.430 earth years, period of rotation=6.39 earth days, aphelion=4.6 x 10^9 miles, perihelion=2.8 x 10^9 miles). It has no known satellites

plu·toc·ra·cy (plu:tɒ́krəsi:) *pl.* **plu·toc·ra·cies** *n.* rule by the rich ‖ a ruling class of rich people **plu·to·crat** (plú:təkræt) *n.* a member of a plutocracy **plu·to·crát·ic** *adj.* [fr. Gk *ploutokratia* fr. *ploutos,* wealth+*kratia,* power]

plu·ton·ic (plu:tɒ́nik) *adj.* (*geol.*) of or relating to the theory that igneous rocks solidified from magmas far below the earth's crust ‖ (of rock) solidified as accounted for by this theory [fr. Gk *Plouton,* Pluto]

plu·to·ni·um (plu:tóuni:əm) *n.* an artificial metallic element (symbol Pu), having up to 15 isotopes (mass of isotope of longest known half-life 242). The most important of these isotopes is Pu 239, which can be produced in large amounts in nuclear reactors. Pu 239 undergoes fission under slow nuclear bombardment and forms uranium 235 (*URANIUM). It is used as nuclear fuel and as a nuclear explosive [after PLUTO, the planet]

plu·vi·al (plú:vi:əl) *adj.* of, relating to or characterized by rain ‖ (*geol.*) due to the action of rain, *pluvial erosion* [fr. L. *pluvialis*]

plu·vi·om·e·ter (plu:vi:ɒ́mitər) *n.* a rain gauge **plu·vi·o·met·ric** (plu:vi:əmétrik), **plu·vi·o·mét·ri·cal** *adjs* **plu·vi·om·e·try** (plu:vi:ɒ́mitri:) *n.* [fr. L. *pluvia,* rain+METER]

plu·vi·ous (plú:vi:əs) *adj.* of or pertaining to rain [fr. L. *pluviosus*]

ply (plai) *pres. part.* **ply·ing** *past* and *past part.* **plied** *v.t.* to use with vigor and diligence, *to ply a needle* ‖ to work busily at, *to ply a trade* ‖ to supply (someone) persistently, *to ply someone with drink* ‖ to keep at (someone) constantly, *to ply someone with questions* ‖ (of boats) to sail or row across (a river etc.) and back more or less regularly ‖ *v.i.* to sail or go, usually regularly, between two places, *the ship plies between London and Rotterdam* ‖ (e.g. of a taxi driver) to have a regular stand where one waits for customers, *to ply for hire* ‖ (*naut.*) to make progress to windward by tacking [M.E. *plye* fr. *aplie, aplyc,* to apply]

ply *pl.* **plies** *n.* one of the lengths of spun fiber which are twisted together to make rope, cord etc., *two-ply wool* ‖ one of the thin wooden layers in plywood ‖ one of several layers of fabric sewn or stuck together [F. *pli,* fold]

Plym·outh (plíməθ) a county borough and port (pop. 255,500) of S.W. Devonshire, England, with a fine harbor: naval base (at adjacent Stonehouse and Devonport), shipbuilding, fishing

Plymouth the town (pop. 35,913) in S.E. Massachusetts where the Pilgrims landed (1620) from the 'Mayflower'

Plymouth Brethren a Christian sect which originated (c. 1830) in Plymouth, England. Its members have no formal creed or regular ministry and regulate their lives solely by their literal interpretation of the Bible

Plymouth Colony a colony founded in 1620 on the coast of Massachusetts by the Pilgrims

Plymouth Rock the rock on which the Pilgrims are said to have landed in 1620

Plymouth Rock a hen of a U.S. breed characterized by its long yellow legs

ply·wood (pláiwud) *n.* a material used in light construction composed of thin layers of wood glued or cemented together, usually having the grain of one layer at right angles to that of the next

Plzen *PILSEN

p.m., P.M. *POST MERIDIEM

PNET (*acronym*) **P**eaceful **N**uclear **E**xplosions **T**reaty, negotiated between the U.S.A. and the U.S.S.R. regulating explosions carried out by both countries in locations other than nuclear-weapon test sites

pneu·mat·ic (numǽtik, njumǽtik) *adj.* of, pertaining to, or using air, wind or gas ‖ operated by pressure of air, *a pneumatic drill* ‖ filled with air, *a pneumatic tire* ‖ (*zool.,* of bones) characterized by air-filled cavities ‖ (*zool.*) of the duct between the swim bladder and the alimentary tract in some fish **pneu·mát·i·cal·ly** *adv.* **pneu·mát·ics** *n.* the branch of physics dealing with the mechanical properties of gases, esp. air, and certain elastic fluids [fr. L. *pneumaticus* fr. Gk]

pneu·ma·tol·o·gy (nu:mətɒ́lədʒi:, nju:mətɒ́lədʒi:) *n.* (*theol.*) the theory of the spirit or of the nature of the spirit ‖ (*theol.*) the doctrine of the Holy Spirit [fr. Gk *pneuma* (*pneumatos*), air+*logos,* discourse]

pneu·ma·tol·y·sis (nu:mətɒ́lisis, nju:mətɒ́lisis) *n.* the formation of ores and rocks by steam or other vapors, or by superheated liquids under pressure [Mod. L. fr. Gk *pneuma (pneumatos),* air+*lusis,* a loosening]

pneu·ma·to·lyt·ic (nu:mətoulítik, nju:mət'litik) *adj.* of ores or rocks formed by pneumatolysis [fr. Gk *pneuma (pneumatos),* air+*lutikos,* able to loose]

pneu·ma·to·phore (nú:mətəfɔr, njú:mətəfɔr, nú:mətəfour, njú:mətəfour) *n.* (*zool.*) the air-filled sac serving as a float on a colony of siphonophores ‖ (*bot.*) a root serving as a breathing organ for various swamp or marsh plants [fr. Gk *pneuma (pneumatos),* air+*-phoros,* bearing]

pneu·mo·coc·cal (nu:məkɒ́k'l, nju:məkɒ́k'l) *adj.* of or caused by pneumococci **pneu·mo·cóc·cic** *adj.*

pneu·mo·coc·cus (nu:məkɒ́kəs, nju:məkɒ́kəs) *pl.* **pneu·mo·coc·ci** (nu:məkɒ́ksai, nju:məkɒ́ksai) *n.* (*med.*) *Diplococcus pneumoniae,* a bacterium that causes one type of pneumonia [fr. Gk *pneumōn,* lung+coccus]

pneu·mo·co·ni·o·sis (nu:məkouni:ousis, nju:məkouni:ósis) *n.* a disease of the lungs caused by the inhalation of particles of dust, metals etc., common among miners [Mod. L. fr. Gk *pneumōn,* lung+*konia,* dust]

pneu·mo·cys·tic (nu:məsístik) *n.* an ice-free body of water formed amid vast ice fields off the coast off Antarctica during winter; believed to be warm-water ventilation from below the surface of the ocean

pneu·mo·gas·tric (nu:mougǽstrik, nju:mougǽstrik) **1.** *adj.* of or pertaining to the lungs and stomach ‖ of or pertaining to the vagus nerve **2.** *n.* the vagus nerve [fr. Gk *pneumōn,* lung+GASTRIC]

pneu·mo·nec·to·my (nu:mənéktəmi:, nju:mənéktəmi:) *pl.* **pneu·mo·nec·to·mies** *n.* the surgical removal of a lung or part of a lung [fr. Gk *pneuma (pneumatos),* air+Mod. L. *-ektomē,* a cutting out]

pneu·mo·nia (numóunjə, njumóunjə, numóuni:ə, njumóuni:ə) *n.* any of several diseases of the respiratory tract characterized by inflammation of the lungs and caused by bacteria, viruses or chemical irritants **pneu·mon·ic** (numɒ́nik, njumɒ́nik) *adj.* [Mod. L. fr. Gk *pneumōn,* lung]

pneu·mo·tho·rax (nu:mouθɔ́ræks, nju:mouθɔ́ræks, nu:mouθóuræks, nju:mouθóuræks) *n.* an accumulation of air or other gas in the pleural cavity, occurring naturally as a result of lung disease or induced artificially in order to collapse a lung in the treatment of pulmonary tuberculosis [fr. Gk *pneumōn,* lung+THORAX]

Po (pou) the longest river (418 miles, navigable for 337) of Italy, and chief river of the N. Italian plain, the country's main industrial and agricultural region. It flows from the Cottian Alps across Piedmont and Lombardy, and between Emilia Romagna and Veneto to the Adriatic. Transported sediment constantly raises its bed, causing disastrous floods

P.O. post office

poach (poutʃ) *v.t.* to cook (fish, chicken etc.) in a liquid that is never allowed to boil ‖ to drop (an egg removed from its shell) into simmering water and let it cook until the white coagulates, or steam it in a special pan [O.F. *pochier,* to enclose in a bag]

poach *v.t.* to take (game or fish) illegally from another person's property ‖ to soften or make holes in (ground) by trampling ‖ *v.i.* (with 'on') to trespass (on another person's property) ‖ to take game or fish illegally from another person's property ‖ (*racket games*) to play a ball that should be played by one's partner ‖ (of ground) to become soggy or full of holes when trampled **póach·er** *n.* someone who trespasses in order to steal or kill game ‖ someone who takes or kills game illegally [F. *pocher* fr. Gmc]

Po·be·do·nos·tsev (pəbjedʌnɔ́stsjəf), Konstantin Petrovich (1827–1907), Russian statesman and jurist. As adviser to Alexander II and Nicholas II, he opposed liberal reforms and strengthened the autocracy

Po·ca·hon·tas (poukəhɒ́ntəs) (c. 1595–1617), a North American Indian princess reputed to have saved the colonist John Smith from being put to death

po·chard (póutʃərd) *pl.* **po·chards, po·chard** *n.* a member of *Aythya,* a genus of European diving sea ducks, esp. *A. ferina.* The male has a dark chestnut head, black breast and pale gray body [etym. doubtful]

pock (pɒk) *n.* a pustule caused by smallpox and other diseases (*POX) [O.E. *pocc*]

pock·et (pɒ́kit) **1.** *n.* a small, baglike receptacle of fabric, leather etc., having the top or side open, inserted in or sewed on a garment, for carrying a handkerchief, small change etc. ‖ a hollow place in which something has collected or could collect, *a pocket in a rock* ‖ a deposit of material (e.g. gold, oil) found on or in the earth ‖ (*football*) a wall of blockers surrounding a passer ‖ financial resources, *living beyond one's pockets* ‖ an air pocket ‖ any of the pouches, usually of netting, at the sides or corners of a billiard table ‖ (*mil.*) a body of soldiers almost completely hemmed in by the enemy, or the area they occupy ‖ the external pouch of some animals **in one's pocket** under one's influence ‖ virtually secured **out of pocket** (esp. *Br.*) in the condition of having lost money on a transaction etc., *he ended up $20 out of pocket on the day's races* **2.** *v.t.* to put into a pocket, *pocket the change* ‖ to take (money etc.) dishonestly, *to pocket the deposits* ‖ (*billiards*) to drive (a ball) into a pocket ‖ to use the pocket veto on (a bill) ‖ to suppress (pride, anger, scruples etc.) ‖ to accept submissively, *to pocket an insult* **3.** *adj.* suitable for or adapted for carrying in a pocket, *a pocket notebook* ‖ small, *a pocket revolution* [A.F. *pokete*]

pocket battleship (*hist.*) one of several fast German battleships of about 10,000 tons, built (1929) of weight-saving materials to come within Treaty of Versailles specifications

pocket billiards any of various games of billiards played usually with 15 object balls on a table having 6 pockets

pock·et·book (pɒ́kitbuk) *n.* a wallet for carrying paper money, papers etc. ‖ a woman's purse or handbag

pocket book a paperback

pocket borough (*Br. hist.*) a parliamentary constituency of which the representation was controlled by a single person or family

pock·et·knife (pɒ́kitnaif) *pl.* **pock·et·knives** (pɒ́kitnaivz) *n.* a small knife having a blade or blades folding into the handle

pocket money money for small personal needs ‖ (*Br.*) a regular allowance to children

pocket veto a method of indirect veto in which the president of the U.S.A. or the governor of a state leaves a bill presented to him within a few days of adjournment unsigned until Congress or the state legislature has adjourned

pock·mark (pɒ́kmɑrk) *n.* the pitlike scar left in the skin by the pustule of esp. smallpox **póck·marked** *adj.* having or as if having pockmarks

po·co (póukou) *adv.* (*mus.*) somewhat, slightly [fr. L. *paucus,* little]

po·co a po·co (póukouɑpóukou) *adv.* (*mus.*) little by little

pod (pɒd) **1.** *n.* a dry dehiscent fruit that is either monocarpellary, e.g. legume, or consists of two or more carpels, e.g. the poppy ‖ a protective envelope, e.g. a cocoon ‖ a streamlined container attached to the wings or fuselage of an aircraft ‖ (*aerospace*) a unit designed to detach from a space craft **2.** *v. pres. part.* **pod·ding** *past* and *past part.* **pod·ded** *v.i.* to swell into pods ‖ to produce pods ‖ *v.t.* to split and empty the pods of (peas etc.) [origin unknown]

pod 1. *n.* a school of seals, whales etc. **2.** *v.t. pres part.* **pod·ding** *past* and *past part.* **pod·ded** to drive (seals) into a pod [origin unknown]

pod *n.* the socket of a brace into which the bit is inserted ‖ the channel or groove of an auger which holds the chips [origin unknown]

pod·a·gra (pɒ́dəgrə) *n.* (*med.*) gout, esp. in the foot **po·dag·ric** (pədǽgrik) *adj.* [fr. Gk *pous (podos),* food+*agra,* a seizure]

podg·i·ness (pɒ́dʒi:nis) *n.* the condition of being podgy [PODGY]

Pod·gor·ny (pɔ́dgʌrni:), Nikolai Viktorovitch (1903–83), Soviet statesman, head of state from 1965

podg·y (pɒ́dʒi:) *comp.* **podg·i·er** *superl.* **podg·i·est** *adj.* short and fat [var. of PUDGY]

po·di·a·trist (poudáiətrist) *n.* a chiropodist [fr. Gk *pous (podos),* foot]

po·di·a·try (poudáiətri:) *n.* chiropody [fr. Gk *pous (podos),* foot]

po·di·um (póudi:əm) *pl.* **po·di·a** (póudi:ə), **po·di·ums** *n.* (*archit.*) a low wall supporting a row of columns or serving as a foundation for the wall of a building ‖ (*hist.*) a low wall surrounding the arena of an ampitheater, serving as a support for the seats ‖ a dais, e.g. for an orchestra conductor ‖ (*zool.*) the foot of an echinoderm [L. fr. Gk *podion,* dim. of *pous (podos),* foot]

pod·o·phyl·lin (pɒdəfílin) *n.* a brown to greenish yellow resin extracted from the roots and rhizomes of *Podophyllum peltatum,* fam. *Berberidaceae,* the mayapple of North America, used esp. as a cathartic [fr. Mod. L. *Podophyllum* fr. Gk *pous (poudos),* foot+*phullon,* leaf]

Poe (pou), Edgar Allan (1809–49), American short-story writer, poet and critic. He was the inventor of the ratio-cinative detective story, his most famous being 'The Murders in the Rue Morgue' (1841). Other stories, e.g. 'Tales of the Grotesque and Arabesque' (1840), are written around motifs that were for him an obsession: death, decay and madness. These motifs also thread through his poetry, which is mainly known for its musicality. The translation of some of his prose works by Baudelaire brought him wide acclaim in France. His critical studies had a powerful effect on Baudelaire's own writing, and served as inspiration for the Symbolists, esp. Mallarmé

po·em (póuəm) *n.* a piece of poetry [F. *poème* L. fr. Gk]

po·e·sy (póuisi:, póuizi:) *n.* (*rhet.*) the art of writing poetry ‖ (*rhet.*) poetry in general [O.F. *poésie* fr. L. fr. Gk]

po·et (póuit) *n.* a person who writes poetry [O.F. *poète* fr. L. fr. Gk]

po·et·as·ter (póuitæstər) *n.* a writer of trivial or bad verse [Mod. L. fr. *poeta,* poet fr. Gk+L. *-aster,* inferior]

po·et·ess (póuitis) *n.* a female poet [POET]

po·et·ic (pouétik) *adj.* of, pertaining to or characteristic of poets or poetry ‖ of the language or meaning of a poem or of poetry ‖ composed in verse ‖ having qualities associated with poetry, *poetic movements* [F. *poétique* fr. L. fr. Gk]

po·et·i·cal (pouétik'l) *adj.* poetic [fr. L. *poeticus*]

po·et·i·cize (pouétisaiz) *pres. part.* **po·et·i·ciz·ing** *past* and *past part.* **po·et·i·cized** *v.t.* to endow with poetic qualities

poetic justice justice which reveals itself in its mode of operation peculiarly appropriate, as though fate had shown itself

poetic license, poetic licence the right of a poet to deviate from the conventional rules of syntax, grammar etc.

po·et·ics (pouétiks) *n.* the theory of poetry ‖ a treatise on poetry [POETIC]

po·et·ize (póuitaiz) *pres. part.* **po·et·iz·ing** *past* and *past part.* **po·et·ized** *v.t.* to treat poetically, *to poetize an experience* ‖ *v.i.* to play the poet [fr. F. *poétiser*]

poet laureate *pl.* **poet laureates, poets laureate** the title given in Britain to a poet appointed to the Royal Household for life and having as his duty the celebrating of national or royal occasions in verse. The laureateship is now largely titular

po·et·ry (póuitri:) *n.* a type of discourse which achieves its effects by rhythm, sound patterns and imagery. Most characteristically, the poetic form evokes emotions or sensations, but it may also serve to convey loftiness of tone, or to lend force to ideas ‖ poems ‖ the quality of a poem ‖ the quality of whatever arouses emotions comparable to those aroused by a poem [O.F. *poétrie*]

Pog·gio Brac·cio·li·ni (pɔ́ddʒɔbrɑttʃɔlí:ni:), Gian Francesco (1380–1459), Italian author. He was lay secretary to the Curia (1404–50), during which time he discovered many valuable Latin manuscripts. He wrote moral essays, a 'History of Florence' and 'Liber Facetiarum', a collection of satiric stories

po·go (póugou) *n.* **1.** (*mil.*) in air intercept, a code meaning 'switch to communications channel number preceding "pogo" and if unable to establish communications, switch to channel number following "pogo" '. **2.** (*music*) a dance step consisting of jumping up and down, esp. by punk rock groups

Po·go·noph·o·ran (pougənɒ́fərən) *n.* (*zool.*) a marine worm of a phylum or class (*Pogonophora*) found at great ocean depths **—po·go·noph·o·ran** *adj.*

po·go stick (póugou) a toy consisting of a single stilt having two pedals and a spring, used to jump around on [origin unknown]

po·grom (pəgrʌ́m, pəgrɒ́m, póugrəm) *n.* an or

ganized massacre, esp. of Jews in Russia (1881, 1903, 1905) [Russ.=devastation]

Po Hai (bóuhái) (formerly Gulf of Chihli) the northwest arm of the Yellow Sea, bordered by Liaoning, Hopei and Shantung, China

poign·an·cy (pɔ́injənsi:) *n.* the quality or state of being poignant [POIGNANT]

poign·ant (pɔ́injənt) *adj.* causing or marked by feelings of sadness ‖ (of grief) deeply felt ‖ stimulating, *of poignant interest* [O. F. *puignant, poignant*]

Poin·ca·ré (pwɛ̃kærei), Jules Henri (1854–1912), French mathematician, physicist and philosopher. He made important discoveries in the field of mathematical functions and wrote 'la Science et l'hypothèse' (1902), 'Science et Méthode' (1909)

Poincaré, Raymond (1860–1934), French statesman, president of France (1913–20). As prime minister (1912–13, 1922–4, 1926–9), he ordered the French occupation of the Ruhr (1923) in order to enforce German payment of reparations

poin·set·ti·a (pɔinséti:ə, pɔinsétə) *n.* any plant of the genus *Euphorbia,* fam. *Euphorbiaceae,* esp. *E. pulcherrima,* a Mexican and South American plant having tapering scarlet leaves surrounding small yellow flowers [Mod. L. after J. R. *Poinsett* (1779-1851), U.S. ambassador to Mexico]

point (pɔint) *n.* a specific place having a definite position in space but no definite size or shape, *a point of intersection* ‖ a measurable position in a scale, *boiling point* ‖ a definite, often decisive, moment in time, *turning point, at the point of death* ‖ (of something spoken or written) the most prominent or important idea, *the point of a story* ‖ the climax of a joke ‖ a particular item in a speech, argument, exposition etc., *there were four main points in his proposal* ‖ a distinguishing characteristic, *generosity is not one of her strong points* ‖ purpose, *is there any point in going on?* ‖ the sharp end of something, *a pencil point* ‖ something having such a sharp end, e.g. a tool used in etching and engraving ‖ a particular place, e.g. on a route, *points of interest* ‖ a period (punctuation mark) ‖ a decimal point ‖ (*games*) a unit of counting in scoring ‖ a unit of value used in quoting variations in cost of living, the prices of stocks etc. ‖ a unit of academic credit ‖ (*printing*) a unit for measuring size of type (1/72 in.) ‖ a unit for assessing performance in boxing etc. ‖ (in Semitic alphabets) a mark for indicating vowels ‖ (*geog.*, esp. in place names) a piece of land projecting into the sea, *Start Point* ‖ (*cricket*) a fielder's position on the off side of the batsman, fairly close to him and roughly in line with the popping crease ‖ (*lacrosse*) the position to the right of the goal ‖ (*securities*) the minimum price fluctuation, equal to 1/100 of one cent in most futures traded in decimal units, to ¼ of one cent in grains, $1 in stocks, $10 in $1,000 bonds ‖ 1% of a sum, sometimes charged for a loan or other service ‖ (*fencing*) a lunge ‖ (*boxing*) the tip of the chin ‖ (*ballet*) the tip of the toe ‖ any of a number of types of lace worked with a needle, esp. needlepoint lace ‖ (of certain gundogs) the act of pointing ‖ (*pl.*) the mane, tail and legs of a horse ‖ a tine of an antler ‖ a physical feature of an animal used esp. as a standard in judging its quality ‖ (*pl.*) the characteristic facial markings of a Siamese cat ‖ (*naut.*) any of the 32 marks around the circumference of a compass ‖ (*naut.*) the difference of 11° 15′ between any such mark and the next to it ‖ (*naut.*) that part of the horizon indicated by one of these marks ‖ (*naut.*) any of the pieces of rope used in reefing a sail ‖ (*hist.*) a cord for lacing parts of a garment together ‖ (*pl.*) the two tapering, movable rails for turning a train from one track to another ‖ (*mil.*) a small party leading an advance guard or following a rear guard ‖ one of the raised dots used in printing for the blind ‖ (*heraldry*) one of the nine divisions of a shield or escutcheon used for locating the position of a charge ‖ (*Br.*) an outlet (of a wiring system) ‖ (*elec.*) either of the two contacts serving to make or break the circuit in a distributor ‖ (*hunting*) a straight run ‖ (*hunting*) the spot to which the run is made ‖ a useful suggestion **at all points** in every respect **beside the point** not relevant **in point of** in the matter of **in point of fact** in reality **to carry one's point** to establish an argument, proposition etc. by persuasion **to come to the point** to discard irrelevancies and get to the heart of the matter **to give points to** (*Br.*) to be better than **to make a point** to establish the force of an idea, argument etc. **to make a point of** (with pres. infin.) to do with marked deliberateness, *to make a point of not answering rude letters* **on the point of** just about to **to stretch a point** to be indulgent in interpreting or applying a rule **to the point** relevant **to win on points** (*boxing*) to win by performance over the rounds fought, not by knockout [F. *point,* a dot and F. *pointe,* a sharp end]

point *v.t.* to give a point to, *to point a pencil* ‖ (often with 'up') to give force or emphasis to, *to point a speech with jokes* ‖ to cause (something) to be turned towards a particular person or object, or in a particular direction, *to point a gun at someone, he pointed the car south* ‖ to fill the joints in (brickwork) with mortar etc. using a special trowel ‖ to mark (Semitic vowels) with points ‖ to mark (a printed text of the Psalms) with indications showing how to phrase when chanting ‖ (of certain gundogs) to indicate the presence of (game) by staring fixedly towards it and assuming a rigid stance with one forepaw upraised and the tail extended ‖ to reef (a sail) with points ‖ *v.i.* (with 'at', 'to', 'towards' etc.) to indicate position or direction with or as if with a finger, *to point at a crack in the ceiling* ‖ to be turned in a particular direction, *an arrow pointing to the south* ‖ (*naut.*) to sail close to the wind ‖ (of certain gundogs) to point game **to point out** to direct attention to ‖ to explain, *he pointed out that it was not his fault* **to point to** (or **towards**) to be an indication of a specified probability, *everything points to his guilt* [O.F. *pointer*]

point balance a statement prepared by futures commodities commission merchants to show profit or loss on all open contracts by computing them to an official closing or settlement price, usu. at calendar month end

point-blank (pɔ́intblǽŋk) **1.** *adv.* with level aim ‖ directly, *he accused her point-blank of lying* **2.** *adj.* (of a shot) fired at a very close target ‖ (of a shooting range) so close that one takes level aim ‖ direct, *a point-blank question* [POINT+BLANK fr. F. *blanc,* white point (center of a target)]

point d'Al·en·con (pwɛ̃dælɑ̃sɔ̃) a needlepoint lace made in Alençon, France. Based on the lace of Venice, it was introduced in the mid 17th c.

point duty (*Br.*) the work of a police officer in directing traffic

Pointe-à-Pi·tre (pwɛ̃tæpi:tr) the largest town (pop. 23,889) of Guadeloupe, a seaport on the southwest coast of Grande Terre Is.

point·ed (pɔ́intid) *adj.* having, or being given, a sharp point ‖ (of a remark) sharply, though obliquely, critical ‖ made deliberately obvious, *his rudeness was very pointed* ‖ lively, piquant, *pointed wit* [POINT]

pointed arch (*archit.*) an arch the top of which forms a point, as in the Gothic style (esp. in contrast to the earlier rounded arch)

pointed fox the fur of the red fox dyed and treated to resemble that of the silver fox

Pointe Noire (pwɛ̃tnwær) the chief port (pop. 141,700) of the Republic of the Congo, linked by rail to Brazzaville: shipyards

point·er (pɔ́intər) *n.* a person or thing that points, *the pointer on a dial* ‖ a rod used for pointing, e.g. by a lecturer ‖ a gundog of a breed having a smooth, usually white coat with brown or black spots, used for pointing game ‖ a useful indication or suggestion [POINT]

Point Four Program a program proposed (1949) by U.S. President Harry Truman, which extended technical assistance and financial aid, previously channeled to rebuild war-torn Europe, to underdeveloped areas. It became a part of the Agency for International Development (AID)

poin·til·lism (pwǽnt'lizəm, pwǽnti:lizəm) *n.* a method of painting developed by Seurat and used by certain other Postimpressionists, in which separated small dots of pure color applied to the picture surface become mixed by the viewer's eye, with an effect of increased luminosity **póin·til·list** *n.* a painter using this method [F. *pointillisme* fr. *pointiller,* to mark with dots]

point lace lace made entirely with a needle

point·less (pɔ́intlis) *adj.* having no point, esp. having no meaning or purpose

point of diminishing return the point after which an increased amount of land, labor or money devoted to a project does not give a proportionate increase in yield, or at which higher prices or charges cease to produce proportionately higher revenue or profit

point of honor, *Br.* **point of honour** a matter to which one chooses to give the force of a principle involving one's honor

point of impact the point hit by a projectile

point of no return the point beyond which one's decisions or actions commit one irrevocably ‖ the point on a cross-country flight after which one is nearer to the destination than to the starting point

point of order a question of debating procedure

point-of-sale (pɔ́intʌfséil) *n.* the place e.g., a retail store, where a product or service is offered to prospective customers. *abbr.* **POS**

point of view a mental position from which something is considered ‖ an opinion

point-to-point (pɔ́inttəpɔ́int) *n.* a cross-country steeplechase for amateur riders from a starting point to a distant but visible point

poise (pwɑz) *n.* (*phys.*) the unit of absolute viscosity of a fluid [after Jean *Poiseuille* (1779-1869), French physicist]

poise (pɔiz) *n.* balance ‖ carriage, bearing ‖ emotional stability, self-possession [M.E. *poys* fr. O.F.]

poise *pres. part.* **pois·ing** *past* and *past part.* **poised** *v.t.* to balance, *to carry a jug poised on one's head* ‖ to hold suspended for a moment, *to poise a javelin before hurling it* ‖ to hold (the head) in a particular way ‖ to put (esp. oneself) in a state of readiness, *to poise oneself for an ordeal* ‖ *v.i.* to be balanced ‖ to hang suspended or as if suspended, *a dancer poised in mid-air* [M.E. *poise* fr. O.F.]

Poi·seuille's law (pwæsə:jz) (*phys.*) the law stating that the rate of flow of a fluid through a tube varies directly with the pressure and the fourth power of the diameter of the tube, and inversely with the length of the tube and the coefficient of viscosity, for laminar (i.e. nonturbulent) flow [after Jean *Poiseuille* (1799-1869), F. physicist who formulated the law in 1844]

poi·son (pɔ́iz'n) **1.** *n.* a substance which, by its direct action on tissues, a mucous membrane etc., or after absorption into the circulatory system, can seriously injure an organism or destroy life completely ‖ anything having a pernicious effect on the mind or character of an individual or individuals **2.** *adj.* poisonous [M.E. *poison, puison* fr. O.F.]

poison *v.t.* to injure or destroy by using a poison ‖ to make poisonous, *to poison a well* ‖ to exert a pernicious influence on (the mind or character of an individual or individuals) [M.E. *poisonen* fr. O.F.]

poison gas a poisonous gas used esp. in chemical warfare

poi·son·ing (pɔ́iz'niŋ) *n.* the condition produced by the application or absorption of a poison

poison ivy a member of *Rhus,* fam. *Anacardiaceae,* a genus of North American shrubs, esp. *R. toxicodendron,* common in the eastern and central U.S.A. These shrubs exude an irritating oil capable of causing a violently itchy skin rash

poison oak a shrubby variety of poison ivy ‖ any of various poison sumacs

poi·son·ous (pɔ́iz'nəs) *adj.* having the properties or effects of a poison ‖ impregnated with, or containing poison ‖ as pernicious or deadly as a poison, *a poisonous influence* ‖ (*pop.*) hateful, *a poisonous fellow*

poi·son-pen (pɔ́iz'npén) *adj.* written anonymously and with deliberate malice, *a poison-pen letter*

poison sumac, poison sumach *Rhus vernix,* fam. *Anacardiaceae,* a North American swamp sumac having pinnate leaves, greenish flowers and greenish-white berries. It produces an irritating oil like that of poison ivy

Pois·son (pwæsɔ̃), Siméon Denis (1781–1840), French mathematician and physicist, noted for his contributions to electrostatics and mechanics

Poisson's ratio (*phys.*) the ratio between the lateral and longitudinal strains in a stretched wire or rod (symbol σ)

Poi·tiers (pwætjei) the chief town (pop. 81,313) of Vienne, France, and historical capital of Poitou. Gothic cathedral (12th–13th cc.), Romanesque and pre-Romanesque churches. University (1431)

Poitiers, Battle of a battle (732) in which Charles Martel repulsed the Moslem invasion of Europe ‖ an English victory (1356) in the Hundred Years' War. The Black Prince fought a brilliant defensive battle against the French, who greatly outnumbered his army

Poi·tou (pwætu:) a former province of W. France between the Paris and Garonne basins, comprising Vienne and Deux-Sèvres departments inland, and Vendée on the Atlantic, with parts of Charente (inland) and Charente-Maritime (coast). It consists largely of limestone plains, partly fertile, partly sandy. The coast is marshy. Agriculture: cereals, market produce, beef cattle, dairy farming. Historic capital: Poitiers. United with Aquitaine, it went to England through Henry II (1152), was taken back by the French, first in 1224, finally in 1369

poke (pouk) **1.** *v. pres. part.* **pok·ing** *past* and *past part.* **poked** *v.t.* to thrust quickly the tip of some object, e.g. a finger, into (someone or something), *to poke someone in the ribs* ‖ to thrust (something) forward, or into or through an aperture, *to poke one's finger into a crack* ‖ to insert (an object) into something soft, *he poked his finger into the clay* ‖ to make (a hole) by doing this ‖ to stir up (a fire in a grate etc.) with a poker ‖ (*pop.*) to hit with a short, jabbing blow of the fist ‖ *v.i.* to make little digs or thrusts with a stick, finger etc. ‖ to be thrust forward through an aperture, *his head poked through the door* ‖ to go slowly, dawdle **to poke around** to examine things in a nosy or desultory way ‖ to busy oneself without any apparent purpose, *he is poking around in the garden* **to poke fun at** to make the object of ridicule **2.** *n.* the act of poking ‖ (*old-fash.*) a poke bonnet ‖ (*pop.*) a short, jabbing blow with the fist ‖ a slow-moving person, slow coach [M.E. *poken*]

poke bonnet (*old-fash.*) a woman's bonnet having a projecting brim in the front

po·ker (póukər) *n.* a gambling game played with 52 cards (each player being dealt 5 or 7 cards), and based on the relative value of certain combinations of cards. To stay in the game a player must either equal or raise the bets made by other players. These bets, in the form of money or chips, constitute the pot, which is won by the possessor of the highest card combination shown. Bluffing plays an important part in the game

poker *n.* a heavy, usually iron, rod used to poke a fire [POKE v.]

poker face a face revealing no emotion whatsoever

poker work the art of making decorative designs on wood, leather, calabashes etc. by burning or scorching with a hot instrument ‖ this decoration, or articles so decorated

poke·sy (póukzi:) *adj.* word combining 'pokey' and 'folksy'; meaning easygoing

poke·weed (póukwi:d) *n. Phytolacca americana,* fam. *Phytolaccaceae,* a North American perennial plant, having greenish-white flowers, poisonous purple berries and edible shoots

pok·y, pok·ey (póuki:) *comp.* **pok·i·er** *superl.* **pok·i·est** *adj.* (of a small room, house etc.) inconveniently small ‖ (esp. of a town) small, drab and dull ‖ (of a person) slow, lazy

Po·land (póulənd) a republic (area 120,733 sq. miles, pop. 36,229,000) of central Europe on the Baltic. Capital: Warsaw. People: 98% Polish, with Ukrainian, Byelorussian and other minorities. Language: Polish. Religion: 95% Roman Catholic, 1.5% Orthodox, 5% Protestant, with smaller Old Catholic and Jewish minorities. The land is 54% arable, 13% pasture and 23% forest. It is largely a plain, rising to a slightly elevated (mainly 600–1,000 ft) plateau in the southwest quarter, the country's richest agricultural district, and to the wooded Sudeten and Carpathian Mtns (*BESKIDS, *TATRA MTNS) along the southern border. The north (with N. East Germany) forms part of the Baltic lake plateau (coastal lagoons, sandy soil, marshes, peat deposits, hundreds of lakes). Climate: continental. The Oder is frozen an average of 40 days a year, the Vistula 60. Average temperatures (F.): (Jan.) 26°, (July) 64°. Rainfall: Warsaw 18 ins, Carpathians 50 ins. Livestock: cattle, hogs, sheep, horses. Agricultural products: cereals, root vegetables, tobacco, hops, flax, silk, dairy goods. Main fisheries: cod, herring. Mineral resources: coal, lignite, iron ore, lead, zinc, petroleum, natural gas, salt, sulfur, potassium salts, silver, nickel, copper, arsenic. Manufactures and industries (rapidly developing): mining, iron and steel, motor vehicles, heavy machinery, rolling stock, electrical and optical equipment, precision instruments, textiles, lumber, chemicals, foodstuffs, leather, rubber goods, paper, cement, shipbuilding, glass, fertilizers, footwear, hydroelectricity. Exports: coal, rolling stock, coke, lignite, ships, chemicals, cement, machinery, iron and steel, sugar, wood and pulp, textiles, eggs. Imports: iron ore, oil and petroleum products, fertilizers, wheat, cotton, wool, zinc concentrates. Chief ports: Gdynia, Gdansk, Szczecin. There are 8 universities, including Krakow (1364) and Warsaw (1816). Monetary unit: zloty (100 groszy). HISTORY. The lower valleys of the Oder and the Vistula, inhabited by Slavs, were united in one duchy (10th c.) and the people became Christians. This territory was expanded to cover most of modern Poland until 1138, when it was split up into a number of duchies. The Teutonic Knights conquered East Prussia (13th c.), cutting off Poland's access to the Baltic. Poland was reunited (14th c.) under Casimir III, and became a refuge for the Jews expelled from W. Europe. Under Ladislaw II, the founder of the Jagiello dynasty, Lithuania was united to Poland (1386) and the Teutonic Knights were decisively defeated at Tannenberg (1410). The kingdom was enlarged to include parts of White Russia and the Ukraine, a constitutional monarchy was established, and a flourishing culture developed. The Reformation made some impact on the nobility, but Catholicism was reestablished by the end of the 16th c. After the death (1572) of the last Jagiello, an elective monarchy was instituted. This weakened the country by provoking civil wars, and involved Poland in wars with the Turks, Sweden and Russia. John III defeated the Turks at Vienna (1683), but by his death (1696) Poland had ceased to be a great power. It was further weakened by the War of the Polish Succession (1733–5) and was finally annihilated when Austria, Russia and Prussia agreed to partition Poland. In the 1st partition (1772) Prussia took northwestern Poland (except Gdansk), Austria took Galicia, and Russia took land east of the Dvina. In the 2nd partition (1793) Prussia and Russia took more than half of what remained. A revolt (1794) led by Kosciusko prompted the 3rd partition (1795), in which Austria, Prussia and Russia annexed all the remainder, and Poland completely disappeared. Napoleon formed the Grand Duchy of Warsaw (1807) but this was abolished (1815) by the Congress of Vienna and the land redistributed to Austria, Prussia and Russia. Polish revolts were harshly put down (1830, 1846, 1848 and 1863) but the independence movement remained strong. In the 1st world war, Pilsudski organized Polish legions to oppose Russia. Poland was reestablished as an independent state (1918) and given access to the Baltic through the Polish Corridor. Frontier disputes caused fighting with the Germans, the Czechs, the Russians and the Ukrainians until 1921. National minorities and the economic backwardness of the country were severe problems. Pilsudski established a dictatorship after a coup d'état (1926). Nazi Germany invaded Poland (Sept 1, 1939), provoking the 2nd world war, and the country was partitioned between Germany and the U.S.S.R. The population, esp. the Jews, were subject to mass deportation and extermination. A large underground resistance movement developed and a government in exile was formed in London. Many Polish exiles fought in the Allied forces. The German army was expelled by the Russians (1945) and the state of Poland was reestablished with the addition of former German territory east of the Oder-Neisse line and Russian territory west of the Curzon line. Communists immediately dominated the Polish government, and took it over completely (1947), establishing a people's republic. After mass riots (1956), Gomulka took power and the regime became more liberal. Poland's eastern frontiers were recognized (1970) 'de facto' by the West German government. A social and economic crisis (Dec. 1970) provoked riots. Gomulka was replaced by Gierek. An industrial boom in the early 1970's was followed by economic difficulties, which led to food-price riots (1976). Increases in food prices (1980) again led to unrest, culminating in a workers' takeover of the Gdańsk shipyards. Strikes spread to include 350,000 workers throughout Poland until the government granted pay increases and the right to form independent unions; the new unions subsequently became Solidarity, a single, nationwide organization. Gierek was replaced by Stanislaw Kania, who announced economic reforms. Solidarity's call for a five-day work week (1981) was agreed to by the government, but following the settlement Premier Jozef Pinkowski (1980–1) was replaced by Defense Minister Gen. Wojciech Jaruzelski, who also replaced Kania as party leader later that year as strikes and protests about food shortages continued. Following a call by Solidarity for a referendum on the competence of the government, Jaruzelski imposed martial law and outlawed Solidarity. Martial law was not lifted until 1983, and the government still retained the power to restrict union activity. After a new parliament was elected (1985), Jaruzelski assumed the office of president, and handed the premiership over to Zbigniew Messner

po·lar (póulər) **1.** *adj.* of or pertaining to the regions of the earth, or of the celestial sphere, located near the poles ‖ of or pertaining to the pole of a magnet, *polar force* ‖ of or pertaining to positive and negative electric charges ‖ (*chem.*) electrovalent ‖ (*chem., phys.*) having a dipole ‖ (*math.*) of a relationship to a fixed point (pole) ‖ opposite in nature, character etc., *polar views* ‖ (*rhet.*) guiding, *a polar principle* **2.** *n.* (*math.*) a polar curve ‖ (*math.*) a line joining the intersections of tangents drawn from a pole to a conic section [fr. M.L. *polaris*]

polar bear *Thalarctos maritimus,* a powerful bear inhabiting the Arctic regions, having a long body (up to 9 ft), a narrow, pointed head, and shaggy yellowish-white fur. It feeds mainly on fish, seals and grasses

polar body a polocyte

polar cap the white region at each pole of the planet Mars

polar circle one of the circular zones parallel to the equator, and at a distance of 23° 27′ from each pole (cf. ARCTIC CIRCLE, cf. ANTARCTIC CIRCLE)

polar climate a climatic regime of the Arctic, Antarctic and high mountain regions, characterized by continuous below-freezing temperatures, low precipitation and little seasonal variation

polar coordinates (*math.*) the distance r of a point from a pole (a fixed point of reference) and the angle θ made by the line joining the point and the pole with a fixed axis passing through the pole

polar curve a curve drawn in polar coordinates

polar distance the angular distance of a point on a sphere from the nearest pole

polar front the boundary between the cold climate of the polar regions and the warmer climate of the temperate latitudes

po·lar·im·e·ter (pǫulərímitər) *n.* an instrument used to measure optical rotation ‖ an instrument used to measure the degree of polarization of light in a partially polarized ray [fr. M.L. *polaris,* polar+METER]

Po·la·ris (pouléəris, poulǽris) *n.* the polestar [Mod. L. short for *stella polaris,* polar star]

Polaris *n.* (*mil.*) an underwater/surface-launched, surface-to-surface solid-propellant, computer-guided ballistic missile (UGM-27), equipped with inertial guidance and nuclear warheads with ranges 1,200 to 2,500 nautical mi. It was replaced by Poseidon

po·lar·i·scope (poulǽriskoup) *n.* a polarimeter used to measure optical rotation

po·lar·i·ty (poulǽriti:) *n.* the quality of having poles ‖ the state of having one or other of two opposite polar conditions, *positive or negative polarity* ‖ the tendency of bodies having magnetic poles to align them with the earth's poles [POLAR]

po·lar·i·za·tion (pǫulərizéiʃən, *Br.* pǫuləraizéiʃən) *n.* the act of polarizing ‖ the state of being polarized, used esp. of light and other transverse wave radiation to signify a special relation between the direction of propagation and the plane of vibration of the waves. In plane or linearly polarized radiation (e.g. light) the vibrations of the waves are confined to a single plane that includes the direction of propagation (as distinguished from nonpolarized light, where the planes of vibration of the waves may be any, including the direction of propagation). Light may be polarized by various means, e.g. by scattering, by its passage through a dichroic material, by its passage through birefringent materials or by reflection from nonmetallic surfaces ‖ the gradual decrease in the voltage of an electrolytic cell associated with the accumula-

CONCISE PRONUNCIATION KEY: **(a)** æ, *cat*; ɑ, *car*; ɔ *fawn*; ei, *snake*. **(e)** e, *hen*; i:, *sheep*; iə, *deer*; ɛə, *bear*. **(i)** i, *fish*; ai, *tiger*; ə:, *bird*. **(o)** o, *ox*; au, *cow*; ou, *goat*; u, *poor*; ɔi, *royal*. **(u)** ʌ, *duck*; u, *bull*; u:, *goose*; ə, *bacillus*; ju:, *cube*. x, *loch*; θ, *think*; ð, *bother*; z, *Zen*; ʒ, *corsage*; dʒ, *savage*; ŋ, *orangutang*; j, *yak*; ʃ, *fish*; tʃ, *fetch*; 'l, *rabble*; 'n, *redden*. Complete pronunciation key appears inside front cover.

tion of gaseous materials on one or both electrodes (also called electrolytic polarization) || the slight shifting of electrons with respect to nuclei in a dielectric or other substance when it is placed in an electric field (also called dielectric or induced polarization) || magnetization

po·lar·ize (póuləraiz) *pres. part.* **po·lar·iz·ing** *past* and *past part.* **po·lar·ized** *v.t.* to produce polarization in or give polarity to || to determine the relative importance of, or to fix the relative direction of, *to polarize the efforts of a team of researchers* || *v.i.* to become concentrated around two opposites or extremes || to serve as a point around which concentration takes place [F. *polariser*]

polarizing microscope a microscope employing polarized light, used to study crystal structure

po·lar·o·graph (pouléərəgræf, pouléərəgrɑf) *n.* an instrument to record the degree of electric polarization in an electrolyte, esp. in microanalysis [after *Polarograph,* a trademark fr. M.L. *polaris,* polar+Gk *graphos,* written]

po·lar·oid (póulərɔid) *n.* a film in which multitudes of polarizing minute crystals are orientated parallel to one another, so that the film polarizes the light it transmits. It is used in sunglasses to prevent glare and in a variety of optical instruments [after *Polaroid,* a trademark]

Polaroid *n.* trademark of Polaroid Corp., producer of Polaroid Land instant-picture cameras and of light-polarizing material, etc.

Po·la·vi·sion (póuləviʒən) *n.* trademark for instant motion picture-making device by Polaroid Corp.

pol·der (póuldər) *n.* an area of low lying land reclaimed from the sea or other large body of water and usually protected by dikes [Du.]

Pole (póul), Reginald (1500–58), English cardinal, archbishop of Canterbury (1556–8). He went into exile (1532) when he opposed Henry VIII's divorce, but returned (1553) as papal legate and attempted to restore Roman Catholicism in England during the reign of Mary I

Pole *n.* a native or inhabitant of Poland [G. fr. Pol. *poljane,* field-dwellers]

pole *n.* (*biol.*) either of two differentiated areas that lie at opposite ends of an axis, e.g. the ends of the spindle in mitosis or the animal and vegetal poles in an egg || either of the terminals of a battery, cell or dynamo etc. between which a current will flow when connected by an external conductor (i.e. between which a potential difference exists) || one of the two or more points in a magnet where most of the magnetic flux is concentrated || one of two extremes, *the poles of an argument* || a point of attraction **Pole** either end of the axis of a sphere, e.g. the North Pole or South Pole of the earth or the celestial sphere [fr. L. *polus* fr. Gk]

pole 1. *n.* a long, usually rounded piece of wood or other material, *tent pole, telegraph pole* || the wooden shaft of a wagon or carriage attached to the front axle and extending between the wheelhorses || a unit of length, esp. one measuring 16 ½ ft || a unit of area measuring 30 ¼ square yards || (*naut.*) a mast, esp. the upper end || the tail of an otter **2.** *v.t. pres. part.* **pol·ing** *past* and *past part.* **poled** to propel (a punt etc.) by using a pole || to furnish with poles, *to pole beans* [O.E. *pāl* fr. L.]

pole·ax, pole·axe (póulæks) **1.** *pl.* **pole·ax·es** *n.* (*hist.*) an ax set in a long handle used as a weapon || (*hist.*) such an ax fitted with a hook, used for grappling an enemy vessel, cutting the ship's tackle etc. || a long-handled, hammer-backed ax used for slaughtering cattle **2.** *v.t. pres. part.* **pole·ax·ing** *past* and *past part.* **pole·axed** to kill or render unconscious by hitting with a poleax [M.E. *pollax* fr. *poll,* the head+*ax,* ax]

pole bean a climbing bean (cf. BUSH BEAN)

pole·cat (póulkæt) *n.* *Mustela putorius,* fam. *Mustelidae,* a European carnivorous mammal about 2 ft long, having brown and black fur and white head markings || (*pop.*) a skunk [M.E. *polcat,* prob. fr. O.F. *pole,* a hen+CAT]

pole lamp lighting fixture with lamps on a pole, often from floor to ceiling

po·lem·ic (pəlémik, poulémik) **1.** *adj.* of or pertaining to controversy **2.** *n.* a disputation || a person who takes part in a controversy, esp. a theological controversy **po·lém·i·cal** *adj.* **po·lém·i·cist** *n.* a person who engages in polemics **po·lém·ics** *n.* (construed as *sing.* or *pl.*) the art or practice of theological disputation [fr. Gk *polemikos* fr. *polemos,* war]

po·lem·ol·ogy (pouləmɒ́lədʒi:) *n.* study of wars

po·len·ta (pouléntə) *n.* meal made of corn || a form of mush made from this [Ital.]

pole position 1. (*sports*) in a race, the position closest to the infield, i.e., the one offering shortest circumference. **2.** by extension, an outstandingly advantageous position

pole·star (póulstɑr) *n.* a bright star in the constellation Ursa Minor

pole strength a measure of the magnetic flux emanating from a given magnetic pole expressed in unit magnetic poles

pole vault a competitive athletic event in which a contestant vaults with the aid of a long pole of bamboo, aluminum etc. over a horizontal bar supported by two upright posts || this vault

po·lice (pəlí:s) *pl.* **po·lice** *n.* a department of government responsible for the preservation of public order, detection of crime and enforcement of civil law || the police force || (*pl.*) members of the police force, *a squad of mounted police* || any body of people whose job is to keep order and enforce regulations || (*mil.*) the act or process of putting and keeping in order (e.g. the grounds of an army camp) || (*mil.*) enlisted men assigned to perform a specific function (*KP) [F.]

police *pres. part.* **po·lic·ing** *past* and *past part.* **po·liced** *v.t.* to control, or maintain law and order in, by means of police || to provide with police || to exercise police control over (an area etc.) || to control, regulate etc. as if by means of police || (*mil.,* esp. with 'up') to clean and put in order (a camp, garrison etc.) [F. *policer* fr. L.L. fr. Gk and POLICE n.]

police constable (*Br.*) a rank-and-file member of the uniformed police force

police court a court of summary jurisdiction, presided over by a magistrate and dealing chiefly with minor offenses, but having the power to bind over for trial those guilty of more serious offenses

police dog a German shepherd (dog) || a dog trained to help the police. e.g. as a tracker

police force the entire body of local or national police

po·lice·man (pəlí:smən) *pl.* **po·lice·men** (pəlí:smən) *n.* a male member of a police force

police state a country in which the government uses its power arbitrarily over citizens mainly through police, esp. secret police

police station the headquarters of a local section of the police force where arrested persons are taken and police reports written

po·lice·wom·an (pəlí:swumən) *pl.* **po·lice·wom·en** (pəlí:swimən) *n.* a female member of a police force

pol·i·cy (pɒ́lisi:) *pl.* **pol·i·cies** *n.* a selected, planned line of conduct in the light of which individual decisions are made and coordination achieved, *advertising policy* || shrewdness in support of an aim, *would it be good policy to accept the invitation?* [O.F. *policie* fr. L. fr. Gk *politeia,* citizenship]

policy *pl.* **policies** *n.* a document containing the contract made between an individual and an insurance company || the numbers (lottery, *NUMBER) [fr. F. *police,* bill of lading]

pol·i·cy·hold·er (pɒ́lisi:houldər) *n.* a person holding an insurance policy

policy matrix the side effects of a policy on other issues and areas, e.g., disarmament on employment, income tax receipts, etc.

Po·lig·nac (pɔli:njæk), Jules Armand, prince de (1780–1847), French statesman, prime minister of France (1829–30). His reactionary government precipitated the revolution of 1830

Polignac Memorandum an assurance given (1823) by the Prince de Polignac, then French ambassador to London, at the request of Prime Minister Canning, to the effect that France would not provide any assistance to Spain if Spain should attempt to recover any of her lost territories in America

pol·i·met·rics (pɒlimétriks) *n.* the study of statistics of political science. **—pol·i·me·tri·cian** *n.*

po·li·o·my·e·li·tis (póuli:oumaiəláitis) *n.* (*pop. abbr.* polio) a serious infectious virus disease, esp. of children, caused by inflammation of the gray matter of the spinal cord, and characterized by fever, motor paralysis and muscular atrophy, often resulting in permanent deformity [Mod. L. fr. Gk *polios,* gray+MYELITIS]

Polisario (*acronym*) Popular Front for the Liberation of Western Sahara, an Algerian- and Libyan-backed guerrilla group seeking the independence of territory in Western Sahara from Morocco

Po·lish (póuliʃ) **1.** *adj.* of or pertaining to Poland, its inhabitants or their language **2.** *n.* the Slavic language of Poland

pol·ish (pɒ́liʃ) **1.** *v.t.* to make smooth and lustrous by rubbing, esp. by exerting a back-and-forth pressure on the waxed surface of || to cause (a person, his speech, behavior etc.) to become more refined or cultivated || to bring (a style, sentence etc.) nearer perfection || *v.i.* to take a polish **to polish off** to consume quickly, *to polish off a meal* || to dispose of completely, *to polish off an opponent* **to polish up** to make brighter by rubbing || to revise and improve, *to polish up one's French* **2.** *n.* a polishing or being polished || the lustrous surface of something polished || a preparation used in polishing || personal refinement or cultivation [F. *polir* (*poliss*)]

Polish Corridor the strip of land which linked Poland to the Baltic Sea between the two world wars. Following the lower Vistula, it separated East Prussia from the rest of Germany, and was a cause of disputes between Germany and Poland on account of its German population and the status of Danzig as a free city

Polish Succession, War of the a war (1733–5) between France, supported by Spain and Sardinia, and Austria, supported by Russia, on behalf of rival candidates for the Polish throne. At the end of the war, France recognized the Austrian candidate, Augustus III, while Stanislaus Leszczynski received the Lorraine duchies until his death, when they were to be annexed to France. Spain regained the Two Sicilies

Po·lit·bu·ro (pəlítbjuərou) *n.* (*hist.*) the former committee of the Russian Communist party for fixing policy between sessions of the Central Committee. It was replaced (1952) by a presidium **politburo** the policy-forming body and executive committee of a Communist party, e.g. of the Chinese [fr. Russ. *politicheskoe buro,* political bureau]

po·lite (pəláit, pouláit) *adj.* having good social manners || characterized by refinement, *polite usage* [fr. L. *polire* (*politus*), to polish]

Po·li·tian (poulíʃən) (Angelo Poliziano or Angelus Politianus 1454–94), Florentine humanist and poet. He translated parts of the Iliad and wrote 'Orfeo' (1475), one of the earliest plays in the Italian language. His poems, written in the Tuscan dialect, are classical in tone

pol·i·tic (pɒ́litik) *adj.* shrewdly judicious in support of an aim [F. *politique*]

po·lit·i·cal (pəlítik'l) *adj.* of or pertaining to politics || engaged in politics, *a political figure* [fr. L. *politicus* fr. Gk]

political animal (*colloq.*) one who thinks and acts like a politician, esp. in relations with others

political economy economics (as an academic study)

political retrogression withdrawal from a political group or organization in protest against its activities

political science the study of the nature and functions of the state and of government

pol·i·ti·cian (pɒlitíʃən) *n.* a person engaged in politics and in the techniques of civil government || (in a derogatory sense) a person engaged in politics merely for personal gain [POLITIC].

po·lit·i·ciz·a·tion (pəlitəsəzéiʃən) *n.* the process of becoming responsive to political forces or issues **—po·lit·i·cize** *v.* **—po·lit·i·cized** *adj.*

pol·i·tics (pɒ́litiks) *n.* the art and science of the government of a state || public affairs or public life as they relate to this || the opinions, principles or policies by which a person orders his participation in such affairs || scheming and maneuvering within a group, *college politics* [POLITIC]

pol·i·ty (pɒ́liti:) *pl.* **pol·i·ties** *n.* organized government || the form or constitution of a nation, state or community || a politically organized nation, state or community [O.F. *politie* fr. L. fr. Gk]

Polk (pouk), James Knox (1795–1849), 11th president of the U.S.A. (1845–9), a Democrat. He reestablished the independent treasury system (1846) and a very low tariff. He accepted the 49th parallel as the Oregon frontier (1846). After the Mexican War (1846–8), he annexed Texas, California and most of Arizona, Colorado, Nevada, Utah, New Mexico and Wyoming

pol·ka (póulkə, póukə) **1.** *n.* a lively dance in

duple time for couples, originating in Bohemia ‖ the music for this type of dance **2.** *v.i.* to dance the polka [F. and G. prob. fr. Czech *pulka,* half step]

polka dot one dot in a regular pattern of dots used as a design, esp. in textiles ‖ a material of this design

poll (poul) **1.** *n.* the number of votes cast in an election, *a heavy poll* ‖ the casting of votes ‖ (esp. *pl.*) the place where votes are cast and recorded ‖ the period of time during which votes may be cast ‖ a poll tax ‖ a canvassing of persons chosen at random or from a sample group in order to discover trends of public opinion ‖ the blunt end of a hammer, miner's pick etc. **2.** *v.t.* to receive (a number of votes) ‖ to record the votes of ‖ to canvass (people) in order to discover their opinions ‖ to cut off the horns of (cattle etc.) ‖ to pollard (a tree) ‖ *v.i.* to cast a vote [M.E. *pol, polle,* head fr. M. Du.]

pol·lack (pɒ́lək) *pl.* **pol·lack, pol·lacks** *n. Pollachius virens,* fam. *Gadidae,* a highly esteemed N. Atlantic food fish related to the cod, but having a longer lower jaw [etym. doubtful]

Pol·lai·uo·lo (pɒllaiwɔ́lɔ), Antonio (1429–98), Florentine painter, sculptor, goldsmith and engraver. He is famous for his muscular figures in action, and is said to have been the first painter to study anatomy by dissection. His brother Piero (1443–96) collaborated on many paintings

pol·lard (pɒ́lərd **1.** *n.* a tree cut back to the trunk so that a thick head of branches is formed by new growth ‖ a hornless variety of goat, ox, sheep etc. ‖ a feed for livestock consisting of a mixture of finely ground bran and coarse flour ‖ a coarse wheat bran **2.** *adj.* pollarded **3.** *v.t.* to cut back the branches of (a tree) so as to make a pollard [POLL]

pol·len (pɒ́lən) *n.* the male reproductive cells or microspores produced by and discharged from the anther of a seed plant [L.=fine flour]

pollen count the amount of pollen of a specific variety in a given volume of air at a specific time and place, useful in determining infective areas for sufferers from hay fever etc.

pol·lex (pɒ́leks) *pl.* **pol·li·ces** (pɒ́lisi:z) *n.* the thumb [L.]

pol·li·nate (pɒ́lineit) *pres. part.* **pol·li·nat·ing** *past* and *past part.* **pol·li·nat·ed** *v.t.* (of insects, wind etc.) to place pollen on the stigma of (a flower) **pol·li·ná·tion** *n.* [fr. L. *poll (pollinis),* fine flour]

polling booth (*Br.*) a voting booth

pol·li·nif·er·ous (pɒlinífərəs) *adj.* bearing or yielding pollen [fr. L. *pollen (pollinis),* fine flour+*-fer,* bearing]

pol·lin·i·um (pəlíni:əm) *pl.* **pol·lin·i·a** (pəlíni:ə) *n.* an agglutinated mass of pollen found esp. in the flowers of orchids [Mod. L. fr. *pollen (pollinis),* fine flour]

pol·li·wog, pol·ly·wog (pɒ́liwɒg) *n.* a tadpole [M.E. *polwygle* fr. *pol,* the head+WIGGLE]

Pol·lock (pɒ́lək), Sir Frederick (1845–1937), British jurist. His works include 'The History of English Law before the Time of Edward I' (with F. W. Maitland, 1895), 'The Principles of Contract' (1876) and 'The Law of Torts' (1887). His correspondence with Oliver Wendell Holmes was published as 'The Holmes-Pollock Letters' (1941)

Pollock, Jackson (1912–56), American painter, an originator of abstract expressionism. Using methods of automatism (e.g. dripping paint on canvas), he painted large, nonobjective compositions of rhythmic intensity

pol·lock (pɒ́lək) *pl.* **pol·lock, pol·locks** *n.* a pollack

poll tax a tax of a fixed amount per head levied on adults. In some states of the U.S.A. payment of a poll tax was formerly a prerequisite of voting but was declared unconstitutional by the U.S. Supreme Court (1966) in state elections, after the xxivth amendment (1964) to the U.S. constitution prohibited the requirement for federal elections

pol·lute (pəlú:t) *pres. part.* **pol·lut·ing** *past* and *past part.* **pol·lut·ed** *v.t.* to make unhealthily impure, *factory waste may pollute rivers* ‖ to corrupt, *books which pollute the mind*‖ to make ritually unclean [fr. L. *polluere (pollutus)*]

pol·lu·tion (pəlú:ʃən) *n.* a polluting or being polluted [fr. L. *pollutio (pollutionis)*]

pol·lut·ive (pəlu̧tiv) *adj.* causing pollution

pollywog *POLLIWOG

Pol·lux (pɒ́ləks) *DIOSCURI

Po·lo (póulou), Marco (1254–1324), Venetian traveler who went overland to China (1271–5) across the Pamirs and the Gobi Desert. After 17 years of itinerant service for Kublai Khan he returned (1292–5) by sea via Sumatra to Persia and thence overland home. His 'Book of Marco Polo' is the earliest firsthand European account of Asia

po·lo (póulou) *n.* a game played on horseback by two teams of three or four players on a ground 300 yds by 160 or 200 yds. Mallets with long flexible handles are used to drive a ball of bamboo or willow root down the field, and through the goalposts ‖ water polo [prob. fr. Tibetan *pulu,* the ball]

po·lo·cyte (póuləsait) *n.* one of the minute cells produced during the first and second meiotic division in maturation [fr. POLE (end of axis)+Gk *kutos,* hollow vessel]

po·lo·naise (pɒlənéiz, poulənéiz) *n.* a dignified dance in 3/4 time, of Polish origin ‖ the music for this dance ‖ a woman's garment consisting of a bodice and a short skirt divided in front and looped back over a longer skirt [F. fem. of *polonais,* Polish]

po·lo·neck (póulounek) *n.* (*Br.*) a turtleneck or sweater with this type of neck

Po·lo·ni·a (pəlóuni:ə) *n.* Poles in diaspora around the world

po·lo·ni·um (pəlóuni:əm) *n.* (radium F) a radioactive element which emits alpha particles as it decays (symbol Po, at. no. 84, at. mass 210), appearing during the disintegration of radium [Mod. L. fr. *Polonia,* Poland (named by Marie Curie)]

po·lo·ny (pəlóuni:) *pl.* **po·lo·nies** *n.* (*Br.*) a cooked, red-skinned sausage filled esp. with pork [corrup. of *Bologna* sausage]

polo shirt a man's knitted cotton sports shirt usually with a collar

Pol·ta·va (pʌltávə) an agricultural center (pop. 279,000) of the N. central Ukraine, U.S.S.R.: food processing, meat packing

pol·ter·geist (póultərgaist) *n.* a mischievous spirit which manifests its presence by throwing objects about noisily [G. fr. *polter,* uproar+*geist,* spirit]

pol·troon (pɒltrú:n) *n.* (*rhet.*) an abject coward **pol·tróon·er·y** *n.* (*rhet.*) cowardice [F. *poltron* fr. Ital.]

pol·y·a·cet·y·lene (pɒli:əsét'li:n) *n.* (*plastics*) a synthetic polymer capable of conducting electricity, used in making paper-thin batteries

pol·y·a·del·phous (pɒli:ədélfəs) *adj.* (*bot.*) having stamens joined by the anthers into three or more bundles [fr. Gk *polu,* many+*adelphos,* brother]

pol·y·an·drous (pɒli:ǽndrəs) *adj.* of or characterized by polyandry ‖ practicing polyandry ‖ (*bot.*) having many separate stamens [fr. Gk fr. *polu,* many+*anēr (andros),* man]

pol·y·an·dry (pɒ́li:ændri:, pɒli:ǽndri:) *n.* the state or practice of having more than one husband at the same time ‖ (*zool.*) the condition of having more than one male mate at a time ‖ (*bot.*) the presence of many separate stamens [fr. Gk *poluandria* fr. *polu,* many+*anēr (andros),* man]

pol·y·an·thus (pɒli:ǽnθəs) *pl.* **pol·y·an·thus·es, pol·y·an·thi** (pɒli:ǽnθai) *n. Primula polyantha,* fam. *Primulaceae,* a hybrid supposedly derived from three primulas ‖ *Narcissus tazetta,* a narcissus having small umbellate yellow or white flowers [Mod. L. fr. Gk *polu,* many+*anthos,* flower]

pol·y·arch·y (pɒ́li:ɑrki:) *n.* a free democratic, literate, decentralized, politically well-organized society with high economic and political mobility. Wealth and power rest with the rank and file

pol·y·ba·sic (pɒli:béisik) *adj.* (*chem..* of acids) having more than one hydrogen atom replaceable by a basic atom or radical ‖ (of a salt) containing two or more atoms of a univalent metal [fr. Gk *polu,* many+BASIC]

pol·y·ben·zim·id·a·zole (pɒli:benzimídəzoul) a synthetic polymer that, as a fiber, creates a textile suitable for clothing, that does not melt, burn in air or become stiff when charred; developed by NASA. *abbr.* **PBI**

Po·lyb·i·us (pəlíbi:əs) (c. 200–c. 125 B.C.), Greek historian. Sent as a hostage to Rome (168 B.C.), he gained the patronage of Scipio Aemilianus. He wrote a 'History' of the period 264–146 B.C. in 40 books, of which five survive complete and the rest in excerpts

pol·y·car·bon·ate (pɒli:kárbəneit) *n.* (*chem.*) any of a group of hard thermoplastics with great resistance to impact and to softening

Pol·y·carp (pɒ́li:kɑrp), St (c. 69–c. 155), bishop of Smyrna (c. 105–55) and martyr. A disciple of St John, he forms a link between the Apostolic period and the early Church Fathers. Feast: Jan. 26

pol·y·cen·trism (pɒli:séntrizəm) *n.* the principle of having many political or management centers. **—pol·y·cen·tric** *adj.* **—pol·y·cen·trist** *n.*

pol·y·chaete, pol·y·chete (pɒ́liki:t) **1.** *adj.* of or relating to *Polychaeta,* a large class of chiefly marine annelid worms, usually having well-developed parapodia and characterized by the numerous bristles on their appendages **2.** *n.* a member of this class [fr. Mod. L. *Polychaeta* fr. Gk *polu,* many+*chaitē,* bristle]

pol·y·cha·sium (pɒli:kéiʒəm) *pl.* **pol·y·cha·sia** (pɒli:kéiʒə) *n.* (*bot.*) a cymose inflorescence in which each main axis produces three or more branches [Mod. L. fr. Gk *polu,* many+*chasis,* division]

polychete *POLYCHAETE

pol·y·chlo·rin·at·ed biphenyl (pɒli:klɔ́rineitid) (*chem.*) highly toxic, very persistent carcinogenic pollutant used in plastics and as an insulator in electrical devices. It has been banned since 1977. *abbr.* **PCB**

pol·y·chro·mat·ic (pɒli:kroumǽtik) *adj.* multicolored [fr. Gk *polu,* many+CHROMATIC]

polychromatic theory concept of seven types of vision color reception: crimson, orange, yellow, green, blue green, blue, and blue violet

pol·y·chrome (pɒ́li:kroum) **1.** *adj.* painted or printed in many colors **2.** *n.* a work of art, esp. a late 6th-c. B.C. Athenian vase, decorated in many colors **pol·y·chróm·ic** *adj.* **pól·y·chrom·y** *n.* [F. fr. Gk *polu,* many+*chrōma,* color]

pol·y·clin·ic (pɒli:klínik) *n.* a clinic or hospital where many sorts of disease are treated

Pol·y·cli·tus (pɒli:kláitəs) Greek sculptor and architect (5th c. B.C.). A contemporary of Phidias, he excelled in bronze sculptures of the male nude. His theory of proportions as applied in the 'Doryphoros' (Spear Bearer) became a standard for other sculptors. No original works survive, but there are many Greek and Roman copies

pol·y·cot·y·le·don (pɒli:kɒt'lí:d'n) *n.* (*bot.*) a plant, e.g. a conifer having more than two cotyledons **pol·y·cot·y·lé·don·ous** *adj.* [Mod. L. fr. Gk *polu,* many+COTYLEDON]

Po·lyc·ra·tes (pəlíkrəti:z) (*d.* c. 522 B.C.), tyrant of Samos (c. 540–c. 522 B.C.). After establishing himself as ruler, he built Samos into a major naval power. He gave Cambyses II strong support against the Egyptians in the Persian Wars

pol·y·crys·tal·line diamond (pɒli:krístəlin) synthetic diamond substitutes bonded to tungsten carbide cutters, used as protective coatings for industrial cutting tools; developed by General Electric Co.

pol·y·dac·tyl (pɒli:dǽkt'l) **1.** *adj.* having more than the normal number of fingers and toes **2.** *n.* a polydactyl person or animal **pol·y·dác·tyl·ism, pol·y·dác·ty·ly** *ns* [fr. Gk *polu,* many+*daktulos,* finger]

pol·y·dae·mon·ism, pol·y·de·mon·ism (pɒli:dí:mənizəm) *n.* the belief in or worship of many divinities, esp. those having evil powers [fr. Gk *polu,* many+*daimon,* divinity]

pol·y·e·lec·tro·lytes (pɒli:iléktrəlaits) *n.* (*chem.*) synthetic chemicals that help solids to clump during sewage treatment

pol·y·em·bry·o·ny (pɒli:émbri:ɒni:) *n.* the condition of giving birth to genetically identical offspring (identical twins, triplets, etc.) **—pol·y·em·bry·on·ic** *adj.*

pol·y·es·tra·di·ol (pɒli:estréidi:əl) *n.* (*pharm.*) estrogen drug used in treatment of carcinoma of the prostate; marketed as Estradurin. *abbr.* **PEP**

pol·y·e·thers (pɒli:í:θərz) *n.* (*plastics*) a group of long-chain dihydric alcohols in a viscous liquid used in producing emulsifying agents, antistatic agents and polyurethane foam

pol·y·ethyl·ene (pɒli:éθəli:n) *n.* one of a group of thermoplastics ($-CH_2CH_2-$)x, lightweight and varying in flexibility and having high resistance to chemicals, and good insulating properties, used in food packaging, insulation etc. [fr. Gk *polu,* many+ETHYLENE]

po·lyg·a·mist (pəlígəmist) *n.* a person who practices polygamy [POLYGAMY]

po·lyg·a·mous (pəlígəməs) *adj.* having more than one wife or husband ‖ (*zool.*) having more than one mate at the same time ‖ (*bot.*) bearing male, female or hermaphrodite flowers on the same plant [fr. Gk *polugamos*]

CONCISE PRONUNCIATION KEY: **(a)** æ, *cat;* ɑ, *car;* ɔ *fawn;* ei, *snake.* **(e)** e, *hen;* i:, *sheep;* iə, *deer;* ɛə, *bear.* **(i)** i, *fish;* ai, *tiger;* ə:, *bird.* **(o)** o, *ox;* au, *cow;* ou, *goat;* u, *poor;* ɔi, *royal.* **(u)** ʌ, *duck;* u, *bull;* u:, *goose;* ə, *bacillus;* ju:, *cube.* x, *loch;* θ, *think;* ð, *bother;* z, *Zen;* ʒ, *corsage;* dʒ, *savage;* ŋ, *orangutang;* j, *yak;* ʃ, *fish;* tʃ, *fetch;* 'l, *rabble;* 'n, *redden.* Complete pronunciation key appears inside front cover.

po·lyg·a·my (pəlígəmi:) *n.* the state or practice of being polygamous [F. *polygamie* fr. L. fr. Gk fr. *polu,* many+*gamos,* marriage]

pol·y·gen·e·sis (pɒli:dʒénisis) *n.* (*biol.*) the theory that the human races originate from a few primitive types taken as species

pol·y·ge·net·ic (pɒli:dʒənétik) *adj.* of or relating to polygenesis

pol·y·glass or polyglas (pɒli:glǽs) *n.* (*plastics*) a polyester fiber cord used in automobile tire belts in order to improve wear

pol·y·glot (pɒ́li:glɒt) **1.** *adj.* speaking or writing several languages ‖ containing or made up of several languages, *a polyglot text* **2.** *n.* a person who knows several languages ‖ a book, esp. the Bible, containing the same text in many languages [fr. Gk *poluglōttos* fr. *polu,* many+*glōtta,* tongue]

Polyglot Bible a Bible in which texts in several languages are printed in parallel columns. Such Bibles were produced by Origen (early 3rd c.), at Alcala (1502–17) by Cisneros, at Antwerp (1569–73), in Paris (1645) and in London (1654–7)

pol·y·gon (pɒ́li:gɒn) *n.* a plane figure enclosed by five or more straight lines **po·lyg·o·nal** (pəlígən'l) *adj.* [fr. L.L. *polygonum* fr. Gk fr. *polu,* many+*gōnia,* angle]

polygon law of vectors the statement that if any number of vectors are represented by straight lines, taken in order and having the same cyclic sense, they are equivalent to a single vector represented by the straight line, drawn in the opposite sense, needed to complete the polygon

polygraph *LIE DETECTOR

po·lyg·y·nous (pəlídʒinəs) *adj.* of, relating to, practicing or characterized by polygyny [fr. Mod. L. *polygynus*]

po·lyg·y·ny (pəlídʒini:) *n.* the state or practice of having several wives at the same time ‖ (*zool.*) the condition of having more than one female mate at a time ‖ (*bot.*) the condition of bearing male, female or hermaphrodite flowers on the same plant [fr. Gk *polu, many+gunē,* woman]

pol·y·he·dral (pɒli:hí:drəl) *adj.* of or relating to, or having the form of, a polyhedron [fr. Gk *poluedros* fr. *polu,* many+*hedra,* base]

pol·y·he·dron (pɒli:hí:drən) *pl.* **pol·y·he·dra** (pɒli:hi:drə), **pol·y·he·drons** *n.* (*geom.*) a figure or solid formed usually by seven or more plane faces [Gk *poluedron*]

Pol·y·hym·ni·a (pɒlihímni:ə) the Muse of sacred song [L. fr. Gk fr. *polu,* many +*humnia,* hymn]

poly I:C *n.* (*physiol.*) chemical resembling a two-stranded RNA that stimulates body production of interferon

pol·y·mer (pɒ́ləmər) *n.* a natural or synthetic substance or mixture, usually of high molecular mass, whose molecules are formed polymerization and consist usually of a linked sequence of identical chemical units (*HIGH POLYMER, *COPOLYMER). Cellulose, lignin, nucleic acids, hair and horn are among a vast number of naturally occurring polymers. Nylon, rayon and rubber are some important synthetic polymers **pol·y·mer·ic** (pɒləmérik) *adj.* **pol·y·mer·ism** (pɒ́ləmərizəm) *n.* [fr. Gk *polu,* many+*meros,* part]

pol·ym·er·ase (púli:mərẹis) *n.* (*physiol.*) any of a group of enzymes that catalyze polymerization assisting in the formation of DNA or RNA

po·lym·er·i·za·tion (pəlịmərizéiʃən) *n.* a chemical reaction in which two or more small molecules react to form larger molecules, eventually resulting in long chains of identical repeating units (*COPOLYMER) ‖ the state of being combined in this way

po·lym·er·ize (pəlíməraiz) *v. pres. part.* **po·lym·er·iz·ing** *past* and *past part.* **po·lym·er·ized** *v.t.* to subject to polymerization ‖ *v.i.* to undergo polymerization

pol·y·mide resin (púli:mạid) (*chem.*) a group of synthetic polymeric resins, strongly heat resistant, used in insulators, coatings, semiconductors and adhesives

pol·y·morph (pɒ́li:mɔrf) *n.* (*biol.*) a leucocyte having the nucleus complexly lobed ‖ (*crystall.*) a substance capable of being crystallized into various forms ‖ one of these forms **pol·y·mór·phic** *adj.* polymorphous **pol·y·mór·phism** *n.* (*biol.*) occurrence of different forms of individuals in the same species ‖ (*biol.*) occurrence of different forms, or different forms of organs, in the same individual at different periods of life (e.g. in some coelenterates) ‖ (*crystall.*) the quality of crystallizing into various forms [fr. Gk *polymorphos,* multiform fr. *polu,* many+*morphē,* form]

pol·y·mor·phous (pɒli:mɔ́rfəs) *adj.* capable of assuming two or more forms [fr. Gk *polymorphos,* multiform]

Pol·y·ne·sia (pɒliní:ʒə, pɒliní:ʃə) the eastern division of Oceania, including French Polynesia, the Hawaiian Is, Samoa, Tonga, the Line, Cook, Phoenix and Ellice Is, and Easter Is.

Pol·y·ne·sian (pɒliní:ʒən, pɒliní:ʃən) **1.** *adj.* of, relating to, or characteristic of Polynesia, its people or its languages **2.** *n.* a native of the Polynesian islands ‖ the group of Austronesian languages spoken there

po·ly·ni·a (pəlíni:ə) *n.* a lakelike patch of clear water in floating ice, esp. if found in the same area every year [Russ. *poluinya*]

pol·y·no·mi·al (pɒlinóumi:əl) **1.** *adj.* (*math.,* of an algebraic expression) having two or more terms **2.** *n.* an expression of this kind [fr. Gk. *polu,* many+NOMIAL]

pol·y·o·ma virus (pɒli:óumə) (*med.*) a DNA virus associated with cancer in mammals. *also* polyoma

pol·y·o·mi·no (pɒli:ɒmí:nou) *n.* a multisided shape capable of covering many squares on a game board *Cf* PENTOMINO

pol·yp (pɒ́lip) *n.* any of various coelenterates, such as those building coral reefs, having tubular, hollow bodies and an anterior mouth surrounded by tentacles ‖ a projecting growth of hypertrophied mucous membrane, e.g. in the nasal passages [F. *polype* fr. L. fr. Gk fr. *polu,* many+*pous (podos),* foot]

pol·y·par·y (pɒ́lipẹri:) *pl.* **pol·y·par·ies** *n.* the common base and connecting tissue of a colony of polyps [fr. Mod. L. *polyparium* fr. *polypus,* polyp]

pol·y·pep·tide (pɒli:péptaid) *n.* any combination of several amino-acid molecules [fr. Gk *polu,* many+PEPTIDE]

pol·y·pet·al·ous (pɒli:pét'ləs) *adj.* (*bot.*) having separate or distinct petals (opp. GAMOPETALOUS) [fr. Gk *polu,* many PETA-LOUS]

pol·y·phase (pɒ́li:fẹiz) *adj.* (*elec.*) having or producing two or more phases [fr. Gk *polu,* many+PHASE]

Pol·y·phe·mus (pɒlifí:məs) a one-eyed giant or Cyclops in Homer's 'Odyssey', who kept Odysseus and his companions prisoners. He ate two of his prisoners each day, until Odysseus made him drunk and blinded him

pol·y·phon·ic (pɒli:fɒ́nik) *adj.* (*mus.*) comprising two or more melodies combined ‖ (of musical instruments, e.g. the piano) able to sound more than one note at a time ‖ consisting of many sounds ‖ (*phon.*) representing more than one vocal sound by the same symbol or group of symbols **po·lyph·o·nous** (pəlífənəs) *adj.* [fr. Gk *poluphōnos* fr. *polu,* many+*phōnē,* sound]

po·lyph·o·ny (pəlífəni:) *n.* (*mus.*) composition in two or more concurrent and harmonizing parts or voices (cf. HOMOPHONY) ‖ (*phon.*) the use of one written character to represent more than one sound [fr. Gk *polyphōnia*]

pol·y·phy·let·ic (pɒli:failétik) *adj.* (*biol.*) combining the characteristics of more than one ancestral line, e.g. by convergence [fr. Gk *polu,* many+*phulētēs,* of the same clan]

pol·y·pide (pɒ́li:paid) *n.* a single polyp, an individual of a zooid colony [POLYP]

pol·y·ploid (pɒ́li:plɔid) **1.** *adj.* with a reduplication of the chromosome number, e.g. triploid, tetraploid etc., i.e. having three, four etc. times the normal haploid or gametic number **2.** *n.* an organism with more than two sets of chromosomes **pol·y·plói·dic** *adj.* **pól·y·ploi·dy** *n.* a manifold arrangement of chromosomes, esp. when this is induced to enhance the size and vigor of plants [fr. Gk *polu,* many+*ploos,* fold]

pol·y·poid (pɒ́li:pɔid) *adj.* of or like a polyp [POLYP]

pol·y·pro·pyl·ene [C_3H_5] (pɒli:próupəli:n) *n.* a thermoplastic resin that is a moisture-resistant, hard, tough plastic used to molded objects in plates, fibers, film, rope and toys; manufactured by Hercules, Inc.

po·lyp·ter·id (pəlíptərid) *n.* a member of fam. *Polypteridae,* primitive, tropical African river fishes having long bodies, ganoid scales and one characteristic dorsal fin separated into a series of spines [fr. Mod. L. *Polypterus,* the type genus, fr. Gk *polu,* many+*pteron,* wing]

pol·y·pus (pɒ́ləpəs) *pl.* **pol·y·pi** (pɒ́ləpai), **pol·y·pus·es** *n.* a polyp (projecting growth) [L. fr. Gk *polu,* many+*pous (podos),* foot]

pol·y·ri·bo·some (pɒli:rúibəsọum) *n.* a cluster of the cell particles held together by a single messenger RNA that synthesize proteins and enzymes. *also* polysome. **—pol·y·ri·bo·som·al** *adj.*

pol·y·sac·cha·ride (pɒli:sǽkəraid) *n.* one of a class of carbohydrates which are decomposable by hydrolysis into two or more molecules of monosaccharides and which include the oligosaccharides as well as high-molecular-weight polymeric substances of complex and often indeterminate structure (e.g. glycogen, starch, cellulose) [fr. Gk *polu,* many+SACCHARIDE]

pol·y·sor·bates (pɒli:sɔ́rbeits) *n.* (*chem.*) group of fatty-acid esters used as emulsifying, dispersing and solubilizing agents in production of certain foods and drugs

pol·y·sty·rene (pɒli:stáiri:n) *n.* a transparent rigid thermoplastic used in making containers and other molded products, e.g. refrigerators [fr. Gk *polu,* many+STYRENE]

pol·y·syl·lab·ic (pɒli:silǽbik) *adj.* having more than three syllables **pol·y·syl·láb·i·cal** *adj.* [fr. M.L. *polysyllabas* fr. Gk *polu,* many+*sullabē,* syllable]

pol·y·syl·la·ble (pɒ́lisiləb'l, pɒlisíləb'l) *n.* a polysyllabic word [fr. M.L. *polysyllaba* fr. Gk fr. *polu,* many+*sullabē,* syllable]

polysystemicism (*linguistics*) *FIRTHIAN

pol·y·tech·nic (pɒli:téknik) **1.** *adj.* of or pertaining to instruction in a number or technical subjects **2.** *n.* a school giving instruction of this kind **pol·y·téch·ni·cal** *adj.* **pol·y·tech·ní·cian** *n.* [F. *polytechnique* fr. Gk fr. *polu,* many+*technē,* an art]

pol·y·the·ism (pɒ́li:θi:ịzəm, pɒliθí:izəm) *n.* belief in or worship of more than one god **pól·y·the·ist** *n.* **pol·y·the·ís·tic** *adj.* [F. *polythéisme* fr. Gk fr. *polu,* many+*theos,* god]

pol·y·thene (pɒ́liθi:n) *n.* polyethylene

pol·y·to·nal·i·ty (pɒli:tounǽliti:) *n.* (*mus.*) the simultaneous use of two or more keys, or the effect of this [fr. Gk *polu,* many+TONALITY]

pol·y·troph·ic (pɒli:trɒ́fik) *adj.* (*bacteriol.*) obtaining nourishment from more than one organic substance or organism [fr. Gk *polutrophos* fr. *polu,* many+*trophos,* feeder]

pol·y·un·sat·u·rate (pɒli:ʌnsǽtʃəreit) *n.* (*chem.*) an oil or fatty acid containing more than one double or triple bond and therefore cholesterol-defensive, e.g., certain fish and vegetable oils. **—pol·y·un·sat·u·rat·ed** *adj.*

pol·y·va·lence (pɒli:véiləns) *n.* the state of being polyvalent

pol·y·va·lent (pɒli:véilənt, pəlívələnt) *adj.* (*bacteriol.*) containing antibodies able to counteract more than one kind of microorganism ‖ (*chem.*) having a valence of more than 1 (cf. MULTIVALENT) [fr. Gk *polu,* many+VALENT]

polyversity *MULTIVERSITY

pol·y·vi·nyl (pɒli:váinil, pɒli:váin'l) *adj.* of a compound made by polymerizing a vinyl compound [fr. Gk *polu,* many+VINYL]

polyvinyl acetal any of several thermoplastic resins made by condensing polyvinyl alcohol with an aldehyde, and used chiefly in molded products and adhesives

polyvinyl acetate a polymer of vinyl acetate used esp. in adhesives, textile processes etc.

polyvinyl alcohol a polymer of vinyl alcohol, esp. a thermoplastic resin used in molded products, emulsifiers etc.

polyvinyl chloride a polymer of vinyl chloride, rigid unless plasticized, used for pipes, electrical insulation, films etc.

pol·y·zo·an (pɒli:zóuən) *n.* a bryozoan [fr. Gk *polu,* many+*zōon,* animal]

pol·y·zo·ar·i·um (pɒli:zouɛ́əri:əm) *pl.* **pol·y·zo·ar·i·a** (pɒli:zouɛ́əri:ə) *n.* (*zool.*) a bryozoan colony or its supporting skeleton [Mod. L. fr. *Polyzoa,* name of the class]

pol·y·zo·ic (pɒli:zóuik) *adj.* (*zool.*) comprising many zooids ‖ producing many sporozoites [fr. *Polyzoa,* name of the class of bryozoans]

pom·ace (pʌ́mis) *n.* a mass of apple pulp crushed for cider-making ‖ some other crushed or pulpy substance, e.g. seeds for oil [fr. L. *pomum,* apple]

po·ma·ceous (pouméiʃəs) *adj.* (*bot.*) of, relating to, or resembling a pome [fr. Mod. L. *pomaceus*]

po·made (pəméid, pəmád) **1.** *n.* a scented ointment for the hair **2.** *v.t. pres. part.* **po·mad·ing** *past* and *past part.* **po·mad·ed** to apply pomade to [F. *pommade*]

po·man·der (poumǽndər, póumændər) *n.* (*hist.*) a ball of fragrant or aromatic substances carried as protection against infection ‖ (*hist.*) a metal ball containing this ‖ an orange pierced with cloves and dried, and hung in a wardrobe etc. for fragrance [earlier *pomamber* fr. O.F. *pomme d'embre,* apple of amber]

po·ma·to (pəméitou) *n.* (*agriculture*) hybrid potato and tomato

po·ma·tum (pəméitəm) *n.* a pomade [Mod. L. fr. L. *pomum,* apple, fruit]

Pom·bal (pɔmbúl), Sebastião José de Carvalho e Mello, marquês de (1699–1782), Portuguese statesman. As foreign secretary (1750–77) to Joseph I, he was the effective ruler of Portugal. In an attempt to modernize the country, he limited the power of the Inquisition and the wealth of the Church, expelled the Jesuits (1759), encouraged trade and replanned Lisbon after the earthquake of 1755

pome (poum) *n.* (*bot.*) a fruit, e.g. an apple, having a seed-containing core enclosed within a cartilaginous capsule and surrounded by the fleshy, edible receptacle [O.F.=apple, fruit]

pome·gran·ate (pɒ́mgrænit, pɒ́migrænit) *n. Punica granatum,* fam. *Punicaceae,* a small shrubby tree, native to Asia and Africa ‖ its edible, orange-sized fruit, consisting of a succulent crimson pulp containing many seeds and enclosed in a tough golden red rind [O.F. *pome grenade, grenate* fr. *pome,* apple, fruit+*grenade, grenate,* seeded, grained]

pom·e·lo (pɒ́məlou) *pl.* **pom·e·los** *n.* a shaddock ‖ a grapefruit [origin unknown]

Pom·er·a·ni·a (pɒməréiniːə) a region bordering the Baltic on both sides of the Oder in N.W. Poland and N.E. East Germany. It was inhabited by German tribes, and conquered by Slavs by the 10th c. The western part was colonized by Germans, became a duchy of the Holy Roman Empire (1181), passed to Sweden (1648) and was taken by Prussia (1720 and 1815). Most of this became the German state of Mecklenburg (1945). The eastern part passed to Prussia (1648) and was taken by Poland (1945)

Pom·er·a·ni·an (pɒməréiniːən) **1.** *adj.* of or relating to Pomerania or its people **2.** *n.* a native or inhabitant of Pomerania ‖ a small black, white or brown dog of a breed having a pointed muzzle, erect ears, upturned tail and long silky hair

pom·mel (pʌ́məl) **1.** *n.* a knob on a sword hilt ‖ a knoblike projection on the front of a saddle **2.** *v.t. pres. part.* **pom·mel·ing,** esp. *Br.* **pom·mel·ling** *past* and *past part.* **pom·meled,** esp. *Br.* **pom·melled to** pummel [O.F. *pomel,* dim. of *pome,* apple]

po·mo·log·i·cal (pɒuməlɒ́dʒik'l) *adj.* of or relating to pomology

po·mol·o·gist (poumɒ́lədʒist) *n.* a person who cultivates fruit professionally [POMOLOGY]

po·mol·o·gy (poumɒ́lədʒiː) *n.* the science and practice of fruit cultivation [fr. Mod. L. *pomologia* fr. *pomum,* apple, fruit+Gk *logos,* word]

pomp (pɒmp) *n.* splendor in display, esp. ceremonial magnificence [F. *pompe* fr. L. fr. Gk *pompē,* procession]

Pom·pa·dour (pɔ̃pæduːr, pɒ́mpədɔr, pɒ́mpədour), Jeanne Antoinette Poisson, marquise de (1721–64), mistress of Louis XV of France (from 1745), over whom and over whose government she wielded great influence. She is thought to have been instrumental in forming the Austrian alliance which involved France in the Seven Years' War. She spent prodigally, but patronized writers and artists, and founded the royal porcelain factory at Sèvres

pom·pa·dour (pɒ́mpədr, pɒ́mpədour, pɒ́mpəduər) *n.* a woman's hairstyle in which the hair is drawn in a high roll up over the forehead ‖ a man's hairstyle in which the hair is brushed straight up and back from the forehead [after the marquise de POMPADOUR]

pom·pa·no (pɒ́mpənou) *pl.* **pom·pa·no, pom·pa·nos** *n. Trachinotus carolinus.* fam. *Carangidae,* an edible fish of the S. Atlantic and Gulf coasts of North America [Span. *pámpano*]

Pom·peii (pɒmpéi, pɒmpéiiː) an ancient Roman port and resort (now inland) in Campania, Italy, near Naples, buried by a sudden eruption of Vesuvius (79). Excavations have uncovered many buildings with their walls nearly intact, wall paintings, mosaics, furniture etc.

Pom·pei·us (pɒmpéiəs), Sextus (75–35 B.C.), Roman soldier, son of Pompey. He attempted to avenge his father's death, was defeated (36 B.C.) by the future Emperor Augustus, and killed

Pom·pey (pɒ́mpiː) (Gnaeus Pompeius Magnus, 106–48 B.C.), Roman soldier and statesman. He distinguished himself as a general and became consul (70 B.C.). He decisively defeated Mithridates VI (66 B.C.) and annexed Syria and Palestine. He formed the lst Triumvirate with Crassus and Caesar (60 B.C.) but broke with Caesar (54 B.C.), was defeated by him at Pharsalus (48 B.C.) and assassinated on arrival in Egypt. He had great military ability but was irresolute in politics

Pom·pi·dou (pɔmpiːduː), Georges (1911–74), French statesman. He was prime minister (1962–8) and president of the republic (1969–74). He died in office

pom·pom (pɒ́mpɒm) *n.* an automatic antiaircraft gun firing explosive shells, mounted on ships' decks in pairs, fours or eights

pom·pon (pɒ́mpɒn, pɔ̃pɔ̃) *n.* a small, brightly colored ball usually of yarn used for ornamenting women's and children's hats, sailors' caps etc. ‖ a dwarf cabbage rose ‖ any of several varieties of chrysanthemum or dahlia bearing small round flowers [F.=a tuft, topknot]

pom·pos·i·ty (pɒmpɒ́sitiː) *pl.* **pom·pos·i·ties** *n.* the quality of being full of self-importance ‖ an instance of behavior revealing this [fr. M.L. *pompositas*]

pomp·ous (pɒ́mpəs) *adj.* (of people) full of ridiculous self-importance ‖ (of language) inflated, pretentious [O.F. *pompeux*]

Pon·ce (pɔ́nθe) the chief Caribbean port (pop. 188,219) of Puerto Rico. Industries: sugar, rum, textiles. Spanish fort, cathedral. University of Santa Maria (Roman Catholic, 1948)

ponce (pɒns) *n.* (*Br., pop.*) a pimp [origin unknown]

Pon·ce de Le·ón (pɔ́nθeðeleɔ́n, pɒ́nsdəlíːoun), Juan (c. 1460–1521), Spanish explorer. He was governor of Puerto Rico (1509–12) and explored the coast of Florida (1513), claiming it for Spain

pon·cho (pɒ́ntʃou) *pl.* **pon·chos** *n.* a Spanish-American cloak like a blanket with a central slit for the head ‖ a waterproof garment made like this [Span. fr. Araucan]

pond (pɒnd) *n.* a small area of still water, in a natural or contrived hollow‖ an area of water smaller than a lake [M.E. *ponde,* var. of POUND]

pon·der (pɒ́ndər) *v.i.* (often with 'on' or 'over') to meditate, be absorbed in thought ‖ *v.t.* to consider carefully, *to ponder a problem* [O. F. *ponderer*]

pon·der·a·bil·i·ty (pɒndərəbíliti:) *n.* the state or quality of being ponderable

pon·der·a·ble (pɒ́ndərəb'l) *adj.* able to be weighed ‖ able to be assessed, *a ponderable influence* [fr. L. L. *ponderabilis*]

pon·der·ous (pɒ́ndərəs) *adj.* (of style or manner) lacking ease and a light touch, *ponderous wit* ‖ (of movement) slow, lumbering ‖ (*rhet.,* of weights) very heavy [fr. F. *pondéreux*]

Pon·di·cher·ry (pɒnditʃéri:) (*F.* Pondichéry) a seaport (pop. 60,000) on the Coromandel coast of India comprising, with Karikal, Mahé and Yanaon, a Union Territory (total area 186 sq. miles, pop. 570,000) of India. Official language: French. Pondicherry was the chief settlement of French India (1674–1954), but was taken by the Dutch (1693–7) and by the British (1761–3, 1778–83, 1793–1802 and 1803–16)

Pon·do·land (pɒ́ndəlænd) *TRANSKEIAN TERRITORIES

pond scum any floating filamentous alga of fam. *Zygnemataceae,* esp. the genus *Spirogyra*

pond·weed (pɒ́ndwiːd) *n.* any of several species of *Potomogeton,* fam. *Potamogetonaceae,* a genus of aquatic plants

pone (poun) *n.* cornmeal bread shaped into ovals, then fried or baked [fr. Algonquian=bread]

pon·gee (pɒndʒíː, pʌndʒíː) *n.* a thin, soft, silk fabric of Chinese origin having its natural écru color [fr. N. Chin. *pun-chi,* domestic loom]

pons (pɒnz) *n.* the pons Varolii [L.=bridge]

pons as·i·no·rum (pɒ́nzæsinɔ́rəm, pɒ́nzæsinóurəm) *n.* the fifth proposition of the first book of Euclid ‖ anything that beginners find hard to understand

pons Va·ro·li·i (pɒ́nzvərɔ́uliai) *n.* that part the brainstem (*BRAIN) at the anterior end of the medulla oblongata transmitting impulses between the cerebrum and cerebellum [Mod. L.=bridge of Varoli, after Costanzo *Varoli* (1542-75), Italian anatomist]

Pon·te·ve·dra (pɒntevédrɑ) a province (area 1,695 sq. miles, pop. 859,897) of N.W. Spain (*GALICIA) ‖ its capital (pop. 47,000)

Pon·ti (pɔ́nti:), Gio (Giovanni Ponti, 1891–1979), Italian architect. He is best known for the Pirelli skyscraper, Milan (1955–9), designed in collaboration with Nervi

Pon·ti·ac (pɒ́ntiːæk) (c. 1720–69), Ottawa Indian chief who led (1763–5) Pontiac's Rebellion. This brought together the most powerful Indian coalition in Indian history to resist the white man. Pontiac signed (1766) a formal peace treaty with the British which permitted peaceful coexistence

Pon·ti·a·nak (pɒntiːɑ́nɑk) the chief port and commercial center (pop. 217,555) of W. Kalimantan, Indonesia

pon·ti·fex (pɒ́ntifeks) *pl.* **pon·tif·i·ces** (pɒntífisiːz) *n.* (*Rom. hist.*) a priest of the principal college of priests (cf. FLAMEN) [L.]

pon·tiff (pɒ́ntif) *n.* the pope ‖ a bishop ‖ a pontifex [F. *pontife*]

pon·tif·i·cal (pɒntífik'l) **1.** *adj.* of or relating to a pontiff ‖ celebrated by a bishop, *pontifical mass* ‖ absurdly dogmatic or pretentious, *pontifical utterances* **2.** *n.* a book setting out the forms for sacraments and rites performed by a bishop ‖ (*pl.*) vestments and insignia worn by a bishop when he celebrates a pontifical mass [fr. L. *pontificalis*]

pon·tif·i·cate 1. (pɒntífikeit) *v.i. pres. part.* **pon·tif·i·cat·ing** *past* and *past part.* **pon·tif·i·cat·ed** (of a pope or bishop) to officiate at a pontifical mass ‖ (of a person) to act in an absurdly solemn and dogmatic way **2.** (pɒntífikit, pɒntífikeit) *n.* the office or term of office of a pope or bishop [fr. L. *pontificare* (*pontificatus*)]

pontifices *pl.* of PONTIFEX

pon·til (pɒ́ntil) *n.* a punty [F. fr. Ital. *pontello,* dim. of *punto,* point]

Pon·tine marshes (pɒ́ntain) (*Ital.* Agro pontino) a narrow plain near the coast of S. Latium, Italy, beginning 25 miles southeast of Rome. The Romans and various popes tried to drain its malarial marshes, but this was not achieved until 1926, under Mussolini

Pon·tius Pilate (pɒ́nʃəs) *PILATE, Pontius

pon·ton (pɒ́ntən) *n.* (*mil.*) a pontoon [F.]

pon·to·nier, pon·to·neer (pɒntəníər) *n.* (*mil.*) a military engineer who builds pontoon bridges [F. *pontonnier*]

pon·toon (pɒntúːn) *n.* a flat-bottomed boat or a metal cylinder used in quantity to support a temporary bridge ‖ in a low, flat boat carrying equipment for sinking shafts at sea, raising sunken ships etc. ‖ a float of an aircraft [F. *ponton*]

pontoon *n.* (*Br.*) blackjack (card game)

pontoon bridge (*mil.*) a temporary bridge supported by pontoons

Pon·tus (pɒ́ntəs) an ancient country of N.E. Asia Minor, occupying what is now the Turkish Black Sea coast east of the Kizil Irmak. It developed in the 4th c. B.C. and, under Mithridates VI (c. 115–63 B.C.), extended its power over all Asia Minor, but was crushed by the Romans (mid-1st c. B.C.)

po·ny (póuniː) *pl.* **po·nies** *n.* a small, sturdy horse of any of several breeds measuring up to 14 to 14 ½ hands in height, or (*Br.*) 13 hands or, in the case of polo ponies, 15 hands ‖ (*pop.*) a literal translation used by students, a crib ‖ (*pop.*) a small liqueur glass, or the amount it holds ‖ (*Br., pop.*) the sum of £25 [Scot. *powny,* prob. fr. F.]

pony car (*automobile*) a small, sporty, two-door hardtop named for an animal, e.g. Mustang, Pinto

pony express (*Am. hist.*) a system of mail transport and delivery by riders on fast ponies (esp. beween St Joseph, Mo. and Sacramento, Calif., 1860-1)

poo·dle (púːd'l) *n.* a dog of a highly intelligent, playful breed, having tight-curling, solid-color hair. They make excellent gundogs, but are usually kept as pets. There are standard, miniature and toy varieties [G. *pudel* fr. L.G. *pudeln,* to splash in water]

pooh (puː) *interj.* used to indicate contempt, impatience, disdain etc.

pooh·pooh (puːpúː) *v.t.* to make light of, *he pooh-poohed her fears* ‖ to dismiss with contempt, *he pooh-poohed the suggestion* [pooh (an expression of contempt or impatience)]

pool (puːl) *n.* a small body of fresh water ‖ a small body of standing water or other liquid, *a pool of blood* ‖ a deep, cool, quiet spot in a stream or river ‖ a swimming pool [O.E. *pōl*]

pool 1. *n.* (*gambling*) the total of sums staked and (sometimes) of fines paid in, all to be taken by the winner, or divided among several winners || pocket billiards || (*Br.*) a game of billiards in which each player contributes to the stake, the winner gaining the whole || (*commerce*) a combination of resources for some common enterprise or for removing competition, manipulating prices etc. || (*commerce*) a fund common to various undertakings on a basis of shared profits and liabilities || a source of supply to which members of a group or organization have access, *a transport pool, a typists' pool* || (*fencing*) a competition in which each member of a team successively engages each member of another team **2.** *v.t.* to contribute (something) to a common fund, *pool resources, to pool ideas* [F. *poule,* stakes in a game]

Pool of London the Thames just below Tower Bridge, the furthest point up the river for oceangoing vessels. The Port of London begins here, with London Docks on the north side

pool·room (pú:lru:m, pú:lrum) *n.* a usually public room where pool and other games are played

pool table a billiard table equipped with pockets, on which various games of pool are played

Poo·na (pú:nə) a commercial center (pop. 856,100) of W. Maharashtra, India, in the Deccan, 80 miles southeast of Bombay. Industries: textiles, paper, chemicals. Maratha palace, temples. University (1948)

poop (pu:p) **1.** *n.* a raised, sometimes enclosed deck at the stern of a ship || the stern of a ship **2.** *v.t.* (of a wave) to break over the stern of (a ship) || to ship (a wave) over the stern [O.F. *pupe,* L.L. *puppa* for L. *puppis,* poop, stern]

poop·er-scoop·er (pú:pərskú:pər) *n.* an instrument for manual removal of dog excrement from a sidewalk or street

Po·o·pó, Lake (pɔ̞ɔpɔ́) a lake (60 miles long) in W. central Bolivia, at 12,000 ft

poor (puər) **1.** *adj.* having little money, few possessions and no luxuries || of, relating to, or characterized by poverty, *a poor place* || meager, *poor attendance* || showing small yield, *a poor harvest* || (of soil) unproductive || inferior, *a poor speaker, poor work* || (of a person) failing to arouse respect || to be pitied, *the poor child cried all night* || in bad condition through underfeeding **2.** *n.* **the poor** poor people collectively [O.F. *povre, poure*]

poor boy a tightly fitting sweater with a ribbed weave

Poor Clares *CLARE, ST, *FRANCISCAN

poor·house (púərhaus) *pl.* **poor·hous·es** (púərhauziz) *n.* (*Am. hist.*) a public institution sheltering and caring for homeless and poor people

Poor Knights of Christ *KNIGHT TEMPLAR

poor·ly (púərli:) **1.** *adv.* inadequately, *poorly fed* **to think poorly of** to have a low opinion of **2.** *adj.* not in good health but not seriously ill

poor-mouth (púərmauθ) *v.* to portray oneself as a poor person

poor white a white person who lives in squalid poverty, esp. in the southern U.S.A.

pop (pɒp) **1.** *n.* a small, sharp, explosive sound, *the pop of a toy pistol* || an effervescent nonalcoholic drink **in pop** (*Br., pop.*) in pawn **2.** *v. pres. part.* **pop·ping** *past* and *past part.* **popped** *v.t.* to cause to make a sharp explosive sound || to cause to burst open with a sharp explosive sound, *to pop corn* || to place quickly, *to pop a peanut into one's mouth* || (*Br., pop.*) to pawn || *v.i.* to move, come, enter etc., suddenly or unexpectedly or for a short time, *to pop in to see someone* || (*of the eyes*) to protrude, or seem to protrude, from the sockets || to explode with a sharp sound **to pop the question** (*pop.*) to propose marriage **3.** *adv.* with a pop || like a pop [imit.]

pop *adj.* of or pertaining to popular music, *pop singer* or pop art [by shortening]

pop *adj.* (*pop.*) father [short for *poppa,* var. of PAPA]

pop art an art style derived from posters and comic strips and depicting objects of everyday life

pop·corn (pɒ́pkɔrn) *n. Zea mays everta,* a variety of corn, the kernels of which burst open with a pop when heated in butter or oil || these popped kernels

Pope (poup), Alexander (1688–1744), English poet. The publication of 'An Essay on Criticism' (1711) established him as a master of didactic poetry and of the heroic couplet. 'The Rape of the Lock' (1712, 1714) is a mock-heroic epic ridiculing the society of his time. 'An Epistle to Dr Arbuthnot' (1735) is a bitter but scintillating attack on Addison and 'The Dunciad' (1728, with an added book IV 1742) is a virulent satire on the literary critics of the day. Pope made the heroic couplet a supremely supple form. The repertory of diction provided e.g. by his translation of Homer (on which he worked 1715–26) was to be predominant up to the Romantic age. His poetry was essentially of the intellect, and in its conversational tone, moral concern and exuberant conceits of fancy it belongs in the tradition of Donne and Marvell. But another side of his work, seen e.g. in 'Windsor Forest' (1713) and 'Eloisa to Abelard', inspired sentiment of a kind which helped to bring in the Romantic movement

pope *n.* the head of the Roman Catholic Church || (*Orthodox Eastern Church*) a parish priest [O.E. *pāpa* fr. L. fr. G k fr. *pappas,* father]

pop·er·y (póupəri:) *n.* a hostile term for the Roman Catholic religion and practices [POPE]

pop·eye (pɒ́pai) *n.* (*mil.*) in air intercept, a code meaning 'in clouds or area of reduced visibility'

pop·eyed (pɒ́paid) *adj.* having protruding eyes

pop·gun (pɒ́pgʌn) *n.* a toy gun which fires corks, pellets etc. by air compression

pop·in·jay (pɒ́pindʒei) *n.* (*rhet.*) a silly, mannered, conceited fop [M.E. *papegai, papejai* fr. O. F. *papegai,* parrot]

pop·ish (póupiʃ) *adj.* a hostile term for Roman Catholic [POPE]

Popish Plot *OATES, TITUS

pop·lar (pɒ́plər) *n.* a member of *Populus,* fam. *Salicaceae,* a genus of trees native to the northern hemisphere || the wood of these trees, used for crates, paper pulp etc. [O.F. *poplier*]

pop·lin (pɒ́plin) *n.* a tightly woven fabric, frequently of mercerized cotton, used for shirts, pajamas etc. [F. *popeline* fr. Ital.]

pop·lit·e·al (pɒplíti:əl) *adj.* (*anat.*) of or relating to the hollow behind the knee joint [fr. L. *poples* (*poplitis*), the ham]

Po·po·ca·te·petl (poupoukɑtéipet'l) a perpetually snowcapped volcano (17,887 ft) of central Mexico, visible from Mexico City 36 miles away

pop·out (pɒ́paut) *n.* book illustration that rises when the page is turned

Po·pov (pʌpɔ́f), Alexandr Stepanovic (1859–1905), Russian physicist, a pioneer in radiotelegraphy. He invented a detector for wireless waves and was the first to use a suspended wire as an aerial

pop·o·ver (pɒ́pouvər) *n.* a puffy, light muffin having a hollow center caused by the intense heat of baking [it pops up over the rim of the baking tin]

pop·pet (pɒ́pit) *n.* (*Br.*) a term of endearment, esp. for a little child (*engin.*) a lathe head || a valve that moves up out of and down into its port || (*naut.*) any of several stout pieces of wood used for various purposes, e.g. to support the hull of a vessel before launching [M.E. *popet, popette* fr. Romanic *puppa* fr. L. *pupa,* a girl]

pop·ping crease (pɒpiŋ) (*cricket*) a line 4 ft in front of the wicket and parallel to it, within which the batsman must stand to receive the ball

pop·ple (pɒ́p'l) **1.** *n.* a heaving or wild tumbling of water **2.** *v.i. pres. part.* **pop·pling** *past* and *past part.* **pop·pled** (of water) to toss or heave, e.g. in a choppy sea [prob. imit.]

pop·py (pɒ́pi:) *pl.* **pop·pies** *n.* a member of *Papaver,* fam. *Papaveraceae,* a genus of annual, biennial and perennial plants usually containing white latex. They have showy white, yellow or red flowers, and many light seeds in a capsule || the flower of any of these plants || an extract made from poppy juice, used in pharmacy || the color of a red poppy [O.E. *popœg* fr. L.]

pop·py·cock (pɒ́pi:kɒk) *n.* (*pop.*) nonsense, foolish talk [etym. doubtful]

pop·py·head (pɒ́pi:hed) *n.* (*archit.*) the raised ornament on the tops of ends of church seats in Gothic carving

poppy seed the seed of the poppy used esp. as a topping for rolls and other baked goods

POPS (*electr. acronym*) pantograph optical projection system, a system for plotting radar data on a board by marking (with a grease pencil) the points of light in a projection of the target. *Cf* DOPS, TOPS

pop top *adj.* of a can with a self-contained ring that creates an opening when pulled. *also* ring top. *Cf* ZIP TOP

pop·u·lace (pɒ́pjuləs) *n.* (*rhet.*) the common people, the masses [F. fr. Ital.]

pop·u·lar (pɒ́pjulər) *adj.* liked or admired by people in general, *a popular actress,* or by a particular group or section, *a popular student* || adapted to the tastes, understanding or needs of people in general, *popular science* || (*commerce*) cheap, *popular prices* || of, relating to or carried on by the people in general, *a popular election* || commonly held, prevalent, *popular opinions* [fr. L. *popularis* fr. *populus,* people]

popular front a coalition of left-wing political parties usually against a common opponent

pop·u·lar·ist (pɒ́pjulərist) *adj.* of someone who appeals to a wide public

pop·u·lar·i·ty (pɒpjulǽriti:) *n.* the state or quality of being popular [F. *popularité*]

pop·u·lar·i·za·tion (pɒpjulərizéiʃən) *n.* a popularizing or being popularized

pop·u·lar·ize (pɒ́pjuləraiz) *pres. part.* **pop·u·lar·iz·ing** *past* and *past part.* **pop·u·lar·ized** *v.t.* to cause (a commercial product) to become widely known and adopted || to cause (a resort etc.) to become popular || to present (e.g. a technical subject) in a form easily understood by people in general [POPULAR]

popular sovereignty the political concept that sovereign power is vested in the people || (*Am. hist.*) the doctrine (introduced by Senator Lewis Cass of Michigan in opposition to the Wilmot Proviso as a means of settling the slavery question) stipulating that the citizens of each territory should decide for themselves whether or not slavery should be permitted in their territory. Its most famous champion was Stephen A. Douglas

pop·u·late (pɒ́pjuleit) *pres. part.* **pop·u·lat·ing** *past* and *past part.* **pop·u·lat·ed** *v.t.* to provide with inhabitants, *an effort to populate Siberia* || to inhabit, *heavily populated bird sanctuaries* [fr. M.L. *populare* (*populatus*)]

pop·u·la·tion (pɒpjuléiʃən) *n.* the inhabitants of a country, town etc. || the total number of these || a specified group of people of a country or area, *the working-class population* || the act or process of supplying with inhabitants || (*statistics*) a group of individuals or items || (*biol.*) all the organisms living in a particular area [fr. L.L. *populatio* (*populationis*)]

population explosion a rapid geometric increase in a population

population inversion (*phys.*) condition in which electrons of an atomic system are more numerous than electrons on an associated lower-energy state

Pop·u·list (pɒ́pjulist) *n.* (*Am. hist.*) a member of a political party (*1891 - c. 1900*) advocating the free coinage of silver, a graduated income tax and government control of railroads || (*Russ. hist.*) a member of a political movement (c. 1870-81) which attempted to spread revolutionary socialist ideas among the peasantry

pop·u·lous (pɒ́pjuləs) *adj.* densely populated [fr. L. *populosus*]

pop wine sweet, fruit-flavored wine

por·bea·gle (pɔ́rbi:g'l) *n. Lamna nasus* or *L. cornubica,* fam. *Lamnidae,* a fierce, viviparous shark reaching 8 ft in length, found in northern seas, and distinguished by its crescent-shaped tail [Cornish, perh. fr. F.]

por·ce·lain (pɔ́rslin, póurslin) **1.** *n.* fine, translucent nonporous ceramic ware made of quartz, feldspar and kaolin, and used esp. for tableware || (*pl.*) articles made of this **2.** *adj.* made of porcelain [F. fr. Ital.]

por·ce·la·ne·ous, por·cel·la·ne·ous (pɔrsəléini:əs, pour səléini:əs) *adj.* of, relating to, or resembling porcelain [fr. Ital. *porcellana,* porcelain]

por·ce·la·nous, por·cel·la·nous (pɔrsəléinəs, poursəléinəs) *adj.* porcelaneous

porch (pɔrtʃ) *n.* the covered entrance of a building jutting out from the main wall || an open, roofed gallery extending along a side of a house, used for sitting out on, or giving access to rooms [O.F. *porche*]

por·cine (pɔ́rsain, pɔ́rsin) *adj.* of, relating to, or resembling a pig

por·cu·pine (pɔ́rkjupain) *n.* any of several vegetarian rodents constituting the Old World terrestrial fam. *Hystricidae* and the New World arboreal fam. *Erthizontidae,* measuring about 2 ft in length, and having the body covered with brown or black barbed spines intermixed with stiff hairs [M.E. *porkepyne, porke despyne* fr. O.F. *porc espin,* spine hog]

pore (pɔr, pour) *pres. part.* **por·ing** *past* and *past part.* **pored** *v.i.* (only in) **to pore over** to study intently, *to pore over a manuscript* || to think deeply about, *to pore over a problem* [origin unknown]

pore *n.* a minute opening or interstice, esp. in mammalian skin, through which fluids, e.g. sweat, pass ‖ a similar opening in plant tissue through which respiration etc. takes place [F. fr. L. fr. Gk]

por·gy (pɔ́rdʒi:) *pl.* **por·gies, por·gy** *n. Pagrus pagrus,* fam. *Sparidae,* a widely distributed edible fish, having a plump, oval body, crimson-colored and blue-spotted ‖ any of various related marine fish [etym. doubtful]

po·rif·er·an (pɔrífərən, pourífərən) **1.** *n.* any of various members of the phylum *Porifera,* comprising the sponges **2.** *adj.* of or belonging to this phylum [fr. L. *porus,* pore+*-fer,* bearing]

pork (pɔrk, pourk) *n.* hog's flesh (fresh or cured) as food [O.F. *porc*]

pork barrel (*pop.*) funds appropriated from the federal treasury, e.g. for local improvements, primarily to ingratiate political representatives with their constituents

pork·er (pɔ́rkər, póurkər) *n.* a hog, esp. one bred and fattened for food

pork·pie (pɔ́rkpai, póurkpai) *n.* a hat with a round flat crown

porn (pɔrn) *n.* (*slang*) short for pornography. — **porn, porno, porny** *adj.*

por·nog·ra·pher (pɔrnɒ́grəfər) *n.* a person who writes etc. pornography

por·no·graph·ic (pɔrnəgrǽfik) *adj.* of, relating to, or characterized by pornography

por·nog·ra·phy (pɔrnɒ́grəfi:) *n.* obscene literature, photographs, paintings etc., intended to cause sexual excitement ‖ the treating of obscene subjects in art, literature etc. [fr. Gk *pornographos,* writing of harlots]

por·no·to·pia (pɔrnətóupi:ə) *n.* (*slang*) an idyllic place for sexual activities

po·ro·mer·ic (pɔrəmérik) *adj.* (*chem.*) of a group of polyurethane-based, synthetic porous leathers used for upper parts of shoes, e.g., Corfam

Po·ron·gos Lakes (pɔrɔ́ŋgɔs) a salt swamp area with no outlet, in N. central Argentina, north of Mar Chiquita

po·ros·i·ty (pɔrɒ́siti:, pourɒ́siti:) *n.* the state or quality of being porous [fr. M.L. *porositas*]

po·rous (pɔ́rəs, póurəs) *adj.* full of pores, permeable [fr. L. *porus,* pore]

por·phy·rin (pɔ́rfərin) *n.* any of a group of naturally occurring complex heterocyclic compounds that play an important role in the respiratory processes of plants and animals. They are found (e.g. in chlorophyll or in the nonprotein portion of hemoglobin) usually in combination with metal ions (e.g. magnesium or iron) [fr. Gk *porphura,* purple]

por·phy·rit·ic (pɔrfərítik) *adj.* of or relating to porphyry ‖ (*geol.*) like porphyry [fr. M.L. *porphyriticus*]

Por·phy·ry (pɔ́rfəri:) (223–305), Greek philosopher. A pupil of Plotinus, he wrote a 15-volume treatise condemning Christianity. Only fragments of this survive

por·phy·ry (pɔ́rfəri:) *pl.* **por·phy·ries** *n.* (*hist.*) a hard rock once quarried in ancient Egypt, made up of white or red feldspar crystals embedded in a compact red or purple glassy base ‖ (*geol.*) any igneous or unstratified rock made up of a homogeneous base in which mineral crystals are embedded [fr. Gk *porphuros,* purple]

por·poise (pɔ́rpəs) *n.* any of various members of *Phocaena,* fam. *Delphinidae,* a genus of toothed whales, 5-8 ft in length, having a blunt snout. *P. phocaena,* inhabiting the N. Atlantic and Pacific, is the most commonly known [M.E. *porpays, porpoys* fr. O.F.]

por·rect (pərékt) **1.** *v.t.* (*eccles. law*) to submit, tender (a document) **2.** *adj.* (*bot.*) extending forward [fr L. *porrigere (porrectus),* to stretch forth]

por·ridge (pɔ́ridʒ, pɒ́ridʒ) *n.* a soft food made by boiling oatmeal or other cereal substance in water or milk [fr. POTTAGE]

por·rin·ger (pɔ́rindʒər, pɒ́rindʒər) *n.* an individual wide shallow bowl, usually having a handle, for porridge, soup etc. [alt. of older *potager*]

Porsena, Lars *LARS PORSENA

port (pɔrt, pourt) *n.* a harbor ‖ a town or place with a harbor ‖ a port of entry [O.E.]

port *n.* (*mil.*) the position taken up in porting arms [fr. the order 'port arms!']

port 1. *n.* the side of a ship or aircraft that is on the left of someone aboard facing the bow (opp. STARBOARD) **2.** *v.t.* to turn (the helm) to the left [etym. doubtful]

port *n.* (*naut.*) a porthole ‖ (*mech.*) an opening in a cylinder through which the lubricating oil can pass ‖ (*mech.*) a valve opening to allow the passage of steam, gases etc. [M.E. *porte, port,* gateway fr. F.]

port *n.* a fortified, sweet, rich red or white wine from Portugal ‖ an imitation of this [fr. *Oporto,* a city in Portugal]

port *v.t.* (*mil.*) to carry (a rifle or other weapon) in an upward-sloping position close to and across the body from right to left, esp. for inspection [F. *porter,* to carry]

port·a·bil·i·ty (pɔrtəbíliti:, pourtəbíliti:) *n.* the condition or quality of being portable **port·a·ble** (pɔ́rtəb'l, póurtəb'l) **1.** *adj.* easily carried or transported, *a portable radio* ‖ that can be carried or transported **2.** *n.* anything easily carried, esp. a portable typewriter [F.]

por·tage (pɔ́rtidʒ, póurtidʒ) **1.** *n.* the carrying of boats or goods by land from one river etc. to another, around falls or rapids etc., or the place or route over which this is done **2.** *v.t. pres. part.* **por·tag·ing** *past* and *past part.* **por·taged** to carry (boats or goods) [F.]

por·tal (pɔ́rt'l, póurt'l) *n.* a door, gateway or other entrance, esp. when large and imposing ‖ a portal vein [obs. F. fr. M.L. *portale* adj. fr. L. *porta,* door]

portal *adj.* (*anat.*) of or relating to the transverse fissure of the liver, where most of the vessels enter ‖ of, relating to, or being any large vein that collects and distributes blood from one part of the body to another [fr. M.L. *portolis,* of a door]

Por·ta·les (pɔrtάles), Diego (1793–1837), Chilean statesman and dictator (1830–7). He unleashed (1836) the war against the Bolivian-Peruvian Confederation

por·tal-to-por·tal (pɔ́rt'ltəpɔ́rt'l, póurt'ltəpóurt'l) *adj.* of or relating to the amount of time a workman spends in getting from the entrance of his place of employment, e.g. a mine, to his work site and, after work, from his work site to the entrance

portal vein a large vein conveying blood from the digestive organs and spleen to the liver

por·ta·men·to (pɔrtəméntou, pourtəméntou) *pl.* **por·ta·men·ti** (pɔrtəménti:, pourtəménti:) *n.* (*mus.*) a smooth gliding from one note to another in singing, or in playing esp. a trombone or a bowed stringed instrument [Ital.]

Port Arthur the chief port (pop. 38,000) for the Canadian prairies on Lake Superior in S.W. Ontario

Port Arthur *LUSHUN

por·ta·tive (pɔ́rtətiv, póurtətiv) *adj.* (*old-fash.*) portable [O.F. *portatif*]

Port-au-Prince (pɔrtouprɛ̃s) the capital and chief port (pop. 862,900) of Haiti. Industries: sugar refining, rum. Cathedral (18th c.). University

port authority a governmental commission in charge of a port

port·cul·lis (pɔrtkʌ́lis, pourtkʌ́lis) *n.* (*hist.*) an iron grating suspended by chains and made to slide in grooves in the sides of a fortified gateway in order to block the entrance [O.F. *porte coleïce,* sliding door]

Porte (pɔrt, pourt) *n.* the title of the government of the Ottoman Empire ‖ the government of Turkey

Port Elizabeth a port (pop. 492,140) of S.E. Cape Province, South Africa: boots and shoes, automobile assembly, fishing, food processing, building materials

por·tend (pɔrténd, pourténd) *v.t.* to give signs of (impending evil or catastrophe) ‖ to indicate broadly (some coming change), *these events perhaps portend a closer link with Europe* [fr. L. *portendere,* to stretch forth]

por·te·ño (pɔrténjɔ) *n.* a monied inhabitant of Buenos Aires, as opposed to a gaucho [Span.]

por·tent (pɔ́rtent, póurtent) *n.* an inexplicable event taken as an omen, esp. as an evil omen ‖ a sign of some coming change for good or bad [fr. L. *portendere (portentus),* to stretch forth]

por·ten·tous (pɔrténtəs, pourténtəs) *adj.* of the nature of a portent ‖ (*rhet.*) highly significant, *portentous happenings* [fr. L. *portentosus*]

Por·ter (pɔ́rtər, póurtər), David (1780–1843), U.S. commodore. As captain of the 'Essex' during the War of 1812, he captured several British ships carrying troops to Halifax. He also attacked British whalers in the Pacific. He was defeated (1814) by British warships when a storm forced the 'Essex' into Valparaiso harbor

Porter, David Dixon (1813–91), U.S. admiral. During the Civil War he led (1862) the mortar flotilla of David Farragut's fleet in the successful assault on New Orleans and aided (1863) Gen. U.S. Grant in the Vicksburg campaign

Porter, Katherine Anne (1890–1980), U.S. novelist and short story writer. Her first full-length novel, 'Ship of Fools' (1962), which is set aboard a German ship shortly before Hitler's rise to power, reflects the mood of impending disaster

Porter, William Sydney *HENRY, O.

por·ter (pɔ́rtər, póurtər) *n.* a dark brown beer brewed from browned or charred malt [short for porter's ale]

porter *n.* (esp. *Br.*) a gatekeeper ‖ (esp. *Br.*) a doorkeeper, e.g. at a school, hotel, college etc. [A.F.]

porter *n.* a person employed in railroad stations, hotels, markets etc. to carry baggage or other loads ‖ a man who cleans or does errands in a store etc. ‖ an attendant in a parlor car or sleeping car [O.F. *porteour*]

por·ter·house steak (pɔ́rtərhaus, póurtərhaus) a choice steak cut from the thick end of the short loin of beef [fr. older *porterhouse,* where steaks and chops and porter were served]

port·fo·li·o (pɔrtfóuli:ou, pourtfóuli:ou) *pl.* **port·fo·li·os** *n.* a case for keeping loose papers, drawings, prints etc. ‖ such a case for carrying state documents ‖ the office and functions of a government minister ‖ the securities etc. held by a bank, investment trust etc. [fr. Ital. *portafogli*]

Port Har·court (hάrkərt) a port (pop. 242,000) and rail terminus of E. Nigeria, on the Niger delta. It is the capital of Rivers State

port·hole (pɔ́rthoul, póurthoul) *n.* an opening in a ship's side to admit light and air ‖ an opening in a tank, fortification etc. to shoot through

por·ti·co (pɔ́rtikou, póurtikou) *pl.* **por·ti·coes, por·ti·cos** *n.* a colonnade or covered passageway in classical architecture [Ital.]

por·tiere, por·tière (pɔrtjέər, pourtjέər) *n.* a door curtain [F.]

Por·ti·na·ri (pɔrti:nάri:), Cândido (1903–62), Brazilian painter of murals. He decorated the entrance to the Hispanic Foundation in the Library of Congress in Washington, D.C.

por·tion (pɔ́rʃən, póurʃən) **1.** *n.* a part of a whole, *a portion of the field was allotted to the sports club* ‖ a helping of food ‖ (*hist.*) a share of an estate received by inheritance or gift ‖ (*old-fash.*) a dowry ‖ (*rhet.*) one's lot in life [O.F. *porcion*]

portion *v.t.* to divide into portions ‖ (with 'out') to share, *he portioned out the estate among his three sons* [O.F. *portionner*].

Port Jackson *SYDNEY

Port·land (pɔ́rtlənd, póurtlənd) the chief city (pop. 366,383) of Oregon, a seaport (on the Columbia 108 miles from the coast) and industrial center: food processing, textiles, sawmilling, pulp and paper, chemicals, aluminum

Portland the largest city (pop. 61,572) of Maine, a seaport

portland cement a cement made by grinding and mixing chalk and clay and burning it in a kiln [after the color of Portland stone, quarried at the Isle of *Portland,* Dorset, England]

port·li·ness (pɔ́rtli:nis, póurtli:nis) *n.* the state or quality of being portly [PORTLY]

Port Louis the capital, chief port and commercial center (pop. 146,844) of Mauritius: sugar refining, tobacco, rum

port·ly (pɔ́rtli:, póurtli:) *comp.* **port·li·er,** *superl.* **port·li·est** *adj.* (of adults) stout, corpulent [PORT n., (obs.) bearing]

port·man·teau (pɔrtmǽntou, pourtmǽntou) *pl.* **port·man·teaus, port·man·teaux** *n.* a traveling case for clothes, opening into two compartments [F. fr. *porter,* to carry+*manteau,* a cloak]

portmanteau word a word in which the sounds and meanings of two other words are combined, e.g. 'smog' (smoke and fog)

Port Mores·by (mɔ́rzbi:, móurzbi:) the capital and chief port (pop. 141,000) of Papua New Guinea, on the southeast coast

Pôr·to A·le·gre (pɔ́rtuəlégrə) the chief port and industrial center (pop. 1,183,500) of S.E. Brazil, at the head of a great lagoon-estuary (Lagoa dos Patos). Industries: meat packing, tanning, wool textiles, food processing. Cathedral. Universities (1934, 1948)

port of call a place at which a ship makes regular stops for supplies, repairs etc.

port of entry a place, not necessarily a port, where foreign goods are cleared through customs offices

por·to·la·no (pɒrt'lɑ́nou, pourt'lɑ́nou) *pl.* **por·to·la·nos, por·to·la·ni** (pɒrt'lɑ́ni:, pourt'lɑ́ni:) *n.* a medieval sailing handbook and guide to harbors, illustrated with charts [Ital.]

Port-of-Spain (pɔ́rtəvspéin, póurtəvspéin) the capital (pop. 11,032) and commercial center of Trinidad and Tobago, a port on the gulf separating Trinidad from Venezuela: sugar refining

Por·to No·vo (pɔ́rtounóuvou, póurtounóuvou) the capital (pop. 104,000) of Benin, a seaport and rail terminus: palm oil refining

Por·to Ri·co (pɔ́rtourí:kou, póurtourí:kou) the former name for Puerto Rico

Por·to·vie·jo (pɒrtɔvjéhɔ) a city (pop. 97,000) of W. Ecuador: Panama hats, baskets

por·trait (pɔ́rtrit, póurtrit) *n.* a painting, photograph, drawing etc. of a person, esp. of his face, usually made from life ‖ a vivid verbal description of someone or something **pór·trait·ist** *n.* a person who makes portraits [F.]

por·trai·ture (pɔ́rtritʃər, póurtritʃər) *n.* the art, act or practice of making portraits ‖ a portrait [O.F.]

por·tray (pɔrtréi, pourtréi) *v.t.* to paint etc. a portrait of ‖ to describe vividly in words, so as to bring out the character of ‖ to represent (a character) on the stage **por·tráy·al** *n.* [O.F. *portraire*]

Port Roy·al (pɔrtrɔ́iəl, pourtrɔ́iəl, pɔrrwæjael) a convent of Cistercian nuns founded in 1204 near Chevreuse, France. It was reformed (1608) by Angélique Arnauld, and transferred (1625) to Paris. It came (1636) under the spiritual direction of Duvergier de Hauranne. It became, with an associated group of scholarly solitaries including Antoine Arnauld living at the Chevreuse convent, a center of Jansenism. A school, the Petites Écoles de Port Royal, was established (1638), and Racine was among the pupils. Some nuns returned to the old convent (1648) and the men took up residence on a nearby farm. It was here that Pascal retired (1654). As one of the measures to suppress Jansenism Louis XIV closed the old convent (1709), and it was razed (1712). The history of Port Royal is vital in the history of French religious thought in the 17th c. and the defense of orthodoxy

Port Sa·id (saí:d) a port and fueling station (pop. 262,760) of Egypt at the Mediterranean end of the Suez canal: fishing, salt works

Ports·mouth (pɔ́rtsməθ, póurtsməθ) a port and county borough (pop. 179,419) of Hampshire, England, on Spithead: naval base, cathedral (12th and 17th cc.)

Port Sudan the port of entry (pop. 132,631) of the Sudan, on the Red Sea, a rail terminus

Port Swet·ten·ham (swét'nəm) a port (pop. 11,000) of Malaysia in W. central Malaya, serving Kuala Lumpur

Por·tu·gal (pɔ́rtʃug'l, póurtʃug'l) a republic (area 34,831 sq. miles, pop. 10,056,000, incl. the Azores and Madeira) in S.W. Europe. Capital: Lisbon. Overseas territory: Macao. Language: Portuguese. Religion: mainly Roman Catholic. The land is 46% arable, 28% forest, 16% pasture. The coastal plain (fertile in delta regions), narrow in the north, widens gradually to cross the country in the far south. East of it is the Meseta, the central plateau (mainly 1,000–3,000 ft) of Iberia, cut by the Minho, Douro, Tagus and Guadiana Rivers. The Meseta is highest north of the Tagus, with mountain ranges (Serra da Estrella, 6,532 ft) running northwest southeast. Average temperatures (F.): (Jan.) 40° in the north, 50° in the south, (July) 70° in the north, 75° in the south. Rainfall: north of the Douro 40–60 ins, Serra da Estrella 110 ins, Lisbon 27 ins, south 20 ins. Principal occupation: agriculture (small holdings and mixed farming in the north, large cereal-growing estates in the center and south). Livestock: sheep, hogs, oxen, goats, donkeys, mules. Crops: cereals, root vegetables, olives, vines, fruit (esp. citrus), almonds. Minerals: coal, copper, kaolin, sulfur, wolfram, cassiterite. Exports: sardines, cork (1st world producer), wine (esp. port, sherry and madeira). olive oil, turpentine, resin, pyrites, wolfram, pulp, tires, embroidery. Other industries: food processing, hydroelectricity, iron and steel, cement, tourism. Imports: iron and steel, machinery, raw cotton, vehicles, wheat, sugar, fuels, oil seeds, coal, tobacco, coffee, chemicals. Chief ports: Lisbon, Oporto. Universities: Coimbra (1290), Lisbon (1911), Oporto (1911). Monetary unit: escudo (100 centavos). HISTORY. Originally inhabited by Iberians, Portugal was visited by Phoenician traders (9th c. B.C.). The Greeks founded colonies (6th–5th cc. B.C.), and the Romans made the area part of the province of Lusitania (2nd c. B.C.–5th c. A.D.). Together with the rest of the Iberian Peninsula, Portugal was overrun by the Visigoths (5th c.) and the Moors (8th c.). It was one of the first areas reconquered from the Moors (11th c.), was made a county (1095) by Alfonso VI, and became a kingdom (1143). By 1249 Portugal had expanded to approximately its modern extent. Under Ferdinand I and John I Portugal was at war with Castile and was supported by England. A permanent alliance was formed (1386) with England. The patronage of Henry the Navigator encouraged Portuguese geographers and navigators to explore the west coast of Africa and parts of South America. Prominent in this age of expansion were Dias, da Gama and Cabral. Portugal and Spain, as the leading colonial powers, divided the undiscovered world between themselves in the Treaty of Tordesillas (1494). By the mid-16th c., Portugal had acquired a vast empire which included Morocco, Brazil, and parts of East Africa and the East Indies. The climax of prosperity was reached under Manuel I and John III, but decline set in rapidly (mid-16th c.) as the economic effects of the expulsion of the Jews (1497) were felt and as Portugal's limited resources and tiny population were unable to compete with the rise of English and Dutch sea power. Philip II of Spain seized the throne (1580). Portugal suffered economically under Spanish rule and lost control of the East Indies to the Dutch. A revolt (1640) brought John IV to the throne. The Methuen Treaty (1703) helped to strengthen the economy, and the marquês de Pombal built up agriculture and trade with a strong mercantilist policy (mid-18th c.). When Portugal refused to obey Napoleon's embargo on trade with Britain, it was invaded by the French, the royal family fled to Brazil (1808) and the Peninsular War broke out. With the restoration of peace, the royal family returned but Brazil declared itself independent (1822). After political struggles between liberals and absolutists throughout the 19th c., Portugal became a republic (1910). The colonization of Mozambique and Angola (late 19th c.) caused ill feeling between Britain and Portugal, but Portugal joined the Allies in the 1st world war. Political and economic chaos worsened until Salazar was appointed finance minister (1928). Salazar became prime minister (1932), established a dictatorship, and kept Portugal neutral in the 2nd world war. Portugal joined NATO (1949), the U.N (1955) and the European Free Trade Association (1959). Attempts were made to modernize industry and agriculture (1950s). Salazar resigned (1968) on grounds of health. Portugal was widely criticized (1960s) for its dealings with Angola and Mozambique. Salazar's successor as premier, Marcello Caetano, was overthrown in a military coup (1974) led by Gen. António de Spínola, and democratic government was restored under a military junta. Portugal granted independence to its African colonies that same year. The constitution of 1976 committed the country to socialist goals and a minority socialist government under Mário Soares came to power (1976–8). After several short-lived successors, the right-centrist Democratic Alliance coalition, headed by Francisco Sá Carneiro, took over the government. After Sá Carneiro's death (1980) Francisco Pinto Balsemão became head of the Democratic Alliance and premier. He remained in office until 1982, and after a six-month political crisis, a new coalition headed by Soares was formed (1983)

Por·tu·guese (pɒrtʃugí:z, pourtʃugí:z, pɒrtʃugí:s, pourtʃugí:s) **1.** *adj.* of or relating to Portugal, its people, language, customs etc. **2.** *n.* a native or inhabitant of Portugal ‖ the Romance languages spoken in Portugal, Madeira, the Azores and Brazil, and in the Portuguese territories, by a total of about 93 million people

Portuguese Guinea *GUINEA-BISSAU

Portuguese man-of-war any of several siphonophore coelenterates of the genus *Physalia,* fam. *Physalidae,* having a large air sac with a sail-like crest on the upper side, enabling them to float on the sea

Portuguese Timor formerly an overseas territory of Portugal, annexed by Indonesia (1976)

POS (*abbr.*) point-of-sale (which see)

pose (pouz) *n.* a way of standing or sitting, esp. the position held by a model etc. in posing ‖ an attitude of mind, or manner of behavior assumed for its effect on others, *his brave words are merely a pose* [F.]

pose *pres. part.* **pos·ing** *past* and *past part.* **posed** *v.t.* to place (an artist's model, a person being photographed etc.) in a certain position for artistic effect ‖ to state or present (a problem etc.) ‖ *v.i.* to assume a certain position, e.g. in having one's portrait made ‖ to represent oneself falsely, *he posed as a successful businessman* [F. *poser,* to place]

Po·sei·don (pəsáid'n) the Greek god of earthquakes, of the sea and of horses, the brother of Zeus and Pluto and identified with the Roman Neptune

Po·sei·don (pousáidən) *n.* (*mil.*) two-stage, solid propellant ICBM [UGM-73] capable of being launched from a specially configured submarine operating on the ocean surface or submerged, equipped with inertial guidance, nuclear warheads, and a maneuverable bus capable of carrying up to 14 reentry bodies that can be directed to many separate targets, with 290-mi range. It replaced Polaris. *Cf* POLARIS, TRIDENT

pos·er (póuzər) *n.* a difficult or baffling question or problem [POSE v.]

po·seur (pouzə́:r) *n.* a person who pretends to be what he is not, out of affectation, insincerity, guile or silliness [F.]

posh (pɒʃ) *adj.* (*pop.*) very smart, *posh clothes* ‖ (*pop.*) high-class, *a posh hotel* [etym. doubtful]

Po·shan (pɔ́ʃɑ́n) *TZEPO

pos·i·grade (pɒ́zəgreid) *adj.* **1.** providing forward thrust. **2.** *n.* (*aerospace*) a supplementary rocket used to provide additional thrust. *Cf* RETROGRADE

pos·it (pɒ́zit) *v.t.* to postulate, assume ‖ to set in context, *the problem posited in this way took on another aspect* [fr. L. *ponere* (*positus*), to place]

po·si·tion (pəzíʃən) **1.** *n.* the place occupied by a person or object in relation to another person or object ‖ (*mil., chess*) strategical advantage, *to maneuver for position* ‖ (*mil.*) a place held by troops, *to attack a position* ‖ a way of looking at things, mental attitude, *to state one's position* ‖ a person's relative rank or standing in the social or business world ‖ exalted rank or standing, *a man of position* ‖ financial circumstances, *in a position to marry* ‖ office or employment, *a position as housemaid* ‖ physical posture, *a comfortable position* ‖ any of the formal postures of the feet and arms upon which all movements in ballet are based ‖ any of the points on the fingerboard of a stringed instrument which when pressed by the fingers control the length of string free to vibrate and so allow various notes to be produced ‖ (*sports*) a place in a team or on the playing field **in a (in no) position to** (not) enabled by circumstances to, *in no position to argue* **in position** normally placed **out of position** abnormally placed **2.** *v.t.* to place in position, *to position troops* **po·si·tion·al** *adj.* [F.]

position paper a statement of opinion on a particular question or issue

pos·i·tive (pɒ́zitiv) **1.** *adj.* leaving no doubt or question, *there is positive proof that he did it* ‖ (of people) given to significant action ‖ (of people) apt to be dogmatic ‖ indicating affirmation, *a positive response* ‖ (*philos.*) constructive as opposed to skeptical ‖ (*photog.*) of a photographic print or transparency in which the distribution of light and dark areas corresponds to that of the original optical image ‖ (*biol.*) moving toward a source of stimulation ‖ (*bacteriol.*) showing the presence of a specific condition, disease etc. ‖ explicit, *he had positive orders to do it* ‖ downright, *he is a positive nuisance* ‖ (*gram.*) designating an adjective or adverb in its simple uncompared degree, e.g. 'good' in contrast to 'better' or 'best' (cf. COMPARATIVE, cf. SUPERLATIVE) ‖ of this degree ‖ (*math.,* symbol +) greater than zero ‖ (*phys.*) of an electric charge of the kind associated with the proton ‖ (*elec.*) of an electrode (anode) of a cell or other electric device that is at the higher potential ‖ of a magnetic pole attracted towards the magnetic north ‖ of a counterclockwise moment or rotation ‖ (*chem.*) of an ion formed by the loss of electrons ‖ acting or moving in a direction conventionally or arbitrarily taken as that of increase, progress or superiority **2.** *n.* that which is positive ‖ (*photog.*) a positive print or transparency ‖ (*gram.*) the positive degree ‖ (*elec.*) the plate of a cell at the higher potential (the anode) [F.]

CONCISE PRONUNCIATION KEY: **(a)** æ, *cat;* ɑ, *car;* ɔ *fawn;* ei, *snake.* **(e)** e, *hen;* i:, *sheep;* iə, *deer;* ɛə, *bear.* **(i)** i, *fish;* ai, *tiger;* ə:, *bird.* **(o)** o, *ox;* au, *cow;* ou, *goat;* u, *poor;* ɔi, *royal.* **(u)** ʌ, *duck;* u, *bull;* u:, *goose;* ə, *bacillus;* ju:, *cube.* x, *loch;* θ, *think;* ð, *bother;* z, *Zen;* ʒ, *corsage;* dʒ, *savage;* ŋ, *orangutang;* j, *yak;* ʃ, *fish;* tʃ, *fetch;* 'l, *rabble;* 'n, *redden.* Complete pronunciation key appears inside front cover.

positive discrimination (*Br.*) *AFFIRMATIVE ACTION
positive eugenics a policy of achieving race improvement by increasing genetic transmission of favorable traits
positive feedback *FEEDBACK
pos·i·tive·ly (pɒzitivli:) *adv.* in a positive way ‖ (pɒzitívli) extremely, certainly
positive prescription (*law*) usage from time immemorial, or for a long period fixed by law, giving right or title ‖ the right or title so acquired
positive ray a stream of positively charged ions traveling towards the cathode in a discharge tube
positive reinforcement (*psych.*) system of employee management technique based on positive rewards, e.g., praise, recognition; developed by Edward J. Feeney. *Cf* BEHAVIOR MODIFICATION, SKINNERISM
pos·i·tiv·ism (pɒ́zitivizəm) *n.* a philosophic system founded by August Comte, based on the assumption that truth is completely represented by observable phenomena and scientifically verified facts [fr. F. *positivisme*]
pos·i·tiv·ist (pɒ́zitivist) *n.* an adherent of positivism [fr. F. *positiviste*]
pos·i·tiv·i·ty (pɒzitíviti:) *n.* the quality or state of being positive [POSITIVE]
pos·i·tron (pɒ́zitrɒn) *n.* (*phys.*) the particle having the same mass and spin as the electron but opposite electric charge (i.e. +1) produced by the interaction of cosmic rays with matter [POSITIVE+ELECTRON]
pos·se (pɒ́si:) *n.* a force of men having legal authority, *a posse of police* [M.L.=power]
pos·sess (pəzés) *v.t.* to have as property, own, *to possess a car* ‖ to have as a faculty, quality etc., *to possess endless patience* ‖ to get control over, *what possessed him to act that way?* ‖ to keep (oneself) in a condition of emotional or mental control, *to possess oneself in patience* ‖ (of an evil spirit) to enter into in order to control, *to be possessed by a devil* ‖ to command (a language other than one's own) **pos·séssed** *adj.* crazy ‖ controlled by an evil spirit [O.F. *possessier*]
pos·ses·sion (pəzéʃən) a possessing or being possessed ‖ that which is possessed ‖ (*pl.*) property ‖ a territory under the political and economic control of another country ‖ (*law*) actual enjoyment of property not founded on any title of ownership **to take possession of** to begin to occupy as owner ‖ to affect so as to dominate [O.F.]
pos·ses·sive (pəzésiv) **1.** *adj.* (*gram.*, of a case, form, or construction) expressing possession or a comparable relationship, *possessive pronoun* (his, ours, yours etc.), *possessive adjective* (my, your, her etc.), *the possessive case of a noun* (expressed by 's, or ' after a plural ending in 's') ‖ tending to want to concentrate all another's affections on oneself ‖ jealously assertive of one's rights over something, *to be possessive about one's toys* **2.** *n.* (*gram.*) a possessive case or form [fr. L. *possessivus*]
pos·ses·sor (pəzésər) *n.* a person who owns or controls ‖ a person who holds property without title of ownership [late M.E. and A.F. *possessour*]
pos·ses·so·ry (pəzésəri:) *adj.* (esp. *law*) arising from, of the nature of, possession ‖ of or being a possessor [fr. L.L. *possessorius*]
pos·set (pɒ́sit) *n.* (*hist.*) a drink made of sweetened hot milk curdled by wine, ale etc. and often spiced, taken as a remedy [M.E. *poshote*, origin unknown]
posset pot a vessel (esp. of the 17th and 18th cc.) with two handles, lid and spout, to make posset in
pos·si·bil·i·ty (pɒsəbíliti:)*pl.* **pos·si·bil·i·ties** *n.* the fact or state of being possible ‖ something that is possible [F. *possibilité*]
pos·si·ble (pɒ́səb'l) **1.** *adj.* that may exist, happen, be done etc. ‖ potential, *a possible enemy* ‖ reasonable, *the only possible explanation* ‖ reasonably satisfactory, *he's quite possible as a bridge partner* **2.** *n.* the highest attainable score, esp. in target shooting ‖ a person whom it is reasonable to consider seriously for some position etc. **pós·si·bly** *adv.* by any possible means, *it can't possibly happen* ‖ perhaps [F.]
pos·sum (pɒ́səm) *n.* (*pop.*) an opossum **to play possum** (*pop.*) to pretend to be asleep or to be dead ‖ to feign ignorance [after the habit of the opossum of feigning death when attacked]
post (poust) **1.** *n.* a strong, usually square or cylindrical piece of wood, metal etc., fixed or meant to be fixed in an upright position, and serving as a support ‖ something resembling this, e.g. one of the stakes in a fence ‖ (*horse racing*) a pole marking the starting point or finishing point **2.** *v.t.* to affix (a public notice, placard etc.) to a post, wall etc. ‖ to put (a list of names etc.) on a bulletin board etc., *to post students' marks* ‖ to warn trespassers to stay off (esp. private property) by placing notices around the boundaries, *to post some woods* ‖ to publish (a name) in a public notice, *posted missing, a ship posted as missing* ‖ to advertise (a show, speaker etc.) by poster [O.E. fr. L.]
post 1. *n.* (esp. *Br.*) the public organization dealing with the collection and delivery of correspondence and other postal matter ‖ (esp *Br.*) the collection of letters etc. taken on one occasion from a collecting point ‖ (esp. *Br.*) the letters etc. delivered on one occasion, *what's in the post?* (*hist.*) one of a series of stations furnishing horses for relays ‖ (*hist.*) the distance between two successive stations in such a series ‖ (*hist.*) one of a relay of men on horseback stationed along a road, each one carrying letters from his own station to the next ‖ (*Br.*) a size of writing paper (16 x 20 ins) **2.** *v.t.* (esp. *Br.*) to mail ‖ (*bookkeeping*) to transfer (an item) from a record to a ledger ‖ (*bookkeeping*, esp. with 'up') to complete (a ledger) by transferring and properly entering all items from preceding records ‖ (*bookkeeping*, esp. with 'up') to transfer entries in (all books) ‖ (often with 'up') to supply (a person) with the latest news, information etc., *to keep someone posted about a situation* ‖ *v.i.* (*hist.*) to travel with relays of horses changed at successive stations [F. *poste* fr. Ital. *posta*, a station]
post 1. *n.* the position a soldier occupies, or the area he patrols when he is on duty ‖ the place at which a soldier or body of troops is stationed ‖ the body of troops occupying this place ‖ a position being held by troops, *advance post*, or the troops themselves ‖ a position to which a person is assigned ‖ a position to which a person is appointed, *a post in the public service* ‖ a trading post ‖ a local branch of an army veterans' organization **first post, last post** (*Br., mil.*) two bugle calls sounded at the hour of retiring to bed (the last post is also sounded at a soldier's grave after burial) **2.** *v.t.* to station in a specific place, *to post men along the route* ‖ (*mil.*) to assign (e.g. a sentry) to a specific station ‖ (*Br., mil.*) to appoint to a particular regiment etc. ‖ (*Br., naval*) to commission as captain [F. *poste* fr. Ital. *posto*, station, employment]
post-*prefix* after ‖ behind [L.]
post·age (póustidʒ) *n.* the charge for conveying a letter or parcel by mail
postage meter (*Am.*=*Br.* franking machine) a machine which automatically stamps letters etc. and records the cost of postage
postage stamp a printed adhesive stamp, or a stamp imprinted on a letter etc., issued by postal authorities for use as evidence of payment of postage
post·al (póustəl) *adj.* of or relating to the post [F.]
postal order (*Br.*) a money order available in fixed denominations, payable at a post office
Postal Union, Universal *UNIVERSAL POSTAL UNION
post·bel·lum (poustbéləm) *adj.* occurring after a war, esp. (*Am. hist.*) after the Civil War [L. *post bellum*=after the war]
post·box (póustbɒks) *n.* a box into which letters etc. are put for collection
post·card (póustkɑrd) *n.* a card for correspondence
post chaise (póustʃéiz) *n.* (*hist.*) a hired covered carriage drawn by two or more horses, changed at successive posting stations
post·code (póustkoud) *n.* (*Br.*) ZIP code
post-com·mun·ion (poustkəmjú:njən) *n.* the prayer in the Mass said by the priest after communion [fr. M.L. *postcommunio* (*posicommunionis*)]
postconciliar (poustkənsíli:ər) *adj.* of the period after the 1962–65 Vatican ecumenical council. *Cf* PRECONCILIAR
post·date (poustdéit) *pres. part.* **post·dat·ing** *past* and *past part.* **post·dat·ed** *v.t.* to assign a later than actual date to (e.g. a check, event etc.) ‖ to be later in time than (a certain date, event etc.)
post·de·ter·min·er (poustditə́:rminər) the limiting modifier of a noun that appears after the noun
post·er (póustər) *n.* a placard displayed in public [POST, a piece of wood]
poste res·tante (póustrestɑ́nt) *n.* (esp. *Br.*) general delivery [F.=remaining post]
pos·te·ri·or (pɒstíəri:ər) **1.** *adj.* located behind (cf. ANTERIOR) ‖ (*anat.*) away from the head ‖ (*human anat.*) dorsal ‖ (*bot.*) facing or on the same side as the axis ‖ (*bot.*) on the side next to the main stem ‖ later in time **2.** *n.* the buttocks [L. comp. of *posterus*, following]
pos·te·ri·or·i·ty (pɒstiəri:ɔ́riti:, pɒstiəri:ɒ́riti:) *n.* the quality or state of being later in time or sequence [fr. M.L. *posterioritas*]
pos·ter·i·ty (postériti:) *n.* the succsive descendants of a person ‖ generations not yet born, *posterity will judge* [F. *postérité*]
pos·tern (póustə:rn) **1.** *n.* (*hist.*, esp. of castles) a back or side door or gate ‖ (*hist., fortification*) an escape tunnel leading to the ditch and outworks **2.** *adj.* (*hist.*, of a door or gate) at the back or side [O.F. *posterne*]
post·ex·il·i·an (poustegzíljən) *adj.* postexilic
post·ex·il·ic (poustegzílik) *adj.* relating to the period after the Babylonian Captivity of the Jews
post·fig·ur·a·tive (poustfígjurətiv) *adj.* of a society in which three generations live together, dominated by the ideas of the older members; defined by American anthropologist Margaret Mead. *Cf* CONFIGURATIVE, PREFIGURATIVE
post·fix 1. (póustfiks) *n.* (*gram.*) a suffix **2.** (póustfíks) *v.t.* to attach as a suffix
post-free (póustfrí:) *adj.* (*Br.*) postpaid
post·gla·cial (poustgléiʃəl) *adj.* occurring after a glacial period, esp. the Pleistocene
post·grad·u·ate (poustgrǽdʒu:it) **1.** *adj.* of or relating to studies that go beyond the first degree ‖ of or relating to a student engaged in such studies **2.** *n.* a student who continues his studies beyond a first degree
post·haste (póusthéist) *adj.* with the greatest possible speed
post·hu·mous (pɒ́stʃuməs) *adj.* published after the death of the author ‖ (of a child) born after the death of the father ‖ occurring after death, *a posthumous award* **pósthu·mous·ly** *adv.* [fr. L. *postumus*, last]
pos·til (pɒ́stil) *n.* a marginal comment, esp. a marginal biblical comment [F. *postille*]
pos·til·ion, pos·til·lion (pəstíljən) *n.* a man who rides the near horse of the leading pair when two pairs or more are used to draw a carriage ‖ a man who rides the near horse of a single pair when there is no driver on the box [F. *postillon*]
Post·im·pres·sion·ism (poustimpréʃənizəm) *n.* the various reactions in painting in the last decade of the 19th c. and the early 20th c. away from Impressionism. Cézanne, Gauguin, Van Gogh and Seurat were, each in his own way, Postimpressionists **Post·im·prés·sion·ist** *adj.* and *n.*
post·in·dus·tri·al society (poustindʌ́stri:əl) late 20th-century society in which theoretical knowledge as a source of innovation and policymaking is centralized in a professional and technical class, such knowledge serving to replace goods as major elements of production; defined by Daniel Bell
post·li·min·i·um (poustlimíni:əm) *n.* postliminy [L. fr. *post*, behind+*limen* (*liminis*), threshold]
post·lim·i·ny (poustlímini:) *n.* (*internat. law*) the law under which persons or property captured by an enemy revert to their original status and the rights relating to them are restored when they come under the jurisdiction of their own country again [fr. POSTLIMINIUM]
post·man (póustmən) *pl.* **post·men** (póustmən) *n.* someone employed to collect and deliver letters and other postal matter
post·mark (póustmɑrk) **1.** *n.* an official post-office mark stamped on a piece of mail, recording the date, place and usually time of mailing, and serving to cancel the stamp **2.** *v.i.* to stamp with a postmark
post·mas·ter (póustmæstər, póustmɑstər) *n.* a man in charge of a post office
postmaster general *pl.* **postmasters general, postmaster generals** the head of a national postal system
post·me·rid·i·an (poustmərídi:ən) *adj.* of or relating to the afternoon
post me·rid·i·em (poustmərídi:əm) *adv.* (*abbr.* p.m., P.M.) after noon and before midnight [L.]
post·mis·tress (póustmistris) *n.* a woman in charge of a post office

CONCISE PRONUNCIATION KEY: (a) æ, *cat*; ɑ, *car*; ɔ *fawn*; ei, *snake*. (e) e, *hen*; i:, *sheep*; iə, *deer*; εə, *bear*. (i) i, *fish*; ai, *tiger*; ə:, *bird*. (o) o, *ox*; au, *cow*; ou, *goat*; u, *poor*; ɔi, *royal*. (u) ʌ, *duck*; u, *bull*; u:, *goose*; ə, *bacillus*; ju:, *cube*. x, *loch*; θ, *think*; ð, *bother*; z, *Zen*; ʒ, *corsage*; dʒ, *savage*; ŋ, *orangutang*; j, *yak*; ʃ, *fish*; tʃ, *fetch*; 'l, *rabble*; 'n, *redden*. Complete pronunciation key appears inside front cover.

post·mor·tem (poustmɔ́rtəm) **1.** *adj.* of or relating to the period after death, *postmortem changes* || after an event, a *postmortem analysis of a campaign* **2.** *n.* a postmortem examination || an analysis after an event, esp. after a hand of bridge [L.]

postmortem examination an autopsy

post·na·tal (poustnéit'l) *adj.* after birth

post·ne·o·na·tal (poustni:ounéit'l) *adj.* of the first year after birth

post·nup·tial (poustnʌ́pʃəl) *adj.* after marriage

post-o·bit (poustóubit) **1.** *adj.* effective after death **2.** *n.* a bond payable after the death of a person from whom the borrower expects to inherit money [fr. L. *post obitum,* after death]

post office an office where the mail is received and sorted for distribution and other postal services are maintained **Post Office** the governmental department or ministry from which this service is administered

Pos·ton (póustən), Charles Debrill (1825–1902), U.S. explorer of the southwestern U.S.A. Advocating territorial organization for Arizona, he served (1863–4) as superintendent of Indian affairs and (1864–5) as the first delegate to Congress from Arizona. His writings include 'Apache Land' (1878)

post-paid (póustpéid) *adj.* (*Am.=Br.* post-free) with the postage prepaid

post·paint·er·ly (poustpéintərli:) *adj.* of a painting style utilizing traditional techniques for nonobjective works with color that tends to blend with the environment. *also* color-field

post·pone (poustpóun, pouspóun) *pres. part.* **post·pon·ing** *past* and *past part.* **post·poned** *v.t.* to put off, defer, *to postpone a holiday* **post·póne·ment** *n.* [fr. L. *postponere* fr. *post,* after+*ponere,* to place]

post·po·si·tion (poustpəzíʃən) *n.* a particle or word placed after another word, esp. a particle or word having the function of a preposition, e.g. 'ward' in 'skyward' **post·pos·i·tive** (poustpɒ́zitiv) *adj.* and *n.* [fr. L. *postponere* (*postpositus*), to place afterwards]

post·pran·di·al (poustprǽndi:əl) *adj.* of or relating to the period following a meal, esp. dinner [fr. POST-+L. *prandium,* meal]

post road (*hist.*) a road, used esp. by mounted mail carriers and mail coaches, having a series of inns that provided refreshment, fresh horses etc.

post·script (póustskript) *n.* (*abbr.* P.S.) a brief afterthought, or series of these, added to a letter below the signature || a short section at the end of a book, often a commentary on what has gone before [fr. L. *postscriptum* fr. *post,* after+*scribere,* to write]

post-traumatic stress disorder psychological disorder following or resulting from trauma. It may develop after any traumatic experience, such as an accident, but it gained prominence in the U.S.A. in the 1970s as a result of the difficulties experienced by Vietnam War veterans in readjusting to civilian life. Symptoms begin with a feeling of numbness as the victim attempts to assimilate the traumatic experience. Other symptoms include irritability, depression, an unreasoned sense of guilt for having survived and emotional difficulties with relationships. Nightmares, flashbacks to the traumatic experience, overreaction to sudden noises and outbursts of violence can also occur. Treatment can include group or individual therapy as well as sedating drugs. *abbr.* **PTSD**

pos·tu·lant (pɒ́stʃulənt) *n.* a candidate for admission to a religious order who is not yet a novice || (*Protestant Episcopal Church*) a candidate for ordination [F.]

pos·tu·late (pɒ́stʃulit) *n.* an assumption || a hypothesis || an essential condition for something || (*geom.*) a statement that a construction etc. can be made [fr. L. *postulatum,* something demanded]

pos·tu·late (pɒ́stʃuleit) *pres. part.* **pos·tu·lat·ing** *past* and *past part.* **pos·tu·lat·ed** *v.t.* to demand, to require as an essential condition || to assume without need to prove || (*eccles. law*) to elect or nominate (a person) subject to acceptance by an ecclesiastical superior **pos·tu·lá·tion** *n.* **pós·tu·la·tor** *n.* [fr. L. *postulare* (*postulatus*)]

pos·ture (pɒ́stʃər) **1.** *n.* the way a person holds himself || the position held by a model in posing **2.** *v.i. pres. part.* **pos·tur·ing** *past* and *past part.* **pos·tured** to assume a physical posture, esp. for effect || to pretend to be something one isn't, *posturing as an intellectual* [F.]

post·war (póustwɔ́r) *adj.* of or relating to the period after a war

po·sy (póuzi:) *pl.* **po·sies** *n.* (esp. *Br.*) a small bunch of flowers, esp. one arranged in a tight bunch so as to form a pattern || a flower [shortened fr. POESY]

pot (pɒt) **1.** *n.* a container of earthenware, glass, metal etc. used for holding liquids or solids, for cooking, boiling etc. || such a container with its contents || a lobster pot || a chamber pot || (*card games,* esp. poker) the total of bets || a large prize or sum to be won, e.g. in a contest || (*pl., pop.*) a lot of, *pots of money* || (*Br., pop.*) a silver cup awarded as a prize || (esp. *Br.*) a chimney pot || (*pop.*) marijuana **to go to pot** to go to ruin **2.** *v. pres. part.* **pot·ting** *past* and *past part.* **pot·ted** *v.t.* to set (e.g. a plant) in a flowerpot || (*Br., billiards*) to pocket (a ball) || to preserve (meat, fish etc.) and pack it in pots || to kill (an animal) by a potshot || (*Br., pop.*) to win, *he potted all the prizes* || (of a potter) to make or shape (earthenware) || *v.i.* to take potshots [O.E. *pott*]

po·ta·ble (póutəb'l) *adj.* suitable for drinking [F. fr. L.L. *potabilis*]

po·tash (pɒ́tæʃ) *n.* potassium carbonate, K_2CO_3, esp. in an impure form || (*loosely*) a potassium salt or compound, *caustic potash* [fr. Du. *potasschen* fr. *pot,* pot+*asch,* ash]

po·tas·sic (pətǽsik) *adj.* of or relating to potassium || containing potassium

po·tas·si·um (pətǽsi:əm) *n.* a silver-white univalent metallic element (symbol K, at. no. 19, at. mass 39.102) that oxidizes rapidly in the air. It occurs in plants and animals, and in combined form in minerals. In the compound potash it is one of the basic mineral fertilizers, and its salts are used extensively in chemical analysis, medicine etc. [Mod. L. fr. POTASH]

potassium alum *ALUM

potassium antimonyl tartrate tartar emetic

po·tas·si·um-ar·gon dating (pətǽsi:əmárgɒn) method of determining the age of geological or archeological specimens based on the measurement of radioactive decay from potassium to argon

potassium bitartrate cream of tartar

potassium carbonate the deliquescent crystalline salt K_2CO_3, used in glass and soap manufacturing || the acid salt potassium bicarbonate. Both are potassium salts of carbonic acid

potassium chlorate $KClO_3$, a crystalline salt of potassium which readily yields oxygen on heating and is a basis of some explosive mixtures

potassium chloride KCl, a crystalline salt used chiefly as a fertilizer and in making other potassium compounds

potassium cyanide KCN, an intensely poisonous salt used chiefly in electroplating and as a weed killer

potassium dichromate $K_2Cr_2O_7$, a red, crystalline, poisonous salt used as an oxidizing agent, e.g. in safety matches, and in textile and leather finishing

potassium hydroxide KOH, a brittle white solid made usually by electrolysis of a solution of potassium chloride and used esp. in making soap and in bleaching

potassium nitrate KNO_3, a soluble crystalline salt used chiefly in curing meat and as a constituent of gunpowder

potassium permanganate $KMnO_4$, a deep purple, crystalline salt used as an oxidizing and bleaching agent, and in solution as a disinfectant

po·ta·to (pətéitou) *pl.* **po·ta·toes** *n.* *Solanum tuberosum,* fam. *Solanaceae,* a plant grown in most temperate regions for its edible tubers || the starchy tuber eaten cooked as a vegetable, and used for stock feed and to produce alcohol || (*loosely*) a sweet potato [Span. *patata,* var. of *batata,* sweet potato fr. Haitian]

potato beetle the Colorado beetle

potato chip (*Am.=Br.* crisp) a thin slice of potato fried until brown and brittle, often sold in quantity in packets || *CHIP

potato ring an 18th-c. stand for a bowl, typically of silver or earthenware, of Irish provenance

Pot·a·wat·a·mi (pɒtəwɒ́təmi:) *pl.* **Pot·a·wat·a·mi, Pot·a·wat·a·mis** *n.* a North American Indian people first encountered (early 17th c.) near Green Bay, Wis. They supported Pontiac's rebellion but sided with the British in the War of 1812. About 1,500 Potawatami live on reservations in Kansas, Michigan, Oklahoma and Wisconsin

pot·bel·lied (pɒ́tbeli:d) *adj.* having a potbelly

pot·bel·ly (pɒ́tbeli:) *pl.* **pot·bel·lies** *n.* a protuberant belly || a person having a protuberant belly || a heating stove having a rounded body

pot·boil·er (pɒ́tbɔilər) *n.* a work of art or literature, usually second-rate, produced merely to make money

pot culture life-style centered on use of marijuana

Po·tem·kin (poutémkin), Grigori Aleksandrovich (1739–91), Russian field marshal and statesman, favorite of Catherine II. He annexed the Crimea (1783), organized the colonization of S. Russia, reformed the army and navy, and wielded great influence in the Russian court

po·ten·cy (póut'nsi:) *pl.* **po·ten·cies** *n.* the state or quality of being potent || degree of being potent || capability [fr. L. *potentia*]

po·tent (póut'nt) *adj.* strong, powerful, *a potent drink* || convincing, *potent arguments* || (of a male) able to perform the act of sexual intercourse [fr. L. *potens* (*potentis*) fr. *posse,* to be able]

po·ten·tate (póut'nteit) *n.* a powerful monarch, ruler [fr. L.L. *potentatus*]

po·ten·tial (pəténʃəl) **1.** *adj.* existing but not fully developed, exploited etc., *a potential source of wealth* || having the capacity to be, *a potential winner* || (*gram.*) expressing possibility **2.** *n.* that which is potential || potentiality || (*gram.*) the mood of a verb which expresses possibility || (*gram.*) a potential construction || (*math.*) a potential function || (*phys.*) electric potential **po·tén·tial·ize** *pres. part.* **po·ten·tial·iz·ing** *past* and *past part.* **po·ten·tial·ized** *v.t.* [fr. L.L. *potentialis*]

potential difference the difference in the electric potential function at two points in an electric field, esp. at two points in a circuit

potential energy (*phys.*) the energy of a body due to its position in a field

potential function (*math., phys.*) a function the difference in whose values at two points in a force field measures the work done in moving a unit of mass, charge or magnetism from one position to the other, from which may be calculated the force at a point

po·ten·ti·al·i·ty (pətenʃi:ǽliti:) *pl.* **po·ten·ti·al·i·ties** *n.* the state or quality of being potential || (*pl.*) possibilities of development [fr. M.L. *potentialitas*]

po·ten·tial·ly (pəténʃəli:) *adv.* with the possibility of becoming actual

po·ten·ti·om·e·ter (pətenʃi:ɒ́mitər) *n.* an instrument for precise measurement of electromotive force employing a voltage divider and a sensitive galvanometer to indicate equality between a standard emf and a known fraction of the unknown emf [fr. POTENTIAL+METER]

pot·head (pɒ́thed) *n.* (*colloq.*) a marijuana smoker

poth·er (pɒ́ðər) *n.* (*old-fash.*) disturbance, commotion [etym. doubtful]

pot·herb (pɒ́tə:rb, pɒ́thə:rb) *n.* a herb, esp. a wild herb, boiled and eaten as a vegetable || a cultivated herb, e.g. mint, used for seasoning

pot·hold·er (pɒ́thouldər) *n.* a square of heavy quilted cotton etc. used for picking up or holding the handles of hot pots, kettles etc.

pot·hole (pɒ́thoul) *n.* a roundish depression in a road surface, bed of a stream etc., caused by local erosion || a deep cavity within a rock formation having its opening at the upper surface **pót·hol·ing** *n.* (*Br.*) spelunking

pot·hol·er (pɒ́thoulər) *n.* amateur cave explorer —**pothole** *v.*

pot·hook (pɒ́thuk) *n.* an S-shaped hook used for hanging pots over an open fire || a stroke with a hook on it copied by children learning to write

po·tion (póuʃən) *n.* a dose of medicine or poison or drug in liquid form [O.F. *pocion, potion*]

pot lead (led) graphite used on the hull of a racing vessel to reduce friction **pot-lead** (pɒ́tled) *v.t.* to apply pot lead to

pot·luck (pɒ́tlʌk) *n.* what can be produced in the way of a meal for an unexpected guest or guests

Po·to·mac (pətóumək) a river (287 miles long) flowing from the Allegheny Mtns, West Virginia, to the Chesapeake Bay, forming the Maryland-Virginia border. Its estuary is navigable by large vessels to Washington, D.C.

Potomac, Army of the a huge Union army in the Civil War, organized (1861) by Gen. George McClellan. It served (1862) in the Peninsular

Campaign and at Antietam. Although defeated (1862) at Fredericksburg and (1863) at Chancellorsville, it captured (1863) Gettysburg

Po·to·sí (pɔtɔsí:) a city (pop. 77,233) of Bolivia at 13,600 ft beside the Cerro (hill) de Potosí, famous for its now exhausted silver lode (worked 1545–19th c.). Tin is mined. Cathedral (16th c.). University

pot·pie (pɒ́tpai) *n.* a meat pie cooked in a deep dish

pot·pour·ri (pouрurí:) *n.* dried flower petals and flavoring herbs stored in jars or displayed in bowls to scent a room ‖ a musical medley ‖ a literary anthology [F. *pot-pourri,* rotten pot, stew, trans. Span. *olla podrida*]

pot roast meat, usually beef, braised with vegetables **pót-roast** *v.t.* to cook (meat) in this way

Pots·dam (pɒ́tsdæm) a city (pop. 125,000) of East Germany 17 miles southwest of Berlin, the historical capital of Brandenburg and the Prussian royal and imperial residence. Industries: mechanical engineering, film making, precision instruments. Palaces and parks (mainly 18th c.) include Frederick II's Sans Souci (1745–7) ‖ the surrounding district (area 4,582 sq. miles, pop. 1,151,000)

Potsdam Conference a meeting (July 17–Aug. 2, 1945) of Truman, Stalin and Churchill (succeeded July 28 by Attlee) after Germany's collapse in the 2nd world war. The conference continued the work of the Yalta Conference in arranging zones of occupation in Germany, reparations and conditions to be imposed on Germany. An ultimatum was issued to Japan. It was agreed that Poland should occupy temporarily land to the east of the Oder-Neisse line

pot·sherd (pɒ́tʃə:rd) *n.* a piece of broken pottery [POT+SHARD]

pot·shot (pɒ́tʃɒt) *n.* an easy shot ‖ a shot at random

pott (pɒt) (*Br.*) *adj.* of a size of printing or writing paper, usually 15½×12½ ins [from the watermark of a pot]

pot·tage (pɒ́tidʒ) *n.* a thick soup made from vegetables or vegetables and meat [M.E. *potage* fr. F., lit.=something put in a pot]

Potter (pɒ́tər), Beatrix (1866–1943) English writer and illustrator of children's books. Best known for 'The Tale of Peter Rabbit' (1901), she wrote and illustrated about 28 children's stories, all involving animal characaters

Pot·ter (pɒ́tər), Paul or Paulus (1625–54), Dutch painter and etcher. He excelled in the painting of animals, e.g. 'The Bear Hunt' and the celebrated life-size 'Young Bull'

pot·ter (pɒ́tər) *v.i.* and *t.* (esp. *Br.*) to putter [O.E. *potian,* to push]

potter *n.* a person who makes pottery

Pot·ter·ies, the a district in N. Staffordshire, the center of the English china and earthenware industry, including the towns of Burslem, Hanley, Fenton, Tunstall, Stoke-on-Trent and Longton

potter's wheel a flat, revolving disk connected by a shaft to a flywheel, for the throwing of round forms in clay

pot·ter·y (pɒ́təri:) *pl.* **pot·ter·ies** *n.* clay vessels, esp. earthenware ‖ the potter's craft ‖ the workshop of a potter [F. *poterie*]

Pott's disease (pɒts) tuberculosis of the spine [after Percivall *Pott* (1714-88), Eng. surgeon]

Pott's fracture a fracture of that part of the fibula nearest the ankle

pot·ty (pɒ́ti:) *comp.* **pot·ti·er** *superl.* **pot·ti·est** *adj.* (*Br., pop.*) trivial, pointless ‖ (*Br., pop.*) slightly crazy [origin unknown]

pouch (pautʃ) **1.** *n.* a small bag, esp. for carrying tobacco or ammunition ‖ an abdominal receptacle for the young of a marsupial ‖ a baglike dilatation of the cheeks of some monkeys and rodents for storing food ‖ any baglike fold of skin, e.g. under the eyes ‖ a bag equipped with a lock for holding first-class mail or diplomatic papers ‖ a baglike plant part, e.g. the seed vessel of certain plants **2.** *v.t.* to put into a pouch, esp. to put (first-class mail etc.) into a locked bag ‖ to store or carry in a cheek pouch ‖ to cause (skin) to form baglike folds, esp. under the eyes ‖ *v.i.* to form a pouch [O.N.F. *pouche*]

pouffe, pouf (pu:f) *n.* a large, tightly wadded cushion used as a seat [F.]

Pouil·let (pu:je), Claude Servais Mathias (1790–1868), French physicist. He invented the tangent galvanometer (1837) and the pyrheliometer (1837)

Pou·lenc (pu:lɑ̃k), Francis (1899–1963), French composer, member of 'Les Six'. He wrote many lyric piano pieces and songs, two operas ('les Mamelles de Tirésias', 1947 and 'Dialogue des Carmélites', 1957) and a ballet ('les Biches', 1924). His religious works include a Mass, many chorales, and the outstanding 'Stabat Mater' (1951)

poult (poult) *n.* a young turkey, pheasant, chicken or other fowl [F. *poulet,* pullet]

poul·ter·er (póultərər) *n.* a poultry dealer [fr. obs. *poulter*]

poul·tice (póultis) **1.** *n.* a warm, soft, moistened mass, e.g. of bread, bran, linseed etc., spread on cloth and applied to a sore or inflamed part of the body to draw pus, act as a counterirritant etc. **2.** *v.t. pres. part.* **poul·tic·ing** *past* and *past part.* **poul·ticed** to apply a poultice to [fr. L. *puls (pultis),* thick pap]

poul·try (póultri:) *n.* chickens, ducks, geese, turkeys and other domesticated birds raised for food

pounce (pauns) *n.* the talon of a bird of prey [etym. doubtful]

pounce *n.* (*hist.*) a fine powder, used to prevent ink from blotting on unsized paper, or to prepare a writing surface on parchment ‖ pulverized charcoal or chalk for transferring a stenciled pattern to a surface [F. *ponce*]

pounce 1. *n.* the act of pouncing ‖ the swooping, grabbing or springing motion made in pouncing **2.** *v.i. pres. part.* **pounc·ing** *past* and *past part.* **pounced** (with 'at', 'on' or 'upon') to make a sudden swoop, spring or grasp, *to pounce on the evening paper* ‖ (with 'on' or 'upon') to seem to swoop, spring or grab, *to pounce on an opponent* [etym. doubtful]

pounce *pres. part.* **pounc·ing** *past* and *past part.* **pounced** *v.t.* to emboss (metal) by beating on the reverse side [M.E. *pounsen,* alt. of *pounsonen* fr. M.F. *poinconer,* to stamp]

pounce *pres. part.* **pounc·ing** *past* and *past part.* **pounced** *v.t.* to sprinkle, rub, or smooth over with pounce ‖ to transfer (a design) with pounce [F. *poncer*]

Pound (paund), Ezra (1885–1972), American poet. Pound began as an imagist, but his work soon transcended the limits of imagism. The most obvious feature is the delicate control of the rhythm, which conveys a tone of subtle witty comment. The element of elaborate artifice, even pedantry and sometime romantic archaism and mystification progressively took control in his work. His masterpiece, the still-unfinished 'Cantos' (begun 1919), is a brilliant though often obscure work woven of myth and legend in which he attempts to reconstruct the history of civilization. Other important works are 'Homage to Sextus Propertius' (1918) and 'Hugh Selwyn Mauberley' (1920)

pound *n.* an enclosure where stray or unlicensed animals are kept until they are claimed or disposed of ‖ an enclosure for trapping animals ‖ an enclosure for fish, esp. the inner compartment of a pound net ‖ a pound net ‖ a place where personal property is held until redeemed by the owner, *a car pound* [O.E. *pundfald,* pinfold]

pound 1. *v.t.* to thump with or as if with repeated blows, *to pound a door with one's fists, to pound a typewriter* ‖ to reduce to small particles by crushing, grinding etc., *to pound cassava* (with 'out') to produce with or as if with vigorous thumps, *to pound out a tune on a piano, to pound out a letter on the typewriter* ‖ (with 'in' or 'into') to cause someone to learn or remember (facts etc.) by constant repetition, *to pound facts into someone's head* ‖ *v.i.* to strike heavy, thumping blows, *to pound on a door* ‖ to make a thumping noise, *the artillery pounded away for an hour* ‖ (of a ship) to hit the water heavily and repeatedly ‖ (of the heart, an engine etc.) to throb violently ‖ to move quickly but heavily or with force or effort and a dull thudding sound **to pound away** to persevere in work calling for effort **2.** *n.* a pounding ‖ a thud or blow or the sound of a thud or blow [O.E. *pūnian*]

pound *pl.* **pounds, pound** *n.* (*abbr.* lb.) the unit of mass equal to 16 oz. avoirdupois or to 12 oz. troy ‖ (symbol £) the pound sterling, the British monetary unit equal to 100 pence ‖ the monetary unit of various countries, e.g. Egypt, Ireland, Syria, Turkey [O.E. *pund* fr. L.]

pound·age (páundidʒ) *n.* charge of a percentage as a fee in pound sterling transactions ‖ payment regulated according to the weight of an object to be handled (e.g. of postal charges)

pound·al (páund'l) *n.* (*phys.*) a unit of force defined as that required to accelerate a mass of 1 lb by 1 ft per sec. per sec.

pound·er (páundər) *n.* (in compounds) something weighing a specific number of pounds, *the fish was a good three-pounder* ‖ a gun firing a shot weighing a specified number of pounds, *a twenty-five pounder* [POUND (unit of mass)]

pound-fool·ish (páundfú:liʃ) *adj.* *PENNY-WISE

pound-force (páundfɔ̀rs, páundfóurs) *n.* (*phys.*) a unit of force in the foot-pound-second system, defined as the force required to accelerate a mass of 1 lb. at a rate equal to the acceleration of gravity

pound net a fish trap consisting of long net fences directing fish into an inner, completely meshed-in compartment from which they cannot escape

pound sterling the pound (British monetary unit)

pound-weight (páundwéit) *n.* the weight of a mass of 1 lb. at a place where the acceleration due to gravity is 32.19 ft per sec. per sec.

pour (pɔr, pour) **1.** *v.t.* to send out in a stream, *pour water over the flowers* ‖ to discharge profusely, *the river poured its waters through the breach* ‖ (esp. with 'out') to send forth (words, music etc.) as if in a stream, *to pour out one's feelings* ‖ *v.i.* to flow in copious streams, *blood poured out of the wound* ‖ to flow out as if in a stream, *the crowd poured out of the theater* ‖ to rain heavily ‖ to preside at a tea table **2.** *n.* the act of pouring ‖ a downpour ‖ (*founding*) a quantity of molten metal poured at one time [M.E. *pouren,* etym. doubtful]

Pous·sin (pu:sɛ̃), Nicolas (1594–1665), French painter who lived mainly in Rome. His early works, based on mythological and elegiac subjects, display dramatic and sensuous beauty, and show the influence of Titian and Veronese. The strict classicism which he went on to develop allowed no compromise with intellectual content: the moral statement of the picture must be fully served by color and composition. His themes are heroic, involving some dramatic moment of classical or biblical inspiration and a central psychological crisis. He sets down a vision of a world of dignity and nobility, with intense power. In landscape painting his ideal is in total contrast with that of Claude Lorrain

pout (paut) *pl.* **pout, pouts** *n. Gadus luscus,* fam. *Gadidae,* a small European cod having a biblike membrane on its head [O.E. *pūta*]

pout 1. *v.i.* to express displeasure, resentment, bad humor etc. by thrusting out the lower lip and looking sulky ‖ to sulk ‖ *v.t.* to thrust out (the lips) ‖ to utter with a pout **2.** *n.* a sulky thrusting out of the lips ‖ (*pl.*) a fit of sulking [M.E. *pouten,* prob. fr. O.N.]

pout·er (páutər) *n.* a person who pouts ‖ a breed of domestic pigeon capable of inflating its crop to a great size [POUT]

po·ver·a (pəvέərə) *adj.* of the art form that emphasizes the idea or process over the product, e.g., collage, fingerpainting

pov·er·ty (pɒ́vərti:) *n.* the condition or quality of being poor ‖ (of soil) unproductiveness ‖ deficiency in or inadequate supply of something, *poverty of ideas* ‖ monastic renunciation of the right to own, *a vow of poverty* [O.F. *pouerte, poverté*]

poverty line the marginal income level at which an adequate living standard is possible

pov·er·ty-strick·en (pɒ́vertistrikən) *adj.* poor ‖ exhibiting poverty, *a poverty stricken town*

pow·der (páudər) **1.** *n.* a dry substance composed of fine particles ‖ a medicine in powdered form ‖ a scented cosmetic for the face or body ‖ gunpowder **2.** *v.t.* to cover, sprinkle or dust with or as if with powder ‖ to convert to powder ‖ to apply cosmetic powder to (the face etc.) ‖ to decorate (a surface) with dots, small figures etc. ‖ *v.i.* to use cosmetic powder ‖ to become powder [F. *poudre*]

powder blue pale blue

powdered sugar confectioners' sugar

powder flask (*Br., hist.*) a case for carrying gunpowder

powder horn (*hist.*) a powder flask made of the horn of an ox or cow

Pow·der·ly (páudərli:), Terence Vincent (1849–1924), U.S. labor leader who headed (1879–93) the Knights of Labor

powder magazine (*hist.*) a place for storing gunpowder

powder metallurgy the process of reducing metals to powder and their use in molding small metal parts

powder monkey (*hist.*) a boy employed on a ship to carry gunpowder to the guns

powder puff a small, soft pad for applying cosmetic powder

powder room a rest room for women in a restaurant, night club etc.

pow·der·y (páudəri:) *adj.* resembling powder, *powdery snow* ‖ covered with powder ‖ apt to become powder

Pow·ell (páuəl), John Wesley (1834–1902), U.S. geologist and ethnologist. His 'Explorations of the Colorado River of the West' (1875) and his 'Canyons of the Colorado' (1895) describe his several expeditions to Arizona and Utah, especially his hazardous voyage through the Grand Canyon. He helped to establish (1879) the U.S. Geological Survey

Powell, Lewis F., Jr. (1907–) U.S. Supreme Court justice. He practiced law in Richmond, Va., beginning in 1932 and was elected president of the American Bar Association (1964). He was appointed to the Supreme Court (1971) by Pres. Richard M. Nixon and usually voted as a moderate conservative. His opinion in 'University of California v. Bakke' (1978) was considered pivotal in the Court's decision on that case

pow·er (páuər) **1.** *n.* an ability or faculty, *the power of motion, intellectual powers* ‖ physical strength ‖ control, *to be in someone's power* ‖ military strength ‖ controlling influence, *political power* ‖ authority, authorization, *the power to sign a document* ‖ a person of great influence or authority ‖ a country having international influence or authority ‖ mechanical or electrical energy ‖ (*phys.*) the rate at which work is done or energy transmitted ‖ (*math.*) the number of times a quantity is multiplied by itself, or the index denoting this, *10 to the power of 3 is 1,000* ‖ the magnifying capacity of a lens measured as the ratio between the dimensions of the image and the object (*MAGNIFICATION) ‖ the reciprocal of the focal length of a lens ‖ (*pl.*) an order of angels (*ANGEL) **in power** in authority or control **2.** *v.t.* to supply with a source of power [M.E. *poer, poeir, pouer* fr. A.F.]

power base the center of support for a person or policy, esp. political support

pow·er·boat (páuərbout) *n.* a motor boat

power broker one who trades in influence, esp. political influence

power component the part of an alternating current which is in phase with the voltage

power dive (*aviation*) a descent with the thrust of the engines added to the pull of gravity

power down *v.* (*astronautics*) to lower the energy level of a spacecraft. *ant.* power up

power elite head of institutional hierarchies (business, military, political, religious) who make decisions of national consequence; originated by sociologist C. Wright Mills in 1956

pow·er·ful (páuərfəl) *adj.* having great power, *a powerful nation* ‖ physically strong ‖ (of drugs, medicine etc.) potent

power function (*math.*) an algebraic function of the form $f(x) = ax^n$ where a and n are constants

pow·er·house (páuərhaus) *pl.* **pow·er·hous·es** (páuərhauziz) *n.* a building in which power is generated

pow·er·less (páuərlis) *adj.* without power ‖ (followed by an infinitive) unable, *powerless to intervene*

power of attorney a written authority, with an attested signature, authorizing a person to act as the attorney or agent of the person granting it

power point (*Br.*) an electrical outlet

power politics international political relations based on the achievement of aims through force or show of force rather than through peaceful negotiations

power station a powerhouse

power steering a steering system in which the engine power automatically amplifies the torque which the driver applies at the steering wheel

power structure where the group that makes basic political and economic decisions for an organization or community. *Cf* ESTABLISHMENT

power sweep (*football*) an end run supported by one or more linemen running interference for the player carrying the ball

POW, P.O.W. prisoner of war

Pow·ha·tan (pauhətǽn, pauhǽt'n) (c. 1550–1618), American Indian chief of the Powhatan tribe in Virginia, and father of Pocahontas

pow·wow (páuwau) **1.** *n.* a North American Indian conjurer or medicine man ‖ a North American Indian ceremony marked by noise and feasting, performed to secure victory in war, the curing of a disease etc. ‖ a conference of or with North American Indians ‖ (*pop.*) any long talk or conference **2.** *v.t.* to take part in a ceremonial powwow ‖ (*pop.*) to confer [fr. Algonquian]

pox (pɒks) *n.* any of various specified diseases characterized by pustules, e.g. chicken pox ‖ (*old-fash.*) syphilis [old pl. of POCK]

pox·vi·rus (pɒksvairəs) *n.* (*med.*) a group of large, chemically complex DNA viruses covered with threads and tubules that cause smallpox, mousepox, and myxomatosis (mucous tumors in rabbits)

Po·yang Hu (póujáŋhú:) a lake (area 1,042 sq. miles) in N. Kiangsi, China, connected by a natural channel to the Yangtze-kiang

Poy·nings' Law (pɔ́iniŋz) (*Br. hist.*) an act of the Irish parliament (1495) extending English jurisdiction to Ireland and requiring English approval for the summoning of an Irish parliament. The law was repealed (1782) [after Sir Edward *Poynings* (1459–1521), English soldier and diplomat, lord deputy of Ireland (1494–6)]

Poyn·ting (pɔ́intiŋ), John Henry (1852–1914), English physicist. He carried out experiments to determine the gravitational constant and mean density of the earth by a balance method, and also did valuable research on electromagnetic energy

Poz·nan (pɔ́znɑn) (*G.* Posen) a commercial and industrial center (pop. 527,000) of W. Poland on the Warta. Main industries: mechanical engineering, chemicals, textiles, food processing. Cathedral (15th–18th cc.), city hall (16th c.), university (1919)

poz·zo·la·na (pɒtsəlɑ́nə) *n.* a volcanic ash used in hydraulic cements [Ital. *pozzuolana* after *Pozzuoli,* a city in Italy near Naples]

poz·zuo·la·na (pɒtswəlɑ́nə) *n.* pozzolana

PPBS or **PPB** (*business acronym*) **p**lanning **p**rogramming **b**udgeting **s**ystems, a procedure for enlarging the information base in budgeting in which benefits are provided in proportion to costs, and alternatives evaluated based on costs

PPLO (*med. abbr.*) **p**leuro**p**neumonia-**l**ike **o**rganism, any of a genus of nonmotile microorganisms without cell walls that are between viruses and bacteria, generally parasitic, found in body fluids (serums) of mammals, *also* mycoplasma

prac·ti·ca·bil·i·ty (præktikəbíliti:) *n.* the quality or condition of being practicable

prac·ti·ca·ble (prǽktikəb'l) *adj.* capable of being done, feasible, *a practicable experiment* ‖ capable of being used, *a practicable route* [F. *praticable*]

prac·ti·cal (prǽktik'l) *adj.* of, relating to, or obtained through practice or action, *practical experience* ‖ that can be put into practice, *a practical suggestion* ‖ able to apply theory, esp. in constructing, repairing etc., *a practical man* **prac·ti·cál·i·ty** *n.* [fr. older *practic* fr. F.]

practical joke a trick played upon a person, often at the expense of his dignity

prac·ti·cal·ly (prǽktik'li:) *adv.* in a practical way ‖ virtually, *she is practically deaf now*

practical nurse a nurse who is experienced but is without the training of a registered nurse

practical unit a unit of measurement which is a multiple or submultiple of an absolute unit, used for arithmetical convenience

prac·tice (prǽktis) **1.** *v.* (*Am.* also **practise,** *Br.* only **practise)** *pres. part.* **prac·tic·ing** *past* and *past part.* **prac·ticed** *v.t.* to make a practice of, *to practice thrift* ‖ to follow or work at as a profession, *to practice medicine* ‖ to study, exercise one's skill in regularly or frequently so as to win greater command, *to practice a circus act, practice the violin* ‖ to drill, *to practice a class in French pronunciation* ‖ *v.i.* to perform an act or exercise a skill repeatedly in order to achieve greater command, *to practice on the flute* ‖ to be active in a profession, *does he still practice?* **2.** *n.* (*Am.* also **practise,** *Br.* only **practice)** a customary action or customary code of behavior, *to make a practice of dining early* ‖ a way of behavior, *evil practices* ‖ repeated performance or systematic exercise for the purpose of learning or acquiring proficiency, *piano practice* ‖ the exercise of a profession, esp. law or medicine ‖ a professional business, *to sell one's practice* ‖ (*law*) the established method of conducting and carrying on suits and prosecutions **in practice** in a condition to be able to perform with skill as a result of exercise and repeated performance **out of practice** not in this condition **to put into practice** to apply (theory etc.) in action **prác·ticed, prác·tised** *adj.* expert through long experience [O.F. *practiser*]

prac·ti·cian (præktíʃən) *n.* a person who practices a skill, art etc. ‖ a practitioner [F. *practicien*]

practise *PRACTICE

prac·ti·tion·er (præktíʃənər) *n.* a person who practices a profession, esp. a doctor [PRACTICIAN]

Pra·do (prɑ́dou) *MADRID

Pra·do y U·gar·te·che (prɑ́ðɔi:u:gɑrtétʃe), Manuel (1889–1967), Peruvian engineer, statesman, and president (1939–45, 1956–62). He was overthrown by a military junta

prae·co·ces, pre·co·ces (prí:kəsi:z) *pl. n.* precocial birds [L., pl. of *praecox,* mature early]

praecocial * PRECOCIAL

prae·mu·ni·re (pri:mju:náiri:) *n.* (*Br. hist.*) a writ charging a sheriff to summon a person accused under the Statutes of Praemunire ‖ the offense of which the person is accused ‖ the penalty incurred by someone found guilty of such an offense [M.L.=to warn, used for L. *praemonire,* to forewarn]

Praemunire, Statute of (*Br. hist.*) any of several statutes enacted (1353, 1365, 1393) with the aim of preventing papal encroachments on royal rights. Charging with praemunire later became a political weapon, notably (1529) in Henry VIII's attack on Wolsey

prae·no·men, pre·no·men (pri:nóumən) *pl.* **prae·no·mens, pre·no·mens, prae·nom·i·na, pre·nom·i·na** (pri:nɒ́minə) *n.* the first of the three names making up an ancient Roman name, e.g. 'Gaius' in Gaius Julius Caesar (cf. AGNOMEN, cf. COGNOMEN, cf. NOMEN) [L.]

praesidium *PRESIDIUM

Praetorian Guard, Pretorian Guard (*Rom. hist.*) a member of the bodyguard of Roman emperors, disbanded (312 A.D.) after its influence had increased to the point where it could make and unmake emperors

praetor, pre·tor (prí:tər) *n.* (*Rom. hist.*) a magistrate, ranking below a consul **prae·to·ri·al, pre·to·ri·al** (pritɔ́ri:əl, pritóuri:əl) *adj.* [L.]

prae·to·ri·an, pre·to·ri·an (pritɔ́ri:ən, pritóuri:ən) **1.** *adj.* of or relating to a praetor **Prae·to·ri·an** of or relating to the Praetorian Guard **2.** *n.* a man of praetorian status **Praetorian** a member of the Praetorian Guard [fr. L. *praetorianus*]

prae·tor·ship, pre·tor·ship (prí:tərʃip) *n.* the office of praetor or period of tenure of the office

prag·mat·ic (prægmǽtik) *adj.* of or relating to pragmatism ‖ dealing with events in the light of practical lessons or applications ‖ of or relating to state affairs **prag·mát·i·cal** *adj.* [fr. L. *pragmaticus* fr. Gk *pragmatikos,* active, businesslike]

prag·mat·ics (prægmǽtiks) *n.* (*semiotics*) the science of relationships between symbols, their interpretation and users

pragmatic sanction a royal decree having the force of fundamental law **Pragmatic Sanction** the Emperor Charles VI's settlement (1713) of the Austrian succession on his daughter Maria Theresa. It was guaranteed by most European sovereigns, but resulted in the War of the Austrian Succession

prag·ma·tism (prǽgmətizəm) *n.* a doctrine which tests truth by its practical consequences. Truth is therefore held to be relative and not attainable by metaphysical speculation. Pragmatism was first formulated by C. S. Peirce (1839-1914) and was developed by William James, John Dewey and others

Prague (prɑg) (*Czech.* Praha) the capital (pop. 1,176,000) and industrial, commercial and cultural center of Czechoslovakia, on the Moldau. Principal industries: metallurgy, heavy machinery, motor vehicles, chemicals, food processing, publishing. The old royal city (14th and 18th cc.) Hradčany castle, mainly 14th-c. Gothic cathedral, baroque palaces and churches) and medieval quarters are on the left bank, and the old town (14th-c. Gothic cathedral, ghetto, medieval monuments) is on the right bank. University (1348), national museums and theaters. The city was occupied (1968) by troops from the U.S.S.R. and other Warsaw Pact countries

Prague Spring (prɑg) political and economic liberalization movement in Czechoslovakia in 1968 under Communist Party Secretary Alexander Dubček. It was opposed by the Warsaw Pact nations by mid-July and crushed by a

Soviet-led invasion in August of the same year

Prague, Treaty of a treaty (May 30, 1635) during the Thirty Years' War, between Emperor Ferdinand II and John George I, elector of Saxony ‖ a treaty (Aug. 23, 1866) between Prussia and Austria, ending the Seven Weeks' War. Italy gained Lombardy-Venetia. Austria was left intact, but had to withdraw from Germany. The North German Confederation was set up

pra·hu (préiu:) *n.* a prau

prai·rie (prέəri:) *n.* a wide tract of treeless and gently undulating grassland in North America, esp. in the Mississippi valley [F. fr. L. *pratum*, meadow]

prairie chicken *Tympanuchus cupido pinnatus*, a North American grouse inhabiting the Mississippi valley from Manitoba to Texas, or a smaller grouse, *T. pallidicinctus*, of W. Texas ‖ *Pedioecetes phasianellus*, a grouse of the western U.S.A. and Canada

prairie dog a member of *Cynomys*, fam. *Sciuridae*, a plump North American rodent, esp. *C. ludovicianus*, having a doglike bark and measuring about 1 ft in length

prairie schooner (*Am. hist.*) a long covered wagon used by the pioneers in traveling westward

prairie wolf a coyote

praise (preiz) **1.** *v.t. pres. part.* **prais·ing** *past* and *past part.* **praised** to speak of with approval or admiration ‖ to glorify (God or a deity) **2.** *n.* a praising or being praised ‖ the act of glorifying God or a deity [O.E. *preisier*]

praise·wor·thi·ly (préizwə̦:rθili:) *adv.* in a praiseworthy manner

praise·wor·thi·ness (préizwə̦:rθi:nis) *n.* the quality of being praiseworthy

praise·wor·thy (préizwə̦:rθi:) *adj.* worthy of praise

Pra·krit (prɑ́krit) *n.* any of the popular ancient Indic languages, including Ardhamagadhi, Maharashtri, Sauraseni and Magadhi (cf. SANSKRIT) ‖ any of the modern Indic languages [fr. Skr. *prākrta*, not refined]

pra·line (prɑ́li:n, préili:n) *n.* a confection of almonds or other nuts browned in boiling sugar [F. after Comte du Plessis-*Praslin* (1598-1675), French marshal]

prall·trill·er (prɑ́ltri̦lər) *n.* (*mus.*) an ornament starting and stopping upon the main note with one sounding of the note above it heard in between, all three notes executed as swiftly as possible [G. fr. *prall*, elastic+*triller*, a trill]

pram (præm) *n.* (*Br., pop.*) a baby carriage [shortened fr. PERAMBULATOR]

prance (præns, prɑns) **1.** *v. pres. part.* **pranc·ing** *past and past part.* **pranced** *v.i.* (of a mettlesome horse) to leap up on the hind legs in a rearing motion, or to move forward by so doing ‖ to ride or drive a horse leaping in this way ‖ (of a person) to move in a gleeful or arrogant way ‖ *v.t.* to cause (a horse) to prance **2.** *n.* a prancing movement [etym. doubtful]

prank (præŋk) *v.t.* (*rhet.*) to deck, adorn [etym. doubtful]

prank *n.* a piece of mischief **prǽnk·ish** *adj.* [perh. fr. PRANK v.]

Pra·sad (prəsɑ́d), Rajendra (1884–1963), Indian statesman, first president of India (1950–62). He was president of the Indian National Congress (1934)

prase (preiz) *n.* a variety of leek-green, translucent quartz [F. fr. L. fr. Gk *prasios*, leek green]

pra·se·o·dym·i·um (pre̦izi:oudími:əm, pre̦isi:oudími:əm) *n.* a trivalent element (symbol Pr, at. no. 59, at. mass 140.907) of the rare-earth group [Mod. L. fr. Gk *prasios*, leek green+*didymium*, a mixture of rare-earth elements containing neodymium and formerly considered as an element]

Pras·lin (prɑlɛ̃) *SEYCHELLES

Prat Cha·cón (prɑ́ttʃɑkɔ́n), Arturo (1848–79), Chilean admiral and hero of the War of the Pacific

prate (preit) **1.** *v.i. pres. part.* **prat·ing** *past* and *past part.* **prat·ed** (*rhet.*) to babble or chatter idly or nonsensically ‖ *v.t.* (*rhet.*) to utter (nonsensical chatter) **2.** *n.* (*rhet.*) foolish talk [M.E. *praten* fr. M. Du.]

prat·in·cole (prǽti̦ŋkoul) *n.* any of several limicoline birds of genus *Glareola*, fam. *Glareolidae*, esp. *G. pratincola*, having a white abdomen, brown breast and brown upper parts, and measuring about 9 ins in length. It is found in parts of Europe, Asia and Africa [fr. Mod. L. *pratincola* fr. *pratum*, meadow+*incola*, inhabitant]

pra·tique (prætí:k) *n.* permission granted to a ship that has complied with quarantine regulations etc. to carry on business with a port [F.]

Pra·to (prɑ́tou) a town (pop. 154,400) of Tuscany, Italy, 10 miles northwest of Florence. Industry: wool textiles. Cathedral (12th c.) with works by Donatello, Lippi and Andrea Della Robbia, palace (13th–14th cc.)

Pratt (præt), Edwin John (1882–1964), the leading Canadian poet of his time. His works include 'The Cachalot' (1926), an imaginative and humorous account of a whale hunt, and 'Brébeuf and His Brethren' (1940), a chronicle of the martyrdom of Jesuit missionaries by the Iroquois. He turned during the 2nd world war to topical themes, esp. 'Dunkirk' (1941)

prat·tle (prǽt'l) **1.** *v. pres. part.* **prat·tling** *past* and *past part.* **prat·tled** *v.i.* to talk incessantly, esp. to gossip ‖ to chatter *v.t.* to babble (gossip, nonsense etc.) **2.** *n.* chatter, esp. childish chatter [PRATE]

prau (prau) *n.* a narrow Malayan boat up to 30 ft long, shaped like a canoe and usually equipped with oars, a large triangular sail, and an outrigger [fr. Malay *prau, prao*]

prawn (prɔn) *n.* any of several decapod crustaceans related to the shrimp and the lobster, having thin legs and long antennae. They are widely distributed in fresh and salt waters of warm and temperate regions and are highly esteemed as food [M.E. *prane*]

prax·is (prǽksis) *pl.* **prax·es** (prǽksi:z) *n.* a customary mode of behavior [Mod. L. fr. Gk *praxis*, doing]

Prax·it·e·les (præksít'li:z) (c. 370–c. 330 B.C.), Athenian sculptor famous for his statues of Aphrodite at Cos and Cnidus. His work survives mainly in Roman copies (*SATYR)

pray (prei) *v.i.* to enter into spiritual communion with God or an object of worship, *he prays constantly* ‖ to implore God or an object of worship, *to pray for better health* ‖ *v.t.* (*archaic*) to implore (God or an object of worship) ‖ (*rhet.*, contr. of 'I pray you') you must tell me, *what, pray, is the meaning of this behavior.?* [O.F. *preier*]

prayer (prɛər) *n.* a humble communication in thought or speech to God or to an object of worship expressing supplication, thanksgiving, praise, confession etc. ‖ that which is prayed for, *God granted him his prayer* ‖ the liturgical formulation of a communication to God or to an object of worship, *the Lord's Prayer* ‖ (esp. *pl.*) a public or private religious service consisting mainly of such formulations, *family prayers* ‖ the act or practice of praying ‖ (*rhet.*) an entreaty made to someone, *a prayer to the king for mercy* [O.F. *preiere*]

prayer book a book containing prayers and usually including set forms of worship

prayer·ful (prέərfəl) *adj.* given to frequent praying ‖ characterized by prayer ‖ expressive of prayer

prayer meeting a religious meeting for offering prayer

prayer rug a mat or small carpet used by Moslems to kneel on when praying

prayer shawl a tallith

prayer wheel a revolving cylinder inscribed with prayers used esp. by Tibetan Buddhists

pray-in (préiín) *n.* a protest gathering characterized by prayers and sermons, usu. held in a house of worship

praying mantis *Mantis religiosa*, the common mantis

pra·ze·pam [$C_{19}H_{17}ClN_2O$] (prɑ́zəpæm) *n.* (*pharm.*) benzodiazepine tranquilizer used as a muscle relaxant and antidepressant; marketed as Verstran

pra·zo·sin [$C_{19}H_{21}N_5O_4$] (prɑ́zousin) *n.* (*pharm.*) a drug used to reduce high blood pressure by relaxing muscles; marketed as Minipress

pre- (pri:) *prefix* earlier than, preceding ‖ beforehand ‖ preparatory to ‖ before, in front of (in location, order of importance or degree etc.) [L. *prae* adv. and prep., before]

preach (pri:tʃ) *v.i.* to deliver a religious address publicly, esp. to expound the gospel ‖ to offer moral advice in a tiresome manner, *he does nothing but preach at his children* ‖ *v.t.* to deliver (a sermon) ‖ to expound (the gospel) ‖ to advocate (*a course or principle*), *to preach moderation and prudence* **préach·er** *n.* someone who preaches, esp. a minister [O.F. *precher, préchier*]

preach·i·fy (prí:tʃifai) *pres. part.* **preach·i·fy·ing** *past* and *past part.* **preach·i·fied** *v.i.* to moralize endlessly [PREACH]

pre·ag·ri·cul·tur·al (pri̦:ægrikʌ́ltʃərəl) *adj.* of the period before human beings began to practice agriculture

pre·am·ble (prí:æmb'l) *n.* an introductory part of a speech or piece of writing, esp. the introductory part of a statute, ordinance etc. stating the reasons and purpose of the text that follows [F. *préambule*]

pre·ar·range (pri̦:əréindʒ) *pres. part.* **pre·ar·rang·ing** *past* and *past part.* **pre·ar·ranged** *v.t.* to arrange in advance

Pre·ax (prí:æks) *n.* trademark of synthetic heat-resistant fabric designed to replace asbestos; created by Gentex Corp. of Carbondale, Pa.

pre·ax·i·al (pri:ǽksi:əl) *adj.* (*anat.*) situated in front of the axis of the body

pre·bend (prébənd) *n.* a stipend paid out of cathedral revenue, e.g. to a member of the chapter ‖ the land or tithe which produces this revenue ‖ a prebendary **pre·ben·dal** (pribénd'l) *adj.* [O.F. *prebende*]

preb·en·dar·y (prébəndəri:) *pl.* **preb·en·dar·ies** *n.* a cleric receiving a prebend ‖ (*Church of England*) an honorary canon (receiving no such stipend) [fr. M.L. *praebendarius*]

pre·bi·o·log·i·cal (pri̦:bai̦əlɔ́dʒik'l) *adj.* of the period before or precursors of the origin of life. —**pre·bi·o·log·ic** or **pre·bi·ot·ic** *adj.*

Pre·cam·bri·an (pri:kǽmbri:ən) *adj.* relating to the eras of geological history prior to the Cambrian (*PROTEROZOIC, *ARCHEOZOIC, *GEOLOGICAL TIME) **the Precambrian** these eras

pre·car·i·ous (prikέəri:əs) *adj.* uncertain, *to earn a precarious living* ‖ dangerous, *falling rocks made the ascent precarious* ‖ not firmly founded, *a precarious line of reasoning* [fr. L. *precarius*]

pre·cast (pri̦:kǽst, pri̦:kɑ́st) *v.t.* (of concrete) to cast in blocks for subsequent construction

prec·a·tive (prékətiv) *adj.* precatory ‖ (*gram.*) of or relating to a verb form expressing a request [L.L. *precativus*]

prec·a·to·ry (prékətɔ̦ri:, prékətouri:) *adj.* of, relating to, or expressing request [fr. L.L. *precatorius*]

precatory trust a trust created by precatory words construed as having binding force

precatory words (*pl.*) words of request employed in a will, not always construed as binding

pre·cau·tion (prikɔ́ʃən) *n.* care with respect to the foreseeable future, *to invest with due precaution* ‖ a measure taken against some possible future evil or calamity or undesirable happening, *fire precautions* **pre·cáu·tion·ar·y, pre·cáu·tious** *adjs* [F. *précaution*]

pre·cede (prisí:d) *pres. part.* **pre·ced·ing** *past* and *past part.* **pre·ced·ed** *v.t.* to go before in rank, importance etc. ‖ to come before in time, *the stillness that precedes a storm* ‖ to go or come before or in front of, *twelve guards on motorcycles preceded the president's car* ‖ (with 'by' or 'with') to preface, *to precede a ceremony with a speech of welcome* ‖ *v.i.* to go or come before, *the days that preceded were filled with activity* [F. *précéder*]

prec·e·dence (présidəns, prisí:d'ns) *n.* the act, fact, right or privilege of preceding another or others, usually according to rank, esp. on ceremonial or highly formal social occasions [PRECEDENT]

prec·e·dent 1. (présidənt) *n.* a previous instance or case that may serve to justify a subsequent act, procedure etc. of a similar kind ‖ (*law*) a previous judicial decision, proceeding etc., taken as a rule in dealing with subsequent similar cases **2.** (prisí:dənt) *adj.* (*rhet.*) coming before in order, time etc., *precedent judgments* **préc·e·dent·ed** *adj.* having an established precedent [F. *précédent*]

pre·cen·sor·ship (pri̦:sénsərʃip) *n.* censorship before publication or other public release, usu. of politically sensitive material. —**pre·cen·sor** *v.*

pre·cen·tor (priséntər) *n.* the leader of congregational singing in some churches ‖ a member of a cathedral staff responsible for all musical arrangements connected with cathedral worship [fr. L.L. *praecentor*]

pre·cept (prí:sept) *n.* a commandment or instruction intended as a rule of action or conduct ‖ a technical instruction [fr. L. *praecipere* (*praeceptus*), to teach]

pre·cep·tive (priséptiv) *adj.* of or relating to a precept ‖ mandatory [L.L. *praeceptivus*]

CONCISE PRONUNCIATION KEY: **(a)** æ, *c*a*t*; ɑ, *c*a*r*; ɔ *f*aw*n*; ei, *sn*a*ke*. **(e)** e, *h*e*n*; i:, *sh*ee*p*; iə, *d*ee*r*; εə, *b*ea*r*. **(i)** i, *f*i*sh*; ai, *t*i*ger*; ə:, *b*i*rd*. **(o)** o, *o*x; au, *c*ow; ou, *g*oa*t*; u, *p*oo*r*; ɔi, *r*oy*al*. **(u)** ʌ, *d*u*ck*; u, *b*u*ll*; u:, *g*oo*se*; ə, *b*a*cillus*; ju:, *c*u*be*. x, *lo*ch; θ, *th*ink; ð, *bo*th*er*; z, *Z*en; ʒ, *cor*s*age*; dʒ, *sava*g*e*; ŋ, *orangu*t*ang*; j, *y*ak; ʃ, *f*ish; tʃ, *fe*tch; 'l, *rabb*le; 'n, *redd*en. Complete pronunciation key appears inside front cover.

pre·cep·tor (priséptər) *n.* (*archaic*) a teacher ‖ (*hist.*) the head of a preceptory [L. *praeceptor*, teacher]

pre·cep·to·ry (priséptəri:) *pl.* **precep·to·ries** *n.* (*hist.*) a subordinate community of the Knights Templars ‖ the manor, estate etc. belonging to this [fr. M.L *praeceptoria*, estate of a preceptor]

pre·ces·sion (priséʃən) *n.* the motion of the axis of rotation of a spinning body (e.g. a gyroscope) about a line that makes an angle with it, so as to describe a cone. It is caused by a torque acting on the rotation axis to change its direction, and is a motion continuously at right angles to the plane of the torque causing it and the angular momentum vector of the spinning body **pre·cés·sion·al** *adj.* [fr. L.L. *praecessio* (*praecessionis*), a preceding]

precession of the equinoxes (*astron.*) the combined effect of lunisolar and planetary precessions on the movement of the equinoctial points, causing a slightly earlier occurrence of the equinoxes each year (a complete to-and-fro swing taking 25,800 terrestrial years)

pre-Chris·tian (pri:krístʃən) *adj.* of, relating to or being a time prior to the birth of Christ ‖ of, relating to or being a time before the introduction of Christianity

pre·cinct (pri:síŋkt) *n.* the space within the boundaries of a church, school or other building or place, *the abbey precinct* ‖ the boundary itself ‖ (*pl.*) the immediate surroundings of a place ‖ a subdivision of a county, city or city ward for police and election purposes [fr. M.L. *praecinctum* fr. *praecingere* (*praecinctus*), to surround]

pre·ci·os·i·ty (preʃi:ɒ́siti:) *n.* excessive refinement, esp. the affected insistence on purity or nicety of language characteristic of a group of fashionable women of 17th-c. French society [O.F. *preciosité*]

pre·cious (préʃəs) **1.** *adj.* of great material value, *precious metals* ‖ of great nonmaterial value, *a precious friendship* ‖ exhibiting preciosity ‖ (used as a term of endearment) beloved ‖ (*pop.*) complete, *you have made a precious fool of yourself* **2.** *adv.* (*pop.*) extremely, *I took precious good care not to let him know* [O.F. *precios*]

precious metal a valuable metal, esp. gold, silver, platinum

precious stone a jewel, e.g. diamond, ruby etc., of great value

prec·i·pice (présəpis) *n.* the very steep or overhanging part of the face of a cliff, side of a mountain etc. [F. *précipice*]

pre·cip·i·tance (prisípitəns) *n.* precipitancy

pre·cip·i·tan·cy (prisípitənsi:) *n.* excessive, violent haste ‖ rashness, or an instance of this [PRECIPITANT]

pre·cip·i·tant (prisípitənt) **1.** *adj.* precipitate **2.** *n.* (*chem.*) that which causes precipitation to occur [fr. L. *praecipitans* (*praecipitantis*) fr. *praecipitare*, to precipitate]

pre·cip·i·tate 1. (prisípiteit) *v. pres. part.* **pre·cip·i·tat·ing** *past* and *past part.* **pre·cip·i·tat·ed** *v.t.* (*rhet.*) to hurl downward, throw violently, *he precipitated himself into the melee* ‖ to hasten, *his illness precipitated the crisis* ‖ (*chem.*) to cause (a soluble substance) to become insoluble and separate from a solution ‖ (*meteorol.*) to cause (vapor) to condense and fall as rain, snow etc. ‖ *v.i.* (*chem.*) to separate from a solution ‖ (*meteorol.*) to condense from a vapor and fall as rain, snow etc. **2.** (prisípitit) *adj.* sudden, hasty, *precipitate action* ‖ rushing violently ‖ rash, headstrong **3.** (prisípitit) *n.* (*chem.*) a solid substance separated from a solution as the result of a chemical reaction, esp. a crystalline solid that can be separated from the solution by filtration [fr. L. *praecipitare* (*praecipitatus*), to rush headlong]

pre·cip·i·ta·tion (prisipitéiʃən) *n.* a precipitating or being precipitated ‖ excessive or reckless haste ‖ (*meteorol.*) a deposit of water in either liquid or solid form, e.g. rain, snow, which reaches the earth from the atmosphere ‖ (*meteorol.*) the quantity deposited ‖ (*chem.*) a precipitate [F. *précipitation*]

pre·cip·i·tat·or (prisípiteitər) *n.* (*envir.*) an air pollution control device that mechanically or electrically collects particles from an emission

pre·cip·i·tin (prisípitin) *n.* (*med.*) an antibody which forms a precipitate when reacting with its antigen [PRECIPITATE]

pre·cip·i·tous (prisípitəs) *adj.* resembling a precipice ‖ containing precipices ‖ hasty [fr. obs. F. *precipiteux*]

pré·cis (préisi:) *pl.* **pré·cis** (préisi:z) *n.* a brief summary of essential points etc. in a speech or writing [F.]

pre·cise (prisáis) *adj.* accurate in every detail, *a precise account* ‖ exact, *precise measurement* ‖ excessively attentive to detail, punctilious, *precise manners* ‖ very, *at that precise moment he came in* **pre·císe·ly** *adv.* [F. *précis*]

pre·ci·sian (prisíʒən) *n.* a person who adheres strictly to rules and forms, esp. in religious observances ‖ (*hist.*) an English Puritan [PRECISE]

pre·ci·sion (prisíʒən) *n.* the quality of being precise ‖ (*computer*) the exactness of a quantity, sometimes expressed in the number of significant digits in the solution [F.]

pre·clas·sic (pri:klǽsik) *adj.* preclassical

pre·clas·si·cal (pri:klǽsik'l) *adj.* of or relating to the period before the classical age, esp. in literature and art

pre·clin·i·cal (pri:klínik'l) *adj.* (*med.*) of or relating to the period before the appearance of symptoms

pre·clude (priklú:d) *pres. part.* **pre·clud·ing** *past* and *past part.* **pre·clud·ed** *v.t.* to prevent, *illness precluded his visit* ‖ to make practically impossible, esp. by anticipatory action, *measures to preclude failure* [fr. L. *praecludere*, to shut off]

pre·clu·sion (priklú:ʒən) *n.* a precluding or being precluded [fr. L. *praeclusio* (*praeclusionis*)]

preclusion order an order providing a choice of alternatives to punishment, e.g., public service

pre·clu·sive (priklú:siv) *adj.* tending to preclude [fr. L. *praeclusus*, shut off]

precoces *PRAECOCES

pre·co·cial, *Br.* **prae·co·cial** (prikóuʃəl) *adj.* designating birds whose young are able to look after themselves as soon as they are hatched [fr. L. *praecox* (*praecocis*), mature early]

pre·co·cious (prikóuʃəs) *adj.* displaying highly developed mental or physical characteristics at an early age, *a precocious child* ‖ done or made by someone having these characteristics, *a precocious work* ‖ (*bot.*) fruiting or flowering earlier than usual [fr. L. *praecox* (*praecocis*), mature early]

pre·coc·i·ty (prikɒ́siti:) *n.* the condition or quality of being precocious [F. *précocité*]

pre·cog·ni·tion (pri:kɒgníʃən) *n.* foreknowledge [fr. L.L. *praecognitio* (*praecognitionis*]

pre-Co·lum·bi·an (pri:kəlʌ́mbi:ən) *adj.* of or relating to the period before the discovery of America by Columbus

pre·con·ceive (pri:kənsí:v) *pres. part.* **pre·con·ceiv·ing** *past* and *past part.* **pre·con·ceived** *v.t.* to form (an idea or opinion) beforehand

pre·con·cep·tion (pri:kənsépʃən) *n.* the act of preconceiving or an instance of this ‖ a prejudice

pre·con·cert (pri:kənsə́:rt) *v.t.* to arrange beforehand by agreement, *preconcerted plans*

pre·con·cil·i·ar (pri:kənsíli:ər) *adj.* of the period before the second Vatican council, 1962–65. *Cf* POSTCONCILIAR

pre·co·nize (prí:kənaiz) *pres. part.* **pre·co·niz·ing** *past* and *past part.* **pre·co·nized** *v.t.* (*Roman Catholicism*) to confirm publicly the appointment of (a bishop etc.) by papal proclamation in consistory ‖ to proclaim, cite or summon publicly [fr. M. L. *praeconizare*]

pre·cur·sive (prikə́:rsiv) *adj.* precursory [fr. L. *praecurrere* (*praecursus*), to run before]

pre·cur·sor (prikə́:rsər) *n.* someone who prepares the way for another or who precedes him in office ‖ something which precedes something else, *Sturm und Drang was a precursor of Romanticism* [L. fr. *praecurrere*, to run before]

pre·cur·so·ry (prikə́:rsəri:) *adj.* preliminary ‖ indicating something to follow [fr. L. *praecursorius*]

pre·da·cious, pre·da·ceous (pridéiʃəs) *adj.* preying upon other animals **pre·dac·i·ty** (pridǽsiti:) *n.* the quality or condition of being predacious [fr. L. *praedari*, to prey upon]

pre·date (pri:déit) *pres. part.* **pre·dat·ing** *past* and *past part.* **pre·dat·ed** *v.t.* to happen before (a certain time or event or set of circumstances) ‖ to inscribe with a date earlier than the date on which the inscribing is done

pred·a·tor (prédətər) *n.* a predatory animal [L. *praedator*]

pred·a·to·ri·ly (prédətɔrili:, prédətouril i:) *adv.* in a predatory way

pred·a·to·ri·ness (prédətɔri:nis, prédətouri:nis) *n.* the quality or state of being predatory

pred·a·to·ry (prédətɔri:, prédətouri:) *adj.* (of persons) given to preying upon others ‖ predacious [fr. L. *praedatorius* fr. *praedator* fr. *praedari*, to prey upon]

pre·de·cease (pri:disí:s) *pres. part.* **pre·de·ceas·ing** *past* and *past part.* **pre·de·ceased** *v.t.* to die before (another person)

pred·e·ces·sor (prédisesər, predisésər, *Br.* esp. prí:disesər, pri:disésər) *n.* a person preceding another in an office, position etc. ‖ something which has been succeeded by something else [fr. F. *prédécesseur*]

pre·del·la (pridélə) *pl.* **pre·del·le** (pridéli:, pridélei) *n.* (*eccles.*) the step or platform on which an altar stands ‖ (*eccles.*) a painting or sculpture on the vertical face of this ‖ (*eccles.*) a secondary painting forming a border or pendant to the principal painting [etym. doubtful]

pre·des·ti·nar·i·an (pri:destinéəri:ən) **1.** *n.* a person who accepts the doctrine of predestination **2.** *adj.* pertaining to predestination [PREDESTINATE]

pre·des·ti·nate 1. (pri:déstineit) *v.t. pres. part.* **pre·des·ti·nat·ing** *past* and *past part.* **pre·des·ti·nat·ed** to predestine **2.** (pri:déstinit) *adj.* determined beforehand [fr. L. *praedestinare* (*praedestinatus*)]

pre·des·ti·na·tion (pri:destinéiʃən) *n.* the act of predestinating ‖ (*theol.*) the doctrine that everything was determined by God from the beginning, esp. with reference to the play of divine omnipotence and human free will in determining the fate of the soul [fr. *praedestinatio* (*praedestinationis*) fr. *praedestinare*, to predestine]

pre·des·tine (pri:déstin) *pres. part.* **pre·des·tin·ing** *past* and *past part.* **pre·des·tined** *v.t.* to destine beforehand, esp. by divine decree [F. *prédestiner*]

pre·de·ter·mi·nate (pri:ditə́:rminit) *adj.* determined beforehand

pre·de·ter·mi·na·tion (pri:ditə:rminéiʃən) *n.* a predetermining or being predetermined

pre·de·ter·mine (pri:ditə́:rmin) *pres. part.* **pre·de·ter·min·ing** *past* and *past part.* **pre·de·ter·mined** *v.t.* to calculate or determine in advance ‖ to predestine ‖ to give a mental bias to, *this predetermined me in his favor* [fr. L. L. *praedeterminare*]

pre·de·ter·min·er (pri:ditə́:rminər) *n.* (*grammar*) a limiting noun modifier placed before a noun in a phrase. *Cf* POSTDETERMINER

pred·i·ca·bil·i·ty (predikəbíliti:) *n.* the state or quality of being predicable

pred·i·ca·ble (prédikəb'l) **1.** *adj.* capable of being predicated **2.** *n.* that which may be predicated ‖ (*logic*) any of Aristotle's five relationships (genus, species, difference, property, accident) used in predication [F. *prédicable*]

pre·dic·a·ment (pridíkəmənt) *n.* a situation involving a hard or unpleasant choice ‖ (*Aristotelian logic*) a category [fr. L. *praedicamentum*]

pred·i·cate 1. (prédikeit) *v. pres. part.* **pred·i·cat·ing** *past* and *past part.* **pred·i·cat·ed** *v.t.* to state as an assumed attribute, quality or property, *to predicate the perfectibility of man* ‖ to imply, connote, *his attitude predicates self-interest* ‖ (*logic*) to affirm or deny (something) about the subject of a proposition ‖ to base (a thesis, statement, attitude etc.) on, *his conclusions are predicated on laboratory tests* ‖ *v.i.* to make a statement **2.** (prédikit) *n.* (*logic*) that which is affirmed or denied about the subject of a proposition ‖ (*gram.*) the words (verb with object or adverbial modifier, or copula with noun or adjective) which express what is stated of the subject of a clause or sentence [fr. M.L. *praedicatum* fr. *praedicare*, to proclaim]

pred·i·ca·tion (predikéiʃən) *n.* a predicating or being predicated [M.E. fr. O.F. *predicaciun*]

pred·i·ca·tive (prédikeitiv) *adj.* constituting a predicate or part of a predicate [fr. L. *praedicativus*]

pre·dict (pridíkt) *v.t.* to make known beforehand, foretell, *to predict rain* ‖ *v.i.* to foretell the future **pre·díct·a·ble** *adj.* [fr. L. *praedicere* (*praedictus*)]

pre·dic·tion (pridíkʃən) *n.* the action of predicting ‖ that which is predicted [fr. L. *praedictio* (*praedictionis*)]

pre·dic·tive (pridíktiv) *adj.* of or relating to prediction

pre·dic·tor (pridíktər) *n.* someone or that which predicts ‖ an instrument used to control antiaircraft guns by allowing for the height and speed of the target

CONCISE PRONUNCIATION KEY: **(a)** æ, *cat*; ɑ, *car*; ɔ *fawn*; ei, *snake*. **(e)** e, *hen*; i:, *sheep*; iə, *deer*; εə, *bear*. **(i)** i, *fish*; ai, *tiger*; ə:, *bird*. **(o)** o, *ox*; au, *cow*; ou, *goat*; u, *poor*; ɔi, *royal*. **(u)** ʌ, *duck*; u, *bull*; u:, *goose*; ə, *bacillus*; ju:, *cube*. x, *loch*; θ, *think*; ð, *bother*; z, *Zen*; ʒ, *corsage*; dʒ, *savage*; ŋ, *orangutang*; j, *yak*; ʃ, *fish*; tʃ, *fetch*; 'l, *rabble*; 'n, *redden*. Complete pronunciation key appears inside front cover.

pre·di·gest (pri:didʒést, prį:daidʒést) v.t. to make (food) more digestible by artificial means **pre·di·gés·tion** n.

pre·di·lec·tion (prį:d'lékʃən, pred'lékʃən) n. a special taste or liking, a predilection for sparkling wines [F. prédilection]

pre·dis·pose (prį:dispóuz) pres. part. **pre·dis·pos·ing** past and past part. **pre·dis·posed** v.i. to make (someone) tend to act, feel, suffer etc. in a particular way or be prone, his constitution predisposes him to colds

pre·dis·po·si·tion (prį:dispəzíʃən) n. the condition of being predisposed || a tendency, susceptibility, a predisposition to quarrelsomeness

pre·dom·i·nance (pridóminəns) n. the quality or state of being predominant

pre·dom·i·nan·cy (pridóminənsi:) n. predominance

pre·dom·i·nant (pridóminənt) adj. most frequent, prevailing, barley is the predominant crop here [F. prédominant]

pre·dom·i·nate (pridómineit) pres. part. **pre·dom·i·nat·ing** past and past part. **pre·dom·i·nat·ed** v.i. to be most frequent, or lead in quality, status etc., small farmers predominate in the region [fr. M.L. praedominari (praedominatus)]

pre·e·mer·gent (prį:imə́:rdʒənt) adj. (botany) of seed below ground

pre·em·i·nence (pri:éminəns) n. the quality or state of being preeminent [fr. L. L. praeeminentia]

pre·em·i·nent (pri:éminənt) adj. superior to others, esp. in some specified quality or sphere, he is preeminent in Shakespearean roles [fr. L. praeeminens (praeemiuentis) fr. praeeminere, to excel]

pre·empt (pri:émpt) v.t. to purchase before others have the opportunity to purchase || (Am. hist.) to settle on (public land) in order to establish the right of preemption || to acquire beforehand || v.i. (bridge) to make a preemptive bid [PREEMPTION]

pre·emp·tion (pri:émpʃən) n. the act or right of purchasing before others have a chance to purchase || (Am. hist.) the preempting of public land || a taking possession before others **pre·emp·tive** (pri:émptiv) adj. (bridge) of, relating to, or constituting a bid that is higher than necessary, in order to discourage one's partner or opponents from bidding [etym. doubtful]

pre·emp·tive adj. occurring before, and in anticipation of, a situation developing, e.g., preemptive attack, preemptive seizure

preen (pri:n) v.t. (of a bird) to trim (the feathers) with the beak || (of a person) to make (oneself) trim in appearance || to congratulate (oneself) mildly [var. of PRUNE v.]

pre·en·gi·neered (prį:endʒiníərd) adj. made of prefabricated units

pre·es·tab·lished harmony (prį:istǽbliʃt) (philos.) a theory of Leibniz stating that a harmony between mind and matter was established eternally at the Creation

pre·ex·ist (prį:igzíst) v.i. to exist previously (esp. of the soul before the birth of the body) || v.t. to exist before (something) **pre·ex·ist·ence** n. previous existence, esp. the life of the soul before birth **pre·ex·ist·ent** adj.

pre·fab (prí:fæb) n. (pop.) a prefabricated building, esp. a house

pre·fab·ri·cate (pri:fǽbrikeit) pres. part. **pre·fab·ri·cat·ing** past and past part. **pre·fab·ri·cat·ed** v.t. to construct sections of (e.g. a house) in a factory for assembly on a site elsewhere **pre·fab·ri·cá·tion** n.

pref·ace (préfis) 1. n. a written introduction to a book or the opening remarks of a speaker intended to elucidate the text or speech to follow || a leading up to something || (eccles.) the part of the Mass before the canon 2. v.t. pres. part. **pref·ac·ing** past and past part. **pref·aced to** introduce by or furnish with a preface || to lead up to [F. préface]

pref·a·to·ri·al (prefətɔ́ri:əl, prefətóuri:əl) adj. prefatory

pref·a·to·ry (préfətɔri:, préfətouri:) adj. of, relating to, or constituting a preface [fr. L. praefari, to say beforehand]

pre·fect (prí:fekt) n. (Rom. hist.) a civil or military commander || the civil governor of a department in France || (in some schools) a senior pupil to whom some disciplinary authority is delegated **pre·fec·tó·ri·al** adj. [O.F.]

pre·fec·tur·al (priféktʃərəl) adj. of or relating to a prefecture

pre·fec·ture (prí:fektʃər) n. the office, official

residence, jurisdiction or term of office of a prefect [fr. L. praefectura]

pre·fer (prifə́:r) pres. part. **pre·fer·ring** past and past part. **pre·ferred** v.t. to like better, I prefer this house to that one || to choose rather, I prefer not to think about it || (law) to place (a charge, complaint etc. against a person) before someone in authority || (law) to give priority to (a creditor) **pref·er·a·ble** (préfərəb'l) adj. **préf·er·a·bly** adv. [fr. L. praeferre, to place before]

pref·er·ence (préfərəns) n. a preferring or being preferred || the person or thing preferred || the right to choose, to be allowed no preference || a system whereby lower import duties are levied on goods from certain countries || (law) priority in the right to demand payment of a debt [F. préférence]

preference shares (Br.) preferred stock

pref·er·en·tial (prefərénʃəl) adj. relating to, or constituting preference [fr. M. L. praeferentia, preference]

preferential primary a presidential primary

preferential shop a firm which gives preference to union members, but is free to hire nonunion workers when the union is unable to supply its own workers

pre·fer·ment (prifə́:rmənt) n. a preferring or being preferred || promotion in office || a position that confers advancement

preferred stock (Am.=Br. preference shares) a corporation's stock which has first claim on the distribution of assets and on the payment of a specified dividend

pre·fig·u·ra·tion (prį:figjəréiʃən) n. something that prefigures || the act of prefiguring or the state of being prefigured [fr. L. praefiguratio (praefigurationis)]

pre·fig·u·ra·tive (prį:fígjərətiv) adj. serving to prefigure || of a society in which the parental role is nurturant until the child reaches the age when he or she can teach the society, and thereafter the child's values predominate; defined by American anthropologist Margaret Mead [fr. M.L. praefigurativus]

pre·fig·ure (prį:fígjər) pres. part. **pre·fig·ur·ing** past and past part. **pre·fig·ured** v.t. to represent beforehand, serve as an image of, Rome in the play prefigures the heavenly city || to picture to oneself beforehand [fr. L.L. praefigurare]

pre·fix 1. (pri:fíks, prí:fiks) v.t. (gram.) to place or put (a syllable, group of syllables or word) in front of a word to modify its meaning or form a new word 2. (prí:fiks) n. (gram.) that which is placed in front in this way, e.g. 'un' in 'unable' [O.F. prefixer]

pre·form (prį:fɔ́rm) v.t. to form beforehand **pre·for·má·tion** n. a forming beforehand || (biol.) a formerly prevalent theory that the ovum of an animal contained a miniature individual and that only nourishment was needed for it to develop into a perfect adult [fr. L. praeformare]

Pregl (preig'l), Fritz (1869–1930), Austrian chemist. He developed microanalysis of organic compounds. Nobel prize (1923)

preg·na·ble (prégnəb'l) adj. capable of being captured [M.E. prenable fr. F.]

preg·nan·cy (prégnənsi:) pl. **preg·nan·cies** n. the condition of being pregnant

preg·nant (prégnənt) adj. (of a female) carrying an unborn child or unborn young within the body || deeply significant, pregnant remarks, or full of implication, a pregnant silence || full ideas, imaginative [fr. L. praegnans (praegnantis)]

pre·hen·sile (prihénsil, prihénsail) adj. (zool.) able to grasp and hold, a prehensile tail **pre·hen·sil·i·ty** (prį:hensíliti:) n. [F. préhensile]

pre·hen·sion (prihénʃən) n. (zool.) the act of seizing or grasping || mental apprehension [fr. L. prehensio (prehensionis) fr. prehendere, to grasp]

pre·his·tor·ic (prį:histórik, prį:histórik) adj. of or relating to the period before recorded history || existing during this period, prehistoric man **pre·his·tór·i·cal·ly** adv.

pre·his·to·ry (prį:hístəri:) n. the study of the period of history before there were written records, esp. the study of prehistoric man || the period of history before there were written records

pre·ig·ni·tion (prį:igníʃən) n. the premature explosion of the gas mixture in the cylinder of an internal-combustion engine

pre·in·i·ti·a·tion (prį:iniʃiéiʃən) n. (mil.) premature initiation of the fission chain reaction in the active material of a nuclear weapon

pre·judge (prį:dʒʌ́dʒ) pres. part. **pre·judg·ing** past and past part. **pre·judged** v.t. to pass judgment on before all the evidence is known || to form a premature opinion of **pre·júdg·ment, pre·júdge·ment** n. [fr. F. préjuger]

pre·ju·di·ca·tion (prį:dʒu:dikéiʃən) n. the act of prejudging [fr. L. praejudicare (praejudicatus), to judge beforehand]

prej·u·dice (prédʒudis) pres. part. **prej·u·dic·ing** past and past part. **prej·u·diced** v.t. to cause (someone) to have a prejudice, to prejudice a jury member || to cause injury to || (law) to impair the validity of (a right) [F. préjuaicier]

prejudice n. a preconceived opinion, usually unfavorable || the holding of such an opinion || an unjustified and unreasonable bias || (law) injury due to some judgment or action of another, e.g. the disregard of a person's rights **without prejudice** (law) without detriment to a person's claims or rights [F. préjudice]

prej·u·di·cial (predʒudíʃəl) adj. injuring, or likely to injure, his political views were prejudicial to his chances of success [F. préjudicial]

prel·a·cy (préləsi:) pl. **prel·a·cies** n. (eccles.) the office, dignity or see of a prelate || prelates collectively || (used in a hostile sense) Church government by prelates [A.F. prelacie]

prel·ate (prélit) n. (eccles.) a high-ranking Church dignitary, e.g. an archbishop, bishop or patriarch **pre·lat·ic** (prilǽtik) adj. [M.E. prelat fr. O.F.]

prelate nullius n. pl. a Roman Catholic ecclesiastic in charge of an independent district not in any diocese

prel·a·ture (prélətʃər) n. the office, dignity or see of a prelate || prelates collectively [F. prélature]

pre·lim·i·nar·i·ly (prilíminerili:) adv. in a preliminary way

pre·lim·i·nar·y (prilíminери:) 1. adj. introductory or preparatory, a preliminary test 2. pl. **pre·lim·i·nar·ies** n. a preliminary step, procedure etc. || a preliminary examination || (pl., abbr. prelims, Br.) front matter [fr. L. prae, before+liminaris, of a threshold]

prel·ude (prélju:d) 1. n. something serving to introduce, or set the mood for, some event, performance, action etc. to follow, the discussions were a prelude to the treaty || a piece of music serving as an introduction to the theme of a fugue, an act of an opera etc. || the title used by some composers for some self-contained pieces for piano and orchestra 2. v.t. pres. part. **prel·ud·ing** past and past part. **prel·ud·ed** to serve as a prelude to [F. prélude]

pre·ma·ture (pri:mətúər, prį:mətjúər, prį:mətʃúər) adj. occurring, done, existing etc. before the proper time, a premature crop || (of an infant) born before the 37th week of pregnancy or weighing less than 5½ lbs **pre·ma·túre·ly** adv. [fr. L. praematurus]

pre·ma·tu·ri·ty (prį:mətúəriti:, prį:mətjúəriti:, prį:mətʃúəriti:) n. the state or quality of being premature [F. prématurité]

pre·max·il·la (prį:mæksílə) pl. **pre·max·il·lae** (prį:mæksíli:), **pre·max·il·las** n. (anat., zool.) one of a pair of bones in the upper jaw of vertebrates, between and in front of the maxillae **pre·max·il·lar·y** (pri:mǽksəleri:) adj.

pre·med·i·cal (pri:médik'l) adj. of or relating to the studies preceding the medical course proper

pre·med·i·tate (priméditeit) v.t. pres. part. **pre·med·i·tat·ing** past and past part. **pre·med·i·tat·ed** to think about and plan beforehand

pre·med·i·ta·tion (priméditéiʃən) n. a premeditating, esp. (law) the degree of planning sufficient to show intent to commit an act [fr. L. praemeditatio (praemeditationis)]

pre·mier (primíər, primjíər, prí:mjər) 1. adj. first in position, importance etc. || bearing the oldest title within a degree of rank, premier earl 2. n. prime minister [F.=first]

pre·miere, pre·mière (primíər, primjíər, primjíər) n. the first public performance of a play or showing of a film || the female star of a theatrical production [F.]

pre·mier·ship (primíərʃip, primjíərʃip, prí:mjərʃip) n. the office of premier or tenure of office of a premier

prem·ise, prem·iss 1. (prémis) n. a fact, statement or assumption on which an argument is based or from which conclusions are drawn || (esp. premiss, logic) one of the two propositions (major and minor) of a syllogism from which the conclusion is drawn || (pl., law) the section of a deed stating the names of the parties involved and giving an explanation of the transaction ||

(*pl.*) a piece of land and the house and buildings on it, *keep off the premises* **2. prem·ise** (primáiz) *v.t. pres. part.* **prem·is·ing** *past* and *past part.* **prem·ised** to state or assume as a premise [F. *prémisse*]

pre·mi·um (prí:mi:əm) *n.* a prize or reward, esp. a sum paid addition to wages or salary ‖ a sum paid, either all at once or periodically, for an insurance contract ‖ the rate above nominal value at which something sells ‖ a fee paid for instruction or training in a trade etc. ‖ a sum given for a loan in addition to interest at a premium worth more than the nominal value ‖ very hard to get and therefore valuable **to put a premium on** to stress the importance of, put a high value on, *to put a premium on honesty* [L. *praemium*, profit, reward]

pre·mo·lar (prí:móulər) **1.** *n.* a premolar tooth **2.** *adj.* situated in front of the molar teeth

pre·mo·ni·tion (prị:məníʃən, prẹməníʃən) *n.* a forewarning ‖ a presentiment [fr. obs. F. *premonicion* fr. L.L. *praemonitio* fr. L. *praemonere*]

pre·mon·i·to·ry (primɒ́nitọri:, primɒ́nitọuri:) *adj.* giving warning beforehand, *premonitory signs of sickness* [fr. *premonitor*, something that forewarns fr. L.]

Pre·mon·stra·ten·sian (pri:mɒnstrəténʃən) **1** *adj.* of a religious order of canons regular founded (1119) by St Norbert at Prémontré in N. France **2.** *n.* a member of this order, or of its order of nuns, or of its third order [after *Prémontré*]

pre·morse (primɔ́rs) *adj.* (of a leaf or root) having the end truncated as if bitten off [fr. L. *praemordere (praemorsus)*, to bite off in front]

Prem·y·slide (prémislid) *n.* a member of the Přemysl family who ruled Bohemia (9th-13th cc.)

pre·na·tal (pri:néit'l) *adj.* occurring or existing before birth

prenomen *PRAENOMEN

pren·tice (préntis) *adj.* of work showing incomplete command or skill ‖ of work done in order to learn, *prentice plays* [APPRENTICE]

pre·oc·cu·pa·tion (pri:ɒkjupéiʃən) *n.* a preoccupying or being preoccupied [fr. L. *praeoccupatio (praeoccupationis)*]

pre·oc·cu·pied (pri:ɒ́kjupaid) *adj.* completely engrossed, esp. in thought ‖ (*biol.*, of a generic or specific name) not available as a designation because already in use [PREOCCUPY]

pre·oc·cu·py (pri:ɒ́kjupai) *pres. part.* **pre·oc·cu·py·ing** *past* and *past part.* **pre·oc·cu·pied** *v.t.* to engage the attention or interest of (someone) almost completely

pre·or·dain (prị:ɔrdéin) *v.t.* to ordain beforehand

pre·or·gas·mic (prị:ɔrgǽzmik) *adj.* **1.** of one who has never had an orgasm. **2.** of the arousal period preceding an orgasm

prep (prep) *n.* (*Br., pop.*) homework (done by a schoolboy or schoolgirl)

prep·a·ra·tion (prẹpəréiʃən) *n.* a preparing or being prepared ‖ that which is prepared, esp. a chemical substance or medicine, for subsequent use ‖ (*pl.*) preparatory measures ‖ the work done in preparing school lessons ‖ (*mus.*) the leading up to a dissonance by sounding the dissonant note as a consonant note in the preceding chord ‖ (*mus.*) the note so sounded [F. *préparation*]

pre·par·a·tive (pripǽrətiv) **1.** *adj.* preparatory **2.** *n.* a preparation [F. *préparatif*]

pre·par·a·tor (pripǽrətər) *n.* someone who prepares specimens for scientific study or for display in a museum [L.L. *praeparator*]

pre·par·a·to·ry (pripǽrətọri:, pripέərətọri:, pripǽrətọuri:, pripέərətọuri:) *adj.* of that which prepares or introduces ‖ undergoing preliminary instruction, *a preparatory student* [fr. M. L. *praeparatorius*]

preparatory school (*abbr.* prep school) a private school for preparing students for college ‖ (*Br.*) a private school bringing children to public secondary school level at age 13½

pre·pare (pripέər) *v.t. pres. part.* **pre·par·ing** *past* and *past part.* **pre·pared** to make the necessary preparations for, *to prepare a meal* ‖ to get ready for by study, work, practice etc., *to prepare a speech, lesson etc.* ‖ to get (someone) ready ‖ to put (someone) in a receptive state of mind, *to prepare someone for a shock* ‖ to make (e.g. a chemical preparation), *to prepare a vaccine* ‖ (*mus.*) to lead up to (a dissonance) by sounding the dissonant note as a consonant note in the preceding chord ‖ (*mus.*) to lead up to (a note or ornament) by a preliminary note ‖ *v.i.* to take necessary previous measures, *to prepare for a journey* ‖ to make oneself ready in one's mind, *to prepare for the worst* **to be prepared to** to be willing to, *to be prepared to apologize* **pre·par·ed·ly** (pripέəridli:) *adv.* **pre·pár·ed·ness** *n.* the state of being prepared, esp. of being prepared for war [F. *préparer*]

pre·pay (pri:péi) *pres. part.* **pre·pay·ing** *past* and *past part.* **pre·paid** *v.t.* to pay for in advance **pre·páy·ment** *n.*

pre·pense (pripéns) *adj.* (in the phrase) **malice prepense** (*law*) malice aforethought [alt. fr. *purpense* fr. O.F. *purpenser*]

pre·pon·der·ance (pripɒ́ndərəns) *n.* the condition of being preponderant

pre·pon·der·ant (pripɒ́ndərənt) *adj.* superior in weight, number, influence, power, importance etc. [fr. L. *praeponderans (praeponderantis)* fr. *praeponderare*, to outweigh]

pre·pon·der·ate (pripɒ́ndəreit) *pres. part.* **pre·pon·der·at·ing** *past* and *past part.* **pre·pon·der·at·ed** *v.i.* to be superior in weight, number, influence, power, importance etc. **pre·pón·der·at·ing·ly** *adv.* [fr. L. *paraeponderare (praeponderatus)*, to outweigh]

prep·o·si·tion (prẹpəzíʃən) *n.* (*gram.*) a word (in some languages) expressing the relationship between a noun, pronoun or noun phrase (which usually follows the preposition and is called the 'object' of the preposition) and another element of the sentence, e.g. a verb ('down' in 'he walked down the street'), a noun ('of' in 'the mother of twins') or an adjective ('for' in 'grateful for favors') ‖ a compound construction which functions as a preposition (e.g. 'on top of') **prep·o·sí·tion·al** *adj.* [fr. L. *praepositio (praepositionis)*]

prepositional phrase a preposition and its object

pre·pos·i·tive (pri:pɒ́zitiv) *adj.* (*gram.*) prefixed or placed before a word [fr. L.L. *praepositivus*]

pre·pos·sess (prị:pəzés) *v.t.* to influence favorably in advance or at the outset

pre·pos·sess·ing (prị:pəzésiŋ) *adj.* making an immediate favorable impression, attractive

pre·pos·ter·ous (pripɒ́stərəs) *adj.* grotesquely or comically ridiculous, *a preposterous hat* ‖ unreasonable, unlikely, *a preposterous proposal, a preposterous story* [fr. L. *praeposterus*, reversed]

pre·po·ten·cy (prị:póut'nsi:) *n.* the quality or condition of being prepotent ‖ (*biol.*) the capacity of one parent to transmit more characteristics to its offspring than the other parent ‖ fertilization of a flower by pollen from another flower in preference to pollen from its own stamens, when both are offered simultaneously [fr. L. *praepotentia*]

pre·po·tent (prị:póut'nt) *adj.* having superior power ‖ (*bot.*, of a flower) exhibiting a preference for cross-pollination ‖ (*biol.*) displaying prepotency [fr. L. *praepotens (praepotentis)* fr. *praeposse*, to be very powerful]

prep·pie (prépi:) *n.* one who attends or has attended a private secondary high school — **prep·pie** *adj.* of the typical appearance or characteristics of such a person

pre·peg (prí:pẹg) *n.* (*chem.*) a synthetic impregnated with resin before processing. —**pre-peg** *adj.*

pre·pref·er·ence (prị:préfərəns) *adj.* (*Br.*, of shares etc.) ranking before preference shares in a claim to dividend or repayment

pre·puce (prí:pju:s) *n.* the foreskin, or a similar fold of skin over the clitoris [F. *prépuce*]

Pre-Raph·a·el·ite (prị:rǽfi:əlait) **1.** *n.* a member or follower of the Pre-Raphaelite Brotherhood **2.** *adj.* pertaining to such an artist or his work

Pre-Raphaelite Brotherhood a group of English painters, including William Holman Hunt, Millais and Dante Gabriel Rossetti, formed in London in 1848. In a broad sense they took their ideals from the painting of Italian masters prior to Raphael. They gave great importance to subject, and often took it from religion. Other characteristics include sensitive painting of elaborate detail, fondness for outdoor settings, and the use of bright color. Ruskin defended their ideas in 'Pre-Raphaelitism' (1851)

pre·req·ui·site (prirékwizit) **1.** *adj.* requisite in an antecedent condition **2.** *n.* that which is prerequisite

pre·rog·a·tive (prirɒ́gətiv) **1.** *n.* an exclusive right or privilege possessed by a person or body of persons ‖ a right attached to an office or rank, *the royal prerogative* ‖ **2.** *adj.* pertaining to a prerogative, arising from special privilege [F. *prérogative*]

pres·age 1. (présidʒ) *n.* that which foretells a future event ‖ a presentiment **2.** (présidʒ, priséidʒ) *v.t. pres. part.* **pres·ag·ing** *past* and *past part.* **pres·aged** to foretell (a future event) [fr. L. *praesagium*, a foreboding]

pre·sanc·ti·fied (prị:sǽŋktifaid) *adj.* (*eccles.*, of the Host) consecrated at a previous celebration of the Mass

pres·by·o·pi·a (prẹzbi:óupi:ə, prẹsbi:óupi:ə) *n.* (*med.*) a failure, due to age, of the muscles of the eye to adjust the focus of the crystalline lens for vision at different distances (*ACCOMMODATION), and to distinguish near objects sharply **pres·by·op·ic** (prẹzbi:ɒ́pik, prẹsbi:ɒ́pik) *adj.* [Mod. L. fr. Gk *presbus*, old+*ops*, eye]

pres·by·ter (prézbitər, présbitər) *n.* (*eccles., hist.*) an elder having lay authority in the early Christian Church ‖ a minister in certain Episcopal churches ‖ an elder in a Presbyterian Church, esp. a member of a presbytery [L.L. fr. Gk]

pres·byt·er·ate (prezbítərit, presbítərit) *n.* the office of a presbyter ‖ a body of presbyters [fr. M.L. *presbyteratus*]

pres·by·te·ri·al (prẹzbitíəri:əl, prẹsbitíəri:əl) *adj.* of or relating to a presbyter, a body of presbyters, or a presbytery [fr. L.L. *presbyterium*]

Pres·by·te·ri·an (prẹzbitíəri:ən, prẹsbitíəri:ən) **1.** *adj.* of or relating to a system of Church polity consisting of a series of four courts composed of ministers and elected elders **2.** *n.* a member of a Church adhering to this form of government **Pres·by·té·ri·an·ism** *n.* [fr. L. *presbyterium*, presbytery]

—Presbyterian polity was first established in Geneva by Calvin, who held that Church government by elders and ministers conformed with New Testament practice. This system was adopted by Knox (*CHURCH OF SCOTLAND) and the Huguenots, and is now found throughout the world. Most Presbyterian Churches also adhere to Calvinist doctrine

pres·by·ter·y (prézbitẹri:, présbitẹri:) *pl.* **pres·by·ter·ies** *n.* (*eccles.*) a district court of ministers and elders of a Presbyterian Church ‖ the district within which this court has jurisdiction ‖ (*archit.*) the eastern part of a church beyond the choir stalls ‖ (*Roman Catholicism*) the residence of a priest [O.F. *presbiterie*, a priest's house]

pre·school (pri:skú:l) *adj.* of or relating to the period of infancy prior to the age of compulsory school attendance

pre·science (prí:ʃi:əns, préʃi:əns, prí:ʃəns, préʃəns) *n.* foreknowledge ‖ an instance of foreknowledge [F.]

pre·scient (prí:ʃənt, préʃənt) *adj.* having foreknowledge [F.]

Pres·cott (préskɒt), William Hickling (1796–1858), American historian. He wrote a 'History of the Conquest of Mexico' (1842) and a 'History of the Conquest of Peru' (1847)

pre·scribe (priskráib) *pres. part.* **pre·scrib·ing** *past* and *past part.* **pre·scribed** *v.t.* to order with the force of authority ‖ to order the use of (a medicine or treatment) ‖ *law*) to state (a prescriptive right or title) ‖ *v.i.* to lay down a rule ‖ to write a medical prescription ‖ (*law*) to claim a title etc. by a prescription [fr. L. *praescribere*, to write before]

pre·script (prí:skript) *n.* a command, rule [fr. L. *praescribere (praescriptus)*, to write before]

pre·scrip·tion (priskrípʃən) *n.* the act of prescribing ‖ that which is prescribed, esp. (*med.*) a written statement, giving directions for making and using a medicine ‖ (*law*) negative prescription ‖ (*law*) positive prescription ‖ ancient custom, esp. when regarded as authoritative [F. or fr. L. *praescriptio (praescriptionis)*, a prescribing]

pre·scrip·tive (priskríptiv) *adj.* that prescribes ‖ arising from, based on, or determined by prescription, *a prescriptive right* [fr. L.L. *praescriptivus*, pertaining to a legal exception]

pres·ence (préz'ns) *n.* the state or fact of being in a certain place, *his presence in the room was not noticed* ‖ the space immediately surrounding a person, *in the royal presence* ‖ distinction of bearing and demeanor ‖ the quality which marks a dominating personality, esp. the quality which enables a performer to dominate his audience, *to lack presence* ‖ an intangible spirit or mysterious influence felt to be present [O.F.]

presence of mind the ability to act quickly, intelligently and calmly in an emergency

pres·ent (préz'nt) *n.* a gift [O.F.]

present 1. *adj.* being in a specified place,

present in the room ‖ existing, being done, or occurring at this time, *the present moment, the present discussion* ‖ used as a form of reference to oneself, *the present writer* ‖ (*gram.*) of or designating a tense that expresses action now taking place, or state in time now existing **2.** *n.* this time ‖ (*gram.*) the present tense ‖ (*gram.*) a verb in the present tense ‖ (*pl., law*) present statements, *let it be known by these presents* **at present** at this time, *I cannot receive him at present* **for the present** at this time and for some little time to come, *that is enough for the present* [O. F.]

pre·sent (prizént) **1.** *v.t.* to bring (someone) to the notice of or into the presence of someone else, esp. a superior, *to present the candidates in Latin* ‖ to introduce (someone) formally at court ‖ to offer as a gift ‖ (with 'with') to make a gift to ‖ (with 'with') to cause to face, *to present with a problem* ‖ to exhibit or offer to view or notice, *to present a fine appearance, to present a bold front* ‖ to offer as a public entertainment ‖ to submit for consideration or action, *to present an argument, to present a bill* ‖ (*law*) to bring a formal charge against ‖ (*law*) to lay (e. g. a charge) before a court etc. ‖ to aim or point (e.g. a gun) at someone or something ‖ to bring (a clergyman) to the notice of a bishop with a view toward his selection for a benefice ‖ to install (a clergyman) in a benefice ‖ *v.i.* (of a fetus) to be directed towards the opening of the womb ‖ (*med.*) to come forward as a patient **to present arms** (*mil.*) to display the rifle perpendicularly in front of the center of the body as a salute while at the position of attention **2.** *n.* the position of presenting arms **pre·sent·a·bíl·i·ty** *n.* the condition or quality of being presentable **pre·sént·a·ble** *adj.* fit to be presented, shown, or offered, *a presentable appearance* **pre·sént·a·bly** *adv.* [O.F. *présenter*]

pres·en·ta·tion (prezentéiʃən, pri:zəntéiʃən) *n.* a presenting or being presented ‖ that which is presented, e.g. a theatrical performance ‖ a formal introduction, esp. an introduction at Court ‖ the act of presenting a benefice to a clergyman ‖ a formal presenting of a gift, usually before a gathering of people, *a presentation to the retiring chairman* ‖ (*med.*) the position of the fetus at birth ‖ (*philos.*) direct awareness (as distinct from association or reflection) as an element of cognition **pres·en·tá·tion·al** *adj.* **pres·en·tá·tion·ism** *n.* (*philos.*) the doctrine that the mind has immediate cognition of the objects of perception [O.F. *presentacion*]

pre·sent-day (préz'ntdéi) *adj.* belonging to the present time, *present-day standards*

pre·sen·tient (pri:sénʃənt) *adj.* (with 'of') feeling or perceiving beforehand [fr. L. *praesentiens* (*praesentientis*) fr. *praesentire,* to feel beforehand]

pre·sen·ti·ment (prizéntəmənt) *n.* a vague, usually uneasy sensing of an impending event [obs. F.]

pre·sen·tive (prizéntiv) *adj.* (of a word) presenting a thing directly to the mind (cf. SYMBOLIC)

pres·ent·ly (préz'ntli:) *adv.* in a short time from now, *I'll write to him presently* ‖ in a short time from then, *presently the room began to fill*

pre·sent·ment (prizéntmənt) *n.* a theatrical presentation or artistic delineation ‖ the act of presenting to the mind, e.g. by statement or suggestion ‖ that which is presented ‖ (*law*) the statement made by members of a grand jury under oath of any offense based on their own knowledge or without any bill of indictment ‖ (*eccles.*) a complaint presented to a bishop by the parish authorities ‖ (*philos.*) presentation [O.F. *presentement*]

present participle (*gram.*) a participle which expresses an action that takes place in the present or at the same time as the finite verb in the sentence, formed in English by adding '-ing' to the verb stem

pres·er·va·tion (prezərvéiʃən) *n.* a preserving or being preserved [F. *préservation*]

pre·serv·a·tive (prizə́:rvətiv) **1.** *adj.* having the ability to preserve, *a preservative coat of lead paint* **2.** *n.* a substance added to preserve, esp. a chemical added to prevent food from decomposition [fr. M.L. *praeservativus*]

pre·serve (prizə́:rv) **1.** *v. pres. part.* **pre·serv·ing** *past* and *past part.* **pre·served** *v.t.* to prepare (fruit, vegetables, meat or fish) by boiling, salting, pickling etc. and packing into containers for future use ‖ to keep up, maintain, prevent from ruin or decay, *to preserve the countryside* ‖ to keep from decomposition by freezing, treating with chemicals etc. ‖ to retain (e.g. a quality), *to preserve one's dignity* ‖ to maintain and protect (fish or game) for private use ‖ *v.i.* to be suitable for preserving ‖ to make preserves **2.** *n.* a large area of land or body of water where game or fish is protected ‖ something, e.g. an occupation, place etc., regarded exclusively as one's own, *to trespass on someone's preserve* ‖ (esp. *pl.*) jam [F. *préserver*]

pre·set (pri:sét) *pres. part.* **pre·set·ting** *past* and *past part.* **pre·set** *v.t.* to set (e.g. a thermostat reading) in advance

pre·side (prizáid) *pres. part.* **pre·sid·ing** *past* and *past part.* **pre·sid·ed** *v.i.* to be in a position of control or authority, *to preside over a meeting* [F. *présider*]

pres·i·den·cy (prézidənsi:) *pl.* **pres·i·den·cies** *n.* the office or function of president ‖ the term of office of a president ‖ the region under the control of a president, esp. (*hist.*) one of the three regions of India administered by the East India Company (presidencies of Bengal, Bombay, Madras) [fr. M.L. *praesidentia*]

pres·i·dent (prézidənt) *n.* the elected head of government in the U.S.A. and many other republics ‖ a person elected to preside over an organization, *the president of the football club* ‖ the chief officer of a bank, company, corporation etc. ‖ the head of a college or university ‖ (*Br.*) the head of certain colleges within a university [F. *président*]

pres·i·den·tial (prezidénʃəl) *adj.* of or relating to a president or a presidency [M.L. *praesidentialis* fr. *praesidentia,* presidency]

presidential primary an election within a state political party in which the voters indicate choices for president of the U.S.A. either by vote or by the selection of delegates to the national nominating convention

Presidential Succession Act a U.S. Congressional act sponsored (1947) by President Harry Truman. It declared that, in the event of the death or incapacity of both the president and the vice president, succession would pass to the Speaker of the House, then to the President pro tempore of the Senate, and then in succession to the cabinet members in the order of the creation of their departments

pre·sid·i·um, prae·sid·i·um (prisídi:əm) *pl.* **pre·sid·i·a, prae·sid·i·a** (prisídi:ə), **pre·sid·i·ums, prae·sid·i·ums** *n.* an executive committee of the Supreme Soviet of the U.S.S.R. which exercises supreme authority between sessions of the latter ‖ a similar body in various administrative districts of the U.S.S.R., or within a Communist party [fr. L. *praesidium*]

Presley (prézli:), Elvis (1935–77) U.S. singer and film actor, credited with popularizing rock 'n' roll music during the 1950s. Known worldwide for his vocal style, sideburns and body gyrations, he was a phenomenal recording artist, receiving 28 gold-record awards, more than any other individual, by the time of his death. Some of his best-known recordings include 'Heartbreak Hotel' (1956), 'Hound Dog,' 'Don't Be Cruel' and 'Love Me Tender.' He also appeared in 33 films and in concerts and on television

pre·soak (pri:sóuk) *v.* to soak clothes prior to washing. —**pre·soak** *n.* the solution in which the clothes are soaked, such a soaking

pre·sort (pri:sɔ́rt) *v.* to sort mail by ZIP code prior to posting, esp. in order to reduce postal costs

press (pres) *v.t.* to exert a steady force upon (something) by applying pressure ‖ to make flat by exerting such pressure, *to press flowers* ‖ to make smooth by applying pressure, *to press clothes* ‖ to try to force or persuade, *to press someone to stay* ‖ to put forward (a claim) with energy ‖ to squeeze (fruit etc.) in order to extract juice ‖ to make more forceful by insistence, *to press a point* ‖ to cause distress to (the mind or spirits), *pressed by poverty* ‖ to clasp or hold in an affectionate embrace, *to press someone's hand* ‖ to make (a phonograph record) ‖ *v.i.* to throng about someone or something, *the crowd pressed against the sentries* ‖ to force one's way ‖ to require immediate action, *the matter does not press* ‖ (of time) to suffice barely for what must be done ‖ (with 'for') to make an insistent demand or recommendation, *to press for higher wages* **pressed for** desperately short of (money, time, space etc.) **to press on** to advance with grim resolution [O.F. *presser*]

press *n.* a pressing or being pressed ‖ an instance of pressing ‖ an instrument or machine by which a substance or material is shaped, smoothed, stamped, compressed etc. by the force of pressure, *a cheese press* ‖ a printing press ‖ an establishment for printing and publishing books etc. ‖ the personnel of such an establishment ‖ newspapers and periodicals collectively ‖ journalists collectively ‖ critical notice in newspapers etc., *the play received a good press* ‖ a cupboard in which linen, clothes etc. are kept ‖ a device for holding a tennis racket etc., in order to keep it from warping ‖ (*old-fash.*) a dense crowd, *the press at the gate* **in press,** *Br.* **in the press** in the process of being printed **off the press** just printed **to go to press** to print off the edition of a newspaper etc. [F. *presse*]

press 1. *v.t.* (*hist.*) to force into military or naval service **to press into service** to make use of (something) through urgent necessity, *a door was pressed into service as a stretcher* **2.** *n.* (*hist.*) forced enlistment ‖ (*hist.*) a commission to press men into the armed forces [fr. older *prest v.,* to hire, giving part payment in advance, fr. O.F. fr. *prester,* to make a loan]

press agent someone whose job is to see to the publicity for a film star, theater, company etc.

press availability in political public relations, an indication that a person will be available for questioning

press box a newspaper reporters' enclosure, esp. at sporting events

Press·burg (présburk) *BRATISLAVA

press·gang (présgæŋ) *n.* (*hist.*) a detachment of men used to compel men into military or naval service

press·ing (présiŋ) *adj.* requiring immediate attention, *a pressing need* ‖ (of a request, invitation etc.) very earnest ‖ very persistent, *pressing demands for payment*

press kit a package of releases, photographs and other material for distribution to the press

press·man (présmən) *pl.* **press·men** (présmən) *n.* a man who operates a printing press ‖ (esp. *Br.*) a journalist

press·mark (présmɑrk) *n.* (*Br.*) a call number

press money (*hist.*) a money reward paid to men enlisting for armed service

press of canvas press of sail

press of sail (*naut.*) as much sail as the wind permits

press·room (présru:m, présrum) *n.* that part of a printing plant which contains the printing presses

press-show (présʃou) *v.* to display for the press before a public opening. —**press show** *n.*

press stud (*Br.*) a snap fastener

press-up (présʌp) *n.* (*Br.*) a push-up

pres·sure (préʃər) **1.** *n.* the action of pressing ‖ (*phys.*) the force acting per unit area ‖ (*elec.*) electromotive force ‖ atmospheric pressure ‖ interference, by an interested party, with someone's freedom in making a decision ‖ (*fig.*) a burden, *pressure of work* **2.** *pres. part.* **pres·sur·ing** *past* and *past part.* **pres·sured** to influence or force by using psychological pressure ‖ to pressurize [obs. F. fr. L. *pressura*]

pressure altitude (*meteor.*) an atmospheric pressure, expressed in terms of the altitude at which that pressure would be duplicated on the earth

pressure cabin a pressurized cabin in an aircraft

pressure cooker an airtight cooking pot for quick cooking by superheated steam under pressure

pressure gauge an instrument used to measure the pressure of a fluid ‖ an instrument used to measure the pressure of an explosive, e.g. in a gun barrel

pressure group a group of persons who cooperate in seeking to influence the policy of a legitive body etc.

pres·sur·ize (préʃəraiz) *pres. part.* **pres·sur·iz·ing** *past* and *past part.* **pres·sur·ized** *v.t.* to cause the air pressure within (an aircraft cabin etc.) to remain equal to atmospheric pressure at ground level whatever the external air pressure may actually be

press·work (préswə:rk) *n.* the work done by a printing press in making an ink impression ‖ the quality of the result of this work

Pres·ter John (préstər) a mythical Christian priest-king supposed by Europeans in the Middle Ages to rule some vast and rich Eastern country, but thought in the 14th c. to be the king of Abyssinia [M.E. *Prestre Johan* fr. O.F. *prestre,* priest + *Jehan,* John]

CONCISE PRONUNCIATION KEY: **(a)** æ, *c*a*t*; ɑ, *c*a*r*; ɔ *f*aw*n*; ei, *sn*a*ke*. **(e)** e, *h*e*n*; i:, *sh*ee*p*; iə, *d*ee*r*; ɛə, *b*ea*r*. **(i)** i, *f*i*sh*; ai, *t*i*ger*; ə:, *b*i*rd*. **(o)** o, *o*x; au, *c*ow; ou, *g*oa*t*; u, *p*oo*r*; ɔi, *r*oy*al*. **(u)** ʌ, *d*u*ck*; u, *b*u*ll*; u:, *g*oo*se*; ə, *bacill*u*s*; ju:, *c*u*be*. x, *lo*ch; θ, *th*ink; ð, *bo*th*er*; z, *Z*en; ʒ, *corsa*g*e*; dʒ, *sava*g*e*; ŋ, *orangutan*g; j, *y*ak; ʃ, *f*ish; tʃ, *fe*tch; 'l, *rabb*le; 'n, *redd*en. Complete pronunciation key appears inside front cover.

pres·ti·dig·i·ta·tion (prestididʒitéiʃən) *n.* sleight of hand [PRESTIDIGITATOR]

pres·ti·dig·i·ta·tor (prestidídʒiteitər) *n.* someone skilled in sleight of hand [fr. F. *prestiaigitateur* fr. *preste*, nimble+L. *digitus*, finger]

pres·tige (prestíːʒ) *n.* widely acknowledged high reputation, as a source of power, credit or influence [F.]

prestige advertising (*Br.*) institutional advertising

pres·tig·ious (prestídzəs, prestídʒiːəs, prestíːdʒəs, prestíːdʒiːəs) *adj.* held in high esteem [fr. L.L. *praestigiosus*, cheating, deceitful, illusory]

pres·tis·si·mo (prestísəmou) *adv.* and *adj.* (*mus.*) extremely fast [Ital. superl. of *presto*, presto]

prest money (prest) (*hist.*) press money [O.F. *prest*, a loan]

pres·to (préstou) *adv.* and *adj.* (*mus.*) fast [Ital.]

Pres·ton (préstən) a sea and river port and county borough (pop. 143,734) of W. central Lancashire, England: textiles, electrical appliances, aircraft

pre·stress (príːstrés) *v.* to process (e.g., steel, concrete) by placing under stress before completing manufacture —**pre·stress** *n.* —**pre·stressed** *adj.*

pre·stressed (príːstrest) *adj.* (of concrete) reinforced with wire strands to which stress has been applied

pre·sum·a·ble (prizúːməb'l) *adj.* that may be presumed **pre·súm·a·bly** *adv.*

pre·sume (prizúːm) *pres. part.* **pre·sum·ing** *past* and *past part.* **pre·sumed** *v.t.* to assume as true, take for granted ‖ (with *infin.*) to take upon oneself boldly or rashly, venture, *he presumed to criticize her performance* ‖ to imply, presuppose ‖ *v.i.* (with 'on', 'upon') to take advantage of or rely on something or someone more than is warranted [F. *présumer*, to usurp or fr. L. *praesumere*, to anticipate assume]

pre·sump·tion (prizʌ́mpʃən) *n.* the act of presuming ‖ something presumed, a supposition ‖ unwarranted taking for granted of someone's approval, acquiescence etc. ‖ a too high opinion of oneself ‖ (*law*) a deduction made from known facts but lacking direct evidence [M.E. fr. O.F. *presumpcion, presompcion*]

pre·sump·tive (prizʌ́mptiv) *adj.* based on or justifying a presumption [F. *présomptif, présomptive*]

presumptive evidence circumstantial evidence

pre·sump·tu·ous (prizʌ́mptʃuːəs) *adj.* displaying excessive self-confidence and taking liberties [O.F. *presuntuex, presumptuoux*]

pre·sup·pose (priːsəpóuz) *v.t. pres. part.* **pre·sup·pos·ing** *past* and *past part.* **pre·sup·posed** to assume beforehand, take for granted ‖ to imply the existence of, *the agreement presupposes certain conditions* [F. *présupposer*]

pre·sup·po·si·tion (priːsʌpəzíʃən) *n.* the act of presupposing ‖ something presupposed [fr. M.L. *praesuppositio (praesuppositionis)*]

prêt á port·er (prétəpɔrtéi) *adj.* (*Fr.*) prepared-to-carry, ready-to-wear, e.g., clothing

pre·tax (príːtǽks) *adj.* (*economics*) of a sum, esp. profit, before making provision for taxes

pre·teen (príːtíːn) *n.* one who is under the age of 13 years, esp. between the ages of 9 and 12 —**preteen** *adj.*

pretence *PRETENSE

pre·tend (priténd) *v.t.* to allege falsely, make deliberately (a false impression), *to pretend ignorance* ‖ to claim, *he did not pretend to know much about it* ‖ to imagine in play or go through motions representing (an imaginary situation), *let's pretend that we're on an island* ‖ *v.i.* to make a pretense **to pretend to (something)** to lay claim to (some honor, quality etc.) [fr. L. *praetendere*, to stretch forth]

pre·tend·ed (priténdid) *adj.* put forward as being something it is not, *pretended kindness*

pre·tend·er (priténdər) *n.* a claimant to a throne without just title ‖ someone who pretends

Pretender, the Old *STUART, James Francis Edward

Pretender, the Young *STUART, Charles Edward

pre·tense, esp. *Br.* **pre·tence** (priténs, príːtens) *n.* the deliberate creating of a false impression, *a pretense of friendship* ‖ something pretended, *his anger was all a pretense* ‖ pretentiousness ‖ a claim, *no pretense to originality* [A. F. *pretensse*]

pre·ten·sion (priténʃən) *n.* a claim, whether true or false ‖ the putting forth of a claim ‖ pretentiousness [prob. fr. M.L. *praetensio (praetensionis)*]

pre·ten·tious (priténʃəs) *adj.* claiming to possess superior qualities or great importance, esp. without justification [fr. F. *prétentieux*]

pret·er·ite, pret·er·it (prétərit) **1.** *adj.* (*gram.*) of the form of a verb which denotes something done or existing in the past **2.** *n.* (*gram.*) the preterite tense of a verb, e.g. 'went' is the preterite of 'go' [fr. L. *praeterire (praeteritus)*, to pass by]

pret·er·i·tion (pretəríʃən) *n.* a passing over or omitting ‖ the state of being so treated ‖ (*law*) the omission of the name of a possible heir by a testator ‖ (*theol.*) the Calvinist doctrine that God passes over all but the elect [fr. L.L. *praeteritio (praeteritionis)*]

pre·ter·mis·sion (priːtərmíʃən) *n.* a pretermitting [fr. L. *praetermissio (praetermissionis)*]

pre·ter·mit (priːtərmít) *pres. part.* **pre·ter·mit·ting** *past* and *past part.* **pre·ter·mit·ted** *v.t.* to pass over or omit ‖ to discontinue temporarily ‖ (*law*) to omit (a possible heir's name) in a will [fr. L. *praetermittere*, to let go by]

pre·ter·nat·u·ral (priːtərnǽtʃərəl) *adj.* beyond what is regarded as natural, *a preternatural gift for remembering faces* ‖ supernatural [fr. M.L. *praeternaturalis*]

pre·text 1. (príːtekst) *n.* a false reason given to conceal the real reason for an action etc. **2.** (pritékst) *v.t.* to advance (a pretext) for one's actions etc. [fr. L. *praetextus*, outward display]

pretor *PRAETOR

Pre·to·ri·a (pritɔ́riːə, pritóuriːə) the capital (pop. 739,043) of South Africa and of the Transvaal, 30 miles northeast of Johannesburg: iron and steel, mechanical engineering, mining, chemicals, cement. Universities (1873, 1930)

pretorian *PRAETORIAN

Pretorian Guard *PRAETORIAN GUARD

Pre·to·ri·us (pritɔ́riːəs, pritóuriːəs), Andries Wilhelmus Jacobus (1799–1853), Boer leader. He led the Great Trek (1835–6), defeated the Zulus in Natal (1838) and laid the foundations of the independent South African Republic, later the Transvaal

Pretorius, Martinus Wessel (c. 1818–1901), Boer statesman, son of Andries Pretorius. He was first president (1857–71) of the South African Republic, later the Transvaal, and president of the Orange Free State (1859–63)

pretorship *PRAETORSHIP

pret·ti·fy (prítifai) *pres. part.* **pret·ti·fy·ing** *past* and *past part.* **pret·ti·fied** *v.t.* to make pretty or depict prettily, esp. inappropriately or vapidly

pret·ti·ly (prítiliː) *adv.* in a way that is charming to see or hear, *she curtsied prettily*

pret·ti·ness (prítiːnis) *n.* the quality of being pretty

pret·ty (prítiː) *comp.* **pret·ti·er** *superl.* **pret·ti·est 1.** *adj.* pleasing to see or hear, esp. on account of grace, delicacy or charm, but less than beautiful ‖ excellent, fine, good (used ironically), *a pretty mess* **2.** *adv.* (used as a mild intensive before another adv. or an adj.) rather, *pretty good, pretty awful* **sitting pretty** (*pop.*) well placed for taking advantage of a situation [O.E. *prœttig*, crafty]

pret·ty·pret·ty (prítiːpriti:) *adj.* insipidly pretty

pret·zel (prétsəl) *n.* a cracker shaped like an open knot, glazed and salted [G. *brezel*]

pre·vail (privéil) *v.i.* (often with 'against', 'over') to be victorious ‖ to be the chief characteristic, predominate, *strong winds prevail in those regions* ‖ to be widespread or current, *strange customs prevail among the inhabitants* ‖ (with 'on', 'upon') to persuade **pre·váil·ing** *adj.* [M.E. *prevaylle, prevaile* fr. L. *praevalere*, to be very strong]

prev·a·lence (prévələns) *n.* the quality, state or fact of being prevalent [F. *prévalence*]

prev·a·lent (prévələnt) *adj.* widespread, generally used, followed, circulated etc., *the prevalent fashion* [fr. L. *praevalens (praevalentis)* fr. *praevalere*, to be very strong]

pre·var·i·cate (privǽrikéit) *pres. part.* **pre·var·i·cat·ing** *past* and *past part.* **pre·var·i·cat·ed** *v.i.* to speak or act evasively, hiding the truth [fr. L. *praevaricari (praevaricatus)*, to walk crookedly]

pre·var·i·ca·tion (priværikéiʃən) *n.* the act of prevaricating ‖ an instance of this [fr. L. *praevaricatio (praevaricationis)*]

pre·var·i·ca·tor (privǽrikeitər) *n.* someone who prevaricates [L. *praevaricator*]

pre·ven·ient (privíːnjənt) *adj.* preceding ‖ anticipating [fr. L. *praeveniens (praevenientis)* fr. *praevenire*, to come before]

prevenient grace (*theol.*) the grace which operates on a person's will and disposes him to repentance

pre·vent (privént) *v.t.* to cause not to do something, *illness prevented him from going* ‖ to cause not to happen, or not to be made or done, *the storm prevented an early departure* [fr. L. *praevenire (praeventus)*, to come before]

pre·vent·a·ble, pre·vent·i·ble (privéntəb'l) *adj.* capable of being prevented

pre·vent·a·tive (privéntətiv) **1.** *adj.* preventive **2.** *n.* a preventive

prevent defense (*football*) deep behind-the-line defense against a long forward pass

preventible *PREVENTABLE

pre·ven·tion (privénʃən) *n.* the act of preventing ‖ something that serves as a preventive [fr. L.L. *praeventio (praeventionis)*]

pre·ven·tive (privéntiv) **1.** *adj.* preventing or intended to prevent something ‖ (*med.*) intended to prevent disease **2.** *n.* something that prevents or is intended to prevent something ‖ a medicament etc. used for preventing disease ‖ (*Br.*) of or pertaining to that department of Customs which is concerned with prevention of smuggling, *a preventive officer* [fr. L. *praevenire (praeventus)*, to come before]

preventive detention holding one suspected of a crime in order to prevent his or her commission of further crime (illegal in the U.S.A.)

pre·view (príːvjuː) **1.** *n.* a presentation of a film, book etc. to critics, press reporters etc. before it is presented to the general public ‖ a brief view or foretaste of something that is to come ‖ (also **prevue**) short extracts from a new film exhibited as advance publicity **2.** *v.t.* to see or show a preview of

pre·vi·ous (príːviːəs) **1.** *adj.* occurring or done earlier, *his previous attempts had been unsuccessful* ‖ (*pop.*) before the right time, *she was a little previous in announcing the engagement* **2.** *adv.* (with 'to') before, *did you test it previous to buying it?* [fr. L. *praevius*, going before]

previous question a motion in a legislative session to put some central matter under discussion to the vote immediately, without more debate or proposal of further amendments. In British usage, if the motion is not carried the matter is shelved, but in the U.S.A. the matter remains a live issue

pre·vi·sion(privíʒən) *n.* foresight **pre·ví·sion·al** *adj.* showing or characterized by prevision [fr. L. *praevidere (praevisus)*, to foresee]

pre·vo·ca·tion·al (priːvoukéiʃən'l) *adj.* of a course of study combining general education with preparation for vocational training

Pré·vost (preivou), l'Abbé (Antoine François Prévost d'Exiles, 1697–1763), French novelist. He is best known for his sentimental masterpiece of psychological analysis, 'Manon Lescaut' (1731)

prevue *PREVIEW

pre·war (príːwɔ́r) *adj.* existing or occurring before a war recently over

prey (prei) (*sing.* and *collect.*) *n.* an animal or animals seized as food by another animal ‖ a victim or victims, *con men and their prey* [M.E. fr. O.F. *preie*, booty]

prey *v.i.* (of an animal, esp. with 'on', 'upon') to seek for or seize prey ‖ (with 'on', 'upon') to make raids in order to take booty ‖ (with 'on', 'upon') to have a destructively wearing effect, *his worries preyed on his mind* [M.E. fr. O.F. *preer, preier*]

Pri·am (práiəm) the last king of Troy, who reigned during its siege and was killed when the city was taken. He was the father of Hector, Paris, Cassandra etc.

pri·a·pism (práiəpizəm) *n.* persistent erection of the penis, caused esp. by disease [fr. L.L. *Priapismus* fr. Gk fr. *Priapizein*, to act the part of Priapus]

Pri·a·pus (praiéipəs) Greek god of fertility, son of Dionysus and Aphrodite, guardian deity of gardens, vineyards and herds. His cult spread to Greece during the time of Alexander. He personified male procreative power

Prib·i·lof (príbəlɔf) (or Fur Seal Islands) a group of hilly islands in the southeast Bering Sea, Alaska, noted as fur-seal grounds

price (prais) *n.* that which is given or demanded in return for a thing, service etc. offered for sale or for barter ‖ (*rhet.*) that which must be done, sacrificed, suffered etc. in return for something,

CONCISE PRONUNCIATION KEY: **(a)** æ, *cat*; ɑ, *car*; ɔ *fawn*; ei, *snake*. **(e)** e, *hen*; iː, *sheep*; iə, *deer*; ɛə, *bear*. **(i)** i, *fish*; ai, *tiger*; əː, *bird*. **(o)** o, *ox*; au, *cow*; ou, *goat*; u, *poor*; ɔi, *royal*. **(u)** ʌ, *duck*; u, *bull*; uː, *goose*; ə, *bacillus*; juː, *cube*. x, *loch*; θ, *think*; ð, *bother*; z, *Zen*; ʒ, *corsage*; dʒ, *savage*; ŋ, *orangutang*; j, *yak*; ʃ, *fish*; tʃ, *fetch*; 'l, *rabble*; 'n, *redden*. Complete pronunciation key appears inside front cover.

his freedom was the price he paid for security **a price on someone's head** a reward offered for the capture or killing of someone **at a price** at an unusually high cost ‖ with great sacrifice **beyond** (or **without**) **price** of so great a value that no buyer could pay for it **to have one's price** to be willing to be bribed if the bribe is big enough **what price (something)?** what is the use or value of (something)?, *what price freedom now?* [M.E. fr. O.F. *pris*]

price *pres. part.* **pric·ing** *past* and *past part.* **priced** *v.t.* to state or ascertain the price or market value of ‖ to set the price of (something one is selling), *he prices his goods very high* [var. of older *prise* fr. O.F. *prisier*, F. *priser*]

price control governmental establishment of ceiling prices on basic commodities to combat inflation etc.

price-earn·ings ratio (práisə́:rniŋz) (*securities*) the ratio of market price to earnings expressed as a simple number, e.g., 9 × earnings. *also* price-earnings multiple

price index (*Br.*) (*economics*) an economic measure based on annual Family Expenditure Surveys for the preceding three yrs. *Cf* CONSUMER PRICE INDEX

price·less (práislis) *adj.* too valuable to carry any price ‖ very valuable ‖ (*pop.*) very funny, ridiculous, *a priceless story*

prick (prik) *v.t.* to make a very small hole in with a sharp point ‖ to make (a hole) in something with a sharp point ‖ to deflate (a balloon etc.) by piercing its surface ‖ to wound by piercing with a sharp implement, *to prick one's finger* ‖ to pain mentally, esp. to goad as if with spurs, *his conscience pricked him* ‖ to mark (a surface) with little punctures or dots, esp. in tracing ‖ to form (a pattern etc.) on a surface with little punctures or dots ‖ to disable (a horse) by driving a nail into the quick in shoeing ‖ (with 'off') to mark (a name or item) on a list by putting a dot etc. next to it ‖ (with 'up') to cause (esp. the ears) to point upward or forward as a sign of sudden attention or interest ‖ (esp. with, 'out') to transplant (seedlings) ‖ *v.i.* (with 'up') to point upward or forward. *his ears pricked up* ‖ to have or cause a feeling of being pierced [O.E. *prician*]

prick *n.* the act or an instance of pricking ‖ a small puncture made by pricking ‖ the pain caused by pricking [O.E. *prica, pricca, price*]

prick-eared (príkiərd) *adj.* (of a dog) having erect pointed ears

prick·er (príkər) *n.* a sharp instrument for pricking, e.g. an awl

prick·et (príkit) *n.* a sharp-pointed spike on which a candle is stuck ‖ a candlestick with such a sharp spike ‖ a buck in its second year when the horns are straight and unbranched [prob. fr. M.L. *prikettus*]

prick·le (prík'l) **1.** *n.* (*bot.*) a pointed process arising from epidermal tissue, e.g. of a bramble, rose etc., and which can be peeled off with the outer skin (cf. THORN) ‖ a tingling or prickling sensation **2.** *v. pres. part.* **prick·ling** *past* and *past part.* **prick·led** *v.i.* to feel a tingling or pricking sensation ‖ *v.t.* to pierce with or as if with a prickle ‖ to cause to feel a tingling or prickling sensation [O.E. *pricel*]

prick·li·ness (príkli:nis) *n.* the quality or state of being prickly

prick·ly (príkli:) *comp.* **prick·li·er** *superl.* **prick·li·est** *adj.* armed with prickles, *prickly leaves* ‖ feeling as if pricked by prickles ‖ causing such a feeling ‖ quick to take offense, very touchy

prickly ash *Zanthoxylum americanum,* fam. *Rutaceae,* a fragrant shrub or small tree with many prickles and yellowish flowers

prickly heat an inflammation of the sweat glands of the skin, accompanied by a rash and itching, common in hot and humid climates

prickly pear a member of *Opuntia,* fam. *Cactaceae,* a genus of jointed cactus with pear-shaped, edible fruit, native to America but widely distributed in warm regions ‖ the fruit of this cactus

prickly poppy a member of *Argemone,* fam. *Papaveraceae,* a genus of American plants with large flowers and prickles, esp. *A. mexicana*

pride (praid) **1.** *n.* excessive self-esteem ‖ behavior that shows this ‖ proper self-respect ‖ a source of great satisfaction for which one feels some responsibility, *he is his mother's pride* ‖ a sense of satisfaction with one's achievements etc. ‖ the best, *this one is the pride of his collection* ‖ (of a bird) the state of having the tail fully displayed, *a peacock in his pride* ‖ (of lions) a group, often a family, in the wild state **to take pride in** to set oneself a high standard in (one's work etc.) for the satisfaction brings ‖ to be proud of (some achievement etc.) **2.** *v. refl. pres. part.* **prid·ing** *past* and *past part.* **prid·ed** to feel pride in some achievement or prowess [O.E. *prȳtu, prȳte*]

pride of place the first or most exalted position

Pride's Purge (*Eng. hist.*) the exclusion (Dec. 6, 1648) by a group of soldiers under Colonel Thomas Pride (*d.* 1658) of more than 100 members (mostly Presbyterians) from the Long Parliament. The remaining members formed the extremist Rump Parliament

prie-dieu (pri:djə́:) *n.* a narrow desk or high-backed chair with a ledge on which one kneels to say prayers [F.]

priest (pri:st) *n.* (*Christian churches*) an ordained person trained and authorized by a bishop to be an intermediary between the people and God by conducting sacred rites. administering the sacraments, making intercession, pronouncing absolution and safeguarding sacred buildings and treasures ‖ any member of the clergy ‖ a minister of a non-Christian religion [O.E. *prēost* fr. L. *presbyter* fr. Gk]

priest·craft (prí:stkræft, prí:stkrɑft) *n.* worldly scheming by priests

priest·ess (prí:stis) *n.* a woman priest

priest·hood (prí:sthud) *n.* the office held by a priest ‖ the collective body of priests in a Church [O.E. *prēosthād*]

Priest·ley (prí:stli:), Joseph (1733–1804), British scientist and clergyman. He discovered oxygen (1774) independently of Scheele. He isolated and identified many new gases. He invented soda water (1772)

priest·ly (prí:stli:) *comp.* **priest·li·er** *superl.* **priest·li·est** *adj.* pertaining to a priest, his office or qualities ‖ like or characteristic of a priest

priest-rid·den (prí:strid'n) *adj.* (of a country or people) harmfully dominated by priests

priest's hole (*hist.*) a hidden room or other hiding place for Catholic priests during the times in which they were persecuted in England

Priests of the Mission, Congregation of the *LAZARIST

priest vicar (*Church of England*) a minor canon in some cathedrals

Pri·e·to (pri:étɔ), Guillermo (1818–97), Mexican politician, orator and romantic poet. His works include 'El romancero nacional', 'Musa callejera', and 'Memorias de mis tiempos'

prig (prig) *n.* a narrow-minded person who makes an annoying parade of being morally or culturally superior to others **príg·gish** *adj.* [origin unknown]

prim 1. *adj.* (prim) *comp.* **prim·mer** *superl.* **prim·mest** (of a person) stiff in manner, too clipped or precise in speech, too formal in dress, or narrow and intolerant in opinion ‖ (of manner or expression) stiff and formal **2.** *v.t. pres. part.* **prim·ming** *past* and *past part.* **primmed** to shape (the face or lips) into a prim expression [etym. doubtful]

pri·ma ballerina (prí:mə) the principal female dancer of a ballet company [Ital.]

pri·ma·cy (práiməsi:) *n.* the state or being first in rank, importance etc. ‖ (*eccles.*) the office or dignity of a primate [O.F. *primacie*]

pri·ma don·na (pri:mədɔ́nə, pri:mədɔ́nə) *pl.* **pri·ma don·nas** *n.* the chief woman singer in an opera [Ital.]

primaeval *PRIMEVAL

pri·ma fa·cie (práiməféiʃi:) *adj.* (*law,* of evidence) having every appearance of proving a fact though it may not constitute certain proof [L.=at first appearance]

pri·mage (práimidʒ) *n.* a percentage of the freight charge, paid to the ship's owner in consideration of satisfactory loading or unloading [etym. doubtful]

pri·mal (práiməl) *adj.* primitive or earliest in history, *primal customs* ‖ first in importance [fr. M.L. *primalis*]

pri·ma·ri·ly (praimέərili:, práimerili:. práiməri:li:) *adv.* principally ‖ originally

pri·ma·ry (práiməri:) **1.** *adj.* first in time of origin or order of development, *primary instincts* ‖ basic, fundamental ‖ first in a succession or series, *primary school* ‖ first in importance, *a primary consideration* ‖ not derived, *his diaries are a primary source for the history of the period* ‖ first in order of production, *gas, coke and tar are primary products of the coal-gas industry* ‖ of or designating the large, stiff feathers on the end joint of a bird's wing ‖ (*elec.*) of or relating to or designating the inducing current, coil or circuit of a transformer or induction motor ‖ (*geol.*) relating to the Paleozoic or earlier eras ‖ (*chem.*) formed by the direct union of two atoms, or by the substitution of only one atom or group, *a primary compound* ‖ (of Latin, Greek or Sanskrit tenses) referring to present or future times **2.** *pl.* **pri·ma·ries** *n.* something which is primary ‖ a primary color ‖ (esp. *pl.*) a primary election ‖ a primary feather ‖ (*astron.*) a primary planet ‖ (*chem.*) a primary compound or product ‖ (*elec.*) a primary cell [fr. L. *primarius,* chief]

primary accent the first and main beat in a musical measure ‖ the strongest stress on a syllable in a polysyllabic word

primary cell (*elec.*) a device for producing by chemical changes an electromotive force which can be used to give an electric current (e.g. Leclanché or Daniell cell)

primary coil (*elec.*) the intake coil of an induction coil or transformer

primary color, *Br.* **primary colour** (*phys.,* of light) one of the three wave bands (red, green, bluish-violet) from which, by suitable combinations, all other colors can be obtained ‖ (of pigments) one of the three colored pigments (red, yellow, blue) which cannot be imitated by mixing other pigments

primary consumer the original primitive plant-eating organism in the food cycle

primary election a direct primary ‖ an election within a political party to choose delegates to a party's nominating convention or to select party officers

primary planet (*astron.*) any of the planets which move in orbit around the sun

primary sere (*botany*) the first plant in an area that has not produced vegetation in recent eras

primary service area (*broadcasting*) area capable of receiving consistently satisfactory broadcast transmission from a station

primary storage (*computer*) the storage unit in the main frame

primary structure (*aerospace*) **1.** the craft components that upon failing could destroy the aircraft, e.g., wings, tail, engine bearers. **2.** (*sculptural*) art reduced to simplest primary form with no embellishment. **—primary structurist** *n.* the artist

pri·mate (práimeit) *n.* (*eccles.*) an archbishop ‖ (*eccles.*) a bishop having authority over other bishops ‖ (*zool.*) a member of the order *Primates,* the highest order of mammals, including man, apes, monkeys, lemurs etc. [fr. L.L. *primas* (*primatis*) adj., first]

pri·ma·tial (praiméiʃəl) *adj.* characteristic of or having to do with a primate [F.]

prime (praim) **1.** *adj.* first in time, importance, quality or rank ‖ fundamental ‖ (*math.,* of a number) divisible only by itself and by 1, not by any other integer **2.** *n.* a minute of angle or the symbol (′) for this ‖ (*math.*) a prime number ‖ a symbol (′) used after a character to distinguish it from another, e.g. to distinguish A′ from A ‖ (*fencing*) the first of eight parrying positions ‖ (*mus.*) the tonic ‖ (*mus.*) a unison ‖ (*mus.*) the fundamental note in a harmonic series [F. *prime* or fr. L. *primus*]

prime *n.* (*eccles.*) the first service of the day, held at sunrise or at 6 o'clock a.m. ‖ the time or hour of this service ‖ the best, most flourishing stage or state, *he has passed his prime* ‖ (*rhet.*) the earliest state, *the prime of the year* ‖ (*rhet.*) the best or chief part or member [O.E. *prīm* fr.L. *prima* (*hora*), first (hour)]

prime *pres. part.* **prim·ing** *past* and *past part.* **primed** *v.t.* to fill (a pump) with water to initiate action ‖ to inject gasoline into the carburetor of (an engine) ‖ to fill pores of (wood etc.) with a first coat of paint etc. ‖ to provide (someone) with information etc. beforehand ‖ to ply (someone) with liquor ‖ (*hist.*) to put the charge in (a gun) ‖ *v.i.* (of a steam cylinder) to carry over water with the steam [etym. doubtful]

prime cost the cost of raw material and labor in producing an article (in contrast to the cost of advertising, distribution etc.)

prime meridian the meridian at 0° longitude, passing through Greenwich, England, from which longitude is measured

prime minister the leader of a government ‖ the leader of a cabinet or of an executive ‖ a chief minister

CONCISE PRONUNCIATION KEY: (a) æ, cat; ɑ, car; ɔ fawn; ei, snake. (e) e, hen; i:, sheep; iə, deer; εə, bear. (i) i, fish; ai, tiger; ə:, bird. (o) o, ox; au, cow; ou, goat; u, poor; ɔi, royal. (u) ʌ, duck; u, bull; u:, goose; ə, bacillus; ju:, cube. x, loch; θ, think; ð, bother; z, Zen; ʒ, corsage; dʒ, savage; ŋ, orangutang; j, yak; ʃ, fish; tʃ, fetch; 'l, rabble; 'n, redden. Complete pronunciation key appears inside front cover.

prime mover (*engin.*) a natural source of power (wind, water pressure etc.) ‖ a machine (a windmill, water wheel etc.) converting this power to useful purposes ‖ the first cause of all movement ‖ the person who originates a corporate action

prim·er (prímər, *Br.* esp. práimər) *n.* a simple book for children learning to read ‖ an elementary textbook, *Latin primer* [fr. M.L. *primarius,* a prayer book for the laity]

prim·er (práimər) *n.* something that primes ‖ a cap, cylinder etc. containing an explosive compound used to fire the charge of a gun

prime rate or **prime interest rate** (*banking*) the lowest rate of interest charged by a lending institution to its best-rated customers

prime time (*broadcasting*) the broadcast period during which the largest audiences are watching or listening, usu. from 6 PM to 10 PM or 11 PM

pri·me·val, pri·mae·vál (praimí:vəl) *adj.* belonging to the earliest era of life on the earth, *primeval forest* [fr. L. *primaevus*]

prim·ing (práimiŋ) *n.* the act of someone who or something that primes ‖ something used for priming, e.g. a first coat of paint

priming of the tides an acceleration of the time of high and low tide occurring during the first and third quarters of the moon

pri·mip·a·ra (praimípərə) *pl.* **pri·mip·a·rae** (praimípəri:) *n.* a woman who or animal that has given birth once only ‖ an individual pregnant for the first time **pri·míp·a·rous** *adj.* [L. fr. *primus,* first+parere, to bring forth]

prim·i·tive (prímitiv) **1.** *adj.* of, pertaining to or characteristic of the earliest period or origin of something ‖ having the characteristics of the earliest stages of civilization, *they are a primitive tribe* ‖ roughly constructed, crude and simple ‖ without civilized accretions, *he lives a primitive life* ‖ (of a work of art or artist) of the period just before the Renaissance ‖ of modern (often deliberately) unsophisticated works of art, or artists painting in such a style ‖ (*math.*) of a figure, line etc. from which another is derived ‖ (*biol.*) of or pertaining to an early stage of development ‖ (*biol.*) showing little change from an early ancestral type ‖ (*geol.*) primary ‖ (*gram.*) of a root form in contrast to a derived word **2.** *n.* a primitive person ‖ a primitive work of art or artist ‖ (*math.*) a primitive line, figure etc. ‖ (*gram.*) a primitive form **prím·i·tiv·ism** *n.* primitivity ‖ primitive practices, customs etc. ‖ a belief in the superiority of a primitive way of life or of things primitive ‖ the style of a primitive (deliberately unsophisticated) artist **prim·i·tív·i·ty** *n.* the quality or stage of being primitive [M.E. *primitif* fr. F. fr. L. *primitivus,* first of its kind]

Pri·mo de Ri·ve·ra (prí:moðeri:vérɑ), Miguel, marqués de Estella (1870–1930), Spanish general and dictator (1923–30). His son, José Antonio (1903–36), founded Falangism (1933)

pri·mo·gen·i·tor (praimoudʒénitər) *n.* the earliest ancestor of whom anything is known ‖ (*loosely*) an ancestor [M.L. fr. L. *primo* adv., first+*genitor,* begetter]

pri·mo·gen·i·ture (praimoudʒénitʃər) *n.* the state or fact of being the firstborn of parents ‖ (*law*) this fact as conferring the right to inherit in the event of intestacy [fr. M.L. *primogenitura* fr. L. *primo* adv., first+*genitura,* birth]

pri·mor·di·al (praimɔ́rdi:əl) *adj.* existing from the beginning, of that which was the first to be created, *primordial matter* ‖ fundamental, underived, *primordial rights* ‖ (*biol.,* of a species, organ, cell etc.) earliest developed [fr. L.L. *primordialis,* first of all]

primordial soup mixture of amino acids, purine, pyrimidine and phosphate, from which life first began. *also* prebiotic soup or protolicotic soup

primp (primp) *v.i.* to busy oneself fussily about one's dress or appearance, *she likes to primp before her mirror* ‖ *v.t.* to fuss over (one's hair, clothes etc.) so as to impress ‖ to put in order (a room etc.), esp. for visitors' eyes [perh. fr. PRIM]

prim·rose (prímrouz) *n. Primula vulgaris,* fam. *Primulaceae,* a plant having a rosette of leaves and a single flower ‖ the flower of this plant ‖ a light yellow color [M.E. *primerose,* rel. to O.F. *primerose* and to M.L. *prima rosa,* earliest rose]

primrose path a way of pleasure ‖ an easy way that leads to destruction etc.

prim·u·la (prímjulə) *n.* a member of *Primula,* fam. *Primulaceae,* a large genus of perennial plants with white, yellow and pink flowers, found in temperate and mountainous parts of the northern hemisphere [M.L.]

pri·mum mo·bi·le (práiməmmóubəli:) *n.* (*Ptolemaic astron.*) a sphere assumed to revolve from east west around the earth, carrying with it the heavenly bodies ‖ a prime mover [M.L. fr. L. *primus,* first+*mobilis* adj., movable]

Prince (prins), Morton (1854–1929), U.S. psychologist and physician who formulated such concepts as neurograms (the neurological record of psychological behavior) and the coconscious (a parallel, possibly rival, well-organized system of awareness comparable with ordinary consciousness). His 'The Dissociation of a Personality' (1906) is a study of a multiple personality

prince (prins) *n.* (*Br.*) a son or son's son of a ruling sovereign ‖ any male member in certain royal families ‖ the ruler of a principality ‖ a courtesy title in some countries, accorded to certain members of noble families ‖ a ruler ‖ a distinguished and powerful person in some walk of life, *a merchant prince* ‖ (*Roman Catholicism*) a cardinal [O.F.]

prince consort the husband of a reigning queen, who is himself a prince **the Prince Consort** *ALBERT

prince·dom (prínsdəm) *n.* a principality (state) ‖ the rank or dignity of a prince

Prince Edward Island an island (area 2, 184 sq. miles, pop. 124,600) in the Gulf of St Lawrence, forming a province of Canada. Capital: Charlottetown. It is a rolling, fertile lowland. Industries: farming (dairying, potatoes, hay, oats, fruit, furs), food processing, tourism. The island was settled by the French (17th c.) but captured by the English (1758). It became a separate colony (1769) and joined the Canadian Confederation (1873)

prince·ling (prínsliŋ) *n.* a minor prince

prince·ly (prínsli:) *comp.* **prince·li·er** *superl.* **prince·li·est** *adj.* worthy of a prince, splendid, *a princely reward* ‖ of or relating to a prince

prince of Wales a title conferred on the eldest son of a British sovereign

Prince of Wales, Cape the most westerly point of the North American mainland, on the Bering Strait at the west tip of the Seward Peninsula

prince regent *pl.* **prince regents** a title conferred on a royal prince appointed to act as regent **the Prince Regent** (*Br. hist.*) the title by which the future George IV was commonly styled while he was regent (1811-20) for George III

Prince Rupert a city (pop. 12,000) of W. British Columbia, Canada. It is the W. terminus of the Canadian National transcontinental railroad (completed 1914). Fisheries, sawmills, shipbuilding

prin·cess (prínsis, prínses, *Br.* also prinsés) *n.* a nonreigning female member of a royal family ‖ a daughter or granddaughter of a sovereign ‖ the wife of a prince [M.E. *princesse* fr. F.]

princess royal *pl.* **princesses royal** a title which may be conferred upon the eldest daughter of the British sovereign

Prince·ton University (prínstən) a private university at Princeton, New Jersey, chartered (1746) as the College of New Jersey. It consists of Princeton College, graduate schools and research centers. It shares facilities with the Institute for Advanced Study

prin·ci·pal (prínsəp'l) **1.** *adj.* first in importance **2.** *n.* a person having the chief authority or responsibility, *the principal of a school* ‖ a person employing another as his agent ‖ (*law*) a person actually committing or directly aiding in a crime ‖ the sum of money on which interest is earned ‖ a person playing a chief role in a play, film, ballet etc. ‖ the soloist in a concert ‖ (*mus.*) the chief metal stop of an organ, giving the octave above the open diapason ‖ (*mus.*) the subject of a fugue ‖ (*mus.*) the first player of any division of orchestral instruments except first violins (*LEADER) ‖ (*law*) someone who is primarily liable, as distinct from someone who stands surety or endorses ‖ (*building*) a roof truss ‖ one of the combatants in a duel [fr. L. *principalis*]

principal diagonal (*math.*) in a square matrix, the diagonal from lower right to upper left

principal focus the point at which a beam of rays parallel to the axis of a lens (*OPTICAL CENTER) is brought to a focus. Its distance from the optical center (i.e. the focal length of the lens) depends upon the algebraic sum of the reciprocals of the radii of curvature of the lens surface and the refractive index of the lens substance

prin·ci·pal·i·ty (prinsəpǽliti:) *pl.* **prin·ci·pal·i·ties** *n.* any of certain small states whose ruler is called a prince, e.g. one which is or was within or subordinate to a kingdom or empire ‖ the rank, office or dignity of a prince ‖ (*pl.*) an order of angels (*ANGEL) [M.E. *principalite* fr. O.F *principalite, principaltee*]

principal parts (*gram.*) the inflected forms of a verb, including in English the infinitive, past tense and past participle, from which other inflected forms can be derived

prin·ci·pate (prínsəpit) *n.* (*Rom. hist.*) a form of government under the early emperors which retained some republican features ‖ the term of office of one of these emperors [fr. L. *principatus,* the first place]

Principe *SÃO TOMÉ AND PRINCIPE

prin·ci·ple (prínsəp'l) *n.* a law of nature as formulated and accepted by the mind, *Archimedes' principle* ‖ an essential truth upon which other truths are based ‖ the acceptance of moral law as a guide to behavior, *a man of principle* ‖ a rule by which a person chooses to govern his conduct, often forming part of a code, *a man of liberal principles* ‖ a fundamental implication, *he objects to the principle of the thing, not to the method* **in principle** as regards essentials, *we agree in principle but we dislike your procedure* **on principle** by virtue of the principles one accepts, *to agree on principle* [fr. F. *principe* or L. *principium*]

principle of inertia *LAW OF MOTION

principle of superposition a theorem in physics that permits the vectorial addition of effects if they are proportional to the causes and if the causes are also vectorially additive. Thus the resultant displacement produced by two or more waves intersecting at a point at a given time is equal to what the sum of the instantaneous displacement of each wave would be if each were acting alone at that point

prink (priŋk) *v.i.* and *t.* (often with 'up') to dress with elaborate care and finery [perh. related to PRANK v.]

print (print) **1.** *n.* a picture or design made by an inked impression of a block, engraved plate etc. ‖ a mark made on something by pressure ‖ a photograph made from a negative ‖ printed matter ‖ handwritten letters imitating typographical forms ‖ an object for making a mark by impression, a stamp, seal ‖ an object which has received such a mark, *a print of butter* ‖ a textile made with an applied colored or black and white pattern ‖ a dress made of this **in print** printed in a publication etc., *to see one's name in print* ‖ still available from the publisher **out of print** no longer available from the publisher [M.E. fr. O.F. *priente,preinte,* impression of a seal etc.]

print *v.t.* to make a mark on (a surface) by pressure or stamping ‖ to make (a mark) on a surface by pressing or stamping ‖ to make an impression on the surface of (paper, fabric etc.) by pressing inked blocks etc. on it ‖ to reproduce (a text, news etc.) by this process ‖ to write or draw (letters) in imitation of type forms ‖ to make (a photograph) from a negative ‖ to fix firmly (a memory, idea etc.) on the mind ‖ *v.i.* to practice the art of making inked impressions on paper etc. ‖ to write in characters resembling type forms **to print off** to go to press with (the edition) after proofing is finished **prínt·a·ble** *adj.* good enough or proper enough to be printed and published **prínt·er** *n.* someone who prints, esp. as a profession [M.E. *prenten, printen* fr. *prente,printe* n., a print]

printer's devil a person employed in a printing business as an apprentice or to do odd jobs

printer's imprint the name or identifying mark on printed matter of the printer, together with the place of printing, usually found on the back of the title page or on the last page of a book, or the foot of the last page of a newspaper

printer's ink a quick-drying ink used in printing newspapers, books etc.

printer's ream a ream of 516 sheets

print·ing (príntiŋ) *n.* the action of someone who or something that prints ‖ the art or business of a printer ‖ the style or quality of that which is printed ‖ the total number of printed copies of a book etc. made at one time.

—The technique of printing was known to the Chinese as early as the 9th c. In the European Middle Ages pictures and playing cards were printed from wood blocks. It was not until c. 1436 that Gutenberg invented the technique of casting single metal letters (types) which could be assembled together to form a continuous text. The first book printed from movable types was probably the celebrated 42-line Bible produced (c. 1452-5) by Gutenberg in Mainz. The art quickly spread to Italy, Venice, Switzerland, France, the Low Countries, Spain and England. The Renaissance and Reformation almost coincided with the development of printing, and were greatly assisted by it. The spread of learning and the production of the works of the Reformers gave printers a crucial importance. At first books remained expensive, and were produced in small numbers, but editions of 1,500-3,000 became common in the 16th c. and prices fell.

Until the early 19th c. printing developed little. The old wooden printing press was improved but not substantially changed. Type was set, and paper made, by hand. In 1802 the first papermaking machine was invented. In 1811 the mechanical press, which could be driven by steam, was invented. In 1804 stereotyping was perfected, enabling casts to be taken of whole pages of type. The mechanization of printing coincided with the movement towards universal education. Vast audiences were thus created at the same time as the craft became one of mass production

printing press a machine used to print from type or metal plates etc.

print·out (príntpυt) *n.* (*computer*) the printed record of the solution to the program or of the contents of the computer memory —**print out** *v.*

Pri·or (práiər), Matthew (1664–1721), English poet and diplomat. His humorous poems and satires include 'Poems on Several Occasions' (1718)

pri·or (práiər) **1.** *adj.* earlier ‖ preceding in order or importance **2.** *adv.* (with 'to') earlier than, *we had not met prior to that occasion* [L.=former, superior]

prior *n.* a superior of a religious order or house, esp. a priory ‖ the officer in a monastic order ranking next below an abbot [O.E. fr. L. *prior* adj., former, superior]

pri·or·ate (práiərit) *n.* the office, term of office or dignity of a prior [fr. L.L. *prioratus*]

pri·or·ess (práiəris) *n.* a nun whose rank in a woman's order or religious house corresponds to that of a prior [M. E. fr. O.F. *prioresse, prieuresse*]

pri·or·i·tize (praiɔ́ritaiz) *v.* to place in an order of priority

pri·or·i·ty (praiɔ́riti:, praiɒ́riti:) *pl.* **pri·or·i·ties** *n.* the quality or state of coming first in time, *priority of claim* ‖ something that comes first or among the first in importance ‖ the right or privilege of precedence over others, *the job must be given top priority* [M.E. fr. F. *priorité*]

prior restraint a court order against publishing, with a contempt citation as the penalty for violation

pri·o·ry (práiəri:) *pl.* **pri·o·ries** *n.* a religious house governed by a prior or prioress, lower in status and smaller than an abbey [M.E. fr. A.F. *priorie*]

Pri·pet (prí:pet) (*Russ.* Pripyat) a river (500 miles long, navigable for 300) rising in the N.W. Ukraine. U.S.S.R., and curving east through Byelorussia to join the Dnieper north of Kiev ‖ a thickly wooded marshland (about 4,200 sq. miles) lying along its central course, largely impassable except when frozen

Pris·ci·an (príʃi:ən) (Priscianus Caesariensis, 6th c.), Latin grammarian who taught in Constantinople. His 'Institutiones grammaticae' was the definitive Latin grammar of the Middle Ages

Pris·cil·lian (prisíljən) (*d.* 385), Spanish bishop. His teaching was suspected of containing Manichaean and Gnostic heresy. His execution, on the order of the Emperor Maximus, was the first instance of capital punishment for heresy by a Christian state

prise *PRIZE (leverage)

prism (prízəm) *n.* (*geom.*) a solid figure having two parallel polygonal faces, the other faces being parallelograms ‖ (*crystall.*) a crystal form having three or more faces parallel to one axis ‖ (*optics*) a device used to disperse light or change its direction, consisting of a transparent solid with two nonparallel plane faces ‖ an electric or magnetic field used to deviate or disperse a beam of charged particles [fr. L.L. *prisma* fr. Gk]

pris·mat·ic (prizmǽtik) *adj.* of or resembling a prism ‖ formed, dispersed, refracted by, or using a prism ‖ orthorhombic [fr. Gk *prisma* (*prismatos*), something sawed]

prismatic compass a compass used in surveying: (a prism supplies an image of the reading in such a way that it can be read while the user sights through a telescope)

prismatic spectrum (*phys.*) a spectrum formed by dispersion by a prism

prism binoculars a pair of binoculars in which the path of the light entering the objective lenses is increased by the use of two totally reflecting prisms, allowing the use of an objective lens of longer focal length than the length of the tube itself would permit

prism spectrum a prismatic spectrum

pris·on (príz'n) *n.* a building used to confine offenders or suspects awaiting trial, or enemy captives ‖ imprisonment. *prison is no cure for first offenders* [M.E. fr. O.F. *prisun, prison,* the act of taking]

pris·on·er (príz'nər) *n.* a person who is confined in a prison ‖ a person who is in custody or under restraint ‖ a person who is captured or held captive [M.E. fr. F. *prisonier*]

prisoner of conscience one imprisoned for political reasons

prisoner of war a member of the armed forces captured by the enemy during a war

pris·sy (prísi:) *comp.* **pris·si·er** *superl.* **pris·si·est** *adj.* (*pop.*) primly precise about little details of dress, behavior etc. ‖ prudish [PRECISE or PRIM+SISSY]

pris·tane [$C_{19}H_{40}$] (prístein) *n.* (*chem.*) hydrocarbon resulting from breakdown of chlorophyll in marine fossils; used as a lubricant and anticorrosion agent. *also* norphytane

pris·tine (prísti:n, prístain, pristí:n) *adj.* unspoiled, still in an uncorrupted state ‖ of or in ancient or original condition [fr. L. *pristinus,* former]

pris·tin·i·ty (pristíniti:) *n.* the quality of being pristine

Pritchett (prítʃət), V. S. (1900–) British author. Best known for his masterfully-crafted, comically ironic short stories, exemplified in 'Collected Stories' (1982) and 'More Collected Stories' (1983). He also wrote novels, literary essays, biographies of Turgenev and Balzac, travel books and several autobiographical works

pri·va·cy (práivəsi:, *Br.* prívəsi:) *n.* the quality or state of being hidden from, or undisturbed by, the observation or activities of other persons, *there is no privacy in a barracks* ‖ freedom from undesirable intrusions, *to respect someone's privacy* [PRIVATE]

pri·vate (práivit) **1.** *adj.* belonging to a particular person or group and not shared with others in any way, *private property* ‖ not holding public office, *private citizen* ‖ having nothing to do with one's official or public character, *private life* ‖ secret, hidden from others, *private thoughts* ‖ not available to or not supported by the general public, *a private library* **2.** *n.* a soldier in the U.S. army one grade above a new or recent recruit ‖ (*Br.*) a private soldier **in private** not openly, without witnesses [fr. L. *privatus,* not holding public office]

private bill a legislative bill conferring particular powers or benefits on an individual or body in excess of, and sometimes in conflict with, the general law (cf. PUBLIC BILL)

private detective a person who hires himself out to make confidential investigations into crime or into people's activities or who patrols a store on the lookout for shoplifters etc.

pri·va·teer (praivətíər) **1.** *n.* (*hist.*) an armed private vessel authorized by a government to engage in hostile acts against the enemy (*LETTERS OF MARQUE) ‖ the captain or a member of the crew of such a vessel **2.** *v.i.* to sail or act as a privateer

private first class a soldier in the U.S. army or Marine Corps ranking next above private

private hotel (*Br.*) a hotel catering esp. to resident guests and usually not having a liquor license

private income private means

private means income from investments etc., not from salary or fees

private member's bill (*Br.*) a parliamentary bill introduced by a member of parliament who does not hold office in the government

private practice practice of a profession (e.g. medicine, architecture) on one's own independent financial account ‖ the goodwill of the patients of a doctor having such a practice, *to buy a private practice*

private school a school owned and run by private individuals, not by the government, and usually charging fees for tuition etc.

private soldier (*Br.*) a soldier ranking below a noncommissioned officer

private view a showing of an exhibition to specially invited people, held before the general public is admitted

pri·va·tion (praivéiʃən) *n.* complete or serious lack of the usual necessities of life (food, shelter, warmth etc.) ‖ an instance of this [fr. L. *privatio* (*privationis*) fr. *privare,* to deprive]

pri·vat·ism (práivətizəm) *n.* **1.** policy of not becoming involved in matters not personally essential. **2.** the desire for privacy —**pri·vat·is·tic** *adj.*

priv·a·tive (prívətiv) **1.** *adj.* causing privation ‖ of that which constitutes a lack ‖ (*gram.*) indicating negation or lack **2.** *n.* (*gram.*) a prefix or suffix denoting a negative meaning, e.g. 'un-' or '-less' [fr. L. *privativus*]

priv·et (prívit) *n. Ligustrum vulgare,* fam. *Oleaceae,* a quick-growing shrub, with small leaves, white flowers and black berries, native to S. Europe and N. Africa but widely grown as hedging ‖ any of several other plants of genus *Ligustrum,* grown as hedging [origin unknown]

priv·i·lege (prívəlidʒ) *n.* a benefit or advantage possessed by one person only or by a minority of the community, *his seniority brings him many privileges* ‖ any of the fundamental rights common to all persons under a modern constitutional government ‖ (*law*) a right or power conferred by a special law [fr. L. *privilegium,* a bill or law in favor of or against an individual]

priv·i·lege *pres. part.* **priv·i·leg·ing** *past* and *past part.* **priv·i·leged** *v.t.* to grant a privilege to [fr. F. *privilégier* fr. M. L. *privilegiare*]

priv·i·leged (prívəlidʒd) *adj.* enjoying a privilege [fr. PRIVILEGE n. or v.]

privileged communication (*law*) a defamatory communication made under circumstances such that it is not actionable as slander or libel ‖ (*law*) a communication made under circumstances such that a witness cannot be compelled to disclose it in court

priv·i·leg·es (prívəlidʒes) *n.* (*securities*) a contract whereby one party acquires the right, but not the obligation, to buy from or sell to another party a specified amount of a commodity or security at a predetermined price. *also* puts and calls

private automatic branch exchange a depot where telephone connections are made automatically or by remote control. *abbr.* **PABX**

priv·i·ly (prívəli:) *adv.* (*rhet.*) privately, esp. secretly [PRIVY]

priv·i·ty (príviti:) *pl.* **priv·i·ties** *n.* (*law*) a relationship between persons, esp. a mutual property interest, that is recognized in law, e.g. between lessor and lessee [M.E. *privite, privete* fr. O.F.]

priv·y (prívi:) **1.** *adj.* (in the phrase) **privy to** (*rhet.*) having private knowledge of, taken into the secret of ‖ (*law*) having a personal interest or part in **2.** *pl.* **priv·ies** *n.* (*pop.*) an outdoor toilet with no flushing mechanism ‖ (*law*) a party to a privity [M.E. *prive, privy,* intimate, familiar fr. F. *privé*]

privy council a British body which advises the Crown on matters of government, nominally comprising all ministers and ex-ministers and several people eminent in public life in the Commonwealth. It developed out of the king's council of the 13th c., and remained powerful until the 18th c., when most of its work was taken over by the cabinet. Its work is now restricted to formal matters, e.g. orders-in-council, royal proclamations etc., mostly carried out in a series of committees. It is presided over by the lord president of the council **privy councillor** a member of this body

privy purse money granted by the British parliament from public revenue for the personal use of the sovereign **Privy Purse** the officer in charge of this

privy seal (*Br. hist.*) the royal seal formerly affixed to documents to authorize the use of the great seal, or to documents not requiring the great seal. It was originally intended for the sovereign's private business (13th c.) but by the mid-14th c. had become a public department and had been replaced by the signet. It was abolished (1884), but the office of lord privy seal remains **Privy Seal** the lord privy seal ‖ his office

prize (praiz) **1.** *n.* something of value or satisfaction received in recognition of distinction ‖ such a thing offered to the winner of a competition, to the drawer of a lucky lottery ticket etc. ‖ something of value or satisfaction that is gained or worth gaining by an effort **2.** *adj.* awarded or worthy of receiving a prize, *a prize bull* ‖ awarded as a prize, *prize money* [M.E. *pris, prise,* price fr. O.F.]

prize *pres. part.* **priz·ing** *past* and *past part.* **prized** *v.t.* to value highly [M.E. fr. O.F. *prisier,* F. *priser,* to regard as worth (something)]

prize 1. *n.* (also **prise**) leverage, *to get a prize on a weight to be lifted* ‖ a vessel or property captured at sea in wartime **2.** *v.t. pres. part.* **priz·ing** *past* and *past part.* **prized** to capture (a ship) as prize ‖ (also **prise** *pres. part.* **pris·ing** *past* and *past part.* **prised**) to leverage, to pry, force open or lift with or as if with a lever [M.E. *prise,* a taking hold fr. O.F.]

prize court (*law*) a court which assesses and distributes the value of a prize taken at sea during wartime

prize·fight (práizfait) *n.* a professional boxing match [back-formation fr. PRIZEFIGHTER]

prize·fight·er (práizfaitər) *n.* a professional boxer, esp. one taking part in a prizefight **príze·fight·ing** *n.* professional boxing

prize money money from the proceeds of a prize captured at sea, formerly distributed among the officers and crew of the vessel that had made the capture ‖ any money offered as a prize

prize ring the roped enclosure within which a boxing match takes place ‖ prizefighting

Pro (prɔ), Miguel Agustín (1891–1927), Mexican Jesuit priest. He was accused of an attempted assassination of President Álvaro Obregón, and was executed

pro (prou) *PRO AND CON [L.=for]

pro *n.* (*pop.*) a professional, esp. a professional athlete or coach

pro- *prefix* favoring or advocating ‖ taking the place of ‖ forward, to the front of ‖ before, in advance [L.]

P.R.O. (*abbr.*) public relations officer

pro·a (próuə) *n.* prau [fr. Malay *prau, prao*]

pro·ac·tive (prouǽktiv) *adj.* (*psych.*) of the dominance of material learned early in life, before the current process of change

pro·am (próuǽm) *adj.* (*sports*) of competition including both professionals and amateurs

pro and con *adv.* for and against **pros and cons** *pl. n.* the arguments for and against ‖ those persons who are, respectively, in favor of or opposed to a proposal or proposition ‖ their respective affirmative and negative votes [L. *pro,* for+*contra,* against]

prob·a·bil·ism (prɒbəb'lizəm) *n.* (*theol.*) the doctrine that where there is reasonable doubt in a matter of conscience, it is lawful to act as one thinks best, esp. when there seems to be some authority for acting thus ‖ (*philos.*) the doctrine that knowledge is uncertain and that probability is a sufficient basis for action [fr. L. *probabilis,* probable]

prob·a·bil·i·ty (prɒbəbíliti:) *pl.* **prob·a·bil·i·ties** *n.* the state or quality of being probable ‖ (*math.*) the likelihood of an event, based on the ratio between its occurrence and the average number of cases favorable to its occurrence, taken over an indefinitely extended series of such cases ‖ something regarded as probable, based on the experience that of two or more possible effects one tends to predominate **in all probability** quite probably [fr. F. *probabilité*]

probability distribution or **probability function** (*math.*) a frequency function, where the function values *f(x)* are interpreted as probabilities that a quantity will take the value *x*

prob·a·ble (prɒ́bəb'l) **1.** *adj.* likely though not certain to occur or to be true, *rain is probable today, it is probable that he was murdered* **2.** *n.* a person, horse etc. likely to participate in a race ‖ a person likely to be selected as a member of a team, or to participate in a competition, or to be a candidate in an election or examination [F. or fr. L. *probabilis*]

probable cause (*law*) reasonable grounds for supposing guilt in a person charged with a crime

prob·a·bly (prɒ́bəbli:) *adv.* very likely, with probability

pro·bate (próubeit) **1.** *n.* (*law*) the official establishing of the legal validity of a will ‖ (*law*) a copy of a will certified to be legally valid **2.** *v.t. pres. part.* **pro·bat·ing** *past* and *past part.* **pro·bat·ed** (*law*) to prove (a will) ‖ to put on probation [fr. L. *probatum,* something proved]

probate court a court for submitting wills to probate and administering estates

pro·ba·tion (proubéiʃən) *n.* a critical testing, esp. to discover a person's suitability for a job, membership of an organization or institution etc. ‖ a period of such testing ‖ the suspension of the sentence of a convicted offender, allowing him his freedom subject to regular supervision by a probation officer ‖ a period of such supervision **on probation** in the condition of being a probationer **pro·bá·tion·ar·y** *adj.* of or relating to probation ‖ undergoing probation **pro·ba·tion·er** *n.* a person undergoing probation [O. F. *probacion*]

probation officer an official who supervises a convicted offender on probation

pro·ba·tive (próubətiv, prɒ́bətiv) *adj.* proving, or tending to prove, *probative evidence* ‖ serving to test [fr. L. *probativus*]

probe (proub) **1.** *n.* a blunt surgical instrument used to explore and examine wounds or cavities in the body ‖ a device, e.g. a space satellite, used for scientific exploration and investigation ‖ an investigation **2.** *v. pres. part.* **prob·ing** *past* and *past part.* **probed** *v.t.* to investigate thoroughly ‖ to examine with a surgical probe ‖ *v.i.* to make a thorough investigation ‖ to make an examination with a surgical probe [fr. L.L. *proba,* proof]

Prob·eye (próubai) *n.* trademark of infrared viewer that creates pictures by sensing heat radiated by objects, e.g., used to locate energy losses

pro·bi·ty (próubiti:, prɒ́biti:) *n.* scrupulous honesty [fr. L. *probitas*]

prob·lem (prɒ́bləm) **1.** *n.* a question whose answer is doubtful or difficult to find ‖ a question for discussion or consideration ‖ a matter that causes worry or perplexity ‖ (*math.*) a statement of what has to be done ‖ (*chess*) an arrangement of chessmen on a chessboard, in which a given result is to be achieved under given conditions, usually a certain number of moves **2.** *adj.* (of a play, novel etc.) presenting or dealing with a human or social problem ‖ that constitutes a problem or is difficult to deal with, *a problem child* [F. *problème*]

prob·lem·at·ic (prɒbləmǽtik) *adj.* constituting a problem ‖ open to question ‖ uncertain, *his success is very problematic* **prob·lem·át·i·cal** *adj.* [F. *problématique*]

pro·bos·cid·e·an, pro·bos·cid·i·an (proubasídi:ən, proubɒsidí:ən) **1.** *adj.* (zool.) pertaining to *Proboscidea,* an order of mammals having an elongated proboscis and some of the teeth adapted as tusks (e.g. the elephant, mammoth) **2.** *n.* a member of this order [fr. Mod. L. fr. Gk]

pro·bos·cis (proubɒ́sis) *pl.* **pro·bos·cis·es, pro·bos·ci·des** (proubɒ́sidi:z) *n.* a trunklike process of the head e.g. in many insects and annelids, and in elephants [L. fr. Gk fr. *pro,* in front+*boskein,* to feed]

proboscis monkey *Nasalis larvatus,* a monkey of Borneo with a long nose

pro·bu·col [$C_{31}H_{48}O_2S_3$] (próubu:kəl) *n.* (*pharm.*) a drug used to lower serum cholesterol; marketed as Lorelco

Pro·bus (próubəs), Marcus Aurelius (232–82), Roman emperor (276–82). He repelled barbarian invasions in many parts of the Roman Empire. He used soldiers on public works in peacetime, and was murdered by mutinous troops

pro·cain·a·mide or **procaine amide** [$C_{13}H_{21}N_3O$] (proukéinəmaid) *n.* (*pharm.*) a cardiac muscle depressant used to treat heart disease; marketed as Pronestyl

pro·cam·bi·al (proukǽmbi:əl) *adj.* of or derived from the procambium

pro·cam·bi·um (proukǽmbi:əm) *n.* (*bot.*) the tissue from which vascular bundles and cambium are developed [Mod. L. fr. Gk *pro,* before+CAMBIUM]

procaryote *PROKARYOTE

pro·ca·the·dral (proukəθí:drəl) *n.* a church or other building used as a cathedral

pro·ce·dur·al (prəsí:dʒərəl) *adj.* of or relating to procedure

pro·ce·dure (prəsí:dʒər) *n.* an act or manner of proceeding, *he agreed with our purpose but criticized our procedure* ‖ a prescribed way of doing something, *legal procedure* ‖ rules of parliamentary practice ‖ a particular course of action [F. *procédure*]

pro·ceed (prəsí:d) *v.i.* to move forward, to go further, *to proceed on one's way* ‖ to continue, *proceed along these same lines* ‖ to begin some action and persist in it, *he proceeded to get angry* ‖ to come forth, arise, *the whole trouble proceeded from a misunderstanding* ‖ (*law,* with 'against') to begin action or take legal measures

pro·céed·ing *n.* the act of someone who or something which proceeds ‖ a course of action, *an illegal proceeding* ‖ (*pl.*) transactions or negotiations ‖ (*pl.*) a record of the activities of a body or organization, *the proceedings of the last meeting* ‖ (*pl.*) a legal action ‖ (*pl.*) legal measures **pro·ceeds** (próusi:dz) *pl. n.* the sum yielded by a sale or other money-raising transaction, *he is entitled to one half of the proceeds* [F. *procéder*]

proc·ess (prɒ́ces, *Br.* esp. próuses) **1.** *n.* a series of acts or changes, proceeding from one to the next ‖ a method of manufacturing or conditioning something ‖ a moving forward, esp. as part of a progression or development, *the historical process* ‖ (*biol.*) an outgrowth or extension of an organ or an organism ‖ (*law*) legal proceedings, or the writ or summons beginning them **in process** in progress **in process of, in the process of** during the course of **2.** *v.t.* to submit (something) to a treatment, preparation or process, *to process milk* ‖ to submit (something) to a routine handling procedure, *his application was quickly processed* ‖ to submit (data etc.) to analysis ‖ (*printing*) to produce by a photomechanical process [F. *procès*]

process *v.t.* (*law*) to take legal action against by serving a writ [O.F. *processer,* to prosecute]

pro·cess (prəsés, prousés) *v.i.* (esp. *Br.*) to go in procession

process art art form involving ideas and effects, sometimes never executed and without completed objects. *also* conceptual art —**processor** *n.*

process engraving any method of engraving printing blocks other than by hand

pro·ces·sion (prəséʃən) *n.* an orderly line of persons, animals or things, singly or in rows, moving together in the same direction ‖ the act of moving thus, *the procession lasted five hours* ‖ (*theol.*) a divine issuing forth, *the procession of the Holy Ghost* [F.]

pro·ces·sion·al (prəséʃən'l) **1.** *adj.* of or pertaining to a procession, *a processional hymn* **2.** *n.* a musical composition, esp. a hymn, which accompanies a procession ‖ a service book containing hymns etc. to be sung in procession [fr. M. L. *processionale*]

processor (*computer*) *CENTRAL PROCESSING UNIT

process printing halftone printing in three or more superimposed colors, giving almost any desired color combination

process server (*law*) a person who serves legal documents, e.g. subpoenas

pro·claim (proukléim) *v.t.* to announce publicly or officially ‖ to declare (someone or something) officially to be, *the new state was proclaimed a republic* ‖ to declare (war, peace) ‖ to announce the accession to the throne of ‖ to reveal as, *his pretentious terminology proclaimed him a charlatan* [fr. L. *proclamare,* to cry out]

proc·la·ma·tion (prɒkləméiʃən) *n.* a proclaiming or being proclaimed ‖ an announcement, esp. an official one [F.]

pro·clam·a·to·ry (prəklǽmətɔri:, prəklǽmətouri:) *adj.* of or resembling a proclamation ‖ resembling the style of a person proclaiming

pro·clit·ic (prouklítik) **1.** *adj.* (*gram.*) of a monosyllabic word or particle with no accent of its own which is pronounced with the following word in ordinary speech (cf. ENCLITIC) **2.** *n.* a proclitic word or particle [fr. Mod. L. *procliticus* fr. Gk *proklinein,* to lean forward]

pro·cliv·i·ty (prouklíviti:) *pl.* **pro·cliv·i·ties** *n.* a tendency or inclination towards some habit, attitude of mind etc., esp. an undesirable one [F. *proclivité*]

Pro·clus (próukləs, prɒ́kləs) (c. 410–85), Greek philosopher. He combined metaphysics with Euclid's geometric method, to present Neoplatonism in its most complete and systematic form

Proc·ne (prɒ́kni:) *PHILOMELA

pro·con·sul (proukɒ́nsəl) *n.* (*Rom. hist.*) a governor of a province, with most of the powers of a consul ‖ a deputy consul **pro·cón·su·lar** *adj.* [L.]

pro·con·su·late (proukɔ́nsəlit) *n.* the office or jurisdiction of a proconsul [fr. L. *proconsulatus*]

pro·con·sul·ship (proukɔ́nsəlʃip) *n.* the office or term of office of a proconsul

Pro·co·pi·us (proukóupi:əs) (c. 500–c. 562), Byzantine historian. His 'History of the Wars' (550–3) is a valuable account of the wars of Justinian I

Procopius 'the Great' (Andrew Prokop, c. 1380–1434), Czech Hussite leader. He succeeded Žižka as leader of the Hussites in Bohemia (1425), won several victories over Imperial forces, and ravaged Hungary, Silesia and Saxony

pro·cras·ti·nate (proukrǽstineit) *pres. part.* **pro·cras·ti·nat·ing** *past* and *past part.* **pro·cras·ti·nat·ed** *v.i.* to keep delaying and putting things off **pro·crás·ti·na·tor** *n.* [fr. L. *procrastinare* (*procrastinatus*)]

pro·cras·ti·na·tion (proukræstinéiʃən) *n.* the act or habit of procrastinating [fr. L. *procrastinatio* (*procrastinationis*)]

pro·cre·ant (proukri:ənt) *adj.* producing young ‖ of procreation [fr. L. *procreans* (*procreantis*) fr. *procreare*, to procreate]

pro·cre·ate (próukri:eit) *pres. part.* **pro·cre·at·ing** *past* and *past part.* **pro·cre·at·ed** *v.t.* to produce (offspring) ‖ *v.i.* to bear offspring **pró·cre·a·tive** *adj.* [fr. L. *procreare* (*procreatus*)]

pro·cre·a·tion (proukri:éiʃən) *n.* a procreating or being procreated [O.F. *procreacion*]

Pro·crus·te·an (proukrʌ́sti:ən) *adj.* of or relating to Procrustes ‖ fitting people, ideas or events forcibly into a rigid preconceived plan or pattern, *Procrustean methods of reform* [after PROCRUSTES]

Pro·crus·tes (proukrʌ́sti:z) (*Gk mythol.*) a brigand who tied his guests to an iron bed and then either stretched them or lopped off their legs to make them fit it

proc·tor (prɔ́ktər) **1.** *n.* (*Am.* = *Br.* invigilator) someone who supervises students at a written examination ‖ (*Br.*) a university official appointed from the academic staff to see that undergraduates observe the regulations ‖ a person who manages another's cause in a court of canon or civil law or admiralty law ‖ (*Br.*) a clergyman elected as a deputy to convocation of the Church of England **2.** *v.t.* (*Am.*=*Br.* invigilate) to supervise students at (a written examination) **proc·tó·ri·al** *adj.* [alt. form of O.F. *procuratour*, procurator]

pro·cum·bent (proukʌ́mbənt) *adj.* (*of* plants) trailing along the ground [fr. L. *procumbens* (*procumbentis*) fr. *procumbere*, to fall forward]

pro·cur·a·ble (proukjúərəb'l) *adj.* able to be procured

pro·cur·ance (proukjúərəns) *n.* the act of procuring or bringing about

proc·u·ra·tion (prɒkjəréiʃən) *n.* procuring ‖ an instance of this ‖ the act of giving someone power of attorney ‖ a fee paid (to a broker) for the negotiation of a loan [F.]

proc·u·ra·tor (prɔ́kjəreitər) *n.* someone who manages another's legal affairs ‖ a proctor in a court of civil or canon law ‖ (*hist.*) a financial administrator in a province of the Roman Empire **proc·u·ra·tó·ri·al** *adj.* [O.F. *procuratour* or fr. L.]

proc·u·ra·to·ry (prɔ́kjərətɒri:, prɔ́kjərətouri:) *n.* legal authorization to act for another [fr. L.L. *procuratorius*, belonging to a procurator]

pro·cure (proukjúər) *pres. part.* **pro·cur·ing** *past* and *past part.* **pro·cured** *v.t.* to obtain, esp. as a result of some degree of effort ‖ to bring about, contrive, *to procure someone's dismissal* ‖ to obtain (women) for prostitution ‖ *v.i.* to obtain women for prostitution **pro·cúre·ment** *n.* [F. *procurer*]

pro·cur·er (proukjúərər) *n.* someone who procures (esp. women for prostitution) **pro·cúr·ess** *n.* a female procurer [A.F. *procurour*, procurator]

prod (prɒd) **1.** *v. pres. part.* **prod·ding** *past* and *past part.* **prod·ded** *v.t.* to poke with a finger, stick or pointed instrument ‖ to goad, rouse, *he occasionally needs prodding into activity* ‖ *v.i.* (with 'at') to poke **2.** *n.* a poke or sharp dig, *she gave him a prod with her stick* ‖ an urge to activity, a sharp reminder, *her memory needs a prod* ‖ a pointed instrument for prodding with [etym. doubtful]

prod·i·gal (prɔ́dig'l) **1.** *adj.* given to reckless spending, wasteful ‖ (*rhet.*) lavishly generous **2.** *n.* (*rhet.*) a spendthrift [obs. F.]

prod·i·gal·i·ty (prɒdigǽliti:) *n.* reckless spending, extravagance ‖ very great generosity ‖ abundance [F. *prodigalité*]

prodigal son a repentant waster [after the biblical parable (Luke xv, 11-32)]

pro·di·gious (prədídʒəs) *adj.* amazing, esp. marvelously great, *a prodigious memory* [fr. L. *prodigiosus*]

prod·i·gy (prɔ́didʒi:) *pl.* **prod·i·gies** *n.* a person, esp. a child, with extraordinary talents ‖ an exceptional instance (of some quality), *a prodigy of patience* [fr. L. *prodigium*, portent]

prod·ro·mal (prɔ́drəməl) *adj.* (*med.*) of or constituting a prodrome

pro·drome (próudroum, *Br.* prɔ́drəm) *n.* (*med.*) a premonitory symptom of a disease [F. fr. Mod. L. fr. Gk *prodromos*, forerunner]

pro·duce 1. (prədú:s, prədjú:s) *v. pres. part.* **pro·duc·ing** *past* and *past part.* **pro·duced** *v.t.* to bring forward, present for inspection, *to produce one's ticket* ‖ to bring forth, cause to appear, *he produced two apples from his pocket* ‖ to create (a work of art), write (books etc.), *this author has produced little in the last few years* ‖ (of land, plants etc.) to bear, yield ‖ to give birth to ‖ to yield as an exportable product, *Australia produces wool and meat* ‖ to manufacture, *the factory produces 1,000 cars a week* ‖ to bring (a play) before the public, arranging financial backing etc. ‖ (*Br.*=*Am.* direct) to supervise the presentation of (a play), directing the actors etc. at rehearsals ‖ to assume overall responsibility for the making of (a film) ‖ (*geom.*) to extend (a line), *produce the base BC of the triangle ABC* ‖ to give rise to, cause, *his arrival produced a sensation* ‖ to cause to accrue, *money invested produces interest* ‖ *v.i.* to yield or manufacture economically valuable products **2.** (prɔ́du:s, prɔ́dju:s, próudu:s, próudju:s) *n.* agricultural or horticultural products, *dairy produce* ‖ a result (of efforts etc.) ‖ an amount produced **pro·dúc·er** *n.* a person who or a thing which produces ‖ a furnace for making producer gas [fr. L. *producere*, to lead forth]

producer gas a fuel gas which is a mixture of carbon monoxide, hydrogen and nitrogen, made by passing air over red-hot coke

producer goods goods, e.g. raw materials and tools, needed by a manufacturer to make other goods (cf. CONSUMER GOODS)

pro·duc·i·ble (prədú:səb'l, prədjú':səb'l) *adj.* capable of being produced

prod·uct (prɔ́dəkt, prɔ́dʌkt) *n.* something produced, esp. something grown or manufactured ‖ an outcome, result, *these evils were the product of laissez-faire* ‖ (*math.*) the number obtained by multiplying numbers together ‖ (*chem.*) a new compound formed as a result of chemical change (cf. EDUCT) [fr. L. *productum*]

product differentiation (*business*) marketing strategy based upon the creation and promotion of product differences, which may be real or imagined, in the physical character of the product or in packaging, name or way it is being promoted

pro·duc·tion (prədʌ́kʃən) *n.* a producing or being produced ‖ something produced, esp. a literary, artistic or dramatic work [F.]

pro·duc·tive (prədʌ́ktiv) *adj.* able to produce or producing in abundance ‖ (with 'of') being the direct or indirect cause, *these laws were productive of great hardship* ‖ yielding results or profit, *productive efforts* ‖ (*econ.*) producing goods which have economic value, *productive labor* **pro·duc·tiv·i·ty** (proudʌktíviti:, prɒdəktíviti:) *n.* ability to produce ‖ productive yield, *productivity and wage increases have not kept in step* [fr. F. *productif* (*productive*)]

pro·em (próuem) *n.* a preface or introduction, e.g. to a book or speech **pro·e·mi·al** (prouí:mi:əl) *adj.* [O.F. *proeme* fr. L. fr. Gk]

prof·a·na·tion (prɒfənéiʃən) *n.* a profaning or being profaned [O.F. *prophanation*]

pro·fane (prəféin) *adj.* blasphemous, irreverent, *profane language* ‖ heathen, *profane rites* ‖ not connected with things sacred or biblical, *sacred and profane literature* ‖ (*rhet.*) not initiated into sacred mysteries, *the profane multitude* ‖ (*rhet.*) not possessing esoteric knowledge or tastes, *his work is too subtle for the profane mass of readers* [F.]

profane *pres. part.* **pro·fan·ing** *past* and *past part.* **pro·faned** *v.t.* to treat (something sacred) with irreverence, desecrate ‖ (*rhet.*) to treat disrespectfully, debase [fr. L. *profanare*]

pro·fan·i·ty (prəfǽniti:) *pl.* **pro·fan·i·ties** *n.* irreverence ‖ an irreverent act or utterance [fr. L. *profanitas*]

pro·fess (prəfés) *v.t.* to claim, *he doesn't profess to be an expert* ‖ to claim or declare falsely, *he professed to be sorry but doesn't look it* ‖ to declare one's faith in by observances and practices, *to profess Christianity* ‖ to follow as one's profession, *to profess medicine* ‖ to accept into a religious order ‖ *v.i.* to make a profession, esp. of religious vows **pro·féssed** *adj.* openly declared, self-acknowledged, *a professed atheist* ‖ pretended, claiming to be, *professed friendship* ‖ having taken religious vows, *a professed nun* **pro·fess·ed·ly** (prəfésidli:) *adv.* according to a person's own claims, *he is professedly an authority on the subject* [L. *profiteri* (*professus*), to profess]

pro·fes·sion (prəféʃən) *n.* one of a limited number of occupations or vocations involving special learning and carrying a certain social prestige, esp. the learned professions: law, medicine and the Church ‖ any vocation or occupation, *a dancer by profession* ‖ the people engaged in such an occupation, *an insult to the profession* ‖ open declaration, avowal, *a profession of loyalty* ‖ a declaration of religious belief ‖ a taking of religious vows **pro·fés·sion·al 1.** *adj.* of or relating to a profession ‖ showing a sound workman's command, *a thoroughly professional novel* ‖ engaging in some activity as a remunerated occupation, *a professional football player* (*cf.* AMATEUR) ‖ following some line of conduct as if it were one's profession, *a professional agitator* ‖ of or done by professionals, *professional golf* **2.** *n.* someone who engages in an activity, esp. a sport, to earn money ‖ someone engaged in one of the learned or salaried professions **pro·fés·sion·al·ism** *n.* [F.]

pro·fes·sor (prəfésər) *n.* a university teacher of the highest rank in a faculty ‖ someone who declares or confesses views, a faith etc. **pro·fés·sor·ate** *n.* the office or term of office of a professor **pro·fes·so·ri·al** (proufəsɔ́ri:əl, prɒfəsɔ́ri:əl, proufəsóuri:əl, prɒfəsóuri:əl) *adj.* **pro·fes·só·ri·ate** *n.* a body of professors **pro·fés·sor·ship** *n.* [fr. L. fr. *profiteri*, to profess]

prof·fer (prɔ́fər) *n.* an offer, *a proffer of help* [A. F. *profre*]

proffer *v.t.* to offer, tender, *to proffer a bribe* [O.F. *proffrir*]

pro·fi·cien·cy (prəfíʃənsi:) *n.* the state or quality of being proficient

pro·fi·cient (prəfíʃənt) *adj.* having or showing effective command in an art, skill, study etc. [fr. L. *proficiens* (*proficientis*) fr. *proficere*, to advance]

pro·file (próufail) **1.** *n.* the shape of something, esp. the face, as seen from a side view ‖ a drawing of the side view of something, esp. the face ‖ a concise biographical description, *a profile of the new prime minister* ‖ any short historical, geographical or other descriptive sketch in writing, *a profile of modern India* ‖ a flat, cutout piece of stage scenery ‖ (*archit.*, *engin.* etc.) a side elevation or a section **2.** *v.t. pres. part.* **pro·fil·ing** *past* and *past part.* **pro·filed** to draw or write a profile of [fr. Ital. *profilo*]

prof·it (prɔ́fit) *n.* advantage, benefit, *he gained a lot of profit from his visit* ‖ financial gain, *he says he writes for profit, not for pleasure* ‖ (*sing.* or *pl.*) an excess of income over expenditure, esp. in a particular transaction or over a period of time ‖ the ratio of this annual excess to the amount of capital invested ‖ (*econ.*) net income [O.F.]

profit *v.i.* (with 'by' or 'from') to obtain financial gain or other benefit, *to profit from an experience* ‖ *v.t.* (*old-fash.*) to be of advantage to, *it will not profit you to start an argument* [F. *profiter*]

prof·it·a·ble (prɔ́fitəb'l) *adj.* yielding profit or a profit **próf·it·a·bly** *adv.* [F.]

profit and loss account (*bookkeeping*) an account in which receipts are credited and expenses debited so as to show the net profit or loss over any given period

profit center (*business*) division providing major source of profit for a company, such as a particular department or product line

prof·it·eer (prɒfitíər) **1.** *n.* someone who makes extortionate profits, esp. in times of scarcity **2.** *v.i.* to make such profits

prof·it·less (prɔ́fitlis) *adj.* yielding or offering no profit

profit sharing a system by which workers share in the profits of a business

prof·li·ga·cy (prɔ́fligəsi:) *n.* the state or quality of being profligate

prof·li·gate (prɔ́fligit) **1.** *adj.* dissolute ‖ wildly extravagant **2.** *n.* a profligate person [fr. L. *profligare (profligatus),* to ruin, destroy]

pro for·ma invoice (proufɔ́rmə) an invoice sent in advance of goods to show that they are being dispatched and what sum will figure on the invoice proper

pro·found (prəfáund) *adj.* searching into the deepest and most subtle problems or truths, *a profound thinker* ‖ possessing particular wisdom and shrewdness, *a profound statesman* ‖ requiring deep thought, *profound difficulties* ‖ very great, intense, *he made a profound impression* ‖ coming as if from a great depth, *a profound sigh of relief* [O.F. *profund, profond,* deep]

pro·fun·di·ty (prəfʌ́nditi:) *pl.* **pro·fun·di·ties** *n.* depth, intensity, *the profundity of his learning* ‖ something profound, *we could not follow him in these profundities* [O.F. *profundite*]

pro·fuse (prəfjú:s) *adj.* (of persons) lavish, very generous, *he was profuse in his thanks* ‖ (of things) very abundant, *profuse apologies* [fr. L. *profundere (profusus),* to pour forth]

pro·fu·sion (prəfjú:ʒən) *n.* the quality or state of being profuse ‖ great abundance, *flowers grew in profusion* [F.]

pro·gen·i·tive (proudʒénitiv) *adj.* able to produce offspring ‖ relating to the production of offspring [fr. L. *progignere (progenitus),* to beget]

pro·gen·i·tor (proudʒénitər) *n.* an ancestor of a person, animal or plant ‖ an originator of an idea, theory etc. [obs. F. *progeniteur*]

pro·gen·i·ture (proudʒénitʃər) *n.* offspring ‖ the begetting of offspring [fr. L. *progignere (progenitus),* to beget]

prog·e·ny (prɒ́dʒəni:) *pl.* **prog·e·nies** *n.* offspring, descendants [obs. F. *progenie*]

pro·ges·ter·one (proudʒéstəroun) *n.* a hormone produced by the ovaries, preparing the uterus for pregnancy [PROGESTIN+STEROL]

pro·ges·tin (proudʒéstin) *n.* progesterone [L. *pro,* for+GESTATION]

pro·glot·tis (prouglɒ́tis) *pl.* **pro·glot·ti·des** (prouglɒ́tidi:z) *n.* a reproductive body segment of a cestode formed by budding from the neck [Mod. L. fr. Gk *pro-,* forward+*glōssa, glōtta,* tongue]

prog·nath·ic (prɒgnǽθik) *adj.* prognathous

prog·na·thism (prɒ́gneθizəm, *Br.* also prɒgnǽθizəm) *n.* the state of being prognathous

prog·na·thous (prɒ́gnəθəs) *adj.* having projecting jaws ‖ (of jaws) projecting [fr. Gk *pro-,* forward+*gnathos,* jaw]

prog·no·sis (prɒgnóusis) *pl.* **prog·no·ses** (prɒgnóusi:z) *n.* a doctor's assessment of the probable course of an illness and the prospects of recovery ‖ the act of making such an assessment ‖ a forecast [L.L. fr. Gk fr. *pro-,* before+*gnōsis,* knowledge]

prog·nos·tic (prɒgnɒ́stik) *n.* an omen, sign ‖ a forecast [O.F. *pronostique* fr. L. fr. Gk]

prognostic *adj.* of or relating to prognosis or a prognostication [fr. M.L. *prognosticus*]

prog·nos·ti·cate (prɒgnɒ́stikeit) *pres. part.* **prog·nos·ti·cat·ing** *past* and *past part.* **prog·nos·ti·cat·ed** *v.t.* to foretell, predict ‖ *v.i.* to make a prediction [fr. Mod. L. *prognosticare (prognosticatus)*]

prog·nos·ti·ca·tive (prɒgnɒ́stikeitiv) *adj.* characterized by prognostication

prog·nos·ti·ca·tion (prɒgnɒstikéiʃən) *n.* a prognosticating ‖ a forecast [O.F. *pronosticacion*]

prog·nos·ti·ca·tor (prɒgnɒ́stikeitər) *n.* someone who prognosticates

pro·gram, esp. *Br.* **pro·gramme** (próugræm, próugrəm) **1.** *n.* a plan or sequence of things to be done, *a research program* ‖ a list of items planned to constitute a concert, dramatic performance, athletic meet etc., esp. a printed list giving the names of the participants etc. ‖ the performance itself, *last night's program was a great success* ‖ a complete item broadcast on radio or television ‖ a plan of the operations to be executed by a computer **2.** *v.t. pres. part.* **pro·gram·ing,** esp. *Br.* and *computer technol.* **pro·gram·ming** *past* and *past part.* **pro·gramed,** esp. *Br.* and *computer technol.* **pro·grammed** to work out a plan of the operations to be executed by (a computer) ‖ to plan the details of, esp. with respect to timing **pró·gram·mer** *n.* someone who programmes a computer [F. and fr. L. fr. Gk *programma,* a public notice]

programmable signal processor (*mil.*) digital computer device for U.S. fighter aircraft capable of performing 7.2 million operations per second, used in radar on F-18A Hornet, F-15 Eagle, and F-14 Tomcat. *abbr.* **PSP**

programmed instruction technique for arranging material to make learning of it easy, and for showing interconnection of the material, esp. with use of a computer. *Cf* TEACHING MACHINE

pro·gram·metry (prougrǽmitri:) *n.* (*computer*) the measurement of the performance of a program

programming language (*computer*) a series of codes to which a computer can respond

program music, esp. *Br.* **programme music** music whose primary intention is to evoke moods, suggest images or tell a story to the listener

prog·ress 1. (prɒ́gres, esp. *Br.* próugrəs) *n.* forward movement ‖ (*fig.*) movement nearer to some aim, *his research made slow progress* ‖ a forward course or development, *the progress of a disease* ‖ improvement, advancement, *he has made good progress in his job* ‖ a supposed gradual advancement or improvement in the condition of mankind, esp. seen from a scientific or material standpoint ‖ (esp. *hist.*) an official or ceremonial journey **in progress** going on now or at the time in question **2. pro·gress** (prəgrés, *Br.* esp. prougrés) *v.i.* to go forward or onward ‖ to go on, continue, *the demolition work progresses steadily* ‖ to develop, show improvement, *how is the boy progressing?* ‖ (*fig.*) to advance, move nearer to some aim, *space research has progressed greatly* [fr. L. *progredi (progressus),* to go forward]

pro·gres·sion (prəgréʃən) *n.* the act or process of going forward ‖ continuing development, *the narrative shows a sense of orderly progression* ‖ (*mus.*) a movement from one note or chord to another, or the series of notes or chords themselves ‖ (*astron.*) movement of the planets from west to east through the zodiac ‖ (*math.*) a series whose terms increase or decrease according to a rule (*ARITHMETIC PROGRESSION, *GEOMETRIC PROGRESSION, *HARMONIC PROGRESSION) ‖ a connected series, esp. showing continuity **pro·grés·sion·ist** *n.* someone who believes in human progress [F.]

pro·gres·sive (prəgrésiv) **1.** *adj.* moving forward or onward ‖ increasing in severity, intensity etc., *the progressive stages of an illness* ‖ increasing or advancing in stages or in series, *progressive taxation* ‖ having to do with, or favoring, political and social progress or reform ‖ of or favoring modern educational ideas which stress informal teaching methods and the encouragement of self-expression, *a progressive headmaster* ‖ (*gram.*) of or being a verbal form designating action going on (e.g. 'he is running') ‖ (*cards*) of a tournament in which there is a movement from table to table after each game so as to effect a change of partners ‖ (of a dance)in which there is a regular change of partners **Pro·gres·sive** (*Am. hist.*) of a Progressive party **2.** *n.* someone who is progressive (*printing, pl.*) progressive proofs **Progressive** (*Am. hist.*) a member of a Progressive party [F. *progressif (progressive)*]

Progressive party (*Am. hist.*) a Republican splinter group (1912–16) led by Theodore Roosevelt in opposition to Taft ‖ a Republican splinter group (1924–46) centered chiefly in Wisconsin ‖ a Democratic splinter group organized (1948) by H. A. Wallace

progressive proofs (*printing*) a set of individual color guides for inking and registration from which a color printer works in order to reproduce exactly the model proposed

pro·hib·it (prouhíbit) *v.t.* to forbid with authority, esp. by law ‖ to prevent or make impossible [fr. L. *prohibere (prohibitus)*]

pro·hi·bi·tion (prouəbíʃən) *n.* a prohibiting by authority ‖ a law that prohibits ‖ the forbidding by law of the manufacture or sale of liquor, or the law itself ‖ (*law*) a high-court writ prohibiting a lower court from proceeding in a case beyond its jurisdiction **Pro·hi·bi·tion** (*Am. hist.*) the forbidding, under the 18th amendment to the constitution, of the manufacture, sale, import or export of liquor throughout the U.S.A. The law was in force 1920-33. In spite of the Volstead Act (1919), the law proved impossible to enforce and was frequently evaded thanks to bootleggers and speakeasies **pro·hi·bí·tion·ist** *n.* an advocate of prohibition of the sale of liquor [F.]

Prohibition party the oldest of U.S. third political parties, founded (1869) in Chicago, Ill., to secure legislation to prohibit the manufacture, transportation and sale of intoxicating liquors. It strongly influenced the presidential election of 1892 and the passage (1919) of the Prohibition Amendment. After that its most effective work was in local and county elections

pro·hib·i·tive (prouhíbitiv) *adj.* serving to prohibit, *prohibitive laws* ‖ (of prices or tax) so high as to discourage purchase or use [F. *prohibitif, prohibitive*]

pro·hib·i·to·ry (prouhíbitɔri:, prouhíbitouri:) *adj.* prohibitive [fr. L. *prohibitorius*]

proj·ect (prɒ́dʒekt) *n.* a course of action intended or considered possible ‖ a systematic planned undertaking, *a research project* ‖ a set task for a class of schoolchildren in which, for a given period of time, subjects are taught with special reference to some chosen topic, and pupils are encouraged to make independent inquiries to supplement formal teaching

pro·ject (prədʒékt) *v.t.* to throw by mechanical means ‖ to cause (light, an image etc.) to fall on a certain surface, *the film was projected onto the screen* ‖ to have in mind as an intention or possibility, *to project a visit* ‖ to direct (the mind etc.), *to project one's thoughts into the future* ‖ to cause (oneself) to enter imaginatively, *to project oneself into the hero's situation* ‖ to externalize (one's own hopes, ideas, frustrations etc.) in something outside oneself or in some other person ‖ (*geom.*) to represent on a given plane or surface a point, line, surface or solid, as viewed from a particular direction or in accordance with a fixed correspondence ‖ to represent (e.g. a map of the earth or heavens) in this way ‖ *v.i.* to stick out, protrude ‖ (of an actor etc.) to establish effective sympathy with the audience [fr. L. *projicere (projectus),* to thrust forward]

project grant a contract with a government or private agency to perform certain tasks, esp. research

pro·jec·tile (prədʒéktil, prədʒéktail) **1.** *n.* a body projected, esp. a missile projected from a gun etc. **2.** *adj.* suddenly thrusting forward, *projectile force* ‖ capable of being projected with force [fr. Mod. L. *projectilis* fr. *projicere,* to thrust forward]

pro·jec·tion (prədʒékʃən) *n.* a projecting or being projected ‖ a system by which lines of longitude and latitude are translated onto a plane surface so as to represent the curved surface of the earth or the celestial sphere ‖ the result of projecting a geometrical figure ‖ (*psych.*) accusation of, or unconscious attribution to another of, one's own thoughts, feelings, or actions [fr. L. *projectio (projectionis)*]

projection booth (*Am.=Br.* projection room) a room at the rear of a movie house from which a movie is projected onto the screen

pro·jec·tion·ist (prədʒékʃənist) *n.* the operator of a movie projector

projection room (*Br.*) a projection booth

pro·jec·tive (prədʒéktiv) *adj.* projecting ‖ of or relating to projection [fr. L. *projicere (projectus),* to thrust forward]

projective geometry the branch of geometry concerned with those properties of figures that are unaltered by projection

pro·jec·tor (prədʒéktər) *n.* an instrument for projecting a beam of light or for throwing an image or a series of images onto a screen

pro·jec·tu·al (prədʒéktʃu:əl) *adj.* of visual material suitable for projection on a screen, e.g., by an instructor. **—projector** *n.* the projectionist or the projecting machine

pro·kar·y·ote or **pro·car·y·ote** (proukǽri:out) *n.* (*biol.*) a primitive single-celled organism with no bound nucleus, e.g., blue-green alga, a bacterium. *Cf* EUCARYOTE

Pro·ko·fiev (prəkɔ́fi:ef), Sergei Sergeyevich (1891–1953), Russian composer and soloist. His work showed great rhythmic and percussive originality and humor. He wrote five piano and two violin concertos, ballet and film music, and seven symphonies, including the 'Classical Symphony' (1916–17). His 'Peter and the Wolf' (1936) is a popular descriptive guide to the orchestra

Pro·ko·pyevsk (prʌkɔ́pjəfsk) a coal-mining center (pop. 267,000) of the R.S.F.S.R., U.S.S.R., in the S. Kuznetsk Basin

pro·lapse (próulæps) **1.** *n.* (*med.*) a slipping down or out of place of some internal organ of the body, esp. the womb **2.** *v.i. pres. part.* **pro·laps·ing** *past* and *past part.* **pro·lapsed** (*med.*) to slip down (as in a prolapse) [fr. L. *prolabi (prolapsus),* to fall forward]

pro·lap·sus (proulǽpsəs) *n.* (*med.*) a prolapse [L.]

CONCISE PRONUNCIATION KEY: **(a)** æ, *cat;* ɑ, *car;* ɔ *fawn;* ei, *snake.* **(e)** e, *hen;* i:, *sheep;* iə, *deer;* ɛə, *bear.* **(i)** i, *fish;* ai, *tiger;* ə:, *bird.* **(o)** o, *ox;* au, *cow;* ou, *goat;* u, *poor;* ɔi, *royal.* **(u)** ʌ, *duck;* u, *bull;* u:, *goose;* ə, *bacillus;* ju:, *cube.* x, *loch;* θ, *think;* ð, *bother;* z, *Zen;* ʒ, *corsage;* dʒ, *savage;* ŋ, *orangutang;* j, *yak;* ʃ, *fish;* tʃ, *fetch;* 'l, *rabble;* 'n, *redden.* Complete pronunciation key appears inside front cover.

pro·late (próuleit) *adj.* (*geom.*, of a spheroid) elongated in the direction of the longer axis (opp. OBLATE) [fr. L. *proferre* (*prolatus*), to extend]

pro·leg (próuleg) *n.* one of the fleshy legs found on the abdominal segments of the larvae of certain insects

pro·le·gom·e·non (proulәgómәnɒn) *pl.* **pro·le·gom·e·na** (proulegómәnә) *n.* (esp. *pl.*) an introductory section, esp. to a learned work **pro·le·góm·e·nous** *adj.* [Gk=what is being said first, fr. *prolegein*, to say before]

pro·lep·sis (proulépsis) *pl.* **pro·lep·ses** (proulépsi:z) *n.* (in rhetoric) the anticipation of objections ‖ the figure of speech by which what is to follow is taken as already effective, e.g. the application for dramatic effect of an adjective to a noun to which it does not yet apply [Gk *prolēpsis* fr. *prolambanein*, to take before]

pro·le·tar·i·an (proulitéәri:әn) **1.** *n.* a member of the proletariat **2.** *adj.* of or relating to the proletariat [fr. L. *proletarius*, lowest-class citizen]

pro·le·tar·i·at (proulitéәri:әt) *n.* the lowest class in a modern society, esp. (in Marxist theory) industrial wage earners possessing neither property nor capital and living by the sale of their labor ‖ (*Rom. hist.*) the lowest class in ancient Rome [F. *prolétariat*]

pro-life movement (próuláif) antiabortion political pressure groups. *ant.* pro-choice movement

pro·lif·er·ate (proulífәreit) *pres. part.* **pro·lif·er·at·ing** *past and past part.* **pro·lif·er·at·ed** *v.i.* (*biol.*) to grow or reproduce rapidly by cell division, budding etc. ‖ to multiply fast, grow by multiplying, *ideas proliferated in his mind* ‖ *v.t.* to cause to increase greatly in number [back-formation fr. PROLIFERATION]

pro·lif·er·a·tion (proulifәréiʃәn) *n.* a proliferating or being proliferated [F. *prolifération*]

pro·lif·er·ous (proulífәrәs) *adj.* (*bot.*) developing buds from a normally terminal organ (e.g. a leaf or flower) ‖ (*biol.*) reproducing by budding [fr. M.L. *prolifer*, bearing offspring]

pro·lif·ic (proulífik) *adj.* reproducing rapidly and in large numbers, *rabbits are very prolific* ‖ producing abundantly, *a prolific writer* ‖ abundant, *a prolific output* ‖ (*rhet.*, with 'in' or 'of') very productive **pro·líf·i·ca·cy** *n.* **pro·líf·i·cal·ly** *adv.* [fr. M. L. *prolificus*]

pro·lif·i·ca·tion (proulifikéiʃәn) *n.* (*biol.*) the quality or state of being proliferous ‖ (*bot.*) a proliferous growth [fr. M.L. *prolificatio* (*prolificationis*), production of offspring]

pro·lix (próuliks, proulíks) *adj.* tediously wordy, long-winded, verbose **pro·líx·i·ty** *n.* [F. *prolixe* or fr. L. *prolixus*, extended]

pro·loc·u·tor (proulókjutәr) *n.* (*rhet.*) a spokesman ‖ a chairman, esp. (*Br.*) of the lower house of a convocation of the Church of England [L. fr. *proloqui* (*prolocutus*), to speak out]

prolog *PROLOGUE

pro·log·ize (proulɔgaiz, proulɒgaiz, prouləd3aiz) *pres. part.* **pro·log·iz·ing** *past and past part.* **pro·log·ized** *v.i.* to write or speak a prologue [fr. Gk *prologizein*]

pro·logue, pro·log (próulɔg, próulɒg) *n.* an introduction or preface, often in verse, to a literary work, esp. a play (cf. EPILOGUE) [O.F. fr. L. fr. Gk]

pro·logu·ize (próulɔgaiz, próulɒgaiz) *pres. part.* **pro·logu·iz·ing** *past and past part.* **pro·logu·ized** *v.i.* to prologize

pro·long (prәlɔ́ŋ, prәlɒ́ŋ) *v.t.* to make longer, extend, draw out (usually in time), *to prolong a visit* ‖ to lengthen the pronunciation of (a syllable etc.) [O.F. *prolonguer*]

pro·lon·ga·tion (proulɔŋgéiʃәn, proulɒŋgéiʃәn) *n.* a prolonging or being prolonged ‖ a linear extension [F.]

prom (prɒm) *n.* ‖ (*pop.*) a ball or dance given by a college or high school group or class ‖ (*Br., pop.*) a promenade concert ‖ (*Br., pop.*) a seafront promenade [shortened fr. PROMENADE]

prom·e·nade (prɒmәnéid, prɒmәnɑ́d) **1.** *n.* a slow walk or ride taken for pleasure, esp. for display or as a social custom ‖ a place suitable for this, esp. a paved walk along the seafront at a resort ‖ a series of walking steps in a square dance ‖ the opening of a formal ball in which all the guests participate in a stately march ‖ (*Am., hist.*) a competitive walk or strut to music by couples **2.** *v. pres. part.* **prom·e·nad·ing** *past and past part.* **prom·e·nad·ed** *v.i.* to take a stroll ‖ to go on a promenade ‖ to perform a promenade in a dance ‖ *v.t.* to take a stroll through, *to promenade the streets* ‖ to take for a stroll or ride so as to display [F.]

promenade concert an orchestral concert where some members of the audience are not seated and may stroll around

promenade deck an upper deck of a liner, where passengers may stroll

Pro·me·the·an (prәmí:θi:әn) *adj.* having to do with Prometheus, or like him in his skill or suffering

Pro·me·the·us (prәmí:θi:әs, prәmí:θju:s) (*Gk mythol.*) son of the Titan Iapetus and brother of Atlas. He stole fire from the gods and gave it to man. In punishment, Zeus chained Prometheus to a rock and sent an eagle or vulture by day to eat out his liver, which was restored every night. He was eventually rescued by Heracles. In some myths, Prometheus appears as the giver of the arts and sciences to mankind

pro·me·thi·um (prәmí:θi:әm) *n.* a metallic element (symbol Pm, at. no. 61, weight of most important isotope 147) of the rare-earth series, produced during the fission of uranium [after PROMETHEUS]

prom·i·nence (próminәns) *n.* the state or quality of being prominent ‖ a hill, elevation etc. ‖ a solar prominence **próm·i·nen·cy** *n.* [F. *prominence*]

prom·i·nent (próminәnt) *adj.* conspicuous, *a prominent landmark* ‖ jutting out, projecting, *a prominent nose* ‖ distinguished, eminent, *a prominent public figure* ‖ leading, *a prominent advocate of reform* [fr. L. *prominens* (*prominentis*) fr. *prominere*, to project, jut out]

prom·is·cu·i·ty (prɒmiskjú:iti:) *pl.* **prom·is·cu·i·ties** *n.* the fact or an instance of being promiscuous [fr. F. *promiscuité*]

pro·mis·cu·ous (prәmískju:әs) *adj.* having sexual relations with many ‖ indiscriminate, *promiscuous borrowing from secondary sources* ‖ made up of various kinds indiscriminately mixed together, *a promiscuous gathering* [fr. L. *promiscuus*, mixed]

prom·ise (prómis) **1.** *n.* an assurance that one will do or refrain from doing a specified thing, *a promise to return soon* ‖ a firm prospect, *a promise of a good harvest* ‖ potential greatness or distinction, *a new writer of great promise* **2.** *v. pres. part.* **prom·is·ing** *past and past part.* **prom·ised** *v.t.* to make a promise (to do something, that something will be done etc.) ‖ to assure (someone) that he will receive, *to promise someone a warm welcome* ‖ to give cause for expectation of, *early mist promises a fine day* ‖ *v.i.* to make a promise ‖ (with 'well') to show potential good quality, *he promises well as a mathematician* [fr. L. *promittere* (*promissum*), to put forth, promise]

promised Land Canaan

prom·is·ee (prɒmisí:) *n.* (*law*) someone to whom a promise is made

prom·is·ing (prɒmisiŋ) *adj.* giving hope of achievement or success in the future, likely to turn out well, *a promising pupil*

prom·i·sor (prómisәr) *n.* (*law*) someone who makes a promise

prom·is·so·ry (prómisɔri:, prómisouri:) *adj.* containing a promise [fr. M.L. *promissorius*]

promissory note a written and signed promise to pay unconditionally to a named person or body, or to bearer, a fixed sum of money either on demand or at some definite future time, e.g. a bank note

pro·mo (próumou) *n.* (*colloq.*) short for advertising promotion —**promo** *adj.*, *v.*

prom·on·to·ry (prómәntɔri:, prómәntouri:) *pl.* **prom·on·to·ries** *n.* a point of high land jutting out into an area of water ‖ (*anat.*) any one of certain protuberances [fr. M.L. *promontorium*]

pro·mote (prәmóut) *pres. part.* **pro·mot·ing** *past and past part.* **pro·mot·ed** *v.t.* to raise in rank or status ‖ to help forward, further, *to promote a scheme* ‖ to push the sales of by intensive advertising etc. ‖ to encourage, *to promote interest* ‖ to organize, present and secure financial backing for, *to promote a boxing match* ‖ to support actively, devote energy and influence to securing the passage of, *to promote a bill in Congress* ‖ (*chess*) to advance (a pawn) to the eighth rank and change it into a piece [fr. L. *promovere* (*promotus*), to move forward]

pro·mot·er (prәmóutәr) *n.* a person who promotes the formation of a company etc. ‖ someone who organizes and secures financial backing (esp. for a sporting event) [A.F. *promotour*]

pro·mo·tion (prәmóuʃәn) *n.* a promoting or being promoted ‖ advancement to higher rank or status, *to work for promotion* ‖ a striving to secure greater sales by intensive advertising etc. ‖ the organization or setting up of an enterprise, *company promotion* **pro·mó·tion·al, pro·mó·tive** *adjs* [F.]

prompt 1. *adj.* quick to respond and act without delay, *prompt to obey* ‖ immediate, instant, *a prompt reply* **2.** *n.* (*commerce*) a time limit given for payment of the account for goods bought [F. or fr. L. *promptus*, at hand]

prompt (prompt) **1.** *v.t.* to move or rouse to action, *his anger prompted him to interrupt* ‖ to give rise to, inspire, *malice prompted that remark* ‖ to whisper to (an actor) words which he has forgotten ‖ to suggest words to (a hesitating speaker) **2.** *n.* the prompting of an actor or speaker ‖ the words said in prompting **prómpt·er** *n.* [fr. PROMPT adj. or fr. F. or L. *promere* (*promptus*), to make ready to do something]

prompt·i·tude (prómptitu:d, prómptitju:d) *n.* the quality of being prompt [F. or fr. L. *promptitudo*]

prompt side (*theater*) the side of the stage closest to the prompter, usually to the actor's right (in the U.S.A.) or left (in Britain) as he faces the audience

prom·ul·gate (prómәlgeit, proumʌ́lgeit) *pres. part.* **prom·ul·gat·ing** *past and past part.* **prom·ul·gat·ed** *v.t.* to proclaim, make publicly known (a statute, decree, dogma etc.) **prom·ul·gá·tion, próm·ul·ga·tor** *ns* [fr. L. *promulgare* (*promulgatus*), to expose to public view]

pro·nate (próuneit) *pres. part.* **pro·nat·ing** *past and past part.* **pro·nat·ed** *v.t.* to turn (a hand) so that the palm is downward (cf. SUPINATE) [fr. L. L. *pronare* (*pronatus*), to bend forward]

pro·na·tion (prounéiʃәn) *n.* a pronating or being pronated [fr. M.L. *pronatio* (*pronationis*), a bending forward]

pro·na·tor (prounéitәr) *n.* a muscle in the forearm which performs pronation [M.L.]

prone (proun) *adj.* lying face down (opp. SUPINE) ‖ flat on the ground, prostrate, *the boxer lay prone for several seconds* ‖ (with 'to') inclined, liable, disposed, *prone to act rashly* [fr. L. *pronus*]

pro·neth·a·lol [$C_{15}H_{19}NO$] (prounéθαlәl) *n.* (*pharm.*) drug that causes a blockage of the receptor of sympathomimetic agent. *also* nethalide

prong (prɔŋ, prɒŋ) **1.** *n.* a tine of a fork ‖ a fork for lifting hay etc. ‖ any thin pointed object, e.g. the point of an antler **2.** *v.t.* to pierce or lift (soil etc.) with a fork or prong [etym. doubtful]

prong·horn (prɔ́ŋhɔrn, prɒ́ŋhɔrn) *pl.* **prong·horn, prong·horns** *n.* *Antilocapra americana*, a North American ruminant mammal whose curved horns have an annually deciduous outer sheath and a short prong in front

pro·nom·i·nal (prounómin'l) *adj.* (*gram.*) of, relating to or acting as a pronoun [fr. L.L. *pronominalis*]

pro·noun (próunaun) *n.* a word used to replace noun. It functions as a noun and represents a person or thing previously mentioned or known, or being asked about. Pronouns may be classified as demonstrative, distributive, indefinite, interrogative, personal, possessive, reflexive and relative

pro·nounce (prәnáuns) *pres. part.* **pro·nounc·ing** *past and past part.* **pro·nounced** *v.t.* to make the sounds of, utter, articulate, *he pronounced every syllable with care* ‖ to utter or declare formally, *to pronounce sentence* ‖ to declare authoritatively, *the doctor pronounced him free from infection* ‖ *v.i.* to produce speech sounds, *she pronounces abominably* ‖ to give one's considered or authoritative opinion, *to pronounce on a matter* **pro·nóunced** *adj.* strongly marked, very noticeable, *a pronounced list to port* **pro·nóunce·ment** *n.* an official statement or announcement ‖ an opinion, decision etc. announced in a formal way [O.F. *pronuncier*]

pronouncing dictionary a dictionary which shows how words are pronounced

PRONTO (*computer acronym*) **pro**gram for **nu**merical **to**ol operation, a computer program utilizing numerical machine tool language translated from drawings in order to position a cutting device; designed by General Electric

pro·nu·cle·us (prounú:kli:әs, prounjú:kli:әs) *pl.* **pro·nu·cle·i** (prounú:kli:ai, prounjú:kli:ai) *n.* (*biol.*) the haploid nucleus of a spermatozoon or egg (ovum) after maturation and fertilization

pro·nun·ci·a·men·to (prәnʌnsi:әméntou, prәnʌnʃi:әméntou) *pl.* **pro·nun·ci·a·men·tos** *n.* a proclamation or pronouncement, esp. one made by revolutionaries or by any self-appointed dictatorial body [fr. Span. *pronunciamiento*]

CONCISE PRONUNCIATION KEY: **(a)** æ, *cat*; ɑ, *car*; ɔ *fawn*; ei, *snake*. **(e)** e, *hen*; i:, *sheep*; iә, *deer*; εә, *bear*. **(i)** i, *fish*; ai, *tiger*; ә:, *bird*. **(o)** o, *ox*; au, *cow*; ou, *goat*; u, *poor*; ɔi, *royal*. **(u)** ʌ, *duck*; u, *bull*; u:, *goose*; ә, *bacillus*; ju:, *cube*. x, *loch*; θ, *think*; ð, *bother*; z, *Zen*; ʒ, *corsage*; dʒ, *savage*; ŋ, *orangutang*; j, *yak*; ʃ, *fish*; tʃ, *fetch*; 'l, *rabble*; 'n, *redden*. Complete pronunciation key appears inside front cover.

pro·nun·ci·a·tion (prənʌnsi:éiʃən) *n.* the act of making the sounds of syllables, words etc. ‖ the way in which a word etc. is sounded ‖ the phonetic transcription of the way in which a word should be or is pronounced [fr. L. *pronuntiatio (pronuntiationis)*]

proof (pru:f) 1. *n.* a proving or being proved ‖ convincing evidence, *his fingerprints were a proof of his guilt* ‖ (*law*) a document receivable as evidence ‖ (*law*) a written version of the evidence a witness is willing to give on oath in court ‖ the alcoholic content of a beverage compared with the standard for proof spirit ‖ (*printing*) an impression of composed type to verify correctness ‖ (*engraving*) an impression carefully taken, for approval before general printing proceeds ‖ (*photog.*) a test print ‖ (*geom.*) the operations which demonstrate and verify a proposition 2. *adj.* (with 'against') able to resist, *proof against temptation* ‖ (in compounds) impenetrable by, *bulletproof* ‖ of proved strength, *proof armor* ‖ (of gold and silver) pure and serving as a standard for comparison (in a mint etc.) ‖ of a standard alcoholic strength, *duty charged on the proof gallon* 3. *v.t.* to make (something) impervious (esp. to water), *to proof tent fabric* ‖ (*printing, engraving* etc.) to take a trial impression of ‖ to proofread [M.E. *preove, proeve, preve* fr. O. F.]

proof·ing (prú:fiŋ) *n.* the act of making proof ‖ a substance used for proofing (fabric) etc., esp. against water

proof·read (prú:fri:d) *pres. part.* **proof·read·ing** *past* and *past part.* **proof·read** (prú:fred) *v.t.* to read and correct (a printer's proof) ‖ *v.i.* to read and correct a printer's proof [back-formation fr. PROOFREADER]

proof·read·er (prú:fri:dər) *n.* a person employed to read and correct printers' proofs

proof spirit a mixture of alcohol and water, containing a standard amount of alcohol of (*Am.*) one half by volume, (*Br.*) 57.10% by volume. The alcoholic content of a drink is measured as a percentage of the standard proof spirit

prop (prop) *n.* (*theater*) a property

prop *n.* a propeller

prop 1. *n.* a support placed under or against something to hold it up ‖ any person or thing serving as a support 2. *v.t. pres. part.* **prop·ping** *past* and *past part.* **propped** (often with 'up') to support with or as if with a prop, keep upright, *to prop up a drunken man* ‖ to make to stand or stay in a specified condition, *to prop a door open with a chair* [origin unknown]

pro·pae·deu·tic (proupi:dú:tik, proupi:djú:tik) 1. *adj.* serving as introduction to higher study 2. *n.* a preliminary study [fr. Gk *propaideuein*, to teach beforehand]

prop·a·gan·da (propəgǽndə) *n.* information and opinions (esp. prejudiced ones) spread to influence people in favor of or against some doctrine or idea ‖ the spreading of such information and opinions **prop·a·gán·dist** *n.* someone who uses or spreads propaganda **prop·a·gán·dize** *pres. part.* **prop·a·gan·diz·ing** *past* and *past part.* **prop·a·gan·dized** *v.t.* to spread (ideas etc.) through propaganda ‖ to expose (a person or people) to propaganda ‖ *v.i.* to spread propaganda [Ital. fr. Mod. L. *Congregatio de propaganda fide*, Congregation for the propagation of the faith, the committee of cardinals formed (1622) by Gregory XV (1554-1623, pope 1621-3) to be in charge of foreign missions]

prop·a·gate (própəgeit) *pres. part.* **prop·a·gat·ing** *past* and *past part.* **prop·a·gat·ed** *v.t.* to cause to multiply by natural reproduction, to reproduce, *to propagate a species* ‖ to transmit from one generation to another ‖ to spread, disseminate, make widely known, *to propagate the gospel of social service* ‖ to transmit (heat, light, sound etc.) ‖ *v.i.* to multiply by natural reproduction, *this plant propagates readily* [fr. L. *propagare (propagatus)*, to multiply (plants) by means of layers]

prop·a·ga·tion (propəgéiʃən) *n.* a propagating or being propagated [F. or fr. L. *propagatio(propagationis)*]

prop·a·ga·tor (própəgeitər) *n.* someone who or something which propagates

pro·pane (próupein) *n.* a gaseous hydrocarbon, $CH_3CH_2CH_3$ [fr. PROPIONIC ACID+METHANE]

pro·par·il ($C_9H_9Cl_2NO$) (próupəril) *n.* (*chem.*) a weed killer, esp. used in rice cultivation

pro·pel (prəpél) *pres. part.* **pro·pel·ling** *past* and *past part.* **pro·pelled** *v.t.* to push or drive forward or onward, *the earliest locomotives were propelled by steam* **pro·pél·lant**, **pro·pél·lent** 1.

adj. able or serving to propel 2. *n.* a propelling agent, esp. a rocket fuel or an explosive which propels a bullet or shell from a gun **pro·pél·ler** *n.* something that propels, esp. a screw propeller [fr. L. *propellere*]

propeller shaft a shaft that transmits power from the engine to the driving device (e.g. wheels, propeller) of an automotive vehicle

pro·pene (próupi:n) *n.* propylene [fr. PROPIONIC ACID]

pro·pen·si·ty (prəpénsiti) *pl.* **pro·pen·si·ties** *n.* a natural disposition, tendency [fr. L. *propensio (propensionis)*, inclination]

prop·er (própər) 1. *adj.* decent, seemly, *proper behavior* ‖ (*Br.*) real, genuine, *he wants a proper gun, not a toy one* ‖ (*Br., pop.*) utter, complete, thorough, *a proper fool* ‖ fitting, suitable, *the proper time to broach the matter* ‖ accurate, in the proper sense of the word ‖ (usually following the noun) strictly so-called, excluding adjuncts etc., *Japan proper excludes the outlying islands* ‖ (with 'to') belonging particularly or exclusively, *the activities proper to a mayor* ‖ (*eccles.*) appointed for a certain day, *the proper Psalms* ‖ (*heraldry*) represented in its natural colors 2. *n.* (*eccles.*) a special office, or part of one, appointed for a certain day [F. *propre*, own]

proper fraction (*math.*) a fraction less than unity in which the numerator is less than the denominator (cf. IMPROPER FRACTION)

prop·er·ly (própərli:) *adv.* correctly, rightly, *she likes to do a thing properly* ‖ in a respectable way, with good manners, *you must learn to behave properly* ‖ (*Br., pop.*) thoroughly, completely, *you've properly messed it up*

proper motion (*astron.*) the motion through space of a star in relation to an imagined position of absolute rest (not to the earth) (cf. TANGENTIAL MOTION)

proper name a proper noun

proper noun a noun designating some single person, place etc. and usually spelled with a capital letter (cf. COMMON NOUN)

prop·er·tied (própərti:d) *adj.* owning property, esp. land, *the propertied classes*

Pro·per·ti·us (proupó:rʃi:əs), **Sextus** (c. 47–c. 15 B.C.), Roman lyric poet. He wrote four books of elegies mainly devoted to love, in the style of the Alexandrian poets

prop·er·ty (própərti:) *pl.* **prop·er·ties** *n.* a thing or things owned ‖ real estate ‖ a piece of real estate ‖ abundant wealth, *a man of property* ‖ ownership, the exclusive right to possess and use something, *is private property in itself wrong?* ‖ an attribute, characteristic, *the properties of a magnet* ‖ virtue, quality, *the soothing property of an ointment* ‖ (*logic*) an attribute common to a whole class but not necessary to distinguish it from others ‖ (*theater, movie*) any piece of furniture or accessory used on the stage or set (excluding only fixed scenery and clothes actually worn by actors) [M.E. *proprete* fr. O.F.]

pro·phase (próufeiz) *n.* (*biol.*) the first events in mitosis and meiosis, consisting of the condensation of the dispersed chromosomes, the replication of these and the formation of the spindle. The prophase of the first meiotic division involves synapsis. That of the second meiotic division occurs without replication (*METAPHASE, *ANAPHASE, *TELOPHASE)

proph·e·cy (prófisi:) *pl.* **proph·e·cies** *n.* a prediction or foretelling of what is to come ‖ the power to speak as a prophet, *the gift of prophecy* ‖ something said by a prophet [O.F. *profecie* fr. L.L. fr. Gk]

proph·e·sy (prófisai) *pres. part.* **proph·e·sy·ing** *past* and *past part.* **proph·e·sied** *v.t.* to foretell by divine inspiration ‖ to predict ‖ *v.i.* to act as a prophet ‖ to make a prediction or predictions [O.F. *profecier*]

proph·et (prófit) *n.* a person who, by divine inspiration, declares to the world the divine will, judgments etc. ‖ a person who foretells the course or nature of future events ‖ a leader, founder or spokesman of a cause or party, *an early prophet of socialism* **Proph·et** one of the Old Testament writers of the prophetic books. The Major Prophets are Isaiah, Jeremiah, Ezekiel and (in Christian versions of the Old Testament) Daniel. The Minor Prophets are Hosea, Joel, Arnos, Obadiah, Jonah, Micah, Nahum, Habakkuk, Zephaniah, Haggai, Zechariah and Malachi **the Prophet** Mohammed **próph·et·ess** *n.* a woman prophet [F. *prophète* fr. L. fr. Gk]

pro·phet·ic (prəfétik) *adj.* foretelling, containing a prediction ‖ of or relating to a prophet or

prophecy **pro·phét·i·cal** *adj.* [F. *prophétique* or fr. L.L. *propheticus* fr. Gk]

pro·phy·lac·tic (proufəlǽktik, profəlǽktik) 1. *adj.* guarding against disease ‖ preventive, protective 2. *n.* a prophylactic medicine ‖ anything which guards against disease [fr. Gk *prophulaktikos*]

pro·phy·lax·is (proufəlǽksis, profəlǽksis) *pl.* **pro·phy·lax·es** (proufəlǽksi:z, profəlǽksi:z) *n.* measures aiming to prevent disease ‖ the prevention of disease [Mod. L. fr. Gk *pro*, against+*phulaxis*, a guarding]

pro·pin·qui·ty (prəpíŋkwiti:) *pl.* **pro·pin·qui·ties** *n.* nearness in place or time ‖ nearness of kinship [O.F. *propinquite*]

pro·pi·on·ic acid (proupi:ónik) a pungent liquid acid, C_2H_5COOH, found in milk and its products. It is used in the form of its esters in the perfume industry and in the form of its salts (esp. of sodium and calcium) as a fungistatic agent [fr. F. *propionique* fr. Gk *pro-*, before+*pion*, fat]

pro·pi·ti·ate (prəpíʃi:eit) *pres. part.* **pro·pi·ti·at·ing** *past* and *past part.* **pro·pi·ti·at·ed** *v.t.* to gain the favor of by appeasement or conciliation [fr. L. *propitiare (propitiatus)*]

pro·pi·ti·a·tion (prəpiʃi:éiʃən) *n.* a propitiating or being propitiated ‖ an atoning sacrifice, esp. Christ as this [fr. L.L. *propitiatio (propitiationis)*]

pro·pi·ti·a·to·ry (prəpíʃi:ətɔri:, prəpíʃi:ətouri:) *adj.* intended or serving to propitiate

pro·pi·tious (prəpíʃəs) *adj.* favorably disposed, *the fates were propitious* ‖ favorable, giving promise of success, *a propitious omen* ‖ advantageous, *a moment propitious for action* [O.F. *propicius*]

prop·o·lis (própəlis) *n.* a sticky red resin which bees obtain from the buds of trees (e.g. the horse chestnut) and use to fix the combs to the hive and to stop up crevices [L. fr. Gk=suburb, bee glue]

pro·po·nent (prəpóunənt) *n.* a person who advocates or supports a proposal or idea ‖ (*law*) someone who propounds a will etc. [fr. L. *proponens (proponentis)* fr. *proponere*, to put forward]

Pro·pon·tis (prəpóntis) *MARMARA, SEA OF

pro·por·tion (prəpɔ́rʃən, prəpóurʃən) *n.* a part, share (in relation to the whole), *a large proportion of the population is illiterate* ‖ relative size or number, ratio, comparative relation, *the proportion of deaths to births* ‖ satisfactory relation between things or parts as regards size, symmetry, balance, *the door is out of proportion with the windows* ‖ (*pl.*) dimensions, *a room of generous proportions* ‖ (*math.*) an equality of ratios between two pairs of numbers, as in the statement 2 is to 4 as 3 is to 6 [F. fr. L.]

proportion *v.t.* to adjust in proportion or suitable relation [O.F. *proporcioner*]

pro·por·tion·al (prəpɔ́rʃən'l, prəpóurʃən'l) 1. *adj.* in proportion ‖ (*math.*) having the same or a constant ratio ‖ used in determining proportions, *proportional compasses* 2. *n.* (*math.*) any number in a proportion **pro·por·tion·ál·i·ty** *n.* [fr. L. *proportionalis*]

proportional representation a system of election by which each party has a number of representatives in the governing body proportional to the number of votes cast for it

pro·por·tion·ate 1. (prəpɔ́rʃənit, prəpóurʃənit) *adj.* being in proportion, proportionally adjusted 2. (prəpɔ́rʃəneit, prəpóurʃəneit) *v.t. pres. part.* **pro·por·tion·at·ing** *past* and *past part.* **pro·por·tion·at·ed** to proportion [fr. L.L. *proportionatus*]

pro·pos·al (prəpóuz'l) *n.* a course of action put forward for consideration ‖ an offer of marriage ‖ the act of proposing

pro·pose (prəpóuz) *pres. part.* **pro·pos·ing** *past* and *past part.* **pro·posed** *v.t.* to offer for consideration, *to propose a plan* ‖ to intend, *she proposes to catch the early train* ‖ to put forward for approval (a person for office or as a new member of a society) ‖ to offer as a toast ‖ to expound the arguments in favor of, *to propose a motion in debate* ‖ *v.i.* to offer marriage [F. *proposer*]

prop·o·si·tion (propəzíʃən) 1. *n.* a proposal ‖ (*logic*) an expression or statement of which the subject can be affirmed or denied ‖ the point to be discussed in formal disputation, usually framed in a single sentence ‖ (*math.*) the statement of a theorem or problem to be demonstrated or solved ‖ a scheme, offer, usually commercial ‖ an invitation to sexual intercourse ‖ (*pop.*) any project, thing or person considered to be difficult to handle, *a tough proposition* **2.** *v.t.* to make a business proposal to ‖ to suggest sexual intercourse to **prop·o·sí·tion·al** *adj.* [F.]

Proposition 13 1978 referendum passed in California that placed a ceiling on local taxes; promoted by Howard Jarvis

Proposition 2½ tax-cutting initiative defeated in Massachusetts in 1980; it limits property tax to 2½% of fair cash value and increases in government expenditures to 4% a year

pro·pound (prəpáund) *v.t.* to set forth (a problem, plan, interpretation etc.) for consideration ‖ (*law*) to produce (a will or other testamentary document) before the probate authority so as to establish its legality [fr. earlier *propone* fr. L. *proponere,* to set forward]

pro·prae·tor, pro·pre·tor (prouprí:tər) *n.* (*Rom. hist.*) a magistrate, having served as praetor in ancient Rome, sent out to govern a province [L.]

pro·pran·o·lol [$C_{16}H_{21}NO_2$] (proupræ̃nələl) *n.* (*pharm.*) a beta-adrenergic blocking drug that lowers the heart rate and increases end-diastolic pressure; marketed as Inderal

pro·pri·e·tar·y (prəpráiiteri:) **1.** *adj.* relating to ownership, *he has a proprietary interest in the business* ‖ owning property, *the proprietary section of the community* ‖ legally made or distributed only by those holding patents or special rights, *proprietary medicines* **2.** *pl.* **pro·pri·e·tar·ies** *n.* a body of owners ‖ right of ownership, *a proprietary over the manufacture of a product* ‖ (*Am. hist.*) the owner of a proprietary colony [fr. L.L. *proprietarius*]

proprietary colony (*Am. hist.*) a colony in which extensive rights of government were granted to a person or persons

pro·pri·e·tor (prəpráiitər) *n.* a person who has legal rights of possession of land, an object, or a process of manufacture or distribution, an owner ‖ a person who has the temporary but not the absolute control and use of property ‖ (*Am. hist.*) a proprietary **pro·prí·e·tress** *n.* a woman proprietor [irregular fr. PROPRIETARY]

pro·pri·e·ty (prəpráiiti:) *pl.* **pro·pri·e·ties** *n.* suitability, correctness, *the propriety of such a move is doubtful* ‖ accepted conventions of behavior or morals, *an offense against propriety* ‖ (*pl.*) details of correct conduct in polite society, *to observe the proprieties* [F. *propriété,* property]

pro·pri·o·cep·tive (prɒupri:ouséptiv) *adj.* (*physiol.*) capable of receiving stimuli from within the organism, used in receiving these, or concerned with receiving these, e.g. through muscles, tendons and joints (cf. EXTEROCEPTIVE, cf. INTEROCEPTIVE) [fr. L. *proprius,* own+RECEPTIVE]

prop root a root growing outwards from the stem close to ground level and serving to support the plant (e.g. mangrove)

prop shaft a propeller shaft

prop·to·sis (prɒptóusis) *n.* (*med.*) protrusion, esp. of the eyeball [L.L. fr. Gk *proptōsis,* a fall forward]

pro·pul·sion (prəpʌ́lʃən) *n.* a propelling or being propelled ‖ a driving force [F.]

pro·pul·sive (prəpʌ́lsiv) *adj.* tending to propel, driving forward [fr. L. *propellere* (*propulsus*), to drive forward]

pro·pyl (próupil) *n.* the monovalent radical, C_3H_7, derived from propane [PROPIONIC ACID]

prop·y·lae·um (prɒpəlí:əm) *pl.* **prop·y·lae·a** (prɒpəlí:ə) *n.* (*archit.*) a porch or vestibule serving as entrance to a temple or public building **the Prop·y·lae·a** the entrance to the Acropolis in Athens [L. fr. Gk *propulaion*]

propyl alcohol a liquid alcohol, C_3H_7OH

pro·pyl·ene (próupəli:n) *n.* an inflammable gaseous hydrocarbon, $CH_3CH{=}CH_2$, obtained by breaking down petroleum hydrocarbons and used in the manufacture of detergents

prop·y·lite (própəlait) *n.* a volcanic rock, an altered form of andesite, found in the vicinity of certain ore deposits, esp. silver [fr. Gk *propylon,* gateway (formerly considered to mark the opening of the Tertiary)]

pro ra·ta (prouréitə, prourɑ́tə) **1.** *adv.* at a proportionate rate, *costs are $100 per thousand and pro rata* **2.** *adj.* calculated at a proportionate rate [L.]

pro·rate (prouréit, prourεit) *pres. part.* **pro·rat·ing** *past* and *past part.* **pro·rat·ed** *v.t.* to assess pro rata ‖ to distribute proportionally ‖ *v.i.* to make a pro rata distribution

pro·ro·ga·tion (prɒurəgéiʃən) *n.* a proroguing or being prorogued

pro·rogue (prouróug) *pres. part.* **pro·rogu·ing** *past* and *past part.* **pro·rogued** *v.t.* to bring a session of (esp. a parliament) to a close by adjourning the next meeting to a particular day ‖ *v.i.* to be prorogued [F. *proroguer*]

pro·sa·ic (prouzéiik) *adj.* commonplace, without great imaginative gifts, *a prosaic young man* ‖ dull, ordinary, *a prosaic career* **pro·sá·i·cal·ly** *adv.* [fr. M.L. *prosaicus*]

pro·sce·ni·um (prousí:ni:əm) *n.* (*theater*) that part of a stage between the curtain and the orchestra ‖ (*theater*) the proscenium arch and surrounding wall ‖ the stage in an ancient Greek or Roman theater [L. fr. Gk *proskēnion*]

proscenium arch (*theater*) the structure which frames the spectators' view of the stage

pro·scribe (prouskráib) *pres. part.* **pro·scrib·ing** *past* and *past part.* **pro·scribed** *v.t.* to outlaw (a person) ‖ to condemn or forbid (a practice) ‖ (*Rom. hist.*) to publish the name of (a person) as being condemned to death and to have his property confiscated [fr. L. *proscribere,* to write in front of]

pro·scrip·tion (prouskrípʃən) *n.* a proscribing or being proscribed ‖ a prohibition [fr. L. *proscriptio* (*proscriptionis*)]

pro·scrip·tive (prouskríptiv) *adj.* pertaining to proscription ‖ tending to proscribe [L. *pro scribere* (*proscriptus*), to write in front of]

prose (prouz) **1.** *n.* the language of ordinary speech ‖ this language artificially heightened for literary effect, in nonmetrical rhythms (*cf.* POETRY) ‖ dull, commonplace discourse or writing ‖ (*rhet.*) humdrum commonplace quality, *the prose of everyday life* ‖ (*eccles.*) a sequence **2.** *v.i. pres. part.* **pros·ing** *past* and *past part.* **prosed** to talk or write boringly and tediously [F.]

pros·e·cute (prɒ́sikju:t) *pres. part.* **pros·e·cut·ing** *past* and *past part.* **pros·e·cut·ed** *v.t.* to start legal proceedings against, *trespassers will be prosecuted* ‖ to start legal proceedings with reference to (a claim etc.) ‖ (*rhet.*) to carry on, *to prosecute a war* ‖ *v.i.* to start and continue legal proceedings ‖ to act as prosecutor [fr. L. *prosequi* (*prosecutus*), to follow, pursue]

prosecuting attorney the attorney who conducts proceedings in a court of law on behalf of the government against accused persons on criminal charges

pros·e·cu·tion (prɒsikjú:ʃən) *n.* a prosecuting or being prosecuted ‖ (*law*) the prosecuting party or his legal representatives ‖ (*law*) the bringing of formal criminal charges against an offender in court [O.F.]

pros·e·cu·tor (prɒ́sikju:tər) *n.* a person who starts legal proceedings against another or others ‖ a prosecuting attorney ‖ (*Br.*) a public prosecutor [M.L.]

pros·e·lyte (prɒ́səlait) **1.** *n.* an individual newly converted from one creed or belief to another, esp. a convert to Judaism **2.** *v.t. pres. part.* **pros·e·lyt·ing** *past* and *past part.* **pros·e·lyt·ed** to proselytize ‖ *v.i.* to proselytize ‖ to induce athletes to attend and play for a certain school

pros·e·lyt·ism (prɒ́səlitizəm) *n.* the practice of making converts ‖ the act, or fact, of becoming a convert **prós·e·lyt·ize** *pres. part.* **pros·e·lyt·iz·ing** *past* and *past part.* **pros·e·lyt·ized** *v.i.* to make or try to make converts ‖ *v.t.* to make a convert of [fr. L.L. *proselytus* fr. Gk]

pros·en·chy·ma (prɒséŋkəmə) *n.* (*bot.*) any of several kinds of tissue, distinguishable in higher plants, consisting of elongated cells with pointed ends, containing little or no protoplasm and serving to support and to conduct (cf. PARENCHYMA) **pros·en·chym·a·tous** (prɒsəŋkímətəs) *adj.* [fr. Gk *pros,* toward+*enchuma,* infusion]

Pro·ser·pi·na (prousə́:rpinə) Persephone

Pros·er·pine (prɒ́sərpain, prousə́:rpini:) Persephone

pros·i·ly (próuzili:) *adv.* in a prosy way

pros·i·ness (próuzi:nis) *n.* the state or quality of being prosy

pro·sod·ic (prəsɒ́dik) *adj.* of or pertaining to prosody

pros·o·dist (prɒ́sədist) *n.* a person skilled in prosody

pros·o·dy (prɒ́sədi:) *pl.* **pros·o·dies** *n.* the rhythmic structure of sound in speech ‖ the study of versification ‖ a particular system of versification [fr. L. *prosodia* fr. Gk]

pro·so·ma (prousóumə) *n.* the anterior part of the body of some mollusks and some other vertebra [Mod. L.]

pros·o·pog·ra·phy (prɒsəpɒ́grəfi:) *n.* biographical study of a group, esp. of an elite group—a method used in quantitative history

pro·so·po·poe·ia (prəsɒupəpí:ə) *n.* (*rhet.*) introduction by an orator of an imaginary speaker, esp. the personification of an abstract concept, e.g. '... at this point Common Sense will retort...' [L. fr. Gk]

pros·pect 1. (prɒ́spekt) *n.* a wide or distant scenic view, *a splendid prospect over the bay* ‖ the scene itself, *admiring the prospect beneath them* ‖ the assumed course of the future, *their probable defeat is a grim prospect* ‖ a view of some specified eventuality, *the prospect for the harvest* ‖ reasonable expectation, *is there any prospect of a meeting?* ‖ a potential client or customer ‖ (*pl.*) social or financial expectations, *a job offering good prospects* ‖ (*mining*) property on which signs of mineral deposit are found ‖ (*mining*) a partly developed mine ‖ (*mining*) mineral extracted from a test sample **in prospect** likely to materialize, *he has a job in prospect* **2.** (prɒ́spekt, prəspékt) *v.i.* to explore a region in search of oil, gold, minerals etc. ‖ *v.t.* to explore (an area, mine) for minerals [fr. L. *prospectus,* view]

pro·spec·tive (prəspéktiv) *adj.* (of payments etc.) relating to the future (cf. RETROSPECTIVE) ‖ destined or expected to be, *her prospective father-in-law* [fr. F. *prospectif*]

pros·pec·tor (prɒ́spektər, prəspéktər) *n.* someone who prospects for oil, gold, minerals etc.

pro·spec·tus (prəspéktəs) *n.* a circular containing information or plans of enterprise, literary work, issue of securities etc., designed to win support [L.=lookout]

pros·per (prɒ́spər) *v.i.* to thrive ‖ to achieve financial success [F. *prospérer*]

pros·per·i·ty (prɒspériti:) *n.* the condition of being prosperous, the condition of high economic activity [F. *prospérité*]

Pros·per of Aquitaine (prɒ́spər), St (c. 390–c. 460), Gallic theologian. He championed St Augustine of Hippo's doctrine of grace against Pelagian tendencies. Feast: July 7

pros·per·ous (prɒ́spərəs) *adj.* financially successful [obs. F. *prospereus*]

pros·ta·glan·din (prɒstəglǽndin) *n.* (*physiol.*) a potent compound that acts like a hormone, produced by enzyme action on fatty acids in mammals, highly concentrated in seminal fluid, important in metabolism reproduction, muscle contraction, transmission of nerve impulses and blood pressure control

pros·tate (prɒsteit) **1.** *adj.* of the partially muscular gland at the neck of the bladder surrounding the beginning of the urethra in male mammals **2.** *n.* this gland **pro·stat·ic** (proustǽtik) *adj.* [fr. M.L. *prostata* fr. Gk *prostatēs,* one who stands before]

pros·the·sis (prɒ́sθisis) *pl.* **pros·the·ses** (prɒ́sθisi:z) *n.* (*gram.*) the prefixing of a letter or syllable to a word, e.g. 'be' in 'bemoan' ‖ (*med.*) an artificial device to replace a missing part of the body (e.g. false teeth, an artificial limb) [L. fr. Gk *prosthesis,* addition]

pros·thet·ic (prɒsθétik) *adj.* of or relating to prosthesis or prosthetics ‖ (*biochem.*) relating to a group or radical of a different kind attached to or substituted in a compound, e.g. the nonprotein portion of a conjugated protein or the vitamin portion of certain enzymes **pros·thét·ics** *n.* the branch of surgery or dentistry which deals with artificial limbs, teeth etc. [fr. Gk *prosthetikos*]

pros·ti·tute (prɒ́stitu:t, prɒ́stitju:t) **1.** *n.* a woman who has promiscuous sexual intercourse for payment ‖ (*hist.*) a woman who has sexual intercourse as part of a religious cult ‖ a person who degrades his talents for money **2.** *v.t. pres. part.* **pros·ti·tut·ing** *past* and *past part.* **pros·ti·tut·ed** to degrade (a science, talents etc.), esp. for money [fr. L. *prostituere* (*prostitutus*), to offer for sale]

pros·ti·tu·tion (prɒstitú:ʃən, prɒstitjú:ʃən) *n.* the act, practice or profession of offering the body for sexual relations for money ‖ the degradation of some science, talent etc. for money [fr. L.L. *prostitutio* (*prostitutionis*)]

pros·trate 1. (prɒ́streit) *v.t. pres. part.* **pros·trat·ing** *past* and *past part.* **pros·trat·ed** to cast to the ground face downwards ‖ to abase (oneself) in submission, worship etc. ‖ (*rhet.*) to reduce to utter submission, *to prostrate an enemy* ‖ to exhaust bodily, wear out ‖ to overcome with shock, grief etc. 2. *adj.* lying full-length face downwards ‖ overcome with shock, grief etc. ‖ physically exhausted ‖ (*rhet.*) utterly defeated, *Carthage lay prostrate* ‖ (*bot.*) lying loosely along the surface of the ground [fr. L. *prosternere* (*prostratus*), to lay flat]

pros·tra·tion (prɒstréiʃən) *n.* a prostrating or being prostrated [F.]

pro·style (próustail) 1. *adj.* (*archit.*, of a classical temple) having a row of free columns in a portico across the whole front 2. *n.* such a temple [L. *prostylos*, having pillars in front, fr. Gk]

pro·sum·er (prousú:mər) *n.* (*slang*) one who consumes what he or she produces

pros·y (próuzi) *comp.* **pros·i·er** *superl.* **pros·i·est** *adj.* dull, tedious, *a prosy speaker* [PROSE]

pro·tac·tin·i·um (proutæktíni:əm) *n.* a radioactive pentavalent element (symbol Pa, at. no. 91, mass of most important isotope 231) which is formed naturally by the radioactive decay of uranium 235, and which on disintegration yields actinium [Mod. fr. Gk *prōtos*, first+ACTINIUM]

pro·tag·o·nist (proutǽgənist) *n.* the principal character in a drama, story etc. ‖ someone who champions a cause [fr. Gk *prōtagōnistēs* fr. *prōtos*, first+*agōnistēs*, actor]

Pro·tag·o·ras (proutǽgərəs) (c. 485–c. 411 B.C.), Greek Sophist and philosopher, famous for his dictum 'Man is the measure of all things'. He was attacked by Plato in 'Protagoras' for his emphasis on rhetoric and his Sophist belief that there is no absolute good

pro·ta·mine (próutəmi:n) *n.* (*biochem.*) any of a class of basic proteins, occurring in the sperm of fish, soluble in ammonia, not coagulating in heat and yielding certain amino acids on hydrolysis [fr. Gk *prōtos*, first+AMINE]

pro·tan·drous (proutǽndrəs) *adj.* (*biol.*) having the male reproductive organs mature before the corresponding female organs are (cf. PROTOGYNOUS) [fr. PROTO- +Gk *anēr* (*andros*), man]

prot·a·sis (prótəsis) *pl.* **prot·a·ses** (prótəsi:z) *n.* (*gram.*) a subordinate clause expressing condition in a conditional sentence (cf. APODOSIS) ‖ the introductory section of a play, preceding the epitasis [L.L. fr. Gk *protasis*, a stretching forward]

pro·te·an (próuti:ən, proutí:ən) *adj.* versatile ‖ extremely variable, often changing, *a protean policy* ‖ able to take on different shapes [after PROTEUS]

pro·te·ase (próuti:eis) *n.* (*biochem.*) any of a class of enzymes which hydrolyze proteins or peptides [PROTEIN]

pro·tect (prətékt) *v.t.* to shield or defend against danger, injury etc. ‖ (*econ.*) to guard (home producers) from foreign competition in the home market by imposing protective tariffs on imported goods ‖ (*commerce*) to guarantee the availability of funds to meet (a draft, note etc.) when it matures [fr. L. *protegere* (*protectus*)]

protected state a state under the protection of another, esp. one retaining its traditional form of government and control over domestic policy, which has signed a treaty with Britain whereby it receives British protection in return for placing its foreign affairs under British control

pro·tec·tion (prətékʃən) *n.* a protecting or being protected ‖ a person who or a thing which protects ‖ (*econ.*) the theory, policy or system of helping home producers to face foreign competition by putting protective tariffs on imported goods ‖ money paid to gangsters under threat of damage to property etc. **pro·téc·tion·ism, pro·téc·tion·ist** *ns* [F.]

pro·tec·tive (prətéktiv) *adj.* giving or intended to give protection ‖ seeking to guard, *protective instincts*

protective coloring, *Br.* **protective colouring** coloring which enables animals to escape notice in their natural surroundings

protective custody detention of a person by the state in order to protect him, or on this pretext

protective tariff a tariff designed to secure protection for domestic producers from foreign competition (cf. REVENUE TARIFF)

pro·tec·tor (prətéktər) *n.* a person who or thing which protects ‖ (*Eng. hist.*) a regent ‖ (*Eng. hist.*) a lord protector **pro·téc·tor·al** *adj.* **pro·téc·tor·ate** *n.* government by a protector ‖ the office of protector ‖ authority assumed by a strong state over a weak or underdeveloped one, without direct annexation, for the defense of the latter from external enemies ‖ a state so

governed, esp. a territory ruled in foreign and domestic affairs by Britain, but not having the legal status of a colony ‖ the period of such government **the Protectorate** (*Eng. hist.*) the period of rule by the Cromwells (1653-9) [O.F. *protectour*]

pro·tec·tress (prətéktris) *n.* a woman protector

pro·té·gé (próutəʒei) *n.* someone who is under the patronage, care or guidance of another, esp. for help in his career **pro·té·gée** (próutəʒei) *n.* a female protégé [F.]

pro·tein (próuti:n) *n.* (*chem.*) any of a class of naturally occurring, usually colloidal, complex combinations of amino acids (containing carbon, hydrogen, oxygen, nitrogen, usually sulfur, occasionally phosphorus) which are essential constituents of all living cells, being responsible for growth and maintenance of all tissue, and the essential nitrogenous constituent of the food of animals. They can be synthesized from inorganic nitrogenous material by plants, but apparently not by animals **pro·tein·a·ceous, pro·téin·ic, pro·téin·ous** *adjs* [F. *protéine* and G. *protein* fr. Gk *prōteios*, primary]

pro·tein·oid (próutənɔid) *n.* (*biol.*) a compound of two or more amino acids united through the peptide linkage (CONH), hypothesized as an early stage in the evolution of life

pro tem·po·re (proutémpəri) *adv.* and *adj.* (*abbr.* pro tem.) for the time being [L.]

pro·te·ol·y·sis (prouti:ólisis) *n.* (*biochem.*) the hydrolysis of proteins to form simpler soluble products, e.g. in digestion **pro·te·o·lýt·ic** *adj.* [PROTEIN+Gk *lusis*, loosening]

pro·te·ose (próuti:ous) *n.* (*biochem.*) any of a class of substances, soluble in water, formed by the partial hydrolysis of proteins by digestive enzymes [PROTEIN]

Prot·er·o·zo·ic (prɒtərəzóuik) *adj.* of the era of geological history between the Archeozoic the Paleozoic, and the rocks formed during this era, whose fossils indicate the contemporary existence of annelid worms and algae (*GEOLOGICAL TIME) **the Proterozoic** this era [fr. Gk *proteros*, former+*zōē*, life]

pro·test (próutest) *n.* a strong affirmation of, dissent from or disapproval of something done or some policy adopted ‖ a written declaration by a notary of an unpaid or unaccepted bill ‖ written declaration by the master of a ship giving details of disaster, accident or injury at sea ‖ (in diplomacy etc.) a solemn declaration of disapproval **to do (something) under protest** to do (something) having first stated one's disapproval [O.F.]

pro·test (prətést) *v.i.* to express strong dissent or objection ‖ *v.t.* to affirm emphatically, *to protest one's innocence* ‖ to write a declaration of nonpayment or nonacceptance of (a bill) ‖ to make a protest against, *to protest a witness* [F. *protester*]

Prot·es·tant (prótistənt) 1. *n.* a member of any Christian body which separated from the Roman Catholic Church at the Reformation, or of any later offshoot of such a body, esp. the Anglican, Baptist, Congregationalist, Evangelical, Lutheran, Methodist, Reformed and Presbyterian Churches ‖ (*hist.*) one of the German princes who protested against an edict of the Diet of Speyer (1529) designed to crush the reform movement in the Church 2. *adj.* relating to the doctrines or organizations of Protestants **prot·es·tant** 1. *n.* someone who protests 2. *adj.* protesting [F.]

Protestant Episcopal Church the religious body which represents the Anglican Communion in the U.S.A. It adopted an organization separate from that of the Church of England in 1789, but is still linked with it through the Lambeth Conference.

Protestant ethic mores of early Americans, involving compliance with the law and placing importance on work, thrift, self-discipline, competition and making a profit

Prot·es·tant·ism (prótistəntizəm) *n.* the beliefs and practices of Protestants. These cover a very wide range, but have common roots in the refusal to accept any external, man-centered, ultimate authority in spiritual matters, and the rejection of any belief which implies the possibility of self-justification before God

Protestant Union an alliance of Protestant German states formed (1608) in opposition to the future Emperor Ferdinand II's attempt to revive and enforce the Peace of Augsburg. It collapsed (1621) early in the Thirty Years' War

prot·es·ta·tion (prɒtistéiʃən, proutestéiʃən) *n.* an emphatic affirmation, *protestations of friendship* ‖ a formal protest [F.]

Pro·te·us (próuti:əs, próutju:s) (*Gk mythol.*) a prophetic sea god who could assume different shapes so as to escape capture. He was shepherd of the flocks of seals for Poseidon

pro·te·us (próuti:əs, próutju:s) *n. Proteus anguinus,* fam. *Proteidae,* a blind, aquatic salamander with a long body and permanent gills, found in caves in S.E. Europe [after PROTEUS]

pro·tha·la·mi·um (prouθəléimi:əm) *n.* a marriage song sung to herald the wedding (cf. EPITHALAMIUM) [coined by Edmund SPENSER]

pro·thal·li·um (prouθǽli:əm) *pl.* **pro·thal·li·a** (prouθǽli:ə) *n.* the gametophyte of a fern, consisting usually of a small, flat, green thallus with rhizoid soil attachment that is differentiated into antheridia and archegonia ‖ any of various structures in seed plants that resemble or correspond to the prothallium of the pteridophytes [Mod. L. fr. Gk *pro,* before+*thallos,* young shoot]

pro·thal·lus (prouθǽləs) *pl.* **pro·thal·li** (prouθǽlai) *n.* a prothallium [L. fr. Gk]

proth·e·sis (próθisis) *n.* (*Orthodox Eastern Church*) preparation and offering of the Eucharistic bread and wine before the liturgy ‖ the table on which this is done ‖ the part of the church where this stands ‖ (*gram.*) prosthesis **pro·thet·ic** (prəθétik) *adj.* [L.L. fr. Gk *prothesis*, placing in public]

proth·et·e·ly (próθətəli) *n.* (*zool.*) a condition in insects between nymph and adult resulting from dysfunction during metamorphosis — **proth·et·e·lic** *adj.*

pro·thon·o·tar·y (prouθónətəri, prɒuθounóutəri) *pl.* **pro·thon·o·tar·ies** *n.* a protonotary

pro·tho·rac·ic (prouθɒrǽsik, prouθourǽsik) *adj.* pertaining to the prothorax

prothoracic gland (*entomology*) one of a pair of glands that produce ecdysome to control molting in some insects

pro·tho·rax (prouθóræks, prouθóu·ræks) *pl.* **pro·tho·rax·es, pro·tho·ra·ces** (prouθórəsi:z, prouθóurəsi:z) *n.* the anterior segment of an insect's thorax

pro·throm·bin (prouθrómbin) *n.* (*biochem.*) a protein produced in the liver in the presence of vitamin K and present in blood plasma. Under the proper conditions (e.g. the presence of activators, *PLATELET) it is converted to thrombin, which initiates clot formation

pro·tist (próutist) *n.* (*biol.*) a member of *Protista,* a group of simple organisms, e.g. protozoans, not distinguished as animals or plants, though having some characters common to both [fr. Gk *prōtistos,* primary]

pro·ti·um (próuti:əm) *n.* (*nuclear physics*) a hydrogen isotope with a mass of 1, consisting of one proton and one electron. *Cf* DEUTERIUM, TRITIUM

proto- (próutou) *prefix* first in time, status or importance ‖ first in a series ‖ original, primitive [Gk *prōtos,* first]

pro·to·ac·tin·i·um (proutouæktíni:əm) *n.* protactinium

pro·to·bi·ont (proutoubáiənt) *n.* an organism extant at the emergence of life on earth

pro·to·col (próutokɒl) 1. *n.* a code of precedence in rank and status and correct procedure in diplomatic exchange and state ceremonies ‖ a preliminary draft or memorandum of a diplomatic document, e.g. of resolutions arrived at in negotiation to be incorporated in a formal treaty, and signed by the negotiators ‖ official formulas at the beginning and end of a charter, papal bull etc. 2. *v. pres. part.* **pro·to·col·ling** *past* and *past part.* **pro·to·colled, pro·to·cole** *v.t.* to record (something) in a protocol ‖ *v.i.* to draw up a protocol [O.F. *protocole* fr. M.L. fr. Gk *prōtokollon,* flyleaf glued to a book]

pro·to·con·ti·nent (proutoukóntinənt) *n.* a hypothetical great landmass existing on the earth 60 million yrs ago, from which contemporary continents were created. *also* supercontinent

pro·to·gal·ax·y (proutougǽləksi) *n.* (*astron.*) gas and dust in the process of hypothetical star formation

pro·tog·y·nous (proutódʒənəs) *adj.* (*biol.*) having the female reproductive organs mature before the corresponding male organs are (cf. PROTANDROUS) [PROTO- +Gk *gunē,* woman]

pro·to·his·to·ry (proutouhístəri) *n.* period after prehistory, sometimes referred to, but not elucidated in, recorded history

CONCISE PRONUNCIATION KEY: **(a)** æ, c**a**t; ɑ, c**a**r; ɔ f**aw**n; ei, sn**a**ke. **(e)** e, h**e**n; i:, sh**ee**p; iə, d**ee**r; ɛə, b**ea**r. **(i)** i, f**i**sh; ai, t**i**ger; ə:, b**i**rd. **(o)** o, **o**x; au, c**ow**; ou, g**oa**t; u, p**oo**r; ɔi, r**oy**al. **(u)** ʌ, d**u**ck; u, b**u**ll; u:, g**oo**se; ə, b**a**cillus; ju:, c**u**be. x, lo**ch**; θ, **th**ink; ð, **b**o**th**er; z, **Z**en; ʒ, cor**s**age; dʒ, sava**g**e; ŋ, ora**n**gutang; j, **y**ak; ʃ, **f**i**sh**; tʃ, fe**tch**; 'l, rabb**le**; 'n, redd**en**. Complete pronunciation key appears inside front cover.

pro·to·lith·ic (proutəlíθik) *adj.* Eolithic [PROTO-+Gk *lithos*, stone]

pro·to·mar·tyr (proutoumártər) *n.* the first martyr in any cause, esp. the first Christian martyr, St Stephen [M.E. *prothomartir* fr. O.F.]

pro·ton (próutɒn) *n.* (*phys.*) a baryon of mass 938.2+ 10^6 eV (1.672 x 10^{-24} gm) and net electric charge +1 that is a constituent of all atomic nuclei (the proton is the nucleus of the lightest hydrogen isotope). The proton is thought to be closely related to the neutron in structure, both having the same positive core of electrical charge, though the proton has a shell of positive charge thus rendering it positive ‖ a hydrogen ion of at. mass 1 [Gk, neuter of *prōtos*, first]

proton decay (*nuclear phys.*) transmutation of one chemical into another by loss of a proton

pro·to·ne·ma (proutəní:mə) *pl.* **pro·to·ne·ma·ta** (proutəní:mətə) *n.* the early stage of the development of the gametophyte of a moss or liverwort. It often consists of a branching system of filaments arising directly from the asexual spore, and develops by budding into the moss plant proper or gives rise to the second stage of the gametophyte [PROTO-+Gk *nēma*, thread]

proton microscope (*nuclear phys.*) a microscope in which a beam of protons passing through a sample is absorbed in proportion to its density, providing an image by the emerging protons that is magnified and displayed on a fluorescent screen or photo film

pro·ton·o·tar·y (proutɒ́nəteri:, proutounóutəri:) *pl.* **pro·ton·o·tar·ies** *n.* (*Br. hist.*) the chief clerk in the courts of Chancery, Common Pleas and King's Bench ‖ (*Roman Catholicism*) a protonotary apostolic ‖ (in some European courts) a chief secretary [fr. L.L. *protonotarius* fr. Gk]

protonotary apostolic (*Roman Catholicism*) one of the seven members of the highest college of prelates, authorized to sign papal bulls and keep papal records

pro·ton-syn·chro·tron (proutɒnsíŋkrətrɒn) *n.* a synchrotron that accelerates protons to extremely high energies by frequency modulation of the accelerating voltage

pro·to·phyte (próutəfait) *n.* a member of *Protophyta,* a division of the lower plants (esp. in former classifications) comprising unicellular plants incl. bacteria, yeasts, slime molds, blue-green algae and various simple green algae [fr. Mod. L. *Protophyta* fr. Gk *prōtos*, first+*phuton*, a plant]

pro·to·plasm (próutəplæzəm) *n.* a viscous, translucent, colloidal substance constituting all living cells. It consists of compounds of oxygen, hydrogen, carbon and nitrogen and is usually differentiated into cytoplasm and nucleoplasm **pro·to·plás·mic** *adj.* [G. *protoplasma* fr. Gk *prōtos*, first+*plasma*, form]

pro·to·plast (próutəplæst) *n.* the first formed example of any type, the original ‖ (*biol.*) a living unit of protoplasm **pro·to·plás·tic** *adj.* [F. *protoplaste* or fr. L.L. fr. Gk *prōtos*, first+*plastos*, shaped]

protoplast *n.* (*cytol.*) the living part of a cell.

pro·to·ste·le (próutəsti:li:, próutəsti:l) *n.* (*bot.*) a solid stele, characteristic of most roots and some young stems (cf. SIPHONOSTELE) **pro·to·sté·lic** *adj.*

pro·to·tract (proutətrǽkt) *v.* to move back and forth, e.g., the jaw

pro·to·troph·ic (proutətrɒ́fik) *adj.* (of bacteria etc.) feeding on inorganic matter

pro·to·typ·al (próutətaip'l, proutətáip'l) *adj.* of or relating to a prototype

pro·to·type (próutətaip) *n.* an original model or pattern from which subsequent copies are made, or improved specimens developed ‖ (*biol.*) an ancestral form or archetype **pro·to·typ·i·cal** (proutətípik'l) *adj.* [F. fr. Mod. L. fr. Gk *prōtos*, first+*tupos*, model, mold]

pro·to·vi·rus (próutəvairəs) *n.* a prototype of a virus that stimulates DNA production

pro·to·zo·an (proutəzóuən) *n.* a member of *Protozoa*, a phylum of small (often microscopic) single-celled or colonial organisms. They are of worldwide distribution and are usually restricted to water. They include flagellates, sporozoans, ciliates and rhizopods **pro·to·zó·ic** *adj.* [PROTO-+Gk *zōē*, life]

pro·to·zo·ol·o·gy (proutouzouɒ́lədʒi:) *n.* the study of protozoans

pro·to·zo·on (proutəzóuən) *pl.* **pro·to·zo·a** (proutəzóuə) *n.* a protozoan

pro·tract (proutrǽkt) *v.t.* to draw out in time, prolong, *bad weather protracted the work* ‖ (*surveying*) to plot to scale **pro·tráct·ed·ly** *adv.*

pro·trac·tile (proutrǽktil) *adj.* (*zool.*, of an organ etc.) capable of being pushed out, extended or lengthened [fr. L. *protrahere (protractus)*, to prolong]

pro·trac·tion (proutrǽkʃən) *n.* a protracting or being protracted [F.]

pro·trac·tor (proutrǽktər) *n.* an instrument for measuring or drawing angles on a flat surface, often in the form of a semicircle graduated in 180 degrees ‖ (*zool.*) a muscle whose function extends a limb or part of the body [M.L. fr. *protrahere*, to prolong]

pro·trude (proutrú:d) *pres. part.* **pro·trud·ing** *past* and *past part.* **pro·trud·ed** *v.t.* to thrust forward or outward ‖ *v.i.* to stick out or project [fr. L. *protrudeve*, to thrust forward]

pro·tru·sile (proutrú:sil) *adj.* (of a limb or organ) so formed that it can be pushed outwards [fr. L. *protrudere (protrusus)*, to thrust forward]

pro·tru·sion (proutrú:ʒən) *n.* a protruding or being protruded ‖ something which protrudes [F.]

pro·tru·sive (proutrú:siv) *adj.* protruding ‖ obtrusive [fr. L. *protrudere (protrusus)*, to thrust forward]

pro·tu·ber·ance (proutú:bərəns, proutjú:bərəns) *n.* something that is protuberant ‖ the condition of being protuberant

pro·tu·ber·ant (proutú:bərənt, proutjú:bərənt) *adj.* bulging, swelling out [fr. L.L. *protuberans (protuberantis)* fr. *protuberare*, to bulge]

proud (praud) *adj.* manifesting inordinate self-esteem ‖ feeling proper satisfaction, *proud of his son's success* ‖ arousing or marked by feelings of great satisfaction, *a proud moment* ‖ having a proper sense of self-esteem, *too proud to give way to self-pity* ‖ (*rhet.*) splendid, glorious, *a proud heritage* ‖ (*rhet.*, of a horse) mettlesome **to do oneself proud** to indulge oneself lavishly **to do someone proud** to honor someone with lavish hospitality or attentioms [O.E. *prūt*, *prūd* fr. O.F.]

proud flesh (*med.*) excessive growth of granulation tissue around a wound or ulcer

Prou·dhon (pru:dɔ̃), Pierre Joseph (1809–65), French anarchist philosopher. In his pamphlet 'Qu'est-ce que la propriété?' (1840) he declared that property was theft. He believed that the State should be replaced by a voluntary contract among individuals, and that labor should be the basis of value. He was strongly opposed to communism and socialism

Proust (pru:st), Joseph Louis (1754–1826), French chemist. He formulated the law of constant composition, stating that every compound always contains the same elements in the same proportion by mass

Proust, Marcel (1871–1922), French novelist. His 'A la recherche du temps perdu' (1913–27), in seven novels, recreates in fictional form Proust's own childhood in Paris and the Normandy countryside. In effect it re-creates the society, especially the upper-class society, of Paris at the turn of the century. Certain themes emerge: above all that of the transforming power of dominant love, and the effects it has on the lover's vision of the beloved and the world. But in a sense the whole work is about the transformation of the universe by the individual perceiving and suffering sensibility. The style reflects this characteristic of personal vision: it is highly poetic and complex, full of elaborate imagery. The work has had a profound influence on the art of the novel

Prout (praut), William (1785–1850), English chemist. He discovered that the stomach contains hydrochloric acid. He proposed (1815) on the basis of the effectively whole number values of the atomic masses of the elements that these were condensed forms of hydrogen

prove (pru:v) *pres. part.* **prov·ing** *past* and *past-part.* **proved,** (*old-fash.* and *legal*) **prov·en** (prú:vən) *v.t.* to establish the truth of by evidence, *they proved his innocence* ‖ to show to be true by reasoning, *to prove a point in argument* ‖ (*math.*) to test (a calculation) ‖ to test for conformity to standard ‖ to test the alcoholic content of ‖ to establish the authenticity of (a legal document) ‖ to obtain probate of (a will) ‖ to test experimentally ‖ (*printing*) to proof, take proofs of (a block etc.) ‖ *v.i.* (sometimes with 'to be') to be shown by later knowledge to be, *the story proved quite false* [O.F. *prover*]

prov·e·nance (prɒ́vənəns) *n.* place of origin ‖ source of supply [F.]

Pro·ven·çal (prɔvɑ̃sæl) **1.** *adj.* of or pertaining to Provence or its inhabitants ‖ of or pertaining to Provençal **2.** *n.* the Romance language spoken in Provence proper, a form of langue d'oc ‖ a native or inhabitant of Provence [F.]

Pro·vence (prɔvɑ̃s) a former province of France in the S.E. Rhône valley and the southern slopes of the Maritime Alps. Provence proper comprises Bouches-du-Rhône (including the Camargue) in the fertile Rhône valley (fruit, market produce, cereals, livestock, wine), Var, largely in the mountains, and Alpes-de-Haute-Provence entirely so (olives, wine, lavender). Comtat-Venaissin (now Vaucluse department) was added in 1791 and the former countship of Nice (coastal Alpes-Maritimes) in 1860. The rich Mediterranean Riviera contrasts with the arid interior. The climate is Mediterranean. Main towns Marseille, Nice, Toulon, Aix-en-Provence (the old capital), Avignon, Arles. Provence was the first part of Gaul subdued by Rome (1st c. B.C.), and the last to surrender to the Germanic invasion (5th c.). It was overrun by the Arabs (8th c.), was reduced and annexed by the Carolingians, and was united with Burgundy. It passed to Aragon and Anjou before being attached to France (1486). Provençal is still spoken, though by few

prov·en·der (prɒ́vəndər) *n.* food for domestic animals [O.F. *provendre*]

pro·ve·ni·ence (prouví:ni:əns) *n.* (esp. *Am.*) provenance [fr. L. *proveniens (provenientis)* fr. *provenire*, to come forth]

pro·ven·tric·u·lus (prouventríkjuləs) *pl.* **pro·ven·tric·u·li** (prouventríkjulai) *n.* the glandular or true stomach of a bird ‖ (in many insects) a dilated part of the alimentary canal, in which food is ground up [Mod. L.]

pro·verb (prɒ́və:rb) *n.* a brief familiar maxim of folk wisdom, usually compressed in form, often involving a bold image and frequently a jingle that catches the memory [F. *proverbe*]

pro·ver·bi·al (prəvə́:rbi:əl) *adj.* characteristic of or expressed in proverbs or mentioned in a proverb, *proverbial wisdom* ‖ very well known, notorious, *his stinginess was proverbial* [fr. L.L. *proverbialis*]

Prov·erbs (prɒ́və:rbz) a book of the Old Testament, containing a collection of didactic sayings

pro·vide (prəváid) *pres. part.* **pro·vid·ing** *past* and *past part.* **pro·vid·ed** *v.t.* to supply, *the trees provide shade* ‖ to equip, *provided with helmets* ‖ (*law*) to stipulate, *the law provides that these buildings may not be demolished* ‖ *v.i.* to make advance preparations (for, against some eventuality), *I think we have provided for every possible hazard* ‖ to ensure a supply of the necessities of life, *to provide for one's family* **pro·víd·ed** *conj.* (sometimes with 'that') on condition that, on the understanding that, *they may swim provided an adult accompanies them* [fr. L. *providere*, to see before]

Prov·i·dence (prɒ́vidəns) the capital (pop. 156,840), chief port and commercial center of Rhode Island. Industries: textiles, jewelry, silverware. Colonial State House (1762). Brown University (1764)

prov·i·dence (prɒ́vidəns) *n.* prudent looking ahead, forethought ‖ thrift **Prov·i·dence** God as prescient guide and guardian of human beings ‖ divine care and guidance [F.]

prov·i·dent (prɒ́vidənt) *adj.* showing providence [fr. L. *providens (providentis)* fr. *providere*, to see before]

prov·i·den·tial (prɒvidénʃəl) *adj.* opportune, as if brought about by divine foresight ‖ of or determined by Providence [fr. L. *providentia*, providence]

Pro·vid·er (prəváidər) (*mil.*) an assault, twin-engine transport aircraft (C-123K or AC-123K) that can operate from short, unprepared landing strips

pro·vid·ing (prəváidiŋ) *conj.* (sometimes with 'that') provided

prov·ince (prɒ́vins) *n.* (*Rom. hist.*) a territory outside Italy ruled by a Roman governor ‖ an administrative division, sometimes overseas, of certain countries ‖ (*eccles.*) an area under the charge of an archbishop or metropolitan ‖ (*eccles.*) an administrative area of a religious order ‖ proper scope of professional or business action, *theater criticism is not my province* ‖ a particular sphere of learning ‖ (*pl.*, with 'the') the parts of a country beyond the capital [F.]

Province Wellesley *PENANG

pro·vin·cial (prəvínʃəl) **1.** *adj.* of or relating to a province ‖ characteristic of the provinces in manner, mode or speech || taking or characterized by a limited view **2.** *n.* a native or inhabitant of a province or of the provinces || (*eccles.*) a superintendent of the daughter houses of a religious order in a province, responsible to the general of the order **pro·vín·cial·ism** *n.* the narrow attitude of mind or the unpolished behavior held to be characteristic of the provinces || a word, pronunciation, custom etc. peculiar to a province || love of one's own region not enlarged into patriotism **pro·vin·ci·al·i·ty** (prəvinʃiːǽliti:) *n.* [F.]

proving ground a site for testing vehicles etc.

pro·vi·sion (prəvíʒən) **1.** *n.* a providing or being provided || preparation, *make provision for six new arrivals* || a clause in a legal document, esp. a proviso || a supply or stock || (*pl.*) food supplies **Pro·vi·sion** (*Eng. hist.*) a law issued (13th and 14th cc.) by the nobility or the king **2.** *v.t.* to supply with provisions **pro·ví·sion·al** *adj.* temporary, filling an interval until a definite decision is made, *a provisional government* || requiring later confirmation, *provisional assent* [F.]

Provisions of Oxford *OXFORD, PROVISIONS OF

pro·vi·so (prəváizou) *pl.* **pro·vi·soes, pro·vi·sos** *n.* a condition, stipulation || a clause containing this in a legal document [L.=it being provided]

pro·vi·so·ry (prəváizəri:) *adj.* conditional, containing a proviso || provisional [fr. F. *provisoire*]

Pro·vo (próuvou) *n.* member of the Provisional Irish Republican Army

prov·o·ca·tion (prɒvəkéiʃən) *n.* a provoking or being provoked || something which provokes [F.]

pro·voc·a·tive (prəvɒ́kətiv) *adj.* tending to provoke || arousing annoyance deliberately || involved in the planning stage of a crime; provocative of a crime [fr. L.L. *provocativus*]

pro·voke (prəvóuk) *pres. part.* **pro·vok·ing** *past* and *past part.* **pro·voked** *v.t.* to rouse to anger || to incite, instigate, esp. deliberately, *their arrival provoked an international crisis* || to excite, call forth, *to provoke an answer* [O.F. *provoker*]

prov·ost (prɒ́vəst, próuvoust) *n.* an administrative officer of high rank in some universities || (*Br.*) the head of any of certain colleges || (*eccles.*) the head of a chapter or religious community || the mayor of a Scottish burgh || (próuvou) a provost marshal || (*Br.*, (prəvóu) an officer in the military police [O E. *prafost, profost* fr. L.]

pro·vost marshal (próuvou) (*mil.*) the head of the military police in camp or in the field

prov·ost·ship (prɒ́vəstʃip, próuvoustʃip) *n.* the office or term of office of a provost || the jurisdiction of a provost

prow (prau) *n.* the forepart of a boat or ship, the bow [F. *proue fr. L. fr. Gk*]

prow·ess (práuis) *n.* dexterity and daring || great ability [O.F. *proece*]

prowl (praul) **1.** *v.i.* to roam stealthily in search of prey, or as if in search of prey || *v.t.* to roam over (a place) in search of prey or as if searching for prey, *to prowl the streets* **2.** *n.* a prowling **on the prowl** prowling [M.E. *prollen*, origin unknown]

prowl car a squad car

prowl·er (práulər) *n.* someone who prowls, esp. a sneak thief

Prowler *n.* a twin-engine, quadruple-crew, all-weather turbojet aircraft (EA-6B), designed to operate from aircraft carriers

prox·em·ics (prɒksíːmiks) *n.* study of the interaction of human beings with their environment

prox·i·mal (prɒ́ksəməl) *adj.* (*anat.*, of a point on a limb or part of the body) situated at the end nearest the point of attachment (opp. DISTAL) [fr. L. *proximus*, nearest]

prox·i·mate (prɒ́ksəmit) *adj.* (in space, time or kinship, or in a series of events) nearest, next || approximate || (of a cause) direct, immediate [fr. L.L. *proximare (proximiatus)*, to approach]

prox·im·i·ty (prɒksímiti:) *n.* the state or quality of being near in space, time or kinship [F. *proximité*]

proximity fuze, esp. *Br.* **proximity fuse** an electronic device for detonating a projectile by means of radio waves reflected back off the target from a transmitter in the nose of the projectile, thus ensuring that detonation takes place only within effective range of the target

prox·i·mo (prɒ́ksəmou) *adj.* (*commerce, abbr.* prox.) in or of the next month, *the meeting proposed for the 18th prox.* [L. *proximo (mense)*, in the next month]

prox·y (prɒ́ksi:) **1.** *pl.* **prox·ies** *n.* authority given by one person to another to act for him, *to vote by proxy* || the person thus authorized || a document empowering a person to act for another **to stand proxy for** to act as proxy for **2.** *adj.* of an act done by a proxy, *a proxy vote* [contr. fr. obs. *procuracy* fr. M.L. *procuratia*, procuration]

PRS-7 (*mil.*) a U.S. Army land-mine detector

prude (pru:d) *n.* a person who affects an excessively rigid attitude in matters of personal modesty and proper conduct [F.]

pru·dence (prúːd'ns) *n.* foresight leading a person to avoid error or danger || the virtue by which the practical reason distinguishes the things useful for salvation (*CARDINAL VIRTUES) || practical discretion [F.]

pru·dent (prúːd'nt) *adj.* (of a person) exercising prudence || (of behavior) guided by prudence [F.]

pru·den·tial (pru:dénʃəl) *adj.* of that which is characterized or actuated by prudence [fr. L. *prudentia*, prudence]

prudent investment 1. standard for investment, esp. for a fiduciary, involving a reasonable income and preservation of capital in a security. **2.** in some jurisdictions, a specified list of securities designated by the state. *Cf* BUSINESSMAN'S RISK

Pru·den·tius (pru:dénʃəs), Aurelius Clemens (348–c. 410), Latin poet born in Spain. He wrote Christian hymns and poems

prud·er·y (prúːdəri:) *n.* the quality or state of being prudish [fr. F. *pruderie*]

Pru·d'hon (prydɔ), Pierre-Paul (1758–1823), French painter, esp. of portraits, to which he gave a mysterious and poetic but rather vapid grace

prud·ish (prúːdiʃ) *adj.* of or relating to a prude or the behavior of a prude

pru·i·nose (prúːinous) *adj.* (*bot.*) covered with a whitish powdery substance or bloom [fr. L. *pruinosus*, frosty]

prune (pru:n) *n.* a plum that has been dried without allowing fermentation to take place and that has a dark, wrinkled, pruinose skin [F.=plum, fr. L. fr. Gk]

prune *pres. part.* **prun·ing** *past* and *past part.* **pruned** *v.t.* to cut off from (a tree or bush) branches, twigs etc. which are diseased or not desired, so as to encourage fruiting or flowering, and to shape || to reduce, cut down, *to prune expenses* || *v.i.* to prune trees or bushes [O.F. *proignier*, to prune the vine]

pru·nus (prúːnəs) *n.* an ornamental shrub of the very large genus *Prunus*, fam. *Rosaceae* (which includes the sloe, plum, greengage, cherry, almond, apricot, peach etc.) [L.]

pru·ri·ence (prúəriːəns) *n.* the state or quality of being prurient **prú·ri·en·cy** *n.*

pru·ri·ent (prúəriːənt) *adj.* (of people) excessively interested in or curious about sexuality || (of ideas, books etc.) tending to excite such interest or curiosity [fr. L. *pruriens* (*prurientis*) fr. *prurire*, to itch]

pru·ri·go (pruráigou) *n.* (*med.*) a skin inflammation characterized by itching papules [L.=an itching]

pru·rit·ic (pruritik) *adj.* of or marked by pruritus

pru·ri·tus (pruráitəs) *n.* (*med.*) itching of the skin [fr. L. *prurire*, to itch]

Prus·sia (prʌ́ʃə) the former largest state of Germany (area in 1939 113,545 sq. miles, pop. 41,762,000). It extended from France and the Low Countries to the Baltic Sea and Poland, and included the provinces of East Prussia, Brandenburg, Berlin, Pomerania, Grenzmark, Silesia, Prussian Saxony, Schleswig-Holstein, Hanover, Westphalia, Hesse-Nassau, Rhine and the district of Hohenzollern. Historic capital: Berlin. HISTORY. The people known from the 10th c. onwards as Prussians were overrun and converted to Christianity (mid-13th c.) by the Teutonic Knights. Rebellion against the Knights (1454) brought Prussia under Polish suzerainty. The Knights' grand master, Albert of Ansbach and Bayreuth, a member of a branch of the Hohenzollern dynasty, became duke of Prussia (1525), which was converted to a secular duchy under the crown of Poland. The duchy passed (1618) to the house of Brandenburg and, under Frederick William, the Great Elector, gained full independence (1660) from Poland. The Reformation and the Treaties of Westphalia (1648) increased Prussian territory. Elector Frederick III of Brandenburg, duke of Prussia, was crowned (1701) King Frederick I of Prussia. Frederick William I (1713–40) built up a unified state founded on Junker power and developed a strong army. Under Frederick the Great (1740–86), Prussia started a policy of ruthless conquest, gaining Silesia from the War of the Austrian Succession (1740–8), and emerging from the Seven Years' War (1756–63) as the chief military power of the Continent. More territory was gained in the partitions of Poland (1772, 1793, 1795). Under Frederick William II (1786–97) Prussia entered the French Revolutionary War, but agreed by the Treaty of Basle (1795) to withdraw from the coalition. Frederick William III (1797–1840) reopened the struggle against France, but met with total defeat at Jena (1806) and humiliation in the Treaty of Tilsit (1807). Prussia was transformed by the social reforms of Stein and Hardenberg, the educational reforms of Humboldt and the army reforms of Scharnhorst and Gneisenau. Prussia again joined (1813) the coalition against France, participating in the defeat of Napoleon at the Battle of the Nations (1813) and Waterloo (1815). The Congress of Vienna increased Prussian territory considerably, notably along the Rhine, and incorporated Prussia in the German Confederation. Prussia's reactionary policy after entering the Holy Alliance was modified only by her organization (1834) of the Zollverein. Under Frederick William IV the 1848 revolution was put down, and the German Confederation revived, although Prussia was granted a constitution. Bismarck, appointed chancellor (1861) by Wilhelm I (1861–88), eliminated Austria from German affairs by fighting Denmark (1864) over Schleswig-Holstein, by the Seven Weeks War (1866), and by the Franco-Prussian War (1870–1). The king of Prussia was proclaimed emperor of the new German Empire (1871), which was dominated by Prussian control of foreign and military affairs. Prussia remained part of Germany until the collapse of the Third Reich (1945), when it was divided among the U.S.S.R., Poland, East Germany and West Germany

Prus·sian (prʌ́ʃən) **1.** *adj.* of or pertaining to Prussia **2.** *n.* (*hist.*) a native or inhabitant of Prussia

Prussian blue a dark blue crystalline salt, ferric ferrocyanide, $Fe_4[Fe(CN)_6]_3 \cdot xH_2O$, used as a pigment and a dye

prus·sic acid (prʌ́sik) hydrocyanic acid [fr. F. *prussique*, hydrocyanic]

Prut (pru:t) a river (500 miles long) flowing south from the E. Carpathians in the S.W. Ukraine, U.S.S.R., to form the border between Moldavia (Rumania) and Moldavia (U.S.S.R.)

pry (prai) *pres. part.* **pry·ing** *past* and *past part.* **pried** *v.i.* to look closely into something which is not one's own concern merely to satisfy one's curiosity, *to pry into someone's affairs* [M.E. *prien*, origin unknown]

pry 1. *v.t. pres. part.* **pry·ing** *past* and *past part.* **pried** to force open or lift with or as if with a lever || (*fig.*) to extract with difficulty, *they pried his secret from him* **2.** *pl.* **pries** *n.* a lever used in prying [PRIZE]

P.S. postscript || Public School

Psalm (sɑm) *n.* any of the sacred songs in the Book of Psalms (*PSALMS) || a metrical version of any of these, for chanting **psalm** (*rhet.*) a song to God [O.E. *psealm, sealm* fr. L. fr. Gk *psalmos*, a song accompaniment]

psalm·ist (sɑ́mist) *n.* an author of sacred songs, esp. of one of the Psalms [fr. L. L. *psalmista*]

psal·mod·ic (sælmɒ́dik, sɑmɒ́dik) *adj.* of or relating to psalmody

psal·mo·dist (sǽlmədist, sɑ́mədist) *n.* a writer or singer of psalms

psal·mo·dy (sǽlmədi:, sɑ́mədi:) *pl.* **psal·mo·dies** *n.* the act or art of singing psalms, esp. in a religious service || a collection of psalms in book form for liturgical use [fr. L.L. *psalmodia* fr. Gk]

Psalms (sɑmz) a book of the Old Testament containing 150 psalms attributed to King David. Most scholars detect a variety of authors, from widely differing periods. The final compilation was probably c. 150 B.C. The Psalms are widely used in both the Jewish and Christian liturgies

psal·ter (sɔ́ltər) *n.* a copy or version of the Psalms for liturgical use [O.E. *psaltere, saltere* fr. L. fr. Gk]

psal·te·ri·um (sɔltíəriːəm) *pl.* **psal·te·ri·a**

(sɔltíəri:ə) *n.* an omasum [L.=psalter (fr. its resemblance to the leaves of a psalter)]
psal·ter·y (sɔ́ltəri:) *pl.* **psal·ter·ies** *n.* an ancient and medieval stringed instrument resembling a dulcimer, played by plucking with the fingers or a plectrum [O.F. *psalterie, sauterie* fr. L. fr. Gk]
pse·phite (sí:fait) *n.* a coarse rock composed of pebbles [fr. Gk *psēphos,* pebble]
pse·phol·o·gist (si:fɔ́lədʒist) *n.* a specialist in psephology
pse·phol·o·gy (si:fɔ́lədʒi:) *n.* the study of elections and the scientific analysis of election results [fr. Gk *psēphos,* pebble+ *logos,* discourse (fr. the Greeks' use of pebbles for voting)]
pseud·ax·is (su:dǽksis) *n.* (*bot.*) a sympodium
pseud·e·pig·ra·pha (su:dipígrəfə) *pl. n.* writing falsely attributed to an author, esp. to a biblical author **pseud·e·píg·ra·phy** *n.* the ascription of false names of authors to writings [fr. Gk *pseudepigrophos* adj., with false title]
pseudo- (sú:dou) *prefix* sham ‖ spurious ‖ unreal ‖ showing a superficial resemblance to ‖ being an abnormal form of [Gk=false, falsely]
pseu·do·carp (sú:dəkɑrp) *n.* (*bot.*) a fruit including parts of the flower other than the ripened ovary (e.g. a pome) [fr. PSEUDO-+Gk *karpos,* fruit]
pseu·do·cho·lin·es·ter·ase (su:doukoulənéstəreis) *n.* (*physiol.*) an enzyme that catalyzes the hydrolosis of choline esters and other esters, present in the human liver and in blood plasma. *also* cholinesterase
Pseu·do-Di·o·ny·si·us (sú:doudaiəníʃi:əs, sú:doudaiənísi:əs) a pseudonym of Dionysius the Areopagite (c. 500)
pseu·do·morph (sú:dəmɔrf) *n.* a mineral resembling another in crystalline form **pseu·do·mór·phic** *adj.* **pseu·do·mór·phism** *n.* **pseu·do·mór·phous** *adj.* [fr. PSEUDO-+Gk *morphē,* form]
pseu·do·nym (sú:d'nim) *n.* a name other than one's own, assumed for some purpose **pseu·do·ným·i·ty** *n.* **pseu·don·y·mous** (su:dɔ́nəməs) *adj.* having or bearing a pseudonym [fr. Gk *pseudōnumos,* falsely named]
pseu·do·pod (sú:dəpɔd) *n.* a pseudopodium
pseu·do·po·di·um (su:dəpóudi:əm) *pl.* **pseu·do·po·di·a** (su:dəpóudi:ə) *n.* (*biol.*) a temporary, blunt protrusion of ectoplasm serving for locomotion and prehension in cain protozoans, e.g. in an amoeba [fr. PSEUDO-+Gk *pōdion,* dim. of *pous* (*podos*), foot]
pseu·do·ran·dom (su:dourǽndəm) *adj.* of numbers selected by a system that duplicates random selection
pshaw (ʃɔ) **1.** *interj.* (*old-fash.*) used as a mild expression of irritation, disbelief etc. **2.** *n.* (*old-fash.*) an exclamation of 'pshaw!'
psi (psai) *n.* the twenty-third letter (Ψ, ψ=psi) of the Greek alphabet
PSI (*computer acronym*) **p**roto **s**ynthex **i**ndexing, a computer program for indexing each word in English based on semantic or morphological similarity; used in IBM 7090 and applied by System Development Corp.
psil·an·thro·pism (sailǽnθrəpizəm) *n.* (*theol.*) psilanthropy **psil·án·thro·pist** *n.* **psil·án·thro·py** *n.* (*theol.*) the doctrine that Christ was only human [fr. Gk *psilos,* bare, mere+*anthrōpos,* man]
psi·lo·cin [$C_{12}H_{16}N_2O$] (sáiləsin) *n.* (*chem.*) hallucinogenic compounds found in mushrooms
psi·lo·cy·bin [$C_{12}H_{17}N_2O_2P$] (sailəsáibin) *n.* (*chem.*) hallucinogenic compound found in mushrooms, *Psilocybe mexicana*
psi·lo·phyt·ic (sailəfítik) *adj.* (*paleobiol.*) of Psilophytales, an order of Paleozoic fossil plants
psi·lop·sid (sailɔ́psid) *n.* a member of *Psilopsida,* a subphylum of mostly very old fossil plants but which includes two living genera of rootless, leafless plants having a branched, primitively vascular stem [fr. Mod. L. *Psilopsida* fr. Gk *psilos,* bare+*Lycopsida* (*LYCOPSID)]
psi particle *J PARTICLE
psit·ta·co·sis (sitəkousis) *n.* (*med.*) a disease of birds, esp. parrots, communicable to man and causing high fever and pulmonary disorders [Mod. L. fr. Gk *psittakos,* parrot]
Pskov (pskɔf) a town (pop. 176,000) in the R.S.F.S.R., U.S.S.R., 160 miles southwest of Leningrad: textiles, rope. Kremlin (12th–16th cc.)
pso·as (sóuəs) *pl.* **pso·ai** (sóuai), **pso·ae** (soui:) *n.* (*anat.*) either of two muscles in the loin [fr. Gk *psoa,* loin muscle]
psor·a·len [$C_{11}H_6O_3$] (sɔ́rəlen) *n.* (*chem.*) a plant derivative, parts of which are used to darken human skin
pso·ri·a·sis (səráiəsis) *n.* (*med.*) a chronic skin disease, characterized by red patches covered with white scales **pso·ri·at·ic** (sɔri:ǽtik, souri:ǽtik) *adj.* [Mod. L. fr. Gk fr. *psōra,* an itch]
PSRO (*acronym*) **P**rofessional **S**tandard **R**eview **O**rganization, created as part of Social Security Amendment in 1972 to oversee health services
P.S.T. Pacific standard time
psych or **psyche** (saik) *v.* to make one receptive for what is to come or not to come. —**psyched** *adj.* of one dominated by an idea
psy·chas·the·ni·a (saikəsθí:ni:ə) *n.* any of a variety of mental disorders involving irrational obsessions and fears
Psy·che (sáiki:) (*Gk mythol.*) a maiden, personifying the soul, loved by Eros
psy·che (sáiki:) *n.* the soul ‖ (*psychol.*) the mind, both conscious and unconscious [Gk *psuchē,* soul]
psych·e·del·ic (saikidélik) *adj.* of a mental condition induced by certain drugs and characterized by an impression of greatly heightened sensory perception. It may be accompanied by feelings of elation or misery, by hallucinations, or by sharp perceptual distortion ‖ of a drug inducing this state ‖ of patterns, images etc. characteristic of this state [fr. PSYCHE+Gk *dēlos,* visible, evident]
psy·chi·at·ric (saiki:ǽtrik) *adj.* of psychiatry ‖ using psychiatry
psychiatric nurse registered nurse trained to assist with mental health patients
psy·chi·a·trist (sikáiətrist, saikáiətrist) *n.* a doctor who specializes in psychiatry
psy·chi·a·try (sikáiətri:, saikáiətri:) *n.* the branch of medicine concerned with the treatment and study of mental and emotional disorders [fr. Gk *psuchē,* soul + *iatreia,* healing]
psy·chic (sáikik) **1.** *adj.* nonphysical, *psychic forces* ‖ of or pertaining to the mind or spirit ‖ apparently able to respond to nonphysical influences, *a psychic medium* **2.** *n.* a person seemingly sensitive to nonphysical influences ‖ a person able to act as a medium **psy·chi·cal** (sáikik'l) *adj.* [fr. Gk *psuchikos,* of the soul]
psychic energizer (*pharm.*) a mental stimulant, e.g., amphetamine
psycho- (sáikou) *prefix* of or concerned with the mind or brain [fr. Gk fr. *psuchē,* soul]
psy·cho·ac·tive (saikouǽktiv) *adj.* (*pharm.*) of a drug or drugs that affect the mind or behavior. —**psy·cho·ac·tiv·i·ty** *n. Cf* PSYCHOCHEMICAL
psy·cho·a·nal·y·sis (saikouənǽlisis) *n.* a technique of psychotherapy which renders conscious the contents of the unconscious mind through a dialogue between analyst and analysand ‖ the psychological system or doctrine elaborated from the results of this technique (both technique and doctrine owe much to Freud) **psy·cho·an·a·lyst** (saikouǽnəlist) *n.* a person who practices psychoanalysis **psy·cho·an·a·lýt·ic, psy·cho·an·a·lýt·i·cal** *adjs* **psy·cho·an·a·lýt·i·cal·ly** *adv.* **psy·cho·an·a·lyze, psy·cho·an·a·lyse** (saikouǽnəlaiz) *pres. part.* **psy·cho·an·a·lyz·ing, psy·cho·an·a·lys·ing** *past* and *past part.* **psy·cho·an·a·lyzed, psy·cho·an·a·lysed** *v.t.* to subject (someone) to psychoanalytic treatment
psy·cho·bi·og·ra·phy (saikoubaiɔ́grəfi:) *n.* a study of a person from a psychodynamic or psychoanalytical viewpoint. *Cf* PSYCHOHISTORY
psy·cho·chem·i·cal (saikoukémik'l) *n.* (*pharm.*) **1.** a chemical that affects the nervous system, esp. to cause temporary ineffectuality, e.g., for chemical warfare. **2.** a psychoactive chemical —**psychochemical** *adj.*
psy·cho·di·ag·nos·tics (saikoudaiəgnɔ́stiks) *n.* (*psych.*) analysis of personality based on mannerisms, gait, facial expressions, handwriting, or on response in inkblots
psy·cho·dra·ma (sáikoudrɑmə, sáikoudræmə) *n.* a form of psychiatric treatment in which the patient obtains emotional release by acting out his problem in an improvised dramatic play
psy·cho·gen·ic (saikoudʒénik) *adj.* belonging to or originating in the mind, mental, *psychogenic disorder* (cf. SOMATOGENIC) [PSYCHO-+Gk *-genēs,* born]
psy·cho·ger·i·at·ric (saikoudʒeri:ǽtrik) *adj.* (*psych.*) of mental illness in old age
psy·cho·his·to·ry (saikouhístəri) *n.* approach to history based in analysis of subconscious and private elements in the lives of participants: a psychodynamic view of the people involved in historic incidents. —**psy·cho·his·to·ri·an** *n.* —**psy·cho·his·to·ri·cal** *adj. Cf* PSYCHOBIOGRAPHY
psy·cho·log·i·cal (saikəlɔ́dʒik'l) *adj.* of or pertaining to psychology ‖ of or relating to the mind
psychological moment the moment when the individual or collective mind is most likely to respond positively to an action, statement, request etc.
psychological warfare actions designed to weaken the morale or loyalty of an enemy
psy·chol·o·gist (saikɔ́lədʒist) *n.* a specialist in psychology
psy·chol·o·gy (saikɔ́lədʒi:) *n.* the scientific study of human or animal behavior ‖ the mental and behavioral characteristics of a person or group, *mob psychology* ‖ the mental characteristics associated with a particular kind of behavior, *the psychology of thieving* [fr. Mod. L. *psychologia* fr. Gk *psuchē,* soul+*logos,* discourse]
psy·cho·met·ric (saikoumetrik) *adj.* of or relating to the measurement of mental data
psy·cho·met·rics (saikoumétriks) *n.* the science of applied psychometric techniques
psy·chom·e·trist (saikɔ́mitrist) *n.* a person who practices psychometrics
psy·chom·e·try (saikɔ́mitri:) *n.* divination, from personal, physical contact with an object, of the character etc. of the object or of people connected with it ‖ psychometrics [fr. PSYCHO-+ Gk *-metria,* measuring]
psy·cho·mi·met·ic (saikoumimétik) *adj.* (*pharm.*) of a drug that creates the symptoms of a hallucinogenic state. *Cf* PSYCHOTOMIMETIC
psy·cho·mo·tor (saikoumóutər) *adj.* (*physiol.*) of a muscular movement which results directly from a mental process
psy·cho·neu·ro·sis (saikounuróusis, saikounjuróusis) *pl.* **psy·cho·neu·ro·ses** (saikounuróusi:z, saikounjuróusi:z) *n.* a nervous disorder of mainly psychic origin **psy·cho·neu·rot·ic** (saikounurɔ́tik, saikounjurɔ́tik) **1.** *adj.* of, relating to, or afflicted by psychoneurosis **2.** *n.* a person suffering from psychoneurosis
psy·cho·path (sáikəpæθ) *n.* a person suffering from a mental disorder (*CHARACTER DISORDER)
psy·cho·path·ic (saikəpǽθik) *adj.* of or characterized by mental disorder
psy·cho·path·o·let·ic (saikoupæθəlétik) *adj.* of a political system without roots or special values, unsure of its goals, usu. functioning at minimum effectiveness, and using force to ensure compliance with its rules
psy·cho·pa·thol·o·gy (saikoupəθɔ́lədʒi:) *n.* the scientific study of the psychological causes of mental illnesses
psy·chop·a·thy (saikɔ́pəθi:) *n.* character disorder
psy·cho·phar·ma·ceu·ti·cal (saikoufɑrməsú:tik'l) *n.* (*pharm.*) a drug that affects one's mental condition
psy·cho·pro·phy·lax·is (saikouproufəlǽksis) *n.* (*med.*) preparing women psychologically for childbirth, esp. natural childbirth. *Cf* LAMAZE
psy·cho·quack·er·y (saikoukwǽkəri:) *n.* the practice of psychology or psychiatry by an unqualified person —**psy·cho·quack** *n.*
psy·cho·sen·so·ry or **psy·cho·sen·so·ri·al** (saikousénsəri:) *adj.* (*psych.*) perceived either as something real or as a hallucination
psy·cho·sis (saikóusis) *pl.* **psy·cho·ses** (saikóusi:z) *n.* serious mental derangement [fr. late Gk *psuchōsis,* animation]
psy·cho·so·mat·ic (saikousəmǽtik) *adj.* of, pertaining to or resulting from the interaction between mind and body
psy·cho·so·mat·o·graph (saikousoumǽtəgræf) *n.* a device for measuring and recording muscular reactions to mental stimuli
psy·cho·sur·ger·y (saikousə́:rdʒəri:) *n.* (*med.*) surgery performed on the brain for the purpose of changing the patient's personality, thought, emotions or behavior, rather than for the treatment of a physical disease
psy·cho·ther·a·pist (saikouθérəpist) *n.* a person who practices psychotherapy
psy·cho·ther·a·py (saikouθérəpi:) *n.* the treatment of mental illness by psychological methods, esp. psychoanalysis
psy·chot·ic (saikɔ́tik) **1.** *adj.* of, relating to or

suffering from psychosis **2.** *n.* a psychotic person

psy·chot·o·gen (saikɒtədʒən) *n.* (*pharm.*) a drug affecting the mind psychotically. —**psy·chot·o·gen·ic**

psy·chot·o·mi·met·ic (saikɒtoumimétik) *adj.* (*psych.*) inducing or mimicking a psychosis. — **psy·chot·o·mi·met·ic** *n.* a psychotomimetic drug. *Cf* PSYCHOMIMETIC

psy·cho·tox·ic (sąikoutɒ́ksik) *adj.* (*pharm.*) of a nonnarcotic drug with harmful effects, esp. on the mind

psy·cho·trop·ic drug (sąikoutróupik) (*pharm.*) a drug affecting psychic function, behavior or experience

psy·chrom·e·ter (saikrɒ́mitər) *n.* (*phys.*) a hygrometer consisting of a wet-and-dry-bulb thermometer. The difference in the thermometer readings is a measure of the relative humidity of the atmosphere

psy-op (sáiɒp) *n.* (*mil.*) a psychological warfare operation

P-3 *ORION

ptar·mi·gan (tɑ́rmigən) *pl.* **ptar·mi·gan, ptar·mi·gans,** *n.* any of several grouse of genus *Lagopus,* of the Arctic and northern temperate zones of Europe and America, characterized by completely feathered feet, and plumage that is brownish or blackish in summer and, in most species, largely white in winter [Gael. *tarmachan,* origin unknown]

PT boat a motor torpedo boat [fr. *patrol torpedo boat*]

pter·i·dol·o·gist (tęridɒ́lədʒist) *n.* a specialist in pteridology

pter·i·dol·o·gy (tęridɒ́lədʒi:) *n.* (*bot.*) the study of ferns [fr. Gk *pteris* (*pteridos*), fern+*logos,* discourse]

pte·rid·o·phyte (tərídəfait) *n.* (in former classifications) a member of *Pteridophyta,* a subdivision of the plant kingdom coordinate with thallophytes, bryophytes and spermatophytes, including the ferns and fern allies (*PTEROPSID) [fr. Mod. L. *Pteridophyta* fr. Gk *pteris* (*pteridos*), fern+*phuton,* a plant]

pter·o·dac·tyl (tęrədǽktil) *n.* one of the pterosaurs. The flying mechanism was a large membrane between the body and a greatly developed fourth digit. Fossilized remains are found in strata from the Lower Jurassic to Late Mesozoic [fr. Mod. L. *Pterodactylus* fr. Gk *pteron,* wing+*daktulos,* finger]

pter·o·pod (térəpɒd) *n.* any of various mollusks of *Pteropoda,* a division of *Tectibranchia,* with the foot expanded into a wing-shaped paddle for swimming [fr. Gk *pteron,* wing+*pous* (*podos*), foot]

pte·rop·sid (tərɒ́psid) *n.* a member of *Pteropsida,* a large subphylum of green vascular land plants, comprising the ferns and flowering plants. The sporophytes possess roots, stems and often large leaves and are independent. In ferns the gametophyte generation is independent, but in the seed plants it is dependent upon the sporophyte for water and nutriment. The subphylum includes ferns, gymnosperms and angiosperms [fr. Gk *pteron,* wing+*opsio,* appearance]

pter·o·saur (térəsɔr) *n.* a member of *Pterosauria,* an extinct order of flying reptiles which included the pterodactyl

pter·y·goid (térigɔid) *adj.* of, pertaining to, or situated in the lower part of the sphenoid bone in the skull of man and other vertebrates [fr. Gk *pterugoeidēs,* like a wing]

Ptol·e·ma·ic (tɒləméiik) *adj.* of or pertaining to Ptolemy or to his theory of the universe ‖ of the Macedonian dynasty which ruled Egypt (304-30 B.C.)

Ptol·e·my (tɒ́ləmi:) (Claudius Ptolemaeus, 2nd c. A.D.), Greek astronomer and geographer of Alexandria, author of the famous 'Geography', which remained the standard geographic work throughout the Middle Ages, of the 'Optics', and of the 'Great Collection' or 'Almagest'. In this he gave a full account of Greek astronomy and propounded his own belief (unchallenged until Copernicus) that the earth is the center of the universe, and the sun, planets and stars revolve around it. Ptolemy divided the degree into minutes and seconds. He also determined the value of [π] (*PI)

Ptolemy I (*d.* 283 B.C.), king of Egypt (304.283 B.C.), founder of the Ptolemaic dynasty. He was a general of Alexander the Great, after whose death (323 B.C.) he seized power in Egypt

Ptolemy II (c. 308–c. 246 B.C.), king of Egypt (c. 285–c. 246 B.C.), son of Ptolemy I. He carried out economic reforms, completed the Pharos, was a patron of art and literature and, according to tradition, commissioned the Septuagint

Ptolemy III (*d.* c. 221 B.C.), king of Egypt (c. 246–c. 221 B.C.), son of Ptolemy II. He made war on Syria and extended his power to the coasts of Asia Minor and E. Greece

Ptolemy XI (*d.* 51 B.C.), king of Egypt (80–58 B.C. and 55–51 B.C.). He was overthrown (58 B.C.) by the Egyptians for misrule, but was restored (55 B.C.) with Roman support, giving Rome complete control of Egypt

pto·maine (tóumein, touméin) *n.* any of a number of alkaloids, some highly poisonous, formed by the action of bacteria on putrefying proteins [fr. Ital. *ptomaina* fr. Gk *ptōma,* corpse]

ptomaine poisoning poisoning by ptomaines ‖ (*pop.*) any food poisoning

pto·sis (tóusis) *n.* (*med.*) the drooping of an upper eyelid due to the paralysis of the muscle which lifts it [Gk *ptōsis,* a falling]

PTV (*acronym*) public television

pty·a·lin (táiəlin) *n.* (*biochem.*) an enzyme in human saliva which promotes the conversion of starch into sugar [fr. Gk *ptualon,* spittle]

pty·a·lism (táiəlizəm) *n.* (*med.*) excessive flow of saliva [fr. Gk *ptualismos* fr. *ptualizein,* to expectorate]

p-type semiconductor (pí:taip) (*electr.*) a crystal material in a semiconductor that has been doped with an impurity that causes electronic holes that move from molecule to molecule, creating a condition as the major carrier of electric current

pub (pʌb) *n.* (*Br., pop.*) a public house

pu·ber·ty (pjú:bərti:) *n.* the period of life when the reproductive glands begin to function ‖ the condition of becoming able to reproduce [F. *puberté*]

pu·bes (pjú:bi:z) *n.* the hair that begins to grow on the lower hypogastric region at puberty ‖ the lower hypogastric region [L.]

pubes pl. of PUBIS

pu·bes·cence (pju:bés'ns) *n.* the reaching of puberty ‖ (*biol.,* of some plants and certain insects) a downy or hairy covering **pu·bés·cent** *adj.* [F.]

pu·bic (pjú:bik) *adj.* of or pertaining to the pubis ‖ of or pertaining to the pubes

pu·bis (pjú:bis) *pl.* **pu·bes** (pjú:bi:z) *n.* the foremost of the three sections of the hipbone [L. (*os*) *pubis,* the groin (bone)]

pub·lic (pʌ́blik) **1.** *adj.* of or pertaining to the community as a whole, *the public good* ‖ for the use of the community at large and maintained at the community's expense, *public amenities* ‖ that is or can be known by all members of the community, *a public scandal* ‖ acting for the people, *public prosecutor* ‖ of or relating to the service of the community, *prominent in public life,* often receiving publicity, *a public figure* **2.** *n.* (usually with 'the') the members of a community in general ‖ a group or section of a community characterized by some common interest etc., *his television program reaches a wide public* **in public** in the state of being visible or accessible to the public [M.E. *publique* fr. F.]

public access 1. access to government-held information under the Freedom of Information Act. **2.** access to broadcast facilities, e.g., CATV, under licensing arrangements

public address system a microphone and amplifier system which enables a speaker etc. to be heard at a distance

pub·li·can (pʌ́blikən) *n.* (*Br.*) a person who manages a public house ‖ (*Rom. hist.*) a tax collector [F. *publicain,* a tax collector of ancient Rome]

pub·li·ca·tion (pʌblikéiʃən) *n.* a publishing or being published ‖ the issue of printed matter for public sale or free distribution ‖ a printed and published book, magazine, pamphlet etc. [M.E. *publicacion* fr. O.F.]

public bill a legislative bill affecting a whole country (cf. PRIVATE BILL)

public domain the realm of collective property (esp. property not protected by patent or copyright) to which any member of the public may lay claim, *Oscar Wilde's plays are in the public domain now* ‖ land belonging to, or controlled by, the government

public enemy a criminal at large whose liberty menaces the community, esp. one widely advertised as sought by the police

public house (*Br.*) an establishment licensed for the sale and consumption of alcoholic beverages on the premises, sometimes also having a license permitting consumption off the premises. There is usually more than one bar, beer is the main drink, and food and lodging are sometimes provided. A public house is often the center of sociability in a community

pub·li·cist (pʌ́blisist) *n.* an expert in international law ‖ a person who writes on public affairs ‖ a person who publicizes ‖ a press agent [F. *publiciste*]

pub·lic·i·ty (pʌblísiti:) *n.* the whole of the methods and materials used in making an enterprise, product etc. known to the public with a view to increasing business ‖ the methods and materials used in making some noncommercial matter similarly known ‖ the disseminating of advertising or informative matter ‖ the condition of being exposed to the knowledge of the general public, esp. through newspaper reports, *the scandal was given full publicity* [fr. F. *publicité*]

pub·li·cize (pʌ́blisaiz) *pres. part.* **pub·li·ciz·ing** *past* and *past part* **pub·li·cized** *v.t.* to bring to public notice

public library a library usually run by a municipality from which books may be borrowed free

public opinion the consensus of people's views on a given issue, usually of a political, social or economic nature and on a national scale

public orator (*Br.*) the official spokesman of a university, who delivers addresses (usually in Latin) on official occasions (such as the conferring of honorary degrees)

public prosecutor an official who investigates and prosecutes a criminal act on behalf of the State ‖ (*Br.*) a legal officer who prosecutes on behalf of the State

public relations the promotion, by a firm, corporation, government department etc., of the goodwill of other organizations or the public by distributing information about policy etc. ‖ the degree of goodwill existing or created between organizations or between an organization and the public

public relations officer (*Br., abbr.* P.R.O.) a person employed to promote good public relations

Public Safety, Committee of (*F. hist.*) the group of 12 men who ruled France Apr. 6, 1793–Oct. 27, 1795. Led (Sept. 1793–July 1794) by Carnot, Danton and Robespierre, the committee developed into a dictatorship under Robespierre, and was responsible for the Terror

public school an elementary or secondary school maintained by taxes, supervised by local authorities and offering education to the children of the district free of charge ‖ (*Br.*) a private secondary school whose headmaster is a member of the Headmasters' Conference, an independent professional body. Such schools are wholly or partly boarding, are administered by a governing body and meet some part of their upkeep from pupils' fees and income from endowments

public servant a person holding public office

public service service of the state ‖ that which serves a need of the public, e.g. a public transport system

pub·lic-spir·it·ed (pʌ́blikspíritid) *adj.* (of people) seeking the public good and acting accordingly ‖ (of actions) prompted by zeal for the public good

public television educational, cultural and informational television programs, without commercials, provided by nonprofit organizations

public trustee (*Br. law*) an official authorized and appointed by the State to act as trustee (e.g. in relation to the investment of charitable funds)

public utility *pl.* **public utilities** a business concern which provides and administers a public service, e.g. water, gas, electricity ‖ a stock or bond issued by such a concern

public works facilities such as roads, playgrounds etc. built with government funds for the use of the general public

pub·lish (pʌ́bliʃ) *v.t.* to arrange the printing and distribution of (books, newspapers etc.) for sale to the public ‖ (*loosely*) to be the author of (a work thus offered to the public), *he has just published his third novel* ‖ to make known to the public ‖ to announce publicly, *to publish banns of marriage* **púb·lish·er** *n.* someone who arranges for the multiplication of copies of a work (a book, record, sheet music etc.) and for their handling by distributive agencies. He remunerates, or is remunerated by, the author (or performer etc.) according to the terms of the contract made between them [M.E. *publisen, publisshen* fr. O.F.]

publisher's imprint the name of the publisher, together with the place and date of publication, e.g. on the title page of a book

Puc·ci·ni (pu:tʃí:ni:), Giacomo (1858–1924), Italian operatic composer. His dramatic sense and his flow of sensuous melody made his operas popular. The best known are 'Manon Lescaut' (1893), 'la Bohème' (1896), 'la Tosca' (1900) and 'Madame Butterfly' (1904). 'Turandot', unfinished at his death, was first performed in 1926

puc·coon (pəkú:n) *n.* any of various North American plants (e.g. the bloodroot) which yield a red or yellow pigment [Algonquian]

puce (pju:s) *n.* and *adj.* brownish purple [F.=flea]

Puck (pʌk) a mischievous goblin believed, esp. in the 16th and 17th cc., to roam the English countryside looking for pranks to play [O.E. *pūca,* a mischievous spirit]

puck *n.* a hard rubber disk used in ice hockey as the object to be shot into the goal [origin unknown]

puck·er (pʌ́kər) **1.** *v.t.* (often with 'up') to gather into narrow folds or wrinkles ‖ *v.i.* to become gathered into narrow folds or wrinkles **2.** *n.* a narrow fold or wrinkle, or a number of them together [prob. fr. POKE, (obs.) a bag]

puck·ish (pʌ́kiʃ) *adj.* mischievous, *puckish humor* [after PUCK]

pud·ding (púdiŋ) *n.* a sweet dessert, thick and soft, typically composed of flour and milk and eggs and sometimes fruit ‖ (*naut.*) a pad of rope etc. used as a fender [M.E. *poding, pudding,* origin unknown]

pudding stone conglomerate

pud·dle (pʌ́d'l) **1.** *n.* a small pool of liquid, esp. rainwater ‖ clay and sand kneaded together with water and used to construct a watertight lining for the bank of a canal, the bottom of a pond etc. **2.** *v. pres. part.* **pud·dling** *past* and *past part.* **pud·dled** *v.t.* to knead (clay, sand and water or concrete etc.) into an impervious mass‖ to stir (molten iron) in order to reduce its carbon content ‖ to make (water etc.) dirty ‖ *v.i.* to dabble in mud etc. ‖ to play about messily with paints, clay etc. **púd·dly** *adj.* having many puddles, *a puddly road* [M.E. *podel, puddel,* prob. dim. of O.E. *pudd,* ditch]

pu·den·da (pju:déndə) *pl. n.* the external genital organs, esp. those of a woman [pl. of L. *pudendum,* that of which one ought to be ashamed]

pudge (pʌdʒ) *n.* (*pop.*) a short, fat person **púdg·i·ness** *n.* the quality of being pudgy **púdg·y** *comp.* **pudg·i·er** *superl.* **pudg·i·est** *adj.* short and fat [etym. doubtful]

Pue·bla (pwéblɑ) a densely populated interior state (area 13,096 sq. miles, pop. 3,285,300) of Mexico, on the Anáhuac Plateau. Capital: Puebla. Main crops: coffee, sugarcane, fibers, corn, cereals. Its mountains yield onyx and gold and other metals. Rivers provide hydroelectric power. Puebla is an important corridor between Mexico City and Veracruz. There are many sites of archaeological interest

Puebla a city (pop. 710,833) of central Mexico, 130 miles southeast of Mexico City. Traditional crafts: pottery and tiles (it was the original center of Moorish style in Mexico), onyx carving. Industries: metallurgy, building materials, textiles. Cathedral (16th–17th cc.). University (1922)

pueb·lo (pwéblou) **1.** *pl.* **pueb·los** *n.* a type of Indian village in the southwest U.S.A. and some parts of Latin America built as communal dwelling houses of adobe or stone **Pueb·lo** a member of certain Indian tribes of Arizona and New Mexico, e.g. the Zuñi and the Hopi, inhabiting such a village ‖ their languages **2. Pueb·lo** *adj.* of the Pueblo Indians or their culture [Span.=village, people]

'Pueblo', U.S.S. a U.S. vessel designed for espionage which became (1968) the center of an international crisis when North Korean vessels intercepted it in the Sea of Japan and escorted it to North Korea, where it was detained. The captain and crew were released (1969) when the U.S.A. agreed to admit what it officially denied: that at the time of capture the vessel was inside North Korean territorial waters

pu·er·ile (pjú:əril, pjú:ərail) *adj.* (*of* an adult's ideas, behavior) not befitting an adult, childish

pu·er·il·i·ty (pju:əríliti:) *n.* [fr. L. *puerilis,* pertaining to a child]

pu·er·per·al (pju:ɜ́:rpərəl) *adj.* (*med.*) relating to the puerperium [fr. L. *puerperus*]

puerperal fever infection of the female reproductive organs following childbirth

pu·er·pe·ri·um (pju:ərpíəri:əm) *n.* the period of confinement immediately after childbirth [L.=childbirth]

Puer·to Ca·be·llo (pwértɔkɑbéjɔ) a seaport (pop. 90,000) in N. Venezuela, 70 miles west of Caracas

Puer·to Ri·can (pwərtourí:kən, pɔ́rtourí:kən, póurtourí:kən) **1.** *adj.* of or pertaining to Puerto Rico or its inhabitants **2.** *n.* a native or inhabitant of Puerto Rico

Puer·to Ri·co (pwértourí:kou, pɔ́rtourí:kou, póurtourí:kou) the easternmost island (area 3,423 sq. miles, pop. 3,196,520) of the Greater Antilles, comprising, with Vieques, Culebra and Mona Is (total pop. 7,800), a territory of the U.S.A. Capital and chief port: San Juan. People: 80% European stock, with African and Mulatto minorities. Language: Spanish, 17% also speak English (both are official). Religion: mainly Roman Catholic, with Protestant and Spiritist minorities. The land is 38% arable, 37% pasture, and 12% forest (palms, tropical hardwoods). Reforestation is proceeding. The coast (sugar plantations) is flat, and the interior mountainous (highest point 4,398 ft). Mean annual temperature (F.) 76°. Rainfall: north 40–60 ins, south 20–40 ins. Exports: sugar, rum, tobacco, molasses, cotton textiles, pineapples, citrus fruit, light manufactures. The tourist industry is important. Territorial university (founded as a normal school, 1900) at Rio Piedras, near San Juan. Some land has been redistributed, but there is heavy emigration to the mainland, esp. New York City. HISTORY. Puerto Rico was inhabited by the Arawak and Carib Indians when Columbus landed there (1493) during his second voyage. The island was explored (1508) by Ponce de León, who founded the city of San Juan de Puerto Rico in the same year. During the colonial period it lay under the authority of the Audiencia de Santo Domingo and was subjected to numerous attacks by pirates, notably Drake, who set fire (1595) to San Juan. During the 18th c. Britain attempted on three occasions to take possession of the island and to annex it to Jamaica. Following several independence movements during the 19th c., the island was occupied by the U.S.A. in the Spanish-American War and was ceded to the U.S.A. (1898) in the Treaty of Paris. Government was at first in the hands of the military. In 1917 Puerto Ricans obtained U.S. citizenship. President Franklin Roosevelt initiated (mid-1930s) a New Deal measure, the Puerto Rico Reconstruction Administration (PRRA), which gave rise (1938) to the Popular Democratic party (PDP), led by Luis Muñoz Marín. It initiated reforms, notably land distribution, enforcement of minimum wage and hour laws and a progressive income tax law, and the establishment of an economic development program known as Operation Bootstrap, initiated in 1942. President Harry Truman named (1946) Jesús T. Piñero as the first Puerto Rican governor. The U.S. government permitted (in the Organic Act, 1947) the election of governors by popular vote, the first of whom (1948) was Muñoz Marín. Endorsing a proposal made by the U.S. government, he drafted a new constitution which went into effect in 1952 and which defined Puerto Rico as an internally self-governing commonwealth or associated free state. Muñoz Marín was reelected in 1956 and 1960 and was succeeded (1964–8) by his PDP lieutenant Roberto Sánchez Vilella. In 1968 the PDP lost to millionaire engineer and industrialist Luis Alberto Ferré, leader of the New Progressive party (NPP) which had been founded only one year earlier. Although Ferré had campaigned for statehood in a 1967 plebiscite which ratified (by about 60–40) the island's status as associated free state, he did not interpret his election as a mandate for statehood, but favored another plebiscite in 1971. By the early 1980s federal budget cuts, a worldwide recession, and an erosion of Puerto Rico's competitive advantages caused an economic slump that led to demands for greater autonomy, with or without change in commonwealth status. Debate continued among factions favoring commonwealth, statehood and independence

Puerto Rico Reconstruction Administration (PRRA), a New Deal agency established (mid-1930s) to readjust the distribution of economic power in Puerto Rico. It placed a restrictive quota on sugar production and enforced a law limiting corporation holdings to 500 acres. It established a cooperative sugar mill to compete with private mills, and catered to the long-neglected coffee and tobacco interests. The PRRA gave birth (1938) to the Popular Democratic party

puff (pʌf) **1.** *v.i.* to breathe quickly, esp. after exertion ‖ to emit steam, smoke etc. in a series of whiffs or puffs ‖ to blow in rapid gusts, whiffs or puffs ‖ (with 'up' or 'out') to swell, become inflated ‖ (with 'at' or 'on') to draw (on a pipe etc.) ‖ *v.t.* to blow or emit in whiffs or puffs ‖ to draw on (a pipe, cigar, or cigarette), emitting puffs of smoke ‖ (with 'out') to extinguish (a candle etc.) by blowing on it ‖ (with 'up' or 'out') to cause to swell, inflate ‖ (with 'out') to arrange (hair etc.) in a loose, fluffy mass ‖ (sometimes with 'up') to praise excessively ‖ (with 'up') to make conceited **2.** *n.* a short, light gust of air, steam, smoke etc. ‖ a small cloud, emission of smoke etc. ‖ a draw on a cigarette etc. ‖ a shell of soft light pastry etc. ‖ a fluffy mass ‖ a powder puff ‖ a quilt ‖ a laudatory critical notice written to publicize a work ‖ publisher's blurb ‖ (*genetics*) an intensely active portion of an enlarged chromosome [M.E. *puffen*]

puff adder a deadly poisonous S. African viper, *Bitis arietans,* which inflates the upper part of its body when excited

puff·ball (pʌ́fbɔl) *n.* any of several fungi of fam. *Lycoperdaceae* with a large round, white spore case which emits dustlike spores when stepped on or struck

puffed (pʌft) *adj.* swollen, puffy ‖ (*Br.*) out of breath

puf·fin (pʌ́fin) *n.* any of various marine birds of genera *Fratercula* or *Lunda,* fam. *Alcidae,* having a brightly colored, laterally flattened bill, which it partially sheds after the breeding season. It lives colonially in rabbit or shearwater burrows on cliffs or grassy islands on the N. Atlantic seaboard [origin unknown]

puff·i·ness (pʌ́fi:nis) *n.* the state or quality of being puffy

puff pastry light flaky pastry

puff·y (pʌ́fi:) *comp.* **puff·i·er** *superl.* **puff·i·est** *adj.* short of breath ‖ puffed out ‖ swollen, *puffy eyelids*

pug (pʌg) **1.** *n.* a large roll of clay prepared for working **2.** *v.t. pres. part.* **pug·ging** *past* and *past part.* **pugged** to mix (clay) into a working consistency ‖ to fill (a hollow floor or wall) with compacted material in order to absorb vibration and sound [etym. doubtful]

pug *n.* a dog of a small, short-haired breed having a broad, flat nose and short, tightly curled tail [origin unknown]

pug *n.* the footprint of a wild beast [Hindi *pag,* foot]

Pu·get (pyʒe), Pierre (1620–94), French sculptor. His classical subjects are treated with often violent realism and are full of power and movement

Pu·get Sound (pjú:dʒit) a branched inlet (80 miles long) of the Pacific in north and central Washington

pu·gil·ism (pjú:dʒəlizəm) *n.* boxing **pú·gil·ist** *n.* a boxer **pu·gil·ís·ti·c** *adj.* [fr. L. *pugil,* boxer]

Pu·gin (pjú:dʒin), Augustus Welby Northmore (1812–52), English architect. He was one of the leaders of the Gothic Revival, esp. in its decorative detail, and was best known for his ecclesiastical architecture and his part in designing the Houses of Parliament in London

pug mark a pug (footprint)

pug mill a machine in which clay is pugged

pug·na·cious (pʌgnéiʃəs) *adj.* fond of fighting, aggressive [fr. L. *pugnax* (*pugnacis*)]

pug·nac·i·ty (pʌgnǽsiti:) *n.* the state or quality of being pugnacious [fr. L. *pugnacitus*]

pug nose a broad snub nose **púg·nosed** *adj.*

puis·ne (pjú:ni:) **1.** *adj.* (*law*) more recent, *a puisne mortgage* ‖ (*law*) of lower rank or importance **2.** *n.* (*law*) a puisne judge [O. F. fr. *puis,* after+*né,* born]

pu·is·sance (pjú:isəns, pju:ís'ns, pwís'ns) *n.* (*rhet.*) might, power [F. fr. *puissant,* puissant]

pu·is·sant (pjú:isənt, pju:ís'nt, pwís'nt) *adj.* (*rhet.*) mighty, powerful [F.]

puke (pju:k) **1.** *v. pres. part.* **puk·ing** *past* and *past part.* **puked** *v.i.* (*pop.*) to vomit ‖ *v.t.* (*pop.*) to vomit **2.** *n.* (*pop.*) vomit [origin unknown]

pul (pu:l) *pl.* **puls, pu·li** (pú:li:) *n.* a monetary unit of Afghanistan equal to one hundredth of an afghani ‖ a coin of the value of one pul [Pers. *pūl* fr. Turk.]

pu·la (púlə) *n.* unit of currency in Botswana

Pu·las·ki (pulǽski:), Kazimierz (Casimir) (1747–79), Polish patriot and U.S. general. He distinguished himself during the Polish anti-Russian insurrection of 1768 and in the American Revolution, when he led his Pulaski legion against the British

pul·chri·tude (pʌ́lkritu:d, pʌ́lkritju:d) *n.* (*rhet.*) physical beauty [fr. L. *pulchritudo*]

pule (pju:l) *pres. part.* **pul·ing** *past* and *past part.* **puled** *v.i.* (*rhet.*) to cry with weak, whimpering sounds [of imit. origin, perh. fr. F. *piauler*]

Pu·litz·er (pú:litsər, pjúlitsər), Joseph (1847–1911), American newspaper publisher of Hungarian birth. He endowed a number of monetary prizes and scholarships which have been awarded annually in the U.S.A. since 1917 for distinction in journalism, letters and music

pull (pul) **1.** *v.t.* to apply a force to (something) in order to make it move towards the person or thing applying the force (opp. PUSH) ‖ to extract, *to pull a tooth* ‖ to strain (a muscle etc.) ‖ (sometimes with 'up') to uproot (vegetables etc.) ‖ to row (a boat) ‖ (*racing*) to check (a horse) by pulling the reins, and so prevent it from winning ‖ (*football*) to pull back from the scrimmage line and toward one side to protect the carrier ‖ (*golf, baseball, cricket* etc.) to hit (the ball) towards the side on which the player is standing ‖ (*printing,* often with 'up') to take (a proof) from the inked type, lithographic stone etc. ‖ to draw out (a knife, gun etc.) ready for use ‖ to draw off (beer) from a container ‖ (*pop.*) to accomplish with daring, *to pull a coup* ‖ (*pop.*) to assert (superiority) in order to obtain an advantage over someone ‖ (*pop.*) to attract (votes, support, an audience etc.) ‖ *v.i.* to apply a force to something in order to make it move towards the person or thing applying the force ‖ to be capable of being so moved, *the drawer won't pull* ‖ (often with 'away', 'ahead', 'into', 'out' etc.) to move by means of physical or mechanical energy ‖ (with 'at') to draw (on a pipe) ‖ (with 'at') to take a drink (from a bottle) ‖ (*golf, baseball, cricket* etc.) to pull the ball ‖ (of a horse) to strain against the bit ‖ to row a boat **to pull around** to handle (a person) roughly **to pull a fast one** to play an unfair trick **to pull apart, to pull to pieces** to tear apart ‖ to find great fault with (a piece of work etc.) **to pull down** to demolish (a building) ‖ to weaken in health **to pull for** (*pop.*) to encourage by shouting or cheering **to pull off** to be finally successful in (something difficult or chancy) **to pull oneself together** to regain control of one's emotions or behavior **to pull one's punches** (of a boxer) to abstain from hitting as hard as one can ‖ to criticize or accuse less forcibly than would be justifiable **to pull one's weight** to take one's full share of work or responsibility **to pull out** (of a vehicle) to move out from the side of the road or from the line of traffic ‖ (*pop.*) to leave, esp. to abandon some group effort **to pull over** (of a vehicle) to move suddenly across the road or move to the edge of the road **to pull through** to survive illness, danger etc. ‖ to enable (someone) to survive illness, danger etc. **to pull together** to cooperate in a task **to pull up** (of a moving vehicle, horse etc.) to come to a stop ‖ (*Br.*) to reprimand, *the manager pulled him up for his carelessness* ‖ to improve one's position relative to other competitors in a race **2.** *n.* the act of pulling ‖ an instance of this ‖ a force which pulls or attracts, *the pull of the tide* ‖ an effort necessary for forward or upward movement, *a hard pull up the hill* ‖ a draw on a cigarette, drink etc. ‖ (*golf, baseball, cricket* etc.) a stroke which pulls the ball ‖ the force needed to pull a bow or the trigger of a firearm ‖ an advantage due to influence, relationship etc. ‖ influence exerted to obtain a privilege or advantage ‖ a knob, handle etc. by which a drawer, bell etc. may be pulled ‖ (*printing*) a proof ‖ the checking of a horse by pulling on the bridle, esp. to prevent it from winning a race ‖ a row (in a boat etc.) ‖ a distance or period of time spent in rowing [O.E. *pullian,* origin unknown]

pull date a date recorded on a food product indicating the latest time at which it should be sold, e.g., on milk

pul·let (púlit) *n.* a hen before the first moult [F. *poulet,* chicken]

pul·ley (púli:) *pl.* **pul·leys** *n.* a wheel with a grooved rim, used to raise or lower a load attached to one end of a rope, chain etc. passing around the groove and pulled from the other end. The mechanical advantage of pulleys, mounted in the same block, enables a small effort exerted over a long distance to raise a heavy load through a short distance ‖ a wheel on a fixed shaft used to transmit power by means of a belt, chain etc. passing over its circumference [O.F. *polie* prob. fr. Gk]

Pullman (púlmən), George Mortimer (1831–97) U.S. industrialist, inventor of the railroad sleeping car. Working in Chicago from 1855, he first remodeled old railroad coaches and then built the first modern sleeping car (1863). Called the 'Pioneer,' it had a folding upper berth and seat cushions that could be extended to form a lower berth. He also developed other types of railroad cars, including the dining car (1868), and formed the Pullman Palace Car Company to manufacture his sleeping cars

Pull·man (púlmən) *n.* a railroad car with luxurious sleeping or dining accommodations [after George Mortimer *Pullman* (1831-97), American inventor who introduced such cars in the U.S.A.]

Pullman Strike a shutdown (1894) in the servicing of Pullman cars in Chicago, Ill., undertaken by the American Railway Union led by Eugene Debs. The strike was broken by the intervention of U.S. troops, and Debs and other leaders were arrested. Although defended at his trial by Clarence Darrow, Debs was convicted (1895) and imprisoned

pull·o·ver (púlǫuvər) *n.* a sweater put on by being pulled over the head ‖ a shirt or blouse put on in this way

pull-through (púlθrụ:) *n.* a weighted cord with an oiled rag or a brush attached, used for cleaning the bore of a gun

pul·lu·late (pʌ́ljuleit) *pres. part.* **pul·lu·lat·ing** *past* and *past part.* **pul·lu·lat·ed** *v.i.* (of a seed) to germinate ‖ to develop in great quantity, to swarm, **pul·lu·lá·tion** *n.* [fr. L. *pullulare* (*pullulatus*), to sprout]

pul·mo·nar·y (púlmənẹri:) *adj.* of, like or affecting the lungs ‖ pulmonate ‖ of the artery conveying blood from the heart to the lungs ‖ of the vein conveying blood from the lungs to the heart [fr. L. *pulmonarius*]

pulmonary valve a valve in the heart of higher vertebrates between the right ventricle and the artery leading blood from the heart to the lungs

pul·mo·nate (púlməneit, púlmənit) **1.** *adj.* (*zool.*) having lungs or the equivalent of lungs ‖ belonging or relating to *Pulmonata,* an order of gastropod mollusks having a lung or respiratory sac **2.** *n.* a pulmonate gastropod [fr. Mod. L. *pulmonatus*]

pul·mon·ic (pulmɒ́nik) *adj.* pulmonary [F. *pulmonique*]

pulp (pʌlp) **1.** *n.* a soft, moist mass of animal or vegetable matter ‖ such a part of a fruit (e.g. of an orange) or of an animal body (e.g. of a tooth) ‖ soft pithy matter found in plant stems ‖ a mixture, made by mechanical or chemical treatment of wood, consisting of water and cellulose fibers, and used as the raw material in papermaking ‖ (*Am., pl.*) pulp magazines ‖ (*mining*) pulverized ore mixed with water ‖ (*mining*) dry crushed ore **2.** *v.t.* to make into a pulp ‖ *v.i.* to become a pulp **púlp·i·ness** *n.* the quality or state of being pulpy [F. *pulpe*]

pul·pit (púlpit, pʌ́lpit) *n.* a small stone or wooden structure reached by a short flight of stairs and from which a preacher preaches, in a church or chapel [fr. L. *pulpitum*]

pulp magazine a magazine, usually sensational, on cheap wood-pulp paper

pulp·wood (pʌ́lpwụd) *n.* the wood of some trees, e.g. spruces, most suitable for converting into pulp for papermaking

pulp·y (pʌ́lpi:) *comp.* **pulp·i·er** *superl.* **pulp·i·est** *adj.* of, like or having the consistency of pulp

pul·que (pú:lke, púlki:) *n.* a Mexican fermented drink prepared from several species of agave, esp. *Agave atrovirens* [Span.]

pul·sar (pʌ́lsạr) *n.* (*meteor.*) a source in space of strong, pulsating radio waves, believed to be the core of an exploded or rotating neutron star. *Cf* QUASAR

pul·sate (pʌ́lseit) *pres. part.* **pul·sat·ing** *past* and *past part.* **pul·sat·ed** *v.i.* to move rhythmically to and fro, esp. to expand and contract in a regular way (e.g. of the heart) ‖ to be as if throbbing or vibrating, *the pulsating enthusiasm of the crowd* [fr. L. *pulsare* (*pulsatus*), to beat]

pul·sa·tile (pʌ́lsətil, pʌ́lsətail) *adj.* pulsating ‖ percussive [fr. M.L. *pulsatilis*]

pul·sa·tion (pʌlséiʃən) *n.* the action of pulsating ‖ a beat, throb [fr. L. *pulsatio* (*pulsationis*)]

pul·sa·tor (pʌ́lseitər, pʌlséitər) *n.* a device that works with a throbbing movement, e.g. a machine which agitates diamond-bearing earth and so separates out the diamonds, or an attachment on milking machinery [fr. L. *pulsare* (*pulsatus*), to beat]

pul·sa·to·ry (pʌ́lsətọri:, pʌ́lsətǫuri:) *adj.* able to pulsate, throbbing

pulse (pʌls) **1.** *n.* the regular expansion and contraction of the arteries due to the rhythmical action of the heart in forcing blood through them ‖ the frequency with which the resultant throbs occur, *a rapid pulse* ‖ a single one of these throbs ‖ the magnitude of the arterial expansions and contractions, *a strong pulse* ‖ the beat in music or verse ‖ any rhythmical beat ‖ a disturbance of brief duration transmitted through a medium ‖ a transitory disturbance of voltage, current, pressure or some other normally constant quantity ‖ a generalized group sentiment divined rather than known by direct experience, *testing the political pulse of the South* **2.** *v. pres. part.* **puls·ing** *past* and *past part.* **pulsed** *v.i.* to pulsate ‖ *v.t.* to emit in a regular succession of pulses or waves [L. *pulsus* fr. *pellere* (*pulsum*), to beat]

pulse *n.* a leguminous plant (pea, bean etc.) ‖ the edible seeds of these plants [O.F. *pols, pouls*]

pulse-jet engine a jet engine to which the intake of air is intermittent (through valves), resulting in a pulsating thrust

pulse-jet or **pulse-jet engine** a jet-propulsion engine containing neither compressor nor turbine, equipped with valves in its front that open and shut and so create thrust intermittently, rather than continuously. *Cf* RAMJET

pul·sim·e·ter (pʌlsímitər) *n.* (*med.*) an instrument used to measure the rate and strength of the pulse

puls·ing (pʌ́lsiŋ) *n.* (*mil.*) in naval mine warfare, a method of operating magnetic and acoustic sweeps in which the sweep is energized by varying or intermittent current in accordance with predetermined schedule

pul·som·e·ter (pʌlsɒ́mitər) *n.* a vacuum pump operating by the intake and condensation of steam at regular intervals ‖ a pulsimeter

pul·ver·i·za·tion (pʌlvərizéiʃən) *n.* a pulverizing or being pulverized

pul·ver·ize (pʌ́lvəraiz) *pres. part.* **pul·ver·iz·ing** *past* and *past part.* **pul·ver·ized** *v.t.* to reduce to a fine powder ‖ to defeat with devastating effect, *to pulverize the opposition* ‖ *v.i.* to become powder **púl·ver·iz·er** *n.* someone who or something which pulverizes ‖ a harrow for breaking soil into a fine tilth [fr. L.L. *pulverizare*]

pul·ver·u·lent (pʌlvérjulənt) *adj.* consisting of fine powder ‖ covered with fine powder ‖ (of a rock) disintegrating with ease into a fine powder [fr. L. *pulverulentus*]

pul·vil·lus (pʌlvíləs) *pl.* **pul·vil·li** (pʌlvílai) *n.* (*zool.*) a process or membrane on an insect's foot sometimes serving as an adhesive organ [L. fr. *pulvinulus,* dim. of *pulvinus,* pillow]

pul·vi·nus (pʌlváinəs) *pl.* **pul·vi·ni** (pʌlváinai) *n.* (*bot.*) a swelling at the base of a petiole [L.=pillow]

pu·ma (pjú:mə) *pl.* **pu·mas, pu·ma** *n.* a cougar ‖ the fur of the cougar [Span.]

pum·ice (pʌ́mis) **1.** *n.* a light, porous volcanic stone formed by the escape of steam or gas from cooling lava, used as an abrasive in cleaning, smoothing and polishing ‖ a piece of this **2.** *v.t. pres. part.* **pum·ic·ing** *past* and *past part.* **pum·iced** to clean, smooth or polish with pumice [O.F. *pomis, pumis*]

pum·mel (pʌ́məl) *pres. part.* **pum·mel·ing,** esp. *Br.* **pum·mel·ling** *past* and *past part.* **pum·meled,** esp. *Br.* **pum·melled** *v.t.* to strike or thump repeatedly, esp. with the fist or fists [var. of POMMEL]

pump (pʌmp) **1.** *n.* a device for raising or moving a liquid or gas by decreasing or increasing the pressure on it ‖ an act or the process of pumping **2.** *v.t.* to raise, move or eject by using a pump or as if with a pump ‖ (sometimes with 'out') to remove a liquid or gas from, *they pumped the well dry* ‖ to supply with air by means of a pump or bellows, *to pump an organ* ‖

(usually with 'up') to inflate by means of a pump, *to pump up car tires* ‖ to inject (someone) with a stream of something, *he pumped him full of shots* ‖ to extract information from (a person) by subtle questions ‖ to move (something) energetically up and down as if working a pump handle, *to pump someone's hand* ‖ to invest (capital) heavily in a business, industry etc., *he pumped funds into the firm* ‖ *v.i.* to work a pump [M.E. *pumpe*]

pump *n.* (*old-fash.*) a man's light shoe fitting without laces or other fastening, esp. one of patent leather worn with evening dress ‖ (*Am.*=*Br.* court shoe) a lady's high-heeled shoe without fastenings [origin unknown]

pumped storage (*electr.*) system for storing energy by using surplus power to lift water into a reservoir so that it may be lowered to turn a generator to produce electricity when needed

pum·per·nick·el (pʌ́mpərnik'l) *n.* a very dark, close-textured German wholemeal rye bread [G.]

pump·kin (pʌ́mpkin) *n.* any of several members of *Cucurbita*, fam. *Cucurbitaceae*, a genus of vines bearing a large, edible, globular fruit with a firm yellowish-orange rind, esp. *C. pepo* ‖ the fruit of such a plant [fr. older *pumpion* fr. F. fr. L. fr. Gk]

pump room a large room in a spa where medicinal waters are supplied

pun (pʌn) **1.** *n.* a witticism involving the playful use of a word in different senses or of words which differ in meaning but sound alike **2.** *v.i. pres. part.* **pun·ning** *past* and *past part.* **punned** to make a pun [etym. doubtful]

pun *pres. part.* **pun·ning** *past* and *past part.* **punned** *v.t.* to pound (earth etc.) in order to form it into a hard, dense mass [var. of POUND]

Pu·na (pu:nú) an island (29 miles long) in the Gulf of Guayaquil, S.W. Ecuador

pu·na (pú:nə) *n.* a cold high plateau between two ranges of the Andes in Peru ‖ the cold prevalent wind of this region [Span. fr. Quechua]

Pu·na de A·ta·ca·ma (pú:nɑðeɑtɑkɑ́mɑ) a highland region (mainly 7,000–13,500 ft) in N.W. Argentina, with border peaks above 21,000 ft

punch (pʌntʃ) **1.** *v.t.* to indent or make a hole in (metal, paper etc.) using a punch ‖ to make (this indentation or hole) ‖ to strike with the closed fist ‖ to herd (cattle) **2.** *n.* the action of punching ‖ a blow with the closed fist ‖ forcefulness, *the story lacks punch* [etym. doubtful]

punch *n.* a tool, usually cylindrical but tapered at one end, used to emboss or make holes in metal, paper etc. ‖ a tool for forcing a bolt from a hole ‖ a tool for driving the head of a nail beneath a surface ‖ a tool used to stamp a die or impress a design [etym. doubtful]

punch *n.* a drink composed of sugar, spice and fruit, usually mixed with wine or liquor, and drunk hot or cold [Hindi *panch*, five (from the original number of ingredients)]

Punch and Judy the hero and heroine of a farcical puppet show, which originated in Italian popular comedy, spread to France and England in the 17th c., gained widespread popularity in the 18th c., and spread to the U.S.A.

punch·ball (pʌ́ntʃbɔl) *n.* (*Br.*) a punching bag ‖ a game resembling baseball in which the ball is struck with the fist

punch card a card having a pattern of perforations representing data for use in a computer

punch-drunk (pʌ́ntʃdrʌŋk) *adj.* (of a boxer) dazed through brain injury after receiving many punches on the head

pun·cheon (pʌ́ntʃən) *n.* a short vertical auxiliary strut used to hold up a roof, esp. in a mine ‖ a slab of wood or split log used in flooring etc. ‖ a patterned die used by goldsmiths, silversmiths etc. to punch an impression in metal [O.F. *poinçon, poinchon*]

puncheon *n.* a cask varying in capacity from 70 to 120 gallons ‖ the amount such a cask holds [O.F. *ponçon, poinchon*]

punching bag (*Am.*=*Br.* punchball) a large leather ball, suspended from or tethered to a flexible upright, used for exercising the muscles of the arm, shoulder and chest

punch press a machine used for working metal by cutting, shaping or various combination dies

punch-up (pʌ́ntʃʌp) *n.* (*Br.*) a street fight

punc·tate (pʌ́ŋkteit) *adj.* (*biol.*) dotted or shallowly pitted ‖ covered with very small dots or holes (e.g. in some skin diseases) [fr. Mod. L. *punctatus* fr. *punctum*, a point]

punc·ta·tion (pʌŋktéiʃən) *n.* the action of making or condition of being punctate ‖ a small dot or depression on a plant, animal etc.

punc·til·i·o (pʌŋktíli:ou) *pl.* **punc·til·i·os** *n.* a point of detail in very correct behavior or in ceremony ‖ careful attention to such details [Span. *puntillo* and Ital. *puntiglio*, dim. of *punto*, point]

punc·til·i·ous (pʌŋktíli:əs) *adj.* paying scrupulous attention to points of detail in behavior, ceremony or matters touching one's honor [fr. F. *pointilleux* fr. Ital.]

punc·tu·al (pʌ́ŋktʃu:əl) *adj.* occurring, arriving etc. at the agreed, right or stated time ‖ of or pertaining to a point ‖ having the nature of a point **punc·tu·ál·i·ty** *n.* the quality of being punctual [fr. M.L. *punctualis*]

punc·tu·ate (pʌ́ŋktʃu:eit) *pres. part.* **punc·tu·at·ing** *past* and *past part.* **punc·tu·at·ed** *v.t.* to mark the divisions of (written matter) into sentences, clauses etc. or to indicate exclamation, interrogation, direct speech etc. by inserting punctuation marks ‖ to interrupt by, or intersperse with, sound or gesture, *his speech was punctuated by cheers* ‖ *v.i.* to use punctuation [fr. M.L. *punctuare* (*punctuatus*), to prick, point]

punc·tu·a·tion (pʌŋktʃu:éiʃən) *n.* a punctuating or being punctuated ‖ the act, practice or system of inserting the correct marks to punctuate written matter ‖ punctuation marks [fr. M.L. *punctuatio* (*punctuationis*)]

punctuation mark one of the marks used to punctuate written matter, esp. the period or full stop (.), comma (,), colon (:), semicolon (;), exclamation mark (!), question mark (?), hyphen (-), dash (—), brackets ([]), parentheses (()), inverted commas or quotation marks (" "), apostrophe (')

punc·ture (pʌ́ŋktʃər) **1.** *n.* the act of making a hole in something by pricking ‖ a small hole made thus, esp. one made accidentally in a tire **2.** *v. pres. part.* **punc·tur·ing** *past* and *past part.* **punc·tured** *v.t.* to make a small hole in by pricking ‖ to make (a hole, perforation etc.) by pricking ‖ to sustain a puncture in, *the cyclist punctured his front tire* ‖ to destroy as if by pricking and deflating, *to puncture someone's self-esteem* ‖ *v.i.* (of a tire etc.) to sustain a puncture [fr. L. *punctura*]

pun·dit (pʌ́ndit) *n.* (*pop.*) an expert [fr. PANDIT]

pun·gen·cy (pʌ́ndʒənsi:) *n.* the quality or condition of being pungent

pun·gent (pʌ́ndʒənt) *adj.* pricking or stinging to the taste or smell ‖ (of speech or writing) sharply biting ‖ (of remarks, a speech etc.) forthright and very much to the point [fr. L. *pungens* (*pungentis*) fr. *pungere*, to prick]

Pu·nic (pjú:nik) **1.** *adj.* (*hist.*) pertaining to the ancient city of Carthage or its inhabitants ‖ (of the Carthaginians as regarded by the Romans) treacherous **2.** *n.* the language of ancient Carthage, related to Phoenician [fr. L. *Punicus*]

Punic Wars three wars between Rome and Carthage in which Rome became the leading power in the W. Mediterranean. Early relations had been friendly, but the Carthaginian occupation of Sicily, prompted by commercial interest, threatened the trade and security of Rome's allies, the Greek cities of S. Italy. Rome's intervention to help Messina led to the lst Punic War (264–241 B.C.). The Romans built a fleet to challenge the naval strength of Carthage and reduced Sicily to a Roman province (241 B.C.). The Carthaginians under Hamilcar and Hannibal conquered Spain (237–219 B.C.). Hannibal's attack (219 B.C.) on Saguntum, a Roman ally in Spain, led to the 2nd Punic War (218–201 B.C.). Hannibal crossed the Rhône and the Alps into Italy and defeated the Romans at Trasimene (217 B.C.) and Cannae (216 B.C.). But worn down by the tactics of Fabius Cunctator, who avoided further pitched battles, and deprived of the help of Hasdrubal, who was defeated and killed on the Metaurus (207 B.C.), Hannibal was recalled (203 B.C.), Scipio Africanus had driven the Carthaginians from Spain (206 B.C.) and invaded Africa. After his defeat by Scipio Africanus at Zama (202 B.C.), Hannibal advised acceptance of the harsh Roman terms of peace. Carthage nevertheless made a quick economic recovery. On the pretext of a Carthaginian attack on one of Rome's allies, Rome opened the 3rd Punic War (149–146 B.C.) landed in Africa and, under Scipio Aemilianus, destroyed Carthage completely (146 B.C.), as Cato the Elder had long urged should be done

pu·ni·ness (pjú:ni:nis) *n.* the condition or quality of being puny

pun·ish (pʌ́niʃ) *v.t.* to cause to suffer for some offense committed ‖ to prescribe a form of suffering in penalty for (an offense), *the crime was punished by death* ‖ (*pop.*) to treat harshly, *to punish an engine* ‖ (*pop.*) to deal (someone) hard blows ‖ *v.i.* to inflict punishment **to take a punishing** to be subjected to rough treatment **pún·ish·a·ble** *adj.* deserving or capable of being, or liable to be, punished **pún·ish·ment** *n.* a punishing or being punished ‖ the suffering given or received, *the punishment was a fine* [F. *punir* (*puniss-*)]

pu·ni·tive (pjú:nitiv) *adj.* concerned with punishing, *a punitive expedition* ‖ harsh or severely discriminatory, *punitive taxation* [F. *punitif* (*punitive*)]

Pun·jab (pʌ́ndʒɑb) (*hist.*) a region of N.W. British India bordering the Himalayas, and consisting mainly of the basin of the Sutlej, Beas, Ravi, Chenab and Jhelum Rivers. It was partitioned (1947) between India and Pakistan ‖ (formerly East Punjab) the state (area 47,205 sq. miles, pop. 47,000,000) of India comprised of the eastern part of the former Punjab with Patiala, crossed by the Beas and Sutlej. Capital: Chandigarh. Products: irrigated crops (cereals, sugarcane, cotton), lumber, resin. This was partitioned (1966) into a Punjabi-speaking state (Punjab) and a Hindi-speaking state (Haryana) ‖ (formerly West Punjab) a region and former province (area 62,245 sq. miles) of Pakistan comprised of the western part of the former Punjab, a rich agricultural area (cereals, sugarcane, cotton) crossed by the Sutlej, Ravi, Chenab and Jhelum. Chief towns: Lahore, Rawalpindi

Pun·ja·bi, Pan·ja·bi (pʌndʒɑ́bi:) **1.** *n.* a native of the Punjab, India ‖ the Indic language spoken in the Punjab **2.** *adj.* of or relating to the Punjab or its inhabitants [Hind.]

pun·ji stick (pʌ́ndʒi:) (*mil.*) a bamboo spike set in camouflaged trap to wound the enemy

punk (pʌŋk) **1.** *n.* wood rotted by a fungus, sometimes used as tinder ‖ amadou [origin unknown]

punk **1.** *n.* a person, esp. a young one, regarded as inferior **2.** *adj.* (*pop.*) worthless, of poor quality [etym. doubtful]

punk rock hard rock music created by and for the working-class English, in the late 1970s and subsequently popular in the U.S.A. — **punk** *adj.* of punk rock music; of the style of dress associated with punk rock musicians and their admirers. *Cf* NEW WAVE

pun·ner (pʌ́nər) *n.* a heavy-headed tool used for punning earth etc.

pun·net (pʌ́nit) *n.* (*Br.*) a chip basket [origin unknown]

pun·ster (pʌ́nstər) *n.* a person who makes puns

punt (pʌnt) **1.** *n.* a long, shallow, square-ended, flat-bottomed boat, usually propelled by thrusting a long pole with a two-pronged iron end on the riverbed **2.** *v.t.* to propel (someone or something) in this way ‖ *v.i.* to go by punt [O.E. fr. L.]

punt **1.** *v.t.* (*football, rugby*) to kick (the ball) as it drops from the hands and before it bounces on the ground ‖ *v.i.* to punt a football **2.** *n.* a kick made in this way [etym. doubtful]

punt **1.** *v.i.* (*gambling*) to bet against the bank ‖ (*Br.*) to gamble **2.** *n.* (*gambling*) a bet made against the bank [fr. F. *ponter*]

Pun·ta A·re·nas (púntɑɑrénɑs) a port (pop. 67,600) of Chile on the Strait of Magellan, the southernmost town in the world

Pun·ta del Es·te (pú:ntɑdeléste) a seaside resort in S. Uruguay, in the state of Maldonado. It served (1961) as site of the Inter-American Economic and Social Council Conference, which created the Alliance for Progress, and (1962) as site of the eighth foreign ministers conference which by a bare two-thirds majority suspended Cuba from membership in the Organization of American States

pun·ty (pʌ́nti:) *pl.* **pun·ties** *n.* an iron rod used in shaping hot glass [perh. fr. F. *pontil*]

pu·ny (pjú:ni:) *comp.* **pu·ni·er** *superl.* **pu·ni·est** *adj.* much below normal in development, size or strength [fr. PUISNE]

pup (pʌp) **1.** *n.* a puppy ‖ a young seal **2.** *v.i. pres. part.* **pup·ping** *past* and *past part.* **pupped** (of a bitch) to bring forth young **to sell someone a pup** to sell someone something which proves to be worthless

pu·pa (pjú:pə) *pl.* **pu·pae** (pjú:pi:), **pu·pas** *n.* the stage in the metamorphosis of an insect between the larva and the imago, in which the insect is enclosed in a hardened case ‖ an insect in this stage **pú·pal** *adj.* **pu·pate** (pjú:peit) *pres. part.* **pu·pat·ing** *past* and *past part.* **pu·pat·ed** *v.i.* to pass into or through the pupal stage **pu·pá·tion** *n.* [Mod. L. fr. L. *pupa,* doll]

pu·pil (pjú:p'l) *n.* a person, esp. a child, receiving tuition ‖ (*Rom. and Scot. civil law*) a child under the age of puberty in the care of a guardian [F. *pupille,* an orphan who is a minor]

pupil *n.* the aperture in the iris of the eye, contracted or dilated by the muscles of the iris to control the amount of light entering the eye [F. *pupille*]

pu·pil·age, pu·pil·lage (pjú:p'lidʒ) *n.* the state or period of being a pupil

Pu·pin (pú:pi:n, pu:pí:n), Michael Idvorsky (1858–1935), U.S. physicist who invented devices to extend the range of long-distance telephony, and discovered (1896) secondary X-ray radiation

pu·pip·a·rous (pju:pípərəs) *adj.* (*zool.,* e.g. of certain parasitic insects) bringing forth young already developed to the pupal stage [fr. PUPA+L. *parere,* to bring forth]

pup·pet (pʌ́pit) *n.* a small model of a human being or an animal with mobile limbs controlled by strings or wires, or made in the form of a glove and operated by a hand inserted in it. Texts are written and miniature stages made for puppet shows ‖ a person whose actions are initiated and controlled by the will of another **pup·pet·eer** (pʌpitíər) *n.* a person who operates puppets **púp·pet·ry** *n.* the art of making or operating puppets [fr. POPPET]

puppet valve a valve operated by the vertical rise and fall of a disk, ball etc.

pup·py (pʌ́pi:) *pl.* **pup·pies** *n.* a young dog ‖ (*old-fash.*) a bad-mannered, selfsatisfied young man as seen by an older person [perh. fr. F. *poupée,* doll]

puppy love calf love

pup tent a simple tent for shelter, without side walls, such as U.S. soldiers carry in their pack

Pu·ra·cé (pu:rɑsé) an active volcano (15,420 ft) in S.W. central Colombia

Pu·ra·nas (purɑ́nəz) a group of 18 sacred Sanskrit poems comprised chiefly of mythical and historical legends concerning the creation of the universe, the gods and the era of the lawgivers and patriarchs, in direct tradition with earlier Vedic literature and law books [Skr. =of former times]

Pur·beck marble (pə́:rbek) a fine-grained, metamorphosed limestone from Purbeck, Dorset, England, used for building

pur·blind (pə́:rblaind) *adj.* partially blind ‖ unable to understand or perceive the obvious truth [M.E. *pur blind,* quite blind]

Pur·cell (pə́:rs'l), Henry (1659–95), English composer. His many vocal and instrumental compositions include much important church music and music for state occasions. His works for the theater include 'King Arthur' (1691), 'The Fairy Queen' (1692) and the opera 'Dido and Aeneas' (c. 1689)

Pur·chas (pə́:rtʃəs), Samuel (c. 1575–1626), English author. His collections of travelers' tales 'Purchas his Pilgrimage' (1613) and 'Hakluytus Posthumus' (1625) are often inaccurate but contain valuable historical material

pur·chase (pə́:rtʃəs) **1.** *v.t. pres. part.* **pur·chas·ing** *past* and *past part.* **pur·chased** to acquire by paying money ‖ to acquire at the cost of sacrifice, work, exposure to danger etc. ‖ (*law*) to become the owner of (real estate) otherwise than by inheritance ‖ to move or raise by means of a lever, pulley etc. **2.** *n.* the act of purchasing ‖ a thing purchased ‖ (in assessing value) annual yield in rent, *worth 20 years' purchase* ‖ mechanical advantages gained by the use of a pulley, lever etc. ‖ a device, e.g. a lever or pulley, by which this may be gained ‖ a hold or position in which leverage may be applied [A.F. *porchacier,* to seek to obtain]

purchase tax (*Br.*) a tax levied at varying percentages on the sale of certain kinds of consumer goods

pur·dah (pə́:rdə) *n.* the practice of secluding women from the sight of all men except the head of the family, by screens and curtains in the home or by veils outside it, maintained esp. in India ‖ a curtain serving to secure this seclusion **in purdah** secluded in this way [Urdu and Pers. *pardah,* veil]

pure (pjuər) *comp.* **pur·er** *superl.* **pur·est** *adj.* (of a substance) free from the presence of any other substance, *pure gold* ‖ free from contamination or admixture, *pure drinking water* ‖ free from moral guilt, *pure intentions* ‖ (*fig.*) unalloyed, *pure stupidity, pure joy* ‖ chaste, *a pure girl* ‖ not lascivious, *pure thought* ‖ not turned or related to practical use, *pure mathematics* (cf. APPLIED) ‖ (*genetics*) homozygous ‖ (of an animal) with an unmixed ancestry ‖ (*phon.,* of a vowel) not diphthongized ‖ (of a language) free from foreign elements ‖ (*philos.*) a priori ‖ (*phys.,* of a note) due to one simple periodic vibration, unmixed with any overtones [O.F. *pur*]

pure·bred 1. (pjúərbréd) *adj.* of a recognized breed, unmixed by crossbreeding **2.** (pjúərbred) *n.* an animal which is pure bred

pure culture (*bot.*) a culture containing one strain of e.g. algae or fungi

pu·rée (pjuréi, pjurí:) **1.** *n.* a thick liquid prepared by forcing cooked fruit or vegetables through a sieve ‖ a thick soup prepared in this way **2.** *v.t.* to make a purée of (fruits or vegetables) [F.]

pure·ly (pjúərli:) *adv.* in a pure way ‖ only, merely, *purely by chance*

pur·ga·tion (pə:rgéiʃən) *n.* a purging or being purged ‖ the purging of sin, esp. the process of spiritual purification in purgatory [O.F. *purgacion*]

pur·ga·tive (pə́:rgətiv) **1.** *adj.* having the quality of purging (esp. the bowels) **2.** *n.* a medicine which has this quality [F. *purgatif (purgative)*]

pur·ga·to·ri·al (pə:rgətɔ́ri:əl) *adj.* serving to expiate sin ‖ of or like purgatory [fr. L.L. *purgatorius*]

pur·ga·to·ry (pə́:rgətɔri:, pə́:rgətouri:) *pl.* **pur·ga·to·ries** *n.* a condition or place of purification, esp. (*Roman Catholicism*) the state or place where the souls of the departed, though in a condition of grace, are purified by suffering before they enter paradise ‖ a condition of suffering, *it was purgatory to have to listen* [M.L. *purgatorium*]

purge (pə:rdʒ) **1.** *v. pres. part.* **purg·ing** *past* and *past part.* **purged** *v.t.* to cause (the bowels) to be evacuated by administering or taking a purgative ‖ to remove undesirable elements from, *to purge a political party* ‖ to make expiation for, *to purge a sin* ‖ to clear (oneself or another) of a charge or suspicion **2.** *n.* a purging or being purged ‖ a purgative [O. F. *purgier*]

Pu·ri (púəri:) (formerly also Jagannath) a port (pop. 72,712) of Orissa, India, on the Bay of Bengal, among the most sacred of Hindu pilgrimage places. Temple (12th c.) to Krishna under the name of Jagannath (*JUGGERNAUT)

pu·ri·fi·ca·tion (pjuərifikéiʃən) *n.* a purifying or being purified **the Purification** the Church festival (Feb. 2 in the Western Church) commemorating the presentation of Christ in the Temple at the end of the ritual time of purification of the Virgin Mary [O.F.]

pu·ri·fi·ca·tor (pjúərifikeitər) *n.* someone who or that which cleanses, esp. (*eccles.*) a cloth used to wipe clean the chalice, the paten, and the fingers and lips of the celebrant of the Eucharist [fr. L. *purificare,* to purify]

pu·ri·fi·ca·to·ry (pjurífikətɔri:, pjurífikətouri:) *adj.* serving to purify [fr. L.L. *purificatorius*]

pu·ri·fy (pjúərifai) *pres. part.* **pu·ri·fy·ing** *past* and *past part.* **pu·ri·fied** *v.t.* to make pure by removing impurities ‖ to free from guilt or sin ‖ to free from corrupting elements [F. *purer*]

Pu·rim (púərim) *pl. n.* (construed as *sing.*) a Jewish festival commemorating the rescue of the Jews by Esther, celebrated on the 14th day of Adar (*JEWISH CALENDAR) [Heb. *pūrīm,* pl. of *pūr,* lot]

pu·rine (pjúəri:n) *n.* a crystalline heterocyclic nitrogen base ($C_5H_4N_4$) related to the pyrimidines and to uric acid ‖ any of a group of derivatives of purine, some of which (e.g. adenine and guanine) are hydrolysis products of nucleic acids [fr. G. *purin* fr. L.]

pur·ism (pjúərizəm) *n.* strict emphasis on purity, esp. in language ‖ an instance of this [fr. F. *purisme*]

pur·ist (pjúərist) *n.* a person who places great emphasis or overemphasis on linguistic purity (freedom from foreign words or bastard forms etc.) ‖ a person, who will admit no departures from some chosen method, technique or ideal of perfection [fr. F. *puriste*]

Pu·ri·tan (pjúəritən) *n.* (*hist.*) a member of a Protestant movement in England (16th and 17th cc.) which sought to purify worship in the Church of England by excluding everything for which authority could not be found in the Bible **pu·ri·tan 1.** *n.* a person who seeks to regulate his own way of life and that of the community by a narrow moral code, esp. someone who intolerantly denounces many usual pleasures as sinful or corrupting **2.** *adj.* of or relating to the Puritans **pu·ri·tán·ic, pu·ri·tán·i·cal** *adjs* **Pú·ri·tan·ism, pú·ri·tan·ism** *ns* [L. *purus,* pure or *puritas,* purity]

—Puritanism arose (1560s) as a protest against the ecclesiastical settlement of Elizabeth I. Puritans objected to the liturgy, vestments and episcopal organization of the Church of England, as not being warranted by the Scriptures. Sharp divisions arose among those Puritans who would be content with moderate reform, the Presbyterians (who wanted to abolish episcopacy), and the Brownists (who favored Congregationalism). Puritanism grew more vociferous and took on political overtones at the end of Elizabeth's reign and under the early Stuarts, culminating in the English Civil War and triumphing under Cromwell. Episcopacy returned with the Restoration (1660) and the Puritans became known as dissenters. Meanwhile in New England the Pilgrims (1620) had founded the first of several successful Puritan settlements

Puritan Revolution (*Eng. hist.*) the constitutional conflicts of the reigns of James I (1603–25) and Charles I (1625–49) and the English Civil War

pu·ri·ty (pjúəriti:) *n.* the state or quality of being pure [O.F. *purte*]

Pur·kin·je (pə:rkíndʒi:), Johannes Evangelista (1787–1869), Czech physiologist and microscopist. He is particularly noted for his ophthalmological studies

purl (pə:rl) **1.** *n.* a stitch in knitting in which the yarn is held in front of the work and the right needle is inserted into a stitch in front of the left needle to form a new stitch (cf. KNIT) ‖ (*Br.*) an edging of small loops on lace, ribbon etc. ‖ an edging of twisted gold or silver thread ‖ the gold or silver thread used in this **2.** *v.t.* to invert (stitches) in knitting ‖ to make (a garment) in purl stitches ‖ to border or decorate with purl ‖ *v.i.* to do purl stitches [etym. doubtful]

purl 1. *v.i.* (of little streams) to flow in eddies, making pleasing soft sounds **2.** *n.* the sound or movement of purling [akin to Norw. *purla,* to bubble up]

purl·er (pə́:rlər) *n.* (*Br., pop.*) a heavy headlong fall

pur·lieu (pə́:rlu:, pə́:rlju:) *n.* (*Eng. hist.*) a tract of royal forest restored to private ownership but still subject to forest laws ‖ (*pl.*) the region immediately surrounding a town, city etc., the outskirts [A.F. *puralée*]

pur·lin, pur·line (pə́:rlin) *n.* a horizontal beam supported by the principals of a roof and itself supporting the common rafters [etym. doubtful]

pur·loin (pə:rlɔ́in, pə́:rlɔin) *v.t.* to steal [A. F. *purloigner*]

pur·ple (pə́:rp'l) **1.** *n.* a composite deep color of red and blue ‖ a pigment, fabric etc. of this color ‖ Tyrian purple **the purple** royal or very noble rank **2.** *adj.* of the color purple **3.** *v. pres. part.* **pur·pling** *past* and *past part.* **pur·pled** *v.i.* to assume a purple color ‖ *v.t.* to make purple [O.E.]

Purple Heart a heart-shaped medal awarded to U.S. servicemen for wounds received in action

purple of Cassius a mixture of stannic oxide and colloidal gold, used as a purple pigment and in making ruby glass

purple passage (in a book, play etc.) a passage overcharged with emotive words and sentiments

purple patch a purple passage

pur·plish (pə́:rpliʃ) *adj.* having a purple tinge

pur·ply (pə:rpli:) *adj.* purplish

pur·port 1. (pə:rpɔ́rt, pə:rpóurt) *v.t.* (*rhet.*) to have as meaning or purpose, *what do his actions purport?* ‖ (with 'to be') to be meant to appear, *the letter purports to be in his writing* **2.** (pə́:rpɔrt, pə́:rpourt) *n.* the meaning of a document, speech etc. [A.F. *purporter*]

pur·pose (pə́:rpəs) *pres. part.* **pur·pos·ing** *past* and *past part.* **pur·posed** *v.t.* (*old-fash.*) to have as intention (to do something) [O.F. *porposer*]

purpose *n.* a result which it is desired to obtain and which is kept in mind in performing an action ‖ (*old-fash.*) willpower, *weak of purpose* **on purpose** deliberately, intentionally ‖ with a specific intention, *he came on purpose to see them* **to no (little, good) purpose** with no (little, good) effect **to the purpose** relevant **púr·pose·ful** *adj.* serving or having a purpose **púr·pose·less** *adj.* **púr·pose·ly** *adv.* on purpose **púr·pos·ive** *adj.* purposeful [A.F.]

pur·po·siv·ism (pə́:rpəsivizəm) *n.* (*psych.*) approach to psychological analysis based on the theory that behavior is purposeful and that a person is responsible for his or her condition and destiny

pur·pu·ra (pə́:rpjərə) *n.* the occurrence of multiple small purplish hemorrhages in the skin and mucous membranes, due to a variety of blood and blood vessel disorders **pur·pu·ric** (pə:rpjúərik) *adj.* [L.=purple]

pur·pure (pə́:rpjər) *n.* (*heraldry*) purple [O.E. fr. L.]

purr (pə:r) **1.** *n.* the soft, intermittent vibratory sound made by a contented cat ‖ a similar sound, *the purr of an engine* **2.** *v.i.* to make this sound [imit.]

purse (pə:rs) **1.** *n.* a small container for coins etc., carried in a pocket or handbag ‖ a handbag ‖ a sum of money collected for a charity, or offered as a gift or prize ‖ (*rhet.*) financial resources ‖ a baglike receptacle **to hold the purse strings** to control the money in a household etc. **2.** *v.t. pres. part.* **purs·ing** *past* and *past part.* **pursed** (sometimes with 'up') to pucker, *she pursed her lips in displeasure* [O.E. *purs*, prob. fr. L.L. *bursa*]

purs·er (pə́:rsər) *n.* a ship's officer responsible for accounts etc. and for the welfare of passengers on a passenger boat [PURSE n.]

purs·lane (pə́:rslin, pə́:rslein) *n.* *Portulaca oleracea*, fam. *Portulacaceae*, a garden annual, eaten raw in salads or boiled [O.F. *porcelaine*]

pur·su·ance (pərsú:əns) *n.* the act of pursuing an end, object etc. ‖ the carrying out of a plan etc.

pur·su·ant (pərsú:ənt) **1.** *adj.* (*rhet.*) pursuing **2.** *adv.* (with 'to') in accordance with, *pursuant to the act* [O.F. *porsuiant, poursuiant*]

pur·sue (pərsú:) *pres. part.* **pur·su·ing** *past* and *past part.* **pur·sued** *v.t.* to follow in order to capture, overtake etc., *to pursue a thief* ‖ to harass (someone) persistently, *bad luck pursued him* ‖ to inflict persistent attentions on (someone) ‖ to continue with, *to pursue one's studies* ‖ to engage in, *to pursue a hobby* ‖ to go on talking about, *we will not pursue the subject* ‖ *v.i.* to go in pursuit ‖ to resume an argument or narrative after interruption [O.F. *poursuir*]

pur·suit (pərsú:t) *n.* the act of pursuing‖ the act of proceeding with or towards an aim ‖ an occupation, *an aimless pursuit* [O.F. *poursuite*]

pur·sui·vant (pə́:rsivənt, pə́:rswivənt) *n.* (*heraldry*) an officer of arms of lower rank than a herald [O.F. *poursuivant*, following]

pur·sy (pə́:rsi:) *adj.* corpulent ‖ shortwinded [fr. PURSE]

pu·ru·lence (pjúərulәns, pjúərjuləns) *n.* the state of being purulent ‖ pus [fr. L.L. *purulentia*]

pu·ru·lent (pjúərulənt, pjúərjulənt) *adj.* consisting of, or exuding pus [fr. L. *purulentus*]

Pu·rús (pu:rú:s) a river (2,000 miles long) flowing from S.E. Peru into E. Brazil, joining the Amazon above Manaus. It is navigable for river steamers for 800 miles, and for small boats for most of its length

pur·vey (pə:rvéi) *v.t.* (*old-fash.*) to supply (groceries) as a commercial activity ‖ to provide (information) [A.F. *porveier, purveier*]

pur·vey·ance (pə:rvéiəns) *n.* the act of purveying ‖ that which is purveyed ‖ (*Eng. hist.*) the royal right to buy provisions, services and supplies at a price fixed by the purveyors [O.F. *porveaunce, purveaunce*]

pur·vey·or (pə:rvéiər) *n.* someone who deals in groceries, esp. on a large scale ‖ (*Eng. hist.*) a royal agent who bought supplies under the right of purveyance [A.F. *purveür, purveour*]

pur·view (pə́:rvju:) *n.* the extent of the meaning of a document ‖ the extent of the knowledge, authority or responsibility etc. of a person, group etc., *the matter lies outside his purview* ‖ (*law*) that part of a statute which includes the enacting clauses [A.F.=provided]

pus (pʌs) *n.* yellowish-white fluid matter, produced by infected body tissue, and composed of bacteria and disintegrated tissue [L.]

Pu·san (pú:sɑ́n) (*Jap.* Fusan) the chief port (pop. 2,879,600) of South Korea, on the east coast, exporting rice, soybeans etc. Industries: shipbuilding, textiles, rubber, food processing. University

Pu·sey (pjú:zi:), Edward Bouverie (1800–82), British churchman. He became the leader of the Oxford movement after Newman had been received into the Roman Catholic Church

Pu·sey·ism (pjú:zi:izəm) *n.* the Oxford movement **Pú·sey·ite** *n.* an adherent of this [after E. B. *Pusey*]

push (puʃ) **1.** *v.t.* to apply a force to (something) in order to make it move away from the person or thing applying the force (opp. PULL) ‖ to move (something) away or forward by applying such a force, *to push a bicycle uphill* ‖ to make (a way) by forcing obstacles aside ‖ (with 'up', 'down', 'along' etc.) to cause to move by exerting pressure ‖ (with 'up') to cause (something) to increase as if under pressure, *the wage increase pushed up prices* ‖ to exert influence upon (someone) so that he acts in a desired way, *they pushed him into doing it* ‖ to force toward or beyond the limits of capacity or endurance, *they pushed the child too hard at school* ‖ to develop (an idea etc.), esp. to an extreme degree ‖ to urge the qualities of (a person or thing) in order to secure some advantage ‖ to stimulate (someone) in his will to succeed ‖ to make a steady effort to secure recognition for (a claim) ‖ *v.i.* to apply a force to something in order to make it move away from the person or thing applying the force ‖ to move by the application of such force ‖ to make a steady effort towards some end, *to push for more pay* ‖ to advance, esp. with persistence or energy **to be pushed for time** (or **money**) to be short of time (or money) **to push off** (*pop.*) to leave **to push on** to proceed, esp. with determination **to push one's luck** to act rashly, take a dangerous risk **2.** *n.* the act of pushing ‖ an instance of this ‖ a force which pushes ‖ (*mil.*) an offensive ‖ the ineluctable moment of decision, *when it came to the push* ‖ influence, *to use push* ‖ self-assertion, aggressive drive **at a push** (*Br.*) if absolutely necessary **to get the push** (*Br.*) to be dismissed **to give (someone) the push** (*Br.*) to dismiss (someone) [F. *pousser*]

push·ball (púʃbɔl) *n.* a game played by two teams of usually 11 each, in which a 50-lb ball, 6 ft in diameter, is pushed toward either of two opposite goals ‖ this ball

push button a device which, when pressed with the finger, makes or breaks an electrical circuit and so controls an electrical mechanism

push-button dialing making a telephone connection by pushing buttons, using Bell System Touch Tone or similar equipment

push·cart (púʃkɑrt) *n.* a hand-pushed cart used esp. by street vendors

push·chair (púʃtʃɛər) *n.* (*Br.*) a stroller (child's wheeled chair)

push·down, pushdown list, or **pushdown stack** (púʃdaun) *n.* (*computer*) a list on which the last item stored is the first item retrieved, and the first item is the second item, the second the third, etc.

push·er (púʃər) *n.* a person who is aggressive in furthering his own career ‖ (*colloq.*) one who sells drugs illegally

push·ing (púʃiŋ) *adj.* aggressively self-assertive, esp. for self-advancement

Push·kin (púʃkin), Alexander Sergeievich (1799–1837), Russian poet. novelist and short-story writer. Some of his most important poetical works are 'The Captive of the Caucasus' (1822), 'Boris Godunov' (1825) and 'Eugene Onegin' (1825–33). His best-known prose work is 'The Captain's Daughter' (1836)

push·o·ver (púʃouvər) *n.* (*pop.*) something very easy to accomplish, or very easily accomplished ‖ (*pop.*) a person easily persuaded, tricked etc.

push·pin (púʃpin) *n.* a short pin with a large, often colored, head, used to mark positions on a map etc.

push shot (*billiards*) a shot in which the cue stays in contact with the cue ball until it strikes the object ball or in which the cue strikes the cue ball twice

Push·tu, Pash·tu (pʌ́ʃtu:) *n.* the principal language of Afghanistan, an Iranian language spoken by about 4 millions [Pers. *Pashtō*]

push-up (púʃʌp) (*Am.*=*Br.* press-up) *n.* an exercise in which a person pushes himself up from a face-down prone position by placing his palms on the ground or floor at shoulder level and straightening his arms (while keeping the trunk and legs rigidly straight) and lets himself down by bending his arms

pu·sil·la·nim·i·ty (pju:sələnímiti:) *n.* the quality of being pusillanimous [F. *pusillanimité*]

pu·sil·lan·i·mous (pju:səlǽnəməs) *adj.* showing a lack of moral courage [fr. eccles. L. *pusillanimis* fr. *pusillus*, very small+*animus*, mind, spirit]

puss (pus) *n.* (pet name for) a cat [origin unknown]

puss·y (púsi:) *pl.* **puss·ies** *n.* (pet name for) a cat

puss·y·foot (púsi:fut) *v.i.* (*pop.*) to avoid committing oneself

pussy willow either of two species of willow bearing large silky catkins, *Salix capera* and *S. discolor*

pus·tu·lar (pʌ́stʃulər) *adj.* like pustules ‖ covered with pustules [fr. Mod. L. *pustularis*]

pus·tu·late 1. (pʌ́stʃulit) *adj.* covered with pustules **2.** (pʌ́stʃuleit) *v. pres. part.* **pus·tu·lat·ing** *past* and *past part.* **pus·tu·lat·ed** *v.t.* to cause to form into pustules ‖ *v.i.* to form into pustules [fr. L.L. *pustulare* (*pustulatus*)]

pus·tule (pʌ́stʃu:l) *n.* a tiny abscess on the skin surface ‖ (*zool.*) a warty excrescence on the skin, e.g. in toads ‖ (*bot.*) a small wart or swelling on a leaf, either natural or caused by parasitic influence [fr. L. *pustula*]

pus·tu·lous (pʌ́stʃuləs) *adj.* pustular [fr. L.L. *pustulosus*]

put (put) **1.** *v. pres. part.* **put·ting** *past* and *past part.* **put** *v.t.* to cause to be in a specified place, position etc., *put the books on the table* ‖ to cause to be in a specified condition, situation, relationship etc., *to put someone's mind at rest* ‖ to submit for attention or consideration, *to put a proposal before a committee* ‖ to cause to be voted on, *to put a motion* ‖ (followed by 'to') to subject, *to put someone to expense* ‖ (usually followed by 'in' or 'into') to formulate, *put it in writing* ‖ (followed by 'at') to cause (a horse) to attempt to clear an obstacle ‖ (followed by 'on', 'upon') to impose, *to put a tax on beer* ‖ (followed by 'to' or 'into') to apply, bring to bear, *to put one's mind to a problem* ‖ (followed by 'on') to lay (blame, responsibility etc.) ‖ (followed by 'to' and pres. part.) to set (someone) to work of a specified kind, *to put the troops to digging trenches* ‖ (followed by 'in' or 'into') to invest, *to put one's money in copper shares* ‖ (followed by 'on') to gamble (money), *he put his last penny on that horse* ‖ to estimate, *he put the price at five pounds* ‖ (followed by 'on' or 'upon') to attribute, ascribe, *to put a high value on someone's service* ‖ to fix (a limit etc.), *to put an end to something* ‖ to throw (the shot) with a thrust from the shoulder ‖ *v.i.* (of a ship) to take a specified course, *to put out to sea* **to put about** to change the course of (a boat) ‖ (of a boat) to go on the contrary tack **to put across** to convey effectively the meaning, dramatic effect etc. of **to put aside** to place to one side, esp. as of no immediate use or importance ‖ to save (money etc.) for later use **to put away** to place (something) where it should be when not in use ‖ to save (money etc.) for later use ‖ (*pop.*) to consume (food or drink) ‖ to have an animal) killed painlessly **to put back** to restore (something) to its former place ‖ to move the hands of (a clock) backwards ‖ (of a boat) to return to harbor **to put by** to save (money etc.) for later use **to put down** to stop (a rebellion etc.) by force ‖ to commit to writing ‖ to pay as deposit ‖ to place (bottled wine) in a cellar for drinking later ‖ (*Br.*) to have (an animal) killed painlessly ‖ (*Br.*) to preserve (eggs) ‖ to attribute, *to put a remark down to bad humor* ‖ to enter (an item) on a bill, account etc. **to put forward** to submit (a proposal etc.) for attention or consideration ‖ to propose (someone or oneself) as a candidate **to put in** to present (a claim) ‖ to do (a specified amount of a specified activity), *to put in two hours' weeding* ‖ (of a boat) to enter a port **to put it across (someone)** (*Br., pop.*) to deceive (someone) **to put it on** to pretend **to put it over on (someone)** (*pop.*) to deceive (someone) **to put it past (someone) to do (something)** (*neg.* and *interrog.*) to consider (someone) morally incapable of doing (something) **to put off** to postpone (something planned) ‖ to postpone an engagement made with (someone) ‖ to cause (someone) to cease to like something ‖ to cause (someone) to be unable to concentrate on something ‖ to avoid giving a direct answer to (someone) or undertaking (something) **to put on** to clothe oneself with ‖ to assume (an attitude, expression etc.) deceptively ‖ to apply (a brake etc.) ‖ to cause (a light etc.) to work || to increase (speed) || to present (an entertainment) to the public || to move the hands of (a clock) forwards || to acquire extra (weight) **to put out** to extinguish (a flame, light or fire) || to cause (someone) to feel affronted || to inconvenience || to produce industrially || to gouge out (eyes) || to publish || (*baseball*) to retire (a batter or a runner) || (*cricket*) to cause (a batsman) to be out || to dislocate (a joint) || to give (work) to be done off the premises **to put over** to convey effectively the meaning, dramatic effect etc. of || to postpone || to succeed in doing (something) by craft or against odds **to put through** to cause to undergo, *he put her through great suffering* || to negotiate (a business deal) || to make (a telephone call) || to connect (a telephone caller) with the person he is calling **to put through it** (*Br.*) to cause (someone) to suffer or to make a great physical or mental effort **to put together** to assemble **to put up** to offer (resistance, a fight etc.) || to increase (a price etc.) || to offer (someone) as candidate || to offer oneself as candidate || to provide (someone) with lodging || to be provided with lodging at a hotel etc. || to provide (financial backing) || to stake (money) || to pack in containers || to publish (banns) || to cause (game) to leave cover || to preserve (fruit, vegetables etc.) || to construct || to offer (for sale, auction etc.) || (with 'to') to incite (a person) to some action, esp. to some mischief or crime **to put upon** to impose on **to put up with** to endure, esp. without resentment or complaint **2.** *n.* a throw of the weight or shot || (*med.*) the outer, darker part of the lenticular nucleus of the brain **3.** *adj.* (in the phrase) **to stay put** to remain in the same position, condition, situation etc. [O.E. *putian*, to thrust]

pu·ta·men (pju:téimin) *pl.* **pu·tam·i·na** (pju:tǽminə) *n.* (*bot.*) the hard stone of a drupe, e.g. of a plum [L.=that which falls off in pruning]

pu·ta·tive (pjú:tətiv) *adj.* commonly thought to be, reputed [F. *putatif* or fr. L.L. *putativus*]

put-down (pʌ́tdaun) *n.* an act or statement to embarrass or denigrate another **—put down** *v.*

put·log (pʌ́tlɔg, pútlɔg, pʌ́tlɒg, pútlɒg) *n.* a short horizontal beam supporting scaffolding planks, with one end resting on the scaffolding and the other in a hole left or made for it in a wall [etym. doubtful]

put-on (pútɔn) *n.* a tease or spoof **—put-on** *adj.* **—put on** *n.*

put on hold *v.* (*colloq.*) to delay momentarily, from the telephone operator's procedure

Pu·to Shan (pú:touʃán) a Buddhist sacred island in the Chushan Archipelago China: temples, monasteries

put-out (pútaut) *n.* (*baseball*) the act of retiring a baserunner or batter

pu·tre·fac·tion (pju:trifǽkʃən) *n.* the chemical decomposition of animal or vegetable tissue, esp. proteins, caused by bacteria, fungi etc. [O. F. or fr. L. *putrefactio (putrefactionis)*]

pu·tre·fac·tive (pju:trifǽktiv) *adj.* of, relating to or causing putrefaction [F. *putréfactif*]

pu·tre·fy (pjú:trifai) *v. pres. part.* **pu·tre·fy·ing** *past* and *past part.* **pu·tre·fied** *v.i.* to become putrid || *v.t.* to cause to become putrid [F. *putréfier*]

pu·tres·cence (pju:trés'ns) *n.* the condition of being putrescent

pu·tres·cent (pju:trés'nt) *adj.* becoming putrid || of or relating to putrefaction [fr. L. *putrescens (putrescentis)*]

pu·tres·ci·ble (pju:trésəb'l) *adj.* liable to be putrefied

pu·tres·cine (pju:trési:n) *n.* a poisonous ptomaine, $NH_2(CH_2)_4NH_2$, formed by the decomposition of animal tissue

pu·trid (pjú:trid) *adj.* rotten, decayed || of, relating to or caused by decay **pu·trid·i·ty** *n.* [fr. L. *putridus*]

puts and calls *PRIVILEGES

putsch (putʃ) *n.* a coup d'etat [G.=push fr. Swiss dial.]

putt (pʌt) **1.** *v.t.* (*golf*) to strike (the ball) gently so that it rolls across the green towards the hole || *v.i.* (*golf*) to play the ball in this way **2.** *n.* (*golf*) a stroke made in this way [akin to PUT v.]

put·tee (pʌ́ti:) *n.* a cloth strip wound firmly around the leg from the ankle to the knee || a leather gaiter [Hind. *paṭṭī*, bandage]

putt·er (pʌ́tər) *n.* (*golf*) a short-shafted wood or iron with an almost vertical face, used for putting

put·ter (pʌ́tər) *v.i.* to busy oneself in an agreeable though somewhat aimless way || to loiter, dawdle [alt. fr. POTTER]

put·ty (pʌ́ti:) **1.** *n.* powdered chalk mixed with linseed oil to form a highly malleable mass which hardens when the oil oxidizes, used e.g. to hold window glass in its frame || any of several other malleable cements made with linseed oil || impure tin oxide used for polishing by jewelers **2.** *v.t. pres. part.* **put·ty·ing** *past* and *past part.* **put·tied** to fix, fill or cover with putty [F. *potée*, a potful]

Pu·tu·ma·yo (pu:tu:májɔ) a tributary (980 miles long) of the Amazon. It flows from W. Colombia. forming most of the southern frontier, into N.E. Brazil (as the Ica)

put·up (pútʌp) *adj.* (*pop.*) prearranged with guile, esp. with the connivance of insiders

Pu·vis de Cha·vannes (pyvi:dʃævæn), Pierre (1824–98), French painter, notably of large-scale murals and decorative panels including 'Life of St Geneviève' (1898)

Puy-de-Dôme (pwi:dədoum) a department (area 3,090 sq. miles, pop. 580,000) of France in the N. Massif Central (*AUVERGNE, *BOURBONNAIS). Chief town: Clermont-Ferrand || the summit (4.806 ft) of les Puys, a chain of volcanic cones in the N. Massif Central

puz·zle (pʌ́z'l) **1.** *v. pres. part.* **puz·zling** *past* and *past part.* **puz·zled** *v.t.* to perplex (someone) || *v.i.* to make a great mental effort to find a solution or meaning, *to puzzle over a problem* **to puzzle out** to find (a solution or meaning) by means of great mental effort **2.** *n.* a question or device which sets a problem to be worked out by ingenuity || something which puzzles || the state of being puzzled [etym. doubtful]

pya (pjɑ, pi:ɑ́) *n.* a monetary unit of Burma equal to one hundredth of a kyat || a coin of the value of one pya [Burmese]

pyaemia *PYEMIA

pyc·nid·i·o·spore (piknídi:əspɔr, pikní di:əspour) *n.* a spore formed in a pycnidium

pyc·nid·i·um (pikníd i:əm) *pl.* **pyc·nid·i·a** (pikníd i:ə) *n.* (*bot.*) a small flasklike organ or spermagonium which forms pycnidiospores and conidiophores, e.g. in various fungi [Mod. L. fr. Gk *puknos*, thick+*-idion*, dim. suffix]

pyc·nom·e·ter, pyk·nom·e·ter (piknómitər) *n.* a graduated glass vessel used to determine the variation of density of a liquid with variation of temperature [fr. Gk *puknos*, thick+METER]

pye-dog, pi-dog (páidɔg, páidɒg) *n.* a mongrel dog which hangs around Indian and other Asian villages

py·e·li·tis (paiəláitis) *n.* (*med.*) inflammation of the pelvis of the kidney [Mod. L. fr. Gk *puelos*, trough]

py·e·mi·a, py·ae·mi·a (paií:mi:ə) *n.* (*med.*) pus in the blood, a condition causing multiple abscesses throughout the body **py·é·mic, py·á·mic** *adj.* [Mod. L. fr. Gk *puon*, pus+*haima*, blood]

py·gid·i·um (paidʒídi:əm) *pl.* **py·gid·i·a** (paidʒídi:ə) *n.* a caudal shield covering the abdomen of certain arthropods || the terminal abdominal segment in certain insects [Mod. L. fr. Gk *pugidion*, dim. of *pugē*, rump]

Pyg·ma·li·on (pigméili:ən) (*Gk mythol.*) Cypriot king and sculptor who fell in love with the statue he had made of a girl. He successfully begged Aphrodite to bring the statue to life

Pygmalion legendary king of Tyre, brother of Dido

pyg·my, pig·my (pígmi:) **1.** *pl.* **pyg·mies, pig·mies** *n.* a person of very small stature **Pyg·my, Pig·my** *pl.* **Pyg·mies, Pig·mies** a member of a Negrillo people of very small stature of equatorial Africa || a member of a mythical race of dwarfs described by ancient Greek authors as inhabiting Ethiopia or India **2.** *adj.* of or relating to a person of very small stature **Pyg·my, Pig·my** of or relating to the Pygmies [fr. L. *pygmaeus* fr. Gk fr. *pugmē*, length from elbow to knuckles]

pyjamas *PAJAMAS

pyk·nic (píknik) *adj.* (*anthrop.*) having an endomorphic physique [fr. Gk *puknos*, compact]

pyknometer *PYCNOMETER

py·lon (páilɒn) *n.* a lofty structure, typically of open steelwork, used esp. to carry electric cables etc. over a long span || (*archit.*) a large monumental gateway having two truncated pyramidal towers, esp. on an ancient Egyptian temple [Gk *pulōn*, gateway]

py·lor·ic (pailɔ́rik, pailɒ́rik) *adj.* of or relating to the pylorus

py·lo·rus (pailɔ́rəs, pailóurəs) *pl.* **py·lo·ri** (pailɔ́rai, pailóurai) *n.* (*anat.*) the opening from the stomach into the intestine of vertebrates, usually including a muscular valve || (in some invertebrates) a posterior division of the stomach [L.L. fr. Gk *pulōros*, gatekeeper]

Py·los (páilɒs) an ancient port of Messenia, S.W. Greece

Pym (pim), John (c. 1583–1643), English parliamentarian, one of the leaders of the opposition to Charles I, notably in the Long Parliament

Pyong·yang (pjɔ́ŋjɑ́ŋ) the capital (pop. 1,700,000) and industrial center of North Korea, founded c. 1122 B.C. Industries: anthracite mining (nearby), iron and steel, mechanical engineering. textiles, sugar, cement, chemicals, railway stock, light manufacturing. Ruins: tombs (1st c. B.C.), gates and Buddhist temples. University (1946)

py·or·rhe·a, py·or·rhoe·a (paiərí:ə) *n.* (*med.*) a discharge of pus, esp. from the gums [Mod. L. Gk *puon*, pus+*rhoia*, a flow]

pyr·a·mid (pírəmid) **1.** *n.* (*geom.*) a solid figure of which the base is a polygon and the other faces are triangles with a common vertex || any of the very large square-based stone monuments of this form, constructed by the ancient Egyptians as royal burial places, esp. during the Old Kingdom (c. 2614-2181 B.C.), and by the Aztecs and Mayas as centers of ritual worship. The huge pyramid of Khufu at Giza was one of the Seven Wonders of the World || anything shaped thus || a group of things piled up or arranged in this form || (*anat.*) any of various parts resembling this form || the shape of a well-organized staffing structure in relation to levels of responsibility or to age distribution, or any comparable organizational structure || (*crystall.*) any crystal form having inclined faces which intersect all three axes of symmetry || the series of buying operations in which a speculator pyramids on an exchange **2.** *v.t.* to build up in the form of a pyramid || *v.i.* to engage in a series of buying operations during a continued rise, buying out of the paper profits made on the transactions **py·ra·mi·dal** (pirǽmid'l) *adj.* [L. *pyramis (pyramidis)*]

Pyramids, Battle of the a victory (July 1798) in which Napoleon defeated the Mamelukes and gained control of Egypt

py·rar·gy·rite (pairárdʒərait) *n.* a naturally occurring silver antimony sulfide, Ag_3SbS_3, having a rhombohedral crystalline form [fr. Gk *pur*, fire+*arguros*, silver]

pyre (páiər) *n.* a heaped mass of material for the burning of a corpse [fr. L. *pyra* fr. Gk]

py·rene (páiri:n) *n.* a yellow, crystalline hydrocarbon, $C_{16}H_{10}$, derived by distillation from coal tar [fr. Gk *pur*, fire]

pyrene *n.* (*bot.*) the seed of a drupelet [fr. Mod. L. *pyrena* fr. Gk]

Pyr·e·nees (pírəni:z) (*F.* les Pyrénées) the mountain range (270 miles long, mainly 6,000–9,000 ft high in the center, lower toward the coasts) separating France from Spain. Two main roads and two railways cross them by passes over 5,000 ft, but other main routes follow the coasts. The higher peaks are rugged, with perpetual snowfields, but the lower slopes serve as cattle and sheep pasture. The Spanish side is drier and less populated than the French. Industries: hydroelectricity, tourism

Pyrénées, Basses- *PYRÉNÉES ATLANTIQUES

Pyrénées, Hautes- *HAUTES-PYRÉNÉES

Py·ré·nées-At·lant·iques (pi:reineizɑtlɑntik) a department (area 2,977 sq. miles, pop. 534,700) of S.W. France (*BÉARN *NAVARE, *BASQUE COUNTRY). Chief town: Pau

Py·ré·nées-O·rien·tales (pi:reineizɔrjɑ̃ntæl) a department (area 1,598 sq. miles, pop. 299,500) of S. France (*ROUSILLON). Chief town: Perpignan

Pyrenees, Treaty of the a treaty (1659) between France and Spain, in which Spain ceded Roussillon and part of Flanders to France and the marriage of Louis XIV and the infanta of Spain was arranged

py·re·thrum (pairí:θrəm) *n.* *Chrysanthemum coccineum*, fam. *Compositae*, which yields insecticide, or any of several garden perennials derived from it || an insecticide obtained from the dried powdered flowers of the pyrethrum [L. fr. Gk *purethron*, feverfew]

py·rex·i·a (pairéksi:ə) *n.* (*med.*) fever **py·réx·i·al, py·réx·ic** *adjs* [Mod. L. fr. Gk *purexis*]

pyr·he·li·om·e·ter (paiərhi:li:ɒ́mitər) *n.* an instrument used to determine the solar constant

CONCISE PRONUNCIATION KEY: **(a)** æ, *cat*; ɑ, *car*; ɔ *fawn*; ei, *snake*. **(e)** e, *hen*; i:, *sheep*; iə, *deer*; ɛə, *bear*. **(i)** i, *fish*; ai, *tiger*; ə:, *bird*. **(o)** o, *ox*; au, *cow*; ou, *goat*; u, *poor*; ɔi, *royal*. **(u)** ʌ, *duck*; u, *bull*; u:, *goose*; ə, *bacillus*; ju:, *cube*. x, *loch*; θ, *think*; ð, *bother*; z, *Zen*; ʒ, *corsage*; dʒ, *savage*; ŋ, *orangutang*; j, *yak*; ʃ, *fish*; tʃ, *fetch*; 'l, *rabble*; 'n, *redden*. Complete pronunciation key appears inside front cover.

of radiation [fr. PYRO-+ Gk *hēlios*, sun+ME-TER]

pyr·i·dine (píridi:n) *n.* a heterocyclic compound, C_5H_5N, with an unpleasant smell and taste, used to make methylated spirit unpalatable, and as the basis of compounds used in medicine [fr. Gk *pur*, fire]

pyr·i·form (pírifɔrm) *adj.* (esp. of the forward aperture of the nasal canal in the skull) pear-shaped [fr. Mod. L. *pyriformis* fr. *pirum.* pear]

py·ri·meth·a·mine [$C_{12}H_{13}C1N_4$] (pairəméθəmi:n) *n.* (*pharm.*) an antimalarial drug; marketed as Daraprim

py·rim·i·dine (pairímidi:n) *n.* a crystalline, weakly basic, heterocyclic compound ($C_4H_4N_2$) ‖ any of a group of derivatives of pyrimidine, some of which (e.g. thymine and cytosine) are hydrolysis products of nucleic acids [altered fr. PYRIDINE]

py·rite (páirait) *n.* iron disulfide, FeS_2 [fr. L. *pyrites*, firestone fr. Gk]

py·ri·tes (pairáiti:z, páiraits) *pl.* **py·ri·tes** *n.* (*mineral.*) one of several disulfides of metals, e.g. of iron or copper occurring as ores **py·rít·ic** *adj.* [L.=firestone fr. Gk]

pyro- (páirou) *prefix* fire ‖ heat ‖ producing or derived from fire or heat ‖ causing fever [fr. Gk fr. *pur*, fire]

py·ro·chem·i·cal (pairoukémik'l) *adj.* pertaining to chemical changes at high temperatures

py·ro·clas·tic (pairouklǽstik) *adj.* (geol., of a rock) formed of igneous material subjected to fragmentation [fr. PYRO-+Gk *klastos*, broken]

py·ro·e·lec·tric (pairouiléktrik) *adj.* of, relating to or acquiring pyroelectricity

py·ro·e·lec·tric·i·ty (pairouilektrísiti:) *n.* the electric charges produced in various crystals by heating

py·ro·gal·lol (pairougǽlɔl) *n.* a crystalline phenol, $C_6H_3(OH)_3$, used as a developer in photography [fr. Gk *pur*, fire+GALLIC ACID]

py·ro·gen·ic (pairoudʒénik) *adj.* producing or produced by heat ‖ igneous in origin ‖ producing or produced by fever [fr. PYRO-+-*genic*, produced]

py·ro·lig·ne·ous (pairoulígni:əs) *adj.* produced by the destructive distillation of wood [F. *pyroligneux* fr. Gk *pur*, fire+L. *lignium*, wood]

pyroligneous acid an acid liquid produced by the destructive distillation of wood, the chief source of commercial acetic acid

py·ro·lu·site (pairoulú:sait) *n.* naturally occurring manganese dioxide, MnO_2 [fr. PYRO-+Gk *lousis*, a washing]

py·rol·y·sis (pairólisis) *n.* chemical decomposition by heat [Mod. L. fr. PYRO-+Gk *lusis*, a loosing]

py·ro·lyt·ic incinerator (pairəlítik) an incinerator that requires little oxygen for burning, reducing pollution and producing gas suitable for burning

py·ro·ma·ni·a (pairouméini:ə) *n.* an irrational compulsion to destroy by fire **py·ro·ma·ni·ac** (pairouméini:æk) *n.* **py·ro·ma·ni·a·cal** (pairoumənáiək'l) *adj.*

py·rom·e·ter (pairómitər) *n.* an instrument used to measure temperatures too high for ordinary thermometers **py·ro·met·ric** (pairoumétrik), **py·ro·mét·ri·cal** *adjs* **py·róm·e·try** *n.*

py·ro·mor·phite (pairoumórfait) *n.* a naturally occurring crystalline, usually colored, double chloride and phosphate of lead, $PbCl\cdot Pb_4(PO_4)_3$ [G. *pyromorphit* fr. Gk *pur*, fire+*morphē*, shape]

py·rone (páiroun) *n.* an unsaturated heterocyclic ring compound, $C_5H_4O_2$, used as the basis of yellow dyes [fr. PYRO-+Gk -*ōnē*, patronymic suffix]

py·rope (páiroup) *n.* a dark red variety of garnet, used as a gem [fr. L. fr. Gk *purōpos*, fiery-eyed]

py·ro·phor·ic (pairəfórik, pairəfórik) *adj.* igniting spontaneously ‖ (of an alloy) emitting sparks when scraped or struck [fr. Gk *purophoros* fr. *pur*, fire+*pherein*, to bear]

py·ro·sis (pairóusis) *n.* (*med.*) heartburn [Mod. L. fr. Gk]

py·ro·some (páirəsoum) *n.* a member of *Pyrosoma*, fam. *Pyrosomaditae*, a genus of highly phosphorescent compound ascidians of tropical seas, which unite into a free-swimming colony in the form of a hollow cylinder closed at one end [fr. Mod. L. *Pyrosoma* fr. Gk *pur*-, fire+*sōma*, body] .

py·ro·stat (páirəstæt) *n.* any mechanical device which automatically warns of a fire, or which sets in operation an extinguisher [fr. PYRO-+Gk *statēs*, one that causes to stand]

py·ro·sul·fu·ric acid, py·ro·sul·phu·ric acid (pairousʌlfjúərik) a crystalline acid, $H_2S_2O_7$, formed by combining sulfur trioxide with sulfuric acid

py·ro·tech·nic (pairoutéknik) *adj.* of or relating to pyrotechnics **py·ro·téch·ni·cal** *adj.*

py·ro·téch·nics *n.* the art of making or displaying fireworks ‖ (*pl.*) a brilliant or witty display **py·ro·téch·nist**, **py·ro·tech·ny** *ns* [fr. PYRO-+Gk *technikos* fr. *technē*, art]

py·ro·tox·in (pairoutóksin) *n.* one of various toxins capable of causing fever

py·ro·tron (páirətrɒn) *n.* device using magnetic mirrors in a tube surrounded by electric coils used to reflect charged particles; prevents end leaks in fusion research

py·rox·ene (pairóksi:n) *n.* any of a class of double silicates (e.g. of calcium and magnesium) occurring widely in igneous rocks **py·rox·en·ic** (pairoksénik) *adj.* **py·rox·e·nite** (pairóksənait) *n.* an igneous rock composed chiefly of pyroxene, with no olivine [fr. Gk *pur*, fire+*xenos*, stranger]

py·rox·y·lin, py·rox·y·line (pairóksəlin) *n.* any of the lower nitrates of cellulose, dissolved in an organic solvent (usually alcohol and ether) and used in making lacquers, celluloid etc. [F. *pyroxyline* fr. Gk *pur*, fire+*xulon*, wood]

pyr·rhic (pírik) *n.* an ancient Greek war dance performed in armor [fr. L. *pyrrhica* or Gk *purrhichē*]

pyrrhic 1. *n.* a metrical foot of two short syllables **2.** *adj.* of or composed of pyrrhics [fr. L. *pyrrhichius* fr. Gk]

Pyrrhic victory a victory won with terrible loss of life or otherwise at too heavy a cost [after the victory of PYRRHUS at Asculum (279 B.C.)]

Pyr·rho (pírou) (c. 360–c. 270 B.C.), Greek philosopher, founder of skepticism. He thought it impossible to arrive at any certain knowledge and held that the wise man should not judge but should aim at a balanced imperturbability

Pyr·rho·nism (pírənizəm) *n.* the skeptical philosophy taught by Pyrrho ‖ philosopical skepticism

pyr·rho·tite (pírətait) *n.* a bronze-colored sulfide of iron, often with some nickel, occurring naturally [fr. Gk *purrhotēs*, redness]

Pyr·rhus (pírəs) (c. 318–272 B.C.), king of Epirus (295–272 B.C.). He invaded Italy to assist Tarentum (modern Tarento) against Rome, and defeated the Romans at Heraclea (280 B.C.) and at Asculum (279 B.C.), although with very heavy loss to his own army. After being defeated by the Romans at Beneventum (275 B.C.) he withdrew to Greece, where he was killed besieging Argos

Pyr·rhus a son of Achilles who killed Priam at the siege of Troy and carried off Andromache

pyr·role, pyr·rol (píroul) *n.* a liquid azole, C_4H_5N, that is both a weak acid and base, found naturally in coal tar [Gk *purros*, reddish]

Py·thag·o·ras (piθǽgərəs) (c. 580–c. 500 B.C.), Greek mathematician and philosopher. He founded the Pythagorean school which believed in metempsychosis, thought that the soul imprisoned in the body could be purified by study, and followed a strict discipline of purity and self-examination. Pythagoras discovered the numerical ratios of intervals in the musical scale, and believed that the elements of numbers were the elements of the world. The so-called Pythagorean theorem, that the square on the hypotenuse of a right-angled triangle is equal to the sum of the squares on the other two sides, is attributed to his school

Py·thag·o·re·an (piθægərí:ən) **1.** *adj.* pertaining to Pythagoras, his followers or his teachings **2.** *n.* a follower of Pythagoras

Pyth·i·an (píθi:ən) *adj.* (Gk *mythol.*) pertaining to the oracle at Delphi or to Apollo as its patron ‖ of the games held every four years near Delphi in honor of Apollo's slaying of the Python [fr. L. *Pythius* fr. Gk fr. *Puthō*, old name for Delphi]

py·thon (páiθon, páiθən) *n.* a member of *Python*, fam. *Boidae*, a genus of nonvenomous snakes up to 30 ft long, which kill their prey by constriction, native to the Old World tropics ‖ any of several large snakes which kill by constriction

Py·thon (Gk *mythol.*) a monstrous serpent which lived in a cave near Delphi and was killed by Apollo [L. fr. Gk fr. *Puthō*, old name for Delphi]

py·tho·ness (páiθənis) *n.* (Gk *mythol.*) a priestess of Apollo at Delphi [O.F. *phitonise* fr. M.L.]

py·u·ri·a (paijúəri:ə) *n.* (*med.*) the presence of pus in the urine, causing pain and frequency of micturition [fr. Gk *puon*, pus+*ouron*, urine]

pyx (piks) *n.* (*eccles.*) a vessel in which the Host is reserved ‖ (also **pix**) a box at a mint in which sample coins are reserved for assay [fr. L. *pyxis*, box fr. Gk]

pyx·id·i·um (piksídi:əm) *pl.* **pyx·id·i·a** (piksídi:ə) *n.* (*bot.*) a fruit capsule (e.g. in plantain) whose upper portion is dehisced transversely [Mod. L. fr. Gk *puxidion*, dim. of *púxis*, a box]

CONCISE PRONUNCIATION KEY: **(a)** æ, c*a*t; ɑ, c*a*r; ɔ f*aw*n; ei, sn*a*ke. **(e)** e, h*e*n; i:, sh*ee*p; iə, d*ee*r; ɛə, b*ea*r. **(i)** i, f*i*sh; ai, t*i*ger; ə:, b*i*rd. **(o)** o, *o*x; au, c*ow*; ou, g*oa*t; u, p*oo*r; ɔi, r*oy*al. **(u)** ʌ, d*u*ck; u, b*u*ll; u:, g*oo*se; ə, b*a*cillus; ju:, c*u*be. x, lo*ch*; θ, *th*ink; ð, bo*th*er; z, *Z*en; ʒ, corsa*g*e; dʒ, sava*g*e; ŋ, ora*n*gutang; j, *y*ak; ʃ, *f*ish; tʃ, fe*tch*; 'l, rabb*le*; 'n, redd*en*. Complete pronunciation key appears inside front cover.

	EARLY NORTH SEMITIC	PHOENICIAN	EARLY HEBREW (GEZER)	EARLY GREEK	CLASSICAL GREEK	ETRUSCAN Early	ETRUSCAN Classical	EARLY LATIN	CLASSICAL LATIN
	φ	φ	φ φ	φ	φ	φ	Q	Q	Q

	CURSIVE MAJUSCULE (ROMAN)	CURSIVE MINUSCULE (ROMAN)	ANGLO-IRISH MAJUSCULE	CAROLINE MINUSCULE	MODERN ITALIC	N. ITALIAN MINUSCULE (ROMAN)
	५	५	q	q	q	q

A. C. SYLVESTER, CAMBRIDGE, ENGLAND

Development of the letter Q, beginning with the early North Semitic letter. Evolution of both the majuscule, or capital, letter Q and the minuscule, or lowercase, letter q are shown.

Q, q (kju:) the seventeenth letter of the English alphabet

Q n. 1. symbol of one quadrillion [10^{18}] 2. British terminal unit of heat equal to 1.055×10^{21} joules

Qaddafi, Muammar al- (mu:amáralkadáfi:) (1942–) Libyan head of state. An army colonel, he assumed power (1969) after leading a coup against King Idris I. He negotiated (1970) the removal of U.S. and British military bases. A Moslem fundamentalist, he instituted a cultural revolution (1973) that established the Koran as the basis of law. He took control of the Libyan oil industry (1973–4) and later abolished all private enterprise. A militant Arab nationalist, he has tried unsuccessfully to effect various mergers with Egypt, Syria, Tunisia, Chad and Morocco. Often accused by neighboring African countries of meddling in their internal political affairs, he also intervened militarily in a civil war in Chad. He has been accused of fostering international terrorism; various terrorist attacks around the world resulted in the U.S. bombing of Libya in 1986

Qajar *KAJAR

qat (kɒt) n. Catha edulis, fam. Celastraceae, a shrub cultivated in Arabia for the narcotic qualities of its leaves [Arab. qāt]

Qa·tar, Ka·tar (kátar) a sovereign independent state (area 4,000 sq. miles, pop. 250,000) occupying the Qatar peninsula on the west coast of the Persian Gulf. Capital: Doha (pop. 190,000). Port: Umm Said. Race and language: Arabic. Religion: Moslem. The land is a flat desert, with few oases. Traditional occupations: fishing, pearl diving. Industry: petroleum extraction (since 1949). Monetary unit: Saudi Arabian rial. Qatar was subject to Bahrain until 1868, and was under British protection (1916–71)

Qaz·vin, Kaz·vin (kɑzví:n) an agricultural market (pop. 138,527) of N.W. Iran at the foot of the Elburz Mtns. It was the capital of Persia (1514–90)

Q band (electromag.) band of radio frequency of 36–46 GHz

QC (abbr.) for 1. quick-change convertible passenger-cargo jets 2. quality control.

Q clearance the highest governmental security clearance, including availability to atomic secrets

Q fever (med.) an acute infectious disease caused by Coxiella burnetii, acquired by inhalation, ingestion, (milk) handling, and symptomized by fever, headache, malaise, and muscle pains

qi·vi·ut (kí:vi:u:t) n. cashmerelike wool of the undercoat of the musk-ox

q-mes·sage (kjúmésidʒ) n. (mil.) a classified message relating to navigational dangers, navigational aids, mine areas, and searched or swept channels

Q point position and direction of a radar target, observed from two or more directions

Q rating system of measurement on tests on audience response to action

Q ratio ratio of the market value of a nonfinancial corporation to replacement cost of net assets

Q scale (geol.) unit of geological measurement of transverse waves of planetary tremors

QSO (astron. acronym) for quasi-stellar object

QSTOL (acronym) for quiet short takeoff and landing. Cf CTOL, STOL, VTOL

Q-switch (kjúswítʃ) n. a device that produces a powerful pulsed output from a laser after first creating a blockage. —**Q-switch** v. —**Q-switched** adj.

qua (kwei, kwɑ) adv. (rhet.) strictly in the capacity or character of, the match qua match was a victory, but as sport it was lamentable [L. abl. fem. sing. of qui, who]

Quaa·lude (kwɑ́lu:d) n. (pharm.) trade name and popular terms for methaqualone (which see). also lude

quack (kwæk) 1. n. the call of a duck 2. v.i. (of ducks) to utter this [imit.]

quack 1. n. a person who pretends to have medical knowledge ‖ a fraudulent person 2. adj. fraudulent, bogus **quack·er·y** n. [shortened fr. quacksalver fr. Du., perh. fr. quacken. to quack+salf, salve]

quad (kwɒd) n. (printing) a piece of type metal used for spacing etc., an em quad [abbr. of QUADRAT]

quad n. a quadrangle (courtyard or courtyard and its buildings) [abbr. of QUADRANGLE]

quad adj. of a size paper that is four times as large as the specified size, quad demy [abbr. or QUADRUPLE]

quad n. a quadruplet

quad·plex (kwɒ́dpleks) n. a multiple dwelling consisting of four apartments. also fourplex

quad·ra·ge·nar·i·an (kwɒdrədʒənéəri:ən) 1. n. a person who is 40 years old or over but not yet 50 2. adj. having such an age [fr. L. quadragenarius]

Quad·ra·ges·i·ma (kwɒdrədʒésimə) n. the first Sunday in Lent [M.L.. the forty days of Lent, fem. of quadragesimus, fortieth]

quad·ran·gle (kwɒ́dræŋg'l) n. a plane figure with four sides, esp. a square or rectangle ‖ a courtyard surrounded by large buildings or the courtyard and its buildings **quad·rán·gu·lar** adj. [F.]

quad·rant (kwɒ́drənt) n. a quarter of a circle's circumference ‖ the area bounded by this and

the two radii drawn from its ends to the center of the circle ‖ a quarter of something, e.g. a sphere ‖ an instrument with a calibrated arc of 90°, used for measuring angles and formerly, before the sextant was developed, for measuring altitudes [fr. L. quadrans (quadrantis), fourth part]

Qua·dran·tids (kwɒdrǽntəds) n. (astronomy) a meteor shower with a small orbit; it occurs annually about January 31

quad·ra·phon·ic (kwɒdrəfónik) adj. of a sound system utilizing four channels to obtain high-fidelity sound reproduction. —**quadraphony** n.

quadraphonic recordings sound recordings made on four channels to provide high fidelity

quad·rat (kwɒ́drit) n. (printing) a quad [var. of older quadraie n., a square]

quad·rate (kwɒ́dreit) 1. v.i. pres. part. **quad·rat·ing** past and past part. **quad·rat·ed** (with 'with') to conform, square, correspond 2. adj. square or rectangular 3. n. a quadrate bone [fr. L. quadrare (quadraius), to square]

quadrate bone a bone in birds and reptiles which articulates the lower jaw with the skull

quad·rat·ic (kwɒdrǽtik) 1. adj. (algebra) of an expression which involves the square but no higher power of a term 2. n. a quadratic expression or equation **quad·rát·ics** n. the branch of algebra dealing with quadratic equations [fr. L. quadratus, squared]

quad·ra·ture (kwɒ́drətʃər) n. (math.) the act of finding a square with an area exactly equal to that of a curvilinear figure ‖ (astron.) a position in which a celestial body is in a relation of 90° or 70° to another celestial body ‖ (astron.) one of two points on an orbit midway between the syzygies [fr. L. quadratura, a square]

quad·ren·ni·al (kwɒdréni:əl) adj. happening every four years ‖ lasting four years [fr. L. quadriennium, four-year period]

quad·ren·ni·um (kwɒdréni:əm) pl. **quad·ren·ni·ums,** **quad·ren·ni·a** (kwɒdréni:ə) n. a four-year period [L. fr. quadri-, four+annus, year]

qua·dri- (kwɒ́dri:) prefix four [=L. quattuor, four]

quad·ric (kwɒ́drik) 1. adj. (math.) of the second degree 2. n. (math.) a quantic of the second degree ‖ (math.) a surface whose equation is of the second degree [fr. L. quadra, square]

quad·ri·ceps (kwɒ́driseps) n. the large extension muscle of the thigh **quad·ri·cip·i·tal** (kwɒdrisípit'l) adj. [Mod. L. fr. QUADRI-+caput (capitis), head]

quad·ri·ga (kwədráigə) pl. **quad·ri·gae** (kwədráidʒi:) n. (Rom. hist.) a two-wheeled chariot drawn by four horses abreast [L.]

quad·ri·lat·er·al (kwɒdrilǽtərəl) **1.** *n.* a plane figure enclosed by four straight lines **2.** *adj.* having four straight sides [fr. L. *quadrilaterus*]
quad·ri·lin·gual (kwɒdrilíŋgwəl) *adj.* written in or involving four languages ‖ speaking or knowing four languages [fr. QUADRI-+L. *lingua*, tongue]
qua·drille (kwədríl) *n.* a square dance for four couples, consisting of five figures ‖ the music for such a dance [F. fr. Span. *cuadrilla* or Ital. *quadriglia*, a troop]
quadrille *n.* a four-handed game played with 40 cards, fashionable in the 18th c. [F.]
quad·ril·lion (kwɒdríljən) *n.* *NUMBER TABLE **quad·ríl·lionth** *n.* and *adj.* [F.]
quad·ri·no·mi·al (kwɒdrinóumi:əl) **1.** *adj.* (*algebra*) consisting of four terms **2.** *n.* (*algebra*) a quadrinomial expression [QUADRI-+BINOMIAL]
quad·ri·par·tite (kwɒdripártait) *adj.* having four parts shared or undertaken by four parties, *a quadripartite agreement* [fr. *quadripartitus*]
quad·ri·syl·lab·ic (kwɒdrisilǽbik) *adj.* having four syllables ‖ of quadrisyllables
quad·ri·syl·la·ble (kwɒdrisíləb'l) *n.* a word of four syllables
quad·ri·va·lent (kwɒdrivéilənt) *adj.* (*chem.*) having four valencies (cf. TETRAVALENT) [fr. QUADRI-+L. *valens* (*valentis*) fr. *valere*, to be strong]
quad·riv·i·um (kwɒdrívi:əm) *pl.* **quad·riv·i·a** (kwɒdrívi:ə) *n.* (in medieval education) arithmetic, geometry, astronomy and music, the higher division of the seven liberal arts, studied for three years between the bachelor's and master's degree (cf. TRIVIUM) [L.=a place where four roads meet]
quad·ro (kwɒ́drou) *n.* in city planning, a section containing residential and commercial entities
quad·roon (kwɒdrú:n) *n.* a person of quarter Negro blood [fr. Span. *cuarteron* fr. *cuarto*, fourth]
qua·dru·ma·nous (kwɒdrú:mənəs) *adj.* (*zool.*, of primates except man) having hind feet as well as forefeet constructed like hands ‖ of or relating to such primates [fr. Mod. L. *quadrumana* fr. *quadrumanus*, four-handed]
quad·ru·ped (kwɒ́druped) **1.** *n.* a four-footed animal, esp. such a mammal **2.** *adj.* four-footed **quad·ru·pe·dal** (kwɒdrú:pid'l) *adj.* [fr. L. *quadrupes* (*quadrupedis*), four-footed]
quad·ru·ple (kwɒ́drup'l, kwɒdrú:p'l) **1.** *adj.* four times as much or as many ‖ having four parts or parties, *Quadruple Alliance* ‖ (*mus.*) having four beats to a measure **2.** *n.* a quantity or amount four times as large as another, 8 *is the quadruple of 2* [F.]
quadruple *pres. part.* **quad·ru·pling** *past* and *past part.* **quad·ru·pled** *v.t.* to multiply by four ‖ *v.i.* to become four times as many or as much [fr. F. *quadrupler* or fr. L. *quadruplare*]
Quadruple Alliance the alliance (1718) of Britain, France, the Netherlands and Austria to oppose Spain's attempt to undo the Treaty of Utrecht (1713) ‖ the alliance (1815) of Britain, Austria, Russia and Prussia to maintain peace after the defeat of Napoleon ‖ the alliance (1834) of Britain, France, Spain and Portugal to support Isabella II against the Carlists
quad·ru·plet (kwɒ́druplit, kwɒdrú:plit) *n.* one of four offspring of a single birth [QUADRUPLE adj.]
quad·ru·pli·cate 1. (kwɒdrú:plikit) *adj.* repeated four times **2.**(kwɒdrú:plikit) *n.* one of four copies or specimens **in quadruplicate** in four copies **3.** (kwɒdrú:plikeit) *v.t. pres. part.* **quad·ru·pli·cat·ing** *past* and *past part.* **quad·ru·pli·cat·ed** to make four copies or specimens of ‖ to quadruple **quad·ru·pli·cá·tion** *n.* [fr. L. *quadruplicare* (*quadruplicatus*), to quadruple]
quaes·tor, ques·tor (kwéstər, kwí:stər) *n.* (*Rom. hist.*) a state official, originally a prosecutor, or judge in certain criminal cases, later a treasurer, paymaster etc. **quaes·to·ri·al, ques·to·ri·al** (kwestɔ́ri:əl, kwi:stɔ́ri:əl, kwestóuri:əl, kwi:stóuri:əl) *adj.* **quaes·tor·ship, qués·torship** *n.* [L. fr. *quaerere*, to seek]
quaff (kwɑf) **1.** *v.t.* (*rhet.*) to drink off or take long drinks at ‖ *v.i.* (*rhet.*) to take copious drinks **2.** *n.* (*rhet.*) a hearty drink [prob. imit.]
quag (kwæg) *n.* a quagmire (shaky, muddy ground) [perh. related to obs. *quag*, to shake]
quag·ga (kwǽgə) *pl.* **quag·gas, quag·ga** *n.* *Equus quagga*, fam. *Equidae*, an extinct ungulate mammal of southern Africa, related to the zebra. It had wide stripes on the head and foreparts [S. African]
quag·gy (kwǽgi:) *comp.* **quag·gi·er** *superl.* **quag·gi·est** *adj.* of or like a quagmire [QUAG]
quag·mire (kwǽgmaiər) *n.* shaky, muddy ground ‖ a piece of firm ground transformed by rain or flooding into a sea of mud ‖ a situation which threatens to become inextricable
qua·hog, qua·haug (kwɒ́hɒg) n. *Mercenaria mercenaria*, fam. *Veneridae*, the common round clam, an edible mollusk found on the North American Atlantic coast [Am. Ind.]
Quai d'Or·say (keidɔrsei) the French ministry of foreign affairs [after the Paris street where it is]
quail (kweil) *pl.* **quail, quails** *n.* *Coturnix coturnix*, fam. *Phasianidae*, a migratory game bird of Europe, Asia and Africa. It is about 7 ins in length and the general color of its upper body is sandy with a reddish breast and white belly ‖ any of various gallinaceous game birds of North America, e.g. the bobwhite [O. F. *quaille*]
quail *v.i.* to flinch, to lose courage, *his spirit quailed at the ordeal ahead* [origin unknown]
Quail (*mil.*) an air-launched decoy missile [ADM-20] carried within the B-52 that is used to lessen the effectiveness of enemy radar, interceptor aircraft, air-defense missiles, etc.
quaint (kweint) *adj.* old and picturesque, *quaint thatched cottages* ‖ amusingly old-fashioned, *a quaint survival* ‖ odd in an interesting way, *a quaint sense of humor* [O.F. *queinte*, *cointe*, wise, crafty]
quake (kweik) **1.** *v.i. pres. part.* **quak·ing** *past* and *past part.* **quaked** to shake violently ‖ to shake inwardly **2.** n. a trembling or quaking ‖ an earthquake [O. E. *cwacian*]
Quak·er (kwéikər) *n.* a member of the Society of Friends (*FRIENDS) **Quák·er·ism** *n.* [a nickname given by a judge to George Fox, who had told him to quake at the word of the Lord]
Quaker meeting a communal meeting of Friends for worship ‖ a congregation of Friends
quak·y (kwéiki:) *comp.* **quak·i·er** *superl.* **quak·i·est** *a* trembling, shaky ‖ having a tendency to quake [QUAKE V.]
qual·i·fi·ca·tion (kwɒlifikéiʃən) *n.* a limiting, narrowing down (e.g. of meaning, application etc.), reservation, the *statement needs some qualification*, or something that does this ‖ a skill, quality etc. fitting a person for particular work or a particular appointment ‖ a requirement which has to be met, *we can waive the qualifications in his case* ‖ a descriptive term, *opportunist is hardly the qualification applicable to their policy* **qual·i·fi·ca·to·ry** (kwɒ́lifikətɔri:, kwɒ́lifikətouri:) *adj.* [fr. M. L. *qualificatio* (*qualificationis*)]
qual·i·fi·er (kwɒ́lifaiər) *n.* someone who or something that qualifies
qual·i·fy (kwɒ́lifai) *pres. part.* **qual·i·fy·ing** *past* and *past part.* **qual·i·fied** *v.t.* to render fit or competent, to entitle, *one experience doesn't qualify him to speak as an authority* ‖ to render legally capable or entitled, *residence qualifies you for membership* ‖ to describe by attributing a quality to, *could you qualify his behavior as offensive?* ‖ to modify, restrict, *to qualify a statement* ‖ to make less severe, mitigate, *to qualify a criticism* ‖ (*gram.*) to limit the meaning of, *adjectives qualify nouns* ‖ *v.i.* to be or become qualified ‖ (*sports*) to reach the required standard in preliminary contests [F. *qualifier*]
qual·i·ta·tive (kwɒ́liteitiv) *adj.* concerned with, relating to or involving quality (cf. QUANTITATIVE) [fr. L.L. *qualitativus*]
qualitative analysis the branch of chemistry concerned with the identifcation of the constituent elements in a compound mixture, e.g. by spectroscopic and spectrographic analysis (cf. QUANTITATIVE ANALYSIS)
qual·i·ty (kwɒ́liti:) *pl.* **qual·i·ties** *n.* grade, degree of excellence, *goods of the first quality* ‖ excellence, worth, *a tobacco of quality* ‖ trait, characteristic, attribute etc. ‖ (*hist.*) high social status, *a man of quality* ‖ (*logic*, of a proposition) the character of being affirmative or negative ‖ (*mus.*) timbre **the quality** (*hist.*) the nobility [M.E. *qualite fr. F. qualité*]
quality control (*business*) system for ensuring quality of output involving inspection, analysis, and action to make required changes
quality of life standard of living including health, entertainment, and subjective factors, e.g., social satisfaction
qualm (kwɑm, kwɔm) *n.* a twinge of guilt, a scruple, *qualms of conscience* ‖ a sudden feeling of anxicty or apprehension, a *qualm of fear* ‖ a sudden sensation of nausea or faintness [etym. doubtful]
quan·da·ry (kwɒ́ndəri:) *pl.* **quan·da·ries** *n.* a dilemma, a state of perplexity [etym. doubtful]
quan·ta·some (kwɒ́ntəsoum) *n.* (*botany*) the chlorophyll granule in chloroplast of plant cells, believed to be site of photosynthesis
quan·tic (kwɒ́ntik) *n.* (*math.*) a rational, integrally homogeneous function of two or more variables [fr. L. *quantus*, how much]
quantic *adj.* of or relating to a quantum
quan·ti·fy (kwɒ́ntifai) *pres. part.* **quan·ti·fy·ing** *past* and *past part.* **quanti·fied** *v.t.* (*logic*) to specify the application of (a term) by the use of 'all', 'many', 'some' etc. ‖ to determine the quantity of [M.L. *quantificare* fr. *quantus*, how much]
quan·ti·ta·tive (kwɒ́ntiteitiv) *adj.* relating to or concerned with quantity ‖ involving measurement or quantity (cf. QUALITATIVE) ‖ of or relating to the quantity of vowels, *quantitative scansion* [fr. M. L. *quantitativus*]
quantitative analysis the branch of chemistry concerned with the determination of the relative quantities of the constituent elements in a compound or mixture, e.g. by gravimetric and volumetric analysis (Cf. QUALITATIVE ANALYSIS)
quan·ti·ty (kwɒ́ntiti:) *pl.* **quan·ti·ties** *n.* an amount, *a small quantity of cement* ‖ a great deal, *a quantity of jewelry was missing* ‖ the property of things that can be measured, *the science of pure quantity* ‖ the relative length or shortness of vowel sounds or syllables ‖ (*logic*) the extent of the application of a proposition ‖ (*math.*) anything which is measurable a figure or symbol used to represent this [O.F. *quantité*]
quantity surveyor someone who estimates the quantities that will be required for a building job, with their costs
quan·tize (kwɒ́ntaiz) *pres. part.* **quan·tiz·ing** *past* and *past part.* **quan·tized** *v.t.* to subdivide (energy) into quanta ‖ to impart a quantum to ‖ to express in multiples of an indivisible unit, e.g., age in whole years ‖ to treat or express in terms of quantum mechanics
Quantrill (kwɑ́ntril), William C. (1837–65) American Confederate guerrilla leader during the Civil War. Known as Quantrill's Raiders, his guerrilla bands burned and looted Union strongholds in Kansas and Missouri, and on Aug. 21, 1863, they pillaged Lawrence, Kans., killing more than 150 civilians. Quantrill was mortally wounded by Union troops (May 1865) and died in prison in Louisville, Ky.
quan·tum (kwɒ́ntəm) *pl.* **quan·ta** (kwɒ́ntə) *n.* amount, quantity ‖ share ‖ one of the very small discrete packets into which many forms of energy are subdivided, and which are always associated with a frequency v such that the product of v and Planck's constant is equal to the quantum ‖ one of the small subdivisions of other quantized physical magnitudes (*QUANTUM NUMBER, *SHELL, *ORBITAL) [L. neut. of *quantus*, how much]
quantum chemistry the study of the mechanics of molecular physics applied to chemistry. — **quantum chemist** *n.*
quantum electronics the application of the mechanics of molecular physics to electronics, e.g., hydrogen maser, atomic beam resonator
quantum leap a sudden large advance or breakthrough
quantum mechanics the formal mathematical methods of wave mechanics and of matrix mechanics applied to physical problems
quantum number an integral or half integral number belonging to a set of four such numbers denoting the energy level, angular momentum, magnetic moment and spin of a particle, esp. an electron in an atom (*PAULI EXCLUSION PRINCIPLE). For such a particle, each of the above-mentioned quantities is quantized, the quantum numbers representing the discrete levels of each quantity in which the particle is to be found (*QUANTUM THEORY, *SHELL, *ORBITAL)
quantum physics an approach to physics based on the quantum theory
quantum theory a theory in physics and chemistry based on the assumption that the energy possessed by a physical system is quantized, i.e. it cannot take on a continuous range of values (permitted in classical physics) but is restricted to discrete ones that depend on its dimensions, masses and charges. This hypothesis, made first in the early 20th c. to explain certain per-

plexing phenomena (*PLANCK RADIATION LAW, *PHOTOEMISSION*, *ATOMIC SPECTRUM), was incorporated in the 1920s into different but equivalent thematical formulations (*WAVE MECHANICS, *MATRIX MECHANICS) which are now regarded as providing a more general theoretical framework than that supporting classical mechanics. Indeed, the latter is considered a special case of quantum mechanics, applying to systems whose dimensions and energy are such as to allow them to exist in quantum states so close together that they may, for purpose of calculation, be regarded as continuous. The quantum theory has progressed to the point where it permeates the whole of physics and chemistry, permitting a unified and often quantitative treatment of a wide range of experimental facts. It has also revealed certain fundamental properties of nature (*UNCERTAINTY PRINCIPLE, *WAVE-PARTICLE DUALITY) that have profoundly affected current epistemology

quantum theory of fields a modern unified theory of force fields in which the field at some distance from its source is thought of as being carried to that point by a messenger or field quantum. For electrostatic fields this messenger is the photon, for gravitational fields it is the hypothetical graviton. Both these particles have 0 rest mass, travel with the speed of light, and therefore extend their effect to infinity. For the short-range forces observed in nuclei by means of scattering experiments, a type of meson with finite rest mass and therefore limited effective distance was postulated. Several such mesons have since been observed

quap (kwɒp) *n.* a hypothetical nuclear particle of a quark plus an antiproton

quar·an·tine (kwɔ́rənti:n, kwɒ́rənti:n) **1.** *n.* a period of isolation imposed to lessen the risk of spreading an infectious or contagious disease ‖ a period of detention during which a ship suspected of carrying contagion is allowed no contact with the shore ‖ such a state of isolation imposed on an individual, ship etc. ‖ the place where the ship is detained ‖ a place, esp. a hospital, where people with contagious diseases are isolated. **2.** *v.t. pres. part.* **quar·an·tin·ing** *past* and *past part.* **quar·an·tined to** put in quarantine, to isolate [fr. Ital. *quarantina* fr. *quaranta,* forty]

quark (kwɒrk) *n.* a hypothetical basic subatomic nuclear particle held to be the basic component of protons, neutrons, etc., or a mathematically convenient parameter of a model; coined by American physicist Murray Gell-Mann *Cf* ATOM SMASHER, BETATRON, PARTICLE ACCELERATOR, PEP, PETA

quar·rel (kwɔ́rəl, kwɒ́rəl) *n.* (*hist.*) a heavy square-headed arrow, esp. one used with a crossbow [O.F.]

quarrel *pres. part.* **quar·rel·ing,** esp. *Br.* **quar·rel·ling** *past* and *past part.* **quar·reled,** esp. *Br.* **quar·relled** *v.i.* to wrangle, to dispute angrily ‖ to find fault, to *quarrel with someone's suggestions* [O.F. *quereler*]

quarrel *n.* an angry dispute, altercation ‖ disagreement, *what is your quarrel with this definition?* ‖ a cause for complaint, *my real quarrel with him is the way he treats dogs* **quár·rel·some** *adj.* quick to quarrel [O.F. *querele, querelle*]

quar·ry (kwɔ́ri:, kwɒ́ri:) *pl.* **quar·ries** *n.* a diamond-shaped pane of glass ‖ a machine-made paving tile [var. of QUARREL (arrow)]

quarry *pl.* **quarries** *n.* the prey of an animal ‖ the victim of a hunt ‖ a person or thing pursued as though the victim of a hunt [fr. O.F. *cuirée, curée* fr. *cuir,* hide]

quarry 1. *pl.* **quar·ries** *n.* an open cavity where stone or slate is extracted **2.** *v.t. pres. part.* **quar·ry·ing** *past* and *past part.* **quar·ried** to take from a quarry ‖ to make a quarry in ‖ to extract (information) from books, records etc. ‖ *v.i.* to search for information **quar·ry·man** (kwɔ́ri:mən, kwɒ́ri:mən) *pl.* **quar·ry·men** (kwɔ́ri:mən, kwɒ́ri:mən) *n.* a person who works in a quarry [fr. M.L. *quareia*]

quart (kwɔrt) *n.* any of various units of liquid or dry capacity esp. (*Am.*) one equal to ¼ liquid gallon or 57.75 cu. ins or (*Br.*) one equal to ¼ imperial gallon or 69.355 cu. ins ‖ a measure of dry capacity equal to 1/32 bushel or 67.200 cu. ins [F. *quart, quarte*]

quart *QUARTE

quar·tan (kwɔ́rt'n) **1.** *n.* a type of fever characterized by a paroxysm reoccurring every 72 hours **2.** *adj.* (of a fever) occurring every 72 hours [F. (*fièvre) quartaine*]

quarte (kart) *n.* (*fencing,* also **quart, carte**) the fourth parrying position ‖ a sequence of four cards in piquet [F.]

quar·ter (kwɔ́rtər) **1.** *n.* one of four equal parts, a fourth part ‖ a fourth part of an hour ‖ the moment marking this ‖ a fourth part of a year ‖ a fourth of a lunar period ‖ the phase of the moon between the first and second quarter, or between the third and fourth quarter ‖ a period for instruction and study, usually equal to one fourth of an academic year ‖ (*sports*) one of the four periods of playing time into which certain games are divided ‖ a race over one fourth of a mile ‖ one of four parts, each including a limb, into which a carcass is divided by a butcher ‖ a district in a town, *the Chinese quarter* ‖ a region or direction corresponding to one of the cardinal points of the compass, *the wind is moving around to the opposite quarter* ‖ any point or direction of the compass, esp. a cardinal point or division ‖ a source of information, help etc.. *don't look for sympathy in that quarter* ‖ (*hist. or fig.*) mercy granted to an enemy or opponent in a contest‖ the fourth part of a hundredweight ‖ (*Br.*) a measure for grain etc. equal to about 8 bushels ‖ 25 cents, a fourth part of a dollar ‖ a coin of this value ‖ the lateral part of a horse's hoof between the heel and the toe ‖ (*naut.*) the fourth part of a fathom ‖ (*naut.*) the afterpart of a ship's side ‖ (*naut.,* esp. *pl.*) one of the stations where men are called for a specified activity, *battle quarters* ‖ (*shoemaking*) the side of a shoe from heel to vamp ‖ (*heraldry*) one of the four divisions of a quartered shield ‖ (*heraldry*) a charge occupying such a division placed in chief ‖ (*pl.,* esp. *mil.*) lodging‖ (of two machine parts) the condition of being at a 90° angle to one another **at close quarters** very near by **from all quarters, from every quarter** from all directions ‖ from everyone **2.** *v.t.* to divide into four equal parts ‖ to lodge, assign accommodation to, *he quartered his troops in the school* ‖ to fix, adjust etc. (two parts of a machine) at right angles ‖ (*heraldry*) to bear or arrange (different coats of arms) quarterly on a shield ‖ (*heraldry*) to add (another's coat) to one's hereditary arms ‖ (*heraldry,* with 'with') to place in alternate quarters to ‖ (*heraldry*) to divide (a shield) into parts ‖ (of dogs) to search (the ground) thoroughly in all directions ‖ (*hist.*) to cut (a corpse) into four pieces **3.** *adj.* consisting of or equal to a quarter ‖ (of a machine part) placed at a right angle to another part [O.F.]

quar·ter·back (kwɔ́rtərbæk) *n.* (*football*) the player whose position is behind the line of scrimmage with the fullback and the halfbacks, and who generally calls the signals for the plays

quarter binding a book binding in which the material covering the spine is different from that covering the sides. The material covering the spine extends over the boards up to a quarter of their width (cf. FULL BINDING, cf. HALF BINDING, cf. THREE-QUARTER BINDING)

quar·ter-bound (kwɔ́rtərbaund) *adj.* bound in quarter binding

quarter day a day on which a quarterly payment (of rent, interest etc.) is due and a quarterly tenancy begins or ends

quar·ter·deck (kwɔ́rtərdek) *n.* the after section of a ship's upper deck usually between stern and after mast

quar·ter·fi·nal (kwɔrtərfáin'l) *n.* the game or round before the semifinal of a tournament

quarter horse a horse of a U.S. breed developed for short-distance racing

quar·ter·ing (kwɔ́rtəriŋ) *n.* (*heraldry*) the arrangement of coats of arms on a shield to show family alliances [QUARTER v.]

Quartering Act of 1764 a British act of parliament during the ministry of George Grenville, which declared that the American colonists were required to pay for housing British troops in the colonies. It was re-enacted (1774) with the passage of the Intolerable Acts, which caused bitter colonial resentment

quar·ter·ly (kwɔ́rtərli:) **1.** *adj.* occurring every quarter of a year **2.** *adv.* once every quarter ‖ (heraldry) in quarters ‖ (*heraldry*) in diagonally opposite quarters **3.** *pl.* **quar·ter·lies** *n.* a publication issued once every quarter

quar·ter·mas·ter (kwɔ́rtərmæstər, kwɔ́rtərmɑstər) *n.* (*naut.*) a petty officer in charge of steering, signals etc. ‖ (*mil., abbr.* Q.M.) an officer who allots quarters to troops, deals with supplies etc.

quartermaster general (*mil., abbr.* Q.M.G.) a staff officer in charge of the department dealing with quarters, supplies etc.

quarter note (*mus., Am.=Br.* crotchet) a note (symbol ♩) equal to half a half note or two eighth notes

quarter plate (*Br.*) a photographic plate or film of the size 4½ x 3½ ins

quar·ter·saw (kwɔ́rtərsɔ) *pres. part.* **quar·ter·saw·ing** *past* **quar·ter·sawed** *past part.* **quar·ter·sawn** (kwɔ́rtərsɔn), **quar·ter·sawed** *v.t.* to saw (a log) into quarters and then each quarter into planks so that the grain shows to advantage i.e. with the growth rings at least 45° to the cut face) and warping is reduced

quarter section (*abbr.* q.s.) one fourth of a section of land

quarter session a local court in certain states, having limited criminal jurisdiction ‖ a British court of limited criminal and civil jurisdiction held quarterly and presided over by two justices of the peace or by a judge sitting with a jury in counties, and by recorders in boroughs

quarter tone (*mus.*) an interval equal to half a semitone

quar·tet, quar·tette (kwɔrtét) *n.* a musical composition for four voices or instruments ‖ a group of performers of such compositions [F. *quartette* fr. Ital.]

quar·tile (kwɔ́rtail, kwɔ́rt'l) *n.* (*statistics*) one of the three values in a frequency distribution which divides the items into four categories [fr. M.L. *quartilis* adj. fr. *quartus,* fourth]

quar·to (kwɔ́rtou) *n.* (*abbr.* 4to, 4°) the size of a sheet of paper folded into four ‖ a book of sheets so folded [L. (*in*) *quarto,* (*in*) fourth]

quartz (kwɔrts) *n.* a common and widely distributed form of silicon dioxide, SiO_2, occurring in hexagonal crystals and massive forms. Usually colorless and transparent (*ROCK CRYSTAL), it is also found in colored, translucent and opaque forms. It is more transparent than glass to ultraviolet waves, but polarizes the light it transmits. Having a very small coefficient of expansion, and high rigidity, it is used for making heat resistant apparatus. It exhibits piezoelectricity and so is used in radio transmitters and the mechanisms of astronomical clocks etc. [G. *quarz*]

quartz-i·o·dine lamp (kwɔ́rtsáiədain) (*electrical eng.*) a high-intensity incandescent lamp with a tungsten filament, and a quartz bulb containing an inert gas of iodine or bromine vapor. It is used in automobile lamps, movie projectors, etc.

quartz·ite (kwɔ́rtsait) *n.* a sandstone, often milky white in color, compacted into a solid rock by a deposit of crystalline quartz around its grains

quartz light (*med.*) a bactericidal cold-light lamp with a quartz lens, used for therapy

qua·sar (kwéizɑr) *n.* any of several very intense celestial radio sources, among the furthest known objects from the earth (10^9 light-years away). The size, optical and radio intensity, frequency of occurrence and distance of quasars are extremely unusual. Quasars are of primary importance in modern cosmological theories [*quasi*-stel*lar* radio source]

quash (kwɒʃ) *v.t.* (*law*) to annul ‖ to dismiss summarily, *to quash an objection* ‖ to put down (a rebellion etc.) [fr. O.F. *quasser*]

qua·si- (kwázi:, kwéizai) **1.** *adj.* seeming, *quasi humor* **2.** *prefix* seemingly, almost real, apparent, *the decision has an appearance of quasi-legality* ‖ semi-, more or less, *in a quasi-official capacity* [L.=if]

Qua·si·mo·do (kwɑzi:mɔ́dɔ), Salvatore (1901–68), Italian lyric poet. His works include 'La Vita non e sogno' (1949) and 'La Terra impareggiabile' (1958)

Qua·si·mo·do Sunday (kwɑzi:mɔ́dɔ) Low Sunday [fr. L. *quasi modo,* the opening words of the introit for this day]

qua·si·par·ti·cle (kwázi:pɑ́rtik'l) *n.* (*phys.*) in solid-state physics, a unit of energy (sound, light, heat) with mass and momentum but that does not exist as a free particle, e.g., phonons

quasi-stellar object *QUASAR

quas·sia (kwɒ́ʃə) *n.* a drug obtained from the heartwood of several members of *Simaroubaceae,* a family of tropical trees. It is used as a tonic, a roundworm cure, and in insect control

quas·sin (kwɒ́s'n) *n.* the bitter essence of quassia [Mod. L. fr. Graman *Quassi,* a Surinam slave, who discovered. c. 1730) this drug]

qua·ter·cen·te·nar·y (kwɒtərséntəneri:) *pl.* **qua·ter·cen·te·nar·ies** *n.* a 400th anniversary [fr. L. *quater*, four times]

qua·ter·na·ry (kwətə́:rnəri:, kwɑ́tərneri:) **1.** *adj.* consisting of four ‖ arranged in groups of four **Qua·ter·na·ry** of the most recent period of geological time **2.** *n.* the number four ‖ a group of four **the Quaternary** the Quaternary period or system of rocks [fr. L. *quaternarius* fr. *quaterni*, by fours]

Quaternary *n.* (*geol.*) time period of the last 2 or 3 million yrs, i.e., the Pleistocene and Holocene eras. —**Quaternary** *adj.*

qua·ter·nate (kwətə́:rnit, kwɑ́tərneit) *adj.* being a set or sets of four ‖ having four parts [fr. L. *quaterni*, by fours]

qua·ter·ni·on (kwətə́:rni:ən) *n.* a set of four ‖ (*math.*) an operator, depending upon four irreducible elements, which changes one vector into another ‖ (*pl.*) the calculus of these [fr. L.L. *quaternio* (*quarternionis*) fr. *quaterni*, by fours]

quat·rain (kwɒ́trein) *n.* a four-line stanza ‖ four lines of verse [F fr. *quatre*, four]

quat·rat (kwɒ́trɑt) *n.* (*envir.*) area, usu. 1 sq m, used to sample vegetation. *Cf* QUODRAT

quat·re·foil (kǽtrəfɔil) *n.* a stylized ornament, used e.g. in tracery, representing a leaf or flower with four lobes [fr. O. F. fr. *quatre*, four+foil, leaf]

quat·tro·cen·to (kwɒtroutʃéntou) n. the 15th c. in Italy, esp. in relation to its art and literature [Ital.=four hundred, used for fourteen hundred]

quat·tu·or·de·cil·lion (kwɒtu:ɔrdisíljən) *n.* *NUMBER TABLE [fr. L. *quattuordim*, fourteen+MILLION]

Quauhtémoc *CUAUHTÉMOC

qua·ver (kwéivər) **1.** *v.i.* (*of* the voice) to shake, tremble ‖ to speak or sing tremulously ‖ *v.t.* to utter or sing with a tremulous voice **2.** *n.* a tremulous unsteadiness in speech ‖ (*mus.*) a trill in singing ‖ (*Br., mus.*) an eighth note **quá·ver·y** *adj.* shaky, tremulous [fr. older *quave* fr. M.E. *cwavier*, to shake]

quay (*ki:*) *n.* an artificially constructed wharf lying parallel to or projecting into the water, for loading and unloading ships **quay·age** (kí:idʒ) *n.* the charge for the use of a quay ‖ mooring space alongside a quay [alt. spelling of older *key*, a quay, after F. *quai*]

quea·si·ly (kwí:zili:) *adv.* uneasily [QUEASY]

quea·si·ness (kwí:zi:nis) *n.* the condition or quality of being queasy

quea·sy (kwi:zi:) *comp.* **quea·si·er** *superl.* **quea·si·est** *adj.* sick, qualmish, inclined to nausea ‖ nauseating, *the queasy rolling of the ship* ‖ fastidious, easily upset ‖ uneasy, uncomfortable in one's mind [perh. rel. to O.F. *coisier*, to hurt]

Que·bec (kwibék, *F.* keibek) the capital (pop. 166,474, with agglom. 576,075) of Quebec province, Canada, a port on the St Lawrence. Industries: textiles, leather, pulp and paper, mechanical engineering. Language: 90% French. Cathedrals (1647 and 1922), 17th-c. city walls. University (*LAVAL). The first French settlement in Canada, Quebec was founded (1608) by Champlain. The battle of the Heights of Abraham was fought here (1759). Quebec was the capital of Lower Canada (1791–1840)

Quebec a province (area 594,860 sq. miles, pop. 6,529,300, about 80% French-speaking of whom a quarter are bilingual) occupying most of E. Canada. Capital: Quebec. Largest city: Montreal. It lies almost wholly within the Canadian Shield, and settlement is concentrated in the fertile St Lawrence valley. Agriculture: beef and dairy cattle, hogs, poultry, fodder crops, fruit and vegetables, maple syrup. Resources: furs, fish, timber, asbestos, copper, iron ore, gold, building materials, hydroelectricity. Industries: pulp and paper, nonferrous-metal processing, wood industries, textiles and clothing, chemicals. food processing, aircraft, rolling stock. The city of Quebec was founded in 1608 and the area was part of New France until ceded to the English (1763). The province of Quebec was set up (1763–90), became Lower Canada (1791–1840) and joined the Canadian Confederation (1867). Its predominantly French culture fostered a separatist spirit which gave rise in the 1960s to both a moderate and a radical movement. The moderate Parti Québécois (founded 1968) demanded political separation from Canada. The radical Front de Libération du Québec (FLQ, founded 1962) sought the same end by terrorism. The Parti Québécois was elected in 1976 with René Lévesque as its leader, but a 1980 referendum defeated the proposal to negotiate the province's sovereignty with the federal government. In 1985, following Lévesque's resignation, Pierre Marc Johnson took office as premier and head of the Parti Québécois

Quebec Act a British act of parliament (1774) which guaranteed freedom of worship and maintenance of the French civil code to the former French colonies of Canada

Quebec Conference a meeting (Aug. 11–24, 1943) at Quebec between F. D. Roosevelt, Churchill, Mackenzie King and Tse-ven Soong. Lord Louis Mountbatten was made supreme Allied commander in S.E. Asia, and plans for the invasion of France were approved

que·bra·cho (keibrɑ́tʃou) *n.* any of various tropical American trees with very hard wood, esp. *Aspidosplierma quebracho*, fam. *Apocynaceae*, the white quebracho of Chile and Argentina, yielding a bark used medicinally and *Schinopsis* (*Lorentzii*, fam. *Anacardiaceae*, the red quebracho of Argentina, whose bark yields tannin used in dyeing the wood of a quebracho [Span. fr. *quebrar*, to break+*hacha* , axe]

Quech·ua (kétʃwə) *n.* a member of a group of Inca tribes ‖ the language of these tribes (still spoken among Indians of Peru and Ecuador)

Quech·uan **1.** *n.* Quechua **2.** *adj.* relating to the Quechuas, their language, culture etc.

queen (kwi:n) **1.** *n.* the wife of a king ‖ a female monarch ‖ (*rhet.*) a woman, creature or thing thought of as the foremost of its kind ‖ the fertile female of social insects, e.g. bees, wasps, ants and termites ‖ a playing card bearing a conventionalized picture of a queen ‖ (*chess*) the most mobile piece, able to move in a straight line in any direction for any number of squares **2.** *v.t.* (*chess*) to convert (a pawn) into a queen by advancing it to the opponent's end of the board ‖ *v.t.* (*chess*, of a pawn) to become a queen **to queen it** to be bossy, put on airs, and assume that other people are there to do one's bidding [O.E. *cwēn*, a woman, wife, queen]

Queen Anne (*archit.*) of an early 18th-c. English style of unpretentious elegance, usually employing red brick with restrained carved classical ornamentation, and used very successfully, esp. in domestic architecture ‖ (*furniture*) of an early 19th-c. English style showing Dutch influence, generally characterized by cabriole legs, generous but elegant comfort in the chairs, use of walnut, affection for marquetry, and use of upholstery

Queen Anne's lace *Dancus carota*, an umbellifer widely distributed in North America. It has large, lacy umbels of white flowers, the central flower often being purple

Queen Anne's War the American aspect (1701–13) of the War of the Spanish Succession, fought by England and her American colonies against the French and the Indians, and settled by the Peace of Utrecht (1713)

Queen Charlotte Islands (ʃɑ́r:lət) a wooded archipelago (land area 3,970 sq. miles, pop. 3,000) of British Columbia, Canada. The islands are mountainous, with the exception of Graham (the largest island). Minerals (largely unexploited): coal, copper, iron, gold. Occupations: fishing, farming, forestry

queen dowager the widow of a king

queen·li·ness (kwí:nli:nis) *n.* the quality of being queenly

queen·ly (kwí:nli:) *comp.* **queen·li·er** *superl.* **queen·li·est** *adj.* befitting a queen of or like a queen

Queen Maud Land (mɔd) a sector of Antarctica between 20° W and 45° E and south of 60° S., claimed by Norway

queen mother a queen dowager who is the mother of a reigning monarch

queen post one of two uprights on a tie beam, supporting the main rafters

Queens (kwi:nz) a residential and industrial borough (pop. 1,891,325) of New York City, on Long Island

Queen's Bench *KING'S BENCH

Queens·ber·ry rules (kwí:nzbəri:) the code of rules governing modern boxing, introduced (1865) by John Sholto Douglas, 8th marquis of Queensberry (1844–1900), British sports enthusiast

Queen's Counsel *KING'S COUNSEL

Queen's county *LAOIGHIS

queen-size (kwí:nsaiz) *adj.* of a bed size, approximately 60 in by 80 in

Queens·land (kwí:nzlənd, kwí:nzlænd) the state (estimated area 667,000 sq. miles, pop. 2,275,700) comprising the northeastern part of Australia. Capital: Brisbane. The Great Dividing Range separates the wet coastal plain from the dry Great Artesian Basin in the south. The northern half is tropical. Agriculture: sugarcane, wheat, corn, sorghum, vegetables, fruits, dairy and meat cattle, sheep and pig farming. Resources: timber, coal, copper, uranium, gold, silver, lead, zinc, petroleum. Industries: agricultural processing, lumber, engineering, copper refining, rubber, clothing. University of Queensland (1909) at Brisbane

Queen's Proctor *KING'S PROCTOR

queen's shilling *KING'S SHILLING

queen substance (*zool.*) a pheromone secreted by queen bees, made up of 9-ketodecanoic acid, that is ingested by worker bees, suppressing their ovary development

Queen's War *DEVOLUTION, WAR OF

queer (kwiər) **1.** *adj.* strange, peculiar ‖ eccentric, odd ‖ arousing suspicion ‖ unwell, sick ‖ (*pop.*) homosexual **2.** *v.t.* to spoil, ruin **to queer someone's pitch** (esp. *Br.*) to spoil someone's plans, chances of success, schemings, etc. **3.** *n.* (*pop.*) a homosexual [origin unknown]

quell (kwel) *v.t.* to subdue, to overcome, *to quell someone's fears* ‖ to crush, to supress, *to quell an uprising* [O.E. *cwellan*, to kill]

Que·moy (kimɔ́i) an island (area 60 sq. miles, pop. 57,500) off the coast of Fukien, China, held by Formosa since 1949

quench (kwentʃ) *v.t.* (*rhet.*) to put out, extinguish, *to quench flames* ‖ to suppress, *to quench enthusiasm* ‖ to slake (thirst) ‖ to cool (heated steel etc.) by immersion in water or oil in order to harden it [M.E. *cwenken*, *quenchen*]

quench tank water tank used to cool hot materials in an industrial plant

Quen·tal (kentɑ́l), Antero de (1842–91), Portuguese poet, whose introspective works, usually in sonnet form, reflect his socialistic political philosophy

Quer·cia (kwértʃɑ), Jacopo della (c. 1367–1438), Italian sculptor. His tombs, fountains and religious works are characterized by vigorous rounded forms

quer·ci·tron (kwə́:rsitrən) *n.* *Quercus velutina*, a black oak of N. America ‖ its bark, yielding a yellow dye ‖ this dye [fr. L. *quercus*, oak+CITRON]

Que·ré·ta·ro (kerétɑrɔ) a central plateau state (area 4,544 sq. miles, pop. 355,000) of Mexico. Capital: Querétaro. The land is divided between mountainous areas (opals and mercury) and plains and fertile southern valleys (fruits, grain, medicinal plants, sweet potatoes). Fighting bulls are bred

Querétaro a town (pop. 680,700) in central Mexico, capital of Querétaro state. It was the site of the execution (1867) of Emperor Maximilian and his generals, and was the seat of the Constituent Congress of 1917

quern (kwə:rn) *n.* (*hist.*) a hand mill for grinding grain ‖a small hand mill for grinding spices [O.E. *cweorn*]

quer·u·lous (kwéruləs, kwérjuləs) *adj.* complaining, peevish, *querulous old age* [fr. L. L. *querulosus*]

que·ry (kwíəri:) **1.** *pl.* **que·ries** *n.* a question ‖ a doubt or objection, mental reservation ‖ a question mark, used to signalize a question about a text etc. **2.** *v.t. pres. part.* **que·ry·ing** *past* and *past part.* **que·ried** to question the truth or accuracy of ‖ to pose as a question ‖ to question (someone), *he queried several doctors on reactions to the drug* ‖ to mark as a query [Anglicized fr. L. *quaere*, imper. of *quaerere*, to ask a question]

Quesada *JIMÉNEZ DE QUESADA

Ques·nay (kenei), François *PHYSIOCRAT

quest (kwest) *n.* (*rhet.*) a pursuit, search, *a quest for riches* ‖ (in medieval romance) a search undertaken by a knight in selfless devotion, *the quest for the Holy Grail* **in quest of** (*rhet.*) in search of (adventure, treasure etc.) [O.F. *queste*]

quest *v.i.* (of gun dogs) to search for game ‖ (*rhet.*) to be on a quest ‖ *v.t.* (*rhet.*) to search for ‖ F. *quester*]

ques·tion (kwéstʃən) *n.* a word, phrase or sentence asking about a particular point, fact etc. ‖ a problem designed to test knowledge, *answer 7 out of 10 questions* ‖ doubt, *there's some question about his qualifications* ‖ a topic, esp. one involving a difficulty, *the question of capital*

CONCISE PRONUNCIATION KEY: **(a)** æ, *cat*; ɑ, *car*; ɔ *fawn*; ei, *snake*. **(e)** e, *hen*; i:, *sheep*; iə, *deer*; ɛə, *bear*. **(i)** i, *fish*; ai, *tiger*; ə:, *bird*. **(o)** o, *ox*; au, *cow*; ou, *goat*; u, *poor*; ɔi, *royal*. **(u)** ʌ, *duck*; u, *bull*; u:, *goose*; ə, *bacillus*; ju:, *cube*. x, *loch*; θ, *think*; ð, *bother*; z, *Zen*; ʒ, *corsage*; dʒ, *savage*; ŋ, *orangutang*; j, *yak*; ʃ, *fish*; tʃ, *fetch*; 'l, *rabble*; 'n, *redden*. Complete pronunciation key appears inside front cover.

punishment is sure to come up || a matter, *it's only a question of time* || the subject for or under discussion || a questioning, interrogation, *he broke down under question* **beyond question, beyond all question** without doubt, certainly **in question** in doubt ||under consideration **out of the question** impossible, not to be thought of **to make no question** to have no doubts in one's mind **to put to the question** (*hist.*) to torture (in the exercise of justice) **without question** without doubt without challenge [A.F. *questium* fr. O.F. *question*]

question *v.t.* to ask (someone) a question or questions, to interrogate || to dispute, to cast doubt upon, *we question the accuracy of the statistics v.i.* to ask a question or questions **qués·tion·a·ble** *adj.* open to doubt of a dubious, shady character **qués·tion·a·bly** *adv.* [O. F. *questionner*]

question mark a punctuation mark (?) after a question

ques·tion·naire (kwestʃənέər) *n.* a set of questions drawn up for answering by a number of people independently, usually to provide statistical information || a paper containing such questions || an inquiry using such questions [F.]

question time (*parliament*) a period in which ministers reply orally to written questions from members

questor *QUAESTER

Quet·ta (kwétə) a trade, road and rail center (pop. 156,000) of Baluchistan, Pakistan, near the passes leading to Iran and Afghanistan: wool textiles. It was largely rebuilt after the earthquake of 1935

quet·zal (ketsúl) *n. Pharomachrus mocino,* fam. *Trogonidae,* a central American bird, with splendid metallic plumage, the male having long, streaming tail feathers. According to tradition, it is the bird of liberty and cannot live in captivity, though its plumage never fades in life or death. It has been taken as the emblem and monetary unit of Guatemala [Span. fr. Nahuatl]

Quet·zal·có·atl (ketsəlkouát'l) ('plumed serpent') a 9th-c. pre-Columbian deity of Mexico, king of the Toltecs, and poet-philosopher who discovered the supreme divine duality. He was deified as Ehecatl ('god of the winds', or 'god of air and water') and was reputed to have the power of giving life by his mere look. He taught men agriculture, metal work, the arts, and the calendar. Because he disapproved of the growing practice of offering human sacrifices he abandoned the Toltecs for the 'land of black and red' to the east (probably Yucatán), promising his faithful that he would return in another age and under a different guise. The Aztecs, who revered him as the animator of nature, regarded Hernán Cortés as the promised reincarnation

queue (kjú:) **1.** *n.* (esp. *Br.*) a line of people etc. awaiting their turn || (*computer*) the line-up of messages waiting to be processed, transmitted, or stored || (*hist.*) a plait of hair hanging at the back of the head, esp. as formerly worn by Chinese men or found on men's wigs in Europe **2.** *v.i. pres. part.* **queu·ing** *past* and *past part.* **queued** (esp. *Br.,* often with 'up') to form a queue (esp. *Br.*) to join a queue [F.]

queuing theory (*math.*) application of the probability theory relating to waiting time, order, and delays at a point where action is delayed in computers, esp. in handling information from diverse sources

Que·ve·do y Vi·lle·gas (kevéðoi:vi:ljégɑs), Francisco Gomez de (1580–1645), Spanish satirical writer, poet and author of political treatises. His picaresque novel 'Historia de la vida del Buscón llamado don Pablos' (1626) is one of the first to trace the psychological development of a hero from his youth

Que·zon (kéisɒn), Manuel Luis (1878–1944), Filipino statesman, first president of the Philippine Commonwealth (1935–44). He led his government-in-exile in the U.S.A. (1942–4) during the Japanese occupation of the Philippines

Quezon City former capital (pop. 1,165,865) of the Philippines, in central Luzon overlooking Manila, which it replaced as capital from 1948–76. University (1908)

quib·ble (kwíb'l) **1.** *n.* an evasion of the point at issue by petty argumentation, raising purely formal difficulties etc. || a piddling piece of fault-finding **2.** *v.i. pres. part.* **quib·bling** *past* and *past part.* **quib·bled** to use a quibble or quibbles [perh. dim. of older *quib* fr. L. *quibus* ablative and dative pl. of *qui,* who, which]

Qui·be·ron Bay, Battle of (ki:brɔ̃) a sea battle (1759) of the Seven Years' War, in which the British under Hawke decisively defeated a French fleet preparing to invade Britain

Qui·che (ki:tʃei) *pl.* **Qui·che, Qui·ches** *n.* a member of an Indian people of S. central Guatemala || their Mayan language [Span. *Quiché*]

quiche (ki:ʃ) *n.* a pastry shell filled with egg custard into which bits of ham and grated cheese have been added

quick (kwik) **1.** *adj.* fast-moving, rapid hurried, *a quick look* || lively, perceptive, alert, responsive, *a quick mind* || prompt, *quick action* || easily aroused, *a quick temper* || hasty, impulsive, *a quick retort* || (*Br.*) quickset **2.** *n.* the sensitive living flesh, esp. the part under the nail **to hurt** (or **touch** or **wound**) **someone to the quick** to hurt someone's feelings very deeply **the quick and the dead** the living and dead **3.** *adv.* quickly, *come as quick as you can* [O.E. *cwicu,* alive]

quick assets (*accounting*) ready cash and goods which can easily be marketed

quick bread a kind of bread, muffin etc. made with a leaven which allows it to be baked as soon as mixed

quick·en (kwíkən) *v.t.* to accelerate, *to quicken one's pace* || (*rhet.*) to restore to life, *to quicken the dead* || to stimulate, rouse, *to quicken someone's interest* || *v.i.* to become faster ||to reach the stage in pregnancy when the fetal movement is perceptible [QUICK adj.]

quick-fire (kwíkfaiər) *adj.* firing or made for firing in quick succession **quíckfir·ing** *adj.*

quick-freeze (kwíkfri:z) *pres. part.* **quick-freez·ing** *past* **quick-froze** (kwikfróuz) *past part.* **quick-fro·zen** (kwikfróuz'n) *v.t.* to deep-freeze

quick grass couch grass

quick·ie (kwíki:) *n.* (*pop.*) anything made, produced or consumed quickly, esp. something not requiring much time or effort, e.g. a hastily made, cheap film

quick kick (*football*) a surprise punt made on the first, second, or third down

quick·lime (kwíklaim) *n.* lime (calcium oxide)

quick·sand (kwíksænd) *n.* a mass of unstable sand saturated with water, tending to suck down into it anyone or anything that comes on to it|| such sand

quick·set (kwíkset) **1.** *n.* live slips esp. of whitethorn or hawthorn, planted closely to make a hedge || *Br.*) a quickset hedee **2.** *adj.* (*Br.,* of a hedge etc.) made up of such slips planted in this way

quick·sil·ver (kwíksilvər) **1.** *n.* mercury **2.** *adj.* (of temperament) changing rapidly and without warning **3.** *v.t.* to treat with quicksilver or a compound of this [O.E. *cwicseolfor* after L. *argentum vivum*]

quick·step (kwíkstep) *n.* (*mil.*) a step used in marching quick time || music with this rhythm || a quick dance step, esp. a fast fox-trot

quick-tem·pered (kwiktémpərd) *adj.* having a temper that flares up easily

quick time (*mil.*) a rate of marching reckoned as (*Am.*) 120 paces of 30 ins to the minute, (*Br.*) 128 paces of 33 ins to the minute

Quick·tran (kwíktræn) *n.* (*computer*) programming language for use on IBM 1050 terminal 7044 for time-sharing for concurrent access to up to 50 remote terminals

quick·trans (kwíktrænz) *n.* (*mil.*) long-term contract airlift service within continental U.S. for the movement of cargo in support of the logistic system for the military services. *Cf* LOGAIR

quick trick (*bridge*) a card or combination of cards that can be expected to win the first or second trick in a suit

quick-wit·ted (kwíkwítid) *adj.* having a ready wit ||quick to understand

quid (kwid) *n.* a piece of chewing tobacco [var. of CUD]

quid *pl.* quid *n.* (*Br., pop.*) a pound sterling **quids in** (*Br., pop.*) full of winnings; a bet or a gamble [origin unknown]

quid·di·ty (kwíditi:) *pl.* **quid·di·ties** *n.* (*old-fash.*) the essence of a thing || a quibble [fr. M.L. *quidaitas* fr. *quid,* what]

quid pro quo (kwídproukwóu) *n.* something said or done in return for something else, esp. by way of retaliation [L.=something for something]

qui·es·cense (kwaiés'ns) *n.* the state or quality of being quiescent [fr. L.L. *quiescentia*]

qui·es·cent (kwaiés'nt) *adj.* at rest, dormant, inactive [fr. L. *quiescens* (*quiescentis*) fr. *quiescere,* to become quiescent]

qui·et (kwáiit) *n.* silence, stillness, the *quiet of the night* || repose, *periods of quiet between bursts of activity* [fr. L. *quies* (*quietis*)]

quiet *adj.* peaceful, calm and undisturbed, *quiet waters* || noiseless, the *machine room was quiet for once* || not speaking at all, *to keep quiet* || making little sound, *quiet footsteps* || having little volume of sound, *a quiet voice* || (of a person or the mind) free from anguish, worry etc. || (of people) having a gentle, reserved manner || (of colors) soft, unobtrusive || (of feeling etc.) private, interior, a *mood of quiet happiness* || tranquil, free from social pressures, *a quiet life* || (of a social function) informal, attended by few people || (*commerce*) characterized by relatively few sales or little business **on the quiet** (*pop.*) secretly || stealthily [fr. L. *quietus* or O.F. *quiet, quiete*]

quiet *v.t.* to make quiet || to soothe, *to quiet someone's fears* || *v.i.* (usually with 'down') to become quiet [fr. M.L. *quietare*]

qui·et·en (kwáit'n) *v.t.* (*Br.*) to make quiet *v.i.* (*Br.*) to become quiet

qui·et·ism (kwáiitizəm) *n.* a Christian mystical doctrine of the 17th c., expounded chiefly by Molinos, Madame Guyon and Fénelon. It stressed the annihilation of the self in contemplation so as to allow free course to the divine will. It was ethically antinomian, and was condemned by Innocent XI (1687) and Innocent XII (1699) **quí·et·ist** *n.* **qui·et·ís·tic** *adj.* [fr. Ital. *quietismo*]

qui·e·tude (kwáiitu:d, kwáiitju:d) *n.* (*rhet.*) stillness, calm [F. *quiétude*]

qui·e·tus (kwaii:təs) *n.* (*rhet.*) death, final dissolution [fr. M.L. *quietus est,* he is released (from a debt)]

quiff (kwif) *n.* (*Br.*) a flat curl on the forehead [origin unknown]

quill (kwil) **1.** *n.* the hard, partly hollow stem of a bird's feather by which the feather is attached to the skin || a long feather of a bird's wing or tail || something, esp. a pen or a plectrum, made from the hard stem of a bird's feather || the hollow spine of a porcupine || (*weaving*) a spindle or bobbin ||(*pharm.*) a roll of dried bark, e.g. of cinnamon or cinchona **2.** *v.t.* (*weaving*) to wind (thread) onto a spindle or bobbin [etym. doubtful]

qui·llai (ki:jái) *n.* soapbark (tree or bark) [Span.]

Qui·lon (ki:lɔ̃) a port (pop. 100,000) of Kerala, India, on the Malabar coast. Industries: textiles, woodworking, chemicals, metallurgy

quilt (kwilt) **1.** *n.* a bedcover made of feathers, flock or other padding between two pieces of fabric, held in place by lines of stitching || an eiderdown || (*esp. Br.*) a bedspread **2.** *v.t.* to put padded material into || to stitch or stitch together like a quilt || to make (a quilt) || *v.i.* to make a quilt **quílt·ing** *n.* the act of quilting || padded material used esp. for making quilts and warm clothes [O.F. *cuilte, coilte*]

quin (kwin) *n.* (esp. *Br.*) a quintuplet [QUINTUPLET]

qui·nate (kwáinit) *adj.* (*bot.,* of a compound leaf) having five leaflets growing from one point [fr. L. *quini,* five each, like BINATE]

Qui·nault (ki:nou), Philippe (1635–88), French dramatist. He wrote libretti for Lully, e.g. 'Cadmus et Hermione' (1673), 'Armide' (1686) and 'Alceste' (1674)

quince (kwins) *n. Cydonia oblonga,* fam. *Rosaceae,* a small tree native to central and eastern Asia and cultivated in temperate climates. It bears solitary white flowers and pear-shaped, astringent yellow fruits, used cooked or preserved. The tree is also used as a dwarfing stock for grafting pears || its fruit (orig. pl. of M.E. *qe,* a quince]

quin·cen·te·nar·y (kwinséntəneri:) *pl.* **quin·cen·te·nar·ies** *n.* a 500th anniversary [fr. L. *quinque,* five+CENTENARY]

quin·cunx (kwíŋkʌŋks) *n.* an arrangement of five objects, e.g. the symbols on playing cards, with one at each corner and one in the center || this as a planting unit, esp. for orchards [L. fr. *quinque,* five+*uncia,* a twelfth]

Quin·cy (kwínzi:, kwínsi:), Josiah (1772–1864), U.S. Federalist statesman and president (1829–45) of Harvard University. Appointed (1822) judge of the Boston Municipal Court, he was the first to rule that the publication of truth with good intent and for a justifiable end is not libel

quin·de·cil·lion (kwịndisíljən) *n.* *NUMBER TABLE [fr. L. *quinque,* five+DECILLION]

Quine (kwɑin), Willard Van Orman (1908–) U.S. philosopher and logician. Although influenced by such positivists as Rudolf Carnap, he deviated sharply from positivism with his denial of the distinction between analytic and synthetic statements and his view on the logical status of the problem of what exists. His belief that logic and language evolve as tools of inquiry reflect the pragmatism of Clarence Irving Lewis. His books include 'From a Logical Point of View' (1953), 'Word and Object' (1960), 'Philosophy of Logic' (1970) and 'Theories and Things' (1981)

quin·es·trol [$C_{25}H_{32}O_2$] (kwínəstrɒl) *n.* (*pharm.*) estrogenic sex hormone; marketed as Estrovis

Qui·net (ki:nei), Edgar (1803–75), French republican writer. He wrote historical and philosophical works, including 'le Génie des religions' (1842), and imaginative works, including 'Ahasvérus' (1833), a prose poem

quin·i·dine [$C_{20}H_{24}N_2O_2$] (kwínədi:n) *n.* (*pharm.*) a cardiac depressant with actions similar to quinine in malaria; marketed as Cardioquin and Quinalglute

qui·nine (kwáinain, *Br.* esp. kwiní:n) *n.* an alkaloid $C_{20}H_{24}N_2O_2$, derived from the bark of the cinchona and used esp. as a febrifuge in antimalarial treatment ‖ a quinine salt [fr. Span. *quina* fr. Quechua *kina,* bark]

qui·no·a (ki:nóuə) *n. Chenopodium quinoa,* fam. *Chenopodiaceae,* a herbaceous plant native to the high Andes ‖ the seeds of this plant which, ground into meal, constitute a staple of the native diet [Span. fr. Quechua *kinua, kinoa*]

quin·o·line (kwínəli:n, kwínəlin) *n.* a colorless pungent, oily liquid, C_9H_7N, obtained from coal tar and bone oil, used in the manufacture of many dyes and medicines [fr. Span. *quina* fr. Quechua *kina,* bark]

qui·none (kwinóun) *n.* one of two compounds, $C_6H_4O_2$, derived from the benzene hydrocarbons, used in dyes [fr. Span. *quima* fr. Quechua *kina,* bark]

quin·qua·ge·nar·i·an (kwịdkwədʒinéəri:ən) **1.** *n.* a person 50 years old or more but not yet 60 **2.** *adj.* having such an age [fr. L. *quinquagenarius* fr. *quinquaginta,* fifty]

Quin·qua·ges·i·ma (kwịŋkwədʒe'simə) *n.* the Sunday before Lent [M.L. fr. *quinquagesimus,* fiftieth]

quin·que- (kwíŋkwei) *prefix* five [L. *quinque,* five]

quin·que·fo·li·o·late (kwịŋkwifóuli:əleit) *adj.* (*bot.*) having five leaflets [QUINQUE-+L. *folium,* a leaf]

quin·quen·ni·al (kwịŋkwéni:əl) **1.** *adj.* taking place every five years ‖ of or lasting for a five-year period **2.** *n.* a five-year period or term [fr. L. *quinquennis*]

quin·quen·ni·um (kwịŋkwéni:əm) *pl.* **quin·quen·ni·ums, quin·quen·ni·a** (kwịŋkwéni:ə) *n.* a five-year period [L. fr. *quinque,* five+*annus,* a year]

quin·que·va·lent, quin·qui·va·lent (kwịŋkwivéilənt) *adj.* (*chem.*) exhibiting five different valencies (cf. PENTAVALENT) [fr. QUINQUE-+L. *valens* (*valentis*) fr. *valere,* to be strong]

quin·sy (kwínzi:) *n.* an abscess of the areas surrounding the tonsils, esp. when these are previously infected, giving rise to a very sore throat, difficulty in swallowing and fever [fr. M.L. *quinancia* fr. Gk *kunanchē* fr. *kun-,* dog+*anchein,* to throttle]

quint (kwint) *n.* a quintuplet [QUINTUPLET]

quint (kwint, kint) *n.* (*piquet*) a sequence of five cards [F. *quinte*]

quint (kwint, kint) *n.* a pipe-organ stop which causes a note to sound a fifth higher than the key depressed [F. *quint, quinte*]

quin·tain (kwíntin) *n.* (*hist.*) a device consisting of a vertical post surmounted by a pivoting horizontal bar with a board at one end and a bag of sand etc. at the other. It was used in a medieval sport in which a rider tilted at the board and tried to avoid being hit by the swinging bag [O.F. *quintaine*]

quin·tal (kwínt'l) *n.* a measure of weight which varies according to the country (in the U.S.A. 100 pounds, in England 112 pounds) ‖ a metric unit of weight equal to 100 kilograms [fr. O.F. fr. Arab. *quintar*]

Quin·ta·na Ro·o (ki:ntɑ́nɑrɔ́ɔ), Andrés (1787–1851), Mexican jurist, poet and patriot. He served as president of the Congress of Chilpancingo (1813)

Quintana Roo a federal territory (area 19,630 sq. miles, pop. 209,858) of Mexico, on the eastern side of the Yucatán peninsula. Capital: Chetumal (pop. 8,000). Main products: chicle, copra. The hardwood forests are largely unexploited. The descendants of the Maya Indians, who form the bulk of the population, practice subsistence farming

quin·tar (kwíntɑr) *n.* one-hundredth of a lek [Albanian]

quinte (kɛ̃t) *n.* (*fencing*) the fifth parrying position [F.]

quin·tes·sence (kwintés'ns) *n.* the chief, purest or best part of anything, *the quintessence of the book is not in the film* ‖ someone or something perfectly exemplifying a quality ‖ (*ancient and medieval philos.*) the fifth and highest essence, present in all things, but distinct from the four elements of earth, water, air and fire **quin·tes·sen·tial** (kwịntisénʃəl) *adj.* [F. or fr. M.L. *quinta essentia,* fifth essence]

quin·tet, quin·tette (kwintét) *n.* (*mus.*) a composition for five performers ‖ a group of five instrumentalists or singers [F. *quintette*]

quin·tile (kwínt'l) *n.* (*astron.*) the aspect of two planets when distant 72° from one another (=360/5°) ‖ (*statistics*) one of the four values in a frequency distribution which divides the items into five categories [fr. L. *quintus,* fifth]

Quin·til·ian (kwintíljən) (Marcus Fabius Quintilianus, c. 35–95), Roman orator and teacher of rhetoric. His 'Institutio oratoria' (c. 95) describes the education of an orator and analyzes the composition, style and delivery of a classical speech

quin·til·lion (kwintíljən) *n.* *NUMBER TABLE **quin·til·lionth** *n.* and *adj.* [fr. L. *quintus,* fifth+MILLION]

quin·tu·ple (kwintjú:p'l, kwintú:p'l, kwintʌ́p'l) **1.** *adj.* five times as much or as many ‖ having five parts (*mus.*) having five beats to a measure **2.** *n.* a quantity or amount five times as large as another 3. *v. pres. part.* **quin·tu·pling** *past* and *past part.* **quin·tu·pled** *v.t.* to multiply by five ‖ *v.i.* to become five times as much or as many [F.]

quin·tu·plet (kwintʌ́plit, kwintú:plit, kwintjú:plit) *n.* one of five children born at a single birth [QUINTUPLE adj.]

quip (kwip) **1.** *n.* a drily witty or sarcastic remark **2.** *v.t. pres. part.* **quip·ping** *past* and *past part.* **quipped** to make (such a remark) ‖ *v.i.* to make such a remark or remarks [fr. older *quippy,* perh. fr. L. *quippe,* indeed]

qui·pu (kí:pu:) *n.* a device used by the ancient Peruvians for recording dates and events by knotting colored threads together [Quechua]

quire (kwáiər) *n.* a set of 24 or 25 matching sheets of paper ‖ four sheets of paper folded to form eight leaves ‖ a group of sheets folded one within the next in a book etc. **in quires** (of a book, manuscript etc.) in unbound folded sheets [O.F. *quaer, quaier,* a quire of six sheets]

Quir·i·nal (kwírin'l) one of the seven hills of Rome ‖ the former royal palace situated on it, now used by the president of Italy

Qui·ri·no (ki:rí:nɔ), Elpidio (1890–1956), second president (1948–53) of the Republic of the Philippines. His administration was marked by great progress in the post-war reconstruction

quirk (kwə:rk) *n.* a peculiar trait of character or kind of imagination ‖ a flourish with a pen in writing ‖ (*archit.*) a deep lengthwise groove in a molding [etym. doubtful]

Qui·ro·ga (ki:rɔ́gɑ), Horacio (1878– 1937), Uruguayan writer, best known for his short stories, notably 'Cuentos de la selva' (1918), 'Anaconda' (1921), 'El desierto' (1924), and 'Los desterrados' (1926)

Quiroga, Juan Facundo (1793–1835), Argentinian federalist. military adventurer, and virtual ruler (1820–30) of northeastern Argentina. His exploits earned him the nickname 'tiger of the llanos'. While governor of Buenos Aires (1834–5) he was assassinated

quirt (kwə:rt) **1.** *n.* a short-handled riding whip, with a plaited leather lash **2.** *v.t.* to lash with such a whip [Span. *cuarta*]

Quis·ling (kwízliŋ), Vidkun (1887–1945), Norwegian fascist politician. He led a puppet regime (1940–5) during the German occupation of Norway, and was executed for treason

quis·ling (kwízliŋ) *n.* person who collaborates with an enemy power occupying his country ‖ (*loosely*) a traitor [after V. QUISLING]

Quis·que·ya (kiskéijɑ) the original name of the island of Hispaniola

quit (kwit) *adj.* (usually followed by 'of') rid, free, *to be quit of an obligation* [M.E. *quite* fr. O.F.]

quit *pres. part.* **quit·ting** *past* and *past part.* **quit, quit·ted** *v.t.* to leave, go away from, *to quit the army* ‖ to resign (one's job) ‖ to discontinue (some activity), *to quit work* ‖ *v.i.* (*Br.,* of a tenant) to leave a rented house, flat etc. ‖ to resign one's job ‖ to discontinue some activity [M.E. *quitten* fr. O.F.]

quitch (kwitʃ) *n.* couch grass [O.E. *cwice,*rh. related to *cwic,* quick]

quit·claim (kwítklẹim) *n.* (*law*) a document by which the signatory renounces his rights to some title, claim or possession and gives this over to another person [M.E. *quitclaymie* fr. O.F.]

quitclaim *v.t.* to renounce one's rights to (a property, title etc.) by quitclaim [M.E. fr. A.F. and O.F. *quiteclamer, quiteclaimer*]

quite (kwait) *adv.* completely, entirely, *are you quite sure?, we are not quite there yet* ‖ very much, *he is quite an artist* rather, to an appreciable extent, *it's quite warm* ‖ (*Br.,* as a response to a question or statement) true, yes **quite a few** a considerable number [M.E. fr. *quite,* quit *adj.*]

Qui·to (kí:tou) the capital (pop. 1,110,248) of Ecuador, in the N. Sierra at 9,300 ft, 170 miles from its port, Guayaquil. Earthquakes are frequent. Industries: textiles, food processing, light manufactures. Handicrafts: leatherwork, stone and wood carving, jewelry. It was a pre-Inca capital (10th–15th cc.). It was founded (1534) by Sebastián de Benalcázar with the name San Francisco de Quito. Cathedral (18th c.). University (1787)

quit·rent (kwítrẹnt) *n.* (*hist.*) a sum paid in commutation of feudal services

quits (kwits) *adj.* equal, on even terms as a result or repayment of a debt or injury, *to be quits* (*with someone*) **to call it quits** to agree to stop squabbling or competing without victory or defeat on either side, and with no ill feeling [QUIT adj.]

quit·tance (kwít'ns) *n.* acknowledgment of payment of a debt or the receipt for this [O.F. *quitance*]

quiv·er (kwívər) **1.** *v.i.* to tremble, to shake with a slight, rapid movement, *leaves quivering in the breeze, to quiver with rage* ‖ *v.t.* to cause to tremble **2.** *n.* a quivering ‖ a tremulous sound, *a quiver in his voice* [perh. imit.]

quiver *n.* a long case, suspended on a strap worn over one shoulder, to hold arrows ‖ the arrows themselves [A.F. *quiveir,* O.F. *quivre* fr. Gmc]

qui vive (ki:ví:v) *n.* (only in the phrase) **on the qui vive** on the alert, on guard or on the watch [F.=(long) live who?, originally a sentry's challenge]

quix·ot·ic (kwiksɒ́tik) *adj.* striving for or characterized by lofty ideals in a way that is ludicrous because totally unrealistic ‖ rashly altruistic **quix·ót·i·cal·ly** *adv.* [after *Don Quixote,* hero of a story by Cervantes]

quiz (kwiz) **1.** *pl.* **quiz·zes** *n.* a short written or oral test of knowledge **2.** *v.t. pres. part.* **quiz·zing** *past* and *past part.* **quizzed** to test (someone) by asking a series of questions [origin unknown]

quiz·zi·cal (kwízik'l) *adj.* interrogative, indicating a state of puzzlement, *a quizzical glance* ‖ teasing, gently mocking, *quizzical remarks* mildly eccentric or odd [QUIZ=(obs.) to make fun of]

Qum·ran (kumrɑ́n) a village of Jordan, northwest of the Dead Sea, the site of the ascetic community (2nd c. B.C.–1st c. A.D.) by whom the Dead Sea Scrolls were written

quo·drat (kwóudrɑt) *n.* (*envir.*) a sampling area, usu. 1 sq mi, used for analyzing vegetation. *Cf* QUATRAT

quoin (kɔin, kwɔin) **1.** *n.* the external corner of a building, or one of the stones or bricks which form it (usually laid with their long axes in alternate directions) and which are distinguished from the material of the walls coming in to form the corner ‖ (*printing*) a wedge keeping type in its form ‖ a wedge used for various purposes, e.g. for raising a gun carriage **2.** *v.t.* to secure or raise with a quoin [var. of COIN=(obs.) quoin, wedge] .

quoit (kɔit, kwɔit) *n.* a ring of rope, wood etc. used in a throwing game (*pl.*) a game in which such a ring is tossed towards a peg or small stake in an attempt to ring it [prob. fr. F.]

quon·dam (kwóndæm) *adj.* (*rhet.*) former, *a quondam colleague* [L.=formerly]

Quon·set hut (kwónsit) a prefabricated structure used for temporary army barracks etc. It has a cylindrical roof of corrugated iron curving down to form walls [Trademark]

quo·rum (kwóɾəm, kwóuɾəm) *n.* a number of people, fixed by rule, that must be present to make valid the proceedings of a committee, society, court etc. [L.=of whom]

quo·ta (kwóutə) *n.* an allotted share, to be either contributed or received, *each has his quota of work for the day* ‖ a numerical limit set on some class of things or persons, *a quota of immigrants* [M.L. *quota (pars)*, how great (a part)]

quo·ta·ble (kwóutəb'l) *adj.* which may be publicly repeated lending itself to quotation [QUOTE V.]

quota post an international post that a particular nation has accepted to fill indefinitely

quo·ta·tion (kwoutéiʃən) **1.** *n.* a passage or phrase quoted, esp. from printed literature ‖ the act of quoting ‖ the amount declared as the current price for a commodity etc. ‖ a contractor's estimate of the cost of a piece of work ‖ (*printing*) a large metal quad used for filling blanks [fr. M.L. *quotatio (quotationis)*, a reference to a passage in a manuscript etc.]

quotation marks single (") or double ("") punctuation marks signalizing direct speech, a quoted passage or phrase, book titles etc.

quote (kwout) **1.** *v. pres. part.* **quot·ing** *past* and *past part.* **quot·ed** *v.t.* to repeat in writing or speech (a passage or phrase previously said or written, esp. by someone else) ‖ to repeat in speech or writing a passage from, *to quote the Scriptures* ‖ to refer to (a person, work etc.) in support of a statement, *she quoted him as her authority* ‖ to enclose (a word or words) within quotation marks ‖ to state (the price) of a commodity etc. ‖ to state the price of (a commodity etc.) ‖ *v.i.* to make a quotation or quotations **2.** *n.* a quotation ‖(*pl.*) quotation marks [fr. M.L. *quotare*, to mark the number of]

quo·tid·i·an (kwoutídiːən) **1.** *adj.* (*rhet.*) daily, occurring each day ‖ (of a fever) which occurs every day **2.** *n.* a quotidian fever [O.F. *cotidien, cotidian* or fr. L. *cotidianus, quotidianus*]

quo·tient (kwóuʃənt) *n.* the result obtained after dividing one number by another [fr. L. *quotiens*, how many times]

quo war·ran·to (kwɒuwɔɹǽntou) *n.* a writ issued by a court commanding a person to show by what warrant he holds an office, franchise etc. [Med. L.=by what warrant]

qu·rush (kʌ́rəʃ) *n.* a monetary unit of Saudi Arabia equal to one twentieth of a rial ‖ a coin of the value of one qurush

Q-val·ue (kjúvǽljuː) *n.* (*phys.*) quantity of energy released in a nuclear reaction, expressed in million electron volts, (MEV), or atomic mass units

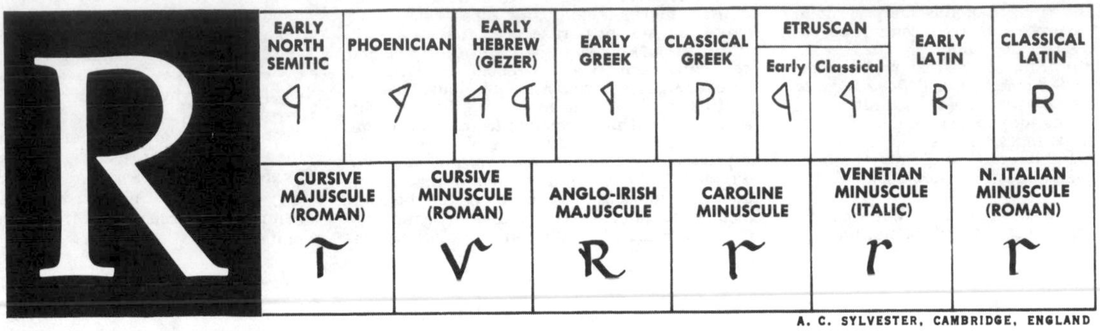
R
EARLY NORTH SEMITIC
PHOENICIAN
EARLY HEBREW (GEZER)
EARLY GREEK
CLASSICAL GREEK
ETRUSCAN
Early
Classical
EARLY LATIN
CLASSICAL LATIN
CURSIVE MAJUSCULE (ROMAN)
CURSIVE MINUSCULE (ROMAN)
ANGLO-IRISH MAJUSCULE
CAROLINE MINUSCULE
VENETIAN MINUSCULE (ITALIC)
N. ITALIAN MINUSCULE (ROMAN)
A. C. SYLVESTER, CAMBRIDGE, ENGLAND

Development of the letter R, beginning with the early North Semitic letter. Evolution of both the majuscule, or capital, letter R and the minuscule, or lowercase, letter r are shown.

R, r (ɑr) the eighteenth letter of the English alphabet

R *adj.* motion picture rating of *restricted,* requiring that a person under the age of 18 (sometimes 17) be accompanied by an adult. *Cf* G, PG, X

Ra (rɑ) (*Egypt. mythol.*) the sun god and chief deity of ancient Egypt. He is usually represented as having the head of a hawk crowned with the solar disk

Raa·be (rɑ́bə), Wilhelm (1831-1910), German novelist, best known for his 'Die Chronik aus der Sperlingsgasse' (1857) and 'Der Hungerpastor' (1864)

Rab (rɑb) a Yugoslav island (area 40 sq. miles, pop. 7,000), in the N. Adriatic: tourism

RABAL (*meteor. acronym*) for radiosonde balloon, a system of balloons at various altitudes that relay information about atmospheric conditions

Ra·ba·nus Mau·rus (rəbéinəsmɔ́rəs) (c. 780-856), German Benedictine theologian and scholar. As abbot of Fulda (822-42), he made the monastery a leading center of the Carolingian revival of learning

Ra·bat (rəbɑ́t) the capital (pop. 518,616) of Morocco, on the Atlantic: cotton spinning, weaving, leatherwork, carpets. Famous mosque (12th c.), palace, university

rab·bet (rǽbit) **1.** *n.* a groove cut in a wooden board, panel etc. to fit the edge or a tongue on another piece of wood **2.** *v.t.* to cut a rabbet in ‖ to join (two pieces of wood) with a rabbet [O.F. *rabat, rabbat* fr. *rabattre,* to beat down]

rab·bi (rǽbai) *n.* (esp. *hist.*) a teacher and scholar of Jewish civil and religious law ‖ an ordained leader of a Jewish congregation [Heb. *rabbī,* my master]

rab·bin (rǽbin) *n.* (esp. *hist.*) a rabbi (teacher) **rab·bin·ate** (rǽbinit, rǽbineit) *n.* the office or term of office of a rabbi ‖ (*collect.*) rabbis **rab·bín·ic** *adj.* of or pertaining to rabbis, their writings etc. ‖ of or pertaining to the rabbinate **Rab·bin·ic 1.** *adj.* of or pertaining to the rabbis of the period of the compilation and exegesis (c. 2nd c.–13th c.) of the Talmud **2.** *n.* Rabbinic Hebrew [F. or fr. M.L. *rabbinus*]

rab·bin·i·cal (rəbínik'l) *adj.* **rabbinic Rab·bin·i·cal** *adj.* Rabbinic

Rabbinic Hebrew the Hebrew language as used by the rabbis in their writings, esp. during the Middle Ages

rab·bit (rǽbit) **1.** *pl.* **rab·bits, rab·bit** *n. Oryctolagus cuniculus,* fam. *Leporidae,* a usually gray-brown, extremely prolific, herbivorous, burrowing lagomorph approximately 16 ins long. Native to W. Europe, it is now found in nearly all temperate regions. It has very long ears, a short round tail, and long hind limbs and feet. It moves about by jumping. Rabbits yield meat good to eat and furs (*CONEY), poorer quality furs being made into felt ‖ the fur or pelt of a rabbit ‖ (*sports*) track-team member who sets a fast pace to induce competition to spend energy early in a long-distance race, to the advantage of a teammate ‖ (*Br., pop.*) someone who is very weak in games **2.** *v.i.* to hunt rabbits [etym. doubtful]

rabbit ears *n. pl.* a V-shape indoor television antenna

rabbit punch (*boxing*) an illegal blow delivered with the outside edge of the hand to the base of the skull

rab·ble (rǽb'l) *n.* a large, disorderly mob of people **the rabble** (used contemptuously) the common people, lowest members of society [etym. doubtful]

rabble *n.* an iron rod bent at one end, used for stirring molten metal [F. *râble*]

Rab·e·lais (rǽblei), François (c. 1494–c. 1553), French writer and scholar. After a time in monasteries, he became a secular priest and a doctor. His great satirical work, usually known as 'Gargantua and Pantagruel', was published in parts (1532-64). 'Rabelaisian' has come to mean joyously coarse, for there is an enormous strain of hyperbolical bawdiness in Rabelais. It combines with his obvious love of life and its good things, and his extraordinary torrential style—punning, neologizing, alternately mock-pedantic and earthy—to produce his special humor. He had a profound reverence and sympathy for the ideal of humanist learning. This is best expressed in the education devised for the philosophic monster Gargantua, and the description of the Abbey of Thelème. In contrast, monkish learning, the pedantries of medieval scholarship, and the bigotry which for Rabelais went with them, are derided. Yet the freedom and art of his grotesque humor places him firmly in the Middle Ages

Rab·e·lai·sian (ræbəléiʒən) *adj.* (of humor) joyously coarse or gross ‖ of or pertaining to Rabelais [after RABELAIS]

Ra·bi (rɑ́:bi:), Isidor Issac (1898-), U.S. physicist and winner of the 1944 Nobel prize in physics for discovering and measuring spectra in the radio-frequency range of atomic nuclei whose magnetic spin has been disturbed

rab·id (rǽbid) *adj.* affected with rabies ‖ pertaining to rabies ‖ violent, unreasoning, *a rabid reactionary* **ra·bid·i·ty** (rəbíditi:) *n.* [fr. L. *rabidus,* mad]

ra·bies (réibi:z) *n.* an acute virus disease of warm-blooded animals, esp. dogs. It is transmitted with infected saliva through the bite of a rabid animal (*HYDROPHOBIA)

Rabin (rabí:n), Yitzhak (1922-), Israeli statesman, prime minister (1974-7). He served as armed forces chief of staff (1964-8), during which time he directed the Six-Day War victory (1967), and as ambassador to the U.S.A. (1968-73) before being made prime minister. Pres. Shimon Peres named him defense minister in 1984

Ra·can (rækã), Honorat de Bueil, marquis de (1589-1670), French classical poet. 'Bergeries' (1625), a pastoral play, is his most important work

rac·coon, ra·coon (rækú:n) *pl.* **rac·coon, rac·coons, ra·coon, ra·coons** *n. Procyon lotor,* fam. *Procyonidae,* a North American carnivore about 32 ins in length, with grayish-brown fur and a bushy tail marked with black rings ‖ its fur [fr. Algonquian *ärähkun* fr. *ärähkuněm,* he scratches with his hands]

race (reis) *n.* a distinct group of people, the members of which share certain inherited physical characteristics (skin color, form of the hair etc.) and transmit them ‖ all descendants of a person, family or a people, *the race of David* ‖ a group of people of the same profession or sharing some binding interest, *the race of actors* ‖ (*biol.*) a subdivision of a species ‖ (*biol.*) a permanent variety ‖ (*biol.*) a particular breed ‖ (*loosely*) a political, linguistic or nationalist group [F.]

race 1. *n.* a contest of speed in which runners, horses or yachts etc. try to reach a set goal first ‖ (*pl.*) a series of such contests for horses on a regular course ‖ (*astron.*) a set orbit ‖ a strong, swift current in water ‖ the channel of a stream, esp. one artificially constructed to create power for industrial use ‖ either of the rings of a ball bearing or a roller bearing between which the bearings rotate ‖ the groove along which a shuttle moves in a loom ‖ a slipstream **2.** *v.i. pres. part.* **rac·ing** *past* and *past part.* **raced** to take part in a contest of speed ‖ to go swiftly ‖ (of an engine) to go very fast, either without the gears being engaged or because the load has been diminished ‖ *v.t.* to compete against in speed ‖ to cause (a horse etc.) to compete in a race ‖ to accelerate (an engine) very fast without engaging the gears ‖ to make (something or someone) move quickly [O.N. *rās,* a running]

racecourse (réiskɔrs, réiskours) *n.* a racetrack

race·horse (réishɔrs) *n.* a horse bred and trained for racing

ra·ceme (rəsí:m) *n.* an unbranched inflorescence having stalked flowers with the youngest growing at the tip (e.g. lupin, hyacinth) [fr. L. *racemus,* bunch of grapes]

race meeting (*Br.*) a number of horse races held at one place on one day or over several days

ra·ce·mic (rəsí:mik, rəsémik) *adj.* (*chem.*) of or pertaining to a compound or mixture having equal amounts of dextrorotatory and levorotatory forms of the same compound and which is therefore optically inactive to polarized light ‖ of or derived from racemic acid [F. *racémique*]

racemic acid racemic tartaric acid, obtained from grape juice

rac·e·mi·za·tion (ræsəmizéiʃən) *n.* the process of changing from an optically active substance to a racemic substance [RACEMIZE]

rac·e·mize (rǽsəmaiz) *pres. part.* **rac·e·miz·ing** *past* and *past part.* **rac·e·mized** *v.t.* to cause to undergo racemization ‖ *v.i.* to undergo racemization [RACEMIC]

rac·e·mose (rǽsəmous) *adj.* bearing a raceme or racemes ‖ of the nature of a raceme [fr. L. *racemosus*]

rac·er (réisər) *n.* a person or animal who races ‖ a car, bicycle etc. made and used for racing ‖ a circular rail on which a heavy coast artillery gun is traversed ‖ any of several snakes, esp. the black racer and the blue racer of North America [RACE]

race riot an outbreak of violence and fighting caused by racial hatred in a community

race suicide the gradual dying out of a race whose members deliberately fail to keep the birthrate as high as the death rate

race·track (réistræk) *n.* a course laid out, typically in an oval, for horse racing

Ra·chel (réitʃəl) (*Bible*) the wife of Jacob, and the mother of Joseph and Benjamin

ra·chis (réikis) *pl.* **ra·chis·es, ra·chi·des** (réikidi:z) *n.* the central stalk which bears the leaflets of a compound leaf ‖ (*bot.*) the axis of an inflorescence ‖ the shaft of a feather ‖ the spinal column [Mod. L. fr. Gk *rhachis,* spine]

ra·chit·ic (rəkítik) *adj.* suffering from or pertaining to rickets

ra·chi·tis (rəkáitis) *n.* rickets [Mod. L. fr. Gk *rhachitis,* inflammation of the spine]

Rach·ma·ni·noff (rækmáninɔf, ræxmáninɔf), Sergei Vassilievich (1873-1943), Russian composer, pianist and conductor who lived in the U.S.A. after 1918. The best-known of his highly romantic compositions are the piano preludes and the Second Piano Concerto (1901)

ra·cial (réiʃəl) *adj.* pertaining to or caused by the distinction between races **rá·cial·ism** *n.* race hatred or race discrimination

rac·i·ly (réisili:) *adv.* in a racy way

Ra·cine (ræsi:n), Jean (1639-99), French dramatist. He was as great a poet as he was a dramatist, developing the Alexandrine as an instrument for the direct expression of intense emotion, in language of great beauty. His plays are based on classical themes and they obey the classical unities and conventions. In the 24 hours of the action the fruit of years, or a lifetime, is reaped, so that the audience is filled with a profound sense of destiny. The motivating force is always love, which is presented as a destructive force dissolving the personality and bringing spiritual disaster. Racine's heroes and heroines analyze their failings with great lucidity, and this lucidity adds to the pathos and feeling of imminent disaster. Racine's greatest plays are: 'Andromaque' (1667), 'Britannicus' (1669), 'Bérénice' (1670) and 'Phèdre' (1677)

rac·i·ness (réisi:nis) *n.* the quality of being racy

racing form information printed in a newspaper or in a separate sheet, comprising data about horses, races, jockeys, odds etc.

rac·ism (réisizəm) *n.* the assumption that the characteristics and abilities of an individual are determined by race and that one race is biologically superior to another ‖ a political program or social system based on these assumptions **rác·ist** *n.* and *adj.*

rack (ræk) **1.** *n.* a mass of clouds driven by the wind **2.** *v.i.* (of scudding clouds) to fly before the wind [prob. fr. Scand.]

rack *n.* a framework of wooden or metal bars, pegs etc. for holding objects, often adapted to objects of a particular type, e.g. hats, plates ‖ a shelf of bars or cord mesh in a railroad car etc. to hold luggage ‖ a framework in a stable, paddock etc. holding hay or fodder ‖ a framework fitted on a wagon for carrying hay, straw etc. ‖ a bar or rail with teeth which gear into those of a cogwheel or worm ‖ (*printing*) a frame holding type cases ‖ a row or box of pigeonholes into which letters etc. are sorted ‖ (*pool games*) a triangular frame for setting up the balls at the beginning of a game [prob. M. Du. *rec* fr. *recken,* to stretch]

rack 1. *v.t.* (*hist.*) to torture by stretching on a rack ‖ to inflict extreme mental or physical pain upon ‖ to shake or strain severely, *a racking cough* ‖ (of a landlord) to exact an unjustly high rent from (a tenant) ‖ (of a landlord) to raise (rents) unjustly and exorbitantly **to rack one's brains** to think very hard ‖ to try very hard to remember **2.** *n.* (*hist.*) an instrument of torture consisting of a frame with rollers at each end, to which the victim's wrists and ankles were tied so that he was stretched as the rollers were turned **on the rack** in physical or mental anguish [prob. fr. M. Du. or Middle L.G. *recken,* to stretch]

rack *n.* (only in the phrase) **rack and ruin** utter destruction or decay [var. of WRACK]

rack 1. *n.* a fast gait in which a horse is supported on the right and left pairs of legs alternately **2.** *v.i.* (of a horse) to go at a rack [etym. doubtful]

rack *v.t.* to draw off (wine etc.) from the lees [fr. Prov. *arracar* fr. *raca,* stems and skins of grapes]

rack and pinion (*mechanics*) method of exchanging linear and rotary force by engagement between a straight-toothed rack and a small gear-wheel (pinion)

rack car a railroad freight car equipped with two or three levels for carrying automobiles

rack·et, rac·quet (rǽkit) *n.* (*games*) a bat formed by a long-handled oval wooden frame across which a mesh of catgut or nylon is stretched. Each game (tennis, squash etc.) played with a racket has its own special kind ‖ (*pl.*) a game not unlike squash played with rackets and a ball in a four-walled court by two or four players [F. *raquette*]

racket *n.* a considerable and usually continued clattering noise or similar disturbance ‖ (*pop.*) a fraudulent means of gaining money on a large or small scale ‖ (*pop.*) an easy way of making money which is lawful but not praiseworthy or respectable **to stand the racket** (*Br.*) to take the blame for an action [prob. imit.]

racket ball a small, hard, kid-covered ball used in rackets

rack·et·eer (rækitíər) *n.* a person who is engaged in fraudulent business or who extorts money by threats, blackmail etc.

rack·e·ty (rǽkiti:) *adj.* noisy, causing a racket

rack railway a railway with an extra, cogged rail between the lines, which engages with a cogged wheel on the railway engine to prevent its sliding back on steep slopes

rack rent an unjustly large sum demanded as rent for property **rack-rent** *v.t.* to subject to such extortion

rac·on·teur (rækɒntə́:r) *n.* a person who tells anecdotes well [F.]

ra·coon *RACCOON

racquet *RACKET

rac·y (réisi:) *comp.* **rac·i·er** *superl.* **rac·i·est** *adj.* spirited, lively, *written in a racy style* ‖ (of stories or conversation) wittily indecent

rad (ræd) *n.* (*phys.*) unit of absorbed radiation equal to 100 ergs per gram of irradiated material

RADAN (*acronym*) for radar doppler automatic navigation, an aircraft radar navigation system depending on Doppler effect, with no ground communication

ra·dar (réidɑr) *n.* a radio system which detects the presence, position and speed of such objects as ships, aircraft, vehicles etc. by emitting microwaves and measuring by electronic devices the speed with which they return after reflection from the object. It is also used e.g. for guiding ships and aircraft in fog etc. or by police for determining the speed of vehicles etc. [*RAdio Detection And Ranging*]

radar astronomy (*meteor.*) study of celestial bodies through use of radar signals sent from earth **—radar telescope** *n.* the instrument used

radar range distance at which a radar sighting may be made with 50% visibility

ra·dar·sonde (reídɑrsɒnd) *n.* **1.** (*meteor.*) a system for measuring atmospheric conditions automatically from high altitudes and transmitting data via a ground command signal **2.** a system to gauge the range, elevation, and azimuth of a radar target

Rad·cliffe (rǽdklif), Mrs Ann (1764-1823), British novelist. Her Gothic novels include 'The Mysteries of Udolpho' (1794)

rad·dled (rǽd'ld) *adj.* (of aging women) grotesquely rouged, haggard under cosmetics [fr. older *raddle,* to ruddle]

Ra·detz·ky (rædétski:) Joseph, Graf Radetzky von Radetz (1766-1858), Austrian field marshal. He led the Austrian army against Sardinia (1848-9), winning brilliant victories at Custozza (1848) and Novara (1849)

Radhakrishnan (radəkríʃnən), Sir Sarvepalli (1888-1976), Indian statesman and educator, president (1962-7). He taught at Oxford (1936-9), Benares Hindu (1938-48) and Delhi (1953-62) universities; headed the Indian UNESCO delegation (1946-52); was ambassador to the U.S.S.R. (1949-52); and was vice-president (1952-62) before becoming president. His works include 'Indian Philosophy' (1923-7), 'An Idealist View of Life' (1932) and 'Indian Philosophy Religions and Western Thought' (1939)

ra·di·ac (reídi:æk) *adj.* (*mil. acronym*) for radioactivity detection, indication, and computation of various types of radiological measuring instruments, or equipment. **—radiac dosimeter** *n.* an instrument used to measure the ionizing radiation absorbed by that instrument

ra·di·al (réidi:əl) **1.** *adj.* pertaining to a radius ‖ arranged like or resembling radii ‖ having radiating lines, *radial engine* ‖ (*anat.*) pertaining to the radius ‖ moving along a radius **2.** *n.* a radial nerve or artery [fr. L.L. *radialis*]

radial, radial-ply tire, or **radial tire** *n.* a pneumatic tire made with ply casing cords parallel at right angles to the center line and rim

radial keratotomy (*med.*) surgical process involving a series of cuts into the transparent corneal tissue, causing a slight bulge, thus improving the focusing ability of nearsighted people; developed by U.S.S.R. scientist Svyatoslav Fydorov in 1980

radial symmetry the state of having an arrangement of similar parts around a median vertical axis, e.g. in jellyfish or starfish

ra·di·an (réidi:ən) *n.* a unit of angular measurement, the angle subtended at the center of a circle by an arc equal in length to the radius. Since the circumference of a circle equals 2π times its radius the total angle in a complete turn (360°) is 2π radians [RADIUS]

ra·di·ance (réidi:əns) *n.* the state or quality of being radiant **rá·di·an·cy** *n.* [fr. L.L. or M.L. *radiantia*]

ra·di·ant (réidi:ənt) **1.** *adj.* emitting energy in the form of electromagnetic waves ‖ shining, bright ‖ bright with, or expressing, great joy, hope etc., *a radiant smile* **2.** *n.* (*astron.*) a point from which a meteor appears to proceed ‖ (*phys.*) a point which is a source of radiant energy [fr. L. *radians* (*radiantis*) fr. *radiare,* to emit rays]

ra·di·ate (réidi:eit) **1.** *v. pres. part.* **ra·di·at·ing** *past* and *past part.* **ra·di·at·ed** *v.t.* to emit (something) in all directions from a central point ‖ *v.i.* to lose energy by emission of waves or particles ‖ to proceed in all directions from a central point, *eight roads radiate from the marketplace* **2.** *adj.* radially symmetrical ‖ having ray flowers [fr. L. *radiare* (*radiatus*), to emit rays]

ra·di·a·tion (reidi:éiʃən) *n.* the act or process of radiating ‖ energy radiated in the form of waves or particles (e.g. the energy in the form of heat and light radiated from an incandescent source) [fr. L. *radiatio* (*radiationis*)]

radiation chemistry the study of the chemical effects of high-energy radiations on matter (cf. RADIOCHEMISTRY)

radiation genetics study of mutations produced by ionizing radiation. *also* radiogenetics

radiation sickness an illness caused by the action of high-energy radiation upon the body, resulting either from radiotherapy or from radioactive debris after an atomic-bomb explosion. Vomiting and fatigue are the first symptoms after exposure, and may be followed later by liability to infection, hemorrhage, prostration and death

ra·di·a·tor (réidi:eitər) *n.* any of various heating or cooling devices which work by radiating heat ‖ any object emitting radiant energy [RADIATE]

rad·i·cal (rǽdik'l) **1.** *adj.* relating to or affecting fundamentals, *a radical change* ‖ existing in the essential character of a person or thing, *radical differences* ‖ (*math.*) relating to the root of a number ‖ (*bot.,* e.g. of basal leaves or peduncles) arising from the rhizome, or rootlike stem ‖ (*gram.*) of or pertaining to a linguistic root ‖ (esp. *politics*) seeking to make drastic reforms in society as it is **2.** *n.* (*math.*) a number or quantity as the root of another number or quantity ‖

(*chem.*) an atom or group of atoms that retains its identity during chemical changes of the rest of the molecule ‖ (*chem.*) a free radical ‖ (*gram.*) the base or root of a word from which other words can be formed ‖ (*politics*) a person of radical views or sympathies [fr. L.L. *radicalis*]

rad·i·cal·ism (rǽdik'lizəm) *n.* the state or quality of being radical, esp. in politics ‖ the doctrines or practices of radicals, esp. political radicals

radical right (*U.S.*) extreme conservative movement in politics, e.g., fascism —**radical rightism** *n.* —**radical rightist** *n.*

radical sign the symbol √ or √‾, indicating that the square root is to be extracted from the quantity that follows the sign

radices alt. *pl.* of RADIX

rad·i·cle (rǽdik'l) *n.* the primary root developing in a seed ‖ a rootlet of a seedling ‖ (*chem.*) a radical ‖ (*anat.*) a small rootlike origin of a bodily part [fr. L. *radicula,* dim. of *radix,* root]

rad·i·es·the·sia (rædi:esθí:ʒə) *n.* **1.** use of a divining rod, e.g., for water **2.** the capability of using a divining rod **3.** the study of the subject

Ra·di·guet (rædi:gei), Raymond (1903-23), French novelist, author of 'le Diable au corps' (1923) and 'le Bal du comte d'Orgel' (published 1924)

radii alt. *pl.* of RADIUS

ra·di·o (réidi:ou) **1.** *n.* the transmission and reception of messages by electromagnetic waves ‖ broadcasting for public entertainment ‖ a radio receiving set ‖ a message sent by radio **2.** *adj.* operated by radiant energy, esp. electromagnetic waves ‖ (of waves) having a frequency between about 10^4 and 3 x 10^{11} cycles ‖ of or relating to radio or a radio receiving set **3.** *v.i.* to communicate by radio ‖ *v.t.* to send (a message) by radio [shortened from RADIOTELEGRAPHY] —Coded signals, speech, music etc. may be transmitted by superimposing the audible signals on an electromagnetic carrier wave of much higher frequency, so that they vary (modulate) the frequency of the amplitude of the carrier wave. In the receiver the superimposed signal is isolated and fed to a loudspeaker. The radio frequency band occupies a range of wavelengths from 10^5 to 10^{-3} meters

radio- *prefix* concerned with radiation ‖ radioactive ‖ radio [fr. L. *radius,* spoke, ray]

ra·di·o·ac·tin·i·um (rẹidi:ouæktíni:əm) *n.* (*phys.*) thorium isotope resulting from natural decay of actinium 227. *abbr.* **RdAc**

ra·di·o·ac·tive (rẹidi:ouǽktiv) *adj.* of, relating to or having radioactivity **ra·di·o·ac·tiv·i·ty** *n.* the property possessed by some natural elements (e.g. radium, uranium) and many synthetic elements (all those with atomic number greater than 92) of spontaneously undergoing nuclear decay, emitting either an alpha particle (reducing their atomic number by 2 and mass number by 4) or a beta particle (increasing their atomic number by 1, leaving their mass number unaltered). Emission of a beta particle is accompanied by the emission of a neutrino, the overall process obeying both energy and momentum conservation. Sometimes emission of either alpha or beta particles leaves the new nucleus in an excited state from which it falls with the emission of a gamma ray. The rates for such nuclear processes, usually indicated by the half-life, vary over a tremendous range (from a microsecond to a billion years or more). The half-life for a radioactive element is an important constant, characteristic of the element (*FISSION, *NUCLEAR ENERGY)

radioactive dating a technique for dating ancient objects by evaluating and comparing the ratio of radioisotopes contained in them —**radiocarbon age** *n. Cf* RADIOCARBON DATING

radioactive decay (*nuclear phys.*) the decrease in the radiation intensity of any radioactive material over time, generally accompanied by the emission of particles and/or gamma radiation

radioactive isotope or **radioisotope** (*nuclear chem.*) any of two or more natural or artifically produced chemical elements with the same atomic number but a different mass number, used for tracing in medicine and industry —**radioisotopic** *adj.* —**radioisotopically** *adv.*

radioactive tracer a preparation consisting of a radioisotope added to a nonradioactive material, to tag it in order that it can be followed in a living system or along an oil pipeline

radio astronomy a branch of astronomy dealing with electromagnetic radiation in the range of radio frequencies received (*RADIO TELESCOPE) from objects or regions outside the earth's atmosphere. Radio astronomy has been able, for example, to elucidate the structure of spiral galaxies, since these contain large quantities of hydrogen which emits a strong signal of wavelength 21 cm.

radio beacon a radio station which transmits a special identifying signal to enable esp. an aircraft to fix its position at night or in fog

radio beam a beam of radio-frequency electromagnetic radiation, emitted from a highly directional antenna, used in location and guidance systems

ra·di·o·car·bon (rẹidi:oukɑ́rbən) *n.* radioactive carbon, esp. carbon 14 (*CARBON)

radiocarbon dating a technique for determining the age of ancient material by measuring the proportion of 12C to residual 14C, a constant ratio formed by cosmic radiation in living organisms. 14C has a half-life of 5,740 yrs. *also* carbon dating, carbon 14 dating. *Cf* RADIOACTIVE DATING

ra·di·o·chem·is·try (rẹidi:oukémistri:) *n.* the chemistry of radioactive elements and compounds ‖ radiation chemistry

ra·di·o·chro·ma·tog·ra·phy (rẹidi:oukrọuma-tɒ́grəfi:) *n.* measurement of isotope-labeled chemicals by their radioactivity —**radiochromatographic** *adj.*

ra·di·o·e·col·o·gy (rẹidi:ouikɒ́lədʒi:) *n.* the study of effects of radiation on plant and animal life —**radioecological** *adj.* —**radioecologically** *adv.* —**radioecologist** *n.*

radio frequency any of a range of electromagnetic wave frequencies used for carrier-wave radio and television transmission

radio galaxy (*astron.*) a group of celestial bodies from which radio energy emissions are detected

ra·di·o·gen·ic (rẹidi:oudʒénik) *adj.* (*nuclear phys.*) produced by radioactive transformation. *Cf* RADIATION GENETICS

ra·di·o·gram (réidi:ougræm) *n.* a radiograph ‖ a message sent by wireless telegraphy ‖ (*Br.*) a radiogramophone [fr. RADIO-+Gk *gramma,* letter]

ra·di·o·gram·o·phone (rẹidi:ougrǽməfoun) *n.* (*Br.*) a cabinet combining radio receiver and a record player

ra·di·o·graph (réidi:ougræf, réidi:ougrɑf) **1.** *n.* an image produced on a fluorescent screen or photographic plate by rays other than those of light, esp. an X-ray photograph **2.** *v.t.* to take an X-ray photograph of **ra·di·og·ra·pher** (rẹidi:ɒ́grəfər) *n.* someone who takes X-ray photographs, esp. for medical purposes **ra·di·o·graph·ic** (rẹidi:ougrǽfik) *adj.* **ra·di·og·ra·phy** (rẹidi:ɒ́grəfi:) *n.* the making of X-ray photographs [fr. RADIO-+Gk *-graphos,* written]

ra·di·o·im·mu·no·as·say (rẹidi:ouịmjunouǽsei) *n.* (*med.*) diagnostic technique utilizing radioisotopes to measure small quantities of hormones and enzymes present in blood and tissue —**radioimmunoassayable** *adj. abbr.* RIA. *Cf* IMMUNOASSAY

ra·di·o·i·so·tope (rẹidi:ouáisətoup) *n.* a radioactive isotope

ra·di·o·la·beled (rẹidi:ouléib'ld) *n.* a material into which a radioactive substance has been added for identification or tracing

ra·di·o·lar·i·an (rẹidi:ouléəri:ən) **1.** *n.* a member of *Radiolaria,* an order of highly organized marine rhizopods, producers of almost indestructible siliceous skeletons. Their remains form an ooze on the Pacific and Indian Ocean bottoms **2.** *adj.* of a radiolarian [fr. L.L. *radiolus,* dim. of *radius,* ray]

ra·di·o·lo·ca·tion (rẹidi:oulouкéiʃən) *n.* the science and practice of identifying distant objects, e.g. aircraft or ships, by radar

ra·di·ol·o·gist (rẹidi:ɒ́lədʒist) *n.* a specialist in radiology

ra·di·ol·o·gy (rẹidi:ɒ́lədʒi:) *n.* the study of radioactive substances and high-energy radiations (e.g. X rays, gamma rays), esp. their use in the diagnosis and treatment of disease [fr. RADIO-+Gk *logos,* word]

ra·di·om·e·ter (rẹidi:ɒ́mitər) *n.* a device to detect or measure electromagnetic radiation, commonly a pivoted set of vanes each with one black and one polished side [fr. L. *radius,* ray+METER]

ra·di·o·paque (rẹidi:oupéik) *adj.* opaque to radiation

ra·di·o·par·ent (rẹidi:oupǽrənt) *adj.* transparent to radiation

ra·di·o·phar·ma·ceu·ti·cal (rẹidi:oufɑ́rməsú:ti-k'l) *n.* a radioactive drug used in therapy, diagnosis, or research

radio pill (*med.*) capsuled radio transmitter used in medical diagnosis for monitoring physiological activity, e.g., pH values in animal digestion

ra·di·o·pro·tec·tive (rẹidi:ouprətéktiv) *adj.* of a shield that reflects or absorbs radiation to protect against exposure —**radioprotection** *n.* —**radioprotector** *n.*

ra·di·o·re·sist·ance (rẹidi:ourizístəns) *n.* capability of resisting the effects of radiation, e.g., certain cells. —**radioresistant,** *adj.*

ra·di·o·re·sist·ant (rẹidi:ourizístənt) *adj.* (esp. of cancer cells) not destroyed by radiation (cf. RADIOSENSITIVE)

ra·di·o·scop·ic (rẹidi:əskɒ́pik) *adj.* of or pertaining to radioscopy

ra·di·os·co·py (rẹidi:ɒ́skəpi:) *n.* the study of opaque material, esp. by X rays [fr. RADIO-+Gk *skopein,* to look at]

ra·di·o·sen·si·tive (rẹidi:ousénsitiv) *adj.* (esp. of cancer cells) able to be destroyed by radiation (cf. RADIORESISTANT)

ra·di·o·sonde (réidi:ousɒnd) *n.* a balloon equipped with a radio transmitter from which information is obtained about atmospheric conditions at high altitudes

radio spectrum the radio-frequency spectrum

radio stars (*astron.*) celestial bodies that are probably made up of turbulent gases and are identified by discrete radio emissions, e.g., a crab nebula, Cygnus A

ra·di·o·sterilization (rẹidi:oustẹrəlizéiʃən) *n.* process of sterilizing by use of radiation —**radiosterilize** *v.*

ra·di·o·tel·e·gram (rẹidi:outéligræm) n. a message sent by radiotelegraphy

ra·di·o·tel·e·graph (rẹidi:outéligræf, rẹidi:outéligrɑf) **1.** *n.* radiotelegraphy **2.** *v.t.* to transmit (a message) by means of radiotelegraphy

ra·di·o·te·leg·ra·phy (rẹidi:outəlégrəfi:) *n.* telegraphy by means of radio waves

ra·di·o·te·lem·e·try (rẹidi:outəlémitri:) *n.* measurement of distance by radio transmission. —**radiotelemetric** *adj. Cf* BIOTELEMETRY

ra·di·o·tel·e·phone (rẹidi:outélifoun) *n.* a transmitter for radiotelephony

ra·di·o·te·leph·o·ny (rẹidi:outəléfəni:) *n.* sound transmitted by radio waves. The sound is converted by a microphone into electrical impulses which are superimposed on a continuous carrier wave, esp. a microwave. The receiver, after amplification and rectification of the carrier wave, passes the resulting direct current through a telephone, which reconverts the impulses into sound

radio telescope an instrument for studying radio signals of cosmic origin (particularly the 21-cm. hydrogen radio line). It consists of an antenna (usually a large paraboloid, mounted on a heavy, vibration-free, mechanically steerable base) for capturing and focusing the cosmic signal, and a receiver for amplifying and rectifying it (*RADIO ASTRONOMY)

ra·di·o·tel·e·type (rẹidi:outélitaip) *n.* communication by radio-operated telegraphy connected to a typewriter *abbr.* RTTY

ra·di·o·ther·a·pist (rẹidi:ouθérəpist) *n.* a specialist in radiotherapy

ra·di·o·ther·a·py (rẹidi:ouθérəpi:) *n.* the treatment of malignant tumors and certain other diseases by means of X rays and radioactive substances

ra·di·o·thon (rẹidi:ouθɒ́n) *n.* a long-continuing radio program in support of a cause, usu. to raise funds

ra·di·o·tox·ic (rẹidi:outɒ́ksik) *adj.* of toxic effects of radiation —**radiotoxin** *n.* the poison in irradiated chemicals —**radiotoxologic** *adj.* of the study of radiotoxins

rad·ish (rǽdiʃ) *n. Raphanus sativus,* fam. *Cruciferae,* an annual plant with a basal rosette of leaves, and a tuberous taproot esteemed for its pungent, crisp flesh ‖ this root [O.E. *rædic, redic* fr. L.]

ra·di·um (réidi:əm) *n.* a shining white, divalent metallic element (symbol Ra, at. no. 88, mass of isotope of longest known half-life 226) which is strongly radioactive, disintegrating into radon. It was first isolated by Pierre and Marie Curie. It is used in radiography and radiotherapy and in the making of luminous paints etc. [Mod. L. fr. *radius,* ray]

ra·di·us (réidi:əs) *pl.* **ra·di·i** (réidi:ai), **ra·di·us·es** *n.* a straight line drawn from the center of a circle or sphere to any point on its periphery, or the length of this line ‖ a radiating part, e.g. a spoke of a wheel ‖ any of a number of lines diverging from a central point ‖ (*pop.*) an area measured or indicated by a radius, *he knows all the bars in a 15-mile radius* ‖ (*anat.*) the shorter of the two bones of the forearm in man, or the corresponding bone in an animal's forelimb or bird's wing. In some vertebrates it is fused with the ulna ‖ the ray or outer zone of petals of a composite flower, e.g. the daisy ‖ an insect-wing vein [L.=spoke, ray]

radius of gyration the square root of the mean squared distance of the particles of a pivoted body from the pivot point (*MOMENT OF INERTIA)

radius vector *pl.* **radii vec·to·res** (vektóri:z, vektóuri:z) (*math.*) a line, or the length of a line, from a fixed point to a variable point ‖ (*astron.*) a straight line between a star or planet and a heavenly body describing an orbit around it

ra·dix (réidiks) *pl.* **rad·i·ces** (rǽdisi:z, réidisi:z), **ra·dix·es** *n.* a number or value used as the basis for a scale of numeration, measurement etc., *10 is the radix of the decimal system* ‖ (*bot.*) the root of a plant ‖ (*anat.*) a radicle [L.=root]

RADNO (*acronym*) (transposed) for *No Radio,* fadeout of reception in arctic areas believed to be the result of solar explosions

Rad·nor·shire (rǽdnərʃiər) (*abbr.* Radnor) a county (area 471 sq. miles, pop. 18,000) in N. Wales. County town: Presteigne (pop. 1,000). Administrative center: Llandrindod Wells (pop. 3,000)

Ra·dom (rádɔm) a town (pop. 183,600) in Poland, 60 miles south of Warsaw: metallurgy, chemicals, tanning, mechanical engineering

ra·dome (*acronym*) for radar dome, a radar antenna housing made of insulation material that permits passage of radio frequency radiation

ra·don (réidɒn) *n.* a radioactive gaseous element (symbol Rn, at. no. 86, mass of isotope of longest known half-life 222) formed by the disintegration of radium ‖ a radioactive gas released from the earth, esp. before an earthquake [RADIUM]

rad·u·la (rǽdʒulə) *pl.* **rad·u·lae** (rǽdʒuli:) *n.* a short broad strip of membrane bearing rows of chitinous teeth, found in the mouths of most gastropod mollusks [L.=scraper]

Rae·burn (réibərn), Sir Henry (1756-1823), Scottish portrait painter who made many paintings of contemporary leading Scottish figures, esp. in Edinburgh

Raetia *RHAETIA

raf·fi·a (rǽfi:ə) *n.* the fiber obtained from the leaves of *Raphia ruffia,* the low-growing raffia palm of Madagascar. It is used for matting, tying up plants etc. [Malagasy]

raf·fi·né (ræfi:néi) *adj.* (*Fr.*) highbrow, ultra-refined

raf·fish (rǽfiʃ) *adj.* (of appearance) flashily attractive without breeding or style ‖ (esp. of men) somewhat disreputable, in a flashy way [fr. older *raff,* a low fellow]

raf·fle (rǽfəl) **1.** *n.* a lottery in which numbered tickets are sold to a large number of people, the holder of a ticket selected at random qualifying for a prize **2.** *v. pres. part.* **raf·fling** *past* and *past part.* **raf·fled** *v.t.* (usually with 'off') to sell by raffle ‖ *v.i.* to take part in or conduct a raffle [F. *rafle,* a dice game]

raffle *n.* (*naut.*) a jumble of ropes, canvas etc. [perh. fr. O.F. *rafle* used in phrase *rifle ou rafle,* anything at all]

Raf·fles (rǽfəlz), Sir Thomas Stamford Bigley (1781-1826), British colonial administrator. He was lieutenant governor of Java (1811-16). He acquired Singapore for Britain (1819)

raft (ræft, rɑft) **1.** *n.* a floating platform used for transportation over water or moored as a diving platform or landing stage ‖ a number of casks, logs etc. lashed together for floating down a river ‖ a mass of floating driftwood, ice etc. **2.** *v.t.* to transport on a raft ‖ to make into a raft ‖ to cross (a river) on a raft ‖ *v.i.* to work a raft ‖ to go by raft [O.N. *raptr,* rafter]

raft *n.* (*pop.*) a lot, large number [fr. older *raff,* a jumble]

raf·ter (rǽftər, rɑ́ftər) *n.* one of the sloping beams forming the framework of a roof [O.E. *ræfter*]

raft·er *n.* a man who forms rafts out of logs

rafts·man (rǽftsmən, rɑ́ftsmən) *pl.* **rafts·men** (rǽftsmən, rɑ́ftsmən) *n.* someone who works a raft or works on a raft

rag (ræg) *n.* a torn, tattered or worn scrap, piece of cloth, article of clothing etc. ‖ (*pl.*) shabby, tattered clothing ‖ a small piece of used cloth for cleaning or polishing ‖ (*pop., pejorative*) a newspaper [M.E. *ragge*]

rag 1. *v. pres. part.* **rag·ging** *past* and *past part.* **ragged** *v.t.* to tease ‖ to scold ‖ (*Br., pop.*) to play practical, esp. rough, jokes upon ‖ *v.i.* (*Br., pop.*) to engage in horseplay **2.** *n.* (*Br., pop.*) a show of horseplay by students, with dressing up and fooling around to get money for some charity [origin unknown]

rag *n.* a large roofing slate with one rough surface ‖ any of various kinds of hard, coarse stone which split into thick, flat slabs [perh. RAG (scrap)]

rag·a·muf·fin (rǽgəmʌfin) *n.* a ragged, disreputable person, esp. a street urchin [prob. fr. RAG (scrap)]

rag-and-bone man (*Br.*) a man who with a cart or car goes through the streets collecting old clothes or junk

rag·a·rock (rǽgərɒk) *n.* a mixture of rock 'n roll and Indian musical forms, often played with a sitar

rag bolt a bolt having barbs on its shaft which prevent its easy withdrawal

rage (reidʒ) *n.* violent and uncontrolled anger, or a fit of this ‖ (*rhet.*) the violence of a natural element ‖ (*rhet.*) passionate desire for something, *the rage for conquest* ‖ intense emotion, passion, *a rage of grief* ‖ an object of modish enthusiasm, *big hats were the rage* [F. *raige, rage*]

rage *v.i. pres. part.* **rag·ing** *past* and *past part.* **raged** (often with 'at', 'over' or 'against') to utter with violent and uncontrolled anger ‖ (of a storm, sea, battle, disease, passion etc.) to be unchecked in its violence [fr. F. *rager*]

rag·ged (rǽgid) *adj.* (of fabric, clothes etc.) torn or frayed ‖ (of hair, fur etc.) rough, hanging in tufts ‖ having a broken, jagged outline or surface ‖ written or performed in an uneven way ‖ (of people) dressed in torn or frayed clothes

ragged robin *Lychnis floscuculi,* fam. *Caryophyllaceae,* a perennial plant with small pink flowers with five narrow-lobed and ragged-looking petals

rag·gee, rag·i (rǽgi:) *n. Eleusine coracana,* fam. *Graminaceae,* a cereal cultivated in India and Africa for flour [Hindi *rāgī*]

Rag·lan (rǽglən), Fitzroy James Henry Somerset, 1st Baron (1788-1855), British field marshal. He commanded (1854-5) the British troops in the Crimean War

rag·lan (rǽglən) *adj.* (of sleeves) made with the seams running from the underarm to the neck so that there are no shoulder seams ‖ (of coats etc.) having such sleeves [after Lord *Raglan*]

rag·man (rǽgmæn, rǽgmən) *pl.* **rag·men** (rǽgmen, rǽgmən) *n.* a man who collects or deals in rags, old newspapers etc.

ra·gout (rægú:) *n.* a highly seasoned dish of stewed meat and vegetables [F.]

rag paper high-quality paper made from rags

rag·pick·er (rǽgpikər) *n.* a person who picks up rags and other refuse for a living

rag·tag (rǽgtæg) *n.* (*pop.*) a crowd of poor, dirty people **ragtag and bobtail** the rabble, the riff-raff

rag·time (rǽgtaim) *n.* a type of early jazz popular in the two decades before the 1st world war. It derived from black folk music and is marked by persistent syncopation [=ragged time]

Ra·gu·sa (rɑgú:zɑ) *DUBROVNIK

rag·weed (rǽgwi:d) *n.* ragwort ‖ a member of *Ambrosia,* fam. *Compositae,* a genus of plants whose pollen may cause hay fever and asthma

rag·wort (rǽgwə:rt) *n.* a member of *Senecio,* fam. *Compositae,* a genus of plants growing in fields and hedgerows, with lyrate leaves and clusters of bright yellow flowers, esp. *S. jacobaea*

Rahman, Tunku Abdul *ABDUL RAHMAN

raid (reid) **1.** *n.* a swift, sudden military attack with a limited objective, esp. by a detachment ‖ air raid ‖ a swift, sudden robbery of money, goods, cattle etc., esp. in broad daylight ‖ a sudden swoop on suspected premises by law-enforcement officers to arrest criminals, seize contraband etc. ‖ (*stock exchange*) an attempt by dealers to force prices down **2.** *v.t.* to make a raid upon ‖ *v.i.* to make a raid [orig. Scot. fr. O.E. *rād,* road]

rail (reil) **1.** *n.* a horizontal bar of wood or metal etc. used e.g. to hang things on or from, for a support in climbing stairs etc. or for a guard or barrier ‖ a horizontal piece in a fence or in paneling ‖ the fence on either side of a racetrack ‖ a line of a track on which, or suspended from which, a vehicle moves ‖ (*naut.*) the wide wooden bar along the top of the bulwarks **by rail** by railroad train **on the rails** progressing satisfactorily, going along well **over the rail** over a ship's side **to go off the rails** (*Br.*) to stop behaving with propriety **2.** *v.t.* (with 'in', 'off') to separate from an adjoining or surrounding space by a rail [O.F. *reille*]

rail *v.i.* (*rhet.,* with 'against' or 'at') to utter curses and lamentations, *to rail against fate* ‖ (with 'at') to shout abuse [F. *railler,* to banter]

rail *n.* any of various wading birds of temperate regions, with thin bodies, strong legs and short wings, constituting a subfamily of fam. *Rallidae.* They have a raucous cry [F. *râle*]

rail chair one of the iron clamps fastened to the sleepers which hold the tracks of a railroad

rail·gun (réilgʌn) *n.* device under development for projecting a plastic missile (bullet, rocket) utilizing a magnetic flux generator with a direct current linear motor fired by a pulse of high-voltage electrical energy with 10 times the power of a rifle

rail·head (réilhed) *n.* the furthest point reached by a railroad under construction ‖ (*mil.*) the point on a railroad at which supplies are unloaded and sent up to front-line troops by other means

rail·ing (réiliŋ) *n.* a fence, barrier, or support consisting of rails or a rail ‖ material for rails

rail·ler·y (réiləri:) *n.* good-humored teasing [F. *raillerie*]

rail·road (réilroud) **1.** *n.* (*Am.=Br.* railway) a road or system of roads of easy gradient on which parallel rails are laid, and held in position by being bolted to ties, for trains to run on **2.** *v.t.* to transport by railroad train ‖ (*pop.*) to rush (something) through quickly so that it cannot receive careful consideration ‖ (*pop.*) to cause (someone) to be sent to prison on a false charge

—The first surface railroad designed for passenger transport was constructed between Stockton and Darlington, in England, in 1825 (*STEPHENSON). U.S. railroads began effectively with the Baltimore and Ohio Railroad (1830)

rail·way (réilwei) *n.* (*Br.*) the organization concerned with running a regional system of railroads ‖ the tracks of such a regional system ‖ a rail line which carries equipment over a relatively small area

rai·ment (réimənt) *n.* (*rhet.*) clothing, esp. of fine quality [fr. older *arrayment* fr. ARRAY]

rain (rein) *n.* a multitude of falling drops of water formed by the coalescing of droplets in a cloud ‖ the fall of such drops ‖ a fall of other liquid drops, dust particles, bullets etc. ‖ (*pl.*) the season of heavy rain, esp. in countries with a monsoon climate [O.E. *regn, rēn*]

rain *v.i.* (usually impersonal) to fall as rain, *it is raining* ‖ to fall like pouring rain ‖ *v.t.* to cause to fall like pouring rain **to rain cats and dogs** to rain very hard [O.E. *regnian*]

rain·bow (réinbou) **1.** *n.* a circle (usually observed as an arc) of concentric bands in the atmosphere in the colors of the spectrum, due to the reflection and refraction of sunlight in drops of water **2.** *adj.* colored like a rainbow ‖ many-colored [O.E. *regnboga*]

rainbow pill (*med.*) a capsule containing drugs of several colors, each of which usually becomes effective at various times

rainbow trout *Salmo gairdnerii,* fam. *Salmonidae,* a brightly colored trout, native to the mountain streams and the rivers of the Pacific coast of North America

rain check a ticket which a spectator can use for readmission to a game, e.g. baseball, which has been called off or stopped because of rain ‖ an agreement that a person can exercise an unfulfilled privilege, favor etc. sometime in the future

rain·coat (réinkout) *n.* a rainproof coat

rain·drop (réindrɒp) *n.* a drop of rain

rain·fall (réinfɔl) *n.* a fall of rain ‖ the precipitation of a given period on a region as measured by the depth (in inches or centimeters) of the water in a rain gauge which collects the rain, snow or hail

rain forest a hot, wet, equatorial forest characterized by high, broadleaved, evergreen trees and absence of undergrowth

rain gauge, rain gage an instrument for measuring the amount of rainfall at a given time and place

CONCISE PRONUNCIATION KEY: **(a)** æ, *cat;* ɑ, *car;* ɔ *fawn;* ei, *snake.* **(e)** e, *hen;* i:, *sheep;* iə, *deer;* εə, *bear.* **(i)** i, *fish;* ai, *tiger;* ə:, *bird.* **(o)** o, *ox;* au, *cow;* ou, *goat;* u, *poor;* ɔi, *royal.* **(u)** ʌ, *duck;* u, *bull;* u:, *goose;* ə, *bacillus;* ju:, *cube.* x, *loch;* θ, *think;* ð, *bother;* z, *Zen;* ʒ, *corsage;* dʒ, *savage;* ŋ, *orangutang;* j, *yak;* ʃ, *fish;* tʃ, *fetch;* 'l, *rabble;* 'n, *redden.* Complete pronunciation key appears inside front cover.

Rai·nier III (reiníər, F. renjei) (1923-), prince of Monaco since 1950

Rai·nier (rəníər, réiniər) the highest peak (14,410 ft) of the Cascade Range, in W. central Washington

rain·out (réinaut) *n.* radioactive material in the atmosphere brought to earth by precipitation

rain·proof (réinpru:f) **1.** *adj.* (of materials) not letting the rain come through **2.** *v.t.* to make rainproof

rain shadow the area to the leeward of mountains where little rain falls

rain·storm (réinstɔrm) *n.* a heavy fall of rain

rain·wa·ter (rainwɔtər, réinwɒtər) *n.* water recently fallen as rain and free of the dissolved salts often present in water which has percolated through chalk, soil, rocks etc.

rain·y (réini) *comp.* **rain·i·er** *superl.* **rain·i·est** *adj.* during or in which much rain falls, *the rainy season* ‖ (of clouds, wind etc.) bringing rain ‖ wet with rain

rainy day a future time or period when one will experience some want or urgent need, *put money away for a rainy day*

Rai·pur (ráipur) a rail center (pop. 140,000) of E. Madhya Pradesh, India: food processing, sawmills, mechanical engineering

raise (reiz) **1.** *v.t. pres. part.* **rais·ing** *past* and *past part.* **raised** to cause to rise or come to a vertical or standing position ‖ to rouse, enliven, *to raise one's spirits* ‖ to incite, *to raise a revolt* ‖ to stir up (a person or persons) to some action ‖ to call up, evoke (the spirit of a deceased person) ‖ to bring back to life ‖ to build up or construct (a building etc.) ‖ to give rise to, *to raise a smile* ‖ to give vent to (a loud cry, shout etc.) ‖ to institute, initiate (a claim, complaint etc.) ‖ to bring up (a question, objection etc.) for consideration ‖ to elevate, cause to be on or at a higher level ‖ to exalt in rank, position etc. ‖ to make rise according to some accepted scale, *to raise the temperature* ‖ to cause (the voice) to rise in pitch or strength ‖ to cause to rise in amount, size, value, price etc., *to raise the cost of living* ‖ to cause (dough) to rise or lighten ‖ (*dyeing*) to make (a color) brighter ‖ to give (cloth) a nap ‖ to collect together, *to raise an army, to raise money* ‖ to abandon, give up (a blockade, siege etc.) ‖ to end (a blockade, siege etc.) by forcing the besieging troops to retire ‖ to remove (an embargo, injunction etc.) ‖ to increase (a bid or wager) ‖ (*cards*) to go one better than (a previous player) ‖ (*naut.*) to come in sight of (land, another ship etc.) ‖ (*naut.*) to make (land, another ship etc.) seem higher by approaching it ‖ to bring up (children) ‖ to breed (animals) ‖ to cause to grow, *to raise corn* ‖ to flush (game) ‖ (*math.*) to multiply (a quantity) by itself a given number of times ‖ to increase fraudulently the face value of (a money order, check etc.) by altering the figures **to raise hell** (or **the devil**) to make a great disturbance ‖ to make a furious protest **to raise one's voice** to give expression to one's disapproval or disagreement **2.** *n.* an act of raising ‖ an increase of stakes or the amount increased ‖ (*Am.=Br.* rise) an increase in salary [O.N. *reisa*]

rai·sin (réiz'n) *n.* any of various kinds of grape dried either in the sun or artificially [O.F. *razin, raizin,* grape]

rai·son d'ê·tre (réizɔndétrə, F. rezɔ̃detr) *n.* the justifying reason for the existence of something [F.]

rai·son·neur (reizɔnə́:r) *n.* (*Fr.*) one who comments on the actions of others, esp. a character in a literary work

raj (rɑdʒ) *n.* (in India) rule, reign [Hindi *rāj*]

ra·ja, ra·jah (rádʒə) *n.* an Indian prince ‖ someone who holds a Hindu title of nobility ‖ the title of an Indian noble or dignitary or of a Malay or Javanese prince [Hindi *rājā*]

Ra·ja·mun·dry (rɑdʒəmúndri:) a city (pop. 130,000) of N.W. Andhra Pradesh, India, on the Godavari River: aluminum, metallurgy, lumber, food processing

Ra·ja·sthan (rádʒəstɑn) a state (area 132,152 sq. miles, pop. 28,401,000) of N.W. India, in the Thar and the central plateau. Capital: Jaipur. Resources: mica, gypsum, salt. Agriculture: livestock, wheat, sugar, cotton, pulses. Industries: sugar refining, cotton textiles. State university (1947) at Jaipur

Raj·kot (rádʒkout) a former princely capital (pop. 300,612) in the Kathiawar Peninsula, Gujarat, India, a rail center: food processing, tanning

Raj·put (rádʒput) *n.* a member of a landowning and military caste of the former Rajputana states of N. India, now part of Rajasthan. The Rajputs ruled much of central India (7th–18th cc.) [Hindi *rājpūt*]

rake (reik) *n.* a hand tool consisting of a pole ending in a short crossbar set with prongs, for smoothing out loose soil or gravel, collecting fallen leaves etc. ‖ a farm machine for collecting hay into lanes ‖ any of a variety of tools similar to a garden rake, used e.g. by a croupier or a bookbinder [O.E. *raca*]

rake *n.* a thoroughly dissolute man, esp. one in fashionable society [shortened fr. older *rakehell*]

rake *pres. part.* **rak·ing** *past* and *past part.* **raked** *v.t.* to collect with a rake, *to rake leaves* ‖ (often with 'up') to gather (e.g. facts) by hard work ‖ to make clean, smooth, loosen etc. with a rake ‖ (with 'up') to search out and expose, *to rake up a scandal* ‖ to bank up (a fire) for slow burning ‖ to search minutely ‖ (*pop.,* usually with 'in') to take in a great deal of (money) ‖ to sweep the length of (a ship, column of troops etc.) with shots ‖ (of a hawk) to attack while flying ‖ *v.i.* to use a rake ‖ to search with a rake or as if with a rake [O.N. *raka,* to scrape]

rake 1. *v. pres. part.* **rak·ing** *past* and *past part.* **raked** *v.t.* to cause to be set off at an angle from the perpendicular ‖ *v.i.* to be at such an angle ‖ (*naut.*) to project at the bow or stern beyond the keel **2.** *n.* a slant from the perpendicular ‖ (*naut.*) the projection of a ship's bow or stern over the keel ‖ an upward slope of the stage or auditorium of a theater from the horizontal ‖ the angle given to the face of a cutting tool [etym. doubtful]

rake-off (réikɔf, réikɒf) *n.* a percentage of profits or winnings kept, often illegally or covertly, by a party to a transaction [RAKE (garden tool)+OFF]

rak·ish (réikiʃ) *adj.* (esp. of ships) looking as though built for speed ‖ jaunty [etym. doubtful]

rakish *adj.* of or like a rake (dissolute man)

rale, *Br.* **râle** (ræl, rɑl) *n.* any abnormal breathing sound heard through a stethoscope, indicating lung disorder [F.]

Ra·leigh, Ra·legh (rɔ́li:), Sir Walter (c. 1552-1618), English courtier, explorer and author. The favorite of Elizabeth I, he sent expeditions (1584-9) to colonize the coast of North America, founding an unsuccessful settlement in Virginia. He led (1595) an expedition to the Orinoco in search of gold. He fell from favor on the accession of James I and was imprisoned (1603-16) in the Tower of London, where he began his 'History of the World'. After the failure of a second expedition to the Orinoco (1617), he was executed

Raleigh the capital (pop. 150,255) of North Carolina: tobacco, cotton, textiles

ral·len·tan·do (rɑlentɑndou) *n.* (*mus.*) a direction to play or sing more slowly ‖ (*mus.*) a passage becoming gradually slower in tempo [Ital.]

ral·ly (ræli:) **1.** *v. pres. part.* **ral·ly·ing** *past* and *past part.* **ral·lied** *v.t.* to gather together (what was disunited or disordered, e.g. troops) ‖ to cause to regain vigor, *to rally one's spirits* ‖ to summon together for a common purpose ‖ *v.i.* to come back to a state of order ‖ to come together for a common purpose, *to rally to a cause* ‖ to regain strength of body or mind ‖ (*tennis*) to take part in a rally ‖ (of stocks etc.) to rise again in price after a fall **2.** *pl.* **ral·lies** *n.* the act of rallying a gathering of persons with a common purpose, *a political rally* ‖ (*tennis*) a sustained to-and-fro succession of strokes by opposing players [F. *rallier*]

ral·ly *pres. part.* **ral·ly·ing** *past* and *past part.* **ral·lied** *v.t.* (*old-fash.*) to tease or chaff [F. *railler*]

ram (ræm) *n.* a male sheep ‖ the dropweight of a pile driver or steam hammer ‖ the compressing piston of a hydrostatic press or force pump ‖ a battering ram ‖ a device for raising water from a running stream ‖ (*hist.*) a steel beak jutting from the prow of a ship for piercing the side of an enemy ship, or a ship thus equipped [O.E. *ram, ramm*]

ram *pres. part.* **ram·ming** *past* and *past part.* **rammed** *v.t.* to pound (earth) so as to make it firm ‖ to crash head-on into ‖ to drive or force down or into by heavy blows, pressure etc. ‖ to fill or stuff with tightly pressed material ‖ to force (a charge) into a gun ‖ to force acceptance of (e.g. an idea), *to ram facts into someone's head* ‖ (*hist.,* of a ship) to attack (another ship) with a ram ‖ *v.i.* (of something in movement) to crash violently into an obstacle ‖ to pound earth in order to make it firm **to ram something down someone's throat** to force someone to accept an unwelcome fact [M.E. *rammen*]

RAM 1. (*computer acronym*) for random-access memory **2.** (*mil. acronym*) for reentry antimissile

Ra·ma (rɑ́mə) (*Hindu mythol.*) the sixth, seventh or eighth avatar of Vishnu, esp. Ramachandra

RAMAC (*acronym*) for random-access method of accounting and control, a computerized accounting system designed by IBM

Ra·ma·chan·dra (rɑmətʃʌ́ndrə) the seventh, most famous avatar of Vishnu [Skr. *Rāmacandra*]

Ram·a·dan (ræmədɑ́n) *n.* the ninth month of the Moslem year, during which strict fasting is observed from dawn until sunset ‖ this fast [Arab. *ramadān*]

Ra·ma·krish·na (rɑməkríʃnə) (1836-86), Hindu reformer and founder of the Ramakrishna Mission. Having practiced Hindu, Moslem and Christian rites, he taught that all religions are one, but suit man's needs differently. His disciples were taught to see God in all men, and to serve mankind accordingly

Ramakrishna Mission an order of monks dedicated to chastity, poverty and charity, founded by Ramakrishna

Ra·man (rɑ́mən), Sir Chandrasekhara Venkata (1888-1970), Indian physicist, who discovered the Raman effect. Nobel prize (1930)

Raman effect (*phys.*) a change in frequency experienced by radiation scattered while traversing a transparent substance. The amount of the change is determined by the substance. The Raman effect is the principle underlying a spectroscopic technique (*SPECTROSCOPY) that employs a monochromatic beam in the infrared, which upon scattering produces new frequencies characteristic of the material [after Sir Chandrasekhara RAMAN]

Ra·ma·nu·ja (rɑmɑ́nujə) Brahmin commentator on the Upanishads, writing c. 1017. He taught, in contrast with the more usual monistic teaching of Hinduism, that individual selves are dependent on the Highest Self for their existence, yet are distinct from him, and can enter into a relationship of love with him

RAMARK (*acronym*) for radar marker, a beacon that emits continuous radar waves as a navigation guide

Ra·ma·ya·na (rɑmɑ́jənə) one of the two great Sanskrit poems of Hinduism (*MAHABHARATA), written c. 5th c. B.C. Its 24,000 couplets in seven books record the deeds of Rama

ram·ble (rǽmb'l) **1.** *v.i. pres. part.* **ram·bling** *past* and *past part.* **ram·bled** to go for a long, unplanned walk purely for enjoyment ‖ to talk or write without any clear thread **2.** *n.* the act of rambling **rám·bler** *n.* someone who rambles ‖ any of several climbing roses having large clusters of small flowers **rám·bling** *adj.* seeming to be constructed on no clear plan, *a rambling house* ‖ wandering, disconnected, *rambling thoughts* [origin unknown]

Ram·bouil·let (rɑ̃bu:jei), Catherine de Vivonne, marquise de (1588-1665), French noblewoman. Her salon, which included Mme de Sévigné, Descartes, La Rochefoucauld and Bossuet, was the first of its kind and influenced the development of the French language and French literature

ram·bunc·tious (ræmbʌ́ŋkʃəs) *adj.* boisterous, noisy ‖ difficult to control [prob. altered fr. RUMBUSTIOUS]

ram·bu·tan (ræmbú:t'n) *n.* *Nephelium lappaceum,* fam. *Sapindaceae,* a Malaysian and Indonesian tree cultivated for its fruit ‖ this fruit, covered with soft, red hair [Malay]

Ra·meau (ræmou), Jean-Philippe (1683-1764), French classical composer. His 'Traité de l'harmonie' (1722) helped to establish the theories of modern harmony. His operas include 'les Indes galantes' (1735) and 'Castor et Pollux' (1737). He also wrote church music, chamber music, cantatas and works for the harpsichord

ram·e·kin, ra·me·quin (rǽməkin) *n.* cheese, with bread crumbs, eggs etc. baked in an individual dish ‖ a dish for baking and serving this [F. *ramequin*]

Ram·e·ses (rǽmsi:z) Ramses

ram·ie (rǽmi:) *n.* a strong, absorbent, lustrous fiber obtained from *Boehmeria nivea,* fam. *Urticaceae,* a bushy plant of E. Asia, now cultivated in the southeastern U.S.A. ‖ this plant [Malay *rāmī*]

CONCISE PRONUNCIATION KEY: (a) æ, *cat;* ɑ, *car;* ɔ *fawn;* ei, *snake.* (e) e, *hen;* i:, *sheep;* iə, *deer;* εə, *bear.* (i) i, *fish;* ai, *tiger;* ə:, *bird.* (o) o, *ox;* au, *cow;* ou, *goat;* u, *poor;* ɔi, *royal.* (u) ʌ, *duck;* u, *bull;* u:, *goose;* ə, *bacillus;* ju:, *cube.* x, *loch;* θ, *think;* ð, *bother;* z, *Zen;* ʒ, *corsage;* dʒ, *savage;* ŋ, *orangutang;* j, *yak;* ʃ, *fish;* tʃ, *fetch;* 'l, *rabble;* 'n, *redden.* Complete pronunciation key appears inside front cover.

ram·i·fi·ca·tion (ræmifikéiʃən) *n.* the process of branching ‖ the way in which branches are arranged ‖ a branch or offshoot ‖ (*biol.*) a branched structure ‖ a development or outgrowth of something which has expanded as though by branching, *the ramifications of the plot are hard to follow* [fr. M.L. *ramificare* (*ramificatus*), to ramify]

ram·i·fy (rǽmifai) *pres. part.* **ram·i·fy·ing** *past* and *past part.* **ram·i·fied** *v.t.* to cause to form or produce branches or subdivisions ‖ *v.i.* to spread out by branching [F. *ramifier*]

Ram·il·lies, Battle of (rǽmili:z, ræmi:ji:) a victory (1706) of Marlborough, commanding allied British, Dutch and Danish armies, during the War of the Spanish Succession

Ra·mí·rez (rɑmí:res), Ignacio (1818-97), Mexican politician, writer and poet, of pure Indian stock, who styled himself 'El nigromante' (the necromancer). When not inflamed by politics he wrote classical love sonnets, notably 'Al amor', 'A sol', and 'A mi musa'

ram·jet (rǽmdʒet) *n.* a jet engine in which the stream of air used for fuel combustion is compressed by the forward motion of the engine ‖ (*mil.*) U.S. missile containing no oxidizer, reaching speeds up to 3,000 mph, with a range of 300–400 mi

Ra·món y Ca·jal (ramóni:kɑhál), Santiago (1852-1934), Spanish physician and biologist, and winner (1906) of the Nobel prize for medicine

ra·mose (ræmóus, rəmóus) *adj.* composed of or having branches [fr. L. *ramosus*]

ramp (ræmp) *n.* a sloping path or way joining different levels of a building, road etc. ‖ (*archit.*) a difference in level in the opposite abutments of a rampant arch ‖ an upward bend in a stair rail etc. ‖ a passenger stairway for boarding or leaving an aircraft [F. *rampe*]

ramp *n.* (*Br., pop.*) a racket, swindle [etym. doubtful]

ramp *v.i.* to slope up or down to a different level ‖ (*heraldry*, of a lion) to stand rampant ‖ *v.t.* to provide with a ramp [O.F. *ramper*, to creep]

ram·page 1. (ræmpéidʒ) *v.i. pres. part.* **ram·pag·ing** *past* and *past part.* **ram·paged** to behave violently, be in a storm of anger **2.** (rǽmpeidʒ) *n.* violent or uncontrolled behavior, esp. in the phrase **on the rampage** furiously active, esp. punitively or destructively **ram·pá·geous** *adj.* [Scot., etym. doubtful]

ram·pan·cy (rǽmpənsi:) *n.* the state or quality of being rampant

ramp·ant (rǽmpənt) *adj.* (*heraldry*, of a lion) on the hind legs with forepaws menacingly or aggressively outstretched and the head in profile ‖ holding extremist views and proclaiming them aggressively, *a rampant militarist* ‖ (of crime, disease etc.) rife ‖ (of roses, weeds etc.) growing unchecked ‖ (*archit.*, of an arch) with one abutment higher than the other [F., pres. part. of *ramper*, to ramp]

ram·part (rǽmpɑrt) **1.** *n.* (*hist.*) a broad-topped embankment, usually with a stone parapet, constructed for defense ‖ something compared to this **2.** *v.t.* to protect with a rampart or as though with a rampart [fr. F. *rempart, rampart*]

Ram·pur (rɑ́mpur) a town (pop. 135,000) of N. Uttar Pradesh, India: damask, chemicals, electrical goods, jewelry

ram·rod (rǽmrɒd) *n.* (*hist.*) a long, straight rod of iron used to force the gunpowder and bullets down the barrel of a muzzle-loading gun ‖ a rod for cleaning the bore of a rifle or gun ‖ a keen disciplinarian

Ram·say (rǽmzi:), Sir William (1852-1916), Scottish chemist. He discovered the line spectrum of helium in uranium and thorium ores. With Lord Rayleigh he discovered argon (1894) and was also one of the discoverers of neon, krypton and xenon. Nobel prize (1904)

Rams·den (rǽmzdən), Jesse (1735-1800), British optician and instrument maker. He devised the equatorial mounting for telescopes and invented a machine for graduating instruments

Ram·ses II (rǽmsi:z) (*d.* c. 1223 B.C.), king of Egypt (c. 1290–c. 1223 B.C.), of the 19th dynasty. He extended Egyptian rule over Ethiopia and part of Arabia, and was at war with the Hittites for 15 years. He had many monuments built, esp. at Thebes

Ramses III (*d.* c. 1158 B.C.), king of Egypt (c. 1190–c. 1158 B.C.) of the 20th dynasty. He won military successes in Nubia and Syria

ram·shack·le (rǽmʃæk'l) *adj.* (of a structure, machine etc.) so old or badly made or in such disrepair that it is in danger of falling to pieces [fr. older *ramshackled*]

ram·son (rǽms'n, rǽmz'n) *n.* *Allium ursinum*, fam. *Liliaceae*, a species of garlic with broad leaves ‖ (*pl.*) the root of this plant, used esp. in salads [O.E. *hramsan*, pl. of *hramsa*, wild garlic]

ram·til (rǽmtil) *n.* *Guizotia abyssinica*, fam. *Compositae*, a plant cultivated in India for its seeds, from which an oil is expressed [Hindi *rāmtil*]

ram·u·lose (rǽmjulous) *adj.* having numerous small branches [fr. L. *ramulosus*]

Ra·mus (réiməs), Petrus (Pierre de la Ramée, 1515-72), French philosopher. He opposed Aristotelian scholasticism and encouraged skeptical thought. He was converted to Calvinism and was killed in the Massacre of St Bartholomew

ra·mus (réiməs) *pl.* **ra·mi** (réimai) *n.* (*biol.*) a branchlike structure, e.g. the barb of a feather, the mandible or its proximal part of a vertebrate, or a branch of a nerve [L.=branch]

ran *past* of RUN

Ran·cé (rɑ̃sei), Armand Jean le Bouthillier de (1626-1700), French religious reformer. His reform of the Cistercian order (c. 1662) gave rise to the Trappists

ranch (ræntʃ) **1.** *n.* a farm, esp in the southwest and western U.S.A. and S.W. central Canada, for breeding and raising cattle, horses or sheep ‖ the people living and working on a ranch **2.** *v.i.* to manage a ranch ‖ *v.t.* to raise (an animal) on a ranch ‖ to use (land) as a ranch **ránch·er** *n.* a person who owns or manages a ranch, or a ranch hand [fr. Span. *rancho*, a mess (group dining together)]

ran·che·ro (ræntʃέərou) *n.* (esp. in the southwest U.S.A. and Mexico) a rancher [Span.]

ranch·ette (ræntʃét) *n.* **1.** a small ranch **2.** small ranch-type house

ranch house a house built on one level, sometimes with adjoining half levels. *Cf* BILEVEL

Ran·chi (rɑ́ntʃi:) a town (pop. 122,000) in Bihar, India, in Chota Nagpur: silk weaving, lacquer

ranch·man (rǽntʃmən) *pl.* **ranch·men** (rǽntʃmən) *n.* a rancher

ran·cid (rǽnsid) *adj.* (esp. of food) smelling or tasting foul because of chemical change, esp. due to age **ran·cíd·i·ty** *n.* [fr. L. *rancidus*]

ran·cor, *Br.* **ran·cour** (rǽŋkər) *n.* bitter, lasting hatred or malignant spite **rán·cor·ous** *adj.* [O.F. *rancour*]

Rand (rænd), Ayn (1905-82), U.S. writer, originator of objectivism, born in Russia. Her philosophy encompassed self-interest as a reason for action, self-fulfillment as a responsibility and productivity as the ultimate. She wrote 'The Fountainhead' (1943) and 'Atlas Shrugged' (1957) and edited her own newsletter (1962-82)

rand (rænd) *n.* the strip of leather or similar material between the heel and sole of a shoe or boot [O.E. *rand, rond*, a border, margin]

rand *n.* (*abbr.*) the basic monetary unit of the republic of South Africa, divided into 100 cents ‖ a coin of the value of one rand

R & B *RHYTHM AND BLUES

R & D (*acronym*) for research and development

rand·i·ness (rǽndi:nis) *n.* the quality or state of being randy

ran·dom (rǽndəm) **1.** *n.* (only in the phrase) **at random** in an unplanned way, without any predetermined direction, purpose or method **2.** *adj.* haphazard, *random bombing* ‖ made or chosen at random, *a random guess* ‖ (*math.*, of numbers) as likely to come up as any others in a set [O.F. *randon* fr. *randir*, to run fast, gallop]

random access (*computer*) capability of obtaining stored information in any order — **random-access** *adj.* —**random-access memory (RAM)** *n.*

R and R (*acronym*) **1.** rest and recreation; **2.** rest and recuperation

Rand, the (rænd) *WITWATERSRAND

Randolph (rǽndɒlf, rǽndəlf), Asa Philip (1889-1979), U.S. labor leader, organizer of the Brotherhood of Sleeping Car Porters (1925), vice-president of the AFL-CIO from 1955. He was a major influence in the organization of the federal Fair Employment Practices Committee and worked for civil rights in industry and government, directing the March on Washington for Jobs and Freedom (1963)

Randolph, Edmund (1753-1813), U.S. statesman. A delegate to the Constitutional Convention of 1787, he presented his Virginia Plan. He served (1789-94) as the first attorney general of the U.S.A.

Randolph, John (1773-1833), U.S. orator and Congressman from Virginia who vigorously supported the cause of states' rights

rand·y (rǽndi:) *comp.* **rand·i·er** *superl.* **rand·i·est** *adj.* lecherous [prob. fr. obs. *rand*, var. of RANT]

ranee *RANI

rang *past* of RING

range (reindʒ) *n.* a row, file or rank of things ‖ a group of mountains considered as forming a connected system ‖ a cooking stove, esp. one fired by solid fuel ‖ grazing land for cattle, sheep etc., usually not fenced in ‖ freedom to roam at will, *to give free range to one's imagination* ‖ a maximum attainable distance, *the missile has a range of 2,000 miles* ‖ field, scope, *within one's range of vision* ‖ the distance of a target from a gun etc. or this as a setting on a sight ‖ the maximum distance which an aircraft etc. can travel without refueling ‖ a place for practicing shooting ‖ (*statistics*) the area of magnitude within which a variable lies ‖ an order or class, *the upper ranges of society* ‖ extent between limits, area of activity, experience or knowledge, *within the income range of $4–5,000, temperature range, a wide range of interests* ‖ the scope of the voice or an instrument ‖ the region over which a plant or animal is distributed ‖ one of the north-south rows of a township numbered east-west from the principal meridian of a public-land survey [O.F.]

range *pres. part.* **rang·ing** *past* and *past part.* **ranged** *v.t.* to place in a line or orderly pattern, *trees were ranged along the roadside* ‖ to wander through, *to range the countryside* ‖ to sail along or through ‖ to pasture (cattle etc.) on a range ‖ (*Br., printing*) to set (type) so that the start or end of the line or word falls directly under some other part of the matter being set, *range the author's name under the last word of the title* ‖ (Br., *printing*) to make (lines of type, margins etc.) straight ‖ to put in a class etc., *he ranged himself with the opposition* ‖ to fire and observe single rounds from (a gun or guns) in an attempt to bracket a target ‖ (*naut.*) to arrange (an anchor cable) so that the anchor can descend without difficulty ‖ *v.i.* to stretch in a line, *the peaks ranged as far as he could see* ‖ to go about, move freely, *they range through the desert, his speech ranged over a number of topics* ‖ (*biol.*) to be found over a specific region ‖ to vary within limits, *the temperature ranges between 0° C and 30° C* ‖ (*Br., printing*) to line up, lie in the same line ‖ (of artillery) to fire and observe single rounds in an attempt to bracket a target ‖ to use a range finder [fr. F. *ranger*]

range finder an instrument for establishing the distance between an observer and a point (e.g. a target) ‖ (*photog.*) a camera attachment for measuring the distance between a camera and what is to be photographed

rang·er (réindʒər) *n.* an officer who patrols a public forest ‖ a soldier trained for close-range fighting ‖ (*Br.*) an official who supervises a royal forest or park ‖ (*Br.*) a senior girl scout

Ran·goon (ræŋgú:n) the capital (pop. 3,662,300) and chief port of Burma, on River Rangoon. Industries: food processing (esp. rice), wood working, oil refining. It is dominated by the gilded pagoda of Shwe Dagon (18th c.). University (1920)

rang·y (réindʒi:) *comp.* **rang·i·er** *superl.* **rang·i·est** *adj.* tall, slim and loose-limbed [RANGE n. or v.]

ra·ni, ra·nee (rɑ́ni:) *n.* an Indian princess ‖ the wife of a raja [Hind. *rānī*]

Ran·jit Singh (rʌ́ndʒitsíŋ) (1780-1839), Sikh ruler. He conquered Kashmir and the Punjab, allied himself with the British and united the Punjab into the most powerful state in India

rank (ræŋk) **1.** *n.* a homogeneous line or row of persons or things ‖ a level of relative excellence, *writing of the very first rank* ‖ position in a hierarchy ‖ high social position, *a man of rank* ‖ a row of soldiers standing or marching abreast ‖ (*pl.*) the body of private soldiers, *to rise from the ranks* ‖ (*chess*) one of the horizontal lines extending across a chessboard **2.** *v.t.* to arrange in a rank or ranks ‖ to ascribe a level or position in a hierarchy to, *to rank something very highly* ‖ to hold a higher rank than, *a major ranks a lieutenant* ‖ *v.i.* to form a rank or ranks ‖ to belong to a category in a hierarchy, *he ranks with our finest poets* ‖ to be in the top rank,

ranking officers of the corporation [obs. O.F. *ranc*, perh. fr. Gmc]
rank *adj.* excessively luxuriant in growth, *rank weeds* || coarse in growth, *rank grass* || gross, crude, *rank behavior* || smelling like damp, partly rotted vegetation || complete, utter, *a rank outsider* [O.E. *ranc*, strong proud]
rank and file private soldiers, as distinguished from their officers || ordinary people, as distinguished from their leaders
Ran·ke (rɑ́ŋkə), Leopold von (1795-1886), German historian. His works include 'German History in the Time of the Reformation' (1839-47), 'The Roman Popes in the Last Four Centuries' (1834-7) and a 'History of the World' (1880-8). He was a pioneer of objective method in historical research
ran·kle (rǽŋk'l) *pres. part.* **ran·kling** *past* and *past part.* **ran·kled** *v.i.* to be a source of prolonged emotional pain or distress, *his unkind remark rankled in her mind* || *v.t.* to cause bitter feelings in, *it rankled him to think of her ingratitude* [O. F. *rancler, raoncler*]
Rann of Kutch (rǽn) a salt marsh (about 9,000 sq. miles) along the frontier between Pakistan and Gujarat, India. It is dry Oct.-Feb. By arbitration c. 300 square miles formerly administered by India passed (Feb. 1968) to Pakistan
ran·sack (rǽnsæk) *v.t.* to search thoroughly, *he ransacked his pockets for the ticket* || to steal everything valuable from [O.N. *rannsake* fr. *rann*, house+*sækja*, to search]
ran·som (rǽnsəm) *v.t.* to secure the release of by paying a ransom || to demand a ransom for || to release on payment of a ransom [O. F. *ransonner, rançonner*]
ransom *n.* money paid or demanded for the release of a person held captive || a release by payment of this **to hold (someone) in** (*Br.* **to**) **ransom** to keep (someone) captive until a ransom is paid [O.F. *rançon, raençon*]
rant (rænt) **1.** *v.i.* to use bombastic language, esp. in public speaking || (of an actor) to be declamatory in a ludicrously exaggerated way || to be noisily angry || *v.t.* to utter with exaggerated emphasis **2.** *n.* a piece of ranting [obs. Du. *randten*, to rave]
ra·nun·cu·lus (rənʌ́ŋkjuləs) *pl.* **ra·nun·cu·lus·es, ra·nun·cu·li** (rənʌ́nkjulai) *n.* a member of *Ranunculus*, fam. *Ranunculaceae*, a genus of plants including about 200 species, e.g. the buttercup, found chiefly in northern temperate latitudes [L. dim. of *rana*, frog]
Ra·oult (ræu:), François Marie (1830-1901), French chemist. He demonstrated for dilute solutions that the depression of the freezing point and the elevation of the boiling point were related to the molecular mass and the concentration of the solute
rap (ræp) **1.** *n.* a sharp, quick blow || the sound of such an impact **to take the rap** to take blame or punishment, esp. unjustly, or agree to be held responsible **2.** *v. pres. part.* **rap·ping** *past* and *past part.* **rapped** *v.t.* to strike with a quick sharp blow || (with 'out') to express (something) quickly and forcefully, *to rap out a command* || *v.i.* (usually with 'at' or 'on') to knock sharply [imit.]
rap *n.* (only in the phrase) **not to care** (or **give**) **a rap** not to care the least bit [fr. its 18th-c. meaning: a counterfeit halfpenny. Origin unknown]
rap *n.* (*colloq.*) **1.** a free, open, and unorganized conversation **2.** a conversation that stimulates spontaneity —**rap** *v.* —**rap group** *n.* —**rapper** *n.* —**rap session** *v.*
ra·pa·cious (rəpéiʃəs) *adj.* grasping, avid for wealth or gain || living by preying || ravenous, *a rapacious appetite* [fr. L. *rapax* (*rapacis*), grasping]
ra·pac·i·ty (rəpǽsiti:) *n.* the quality of being rapacious [fr. L. *rapacitas, rapacitatis*]
Ra·pal·lo, Treaty of (rəpǽlou) a treaty (1920) between Italy and Yugoslavia, agreeing to establish a free state of Fiume || a treaty (1922) between Germany and the U.S.S.R. canceling pre-war debts and war claims and providing for trade agreements
rape (reip) *n.* (*law*) illicit sexual intercourse with a woman without her consent (by force, deception, while she is asleep etc.) || (*rhet.*) the doing of violence, e.g. to a city or country, esp. in war [A.F. *rap, rape*]
rape *pres. part.* **rap·ing** *past* and *past part.* **raped** *v.t.* to commit rape on [prob. fr. L. *rapere*, to seize]
rape *n. Brica napus*, fam. *Cruciferae*, an annual plant cultivated in Europe and America as forage for sheep and hogs and for the oil expressed from rapeseeds [fr. L. *rapa, rapum*, turnip]
rape *n.* (often *pl.*) the substance which remains after the juice has been pressed out of grapes, used as a filter in making vinegar [F. *rape*, grape stalk]
rape cake cattle food made of the compressed residue when the oil from rapeseed has been extracted
rape oil an oil obtained from rapeseed and turnip seed, used e.g. as a lubricant and food
rape·seed (réipsi:d) *n.* the seed of rape
Raph·a·el (rǽfi:əl, réifi:əl) (Raffaello Sanzio, 1483-1520), Italian Renaissance painter and architect. He was a pupil of Perugino. His greatest paintings were done in Florence and Rome. By 1511 he had finished the frescos for the Stanza della Segnatura of the Vatican, and at the age of 28 he ranked with the greatest painters of the time. In 1514 he was appointed chief architect of St Peter's. He also worked on paintings for the Vatican and designed tapestries for the Sistine Chapel. His finely drawn compositions, though sometimes elaborate, are subtly unified and the poses of his figures are profoundly expressive. His colors are of extreme delicacy. His portraits are perhaps the first in European art in which the spirituality of the sitter is expressed as well as his likeness. Raphael expresses, in both his religious and classical subjects, a vision of idealized beauty in a harmoniously ordered universe
ra·phe (réifi:) *n.* (*anat.*) a line of union like a seam, e.g. in the perineum, scrotum, tongue, medulla oblongata etc. || (*bot.*) a line of junction, suture || (*biol.*) the slitlike median line in a diatom valve [Mod. L. fr. Gk *raphē*, seam]
ra·phide (réifid) *n.* (*bot.*) a needleshaped crystal, usually of calcium oxalate, developed as a metabolic by-product in plant cells [F. fr. Gk *rhaphis* (*rhaphidos*), a needle]
rap·id (rǽpid) **1.** *adj.* occurring, done or acting with speed || characterized by speed **2.** *n.* (esp. *pl.*) that part of a river where the water flows swiftly and turbulently over a shallow, usually rocky, bed **ra·pid·i·ty** (rəpíditi:) *n.* the state or quality of being rapid [fr. L. *rapidus*]
ra·pi·er (réipi:ər) *n.* a light, straight, thin, two-edged sword [F. *rapière*, origin unknown]
ra·pine (rǽpin) *n.* (*rhet.*) plundering, despoiling others of their property [F.]
rap·ist (réipist) *n.* a person who has committed rape
rap music (*music*) personal lyrics sung with no melody in a syncopated beat —**rapper** *n.*
RAPCON (*acronym*) for radar approach control, a system of radar control of aircraft in their approach to the airport
rapid eye movement *n.* a rapid movement of the eyes during sleep when dreams occur and special forms of relaxation occur. *acronym* REM. *Cf* REM SLEEP
rap·pen (rǽpin) *pl.* **rap·pen** *n.* a Swiss centime [G. fr. *rappe*, raven]
rap·port (ræpɔ́r, ræpóur) *n.* sympathetic connection, harmony, *to be in rapport with one's surroundings* [F.]
rap·proche·ment (ræprɔʃmã) *n.* a renewal of friendly relations, esp. between states or parties [F.]
rap·scal·lion (ræpskǽljən) *n.* (*old-fash.*) a rascal, good-for-nothing [earlier *rascallion* fr. RASCAL]
rapt (ræpt) *adj.* carried away in imagination from the reality of one's environment || of the mental or emotional state or activity accompanying this condition, *rapt attention* [fr. L. *rapere* (*raptus*), to seize]
rap·to·ri·al (ræptɔ́ri:əl, ræptóuri:əl) *adj.* (of claws) adapted for seizing prey || of or relating to birds of prey [fr. L. *raptor*, one that seizes]
rap·ture (rǽptʃər) *n.* an emotional state in which intense joy, love etc. possesses the mind to the exclusion of every other emotion or consideration || a fulsome expression of approval or satisfaction **ráp·tur·ous** *adj.* characterized by rapture [fr. past part. of obs. *rapt*, to carry away]
rare (rɛər) *adj.* infrequently found, seen or experienced, *a rare event, a rare species* || (of a gas, air etc.) not dense, not having the components massed closely together || unusually good, appealing etc. || (*pop.*) intense, extreme, *a rare fright* [fr. L. *rarus* or F. *rare*]
rare *adj.* (of meat) cooked very lightly [fr. older *rear* fr. O.E. *hrēr*, lightly boiled]
rare·bit (rέərbit) *n.* Welsh rabbit
rare earth any of a group of oxides of the lanthanide elements that usually occur together naturally and have very similar properties (*PERIODIC TABLE)
rare-earth element one of the lanthanide series (*PERIODIC TABLE)
rare-earth metal a rare-earth element
rar·e·fac·tion (rɛərəfǽkʃən) *n.* a rarefying or being rarefied [fr. L. *rarefacere* (*rarefactus*), to rarefy]
rar·e·fac·tive (rɛərəfǽktiv) *adj.* causing rarefaction || characterized by rarefaction [fr. L. *rarefacere* (*rarefactus*), to rarefy]
rar·e·fy, rar·i·fy (rέərəfai) *pres. part.* **rar·e·fy·ing, rar·i·fy·ing** *past* and *past part.* **rar·e·fied, rar·i·fied** *v.t.* to make (a gas etc.) rare || to refine, make more subtle, *rarefied notions* || *v.i.* (of gases etc.) to become rare [F. *raréfier*]
rare gas an inert gas belonging to group 0 of the periodic table
rare·ly (rέərli:) *adv.* very infrequently
rarity *RAREFY
rar·ing (rέəriŋ) *adj.* (*pop.*, used with an infinitive) full of eagerness, *raring to go*
rar·i·ty (rέəriti:) *pl.* **rar·i·ties** *n.* something which is rare || something highly valued because it is rare || the quality or fact of being rare [fr. L. *raritas*]
ras·cal (rǽskəl) **1.** *n.* a rogue, trickster || an endearingly mischievous person, esp. a child **ras·cal·i·ty** (ræskǽliti:) **2.** *n.* the quality of being a rascal or behaving like a rascal [O.F. *rascaille*, rabble]
ra·schel knit (rǽʃəl) fabric made on latch needles, with 1 to 32 warp or thread systems, with warps mounted in a stationary position
rase *RAZE
rash (ræʃ) *adj.* made or done hastily without considering the possible consequences or attendant risks || acting in a hasty inconsidered manner, or given to acting in this way [M.E. *rasch*, active, vigorous]
rash *n.* an eruption or collection of spots or small red patches on the skin [perh. fr. O.F. *rache, rasque*]
rash·er (rǽʃər) *n.* a thin slice of bacon or ham, usually for frying [etym. doubtful]
rasp (ræsp, rɑsp) *v.t.* to remove unevennesses etc. from by rubbing with a rasp || to grate harshly upon (the nerves) || *v.i.* to make a rough scraping sound || to grate [prob. O.F. *rasper*]
rasp *n.* a type of coarse file with individual, hard, raised teeth set very close together || a machine used for rasping || a noise made by rasping or as if by rasping || a machine that grinds waste into a manageable material and helps prevent odor [O.F. *raspe* fr. *rasper*, to rasp]
ras·pa·to·ry (rǽspətɔri:, rǽspətouri:) *pl.* **ras·pa·to·ries** *n.* a surgical rasp [fr. M.L. *raspatorium* fr. *raspare*, to rasp]
rasp·ber·ry (rǽzberi:, rɑ́zberi:) *pl.* **rasp·ber·ries** *n.* any of several members of *Rubus*, fam. *Rosaceae*, a genus of tall-growing shrubs having annually renewed canes usually covered with fine, prickly hairs, and bearing succulent red or black aggregate fruits, each composed of many small drupes and set on a conical receptacle || the fruit of this shrub || the color or flavor of the fruit of the red raspberry || (*pop.*) a rude sound made by vibrating the tongue between the lips, to show contempt or derision [fr. older *rasp*, raspberry+BERRY]
raspberry sawfly *Blennocampa rubi*, fam. *Tenthredinidae*, a small, black sawfly with a reddish abdomen. Its pale green larvae feed on the leaves of raspberries and blackberries
Ras·pu·tin (ræspjú:tin), Grigori Yefimovich (1871-1916), Russian monk and adventurer. He exercised a hypnotic fascination on the czarina and influenced the policies of Nicholas II. Hated by the nobility for his debauchery and abuse of power, he was assassinated
Ras-Sham·ra (rɑ́sʃǽmrə) *UGARIT
Ras Ta·fa·ri (rǽstəfɑ́ri:) a black, back-to-Africa movement in Jamaica organized by Marcus Garvey. It makes Ethiopia's Emperor Haile Selassie (Ras Tafari is the original name of Haile Selassie) the object of a cult, and compares the 'heaven' of Ethiopia with the 'hell' of Jamaica
Ras Ta·fa·ri·an (rǽstəfέəri:ən) *n.* an adherent of the Ras Tafari movement
Rastafarian *n.* Jamaica-based sect devoted to Haile Selassie (former Emperor of Ethiopia) espousing love, peace, ganja (marijuana); noted for reggae music and for members' hair worn in dread locks, ropelike boyo strands

CONCISE PRONUNCIATION KEY: **(a)** æ, *cat*; ɑ, *car*; ɔ *fawn*; ei, *snake*. **(e)** e, *hen*; i:, *sheep*; iə, *deer*; εə, *bear*. **(i)** i, *fish*; ai, *tiger*; ə:, *bird*. **(o)** o, *ox*; au, *cow*; ou, *goat*; u, *poor*; ɔi, *royal*. **(u)** ʌ, *duck*; u, *bull*; u:, *goose*; ə, *bacillus*; ju:, *cube*. x, *loch*; θ, *think*; ð, *bother*; z, *Zen*; ʒ, *corsage*; dʒ, *savage*; ŋ, *orangutang*; j, *yak*; ʃ, *fish*; tʃ, *fetch*; 'l, *rabble*; 'n, *redden*. Complete pronunciation key appears inside front cover.

Ras·tatt, Treaty of (rɑ́ʃtɑt) a treaty (1714) between Austria and France at the end of the War of the Spanish Succession, complementing the Peace of Utrecht (1713)

rast·er (rǽstər) *n.* the part in the cathode-ray tube of a television set on which the image is reproduced [G.=screen]

raster display (*computer*) a graphic presentation of data created on a screen in fixed sequence, usu. from left to right

rat (ræt) **1.** *n.* any of various omnivorous rodents of *Rattus* and related genera of fam. *Muridae.* They are approximately 8 ins long with a scaly tail 8–9 ins in length. Rats live in drains, sewers and rubbish piles and have spread throughout the world on ships. They are highly destructive and are the carriers of many diseases, esp. bubonic plague ‖ (*pop.*) a contemptible person, esp. one who betrays or deserts associates ‖ a tapered coil, esp. of hair, over which a woman's hair may be arranged ‖ **to smell a rat** to suspect some trap, piece of trickery, treachery etc. **2.** *v. pres. part.* **rat·ting** *past* and *past part.* **rat·ted** *v.i.* to hunt rats ‖ (often with 'on') to desert or betray one's associates [O.E. *rœt*]

ra·ta (rɑ́tə) *n.* either of two New Zealand trees, *Metrosideros robusta* and *M. lucida,* fam. *Myrtaceae,* yielding a hard, red wood ‖ this wood [Maori]

rat·a·ble, rate·a·ble (réitəb'l) *adj.* liable to be rated ‖ able to be rated in accordance with some scale **rát·a·bly, ráte·a·bly** *adv.*

rat·a·fi·a (rætəfíːə) *n.* a liqueur flavored with almonds or with peach, apricot or cherry kernels [F., origin unknown]

rat·al (réit'l) *n.* (*Br.*) the amount on which local property taxes are assessed

ratan *RATTAN

rat-bite fever a febrile disease caused by the bacterium *Spirillum minus* and transmitted by the bite of a rat. An ulcer forms at the site of the wound, the lymph glands swell, and there is usually a bluish-red rash

ratch (rætʃ) *n.* a ratchet ‖ a toothed bar with which a pawl engages to prevent reverse motion

ratch·et (rǽtʃit) *n.* a detent, catch or pawl for retaining or activating a ratchet wheel ‖ a ratchet wheel and pawl working together ‖ (*Br.*) the notched, tapering teeth set on certain wheels and bars which may engage with a pawl to prevent reverse motion [F. *rochet,* lance head, bobbin]

ratchet wheel a wheel having teeth with which a detent, catch or pawl engages to prevent reverse motion or to activate forward motion

rate (reit) **1.** *n.* the amount of something in relation to some other thing, *absentee rate of 2 men and 5 women per 1,000 employees* ‖ a fixed ratio between two things, quantities etc., *rate of exchange* ‖ speed of motion or change, *drive at a moderate rate* ‖ (*pl., Br.*) a local property tax levied on buildings etc. in proportion to an estimated annual rental value ‖ a fixed charge per unit of a commodity, service etc. ‖ (*insurance*) a premium charge per unit ‖ a charge asked or paid for a service etc. ‖ (*naut.*) a class of vessel, esp. of warships **at any rate** at least, in any case, *at any rate he didn't forget* **at this** (or **that**) **rate** given the present (or those) conditions **2.** *v. pres. part.* **rat·ing** *past* and *past part.* **rat·ed** *v.t.* to assess the quality or worth of ‖ (*Br.*) to assess (property) for local tax purposes ‖ to consider (someone or something) as something, *they rate him as a public menace* ‖ to deserve, merit, *this essay rates a low grade* ‖ (*naut.*) to determine the relative rank or class of ‖ *v.i.* to be considered, *he rates as a fine workman* [O.F.]

rate (reit) *pres. part.* **rat·ing** *past* and *past part.* **rat·ed** *v.t.* to scold severely ‖ *v.i.* (usually with 'at') to deliver a scolding [etym. doubtful]

rateable *RATABLE

ra·tel (réit'l) *n.* a member of *Mellivora,* fam. *Mustelidae,* a genus of burrowing carnivores, esp. *M. capensis* of S. Africa and *M. indica* of India. Ratels are about 3 ft long, including an 8–9-in. tail, and have thick coarse fur, gray on top and black underneath. They destroy wild bees' nests for their honey [Afrik.]

rate·me·ter (réitmiːtər) *n.* an instrument that indicates the rate at which radiation is being absorbed by a human

rat·er (réitər) *n.* (only in compounds) a person of a certain class or rating, *a second-rater*

rath·er (rǽðər, rɑ́ðər) *adv.* more willingly, preferably, *we would rather go for a walk than stay indoors* ‖ more truthfully, more exactly, *it was a foolish rather than a malicious remark* ‖ on the contrary, *it wasn't damp, rather it was too dry* ‖ in some measure, *he is rather tiresome* ‖ (ræðə́ːr, rɑðə́ːr) (*Br., pop.,* in answering a question) yes, most certainly [comp. of older *rathe,* quickly]

rat·i·cide (rǽtisaid) *n.* a chemical or other preparation for exterminating rats [fr. RAT+L. *caedere,* to kill]

rat·i·fi·ca·tion (rætifikéiʃən) *n.* a ratifying or being ratified

rat·i·fy (rǽtifai) *pres. part.* **rat·i·fy·ing** *past* and *past part.* **rat·i·fied** *v.t.* to confirm (something done or promised), esp. formally, *to ratify a treaty* [F. *ratifier*]

ra·tine (rætíːn) *n.* ratiné

rat·i·né (rætnéi) *n.* a coarse woolen, cotton or rayon cloth, woven so as to have a rough, knotted surface [F.=tufted]

rat·ing (réitiŋ) *n.* a man's class in a warship's crew, or in the army ‖ (*Br.*) a sailor below commissioned rank ‖ classification, e.g. of engines by horsepower, yachts by tonnage etc. ‖ (*commerce*) the estimated credit and reliability of a business concern ‖ an estimate of achievement, status etc. ‖ (*Br.*) the amount fixed as a rate to be paid on property

ra·ti·o (réiʃiːou, réiʃou) *n.* the relation between two quantities which is expressed by dividing the magnitude of one by that of the other, *the ratio between selling price and cost price is 3 to 1* [L.=reason]

ra·ti·oc·i·nate (ræʃiːɒ́sineit) *pres. part.* **ra·ti·oc·i·nat·ing** *past* and *past part.* **ra·ti·oc·i·nat·ed** *v.i.* (*rhet.*) to reason, argue logically [fr. L. *ratiocinari* (*ratiocinatus*)]

ra·ti·oc·i·na·tion (ræʃiːɒsinéiʃən) *n.* (*rhet.*) the reasoning process [fr. L. *ratiocinatio* (*ratiocinationis*)]

ra·ti·oc·i·na·tive (ræʃiːɒ́sineitiv) *adj.* (*rhet.*) of or marked by ratiocination [fr. L. *ratiocinativus*]

ra·tion (rǽʃən, réiʃən) **1.** *n.* an amount (of food, time etc.) which one permits oneself or which one is permitted ‖ (*pl.*) provisions (esp. of food or drink) allotted **2.** *v.t.* to fix the amount of (something) which each individual is permitted to consume ‖ to allow to consume only a certain amount of something ‖ (with 'out') to give out as a ration [F. or fr. L. *ratio* (*rationis*), ratio]

ra·tion·al (rǽʃən'l) *adj.* of or relating to reason ‖ based on and in accordance with reason or reasoning ‖ well suited to its purpose, *rational dress* ‖ endowed with reason, *man is a rational animal* ‖ (*pop.*) sensible, sound-minded ‖ (*math.*) not requiring a radical for its expression [fr. L. *rationalis*]

ra·tion·ale (ræʃənǽl) *n.* the logical justifying grounds for something ‖ a statement or exposition of principles or reasons [L. neut. of *rationalis,* rational]

ra·tion·al·ism (rǽʃən'lizəm) *n.* the belief that all knowledge and truth consist in what is ascertainable by rational processes of thought and that there is no supernatural revelation ‖ (*philos.*) the doctrine that true and absolute knowledge is found only in reason **rá·tion·al·ist** *adj.* and *n.* **ra·tion·al·ís·tic** *adj.*

ra·tion·al·i·ty (ræʃənǽliti:) *n.* the quality or state of being rational [fr. L.L. *rationalitas*]

ra·tion·al·i·za·tion (ræʃən'lizéiʃən) *n.* a rationalizing or the result of this ‖ (*business*) reducing costs of industrial production to meet competition, esp. in world markets

ra·tion·al·ize (rǽʃən'laiz) *pres. part.* **ra·tion·al·iz·ing** *past* and *past part.* **ra·tion·al·ized** *v.t.* to discover and express the reason for (conduct etc.), esp. in order to justify ‖ to put a natural explanation in place of a supernatural one for (something) ‖ to make (a production or an industry) more efficient and less costly ‖ (*math.*) to reduce (an expression) to finite terms

Rat·is·bon (rǽtizbɒn) *REGENSBURG

rat·ite (rǽtait) **1.** *adj.* of a member of *Ratitae,* a group of flightless, running birds with a flat sternum and rudimentary wings (e.g. emu, ostrich) **2.** *n.* a member of *Ratitae* [fr. L. *ratis,* raft]

rat·line (rǽtlin) *n.* (*naut.,* esp. *pl.*) one of the small lines rope across the shrouds of a ship, forming a ladder ‖ the thin rope so used ‖ (*mil.*) an organized effort for clandestine movement of personnel and/or material across a denied area or border [etym. doubtful]

rat·o·mor·phic (rætəmɔ́rfik) *adj.* research conclusions based on the reactions of rats

ra·toon, rat·toon (rætúːn) **1.** *n.* a new shoot growing from the root or crown of a perennial, e.g. sugarcane, after the old growth has been cut down **2.** *v.i.* to send up new shoots in this way ‖ *v.t.* to cut back (a plant) to encourage ratoons to sprout [fr. Span. *retoño,* a sprout]

rat race (*pop.*) a hectic rush, frantic scramble (used esp. of the struggle to earn a living in an industrial economy under conditions which tend to dehumanize)

rat racer *n.* (*colloq.*) participant in competitive society

rat·tan, ra·tan (rætǽn) *n.* any of various climbing palms, esp. of genera *Calamus* and *Daemonothops,* growing in India and S.E. Asia ‖ a part of the long stem of this plant used for wickerwork, chair seats, rope etc. ‖ a walking stick fashioned from such a stem [Malay *rōtan* fr. *rāut,* to pare]

rat·ter (rǽtər) *n.* a dog good at catching rats

rat·tle (rǽt'l) **1.** *v. pres. part.* **rat·tling** *past* and *past part.* **rat·tled** *v.i.* to emit a rapid succession of short, sharp sounds, *the shutter rattled in the wind* ‖ to move emitting such sounds, *the old car rattled down the road* ‖ to move rapidly, *the car rattled along at great speed* ‖ (often with 'on') to talk rapidly, incessantly and often rather foolishly ‖ *v.t.* to cause (something) to make a rattling sound ‖ (often with 'off') to express in rapid, usually emotionless, speech, *he rattled off the poem* ‖ to cause to become confused and lacking in confidence, *the questions rattled the witness* **2.** *n.* the sound made by something which rattles ‖ such a sound made in a mucus-clogged throat ‖ a contrivance or baby's toy designed to make this sound ‖ the horny rings on a rattlesnake's tail [M.E. *ratelen,* prob. imit.]

rat·tle·brain (rǽt'lbrein) *n.* an emptyheaded person **rát·tle·brained** *adj.*

rat·tler (rǽtlər) *n.* a rattlesnake

rat·tle·snake (rǽt'lsneik) *n.* a member of *Sistrurus* or *Crotalus,* fam. *Crotalidae,* genera of North American poisonous snakes having horny sheaths towards the end of the tail which make a rattling sound

rat·tle·trap (rǽt'ltræp) **1.** *n.* something old and dilapidated, esp. a noisy, rattling automobile, wagon etc. ‖ (*Br., old-fash.*) someone who chatters incessantly **2.** *adj.* old and dilapidated

rat·tling (rǽtliŋ) *adj.* (*pop.*) decidedly good, *a rattling success* ‖ (*pop.*) lively, brisk, *a rattling pace*

rat·tly (rǽtli:) *adj.* tending to rattle ‖ having a noisy sound like a rattle

rattoon *RATOON

rat·trap, rat-trap (rǽttræp) *n.* a trap for catching rats

rau·cous (rɔ́kəs) *adj.* hoarse, grating, rough-sounding, *raucous laughter* [fr. L. *raucus*]

raun·chy (rɔ́ntʃi:) *adj.* bawdy —**raunchiness** *n.*

Rau·schen·berg (ráuʃənbəːrg), Robert (1925-), U.S. painter, known esp. for his 'combine-drawings' depicting themes drawn from American folklore and using a juxtaposition of collage, ink, pencil and photography

rav·age (rǽvidʒ) *n.* devastation ‖ (*pl.*) ill effects, *the ravages of time* [F.]

rav·age *pres. part.* **rav·ag·ing** *past* and *past part.* **rav·aged** *v.t.* to lay waste to ‖ *v.i.* to do ruinous damage [F. *ravager*]

rave (reiv) **1.** *v.i. pres. part.* **rav·ing** *past* and *past part.* **raved** to talk or act wildly or incoherently, *he raved in his delirium* ‖ (with 'about' or 'over') to express or feel exaggerated admiration, *she raves about that singer* ‖ *v.t.* to express wildly or incoherently, *to rave obscenities* **2.** *n.* the act of raving or an instance of this ‖ (*pop.*) an excessively enthusiastic criticism, esp. of a play [perh. O.F. *raver*]

Ra·vel (rævel), Maurice (1875-1937), French composer. He explored a highly chromatic and sensuous harmony. His art is rigorously precise, but also full of tenderness and fantasy, e.g. 'Ma mère l'Oye' (1908) and the operas 'l'Heure espagnole' (1907) and 'l'Enfant et les sortilèges' (completed in 1925). His mastery of orchestration, e.g. the suites from the ballet 'Daphnis and Chloe' (1908), is famous. Other works include the piano suite 'Gaspard de la nuit' (1908), two piano concertos, chamber music and songs

rav·el (rǽvəl) **1.** *v. pres. part.* **rav·el·ing,** esp. *Br.* **rav·el·ling** *past.* and *past part.* **rav·eled,** esp. *Br.* **rav·elled** *v.t.* to separate the threads of ‖ to cause (the edge of a fabric) to fray ‖ *v.i.* to become tangled or confused ‖ to become untwisted ‖ to fray **2.** *n.* a frayed end or loose thread ‖ something tangled, esp. a tangled situation [prob. fr. Du. *ravelen, rafelen,* to make tangled]

rave·lin (rǽvlin) *n.* (*hist.*) a detached part of a system of fortifications (15th–16th cc.) outside the curtain, its two embankments forming a salient [F. fr. Ital.]

rav·el·ing, esp. *Br.* **rav·el·ling,** (rǽvəliŋ) *n.* a thread that has come loose from a fabric and hangs from the surface

ra·ven (réivən) **1.** *n. Corvus corax,* fam. *Corvidae,* a large, black, omnivorous and occasionally predatory bird about 2 ft long with a wingspread of 3 to 4 ft. It has a black bill, a wedge-shaped tail and a deep, harsh croak. It nests on cliffs or in very tall trees **2.** *adj.* glossy black [O.E. *hræfn*]

rav·en·ing (rǽvəniŋ) *adj.* (*rhet.*) hungrily searching for prey [pres. part. of *raven,* to search for prey, fr. O.F. *raviner*]

Ra·ven·na (rəvénə) a town (pop. 137,093) of Emilia Romagna, Italy, an ancient port, now 6 miles from the Adriatic. Industries: sugar refining, textiles, oil refining. Cathedral (18th c.). Romano-Byzantine and Byzantine mausoleums, baptistry and churches (5th-11th cc.), some containing celebrated mosaics (esp. those of San Vitale and Sant' Apollinare Nuovo, both 6th c.). Ravenna was the capital of the Western Roman Empire (402-76), of the Ostrogoths (493-526), and of an exarchate (584-751). It was given to the papacy (754) by Pépin III

rav·en·ous (rǽvinəs) *adj.* fiercely hungry ‖ consuming or devouring greedily [O.F. *ravineux,* addicted to plundering]

Ra·vens·brück (réivənzbruk, rɑvənsbryk) the site in S. Mecklenburg, East Germany, of a Nazi concentration camp for women (1934-45)

Ra·vi (rɑ́vi:) a tributary (400 miles long) of the Chenab, rising in S. Kashmir and forming part of the border between the Indian Punjab and the Pakistani Punjab. It joins the Chenab above Multan

ra·vine (rəví:n) *n.* a long, deep, narrow hollow, usually made by a torrent deepening its bed [F.=flood, torrent]

rav·ing (réiviŋ) **1.** *adj.* talking wildly or incoherently, *a raving lunatic* ‖ worthy of being raved about, *a raving beauty* **2.** *adv.* to the extent of raving, *raving mad* **3.** *n.* (esp. *pl.*) incoherent talk or an item of such talk, *lucid moments in her ravings* [RAVE]

ra·vi·o·li (rævi:óuli:, rɑvi:óuli:) *pl. n.* small cases of pasta filled with meat, spinach etc. cooked and served with a sauce [Ital.]

rav·ish (rǽviʃ) *v.t.* (*rhet.*) to rape **ráv·ish·ing** *adj.* so beautiful as to cause rapture [F. *ravir* (*ravis-*)]

raw (rɔ) **1.** *adj.* (of foodstuffs) uncooked ‖ (of other material) unprocessed, unrefined, or unfinished, *raw silk, raw spirit* ‖ untrained, inexperienced, *raw recruits* ‖ (of a wound or part of the body) having the skin partly or wholly removed ‖ (of weather) cold and damp ‖ (*pop.*) indecent, *a raw joke* ‖ (*photog.*) unexposed **2.** *n.* (in the phrases) **to touch on the raw** (*Br.*) to cause painful emotions to **in the raw** in the original state, *nature in the raw* ‖ (*pop.*) naked [O.E. *hrēaw* fr. Gk]

Ra·wal·pin·di (rɔlpíndi:) a city (pop. 928,000) of Pakistan in the N. Punjab, a commercial center and military base, temporary headquarters of the national government (1959-60): oil refining, chemicals, rail yards

raw·boned (rɔ́bound) *adj.* having little flesh covering the bones

raw deal an instance of unfair or unjust treatment

raw·hide (rɔ́haid) *n.* untanned cattle hide ‖ a whip made of this

ra·win (reíwən) *n.* (*meteor. acronym*) for radar wind sounding, **1.** a radar system for determining wind direction and velocity above a station utilizing a balloon-borne radiosonde and radio; or **2.** the information so collected

ra·win·sonde (reíwənsɒnd) *n.* (*meteor.*) a method of determining and evaluating wind speed, direction, air pressure and humidity

Rawlings (rɔ́liŋz), Jerry (1947-), leader of Ghana (1979, 1981-). An armed forces officer, he overthrew Lt.-Gen. Frederick W. K. Akuffo (1979), briefly led the country before installing a civilian government and then staged another coup in 1981

Raw·lin·son (rɔ́linsən), Sir Henry Creswicke (1810-95), British administrator and Orientalist. He deciphered (1835-46) the Assyrian cuneiform inscription of Darius I at Behistun and was a founder of Assyriology

raw material the basic matter from which processed or manufactured goods are made

RAWOL (*mil. acronym*) for radar without line of sight, a system of radar detection of targets obscured by intervening hills.

raw sienna sienna that has not been calcined ‖ the brownish-orange color of this

Raws·thorne (rɔ́sθɔrn), Alan (1905-71), English composer. His works include three symphonies, piano and violin concertos, chamber music etc.

raw umber umber that has not been calcined ‖ the dark yellowish-brown color of this (cf. BURNT UMBER)

Ray (rei), John (1627-1705), English naturalist. He and Willughby planned a complete classification of animal and vegetable life. His 'Catalogus plantarum Angliae' (1670) was the first systematic account of English flora

Ray, Man (1890-1976), U.S. painter of the Dada movement, and photographer. He invented the 'rayograph', a photograph obtained by the direct application of objects of varying opacity to a light-sensitive plate

ray (rei) **1.** *n.* a line constructed perpendicular to a wave front in which light is propagated, representing the path of light in geometrical optics. It is considered a beam of infinitesimally small cross section ‖ a line of light that appears to radiate from some light-producing or light-reflecting objects ‖ a stream of particles traveling along the same path ‖ any of several lines radiating from a center (e.g. the radii of a circle) ‖ a portion or organ of a plant or animal having a number of like parts diverging from a common center, e.g. a vascular ray, the arm of a starfish or any of the supporting bones of the fins of some fishes ‖ a slight manifestation, e.g. of hope or intelligence ‖ (*bot.*) the outer whorl of florets of a composite flower **2.** *v.i.* to issue in rays [O.F. *rai*]

ray *n.* a member of *Hypotremata,* an order of flattened, cartilaginous fish similar to the skate (*STING RAY, ELECTRIC RAY)

ray (*mus.*) *RE

Rayburn (reíbərn), Samuel Taliaferro (1882-1961), U.S. politician, Speaker of the House of Representatives (1940-7; 1949-53; 1955-61). A Democrat from Texas, he served in the House (1913-61) and was elected majority leader in 1937. He was instrumental in the drafting of New Deal legislation

ray·dist (reídist) *n.* a navigation system involving a continuous signal to several ground stations, which compare, compute, and report position

ray floret one of the marginal flowers going around the head of disk florets in e.g. the daisy, or making up the head in composites having no disk florets

ray flower a ray floret

Ray·leigh (réili:), John William Strutt, 3rd Baron (1842-1919), English physicist. He contributed largely to the study of vibratory motion. With Ramsay he discovered argon, and he worked on the standardizing of electrical units. Nobel prize (1904)

Ray·leigh wave or **R wave** (reíli:) **1.** (*seismology*) surface vibrations with retrograde, elliptical ground motion. **2.** (*mechanics*) parallel waves in the surface of a solid

Ray·naud's phenomenon (reinóuz) (*med.*) obstruction in bloodstream resulting in discoloration (white or blue) of hands

ray·on (réiɒn) *n.* a textile fiber made by forcing various solutions of naturally occurring cellulose through fine holes and solidifying in a chemical bath or warm air ‖ any of various textiles made of such fibers [coined fr. RAY]

raze, rase (reiz) *pres. part.* **raz·ing, ras·ing** *past* and *past part.* **razed, rased** *v.t.* to destroy completely, *to raze a city* [F. *raser,* to shave]

ra·zor (réizər) *n.* an instrument with a very sharp rigid cutting edge, or fitted with a blade having this, used esp. to shave hair from the skin (*STRAIGHT RAZOR) [O.F. *rasor, rasour*]

ra·zor·back (réizərbæk) *n.* a rorqual whale ‖ a thin, long-legged, semiwild hog of the southern U.S.A.

ra·zor·bill (réizərbil) *n. Alca torda,* fam. *Alcidae,* a black and white auk of the N. Atlantic, approx. 16 ins long with a very sharp bill

razor clam a member of *Solenidae,* a family of bivalve mollusks having a very long, narrow, curved shell

razor cut a haircut given with a razor

razor fish a razor clam

razor shell a razor clam ‖ the shell of a razor clam

razz (ræz) *v.t.* (*pop.*) to tease

RBE (*abbr.*) for relative biological effectiveness, a factor for comparison of radiation effects on organisms

R.C. Roman Catholic

RC-135 *n.* (*mil.*) U.S. strategic reconnaissance plane with altitude capability of 40,000 ft, replacing the U-2

Rd. Road

R.D. rural free delivery

RDX *CYCLONITE

Re (rei) Ra

re (ri:) *prep.* (*law, commerce,* etc.) in the matter of, as regards [L. ablative of *res,* thing]

re, *Br.* also **ray** (rei) *n.* (*mus.*) the note D in the fixed-do system of solmization ‖ the second note of any diatonic scale in movable-do solmization [Ital.]

re- (ri:) *prefix* again, another time. Re-compounds are hyphenated when confusion might occur between identical forms, e.g. re-ally and really. The hyphen is also employed when the second part of the word begins with a capital letter, e.g. re-Christianize ‖ back, to a former state or condition [L.]

reach (ri:tʃ) **1.** *v.t.* to arrive at, *to reach the end of a journey, to reach the age of 30* ‖ to extend so as to touch (a particular point or place), *the rubber plant reaches the ceiling* ‖ to extend, *to reach out one's hand* ‖ to succeed in touching or grasping with an outstretched limb ‖ to pass with the hand, *just reach me that book* ‖ to get in touch with, *we tried to reach them by cable* ‖ to touch the mind or feelings of, *her words failed to reach him* ‖ *v.i.* to extend in dimension, scope etc., *the woods reach as far as the river* ‖ (of the voice, eye etc.) to carry, penetrate, *as far as the eye can reach* ‖ to put or stretch out a hand or foot, *reach for the bell* ‖ (*naut.*) to sail on a reach **2.** *n.* the act of stretching out or reaching, or an instance of this ‖ the extent of such a reach ‖ intellectual or imaginative range, *an idea not within his reach* ‖ an uninterrupted expanse, e.g. a straight part of a river or a length of canal between locks ‖ (*naut.*) a tack sailed with the wind abeam ‖ the pole coupling the rear axle of a wagon to the transverse bar over the front axle [O.E. *rǣcan*]

re-act (ri:ǽkt) *v.t.* to act again

re·act (ri:ǽkt) *v.i.* to act in response to a stimulus etc., *he did not react to the treatment* ‖ to act contrary to a stimulus etc., *he reacted against my suggestion* ‖ to undergo chemical change

re·ac·tance (ri:ǽktəns) *n.* (*elec.*) the portion of impedance in an alternating current circuit that results from capacitance or inductance or both. It is expressed in ohms [REACT]

re·ac·tion (ri:ǽkʃən) *n.* a response to a stimulus ‖ opposition caused by an act, proposal etc., *the workers' reaction against automation* ‖ the tendency to favor extremely conservative social or political policies ‖ (*phys.*) the equal and opposing force which is always called into play by a force ‖ a chemical change involving two or more substances **re·ác·tion·ar·y 1.** *adj.* characterized by reaction, esp. in politics **2.** *n. pl.* **re·ác·tion·ar·ies** a reactionary person **re·ác·tion·ist** *n.* a reactionary

reaction time (*psychol.*) the time which elapses between the start of the application of a stimulus and the start of the response it evokes

re·ac·ti·vate (ri:ǽktəveit) *pres. part.* **re·ac·ti·vat·ing** *past* and *past part.* **re·ac·ti·vat·ed** *v.t.* to cause to be active again ‖ *v.i.* to be active again

re·ac·tive (ri:ǽktiv) *adj.* of or characterized by reaction or reactance ‖ tending to react

re·ac·tor (ri:ǽktər) *n.* a person or thing that reacts (e.g. a chemical reagent or a subject of a physiological test reacting to a stimulus) ‖ a low-resistance coil of high inductance used to suppress alternating current or change its phase ‖ a vessel or other piece of equipment in which a chemical reaction is carried out, esp. on a large scale ‖ a device in which a fission chain reaction is initiated and controlled. In general it includes a fuel (a source of neutrons) such as uranium or plutonium, a moderator such as graphite or heavy water (which slows the neutrons to a speed permitting the maximization of capture by other nuclei) and a set of control rods (usually made of cadmium or boron) which absorb neutrons readily and which are brought into play to arrest the reaction if and when there is a danger of its going out of control. The energy produced (*NUCLEAR ENERGY) in a reactor may be converted to electricity (via steam turbines) or to mechanical energy (e.g. in nuclear ships). The nuclear reaction can be used as a source of neutrons producing further radioactive material (*BREEDER REACTOR) [REACT]

read (ri:d) **1.** *v. pres. part.* **read·ing** *past* and *past part.* **read** (red) *v.t.* to understand the meaning of (symbols, signs, gestures etc.) by looking at them and assimilating them mentally, *to read a book, to read music, to read French* ‖ to learn in this way, *he read that sterling had been protected* ‖ to say aloud (written or printed material that one sees and understands in this way), *read this story to us* ‖ (*Br.*) to study (a subject) at a university ‖ to touch (Braille symbols) and understand them ‖ to observe a measurement shown by (an instrument), *to read a pressure gauge* ‖ (of an instrument) to show (a measurement), *the thermometer reads 30 degrees* ‖ to consider (something) to have a certain meaning, *she read his letter to mean that he didn't intend to come* ‖ to give (a word, phrase etc.) as a reading in a particular passage, *for 'marry' this copy reads 'merry'* ‖ to cause (a word, phrase etc.) to be substituted in a particular passage, *read 'marry' for 'merry'* ‖ to discover the meaning of (someone's thoughts, expressions etc.) by observation ‖ to predict (the future, someone's fortune etc.) ‖ to explain or interpret (riddles, magic symbols, palms etc.) ‖ to go over (printer's proofs), marking corrections on them ‖ *v.i.* to be engaged in reading something ‖ to be able to read books etc. ‖ to say audibly what one is reading, *he is reading to the children* ‖ to make a specified impression on a reader, *his letter reads well* ‖ to contain certain words, *the constitution reads as follows . . .* ‖ to suggest a meaning, *his letter reads as if he doesn't intend to come* ‖ to learn or study by reading, *he likes reading about ancient peoples* ‖ to have a specified stylistic quality, *it reads jerkily* **to read out** to read (something) aloud ‖ to expel (someone) from an organization by publicly reading the notice of dismissal **to read (someone) like a book** to understand perfectly the intentions, motives etc. of (someone) without his explaining them or even if he tries to hide them **to read into** to attach to (something) a meaning which is neither stated nor intended **to read oneself in** (*Church of England*) to assume the office of incumbent by reading aloud publicly the Thirty-nine Articles ‖ (*Br.*) to familiarize oneself with the files etc. before attempting to make decisions, initiate work etc. **2.** *n.* (*Br.*) a period of reading, *to enjoy a read after dinner* **read** (red) *adj.* (often in compounds) learned or informed through reading, *a well-read critic* **to take as read** to accept as accurate without having read aloud, *to take the minutes as read* ‖ to assume to be true **réad·a·ble** *adj.* easy or pleasant to read ‖ legible [O.E. *rǣdan*]

re·ad·dress (ri:ədrés) *v.t.* to alter the address on (e.g. a letter)

Reade (ri:d), Charles (1814-84), British novelist. His works include the historical novel 'The Cloister and the Hearth' (1861)

read·er (rí:dər) *n.* a person able to read ‖ a book for children learning to read ‖ a book containing selections for reading for a beginner, esp. in another language ‖ a person who reads, esp. one who reads a particular book or periodical, *this newspaper has over a million readers* ‖ a person very fond of reading ‖ someone who reads and criticizes manuscripts for a publisher, literary agent etc. ‖ a proofreader ‖ someone, esp. a graduate student, who marks examination papers ‖ a person selected to read aloud, e.g. in a religious service ‖ (*Br.*) a member of a university staff ranking between a senior lecturer and a professor **réad·er·ship** *n.* the office of a university reader ‖ the collective body of readers of a newspaper or periodical

read·i·ly (rédili:) *adv.* easily, *one can readily imagine this* ‖ willingly, *to admit a mistake readily* [READY]

read·i·ness (rédi:nis) *n.* the state of being ready ‖ willingness, lack of hesitation, *readiness to offer help*

Read·ing (rédiŋ) the county town (pop. 132,037) of Berkshire, England. Industries: biscuit-making, brewing, mechanical engineering, seed nurseries. University (1926)

read·ing (rí:diŋ) **1.** *n.* the act of one who reads ‖ the ability to read, *reading comes slowly* ‖ the material a person is reading, means to read or has read ‖ the extent to which a person has read, *a man of wide reading* ‖ a public entertainment at which passages from a book, stories, poems etc. are read aloud ‖ a textual version, *the manuscripts offer four variant readings of the passage* ‖ a measurement shown by an instrument, *the reading is 30°C* ‖ understanding, *my reading of the situation differs somewhat* ‖ (*parliament*) the presentation of a bill for debate. The first reading serves as a general and formal introduction. The second reading provides an opportunity for debate on the purpose of the measure and the means proposed to put it into effect. The third reading is a review of the final form of the bill **2.** *adj.* of or for reading or readers

reading desk a raised stand on which a book etc. being read is placed

re·ad·just (ri:ədʒʌ́st) *v.t.* to adjust or arrange again ‖ to change or rearrange (the terms of a company's debts, stocks etc.) through the voluntary action of shareholders, esp. so as to take advantage of new business opportunities **re·ad·júst·ment** *n.* a readjusting or being readjusted

read-on·ly (rí:dóunli:) *n.* (*computer*) device that stores basic operational data that cannot be altered by programmed instructions

read·out (rí:daut) *n.* (*computer*) **1.** information taken from storage for transcription and recording **2.** the processor output. **—readout** *v.* to produce a readout. **—read-out device** *n.* the device

read·y (rédi:) **1.** *adj. comp.* **read·i·er** *superl.* **read·i·est** in a state fit for immediate action, use etc. ‖ immediately available whenever needed, *a ready source of supplies* ‖ in an emotional state adapted to a possible set of circumstances, willing, *she is ready to suffer in order to stay slim* ‖ quick and easy, *a ready wit* ‖ forward, prompt, *he is very ready with his criticism* ‖ reduced to the point of being likely (to do something indicated), *she looked ready to drop* **2.** *n.* (*mil.*, esp. of firearms) the state of being fit or poised for immediate action or use, *rifles at the ready* **3.** *v.t. pres. part.* **read·y·ing** *past* and *past part.* **read·ied** (esp. *reflex.*) to prepare, *he readied himself for the blow* [M.E. *rǣdi, readi, redi,* prob. fr. O.E. *rǣde*]

ready cap (*mil.*) fighter aircraft in condition of 'standby.'

read·y-made (rédi:méid) *adj.* (of clothes) made to a stock size, not to individual requirements ‖ lacking freshness and originality, *ready-made excuses*

ready reckoner a book of mathematical tables

read·y-to-wear (redi:təwέər) *adj.* (of clothes) ready-made

re·af·firm (ri:əfə́:rm) *v.t.* to affirm again

re·af·for·est (ri:æfɔ́rist, ri:æfɔ́rist) *v.t.* (*Br.*) to reforest **re·af·for·est·á·tion** *n.*

Reagan (réigən), Ronald Wilson (1911-), U.S. statesman and actor, 40th president (1981-). Born in Tampico, Ill., he went to Eureka College and then to Hollywood (1937) where he appeared in 53 films and also served as president of the Screen Actors' Guild (1952, 1959-60). He also hosted the TV series 'Death Valley Days' (1961-2). Finding that his views had become more conservative, he ran for governor of California on the Republican ticket in 1966 and, defeating incumbent Democrat Pat Brown, served in that post for eight years (1967-75). He opposed tax increases and government spending and left office with a considerable budget surplus. The Republican nominee in the 1980 presidential election, he chose George Bush as his running mate, won by a near-landslide victory and was decisively reelected in 1984. As president he worked to revamp the U.S. economy, stem inflation, produce tax cuts and increase the country's defenses, and he took a firm stand against the Soviet Union and terrorist tactics. An assassination attempt (1981) by John W. Hinckley, Jr., hospitalized him briefly, as did the early discovery of intestinal cancer in 1985. He was married to actress Jane Wyman (1940-9) and Nancy Davis (1952-)

re·agent (ri:éidʒənt) *n.* a substance used to bring about a chemical reaction in another substance

re·al (rí:əl, ríəl) **1.** *adj.* existing in fact, not merely seeming, *his pain is real, not imaginary* ‖ natural, not artificial, *a real pearl* ‖ proper, *this is real summer weather* ‖ (used merely for emphasis) great, *a real surprise* ‖ (*philos.*) relating to objective things in the physical world ‖ (*law*) of or relating to real estate ‖ (*math.*, of numbers) not imaginary ‖ (of wages) measured by their purchasing power (cf. NOMINAL) **2.** *adv.* (*pop.*) really, *a real good time* **3.** *n.* **the real** that which exists objectively in the physical world [O.F. *real, réel* or L.L. *realis*]

re·al (reiál) *pl.* **re·als, re·a·les** (reiáleis) *n.* a former Spanish silver coin and money of account [Span.=royal]

real estate (*law*) immovable property, e.g. land or houses, as opposed to temporary, movable personal property

real estate investment trusts mutual funds holding real property or mortgages on real property as principal assets. *acronym* REIT

re·al·gar (ri:ǽlgar) *n.* a naturally occurring mineral, As_4S_4 or AsS, arsenic sulfide, used in fireworks [M.L. fr. Arab. *rehj al-ghār*, powder of the cave]

real image an optical image formed of the points of convergence of light coming from an object

realise *REALIZE

re·al·ism (rí:əlizəm) *n.* an attitude based on facts and reality as opposed to emotions, imaginings etc. ‖ (*philos.*) the doctrine that ideas, or universals, have an absolute existence outside the mind ‖ (*philos.*) the belief that the objects of sense perception have real existence ‖ (in art, literature etc.) fidelity to life as perceived and experienced (cf. NATURALISM)

re·al·ist (rí:əlist) *n.* an exponent of realism in art, philosophy etc. ‖ a practical person who concerns himself with facts as they are known to him rather than with things as they might be **re·al·ís·tic** *adj.* of, characterized by, or relating to, realism **re·al·ís·ti·cal·ly** *adv.*

re·al·i·ty (ri:ǽliti:) *pl.* **re·al·i·ties** *n.* the state or quality of being real or of existing in fact ‖ someone or something that is real or exists in fact ‖ (*collect.*) the real world, e.g. considered as a force or pressure ‖ the true or actual nature of something **in reality** actually, in fact, really [fr. M.L. *realitas* or F. *realité*]

re·al·iz·a·ble (rí:əlaizəb'l) *adj.* able to be realized

re·al·i·za·tion (ri:əlaizéiʃən) *n.* a realizing or being realized ‖ that which is realized

re·al·ize (rí:əlaiz) *pres. part.* **re·al·iz·ing** *past* and *past part.* **re·al·ized** *v.t.* to be aware of the truth of, recognize as real, *he realized that she was in danger* ‖ to make real or actual (something imagined, hoped for etc.), *her wish was realized at last* ‖ to convert (other forms of property) into money, *to realize investments* ‖ to acquire, gain, *to realize profits* ‖ (of property) to bring as proceeds, *the sale of the house realized a large profit* [fr. REAL after F. *réaliser*]

re·al·ly (rí:əli:, rí:li:) *adv.* in reality ‖ (emphatic) truly, *a really steep hill*

realm (relm) *n.* (*hist., law* or *rhet.*) kingdom, *the laws of the realm* ‖ province, domain, *the realm of fancy* [O.F. *realme, reaume*]

re·al·po·li·tik (reiálpoulití:k) *n.* politics which deal solely in terms of national interests and the realities of the situation, being neither doctrinaire nor idealistic and not concerned with ethics [G.=real politics]

real property real estate

real tennis (*Br.*) court tennis

real time *n.* (*computer*) **1.** (*mil.*) the absence of delay, except for the time required for transmission by electromagnetic energy, between the occurrence of an event or the transmission of data, and the knowledge of the event, or reception of the data at some other location **2.** (*computer*) the actual time for a physical operation or process to take place **3.** the adequate performance of a computation in the actual time to solve a problem. **—real-time** *adj.* **1.** of the time necessary to perform a computation **2.** of a data-processing system that produces data not later than is required, e.g., a reservations system

re·al·tor (rí:əltər) *n.* (*Am.=Br.* estate agent) someone who sells or lets land or houses on behalf of the owner, manages estates, collects rents, draws up leases etc. and often surveys and values properties, esp. someone who is a member of the National Association of Real Estate Boards [REALTY]

re·al·ty (rí:əlti:) *n.* real estate

real wage insurance President Carter's proposed anti-inflation program (October 1978) providing bonus of up to 3% of annual wage, to be paid by the government to offset the difference between the percentage increase in the consumer price index over 7% and any proposed wage settlement

re·an·i·mate (ri:ǽnəmeit) *pres. part.* **re·an·i·mat·ing** *past* and *past part.* **re·an·i·mat·ed** *v.t.* to cause to be animate again ‖ to cause to be animated again, put fresh spirit into

ream (ri:m) *n.* a unit of measure for paper usually equal to 20 quires or 480 sheets ‖ a unit of measure for paper for printing, being 211 quires or 516 sheets ‖ (usually *pl.*) a huge amount (esp. of written matter), *to write reams* [M.E. *rem, rim* fr. Arab. *rizmah*, bundle]

ream *v.t.* to widen or shape (an opening of a hole in metal) with a reamer ‖ to widen the bore of (a gun) with a reamer ‖ (*naut.*) to open (a seam) for caulking ‖ to extract (fruit juice) with a reamer ‖ to extract the juice of (fruit) with a reamer ‖ (*Br.*) to turn over the edge of (a metal cap) **réam·er** *n.* a rotating tool with cutting edges for reaming a gun's bore or a hole ‖ a lemon squeezer ‖ (*Br.*) a tool used to turn over the edge of a metal cap [etym. doubtful]

reap (ri:p) *v.t.* to cut (ripe grain etc.) ‖ to gather (a crop) ‖ to cut the crop of (a field) ‖ to receive as the result of one's own acts **réap·er** *n.* someone who reaps ‖ a machine for reaping grain without binding into sheaves [O.E. *rīpan, reopan*]

rear (ríər) **1.** *n.* the back of something ‖ the position or space behind something ‖ the part of a procession, army, fleet, military column etc. furthest from the front ‖ (*pop.*) the buttocks ‖ (*Br., pop.*) a latrine **to bring up the rear** to be the last person in a line etc. **2.** *adj.* located at or toward the rear [fr. older *arrear*, that which is behind]

rear (ríər) *v.t.* to erect, *to rear a monument* ‖ to raise, esp. to great or unusual height, *to rear one's head* ‖ to bring up, *to rear a family* ‖ to cultivate, *to rear a crop* ‖ to breed, *to rear dogs* ‖ *v.i.* (of a horse) to rise up on its hind legs ‖ (*rhet.*) to rise high up, *the mountain reared above the village* [O.E. *rǣran*]

rear admiral a naval officer ranking below a vice admiral and above a commodore

rear guard a body of troops protecting the rear of a military force, esp. in a withdrawal

re·arm (ri:ɑ́rm) *v.t.* (*mil.*) to arm again, esp. with new or better arms ‖ *v.i.* to become so equipped **re·ár·ma·ment** *n.*

rear·most (ríərmoust) *adj.* farthest behind

re·ar·range (rí:əréindʒ) *v.t. pres. part.* **re·ar·rang·ing** *past* and *past part.* **re·ar·ranged** to arrange again, esp. in a different way **re·ar·ránge·ment** *n.*

rear·ward (ríərwərd) **1.** *adj.* being at or towards the rear **2.** *adv.* towards the rear **réar·wards** *adv.*

rea·son (rí:z'n) *n.* the ability to think logically, to understand, and to draw inferences, *his reason has shown him the right course* ‖ the cause that makes a phenomenon intelligible, *she understands the reason for his behavior* ‖ sound thinking, *it is contrary to reason* ‖ (*Kantian philos.*) the faculty which provides a priori principles (as opposed to the understanding, which is the mere ability to think logically) **in reason** reasonably ‖ within reasonable limits **to have (good) reason to** to have sufficient (strong) cause for **to listen to reason** to be persuaded out of one's obstinacy **to stand to reason** to be obviously true **within reason** within reasonable limits [O.F. *resun, reisun, reson, reison*]

reason *v.i.* to think or talk logically ‖ to argue persuasively with someone ‖ *v.t.* to analyze by reasoning (usually with 'out') ‖ to think out (something) by reasoning ‖ to persuade (someone) by reasoning [fr. O.F. *raisonner*]

rea·son·a·ble (rí:z'nəb'l) *adj.* ready to listen to reason or act according to reason, *a reasonable person* ‖ in accord with reason, *a reasonable excuse* ‖ not expensive, *a reasonable rent* ‖ neither more nor less than normal or expected, *the book had a reasonable success* **réa·son·a·bly** *adv.* [O.F. *raisonable, raisonnable*]

rea·son·ing (rí:z'niŋ) *n.* the act of someone who reasons or an instance of this

re·as·sem·ble (rí:əsémb'l) *pres. part.* **re·as·sem·bling** *past* and *past part.* **re·as·sem·bled** *v.t.* to put together again ‖ *v.i.* to come together again

re·as·sur·ance (ri:əʃúərəns) *n.* a reassuring or being reassured ‖ something which reassures

re·as·sure (ri:əʃúər) *pres. part.* **re·as·sur·ing** *past* and *past part.* **re·as·sured** *v.t.* to restore confidence to (someone), esp. in a matter of judgment ‖ to reinsure

Ré·au·mur scale (réiəmjuər) (*abbr.* R) a temperature scale on which the freezing point of water at 1 atmosphere is 0° and its boiling point 80° at the same pressure, i.e. 1°C=0.8°R [after René Antoine Ferchault de *Réaumur* (1683–1757), French physicist]

re·bate (rí:beit, ribéit) *n.* a deduction from an amount to be paid, usually as a courtesy discount [fr. F. *rabat* fr. *rebattre*, to rebate]

rebate *pres. part.* **re·bat·ing** *past* and *past part.* **re·bat·ed** *v.t.* to make a rebate of (a sum) ‖ to give a rebate to (a person) ‖ (rǽbit) (*heraldry*) to remove a portion of (a charge) [O.F. *rabattre*]

rebate (rí:beit, rǽbit) **1.** *n.* a rabbet **2.** *v.t. pres. part.* **re·bat·ing** *past* and *past part.* **re·bat·ed** to rabbet

Re·bec·ca-Eu·re·ka system (ri:békə ju:rí:kə) a preset homing aircraft system utilizing a ground beacon (Eureka) and an airborne interrogator (Rebecca)

reb·el (réb'l) **1.** *n.* a person who resists authority ‖ a person who opposes the lawful government by force of arms **2.** *adj.* rebellious of or pertaining to rebels [F. *rebelle*]

re·bel (ribél) *pres. part.* **re·bel·ling** *past* and *past part.* **re·belled** *v.i.* to disobey or oppose someone in authority ‖ to resist the lawful government by force of arms ‖ to feel or show aversion [fr. F. *rebeller*]

re·bel·lion (ribéljən) *n.* an organized attempt to overthrow a lawful government by force of arms ‖ open opposition to any authority [F. *rébellion*]

re·bel·lious (ribéljəs) *adj.* defying authority or control ‖ engaged in rebellion ‖ stubbornly defying control or treatment, *rebellious curly hair* [fr. L. *rebellis*]

re·birth (ri:bə́:rθ) *n.* a second birth ‖ a renewal, e.g. of energy or strength ‖ a renaissance

re·bound 1. (ribáund) *v.i.* to reverse direction after an impact ‖ to bounce back as if on impact **2.** (rí:baund) *n.* a rebounding ‖ a rebounding ball **on the rebound** in a state of hasty emotional reaction to some setback or blow to one's pride etc. [fr. O.F. *rebondir*]

re·buff (ribʌ́f) *v.t.* to give a rebuff to (someone or someone's suggestion, idea etc.) [fr. obs. F. *rebuffer* fr. Ital.]

re·buff (ribʌ́f, rí:bʌf) *n.* a curt rejection (esp. of an expressed desire) causing injury to a person's self-esteem, *his suggestion met with a rebuff* [obs. F. *rebuffe* fr. Ital.]

re·buke (ribjú:k) **1.** *v.t. pres. part.* **re·buk·ing** *past* and *past part.* **re·buked** to tell (someone) severely that his conduct or action is wrong or unsatisfactory **2.** *n.* a rebuking or being rebuked, or the words uttered or written [A.F. *rebuker*]

re·bus (rí:bəs) *n.* a word or series of words represented by pictures of objects, symbols etc. ‖ a puzzle or riddle made up of such pictures, symbols etc. [ablative pl. of L. *res*, thing]

re·but (ribʌ́t) *pres. part.* **re·but·ting** *past* and *past part.* **re·but·ted** *v.t.* to refute, esp. in formal or legal argument **re·bút·tal** *n.* a rebutting **re·bút·ter** *n.* (*law*) a defendant's answer in matters of fact to a plaintiff's surrejoinder [A.F. *reboter*]

re·cal·ci·trance (rikǽlsitrəns) *n.* the quality or state of being recalcitrant ‖ recalcitrant behavior

re·cal·ci·trant (rikǽlsitrənt) **1.** *adj.* refusing to submit to authority, rules etc. ‖ (of a substance or a machine) resisting efforts at control ‖ (*med.*) unresponsive to treatment **2.** *n.* a recalcitrant person [F. fr. L. *recalcitrans* (*recalcitrantis*) fr. *recalitrare*, to kick back]

re·ca·les·cence (ri:kəlés'ns) *n.* the process of becoming hot again, esp. in iron and steel which, when allowed to cool from white heat, suddenly glow more brightly for a short time at their critical temperature [fr. L. *recalescere*. to grow hot again]

re·call 1. (rikɔ́l) *v.t.* to order to return, *to recall an ambassador* ‖ to cause to return, *the edition was recalled from the booksellers* ‖ to recollect, remember, *she recalls meeting him last year* ‖ to revive the memory or thought of, *the scene recalled her childhood* **2.** (rikɔ́l, rí:kɔl) *n.* the act of recalling or an instance of this ‖ the process or right of removal of a public official from office before the end of his term by a vote of the people ‖ (*business*) offer by a manufacturer to repair or replace a defective part of a product ‖ (*mil.*) a signal to call troops back to ranks or camp ‖ (*naut.*) a flag used to signal a ship to return to a squadron **beyond recall** impossible to undo, revoke, rescind etc.

recall ratio (*computer*) ratio of data retrieved to the total

re·cant (rikǽnt) *v.t.* to retract or renounce (an opinion, belief, statement etc.) ‖ *v.i.* to declare publicly that one has been wrong, or held a mistaken belief, esp. religious or political **re·can·ta·tion** (ri:kæntéiʃən) *n.* [fr. L. *recantare*]

re·cap (ri:kǽp, ri:kǽp) *pres. part.* **re·cap·ping** *past* and *past part.* **re·capped** *v.t.* (*pop.*) to recapitulate [by shortening]

re·cap (rí:kæp) *n.* a recapitulation [by shortening]

re·cap 1. (ri:kǽp) *v.t.* to put a strip of prepared rubber on the worn tread of (a tire) and vulcanize it **2.** (rí:kæp) *n.* a tire refurbished in this way (cf. RETREAD)

re·ca·pit·u·late (ri:kəpítʃuleit) *v.t. pres. part.* **re·ca·pit·u·lat·ing** *past* and *past part.* **re·cap·it·u·lat·ed** to repeat or go over again briefly, summarize [RE-+CAPITULATE, (obs.) to draw up under headings]

re·ca·pit·u·la·tion (ri:kəpitʃuléiʃən) *n.* a recapitulating or an instance of this ‖ (*biol.*) the repetition of phylogenetic development in an individual ‖ (*mus.*, esp. of sonata form) a repetition of themes introduced earlier but which in the interval have undergone development [O.F. *recapitulacion* or fr. L. *recapitulatio* (*recapitulationis*)]

re·cap·ture (ri:kǽptʃər) **1.** *v.t. pres. part.* **re·cap·tur·ing** *past* and *past part.* **re·cap·tured** to capture again ‖ to get or give the illusion of by remembering or imitating, *to recapture the atmosphere of the past* **2.** *n.* a recapturing or being recaptured ‖ the taking by a government of a certain portion of earnings or profits over a fixed amount

re·cast 1. (ri:kǽst, ri:kɑ́st) *v.t.* to cast (metal) again ‖ to get a new cast for (a play etc.) ‖ to put into a new form, to remodel, *to recast the plot of a novel* ‖ to add up again **2.** (rí:kæst, rí:kɑst) *n.* a recasting ‖ that which is obtained by recasting

re·cede (ri:sí:d) *pres. part.* **re·ced·ing** *past* and *past part.* **re·ced·ed** *v.i.* to draw back, *the floods slowly receded from the fields* ‖ to become more distant, *the shore gradually receded* ‖ to slope backwards, *a receding chin* ‖ to become less, *the volume of trade has receded* ‖ (usually with 'from') to withdraw from a position, promise etc. [fr. L. *recedere*]

re·ceipt (ri:sí:t) **1.** *n.* the act of receiving ‖ a formal written acknowledgment that something has been received, *a receipt for payment* ‖ (*old-fash.*) a recipe ‖ (esp. *pl.*) something received, e.g. goods, money **2.** *v.t.* to sign a receipt for ‖ to sign (a bill) as a receipt ‖ *v.i.* (with 'for') to give a signed receipt [M.E. *receit, receite*]

re·ceiv·a·ble (risí:vəb'l) *adj.* that can be accepted or received, esp. as legal, *receivable bonds* ‖ (of bills etc.) on which money is due or callable, *accounts receivable* **re·céiv·a·bles** *pl. n.* accounts, bills or business notes becoming due on a fixed date, or due from others

re·ceive (risí:v) *pres. part.* **re·ceiv·ing** *past* and *past part.* **re·ceived** *v.t.* to be given, awarded or sent, *to receive a good education, to receive a letter through the mail* ‖ to take into one's hands or one's mind ‖ to accept (something offered) ‖ to be subjected to, *to receive bad advice*, or have inflicted on one, *to receive a wound* ‖ to experience, undergo, *to receive a shock to the nerves* ‖ to be accorded, *to receive acceptance* ‖ to welcome (someone as a visitor or guest) into one's presence, one's home etc. ‖ to admit into membership, *to be received into a club* ‖ to give a reception of a specified kind to, *they received him with cheers* ‖ to act as a receptacle for, *this pit receives the juice from the grapes* ‖ to accept and pay for (stolen goods), esp. in order to resell them ‖ to take the force of, *the buttresses receive the weight of the stone roof* ‖ (esp. *past part.*) to accept as authoritatively sound and valid ‖ to take (Communion) from the priest ‖ *v.i.* to be a recipient or receiver ‖ to take Communion ‖ to act as host or hostess, *to receive on Thursday* ‖ (*radio, television*) to transform incoming electromagnetic waves into sound or light [O.N.F. *receivre*]

re·ceiv·er (risí:vər) *n.* a person who receives, e.g. a fence ‖ something that receives, e.g. a receptacle for collecting and containing a chemical distillate ‖ (*law*) a person appointed by a court to administer a bankrupt's property or property under litigation ‖ the earpiece of a telephone ‖ a television or radio receiving set [M.E. fr. A.F. *receivour*]

re·ceiv·er·ship (risí:vərʃip) *n.* (*law*) the condition of being in the receiver's hands ‖ (*law*) the position of being a receiver

re·cen·cy (rí:s'nsi:) *n.* the state or quality of being recent

re·cen·sion (risénʃən) *n.* a revising of a text ‖ a version thus produced [fr. L. *recensio (recensionis)*, a review]
re·cent (ríːs'nt) *adj.* of or pertaining to a time not long before the present, *in recent months, footprints of recent origin* ‖ done or made during such a time, *a recent housing development* **Recent** (*geol.*) Holocene [fr. L. *recens (recentis)* or F. *récente*]
re·cep·ta·cle (riséptək'l) *n.* a container, *have a receptacle ready before you open the vent* ‖ (*bot.*) the part of a plant stem containing germinal buds, sporangia etc. [fr. L. *receptaculum*]
re·cep·tion (risépʃən) *n.* a receiving or being received ‖ the admission of a person into a religious organization, hospital, club etc. ‖ a formal social gathering during which guests are received ‖ a welcoming or greeting in a specified manner ‖ the receiving of radio or television signals or the quality of these **re·cép·tion·ist** *n.* a person, usually a woman, whose job is to fix appointments for, and receive, the patients or clients of her employer [F.]
reception room a room used for receiving the patients of a doctor, dentist etc. ‖ a room for receiving guests, e.g. in a hotel, institution etc. ‖ (*Br.*, realtor's term) a living room as distinct from a bedroom
re·cep·tive (riséptiv) *adj.* markedly able and willing to receive and retain impressions, ideas etc. ‖ (of a sensory end organ) able to receive and send stimuli ‖ of or relating to sense organs **re·cep·tiv·i·ty** (riːseptíviti:) *n.* [fr. M.L. *receptivus*]
re·cep·tor (riséptər) *n.* (*physiol.*) a specialized cell or tissue sensitive to a specific stimulus, e.g. a sense organ or sensory nerve ending [M.E. *receptour*]
receptor *n.* (*cytol.*) a specialized structure portion of a cell that is capable of combining with molecules (hormones, toxins, etc.) in a physiological process, e.g., in a nerve terminal
re·cess (risés, ríːses) **1.** *n.* an alcove, *window recess*, or a natural feature suggesting this ‖ (esp. *fig.*) an obscure or secret place, *the recesses of the mind* ‖ an interval of time during which an activity ceases, e.g. in business or parliament ‖ a period between school classes, usually devoted to play ‖ (*anat.*) a fossa, sinus, cleft or hollow space **2.** *v.t.* to construct a recess in (a wall) ‖ to put into a recess, set back ‖ *v.i.* to go into recess [fr. L. *recedere (recessus)*, to recede]
re·ces·sion (riséʃən) *n.* a receding or withdrawing ‖ a receding part ‖ a return procession, esp. of clergy and choir after a service ‖ (*econ.*) a temporary falling off of business activity, less serious than a depression **re·cés·sion·al 1.** *adj.* of or relating to the recession of the clergy and choir from the chancel after a service ‖ (*Br.*) of or relating to a parliamentary recess **2.** *n.* a hymn sung during the recession of the clergy and choir [fr. L. *recessio (recessionis)*]
re·ces·sive (risésiv) **1.** *adj.* receding or tending to recede ‖ (of stress or accent) tending to move from the last toward the first syllable of a word ‖ (*biol.*) of a character possessed by one parent which in a hybrid is masked by the corresponding alternative or dominant character derived from the other parent (opp. DOMINANT) **2.** *n.* (*biol.*) a recessive character ‖ (*biol.*) an organism having such characters [fr. L. *recedere (recessus)*, to recede]
re·cher·ché, re·cher·che (rəʃéərʃei) *adj.* uncommon, out of the ordinary ‖ affected, precious, *recherché language* [F.]
re·cid·i·vism (risídivizəm) *n.* constant falling back or the tendency to fall back into criminal, delinquent or antisocial habits in spite of punishment or treatment [RECIDIVIST]
re·cid·i·vist (risídivist) *n.* a person marked by recidivism [fr. F. *récidiviste*]
Re·ci·fe (rəsíːfə) (formerly Pernambuco) a port (pop. 1,249,800) in Brazil, the commercial center of the northeast, founded in 1548. Food industry, university (1946)
rec·i·pe (résəpiː) *n.* a list of ingredients and set of cooking directions for a dish ‖ a course of action recommended for producing some result, *a recipe for fitness* [L. imper. of *recipere*, to receive, take]
re·cip·i·ence (risípiːəns) *n.* the quality of being recipient
re·cip·i·en·cy (risípiːənsiː) *n.* recipience
re·cip·i·ent (risípiːənt) **1.** *n.* someone who or something which receives **2.** *adj.* receiving or able to receive [fr. L. *recipiens (recipientis)* fr. *recipere*, to receive]
re·cip·ro·cal (risíprək'l) **1.** *adj.* mutual, *reciprocal feelings of affection* ‖ of something in an inverse relationship to something else ‖ (of two things) corresponding, complementary ‖ (*gram.*) expressing mutual relation, *one another is a reciprocal pronoun* ‖ (*math.*) of a quantity which is reciprocal **2.** *n.* a thing that has a reciprocal relation to something else ‖ (*math.*) a quantity which when multiplied by a given quantity produces unity, *1/6 is the reciprocal of 6* [fr. L. *reciprocus*]
reciprocal ohm the mho
re·cip·ro·cate (risíprəkeit) *pres. part.* **re·cip·ro·cat·ing** *past* and *past part.* **re·cip·ro·cat·ed** *v.t.* to give in return (affection, good wishes etc.) ‖ (*mech.*) to cause to move backwards and forwards alternately ‖ to give and receive mutually, *the negotiators reciprocated formal expressions of goodwill* ‖ *v.i.* to return in kind something done, given etc. ‖ to be correspondent ‖ (*mech.*) to move backwards and forwards [fr. L. *reciprocare (reciprocatus)*]
reciprocating engine an engine in which a piston or pistons move to and fro (*ROTARY ENGINE)
re·cip·ro·ca·tion (risiprəkéiʃən) *n.* a reciprocating or an instance of this [fr. L. *reciprocatio (reciprocationis)*]
rec·i·proc·i·ty (resəprósitiː) *n.* the state of being reciprocal ‖ an exchange of trade between nations etc., based upon privileges granted to both [fr. F. *réciprocité*]
re·cit·al (risáit'l) *n.* an enumerating or relating of facts, events etc. ‖ something which is so enumerated or related ‖ a reciting of poetry before an audience ‖ (*mus., dancing*) a performance given by one person or a small group ‖ (*law*) the reciting of facts in a document [RECITE]
rec·i·ta·tion (resitéiʃən) *n.* an enumerating of facts, events etc. ‖ a reciting, esp. before an audience, or an instance of this ‖ (*old-fash.*) the reciting of a lesson to satisfy the teacher or the answering of the teacher's questions on a prepared lesson [fr. L. *recitatio (recitationis)*]
rec·i·ta·tive (resitətíːv) **1.** *n.* musical declamation of the narrative parts of opera and oratorio **2.** *adj.* of or in this style [fr. Ital. *recitativo*]
re·cite (risáit) *pres. part.* **re·cit·ing** *past* and *past part.* **re·cit·ed** *v.t.* to repeat aloud (something memorized), esp. before an audience ‖ (*old-fash.*) to repeat aloud or answer the teacher's questions about (a lesson) ‖ to enumerate ‖ (*law*) to set out (facts) in a document ‖ *v.i.* to repeat aloud something memorized, esp. before an audience ‖ (*old-fash.*) to repeat aloud or answer the teacher's questions about a lesson [F. *réciter* or fr. L. *recitare*]
reck (rek) *v.t.* (*archaic*, neg. or quasi-neg. and interrog. only) to take heed of (danger, expense etc.), or to care about, *he little recks what the outcome may be* [O.E. *reccan*]
reck·less (réklis) *adj.* wildly careless, *reckless driving* ‖ indifferent to danger, *reckless courage* [O.E. *recceléas, rēceléas*]
Reck·ling·hau·sen (réklinhauz'n) a town (pop. 119,600) of North-Rhine-Westphalia, West Germany, in the Ruhr: coal mining, mechanical engineering, textiles, chemicals
reck·on (rékən) *v.t.* (often with 'up') to work out, calculate, *reckon how much you have spent* ‖ to arrive at (a number, answer etc.) by calculating, *he reckoned 400 persons attended* ‖ to include as one of a number, *she reckons him among her best friends* ‖ (*pop.*) to think, suppose ‖ to estimate, *they reckon him to be the best worker* ‖ *v.i.* (with 'with') to make a reckoning, *he'll reckon with you later* ‖ to count, calculate, *she reckoned on her fingers* ‖ (with 'on' or 'upon') to count on having something or on some event, *we are reckoning on a devaluation of the franc* **to reckon with (without)** to take into (leave out of) account [O.E. *gerecenian, recenian*]
reck·on·er (rékənər) *n.* someone who reckons ‖ a ready reckoner
reck·on·ing (rékəniŋ) *n.* the act of counting or calculating, or an instance of this ‖ the manner of doing this ‖ the process of doing this or the result arrived at ‖ (*naut.*) a calculation of a ship's position by astronomical observations and reference to logged information ‖ (*naut.*) a position so determined ‖ a settling of accounts, differences etc., or an instance of this
re·claim (rikléim) **1.** *v.t.* to reform, salvage from a life of vice, crime etc. ‖ to bring back (land suitable for human use) into service, e.g. by draining or irrigation ‖ to obtain (something useful) from a waste product **2.** *n.* a reclaiming or being reclaimed [fr. O.F. *recalmer*]
re·claim (riːkléim) *v.t.* to claim back, to recover possession of
re·clam·a (riklǽmə) *n.* (*mil.*) a request to authority to reconsider a decision or proposed action
rec·la·ma·tion (rekləméiʃən) *n.* a reclaiming or being reclaimed [F.]
rec·li·nate (réklineit) *adj.* (*bot.*) curving downward, *a reclinate leaf* [fr. L. *reclinare (reclinatus)*, to recline]
re·cline (rikláin) *pres. part.* **re·clin·ing** *past* and *past part.* **re·clined** *v.i.* (usually with 'on' or 'upon') to lie at ease ‖ to lean back comfortably ‖ *v.t.* to lay (one's head etc.) back [fr. L. *reclinare*]
re·cluse (riklúːs, rékluːs) *n.* someone who lives alone and avoids the company of others ‖ such a person acting out of self-discipline on religious grounds [fr. F. *reclus, recluse* fr. *reclure*, to shut up]
rec·og·ni·tion (rekəgníʃən) *n.* a recognizing or being recognized ‖ acknowledgment, *in recognition of his services* ‖ (*internat. law*) acknowledgment of the status of an independent state [fr. L. *recognitio (recognitionis)*]
rec·og·niz·a·ble (rékəgnaizəb'l) *adj.* able to be recognized **rec·og·niz·a·bly** *adv.*
re·cog·ni·zance (rikógnizəns) *n.* (*law*) a bond entered into before a court or magistrate by which one undertakes to do something ‖ the sum pledged as a surety for the performance of such an obligation [O.F. *reconissance, reconuissance, recognussance*]
rec·og·nize (rékəgnaiz) *pres. part.* **rec·og·niz·ing** *past* and *past part.* **rec·og·nized** *v.t.* to identify (something known or perceived before), *to recognize a handwriting* ‖ to acknowledge, *to recognize a debt* ‖ to admit acquaintance with (someone) by a sign etc., *he recognized us with a wave* ‖ (*law*) to acknowledge the status of (e.g. a newly independent state or a new government) ‖ to give (someone) the opportunity to speak in a legislature, public meeting etc. ‖ (*law*) to obligate (someone) by a recognizance ‖ *v.i.* (*law*) to enter into a recognizance [O.F. *reconoistre (reconuiss-, recognoiss-)*]
re·coil 1. (rikóil) *v.i.* to start back in repugnance ‖ to shrink away ‖ (of a piece of artillery) to slide back when the charge explodes ‖ (of a rifle or shotgun) to kick ‖ (of a spring) to spring back when released ‖ to retreat, to fall back before the enemy **2.** (rikóil, ríːkɔil) *n.* the sliding back or kick of a gun when the charge explodes ‖ the distance of such a backward movement ‖ a physical or mental shrinking away [fr. O.F. *reculer*]
rec·ol·lect (rekəlékt) *v.t.* to call to mind, remember [fr. L. *recolligere (recollectus)*, to gather again]
re·col·lect (riːkəlékt) *v.t.* to gather together again ‖ to regain control of, collect (oneself, one's thoughts etc.) [fr. L. *recolligere (recollectus)*, to gather again]
rec·ol·lec·tion (rekəlékʃən) *n.* the act of remembering ‖ a memory ‖ the span or power of a person's memory, *within my recollection* ‖ a spiritual gathering of oneself together **rec·ol·léc·tive** *adj.* [F. *récollection*]
re·com·bi·nant DNA (riːkómbənənt) (*genetics*) a technique for splicing strands of genetic material (DNA) from different organisms and inserting the resultant combination into a host virus or bacterium. *Cf* GENE SPLICING
re·com·mence (riːkəméns) *pres. part.* **re·com·menc·ing** *past* and *past part.* **re·com·menced** *v.i.* to begin again ‖ *v.t.* to cause to begin **re·com·ménce·ment** *n.* [fr. F. *recommencer*]
rec·om·mend (rekəménd) *v.t.* to write or speak in favor of (someone, something) to another person, as deserving employment, patronage etc. ‖ to advise, *he recommended a long holiday* ‖ to render pleasing, *the property has little to recommend it* ‖ (*rhet.*) to commend, *he recommended his soul to God* [M.L. *recommendare*]
rec·om·men·da·tion (rekəmendéiʃən) *n.* the act of recommending a person or thing ‖ a letter which recommends a person to a prospective employer ‖ advice ‖ a quality which predisposes in favor of someone or something, *ease of access is a strong recommendation for the site* [O.F. or fr. M.L. *recommendatio (recommendationis)*]
rec·om·pense (rékəmpens) *n.* a gift or remuneration in recognition of a service rendered ‖ a payment or compensation for an injury done or received [O.F.]
recompense *pres. part.* **rec·om·pens·ing** *past* and *past part.* **rec·om·pensed** *v.t.* to give a recompense to [fr. O.F. *recompenser*]

rec·on·cil·a·ble (rȩkənsáiləb'l) *adj.* able to be reconciled **rec·on·cíl·a·bly** *adv.*

reconcilable neglect governmental and political practices based on disregard of new conditions and ideas, and the belief that inadequacies will somehow be self-correcting; suggested by American journalist Walter J. Raymond

rec·on·cile (rékənsail) *pres. part* **rec·on·cil·ing** *past* and *past part.* **rec·on·ciled** *v.t.* to bring together again in love or friendship ‖ to induce (someone) to accept something disagreeable ‖ to make or show to be consistent ‖ to reach a compromise agreement about (differences) **réc·on·cile·ment** *n.* [fr. F. *réconcilier* or L. *reconciliare*]

rec·on·cil·i·a·tion (rȩkənsįli:éiʃən) *n.* a reconciling or being reconciled [F. or fr. L. *reconciliatio (reconciliationis)*]

rec·on·dite (rékəndait, rikɒ́ndait) *adj.* obscure, little known ‖ concerned with something obscure and little known ‖ difficult to understand [fr. L. *recondere (reconditus)*, to put away]

re·con·di·tion (rį:kəndíʃən) *v.t.* to restore (something) to sound condition by cleaning, repairing etc.

re·con·fig·ure (rį:kənfígjər) *v.* to rearrange

re·con·nais·sance (rikɒ́nisəns) *n.* a survey of an enemy-held area to procure military information concerning the enemy's position, strength, intentions etc. ‖ any preliminary survey ‖ (*engin.*) a general survey of a territory before proceeding with a more specialized one ‖ (*geol.*) a preliminary examination of a particular region [F.]

re·con·noi·ter, esp. *Br.* **re·con·noi·tre** (rį:kənɔ́itər) **1.** *v. pres. part.* **re·con·noi·ter·ing,** esp. *Br.,* **re·con·noi·tring** *past* and *past part.* **re·con·noi·tered,** esp. *Br.* **re·con·noi·tred** *v.t.* to make a reconnaissance of ‖ *v.i.* to make a reconnaissance **2.** *n.* a reconnaissance [obs. F. *reconnoitre,* to recognize]

re·con·sid·er (rį:kənsídər) *v.t.* to consider again, esp. with a view to changing one's opinion, *to reconsider a decision* ‖ *v.i.* to consider a matter again **re·con·sid·er·á·tion** *n.*

re·con·sti·tute (ri:kɒ́nstitu:t, ri:kɒ́nstitju:t) *pres. part.* **re·con·sti·tut·ing** *past* and *past part.* **re·con·sti·tut·ed** *v.t.* to reconstruct, *to reconstitute an ancient poem from fragments* ‖ to reorganize in a changed form, *to reconstitute the cabinet* ‖ to restore the composition of (dried or concentrated foods or juices) by adding water **re·con·sti·tú·tion** *n.*

re·con·struct (rį:kənstrʌ́kt) *v.t.* to rebuild ‖ to re-create mentally or in fact the known conditions, actions etc. surrounding (a crime, battle etc.) in the hope that this will lead to better understanding

re·con·struc·tion (rį:kənstrʌ́kʃən) *n.* a reconstructing ‖ something reconstructed **Re·con·struc·tion** (*Am. hist.*) the period in the Southern states between the end of the Civil War (1865) and the withdrawal of federal troops (1877)

Reconstruction Finance Corporation (RFC), a U.S. government agency created (1932) by President Herbert Hoover to revive economic activity in the Depression by granting loans totaling $50 billion. It was abolished (1953) by act of Congress, on the grounds that it had been used for political favoritism

re·con·ver·sion (rį:kənvə́:rʒən) *n.* a reconverting or being reconverted, esp. a going back from a wartime to a peacetime basis ‖ a period of reconverting

re·con·vert (rį:kənvə́:rt) *v.t.* to convert back to a former state ‖ *v.i.* to go back, esp. from a wartime to a peacetime basis

rec·ord (rékərd) **1.** *n.* a recording or being recorded ‖ a document or other piece of historical evidence ‖ an account made in permanent form, *he will not keep records of his telephone conversations* ‖ a minute or official text, *he keeps the records of the society's proceedings, he asked for it to go on record that he took no part in the discussion* ‖ (*law*) an official copy of the proceedings of a case which will be accepted as authentic evidence subsequently ‖ a public register, monument etc. where historical or legal evidence is recorded ‖ the facts concerning the past performance etc. of a person or thing, *he has an excellent war record* ‖ a memento, *he gave it to her as a record of her visit* ‖ the best performance so far recorded ‖ a circular plate to which sound has been transferred, esp. electronically. When the record is played through a phonograph, the sound is reproduced **off the record** private and not to be repeated or made publicly known **on record** recorded or publicly declared **to go on record** to keep a written statement of a decision, opinion etc. **2.** *adj.* of that which is the best so far officially recorded, *a record jump* [O.F.]

re·cord (rikɔ́rd) *v.t.* to set down in some permanent form, esp. in writing ‖ (*law*) to commit to writing as authentic evidence of ‖ to transcribe (sound) in some permanent form, e.g. on tape ‖ (esp. of an instrument) to make a graph or chart of ‖ to serve as evidence of, *this gift will serve to record our appreciation* ‖ to register, *to record a vote* ‖ *v.i.* to make a record, esp. a phonograph record ‖ to be able to be recorded [fr. O.F. *recorder*]

re·cord·er (rikɔ́rdər) *n.* someone who or something which records ‖ an official appointed or elected to keep records of deeds etc. ‖ (*Br.*) a magistrate of a city or borough who presides over the court of quarter sessions and has a limited criminal and civil jurisdiction ‖ (*mus.*) a simple woodwind instrument somewhat similar to a flute and popular, esp. in the 16th–18th cc. It is blown from an end mouthpiece and held downwards not transversely ‖ the recording device in certain machines, e.g. in a cash register

re·cord·er·ship (rikɔ́rdərʃip) *n.* the office or duration of office of a recorder

re·cord·ing (rikɔ́rdiŋ) *n.* the act of making a record ‖ the process of preserving sound on a record, cylinder, tape etc. ‖ a phonograph record or a tape etc. on which something is recorded ‖ that which is recorded

Record Office (*Br.*) a state department responsible for the safe custody of public documents ‖ (*Br.*) the place housing these documents

record player an instrument for playing phonograph records by means of a pickup and one or more amplifiers

re·count (rikáunt) *v.t.* to relate, narrate in detail [A.F. *reconter*]

re-count 1. (ri:káunt) *v.t.* to count again **2.** (rí:kaunt, ri:káunt) *n.* a second or additional counting, esp. of votes

re·coup (rikú:p) *v.t.* to make good, get back the equivalent of (a loss) ‖ to compensate (oneself) for losses, expenses etc. ‖ to get back, *to recoup one's fortune* ‖ (*law*) to deduct or withhold (part of a sum due) **re·cóup·ment** *n.* [fr. F. *recouper,* to cut back]

re·course (ri:kɔ́rs, ri:kóurs, rí:kɔrs, rí:kours) *n.* someone or something to which one turns for help, *the only recourse was prayer* ‖ a turning to someone or something for help **to have recourse to** to turn to when in need of help **without recourse** the words added to a bill by the endorser to show that he does not take responsibility for nonpayment [F. *recours*]

re·cov·er (rikʌ́vər) **1.** *v.t.* to get back possession of, *to recover a stolen car, to recover consciousness* ‖ to regain the composure, control, balance etc. of (oneself) ‖ to make good (a loss) ‖ (*law*) to obtain by a court decision etc. ‖ to reclaim (e.g. land from the sea) ‖ to obtain (a useful substance) from a waste product ‖ *v.i.* to return to normal health after illness ‖ to return to a normal condition of prosperity etc., *to recover from civil war* ‖ to regain one's composure, balance etc. ‖ (*law*) to obtain a favorable judgment in a suit ‖ (*fencing*) to return to the normal posture of defense ‖ (*rowing*) to return to a position of readiness for the succeeding stroke **2.** *n.* (*fencing, rowing*) a recovery [A.F. *recouvrer*]

re-cov·er (ri:kʌ́vər) *v.t.* to provide with a new cover

re·cov·er·y (rikʌ́vri:) *pl.* **re·cov·er·ies** *n.* the act or an instance of recovering ‖ a returning to normal health or prosperity ‖ the regaining of one's balance or control after e.g. a stumble or mistake ‖ a return to financial well-being after a depression ‖ (*fencing*) the return to a position of guard after a thrust ‖ (*rowing*) the return to a position of readiness in preparation for the next stroke ‖ (*law*) the obtaining of a right to something by verdict or judgment ‖ the salvaging of useful material from waste products [A.F. *recoverie*]

rec·re·an·cy (rékri:ənsi:) *pl.* **rec·re·an·cies** *n.* (*rhet.*) the quality of being recreant or an instance of this

rec·re·ant (rékri:ənt) **1.** *adj.* (*rhet.*) cowardly ‖ (*rhet.*) apostate, unfaithful **2.** *n.* (*rhet.*) a coward ‖ (*rhet.*) a deserter ‖ (*rhet.*) a betrayer [O.F.=one who gives up his cause]

rec·re·ate (rékri:eit) *pres. part.* **rec·re·at·ing** *past* and *past part.* **rec·re·at·ed** *v.t.* (*rhet.*) to put fresh life into, esp. by some kind of amusement or relaxation after work [fr. L. *recreare (recreatus)*, to refresh]

re-cre·ate (rį:kri:éit) *pres. part.* **re-cre·at·ing** *past* and *past part.* **re-cre·at·ed** *v.t.* to create again

rec·re·a·tion (rȩkri:éiʃən) *n.* a leisure-time activity engaged in for the sake of refreshment or entertainment ‖ (*loosely*) a pastime, *her favorite recreation is spying on her neighbors* [fr. L. *recreatio (recreationis)*]

re-cre·a·tion (rį:kri:éiʃən) *n.* a re-creating or being re-created ‖ that which is re-created

re·crim·i·nate (rikrímineit) *pres. part.* **re·crim·i·nat·ing** *past* and *past part.* **re·crim·i·nat·ed** *v.i.* to make counter accusations [fr. L. *recriminari (recriminatus)*]

re·crim·i·na·tion (rikrįminéiʃən) *n.* a recriminating ‖ a counter accusation [F. *récrimination*]

re·cri·mi·na·tive (rikrímineįtiv) *adj.* recriminating **re·crim·i·na·to·ry** (rikríminətɔri:, rikríminətouri:) *adj.*

re·cru·desce (rį:kru:dés) *pres. part.* **re·cru·desc·ing** *past* and *past part.* **re·cru·desced** *v.i.* (of an illness, sore etc.) to break out afresh **re·cru·dés·cence** *n.* **re·cru·dés·cent** *adj.* [fr. L. *recrudescere*]

re·cruit (rikrú:t) *v.t.* to enlist (recruits) ‖ to enlist men for (an army) ‖ to recover (strength, health etc.) ‖ to recover the strength, health etc. of (oneself) ‖ *v.i.* to enlist recruits ‖ to recuperate, recover strength, health **re·cruit·ment** *n.* [fr. F. *recruter*]

recruit *n.* a newly enlisted member of the armed forces, esp. of the army ‖ a new member or supporter of a society, cause etc. [fr. obs. F. *recrute*]

rec·tal (réktəl) *adj.* of, relating to, or near the rectum

rec·tan·gle (réktæŋg'l) *n.* a plane quadrilateral figure with four right angles **rec·tan·gu·lar** (rektǽŋgjulər) *adj.* shaped like a rectangle ‖ right-angled ‖ at right angles **rec·tan·gu·lar·i·ty** (rəktæŋgjulǽriti:) *n.* [fr. L.L. *rectiangulum,* a right-angled triangle]

rec·ten·na (rekténə) *n.* an antenna used to convert microwave power to DC power, including rectifying elements

rec·ti·fi·a·ble (rȩktifáiəb'l) *adj.* able to be rectified

rec·ti·fi·ca·tion (rȩktifikéiʃən) *n.* a rectifying or being rectified [F. or fr. L.L. *rectificatio (rectificationis)*]

rec·ti·fi·er (réktifąiər) *n.* someone who or something that rectifies ‖ (*elec.*) a device for converting an alternating current into a direct current

rec·ti·fy (réktifai) *pres. part.* **rec·ti·fy·ing** *past* and *past part.* **rec·ti·fied** *v.t.* to put right, *to rectify an error* ‖ to set (a trajectory, orbit etc.) right by computation and mechanical adjustment ‖ to replace by something more right or just, *he rectified the earlier judgment* ‖ (*chem.*) to purify by repeated distillation ‖ (*elec.*) to convert (an alternating current) to a direct current ‖ (*math.*) to measure (the length of a curve) [fr. F. *rectifier*]

rec·ti·lin·e·al (rȩktilíni:əl) *adj.* rectilinear [fr. L.L. *rectilineus*]

rec·ti·lin·e·ar (rȩktilíni:ər) *adj.* in a straight line ‖ bounded by straight lines ‖ characterized by straight lines [fr. L.L. *rectilineus*]

rec·ti·tude (réktitu:d, réktitju:d) *n.* moral uprightness, integrity [F.]

rec·to (réktou) *n.* (*printing*) the righthand page of an open book ‖ (*printing*) the front of a leaf (opp. VERSO) [fr. L. *recto (folio)*, on the right (leaf)]

rec·tor (réktər) *n.* (*Church of England*) a clergyman to whom the parish tithes were formerly payable (cf. VICAR) ‖ (*Protestant Episcopal Church* and *Episcopal Church of Scotland*) a minister in charge of a parish ‖ (*Roman Catholicism*) the head priest of a parish ‖ the head of some universities, colleges, schools or religious institutions **réc·tor·ate** *n.* **rec·tor·i·al** (rektɔ́ri:əl, rektóuri:əl) *adj.* **rec·tor·ship** (réktərʃip) *n.* [L.=one who rules]

rec·to·ry (réktəri:) *pl.* **rec·to·ries** *n.* a rector's house ‖ the benefice of a rector [fr. M.L. *rectoria*]

rec·trix (réktriks) *pl.* **rec·tri·ces** (réktrisi:z) *n.* (usually *pl.*) one of a bird's long stiff tail feathers used in steering [L. fem. of *rector*=one who rules]

rec·tum (réktəm) *pl.* **rec·tums, rec·ta** (réktə) *n.* (*anat.*) the portion of the large intestine nearest to the anus [L. neut. of *rectus,* straight]

CONCISE PRONUNCIATION KEY: **(a)** æ, *cat*; ɑ, *car*; ɔ *fawn*; ei, *snake*. **(e)** e, *hen*; i:, *sheep*; iə, *deer*; ɛə, *bear*. **(i)** i, *fish*; ai, *tiger*; ə:, *bird*. **(o)** o, *ox*; au, *cow*; ou, *goat*; u, *poor*; ɔi, *royal*. **(u)** ʌ, *duck*; u, *bull*; u:, *goose*; ə, *bacillus*; ju:, *cube*. x, *loch*; θ, *think*; ð, *bother*; z, *Zen*; ʒ, *corsage*; dʒ, *savage*; ŋ, *orangutang*; j, *yak*; ʃ, *fish*; tʃ, *fetch*; 'l, *rabble*; 'n, *redden*. Complete pronunciation key appears inside front cover.

re·cum·ben·cy (rikʌ́mbənsi:) *n.* the state or position of being recumbent

re·cum·bent (rikʌ́mbənt) *adj.* lying down, reclining ‖ (*biol.*) of or relating to a part which leans on the part from which it grows [fr. L. *recumbens* (*recumbentis*) fr. *recumbere,* to lie down]

re·cu·per·ate (rikú:pəreit, rikjú:pəreit) *pres. part.* **re·cu·per·at·ing** *past* and *past part.* **re·cu·per·at·ed** *v.t.* to regain (esp. one's health, one's losses) ‖ *v.i.* to make such a recovery [fr. L. *recuperare* (*recuperatus*)]

re·cu·per·a·tion (riku:pəréiʃən, rikju:pəréiʃən) *n.* the restoration of health ‖ the recovery of losses [fr. *L. recuperatio* (*recuperationis*)]

re·cu·per·a·tive (rikú:pərətiv, rikjú:pərətiv) *adj.* of or promoting recuperation [fr. L.L. *recuperativus*]

re·cur (rikə́:r) *pres. part.* **re·cur·ring** *past* and *past part.* **re·curred** *v.i.* to return, come back, *the idea recurred to my mind* ‖ to occur again, esp. after some lapse of time ‖ (of a problem etc.) to present itself repeatedly for consideration [fr. L. *recurrere*]

re·cur·rence (rikə́:rəns, rikʌ́rəns) *n.* the act or fact of recurring [RECURRENT]

re·cur·rent (rikə́:rənt, rikʌ́rənt) *adj.* recurring from time to time, *a recurrent fever* ‖ (*anat.,* of a vein, nerve etc.) running back in the opposite direction [fr. L. *recurrens* (*recurrentis*) fr. *recurrere,* to run back]

recurring clause (*insurance*) a provision in a health insurance policy that specifies a period of time during which the recurrence of a condition is considered a continuation of a former disability or hospital confinement rather than a separate illness

recurring decimal a decimal fraction with the same figure or figures repeated indefinitely in the same order, e.g. 1.6666 (also written 1.6)

re·cur·sion formula or **recursion relation** (rikə́:rʒən) (*math.*) an algorithm that allows a series of quantities to be computed —**recursive** *adj.*

re·cur·sive (rikə́:rsiv) *adj.* **1.** capable of being used again, or of being returned to after an interruption **2.** (*computer*) of a method of calculation in steps, each of which establishes more elementary values, used in ALGOL and LISP, but otherwise not acceptable as a procedure

re·cur·vate (rikə́:rveit) *adj.* recurved [fr. L. *recurvatus*]

re·curved (rikə́:rvd) *adj.* curved backward

rec·u·san·cy (rékjuzənsi:) *n.* the state or condition of being a recusant

rec·u·sant (rékjuzənt) **1.** *n.* someone who refuses to conform ‖ (*Eng. hist.*) a person, esp. a Roman Catholic, who refused to attend Church of England services when attendance was compulsory **2.** *adj.* refusing to conform or submit to authority ‖ (*Eng. hist.*) refusing to attend the services of the Church of England [fr. L. *recusans* (*recusantis*) fr. *recusare,* to refuse]

re·cy·cle (ri:sáik'l) *v.* **1.** to process so that basic raw material may be used again, e.g., to recycle aluminum cans to obtain the metal for reuse **2.** to repeat a series of operations —**recyclable** *n.* —**recyling** *n.*

red (red) **1.** *comp.* **red·der** *superl.* **red·dest** *adj.* of the color sensation stimulated by the wavelengths of light in that portion of the spectrum, ranging from orange to infrared, being the color e.g. of blood flowing from a vein ‖ flushed with blood, *red cheeks* ‖ (of the eyes) bloodshot or with sore or swollen lids ‖ of the tawny or chestnut color of the coat of some animals or the hair of some persons **Red** of or pertaining to a Red or to a country, group etc. of communist political persuasion **2.** *n.* a red color, pigment, fabric etc. ‖ a red object, e.g. the red ball in billiards **Red** a communist **in (out of) the red** (*pop.*) in (not in) debt **to see red** to be made suddenly very angry [O.E. *rēad*]

re·dact (ridǽkt) *v.t.* to edit, to prepare for publication ‖ to draw up (a document etc.) [fr. L. *redigere* (*redactus*), to bring back]

re·dac·tion (ridǽkʃən) *n.* the preparing of written material for publication, or an instance of this ‖ the work so prepared [F. *rédaction*]

re·dac·tor (ridǽktər) *n.* an editor [F. *rédacteur*]

red admiral *Vanessa atlanta,* fam. *Nymphalidae,* a purplish-black butterfly, with white spots on the front wings, and orange bands across the front wings and bordering the hind wings

red alert **1.** signal of imminent danger **2.** the period of such danger

re·dan (ridǽn) *n.* a fortification with two parapets forming a salient angle [F.]

Red Army faction guerrilla group responsible for terrorism in West Germany, 1976–1980. *Cf* BAADER-MEINHOF GANG

Red Basin of Szechwan *SZECHWAN

red·bird (rédbə:rd) *n. Richmondena cardinala,* the cardinal

red blood cell an erythrocyte

red-blood·ed (rédblʌ́did) *adj.* (of writing) full of strong action ‖ (of people) vigorous, lusty

red·breast (rédbrest) *n.* a European or American robin ‖ an American knot (sandpiper)

Red Brigade Italian left-wing terrorist organization

red·cap (rédkæp) *n.* a porter in a railroad station etc. ‖ (*Br., pop.*) a military policeman

Red Cat theory hypothesis of Chinese political economy that the source of technical know-how is unimportant, from *It is irrelevant if the cat is red or not, as long as it catches the mouse;* expressed by Deng Xiaoping, Chinese leader

red cent (*pop.*) a trifling sum of money, *it isn't worth a red cent*

Red Cloud (red klaud) (1822-1909), U.S. Indian chief of the Sioux Oglala Lakota tribe, born as Makhpiya Luta. He fought the white settlers of the West, esp. around Ft. Laramie, Wy., and along the Bozeman Trail so that by 1868 the trail was no longer used by the whites. He signed a peace treaty (1868), settled on a reservation and, after accusations that he had 'sold out' to the whites, stepped down as head chief

red·coat (rédkout) *n.* (*hist.*) a British soldier, esp. during the Revolutionary War

red cross St George's cross, the national emblem of England **Red Cross** a red Greek cross on a white ground, adapted from the Swiss flag, used to mark hospitals, ambulances etc. as a symbol of neutrality in time of war ‖ the International Red Cross

red currant a shrub of genus *Ribes,* bearing red, edible berries ‖ its fruit

red deer *Cervus elaphus,* the common European and Asian deer related to the wapiti, measuring about 4 ft from shoulders to ground and weighing about 300 lbs. ‖ the Virginia deer in its summer markings

red·den (réd'n) *v.i.* to become red ‖ to become flushed ‖ *v.t.* to make red

red·dish (rédiʃ) *adj.* somewhat red, tinged with red

red·dle (réd'l) **1.** *n.* ruddle **2.** *v.t. pres. part.* **red·dling** *past* and *past part.* **red·dled** to ruddle

red dye #2 a former food and cosmetic coloring agent made from coal, found to be carcinogenic and now banned for any use

re·deem (ridí:m) *v.t.* to get back full possession of, esp. by repaying the sum of money secured by the thing being recovered, *to redeem a pawned ring* ‖ to change or convert (bonds etc.) into cash ‖ to fulfill (a promise) ‖ to recover from captivity, by ransom ‖ (*theol.*) to free from the bondage of sin ‖ to save from being a total failure, *this quality redeemed him in her opinion* **re·déem·a·ble** *adj.* **the Re·déem·er** Jesus Christ [fr. F. *rédimer* or L. *redimere*]

re·demp·tion (ridémpʃən) *n.* a redeeming or being redeemed ‖ something which redeems ‖ (*theol.*) salvation from sin and its consequences **re·démp·tive** *adj.* [F. or fr. L. *redemptio* (*redemptionis*)]

Re·demp·tor·ist (ridémptərist) *n.* a member of the Congregation of the Most Holy Redeemer, a Roman Catholic order founded (1732) by St Alphonsus Liguori for missionary work among the poor [F. *Rédemptoriste*]

red ensign a red flag with the Union Jack in one corner, flown by British merchant ships

Red·eye [M4 1E2] (rédai) *n.* (*mil.*) a lightweight, portable, shoulder-fired air defense artillery weapon with infrared guidance for low altitude air defense, widely used in NATO

red·fish (rédfiʃ) *pl.* **red·fish, red·fish·es** *n.* any of various reddish fishes, esp. the sockeye ‖ (*Br.*) a male salmon in spawning condition, when it assumes a red color

red fox a fox, esp. *Vulpes vulpes,* having reddish-brown fur, with considerable variation in color (*SILVER FOX)

red giant (*astron.*) a large star, hundreds of times the size of the sun, with a cool, low density (less than the air on earth), that is nearing the end of its life, e.g., Betelgeuse in the constellation Orion

red grouse *Lagopus scoticus,* fam. *Tetraonidae,* a ptarmigan of the British Isles which does not turn white in winter

Red Guard **1.** the masses of young Chinese who actively promoted the Great Proletarian Cultural Revolution, Mao Zedong's movement during 1965–1968 to reestablish the egalitarian values of the Chinese revolution **2.** a member of the group —**Red Guardism** *adj. Cf* CULTURAL REVOLUTION

red-hand·ed (rédhǽndid) *adj.* actually engaged in a crime or bearing clear signs of having just committed a crime

red·head (rédhed) *n.* a person with red hair **réd·head·ed** *adj.*

redheaded woodpecker *Melanerpes erythrocephalus,* fam. *Picidae,* a North American woodpecker with chiefly black and white plumage and a red head and neck

red herring a dried, salted smoked herring ‖ a subject introduced into talk to divert attention from the truth or from the matter at issue

red-hot (rédhɒ́t) *adj.* (of a metal) so hot as to emit red light ‖ (of news etc.) the very latest ‖ (of a story) sensational ‖ (*pop.*) full of pep, *a red-hot band*

re·di·a (rí:di:ə) *pl.* **re·di·ae** (rí:di:i:) *n.* a larva of some trematodes growing inside the sporocyst [Mod. L. after Francesco *Redi* (1626–98), Italian naturalist]

Red Indian a North American Indian

red·in·gote (rédiŋgout) *n.* (*hist.*) a long double-breasted overcoat formerly worn by men ‖ a woman's lightweight coat which is cut away below the waist or worn open [F. fr. Eng. *riding coat*]

re·di·rect examination (ri:dirékt) the further questioning of one's own witness after his cross-examination by the opposing lawyer

re·dis·trict (ri:dístrikt) *v.t.* to divide into new districts, esp. into new political divisions

red lead the tetroxide Pb_3O_4 (*LEAD OXIDE)

red-letter day a very fortunate day [from the marking of festivals and holy days in red letters on Christian calendars]

red-light district a district where brothels are situated in a town

red-lin·ing (rédlainiŋ) *n.* a policy of many financial institutions of refusing to lend money on properties in certain areas, esp. those with a predominantly black and/or Hispanic population

red man (*rhet.*) a North American Indian

red mullet any of several small fish of fam. *Mullidae,* usually red or gold in color, with two long barbels on the chin. They are highly valued as food

red ocher, red ochre a red form of hematite, used as a pigment ‖ the color of this

red·o·lence (réd'ləns) *n.* the quality or state of being redolent [O.F.]

red·o·lent (réd'lənt) *adj.* (of an odor) sweet or aromatic ‖ (with 'of' or 'with') smelling, having a strong fragrance ‖ (*rhet.,* with 'of' or 'with') suggestive, evocative, *the place was redolent of vanished glories* [O.F.]

Re·don (rədɔ̃), Odilon (1840-1916), French symbolist painter and illustrator

Re·don·da (rədóndə) an island (area 1 sq. mile) of the Leeward Is, a dependency of Antigua

re·dou·ble (rí:dʌ́b'l) **1.** *v. pres. part.* **re·dou·bling** *past and past part.* **re·dou·bled** *v.t.* (*bridge*) to double (one's opponent's double) ‖ *v.i.* (*bridge*) to double a bid which one's opponent has already doubled **2.** *n.* (*bridge*) an instance of redoubling

re·dou·ble (ridʌ́b'l) *pres. part.* **re·dou·bling** *past* and *past part.* **re·dou·bled** *v.t.* to intensify, *to redouble one's efforts* ‖ *v.i.* to become more intense, more frequent etc. [F. *redoubler*]

re·doubt (ridáut) *n.* a temporary isolated fortification without flanking defenses [F. *redoute, ridotte*]

re·doubt·a·ble (ridáutəb'l) *adj.* formidably hard to resist or conquer, *a redoubtable adversary* [F. *redoutable*]

re·dound (ridáund) *v.i.* (with 'to') to contribute (to someone's credit or discredit) ‖ (with 'on' or 'upon', of honor, disgrace etc.) to recoil [fr. F. *rédonder,* to overflow]

re·dox (rí:dɒks) *n.* (*chem.*) oxidation reduction [REDUCTION+OXIDATION]

red pepper cayenne pepper ‖ any pepper which is red when ripe

red·poll (rédpoul) *n.* any of several small finches of genus *Carduelis* of N. Europe, Asia and America. They are streaked gray-brown on the back and sides and the males have a red crown and sometimes a reddish breast [RED+M.E. *pol, polle,* head]

CONCISE PRONUNCIATION KEY: **(a)** æ, *cat;* ɑ, *car;* ɔ *fawn;* ei, *snake.* **(e)** e, *hen;* i:, *sheep;* iə, *deer;* ɛə, *bear.* **(i)** i, *fish;* ai, *tiger;* ə:, *bird.* **(o)** o, *ox;* au, *cow;* ou, *goat;* u, *poor;* ɔi, *royal.* **(u)** ʌ, *duck;* u, *bull;* u:, *goose;* ə, *bacillus;* ju:, *cube.* x, *loch;* θ, *think;* ð, *bother;* z, *Zen;* ʒ, *corsage;* dʒ, *savage;* ŋ, *orangutang;* j, *yak;* ʃ, *fish;* tʃ, *fetch;* 'l, *rabble;* 'n, *redden.* Complete pronunciation key appears inside front cover.

Red Power American Indian slogan urging political unity, comparable to Black Power. *Cf* BROWN POWER

re·draft 1. (ri:drǽft, ri:drɑ́ft) *v.t.* to make another draft of **2.** (rí:dræft, rí:drɑft) *n.* a second or later draft ‖ a draft on the endorser of a protested bill of exchange for the amount of the bill plus charges

re·dress (ridrés) *v.t.* to put right (e.g. a fault) ‖ to make amends for, *to redress wrongs* ‖ to readjust, *to redress the balance* [fr. F. *redresser*]

re·dress (rí:dres, ridrés) *n.* the reparation of a wrong ‖ a redressing [A.F. *redresse*]

Red River (*Vietnamese* Songkoi) a river (500 miles long) flowing from Yunnan, China, across northern Vietnam to the Gulf of Tonkin, navigable to the Chinese border. Chief port: Hanoi

Red River a river (1,020 miles long) flowing from N.W. Texas (forming the Texas borders with Oklahoma and Arkansas) through S.W. Arkansas and across Louisiana to the Mississippi. It is navigable to Shreveport

Red River of the North a river (about 310 miles long) flowing north from W. Minnesota to form the Minnesota-North Dakota boundary, crossing the Canadian border and continuing north to Lake Winnipeg, Canada

Red Sea a long arm (area 178,000 sq. miles) of the Arabian Sea between Arabia and Africa, joined to the Mediterranean by the Suez Canal

red·shank (rédʃæŋk) *n. Tringa totanus,* fam. *Scolopacidae,* a European shore bird about 11 ins long, with pale red legs and feet

red shift (*astron.*) the shift of light of receding galaxies toward the red end of the spectrum. This is interpreted as a Doppler effect or shift, lending confirmation to the theory of an expanding universe

red·shirt (rédʃə:rt) *n.* (*sports*) a college athlete whose eligibility to play is extended by exclusion for varsity competition for a year — **redshirt** *v.* —**redshirting** *n.*

red·skin (rédskịn) *n.* a North American Indian

red snow arctic or alpine snow reddened by the presence of various algae, esp. *Chlamydomonas nivalis*

red·start (rédstɑrt) *n. Setophaga ruticilla,* a N. American warbler. The male has black plumage with white belly and bright orange on the sides, wings and tail ‖ *Phoenicurus phoenicurus,* fam. *Sylviidae,* a small European singing bird about 5 ½ ins long. It has a black face with white forehead and a chestnut breast and tail [fr. RED+O.E. *steort,* tail]

red tape the rigid application or observance of rules and regulations in all their minute detail without regard for the end they were designed to achieve ‖ such rules and regulations [fr. the tape tied around legal documents]

red tide (*zool.*) seawater discolored by a proliferation of plankton, usu. red in color, that kills large numbers of fish and other marine life. The proliferation is sometimes stimulated by the addition of nutrients

re·duce (ridú:s, ridjú:s) *pres. part.* **re·duc·ing** *past* and *past part.* **re·duced** *v.t.* to make smaller or less in size, weight, condition etc., *to reduce prices* ‖ to change to a different form, *to reduce a stone to powder, to reduce one's ideas to writing* ‖ to separate into its elements ‖ to bring to a certain state, *to reduce to silence* ‖ to lower in rank ‖ to conquer by assault, or bring under control ‖ to compel by force of circumstances, *reduced to begging* ‖ to make physically weak ‖ to thin (paint etc.) ‖ to reduce the volume of (a sauce etc.) by boiling ‖ (*chem.*) to combine with or subject to the action of hydrogen ‖ to add one or more electrons to (a compound, radical or ion) and thus change the oxidation state to a lower positive or higher negative number ‖ (*math.*) to express in another form without changing the value of, *to reduce acres to square yards* ‖ (*surg.*) to restore (a broken or dislocated bone or organ) to its original position ‖ (*biol.*) to cause (a cell) to undergo meiosis ‖ (*photog.*) to make (a negative) less dense ‖ *v.i.* to become reduced ‖ to lose weight by dieting ‖ to limit the air intake into a kiln so that fuel gases are not completely burned ‖ to undergo meiosis **re·dúced** *adj.* decreased in size, cost etc. ‖ (*phys., chem.*) of a variable (e.g. temperature, pressure, volume) of the state of a system or substance divided by the critical value of that variable [fr. L. *reducere,* to lead back]

reduced circumstances comparative poverty experienced by someone used to having plenty of money

re·duc·er (ridú:sər, ridjú:sər) *n.* (*chem.*) a substance that acts as a reducing agent ‖ (*mech.*) a pipe fitting for connecting two different sizes of pipe ‖ (*photog.*) a developing agent ‖ (*photog.*) an agent that reduces the density of negatives ‖ a paint thinner

re·duc·i·bil·i·ty (ridụ:səbíliti:, ridjụ:səbíliti:) *n.* the quality of being reducible

re·duc·i·ble (ridú:səb'l, ridjú:səb'l) *adj.* able to be reduced

re·duc·tion (ridʌ́kʃən) *n.* a reducing or being reduced ‖ the result of reducing, e.g. a lower price ‖ the amount by which something is reduced ‖ limitation of the air intake into a kiln so that there is incomplete combustion of fuel gases ‖ (*chem.*) the process by which electrons are added to a substance to reduce it, e.g. the conversion of a metallic oxide or sulfide to the free metal (cf. OXIDATION, *OXIDATION-REDUCTION) ‖ (*math.*) an expression in simpler form or in another denomination ‖ (*photog.*) the lessening of the opacity of a negative ‖ (*biol.*) meiosis [F. *réduction* or fr. L. *reductio* (*reductionis*)]

reduction division the first of two meiotic divisions in maturation

re·duc·tion·ism (ridʌ́kʃənịzəm) *n.* (*biol.*) theory that all biological processes follow the same laws as do chemistry and physics

reductivism *MINIMAL ART

re·dun·dance (ridʌ́ndəns) *n.* redundancy [fr. L. *redundantia*]

re·dun·dan·cy (ridʌ́ndənsi:) *pl.* **re·dun·dan·cies** *n.* the state or quality of being redundant ‖ something or (*Br., administration*) someone redundant [fr. L. *redundantia*]

re·dun·dant (ridʌ́ndənt) *adj.* unnecessarily repetitive or superfluous, *redundant phrases* ‖ of a back-up system duplicating the function of a device, e.g., in a space vehicle ‖ (*Br., administration,* of a workman or his work) surplus to requirements [fr. L. *redundans* (*redundantis*) fr. *redundare,* to redound]

re·du·pli·cate (ridú:plikeit, ridjú:plikeit) *pres. part.* **re·du·pli·cat·ing** *past* and *past part.* **re·du·pli·cat·ed** *v.t.* to repeat, esp. unnecessarily ‖ (*gram.*) to repeat (a letter or syllable) so as to form an inflected or derived form, sometimes with change of vowel etc., e.g. 'dilly-dally' ‖ (*gram.*) to form (words) in this way [fr. M.L. *reduplicare* (*reduplicatus*)]

re·du·pli·cate (ridú:plikit, ridjú:plikit) *adj.* reduplicated ‖ (*bot.,* of petals) having the edges curving outward [fr. L.L. *reduplicatus*]

re·du·pli·ca·tion (ridụ:plikéiʃən, ridjụ:plikéiʃən) *n.* a reduplicating or being reduplicated ‖ a word produced by reduplicating ‖ the part of the word added in reduplicating [fr. L.L. *reduplicatio* (*reduplicationis*)]

re·du·pli·ca·tive (ridú:plikẹitiv, ridjú:plikẹitiv) *adj.* of, relating to, formed or characterized by reduplication [fr. L. *reduplicare* (*reduplicatus*), to double]

red warbler *Acrocephalus scirpaceus,* a small brown and white European warbler frequenting the reeds of a river's edge or marsh

red·wing (rédwịŋ) *n. Turdus musicus* (or *T. iliacus*) the smallest common European thrush, having chestnut-red feathers on the underpart of its wings and tail ‖ the redwing blackbird

redwing blackbird *Agelaius phoeniceus,* fam. *Icteridae,* a North American bird about 9 ins in length. The male is jet black, with a bright red patch on the upper part of each wing

red·wood (rédwụd) *n. Sequoia sempervirens,* fam. *Taxodiaceae,* a giant Californian conifer often reaching a height of 300 ft and having a diameter of up to 28 ft ‖ the hard reddish wood of this tree ‖ any of various trees with reddish wood, or their wood

Reed (ri:d), Thomas Brackett (1839-1902), U.S. legislator. As Speaker of the House (1889-91, 1895-9), he introduced the 'Reed Rules' (1890). One of these determined the House quorum by the count of members present rather than by the count of those voting. His use of the Speaker's power of recognition to thwart obstructive tactics by the minority earned him the nickname 'Tsar Reed'

Reed, Walter (1851-1902), U.S. army surgeon. He proved that yellow fever was caused by a virus transmitted by a mosquito. His findings enabled W. C. Gorgas to eradicate the disease in Cuba and in the Canal Zone. His name is given to the army medical center in Washington, D.C.

reed (ri:d) **1.** *n.* any of several varieties of tall-growing, erect grasses, found in water or swamps ‖ (*collect.*) a quantity of these growing or cut and dried ‖ material of cut reeds used as a thatch etc. ‖ a musical pipe made of one or more hollow reed stems ‖ a thin strip of cane or metal which vibrates when agitated by air pressure and thus emits sound, e.g. in a harmonium, or when attached to a pipe, e.g. in a clarinet ‖ a musical instrument fitted with a reed or reeds ‖ (*archit.*) a semicircular molding, usually one of a number set parallel in a line ‖ (*weaving*) a device for separating the threads of the warp and beating up the weft **2.** *v.t.* to thatch with reed ‖ to furnish with reed or reeds ‖ (*weaving*) to draw (yarn) through a reed **réed·ing** *n.* (*archit.*) a reed ‖ (*collect.*) decoration made with a series of these ‖ the grooves around the edge of a coin [O.E. *hrēod*]

reed mace the cattail

reed organ a keyboard wind instrument in which the sound is produced by the action of wind on free metal reeds

reed pipe the pipe of a pipe organ in which the tone is produced by an air current striking a vibrating reed (cf. FLUE PIPE)

reed stop a set of reed pipes (usually imitating some instrument of the orchestra) controlled by a single stop of a reed organ

re·ed·u·cate (ri:édʒukeit, ri:édjukeit) *pres. part.* **re·ed·u·cat·ing** *past* and *past part.* **re·ed·u·cat·ed** *v.t.* to educate again, esp. to rehabilitate by special training

reeducation camps a euphemism for detention camps in which some nations 'reorient' certain members of their population to the government's political and social philosophy, e.g., Cambodia, China

reed·y (rí:di:) *comp.* **reed·i·er** *superl.* **reed·i·est** *adj.* abounding in reeds ‖ thin, reedlike in form ‖ like a reed instrument in quality

reef (ri:f) *n.* a line of rocks, sand, small stones etc., just above or near the surface of the water ‖ (*mining*) a vein of ore [akin to O.N. *rif,* reef of a sail]

reef 1. *n.* a part of a sail which can be rolled up to expose less surface to the wind **2.** *v.t.* to take in or roll up a reef in (a sail) ‖ to shorten (a topmast) by taking part of it down or (a bowsprit) by taking part of it in ‖ to fold up or roll, as though folding a sail [O.N. *rif*]

reef·er (rí:fər) *n.* **1.** a refrigerator **2.** a railroad freight car, ship, aircraft, or other conveyance, so constructed and insulated as to protect commodities from either heat or cold **3.** a thick, close-fitting, double-breasted jacket **4.** (*pop.*) a cigarette containing marijuana

reef knot (*naut.*) a square knot used in reefing a sail

reek (ri:k) *n.* a very strong, unpleasant smell ‖ mist, vapor [O.E. *rēc*]

reek *v.i.* to give off thick smoke ‖ to give off an unpleasant smell ‖ to have an undesirable quality in abundance, *it reeks of hypocrisy* [O.E. *rēocan, rēcan*]

reel (ri:l) **1.** *n.* a revolving, often cylindrical device for winding up or letting out yarn, cord, wire etc. ‖ the quantity of material contained on such a device ‖ a small revolving device attached to a fishing rod for winding in and letting out the line ‖ the quantity of line contained on it ‖ (*Br.*) a spool or bobbin for sewing thread ‖ a spool onto which photographic film is wound for use in a camera ‖ a strip of film of given length so wound or able to be so wound **off the reel** straight off, without interruption, *he recited their names and dates off the reel* **2.** *v.t.* to wind on a reel ‖ (with 'in') to bring in by reeling **to reel off** to recite easily without pause or interruption, *he reeled off the verses* [O.E. *hrēol*]

reel 1. *v.i.* to sway unsteadily (from a blow, drunkenness etc.) ‖ to be attacked by vertigo ‖ to be shaken physically or mentally by the shock of grief or astonishment ‖ to whirl around or to seem to whirl around **2.** *n.* a reeling movement [perh. fr. REEL, to wind]

reel 1. *n.* a lively Scottish dance, performed by facing couples who move around one another in a series of figures of eight ‖ the Virginia reel ‖ the music for these dances **2.** *v.i.* to dance a reel [perh. fr. REEL, to wind]

re·e·lect (rị:ilékt) *v.t.* to elect for another term **re·e·léc·tion** *n.*

re·en·force (rị:enfɔ́rs, rị:enfóurs) *pres. part.* **re·en·forc·ing** *past* and *past part.* **re·en·forced** *v.t.* to reinforce

re·en·ter (ri:éntər) *v.t.* to enter again

CONCISE PRONUNCIATION KEY: **(a)** æ, *cat;* ɑ, *car;* ɔ *fawn;* ei, *snake.* **(e)** e, *hen;* i:, *sheep;* iə, *deer;* ɛə, *bear.* **(i)** i, *fish;* ai, *tiger;* ə:, *bird.* **(o)** o, *ox;* au, *cow;* ou, *goat;* u, *poor;* ɔi, *royal.* **(u)** ʌ, *duck;* u, *bull;* u:, *goose;* ə, *bacillus;* ju:, *cube.* x, *loch;* θ, *think;* ð, *bother;* z, *Zen;* ʒ, *corsage;* dʒ, *savage;* ŋ, *orangutang;* j, *yak;* ʃ, *fish;* tʃ, *fetch;* 'l, *rabble;* 'n, *redden.* Complete pronunciation key appears inside front cover.

re·en·trant (ri:éntrənt) **1.** *adj.* pointing inward, *a reentrant angle* **2.** *n.* something reentrant, esp. (*mil.*) a part of a defense line which projects away from the enemy ‖ an angle at the side of a valley where a secondary valley joins the main one

re·en·try (ri:éntri:) *pl.* **re·en·tries** *n.* the act of entering again ‖ (*law*) the act of taking possession again, esp. of leased property ‖ (*bridge*) a card with which a player is assured of recapturing the lead ‖ (of a rocket, spaceship etc.) the act of returning from space to the earth's atmosphere

reeve (ri:v) *n.* (*Eng. hist.*) a royal agent in Anglo-Saxon times ‖ (*Eng. hist.*) the chief magistrate of a town or district ‖ (*Eng. hist.*) an officer of a medieval manor ranking below a bailiff ‖ (*Canada*) the president of a local council [O.E. *gerēfa*]

reeve *n.* the female of the ruff (sandpiper) [etym. doubtful]

reeve *pres. part.* **reev·ing** *past* and *past part.* **rove** (rouv), **reeved** *v.t.* (*naut.*) to pass (the end of a rope) through a hole in a block, cleat etc. ‖ to thread (a block, cleat etc.) with a rope ‖ to attach a rope, block etc. to by reeving [etym. doubtful]

re·ex·am·i·na·tion (ri:igzæminéiʃən) *n.* a reexamining or being reexamined

re·ex·am·ine (ri:igzǽmin) *pres. part.* **re·ex·am·in·ing** *past* and *past part.* **re·ex·am·ined** *v.t.* to examine again ‖ (*law*) to examine a witness after cross-examination

re·ex·port (ri:ikspɔ́rt, ri:ikspóurt, ri:ékspɔrt, ri:ékspourt) **1.** *v.t.* to export (something previously imported) **2.** *n.* something reexported ‖ a reexporting

re·face (ri:féis) *pres. part.* **re·fac·ing** *past* and *past part.* **re·faced** *v.t.* to renew the front surface of (e.g. a building)

re·fec·tion (rifékʃən) *n.* (*rhet.*) a light meal [F. *réfection*]

re·fec·to·ry (riféktəri:) *pl.* **re·fec·to·ries** *n.* a room used for meals by a religious community [fr. M.L. *refectorium*]

refectory table a long, narrow dining table, massively built

re·fer (rifə́:r) *pres. part.* **re·fer·ring** *past* and *past part.* **re·ferred** *v.i.* to speak or write of something in the course of dealing with some other or larger topic ‖ to relate, *this statement refers to remarks by his opponent* ‖ to turn for information etc., *to refer to the dictionary* ‖ *v.t.* to transfer (something) for the attention or action of someone else ‖ to direct (someone) to a source of information etc. ‖ to assign to a specific place, period etc., *historians refer the fall of Rome to 410 A.D.* ‖ to regard as caused by, *he referred his depressions to his childhood illness* **ref·er·ee** (refəri:) **1.** *n.* a person to whom something in dispute is referred for his opinion or decision ‖ (*law*) a person appointed to examine, take testimony and give judgment on a matter ‖ (*Br.*) someone who furnishes a character reference etc. for another ‖ (*in many sports*) a person appointed to make sure that a game is played or match fought according to the rules **2.** *v.i. pres. part.* **ref·er·ee·ing** *past* and *past part.* **ref·er·eed** to act as a referee ‖ *v.t.* to be the referee of

ref·er·ence (réfrəns, réfərəns) **1.** *n.* a referring or being referred or an instance of this ‖ the state of being related, *all the parts have reference to one another* ‖ an indication in a work of some other work to be consulted ‖ the work cited ‖ a mark directing the reader to a footnote etc. ‖ a person who, on request, will testify to the ability, qualities, character etc. of an applicant e.g. for employment ‖ a written testimony as to the character, ability etc. of another person ‖ a source of information taken as authoritative **in** (or **with**) **reference to** concerning **2.** *v.t. pres. part.* **ref·er·enc·ing** *past* and *past part.* **ref·er·enced** to furnish (a book etc.) with references [fr. O.F. *referer* or L. *referre*, to carry back]

reference beam (*holography*) guiding laser beam aimed at the film

reference book a book consulted for information, e.g. a dictionary ‖ a book in a library to be used only on the premises

reference library a library in which books may be consulted on the premises but not taken away

ref·er·en·dum (refəréndəm) *pl.* **ref·er·en·da** (refəréndə), **ref·er·en·dums** *n.* the submission of a particular measure or question of national importance to the whole electorate (rather than just to their representatives) as a single issue on which to vote ‖ such a vote ‖ a similar procedure in an organized group for discovering its general will ‖ a note sent by a diplomat to his government asking for instructions [L.=a carrying back]

re·fill 1. (rí:fil) *n.* a replacement for the expendable contents of a container intended for reuse **2.** (ri:fíl) *v.t.* to fill again

re·fine (rifáin) *pres. part.* **re·fin·ing** *past* and *past part.* **re·fined** *v.t.* to remove impurities or coarse elements from ‖ to make (manners, language, taste, expression etc.) more delicate or polished ‖ to make more subtle and efficient, *refined methods of cataloging* ‖ *v.i.* (with 'on' or 'upon') to achieve greater subtlety or purity in meaning or effect, *to refine on a definition* **re·fined** *adj.* **re·fine·ment** *n.*

re·fin·er·y (rifáinəri:) *pl.* **re·fin·er·ies** *n.* a place or apparatus for refining or for purifying e.g. sugar, petroleum or pig iron

re·fit 1. (ri:fít) *v. pres. part.* **re·fit·ting** *past* and *past part.* **re·fit·ted** *v.t.* to supply (a ship) with new equipment, appointments etc. ‖ *v.i.* (of a ship) to be reequipped and made fit for service again **2.** (rí:fit) *n.* a refitting or being refitted

re·flect (riflékt) *v.t.* to cause or permit the collision of (a beam of particles or a wave) with a surface, resulting in its partial or complete return into the medium originally traversed (*LAW OF REFLECTION) ‖ to show as an image, *they gazed at the stars reflected in the lake* ‖ (with 'on', 'upon') to cause (contributory credit or discredit) to be ascribed to, *his success reflects credit on his trainer* ‖ to be in accordance with and give an insight into, *his behavior reflects his upbringing* ‖ (*biol.*) to bend back, *reflected petals* ‖ *v.i.* (of a beam of particles or wave) to become reflected ‖ to act as a reflector ‖ (with 'on' or 'upon') to think back, *to reflect on one's past* ‖ to ponder, meditate, *give them time to reflect* ‖ (with 'on' or 'upon') to bring discredit, *such an act reflects upon him* [O.F. *reflecter* or L. *reflectere*]

re·flect·ance (rifléktəns) *n.* (*phys.*) a measure of a surface's ability to reflect radiant energy, equal to the ratio of the intensity of the reflected radiation to that of the incident radiation

reflecting telescope a telescope whose objective is a mirror (*NEWTONIAN TELESCOPE, *CASSEGRAINIAN TELESCOPE). Since there is no refractive medium through which the light from the object must pass, chromatic aberrations are eliminated. By utilizing a paraboloidal mirror rather than a spherical one, the spherical aberrations are eliminated as well. Reflecting telescopes are used mainly as astronomical telescopes (cf. REFRACTING TELESCOPE)

re·flec·tion, re·flex·ion (riflékʃən) *n.* a reflecting or being reflected ‖ something (e.g. light, heat or an image) reflected ‖ an organ or tissue bent or folded back ‖ an opinion arrived at after consideration, *we are waiting to hear his reflections on the book's merits* ‖ (often *pl.*) adverse criticism, *to cast reflections on someone* **on reflection** after consideration [F. *réflexion*]

reflection coefficient reflectance

reflection factor reflectance

re·flec·tive (rifléktiv) *adj.* inclined to be thoughtful, meditative ‖ concerning thinking habits or faculties ‖ causing, relating to, or caused by reflection, *reflective surfaces*

re·flec·tor (rifléktər) *n.* any surface which reflects, esp. a highly polished curved surface which reflects light or heat as a coherent beam ‖ a reflecting telescope

re·flex (rí:fleks) **1.** *n.* (*physiol.*) an automatic or involuntary response to a stimulus (*REFLEX ARC) ‖ (*pl.*) the ability to respond in this way, *his reflexes are failing* ‖ an automatic mental reaction, *it had become a reflex to say 'no'* **2.** *adj.* reflected, bent back ‖ (*math.*) of an angle greater than 180° but less than 360° ‖ (*physiol.*) of an automatic or involuntary response to a stimulus, *a reflex action* [fr. L. *reflectere* (*reflexus*), to bend back]

reflex arc the complete nerve path of a reflex action. The simplest is a sensory impulse conducted by an afferent neuron to a nerve center and a motor impulse conducted by an efferent neuron to an effector, e.g. a muscle, e.g. in the case of a hand touching a hot iron

reflex camera a camera equipped with two objective lenses (or with one objective lens and a movable mirror), one of which forms an image on the film and the other forms an image on a ground-glass plate. The latter is identical with the former and is used to focus and compose the image

reflex force (*mil.*) the part of the Air Force alert forces maintained overseas or domestic forward bases by scheduled rotations

reflexion *REFLECTION

re·flex·ive (rifléksiv) **1.** *adj.* (*gram.*) denoting an action by the subject upon itself, e.g. of a verb whose subject and direct object are the same ('dressed' in 'he dressed himself'), or of a pronoun which is the object of such a verb ('himself' in 'he dressed himself') ‖ of or relating to or consisting of a reflex or reflexes ‖ able to bend back **2.** *n.* a reflexive verb or pronoun [M.L. *reflexivus*, reflected fr. L. *reflectere* (*reflexus*), to bend back, reflect]

reflexology *FOOT REFLEXOLOGY

ref·lu·ence (réflu:əns) *n.* reflux [fr. L. *refluere*, to flow back]

ref·lu·ent (réflu:ənt) *adj.* flowing back ‖ ebbing [fr. L. *refluens* (*refluentis*) fr. *refluere*, to flow back]

re·flux (rí:flʌks) *n.* a flowing back, *the flux and reflux of the tide*

re·for·est (ri:fɔ́rist, ri:fórist) *v.t.* (*Am.*=*Br.* reafforest) to plant (denuded land) with trees again **re·for·est·á·tion** *n.*

re·form (rifɔ́rm) *v.t.* to improve by removing faults and weaknesses or by strengthening good qualities ‖ to put an end to (an evil, abuse etc.) ‖ to correct, *Pope Gregory reformed the calendar* ‖ to persuade (a person) to change his ways for the better ‖ *v.i.* to become reformed [fr. O.F. *reformer* or L. *reformare*]

reform 1. *n.* a reforming ‖ a measure intended to reform something **2.** *adj.* of, pertaining to or advocating reform [REFORM v. or fr. F. *réforme*]

re·form (ri:fɔ́rm) *v.t.* to form again ‖ *v.i.* to take form again ‖ to form up or gather together again

Re·for·ma, Guer·ra de la (gérɑðelɑrefɔ́rmɑ) the internal struggle (1858-61) in Mexico between the conservatives and the liberals under Benito Juárez, victory going to the latter. The 'Leyes de Reforma' refer to the laws establishing the separation of Church and State

ref·or·ma·tion (refərméiʃən) *n.* a reforming or being reformed **the Reformation** a 16th-c. religious movement against abuses in the Roman Catholic Church, ending in the formation of the Protestant Churches [fr. L. *reformatio* (*reformationis*)]

—Although the Reformation was a religious movement in origin, its course was much influenced by political and economic factors. Wyclif and Hus had prepared the way for it, and by the end of the Middle Ages many were convinced that the Church needed reforming. Circumstances favorable to the Reformation included: humanism and the Renaissance (which encouraged a new critical spirit), the invention of printing (which aided the spread of ideas), the reaction of princes and jurists against the temporal encroachments of the papacy, the growing wealth of the clergy (esp. in Germany) and the religious and moral shortcomings of certain sections of the clergy. The leaders of the Reformation sought to restore Christianity to its early purity by submitting ecclesiastical tradition to the test of Scriptural authority.

The Reformation was begun in Germany (1517) by Luther, who at first thought reform possible without schism. His attack on the papacy and his refusal to recant led to his excommunication (1521). The Augsburg Confession (1530) defined Lutheran doctrine, of which the main points were justification by faith and the sovereign authority of the Scriptures in matters of faith. The German nobles adopted the new ideas, enabling themselves to appropriate Church property and to challenge the authority of the Emperor as members of the Schmalkaldic League. On Luther's death (1546), his followers were condemned by the Council of Trent and defeated in the Schmalkaldic War. The Peace of Augsburg (1555) recognized the legal existence of Lutheranism in Germany. The conflict later became merged in the Thirty Years' War.

From Saxony, Lutheranism spread into Prussia and the Slav provinces of the Baltic, and was adopted by Denmark, Sweden, Norway and Iceland. The Reformation was preached in Switzerland by Zwingli and in France by Calvin, who added to it the doctrine of predestination. Protestants did not win religious freedom in France until the end of the Wars of Religion. Calvinism was victorious in the Protestant cantons of Switzerland, in Scotland under Knox, and in Flanders and the Netherlands despite

CONCISE PRONUNCIATION KEY: **(a)** æ, *cat*; ɑ, *car*; ɔ *fawn*; ei, *snake*. **(e)** e, *hen*; i:, *sheep*; iə, *deer*; ɛə, *bear*. **(i)** i, *fish*; ai, *tiger*; ə:, *bird*. **(o)** o, *ox*; au, *cow*; ou, *goat*; u, *poor*; ɔi, *royal*. **(u)** ʌ, *duck*; u, *bull*; u:, *goose*; ə, *bacillus*; ju:, *cube*. x, *loch*; θ, *think*; ð, *bother*; z, *Zen*; ʒ, *corsage*; dʒ, *savage*; ŋ, *orangutang*; j, *yak*; ʃ, *fish*; tʃ, *fetch*; 'l, *rabble*; 'n, *redden*. Complete pronunciation key appears inside front cover.

the persecutions of Philip II. England rejected papal control (1534) under Henry VIII, veered towards Calvinism under Edward VI, and, after the Catholic reaction under Mary I, adopted the compromise of the Elizabethan Church settlement (*CHURCH OF ENGLAND).

The Reformation tended to increase the growth of nationalism and to strengthen the economic position of the mercantile class. Within the Roman Catholic Church it led to the Counter-Reformation

re·form·a·tive (rifɔ́rmətiv) *adj.* producing or likely to produce reform [fr. L. *reformare (reformatus)*, to reform]

re·form·a·to·ry (rifɔ́rmətɔri:, rifɔ́rmətouri:) **1.** *n. pl.* **re·form·a·to·ries** an institution to which young offenders may be sent for rehabilitation **2.** *adj.* reformative [fr. L. *reformare (reformatus)*, to reform]

Re·formed (rifɔ́rm'd) *adj.* of or relating to Protestant theology || of or relating to a Reformed Church

Reformed Church any of the group of Protestant Churches which follow the doctrines of Zwingli and Calvin rather than those of Luther, and which are Presbyterian in Church government. The first Reformed Church was set up by Zwingli in Zurich (1519) under the influence of Erasmus. Zurich broke with Roman Catholicism in 1523, followed by Geneva (site of Calvin's theocracy) in 1541. The movement spread to Strasbourg (1521) and thence to Germany, the Netherlands (1522), France and England. Its doctrine and orders were defined by the Heidelberg Catechism (1563). The French Huguenots were the first to apply Presbyterian Church polity on a national scale, closely followed by Scotland (1561-7 under Knox), Hungary (1567) and the Netherlands (1584). The movement reached the U.S.A. in the 1640s. Politically the movement lost ground in England (from 1660) and was crushed by the Counter-Reformation in Bohemia (1620). Hungary (mid-17th c.) and France (1685). Its religious influence dwindled under the incursions of rationalism in the successive forms of Socinianism, Arminianism and Unitarianism, but in the 20th c. its orthodoxy was redefined by Karl Barth. There are about 50 million adherents of the Reformed or Presbyterian Churches. They are strong in North America (16 million), Scotland (1 million), the Netherlands (4 million), Switzerland (3 million), and South Africa (1½ million). They form important minorities in Hungary (2 million), Rumania (800,000), Czechoslovakia (530,000), France (750,000), Indonesia (2 million), Korea (500,000), Australasia (1½ million), Brazil (500,000), Lesotho (200,000), Cameroun (300,000), Central Africa (500,000), and Ghana (200,000), and smaller ones in Italy (Waldensians), Poland, the Malagasy Republic and Togo. In Germany they are united with the Lutherans

Reformed Episcopal Church a U.S. Protestant community formed (1873) as a result of a division in the Protestant Episcopal Church. It was established by George David Cummings, a leader of the evangelical episcopalians, who stressed the difference in points of faith between Anglicanism and Roman Catholicism

re·form·er (rifɔ́rmər) *n.* someone who reforms or favors reform **Re·form·er** a leader of the 16th-c. Protestant Reformation

reform school a reformatory

re·fract (rifrǽkt) *v.t.* to subject (waves of light, sound etc.) to refraction || to measure the refraction of (an eye or a lens) [fr. L. *refringere (refractus)*]

refracting telescope a telescope whose objective is a lens or lens system (*GALILEAN TELESCOPE). Modern refractors are equipped with compound achromatic objective lenses and are used for astronomical and terrestrial observations (cf. REFLECTING TELESCOPE)

re·frac·tion (rifrǽkʃən) *n.* a refracting or being refracted || the ability of the eye to refract light || the technique of determining the refractive condition of the eye || the change in direction of the path followed by electromagnetic waves (e.g. a ray of light) or other energy-bearing waves in passing obliquely from one medium to another in which its velocity is different (*SNELL'S LAW OF REFRACTION) || the change in the apparent position of a celestial body caused by the passage of light from it through the earth's atmosphere || the determination of the refractive index of the eye or a lens [fr. L.L. *refractio (refractionis)*]

re·frac·tive (rifrǽktiv) *adj.* of or pertaining to refraction || caused by refraction || able to refract [fr. L.L. *refractivus* or REFRACT]

refractive index (*phys.*) the ratio of the velocity of light, or other radiation, in one medium (usually taken to be a vacuum) to its velocity in a second medium (*SNELL'S LAW)

re·frac·tom·e·ter (ri:frǽktɒ́mitər) *n.* (*phys.*) an instrument for measuring refractive indices

re·frac·tor (ri:frǽktər) *n.* a device (e.g. a refracting telescope) that causes refraction, i.e. one utilizing a lens as the focusing device

re·frac·to·ry (rifrǽktəri:) **1.** *adj.* resisting discipline, *a refractory child* || (of injuries, diseases etc.) not benefiting from treatment || (of substances) resisting high temperature **2.** *pl.* **re·frac·to·ries** *n.* any of various nonmetallic ceramic substances that resist great heat, e.g. oxides of silicon, aluminum or magnesium and certain plastics [older *refractary* fr. L. *refractarius*]

re·frain (rifréin) *n.* a phrase or line in poetry or song repeated at regular intervals || the music for such a phrase or line [O.F. *refrein, refrain*]

refrain *v.i.* to abstain from doing something, *he refrained from making any criticism* [O.F. *refrener*, to hold back]

re·fran·gi·bil·i·ty (rifrændʒəbíliti:) *n.* the quality of being refrangible

re·fran·gi·ble (rifrǽndʒəb'l) *adj.* able to be refracted [altered fr. L. *refringere*, to bend]

re·fresh (rifréʃ) *v.t.* to make (someone) feel restored and freshened, e.g. by rest or food || to recall to (the mind) **re·frésh·er** *n.* something that refreshes, e.g. a cool drink || (*Br.*) an extra fee paid to counsel in a prolonged law case || a refresher course [O.F. *refrescher*]

refresher course a course of study to bring one's knowledge of something up to date

re·fresh·ment (rifréʃmənt) *n.* a refreshing or being refreshed || something that refreshes || (*pl.*) light food and drink, *refreshments will be served after the meeting* [O.F. *refreschement*]

re·frig·er·ant (rifrídʒərənt) **1.** *adj.* cooling || alleviating fever or bodily heat **2.** *n.* a substance used in a refrigerating cycle or directly (e.g. ice) for cooling || a medicine, ointment etc. used in reducing fever [F. *réfrigérant* or fr. L. *refrigerans (refrigerantis)* fr. *refrigerare*, to cool]

re·frig·er·ate (rifrídʒəreit) *pres. part.* **re·frig·er·at·ing** *past* and *past part.* **re·frig·er·at·ed** *v.t.* to cool, make or keep cold || to keep (food) at a low temperature in order to preserve it [fr. L. *refrigerare (refrigeratus)*]

re·frig·er·a·tion (rifridʒəréiʃən) *n.* a refrigerating or being refrigerated [fr. L. *refrigeratio (refrigerationis)*]

refrigeration cycle a sequence of compression and expansion stages of a working substance (e.g. freon, ammonia) induced by mechanical means that permits the continuous transfer of heat from one region (the source) to another region (the sink), where it is either dissipated (e.g. in a refrigerator) or is utilized for heating (e.g. in a heat pump)

refrigeration machine a refrigerator utilizing a refrigeration cycle

re·frig·er·a·tive (rifrídʒəreitiv, rifrídʒərətiv) *adj.* refrigerating, used to refrigerate

re·frig·er·a·tor (rifrídʒəreitər) *n.* any of several devices used to maintain a low temperature in a container or a room, for preserving food or other articles

re·frig·er·a·to·ry (rifrídʒərətɔri:, rifrídʒərətouri:) *adj.* refrigerative [fr. L. *refrigeratorius*]

re·frin·gent (rifríndʒənt) *adj.* refractive [fr. L. *refringens (refringentis)* fr. *refringere*, to refract]

ref·uge (réfju:dʒ) *n.* shelter or protection from danger, distress or difficulty || a place offering this || a person, thing, or course of action offering protection, *tears were her usual refuge* **to take refuge** to put oneself in a place or state that affords protection [F.]

ref·u·gee (refju:dʒí:, réfju:dʒi:) *n.* a person who flees, esp. to a foreign country, to escape e.g. an oppressive government, religious persecution or an invading army [fr. F. *réfugié*]

re·ful·gence (rifʌ́ldʒəns) *n.* the state or quality of being refulgent [fr. L. *refulgentia*]

re·ful·gent (rifʌ́ldʒənt) *adj.* shining brightly [fr. L. *refulgens (refulgentis)* fr. *refulgere*, to shine]

re·fund 1. (rifʌ́nd) *v.t.* to pay back (money spent) || to reimburse (someone) || *v.i.* to make repayment **2.** (rí:fʌnd) *n.* a repayment [fr. O.F. *refunder* or L. *refundere*, to pour back]

re·fur·bish (ri:fʌ́rbiʃ) *v.t.* to make bright or fresh again, renovate

re·fus·al (rifjú:z'l) *n.* the act of refusing || the right or opportunity to have the offer of something before it is offered to another, *he has the refusal of the property*

re·fuse (rifjú:z) *pres. part.* **re·fus·ing** *past* and *past part.* **re·fused** *v.t.* to decline to accept, *he refused my offer*, or to submit to, *he refused the lie-detector test* || to decline to grant or give (something) to someone, *to refuse readmittance to former members* || to decline (to do something), *he refused to shake hands* || (of a fabric) to fail to be affected by (a dye) || (of a horse) to decline to jump (a fence etc.) || (*cards*) to be unable to play a card of (the suit led) || *v.i.* to make a refusal || (*cards*) to fail to play a card of the suit led [fr. F. *refuser*]

re·fuse (réfju:s) **1.** *n.* remains having no value or use **2.** *adj.* rejected as of no value or use [fr. O.F., past part. of *refuser*, to refuse]

ref·u·ta·ble (réfjutəb'l, rifjú:təb'l) *adj.* able to be refuted **réf·u·ta·bly** *adv.* [fr. L.L. *refutabilis*]

re·fut·al (rifjú:t'l) *n.* a refutation [REFUTE]

ref·u·ta·tion (refjutéiʃən) *n.* a refuting || something which refutes [fr. L. *refutatio (refutationis)*]

re·fute (rifjú:t) *pres. part.* **re·fut·ing** *past* and *past part.* **re·fut·ed** *v.t.* to prove (an assertion or argument) to be untrue or incorrect || to prove (a person) wrong [fr. L. *refutare*]

re·gain (rigéin, ri:géin) *v.t.* to get back (something lost), *to regain one's composure* || to get back to (a place) [fr. F. *regagner*]

re·gal (rí:g'l) *adj.* befitting a king || of or pertaining to a king [O.F. or L. *regalis*]

re·gale (rigéil) *pres. part.* **re·gal·ing** *past* and *past part.* **re·galed** *v.t.* to entertain (someone) richly || to amuse and entertain, *he regaled her with the latest gossip* || to feast (oneself) || *v.i.* to feast [fr. F. *régaler*, Ital. *regalare*]

re·ga·lia (rigéiljə) *pl. n.* objects symbolizing kingship || emblems of office

re·gal·i·ty (rigǽliti:) *n.* royal jurisdiction [O.F. *regalité*]

re·gard (rigárd) *n.* esteem, *he stands high in their regard* || consideration, sympathetic concern, *he shows little regard for others* || (*old-fash.*) a long, steady look || attention, heed, *without regard for danger* || (*pl.*) a conventional expression of kindly feeling, esteem etc., *give him my best regards* **in** (or **with**) **regard to** concerning [F.]

regard *v.t.* (usually with 'as') to consider (someone or something) as being a specified thing, possessing specified qualities etc. || to concern, *insofar as it regards them . . .* || to look closely at [F. *regarder*]

re·gard·ant (rigárd'nt) *adj.* (*heraldry*) looking backward [F.]

re·gard·ful (rigárdfəl) *adj.* (*old-fash.*) heedful, mindful || (*old-fash.*) respectful

re·gard·ing (rigárdiŋ) *prep.* in or with regard to, concerning

re·gard·less (rigárdlis) **1.** *adj.* (usually with 'of') paying no heed or attention, *he went regardless of the risk* **2.** *adv.* (*pop.*) without consideration of the situation, consequences etc., *we'll go regardless*

re·gat·ta (rigǽtə, rigátə) *n.* a series of rowing or sailing races, organized as a sporting and social event [Ital.=gondola race]

re·ge·late (rí:dʒileit) *pres. part.* **re·ge·lat·ing** *past* and *past part.* **re·ge·lat·ed** *v.i.* (of water or ice) to freeze again when the pressure is released after partial, local melting due to pressure **re·ge·lá·tion** *n.* [fr. RE-+L. *gelare (gelatus)*, to freeze]

re·gen·cy (rí:dʒənsi:) **1.** *pl.* **re·gen·cies** *n.* the office of a regent || the authority of a regent || the period of power of a regent || a commission exercising such power || the region controlled by a regent or body of regents **Re·gen·cy** (*Br. hist.*) the period (1811–20) during which the future George IV was regent for George III || (*F. hist.*) the period (1715–23) during which Philippe, duc d'Orléans was regent for Louis XV **2. Re·gen·cy** *adj.* of a transitional style of French furniture developed c. 1715–23 and characterized by scrollwork, curves and graceful decorative motifs || of a style of English furniture, architecture etc. prevalent c. 1811–30, characterized by fine proportions, classical elements, the use of stucco in buildings and often decorative use of iron [fr. M.L. *regentia*]

re·gen·er·a·cy (ridʒénərəsi:) *n.* the state or quality of being regenerate

CONCISE PRONUNCIATION KEY: **(a)** æ, cat; ɑ, car; ɔ fawn; ei, snake. **(e)** e, hen; i:, sheep; iə, deer; ɛə, bear. **(i)** i, fish; ai, tiger; ə:, bird. **(o)** o, ox; au, cow; ou, goat; u, poor; ɔi, royal. **(u)** ʌ, duck; u, bull; u:, goose; ə, bacillus; ju:, cube. x, loch; θ, think; ð, bother; z, Zen; ʒ, corsage; dʒ, savage; ŋ, orangutang; j, yak; ʃ, fish; tʃ, fetch; 'l, rabble; 'n, redden. Complete pronunciation key appears inside front cover.

re·gen·er·ate 1. (ridʒénəreit) *v. pres. part.* **re·gen·er·at·ing** *past* and *past part.* **re·gen·er·at·ed** *v.t.* to give new life or vigor to ‖ to restore to moral or spiritual health ‖ (*biol.*) to grow (a new part) to replace a lost or injured one ‖ *v.i.* to become regenerate **2.** (ridʒénərit) *adj.* having new life or vigor ‖ spiritually or morally revived or restored ‖ (*biol.*) reformed or grown again [fr. L. *regenerare* (*regeneratus*), to be reborn]

re·gen·er·a·tion (ridʒenəréiʃən) *n.* a regenerating or being regenerated ‖ a spiritual rebirth ‖ (*biol.*) the regrowth or renewal of an organ, tissue or substance that has been lost or damaged [fr. F. *régénération* or L. *regeneratio* (*regenerationis*)]

re·gen·er·a·tive (ridʒénərətiv, ridʒénəreitiv) *adj.* of regeneration ‖ regenerating [fr. F. *régénératif* or M.L. *regenerativus*]

re·gen·er·a·tor (ridʒénəreitər) *n.* a device which uses the heat of combustion in a furnace to raise the temperature of the inflowing air or combustible gas

Re·gens·burg (réigənsbu:rx) (*Eng.* formerly Ratisbon) a communications center (pop. 131,800) of E. Bavaria, West Germany, on the Danube. Industries: mechanical engineering, light manufactures. Gothic cathedral (13th-16th cc.), town hall (14th c.). University

re·gent (rí:dʒənt) **1.** *adj.* (placed after the noun) acting as regent, *a prince regent* **2.** *n.* a person appointed to rule during the minority, absence or physical or mental disability of a monarch ‖ one of a governing board, esp. of a university [F. *régent* or fr. L. *regens* (*regentis*) fr. *regere,* to rule]

Re·ger (réigər), Max (1873-1916), German composer, esp. for the organ. He also wrote chamber and orchestral music. He adapted classical forms to the Romantic idiom

reg·gae (régei) *n.* Jamaican rock music with pulsating blues style, often with a political or religious message derived from Rastafarian beliefs. *Cf* RASTAFARIAN

Reg·gio di Ca·la·bria (réddʒɔdi:kɑlɑ́brjɑ) a port (pop. 150,000) of Calabria, Italy, on the Straits of Messina, rebuilt after an earthquake (1908). Manufactures: perfumes, silk goods

Reg·gio nell' E·mi·lia (réddʒɔnelemí:ljɑ) an agricultural market (pop. 130,159) of Emilia-Romagna, Italy, in the Po Valley: food processing, mechanical engineering, clothing

reg·i·cid·al (redʒisáid'l) *adj.* pertaining to regicide or a regicide

reg·i·cide (rédʒisaid) *n.* a person who kills a monarch, esp. the monarch to whom he is subject ‖ the crime of killing a monarch **Reg·i·cide** (*Eng. hist.*) any of the judges who condemned Charles I to death (1649) ‖ (*F. hist.*) any of the members of the National Convention who voted (1792) for the execution of Louis XVI [fr. L. *rex* (*regis*), king + *caedere,* to kill]

re·gime, ré·gime (reiʒí:m, rəʒí:m) *n.* a system of rule or government, *a republican regime* ‖ any systematic organizational control ‖ the length of time during which such a system or organization is in force ‖ a recurring pattern of prevailing conditions, activity etc., *climatic regime* ‖ the character of a river with respect to its rate of flow ‖ a regimen [F.]

reg·i·men (rédʒəmen, rédʒəmən) *n.* (*med.*) a regulated course of diet, exercise etc. for restoring strength and health or for keeping the body fit [L.=rule]

reg·i·ment 1. (rédʒəmənt) *n.* (*mil.*) an army unit, commanded by a colonel, and containing subunits: troops, batteries, battalions etc. ‖ a large number, *a regiment of ants* **2.** (rédʒiment) *v.t.* (*mil.*) to form into a regiment ‖ to assign to a regiment ‖ to subject to stultifying organization, *children should not be regimented* [fr. L. L. *regimentum,* rule, government]

reg·i·men·tal (redʒəmént'l) **1.** *adj.* of a military regiment **2.** *n.* (*pl.*) the uniform worn by a regiment [REGIMENT n.]

reg·i·men·ta·tion (redʒəmentéiʃən) *n.* the act of regimenting, esp. so as to produce a dull uniformity and stifle individual initiative ‖ a being so regimented

Re·gi·na (ridʒáinə) the capital (pop. 162,613) of Saskatchewan, Canada, an agricultural market: farm machinery, oil refining

Re·gi·o·mon·ta·nus (ri:dʒi:oumɒntéinəs) (Johann Müller, 1436-76), German astronomer. He advanced the study of algebra and trigonometry and introduced the use of tangents. He published his astronomical observations and calculations in his 'Ephemerides' for the years 1474-1506

re·gion (rí:dʒən) *n.* a large part of space, land, sea or air which has certain distinctive characteristics (e.g. of boundary, temperature, fauna or flora, configuration), *the solar regions, the arctic region* ‖ the space or area surrounding a specified place, *the London region* ‖ an area which is a unit of administration ‖ an area surrounding an organ of the body, *the lumbar region* **ré·gion·al** *adj.* **ré·gion·al·ism** *n.* [A.F. *regiun*]

regional planning coordination of more than one governmental agency in an area to meet common problems

reg·is·ter (rédʒistər) *n.* an official or formal list, *Lloyd's Register of Ships* ‖ an official record of births, marriages and deaths ‖ a book in which a record is kept, *a hotel register* ‖ an official document issued to the owner of a ship as evidence of her nationality etc. ‖ an automatic cash till, recording sums as they are paid in ‖ (*mus.*) the range of a voice or an instrument, or a part of this, *the chest register* ‖ (*mus.*) a set of pipes in an organ controlled by one stop ‖ a movable plate for regulating the draft into a furnace, fire grate etc. ‖ registration, registry, *port of register* ‖ an instrument recording speed, force etc. ‖ (*computer*) a short-term storage of limited capacity used to facilitate operations ‖ (*printing*) the correctness of fall in relation to one another of successive printings on a single sheet, or of the recto and verso of a leaf in relation to each other ‖ (*photog.*) correspondence in position between the focusing screen and the surface of the sensitive film or plate ‖ (*art, archit.*) a strip or layer e.g. of sculptural relief [F. *registre* or M.L. *registrum, regestrum*]

register *v.t.* to place on formal or official record ‖ to express or show (a feeling or emotion) ‖ to send (a letter etc.) through the mail under a system whereby for a fee the postal authority gives the sender a certificate of receipt and demands a certificate of receipt on delivery ‖ (of gauges, meters etc.) to record ‖ (*printing, photog.*) to make correspond exactly ‖ *v.i.* to enter one's name on a formal or official record ‖ to have one's name entered on a voters' list by following the procedure prescribed ‖ (*mus.*) to select pipe organ stops suitable for the piece to be played ‖ (*pop.*) to penetrate the mind, *he heard, but did it register?* ‖ (*printing, photog.*) to be in register, correspond exactly [fr. F. *registrer* or M.L. *registrare*]

registered nurse (*abbr.* R.N.) a fully qualified nurse who has passed a state examination ‖ (*Br.*) a state-registered nurse

register office a place where registration is made

register ton a unit of internal capacity for ships equal to 100 cu. ft

reg·is·tra·ble (rédʒistrəb'l) *adj.* able to be registered

reg·is·trar (rédʒistrɑr, redʒistrɑ́r) *n.* an official in charge of a register, e.g. in a university, or one responsible for recording births, marriages, deaths **rég·is·trar·ship** *n.*

reg·is·trate (rédʒistreit) *pres. part.* **reg·is·trat·ing** *past* and *past part.* **reg·is·trat·ed** *v.i.* to register pipe organ stops [fr. M.L. *registrare* (*registratus*)]

reg·is·tra·tion (redʒistréiʃən) *n.* a registering or being registered ‖ an entry in an official register ‖ a number of persons registered ‖ the selecting and adjusting of organ stops for a piece of music to be performed, or the selection made [fr. M.L. *registratio* (*registrationis*)]

reg·is·try (rédʒistri:) *pl.* **reg·is·tries** *n.* registration ‖ a register office ‖ (*Br.*) a registry office

registry office (*Br.*) a place where registration is made and where civil marriages take place

re·gius (rí:dʒəs) *adj.* (of a professorship at Oxford or Cambridge or certain Scottish universities) founded by the monarch, or requiring royal consent for an appointment to it to be made ‖ designating a professor holding such a chair [L.=royal]

reg·let (réglit) *n.* (*archit.*) a flat, thin molding [F. *réglet*]

reg·nal (régnəl) *adj.* of or pertaining to a reign or a monarch [fr. M.L. *regnalis*]

regnal day the anniversary of a monarch's accession to the throne

regnal year (used in dating State documents) the year dating from a monarch's accession

reg·nant (régnənt) *adj.* (of a queen, always following the noun) reigning as sovereign in her own right, not as consort [fr. L. *regnans* (*regnantis*) fr. *regnare,* to rule]

Re·gnard (renjær), Jean-François (1655-1709), French dramatist. His lively comedies include 'le Joueur' (1696)

Re·gnault (renjou), Victor (1810-78), French physicist and chemist. He made extremely precise measurements for his study of the physical, esp. thermal, properties of fluids. He also worked in the field of organic chemistry

Ré·gnier (reinjei), Henri de (1864-1936), French writer. His volumes of poetry include 'Sites' (1887) and 'les Médailles d'argile' (1900). His best known novel is 'la Double Maîtresse' (1900)

Régnier, Mathurin (1573-1613), French poet. His satires imitated the Latin poets, esp. Horace and Juvenal

reg·o·lith (régəliθ) *n.* mantlerock [fr. Gk *rhēgos,* blanket+*lithos,* stone]

re·gress 1. (rí:gres) *n.* a going back or returning ‖ a tendency to decline **2.** (rigrés) *v.i.* to move backwards ‖ to retrogress [fr. L. *regredi* (*regressus*), to go back]

re·gres·sion (rigréʃən) *n.* a regressing ‖ a reversion to earlier stages of personality development or to objects of infantile attachment ‖ (*biol.*) the return to an earlier or less complex form ‖ (*astron.*) movement of a heavenly body in a direction contrary to normal, esp. movement of a planet from east to west in the solar system [fr. L. *regressio* (*regressionis*)]

re·gres·sive (rigrésiv) *adj.* regressing or tending to regress ‖ (*biol.*) of, marked by, or caused by regression

re·gret (rigrét) *n.* the emotion arising from a wish that some matter or situation could be different from what it is. The emotion may be accompanied by sadness, remorse, disappointment, dissatisfaction etc., and may arise from something done or said or from some failure to do or say something, or be a response to a general situation, or be felt on behalf of someone else ‖ an expression of this emotion ‖ (*pl.*) a conventional expression of disappointment, esp. at refusing an invitation [F.]

regret *pres. part.* **re·gret·ting** *past* and *past part.* **re·gret·ted** *v.t.* to feel or express regret for **re·grét·ful, re·grét·ta·ble** *adjs.* [fr. F. *regretter,* origin unknown]

reg·u·lar (régjulər) **1.** *adj.* conforming to a rule of equal disposition in space or time, *houses built at regular distances from one another, occurring at regular times of the day* ‖ conforming to some standard pattern of proportion or symmetry *the crystal has a regular form* ‖ conforming to rules of procedure etc. ‖ customary, *this is not his regular job* ‖ disciplined, *regular habits* ‖ (*pop.*) real, complete, *a regular nuisance* ‖ (*eccles.*) subject to monastic vows or discipline, *the regular clergy* ‖ (*gram.*) having the normal type of inflection, formation etc., *a regular verb* ‖ (*math.*) obeying the same law throughout ‖ (*math.*) having equal sides and angles ‖ (of a customer, visitor etc.) frequently received over a long period ‖ (*bot.*) radially symmetrical, actinomorphic ‖ not varying, *keep up a regular stroke* ‖ (*internat. law,* of soldiers) recognized as legitimate combatants in warfare ‖ (*mil.*) of the standing army of a country **2.** *n.* one of the regular clergy ‖ a regular soldier **reg·u·lar·i·ty** (regjulǽriti:) *n.* [O.F. *reguler* fr. L. *regularis* fr. *regula,* rule]

reg·u·lar·i·za·tion (regjulərizéiʃən) *n.* a regularizing or being regularized ‖ an instance of regularizing

reg·u·lar·ize (régjuləraiz) *pres. part.* **reg·u·lar·iz·ing** *past* and *past part.* **reg·u·lar·ized** *v.t.* to make regular, cause to conform to a rule, principle etc.

reg·u·late (régjuleit) *pres. part.* **reg·u·lat·ing** *past* and *past part.* **reg·u·lat·ed** *v.t.* to control by rule, system etc. ‖ to adjust so as to make accurate, *to regulate a watch* ‖ to adjust as regards amount, rate etc., *they regulate the flow of water by the sluice gate* ‖ to arrange so as to adapt, *she regulates her hours to fit in with his* **reg·u·lá·tion 1.** *n.* a regulating or being regulated ‖ a rule **2.** *adj.* correct, prescribed, *regulation dress* **rég·u·la·tive** *adj.* **rég·u·la·tor** *n.* something which regulates ‖ a device in a timepiece for making it run faster or slower ‖ a mechanical device controlling temperature, pressure, the admission of steam or water etc. **rég·u·la·to·ry** *adj.* [fr. L.L. *regulare* (*regulatus*)]

regulatory gene (*genetics*) class of genes that specify whether a structural gene will function. *Cf* OPERATOR

Reg·u·lus (régjuləs), Marcus Atilius (*d.* c. 250 B.C.), Roman general, consul (267 B.C. and 256

B.C.). Captured (255 B.C.) by the Carthaginians in the 1st Punic War, he is said to have been sent on parole to Rome to negotiate peace but to have advised the senate against accepting the Carthaginian terms. On his return to Carthage he was tortured to death

reg·u·lus (régjuləs) *pl.* **reg·u·lus·es, reg·u·li** (régjulai) *n.* the impure metallic mass formed under the slag when ores are smelted ‖ the substance of such a mass [L. dim. of *rex* (*regis*), king]

re·gur·gi·tate (rigə́:rdʒiteit) *pres. part.* **re·gur·gi·tat·ing** *past* and *past part.* **re·gur·gi·tat·ed** *v.t.* to bring up (what has been swallowed) ‖ *v.i.* (*rhet.*) to gush or surge back

re·gur·gi·ta·tion (rigə:rdʒitéiʃən) *n.* a regurgitating or being regurgitated [fr. M.L. *regurgitatio* (*regurgitationis*)]

re·hab (rí:hæb) *v.* to rehabilitate a real property as a business or for one's own use. **—rehab·bing** *n.*

re·ha·bil·i·tate (ri:həbíliteit, ri:əbíliteit) *pres. part.* **re·ha·bil·i·tat·ing** *past* and *past part.* **re·ha·bil·i·tat·ed** *v.t.* to restore to rank, privileges, rights etc. lost or forfeited ‖ to vindicate, restore the reputation of ‖ to restore (e.g. something damaged, decayed or not functioning) to its previous good condition ‖ to restore (e.g. a disabled person or a criminal) to physical or mental health through training **re·ha·bil·i·tá·tion** *n.* [fr. M.L. *rehabilitare* (*rehabilitatus*)]

re·hash 1. (ri:hǽʃ) *v.t.* to serve up the same (food, arguments, ideas etc.) in a new guise **2.** (rí:hæʃ) *n.* the act or process of rehashing ‖ something which is the result of rehashing

re·hears·al (rihə́:rs'l) *n.* a rehearsing ‖ a trial performance

re·hearse (rihə́:rs) *pres. part.* **re·hears·ing** *past* and *past part.* **re·hearsed** *v.t.* to practice (a play etc.) before performing it for an audience ‖ to enumerate, *to rehearse a list of complaints* ‖ *v.i.* to practice a play etc. [O.F. *rehercer*, to harrow again]

Rehnquist (rénkwist), William Hubbs (1924-), U.S. Supreme Court associate justice (1971-86) and chief (1986-) justice. He graduated from Stanford Law School (1952) and practiced law privately in Phoenix, Ariz. from 1953. An assistant U.S. attorney general (1969-71), he was nominated to the Supreme Court by Pres. Richard M. Nixon in 1971. A conservative, Pres. Ronald Reagan nominated him to be chief justice in 1986, upon the retirement of Chief Justice Warren Burger. As an associate justice he wrote the majority opinions in 'Edelman v. Jordan' (1974) and 'Fitzpatrick v. Bitzer' (1976), both of which denied retroactive benefits for welfare recipients, and in 'Rostker v. Goldberg' (1981), which dealt with excluding women from the draft. In 'New York v. Quarles' (1984) and 'Hunter v. Underwood' (1985) he wrote for the Court regarding civil rights

Re·ho·bo·am (ri:əbóuəm) (*d.* c. 914 B.C.), king of the Hebrews (c. 932–c. 914 B.C.), son of Solomon. During his reign, the northern tribes seceded under Jeroboam I to form the kingdom of Israel

Reich (raik), Wilhelm (1897-1957), Austrian psychoanalyst known for his controversial theory of orgastic potency—that emotions of love and the pleasurable sensations form the basis of mental health. He taught in Vienna and Berlin (1927-33). During the 1940s and 1950s, in the U.S.A., he maintained that orgone energy was the basis of life energy and invented the orgone energy accumulator, a device that was banned. When he defied the ban he was arrested, convicted and imprisoned. He wrote 'Character Analysis' (1933) and 'The Mass Psychology of Fascism' (1933)

Reich *THIRD REICH

Reichs·rat (ráixsrɑt) the lower chamber of the German parliament (1871-1934)

Reich·stadt (ráixʃtɑt), duke of *NAPOLEON II

Reich·stag (ráixstɑx) the diet of the Holy Roman Empire ‖ the lower chamber of the parliament of the North German Confederation ‖ the lower chamber of the German parliament (1871-1945). The deliberate destruction by fire (1933) of the building in which this met was used by Hitler as a pretext for measures against the Communist party

Reid (ri:d), Thomas (1710-96), British philosopher. His teaching opposed both the idealism of Berkeley and the skepticism of Hume. His main work is 'Inquiry into the Human Mind on the Principles of Common Sense' (1764)

re·i·fy (rí:ifai) *pres. part.* **re·i·fy·ing** *past* and *past part.* **re·i·fied** *v.t.* to treat (an abstraction) as a real thing [fr. L. *res*, thing]

reign (rein) *n.* the power of a monarch ‖ some other power compared with this, *the reign of law* ‖ the period during which a monarch reigns [O.F. *regne, reigne*]

reign *v.i.* to hold royal office, to be monarch ‖ to be predominant, prevail, *confusion reigned* [O.F. *regner*]

re·ig·ni·tion (ri:igníʃən) *n.* (*electr.*) **1.** a process by which several counts are generated within a radiation-counter tube by a single ionization **2.** renewal of ionization after cessation of conduction

Reign of Terror *TERROR, the

re·im·burse (ri:imbə́rs) *pres. part.* **re·im·burs·ing** *past* and *past part.* **re·im·bursed** *v.t.* to compensate (a person) for money expended ‖ to repay (expenses) **re·im·búrse·ment** *n.* [fr. RE- + L. *inbursare*, to put into a purse]

re·im·port (ri:impɔ́rt, ri:impóurt) **1.** *v.t.* to import again (something previously exported in a raw state) **2.** *n.* a reimporting ‖ something reimported **re·im·por·tá·tion** *n.*

re·im·pres·sion (ri:impréʃən) *n.* a reprint from the original plates or type without correction

Reims (rɛ̃s) (*Eng.* Rheims, ri:mz) the chief town (pop. 177,369) of Marne department, France. Industries: champagne, wool textiles, mechanical engineering. Gothic cathedral (12th–late 13th cc.), Romanesque and Gothic abbey (11th-12th cc.), both damaged during the 1st world war. University (1547-1793, refounded 1961)

rein (rein) **1.** *n.* one of the two leather straps or ropes fastened to the sides of a horse's bit as a means of control ‖ a similar device used to control other animals ‖ (*Br., pl.*) a harness used to keep a small child close to its mother etc. when walking ‖ (*pl.*) a means of control or restraint, *the reins of government*, or power to control, *to hold the reins* **to draw rein** to halt one's horse **to give rein to** to allow (a horse, a person, one's imagination or desire etc.) to proceed without restraint **to keep a tight rein on** to keep under one's strict control **2.** *v.t.* (usually with 'in', 'up') to bring (a horse) to a halt or to a slower gait [O.F. *rene*]

re·in·car·nate 1. (ri:inkárneit) *pres. part.* **re·in·car·nat·ing** *past* and *past part.* **re·in·car·nat·ed** *v.t.* to cause to be reborn in a new body or a new form **2.** (ri:inkárnit) *adj.* born again in a new form **re·in·car·ná·tion** *n.* a reincarnating or being reincarnated

rein·deer (réindiər) *pl.* **rein·deer, rein·deers** *n.* any of several large subarctic deer of the genus *Rangifer*, inhabiting Northern Europe, Asia and America. They are domesticated, esp. in Lapland, and are used to draw sleighs and to provide meat and leather. Both the male and female have antlers, those of the male being broader and more sweeping [O.N. *hreindýri*]

Reindeer Lake (réindiər) a lake (area 2,436 sq. miles) on the northern section of the Saskatchewan-Manitoba boundary in central Canada

reindeer moss *Cladonia rangiferina*, fam. *Cladoniaceae*, a gray, tufted lichen that is the main food of reindeer and caribou in winter and is sometimes eaten by man

re·in·dus·tri·al·i·za·tion (ri:indʌstri:əlizéiʃən) *n.* 1980 government policy designed to make American industry competitively more efficient

re·in·force (ri:infɔ́rs, ri:infóurs) *pres. part.* **re·in·forc·ing** *past* and *past part.* **re·in·forced** *v.t.* to strengthen by the addition of something ‖ to support (an argument, suggestion) with facts, evidence etc. ‖ (*behavioral psych.*) to strengthen a tendency to act in a desired manner, esp. by a system of rewards

reinforced concrete concrete strengthened by having wire mesh, metal bars etc. embedded in it

re·in·force·ment (ri:infɔ́rsmənt, ri:infóursmənt) *n.* a reinforcing or being reinforced ‖ something that reinforces ‖ (*pl.*) extra men or material to strengthen a military force

Rein·hardt (ráinhɑrt), Max (1873-1943), Austrian theatrical producer, naturalized American (1943). He led (c. 1903-32) the German romantic school of producers and directed works by Shakespeare, Molière, Goethe, Strindberg, Ibsen and Shaw. His spectacular production of 'The Miracle', first presented in 1911, was one of his greatest successes

Reinsch (rainʃ), Paul Samuel (1869-1923), U.S. educator and diplomat. As U.S. minister to China (1913-9), he was highly respected by the new republican regime, which appointed him (1919) legal adviser

re·in·state (ri:instéit) *pres. part.* **re·in·stat·ing** *past* and *past part.* **re·in·stat·ed** *v.t.* to restore to a former position, state etc. **re·in·státe·ment** *n.*

re·in·sur·ance (ri:inʃúərəns) *n.* a reinsuring ‖ insurance taken out by an insuring company against loss ‖ the amount of this

re·in·sure (ri:inʃúər) *pres. part.* **re·in·sur·ing** *past* and *past part.* **re·in·sured** *v.t.* to insure again by transferring (a risk) to another company in whole or in part ‖ to insure again by accepting (such a transferred risk)

REIT (*acronym*) for real estate investment trusts (which see)

re·it·er·ate (ri:ítəreit) *pres. part.* **re·it·er·at·ing** *past* and *past part.* **re·it·er·at·ed** *v.t.* to repeat several times [fr. L. *reiterare* (*reiteratus*)]

re·it·er·a·tion (ri:itəréiʃən) *n.* a reiterating or being reiterated [fr. L. *reiteratio* (*reiterationis*)]

re·it·er·a·tive (ri:ítərətiv, ri:ítəreitiv) *adj.* repetitious [REITERATE]

re·ject 1. (ridʒékt) *v.t.* to refuse to accept, *to reject an offer* ‖ to cast or set aside as being unacceptable, faulty or useless, *the machine rejects badly worn coins* ‖ to eject from the stomach **2.** (rí:dʒekt) *n.* someone or something rejected [fr. L. *reicere, rejicere* (*rejectus*), to throw back]

re·ject·ant (ridʒéktənt) *n.* a natural insect-repellent substance in plants

re·jec·tion (ridʒékʃən) *n.* a rejecting or being rejected ‖ something rejected ‖ the action of the body to destroy foreign matter, e.g., transplanted tissue [F. *réjection* or fr. L. *rejectio* (*rejectionis*)]

rejectivism *MINIMALISM **—rejectivist** *n.*

re·joice (ridʒɔ́is) *pres. part.* **re·joic·ing** *past* and *past part.* **re·joiced** *v.i.* to feel joy ‖ *v.t.* to cause to feel joy **re·jóic·ing** *n.* joyfulness, esp. shared with others ‖ the action of someone who rejoices ‖ (esp. *pl.*) an instance or expression of joyfulness [O.F. *rejoir* (*rejoiss*-)]

re·join (ri:dʒɔ́in) *v.t.* to join again [fr. F. *rejoindre* (*rejoign*-) or fr. RE-+JOIN]

re·join (ridʒɔ́in) *v.t.* to reply, to retort ‖ *v.i.* (*law*) to reply to a charge, esp. to the plaintiff's replication [fr. F. *rejoindre* (*rejoign*-)]

re·join·der (ridʒɔ́indər) *n.* a reply, retort ‖ (*law*) the defendant's answer to the replication of the plaintiff [F. *rejoindre*, to join again]

re·jus·ti·fy (ri:dʒʌ́stifai) *n.* (*computer*) a command to justify the margins of the input after additions and deletions have been made

re·ju·ve·nate (ridʒú:vineit) *pres. part.* **re·ju·ve·nat·ing** *past* and *past part.* **re·ju·ve·nat·ed** *v.t.* to make as though young again ‖ (*geol.*) to restore (a stream), e.g. by uplift of the surrounding land, to a state of active erosion ‖ *v.i.* to become as though young again **re·ju·ve·ná·tion** *n.*

re·ju·ve·nes·cence (ridʒu:vinés'ns) *n.* a reviving, renewing of youthful characteristics **re·ju·ve·nés·cent** *adj.* [fr. older *rejuvenesce*, to become young again]

re·lapse 1. (rilǽps) *v.i. pres. part.* **re·laps·ing** *past* and *past part.* **re·lapsed** to fall back into ill health, crime or heresy **2.** (rilǽps, rí:læps) *n.* a relapsing or an instance of this [fr. L. *relabi* (*relapsus*), to slip back]

relapsing fever any of several related acute infectious diseases characterized by recurring fever and muscular pains. The fever occurs esp. in the tropics and is caused by a spirochete transmitted by lice and tick bites

re·late (riléit) *pres. part.* **re·lat·ing** *past* and *past part.* **re·lat·ed** *v.t.* to tell the story of, recount, narrate ‖ to show or establish a relation between ‖ *v.i.* to have or be in relation, *anything relating to his welfare concerns you* **re·lát·ed** *adj.* (of two or more things) having or bearing a relationship, *related subjects* ‖ in the same family through birth or by marriage, *distantly related* ‖ (*mus.*, of one key, chord etc. and another) in harmonic relation [fr. L. *referre* (*relatus*), to carry back, refer]

re·la·tion (riléiʃən) *n.* a recounting or narrating ‖ that which is recounted or narrated ‖ a relative by birth or marriage ‖ relationship by blood or marriage ‖ the way in which one thing is associated with another, *the two are in a simple relation numerically* ‖ the fact of being so associated, *he sees no relation between the two events* ‖ (*Br. law*) the laying of information before the attorney general by a plaintiff ‖ (*pl.*) the terms on which one person (state etc.) has dealings

CONCISE PRONUNCIATION KEY: **(a)** æ, *cat*; ɑ, *car*; ɔ *fawn*; ei, *snake*. **(e)** e, *hen*; i:, *sheep*; iə, *deer*; ɛə, *bear*. **(i)** i, *fish*; ai, *tiger*; ə:, *bird*. **(o)** o, *ox*; au, *cow*; ou, *goat*; u, *poor*; ɔi, *royal*. **(u)** ʌ, *duck*; u, *bull*; u:, *goose*; ə, *bacillus*; ju:, *cube*. x, *loch*; θ, *think*; ð, *bother*; z, *Zen*; ʒ, *corsage*; dʒ, *savage*; ŋ, *orangutang*; j, *yak*; ʃ, *fish*; tʃ, *fetch*; 'l, *rabble*; 'n, *redden*. Complete pronunciation key appears inside front cover.

with another person (state etc.) **in** (or **with**) **relation to** concerning, so far as concerns **re·lá·tion·al** *adj.* (*gram.*, of conjunctions, prepositions etc.) showing syntactic relation [F.]

re·la·tion·ship (riléiʃənʃip) *n.* the state of being related ‖ the mutual exchange between two people or groups who have dealings with one another ‖ kinship

rel·a·tive (rélətiv) **1.** *adj.* of something (a quantity, quality, truth, idea etc.) considered in reference to something else, *the mass of the earth, relative to that of the sun, is very small* ‖ comparative, not absolute ‖ pertinent ‖ (*gram.*) of a word that introduces a subordinate clause and refers to an antecedent (e.g. 'whom' is a relative pronoun in the phrase 'the man whom she saw') ‖ (*gram.*) of a clause introduced by such a word ‖ (*mus.*, of a minor key or scale) having the same key signature as a specified major key or scale ‖ (*mus.*, of a major key or scale) having the same key signature as a specified minor key or scale **2.** *n.* a person connected by birth or marriage with another person ‖ something that is relative ‖ (*gram.*) a relative pronoun [fr. F. *relatif* or L. *relativus*]

relative aperture the effective diameter of a camera lens expressed as a fraction of its focal length (*F-NUMBER) or as the ratio of the aperture to the focal length. Thus a lens with an aperture that is one eleventh of its focal length has a relative aperture of f/11 or 1:11

relative humidity the ratio between the actual amount of moisture in the air and that which would be needed to saturate the air at the same temperature, expressed as a percentage

rel·a·tive·ly (rélətivli:) *adv.* in a relative way, to a qualified degree or extent

rel·a·tiv·ism (rélətivizəm) *n.* (*philos.*) the doctrine that all we can know about things is the relations between them, i.e. that all knowledge is relative

rel·a·tiv·i·ty (relətíviti:) *n.* the state or quality of being relative ‖ a theory first formulated by Einstein (1905), and usually called the special theory of relativity (special relativity), which deals with the question of what may properly be understood by space and time, restricting the analysis to systems at rest or those moving with uniform motion (nonaccelerated) in a region free from gravitation. Its fundamental assumptions are (a) that the laws of physics are the same in any system regardless of its velocity and (b) that the velocity of light is a constant, independent of its source and of the system in which it is measured. By defining two systems, one at rest and one in motion, in terms of their space coordinates and their time coordinates, Einstein was able to show the relation between the usual physical quantities in the two systems, i.e. the effect of relative motion on observations of time, length etc. He found that; (1) the mass of a body depends upon its velocity (2) mass and energy are interconvertible (*MASS-ENERGY EQUATION) (3) a body moving with a given velocity appears to an observer at rest to be shortened in the direction of motion (*FITZGERALD CONTRACTION). The condition of nonaccelerated and hence gravitation-free systems in the special theory is too restrictive. When applied to gravitational systems it is found that no set of coordinates exists in which special relativity holds throughout a finite region. Einstein therefore sought to present the theory in a form that would include gravitation and be independent of the choice of coordinates. The result, the general theory of relativity (general relativity), presents a set of equations which meet these requirements and which show that the space described by them is curved in a way which depends upon the distribution of mass and energy in it, so that space and time near concentrations of mass differ from space and time great distances away. The general theory has been confirmed in a number of its predictions, esp. in astrophysics and astronomy

re·lax (rilǽks) *v.t.* to loosen, *to relax a hold* ‖ to make less strict, *to relax discipline* ‖ to lower nervous tension in, *to relax the upper torso* ‖ to diminish, *to relax one's efforts* ‖ *v.i.* to become less tense, esp. in nerves and muscles ‖ to become less strict, esp. in matters of discipline ‖ (of a person) to become less restrained, esp. in social relationships ‖ to cease to work, take relaxation [fr. L. *relaxare*]

re·lax·a·tion (ri:lækséiʃən) *n.* a relaxing or being relaxed ‖ a partial remission of a duty, punishment etc. ‖ a recreation, *driving fast cars was his main relaxation* [fr. L. *relaxatio* (*relaxationis*)]

re·lax·er (rilǽksər) *n.* a curly-hair straightener

re·lay (rí:lei) *n.* a fresh supply of people, animals or materials used to take the place of others when these are exhausted or have completed their assigned tasks ‖ (*elec.*) a device which enables a current in one circuit to open or close another circuit to the flow of a current ‖ a local battery used to enable telegraphic or telephonic signals to be transmitted over long distances ‖ a relaying, passing on ‖ a relay race or one of its divisions [fr. O.F. *relais*, a fresh supply of hunting hounds or horses]

re·lay (rí:lei, riléi) *v.t.* to pass on, *relay the news* ‖ (*radio*) to transmit (a program received from another transmitting station) ‖ (*elec.*) to control by using a relay ‖ to arrange in or supply with relays [fr. F. *relayer*]

re-lay (ri:léi) *pres. part.* **re-lay·ing** *past* and *past part.* **re-laid** *v.t.* to lay again

relay race a race between teams in which each team member, after covering a certain distance, is relieved by another team member

re·lease (rilí:s) *n.* a setting free or being set free from e.g. pain, duty or imprisonment ‖ a document stating that one is free, e.g. from prison ‖ a putting of information or a new film before the public ‖ something (e.g. information or a new film) put before the public ‖ (*law*) the surrender of a claim, right etc. to someone else ‖ (*law*) the document containing this surrender ‖ something which releases, e.g. a mechanical contrivance, *the release in an alarm clock* [O.F. *reles*, *relais*]

release *pres. part* **re·leas·ing** *past* and *past part.* **re·leased** *v.t.* to free (someone or something) from whatever had limited his or her freedom to act, move etc., *to release a prisoner* ‖ to free from care, pain, anxiety etc. ‖ (*law*) to surrender (property, a right etc.) to another ‖ to put (information, a new film etc.) before the public [fr. O. F. *relesser*, *relaissier*]

releasing factor (*physiol.*) a hormone that triggers the secretion of other hormones

rel·e·gate (réligeit) *pres. part.* **rel·e·gat·ing** *past* and *past part.* **rel·e·gat·ed** *v.t.* to demote to some inferior or obscure place, *the officer was relegated to the ranks* ‖ to pass (a matter requiring a decision) to someone else ‖ to assign or refer to a particular class or kind [fr. L. *relegare* (*relegatus*) fr. *re-*, again + *legare*, to send with a commission]

rel·e·ga·tion (religéiʃən) *n.* a relegating or being relegated ‖ an instance of relegating [fr. L. *relegatio* (*relegationis*) fr. *re-*, again + *legare*, to send with a commission]

re·lent (rilént) *v.i.* to become less severe in one's attitude, intention, judgment etc., esp. under the influence of love or pity **re·lént·less** *adj.* unmoved by love or pity ‖ unceasing, as if without mercy, *relentless pressure of work* [fr. L. *re-*, again + *lentus*, pliable]

rel·e·vance (rélivəns) *n.* the state or quality of being relevant **rél·e·van·cy** *n.*

relevance or **relevance ratio** (*computer*) the ratio of the number of items retrieved by an instruction to the number retrieved by a standard query. *Cf* RECALL RATIO

rel·e·vant (rélivənt) *adj.* closely related to a matter under consideration [fr. M.L. *relevans* (*relevantis*) fr. *relevare*, to raise again]

re·li·a·bil·i·ty (rilaiəbíliti:) *n.* the state or quality of being reliable

re·li·a·ble (riláiəb'l) *adj.* able to be relied on **re·lí·a·bly** *adv.*

re·li·ance (riláiəns) *n.* a relying ‖ readiness to believe in and depend on the good qualities of someone or something, *do not put too much reliance on his honesty*

re·li·ant (riláiənt) *adj.* having reliance ‖ trusting [RELY]

rel·ic (rélik) *n.* the material evidence of something which has ceased to exist ‖ a trace of something no longer in existence, practiced, believed etc. ‖ the body or a part of the body of a saint or martyr or something associated with him, set apart after his death for veneration ‖ (*pl.*, *rhet.*) the remains of a dead person [F. *relique*]

rel·ict (rélikt) *n.* (*rhet.*) a widow ‖ (*ecology*) a species which has the characteristics of an earlier stage of evolution and has survived unchanged [fr. L. *relinquere* (*relictus*), to relinquish]

re·lief (rilí:f) *n.* a freeing from military siege ‖ a freeing from or alleviating of oppression, danger, distress, pain etc. ‖ the sensation of being set free from emotional tension, anxiety, fear etc., *a sigh of relief* ‖ something which breaks or relieves monotony, emotional tension etc. ‖ a release from work or duty ‖ someone to whom a person's work is handed over, esp. to insure continuity ‖ something, esp. money, food or clothing, given by state agencies or private persons to alleviate privation, *famine relief* [O.F.]

relief *n.* the extent to which, in a three-dimensional carving, sculpture, map etc., features are represented as raised above the general plane, *low relief* ‖ the quality of being or appearing to be raised thus, *lettering in relief* ‖ a carving etc. having this quality ‖ the appearance of solidity and spatial dimension in a painting ‖ (*geog.*) the parts of a land surface raised above the surrounding lowlands ‖ the difference of level between the top of the works and the bottom of the ditch in a fortification [fr. Ital. *rilievo* and F. *relief*]

relief map a map which indicates altitude, either by actual three-dimensional representation or by using colors, shading etc.

re·lieve (rilí:v) *pres. part.* **re·liev·ing** *past* and *past part.* **re·lieved** *v.t.* to alleviate (pain, distress, anxiety etc.) ‖ to free (someone) from pain, distress, anxiety etc. ‖ to rescue (a besieged city) ‖ (*pop.*, with 'of') to rob, *to relieve someone of his wallet* ‖ to provide a contrast, make less monotonous ‖ to replace (someone on duty), *to relieve a sentry* ‖ to give relief to (oneself) by passing water or emptying the bowels [fr. O.F. *relever*]

re·li·gion (rilídʒən) *n.* man's expression of his acknowledgment of the divine ‖ a system of beliefs and practices relating to the sacred and uniting its adherents in a community, e.g. Judaism, Christianity ‖ adherence to such a system, *a man without religion* ‖ something which has a powerful hold on a person's way of thinking, interests etc., *football is his religion* ‖ monastic life, *his name in religion was Damian* [A.F. *religiun* and O.F. *religion* or fr. L. *religio* (*religionis*)]

—The major extant religions emerged in the following order: Hinduism (in India) and Shintoism (in Japan) 3rd millennium B.C., Judaism (in Palestine) 13th c. B.C., Zoroastrianism (in Persia) 7th c. B.C., Taoism and Confucianism (in China) and Jainism and Buddhism (in India, with roots in Hinduism) 6th c. B.C., Christianity (in Palestine with roots in Judaism) 1st c. A.D., Islam (in Arabia, with roots in Judaism) 7th c., Sikhism (in India, with roots in Hinduism) 16th c., Bahaism (in Persia, with roots in Islam) 19th c.

Religion, Wars of a series of civil wars (1562-3, 1567-8, 1568-70, 1572-3, 1574-6, 1576-7, 1580, 1585-98) in France. Basically a Huguenot struggle for freedom of worship, they developed into political wars between the monarchy and the houses of Guise and Bourbon. The main Huguenot leaders were Condé, Coligny and Henri de Navarre (later Henri IV). The Catholics were led by Henri, duc de Guise, who formed (1576) the Holy League. Catherine de' Medici and her sons, François II, Charles IX and Henri III, intrigued mainly on behalf of the Catholics. Many Huguenots were killed in the Massacre of St Bartholomew (1572), but the Huguenot cause triumphed after Henri IV succeeded to the throne (1589). Freedom of worship was granted in the Edict of Nantes (1598)

re·lig·i·os·i·ty (rilidʒi:ɔ́siti:) *n.* morbid or excessive concern with religion in its formal expressions, or the practice of a merely superficial religion [fr. L.L. *religiositas*]

re·li·gious (rilídʒəs) **1.** *adj.* of, pertaining to, or concerned with religion ‖ faithful in religion ‖ associated with the practice of religion, *a religious rite* ‖ (of behavior) governed by principles adhered to as strictly as if they were those of a religion, *a religious regard for accuracy* ‖ of or pertaining to a monastic order **2.** *pl.* **re·li·gious** *n.* someone who has made monastic vows [A.F. *religius*, O.F. *religious* or fr. L. *religiosus*]

re·lin·quish (rilíŋkwiʃ) *v.t.* to give up, renounce, *to relinquish a right* ‖ to let go of, cease to hold in the hand **re·lín·quish·ment** *n.* [fr. O.F. *relinquir* (*relinquiss-*)]

rel·i·quar·y (rélikweri:) *pl.* **rel·i·quar·ies** *n.* a receptacle in which a sacred relic or relics are kept [F. *reliquaire*]

rel·ish (réliʃ) **1.** *v.t.* to take pleasure in (food or drink) ‖ to enjoy heartily, *to relish a good joke* **2.** *n.* keen enjoyment, *to do something with relish* ‖ a savory embellishment (e.g. chutney, pickles) to a dish [O.F. *reles, relais,* something remaining]

re·luc·tance (rilʌ́ktəns) *n.* an emotional or mental opposition to a course of action, *he did it with reluctance* ‖ the property of a magnetic circuit expressed by the ratio of the magnetic potential difference to the magnetic flux. It is analogous to the resistance of an electric circuit

re·luc·tant (rilʌ́ktənt) *adj.* marked by or showing reluctance [fr. L. *reluctans* (*reluctantis*) fr. *reluctari,* to resist]

re·ly (rilái) *pres. part.* **re·ly·ing** *past* and *past part.* **re·lied** *v.i.* (with 'on' or 'upon') to depend absolutely, *they relied on the weekly boat for their supplies* ‖ to place one's complete confidence in and make no alternative provision, *he relied on his subordinate to prepare the report* [fr. O.F. *relier,* to bind together]

rem (*acronym*) for roentgen equivalent man, a unit of measurement of ionizing radiation that, when absorbed by a human being or other mammal, produces a physiological effect equivalent to that produced by the absorption of one roentgen of X-ray or gamma radiation

REM (*acronym*) for rapid eye movement (which see)

re·main (riméin) *v.i.* to stay behind ‖ to stay in the same place ‖ to be left, *nothing remains to be done* ‖ to continue in a certain state, *to remain calm in a crisis* [A.F. *remeyn-, remayn-,* stem of O.F. *remanoir*]

re·main·der (riméindər) **1.** *n.* the portion which remains when part has been taken away ‖ (*math.*) the number remaining after subtraction or division ‖ (*law*) the right to inherit a title, rank etc. upon the death of the holder ‖ (*law*) an interest in property which comes to someone upon the termination of a previous estate and that was devised at the same time as the estate ‖ a copy of a book withdrawn from normal sale and offered for sale at a reduced price **2.** *v.t.* to withdraw (books) from normal sale and offer them for sale at a reduced price [A.F.]

re·mains (riméinz) *pl. n.* the part which is left after the ravages of e.g. time, weather or destruction, *the remains of an ancient fort* ‖ the part which is left over, *the remains of a meal* ‖ (in funeral contexts) a dead human body ‖ the writings left unpublished at the time of an author's death, *literary remains* [O.F. *remain*]

re·make 1. (ri:méik) *v.t. pres. part.* **re·mak·ing** *past* and *past part.* **re·made** (ri:méid) to make again, esp. in a new form or to a new plan ‖ (*movies*) to make (a film) using the same story as that of an old film **2.** (rí:meik) *n.* (*movies*) a remade film

re·man (ri:mǽn) *pres. part.* **re·man·ning** *past* and *past part.* **re·manned** *v.t.* to furnish (e.g. a ship) with a new complement of men

re·mand (ri:mǽnd, ri:mánd) **1.** *v.t.* to order back into custody until brought before a court of law for trial ‖ to release on bail pending trial ‖ (*law*) to order back for further action, *the appellate court remanded the case to the trial court* **2.** *n.* a remanding or being remanded ‖ an order to remand a person [fr. F. *remander*]

rem·a·nence (rémənəns) *n.* (*phys.*) the residual magnetism of a ferromagnetic substance when the magnetizing field is reduced to zero (cf. COERCIVE FORCE) [fr. L. *remanens* (*remanentis*) fr. *remanere,* to remain]

re·mark (rimárk) *n.* a brief spoken or written statement expressing an opinion on something noticed or observed **to escape remark** to pass unnoticed [fr. F. *remarque*]

remark *v.t.* to make as a remark ‖ *v.i.* (with 'on' or 'upon') to make a remark [fr. F. *remarquer*]

re·mark·a·ble (rimárkəb'l) *adj.* exceptional, unusual enough to arouse notice, *remarkable linguistic ability, remarkable obstinacy* **re·márk·a·bly** *adv.* [fr. F. *remarquable*]

Remarque (rəmárk), Erich Maria (1898-1970), German writer whose well known work 'All Quiet on the Western Front' (1929) dealt with the 1st world war. The Nazis banned his books in 1933, and when they revoked his citizenship in 1938, he emigrated to the U.S.A. His other works include 'The Road Back' (1931), 'Three Comrades' (1938), 'Arc de Triomphe' (1946), 'Spark of Life' (1952) and 'The Night in Lisbon' (1963)

re·marque (rimárk) *n.* a mark, usually a marginal sketch, indicating the stage reached in engraving a plate ‖ an impression taken from a plate bearing such a mark [F.]

Rem·brandt (rémbrænt, rémbrɑnt) (Rembrɑndt Harmenszoon van Rijn, 1609-69), Dutch baroque painter and etcher, one of the greatest masters of European art. He became famous and successful esp. as a portrait painter in the rich bourgeois society of 17th-c. Holland. But as his art matured the portraits became less flattering, less obviously brilliant, and patronage declined. The most obvious characteristic of Rembrandt's art is the use of a single, hidden source of light falling like a shaft into spacious shadows, creating a single focus, or reflected from a few highlights. The tones are somber but more jewellike because of the contrast of light and shade. The subject is often motionless, but again made more dramatic by this contrast. There is a love of exotic costume (turban, golden helmet, plume, rich robe) and of striking architecture (vault or pillar lost in shadow at the top of the picture and dramatically defining the human groups below), but these are used as settings for human experience. No artist saw more clearly or realized more deftly the poignant human meaning of a biblical scene. The drama is never merely theatrical. It is felt as truth and marvelously captured, especially in the easy, amazingly fast line of the drawing, or the etchings. The bodily pose and facial expression belie in their homeliness and truth the grandeur of the trappings. Especially in portraits of the aging, and in his many self-portraits, he saw the battered vessel of a hard-won spirituality, beyond pity

re·me·di·a·ble (rimí:di:əb'l) *adj.* able to be remedied [fr. F. *remédiable* or fr. L. *remediabilis*]

re·me·di·al (rimí:di:əl) *adj.* of that which serves to remedy, *remedial treatment*

rem·e·dy (rémidi:) *pl.* **rem·e·dies** *n.* something which corrects a fault, error or evil ‖ a medicine or application which relieves or cures a disease or other physical affliction ‖ (*coinage*) the margin of tolerance permitted as to weight or purity ‖ (*law*) legal redress, restitution [A.F. *remedie*]

rem·e·dy (rémidi:) *pres. part.* **rem·e·dy·ing** *past* and *past part.* **rem·e·died** *v.t.* to correct by removing a fault, error or evil ‖ to heal or cure [O.F. *remedier*]

re·mem·ber (rimémbər) *v.t.* to bring back to mind by an effort of will, *he could not remember your name* ‖ to have (something) come into one's memory again by chance, *she suddenly remembered that the kettle was on* ‖ to retain in the conscious mind, *remember to keep your shoulders back* ‖ to bear (a person) in mind as deserving a gift, attention etc., *to remember a friend on his birthday* ‖ to leave (a person) a legacy, *he remembered her in his will* ‖ to mention (a person) to another as sending greetings, *please remember me to him* ‖ to give a gratuity to [fr. O.F. *remembrer*]

re·mem·brance (rimémbrəns) *n.* a remembering ‖ the condition of retaining in the conscious mind, *to have something in remembrance* ‖ memory, the ability to recall the past ‖ the period over which the memory extends ‖ something which recalls a person, event etc. to the memory, *please accept this as a remembrance of me* ‖ (*pl.*) greeting conveyed on one's behalf [F.]

Re·mem·branc·er (rimémbrənsər) *n.* (*Br.*) an officer of the Supreme Court of Judicature whose duty is to collect debts owed to the sovereign

Rem·en·dur (rémendər) *n.* a cobalt-iron-vanadium alloy with high magnetic retention (remanence) that is malleable and ductible, developed by Bell Laboratories

re·mex (rí:meks) *pl.* **rem·i·ges** (remidʒi:z) *n.* one of the primary or secondary quill feathers of a bird's wing [L.= a rower]

Re·mi (reimi:), St (c. 437–c. 533), bishop of Reims (c. 458–c. 533), apostle of the Franks. He baptized Clovis (c. 496). Feast: Oct. 1

re·mind (rimáind) *v.t.* to cause (a person) to remember **re·mínd·er** *n.*

Rem·ing·ton (rémiŋtən), Eliphalet (1793-1861), U.S. inventor, gunsmith, and arms manufacturer. He supplied the U.S. army with rifles in the Mexican War and his firm held many government contracts during the Civil War. The firm began (1870) to manufacture sewing machines and (1873) typewriters

Remington, Frederic Sackrider (1861-1909), U.S. artist whose works depicted the Wild West. After traveling through the West as a young man, he settled (1891) in New Rochelle, N.Y., and painted and sculpted in clay for bronze casting, taking time out to serve as an illustrator and correspondent in Cuba for a magazine during the Spanish-American War (1898). His works include numerous book illustrations and the sculptures 'Trooper of the Plains' (1868), 'Bronco Buster' (1895) and 'Comin' through the Rye' (1902)

rem·i·nisce (reminís) *pres. part.* **rem·i·nisc·ing** *past* and *past part.* **rem·i·nisced** *v.i.* to recall memories of past events, esp. in relating them to others [REMINISCENCE]

rem·i·nis·cence (reminís'ns) *n.* something which is remembered ‖ (*pl.*) personal memories of past events ‖ reminiscing, *evenings given up to reminiscence* ‖ something which reminds one of someone or something else [F. *réminiscence* or fr. L.L. *reminiscentia*]

rem·i·nis·cent (reminís'nt) *adj.* indulging in memories ‖ (with 'of') apt to call up memories, *it is reminiscent of his earlier book* [fr. L. *reminiscens* (*reminiscentis*) fr. *reminisci,* to remember]

re·mise (rimí:z) **1.** *n.* (*fencing*) the second of two thrusts made on one lunge **2.** *v. pres. part.* **re·mis·ing** *past* and *past part.* **re·mised** *v.i.* (*fencing*) to make a remise ‖ (rimáiz) *v.t.* (*law*) to give or release (property) to another person [F.=restoration]

re·miss (rimís) *adj.* neglectful of doing one's duty or work efficiently ‖ marked by such negligence [fr. L. *remittere* (*remissus*), to send back]

re·mis·si·ble (rimísəb'l) *adj.* able to be remitted [F. *rémissible* or fr. L. *remissibilis*]

re·mis·sion (rimíʃən) *n.* forgiveness, *the remission of sins* ‖ a decrease in the magnitude of a force etc. ‖ a remitting of a debt, fine etc. [O.F.]

re·mis·sive (rimísiv) *adj.* characterized by remission [fr. M.L. *remissivus*]

re·mit (rimít) *pres. part.* **re·mit·ting** *past* and *past part.* **re·mit·ted** *v.t.* to send (e.g. a decision or a report) to an authority for further consideration ‖ to return (a case) to a lower court ‖ to postpone ‖ to forgive (a sin) ‖ to waive (a debt, fine, penalty etc.) ‖ to send (money) by mail or other means ‖ *v.i.* to become less in force, intensity etc. [fr. L. *remittere,* to send back]

re·mit·tal (rimít'l) *n.* a remission [REMIT]

re·mit·tance (rimít'ns) *n.* the sending of money ‖ the money sent [REMIT]

remittance man (esp. *Br.*) a man living abroad on money sent to him from home

re·mit·tent (rimít'nt) *adj.* abating at intervals; *a remittent fever* [fr. L. *remittens* (*remittentis*) fr. *remittere,* to send back]

re·mit·ter (rimítər) *n.* (*law*) the substitution of a more valid claim to property than the claim under which a person is holding it ‖ (*law*) the remitting of a case to another court [fr. REMIT, (obs.) to surrender (a claim or property)]

rem·nant (rémnənt) *n.* a small remaining part, number, amount etc., *the last remnants of his self-control* ‖ a piece, esp. the end piece, of a roll of fabric remaining unused or unsold [fr. older *remenant* fr. O.F. *remenoir,* to remain]

re·mod·el (ri:mɒ́d'l) *v.t. pres. part.* **re·mod·el·ing,** esp. *Br.* **re·mod·el·ling** *past* and *past part.* **re·mod·eled,** esp. *Br.,* **re·mod·elled** to give new shape or form to

Re·món Can·te·ra (remɔ́nkɑntéru), José Antonio (1908-55), Panamanian soldier and president of the Republic (1952-5). He was assassinated

re·mon·e·ti·za·tion (ri:mʌnitizéiʃən, ri:mɒnitizéiʃən) *n.* a remonetizing or being remonetized

re·mon·e·tize (ri:mʌ́nitaiz, ri:mɒ́nitaiz) *pres. part.* **re·mon·e·tiz·ing** *past* and *past part.* **re·mon·e·tized** *v.t.* to make (a metal) legal again as the basis of coinage

re·mon·strance (rimɒnstrəns) *n.* a remonstrating or an instance of this ‖ (*Br. hist.*) a formal public statement of protest against wrongs (*GRAND REMONSTRANCE) **Re·mon·strance** (*hist.*) the document in which 46 Dutch Arminians set out their differences from the Reformed Church, addressing it to the States General of the Netherlands (1610) [O.F.]

Re·mon·strant (rimɒ́nstrənt) **1.** *n.* an Arminian of the Dutch Reformed Church deriving from those who presented the Remonstrance of 1610. The Remonstrants were banned in the Netherlands (1619–25) and were recognized as an independent Church (1795) **2.** *adj.* of or pertaining to these Arminians [fr. M.L. *remonstrans* (*remonstrantis*) fr. *remonstrare,* to remonstrate]

re·mon·strate (rimɒ́nstreit) *pres. part.* **re·mon·strat·ing** *past* and *past part.* **re·mon·strat·ed**

v.i. to express opposition or disapproval ‖ *v.t.* to say or urge in protest **re·mon·stra·tion** (ri:mɒnstréiʃən) *n.* **re·mon·stra·tive** (rimɒ́nstrətiv) *adj.* [fr. M.L. *remonstrare* (*remonstratus*), to remonstrate]

re·mon·tant (rimɒ́ntənt) **1.** *adj.* (of a rose bush) blooming more than once in a year **2.** *n.* a remontant rose bush [F. fr. *remonter,* to climb back up]

rem·o·ra (rémərə) *n.* any of several carnivorous fishes of *Echeneis* and related genera which attach themselves by a sucking disk to sharks and other large fishes and to ships. They inhabit warm seas [L. fr. *re,* back+ *mora,* delay]

re·morse (rimɔ́rs) *n.* the emotion associated with painful recollection of something one would prefer not to have done or said, usually because it hurt others **re·mórse·ful** *adj.* **re·mórse·less** *adj.* without remorse, without mercy ‖ not ceasing to cause pain or discomfort, *a remorseless wind* [O.F. *remors*]

re·mote (rimóut) *adj.* at a great distance in space or time ‖ far removed from a place, person etc. ‖ out-of-the-way, rarely frequented ‖ exhibiting great differences, *remote theories* ‖ (of an idea, intention, possibility etc.) very slight ‖ not closely related, *a remote cousin* [fr. L. *removere* (*remotus*), to move back]

remote bath (*computer*) data stored in peripheral units

remote control control exercised from some distance, usually by using an electrical circuit or radio waves ‖ a device by which this is effected

remote sensing data gathering from a great distance by infrared photography, radar, and other techniques

re·mount 1. (ri:máunt) *v.t.* to mount again **2.** (rí:maunt, ri:máunt) *n.* a fresh horse

re·mov·a·bil·i·ty (rimu:vəbíliti:) *n.* the state or quality of being removable

re·mov·a·ble (rimú:vəb'l) *adj.* able to be removed from a place or office

re·mov·al (rimú:vəl) *n.* a removing or being removed ‖ a discharge from office ‖ (*Br.*) the moving of furniture and possessions out of one's old home to a new one ‖ a change of residence

re·move (rimú:v) **1.** *pres. part.* **re·mov·ing** *past* and *past part.* **re·moved** *v.t.* to move from a place ‖ to eliminate, *he removed all traces of having been there* ‖ to take off, *remove your hat* ‖ to dismiss from office or to transfer to another post ‖ (*Br.*) to transfer (one's personal effects) from one dwelling to another ‖ *v.i.* (*Br.*) to change one's place of residence **2.** *n.* (*fig.*) a degree of difference, *it is many removes from what he would like* ‖ a specified distance in relationship, *a cousin at first remove* **re·móved** *adj.* distant by a specified number of degrees of relationship, a *second cousin once removed* ‖ remote, distant **re·móv·er** *n.* [O.F. *remeuvoir, remouvoir*]

Rem·scheid (rémʃait) a town (pop. 129,300) of North Rhine-Westphalia, West Germany, in the Ruhr: tool and dye making, cutlery, metallurgy, chemicals

Rem·sen (rémsən), Ira (1846-1927), U.S. chemist, best known for his research in organic chemistry, esp. on saccharin. He founded the department of chemistry at Johns Hopkins and served (1901-13) as the university's second president

REM sleep (*physiol.*) deep sleep pattern in which rapid eye movement takes place, characterized by sudden electroencephalograph arousal, slowing of heart rate, and dreams. *also* paradoxical sleep

re·mu·ner·ate (rimjú:nəreit) *pres. part.* **re·mu·ner·at·ing** *past* and *past part.* **re·mu·ner·at·ed** *v.t.* to pay money, or make a gift, to (someone) in return for his services ‖ to compensate for (an expenditure of time, trouble or money) **re·mu·ner·á·tion** *n.* a remunerating ‖ the money or gift received by the person remunerated **re·mú·ner·a·tive** *adj.* paying, producing a good profit or carrying a good salary [fr. L. *remunerari* (*remuneratus*), to reward]

Remus *ROMULUS AND REMUS

ren·ais·sance (rénisɑns, rẹnisɑ́ns, rənesɑ̃s) *n.* a revival or rebirth **Ren·ais·sance 1.** *n.* the artistic, literary and scientific revival which originated in Italy in the 14th c. and which influenced the rest of Europe in a great variety of ways in the next two centuries. Broadly, it was typified by the spread of humanism, a return to classical values and the beginning of objective scientific inquiry ‖ this period of history, considered as intermediate between the Middle Ages and modern times **2.** *adj.* of or relating to the Renaissance or its style in art, architecture, music etc. [F.]

—The term 'Renaissance' was given currency in the 19th c. by Burckhardt, who emphasized the contrast between the Church-centered culture of the Middle Ages and the new sense of the primacy of personality of 14th-c. Italy. More recent research sees the Italian Renaissance as the result of gradual change rather than as a break with the past, and emphasizes earlier cultural revivals in the Middle Ages. The political and economic situation of Italy in the 14th c. was peculiarly favorable to the development of the Renaissance. The presence of a wealthy leisured class of merchants and bankers made secular patronage of men of genius possible. The city-states were ruled by families (e.g. Medici, Sforza, Este) for whom lavish patronage of the arts was often a means of justifying their otherwise weak title to political power. In Florence in the 14th c., Petrarch and Boccaccio revived interest in humanist and classical learning, while Giotto brought a new realism to art. In the 15th c. the invention of printing, and the founding of libraries and academies by princes and popes, helped to spread the new ideas. Uccello, Fra Angelico, Botticelli and Pollaiuolo excelled in painting, Donatello and Ghiberti in sculpture and Brunelleschi in architecture. The Renaissance reached its height in the 16th c., esp. under the patronage of Julius II and Leo X, with Michelangelo, Leonardo da Vinci and Raphael in Rome and Giovanni Bellini and Titian in Venice. Ariosto and Tasso used Italian for epic poetry, and Machiavelli brought a new approach to political thought. Palestrina was the glory of Renaissance music. The Italian Wars (1494–1559) ended political stability, but were effective in spreading the Renaissance to other parts of Europe. In France the Renaissance gave rise, under the patronage of François I, to the chateaus of the Loire valley and to the writings of Ronsard and Rabelais, and, later, to those of Montaigne. In Germany and the Netherlands, the dominant literary figure was Erasmus, while the critical spirit of the Renaissance may be said to have contributed to the development of the Reformation. Dürer, Holbein and the Bruegel family dominated in the arts. In Spain the leading figures were El Greco, Cervantes and Lope de Vega. In England the influence of the Renaissance is seen in Colet and More as well as in Shakespeare and Marlowe. The new scientific spirit of inquiry was fruitful esp. in astronomy with the work of Copernicus and Galileo, and in the new studies of psychology, ethics, anatomy and philology. The Renaissance created a culture which, though based in large part on the imitation of the ancients, freed men to prove and enjoy the world in a way not possible under the medieval Church's dispensation. In this release lay the way of development of the modern world

Renaissance man a man of wide knowledge in many fields

Renaissance woman a woman of wide knowledge in many fields

re·nal (rí:n'l) *adj.* pertaining to or near the kidneys [F. *rénal* or fr. L.L. *renalis*]

Re·nan (rənɑ̃), Joseph Ernest (1823-92), French historian and critic. He studied for the priesthood but lost his faith and instead devoted himself to the history of languages and religions, and to scientific studies. His exegetical work strengthened him in his rationalism and his faith in science ('l'Avenir de la science', 1890, 'Histoire des origines du Christianisme', 1863-81). In his 'Vie de Jésus' (1863) he describes Christ as an 'incomparable man', but man only, not divine. He had great influence on students and young writers in the 1880s. He also wrote the autobiographical 'Souvenirs d'enfance et de jeunesse' (1883)

Re·nard (rənær), Jules (1864-1910), French writer. His bitter attacks on middle-class society are relieved by passages of poignant tenderness. His best-known novel is 'Poil de carotte' (1894)

re·nas·cence (rinǽs'ns) *n.* a renaissance, revival **Re·nas·cence** the Renaissance **re·nás·cent** *adj.* coming into existence again, *renascent militarism* [fr. L. *renascens* (*renascentis*) fr. *renasei,* to be born again]

rend (rend) *pres. part.* **rend·ing** *past* and *past part.* **rent** (rent) *v.t.* to split or tear violently ‖ to pull away, wrench out with great force ‖ to cause emotional pain to ‖ to divide into bitter factions ‖ *v.i.* to become torn or split **to rend the air** (of screams, bullets etc.) to pierce or shatter the silence [O.E. *rendan*]

rend·er (réndər) **1.** *v.t.* to give (what is due), *to render thanks to God* ‖ to submit (a bill) for payment ‖ to do (a service) ‖ to cause to become, *the blow rendered him unconscious* ‖ to melt (fat) ‖ to clarify (a fat) by melting ‖ to extract the fat from by melting ‖ (*building*) to cover with a render ‖ to translate ‖ to interpret, express artistically **2.** *n.* (*building*) a first thin coat of plaster or cement applied to a wall ‖ (*hist.*) a return in money, kind or service made by a tenant to his lord **rénd·er·ing** *n.* the process of melting or extracting fat ‖ (*building*) the application of a render ‖ an artistic version or interpretation ‖ a translation ‖ an architect's perspective drawing for a building [A.F.=to give back]

ren·dez·vous (rɑ́ndivu:, rɑ́ndeivu:) **1.** *pl.* **ren·dez·vous** (rɑ́ndivu:z, rɑ́ndeivu:z) *n.* an agreement to meet ‖ a place agreed upon for a meeting ‖ a meeting at an agreed time and place ‖ a place where people habitually gather, *a gourmets' rendezvous* **2.** *v.i.* to meet at an agreed time and place ‖ *v.t.* (esp. *mil.*) to assemble (e.g. troops, ships) at an agreed time and place [F. *rendez vous,* present or take yourselves]

ren·di·tion (rendíʃən) *n.* a translation ‖ an artist's interpretation of a dramatic part or piece of music [obs. F. fr. *rendre,* to render]

ren·e·gade (rénigeid) *n.* (used esp. in apposition) someone who throws over authority or allegiance and gives himself to another, usually opposed, allegiance, *a renegade priest, a renegade socialist* [fr. Span. *renegado,* an apostate]

re·nege (riníg, riní:g, rinég) **1.** *v.i. pres. part.* **re·neg·ing** *past* and *past part.* **re·neged** to go back on a promise ‖ to go back on an agreement, position etc. ‖ (*cards*) to revoke **2.** *n.* (*cards*) a revoke [fr. M.L. *renegare,* to deny]

re·new (rinú:, rinjú:) *v.t.* to make new again or as if new ‖ to begin again after an interval of time, *to renew one's efforts* ‖ to revive, reawaken, *to renew one's interest* ‖ to make (a contract) valid for a further period, *to renew a lease* ‖ to replace, replenish, *to renew stock* ‖ *v.i.* to become new or as if new again **re·néw·al** *n.* a renewing or being renewed

re·new·a·ble (rinú:əb'l) *adj.* replaceable naturally or by human activity, e.g., of forests

Ren·frew (rénfru:) a county (area 239 sq. miles, pop. 339,000) of S.W. Scotland. County town: Renfrew (pop. 18,000). Administrative center: Paisley

Reni *GUIDO RENI

re·ni·form (rí:nifɔrm, rénifɔrm) *adj.* (*bot.*) kidney-shaped [fr. Mod. L. *reniformis* fr. L. *ren* (*renis*), kidney + *forma,* form]

re·nin (rí:nin) *n.* a protein occurring in the kidney thought to increase blood pressure [fr. L. *ren* (*renis*), kidney]

Rennes (ren) the chief town (pop. 234,000) in Ille-et-Vilaine, France, the old capital in Brittany. Industries: mechanical engineering, textiles, food processing. Courthouse (17th c.), the former parliament of Brittany. University (1735)

ren·net (rénit) *n.* curdled milk from the stomach of an unweaned calf, used to curdle milk by coagulating the protein ‖ the membrane lining the stomach, esp. the abomasum of some young animals, esp. the calf, or a prepared extract of such a membrane. They are both used for curdling milk ‖ any natural or artificial product used for this purpose ‖ rennin [fr. obs. *renne* fr. RUN]

rennet casein casein (insoluble protein)

Ren·nie (réni:), John (1761-1821), Scottish civil engineer. He designed and built several bridges and docks in London

ren·nin (rénin) *n.* an enzyme of the gastric juice of young animals which coagulates the protein in milk [RENNET]

Re·no (rí:nou) a city (pop. 100,756) in Nevada on the Truckee River. Industries: mining, gambling, tourism (largely owing to the relative liberality of the state divorce laws). University of Nevada (1886)

re·no·gram (rí:nəgræm) *n.* a photographic record of the movement of a tagged radioactive renal excretion. *also* nephrogram **—renography** *n.* the process

Re·noir (rənwær), Jean (1894-1979), French film director. Among his films are: 'la Grande

CONCISE PRONUNCIATION KEY: **(a)** æ, *c*a*t*; ɑ, *c*a*r*; ɔ *f*aw*n*; ei, *sn*a*ke*. **(e)** e, *h*e*n*; i:, *sh*ee*p*; iə, *d*ee*r*; ɛə, *b*ea*r*. **(i)** i, *f*i*sh*; ai, *t*i*ger*; ə:, *b*i*rd*. **(o)** o, *o*x; au, *c*ow; ou, *g*oa*t*; u, *p*oo*r*; ɔi, *r*oy*al*. **(u)** ʌ, *d*u*ck*; u, *b*u*ll*; u:, *g*oo*se*; ə, *bacill*u*s*; ju:, *c*u*be*. x, *lo*ch; θ, *th*ink; ð, *bo*th*er*; z, *Z*en; ʒ, *cor*s*age*; dʒ, *sava*g*e*; ŋ, *oranguta*ng; j, *y*ak; ʃ, *f*i*sh*; tʃ, *fe*tch; 'l, *rabbl*e; 'n, *redd*en. Complete pronunciation key appears inside front cover.

Illusion' (1937), 'la Bête humaine' (1939), 'la Règle du jeu' (1941), 'The River' (1952)

Renoir, Pierre Auguste (1841-1919), French Impressionist painter. Working with Monet in the late 1860s, he painted from nature and also developed the broken-color technique (*MONET). His early paintings include many kinds of subject: portraits, flowers, nudes, modern life, landscapes. After 1882, when he first went to Italy, he supplemented the techniques of Impressionism with much careful working out of the elements of the picture, exploitation of limited (pink and red) color ranges etc. His later subjects are mostly female nudes. These differ from other Impressionist nudes in that there is a fine fleshiness in them, a solidity, and indeed sensuality

re·nounce (rináuns) **1.** *v. pres. part.* **re·nounc·ing** *past* and *past part.* **re·nounced** *v.t.* to refuse to have anything to do with, repudiate ‖ to give up, *to renounce a claim* ‖ to decline or abandon (a legal right) ‖ *v.i.* (*cards*) to fail to follow suit through inability to do so ‖ (*cards*) to revoke **2.** *n.* (*cards*) an instance of renouncing ‖ (*cards*) a revoking [fr. F. *renoncer*]

ren·o·vate (rénəveit) *pres. part.* **ren·o·vat·ing** *past* and *past part.* **ren·o·vat·ed** *v.t.* to make as good as new, *to renovate a house* [fr. L. *renovare* (*renovatus*)]

ren·o·va·tion (rənəvéiʃən) *n.* a renovating or being renovated [F. *rénovation* or fr. L. *renovatio* (*renovationis*)]

ren·o·va·tor (rénəveitər) *n.* someone who renovates or restores (e.g. paintings or furniture)

re·nown (rináun) *n.* public recognition, fame [A.F. *renoun, renun*]

re·nowned (rináund) *adj.* famous ‖ widely known, *renowned for his generosity* [fr. O. F. *renoumer*, to make famous]

rent (rent) *n.* a payment made usually at fixed intervals to an owner of land or property in return for the right to occupy or use it [O.F. *rente*]

rent *v.t.* to occupy or use (land or property owned by another), paying rent for doing so ‖ to allow another to occupy or use (one's land or property) in return for payment ‖ *v.i.* to command rent, *the house rents at a high sum* [fr. O.F. *renter*]

rent *past* and *past part.* of REND

rent *n.* the result of rending, e.g. a tear, hole or gap ‖ a schism [fr. obs. *rent* v., *var.* of REND]

rent·al (rént'l) **1.** *n.* a sum paid as rent ‖ income from rents ‖ a house etc. offered for rent ‖ a renting **2.** *adj.* pertaining to rent [A.F.]

rental library a library lending books for a fee

rent·er (réntər) *n.* someone who pays rent ‖ someone who permits occupation or use of his land or property in return for rent ‖ (*Br.*) a distributor in the movie business

rent-free (réntfrí:) **1.** *adv.* without payment of rent **2.** *adj.* occupied or used without payment of rent

ren·tier (rɑ̃tjei) *n.* someone whose income is drawn from his investments or from rents on property [F.]

rent-roll (réntroul) *n.* a list of properties which bring in an income from rent ‖ the total of this income, esp. as an indication of market value

Rentsch·ler (réntʃlər), Harvey Clayton (1881-1949), U.S. physicist. He pioneered (1922) in refining pure uranium from uranium salts. During the 2nd world war, while employed at Westinghouse Electric Corporation, he was the only man who could provide the three tons of pure uranium needed for the atomic bomb project

rent strike a protest action (as against lack of services) by tenants by withholding rents or placing the rents into a special fund, such rents to be paid upon the landlord's compliance with tenants' demands

re·nun·ci·a·tion (rinʌnsi:éiʃən) *n.* a renouncing, esp. the giving up of a pleasure or of a claim, right etc. ‖ very strict self-denial ‖ (*Br.*) a written statement embodying the giving up of a claim or right **re·nun·ci·a·to·ry** (rinʌ́nsi:ətəri:, rinʌ́nsi:ətouri:) *adj.* [fr. L. *renunciatio* (*renunciationis*)]

Ren·wick (rénwik), James (1792-1863), U.S. educator and engineer who became (1853) the first professor emeritus of Columbia University. He constructed the Morris Canal, connecting the Hudson and Delaware Rivers, and surveyed (1840) the disputed boundary between the U.S.A. and New Brunswick, Canada, which led to the Webster-Ashburton Treaty

re·o·pen (ri:óupən) *v.t.* to open again ‖ to make a fresh start on

re·or·der (rí:ɔ́rdər) **1.** *v.t.* to give as a reorder ‖ to reorganize ‖ *v.i.* to give a reorder **2.** *n.* a repeat order for goods previously supplied

re·or·gan·i·za·tion (ri:ɔrgənizéiʃən) *n.* a reorganizing or being reorganized

re·or·gan·ize (ri:ɔ́rgənaiz) *pres. part.* **re·or·gan·iz·ing** *past* and *past part.* **re·or·gan·ized** *v.t.* to organize again, usually by rearranging

re·o·vi·rus (ri:ouváirəs) (*med. acronym*) for respiratory enteric orphan virus, any of a group of relatively large (72 millimicrons) RNA viruses, that are parasitic for humans and most animals, and believed to cause intestinal ailments and tumors

rep, repp (rep) *n.* a strong fabric with a finely corded surface, used chiefly in upholstery [fr. F. *reps*, origin unknown]

re·paint 1. (ri:péint) *v.t.* to paint again **2.** (rí:peint) *n.* a repainting ‖ something repainted ‖ a repainted golf ball

re·pair (ripɛ́ər) *v.i.* (*rhet.*) to go to a specified place, esp. often or as a party [O. F. *repeirer, repairer*]

repair 1. *v.t.* to make (something) good, strong, whole etc. after damage, injury etc. ‖ to right (a wrong) or make good (a loss) **2.** *n.* a repairing or being repaired ‖ (often *pl.*) an instance of repairing or the result of this ‖ a state of good condition, *to keep in repair* **in good (bad) repair** in good (bad) condition [O.F. *reparer*]

re·pand (ripǽnd) *adj.* (of a leaf) having a wavy margin [fr. L. *repandus*, bent back]

rep·a·ra·ble (répərəb'l) *adj.* able to be repaired or remedied

rep·a·ra·tion (repəréiʃən) *n.* a putting into good condition again or being so repaired ‖ a righting of a wrong ‖ something done or paid as compensation for a wrong ‖ (*pl.*) the money or services paid by a defeated nation as compensation for the destruction and loss it has inflicted [O.F. *reparacion*]

rep·ar·tee (repɑrtí:, repɑrtéi) *n.* quick, witty exchange between two speakers, in which each speaker makes a reply which neatly destroys the force of what the other has just said ‖ the practice or art of making such replies [fr. F. *repartie* fr. *repartir*, to set out again]

re·par·ti·mien·to (repɑrti:mjéntɔ) *n.* an official act of distribution of Indian workers to Spanish colonists in Latin America, after the decline of the encomienda [Span.]

re·par·ti·tion (ri:pɑrtíʃən) *n.* distribution ‖ a fresh distribution

re·pass (ri:pǽs, ri:pɑ́s) *v.t.* to pass again ‖ to cause to pass again ‖ *v.i.* to pass again, esp. in the opposite direction **re·pas·sage** (ri:pǽsidʒ) *n.* a repassing ‖ the right to repass [F. *repasser*]

re·past (ri:pǽst, ri:pɑ́st) *n.* (*rhet.*) a meal ‖ (*rhet.*) the food eaten at a meal [O.F.]

re·pa·tri·ate 1. (ri:péitri:eit, ri:pǽtri:eit) *v. pres. part.* **re·pa·tri·at·ing** *past* and *past part.* **re·pa·tri·at·ed** *v.t.* to send back to the country of origin ‖ *v.i.* to go back to the country of origin **2.** (ri:péitri:it, ri:pǽtri:it) *n.* a repatriated person **re·pa·tri·á·tion** *n.* [fr. L.L. *repatriare* (*repatriatus*)]

re·pay (ri:péi) *pres. part.* **re·pay·ing** *past* and *past part.* **re·paid** (ri:péid) *v.t.* to pay back (money) ‖ to pay (someone) back ‖ to return (e.g. a service), *to repay someone's kindness* ‖ to recompense, *to be repaid for one's trouble* ‖ to requite, *he repaid the trick by setting his dog on them* ‖ *v.i.* to make repayment **re·páy·a·ble** *adj.* able or due to be repaid **re·páy·ment** *n.* a paying back or an instance of this ‖ the sum repaid [fr. O.F. *repaier, rapaier*]

re·peal (ripí:l) *n.* a repealing or an instance of this [A.F. *repel*]

repeal *v.t.* to cancel, revoke (a decision or enactment previously made) [fr. A.F. *repeller, repeler*]

re·peat (ripí:t) **1.** *v.t.* to say again, *to repeat a statement* ‖ to do or make again, *to repeat a visit* ‖ to say from memory or after someone else ‖ to say to another (what one has oneself been told), *to repeat gossip* ‖ to undergo again, *to repeat an experience* ‖ to cause or allow to recur, *the second room repeats the decorative motif* ‖ (of a student) to take (a course or term) again because of previous failure ‖ *v.i.* to say or do something again ‖ to occur again ‖ to vote more than once in an election **not to bear repeating** to be unworthy of being repeated **to repeat oneself** to say, write or do again what one has already said etc., or something very like it **2.** *n.* a repeating ‖ something repeated ‖ (*mus.*) a passage to be played twice ‖ (*mus.*) the symbol for this (:‖) **re·péat·ed·ly** *adv.* over and over again, *she told him repeatedly* **re·péat·er** *n.* someone or something that repeats ‖ a repeating watch or clock which strikes the last hour, quarter hour and the subsequent number of minutes when a spring is released ‖ a rifle, shotgun or pistol which can fire a number of times without reloading ‖ a person who repeats in an election ‖ a student who has to repeat a class or term ‖ (*telegraphy*) an automatic relay for switching a message from a weak circuit to a strong one [fr. F. *répéter*]

repeating decimal a recurring decimal

re·pel (ripél) *pres. part.* **re·pel·ling** *past* and *past part.* **re·pelled** *v.t.* to exert a force tending to move (a body) further away, *like magnetic poles repel one another* ‖ to drive back, *to repel an attack* ‖ to repress, *to repel a desire to turn and run* ‖ to discourage, *to repel an offer of friendship* ‖ to cause not to adhere, penetrate etc., *to repel moisture* ‖ to cause to feel aversion, to repulse, *the sight of such luxury repelled him* [fr. L. *repellere*]

re·pel·lent (ripélənt) **1.** *adj.* repelling, driving back ‖ causing aversion **2.** *n.* a preparation for repelling insects or pests ‖ a solution which makes a fabric resist moisture, liquids, etc. [fr. L. *repellens* (*repellentis*) fr. *repellere*, to drive back]

re·pent (rí:pənt) *adj.* (*bot.*) creeping ‖ (*zool.*) crawling [fr. L. *repens* (*repentis*) fr. *repere*, to crawl]

re·pent (ripént) *v.i.* to grieve for sins committed or for things sinfully left undone ‖ (often with 'of') to feel extreme regret for what one has done or forgotten or omitted to do, *he repented of his decision to lend the boy his car* ‖ to change one's mind and regret the original decision, *he thinks he has been clever but he will live to repent* ‖ *v.t.* to think with contrition of or do penance for, *to repent one's sins* [fr. F. *repentir*]

re·pent·ance (ripéntəns) *n.* the act of repenting ‖ a feeling of contrition or act of penance for sins committed [F.]

re·pent·ant (ripéntənt) *adj.* feeling repentance ‖ indicating repentance [F.]

re·peo·ple (ri:pí:p'l) *pres. part.* **re·peo·pling** *past* and *past part.* **re·peo·pled** *v.t.* to furnish (a region) again with people

re·per·cus·sion (ri:pərkʌ́ʃən) *n.* a recoil, e.g. of a gun ‖ a reverberation, echo ‖ a usually unanticipated and indirect reaction to some event, *nonratification of the treaty would have grave repercussions* ‖ (*mus.*, in a fugue) the reappearance of the subject and answer after an episode [F. *répercussion* or fr. L. *repercussio* (*repercussionis*)]

rep·er·toire (répərtwɑr, répərtwər) *n.* a collection of anecdotes, songs, plays, pieces of music etc. which a person or group of persons is able to present or perform ‖ an inventory of capabilities ‖ (*computer*) the operations that can be contained in a specific code [F. *répertoire*]

rep·er·to·ry (répərtɔri:, répərtouri:, *Br.* répətri) *pl.* **rep·er·to·ries** *n.* a repertoire ‖ any store or stock (e.g. of information) that can be drawn on [fr. L. *repertorium*, catalog, storehouse]

repertory theater, *Br.* **repertory theatre** a theater where a permanent acting company presents its repertoire of plays

rep·e·ti·tion (repitíʃən) *n.* a repeating or being repeated ‖ something done or said again ‖ the ability of a keyboard instrument to respond to the striking of the same note in rapid succession [O.F. *repeticion* or fr. L. *repetitio* (*repetitionis*)]

rep·e·ti·tious (repitíʃəs) *adj.* full of repetition, esp. boringly so [fr. L. *repetere* (*repetitus*), to repeat]

re·pet·i·tive (ripétitiv) *adj.* repeating or tending to repeat ‖ repetitious [fr. L. *repetere* (*repetitus*), to repeat]

re·phrase (ri:fréiz) *pres. part.* **re·phras·ing** *past* and *past part.* **re·phrased** *v.t.* to express again in a different way

re·pine (ripáin) *pres. part.* **re·pin·ing** *past* and *past part.* **re·pined** *v.i.* (*rhet.*, often with 'at') to feel or express discontent

re·pique (ri:pí:k) **1.** *n.* (*piquet*) the scoring of 30 points from the cards held before play begins **2.** *v. pres. part.* **re·piqu·ing** *past* and *past part.* **re·piqued** *v.t.* (*piquet*) to make this score against ‖ *v.i.* (*piquet*) to make this score [fr. F. *repic*]

re·place (ripléis) *pres. part.* **re·plac·ing** *past* and *past part.* **re·placed** *v.t.* to put back (something) in its original place || to take the place of (someone or something), *Smith replaced Brown* || to fill the place of (someone or something) with another, *he replaced Brown by Smith* **re·pláce·ment** *n.* a replacing or being replaced || someone or something that replaces || a person immediately available for assignment to a military or naval unit

re·plead·er (ri:plí:dər) *n.* (*law*) a second pleading || (*law*) the right to a second pleading

re·plen·ish (ripléniʃ) *v.t.* to fill again, *to replenish a glass* || to get a new supply of, *to replenish one's stores* **re·plén·ish·ment** *n.* [fr. O.F. *re-pliner* (*repleniss-*)]

re·plete (riplí:t) *adj.* gorged, *replete with food* || richly supplied or imbued, *replete with humor* || completely filled **re·plé·tion** *n.* [F. *replet* or fr. L. *replere* (*repletus*), to fill again]

re·plev·in (riplévin) **1.** *n.* (*law*) a replevying || (*law*) an action for replevying || (*law*) the writ by which goods or property are replevied **2.** *v.t.* (*law*) to replevy [A.F.]

re·plev·y (riplévi:) **1.** *v. pres. part.* **re·plev·y·ing** *past* and *past part.* **re·plev·ied** *v.t.* (*law*) to take possession of (disputed goods or property) subject to an undertaking to submit the dispute to a court and surrender the property if the court so decrees || *v.i.* (*law*) to take possession of goods, or property by replevin **2.** *n.* (*law*) a replevin

rep·li·ca (réplikə) *n.* an accurate copy of a painting, statue etc., esp. one made by the artist who made the original || someone or something very closely resembling someone or something else [Ital.]

rep·li·case (réplikeis) *n.* an enzyme that synthesizes RNA from DNA. **also** RNA polymerase —**replicate** *v.* —**replicative** *adj.* *Cf* DNA POLYMERASE, RIBONUCLEASE

rep·li·cate 1. (réplikit) *adj.* folded back on itself **2.** (réplikit) *n.* (*mus.*) a tone which is one or more octaves above or below another **3.** (réplikeit) *v.t. pres. part.* **rep·li·cat·ing** *past* and *past part.* **rep·li·cat·ed** (*biol.*) to repeat or duplicate (e.g. a procedure or experiment) **rép·li·cat·ed** *adj.* replicate [fr. L. *replicare* (*replicatus*), to fold back]

rep·li·ca·tion (replikéiʃən) *n.* (*law*) the plaintiff's reply to the defense || (*biol.*) a replicating or being replicated || repetition of an experiment under the same conditions, e.g., to verify the results || (*biol.*) reproduction of bacteriophage in order to enlarge itself || (*biol.*) division of cells for reproduction [O.F.]

rep·li·somes (réplisoumz) *n.* (*genetics*) fixed points in chromosomes at which genetic factors are transferred

re·ply (ripláí) **1.** *v. pres. part.* **re·ply·ing** *past* and *past part.* **re·plied** *v.t.* to say or write (something) in return, after a question, letter etc. || *v.i.* to say or write something in return || to act by way of a return, *he replied with a round of shots* || (*law*) to plead so as to deal with the case put forward by a defendant **2.** *pl.* **re·plies** *n.* a replying || something said, written or done in replying to a question, letter, action etc. || (*law*) the plaintiff's reply to the defense [fr. O.F. *replier*]

re·ply-paid (ripláipéid) *adj.* (of a telegram) having a reply by telegram paid for in advance by the sender || (of a letter or postcard, used esp. in publicity drives) for which the person to whom it is addressed bears the postage

re·port (ripɔ́rt, ripóurt) *n.* something reported, esp. a formal account of what has been said, seen or done || an unsubstantiated item of information or news || (*rhet.*) repute, *of good report* || a loud explosive noise, *the report of a firearm* || a periodic statement of a student's academic rating and sometimes his school conduct, sent to his parents [O.F. *report, raport*]

report 1. *v.t.* to give information about or relate (e.g. what one has seen or heard) || to repeat (a message) || to register a complaint about to someone in authority, *he reported the driver to the foreman* || to make known to the correct authority, *to report a theft to an insurance company* || to write an account of (some event etc.), esp. for publication || to tell about following inquiry, investigation etc., *to report the results of research* || to give a formal statement of || *v.i.* to make a report || to work as a reporter || to make one's arrival or presence known by presenting oneself, *he reported to the office at noon* [O.F. *reporter*]

report card a periodic report on a student's academic achievement etc. sent to his parents

re·port·ed·ly (ripɔ́rtidli:) *adv.* on the authority of what people are saying

re·port·er (ripɔ́rtər, ripóurtər) *n.* a person who reports, esp. one who writes an account of formal proceedings for the record || a person who writes accounts of events for publication, esp. in a newspaper

report stage the stage reached in parliamentary practice when a committee has considered a bill and reports its findings to the full assembly, between the second and third readings

re·pose (ripóuz) *n.* a state or condition of rest, esp. after work, activity or excitement || sleep || a state of tranquillity || a restful attitude || a restful effect, e.g. in painting [F. *repos*]

repose *pres. part.* **re·pos·ing** *past* and *past part.* **re·posed** *v.i.* to rest || to lie in a restful position || (*rhet.*) to lie in death, *to repose in state* || (with 'on' or 'upon') to have as a support or basis [fr. F. *reposer*]

repose *pres. part.* **re·pos·ing** *past* and *past part.* **re·posed** *v.t.* (usually with 'in') to place (trust, confidence etc.) in someone or something [fr. L. *reponere* (*repositus*), to replace]

re·pos·i·tor·y (ripɔ́zitɔri:, ripɔ́zitouri:) *pl.* **re·pos·i·tor·ies** *n.* a place where things are put for safekeeping || (*rhet.*) a burial vault || anything thought of as a place of storage [fr. obs. F. *repositoire* or L. *repositorium*]

re·pos·sess (ri:pəzés) *v.t.* to possess again || to put in possession again **re·pos·ses·sion** (ri:pəzéʃən) *n.*

re·pous·sé (rəpu:séi) **1.** *adj.* (of sheet metal) having a pattern in relief made by hammering the reverse face || of a pattern or design formed in this way **2.** *n.* metalwork so ornamented || the art of ornamenting metal in this way [F.]

repp *REP

rep·re·hend (reprihénd) *v.t.* to reprimand || to blame, be critical of [fr. L. *reprehendere*]

rep·re·hen·si·ble (reprihénsib'l) *adj.* (of an act or of conduct) that ought to be blamed or punished [fr. L.L. *reprehensibilis*]

rep·re·hen·sion (reprihénʃən) *n.* a reprehending [fr. L. *reprehensio* (*reprehensionis*)]

rep·re·sent (reprizént) *v.t.* to present an image of, *this drawing represents a rocking horse* || to describe as being of a certain kind, *he represented the hovel as 'a desirable residence'* || (*rhet.*) to point out, *he represented to them the folly of such a move* || to act on behalf of, *a lawyer represents his client* || to be the delegate of, esp. to a legislative assembly || to be a fair sample of, *his opinion represents that of the majority* || to be a symbol for, *∞ represents infinity* || to correspond to, *these notes represent eight hours' work* [fr. O. F. *représenter* or L. *repraesentare*]

re·pre·sent (ri:prizént) *v.t.* to present again

rep·re·sen·ta·tion (reprizentéiʃən) *n.* a representing or being represented || something which represents || (*law*) a statement accepted as true and as a reason for entering into a contract **rep·re·sen·tá·tion·al** *adj.* [F. or fr. L. *repraesentatio* (*repraesentationis*)]

rep·re·sen·ta·tive (reprizéntətiv) **1.** *adj.* serving to represent, esp. as being an example of or having the general character of some whole, *this painting is representative of his work* || of, marked by or based on a system of representation by elected delegates, *representative government* **2.** *n.* someone or something regarded as characteristic or serving to exemplify || a person who is appointed to act and speak for another person or for a country, company, group etc. || a traveling salesman || in the U.S.A., a member of the elected lower house of Congress (House of Representatives) or of a state legislature (capitalized when used with the representative's name) [fr. F. *représentatif* or M.L. *repraesentativus*]

re·press (riprés) *v.t.* to put down, *to repress an uprising* || to keep back, *to repress tears* || to hinder the natural expression or development of, *to repress a child* || (*psychol.*) to prevent (an idea, desire, memory etc.) from reaching the consciousness [fr. L. *reprimere* (*repressus*)]

re·pres·sion (ripréʃən) *n.* a repressing or being repressed || an instance of repressing || (*psychol.*) a process by which unattainable or unacceptable desires, impulses etc. are repressed || (*psychol.*) a desire, impulse etc. so repressed [fr. L. *repressio* (*repressionis*)]

re·pres·sive (riprésiv) *adj.* repressing or tending to repress

re·pres·sor (riprésər) *n.* (*genetics*) the product of a metabolic process between a regulator gene and a genetic operator that tends to halt synthesis of enzymes —**repress** *v.* —**repressible** *adj.* —**repressibility** *n.* *Cf* ENDUCER

re·prieve (riprí:v) **1.** *v. pres. part.* **re·priev·ing** *past* and *past part.* **re·prieved** *v.t.* to suspend the punishment of (a person), esp. punishment by death || to give temporary relief or respite to, e.g. from pain **2.** *n.* a reprieving or being reprieved || a revoking or commuting of a punishment, esp. of a death sentence || a document authorizing such a revocation or commutation || a temporary relief from pain or other ill [fr. older *repry*, prob. fr. F. *repris*, past part. of *reprendre*, to take back]

rep·ri·mand (réprimænd, réprimɑnd) *n.* a severe rebuke, esp. by someone in authority [fr. F. *réprimande*]

reprimand *v.t.* to rebuke severely, esp. using authority [fr. F. *réprimander*]

re·print 1. (ri:prínt) *v.t.* to print again **2.** (rí:print) *n.* a new copy of an article, book etc. made by printing it again without altering the type || an impression in quantity of a work made in this way || an edition of a work printed by a publisher other than the original one and made without alteration of the text || an offprint

re·pris·al (ripráiz'l) *n.* an injury inflicted in return for one suffered, or as vengeance || the act or practice of using some means of coercion other than war against another nation in order to secure redress against real or imagined injustices an instance of this [O.F. *reprisaille*]

re·prise (ripráiz, riprí:z) *n.* (*law*) an annual payment made as rent or other charge on an estate || (*mus.*) a repeated phrase, after an intervening section has been played [F.]

re·proach (ripróutʃ) *v.t.* to tell (someone) that he has acted wrongly, esp. when one would not have expected him to do so or because one feels hurt [F. *reprocher*]

reproach *n.* a reproaching || an expression of such reproaching || something which merits reproaching **to bring reproach on** to cause to feel disgraced **the Reproaches** part of the Good Friday ceremonies in Roman Catholic and some Anglican churches, consisting of antiphons and responses which recall what Christ did for man **re·próach·ful** *adj.* [F. *reproche*]

rep·ro·bate (réprəbeit) **1.** *adj.* of someone who pursues evil in preference to good || (*theol.*) condemned by God to eternal damnation **2.** *n.* a reprobate person **3.** *v.t. pres. part.* **rep·ro·bat·ing** *past* and *past part.* **rep·ro·bat·ed** to condemn severely, esp. as being evil || (*theol.*, of God) to condemn to eternal damnation **rep·ro·bá·tion** *n.* [fr. L. *reprobare* (*reprobatus*), to reprove]

re·pro·duce (ri:prədú:s, ri:prədjú:s) *pres. part.* **re·pro·duc·ing** *past* and *past part.* **re·pro·duced** *v.t.* to repeat exactly or very closely, *to reproduce Georgian furniture* || to produce (a new individual or new individuals of the same species) by sexual or asexual methods || to cause (a lost part or organ) to be replaced by the growth of a new one || to re-create (e.g. a memory) mentally || to quote the exact text of in writing or printing, *he reproduces extracts from her letters in his autobiography* || to make a copy of, esp. by mechanical means, and use the copy e.g. to illustrate a text || *v.i.* to produce a new individual or new individuals of the same species || (of music, paintings etc.) to be susceptible of recording, printing etc. by mechanical means, *the second movement reproduces very well*

re·pro·duc·i·ble (ri:prədú:sib'l, ri:prədjú:sib'l) *adj.* able to be reproduced

re·pro·duc·tion (ri:prədʌ́kʃən) *n.* a reproducing or being reproduced || a painting, piece of furniture etc. which is a replica of an original || the sexual or asexual process by which animals or plants produce new individuals

reproduction factor the ratio in a nuclear reactor between the number of neutrons produced and the number which vanish. If the factor exceeds unity, the chain reaction builds up until it is maintained at a constant level by reducing the factor to unity again

re·pro·duc·tive (ri:prədʌ́ktiv) *adj.* of or concerned with reproducing or reproduction [REPRODUCE]

reproductive system the system in man and other vertebrates, plants and some invertebrates relating to and effecting reproduction. In the human male it comprises the following organs: the testicles, the two epididymides and vasa deferentia and the penis. In the human

female it comprises the two ovaries, the Fallopian tubes, the uterus and the vagina
re·pro·graph·ics (ri:prəgrǽfiks) *n.* the field of reproduction of documents, including input, editing, photocomposing, and reproduction; esp. for official use
re·prog·ra·phy (riprɒ́grəfi:) *n.* document reproduction by electronic techniques, e.g., by photocopying —**reprographic** *adj.*
re·proof (riprú:f) *n.* a reproving or an instance of this [O.F. *reprove, reprouve*]
re·prove (riprú:v) *pres. part.* **re·prov·ing** *past* and *past part.* **re·proved** *v.t.* to rebuke (someone) [fr. O.F. *reprover*]
rep·tant (réptənt) *adj.* (*biol.*) creeping or crawling [fr. L. *reptans* (*reptantis*)]
rep·tile (réptail, réptil) **1.** *n.* a member of *Reptilia,* a class of cold-blooded vertebrates incl. snakes, lizards, crocodiles and turtles etc. They have lungs, a heart with three chambers, and a skin covered with tough scales or plates. Some creep on their bellies, others crawl on very short legs **2.** *adj.* of, like or having the characteristics of a reptile **rep·til·i·an** (reptíljən, reptília:n) *adj.* and *n.* [fr. L.L. *reptilis,* creeping]
re·pub·lic (ripʌ́blik) *n.* a form of government in which the head of state is an elected president rather than a monarch ‖ a form of government in which the sovereign power is widely vested in the people either directly or through elected representatives ‖ a state with either of these forms of government ‖ a society whose members are equally engaged in the same activity, *the republic of letters* [fr. F. *république* or L. *respublica* fr. *res,* affair +*publicus,* public]
re·pub·li·can (ripʌ́blikən) **1.** *adj.* pertaining to, characteristic of or having the nature of, a republic ‖ favoring a republic **Re·pub·li·can** of or belonging to the Republican party **2.** *n.* a person who supports the form of government of a republic **Re·pub·li·can** a member of the Republican party
Republican party one of the two main political parties of the U.S.A. (cf. DEMOCRATIC PARTY). It was formed (1854) by antislavery groups to oppose the Kansas-Nebraska Act, and attracted many Whigs, Free-Soilers and those Know-Nothings who opposed slavery. It rapidly gained power in the North and held its first national convention in 1856. Lincoln became the first Republican president (1861). The Republicans held the presidency from then until 1913, with the exception of the administrations (1885-9 and 1893-7) of Cleveland. They were weakened by the secession of the Liberal Republicans (1872) and the Mugwumps (1884). In the late 19th c. the Republican party favored protective tariffs and the gold standard. After the administrations of Theodore Roosevelt and Taft, the secession of the Progressive party split the Republicans (1912). They returned to power (1921-33) under Harding, Coolidge and Hoover, but were blamed for the economic crisis of 1929 and were out of office until the administration (1953-61) of Eisenhower. They lost (1961-9) the presidency, regaining it with the administration (1969-74) of Richard Nixon. Vice President Gerald Ford assumed the presidency following Nixon's resignation but lost the 1976 election to Democrat Jimmy Carter. The Republicans regained the presidency with Ronald Reagan's landslide victory in 1980, and they controlled the Senate for the first time since 1955. Democrats held control of the House through the 1984 elections, when Reagan was reelected
Republic of Ireland *IRISH REPUBLIC
re·pu·di·ate (ripjú:di:eit) *pres. part.* **re·pu·di·at·ing** *past* and *past part.* **re·pu·di·at·ed** *v.t.* to refuse to be concerned with or responsible for (someone) ‖ to refuse to accept (something) as valid or true ‖ to refuse to pay (e.g. a debt or claim) [fr. L. *repudiare* (*repudiatus*), to divorce]
re·pu·di·a·tion (ripjụ:di:éiʃən) *n.* a repudiating or being repudiated [fr. L. *repudiatio* (*repudiationis*)]
re·pug·nance (ripʌ́gnəns) *n.* extreme dislike, aversion [F. *répugmance* or fr. L. *repugnantia*]
re·pug·nant (ripʌ́gnənt) *adj.* producing the feeling of repugnance [F. or fr. L. *repugnans* (*repugnantis*)]
re·pulse (ripʌ́ls) *n.* a repulsing or being repulsed [fr. L. *repulsa* or *repulsus* fr. *repellere* (*repulsus*), to drive back]
repulse *pres. part.* **re·puls·ing** *past* and *past part.* **re·pulsed** *v.t.* to drive back by force ‖ to refuse or reject, *to repulse an offer of help* ‖ to fill with repulsion [fr. L. *repellere* (*repulsus*), to drive back]
re·pul·sion (ripʌ́lʃən) *n.* a repulse ‖ a feeling of repugnance ‖ (*phys.*) the force tending to drive two bodies further apart [fr. L. L. *repulsio* (*repulsionis*)]
re·pul·sive (ripʌ́lsiv) *adj.* causing feelings of repulsion ‖ (*phys.*) tending to repel [REPULSE v.]
rep·u·nit (répju:nit) *n.* (*math.*) a number consisting entirely of integers, 11, 111, etc., or 99, 999, etc.
re·pur·chase (rị:pə́:rtʃəs) *pres. part.* **re·pur·chas·ing** *past* and *past part.* **re·pur·chased 1.** *v.t.* to buy back **2.** *n.* a repurchasing
rep·u·ta·bil·i·ty (rẹpjutəbíliti:) *n.* the state or quality of being reputable
rep·u·ta·ble (répjutəb'l) *adj.* having a good reputation ‖ reliable, *a reputable source* **rép·u·ta·bly** *adv.* [fr. older *repute,* to consider fr. F. *réputer* or L. *reputare*]
rep·u·ta·tion (rẹpjutéiʃən) *n.* the general opinion held by people about the merits or demerits of a person or thing ‖ the state or fact of being highly thought of or esteemed ‖ the good name of a person or thing earned through merit and distinction ‖ (usually with 'of') a specified manner, quality etc. generally ascribed to someone or something, *he has the reputation of being an excellent horseman* [fr. L. *reputatio* (*reputationis*), consideration]
re·pute (ripjú:t) **1.** *n.* reputation, esp. good reputation, *a writer of repute* **2.** *v.t. pres. part.* **re·put·ing** *past* and *past part.* **re·put·ed** (esp. used passively) to consider, accord a certain character etc. to, *he is reputed to be rich* **re·pút·ed** *adj.* held in high esteem ‖ generally supposed, *its reputed origin goes back to Roman times* **re·pút·ed·ly** *adv.* by or according to reputation [fr. older *repute,* to consider fr. F. *réputer* or L. *reputare*]
re·quest (rikwést) *n.* an act of requesting something or an instance of this ‖ something requested ‖ the fact or state of being requested, *available on request* **by request** because of or following a request or requests **in request** asked for by many persons, popular [O.F. *requeste*]
request *v.t.* attempt to obtain (something) by making one's wants or desires known in speech or writing ‖ to attempt to get (someone) to do or give something that one wants by making this known in speech or writing ‖ to attempt in speech or writing to obtain permission (to do something) [fr. O.F. *requester*]
req·ui·em (rékwi:əm, rí:kwi:əm) *n.* a Mass for the repose of a deceased person ‖ the musical setting of such a Mass [L., accusative of *requies,* rest (the first word of the introit of the Roman Catholic requiem)]
re·quire (rikwáiər) *pres. part.* **re·quir·ing** *past* and *past part.* **re·quired** *v.t.* to stipulate, *the law requires that the report must be made annually* ‖ to place an obligation on (someone), *the law requires you to report annually* ‖ to need, *this requires careful consideration* **re·quíre·ment** *n.* something stipulated or demanded ‖ something needed [O. F. *requerre* (*requer-, requier-*)]
req·ui·site (rékwizit) **1.** *adj.* required **2.** *n.* something required or necessary [fr. L. *requirere* (*requisitus*)]
req·ui·si·tion (rẹkwizíʃən) **1.** *n.* a formal taking of control over goods or services under authority, esp. by an army in the field or by the State in a war or other catastrophe ‖ the condition of being taken over for use in this way, *to be on requisition* ‖ a written request or formal demand for goods or supplies under a centralized system of supply **2.** *v.t.* to take control of under authority, *to requisition a house* ‖ to require (someone or something) to provide, *householders were requisitioned to provide shelter for the victims* ‖ to request (goods, supplies etc.) under a centralized system of supply [F. *réquisition* or L. *requisitio* (*requisitionis*)]
re·quit·al (rikwáit'l) *n.* a requiting or being requited ‖ something given in return for services or retaliation
re·quite (rikwáit) *pres. part* **re·quit·ing** *past* and *past part.* **re·quit·ed** *v.t.* to repay (someone) for a benefit, injury etc. ‖ to give (something) in return for a benefit, injury etc., *to requite good for evil* [fr. RE- + *quite,* var. of QUIT]
re·ra·di·a·tion (rị:rẹidi:éiʃən) *n.* (*communications*) unwanted radio signals in a receiving instrument
re·ra·di·a·tive (rị:réidi:ətiv) *adj.* having the ability to reflect radiation
rere·dos (ríərdɒs) *n.* an ornamental screen behind an altar [A.F. fr. *rere,* back + *dos,* back]
re·run 1. (ri:rʌ́n) *v. pres part.* **re·run·ning** *past* **re·ran** (ri:rǽn) *past part.* **re·run** *v.t.* to run (esp. a race, movie or television show) again **2.** (rí:rʌn) *n.* a replayed T.V. show ‖ the public showing of a movie after withdrawing it from circulation for a time, or the movie itself
Re·sa·ca de la Pal·ma (resákaðelapálmɑ), a valley of the Rio Grande in Texas, site of the second battle (1846) of the Mexican War. Mexican troops under Gen. Mariano Arista, retreating south after the battle of Palo Alto, were defeated by U.S. forces under Gen. Zachary Taylor
re·sale (rí:sẹil, ri:séil) *n.* a selling again or an instance of this
re·scind (risínd) *v.t.* to cancel (a previous decision, regulation etc.) **re·scínd·a·ble** *adj.* [fr. L. *rescindere*]
re·scis·sion (risíʒən) *n.* the act of rescinding [fr. L. *rescissio* (*rescissionis*)]
re·scis·so·ry (risísəri:, risíʒəri:) *adj.* rescinding [fr. L.L. *rescissorius*]
re·script (rí:skrịpt) *n.* (*hist.*) a written reply by a Roman emperor or a pope to a question of jurisprudence ‖ any official order or announcement by a ruler or government ‖ a rewriting ‖ something rewritten [fr. L. *rescribere* (*rescriptus*), to rewrite, to write back]
res·cue (réskju:) **1.** *pres. part.* **res·cu·ing** *past* and *past part.* **res·cued** *v.t.* to deliver from danger, harm, evil, violence, imprisonment etc. or the threat of any of these ‖ (*law*) to free from legal custody by force **2.** *n.* the act of rescuing ‖ (*law*) release by force from legal custody [O.F. *rescourre*]
re·search (risə́:rtʃ) *v.i.* to engage in research [fr. obs. F. *recercher*]
research (risə́:rtʃ, rí:sə:rtʃ) *n.* a systematic search for facts ‖ scientific investigation [fr. obs. F. *recerche*]
re·seat (ri:sí:t) *v.t.* to seat (oneself, a person) again ‖ (*mech.*) to refit in its setting, *to reseat a valve* ‖ to provide (a chair) with a new seat
re·sect (risékt) *v.t.* (*surg.*) to remove a portion of (an organ etc.) [fr. L. *resecare* (*resectus*), to cut off]
re·se·da (risí:də) *n.* a member of *Reseda,* fam. *Resedaceae,* a genus of plants including mignonette, chiefly native to the Mediterranean region, having cleft petals and numerous stamens in their racemose flowers ‖ (also rézidə) the greenish-yellow color of some mignonette flowers [fr. L. *resedare,* to assuage (fr. the use of the plants as a charm for curing tumors)]
re·seg·re·ga·tion (rị:sẹgrigéiʃən) *n.* to segregate after having desegregated
re·sem·blance (rizémbləns) *n.* the state, fact or quality of resembling, similarity
re·sem·ble (rizémb'l) *pres. part.* **re·sem·bling** *past* and *past part.* **re·sem·bled** *v.t.* to be similar to, have the same appearance or nature as [fr. O.F. *resembler*]
re·sent (rizént) *v.t.* to take strong exception to (what is thought to be unjust, interfering, insulting, critical etc.) **re·sént·ful** *adj.* **re·sént·ment** *n.* [fr. F. *ressentir,* to feel the result of]
res·er·va·tion (rẹzərvéiʃən) *n.* a reserving ‖ something that is reserved ‖ a limitation or qualification, *mental reservation* ‖ (*eccles.*) the practice of keeping in the sanctuary a portion of the consecrated Host ‖ (*eccles.*) the keeping back of the right of granting absolution in certain cases ‖ the engaging in advance of a hotel room, theater seat etc. ‖ a record of such an engaging ‖ a tract of land set aside for some special use [O.F.]
re·serve (rizə́:rv) *n.* something set aside for future use ‖ limitation, reservation or qualification, *to accept a statement with reserve* ‖ an instance of this ‖ avoidance of familiarity in social relationships ‖ self-restraint in action or speech ‖ (in religious instruction and casuistry) suppression of a part of the truth ‖ (*mil.,* usually *pl.*) troops temporarily withheld from action so that they may be available for special use ‖ (*mil.*) the trained men of a country not in active service, but subject to call in case of war or emergency ‖ one of these men ‖ (*finance*) profit added to capital rather than being paid out to shareholders ‖ (*banking*) assets kept available as cash ‖ (*central banks*) assets held as gold or foreign exchange ‖ a reservation (tract of land) **in reserve** put aside for future use **without**

reserve (of something sold by auction) not subject to a fixed minimum price [F. *réserve*]

reserve *pres. part.* **re·serv·ing** *past* and *past part.* **re·served** *v.t.* to keep back for future use, *to reserve part of profit for reinvestment* || (esp. with 'for') to set aside or apart for a specific use, *this room is reserved for chess players* || to retain legal control of, *author's rights reserved* || to book in advance, *to reserve train seats* || (*eccles.*) to set apart (a portion of the consecrated Host), e.g. for communion of the sick || to retain control of (some power, e.g. to pronounce absolution) [O.F. *reserver*]

reserve bank one of the 12 principal banks of the Federal Reserve System in the U.S.A.

reserve clause (*sports*) provision in a professional athlete's contract that gives a renewal option to the club for the athlete's effective playing life until he or she is traded, sold, etc.

re·served (rizə́:rvd) *adj.* disciplined not to exhibit emotion or to express opinions or to welcome intimate contact with others || set apart or retained for future use || booked in advance

Reserve Officers Training Corps (ROTC), an organization of the U.S. Department of Defense, established (1916) by the National Defense Act to develop a reserve of trained officers available for service in national emergencies

re·serv·ist (rizə́:rvist) *n.* a member of a military reserve force

res·er·voir (rézərvwɑr, rézərvwɔr) *n.* a place, esp. an artificial lake, where a large quantity of water is collected and stored to be piped to a city or used for irrigation, hydroelectric power etc. || any container for a store of liquid or gas, *the ink reservoir of a fountain pen* || a sac or cavity in a plant or animal in which fluid collects or is secreted [F. *réservoir*]

re·set 1. (ri:sét) *pres. part.* **re·set·ting** *past* and *past part.* **re·set** *v.t.* to set anew (a diamond, broken arm, hair etc.) || (*printing*) to compose (a book, type) afresh 2. (rí:sęt) *n.* a resetting || something that is reset

re·ship (ri:ʃíp) *pres. part.* **re·ship·ping** *past* and *past part.* **re·shipped** *v.t.* to put on board again (goods which had been unloaded from the same or another ship) *v.i.* to go on board again, after disembarking from the same or another ship || to sign up again as a member of a ship's crew

re·sid or **residual oil** (rizíd) *n.* the elements of petroleum remaining after its valuable portions are removed

re·side (rizáid) *pres. part.* **re·sid·ing** *past* and *past part.* **re·sid·ed** *v.i.* to have one's home in a particular place for a considerable length of time || (of qualities) to lie, be present, *its virtue resides in its clarity and brevity* || (of rights etc.) to be vested [fr. F. *résider* or L. *residere*]

res·i·dence (rézidəns) *n.* the act or fact of living in a particular place for a considerable length of time || the period during which one lives at a place || the act or fact of residing || the place where one lives, esp. the official house of a dignitary, or a dwelling house of some size or pretension **in residence** living in a place where one fulfills certain duties, e.g. at a hospital inhabiting an official residence, *the palace flag flies when the queen is in residence* || (*chem.*) the persistence of an undesired element in a solution [F. *résidence*]

res·i·den·cy (rézidənsi:) *pl.* **res·i·den·cies** *n.* (*hist.*) a territory in a protected state where a resident agent of the protecting power has authority || (*hist.*) the official residence of such an agent || (*med.*) the position of a resident in a hospital, or the period during which he holds the position [fr. L. *residentia*]

res·i·dent (rézidənt) 1. *adj.* residing || involving residence, *a resident year in college* || living in residence, *a resident teacher* || (of birds etc.) nonmigratory 2. *n.* a person who resides for a considerable length of time in a certain place, *the local residents* || (*hist.*) the governor of a residency || a qualified physician in residence at a hospital, usually as the final part of his medical training [fr. L. *residens* (*residentis*) fr. *residere*, to reside]

res·i·den·tial (ręzidénʃəl) *adj.* occupied mainly by private houses, esp. of some standing || (esp. *Br.*) requiring the holder of a post to reside at his place of work, a residential post || of or relating to residence, *residential qualifications* [RESIDENCE]

res·i·den·tiar·y (ręzidénʃəri:, ręzidénʃi:ęri:) 1. *adj.* (esp. *eccles.*, usually following the noun) obliged to be in residence for a stipulated period, *a canon residentiary* 2. *pl.* **res·i·den·tiar·ies** *n.* an ecclesiastic bound to live in residence for a certain period [fr. M.L. *residentiarius*]

re·sid·u·al (rizídʒu:əl) 1. *adj.* remaining, left over || of or relating to something which so remains || remaining in a body cavity after maximum elimination || (*math.*) remaining after subtraction 2. *n.* (*phys.*) the difference between a theoretical and an experimental value, an *error in the residual* || a substance or product left over after a chemical process, distillation etc. || fee for each repetition (after its first showing) of a performance paid to a participant, esp. in television commercials [fr. L. *residuum*, residue]

re·sid·u·ar·y (rizídʒu:ęri:) *adj.* of, relating to, or consisting of a residuum [RESIDUUM]

residuary legatee (*law*) someone who inherits what remains of an estate after specific bequests and charges on the estate have been met

res·i·due (rézidu:, rézidju:) *n.* that which remains after something has been taken away, separated out etc., *evaporation left a white residue in the dish* || (*law*) that part of an estate remaining after the paying of all debts, bequests etc. [fr. F. *résidu*]

re·sid·u·um (rizídʒu:əm) *pl.* **re·sid·u·a** (rizídʒu:ə), **re·sid·u·ums** *n.* that which remains, esp. (*chem.*) that which remains after other substances have been removed by evaporation, filtration etc. || (*law*) the residue of an estate [L. neuter of *residuus*, remaining]

re·sign (rizáin) *v.t.* to leave (an occupation, office, post) of one's own volition, *he resigned his post last week* || to relinquish, *he resigned his rights under the patent* || *v.i.* (esp. with 'as' or 'from') to leave an office, post etc. of one's own volition, *to resign as chairman* **to resign oneself to** to accept as unavoidable, *he resigned himself to a long wait* [fr. O.F. *resigner*]

re·sign (ri:sáin) *v.t.* to sign again

res·ig·na·tion (ręzignéiʃən) *n.* the act of resigning || a formal letter, notice etc. affirming that one has resigned or wishes to resign a position, office etc. || the state of being mentally resigned, *to accept a situation with resignation* [F. *résignation*]

re·signed (rizáind) *adj.* accepting what cannot be avoided [RESIGN]

re·sil·ience (rizíljəns) *n.* the quality of being resilient

re·sil·ien·cy (rizíljənsi:) *n.* resilience

re·sil·ient (rizíljənt) *adj.* (of a body or material) capable of resuming its shape, position etc. after being subjected to stress, elastic || (of human temperament) capable of recovering rapidly, esp. from an emotional shock [fr. L. *resiliens* (*resilientis*) fr. *resilire*, to spring back]

res·in (rézin) 1. *n.* any of various amorphous plant secretions (e.g. from pine, fir and tropical trees) used chiefly in varnishes, printing ink, plastics etc. as a binder || any of a large class of synthetic products usually with some physical properties similar to the natural resins but which are different chemically. The synthetic resins are prepared by polymerization and are used as plastics, varnishes, in adhesives and in ion exchange 2. *v.t.* to treat with resin **rés·in·ate** *pres. part.* **res·in·at·ing** *past* and *past part.* **res·in·at·ed** *v.t.* to impregnate with resin || to flavor with pine resin **res·in·if·er·ous** (ręziníførəs) *adj.* of a tree or plant which secretes resin **rés·in·oid** 1. *adj.* somewhat resinous 2. *n.* a gum resin **rés·in·ous** *adj.* of, pertaining to or obtained from resin [fr. F. *résine*]

re·sist (rizíst) 1. *v.t.* to oppose (a physical force, chemical change, mental influence etc.) || *v.i.* to oppose a physical force etc. 2. *n.* a substance used to protect a surface from change, e.g. wax to protect parts of a piece of pottery not to be affected by a glaze or slip [fr. F. *résister* or L. *resistere*]

re·sist·ance (rizístəns) *n.* a resisting || the opposing force used in resisting, *the resistance of the air to a body moving through it* || (*elec.*) opposition offered by a substance (e.g. a conductor) to the flow of an electric current (*OHM'S LAW) or that which offers such resistance (e.g. a coil of wire) **Re·sist·ance** (often with 'the') an organized, usually underground, movement of fighters engaged in acts of sabotage etc. against occupying forces [F. *résistance*]

resistance, resistance level, or **resistance area** (*securities*) trading price range at which notable amounts of buying or selling appear

resistance thermometer a temperature-measuring device that depends upon the known variation of the electrical resistance of a substance (usually a platinum wire) with temperature, to give temperature readings by measurements of electrical resistance

re·sist·ant, re·sist·ent (rizístənt) 1. *adj.* resisting 2. *n.* someone who resists

re·sist·i·bil·i·ty (rizįstəbíliti:) *n.* the quality or state of being resistible

re·sist·i·ble (rizístəb'l) *adj.* capable of being resisted

re·sis·tive (rizístiv) *adj.* resistant || of, relating to, or having electrical resistance

re·sis·tiv·i·ty (ri:zistíviti:) *n.* (*elec.*) the property of a substance that determines the electrical resistance of a body made of that substance || the electrical resistance per unit length of a uniform bar of unit cross-sectional area || the ability to resist

re·sist·less (rizístlis) *adj.* of that which cannot be resisted, *the resistless onset of age* || unable to resist

re·sis·to·jet (rizístədʒęt) *n.* (*aerospace*) engine fueled by electrically heated hydrogen or ammonia, used to change a spacecraft's direction

re·sis·tor (rizístər) *n.* (*elec.*) an electrical resistance used in a circuit to control the current

re·sol·u·ble (ri:sɔ́ljub'l) *adj.* able to be dissolved again (e.g. silver oxide when excess of ammonium hydroxide is added)

re·sol·u·ble (rizɔ́ljub'l) able to be resolved [fr. L.L. *resolubilis*]

res·o·lute (rézəlu:t) *adj.* not turned from a purpose by difficulties or opposition or risk etc. [fr. L. *resolvere* (*resolutus*), to resolve]

res·o·lu·tion (ręzəlú:ʃən) *n.* a resolving or being resolved || something resolved || the quality of not allowing difficulties or opposition to affect one's purpose || the degree to which an analysis (e.g. in chemical, spectral, optical or statistical analysis) is capable of distinguishing between similar substances, properties, events, adjacent parts etc. (*RESOLVING POWER) || a formal statement of opinion or decision, agreed to after the consideration of a motion || (*med.*) dissipation, e.g. of an inflammation || (*mus.*) the consonance in which a dissonance is resolved (O.F.]

Resolution 242 a resolution of the United Nations Security Council adopted November 22, 1967, advocating Israeli withdrawal from occupied territories, acknowledgment of the sovereignty of each state in the area, an end to belligerency, and settlement of the Palestinian refugee problem

re·solve (rizɔ́lv) 1. *v. pres. part.* **re·solv·ing** *past* and *past part.* **re·solved** *v.t.* to separate (something) into component parts, *to resolve a compound or mixture into its constituents* || to render (adjacent parts, e.g. lines of a spectrum, or objects or light sources imaged by a microscope or telescope) distinguishable || to decompose (a vector) into two or more components along specific (usually orthogonal) directions || (*med.*) to cause (e.g. an inflammation) to dissipate || to find a solution to (a question or problem) || to convert by resolution, *the assembly resolved itself into a committee* || (*mus.*) to convert (a discord) into a concord || to decide, determine, *to resolve not to go* || (of a committee) to agree to (a course of action or expression of opinion) by formal resolution || *v.i.* (with 'on' or 'upon') to determine, *to resolve on a less violent course of action* || to become separated into constituent parts || (*mus.*) to pass from discord to concord 2. *n.* something resolved || firmness of purpose || a formal resolution [fr. L. *resolvere*]

resolving power the ability of an optical system or instrument (e.g. a microscope, telescope, or the lenses of a camera) to form distinct magnified images of adjacent features on the object being observed || the degree to which photographic film is able to reproduce the fine features of an optical image

res·o·nance (rézənəns) *n.* the prolongation, amplification or modification of a sound by vibration || (*phys.*) the increase in amplitude of an oscillation in a mechanical or electrical system, under the influence of an external periodic impulse of similar frequency to the original vibration || this modified oscillation || the state of adjustment of a system that results in this || (*med.*) the sound produced by the chest on percussion || (*chem.*) the phenomenon in certain molecules, ions or radicals to which two or more structures that differ in their electron distribution can be assigned, that results in greater stability and different bond lengths than in the

CONCISE PRONUNCIATION KEY: (a) æ, cat; ɑ, car; ɔ fawn; ei, snake. (e) e, hen; i:, sheep; iə, deer; εə, bear. (i) i, fish; ai, tiger; ə:, bird. (o) o, ox; au, cow; ou, goat; u, poor; ɔi, royal. (u) ʌ, duck; u, bull; u:, goose; ə, bacillus; ju:, cube. x, loch; θ, think; ð, bother; z, Zen; ʒ, corsage; dʒ, savage; ŋ, orangutang; j, yak; ʃ, fish; tʃ, fetch; 'l, rabble; 'n, redden. Complete pronunciation key appears inside front cover.

hypothetical structures, and that is attributed to the fact that the electrons in the system are no longer localized ‖ (*particle phys.*) a short-lived elementary particle or group of particles, e.g., rho mesons; undetectable temporary state of mesons or hyperons during a nuclear reaction; the particles themselves [O.F.]

resonance particle any of a group of extremely short-lived fundamental particles of high mass and variable charge and angular momentum that are as yet incompletely understood, but which appear to play the role of field quanta (*QUANTUM THEORY OF FIELDS)

res·o·nant (rézənənt) *adj.* resounding ‖ causing sound to be reinforced or prolonged ‖ (of a sound) loud and rich in overtones ‖ (*phys.*) of or exhibiting resonance [fr. L. *resonans (resonantis)* fr. *resonare,* to resound]

res·o·nate (rézəneit) *pres. part.* **res·o·nat·ing** *past* and *past part.* **res·o·nat·ed** *v.i.* to exhibit resonance ‖ to react as if by resonance ‖ *v.t.* to make resonant **rés·o·na·tor** *n.* a device used to give resonance to sounds ‖ (*radio*) the system of antennae, or other high-frequency circuit, of a receiver [fr. L. *resonare,* to resound]

re·sorb (risɔ́rb, rizɔ́rb) *v.t.* to absorb again **re·sórb·ent** *adj.* [fr. L. *resorbere*]

res·or·cin·ol (rezɔ́rsinɔl, rezɔ́rsinoul) *n.* a crystalline phenol, $C_6H_4(OH)_2$, obtained in its natural state from various resins and tannins, and also prepared synthetically. It is used in the manufacture of dyes and in lotions for some skin diseases [RESIN +ORCIN]

re·sorp·tion (risɔ́rpʃən, rizɔ́rpʃən) *n.* a resorbing or being resorbed [fr. L. *resorbere (resorptus),* to resorb]

re·sort (rizɔ́rt) *v.i.* (often with 'to') to have recourse, *to resort to violence* ‖ (often with 'to') to go, esp. to go often and in great numbers [fr. O.F. *resortir,* to rebound]

resort *n.* a place to which people go frequently or habitually for rest, pleasure etc., *a seaside resort* ‖ a habitual or general going to a place, *a place of public resort* ‖ a person to whom or a thing to which one applies for aid ‖ the action of applying for aid [O.F.]

re·sound (rizáund) *v.i.* to sound loudly and with rich quality ‖ to re-echo ‖ to be filled with sound, *the hall resounded with applause* ‖ *v.t.* to utter with enthusiasm (someone's praises etc.) [fr. L. *resonare*]

re·source (risɔ́rs, risóurs, rí:sɔrs, rí:sours) *n.* a source of supply or support ‖ quick-wittedness in mastering a difficult situation ‖ something to which one resorts for comfort or help or to gain an end, *tears are her main resource when she is thwarted* ‖ (*pl.*) means of diversion, *he soon exhausted the resources of the place* ‖ (*pl.*) natural assets (of a country) ‖ (*pl.*) assets, wealth **without resource** having nothing to fall back on **re·sóurce·ful** *adj.* [fr. F. *ressource*]

re·spect (rispékt) **1.** *n.* the special esteem or consideration in which one holds another person or thing ‖ the state or quality of being esteemed etc., *to be held in respect* ‖ aspect, detail, *the plan is faulty in every respect* ‖ (*pl.*) conventional expressions of esteem, sympathy etc. **in respect of, with respect to** as regards, concerning, *he wants to talk to you with respect to your journey* **2.** *v.t.* to feel or show respect or consideration for [fr. L. *respicere (respectus),* to look (back) at]

re·spect·a·bil·i·ty (rispektəbíliti:) *n.* the state or quality of being respectable

re·spect·a·ble (rispéktəb'l) *adj.* conforming to the standards of what one considers proper, socially acceptable etc. ‖ fairly large in amount, size, quantity etc., *a respectable sum of money* ‖ tolerably good, *a respectable performance* ‖ of good standing or acceptable appearance etc., *a respectable hotel* **re·spéct·a·bly** *adv.*

re·spect·ful (rispéktfəl) *adj.* showing respect, *a respectful silence*

re·spect·ing (rispéktiŋ) *prep.* considering ‖ regarding

re·spec·tive (rispéktiv) *adj.* concerning each of two or more persons or things taken in relationship to the other or others, *check the respective parts of the ignition according to the procedure laid down* ‖ proper to each individual of two or more persons or things of a group under consideration, *they all went off to their respective jobs* **re·spéc·tive·ly** *adv.* each considered in the order indicated, *Dick, John and Bill made the journey by car, train and on foot respectively* ‖ in a way which regards each of two or more persons or things in relation to the other or others, *consider respectively their prices and the uses they can be put to* [fr. L.L. *respectivus*]

re·spell (ri:spél) *pres. part.* **re·spell·ing** *past* and *past part.* **re·spelled,** (esp. *Br.*) **re·spelt** (ri:spélt) *v.t.* to spell again, e.g. in a phonetic system so as to indicate pronunciation

Re·spi·ghi (respí:gi:), Ottorino (1879-1936), Italian composer. He is mainly known for his orchestral suites, esp. 'Fontane di Roma' (1917) and for his ballet music for 'la Boutique fantasque' (1917-18) arranged from airs by Rossini

re·spir·a·ble (résparəb'l, rispáiərəb'l) *adj.* capable of, or suited for, being respired

res·pi·ra·tion (rèspəréiʃən) *n.* any of various processes by which an organism takes in air or dissolved gases, uses one or more of them in energy-producing chemical changes, and expels both the gaseous by-products of the changes and the unused part of the air or gas. Animals and plants use oxygen, expelling carbon dioxide formed by the oxidation of carbon compounds in the system. Green plants in daylight can use the carbon dioxide of the air to form starch, expelling oxygen as a by-product [fr. L. *respiratio (respirationis)*]

res·pi·ra·tor (réspərèitər) *n.* a device worn over the mouth and nose to filter poisonous substances from the air breathed in ‖ (*Br.*) a gas mask ‖ a device for inducing artificial respiration [fr. L. *respirare,* to breathe]

res·pi·ra·to·ry (réspərətɔri:, réspərətouri:, rispáiərətɔri:, rispáiərətouri:) *adj.* of or relating to respiration ‖ serving for respiration [fr. Mod L. *respiratorius*]

re·spire (rispáiər) *pres. part.* **re·spir·ing** *past* and *past part.* **re·spired** *v.i.* to breathe ‖ *v.t.* to breathe (air etc.) in and out [L. *respirare,* to breathe]

res·pite (réspit) *n.* an interval of relief during a period of work, suffering etc. ‖ the postponement of the fulfilling of some obligation ‖ the postponement of the carrying out of a death sentence [O.F. *respit*]

respite *pres. part.* **res·pit·ing** *past* and *past part.* **res·pit·ed** *v.t.* to grant a respite to (someone) ‖ to delay the execution of (a sentence or punishment etc.) [O.F. *respiter*]

re·splend·ence (rispléndəns) *n.* the state or quality of being resplendent

re·splend·en·cy (rispléndənsi:) *n.* resplendence

re·splend·ent (rispléndənt) *adj.* brightly glowing with light or color [fr. L. *resplendens (resplendentis)*]

re·spond (rispɔ́nd) *n.* (*archit.*) a half-column or half-pier in a wall, used to support an arch ‖ (*eccles.*) a response (words said or sung by the congregation in answer) [O.F.]

respond *v.i.* to reply ‖ to show an effect due to a force, influence or stimulus, *the illness responded to treatment* ‖ (*eccles.*) to make a response in a liturgy [fr. L. *respondere*]

re·spond·ent (rispɔ́ndənt) **1.** *adj.* (*law*) in the position of a defendant **2.** *n.* (*law*) a defendant, esp. in a divorce case [fr. L. *respondens (respondentis)* fr. *respondere,* to answer]

re·sponse (rispɔ́ns) *n.* a reply, *he failed to make any response, a good response to the appeal* ‖ something answered, esp. (*eccles.*) words said or sung by the congregation or choir in answer to the priest ‖ (*eccles.*) a responsory ‖ (*mus.*) an answer ‖ the reaction to a stimulus **in response to** in answer to [O.F. *respons, response* and L. *responsum*]

re·spon·si·bil·i·ty (rispɔnsəbíliti:) *pl.* **re·spon·si·bil·i·ties** *n.* the state or quality of being responsible ‖ a person for whom or a thing for which one is responsible **to take responsibility for** to consider oneself answerable for

re·spon·si·ble (rispɔ́nsəb'l) *adj.* (of a person or persons) placed in control and having to give satisfaction, *he is responsible for the success or failure of the experiment* ‖ (of a position) held by such a person or persons ‖ fit to be placed in control, *a responsible man* ‖ capable of acting rationally, *he is not responsible* ‖ causing a particular result, *the rain was responsible for the poor attendance* **re·spón·si·bly** *adv.* [obs. F. fr. L. *respondere (responsus),* to pledge in return]

Re·spon·sions (rispɔ́nʃənz) *pl. n.* the first examination for a B.A. degree at Oxford University in certain faculties [F. or fr. L. *responsio (responsionis),* answer]

re·spon·sive (rispɔ́nsiv) *adj.* giving a response, e.g. to a stimulus ‖ (of persons and things) quick to respond ‖ (*eccles.*) involving or consisting of responses [F. *responsif*]

re·spon·so·ry (rispɔ́nsəri:) *pl.* **re·spon·so·ries** *n.* (*eccles.*) an anthem said or sung by soloist and choir alternately after a reading from the Bible [fr. L.L. *responsoria*]

rest (rest) *n.* the state of being motionless ‖ the state of being inactive, esp. after physical exertion ‖ a period of being inactive, during which one gets back one's energy ‖ a period of sleep, *a good night's rest* ‖ (*mus.*) a short period of silence of an indicated time value ‖ (*mus.*) any of various symbols indicating this period and the length of the period ‖ something serving as a support for something else, *the fork of a tree made a rest for his back* ‖ a caesura ‖ (*billiards*) a bridge ‖ (*rhet.*) mental tranquillity **at rest** having no motion ‖ free from worries etc. ‖ in a state of repose **to come to rest** to cease moving, *the ball came to rest at the edge of the hole* **to lay to rest** to bury (a dead person) **to set (someone's) mind at rest** to cause (someone) to be free of worries etc. [O.E. *ræste, reste*]

rest *v.i.* to be motionless, *the ball rested at the edge of the hole* ‖ to refrain from activity, esp. in order to recover energy ‖ (of the mind etc.) to be or become tranquil ‖ to be fixed or supported, *the vase rests on a pedestal* ‖ (with 'on' or 'upon') to be founded, *the charge rests on the evidence of one witness* ‖ to remain in abeyance, *to let a matter rest* ‖ (with 'on' or 'upon') to be steadily directed, *his eyes rested on the ceiling* ‖ *v.t.* to place on or against a support, *to rest a ladder against a wall* ‖ to direct (e.g. the eyes), *to rest one's gaze on the ceiling* ‖ to give a period of rest to, *to rest one's feet after a march* ‖ to give tranquillity to, *to rest one's mind* ‖ to base (e.g. a case), *to rest one's defense on a plea of insanity* ‖ (*law*) to cease voluntarily the introduction of evidence in (a case) [O.E. *ræstan, restan*]

rest *n.* the portion which remains after part has been taken away ‖ (constr. as *pl.*) the others, the remaining group, *some of the guests went to church, the rest stayed at home* [F. *reste*]

rest *n.* (*hist.,* of armor) an attachment projecting from the right side of the cuirass for supporting the butt end of the lance [older *arest, arrest n.*]

re·state (ri:stéit) *pres. part.* **re·stat·ing** *past* and *past part.* **re·stat·ed** *v.t.* to state again or in other words **re·státe·ment** *n.*

res·tau·rant (réstərənt, réstərɑnt) *n.* a place where meals are served, for payment, to members of the public [F.]

res·tau·ra·teur (rèstərətə́:r) *n.* a person who owns or manages a restaurant [F.]

rest·ful (réstfəl) *adj.* enabling a person to rest his body or mind, *a restful holiday* ‖ having a calming effect, esp. on the senses, *restful colors*

Res·tif (or **Re·tif) de la Bre·tonne** (reiti:fdəlæbretɔn), Nicolas Edmé (1734-1806), French writer. He wrote some 250 volumes, many of which he illustrated and most of which were pornographic. They provide insight into the life of the poor in 18th-c. France

res·ti·form body (réstifɔrm) (*anat.*) one of the two cordlike bundles of fibers which connect the medulla oblongata with the cerebellum [Mod. L. *restiformis* fr. *restis,* cord+*-forma,* form]

rest·ing (réstiŋ) *adj.* (*biol.*) dormant ‖ (of actors) temporarily without an engagement

res·ti·tu·tion (rèstitú:ʃən, rèstitjú:ʃən) *n.* the act of giving back to a rightful owner ‖ a giving of something as an equivalent for what has been lost, damaged etc. ‖ a returning of something to its original state or condition ‖ (*phys.,* of an elastic body) a going back to its original form after deformation [O.F.]

res·tive (réstiv) *adj.* (of a person) having too much energy to be willing to remain at rest or to submit to control ‖ (of a horse) resisting control ‖ (of a crowd, audience etc.) uneasy or beginning to show displeasure [O.F. *restif*]

rest·less (réstlis) *adj.* agitatedly moving about, not composed ‖ not accompanied by unbroken sleep, *a restless night* ‖ in continual motion, *the restless sea* ‖ (of a person) constantly seeking change

rest mass the mass of a body which has no relative motion in regard to the observer ‖ (*nuclear phys.*) the mass of a particle (exclusive of mass acquired in movement) while moving at less than the speed of light

res·to·ra·tion (rèstəréiʃən) **1.** *n.* a restoring or being restored ‖ a representation of what the original form of a building etc. may be supposed to have been **the Restoration** (*Eng. hist.*) the reestablishment of the monarchy on the accession (1660) of Charles II ‖ the period immediately following this || (*F. hist.*) the reestablishment of the monarchy on the accession (1814) of Louis XVIII || (*F. hist.*) the period 1814–30, interrupted by the Hundred Days (Mar. 20–June 18, 1815) **2.** *adj.* **Res·to·ra·tion** of or belonging to the Restoration

re·stor·a·tive (ristɔ́rətiv, ristóurətiv) **1.** *adj.* capable of restoring one's health or strength **2.** *n.* something which restores someone to consciousness, health etc. [O.F. *restoratif*]

re·store (ristɔ́r, ristóur) *pres. part.* **re·stor·ing** *past* and *past part.* **re·stored** *v.t.* to give back, *to restore stolen jewels to the owner* || to make (something) look as it looked originally by repairing, retouching etc., *to restore a painting* || to re-create the original form of (something no longer existing, or existing as a ruin), *to restore an amphora* || to put back (a deposed monarch) on the throne or bring back (the monarchy) || to bring back to a previous rank, dignity etc. || to bring back to a healthy state || to bring into use or being again, *the old custom has been restored, to restore order* || (*rhet.*) to put back into place || to add or correct (missing or illegible words or letters) to or in a text **re·stór·er** *n.* someone who restores || an agent said to promote growth or activity, *a hair restorer* [O.F. *restorer*]

re·strain (ristréin) *v.t.* to prevent from doing something, *the dog was restrained from attacking the man* || to set limits to (expansion, ambition etc.) || to repress (emotions, a sigh etc.) || to deprive of physical liberty, *restrained by a straitjacket* [O.F. *restraindre* (*restraign, restrain*)]

re·straint (ristréint) *n.* a restraining or being restrained || something which restrains, *the natural restraints on conduct imposed by small communities* || confinement, esp. because of madness, *to be placed under restraint* || avoidance of exaggeration, shocking effects etc. in any form of expression **without restraint** freely, with no holding back [O.F. *restrainte*]

Res·tre·po (restrépɔ), Carlos E. (1868-1937), Colombian politician and president of the Republic (1910-14). He reformed (1910) the constitution and briefly restored constitutional government

re·strict (ristríkt) *v.t.* to keep within certain limits, *to restrict someone's movements, to restrict someone's freedom of choice* **re·stríct·ed** *adj.* limited, *restricted supply* || limited to a certain group or groups, esp. (used as a racist euphemism) limited e.g. to white non-Jews || (of documents) not for general circulation, for reasons of security, although not classified as secret || (*mil.*) of or relating to an area from which military personnel are excluded for reasons of security [fr. L. *restringere* (*restrictus*)]

re·stric·tion (ristríkʃən) *n.* a restricting or being restricted || something which restricts [F.]

re·stric·tive (ristríktiv) *adj.* restricting or tending to restrict [F. *restrictif*]

restrictive clause (*gram.*) a relative clause, usually not set off by commas in English, which identifies the antecedent

rest room a room equipped with toilets, washbasins etc. for the use of employees, clients etc. in a department store or other building

result (rizʌ́lt) **1.** *v.i.* (with 'from') be the effect of something, *his death resulted from injuries* || (with 'in') to have a specified effect, *his injuries resulted in his death* **2.** *n.* an effect arising from something || a solution arrived at by calculation or reasoning || the success or benefit obtained from a course of action, *his efforts had some result* || the outcome of an examination, election or similar contest || (*pl.*, of sports) published or announced scores and winners etc. [fr. L. *resultare*, to spring back]

re·sult·ant (rizʌ́ltənt) **1.** *adj.* resulting, being a result **2.** *n.* that which is a result || (*phys.*) a vector which is equivalent to or the sum of two or more other vectors taken together [fr. L. *resultans* (*resultantis*) fr. *resultare*, to spring back]

resume (rizú:m) *pres. part.* **re·sum·ing** *past* and *past part.* **re·sumed** *v.t.* to take back, or again, *to resume possession of property* || to begin again, *to resume occupation of a house* || to go back to using, *to resume a maiden name* || to sum up, *to resume the main points of an argument* [fr. O.F. *resumer* or L. *resumere*, to take back]

ré·su·mé (rézumei, rezuméi) *n.* a summary || a curriculum vitae [F.]

re·sump·tion (rizʌ́mpʃən) *n.* the act or fact of beginning again, *a resumption of work* [F. *résumption*]

re·su·pi·nate (risú:pineit) *adj.* (*bot.*) so arranged that parts appear upside down, e.g. the flower of an orchid [fr. L. *resupinare* (*resupinatus*), to bend back]

re·sur·face (ri:sə́:rfis) *pres. part.* **re·sur·fac·ing** *past* and *past part.* **re·sur·faced** *v.t.* to give a new surface to

re·sur·gence (risə́:rdʒəns) *n.* a rising again, *a resurgence of anger in the crowd*

re·sur·gent (risə́:rdʒənt) *adj.* rising or seeming to rise again [fr. L. *resurgens* (*resurgentis*) fr. *resurgere*, to rise again]

res·ur·rect (rezərékt) *v.t.* to bring back to life || to bring back to memory or into use, *don't resurrect that old tale, to resurrect an old custom* || to bring back to the surface by erosion || (*hist.*) to steal (a body) from the grave || *v.i.* to rise from the dead [RESURRECTION]

res·ur·rec·tion (rezərékʃən) *n.* the act of rising again after death || a bringing back into use, memory etc. **the Resurrec·tion** (*theol.*) the rising of Christ from the dead || (*theol.*) the rising of all the dead at the Last Judgment **res·ur·réc·tion·ist** *n.* (*hist.*) a body snatcher [O.F.]

re·sur·vey (ri:sɔ:rvéi) **1.** *v.t.* to survey again **2.** (also ri:sə́:rvei) *n.* a fresh survey

re·sus·ci·ta·tion (risʌsitéiʃən) *n.* a resuscitating or being resuscitated [fr. L.L. *resuscitatio* (*resuscitationis*)]

re·sus·ci·tate (risʌ́siteit) *pres. part.* **re·sus·ci·tat·ing** *past* and *past part.* **re·sus·ci·tat·ed** *v.t.* to bring (someone unconscious or seemingly dead) to life or consciousness again || (*fig.*) to revive (what had been discarded or forgotten), *to resuscitate old rumors* || *v.i.* (esp. *fig., rhet.*) to come to life again, revive **re·sús·ci·ta·tor** *n.* someone who or something that resuscitates || an apparatus which, by forcing oxygen (or oxygen and carbon dioxide) into the lungs of an asphyxiated person induces respiration

ret (ret) *pres. part.* **ret·ting** *past* and *past part.* **ret·ted** *v.t.* to soak (flax etc.) in water in order to loosen the fibers from the woody stem by the action of bacteria || *v.i.* (of flax) to undergo this soaking [etym. doubtful]

re·ta·ble (rí:teib'l) *n.* (*eccles.*) a ledge or shelf above the back of an altar, used for supporting the ornaments || (*eccles.*) a framework behind the altar enclosing a decorated panel [F. *rétable, retable*]

re·tail (rí:teil) **1.** *n.* the sale of goods in small quantities directly to consumers (opp. WHOLESALE) **2.** *adj.* of, relating to, or engaged in the sale of goods in this way, *retail price* **3.** *adv.* by retail sale **4.** (ri:téil) *v.t.* to sell in small quantities || to repeat (a story) in detail to others || *v.i.* to be sold in small quantities directly to consumers, *these goods retail at 20 francs a dozen* [O.F.]

re·tain (ritéin) *v.t.* to keep in one's possession or control, *he retained his vitality to the end* || (*law*) to keep available the services of (an attorney or barrister) in case of need by paying a preliminary fee || to keep securely in place || to keep in one's memory, *to have difficulty in retaining names* **re·táin·er** *n.* something which retains, e.g. a device for keeping the balls or rollers of a bearing spaced correctly || (*hist.*) a person serving someone of high rank || (used to connote long and faithful service) a servant || (*law*) the engaging by a client of the services of an attorney || (*law*) a fee paid to an attorney or barrister to retain his services in case of need || a similar fee or salary paid to any professional adviser [fr. O.F. *retenir*]

retaining fee a retainer (fee paid)

retaining wall a wall built to hold back water or the earth of an embankment

re·take (ri:téik) *v.t. pres. part.* **re·tak·ing** *past* **re·took** (ri:túk) *past part.* **re·tak·en** (ri:téikən) to take back || to recapture, *the fugitive was retaken* || (*movies*) to rephotograph (a scene) **2.** (rí:teik) *n.* (*movies*) a refilming of a scene or the scene refilmed

re·tal·i·ate (ritǽlieit) *pres. part.* **re·tal·i·at·ing** *past* and *past part.* **re·tal·i·at·ed** *v.i.* to return blow for blow, insult for insult, harm for harm || *v.t.* to return (a blow, insult etc.) **re·tal·i·á·tion** *n.* **re·tál·i·a·tive, re·tal·i·a·to·ry** (ritǽli:ətɔri:, ritǽli:ətouri:) *adjs.* [fr. L. *retaliare* (*retaliatus*)]

re·tard (ritárd) *v.t.* to slow down the advance of, delay, *the storm retarded his arrival by an hour, solitude retarded her mental development* || (*mech.*) to adjust the timing of (ignition) so that the spark ignites the fuel later in the stroke with respect to top dead center || *v.i.* (of tides, or the movement of heavenly bodies) to occur later than the normal or calculated time [fr. F. *retarder*]

re·tard·ate (ritárdeit) *n.* someone who is mentally retarded [fr. L. *retardare* (*retardatus*), to retard, delay]

re·tard·a·tion (ri:tardéiʃən) *n.* a retarding or being retarded || the amount by which something is retarded || the state of being backward in mental development || (*mus.*) a suspension || (*mus.*) a slowing down of the tempo [F.]

re·tard·a·tive (ritárdətiv) *adj.* relating to or causing retardation

re·tard·a·to·ry (ritárdətɔri:, ritárdətouri:) *adj.* tending to retard

re·tard·ed (ritárdid) *adj.* (esp. of children) physically or mentally backward

re·tard·er (ritárdər) *n.* (*photog.*) a chemical which retards the action of a developer || a substance which delays the setting of cement etc.

retch (retʃ) **1.** *v.i.* to try to vomit but fail to do so **2.** *n.* the act of retching [var. of *reach* fr. O.E. *hrǣcan*]

re·ten·tion (riténʃən) a retaining or being retained || the capacity of retaining || (*med.*) the retaining in a bodily sac, canal etc. of some fluid meant to be eliminated || a remembering or a keeping in the memory [O.F. *retencion*]

re·ten·tive (riténtiv) *adj.* tending or serving to retain or having the power or capacity of retaining || having the ability to remember **re·ten·tiv·i·ty** (ri:tentíviti:) *n.* [O.F. *retentif, retentive*]

re·think (ri:θíŋk) *v.* to reconsider in depth

ret·i·cence (rétisəns) *n.* an inclination to be reserved in speech or behavior || an instance of this [F.]

ret·i·cent (rétisənt) *adj.* characterized by reticence [fr. L. *reticens* (*reticentis*) fr. *reticere*, to be silent]

ret·i·cle (rétik'l) *n.* a system of fine lines, cross hairs etc. in the focus of the lens of an optical instrument to assist observation [fr. L. *reticulum*, a little net]

re·tic·u·lar (ritíkjulər) *adj.* netlike || (*rhet.*) intricate [fr. Mod. L. *reticularis*]

re·tic·u·late (ritíkjuleit) **1.** *v. pres. part.* **re·tic·u·lat·ing** *past* and *past part.* **re·tic·u·lat·ed** *v.t.* to divide so as to look like or form a mesh or network || to construct with a reticle || *v.i.* to be divided into a mesh or network or so divided as to resemble a mesh or network **2.** *adj.* (*biol.*) possessing crossing veins or fibers resembling a network **re·tíc·u·lat·ed** *adj.* **re·tic·u·la·tion** (ritikjuléiʃən) *n.* [fr. L. *reticulatus* fr. *reticulum*, a little net]

ret·i·cule (rétikju:l) *n.* a reticle || (*old-fash.*) a lady's small handbag [F. *réticule*]

re·tic·u·lum (ritikjuləm) *pl.* **re·tic·u·la** (ritíkjulə) *n.* the second stomach of a ruminant mammal || a network structure, esp. in the dense protoplasm of cells [L.=a little net]

re·ti·form (rí:tifɔrm, rétifɔrm) *adj.* having the form of a net [fr. Mod. L. *retiformis*]

ret·i·na (rét'nə) *pl.* **ret·i·nas, ret·i·nae** (rét'ni:) *n.* the membrane which forms the inner lining of the back wall of the vertebrate eye, constituted of two kinds of cell which respond to the stimulus of light and send nervous impulses to the brain through the optic nerve **rét·i·nal** *adj.* **ret·i·ni·tis** (ret'náitis) *n.* (*med.*) inflammation of the retina [M.L.]

ret·i·nal [$C_{20}H_{28}O$] (rét'n'l) *n.* the visual pigment (derived from retinol, or vitamin A) in the disk of the retina essential to color perception

retinol *RETINAL

ret·i·nue (rét'nju:, rét'nu:) *n.* the persons following someone as attendants [O.F. *retenue*]

re·tire (ritáiər) *pres. part.* **re·tir·ing** *past* and *past part.* **re·tired** *v.i.* to give up active participation in a business or other occupation, esp. because of advanced age || to draw back or seem to do so || to draw back from an area of combat, danger etc. || (*cricket*) to cease batting although not out, e.g. because of being hurt || to seek privacy || to go to bed || *v.t.* to withdraw (money) from circulation or (bonds, stocks) from the market || to cause (troops) to fall back || (*baseball*) to put out (a batter, side etc.) || to cause to go into retirement **re·tíred** *adj.* no longer taking an active part in a profession or other occupation, *a retired actress* || of or relating to a person or persons no longer active in a profession etc., *the retired list, retired pay* || (*old-fash.*) secluded, *a retired corner of the garden* **re·tíre·ment** *n.* a retiring or being retired **re·tír·ing** *adj.* (of persons) reserved, preferring seclusion [fr. F. *retirer*, to draw back]

retook *past* of RETAKE

CONCISE PRONUNCIATION KEY: **(a)** æ, *cat*; ɑ, *car*; ɔ *fawn*; ei, *snake*. **(e)** e, *hen*; i:, *sheep*; iə, *deer*; ɛə, *bear*. **(i)** i, *fish*; ai, *tiger*; ə:, *bird*. **(o)** o, *ox*; au, *cow*; ou, *goat*; u, *poor*; ɔi, *royal*. **(u)** ʌ, *duck*; u, *bull*; u:, *goose*; ə, *bacillus*; ju:, *cube*. x, *loch*; θ, *think*; ð, *bother*; z, *Zen*; ʒ, *corsage*; dʒ, *savage*; ŋ, *orangutang*; j, *yak*; ʃ, *fish*; tʃ, *fetch*; 'l, *rabble*; 'n, *redden*. Complete pronunciation key appears inside front cover.

re·tool (ri:tú:l) *v.t.* to reequip (a factory) with tools and machine ‖ *v.i.* to reequip a factory with tools and machines

re·tort (ritɔ́rt) *n.* a vessel of metal etc. used for distilling metals, e.g. for extracting zinc from zinc ore ‖ a refractory chamber in which coal is carbonized by heating the outside of the chamber ‖ a vessel usually of glass with a long slanting tube, used in distillation [F. *retorte*]

retort 1. *v.i.* to make a retort ‖ to retaliate ‖ *v.t.* to turn (an argument, insult etc.) against the user **2.** *n.* a quick witty or sarcastic reply countering a remark by a previous speaker [fr. L. *retorquere* (*retortus*), to bend back]

re·tor·tion (ritɔ́rʃən) *n.* the act of retorting ‖ a bending back ‖ (*internat. law*) retaliation in kind by a country against the citizens of the state which has provoked it [fr. M.L. *retortio* (*retortionis*), a bending back]

re·touch 1. (ri:tʌ́tʃ) *v.t.* to improve by making small alterations in ‖ to change the details on (a photographic print or negative or an engraved plate), esp. so as to hide blemishes or allow for process effects **2.** (ri:tʌtʃ, rit:ʌ́tʃ) *n.* a retouching ‖ a detail which has been changed in retouching ‖ a photograph etc. which has been retouched [F. *retoucher*]

re·trace (ritréis) *pres. part.* **re·trac·ing** *past* and *past part.* **re·traced** *v.t.* to go over again, *to retrace one's path* ‖ to discover by going back in time step by step, *to retrace a genealogy* ‖ to review step by step in memory, *to retrace one's childhood* [F. *retracer*]

re·tract (ritrǽkt) *v.t.* to take back, withdraw (a criticism, accusation etc.) ‖ *v.i.* to draw back, shrink back ‖ to recant [fr. L. *retractare*, to draw back]

retract *v.t.* (*zool.*) to draw (the head, body or limbs) back into the shell ‖ (*zool.*) to draw (the claws) back into their sheaths ‖ (*mach.*) to draw (e.g. wheels) up into the body ‖ *v.i.* (*zool.*, of a head, body or limb) to able to be drawn back into the shell ‖ (*zool.*, of claws) to be able to be drawn back into their sheaths ‖ (*mach.*, of a wheel) to go up into the body [fr. L. *retrahere* (*retractus*), to draw back]

re·trac·tile (ritrǽktil) *adj.* (of claws etc.) that can be retracted [F. *rétractile*]

re·trac·tion (ritrǽkʃən) *n.* a retracting or being retracted ‖ the act of withdrawing something said or promised etc. ‖ the statement made in doing this [fr. L. *retractio* (*retractionis*)]

re·trac·tor (ritrǽktər) *n.* a muscle which causes an organ or part to retract ‖ a surgical instrument for holding back the tissues around an incision during an operation

re·tral (rí:trəl) *adj.* at the back, posterior [fr. L. *retro*, backward]

re·tread 1. (ri:tréd) *v.t.* to supply (a tire) with a new tread after removing the old **2.** (rí:tred) *n.* a tire thus renewed (cf. RECAP)

re·treat (ritrí:t) *n.* (*mil.*) the withdrawal of troops from enemy territory or before invading forces after a defeat or when defeat appears imminent ‖ (*hist.*) the signal for this ‖ the act of absenting oneself temporarily from the dangers or difficulties of life ‖ something which allows one to do this, *the world of books was his retreat* ‖ a place to which one withdraws for peace, safety etc., *a country retreat* ‖ (*mil.*) a signal given by a bugle (sometimes accompanied by drums) at sunset, announcing the ceremony of flag lowering ‖ (*mil.*) this ceremony ‖ (*eccles.*) a period during which a person or group of persons withdraws from worldly activities to e.g. a monastery for spiritual recollection under instruction and discipline [O. F. *retret, retrete*]

retreat *v.i.* to make a retreat ‖ (esp. of the wing tip of an airplane) to slope backward ‖ *v.t.* (*chess*) to move (a piece) back [fr. O.F. *retraiter*]

re·trench (ritréntʃ) *v.i.* to cut down expenses, live more cheaply ‖ *v.t.* to reduce amount of, curtail, esp. in order to economize, *the government retrenched its expenditure on education* ‖ (*mil.*) to furnish with a retrenchment **re·trénch·ment** *n.* a retrenching ‖ (*mil.*) an inner line of defense (e.g. a ditch and parapet) to which troops can retreat if the outer line is breached [fr. F. *retrencher*]

ret·ri·bu·tion (rętrəbjú:ʃən) *n.* merited punishment ‖ the meting out of reward or punishment according to one's deserts, esp. (*theol.*) in the hereafter ‖ something given in recompense [O.F.]

re·tri·bu·tive (ritríbjutiv) *adj.* of, relating to or involving retribution, *retributive justice* [fr. L. *retribuere* (*retributus*), to give, assign]

re·triev·al (ritrí:vəl) *n.* a retrieving **beyond** (or **past**) **retrieval** lost without chance of recovery

re·trieve (ritrí:v) **1.** *pres. part.* **re·triev·ing** *past* and *past part.* **re·trieved** *v.t.* (of dogs) to find and bring back (fallen game) ‖ to get back possession of ‖ to win back (something almost lost), *to retrieve a reputation* ‖ to save, *to retrieve a situation* ‖ to put right, *to retrieve a mistake* ‖ (*games*) to return (a difficult ball) ‖ *v.i.* (of dogs) to bring back fallen game **2.** *n.* (*games*) the return of a difficult ball **beyond** (or **past**) **retrieve** beyond (or past) retrieval **re·tríev·er** *n.* a dog of any of various breeds trained to recover fallen game [fr. O.F. *retrover, retrouver*]

ret·ro·act (rętrouǽkt) *v.i.* to have effect as from a stipulated date in the past ‖ to act in a way which affects the past **ret·ro·ác·tion** *n.* **ret·ro·ác·tive** *adj.* [fr. L. *retroagere* (*retroactus*)]

ret·ro·cede (rętrousí:d) *pres. part.* **ret·ro·ced·ing** *past* and *past part.* **ret·ro·ced·ed** *v.t.* to cede (territory) back to a country [fr. F. *rétrocéder*]

retrocede *pres. part.* **ret·ro·ced·ing** *past* and *past part.* **ret·ro·ced·ed** *v.i.* to recede, move back [fr. L. *retrocedere*]

ret·ro·ces·sa·tion (rętrouseséiʃən) *n.* a ceding back [fr. F. *rétrocession*]

ret·ro·ces·sion (rętrouséʃən) *n.* a moving backward [fr. L.L. *retrocessio* (*retrocessionis*)]

ret·ro·choir (rétrəkwaiər) *n.* the area behind the high altar in a large church or cathedral [fr. M.L. *retrochorus*]

ret·ro·en·gine (rętrouéndʒin) *n.* (*aerospace*) a reverse thrust engine

ret·ro·fit (rętroufít) *v.* **1.** to modify equipment to include improvements in design and use **2.** to install new equipment in an old structure

ret·ro·flex (rétrəflęks) *adj.* (*biol.*) bent sharply backwards ‖ (*phon.*, of the tip of the tongue) raised and bent back ‖ (*phon.*, of a vowel) articulated in this manner **rét·ro·flexed** *adj.* [fr. M.L. *retroflectere* (*retroflexus*), to bend back]

ret·ro·flex·ion (rętrəflékʃən) *n.* the act of bending back ‖ the state of being bent backwards, esp. (*med.*) of the uterus upon the cervix ‖ (*phon.*) retroflex articulation [fr. Mod. L. *retroflexio* (*retroflexionis*)]

ret·ro·gra·da·tion (rętrougreidéiʃən) *n.* retrogression ‖ (*astron.*) regression [fr. L. *retrogradatio* (*retrogradationis*)]

ret·ro·grade (rétrəgreid) **1.** *v.i. pres. part.* **ret·ro·grad·ing** *past* and *past part.* **ret·ro·grad·ed** to go from a better to a worse condition ‖ (*astron.*) to move in a direction contrary to normal, esp. (of a planet) to appear to move from east to west in the solar system **2.** *adj.* moving or directed backwards ‖ involving something worse or less desirable, *a retrograde step* ‖ inverse, esp. of an alphabet that is written from right to left ‖ (*astron.*) showing regression ‖ (*aerospace*) of rotation of more than 90 degrees in the opposite direction to that of the launching point [fr. L. *retrogradi* or *retrogradare*, to go backward]

ret·ro·gress (rętrəgrés) *v.i.* to revert to an inferior state [fr. L. *retrogradi* (*retrogressus*), to go backwards]

ret·ro·gres·sion (rętrəgréʃən) *n.* (*astron.*) regression ‖ a reversion to an inferior state, esp. (*biol.*) a reverting to a lower state in the evolutionary process of the individual or race ‖ the subsiding of symptoms of a disease [fr. L. *retrogradi* (*retrogressus*), to retrograde]

ret·ro·gres·sive (rętrəgrésiv) *adj.* retrograde

ret·ro·pack (rétroupæk) *n.* (*aerospace*) a group of retroengines on a spacecraft

ret·ro·re·flec·tive (rętrouriflέktiv) *adj.* of reflection of light to its source —**retroreflect** *v.* —**retroflection** *n.* —**retroflector** *n.* the device

ret·ro·rock·et (rétrourǫkit) *n.* a spacecraft's auxiliary rocket engine with a thrust opposing the vehicle's motion, so as to bring about deceleration, or for separating rocket stages, etc.

retro-rocket *n.* (*aerospace*) a rocket on an aircraft that provides reverse thrust for deceleration —**retrofire** *v.*

re·trorse (ritrɔ́rs) *adj.* (*biol.*) turned or directed backwards or downwards [fr. L. *retrorsus*]

ret·ro·spect (rétrəspekt) *n.* an instance of looking back on past activities or events (cf. PROSPECT) **in retrospect** the past being looked at afresh, *in retrospect, the meeting was more successful than we had imagined* **ret·ro·spéc·tion** *n.* the act or process of reviewing the past ‖ an instance of this **ret·ro·spéc·tive** *adj.* of, relating to or indulging in retrospection, *a retrospective exhibition* ‖ (of payments etc.) retroactive, applying to past enactments (cf. PROSPECTIVE) [fr. L. *retrospicere* (*retrospectus*), to look back upon]

retrospective *n.* a comprehensive presentation of accomplishments over a period of years, esp. of an artist —**retrospective** *adj.*

ret·rous·sé (rətrú:sei, rętru:séi) *adj.* (of a nose) turned up at the tip [F.]

ret·ro·ver·sion (rętrəvə́:rʒən, rętrəvə́:rʃən) *n.* the act or process of turning back ‖ (*med.*) a retroflexion of the uterus ‖ a retrogression in development or condition [fr. L. *retrovertere* (*retroversus*), to turn backward]

re·turn (ritə́:rn) **1.** *n.* the act of returning to or from another place or condition ‖ the act of returning something to a former place or condition ‖ something returned, e.g. (*pl.*) unsold newspapers sent back to the publisher for refund ‖ profit from business etc., esp. this in relation to its source ‖ (*pl.*) an official report, announced or printed, of the results of balloting ‖ a report of statistics, *tax returns* ‖ (*Br.*) election, *the return of the same members is likely* ‖ (*pl.*) the mail received in answer to an advertising campaign ‖ (*archit.*) a wall etc. made to run in a different direction from the facade or from the direct line of building, esp. one turned back through 90° ‖ (*card games*) a card played in answer to a partner's lead ‖ (*fencing*) a riposte ‖ (*tennis, handball* etc.) the act of returning a ball ‖ (*baseball* and *cricket*) the sending back of a fielded ball ‖ a pipe, channel etc. for conveying liquid etc. back to its starting point ‖ (*Br.*) a return ticket **in return** by way of reward or retaliation **many happy returns (of the day)** a birthday greeting wishing the person greeted a long, happy life **2.** *adj.* of or pertaining to a return or a returning, *a return trip* ‖ given or done in return, *a return blow* ‖ used for returning, *a return pipe* [A.F. *retorn, retourn*]

return *v.i.* to go or come back to the same place, condition, person etc. ‖ to go back mentally, *thoughts constantly returning to childhood* ‖ to revert, *to return to my original theme* ‖ to occur again, *the fits return at intervals* ‖ *v.t.* to bring, give, put etc. (someone or something) back to a former place, condition or person, *return the book to the library, his departure returned us to normalcy, return the pipe to its owner* ‖ to give back by way of thanks or retaliation, *to return a call* ‖ to express as an answer or retort, *to return an oath* ‖ to repay (a loan) ‖ to pronounce (a verdict) ‖ (*Br.*) to elect by voting ‖ to yield (e.g. a profit) ‖ to cast back (e.g. sound) ‖ to submit (a set of statistics) required by authority ‖ to render (thanks) in prayer ‖ to cause (a wall etc.) to change in direction, esp. back through 90° ‖ (*card games*) to respond to (a partner's lead) by the expected lead ‖ (esp. *tennis*) to play back (the ball) ‖ (esp. *baseball* and *cricket*) to send back (a fielded ball) ‖ (*mil.*) to put (e.g. a weapon) back in its proper place [fr. O.F. *retorner, retourner*]

re·turn·a·ble (ritə́:rnəb'l) *adj.* that may be returned ‖ (*law*) required to be returned [A.F. *retournable*, O.F. *retournable*]

re·turn·ee (ritə:rní:, ritə́:rni:) *n.* a soldier returning to the U.S.A. after service overseas

return game a return match

return match a second game played between the same opposing teams or players so that the loser of the first game may have a chance to recoup the loss

return ticket (*Br.*) a round-trip ticket, i.e. for a journey to a destination and back over the same route ‖ the part of such a ticket valid for the trip back to the point of departure

re·tuse (ritú:s, ritjú:s) *adj.* (*biol.*) obtuse, with a broad shallow notch in the middle [fr. L. *retundere* (*retusus*), to beat]

re·type (ri:táip) *pres. part.* **re·typ·ing** *past* and *past part.* **re·typed** *v.t.* to type again

Retz (rets), Jean-François Paul de Gondi, cardinal de (1613-79), French politician and prelate. An enemy of Mazarin, he was a leader of the Fronde. He was nominally archbishop of Paris (1654-62) but was in exile until the death of Mazarin (1661), after which he was reconciled with Louis XIV. His 'Mémoires' vividly touch off men and situations

Reu·ben (rú:bən) Hebrew patriarch, the eldest son of Jacob ‖ the Israelite tribe of which he was the ancestor

Reu·ben sandwich (rú:bən) three-deck sandwich with corned beef, turkey, and Swiss cheese

Reuch·lin (rɔ́ixlən), Johann (1455-1522), German humanist. His 'De rudimentis Hebraicis'

CONCISE PRONUNCIATION KEY: **(a)** æ, *cat*; ɑ, *car*; ɔ *fawn*; ei, *snake*. **(e)** e, *hen*; i:, *sheep*; iə, *deer*; εə, *bear*. **(i)** i, *fish*; ai, *tiger*; ə:, *bird*. **(o)** o, *ox*; au, *cow*; ou, *goat*; u, *poor*; ɔi, *royal*. **(u)** ʌ, *duck*; u, *bull*; u:, *goose*; ə, *bacillus*; ju:, *cube*. x, *loch*; θ, *think*; ð, *bother*; z, *Zen*; ʒ, *corsage*; dʒ, *savage*; ŋ, *orangutang*; j, *yak*; ʃ, *fish*; tʃ, *fetch*; 'l, *rabble*; 'n, *redden*. Complete pronunciation key appears inside front cover.

(1506), a grammar and dictionary, was a major contribution to Hebrew scholarship. His defense of Hebrew literature caused a bitter feud between reformers and conservatives in the Church

re·u·ni·fi·ca·tion (ri:ju̜:nifikéiʃən) *n.* the restoration of a divided country to unity

re·u·ni·fy (ri:jú:nifai) *pres. part.* **re·u·ni·fy·ing** *past* and *past part.* **re·u·ni·fied** *v.t.* to restore (e.g. a divided country) to unity

Ré·u·nion (reiynjɔ̃) a mountainous, volcanic island (area 970 sq. miles, pop. 515,814) in the Indian Ocean between Mauritius and Madagascar, forming an overseas department of France. Chief town: Saint-Denis. People: Creole, with mulatto, Indian and African minorities. Highest point: Piton des Neiges (10,069 ft). Mean annual temperature: 69°. Rainfall: windward side over 100 ins, leeward side 30 ins. Exports: sugar (80% of exports, grown on coastal plantations), rum, tobacco, essential oils, fruit. Subsistence crops: corn, vegetables, vines. The island was discovered by the Portuguese (1513) and occupied by the French (17th c.). It became an overseas department in 1946

re·un·ion (ri:jú:njən) *n.* a reuniting or being reunited ‖ a meeting of former associates or of members of a family separated for a long time ‖ any social gathering held more or less regularly

re·u·nite (ri̜:ju:náit) *pres. part.* **re·u·nit·ing** *past* and *past part.* **re·u·nit·ed** *v.t.* to unite again after a period of separation ‖ *v.i.* to be united again [fr. M.L. *reunire (reunitus)*]

Reu·ters (rɔ́itərz) an independent international news agency founded (1851) in London by Baron Paul Julius von Reuter

Reuther (rú:θər), Walter Philip (1907-70), U.S. labor leader, president of the United Auto Workers (UAW) (1946-70). As a factory worker he became involved in the unions and quickly rose in the ranks. He also served as president of the Congress of Industrial Organizations (CIO) (1952-5) and, after its merger with the American Federation of Labor (AFL), as vice-president of the AFL-CIO (1955-68)

rev (rev) **1.** *n. (pop.)* a revolution of an engine **2.** *v. pres. part.* **rev·ving** *past* and *past part.* **revved** *v.t. (pop.,* usually with 'up') to increase the number of revolutions per minute of (an engine) ‖ *v.i. (pop.,* of an engine, usually with 'up') to turn over faster [REVOLUTION]

Re·val (réivɑl) *TALLINN

re·val·or·i·za·tion (ri:væləri̇zéiʃən) *n.* a revalorizing or being revalorized **re·vál·or·ize** *pres. part.* **re·val·or·iz·ing** *past* and *past part.* **re·val·or·ized** *v.t.* to alter the value of (a currency or assets)

re·val·ue (ri:vǽlju:) *pres. part.* **re·val·u·ing** *past* and *past part.* **re·val·ued** *v.t.* to give a new value to (e.g. currency) ‖ to set a new estimate of worth on

re·vamp (ri:vǽmp) *v.t.* to put a new vamp on (an old shoe) ‖ to refurbish, revise and improve, *to revamp a play*

re·vas·cu·lar·ize (ri̜:vǽskjuləri:z) *v. (med.)* **1.** to substitute arteries from other parts of the body for clogged or diseased arteries **2.** to reestablish of blood supply, esp. after destruction of arteries —**revascularization** *n. Cf* CORONARY BYPASS

re·veal (ri:ví:l) *n. (archit.)* the thickness of a wall as shown by a doorway, aperture or window [fr. M.E. *revale*, to bring down]

reveal *v.t.* to make known, manifest, *to reveal one's real intention, God revealed his will to the Israelites* ‖ to expose to view (something that was hidden) ‖ to divulge (a secret) [fr. O.F. *reveler* or L. *revelare*]

revealed religion a religion based upon divine revelation (cf. NATURAL RELIGION)

rev·eil·le (révəli:) *n. (mil.)* as signal sounded esp. by a bugle, to wake members of the forces in the morning ‖ *(mil.)* the first assembly of the day [fr. F. *réveillez (-vous)*, wake up]

Re·vel (réivəl) *TALLINN

rev·el (révəl) *n. (hist., pl.)* the games and dances etc. of a festive occasion [O.F.]

revel *pres. part.* **rev·el·ing,** esp. *Br.* **rev·el·ling** *past* and *past part.* **rev·eled,** esp. *Br.* **rev·elled** *v.i.* (with 'in') to take intense pleasure, *she revels in ballet* ‖ to be festive, *to revel all night long* [O.F. *reveler*]

Rev·e·la·tion (re̜vəléiʃən) the 27th and last book (late 1st or early 2nd c.) of the New Testament, of uncertain authorship. It contains apocalyptic visions of the victory of God over Satan and was apparently written to strengthen persecuted Christians

rev·e·la·tion (re̜vəléiʃən) *n.* a revealing ‖ something revealed ‖ *(theol.)* God's manifestation of himself to man ‖ something revealed to man by God ‖ something which brings a shock of surprise, *the revelation of hearing one's recorded voice* [O.F.]

rev·el·ry (révəlri:) *pl.* **rev·el·ries** *n.* the act of reveling

re·ven·di·ca·tion (rive̜ndikéiʃən) *n. (law)* a formal claim for the recovery of property ‖ *(law)* the recovery of property by formal claim [F.]

re·venge (rivéndʒ) **1.** *v.t. pres. part.* **re·veng·ing** *past* and *past part.* **re·venged** to inflict injury etc. in return for (injury etc.) ‖ to avenge (oneself or another person) **2.** *n.* a revenging ‖ something done in revenging, *his revenge was to set the papers on fire* ‖ a desire to inflict injury etc. in return for an injury etc. suffered, *to be full of revenge* ‖ *(games)* a chance to win after a previous defeat, e.g. in a return match [obs. F. *revenger*]

rev·e·nue (révənu:, révənju:) *n.* return from investments, property etc. ‖ *(pl.)* items of income collectively ‖ the annual or periodic income, e.g. from taxes, customs and excise etc., collected by a government, state etc. for public use ‖ a government department in charge of collecting such income [O.F.]

revenue sharing policy of subsidizing taxes received by the federal government with states and/or municipalities

revenue stamp a stamp used on documents etc. as evidence that a tax has been paid

revenue tariff a tariff designed primarily to secure public revenue (cf. PROTECTIVE TARIFF)

re·verb (rivə́:rb) *n.* an echo effect in a musical recording —**reverb** *n.* device for creating an echo effect

re·ver·ber·ate (rivə́:rbəreit) *pres. part.* **re·ver·ber·at·ing** *past* and *past part.* **re·ver·ber·at·ed** *v.t.* to reflect (light etc.) ‖ to throw back (sound) ‖ to deflect (e.g. heat in a furnace) ‖ to subject to the heat of a reverberatory furnace ‖ *v.i.* to reecho ‖ to be reflected ‖ *(metall.,* of flame or heat, with 'upon' or 'over') to be forced to strike [fr. L. *reverberare (reverberatus)*]

re·ver·ber·a·tion (rivə̜:rbəréiʃən) *n.* a reechoing of sound ‖ a reflecting of light etc. ‖ a deflection of heat etc. ‖ subjection to the action of a reverberatory furnace ‖ something reverberated [O.F.]

re·ver·ber·a·tive (rivə́:rbərətiv, rivə́:rbəre̜itiv) *adj.* reverberating or tending to reverberate ‖ of the nature of reverberation

re·ver·ber·a·tor (rivə́:rbəre̜itər) *n.* something that produces reverberation, e.g. a reflector **re·ver·ber·a·to·ry** (rivə́:rbərətɔ̜ri:, rivə́:rbərətɔ̜uri) **1.** *adj.* acting by reverberation **2.** *pl.* **re·ver·ber·a·to·ries** *n.* a reverberatory furnace

reverberatory furnace a furnace or kiln in which the ore, metal etc. is melted not by direct contact with flame, but by the heat of flames radiated from the roof

Re·vere (rivíər), Paul (1735-1818), American patriot. By a famous night ride (Apr. 18, 1775) he warned the Massachusetts colonists of the arrival of British troops at the start of the Revolutionary War

re·vere (rivíər) *pres. part.* **re·ver·ing** *past* and *past part.* **re·vered** *v.t.* to regard with affectionate awe or veneration [fr. F. *révérer* or L. *revereri*]

rev·er·ence (révərəns, révrəns) **1.** *n.* a revering, *teach them reverence for truth* ‖ the condition or state of being revered, *to be held in reverence* ‖ *(old-fash.)* a bow or curtsy **2.** *v.t. pres. part.* **rev·er·enc·ing** *past* and *past part.* **rev·er·enced** to revere [O. F.]

Rev·er·end (révərənd, révrənd) *adj. (abbr.* Rev., preceded by 'the') used as a title for a clergyman (his surname being preceded by Mr. or Dr. or by his Christian name) [O.F.]

rev·er·ent (révərənt, révrənt) *adj.* feeling or showing due reverence [fr. L. *reverens (reverentis)* fr. *revereri*, to revere]

rev·er·en·tial (re̜vərénʃəl) *adj.* showing reverence [fr. L. *reverentia*, reverence]

rev·er·ie (révəri:) *n.* the state of being absorbed in dreamlike contemplation ‖ an idea, theory etc. characteristic of such contemplation [F.]

re·vers (rivíər) *pl.* **re·vers** (rivíərz) *n.* a fold in a piece of tailoring work showing the inside lining of a facing ‖ a lapel on women's jackets, coats etc. [F.]

re·ver·sal (rivə́:rsəl) *n.* a reversing or being reversed ‖ *(law)* a revoking or overthrowing of a legal proceeding

re·verse (rivə́:rs) *pres. part.* **re·vers·ing** *past* and *past part.* **re·versed** *v.t.* to change the direction, arrangement, nature etc. of (something) to its opposite ‖ to turn (a reversible garment) inside out ‖ to turn upside down, *to reverse an hourglass* ‖ to change (a trend, opinion etc.) to the opposite ‖ to cause to go or move backwards, *to reverse a car* ‖ *(law)* to annul, make void (a decision etc.) ‖ *v.i.* to move, turn or go backwards ‖ *(dancing)* to go in the opposite direction ‖ to put an engine etc. in reverse [F. *reverser*]

reverse 1. *adj.* opposite, *the reverse side of the cloth* ‖ backward, *reverse motion* ‖ causing backward movement, *reverse gear* **2.** *n.* the opposite of something, *what you say is the reverse of what I believed* ‖ the back side of a coin, medal etc. (opp. OBVERSE) ‖ a change from good fortune to bad, *a financial reverse* ‖ *(mil.)* a defeat ‖ a mechanism, e.g. a gear, for causing a motor etc. to run backwards **in reverse** in reverse gear ‖ (of a vehicle) moving backwards ‖ in the reverse order [O.F. *revers, reverse*]

reverse discrimination discrimination against one group (e.g., white people) alleged to result from affirmative action for another group (e.g., black people)

reverse mortgage mortgage funds withdrawn in installments from a lender, e.g., as a source of living expenses

reverse osmosis the pumping of a solvent through a semipermeable membrane to counter osmosis

re·vers·i·bil·i·ty (rivə̜:rsəbíliti:) *n.* the state or quality of being reversible

re·vers·i·ble (rivə́:rsəb'l) *adj.* able to be reversed ‖ (of a fabric) having the full pattern on both sides ‖ (of a garment) made so that either the inside or outside can be worn outermost ‖ *(chem.)* of a reaction in which a change from one state to another can occur in either direction **re·vérs·i·bly** *adv.*

re·ver·sion (rivə́:rʒən, rivə́:rʃən) *n.* return to a former condition, belief etc. or an instance of this ‖ *(biol.)* atavism ‖ *(biol.)* an atavistic organism or individual ‖ *(law)* the right to own something when it is relinquished by the present owner ‖ *(law)* the returning of property to its previous owner at the end of a period during which it was the temporary possession of someone else ‖ a reversionary annuity **re·vér·sion·al** *adj.* **re·ver·sion·ar·y** (rivə́:rʒəne̜ri:, rivə́:rʃəne̜ri:) *adj.* **re·vér·sion·er** *n. (law)* someone who has a reversion [O.F.]

re·vert (rivə́:rt) *v.i.* to return to a former belief, opinion, condition etc., *the tribe reverted to paganism* ‖ to return to a topic, *to revert to your earlier remark...* ‖ *(law)* to return to a former owner by reversion ‖ *(biol.)* to undergo reversion **re·vért·i·ble** *adj.* subject to reversion [O.F. *revertir*]

re·ver·tant (rivə́:rtənt) *n. (genetics)* a mutated organism that returns to a previous condition, e.g., a hybrid returning to a wild form —**revertant** *adj.*

re·vet (rivét) *pres. part.* **re·vet·ting** *past* and *past part.* **re·vet·ted** *v.i.* to face (an embankment, trench etc.) with supporting material **re·vét·ment** *n.* a retaining wall or other support for a trench or embankment [fr. F. *revétir*]

re·view (rivjú:) **1.** *n.* a looking over, considering, studying etc. again ‖ a general consideration of past events or situations, *a review of one's life* ‖ a ceremonial inspection of troops etc. ‖ *(law)* a reexamination of a decision etc. ‖ a critical evaluation of a book, concert, theatrical performance etc. in mass media ‖ a periodical containing critical evaluations and articles on specific subjects, *a science review* ‖ a brushing up (on work learned earlier) **re·víew·al** *n.* **re·víew·er** *n.* a person who writes reviews of books, plays etc. for publication **2.** *v.t.* to consider again, *to review a manuscript in the light of criticism* ‖ to inspect ceremonially, *to review troops* ‖ to pass over (past events etc.) in one's mind ‖ to write a critical evaluation of (a book, theatrical performance etc.) ‖ *(law)* to reexamine judicially ‖ to brush up (something learned earlier) ‖ *v.i.* to write reviews of books, plays etc.

re·vile (riváil) *pres. part.* **re·vil·ing** *past* and *past part.* **re·viled** *v.t.* to use abusive language to or about ‖ *v.i.* to speak abusively [O.F. *reviler*]

re·vis·al (riváiz'l) *n.* a revising or being revised

re·vise (riváiz) **1.** *v.t. pres. part.* **re·vis·ing** *past* and *past part.* **re·vised** to reexamine, esp. in order to discover and amend errors in (a text etc.) || to brush up (something learned earlier) so as to refresh the memory **2.** *n.* (*printing*) a proof of corrected type [F. *reviser*]

Revised Standard Version a revision (1946-57) by a committee of American biblical scholars of the American Standard edition (1901) of the Revised Version of the Bible. Designed for use in public worship, it succeeded largely in preserving the beauty of the Authorized (King James) Version

Revised Version (*abbr.* R.V., Rev. Ver.) a revision of the Authorized (King James) Version (1611) of the Bible, made by a committee of English and American scholars. The New Testament was published in 1881 and the Old Testament in 1885

re·vi·sion (rivíʒən) *n.* a revising or being revised || the result of revising, e.g. a revised text **re·ví·sion·al** *adj.* [fr. L.L. *revisio* (*revisionis*)]

re·vi·sion·ism (rivíʒənizəm) *n.* a movement among socialists to modify Marxian revolutionary doctrine **re·vi·sion·ist** *n.*

re·vi·so·ry (riváizəri:) *adj.* of or relating to revision || having the power to revise, *a revisory body*

re·viv·al (riváivəl) *n.* a reviving or being revived || (of the mind or body) a coming back to health or consciousness || an awakening of religious fervor, esp. by evangelism || an evangelistic meeting or series of meetings || the reappearance of a past mode, esp. the reappearance of Gothic architecture in the 19th c. || a restaging of a play, esp. of one long neglected **re·vív·al·ism, re·vív·al·ist** *ns.*

Revival of Learning the literary aspect of the Renaissance

re·vive (riváiv) *pres. part.* **re·viv·ing** *past* and *past part.* **re·vived** *v.i.* to come back to consciousness || to recover strength, vigor, spirits etc., *he revived after a rest and some food* || (*chem.*, of a metal) to recover the metallic state || *v.t.* to restore to consciousness, strength, vigor, spirits etc. || to produce (an old play) again || to make valid again, *why revive harsh laws?* || to bring (old memories) to mind again || to bring back into fashion || (*chem.*) to restore (a metal) to the metallic state [fr. F. *revivre*]

re·viv·i·fi·ca·tion (rivivifikéiʃən) *n.* a revivifying or being revivified

re·viv·i·fy (rivívifai) *pres. part.* **re·viv·i·fy·ing** *past* and *past part.* **re·viv·i·fied** *v.t.* to restore to strength or vigor [fr. F. *revivifier*]

re·vi·vor (riváivər) *n.* (*Br., law*) proceedings to revive a lawsuit after its lapsing (due to a death etc.)

rev·o·ca·bil·i·ty (revəkəbíliti:) *n.* the state or quality of being revocable

rev·o·ca·ble, rev·o·ka·ble (révəkəb'l, rivóukəb'l) *adj.* that can be revoked [O.F. or fr. L. *revocabilis*]

rev·o·ca·tion (revəkéiʃən) *n.* a revoking or being revoked || a repealing or annulling [O.F.]

rev·o·ca·to·ry (révəkətɔri:, révəkətouri:) *adj.* revoking, tending to revoke [fr. L. L. *revocatorius*]

revokable *REVOCABLE

re·voke (rivóuk) **1.** *v. pres. part.* **re·vok·ing** *past* and *past part.* **re·voked** *v.t.* to cancel, withdraw, *to revoke permission* || *v.i.* (*cards*) to fail to follow suit when one can and should do so **2.** *n.* (*cards*) a failure to follow suit when one could have done so [O.F. *revoquer*]

re·volt (rivóult) *n.* an opposing of authority, esp. by armed rebellion || such rebellion || the mental state of a person or group of persons likely to express itself by rebellion **in revolt** (of a person or group) in a state of rebellion [F. *révolte*]

revolt *v.i.* to turn actively against the government, esp. in armed rebellion || to rebel against other authority || (with 'at' or 'against') to feel disgust, *the mind revolts at such an idea* || *v.t.* to disgust, the *scene revolted him* **re·vólt·ing** *adj.* disgusting || rebelling [fr. F. *révolter*]

rev·o·lute (révəlu:t) *adj.* (*bot.*, esp. of leaves) having the margins or tips rolled backward or downward [fr. L. *revolutus*, rolled back]

rev·o·lu·tion (revəlú:ʃən) *n.* the act of revolving || one complete turn in the action of revolving, *45 revolutions a minute* || an unconstitutional overthrow of an established government || a fundamental social change, *the Industrial Revolution* || any fundamental complete change || (of heavenly bodies) the action of going around in an orbit || (of heavenly bodies) the time taken to complete this action **rev·o·lú·tion·ar·y 1.** *adj.* of or relating to a revolution, esp. a political or social revolution || tending toward, or seeming to tend toward, a revolution, *a revolutionary speech* **2.** *pl.* **rev·o·lu·tion·ar·ies** *n.* a revolutionist [O.F.]

Revolutionary War (*Am.=Br.* War of American Independence) the struggle (1775-83) of the Thirteen Colonies of America for independence from British rule. The war was caused by British attempts to tax the colonies for revenue without representation in Parliament and to make them pay for a standing army. The colonies' dependence on Britain was lessened when the Treaty of Paris (1763) removed the French and Indian threat. The colonies revolted (1775) under Washington and declared their independence (1776). Burgoyne's surrender at Saratoga (1777) encouraged France to declare war on Britain (1778), followed by Spain (1779) and the Netherlands (1780). Britain lost command of the sea, and her army was finally defeated at Yorktown (1781). Britain regained naval supremacy (1781-2) and the war ended with the Treaty of Paris (1783), in which the independence of the U.S.A. was recognized. The war discredited George III's government, weakened France financially, and served as an inspiration for the French Revolution and for revolutions in Spanish colonies in America

rev·o·lu·tion·ist (revəlú:ʃənist) *n.* a person who takes part in a revolution or who advocates revolution

rev·o·lu·tion·ize (revəlú:ʃənaiz) *pres. part.* **rev·o·lu·tion·iz·ing** *past* and *past part.* **rev·o·lu·tion·ized** *v.t.* to change completely as if by a revolution, *the invention of the reaper revolutionized harvesting*

Revolution of 1789 *FRENCH REVOLUTION

Revolution of 1830 *FRANCE

Revolution of 1848 *FRANCE, *GERMANY, *HUNGARY, *ITALY

Revolution of 1905 *RUSSIA

Revolution of 1917 *RUSSIA

re·volve (rivɔ́lv) *pres. part.* **re·vol·ving** *past* and *past part.* **re·volved** *v.t.* to cause to turn around an axis or center, *to revolve a prayer wheel* || (*rhet.*) to ponder, *to revolve a problem* || *v.i.* to move around or as if around an axis or center || to recur, *the revolving seasons* || (*rhet.*, of a problem etc.) to present itself for consideration under various aspects, *the subject was revolving in his mind* [fr. L. *revolvere*]

re·volv·er (rivɔ́lvər) *n.* a pistol with a revolving feeding mechanism enabling several cartridges to be discharged without reloading

revolving door a door, e.g. of a public building, consisting of two or more panels, normally of glass, attached to a central axis to allow free rotation usually in one direction

re·vue (rivjú:) *n.* a stage spectacle consisting of sketches, songs etc. in which parody and satire predominate [F.]

re·vul·sion (rivʌ́lʃən) *n.* a sudden, violent antipathy, *a revulsion against a person* || disgust, *he shrank away in revulsion* [F.]

rev up or **rev** *v.* to get started by turning an airplane propeller

re·ward (riwɔ́rd) *n.* something given or promised in recognition of service rendered or in requital for ill-doing || money offered for information leading to the capture of a criminal, the recovery of lost property etc. [O.N.F.]

reward *v.t.* to give a reward to (a person) || to give a reward for (a service, merit etc.) **re·wárd·ing** *adj.* giving personal satisfaction, *a rewarding occupation* [O.N.F. *rewarder*]

re·wire (ri:wáiər) *pres. part.* **re·wir·ing** *past* and *past part.* **re·wired** *v.t.* to furnish (an electric circuit) with new wires || to furnish (a house etc.) with a rewired electric circuit

re·word (ri:wɔ́:rd) *v.t.* to express in other words

re·write 1. (ri:ráit) *v.t. pres. part.* **re·writ·ing** *past* **re·wrote** (ri:róut) *past part.* **re·writ·ten** (ri:rít'n) to alter or improve the style or wording of, *rewrite the section on accountancy*, esp. (*journalism*) to make (material turned in by a reporter) suitable for publication **2.** (rí:rait) *n.* a piece of writing treated in this way

Re·yes (réjes), Alfonso (1889-1959), Mexican humanist writer and diplomat. He exerted a major influence on the intellectual life of Latin America. His prose works, inspired by Greek and Roman civilization and by national themes, include 'Cuestiones estéticas', 'Homero en Cuernavaca', and 'Visión de Anáhuac'

Reyes, Neftalí *NERUDA

Reyes syndrome (raiz), a children's disease, first described (1963) by Australian pathologist R.D.K. Reye, that occurs most often as a result of influenza or chicken pox. Symptoms include high fever, headache, vomiting and central nervous system disorders. It is thought that aspirin, often prescribed for the initial sickness, can trigger Reyes syndrome

Rey·kja·vik (réikjəvi:k) the capital and chief port (pop. 87,309) of Iceland, on the southwest coast. Industries: fishing, fish processing, codliver oil refining, shipbuilding. University (1911), national museums. It was settled by Vikings (late 9th c.) and became the capital of Iceland in 1918

Rey·les (réiles), Carlos (1868-1938), Uruguayan novelist, the author of 'Beba', 'La Raza de Caín', 'El embrujo de Sevilla', 'El gaucho Florido', and 'El terruño'

Rey·naud (reinou), Paul (1878-1966), French statesman. Appointed prime minister (Mar. 1940), he resigned (June 1940) when the Germans invaded France. He was a prisoner in Germany (1943-5)

Reyn·olds (rénəldz), Sir Joshua (1723-92), English portrait painter. He was a founding member and first president (1769) of the Royal Academy of Arts, London. His annual addresses to the Academy, published as his 'Discourses', have become classics in the field of art criticism. His portraits and historical paintings are notable for their richness of color. Reynolds was a member of the famous dining club which included Johnson, Gibbon, Burke, Garrick, Sheridan, Goldsmith and others

Reynolds, Osborne (1842-1912), British engineer. He developed the theory of the radiometer, and invented a high-lift centrifugal pump

Re·zai·yeh (rezɑjá) (formerly Urmia) a salt lake (area 1,500-2,300 sq. miles, depending on season) in N.W. Iran, near Tabriz

Reza Shah Pahlavi *PAHLAVI, REZA SHAH

R factor unit of measurement of **1.** a material's resistance to heat loss, used in stating the effectiveness of insulation, e.g., 6 in of fiberglass equals R-19 **2.** bacterial resistance to antibiotics in cells

R.F.D. rural free delivery

RF energy the energy of alternating current in the frequency range to 10 kHz and 300 GHz

RF-4 *PHANTOM II

RGM-84 *HARPOON

RGM-66D *STANDARD SSM (ARM)

rhab·do·vi·rus (ræbdouváirəs) *n.* (*med.*) any of a group of viruses associated with animal-bite diseases, e.g., rabies

rhachis *RACHIS

Rhad·a·man·thine (rædəmǽnθain, rædəmǽnθin) *adj.* (*rhet.*) sternly just [after *Rhadamanthus*, (Gk mythol.) son of Zeus and Europa and a judge in the lower world]

Rhae·ti·a, Rae·ti·a (rí:ʃi:ə) (*hist.*) a region of what is now E. Switzerland and W. Austria, annexed (c. 15 B.C.) as a province by the Romans

Rhae·tic (rí:tik) *n.* (*geol.*) the uppermost division of the European Triassic, disclosed in the Rhaetian Alps [fr. L. *Rhaeticus*, Rhaetian]

Rhae·to-Ro·man·ic (ri:tourouмǽnik) *n.* a Romance language of the Tyrol and the cantons of S.E. Switzerland and N. Italy

rhap·sod·ic (ræpsɔ́dik) *adj.* of, resembling or having the form of rhapsody || extravagantly enthusiastic **rhap·sód·i·cal** *adj.* [fr. Gk *rhapsōdikos*]

rhap·so·dist (rǽpsədist) *n.* a professional reciter of epic poetry in ancient Greece [fr. Gk *rhapsōdos* fr. *rhaptein*, to put together and *ōdē*, an ode]

rhap·so·dize (rǽpsədaiz) *pres. part.* **rhap·so·diz·ing** *past* and *past part.* **rhap·so·dized** *v.i.* to speak or write in an extravagantly enthusiastic manner

rhap·so·dy (rǽpsədi:) *pl.* **rhap·so·dies** *n.* an epic poem of ancient Greece, or a portion of one, suitable for recitation || extravagant enthusiasm in speaking or writing || (*mus.*) a title given to some usually single-movement compositions having no fixed form and often based on existing themes [fr. L. *rhapsodia* fr. Gk]

rhat·a·ny (rǽt'ni:) *pl.* **rhat·a·nies** *n.* the dried root of *Krameria triandra* or *K. argentea*, fam. *Papilionaceae*, two South American shrubs, used in medicine as an astringent || either of these shrubs [fr. Mod. L. *rhatania*]

Rhe·a (rí:ə) (*Gk mythol.*) one of the Titans, wife of Cronus, mother of Zeus, Poseidon etc. She was identified with Cybele

rhe·a (rí:ə) *n.* a member of *Rhea*, order *Rheiformes*, a genus of ostrichlike, flightless South

American birds, esp. *R. americana* [L. after RHEA]

Rhee (ri:), Syngman (1875-1965), South Korean leader. He campaigned for self-rule (1910-19) and was president of the exiled provisional government. He was president of the Republic of South Korea (1948-60). He opposed the truce of 1953 which partitioned Korea. In Apr. 1960 riots and the resignation of his cabinet forced him to resign

Rheims (ri:mz) *REIMS

Rhen·ish (réniʃ) *adj.* of or pertaining to the Rhine or the Rhine valley [fr. L. *Rhenus*, Rhine]

rhe·ni·um (rí:ni:əm) *n.* a rare, heavy polyvalent metallic element (symbol Re, at. no. 75, at. mass 186.2) having a high melting point (3,167°C.), used esp. in thermocouples [Mod. L. fr. *Rhenus*, Rhine]

rhe·ol·o·gy (ri:ɒlədʒi:) *n.* the study of the deformation and flow of matter [fr. Gk *rheos*, stream + *logos*, word]

rhe·o·stat (rí:əstæt) *n.* a variable resistance for the strength of an electric current **rhe·o·stát·ic** *adj.* [fr. Gk *rheos*, stream + *statos*, standing still]

rhe·o·tax·is (ri:ətæksis) *pl.* **rhe·o·tax·es** (ri:ətæksi:z) *n.* (*biol.*) a locomotor response to the stimulus of a current, usually of water [Mod. L. fr. Gk *rheos*, stream + *taxis*, arrangement]

rhe·o·trope (rí:ətroup) *n.* an instrument for changing the direction of an electric current [fr. Gk *rheos*, stream + *tropos*, a turning]

rhe·ot·ro·pism (ri:ɒtrəpizəm) *n.* (*biol.*) curvature or growth response to the influence of a water current [fr. Gk *rheos*, stream + TROPISM]

rhe·sus (rí:səs) *n.* *Macaca mulata*, a small light brown Indian monkey [Mod. L. fr. a proper name]

rhesus factor (*abbr.* Rh factor) an inherited sex-linked agglutinating factor sometimes present in human red blood cells, which is capable of causing an intense antigenic reaction in certain circumstances (a Rh negative mother carrying a Rh positive fetus). Those having this factor are Rh positive. Those not having it are Rh negative

rhe·tor (rí:tər) *n.* a teacher of rhetoric, esp. in ancient Greece and Rome [L. fr. Gk *rhētōr*]

rhet·o·ric (rétərik) *n.* the art or science of communication in words ‖ this art or science practiced or taught as a formal discipline, esp. the doctrine formulated by Aristotle and taught throughout the Middle Ages ‖ overornate or ostentatious language ‖ language held by many to be proper to elevated written style but not normally used in everyday speech (indicated by *rhet.* in this book) **rhe·tor·i·cal** (ritɔ́rik'l, ritɒ́rik'l) *adj.* [O.F. *rethorique* fr. L. fr. Gk]

rhetorical question a question posed for rhetorical effect, emphasis etc. and not meant to be answered. Its context supplies its own answer by suggestion and admits of no others

rhet·o·ri·cian (retəríʃən) *n.* a teacher of or expert in the art of rhetoric ‖ a rhetorical speaker or writer [O.F. *rethoricien*]

rheum (ru:m) *n.* a discharge from the mucous membranes of the eyes or nose [O.F. *reume* fr. L. fr. Gk]

rheu·mat·ic (rumætik) **1.** *adj.* relating to rheumatism ‖ affected by or suffering from rheumatism **2.** *n.* someone afflicted with rheumatism [O.F. *reumatique* fr. L. fr. Gk]

rheumatic fever a disease, often recurrent, which sometimes follows an infected throat, occurring mainly in children or young adults. It is characterized by fever, pains and swelling in and around the joints and inflammation of the pericardium and valves of the heart

rheu·ma·tism (rú:mətizəm) *n.* any of various conditions characterized by pain and swelling in and around the muscles and joints [fr. L.L. *rheumatismus*]

rheu·ma·toid (rú:mətɔid) *adj.* of or resembling rheumatoid arthritis ‖ affected with rheumatoid arthritis [fr. Gk *rheuma* (*rheumatos*), catarrh]

rheumatoid arthritis a chronic relapsing disease of unknown cause, characterized by pain and stiffness of the joints, esp. those of the limbs. It tends to be a progressive disease and may cause permanent deformity

rheumatoid factor (*med.*) an antiglobulin (gamma globulin) often found in the blood serum of rheumatoid arthritics

RH-53 *SEA STALLION

rheum·y (rú:mi:) *comp.* **rheum·i·er** *superl.* **rheum·i·est** *adj.* exuding rheum ‖ (of weather) damp and tending to cause rheumatic troubles, catarrh etc.

Rheydt (rait) a textile manufacturing town (pop. 101,500) in North Rhine-Westphalia, West Germany, adjoining München-Gladbach

Rh factor *RHESUS FACTOR

rhi·nal (ráin'l) *adj.* (*anat.*) of or relating to the nose [fr. Gk *rhis* (*rhinos*), nose]

Rhin (Bas-) *BAS-RHIN

rhi·nen·ceph·a·lon (rainenséfəlɒn) *pl.* **rhi·nen·ceph·a·la** (rainenséfələ) *n.* (*anat.*) the part of the forebrain forming most of the cerebral hemispheres in fishes, amphibia and reptiles, and comprising chiefly the olfactory lobes in man [fr. Gk *rhis* (*rhinos*), nose + ENCEPHALON]

rhine·stone (ráinstoun) *n.* a colorless artificial gem usually cut to resemble a diamond [trans. F. *caillou du Rhin*]

Rhine wine any of the light, dry, white wines produced in the valley of the Rhine

Rhin (Haut-) *HAUT-RHIN

Rhine (rain) (*G.* Rhein, *Du.* Rijn) the chief river (824 miles long) of W. Europe, flowing from the Swiss Alps south of Lake Constance, through W. West Germany and the Netherlands to a delta on the North Sea, forming the frontiers of Switzerland with Liechtenstein, Austria and West Germany, and of West Germany with E. France. It is navigable to Basle. Chief ports: Strasbourg, Mannheim, Cologne, Duisburg, Rotterdam. Principal tributaries: the Aar, Main, Moselle, Ruhr and Meuse. Canals link it to the Danube, Rhône, Marne, Ems, Weser and Elbe. It flows through mountains between Bonn and Mainz, in a gorge of great scenic splendor, lined with vineyards and topped with castles

Rhine, Confederation of the a military and political confederation (1806-13) created by Napoleon, including Bavaria, Württemberg, Baden, Hesse-Darmstadt and other German states, as a bastion against Prussia and Austria

Rhine·land (ráinlænd, ráinlənd) the region of West Germany along both banks of the middle Rhine

Rhine·land-Pa·lat·i·nate (ráinlænd-pəlǽt'nit) (*G.* Rheinland-Pfalz) a state (area 7,654 sq. miles, pop. 3,638,700) of West Germany between the middle Rhine and the western frontier, partly wooded and largely mountainous. Agricultural products: wine (Moselle valley), cereals, root vegetables, fruit, tobacco (Rhine plain). Main industries: hydroelectricity, mining, chemicals. Chief towns: Mainz (the capital), Ludwigshafen, Koblenz. The state was formed (1945) out of the S. Prussian Rhine province (*NORTH RHINE-WESTPHALIA), the Rhine Palatinate and W. Hesse-Nassau

Rhine Palatinate *PALATINATE

rhi·ni·tis (raináitis) *n.* inflammation of the mucous membrane of the nose [fr. Gk *rhis* (*rhinos*), nose]

rhi·no (ráinou) *n.* (*pop.*) a rhinoceros

rhi·noc·er·os (rainɒ́sərəs) *pl.* **rhi·noc·er·os·es, rhi·noc·er·os** *n.* any of various herbivorous mammals of fam. *Rhinocerotidae*, native to Africa and S.E. Asia, weighing from 2 to 3½ tons and having a very thick gray or blackish gray knobby hide and either one or two horns curving up from the snout [Mod. L. fr. Gk fr. *rhis* (*rhinos*), nose + *keras*, horn]

rhi·nol·o·gist (rainɒ́lədʒist) *n.* a physician specializing in rhinology

rhi·nol·o·gy (rainɒ́lədʒi:) *n.* the study of the nose and its diseases [fr. Gk *rhis* (*rhinos*), nose + *logos*, word]

rhi·no·plas·tic (rainouplǽstik) *adj.* of or relating to rhinoplasty

rhi·no·plas·ty (ráinouplæsti:) *n.* plastic surgery of the nose [fr. Gk *rhis* (*rhinos*), nose +*-plastia*, formation]

rhi·no·scope (ráinəskoup) *n.* an instrument for examining the interior of the nose **rhi·nos·co·py** (rainɒ́skəpi:) *n.* examination of the nasal cavity and passages [fr. Gk *rhis* (*rhinos*), nose + *skopein*, to observe]

rhi·no·vi·rus (rainouváirəs) *n.* (*med.*) one of the small viruses in the picornavirus group, associated with the common cold. *Cf* PICORNOVIRUS

rhi·zo·bi·um (rizóubi:əm) *pl.* **rhi·zo·bi·a** (rizóubi:ə) *n.* a rod-shaped nitrogen-fixing bacterium living in the nodules of certain leguminous plants, e.g. the bean [Mod. L. fr. Gk *rhiza*, root + *bios*, life]

rhi·zo·car·pous (raizoukárpəs) *adj.* having a perennial root or rootlike process but annual stems and foliage [fr. Gk *rhiza*, root + *karpos*, fruit]

rhi·zo·ceph·a·lous (raizouséfələs) *adj.* of or relating to a parasitic crustacean of the order *Rhizocephala*, allied to the cirripeds [fr. Gk *rhiza*, root+ *kephalē*, head]

rhi·zo·gen·ic (raizoudʒénik) *adj.* (*bot.*) producing roots indigenously (from the pericycle of seed plants) [fr. Gk *rhiza*, root + *genes*, born of]

rhi·zog·e·nous (raizɒ́dʒənəs) *adj.* rhizogenic

rhi·zoid (ráizɔid) **1.** *n.* a rootlike filamentous outgrowth of the thallus of the gametophyte generation of many pteridophytes that serves to anchor the organism to the soil and function as an absorptive organ ‖ a similar organ in some thallophytes **2.** *adj.* rootlike [fr. Gk *rhiza*, root]

rhi·zom·a·tous (raizɒ́mətəs, raizóumətəs) *n.* of or having rhizomes

rhi·zome (ráizoum) *n.* a thickened, usually horizontal underground stem or branch of a plant that stores food, producing roots below and leafy shoots above, and that differs from a root in having buds and scaly leaves [fr. Mod. L. *rhizoma* fr. Gk]

rhi·zo·morph (ráizəmɔrf) *n.* a twisted strand of fungal hyphae that in many basidiomycetes serves for the transport of liquids and as a means by which the fungus spreads **rhi·zo·mór·phous** *adj.* formed like a root, rootlike [fr. Gk *rhiza*, root+ *morphē*, shape, form]

rhi·zo·pod (ráizəpɒd) *n.* a member of *Rhizopoda*, a subclass of protozoans characterized by pseudopodia. Some form external shells or internal stiffening skeletons. Most are free-living, some parasitic. The subclass includes foraminifers, radiolarians, amoebas etc. **rhi·zop·o·dan** (raizɒ́pədən) *n.* and *adj.* **rhi·zóp·o·dous** *adj.* [fr. Gk *rhiza*, root + *pous* (*podos*), foot]

rho (rou) *n.* the seventeenth letter (Ρ, ρ = r) of the Greek alphabet

Rhode Island (roud) (*abbr.* R.I.) the smallest state (area 1,214 sq. miles, pop. 958,000) of the U.S.A., on the northeast coast. Capital: Providence. The indented coastline is backed by a wooded coastal plain and hilly upland in the northwest. It is primarily industrial (textiles, machinery and metalwork, electronics, jewelry). Agriculture: dairy farming, poultry, nurseries. Resources: building materials. Chief universities: Brown (1764) at Providence, University of Rhode Island (1892) at Kingston. Rhode Island was settled by the English (17th c.), was one of the Thirteen Colonies, and became (1790) the 13th state of the U.S.A.

Rhodes (roudz) (*Gk* Rhodos) a mountainous Greek island (area 538 sq. miles, pop. 66,606), southernmost and largest of the Dodecanese. Products: barley, oranges, olives, wine ‖ its chief town and port (pop. 27,000): medieval city walls, palaces of the Knights Hospitalers. The island was settled (c. 1000 B.C.) by Dorian Greeks and reached the height of its prosperity in the 3rd c. B.C. Rhodes was ruled by Rome (1st c. B.C.-395 A.D.), the Byzantine Empire (395-1204), local lords (1204-48), Genoa (1248-50), Nicaea (1256-82), the Seljuk Turks (1282-1309), the Knights Hospitalers (1309-1522), the Ottoman Empire (1522-1912) and Italy (1912-47), after which it was ceded to Greece (*COLOSSUS OF RHODES)

Rhodes, Cecil John (1853-1902), British statesman and financier. After emigrating to South Africa (1870), he amassed a fortune from the Kimberley diamond mines and the Transvaal gold mines. He became a leading advocate of British imperialist expansion in Africa, entered the Cape Colony parliament (1881), obtained the British annexation of Bechuanaland (1884), and gained a monopoly of mineral rights (1888) in the Matabele lands later known as Southern Rhodesia. He was prime minister of Cape Colony (1890-6), resigning after popular criticism of the Jameson Raid. His connection with the raid was censured by the British House of Commons and he retired to Southern Rhodesia

Rhodes, James Ford (1848-1927), U.S. historian, author of 'History of the United States from the Compromise of 1850' (7 vols, 1893-1906)

Rho·de·sia former colony of Britain, then an independent country *ZIMBABWE

Rhodesia and Nyasaland, Federation of the Central African Federation

CONCISE PRONUNCIATION KEY: **(a)** æ, *cat*; ɑ, *car*; ɔ *fawn*; ei, *snake*. **(e)** e, *hen*; i:, *sheep*; iə, *deer*; ɛə, *bear*. **(i)** i, *fish*; ai, *tiger*; ə:, *bird*. **(o)** o, *ox*; au, *cow*; ou, *goat*; u, *poor*; ɔi, *royal*. **(u)** ʌ, *duck*; u, *bull*; u:, *goose*; ə, *bacillus*; ju:, *cube*. x, *loch*; θ, *think*; ð, *bother*; z, *Zen*; ʒ, *corsage*; dʒ, *savage*; ŋ, *orangutang*; j, *yak*; ʃ, *fish*; tʃ, *fetch*; 'l, *rabble*; 'n, *redden*. Complete pronunciation key appears inside front cover.

rho·di·um (róudiːəm) *n.* a metallic element (symbol Rh, at. no. 45, at. mass 102.905) resembling platinum, used in very hard alloys, as a catalyst, and in thermocouples [Mod. L. fr. Gk *rhodon,* a rose (from the reddish color of some of its compounds)]

rho·do·den·dron (roudədéndrən) *n.* a member of *Rhododendron,* fam. *Ericaceae,* a genus of evergreen shrubs bearing large pink, red, purplish or white flowers, native to the cool areas of the northern hemisphere [L. fr. Gk fr. *rhodon,* rose + *dendron,* tree]

rho·do·nite (róud'nait) *n.* a rose-red silicate of manganese ($MnSiO_3$), used as an ornamental stone [G. *rhodonit* fr. Gk *rhodon,* rose]

Rhod·o·pe Mountains (ródəpiː) a wooded mountain range running along the Bulgarian-Greek frontier. Occupations: livestock, mining (iron, lead, zinc). Highest peak: Musala (9,595 ft), in S.W. Bulgaria

rho·dop·sin (roudópsin) *n.* (*physiol.*) a red or purple photosensitive pigment occurring in the rods of the retina of marine fishes and most higher vertebrates, facilitating vision in dim light. Absence of it causes night blindness (*NYCTALOPIA). Vitamin A favors its formation [fr. Gk *rhodon,* rose + *opsis,* appearance]

rhomb (rɒm, rɒmb) *n.* a rhombus ‖ a rhombohedron [fr. L. *rhombus* fr. Gk]

rhom·ben·ceph·a·lon (rómbensέfəlɒn) *pl.* **rhom·ben·ceph·a·la** (rómbensέfələ) *n.* the developed hindbrain

rhom·bic (rómbik) *adj.* having the shape of a rhombus ‖ orthorhombic

rhom·bo·he·dral (rɒmbəhíːdrəl) *adj.* of or having the form of a rhombohedron

rhom·bo·he·dron (rɒmbəhíːdrən) *pl.* **rhom·bo·he·drons, rhom·bo·he·dra** (rɒmbəhíːdrə) *n.* a six-sided figure whose faces are equal rhombuses ‖ a crystal having this form [fr. Gk *rhombos,* rhomb + *hedra,* seat, base]

rhom·boid (rómbɔid) **1.** *n.* a parallelogram having unequal adjacent sides and oblique angles **2.** *adj.* shaped like a rhombus ‖ rhomboidal [fr. F. *rhomboide* fr. L. fr. Gk]

rhom·boi·dal (rɒmbɔ́id'l) *adj.* shaped like a rhomboid [fr. Mod. L. *rhomboidolis*]

rhom·bus (rómbəs) *pl.* **rhom·bus·es, rhom·bi** (rómbai) *n.* an equilateral parallelogram other than a square [L.]

rho meson (*particle phys.*) a short-lived vector meson with isospin of 1, hypercharge 0, negative charge, mass of 750 MEV, detected in high-energy colliscope, reclassified principally as mu meson as a result of additional research. *Cf* MU MESON

rho·met·al (róumetəl) *n.* an alloy of iron and nickel highly resistant to magnetism and used in high-frequency electrical circuits

rhon·chal (róŋk'l) *adj.* of or relating to a rhonchus ‖ caused by a rhonchus or by rhonchi

rhon·chi·al (róŋkiːəl) *adj.* rhonchal

rhon·chus (róŋkəs) *pl.* **rhon·chi** (róŋkai) *n.* a whistling or wheezing sound heard on auscultation of the chest, due to partial blockage of the bronchi [L.=a snoring, fr. Gk]

Rhon·dda (róndə, hrɒnðæ) the chief town (pop. 100,000) of a coal-mining valley (the Rhondda Valley) of Glamorganshire, Wales

Rhône (roun) a department (area 1,104 sq. miles, pop. 1,429,600) in E. central France (*LYONNAIS, *BEAUJOLAIS). Chief town: Lyon

Rhône a river (505 miles long) flowing from a glacier on the St Gotthard massif, Switzerland, through the Lake of Geneva and the S. Jura into France, where it flows south between the Massif Central and the Alps to a delta on the Mediterranean. It receives the Saône at Lyon. Rapidity and shifting sandbanks make navigation difficult, but it is a great source of hydroelectric power

rhu·barb (rúːbɑrb) *n.* a member of *Rheum,* fam. *Polygonaceae,* a genus of perennial, large-leaved plants. The cultivated garden varieties, esp. *R. rhaponticum,* have large, fleshy, reddish stems which are peeled and cooked and used in making pies, preserves etc. [O.F. *reubarbe, rubarbe*]

rhu·barb·ing (rúːbɑrbiŋ) *n.* (*Br.*) the mutterings of actors to simulate background talk

rhumb (rʌm) *n.* a rhumb line ‖ the angular distance (11° 15') between two successive compass points [fr. F. *rumb* or Span. *rumbo,* Port. *rumbo, rumo*]

rhumba *RUMBA

rhumb line the curve followed by a ship keeping to one course, cutting all meridians at the same angle ‖ a line of the surface of the earth cutting all meridians at the same angle

rhyme (raim) *n.* identity or similarity in the sounds of word endings, employed usually at the ends of lines in order to please the ear and to assist in the construction of a poem ‖ verse in which this occurs ‖ a word presenting such identity with or similarity to another, *cat is a rhyme for rat* **without rhyme or reason** having no system or sense [O.F. *rime* fr. L. fr. Gk]

rhyme *pres. part.* **rhym·ing** *past* and *past part.* **rhymed** *v.i.* to form a rhyme, *'stoat' rhymes with 'moat'* ‖ to use or embody a technique or pattern of rhymes, *how do Milton's sonnets rhyme?* ‖ (*old-fash.*) to write verse ‖ *v.t.* to use as a rhyme ‖ (*old-fash.*) to put into verse [fr. O.F. *rimer*]

rhyme royal a stanza of 7 decasyllabic lines rhyming a b a b b c c

rhyming dictionary a dictionary which groups words by the rhymes which their last syllables provide

rhyming slang a kind of slang spoken by cockneys in which monosyllabic words are replaced by pairs of words (totally unrelated in meaning), the second of which rhymes with the original word, e.g. 'trouble and strife' = wife, 'butcher's hook'=look. In practice when rhyming slang is spoken the first, non-rhyming word is usually the only one pronounced

rhyn·cho·ce·pha·lian (riŋkousiféiljən) **1.** *adj.* of or relating to *Rhynchocephalia,* an order of lizardlike reptiles now extinct except for the tuatara **2.** *n.* a reptile of this order [fr. M.L. fr. Gk *rhunchos,* snout + *kephalē, head*]

rhy·o·lite (ráiəlait) *n.* an acid volcanic rock showing the effect of lava flow and containing quartz, orthoclase etc. [fr. G. *ryholit* fr. Gk *rhuax,* stream + *lithos,* rock]

rhythm (ríðəm) *n.* (in language) the irregular alternation of stress, duration or pitch, tending with heightened emotion towards meter ‖ a particular instance of such a pattern, *Skeltonic rhythm* ‖ (in music) the pattern produced by the relative duration and stress of notes ‖ (in art) the pattern of movement produced by the relationships between the parts of a work ‖ such a pattern in the movements of nature, the course of events etc., *the rhythm of the seasons* [fr. L. *rhythmus*]

rhythm and blues a mixture of rock 'n' roll and blues music. *abbr.* **R & B**

rhyth·mic (ríðmik) *adj.* having or using rhythm [fr. F. *rhythmique*]

rhyth·mi·cal (ríðmik'l) *adj.* of or relating to rhythm ‖ rhythmic

rhyth·mics (ríðmiks) *n.* the science or theory of rhythm

rhythm method a method of birth control in which continence is practiced during the period when fertilization is most likely to occur

rhythm section the instruments of a dance or jazz band which beat out the rhythm, e.g. drums, piano, double bass, guitar

R.I. Rhode Island

ri·al (riːúl, riːɔ́l) *n.* the basic monetary unit of Iran and Saudi Arabia ‖ a coin or note representing one rial [Pers. fr. Arab.]

Ri·al·to (riːǽltou) an island in Venice, Italy where the exchange was located ‖ the bridge (1590) spanning the middle of the Grand Canal in Venice

Riau *RIOUW ARCHIPELAGO

rib (rib) **1.** *n.* one of the paired, curved bones that form the bony cage which encloses and protects the thoracic cavity of most vertebrates. The ribs are articulated with the spine at the dorsal end, and are either joined to the sternum at the ventral end or free to move with the expansion and contraction of the lungs. In man there are normally 12 pairs ‖ (*archit.*) a raised molding on a ceiling, esp. of an arched roof ‖ (*Gothic* and *Romanesque archit.*) any of the intersecting arches of a vault ‖ (*bot.*) the principal vein of a leaf ‖ (*zool.*) a vein in an insect's wing ‖ (*zool.*) the quill of a feather ‖ a hinged, usually metal, rod supporting and shaping the fabric of an umbrella ‖ a vertical ridge in a woven or knitted fabric ‖ a curved timber supporting the frame of a ship ‖ any of the light, transverse pieces placed along the length of an airplane wing ‖ a pillar of ore or coal serving to support the roof of a mine ‖ a vein of ore ‖ (*bookbinding*) one of the raised bands where stitching goes across the spine of a book or such a band used ornamentally ‖ a cut of meat including a rib or ribs **2.** *v.t. pres. part.* **rib·bing** *past* and *past part.* **ribbed** to furnish or strengthen with a rib or ribs ‖ to make (a rib) in knitting ‖ (*pop.*) to tease (someone) [O.E. *rib, ribb*]

rib·ald (ríbəld) *adj.* (of wit or language) broad, indecent ‖ (of a person) wittily indecent or coarse **rib·ald·ry** (ríbəldriː) *n.* ribald wit or language [fr. O.F. *ribaud, ribault* n., a menial]

Ri·baut, Ri·bault (riːbou), Jean (c. 1520-65), French colonist. On the orders of Coligny, he established a Huguenot colony in South Carolina (1562)

rib·band (ríbənd, ríbbænd) *n.* a narrow flexible slat of wood or metal fastened to a ship's frame while it is being built, to hold the ribs in position

Rib·ben·trop (ríbəntrɒp), Joachim von (1893-1946), German foreign minister (1938-45). He helped to form the Rome-Berlin Axis and to plan Nazi aggression, and negotiated the RussoGerman nonaggression pact of 1939. He was convicted as a war criminal and hanged

rib·bing (ríbiŋ) *n.* ribs collectively, esp. ribbed fabric ‖ (*pop.*) a teasing

rib·bon (ríbən) *n.* a narrow strip of satin, silk, velvet etc. used e.g. for tying the hair, or for trimming or decoration, or as a bookmark, or made up into a badge etc. as a symbol of achievement in a competition ‖ material sold in such strips ‖ anything resembling such a strip, *ribbons of light* ‖ (*pl.*) torn or ragged strips of anything, *the flag was in ribbons* ‖ a narrow strip used as a badge of a knightly order or to indicate membership in an athletic team etc. ‖ (*mil.*) a colored strip of material indicating that the wearer has received a particular medal or decoration ‖ a roll of narrow inked fabric used in a typewriter ‖ a radula [O.F. *riban, ruban,* perh. fr. Gmc]

ribbon development urban expansion along a highway

rib·bon·fish (ríbənfiʃ) *pl.* **rib·bon·fish, rib·bon·fish·es** *n.* any of various members of *Equetus,* fam. *Sciaenidae,* a genus of fishes having gray and black ribbonlike markings ‖ any of various fishes of fam. *Cepolidae,* having narrow elongated bodies

ribbon foil a cheaper substitute for gold leaf etc. applied in decorative work, e.g. in bookbinding

Ri·be·ra (riːbéra), José (called Spagnoletto, 1588-1652), Spanish painter. After 1616 he lived mainly in Naples. His early work depends much on chiaroscuro for its effects, and its subjects are often brutal. Later his style softened and his subjects are devotional with the fervor typical of the Counter-Reformation

ri·bo·fla·vin (raiboufléivən) *n.* vitamin B_2 (*DIET)

ri·bo·nu·cle·ase (raibounúːkliːeis) *n.* (*physiol.*) enzyme, present in body tissue, that polymerizes ribonucleic acid. *abbr.* RNase or RNAse

ri·bo·nu·cle·ic acid (ráibounuːklíːik, ráibounjuːklíːik) (*abbr.* RNA) a nucleic acid similar to deoxyribonucleic acid but having a sugar residue, ribose (containing an additional oxygen atom) instead of deoxyribose. It serves as an intermediary in protein synthesis

ri·bose (ráibous, ráibouz) *n.* a pentose sugar, $C_5H_{10}O_5$, obtained by hydrolysis from certain nucleic acids (*RIBONUCLEIC ACID, *DEOXYRIBONUCLEIC ACID) [fr. *ribonic* fr. G.]

ri·bo·som·al RNA (raibəsóum'l) the part of RNA that combines with proteins to form cell ribosomes linked to messenger RNA to help synthesize proteins and enzymes —**ribosomal** *adj. Cf* MESSENGER RNA, RIBONUCLEIC ACID, TRANSFER RNA

Ri·car·di·an (rikárdiːən) **1.** *adj.* of or concerned with the political economist Ricardo **2.** *n.* a supporter of Ricardo's economic theories

Ri·car·do (rikárdou), David (1722-1823), British economist. He applied the deductive logic of his mentor, James Mill, to the analysis of monetary principles and in 'Principles of Political Economy and Taxation' (1817) elaborated the labor theory of value, the division of incomes, and the function of wages, rent and trade. He was the founder of the classical school of economics, and his philosophy influenced Marx, Malthus, J. S. Mill, Henry George, Alfred Marshall and many others

Rice (rais), Elmer (1892-1967), American dramatist whose plays include 'The Adding Machine' (1923) and 'Street Scene' (1929)

rice (rais) **1.** *n. Oryza sativa,* fam. *Gramineae,* an annual cereal grass widely cultivated for its seed, used for human food. It is one of the world's most important food crops. Rice is grown in Asian countries, esp. China and India, in parts of the Middle East (e.g. Egypt), in Rus-

CONCISE PRONUNCIATION KEY: **(a)** æ, *cat;* ɑ, *car;* ɔ *fawn;* ei, *snake.* **(e)** e, *hen;* iː, *sheep;* iə, *deer;* εə, *bear.* **(i)** i, *fish;* ai, *tiger;* əː, *bird.* **(o)** o, *ox;* au, *cow;* ou, *goat;* u, *poor;* ɔi, *royal.* **(u)** ʌ, *duck;* u, *bull;* uː, *goose;* ə, *bacillus;* juː, *cube.* x, *loch;* θ, *think;* ð, *bother;* z, *Zen;* ʒ, *corsage;* dʒ, *savage;* ŋ, *orangutang;* j, *yak;* ʃ, *fish;* tʃ, *fetch;* 'l, *rabble;* 'n, *redden.* Complete pronunciation key appears inside front cover.

sia, South America, Canada and the U.S.A. It is produced mainly in the deltas of rivers, on irrigated or flooded coastal plains, or on terraced hillsides. In Asia, dried rice stalks are used to make paper, sandals, hats etc., and to thatch roofs. Fermented rice kernels are sometimes used in making spirits, wine and beer, and in some countries rice hulls are fed to livestock || the seeds or grains of this grass **2.** *v.t. pres. part.* **ric·ing** *past* and *past part.* **riced** to pass through a ricer [M.E. *ris, rys* fr. O.F. fr. Ital. fr. L. fr. Gk fr. an Oriental source]

rice paddy *pl.* **rice paddies** a field in which rice is grown

rice paper paper made from the pith of the shrub *Tetrapanax papyriferum,* fam. *Araliaceae.* It is widely used in China, Japan etc.

ric·er (ráisər) *n.* a utensil with a sievelike container through which boiled potatoes etc. are pressed so that they emerge in small strings about the thickness of a rice grain

Rich (ritʃ), Edmund *EDMUND RICH

rich 1. *adj.* possessing great wealth, *a rich man* || having many natural resources, *a rich country* || abundant, *a rich harvest* || costly, precious, *rich jewels* || (with 'in') abounding, *rivers rich in fish* || fertile, *rich soil* || (of food) containing a high proportion of fat, esp. butter, *a rich cake* || (of voices) deep and mellow || (of colors) vivid, deep and intense || (of odors) strongly redolent || producing abundantly, *a rich mine* || (of materials or workmanship) elaborate, *rich brocade, rich carving* || (*pop.*) humorous || (*pop.*) absurd **2.** *n.* **the rich** rich people in general [O.E. *rice*]

Rich·ard I (rítʃərd) 'Cœur de Lion' (1157-99), king of England (1189-99), son of Henry II, with whom he was at war (1173 and 1189). He spent almost his entire reign outside England. Returning from the 3rd Crusade (1190-2), he was imprisoned (1192-4) by the emperor of Austria, and ransomed (1194). He prevented his brother John from usurping his throne (1194), and was at war (1194-9) with Philippe II of France. His continual wars and huge ransom necessitated heavy taxation in England. Many acts of cruelty marred his reputation for chivalry

Richard II (1367-1400), king of England (1377-99), son of Edward the Black Prince. During his minority (1377-83), the government was in the hands of his uncle, John of Gaunt, but the young king showed great courage in dealing with the Peasants' Revolt (1381). He was forced to submit to a baronial faction known as the lords appellant (1387-8), whom he eliminated (1397). His subsequent tyrannical rule alienated his supporters, who deserted him when his cousin Henry of Lancaster forced him to abdicate (1399) and succeeded him as Henry IV. Richard died or was murdered shortly afterwards in prison

Richard III (1452-85), king of England (1483-5), younger brother of Edward IV, on whose death (1483) he was appointed protector of his nephews Edward V and his brother Richard. He usurped the throne (1483) and the young princes were murdered shortly afterwards in the Tower of London, almost certainly at his instigation. A rebellion under Stafford was put down (1483), but Henry Tudor, the Lancastrian claimant to the throne, invaded (1485), defeating and killing Richard at Bosworth Field. Henry assumed the crown as Henry VII

Richard, earl of Cornwall (1209-72), titular king of the Romans (1257-72), son of King John of England

Rich·ards (rítʃərdz), Dickinson Woodruff (1895-1973), U.S. physician, co-winner (with Werner Forssman and André Cournand) of the 1965 Nobel prize in medicine and physiology

Richards, Theodore William (1868-1928), U.S. chemist. He received the 1914 Nobel prize in chemistry for his research on atomic weights

Rich·ard·son (rítʃərdsən), Henry Hobson (1838-86), U.S. architect, known both as an initiator of the Romanesque revival, epitomized in his Trinity Church, Boston (1872-7), and as a pioneer of an indigenous, modern American style, exemplified by parts of the capitol at Albany, N.Y.

Richardson, Sir Owen Willans (1879-1959), English physicist, noted for his researches on the emission of charged particles by hot bodies. Nobel prize (1928)

Richardson, Samuel (1689-1761), English novelist. He wrote 'Pamela' (1740-1), the enormously popular 'Clarissa' (1747-8) and 'The History of Sir Charles Grandison' (1753-4). Unlike his contemporaries, who were principally interested in simple narrative, social criticism and the humorous aspects of character, Richardson used the novel as a way of exploring psychological subtleties and moral issues

Rich·e·lieu (ri:ʃljə:), Armand-Jean du Plessis de (1585-1642), French cardinal and statesman. Through the influence of Marie de' Medici, he was appointed secretary of state (1616), cardinal (1622) and chief minister (1624) to Louis XIII. His domestic policy aimed at destroying the political power of the Huguenots, whom he successfully besieged (1628) in their stronghold of La Rochelle. Feudal nobles were suppressed, and their fortresses demolished. He obtained (1630) Marie de' Medici's banishment from court. Richelieu's foreign policy aimed at humbling the Hapsburgs in the Thirty Years' War. He made alliances with the Netherlands, the German states and Sweden, and took France into the war (1635), which caused financial crises but gained Catalonia and Roussillon from Spain. One of France's greatest statesmen, Richelieu carried out financial, military and legal reforms, encouraged manufactures, colonial trade and commerce, patronized the arts and founded the French Academy (1635)

rich·es (rítʃiz) *pl. n.* wealth, abundance || precious possessions [orig. sing. fr. O.F. *richesse*]

Richler, (rítʃlər) Mordecai (1931-), Canadian writer whose novels concentrate on being Jewish in Montreal. His works include 'The Acrobats' (1954), 'The Apprenticeship of Duddy Kravitz' (1959), 'Saint Urbain's Horseman' (1971), 'Joshua Then and Now' (1980) and 'Home Sweet Home' (1984)

rich·ly (rítʃli:) *adv.* in a rich way || thoroughly, *he richly deserved the punishment*

Rich·mond (rítʃmənd) an industrial and residential borough (pop. 219,214) of New York City, consisting of Staten Island and adjacent islets

Richmond the capital (pop. 220,000) of Virginia, a river port and industrial center (tobacco, paper, printing, textiles, chemicals). It figured prominently during the Revolution, and was the Confederate capital during the Civil War

Rich·ter (ríxtər) *JEAN-PAUL

Rich·ter scale (ríktər) (*seismology*) a logarithmic scale for measuring the magnitude of a seismic disturbance in which the smallest detectable movement is 1.5 and 8.5 is the most devastating; after American seismologist Charles R. Richter

rick (rik) **1.** *n.* an outdoor stack of hay or straw etc., usually thatched **2.** *v.t.* to stack into a rick [O.E. *hrēac*]

rick 1. *v.t.* (*Br.*) to sprain or twist (an ankle, knee etc.) **2.** *n.* (*Br.*) a sprain or twist [M.E. *wrikken,* to move jerkily]

Rick·en·back·er (ríkənbækər), Edward Vernon (1890-1973), U.S. adventurer and airline executive. As a racing driver he set (1917) a world speed record of 134 m.p.h. at Daytona Beach, Fla. During the 1st world war he became America's 'ace' fighter pilot. He developed (from 1935) Eastern Air Lines into a major international air-transport system

rick·ets (ríkits) *pl. n.* (*sing.* in construction) a disease characterized by a softening and sometimes bending of bone structure in the pelvis and leg bones of infants and children. It is caused by a deficiency of vitamin D or lack of sunlight [etym. doubtful]

rick·ett·si·a (rikétsi:ə) *pl.* **rick·ett·si·ae** (rikétsi:i:) *n.* a member of *Rickettsia,* fam. *Rickettsiaceae,* a genus of microorganisms inhabiting the cells of certain biting arthropods. When transmitted to man by the bite of the host they can cause typhus and other serious diseases **rick·étt·si·al** *adj.* [after H.T. *Ricketts* (1871–1910), U.S. pathologist]

rick·et·y (ríkiti:) *adj.* suffering from rickets || weak in the joints, *a rickety old man* || shaky, insecure, *a rickety chair*

rick·rack (ríkræk) *n.* a zigzag braid trimming

rick·shaw, rick·sha (ríkʃɔ) *n.* a jinricksha

rick·yard (ríkjɑrd) *n.* a stackyard

rick·y-tick (ríki:tík) *n.* a jazz music style of the 1920s —**ricky-ticky** *adj.*

ric·o·chet (ríkəʃei, rikəʃéi) **1.** *n.* the skipping or glancing off at a tangent of a bullet or other missile after hitting a flat surface which it does not penetrate **2.** *v.i. pres. part.* **ric·o·chet·ing,** esp. *Br.* **ric·o·chet·ting** (ríkəʃeiiŋ, rikəʃéiiŋ) *past* and *past part.* **ric·o·cheted,** esp. *Br.* **ric·o·chetted** (ríkəʃeid, rikəʃéid) (of a missile) to glance off, to rebound [F.]

ric·tus (ríktəs) *pl.* **ric·tus, ric·tus·es** *n.* the gape of a mouth, beak etc. [L.=open mouth]

rid (rid) *v.t. pres. part.* **rid·ding** *past* and *past part.* **rid, rid·ded** to free of a nuisance or something unwelcome, *to rid a house of rats* **to be rid of** to be freed from **to get rid of** to get free from || to do away with || (*pop.*) to cause (someone) to go away **rid·dance** (ríd'ns) *n.* a ridding or being rid **good riddance!** an expression of satisfaction or relief at getting rid of someone or something [O.N. *rythja*]

rid·a·ble, ride·a·ble (ráidəb'l) *adj.* capable of being ridden || able to be ridden over, *a ridable track*

rid·del (ríd'l) *n.* one of the side curtains of an altar [M.E. *ridel, riddel,* perh. fr. *riddil, a riddle* (sieve)]

ridden *past part.* of RIDE

rid·dle (ríd'l) **1.** *n.* a question or problem phrased obscurely but correctly and posed to test the ingenuity of the person trying to find the answer || a puzzling person or thing **2.** *v. pres. part.* **rid·dling** *past* and *past part.* **rid·dled** *v.i.* to speak in riddles || *v.t.* to solve, explain (a riddle) [O.E. *rǣdels, rǣdelse*]

riddle 1. *n.* a coarse sieve for gravel, cinders etc. **2.** *v.t. pres. part.* **rid·dling** *past* and *past part.* **rid·dled** to sieve through a riddle || to fill with holes, esp. by shooting || to find flaws in (an argument etc.) [O.E. *hriddel*]

Ride, (raid) Sally Kirsten (1951–), U.S. astronaut, the first American woman in space. She graduated from Stanford University (1977) and became an astronaut in 1978. Her first space flight (June 18–24, 1983) was followed by the 13th shuttle mission (Oct. 5–13, 1984)

ride (raid) **1.** *v. pres. part.* **rid·ing** *past* **rode** (roud) *past part.* **rid·den** (ríd'n) *v.i.* to sit in a car, train etc. and be carried along || to sit on and be carried along by a horse or other animal while controlling its movements || to be carried as if on a horse, *to ride on someone's back* || to turn or move on or in something, *the stud rides in the groove* || (of a ship) to lie at anchor || (of a ship) to move over or float on water || (of the moon, sun etc.) to seem to float through the sky || to be in a specified condition for riding or being ridden, *the ground rides hard* || (of clothing, with 'up') to work upward out of place, *trousers that tend to ride up* || (*pop.*) to continue without change, solution, interference etc., *to let a problem ride* || (of a male animal) to mount in copulation || *v.t.* to sit on (an animal) or on or in (a vehicle) and be carried along while controlling its movements || to move along on and be supported by, *to ride the waves* || to give a ride to, *to ride a baby on one's back* || to engage in or do by riding, *to ride a race* || (*horse racing*) to urge (a horse) to the point of exhaustion || to keep (a ship) at anchor || to rest on (something), e.g. by overlapping || (esp. *past part.* in combination) to dominate completely, *fear-ridden* || (*pop.*) to tease || (of a male animal) to mount (the female) in copulation || (*lacrosse*) to charge (an opponent in possession of the ball) legally **to ride down** (*horse racing*) to exhaust (a horse) by riding it too hard || to overtake by riding || to allow one's mount or vehicle to hit and knock down (a person or thing) **to ride for a fall** to court disaster **to ride out** to come through safely, *to ride out a storm, to ride out a crisis* **to ride (someone) on a rail** to cause (someone) to leave town **2.** *n.* a riding, esp. a journey made by riding || a road for horseback riding, esp. one cut through a forest || a machine to ride on for fun in an amusement park etc., e.g. a Ferris wheel **to take (someone) for a ride** (*pop.*) to deceive or trick (someone) by fooling or cheating him [O.E. *rīdan*]

rideable *RIDABLE

rid·er (ráidər) *n.* someone who rides, esp. someone who rides a horse || an additional clause or amendment added to a legislative bill, document etc. || (*Br., law*) an opinion, recommendation etc. added to a verdict || (*math.*) a problem which is subsidiary to a theorem || a piece of machinery, apparatus etc. that rests on or surmounts another, e.g. the movable weight on a balance beam || (*naut., pl.*) an extra set of timbers or plates used to strengthen a ship's frame [O.E. *rīdere*]

ri·der·ship (ráidərʃip) *n.* those who ride in a particular vehicle or system

ride shotgun *v.* to protect or ensure, e.g., the successful completion of a project, from the stage-coach riders in the Old West

ridge (ridʒ) **1.** *n.* the horizontal angle at the junction of two slopes || the top edge of a roof where two sloping sides meet || a long, narrow elevation of land, *a ridge of hills* || a narrow, raised line on the surface of cloth etc. || the raised earth thrown up between furrows || (*Br.*) a raised hotbed for the cultivation of cucumbers, melons etc. || (*meteorol.*) a wedge-shaped area of high atmospheric pressure (cf. TROUGH) **2.** *v. pres. part.* **ridg·ing** *past* and *past part.* **ridged** *v.t.* to form into a ridge or ridges || to mark with ridges || (*Br.*) to plant (cucumbers etc.) in ridges || *v.i.* to form into ridges [O.E. *hrycg*]

ridge·piece (rídʒpi:s) *n.* (*Br.*) a ridgepole (beam in a roof)

ridge·pole (rídʒpoul) *n.* the horizontal beam in a roof supporting the upper ends of the rafters || the pole supporting the roof of a tent

ridge tile a curved tile used in quantity to form the ridge covering of a roof

Ridg·way (rídʒwei), Matthew Bunker (1895-), American general. He commanded the U.N. forces in Korea (1951-2)

rid·i·cule (rídikju:l) **1.** *n.* contemptuous laughter, *his suggestion met with ridicule by the others* **2.** *v.t. pres. part.* **rid·i·cul·ing** *past* and *past part.* **rid·i·culed** to treat with ridicule, cause (someone, something) to be an object of ridicule [F.]

ri·dic·u·lous (ridíkjuləs) *adj.* provoking derisive laughter, *a ridiculous fellow* || unworthy of consideration, unreasonable, *a ridiculous excuse, a ridiculous charge* [fr. L. *ridiculus*]

rid·ing (ráidiŋ) *n.* one of the three administrative divisions (East, West, North) of Yorkshire, England [fr. O.N. *thrithjungr*, third part]

riding 1. *n.* the act of a person who rides || (*Br.*) a track for riders, esp. a grassy one through or along woods **2.** *adj.* used in or for riding, *riding horses, a riding habit*

riding master a man who teaches horsemanship

Rid·ley (rídli:), Nicholas (c. 1500-55), English bishop. A Protestant, he helped to revise the liturgy under Edward VI and, refusing to recant after the accession of Mary I, was burned at the stake as a heretic

Rie·go y Núñ·ez (rjégɔi:nú:njeθ), Rafael del (1785-1823), Spanish general. He and his force of 22,000, about to sail for America, mutinied (1820) at Cabezas de San Juan near Seville, forcing Ferdinand VII to capitulate. Following the French intervention (1823) he was hanged and quartered. The 'Hymn of Riego' became the national anthem of the Second Spanish Republic

Rieka *RIJEKA

Riel (rjel), Louis (1844-85), French-Canadian political leader. He led (1869) a rebellion composed of Franco-Scottish métis of the Hudson Bay Company's territories, who opposed attempts (1868-9) by the Canadian government to transfer the area to Canada. He presided over a provisional government which established (1870), by an act of Parliament, the province of Manitoba. He led (1884) the Second Riel Rebellion of métis of the Saskatchewan Valley but was defeated (1885) by Canadian government forces, convicted of treason, and executed. His death increased racial and religious tensions in Canada, severely damaged the Conservative party in Quebec, and gave rise to a French-Canadian nationalist movement

ri·el (rí:əl) *n.* the basic monetary unit of Cambodia, divided into 100 sen [origin unknown]

Rie·mann (rí:mɑn), Georg Friedrich Bernhard (1826-66), German mathematician. He is best known for his discussion of the foundations of geometry and his development of forms of geometry which do not assume Euclid's axiom about parallel lines

Rie·men·schnei·der (rí:mənʃnaidər), Tilmann (c. 1460-1531), German sculptor in stone and wood. His work can be seen in tombs and altars at Würzburg, Bamberg and other cathedrals and churches

rif·am·pi·cin or **rif·am·pin** (rifǽmpisin) *n.* (*pharm.*) any of a group of semisynthetic antibiotic and antiviral drugs that inhibit enzyme action; used in the treatment of pulmonary tuberculosis; marketed as Rifadin, Rimactane; and others

rif·a·my·cin (rifəmáisin) *n.* any of a group of substances resulting from fungal fermentation, some of which have antibiotic and antiviral capacity

rife (raif) *adj.* (*rhet.*, used only predicatively) widespread, prevalent [O.E. *rȳfe*]

Riff, Rif (rif) *n.* a Berber inhabitant of the Rif

riffed (rift) *adj.* dismissed from a job on the basis of reduction in force. —**riff** *v.*

riffle zone (*envir.*) shallow rapids in an open stream caused by submerged obstructions

riff·raff (rífræf) *n.* people regarded as worthless or disreputable [fr. M.E. *riff and raff* fr. O.F. *rif et raf*, one and all]

rif·fle (rífəl) **1.** *n.* any of various devices, e.g. slats or blocks of wood, stones etc. which, when laid across the bottom of a mining sluice, form a series of grooves or ridges serving to catch and hold gold particles as the ore is washed || one of these grooves or ridges || a shallow in the bed of a stream across which the water flows rapidly, producing small choppy waves || one of these waves || the act or practice of riffling cards || the sound of cards being riffled **2.** *v. pres. part.* **rif·fling** *past* and *past part.* **rif·fled** *v.t.* to put (e.g. ore) through a riffle || to form a riffle or riffles in (water) || to leaf through (e.g. the pages of a book) rapidly, causing a slight rustling sound || to shuffle (cards) by holding part of the pack in each hand and letting some cards slip between others as the two sets are quickly flicked together [fr. F. *riffler*]

ri·fle (ráifəl) **1.** *v.t. pres. part.* **ri·fling** *past* and *past part.* **ri·fled** to steal everything of value from (a safe, a pocket etc.) || to carry off as booty || to cut spiral grooves in (the bore of a gun) so as to make the bullet spin in flight **2.** *n.* a gun (usually fired from the shoulder) having spiral grooves cut in the bore || (*pl.*, in regimental names) troops armed with rifles [O.F. *rifler, rifler*, to scratch]

ri·fle·man (ráifəlmən) *pl.* **ri·fle·men** (ráifəlmən) *n.* a soldier armed with a rifle || a person with respect to his skill in using a rifle

rifle range a place for rifle practice

ri·fling (ráifliŋ) *n.* the act or process of cutting spiral grooves into a gun bore || the spiral grooving itself

Rif, Riff (rif) the coastal strip of N. Morocco

rift (rift) *n.* a crack, fissure, e.g. in the earth || a clearing or opening, e.g. in clouds or mist || (*geol.*) a fault || a break in friendship [of Scand. origin]

rift saw a saw for cutting lumber into planks

rift valley a valley which has been formed by the sinking of land between two roughly parallel faults. The best known example is the Great Rift Valley

Rift Valley fever (*med.*) livestock disease carried by mosquitoes that can cause blindness in humans; discovered in Africa in 1978

rift zone (*geol.*) a zone where plates of earth's crust tend to separate

rig (rig) **1.** *v.t. pres. part.* **rig·ging** *past* and *past part.* **rigged** to fit (a ship) with ropes, spars and all necessary tackle || to fit (shrouds, stays etc.) to a mast or yard || to assemble and align the wings, fuselage etc. of (an airplane) || (esp. with 'out') to provide with clothes, esp. outlandish clothes, *to rig someone out like a gypsy* || (esp. with 'up') to put (something) together quickly as a temporary arrangement, *to rig up a hut in the garden* || to provide with proper equipment, tools etc., *a boat rigged for trawling* **2.** *n.* the manner in which a ship's sails, masts etc. are arranged, *schooner rig* || (*pop.*) distinctive dress, esp. when designed for a special purpose, *a beefeater's rig* || any specific tackle or machinery, esp. the equipment used in drilling an oil well [origin unknown]

rig *pres. part.* **rig·ging** *past* and *past part.* **rigged** *v.t.* to prearrange fraudulently, *the fire was rigged to make suspicion fall on the caretaker* || to manipulate dishonestly, *to rig an election* [origin unknown]

Ri·ga (rí:gə) the capital, chief port and industrial center (pop. 835,000) of Latvia, U.S.S.R., on the Western Dvina near the head of the Gulf of Riga, an inlet (approx. 100 miles long, 60 miles wide) of the Baltic. Industries: mechanical engineering, metallurgy, textiles, oil refining, wood, fishing, fish packing. University (1919)

rig·a·doon (rigədú:n) *n.* a spirited dance popular in the 17th and 18th cc. || the music for this dance [etym. doubtful]

rig·a·ma·role (rígəmərəul) *n.* rigmarole

Ri·gaud (ri:gou), Hyacinthe (1659-1743), French painter. He specialized in portraits and in historical paintings. He is best known for his portraits of Bossuet and Louis XIV

rig·ger (rígər) *n.* someone who rigs, esp. someone who rigs ships or aircraft || (in combination) a ship rigged in a specified way, *a square-rigger*

rig·ging (rígiŋ) *n.* all the ropes, chains etc. used for supporting a ship's masts and spars and for hoisting and lowering the sails

right (rait) **1.** *adj.* obeying the moral law, *in the circumstances his conduct was right* || correct, *the right answer* || true, logically sound, *the right conclusion* || appropriate, opportune, *the right time to act* || suitable, *the right man for the position* || of or on the side of the body away from the location of the heart, or on this side of a person's vertical axis of symmetry || on or to this side as perceived by an observer || (of a river bank) on this side of an observer facing downstream || (of solid figures) involving a right angle || of or pertaining to the finished side or surface of something, *the right side of the chintz* || mentally sound || physically healthy **Right** belonging to or associated with the Right **in one's right mind** in full possession of one's mental faculties **2.** *n.* that which is morally right, *to fight for the right* || that to which one is morally or legally entitled || that which one judges to be the most suitable, correct etc. || the right side or direction || (*boxing*) the right hand or a blow with this hand || (*marching, dancing* etc.) the right foot **the Right** that section of a political party, system of political parties, organization, group etc. which associates itself with traditional authority or opinion and which in legislative bodies is seated traditionally to the right of the presiding officer **in one's own right** through one's own authority, title etc. **in the right** having justice, legality or the facts on one's side **to put** (or **set**) **to rights** to make orderly or correct [O.E. *riht*]

right *adv.* in conformity with the moral law || correctly, accurately, *to add a column of figures right* || in a right-hand direction, *turn right* || completely, *right on to the end* || immediately (in time), *right after breakfast* || immediately (in position), *right by the church* || in a suitable way, *to turn out right* || directly, *go right home* **right away** immediately **right off** right away [O.E. *rehte, rihte*]

right *v.t.* to restore to, or set in, the proper position, *to right a boat* || to put (oneself) back into balance, *to right oneself after stumbling* || to redress (a wrong) || to put to rights || *v.i.* to return to a correct or upright position, *the boat righted on the next wave* [O.E. *rihtan*]

right about, right-a·bout (ráitəbaut) **1.** *n.* the position reached by turning to the right so as to face in the opposite direction || a right-about-face **2.** *adj.* pertaining to this movement **3.** *adv.* in a right-about way, *to turn right about*

right-a·bout-face (ráitəbautféis) **1.** *n.* (*mil.*) a turning to the opposite direction || a reversal of opinion, attitude etc. **2.** *interj.* turn right about! **3.** *v.i.* to execute a right-about-face

right angle the angle (90°) between two radii which bound one quarter of a circle || the angle between two lines perpendicular to one another **at right angles** perpendicularly **right-án·gled** *adj.*

right ascension (*astron.*) the angular distance eastwards along the celestial equator (or equinoctial) between the first point of Aries and the point where the circle of declination of a heavenly body cuts the equinoctial. It is one of the two data which determine position in the celestial sphere, corresponding with terrestrial longitude (*DECLINATION)

right·eous (ráitʃəs) *adj.* conforming to or in conformity with the moral law, *a righteous ruler, a righteous cause* || caused by outrage against injustice, *righteous anger* [O.E. *rihtwīs*]

right field (*baseball*) the right-hand part of the outfield (as seen from home plate) || the position of the player defending this

right·ful (ráitfəl) *adj.* having a just claim, *the rightful heir* || owned by just claim, *rightful inheritance* || proper, as befits a person's rank, merit etc., *to take one's rightful place in society* [late O.E. *rihtful* fr. *riht*, right]

right-hand (ráithænd) *adj.* on or to the right side || (of a screw or thing to be used by a right-handed person) right-handed

right-hand·ed (ráithǽndid) **1.** *adj.* using the right hand more efficiently than the left hand || of or for someone who does this || (of a screw) having a clockwise thread || (of a rope) right-laid **2.** *adv.* with the right hand

right-hand man someone's most relied-on assistant

Right Honourable (*Br.*) a title used in referring to a peer holding a rank lower than marquis, or to a privy councillor etc.

Right·ist (ráitist) **1.** *n.* someone who belongs to the Right or tends to hold the views of the Right **2.** *adj.* of, associated with or belonging to the Right

right-laid (ráitléid) *adj.* (of a rope) having strands twisted counterclockwise

right·ly (ráitli:) *adv.* correctly ‖ in the right way ‖ justly, fairly [O.E. *rihtlīce*]

right-mind·ed (ráitmáindid) *adj.* thinking and judging according to correct principles

right of search (*maritime law*) the right of a nation at war to stop any neutral vessel at sea to search her for contraband etc.

right-of-way, *Br.* also **right of way** (ráitəvwéi) *n.* the right of one vehicle to take precedence over another as laid down by traffic regulations ‖ the right of using a path or thoroughfare over another person's property ‖ the path or thoroughfare used ‖ the land over which an electric power line or natural-gas pipeline etc. passes

right-on (raítɒn) *adj.* (*slang*) correct; honest; real —**right on** interjection indicating approval or encouragement

Right Reverend a title used in referring to a bishop

Rights, Bill of *BILL OF RIGHTS

Rights of Man, Declaration of the (*F. hist.*) a statement of the basic principles of civil society, drawn up (Aug. 17-26, 1789) by the Constituent Assembly

right-to-die (ráittədái) *n.* concept of patient's right to refuse life-prolonging measures if he or she is terminally ill

right-to-know law *FREEDOM OF INFORMATION ACT

right-to-life (ráittəláif) *n.* slogan of antiabortion proponents indicating a supposed right of the unborn from the moment of conception

right-to-work law (ráittəwə́:rk) law forbidding the refusing of employment to one who does not belong to a union

right whale *Balaena mysticetus,* fam. *Balaenidae,* a genus of whalebone whales having no dorsal fin and no furrows on the throat

right wing the section of a political party, government, group etc. holding the views of the Right **right-wing** *adj.* **right-wing·er** *n.*

rig·id (rídʒid) *adj.* (*phys.*) strongly resisting deformation ‖ stiffly set, *a rigid stare* ‖ rigorous, *rigid discipline* ‖ inflexible, *too rigid a regard for the rules* ‖ (of an airship) having the gas chambers enclosed within a fixed framework **ri·gíd·i·ty** *n.* the state or quality of being rigid (*MODULUS OF RIGIDITY) [fr. L. *rigidus*]

rig·ma·role (rígməroul) *n.* a long, disconnected narration, with no clear meaning ‖ a protracted, tiresome procedure or ceremonial, *I'm not going through all that rigmarole again just to get a visa* [etym. doubtful]

rig·or (rígər) *n.* (*med.*) a shivering fit often preceding an onset of fever ‖ (*physiol.*) a state of rigidity affecting living organs or tissues, due e.g. to shock or an accumulation of toxic substances [L. =stiffness]

rig·or, *Br.* **rig·our** (rígər) *n.* uncompromising firmness ‖ an instance of this ‖ extreme precision in the application of a rule, principle etc., *the rigor of the law* ‖ (of climate and season) extreme harshness ‖ (*pl.*) hardships ‖ (*math., logic*) severe precision of method [O.F. *rigor, rigour*]

rig·or mor·tis (rígərmɔ́rtis, ráigɔrmɔ́rtis) *n.* the stiffening of the muscles after death [L.]

rig·or·ous (rígərəs) *adj.* characterized by rigor ‖ (of climate or season) inclement ‖ precise, accurate [O.F.]

rigour *RIGOR

Rig-Ve·da (rɪgvéidə) the oldest and most important of the sacred Vedas

Ri·je·ka, Ri·e·ka (ri:jékə) (*Ital.* Fiume) the chief port (pop., with adjacent Sušak, 132,600) of Yugoslavia, in N.W. Croatia. Industries: shipbuilding, paper, oil refining, electrical engineering, food processing. Roman arch (1st c.), 18th-c. churches and palace. It was Austro-Hungarian before the 1st world war, but in 1919 was seized by d'Annunzio for Italy, whose possession was confirmed only in 1924. It passed to Yugoslavia in 1947

Rijswijk, Treaty of *RYSWICK, TREATY OF

rile (rail) *pres. part.* **ril·ing** *past* and *past part.* **riled** *v.t.* to arouse anger or resentfulness in ‖ to roil (a liquid) [var. of ROIL]

Ri·ley (ráili:), James Whitcomb (1849-1916), U.S. poet who wrote in the dialect of his native Indiana

Ril·ke (rílkə), Rainer Maria (1875-1926), German lyric poet born in Czechoslovakia of German parents. One of his great preoccupations was the quality of European life, which he saw as menaced by an encroaching mechanistic utilitarianism symbolized by the U.S.A. The two greatest of his works were the 'Sonnets to Orpheus' (1923) and the 'Duino Elegies' (1923), which are both a sustained meditation and a series of variations on certain themes, or indeed on the whole of life: a life without the Christian god, in which a religious attitude has to be recreated. Meaning and value are restored through the contemplation in particular of what artists, lovers and the great dead have made of life and of death, by the contemplation at the humbler level of the accumulated treasure of significance with which all the past has loaded every object in an old continent, and by the acceptance of death as the other side of life. But the themes are not to be divorced from the verse, which is richly metaphorical, the originality of the language springing directly from the forms and natural workings of German. He surrendered himself, he thought, to visitations in his verse, and he was perhaps the last and one of the greatest exponents of the romantic theory of inspiration

rill (ril) *n.* a small brook or stream [of Gmc origin]

rille, rill (ril) *n.* (*astron.*) a long narrow valley on the moon's surface [G. *rille,* groove]

rill·et (rílet) *n.* a little rill

rim (rim) **1.** *n.* the outer edge of a circular, oval or otherwise curved object, often beveled, thickened etc. ‖ a curved frame, e.g. of a wheel or surrounding a lens in a pair of glasses etc. **2.** *v.t. pres. part.* **rim·ming** *past* and *past part.* **rimmed** to furnish with a rim ‖ (of a ball) to roll around the rim of (esp. a golf hole) [O.E. *rima*]

RIM-8 *TALOS

RIM-7 *SPARROW

RIM-67 *STANDARD MISSILE

RIM-66 *STANDARD MISSILE

RIM-24 *TARTAR

RIM-2 *TERRIER

Rim·baud (rɛ̃bou), Arthur (1854-91), French poet. His literary works, including 'le Bateau ivre' (1871), 'les Illuminations' (published in 1886) and 'Une saison en enfer' (1873), were all written before he was 20. The last 16 years of his life were spent mainly in Ethiopia, where he became a trader. His influence has been profound: as a type of the world-forsaking visionary artist, of the inspired youthful genius, of the 'outcast' or scandalous bohemian, and of the poet as oracle. His poetry sprang from, as he said, a systematic transformation of the function of the senses, and a naturally oblique and figurative habit of expression

rime (raim) **1.** *n.* white hoarfrost **2.** *v.t. pres. part.* **rim·ing** *past* and *past part.* **rimed** to cover with or as if with rime [O.E. *hrīm*]

Rim·i·ni (rí:mini:) a resort and fishing port (pop. 125,800) of Emilia-Romagna, Italy, on the Adriatic: Roman bridge and arch (1st c.), 15th-c. cathedral (the Malatesta temple)

ri·mose (ráimous) *adj.* (*bot.,* esp. of bark) having many intersecting clefts or fissures **ri·mous** (ráiməs) *adj.* rimose [fr. L. *rimosus*]

Rim·sky-Kor·sa·kov (rímski:kɔ́rsəkɔf), Nikolay Andreyevich (1844-1908), Russian composer. One of his best-known works is the orchestral suite 'Schéhérazade' (1888). His operas on Russian themes, e.g. 'le Coq d'or' (performed 1910), brought him great acclaim in Russia

rim·y (ráimi:) *comp.* **rim·i·er** *superl.* **rim·i·est** *adj.* covered with rime

rind (raind) *n.* peel ‖ the outer layer of tree bark ‖ a hard skin or outer covering, e.g. of bacon or cheese [O.E.]

rin·der·pest (ríndərpest) *n.* a virulent infectious disease, affecting ruminant mammals, esp. cattle. It is characterized by fever, dysentery and inflammation of the mucous membranes [G. fr. *rinder* pl. of *rind,* ox]

ring (riŋ) **1.** *v. pres. part.* **ring·ing** *past* **rang** (ræŋ) *past part.* **rung** (rʌŋ) *v.i.* to cause a bell to ring ‖ to give a sound suggestive of a bell ‖ to sound a bell as a summons, *to ring for a servant* ‖ to resound, *the room rang with laughter,* or seem to resound, *the country rang with his praise* ‖ (of the ears or head) to have or seem to have a buzzing sensation ‖ *v.t.* to cause (a bell) to sound ‖ (esp. *Br.,* often with 'up') to telephone ‖ (with 'in' or 'out') to usher by the sound of bells, *to ring in the New Year* ‖ to test the purity of (a coin etc.) by striking it against a hard object **to ring a bell** to evoke a vague memory, sound remotely familiar **to ring down the curtain** to lower the curtain or give a signal for lowering the curtain in a theater etc. **to ring false (true)** to sound false (true) **to ring off** (esp. *Br.*) to end a telephone call **to ring the bell** to be successful **to ring up** to record (a sale etc.) on a cash register **to ring up the curtain** to raise the curtain or give a signal for raising the curtain in a theater etc. **2.** *n.* the sound of a bell ‖ a sound resembling this, *the ring of laughter* ‖ a sound or tone suggesting a specified quality, *a ring of pride* ‖ a telephone call, *to give someone a ring* ‖ a set of church bells ‖ the act of ringing a bell [O.E. *hringan*]

ring 1. *n.* a circular band, usually of precious metal and often set with precious or semiprecious stones, worn on a finger as an ornament or symbol, *wedding ring* ‖ a circular band worn as an ornament elsewhere on the body, *nose ring* ‖ a circular band of metal, wood, plastic etc. used for holding, attaching etc., *key ring* ‖ anything having a more or less circular form, *smoke ring* ‖ the rim of a circular object ‖ the circular arena in which the acts of a circus are performed ‖ the square enclosure in which boxing and wrestling matches are held ‖ a bullring ‖ a piston ring ‖ an annual ring ‖ a cut around the trunk or limb of a tree ‖ (*horse racing*) an enclosure in which betting takes place ‖ a group of persons or things arranged in a circle ‖ a circular course ‖ a group of persons working together, often illicitly, e.g. in order to gain control of a market, political party etc. ‖ (*chem.*) a number of atoms united in such a way that they can be represented graphically in cyclic form **to make** (or **run**) **rings around** to surpass with ease **to throw one's hat in the ring** to announce that one is a candidate in a political contest **2.** *v.t.* to encircle, *a lake ringed by trees* ‖ to fit with a ring, *to ring a bull* ‖ to prevent (cattle, game etc.) from straying or escaping by riding around them in a circle ‖ to cut a ring in the bark of (a tree) ‖ (in some games, e.g. quoits) to encircle (a peg etc.) with a ring ‖ *v.i.* to form into a ring or rings ‖ to move in a ring ‖ (esp. of a bird) to rise in a spiral [O.E. *hring*]

ring·bolt (ríŋboult) *n.* (*naut.*) an iron bolt having a ring through an eye at one end, through which a rope can be passed and tied

ring·bone (ríŋboun) *n.* (*vet.*) a deposit of bony matter on the pastern bones of a horse, usually causing lameness

ring compound (*chem.*) a compound in which some or all of the atoms of the molecule are linked to form a closed ring, e.g. benzene

ring·dove (ríŋdʌv) *n.* *Columba palumbus,* a European pigeon having a patch of white on each side of its neck ‖ *Streptopelia risoria,* a turtledove native to Asia and S.E. Europe having a ring of black around its neck

ringed (riŋd) *adj.* encircled by or as if by a ring or rings ‖ shaped like a ring or rings ‖ wearing a ring or rings ‖ decorated with a ring or rings

Ring·el·mann chart (ríŋgəlmɒn) (*envir.*) a series of shaded illustrations used to measure the opacity of air-pollution emissions, ranging from light gray (number 1) through black (number 5), used to set and enforce emission standards

ring·er (ríŋər) *n.* a person who, or thing which, rings a bell ‖ (*pop.,* often with 'dead') a person who strongly resembles another, *he is a dead ringer for his brother* ‖ a person or horse etc. entered in a competition under false identity or false representation

ringer *n.* a quoit that lodges correctly around a pin or peg

ring fence a fence completely enclosing a large piece of land, esp. grazing land

ring·lead·er (ríŋli:dər) *n.* a leader of a group of people engaged in unlawful or objectionable acts

ring·let (ríŋlit) *n.* a long lock of curly hair

ring·mas·ter (ríŋmæstər, ríŋmɑstər) *n.* an official in charge of the various acts in a circus

ring ou·zel (ú:z'l) *Turdus torquatus,* fam. *Turdidae,* a thrushlike bird allied to the European blackbird and American robin, having a white band on the breast. It breeds in the mountainous areas of N. Europe

ring-pull (ríŋpul) *n.* a metal ring on the top of a can that creates an opening when pulled off —**ring-pull** *adj.* *Cf* POP-TOP, ZIP-TOP

CONCISE PRONUNCIATION KEY: **(a)** æ, cat; ɑ, car; ɔ fawn; ei, snake. **(e)** e, hen; i:, sheep; iə, deer; ɛə, bear. **(i)** i, fish; ai, tiger; ə:, bird. **(o)** o, ox; au, cow; ou, goat; u, poor; ɔi, royal. **(u)** ʌ, duck; u, bull; u:, goose; ə, bacillus; ju:, cube. x, loch; θ, think; ð, bother; z, Zen; ʒ, corsage; dʒ, savage; ŋ, orangutang; j, yak; ʃ, fish; tʃ, fetch; 'l, rabble; 'n, redden. Complete pronunciation key appears inside front cover.

ring road (*Br.*) a belt highway
ring·side (ríŋsaid) *n.* the area immediately outside a boxing or circus ring where a good view is afforded
ring vaccination (*med.*) universal inoculation of those who have been in the close vicinity of a sick person
ring·way (ríŋwei) *n.* (*Br.*) beltway; a road around a community, avoiding the city center
ring·worm (ríŋwə:rm) *n.* any of various contagious diseases of hair, skin and nails caused in man and domestic animals by fungi, esp. genera *Trichophyton* and *Microsporum*, marked by ring-shaped patches of discoloration in the skin
rink (riŋk) *n.* an area of natural or artificial ice used for ice-skating ‖ a wooden or asphalt floor used for roller-skating ‖ a building or enclosure containing an area for ice-skating or roller-skating ‖ a stretch of ice used for the game of curling or hockey ‖ a section of a bowling green wide enough for a match ‖ (*curling* and *bowling*) a team of four players [prob. O.F. *renc*, row, rank]
rink·y-dink or **rinky-tinky** (ríŋki:díŋk) *adj.* (*slang*) old-fashioned and dilapidated —**rinky dink, rinky tink** *n.*
rinse (rins) **1.** *v.t. pres. part.* **rins·ing** *past* and *past part.* **rinsed** to remove the soap, dirt etc. from (clothes etc.) with clear water ‖ to remove (soap etc.) in this way ‖ to wash superficially in clear water **2.** *n.* a rinsing or being rinsed ‖ a solution that tints the hair temporarily [F. *rincer*, origin unknown]
Ri·o·bam·ba (ri:əbámbɑ) a city (pop. 61,000) in central Ecuador. The first constitution of the Republic of Ecuador was proclaimed (1830) here
Río Bravo *RIO GRANDE
Rí·o de Ja·nei·ro (rí:oudədʒənéərou) the chief port of entry (pop. 4,857,700) of Brazil, on the southeast coast. Manufactures and industries: chemicals, pharmaceuticals, food processing, consumer goods. Built on the coastal plain and hills rising from Guanabara Bay, and flanked by crescent beaches, it is backed by a row of steep granite peaks, notably Pão de Açúcar (Sugarloaf, 1,296 ft) jutting into the bay, and Corcovado (Hunchback, 2,310 ft). Its modern architecture is often spectacular. Its colonial monuments include the 18th-c. cathedral and churches, botanical gardens (1808), National University (1920), library, museums and academies. The site was explored (1502) by the Portuguese, and settlement was begun by French Huguenots (1555). Rio de Janeiro was the capital of Brazil (1763-1960)
Rí·o de la Pla·ta (rí:ɔðelɑplɑ́tɑ) (*Eng.* River Plate) an estuary (170 miles long, 20-120 miles wide) between Uruguay and Argentina, formed by the Paraná and Uruguay Rivers. Chief ports: Montevideo, Buenos Aires. Its basin is one of the most fertile regions of South America
Ri·o de O·ro (rí:ɔðeɔ́rɔ) *SPANISH SAHARA
Rí·o Gran·de (rí:ugrɑ́ndə) a headstream (680 miles long) of the Paraná, rising in the coastal highlands of S.E. Brazil
Ri·o Gran·de (rí:ougrǽndi:, ri:ougrǽnd) (*Span.* Río Bravo or Río Grande del Norte) a river (1,800 miles long) flowing south from the Rocky Mtns in S. Colorado, through New Mexico to El Paso, Texas, then southeast, forming the Texas-Mexico border, to the Gulf of Mexico
Rio Grande de Santiago *SANTIAGO
ri·om·e·ter (ri:ɒ́mitər) (*acronym*) for relative ionospheric opacity meter, a device that records cosmic radio noise through changes in absorption rate of electromagnetic waves in the ionosphere
Rí·o Mu·ni (rí:oumú:ni:), or Mbini, the mainland (area incl. offshore islands 10,047 sq. miles, pop. 183,000) part of Guinea-Bissau. Capital: Bata. People: Fang (Bantu-speaking), 2% European. It is mountainous except for a narrow coastal strip. Highest point: 4,920 ft. Exports: cocoa, palm oil, coffee, hardwoods, fruit. Río Muni was occupied by Spain (1844) and became part of Equatorial Guinea (now Guinea-Bissau) (1959)
Rí·o Ne·gro (rí:ɔnégrɔ) a river (1,400 miles long) rising (as the Guainía) in E. Colombia, flowing southwest along the Venezuelan border, then west through Brazil to the Amazon at Manaus
Ri·o Pie·dras (rí:ɔpjeðrɑs) a town (pop. 132,000) in N. Puerto Rico, main seat of the University of Puerto Rico
Ri·os Mo·ra·les (rí:ɔsmɔrɑ́les), Juan Antonio (1888-1946), Chilean statesman, president (1942-6). He followed a policy of neutrality in the 2nd world war
ri·ot (ráiət) *n.* a public tumult, often in defiance of authority and the law and sometimes destructive of life or property ‖ a profuse display or growth, *a riot of color, a riot of tropical vegetation* ‖ a hound's following of a scent other than that of the animal being hunted ‖ (*pop.*) a very funny person or entertainment **to read the riot act** to order someone to desist peremptorily on pain of punishment **to run riot** to act without control or restraint ‖ (of plants) to grow in wild profusion [O.F. *riote, riot*]
riot *v.i.* to take part in a riot ‖ to grow in undisciplined profusion, *roses rioted everywhere in the garden* ‖ (of a hound) to follow the scent of an animal other than the one it is supposed to be hunting ‖ *v.i.* (with 'away') to spend (time, money etc.) wantonly [O.F. *rioter*]
Riot Act an act of the British parliament, passed (1715) as a result of the rioting which followed the accession of George I. The act made it a felony if an unlawful assembly of 12 or more people fails to disperse within an hour of the reading of a prescribed proclamation by a magistrate or other law officer
Rí·o Tin·to (rí:ɔtí:ntɔ) a town (pop. 7,000) in Huelva, Spain, the site of copper mines (Minas de Río Tinto) exploited by the Phoenicians and Romans and, in modern times, since the 18th c., but now nearly exhausted
ri·ot·ous (ráiətəs) *adj.* marked by rioting ‖ noisy and disorderly ‖ profligate, *riotous living* ‖ profuse, *riotous color* [O.F.]
Rio Treaty *INTERAMERICAN TREATY OF RECIPROCAL ASSISTANCE
Ri·ouw Archipelago (rí:ou) (*Indonesian* Riau) a group of islands (land area 2,279 sq. miles, pop. 77,000) in Indonesia, of S.E. Malaya. Main islands: Bintan, Bantam, Rempang. Chief town: Pakan Baru. Products: copra, bauxite
rip (rip) **1.** *v. pres. part.* **rip·ping** *past* and *past part.* **ripped** *v.t.* to break the fibers of (e.g. cloth) by a sudden pull, tear, cut etc. ‖ (with 'off', 'out', 'away') to remove by pulling suddenly, *they ripped off his medals* ‖ to give a sudden pull or pulls to so as to bring into a specified condition, *to rip open a parcel* ‖ to split or saw (wood) in the direction of the grain ‖ *v.i.* to be suddenly torn, cut, split etc. ‖ (*pop.*) to move at a great speed **to rip into** (*pop.*) to attack suddenly with angry words **to rip out** to utter (an oath, threat etc.) violently **2.** *n.* the act of ripping ‖ a tear or rent made by ripping [etym. doubtful]
rip *n.* a tide rip ‖ a tidal or river current caused by water moving over an irregular bottom [perh. fr. RIP v.]
rip *n.* (*pop.*) a dissolute person [perh. var. of REP]
ri·par·i·an (raipéəri:ən, ripéəri:ən) *adj.* of or relating to a riverbank, *riparian rights* ‖ located on a riverbank, *riparian land* [L. *riparius*]
rip cord a cord for opening a parachute ‖ a cord for opening the gasbag of a balloon for a rapid descent
ripe (raip) *adj.* ready to be harvested, *the corn is ripe* or to be eaten, *a ripe plum* ‖ having reached full flavor, e.g. by aging, *a ripe cheese* ‖ (of a plan etc.) ready to be put into action, execution etc. ‖ (of time) at a propitious juncture ‖ mature, *ripe judgment* ‖ far on in years, *the ripe age of 82* ‖ (of a boil etc.) ready to open **rí·pen** *v.i.* to become ripe ‖ *v.t.* to cause to become ripe [O.E. *rīpe*]
rip-off (rípɔf) *n.* (*slang or colloq.*) an unethical, cheating practice —**rip off** *v.* —**rip-off** *adj.*
Rip·on Falls (rípən) a low waterfall marking the exit of the Nile from its source in Lake Victoria, Uganda. It has become virtually submerged by the nearby hydroelectric scheme at Owens Falls
Ripon Society an organization of liberal Republicans founded (1960s) to research for liberal Republican candidates. It is privately financed
ri·poste, ri·post (ripóust) *n.* a quick return thrust in fencing ‖ a quick, sharp retort [F. *riposte* fr. Ital. *risposta*, reply]
riposte, ripost *pres. part.* **ri·post·ing** *past* and *past part.* **ri·post·ed** *v.i.* to make a riposte [fr. F. *riposter*]
rip·per (rípər) *n.* a device for ripping, e.g. a ripsaw ‖ the operator of a ripsaw
rip·ple (ríp'l) **1.** *v. pres. part.* **rip·pling** *past* and *past part.* **rip·pled** *v.i.* (of water) to have the surface disturbed by ripples ‖ to make the sound of ripples ‖ to cause ripples, *the rippling movement of the boat* ‖ (of fabric etc.) to fall in ripplelike folds ‖ *v.t.* to cause ripples in, give a wavy appearance to **2.** *n.* a small wave spreading outwards from a point where the surface of water etc. is disturbed ‖ a small wave made by the action of wind on water ‖ anything resembling this in appearance, *ripples in the grass* ‖ the sound made by small waves or the action of the wind on waves ‖ a sound compared with this, *a ripple of laughter* ‖ a ripple mark [etym. doubtful]
ripple 1. *v.t. pres. part.* **rip·pling** *past* and *past part.* **rip·pled** to draw (flax etc.) through a ripple in order to separate out the seeds **2.** *n.* a comb used for separating the seeds from flax [M.E. *ripelen*]
ripple mark a wavy line or ridge produced by the action of wind or waves or both on the surface of sand etc.
rip·plet (ríplit) *n.* a little ripple
rip·ply (rípli:) *comp.* **rip·pli·er** *superl.* **rip·pli·est** *adj.* having ripples ‖ rippling
rip·rap (ríprӕp) **1.** *n.* a foundation or wall of stones thrown together loosely and irregularly, used e.g. on slopes to prevent erosion ‖ stones used for this purpose **2.** *v.t. pres. part.* **rip·rap·ping** *past* and *past part.* **rip·rapped** to strengthen with a riprap ‖ to build a riprap in or upon
rip-roar·ing (ríprɔriŋ, ríprouriŋ) *adj.* (*pop.*) (used as an intensive) very great, *a rip-roaring success, a rip-roaring time*
rip·saw (rípsɔ) *n.* a coarse-toothed saw for cutting wood along the grain
rip·snort·er (rípsnɔ́rtər) *n.* something very powerful, impressive or remarkable **ríp·snórt·ing** *adj.*
rip·tide (ríptaid) *n.* a powerful surface current flowing away from shore
Rip·u·ar·i·an (ripju:éəri:ən) **1.** *adj.* of or relating to the southern division of the Franks, united (late 5th c.) with the Salian Franks under Clovis **2.** *n.* a Ripuarian Frank [M.L. *Ripuarius*]
rise (raiz) **1.** *v. pres. part.* **ris·ing** *past* **rose** (rouz) *past part.* **ris·en** (ríz'n) *v.i.* to come to a vertical position after sitting, kneeling, lying etc. ‖ to get up after sleeping, *to rise early* ‖ to extend upwards, *the mountain rises abruptly* ‖ to move upwards, *the balloon rose in the air* ‖ to be restored to life, *to rise from the dead* ‖ (of birds) to soar up from the ground in alarm ‖ (of a heavenly body) to appear above the horizon, *the moon rose* ‖ to increase in degree, quantity, volume, price etc., ‖ to become louder, *her voice rose in indignation* ‖ (of emotions) to become intensified, *indignation rose in him* ‖ to swell, puff up, *a blister rose on his thumb, the bread is rising* ‖ to advance in rank, acquire a higher social status etc., *to rise in a profession* ‖ to become elated, stirred, animated etc., *his spirits rose when he heard the news* ‖ to begin, *the river rises in the mountains* ‖ to revolt, *to rise against a king* ‖ to come into being, *the idea rose from my knowledge of him* ‖ (of the wind) to begin to blow ‖ (of the wind) to blow with greater force ‖ (of fish) to come towards the surface of the water to take food or bait ‖ to end a meeting, *the committee rose at 7* ‖ to be in the process of being erected, *a skyscraper is rising in the river area* ‖ to become, or seem to become, erect, *fear caused his hair to rise* ‖ *v.t.* to cause (birds) to soar up from the ground ‖ to cause (fish) to come towards the surface of the water **to rise above** to dominate by moral effort, *to rise above one's misfortunes* **to rise to** to show oneself capable of meeting (challenging circumstances, occasions etc.) **2.** *n.* an upward-sloping piece of ground ‖ advancement in rank, social status etc. ‖ the original source of something, e.g. a river ‖ the emergence and early growth of something, e.g. a civilization or industry, *the rise of the Roman Empire* ‖ an increase in price, rate, value, volume etc. ‖ (of a body of water) a coming to a higher level or the amount of this ‖ (*Br.*) a raise (increase in salary or wages) ‖ the appearance of fish near the surface of water **to get a rise out of (someone)** to get a hoped-for reaction from (someone) by teasing or otherwise provoking
rís·er *n.* the vertical piece connecting two stair treads **an early (late) riser,** a person who gets up early (late) in the morning [O.E. *rīsan*]
rise time (*telecommunications*) the time required for a pulse signal to go from 10% to 90% of maximum amplitude. *also* build-up time
ris·i·bil·i·ty (rizəbíliti:) *pl.* **ris·i·bil·i·ties** *n.* (*rhet.*) laughter, *to excise risibility* ‖ (*pl., rhet.*) responsiveness to what excites laughter

CONCISE PRONUNCIATION KEY: **(a)** æ, *cat*; ɑ, *car*; ɔ *fawn*; ei, *snake*. **(e)** e, *hen*; i:, *sheep*; iə, *deer*; ɛə, *bear*. **(i)** i, *fish*; ai, *tiger*; ə:, *bird*. **(o)** o, *ox*; au, *cow*; ou, *goat*; u, *poor*; ɔi, *royal*. **(u)** ʌ, *duck*; u, *bull*; u:, *goose*; ə, *bacillus*; ju:, *cube*. x, *loch*; θ, *think*; ð, *bother*; z, *Zen*; ʒ, *corsage*; dʒ, *savage*; ŋ, *orangutang*; j, *yak*; ʃ, *fish*; tʃ, *fetch*; 'l, *rabble*; 'n, *redden*. Complete pronunciation key appears inside front cover.

ris·i·ble (rízəb'l) *adj.* (*rhet.*) exciting laughter ‖ (*rhet.*) of or relating to laughter ‖ (*rhet.*) used in laughing, *risible muscles* ‖ (*rhet.*) easily disposed to laugh [fr. L.L. *risibilis*]

ris·ing (ráiziŋ) **1.** *adj.* of or relating to someone who, or something which, rises, *the rising sun, a rising man in his profession, the rising generation* ‖ (*Br.*) nearing a stated age, *he must be rising 12 by now* **2.** *n.* the act or process of someone who, or something which, rises ‖ a rebellion ‖ (*naut.*) one of the narrow strakes of wood on which the thwarts rest

risk (risk) **1.** *n.* the possibility of danger, injury, loss etc. ‖ (*insurance*) the possibility of loss in the case of goods covered by an insurance policy ‖ (*insurance*) the probability of such loss ‖ (*insurance*) a person or thing with reference to the hazard involved in insuring him or it, *a good risk* **at owner's risk** (*commerce*) on condition that the owner bears the risk in case of loss etc. **to run** (or **take**) **a risk** to expose oneself or be exposed to danger, injury, loss etc. **2.** *v.t.* to expose to danger, injury, loss etc., *to risk one's neck* ‖ to run or take the risk of, *to risk a battle* [F. *risque* fr. Ital.]

risk·i·ly (rískili:) *adv.* in a risky way

risk·i·ness (ríski:nis) *n.* the state or quality of being risky

risk retention self insurance, esp. by a cooperating group in a common situation

risk·y (ríski:) *comp.* **risk·i·er** *superl.* **risk·i·est** *adj.* involving risk

Ri·sor·gi·men·to (ri:sɔrdʒi:méntɔ) the rising (1815-70) of the people of Italy against Austrian domination. Among its leaders were Mazzini, who founded (1831) the 'Young Italy' movement, Garibaldi and Cavour

ri·sot·to (risɔ́tou, risɔ́tou) *n.* rice cooked in meat stock, with onions, bits of cooked meat etc. [Ital.]

ris·qué (riskéi) *adj.* close to being indecent, *a risqué story* [F.]

ris·sole (rísoul, risóul) *n.* a small ball of minced meat or fish coated with bread crumbs etc. and fried [O.F.]

ri·tar·dan·do (ri̧tardɑ́ndou) *n.* (*mus., abbr.* rit., ritard.) a direction to go gradually slower [Ital.]

rite (rait) *n.* a religious ceremony or formal act of worship ‖ any ceremonial observance or procedure ‖ (often **Rite**) the liturgical form adopted by a church, *the Roman Rite* ‖ (often **Rite**) a division of a Church using such liturgical form [fr. L. *ritus*, ceremony]

ri·tor·nel·lo (ri̧tɔrnélou) *pl.* **ri·tor·nel·li** (ri̧tɔrnéli:) *n.* (*mus.*) a purely orchestral passage, esp. a refrain, in a vocal composition [Ital.]

rit·u·al (rítʃu:əl) **1.** *adj.* of or relating to or practiced as a rite or rites **2.** *n.* a strictly ordered traditional method of conducting and performing an act of worship or other solemn ceremony ‖ a book setting out this method ‖ (*loosely*) any method of doing something in which the details are always faithfully repeated, *to make a ritual of welcoming one's guests* **rít·u·al·ism** *n.* excessive observance of religious ritual ‖ the study of religious ritual **rít·u·al·ist** *n.* a person who practices or advocates ritualism **rit·u·al·ís·tic**, *adj.* **rit·u·al·ís·ti·cal·ly** *adv.* [fr. L. *ritualis*]

ritz wrap (rítzræ̀p) (*cosmetology*) hair-styling device made with fabric-covered wire, to put up long hair into an elevated style

Ri·va·da·via (ri̧:vadɑ́vjɑ), Bernardino (1780-1845), Argentinian politician and first president of the Republic (1826-7). He was forced to resign, and lived the remainder of his life in exile

ri·val (ráivəl) **1.** *n.* a person in competition with another or others, e.g. in love or business ‖ someone who or something which equals or nearly equals another in some desirable quality, *he has no rival in Shakespearean roles* **2.** *adj.* competitive, *rival firms* **3.** *v.t. pres. part.* **ri·val·ing,** esp. *Br.* **ri·val·ling** *past* and *past part.* **ri·valed,** esp. *Br.* **ri·valled** to be in competition with ‖ to equal or approach equality with, *to rival someone in intelligence* **rí·val·ry** *pl.* **ri·val·ries** *n.* competition ‖ an instance of this [fr. L. *rivalis*, orig. a person living on the opposite riverbank from another person]

Ri·va Pa·la·cio (rí:vɑpɑlásjɔ), Vicente (1832-96), Mexican historical novelist and patriot. His 'Calvario y tabor' depicts the French intervention, against which he fought. His 'Mexico a través de los siglos' is an epic history of Mexico from its origins

rive (raiv) *pres. part.* **riv·ing** *past* **rived** *past part.* **rived, riv·en** (rívən) *v.t.* (rare except in *past part.*) to split apart, a *riven oak* [O.N. *rífa*]

riv·er (rívər) *n.* a usually voluminous stream of fresh water flowing either permanently or seasonally in a natural channel into another body of water, e.g. a sea or a lake ‖ a voluminous flow of something, *a river of mud* **to sell (someone) down the river** to cause (someone) to come to ruin or near ruin by some kind of betrayal [O.F. *rivere, riviere*]

Ri·ve·ra (ri:véra), Diego (1886-1957), Mexican painter, esp. of murals depicting past and present social injustices and the reform achievements of the Mexican Revolution (1910-19)

Rivera, José Eustasio (1889-1928), Colombian writer, author of a collection of sonnets, 'Tierra de promisión' (1921), and of the novel 'La vorágine' (1924). The latter depicts Amazon jungle life, centered around the rubber industry, as one which debases all who come into contact with it, but which presents a challenge to the hero

Rivera, José Fructuoso (1788-1854), Uruguayan general, independence leader, and first president (1830-4, 1839-43)

Rivera, Primo de *PRIMO DE RIVERA

Rivera a town (pop. 40,000) in N. Uruguay on the Brazilian border

riv·er·bank (rívərbæŋk) *n.* the bank of a river

riv·er·bed (rívərbȩd) *n.* the channel in which a river flows or formerly flowed

Riv·er·i·na (ri̧vərí:nə) an extensively irrigated district in New South Wales, Australia, watered by the Lachlan, Murrumbidgee and Murray Rivers: wheat, wool, fruit, vegetables, cattle

riv·er·ine (rívərain, rívərin) *adj.* situated on or living on the banks of a river ‖ of or relating to a river, *riverine traffic*

ri·ver·side (rívərsaid) *n.* the ground beside a river

riv·et (rívit) **1.** *n.* a metal pin or bolt, with a large head at one end, inserted into two or more metal plates etc., the headless end then being hammered out flat (often while hot) to hold the plates etc. firmly together **2.** *v.t. pres. part.* **riv·et·ing, riv·et·ting** *past* and *past part.* **riv·et·ed, riv·et·ted** to join with rivets ‖ (with 'on') to fix (the attention eyes, gaze etc.) [O.F. fr. *river*, to clinch]

Riv·i·er·a (ri̧vi:éərə) the Mediterranean coast between Toulon, France and La Spezia, Italy, a famous resort area

ri·vière (rivjéər, ri̧vi:éər) *n.* a necklace of precious stones, esp. a necklace of diamonds [F. = a river]

riv·u·let (rívjulit) *n.* a small stream [perh. fr. Ital. *rivoletto*]

Ri·yadh (ri:jɑ́d) the chief city (pop. 667,000) of Nejd and capital of Saudi Arabia, and principal commercial center or the interior, in a cultivated oasis on the pilgrimage road from Iran to Mecca: Great Mosque (center for the Wahhabi sect), royal palace. University

ri·yal (ri:ɑ́l, ri:ɔ́l) *pl.* **ri·yal, ri·yals** *n.* the basic monetary unit of the Yemen ‖ a coin of the value of one riyal

Riz·zio (rítsi:ou), David (c. 1533-66), Italian musician and favorite of Mary Queen of Scots. He was murdered by Darnley, Mary's husband

RM-47 *U-2

RNA *RIBONUCLEIC ACID

RNA polymerase *REPLICASE

RNAse or **RNAase** (*physiol. abbr.*) for ribonuclease (which see)

RO *adj.* (*computer abbr.*) for receive only, used in reference to a printer that only receives data

roach (routʃ) *n.* a cockroach

roach *pl.* **roach, roach·es** *n.* *Rutilus rutilus*, fam. *Cyprinidae*, a European freshwater fish about 10-12 ins long and weighing up to 1 lb ‖ any of various American sunfishes of fam. *Centrarchidae* [O.F. *roche*]

roach *n.* (*naut.*) a curving edge at the foot of a square sail [origin unknown]

road (roud) *n.* a strip of smoothed, cleared land, usually provided with a hard surface, for the passage from place to place of vehicles, riders, pedestrians etc. ‖ a roadstead ‖ the way to get somewhere, *the road to Rome, the road to success* ‖ (*pop.*) a railroad **on the road** (of a salesman) traveling from place to place selling goods ‖ (esp. of a theatrical company) touring [O.E. *rād*]

road agent (*Am. hist.*) a highwayman on the stagecoach routes

road·bed (róudbȩd) *n.* the foundation of a road ‖ that part of a road surface upon which vehicles travel ‖ the bed of a railroad on which rails and sleepers are laid

road·block (róudblɒk) *n.* (*mil.*) a barricade constructed to impede the advance of an enemy ‖ a barrier set up by police to halt traffic

road·craft (róudkræft) *n.* (*Br.*) autodriving skill

road hog a driver of a vehicle who stays in or near the middle of the road and so prevents others from passing him

road·house (róudhaus) *pl.* **road·hous·es** (róudhauziz) *n.* a country inn ‖ a nightclub located outside the limits of a city

road·ie (róudi:) *n.* a road-show manager

road·man (róudmən) *pl.* **road·men** (róudmən) *n.* a worker employed in building and maintaining roads

road metal the broken stone etc. used in constructing a road

road racing (*sports*) motorcycle or auto racing on public roads or on simulations of public roads

road·run·ner (róudrʌnər) *n.* the chaparral cock

road·side (róudsaid) **1.** *n.* the side of a road **2.** *adj.* located along a roadside, *a roadside inn*

road·stead (róudstȩd) *n.* a sheltered water where ships may ride at anchor

road·ster (róudstər) *n.* an open car, with a front seat only, and room for luggage in the back or a rumble seat

road·way (róudwei) *n.* a road, esp. its central area ‖ the part of a bridge used by vehicular traffic

road·wor·thy (róudwə:rði:) *adj.* fit for being driven on the road

roam (roum) **1.** *v.i.* to walk or travel with no particular goal ‖ *v.t.* to wander through, *to roam the streets* **2.** *n.* a roaming, ramble [etym. doubtful]

roan (roun) **1.** *adj.* (of an animal's coat, esp. a horse's coat) having the prevailing color, esp. when this is reddish-brown, deeply flecked with white or gray hairs **2.** *n.* a roan horse or other animal ‖ a reddish-brown color [O.F. *roan, rouen*, origin unknown]

roan *n.* a sheepskin tanned to resemble morocco, used esp. for bookbinding [perh. F. *Roan*, old form of ROUEN]

roar (rɔr, rour) **1.** *v.i.* to emit the loud, deep sound characteristic of some savage or enraged beasts, e.g. a lion or bull ‖ to talk, sing or laugh loudly and boisterously ‖ (e.g. of flood water or the sea) to emit a loud, deep, confused, sometimes rumbling, noise ‖ (of a tunnel or other confined place) to resound noisily ‖ to go with a roaring noise, *cars roar past their houses* ‖ (of a horse afflicted with roaring) to breathe raspingly ‖ *v.t.* to utter or express with a roar ‖ (with 'down') to silence by roaring **2.** *n.* a roaring noise **róar·ing 1.** *n.* the sound made by someone who or something which roars ‖ (*vet.*) a disease of horses causing them to emit rasping breathing sounds during exercise **2.** *adj.* that roars ‖ (*pop.*) extremely successful, *a roaring trade* [O.E. *rārian*]

roaring forties either of two ocean areas between latitudes 40° and 50° N. and S., where very strong westerly winds prevail

roast (roust) **1.** *v.t.* to cook (meat etc.) by exposing it to the radiant heat from a fire, or the dry heat of an oven ‖ to cook (e.g. potatoes) in hot ashes etc. ‖ to dry and partly scorch (esp. coffee beans) ‖ to heat excessively, *the sun was roasting us* ‖ (*metall.*) to heat without melting, in order to burn away impurities ‖ (*pop.*) to criticize mercilessly, *to roast a performance* ‖ *v.i.* to be roasted ‖ to feel extremely hot **2.** *n.* a cut of meat roasted or ready for roasting ‖ a roasting or being roasted ‖ an outdoor social gathering in which the principal item of food is roasted, usually over an open fire, *a wiener roast* **róast·er** *n.* a chicken, pig, rabbit etc. suitable for roasting ‖ an oven for roasting ‖ a furnace used for roasting coffee etc. [fr. O.F. *rostir*]

rob (rɒb) *pres. part.* **rob·bing** *past* and *past part.* **robbed** *v.t.* to take property from (a person) illegally ‖ (*law*) to do this to (someone) with force or threat of force ‖ to take money, valuables etc. from (a place) illegally, *to rob a bank* ‖ to deprive (a person) of something desired or due, *fear robbed him of speech* ‖ *v.i.* to engage in robbery [fr. O.F. *robber, rober* fr. Gmc]

rob·a·lo (roubɑ́lou, róubəlou) *pl.* **rob·a·los, rob·a·lo** *n.* the snook (*Centropomus undecimalis*) [Span. *róbalo*]

rob·ber (rɒ́bər) *n.* a person who robs

robber baron (*hist.*) a feudal noble who lived by robbing people passing through his territory or holding them for ransom ‖ (*Am. hist.*) any late 19th-c. capitalist who grew rich by exploitation

rob·ber·y (rɒ́bəri:) *pl.* **rob·ber·ies** *n.* the act or practice of robbing [O.F. *roberie*]

Rob·bia (rɔ́bbjɑ), Luca della (c. 1400-82), Florentine sculptor, one of a large and distinguished family. His most famous work was a series of singing angels and dancing boys, called the 'Cantoria' ('The Singing Gallery') made for the cathedral in Florence, Italy. He perfected a technique of applying colored lead glazes to terra cotta: typically, white figures on a clear blue ground. His work was continued by other members of the family, notably by his nephew, Andrea della Robbia (1435-1528)

Rob·bins (rɒ́binz), Frederick Chapman (1916-), U.S. pediatrician and co-winner (with J. F. Enders and T. H. Weller) of the 1954 Nobel prize in medicine and physiology for cultivation of the poliomyelitis viruses in tissue culture

robe (roub) **1.** *n.* a long, loose outer garment worn as a symbol of profession or position, *academic robes, judge's robe* ‖ a skin or rug tucked around the legs while riding in a car etc. ‖ a dressing gown **2.** *v. pres. part.* **rob·ing** *past* and *past part.* **robed** *v.t.* to put a robe or robes on ‖ *v.i.* to put on robes or a robe [O.F.]

Rob·ert I (rɒ́bərt) (c. 865-923), French king (922-3)

Robert II (c. 970-1031), king of France (996-1031), son of Hugh Capet. He ruled jointly with his father after 987

Robert I (*d.* 1035), duke of Normandy (1027-35). He was the father of William the Conqueror

Robert II 'Curthose' (c. 1054-1134), duke of Normandy (1087-1106), son of William I of England. He rebelled against his father, was at war (1091-6) with his brother William II, and was defeated and captured by Henry I at Tinchebrai (1106)

Robert I 'the Bruce' (1274-1329), king of Scotland (1306-29). He was crowned in defiance of Edward I, and consolidated his hold on Scotland during the weak reign of Edward II, whom he heavily defeated at Bannockburn (1314). His title to the throne and the independence of Scotland were officially recognized (1328)

Robert II (1316-90), king of Scotland (1371-90), founder of the Stuart dynasty, grandson of Robert I. He was regent (1334-41 and 1346-57) for David II. His reign was spent in war with England

Ro·bert (rɔber), Hubert (1733-1808), French painter. His landscapes usually incorporated architectural features, often ruins, in the standard romantic vein

Ro·bert Guis·card (rɔbergi:skær) (c. 1015-85), Norman conqueror of Naples and Sicily. Between attempts (1081-2 and 1085) to conquer the Byzantine Empire, he defended (1084) Pope Gregory VII from a siege by Henry IV of Germany

Rob·erts (rɒ́bərts), Sir Charles George Douglas (1860-1943), Canadian writer. His prose works include 'History of Canada' (1897) and animal stories, notably 'The Kindred of the Wild' (1902) and 'Neighbours Unknown' (1911). His verse includes 'In Divers Tones' (1887) and 'The Vagrant of Time' (1927)

Roberts, Frederick Sleigh, 1st Earl Roberts of Kandahar, Pretoria and Waterford (1832-1914), British field marshal. He relieved Kandahar (1880) during the war between Britain and the Afghans (1878-80), was commander in chief in India (1885-93) and commanded (1899-1900) the British forces in the Boer War

Roberts, Owen Josephus (1875–1955), U.S. associate justice of the Supreme Court (1930–45). He was a special U.S. attorney (1924–30) during which time he was involved in the investigation of the Teapot Dome scandal before being appointed to the Court by Pres. Herbert Hoover. He was known as a conservative, generally opposed to Pres. Roosevelt's New Deal programs. He wrote the majority opinions in 'Nebbia v. New York' (1934), 'Railroad Retirement Board v. Alton Railroad Co.' (1935), 'Grovey v. Townsend' (1935) and 'United States v. Butler' (1936). After his resignation from the Court in 1945 he served as president of the University of Pennsylvania Law School (1948–51)

Robert (the) Bruce *ROBERT I

Robe·son (róubsən), Paul (1898–1976) U.S. black singer and actor. His rich bass voice is esp. associated with his repertory of spirituals. He was the star of New York productions 'Emperor Jones' (1924) and (1943) 'Othello', which established the longest Shakespearean run in the U.S.A.

Robes·pierre (rɔbzpjɛər), Maximilien François Marie-Isidore de (1758-94), French revolutionist. A provincial lawyer, he became the leader of the Jacobins during the French Revolution, and led the Mountain in overthrowing the Girondists (1793). As a member of the Committee of Public Safety (July 1793-July 1794) he was the virtual dictator of France, establishing the Terror, and eliminating his rivals Hébert and Danton. His measures, based on the doctrines of Rousseau, became increasingly extremist. He instituted the Cult of the Supreme Being (a mixture of deism and nationalism). He was overthrown and executed in the coup d'état of Thermidor (1794)

rob·in (rɒ́bin) *n. Erithacus rubecola,* fam. *Turdidae,* a small, plump European thrush having a dark olive-colored back and a yellowish red throat and breast ‖ *Turdus migratorius,* fam. *Turoidae,* a large (9-10 ins in length) North American thrush having an olive-gray back, a black throat streaked with gray, and a dull-red breast [O.F. familiar form of ROBERT]

Rob·in Good·fel·low (rɒ́bingúdfelou) Puck

Robin Hood (rɒ́binhud) a medieval English outlaw of Sherwood Forest, the subject of many legends. His exploits are sometimes associated with the reign of Richard I

Rob·in·son (rɒ́binsən), Edward (1794-1863), U.S. biblical scholar. His 'Biblical Researches in Palestine, Mount Sinai, and Arabia Petraea' (1841) and 'Later Biblical Researches in Palestine and the Adjacent Regions' (1856) were pioneer efforts in biblical geography

Robinson, Edwin Arlington (1869-1935), U.S. narrative poet. His best known works are 'The Man Against The Sky' (1916), 'Tristram' (1927) and 'Cavender's House' (1929). The residents of his 'Tilbury Town' are modeled after his boyhood hometown in Maine

Robinson, Henry Crabb (1775-1867), English diarist. He was a friend of Wordsworth, Southey, Coleridge, Lamb etc. and his vivid recollections make his 'Diary, Reminiscences and Correspondence' (1869) a valuable source book

Robinson, Jackie (Jack Roosevelt Robinson, 1919–72), U.S. baseball player, the first black to play (1947) in the major leagues. He became (1962) the first black to gain admission to the National Baseball Hall of Fame

ro·bot (róubɒt róubət) *n.* a mechanical device designed to do the work or part of the work of one or more human beings, esp. such a device activated by radiant energy, sound waves etc. ‖ an efficient but unfeeling person [fr. Czech *robota,* compulsory service, used in Karel Capek's play 'R.U.R.']

ro·bot·ics (roubɒ́tiks) *n.* the science of automated devices (robots) used to replace live workers, esp. in factories

ro·bot·o·mor·phic (roubɒtəmɔ́rfik) *adj.* of robotlike behavior

Rob Roy (rɒ́brɔ́i) (Robert MacGregor, 1671-1734), Scottish outlaw. He ran an extortion racket, demanding money from his neighbors for the return of stolen cattle

Rob·son, Mt (rɒ́bsən) the highest point (12,972 ft) of the Canadian Rocky Mtns, in E. British Columbia

ro·bust (roubʌ́st, róubʌst) *adj.* strong, esp. in resisting fatigue, illness etc. ‖ requiring muscular strength, *a robust game* ‖ coarse, *robust humor* ‖ (esp. of a plant) hardy [fr. L. *robustus*]

roc (rɒk) *n.* an enormous legendary bird thought to inhabit the region around the Indian Ocean [fr. Arab. *rokh, rukhkh*]

Ro·ca (rɔ́kɑ), Julio Argentino (1843-1914), Argentinian general, leader in the Paraguay Campaign, conqueror (1879) of Patagonia, and president (1880-6, 1898-1904)

roc·am·bole (rɒ́kemboul) *n. Allium scorodoprasum,* fam. *Liliaceae,* a European leek, used as a seasoning [etym. doubtful]

Ro·cham·beau (rɔʃɑ̃bou), Jean-Baptiste Donatien de Vimeur, Comte de (1725–1807), French marshal. As commander of the French troops sent to aid the American patriots during the Revolutionary War, he contributed to the victory at Yorktown (1781)

Ro·chelle salt (rɔʃél) $KNaC_4H_4O_6 4H_2O$, a crystalline salt used as a mild laxative and in the silvering of mirrors [after *La Rochelle,* France, where it was discovered]

roches mou·ton·nées (rɔ́ʃmu:tɔnéi) *pl. n.* knobs or hillocks of rock commonly occurring in upland regions, which have been formed and smoothed by glacial action [F. = sheeplike rocks]

Roch·es·ter (rɒ́tʃistər) a port (pop. 241,741) in N.W. New York State, on Lake Ontario. Industries: optical and other precision instruments, electrical equipment. University (1848)

Rochester, John Wilmot, 2nd earl of (1647-80), English poet and satirist. His best-known work is 'A Satire Against Mankind' (1675)

roch·et (rɒ́tʃit) *n.* (*eccles.*) a white linen vestment resembling a surplice. It is worn chiefly by bishops [O.F.]

rock (rɒk) *n.* (*geol.*) an aggregate of particles composed of one or more minerals, forming the major part of the earth's crust (*IGNEOUS ROCK, *METAMORPHIC ROCK, *SEDIMENTARY ROCK) ‖ a large, usually jagged, mass of this material protruding from the surface of the land or from a body of water ‖ a piece broken off from such a mass ‖ (*fig.*) a firm foundation or support ‖ (*Br.*) a stick of candied sugar flavored with peppermint etc. **on the rocks** in desperate financial straits ‖ (of drinks, esp. whiskey) served neat over ice cubes ‖ in or into a condition of disruption or ruin, a *marriage going on the rocks* ‖ short for rock 'n roll [O.F. *roke*]

rock 1. *v.t.* to cause to move to and fro, *to rock a baby's cradle* ‖ to bring into a specified condition by doing this, *to rock a baby to sleep* ‖ to cause to shake, vibrate, sway etc. violently ‖ to disturb emotionally ‖ (*mining*) to wash (sand or gravel) in a rocker ‖ (in mezzotint engraving) to prepare the surface of (a plate) by scraping it with a cradle ‖ *v.i.* to move to and fro ‖ to sway violently **2.** *n.* the act of rocking ‖ the movement involved in this act [O.E. *roccian*]

rock·a·bil·ly (rɒ́kəbili:) *n.* a combination of pop, rock, and country and western music styles

rock and roll, rock-'n-roll (rɒ́kənroul) a style of popular music of Afro-American origin, characterized by an insistent, heavily accented syncopated rhythm and the obsessive repetition of short musical phrases, tending to build up tension in an audience and induce a state of group frenzy when played very loud

rock bass *Ambloplites rupestris,* fam. *Centrarchidae,* a North American sunfish found esp. in the Great Lakes region and the upper Mississippi valley ‖ the striped bass ‖ any of several sea basses of genus *Paralabrax* widely distributed in the coastal waters of California and Mexico

rock bottom the lowest point or level, *sales have reached rock bottom* **at rock bottom** fundamentally **róck-bót·tom** *adj.*

rock candy sugar in large, hard, clear crystals

rock crystal the purest and most transparent form of quartz

rock dove the rock pigeon

Rock·e·fel·ler (rɒ́kifelər), John Davison (1839-1937), American industrialist and philanthropist. He acquired a near-monopoly of oil refining in the U.S.A. He endowed an institute for medical research with 500 million dollars (1901), and also gave generously to educational, scientific and religious funds

Rockefeller, Nelson Aldrich (1908–79), U.S. statesman, vice-president (1974–7), governor of New York (1959–73), grandson of John D. Rockefeller. He served as coordinator of inter-American affairs (1940–4), assistant secretary of state (1944–5), head of the International Development Advisory Board (1953–4) and special assistant to Pres. Dwight D. Eisenhower (1954–5). As New York's governor he expanded social welfare and education programs. He was appointed vice-president when Gerald Ford succeeded Richard Nixon as president

Rockefeller Foundation a philanthropic organization chartered (1913) by John D. Rockefeller, Sr. Its objectives are the conquest of hunger, the solution to the problems of population, university development, equality of opportunity, and cultural development

rock·er (rɒ́kər) *n.* either of the curved pieces on which a rocking chair or cradle rocks ‖ a rocking chair ‖ a cradle for washing sand or gravel ‖ a cradle used by a mezzotint engraver ‖ a skate with a curved blade

rocker *n.* a rock musician

rocker arm a lever, usually pivoted near its midpoint, used to transmit motion to a valve stem from a cam

rock·er·y (rɒ́kəri:) *pl.* **rock·er·ies** *n.* a rock garden

rock·et (rɒ́kit) **1.** *n.* a projectile driven by the reaction to the rearward expulsion of gases which are produced by burning a fuel inside it. It is the only known form of propulsion which can operate in a vacuum, and is therefore used in space vehicles. Rockets range in size from toy fireworks up to the very large ones used to launch earth satellites etc. Rockets are also used to throw the line in marine lifesaving appliances and to propel military warheads **2.** *v.i.* to rise very rapidly, *prices rocketed when the news was heard* ‖ (of game birds) to fly straight when flushed [F. *roquet* or fr. Ital. *rocchetta*]

rocket *n.* a member of *Hesperis,* fam. *Cruciferae,* a genus of plants having spikes of white or purple flowers which are fragrant at night, esp. *H. matronalis* ‖ *Eruca sativa,* fam. *Cruciferae,* a European annual grown mainly for salad [F. *roquette* fr. Ital.]

rocket astronomy the science involving analysis of high-altitude data accumulated by rocket instruments

rock·et·drome (rɒ́kitdroum) *n.* a rocket airport

rock·et·ry (rɒ́kitri:) *n.* the study of or use of rockets

rock·fish (rɒ́kfiʃ) *pl.* **rock·fish, rock·fish·es** *n.* any of several food fishes living among rocks in deep or shallow water, e.g. the striped bass and various groupers

rock garden an arrangement of large stones set in soil, in which various alpine plants, dwarf shrubs etc. are grown

Rock·ies (rɒ́ki:z) the Rocky Mtns

rock·i·ness (rɒ́kinis) *n.* the state or quality of being rocky

rocking chair a chair mounted on rockers

Rock·ing·ham (rɒ́kiŋəm), Charles Watson-Wentworth, 2nd marquis of (1730-82), English statesman who led Whig ministries (1765-6 and 1782)

rocking horse a wooden horse mounted on rockers, for children to ride on

rock·oon (rɒkkú:n) *n.* (*aerospace*) a system for high-altitude exploration utilizing a balloon from which a small, solidpropellant research rocket is launched near maximum altitude

rock pigeon *Columba livia,* fam. *Columbidae,* a bluish-gray European and Asian wild pigeon living along rocky coasts

rock rabbit the hyrax

rock·rose (rɒ́krouz) *n.* any of various low-growing plants of fam. *Cistaceae,* esp. of genera *Cistus, Helianthemum* and *Crocantheum,* growing mainly on rocky slopes and bearing roselike single flowers ‖ the flower of any of these plants

rock salmon any of various tropical fishes, esp. *Lutjanus argentimaculatus,* fam. *Lutjanidae,* a variety of red or pink snapper of the Pacific ‖ (*Br.*) the dogfish as sold by fish dealers

rock salt common salt occurring in stratified layers

rock·shaft (rɒ́kʃæft, rɒ́kʃɑft) *n.* a shaft that rocks back and forth on its journals (rather than revolving)

Rockwell (rɒ́kwel), Norman (1894–1978), U.S. illustrator, known for his 'Saturday Evening Post' covers (1916–63) depicting whimsical, humorous views of Middle America as well as events of the day. His best-known work is the 'Four Freedoms' mural, which was used on posters during the 2nd world war

rock wool a fibrous material formed by passing a jet of steam through limestone, siliceous rock etc. It is used for heat and sound insulation

rock·y (rɒ́ki:) *comp.* **rock·i·er** *superl.* **rock·i·est** *adj.* full of rocks ‖ made of rock ‖ hard as rock

rocky *comp.* **rock·i·er** *superl.* **rock·i·est** *adj.* (of something which ought to be firm) shaky or weak, *a rocky table* ‖ (*pop.*) feeling unwell

Rocky Mountain goat the mountain goat

Rocky Mountains a mountain system of W. North America, running from British Columbia and Alberta, Canada, through Montana, Idaho, Wyoming, Utah and Colorado to Arizona and New Mexico. The peaks are characteristically massive and barren, only lower slopes being forested. The system is rich in minerals. Highest point: Mt Elbert (14,431 ft) in Colorado ‖ the entire axial mountain system of North America, running from the Bering Strait to the Andes, including, with the Rocky Mtns proper, the Alaska, Cascade, Sierra Nevada, Sierra Madre, Central American and lesser ranges

Rocky Mountain spotted fever a serious febrile disease characterized by chills, fever, pains in the muscles and joints, and a dark reddish-purple rash. It is caused by rickettsia transmitted by the bite of the Rocky Mountain wood tick

ro·co·co (rəkóukou, roukóukou) **1.** *n.* a highly ornamental style in architecture, interior decoration etc., characterized by asymmetrical arrangements of curved lines and elaborate scrollwork, developed in Europe from the baroque, and prevalent in Europe in the 18th c. **2.** *adj.* of or relating to painting, music, literature etc. of this same period having similar ornately decorative characteristics [F.]

Roc·roi, Battle of (rɔkrwæ) a battle (1643), during the Thirty Years' War. The French army under Louis II de Condé decimated the Spanish infantry

rod (rɒd) a slender, sometimes extensible bar, shaft, pole, staff etc. in wood, cane, metal, glass etc., *a curtain rod, a fishing rod* ‖ a connecting rod ‖ a staff or wand carried as a symbol of office, authority etc. ‖ a stick used to measure with ‖ a measure of length equal to 5 ½ yds or 16 ½ ft ‖ a square rod ‖ one of the rod-shaped cells in the retina of the eye sensitive to dim light ‖ a rod-shaped bacterium **the rod** corporal punishment [O. E. *rodd*]

rode past of RIDE

ro·dent (róud'nt) **1.** *n.* a small gnawing mammal of the order *Rodentia* including rats, mice, squirrels, marmots etc. All rodents have a single pair of large chisellike incisors in the upper jaw. These keep growing from the roots as they wear away at the tips **2.** *adj.* of or relating to a rodent [fr. L. *rodens* (*rodentis*) fr. *rodere,* to gnaw]

ro·de·o (róudi:ou, roudéiou) *n.* a roundup (of cattle) ‖ an area where cattle are enclosed ‖ a public exhibition of skill by cowboys, e.g. in riding, lassoing etc., often in competition [Span.=a going around]

Rod·er·ick (rɒ́dərik) (*d.* c. 711), last king of the Visigoths in Spain (c. 710–c. 711). He was killed fighting the Moors

Ro·dil (rɔdí:l), José Ramón (1789-1853), Spanish general. In spite of the definitive defeat of Spanish forces at Ayacucho, he held the port of El Callao until the following year (1825)

Ro·din (rɔdɛ̃), Auguste (1840-1917), French sculptor. The sensitive, almost flickering surfaces of his bronzes render both the internal life and energy of the subject and the modeler's own creative energy. The subjects start from the human form, but tend toward a more abstract 'thought'. They thus form a bridge between the 'literary' symbolism of Rodin's own time and the more abstract formal art of the 20th c. His most frequent themes are human aspiration and creativity ('The Thinker', 'Balzac'), the anguish of humanity which knows its own mortality ('The Burghers of Calais'), and the related theme of erotic love ('The Kiss' etc.)

Rod·ney (rɒ́dni:), George Brydges, 1st Baron Rodney (1718-92), British admiral. He won victories over the Spanish and French fleets in the Revolutionary War

Ro·dó (roudóu), José Enrique (1872-1917), Uruguayan essayist and moralist. His most important works are his essay on Rubén Darío (1899), 'Ariel' (1900) and 'Motivos de Proteo' (1909)

rod·o·mon·tade (rɒdəmɒntéid, rɒdəmɒntɑ́d, roudəmɒntéid, roudəmɒntɑ́d) **1.** *n.* bluster, boasting **2.** *adj.* boastful **3.** *v.i. pres. part.* **rod·o·mon·tad·ing** *past* and *past part.* **rod·o·mon·tad·ed** to boast [F. fr. Ital. after the character *Rodomonte* in Ariosto's 'Orlando Furioso']

Rod·rí·guez (rɔdri:ges), José Gaspar *FRANCIA

rod storage (*computer*) cylindrical rods or wires, 1/10th-in long, utilized as a static magnetic storage unit in some computers in place of ring-shape cores

roe (rou) *n.* a mass of fish eggs, esp. when enclosed in the ovarian membrane ‖ the eggs or ovaries of certain crustaceans, e.g. the coral of a lobster [prob. fr. O.N. *hrogn*]

roe *pl.* **roe, roes** *n.* a roe deer [O.E. *rāha, rǣge*]

Roeb·ling (róubliŋ), John Augustus (1806-69), U.S. civil engineer and designer of suspension bridges, notably the Brooklyn Bridge in New York

roe·buck (róubʌk) *n.* the male roe deer

roe deer *Capreolus capreolus,* a species of small, graceful, European and Asian deer, having forked antlers. They are reddish-brown in summer, grayish in winter

roent·gen, rönt·gen (réntgən, réntʃən) *n.* (*phys.*) a unit of X-ray or gamma radiation, defined as the amount which will produce ions in 1 cc. of dry air at standard temperature and pressure that carry 1 electrostatic unit of charge [after Wilhelm Konrad *Roentgen* (1845-1923), G. discoverer of X rays]

roent·gen·o·gram (réntgənəgræm, réntʃənəgræm) *n.* an X-ray picture, radiograph

Roentgen ray an X-ray

ro·ga·tion (rougéiʃən) *n.* (*eccles., pl.*) the litanies sung on Rogation Days ‖ (*Rom. hist.*) a law proposed by consuls or tribunes for ratification by the people [fr. L. *rogatio* (*rogationis*), supplication]

Rogation Days the three days preceding Ascension Day

rog·a·to·ry (rɒ́gətɔri:, rɒ́gətouri:) *adj.* (*law*) demanding information, esp. authorized to question witnesses [fr. F. *rogatoire*]

rog·er (rɒ́dʒər) *interj.* (in radio communication) your message has been received and understood ‖ your instruction will be complied with

Rog·er I (rɒ́dʒər) (c. 1031-1101), Norman count of Sicily (1072-1101), brother of Robert Guiscard. He conquered Sicily from the Arabs and made it a strong feudal state

Roger II (c. 1095-1154), count (1101-30) and king (1130-54) of Sicily, son of Roger I. He defeated (1139) the forces of Innocent II and extended his conquests to N. Africa

Rog·ers (rɒ́dʒərz), Robert (1731-95), American frontiersman. A popular hero during the French and Indian Wars, he led daring expeditions in the British cause. He directed (1760s) a secret expedition to discover the Northwest Passage, was arrested on a charge of conspiring with foreign governments to establish an independent state, but was acquitted

Rogers, Will (William Penn Adair Rogers, 1879-1935), U.S. humorist, known as the 'cowboy philosopher' for his freewheeling comments on the political and social scene through the media of radio, movies, books, and a syndicated newspaper column

rogue (roug) **1.** *n.* a man who gets along in life by cheating, deceiving, and taking advantage of others ‖ a mischievous child or person ‖ (*hort.*) an abnormal or inferior plant displaying a variation from the standard ‖ a rogue elephant ‖ any enraged, large animal which has left the herd **2.** *adj.* resembling a rogue elephant [16th-c. thieves' slang]

rogue elephant an enraged elephant which leaves the herd to live alone

ro·guer·y (róugəri:) *pl.* **ro·guer·ies** *n.* roguish behavior ‖ a roguish act

rogues' gallery a collection of photographs of criminals, used by police for purposes of identification

ro·guish (róugiʃ) *adj.* of, relating to or acting like a rogue ‖ mischievous, *a roguish look*

roil (rɔil) *v.t.* to stir up sediment in (a liquid) and make it turbid ‖ to vex, irritate **róil·y** *comp.* **roil·i·er** *superl.* **roil·i·est** *adj.* turbid [etym. doubtful]

roist·er (rɔ́istər) *v.i.* (*rhet.*) to engage in noisy, carefree, drunken revelry [fr. F. *rustre*]

Ro·kos·sov·sky (rɒkɔssɔ́fski:), Konstantin Konstantinovitch (1896-1968), Russian army officer. He commanded the defense of Moscow (1941-2) and Stalingrad (1943). He was minister of defense in Poland (1949-56)

ro·la·mite (róuləmait) *n.* a device for minimizing sliding friction on rollers by use of a flexible loop over the rollers, used in miniaturized nuclear weapons, developed by American physicist Donald F. Wilkes

Ro·land (róulənd) *n.* (*mil.*) U.S. air-launched cruise missile made by Boeing

Ro·land, Chanson de (rɔlɑ̃) a *Chanson* (*CHANSON DE GESTE), written two or three hundred years after the event, describing the death of Roland (who was a historical character, one of Charlemagne's knights) at Roncesvalles. Charlemagne had invaded Spain in 778 and, after capturing Pamplona, had been recalled home by news of a Saxon revolt on the Rhine. Roland was in charge of the rear, which was ambushed by the Saracens in a pass in the Pyrenees and destroyed. He blew his magic horn, which Charlemagne duly heard, but by the time he had returned Roland was dead. The *Chanson* is one

CONCISE PRONUNCIATION KEY: **(a)** æ, *cat;* ɑ, *car;* ɔ *fawn;* ei, *snake.* **(e)** e, *hen;* i:, *sheep;* iə, *deer;* ɛə, *bear.* **(i)** i, *fish;* ai, *tiger;* ə:, *bird.* **(o)** ɒ, *ox;* au, *cow;* ou, *goat;* u, *poor;* ɔi, *royal.* **(u)** ʌ, *duck;* u, *bull;* u:, *goose;* ə, *bacillus;* ju:, *cube.* x, *loch;* θ, *think;* ð, *bother;* z, *Zen;* ʒ, *corsage;* dʒ, *savage;* ŋ, *orangutang;* j, *yak;* ʃ, *fish;* tʃ, *fetch;* 'l, *rabble;* 'n, *redden.* Complete pronunciation key appears inside front cover.

of the finest examples of the heroic French epic

Ro·land de la Pla·tière (rɔlɑ̃dəlæplætjɛər), Manon (Manon Phlipon, 1754-93), French revolutionist. She influenced Girondist policy through her salon, a brilliant intellectual center

role, rôle (roul) *n.* the part in which an actor or singer is cast in a play, opera etc. ‖ the part a person or thing plays in a specific situation, operation etc., *the role of cement in modern building* [F. *rôle,* a roll, the scroll on which an actor's part was written]

Rolfe (rɒlf), John (1585–1622), English settler in America. He settled in Jamestown, Va., married Pocahontas, an Indian princess, in 1614 and worked at farming tobacco, which became the main crop of Virginia. He died fighting the Powhatan Indians

roll (roul) *n.* a quantity of cloth, wrapping paper, wallpaper etc., rolled up in the form of a cylinder ‖ a rounded mass of something, *rolls of fat, a roll of hair* ‖ any of variously shaped pieces of baked dough ‖ a scroll (of parchment or paper) ‖ an official list of names or catalog of items ‖ a muster roll ‖ (*Br.,* esp. *pl.*) a list of solicitors qualified to practice ‖ (*bookbinding*) a wheel-like tool for making decorative lines on book covers ‖ (*bookbinding*) the decoration produced ‖ a tobacco twist done up in cylindrical form ‖ (*archit.*) a curved molding ‖ (*pop.*) a wad of paper money **to strike off the rolls** (*Br.*) to disqualify (a solicitor) from practicing ‖ to disqualify (someone) from membership [O.F. *role, rolle*]

roll 1. *v.i.* to move along a surface by turning over and over, *the marble rolled across the floor* ‖ (of a wheeled vehicle) to move, *the car rolled down the slope* ‖ to flow forward in undulations, streams, etc., *the smoke rolled across the sky* ‖ (esp. of land) to have an undulating surface ‖ to make a long, deep sound varying in loudness, *the thunder rolled* ‖ (of a bird) to trill ‖ (of a ship) to move with a heavy side-to-side motion ‖ (of a person) to walk in this manner ‖ to acquire a spherical or cylindrical shape by curling over and over on itself or on something else ‖ (of the eyes) to turn from side to side and seem to rotate in their sockets ‖ to move or proceed smoothly, *the work keeps rolling along* ‖ *v.t.* to make (something) move along a surface by causing it to turn over and over, *to roll a marble* ‖ to cause to move on wheels, rollers etc., *to roll a wheelbarrow down a road* ‖ to shape by movements inducing roundness, *to roll a cigarette* ‖ to move (the eyes) from side to side, causing them to seem to rotate ‖ to level, smooth, flatten etc. with a roller or something resembling a roller ‖ to beat a roll upon (a drum) ‖ to throw (dice) ‖ to envelop (someone or something) in a covering, *to roll a baby in a blanket* ‖ (*printing*) to ink (a form etc.) with a roller ‖ to utter (the letter 'r') with a trill-like sound ‖ to drive forward with a sweeping motion, *the waves rolled the bathers toward the shore* ‖ (*pop.*) to rob (someone) while he is asleep, unconscious etc. **to roll around** (of a cyclical event) to recur, *spring rolled around again* **to roll back** to reduce (a price or prices) by government control ‖ to cause (a crowd etc.) to retreat **to roll in** to arrive in large numbers ‖ (*pop.*) to have a great deal of (money) **to roll out** to make flat or thin by using a roller, *to roll out pastry* ‖ to unroll **2.** *n.* a rolling movement, e.g. of a ship in heavy seas ‖ (of a person) a rolling walk ‖ a long, deep sound varying in loudness, *the roll of thunder* ‖ a succession of rapid beats on a drum ‖ (*aeron.*) a complete revolution of an aircraft around its longitudinal axis with little or no change in the horizontal direction of flight ‖ the trill of some birds ‖ one of a set of grooved cylinders in a steel mill used for shaping white-hot ingots [fr. O.F. *roler*]

Rol·land (rɔlɑ̃), Romain Edmé Paul Emile (1866-1944), French author. In his works he exalts an ideal of energy without violence. His best-known work is 'Jean Christophe' (10 vols, 1904-12), the fictitious biography of a German-born musician

roll·a·thon (róuləθɒn) *n.* (*sports*) marathon race in which participants roller skate

roll·a·way bed (róuləwei) a bed that folds up and can be rolled out of sight when not in use

roll·back (róulbæk) *n.* a reduction in prices by government control

roll bar a heavy steel bar on top of a motor vehicle, esp. a convertible, to protect riders from being crushed should the vehicle overturn —**roll cage** *n.* a roll bar for a racing car

roll call the act of calling out names from a list in order to ascertain those present ‖ the fixed time at which this is done ‖ (*mil.*) the signal for a roll call

Rolle (roul), Richard, of Hampole (c. 1300–c. 1349), English hermit and mystic. He was one of the first religious authors to write in the vernacular as well as in Latin. He is the author of 'Meditation of the Passion'

roll·er (róulər) *n.* a revolving cylinder over or on which something is rolled, e.g. the cylinder on which a roller towel is placed ‖ a revolving cylinder used for pressing, crushing or smoothing a road surface, soil etc. ‖ a cylinder on which heavy objects are moved ‖ a revolving cylinder for applying paint to a flat surface or (*printing*) for spreading ink on a form ‖ either of the revolving cylinders in a mangle or wringer between which linen is pressed flat or wrung out ‖ someone who operates rolling machinery ‖ a large, long wave that rolls over as it breaks ‖ a roll for flattening metal etc. ‖ a tumbler pigeon [ROLL V.]

roller *n.* any of various nonpasserine Old World birds of fam. *Coraciidae,* esp. *Coracius garrulus,* a European species having blue or green plumage and a reddish-brown back [G. fr. *rollen,* to roll]

roller bearing a bearing consisting of hardened steel cylinders revolving in a cylindrical housing

roller coaster (*Am.=Br.* switchback) a usually circular railway high up in an amusement park, consisting of very steep alternate ascents and descents, along which small, open cars hurtle

roller hockey (*sports*) hockey played on roller skates

roller skate a skate mounted on small wheels **róll·er-skate** *pres. part.* **roll·er-skat·ing** *past and past part.* **roll·er-skat·ed** *v.i.* to skate on a pair of these

roller towel an endless towel suspended from a rotating roller

rol·lick (rɒ́lik) **1.** *v.i.* to move or act with exuberant gaiety **2.** *n.* a burst of exuberant gaiety **ról·lick·ing** *adj.* [origin unknown]

rolling mill a plant where metal etc. is rolled into sheets, bars etc. ‖ the machine used for this purpose

rolling pin a usually wooden cylinder used for rolling out pastry, dough etc.

rolling stock the wheeled vehicles of a railroad, collectively ‖ a road carrier's fleet of vehicles

Rol·lo (rɒ́lou) (or Hrolf, c. 860–c. 931), first duke of Normandy (911-27). A Viking leader, he was granted (911) the fief of Normandy by Charles III of France

roll-on (róulɒn) *adj.* of a movable ball-shaped applicator in the top of a container that dispenses a substance, e.g., deodorant

roll·out (rouláut) *v.* (*football*) to carry the ball behind the scrimmage line to one flank separating from blockers in order to throw a pass or feint for a pass —**rollout** *n.*

roll·top desk (róultɒp) a writing desk having a slatted cover which slides open and shut

roll·way (róulwei) *n.* a road or path used esp. for rolling logs down to a stream ‖ a pile of logs by a stream awaiting transport

ro·ly-po·ly (róuli:póuli:) **1.** *adj.* (of a person or an animal) round and plump **2.** *pl.* **ro·ly-po·lys, ro·ly-po·lies** *n.* a roly-poly person or animal ‖ a dough spread with jam etc., rolled up and steamed or baked ‖ a weighted toy which, when pushed down, returns to an erect position [etym. doubtful]

ROM (*computer abbr.*) for read-only memory

Ro·ma·gna (roumánjə) (*hist.*) a region on the Adriatic coast of Emilia-Romagna, Italy, under the rule of the Papal States (early 13th c.–1860)

Ro·ma·ic (rouméiik) **1.** *adj.* of or pertaining to modern Greece ‖ of or pertaining to the language of modern Greece **2.** *n.* modern Greek [fr. Gk *Rhōmaïkos,* Roman]

ro·maine (rouméin) *n.* (*Am.* = *Br.* cos) a variety of crisp lettuce with long leaves [F.]

Ro·mains (rɔmɛ̃), Jules (Louis Farigoule, 1885–1972), French poet, novelist and playwright. His works include the farce 'Knock' (1923) and the cycle of novels 'les Hommes de bonne volonté' (1932-47)

Ro·man (róumən) **1.** *adj.* of or pertaining to the city of Rome, its history, its people, its language etc. ‖ of or pertaining to the Roman Catholic Church or the Latin rite ‖ of or pertaining to the type normally used for printed narrative and based on the forms used in Roman inscriptions (cf. ITALIC, cf. BOLDFACE) ‖ (of a nose) having a highly arched bridge **2.** *n.* a resident or native of Rome ‖ (used disparagingly) a member of the Roman Catholic Church ‖ (*printing*) Roman type ‖ the dialect spoken in Rome [O.E. fr. L.]

Roman alphabet an alphabet of the classical Latin period consisting of 23 letters (J, U and W were added later) from which most modern European alphabets are derived

Roman arch a semicircular arch

Roman candle a candle-shaped firework emitting sparks and globes of fire

Roman Catholic 1. *adj.* of or pertaining to the Roman Catholic Church **2.** *n.* a member of this Church

Roman Catholic Church that part of the Christian Church which accepts the authority of the pope, in distinction to the Orthodox Eastern Church, which separated from it in 1054, and to the Protestant Churches, which broke away in the 16th c. (For the early history of the Church *CHRISTIANITY.) The Roman Catholic Church rose to be a great political force in the Roman Empire (4th c.) and dominated Western Europe throughout the Middle Ages. Attacks on the Church culminated in the Reformation. The Counter-Reformation produced administrative and educational reforms within the Church, and missionary activities were extended under the Jesuits in the Far East and America. From the Council of Trent (1545-63) to the Vatican Council (1869-70) the Church was on the defensive against the incursions of rationalism, enlightenment, liberalism and revolution. In the 20th c. it has begun to reconsider its ideological traditions and to participate in the ecumenical movement. The excommunication of the Orthodox Eastern Church was annulled (1965). Distinctive tenets of Roman Catholicism are the authority of ecclesiastical tradition, transubstantiation, the seven sacraments, papal infallibility, purgatory, the Immaculate Conception (1854) and the Assumption (1950) of the Virgin Mary. Theology is based on natural and divine law as established by Thomas Aquinas. The clergy are celibate, though in E. Europe and the Middle East there are Roman Catholic Churches with Uniate rites and noncelibate clergy. Many religious orders exist. There are several hundred million Roman Catholics in the world. They preponderate (over 85%) in Spain, Ireland, Luxembourg, Belgium, Portugal, Italy, Latin America, Austria, Poland and France. They form large minorities (over 30%) in the Netherlands, Czechoslovakia, Hungary, Switzerland, West Germany, Lebanon, Yugoslavia, the Philippines, Canada and the U.S.A. Smaller minorities exist in Australia, New Zealand, East Germany, Rumania, Great Britain and the U.S.S.R.

Roman Catholicism the doctrine and organization of the Roman Catholic Church

ro·mance (roumǽns, róumæns) **1.** *n.* a medieval literary form, initially old French or Provençal, dealing with deeds of chivalry or with historical or mythological events seen in the perspective of a medieval court ‖ an example of this ‖ an imaginative story of idealized love ‖ the type of literature comprising such stories ‖ a love affair ‖ the quality of being romantic ‖ a pure exaggeration, falsehood ‖ (*mus.*) a term loosely used for various sorts of composition predominantly tender or intimate in mood **2.** *v. pres. part.* **ro·manc·ing** *past* and *past part.* **ro·manced** *v.i.* to indulge in highly exaggerated stories ‖ *v.t.* to give a made-up version of, *romanced biography* **Ro·mance** *adj.* of or relating to the Romance languages [O.F. *romans, romanz*]

Romance languages a group of languages developed from Latin, incl. French, Italian, Provençal, Portuguese, Rumanian, Spanish, Catalan, Rhaeto-Romanic, Sardinian and the now-extinct Dalmatian

ro·man cour·tois (rɔmɑ̃ku:rtwæ) *pl.* **ro·mans cour·tois** (rɔmɑ̃ku:rtwæ) a medieval romance, based on classical or legendary themes. They were usually in verse and were intended to be read aloud, whereas the Chansons de Geste were written to be sung [F.]

Roman de la Rose *LORRIS, GUILLAUME DE, *JEAN DE MEUNG

Ro·man de Re·nart (rɔmɑ̃dərənær) a collection of verse stories by unknown authors, in which animals—and their 'wives'—have experiences which satirize or parallel human behavior. The stories, of which the best date from the 13th c., seem to have originated near the borders of modern France, but there are Flemish, Dutch and German versions

Roman Empire *ROME

Ro·man·esque (roumənésk) **1.** *n.* (*archit.*) a style developed between the Roman and Gothic periods in former Roman European territories. It is characterized by round arches, decorative arcades, and elaborately carved ornament, esp. on capitals and moldings **2.** *adj.* of, relating to, or constructed in the Romanesque style [F.]

Romania *RUMANIA

Ro·man·ic (roumǽnik) **1.** *adj.* of or relating to the Romance languages **2.** *n.* the Romance languages [fr. L. *Romanicus*]

Ro·man·ism (róumənizəm) *n.* (used disparagingly) the doctrine and usages of the Roman Catholic faith **Ró·man·ist** *n.* and *adj.*

Roman law the system of jurisdiction of ancient Rome and of the Roman and Byzantine Empires, esp. to the death (565) of Justinian I

Roman numerals letters of the Roman alphabet used as symbols for numbers until the 10th c. A.D. Those still used, e.g. on clock faces or in classifications, are I = 1, V=5, X= 10, L= 50, C = 100, D = 500, M = 1,000. A letter placed in front of one of greater value is subtracted from it, a letter placed after it is added, e.g. XCIV=94

Ro·ma·nov (róumənɔf) the Russian ruling dynasty from the accession (1613) of Michael until the enforced abdication (1917) of Nicholas II

Romans, Epistle to the the sixth book of the New Testament, written (c. 58) by St Paul to the Church at Rome. It proclaims the possibility of salvation for all men through Christ

Ro·mansh, Ro·mansch (roumǽnʃ, roumάnʃ) *n.* Rhaeto-Romanic as spoken esp. in Graubünden, Switzerland [native name]

ro·man·tic (roumǽntik) **1.** *adj.* of or pertaining to romance, *a romantic novel, a romantic situation* ‖ susceptible to romance, *a romantic person* ‖ not based on fact, fanciful or exaggerated, *a romantic rendering of the facts* ‖ (*loosely*) far-fetched, not very practical, *a romantic scheme* **Ro·man·tic** of, relating to or having the characteristics of Romanticism **2.** *n.* a romantic person **Ro·man·tic** an exponent of Romanticism **ro·mán·ti·cal·ly** *adv.* **ro·mán·ti·cism** *n.* the quality or state of being romantic **Ro·man·ti·cism** a movement in literature, philosophy and art which developed in Europe in the late 18th and early 19th cc. Starting from the ideas and attitudes of Rousseau in France and from the Sturm und Drang movement in Germany, it held that classicism, dominant since the 16th c., denied expression to man's emotional nature and overlooked his profound inner forces. Romanticism is above all an exaltation of individual values and aspirations above those of society. The movement looked to the Middle Ages and to direct contact with nature for inspiration, and it was responsible for the national liberation movement of 19th-c. Europe. The leading Romantic poets were Byron, Keats, Shelley, Wordsworth, Hugo, Musset, Heine and Novalis. In painting its chief exponent was Delacroix. Beethoven, Schubert, Berlioz and Bizet were great Romantic composers. Through its concern with the hidden forces in man, Romanticism exerted a profound influence on modern thought, and opened the way e.g. to psychoanalysis. In art, the same current led to expressionism and surrealism **ro·mán·ti·cist** *n.* **Ro·man·ti·cist** a Romantic **ro·mán·ti·cize** *pres. part.* **ro·man·ti·ciz·ing** *past* and *past part.* **ro·man·ti·cized** *v.t.* to treat or interpret romantically, esp. to falsify so as to make more pleasing [fr. obs. *romant,* romance fr. O.F.]

Ro·ma·nus II (rouméinəs) (939-63), Byzantine emperor (959-63), son of Constantine VII. His reign was notable for the military successes of Nicephorus II Phocas

Rom·a·ny (rómәni:, róumәni:) *pl.* **Rom·a·nies** **1.** *n.* a gypsy ‖ the Indic language of the gypsies **2.** *adj.* of or relating to gypsies, or to their language

Rome (roum) (*Ital.* Roma) the capital (pop. 2,897,800) of Italy and ancient capital of the Roman Empire, in Latium, 16 miles up the Tiber. Industries: light manufacturing, esp. luxury goods (haute couture, leatherwork etc.), chemicals, food processing, printing and publishing, film making, tourism. The left bank (with Trastevere, a section of the right bank included by the Aurelian wall, 2nd c.), now a region of narrow streets opening on to squares cut by occasional wide avenues, is still the center of the city. The Vatican City is on the upper right bank. Surviving ancient structures include the Forum (remains of temples, 5th c. B.C.–3rd c. A.D., triumphal arches and columns of the emperors), the Pantheon, and the Colosseum or amphitheater (1st c.). Each age has employed, in its buildings, elements left by past ones. Monuments of the Romano-Byzantine period (4th-9th cc.) include numerous churches and basilicas, many partially restored, e.g. St John Lateran (4th c.), and Santa Maria Maggiore (4th-5th cc., with 5th-c. mosaics). Renaissance Rome survives in churches, palaces and piazza architecture, e.g. the Vatican, the Farnese Palace (1514–mid-16th c.), St Peter's and the Square of the Capitol (designed by Michelangelo). The baroque period (16th-late 18th c.) is rich in churches, squares, fountains and facades, e.g. the church of Il Gesù (1568-84, the first of the Jesuit style), the portico (1667) of St Peter's, the Trevi fountain (1632-62), the Spanish Steps (completed in 1725), the facades of St Peter's, St John Lateran etc. Principal cultural institutions: the Vatican Museum, Gallery and Library, the National Library, galleries, and museums of antiquities (the Terme and Villa Giulia), the university (1303), and numerous academies. HISTORY. Traditionally founded by Romulus in 753 B.C., Rome grew as a group of villages on seven hills on the east bank of the Tiber, and was ruled until 510 B.C. by seven kings, of whom the last three are thought to have been Etruscan. After the last of these, Tarquinius Superbus, had been expelled, a republic was set up (510 B.C.), ruled by a senate and two consuls. The dominant power of the patricians was increasingly challenged by the plebeians, until by 300 B.C. the latter had obtained the right to hold any office. The political organization was expanded to include tribunes, quaestors, aediles, censors and praetors. A code of law was drawn up (451 B.C.) by the decemvirs. Rome extended its power to neighboring peoples in Italy (5th-3rd cc. B.C.), defeated Carthage in the Punic Wars (264-241 B.C., 218-201 B.C. and 149-146 B.C.) and gained territory in Spain, Sicily, Sardinia, Corsica and N. Africa. Macedon was made a Roman province (146 B.C.) and the whole of Greece was subdued by 27 B.C. The task of governing the Mediterranean world resulted in class dissension in Rome, notably when the brothers Gracchus attempted to reform the agrarian laws (2nd c. B.C.). Civil war broke out, and the republic was further weakened by the rivalry between Marius and Sulla and by that between Pompey and Caesar. After the collapse of the 1st Triumvirate, Caesar established a dictatorship (48-44 B.C.). On his assassination, civil war was resumed and the 2nd Triumvirate was formed. This dissolved in war between Antony and Octavian, and the republic collapsed when the latter took absolute power as emperor with the title of Augustus (27 B.C.). In the two centuries after the reign of Augustus the Roman Empire reached its greatest extent, encircling the Mediterranean, reaching north to the Rhine, the Danube and central Scotland and spreading into Armenia and Mesopotamia. The empire was united by a well-developed system of communications, the use of Latin as a universal language, and the growth of trade and industry. Augustus' successors, Tiberius, Caligula, Claudius and Nero, continued to develop the civil service and provincial administration (14-68). In the civil war of 68-9, provincial armies successively made Galba, Otho and Vitellius emperors. Stability was restored by Vespasian and his sons Titus and Domitian. Rome reached the height of its prosperity under Trajan, Hadrian, Antoninus Pius and Marcus Aurelius, but decline set in during the reign (180-92) of Commodus. Civil war followed his murder and the Praetorians began to exercise the dominating influence in the choice of emperors. Septimius Severus established a new dynasty (193) supported by the army, and under Caracalla, his son, Roman citizenship was extended to free men throughout the empire. Military anarchy followed the murder (235) of Alexander Severus and provincial armies made emperors in rapid succession. The frontiers came under increasing pressure from the Sassanids in Persia, and from the Alemanni, the Franks and the Goths in the north. These incursions were halted by the capable emperors Claudius II, Aurelian and Probus. During the reign (284-305) of Diocletian, the empire was divided into four administrative units. It was temporarily reunited by Constantine I, who moved its capital to Constantinople (330). Christianity, which had spread throughout the empire, won toleration (313) and became official (380) under Theodosius I. On Constantine's death (337) the division between east and west reappeared. It became final on the death (395) of Theodosius I, Arcadius inheriting the east (*BYZANTINE EMPIRE) and Honorius the west. To deal with increasing barbarian attacks, the capital of the Western Roman Empire was moved to Ravenna (402). Rome was sacked by the Visigoths under Alaric I (410) and by the Vandals under Genseric (455). Attila was prevented from sacking it by Pope Leo I, and papal influence over the city began to increase. The last Roman emperor, Romulus Augustulus was deposed (476) by Odoacer. The Roman Empire had brought urban civilization and a high degree of material prosperity as well as Roman law, the Latin language and the Christian religion to a large part of Europe. Rome now came to be disputed between the Byzantine Empire and the barbarians, and later between the papacy and the Holy Roman Empire. As capital of the Papal States (after 756), it became the spiritual center of W. Europe during the Middle Ages. It was several times devastated by invading armies but began to recover in the second half of the 15th c. and became a center of the Renaissance. It became the capital of Italy (1871)

Ro·me·ro (rɔmérɔ), Francisco (1891-1962), Argentinian philosopher, author of 'Filosofía de la persona' (1944), 'El hombre y la cultura' (1950), and 'Teoría del hombre' (1952)

Rom·il·ly (rómili:, rʌ́mili:), Sir Samuel (1757-1818), British lawyer and social reformer. He worked all his life for the reform of the criminal code. Many of his proposals were put into effect later in the 19th c.

Rom·mel (rɔ́mel), Erwin (1891-1944), German field marshal. He led the German army in N. Africa (1941) and drove the British army back to Alamein (1942), but was then forced to retreat to Tunisia. He was briefly commander in chief of the German armies in N. Europe (1944). His sympathy with the July 1944 plot against Hitler led to his enforced suicide

Rom·ney (rómni:, rʌ́mni:), George (1734-1802), English portrait painter. He was esp. famous for his paintings of Lady Hamilton

romp (rɒmp) **1.** *v.i.* to be in high spirits and play boisterously **to romp home** (or in) (esp. of a racehorse) to win easily **2.** *n.* the act of romping **rómp·ers** *pl. n.* a child's one-piece garment combining top and bloomers [perh. var. of RAMP]

Rom·u·lus and Re·mus (rómjuləs, rí:məs) (*Rom. mythol.*) twin sons of Mars. They were exposed in infancy, but were suckled by a she-wolf and then brought up by a shepherd. According to tradition, Romulus was the founder of Rome (753 B.C.)

Romulus Au·gus·tu·lus (ɔgʌ́stjuləs) (*d.* after 476), last Roman emperor (475-6). He was deposed by Odoacer and spent the rest of his life in retirement

Ron·ces·valles (rɔnθesváljes, *Eng.* rónsəvælz) a pass in the Pyrenees, where, according to the Chanson de Roland, the rear of Charlemagne's army was attacked and Roland was killed (778)

ron·deau (róndou, rɒndóu) *pl.* **ron·deaux** (róndouz, rɒndóuz) *n.* a form of verse consisting of 15 usually octosyllabic lines arranged in three stanzas. It uses the opening words twice as a refrain and permits only two rhymes: aabba, aab refrain, aabba refrain ‖ a poem in this form [F.]

ron·del (rónd'l) *n.* a form of verse having two rhymes only, consisting of usually 14 lines arranged in three stanzas. The first two lines of the first stanza serve as a refrain for the second and third stanzas ‖ a poem in this form [F.]

ron·do (róndou, rɒndóu) *pl.* **ron·dos** *n.* a musical composition in which the principal theme is repeated three or more times. It often forms the last movement of a sonata [Ital.]

Ron·dón (rɔndɔ́n), Cândido (1865-1957), Brazilian general who opened up vast regions of the Brazilian interior. An Indian himself, he founded the Service for the Protection of the Indians, which forbade its personnel to carry arms into the interior

Ron·sard (rɔ̃sær), Pierre de (1524-85), French poet, leader of the Pléiade. Ronsard and his fol-

CONCISE PRONUNCIATION KEY: **(a)** æ, *cat;* ɑ, *car;* ɔ *fawn;* ei, *snake.* **(e)** e, *hen;* i:, *sheep;* iə, *deer;* εə, *bear.* **(i)** i, *fish;* ai, *tiger;* ə:, *bird.* **(o)** o, *ox;* au, *cow;* ou, *goat;* u, *poor;* ɔi, *royal.* **(u)** ʌ, *duck;* u, *bull;* u:, *goose;* ə, *bacillus;* ju:, *cube.* x, *loch;* θ, *think;* ð, *bother;* z, *Zen;* ʒ, *corsage;* dʒ, *savage;* ŋ, *orangutang;* j, *yak;* ʃ, *fish;* tʃ, *fetch;* 'l, *rabble;* 'n, *redden.* Complete pronunciation key appears inside front cover.

lowers wished to make French—as Petrarch had made Italian—a literary language, rich, supple and elegant, capable of a poetry which would rival that of Greece and Rome. Though Ronsard's verse is characterized by a Renaissance courtliness and elegance, it also retains some of the directness and naïve freshness of the Middle Ages

röntgen *ROENTGEN

rood (ru:d) n. a crucifix, esp. one mounted on a rood screen ‖ (in England and Scotland) a quarter of an acre [O.E. *rōd*]

rood loft a gallery above the rood screen

rood screen a carved wooden or stone screen separating the nave from the choir in a church and usually having a crucifix raised up on it

roof (ru:f, ruf) **1.** *pl.* **roofs** *n.* the structure which covers the top of a building, typically of shingles, slates, tiles, concrete etc., together with the load-carrying elements above the walls ‖ something compared to this, *the roof of a cave, the roof of the mouth* ‖ the hard or canvas top of an automobile etc. ‖ (*rhet.*) a home or house as affording shelter and hospitality ‖ (*mining*) the overhanging part of an excavation or tunnel ‖ (*mining*) the rock above a bed of coal etc. **to raise the roof** (*pop.*) to create a noisy disturbance due to anger, discontent, enthusiasm etc. **2.** *v.t.* to furnish with a roof **roof·age** (rú:fidʒ) *n.* roofing [O.E. *hrōf*]

roof garden a restaurant on the roof of a building ‖ a flat roof of a building used as a terrace

roof·ing (rú:fiŋ, rúfiŋ) *n.* the material used to surface a roof

roof·less (rú:flis, rúflis) *adj.* having no roof ‖ without a home or any shelter

roof·tree (rú:ftri:, rúftri:) *n.* the ridgepole of a roof

rook (ruk) **1.** *n. Corvus frugilegus,* fam. *Corvidae,* an Old World bird (about 18 ins in length), resembling a crow in color, form and habits. With age, the skin around the base of its bill becomes gray and scabby ‖ (*pop.*) a cheat, esp. in gambling **2.** *v.t.* (*pop.*) to cheat, esp. in gambling ‖ (*Br.*) to overcharge [O.E. *hrōc*]

rook *n.* (*chess*) a castle-shaped piece having the power to move over any number of unoccupied, consecutive squares either horizontally or vertically [O.F. *roc* fr. Pers.]

rook·er·y (rúkəri:) *pl.* **rook·er·ies** *n.* a colony of rooks or the group of trees containing their nests ‖ a breeding place or colony of seals, penguins and other gregarious birds or beasts

rook·ie (rúki:) *n.* (*pop.*) a raw army recruit ‖ a raw recruit of any sort ‖ (*baseball*) a player in his first season with a major league team

room (ru:m, rum) **1.** *n.* a space within a building enclosed by its own walls, ceiling and floor, *hotel room, assembly room* ‖ space regarded as available to contain something, or something more, *make some room on the shelf,* or as affording the opportunity to act, move etc., *scarcely room to breathe* ‖ opportunity or scope, *room for improvement, room to expand* ‖ (*pl.*) a suite in a private house, boarding house etc., rented for a period ‖ a roomful of people, *the room was hushed* ‖ one of the chambers where coal is mined **to make room for** to move so as to leave space for **2.** *v.i.* to lodge in someone's house, or with someone else, sharing accommodation [O.E. *rūm*]

room·er (rú:mər, rúmər) *n.* someone who rents a room in someone else's house

room·ful (rú:mful, rúmful) *n.* as much as a room will contain ‖ the people, objects etc. in a room

room·i·ness (rú:mi:nis, rúmi:nis) *n.* the quality or state of being roomy

rooming house a lodging house

room·mate (rú:mmeit, rúmmeit) *n.* someone with respect to a person with whom he shares a room

room·y (rú:mi:, rúmi:) *comp.* **room·i·er** *superl.* **room·i·est** *adj.* having plenty of room, *a roomy trunk*

Roon (ru:n), Albrecht Theodor Emil, Graf von (1803-79), Prussian general and minister of war (1839-73). His army reforms provoked parliamentary hostility, but were largely responsible for the victories of Prussia over Austria (1866) and France (1870-1)

Roosevelt (róuzəvelt, rú:zəvelt), Anna Eleanor (1884–1962), U.S. First Lady (1933–45) and social activist. She married her cousin, Franklin D. Roosevelt, and when he became crippled (1921) by polio she represented him on the campaign trail. As First Lady she undertook her special causes, esp. youth employment and civil rights for minorities, and continued working for these causes after her husband's death. She was a U.S. delegate to the U.N. (1945–52, 1961–2) and was instrumental in drafting the U.N. Declaration of Human Rights. She wrote 'This I Remember' (1949) and 'The Autobiography of Eleanor Roosevelt' (1961)

Roo·se·velt, Franklin Delano (1882-1945), 32nd president (1933-45) of the U.S.A., a Democrat. Beginning with a general 'bank holiday', he initiated the New Deal in order to restore the economy after the great depression of 1929. His 'fireside chats', broadcast by radio to the nation, helped him to maintain the support and confidence of the American people. He led the U.S.A. away from isolationism with his good-neighbor policy toward Latin America, his recognition (1933) of the U.S.S.R., and his lend-lease support (1941) for Britain. He became (1940) the first U.S. president to run for a third term in office. With Churchill he drafted (1941) the Atlantic Charter and, as the power of the Axis increased, he augmented U.S. military strength and preparedness, issuing the first peacetime selective service act in U.S. history. With the Japanese attack (1941) on Pearl Harbor, he brought the U.S.A. into the 2nd world war. He attended conferences with Allied leaders at Casablanca (1943), Quebec (1943 and 1944), Cairo (1943), Tehran (1943) and Yalta (1945). He has been criticized for making too many territorial concessions to the U.S.S.R. at Yalta. He died a month before Germany's surrender. His wife Eleanor (1884-1962) continued his humanitarian policies as a delegate to the U.N.

Roosevelt, Theodore (1858-1919), 26th president (1901-9) of the U.S.A., following the assassination of President McKinley. He was a Republican. During the Spanish-American War he organized the regiment of volunteers known as the Rough Riders, and gained wide fame as a cavalry colonel in Cuba (1898). As president he launched an extensive 'trust-busting' campaign, promoted the conservation of natural resources, and through his Roosevelt Corollary to the Monroe Doctrine he maintained the right of the U.S.A. to intervene in the internal affairs of Latin American countries for the maintenance of law and order. He also pursued a policy of 'dollar diplomacy', notably in the Caribbean. He used the U.S. Navy (1903) to ensure that Panama gained independence from Colombia, and secured the right to construct the Panama Canal. He received the Nobel peace prize (1906) for his mediation in the Russo-Japanese War (1904-5). At his initiative the Algeciras Conference (1906) was called. Opposed to the reelection of conservative Republican President Taft, he organized (1912) the Progressive or 'Bull Moose' party, running as its candidate in the 1912 presidential elections and thus splitting Republican ranks, which allowed a Democratic victory. During the 1st world war he vigorously attacked President Wilson's initial policy of neutrality

Roosevelt Corollary an extension of the Monroe Doctrine issued (1904) by President Theodore Roosevelt and Elihu Root. It asserted U.S. right to intervene in the internal affairs of Latin America to maintain peace and order. It is the most imperialistic interpretation of the Monroe Doctrine

roost (ru:st) **1.** *n.* the perch of a bird or fowl ‖ the part of a hen house or other building where fowls roost **to rule the roost** to be the dominating person (esp. in a household) **2.** *v.i.* to be perched for the night ‖ to settle down as if on a perch, *to roost on a park bench* **róost·er** *n.* a male domestic fowl [O.E. *hrōst*]

Root (ru:t), Elihu (1845-1937), U.S. lawyer, political leader and diplomat. As secretary of war (1899-1903) under Presidents McKinley and T. Roosevelt he strongly influenced the Foraker Act of 1900 and the Organic Act of 1902. His military reforms included the transformation of the state National Guard into the organized militia of the U.S.A. and the creation of the Army War College. As secretary of state (1905-9) under President Theodore Roosevelt, he negotiated the Root-Takahira agreement and settled the dispute with the British over the North Atlantic coast fisheries. He received the 1912 Nobel prize for peace

root (ru:t, rut) **1.** *n.* that part of a plant which in most species penetrates the earth. It absorbs moisture, stores food, and also serves as an anchor and support ‖ a plant, e.g. a carrot, in which this part is fleshy and edible ‖ (*Br.*) a young, esp. herbaceous, plant suitable for transplanting ‖ (*physiol.*) the part of an organ etc. by which it is attached to the body, *the root of a tooth* ‖ a fundamental or essential part, *the root of a problem* ‖ the original cause of something, *his selfishness was the root of the trouble* ‖ (*math.*) a quantity which, when multiplied by itself a certain number of times, produces a given quantity, *2 is the square root of 4 or the cube root of 8* ‖ (*math.*) a value of an unknown which satisfies an equation ‖ (*linguistics*) that part of a word remaining after removal of prefixes, suffixes, inflectional endings etc. ‖ (*mus.*) the lowest note of a chord when the chord is in its normal position **to take root** to grow roots ‖ to become firmly fixed by or as if by roots, *the idea gradually began to take root* **2.** *v.i.* to grow roots ‖ to become firmly fixed by or as if by roots ‖ *v.t.* to cause to root ‖ (*fig.*) to fix firmly, *rooted in one's memory* ‖ to attach by or as if by roots **to root out** (or **up**) to remove (a plant) completely by pulling it, with its roots, out of the ground ‖ to remove (a habit, idea etc.) completely [O.E. *rōt* fr. O.N.]

root *v.i.* (esp. of swine) to turn up the earth with the snout looking for food ‖ to search around (among papers, in closets etc.) for something ‖ *v.t.* (with 'up') to turn up with the snout [O.E. *wrōtan*]

root *v.i.* (*pop.*) to give encouragement by shouting or cheering, *to root for one's team* or simply give moral support [perh. fr. *rout,* to shout]

root beer a carbonated soft drink made of various roots and herbs and flavored with cloves, anise etc.

root cap the protective cap of tissue at the apex of a root

root hair (*bot.*) one of many epidermal outgrowths behind the root cap, having absorptive functions

roo·tle (rú:t'l, rút'l) *pres. part.* **roo·tling** *past* and *past part.* **roo·tled** *v.i.* (*pop.,* esp. of swine) to root

root·let (rú:tlət, rútlət) *n.* a small root

root nodule a small swelling on the root of a leguminous plant, containing nitrogen-fixing bacteria

root pressure the force by which water is made to rise from the roots to the stem of a plant

root·stalk (rú:tstɔk, rútstɔk) *n.* a rhizome

root·stock (rú:tstɒk, rútstɒk) *n.* the rhizomatous underground part of a stem

Root-Takahira Agreement (1908), a U.S.-Japanese agreement, under which the U.S.A. acknowledged Japan's right to annex Korea and its special position in Manchuria in return for Japan's promise not to grant exit visas to laborers

rope (roup) **1.** *n.* a thick cord made of twisted strands of hemp, flax, wire etc. ‖ (*pl.*) the ropes enclosing a boxing ring ‖ a row of things strung together, *a rope of pearls, a rope of onions* ‖ a viscous stringy formation in wine, beer etc. caused by contamination by bacteria ‖ a lasso **at the end of one's rope** at the limit of what one can bear **to know the ropes** to know how an organization works, what procedures to follow etc., in circumstances which would be strange to the uninitiated **to give someone plenty of rope, to give someone enough rope to hang himself** to allow someone to continue unchecked until he brings about his own downfall **2.** *v. pres. part.* **rop·ing** *past* and *past part.* **roped** *v.t.* to fasten or secure with a rope ‖ (with 'off') to mark off or enclose with ropes ‖ to lasso ‖ (of climbers) to link together by attachment to a common rope ‖ *v.i.* to become viscous **to rope somebody in** to secure somebody's help or support (usually in spite of his reluctance) [O.E. *rāp*]

rope·danc·er (róupdænsər, róupdɑnsər) *n.* a dancer who performs on a tightrope

rope ladder a ladder having rope sides and rope, wood or metal rungs

rope walk a long covered walk where ropes are twisted ‖ a building containing a rope walk

rope·walk·er (róupwɔkər) *n.* an acrobat who walks on a tightrope

rop·y (róupi:) *comp.* **rop·i·er** *superl.* **rop·i·est** *adj.* viscous like rope, stringy

Roque·fort (róukfərt) *n.* a cheese made from ewes' milk, impregnated with a special mold, and ripened in caves [after *Roquefort,* French town in the Aveyron]

ro·quet (roukéi) **1.** *v.t. pres. part.* **ro·quet·ing** (roukéiiŋ) *past* and *past part.* **ro·queted**

CONCISE PRONUNCIATION KEY: **(a)** æ, *cat;* ɑ, *car;* ɔ *fawn;* ei, *snake.* **(e)** e, *hen;* i:, *sheep;* iə, *deer;* ɛə, *bear.* **(i)** i, *fish;* ai, *tiger;* ə:, *bird.* **(o)** o, *ox;* au, *cow;* ou, *goat;* u, *poor;* ɔi, *royal.* **(u)** ʌ, *duck;* u, *bull;* u:, *goose;* ə, *bacillus;* ju:, *cube.* x, *loch;* θ, *think;* ð, *bother;* z, *Zen;* ʒ, *corsage;* dʒ, *savage;* ŋ, *orangutang;* j, *yak;* ʃ, *fish;* tʃ, *fetch;* 'l, *rabble;* 'n, *redden.* Complete pronunciation key appears inside front cover.

(roukéid) (*croquet*) to make one's ball hit (another ball) || (*croquet, of a ball*) to hit (another ball) **2.** *n.* (*croquet*) the act of roqueting [formed fr. CROQUET]

Ro·rai·ma, Mt (ruráimə) *PACARAIMA

ro·ro ship (róuróu) a freighter that carries loaded trucks and trailers

ror·qual (rɔ́rkwəl) *n.* a member of *Balaenoptera,* fam. *Ballaenopteridae,* a genus of whalebone whales having a dorsal fin and many furrows on the throat [F. fr. Norw. *røyrkval*]

Ror·schach test (rɔ́rʃæk, róurʃæk) a psychological test in which the subject is presented with a series of blots of ink of standard designs. The responses of the subject yield useful, if not always specific, information about his intelligence and emotional state [after Hermann *Rorschach* (1884–1922), Swiss psychiatrist]

Ro·sa (rɔ́zɑ), Salvator (1615-73), Italian painter, etcher and poet. He is best known for his large battle scenes and romantic landscapes

Rosa a massif in the Pennine Alps on the Swiss-Italian border. Summit: Dufourspitze (15,217 ft), the highest point in Switzerland

Ro·sa·rio (rɔsárjɔ) a port and commercial center (pop. 750,455) in N. Argentina on the Paraná. Industries: meat packing, flour milling, sugar refining, tanning. University (1920)

ro·sa·ry (róuzəri:) *pl.* **ro·sa·ries** *n.* a rose garden || a string of beads for keeping count of the prayers of the Rosary **the Rosary** a Roman Catholic devotion to the Virgin Mary consisting of 5 or 15 decades of Aves, each preceded by a paternoster and ended by a gloria (Gloria Patri) [fr. L. *rosarium*]

Ro·sas (rɔ́sɑs), Juan Manuel de (1793-1877), Argentinian general and dictator, leader (after 1828) of the Federal Party. With the aid of a force of vaqueros, which he made the most efficient fighting force in Argentina after independence, he served as governor and dictator (1829-32 and 1835-52) of the province of Buenos Aires. Despite hostilities with Paraguay, Chile, Peru, Brazil, Uruguay, France, and England, from which he had scarcely a moment's freedom, he waged a war of extermination against the leaders of the interior provinces who sought to combine against him or to set themselves up as independent rulers. A coalition of his disaffected generals and Brazil brought about his defeat (1852) at Monte Caseros. He fled to exile in England (*SARMIENTO). He was dictatorial, but greatly contributed to the unification of Argentina

Ros·ce·lin (rɔslɛ̃) (*Lat.* Roscellinus, c. 1050–c. 1120), French scholastic philosopher, the founder of nominalism

Ros·com·mon (rɒskɒ́mən) an island county (area 951 sq. miles, pop. 53,519) in Connacht, Irish Republic || its county seat (pop. 2,000)

rose (rouz) **1.** *n.* a member of *Rosa,* fam. *Rosaceae,* a genus of erect, climbing or creeping shrubs, usually with prickles, native to the northern hemisphere, but grown throughout the temperate regions in hundreds of varieties. They have compound leaves and usually fragrant red, rose, pink, yellow or white flowers || the flower of any of these shrubs || the dark pinkish color characteristic of some of these flowers || a representation of the flower, e.g. in heraldry or (*Eng. hist.*) as an emblem of the houses of York and Lancaster (*ROSES, WARS OF THE) || a form in which many gems are cut, consisting of a double tier of triangular facets rising to a point from a round, flat base || a gem, esp. a diamond, cut in this way || the perforated nozzle of a hose, watering can etc. || (*naut.*) the card of the mariner's compass || a rose window || a rosette (ornamental fixture or other decoration) || (*pl.*) a healthy glow, esp. in the cheeks **2.** *adj.* of or relating to a rose || scented or flavored with roses || having a rose color [O.E. fr. L. fr. Gk]

rose *past* of RISE

ro·se·ate (róuzi:it, róuzi:eit) *adj.* (*rhet.*) flushed pink, *the roseate hue of dawn* || (*rhet., of a viewpoint etc.*) optimistic [fr. L. *roseus*]

Rose·ber·y (róuzbəri:), Archibald Philip Primrose, 5th earl of (1847-1929), British Liberal statesman. As foreign secretary (1886 and 1892-4) and prime minister (1894-5) he advocated imperial federation

Rose Bowl (*football*) postseason college game played in Pasadena, CA

rose·bud (róuzbʌd) *n.* the bud of a rose

rose·bush (róuzbuʃ) *n.* a shrub bearing roses

rose-col·ored, rose-col·oured (róuzkʌlərd) *adj.* of a warm pink color || (of opinions etc.) optimistic, hopeful **to see life through rose-colored glasses** (or **spectacles**) to view things optimistically

Rose·crans (róuzkræns), William Starke (1819-98), U.S. Union general during the Civil War. His excessive cautiousness earned him official displeasure. Pressured to assume the offensive, he was saved from complete disaster at Chickamauga and Chattanooga only by the stand of Gen. George Thomas

rose geranium any of several S. African plants of the genus *Pelargonium,* fam. *Geraniaceae,* esp. *P. graveolens,* having fragrant leaves and small pink flowers

rose mallow the hibiscus || the hollyhock

rose·mar·y (róuzmɛəri:) **rose·mar·ies** *n.* *Rosmarinus officinalis,* fam. *Labiatae,* an evergreen shrub grown esp. in the Mediterranean area. The pungent leaves are used as a culinary herb and in making perfume, soap etc.

Ro·sen·bach (róuz'nbæk), Abraham Simon Wolf (1876-1952), U.S. book and manuscript collector and dealer. He founded (1902) the Rosenbach Company which became probably the largest book dealer in the world. He willed his estate to the Rosenbach Foundation, established (1950) to foster interest in books, paintings, and objets d'art

Ro·sen·berg Trial (róuz'nbə:rg) a U.S. federal espionage trial, in which Julius and Ethel Rosenberg and their associates were convicted (1951) of revealing to the Soviet Union secret information concerning the construction of the atomic bomb. The Rosenbergs were executed (1953). They were the first U.S. civilians to receive the death penalty for treason

Ro·sen·wald (róuz'nwɔld), Julius (1862-1932), U.S. merchant and philanthropist. As president (1910-25) of Sears Roebuck & Company, he created a fund (1917) for the education of blacks which helped to construct more than 5,000 schools in 15 Southern states. His donations exceeded $22 million

rose of Jericho *Anastatica hierochuntica,* fam. *Cruciferae,* an Asiatic plant which curls up in a dry wickerlike ball when dry and opens out when moistened

rose oil an essential oil distilled from roses, esp. attar of roses

ro·se·o·la (rouzí:ələ) *n.* (*med.*) a mild disease affecting babies and very young children, characterized by a three-day fever followed by a rose-colored rash [Mod. L. fr. *roseus,* rosy]

Roses, Wars of the (*Eng. hist.*) an intermittent civil war (1455-85) between the houses of York and Lancaster for possession of the throne, so called because of the white rose emblem of York and the red rose of Lancaster. Prompted by the incapacity and French failures of the Lancastrian Henry VI, the Yorkists took up arms (1455), deposed Henry (1461) and replaced him by the Yorkist Edward IV. Henry was briefly restored (1470-1) by Warwick 'the Kingmaker', but Edward regained the throne (1471). His son Edward V was overthrown (1483) by Richard III, who was defeated and killed (1485) at Bosworth Field by the Lancastrian claimant Henry Tudor. The latter, as Henry VII, married (1486) the daughter of Edward IV, thus uniting the rival houses. The wars demonstrated the danger of allowing too powerful nobles to build up private armies

Ro·set·ta stone (rouzétə) a large piece of black basalt bearing an inscription in Egyptian hieroglyphics, in demotic script and in Greek. Jean-François Champollion and Thomas Young, working independently, found the key to the deciphering of ancient Egyptian hieroglyphics from it. The stone was found by some of Napoleon's soldiers in 1799 near Rosetta, on the western mouth of the Nile. It is in the British Museum

ro·sette (rouzét) *n.* a knot of ribbon or other small decoration in the shape of a rose || (*archit.*) a formal representation of the wild rose used as an ornament || (*Br.*) a rose window || (*bot.*) a cluster of leaves arising in close circles from a central axis || (*bot.*) any of several plant diseases affecting the leaves and due to an attack of fungi, nutritional deficiencies etc. || any of various ornamental fixtures resembling a rose, e.g. the head of a screw for fastening mirrors [F.]

rose water a solution distilled from rose petals and used as a perfume

rose window (*archit.*) a circular window with radiating tracery

rose·wood (róuzwud) *n.* a dark red cabinet wood obtained from various tropical trees || a tree producing such wood, esp. *Dalbergia nigra,* fam. *Papilionaceae*

Rosh Ha·sha·nah (rouʃhəʃúnə, rouʃhəʃɔ́nə) the Jewish New Year celebrated on the first two days of Tishri (cf. JEWISH CALENDAR) [Mishnaic Heb. *rosh hashānāh,* beginning of the year]

Ro·si·cru·cian (rouzikrú:ʃən, rɒzikrú:ʃən) **1.** *n.* a member of a secret society which flourished in the 17th and early 18th cc. and was concerned with occult symbols and other secret lore, the transmutation of metals etc. It is said to have been founded in the late 15th c. by a man named Christian Rosenkreuz || a member of any of several groups descended from this society **2.** *adj.* of or pertaining to Rosicrucians or Rosicrucianism **Ro·si·crú·cian·ism** *n.* [fr. L. *rosa,* rose and *crucis,* of the cross (to give a Latinized form of *Rosenkreuz*)]

ros·i·ly (róuzili:) *adv.* with a rosy color || brightly, cheerfully

ros·in (rɒzin) **1.** *n.* the resin obtained from the oleoresin of pine by the removal of the volatile turpentine or as a by-product in the production of chemical pulp **2.** *v.t.* to rub (esp. a violin bow) with rosin || to add rosin to [O.F. *rosine, resine,* resin]

ros·i·ness (róuzi:nis) *n.* the state or quality of being rosy

Ross (rɔs, rɒs), Betsy (Elizabeth Griscom Ross, 1752-1836), American flagmaker at the time of the American Revolution. She was for long credited with designing and creating the first U.S. national flag, but this is now generally refuted

Ross, Edward Alsworth (1866-1951), U.S. pioneer sociologist, best known for his 'Social Control' (1901) and 'Social Psychology' (1908)

Ross, Harold Wallace (1892-1951), U.S. journalist, founding-editor (from 1925) of 'The New Yorker'

Ross, Sir James Clark (1800-62), British explorer. He located the North magnetic pole (1831). He led an expedition to Antarctica (1839-43), during which he discovered Ross Sea and explored the Ross Ice Shelf

Ross, Sir Ronald (1857-1932), British physician. He established (1897) the presence of the malarial parasite in the stomach of the anopheles mosquito. Nobel prize (1902)

Ross and Crom·ar·ty (krɒmərti:) a former county (area 3,089 sq. miles, pop. 57,000) in N. Scotland. County town: Dingwall (pop. 4,000)

Ross Barrier *ROSS SEA

Ross·by (rɔ́sbi:, rɒsbi:), Carl-Gustaf Arvid (1898-1957), Swedish-U.S. meteorologist, best known for his research in atmospheric circulation, for his discovery of the 'Rossby Waves' (the long waves in the upper westerlies) and of the jet stream, and as a leader of international research teams in atmospheric chemistry and radioactivity

Ross Dependency a sector of Antarctica between 160° E. and 150° W. south of 60° S., claimed by Britain under New Zealand jurisdiction

Ros·sel·li·no (rɔsəlí:nou), Antonio (c. 1427–c. 1478), Italian sculptor. His greatest work (1459-61) is the tomb of the cardinal prince of Portugal in the church of San Miniato, Florence, Italy

Rossellino, Bernardo (1409-64), Italian sculptor, eldest brother of Antonio. His principal work (c. 1444) is the tomb of Leonardo Bruni in Santa Croce, Florence, Italy

Ros·set·ti (rouséti:), Christina Georgina (1830-94), English Pre-Raphaelite poet. Her work, mainly lyrical, is combined with a strong element of mystical or religious feeling. She shared her sense of color and atmosphere with her brother Dante Gabriel and other Pre-Raphaelites. 'Goblin Market and other Poems' was published in 1862

Rossetti, Dante Gabriel (Gabriel Charles Dante, 1828-82), English poet and painter, son of an Italian exile, brother of Christina. With Millais and Holman Hunt he formed the Pre-Raphaelite Brotherhood. In its passionate feeling, its sense of color and its preoccupation with medieval themes and atmosphere, his poetry creates the haunted, autumnal dream world of a group of artists who had turned away from society. Among his best poems are 'The Blessed Damozel' (1847), 'Sister Helen' (1870) and the sonnet sequence 'The House of Life', included in his collection 'Ballads and Sonnets' (1881). His best-known paintings are 'Ecce Ancilla Domini'

(1849), 'Beata Beatrix' (1863), 'Dante's Dream' (1871)

Ross Ice Shelf *ROSS SEA

Ros·si·ni (rɒsíːniː, rɔssíːniː), Gioacchino Antonio (1792-1868), Italian composer. He began to compose when he was 18 and it is said that he wrote 40 operas in as many years. Some of the best known of these are 'The Barber of Seville' (1816), 'La Cenerentola' (1817), 'Semiramis' (1823) and 'William Tell' (1829). After 1829 he wrote no more operas, and few works of any kind apart from the 'Stabat Mater' oratorio (1842). Rossini's greatest gifts were his feeling for the theater and his brilliant bravura pieces

Ross Sea an arm of the S. Pacific in Ross Dependency, Antarctica, ending at about 78° S. in the Ross Ice Shelf or Ross Barrier, a permanent layer of ice (50-200 ft high) ending in mountains at about 85° S.

Ros·tand (rɔstɑ̃), Edmond (1868-1918), French playwright. 'Cyrano de Bergerac' (1897) and 'l'Aiglon' (1900), his best-known works, are distinguished by their wit and brilliance

ros·tel·late (rɒ́steleit, rɒ́stəlit) *adj.* (*biol.*) having a rostellum

ros·tel·lum (rɒstéləm) *pl.* **ros·tel·la** (rɒstélə) *n.* (*biol.*) a small rostrum ‖ a beaklike structure developed from the stigmatic surface of an orchid ‖ a round prominence on the scolex of the tapeworm ‖ the sucking mouthpart of a louse [L. dim. of *rostrum*, beak]

ros·ter (rɒ́stər) *n.* a list, esp. of officers or men, setting out the duties of groups or individuals, together with the times or dates for performing these ‖ any itemized list or roll [fr. Du. *rooster*, a list]

Ros·tock (rɔ́stɔk) the chief port (pop. incl. Warnemünde, its outport, 220,900) of East Germany, in former Mecklenburg. Industries: shipbuilding, fishing, mechanical engineering, chemicals. University (1419) ‖ the surrounding district (area 2,730 sq. miles, pop. 849,000)

Ros·tov-on-Don (rɒstɔ́fɒndɒ́n, rɔstɔ́fɔndɔ́n) (*Russ.* Rostov-na-Donu) a seaport and communications center (pop. 934,000) in the R.S.F.S.R., U.S.S.R., on the Don 25 miles above the Sea of Azov. Industries: textiles, shipbuilding, heavy engineering, metallurgy, chemicals, food processing. University

ros·tral (rɒ́strəl) *adj.* (*zool.*) of, relating to, resembling or being a rostrum ‖ (*Rom. hist.*, of historical monuments) adorned with rostrums [fr. L.L. *rostralis*]

ros·trate (rɒ́streit, rɒ́strit) *adj.* (*zool.*) having a rostrum ‖ (*Rom. hist.*, of historical monuments) rostral **ros·trat·ed** (rɒ́streitid) *adj.* (*zool.*) rostrate [fr. L. *rostratus* fr. *rostrum*, beak]

Rostropovich (rɒstrəpóuvitʃ), Mstislav (1927–), Russian-American cellist and conductor. After establishing his career as a cellist in the U.S.S.R., he was forced to flee to the U.S.A. because his association with dissidents and his outspokenness had put him in disfavor with the Soviet government. He directed (1974–) the National Symphony Orchestra in Washington, D.C.

ros·trum (rɒ́strəm) *pl.* **ros·trums, ros·tra** (rɒ́strə) *n.* a platform from which a speaker addresses his audience ‖ (*Rom. hist.*) the beaked prow of an ancient war galley ‖ (*biol.*) a beak or a beaklike process, esp. of many insects and arachnids [L. = beak]

ros·y (róuziː) *comp.* **ros·i·er** *superl.* **ros·i·est** *adj.* like a rose ‖ having a healthy, rose-colored complexion ‖ hopeful, promising, *a rosy future* ‖ optimistic, *to take a rosy view*

rot (rɒt) *pres. part.* **rot·ting** *past* and *past part.* **rot·ted** *v.i.* to decay ‖ (with 'away', 'off' etc.) to become impaired or detached by decay ‖ to degenerate morally ‖ (esp. of plants) to suffer from rot ‖ *v.t.* to cause to decay ‖ to affect (sheep) with rot ‖ to ret (flax etc.) [O.E. *rotian*]

rot 1. *n.* a rotting or being rotten ‖ something rotting or rotten ‖ a parasitic liver disease in sheep caused by the liver fluke ‖ (*pop.*) rubbish, nonsense ‖ a process of decline **2.** *interj.* rubbish [prob. Scand.]

ro·ta (róutə) *n.* (*Br.*) a roster **Ro·ta** the supreme court of the Curia [L. = wheel]

Ro·tar·i·an (routέəriːən) *n.* a member of the Rotary movement of international clubs (*ROTARY INTERNATIONAL)

ro·ta·ry (róutəriː) **1.** *adj.* rotating, turning on an axis ‖ working by rotation **2.** *pl.* **ro·ta·ries** *n.* a rotary machine, e.g. a rotary press ‖ a traffic circle [fr. L.L. *rotarius*]

Rotary Club a local branch of the Rotary International

rotary engine an engine, e.g. a turbine, in which the turning movement results from the direct application of a force to vanes etc. (cf. RECIPROCATING ENGINE)

Rotary International an international organization of clubs for business and professional men. It was founded in Chicago, Illinois (1905). Local club members each represent a different business or profession. It aims at serving the community and promoting international friendship

rotary press a printing press on which the type, in the form of a curved plate, is mounted on a cylinder rotating at high speed against a continuously moving reel of paper

ro·tate (róuteit) *adj.* having flat, radiating, spokelike parts [fr. L. *rota*, wheel]

rotate *pres. part.* **ro·tat·ing** *past* and *past part.* **ro·tat·ed** *v.i.* to turn around an axis ‖ to turn on a pivot with a circular movement ‖ to happen in regular cyclical succession, *the rotating seasons* ‖ *v.t.* to cause to revolve ‖ to cause to move on a pivot in a circular movement ‖ to cause to recur in a cycle, *to rotate crops* [fr. L. *rotare* (*rotatus*)]

ro·ta·tion (routéiʃən) *n.* a rotating or being rotated ‖ a repetitive arrangement or occurrence, *each becomes chairman in rotation* **ro·tá·tion·al** *adj.* [fr. L. *rotatio* (*rotationem*)]

rotation of crops the order in which different crops are grown so that each contributes to the soil constituents or conditions needed by its successors

ro·ta·tive (róuteitiv) *adj.* causing rotation ‖ characterized by rotation ‖ occurring in regular succession

ro·ta·tor (routéitər, róuteiter) *n.* anything that rotates ‖ (*anat.*, *pl.* **ro·ta·tors, ro·ta·to·res** (rǫutətɔ́riːz, rǫutətóuriːz) a muscle that rotates a limb etc. [L.]

ro·ta·to·ry (róutətɔriː, róutətǫuriː) *adj.* of, relating to or causing rotation

rote (rout) *n.* (only in) **by rote** (of the process of learning) by memory only, without intelligent understanding and assimilation [etym. doubtful]

Roth (rɔθ), Philip Milton (1933–), U.S. writer, known for his stories of American Jewish life. His novels include 'Letting Go' (1962), 'When She Was Good' (1967), 'Portnoy's Complaint' (1969), 'The Great American Novel' (1973), 'The Professor of Desire' (1977), 'The Ghost Writer' (1979), 'Zuckerman Unbound' (1981) and 'The Anatomy Lesson' (1983). His short stories are collected in 'Goodbye, Columbus' (1959)

Roth·er·mere (rɒ́ðərmiər) * NORTHCLIFFE

Roth·ko (rɒ́θkou), Mark (1903-70), American painter born in Russia, an originator of abstract expressionism. His vast compositions, usually employing two or three colors, achieve intensity by their strong tones and extreme simplicity of form

Roth·schild (rɔ́θtʃaild, rɔ́θstʃaild, rɒ́θtʃaild, rɒ́θstʃaild), Meyer Anselm (1743-1812), German Jewish banker. He founded a family of international bankers who dominated European finance in the 19th c.

ro·ti·fer (róutifər) *n.* a member of *Rotifera*, a class of usually microscopic, many-celled aquatic animals of phylum *Aschelminthes.* The anterior end bears one or two rings of cilia, used esp. for swimming, which seem to rotate like spinning wheels [Mod. L. fr. *rota*, wheel+*-fer*, bearing]

ro·tis·ser·ie (routísəriː) *n.* an electric cooking appliance fitted with a rotating spit for broiling fowl etc. [F.]

ro·to·flec·tor (róutəflęktər) *n.* a radar reflector shaped elliptically so that it reflects radar beams at a right angle

ro·to·gra·vure (rǫutəgrəvjúər) *n.* a process of photogravure using etched cylinders fixed to the rollers of a rotary press ‖ a print reproduced by this method ‖ the section of a newspaper containing these reproductions [fr. L. *rota*, wheel+ GRAVURE]

ro·tor (róutər) *n.* the rotary part of an electrical machine ‖ (*aeron.*) a system of rotating airfoils producing lift

ro·to·va·tor (róutəvęitər) *n.* (*Br.*) a power-driven soil tiller —**rotovate** *v.*

Ro·trou (rɔtruː), Jean de (1609-50), French poetic dramatist. A contemporary of Corneille, he contributed to the founding of French classical drama. His best-known works are 'Saint Genest' (1646) and 'Venceslas' (1647)

rot·ten (rɒ́t'n) *adj.* decayed, decomposed ‖ having a bad smell because of decay ‖ (of rocks) friable ‖ morally corrupt ‖ (of a sheep) affected with rot ‖ (*pop.*) completely unsatisfactory, *a rotten idea!* ‖ (*pop.*) very unpleasant, *rotten weather* [O.N. *rotinn*]

rotten borough (*Br. hist.*) a parliamentary constituency which possessed the right to elect members of parliament even though its population had dwindled or was nonexistent. The rotten boroughs were abolished in 1832

rot·ten·stone (rɒ́t'nstǫun) *n.* a friable siliceous limestone, used for polishing metals

rot·ter (rɒ́tər) *n.* a person having no moral integrity whatsoever

Rot·ter·dam (rɒ́tərdæm, rǫtərdǽm) the second largest city (pop. 568,167) and chief port of the Netherlands, serving much of W. Europe, on the Rhine delta in South Holland. Industries: oil refining, mechanical engineering, distilling, shipbuilding, chemicals, food processing. The city has been rebuilt in modern style after being almost totally destroyed (May 14, 1940) in a German bombing attack

ro·tund (routʌ́nd) *adj.* round, plump ‖ (of speech) florid, rhetorical [fr. L. *rotundus*, round]

ro·tun·da (routʌ́ndə) *n.* a circular building, esp. one with a dome or cupola ‖ a large circular room [fr. earlier *rotonda* fr. Ital. *rotonda* fem. adj., round]

ro·tun·di·ty (routʌ́nditiː) *pl.* **ro·tun·di·ties** *n.* the state or quality of being rotund ‖ a rotund phrase [fr. L. *rotunditas*]

Rou·ault (ruːou), Georges (1871-1958), French expressionist painter, etcher and lithographer, briefly associated with Fauvism. His works, ranging in subject from Christ's Passion and biblical themes to grotesque judges, clowns and prostitutes, reveal his love of Christ and his compassion for his fellow men in the face of social injustice and human suffering. He knew the technique of making stained glass, and his style was greatly influenced by this. He designed (1945) windows for the church at Assy, Haute-Savoie, France. His 'Miserere' etchings (1917-27) were published in 1948

Rou·baix (ruːbei) a textile manufacturing center (pop. 109,797) of Nord department, France

Rou·bi·liac (ruːbiːljæk) (Louis François Roubillac, c. 1695-1762), French sculptor. He lived in England from about 1720. His works include many fine tombs in Westminster Abbey, and busts in Trinity College Library, Cambridge

rouble *RUBLE

rou·é (rúːei, ruːéi) *n.* a sexually debauched man, esp. one who is no longer young [F. past part. of *rouer*, to break on the wheel]

Rou·en (rwɑ̃) the chief town (pop. 114,925) of Seine-Maritime, France, and historic capital of Normandy, a sea and river port on the Lower Seine. Main industries: metallurgy, shipbuilding, mechanical engineering. Half the town was destroyed (1944) in the 2nd world war, but the cathedral (12th-16th cc.), churches (14th and 15th cc.) and other monuments remain, partly restored

rouge (ruːʒ) **1.** *n.* a cosmetic for heightening the color of the cheeks ‖ jewelers' rouge **2.** *v. pres. part.* **roug·ing** *past* and *past part.* **rouged** *v.t.* to color with rouge ‖ *v.i.* to use rouge [F.=rouge, red]

rouge et noir (rúːʒeinwǽr) (*gambling*) a card game in which two rows of cards are dealt, one row designated as red, the other as black. The players bet on which row will come closer to the count of 31 [F.=red and black]

Rou·get de Lisle (ruːʒeidəliːl), Claude Joseph (1760-1836), French army officer. He wrote both words and music of the 'Marseillaise' (1792)

rough (rʌf) **1.** *adj.* having a surface which is uneven or marked by protuberances or other irregularities ‖ difficult to make one's way over or through, *rough country* ‖ (of cloth) having a coarse texture ‖ (of an animal's coat) coarse and shaggy ‖ turbulent, *a rough sea, a rough crossing* ‖ (of sound) harsh and rasping ‖ (of wine, cider etc.) harsh and acid to the taste ‖ approximate, *a rough guess* ‖ hasty and not worked up, *rough notes* ‖ unrefined, *a rough manner* ‖ full of oaths, *rough language* ‖ boisterous, *rough play* ‖ requiring strength rather than intelligence, *rough work* ‖ (of behavior) characterized by violence ‖ crudely executed, *rough garden furniture* ‖ (*pop.*) severely trying, *a rough time* ‖ (esp.

of gems) unpolished || lacking luxuries, comfort etc., *a rough camping holiday* || (*phon.*) aspirate **to be rough on** to be harsh with || (*impers.*) to involve hardship for, *it was rough on her having to work on Saturdays* **2.** *adv.* (esp. with *past part.*) roughly, *rough shaped* **3.** *n.* uneven, stony ground || (*golf*) the ground bordering the fairway || anything in a rough, unfinished state, esp. an uncut gem || a tough || a spike in a horseshoe to prevent the horse from slipping **in the rough** in a crude, unfinished state **to take the rough with the smooth** to accept life as it comes, good or bad **4.** *v.t.* to make rough || (esp. with 'up') to treat roughly || to put a spike or spikes into (a horseshoe) **to rough in** to add (provisional detail) to a sketch, plan etc. **to rough it** to live without the comforts and amenities of civilized life **to rough out** to make (a diagram, plan etc.) in broad outline, without detail **róugh·age** *n.* the rough or refuse part of grain etc. used as food for domestic animals || (*dietetics*) the bran of cereals or vegetable fibers, which stimulates the action of the alimentary canal [O.E. *rūh*]

rough-and-read·y (rʌ́fənrédi:) *adj.* (of a thing) good enough for its purpose, though not well designed or finished || (of a person) crude, vigorous and outspoken || (of method) crude but adequate

rough-and-tum·ble (rʌ́fəntʌ́mb'l) *n.* an unorganized fight, brawl or scuffle in which anyone joins who wants to

rough breathing *BREATHING

rough·cast (rʌ́fkæst, rʌ́fkɑst) **1.** *n.* a coarse plaster usually of mortar and small stones used on outside walls || a rough, preliminary model **2.** *v.t.* to coat (a wall) with roughcast || to construct in a rough preliminary form

rough diamond an uncut diamond || (*Br.*) a diamond in the rough

rough·dry (rʌ́fdrái) **1.** *v.t. pres. part.* **rough·dry·ing** *past* and *past part.* **rough·dried** to dry (laundry) without ironing it **2.** *adj.* (of laundry) dried but not ironed

rough·en (rʌ́fən) *v.t.* to make rough || *v.i.* to become rough

rough·hew (rʌ́fhjú:) *pres. part.* **rough·hew·ing** *past* **rough·hewed** *past part.* **rough·hewn** (rʌ́fhjú:n), **rough·hewed** *v.t.* to cut into shape without smoothing or polishing || to make a preliminary shape or rough model of **róugh·héwn** *adj.* left as it was hewn, not smoothed or polished || (of a person) uncultivated

rough·house (rʌ́fhaus) **1.** *n.* play that has gotten out of hand and turned into brawling **2.** *v. pres. part.* **rough·hous·ing** (rʌ́fhausiŋ, rʌ́fhauzing) *past* and *past part.* **rough·housed** (rʌ́fhaust, rʌ́fhauzd) *v.i.* to create or take part in a roughhouse || *v.t.* to give (someone) a rough handling (sometimes in fun, sometimes in earnest)

rough·ly (rʌ́fli:) *adv.* in a rough way || approximately, *the price is roughly 600 francs*

rough·neck (rʌ́fnek) *n.* (*pop.*) a tough, rowdy man or boy || the lowest member of an oil-rig crew, doing manual work only

rough·rid·er (rʌ́fraidər) *n.* a person who rides untrained horses, or breaks them to the saddle

Rough·rid·er (*Am. hist.*) a member of the 1st U.S. Volunteer Cavalry regiment in the Spanish-American War (1898), commanded by Theodore Roosevelt

rough·shod (rʌ́fʃód) *adj.* (of a horse) having shoes with spikes in them to prevent slipping **to ride roughshod over** to show no regard for

rough-spo·ken (rʌ́fspoukən) *adj.* using blunt or coarse language

rou·lade (ru:lɑ́d) *n.* (*mus.*) an ornamental passage of running notes usually sung to one syllable [F.]

rou·leau (ru:lou) *pl.* **rou·leaus, rou·leaux** (ru:lóuz) *n.* a roll of coins packeted in paper [F.]

rou·lette (ru:lét) **1.** *n.* a gambling game played with a ball on a revolving disk which brings a ball to rest against a numbered red or black compartment || a toothed wheel for making dots or incisions, e.g. in engraving || a series of small slits separating rows of postage stamps **2.** *v.t. pres. part.* **rou·let·ting** *past* and *past part.* **rou·let·ted** to make incisions in or on with a roulette [F.]

Roumania *RUMANIA

Roumanian *RUMANIAN

round (raund) **1.** *adj.* having a circular or roughly circular shape || having a spherical or roughly spherical shape || having a circular cross section, cylindrical || involving a circular movement || plump, *round cheeks* || pronounced with the lips rounded || brisk, *a round pace* || (of the voice, a sound etc.) full-toned and even || (of handwriting) curved rather than angular || expressed in tens, hundreds, thousands etc. || expressed as a whole number, not fractional || full, complete, *a round dozen* || approximate, *a round estimate* || loud and clear, *a round oath* || (of a blow) delivered with a swinging motion of the arm **2.** *n.* the rung of a ladder || (esp. *pl.*) a route or course habitually taken. e.g. by a milkman, watchman, a doctor visiting patients in a hospital etc. || (*mil.*) a patrol whose main function is to keep the sentinels alert, esp. at night || (*mil.*) the route taken by this patrol || (*mil.*) a single shot fired from a weapon or from each gun of a troop, battery etc. || a single outburst of applause, cheers etc. || a circular movement || a succession of events, actions etc., *a round of parties* || the rounded part of the thigh of beef, or a slice cut from this || a round slice of bread, sausage etc. || (*archery*) a given number of arrows shot from a given distance at the target || (*boxing*) one of the periods into which a match is divided || (*golf*) the playing of all the holes of the course || (*mus.*) a usually short vocal canon in which the voices enter in turn and sing the melody at the same pitch or at the octave || (*card games*) a unit of play in which each player has a turn || a drink of liquor served at the same time to each member of a group of people || (*archit*) a rounded molding **in the round** in which sculptured figures are three-dimensional and not attached to a background || (*theater*) with a central stage, surrounded by seats **out of round** distorted from true roundness **to go the round of** to go, ask etc. all through (a group of people), *he went the round of the class asking the same question* **to go the round** (or **rounds**) (of gossip, rumor etc.) to be circulated about and widely repeated **3.** *v.t.* to make round || to pronounce with rounded lips || to pass esp. by making a circuit of, *to round the Cape, to round a corner* || to make full or plump || to polish (phrases or style) || *v.i.* to become round || to make a circular course || to become full or plump || (with 'into') to develop fully, *the plan rounded into shape* || to reverse direction by turning around, *he rounded on his heel* **to round off** to complete, put the finishing touches to **to round on** to betray, inform against || to make an unexpected verbal attack on **to round out** to make full or round || to furnish with detail **to round to** (*naut.*) to come about in order to heave to **to round up** to drive (cattle) together || (*pop.*) to collect (people) together || to bring in (e.g. criminals or suspects) for questioning **4.** *adv.* in a circle or in a circular course, *to run round* || on every side, *gather round* || from beginning to end, *all year round* || in various places, *scattered round* || with a revolving movement, *the wheel whirled round* || in circumference, *the tower is 60 ft round* || on a circuit, *the milkman comes round at 10* || so as to face, go etc. in the opposite direction, *turn round,* or so as to hold an opposite or different view, *to talk someone round* || to everyone present, *pass the muffins round* || to someone or some place understood, *send round for more beer* || in the area, *search round* || so as to encircle, *wrap round* || so as to see the sights, inspect a property etc., *to show someone round* || back to consciousness, *to bring someone round* **5.** *prep.* on every side of, *the wind blew round the house* || so as to encircle, *put it round your wrist* || so as to revolve about, *the earth turns round its axis* || near, *he lives round here somewhere* || on a circuit of, *he went round his diocese* || throughout, *it works all round the clock* || here and there in, *he looked round the room* || on the border, edge or outer part of, *a pattern of roses round the saucers* || so as to go in a curved or circular path about, *ski round the trees* || located beyond the circuit of, *the house round the corner* || (of a specified time, date or season) at about, *round 1830* || in different parts of, *public telephones were put all round the town* **round the clock** for 24 hours nonstop [O.F. *rund-, rond-, round-*]

round·a·bout (ráundəbaut) **1.** *adj.* circuitous, indirect, *a roundabout way of getting somewhere* || circumlocutory, *a roundabout way of saying something* **2.** *n.* (*Br.*) a merry-go-round || (*Br.*) a traffic circle

roun·del, roun·dle (ráund'l) *n.* a small, round disk, form or figure || (*poetry*) an English version of the French rondeau || a circular medallion, panel or window [O. F. *rondel*]

roun·de·lay (ráundəlei) *n.* a short song, part of which is repeated as a refrain [fr. F. *rondelet*]

round·ers (ráundərz) *n.* (*Br.*) a game resembling baseball played esp. by children [ROUND n. and v.]

Round·head (ráundhed) *n.* (*Br. hist.*) a Puritan or parliamentarian in the English Civil War, 1642-52 (cf. CAVALIER)

round·house (ráundhaus) *pl.* **round·hous·es** (ráundhauziz) *n.* (*hist.*) a cabin on the afterpart of the quarterdeck of a ship || (*hist.*) a building where prisoners were kept temporarily || a circular building where railroad engines are stored or repaired

roundle *ROUNDEL

round·ly (ráundli:) *adv.* violently, *to abuse someone roundly* || openly, without circumlocution, *he roundly declared himself satisfied* || thoroughly, completely, *roundly condemned*

round robin a letter, petition or protest bearing a number of signatures in a circle so that none heads the list || a letter addressed to a group. When the first person to receive it has read it he sends it on to the next, perhaps adding information or comment, and so on until all have seen it

round-shoul·dered (ráundʃouldərd) *adj.* having the shoulders slouched forward and the upper part of the back rounded

rounds·man (ráundzmən) *pl.* **rounds·men** (ráundzmən) *n.* (*Br.*) a man employed to deliver milk, bread etc. to customers

Round Table King Arthur's assembly of knights, in the Arthurian legend

round table conference a conference so arranged that none of the participants takes precedence

round trip a journey to and from a place over the same route || (*Br.*) a circular journey, not covering the same ground twice

round turn (*naut.*) a single turn of a rope around a post or bollard made in order to check the motion of a ship abruptly

round-up (ráundʌp) *n.* the collecting of scattered cattle || men and horses who collect such cattle || a collecting of scattered people, esp. of criminals by police

round·worm (ráundwə:rm) *n.* a nematode worm, as distinguished from a flatworm or tapeworm

roup (ru:p) *n.* one of various poultry diseases, esp. fowl pox [etym. doubtful]

rouse (rauz) *pres. part.* **rous·ing** *past* and *past part.* **roused** *v.t.* to awaken from sleep || to cause to become active || to provoke, *the sight roused him to anger* || (*naut.*, with 'in', 'out' or 'up') to pull with great force

rouse·a·bout (ráuzəbaut) *n.* (*Austral.*) a handyman on a sheep farm

rous·ing (ráuziŋ) *adj.* exciting, *a rousing speech* || very enthusiastic, *a rousing welcome*

Rous·seau (ru:sou), Henri 'le Douanier' (1844-1910), French painter. Much of his work re-creates a childish vision of a luxuriant, strangely ordered jungle, through which elegant beasts menacingly approach the spectator. His view of contemporary France and his portraits have the same direct, naïve character

Rousseau, Jean-Jacques (1712-78), French writer born in Geneva. A man of volatile emotions but keen mind, he rebelled against many dominant values of his time and quarreled with a striking number of contemporaries, e.g. Voltaire, Grimm, Diderot and Hume. He rejected absolutism, rationalism, the moderation as well as the rigidity of waning classicism, coercive education and formal gardens. Prefiguring the main trends which were to converge in Romanticism, he glorified nature, including human nature (the greater part of his work stems from his belief in the natural goodness of men), favored feeling and emotion as against reason, and advocated a method of education in which the pupil would be helped to develop freely in accordance with his own inborn nature. In 'le Contrat social' (1762), he developed a theory of the State based on a contract by which free individuals freely entrust a part of their freedom to the body politic. His political ideas played an important part in the development of modern democracy. Other important works are: 'Discours sur l'origine de l'inégalité' (1755), 'Julie ou la Nouvelle Héloïse' (1761), 'Emile ou Traité de l'Education' (1762) and 'Confessions' (published posthumously)

CONCISE PRONUNCIATION KEY: **(a)** æ, *cat*; ɑ, *car*; ɔ *fawn*; ei, *snake*. **(e)** e, *hen*; i:, *sheep*; iə, *deer*; εə, *bear*. **(i)** i, *fish*; ai, *tiger*; ə:, *bird*. **(o)** o, *ox*; au, *cow*; ou, *goat*; u, *poor*; ɔi, *royal*. **(u)** ʌ, *duck*; u, *bull*; u:, *goose*; ə, *bacillus*; ju:, *cube*. x, *loch*; θ, *think*; ð, *bother*; z, *Zen*; ʒ, *corsage*; dʒ, *savage*; ŋ, *orangutang*; j, *yak*; ʃ, *fish*; tʃ, *fetch*; 'l, *rabble*; 'n, *redden*. Complete pronunciation key appears inside front cover.

Rousseau, Théodore (1812-67), French landscape painter, one of the leaders of the Barbizon school

Rous·sel (ru:sel). Albert (1869-1937), French composer. He wrote four symphonies (of which the second is the best known). Of his four ballets, the most famous is 'le Festin de l'araignée'(1912). Other works include the symphonic poem 'Evocations' (1910-11), chamber music, songs etc.

Rous·sil·lon (ru:si:jɔ̃) a former province of France in the Pyrenees, bordering Spain and the Mediterranean, forming the modern Pyrénées-Orientales. Historic capital: Perpignan. Industries: agriculture (early vegetables, fruit, wine), fishing, tourism. It was disputed by French and Spanish powers from the 8th c., when the Franks took it from the Arabs, until 1659, when France definitively annexed it. Catalan is widely spoken

roust·a·bout (ráustəbaut) *n.* a dock laborer ‖ a deckhand ‖ an unskilled laborer ‖ a laborer in a circus ‖ (*Austral.*) a rouseabout [ROUSE+ ABOUT]

rout (raut) **1.** *n.* a disorderly flight, e.g. of defeated troops **to put to rout** to defeat utterly **2.** *v.t.* to put (an army) to rout. [obs. F. *route*]

rout *v.i.* (of swine) to root ‖ to rummage, *to rout about in a drawer* ‖ *v.t.* (with 'out') to make (someone) come out or get up ‖ (with 'out') to search for and discover ‖ to dig out (metal or wood) with a router

route (ru:t, raut) **1.** *n.* a course of travel, esp. between two distant points ‖ a way of progress, *to reconnoiter a route through a minefield* ‖ a regularly followed course, *a map of the main shipping routes to Africa* ‖ a specific area covered regularly by a specific person, *postal route* **2.** *v.t. pres. part.* **rout·ing** *past* and *past part.* **rout·ed** to send (goods, troops etc.) by a certain route, or to plan such a route for (someone or something) [F.]

rout·er (ráutər) *n.* a carpenter's plane used to cut grooves, moldings etc. ‖ a machine for routing out wooden or metal surfaces

rou·tine (ru:tí:n) **1.** *n.* a regularly repeated course of action or standard practice, *a hospital routine* ‖ (*dancing*) a set series of steps ‖ an act (feature in a show), *a comedy routine* **2.** *adj.* in accordance with a routine, *routine duties* [F.]

roux (ru:) *pl.* **roux** *n.* a mixture of fat and flour browned together and used to thicken sauces [F. = red, browned]

rove (rouv) *pres. part.* **rov·ing** *past* and *past part.* **roved** *v.i.* and *t.* to roam [etym. doubtful]

rove *n.* a small metal plate or ring, through which a screw or nail is passed and held fast, used in boat building ‖ a burr (small washer) [O.N. *rō*]

rove 1. *v.t. pres. part.* **rov·ing** *past* and *past part.* **roved** to form into roves **2.** *n.* a thin strand of cotton, wool or silk drawn out and slightly twisted [etym. doubtful]

rove *past* and *past part.* of REEVE

rove beetle a member of *Staphylinidae,* a large family of swift-running, long-bodied beetles having very short wing cases. They are found in decaying animal and vegetable matter

rov·er (róuvər) *n.* a person who shuns a settled life ‖ (*Br.*) a senior boy scout ‖ (*archery*) a fixed mark for long-distance shooting, also one chosen at random ‖ (*croquet*) a ball that has passed through all its wickets, but is continued in play rather than being allowed to peg out ‖ (*croquet*) the person playing this ball

ro·ver·back (róuvərbæk) *n.* (*football*) linesman who plays linebacker and cornerback

rov·ing (róuviŋ) *n.* a rove (thin strand of cotton etc.)

row (rou) **1.** *v.t.* to propel (a boat) by using oars ‖ to participate in (a race) by doing this ‖ to compete against in a race ‖ to employ (a specified number of oars) ‖ to take (passengers) in an oar-propelled boat, *to row someone across a river* ‖ *v.i.* to use oars ‖ to be an oarsman ‖ to be propelled by or as if by oars **2.** *n.* a journey in a rowboat [O.E. *rōwan*]

row (rou) *n.* an orderly line of persons or things near, or touching, one another, *a row of houses* ‖ a line of seats in a theater etc. ‖ (esp. *Br.*, used chiefly in street names) a small street each side of which is lined with houses **a hard** (or **long**) **row to hoe** a wearisome, difficult task to perform [perh. O.E. *rāw*]

row (rau) *n.* (esp. *Br.*) a loud, harsh noise ‖ a quarrel or disturbance, esp. a noisy one **to make** (or **kick up**) **a row** to make a lot of noise ‖ to protest strongly [origin unknown]

row·an (róuən, ráuən) *n. Sorbus aucuparia,* a tree of Europe and Asia bearing corymbs of small white flowers. The fruits are red, berry-like pomes [of Scand. origin]

row·boat (roubout) *n.* (*Am.*= *Br.* rowing boat) a small, shallow boat propelled by oars

row·di·ness (ráudi:nis) *n.* the state or quality of being rowdy

row·dy (ráudi:) **1.** *comp.* **row·di·er** *superl.* **row·di·est** *adj.* disorderly and noisy **2.** *pl.* **row·dies** *n.* a disorderly, noisy person **rów·dy·ism** *n.* [etym. doubtful]

row·el (ráuəl) *n.* the spiked wheel on a spur [fr. O.F. *roel, rouel*]

row·ing boat (róuiŋ) *n.* (*Br.*) a rowboat

Row·land (róulənd), Henry Augustus (1848-1901), American physicist. He made valuable experiments in electricity and invented a dividing apparatus for ruling diffraction gratings

Row·land·son (róuləndsən), Thomas (1756-1827), English painter and caricaturist. Though his drawings reveal a brutal and gross world, the seamy side of 18th-c. civilization, they display a sublime sense of the ridiculous coupled with delicate tone and brilliant line

row·lock (rólək, róulɒk) *n.* an oarlock

Ro·xas y A·cu·ña (rɔ́jɑsi:ɑkú:njɑ), Manuel (1892-1948), first president (1946-8) of the Republic of the Philippines

Rox·burgh (róksbrə) a former county (area 670 sq. miles.) of S. Scotland. County town: Jedburgh. Administrative center: Newtown St Boswells

roy·al (rɔ́iəl) **1.** *adj.* of or relating to a king or queen ‖ of or belonging to the family of a king or queen, *the royal governess* ‖ having the rank of a king or queen ‖ fit for a king or queen, *a royal welcome* ‖ very imposing, splendid, majestic etc. ‖ (of a mast, sail or yard) next above the topgallant ‖ (*printing*) folded from royal paper, *royal octavo* **Roy·al** (*Br.*) the descriptive title of a place or institution under the patronage of a king or queen or given a charter under the monarch's hand etc., *the Royal Borough of Tunbridge Wells, the Royal College of Physicians* **2.** *n.* a stag at least 8 years old having 12 or more points on its antlers ‖ a sail set on the royal mast ‖ (*Br.*) a size of paper measuring 24 ins x 19 ins (for writing) or 25 ins × 20 ins (for printing) [O.F. *roial*]

Royal *n.* U.S. government secrecy classification more restrictive than 'top secret,' established September 1980

royal assent the British sovereign's formal ratification of an act of parliament

royal blue a deep, vivid blue

Royal Canadian Mounted Police (RCMP) the federal police force of Canada, originally instituted (1873) to establish law and order between the Manitoba border and the Rocky Mtns. In the 1900s it tracked down murderers, horse thieves, and desperadoes, contained the Sioux Indians, and assisted thousands of new settlers unfamiliar with the wilderness. It is the only police force in the Yukon and Northwest Territories. In the 1930s the marine and air divisions and the first crime detection laboratories were added. Its many duties include ceremonial parades and national security

roy·al·ism (rɔ́iəlizəm) *n.* monarchism

roy·al·ist (rɔ́iəlist) **1.** *n.* a person who supports the institution of monarchy ‖ (*Br. hist.*) a Cavalier, or supporter of the king in the English Civil War, 1642–52 (cf. PARLIAMENTARIAN) ‖ (*hist.*) a supporter of George III's government at the time of the Revolutionary War ‖ (in France) a supporter of the Bourbons at any time during and since the French Revolution **2.** *adj.* of royalism or pertaining to a royalist

royal jelly a jellylike substance secreted from the pharyngeal glands of the honey bee and fed to very young larvae and to all queen larvae

royal palm a member of *Roystonea,* fam. *Palmaceae,* a genus of tall, ornamental palms, esp. *R. regia,* a native to Florida and Cuba, grown in many tropical regions

royal purple a rich reddish-purple color

Royal Society British scientific society. It is an independent, private body of scientific scholars, founded in 1660. There are more than 900 fellows and foreign members; elections of new members are made each year. The Royal Society promotes scientific research, advises the government, and represents Britain internationally in scientific matters. It publishes its learned 'Proceedings' and 'Philosophical Transactions'. It receives an annual government subsidy

royal standard a square banner bearing the royal arms, flown to indicate the presence of the sovereign in a castle or on a ship and as a naval flag of command

roy·al·ty (rɔ́iəlti:) *pl.* **roy·al·ties** *n.* the office or dignity of a sovereign ‖ a person having royal rank ‖ royal persons collectively ‖ the sum, e.g. a percentage of the sales figure, paid to the owner of a literary etc. property by the person who exploits it commercially, or the sum paid to the owner of a patent for the use of his patent ‖ (*pl., hist.*) a right or prerogative granted by a sovereign [O.F. *roialté*]

Royce (rɔis), Josiah (1855-1916), U.S. philosopher. Espousing a monistic idealism, he held that moral order in the world takes the form of man's loyalty to the great community, or to collective individuals

RPG (*computer abbr.*) for report program generator, a computer language used to display data or prepare a desired business report

rpm, r.p.m revolutions per minute

R.R. railroad

R.S.F.S.R. *RUSSIAN SOVIET FEDERAL SOCIALIST REPUBLIC

R.S.V.P. (used in formal invitations) please reply [F. *répondez s'il vous plait*]

Ru·an·da-U·run·di (ru:ándəu:rú:ndi:) a former territory of central Africa. It was incorporated in German East Africa (1890) and was administered by Belgium as a mandate (1919-46) and as a trustee territory (1946-62). It divided (July 1, 1962) into the separate independent states of Rwanda and Burundi

rub (rʌb) **1.** *v. pres. part.* **rub·bing** *past* and *past part.* **rubbed** *v.t.* to move (something), using pressure, over a surface, *to rub ointment on one's leg* ‖ to apply such moving pressure to, *to rub one's leg with ointment* ‖ to clean or polish with a pressing motion ‖ to chafe, *to rub one's shin on a rail* ‖ to take a rubbing of (an incised design) ‖ to move in contact causing friction, *to rub one's hands together* ‖ *v.i.* to be subjected to friction ‖ to chafe, *shoes that rub* ‖ (*lawn bowling*) to be deflected or slowed down by an uneven piece of ground **to rub along** to make a barely adequate living ‖ to manage to avoid undue friction in social relationships **to rub down** to dry the sweat off (a horse) after exercise or a race **to rub in** to cause to penetrate by rubbing **to rub it in** to emphasize, and continue to emphasize, a person's shortcomings, failures, mistakes etc. **to rub off** to remove (something) by rubbing ‖ to be removable by rubbing **to rub out** to erase ‖ to become erased **to rub shoulders (elbows)** (esp. with 'with') to associate with someone whom one would not normally expect to associate with, *to rub shoulders with the gentry* **to rub (someone) the wrong way,** *Br.* also **to rub (someone) up the wrong way,** to offend the susceptibilities of (someone) and so irritate him **to rub up** (*Br.*) to refresh one's memory of, *to rub up one's French* **2.** *n.* a rubbing, *give the silver a rub* ‖ (*lawn bowling*) unevenness or inequality in the surface of the ground affecting the course of a bowl ‖ a hindrance or obstacle, esp. one having metaphysical overtones [origin unknown]

Rub al Kha·li (rubælxɑ́li:) *GREAT SANDY DESERT

ru·ba·to (ru:bɑ́tou) **1.** *adj.* (*mus.*) played with some freedom as regards tempo **2.** *pl.* **ru·ba·ti** (ru:bɑ́ti:), **ru·ba·tos** *n.* (*mus.*) a tempo varied at discretion to express changes of mood [Ital.]

rub·ber (rʌ́bər) *n.* an elastic substance obtained from the latex of many tropical plants, esp. *Hevea brasiliensis,* fam. *Euphorbiaceae,* and *Ficus elastica,* fam. *Moraceae* ‖ a substitute for this made synthetically ‖ (*Am.*=*Br.* galosh) a low rubber overshoe worn in wet weather ‖ someone who or something which rubs ‖ (*Br.*) an eraser ‖ an overshoe [RUB v.]

rubber *n.* three successive games of bridge or of certain other games, or the first two only if the same side wins both

rubber band an endless band of rubber used to hold bundles, papers etc. together

rub·ber·ize (rʌ́bəraiz) *v.t. pres. part.* **rub·ber·iz·ing** *past* and *past part.* **rub·ber·ized** to coat with rubber, impregnate with rubber solution

rub·ber·neck (rʌ́bərnek) **1.** *n.* (*pop.*) a very inquisitive person ‖ an indefatigable sightseer **2.** *v.i.* (*pop.*) to stare out of curiosity

rubber plant any of several plants which yield rubber, esp. *Ficus elastica,* fam. *Moraceae,* an Asian tree which grows to 100 ft or more and is the source of Assam rubber. A dwarfed variety is popular as an indoor plant

rubber ring (*Br.*) a rubber band || (*Br.*) a rubber washer for a jar || (*Br.*) an inflatable device worn around the waist by someone learning to swim

rubber stamp a rubber device which is inked and used on documents etc. for dating, endorsing, signing etc. **rúb·ber stámp** *v.t.* to stamp with this || (*pop.*) to approve as a matter of routine, without real consideration

rub·ber·y (rʌ́bəri:) *adj.* like rubber in consistency, appearance etc.

rub·bish (rʌ́biʃ) *n.* waste material, refuse || worthless or inferior ideas, goods etc. || (*pop.*) nonsense **rúb·bish·y** *adj.* [etym. doubtful]

rub·ble (rʌ́b'l) *n.* pieces of broken brick, stone etc., usually from demolition and used for foundations etc. || (*masonry*) rough stones for filling in || rubblework|| (*geol.*) loose fragments of stone or rock lying beneath alluvium [M.E., etym. doubtful]

rub·ble·work (rʌ́b'lwə:rk) *n.* coarse masonry of roughly dressed stones

Rub·bra (rʌ́brə), Edmund (1901-), English composer and pianist. His works include seven symphonies, two masses, much chamber music, songs and choral works

rub·down (rʌ́bdaun) *n.* the act of rubbing down the body, e.g. a brisk toweling after swimming or bathing || a massage given to athletes to improve circulation

rube (ru:b) *n.* (*pop.*) a bumpkin [shortened fr. *Reuben,* a man's name]

ru·be·fa·cient (ru:biféiʃənt) **1.** *adj.* causing redness **2.** *n.* (*med.*) a salve etc. which causes the skin to redden **ru·be·fac·tion** (ru:bifǽkʃən) *n.* [fr. L. *rubefaciens* (*rubefacientis*) fr. *rubefacere,* to redden]

ru·bel·la (ru:bélə) *n.* German measles [Mod. L.]

ru·bel·lite (rú:belait, ru:bélait) *n.* a variety of tourmaline in various shades of red [fr. L. *rubellus,* reddish]

Ru·bens (rú:binz), Sir Peter Paul (1577-1640), Flemish painter. His patrons included the Gonzaga family, Marie de' Medici, Philip IV of Spain, and Charles I of England. After work and study in Italy (1600-3, 1604-8), where he steeped himself in the classic style of the high Renaissance and the naturalism of Caravaggio, he returned to Antwerp and established himself as a portrait painter and master of allegorical and mythological subjects. His large compositions reduce an enormous number of component parts to a unified composition, and yet remain full of light and air and above all of life and energy. His swift brushwork was extraordinarily fluent in rendering surface textures, above all that of flesh. The breadth of his drawings, the freedom of his technique and the warmth of his color make him one of the greatest of decorative painters. Among his masterpieces are 'The Raising of the Cross' (1610) and 'The Descent from the Cross' (1612) both in Antwerp Cathedral

ru·be·o·la (ru:bí:ələ, ru:bi:óulə) *n.* measles [Mod. L., neut. pl. of *rubeolus,* reddish]

ru·bes·cent (ru:bésənt) *adj.* growing or becoming red [fr. L. *rubescens* (*rubescentis*) fr. *rubescere,* to redden]

ru·bi·celle (rú:bisel) *n.* a yellow or reddish-orange ruby spinel [F.]

Ru·bi·con (rú:bikɒn) a small river which marked the boundary between Italy and Cisalpine Gaul. Caesar's crossing of the Rubicon into Italy against the orders of the senate (49 B.C.) marked the opening of the civil war with Pompey

ru·bi·cund (rú:bikənd) *adj.* (of complexions) ruddy [F. *rubicond* or fr. L. *rubicundus*]

ru·bid·i·um (ru:bídi:əm) *n.* a soft silvery metallic element (symbol Rb, at. no. 37, at. mass 85.47) resembling sodium both physically and chemically [Mod. L. fr. *rubidus,* red]

ru·big·i·nous (ru:bídʒinəs) *adj.* rust-colored [fr. L. *rubiginosus*]

Rubinstein (rú:bənstain) Arthur (1887-1982), U.S. pianist, born in Poland. He debuted in Berlin (1899) and gave concerts in Europe and Russia, debuting in the U.S.A. in 1906. He was esp. known for his interpretation of such composers as Chopin, Brahms, Mozart and Grieg. A world concert tourer, he became a U.S. citizen in 1946

ru·ble, rou·ble (rú:b'l) *n.* the Russian monetary unit || a coin representing a ruble [F. fr. Russ. *rubli*]

ru·bric (rú:brik) *n.* the heading of a chapter or section printed or written in special lettering (originally red), or a section so indicated || a liturgical direction in a prayer book **rú·bri·cal** *adj.* [fr. F. *rubrique* or L. *rubrica*]

ru·bri·cate (rú:brikeit) *pres. part.* **ru·bri·cat·ing** *past* and *past part.* **ru·bri·cat·ed** *v.t.* to mark with red || to print or write in red || to provide with rubrics **ru·bri·cá·tion, rú·bri·ca·tor** *ns* [fr. L. *rubricare* (*rubricatus*)]

ru·bri·cian (ru:bríʃən) *n.* an expert in liturgical rubrics

ru·by (rú:bi:) **1.** *pl.* **ru·bies** *n.* a precious stone of red corundum || something made of this, e.g. the jewel of a watch || the red wine cr of ruby || (*Br., printing*) agate **2.** *adj.* of the color of ruby [O.F. *rubi, rubis*]

ruby laser a laser based on a rod-shape ruby crystal to which optical pumping is applied, producing a narrow beam of red light

ruby maser a maser utilizing a ruby crystal

ruby spinel a spinel used as a gem

ruche (ru:ʃ) **1.** *n.* a frill, pleat or ruffle of lace, net etc. **2.** *v.t. pres. part.* **ruch·ing** *past* and *past part.* **ruched** to trim with ruching [F.]

ruch·ing (rú:ʃiŋ) *n.* material used in making a ruche or ruches

ruck (rʌk) *n.* the ordinary run of persons or things [prob. of Scand. origin]

ruck **1.** *n.* a crease, wrinkle **2.** *v.i.* (esp. with 'up') to become wrinkled || *v.t.* (esp. with 'up') to wrinkle [O.N. *hrukka*]

ruck *v.* (*Br.*) to seek the ball aggressively in rugby

Rück·ert (rýkərt), Friedrich (1788-1866), German poet and Orientalist. He wrote many imitations of Oriental poetry, as well as 'Kindertotenlieder' (1834) set to music by Mahler

ruck·sack (rʌ́ksæk, rúksæk) *n.* a knapsack [G.]

ruck·us (rʌ́kəs) *n.* a noisy disturbance, argument etc. [prob. fr. RUCTION + RUMPUS]

ruc·tion (rʌ́kʃən) *n.* (*pop.,* often *pl.*) a row, noisy disturbance [origin unknown]

rud·beck·i·a (rʌdbéki:ə) *n.* a member of *Rudbeckia,* fam. *Compositae,* a genus of North American perennial plants cultivated for their showy, usually yellow, flowers || one of these flowers [after Olof *Rudbeck* (1630–1702), Swedish botanist]

rudd (rʌd) *n.* *Scardinius erythrophthalmus,* fam. *Cyprinidae,* a small common European freshwater fish having red irises and red fins [perh. O.E. *rudu,* red]

rud·der (rʌ́dər) *n.* a flat piece of wood or metal hinged vertically to a vessel's sternpost, used for steering || a similar device for controlling the direction of an aircraft's flight [O.E. *rōther*]

rud·di·ly (rʌ́dili:) *adv.* with a ruddy color

rud·di·ness (rʌ́di:nis) *n.* the quality or state of being ruddy

rud·dle (rʌ́d'l) **1.** *n.* red ocher, esp. that used for marking sheep **2.** *v.t. pres. part.* **rud·dling** *past* and *past part.* **rud·dled** to mark or color with ruddle [fr. older *rud,* red color, redness]

rud·dy (rʌ́di:) *comp.* **rud·di·er** *superl.* **rud·di·est** *adj.* red-tinted || glowing healthily, *ruddy cheeks* [O.E. *rudig*]

ruddy duck *Oxyura jamaicensis rubida,* an American broad-billed duck having a wedge-shaped tail and, in the drake, reddish upper parts

rude (ru:d) *comp.* **rud·er** *superl.* **rud·est** *adj.* very impolite, *rude behavior* || vulgar, *a rude story* || roughly put together, *rude carpentry* || crude, *a rude plow* || unexpectedly unpleasant, *a rude awakening, a rude shock* || (*rhet.*) uneducated, uncivilized || (*rhet.,* esp. of the wind or the sea) violent || (of health) vigorous [O.F. *ruide, rude*]

ru·di·ment (rú:dəmənt) *n.* (esp. *pl.*) a basic principle of a subject, *the rudiments of orchestration* || (esp. *pl.*) the merest beginning of something capable of being developed, *the rudiments of a plot* || (*biol.*) a part or organ beginning to develop || (*biol.*) a part or organ whose development has been arrested || (*biol.*) a vestigial part or organ **ru·di·men·ta·ri·ly** (ru:dəménterili:) *adv.* **ru·di·men·ta·ri·ness** (ru:dəméntəri:nis) *n.* **ru·di·men·ta·ry** (ru:dəméntəri:, ru:dəméntri:) *adj.* very elementary || (*biol.*) in an early or arrested stage of development || (*biol.*) vestigial [fr. L. *rudimentum,* beginning]

Ru·dolf (rú:dɒlf) a lake (area 3,500 sq. miles) extending from the southwest corner of Ethiopia through N.W. Kenya. It has no outlet and is surrounded by desert

Rudolf I (1218-91), king of Germany (1273-91), founder of the Hapsburg dynasty. He enlarged his kingdom at the expense of Ottocar II of Bohemia, whom he defeated (1278)

Rudolf II (1552-1612), Holy Roman Emperor (1576-1612), king of Hungary (1572-1608) and of Bohemia (1575-1611), son of Maximilian II. Unable to deal with attacks from Turkey and revolts in Hungary and Bohemia, he ceded his kingdoms to his brother Matthias

rue (ru:) *n.* *Ruta graveolens,* fam. *Rutaceae,* a perennial evergreen European shrub bearing yellow flowers. Its strongly scented, bitter leaves were formerly used as a narcotic and stimulant [F. fr. L. fr. Gk]

rue *pres. part.* **ru·ing** *past* and *past part.* **rued** *v.t.* (*old-fash.*) to regret, to repent of **to rue the day** to regret bitterly a particular moment, *you'll live to rue the day you left him* **rúe·ful** *adj.* regretful, sorrowful || arousing sorrow or regret [O.E. *hrēowan,* to grieve]

ru·fes·cence (ru:fés'ns) *n.* the state or quality of being rufescent

ru·fes·cent (ru:fés'nt) *adj.* red-tinged [fr. L. *rufescens* (*rufescentis*) fr. *rufescere,* to become red]

ruff (rʌf) *n.* a natural growth of hair or feathers around the neck of a bird or beast || (*hist.*) a broad starched collar of fluted linen or muslin worn by both men and women, esp. in the 16th c. [perh. fr. ROUGH adj.]

ruff *n.* *Acerina cernua,* fam. *Percidae,* a small, freshwater European fish [perh. fr. ROUGH because of its prickly scales]

ruff *n.* *Philomachus pugnax,* fam. *Scolopacidae,* a sandpiper of Europe and Asia. The male is about 11 ins long, the female (reeve) is smaller. In the breeding season, the male develops an enormous ruff of erectile feathers [perh. rel. to RUFF (growth of hair or feathers)]

ruff **1.** *n.* (*card games*) the act of trumping **2.** *v.i.* to play a trump card || *v.t.* to trump [fr. O.F. *roffle, rouffle,* a card game]

ruffed grouse (rʌft) *Bonasa umbellus,* fam. *Tetraonidae,* a North American reddish-black and gray game bird. The male (about 17 ins in length) has tufts of long black feathers on each side of its neck, and drums loudly with its wings during the mating season

ruf·fi·an (rʌ́fjən, rʌ́fi:ən) *n.* a man who is coarse, tough, brutal, and prepared to break the law || a boisterous, rascally boy **rúf·fi·an·ism** *n.* **rúf·fi·an·ly** *adj.* [O.F. *rufien, ruffian*]

ruf·fle (rʌ́fəl) **1.** *v. pres. part.* **ruf·fling** *past* and *past part.* **ruf·fled** *v.t.* to destroy the smoothness or regularity of, *the breeze ruffled her hair* || to disturb the self-possession of || (of a bird) to stiffen and to raise (the feathers) e.g. in fright or astonishment || to pucker up, gather (cloth, ribbon etc.) into a ruffle || *v.i.* to become disordered, broken up into little waves etc. || to become disturbed or confused **2.** *n.* an ornamental frill attached to a garment, esp. at the neckline or wrists || something resembling this, e.g. the ruff of a bird || a ripple on the surface of water [etym. doubtful]

ruffle **1.** *n.* (*mil.*) a low throbbing drumbeat **2.** *v.i. pres. part.* **ruf·fling** *past* and *past part.* **ruf·fled** (of a drum) to beat a ruffle [prob. imit.]

ru·fous (rú:fəs) *adj.* reddish-brown (used esp. of the color of animals) [fr. L. *rufus*]

rug (rʌg) *n.* a mat usually of thick wool used esp. to cover part of a floor || a mat made of an animal pelt placed directly on the floor or over a carpet || a thick blanket used as a bed covering or for wrapping around the knees when traveling etc. [perh. of Scand. origin]

rug·by (rʌ́gbi:) *n.* rugby football

rugby football a game which originated (1823) at Rugby School, England. It is played by two teams of 15 men (in Rugby Union) or 13 men (in Rugby League), with an elliptical football, on a rectangular field (110 yds by 75 yds) having an H-shaped goal at either end. Players may kick the ball or run with it in their hands, but may not pass, throw or knock it forwards. Tackling is allowed, and scrums are a feature of the game. Scoring is by points: in Rugby Union, 3 for a try, 5 for a try converted into a goal (the 3 for the try being discounted) and 3 for any other goals; in Rugby League, 3 for a try and 2 for any goal

Rü·gen (rýgən) an island (area 358 sq. miles, pop. 86,216) of Rostock district, East Germany. Industries: agriculture (livestock, cereals, sugar beets), fishing, tourism

rug·ged (rʌ́gid) *adj.* (of country) wild and broken || (of ground) very rough-surfaced || (of men's faces) having well-marked, usually irregular features suggesting a strong, generous character ‖ (of style) lacking polish ‖ (of a way of life) hard and austere ‖ hardy and vigorous, *rugged pioneers* [prob. of Scand. origin]

rug·ger (rʌ́gər) *n.* (*Br.*) rugby football

ru·gose (rú:gous) *adj.* (*bot.*, of leaves) wrinkled-looking because of having sunken veins and the spaces between them elevated **ru·gos·i·ty** (ru:gɔ́siti:) *n.* [fr. L. *rugosus*]

Ruhr (rúər, ru:r) a tributary (144 miles long) of the lower Rhine ‖ the district of North Rhine-Westphalia, West Germany, through which it flows, containing the largest concentration of industry on the mainland of Europe, based on vast local hard-coal deposits and iron ore from Sweden, Spain and France (Lorraine). Centers: Essen, Düsseldorf, Dortmund, Duisburg, Wuppertal, Gelsenkirchen, Bochum, Oberhausen, Cologne. The Ruhr was occupied (1923-5) by the French as a result of the Franco-German dispute over reparations

ru·in (rú:in) *n.* a state of advanced destruction or decay (physical or moral), *the house fell into ruin, drink led to his ruin* ‖ something or someone in this state, *the mansion is now a ruin* ‖ something which causes such a state, *this flood will be the ruin of the harvest* ‖ (*pl.*) the remains of something which has been destroyed or fallen into decay, *they wandered among the ruins of the old city* ‖ financial disaster [O.F *ruine*]

ruin *v.t.* to cause to become a ruin, *an earthquake ruined the city* ‖ to destroy, *it ruined his chances of success* ‖ (*loosely*) to spoil, *the rain ruined her hair* ‖ to wreck financially, *the inflation ruined him* [fr. F. *ruiner*]

ru·in·a·tion (rụ:inéiʃən) *n.* a ruining or being ruined ‖ a cause of ruin

ru·in·ous (rú:inəs) *adj.* causing or likely to cause ruin, *ruinous expense* ‖ ruined, dilapidated, *a ruinous estate* [F. *ruineux*]

Ruis·dael, Ruys·dael (ráizdɑl, ráisdɑl), Jacob van (c. 1628-82), Dutch landscape painter. He excelled in the painting of trees and woodlands beneath skies in which dark clouds are a foil to bright light. Little appreciated in his lifetime, his work was deeply influential on later Romantic landscape painting

Ru·iz (ru:í:θ), José Martinez *AZORIN

Ru·iz de A·lar·cón y Men·do·za (ru:í:sðeɑlɑrkɔ́ni:mendɔ́sɑ), Juan (c. 1581-1639), Mexican dramatist. His works include 'comedias de caracteres' (notably 'La verdad sospechosa', which was the inspiration of Corneille's 'le Menteur', and 'Las paredes oyen'), plays depicting social vices, and plays portraying the national herofigure

rule (ru:l) *n.* control by authority ‖ the reign of a monarch ‖ an accepted method of behavior or procedure, *rules of conduct, the rules of arithmetic* ‖ something which prevails generally or occurs normally, *after a victory, free drinks are the rule* ‖ a code of regulations setting forth the discipline under which members of a religious order live, *the Benedictine rule* ‖ (*pl.*) the body of official regulations setting forth the method of play in a sport, or the method of procedure in some other group activity ‖ (*law*) a regulation governing court procedure ‖ a ruler (strip of wood etc.) ‖ (*printing*) a thin metal strip used for making ornamental borders, separating headings etc. **as a rule** usually **to work to rule** (*Br.*, of organized labor) to obey in detail all the rules laid down, e.g. on safety, as a method of slowing production and so bringing force to bear on an employer [O.F. *riule, rule*]

rule *pres. part.* **rul·ing** *past* and *past part.* **ruled** *v.t.* to exercise authority or dominion over, *to rule a country* ‖ to exercise power over, esp. in enforcing obedience to one's own ideas of what is desirable, *to rule a household, to rule one's life with austerity* ‖ to decide or decree with authority ‖ to mark with straight lines, *ruled paper* ‖ to draw (a line) with a ruler ‖ *v.i.* to exercise authority or power ‖ to be the governing condition, *silence ruled in the assembly* ‖ (of prices) to be prevalent ‖ to decide a point of law or lay down a formal ruling **to rule (something) out** to exclude (something) from further consideration [O.F. *riuler, ruler*]

rule·mon·ger (rú:lmʌŋgər) *n.* a strict constructionist and strong enforcer of written rules, esp. in an authoritarian regime

rule-of-rum·mage (rú:ləvrʌ́midʒ) *n.* Supreme Court decision permitting police with warrants to search newspaper offices, etc., for information

rule of the road the rules governing vehicles or ships in their movements

rule of three a rule for finding the fourth term of a proportion where only three are given. The rule states that the product of the means equals the product of the extremes

rule of thumb a rough guide or principle, adequate working method

ru·ler (rú:lər) *n.* a sovereign ‖ someone who commands or dominates ‖ a strip of wood, metal etc., marked off in inches or centimeters, used in drawing straight lines, measuring etc.

ru·ling (rú:liŋ) **1.** *adj.* exercising sovereignty ‖ predominant, controlling, *a ruling passion* **2.** *n.* the act of someone who rules ‖ the drawing of a line or lines ‖ the line or lines drawn ‖ an authoritative decision, esp. (*law*) a decision of a judge or court

ru·ly English (rú:li:) English language adapted so that each word has a single meaning and each meaning a single word, utilized with a set of ambiguity-avoiding rules, esp. for patents, computer commands

rum (rʌm) *n.* an alcoholic liquor prepared by fermenting molasses, sugarcane etc. and distilling it. It is produced mainly in the West Indies [etym. doubtful]

rum *comp.* **rum·mer** *superl.* **rum·mest** *adj.* (*Br., pop.*) odd, queer [etym. doubtful]

Ru·ma·nian, Rou·ma·nian (ru:méinjən, ru:méini:ən) **1.** *n.* the Romance language of Rumania ‖ a native or inhabitant of Rumania **2.** *adj.* of or pertaining to Rumania, Rumanians or the Rumanian language

Ru·ma·nia, Rou·ma·nia (ru:méinjə, ru:méini:ə) a republic (area 91,671 sq. miles, pop. 22,510,000) in S.E. Europe. Capital: Bucharest. People and languages: 86% Rumanian, 9% Magyar, 2% German, Ukrainian, Gypsy, Yugoslav, Russian and other minorities. Religion: 80% Orthodox, 6% Roman Catholic, 5% Calvinist, 2% Lutheran, small Jewish, Moslem and Protestant minorities. The land is 44% arable, 17% pasture and 27% forest (mainly evergreen). The E. Carpathians (Pietros, 7,568 ft) and the Transylvanian Alps (Negoi, 8,346 ft) cross the country diagonally from north and south meeting in the east center. With the Bihor massif (6,000 ft) in the west they enclose the cultivated Transylvanian plateau (1,000–1,600 ft). The mountains are surrounded north-west, west, south, and east, by the Hungarian, Banat, Walachian and Moldavian plains. The Black Sea coast (Dobruja) is flat. The Danube, cutting through the Transylvanian Alps at the Iron Gate, forms most of the southern border. Average temperatures (F.): Bucharest 9° (Jan.) and 72° (July). Rainfall: 10-20 ins in Dobruja, Moldavia and Walachia, 20-30 ins in the west and the central basin, 30-60 ins in the mountains. Livestock: cattle, sheep, hogs, poultry, horses. Agricultural products: cereals, potatoes, root vegetables, tobacco, grapes, plums and other fruit. Fishing is important in the Danube delta and the Black Sea. Mineral resources: oil (esp. Ploesti), coal, natural gas, salt, iron ore, lignite, copper, bauxite, chromium, other metals. Other resources: timber, hydroelectricity. Manufactures and industries: iron and steel, mining, machinery, oil refining, shipbuilding, chemicals, paper, cement, sugar, edible oils, textiles, light manufactures, electrical equipment, vehicles. Exports: oil, cement, lumber, tractors, machinery, ships, oilfield and factory equipment, corn, foodstuffs. Imports: iron ore, metals, industrial plant, coke, electric cables, diesel engines. Chief ports: Constanta, Galati. Universities: Iasi (1860), Bucharest (1864), Cluj (1872), Timisoara (1945). Monetary unit: leu (100 bani). HISTORY. The region formed the Roman province of Dacia (2nd-3rd cc.), was invaded by Visigoths, Huns, Lombards and Avars (4th-5th cc.) and was settled by Slavs (6th c.) and Bulgarians (7th c.). It became divided (late 13th c.) into the principalities of Moldavia and Walachia, which became vassals of the Ottoman Empire (15th and 16th cc.), were briefly united (early 17th c.) and were involved in the Russo-Turkish Wars. Revolutions were put down (1821) by the Turks and the principalities were occupied (1829-34) by the Russians after the Treaty of Adrianople. More revolutions failed (1848) and the principalities were jointly occupied by the Turks and the Russians. Conflicts over navigation rights on the Danube were a cause of the Crimean War. Moldavia and Walachia formed a personal union (1859) and were officially united as Rumania (1861). Under Carol I constitutional and economic progress was made and, after the Congress of Berlin (1878), the country became an independent kingdom (1881). Rumania gained S. Dobruja after the 2nd Balkan War (1913) and joined the Allies (1916) in the 1st world war, after which it received Transylvania, Bukovina, Banat and Bessarabia. Agrarian reforms broke up most of the large estates, but political chaos weakened the country. Carol II established (1930) a fascist dictatorship, but was deposed (1940) and Antonescu became dictator, supporting the Axis in the 2nd world war. King Michael overthrew Antonescu (1944) and formed an alliance with the Allies. Communists gained a majority (1946), Michael abdicated (1947) and Rumania became a people's republic. It joined the U.N. and the Warsaw Pact (1955); it is also a member of COMECON. It became a socialist republic (1965) but maintains a foreign policy independent of the Soviet Union

rum·ba, rhum·ba (rʌ́mbə, rúmbə) *n.* an Afro-Cuban dance ‖ a ballroom version of this ‖ the music for this dance [Span.]

rum·ble (rʌ́mb'l) **1.** *v. pres. part.* **rum·bling** *past* and *past part.* **rum·bled** *v.i.* to make a dull, rolling sound, *the thunder rumbled in the distance* ‖ to move with such a sound, *the cart rumbled slowly down the street* ‖ *v.t.* to utter in a deep, gruff voice, *to rumble a reply* ‖ to polish (small metal parts) in a tumbling box **2.** *n.* a rumbling sound ‖ a tumbling box [imit.]

rumble seat (*Am.*=*Br.* dickey) an open-air seat at the back of some automobiles

rum·bus·tious (rʌmbʌ́stʃəs) *adj.* (*pop.*) rambunctious [fr. earlier *robustious*, robust]

Ru·me·lia (ru:mí:ljə, ru:mí:li:ə) a former region of the Ottoman Empire, comprising the provinces of Thrace and Macedonia. Eastern Rumelia was made an autonomous province (1878) and was annexed (1885) by Bulgaria

ru·men (rú:min) *pl.* **ru·mi·na** (rú:minə), **ru·mens** *n.* the first chamber of a ruminant's stomach [L.=throat]

Rum·ford (rʌ́mfərd), Benjamin Thompson, Count (1753-1814), American scientist who spent the major part of his life in England. He is known chiefly for his measurements on the production of heat by mechanical work

Ru·mi·ña·hui (rụ:minjáwi:) (*d.* 1534), Inca cacique, adviser and general of Atahualpa, upon whose death he proclaimed himself sovereign. His stubborn resistance to the conquistadores ended in his execution

ru·mi·nant (rú:minənt) **1.** *n.* any member of the order *Artiodactyla*, suborder *Ruminantia*, e.g. the sheep, cow, camel, llama, goat, giraffe, deer. These animals are all even-toed and hoofed, and all chew the cud and have a stomach consisting of four chambers **2.** *adj.* of or relating to one of these animals ‖ meditative [fr. L. *ruminans* (*ruminantis*) fr. *ruminare*, to ruminate]

ru·mi·nate (rú:mineit) *pres. part.* **ru·mi·nat·ing** *past* and *past part.* **ru·mi·nat·ed** *v.i.* to chew the cud ‖ to reflect at length ‖ *v.t.* to ponder over [fr. L. *ruminari* (*ruminatus*)]

ru·mi·na·tion (rụ:minéiʃən) *n.* the act or process of ruminating [fr. L. *ruminatio* (*ruminationis*)]

ru·mi·na·tive (rú:minẹitiv) *adj.* ruminating or apt to ruminate

rum·mage (rʌ́midʒ) **1.** *v. pres. part.* **rum·mag·ing** *past* and *past part.* **rum·maged** *v.i.* to make a search, esp. by turning things over or otherwise creating disorder, *to rummage in a drawer* ‖ *v.t.* to search through (a place etc.) thoroughly, ransack **2.** *n.* things found or turned up by rummaging, odds and ends ‖ a search made by rummaging [origin unknown]

rummage sale a sale of odds and ends, usually to raise money for charity

rum·mer (rʌ́mər) *n.* a large upright drinking vessel, esp. for wine [Du. *romer, roemer*]

rum·my (rʌ́mi:) *n.* a simple card game won by the first player to match all his cards into sets, sequences of three etc. by drawing cards from the stock and discarding others and declaring the sets he has made

ru·mor, *Br.* **ru·mour** (rú:mər) **1.** *n.* an unauthenticated story or report put into circulation, *an idle rumor* **2.** *v.t.* to spread or report by rumor [O.F.]

rump (rʌmp) *n.* the upper hindquarters of an animal ‖ the posterior of a bird ‖ a cut of beef between the loin and the round ‖ the buttocks ‖ a remnant, esp. of a parliament or other body [prob. of Scand. orig.]

rum·ple (rʌ́mp'l) **1.** *v. pres. part.* **rum·pling** *past* and *past part.* **rum·pled** *v.t.* to make (hair, clothes etc.) disorderly, wrinkled etc. ‖ *v.i.* to become wrinkled **2.** *n.* a wrinkle in clothes etc. [fr. M. Du. *rompelen*]

Rump Parliament (*Eng. hist.*) the name given to the Long Parliament after Pride's Purge (1648) had reduced it to about 50 antiroyalists who ordered the execution (1649) of Charles I

rum·pus (rʌ́mpəs) *n.* (*pop.*) an uproar, disturbance, row [origin unknown]

run (rʌn) **1.** *v. pres. part.* **run·ning** *past* **ran** (ræn) *past part.* **run** *v.i.* (of persons and animals) to move rapidly over the ground with long, usually even, strides in such a way that for a moment the feet are off the ground ‖ to escape by moving in this way, *he grabbed the gun and ran* ‖ to go rapidly, *run for the doctor* ‖ to move about without restraint, *the lions ran loose in the streets* ‖ to compete in a race‖ to finish a race in a specified place, *who ran third?* ‖ to be a candidate in an election ‖ (with 'up', 'down' etc.) to make a quick, casual trip, *to run up to London for a day* ‖ to move on or as if on wheels ‖ to move with a smooth, gliding motion, *the rope runs in the pulley* ‖ to go regularly between two places, *the ferry runs every three hours* ‖ to circulate, *rumors ran through the crowd* ‖ to flow rapidly, *water ran down the pipe* ‖ to melt and flow, *the ice cream is starting to run* ‖ to be covered with a flow, *her eyes were running with tears, the gutters are running with water* ‖ (of a sore etc.) to discharge pus etc. ‖ (of the nose) to exude mucus ‖ (esp. with 'through' or 'in') to force itself again and again into the conscious mind, *the song kept running through his head* ‖ (of a theatrical production) to be presented, *the play ran for six months* ‖ (of fish) to swim in migration ‖ to be in operation, *the motor is still running* ‖ (with 'by' or 'into') to elapse, *the years ran by, the weeks ran into months* ‖ to be impelled, *the ship ran on a rock* ‖ to continue in effect, *the contract has two more years to run* ‖ to average a specified size, *trout are running large this year* ‖ to be at a specified level or average, *casualties are running high, sales are running just above last year's figures* ‖ (with 'in') to be a hereditary feature, *insanity runs in the family* ‖ (of liquids, e.g. ink) to spread on being applied to a surface ‖ (of colors in a fabric) to spread or become mixed together when washed or moistened ‖ to extend in time, *the holiday ran into a third week* ‖ to proceed, *the poem runs like this* ‖ to merge, *the two towns run into one another* ‖ to extend in a certain direction or course, *bookshelves run across the left side of the room, the road runs through mountains* ‖ to proliferate unchecked, *dry rot ran all through the roof* ‖ (of vines) to creep and climb ‖ to pass lightly and rapidly, *fire ran through the stubble* ‖ (with 'into') to pass into a specified situation, condition etc., *to run into trouble, to run into debt* ‖ (of a stocking etc.) to develop a vertical flaw because of the breaking of a longitudinal thread ‖ *v.t.* to cause to move, operate etc., *to run a tractor* ‖ to cause (e.g. a vehicle) to go in a specified direction, *to run a car into a ditch* ‖ to enter (a horse) in a race ‖ to enter (someone) as a candidate in an election ‖ to do by or as if by running, *to run a race, to run an errand* ‖ to traverse by or as if by running, *he ran the full length of the room, let the situation run its course* ‖ to roam about in, *to run the streets* ‖ to hunt, *to run a fox to earth*‖ to smuggle ‖ (with 'into' or 'through') to cause to pierce, *to run a needle into one's finger* ‖ (with 'into' or 'against') to cause to be thrust, *to run one's head into a wall* ‖ to force or contrive one's way through, or attempt to get through (a blockade etc.) ‖ (of a newspaper) to publish (e.g. a story) ‖ to cause (a liquid) to flow, *run the water into that ditch* ‖ to manage or control, *to run a factory* ‖ to cause to extend in a particular direction or manner, *run the rope between those two trees* ‖ to cause to pass quickly over, along etc., *to run one's fingers over a shelf* ‖ to cast (e.g. bullets) in a mold ‖ to convey in a ship or vehicle ‖ to bring to a specific state by or as if by running, *to run oneself to death, to run someone into debt* ‖ to sew with rapid stitches, *run a hem around the cuff* ‖ to have (an account) which is allowed to accumulate for a certain length of time **to run across** to meet by chance **to run after** to chase, *to run after a thief* ‖ (*pop.*) to pursue amorously, *to run after girls* **to run around** to go out a great deal, esp. in pursuit of pleasures, esp. through casual sexual adventures **to run a temperature** to have a fever **to run away** to flee ‖ to elope ‖ (esp. of children) to leave home without parental consent ‖ (esp. of a horse being driven or ridden) to get completely out of control **to run away with** to take over emotional control of, *his temper ran away with him* **to run down** (of a clock) to become in need of winding ‖ to run against and knock down ‖ (*pop.*) to disparage or abuse ‖ (*baseball*) to tag out (a base runner) between bases **to run dry** to become empty of water or other liquid ‖ to cease to have ideas, inspiration etc. **to run foul of** to come into conflict with, *to run foul of the law* **to run free** (*naut.*) to sail with the wind coming from behind the beam **to run in** (*pop.*) to arrest ‖ to operate (new machinery, e.g. an automobile engine) over a specified period at restricted speed so as to adjust bearing surfaces to one another ‖ (*printing*) to run on ‖ to pay a quick, usually casual, visit **to run into** to collide with ‖ to meet by accident, *to run into an old classmate* ‖ to amount to, *it ran into hundreds of dollars* **to run low** to become depleted or scarce, *money was running low* **to run off** to print (an edition or specified number of copies) ‖ to cause (a race) to be run ‖ to flee, *he snatched the package and ran off* **to run on** to continue ‖ to talk continuously ‖ (*printing*) to set (typeset matter) on the same line as what precedes **to run out** to come to an end, *his patience has run out* ‖ to cause to leave by force ‖ (*cricket*) to put (a batsman) out while he is running between the wickets ‖ (*cricket*, of a batsman) to leave the crease and go up the pitch to hit a ball being bowled **to run out of** to come to the end of, esp. prematurely **to run out on** (*pop.*) to desert, leave, forsake, *to run out on one's wife* **to run over** to drive or ride over, *to run over a dog* ‖ to flow over the edge of ‖ to make a rapid review of, *to run over some notes* ‖ to flow over the edge of a container **to run short** to begin to cease to be plentiful ‖ to be left with less than enough **to run short of** to come to have less than enough of **to run (someone) ragged** to exhaust (someone) physically **to run through** to transpierce ‖ to spend quickly and completely, *to run through a fortune* ‖ to examine rapidly, *to run through the accounts* ‖ to rehearse (e.g. a play) without pausing **to run to** (*Br.*) to be sufficient for, *his income won't run to two holidays a year* ‖ (*Br.*) to be able to afford, *we can't run to a new car this year* **to run up** to make rapidly (by sewing), *to run up a skirt in an afternoon* ‖ to add (figures) rapidly ‖ to construct hastily, *to run up a shed in the garden* ‖ to accumulate, *his debts ran up over the years* **to run wild** to run riot ‖ to grow in disorderly confusion, *roses running wild* **2.** *n.* an act or period of running ‖ the distance covered in running ‖ the time spent in running ‖ (of a theatrical production) a continuous succession of performances ‖ a prolonged period of being in a specified condition, *a run of good luck* ‖ a continuous series or sequence of similar or identical things, *a run of misprints* ‖ a mass withdrawal of funds by depositors, usually provoked by panic, *a run on a bank* ‖ an abnormally high demand from buyers for some article or class of articles, *a run on sugar* ‖ a kind or class, e.g. of goods, *the ordinary run of ski boots* ‖ the average or usual level of people or things, *he is above the run of politicians* ‖ (with 'the') unrestricted access to a place, *he gave them the run of the library* ‖ a track used habitually by animals, *a rat run* ‖ an enclosure for livestock large enough for them to exercise in ‖ a number of fish migrating together ‖ a vertical flaw in a stocking caused by the breaking of a longitudinal thread ‖ a short, usually quick, journey ‖ the regularly traveled route or course covered by a train, ship etc. ‖ the distance covered in a period of sailing etc. ‖ general tendency, *the run of the market* ‖ general direction, *the run of the streets is away from the river* ‖ a rush of tidal water ‖ a small stream ‖ the period in which a machine is in operation ‖ an amount of work turned out in one operation ‖ (*printing*) an edition size, *a run of 20,000 copies* ‖ (*baseball*) the point scored by a player in completing a circuit of the bases ‖ (*cricket*) the point scored by a batsman in moving without penalty from one popping crease to the other ‖ (*mil.*) the part of a bombing sortie during which the bomber approaches the target and releases its bombs ‖ (*naut.*) the bottom of a ship where it rises from the keel and bilge, narrowing in to the stern ‖ (*mining*) a sudden fall of a mass of earth ‖ (*mining*) an inclined passage between levels ‖ a downward course, e.g. for skiing ‖ a track, course, channel etc. on or along which something moves ‖ the bower of a bower-bird **in the long run** measured over a prolonged period of time **on the run** retreating in disorderly haste ‖ trying to escape capture, e.g. by police [partly fr. O.E. *rinnan*, partly fr. O.N. *rinna, renna*]

run·a·bout (rʌ́nəbaut) *n.* a small, easily parked, economical automobile used for short journeys, shopping expeditions etc. ‖ a small motorboat used for pleasure trips ‖ a person who goes out a great deal in pursuit of pleasure, esp. through casual sexual adventures

run·a·way (rʌ́nəwei) **1.** *n.* a fugitive ‖ a horse running out of control ‖ a runaway race, victory etc. **2.** *adj.* escaping ‖ (of a marriage) achieved by eloping ‖ (of a race, victory etc.) easily won ‖ (of prices etc.) rising very rapidly

runaway shop business that relocates in a distant area to avoid labor difficulties, esp. with unions

run·ci·nate (rʌ́nsinit, rʌ́nsineit) *adj.* (of leaves) pinnate with their other divisions pointing towards the base (e.g. in the dandelion) [fr. L. *runcina*, a plane]

run·down (rʌ́ndáun) *adj.* in poor health ‖ exhausted ‖ dilapidated ‖ (of clocks) stopped because not wound **run·down** (rʌ́ndaun) *n.* a summary ‖ (*baseball*) the act of running down a base runner

Rund·stedt (rúntʃtet), Karl Rudolf Gerd von (1875-1953), German field marshal. He commanded a group of armies in Poland, France and Russia (1939-41). In command of the German western front (1942-4), he was the effective military ruler of France. His Ardennes counteroffensive (Dec. 1944) failed

rune (ru:n) one of the characters of an ancient alphabet used for making inscriptions and magic signs by the Germanic peoples, esp. the Scandinavians and Anglo-Saxons. The characters were supposedly formed by adapting Greek or Roman letters for carving on wood ‖ a Finnish poem or a division of one ‖ an ancient Norse poem [O.N. *rūn*]

rung (rʌŋ) *n.* a crosspiece in a ladder ‖ a bar joining the legs of a chair ‖ a spoke in a wheel [O.E. *hrung*]

rung *past part.* of RING

ru·nic (rú:nik) *adj.* of or relating to a rune or runes ‖ consisting of runes, *runic poetry* [fr. Mod. L. *runicus* fr. O.N. *rūn*, a rune]

run-in (rʌ́nin) *n.* (*pop.*) a minor altercation, *a run-in with the milkman* ‖ (*printing*) an additional insertion in copy or typeset material

run·let (rʌ́nlit) *n.* a small stream

run·nel (rʌ́n'l) *n.* a small channel ‖ a small stream [O.E. *rynel*]

run·ner (rʌ́nər) *n.* a person who or animal which runs, esp. in a race ‖ a person who runs errands, esp. for a brokerage house ‖a smuggler ‖ a ship carrying smuggled goods ‖ (*bot.*) a stolon ‖ (*bot.*) a plant that creeps by means of these ‖ (*loosely*) any of various twining plants ‖ the blade of an ice skate ‖ a decorative strip of cloth, lace etc. to be laid on a table, dresser etc. ‖ a long strip or carpet for a corridor, staircase etc. ‖ either of the pieces on which a sled or sledge slides ‖ (*naut.*) a rope with a hook at one end rove through a single block and run around a tackle block ‖ a groove along which something (e.g. a drawer) slides ‖ a roller for moving a heavy object ‖ (*metall.*) the trough through which molten metal flows on its way to the mold ‖ a run in a stocking ‖ the water rail ‖ the revolving stone of a pair of millstones [M.E. *rennere* fr. *rennen*, to run]

runner bean (*Br.*) a string bean

run·ner-up (rʌ́nərʌ́p) *pl.* **run·ners-up** *n.* a competitor or team coming second in a contest etc.

run·ning (rʌ́niŋ) **1.** *n.* the act of a person or thing that runs **in (out of) the running** having a good chance (no chance) of winning a competition **2.** *adj.* moving at a run ‖done while running, *a running fight* ‖ performed with a run, *a running play* ‖ uninterrupted, *running fire* ‖ flowing, *running water* ‖ sliding, able to slip, *a running knot* ‖ (of machines) operating ‖ discharging pus, *a running sore* ‖ measured in a straight line, *per running foot* **3.** *adv.* successively, *three months running*

running board a footboard on either side of a vehicle

running commentary a verbal (esp. broadcast) description of the events of a game etc. as they occur

running dog lackey; collaborator

running fix (*mil.*) the intersection of two or more position lines, not obtained simultaneously, adjusted to a common time
running head a running title
running mate a horse entered in a race to set the pace for another expected to win ‖ a candidate competing for a subordinate place, esp. the office of vice-president
running title a short heading or title printed at the top of each text page or at the top of each left-hand text page
Run·ny·mede (rʌ́nimi:d) a meadow on the south bank of the Thames, three miles downstream from Windsor, where Magna Carta was signed (1215)
run·off (rʌ́nɔf, rʌ́nɒf) *n.* a final contest, made necessary because a previous contest was drawn or without a result ‖ water drained from surface soil
run-of-the-mill (rʌ́nəvðəmíl) *adj.* not outstanding in quality, ordinary, *a run-of-the-mill group of students*
run-on (rʌ́nɔn, rʌ́nɒn) *adj.* (*printing*) immediately appended without any break ‖ (*poetry*) continuing without pause from one line into the next
runt (rʌnt) (*Br.*) an ox or cow of a small breed ‖ any small animal, esp. the smallest in a litter of pigs ‖ (*pop.*, used disparagingly) an undersized person [etym. doubtful]
run-up (rʌ́nʌp) *n.* (*Br.*) prelude
run-up area (*mil.*) a zone within the maneuvering area reserved for testing aircraft engines prior to take-off
run·way (rʌ́nwei) *n.* a strip on an airfield for taking off or landing ‖ a gangway ‖ a slope down which logs are slid ‖ the trail made by animals in going to and from their regular feeding places ‖an enclosed area in which chickens etc. are kept
Run·yon (rʌ́njən), (Alfred) Damon (1884-1946), U.S. writer of humorous short stories, notably 'Guys and Dolls' (1931), 'Blue Plate Special' (1934), and 'Money from Home' (1935), which portray underworld characters in New York City
ru·pee (ru:pí:, rú:pi:) *n.* the monetary unit of India, Pakistan, Ceylon and Nepal ‖ the monetary unit of Mauritius, Seychelles and some areas of the Arabian peninsula ‖ a coin worth one rupee [fr. Urdu *rūpiyah*]
Ru·pert (rú:pərt), Prince (1619-82), count palatine of the Rhine, duke of Bavaria, nephew of Charles I of England. He distinguished himself as a royalist cavalry leader in the English Civil War and, later, as an admiral in the Dutch Wars
ru·pi·ah (ru:pí:ə) *pl.* **ru·pi·ah, ru·pi·ahs** *n.* the basic monetary unit of Indonesia ‖ a note worth one rupiah [Hindi *rūpaiyā*, rupee]
rup·ture (rʌ́ptʃər) **1.** *n.* a drastic break in harmonious relations between individuals or nations ‖ a hernia ‖ the tearing apart of a muscle or other bodily part ‖ a breaking apart ‖ the state of being broken apart **2.** *v. pres. part.* **rup·tur·ing** *past* and *past part.* **rup·tured** *v.t.* to cause a break in ‖ to cause a hernia in ‖ *v.i.* to suffer a rupture [F.]
rupture zone (*mil.*) the region immediately adjacent to the crater boundary after an explosion characterized by the appearance of numerous radial cracks of various sizes. *Cf* PLASTIC ZONE
RUR-5A *ANTISUBMARINE ROCKET
ru·ral (rúərəl) *adj.* of, relating to, or characteristic of the country or of people living in the country (opp. URBAN) [F. or fr. L. *ruralis*]
rural dean a clergyman ranking below an archdeacon and responsible for a district containing a number of rural parishes
rural free delivery (*abbr.* R.F.D., R.D.) the free delivery, by postal employees, of mail in rural areas
ru·ri·de·ca·nal (ruəridikéin'l, ruəridékən'l) *adj.* of or relating to a rural dean or rural deanery [fr. L. *rus* (*ruris*), country+DECANAL]
Ru·rik (rúərik) (*d.* 879), Varangian chief. He established control over Novgorod (c. 862). His descendants ruled Russia until 1598
Ru·ri·ta·nian (ruəritéinjən, ruəritéini:ən) *adj.* of or like the imaginary European kingdom of Ruritania, where all is romantic gaiety and adventure, court intrigue and royal splendor [after the setting of two novels by Anthony Hope (Sir Anthony Hope Hawkins, 1863–1933), Eng. novelist]
rurp (*acronym*) for released ultimate reality piton, a sharp, pointed tool, used in mountaineering
Ru·se (rú:sei) (formerly Ruschuk) the chief inland port (pop. 170,594) of Bulgaria, on the Danube
ruse (ru:z) *n.* a piece of cunning, *a ruse to escape taxation* ‖ cunning, *ruse and influence got him the appointment* [F.]
Rush (rʌʃ), Benjamin (1745-1813), U.S. physician. He became (1769) the first professor of chemistry in the U.S.A., at what became the University of Pennsylvania, where he introduced clinical instruction. He pioneered in the treatment and care of mental patients, and his 'Medical Inquiries and Observations Upon the Diseases of the Mind' (1812) was the first systematic U.S. work on the subject
Rush, Richard (1780-1859), U.S. statesman and diplomat, son of Benjamin Rush. Attorney general (1814-17) under President James Madison, and temporary secretary of state (1817), he negotiated with Charles Bagot the Rush-Bagot Treaty providing for the demilitarization of the Great Lakes. As minister to Great Britain (1817-25), he negotiated the Convention of 1818. He helped to found (1836) the Smithsonian Institution
rush (rʌʃ) **1.** *v.i.* to move with speed and violence, *the boys rushed down the corridor* ‖ to hasten, *he rushed to help her* ‖ to appear or seem to appear swiftly, *tears rushed to her eyes, the idea rushed into his mind* ‖ to act swiftly with too little reflection, *don't rush into divorce* ‖ *v.t.* to cause to move or be moved with great speed, *they rushed the child to the doctor* ‖ to cause to decide or act hastily, *to rush someone into marriage* ‖ to get past or over with violent movement, *they rushed the barrier* ‖ to take by sudden attack, *to rush an enemy position* ‖ (*football*) to carry (the ball) forward in a running play ‖ (*football*) to move in on (a player) in order to block a kick or pass ‖ (*pop.*) to court (a girl) assiduously ‖ to entertain (a prospective member of a sorority or fraternity) as a means of persuasion into membership **to rush at** to charge **to rush into print** to publish after too little work or experience **to rush someone off his feet** to make a person do too much in too short a time ‖ to upset or try to upset a person's judgment by harrying him **2.** *n.* a violent forward movement or the sound of it, *the rush of water* ‖ a movement of many people to a place or region to be occupied or exploited, *a rush for the corner seats* ‖ feverish movement, *the rush of city life* ‖ a sudden burst of activity, *a rush of work* ‖ the state of being busy and pressed for time, *she was always in a rush* ‖ violent inflow, *a rush of blood to the head* ‖ (of an emotion) a sudden access, *a rush of tenderness* ‖ the first surge of pleasures produced by a drug ‖ (with 'on') a great demand for a commodity ‖ (*soccer*) a sudden attack by several players ‖ (*football*) the act of carrying the ball during a game ‖ (*movies*, esp. *pl.*) the first print of a sequence of filming, for inspection by the director etc. **3.** *adj.* needing to be dealt with or done very quickly, *a rush order* ‖ characterized by enormous bustle and activity, *the rush hour* [A.F. *russher*]
rush *n.* any of various members of *Juncus*, fam. *Juncaceae*, or *Scirpus*, fam. *Cyperaceae*, plants having cylindrical and often hollow stems which are used for making chair seats, mats, baskets etc. [O. E. *risc, rìsce*]
rush·light (rʌ́ʃlait) *n.* a rude candle made by dipping the peeled pith of various rushes in grease
Rush·more, Mount (rʌ́ʃmɔr, rʌ́ʃmour) a peak in the Black Hills of South Dakota which has 60-ft busts of Washington, Jefferson, Lincoln and Theodore Roosevelt carved in it by John Gutzon Borglum (1867-1941)
Rusk (rʌsk), (David) Dean (1909–), U.S. secretary of state (1961-8) under Presidents John Kennedy and Lyndon Johnson. He advocated negotiation with Communist powers from a position of national strength and more extensive aid to underdeveloped countries
rusk (rʌsk) *n.* a slice of crisp, twice-baked bread often sweetened [Span. *rosca*, a twisted roll of bread]
Rus·kin (rʌ́skin), John (1819-1900), English critic and essayist. He made his name as an art critic with the first part of 'Modern Painters' (1843), begun as a defense of Turner. Visits to Switzerland and Italy—esp. to Venice—led to 'The Seven Lamps of Architecture' (1849) and 'The Stones of Venice' (1851-3). 'Modern Painters' continued to appear until 1860. In 1853 Ruskin began his career as a lecturer, mainly on art but later also on economic, social and general cultural subjects. 'Sesame and Lilies' (1865) was the most popular collection. Later works include 'Fors Clavigera' (1871-84), a series of letters to the working men of England, and 'Praeterita' (1885-9), his autobiography. He was a profound critic of art, and his range was wide, though he had little sympathy for 'advanced' contemporary work. He was also a profound social critic, emphasizing the distinction between mere wealth and true social welfare, and between mechanical labor and craftsmanship. Like Dickens and Morris, he laid his finger on the defects of the new industrial society
Rus·sell (rʌ́s'l), Bertrand, 3rd Earl Russell (1872-1970), British philosopher. His 'Principles of Mathematics' (1903) led to 'Principia Mathematica' (1910-13, in collaboration with Whitehead), a research into symbolic logic. Other writings include 'An Outline of Philosophy' (1927) and 'Philosophy and Politics' (1947)
Russell, Henry Norris (1877-1957), U.S. astronomer. He invented (1913, with Ejnar Hertzsprung of Denmark) the Russell diagram, which determined the distances from the solar system of double stars which are telescopically observed to be in revolution about their common center of gravity
Russell, Lord John, 1st Earl Russell (1792-1878), British Whig statesman. A liberal reformer, he supported the Catholic Emancipation Act (1829) and was largely responsible for the Reform Act of 1832. He brought in other reforms as home secretary (1835-9) and was prime minister (1846-52 and 1865-6)
Russell, Lord William (1639-83), English statesman. One of the leaders of the Whig campaign to exclude the future James II from the succession, he was unjustly executed for alleged complicity in the Rye House Plot
rus·set (rʌ́sit) **1.** *n.* a color between red and brown ‖ a variety of rough-skinned russet-colored eating apple ‖ (*hist.*) coarse homespun cloth worn by peasants **2.** *adj.* reddish-brown [O.F. *rousset*]
Rus·sia (rʌ́ʃə) a former country of E. Europe and Asia which developed out of the grand duchy of Moscow, and which became (1917) the Union of Soviet Socialist Republics. The name is loosely used for the U.S.S.R., but is properly applied only to the R.S.F.S.R., esp. the European part. HISTORY. The Scythians, inhabiting the steppes from before the 7th c. B.C., were displaced (3rd c. B.C.) by the Sarmatians. The steppes were successively invaded by the Goths (3rd c. A.D.), the Huns (4th c.) and the Avars (6th c.). The Khazars established an empire in the southeast (7th–early 11th cc.) and the Bulgars founded a state (8th-13th cc.) in the region of the Volga. The Eastern Slavs settled in the Ukraine (c. 9th c.). A Russian state originated in the conquests (9th c.) of the Varangians, Viking warriors who established their capital at Kiev. Greek Orthodox Christianity became the official religion (c. 988). Trade with Scandinavia, Byzantium and the Middle East prospered but, after the attacks of the Cumans (11th c.), Kiev declined (12th c.). Russia was overrun (1237-40) by the Golden Horde and under the rule of the Tatars Moscow emerged as the dominant principality (14th c.). During the reign (1462-1505) of Ivan III, Novgorod and much of N. Russia were conquered, and Moscow asserted its independence against the Tatars (1480). Ivan IV's reign (1533-84) brought conquests in the lower Volga, extending Muscovite territory south to the Caspian. Ivan took the title of czar, established an autocracy, and did much to reduce the power of the boyars. Boris Godunov seized power on the death (1598) of Ivan's weak-minded son, and faced the opposition of the boyars and the Cossacks, and the threat of pretenders to the throne. Disorder followed Godunov's death (1605) and Sigismund III of Poland, in alliance with the boyars and the Cossacks, occupied Moscow (1610-12). After a national uprising (1612), Michael Romanov was elected czar (1613). Order was restored but, despite the growth of trade with the West, Moscow remained largely isolated from Europe. Colonization began to spread toward the Pacific. The nobles' rights over the serfs were increased, until serfdom was little better than slavery (17th c.). The rule of the czars became even more absolute. Peter I, who had traveled widely in Europe, began to westernize and modernize the country during his reign (1689-

1725). The army was reorganized and a navy founded. The Church was made subject to the State, and the capital was moved from Moscow to St Petersburg (1713). The upper classes were forced to adopt Western clothes, and educational institutions were founded on Western lines. The Northern War (1700-21) resulted in the acquisition of Livonia and other Baltic territories. The Russo-Turkish Wars enabled Russia to expand toward the Balkans. After Peter's death (1725), Russian participation in European affairs continued to increase. Russia supported Austria in the War of the Polish Succession (1733-5) and, under Elizabeth, fought Prussia in the Seven Years' War (1756-63). During the reign (1762-96) of Catherine II, Russia became a leading European power, gaining vast territories in the partitions of Poland (1772, 1793, 1795), by the Treaty of Kuchuk Kainarji (1774), and by the annexation of the Crimea (1783). After a rising of Cossacks and serfs (1773), the central autocracy was strengthened. Under the influence of the French Enlightenment, literature and the arts flourished. Catherine's son and successor, the mentally unstable Paul I, was assassinated (1801), and succeeded by Alexander I. Russia opposed France in the Napoleonic Wars, but was forced to make peace at Tilsit (1807). Russian territory expanded with the acquisition of Finland (1809), Bessarabia (1812) and Caucasia (1813). Russian reluctance to adhere to the Continental System led to an unsuccessful Napoleonic invasion (1812). Russia took a leading part in the Congress of Vienna (1814-15) and in the establishment of the reactionary Holy Alliance (1815). On Alexander's death (1825), the liberal Decembrist movement failed in its attempt to prevent his brother Nicholas I from succeeding to the throne, and a period of repression began. Russian troops put down risings in Poland (1830-1) and revolution in Hungary (1848-9), but Russia's attempt to extend its influence toward Constantinople met with a severe defeat in the Crimean War (1853-6). This was followed by a period of liberal reform during the reign (1855-81) of Alexander II. The serfs were emancipated (1861), but agrarian conditions failed to improve. The courts were reformed, and a limited form of self-government was provided by the introduction of zemstvos (1864). Under Gorchakov, Russia's foreign policy concentrated on expansion into Caucasia and central Asia, but renewed attempts to expand at the expense of Turkey were crushed at the Congress of Berlin (1878). The late 19th c. saw rapid industrial progress as the construction of railroads enabled Russia's vast resources to be brought into use. Siberia was opened up by the Trans-Siberian Railroad, begun in 1891. A Populist conspiracy resulted in the assassination (1881) of Alexander II, but his successor, Alexander III, proved more reactionary. Increasing rivalry led to the Russo-Japanese War (1904-5). Marxist doctrines spread among the small but rapidly growing urban proletariat, and a revolution broke out (1905) in St Petersburg, spreading to the Black Sea fleet. It was followed by a series of strikes and peasant riots, and by the formation of soviets. Police repression included pogroms of the Jews. The czar granted a measure of parliamentary government by creating a duma, but its meetings were dissolved when it opposed the regime. Stolypin brought in belated agrarian reforms to distribute land to the peasants. Russia allied with France and Britain in the Triple Entente. Russian support of Pan-Slavism contributed to the outbreak of the 1st world war, which Russia entered very ill-prepared. Its first offensive against the Germans was halted at Tannenberg (Aug. 1914) and a series of reverses followed, with heavy casualties. Popular feeling turned against Nicholas II and his court. A revolution took place in Petrograd and spread throughout the country (Feb. 1917), the duma assumed real power, and the czar was forced to abdicate (Mar. 15, 1917). A provisional government was organized under the leadership (July-Nov. 1917) of Kerenski. This was overthrown (Nov. 7, 1917) by the Bolsheviks, led by Lenin, who had been allowed to return to Russia by the German government. The dictatorship of the proletariat was announced, and Russia went out of the 1st world war under the humiliating terms of the Treaty of Brest-Litovsk (1918). (For subsequent history *UNION OF SOVIET SOCIALIST REPUBLICS)

Russia leather a hard-wearing leather used esp. for bookbinding and made by tanning skins of various kinds with the barks of birch, willow or oak and then soaking them in birch-tar oil to protect them against insects

Rus·sian (rʌʃən) **1.** *adj.* of or relating to Russia, its inhabitants, language, customs etc. **2.** *n.* a native or inhabitant of Russia ‖ a member of the Slavic-speaking Great Russian ethnic group ‖ the official language of the U.S.S.R.

Russian Orthodox Church the largest of the Orthodox Eastern Churches. It dates officially from the baptism in 988 of Vladimir, grand duke of Kiev. Its life from 1051-1240 was centered in the monastic stronghold of Kiev. After the fall of Constantinople (1453), the patriarchate of Moscow assumed the leadership of Orthodoxy. Peter I abolished the patriarchate (1721) and put the Church under State control. It thus became associated with czarism, to its cost in the Communist revolution. But thanks to its patriotic action during the 2nd world war the patriarchate was restored (1943)

Russian Soviet Federal Socialist Republic (*abbr.* R.S.F.S.R.) the chief constituent republic (area 6,500,000 sq. miles, pop. 137,552,000) of the U.S.S.R. Capital: Moscow. The Urals divide the European R.S.F.S.R., or European Russia (pop. 100,000,000), from Siberia, the Asian section (area approx. 4,887,000 sq. miles), whose native Finnic, Turkic and Mongol tribal peoples are outnumbered by Russian and Ukrainian settlers. The western half of the republic, comprising the rolling plain of the European R.S.F.S.R. (drained by the Volga and Pechora systems) and the flat plain of W. Siberia (drained by the Ob), rises above 1,000 ft only in the Kola Peninsula, the Caucasus and the Urals. The north is tundra and forest (mixed evergreen and deciduous), the center (the 'Black Earth' region) and south are steppe, largely cultivated. Central (or Eastern) Siberia, between the Yenisei and the lower Lena and Amur, is a plateau (1,000–3,000 ft), largely evergreen forest, with tundra in the north and scattered steppe lands in the south. The Pacific coast region (or Far East) is mountainous (few peaks over 7,000 ft), with tundra covering half the country in the east. The center and south are heavily forested. Climate: *U.S.S.R. Crops: (European R.S.F.S.R. and W. Siberia) cereals, flax, root vegetables, hemp, sunflower seed, (central Siberia) cereals, (Pacific region, south of the Amur) cereals, incl. rice, soybeans, kaoliang. Livestock: dairy and beef cattle (mainly European R.S.F.S.R.), sheep, reindeer. Resources (fully exploited only in European R.S.F.S.R. and W. Siberia): coal (esp. Kuznetsk Basin), iron (esp. E. Volga basin and Urals), oil (esp. E. Volga basin and Urals, N. Caucasia, E. Siberia), lead, zinc, tin, tungsten, salt, gold and most other known minerals, fish, furs. timber, hydroelectricity. The R.S.F.S.R. contains two thirds of Soviet industry (expanding in Siberia as hydroelectricity is developed). Main industries: chemicals, building materials, iron and steel, oil refining, mechanical and aeronautical engineering. Industrial centers: Moscow, Leningrad, Volga basin, Urals, Novosibirsk, Omsk, Novokuznetsk, Krasnoyarsk, Irkutsk, Khabarovsk, Vladivostok. Ports: Leningrad, Vladivostok

Russian wolfhound a dog of a tall (28 to 31 ins), long-haired, long-legged breed of Russian origin, originally bred for coursing wolves

Rus·si·fi·ca·tion (rʌsəfikéiʃən) *n.* practice of requiring study of Russian language and culture by all ethnic groups in the U.S.S.R.

Rus·so-Jap·an·ese War (rʌ́soudʒæpəní:z, rʌ́soudʒæpəní:s) a war fought (1904-5) between Russia and Japan over a conflict of interests in Manchuria and Korea. Rapid Japanese victories gave Japan control of Manchuria and Korea, and established her as a world power. Russia's loss of prestige was a chief cause of the Russian revolution of 1905

Rus·so·phil (rʌ́səfil) *n.* a Russophile

Rus·so·phile (rʌ́səfail) *n.* a person who admires Russia or Russian civilization

Rus·so·phobe (rʌ́səfoub) *n.* a person who dislikes Russia or Russian civilization

Rus·so-Tur·kish Wars (rʌ́soutə́:rkiʃ) a series of wars (17th-19th cc.) between Russia and Turkey, caused by Russia's desire to take advantage of Turkey's weakness and to expand toward the Black Sea and the Balkans. The main wars were those of 1677-81, 1686-1700, 1736-9, 1768-74 (settled by the Treaty of Kuchuk Kainarji), 1787-92, 1806-12, 1828-9 (settled by the Treaty of Adrianople), 1853-6 (the Crimean War) and 1877-8 (settled by the Treaty of San Stefano and the Congress of Berlin) (*EASTERN QUESTION)

rust (rʌst) **1.** *n.* a hydrated oxide of iron, $Fe_2O_3 \cdot H_2O$, formed when iron is exposed to air and moisture ‖ the reddish-brown color of this substance ‖ a stain that looks like iron rust ‖ any of several diseases of grasses and other plants caused by phycomycetes ‖ the parasitic fungus producing rust **2.** *v.i.* to become coated with, or converted into, rust ‖ to deteriorate through lack of use ‖ *v.t.* to cause to be coated with or converted into rust [O.E. *rūst*]

rus·tic (rʌ́stik) **1.** *adj.* of, relating to, or characteristic of the country or countryside, *a rustic scene* ‖ characteristic of the qualities ascribed to country life, country people etc., *rustic simplicity, rustic speech* ‖ robust and simple in workmanship ‖ made of untrimmed wood, *a rustic seat* ‖ (*archit.*) with roughened surface or chamfered joints ‖ (*rhet.*) rural **2.** *n.* (*rhet.*) a person born and bred in the country and quite unsophisticated **rús·ti·cal·ly** *adv.* [fr. L. *rusticus*]

rus·ti·cate (rʌ́stikeit) *pres. part.* **rus·ti·cat·ing** *past* and *past part.* **rus·ti·cat·ed** *v.i.* (*rhet.*) to retire to live in the country ‖ *v.t.* (*Br.*) to suspend for a time from a university or college as punishment ‖ (*archit.*) to produce a rustic effect by roughening the surface or sinking the joints of (stone) **rus·ti·cá·tion** *n.* [fr. L. *rusticari* (*rusticatus*), to live in the country]

rus·tic·i·ty (rʌstísiti:) *n.* the state or quality of being rustic [fr. F. *rusticité* or L. *rusticitas*]

rus·tle (rʌ́s'l) **1.** *v. pres. part.* **rus·tling** *past* and *past part.* **rus·tled** *v.i.* to make light sounds like those of stirring leaves etc., *her dress rustled as she moved* ‖ (*pop.*) to move busily and energetically ‖ to steal cattle ‖ *v.t.* to cause to make light sounds like those of stirring leaves, *he rustled his newspaper* ‖ to get by making energetic efforts ‖ to steal (cattle) **to rustle up** (*pop.*) to get together by or as if by foraging, *to rustle up a meal* **2.** *n.* the sound made by something that rustles **rús·tler** *n.* a cattle thief [imit.]

rus·ty (rʌ́sti:) *comp.* **rus·ti·er** *superl.* **rus·ti·est** *adj.* coated with rust, a *rusty knife* ‖ having the color of rust ‖ deteriorated by disuse, *his French has grown rusty* ‖ (of a voice) hoarse, esp. from old age ‖ stiff from age or neglect ‖ (of black clothes) discolored by age ‖ out-of-date, behind the times

rut (rʌt) **1.** *n.* a groove made by wheels in soft ground ‖ a way of life so fixed in routine as to be dreary, *to get into a rut* **2.** *v.t. pres. part.* **rut·ting** *past* and *past part.* **rut·ted** to make a rut or ruts in [etym. doubtful]

rut 1. *n.* the periodic sexual excitement of male deer and some other animals ‖ (often with 'the') the period during which this occurs **2.** *v.i. pres. part.* **rut·ting** *past* and *past part.* **rut·ted** to be affected with this [O.F.]

ru·ta·ba·ga (ru:təbéigə) *n.* (*Am.*=*Br.* swede) *Brassica napobrassica*, fam. *Cruciferae*, a turnip having a large yellowish root used as food by humans and livestock [Swed. dial. *rotabagge*]

Ru·te·beuf (rytəbə:f) 13th-c. French trouvère. He wrote fabliaux and satires, mainly in vigorous rhyming octosyllabics, and some plays

Rut·gers University (rʌ́tgərz) the State University of New Jersey, the eighth colonial college in British America, at New Brunswick, N. J. It was chartered (1776) by George III in response to a petition of the Dutch Reformed Church. It became a university in 1924

Ruth (ru:θ) a book of the Old Testament which tells the story of Ruth, a Moabite widow who accompanied her mother-in-law, Naomi, to Bethlehem and married Boaz, a Hebrew

Ruth (ru:θ), 'Babe' (George Herman Ruth, 1895-1948), the most popular baseball player in U.S. history and holder (1927) of the home-run record of 60 in a 154-game season

Ru·the·ni·a (ru:θí:ni:ə) a former region of E. Europe. It became a province of Czechoslovakia (1919) and part of the Ukraine (1945)

Ru·the·ni·an (ru:θí:ni:ən) *n.* a member of a people living in the former region of Ruthenia, now part of the Ukraine ‖ the Ukrainian language, esp. as spoken in the former region of Ruthenia

ru·then·ic (ru:θí:nik, ru:θénik) *adj.* of or relating to ruthenium ‖ derived from ruthenium

ru·the·ni·um (ru:θí:ni:əm) *n.* a rare metallic element of the platinum group (symbol Ru, at. no.

44, at. mass 101.07) [Mod. L. fr. *Ruthenia,* Russia]

Ruth·er·ford (rʌðərfərd), Ernest, Baron (1871-1937), British physicist, born in New Zealand. His major achievements included the identification of the alpha and beta particles and gamma rays formed in radioactive decay, the discovery of the atomic nucleus (1919) and the artificial transmutation of one element into another. Nobel prize in chemistry (1908)

ruth·er·ford·i·um (rʌðərfərdi:əm) *n.* element 104 as proposed to honor English physicist Lord Ernest Rutherford. *Cf* KURCHOTOVIUM

ruth·less (rú:θlis) *adj.* merciless, *a ruthless tyrant* [fr. older *ruth,* compassion]

ru·tile (rú:ti:l, rú:tail) a crystalline mineral, titanium dioxide, that is usually reddish-brown with a brilliant metallic luster ‖ a synthetic gem of the same composition as the mineral [F. or G. *rutil* fr. L.]

ru·tin (rú:t'n) *n.* a glycoside ($C_{27}H_{30}O_{16}$), found in buckwheat, tobacco leaves and other plants, used mainly for treating hypertension and radiation injuries [G. fr. L.]

Rut·land (rʌtlənd) a county (area 152 sq. miles, pop. 24,000) of England, in the E. Midlands. County town: Oakham

Rut·ledge (rʌtlidʒ), Ann (c. 1813-35), daughter of an innkeeper of New Salem, Illinois. Evidence for the story of Abraham Lincoln's romance with her is generally thought too slight to be taken seriously

Rutledge, John (1739-1800), U.S. political leader and jurist. He served (1776-8) as president and (1779-82) as the first governor of South Carolina. At the Constitutional Convention he championed slavery, the division of society into classes as a basis for representation, and the restriction of office-holders to those owning large property. Nominated (1795) chief justice of the Supreme Court, he failed to win confirmation by the Senate

rut·ty (rʌti:) *comp.* **rut·ti·er** *superl.* **rut·ti·est** *adj.* full of ruts

Ru·vu·ma (ru:vú:mə) a river (400 miles long) rising in S.W. Tanganyika, Tanzania, and flowing east, forming the border with Mozambique, to the Indian Ocean

Ru·wen·zo·ri (ru:wənzóri:, ru:wənzóuri:) a snow-capped massif on the border between Uganda and Zaïre. Highest peak: Mt Stanley, with two summits (16,750 ft and 16,791 ft)

Ruys·broeck (róisbryk), Jan Van (1293-1381), Flemish mystic. Among his best-known writings are 'The Seven Steps of the Ladder of Spiritual Love', 'The Adornment of the Spiritual Marriage', 'The Book of the Highest Truth', 'The Mirror of Blessedness'

Ruysdael *RUISDAEL

Ruy·ter (róitər), Michiel Adriaanszoon de (1607-76), Dutch admiral. He distinguished himself in the Dutch Wars, notably by leading a fleet up the Thames (1667)

RV (*abbr.*) **1.** reentry vehicle, i.e., from space **2.** recreational vehicle, e.g., a trailer

R-val·ue (órvælju:) **1.** (*phys.*) unit of measure of resistance to heat flow **2.** (*nuclear phys.*) decrease in the density of reactor fuel for 1% burn-up. *Cf* S-VALUE

Rwan·da (rwándə) (formerly Ruanda) a republic (area 10,169 sq. miles, pop. 5,111,000) in central Africa. Capital: Kigali. People: mainly Bahutu, with Watutsi and Batwa (pygmy) minorities. Languages: Kinyarwanda (Bantu) and French (both official), Swahili for trading. Religion: mainly local African and Roman Catholic, with a Moslem minority. The Nile-Congo dividing range (rising to 9,000 ft) and a volcanic chain (Karisimbi, 14,825 ft) rise sharply from the Great Rift Valley (Lake Kivu) in the west. The east (5,000–7,000 ft) is part of the E. African plateau. Little woodland remains. Average temperature (F.): 63°-80°. Rainfall: northeastern plateau 40 ins, Lake Kivu 70 ins. Main industries: subsistence agriculture (beans, palm products, peanuts, cassava, cereals), coffee growing, cattle raising, mining (cassiterite, tin, gold), hydroelectricity, brewing. Exports: coffee, cassiterite. University college at Butare (1963). Monetary unit: Rwanda-Burundi franc. Formerly part of Ruanda-Urundi, Rwanda became independent July 1, 1962. The Bahutu had risen against Watutsi domination (1959). They massacred several thousand (1964) and caused thousands of others to emigrate to neighboring countries. Habyarimana led a coup that put him in power July 5, 1973 and he has since been reelected to successive 5-year terms

ry·a (ráiə) *n.* **1.** a colorful, handwoven, flat pile Scandinavian rug with characteristic patterns **2.** a similarly made bed cover —**rya** *adj.* of the weave typical of the rug

Ry·a·zan (ri:əzǽn) a city (pop. 453,000) of the central European R.S.F.S.R., U.S.S.R.: mechanical engineering, food processing, shoes

Ry·binsk (ríbinsk) (called Shcherbakov 1946-57) an inland port (pop. 243,000) of the N. European R.S.F.S.R., U.S.S.R., on the Rybinsk Reservoir (formed by damming the upper Volga). Industries: engineering, shipbuilding, food processing, sawmilling

Ry·der (ráidər), Albert Pinkham (1847-1917), U.S. painter, best known for his moonlit landscapes, seascapes and allegorical scenes, notably 'Siegfried', 'The Race Track' and 'Toilers of the Sea'

rye (rai) *n. Secale cereale,* fam. *Gramineae,* a tall-growing cereal with dark-colored grain. It is cultivated mainly in N. Europe and North America ‖ its grain, used in making bread and for the distilling of rye whiskey, and fed to poultry and farm animals ‖ rye whiskey [O.E. *ryge*]

rye·grass (ráigræs, ráigrɔs) *n.* a member of *Lolium,* fam. *Gramineae,* a genus of European perennial grasses used for lawn grass, hay and pasture

Rye House Plot (*Eng. hist.*) an unsuccessful conspiracy (1683) to assassinate Charles II and his brother, the future James II. The Whig leaders Russell and Sidney were unjustly held responsible for the plot, and executed

ry·o·kan (ri:óukɑn) *n.* (*slang*) a traditional Japanese inn

Rys·brack (ráisbræk), John Michael (1693-1770), sculptor. He was Dutch by parentage but worked in England from 1720. His works include tombs in Westminster Abbey and of the Marlboroughs at Blenheim

Rys·wick, Treaty of (ráizwik) the treaty (1697) which ended the War of the Grand Alliance. Louis XIV lost most of his conquests and William III was recognized king of England. Spain acknowledged the French invasion of Hispaniola and ceded the western part of the island (Haiti) to France. England's promise to refrain from sacking Spanish towns put an end to buccaneering in the West Indies

Ryu·kyu Islands (ri:ú:kju:) a volcanic archipelago (land area excluding islands included in Japan 848 sq. miles, pop. 1,118,000) in the N.W. Pacific, stretching 600 miles between Kyushu, Japan and Formosa. Chief town: Naha, on Okinawa. Language: Ryukyu (akin to Japanese). The larger of the several dozen islands are mountainous, the smaller are coral atolls. Climate: tropical, with typhoons. Products: fish, sugarcane, sweet potatoes, rice, pineapples, market produce. University at Shuri, Okinawa (1949). The islands were invaded (7th c.) by the Chinese. They were tributary to China (14th-17th cc.). Japan and China have disputed them since the 17th c. They were formally incorporated (1879) with Japan. They were placed (1945) under a U.S. military governor. The Japanese were given sovereignty (1951) over the islands, but the U.S.A. retained actual control. The islands were returned (by 1968) to Japan, with the exception of Okinawa, which the U.S.A. handed back in 1972, maintaining bases

	EARLY NORTH SEMITIC	PHOENICIAN	EARLY HEBREW (GEZER)	EARLY GREEK	CLASSICAL GREEK	ETRUSCAN		EARLY LATIN	CLASSICAL LATIN
						Early	Classical		
S	干 (s) ⑽(sh-s)	丰 (s) W (sh-s)	丰 (s) W W (sh — s)	ʃ	Σ	ϟ	ϟ	ϟ	S

CURSIVE MAJUSCULE (ROMAN)	CURSIVE MINUSCULE (ROMAN)	ANGLO-IRISH MAJUSCULE	CAROLINE MINUSCULE	VENETIAN MINUSCULE (ITALIC)	N. ITALIAN MINUSCULE (ROMAN)
ʃ	ʋ	S	ſ	δ	S

A. C. SYLVESTER, CAMBRIDGE, ENGLAND

Development of the letter S, beginning with the early North Semitic letter. Evolution of both the majuscule, or capital, letter S and the minuscule, or lowercase, letter s are shown.

S, s (es) the 19th letter of the English alphabet ‖ an object shaped like this letter

S, S. South, Southern

's (es *after a vowel and after most voiced consonant sounds*, z *after most unvoiced consonant sounds*, iz *after* s, ʃ, tʃ, z, ʒ, dʒ) possessive ending for singular nouns, *Brown's dog*, some pronouns, *anyone's*, noun word groups, *the man in the corner's hat*, and of plural nouns not ending in s, *the children's toys* [older -es, genitive sing. suffix of many masculine and feminine nouns and adjectives]

S (*abbr.*) for siemens, a unit of electrical conductance

Saa·le (zálə) a tributary (226 miles long, navigable for 100 miles) of the Elbe, flowing from the Thüringer Wald through Thuringia and Saxony-Anhalt, East Germany

Saar, the (zɑr, sɑr) the industrial region of Saarland

Saar·brück·en (zɑrbrýkən) the capital (pop. 198,900) of Saarland, West Germany, center of its coal basin: iron and steel

Saa·ri·nen (sárinən), Eero (1910-61), naturalized American architect, born in Finland. He experimented with modern materials and techniques, attempting to reconcile external forms of maximum simplicity and originality with complex functional requirements. Among his best-known works are General Motors Technical Center, Warren, Michigan (1951-5), Kresge Auditorium, Massachusetts Institute of Technology, Cambridge, Massachusetts (1955), and Trans World Airlines Terminal Building, Kennedy International Airport, New York City (1962)

Saar·land (zárlǫnt) a state (area 991 sq. miles, pop. 1,081,000) of West Germany in the southwestern hills bordering France (Lorraine), a great industrial region based on coal reserves. Industries: coal mining, iron and steel (using iron ore from Lorraine), engineering. Capital: Saarbrücken. It was formed (1919) from Bavarian and Prussian territories and put under League of Nations control, but reverted to Germany after a plebiscite (1935). Part of the French zone from 1945, it was attached economically to France (1948) but returned under Franco-German agreement to West Germany (1957)

Sa·a·ve·dra (sǫavéðrɑ), Cornelio de (1761–1829), Argentinian soldier. Following the declaration (1810) in Buenos Aires by a cabildo abierto that the viceroyalty was now vacant, he served as president of a junta acting in the name of the king

Saavedra La·mas (lámas), Carlos (1880-1959), Argentine lawyer, professor, diplomat, who received the 1936 Nobel peace prize. He is best known for his 'Por la Paz de las Américas' (1937)

Sa·ba (séibə) (*Bible* Sheba) an ancient country of S. Arabia, including modern Yemen and Hadhramaut (*SABAEAN)

Sa·ba (séibə, sábə) an island (area 5 sq. miles, pop. 1100) in the N.W. Leeward Is, part of the Netherlands Antilles. It is the cone (2,851 ft) of an extinct volcano

Sa·ba·dell (sǫbadél) a textile-manufacturing center (pop. 159,408) in Barcelona Province, Spain

Sa·bae·an, Sa·be·an (səbíːən) 1. *adj.* of or relating to Saba, its people or its language 2. *n.* an inhabitant of Saba. The Sabaeans developed a flourishing kingdom (c. 930–c. 115 B.C.) and acquired great wealth from a monopoly of the spice trade through S. Arabia. Many inscriptions from the 7th c. B.C. in an alphabet resembling the Phoenician have been found ‖ the language of the Sabaeans

Sa·bah (sábɑ) (formerly North Borneo) a state (area 29,545 sq. miles, pop. 967,000, incl. adjacent islands) of Malaysia, occupying the northeast corner of Borneo. Capital: Kota Kinabalu. The population includes a large Chinese minority (23%). Languages: Malay, Chinese, English, Dusun. Religions: Animist, Moslem, with a 17% Christian minority. Highest point: Mt Kinabulu (13,455 ft). Exports: hardwoods, rubber, cutch, hemp, tobacco, fish. Other products: building materials. Imports: foodstuffs (incl. rice), machinery, textiles. Chief ports: Victoria (on Labuan Is.), Kota Kinabalu. HISTORY. Britain established trading links with the area (19th c.) and proclaimed it a protectorate as North Borneo (1888). Rubber cultivation was introduced (late 19th c.). North Borneo was occupied by the Japanese (1942-5), and became a British colony (1946). It became independent and, as Sabah, joined Malaysia (1963)

Sa·ba·tier (sæbætjei), Paul (1854-1941), French chemist known for his method of hydrogenating organic compounds. Nobel prize (1912)

sab·ba·tar·i·an (sæbətéəriːən) 1. *adj.* of the sabbath or its observance ‖ of the doctrines of the sabbatarians 2. *n.* a Jew who observes Saturday as holy ‖ a Christian who keeps strict observance of Sunday as the holy day of the week **sab·ba·tar·i·an·ism** *n.* [L. *sabbatarius*]

sab·bath (sæbəθ) *n.* the seventh day of the Jewish week (from sundown on Friday until sundown on Saturday), set apart by Moses (Exodus xx, 8–9) as a holy day of rest and worship commemorating the completion of the Creation (Genesis ii, 1–3) ‖ Sunday, the first day of the Christian week, set apart for worship in memory of Christ's resurrection ‖ a day of the week set apart regularly for worship in any of certain other religions, e.g. Friday in the Moslem week [fr. L. *sabbatum* fr. Gk fr. Heb.]

sab·bat·i·cal (səbætik'l) 1. *adj.* of, relating to or characteristic of the sabbath ‖ of an extended period of free time, esp. one available for special study given to teachers by some schools etc. 2. *n.* such an extended period

Sabean *SABAEAN

sa·ber, *Br.* **sa·bre** (séibər) 1. *n.* a heavy cavalry sword with a curved blade ‖ (*fencing*) a light weapon heavier than a foil 2. *v.t. pres. part.* **sa·ber·ing,** *Br.* **sa·bring** *past* and *past part.* **sa·bered,** *Br.* **sa·bred** to wound or kill with a saber [F. fr. older G. *sabel*]

sa·ber-toothed tiger, *Br.* **sa·bre-toothed tiger** (séibərtúː.θt) one of several large, extinct felines with long, swordlike, curved upper canine teeth

sab·il·iz·ing (séibəlaiziŋ) *n.* (*cosmetology*) hair coloring technique that darkens the ends of light-colored hair

Sa·bin (séibin), Albert Bruce (1906-   ), U.S. physician who developed (c. 1959) a live-virus vaccine against poliomyelitis. It protects not only against paralyzation (as with the Salk vaccine) but also infection, and provides longer immunity

Sa·bine (séibain), Sir Edward (1788-1883), British physicist and astronomer. The discovery of the effect of sunspots on the earth's magnetic field arose from his work

Sabine 1. *n.* (*hist.*) a member of an ancient people of the Apennines northwest of Rome. It was said that during a festival the Sabine women were seized by the men of Romulus, and that when the Sabines attacked Rome the women placed themselves between the armies to stop the battle. By the 3rd c. B.C. the Sabines had become fully Romanized ‖ their Italic language 2. *adj.* of the Sabines or their language [fr. L. *Sabinus*]

sa·ble (séib'l) *n. Martes zibellina*, fam. *Mustelidae*, a small carnivorous mammal related to the weasel, native to arctic and subarctic Europe and Asia, highly valued for its lustrous dark brown fur ‖ the fur or pelt of this animal ‖ any of several related animals ‖ a garment of sable fur [O.F. prob. fr. Slavonic]

sable 1. *n.* (*heraldry*) black ‖ (*rhet.*) black clothing, esp. as a sign of mourning 2. *adj.* (*heraldry*) of the color sable [F.]

sable antelope *Hippotragus niger*, a large antelope of E. and S. Africa having long curved horns and a little mane. The male is shiny black

Sa·ble, Cape (séib'l) a swampy, mangrove-covered peninsula (c. 20 miles long, 5-10 miles wide) in S.W. Florida, the southernmost point of the U.S. mainland

---

CONCISE PRONUNCIATION KEY: (a) æ, cat; ɑ, car; ɔ fawn; ei, snake. **(e)** e, hen; iː, sheep; iə, deer; ɛə, bear. **(i)** i, fish; ai, tiger; əː, bird. **(o)** o, ox; au, cow; ou, goat; u, poor; ɔi, royal. **(u)** ʌ, duck; u, bull; uː, goose; ə, bacillus; juː, cube. x, loch; θ, think; ð, bother; z, Zen; ʒ, corsage; dʒ, savage; ŋ, orangutang; j, yak; ʃ, fish; tʃ, fetch; 'l, rabble; 'n, redden.   Complete pronunciation key appears inside front cover.

sa·bot (sǽbou) *n.* a clog made from a single piece of wood, worn esp. in rural France, Belgium, the Netherlands and Germany ‖ a leather work shoe with a wooden sole ‖ (*mil.*) a disk of wood or metal attached to a spherical projectile to make it fit the bore [F.]
Sabot *n.* (*mil.*) lightweight carrier in which a subcaliber projectile is centered to permit firing the projectile in a larger caliber weapon, the carrier filling the bore of the weapon from which the projectile is fired
sab·o·tage (sǽbətɑʒ, sæbətɑ́ʒ) **1.** *n.* deliberate damage done to property, installations etc., e.g. by enemy agents or by hostile employees, or (*fig.*) to plans, enterprises etc. **2.** *v.t. pres. part.* **sab·o·tag·ing** *past* and *past part.* **sab·o·taged** to commit sabotage upon [F.]
sab·o·teur (sæbətə́:r) *n.* a person who commits sabotage [F]
sabre *SABER
SABRE *n.* an electronic seat-reservation system created for American Airlines by IBM
sa·bre·tache (séibərtæʃ, sǽbərtæʃ) *n.* a leather case hung on the left side from a cavalry officer's sword belt [F. fr. G. *säbeltasche* fr. *säbel,* saber + *tasche,* pocket]
sabre-toothed tiger *SABER-TOOTHED TIGER
Sac (sæk, sɔk) *n.* a Sauk Indian
sac (sæk) *n.* (*biol.*) a part shaped like a pouch in an animal or plant, often filled with a fluid [F. or fr. L. *saccus,* sack]
SAC *n.* (*mil. acronym*) for Strategic Air Command, U.S. Air Force agency charged with air-defense strategy and maintenance of long-range aircraft and missiles
Sacagawea (sækədʒəwí:ə) (c. 1788–1884), American Shoshoni Indian woman, interpreter and guide for the Lewis and Clark expedition (1804–5). A captive of the Hidatsa tribe of North Dakota, she and her baby accompanied the expedition party in the Pacific Northwest and, on the return journey, remained with Shoshoni in Wyoming
sac·cade (sækɑ́d) *n.* a jerky eye movement
sac·cate (sǽkit, sǽkeit) *adj.* (*biol.*) shaped like a sac ‖ encysted [fr. M.L. *saccatus*]
sac·cha·rate (sǽkəreit) *n.* (*chem.*) a salt of saccharic acid
sac·char·ic (səkǽrik) *adj.* of or obtained from saccharine compounds [fr. M.L. *saccharum,* sugar]
saccharic acid a solid diacid, $HOOC(CHOH)_4COOH$, obtained from glucose and its derivatives
sac·cha·ride (sǽkəraid, sǽkərid) *n.* a sugar, polymerized sugar or combination of sugars [fr. M.L. *saccharum,* sugar]
sac·cha·rim·e·ter (sækərímitər) *n.* an instrument used to find the concentration of sugar in a solution by measuring the angle through which the plane of vibration of polarized light is turned by the solution [F. *saccharimètre* fr. Gk *sakchari, sakcharon,* sugar + *metron,* measure]
sac·cha·rin (sǽkərin) *n.* a white crystalline extremely sweet substance, $C_6H_4(SO_2)(CO)NH$, prepared from toluene, and used as a sugar substitute, e.g. by diabetics. It has no food value
sac·cha·rine (sǽkərin, sǽkərain) *adj.* very sweet, esp. (*fig.*) sickeningly cloying, *saccharine sentiment* **sac·cha·rin·i·ty** (sækəríniti:) *n.* [fr. M.L. *saccharum* or Gk *sakcharon,* sugar]
sac·cha·roid (sǽkərɔid) *adj.* (*geol.,* of rocks) granular in structure, like sugar [fr. Gk *sakcharon,* sugar]
sac·cha·rom·e·ter (sækərɒ́mitər) *n.* a hydrometer calibrated to show the concentration of sugar in a solution as it affects the density [fr. Gk *sakcharon,* sugar + *metron,* measure]
sac·cha·rose (sǽkərous) *n.* sucrose [fr. Gk *sakcharon,* sugar]
Sac·co-Van·zet·ti Case (sǽkouvænzéti:) a U.S. murder trial held (1920-7) in Massachusetts. The defendants, Nicola Sacco and Bartolomeo Vanzetti, two Italian immigrants, were accused of murdering F. A. Parmenter, paymaster of a shoe factory, and Alessandro Berardelli, the accompanying guard, to secure the payroll they were carrying. After their conviction and execution, worldwide demonstrations protested that they were convicted for their radical, anarchist beliefs, and not because there was clear evidence of guilt on the murder charge. Subsequent investigations suggested that others might have committed the crime, but their convictions were never overturned
sac·cu·late (sǽkjuleit) *adj.* formed of or divided into saccules **sác·cu·lat·ed** *adj.* [SACCULUS]
sac·cule (sǽkju:l) *n.* a small sac, esp. the smaller division in the membranous labyrinth of the ear [SACCULUS]
sac·cu·lus (sǽkjuləs) *pl.* **sac·cu·li** (sǽkjulai) *n.* a saccule [L. dim. of *saccus,* sack]
sac·er·do·tal (sæsərdóut'l) *adj.* pertaining to priests or the priesthood ‖ of doctrines asserting great or excessive spiritual authority in priests **sac·er·dó·tal·ism** *n.* the assuming of spiritual powers by priests as intermediaries between man and God, or the ascribing of excessive authority to priests [F.]
sa·chem (séitʃəm) *n.* (among certain peoples) a North American Indian chief ‖ an officer of the Tammany Society [Algonquian]
sa·chet (sæʃéi, sǽʃei) *n.* a small bag, esp. one containing perfumed powder or dried herbs, placed among clothes and linen [F., dim. of *sac,* bag]
Sachs (zɑks), Hans (1494-1576), German meistersinger and playwright. Wagner made him the central figure of 'Die Meistersinger von Nürnberg'
Sachs (sæks), (Leonie) Nelly (1891–1970), German poet whose poetry spoke out against Nazism and the Holocaust, co-winner of the Nobel Prize for literature (1966). She fled from Germany to Sweden in 1940. Her poems are collected in 'O the Chimneys' (1967)
sack (sæk) **1.** *n.* a large receptacle, typically oblong and made of a coarse fabric, for storing or conveying goods ‖ such a receptacle with its contents ‖ the amount it holds, sometimes used as a unit of measurement ‖ a woman's loose-fitting straight dress ‖ (*hist., also* **sacque**) a woman's loose gown, or a train hanging from its shoulders ‖ (*pop.*) summary dismissal, esp. from employment, *to get the sack* **2.** *v.t.* to put into a sack or sacks ‖ (*pop.*) to dismiss, esp. from employment [O.E. *sacc* fr. L. *saccus* fr. Gk fr. Heb.]
sack *n.* (*hist.*) any of various kinds of dry white wine imported into England from Spain and the Canary Islands in the 16th and 17th cc. [earlier (*wyne*) *seck* fr. F. (*vin*) *sec,* dry (wine)]
sack **1.** *n.* the violent plundering by soldiers of a captured town, city etc. **2.** *v.t.* to plunder and lay waste (a captured town, city etc.) [F. *sac* fr. Ital.]
sack·but (sǽkbʌt) *n.* a medieval wind instrument, ancestor of the trombone ‖ (*Bible*) a trigon (harp) [F. *saquebute,* prob. fr. O.N.F. *saqueboute,* a hooked lance]
sack·cloth (sǽkklɔθ, sǽkklɒθ) *n.* sacking ‖ penitential or mourning clothing of coarse cloth
sack·ful (sǽkful) *pl.* **sack·fuls** *n.* the amount a sack will hold
sack·ing (sǽkiŋ) *n.* coarse cloth, e.g. of hemp or jute, for making sacks
sack race a race in which each contestant has his legs or the lower half of his body in a sack
sacque *SACK (loose gown)
sa·cral (séikrəl) *adj.* (*anat.*) of or near the sacrum [fr. Mod. L. *sacralis*]
sacral *adj.* of or for sacred ceremonies [fr. L. *sacrum,* sacred thing]
sac·ra·ment (sǽkrəmənt) *n.* any of certain Christian rites held to have been instituted by Christ and to convey God's grace to man. In the Roman Catholic and Orthodox Eastern Churches these are: baptism, penance, the Eucharist, confirmation, ordination, matrimony and Extreme Unction. In most Protestant Churches, baptism and the Eucharist are the only sacraments **the Sacrament** the Eucharist ‖ any ceremony or act symbolizing a deep spiritual reality ‖ a solemn oath or pledge ‖ (*Roman Catholicism*) the Host [F. *sacrement* fr. L. *sacramentum* fr. *sacrare,* to consecrate]
sac·ra·men·tal (sækrəmént'l) **1.** *adj.* of, relating to or having the nature of a sacrament ‖ (of religious doctrine) affirming the validity and indispensability of the sacraments **2.** *n.* a religious rite resembling a sacrament but not regarded as having been instituted by Christ **sac·ra·mén·tal·ism, sac·ra·mén·tal·ist** *ns.* [obs. F. or fr. L.L. *sacramentalis*]
sac·ra·men·tar·i·an (sækrəmentέəri:ən) **1.** *adj.* pertaining to the sacraments or a sacrament ‖ pertaining to the sacramentarians **2.** *n.* (*hist.*) Luther's name for Zwingli and other Protestant theologians who claimed that God was present in the bread and wine of the Eucharist only in a symbolic sense ‖ someone who asserts the inherent efficacy of the sacraments in conveying grace to the soul of a recipient [fr. eccles. L. *sacramentarius*]
Sac·ra·men·to (sækrəméntou) the capital (pop. 275,741) of California, in the central valley, a distributing center of a rich agricultural region. The discovery of gold nearby (1848) started the California gold rush
Sacramento the largest river (382 miles long) in California, rising in N. California and flowing into the east arm of San Francisco Bay. It is navigable for 180 miles. Its valley was the site of the Gold Rush of 1848
sa·cred (séikrid) *adj.* consecrated, holy ‖ set apart, esp. for the service or worship of God or a deity ‖ hallowed by religious association ‖ having a religious, not a profane character, *a sacred picture* ‖ to be held in reverence ‖ (of a person or his office) inviolate [past part. of obs. *sacre,* to consecrate fr. F. *sacrer*]
Sacred College the College of Cardinals
sacred mushroom any hallucinogenic mushroom used in ceremonies by some American Indians
sac·ri·fice (sǽkrəfais) **1.** *n.* an offering, e.g. of animal life, food or incense, made to a deity etc. as propitiation, thanksgiving etc. ‖ the act or practice of making such an offering ‖ (*theol.*) Christ's offering of himself in the Crucifixion ‖ the act of depriving oneself of something for the sake of attaining some goal or for the sake of someone else, *he made many sacrifices for his son's education* ‖ the thing given up in this way ‖ (*baseball*) a sacrifice bunt or fly which does not count as an official time at bat **2.** *v. pres. part.* **sac·ri·fic·ing** *past* and *past part.* **sac·ri·ficed** *v.t.* to offer as a sacrifice ‖ to deprive oneself of (something valued) for the sake of another person, purpose or ideal ‖ *v.i.* to make a sacrifice [F.]
sacrifice bunt (*baseball*) a bunt which enables a base runner to advance although the batter is put out
sacrifice fly (*baseball*) a fly ball to the outfield which enables a base runner to advance although the batter is put out
sa·cri·fi·cial (sækrifíʃəl) *adj.* of or pertaining to sacrifice [fr. *sacrificium* + Eng. *-al* fr. L. *-alis,* of the kind of]
sac·ri·lege (sǽkrəlidʒ) *n.* the violation of a sacred building, or stealing, misuse, destruction etc. of a sacred object [O.F.]
sac·ri·le·gious (sækrəlídʒəs, sækrəlí:dʒəs) *adj.* guilty of sacrilege ‖ having the nature of sacrilege [fr. L. *sacrilegium*]
sa·cring bell (séikriŋ) a small bell rung at the Elevation during the Mass ‖ the tolling of the church bell at the moment of the Elevation [fr. obs. *sacre,* to consecrate fr. F. *sacrer*]
sac·rist (sǽkrist, séikrist) *n.* a sacristan [O.F. *sacriste*]
sac·ris·tan (sǽkristən) *n.* the official who looks after the sacristy of a church [fr. M. L. *sacristanus*]
sac·ris·ty (sǽkristi:) *pl.* **sac·ris·ties** *n.* a room in or attached to a church, in which the sacred vessels, vestments etc. are kept [F. *sacristie*]
sac·ro·il·i·ac (sækrouíli:æk, seikrouíli:æk) **1.** *n.* the region of juncture of the sacrum and the ilium of the spinal column **2.** *adj.* of or pertaining to the sacroiliac
sac·ro·sanct (sǽkrousæŋkt) *adj.* (of a person, place, oath, right etc.) most holy, inviolable **sac·ro·sánc·ti·ty** *n.* [fr. L. *sacrosanctus*]
sac·rum (sǽkrəm, séikrəm) *pl.* **sac·ra** (sǽkrə, séikrə), **sac·rums** *n.* a triangular bone composed of fused vertebrae that is part of the spinal column and forms the back of the pelvis [fr. L. (*os*) *sacrum,* sacred (bone), because it was used in religious rites]
Sac·sa·hua·mán (saksɑwɑmɑ́n) an Inca fortress and arsenal on a hill north of Cuzco, Peru
sad (sæd) *comp.* **sad·der** *superl.* **sad·dest** *adj.* grieving ‖ depressed in spirits ‖ causing sorrow or depression ‖ showing sorrow, *a sad expression* ‖ deplorable, *a sad example to set* ‖ (of color) dark, drab **sad·den** (sǽd'n) *v.t.* to make sad ‖ *v.i.* to become sad [O.E. *sæd,* sated, weary]
Sadarm System (sǽdɑrm) *n.* U.S. sense and destroy missile guidance system, in development as of 1981
Sa·dat (sɑdɑ́t), Anwar (1918-81), Egyptian statesman. He succeeded (1970) Nasser as president of the United Arab Republic. He expelled about 20,000 Soviet advisers and military personnel from the country (1972) and launched a war against Israel (1973). In 1977 he flew to Israel to initiate peace negotiations, which culminated (1979) in an historic Egypt-Israel peace treaty, for which he shared the Nobel peace prize (1978) with Manachem Begin, but

CONCISE PRONUNCIATION KEY: **(a)** æ, *cat;* ɑ, *car;* ɔ *fawn;* ei, *snake.* **(e)** e, *hen;* i:, *sheep;* iə, *deer;* εə, *bear.* **(i)** i, *fish;* ai, *tiger;* ə:, *bird.* **(o)** ɒ, *ox;* au, *cow;* ou, *goat;* u, *poor;* ɔi, *royal.* **(u)** ʌ, *duck;* u, *bull;* u:, *goose;* ə, *bacillus;* ju:, *cube.* x, *loch;* θ, *think;* ð, *bother;* z, *Zen;* ʒ, *corsage;* dʒ, *savage;* ŋ, *orangutang;* j, *yak;* ʃ, *fish;* tʃ, *fetch;* 'l, *rabble;* 'n, *redden.* Complete pronunciation key appears inside front cover.

which made Egypt unpopular with the Arab world. Sadat was assassinated (1981) by members of a militant Moslem fundamentalist group

sad·dle (sǽd'l) *n.* a seat, generally of padded leather, for the rider of a horse, camel etc. ‖ the seat on a bicycle, tractor etc. ‖ the part of a draft horse's harness to which the shafts are attached ‖ an object resembling a riding saddle, esp. a ridge between two mountain peaks ‖ a marking resembling a horse's saddle, on the back of an animal ‖ a cut of mutton or venison including both loins and part of the back ‖ the movable tool carriage of a lathe [O.E. *sadol, sadul*]

saddle *pres. part.* **sad·dling** *past* and *past part.* **sad·dled** *v.t.* to put a saddle on ‖ to place a burdensome duty, responsibility etc. on [O.E. *sadolian*]

sad·dle·back (sǽd'lbæk) *n.* (*archit.*) a roof with a gable at each end or one sloping upwards at each end ‖ a saddlebacked hill ‖ an animal with markings which suggest a saddle, e.g. a black hog of either of two British breeds with a white saddle across the shoulders **sád·dlebacked** *adj.* (*archit.*) having a saddleback ‖ (of a horse) having a hollow in the back behind the withers ‖ having a concave upper outline

sad·dle·bag (sǽd'lbæg) *n.* a large bag or one of a pair, hanging from a saddle ‖ a small bag or one of a pair, hung at the rear wheel of a bicycle or motorcycle

sad·dle·bow (sǽd'lbou) *n.* the arched front of a saddle

sad·dle·cloth (sǽd'lklɔθ, sǽd'lklɒθ) *pl.* **sad·dle·cloths** (sǽd'lklɔθz, sǽd'lklɒθz, sǽd'lklɔðs, sǽd'lklɒðs) *n.* a cloth placed underneath a saddle

saddled prominent a moth (*Heterocampo guttivitta*) that in the larval state, defoliates hardwood trees in the eastern and midwestern U.S.

saddle horse a horse used for riding

sad·dler (sǽdlər) *n.* someone who makes, repairs or sells saddles, harness etc. **sád·dler·y** *pl.* **sad·dler·ies** *n.* the saddles, harness etc. sold by a saddler ‖ a saddler's trade or shop

saddle roof a saddleback roof

saddle shoe an oxford, usually white, having a band of contrasting leather (usually brown or black) across the instep

saddle soap a mild soap for cleaning and treating leather

sad·dle·tree (sǽd'ltri:) *n.* the framework of a saddle ‖ *Liriodendron tulipifera,* the tulip tree

Sad·du·ce·an (sædʒusí:ən, sædjusí:ən) *adj.* of or characteristic of the Sadducees [fr. L. L. *Sadducaeus,* Sadducee]

Sad·du·cee (sǽdʒusi:, sǽdjusi:) *n.* a member of a Jewish religious sect (2nd c. B.C.–1st c. A.D.) believing in free will and denying belief in the resurrection of the dead or the existence of spirits. The Sadducees were the opponents of the Pharisees [fr. L.L. *Saddacaeus* fr. Gk fr. Heb. *Çaddūqī*]

Sade (sæd), Donatien Alphonse François, comte de (known as the marquis de Sade, 1740-1814), French writer after whom sadism was named. His works contain descriptions of sexual perversions

sad·hu (sɑ́du:) *n.* a Hindu ascetic holy man [Skr.=holy man]

Sa'di (sɑdí:) (c. 1184-1291), one of the most popular Persian poets, author of the long didactic works 'Būstān' (Fruit Garden, 1257) and 'Gulistān' (Rose Garden, 1258), partly in verse and partly in prose, containing stories, lyrics, aphorisms etc.

sad·i·ron (sǽdaiərn) *n.* a solid flatiron pointed at each end [SAD, (obs.) heavy]

sad·ism (sǽdizəm, séidizəm) *n.* the deriving of pleasure from inflicting pain on another, esp. as a form of sexual perversion (cf. MASOCHISM) **sád·ist** *n.* **sa·dis·tic** (sədístik, sædístik, seidístik) *adj.* **sa·dís·ti·cal·ly** *adv.* [fr. F. *sadisme* after the marquis de SADE]

Sa·do (sɑ́dou) an island (area 331 sq. miles, pop. 126,000) of Japan off W. Honshu: gold and silver mines

Sa·do·wa, Battle of (sɑ́dɔvɑ) a decisive Prussian victory over Austria (July 3, 1866), also known as the Battle of Königgrätz, fought near Hradec Králové on the upper Elbe, Czechoslovakia

Sá·enz (sɑ́ens), Manuela ('La Sáenz', 1793-1859), a patriot of Quito and mistress of Simón Bolívar. In 1828 she saved Bolívar from conspirators in Bogotá. On his death she remained in Bogotá and protected his papers

sa·fa·ri (səfɑ́ri:) *pl.* **sa·fa·ris** *n.* a hunting expedition, esp. in E. Africa [Swahili fr. Arab. *safara,* to travel]

Sa·fa·vid (sɑfɑ́wi:d) a member of a Moslem dynasty which ruled Persia (1502-1736)

safe (seif) *comp.* **saf·er** *superl.* **saf·est** *adj.* out of danger ‖ not presenting or involving any danger or risk, *a safe policy* ‖ uninjured, *the car crashed but they were safe* ‖ (*baseball*) of a batter or base runner who reaches a base without being put out **on the safe side** covered so as to reduce or avoid risk ‖ (of an estimate etc.) conservative, with a margin in hand [M.E. *sauf* fr. F.]

safe *n.* a fireproof and burglarproof container for valuables ‖ a ventilated cupboard or chest in which foods are stored [older *save* fr. SAVE v.]

safe·break·er (séifbreikər) *n.* (*Br.*) a safecracker

safe-con·duct (séifkɒ́ndʌkt) *n.* the privilege granted by an authority to an otherwise unauthorized person of traveling through a zone or territory without being arrested or molested ‖ the document conveying this authorization

safe·crack·er (séifkrækər) *n.* a person who breaks open and robs safes

safe·crack·ing (séifkrækiŋ) *n.* the breaking open and robbing of safes

safe deposit (*Br.*) a place, e.g. the vault of a bank, where individual safes can be hired for the deposit of valuables

safe-deposit box a metal container for the safe storage of valuables, e.g. one kept in a bank

safe·guard (séifgɑrd) **1.** *n.* someone who or something that serves as protection **2.** *v.t.* to provide with something intended as a protection against a possible risk or danger [M.E. *savegarde* fr. F. *sauvegarde*]

safe haven (*mil.*) **1.** designated area to which noncombatants, commercial vehicles, and matériel can be evacuated during an emergency **2.** temporary storage provided the Department of Energy for classified shipments of nuclear material, including parking for commercial vehicles containing Class A or Class B explosives

safe·keep·ing (séifki:piŋ) *n.* the act of keeping safe or secure ‖ the state of being kept safe or secure ‖ custody, *the money is in his safekeeping*

safe·ty (séifti:) *pl.* **safe·ties** *n.* the condition of being safe from risk or danger ‖ the quality or state of not presenting or involving risk or danger ‖ the condition of a weapon when the safety catch is on, *at safety* ‖ (*baseball*) a base hit ‖ (*football*) a play in which the player grounds the ball behind his goal line (cf. TOUCHDOWN) [M.E. *sauvete* fr. F. *sauveté*]

safety belt a belt or strap fastening an occupant to the seat of an aircraft or vehicle, to prevent or minimize injury if there is an accident ‖ a strong belt securing a man working high above ground, fastened to a rigid support

safety catch a device fitted to a firearm, which, when engaged, prevents the trigger from releasing the firing pin ‖ any of various safety devices on machinery

safety curtain a fireproof curtain which can cut off the stage of a theater from the auditorium in case of fire

safety fuse a fuse made of a slow-burning material, for exploding detonators from a safe distance ‖ (*elec.*) a fuse (short length of wire in an electric circuit)

safety glass strong, tempered glass, treated in such a way that, if broken, it will not shatter or produce jagged fragments

safety lamp a lamp, esp. a Davy lamp, constructed so as not to ignite gas in the surrounding atmosphere

safety man or **safety** (*football*) a defense back whose function is to prevent a long gain by the opposing team

safety match a match which lights only when rubbed on a specially prepared surface

safety net U.S. federal assistance programs designed to assure minimum subsistence for the very poor even under the budget cutbacks proposal by Pres. Ronald Reagan

safety pin a pin for fastening clothing, doubled back on itself so as to form a spring, and having its point secured and covered by a guard

safety razor a razor fitted with a guard so that the blade cannot cut deeply

safety valve a valve automatically opening to release steam or gas from a boiler etc. when the pressure reaches a certain point ‖ something which serves to release excess emotion, energy etc. in a harmless way

safety zone an island in the middle of a busy street where pedestrians can stand until it is safe to cross

saf·flow·er (sǽflauər) *n.* *Carthamus tinctorius,* fam. *Compositae,* a thistlelike plant cultivated esp. in Asia, bearing large orange or red flowers which yield a light red dye ‖ this dye [Du. *saffloer* fr. O.F. *saffleur* fr. Ital.]

saf·fron (sǽfrən) *n.* *Crocus sativus,* a crocus cultivated for its flowers, whose stigmas yield an orange substance used for coloring and flavoring food ‖ this substance ‖ the color of this substance [O.F. *safran* fr. Arab.]

saf·ing (séifiŋ) *v. pres. part* (*mil.*) as applied to weapons and ammunition, the changing from a state of readiness to fire to a safe condition

saf·ra·nin (sǽfrənin) *n.* safranine

saf·ra·nine (sǽfrəni:n, sǽfrənin) *n.* any of several aniline dyes [fr. F. *safran,* saffron]

saf·role (sǽfroul) *n.* a poisonous oil, $C_{10}H_{10}O_2$, obtained from oil of sassafras, and used for perfuming and flavoring [fr. F. *safron,* saffron]

sag (sæg) **1.** *v.i. pres. part.* **sag·ging** *past* and *past part.* **sagged** to bend, hang or sink in the center as a result of weight or pressure, *the plank sagged under his weight* ‖ to bend, hang or sink as if giving way to pressure, *his shoulders sagged from weariness* ‖ (of sales or market prices) to fall ‖ (*naut.*) to drift, *to sag to leeward* ‖ to cease to hold interest **2.** *n.* a sagging ‖ a depression, *a sag in the road* ‖ the amount by which a thing sags from normal position ‖ (*naut.*) a drift to leeward [perh. related to M. Du. *zakken,* Norw. *sakka,* to subside]

sa·ga (sɑ́gə) *n.* a prose epic narrating the history of the early heroes or families of Iceland or Norway ‖ any long narrative story tracing the fortunes of a family through several generations [O.N.=narrative]

—The Icelandic sagas were passed on orally for generations by the descendants of the 9th-c. exiles from Norway, before they began to be written down in the 12th c. By this time their character had become established: the terse simplicity of the language, free from the influence of Latin literature, and the anonymity of the narration, free from subjective commentary, lent great power to the violent, often tragic events related. By the late 13th c. the saga began to decline, depending increasingly upon foreign influences and fictional subjects. The great sagas include the 'Egilssaga' (c. 1200), the 'Laxdaelasaga' (mid-13th c.), the 'Njálssaga' (late 13th c.) and the 'Völsungasaga' (late 13th c.). The 'Heimskringla' was probably by Snorri Sturluson (1179–1241)

sa·ga·cious (səgéiʃəs) *adj.* keen and perceptive, having or showing discernment in judgment [fr. L. *sagax* (*sagacis*)]

sa·gac·i·ty (səgǽsiti:) *n.* the quality of being sagacious [fr. F. *sagacité*]

sag·a·more (sǽgəmɔr, sǽgəmour) *n.* a secondary chief of certain North American Indian tribes [fr. Penobscot *sagamo*]

Sa·gan (séigən) Carl Edward (1934-), U.S. scientist, known for popularizing science and for his research on the possibility of extraterrestrial life. He was a professor of astronomy and director of the Laboratory for Planetary Studies at Cornell University (1968–). He wrote 'Life in the Universe' (1966), with Josif Shlovsky, 'The Cosmic Connection' (1973), 'The Dragons of Eden' (1977, Pulitzer Prize), 'Broca's Brain' (1979), 'Cosmos' (1980) and 'Contact' (1985)

Sage (seidʒ), Russell (1816-1906), U.S. financier. In association with Jay Gould, he amassed a fortune by his control of railroad systems in New York City and the western U.S.A., and of the Western Union Telegraph Company. His wife Margaret Olivia Slocum Sage (1828-1918), to whom he left his fortune, established (1907) the Russell Sage Foundation in New York City, for 'the improvement of social and living conditions' in the U.S.A.

sage (seidʒ) *n.* *Salvia officinalis,* fam. *Labiatae,* an aromatic herb native to Europe and North America, whose leaves are used to flavor food [M.E. *sauge* fr. F.]

sage **1.** *comp.* **sag·er** *superl.* **sag·est** *adj.* having or showing great wisdom and sound judgment **2.** *n.* a very wise man, e.g. a philosopher of ancient times [F.]

SAGE *n.* (*mil. acronym*) for semiautomatic ground environment, a system that correlates surveillance data for air defense and guides interceptor aircraft

sage·brush (séidʒbrʌʃ) *n.* a member of *Artemisia,* fam. *Compositiae,* a genus of bushy, aromatic plants growing wild on the western plains of North America, esp. *A. tridentata*

sagebrush rebellion campaign by Western states in 1970s and 1980s to force federal relinquishment of public lands to states —**sagebrush rebel** *n.*

Sagger AT-3 *n.* U.S.S.R. anti-tank missile with 2 clusters of 3 missiles

sag·ger, sag·gar (sǽgər) *n.* a fireclay container in which porcelain or stoneware is enclosed during firing ‖ the clay of which this container is made [prob. contr. of SAFEGUARD]

Sag·i·naw Bay (sǽginɔ) an inlet (60 miles long, 15-25 miles wide) of Lake Huron on the coast of E. central Michigan

sa·git·ta (sədʒítə) *n.* (*math.*) the distance from the midpoint of an arc to that of its chord [Mod. L. fr. L. =arrow]

sag·it·tal (sǽdʒit'l) *adj.* of, pertaining to or lying in the median plane dividing any animal body into right and left halves, or any plane parallel to this ‖ of or relating to the median suture between the parietal bones of the skull ‖ of or resembling an arrow or arrowhead [fr. Mod. L. *sagittalis* fr. L. *sagitta,* arrow]

Sag·it·ta·ri·us (sædʒitéəriːəs) a southern constellation ‖ the ninth sign of the zodiac, represented as an archer

sag·it·tate (sǽdʒiteit) *adj.* (*bot., of a leaf*) shaped like an arrowhead [fr. Mod. L. *sagittatus* fr. L. *sagitta,* arrow]

sa·go (séigou) *n.* a starch extracted from the pith of certain tropical palms, esp. of genus *Metroxylon,* used as a food and for textile finishing ‖ a plant yielding this starch [Malay *sāgū*]

sa·gua·ro (səgwárou, səwárou) *pl.* **sa·gua·ros** *n.* *Carnegiea gigantea,* a large cactus of Mexico and the southwestern U.S.A., growing to a height of 60 ft. It has white flowers and an edible fruit [Span. fr. native name]

sag wagon (*cycling*) vehicle which follows a race and picks up those who fall behind

Sa·ha·gún (sɑgúːn), Fray Bernardino de (c. 1499-1590), a Spanish Franciscan missionary and historian in Mexico. His chief work is 'A History of Ancient Mexico' (published 1829, Eng. trans. Vol. I, 1932)

Sa·har·a (səhǽrə, səhárə) the largest desert (area about 3,500,000 sq. miles) in the world, covering most of N. Africa (the bulk of Mauritania, Morocco, Western Sahara, Tunisia, Algeria, Libya and Egypt, with the north of Mali, Niger, Chad and the Sudan). It includes the Libyan, Arabian and Nubian deserts. Average elevation: 1,000 ft. A mountain system, running from the Ahaggar Mtns, S.E. Algeria, to the W. Sudan, rises over 11,000 ft (*TIBESTI MTNS). Surface types: *erg* (sandy desert), *reg* (gravel plains), *hammada* (rocky plateaus). Highest recorded temperature: 133° F. Rainfall: mainly under 5 ins. Large oases are mainly in the north, but there are skeletal river systems. Principal resources: natural gas, oil, salt (all mainly in the south). Population is estimated at 2,000,000 incl. nomads and oasis farmers

Sa·ha·ran·pur (səhárənpur) a town (pop. 185,000) in N. Uttar Pradesh, India: railroad shops, paper, wood carving

sa·hel (sáhel) *n.* a climatic transition zone of tropical Africa south of the Sahara, between the desert and the savanna. It is characterized by low, scattered vegetation (tamarisk, gum acacia etc.) and supports a limited agriculture (millet, peanuts) [F. fr. Arab. *sahil*]

sa·hib (sáib, sáiːb) *n.* (*hist.*) a title of address used by Indians to European men

said *past* and *past part.* of SAY

Sa·i·da (sáiːdɑ) *SIDON

Sai·gon *HO CHI MINH CITY (saigón, sæiːgɔ̃) a city (pop. with its mainly Chinese suburb of Cholon 1,825,297) of Vietnam, a seaport (Saigon River) 60 miles from the sea, European in aspect. Industries (largely concentrated in Cholon): shipbuilding, food (esp. rice, sugar) and rubber processing, textiles. University

sail (seil) *n.* a piece of canvas or other cloth suspended from the spars of a boat or ship to catch or deflect the wind and drive the vessel along ‖ such sails collectively ‖ a ship, esp. a sailing ship, *not a sail in sight* ‖ a voyage by ship, *a five-day sail from the nearest port* ‖ something like a ship's sail in form or purpose, *the sails of a windmill* ‖ (*zool.*) a fin, tentacle or wing ‖ a windsail **in full sail** with all sails spread **to set sail** to hoist a boat's sails ‖ to begin a sea voyage **to take in sail** to reduce the amount of sail spread ‖ to curb one's ambitions **under sail** with sails spread [O.E. *segl, segel*]

sail *v.i.* to travel in a boat or ship with sails ‖ to make or start a sea voyage, *the liner sails tomorrow* ‖ to move or glide effortlessly in the air ‖ to walk in a stately manner, *the duchess sailed into the room* ‖ *v.t.* to travel over (a body of water) in a ship ‖ to manage (a boat or ship with sails) ‖ to cause to move or glide through the air **to sail against the wind** to sail in a direction other than or contrary to that of the wind ‖ to act or work under difficulties or opposition **to sail in** to sail into a task etc. **to sail into** to begin (a task etc.) with energy and enthusiasm ‖ to attack with words or blows **to sail near** (or **close to**) **the wind** to sail against the wind ‖ (*Br.*) to come close to breaking a law or rule, e.g. in a business deal [O.E. *siglan, seglian*]

sail arm an arm of a windmill

sail·board (séilbɔrd) *n.* (*sports*) an unsinkable flat boat with a single mast, usu. with no cockpit, for one or two passengers

sail·boat (séilbout) *n.* (*Am.=Br.* sailing boat) a boat normally propelled by sail, though often having an auxiliary engine

sail·cloth (séilklɔθ, séilklɒθ) *n.* canvas cloth used for sails, tents, casual clothes etc.

sail·er (séilər) *n.* a ship considered with reference to the way it sails, *a fast sailer*

sail·fish (séilfiʃ) *pl.* **sail·fish, sail·fish·es** *n.* any of various large fishes of genus *Istiophorus,* fam. *Istiophoridae,* related to the swordfish, and having a large dorsal fin ‖ the basking shark

sail·ing (séiliŋ) *n.* the act or skill of navigating a boat under sail ‖ the sport of navigating a boat under sail ‖ a ship's scheduled departure on a voyage

sailing boat (*Br.*) a sailboat

sailing orders instructions about a voyage given to the ship's captain

sailing ship a ship with sails

sail·or (séilər) *n.* a man professionally trained in the operating of a ship, or a member of a ship's crew below the rank of officer **a good (bad) sailor** a person who is rarely (often) seasick [alt. of older *sailer*]

sailor hat a round, flat-topped straw hat with a narrow brim

sail·plane (séilplein) **1.** *n.* a light glider **2.** *v.i. pres. part.* **sail·plan·ing** *past* and *past part.* **sail·planed** to glide in a sailplane

sain·foin (séinfɔin) *n.* *Onobrychis viciaefolia,* fam. *Papilionaceae,* a pink-flowered perennial Eurasian plant grown for fodder [F. fr. *sain,* wholesome+*foin,* hay]

saint (seint, *Br., when used in combination,* s'nt) **1.** *n.* a soul gone to heaven, esp. (*Roman Catholic and Orthodox Churches*) a person whose holiness has been attested by miracles after his death and who has been officially recognized (canonized) by the Church as worthy of veneration and to receive intercession ‖ (*abbr.* S. or St, *pl.* SS. or Sts) the title of a canonized person or of one receiving the same veneration ‖ (*pop.*) a person of great charity, patience, purity and meekness **2.** *v.t.* to canonize [O.F.]

SAINT *n.* (*mil.*) U.S. satellite inspector system. U.S.S.R. equivalent is ASAT

St Agnes's Eve the night of Jan. 20, when a young girl, upon performing certain ceremonies, expected to have a vision of her future husband

St Al·bans (ɔ́lbənz) a city (pop. 125,600) in Hertfordshire, S.E. England: Roman mosaics and theater. Norman abbey (793, largely rebuilt late 11th c.)

St An·drews (ǽndruːz) a town (pop. 13,100) on the northeast coast of Fife, Scotland. It contains Scotland's oldest university (1411). Famous golf courses

St Andrew's cross a cross in the shape of an X ‖ (*heraldry*) an ordinary consisting of such a cross, usually white on a blue ground. It is the cross of Scotland

St Anthony's cross a cross in the shape of a T

St Anthony's fire any of certain diseased conditions of the skin, esp. erysipelas or ergotism

St Au·gus·tine (ɔ́gəstiːn) a city (pop. 11,985) in N.E. Florida, the oldest in the U.S.A. It was founded in 1565 by the Spanish

St Bartholomew a mountainous island (area 9.5 sq. miles, pop. 2,200) in the Antilles, a dependency of Guadeloupe

St Bartholomew, Massacre of *BARTHOLOMEW, MASSACRE OF ST

St Ber·nard (bəːrnárd, *Br.* esp. bɔ́ːnəd) *n.* a dog of a large, powerful breed, famous for its use esp. at the hospice of Great St Bernard in the Swiss Alps for rescuing lost travelers

St Bernard, Great and Little two passes over the Alps. The Great St Bernard (8,111 ft), in the Pennine Alps 15 miles east of Mont Blanc, links the Rhône valley and Valais, Switzerland, with Valle d'Aosta, Italy. The Little St Bernard (7,178 ft), in the Graian Alps 10 miles south of Mont Blanc, links the Isère valley, Savoie, France, with Valle d'Aosta. Each shows traces of a Roman road and has a hospice and monastery founded by St Bernard de Menthon (11th c.)

St Christopher and Nevis *ST KITTS–NEVIS

Saint Clair, Lake (klεər) a lake (area 460 sq. miles) between S.E. Michigan and S. Ontario, Canada. The U.S.A.-Canadian boundary passes through it. Rivers join it to Lake Huron and Lake Erie

St Croix (krɔi) (or Santa Cruz) the largest island (area 82 sq. miles, pop. 49,013) of the Virgin Is of the U.S.A., south of St. Thomas Is. West Indies. It was purchased (1917) from Denmark by the U.S.A.

Saint-Cy·ran (sɛ̃siːrɑ̃), l'abbé de *DUVERGIER DE HAURANNE

St-De·nis (sɛ̃dəniː) a northern industrial suburb (pop. 90,000) of Paris, with a Gothic abbey church (12th-13th cc.), the burial place of the majority of French sovereigns

Sainte-Beuve (sɛ̃tbəːv), Charles-Augustin (1804-69), French critic. He is best known for his articles on French literature collected in 'Causeries du Lundi' (1851-62) and 'Nouveaux Lundis' (1863-70). His 'Port Royal' (1840-59) is a classic study in depth of the relation, in Jansenism, of literature, society and religion

St E·li·as, Mt (iláiəs) a peak (18,008 ft) in the St Elias Range on the boundary between S.E. Alaska and the S.W. Yukon Territory, Canada

St Elias Range a mountain range (c. 250 miles long) in E. Alaska and the S.W. Yukon Territory, Canada, containing great glaciers on its Alaskan slopes. Highest peak: Mt Logan (19,850 ft)

St El·mo's fire (élmouz) a flamelike discharge sometimes seen on ships' masts etc. during storms, similar in cause to brush discharge

St-É·tienne (sɛ̃teitjen) the chief town (pop. 218,289) of Loire department, France: coal mining, iron and steel, mechanical engineering, metalwork, textiles

St Eu·sta·tius (juːstéiʃəs) an island (area 11.8 sq. miles, pop. 1020) in the Leeward Is, part of the Netherlands Antilles

Saint-Ev·re·mond (sɛ̃tevrəmɔ̃), Charles de Marguetel de Saint-Denis de (c. 1614-1703), French satirical writer and essayist. His writings include literary and dramatic criticism and a voluminous correspondence

Saint-Ex·u·pé·ry (sɛ̃tegzypeiriː), Antoine de (1900-44), French writer and pilot, author of 'Vol de nuit' (1931), 'Terre des hommes' (1939), 'Pilote de guerre' (1942), 'le Petit Prince' (1943) and 'Citadelle' (1948)

St Gal·len (gǽlən) (*G.* Sankt Gallen, *F.* St Gall) a German-speaking canton (area 777 sq. miles, pop. 391,995) of N.E. Switzerland ‖ its capital (pop. 75,847): cathedral (14th c., restored in the 18th c.), formerly part of the Benedictine abbey of St Gall, famous (9th-11th cc.) as a leading center of art and literature

Saint-Gau·dens (seintgɔ́d'nz) Augustus (1848–1907), U.S. sculptor, born in Ireland, known for his monuments of heroic figures. He came to the U.S.A. at a young age and learned the art of cameo cutting to support his art lessons. After studying with François Jouffroy in Paris (1867) he began sculpting; by 1881 his bronze sculpture 'Admiral David Farragut' stood in Madison Square Park in New York City. Other works include 'Abraham Lincoln' (1887, Lincoln Park, Chicago), a shrouded seated woman in Rock Creek cemetery, Washington, D.C., (1886-91) and 'General William Tecumseh Sherman' (1897-1903, Central Park, New York City)

St George's cross a Greek cross, red on a white ground, the cross of England

St-Ger·main, Treaty of (sɛ̃ʒermɛ̃) a treaty (1919) between the Allies and Austria, dissolving the dual monarchy of Austria-Hungary. It recognized the independence of Hungary, Czechoslovakia, Poland and the country that was later called Yugoslavia, and made Austria a republic

St Got·thard (gɒtərd) a massif (highest peak 10,490 ft) in the Lepontine Alps, where the Rhône, Rhine and Ticino rise. The St Gotthard pass (6,808 ft) links Lake Lucerne (Switzerland) with Lake Maggiore (Italy), and the St Gotthard tunnel (completed 1882) links the Swiss and Italian railroads

St He·le·na (həlí:nə) a mountainous volcanic island (area 47 sq. miles, pop. 5,584) in the S. Atlantic 1,200 miles west of Angola, forming, with Ascension I. and Tristan da Cunha, a British Crown Colony. Capital: Jamestown. It was discovered by the Portuguese (1502), then from 1659 held by the East India Company under charter until 1834, when it came directly under the Crown. Napoleon was imprisoned here from 1815 until his death

St Hel·ens (hélinz) a town (pop. 98,769) and county borough in S.W. Lancashire, England: glass, metallurgy, chemicals

saint·hood (séinthud) *n.* the state or quality of being a saint ‖ saints collectively

St James's Palace the London residence of British sovereigns from 1697 to 1837. The British court, to which ambassadors are accredited, is still officially called the Court of St James's

St John (síndʒən), Henry, 1st Viscount Bolingbroke *BOLINGBROKE

St John (seintdʒɔ́n, *Br.* s'ntdʒɔ́n) the chief town (pop. 80,521) of New Brunswick, one of Canada's chief winter ports

St John (seintdʒɔ́n) a river (450 miles long) rising in N.W. Maine and flowing northeast to form a section of the Maine-New Brunswick boundary, then bending southeasterly to the Bay of Fundy. It was named by Champlain on the day of St John the Baptist (1604)

St John of Jerusalem, Order of the Hospital of *KNIGHT HOSPITALER

Saint-John Perse (síndʒənpé:rs, sɛ̃dʒɔnpɛərs) (Alexis Saint-Léger Leger, 1887-1975), French lyric poet. His works included 'Eloges' (1911), 'Anabase' (1924), 'Exil' (1942), 'Vents' (1946), 'Amers' (1957) and 'Oiseaux' (1962). His work is extremely difficult for the reader, full of obscurities, but the nobility and musicality of the language and the force of imagination in the poetry have irresistible power. He wrote a cadenced prose, using forms peculiar to himself. 'Anabase' is generally considered his masterpiece. He received the Nobel prize for literature (1960)

St John's (seintdʒɔ́nz, *Br.* s'ntdʒɔ́nz) the capital (pop. 80,000) of Newfoundland, Canada, a fishing port

St-John's-wort (seintdʒɔ́nzwə:rt) *n.* a member of *Hypericum,* fam. *Gutiferae,* a genus of wild and garden plants with bright yellow flowers

Saint-Just (sɛ̃ʒyst), Louis de (1767-94), French revolutionist. A fervent believer in the teachings of Rousseau, he collaborated with Robespierre in the Committee of Public Safety (1793-4), and shared Robespierre's fall

St Kitts-Ne·vis (kits-ní:vis), officially Saint Christopher and Nevis, independent state (area 103 sq. miles, pop. 44,000) in the Leeward Islands, West Indies. Capital: Basseterre (pop. 14,725). Language: English. People: African descent. Mountainous islands with volcanic peaks (Mount Misery, St Kitts, 3,793 ft. and Nevis Peak, Nevis, 3,232 ft.), the country has dense vegetation surrounded by beaches. Products: sugar processing, cotton, salt, copra. Exports: sugar, molasses, cotton. HISTORY. First settled by English colonists in the 1620s, it became, with Anguilla, a state in association with Britain (Feb. 27, 1967). Anguilla subsequently declared its independence and St Kitts-Nevis became an independent state within the Commonwealth in 1983

Saint-Lau·rent (sɛ̃lɔrã), Louis Stephen (1882-1973), Canadian statesman, Liberal prime minister of Canada (1948-57)

St Law·rence the river system joining the Great Lakes (U.S.A. and Canada) and linking them with the Atlantic, to form in all a waterway 2,100 miles long from the source of its headstream in N. Minnesota. Chicago, Detroit and Montreal are the chief ports. The St Lawrence was opened to oceangoing traffic (1959) by the St Lawrence Seaway (114 miles long), a canal system bypassing shoals and rapids between Lake Ontario and Montreal. The St Lawrence River proper (760 miles long) flows from Lake Ontario, forming the Ontario-New York state border, to the Gulf of St Lawrence. It was discovered by Cartier (1534)

St Lawrence, Gulf of a gulf of the Atlantic Ocean off the east coast of Canada, bounded by Cape Breton Is. and Newfoundland. It receives the St Lawrence

St Lawrence Seaway *ST LAWRENCE

St Leg·er (lédʒər) an annual English horse race run at Doncaster, Yorkshire, in September

saint·li·ness (séintli:nis) *n.* the quality or state of being saintly

St Lou·is (lú:is, lú:i:) the largest city (pop. 453,085, with agglom. 2,355,276) in Missouri, on the Mississippi, 16 miles below its confluence with the Missouri. It is a river port, rail center and market (furs, hides, wheat). Industries: mechanical engineering, automobiles, shoes, chemicals, food processing. Washington University (1857)

St Louis (sɛ̃lwi:) a port (pop. 81,204) of Senegal, on St Louis I., at the mouth of the Senegal River

St Lu·cia (lú:ʃə, lu:sí:ə) a mountainous, largely jungle-covered island republic (area 238 sq. miles, pop. 120,000) of the Windward group, West Indies. Capital: Castries (pop. 45,000). Highest point: 3,145 ft. People: mainly of African origin. Exports: bananas, copra, cocoa, coconut oil. The island was visited by the English (1605), claimed by the French (1642) and ceded to Britain (1814). It became a state in association with Britain (Mar. 3, 1967) and gained its independence in 1979

saint·ly (séintli:) *comp.* **saint·li·er** *superl.* **saint·li·est** *adj.* holy, like a saint ‖ of or pertaining to a saint

St Ma·lo (sɛ̃mælou) a walled fishing port (pop. 46,270) on an island joined to the coast of Ille-et-Vilaine, France: tourism

St Mar·tin (sɛ̃mɑrtɛ̃) (*Du.* Sint Maarten) an island (area 37 sq. miles, pop. 10,300) of the Leeward group, West Indies. Two thirds belong to the French department of Guadeloupe, the remainder to the Netherlands Antilles. Chief port: Marigot (French), a free port

Saint-Mi·hiel (sɛ̃mi:jel) a town (pop. 5,000) in the Meuse department of France, site of a 1st world war battle in which U.S. forces under Gen. Pershing defeated (1918) the Germans, capturing the vital Verdun-Toul-Nancy rail link. It was the first victory in the 1st world war of the U.S. army fighting as an independent unit

St Mo·ritz (mɔríts) a health and winter sports resort (elevation approx. 6,000 ft, pop. 7,400) in the upper Engadine, S.E. Graubünden, Switzerland

St Na·zaire (sɛ̃næzɛər) a port (pop. 69,251) of Loire-Atlantique, France, at the mouth of the Loire, the outport for Nantes

Sain·tonge (sɛ̃tɔ̃ʒ) a former province of France in the N. Aquitaine basin, largely forming Charente-Maritime. It is mainly pasture (dairy cattle, sheep), with salt marshes and oyster beds along the Atlantic. Crops: cereals, vines (for cognac). Old capital: Saintes. Included in Aquitaine, it was recovered from England in 1371 and annexed by the Crown (1375)

St Paul the capital (pop. 270,230) of Minnesota, on the Mississippi opposite Minneapolis, a rail center and livestock market. Industries: meat packing, automobiles, mechanical engineering

saint·pau·lia (seintpɔ́li:ə) *n.* a member of *Saintpaulia,* fam. *Gesneriaceae,* a genus of E. African plants, esp. *S. ionantha,* which is much cultivated as a house plant [Mod. L. fr. Baron Walter von *Saint Paul* (*d.* 1910), G. colonial administrator]

St Peter's the basilica (1450-1626) of Vatican City, Rome: floor plan by Bramante and Raphael, dome by Michelangelo, portico by Bernini

St Pe·ters·burg (pí:tərzbə:rg) *LENINGRAD

St Petersburg a winter resort city (pop. 236,893) in W. central Florida: fruit, vegetables, fish

Saint-Pierre (sɛ̃pjer) a town (pop. 6,000, formerly 26,000) in Martinique, destroyed (1902) by the eruption of Mt Pelée

St Pierre and Mi·que·lon (pjɛər, mikəlɔ́n, *F.* sɛ̃pjer, mi:klɔ̃) an overseas territory of France off S. Newfoundland, consisting of 2 main islands and 6 islets (total area 93 sq. miles, pop. 6,272), mainly bare rock. Industries: cod fishing, fur farming. The islands were claimed for France (1536) by Cartier

Saint-Saëns (sɛ̃sãs), Camille (1835-1921), French composer. His works include five symphonies, five piano concertos, three violin concertos, the opera 'Samson and Delilah' (1877), 'Carnival of Animals' (1886) for two pianos and orchestra, 'Dance Macabre' (1874) for orchestra, symphonic poems, chamber and church music, songs etc.

Saints, Battle of the a battle fought (1782) off Antigua, in which Admiral Rodney defeated the French admiral, François de Grasse (1722-88)

saint's day a day of commemoration in honor of a saint

Saint-Si·mon (sɛ̃si:mɔ̃), Claude-Henri, comte de (1760-1825), French philosopher and political economist. He was opposed to political authority and believed that society should be organized along the principles of a workshop, individual reward being strictly in proportion to productive merit. One of his principal works is 'le Système industriel' (1823-4)

Saint-Simon, Louis de Rouvroy, duc de (1675-1755), French courtier and writer. His 'Mémoires' provide a penetrating description of the French court (1691-1723)

Saint-Si·mo·ni·an (seintsimóuni:ən) **1.** *adj.* of or advocating the ideas of Claude-Henri Saint-Simon **2.** *n.* an advocate of these ideas **Saint-Si·mó·ni·an·ism** *n.*

St So·phi·a (sɔfáiə) *ISTANBUL

St Thomas *VIRGIN ISLANDS OF THE UNITED STATES

St Tro·pez (sɛ̃trɔpei) a popular resort (pop. 6,000) in Var, France, on the Riviera

St Vin·cent and the Gren·a·dines (seint vínsənt; grénədi:nz) independent state (area 153 sq. miles, pop. 138,000) consisting of St Vincent Island and the northern Grenadine Islands in the Caribbean Sea. Capital: Kingstown (pop. 23,959). Language: English. People: African descent. Wooded, mountainous islands, originally volcanic, the highest point is 4,048 ft. Products: arrowroot, bananas, coconuts. Exports: processed food. HISTORY. The island of St Vincent, whose inhabitants were Carib Indians, was disputed between the French and British (18th c.), ceded to Britain (1783), made a Crown Colony (1877) and part of the Windward Is colony (1885). It became a separate colony (1960), then a state in association with Britain and gained independence in 1979. A volcanic eruption in 1979 destroyed most of the banana crop and much of the agricultural land

St Vitus's dance chorea

Sai·pan (saipǽn) *U.S. TRUST TERRITORY OF THE PACIFIC

Saipan Island, Battle of a 2nd world war engagement in the W. Pacific, in which U.S. forces defeated (1944) the Japanese. Afterwards the island was used as a base for air attacks on the Japanese mainland

Sa·ïs (séiis) an ancient city of Egypt on the Nile delta. Princes of Saïs governed Egypt under the 24th, 26th and 28th-30th dynasties. It was the center of a brilliant civilization

Sa·ite (séiait) *adj.* of or pertaining to Saïs ‖ of or pertaining to the 26th dynasty of Egypt, founded by a native of Saïs

saith (seθ) *archaic 3rd pers. sing. pres.* of SAY

Sa·it·ic (seiítik) *adj.* Saite

Sa·kai (sɑkai) a town (pop. 810,000) in S. Honshu, Japan, on Osaka Bay: engineering, chemicals, textiles

sa·ke, sa·ké, sa·ki (sɑ́ki:) *n.* a Japanese liquor made from fermented rice [Jap.]

sake (seik) *n.* (in phrases) **for the sake of (someone** or **something)** and **for (someone's** or **something's) sake** for the benefit of (someone or something), *she did it for the sake of her health* ‖ for the purpose of attaining, achieving etc. (something), *he said it just for argument's sake* [O.E. *sacu,* cause lawsuit]

sa·ker (séikər) *n. Falco cherrug* (or *F. sacer),* a large falcon used in hawking, esp. the female [F. *sacre* fr. Span. and Port. *sacro* fr. Arab.]

sa·ker·et (séikərit) *n.* the male saker, smaller than the female [F. *sacret,* dim. of *sacre,* saker]

Sa·kha·lin (sǽkəli:n, sɑxɑlí:n) a wooded mountainous island (area 24,560 sq. miles, pop. 655,000) off S.W. Siberia, U.S.S.R., 25 miles north of Hokkaido, Japan, part of the R.S.F.S.R. Products: coal, oil, gold, fish. The southern half

CONCISE PRONUNCIATION KEY: **(a)** æ, *cat;* ɑ, *car;* ɔ *fawn;* ei, *snake.* **(e)** e, *hen;* i:, *sheep;* iə, *deer;* ɛə, *bear.* **(i)** i, *fish;* ai, *tiger;* ə:, *bird.* **(o)** o, *ox;* au, *cow;* ou, *goat;* u, *poor;* ɔi, *royal.* **(u)** ʌ, *duck;* u, *bull;* u:, *goose;* ə, *bacillus;* ju:, *cube.* x, *loch;* θ, *think;* ð, *bother;* z, *Zen;* ʒ, *corsage;* dʒ, *savage;* ŋ, *orangutang;* j, *yak;* ʃ, *fish;* tʃ, *fetch;* 'l, *rabble;* 'n, *redden.* Complete pronunciation key appears inside front cover.

of the island was administered (1905-45) by Japan, but was ceded to the U.S.S.R. in 1945

Sa·kha·rov (səkɔ́rɔf) Andrei Dimitriyevich (1921-), Soviet scientist, whose advocacy of nuclear disarmament and democracy brought internal exile to Gorky, winner of the Nobel peace prize (1975). A physicist, he helped to develop the Soviet H-bomb but was ostracized when he criticized the Soviets' violation of the Nuclear Test Ban Treaty in 1961. In following years he criticized the Soviet government's treatment of political prisoners and dissidents and called for nuclear arms reduction. He and his wife Dr. Yelena G. Bonner were sent into exile at Gorky in 1980 but his criticisms continued. They were released in Dec. 1986.

Sa·ki (sɑ́ki:) (Hector Hugh Munro, 1870-1916), British writer, best known for his witty, ironic short stories. Collections of these include 'Reginald' (1904), 'Reginald in Russia' (1910), 'Beasts and Superbeasts' (1914) etc.

sa·ki (sǽki:, sɑ́ki:) *n.* any of certain South American monkeys of fam. *Cebidae,* with long, nonprehensile tails, well-developed thumbs and neck ruffs. They are gregarious and nocturnal [F. fr. Tupi]

saki *SAKE

sal (sɑl) *n. Shorea robusta,* fam. *Dipterocarpaceae,* a tree of E. India, whose resin is used in varnishes ‖ its valuable hardwood [Hindi *sāl*]

sa·laam (səlɑ́m) **1.** *n.* an Oriental greeting, in India usually accompanied by a low bow and the placing of the right palm on the forehead ‖ this bow **2.** *v.i.* to make a salaam ‖ *v.t.* to greet with a salaam [Arab. *salām* fr. Heb. *shalom,* peace]

sal·a·bil·i·ty, sale·a·bil·i·ty (seiləbíliti:) *n.* the quality or state of being salable

sal·a·ble, sale·a·ble (séiləb'l) *adj.* capable of being sold or fit to be sold

sa·la·cious (səléiʃəs) *adj.* arousing lewd thoughts ‖ lewd in character [fr. L. *salax (salacis),* fond of leaping, lustful]

sa·lac·i·ty (səlǽsiti:) *n.* the quality or state of being salacious [fr. L. *salacitas*]

sal·ad (sǽləd) *n.* a cold dish of (esp. raw, green) vegetables etc., usually with a salad dressing ‖ a cold dish of which this forms a substantial part, *lobster salad* ‖ vegetables grown for salad, esp. lettuce [O.F. *salade* fr. Prov.]

salad days days of raw, inexperienced youth [after Shakespeare's 'Antony and Cleopatra' I, v]

salad dressing a sauce of oil, vinegar, mustard etc. for salad

Sal·a·din (sǽlədin) (Salāh-al-Dīn, 1138-93), sultan of Egypt and Syria, founder of the Ayyubid dynasty. His capture (1187) of Jerusalem led to the 3rd Crusade, in which he distinguished himself as the adversary of Richard I of England

Sa·la·do del Nor·te (sɑlɑ́ðɔðelnɔ́rte) (or Salado) a river (1,120 miles long) of N. Argentina, flowing from the Andes across the eastern plain to the Paraná at Santa Fé

Sa·la·do del Sud (sɑlɑ́ðɔðelsú:d) (or Salado) a river (850 miles long) of central Argentina, rising (as the Desaguadero) in the Andes and flowing the length of the Pampas. It joins the smaller Colorado before reaching the Atlantic

Sal·a·man·ca (sæləmǽŋkə, sɑlɑmɑ́ŋkɑ) a province (area 4,829 sq. miles, pop. 368,055) of W. Spain (*LEÓN) ‖ its capital (pop. 167,131): Roman bridge, two cathedrals (12th-13th and 16th-18th cc.), medieval and Renaissance monasteries, churches etc., central square (18th c.). University (early 13th c.)

sal·a·man·der (sǽləmændər) *n.* a mythical creature believed to live in fire and delight in it ‖ a member of *Caudata,* an order of amphibians superficially like lizards but with a soft, moist, brightly colored skin and no scales. The order includes newts and hellbenders. The adults are terrestrial and many are viviparous ‖ a hot iron plate for browning the tops of puddings, pastries etc. **sal·a·mán·dri·an** *adj.* [F. *salamandre* fr. L. fr. Gk]

sal·a·man·drine (sæləmǽndrin) *adj.* of or like a salamander [fr. L. *salamandra,* salamander]

sa·la·mi (səlɑ́mi:) *n.* a highly seasoned sausage of pork and beef [Ital.]

Sal·a·mis (sǽləmis, sɑlɑmí:s) an island (area 36 sq. miles, pop. 18,317) just off the coast of Attica, Greece, west of Piraeus

Salamis, Battle of the decisive victory (480 B.C.) of the Greek fleet over the Persians, fought off Salamis during the Persian Wars

sal ammoniac (sæl) *n.* ammonium chloride [L. *sal,* salt+AMMONIAC]

sal·an·gane (sǽləŋgæn) *n.* any of several swifts of Asia and Oceania, which make edible nests (*BIRD'S NEST SOUP) [F. or fr. Mod. L. *salangana* fr. *salamga,* the birds' name in Luzon]

sa·lar·i·at (səlǽri:æt) *n.* salary earners as a class

sal·a·ried (sǽləri:d) *adj.* receiving a salary

sal·a·ry (sǽləri:) *pl.* **sal·a·ries** *n.* a fixed regular payment made esp. to nonmanual workers (cf. WAGE, cf. FEE) [A.F. *salarie*]

Sa·la·zar (səlɑzɑ́r), Antonio de Oliveira (1889-1970), Portuguese statesman. As finance minister (1928-32), he restored economic order. As prime minister (1932-68), he established a dictatorship on fascist lines (1933)

Sa·la·zar y Es·pi·no·za (sɑlɑθɑ́ri:espi:nɔ́θɑ), Juan de (*b.* 1508), Spanish conquistador. With Gonzalo de Mendoza he founded (1537) Asunción, Paraguay

sale (seil) *n.* a selling or being sold, *to arrange for the sale of one's books* ‖ the amount of goods sold, *sales of wine have gone up* ‖ a public selling by auction ‖ a selling of surplus or out-of-date stock at reduced prices **for sale** offered for purchase **on sale** displayed for purchase [O.E. *sala* prob. fr. O.N.]

saleability *SALABILITY

saleable *SALABLE

Sa·lem (séiləm) a town (pop. 308,716) in N. central Madras, India: textiles, paper, mining (iron ore, manganese)

Salem a seaport and seaside resort (pop. 38,220) in the northeast corner of Massachusetts. Witchcraft trials (1692) led to the execution of 19 'witches'

Salem the capital (pop. 89,233) of Oregon. It is a processing center for the area's livestock, fruit, nut and vegetable farms. Paper and textiles are also produced. Site of Willamette University (1842)

sa·lep (sǽlep) *n.* a starchy food prepared from the dried tubers of certain orchids, esp. *Orchis mascula* [F. fr. Turk. fr. Arab. fr. *khus.a aththa'lab,* the fox's testicles]

sal·e·ra·tus (sæləréitəs) *n.* sodium bicarbonate, $NaHCO_3$, or potassium bicarbonate, $KHCO_3$, used for leavening [Mod. L. *sal,* salt+*aeratus,* aerated]

Sa·ler·no (sɑlérnə, *Eng.* səlɜ́:rnou) a port and agricultural market (pop. 161,997) of Campania, Italy, 32 miles south of Naples on the Gulf of Salerno, a wide inlet of the Tyrrhenian Sea. Cathedral (11th c.). It had a famous school of medicine (flourished 9th-13th cc.). During the 2nd world war it was the site (1943) of a flanking maneuver by Allied landing forces that was bitterly resisted by German forces

sale·room (séilru:m, séilrum) *n.* (*Br.*) a room where goods are displayed and sold esp. by auction

sales clerk a man or woman who sells goods in a store

sales·girl (séilzgɜ:rl) *n.* a saleswoman

Sa·le·sian (səlí:ʒən, səlí:ʃən) **1.** *n.* a member of the Society of St Francis of Sales, founded (c. 1851) by St John Bosco to educate poor children **2.** *adj.* of or pertaining to this order

sales·la·dy (séilzleidi:) *pl.* **sales·la·dies** *n.* a saleswoman

sales·man (séilzmən) *pl.* **sales·men** (séilzmən) *n.* someone whose job is to sell goods, whether in a store or by traveling to visit potential buyers

sales·man·ship (séilzmənʃip) *n.* skill in the technique of selling goods

sales resistance resistance by a potential customer to the persuasive influence of a salesman or of advertisements etc.

sales·room (séilzru:m, séilzrum) *n.* any room where goods are displayed and sold ‖ (*Br.*) a saleroom

Sales, St Francis of *FRANCIS OF SALES, ST

sales tax a tax levied on retail sales and collected by the retailer

sales·wom·an (séilzwumən) *pl.* **sales·wom·en** (séilzwimən) *n.* a girl or woman employee who sells goods, esp. in a store

Sal·ford (sǽlfərd, sɔ́lfərd) a port and county borough (pop. 98,024) in S.E. Lancashire, England, adjoining Manchester, on the Manchester Ship Canal: textiles, engineering, dyeing, rubber goods, paper

Sa·li·an (séili:ən, séiljən) **1.** *adj.* of or relating to the northern division of the Franks, united (late 5th c.) with the Ripuarian Franks under Clovis **2.** *n.* a Salian Frank [fr. L.L. *Salii,* a division of Franks, fr. R. Sala (now the IJssel)]

Sal·ic (sǽlik, séilik) *adj.* Salian [fr. F. *salique* or Med. L. *Salicus*]

sal·i·cet (sǽliset) *n.* an organ stop of soft tone, resembling the salicional but of 4-ft or 2-ft pitch [G. fr. L. *salix (salicis),* willow, with reference to the tone of a willow pipe]

sal·i·cin (sǽlisin) *n.* a bitter white crystalline substance, $C_{13}H_{18}O_7$, obtained from the bark of the willow and poplar and used in the treatment of rheumatism and neuralgia [fr. F. *salicine*]

sa·li·cion·al (səlíʃən'l) *n.* a soft-toned organ stop, sounding somewhat like the strings of the orchestra and usually of 8-ft pitch [G. fr. L. *salix (salicis),* willow, with reference to the tone of a willow pipe]

Salic law a law excluding succession by or through females, adopted in the Middle Ages by several European royal and noble houses and mistakenly thought to have been part of the laws of the Salian Franks. It was invoked (14th c.) in France and contributed to the outbreak of the Hundred Years' War. It was also responsible for the separation of Hanover and Britain on the accession (1837) of Queen Victoria

sa·lic·y·late (səlísəleit, sælisíleit) *n.* a salt or ester of salicylic acid [SALICYLIC ACID]

sal·i·cyl·ic acid (sælisílik) a colorless crystalline acid, HOC_6H_4COOH, formerly obtained from willow bark but now manufactured from phenol. It is used in the preparation of dyestuffs, and as a strong antiseptic, and in medicine as an analgesic and antirheumatic, usually in the form of its acetyl ester, aspirin [fr, F. *salicyle* fr. L. *salix (salicis),* willow]

sa·li·ence (séili:əns, séiljəns) *n.* the quality or state of being salient ‖ a striking feature, detail etc. **sá·li·en·cy** *pl.* **sa·li·en·cies** *n.*

sa·li·ent (séili:ənt, séiljənt) **1.** *adj.* being most prominent or of the most importance, *the salient points in a speech* ‖ pointing outwards, *a salient angle* ‖ (*heraldry*) shown in a leaping posture **2.** *n.* that which is salient, esp. (*mil.*) a part of a defense line which projects into enemy territory [fr. L. *saliens (salientis)* fr. *sal,* to leap]

sa·li·en·ti·an (seili:éntʃi:ən) **1.** *n.* a member of *Salientia,* an order of amphibians which are tailless in the adult stage, with powerful long hind limbs for swimming and leaping. The order includes frogs, toads and tree toads **2.** *adj.* pertaining to salientians [fr. Mod. L. fr. L. *saliens (salientis)* fr. *salire,* to leap]

sa·lif·er·ous (səlífərəs) *adj.* (*e.g.* of geological strata) impregnated with salt [fr. L. *sal,* salt+*ferre,* to bear]

sal·i·fy (sǽlifai) *pres. part.* **sal·i·fy·ing** *past* and *past part.* **sal·i·fied** *v.t.* to cause to become a salt ‖ to combine or impregnate with salt ‖ *v.i.* to become a salt [fr. F. *salifier*]

sa·li·na (səláinə, səlí:nə) *n.* a salt lake or marsh (e.g. in the Argentine plains) [Span.]

sa·line (séilain, séili:n) **1.** *adj.* of or containing salt, *a saline solution* ‖ salty in taste ‖ relating to or having the nature of chemical salts ‖ (*med.*) containing salts of alkaline metals or magnesium **2.** *n.* a salina ‖ a salt spring ‖ a natural deposit of salt ‖ a saline solution ‖ a saline cathartic or other metallic salt **sa·lin·i·ty** (səlíniti:) *n.* [fr. L. *sal,* salt]

Sal·in·ger (sǽlindʒər), J(erome) D(avid) (1919-), U.S. novelist. He is best known for his 'The Catcher in the Rye' (1951). Other works include 'Franny and Zooey' (1961) and 'Raise High the Roof Beam, Carpenters' and 'Seymour: An Introduction' (1963, published in one volume)

sal·i·nom·e·ter (sælinɔ́mitər) *n.* an instrument for determining salinity, e.g. the salinity of the seawater in marine boilers, by measuring the density

Salis·bur·y (sɔ́lzberi:, sɔ́lzbəri:), Robert Arthur Talbot Gascoyne-Cecil, 3rd marquis of (1830-1903), British Conservative statesman. As foreign secretary (1878-80), he attended the Congress of Berlin (1878). He was prime minister (1885-6, 1886-92, 1895-1902) and was also foreign secretary during most of the period. At home, he led the opposition to Irish Home Rule, and abroad was primarily concerned with African affairs, notably the Fashoda crisis (1898-9) and the Boer War (1899-1902). His avoidance of major foreign alliances has been described as 'splendid isolation'

Salisbury *HARARE

Salisbury a city (pop. 100,929) in Wiltshire, England, at the southern end of Salisbury Plain. Early Gothic cathedral (1220-58)

Salisbury Plain a treeless chalk plateau (area 300 sq. miles) in Wiltshire, England, the site of Stonehenge and other ancient monuments

sa·li·va (səláivə) *n.* a colorless viscous fluid secreted into the mouth from special glands, helping by its chemical composition to predigest food and, by keeping the mouth and throat moist, to facilitate swallowing **sal·i·vant** (sǽlivənt) **1.** *adj.* promoting the secretion of saliva **2.** *n.* an agent that promotes secretion of saliva [L.]

sal·i·var·y (sǽliveri:) *adj.* pertaining to or secreting saliva [fr. L. *salivarius*]

sal·i·vate (sǽliveit) *pres. part.* **sal·i·vat·ing** *past* and *past part.* **sal·i·vat·ed** *v.i.* to secrete saliva (esp. in excess) ‖ *v.t.* to cause an excessive flow of saliva in, e.g. by the use of mercury **sal·i·vá·tion** *n.* [fr. L. *salivare (salivatus)*]

Salk (sɔlk, sɔk), Jonas Edward (1914-), U.S. authority on virus diseases. He developed (1947) a dead-virus vaccine which protects against paralyzation in poliomyelitis. His research was further developed by Albert Sabin (1906-), whose live-virus oral vaccine largely replaced Salk's

sal·let (sǽlit) *n.* a light helmet of the 15th c. [F. *salade* fr. Span. or Ital. perh. fr. L. *(galea) caelata,* an engraved (helmet)]

sal·low (sǽlou) **1.** *adj.* (esp. of complexion) dull yellow or pale brown **2.** *v.t.* to make sallow [O.E. *salo*]

sallow *n.* any of several low, shrubby Old World varieties of willow, esp. *Salix caprea* ‖ a willow shoot [O.E. *sealh*]

Sal·lust (sǽləst) (Gaius Sallustius Crispus, 86–c. 34 B.C.), Roman historian. His 'Bellum Catilinarium' (43 B.C.) and his 'Bellum Jugurthinum' (c. 41 B.C.) are important for the character sketches they contain, rather than as accurate history

sal·ly (sǽli:) **1.** *pl.* **sal·lies** *n.* a brief and clever or fanciful witticism ‖ a burst of activity or outburst expressing emotion ‖ *(mil.)* a sudden attack made from a fortified position ‖ a little trip, *a sally into the hills* **2.** *v.i. pres. part.* **sal·ly·ing** *past* and *past part.* **sal·lied** (with 'forth' or 'out') to leave home, or a temporary stopping place, for a short journey ‖ *(mil.)* make a sally [F. *saillie* fr. *saillir,* to rush forth]

Sal·ly Lunn (sǽli:lʌ́n) a sweet tea cake, eaten hot and buttered [perh. after *Sally Lunn,* a street hawker in Bath, c. 1800]

sal·ma·gun·di (sælməgʌ́ndi:) *n.* a mixed dish of chopped meat, anchovies, eggs, oil, vinegar etc. [F. *salmigondis,* origin unknown]

sal·mi, sal·mis (sǽlmi:) *n.* a seasoned stew of game birds in wine or rich brown sauce [F. *salmis* perh. fr. *salmigondis,* salmagundi]

salm·on (sǽmən) *pl.* **salm·on, salm·ons** *n.* *Salmo salar,* fam. *Salmonidae,* a large N. Atlantic game fish prized for its flesh as food ‖ the orange-pink color of its flesh ‖ any fish of fam. *Salmonidae,* esp. of genus *Oncorhynchus,* living and breeding in N. Pacific waters ‖ any of certain fishes of families other than *Salmonidae,* having the reddish flesh of a true salmon [A.F. *salmoun, saumoun*]

—The silvery salmon adults feed in the sea, but ascend rivers in winter to spawn in shallow, gravel-based streams. In 120–140 days the newly hatched salmon escape. In the second or third spring after hatching, when uniformly bluish-silver and about 7 ins long, they descend to the sea and feed voraciously. They may return to spawn 18 months after descent (*GRILSE, * PARR, *SMOLT)

salmon ladder a fish ladder

salmon leap a fish ladder

salmon stair a fish ladder

salmon trout *Salmo trutta,* a European sea trout ‖ any of certain other trout or salmon

Sa·lo·me (səlóumi:) (c. 14–c. 62), daughter of Herodias. Herodias prompted her to ask Herod Antipas to consent, in reward for her dancing, to the death of John the Baptist (Matthew xiv, 8)

sa·lon (səlɔ́n, sælɔ) *n.* a living room or drawing room in a French home ‖ an assembly of wits, artists, writers or other men and women of society, meeting in the house of a society lady, esp. *(hist.)* in 17th-c. and 18th-c. France ‖ a room in which hairdressers, dressmakers etc. receive their clients ‖ an exhibition of paintings etc., esp. in Paris [F.]

Sa·lon·i·ca (səlɔ́nikə) *(Gk* Thessaloniki) a port (pop. 406,413) of central Macedonia, Greece, at the head of the Gulf of Salonica, a narrow inlet of the Aegean. Industries: textiles, tobacco. Greek and Roman ruins, Byzantine churches and fortifications. University

sa·lon·ist (səlɔ́nist) *n.* one who frequents social gatherings of interesting people *syn.* sallonard

sa·loon (səlú:n) *n.* a room, usually public, for some special purpose, *a billiards saloon* ‖ a lounge or other public room on a passenger ship ‖ *(Br.)* a large cabin for a first-class passenger ‖ a public room or establishment where alcoholic drinks are served ‖ *(Br.)* a saloon bar ‖ *(Br.)* a luxurious railroad car without compartments, often having a specified function, *dining saloon* ‖ *(Br.)* a sedan (automobile) [F. *salon* fr. Ital.]

saloon bar *(Br.)* a well-appointed bar in a public house, where prices are higher than in the public bar

saloon deck a ship's deck reserved for first-class passengers occupying saloon cabins, or the deck on which a saloon is located

sa·loon·keep·er (səlú:nki:pər) *n.* the owner or manager of a public bar

Sal·op (sǽləp) Shropshire [fr. A.F. *Sloppesberie* fr. O. E. *Scrobbesbyrig* Shrewsbury (the county town)]

sal·pi·glos·sis (sælpiglɔ́sis, sælpiglɔ́sis) *n.* a member of *Salpiglossis,* fam. *Solanaceae,* a genus of Chilean plants bearing handsome variegated flowers superficially resembling petunias [Mod. L. fr. Gk *salpinx,* trumpet+*glōssa,* tongue]

sal·pinx (sǽlpiŋks) *pl.* **sal·pin·ges** (sælpíndʒi:z) *n.* a Eustachian tube ‖ either of the Fallopian tubes [Gk=trumpet]

sal·si·fy (sǽlsəfi:) *pl.* **sal·si·fies** *n.* *Tragopogon porrifolius,* a European biennial composite plant, whose tubular white roots are eaten as a vegetable [F. *salsifis* prob. fr. Ital.]

sal soda (sæl) crystallized sodium carbonate, $Na_2CO_3 \cdot 10H_2O$, used in washing and bleaching fabrics

salt (sɔlt) **1.** *n.* a white crystalline compound, NaCl, which occurs widely in nature both as a solid and in seawater (2.6%). It is used as a food seasoning, as a preservative for meat and fish, as a raw material for the manufacture of many chemicals and in the manufacture of glass and soap. Salt is found in all animal fluids and plays an important role in maintaining the health of the animal and plant body. It is obtained commercially by the evaporation of brine or from solid deposits ‖ (esp. *pl.*) any of various naturally occurring substances, either mineral or saline mixtures, used as aperients or cathartics ‖ *(chem.)* one of a class of compounds derived from acids by the replacement of one or more acid hydrogens by a metal or by a radical acting like a metal. It may be produced by the reaction of an acid with a base or with a metal or metal oxide, or by the direct combination of its elements. Salts are usually crystalline solids that melt at high temperatures and that in the fused state or in solution conduct electricity ‖ a saltcellar ‖ *(pop.)* an experienced sailor ‖ something that adds piquancy, interest etc. **the salt of the earth** people or a person of simple goodness whom one regards as eminently worthy of respect **to take with a grain** (or **pinch**) **of salt** to have doubts about, regard as exaggerated **2.** *adj.* impregnated with or preserved in salt ‖ tasting of salt ‖ of or relating to salt water [O.E. *sealt*]

salt *v.t.* to flavor, treat or preserve with salt ‖ to enliven, *to salt a speech with racy anecdotes* ‖ to make (a mine) seem richer than it is by scattering valuable bits of ore in it **to salt down** (or **away**) to preserve in salt ‖ to store away (money etc.) [O.E. *sealtan*]

SALT *n. (acronym)* for strategic arms limitation talks, extensive negotiating sessions between the U.S. and the U.S.S.R. on the limitations on strategic nuclear weapons. SALT I opened in Helsinki in November 1969 and expired in 1970 without violation. SALT II, begun in Geneva in November 1972, attempted to achieve a comprehensive agreement on limiting strategic weapons, but it was not approved by the U.S. SALT III is the name for the prospective negotiations for qualitative and quantitative reduction in offensive nuclear arms

sal·ta·rel·lo (sæltərélou, sɔltərélou) *pl.* **sal·ta·rel·los** *n.* an Italian dance characterized by a skip at the beginning of each measure ‖ the music for this dance [Ital.]

sal·ta·tion (sæltéiʃən) *n. (rhet.)* a leaping ‖ a sudden change in the course of evolution [fr. L. *saltatio (saltationis)*]

sal·ta·to·ri·al (sæltətɔ́ri:əl, sæltətóuri:əl) *adj.* saltatory ‖ *(zool.)* adapted for leaping [fr. L. *saltatorius*]

sal·ta·to·ry (sǽltətɔri:, sǽltətouri) *adj. (rhet.)* of or relating to dancing ‖ proceeding by or characterized by sudden changes [fr. L. *saltatorius*]

salt·box (sɔ́ltbɒks) *n.* a New England frame house, esp. in colonial times, usually having two stories in front but only one at the back, the back slope of the gable roof continuing down over this lower part

salt cake sodium sulfate, Na_2SO_4, used in processing wood pulp and in making glass and chemicals

salt·cel·lar (sɔ́ltselər) *n.* a vessel for containing salt, used at table

salted weapon *(mil.)* a nuclear weapon that has certain elements or isotopes capturing neutrons at the time of explosion and producing radioactive products in excess of the usual debris *Cf* MINIMUM RESIDUAL RADIOACTIVITY WEAPON, NEUTRON BOMB

salt·er (sɔ́ltər) *n.* a person who handles, sells or makes salt ‖ a person who salts meat, fish etc.

salt·ern (sɔ́ltərn) *n.* a place where salt is obtained by evaporation or by boiling salt water [O.E. *sealtærn*]

salt glaze a stoneware glaze formed by the reaction of sodium chloride and silica when common salt is burned in the kiln towards the end of the firing

sal·ti·grade (sǽltəgreid) **1.** *adj.* having legs adapted for leaping **2.** *n.* a member of *Salticidae,* a family of saltigrade spiders [fr. L. *saltus,* a leap+*gradi,* to walk]

Sal·ti·llo (sɑltí:jɔ) the capital (pop. 245,738) of the Mexican state of Coahuila, 430 miles north of Mexico City, a commercial and communications center. Manufactures: woolen fabrics, knitted goods. Gold, silver, lead, zinc, copper, iron and coal are mined

sal·tine (sɔltí:n) *n.* a thin cracker baked with a salt topping [fr. SALT+-INE]

salt·i·ness (sɔ́lti:nis) *n.* the quality or state of being salty

sal·tire (sǽltiər, sǽltaiər, sɔ́ltiər, sɔ́ltaiər) *n. (heraldry)* an ordinary having the form X [O.F. *sautoir, salteur*]

Salt Lake, Great *GREAT SALT LAKE

Salt Lake City the capital (pop. 163,033) of Utah, in the W. Rocky Mtns near Great Salt Lake, a communications center and market for the Great Basin. Industries: metallurgy (esp. copper), meat packing, food processing. Mormon Tabernacle (1863-7). University of Utah (1850)

salt lick a place where salt occurs naturally or is placed, and which is visited by animals when they crave salt

salt marsh a marsh impregnated with salt water and partly covered by it at high tide

salt mine a mine where rock salt is hewn from a natural deposit

Sal·to (sɑ́ltɔ) a commercial and shipping center (pop. 80,000) in N.W. Uruguay, at the head of the Uruguay River: meat salting and canning

salt pan a natural depression near the sea, or a shallow vessel, in which salt water gathers and from which salt is obtained by evaporation

salt·pe·ter, salt·pe·tre (sɔltpí:tər) *n.* potassium nitrate ‖ chile saltpeter [older *salpetre* fr. O.F.]

salt pit a pit into which seawater comes and from which salt is obtained by evaporation

Salt Range a mountain range (average elevation 3,500 ft) in Pakistan between the Jhelum and the Indus

salt·shak·er (sɔ́ltʃeikər) *n.* a container having a perforated top for sprinkling salt on food

salt spoon a tiny spoon used for helping oneself to salt at the table

salt water water containing salt, esp. seawater

salt·water (sɔ́ltwɔ́tər, sɔ́ltwɒ́tər) *adj.* of or pertaining to or living in salt water

salt·wort (sɔ́ltwə:rt) *n.* a member of *Salsola,* fam. *Chenopodiaceae,* a genus of plants with sessile succulent leaves, growing in saline habitats, and used for making soda ash ‖ any of several other plants growing in saline soil

salt·y (sɔ́lti:) *comp.* **salt·i·er** *superl.* **salt·i·est** *adj.* containing or tasting of salt ‖ smelling like the sea ‖ *(fig.)* pungent, piquant

sa·lu·bri·ous (səlú:bri:əs) *adj.* good for the health, *a salubrious climate* ‖ morally wholesome [fr. L. *salubris*]

CONCISE PRONUNCIATION KEY: **(a)** æ, *c*a*t*; ɑ, *c*a*r*; ɔ *f*a*wn*; ei, *sn*a*ke*. **(e)** e, *h*e*n*; i:, *sh*ee*p*; iə, *d*ee*r*; ɛə, *b*ea*r*. **(i)** i, *f*i*sh*; ai, *t*i*ger*; ə:, *b*i*rd*. **(o)** o, *o*x; au, *c*ow; ou, *g*oa*t*; u, *p*oo*r*; ɔi, *r*oy*al*. **(u)** ʌ, *d*u*ck*; u, *b*u*ll*; u:, *g*oo*se*; ə, *bacill*u*s*; ju:, *c*u*be*. x, *lo*ch; θ, *th*ink; ð, *bo*th*er*; z, *Z*en; ʒ, *cor*sa*ge*; dʒ, *sava*ge; ŋ, *orangu*tan*g*; j, *y*ak; ʃ, *f*i*sh*; tʃ, *fe*tch; 'l, *rabb*le; 'n, *redd*en. Complete pronunciation key appears inside front cover.

sa·lu·bri·ty (səlú:briti:) *n.* the quality of being salubrious [fr. L. *salubritas*]

Sa·lu·ki (səlú:ki:) *n.* a dog of a swift, tall, slender Middle Eastern breed, used for hunting gazelles [Arab.]

sal·u·re·sis (sæljurí:sis) *n.* (*med.*) excretion of salt in urine —**saluretic** *n.* the drug which facilitates —**saluretic** *adj.* —**saluretically** *adv.*

sal·u·tar·i·ly (sæljutɛ̨rəli:, sæljutéərili:) *adv.* in a salutary way

sal·u·tar·i·ness (sæljutɛ̨ri:nis) *n.* the quality of being salutary

sal·u·tar·y (sæljutɛ̨ri:) *adj.* producing a good result, beneficial, esp. to the health ‖ designed to effect improvement, *salutary punishment* [fr. F. *salutaire* or L. *salutaris*, good for the health]

sal·u·ta·tion (sæljutéiʃən) *n.* the act of saluting, or of giving greeting ‖ something done or said in greeting ‖ the conventional opening of a letter or speech, e.g. 'Dear Sir', 'Ladies and Gentlemen' [O.F. *salutacion*]

sa·lu·ta·to·ri·an (səlu:tətɔ́ri:ən, səlu:tətóuri:ən) *n.* a student, usually the one with the second highest marks, who delivers an oration opening the graduating exercises in high school or college (cf. VALEDICTORIAN)

sa·lu·ta·to·ry (səlú:tətɔ̨ri:, səlú:tətɔ̨uri:) **1.** *adj.* having the nature of a salutation ‖ relating to or designating the oration of a salutatorian **2.** *pl.* **sa·lu·ta·to·ries** *n.* the oration of a salutatorian [fr. L. *salutatorius* fr. *salutare*, to salute]

sa·lute (səlú:t) *pres. part.* **sa·lut·ing** *past* and *past part.* **sa·lut·ed** *v.t.* to address with some sign of respect or spoken formula of greeting ‖ to make a prescribed gesture of respect to (a military superior), esp. by raising the right hand to the cap ‖ *v.i.* to make a salute [fr. L. *salutare* fr. *salus* (*salutis*), health]

salute *n.* the gesture, position, act or form of words used in saluting ‖ (*fencing*) a set of movements made before engaging [F. *salut*]

Sal·va·dor (sælvədɔr) (or Bahía) a port (pop. 1,027,100) of Brazil, 750 miles northeast of Rio de Janeiro, the country's oldest city and first capital (1549-1763). Industries: tanning, tobacco and food processing. Cathedral (16th c.), colonial churches and houses. University (1946)

Salvador, El *EL SALVADOR

sal·vage (sælvidʒ) **1.** *v.t. pres. part.* **sal·vag·ing** *past* and *past part.* **sal·vaged** to rescue from ruin, fire, shipwreck etc. **2.** *n.* things salvaged ‖ the act of salvaging ‖ the value of insured goods saved from a catastrophe etc. ‖ the money paid for saving a ship or cargo from loss at sea [F.]

sal·va·tion (sælvéiʃən) *n.* the act of saving from destruction or catastrophe, esp. the saving of the soul from sin or its consequences ‖ the condition of being saved ‖ something that saves, *the hut was his salvation in the storm* [O.F. *salvatiun*]

Salvation Army a worldwide Christian organization, founded by William Booth in 1865, devoted to evangelism and social work among the poorest and most wretched. It has a quasi-military form of organization

Salvation Islands three islands off the coast of French Guiana. With the mainland prison of St Laurent, they served (up to 1946) as an escape-proof exile center. About 75,000 of France's worst criminals were sent there. The islands include Devil's Is (used for political prisoners, of whom Alfred Dreyfus was the most famous), Ile Royale (for dangerous prisoners), and Ile St Joseph (for incorrigibles who, if they continued to make trouble, were guillotined and tossed to the sharks)

Sal·va·tion·ist (sælvéiʃənist) *n.* a member of the Salvation Army

salve (sæv, sɑv, *Br.* esp. sælv) *n.* a healing ointment ‖ something that soothes hurt feelings or a guilty conscience [O.E. *sealf*]

salve *pres. part.* **salv·ing** *past* and *past part.* **salved** *v.t.* to soothe or set at ease (feelings or the conscience) [O.E. *sealfian*, to apply a salve to (a wound etc.)]

sal·ver (sælvər) *n.* a tray, esp. an ornamental one of silver etc., used for presenting letters, drinks etc. [fr. F. *salve* fr. Span. *salva*, the tasting of food before serving]

Sal·ve Re·gi·na (sálveiridʒí:nə) *n.* (*Roman Catholicism*) an antiphon to the Virgin Mary, recited after Divine Office from Trinity Sunday to Advent ‖ the music for this [L.=hail, queen (the opening words)]

sal·vi·a (sælvi:ə) *n.* a member of *Salvia*, fam. *Labiatae*, a large genus of widely distributed annual or perennial plants of warm and temperate climates. They have lipped flowers, and are protandrous. Many varieties are cultivated, e.g. sage [L.=sage]

sal·vo (sælvou) *pl.* **sal·vos, sal·voes** *n.* a simultaneous discharge of guns, explosion of bombs, or burst of cheers [earlier *salva* fr. Ital.]

sal vo·la·ti·le (sælvoulæt'li:) *n.* ammonium carbonate ‖ an aromatic solution of this used as smelling salts [Mod. L.=volatile salt]

sal·vor (sælvər) *n.* a person or ship effecting a salvage [SALVAGE]

Sal·ween (sælwį:n) a river (1,750 miles long) rising in E. Tibet and flowing through Yunnan, China, and E. Burma to the Indian Ocean

Salz·burg (zɑ́ltsbu:rk, sɔ́lzbə:rg) a city (pop. 138,213) of N. central Austria in the lower Alps. Industries: chemicals, metallurgy, tourism. It was Mozart's birthplace, and is esp. famous for its annual music festival. Castle (11th-17th cc.), baroque cathedral (17th c.), medieval, Renaissance and baroque churches etc. University (1928) ‖ the province (area 2,762 sq. miles, pop. 347,000) of which it is the capital

SAM *n.* (*mil.*) U.S.S.R. surface-to-air missile. SAM-3, named Sandal by NATO, with a range of 1,500 miles; involved in the 1958 Cuban missile crisis. SAM-6, battlefield missile with a range of 20 miles. SAM-9, mobile-mounted, heat-seeking missile with a range of 5 miles

Sa·main (sæmɛ), Albert Victor (1858-1900), French poet. His verse (e.g. 'Au jardin de l'infante,' 1893) showed symbolist influence

Sa·mar (sɑ́mɑr) an island (area 5,050 sq. miles, pop. 1,019,358) of the central Philippines (Visayas)

Sa·ma·ra (səmɑ́rə) * KUIBYSHEV

sam·a·ra (sæmərə, səmǽrə) *n.* (*bot.*) a dry, winged, indehiscent fruit, usually having one seed, e.g. the fruit of the ash or elm [Mod. L. fr. L.=elm seed]

Sa·mar·i·a (səmɛ́əri:ə) the ancient capital (c. 932–c. 722 B.C.) of Israel. It is modern Sebastyeh (pop. 800) in Jordan, near Nablus, with Israelite, Assyrian and Roman ruins ‖ the region of W. Jordan containing this

Sa·mar·i·tan (səmǽrit'n) **1.** *adj.* pertaining to Samaria **2.** *n.* a native of Samaria, esp. a member of a Hebrew sect differing from the Jews in accepting only the Pentateuch. A dwindling number survive in Nablus, Jordan ‖ a Good Samaritan [O.E. fr. L.L. fr. Gk]

sa·mar·i·um (səmɛ́əri:əm) *n.* a metallic element in the rare-earth group (symbol Sm, at. no. 62, at. mass 150.35), discovered spectroscopically in 1879 [Mod. L. fr. SAMARSKITE]

Sam·ar·kand (sæmərkǽnd, sɑ̨mɑrkɑ́nt) (ancient Marcanda) a city (pop. 476,000) of W. Uzbekistan, U.S.S.R., the commercial center of an oasis region. Industries: food processing, cotton and silk spinning. Medieval city walls, Moslem colleges, tombs and mosques of Timur and his successors. From ancient times, Samarkand dominated the trade route between the Near East and China. It was taken (1220) by Genghis Khan, and became the capital of the empire of Timur (14th c.), who made the city splendid with gardens, palaces and mosques

sa·mar·skite (səmɑ́rskait) *n.* a velvet-black orthorhombic mineral with a vitreous luster [after Col. *Samarski*, 19th-c. Russ. mining official]

sam·ba (sǽmbə, sɑ́mbə) *n.* a lively Brazilian dance of African origin ‖ a ballroom dance derived from it [Port.]

sam·bar, sam·bur (sǽmbər, sɑ́mbər) *n.* any of certain large Asiatic deer with strong antlers, esp. *Cervus unicolor unicolor* of India [Hindi *sābar, sāmbar*]

sam·bo (sǽmbou) *n.* (*sports*) wrestling judo style

Sam Browne belt (sǽmbráun) an army officer's light leather belt with an attached shoulder strap [after Gen. Sir *Samuel* J. *Browne* (1834–1901), Br. army officer]

sambur *SAMBAR

Sam D *n.* (*mil.*) an army air-defense artillery surface-to-air missile system under development to replace Nike Hercules and the improved Hawk systems

same (seim) **1.** *adj.* (with 'the' or a demonstrative adjective having one individuality or self, *she wore the same dress all week, the cooking and the eating took place in that same small room* ‖ (with 'the') being of one kind, having one nature or set of characteristics, *several women had on the same dress at the party, the two houses look very much the same* ‖ (with 'the') corresponding, *it was hotter at the same time last year* ‖ (with 'the') not changing or showing change, *the same old routine* ‖ (with 'the' or a demonstrative adj.) being the one already mentioned, *that same boy was to become prime minister* **2.** *adv.* (with 'the') in the same way, *they both feel the same about it* **all the same** nevertheless, *all the same you should apologize* ‖ a matter of indifference, *if it's all the same to you, let's go tomorrow* **just the same** nevertheless ‖ exactly alike ‖ in the same way **3.** *pron.* (with 'the') the same person or thing, *the same applies to the rest of you, I'll have some more of the same, please* [M.E. fr. O.N.]

sam·el (sǽməl) *adj.* (of bricks, tiles etc.) soft, from being fired in the outer part of the kiln and hence insufficiently fired [etym. doubtful]

sameness (séimnis) *n.* the state or quality of being the same ‖ monotonous lack of variety

Sa·mi·an (séimi:ən) **1.** *adj.* of Samos or its people **2.** *n.* a native or inhabitant of Samos [fr. L. *Samius*]

sam·iel (səmjél) *n.* the simoom [Turk. *samyel* fr. Arab.]

sam·i·sen (sǽmisen) *n.* a Japanese three-stringed musical instrument played by plucking [Jap. fr. Chin. *san hsien*, three strings]

sam·ite (sǽmait, séimait) *n.* (*hist.*) a medieval heavy silk fabric, sometimes interwoven with gold or silver thread [O.F. *samit* fr. Gk]

sa·miz·dat (sǽmi:zdæt) *n.* (Russian, *self-publication*) unauthorized, typewritten works, clandestinely circulated to avoid legal censorship, e.g., *The First Circle*, by Alexander Solzhenitsyn —**samizdat** *n.* the system for publishing and circulating

sam·let (sǽmlit) *n.* a young salmon [contr. and dim. of SALMON]

Sam·nite (sǽmnait) **1.** *n.* an inhabitant of ancient Samnium, subjugated (4th–3rd cc. B.C.) by the Romans **2.** *adj.* pertaining to the Samnites [fr. L. *Samnites*]

Sam·ni·um (sǽmni:əm) an ancient country of central and S. Italy inhabited by the Samnites

Sa·mo·a (səmóuə) a mountainous archipelago (14 inhabited islands, with offshore islets) of volcanic origin in the central Pacific (Polynesia), divided into Western Samoa and American Samoa. The larger islands are circled by coral reefs and largely covered by rain forest. Average temperature (F): 70°-90°. Rainfall: 193 ins (esp. Dec.-Mar.). Main occupations: agriculture (yams, taro, breadfruit, pineapples, oranges, bananas), fishing. Livestock: hogs, cattle, poultry. The islands, inhabited by Polynesians, were discovered (1722) by the Dutch. Possession was disputed (19th c.) by the U.S.A., Britain and Germany until 1899

Samoa, American an overseas territory (land area 76 sq. miles, pop. 32,395) of the U.S.A., comprising E. Samoa. Chief port and capital: Pago Pago (pop. 1,500), on the largest island, Tutuila. Highest point: 2,141 ft. Exports: canned tuna, copra, handicraft products (*SAMOA). The islands came under U.S. control in 1899. A local legislature was established (1960). In 1977, American Samoa voters elected their own governor

Sa·mo·an (səmóuən) **1.** *n.* a native of Samoa ‖ the Polynesian language of Samoa **2.** *adj.* pertaining to Samoa, its language, people etc.

Samoa, Western an independent state (land area 1,097 sq. miles, pop. 159,000) comprising the westernmost and largest islands (Savai'i and Upolu) of Samoa, with offshore islets. Chief port and capital: Apia. People: Polynesian, with 7% of mixed race, and small European and Chinese minorities. Official languages: Samoan, English. Religion: about 80% Protestant, 20% Roman Catholic. Highest point: 6,094 ft, on Savai'i. Main exports: copra, bananas, cocoa. Main imports: meat, sugar, cotton textiles. Monetary unit: Samoan pound (*SAMOA). The islands were under German control (1899-1914) and then under New Zealand trusteeship (1920-61). They gained independence Jan. 1, 1962, but maintain special treaty relations with New Zealand. Western Samoa became (1970) a member of the Commonwealth

Sa·mos (séimɒs, sǽmous, sɑ́mɔs) a mountainous Greek island (area 180 sq. miles, pop. 41,709) in the Aegean, 1 mile off W. Turkey. Products: wine, tobacco, olives, fruit. Remains of the temple of Hera (16th c. B.C.). It was at the height of its prosperity in the 6th c. B.C.

Sam·o·thrace (sǽməθreis) (*Gk* Samothraki) a

mountainous Greek island (area 70 sq. miles, pop. 3,012) in the N.E. Aegean. The famous marble Winged Victory of Samothrace (now in the Louvre) was erected here c. 305 B.C. to mark a naval victory by Demetrius I Poliorcetes

sam·o·var (sǽməvɑr, sæməvɑ́r) *n.* a Russian tea urn in which the water is heated by charcoal burning slowly in an inner container [Russ.=self-boiler]

Sam·o·yed (sæməjéd) *n.* a member of a Mongolian people of the northern U.S.S.R. || a group of Uralic languages spoken by these people || any of these languages || (səmɔ́ied) a dog of a medium-sized, white, Siberian breed used for pulling sleds **Sam·o·yéd·ic** *adj.* of or relating to the Samoyed people or languages [Russ.=self-eater]

samp (sæmp) *n.* coarsely ground corn || porridge made of this [Algonquian *nasaump,* softened by water]

sam·pan (sǽmpæn) *n.* a flat-bottomed boat used on rivers and in harbors in China, Japan, Vietnam etc., usually propelled by oars [Chin. *sanpun,* boat]

sam·phire (sǽmfaiər) *n.* *Crithmum maritimum,* fam. *Umbelliferae,* a plant which grows in crevices in sea cliffs and has aromatic fleshy leaves which can be pickled for use as a condiment [earlier *sampere, sampire* fr. F. (*herbe de*) *St. Pierre,* St Peter's (herb)]

sam·ple (sǽmp'l, sɑ́mp'l) **1.** *n.* an individual portion by which the quality of more of the same sort is to be deduced or judged, *to examine a sample of dress material* **2.** *v.t. pres. part.* **sam·pling** *past* and *past part.* **sam·pled** to judge the quality etc. of (the whole) by examining a part [earlier *essample,* example]

sampler (sǽmplər, sɑ́mplər) *n.* a decorative piece of embroidery showing samples of different kinds of stitches and exhibited as evidence of the embroiderer's skill || someone who tests quality by inspecting samples [fr. O.F. *essamplaire,* model]

sam·pling (sǽmpliŋ, sɑ́mpliŋ) *n.* the act or process of selecting a sample || the sample selected || a system of statistical analysis in which samples are assumed to give a reasonably accurate picture of the whole

Samp·son (sǽmpsən), William Thomas (1840-1902), U.S. admiral who commanded the U.S. North Atlantic squadron during the Spanish-American War. He conducted the blockade of Cuba and ordered the destruction of Spanish vessels at Santiago

Sam·son (sǽmsən) an Israelite Judge, of the tribe of Dan. A man of phenomenal physical strength, he was betrayed to the Philistines by Delilah, his mistress (Judges xiii-xvi)

Sam·u·el (sǽmju:əl) a Hebrew Judge and prophet (11th c. B.C.) who chose Saul as first king of the Hebrews and David as his successor || either of two books of the Old Testament which relate the history of the Hebrews from the birth of Samuel to the death of David

Sam·u·el·son (sǽmju:əlsən), Paul Anthony (1915-), U.S. economist. He was awarded the 1970 Nobel prize for economics for his 'outstanding efforts to raise the level of scientific analysis in economic theory'

sam·u·rai (sǽmurai) *pl.* **sam·u·rai** *n.* (*hist.*) a member of a class of knights of feudal Japan who served their clan chiefs according to the bushido code of loyalty, honor and self-sacrifice. They were prominent in the overthrow of the Tokugawa shogunate (1867) and in the creation of modern Japan [Jap.]

Sa·n'a (sanɑ́) the capital (pop. 277,817) of Yemen, an ancient, walled trading center on the central plateau at 7,260 ft, 90 miles northeast of its port, Hodeida. Crafts: weaving, metalwork

San An·to·ni·o (sænæntóuni:ou) the commercial and communications center (pop. 785,410) of S. Texas, in a rich agricultural region and oilfield. Industries: oil refining, meat packing, chemicals, metallurgy, cotton textiles, tobacco. Spanish mission churches, palace (18th c.), the Alamo

san·a·tar·i·um (sænətéəri:əm) *pl.* **san·a·tar·i·ums, san·a·tar·i·a** (sænətéəri:ə) *n.* a sanatorium (residential building for patients)

san·a·tive (sǽnətiv) *adj.* (*rhet.*) healing [O.F. *sanatif* or M.L. *sanativus*]

san·a·to·ri·um (sænətɔ́ri:əm, sænətóuri:əm) *pl.* **san·a·to·ri·ums, san·a·to·ri·a** (sænətɔ́ri:ə, sænətouri:ə) *n.* a residential establishment for patients undergoing treatment (e.g. for alcoholism or tuberculosis), or one for convalescents || (*Br.*) an infirmary in a school etc. [Mod. L. fr. L. *sanare,* to heal]

san·a·to·ry (sǽnətɔri:, sǽnətouri:) *adj.* (*rhet.*) sanative [fr. L.L. *sanatorius*]

san·be·ni·to (sænbəní:tou) *pl.* **san·be·ni·tos** *n.* (*hist.,* Spanish Inquisition) either of two robes: one marked with a red St Andrew's cross, worn by heretics who renounced their heresy and were reconciled to the Church, or a black one bearing a design of devils and flames, worn by an impenitent heretic at the auto-da-fé [Span. fr. *San Benito,* St Benedict]

Sán·chez (sɑ́ntʃes), Francisco del Rosario (1817-61), Dominican general, patriot, and (with Juan Pablo Duarte and Ramón Matías Mella) a hero of Dominican independence. He rebelled against Santana and was executed

Sán·chez Car·ro (sɑ́ntʃeskɑ́rrɔ), Luis Miguel (1894-1933), Peruvian general and president (1930-3). He was assassinated by shock troops (*búfalos*) of the APRA movement, which he had persecuted

San·chi (sǽntʃi:) a village near Bhopal, Madhya Pradesh, India, celebrated for several Buddhist stupas, with elaborate carving, built about 250 B.C.

San Cris·tó·bal (sɑnkristɔ́bɑl) a city (pop. 241,000) in W. Venezuela, 100 miles south of Lake Maracaibo near the Colombian border. It is a commercial center

sanc·ti·fi·ca·tion (sæŋktifikéiʃən) *n.* a sanctifying or being sanctified [fr. eccles. L. *sanctificatio* (*sanctificationis*)]

sanc·ti·fy (sǽŋktifai) *pres. part.* **sanc·ti·fy·ing** *past* and *past part.* **sanc·ti·fied** *v.t.* to make holy || to reverence as holy || to give authority to, *sanctified by long custom* [M.E. *seintefie* fr. O.F. *saintifier* fr. eccles. L. *sanctificare* fr. L. *sanctus,* holy]

sanc·ti·mo·ni·ous (sæŋktəmóuni:əs) *adj.* making a pretense of holiness [fr. L. *sanctimonia,* sanctimony]

sanc·ti·mo·ny (sǽŋktəmouni:) *n.* the quality of being sanctimonious [O.F. *sanctimonie*]

sanc·tion (sǽŋkʃən) **1.** *n.* explicit permission given by someone in authority || a measure taken by a state or states with a view to coercing another state which has failed to comply with internationally agreed forms || a factor, e.g. a penalty for violation, tending to secure obedience to a rule of conduct or law || ratification of a law by a supreme authority || (*hist.*) a law or ecclesiastical decree **2.** *v.t.* to permit || to approve of, give encouragement to || to ratify || to attach a penalty to the violating of (a law) [F. or fr. L. *sanctio* (*sanctionis*), law or decree]

sanc·ti·ty (sǽŋktiti:) *pl.* **sanc·ti·ties** *n.* holiness || the quality of being sacred, *the sanctity of an oath* || (*pl.*) things held sacred, esp. rights and obligations or feelings [O.F. *saintété* fr. L. *sanctitas*]

sanc·tu·ar·y (sǽŋktʃu:eri:) *pl.* **sanc·tu·ar·ies** *n.* a sacred place || (*eccles.*) that part of a church which contains the altar || a place set apart as a refuge, *a bird sanctuary* || (*hist.*) a church or other building where, in the Middle Ages, certain categories of lawbreaker could take refuge from pursuers and be inviolate || the immunity thus taken or given [O.F. *saintuarie*]

sanc·tum (sǽŋktəm) *pl.* **sanc·tums, sanc·ta** (sǽŋktə) *n.* a sacred place || a private room where someone can be undisturbed [L. neut. of *sanctus,* holy]

sanc·tum sanc·to·rum (sǽŋktəmsæŋktɔ́rəm, sǽŋktəmsæŋktóurəm) *n.* the holy of holies in the temple in Jerusalem || a sanctum (private room) [L.=holy of holies, trans. of Heb.]

Sanc·tus (sǽŋktəs) *n.* the last phase of the preface of the Mass or Eucharist, beginning with the words 'sanctus, sanctus, sanctus' or 'holy, holy, holy' || the music for this [L.=holy]

Sanctus bell a bell rung at the Sanctus

Sand (sænd, *F.* sɑ̃), George (Aurore Dupin, baronne Dudevant, 1804-76), French writer. Her best-known novels are the 'rustic' or pastoral ones, e.g. 'la Mare au diable' (1846) and 'François le Champi' (1847-8), and those reflecting her mystical humanitarianism, e.g. 'Consuelo' (1842-5)

sand (sænd) **1.** *n.* small grains of quartz resulting from the breaking down of siliceous rocks, the grains being often rounded by the action of water or wind. It is used as an abrasive, is mixed with lime or cement in making mortar or concrete, and is a constituent of glass || (often *pl.*) a stretch of this, e.g. on the seashore || (*pl.*) a sandbank **2.** *v.t.* to abrade with sand or sandpaper || to sprinkle with sand, e.g. (*hist.*) as a way of drying the ink on a document || to cover, fill or treat with sand || to add sand to for purposes of fraud, *to sand sugar* [O.E. *sand, sond*]

san·dal (sǽnd'l) *n.* sandalwood [M.L. *sandalum* fr. Skr. *candana*]

sandal *n.* a sole attached to the foot by straps || an openwork slipper **sán·daled,** esp. *Br.* **sán·dalled** *adj.* wearing sandals [fr. L. *sandalium* fr. Gk]

san·dal·wood (sǽnd'lwud) *n.* the fragrant, close-grained wood of *Santalum album,* fam. *Santalaceae,* an Indian parasitic tree, used in cabinetmaking || the fragrant wood of various other trees resembling this || one of these trees

sandalwood oil a fragrant oil extracted from sandalwood and used in perfumery

san·da·rac, san·da·rach (sǽndəræk) *n.* *Callitris articulata,* fam. *Pinaceae,* a large Moroccan evergreen tree whose wood is used in building and is the source of a resin used in making varnishes || this resin [fr. L. *sandaraca* fr. Gk prob. fr. Assyrian]

sand·bag (sǽndbæg) **1.** *n.* a bag filled with sand or soil. Such bags are used in quantity to give protection from bullets, flood water or drafts, or for ballast etc. || a bag filled with sand used to stun a person **2.** *v.t. pres. part.* **sand·bag·ging** *past* and *past part.* **sand·bagged** to stun with a sandbag || to put sandbags against, bank up with sandbags || (*pop.*) to coerce, *to sandbag someone into doing something*

sand·bank (sǽndbæŋk) *n.* a bank or raised portion of the bed of a sea or river, made of sand accumulated by waves or currents

sand·bar (sǽndbɑr) *n.* a bank of sand built up at the mouth of a river or along a shore

sand bath a shallow vessel containing heated sand, used for heating glass vessels evenly, and in the tempering of steel

sand·blast (sǽndblæst, sǽndblɑst) **1.** *n.* a high-speed jet of sand used to engrave or cut glass, polish a metal surface or strip a surface of paint, rust etc. || the machine used for this **2.** *v.t.* to clean, polish, cut or engrave with a sandblast

sand·box (sǽndbɒks) *n.* a box containing sand, e.g. one carried in a locomotive for sprinkling sand on slippery rails || (*Am.*=*Br.* sandpit) a large container of sand in which little children can play

Sand·burg (sǽndbə:rg), Carl (1878-1967), American poet and biographer. His poetry catches the primitive quality of a rapidly expanding America. His biography of Abraham Lincoln (6 vols, 1926-39) won wide acclaim

sand-cast (sǽndkæst, sǽndkɑst) *pres. part.* **sand-cast·ing** *past* and *past part.* **sand-cast** *v.t.* to make (a casting) by pouring molten metal into a sand mold

Sand Creek the site in Colorado of an atrocity committed (1864) by U.S. troops. Cheyenne and Arapaho women and children were bayoneted, although they were friendly toward the U.S.A.

sand dollar any of several varieties of flat, round sea urchins, esp. *Echinarachnius parma,* which lives on the sandy bed of the sea on the east coast of the U.S.A.

sand dune a dune

San·deau (sɑ̃dou), Jules (1811-83), French novelist, author of 'Mademoiselle de la Seiglière' (1848)

sand eel a member of *Ammodytes,* fam. *Ammodytidae,* a genus of small, narrow marine fishes that bury themselves in the sand when the tide goes out

sand·er (sǽndər) *n.* a machine that sprinkles sand or abrades with sand || a person who operates such a machine or who cleans, polishes etc. by hand with sand or sandpaper

sand·er·ling (sǽndərliŋ) *n.* *Crocethia alba,* a small sandpiper with chiefly gray and white plumage. It breeds in the Arctic but migrates south and is common on most shores [etym. doubtful]

sand flea a flea found on beaches || *Tungo penetrans,* the chigoe

sand fly any of several biting flies, esp. a member of genus *Phlebotomus,* fam. *Psychodidae*

sand·fly fever a disease of short duration caused by a virus introduced by the bite of *Phlebotomus papatasii,* a sand fly

sand·glass (sǽndglæs, sǽndglɑs) *n.* a device similar to an hourglass, designed to measure a specific amount of time

CONCISE PRONUNCIATION KEY: **(a)** æ, *cat;* ɑ, *car;* ɔ *fawn;* ei, *snake.* **(e)** e, *hen;* i:, *sheep;* iə, *deer;* ɛə, *bear.* **(i)** i, *fish;* ai, *tiger;* ə:, *bird.* **(o)** o, *ox;* au, *cow;* ou, *goat;* u, *poor;* ɔi, *royal.* **(u)** ʌ, *duck;* u, *bull;* u:, *goose;* ə, *bacillus;* ju:, *cube.* x, *loch;* θ, *think;* ð, *bother;* z, *Zen;* ʒ, *corsage;* dʒ, *savage;* ŋ, *orangutang;* j, *yak;* ʃ, *fish;* tʃ, *fetch;* 'l, *rabble;* 'n, *redden.* Complete pronunciation key appears inside front cover.

san·dhi (sǽndi:, sʌ́ndi:) *pl.* **san·dhis** *n.* (*linguistics*) modification of the sound of a word or affix because of phonetic context (e.g. 'the' in 'the girl' and 'the only girl for me') [Skr. *sandhī,* a placing together]

Sand·hoff's disease (sǽndhɒfs) a form of lipidosis affecting the nervous system, similar to Tay-Sachs disease, characterized by paralysis, dementia, occasionally blindness

sand·hog (sǽndhɒg, sǽndhɔg) *n.* a workman employed in underground or underwater construction projects which use pneumatic caissons

sand hopper any of several small crustaceans of fam. *Orchestiidae,* commonly found leaping in great numbers on the sand of a seashore after the tide has gone out

Sand·hurst (sǽndhə:rst) the popular name for the Royal Military Academy (1802) of Great Britain, formerly at Sandhurst, Berkshire, now (since 1947) at Camberley, Surrey

San Di·e·go (sændi:éigou) a port and naval base (pop. 875,504) in S. California, on a protected bay: aeronautical engineering, tuna fishing and packing. Spanish mission church (1769)

San·di·nis·ta (sɑndi:ní:stɑ) *n.* revolutionary group, Sandinista National Liberation Front [FSLN], that replaced the government of Anastasio Debayl Samoza in Nicaragua in 1979; named for General Augusto Cesar Sandino

San·di·no (sɑndí:nɔ), Augusto César (1895-1934), Nicaraguan farmer, mining engineer, and caudillo who led (1927-33) Nicaraguan resistance to the U.S. occupation. He was murdered by agents of Gen. Anastasio Somoza

sand launce, sand lance a sand eel

sand·lot (sǽndlɒt) *n.* a vacant lot, sometimes sand-covered, where city children often play

S and M (*abbr.*) for sadomasochism

sand·man (sǽndmæn) *pl.* **sand·men** (sǽndmen) *n.* an imaginary man of folklore, who puts children to sleep at night by sprinkling sand in their eyes

sand martin (*Br.*) the bank swallow

sand mold, esp. *Br.* **sand mould** a mold for casting, made of sand

sand painting a ceremonial design made of colored sands and finely powdered minerals, used by some Navaho and Pueblo Indian tribes in healing rites and other ceremonies

sand·pa·per (sǽndpeipər) **1.** *n.* stiff paper covered with sharp grains of sand which are bound to it by an adhesive, used as an abrasive **2.** *v.t.* to scour with sandpaper

sand·pi·per (sǽndpaipər) *n.* a small shore bird resembling the plover but having a longer bill, esp. the European *Actitis hypoleucos* and *A. macularia,* the spotted sandpiper of North America

sand·pit (sǽndpit) *n.* (*Br.*) a sandbox

sand·shoe (sǽndʃu:) *n.* (*Br.*) a light canvas shoe with a sole usually of rubber

sand sink *n.* technique for removing oil spills at sea by adding chemically treated sand that adheres to oil, causing it to sink

sand·stone (sǽndstoun) *n.* a porous rock consisting of grains of sand cemented together by substances such as clay or silica which give it characteristic colors. Some sandstones containing considerable quartz are used as grindstones, building stones and furnace linings. If soft they are crushed to sand for commercial purposes

sand·storm (sǽndstɔrm) *n.* a storm of sand-laden wind

sand table a table with raised edges, having a layer of sand which can be manipulated to create landscapes, used to study military tactics etc.

sand·wich (sǽndwitʃ, sǽnwitʃ) **1.** *n.* two slices of buttered bread put face together with meat, fish, salad or vegetables etc. between them **2.** *v.t.* insert between two other things, places, persons etc., *he sandwiched a visit to them in between two jobs* [after John Montagu, 4th earl of *Sandwich* (1718–92), who was said to have eaten these to avoid leaving the gaming table]

sandwich bar restaurant counter specializing in sandwiches

sandwich board the two boards worn by a sandwich man

sandwich course (*education*) technical college courses programmed to alternate with a period of practical work experience

Sandwich Islands the former name of Hawaii

sandwich man a man hired to walk through the streets wearing advertising boards slung one in front of him and one behind him

sandwich shop small restaurant serving a limited menu of light meals

sand·y (sǽndi:) *comp.* **sand·i·er** *superl.* **sand·i·est** *adj.* full of or covered with sand ‖ like sand ‖ (esp. of hair) of the color of sand

sand yacht a beach vehicle with sails, usu. with three wheels *also* land yacht —**sand yachting** *n.*

sane (sein) *comp.* **san·er** *superl.* **san·est** *adj.* (of a person) in full possession of the mental faculties, not insane ‖ (of the mind) sound ‖ (of opinions, plans etc.) sensible [fr. L. *sanus,* healthy]

SA-N-4 U.S.S.R. ship-to-air missile. SA-N-6, named Gainful by NATO

San Fran·cis·co (sænfrænsískou) the chief port and financial and commercial center (pop. 678,974, with agglom. 3,252,721) of the western U.S.A. in N. California, on the southernmost of two hilly peninsulas protecting San Francisco Bay, which ranks among the world's largest natural harbors (area 456 sq. miles). Industries: food processing, chemicals, mechanical engineering, printing and publishing, metal goods. White-collar industries very much predominate, however, and the city's skyline has many high-rise office buildings, notably the Transamerica Building and the Bank of America tower. The city is also a major cultural and educational center, with three universities and three museums. Spanish mission church (1782). San Francisco was founded by the Spanish (1776) and grew rapidly at the time of the California gold rush (1849). It was the scene of the conference which established the U.N. and the International Court of Justice (1945) and of the treaty of peace between the Allies and Japan (1951) after the 2nd world war. Its Haight-Ashbury district was the home of the 'flower children' of the 1960s

San Francisco Bay a large landlocked bay (40 miles long, 3-12 miles wide) on the west central coast of California, connecting with the Pacific through the Golden Gate. San Francisco is situated at its entrance and Oakland on its northeast shore

San Francisco Conference the conference held (1945) in San Francisco, Calif., which promulgated the charter of the United Nations

sang *past* of SING

San·gal·lo (sɑngɑ́llɔ), Antonio 'the Younger' (1483-1546), Italian architect, nephew of Giuliano. He built the Farnese palace in Rome

Sangallo, Giuliano da (1445-1516), Italian architect. He worked with Raphael on the building of St Peter's in Rome

san·ga·ree (sæŋgərí:) *n.* a sweetened, spiced, usually iced drink of wine and water [fr. Span. *sangria*]

Sang·er (sǽŋər), Margaret (1883-1966), U.S. social activist, founder of the National Birth Control League (1914). A nurse in the slums of New York City, she saw the consequences of self-induced abortions and pioneered the birth-control movement in the U.S.A., eventually winning the right for doctors to inform their patients of birth-control methods. She was the first president of the International Planned Parenthood Federation (1953)

sang·froid (sɑ̃frwæ) *n.* calm self-possession at a time of danger or stress [F. fr. *sang,* blood+*froid,* cold]

San·grail (sæŋgréil) *n.* the Holy Grail (*GRAIL) [O.F. *Saint Graal*]

san·gri·a (sæŋgrí:ə) *n.* a wine punch with fruit juices

Sang·ster (sǽŋstər), Sir Donald B. (1911-67), Jamaican statesman, leader of the Jamaican Labor party, minister of finance (1963), acting prime minister (1965-7) and prime minister (Feb.-Mar. 1967)

san·gui·nar·i·ly (sǽŋgwinerili:) *adv.* in a sanguinary way

san·gui·nar·i·ness (sǽŋgwəneri:nis) *n.* the quality or state of being sanguinary

san·gui·nar·y (sǽŋgwəneri:) *adj.* accompanied by much bloodshed ‖ wanting to shed blood, murderous, *a sanguinary nature* ‖ (of laws) exaggerating the use of the death penalty [fr. L. *sanguinarius* fr. *sanguis,* blood]

san·guine (sǽŋgwin) **1.** *adj.* (esp. of complexion) ruddy ‖ cheerfully optimistic **2.** *n.* a reddish drawing crayon, esp. of red hematite ‖ a drawing made with red crayon or chalk [F. *sanguin*]

san·guin·e·ous (sæŋgwíni:əs) *adj.* pertaining to blood ‖ blood-red ‖ bloodthirsty [fr. L. *sanguineus*]

San·he·drim (sǽnhidrim, sǽnidrim) the Sanhedrin

San·hed·rin (sænhédrin, sænhí:drin, sǽnhidrin, sǽnidrin) (*hist.*) the Jewish supreme council and court of justice in New Testament times, consisting of 71 priests, scribes and elders

san·i·cle (sǽnik'l) *n.* a member of *Sanicula,* fam. *Umbelliferae,* a genus of perennial plants found in woods. Its roots were formerly used medicinally ‖ any of several other plants supposed to have healing powers [O.F.]

sa·ni·es (séini:i:z) *n.* a watery discharge of blood and pus from ulcers or infected wounds **sá·ni·ous** *adj.* [L.]

San Il·de·fon·so, Treaty of (sænildifɔ́nsou, sɑni:ldefɔ́nsɔ) a Franco-Spanish treaty (1800) dictated by Napoleon Bonaparte in Segovia, Spain. France regained Louisiana from Spain in exchange for a promise that Napoleon would give an Italian kingdom to a member of the Spanish royal family. Napoleon planned to use the Louisiana territory as a supply base in his drive to reconquer the French West Indies and revive the French New World empire. Disregarding the treaty's provision never to cede Louisiana, he abandoned his designs with the Louisiana Purchase (1803)

san·i·tar·i·um (sænitέəri:əm) *pl.* **san·i·tar·i·ums, san·i·tar·i·a** (sænitέəri:ə) *n.* a sanatorium (residential establishment for patients) [fr. L. *sanitas,* health]

san·i·tar·y (sǽniteri:) *adj.* concerned with, promoting or conducive to the preservation of health [fr. F. *sanitaire*]

sanitary napkin (*Am.=Br.* sanitary towel) a pad of absorbent cotton worn by women during menstruation to absorb the menstrual flow

sanitary towel (*Br.*) a sanitary napkin

san·i·ta·tion (sænitéiʃən) *n.* the provision of means whereby health is protected, esp. the arrangements for the disposal of sewage

san·i·tize (sǽnitaiz) *v.* to revise a report or document in order to prevent identification of information sources, of the actual persons and places with which it is concerned, or of the means by which it was acquired

san·i·ty (sǽniti:) *n.* the quality or state of being sane [F. *sanité*]

San Ja·cin·to, Battle of (sændʒəsíntou) an engagement (1836) in S. Texas, in which Gen. Sam Houston's Texan troops defeated the Mexicans under Gen. Santa Anna, and so won independence for Texas

San Jor·ge, Gulf of (sɑnhɔ́rhe) an inlet (145 miles long, 100 miles wide) of the Atlantic on the east coast of S. Argentina

San Jo·se (sænhouzéi) a computer center and agricultural market (pop. 636,550) in N. central California: fruit canning and packing, wine making, and the U.S.A.'s largest computer and electronics industry, which has led to the San Jose area's being nicknamed 'Silicon Valley'

San Jo·sé (sɑnhɔsé) the capital (pop. 250,079) of Costa Rica, in the central plateau, commercial center of an agricultural region. Spanish cathedral, palace (18th c.). University (1843), national theater

San José Declaration a declaration issued at a meeting of consultation of foreign ministers of the American Republics under the Rio Treaty, held (1960) at San José, Costa Rica. It condemned 'the intervention, or the threat of intervention, even when conditional, by an extra-continental power in the affairs of the American Republics'. It was aimed at the Sino-Soviet powers

San Jose scale *Aspidiotus perniciosus,* a scale insect of warm and temperate climates which destroys fruit trees [after SAN JOSE, California, the first place of entry into the country]

San Juan (sɑnhwɑ́n, sænwɑ́n) a commercial center (pop. 112,582) of N.W. Argentina at the foot of the Andes in a rich farming and mining region, founded in 1562 but rebuilt after an earthquake in 1944

San Juan the capital and chief port (pop. 424,600) of Puerto Rico, on two islets joined to the northeast coast, founded (1521) by the Spanish. Industries: sugar refining, tobacco, plastics, light manufacturing. Spanish cathedral (16th-19th cc.), castle (17th c.)

San Juan del Nor·te (sɑnhwɑ́ndelnɔ́rte) the settlement in Nicaragua, at the mouth of the San Juan River, where a British force laid claim (1740) to sovereignty over Nicaragua

CONCISE PRONUNCIATION KEY: **(a)** æ, c*a*t; ɑ, c*a*r; ɔ f*aw*n; ei, sn*a*ke. **(e)** e, h*e*n; i:, sh*ee*p; iə, d*ee*r; εə, b*ea*r. **(i)** i, f*i*sh; ai, t*i*ger; ə:, b*i*rd. **(o)** o, *o*x; au, c*ow*; ou, g*oa*t; u, p*oo*r; ɔi, r*oy*al. **(u)** ʌ, d*u*ck; u, b*u*ll; u:, g*oo*se; ə, bacill*u*s; ju:, c*u*be. x, lo*ch*; θ, *th*ink; ð, bo*th*er; z, *Z*en; ʒ, corsa*g*e; dʒ, sava*g*e; ŋ, orang*u*tang; j, *y*ak; ʃ, fi*sh*; tʃ, fe*tch*; 'l, rabb*le*; 'n, redd*en*. Complete pronunciation key appears inside front cover.

San Juan Hill, Battle of an engagement (1898) in E. Cuba during the Spanish-American War, in which Spanish troops were routed by Theodore Roosevelt and his Rough Riders

sank *past* of SINK

San·ka·ra (sʌ́ŋkərə) a commentator on the Upanishads and the Bhagavadgita, writing c. 800 A.D. An upholder of traditional monistic Hinduism, he developed the doctrine of illusion (maya): not only the variety of sense apprehensions is illusory, but sense apprehension itself, and all human 'knowing' is mere hallucination

San·khya (sǽŋkjə) *n.* a dualistic system of Hindu philosophy [Skr. *sāmkhya*]

San Lo·ren·zo, Cape (sɑnlɔrénsɔ) a cape on the west central coast of Ecuador

San Lu·is Po·to·sí (sɑnlu:íspɔtɔsí:) a leading mining state (area 24,266 sq. miles, pop. 1,670,637) in Mexico, in the central high plateau region. Capital: San Luis Potosí. Agriculture: wheat, corn, beans, cotton, sugar, coffee, tobacco and fruit. Mining: primarily silver (also gold, copper, zinc and bismuth). Stock raising

San Luis Potosí the capital (pop. 327,333) of the state of San Luis Potosí, Mexico, 215 miles northwest of Mexico City. It is the hub of a rich silver-mining and agricultural region and a leading manufacturing center: rope, brushes, shoes, cotton, woolen textiles, clothing

San Mar·cos, University of *UNIVERSIDAD DE SAN MARCOS

San Ma·ri·no (sæ̜nmərí:nou) a republic (area 23 sq. miles, pop. 21,622) in the E. Apennines, forming an enclave in Italy between Emilia-Romagna and the Marches. Language: Italian. Industries: agriculture, tourism. Exports: wine, postage stamps. The republic dates probably from the mid-4th c. It entered into a customs union and treaty of friendship with Italy (1862) ‖ its walled capital (pop. 1,500): 14th-c. church

San Mar·tín (sɑnmɑrtí:n), José de (1778-1850), Argentinian general and politician. He fought as general in the struggles for independence of Argentina (1814-6) and led across the Andes the army which liberated Chile (1817) and Peru (1821) from Spanish rule. As Protector of Peru (1821-2), he abolished slavery. He retired in favor of Bolívar

San Ma·tí·as, Gulf of (sɑnmɑtí:ɑs) an inlet (115 miles long, 60-100 miles wide) of the Atlantic in S. central Argentina

San·ni *GOA

San Pe·dro Su·la (sɑnpéðrɔsú:lɑ) a town (pop. 342,800) in N. Honduras, the economic center of Honduras

San Re·mo (sæ̜nrí:mou, sæ̜nréimou, sɑnrémɔ) a resort (pop. 53,200) of Liguria, Italy, on the Riviera near the French frontier: Romanesque cathedral (13th c.)

San Sal·va·dor (sænsǽlvədɔr, sɑnsɑlvɑðɔ́r) the capital (pop. 500,000) of El Salvador, at the foot of a volcano in the central highlands. Industries: textiles, food processing, tobacco. University. Founded in 1525, the city has been destroyed several times by earthquakes and floods

San Sal·va·dor (sænsǽlvədɔr) (or Watling Is.) an island (area 60 sq. miles, pop. 776) of the Bahamas, southeast of Cat Is. Columbus first made landfall (1492) in the New World here

sans-cu·lotte (sãkylɔt) *n.* (*F. hist.*) a working-class republican in Paris during the French Revolution [F.=without breeches. (Breeches were discarded in favor of long pants by this class)]

San Se·bas·tián (sæ̜nsibǽstʃən, sɑnsebɑstjɑ́n) the capital (pop. 175,576) of Guipúzcoa, Spain, and summer capital of the country, a port and resort on the Bay of Biscay. Industries: chemicals, metallurgy, glass

san·sei (sɑ́nséi) *pl.* **san·sei, san·seis** *n.* an American citizen whose grandparents were Japanese immigrants to the U.S.A. and who is educated mostly in the U.S.A. (cf. NISEI, cf. KIBEI, cf. ISSEI) [Jap. = third generation]

sanserif *SANS SERIF

San·skrit (sǽnskrit) *n.* the ancient language of India, belonging to the Indo-European family. The oldest literary period of Sanskrit is the Vedic (c. 1500–c. 200 B.C.). The classic period was c. 200 B.C.–c. 1100 A.D. Some of the oldest Indo-European texts are in Sanskrit. The comparison of Sanskrit with European languages at the end of the 18th c. was the starting point of scientific language study

sans ser·if, san·ser·if (sǽnsérif) *n.* a printing type with no serifs [fr. F. *sans,* without+SERIF]

San Ste·fa·no, Treaty of (sɑnstéfɑnɔ) a treaty (1878) ending the Russo-Turkish War (1877-8). It created a large independent state of Bulgaria, and confirmed the independence of Serbia, Montenegro and Rumania. Russia gained land in the Caucasus and a large war indemnity. The treaty roused British and Austrian opposition, and was rapidly quashed by the Congress of Berlin (1878)

San·ta An·a (sɑ́ntɑɑ́nɑ) a commercial center (pop. 109,300) of N. central El Salvador: textiles, tobacco

Santa Ana the highest volcanic peak (8,300 ft) in El Salvador

San·ta An·na (sɑ́ntɑɑ́nɑ, sǽntəǽnə), Antonio Lopez de (c. 1794-1876), Mexican general and politician. By political opportunism he became president of Mexico (1833-6, 1841-4, 1846-7 and 1853-5)

San·ta Bar·ba·ra Islands (sǽntəbɑ́rbərə, sǽntəbɑ́rbrə) a chain of islands and islets extending about 160 miles along the S. California coast, divided into a northern and a southern group. They are separated from the mainland by channels and are sometimes called the Channel Islands

San·ta Cla·ra (sɑ́ntɑklɑ́rɑ, sǽntəklǽrə) a city (pop. 525,402) of W. central Cuba. It is the capital of its province and an important railroad, sugar, and tobacco center. Port: Cienfuegos

San·ta Claus (sǽntəklɔz) the legendary friend of children, identified with St Nicholas, now usually depicted as a fat, jolly old man with a white beard wearing red, who brings children presents on Christmas Eve (or on St Nicholas' Day in some European countries) [fr. Du. dial. *Sante Klaas* fr. *Sant Nikolaas,* St Nicholas]

San·ta Cruz (sɑ́ntɑkrú:s), Andrés de (c. 1792-1865), Bolivian marshal and president of the Republic (1829-36). He created (1836) the Peru-Bolivian Federation and served (1836-9) as its Protector. He was defeated (1839) at Yungay by Chilean forces

Santa Cruz an agricultural market (pop. 255,568) of central Bolivia on the plain and the terminus of a railroad to São Paulo, Brazil

San·ta Cruz de Te·ne·ri·fe (sɑ́ntɑkrú:sðetẹnerí:fe) a province (area 1,528 sq. miles, pop. 653,833) of Spain comprising the W. Canary Is ‖ its capital (pop. 179,600), the chief port of Tenerife: oil refining

Santa Cruz Is. *ST CROIX

San·ta Cruz y Es·pe·jo (sɑ́ntɑkrú:si:espéhɔ), Francisco Javier Eugenio de (1740-95), Ecuadorian encyclopedist, physician and patriot, the author of 'El nuevo Luciano o Despertador de los ingenios'

San·ta E·le·na (sɑ́ntɑelénɑ) a peninsula in W. Ecuador, on the north side of the Gulf of Guayaquil. Its tip is La Puntilla

Santa Elena Bay a bay in W. Ecuador on the north side of the Santa Elena peninsula: the site of most of Ecuador's oil fields

San·ta Fé (sɑ́ntɑfé) a river port (pop. 244,655) in Argentina on the eastern edge of the Pampa at the confluence of the Paraná and the Salado del Norte, founded in 1573. University (1920)

San·ta Fe (sǽntəféi) the capital (pop. 48,899) of New Mexico, in the upper Rio Grande valley, founded by the Spanish c. 1610. Spanish churches (17th and 18th cc.). Indian pueblos. It is a health resort and tourist center

Santa Fe Trail an overland trade route from W. Missouri to Santa Fe, New Mexico, which flourished from 1822 until the coming of the railroad in the 1880s

San·ta I·sa·bel (sɑ́ntɑi:sɑbél) the capital (pop. 37,237) of Equatorial Guinea, a port on Fernando Poo exporting cacao and coffee

Santa María la Antigua del Darién *DARIÉN

San·ta Mar·ta (sɑ́ntɑmɑ́rtɑ) the oldest city (pop. 128,577) in Colombia, on the Caribbean, founded by the Spanish in 1525, now among the world's largest banana ports. Simón Bolívar died here

San·ta·na (sɑntɑ́nɑ), Pedro (1801-64), Dominican general who led the liberation (1844) from Haiti and served (1844-8, 1853-6, 1858-61) as president of the Republic. In 1861 he decreed the reannexation of his country to Spain as a province. This lasted until 1865

San·tan·der (sɑntɑndér), Francisco de Paula (1792-1840), Colombian general and politician. He joined Bolívar's army and won victories at Paya, Pantano de Vargas, and Boyacá. As vice-president of Cundinamarca (1819-26), he participated in a rebellion against Bolívar for which he was condemned to death, but the sentence was commuted to exile. As president of Nueva Granada (1832-7) he initiated advances in education and civics

Santander a province (area 2,108 sq. miles, pop. 432,000) of N. Spain (*OLD CASTILE) ‖ its capital (pop. 170,700) a port and resort on the Bay of Biscay. Industries: fishing, metallurgy, dairy processing. Gothic cathedral (14th-15th cc.)

San·ta·ya·na (sɑnti:ǽnə, sɑntɑjɑ́nɑ), George (1863-1952), American philosopher and poet. In 'The Life of Reason' (1905), 'Scepticism and Animal Faith' (1923) and 'The Realm of Essence' (1928) he restated Aristotelian principles in mechanistic materialist terms. He wrote one novel, 'The Last Puritan' (1935)

San·tia·go (sɑntjɑ́gɔ, sɑnti:ɑ́gou) the capital and economic center (pop. 3,448,700, with agglom. 4,111,800) of Chile, in the center, at the foot of the W. Andes. It was founded (1541) by the Spanish. Industries (over 50% of national production): textiles, food processing, light manufacturing. Cathedral (1748). National university (1747), museum and library. One quarter of the population of Chile lives here

Santiago (Río Grande de Santiago) a river rising 18 miles west of Mexico City and flowing through Lake Chapala into the Pacific (340 miles long below Lake Chapala). It is called the Lerma River above Lake Chapala

Santiago a port (pop. 276,000) of S.E. Cuba, the capital of Oriente province: metallurgy, tobacco, sugar refining. Spanish cathedral (16th c.)

Santiago, Declaration of a declaration (1959) drafted by the Fifth Meeting of Consultation of Foreign Ministers, in Santiago, Chile. It proclaimed that the existence of anti-democratic regimes violated the principles on which the Organization of American States was founded and represented a threat to the peace of the hemisphere. It resulted in the creation of the Inter-American Commission on Human Rights

San·tia·go de Com·po·ste·la (sɑntjɑ́gɔðekɔmpɔstélɑ) a town (pop. 65,000) in La Coruna, Spain. Its cathedral (mainly 1078-1188, now with a baroque facade), built over the supposed grave of St James the Greater, was one of the chief pilgrimage places of medieval Christianity

Santiago de Cuba, Battle of a naval engagement (1898) outside Santiago, Cuba, during the Spanish-American War, in which a U.S. squadron destroyed a Spanish fleet

San·tia·go de los Ca·ba·lle·ros (sɑntjɑ́gɔðelɔskɑbɑjérɔs) a commercial center (pop. 242,000) of the N. central Dominican Republic, founded in 1524 but often destroyed by earthquakes: tobacco industries

San·ti·lla·na (sɑnti:ljɑ́nɑ), Iñigo López de Mendoza, marqués de (1398-1458), Spanish soldier, scholar, statesman and writer. He introduced the Italian sonnet into Spain

Santo Do·min·go (sɑ́ntɔdɔmí:ŋgɔ) (1930-61 Ciudad Trujillo) the capital, chief port and economic center (pop. 1,103,425) of the Dominican Republic, on the southeast coast, the oldest European town of the Americas, founded in 1496 by Bartolomé Colón. It was made (1511) the seat of an audiencia embracing the Caribbean and Venezuela. Industries: sugar refining, brewing, distilling. Spanish cathedral and churches (16th c.). University (1538)

san·ton·i·ca (sæntɔ́nikə) *n.* *Artemisia pauciflora,* fam. *Compositae,* a European wormwood ‖ its dried unopened flower buds used as a drug to destroy intestinal worms [L. fr. *(herba) Santonica,* (herb) of the Santones, a people of Aquitania]

san·to·nin (sǽntənin) *n.* a poisonous crystalline compound, $C_{15}H_{18}O_3$, derived from santonica and related plants and used to destroy intestinal worms [fr. L. *(herba) Sontonica,* santonica]

San·to·rin (sæ̜ntərí:n) (*Gk* Thera) the southernmost inhabited island (area 27 sq. miles, pop. 20,000) of the Cyclades, Greece, consisting largely of a volcanic cone (last active 1866): Mycenaean remains

San·tos (sǽntəs, sɑ́ntus) the chief export port (pop. 395,700) of Brazil, 45 miles southeast of São Paulo: iron and steel. It is the world's leading port for the exportation of coffee

CONCISE PRONUNCIATION KEY: **(a)** æ, *cat;* ɑ, *car;* ɔ *fawn;* ei, *snake.* **(e)** e, *hen;* i:, *sheep;* iə, *deer;* εə, *bear.* **(i)** i, *fish;* ai, *tiger;* ə:, *bird.* **(o)** o, *ox;* au, *cow;* ou, *goat;* u, *poor;* ɔi, *royal.* **(u)** ʌ, *duck;* u, *bull;* u:, *goose;* ə, *bacillus;* ju:, *cube.* x, *loch;* θ, *think;* ð, *bother;* z, *Zen;* ʒ, *corsage;* dʒ, *savage;* ŋ, *orangutang;* j, *yak;* ʃ, *fish;* tʃ, *fetch;* 'l, *rabble;* 'n, *redden.* Complete pronunciation key appears inside front cover.

San·tos-Du·mont (sɑ́tusdymɔ̃), Alberto (1873-1932), Brazilian aviation pioneer. He made (1901) the first roundtrip flight from Saint-Cloud to the Eiffel Tower, erected (1903) at Neuilly the first airship station, and designed (1909) his 'demoiselle' or 'grasshopper' monoplane, the forerunner of the modern light plane

SA-N2 *GUIDELINE

Sa·nu·si, Se·nus·si (sənú:si:) *pl.* **Sa·nu·si, Sa·nu·sis, Se·nus·si, Se·nus·sis** *n.* a member of a militant Moslem sect founded in 1837 in N. Africa by Mohammed Ibn Ali as-Sanusi (*d.* 1859), Algerian religious leader

São Fran·cis·co (sáufrɑnsí:sku) a river (1,600 miles long) flowing north and east from the highlands of E. central Brazil to the Atlantic 300 miles below Recife, navigable, between rapids, for most of its length

São Francisco an island (20 miles long) off the southeast coast of Brazil

São Luis (sáulwí:s) a port (pop. 330,311) of N. Brazil: textiles, food processing. Portuguese cathedral (17th c.)

Saône (soun) the chief tributary (280 miles long, navigable for 190) of the Rhône, flowing from the Vosges to Lyon, E. France

SA-1 *GUILD

Saône, Haute- *HAUTE-SAÔNE

Saône-et-Loire (souneilwɑr) a department (area 3,330 sq. miles, pop. 569,800) of E. central France (*BURGUNDY). Chief town: Mâcon

São Pau·lo (sáupáulu) the chief industrial center (pop. 7,033,529, increasing rapidly) of Brazil, on a hilly plateau (2,500 ft) 200 miles south of Rio de Janeiro, and the market for a great agricultural region (coffee). Main industries: textiles, machinery, automobiles, chemicals, food processing. Port: Santos. University (1934). São Paulo was founded (c. 1552) by Jesuits

São Ro·que, Cape (sɑurɔ́kə) a cape in N.E. Brazil, north of Natal

São To·mé and Prin·ci·pe (sáutɔmé, pri:nsi:pə) an African country consisting of two mountainous, fertile volcanic islands in the E. Gulf of Guinea with offshore islets (area 372 sq. miles, pop. 89,000). Capital: São Tomé. People: mulatto (native inhabitants), African (contract laborers), small European minority. Products: cocoa, copra, coconuts, coffee, palm oil, bananas, fish. Exports: cocoa, copra, coffee, palm oil. HISTORY. The islands were discovered by the Portuguese in 1471. São Tomé became a Portuguese colony in 1522 and Principe in 1573. The islands were a Portuguese overseas territory from 1951 until they achieved their independence in 1975

São Vi·cen·te (sɑuvi:sénte) the first Portuguese colony in America, established (1532) on the coast near Santos, in the state of São Paulo, Brazil

sap (sæp) **1.** *n.* the solution of raw materials and organic products of metabolism which circulates in a plant or tree ‖ (*pop.*) a stupid person easily fooled **2.** *v.t. pres. part.* **sap·ping** *past* and *past part.* **sapped** to drain (a tree) of its sap [O.E. *sæp*]

sap *n.* a deep trench or tunnel dug in order to undermine [older *zappe, sappe* fr. Ital. *zappa* and F. *sappe*, sap, spade]

sap *pres. part.* **sap·ping** *past* and *past part.* **sapped** *v.t.* to dig beneath, e.g. in order to lay an explosive beneath (an enemy fortification) ‖ to undermine (strength, energy etc.) [F. *saper*]

sap·a·jou (sǽpədʒu:) *n.* a capuchin monkey ‖ a spider monkey [F. fr. Tupi]

sapanwood *SAPPANWOOD

sap·head (sǽphęd) *n.* (*pop.*) a sap (stupid person)

sap·id (sǽpid) *adj.* (*rhet.*) having a strong, agreeable taste [fr. L. *sapidus* fr. *sapere*, to taste]

sa·pi·ence (séipi:əns) *n.* (*rhet.*) wisdom [O.F.]

sa·pi·ent (séipi:ənt) *adj.* (*rhet.*) wise, knowledgeable [O.F. or fr. L. *sapiens* (*sapientis*) fr. *sapere*, to be wise]

sapient *n.* any early ancestor of man

sa·pi·en·tial (sęipi:énʃəl) *adj.* characterized by knowledge or wisdom [F.]

sapiential books the biblical books Proverbs, Ecclesiastes, Ecclesiasticus, Wisdom, Song of Solomon

Sa·pir (səpíər), Edward (1884-1939), U.S. linguist, anthropologist, and specialist in American Indian languages, best known for his 'Language: an Introduction to the Study of Speech' (1921)

sap·ling (sǽpliŋ) *n.* a young tree ‖ a greyhound less than 12 months old

sap·o·dil·la (sæpədílə) *n.* *Achras zapota*, fam. *Sapotaceae*, a tropical American evergreen tree, yielding chicle ‖ its durable reddish wood ‖ its edible, sweet-fleshed fruit [Span. *zapotilla* fr. Nahuatl]

sap·o·na·ceous (sæpənéiʃəs) *adj.* of, pertaining to, consisting of or resembling soap [fr. Mod. L. *saponaceus* fr. *sapo* (*saponis*), soap]

sa·pon·i·fi·ca·tion (səpɒnifikéiʃən) *n.* the chemical process of converting fats into soap, involving the hydrolysis of a fat, usually accomplished by the action of alkali with the formation of glycerol and fatty acid salts ‖ the hydrolysis by alkali of any ester with an alcohol and an acid or its salt [F.]

sa·pon·i·fy (səpɒ́nifai) *pres. part.* **sa·pon·i·fy·ing** *past* and *past part.* **sa·pon·i·fied** *v.t.* to convert into soap by saponification ‖ *v.i.* to undergo the process of saponification [fr. F. *saponifier*]

sap·o·nin (sǽpənin) *n.* any of several naturally occurring water-soluble glucosides, able to form a lather. A mixture of saponins is used as a foam producer in fire extinguishers, as a detergent, in beverages etc. [F. *saponine*]

sap·o·nite (sǽpənait) *n.* hydrated aluminum magnesium silicate, occurring in soft, soapy masses in the veins of serpentine etc. [fr. L. *sapo* (*saponis*), soap]

sa·por, *Br.* also **sa·pour** (séipər, séipɔr) *n.* (in scientific contexts) a distinctive flavor ‖ a quality which affects the sense of taste, e.g. sweetness **sap·o·rous** (sǽpərəs) *adj.* [L. fr. *sapere*, to have a taste]

sap·pan·wood, sap·an·wood (səpǽnwųd) *n.* *Caesalpinia sappan*, fam. *Papilionaceae*, an East Indian tree ‖ its red dyewood [fr. Malay *sapang*+ WOOD]

sap·per (sǽpər) *n.* (*mil.*) any member of a corps of engineers, trained in sapping and in other forms of military engineering ‖ (*Br.*) a private in a corps of engineers

Sap·phic (sǽfik) **1.** *adj.* pertaining to Sappho ‖ of the poetic meter used by Sappho (esp. three pentameters followed by a verse in two feet) **2.** *n.* this meter ‖ (*pl.*) verse in Sapphic meter [F. *saphique* fr. L. *Sapphicus* fr. Gk]

sap·phire (sǽfaiər) **1.** *n.* a precious stone of transparent blue corundum, whose color is due to traces of cobalt ‖ any of certain other varieties of corundum of various colors, some of which are used commercially to tip the needles of record players ‖ the deep blue color of the true sapphire **2.** *adj.* of this blue color **sap·phir·ine** (sǽfirain) **1.** *adj.* resembling the sapphire in color **2.** *n.* a pale blue or green magnesium aluminum iron silicate [M.E. *saphyr, safir* fr. O.F. *safir*]

Sap·pho (sǽfou), Greek lyric poetess of Lesbos (late 7th–early 6th c. B.C.). Only very little of her work survives, written in a variety of meters, using vivid language, and showing great love of nature. It includes love poems of passionate intensity, some of which are addressed to women, and a hymn to Aphrodite

Sap·po·ro (sɑpɔrɔ) the chief town (pop. 1,307,600) of Hokkaido, Japan, near the east coast. Industries: food processing, flax, hemp, rubber manufactures. University (1918)

sap·py (sǽpi:) *comp.* **sap·pi·er** *superl.* **sap·pi·est** *adj.* (of a plant) full of sap ‖ (*pop.*) foolish or foolishly sentimental

sap·ro·gen·ic (sæproudʒénik) *adj.* of, pertaining to, or producing putrefaction [fr. Gk *sapros*, putrid+*genēs* fr. *gignesthai*, to become]

sap·ro·phyte (sǽprəfait) *n.* a plant living on nonliving organic matter (opp. AUTOPHYTE, cf. HETEROPHYTE, cf. HETEROTROPH, cf. PARASITE) **sap·ro·phyt·ic** (sæprəfítik) *adj.* pertaining to an organism, usually a plant, that obtains its food by absorbing nonliving organic matter [fr. Gk *sapros*, rotten+*phuton*, plant]

sap·suck·er (sǽpsʌkər) *n.* any of several small American woodpeckers, esp. of genus *Sphyrapicus*, which feed partly on the sap of trees

sap·wood (sǽpwųd) *n.* the outer living portion of the xylem of vascular plants. It consists of radial vascular rays and longitudinal systems of tracheid fibers and vessels and associated parenchyma (cf. HEARTWOOD)

sar·a·band, sar·a·bande (sǽrəbænd) *n.* a slow, stately court dance of the 17th and 18th cc., originating from a lively Spanish dance ‖ the music for this, in triple time with a stress on the second beat, esp. as a movement in the classical suite [fr. F. *sarabande* fr. Span.]

Sar·a·cen (sǽrəs'n) *n.* (*ancient hist.*) one of the nomads of the Syro-Arabian desert ‖ (*hist.*) a Moslem, esp. an Arab. The Saracens invaded France (8th c.) and Sicily (9th c.), and fought against the Crusaders to retain Jerusalem [O.F. *Sarazin* fr. L.L. fr. Gk]

Sar·a·gos·sa (særəgɒ́sə) (*Span.* Zaragoza) a province (area 6,726 sq. miles, pop. 760,000) of E. central Spain (*ARAGON) ‖ its capital (pop. 547,300), the ancient capital of Aragon, on the Ebro. Industries: mechanical and electrical engineering, textiles, food processing. Medieval city walls, bridges. Romanesque-Gothic and baroque cathedrals. University (1474)

Sar·ah (séərə) (*Bible*) the wife of Abraham and mother of Isaac

Sarah Lawrence College a U.S. educational institution chartered (1926) at Bronxville, N.Y., originally for women only, now coeducational. It is known for its creative arts program

Sa·ra·je·vo (særəjéivou, sɑ́rɑjəvɔ) the capital (pop. 244,000) of Bosnia-Herzegovina, Yugoslavia. Industries: food processing, building materials. Crafts: carpetmaking, metalwork. Mosques (16th c.), old Moslem quarters. The assassination here (June 28, 1914) of Archduke Franz Ferdinand precipitated the 1st world war

Sar·a·kolle (sǽrəkɒl, særəkól) *n.* a light-skinned people of W. Africa, speaking a Mandingo dialect ‖ a member of this people

Sa·ra·mac·ca (sɑrɑmákɑ) a river (c. 250 miles long) in central and north central Suriname, flowing into the Atlantic

sarangi (sərǽndʒi:) *n.* Indian stringed instrument played with a bow, controlled with fingernails

Sar·a·to·ga, Battle of (særətóugə) the first major American victory (1777) of the Revolutionary War. Burgoyne's surrender with 5,000 British troops heartened the American patriots and encouraged France to enter the war

Saratoga Springs a health resort (pop. 23,906) and sporting center (horse racing) in E. New York state: over 150 mineral springs and wells. Skidmore College (1911)

Sa·ra·tov (sɑrɑ́tʌf) a city (pop. 864,000) of the W. central R.S.F.S.R., U.S.S.R., on the Volga: shipbuilding, engineering, oil, printing. Baroque cathedral (1697). University

Sa·ra·wak (sərɑ́wɑk, sərɑ́wɑ) a state (area 48,342 sq. miles, pop. 1,294,753) of Malaysia in N. central Borneo. Capital: Kuching. People: 33% Chinese, 29% Sea Dyaks (Iban), 18% Malays, 8% Land Dyaks, with minorities of other indigenous tribes, Asians and Europeans. Languages: Iban, Chinese, Malay, English. Religion: Moslem, Buddhist, Christian, Animist. Rivers are the chief thoroughfares. Highest peak: 7,950 ft. Industries: oil refining, rubber and food processing. Exports: oil, rubber, sago, pepper, cutch, lumber. Other products: fish, rice, gold, bauxite, coal. Imports: crude oil (from Brunei), foodstuffs, machinery. Ports: Miri, Kuching. HISTORY. Sarawak formed part of the sultanate of Brunei until ceded (1841) by the sultan to James Brooke. He and his descendants administered it as an independent state until 1888, and then as a British protectorate until the Japanese occupation (1942-5). It became a British colony (1946) and joined Malaysia (1963)

sar·casm (sɑ́rkæzəm) *n.* a cruelly humorous statement or remark made with the intention of injuring the self-respect of the person to whom it is addressed, usually by drawing attention to one of his weaknesses and often associated with irony ‖ the making of such remarks ‖ the character of such remarks [fr. L.L. *sarcasmus* fr. Gk fr. *sarkazein*, to tear flesh, speak bitterly]

sar·cas·tic (sɑrkǽstik) *adj.* having the nature of or involving sarcasm ‖ using or given to using sarcasm **sar·cás·ti·cal·ly** *adv.* [fr. Gk fr. *sarkazein*, to tear flesh, speak bitterly]

sarce·net, sarse·net (sɑ́rsnit) *n.* a fine fabric of soft silk, used esp. for ribbons and linings [A.F. *sarzinet*, prob. dim. of *sarzin*, Saracen]

sar·co·carp (sɑ́rkoukɑrp) *n.* (*bot.*) the fleshy part of a fruit ‖ a fleshy fruit [fr. Gk *sarx* (*sarkos*), flesh+*karpos*, fruit]

Sar·co·di·na (sɑrkoudí:nə) *pl. n.* a class of protozoans characterized by pseudopodia [Mod. L. fr. Gk *sarkōdes*, fleshy part]

sar·co·ma (sɑrkóumə) *pl.* **sar·co·mas, sar·co·ma·ta** (sɑrkóumətə) *n.* a malignant growth or tumor developing in bony or fibrous tissues

CONCISE PRONUNCIATION KEY: **(a)** æ, *cat*; ɑ, *car*; ɔ *fawn*; ei, *snake*. **(e)** e, *hen*; i:, *sheep*; iə, *deer*; εə, *bear*. **(i)** i, *fish*; ai, *tiger*; ə:, *bird*. **(o)** o, *ox*; au, *cow*; ou, *goat*; u, *poor*; ɔi, *royal*. **(u)** ʌ, *duck*; u, *bull*; u:, *goose*; ə, *bacillus*; ju:, *cube*. x, *loch*; θ, *think*; ð, *bother*; z, *Zen*; ʒ, *corsage*; dʒ, *savage*; ŋ, *orangutang*; j, *yak*; ʃ, *fish*; tʃ, *fetch*; 'l, *rabble*; 'n, *redden*. Complete pronunciation key appears inside front cover.

sar·co·ma·tous (sɑrkóumətəs, sɑrkómətəs) *adj.* [Mod. L. fr. Gk *sarkōma* fr. *sarkoun,* to become fleshy]

sar·coph·a·gus (sɑrkófəgəs) *pl.* **sar·coph·a·gi** (sɑrkófədʒai), **sar·coph·a·gus·es** *n.* a stone coffin usually ornamented [L. fr. Gk *sarkophagos,* flesh-eating (fr. the idea that the limestone of which it was made decomposed the corpse)]

sar·co·plasm (sárkəplæzəm) *n.* the cytoplasmic mass in which fibrils of striated muscle are embedded [Mod. L. fr. Gk *sarx* (*sarkos*), flesh+*plasma,* form]

sar·cous (sárkəs) *adj.* (*anat.*) pertaining to flesh or muscle [fr. Gk *sarx* (*sarkos*), flesh]

sard (sɑrd) *n.* a yellow or orange-red variety of chalcedony used as a gem [prob. F. *sarde* fr. L. *sarda,* sardius]

sar·dine (sɑrdí:n) *pl.* **sar·dines, sar·dine** *n.* *Sardinia pilchardus,* a young pilchard cured and preserved in oil ‖ any of several related small or immature fishes treated in the same way [F. fr. Ital.]

Sar·din·i·a (sɑrdíni:ə, sɑrdínjə) (*Ital.* Sardegna) a mountainous deforested island (area 9,302 sq. miles, pop. 1,568,000) in the Mediterranean, just south of Corsica, forming an autonomous region of Italy. Capital: Cagliari. Language: Sardinian and Italian. Highest peak: 4,468 ft. Except for fertile plains in the southwest and along the coasts it is largely scrub-covered. Industries: mining (a quarter of Italian production, esp. lead, zinc, antimony, copper, manganese, coal), fishing, agriculture (cork, beans, cereals, fruit, olives, vines). Livestock: sheep. Universities: Cagliari (1626), Sassari (1677). HISTORY. Sardinia was conquered by Rome (238 B.C.), by Vandals (5th c.) and Saracens (8th c.), by Genoa and Pisa (1022), and by Aragon (1323). It passed (1720) to the dukes of Savoy, who took the title of king of Sardinia. After the Napoleonic Wars the kingdom was reconstituted (1815) to include Sardinia, Piedmont, Savoy, Nice and Liguria. The reign (1831-49) of Charles Albert saw the granting of a liberal constitution (1848) and an unsuccessful attempt (1848-9) to free northern Italy from the Austrians. Victor Emmanuel II and Cavour obtained French help in defeating (1859) the Austrians. Other Italian states then allied with Sardinia to form (1861) the kingdom of Italy

Sar·din·i·an (sɑrdíni:ən, sɑrdínjən) **1.** *n.* a native or inhabitant of Sardinia ‖ the Romance language of Sardinia **2.** *adj.* of Sardinia, its inhabitants, culture etc.

Sar·dis (sárdis) the ancient capital of Lydia. It flourished (7th c. B.C. to mid-6th c. B.C.) and was taken by the Persians (546 B.C.)

sar·di·us (sárdi:əs) *n.* (*hist.*) one of the gems worn by the Jewish high priest, possibly a sard or sardonyx ‖ a sard [L. fr. Gk *sardios* fr. *Sardeis,* Sardis]

sar·don·ic (sɑrdónik) *adj.* expressing bitterness or ironic mockery under laughter **sar·dón·i·cal·ly** *adv.* [F. *sardonique* fr. L. fr. Gk]

sar·don·yx (sɑrdóniks, sárd'niks) *n.* a variety of onyx in which there are layers of orange-red sard and of a white chalcedony, used as a gem [L. fr. Gk]

Sar·dou (særdu:), Victorien (1831-1908), French dramatist. His successes included the popular historical dramas 'Fedora' (1887) and 'Robespierre' (1902)

sar·gas·so (sɑrgǽsou) *pl.* **sar·gas·sos** *n.* gulfweed ‖ a floating mass of this [Port. *sargaço*]

Sargasso Sea a part (area 2,000,000 sq. miles) of the Atlantic Ocean between the West Indies and the Azores, a calm center in the midst of the Gulf Stream. Its name derives from the sargasso floating on it, in which many varieties of marine life thrive

sar·gas·sum (sɑrgǽsəm) *n.* gulfweed [Mod. L. fr. Port.]

Sar·gent (sárdʒənt), John Singer (1856-1925), American painter who lived in England from 1885. He is best known for his many society portraits

Sar·gon I (sárgɒn) (c. 2600 B.C.), founder of the Semitic kingdom of Akkad in Babylonia

Sargon II (*d.* 705 B.C.), king of Assyria (721-705 B.C.), founder of the last Assyrian dynasty. He destroyed the kingdom of Israel (c. 722 B.C.), captured Samaria (721-717 B.C.), deported its inhabitants and devastated Armenia (714 B.C.)

sa·ri (sá:ri) *pl.* **sa·ris** *n.* the robe of a Hindu woman, consisting of a long piece of cotton or silk fabric wrapped around the body and draped over the head or shoulder [Hindi *sārhī, sārī*]

Sark (sɑrk) the smallest island (area 2 sq. miles, pop. 600) of Great Britain's Channel Islands, comprising Great and Little Sark, connected by an isthmus. It is an autonomous dependency of Guernsey under a hereditary seigneur

Sar·ma·ti·an (sɑrméiʃi:ən, sɑrméiʃən) **1.** *n.* a member of the nomadic Indo-European people who displaced the Scythians (3rd c. B.C.) on the lower Don. First the enemies and then the allies of Rome, they were displaced by the Goths (3rd c. A.D.) **2.** *adj.* of the Sarmatians or the area they inhabited

sar·men·tose (sɑrméntous) *adj.* (*bot.*) having or producing prostrate shoots which root at their nodes [fr. L. *sarmentum,* pruned twig]

Sar·mien·to (sɑrmjéntɔ), Domingo Faustino (1811-88), Argentinian writer, politician, and president of the Republic (1868-74). During the dictatorship of Rosas, which he depicts in his masterpiece 'Facundo o Civilización i barbarie' (1845), he lived in Chile. He returned to join the ranks of Urquiza, but again went into exile (1852-5). Succeeding Mitre as president, he brought the war with Paraguay to an end. He founded the Astronomical Observatory of Córdoba and the military and naval academies

sa·rong (sərɔ́ŋ, sərɒŋ) *n.* an ankle-length garment worn by men and women in the Malay Archipelago, consisting of one long strip of cotton or silk wrapped around the body and tucked in at the waist [Malay *sārung*]

Sa·roy·an (sərɔ́iən), William (1908-81), U.S. writer. His works include the plays 'My Heart's in the Highlands' (1939) and 'The Time of Your Life' (1939); a novel, 'The Human Comedy' (1943); short stories collected in 'The Daring Young Man on the Flying Trapeze' (1934); and his autobiographical works 'My Name is Aram' (1940), 'Places Where I've Done Time' (1972), 'Chance Meeting' (1978) and 'Obituaries' (1979)

sar·ra·ce·ni·a (særəsí:ni:ə) *n.* a member of *Sarracenia,* fam. *Sarraceniaceae,* a genus of pitcher plants [Mod. L. after D. *Sarrazin* (17th c.), Canadian physician]

sar·sa·pa·ril·la (sɑrsəpərílə, sɑrspərilə, sæspərílə) *n.* any of several members of *Smilax,* fam. *Liliaceae,* a genus of American vines ‖ an extract from the dried roots of these, used as a tonic and as a flavoring in beverages ‖ a carbonated beverage flavored with this [Span. *zarzaparrilla*]

sarsenet *SARCENET

Sarthe (sært) a department (area 2,410 sq. miles, pop. 490,400) of N.W. France (*MAINE). Chief town: Le Mans

Sar·to (sártɔ), Andrea del (1486-1531), Florentine painter. Both in his splendid color and in his composition he was exceptional in the Florence of his period. His frescos include the 'Birth of the Virgin' in the cloister of SS. Annunziata, Florence. His paintings include the 'Holy Family' in the Louvre, 'Madonna of the Harpies' in the Uffizi, and the 'Holy Family' in the Metropolitan Museum, New York

sar·to·ri·al (sortɔ́ri:əl, sɑrtóuri:əl) *adj.* of or pertaining to men's clothes ‖ of tailors or their trade [fr. L. *sartorius* fr. *sartor,* tailor]

sar·to·ri·us (sɑrtɔ́ri:əs, sɑrtóuri:əs) *pl.* **sar·to·ri·i** (sortɔ́ri:ai, sɑrtóuri:ai) *n.* the long thigh muscle, the longest in man, which enables the knee to be flexed and adducted [Mod. L. fr. L. *sartor,* tailor (fr. the tailor's traditional cross-legged posture when stitching)]

Sar·tre (særtr), Jean-Paul (1905-80), French philosopher, novelist and playwright. Sartre was the leading French exponent of existentialism (strictly speaking, the proposition that existence, i.e. the concrete historical situation, precedes essence). Among his philosophical works are 'l'Etre et le Néant' (1943), and 'Critique de la raison dialectique' (1960). His novels include 'la Nausée' (1938), 'les Chemins de la liberté' (1945). His plays include 'Huis clos' (1944), 'les Mouches' (1943), 'les Mains sales' (1948) and 'Nekrassov' (1955). His works explore the situation of 'anguish' which precedes 'commitment' to a course of action. He won but declined to accept the Nobel prize for literature (1964)

Sar·um use (sέərəm) *n.* (*eccles.*) the order of divine service used before the Reformation in the diocese of Salisbury, England, and currently followed in some Anglican churches [M.L. *Sarum,* Salisbury]

SAS (*abbr.*) for British Special Air Service, an antiterrorist commando unit

SASE (*abbr.*) for self-addressed stamped envelope

Sa·se·bo (sásəbɔ) a port (pop. 254,313) and naval base of N.W. Kyushu, Japan

sash (sæʃ) *n.* a framework holding glass, in a window or greenhouse etc. ‖ a movable frame of a sash window [fr. F. *châssis,* frame]

sash *n.* a broad ribbon, often of silk, worn as a sign of office or honor ‖ a broad ribbon worn as an adornment around the waist [older *shash* fr. Arab. *shāsh,* turban, muslin]

sa·shay (sæʃéi) *v.i.* (*pop.*) to walk nonchalantly ‖ (*pop.*) to swagger about in an attention-catching way ‖ (*pop.*) to move sideways or in a zigzag course [fr. *chassé,* a gliding sideways dance step, fr. F.]

sash cord a strong cord attached to the sash of a sash window, passing over a pulley and carrying a counterweight, by means of which the sash is held in equilibrium in any position

sash window a window having glazed frames that slide up and down

sa·sin (séisin) *n.* the black buck [Nepalese]

Sask. Saskatchewan

Sas·katch·e·wan (sæskǽtʃəwɒn) a province (area 251,700 sq. miles, pop. 1,000,000) of central Canada. Capital: Regina. The north is part of the Canadian Shield and has important mineral resources. The south consists of fertile prairies. Agriculture: wheat (leading producer) and other cereals, beef and dairy cattle. Resources: copper, uranium, cadmium, zinc, gold, oil, coal, sodium sulfate, salt, potash. Industries: food processing, oil refining. University: Saskatoon. The Hudson's Bay Company promoted trade in furs with the Indians of the area (17th c.) and established permanent settlements (1774). The area was included in the Northwest Territories (1870) and became a province of Canada (1905)

Saskatchewan a navigable river (340 miles long) flowing from E. Saskatchewan, Canada, into Lake Winnipeg. It is formed by the confluence of the North Saskatchewan (760 miles long) and the South Saskatchewan (865 miles long), both rising in the Rocky Mtns in Alberta

Sas·ka·toon (sæskətú:n) a communications center and market (pop. 154,210) of central Saskatchewan, Canada, on the South Saskatchewan River: agricultural machinery, flour milling, meat packing. University (1907)

sas·ka·toon (sæskətú:n) *n.* a Juneberry, esp. *Amelanchier alnifolia* of Canada and the northern and western U.S.A.

Sas·quatch (sáskwɑtʃ) *n.* hypothetical human-like animal said to inhabit the Pacific Northwest

sass (sæs) **1.** *n.* (*pop.*) impudent talk **2.** *v.t.* (*pop.*) to speak impudently to [SASSY]

sas·sa·by (sǽsəbi:) *pl.* **sas·sa·bies** *n.* *Damaliscus lunatus,* a large S. African antelope [Bantu]

sas·sa·fras (sǽsəfræs) *n.* a member of *Sassafras,* fam. *Lauraceae,* a genus of North American and Asian trees, esp. *S. albidum* of E. North America ‖ the dried bark of the roots of *S. albidum,* used as an aromatic stimulant and yielding a volatile oil used in perfumes [Span. *sasafras*]

Sas·sa·ni·an (səséini:ən) **1.** *n.* a member of the Sassanid dynasty **2.** *adj.* of or relating to the Sassanids

Sas·sa·nid (səsánid, səsǽnid) *pl.* **Sas·sa·nids, Sas·sa·ni·dae** (səsánidi:, səsǽnidi:) a member of a Persian dynasty of kings (c. 226–c. 641) who overthrew (c. 226) the kingdom of Parthia, and who were conquered (c. 641) by the Arabs. The dynasty's capital was Ctesiphon

Sas·sa·ri (sássɑri:) a commercial center (pop. 117,300) in N.W. Sardinia, Italy. Romanesque church (13th c.). University (1677)

Sas·se·nach (sǽsənəx, sǽsənæk) *n.* (the Gaelic or Erse term for) an Englishman, Saxon or Lowlander [fr. Gael. *Sasunnach*]

Sas·set·ta (sassétta), Stefano di Giovanni (c. 1392-1450), Italian painter. He worked in Siena and continued the mystical tradition of 14th–c. Sienese painting, but was influenced by the new Renaissance modes. His main work, now scattered, is the St Francis altarpiece painted for S. Francesco, Sansepolcro (1437-44)

sas·sy (sǽsi:) *comp.* **sas·si·er** *superl.* **sas·si·est** *adj.* (*pop.*) impudent, sometimes with coyness, *a sassy answer* [var. of SAUCY]

sat *past* and *past part.* of SIT
Sat. Saturday
Sa·tan (séit'n) *n.* the chief of the rebel angels (*LUCIFER) and the anthropomorphic personification of evil, the Devil
sa·tang (sətǽŋ) *n.* a monetary unit of Thailand, one hundredth of a baht ‖ a coin of the value of one satang [Thai *satān*]
sa·tan·ic (seitǽnik, sətǽnik) *adj.* of, pertaining to or characteristic of Satan [fr. SATAN fr. Heb. *sātān,* enemy]
Sa·tan·ism (séit'nizəm) *n.* worship of Satan, using rites which travesty Christian rites
satch·el (sǽtʃəl) *n.* a bag of leather or stout canvas, usually fastened by a strap and buckle, carried by hand or slung over the shoulder by strap [O.F. *sachel*]
Sat·com *n.* (*acronym*) for satellite communications center *Cf* EARTH STATION
sate (seit) *pres. part.* **sat·ing** *past* and *past part.* **sat·ed** *v.t.* to satisfy totally (the appetite or a desire) ‖ to satisfy so fully as to induce a revulsion of feeling [prob. fr. *sade,* to become or make weary fr. O.E.]
sa·teen, sa·tine (sætíːn) *n.* a cotton fabric given a glossy surface in imitation of satin [fr. SATIN]
sat·el·lite (sǽt'lait) *n.* a natural or man-made body moving in orbit around the moon or one of the planets etc. ‖ a state economically and politically dependent on another, although apparently independent ‖ a person in constant servile attendance upon another [F.]
satellite city an urban area outside a larger urban area, usu. created by municipal plan
satellite town separated residential (sometimes industrial) center associated with an urban center that provides jobs, services, entertainment *Cf* SATELLITE CITY
sa·ti·ate (séiʃiːeit) *pres. part.* **sa·ti·at·ing** *past* and *past part.* **sa·ti·at·ed** *v.t.* to satisfy (a desire or someone), esp. so fully that desire gives place to a revulsion of feeling **sa·ti·a·tion** *n.* [L. *satiare (satiatus),* to satisfy]
Sa·tie (sæti:), Erik Alfred Leslie (1886-1925), French composer. He was an experimentalist, analyzing the elements of music and reassembling them in a way which naturally associated him with cubism in art. His work includes piano solos and duets, the symphonic drama 'Socrates', ballets and a Mass
sa·ti·e·ty (sətáiitiː) *n.* the state of being sated [fr. F. *saiété*]
sat·in (sǽt'n) **1.** *n.* a fabric of silk with a glossy surface on one side ‖ a fabric of nylon, rayon etc. resembling this **2.** *adj.* made of satin ‖ smooth and glossy, like satin [F. perh. fr. Ital. fr. L. *seta,* silk]
SATIN sage air traffic integration, air traffic control system that coordinates with SAGE; designed by Mitre Corporation
sat·i·net, sat·i·nette (sæt'nét) *n.* a glossy fabric of cotton with silk or wool, or of synthetic fiber, made to imitate satin [F. *satinet*]
satin stitch a long embroidery stitch worked in close, parallel bands to give a smooth, satiny appearance
sat·in·wood (sǽt'nwud) *n. Cloroxylon Swietenia,* fam. *Meliaceae,* an East Indian tree, the lustrous, light-colored wood of which is used in cabinetmaking ‖ this wood ‖ any of several trees whose wood resembles this ‖ the wood of these trees
sat·in·y (sǽt'niː) *adj.* like satin in glossy smoothness or softness
sat·ire (sǽtaier) *n.* a literary genre in which ridicule is thrown upon something by stressing its worst features, often by the use of irony, thus assuming or affirming a norm by which aberrations are judged ‖ a literary work in this genre [F. or fr. L. *satira*]
sa·tir·ic (sətírik) *adj.* of, containing or characterized by satire ‖ writing satire, *a satiric poet* [fr. F. *satirique*]
sa·tir·i·cal (sətírik'l) *adj.* of, containing or characterized by satire ‖ given to the use of irony, ridicule or sarcasm [fr. L.L. *satiricus*]
sat·i·rist (sǽtərist) *n.* a writer of satires
sat·i·rize (sǽtəraiz) *pres. part.* **sat·i·riz·ing** *past* and *past part.* **sat·i·rized** *v.t.* to treat in a satirical way [fr. F. *satiriser*]
sat·is·fac·tion (sætisfǽkʃən) *n.* a satisfying or being satisfied ‖ a source or cause of pleasure, fulfilment or gratification ‖ a payment or other compensation for damage, injury etc. ‖ an opportunity to vindicate one's honor by fighting a duel, *he demanded satisfaction for the insult* ‖ (*theol.*) performance of the penance imposed by the priest on a penitent [F.]
sat·is·fac·to·ri·ly (sætisfǽktəriliː) *adv.* in a satisfactory manner
sat·is·fac·to·ri·ness (sætisfǽktəriːnis) *n.* the quality or state of being satisfactory
sat·is·fac·to·ry (sætisfǽktəriː) *adj.* adequate ‖ giving satisfaction [fr. F. *satisfactoire*]
sat·is·fy (sǽtisfai) *pres. part.* **sat·is·fy·ing** *past* and *past part.* **sat·is·fied** *v.t.* to cause (someone) to be happy or free from some desire or need by supplying what he desires, needs or demands ‖ to provide what is required by (a need, obligation, standard etc.), *to satisfy the requirements for graduation* ‖ to provide all that is needed by (appetite, thirst etc.), *the meal did not satisfy his hunger* ‖ to pay (a creditor) ‖ to counter (misgiving, arguments etc.) convincingly ‖ to convince or persuade of some specified fact, *he satisfied the police that he was innocent* ‖ (*math.*) to be, or provide, the solution for (an equation) ‖ *v.i.* to give satisfaction [O.F. *satisfier* fr. L. *satisfacere* fr. *satis,* enough+*facere,* to do]
Sa·to (sɑtou), Eisaku (1901-75), Japanese statesman, prime minister of Japan (1964-75)
Sat·pu·ra Range (sútpurə) a range of hills (average height 3,000 ft) in Madhya Pradesh, India, between the Narbada and Tapti Rivers
sa·trap (séitræp, sǽtræp) *n.* (*hist.*) a provincial ruler in ancient Persia ‖ (*rhet.*) a subordinate ruler or petty official, esp. one who is tyrannical [fr. L. *satrapes* fr. Gk fr. O. Pers.]
sa·trap·y (séitrəpiː, sǽtrəpiː) *pl.* **sa·trap·ies** *n.* the dignity, office or jurisdiction of a satrap [F. *satrapie*]
Sa·tsu·ma (sútsumə) *n.* a cream-colored variety of Japanese pottery [after *Satsuma,* former province of Kyushu]
sat·u·rate (sǽtʃəreit) *pres. part.* **sat·u·rat·ing** *past* and *past part.* **sat·u·rat·ed** *v.t.* to fill completely, *to saturate a market with orders* ‖ to transform some or all of the multiple bonds in (an unsaturated substance) by chemical addition ‖ to cause (a substance) to become impregnated to the point where it can absorb no more ‖ to steep or soak, esp. by immersion ‖ to destroy (an area) with a very high concentration of bombs or projectiles ‖ to magnetize (a substance) till further increase in magnetizing force produces no further increase in magnetization ‖ to increase the voltage to (an electron tube) to the point where further increase of voltage produces no change of current ‖ to dissolve in (a solvent) as much of a solute as can be held in solution at a given temperature and pressure **sát·u·rat·ed** *adj.* (*chem.,* of a solution) having the highest concentration of a solute possible at a given temperature and pressure ‖ (*chem.,* of a compound) having only single bonds between adjacent atoms (used esp. of carbon compounds) and hence not tending to form additional compounds ‖ (of a rock) having the greatest possible amount of combined silica [fr. L. *saturare (saturatus)*]
saturated vapor, esp. *Br.* **saturated vapour** (*phys.*) a vapor which is in equilibrium with its own liquid form
sat·u·ra·tion (sætʃəréiʃən) *n.* a saturating or being saturated ‖ the quality of a color that depends on the amount of achromatic color mixed with it (*COLOR)
saturation diving or **saturated diving** remaining underwater for a maximum period, thus requiring maximum decompression at the time of return to the surface —**saturation dive** *v.* —**saturated diver** *n.*
Sat·ur·day (sǽtərdiː, sǽtərdei) *n.* the seventh and last day of the week [O.E. *Sæterndæg,* Saturday, the day of Saturn]
Saturday night special *n.* (*slang*) an inexpensive, easily obtained handgun
Sat·urn (sǽtərn) (*Rom. mythol.*) the god of agriculture, father of Jupiter ‖ the sixth planet from the sun (mean orbital diameter=8.87 X 10^8 miles) and the second largest in the solar system (mass = 5.58 X 10^{23} tons, diameter=approx. 74,500 miles), 95 times more massive than the earth. It revolves about the sun with a sidereal period of 29.6 years and rotates on its axis with a period that depends on latitude (between 10 hrs 14 mins and 10 hrs 38 mins). In the telescope it appears as a yellowish disk, with belts similar to those of Jupiter but less well defined and yellow to green in color. Its atmosphere consists mostly of hydrogen and helium, with traces of methane, ammonia, ethine, phosphine and acetylene. The gas density gradually decreases downward and the gas becomes a liquid and then metallic. A small core of silicate material probably is at the center. Saturn has a system of seven thin, concentric rings lying in the plane of its equator and varying in width (between 10,000 and 16,000 miles). The rings are composed of dust, of a density varying with the ring, orbiting about the planet. The dust is thought to be the remains of satellites or comets, which, when in the molten state, were disintegrated by tidal motions on approaching the planet. Saturn has at least 22 satellites
sat·ur·na·li·a (sætərnéiliːə, sætərnéiljə) *pl.* **sat·ur·na·li·a, sat·ur·na·li·as** *n.* a period of orgiastic revelry **Sat·ur·na·li·a** (*hist.*) the festival of Saturn, held in December in ancient Rome and characterized by unrestrained revelry **sat·ur·ná·li·an** *adj.* orgiastic **Sat·ur·na·li·an** of or characteristic of the Saturnalia [L., neut. pl. of *Saturnalis,* pertaining to Saturn]
Sa·tur·ni·an (sətə́ːrniːən) *adj.* pertaining to Saturn, esp. to his supposed former reign, thought by ancient Romans to have been marked by peace and prosperity [fr. L. *Saturnius*]
sat·ur·nine (sǽtərnain) *adj.* gloomy, surly [fr. M.L. fr. *Saturnus,* Saturn. People born under the planet's influence were thought to be cold and gloomy in temperament]
sa·tyr (séitər, sǽtər) *n.* (*Gk* and *Rom. mythol.*) a god of the woods given to Bacchic revelry and lechery, often depicted with a horse's or goat's tail and a goat's legs and ears ‖ (*rhet.*) a lecher ‖ any of several butterflies of fam. *Satyridæ,* usually brown and gray and often having ocelli on the wings [fr. L. *satyrus* fr. Gk]
sa·tyr·ic (sətírik) *adj.* of or like a satyr **sa·týr·i·cal** *adj.* [fr. L. *satyricus* and Gk *saturikos*]
sauce (sɔs) **1.** *n.* a preparation, usually liquid or soft, added to food e.g. to make it more piquant ‖ (*fig.*) something which lends piquancy ‖ (*pop.*) impertinence, impudence **2.** *v.t. pres. part.* **sauc·ing** *past* and *past part.* **sauced** to add sauce to ‖ (*pop.*) to be impertinent to [F.]
sauce·boat (sɔ́sbout) *n.* a vessel in which sauce is served
sauce·pan (sɔ́spæn) *n.* a metal pot with a long handle, used to boil or stew food
sau·cer (sɔ́sər) *n.* a small, shallow dish, used as a stand in which to place a cup and to receive any overspill ‖ anything of this shape [O.F. *saussier,* dish for serving sauces]
sau·ci·ly (sɔ́siliː) *adv.* in a saucy manner
sau·ci·ness (sɔ́siːnis) *n.* the quality of being saucy
sau·cy (sɔ́siː) *comp.* **sau·ci·er** *superl.* **sau·ci·est** *adj.* impudent, sometimes with coyness, *a saucy answer* ‖ smart, gaily stylish
Sa·u·di Arabia (saúːdiː, sáudiː, sɔ́diː) a kingdom (area approx. 600,000 sq. miles, pop. approx. 9,795,000, 50% Beduins) occupying most of Arabia and comprising the former kingdom of Hejaz (capital: Mecca) and former sultanate of Nejd (capital: Riyadh), with their dependencies. It has joint control with Iraq over 7,000 sq. miles and with Kuwait over 5,770 sq. miles of neutral territory. Language: Arabic. Religion: Islam (official), mainly Sunnites (Wahhabi sect in Nejd), with a Shi'ite minority in al-Hasa. It is largely an arid plateau (1,500–6,000 ft), with a lowland strip along the Red Sea coast and a wider plain along the Persian Gulf and in the southeast. Mountains between the western coastal strip and the interior rise to 5,000 ft north of Jedda and to 9,000 ft south of Mecca (highest in Asir). The Nafud and Great Sandy deserts occupy the northern center and the southeast. The rest of the country has seasonal vegetation. Average temperatures Jan. and July (F.): Jedda 70° and 90°, Riyadh 60° and 80°. Rainfall: 10 ins in oases, 4 ins and under elsewhere. Exports: crude and refined petroleum (the country contains 10% of known world deposits). Other industries: oasis farming (dates and other fruits, cereals), livestock raising (camels, horses, donkeys, sheep), the Mecca pilgrimage trade, building materials, food processing. Imports: piece goods, cereals, foodstuffs, vehicles, building materials, machinery, chemicals. Communications: chiefly by air services or by camel caravan. Ports: Dammam and Ras Tanura on the Persian Gulf, Jedda on the Red Sea. The trans-Arabian pipeline connects the oil fields with the Mediterranean. Universities: Riyadh, Mecca and Medina. Monetary unit: rial (20 qurush). HISTORY. (For early history *ARABIA) Hejaz and Nejd were united (1925) as a result of the Wahhabi conquest under ibn Saud, and adopted the name of Saudi

Arabia (1932). Vast oil reserves were discovered (1930s) and were developed by an American firm. Saudi Arabia joined the U.N. and the Arab League (1945) and formed a military, economic and political alliance with Jordan (1962). Saud, son of ibn Saud, ruled the country (1953-64), and was succeeded by Faisal. Profits from the oil industry made possible improvements in irrigation, education and communications. Faisal was assassinated (1975) and was succeeded by Khalid, who ruled until his death (1982) and was succeeded by Crown Prince Fahd. Saudi Arabia acts as a 'conservative' force in the Middle East and is a leader of OPEC

Sa·ud ibn Ab·dul A·ziz (saú:di:b'nabdúlazí:z) (1902-69), king of Saudi Arabia (1953-64), son of ibn Saud. He was deposed in favor of Faisal

sau·er·kraut (sáuərkraut) *n.* shredded cabbage fermented under pressure in its own juices, with added salt, in large stone jars [G. fr. *sauer,* sour+*kraut,* cabbage]

sau·ger (sɔ́gər) *n.* *Stizostedion canadense,* a small North American pike perch, valued as a food fish

Sauk (sɔk) *pl.* **Sauk, Sauks** *n.* a North American Indian people from the Fox River valley and Green Bay area in Wisconsin ‖ a member of this people ‖ the dialect

Saul (sɔl) (*d.* c. 1012 B.C.), first king of the Hebrews (c. 1040–c. 1012 B.C.). A Benjamite, he was anointed king by Samuel, and successfully united the Hebrews against the Philistines. He committed suicide after a military defeat, and was succeeded by his son-in-law David (I Samuel x-xxxi)

Saul of Tarsus *PAUL, ST

Sault Sainte Ma·rie (sú:seintməri:) an industrial city (iron and steel, shipbuilding, pulp and paper mills), port of entry and resort (pop. 14,448) in S. Ontario, Canada

Sau·mur (soumyr) a town (pop. 34,191) in Maine-et-Loire, France, on the lower Loire: castle (15th c.), cavalry school

sau·na (sɔ́nə, sáunə, sáunɑ) *n.* a Finnish steam bath ‖ the building in which such baths are taken [Finn.]

saun·ter (sɔ́ntər, sántər) **1.** *v.i.* to walk in a leisurely manner, with no particular aim in view **2.** *n.* a leisurely walk ‖ the leisurely gait at which one saunters [etym. doubtful]

Sau·ra·se·ni (saurəséini:) *n.* one of the Prakrit languages of India

sau·ri·an (sɔ́ri:ən) **1.** *adj.* pertaining to lizards **2.** *n.* a lizard ‖ a reptile resembling a lizard [fr. Mod. L. *Sauria,* former name of a division of reptiles, fr. Gk *saura,* lizard]

sau·ro·pod (sɔ́rəpɒd) *n.* a member of *Sauropoda,* order *Saurischia,* a suborder of gigantic herbivorous dinosaurs of the Jurassic and Cretaceous [fr. Mod. L. *Sauropoda* fr. Gk *sauru,* lizard+*pous (podos),* foot]

sau·ry (sɔ́ri:) *pl.* **sau·ries** *n.* *Scombresox saurus,* fam. *Scombresocidae,* a marine fish with a long body and long beak, found in temperate parts of the Atlantic, off S. Africa, and elsewhere [prob. fr. Mod. L. *saurus,* lizard]

sau·sage (sɔ́sidʒ) *n.* a quantity of finely minced meat, salted and spiced and forced into a thin-walled tube (usually a prepared intestine) which is hermetically sealed by tying its ends and may be divided into short lengths by twisting ‖ one such short length [M.E. *sausige* fr. O.N.F. *saussiche*]

sausage meat the mixture used to make sausages

sausage roll (*Br.*) a small quantity of sausage meat enclosed in flaky pastry and baked

Saus·sure (sousyr), Ferdinand de (1857-1913), Swiss Indo-European scholar and teacher, founder of modern linguistics

Saussure, Horace Bénédict de (1740-99), Swiss physicist and alpine traveler. He did important research in alpine metereology and geology

sau·té (soutéi, sɔtéi) **1.** *adj.* fried quickly in a pan with a little hot butter or other fat **2.** *v. t. pres. part.* **sau·tée·ing** (soutéiiŋ, sɔtéiiŋ) *past* and *past part.* **sau·téed** (soutéid, sɔtéid) to fry in this way **3.** *n.* a dish prepared in this way [F. past part. of *sauter,* to leap]

Sau·terne, Sau·ternes (soutə́:rn, sɔtə́:rn, *F.* soutern) *n.* a white wine, usually semi-sweet, from Sauternes, a region north of Bordeaux, France

Sau·veur (souvə́:r), Albert (1863-1939), U.S. metallurgist whose research into the crystal structure of metals produced methods of improving the quality of steel. He devised (late 1800s) the technique of making photomicrographs

Sa·va (sɑ́vɑ) the chief river (450 miles long, navigable for 360) of Yugoslavia, flowing from the Julian Alps (Italian border) across Slovenia and Croatia (forming the border with Bosnia-Herzegovina) to the Danube at Belgrade

Sava, St (c. 1175-1235), Serbian monk, patron saint of Serbia, son of Stevan Nemanja. Feast: Jan. 14

sav·age (sǽvidʒ) **1.** *adj.* primitive, uncivilized, *a savage tribe* ‖ characteristic of a primitive, uncivilized people, *savage customs* ‖ uncultivated, *savage country* ‖ wild and ferocious, *a savage beast* ‖ extremely cruel, *savage criticism* ‖ (*pop.*) violently angry **2.** *n.* an uncivilized human being, esp. one who has not learned the art of cultivating the soil ‖ a person who behaves in a violent, cruel or uncultivated way **3.** *v.t. pres. part.* **sav·ag·ing** *past* and *past part.* **sav·aged** to attack and bite, claw, rend etc. [F. *sauvage*]

sav·age·ry (sǽvidʒri:) *pl.* **sav·age·ries** *n.* a savage act ‖ savage behavior ‖ the quality or state of being savage

Sa·van·nah (səvǽnə) the oldest and second largest city (pop. 141,390) in Georgia, in the southeast part of the state. It is an important shipping point for cotton, naval stores, and tobacco. Georgia State College (1890)

Savannah a navigable river (314 miles long) rising in N.W. South Carolina and flowing into the Atlantic at Savannah, forming the Georgia-South Carolina boundary: hydroelectric power

sa·van·na, sa·van·nah (səvǽnə) *n.* tropical or subtropical grassland containing scattered trees or bushes characteristic of tropical America and much of tropical Africa ‖ a treeless plain, esp. in the southeastern U.S.A. [older *zavanna* fr. Span. perh. fr. Carib]

sa·vant (sævɑ́nt, sǽvənt, sævã) *n.* (*rhet.*) a man of great erudition [F.]

save (seiv) **1.** *v. pres. part.* **sav·ing** *past* and *past part.* **saved** *v.t.* to keep alive, free, safe or in good condition, esp. when this state is in danger of being changed, *the gifts saved many from starvation* ‖ to make unnecessary or avoidable, *it will save trouble if we start early* ‖ to economize, *he saves his bus fares and walks* ‖ to work the spiritual salvation of ‖ (sometimes with 'up') to reserve for future use, enjoyment etc., *I'm saving that last chapter for tomorrow* ‖ to prevent (a game) from being lost ‖ *v.i.* to put aside for future use money that one would otherwise spend **to save face** to avoid injury to one's pride or public disgrace in some difficult situation **to save the situation** to act in a way which averts disaster or embarrassment **2.** *n.* (*games*) an action which directly prevents the opposing side from scoring [M.E. *salve, sauve* fr. O.F. *salver, sauver*]

save 1. *prep.* except, *they were all unhurt save the pilot* **2.** *conj.* (with 'that') except [fr. SAFE adj. and F. *sauf*]

Sav·ile (sǽvil), George, 1st marquis of Halifax *HALIFAX

sav·in, sav·ine (sǽvin) *n.* *Juniperus sabina,* a small, bushy juniper native to Europe and W. Asia, bearing bluish-green berries. The bitter tops yield an oil, used medicinally [O.F. *savine*]

sav·ing (séiviŋ) **1.** *adj.* making an exception, *a saving clause* ‖ outweighing faults, *a saving grace* ‖ securing salvation for the soul **2.** *n.* the act of someone who or something that saves ‖ a desirable economy in time, money etc. ‖ (*pl.*) money saved ‖ (*law*) a reservation **3.** *prep.* excepting **4.** *conj.* (esp. with 'that') except

savings account (*Am.=Br.* deposit account) a bank account on which checks are not drawn and which earns some interest (cf. CHECKING ACCOUNT)

savings and loan association a financial organization under federal or state law for the promotion of thrift and private home ownership, first organized in 1831 after the pattern of the British building societies

savings bank a public or private bank which accepts small savings on deposit and pays interest on them

savings bond a nontransferable U.S. government bond in denominations of $25 to $1,000

sav·ior, esp. *Br.* **sav·iour** (séivjər) *n.* someone who saves a person or thing from destruction or injury **the Sav·ior,** esp. *Br.* **the Sav·iour** Christ [M.E. fr. O.F. *sauveour*]

Sa·voie (sævwɑ) a department (area 2,388 sq. miles, pop. 305,100) of E. France (*SAVOY). Chief town: Chambéry

Savoie, Haute- *HAUTE-SAVOIE

sa·voir faire (sævwɑrfέər) *n.* tact and easy assurance in social relationships [F.]

Sav·o·na·ro·la (sævənəróulə), Girolamo (1452-98), Italian religious reformer. Prior of the Dominican monastery of St Mark in Florence (1491-8), he preached with great ardor against the moral corruption in Church and State that was an aspect of the Renaissance. When the Medici were exiled from the town (1494), he instituted a republic of terrifying severity until he was excommunicated by Alexander VI (1497) and lost the confidence of the citizens. He was hanged and burned for heresy

sa·vor, esp. *Br.* **sa·vour** (séivər) *n.* tastiness ‖ a smell of cooking which promises well ‖ the taste of something ‖ the characteristic quality of something [O.F. *savur, savour*]

savor, esp. *Br.* **savour** *v.t.* to give a distinctive taste to ‖ to have the distinctive taste of ‖ to have the characteristic quality of ‖ to have experience of ‖ to take pleasure in the taste, smell or characteristic quality of ‖ *v.i.* to have a distinctive taste or smell ‖ (with 'of') to have a quality suggestive of something specified, *his criticisms savor of jealousy* [O.F. *savourer*]

sa·vor·y, esp. *Br.* **sa·vour·y** (séivəri:) **1.** *adj.* having a pleasant and piquant taste and smell, *a savory dish* ‖ (esp. in negative constructions) morally edifying, *it is not a very savory affair* **2.** *n. pl.* **sa·vou·ries** (*Br.*) a small portion of savory food taken esp. as the last course of a dinner [M.E. *savure* prob. fr. O.F. *savouré*]

savory *n.* any of several members of *Satureia,* fam. *Labiatae,* a genus of aromatic mints native to S. Europe, esp. *S. hortensis* (summer savory) and *S. montana* (winter savory), the leaves of which are used in cooking [fr. L. *satureia*]

savour *SAVOR

savoury *SAVORY

Sa·voy (səvɔ́i) (*F.* Savoie) an alpine region forming the French departments of Savoie and Haute-Savoie, on the Italian and Swiss borders. It includes Mont Blanc. Occupations: cattle breeding, farming (cereals, vines), forestry, varied industry (based on abundant hydroelectricity), tourism. Historic capital: Chambéry. Principal resorts: Megève, Saint-Gervais, Chamonix, Annecy. Savoy was an independent county (11th c.) then a duchy (1416), including large regions of modern France and Switzerland which were lost in the 15th and 16th cc. Attached to Sardinia (1720), it was annexed by France (1792-1815) and finally ceded in 1860. The house of Savoy ruled Italy 1861-1946

sa·voy (səvɔ́i) *n.* a hardy cabbage with rough, wrinkled leaves and a compact head [F. (*chou de) Savoie,* (cabbage of) Savoy]

Sa·voy·ard (səvɔ́iərd, sævɔiɑ́rd) *n.* a native of Savoy [F.]

Savoyard *n.* an actor in or producer of the Gilbert and Sullivan operas ‖ a devotee of these operas [after the *Savoy,* London theater where most of the operas were first produced]

saw (sɔ:) **1.** *n.* a steel cutting tool with a toothed edge ‖ (*zool.*) a part of an animal which consists of a series of teeth like this tool, e.g. the snout of a sawfish or the ovipositor of a sawfly **2.** *v. pres. part.* **saw·ing** *past* **sawed** *past part.* **sawed, sawn** (sɔn) *v.t.* to cut with a saw ‖ to make by using a saw, *to saw a keyhole* ‖ to make movements as if using a saw, *to saw the air* ‖ (*pop.*) to play (a tune) on a bowed stringed instrument ‖ (*bookbinding*) to make cuts in (the leaves) to receive the threads with which they are sewn together ‖ *v.i.* to use a saw ‖ (of a saw) to cut ‖ to be able to be cut with a saw, *this wood saws easily* ‖ (*pop.*) to play with a bow on a stringed instrument [O.E. *sage*]

saw *n.* a maxim [O.E. *sagu*]

saw *past* of SEE

saw·bill (sɔ́bil) *n.* any of several birds with a serrated bill, esp. the merganser

saw·buck (sɔ́bʌk) *n.* a sawhorse [Du. *zaagbok*]

saw·dust (sɔ́dʌst) *n.* the small particles of wood torn off by the teeth of a saw as it cuts through wood, used esp. as packing material

saw·fish (sɔ́fiʃ) *pl.* **saw·fish, saw·fish·es** *n.* any of several viviparous fishes of fam. *Pristidae,* having an elongated snout with teeth on both edges. They are found in shallow seas of tropical Africa and America

saw·fly (sɔ́flai) *pl.* **saw·flies** *n.* any of several members of *Tenthredinoidea,* a superfamily of hymenopterous insects. The female has an ovi-

CONCISE PRONUNCIATION KEY: **(a)** æ, *cat;* ɑ, *car;* ɔ *fawn;* ei, *snake.* **(e)** e, *hen;* i:, *sheep;* iə, *deer;* εə, *bear.* **(i)** i, *fish;* ai, *tiger;* ə:, *bird.* **(o)** o, *ox;* au, *cow;* ou, *goat;* u, *poor;* ɔi, *royal.* **(u)** ʌ, *duck;* u, *bull;* u:, *goose;* ə, *bacillus;* ju:, *cube.* x, *loch;* θ, *think;* ð, *bother;* z, *Zen;* ʒ, *corsage;* dʒ, *savage;* ŋ, *orangutang;* j, *yak;* ʃ, *fish;* tʃ, *fetch;* 'l, *rabble;* 'n, *redden.* Complete pronunciation key appears inside front cover.

positor with sawlike teeth for cutting slits in leaves, within which the eggs are laid

saw·horse (sɔ́hɔrs) *n.* a wooden rack resting on splayed end supports, on which lumber is laid for sawing

saw·mill (sɔ́mil) *n.* a factory furnished with power-driven machines which saw and plane lumber

sawn alt. *past part.* of SAW

saw·pit (sɔ́pit) *n.* a pit across which a log is laid to be sawed by a two-man saw, one man standing in the pit and the other raised above the log

saw set a tool used to slant a saw's teeth at desired angles

saw·tooth (sɔ́tu:θ) *pl.* **saw·teeth** (sɔ́ti:θ) **1.** *n.* a tooth of a saw or of a sawlike formation **2.** *adj.* saw-toothed **sáw-toothed** *adj.*

saw·yer (sɔ́jər) *n.* a man whose craft is sawing logs into planks or sawing up lumber in other ways ‖ (*zool.*) any woodboring insect larva, esp. any of several large beetles [altered fr. *sawer,* someone who saws]

sax (sæks) *n.* a tool for trimming slates, with a pointed end for making nail holes in them [O.E. *seax,* knife]

sax *n.* (*pop.*) a saxophone

sax·a·tile (sǽksətil) *adj.* (*biol.*) saxicolous [F. or fr. L. *saxitilis* fr. *saxum,* rock]

Saxe (sæks), Hermann Maurice, comte de (1696-1750), marshal of France. He distinguished himself in the War of the Austrian Succession, notably at Fontenoy (1745)

Saxe blue a light, slightly greenish-blue color [F. *Saxe,* Saxony]

Saxe-Co·burg-Go·tha (sǽkskóubər:ggóuθə) the name (1901-17) of the British royal house, after the German duchy from which Albert, Victoria's consort, took his title. The name was changed (1917) to Windsor by George V

sax·horn (sǽkshɔrn) *n.* one of a family of brass wind instruments ranging from soprano to bass, having a long winding tube and valves. They are used in bands [after Antoine Joseph *Sax* (1814–94), Belgian inventor of the instrument]

sax·ic·o·lous (sæksíkələs) *adj.* (*biol.*) living among or growing on rocks [fr. Mod. L. *saxicola* fr. *saxum,* rock]

sax·i·frage (sǽksifridʒ) *n.* a member of *Saxifraga,* fam. *Saxifragaceae,* a large genus of usually perennial plants native to northern temperate and arctic regions, and widely cultivated in rock gardens [O.F. fr. L. *saxifraga* (*herba*), rockbreaking (plant)]

sax·i·tox·in [$C_{10}H_{17}N_7O_42HCl$] (sæksətúksən) *n.* (*chem.*) nonprotein poison found in red tide algae and mollusks

Sax·on (sǽksən) **1.** *n.* a member of a north-central German race living near the mouth of the Elbe early in the Christian era. They spread over N.W. Germany (6th–9th cc.) ‖ a member of that part of the race which settled in England in the 5th and 6th cc. A.D., an Anglo-Saxon ‖ a native of Saxony ‖ Old Saxon ‖ the German dialect of modern Saxony **2.** *adj.* pertaining to the ancient Saxons ‖ English or Anglo-Saxon ‖ of modern Saxony [F.]

Sax·o·ny (sǽksəni:) (*G.* Sachsen) a former state of East Germany on the central plateau, bordering Czechoslovakia on the south (Erzgebirge Mtns), now included in Leipzig, Dresden and Karl-Marx-Stadt districts. The north is a loess-covered agricultural region (cereals, root vegetables). Minerals: lignite, hard coal, uranium, salt. It is the most densely populated part of the republic, highly industrialized (chiefly textiles, chemicals, metallurgy) since the 19th c. The old duchy of Saxony (9th-12th cc.) included most of the land between the Rhine and the Elbe (largely modern Lower Saxony). It was broken (1180) into smaller fiefs. One of these, Saxe-Wittenberg (on the middle Elbe), became an electorate (1356). With the land south of it it became the basis of the later duchy, which became a kingdom (1806-1918) but lost large territories to Prussia (1815). It joined the German Empire in 1871. Historic capital: Dresden

sax·o·ny (sǽksəni:) *n.* a fine knitting yarn ‖ a fine woolen cloth woven from this, originally made in Saxony

Sax·o·ny-An·halt (sǽksəni:ánhalt) (*G.* Sachsen-Anhalt) a former state of East Germany in the northern plain around the middle Elbe, now included in the districts of Halle, Magdeburg and Erfurt. Crops: root vegetables, hops. Minerals: potash (world's biggest known deposits, in the Harz Mtns), salt, lignite (around Halle), supporting large chemical industries. The state was formed (1945) from the Prussian province of Saxony (the region gained from Saxony in 1815) and the small state (former duchy) of Anhalt, around Dessau

Saxony, Lower (*G.* Niedersachsen) a state (area 18,290 sq. miles, pop. 6,732,000) of West Germany, extending from the North Sea and lower Elbe to the central highland (Harz Mtns in the southeast). The partly reafforested plain, crossed by the Ems and Weser, produces cereals, potatoes and sugar beets. Industry (mechanical and electrical engineering, textiles) is now more important than agriculture. Main towns: Hanover (the capital), Brunswick. It was formed (1945) from the states of Hanover, Oldenburg, Brunswick and Schaumburg-Lippe

sax·o·phone (sǽksəfoun) *n.* (*abbr.* sax) any of a family of instruments classified as woodwinds because they have a reed like a clarinet's, but having a long, usually curved metal body. They have finger keys, range from soprano to bass, and are used mainly in military, jazz and dance bands **sáx·o·phon·ist** *n.* [after Antoine Joseph *Sax* (1814–94), Belgian inventor of the instrument+Gk *phonos,* voiced]

Say (sei), Thomas (1787-1834), U.S. Quaker naturalist. His books include 'American Entomology' (1824-8) and 'American Conchology' (1830-4)

say (sei) **1.** *v. pres. part.* **say·ing** *past* and *past part.* **said** (*sed*) *v.t.* to utter (specified words), *'it's time to go home', he said* ‖ to express (an idea, meaning or statement) vocally, in writing etc., *the papers say exports are down, the clock says 11:10* ‖ to promise, *he said he would come today* ‖ to allege, *don't believe everything people say* ‖ (*imperative*) to assume, suppose, *say x equals the unknown quantity* ‖ to declare, assert, *she says it is true* ‖ to order (something), *do as he says you are to do* ‖ to recite in words, *to say one's prayers* ‖ *v.i.* to make a statement, *you don't say so* ‖ (*imperative*) used parenthetically to indicate that what has just been said is a supposition or estimate, *a third of the population, say, is illiterate* **to go without saying** to be assumed because self-evident, *it goes without saying that they will both come* **to say nothing of** without mentioning or considering (something even more important), *the place is full of insects, to say nothing of the snakes* **2.** *n.* what one wants to say, *let him say his say now* ‖ the opportunity to express one's ideas etc., *it is time I had my say* ‖ a role in the making of a decision, *he had no say in the matter* ‖ (with 'the') the power to decide, *he's the one with the say* **sáy·ing** *n.* a maxim [O.E. *secgan*]

say-so (séisou) *pl.* **say-sos** *n.* (*pop.*) the right to decide or the exercise of this right ‖ (*pop.*) an unsupported assertion

SBA (*abbr.*) for Small Business Administration

S-band *n.* ultrahigh radio frequencies (1,550 to 5,200 MHz) *Cf* L-BAND

SBIC (*abbr.*) for Small Business Investment Corporation

SBN (*abbr.*) for Standard Book Number

scab (skæb) **1.** *n.* a tough crust of dried serum and blood formed over a sore or wound ‖ a form of scabies affecting some animals, esp. sheep ‖ any of certain fungoid or bacterial diseases of plants in which rough spots are formed ‖ one of these spots ‖ a worker who refuses to join the union or who works for less than union pay or conditions ‖ a person who works when his fellow workers are on strike or who works in the place of a striking worker **2.** *v.i. pres. part.* **scab·bing** *past* and *past part.* **scabbed** to become covered with a scab ‖ to work or act as a scab [M.E. fr. O.N.]

scab·bard (skǽbərd) *n.* the sheath of a sword, dagger or similar weapon [A.F. *escauberge* prob. fr. Gmc]

scab·ble (skǽb'l) *pres. part.* **scab·bling** *past* and *past part.* **scab·bled** *v.t.* to work, shape or dress (stone) roughly [older *scapple* fr. O.F. *escapeler*]

scab·by (skǽbi:) *comp.* **scab·bi·er** *superl.* **scab·bi·est** *adj.* encrusted with or consisting of scabs ‖ (of an animal) having scab

sca·bies (skéibi:z) *n.* a contagious skin disease caused by a mite [L. fr. *scabere,* to scratch]

sca·bi·ous (skéibi:əs) *n.* a member of *Scabiosa,* fam. *Dipsacaceae,* a genus of Old World plants bearing showy flowers at the end of tall stalks [fr. M.L. *scabiosa,* fem. of *scabiosus,* mangy (from its being thought effective as a remedy for scabies)]

scab·rous (skǽbrəs, esp. *Br.* skéi:brəs) *adj.* salacious, indecent ‖ (*biol.*) having a rough surface with raised points, scales etc. [fr. L. *scaber,* rough]

scads (skædz) *pl. n.* (*pop.*) a great number or amount, *scads of money* [prob. altered fr. dial. *scald*]

scaf·fold (skǽfəld, skǽfould) **1.** *n.* a platform put on a temporary structure of poles or suspended by ropes, used by men building, repairing etc. at a height ‖ a raised platform constructed for the execution of criminals **2.** *v.t.* to provide with a scaffold or scaffolding **scáf·fold·ing** *n.* a scaffold or number of connected scaffolds ‖ the poles, planks and ties used in constructing a scaffold [Northern F. related to O.F. *shaffaut, eschafaut*]

scagl·io·la (skæljóulə) *n.* an imitation of marble, made of gypsum and glue with marble or granite dust etc. set in it and polished [Ital. *scagliuola*]

scal·a·ble (skéiləb'l) *adj.* able to be scaled

scal·age (skéilidʒ) *n.* the margin allowed for loss by shrinkage ‖ the act of scaling in dimensions, quantity etc. ‖ the estimated yield in board feet of logs or timber [SCALE (arrangement of marks in measuring)]

sca·lar (skéilər) **1.** *adj.* (*math., phys.*) of a quantity which is fully described by a number **2.** *n.* a quantity that has magnitude but is undirected, e.g. mass, temperature etc. (cf. VECTOR) [fr. L. *scalaris,* of a ladder]

sca·lar·i·form (skəlǽrifɔrm) *adj.* (*biol.,* e.g. of some structures of cells, veins, etc.) having the appearance of a ladder or markings like a ladder's rungs ‖ (*biol.*) of or designating conjugation between parallel filaments in an alga [fr. Mod. L. *scalariformis* fr. L. *scalaris,* of a ladder]

scal·a·wag (skǽləwæg) *n.* a scallywag

scald (skɔld) **1.** *v.t.* (of a very hot liquid or vapor) to burn, *the escaping steam scalded his hand* ‖ to heat (liquid) almost to boiling ‖ to cook (food) lightly in steam or hot water ‖ to clean (a vessel) by using boiling water ‖ *v.i.* to be heated almost to boiling, *heat the milk till it scalds* **2.** *n.* the injury to the skin caused by scalding [O.N.F. *escalder, escauder*]

scale (skeil) **1.** *n.* an arrangement of accurately spaced marks representing a series of numerical values, used in measuring lengths, angles, temperature etc. ‖ a measuring instrument having such marks ‖ an ordered series of graduated quantities, values, degrees etc., *scale of salaries, decimal scale* ‖ the proportion of a representation to the object it represents, *a map to the scale of one inch to the mile* ‖ a line on a map etc. with marks dividing it to show this proportion ‖ relative magnitude, *business on a large scale* ‖ (*mus.*) a series of notes in ascending or descending order of pitch in accordance with a system of successive intervals, *minor scale* ‖ the notes of such a series covering the range of an octave, *the scale of F sharp* **2.** *v. pres. part.* **scal·ing** *past* and *past part.* **scaled** *v.t.* to apply a scale to ‖ (with 'down' or 'up') to reduce or increase in magnitude according to a fixed scale ‖ to ascend by or as if by a ladder, *to scale a cliff* ‖ to measure or estimate the yield in board feet of (logs or standing timber) ‖ *v.i.* (of two or more things) to have the same scale [fr. Ital. *scala* or L. *scala,* ladder]

scale **1.** *n.* the suspended dish or pan of a simple beam balance ‖ a balance (instrument for measuring weight) ‖ (*pl.*) a pair of scales **to turn the scales** to decide an issue previously in doubt, *his past record turned the scales in his favor* **2.** *v.t. pres. part.* **scal·ing** *past* and *past part.* **scaled** to amount to (a certain weight) ‖ to weigh on scales [O.N. *skāl,* bowl, weighing pan]

scale **1.** *n.* one of the thin, horny, bony or chitinous plates serving to protect the skin of fishes or reptiles or the legs of birds etc. ‖ a modified part of a leaf, bract etc. resembling this ‖ a small, loosely adhering, hardened flake or flat piece, e.g. of skin ‖ a scale insect ‖ a flaky deposit, e.g. of tartar on the teeth, of oxide formed on the surface of metal, or of lime deposited on the inner surface of a boiler **2.** *v. pres. part.* **scal·ing** *past* and *past part.* **scaled** *v.t.* to remove scale or the scales from ‖ to throw (a flat stone) at a body of water in such a way that it skips on the water's surface ‖ *v.i.* to form scales ‖ to come off in scales ‖ to shed scales [O.F. *escale*]

scale·board (skéilbɔrd, skéilbourd, skǽlbərd) *n.* thin board used for veneers ‖ the thin wooden sheet protecting the back of a picture in its frame

scale insect any of several homopterous insects which suck the sap of plants and have the appearance of small scales on the plant's surface

scale leaf (*bot.*) a leaf resembling a scale, e.g. a bud scale

sca·lene (skéili:n) *adj.* (of a triangle) having unequal sides ‖ of or relating to the scaleni [fr. L.L. *scalenus*, scalenus]

sca·le·nus (skeilí:nəs) *pl.* **sca·le·ni** (skeilí:nai) *n.* (*anat.*) any of a set of triangular muscles on either side of the neck, extending from the cervical vertebrae to the first or second rib [Mod. L. fr. Gk *skalēnos*]

scal·er (skéilər) *n.* an electronic instrument used for recording high-speed impulses ‖ someone who scales logs or timber ‖ (*computer*) a circuit that requires a directed number of inputs for each output

scal·er-ten·sor theory (skéilərténsər) (*phys.*) hypothesis that electromagnetic waves passing through a gravitational field should slow and curve less than indicated by Einstein's general theory

Scal·i·ger (skǽlidʒər) (Giulio Cesare Scaligero, 1484-1558), Italian Renaissance scholar, philologist and doctor. His son Joseph Justus (1540-1609) was also a great scholar and established a scientific basis for ancient chronology in his 'De emendatione temporum' (1583)

scal·i·ness (skéili:nis) *n.* the quality or state of being scaly

scaling ladder a ladder used in climbing walls, e.g. by firemen

scal·la·wag (skǽləwæg) *n.* a scallywag

scal·lion (skǽljən) *n.* the shallot ‖ the leek ‖ a green onion, pulled for eating before the bulb has swollen [A.F. *scalun, scaloun* fr. O.F. *eschaloigne*]

scal·lop (skɒ́ləp, skǽləp) **1.** *n.* any of several marine bivalve mollusks of fam. *Pectinidae* having a fan-shaped fluted shell with an undulating margin ‖ the edible adductor muscle of such a mollusk ‖ a single shell of one of these mollusks, used for serving certain fish dishes ‖ (*hist.*) this shell worn as a badge by pilgrims returning from the Holy Land ‖ a thin, boneless slice of white meat, e.g. veal, turkey ‖ one of the rounded projections forming an undulating edging of cloth, metal etc. **2.** *v.t.* to ornament with an edging of scallops ‖ to cook in a casserole etc. with sauce and a topping of bread crumbs **scál·lop·ing** *n.* a scalloped edging [O.F. *escalope* Gmc]

scal·ly·wag (skǽli:wæg) *n.* a scamp, rogue ‖ (*Am. hist.*) a Southerner willing to fraternize with the victorious enemy after the Civil War [etym. doubtful]

scalp (skælp) **1.** *n.* the skin on the top and back of the head ‖ (*hist.*) this skin, with the hair attached, torn from an enemy by a North American Indian as a trophy ‖ a small profit made by scalping **2.** *v.t.* to tear off the scalp from ‖ to buy and sell (securities and commodities) in order to make small profits on quick returns ‖ (*pop.*) to sell (theater tickets etc.) as a scalper ‖ *v.i.* to buy and sell stocks (or theater tickets etc.) in order to make quick returns [M.E. prob. of Scand. origin]

scal·pel (skǽlpəl) *n.* a small very sharp precision knife used in surgery [fr. L. *scalpellum*]

scalp·er (skǽlpər) *n.* a person who buys and sells for quick profit, esp. one who buys up theater tickets and sells them for more than the established price

scalp lock a tuft of hair left on the shaved crown by certain North American Indian warriors

scal·y (skéili:) *comp.* **scal·i·er** *superl.* **scal·i·est** *adj.* having, covered with or consisting of scales or a scale ‖ shedding scales or flakes ‖ resembling scales or a scale ‖ infested with scale insects

scaly anteater a pangolin

scam (skæm) *n.* (*slang*) an illegal operation, usu. a confidence racket, involving a sum of money

scam·mo·ny (skǽməni:) *pl.* **scam·mo·nies** *n.* *Convolvulus scammonia*, fam. *Convolvulaceae*, an Asiatic twining plant ‖ the dried root of this plant ‖ gum resin obtained from this root, used as a purgative [fr. L. *scammonia, scammonium* fr. Gk]

scamp (skæmp) *n.* a mischievous rogue [prob. fr. older *scamp* v., to rob on the highway, prob. related to SCAMPER]

scamp *v.t.* to perform (work etc.) carelessly [etym. doubtful]

scamp·er (skǽmpər) **1.** *v.i.* to dart about with nimble, precipitous movements, esp. playfully ‖ to make a dash, *they scampered for shelter* **2.** *n.* a scampering [perh. fr. Ital. *scampare*, to decamp]

scam·pi (skǽmpi:) *n., s. & pl.* Italian shrimp dish

scan (skæn) *pres. part.* **scan·ning** *past* and *past part.* **scanned** *v.t.* to examine closely or carefully, *to scan the horizon* ‖ to determine the meter of (verse) by analyzing it ‖ the path periodically followed by a radiation beam ‖ (*med.*) to examine a body by X-ray or other radioactive material ‖ (*computer*) to examine stored material for a purpose ‖ (*computer*) to examine channels for input-output activity ‖ to glance at hastily, *scan the headlines* ‖ *v.i.* to have the correct meter, *these lines do not scan* ‖ to examine verse in order to determine the meter ‖ (*television*) to pass a beam of light or electrons over a surface in order to transmit and reproduce the picture [fr. L. *scandere*, to climb]

scan·dal (skǽnd'l) *n.* a serious breach of the moral or social code which becomes widely known ‖ someone who or something that causes general indignation ‖ the indignation so caused ‖ malicious gossip [M.E. *scandle* fr. O.N.F. *escandle* fr. L. fr. Gk]

scan·dal·ize (skǽnd'laiz) *pres. part.* **scan·dal·iz·ing** *past* and *past part.* **scan·dal·ized** *v.t.* to give offense to (others) by acting contrary to their ideas of what is morally or socially right [F. *scandaliser*]

scan·dal·mon·ger (skǽnd'lmʌŋgər, skǽnd'lmɒŋgər) *n.* a person who makes up scandal or who passes it on [fr. SCANDAL+*monger*, a dealer]

scan·dal·ous (skǽnd'ləs) *adj.* of the nature of scandal, offensive and shocking [F. *scandaleux*]

Scan·der·beg (skǽndərbeg) (George Castriota, c. 1404-68), Albanian national hero who led his country's resistance (1443-68) against the threat of Turkish domination

Scan·di·na·vi·a (skændinéivi:ə) the region of N.W. Europe embracing Sweden, Norway and Denmark. Iceland is often included, on ethnic grounds, and Finland sometimes, on geographical and historical grounds ‖ the peninsula formed by Norway and Sweden

Scan·di·na·vi·an (skændinéivi:ən) **1.** *adj.* pertaining to Scandinavia, its inhabitants, languages etc. **2.** *n.* a native of Scandinavia ‖ the North Germanic group of languages spoken in Scandinavia (*SWEDISH, *NORWEGIAN, *DANISH, *ICELANDIC)

scan·di·um (skǽndi:əm) *n.* a metallic element (symbol Sc, at. no. 21, at. mass 44.956) occurring in some Scandinavian minerals [fr. L. *Scandia*, Scandinavia]

scan·ner (skǽnər) *n.* someone who or something that scans ‖ (*television*) a device used for scanning ‖ (*radar*) an electronic apparatus for traversing a region with a beam

scanning electron microscope *n.* a device for providing a three-dimensional image on a screen of an irregular surface, used for examining and photographing tissue

scan·sion (skǽnʃən) *n.* the scanning of verse [fr. L. *scansio (scansionis)* fr. *scandere*, to climb]

scan·so·ri·al (skænsɔ́ri:əl, skænsóuri:əl) *adj.* (*zool.*, esp. of the feet of certain birds) adapted for climbing ‖ (*zool.*) having such feet [fr. L. *scansorius*, used for climbing]

scant (skænt) **1.** *adj.* meager ‖ less than enough ‖ barely enough ‖ just short of a specific measure, quantity etc., *a scant cup of sugar* **2.** *v.t.* to provide (someone or something) with too small a supply or quantity ‖ to be stinting in the supply of (something) ‖ to treat inadequately [O.N. *skamt*, short]

scant·i·ly (skǽntili:) *adv.* in a scanty way

scant·i·ness (skǽnti:nis) *n.* the quality or state of being scanty

scant·ling (skǽntliŋ) *n.* a beam or timber of small cross section, esp. one less than 2–4 ins. wide and 2–4½ ins. thick ‖ small beams or timbers collectively ‖ (*shipbuilding*) a set of fixed dimensions [fr. older *scantillon*, a measuring rod fr. O. F. *escantillon*]

scant·y (skǽnti:) *comp.* **scant·i·er** *superl.* **scant·i·est** *adj.* barely enough ‖ meager ‖ not quite enough

Sca·pa Flow (skɑ́pə, skǽpə) a protected harbor (15 miles long, 8 miles wide) formed by Great Britain's S. Orkney Is. It was the main British naval base during the 1st world war, and the scene of the scuttling of the German fleet in 1919

scape (skeip) *n.* (*archit.*) the shaft of a column, or a hollow curve in the shaft at the top or base, where it expands to meet the fillet ‖ (*biol.*) the basal joint of the antenna of an insect ‖ (*bot.*) a leafless peduncle arising at the surface of the ground or underground ‖ (*zool.*) the shaft of a feather [fr. L. *scapus*, stem, column shaft]

scape·goat (skéipgout) *n.* a person made to bear the blame which should fall on others ‖ (in ancient Jewish ritual) a goat on whose head the high priest symbolically laid the sins of the people on Yom Kippur, and which was then allowed to escape into the wilderness [fr. obs. *scape*, contr. of ESCAPE+GOAT]

Scapegoat *n.* (*mil.*) U.S.S.R. two-stage strategic, solid-fuel 32-ft-long nuclear missile (SS-14) with a 2,500-mi range

scape·grace (skéipgreis) *n.* a person who is always getting into trouble [fr. *scape*, obs. contr. of ESCAPE+GRACE]

scape wheel an escape wheel [fr *scape*, obs. contr. of ESCAPE]

scaph·oid (skǽfɔid) **1.** *adj.* (*anat.*) navicular **2.** *n.* a navicular bone [fr. Mod. L. *scaphoides* fr. Gk *skaphoeidēs* fr. *skaphē*, a boat+*eidos*, shape]

sca·pose (skéipous) *adj.* of, relating to or resembling a scape

scap·u·la (skǽpjulə) *pl.* **scap·u·lae** (skǽpjuli:), **scap·u·las** *n.* (*anat.*) either shoulder blade ‖ (*zool.*) any of several structures in insects suggestive of a shoulder blade [L.=shoulder, shoulder blade]

scap·u·lar (skǽpjulər) *n.* (*zool.*) any of a bird's feathers lying over the base of the wing ‖ (*zool.*) a scapula ‖ a sleeveless coat worn by certain monks, falling from the shoulders (usually almost to the feet) at the front and back ‖ a badge of membership of some religious orders, consisting of two pieces of cloth worn on the chest and back and joined by strips over the shoulders [fr. L. *scapulare* fr. *scapula*, shoulder]

scapular *adj.* of or relating to a scapula ‖ designating the scapulars of a bird [fr. Mod. L. *scapularis* fr. L. *scapula*, scapula]

scap·u·lar·y (skǽpjuləri:) *pl.* **scap·u·lar·ies** *n.* (*eccles.*) a scapular ‖ a scapular feather [fr. M.L. *scapularium* var. of *scapulare*, a scapular]

scar (skɑr) **1.** *n.* a permanent mark on the skin or other tissue, consisting of fibrous tissue formed where a wound, ulcer etc. heals ‖ a permanent effect left by an emotional wound ‖ (*bot.*) a mark left on a stem etc. by the fall of a leaf or on a seed by the separation of the funicle **2.** *v. pres. part.* **scar·ring** *past* and *past part.* **scarred** *v.t.* to mark with a scar ‖ *v.i.* to form a scar [prob. fr. O.F. *escare* fr. L.L. fr. Gk]

scar *n.* a bare rocky side of a mountain [prob. fr. O.N. *sker*, a rock in the sea]

scar·ab (skǽrəb) *n.* any of several stout-bodied, lamellicorn beetles of fam. *Scarabaeidae*, esp. *Scarabaeus sacer*, a dung beetle of Mediterranean regions ‖ a conventionalized carving of *S. sacer*, common in ancient Egypt as a symbol of resurrection and worn as a charm or for ornament, or buried with the dead [fr. F. *scarabée*]

scar·a·bae·id (skærəbí:id) *n.* a scarab or related beetle [fr. Mod. L. *scarabaeidae* fr. L. *scarabaeus*, scarab]

scarce (skɛərs) *comp.* **scarc·er** *superl.* **scarc·est** *adj.* present or available in very limited or insufficient amount, *food was scarce in the region* **to make oneself scarce** (*pop.*) to keep away from others or go away **scárce·ly** *adv.* barely, only just, *he is scarcely 21* ‖ not at all, *I scarcely think he could have done it* ‖ most improbably, *he will scarcely come at this hour* [M.E. *scars* fr. O.N.F.]

scarce·ment (skɛ́ərsmənt) *n.* a setback in the thickness of a wall or bank of earth [prob. fr. obs. *scarce*, to become or make less]

scar·ci·ty (skɛ́ərsiti:) *pl.* **scar·ci·ties** *n.* the quality or state of being scarce ‖ a limited or insufficient supply [O.N.F. *escarceté*, frugality]

scare (skɛər) **1.** *v. pres. part.* **scar·ing** *past* and *past part.* **scared** *v.t.* to arouse fear in, *the idea scares her* ‖ (with 'away', 'off') to cause to flee in fear, *the noises scared them off* ‖ *v.i.* to become afraid, *he doesn't scare easily* **to scare up** (*pop.*)

CONCISE PRONUNCIATION KEY: **(a)** æ, cat; ɑ, car; ɔ fawn; ei, snake. **(e)** e, hen; i:, sheep; iə, deer; ɛə, bear. **(i)** i, fish; ai, tiger; ə:, bird. **(o)** o, ox; au, cow; ou, goat; u, poor; ɔi, royal. **(u)** ʌ, duck; u, bull; u:, goose; ə, bacillus; ju:, cube. x, loch; θ, think; ð, bother; z, Zen; ʒ, corsage; dʒ, savage; ŋ, orangutang; j, yak; ʃ, fish; tʃ, fetch; 'l, rabble; 'n, redden. Complete pronunciation key appears inside front cover.

to manage to find or get quickly, *see if you can scare up some matches* **2.** *n.* an instance of being scared, *to give someone a scare* ‖ a widespread alarm, panic [M.E. *skerre* fr. O.N. *skirra*]

scare·crow (skέərkrou) *n.* a figure stuffed with straw and dressed in ragged old clothes, set up on a pole in a field to scare birds away from the crops ‖ a shabbily and untidily dressed person, esp. a very thin one

scared straight program for exposing experimental students to life in prison, as a crime deterrent

scare·head (skέərhed) *n.* (*pop.*) an extravagant, sensational newspaper headline in very large print, esp. one meant to cause alarm

scare·mon·ger (skέərmʌŋgər, skέərmɒŋgər) *n.* a person who spreads alarming false or exaggerated reports [fr. SCARE+*monger*, a dealer]

scarf (skɑrf) *pl.* **scarfs,** esp. *Br.* **scarves** (skɑrvz) *n.* a piece of material wrapped around the neck, head or shoulders for warmth or decoration ‖ a strip of cloth placed on a dresser or table ‖ (*mil.*) a sash [prob. fr. O.N.F. *escarpe*]

scarf 1. *pl.* **scarves** (skɑrvz), **scarfs** *n.* a joint made by scarfing lumber, metal or leather ‖ a groove cut along a whale's body **2.** *v.t.* to join (two pieces of lumber, metal or leather) by beveling or chamfering etc. so that they overlap, and then securing them, e.g. by bolting, gluing, brazing or sewing them together ‖ to cut scarfs in and remove the skin and blubber of (a whale) [perh. fr. Swed. *skarf* and Norw. *skarv,* piece added to lengthen a board or garment]

scar·i·fi·ca·tion (skærifikéiʃən) *n.* a scarifying or being scarified ‖ a mark or marks made by scarifying [fr. L.L. *scarificatio* (*scarificationis*) fr. *scarificare,* to scarify]

scar·i·fi·ca·tor (skǽrifikeitər) *n.* a surgical instrument for making superficial cuts in the skin [Mod. L. fr. L.L. *scarificare,* to scarify]

scar·i·fi·er (skǽrifaiər) *n.* a machine for loosening soil ‖ a machine for breaking up a road surface before resurfacing ‖ a scarificator

scar·i·fy (skǽrifai) *pres. part.* **scar·i·fy·ing** *past* and *past part.* **scar·i·fied** *v.t.* (*surgery*) to make superficial cuts in (the skin) ‖ to loosen (topsoil) with a scarifier ‖ to make incisions in the coat of (a seed) to bring on germination faster [F. *scarifier* fr. L.L. *scarificare*]

scar·i·ous (skέəri:əs) *adj.* (*bot.,* of some bracts) thin, dry and membranous in texture [fr. F. *scarieux*]

scar·la·ti·na (skɑrləti:nə) *n.* scarlet fever ‖ (*pop.*) a mild form of this [Mod. L. fr. Ital. *scarlattina* fr. *scarlatto,* scarlet]

Scar·lat·ti (skɑrlάtti:), Alessandro (1660-1725), Italian composer, one of the founders of 18th-c. Italian opera. He wrote over 100 operas, 600 cantatas for solo voice and continuo, oratorios, Masses etc.

Scarlatti, Domenico (1685-1757), Italian composer, son of Alessandro. He wrote over 550 harpsichord 'sonatas', single-movement works in binary form, often characterized by harmonic and rhythmic variety and by brilliance

scar·let (skάrlit) **1.** *n.* a brilliant red color ‖ red cloth or clothes, e.g. the red coat traditionally worn at a hunt **2.** *adj.* of the color scarlet ‖ (*rhet.,* of a sin or crime) flagrantly wicked [fr. O.F. *escarlate,* perh. fr. Pers. *saqalāt,* a kind of rich cloth]

scarlet fever an acute contagious disease caused by a streptococcus and characterized by fever, inflammation of the nose and throat and a reddish skin rash

scarlet pimpernel *PIMPERNEL

scarlet runner *Phaseolus coccineus,* fam. *Papilionaceae,* a climbing bean of tropical American origin, having large red flowers and red and black edible seeds in edible pods, cultivated esp. in Great Britain

scarlet tanager *Piranga olivacea,* a common tanager of the U.S.A., the male of which has a scarlet body and black wings and tail, the female and young being mainly olive in color

scarp (skɑrp) **1.** *n.* a steep slope ‖ the inner wall of a fortified ditch (cf. COUNTERSCARP) **2.** *v.t.* to cut so as to form a scarp [fr. Ital. *scarpa*]

Scar·ron (skærɔ̃), Paul (1610-60), French novelist, best known for his 'le Roman comique' (1651). His wife later became Mme de Maintenon

scarves alt. *pl.* of SCARF (piece of material)

scar·y (skέəri:) *comp.* **scar·i·er** *superl.* **scar·i·est** *adj.* (*pop.*) alarming, causing fright ‖ (*pop.*) easily frightened, timid

scat (skæt) *pres. part.* **scat·ting** *past* and *past part.* **scat·ted** *v.i.* (used esp. in *imperative*) to go away quickly [origin unknown]

scat *n.* (*zool.*) fecal droppings of animals

scathe (skeið) *pres. part.* **scath·ing** *past* and *past part.* **scathed** *v.t.* to attack with bitterly severe criticism, invective or denunciation **scáth·ing** *adj.* [O.N. *skatha,* it hurts]

scat·o·log·i·cal (skæt'lɒdʒik'l) *adj.* of, pertaining to or characterized by scatology

sca·tol·o·gy (skətɒlədʒi:) *n.* preoccupation with or treatment of excrement, defecation etc., esp. in literature ‖ literature characterized by this ‖ the scientific study of animal droppings or coprolites [fr. Gk *skôr* (*skatos*), dung+*logos,* discourse]

scat·ter (skǽtər) **1.** *v.t.* to cause to break up and go in different directions or be widely separated or distributed, esp. at random, *mud was scattered all over their clothes, his dog scattered the flock* ‖ to sow or distribute by handfuls, *to scatter fertilizer* ‖ to distribute or sprinkle something in or over (something), *she scatters her novels with French words* ‖ (*phys.*) to reflect diffusely ‖ (*phys.*) to diffuse (a radiation beam) in a random fashion as a result of collision ‖ (of a gun or cartridge) to cause (shot) to spread ‖ *v.i.* to separate widely in different directions, esp. at random, *the crowd scattered when the police charged* **2.** *n.* something scattered, *a scatter of foam on the sand* ‖ the extent of scattering, e.g. of shot [etym. doubtful]

scat·ter·brain (skǽtərbrein) *n.* a flighty person whose ideas are not properly organized and who forgets or confuses detail **scát·ter·brained** *adj.*

scat·tered (skǽtərd) *adj.* of objects placed at some distance from one another and at random, *a few scattered villages survived*

scat·ter·ing (skǽtəriŋ) **1.** *adj.* dispersed and in no order ‖ going in different directions, widely separated **2.** *n.* a small number of scattered individuals ‖ (*phys.*) the process of being scattered

scat·ter·om·e·ter (skætərɒmitər) *n.* radar equipment with many aerials to receive from a wide area

scatter rug one of a number of small rugs placed here and there in a room

scat·ter·site housing (skǽtərsait) low-income public housing dispersed to avoid concentration in one area

scaup (skɔp) *pl.* **scaup, scaups** *n.* a scaup duck [perh. var. of SCALP]

scaup duck a duck of genus *Aythya,* esp. *A. marila nearctica,* the greater scaup, and *A. affinis,* the lesser scaup, both native to North America

scav·enge (skǽvindʒ) *pres. part.* **scav·eng·ing** *past* and *past part.* **scav·enged** *v.t.* to gather up and remove (refuse) ‖ (of animals) to seek out and devour (refuse or dead organic matter) ‖ to remove refuse or impurities from ‖ to search for usable refuse in (a place) ‖ to remove the burned gases from (an internal-combustion machine) ‖ *v.i.* to seek among refuse for objects of some use ‖ to remove refuse, waste, impurities etc. from a place or thing [back-formation fr. SCAVENGER]

scav·en·ger (skǽvindʒər) *n.* an animal which feeds on dead organic matter ‖ (esp. *Br.*) a person employed to remove refuse [older *scavager* fr. *scavage,* toll levied on nonresident merchants, fr. A.F. *scawage, schawage,* inspection]

sca·zon (skéiz'n) *n.* a limping satiric meter in classical verse, esp. an iambic trimeter ending with a spondee or trochee [L. fr. Gk fr. *skazein,* to limp]

sce·na (ʃéinə,ʃéinɑ) *n.* a scene from an opera ‖ a composition for solo voice with accompaniment, usually a dramatic recitative. It may be either part of an opera or an independent entity [Ital.]

sce·nar·i·o (sinέəri:ou, sinάri:ou) *n.* a brief summary of the scenes and story of a play, opera etc. ‖ a synopsis of a plan of action in specified situation ‖ a detailed outline of a movie, giving directions for actors etc. **sce·nár·ist** *n.* a writer of movie scenarios [Ital. fr. *scena,* scene]

scene (si:n) *n.* the place where some event occurs ‖ the place where the action of a play, novel etc. is supposed to take place ‖ a division of an act in a play ‖ theater scenery ‖ a display of strong emotion, e.g. of anger, *don't make a scene* ‖ (*colloq.*) the situation; the world of activity ‖ a view, episode etc. seen by an observer as though in a theater **behind the scenes** where the public cannot see or know what goes on ‖ in the discreet absence of all publicity [F. *scène* fr. L. *scena* fr. Gk *skēnē,* tent, stage]

scen·er·y (sí:nəri:) *pl.* **scen·er·ies** *n.* the painted flats etc. used in a theater to represent the place of action ‖ natural geographical features with regard to their beauty or picturesqueness [fr. obs. *scenary,* scenario fr. Ital. *scenario*]

scene·shift·er (sí:nʃiftər) *n.* someone who changes scenes during a theatrical production

sce·nic (sí:nik, sénik) *adj.* of or connected with stage scenery or effects ‖ of natural scenery ‖ (of a landscape etc.) beautiful or picturesque **scé·ni·cal·ly** *adv.* [F. *scénique* fr. L. *scenicus*]

scenic easement (*envir.*) right to use, or control use of, an area in order to preserve its natural characteristics

scenic railway a short railway of small gauge constructed to pass between artificial scenic views as an amusement at fairs, amusement parks etc.

scent (sent) **1.** *v.t.* to perceive by the sense of smell, *the buffalo scented our approach* ‖ to begin to have an awareness or suspicion of, *to scent a mystery* ‖ to give an odor to, *scented soap* **2.** *n.* a smell, usually pleasing ‖ (esp. *Br.*) perfume ‖ the smell remaining after an animal has passed ‖ a trace followed in hunting ‖ the way leading to detection of a crime ‖ the power of smelling or of detecting or discovering, *a keen scent* ‖ the paper trail laid in hare and hounds [M.E. *sent,* to scent game fr. F. *sentir,* to feel, smell]

scent·om·e·ter (sentɒmitər) *n.* breath-analyzing instrument for measuring pollutants in the breath

scepsis *SKEPSIS

scep·ter, esp. *Br.* **scep·tre** (séptər) *n.* a staff carried by a sovereign as symbol of authority **scép·tered,** esp. *Br.* **scép·tred** *adj.* [M.E. *ceptre, septre, sceptre* fr. O.F. fr. L. *sceptrum* fr. Gk]

sceptic *SKEPTIC

scepticism *SKEPTICISM

sceptre *SCEPTER

schad·en·freud·e (ʃάd'nfrɔidə) *n.* delight at the misfortune of another person [G. fr. *schaden,* damage+*freude,* joy]

Schaff (ʃæf, ʃɑf), Philip (1819-93), U.S. theologian and advocate of church unity. He believed that Roman Catholicism and Protestantism would blend eventually into an evangelical Catholicism. His works include 'History of the Christian Church' (7 vols, 1858-92)

Schaff·hau·sen (ʃɑfháuz'n) the northernmost canton (area 115 sq. miles, pop. 148,000) of Switzerland, German-speaking and mainly Protestant, and heavily industrialized ‖ its capital (pop. 69,413), near celebrated Rhine waterfalls (hydroelectricity). Industries: mechanical and precision engineering, watchmaking, metallurgy, textiles. Romanesque abbey (11th c.)

Scharn·horst (ʃάrnhɔrst), Gerhard Johann David von (1755-1813), Prussian general. He reformed the Prussian army after the Treaty of Tilsit, basing it on universal conscription and a national reserve

Schech·ter (ʃéktər), Solomon (1847-1915), U.S. Jewish theologian and talmudist. He discovered (1896) in Cairo over 90,000 manuscripts of great significance to biblical and rabbinical research. He served (1902-15) as president of the Jewish Theological Seminary of America in New York City, which he made a center of Jewish research, and founded (1913) the United Synagogue of America

Schechter Poultry Corp. v. United States a unanimous decision (1935) of the U.S. Supreme Court led by Charles Evan Hughes. It ruled that the codes concerning wages and hours outlined in the National Industrial Recovery Act of President Franklin Roosevelt exceeded the powers of Congress under the interstate commerce clause, and that the National Recovery Administration was thus illegal

sched·ule (skédʒu:l, skédʒul, skédʒu:əl, *Br.* ʃédju:l) **1.** *n.* a written or printed list, often appended to a document such as a will ‖ a timed program of procedure ‖ a timetable for trains etc. ‖ the list of occupations the Department of Labor considers to be in short supply throughout the U.S., and for which it grants certification for immigration **2.** *v.t. pres. part.* **sched·ul·ing** *past* and *past part.* **sched·uled** to make a list of ‖ to work out a program or timetable for ‖ to assign in advance a time or date for (an event), *their departure was scheduled for 5:00 p.m.* [O. F. *cedule, sedule,* written slip fr. L.L.]

CONCISE PRONUNCIATION KEY: **(a)** æ, *cat*; ɑ, *car*; ɔ *fawn*; ei, *snake*. **(e)** e, *hen*; i:, *sheep*; iə, *deer*; εə, *bear*. **(i)** i, *fish*; ai, *tiger*; ə:, *bird*. **(o)** o, *ox*; au, *cow*; ou, *goat*; u, *poor*; ɔi, *royal*. **(u)** ʌ, *duck*; u, *bull*; u:, *goose*; ə, *bacillus*; ju:, *cube*. x, *loch*; θ, *think*; ð, *bother*; z, *Zen*; ʒ, *corsage*; dʒ, *savage*; ŋ, *orangutang*; j, *yak*; ʃ, *fish*; tʃ, *fetch*; 'l, *rabble*; 'n, *redden*. Complete pronunciation key appears inside front cover.

Schee·le (ʃéilə), Karl Wilhelm (1742-86), Swedish chemist who discovered oxygen (1773) independently of Priestley. He produced phosphorus from bone ash, studied the reduction of silver salts by light, and studied photosynthesis

Scheele's green a yellowish-green compound of copper and arsenic used as an insecticide and as a pigment

scheel·ite (ʃéilait, ʃí:lait) *n.* native calcium tungstate, $CaWO_4$, one of the sources of tungsten [after K. W. SCHEELE]

Scheldt (skelt, ʃelt) (*Flem.* Schelde, *F.* Escaut) a river (270 miles long, navigable for 200) rising in Aisne, N.E. France, and flowing across W. Belgium through a double estuary in the S.W. Netherlands to the North Sea. By the Treaties of Westphalia (1648) the Dutch obtained the right to close the mouth of the Scheldt, with disastrous effects on Antwerp. Navigation was made free in 1863

Sche·ler (ʃéilər), Max (1874-1928), German phenomenologist philosopher. His main works include 'Der Formalismus in der Ethik und die materiale Wertethik' (1913-16), 'Wesen und Formen der Sympathie' (1923) and 'Die Stellung des Menschen im Kosmos' (1927, 1928)

Schel·ling (ʃéliŋ), Friedrich Wilhelm Joseph von (1775-1854), German idealist philosopher. He was profoundly influential in German thought. In 'Vom Ich als Prinzip der Philosophie' (1795) he follows Fichte, acknowledging only one reality, the infinite and absolute Ego, of which the universe is the expression. In the 'natural philosophy' that marks his middle period he makes nature an absolute being, working unconsciously though purposively toward self-consciousness, man alone being in full possession of this faculty. His later writings were marked by Neoplatonist and theosophist speculations

sche·ma (skí:mə) *pl.* **sche·ma·ta** (skí:mətə) *n.* a plan, outline ‖ a diagram ‖ (*logic*) a syllogistic abstract figure ‖ (*Kantian philos.*) the imaginative form through which a particular perception is taken up into a category [Gk *schēma*, form, figure]

sche·mat·ic (ski:mǽtik) *adj.* of, like or having the nature of a schema **sche·mát·i·cal·ly** *adv.* [fr. Mod. L. *schematicus*]

sche·ma·ti·za·tion (ski:mətizéiʃən) *n.* a schematizing or being schematized ‖ an instance of this

sche·ma·tize (skí:mətaiz) *pres. part.* **sche·ma·tiz·ing** *past* and *past part.* **sche·ma·tized** *v.t.* to arrange in a scheme ‖ to conventionalize, stylize [fr. Gk *schēmatizein*]

scheme (ski:m) **1.** *n.* a detailed plan or system, *a scheme for lodging the extra guests* ‖ a carefully constructed arrangement, *a color scheme* ‖ a secret, dishonest or malicious plot or plan (esp. *Br.*) an official project or plan, *a governmental hydroelectric scheme* **2.** *v.i. pres. part.* **schem·ing** *past* and *past part.* **schemed** to form plans or schemes **schém·er** *n.* someone who devises secret, dishonest or malicious plans **schém·ing** *adj.* intriguing, full of guile [M.L. *schema* fr. Gk]

Scher·ba·kov *RYBINSK

scher·zan·do (skertsándou, skertsǽndou) **1.** *adv.* (*mus.*) in a lively, playful manner **2.** *adj.* (*mus.*) lively, playful **3.** *n.* (*mus.*) a scherzando movement or passage [Ital.]

scher·zo (skértsou) *pl.* **scher·zos, scher·zi** (skértsi:) *n.* (*mus.*) a lively composition, esp. one in ternary form and in triple time, often constituting a movement following a slow movement in a classical sonata or symphony etc. [Ital.= a jest, scherzo]

Schia·pa·rel·li (skjɑparélli:), Giovanni Virginio (1835-1910), Italian astronomer who discovered the canals on Mars, the asteroid Hesperia and the connection between comets and meteorites

Schick Gu·tiér·rez (ʃíkgu:tjérres), René (1910-66), Nicaraguan lawyer, politician, and president of the Republic (1963-6). He died in office

Schick test (ʃik) a test for diphtheria immunity, in which diphtheria toxin is injected into the skin. If the skin reacts by reddening etc., then the subject is susceptible to the disease [after Béla *Schick* (1877–1967), U.S. pediatrician]

Schie·dam (sxi:dám) a town (pop. 74,223) of South Holland, Netherlands, near Rotterdam

Schil·ler (ʃílər), Johann Christoph Friedrich von (1759-1805), German poet, playwright, historian and critic. He achieved instant fame with his Romantic drama 'Die Räuber' (1781). His historical works include 'The History of the Thirty Years' War' (1791-3). The later historical dramas, e.g. 'Wallenstein' (1799), 'Maria Stuart' (1800) and 'Wilhelm Tell' (1804), showed a mature treatment of the themes of freedom, idealism and heroic achievement, and the same idealism is found in the poems (e.g. the 'Hymn to Joy', which Beethoven set to music in the last movement of the 9th Symphony). Collaboration with Goethe at Weimar produced important work in the editing of literary journals and in aesthetic philosophy

schil·ler (ʃílər) *n.* the sheen or iridescence of some minerals [G.=color play]

schil·ling (ʃíliŋ) *n.* the basic monetary unit of Austria, subdivided into 100 groschen [G.]

schip·per·ke (skípərki:, skípərkə) *n.* a small, black dog of a Belgian breed, with a pointed head, prick ears and a piercing bark [Du. dial.=little boatman (fr. its use as a barge watchdog)]

schism (sízəm) *n.* a destruction of the unity of a Church through disagreement on doctrine or practice, resulting in the Church's regrouping into separate parts ‖ one of the sects so formed ‖ the offense of causing this to occur ‖ a division of any party etc. into differing factions [M.E. *scisme* fr. O.F. fr. eccles. L. *schisma* fr. Gk]

schis·mat·ic (sizmǽtik) **1.** *adj.* of the nature of schism ‖ causing schism **2.** *n.* a person who causes or fosters schism **schis·mát·i·cal** *adj.* [M.E. *cysmatyke, scismatik* fr. O.F. fr. eccles. L. *schismaticus* fr. Gk]

schist (ʃist) *n.* a metamorphic crystalline rock, much coarser than gneiss. It contains minerals such as mica and talc but no essential feldspar, and is easily split into thin flakes **schis·tose** (ʃístous) *adj.* of, relating to or having the characteristics of schist [F. *schiste* fr. L. *schistos*, easily split fr. Gk]

Schis·to·so·ma ja·pon·i·cum (skitəsóuməjæpónikəm) (*med.*) species of flukes that are found in the veins of the intestines, esp. in China and Japan

schis·to·some (ʃístəsoum) *n.* a fluke of fam. *Schistosomatidae*, esp. of genus *Schistosoma*, living as a parasite in mammals, snails and mollusks **schis·to·so·mi·a·sis** (ʃistəsoumáiəsis) *n.* bilharzia [fr. Mod. L. *Schistosoma* fr. Gk *schistos*, cleft+*sōma*, body]

schiz·an·thus (skizǽnθəs) *n.* a member of *Schizanthus*, fam. *Solanaceae*, a genus of plants native to Chile, with divided leaves and white, red or violet showy flowers [Mod. L. fr. Gk *schizein*, to split+*anthos*, flower]

schiz·o·carp (skízəkɑrp) *n.* (*bot.*) a compound fruit which splits when ripe into several indehiscent portions, each having one seed **schiz·o·cár·pous** *adj.* [fr. Gk *schizein*, to split+*karpos*, fruit]

schiz·o·gen·e·sis (skizədʒénisis) *n.* (*biol.*) reproduction by fission [Mod. L. fr. Gk *schizein*, to split+*genesis*, origin]

schiz·oid (skítsɔid, skízɔid) **1.** *adj.* characteristic of schizophrenia or of split personality ‖ having personality traits associated with schizophrenia, e.g. reserve, emotional inhibition, introversion etc. **2.** *n.* a schizoid person [fr. Gk *schizein*, to split]

schiz·o·my·cete (skizoumaisí:t) *n.* (in some classifications) a member of *Schizomycetes*, a class of unicellular or noncellular organisms comprising the bacteria grouped usually with the fungi [fr. Mod. L. *Schizomycetes* fr. Gk *schizein*, to split+*mukēs* (*pl. mukētes*), fungus]

schiz·o·my·co·phyte (skizəmáikəfait) *n.* a thallophyte of the phylum *Schizomycophyta* comprising the bacteria and sometimes the blue-green algae [fr. Mod. L. *Schizomycophyta* fr. Gk *schizein*, to split+*mukēs*, fungus+*phuton*, plant]

schiz·o·phrene (skítsəfri:n, skízəfri:n) *n.* a person who has schizophrenia

schiz·o·phre·ni·a (skitsəfrí:ni:ə, skizəfrí:ni:ə) *n.* a common mental disease whose characteristics may include separation of the intellect from the emotions, inappropriate emotional reactions, distortions in normal logical thought processes, withdrawal from social relationships, delusions and hallucinations (*CATATONIA, *HEBEPHRENIA, *PARANOIA) **schiz·o·phren·ic** (skitsəfrénik, skizəfrénik) *adj.* and *n.* [Mod. L. fr. Gk *shizein*, to split+*phrēn*, mind]

schiz·o·phyte (skízəfait) *n.* a schizomycophyte [fr. Mod. L. *Schizophyta* fr. Gk *schizein*, to split+*phuton*, plant]

schiz·zy or **schiz·y** (skítsi:) *adj.* (*slang*) schizophrenic

Schle·gel (ʃléig'l), August Wilhelm von (1767-1845), German translator and critic, one of the earliest of the Romantics. He translated Shakespeare, Calderón, Tasso, Petrarch, Ariosto and others

Schlegel, Friedrich von (1772-1829), younger brother of August, poet and scholar and one of the founders of German Romanticism

Schlei·er·mach·er (ʃláiərmɑxər), Friedrich Daniel Ernst (1768-1834), German mystical theologian who strongly influenced Protestant thought. Under the impetus of the Romantic movement he defined religion in terms of feeling and intuition and rejected dogma ('Discourse on Religion', 1799)

schlepp (ʃlep) (*slang*) (from the Yiddish) *v.* to move with difficulty or reluctance —**schlepper** *n.*

Schles·in·ger (slésiŋgər), Frank (1871-1943), U.S. astronomer. His use of long-focus telescopes for photographic measurements of the distances of stars was a major contribution to knowledge of the scale of the universe beyond the solar system

Schles·wig-Hol·stein (ʃléisvixhɔ́lʃtain) the northernmost state (area 6,057 sq. miles, pop. 2,276,000) of West Germany: Main towns: Kiel (the capital), Lübeck. It is a largely marshy and sandy lowland, forming the neck of the Jutland peninsula (between the Elbe and Denmark), and includes the North Frisian Is. It is heavily industrialized (shipbuilding, mechanical engineering, textiles, fishing). Crops: cereals, root vegetables. HISTORY. The duchies of Schleswig and Holstein became the personal possessions of the king of Denmark in 1460, though the population was largely German. Holstein was included in the German Confederation (1815). Prussia intervened (1848) to stop a Danish attempt to annex the duchies and, with Austria, forced Denmark to give them up (1864), Austria taking Holstein and Prussia Schleswig. A dispute in Holstein was used by Bismarck as a pretext for the Seven Weeks' War against Austria (1866), after which Prussia took both Schleswig and Holstein. N. Schleswig was returned to Denmark (1920)

Schlief·fen (ʃlí:fən), Alfred, graf von (1833-1913), German field marshal. As chief of the German general staff (1891-1906), he devised (1905) a plan for defeating France by a massive flanking movement through the Low Countries. This was put into effect in a modified form in 1914, and was also followed in 1940

Schlie·mann (ʃlí:mɑn), Heinrich (1822-90), German archaeologist. On a private expedition (1870-2) he first excavated Troy. He also excavated Mycenae (1876-8)

schlie·ren (ʃlí:rən) *pl. n.* streaks of different composition within an igneous rock ‖ (*phys.*) layers of differing refractive index, due to differences of pressure within a medium, esp. within the air, which enable sound waves and the air disturbances due to a fast-moving body to be photographed [G.]

schlieren photography technique for photographing changes in gas density occurring in wind tunnels as a result of shock or sound

schlock (ʃlɒk) (from the Yiddish) *n.* (*slang*) something of poor quality —**schlock** *adj.*

Schmal·kal·dic League (ʃmɑlkóldik) a league of Protestant German princes formed (1531) at Schmalkalden, Thuringia, for the defense of the Reformation after the Augsburg Confession. It was crushed during the Schmalkaldic War (1546-7) by Emperor Charles V

schmaltz (ʃmɑlts, ʃmɔlts) *n.* (*pop.*) extremely sentimental music ‖ (*pop.*) anything extremely sentimental **schmáltz·y** *comp.* **schmaltz·i·er** *superl.* **schmáltz·i·est** *adj.* [Yiddish *shmalts*, rendered fat]

schmeer or **schmear** (from the Yiddish) (ʃmiər) *n.* (*slang*) the package, e.g., 'the whole schmeer'

Schmidt (ʃmit), Helmut (1918-), West German statesman, chancellor (1974-82). He joined the Social Democrat party in 1946, was elected to the lower house of parliament (Bundestag) in 1953 and was his party leader in the Bundestag (1967-9). He served as defense minister (1969-72) and finance minister (1972-4). He worked for better relations between the U.S.S.R. and the West and to strengthen West Germany's economy

Schmitt (ʃmit), Florent (1870-1958), French composer. His works, dense in texture, include a choral setting of Psalm XLVI, a piano quintet, and much other symphonic, vocal and chamber music

schmuck (ʃmʌk) *n.* (*slang*) usu. considered vulgar (from the Yiddish) a stupid, or ignorant person

Schmuck·er (ʃmʌ́kər), Samuel Simon (1799-1873), U.S. liberal Lutheran theologian. He established (1820) the General Synod, a first united Lutheran Church of district synods in America, and published (1834) 'Elements of Popular Theology', a first systematic treatment in English of American Lutheran theology. He and his liberal movement were undermined (mid-19th c.) by pressure groups of conservative Lutheran immigrants

schnapps (ʃnɑps, ʃnæps) *n.* any of several distilled liquors of high alcoholic content, e.g. hollands [G.]

schnau·zer (ʃnáuzər) *n.* a short-haired terrier of a German breed, with a heavy head, heavy eyebrows and beard, and small ears [G.]

Schnitz·ler (ʃnítslər), Arthur (1862-1931), Austrian writer, author of novels, short stories, and of 'Anatol' (1893), a series of short dramatic sketches

schnook (ʃnuk) *n.* (*slang*) an easy mark

schnor·kel (ʃnɔ́rk'l) *n.* a snorkel

Schoel·cher (ʃelʃer), Victor (1804-93), French statesman. As Deputy from Martinique and Guadeloupe, he drafted (1848) the decree abolishing slavery in all French territories

Schoenberg, Arnold *SCHÖNBERG

schol·ar (skɒlər) *n.* a learned person ‖ a person who has made a thorough study and acquired a wealth of knowledge of a subject ‖ (esp. *Br.*) a student at a school, college or university who is supported financially, usually as the result of distinction in examination ‖ a school pupil **schól·ar·ly** *adj.* of or like a scholar ‖ having the quality characteristic of the work of a scholar, *a scholarly essay* **schól·ar·ship** *n.* the command of learning displayed by a scholar ‖ the methods by which scholars work ‖ the body of learning with which a subject is invested, *historical scholarship* ‖ a financial award to someone seeking to pursue his studies, usually on the result of a competitive examination [O.E. *scolere, scoliere* fr. L.L. *scholaris adj.*, of a school]

scho·las·tic (skəlǽstik) *adj.* pertaining to school education **Scho·las·tic 1.** *adj.* pertaining to the Schoolmen and to their methods of discussion **2.** *n.* a Schoolman **Scho·lás·ti·cism** *n.* the synthesis of Aristotelian philosophy and Christian revelation in medieval European thought. It sought to resolve the conflicts of faith and reason and of nominalism and realism, and to establish proof of the existence of God. St Augustine of Hippo, in seeking to reconcile Platonic thought and Christian dogma, had stressed the illumination of faith by reason. The philosophical implications of Christianity were actively explored in Europe from the 11th c. onwards, notably by Anselm and Abelard. The debate was increased by the arrival (12th c.) in the universities of the work of Aristotle through the Arabian commentators Avicenna and Averroes. The Averroist doctrine that faith and reason might not be complementary brought Aristotelianism into disrepute until St Thomas Aquinas powerfully vindicated it in his 'Summa theologica', separating philosophy and theology and exploring the relationship between them. Other defenders of Aristotle were St Albertus Magnus and St Bonaventura. Thomism was opposed notably by Duns Scotus and William of Occam. By the time of the Renaissance, philosophy and theology had become separate studies. A Thomist revival took place in the late 19th and 20th cc. (*NEOTHOMISM)

scho·li·ast (skóuliːæst) *n.* a commentator, esp. one of ancient times who annotated the classics [fr. L.L. *scholiasta* fr. Gk]

scho·li·um (skóuliːəm) *pl.* **scho·li·a** (skóuliːə) *n.* an explanatory note, esp. one made to a classic by a scholiast [M.L. fr. Gk]

Schön·berg, Schoen·berg (ʃɔ́ːnbəːrg), Arnold (1874-1951), Austrian composer, who lived in the U.S.A. after 1933 and became a U.S. citizen (1940). After a period as a romantic, showing the influence of Wagner, Brahms and Mahler (e.g. in 'Verklärte Nacht', 1899, a tone poem for string sextet), he began to explore the possibilities of atonal music, e.g. in the song cycle with instruments 'Pierrot Lunaire' (1912). By the early 1920s he had developed the theory and practice of twelve-tone music, which was to have a profound influence. Those he influenced include Berg and Webern. His works comprise lieder, four string quartets, a piano concerto, a violin concerto, operas and many other chamber and orchestral works

Schon·gau·er (ʃóungauər), Martin (c. 1450-92), German engraver and painter. His work showed the influence of the Flemish painters, esp. of Van der Weyden. His 115 engravings on religious subjects had a great influence on the development of the art of engraving and of German art. His only certain extant painting is the 'Madonna of the Rosehedge' (1473, St Martin's Church, Colmar)

school (skuːl) **1.** *n.* a community of those who teach and those who are taught, esp. one for the education of children, usually housed in a building designed and equipped for this purpose ‖ the building itself ‖ the pupils as distinct from the teachers, *the school will assemble in the hall* ‖ the period or session during which classes occur, *school is over at 4:30* ‖ a teaching community devoted to particular studies, often part of a university, *medical school* ‖ formal education, *he only had three years of school* ‖ the conditions of gaining skill or knowledge, *brought up in a hard school* ‖ a group sharing methods, opinions, teachings etc., *painters of the Impressionist school, a gentleman of the old school* ‖ (*pl.*) the medieval universities ‖ (*Br.*, *pl.*) the honors courses of study at Oxford University or the examinations taken at the end of them **to teach school** to be a professional schoolteacher **2.** *v.t.* to train or discipline, *he schooled himself to keep silent* [O.E. *scōl* fr. L. *schola* fr. Gk *schole*, school, leisure]

school *n.* a number of fish or aquatic mammals keeping together while feeding or migrating [Du.]

school·book (skúːlbuk) *n.* a book written for and used by those attending school

school·boy (skúːlbɔi) *n.* a boy attending school

school·child (skúːltʃaild) *pl.* **school·children** (skúːltʃildrən) *n.* a boy or girl attending school

School·craft (skúːlkræft, skúːlkrɑft), Henry Rowe (1793-1864), U.S. ethnologist, explorer, and early specialist of the American Indian. He discovered (1832) Lake Itasca, then thought to be the source of the Mississippi

school·girl (skúːlgəːrl) *n.* a girl attending school

school·house (skúːlhaus) *pl.* **school·hous·es** (skúːlhauziz) *n.* the building in which a school is conducted, esp. a school for children ‖ (*Br.*) the house in which the schoolmaster or schoolmistress of a small school lives

school·ing (skúːliŋ) *n.* the act of someone who schools ‖ school education, *he had little schooling* ‖ disciplined training acquired elsewhere than in a school

School·man (skúːlmən) *pl.* **School·men** (skúːlmən) *n.* (*hist.*) an exponent of Scholasticism in a medieval university

school·mas·ter (skúːlmæstər, skúːlmɑstər) *n.* a man who teaches in a school

school·mate (skúːlmeit) *n.* a person who is educated at the same school as another

school·mis·tress (skúːlmistris) *n.* a woman who teaches in a school

school of thought an opinion or point of view on a subject, held by some but not constituting the only reasonable opinion or point of view, *there are several schools of thought on how to make coffee* ‖ the group holding such an opinion or point of view

school·room (skúːlruːm, skúːlrum) *n.* a room in which pupils are taught, in school or in a private house

school·teach·er (skúːltiːtʃər) *n.* a person who teaches in a school

school·work (skúːlwəːrk) *n.* work done to a schoolteacher's requirements, either at home or at school

school year the academic period making up one year of a school's administration

schoon·er (skúːnər) *n.* (*naut.*) a fore-and-aft vessel with two or more masts [etym. doubtful]

schooner *n.* a tall beer glass [origin unknown]

Scho·pen·hau·er (ʃóupənhauər), Arthur (1788-1860), German philosopher. In 'The World as Will and Idea' (1818), he stated that the will is the key to reason. His statement that without the will 'before us there is nothing' is regarded as a classic expression of pessimism. He counted Buddhism and a world-denying mysticism as superior to current Christian theology

schorl (ʃɔrl) *n.* tourmaline, esp. of a black variety [G. *schörl*]

schot·tische (ʃótiʃ) *n.* a round dance in duple time resembling a slow polka ‖ the music for this dance [G. *schottische* (*tanz*), Scottish (*dance*)]

Schrö·ding·er (ʃrɔ́ːdiŋər), Erwin (1887-1961), Austrian physicist who developed the theory of wave mechanics. Nobel prize (shared with Dirac, 1933)

Schrödinger equation the wave equation

schtick or **shtick** (ʃtik) *n.* (*slang*) (from the Yiddish) **1.** a piece, esp. a theatrical piece **2.** a hobby or characteristic

Schu·bert (ʃúːbəːrt), Franz Peter (1797-1828), Austrian composer. His early work shows a debt to Beethoven but he soon acquired his own style, marked everywhere by abundant lyrical invention and a great gift for sustained melody, with a characteristically subtle use of harmony and modulation. He wrote over 600 incomparable songs (*LIED), 9 symphonies, 15 complete string quartets, a quintet with viola, the 'Trout' piano quintet, piano sonatas and much other chamber and piano music as well as orchestral, choral and operatic works

Schu·man (ʃuːmã), Robert (1886-1963), French statesman. French prime minister (1947-8) and foreign minister (1948-53), he proposed (1950) the establishment of a coal and steel pool in W. Europe, and is regarded as a founder of the European Economic Community

Schu·mann (ʃúːmɑn), Robert Alexander (1810-56), German composer. His most characteristic music is for the piano. It is spontaneous, lyrical and in the main exquisitely brief: most often melancholy, nostalgic and tender. In addition to his many piano works he wrote many deeply expressive songs (*LIED) incl. the cycle 'Dichterliebe' (1840), 4 symphonies, 3 string quartets, a piano concerto, other chamber works etc.

Schurz (ʃuərts), Carl (1829-1906), U.S. political leader and reformer. He led (1884) the Mugwumps, who opposed the Republican party's nomination of James G. Blaine as presidential candidate

schuss (ʃus) **1.** *n.* a straight run in skiing **2.** *v.i.* to ski at high speed on a straight course [G.]

Schütz (ʃyts), Heinrich (1585-1672), German composer, one of the great masters of the German school. His work shows the influence of Gabrieli and Monteverdi. It includes the first German opera, 'Daphne' (1627, no longer extant), and noble and moving church music, notably four 'Passions' (1665-88)

Schutz·pan·zer Marder (ʃútzpɑnzer) *n.* (*mil.*) armored personnel carrier of the German Federal Republic

schwa (ʃwɑ) *n.* (*phon.*) an unstressed mid-central vowel, e.g. the 'o' in 'atom' ‖ the symbol ə used to represent this quality [G. fr. Heb.]

Schwann (ʃvɑn), Theodor (1810-82), German physiologist. He founded the cell theory of living organisms and recognized that the ovum is a cell

Schwarz·en·berg (ʃvɑ́ːrtsənberk), Felix, Fürst zu (1800-52), Austrian statesman. With the aid of Windischgrätz he put down revolutions in Austria and Bohemia (1848) and restored the authority of the Hapsburgs. As prime minister (1848-52) he humiliated Prussia in the Treaty of Olmütz (1850)

Schwarz·schild radius (ʃvártsʃild) (*astron.*) twice the minimum black hole mass times a gravitational force, divided by the speed of light. It is hypothesized in a solution to theory of general relativity concept of a nonrotating black hole *Cf* BLACK HOLE

Schweit·zer (ʃwáitsər, ʃváitsər), Albert (1875-1965), French physician, theologian and musician. He devoted his life after 1913 to a medical mission at Lambaréné, Gabon, originally financing it largely by organ recitals of Bach's music. His theological writings gave a new emphasis to the study of eschatology in New Testament interpretation. Nobel peace prize (1952)

Schweitzer's reagent cuprammonium solution [after Matthias *Schweitzer* (19th c.), G. chemist]

Schwe·rin (ʃveiríːn) the former capital (pop. 113,000) of Mecklenburg, East Germany. Gothic cathedral (15th c.), palace (19th c.) ‖ the surrounding district (area 3,343 sq. miles, pop. 623,000)

Schwit·ters (ʃvítərs), Kurt (1887-1948), German painter and poet, active in dada. He produced collages of considerable beauty out of scraps of wastepaper and rubbish

Schwyz (ʃvi:ts) a German-speaking, mainly Catholic canton (area 350 sq. miles, pop. 97,354) of Switzerland on the Lake of Lucerne ‖ its capital (pop. 11,000)

sci·at·ic (saiǽtik) *adj.* pertaining to the hip, esp. to the great nerve at the back of the thigh [F. *sciatique* fr. M.L. *sciaticus*]

sci·at·i·ca (saiǽtikə) *n.* pain due to irritation of the sciatic nerve [M.L. fr. *sciaticus,* sciatic]

sci·ence (sáiəns) *n.* knowledge acquired by careful observation, by deduction of the laws which govern changes and conditions, and by testing these deductions by experiment ‖ a branch of study, esp. one concerned with facts, principles and methods, *the science of language* ‖ a technique based on training, *the science of fencing* ‖ natural science or a branch of this [F. fr. L. *scientia,* knowledge]

science fiction fiction in which scientific fancy provides plots for adventure stories concerning esp. the future condition of man and society

sci·en·tial (saiénʃəl) *adj.* of or relating to knowledge or science [fr. M.L. *scientialis*]

sci·en·tif·ic (saiəntífik) *adj.* pertaining to science, esp. to natural science ‖ of or using methods based upon well-established facts and obeying well-established laws, *scientific management* ‖ using the knowledge made available by scientists, *scientific farming* ‖ (*loosely*) thorough and accurate **sci·en·tif·i·cal·ly** *adv.* [fr. L.L. *scientificus* fr. L. *sciens* (*scientis*), knowing+*facere,* to make]

sci·en·tist (sáiəntist) *n.* a specialist in science, esp. in a natural science

Sci·en·tol·o·gy (saiəntɒ́lədʒi:) *n.* founded 1952 by L. Ron Hubbard, a religious movement that teaches immortality and reincarnation and claims a psychotherapeutic method for freeing the individual from personal problems

sci-fi (sáifái) *adj.* of science fiction

scil·i·cet (síliset) *adv.* (*abbr.* sc., scil.) namely [L. fr. *scire licet,* it is permitted to know]

scil·la (sílə) *n.* a member of *Scilla,* fam. *Liliaceae,* a genus of wild and cultivated bulbous plants native to N. Europe and Asia, having esp. blue flowers [L.]

Scil·ly Isles (síli:) a group of 140 islets (total area 10 sq. miles, pop. 2,428), five of them inhabited, off S.W. England. Capital: Hugh Town. Products: early fruit, vegetables, flowers

scim·i·tar (símitər) *n.* a short, curved, Oriental sword, with a sharp edge on the convex side only [F. *cimeterre* and Ital. *scimitarra,* origin unknown]

scin·til·la (sintílə) *n.* (*fig.*) a light trace ‖ a spark [L.=spark]

scin·til·lant (sínt'lənt) *adj.* scintillating [fr. L. *scintillans* (*scintillantis*)]

scin·til·late (sínt'leit) *pres. part.* **scin·til·lat·ing** *past* and *past part.* **scin·til·lat·ed** *v.i.* to sparkle or twinkle like a star ‖ to be brilliant in conversation ‖ to emit sparks ‖ *v.t.* to give off in the form of sparks, twinkles etc. **scin·til·lá·tion** *n.* a sparkling, esp. (*astron.*) the sparkling of a celestial body as the result of turbulence in the earth's atmosphere ‖ (*phys.*) a quantum of electromagnetic radiation as emitted e.g. by radioactive material [fr. L. *scintillare* (*scintillatus*)]

scintillation camera device for detecting and recording discrete emissions of radioactive substances, esp. in following isotopes in body scanning

scintillation counter a device for detecting and recording the presence of ionizing radiation, e.g. radioactive material (*GEIGER COUNTER)

sci·o·lism (sáiəlizəm) *n.* pretension to scholarship supported only by superficial knowledge [SCIOLIST]

sci·o·list (sáiəlist) *n.* someone who has only superficial knowledge but who pretends to have more **sci·o·lís·tic** *adj.* [fr. L. L. *sciolus*]

sci·on (sáiən) *n.* a shoot or branch used for grafting ‖ a young member or a descendant of a family, esp. of a noble family [O.F. *cion, sion,* etym. doubtful]

Scip·i·o Ae·mil·i·a·nus (sípi:oui:mili:éinəs), Publius Cornelius (185-129 B.C.), Roman soldier and statesman, adopted by the eldest son of Scipio Africanus. Commander in the 3rd Punic War, he destroyed Carthage (146 B.C.), making Africa a province. He subsequently destroyed Numantia (133 B.C.). At Rome he opposed the agrarian reforms of his brother-in-law Tiberius Gracchus

Scip·i·o Af·ri·ca·nus (sípi:ouæfrikéinəs), Publius Cornelius (c. 235-183 B.C.), Roman statesman and soldier. He defeated the Carthaginians in Spain during the 2nd Punic War, invaded Africa, and finally defeated Hannibal at Zama (202 B.C.). He trained the Roman army in new tactics and made it more professional

scir·rhoid (skírɔid, sírɔid) *adj.* like a scirrhus

scir·rhous (skírəs, sírəs) *adj.* of or having the nature of a scirrhus [fr. F. *scirreux, scirrheux*]

scir·rhus (skírəs, sírəs) *pl.* **scir·rhi** (skírai, sírai), **scir·rhus·es** *n.* a hard, cancerous tumor, esp. characterized by much fibrous tissue [Mod. L. fr. Gk *skiros, skirros,* hard covering, hard tumor]

scis·sile (sísil) *adj.* able to be cut or split with ease [fr. L. *scissilis* fr. *scindere,* to split]

scis·sion (síʒən, síʃən) *n.* a cutting or splitting ‖ a division or split [F.]

scis·sor (sízər) *v.t.* to cut with scissors

scis·sors (sízərz) *pl. n.* a cutting tool consisting of two sharp-edged beveled blades which are pivoted near two handles through which finger and thumb are passed ‖ gymnastic movement of the legs like those of scissors in use ‖ (*wrestling*) a hold, by the legs, of the opponent's head or body [M.E. *sisours, cysowres* fr. O.F. *cisoires*]

scissors kick (*swimming*) a kick used in the sidestroke and trudgen. The upper leg is swung forward from the hip and the lower leg bent back from the knee, both legs then being sharply brought together

SCLC (*abbr.*) for Southern Christian Leadership Conference

scle·ra (sklíərə) *n.* the outer fibrous capsule of the eye, forming the white (*EYE) [Mod L. fr. Gk *sklēros,* hard]

scle·re·id (sklíəri:id) *n.* (*bot.*) a cell, composing one kind of sclerenchyma, that is roughly spherical. Sclereids occur throughout the plant body but esp. in the cortex, phloem, and in both hard and fleshy fruits (*FIBER) [fr. Gk *sklēros,* hard]

scle·ren·chy·ma (skliréŋkəmə) *pl.* **scle·ren·chy·mas, scle·ren·chy·ma·ta** (skliréŋkímətə) *n.* (*bot.*) a simple plant tissue (*PARENCHYMA, *COLLENCHYMA) that consists of thick-walled cells serving in support and protection. There are two principal types: fibers and sclereids ‖ the calcareous walls of certain coral cells [Mod. L. fr. Gk *sklēros,* hard+*enchuma,* infusion]

scle·rite (sklíərait, sklérait) *n.* (*zool.*) a chitinous plate ‖ (*zool.*) a calcareous plate or spicule [fr. Gk *sklēros,* hard]

scle·ro·der·ma·tous (skliərədə́:rmətəs, sklerədə́:rmətəs) *adj.* (*zool.*) covered with hard outer scales or plates [fr. Gk *sklēros,* hard+*derma* (*dermatos*), skin]

scle·roid (sklíərɔid, sklérɔid) *adj.* (*biol.*) hard in texture [fr. Gk *sklēros,* hard]

scle·rom·e·ter (sklirɒ́mətər) *n.* a device used to determine the hardness of a material [fr. Gk *sklēros,* hard+*metron,* measure]

scle·ro·pro·tein (skliərouprόuti:n, skliərouprόuti:in) *n.* one of a class of fibrous proteins which constitute many animal tissues, e.g. hair, horn, nail (*KERATIN, *COLLAGEN) [fr. Gk *sklēros,* hard+PROTEIN]

scle·rosed (sklirόust, sklíərouzd, sklérouzd) *adj.* suffering from sclerosis [SCLEROSIS]

scle·ro·sis (sklirόusis) *pl.* **scle·ro·ses** (sklirόusi:z) *n.* (*med.*) the pathological hardening of tissue produced by the overgrowth of connective tissue (*ARTERIOSCLEROSIS, *MULTIPLE SCLEROSIS) [Mod. L. fr. Gk fr. *sklēros, hard*]

scler·o·tes·ta (skliroutéstə) *n.* (*botany*) the middle layer of the outer covering (the pit in a fruit) of a seed

scle·rot·ic (sklirɒ́tik) **1.** *n.* (*anat.*) the sclera (*EYE) **2.** *adj.* of, relating to or having sclerosis ‖ of the sclera [fr. Mod. L. and M.L. *scleroticus* fr. Gk]

sclerotic coat the sclera

scle·rous (sklíərəs, sklérəs) *adj.* hardened, *sclerous tissue* [fr. Gk *sklēros,* hard]

scoff (skɔf, skɑf) **1.** *v.i.* to adopt a disbelieving or contemptuously mocking attitude towards something, *to scoff at old wives' tales* **2.** *n.* an expression of such mockery [M.E. *scof, skof* n., etym. doubtful]

scold (skould) **1.** *v.t.* to rebuke angrily and often noisily, *to scold a child* ‖ *v.i.* (often with 'at') to utter angry, noisy language or expressions **2.** *n.* (*old-fash.*) a person, esp. a woman, who habitually scolds [prob. fr. O.N. *skāld* n., poet]

sco·lex (skóuleks) *pl.* **sco·le·ces** (skoulí:si:z), **scol·i·ces** (skɒ́lisi:z, skóulisi:z) *n.* the head of a larval or adult tapeworm [Mod. L. fr. Gk *skōlēx,* worm]

sco·li·o·sis (skouli:óusis, skɒli:óusis) *n.* lateral curvature of the spine (*KYPHOSIS, *LORDOSIS) **sco·li·ot·ic** (skouli:ɒ́tik) *adj.* [Mod. L. fr. Gk fr. *skolios,* bent]

scol·lop (skɒ́ləp) **1.** *n.* a scallop **2.** *v.t.* to scallop

sconce (skɒns) **1.** a holder attached to a wall, for a candle or candles ‖ a flat candlestick with a handle [fr. O.F. *esconse,* lantern]

sconce 1. *n.* (*Br.,* at Oxford University) a fine, to be paid in beer or ale, for an offense against good form when dining in hall, imposed by fellow students **2.** *v.t. pres. part.* **sconc·ing** *past* and *past part.* **sconced** to impose this fine upon [origin unknown]

scone (skoun, skɒn) *n.* a small, soft cake of wheat or barley flour (baked originally on a griddle) [perh. fr. M.Du. *schoonbrot* and M.L.G. *schonbrot,* fine bread]

scoop (sku:p) **1.** *n.* any implement for holding or removing liquids or loose solids, e.g. the bucket of an earth-moving machine or dredge or a little shovel for flour etc. ‖ a small concave holder with a handle for serving ice cream etc. ‖ a cutting or gouging instrument with a spoon-shaped blade ‖ (*geog.*) a basin-shaped depression ‖ a surgical implement used to gather and remove matter from the body ‖ a quantity gathered by using a scoop, *a large scoop of ice cream* ‖ (*surfing*) the upturned nose of the surfboard ‖ the act of scooping ‖ (*pop.*) a large profit made by a single transaction ‖ a piece of news obtained and published by a journalist or newspaper exclusively or before it has been published by a rival **2.** *v.t.* to dip into, gather and transfer, by using a scoop ‖ to make (a hole etc.) by scooping ‖ to hollow out ‖ to empty out (water) by bailing ‖ (*pop.*) to get and publish a piece of news before (one's rivals) [M.E. *scope* fr. M.Du. *schôpe, schoepe,* vessel for bailing out water, and M.Du. *schoppe,* shovel]

scoot (sku:t) *v.i.* (*pop.*) to go quickly or go away quickly **scóot·er** *n.* a child's vehicle consisting of a low board fitted with a wheel at each end and a steering handle attached to the axle of the front wheel. The child stands with one foot on the board, thrusting against the ground with his other foot ‖ a low-powered, small-wheeled motorcycle, the driver of which sits as if on a chair, not astraddle [etym. doubtful]

sco·pa (skóupə) *pl.* **sco·pae** (skóupi:), **sco·pas** *n.* (*zool.*) a bunch of small hairs, e.g. the hairs which gather pollen on a bee's legs [L. *scopae* pl., twigs, broom]

Sco·pas (skóupəs) (4th c. B.C.), Greek sculptor who rebuilt the temple of Athena at Tegea and made the sculptures for it

sco·pate (skóupeit) *adj.* (*zool.*) brushlike [fr. L. *scopae* pl., twigs, broom]

scope (skoup) *n.* the area covered by an activity, plan, study etc., *such subjects are not within the scope of this book* ‖ room or opportunity for free activity, thought etc., *he needs more scope for displaying his gifts* ‖ (*fig.*) limit of capacity, *beyond the scope of his imagination* [fr. Ital. *scopo,* aim, fr. Gk *skopos,* mark for shooting at]

Scopes Trial (skoups) a U.S. civil liberty trial in which John Scopes, a Tennessee schoolteacher of biology, was indicted (1925) for teaching the doctrine of evolution. The trial attracted the participation of fundamentalist William Jennings Bryan for the prosecution and of Clarence Darrow for the defense. Scopes was convicted. In an appeal to the state supreme court Scopes was cleared, although the 1925 law was held constitutional

sco·pol·a·mine (skəpɒ́ləmi:n, skəpɒ́ləmin, skoupəlǽmin) *n.* an alkaloid, $C_{17}H_{21}NO_4$, extracted from certain plants of fam. *Solanaceae,* esp. of genus *Scopolia,* and used as a sedative in surgery and obstetrics in conjunction with morphine and in the prevention of airsickness, seasickness etc. [fr. Mod. L. *Scopolia,* plant genus]

scop·u·la (skɒ́pjulə) *pl.* **scop·u·las, scop·u·lae** (skɒ́pjuli:) *n.* (*zool.*) the tuft of hairs on the feet and chelicerae of spiders used in making the web ‖ (*zool.*) a scopa **scop·u·late** (skɒ́pjuleit, skɒ́pjulit) *adj.* [L.L. dim. of *scopa,* broom]

scor·bu·tic (skɔrbjú:tik) *adj.* of, pertaining to or affected by scurvy [fr. Mod. L. *scorbuticus* fr. *scorbutus,* scurvy]

scorch (skɔrtʃ) **1.** *v.t.* to apply such intense heat to (something) as to dry it up, *fields scorched by*

CONCISE PRONUNCIATION KEY: **(a)** æ, *cat;* ɑ, *car;* ɔ *fawn;* ei, *snake.* **(e)** e, *hen;* i:, *sheep;* iə, *deer;* ɛə, *bear.* **(i)** i, *fish;* ai, *tiger;* ə:, *bird.* **(o)** ɒ, *ox;* au, *cow;* ou, *goat;* u, *poor;* ɔi, *royal.* **(u)** ʌ, *duck;* u, *bull;* u:, *goose;* ə, *bacillus;* ju:, *cube.* x, *loch;* θ, *think;* ð, *bother;* z, *Zen;* ʒ, *corsage;* dʒ, *savage;* ŋ, *orangutang;* j, *yak;* ʃ, *fish;* tʃ, *fetch;* 'l, *rabble;* 'n, *redden.* Complete pronunciation key appears inside front cover.

the summer sun || to burn (something) just enough to affect its color or taste, *the iron scorched the sheet* || to criticize very harshly || *v.i.* to become slightly discolored by being partially burned || to become dried up by intense heat || (*pop.*) to drive a vehicle very fast **2.** *n.* a discoloration caused by scorching [etym. doubtful]

scorched-earth policy the policy of destroying everything (buildings, bridges, crops etc.) that could help an enemy force to advance

scorch·er (skɔ́rtʃər) *n.* (*pop.*) a very hot day || (*pop.*) a biting criticism || (*pop.*) a very fast driver

score (skɔr, skour) *n.* a notch or line cut or scratched in the surface of something, *the scores of tribal markings* || the number of points gained by a player or team in a game, or by the respective teams, *the score is 20 to 5 in our favor* || a record of this || the making of a point in a game or competition || the point so made || an act or remark which puts an opponent at a disadvantage || a reason, motive, *he stayed away on the score of ill health* || (*pl.* **scores, score**) a set of twenty (things, people etc.) || (*pl.*) a great number, *scores of people had to be shut out* || (*mus.*) a copy of a piece of music showing all the parts || a number symbolizing the degree of success in a test || (*pop.*) the facts and prospects of a situation, *to know the score* **to pay off** (or **settle**) **a score** to avenge a wrong [O.E. *scoru* fr. O.N. *skor*, notch, tally, four hundred, Icel. twenty]

score *pres. part.* **scor·ing** *past* and *past part.* **scored** *v.t.* to mark with cuts, lines, scratches etc. || to make (a point) or win (a goal etc.) in a game || to keep a record or account of by or as if by making notches or marks in a tally || to count as, *an ace scores 10* || (*mus.*) to arrange (a composition) for performance by certain instruments etc., *the piece is scored for two flutes and viola* || to grade (an examination or a candidate) || to criticize harshly || *v.i.* to keep a score || to win a point or points in a game || to gain an advantage, *to score over a rival* || (*pop.*) to make a success, be a hit, *an actor who scores every time* [O.N. *skora*, to make an incision, count by tallies]

score·board (skɔ́rbɔrd, skóurbourd) *n.* a large board visible to the spectators at a match, setting out the state of play

score·card (skɔ́rkɑrd, skóurkɑrd) *n.* a card identifying players and giving relevant information about a match and which can be used to record the score

score·keep·er (skɔ́rki:pər, skóurki:pər) *n.* an official who records the score throughout the progress of a sports contest

sco·ri·a (skɔ́ri:ə, skóuri:ə) *pl.* **sco·ri·ae** (skɔ́ri:i:, skóuri:i:) *n.* lava with a cellular structure || a piece of such lava || the residue from molten metals || clinker **sco·ri·a·ceous** (skɔri:éiʃəs, skouri:éiʃəs) *adj.* [L. fr. Gk *skōria*, refuse]

sco·ri·fi·ca·tion (skɔrifikéiʃən, skourifikéiʃən) *n.* a scorifying or being scorified || something scorified

sco·ri·fy (skɔ́rifai, skóurifai) *pres. part.* **sco·ri·fy·ing** *past* and *past part.* **sco·ri·fied** *v.t.* to convert into [SCORIA]

scorn (skɔrn) *n.* a feeling of extreme contempt, often accompanied by anger or irritation || a manifesting of this feeling, *her scorn wounded him deeply* **to laugh (someone** or **something) to scorn** to ridicule (someone or something) [M.E. *skarn, scharne* fr. O.F. *escarn, escharn* fr. Gmc]

scorn *v.t.* to reject with scorn, *to scorn an offer* || to feel scorn for || (with *infin.*) to refuse, out of a feeling of scorn or self-respect, *he scorned to answer their insults* [M.E. *scarne, schorne* fr. O.F. *escarnir, escharnir* fr. Gmc]

scorn·ful (skɔ́rnfəl) *adj.* feeling or showing scorn

Scor·pi·o (skɔ́rpi:ou) a southern constellation || the eighth sign of the zodiac, represented as a scorpion [L.= scorpion]

scor·pi·oid (skɔ́rpi:ɔid) *adj.* (*bot.*, of an inflorescence) circinate || like a scorpion [fr. Gk *skorpioeidēs*, like a scorpion]

scor·pi·on (skɔ́rpi:ən) *n.* a member of *Scorpionida*, an order of viviparous, carnivorous nocturnal arachnids of warm and tropical regions. They have an elongated abdomen forming a tail with a terminal poisonous sting which is rarely fatal to man. They may be as long as 6 or 8 ins [O.F. fr. L. fr. Gk]

scor·zo·ne·ra (skɔrzəníərə) *n.* a member of *Scorzonera*, fam. *Compositae*, a genus of European plants with solitary heads of yellow flowers on very long peduncles. The roots of some species are edible, esp. those of black salsify [Ital.]

Scot (skɒt) *n.* a native of Scotland || (*pl.*) the Gaelic-speaking tribe which emigrated from N. Ireland to Scotland (early 6th c. A.D.) [O.E. *Scottas* pl., fr. L.L. *Scottus*]

scot (skɒt) *n.* (*hist.*) a sum of money levied as a tax or imposed as an assessment || one's share in the entertainment expenses of a group, *to pay one's scot* [a form of O.E. *sceot, gesceot*, shot]

Scotch (skɒtʃ) **1.** *adj.* (used esp. outside Scotland) Scottish **2.** *n.* (usually **scotch**) whiskey distilled in Scotland or a drink of this || (non-Scottish term for) the Scottish variety of English **the Scotch** (non-Scottish term for) the Scots [contr. of SCOTTISH]

scotch *v.t.* to put down, crush, *to scotch a conspiracy* || to wound without killing, disable [etym. doubtful]

scotch 1. *n.* a block or wedge used to prevent a wheel, barrel etc. from rolling **2.** *v.t.* to prevent from rolling by inserting a scotch [etym. doubtful]

Scotch-I·rish (skɒ́tʃáiriʃ) *adj.* of mixed Scotch and Irish descent || of a group of people of Scottish descent living in N. Ireland || of a group of people of Scottish descent who emigrated from N. Ireland to the U.S.A. prior to 1846, or of their descendants

Scotch·man (skɒ́tʃmən) *pl.* **Scotch·men** (skɒ́tʃmən) *n.* (non-Scottish term for) a Scot

Scotch terrier a Scottish terrier

Scotch whisky *SCOTCH

Scotch·wom·an (skɒ́tʃwumən) *pl.* **Scotch·wom·en** (skɒ́tʃwimin) *n.* (non- Scottish term for) a Scotswoman

sco·ter (skóutər) *pl.* **sco·ters, sco·ter** *n.* any of several large sea ducks of genera *Melanitta* and *Oidemia*, native to the northern coasts of Europe and North America [etym. doubtful]

scot·free (skɒ́tfri:) *adj.* not sentenced to any punishment || quite unhurt [SCOT (sum of money)+FREE]

sco·tia (skóuʃə) *n.* a hollow molding near or at the base of a column [L. fr. Gk *skotia* fr. *skotos*, darkness (fr. the shadow in the molding)]

Sco·tism (skóutizəm) *n.* the philosophy of Duns Scotus [SCOTIST]

Sco·tist (skóutist) **1.** *n.* a follower of the philosophy of Duns Scotus **2.** *adj.* of or pertaining to this philosophy or its followers [fr. M.L. *Scotista*]

Scot·land (skɒ́tlənd) a country (area 30,405 sq. miles, pop. 5,130,735) occupying the north of Great Britain. It is a division of the United Kingdom. Capital: Edinburgh. Largest town: Glasgow. Language: English, with 1.5% also speaking Gaelic. Church membership: 25% Church of Scotland (Presbyterian), 15% Roman Catholic, with Nonconformist and Church of England minorities. The educational, judicial and financial systems retain many distinctive features. The land is 17% arable, 8% pasture, 16% forest, and much of the rest is rough grazing land. It is divisible into three natural zones: the Highlands, the Lowlands and the southern uplands. The Highlands in the north (1,000–over 4,000 ft, highest point: Ben Nevis, 4,406 ft) are a rocky, sparsely inhabited mountainous plateau (*CAIRNGORM MTNS, *GRAMPIANS), largely moorland, with a coastline deeply indented, esp. in the west, by firths. The Lowlands in the center are comprised mostly of the Forth and Clyde valleys (coal and iron fields, dairy pasture) and contain most of the industry and population. The southern uplands, a rolling moorland (mainly 800–2,000 ft), are cut by small fertile river valleys. Scotland has about 800 islands, including the Orkneys, Shetlands and Hebrides, and hundreds of lakes. Average temperatures (F.): (Jan.) 40°, (Jul.) 56°. Rainfall: under 30 ins along the east coast, over 80 ins along the west coast. Chief ports: Glasgow, Greenock, Leith, Aberdeen. Universities: St Andrews (1411), Glasgow (1451), Aberdeen (1494), Edinburgh (1582), Strathclyde (1964). HISTORY. The earliest inhabitants of Scotland are thought to have been of Iberian stock, and to have mingled with invading Celts (7th c. B.C.). The Romans, who named the northern part Caledonia and its inhabitants Picts, conquered the south (c. 80 A.D.) under Agricola, but were forced to withdraw behind Hadrian's Wall (early 2nd c.). The Scots, a Celtic tribe from Ireland, settled in the west (early 6th c.) and conquered the southern Picts (9th c.). The east coast was raided by Germanic tribes (4th and 5th cc.) and formed part of Northumbria. After the Roman evacuation of Britain, a Romanized British kingdom was left in Strathclyde on the west coast. St Columba brought Christianity to the Picts (6th c.). The Scots, under Kenneth I, defeated the Picts (c. 841) and established a kingdom covering most of Scotland. He and his successors were involved in warfare with raiding Vikings, with Northumbria and with Strathclyde until the 10th c. Norse kingdoms were established in the Hebrides until 1266 and in Orkney and Shetland until 1472. During the reign (1057-93) of Malcolm III and his wife, St Margaret, the Scottish Church was reorganized. Feudalism was introduced in the Lowlands, while the Highlands maintained the clan system (11th c.). Scotland remained united despite sporadic wars with England caused by Norman claims to sovereignty over Scotland and by the intervention of David I in the war between Matilda and Stephen. Scotland became the feudal vassal of England (1174-89). A disputed succession to the throne (1290) enabled Edward I of England to intervene on behalf of John de Baliol, but when Baliol formed an alliance with France (1295) Edward deposed him (1296) and proclaimed himself king. The Scots revolted under Wallace and under Robert the Bruce, who claimed the throne (1306), defeated Edward II at Bannockburn (1314), and gained recognition of Scottish independence (1328). On the death (1371) of David II, Robert II became king, founding the Stuart dynasty. During the Hundred Years' War the Scots supported the French against the English. Scotland was weakened by baronial feuds and was heavily defeated at Flodden Field (1513), when James IV attempted to invade England. During the regency (1554-60) of Mary of Guise, many of the nobility became converted to Protestantism as a result of the work of Knox, and political and religious issues forced Mary Queen of Scots to abdicate (1567) in favor of her Protestant son, James VI. The latter inherited the throne of England (1603) as James I, by virtue of his descent from Margaret Tudor. The union of the two thrones remained a personal one, Scotland maintaining its own institutions and its Presbyterian religious tradition. Charles I's attempt to force the English liturgy on the Presbyterian Scots provoked the formation (1638) of the National Covenant and the outbreak of the Bishops' Wars (1639 and 1640). The Covenanters supported Cromwell in the English Civil War, but Cromwell's forced union of England and Scotland (1654) caused much resentment among the Scots, and a personal union was resumed at the Restoration. The religious policy of Charles II and James II was unpopular in Scotland. To guarantee the Hanoverian succession, Scotland and England were united by the Act of Union (1707), under which Scottish representatives would sit in the British parliament, but Scotland would keep its own laws and the Presbyterian Church. Scotland remained a center of the Jacobite cause until the mid-18th c. (For subsequent history *GREAT BRITAIN)

Scotland Yard the familiar name for the British Criminal Investigation Department of the Metropolitan Police

sco·to·ma (skoutóumə) *pl.* **sco·to·mas, sco·to·ma·ta** (skoutóumətə) *n.* a dark or blind spot in the field of vision [L.L. fr. Gk fr. *skotos*, darkness]

sco·to·pho·bin (skoutoufóubin) *n.* (*biochem.*) substance believed to encode fear-of-the-dark in the brain

sco·to·phor (skóutoufɔr) *n.* (*chem.*) a material that darkens or bleaches when exposed to X-rays, cathode rays, heat, or photons

Scots (skɒts) **1.** *adj.* Scottish **2.** *n.* the English spoken in Scotland [older *Scottis*, var. of Scottish]

Scots·man (skɒ́tsmən) *pl.* **Scots·men** (skɒ́tsmən) *n.* a Scot

Scots·wom·an (skɒ́tswumən) *pl.* **Scots·wom·en** (skɒ́tswimən) *n.* a Scottish woman

Scott (skɒt), Dred (c. 1795-1858), American Negro slave whose suit for freedom, based on his having spent a period in a non-slave state, led the U.S. Supreme Court to declare the Missouri Compromise unconstitutional (*DRED SCOTT DECISION). Scott himself was set free (1857) although technically he had lost his suit

Scott, Sir George Gilbert (1811-78), English architect. His work includes the Martyrs' Memorial at Oxford (1841), and the Albert Memorial

(1863-72) and St Pancras station (1865) in London. He is known chiefly for his restoration work in cathedrals and churches. He was foremost in the Victorian neo-Gothic revival

Scott, Sir Giles Gilbert (1880-1960), English architect, grandson of Sir George. His most striking work is the neo-Gothic Anglican cathedral at Liverpool, England

Scott, James Brown (1866-1943), U.S. jurist, publicist, and educator, and an influential leader in the international peace movement of the 20th c. He became (1906) founding editor of the first English-language international law periodical, and helped to establish (1914) the Academy of International Law at The Hague and (1921) the Permanent Court of International Justice

Scott, Robert Falcon (1868-1912), British naval officer and Antarctic explorer. He led two expeditions to Antarctica (1901-4 and 1909-12). On the first he carried out surveys of the Ross Sea and on the second he led a sledge journey from the Ross Sea to the South Pole, which he reached Jan. 18, 1912, shortly after Amundsen. He and his four companions died on the return journey

Scott, Sir Walter (1771-1832), Scottish poet and novelist. His work displayed his passion for the history of his country. His narrative poems, e.g. 'The Lay of the Last Minstrel' (1805), 'Marmion' (1808) and 'The Lady of the Lake' (1810), were immensely popular. The novel 'Waverley' (1814) was the first of a long series, published anonymously, including 'The Heart of Midlothian' (1818), 'Ivanhoe' (1820) and 'The Talisman' (1825). His influence can be traced in all romantic art of the early 19th c. which took balladry and folklore as its theme

Scott, Winfield (1786-1866), U.S. general, and Whig candidate for the presidency in 1852. As general officer commanding (1841-61) the U.S. Army, he won several victories during the Mexican War, notably at Veracruz, Cerro Gordo, and Chapultepec, by which he forced (1858) Mexico's surrender

Scot·ti·cism (skɔ́tisizəm) *n.* a turn of phrase, use of a word etc. characteristically Scottish [fr. L.L. *Scoticus*]

Scot·tish (skɔ́tiʃ) **1.** *adj.* of or pertaining to Scotland, its people or customs, the variety of English spoken there etc. **2.** *n.* the English language as spoken in Scotland [O.E. *Scottisc*]

Scottish Gaelic *GAELIC

Scottish terrier a terrier of a breed having a strong stocky build, with a large head, prick ears, short legs and thick, rough coat

Scotus, Duns *DUNS SCOTUS

scoun·drel (skáundrəl) *n.* a man who acts with shameful lack of principle **scóun·drel·ly** *adj.* [origin unknown]

scour (skáuər) **1.** *v.t.* to clean by rubbing hard, esp. with an abrasive, or by flushing with a rapid flow of water ‖ to remove (dirt etc.) in this way ‖ to free from impurities, *to scour raw wool* ‖ to purge ‖ to wear away by erosion etc., *the torrent scoured a channel in the hillside* ‖ *v.i.* to perform a cleaning, removing or eroding action **2.** *n.* a scouring ‖ a place eroded by scouring, *a scour in the hillside* ‖ (*pl.*) diarrhea, esp. in cattle [prob. M. Du. or M.L.G. *schuren*]

scour *v.t.* to move rapidly through or over, esp. in search of something, *she scoured the whole town for it* ‖ *v.i.* to move in this way, *scouring over the hills for bluebells* [etym. doubtful]

scourge (skə:rdʒ) *n.* (*rhet.*) a whip used to punish people ‖ someone or something causing misery, esp. on a large scale ‖ any cause of distress thought of as divine punishment [A.F. *escorge, escurge*]

scourge *pres. part.* **scourg·ing** *past* and *past part.* **scourged** *v.t.* (*rhet.*) to whip ‖ (*rhet.*) to cause extreme misery to [O.F. *escorgier*]

scout (skaut) **1.** *n.* a soldier sent ahead to reconnoiter or gain information ‖ anyone whose job is to search, *a talent scout* ‖ a boy scout ‖ a girl scout ‖ a person who observes and reports on the abilities of players of rival professional or university teams ‖ the act of scouting, lookout, *on the scout for good young players* ‖ (*Br.*) a man employed by a motorists' association to assist motorists on the road ‖ (*pop.*) a fellow, *be a good scout* **2.** *v.i.* to make a reconnaissance ‖ to make a search ‖ *v.t.* to observe as a scout ‖ to reconnoiter (a territory etc.) [F. *escoute,* the action of listening]

scout *n.* (*Br., hist.*) a college student's manservant at Oxford University [origin unknown]

scout *v.t.* to reject (a suggestion, statement etc.) as being absurd or clearly untrue [of Scand. origin]

scout·ing (skáutiŋ) *n.* scouts' activities

scout·mas·ter (skáutmæstər, skáutmɑstər) *n.* a man responsible for training a troop of boy scouts

scow (skau) *n.* a large flat-bottomed boat with square ends, used esp. to transport gravel, sand etc. in bulk [Du. *schouw*]

scowl (skaul) **1.** *v.i.* to frown angrily or sullenly ‖ *v.t.* to express by frowning, *he scowled his dissatisfaction* **2.** *n.* an angry or sullen frown [prob. of Scand. origin]

SCP (*biol. abbr.*) for single-celled protein

scrab·ble (skrǽb'l) *pres. part.* **scrab·bling** *past* and *past part.* **scrab·bled** *v.i.* to make scratching movements with the fingers, hands or feet ‖ to make random, scrawling marks ‖ to climb with hasty struggling movements [Du. *schrabbelen*]

Scrabble *n.* word game played with evaluated lettered disks on a board with the object of forming words adjoining those already melded, utilizing maximum evaluations

scrag (skræg) **1.** *n.* a scrawny person or animal ‖ the lean end of a neck of mutton or veal **2.** *v.t. pres. part.* **scrag·ging** *past* and *past part.* **scragged** (*pop.*) to kill by hanging or by wringing or breaking the neck ‖ (*pop.*) to tackle by the neck or handle (someone) roughly [prob. altered fr. older *crag,* the neck]

scrag·gi·ly (skrǽgili:) *adv.* in a scraggy manner

scrag·gi·ness (skrǽgi:nis) *n.* the quality of being scraggy

scrag·gly (skrǽgli:) *comp.* **scrag·gli·er** *superl.* **scrag·gli·est** *adj.* sparse and unkempt, *a scraggly beard* ‖ rough and uneven, *a scraggly path* [SCRAG]

scrag·gy (skrǽgi:) *comp.* **scrag·gi·er** *superl.* **scrag·gi·est** *adj.* scrawny ‖ rough and rugged, *scraggy rocks* [SCRAG]

scram (skræm) *pres. part.* **scram·ming** *past* and *past part.* **scrammed** *v.i.* (*pop.*) to go away quickly [perh. shortened fr. SCRAMBLE]

scram·ble (skrǽmb'l) **1.** *v. pres. part.* **scram·bling** *past* and *past part.* **scram·bled** *v.i.* to climb or move about with hasty or struggling movements, esp. on all fours, *he scrambled up the steep bank* ‖ to engage in a hasty struggle in order to obtain something desired also by others, *they scrambled for the best seats* ‖ (*football*) to carry the ball without blocker protection ‖ *v.t.* to jumble ‖ to mix thoroughly together, *scramble the cards* ‖ to superimpose other frequencies (a radio signal etc.) so that the message cannot be understood by an enemy etc. ‖ to cook (eggs) by beating them and then stirring them in a pan while they cook **2.** *n.* the act or an instance of scrambling, *the way down is quite a scramble, a scramble for coins* **scrám·bler** *n.* someone who or something that scrambles, esp. a device which scrambles radio signals [etym. doubtful]

scram·jet (skrǽmjet) *n.* jet engine that depends on air pressure created by its high speed to mix with fuel to produce thrust

Scran·ton (skrǽntən) a commercial and industrial city (pop. 88,117) in N.E. Pennsylvania: textiles (esp. silk), laces, shoes, mattresses, furniture, mining machinery. It is an anthracite coal-mining center

scrap (skræp) **1.** *n.* a small bit or piece torn out or broken off something, *a scrap of paper* ‖ (*pl.*) paragraphs, pictures etc. cut out of a newspaper etc. as worth keeping or suitable for pasting into an album ‖ a written or printed excerpt ‖ pieces, chips etc. of material left over or discarded, *the floor was littered with scrap* ‖ metal or other raw material recovered from old ships, cars etc. ‖ a least bit, *not a scrap of truth in it* ‖ (*pl.*) leavings, esp. leftovers of food ‖ (*pl.*) residue from fats after the oil has been pressed out **2.** *v.t. pres. part.* **scrap·ping** *past* and *past part.* **scrapped** to discard as useless ‖ to break up into scrap [O.N. *skrap,* scraps, trifles]

scrap **1.** *n.* (*pop.*) a fight, struggle or quarrel of short duration **2.** *v.i. pres. part.* **scrap·ping** *past* and *past part.* **scrapped** (*pop.*) to engage in a scrap [origin unknown]

scrap·book (skrǽpbuk) *n.* a book with blank pages, usually with a hard cover, in which one pastes photos, clippings etc.

scrape (skreip) **1.** *v. pres. part.* **scrap·ing** *past* and *past part.* **scraped** *v.t.* to remove by rubbing with a rough or sharp-edged object, *scrape the paint off the door* ‖ to bring into contact with something hard or rough in such a way as to injure or graze, *he scraped his knee* ‖ to rub the surface of with a rough or sharp object ‖ to make smooth or clean by rubbing with an abrasive or sharp tool, *scrape the floor before applying the varnish* ‖ to cause (something) to make a harsh sound while pulling or rubbing it along a surface, *to scrape furniture across the floor* ‖ (esp. with 'out') to play (music, a tune) on a bowed stringed instrument, producing harsh, grating sounds ‖ to dig (e.g. a hole) with great difficulty, esp. with the nails ‖ (esp. with 'up' or 'together') to gather in small amounts or with difficulty, *to scrape up a team* ‖ *v.i.* to move against something roughly or graze it ‖ to clean or smooth something with an abrasive or sharp tool ‖ to make a harsh grating noise, *his chalk scraped on the blackboard* ‖ to draw back the foot in making a bow ‖ to make or save money in small amounts, with a struggle ‖ (with 'along', 'by' or 'through') to succeed barely or proceed with difficulty, *he scraped through his examination* **to bow and scrape** to make a display of deference, be obsequious **2.** *n.* the act or noise of scraping ‖ an awkward or unpleasant situation, *he's always in scrapes at school* ‖ a scraped place, spot, hole etc., *a scrape on the elbow* **scráp·er** *n.* a tool used to scrape ‖ a device for scraping mud off one's shoes before going indoors ‖ (*archaeol.*) a flint implement used by prehistoric man for scraping the flesh and hair from skins [M.E. perh. fr. O.E. *scrapian*]

scrap·ple (skrǽp'l) *n.* a dish made by boiling together meat scraps, chopped vegetables and corn meal. They are then cooled in a mold, and fried before serving [SCRAP (small bit or piece)]

scrap·py (skrǽpi:) *comp.* **scrap·pi·er** *superl.* **scrap·pi·est** *adj.* assembled from bits and pieces, disconnected and insubstantial, *a scrappy speech* [SCRAP (small bit or piece)]

scrappy *adj.* fond of a scrap (fight or quarrel) [SCRAP n., fight, struggle]

scratch (skrætʃ) **1.** *v.t.* to cut into (a surface) by forcing something hard and sharp along it ‖ to mark (something) on a surface by doing this, *he scratched his name on the post* ‖ to draw claws or nails over (the skin etc.) lightly, *to scratch one's head* ‖ to scrape with a grating noise ‖ to remove (writing etc.) by crossing out etc., *scratch his name from the list* ‖ to cancel (a match, race etc.) or to withdraw (a horse or competitor) from a race or competition ‖ (with 'together' or 'up') to gather with difficulty ‖ to divide (one's vote) or mark (a ballot) so as to divide one's vote between parties ‖ to reject (a candidate) by crossing out his name on a ballot ‖ *v.i.* to dig with the nails or claws ‖ to draw the nails etc. lightly over the skin, e.g. to relieve itching ‖ to give out a scraping noise ‖ to withdraw from a race or contest ‖ (*billiards*) to make a scratch ‖ (with 'along', 'by' or 'through') to manage with difficulty to get along or succeed **2.** *n.* a mark or long, irregular, shallow cut made by scratching ‖ the noise made when a surface is scratched ‖ a slight wound, *it is only a scratch* ‖ the act of scratching, *dogs enjoy a good scratch* ‖ a line from which non-handicapped competitors start in a race etc. ‖ (*pl.*) a disease of horses resulting in scabs between the heel and pastern joint ‖ (*billiards*) a shot resulting in a penalty ‖ a meaningless mark made by a pen, pencil etc. **to start from scratch** to begin from nothing with no advantage, *he started his business from scratch* **up to scratch** reaching the required standard, *her performance was not up to scratch* **3.** *adj.* assembled in a haphazard way, *a scratch team* ‖ of a competitor who has no handicap, allowance etc. [prob. fr. obs. *scrat,* to scratch+obs. *cratch,* to scratch]

scratch paper rough paper on which one jots messages, notes etc.

scratch test a test for allergy made by applying the suspected substance to a scratch in the skin

scratch·y (skrǽtʃi:) *comp.* **scratch·i·er** *superl.* **scratch·i·est** *adj.* covered with scratches ‖ causing surface irritation or itching, *scratchy wool* ‖ making a harsh, grating noise

scrawl (skrɔl) **1.** *v.* to write (something) with badly formed letters, esp. hurriedly ‖ (esp. with 'over') to cover with irregular marks or badly shaped writing **2.** *n.* a piece of scrawled writing, *his signature is just a scrawl* ‖ scrawled writing **scráwl·y** *comp.* **scrawl·i·er** *superl.* **scrawl·i·est** *adj.* [perh. fr. obs. *scrawl,* to spread the limbs in a sprawling manner]

scrawn·y (skrɔ́ni:) *comp.* **scrawn·i·er** *superl.* **scrawn·i·est** *adj.* thin and rawboned or undernourished-looking [var. of dial. *scranny,* rel. to Norw. *skran,* lean]

scream (skri:m) **1.** *v.i.* to utter a sudden high-pitched, loud cry because of fear, pain or shock ‖ to make a similar sound in laughter etc. ‖ to speak in a shrill, loud manner, esp. in anger or hysteria ‖ to produce a strident effect, *posters screamed outside the theater* ‖ *v.i.* to utter in a loud, high-pitched tone, esp. in anger or hysteria, *to scream insults* ‖ (often *refl.*) to bring to a specified state by uttering loud, high-pitched cries, *the baby screamed itself to sleep* **2.** *n.* the sound made in screaming ‖ (*pop.*) someone who or something which is very funny **scréam·ing** *adj.* uttering screams ‖ strident or sensational in effect ‖ extremely funny, *a screaming farce* [M.E. *scrœmen, screamen* perh. fr. O.E.]

scree (skri:) *n.* loose fallen fragments of rock piled up against a hillside ‖ a pile of this [O.N. *skritha,* landslide]

screech (skri:tʃ) **1.** *v.i.* to give a short, shrill scream ‖ to make a noise like a scream, *the brakes screeched* ‖ *v.t.* to utter with such a scream **2.** *n.* the act or sound of screeching ‖ an instance of this [var. of older *scritch,* of imit. origin]

screech owl the barn owl ‖ any of several owls which screech and do not hoot

screed (skri:d) *n.* a tiresomely long discourse ‖ a long, chatty letter or other informal piece of writing ‖ a long list ‖ a strip of plaster put on a surface as a guide to the thickness of the whole plaster layer to be applied ‖ an implement of wood or metal used as a guide in surfacing a concrete pavement [var. of SHRED]

screen (skri:n) **1.** *n.* a movable partition, often folding, made of wood, metal, cloth on a frame etc., used to shut off drafts etc. or to subdivide an area ‖ a fixed structure of wood, metal etc. partly separating one room or section of a building from another, e.g. a rood screen ‖ a window screen ‖ anything giving protection, esp. from observation, *a smoke screen* ‖ (*mil.*) a body of men covering the movement of troops etc. ‖ (*navy*) a formation of smaller vessels serving as a protection to a formation of larger vessels ‖ (*phys.*) a device for shielding from electric, magnetic or other interference ‖ a mesh for separating coarse and fine parts ‖ a transparency with very fine ruled lines used in halftone printing ‖ (*Br.*) a bulletin board ‖ a white surface on which filmstrips, movies etc. are projected ‖ the movie industry, *stars of stage and screen* ‖ the surface on which a television image or radar pattern is produced in a television or radar receiver ‖ (*cricket*) a large, white movable structure placed on or behind the boundary to enable the batsman to get a clear view of the ball as it leaves the bowler's hand **2.** *v.t.* to shelter or conceal with or as if with a screen ‖ (*mil.* and *navy*) to protect with a screen ‖ to sift with a coarse mesh ‖ to make (a story etc.) into a movie ‖ to project (a movie) ‖ to subject (candidates) to exhaustive tests in order to be satisfied as to reliability, capability etc. ‖ (esp. with 'out') to separate (candidates) in this way ‖ to subject (letters, books etc.) to a similar test, e.g. for censorship purposes ‖ *v.i.* to be capable of being made into a film, *this book will screen well* **scréen·ings** *pl. n.* material separated during screening of coal, coke etc. [M.E. *skrene, skreene* perh. fr. F. *écran* and O.F. *escran*]

screen·play (skrí:nplei) the script for a movie, including stage directions, dialogue etc.

screen·wash·er (skrí:nwɒʃər) *n.* (*Br.*) a windshield wiper

screw (skru:) **1.** *n.* a device for fastening things, consisting of a cylindrical or conical pin, with its surface cut in a spiral groove, which fits into a nut or bites securely into wood etc. by being turned ‖ one turn of this device ‖ a female screw ‖ a screw propeller ‖ (*games*) a turn or swerve of a ball struck so that it rotates in addition to its forward motion ‖ (*Br., pop.*) a miser ‖ (*Br., pop.*) salary, wages ‖ (*pop.*) an old broken-down horse **to have a screw loose** to be a little crazy **to put the screws** (*Br.* **screw**) **on** to increase coercive pressure on (someone) **2.** *v.t.* to fasten, compress or tighten, using a screw or screws ‖ to twist ‖ (often with 'up') to contort, *to screw up one's face* ‖ (*pop.*) to extract forcefully or with difficulty, *to screw a dollar out of someone* ‖ *v.i.* to be put together or taken apart with a screw or screws, *the rack screws on to the wall* ‖ to be joined to or separated from something in the manner of a screw, *the top screws on to the jar* ‖ to rotate like a screw **to screw up one's courage** to brace oneself in order to face an ordeal, danger etc. [prob. O.F. *escroue,* female screw, nut]

screw·ball (skrú:bɔl) **1.** *n.* (*baseball*) a pitched ball which breaks in the opposite way to a curve ‖ (*pop.*) a person who is a little crazy in his behavior **2.** *adj.* (*pop.*) somewhat crazy

screw coupling a collar with a female screw used to join pipes furnished with male screws (right-handed and left-handed) at their ends

screw·driv·er (skrú:draivər) *n.* a tool for tightening or loosening screws, having a thin, wedge-shaped end which fits into the groove in a screw's head

screw pine a member of *Pandanus,* fam. *Pandanaceae,* a widespread genus of trees native to tropical Asia. They have prominent prop roots, stems like those of palms, and branches with a terminal crown of long leaves

screw propeller the propeller of a ship, aircraft etc., consisting of a number of blades, each forming part of a helical surface, mounted symmetrically on a central hub at the end of a rotating shaft, so that their pressure on the water or air has a driving reaction on the vessel

screw thread the spiral ridge between the grooves of a screw ‖ the length of one turn of this ridge

screw·y (skrú:i:) *comp.* **screw·i·er** *superl.* **screw·i·est** *adj.* (*pop.*) crazy ‖ (*pop.*) fantastically absurd

Scria·bin (skri:ábin, skrjábin), Alexander Nicholaevich (1872-1915), Russian composer. His work is emotionally highly charged, and he developed advanced theories of harmony to express his theosophical beliefs. His piano music includes 10 sonatas and many other works. His orchestral work includes 'Prometheus, the Poem of Fire' (1909-10)

scrib·ble (skrib'l) **1.** *v.t.* and *i. pres. part.* **scrib·bling** *past* and *past part.* **scrib·bled** to write hastily and carelessly or in a hurried, badly constructed style **2.** *n.* a piece of hasty writing ‖ bad handwriting or literary composition [prob. fr. M.L. *scribillare*]

scribble *pres. part.* **scrib·bling** *past* and *past part.* **scrib·bled** *v.t.* to card (wool) coarsely [prob. fr. L.G.]

scrib·bler (skríblər) *n.* a person who writes rapidly and in great quantities ‖ (*old-fash.*) a worthless writer

scribbler *n.* a machine that scribbles wool

Scribe (skri:b), Augustin Eugène (1791-1861), French playwright, master of light drama. He wrote 350 plays, as well as opera librettos for Auber, Meyerbeer etc.

scribe (skraib) **1.** *n.* a person skilled in handwriting, esp. one who copied out manuscripts before the invention of printing ‖ a professional copyist or clerk ‖ an ancient Jewish interpreter of the Law ‖ a scriber **2.** *v.t. pres. part.* **scrib·ing** *past* and *past part.* **scribed** to mark with a scriber ‖ to make (a line) with a scriber ‖ *v.i.* to act as a scribe **scrib·er** *n.* a pointed tool for marking wood, metal etc. with lines showing where it is to be cut [fr. L. *scriba* fr. *scribere,* to write]

scrim (skrim) *n.* a loosely woven, thin cotton fabric used in upholstering, clothing, curtains etc. ‖ (*theater*) a transparent drop curtain [etym. doubtful]

scrim·mage (skrímidʒ) **1.** *n.* a confused struggle ‖ (*football*) the struggle for possession of the ball after it has been put into play by the center ‖ (*football*) practice between teams **2.** *v.i. pres. part.* **scrim·mag·ing** *past* and *past part.* **scrim·maged** to engage in a scrimmage [altered fr. SKIRMISH]

scrimp (skrimp) *v.t.* to make too small, short etc. ‖ to treat stingily ‖ *v.i.* to be frugal **scrimp·y** *comp.* **scrimp·i·er** *superl.* **scrimp·i·est** *adj.* excessively meager [etym. doubtful]

scrim·shaw (skrímʃɔ) **1.** *v.t.* to carve (whalebone, ivory, shells etc.) or decorate (these) with carved designs ‖ *v.i.* to engage in this work **2.** *n.* a piece of such work ‖ the art or practice of scrimshawing [etym. doubtful]

scrip (skrip) *n.* (*hist.*) a small bag or satchel carried by a pilgrim or traveler [prob. O.F. *escrepe*]

scrip *n.* a provisional certificate of ownership of stock, property etc. ‖ such certificates collectively [SUBSCRIPTION]

scrip *n.* (*hist.*) paper money having a face value of less than a dollar, formerly in circulation [prob. alt. of SCRAP (small bit or piece)]

scrip dividend a dividend paid in the form of scrip (provisional certificates), not money

scrip·oph·i·ly (skripáfəli:) *n.* (*securities*) the collection and care of bonds and stock certificates

Scripps (skrips), Edward Wyllis (1854-1926), U.S. newspaper publisher whose Cleveland Penny Press introduced (1878) into the U.S.A. the low-priced 'chain' newspaper. With his partners George Scripps and Milton McRae, he organized (1897) what eventually became the United Press. He established the Newspaper Enterprise Association, the first newspaper syndicate to serve a chain of newspapers

script (skript) *n.* handwriting as distinguished from print ‖ printer's type which imitates handwriting ‖ a style of handwriting, *Carolingian script* ‖ the printed or written text of a play, broadcast etc. ‖ (*Br.*) the written work of an examination candidate [fr. L. *scriptun,* something written]

scrip·to·ri·um (skriptɔ́ri:əm, skriptóuri:əm) *pl.* **scrip·to·ri·ums, scrip·to·ri·a** (skriptɔ́ri:ə, skriptóuri:ə) *n.* a room set apart for the scribes in a monastery [M.L.]

scrip·tur·al (skríptʃərəl) *adj.* pertaining to or contained in the Bible, *scriptural authority* [fr. Mod. L. *scripturalis*]

Scrip·ture (skríptʃər) *n.* (often in *pl.*) the Bible (usually omitting the Apocrypha) ‖ a passage in the Bible ‖ the study of the Bible ‖ the sacred writing or books of any religion [fr. L. *scriptura,* a writing]

script·writ·er (skríptraitər) *n.* a writer of radio or television programs or of dialogue for films

scrive·ner (skrívnər) *n.* (*hist.*) a notary ‖ (*hist.*) a professional scribe [fr. obs. *scrivein,* professional scribe fr. O.F. *escrivein*]

scro·bic·u·late (skroubíkjulit, skroubíkjuleit) *adj.* (*biol.*) having many small furrows or depressions [fr. Mod. L. *scrobicula* or L.L. *scrobiculus,* small pit or depression]

scrod (skrɒd) *n.* a young cod. esp. one cut into strips for cooking [perh. fr. obs. Du. *schrood* and M. Du. *schrode,* a piece cut off]

scrof·u·la (skrɔ́fjulə) *n.* (*hist.*) tuberculosis of the lymph glands, esp. of the neck **scrɔ́f·u·lous** *adj.* afflicted with scrofula ‖ morally corrupt [after L.L. *scrofulue,* swelling of the glands, and after M. L. *scrofula*]

Scroggs (skrɒgz, skrɒgz) Sir William (c. 1623-83), English jurist. As lord chief justice (1678-81), he was notorious for his brutal judgments on the victims of the Popish Plot

scroll (skroul) **1.** *n.* a length of parchment or paper rolled into a cylinder, esp. an ancient manuscript preserved in this form ‖ anything, esp. an ornament, having the form of a partly opened scroll of paper, e.g. the head of a violin, the legend of a decorative map etc. ‖ the volute of an Ionic or Corinthian capital **2.** *v.t.* to form into a scroll ‖ to decorate with scrolls ‖ *v.i.* to roll up like scroll [earlier *scrowle, scrow* fr. O.F. *escrowe*]

scroll saw a saw consisting of a taut ribbon of steel with a toothed edge, used for sawing curves

scroll·work (skróulwə:rk) *n.* ornamental work having scrolls as its chief feature ‖ thin wood cut into designs with a scroll saw

Scrooge (skru:dʒ) *n.* (*mil.*) U.S.S.R. strategic solid-fuel nuclear missile (SS-15) with a 3,700-mi range

scro·tal (skróut'l) *adj.* of the scrotum [fr. Mod. L. *scrotalis*]

scro·tum (skróutəm) *pl.* **scro·ta** (skróutə), **scro·tums** *n.* the muscular sac containing the testicles [L.]

scrounge (skraundʒ) *pres. part.* **scroung·ing** *past* and *past part.* **scrounged** *v.t.* (*pop.*) to get by cadging ‖ (*pop.*) to get by hunting around for ‖ (*pop.*) to pilfer ‖ *v.i.* (*pop.,* esp. with 'around') to search around [etym. doubtful]

scrub (skrʌb) *n.* thick undergrowth and stunted trees etc. growing together, generally in poor soil or sand ‖ land covered with such growth ‖ a tract of such land ‖ a stunted tree or shrub ‖ (*sports*) a player not one regular team, or a team made up of such players ‖ an undersized, insignificant person or animal [var. of SHRUB]

scrub 1. *v. pres. part.* **scrub·bing** *past* and *past part.* **scrubbed** *v.t.* to clean by rubbing hard, esp. with a brush, soap and water ‖ to cleanse (a gas) so as to remove impurities ‖ *v.i.* to engage in scrubbing **2.** *n.* an act or instance of scrubbing **scrub·ber** *n.* a person or thing that scrubs, esp. a device for cleansing gases, e.g. by passing them through a liquid [etym. doubtful]

scrub·ber (skrʌ́bər) *n.* an air-pollution-control

device that uses a spray of water to trap pollutants and to cool emissions

scrub oak any of several North American oaks of shrubby habit that grow on dry, rocky soil

scrub·by (skrʌ́bi:) *comp.* **scrub·bi·er** *superl.* **scrub·bi·est** *adj.* stunted ‖ covered with scrub ‖ inferior, shabby

scruff (skrʌf) *n.* the nape of the neck [corrup. of older *scuff* etym. doubtful]

scruff·y (skrʌ́fi:) *comp.* **scruff·i·er** *superl.* **scruff·i·est** *adj.* unkempt, grubby and neglected-looking ‖ (of terrain) dry, with a loose, flaky, dusty topsoil and without vegetation [var. of SCURF]

scrum (skrʌm) *n.* (*rugby*) a formation of the forwards of each team, crouching so that the two front rows meet shoulder to shoulder, and pushing in order to gain possession of the ball [abbr. of SCRUMMAGE]

scrum half (*rugby*) the halfback who puts the ball into the scrum .

scrum·mage (skrʌ́midʒ) **1.** *n.* (*rugby*) a scrum **2.** *v.i. pres. part.* **scrum·mag·ing** *past* and *past part.* **scrum·maged** (often with 'down') to form a scrum [var. of SCRIMMAGE]

scrump·tious (skrʌ́mpʃəs) *adj.* (*pop.*) delicious ‖ (*pop.*) delightful [etym. doubtful]

scrunch (skrʌntʃ, skruntʃ) **1.** *v.t.* to crunch ‖ *v.i.* to make a crunching sound ‖ to crouch, esp. in a confined space **2.** *n.* the sound of scrunching, *the scrunch of footsteps on gravel* [var. of CRUNCH]

scru·ple (skrú:p'l) **1.** *n.* a feeling of uneasiness, doubt, objection or reluctance based on principle or propriety **2.** *v.i. pres. part.* **scru·pling** *past* and *past part.* **scru·pled** (usually with *infin.*) to hesitate because of scruples, *he would not scruple to lie* [fr. F. *scrupule* fr. L. *scrupulus*]

scruple *n.* a unit of apothecaries' weight (=20 grains or one-third dram) [fr. L. *scrupulus*]

scru·pu·los·i·ty (skru:pjulɔ́siti:) *pl.* **scru·pu·los·i·ties** *n.* the quality of being scrupulous, esp. to excess ‖ an instance of this [F. *scrupulosité* or fr. L. *scrupulositas*]

scru·pu·lous (skrú:pjuləs) *adj.* strictly honest and adhering to moral principles ‖ painstakingly thorough [fr. F. *scrupuleux* or L. *scrupulosus*]

scru·ti·neer (skru:t'níər) (*Br.*) a canvasser (person who checks the validity of ballot papers)

scru·ti·nize (skrú:t'naiz) *pres. part.* **scru·ti·niz·ing** *past* and *past part.* **scru·ti·nized** *v.t.* to examine with care and in detail [SCRUTINY]

scru·ti·ny (skrú:t'ni:) *pl.* **scru·ti·nies** *n.* close, searching examination ‖ an instance of this ‖ a steady, penetrating gaze ‖ (*Br.*) a fresh count and examination of ballot papers in an election [fr. L.L. *scrutinium* fr. L. *scrutari*, to search carefully, examine]

scu·ba (skú:bə) *n.* a breathing apparatus for free-swimming divers, consisting of a tank of compressed air strapped to the back and connected by a hose to the diver's mouth [SELF-CONTAINED UNDERWATER BREATHING APPARATUS]

scud (skʌd) **1.** *v.i. pres. part.* **scud·ding** *past* and *past part.* **scud·ded** (esp. of a ship running before a gale) to go swiftly **2.** *n.* a scudding ‖ thin clouds driven by a strong wind ‖ a gust of wind ‖ a brief shower of rain ‖ ocean spray etc. driven by the wind [etym. doubtful]

Scud (skʌd) *n.* (*mil.*) NATO name for SS-1, a U.S.S.R. mobile land missile with nuclear capability

Scu·dé·ry (skydeiri:), Madeleine de (1607–1701), French novelist. She collaborated with her brother Georges (1601–68) in sentimental novels with historical backgrounds, e.g. 'Clélie' (1654–61). The characters give an insight into 17th-c. society

scuff (skʌf) **1.** *v.i.* to walk by scraping or dragging the feet along the ground instead of lifting them ‖ to become worn, chipped etc. ‖ repeated friction, *this surface scuffs easily* ‖ *v.t.* to scrape or drag (the feet) in walking ‖ to cause wear to by repeated friction, *to scuff one's shoes* **2.** *n.* a scuffling or a scuffling sound ‖ a worn spot ‖ a soft, flat house slipper without a heel [perh. imit. or rel. to SCURF]

scuf·fle (skʌ́f'l) **1.** *v.i. pres. part.* **scuf·fling** *past* and *past part.* **scuf·fled** to struggle or scrap in a confused way at close quarters ‖ to move about hurriedly with confused sounds **2.** *n.* a confused struggle or scrap at close quarters ‖ the act or sound of scuffling [perh. fr. Scand.]

scuffle hoe a hoe sharpened on both front and rear edge for cutting by pushing or pulling under the surface of soil

scull (skʌl) **1.** *n.* one of a pair of short oars used by one person in rowing a boat ‖ a single oar used at the stern in propelling a boat ‖ a sculler (boat) **2.** *v.t.* to propel (a boat) using sculls or a scull ‖ to convey (a person etc.) in a boat which one sculls, *he sculled them back to shore* ‖ *v.i.* to use sculls or a scull in propelling a boat ‖ (of a boat) to be able to be propelled with a scull or sculls **scúll·er** *n.* a person who sculls ‖ a boat designed for sculling [etym. doubtful]

scul·ler·y (skʌ́ləri:) *pl.* **scul·ler·ies** *n.* a room adjacent to a kitchen, equipped and used for washing and cleaning cooking utensils, cleaning and preparing vegetables etc. [O.F. *escuelerie*]

scul·lion (skʌ́ljən) *n.* (*hist.*) a servant of low status who did the work in a scullery [perh. alt. of F. *souillon*, dirty person]

scul·pin (skʌ́lpin) *pl.* **scul·pin, scul·pins** *n.* any of several Atlantic sea fishes of fam. *Cottidae*, order *Scleroparei*, having large, spiny heads [etym. doubtful]

sculpt (skʌlpt) *v.i.* to make a sculpture or practice sculpture ‖ *v.t.* to sculpture (a figure etc.) [fr. F. *sculpter*]

sculp·tor (skʌ́lptər) *n.* a person who makes sculptures **sculp·tress** *n.* a female sculptor [L.]

sculp·tur·al (skʌ́lptʃərəl) *adj.* of or pertaining to sculpture ‖ having the qualities of sculpture

sculp·ture (skʌ́lptʃər) **1.** *n.* the making of three-dimensional works of art in stone, clay, metal, wood etc. ‖ one of these works ‖ such works collectively ‖ (*biol.*) markings in relief **2.** *v.t. pres. part.* **sculp·tur·ing** *past* and *past part.* **sculp·tured** to represent by, or ornament with, sculpture ‖ to make sculpture out of (stone, clay, metal etc.) [fr. L. *sculptura* fr. *sculpere*, to carve]

scum (skʌm) **1.** *n.* impurities which rise to the surface of a liquid and collect on it, esp. during fermentation or boiling ‖ the light, floating skinlike mass so formed ‖ the residue of oxides etc. which floats on a molten metal ‖ people of a class that one regards with profound contempt **2.** *v. pres. part.* **scum·ming** *past* and *past part.* **scummed** *v.i.* to become covered with scum ‖ *v.t.* to cover with scum [M.L.G. *schûm* and M. Du. *schume*]

scum·ble (skʌ́mb'l) **1.** *v.t. pres. part.* **scum·bling** *past* and *past part.* **scum·bled** to lay a thin coat of opaque or nearly opaque color on (color or a painting) in order to break up the surface and render it less brilliant ‖ to apply (color) for this purpose ‖ to soften the lines or colors of (a drawing) by lightly rubbing them **2.** *n.* the effect produced by scumbling ‖ the material used for scumbling [perh. fr. SCUM]

scum·my (skʌ́mi:) *comp.* **scum·mi·er** *superl.* **scum·mi·est** *adj.* of, like or covered with scum

scun·cheon (skʌ́ntʃən) *n.* (*archit.*) an arch etc. put across the corners of a square tower to give the additional supports for an octagonal spire ‖ (*archit.*) a splay etc. in an embrasure [O.F. *escoinson*]

scup (skʌp) *n.* either of two edible sea fish, *Stenostomus chrysops* and *S. aculeatus*, fam. *Sparidae*, found on the Atlantic coast of the U.S.A. [fr. Narragansett *mishcup*]

scup·per (skʌ́pər) **1.** *n.* an aperture which enables water to escape overboard from the deck of a ship **2.** *v.t.* (*Br., pop.*) to sink (a ship) ‖ (*Br., pop.*) to wreck or spoil (a plan etc.) [etym. doubtful]

scup·per·nong (skʌ́pərnɔŋ, skʌ́pərnɒŋ) *n.* any of several large, yellowish-green muscadine grapes of the southeastern U.S.A., esp. the fruit of *Vitis rotundifolia* ‖ a wine made from these grapes [after the *Scuppernong* River, North Carolina]

scurf (skə:rf) *n.* small flakes of dry skin, easily becoming detached, esp. on the scalp ‖ any scaly surface matter **scúrf·y** *comp.* **scurf·i·er** *superl.* **scurf·iest** *adj.* like scurf ‖ covered with scurf [O.E.]

scur·ril·i·ty (skəríliti:) *pl.* **scur·ril·i·ties** *n.* the quality of being scurrilous ‖ scurrilous language or a scurrilous remark [F. *scurrilité* or fr. L. *scurrilitas*]

scur·ril·ous (skə́:riləs) *adj.* expressed in or using language which is offensively or indecently abusive [fr. obs. *scurrile* fr. F. or fr. L. *scurrilis*, like a buffoon]

scur·ry (skə́:ri:, skʌ́ri:) **1.** *v.i. pres. part.* **scur·ry·ing** *past* and *past part.* **scur·ried** to move along quickly, esp. with hurried little steps **2.** *pl.* **scur·ries** *n.* a hurried moving along, or an instance of this ‖ gust, a *scurry of rain* [perh. fr. HURRY-SCURRY]

scur·vi·ly (skə́:rvili:) *adv.* in a scurvy manner

scur·vi·ness (skə́:rvi:nis) *n.* the quality of being scurvy

scur·vy (skə́:rvi:) **1.** *comp.* **scur·vi·er** *superl.* **scur·vi·est** *adj.* (*rhet.*) meriting contempt, vile, *a scurvy trick* **2.** *n.* a disease characterized by skin spots, swollen gums, bleeding in the mucous membranes and general debility, caused by a deficiency of vitamin C in the diet for a long period of time [SCURF]

scurvy grass *Cochlearia officinalis*, an Arctic cress with pleasantly sharp-tasting leaves, said to prevent scurvy

scut (skʌt) *n.* the short tail of a rabbit, hare, deer etc. [etym. doubtful]

scu·tage (skjú:tidʒ) *n.* (*hist.*) a feudal tax paid by the tenant of a knight's fee in lieu of military service [fr. M.L. *scutagium*]

scu·tal (skjú:t'l) *adj.* (*zool.*) of or having the nature of a scute or scutum [fr. Mod. L. *scutalis* fr. L. *scutum*, shield]

Scu·ta·ri (skú:tɑri:) (*Turk.* Uskudar) *ISTANBUL

Scutari *SHKODËR

Scutari, Lake *SHKODËR

scu·tate (skjú:teit) *adj.* (*zool.*) protected by large scales or horny plates ‖ (*bot.*) shaped like a shield [fr. L. *scutatus* fr. *scutum*, shield]

scutch (skʌtʃ) *v.t.* to remove the woody fibers from (flax, hemp etc.) by beating [O.F. *escousser*, to shake]

scutch *n.* a scutcher ‖ a tool used by bricklayers in cutting and shaping [O.F. *escouche*]

scutch·eon (skʌ́tʃən) *n.* an escutcheon ‖ a scute ‖ the frame or cover of a keyhole [ESCUTCHEON]

scutch·er (skʌ́tʃər) *n.* a tool or machine for scutching [SCUTCH v.]

scute (skju:t) *n.* (*zool.*) an external hard scale, esp. of a reptile, fish or scaly insect (cf. SCUTUM) [fr. L. *scutum*, shield]

scu·tel·late (skju:télit, skju:téleit, skjú:t'leit) *adj.* (*biol.*) flat, with a round or oval shape like a shield ‖ (*zool.*) having small plates or scales **scu·tel·lat·ed** (skjú:t'leitid) *adj.* (*zool.*) scutellate **scu·tel·la·tion** (skju:t'léiʃən) *n.* (*zool.*) the manner in which scales or plates are arranged [fr. Mod. L. *scutellatus* fr. L. *scutella*, platter]

scu·tel·lum (skju:téləm) *pl.* **scu·tel·la** (skju:télə) *n.* (*zool.*) a small scale or plate, e.g. one of the tarsal scales of a bird ‖ (*bot.*) the shield-shaped cotyledon which separates the embryo from the endosperm in the seeds of grasses [Mod. L. fr. L. *scutella*, platter]

scu·ti·form (skjú:tifɔrm) *adj.* (*biol.*) shaped like a shield [fr. Mod. L. *scutiformis* fr. L. *scutum*, shield]

scut·ter (skʌ́tər) **1.** *v.i.* (*Br.*) to scurry **2.** *n.* (*Br.*) a scurrying [perh. fr. SCUTTLE]

scut·tle (skʌ́t'l) **1.** *v.i. pres. part.* **scut·tling** *past* and *past part.* **scut·tled** to scurry **2.** *n.* a scuttling pace [etym. doubtful]

scuttle *n.* a small container holding coal, coke etc. for replenishing a fire [O.E. *scutel*, a dish, fr. M.L. *scutila* and L. *scutella*]

scuttle **1.** *n.* (*naut.*) a hole in the side or deck of a ship, furnished with a movable cover ‖ the cover itself ‖ a similar opening in the roof or floor of a building, or the cover for this **2.** *v.t. pres. part.* **scut·tling** *past* and *past part.* **scut·tled** to make or open holes in (a ship) below water level in order to sink it [etym. doubtful]

scu·tum (skjú:təm) *pl.* **scu·ta** (skjú:tə) *n.* (*zool.*) a horny, bony or chitinous plate, esp. the second of four parts which make up the upper surface of a thoracic segment in an insect (cf. SCUTE) [L.=shield]

scut work (skʌt) (*slang*) hospital staff term for unpleasant work, esp. trivial chores, paperwork, or work that could be done by someone else

Scyl·la and Charybdis (sílə) (*Gk mythol.*) the personification of a rock (Scylla) and a whirlpool (Charybdis), navigation hazards flanking Italy's narrow straits of Messina **between Scylla and Charybdis** in great difficulties no matter which of two alternative courses of action is chosen

scy·pho·zo·an (saifəzóuən) **1.** *n.* a member of *Scyphozoa*, a class of coelenterates including many jellyfish of large size **2.** *adj.* of or relating to this class [fr. Mod. L. *Scyphozoa* fr. Gk *skuphos*, cup + *zōon*, animal]

scy·phus (sáifəs) *pl.* **scy·phi** (sáifai) *n.* an an-

CONCISE PRONUNCIATION KEY: **(a)** æ, *cat*; ɑ, *car*; ɔ *fawn*; ei, *snake*. **(e)** e, *hen*; i:, *sheep*; iə, *deer*; εə, *bear*. **(i)** i, *fish*; ai, *tiger*; ə:, *bird*. **(o)** o, *ox*; au, *cow*; ou, *goat*; u, *poor*; ɔi, *royal*. **(u)** ʌ, *duck*; u, *bull*; u:, *goose*; ə, *bacillus*; ju:, *cube*. x, *loch*; θ, *think*; ð, *bother*; z, *Zen*; ʒ, *corsage*; dʒ, *savage*; ŋ, *orangutang*; j, *yak*; ʃ, *fish*; tʃ, *fetch*; 'l, *rabble*; 'n, *redden*. Complete pronunciation key appears inside front cover.

cient Greek drinking cup with two handles || (*bot.*) a cup-shaped part, e.g. the corona of certain flowers [L. fr. Gk *skuphos*]
scythe (saið) **1.** *n.* a long, curved blade with a sharp edge on the inner side of the curve, fitted to a long wooden handle, used by a person standing up to cut long grass etc. with steady, sweeping pulls **2.** *v.t. pres. part.* **scyth·ing** *past* and *past part.* **scythed** to cut with a scythe [O.E. *sīthe*]
Scyth·i·a (síθi:ə) an ancient region of S.E. Europe and Asia, inhabited by the Scythians, centered north of the Black Sea on the lower Don and Dnieper
Scyth·i·an (síθi:ən) **1.** *n.* a member of a nomadic Indo-European people who settled in Scythia before the 7th c. B.C. and were displaced (3rd c. B.C.) by the Sarmatians. They were specially noted in warfare for their mounted archers and in art for their rich gold ornaments || their Iranian language **2.** *adj.* of Scythia, its people or its language
S. D. South Dakota
S. Dak. South Dakota
SDI (*computer abbr.*) for selective dissemination of information, program to distribute material based on recipient's declaration of interests
SDR (*economics abbr.*) of special drawing rights by nations from the International Monetary Fund *Cf* PAPER GOLD
SDS (*abbr.*) for Students for a Democratic Society, a radical organization originally formed in 1962 at the University of Michigan and later on college campuses throughout the U.S.; active during the late 1960s and early 1970s *Cf* NEW LEFT, WEATHERMAN
SE, S.E. Southeast, Southeastern
sea (si:) *n.* the continuous body of salt water covering most of the earth's surface || a named portion of this body of water, smaller than an ocean, sometimes partly or wholly enclosed by land || (only in names) a vast inland lake of salt or fresh water, e.g. the Sea of Galilee || the surface condition of the ocean with respect to the degree or type of movement of the waves, *a rough sea* || movement of the ocean's surface, *there is a strong sea running between the islands* || a heavy swell or wave || a vast expanse, quantity or mass, *a sea of memoranda* **at sea** on the sea || not knowing how to act or proceed, bewildered **to go to sea** to become a sailor [O. E. *sǣ*]
sea anchor a drag anchor
sea anemone a member of *Actiniaria,* an order of polyps of varied, often brilliant colors, living fixed to shore rocks. They have tentacles around the mouth which are armed with stinging cells for preying on small animals
sea bass any of many sea fishes of fam. *Serranidae,* esp. *Centropristes striatus,* of the Atlantic coast of the U.S.A., which is valued as a food fish
Sea·bee (sí:bi:) *n.* a member of any of the construction battalions of the Civil Engineer Corps of the U.S. Navy, responsible for building bases, harbors etc. [fr. the pronunciation of the initials of 'construction battalion']
sea-bird (si:bə̞:rd) *n.* any of various birds, e.g. gulls and petrels, that fly over the open sea and frequent the seashore
sea·board (sí:bɔrd, sí:bo̞urd) **1.** *n.* the strip of land nearest to a seacoast **2.** *adj.* bordering on the sea
Sea·borg (sí:bɔrg), Glenn Theodore (1912-), U.S. physical chemist and cowinner (with Edwin M. McMillan) of the 1951 Nobel prize in chemistry for the discovery of eight new elements with atomic numbers 94-101, notably plutonium (94)
sea·borne (sí:bo̞rn, sí:bo̞urn) *adj.* carried on or conveyed by the sea
sea bream any of several edible seafishes of the suborder *Percoidea,* order *Percomorphi*
sea breeze a cool breeze from over the sea, replacing hotter air rising over the land
sea calf *Phoca vitulina,* a common seal of the N. Atlantic coasts, about 4 ft long
sea coal (*hist.*) coal (so called because it was transported by sea, esp. to London, from the mines of N.E. England)
sea·coast (sí:ko̞ust) *n.* the edge or strip of land adjacent to the sea
Sea Cobra (*mil.*) a single-rotor light attack helicopter (AH-1) armed with a variety of machine guns, rockets, grenade launchers, and antitank missiles
sea cow any large herbivorous aquatic mammal of the order *Sirenia,* e.g. the manatee and the dugong || a walrus || a hippopotamus
sea cucumber a holothurian
sea dog an old, experienced sailor || (*hist.*) a pirate || a dogfish || the sea calf
Sea Dyak *DYAK
sea eagle any of several eagles which feed on fish, e.g. *Haliaëtus albicilla* || the osprey
sea-ear (sí:iər) *n.* a haliotis
sea elephant an elephant seal
sea fan a member of *Gorgonia,* fam. *Gorgoniidae,* a genus of corals with fanlike branches
sea·far·er (sí:fɛ̞ərər) *n.* a mariner, or anyone traveling by sea
sea·far·ing (sí:fɛ̞əriŋ) **1.** *n.* the occupation of a sailor || travel by sea **2.** *adj.* working as a sailor || traveling on the sea || relating to seafaring
sea farming *v. pres. part.* cultivation of plants and animals in the ocean *also* mariculture
sea·flow·er (sí:fla̞uər) *n.* a sea anemone
sea-foam (sí:fo̞um) *n.* the foam formed by turbulent seawater || meerschaum
sea·food (sí:fu:d) *n.* food extracted from the sea, esp. shellfish
sea·front (sí:frʌnt) *n.* that part of a town etc. directly facing the sea
Se·aga (si:ágə), Edward Phillip George (1930-), Jamaican politician, prime minister (1980-). As a member of the House of Representatives he was minister of development and welfare (1962-7) and of finance and planning (1967-72). He worked to stabilize the economy and fostered ties with the U.S.A.
sea·girt (sí:gə̞:rt) *adj.* (esp. *rhet.*) surrounded by sea
sea·go·ing (sí:go̞uiŋ) *adj.* (of a vessel) designed for sailing on the sea, not built only for river or harbor use
sea grass any of certain plants growing by or in the sea, esp. eelgrass
sea green a bluish-green or yellow-green color
séa-green *adj.* having such a color
sea gull a gull
sea hare a number of *Tethys,* fam. *Tethyidae,* a genus of large gastropod mollusks of sluglike appearance, with a prominent front pair of tentacles
sea holly *Eryngium maritimum,* fam. *Umbelliferae,* a prickly evergreen plant common among sand dunes
sea horse a member of *Hippocampus,* fam. *Syngnathidae,* a genus of small tropical or subtropical bony, lophobranch fishes having a body shaped like the head and arched neck of a horse, ending with a prehensile tail || a walrus || (*mythol.*) a creature half horse and half fish
Sea Island cotton a long-fibered cotton originally grown in the Sea Islands of the Atlantic, off the southern U.S.A., now also grown in the West Indies and on the southern U.S. coast
sea kale *Crambe maritima,* a European cruciferous perennial plant, native to northern temperate coasts. It is cultivated for its large leaves which are eaten as a vegetable
sea king a Norse pirate chief in the Middle Ages
Sea-King *n.* (*mil.*) a single-rotor medium-lift helicopter (SH-3) utilized for air/sea rescue and personnel/cargo transport
seal (si:l) **1.** *pl.* **seals, seal** *n.* any of several fish-eating mammals of fam. *Phocidae* (lacking external ears) and fam. *Otariidae* (having external ears), suborder *Pinnipedia.* They have a thick, smooth coat and limbs like flippers adapted for swimming. They are hunted for their hide, for their pelt, and for their oil-yielding blubber || the valuable pelt of one of these animals, used for coats etc. || leather made from their hide **2.** *v.i.* to hunt seals [O. E. *seolh*]
seal *n.* a device, e.g. a metal die or semiprecious stone, having a design which can be impressed into a plastic material (wax, lead etc.) || the design on this device used as a personal or official emblem || the piece of plastic material thus impressed, attached to a document as a sign of its authenticity, or covering a join in an envelope or wrapping so that it cannot be opened without the seal being broken || anything which serves to keep something secured or closed, e.g. a water seal in a pipe || an absolute obligation, *to put someone under the seal of secrecy* || a decorative adhesive stamp other than a postage stamp, put on an envelope etc. || a sign or guarantee of authority, approval etc., *he gave it the seal of his consent* [O.F. *seel*]
seal *v.t.* to attach or mark with a seal, *to sign and seal a document* || to close up thoroughly, *to seal a crack with putty* || to confirm the validity, authenticity etc. of, *they sealed the bargain with a handshake* || (*fig.*) to make certain, irrevocable etc., *that fact sealed his doom* || to stamp (e.g. merchandise) as official evidence of standard quality, weight, capacity etc. [O.F. *seeler, seieler*]
Sealab *n.* underwater habitat for U.S. navy researchers
seal·ant (sí:lənt) *n.* (*dentistry*) liquid plastic filler
sea lavender a member of *Limonium,* fam. *Plumbaginaceae,* a genus of maritime plants having spikes or panicles of white, pink or yellow flowers
sea lawyer (*pop.*) someone subject to discipline, esp. a sailor, who is given to quoting glibly from the regulations to avoid work or protect his own rights or privileges
sealed orders orders, e.g. to a ship's captain, which must not be opened or read until a fixed place or time has been reached
sea legs the ability to maintain balance and feel well on board ship at sea
seal·er (sí:lər) *n.* a person or vessel engaged in seal hunting
sealer *n.* someone who or something which seals || an official who sets a seal on an article he has judged acceptable as to quality, weight etc. || a coat of material applied to a surface to prevent the top layer of paint or varnish from sinking in
sea level the horizontal line midway between high and low water, used as a line of reference from which to measure the altitude of positions on land
sea lily any crinoid, esp. one having a stalk
sealing wax a mixture of shellac, turpentine and pigment which is hard and brittle at room temperature but softens and becomes plastic when heated. It is used to seal documents, letters etc.
sea lion any of several large seals of the Pacific Ocean, having ears
seal point a Siamese cat of a strain having a fawn or creamy body and brown points (cf. BLUE POINT)
seal ring a signet ring
seal·skin (sí:lskin) *n.* the skin of a seal, esp. with the soft fur || a coat or jacket made from this
Seal·y·ham (sí:li:hæm, sí:li:əm) *n.* a terrier of a Welsh breed with short legs, long head and long body, noted for its high spirits [after *Sealyham,* Wales]
seam (si:m) **1.** *n.* a line of stitches where two pieces of cloth have been sewn together || any visible line, fold or ridge showing where two parts of a surface are joined || such a line etc. showing where two surfaces have been divided, e.g. a thin layer of coal etc. between two strata of rock || a scar or wrinkle of the skin || (*knitting*) a line of purled stitches making or resembling a seam **2.** *v.t.* to join by a seam || to make an ornamental seam in, e.g. with purl stitch in knitting || to mark with a scar or wrinkle, *a face seamed with care* [O. E. *sēam*]
sea·man (sí:mən) *pl.* **sea·men** (sí:mən) *n.* a sailor below the rank of officer **séa·man·like** *adj.* characteristic of or like a good seaman **séa·man·ship** *n.* the art and skill of handling a vessel, esp. of navigating
sea·mark (sí:ma̞rk) *n.* an object on land, visible from the sea, serving to guide navigators of vessels || a line on the shore marking the upper limit of the tide
sea mew a gull, esp. *Larus canus,* a common gull of Europe
sea mile a nautical mile
sea mouse a member of *Aphrodite,* fam. *Aphroditidae,* a genus of marine polychaete worms, inhabiting deep water. They have iridescent setae fringing the sides of their bodies
seam·stress (sí:mstris, *Br.* esp. sémstris) *n.* a woman who makes her living by sewing [O.E. *sēamestre*]
seam·y (sí:mi:) *comp.* **seam·i·er** *superl.* **seam·i·est** *adj.* having seams **the seamy side** the sordid aspect of something
Sean·ad Éir·eann (sǽnədɛ́ərən) the Senate of the Irish Republic, the upper house of the legislature
sé·ance (séiɑns) *n.* a meeting of persons for some purpose, esp. a spiritualist meeting [F. = a sitting]
sea onion a squill
sea otter *Enhydra lutris,* fam. *Mustelidae,* a rare marine mammal, sometimes reaching 6 ft in length, living on some coasts of the N.

Pacific. It has short legs, webbed hind feet and feeds on shellfish || its extremely valuable dark brown fur

sea pen a member of *Pennatula,* fam. *Pennatulidae,* or related genera of alcyonarians, the colonies of which have a feathery form

sea·plane (sí:plèin) *n.* an airplane having floats which enable it to rest on, take off from, and come down on water

sea·port (sí:pɔrt, sí:pourt) *n.* a town on a seacoast, or connected by river with the coast, having a harbor, docks etc., used by seagoing vessels

sea power naval strength || a nation which has great naval strength

sea purse the horny egg case of certain rays, sharks or skates. It has filaments by which it becomes attached, e.g. to seaweed

sear (siər) *v.t.* to wither by applying heat and thus drying || to burn or scorch || to brown quickly the outside of (a piece of meat) so as to seal in the juices || to cauterize [O.E. *sēarian*]

sear *n.* the catch which holds the hammer of a firearm at half cock or full cock [etym. doubtful]

sear *adj.* *SERE

search (sə:rtʃ) *n.* an investigation or scrutiny, in order to find something, gain information etc. || (*maritime law*) the exercise of the right of search **in search of** looking for, searching for [A.F. *serche* and O.F. *cerche*]

search *v.t.* to go or look into, over or through in order to find something, gain information etc., *he searched the records for their address* || to examine the clothing and body of (a person) to see if he is concealing something || *v.i.* to make a search **séarch·ing** *adj.* thorough, *a searching examination* || (*fig.*) penetrating, *searching glances* [O.F. *cerchier*]

search-and-de·stroy (sə́:rtʃænddistrɔ́i) *adj.* of the antiguerrilla warfare tactic of clearing an area of the enemy forces

search·light (sə́:rtʃlait) *n.* a device whereby light from a source of great illuminating power is reflected from a paraboloidal mirror as an almost parallel beam, losing little intensity by spreading and thus brightly illuminating an object in the area which it sweeps. It is used to discover hostile aircraft, ships etc. at night

search warrant a written authorization, given to the police by a court, to enter specified private premises in order to make a search for stolen goods, fugitives from justice etc.

Seasat *n.* 5,000-lb research satellite devoted to ocean observation, with 14 daily orbits of earth

sea·scape (sí:skeip) *n.* a painting or drawing in which the sea is a prominent feature

sea scout (*Br.*) a boy scout in a unit which gives training in seamanship

sea serpent a sea snake || a mythological sea monster

sea·shell (sí:ʃel) *n.* the shell of any marine animal

sea·shore (sí:ʃɔr, sí:ʃour) *n.* the land immediately adjacent to the sea || (*law*) the ground between low-water and high-water marks

sea·sick (sí:sik) *adj.* suffering from seasickness **séa·sick·ness** *n.* nausea and vomiting caused by reaction to the motion of a vessel at sea

sea·side (sí:said) **1.** *n.* the seacoast, esp. as a place for holidays **2.** *adj.* at or pertaining to the seaside

sea skimmer *n.* (*mil.*) a missile designed to transit at less than 50 ft above the surface of the sea

sea slug a holothurian || a nudibranch

sea snail any marine gastropod mollusk with a spiral shell, e.g. a whelk || any of several small slimy fishes of fam. *Liparididae* having a sucker

sea snake any of several poisonous aquatic fish-eating snakes of fam. *Hydrophidae,* inhabiting esp. tropical seas

sea·son (sí:z'n) *n.* a period in the year regarded as having its own characteristic weather, length of days etc., esp. any of the four divisions of the year (spring, summer, autumn and winter) running from equinox to solstice and from solstice to equinox || a period during which something flourishes, or the period most favorable or suitable for something, *the strawberry season, this is not the season for harvesting* || the period during which a specified activity is or may be engaged in, in which a specified event, festival etc. takes place, or during which something is active, *hunting season, Christmas season, the orchestra's season lasts 40 weeks* || a period of great activity of a specified nature, *the social season* || the period of greatest social activity in a specified place, *the London season* || (*Br.*) a season ticket **in good season** early enough **in season** (of fruit, vegetables, shellfish etc.) being harvested after growing under natural climatic conditions and hence available fresh at relatively cheap prices || (of game) legally open to hunting || (of a bitch etc.) in heat || at the proper time **out of season** not in season [M.E. *seson* fr. O.F. *seson, seison*]

season *v.t.* to dry out and harden (lumber) for use, by exposure or heat || to make more suitable for efficient use or bring into good condition by long, slow usage, *a seasoned pipe* || to give long experience to, *a seasoned veteran* || to add condiments or spices to (food) in order to enhance the flavor || to make more tolerable or pleasant, *to season adverse comments with compliments* || *v.i.* to go through the process of being seasoned by exposure, heat etc. [O.F. *saisonner*]

sea·son·a·ble (sí:zənəb'l) *adj.* suitable to the season, *seasonable weather* || opportune, *seasonable advice* **séa·son·a·bly** *adv.*

sea·son·al (sí:zən'l) *adj.* characteristic of a season or the seasons, *seasonal storms* || occurring at, determined by or active during a certain season or seasons, *seasonal work*

sea·son·ing (sí:zəniŋ) *n.* something (e.g. salt, spices etc.) added to food to enhance the flavor || something which seasons

season ticket a ticket entitling one to admission, service etc., for use over an extended specified period

Sea Sparrow *n.* (*mil.*) Navy solid-fuel, radar-directed 500-lb missile, with a 25-mi range *Cf* SPARROW

Sea Sprite *n.* (*mil.*) a single-rotor light-lift helicopter (SH-2), utilized for air/sea rescue, personnel/cargo transport and antisubmarine operations from ships

sea squirt a simple ascidian (so called because it contracts and squirts water when touched)

Sea Stallion *n.* (*mil.*) a single-rotor heavy-lift helicopter (CH-53 and RH-53) utilized for personnel/cargo transport

seat (si:t) **1.** *n.* anything on which one sits or may sit || that part of a chair etc. which supports the weight of the person sitting || the place where one habitually sits, *that is the old man's seat* || that part of a structure which acts as a support || the buttocks || the part of a pair of pants or skirt which covers the buttocks || posture on horseback, *he has a good seat* || a country mansion || a center of some activity etc., *a seat of learning* || the place at which some condition originates, *the seat of the trouble* || the right of membership in an administrative or legislative body, *a seat on the board* **to take a seat** to sit down **to take one's seat** to sit down in the seat allotted to one (at table, in a theater etc.) || to assume membership formally in Parliament **2.** *v.t.* to cause to sit down || to provide seats for, *the theater seats 1,000 people* || to allot a seat or seats to in a certain place, *they had been seated behind a pillar* || to furnish (a chair etc.) with a seat, or a new seat || (*mech.*) to give a seating to, *to seat an axle* **to be seated** to sit down || to be sitting **séat·ed** *adj.* sitting || situated or established in a specified way or place **séat·er** *n.* (in compounds) something having a specified number of seats, *his new car is a two-seater* **séat·ing** *n.* the provision made for people to sit || material for covering chair seats etc. || the arrangement of seats || (*mech.*) a surface on which something is supported [O.N. *sǽti*]

seat belt a strap by which a passenger in a vehicle can secure himself to his seat as a safety precaution

SEATO (sí:tou) *SOUTH EAST ASIA TREATY ORGANIZATION

sea trout any of several trouts that live in the sea as adults but ascend rivers to spawn

Se·at·tle (si:ǽt'l) the chief city and port (pop. 490,077) of the northwestern U.S.A., on Puget Sound in W. central Washington, dominated by Mt Rainier. Industries: aeronautical and mechanical engineering, shipbuilding, food processing, brewing, fishing, lumber, pulp and paper. University of Washington (1861)

sea urchin an echinoderm of the class *Echinoidea,* possessing a calcareous boxlike exoskeleton with movable spines used for walking. The edible sea urchin is *Echinus esculenta*

sea·van (sí:væn) *n.* commercial or government-owned (or -leased) shipping containers without bogey wheels attached, i.e., lifted on and off the ship

sea·wall (sí:wɔl) *n.* a wall built to prevent encroachment by the sea

sea walnut a ctenophore, e.g. of genus *Mnemiopsis,* shaped like a walnut

sea·ward (sí:wərd) **1.** *n.* the direction from a coast towards the open sea **2.** *adj.* directed or situated toward the sea **3.** *adv.* in the direction of the sea **séa·wards** *adv.*

sea·wa·ter (sí:wɔtər, sí:wɒtər) *n.* the water of the sea, containing in solution, on the average, 2.8% sodium chloride and other salts

sea·way (sí:wei) *n.* a route over the sea || a deep inland river up which an oceangoing vessel can sail || (*naut.*) a vessel's progress || a rough sea

sea·weed (sí:wi:d) *n.* any marine plant, esp. a marine alga. Seaweeds are widely distributed in the oceans and are found floating or attached at considerable depth by specialized anchoring attachments. They are an important source of food, fertilizer and minerals (esp. iodine) || seaweeds collectively

sea·wor·thi·ness (sí:wə:rθi:nis) *n.* the quality or state of being seaworthy

sea·wor·thy (sí:wə:rθi:) *adj.* (of a vessel) in a fit condition to go to sea and to survive storms

sea wrack a mass of coarse seaweed || a plant tending to form such a mass || eelgrass

se·ba·ceous (sibéiʃəs) *adj.* (of glands, ducts etc.) containing or secreting fatty oily matter || consisting of such matter, *sebaceous secretions* [fr. L. *sebaceus* fr. *sebum,* tallow]

Se·bas·tian (sibǽstʃən), St (*d.* c. 288), Christian martyr in Rome, usually depicted as a nude youth pierced by arrows. Feast: Jan. 20

Sebastian (*Port.* Sebastião, 1554-78), king of Portugal (1557-78), grandson of John III. He was killed, and his army massacred, in a disastrous battle against the Moors in N. Africa

Se·bas·tia·no del Piom·bo (sebastjánədelpjómbɔ) (1485-1547), Italian painter. He was a Venetian, but worked in Rome after 1511, much influenced by Michelangelo

Se·bas·to·pol (sibǽstəpoul) Sevastopol

se·bum (sí:bəm) *n.* the fatty matter secreted by the sebaceous glands to keep the skin and hair supple [L.=tallow, grease]

SECAM *n.* a color television system developed in France and used in U.S.S.R., East Germany, Czechoslovakia, and Lebanon in which each color is broadcast separately on 650 sequential lines

se·cant (sí:kænt, sí:kənt) **1.** *adj.* (*math.*) intersecting **2.** *n.* a straight line which intercepts a curve || (*math., abbr.* sec) the reciprocal of the cosine [fr. L. *secans* (*secantis*) fr. *secare,* to cut]

sec·a·teurs (sékətə:rz) *pl. n.* (*Br.*) steel shears used for pruning, cutting roses and grapes etc. [F. *sécateur*]

Sec·chi Disk (séki:) device to determine clarity of seawater, usu. on underwater sites

se·cede (sisí:d) *pres. part.* **se·ced·ing** *past* and *past part.* **se·ced·ed** *v.i.* to withdraw formally from membership of some body, esp. from a state, federation etc. [fr. L. *secedere,* to go away]

se·ces·sion (siséʃən) *n.* the act of seceding **se·cés·sion·ism** *n.* the doctrines of those who favor secession from some body **se·cés·sion·ist** *n.* [fr. L. *secessio* (*secessionis*)]

se·clude (siklú:d) *pres. part.* **se·clud·ing** *past* and *past part.* **se·clud·ed** *v.t.* to keep (someone) apart from others, isolate **se·clúd·ed** *adj.* shut off, isolated, *a secluded garden, she lives a secluded life* [fr. L. *secludere,* to shut up apart]

se·clu·sion (siklú:ʒən) *n.* a secluding or being secluded [fr. M.L. *seclusio* (*seclusionis*)]

se·clu·sive (siklú:siv) *adj.* tending to seclude || seeking seclusion [fr. L. *secludere* (*seclusus*), to seclude]

SECO *n.* (*computer acronym*) for sequential control, a system for controlling the sequence of teletype message transmissions of stored data

se·cond (sékənd) *n.* a unit of time equal to 1/60 of a minute or 1/86,400 of a mean solar day || a unit of angular measure (symbol ″) equal to 1/60 of a minute or 1/3,600 of a degree || an undefined very short time, *it will just take me a second* [F. *seconde* fr. M.L. *secunda* (*minuta*), second (minute), denoting the second operation of sexagesimal division]

second 1. *adj.* being number two in a series (*NUMBER TABLE) || next after the first in importance, quality, rank etc. || being another of the

CONCISE PRONUNCIATION KEY: (a) æ, *cat*; ɑ, *car*; ɔ *fawn*; ei, *snake*. (e) e, *hen*; i:, *sheep*; iə, *deer*; ɛə, *bear*. (i) i, *fish*; ai, *tiger*; ə:, *bird*. (o) o, *ox*; au, *cow*; ou, *goat*; u, *poor*; ɔi, *royal*. (u) ʌ, *duck*; u, *bull*; u:, *goose*; ə, *bacillus*; ju:, *cube*. x, *loch*; θ, *think*; ð, *bother*; z, *Zen*; ʒ, *corsage*; dʒ, *savage*; ŋ, *orangutang*; j, *yak*; ʃ, *fish*; tʃ, *fetch*; 'l, *rabble*; 'n, *redden*. Complete pronunciation key appears inside front cover.

same kind as the first, *a second Shakespeare* ‖ (*mus.*, of an instrument or voice) having a part generally lower in pitch than that of the first instrument or voice of the same kind, *second violin* ‖ of the gear immediately above first in a vehicle **2.** *n.* the person or thing next after the first ‖ someone who attends a principal in a boxing match, duel etc. ‖ (*Br.*) a grading in the second class of an examination ‖ a second prize in a race or other contest ‖ the gear immediately above first in a vehicle ‖ the second day of a month ‖ (*mus.*) the interval between two successive diatonic notes ‖ (*mus.*) one of these notes in relation to the other ‖ (*mus.*) a combination of these notes ‖ (*pl.*) substandard or inferior goods ‖ (*pl., pop.*) a second helping of food **3.** *v.t.* to give formal support to (a motion) before it is open to general discussion ‖ to express one's agreement with (a remark) ‖ to aid or encourage (someone's efforts) ‖ (sikɔ́nd, *Br., mil.*) to transfer (an officer) temporarily to another post, unit or rank **4.** *adv.* in the second place ‖ (followed by a superlative) except one, *the second biggest* [F. fr. L. *secundus*, following, next, second]

Second Advent the return of Christ to the world as judge on the last day **Sécond Adventist** a member of a Protestant sect which stresses this day of judgment

Second Amendment (1791) amendment to the U.S. Constitution, part of the Bill of Rights, that protects the right of citizens to maintain a state militia and to 'keep and bear arms.' State militias are represented by National Guard units, regulated by the state governments. The right to keep and bear arms does not necessarily apply to individuals for individual purposes and does not preclude state regulation of arms

sec·ond·ar·y (sékənderi:) **1.** *adj.* being second in succession, rank importance etc. ‖ immediately derived from what is primary, *secondary colors* ‖ (*gram.*, of a tense in Greek etc.) referring to time in the past ‖ (*chem.*) formed by replacing two atoms or radicals, *a secondary compound* ‖ (*geol.*) Mesozoic ‖ (*bot.*) originating from elsewhere than the chief growing point ‖ (*zool.*) of or designating a quill on the second section of a bird's wing, or this section itself **2.** *pl.* **sec·ond·ar·ies** *n.* a secondary person or thing ‖ (*zool.*) a secondary quill of a bird ‖ (*zool.*) an insect's hind wing [fr. L. *secundarius*, of the second class]

secondary accent a stress (shown in this book under the line) weaker than the primary stress

secondary cell (*elec.*) a storage cell

secondary color, *Br.* **secondary colour** a color made by a mixture of two primary colors

secondary education formal education below university level, following elementary education

secondary emission (*phys.*) the emission of electrons by a metal surface (e.g. the anode of a thermionic valve) when it is bombarded by rapidly moving electrons

secondary planet a celestial satellite that revolves around a planet

secondary school a school offering secondary education

second base (*baseball*) the base that must be touched second by the runner ‖ the player stationed at this base

second best something next below the best in quality, desirability etc. ‖ something inferior accepted or offered as a substitute for what is preferred **to come off second best** to be the loser in a dispute **séc·ond-bést** *adj.*

second chamber the upper house in a two-chamber parliament

second childhood dotage

sec·ond-class (sékəndklǽs, sékəndklɑ́s) **1.** *adj.* of or in a class next below the first ‖ of mediocre quality **2.** *adv.* by second-class accommodation etc., *to travel second-class*

Second Coming the Second Advent

second cousin the grandchild of a brother or sister of one of one's grandparents

second cousin once removed the child of one's second cousin

sec·ond-de·gree burn (sékənddigrí:) a burn involving blistering and superficial destruction of the dermis

se·conde (sikɔ́nd, səgɔ̃d) *n.* (*fencing*) the second of eight parrying positions [F.]

Second Empire (of style in furniture, dress etc.) characteristic of the style of Napoleon III's French empire of 1852–71, or imitating that ornate style

second fiddle (in phrase) **to be** (or **play**) **second fiddle** to have a secondary position or role

second hand (in the phrase) **at second hand** (of getting information) through an intermediary, *to hear an account at second hand* **séc·ond·hánd 1.** *adj.* used by a previous owner or owners, *secondhand clothes* ‖ not original, *derivative, secondhand ideas* **2.** *adv.* after use by someone else, *we bought it secondhand* ‖ (*pop.*) indirectly, *he acquired his education secondhand*

second hand the hand marking the seconds on a clock or watch

second intention (*med.*) the healing of a wound slowly and with much scar formation

second lieutenant an officer of the U.S. army, air force or marine corps ranking below a first lieutenant ‖ (*Br.*) an army officer ranking below a lieutenant

sec·ond·ly (sékəndli:) *adv.* (used in enumeration) in the second place

second mortgage a mortgage secured on what will remain of the property when the first mortgage is redeemed

second nature acquired habits or characteristics that have become automatic

second papers an alien's final application papers for U.S. citizenship

second person (*gram.*) the person spoken to as shown in the form of a verb or pronoun

sec·ond-rate (sékəndréit) *adj.* inferior, of poor quality

second sight ability to look into the future

sec·ond-strike (sekəndstráik) *adj.* (*mil.*) of a capacity to withstand an initial nuclear attack and retaliate

sec·ond-string (sékəndstríŋ) **1.** *adj.* serving as a replacement, e.g. for another player in a game ‖ inferior or minor **2.** *n.* (*Br.*) an alternative recourse, esp. one kept in reserve

second thought (*pl.*) a change of mind as a result of thinking again about a matter, *to have second thoughts* on (or **upon**) **second thought** on reconsideration, *on second thought, he decided to wait*

second wind the recovery of breath after initial exhaustion during exercise ‖ (*fig.*) the strength for a renewed effort

SECOR *n.* (*acronym*) for sequential collation of range, navigation and surveying system for locating points on earth, utilizing an orbiting satellite and four ground stations

se·cre·cy (sí:krisi:) *pl.* **se·cre·cies** *n.* the state of being secret, *done in secrecy* ‖ the ability to keep a secret, *you can rely on his secrecy* ‖ the habit of being secretive [alt. of obs. *secretee, secretie* prob. fr. obs. *secre*, secret or SECRET *adj.*]

se·cret (sí:krit) **1.** *adj.* kept from the knowledge of others, *a secret agreement* ‖ hidden, *a secret drawer* ‖ known only to the initiated, *secret signs* **2.** *n.* something kept from the knowledge of others, *the process is a secret* ‖ something which has not been explained ‖ a hidden or not obvious explanation, *what is the secret of his success?* ‖ (*eccles.*) a prayer said very quietly by the celebrant just before the preface at Mass **in secret** secretly **to keep a secret** to refrain from communicating a secret to others [F.]

secret agent a person engaged in espionage or similar undercover work, esp. for a government

se·cre·taire (sekritéər) *n.* a secretary (desk) [F.]

sec·re·tar·i·al (sekritéəri:əl) *adj.* of or relating to a secretary ‖ characteristic of a secretary's work [fr. M.L. *secretarius*]

sec·re·tar·i·at, sec·re·tar·i·ate (sekritéəri:ət) *n.* that department of a large concern, administrative body etc. which handles the paper work ‖ the persons, collectively, who work in this department ‖ the position of secretary [F. *secrétariat*]

sec·re·tar·y (sékriteri:, *Br.* sékrətri) *pl.* **sec·re·tar·ies** *n.* a person responsible for dealing with the correspondence and records of an organization or individual employer ‖ (in titles) a minister in charge of a government department, *secretary of state* ‖ a desk fitted with drawers, having a shelf which hinges forward to work on [fr. M.L. *secretarius*, confidant, secretary]

secretary bird *Sagittarius serpentarius*, fam. *Sagittariidae*, a long-legged S. African bird which eats reptiles. It has a strong beak and long tail, and has a crest of long feathers which look like pens stuck in behind the ears

secretary-general *pl.* **secretaries-general** *n.* the principal administrative officer of a secretariat

Secretary of State, U.S. the chief adviser to the president on foreign affairs, in charge of the State Department, and responsible for the execution of foreign policy

se·crete (sikrí:t) *pres. part.* **se·cret·ing** *past* and *past part.* **se·cret·ed** *v.t.* (*physiol.*) to produce and emit (a secretion) ‖ *v.i.* (*physiol.*) to produce and emit a secretion [fr. L. *secernere* (*secretus*), to separate]

secrete *pres. part.* **se·cret·ing** *past* and *past part.* **se·cret·ed** *v.t.* to conceal [alteration of obs. *secret* v.]

se·cre·tin (sikrí:tin) *n.* a hormone secreted in the intestine, which stimulates the pancreas and the liver [prob. fr. SECRETION]

se·cre·tion (sikrí:ʃən) *n.* a substance (e.g. saliva) elaborated by a gland or other organ or by a plant, for use by the organism or for excretion ‖ the act of elaborating such a substance [F. *sécrétion*]

secretion *n.* a hiding or concealing

se·cre·tive (sí:kritiv, sikrí:tiv) *adj.* fond of or given to having secrets ‖ unduly reticent [back-formation fr. *secretiveness*, the quality of being secretive, after F. *secrétivité*]

se·cre·tor (sikrí:tər) *n.* a gland etc. which secretes

se·cre·to·ry (sikrí:təri:) *adj.* producing or having to do with a secretion or secretions ‖ produced by secretion [fr. L. *secernere* (*secretus*), to separate]

secret service government investigation or espionage

Secret Service, U.S. a bureau of the treasury department created in 1865. Its duties include the protection of the U.S. president and his family, the president-elect, and the vice-president, as well as the solution of crimes relating to coins, paper money, checks and securities of U.S. or foreign governments, and of violations of laws relating to the Federal Deposit Insurance Corporation, federal land banks, joint-stock land banks and national farm loan associations

secret society a group of people associated together for some common interest (e.g. religious, magical, social or political) under conditions of secrecy

sect (sekt) *n.* a body of people, sharing religious, philosophic or political opinions, who have broken away from a larger body (often used as a term of disapproval) ‖ a particular school of thought in politics etc. [F. *secte* or fr. L. *secta*]

sec·tar·i·an (sektéəri:ən) **1.** *adj.* of or relating to a sect or sects ‖ narrow-minded and ready to quarrel over petty differences of opinion **2.** *n.* a member of a sect ‖ a narrow-minded or bigoted adherent of a sect **sec·tár·i·an·ism** *n.* adherence to the interests of a sect rather than to those requiring wider sympathies [SECTARY]

sec·ta·ry (sékteri:) *pl.* **sec·ta·ries** *n.* a sectarian **Sec·ta·ry** (*Eng. hist.*) a Nonconformist of the 17th and 18th cc. [fr. F. *sectaire* or M.L. *sectarius*]

sec·tion (sékʃən) **1.** *n.* a part cut off or separated by cutting, splitting etc., *a section of an orange* ‖ a division or part, *the woodwind section of an orchestra* ‖ (esp. *med.*) separation by cutting ‖ a division of written or printed matter, *a section of an act* ‖ the symbol (§) denoting this division ‖ a part joined or designed to be joined to others to make a complete structure, *the hut consists of five sections to be bolted together* ‖ a distinct part of a community, country etc., *the industrial section of the nation* ‖ a thin slice prepared for study through a microscope ‖ (*mil.*) a subdivision of a platoon etc. ‖ (*geom.*) the plane figure produced by the cutting of a solid by a plane ‖ a drawing or description of any object as it would look if cut through by a plane ‖ one square mile of land forming 1/36 of a township ‖ (*rail.*) a division of a sleeping car, consisting of an upper and a lower berth ‖ (*bookbinding*) a signature (sheet of pages) **2.** *v.t.* to cut into or arrange in sections [F. or fr. L. *sectio* (*sectionis*), a cutting]

sec·tion·al (sékʃən'l) *adj.* relating to or characteristic of a particular section of something ‖ divided into sections **séc·tion·al·ism** *n.* exaggerated loyalty to a particular section of a country, inordinate local fervor

sec·tor (séktər) **1.** *n.* the plane figure bounded by two radii of a circle and the intercepted arc ‖ a mathematical instrument consisting of two rulers marked off in several scales and hinged together || a division or section, e.g. a subdivision of a military zone, or a distinct part of an economy || an astronomical instrument for measuring angles, consisting of a graduated arc with a telescope at its center **2.** *v.t.* to divide into sectors || *v.i.* (of bacteria and fungi) to form colonies of different sectors [L.L.]

sec·to·ri·al (sektɔ́ri:əl, sektóuri:əl) **1.** *adj.* (esp. of one of the premolar teeth) designed for cutting **2.** *n.* a sectorial tooth [fr. Mod. L. *sectorius*]

sectorial *adj.* of, relating to or consisting of a sector || (*biol.*, of a chimera) made up of different tissues, a section of one kind of tissue being inserted in the main body [SECTOR]

sec·u·lar (sékjulər) **1.** *adj.* of or concerned with temporal, worldly matters rather than with religion || profane (as distinct from sacred), *secular music* || (*eccles.*) not belonging to a religious order (cf. REGULAR) || not under the control of a religious body, *secular schools* || of a change or event which occurs once during a century or other long period of time || lasting or continuing over such a long period **2.** *n.* (*eccles.*) a member of the secular clergy **séc·u·lar·ism** *n.* the belief that religious influence should be restricted, and in particular that education, morality, the state etc. should be independent of religion **séc·u·lar·ist** *n.* **sec·u·lar·is·tic** *adj.* [O.F. *seculer* and fr. L. *saecularis*]

secular humanism belief in rational man as a source of his own salvation and a rejection of the supernatural; used esp. by the so-called New Right during the early 1980s

sec·u·lar·i·ty (sekjulǽriti:) *pl.* **sec·u·lar·i·ties** *n.* the quality or state of being secular || a matter or affair that is secular [F. *sécularité* or fr. M.L. *saecularitas*]

sec·u·lar·i·za·tion (sekjulərizéiʃən) *n.* a secularizing or being secularized [fr. F. *sécularisation*]

sec·u·lar·ize (sékjuləraiz) *pres. part.* **sec·u·lar·iz·ing** *past* and *past part.* **sec·u·lar·ized** *v.t.* to make secular, e.g. to transfer from the control or use of the Church to that of the State [A.F. *séculariser*]

se·cund (sí:kʌnd, sékʌnd) *adj.* (*biol.*, e.g. of a plant's flowers) arranged on one side only || (*biol.*) having some part (e.g. the flowers) on one side only [fr. L. *secundus*, following]

se·cure (sikjúər) **1.** *adj.* completely safe || sure, certain || fixed firmly **2.** *v. pres. part.* **se·cur·ing** *past* and *past part.* **se·cured** *v.t.* to make secure against injury, loss etc., *he secured the prisoner with ropes* || to make firm, *to secure a fastening* || to guarantee, *to secure a loan* || to get possession of, *to secure a good seat* || *v.i.* (of a ship) to tie up, berth [fr. L. *securus*]

Securities and Exchange Commission (*abbr.* SEC) (1934) U.S. federal agency that oversees the securities and financial markets. Mandated by the Securities Act of 1933, the SEC requires registration statements with 'full and fair disclosure' for all offerings. It regulates securities exchanges and sets the rules for activities such as selling short, stock options, floor trading and specialists' and odd-lot dealers' transactions. The SEC was empowered to regulate electric and gas utility holding companies by the Public Utility Holding Company Act (1935), mutual funds by the Investment Company Act (1940) and investment counselors' practices by the Investment Advisers Act (1940). It is governed by five commissioners (one of whom is appointed chairman), appointed by the President with Senate approval

se·cu·ri·ty (sikjúəriti:) *pl.* **se·cu·ri·ties** *n.* freedom from danger or anxiety || something given or pledged as a guarantee, esp. for the payment of a debt || a person who stands as guarantor || something which guarantees or safeguards || protective measures against espionage || (esp. *pl.*) a bond, stock certificate etc. given as evidence of a debt or of property [fr. L. *securitas*]

Security Council the executive organ of the U.N., with primary responsibility for international peace and security. It has 11 members, of which China, France, Britain, the U.S.A. and the U.S.S.R. are permanent and the other six are elected for terms of two years. On all matters other than procedural ones, its decisions must not have a negative vote of any of the five permanent members

Se·daine (sədɛn), Michel-Jean (1719-97), French dramatist. His best-known play is 'le Philosophe sans le savoir' (1765)

Se·dan (sədã) a town (pop. 22,000) of N.E. France, in Ardennes department. It was the scene of the surrender (1870) of the French army to the Prussians in the Franco-Prussian War. The German army broke through here (1940), turning the Maginot line

se·dan (sidǽn) *n.* (*Am.*=*Br.* saloon) an automobile with a large closed body, a hard roof, and no internal partitions || (*hist.*) a sedan chair [etym. doubtful]

sedan chair (*hist.*) a canopied chair for one person, carried on poles by two bearers, one before the passenger and one behind, in use in the 17th and 18th cc.

se·date (sidéit) *adj.* characterized by or showing calm dignity, without any appearance of haste, excitement or confusion [fr. L. *sedare* (*sedatus*), to settle]

se·da·tion (sidéiʃən) *n.* (*med.*) a calming or being calmed, esp. by the use of a sedative [F. *sédation* or fr. L. *sedatio* (*sedationis*)]

sed·a·tive (sédətiv) **1.** *adj.* soothing, reducing excitement or nervousness **2.** *n.* something that soothes in this way, esp. a drug [F. *sédatif* or fr. M.L. *sedativus*]

sed·en·tar·i·ly (sęd'ntéərilí:, séd'ntęrili:) *adv.* in a sedentary way

sed·en·tar·i·ness (séd'ntęrí:nis) *n.* the quality or state of being sedentary

sed·en·tar·y (séd'ntęrí:) *adj.* involving a great deal of sitting, *a sedentary occupation* || accustomed, or compelled to sit for much or all of the time, *the accident made him sedentary* || (*zool.*, e.g. of a mollusk) remaining attached by a base to a solid surface || (*zool.*) remaining in the same region, not migratory [fr. F. *sédentaire*]

Se·der (séidər) *n.* a Jewish ceremonial dinner held esp. at home, on the first night of Passover, to commemorate the Exodus. It is repeated on the second night by most Orthodox Jews [Heb. *sēdher*, order, division]

sedge (sedʒ) *n.* any of several members of *Cyperaceae*, a family of coarse, solid-stemmed grasses growing in swampy places, esp. a member of genus *Carex* || these plants collectively [O.E. *secg*]

Sedge·moor, Battle of (sédʒmųər) a battle (1685) in which James II of England defeated a rebellion led by the duke of Monmouth

sedge warbler *Acrocephalus schoenobaenus*, a small, brown and white warbler of Europe and Asia, nesting in dense, swampy thickets. Its song is loud and sweet

se·dil·i·a (sedíli:ə) *sing.* **se·di·le** (sedą·ili:) *pl. n.* a set of (usually three) seats on the south side of the chancel of a church, for the use of officiating clergy during intervals of the service [L. fr. *sedere*, to sit]

sed·i·ment (sédəmənt) *n.* matter that, because of its greater density, sinks to the bottom of an undisturbed liquid with which it was previously mixed || (*geol.*) matter or a mass of matter deposited by wind, glaciers etc. **sed·i·men·ta·ry** (sędəméntəri:) *adj.* of matter thus deposited [F. *sédiment*]

sedimentary rock rock formed from fragments of other rocks, by precipitation from solutions, or by organic secretion (cf. IGNEOUS ROCK, cf. METAMORPHIC ROCK)

sed·i·men·ta·tion (sędəmentéiʃən) *n.* the act or process of settling as a sediment || the movement of finely divided solid particles through a fluid, under the influence of a gravitational or other force (*CENTRIFUGE)

se·di·tion (sidíʃən) *n.* the inciting of hostility against the government, likely to cause rebellion or insurrection, but not amounting to treason [O.F. fr. L. *seditio* (*seditionis*)]

se·di·tious (sidíʃəs) *adj.* of, tending toward or guilty of sedition [fr. O.F. *séditieux*]

se·duce (sidú:s, sidjú:s) *pres. part.* **se·duc·ing** *past* and *past part.* **se·duced** *v.t.* to cause by persuasion or enticement (someone, esp. a girl who is a virgin) to have sexual intercourse with one || to persuade (a person) to act contrary to the principles by which he normally abides [fr. L. *seducere*, to lead aside or away]

se·duc·tion (sidʌ́kʃən) *n.* a seducing or being seduced || something seductive, *the seductions of wealth* [F. *séduction* or fr. L. *seductio* (*seductionis*)]

se·duc·tive (sidʌ́ktiv) *adj.* tempting [fr. L. *seducere* (*seductus*), to lead aside or away]

se·du·li·ty (sidú:liti:, sidjú:liti:) *n.* the quality of being sedulous || sedulous behavior [fr. L. *sedulitas*]

sed·u·lous (sédʒuləs) *adj.* diligent, painstaking, assiduous [fr. L. *sedulus*]

se·dum (sí:dəm) *n.* a member of *Sedum*, fam. *Crassulaceae*, a genus of fleshy-leaved plants, cultivated for their foliage and their yellow, pink or white flowers [L. = houseleek]

see (si:) *n.* a bishop's diocese, or his office [O.F. *sé*, *sed*]

see *pres. part.* **see·ing** *past* **saw** (sɔ) *past part.* **seen** (si:n) *v.t.* to perceive with the eye || to form a mental picture of || to understand, *I see your point* || to imagine as having the character or capacities necessary for some specified activity, position etc., *I can't see her as an actress* || to find out, *go and see what he wants* || to attend as a spectator, *to see a baseball game* || to watch on television, *did you see the fight last night?* || to examine, *let me see your papers* || to receive (a person), *the doctor will see you now* || to call on, arrange to be received by (a person), *you must see your dentist* || to meet, *I'll see you at the races* || (with 'that') to make sure by taking care, *see that you pay attention* || to escort, *to see someone home* || to have or obtain knowledge or experience of, *she has seen a lot of life* || (*cards*) to accept (a bet) by betting an equal sum || (*cards*) to meet the bet of (another player) in this way || *v.i.* to have the power of perceiving things with the eye || to perceive objects, colors etc., e.g. at a given distance || to understand, *now do you see?* || to try to find out something to reflect about something, *let me see* **to see about** to attend to || to make inquiries about **to see after** to attend to, *see after the dinner* **to see into** to investigate || to perceive true nature of **to see (someone) off** to escort (someone) to the point of departure **to see out** to wait till the end of || to finish, complete **to see through** to be undeceived and understand the true meaning or nature of (something)´ without being misled, *to see through someone's fine phrases* || to help (someone) to overcome a difficulty, *he promised to see his client through the lawsuit* || to finish, *you must see the task through, once you start* [O.E. *sēon*]

See·beck effect (sí:bek, zéibek) (*phys.*) the generation of an electric current in a circuit consisting of two different metals in successive contact when the junctions are at different temperatures. It is the principle of the thermoelectric thermometer, thermopile etc. [after Thomas Johann *Seebeck*, G. physicist and inventor of the thermocouple]

seed (si:d) **1.** *pl.* **seed, seeds** *n.* the fertilized ovule of a plant and its covering. The seed contains a miniature plant capable of independent development into a plant similar to the one which produced it || a spore or dry seedlike fruit || seeds collectively || (*rhet.*) semen || a beginning or source, *seeds of discontent* || (*Bible*) descendants, *the seed of David* || seed oysters || (*chem.*) a small crystal added to a solution to induce crystallization **to go** (or **run**) **to seed** (of a plant) to develop seeds at the expense of foliage or further flowers || (of a person) to become lazy, feckless, slovenly etc. by gradual loss of self-respect **2.** *v.t.* to take the seeds out of (fruit) || to sow with seed || to sprinkle with seed || to sprinkle chemicals in (clouds) in order to induce rain to fall || (*sports*, esp. *tennis*) to select (players) so that those likely to be matched in the later stages do not play against one another in the early stages of a tournament || *v.i.* (of a plant) to arrive at the stage when seed matures || to shed seed **3.** *adj.* (of a crop) grown for production of seed or set aside for use as seed [O.E. *sǣd*]

seed·bed (sí:dbęd) *n.* a bed of soil in which seedlings are raised

seed·cake (sí:dkęik) *n.* cake flavored with caraway or other seeds

seed·case (sí:dkęis) *n.* a pod

seed coat the covering of a seed

seed drill a drill (agricultural machine)

seed·er (sí:dər) *n.* a device that sows seed || a device used to remove seed from fruit

seed·i·ly (sí:dilí:) *adv.* in a seedy manner

seed·i·ness (sí:dí:nis) *n.* the quality or state of being seedy

seed leaf a cotyledon

seed·ling (sí:dliŋ) *n.* a young plant grown from seed (rather than from a cutting etc.) || a young tree under 3 ft in height

seed·man (sí:dmən) *pl.* **seed·men** (sí:dmən) *n.* a seedsman

seed money funds to initiate a business or nonprofit undertaking under the assumption that major financing will be forthcoming later

seed oyster a young oyster ready for transplanting

seed pearl a pearl weighing less than ¼ grain

CONCISE PRONUNCIATION KEY: **(a)** æ, *cat*; ɑ, *car*; ɔ *fawn*; ei, *snake*. **(e)** e, *hen*; i:, *sheep*; iə, *deer*; ɛə, *bear*. **(i)** i, *fish*; ai, *tiger*; ə:, *bird*. **(o)** o, *ox*; au, *cow*; ou, *goat*; u, *poor*; ɔi, *royal*. **(u)** ʌ, *duck*; u, *bull*; u:, *goose*; ə, *bacillus*; ju:, *cube*. x, *loch*; θ, *think*; ð, *bother*; z, *Zen*; ʒ, *corsage*; dʒ, *savage*; ŋ, *orangutang*; j, *yak*; ʃ, *fish*; tʃ, *fetch*; 'l, *rabble*; 'n, *redden*. Complete pronunciation key appears inside front cover.

seed plant a spermatophyte
seeds·man (sí:dzmən) *pl.* **seeds·men** (sí:dzmən) *n.* a dealer in seeds and other horticultural supplies
seed vessel a pericarp
seed·y (sí:dí:) *comp.* **seed·i·er** *superl.* **seed·i·est** *adj.* having abundant seeds ‖ having run to seed ‖ shabby and in an uncared-for state ‖ in rather poor health
see·ing (sí:iŋ) **1.** *n.* the power or faculty of vision ‖ the act of someone who sees **2.** *adj.* able to see **3.** *conj.* (usually with 'that') since, considering, *seeing that it is so late you had better go*
seek (si:k) *pres. part.* **seek·ing** *past* and *past part.* **sought** (sɔt) *v.t.* to try to find, *to seek shelter* ‖ to ask for, *to seek advice* ‖ to try to obtain, *he seeks recognition of his work* ‖ (with *infin.*) to try, *to seek to establish a fact* ‖ *v.i.* (with 'for') to try to find, *I am seeking for information* [O.E. *sēcan*]
Seek Bus (*mil.*) a coordinated communications system for all U.S. armed forces linking intelligence and weapons systems for tactical purposes
seeker *n.* (*mil.*) a homing device that locates its target by heat or other radiation
seem (si:m) *v.i.* to give the impression of being something of a specified kind or of having a specified attribute, *she seems a complete fool, he seems happy* ‖ (with *infin.*) to give an impression of something specified, *he seems to have a cold* ‖ (with *infin.*) to have an impression that one is doing or being something specified, *I seem to smell something burning, I seem to be tired today* ‖ to have the appearance of being true, *it seems he died rich* ‖ (in constructions beginning with 'there') to have the appearance of existing, *there seems no reason for believing him* **séem·ing 1.** *adj.* having the false appearance of being, *a seeming friend though a secret enemy* **2.** *n.* appearance, esp. false appearance **séem·ing·ly** *adv.* truly as far as can be judged [M.E. *seme* fr. O.N. *sœma*]
seem·li·ness (sí:mlí:nis) *n.* the quality or state of being seemly
seem·ly (sí:mlí:) *comp.* **seem·li·er** *superl.* **seem·li·est** *adj.* conforming to accepted standards of behavior or appearance [M.E. fr. O.N. *sœmiligr*]
seen *past part.* of SEE
seep (si:p) **1.** *v.i.* (of a fluid) to pass slowly through a porous body **2.** *n.* a place where water or petroleum seeps up out of the ground to form a pool **séep·age** *n.* the act or an instance of seeping ‖ fluid that has seeped through something [perh. fr. O.E. *sipian*, to soak]
se·er (sí:ər, sír) *n.* (*rhet.*) a wise man gifted with powers of divination [SEE v.]
seer·suck·er (síərsʌkər) *n.* a thin linen, cotton or rayon fabric with a crinkly surface, often having thin stripes with a flat surface [E. Indian corrup. of Pers. *shīr o shakkar*, milk and sugar, a striped linen garment]
see·saw (sí:sɔ) **1.** *n.* a plank balanced in the center with its ends free to rise and fall alternately so that a person sitting at one end rises up in the air as one sitting at the other end sinks towards the ground ‖ this alternate rising and falling as a children's amusement ‖ a back-and-forth or up-and-down movement ‖ any situation in which two factors alternately rise and fall or take leading and inferior positions, *the seesaw of supply and demand* **2.** *v.i.* to rise and fall alternately on or as if on a seesaw ‖ *v.t.* to cause to do this **3.** *adj.* moving up and down as if on a seesaw [reduplication of SAW v.]
see-saw principle (*mil.*) tendency of defensive weapons development to overtake offensive weapons development, and vice versa
seethe (sí:ð) *pres. part.* **seeth·ing** *past* and *past part.* **seethed** *v.i.* to bubble violently as if boiling, *seething waters* ‖ to be in a state of rage or turmoil ‖ to be in restless commotion, *seething crowds* [O.E. *sēothan*]
seg academies (seg) *n.* private secular schools established to evade desegregation laws affecting public schools
Se·gal (sí:gəl), George (1924-), U.S. sculptor known for his life-sized, lifelike, white plaster figures of people, usually set in everyday situations. Part of the 'New Realist' school of artists of the 1960s, he exhibited in significant shows of that time. His works include 'Cinema' (1963), a man changing a movie marquee, and 'The Diner' (1964-6), figures on stools at a counter
seg·gar (ségər) *n.* (*Br.*) a saggar
seg·ment (ségmənt) **1.** *n.* a part, esp. a part separable at a natural junction (e.g. at a joint) ‖ (*geom.*) the part of a circle cut off by a chord, or of a sphere cut off by a plane ‖ (*geom.*) the finite part of a line between two points in the line **2.** *v.t.* to separate (something) into segments ‖ *v.i.* to separate into segments ‖ (*biol.*) to undergo cleavage **seg·men·tal** (segmént'l), **seg·men·tar·y** (ségməntẹri:) *adjs* **seg·men·ta·tion** (sẹgməntéiʃən) *n.* separation into segments, e.g. in the cleavage of a cell or ovum [fr. L. *segmentum*]
Se·go·vi·a (segóvjɑ) a province (area 2,635 sq. miles, pop. 149,286) of N. Central Spain (*OLD CASTILE) ‖ its capital (pop. 41,880): Roman aqueduct. Romanesque churches, 16th-c. cathedral
Se·grè (səgrèi), Emilio Gino (1905-), U.S. physicist and co-winner (with Owen Chamberlain) of the 1959 Nobel prize in physics for his discovery of the antiproton
seg·re·gate (ségrəgeit) *pres. part.* **seg·re·gat·ing** *past* and *past part.* **seg·re·gat·ed** *v.t.* to separate from others of a group, esp. to oblige (racial groups) to carry on their activities, schooling etc. separately ‖ *v.i.* to be or become segregated ‖ (*biol.*, of chromosome genes) to separate in meiosis **ség·re·gat·ed** *adj.* conforming to a policy of racial segregation [fr. L. *segregare* (*segregatus*), to set apart from the flock]
seg·re·ga·tion (sẹgrigéiʃən) *n.* a segregating or being segregated ‖ a segregated part, group etc. ‖ (*biol.*) the separation of genes of chromosomes at meiosis **seg·re·gá·tion·ist** *n.* a person who believes in racial segregation [fr. L.L. *segregatio* (*segregationis*), a setting apart]
seg·re·ga·tive (ségrigeitiv) *adj.* relating to, causing or characterized by segregation [fr. M.L. *segregativus*]
se·gui·dil·la (sẹigədí:ljə, sẹigədí:jə) *n.* a Spanish poem of a form employing four to seven short lines ‖ a Spanish dance accompanied by castanets ‖ the music for it, in triple time [Span. fr. *seguida*, sequence]
sei·cen·to (seitʃéntou, setʃéntɔ) *n.* the 17th century in Italian art or literary history [Ital.=six hundred, used for sixteen hundred]
seiche (seiʃ) *n.* an oscillation of the surface in a lake, caused by barometric pressure changes [F. perh. fr. G.]
Seid·litz powder (sédlits) a preparation consisting of two powders, one of tartaric acid, the other of a mixture of sodium bicarbonate and Rochelle salt, which effervesce when mixed together in water, the effervescing liquid being drunk as a mild aperient **Seid·litz powders** Seidlitz powder [after *Seidlitz*, town in Czechoslovakia]
sei·gneur (senjə́:r, senjə:r) *n.* (*hist.*) a feudal lord in France or Canada ‖ a lord of the manor in the Channel Is **sei·gneur·i·al** (seinjə́:rí:əl) *adj.* [F.]
sei·gneur·y (séinjərí:) *pl.* **sei·gneur·ies** *n.* (*hist.*) the territory or estate of a feudal lord, esp. an estate held in Canada by feudal tenure (up to 1854), or the manor house itself ‖ the domain of a seigneur in the Channel Is [fr. F. *seigneurie*]
sei·gnior (séinjɔr) *n.* (*hist.*) the feudal lord of a manor [A.F. *segnour*, O.F. *seignor*]
sei·gnior·age, sei·gnor·age (séinjəridʒ) *n.* (*hist.*) seigniorial prerogative, e.g. the royal right to a percentage levy on bullion used for coinage ‖ the profit made in coining, resulting from the difference between a coin's intrinsic and its face value, as a source of revenue to a government [O.F. *seignorage*]
sei·gnio·ri·al, sei·gno·ri·al (seinjɔ́rí:əl, seinjóurí:əl) *adj.* of or pertaining to a seignior or sovereign
sei·gnior·y, sei·gnor·y (séinjərí:) *pl.* **sei·gnior·ies, sei·gnor·ies** *n.* (*hist.*) the dominion or rights of a seignior [O.F. *seignorie*]
seignorage *SEIGNIORAGE
seignorial *SEIGNIORIAL
Seine (sen, *Eng.* sein) a river (485 miles long) rising near Dijon, E. France, and flowing northwest to the English Channel. Canals link it with the Scheldt, Meuse, Rhine, Saône, Rhône and Loire. Ports: Le Havre, Rouen, Paris
seine (sein) **1.** *n.* a large fishing net, with floats on one edge and weights on the other to make it hang upright in the water. The fish are enclosed in the net when the ends are brought together **2.** *v.t.* and *i. pres. part.* **sein·ing** *past* and *past part.* **seined** to fish with a seine [O.E. *segne*]
Seine-et-Marne (seneimærn) a department (area 2,275 sq. miles, pop. 755,800) in N. France (*ILE-DE-FRANCE). Chief town: Melun
Seine-Ma·ri·time (senmɑri:ti:m) a department (area 2,448 sq. miles, pop. 1,082,300) in N. France (*NORMANDY). Chief town: Rouen
seise (*law*) *SEIZE
seisin *SEIZIN
seis·mal (sáizməl, sáisməl) *adj.* seismic
seis·mic (sáizmik, sáismik) *adj.* relating to, characteristic of or produced by an earthquake or earthquakes **séis·mi·cal** *adj.* **séis·mism** *n.* phenomena characteristic of earthquakes [fr. Gk *seismos*, earthquake]
seis·mo·gram (sáizməgræm, sáisməgræm) *n.* a record made by a seismograph [fr. Gk *seismos*, earthquake +*gramma*, a letter]
seis·mo·graph (sáizməgræf, sáizməgrɑf, sáisməgræf, sáisməgrɑf) *n.* an instrument for recording the period, magnitude and direction of earth tremors **seis·mo·graph·ic** (sạizməgræ̀fik, sạisməgræ̀fik) *adj.* **seis·mog·ra·phy** (saizmɔ́grəfi, saismɔ́grəfi:) *n.* [fr. Gk *seismos*, earthquake + *graphos*, written]
seis·mo·log·ic (sạizməlɔ́dʒik, sạisməlɔ́dʒik) *adj.* of or relating to seismology **seis·mo·lóg·i·cal** *adj.*
seis·mol·o·gy (saizmɔ́lədʒi:, saismɔ́lədʒi:) *n.* the scientific study of earthquakes or of artificially induced earth tremors [fr. Gk *seismos*, earthquake+*logos*, discourse]
seis·mom·e·ter (saizmɔ́mitər, saismɔ́mitər) *n.* an instrument, usually part of a seismograph, which supplies data for measurement of actual ground movements of an earthquake [fr. Gk *seismos*, earthquake + *metron*, measure]
seiz·a·ble (sí:zəb'l) *adj.* able to be seized (used esp. of goods that may lawfully be seized)
seize (si:z) *pres. part.* **seiz·ing** *past* and *past part.* **seized** *v.t.* to take suddenly and hold firmly ‖ to take by force, *he seized his sister's toy* ‖ (*law*) to take legal possession of, *to seize contraband* ‖ (*law*) to put in possession of ‖ to overwhelm mentally, take sudden mental possession of, *panic seized him* ‖ (often with 'on' or 'upon') to make instant use to one's advantage of (some chance, occasion, opportunity etc.), *to seize upon an excuse* ‖ to arrive at an immediate or sudden understanding of (a meaning etc.), *to seize a point* ‖ (*naut.*) to fasten with ropes **to seize up** (of moving mechanical parts) to become locked together because of undue heat, pressure or friction [O.F. *saisir, seisir*]
sei·zin, sei·sin (sí:zin) *n.* (*law*) possession or taking possession of land by freehold ‖ (*law*) the land so possessed [F. *saisine*]
seiz·ing (sí:ziŋ) *n.* (*naut.*) a fastening together with cords ‖ (*naut.*) cords used for this
sei·zor (sí:zər, sí:zɔr) *n.* (*law*) a person who takes possession of a freehold estate
sei·zure (sí:ʒər) *n.* a seizing or being seized ‖ a sudden attack of an illness, e.g. of epilepsy
se·jant (sí:dʒənt) *adj.* (*heraldry*, of an animal) sitting with the forelegs upright [older *seiant* fr. O.F.]
Sek·on·di-Ta·ko·ra·di (sẹkəndí:tạkərάdi:) a seaport and commercial center (pop. 160,900) of W. Ghana with an artificial deep-water harbor
se·lah (sí:lə, sélə) *n.* (*Bible*) a word, possibly denoting a musical rest, found at the end of a stanza in Psalms and in Habakkuk [Heb.]
Se·lan·gor (səlάngɔr, səlάŋgour) a state (area 3,167 sq. miles, pop. 1,467,441) of Malaysia in W. Malaya. Capital: Kuala Lumpur. Selangor came under British protection (1874) and joined the Federation of Malaya (1948)
sel·dom (séldəm) *adv.* not often, rarely, *seldom at a loss* [O.E. *seldan*]
se·lect (silékt) **1.** *v.t.* to take (something or someone preferred, most suitable etc.) from among a number, *to select a book from the shelf* **2.** *adj.* having been selected as the most preferred ‖ socially exclusive, *a select resort* ‖ selecting carefully, discriminating, *select in his choice of books* [fr. L. *seligere* (*selectus*), to collect]
select committee a group of members of a legislative body chosen to study and report on a particular matter
Selected Reserve (*mil.*) the portion of the Ready Reserve consisting of units and individual Reservists required to participate in paid inactive-duty training periods and annual training
se·lec·tion (silékʃən) *n.* a selecting or being selected ‖ something selected ‖ (*biol.*) the natural or artificial process by which some members of a species reproduce while others do not, the result being a perpetuation of the characteristics of those who do reproduce (*NATURAL SELECTION) [fr. L. *selectio* (*selectionis*)]
selection fee a finder's fee

CONCISE PRONUNCIATION KEY: **(a)** æ, *cat*; ɑ, *car*; ɔ *fawn*; ei, *snake*. **(e)** e, *hen*; i:, *sheep*; iə, *deer*; εə, *bear*. **(i)** i, *fish*; ai, *tiger*; ə:, *bird*. **(o)** o, *ox*; au, *cow*; ou, *goat*; u, *poor*; ɔi, *royal*. **(u)** ʌ, *duck*; u, *bull*; u:, *goose*; ə, *bacillus*; ju:, *cube*. x, *loch*; θ, *think*; ð, *bother*; z, *Zen*; ʒ, *corsage*; dʒ, *savage*; ŋ, *orangutang*; j, *yak*; ʃ, *fish*; tʃ, *fetch*; 'l, *rabble*; 'n, *redden*. Complete pronunciation key appears inside front cover.

selection pressure the magnitude of evolutionary pressure, separately measured as the rate at which one allele replaces another; coined by J. B. S. Haldane and R. A. Fisher

se·lec·tive (siléktiv) *adj.* discriminating, tending to select, *he is selective in the towns he visits* ‖ (*radio*) of or designating the ability of a circuit to eliminate all unwanted frequencies

selective service compulsory military service according to age, physical fitness, occupation etc.

Selective Training and Service Act (1940), a U.S. Congressional act which adopted peacetime conscription for the first time in the U.S.A.

se·lec·tiv·i·ty (silektíviti:) *n.* the quality of being select ‖ the extent to which a radio is selective

se·lect·man (siléktmən) *pl.* **se·lect·men** (siléktmən) *n.* an elected member of an administration board in towns of New England

Se·le·ne (silí:ni:) (*Gk mythol.*) the goddess of the moon, identified with the Roman Luna, and later with Artemis

se·le·nic (silí:nik, silénik) *adj.* of or containing selenium, esp. of compounds where this has a higher valence than in selenious compounds

selenic acid an acid, H_2SeO_4, resembling concentrated sulfuric acid in appearance, but so powerful an oxidizer when concentrated that it attacks gold and platinum

se·le·ni·ous (silí:ni:əs) *adj.* of or containing selenium, esp. of compounds where this has a valence lower than in selenic compounds

selenious acid a colorless crystalline acid, H_2SeO_3, an oxidizing agent yielding selenium

sel·e·nite (sélənait, silí:nait) *n.* a transparent crystalline variety of gypsum [fr. L. *selenites* fr. Gk *selēnitēs* (*lithos*), moon (stone)]

selenite *n.* a salt or ester of selenious acid [SELENIUM]

se·le·ni·um (silí:ni:əm) *n.* a nonmetallic element (symbol Se, at. no. 34, at. mass 78.96) obtained as a by-product of the refining of copper by electrolysis, and used in its crystalline form in the photoelectric cell, since its electrical resistance varies with the intensity of its illumination [Mod. L. fr. Gk *selēnē*, moon]

sel·en·o·de·sy (sələnɒ́dəsi:) *n.* (*math.*) the branch of applied mathematics that determines, by observation and measurement, the positions of points and areas of portions of the moon's surface and the shape and size of the moon —**selenodetic** *adj.* —**selenodesist** *n.*

sel·e·nog·ra·pher (sələnɒ́grəfər) *n.* a specialist in selenography

se·le·no·graph·ic (sili:nəgrǽfik) *adj.* relating to selenography

se·le·nog·ra·phy (sələnɒ́grəfi:) *n.* the scientific study of the moon's physical features [fr. Mod. L. *selenographia* fr. Gk *selēnē*, moon + *-graphos*, written]

sel·e·nol·o·gy (sələnɒ́lədʒi:) *n.* the branch of astronomy dealing with the moon [fr. Gk *selēnē*, moon +*logos*, discourse]

Se·leu·cia (silú:ʃə) the ancient capital of the Seleucids, and then of the Parthians, near Baghdad. It was founded (c. 312 B.C.) by Seleucus I

Se·leu·cid (silú:sid) a member of a Macedonian dynasty (312-65 B.C.) in Syria and western Asia, founded by Seleucus I. Under the Seleucids, Greek language and culture were introduced into Syria. Their rule ended when Antiochus XIII was defeated by Pompey (65 B.C.) and Syria became a Roman province

Se·leu·cus I (silú:kəs) (*d.* 280 B.C.), king of Syria (312-280 B.C.). One of Alexander the Great's generals, he received Babylonia when the Macedonian Empire broke up (312 B.C.), extended his power over much of Asia Minor and Syria, and founded the Seleucid dynasty

self- (self) *prefix* of, by, to, with or for oneself or itself ‖ automatic ‖ independent [O.E. *self-, sylf-*]

self 1. *adj.* (*bot.*) being of the same color throughout ‖ of the same kind, material, color etc. as the rest **2.** *n. pl.* **selves** (selvz) the individuality or nature of a person or thing ‖ a person's nature or an aspect of it, as revealed by his behavior etc., *he showed his true self* ‖ a person with respect to his full mental or physical health, *he is his old self again* ‖ personal advantage, *to put service to others before self* ‖ (*biol.*) an individual resulting from self-fertilization ‖ (*biol.*) a self-colored individual **3.** *pron.* myself, himself or herself, *a struggle to keep self and family going* [O.E. *self, selfa*]

self-a·ban·don·ment (sélfəbǽndənmənt) *n.* the act or state of forgetting selfish desires ‖ an emotional state in which the self is heedless of its proper good

self-a·base·ment (sélfəbéismənt) *n.* a humbling of oneself

self-ab·ne·ga·tion (sélfæbnəgéiʃən) *n.* the quality of acting counter to one's desires for oneself in order to serve someone else, others, a cause etc.

self-a·buse (sélfəbjú:s) *n.* masturbation

self-act·ing (sélfǽktiŋ) *adj.* automatic, acting by itself

self-ac·tu·al·i·za·tion (selfæktʃu:əlizéiʃən) *n.* (*psych.*) the process of understanding oneself and developing one's capacities and talents; coined by Abraham Maslow

self-ad·dressed (sélfədrést) *adj.* (of an envelope) addressed by the sender to himself, and enclosed with a letter so as to facilitate or solicit a reply

self-ad·he·sive (sélfədhí:siv) *adj.* (of an envelope) able to be sealed without any moistening of the surfaces treated with an adhesive

self-ap·point·ed (sélfəpɔ́intid) *adj.* acting without outside authority, usually for the pleasure of bestowing blame or criticism

self-as·ser·tion (sélfəsə́:rʃən) *n.* behavior asserting one's claims or rights, expressing confidence in one's proper merit or aggressively asserting the superior quality of one's own mind or body **sélf-as·sér·tive** *adj.*

self-as·sur·ance (sélfəʃúərəns) *n.* self-confidence **sélf-as·súred** *adj.*

self-cen·tered *Br.* **self-cen·tred** (sélfséntərd) *adj.* thinking primarily or solely of what concerns oneself, seeing oneself as at the center of a situation

self-col·ored *Br.* **self-col·oured** (sélfkʌ́lərd) *adj.* (of animals, flowers, fabrics etc.) of one color throughout

self-com·mand (sélfkəmǽnd, sélfkəmɑ́nd) *n.* self-control

self-com·pla·cen·cy (sélfkəmpléis'nsi:) *n.* self-satisfaction **sélf-com·plá·cent** *adj.*

self-com·posed (sélfkəmpóuzd) *adj.* having one's emotions under control

self-con·ceit (sélfkənsí:t) *n.* the quality of having too high an opinion of oneself

self-con·fi·dence (sélfkɒ́nfidəns) *n.* reliance on one's capacities **sélf-cón·fi·dent** *adj.*

self-con·scious (sélfkɒ́nʃəs) *adj.* thinking of one's own appearance or behavior as these may be assessed by others ‖ embarrassed at the thought that one is making a poor impression in one's social relations ‖ (of artistic style) knowingly artificial

self-con·tained (selfkəntéind) *adj.* complete in itself ‖ (*Br.*, of an apartment etc.) having its own entrance and all necessary living facilities ‖ (of a person) not offering or dependent on contact with others

self-con·tra·dic·tion (sélfkɒntrədíkʃən) *n.* a proposition which contains within itself two statements which contradict one another ‖ contradiction of oneself **sélf-con·tra·díc·to·ry** *adj.*

self-con·trol (sélfkəntróul) *n.* the ability to exercise the will so as to prevent oneself from expressing strong emotion or acting impulsively

self-de·ceit (sélfdisí:t) *n.* self-deception

self-de·cep·tion (sélfdisépʃən) *n.* the act or state of deceiving oneself

self-de·feat·ing (sélfdifí:tiŋ) *adj.* initiated by oneself but having the effect of making one's purposes hard or impossible to attain

self-de·fense, *Br.* **self-de·fence** (sélf-diféns) *n.* a defending of one's life, property or reputation ‖ (*law*) the right to defend oneself with the necessary force against violence or a threat of violence **sélf-defén·sive** *adj.*

self-de·lu·sion (sélfdilú:ʒən) *n.* self-deception

self-de·ni·al (sélfdináiəl) *n.* the deliberate refusal to satisfy one's desires, as a method of disciplining oneself or making it possible to help others, e.g. financially

self-de·ny·ing (sélfdináiiŋ) *adj.* showing self-denial

self-de·struct *v.* to destroy itself —**self-de·struct** *adj.*

self-de·struc·tion (sélfdistrʌ́kʃən) *n.* destruction of oneself, esp. suicide

self-de·ter·mi·na·tion (sélfditə:rminéiʃən) *n.* (*internat. law*) the right of a people to decide its own form of government or political status ‖ the free determining of one's own actions **sélf-de·tér·min·ing** *adj.*

self-de·vo·tion (sélfdivóuʃən) *n.* devotion of oneself to some cause or to the needs, comfort etc. of some other person, usually involving personal sacrifice

self-dis·ci·pline (sélfdísəplin) *n.* the process of training one's emotions and impulses so that they conform to a certain standard of behavior in all circumstances

self-dis·trust (sélfdistrʌ́st) *n.* lack of confidence in one's own abilities, judgment etc.

self-driv·en (sélfdrívən) *adj.* driven by its own motive power

self-ed·u·cat·ed (sélfédʒukeitid) *adj.* having been educated by one's own efforts, without formal teaching

self-ef·face·ment (sélfiféismənt) *n.* the quality or practice of keeping modestly or discreetly in the background

self-em·ployed (sélfemplɔ́id) *adj.* earning a living by working directly for oneself, without being tied to a regular employer by wage or salary

self-es·teem (sélfistí:m) *n.* one's good opinion of one's dignity or worth

self-ev·i·dent (sélfévidənt) *adj.* needing no proof of its truth

self-ex·am·i·na·tion (sélfigzæminéiʃən) *n.* thinking about one's own behavior and motives, esp. to judge them according to an ideal standard

self-ex·e·cut·ing (sélféksikju:tiŋ) *adj.* (of laws) coming into operation independently of any other legislation

self-ex·ist·ence (sélfigzístəns) *n.* the quality of being self-existent

self-ex·ist·ent (sélfigzístənt) *adj.* (of God) existing independently of any other cause or circumstance

self-ex·plain·ing (sélfikspléiniŋ) *adj.* self-explanatory

self-ex·plan·a·to·ry (sélfiksplǽnətɔri:, sélfiksplǽnətouri:) *adj.* (of a statement) containing within itself all that is necessary for the understanding of it

self-ex·pres·sion (sélfikspréʃən) *n.* expression of one's personality, e.g. in artistic form or through educational technique etc., esp. as a way of realizing one's individuality more fully

self-fer·ti·li·za·tion (sélffə:rt'lizéiʃən) *n.* fertilization of a hermaphrodite plant or animal by its own male elements

self-for·get·ful (sélffərgétfəl) *adj.* unselfish ‖ characterized by self-abandonment

self-ful·fill·ment, *Br.* **self-ful·fil·ment** (sélfful-fílmənt) *n.* the complete realization of the potentialities of one's personality ‖ (*loosely*) the satisfaction of one's creative impulses

self-gov·ern·ing (sélfgʌ́vərniŋ) *adj.* (of a state) administering its own government without interference from any other state **sélf-góv·ern·ment** *n.*

self-grat·i·fi·ca·tion (sélfgrætifikéiʃən) *n.* the act of satisfying one's desires

self-hard·en·ing (sélfhɑ́rd'niŋ) *adj.* (*metall.*, of steel) that hardens when raised to a high temperature and then cooled in air

self-help (sélfhélp) *n.* the practice of satisfying one's needs by one's own efforts, without drawing from the resources of the community or state

self·hood (sélfhud) *n.* unique identity, individuality

self-im·por·tance (sélfimpɔ́rt'ns) *n.* an exaggerated estimate of one's worth ‖ behavior manifesting this **sélf-im·pór·tant** *adj.*

self-im·prove·ment (sélfimprú:vmənt) *n.* cultivation of the mind by steady application

self-in·duced (sélfindú:st, sélfindjú:st) *adj.* resulting from one's own or its own activity ‖ (*elec.*) produced by self-induction

self-in·duc·tion (sélfindʌ́kʃən) *n.* (*elec.*) the production of an induced electromotive force in a circuit by changes in the magnetic field resulting from changes in the current flowing in the circuit. The induced electromotive force is proportional to the rate of change of the current

self-in·dul·gence (sélfindʌ́ldʒəns) *n.* a weakening of one's moral strength by satisfying one's desires and appetites too readily **sélf-in·dúl·gent** *adj.*

self-in·ter·est (sélfíntərist, sélfíntrist) *n.* primary concern for what is to one's own advantage, as a motive of behavior **sélf-in·ter·est·ed** *adj.*

sel·fish (sélfiʃ) *adj.* concerned only to satisfy one's own desires and prepared to sacrifice the feelings, needs etc. of others in order to do so ‖ caused by such concern

self-knowl·edge (sélfnɒ́lidʒ) *n.* knowledge of one's own nature, abilities, weaknesses etc.

CONCISE PRONUNCIATION KEY: **(a)** æ, *c*a*t*; ɑ, *car*; ɔ *fawn*; ei, *snake*. **(e)** e, *hen*; i:, *sheep*; iə, *deer*; εə, *bear*. **(i)** i, *fish*; ai, *tiger*; ə:, *bird*. **(o)** ɒ, *ox*; au, *cow*; ou, *goat*; u, *poor*; ɔi, *royal*. **(u)** ʌ, *duck*; u, *bull*; u:, *goose*; ə, *bacillus*; ju:, *cube*. x, *loch*; θ, *think*; ð, *bother*; z, *Zen*; ʒ, *corsage*; dʒ, *savage*; ŋ, *orangutang*; j, *yak*; ʃ, *fish*; tʃ, *fetch*; 'l, *rabble*; 'n, *redden*. Complete pronunciation key appears inside front cover.

self·less (sélflis) *adj.* concerned for others and not for one's own advantage, pleasure, comfort etc.
self-liq·ui·dat·ing (sélflíkwideitiŋ) *adj.* of a business transaction in which stock is swiftly turned into money or in which the original investment is quickly paid off
self-load·ing (sélflóudiŋ) *adj.* (of firearms) semiautomatic
self-love (sélflʌv) *n.* love of oneself ‖ (*philos.*) proper concern for one's own well-being
self-made man (sélfmeid) a man who has materially succeeded in life by his own efforts and capacity without advantages of influential connections etc.
self-mas·ter·y (sélfmǽstəri:, sélfmɑ́stəri:) *n.* self-control
self-mov·ing (sélfmú:viŋ) *adj.* able to move under its own power
self-o·pin·ion·at·ed (sélfəpínjəneitid) *adj.* maintaining one's opinions in conceited obstinacy
self-or·dained (sélfɔrdéind) *adj.* designated by oneself, not by anyone else
self-pit·y (sélfpíti:) *n.* pity for oneself, esp. the belief that one is suffering as the innocent victim of circumstances
self-pol·li·nat·ed (sélfpɒ́lineitid) *adj.* pollinated by the transfer of pollen from anther to stigma of the same flower
self-pos·sessed (sélfpəzést) *adj.* having or showing self-possession
self-pos·ses·sion (sélfpəzéʃən) *n.* serene self-control ‖ presence of mind
self-pres·er·va·tion (sélfprezərvéiʃən) *n.* the instinct to avoid being injured or killed
self-pro·nounc·ing (sélfprənáunsiŋ) *adj.* having diacritical marks of pronunciation applied to the original spelling instead of being rewritten in a phonetic transcription
self-pro·pelled (sélfprəpéld) *adj.* (of a gun) mounted on a tank or other armored vehicle and fired from it ‖ (of a missile) propelled by its own fuel ‖ (of a vehicle) driven by its own motor
self-pro·tec·tion (sélfprətékʃən) *n.* protection of oneself or one's interests
self-rais·ing (sélfréiziŋ) *adj.* (*Br.*) self-rising
self-re·al·i·za·tion (sélfri:əlizéiʃən) *n.* self-fulfillment
self-re·cord·ing (sélfrikɔ́rdiŋ) *adj.* (of an instrument) making an automatic record of its own operations
self-re·gard (sélfrigɑ́rd) *n.* concern for oneself
self-re·li·ance (sélfriláiəns) *n.* confidence in one's own abilities, power of judgment etc. **sélf-re·lí·ant** *adj.*
self-re·nun·ci·a·tion (sélfrinʌnsi:éiʃən) *n.* a sacrificing of one's own wishes or interests
self-re·proach (sélfripróutʃ) *n.* a reproaching or blaming of oneself, or an expression of this
self-re·spect (sélfrispékt) *n.* the proper esteem in which one holds oneself **sélf-re·spéct·ing** *adj.*
self-re·straint (sélfristréint) *n.* the ability to keep one's temper or desires in check
self-right·eous (sélfráitʃəs) *adj.* regarding oneself as more virtuous than others, or revealing this attitude
self-ris·ing (sélfráiziŋ) *adj.* (*Am.*=*Br.* self-raising, of flour) needing no further addition of baking powder etc.
self-sac·ri·fice (sélfsǽkrəfais) *n.* action intended to benefit others or to further an ideal, done in the knowledge that it is to one's own disadvantage **sélf-sác·ri·fic·ing** *adj.*
self·same (sélfseim) exactly the same, *both accidents happened at the selfsame spot*
self-sat·is·fac·tion (sélfsætisfǽkʃən) *n.* the belief that one's own actions, achievements or qualities are excellent
self-sat·is·fied (sélfsǽtisfaid) *adj.* having or showing self-satisfaction
self-seal·ing (sélfsí:liŋ) *adj.* made of a substance that automatically seals itself if holed, punctured etc. ‖ (of envelopes etc.) having two treated surfaces which adhere on contact
self-seek·er (sélfsí:kər) *n.* a person who puts his own advantage above other considerations
self-seek·ing (sélfsí:kiŋ) **1.** *adj.* characteristic of a self-seeker **2.** *n.* the behavior of a self-seeker
self-serv·ice (sélfsə́:rvis) **1.** *adj.* of a restaurant or shop where the customer selects and himself takes what he wants from the counter or shelf, paying when he leaves the counter or at the exit ‖ of this method of supplying goods to customers **2.** *n.* such a restaurant or shop
self-sown (sélfsóun) *adj.* sown by some natural process of dispersal, not by man
self-start·er (sélfstɑ́rtər) *n.* a device for starting an engine without having to crank it ‖ (*pop.*) someone who can be relied on to act on his own initiative
self-styled (sélfstáild) *adj.* (of a title etc.) assumed by oneself without authorization
self-suf·fi·cien·cy (sélfsəfíʃənsi:) *n.* the quality of being self-sufficient
self-suf·fi·cient (sélfsəfíʃənt) *adj.* accepting or needing no outside help
self-suf·fic·ing (sélfsəfáisiŋ) *adj.* self-sufficient
self-sup·port (sélfsəpɔ́rt, sélfsəpóurt) *n.* financial support of oneself without outside help **sélf-sup·pórt·ing** *adj.* earning one's own living ‖ (of an enterprise) economically viable
self-sur·ren·der (sélfsəréndər) *n.* spiritual or passionate abandonment of oneself
self-sus·tain·ing (sélfsəstéiniŋ) *adj.* maintaining life or livelihood by oneself or itself
self-taught (sélftɔ́t) *adj.* taught by oneself with no formal instruction
self-will (sélfwíl) *n.* determination to follow one's own wishes, esp. when opposed to those of others **sélf-wílled** *adj.*
self-wind·ing (sélfwáindiŋ) *adj.* (of a watch) winding itself automatically as the result of the kinetic energy imparted to it by moving it
Se·lim I (sí:lim, selí:m) (1467-1520), Ottoman sultan (1512-20). He massacred 40,000 of his own Shi'ite subjects for political reasons and conquered Persia (1514), Syria and Egypt (1516-17). He assumed the caliphate, was an able ruler, and was a patron of writers
Sel·juk (seldʒú:k, séldʒu:k) a member of any of several Turkish dynasties who ruled in Persia (11th-12th cc.), Syria (11th-12th cc.) and Asia Minor (11th-13th cc.)
Sel·kirk (sélkə:rk) a former county (area 267 sq. miles) of S.E. Scotland. Major towns: Selkirk, Galashiels
sell (sel) **1.** *v. pres. part.* **sell·ing** *past* and *past part.* **sold** (sould) *v.t.* to dispose of the ownership of (goods, property or rights) to another or others in exchange for money, *he sold his house to them* ‖ to effect such a transfer as an agent, *he sold their house for them* ‖ to offer for sale, *he sells antiques* ‖ to lead to the sale of, *advertising sold a million copies* ‖ to betray for a reward, *he sold them to the police* ‖ (*pop.*) to persuade others to accept, *to sell an idea* ‖ (*pop.*) to cheat, deceive, *he was sold over the deal* ‖ *v.i.* to offer something for sale, *is he thinking of selling?* ‖ to find a buyer, *these goods sell quickly* **to sell off** to sell (what remains) at a reduced price **to sell out** to sell all the goods one has ‖ to be completely sold, *the edition sold out overnight* ‖ to sell one's stocks or shares, *to sell out before the market falls* ‖ (*pop.*) to betray (a cause, partners in crime etc.) **to sell up** (*Br.*) to sell one's property, esp. in order to pay off debts **2.** *n.* (*Br., pop.*) a deception or disappointment, *the scheme proved a sell* ‖ (*pop.*) salesmanship or sales appeal **séll·er** *n.* a person who sells ‖ a product with respect to its rate of sale, *a poor seller* [O.E. *sellan*]
sellers' market a market in which, because of the scarcity of goods and intense demand, prices are generally high
selling plate a selling race
selling race a horse race in which the winning horse is sold by auction
sell·out (sélaut) *n.* (*pop.*) a betrayal ‖ (*pop.*) a show etc. for which all the tickets are sold ‖ (*pop.*) the sale of the entire stock of something as a result of popular demand
sel·vage, sel·vedge (sélvidʒ) *n.* the edge of cloth so woven as to prevent unraveling ‖ the edge plate of a lock which permits the bolt to obtrude and engage [SELF+EDGE]
selves *pl.* of SELF
se·man·tic (simǽntik) *adj.* of meaning in language ‖ of or in accordance with the science of semantics **se·man·tics** *n.* the branch of linguistic science which deals with the meanings of words and esp. with development and change in these meanings [fr. Gk *sēmantikos,* significant]
sem·a·phore (séməfɔr, séməfour) **1.** *n.* a signaling device using movable arms ‖ a system of signaling by flags or lights **2.** *v. pres. part.* **sem·a·phor·ing** *past* and *past part.* **sem·a·phored** *v.t.* to send (a message) by semaphore ‖ *v.i.* to signal using semaphore **sem·a·phor·ic** (seməfɔ́rik, seməfɒ́rik) *adj.* [fr. Gk *sēma,* sign +*pherein,* to bear]
Se·ma·rang (səmɑ́rɑŋ) the chief port and commercial center (pop. 646,590) of central Java, Indonesia, on the Java Sea: shipbuilding, textiles, mechanical and electrical engineering. University
se·ma·si·o·log·i·cal (simeisi:əlɒ́dʒikəl, simeizi:əlɒ́dʒikəl) *adj.* semantic
se·ma·si·ol·o·gy (simeisi:ɒ́lədʒi:, simeizi:ɒ́lədʒi:) *n.* (*linguistics*) semantics [fr. Gk *sēmasia,* meaning of a word + *logos,* discourse]
se·mat·ic (simǽtik) *adj.* (*biol.*) of color, marking, odor etc. serving as a signal to attract or warn off [fr. Gk *sēma* (*sēmatos*), a sign]
sem·blance (sémbləns) *n.* just enough outward show to be plausible, *a semblance of gratitude* ‖ a wilfully deceptive appearance, *under a semblance of friendship* [F.]
se·mé (səméi) *adj.* (*heraldry*) covered or sprinkled with many small bearings, e.g. flowers or stars [F.]
se·mei·ol·o·gy (si:maiɒ́lədʒi:) *n.* (*philos.*) the science of signs or sign language ‖ (*med.*) symptomatology [fr. Gk *sēmeion,* sign + *logos,* discourse]
se·mei·et·ic (si:maiɒ́tik, si:mi:ɒ́tik, semaiɒ́tik, semi:ɒ́tik) *adj.* (*med.*) of or relating to symptoms [fr. Gk *sēmeiōtikos* fr. *sēmeion,* a sign]
se·men (sí:men) *n.* the fluid secreted by the male's testes and accessory glands, containing spermatozoa [L.=a seed]
se·mes·ter (siméstər) *n.* one of the two divisions of the academic year in some universities, esp. in Germany and the U.S.A. [G. fr. L. (*cursus*) *semestris,* (period) of six months]
semi- (sémi:, sémai) *prefix* half ‖ in part, to some extent ‖ partial, not complete, full or perfect ‖ partially, not completely, fully or perfectly ‖ occurring twice within a specified period [L.]
sem·i·an·nu·al (semi:ǽnju:əl) *adj.* occurring every half year
sem·i·ar·id (semi:ǽrid) *adj.* receiving little annual rainfall, usually 10 to 20 ins
sem·i·au·to·mat·ic (semi:ɔtəmǽtik) *adj.* partly automatic ‖ (of a firearm) that ejects spent cartridges and reloads automatically but that requires the trigger to be released and pressed for each shot
sem·i·breve (sémi:bri:v) *n.* (*Br., mus.*) a whole note
sem·i·cir·cle (sémi:sə:rk'l) *n.* half a circle as divided by a diameter, or half a circle's circumference ‖ an arrangement of objects roughly in this way, *a semicircle of chairs* [fr. L. *semicirculus*]
sem·i·cir·cu·lar (semi:sə́:rkjulər) *adj.* having the shape of a semicircle [fr. M.L. *semicircularis*]
semicircular canal any of the curved tubes of the inner ear that serve to maintain bodily equilibrium
sem·i·co·lon (sémi:koulən) *n.* a punctuation mark (;) separating two related sentences, esp. of some length or complexity, without suggesting the nature of the relationship
sem·i·con·duc·tor (semi:kəndʌ́ktər) *n.* any of a group of materials (e.g. germanium, selenium, copper oxide, cadmium sulfide) having an electrical conductivity between that of metals and insulators. They are used in transistors, rectifiers, photoelectric cells and as thermometers
sem·i·con·scious (semi:kɒ́nʃəs) *adj.* not fully conscious
sem·i·con·serv·a·tive (semi:kənsə́:rvətiv) *adj.* (*genetics*) of replication in which some molecular strands separate and combine with other molecules
sem·i·de·tached (semi:ditǽtʃt) *adj.* (of a house) having a common dividing wall with one other house
sem·i·di·ur·nal (semi:daiə́:rn'l) *adj* occurring twice a day ‖ lasting half a day
sem·i·farm·ing (sémi:fɑrmiŋ) *n.* part-time farming activity
sem·i·fi·nal (semi:fáin'l) **1.** *adj.* of a game or match played immediately before the final one of an eliminating series **2.** *n.* such a game or match **sem·i·fí·na·list** *n.* a contestant in a semifinal
sem·i·flu·id (semi:flú:id) **1.** *adj.* viscous **2.** *n.* a viscous fluid
sem·i·lu·nar (semi:lú:nər) *adj.* crescent-shaped
sem·i·month·ly (semi:mʌ́nθli:) **1.** *adj.* occurring, appearing, etc. twice a month **2.** *pl.* **sem·i·month·lies** *n.* a paper, magazine etc. issued twice a month **3.** *adv.* twice a month
sem·i·nal (sémin'l) *adj.* of seed or semen ‖ constituting a source of later developments, *Coleridge was one of the seminal minds of the 19th century* [F. *séminal*]

CONCISE PRONUNCIATION KEY: **(a)** æ, *cat*; ɑ, *car*; ɔ *fawn*; ei, *snake*. **(e)** e, *hen*; i:, *sheep*; iə, *deer*; ɛə, *bear*. **(i)** i, *fish*; ai, *tiger*; ə:, *bird*. **(o)** o, *ox*; au, *cow*; ou, *goat*; u, *poor*; ɔi, *royal*. **(u)** ʌ, *duck*; u, *bull*; u:, *goose*; ə, *bacillus*; ju:, *cube*. x, *loch*; θ, *think*; ð, *bother*; z, *Zen*; ʒ, *corsage*; dʒ, *savage*; ŋ, *orangutang*; j, *yak*; ʃ, *fish*; tʃ, *fetch*; 'l, *rabble*; 'n, *redden*. Complete pronunciation key appears inside front cover.

seminal fluid semen excepting the spermatozoa ‖ semen
sem·i·nar (séminɑr) *n.* a group of advanced students working in association under the guidance of a teacher ‖ a course for or meeting of such a group [G. fr. L. *seminarium,* seedbed]
sem·i·nar·i·an (seminéəriːən) *n.* a seminarist
sem·i·nar·ist (séminerist) *n.* a student at a seminary
sem·i·nar·y (séminəriː) *pl.* **sem·i·nar·ies** *n.* a place where intending priests, ministers or rabbis are trained ‖ (*old-fash.*) an educational institution [fr. L. *seminarium,* seedbed]
sem·i·nif·er·ous (seminífərəs) *adj.* bearing seed ‖ producing or carrying semen [fr. L. *semen* (*seminis*), seed +*-fer,* bearing]
Sem·i·nole (séminoul) *pl.* **Sem·i·nole, Sem·i·noles** *n.* a member of a Muskogean tribe of American Indians, which separated (18th c.) from the Creeks and settled in Florida. They were at war with the U.S.A. (1817–18 and 1835–42)
sem·i·of·fi·cial (semiːəfíʃəl) *adj.* derived from official sources but not having official authority
se·mi·ol·o·gy (siːmiːɒ́lədʒiː, siːmaiɒ́lədʒiː, semiːɒlədʒiː, semaiɒ́lədʒiː) *n.* semeiology
se·mi·ot·ic (siːmiːɒ́tik, siːmaiɒ́tik, semiːɒ́tik, semaiɒ́tik) **1.** *adj.* (*mathematical logic*) relating to the theory of symbols ‖ semeiotic **2.** *n.* the theory of symbols **se·mi·ót·ics** *n.* semiotic
semiotics study of patterned human communication behavior, including auditory/vocal and facial expression, body talk (kinestics), touch (proxemics), signs, symbols (semiology) *Cf* ZOOSEMIOTICS
sem·i·o·vip·a·rous (semiːouvípərəs) *adj.* bearing young which are incompletely developed when born
sem·i·pal·mate (semiːpǽlmeit, semiːpǽlmit) *adj.* (*zool.*, of some shore birds) having the anterior toes only partly webbed
sem·i·per·me·a·ble (semiːpə́ːrmiːəb'l) *adj.* (*phys.*) of a membrane through which some substances (e.g. solvents) can pass, but not others (e.g. solutes) (*OSMOSIS)
sem·i·po·lar bond (semiːpóulər) a coordinate bond
sem·i·por·ce·lain (semiːpɔ́rsəlin, semiːpóursəlin) *n.* a coarse type of porcelain
sem·i·pre·cious (semiːpréʃəs) *adj.* (of a gem) valued for use in ornaments, but not having the commercial value of precious stones
sem·i·qua·ver (sémiːkweivər) *n.* (*Br., mus.*) a sixteenth note
Se·mir·a·mis (simírəmis) legendary Assyrian queen, traditionally the founder of Babylon and Nineveh, worshiped as a dove and later identified with Ishtar
sem·i·sol·id (semiːsɒ́lid) **1.** *adj.* having a thick viscous consistency **2.** *n.* such a substance
Sem·ite (sémait, esp. *Br.* síːmait) *n.* a member of any of the peoples speaking Semitic languages [fr. Mod. L. *semita* fr. L.L. fr. Gk *Sēm,* Shem (Noah's eldest son, eponymous ancestor of the Semites)]
Se·mit·ic (səmítik) *adj.* of, like, or concerning the Semites ‖ belonging to or concerned with the group of languages including E. Semitic (Akkadian), N.W. Semitic (Phoenician, Punic, Aramaic, Hebrew, Modern Hebrew etc.) and S.W. Semitic (Arabic, Amharic) **Se·mít·ics** *n.* the study of the Semitic languages, cultures etc. **Sem·i·tism** (sémitizəm) *n.* a Semitic characteristic ‖ a Semitic expression or idiom ‖ ideas, cultural ideals etc., thought of as essentially Jewish [fr. Mod. L. *semiticus*]
sem·i·tone (sémiːtoun) *n.* (*mus.*) the smallest interval in a diatonic scale, represented on a keyboard instrument by the interval between any two adjacent keys, e.g. between C and D♭
sem·i·trop·i·cal (semiːtrɒ́pik'l) *adj.* subtropical
sem·i·vow·el (sémiːvauəl) *n.* a vowel sound which functions as a consonant, e.g. w and y in English
sem·i·week·ly (semiːwíːkliː) **1.** *adj.* occurring twice a week **2.** *pl.* **sem·i·week·lies** *n.* a paper, magazine etc. issued twice a week **3.** *adv.* twice a week
sem·o·li·na (seməlíːnə) *n.* the small hard grains of *Triticum durum* or other hard wheat left after sieving and used to make macaroni, puddings etc. [fr. Ital. *semolino*]
sem·pi·ter·nal (sempitə́ːrn'l) *adj.* (*rhet.*) eternal [F. *sempiternel*]
semp·stress (sémpstris, sémstris) *n.* a seamstress
sen (sen) *pl.* **sen** *n.* one hundredth of a yen, or a coin representing this [Jap. fr. Chin.]
sen *pl.* **sen** *n.* one hundredth of a riel [native Cambodian name]
sen *pl.* **sen** *n.* one hundredth of a rupiah, or a coin representing this [native name in Indonesia]
Se·nan·cour (sənãkuːr), Etienne Pivert de (1770-1846), French writer. His introspective epistolary novel 'Obermann' influenced other Romantic writers
sen·ate (sénit) *n.* (*hist.*) the governing body in ancient Athens, ancient Rome, and of certain medieval free cities etc. ‖ the upper legislative assembly in France, the U.S.A. etc. ‖ the governing body of certain U.S. universities and of the Universities of Cambridge (England) and London [O.F. *senat. senaz*]
sen·a·tor (sénətər) *n.* a member of a senate [O.F. *senateur*]
sen·a·to·ri·al (senətɔ́riːəl, senətóuriːəl) *adj.* of, relating to, or befitting a senate or senator [fr. L. *senatorius*]
sen·a·tor·ship (sénətərʃip) *n.* the office or dignity of a senator
send (*send*) *v. pres. part.* **send·ing** *past* and *past part.* **sent** (sent) *v.t.* to cause (a person) to go to a specified place, in a specified direction or for a specified purpose, *she sent him to the store for some milk* ‖ to cause (a thing) to go or to be taken to another place, *to send a letter* ‖ (of God, fate etc.) to cause to happen, *trials sent from above* ‖ to cause to be on a divine mission, *a prophet sent to lead his people* ‖ to cause to behave or move in a specified way, *the blow sent him spinning* ‖ (*Br.*) to drive, cause to be in a specified state, *the noise sent him crazy* ‖ (*radio*) to transmit, *send it in code* ‖ *v.i.* (often with 'away', 'off') to send a letter asking for something ‖ (often with 'out') to send someone to fetch something, *he sent out for some beer* ‖ to send someone as a messenger, *she sent to inquire after you* ‖ (*radio*) to transmit a message **to send down** (*Br.*) to suspend or expel from a university **to send for** to ask for (someone or something) to come or be brought **to send in** to cause (a letter, bill etc.) to be delivered esp. to some large or central organization etc. **to send off** to dispatch ‖ to cause to go away ‖ to give a send-off to **to send on** to cause to be forwarded to someone after his departure to another place **to send out** to emit ‖ to put forth ‖ to distribute, dispatch **to send packing** to dismiss without ceremony [O.E. *sendan*]
Sen·dai (séndái) a city (pop. 618,700) of N. Honshu, Japan, a handicraft center (silk, pottery, lacquerware, woodwork). Castle (17th c.). University (1907)
sen·dal (sénd'l) *n.* (*hist.*) a fine silk fabric of medieval times [O. F. *cendal*]
send·er (séndər) *n.* a person who sends something ‖ (*radio*) a transmitter
send-off (séndɔf, séndɒf) *n.* a friendly demonstration of good wishes to a person or people going away
Sen·e·ca (sénikə), Lucius Annaeus 'the Elder' (c. 55 B.C.–c. 39 A.D.), Roman writer on rhetoric
Seneca, Lucius Annaeus (c. 4 B.C.–65 A.D.), Roman orator, statesman and philosopher, son of Seneca the Elder. He was tutor to Nero from 49 and an influential adviser during the early part of Nero's reign. Implicated in a conspiracy against Nero, he was forced to commit suicide. He wrote works on Stoic philosophy, the 'Apocolocyntosis' (a satire on the deification of Claudius) and nine tragedies on classical subjects
Sen·e·ca (sénəkə) *n.* a member of a tribe of Iroquois Indians who lived in W. New York State
Sen·e·gal (senigɔ́l) a republic (area 76,124 sq. miles, pop. 6,541,000) and member of the French Community, in W. Africa. Capital: Dakar. People: Wolof (24%), Fulani (10%), Serer, Toucouleur, Mandingo, Sarakolle and other African groups, 2% European. Languages: French, tribal languages (mainly Sudanic). Religion: 80% Moslem, 15% local African, 5% Christian. Coastal dunes give way to a rolling plain (rising above 700 ft only in the southeast near the Fouta Djallon of Guinea), semi-desert in the north, savanna and desert in the center and rain forest south of the Gambia. Average temperature (F.): 84° (higher in the northeast). Rainfall: under 20 ins in the north, over 20 ins in the center, tropical in the south. Livestock: cattle, sheep, goats, donkeys, horses, hogs, camels. Agricultural products: peanuts, millet, corn, rice, gum, palm nuts, manioc, beans. Mineral resources: phosphates, titanium, bauxite, iron ore. Industries: fishing (esp. tuna), peanut oil refining, chemicals, textiles building materials, engineering. Exports: peanuts (85% of exports), peanut oil, oil cake, phosphates, hides and skins. Imports: wheat, rice, sugar, petroleum products, cement, textiles, machinery, chemicals. University: Dakar (1957). Monetary unit: CFA franc. HISTORY. A native kingdom developed (c. 9th c.) and was converted to Islam (11th c.). The area formed part of the empire of Mali (13th-15th cc.). The coast was explored by the Portuguese (late 15th c.) and the French established trading posts (17th c.). French control was strengthened (19th c.) and Senegal became part of French West Africa (1895). It became an autonomous republic within the French Community (1958) and was briefly part of the Mali Federation (1959-60). It became fully independent (Aug. 20, 1960) and joined the U.N. (1960). Senegal and Gambia formed the federation of Senegambia (1981) to coordinate their defense and economic and foreign policies
Senegal a river (1,000 miles long, navigable for 600 miles in the rainy season) flowing from S.W. Mali to the Atlantic at St Louis, Senegal, forming the Senegal-Mauritania frontier. Railroads link it to the Niger system
Sen·e·ga·lese (senigɔlíːz, senigɔlíːs, senəgəlíːz, senəgəlíːs) **1.** *adj.* of or pertaining to Senegal or its people **2.** *pl.* **Sen·e·ga·lese** *n.* a native or inhabitant of Senegal
se·nes·cence (sənésəns) *n.* the process or state of growing old [SENESCENT]
se·nes·cent (sənésənt) *adj.* growing old [fr. L. *senescens* (*senescentis*) fr. *senescere,* to grow old]
sen·e·schal (sénəʃəl) *n.* (*hist.*) the majordomo of a great medieval household or steward of an estate [O.F. fr. Gmc]
Sen·ghor (sãgɔr), Léopold Sédar (1906-), Senegalese statesman, poet and essayist. He was president of Senegal (1960-80). In 1984 the Académie Français admitted him as the first black
se·nile (síːnail, sénail) *adj.* of old age ‖ arising from old age, *senile decay* ‖ having the infirmities of old age ‖ (*geog.*) (of a river valley etc.) nearing the end of an erosion cycle **se·nil·i·ty** (siníliti:) *n.* [fr. L. *senilis*]
sen·ior (síːnjər) **1.** *adj.* indicating the older of two, *John Brown senior* (as distinguished from a younger John Brown, esp. a son) ‖ of higher rank, longer service etc., *the senior staff of a school* ‖ of or relating to a student in the graduating class of a school **2.** *n.* someone who is senior by age, rank, length of service etc. ‖ a student in the graduating class of a school [L. comp. of *senex,* old]
senior citizen **1.** a retired person **2.** one over age 65, in some situations over age 55
senior high school a high school comprising the 10th, 11th and 12th grades, which follows junior high school
sen·ior·i·ty (siːnjɔ́riti:, siːnjɒ́riti:) *n.* the quality or state of being senior
senior wrangler (*Br.,* Cambridge University) the person winning the highest first-class honors in the mathematical tripos
sen·na (sénə) *n.* a member of *Cassia,* fam. *Papilionaceae,* a genus of tropical shrubs and trees, whose leaves are dried for use as a laxative ‖ the dried leaves of these plants [Mod. L. fr. Arab.]
Sen·nach·er·ib (senǽkərib) king of Assyria (705-681 B.C.), son of Sargon II. He ravaged Judah (701 B.C.), destroyed Babylon (689 B.C.) and rebuilt Nineveh
se·ñor (seinjɔ́r, *Span.* senjɔ́r) *pl.* **se·ñors,** *Span.* **se·ñor·es** (senjɔ́res) *n.* a courtesy title for a Spanish man (the equivalent of 'Mr') and (without the surname) a term of address [Span.]
se·ñor·a (seinjɔ́rə, *Span.* senjɔ́rɑ) *pl.* **se·ñor·as** (seinjɔ́rəz, *Span.* senjɔ́rɑs) *n.* a courtesy title for a married Spanish woman (the equivalent of 'Mrs') and (without the surname) a term of address [Span.]
se·ñor·i·ta (seinjəríːtə, *Span.* senɔríːtɑ) *pl.* **se·ñor·i·tas** (seinjəríːtəz, *Span.* senjɔríːtɑs) *n.* a courtesy title for an unmarried Spanish girl or woman (the equivalent of 'Miss') and (without the surname) a term of address [Span.]
sen·sa·tion (senséiʃən) *n.* the activity of the senses ‖ (*philos.*) the immediate result of this activity before the combination with other data (cf. PERCEPTION) ‖ a state of emotional excitement, *the news caused a sensation* ‖ the cause of such a state of emotional excitement, *she was a sensation as Cleopatra* **sen·sá·tion·al** *adj.* **sen·-**

sá·tion·al·ism *n.* the use of methods, e.g. in journalism, by which inordinate, foolish or harmful emotional responses are produced ‖ (*philos.*) the doctrine that all knowledge is acquired through the senses **sen·sá·tion·al·ist** *n.* [fr. M.L. *sensatio (sensationis)*]

sense (sens) **1.** *n.* any of the bodily faculties (hearing, sight, smell, taste or touch) by which an organism becomes aware of certain elements in its surroundings, when impulses are conveyed through the nervous system to the brain ‖ a conscious perception or sensation derived through these senses or through the intellect, *a sense of danger* ‖ the ability to judge external conditions, *a sense of direction* ‖ an ability to appreciate some quality, *a sense of honor* ‖ the meaning, nature or significance of a thing or idea, *the sense of someone's remarks* ‖ practical wisdom, the ability to perceive and act or judge soundly ‖ an apparent majority opinion, *the sense of the meeting* ‖ a meaning of a word, expression etc., as distinguished from its other meanings, *he was using the word in a different sense* ‖ (*pl.*) normal control of mental processes, *to bring someone to his senses* **in a sense** from one point of view **to make sense** to have a clear meaning or be rational **to make sense of** to understand the meaning of **2.** *v.t. pres. part.* **sens·ing** *past* and *past part.* **sensed** to perceive, esp. by intuition, *she sensed that he was hiding something* ‖ to read (computer data etc.) mechanically, electrically etc. **sénse·less** *adj.* unconscious, *he knocked her senseless* ‖ foolish, irrational, *a senseless thing to do* [F. *sens*]

sen·sei (sensei) *n.* a teacher of judo and karate

sense organ an organ, e.g. the eye, ear etc., adapted to receive stimuli

sense perception perception resulting from a stimulus received by a sense organ

sen·si·bil·i·ty (sensəbíliti:) *pl.* **sen·si·bil·i·ties** *n.* the ability to respond to a sense stimulus ‖ emotional responsiveness, esp. to the pathetic ‖ extreme refinement of taste ‖ (*pl.*) feelings easily hurt [fr. L. *sensibilitas*]

sen·si·ble (sénsəb'l) *adj.* showing good sense, being reasonable, practical, *a sensible precaution* ‖ appreciable, large enough to be perceived, *a sensible improvement,* ‖ capable of being perceived, *sensible phenomena* ‖ (*old-fash.*) sensitively aware, *he was sensible of the honor being done to him* [F.]

sen·si·bly (sénsəbli:) *adv.* in a sensible way

sen·si·tive (sénsitiv) *adj.* able to respond to a stimulus, *sensitive to light* ‖ able to respond to a very slight stimulus, *a sensitive instrument* ‖ keenly aware of the moods and feelings of others ‖ easily hurt emotionally, too readily affected by the feelings or imagined feelings of others with regard to oneself, *sensitive to criticism* ‖ (of a part of the body) liable to be painful ‖ quick to react to external influences, *a sensitive market* [F. *sensitif (sensitive)*]

sensitive plant *Minos pudica,* a common tropical American weed whose leaves droop and leaflets temporarily close when they are touched, due to changes in the pulvinus

sen·si·tiv·i·ty (sensitíviti:) *pl.* **sen·si·tiv·i·ties** *n.* the state or quality of being sensitive

sensitivity group (*psych.*) participants in a therapeutic group designed to promote understanding of personal emotions

sensitivity training (*psych.*) program designed to sharpen individual self-awareness

sen·si·ti·za·tion (sensitizéiʃən) *n.* a sensitizing or being sensitized

sen·si·tize (sénsitaiz) *pres. part.* **sen·si·tiz·ing** *past* and *past part.* **sen·si·tized** *v.t.* (*photog.*) to render (film, paper etc.) sensitive to light ‖ (*med.*) to render sensitive to a serum by using a series of injections

sen·si·tom·e·ter (sensitómitər) *n.* an instrument for measuring sensitivity, e.g. of the eye, of a film etc.

sen·so·ri·um (sensóri:əm) *n.* (*biol.*) the sensory system

sen·so·ry (sénsəri:) *adj.* of or relating to sensation ‖ (*physiol.*) carrying nerve impulses from the sense organs to the central nervous system

sen·su·al (sénʃu:əl) *adj.* pertaining to the body and the senses as distinct from the intellect ‖ pertaining to the satisfaction of bodily desires, *sensual pleasures* ‖ (of people) having great liking for bodily pleasure, esp. sexual pleasure ‖ showing sensuality, *a sensual mouth* ‖ (*philos.*) relating to the doctrine of sensationalism **sén·su·al·ism** *n.* sensuality ‖ (*philos.*) sensationalism ‖ (*aesthetics*) the view that the beauty of an object depends mainly on its sensuous qualities ‖ (*ethics*) the belief that the gratification of the senses is the highest good **sén·su·al·ist** *n.* **sen·su·al·is·tic** *adj.* [fr. L.L. *sensualis*]

sen·su·al·i·ty (senʃu:ǽliti:) *n.* great liking for sensual pleasures [F. *sensualité*]

sen·su·ous (sénʃu:əs) *adj.* relating to, derived from, or affected by, the senses [fr. L. *sensus,* sense]

sent *past* and *past part.* of SEND

sen·tence (séntəns) **1.** *n.* (*gram.*) a word or group of words which states, asks, commands or exclaims something. It usually includes a subject and a predicate, is conventionally written with a capital letter at the beginning, and ends with a punctuation mark (period, question mark etc.) ‖ (*law*) the statement of a judicial decision to punish, *to pronounce sentence* ‖ the penalty which forms a part of such a statement, *he has served half his sentence* ‖ (*mus.*) a period [F.]

sentence *pres. part.* **sen·tenc·ing** *past* and *past part.* **sen·tenced** *v.t.* to state the penalty to be paid by (a person) [fr. F. *sentencier*]

sentence bargaining arrangement to have a defendant plead guilty in return for a lighter sentence

sentence stress the vocal stress put upon words in a sentence in order to make the meaning more clear. In English it is usually placed on the noun elements of the subject and on the object or complement

sen·ten·tious (senténʃəs) *adj.* making excessive or pompous use of statements of moral principles or of high-sounding phrases ‖ terse, pithy [fr. L. *sententiosus*]

sen·ti (sénti:) *n.* unit of currency in Tonga, equal to 1/100th pa'anga

sen·tience (sénʃəns) *n.* the state or quality of being sentient

sen·tien·cy (sénʃənsi:) *n.* sentience

sen·tient (sénʃənt) *adj.* capable of feeling, having the power of sense perception [fr. L. *sentiens (sentientis)* fr. *sentire,* to feel]

sen·ti·ment (séntəmənt) *n.* a group of emotions and opinions associated with and aroused by an idea ‖ susceptibility to emotional appeal ‖ expression of emotional ideas in art, music or literature ‖ (*loosely*) sentimentality ‖ a short, usually banal, expression of feeling, e.g. on a greeting card **sen·ti·men·tal** (sentəmént'l) *adj.* characterized by excessive emotional show ‖ influenced by feeling rather than reason ‖ feeling, or characterized by, tenderness **sen·ti·mén·tal·ism, sen·ti·mén·tal·ist, sen·ti·men·tal·i·ty** (sentəmentǽliti:) *ns* **sen·ti·mén·tal·ize** *pres. part.* **sen·ti·men·tal·iz·ing** *past* and *past part.* **sen·ti·men·tal·ized** *v.i.* and *t.* [O.F. *sentement*]

sen·ti·nel (séntən'l) *n.* a soldier posted on guard ‖ someone who keeps watch **to stand sentinel** to guard [F. *sentinelle* fr. Ital.]

Sentinel *n.* (*mil.*) proposed system for defense of 50 states against ICBMs utilizing radar-directed antiballistic missiles for interception

sen·try (séntri:) *pl.* **sen·tries** *n.* a soldier on guard duty [perh. fr. *centrinel,* older var. of SENTINEL]

sentry box a tall wooden box to shelter a sentry

sentry go duty as a sentry

Se·nu·fo (sinú:fou) *pl.* **Se·nu·fo, Se·nu·fos** *n.* a member of a W. African people of Mali and the Ivory Coast

Se·nus·si (senú:si:) *pl.* **Se·nus·sis** *SANUSI

sen·za·la (sénzələ) *n.* a set of slave quarters near the master's house in N.E. Brazil [Port.]

Seoul (soul, sɑú:l) the capital (pop. 9,454,825) and commercial and industrial center of South Korea, near the northwest coast. Industries: mechanical and railroad engineering, automobiles, textiles, tobacco, food processing, brewing. Port: Inchon. Palaces (14th c.). University

se·pal (sí:p'l) *n.* (*bot.*) a protective leaflike division of the calyx of a flower [fr. F. *sépale*]

sep·a·ra·bil·i·ty (sepərəbíliti:) *n.* the state or quality of being separable

sep·a·ra·ble (sépərəb'l) *adj.* capable of being separated [F. *séparable*]

sep·a·rate 1. (sépəreit) *v. pres. part.* **sep·a·rat·ing** *past* and *past part.* **sep·a·rat·ed** *v.t.* to cause (things or people which were joined together or mixed) to be no longer joined or mixed, *to separate wheat from chaff* ‖ to form a boundary between, *the fence separates the two gardens* ‖ to distinguish between, *you can't separate the rights and wrongs of the case* ‖ to cause (man and wife) to cease to live together ‖ *v.i.* to cease to be connected or associated, go in different directions, *they separated when they reached the crossroads* ‖ (of man and wife) to cease to live together ‖ (with 'from') to withdraw ‖ to become disconnected ‖ to become separate **2.** (sépərit) *adj.* not joined to or mixed with something else ‖ existing independently of other things ‖ regarded as being individual ‖ isolated ‖ not shared **3.** (sépərit) *n.* an offprint ‖ (*pl.*) women's clothes (blouses, skirts etc.) meant for wearing either in combination with one another or with other alternatives [fr. L. *separare (separatus)*]

sep·a·ra·tion (sepəréiʃən) *n.* a separating or being separated ‖ a place where a division occurs ‖ something that separates ‖ a legal agreement by which man and wife do not live together [O.F.]

separation of powers the division of constitutional government in a democracy between three separate, independent branches: legislative, executive and judicial

sep·a·ra·tist (sépərətist, sépəreitist) *n.* someone in favor of separation (e.g. of a minority group from a large body) ‖ a member of a political or religious minority favoring secession **Sep·a·ra·tist** (*hist.*) a Brownist

sep·a·ra·tive (sépəreitiv, sépərətiv) *adj.* tending to separate or to cause separation [F. *séparatif (séparative)*]

sep·a·ra·tor (sépəreitər) *n.* a device which separates a mixture into constituent parts, e.g. a machine which separates cream from milk centrifugally [L.L.]

Se·phar·dic (səfɑ́rdik) *adj.* of or relating to the Sephardim

Se·phar·dim (səfɑ́rdim, səfɑrdí:m) *pl. n.* (*hist.*) the Jews who settled in Spain and Portugal before the Inquisition and who spread to England, Greece, the Americas etc. (cf. ASHKENAZIM) ‖ their descendants [Heb.]

se·pi·a (sí:pi:ə) *n.* the black inky secretion of cuttlefish ‖ a dark brown pigment prepared from this and used in inks and watercolors ‖ a rich dark brown color ‖ a photograph reproduced in this color ‖ or drawing made in sepia ink [L. fr. Gk]

se·poy (sí:pɔi) *n.* (*hist.*) an Indian soldier in the British-Indian army [fr. Urdu]

Sepoy Rebellion the Indian Mutiny

sep·pu·ku (sepú:ku:) *n.* hara-kiri [Jap. fr. Chin.]

sep·sis (sépsis) *n.* pus formation in an infected part of the body resulting in blood poisoning [Mod. L. fr. Gk *sepsis,* putrefaction]

sept (sept) *n.* a clan, esp. one of ancient Ireland [prob. var. of SECT]

Sept. September

septa *pl.* of SEPTUM

sep·tal (séptəl) *adj.* of a septum or septa

sep·tar·i·um (septɛ́əri:əm) *pl.* **sep·tar·i·a** (septɛ́əri:ə) *n.* (*geol.*) a nodule, esp. of limestone, crisscrossed by cracks which are filled with other deposits [Mod. L. fr. *septum,* partition]

sep·tate (sépteit) *adj.* (*biol.*) partitioned by or provided with a septum or septa [fr. Mod. L. *septatus*]

sep·ta·va·lent (septəvéilənt) *adj.* having seven valences [fr. *septa-* fr. L. *septem,* seven + *valens (valentis)* fr. *valere,* to be strong]

Sep·tem·ber (septémbər) *n.* (*abbr.* Sept., Sep.) the ninth month of the year, having 30 days [L. fr. *septem,* seven (being the seventh month in the Roman year)]

September massacres (*F. hist.*) the slaughter of political prisoners in French prisons Sept. 2-6, 1792, provoked partly by the news of the Prussian invasion

Sep·tem·brist (səptémbrist) *n.* (*F. hist.*) a person who took part in the September massacres

sep·te·nar·y (séptəneri:) **1.** *adj.* of or relating to seven ‖ numbered in sevens **2.** *pl.* **sep·te·nar·ies** *n.* a seven-foot verse [fr. L. *septenarius*]

sep·ten·de·cil·lion (septendisíljən) *n.* *NUMBER TABLE [fr. L. *septendecim,* seventeen + MILLION]

sep·ten·ni·al (septéni:əl) *adj.* lasting seven years ‖ occurring once every seven years [fr. L. *septennium,* period of seven years]

sep·tet, sep·tette (septét) *n.* a set of seven objects or people, esp. musicians ‖ a musical composition for seven instruments or voices [Gk fr. L. *septem,* seven]

sep·tic (séptik) *adj.* causing to putrefy, *septic activity of bacteria* ‖ due to putrefaction, *septic poisoning* [fr. L.L. *septicus* fr. Gk]

sep·ti·ce·mi·a, sep·ti·cae·mi·a (septəsí:mi:ə) *n.* blood poisoning **sep·ti·cémic, sep·ti·cæ·mic**

adj. [Mod. L. fr. Gk *sēptikos,* putrefactive+*haima,* blood]
septic tank a tank in which sewage is broken down by anaerobic bacterial activity
sep·til·lion (septíljən) *n.* *NUMBER TABLE [fr. F. fr. L. *septem,* seven+MILLION]
sep·time (sépti:m) *n.* (*fencing*) the seventh of eight parrying positions [fr. L. *septimus*]
Septimius Severus *SEVERUS
sep·tu·a·ge·nar·i·an (septʃu:ədʒənéəri:ən) **1.** *adj.* between 70 and 80 years of age **2.** *n.* someone of this age [L. *septuagenarius*]
Sep·tu·a·ges·i·ma (septʃu:ədʒésəmə) *n.* the third Sunday before Lent [L. (fem.)=seventieth (this Sunday is about 70 days before Easter)]
Sep·tu·a·gint (séptʃu:ədʒint) *n.* (symbol LXX) the Greek version of the Old Testament, including the Apocrypha, traditionally said to have been made by about 70 translators. Produced for the library of Alexandria in the 3rd and 2nd cc. B.C., this translation was popular with the Jews of the Diaspora, whose language was Greek, and it was often preferred to the Hebrew version by the early Fathers of the Christian Church. It was the first vernacular version of the Bible and is still used in the Orthodox Eastern Church [fr. L. *septuaginta,* seventy]
sep·tum (séptəm) *pl.* **sep·ta** (séptə), **sep·tums** *n.* (*biol.*) a partition separating two cavities (e.g. the nostrils) or masses of tissue (e.g. in fruits) [L.=a partition]
sep·tu·ple (séptup'l, séptjup'l, septú:p'l, septjú:p'l, septʌ́p'l) **1.** *adj.* sevenfold **2.** *v. pres. part.* **sep·tu·pling** *past* and *past part.* **sep·tu·pled** *v.t.* to make seven times as great ‖ *v.i.* to become seven times as great [fr. L. L. *septuplus*]
sep·ul·cher, esp. *Br.* **sep·ul·chre** (sépəlkər) *n.* a tomb, esp. one cut in rock, a burial vault [O.F. *sepulcre*]
se·pul·chral (sipʌ́lkrəl) *adj.* relating to the burial of the dead, *sepulchral rites* ‖ suggestive of the tomb, a *sepulchral voice* [fr. L. *sepulcralis*]
sepulchre *SEPULCHER
sep·ul·ture (sépəltʃər) *n.* (*rhet.*) burial, entombment [O.F.]
se·quel (sí:kwəl) *n.* something which follows a continuation (esp. of a story) ‖ a result or aftereffect [O.F. *sequelle*]
se·que·la (sikwí:lə) *pl.* **se·que·lae** (sikwí:li:) *n.* that which follows as a consequence, esp. (*med.*) the aftermath of a disease [L.]
se·quence (sí:kwəns) *n.* a succession of things which are connected in some way, *the sequence of events which led to his downfall* ‖ a series of poems connected by form and theme, *a sonnet sequence* ‖ (*cards*) three or more consecutive cards in a suit ‖ (*movies*) one complete scene in a film ‖ (*eccles.*) a hymnlike non-biblical text preceding the reading of the Gospel at High Mass or a Requiem Mass ‖ (*mus.*) a succession of phrases repeated at different pitches [fr. L.L. *sequentia*]
se·quent (sí:kwənt) **1.** *adj.* succeeding, following in time or order ‖ following as a natural result **2.** *n.* a result, consequence [O.F. fr. L. *sequens* (*sequentis*) fr. *sequi,* to follow]
se·quen·tial (sikwénʃəl) *adj.* characterized by or constituting a sequence ‖ occurring as a result [fr. L.L. *sequentia,* sequence]
sequential marketing (*business*) marketing strategy involving introduction of a product or service in one market segment at a time
sequentials *n.* (*pharm.*) estrogen-based pills prescribed in series to minimize side effects *also* sequential contraceptive pills
se·ques·ter (sikwéstər) *v.t.* (*law*) to seize (property etc.) until the owner pays a debt or satisfies some other demand ‖ to seize, confiscate by public authority ‖ (*rhet.*) to place apart from society **se·qués·tered** *adj.* withdrawn from social intercourse, *a sequestered life* ‖ in rural isolation, *a sequestered cottage* [fr. L.L. *sequestrare,* to commit for safekeeping]
se·ques·trate (sikwéstreit) *pres. part.* **se·ques·trat·ing** *past* and *past part.* **se·ques·trat·ed** *v.t.* to sequester ‖ (*Br., law*) to divert income from (property) from the owner or owners to another or others for a period of time [fr. L.L. *sequestrare* (*sequestratus*), to commit for safekeeping]
se·ques·tra·tion (si:kwestréiʃən, sikwestréiʃən) *n.* a sequestering or being sequestered [fr. L.L. *sequestratio* (*sequestrationis*)]
se·ques·tra·tor (sí:kwestreitər, sikwéstreitər) *n.* someone who sequestrates ‖ (*law*) a person appointed to administer sequestrated property [L.L.]
se·ques·trum (sikwéstrəm) *pl.* **se·ques·tra** (sikwéstrə), **se·ques·trums** *n.* (*med.*) a piece of dead tissue, esp. bone, which remains in its place although separated from the living tissue [Mod. L. = something separated, neut. of *sequester,* standing apart]
se·quin (sí:kwin) *n.* a small circular piece of glittering metal etc. sewn on to cloth for ornamentation ‖ (*hist.*) a Venetian gold coin [F. fr. Ital. fr. Arab.]
se·quoi·a (sikwɔ́iə) *n.* a member of *Sequoia,* fam. *Taxodiaceae,* a genus of very large North American coniferous trees including the redwood. The tallest reach more than 300 ft and the thickest have a trunk diameter of up to 35 ft [Mod. L. after *Sequoya,* Cherokee Indian leader who reduced the Cherokee language to writing]
Sequoia National Park a reservation (386,863 acres) in the Sierra Nevada Mtns of California, established (1890) by a U.S. Congressional act to protect giant sequoia groves
Se·quoya (səkwɔ́iə), (c. 1760-1843), American Cherokee Indian warrior credited with inventing the Cherokee written language (talking leaves), born George Guess. Having learned Spanish, French and English, and resenting the takeover of tribal lands by the whites, he developed a Cherokee alphabet to record and preserve the Cherokee culture. By 1821 he had developed 86 symbols for sounds. The syllabary was used in the newspaper 'Cherokee Phoenix' from 1828
se·rac (siræ̃k) *n.* (*geol.*) a pinnacle of ice formed by the crossing of crevasses where a glacier breaks at a fall [Swiss F. *sérac,* orig. the name of a cheese]
se·ragl·io (siræ̃ljou, sirɑ́ljou) *pl.* **se·ragl·ios** *n.* a harem ‖ a Turkish palace enclosed by walls [Ital. *serroglio,* enclosure]
se·ra·i (sərɑ́i:, serɑ́i) *pl.* **se·ra·is** *n.* a caravanserai [Turk.]
Se·ram·pur (serəmpúr) (or Serampore) a resort (pop. 75,000) in West Bengal, India, on the Hooghly River near Calcutta. It was a Danish settlement (Frederiksnagar), 1755-1845
se·ra·pe (sərɑ́pi:) *n.* a woolen blanket, often brightly colored, worn as a cloak by Spanish-Americans [Span.]
ser·aph (sérəf) *pl.* **ser·aphs, ser·a·phim** (sérəfim) *n.* a member of the highest order of angels (*ANGEL) [M.L. fr. Heb.]
se·raph·ic (siræ̃fik) *adj.* of or like a seraph ‖ angelic, *a seraphic smile* **se·ráph·i·cal** *adj.* [fr. eccles. L. *seracus*]
Se·ra·pis (siréipis) Egyptian deity whose cult flourished in the Ptolemaic and Roman periods. He was a god of healing, frequently identified with Osiris, Asclepius, Zeus and Dionysus
ser·a·ton·in [$C_{10}H_{12}ON_2$] (seratóunin) *n.* (*biochem.*) sleep-related hormone, derived from L-tryptophan, present in blood and nerve tissue, used to stimulate smooth muscles and nerves. Seratonin is believed to affect neurotransmission
Serb (sə:rb) **1.** *adj.* Serbian **2.** *n.* a member of a Slavic people of Serbia and adjacent regions ‖ their language
Ser·bi·a (sə́:rbi:ə), the largest and most populous constituent republic (area including Vojvodina and Kosovo-Metohija 36,937 sq. miles, pop. 8,860,000) of Yugoslavia. Capital: Belgrade. Serbia proper (pop. 4,900,000) is mainly mountainous, broken up by the broad valleys of the Morava and its tributaries. Crops: corn, cereals. Livestock: cattle. Mineral resources: lignite, copper, antimony. Hydroelectricity. HISTORY. Serbia emerged as a principality in the 9th c., but remained subject to the Byzantine Empire until consolidated (12th c.) by Stevan Nemanja. His son was crowned the first king of Serbia (1217). During the reign (1331-55) of Stevan Dušan, Serbia became the dominant power in the Balkans, but it was overthrown (1389) by the Turks at Kosovo Polje, and made a vassal state. It was fully incorporated in the Ottoman Empire (1459). Serbia revolted (1804) under Karageorge and was recognized by Turkey as independent (1828). Its independence was fully guaranteed by the Congress of Berlin (1878). Serbia acquired much of Macedonia after the Balkan Wars (1912-13), and became (1918) part of the kingdom later called Yugoslavia
Ser·bi·an (sə́:rbi:ən) **1.** *adj.* of or relating to Serbia, the Serbs, or their language **2.** *n.* Serbo-Croatian as spoken in Serbia
Ser·bo-Cro·a·tian (sə:rboukrouéiʃən) **1.** *n.* a S. Slavic language spoken by about 8,500,000 people in Yugoslavia and by minorities in Italy, Rumania and Hungary. Serbo-Croatian is divided into three main dialects. The literary language shows a strong Italian influence. The Croats use the Latin alphabet and the Serbs use the Cyrillic **2.** *adj.* of this language ‖ of the people who speak it
sere, sear (siər) *adj.* (*rhet.*) withered, dried up [O.E. sēar]
ser·e·nade (serənéid) **1.** *n.* a piece of music played or sung at night (cf. AUBADE) in the open air, esp. by a lover beneath his mistress' window ‖ a musical composition for several instruments in a number of movements **2.** *v. pres. part.* **ser·e·nad·ing** *past* and *past part.* **ser·e·nad·ed** *v.t.* to entertain with a serenade ‖ *v.i.* to perform a serenade [F. fr. Ital.]
se·re·na·ta (serənɑ́tə) *pl.* **ser·e·na·tas, ser·e·na·te** (serənɑ́tei) *n.* (*hist.*) a semioperatic cantata ‖ an orchestral serenade [Ital.]
ser·en·dip·i·ty (serəndípiti:) *n.* the gift of being able to make delightful discoveries by pure accident [coined by Horace Walpole after 'The Three Princes of Serendip', a fairy tale]
se·rene (sərí:n) *adj.* (of the weather) fine, clear and calm ‖ (of a person) tranquil, at peace with himself ‖ (of facial expression) expressing tranquility, inner calm ‖ used in the titles of certain members of some royal families, *His Serene Highness* [fr. L. *serenus*]
se·ren·i·ty (səréniti:) *n.* the state or quality of being serene ‖ calmness ‖ clearness **Se·ren·i·ty** *pl.* **Se·ren·i·ties** a title of respect used for certain members of some royal families [F. *sérénité*]
serf (sə:rf) *n.* (*hist.*) a feudal laborer bound to an estate **sérf·age, sérf·dom, sérf·hood** *ns.* [O.F.]
serge (sə:rdʒ) *n.* a hard-wearing twilled worsted fabric used for clothing [O.F. *serge, sarge,* a silk stuff]
ser·geant (sɑ́rdʒənt) *n.* (*mil.*) a noncommissioned officer ranking immediately above a corporal ‖ a police officer ranking immediately below (*Am.*) captain or lieutenant or (*Br.*) inspector ‖ a sergeant-at-arms [O.F. *sergent, serjant,* a servant]
Sergeant *n.* (*mil.*) a mobile, inertially guided, solid-propellant, surface-to-surface missile (MGM-29A), with nuclear warhead capability and a range of 75 nautical miles
ser·geant-at-arms, *Br.* **ser·jeant-at-arms** (sɑ́rdʒəntətɑ́rmz) *n.* an officer in a legislature whose main responsibility is the preservation of order
sergeant first class a noncommissioned army officer ranking below a master sergeant and above a staff sergeant
sergeant major the highest-ranking noncommissioned army or Marine Corps officer
se·ri·al (síəri:əl) **1.** *adj.* being, being arranged as, or forming a series ‖ (of a story, radio or television program etc.) appearing regularly in a series of parts ‖ of a serial or serials, *serial rights* ‖ (*mus.*) pertaining to twelve-tone composition **2.** *n.* a serial story, radio or television program etc. **sé·ri·al·ize** *v.t. pres. part.* **se·ri·al·iz·ing** *past* and *past part.* **se·ri·al·ized** [fr. Mod. L. *serialis* fr. *series,* a row, order]
serial access *n.* (*computer*) method of access to information based on physical location of the data
serial number the separate item number given to a unit of a series for identification
serial printer *n.* (*computer*) an output printer in which each character is printed in sequence by type bars, type balls, daisy wheel, etc. *also* character printer *Cf* LASER PRINTER, LINE PRINTER
se·ri·ate (síəri:it, síəri:eit) *adj.* arranged in a series [fr. Mod. L. *seriatus* fr. *series,* row, order]
se·ri·a·tim (siəri:éitim, seri:éitim) *adv.* point by point, one after another in order [M.L.]
se·ri·a·tion (siəri:éiʃən) *n.* arrangement in an order
se·ri·ceous (siríʃəs) *adj.* (*biol.*) covered with fine silky hairs [fr. L. *sericus*]
ser·i·cin (sérisin) *n.* a gelatinous protein that cements together the fibroin filaments in silk [L. *sericum,* silk]
ser·i·cul·ture (sérəkʌltʃər) *n.* the breeding of silkworms for the production of raw silk [shortened fr. F. *sériciculture*]
ser·i·e·ma (seri:í:mə, seri:éimə) *n.* *Cariama cristata,* fam. *Cariamidae,* a long-legged, crested S. Brazilian bird feeding on snakes, lizards etc. ‖

Chunga burmeisteri, a related bird of Argentina [Mod. L. fr. Tupi]

se·ries (síəri:z) *pl.* **se·ries** *n.* a number of similar things occurring one after another, in space or time, in an orderly way, esp. in such a way that each has a similar relation to the one preceding it, *a pagoda with a series of six progressively narrower roofs* || a number of successive events of the same kind, *a series of accidents* || (*bibliography*) a number of volumes, articles etc. published successively and falling under one general title || (of stamps and coins) a complete set || (*chem.*) a group of substances (usually compounds) related by structure and properties, *a homologous series* || (*geol.*) a division of rocks, formed during an epoch || (*math.*) the sum obtained by adding the terms of a mathematical sequence || (*chem.*) a period or a portion of a period of the periodic table, e.g. the lanthanide series **in series** (*elec.*) of cells or circuits so arranged that the current flows through each in succession (cf. PARALLEL) [L.=row, order]

ser·if (sérif) *n.* a small terminal line across the top or bottom of a main stroke of a printed or written letter [etym. doubtful]

ser·in (sérin) *n. Serinus canarius,* fam. *Fringillidae,* a small finch of central Europe related to the canary [F.]

se·rin·ga (səríŋgə) *n.* a member of *Hevea,* fam. *Euphorbiaceae,* a genus of Brazilian rubber trees || syringa [F.]

se·ri·o·com·ic (sɪəri:oukómik) *adj.* neither wholly serious nor wholly comic but partly both **se·ri·o·cóm·i·cal** *adj.*

se·ri·ous (síəri:əs) *adj.* of great importance, *a serious decision* || (of people) grave and thoughtful in manner || scholarly and thought-provoking, *a serious book* || in earnest || firmly devoted, *a serious bridge player* || alarming, critical, *a serious situation* [fr. F. *sérieux*]

ser·jeant (súrdʒənt) *n.* a sergeant-at-arms || a serjeant at law [O.F. *sergent, serjant,* a servant]

serjeant-at-arms *SERGEANT-AT-ARMS

serjeant at law (*hist.*) a member of the highest rank of barristers, prior to 1880, from which Common Law judges were appointed

ser·mon (sə́:rmən) *n.* an address delivered by a priest or minister to instruct or exhort a congregation || (*pop.*) a serious reproof or exhortation expressed at tedious length **sér·mon·ize** *pres. part.* **ser·mon·iz·ing** *past* and *past part.* **ser·mon·ized** *v.t.* and *i.* [A.F. *sermun*]

Sermon on the Mount Christ's discourse on the Mosaic Law. It includes the Beatitudes and the Lord's Prayer (Matthew v, vi, vii)

se·rol·o·gy (siróledʒi:) *n.* the scientific study of serums and their reactions, esp. the behavior of antibodies and antigens [fr. SERUM + Gk *logos,* word]

se·ros·i·ty (sirósiti:) *n.* the quality or state of being serous

se·rot·i·nous (sirót'nəs) *adj.* (*biol.*) appearing or blooming late in the season [fr. L. *serotinus* fr. *sero,* late]

se·ro·type (síərətaip) *v.* to classify microorganisms according to their antigens

se·rous (síərəs) *adj.* of or like serum || thin, watery [fr. F. *séreux*]

serous membrane a thin tissue that lines or encloses some organs and that produces serum, e.g. the pericardium

Se·row·e (seiróuei) a trade center (pop. 30,000) of E. Botswana

ser·pent (sə́:rpənt) *n.* a snake || (*Bible*) the devil, Satan || (*mus., hist.*) an early bass wind instrument with a long, coiled tube [O.F.]

ser·pen·tine (sə́:rpənti:n, sə́:rpəntain) **1.** *adj.* of or like a serpent || twisting, winding **2.** *n.* a hydrated magnesium silicate, usually dark green, with mottled coloring, used for ornaments [O.F. *serpentin* fr. L. *serpentinus*]

Ser·ra (sérrɑ), Miguel José (in religion, Junípero, 1713-84) Spanish Franciscan priest, apostle to California

Ser·ra A·ca·ra·hy (sérrɑqkɑrɑí:) (Serra Acaraí) a mountain range rising to 2,500 ft and forming the boundary between Guyana and Brazil

Ser·ra da Es·trel·la (sérrədəistrélə) a mountain range in N. central Portugal: highest point 6,532 ft

ser·rate (sérit, séreit) *adj.* (of the edge of a leaf or other structure) having notches or teeth like the cutting edge of a saw **ser·rat·ed** (seréitid) *adj.* **ser·rá·tion** *n.* [fr. L. *serratus* fr. *serra,* a saw]

ser·ried (séri:d) *adj.* close set, arranged closely side by side, *serried ranks of spectators* || ridged [*past part.* of older *serry* v. fr. F. *serrer,* to close]

ser·ro·dyn·ing (sȩrədáiniŋ) *n.* (*mil.*) technique to prevent enemy radar from discerning the velocity of approaching craft, achieved by varying the voltage of communications in a saw-tooth pattern and varying frequency, so that counter equipment loses contact

ser·ru·late (sérjulit, sérjuleit, sérəlit, sérəleit) *adj.* (*biol.*) finely notched, finely serrate **sér·ru·lat·ed** *adj.* **ser·ru·lá·tion** *n.* [fr. Mod. L. *serrulatus* fr. *serrula,* a little saw]

ser·tão (sertãu) *n.* the semi-arid, thinly populated interior of N.E. Brazil [Port.]

Ser·to·ri·us (sərtɔ́ri:əs, sərtóuri:əs), Quintus (c. 123-72 B.C.), Roman general, a supporter of Marius in the civil war against Sulla. He gained control of most of Spain (83-76 B.C.), and organized a senate and a school for the sons of native chiefs. Checked by Pompey, he was murdered at Huesca

Ser·tür·ner (zertýrnər), Friedrich Wilhelm (1783-1841), German chemist. He discovered morphine (1805), isolating it from opium

se·rum (síerəm) *pl.* **se·rums, se·ra** (síərə) *n.* the colorless liquid remaining after blood has clotted || the watery part of any animal fluid after coagulation (cf. PLASMA) || blood serum. In serum therapy an animal serum with specific antibodies is injected into the bloodstream of a human being to immunize him against a particular disease [L.=watery fluid]

ser·val (sə́:rvəl) *n. Felis capensis* or *F. serval,* fam. *Felidae,* a long-legged, blackspotted African wildcat [Mod. L. fr. Port. *lobo cerval,* lynx]

serv·ant (sə́:rvənt) *n.* a person paid to wait on another or others, esp. to do work in or around a house || an official, *a public servant* || someone devoted to a cause etc., *a faithful servant of the Church* [F.]

serve (sə:rv) **1.** *v. pres. part.* **serv·ing** *past* and *past part.* **served** *v.t.* to be a servant to || to satisfy the needs or requirements of (a person, organization etc.), *his old car has served him well* || to render service to (one's country) under arms || (of store employees) to supply (customers) with goods || (of store employees) to supply (goods) to customers || (*law*) to deliver (a writ, summons etc.) || (*law*) to present (someone) with a writ, summons etc. || to bring (food etc.) to the table for distribution, *lunch is served* || to distribute (food etc.) at a meal, *to serve the vegetables* || to distribute food etc. to, *to serve one's guests* || to undergo (a term of imprisonment) || to work through (a term of apprenticeship, training etc.) || to act as server at (Mass) || to assist (a priest) as server || to fulfill (a requirement), *any heavy object will serve the purpose* || to supply a service to, *two libraries serve the town* || to treat, *fate served her badly* || (*animal husbandry*) to mate with (a female animal) || to keep in operation (a large gun) || (*naut.*) to protect (a rope) with a binding || (*tennis* etc.) to hit (the ball) to an opponent to start play || *v.i.* to be a servant || to do military service || to carry out orders or duties, *to serve is to learn how to command* || to act as server at the Eucharist || to function, *this box can serve as a table* || to be sufficient for a particular need, *this cushion will serve* || to distribute food etc. at the table || to wait on the table || (of store employees) to supply goods to customers || (*tennis* etc.) to start play by hitting the ball to an opponent **to serve someone right** to be the punishment someone deserves **2.** *n.* (*tennis* etc.) a service **sérv·er** *n.* someone who serves. esp. an assistant to the celebrant at the Eucharist || (*tennis* etc.) the player whose turn it is to serve || a salver, spoon etc. used in serving [O.F. *servir*]

Ser·ve·tus (sərví:təs), Michael (Miguel Serveto, 1511-53), Spanish doctor and theologian, burned alive on the orders of Calvin at Geneva for denying Christ's divinity and the Christian doctrine of the Trinity

Ser·vice (sə́:rvis), Robert William (1874-1958), Canadian writer, born in England. Known for his ballads, he wrote 'The Spell of the Yukon' (1907) in which were the ballads 'The Shooting of Dan McGrew' and 'The Cremation of Sam McGee'; 'Ballad of a Cheechako' (1909); 'Rhymes of Rolling Stone' (1912) and 'Rhymes of a Red Cross Man' (1916). His autobiography is a two-volume work, 'Ploughman of the Moon' (1945) and 'Harper of Heaven' (1948)

serv·ice (sə́:rvis) **1.** *n.* the occupation of being a servant || government employment || a branch of government employment, *the diplomatic service* || a branch (army, navy etc.) of the armed forces, or the armed forces as a career or occupation || the performance of military duties, esp. in war, *he saw service on several fronts* || (*pl.*) the products of an employee's or professional man's paid activities, *to dispense with someone's services* || assistance or advantage given to another || the benefit derived from this || use, *still in service* || a set form of public worship or the music written for this || (*law*) notification of legal action by delivery of a summons, writ etc. || (*tennis* etc.) the act or manner of serving the ball || (*tennis* etc.) a turn to serve || (*tennis* etc.) a ball served || (*Br., pl.*) utilities, e.g. gas, water and electricity, as supplied to a building || the act or manner of serving food, esp. in a restaurant || maintenance, repairs etc. provided by a dealer for items bought from him || the cups, plates, dishes etc. used in serving a particular meal, drink etc., *a tea service* || (*econ.,* esp. *pl.*) a product of human activity (e.g. transport, research) meant to satisfy a human need but not constituting an item of goods || scheduled public transportation, *an hourly bus service* || the time and route of a bus, airplane etc. operating to a public transportation schedule, *summer services resume next week* || attendance on a client, esp. with respect to quality || (*animal husbandry*) the serving of a female animal by a male **2.** *adj.* of or for servants or service, *service entrance* || of or for the armed forces || (*mil.,* of a uniform) for use in ordinary service || providing services **3.** *v.t. pres. part.* **serv·ic·ing** *past* and *past part.* **serv·iced** to provide maintenance facilities for (cars, machinery etc.) || to provide a service for [O.F. *servise, service*]

service *n.* the service tree || its fruit [O.E. *syrfe* fr. L. *sorbus*]

serv·ice·a·bil·i·ty (sə:rvisəbíliti:) *n.* the quality of being serviceable

serv·ice·a·ble (sə́:rvisəb'l) *adj.* able to be of use though old, damaged etc. || durable, suited for hard use [O.F. *serviçable, servisable*]

serv·ice·ber·ry (sə́:rvisbȩri:) *pl.* **serv·ice·ber·ries** *n.* a Juneberry plant || its fruit

serv·ice·man (sə́:rvismæ̜n, sə́:rvismən) *pl.* **serv·ice·men** (sə́:rvismȩn, sə́:rvismən) *n.* a member of the military forces || a man who services machinery, equipment etc.

service medal a medal awarded for long military service or service in a particular war or campaign

service module in a spacecraft, the area containing propulsion, fuel, and other consumables *abbr.* **SM** *Cf* COMMAND MODULE, LUNAR MODULE

service pipe a pipe which links a main pipe, e.g. a gas or water main, to a building

service road a road branching off a main road and usually running parallel to it, providing access to stores, houses etc. and used exclusively by such local traffic

service station a filling station with a staff for servicing, but without garage or workshop facilities

service stripe (*mil.*) a stripe worn on the sleeve to indicate length of service

service tree *Sorbus domestica,* fam. *Rosaceae,* a European tree bearing small, edible, pear-shaped fruit || *S. torminalis,* fam. *Rosaceae,* a similar tree bearing bitter fruit

ser·vi·ette (sə:rvi:ét) *n.* (esp. *Br.*) a table napkin [F.]

ser·vile (sə́:rvil, sə́:rvail) *adj.* like a slave or like the state of slavery || showing oneself to be in complete submission to another || having or showing no originality whatever, *servile imitation* **ser·vil·i·ty** (sə:rvíliti:) *n.* [fr. L. *servilis*]

serv·ing (sə́:rviŋ) **1.** *n.* the act of one who or that which serves || a portion of food or drink **2.** *adj.* used in holding or passing out food or drink, *a serving table*

Ser·vite (sə́:rvait) *n.* a member of a mendicant order of friars founded (1233) in Florence and devoted to the service of the Virgin Mary

ser·vi·tor (sə́:rvitər) *n.* (*hist.*) a male attendant or servant [O.F.]

ser·vi·tude (sə́:rvitu:d, sə́:rvitju:d) *n.* slavery, bondage || (*law*) a right in respect of land or other property in virtue of which the property is subject to use or enjoyment in a specified way by another person [F.]

ser·vo control (sə́:rvou) an automatic device which aids a pilot's effort in controlling the airfoils of an aircraft

ser·vo·mech·an·ism (sə́:rvoumekənizəm, sə:rvoumékənizəm) *n.* a device by which one mechanism controls the movement of another, independently powered one. Its operation depends on feedback: a signal proportional to the difference in action between master and slave mechanisms is amplified and applied as a correction to reduce the difference || (*eng.*) a control device that operates automatically to adjust to the desired end when input varies, e.g., a thermostat || (*eng.*) a double-sided vacuum-based device to provide pressure in hydrostatic brakes || (*computer*) the mechanical motion device in a computer system used to control the position of the output

ses·a·me (sésəmi:) *n. Sesamum indicum*, fam. *Pedaliaceae*, a herbaceous tropical and subtropical plant with small flat seeds, used as food and yielding a bland, pale yellow oil used in salads, margarine and soap and as a laxative [fr. L. *sesamum*]

ses·a·moid (sésəmɔid) **1.** *adj.* (of a bone or cartilage) of or being a nodular mass in a tendon passing over a joint (e.g. the patella) or bony structure **2.** *n.* such a bone or cartilage [fr. L. *sesamoides*, shaped like a sesame seed, fr. Gk]

ses·qui·cen·ten·ni·al (seskwisenténi:əl) **1.** *adj.* of or relating to a century and a half **2.** *n.* a 150th anniversary [fr. L. *sesqui-*, a half in addition+ CENTENNIAL]

ses·qui·ox·ide (seskwi:ɒ́ksaid, seskwi:ɒ́ksid) *n.* an oxide containing three atoms of oxygen in combination with two of the other atoms constituting the molecule

ses·sile (sésil, sésail) *adj.* (*bot.*, of leaves etc.) attached directly at the base, with no intervening support such as a pedicel, peduncle or stalk || (*anat.*, *zool.*) stationary, permanently fixed || (*anat.*, *zool.*) attached directly by its base [L. *sessilis*, sitting down]

ses·sion (séʃən) *n.* the sitting of a court, parliament or other assembly for official business || a single meeting of such a body || the period between the opening and prorogation of parliament || an academic year or term || a period of time spent in some activity || (in Presbyterian churches) the governing body of an individual congregation composed of elders and the minister **sés·sion·al** *adj.* [F.]

Ses·sions (séʃənz), Roger (1896-1985), American composer. He wrote three symphonies, chamber music, songs, the opera 'The Trial of Lucullus' and the cantata 'Turn O Libertad'

ses·terce (séstə:rs) *n.* an ancient Roman coin worth a quarter of a denarius [L.]

ses·ter·ti·um (sestə́:rʃi:əm, sestə́:rʃəm) *pl.* **ses·ter·ti·a** (sestə́:rʃi:ə, sestə́:rʃə) *n.* an ancient Roman monetary unit equal to 1,000 sesterces [L.]

ses·tet (sestét, séstet) *n.* the last six lines of a sonnet [fr. Ital. *sestetto*]

ses·ti·na (sestí:nə) *pl.* **ses·ti·nas, ses·ti·ne** (sestí:nei) *n.* a poem with six six-line stanzas, each having the same six line-end words though not in the same order, and a three-line envoy containing these six words [Ital.]

Set (set) (*Egypt. mythol.*) the god of evil, represented with an animal's head and long snout

set 1. *v. pres. part.* **set·ting** *past* and *past part.* **set** *v.t.* to cause to occupy a certain position, *set the bowl in the center* || to put (a hen etc.) on eggs to hatch them || to put (eggs) to hatch || (often with 'out') to plant (seedlings, bulbs etc.) || to put (one's jaw or shoulders) into a position showing determination, *he set his shoulders squarely* || to decorate, encrust e.g. with gems || to bring (a lighted match) into contact with something else, *set a match to the leaves* || to cause to be in a specified condition or state, *to set leaves on fire, to set someone thinking* || to cause to be arranged in readiness or in working order, *to set a trap* || to adjust, regulate, *to set a clock* || to fix in a desired position, *set the pointer at 20* || to bring together the parts of (a broken bone) in a position for healing, mending etc. || to curl or wave (hair) by arranging it damp with hairpins or curlers and letting it dry || to put (a seal) on paper || to put (words) to music || (*printing*, often with 'up') to compose (type) || (*printing*, often with 'up') to put (manuscript) into type || to lay (a table) || to fix (a sail) so as to catch the wind || to cause (a blade) to have a sharp edge || to adjust the teeth of (a saw) || to fix (e.g. one's mind, purpose or heart) firmly on something || to cause (e.g. a jelly) to become firm in consistency || to make (a color) fast || to cause to go in a specified direction, *they set their horses towards home* || to fix (a time, date etc.) for something, *they set midnight for the escape* || to fix (limits etc.), *to set a term for a project* || to establish (a standard in performance or a record in competition) || to furnish (a precedent or an example) || to station (someone) for a specific duty, *to set sentries at the gate* || to put (someone) to work on a specified task || to assign or allot (a lesson, task etc.) || (*Br.*) to stipulate the written or practical work for (an examination, homework etc.) || to fix (an amount of work etc.) || to begin to apply (oneself) to a task etc., *he set himself to his chores* || to fix (an amount, price etc.), *the club set $100 as the membership fee* || to fix at an amount, price etc., *they set the goal at $1,000* || to place (value) on something or someone, *she sets great store by him* || to value (someone or something) in a certain way, *to set honor before glory* || to place (a scene of a play, novel etc.) in some locality || to arrange (scenery) in a certain way on the stage || to arrange scenery on (the stage) || (*baking*) to put aside (dough) to rise || *v.i.* to become firm in consistency || (of colors) to become fast || (of a hen) to sit on eggs || (of the sun etc.) to appear to descend below the horizon || to go in a specified direction, *the current sets to the north* || (of a broken bone) to become whole again, mend || (of clothes) to fit in a specified way || (of a flower, seed or fruit) to develop while still attached to the parent plant || (of a gundog) to indicate the presence of game by assuming a rigid attitude || (*square dancing*) to dance facing one's partner **to set about** to begin to cope with **to set against** to make unsympathetic or hostile toward || to place (something) in juxtaposition to something else for contrast or balance **to set apart** to put to one side, reserve || to cause to be seen to be different, outstanding etc. **to set aside** to put aside, esp. temporarily || to reject, dismiss, esp. from the mind || to annul **to set back** to check the progress of || to put (a timepiece) to an earlier time **to set down** to put in writing or in print || (with 'as') to record one's opinion of (someone or something), *they set him down as unfit* **to set forth** to give an account of || to begin a journey **to set in** to insert || (*naut.*) to sail (a boat) toward land || (of weather or a natural catastrophe) to begin to be prevalent || (*naut.*) to go toward land **to set off** to start (on a journey) || to bring into prominence by contrast, *the red scarf set off the dark tweed* || to cause to explode || to cause (someone) to begin an activity (e.g. laughing or talking) **to set on** to attack || to cause to attack, pursue etc. **to set out** to begin a journey || to have a specified intention in beginning some undertaking, *he sets out to prove that Shakespeare was a woman* || to arrange as a display, *to set out merchandise on a counter* **to set to** to begin a fight || to begin a piece of work with determination **to set up** to start in business etc., *to set up as a grocer* || to institute, establish (e.g. an organization) || to put (a drink) in front of a customer || to treat (somebody) to something, *he set them all up with ice cream* || to place in an upright position || to arrange (a machine etc.) in a state in which it can be used, *to set up a sewing machine* || to elate, make happy, *the compliment set her up for the day* **to set upon** to attack with murderous violence **2.** *adj.* located, *a house set in a hollow* || fixed, *a set date* || determined, *a set purpose, set on becoming an actress* || routine, invariable, *a set practice* || rigid, immovable || (of opinions) tenaciously held || firm in consistency || (of a book) prescribed for examination || (of a topic) specified || (of someone's ways) inflexible, unchanging || (of a speech, answer etc.) prepared beforehand || stereotyped, *a set formula* || ready, *set for trouble* || ready and keen, *all set to go* || (of a fight or battle) pitched **3.** *n.* a number of things related to one another by similarity (e.g. of nature, appearance or use), considered as a whole and without regard to the order in which they are arranged in space or time, *a set of carpenter's tools, a tea set, a set of teeth* || a number of people having similar interests, occupations etc. or the same friends || a television or radio receiver || (*tennis*) a group of games counting as a unit toward a match. It is constituted by the winning of six games before the opponent has won more than four. If the opponent wins more than four, play continues until one side is two games up || the direction of motion e.g. of a current or wind || the way clothing fits or hangs || the posture or position of the body or a part of the body, *the set of his jaw* || a deflection from a straight line or usual form because of some sort of strain or pressure || the deflection in alternate directions of the teeth of a saw, or the amount of this || the setting of hair by arranging it damp with hairpins or curlers and letting it dry || a young plant or rooted cutting ready for transplanting || a little bulb, corm or tuber for planting out || (*printing*) the spacing between words with regard to closeness || (*printing*) the width of the shank of a piece of type || a badger's burrow || a clutch of eggs || the act of a gundog that sets || the flats, drops, furniture, props etc. used in the theater or in film making to set a scene || (*square dancing*) the number of persons required to execute the figures in a dance || (*square dancing*) the figure formed at the start of a dance [O.E. *settan*]

se·ta (sí:tə) *pl.* **se·tae** (sí:ti:) *n.* (*biol.*) any of various bristlelike structures || (*bot.*) the stalk of the sporogonium of mosses and liverworts || (*zool.*) a bristle or stiff hair, e.g. in earthworms [L. = a bristle]

se·ta·ceous (sitéiʃəs) *adj.* (*biol.*) having or resembling bristles [fr. Mod. L. *setaceus*]

set-a·sides (sétəsaids) *n.* minimum quotas for special groups, esp. black, small business, in affirmative action programs

set·back (sétbæk) *n.* an unwelcome reversal of fortune || an impeding of progress || (*archit.*) a setting back of a building or part of a building behind the building line to give adequate daylight to adjacent buildings or streets

Se·ti I (sí:tai, séiti:) (*d.* c. 1290 B.C.), king of Egypt (c. 1303–c. 1290 B.C.), of the 19th dynasty. He conquered Palestine and Libya, and built a temple to Osiris at Abydos

Se·tif (seití:f) a commercial center (pop. 94,000) in Algeria in the northeastern plateau at 3,600 ft

set·line (sétlain) *n.* a strong fishline having hooks on short lines attached to it at frequent intervals. It is put out at low tide, or strung out in a river

set·off (sétɔf, sétɒf) *n.* something counterbalancing something else || (*law*) the balancing of a debt by money owed by the creditor to the debtor || (*archit.*) an offset || (*printing*) an image smudged on the back of a printed sheet from the freshly printed sheet beneath it, through failure of the ink to dry

Se·ton (sí:t'n), Elizabeth Ann (née Bayley, 1774-1821), U.S. founder (1812) of the American Sisters of Charity, an organization of Catholic nuns, which laid the foundations of the parochial school system in the U.S.A. She was canonized (1975), becoming the first native-born American to be named a saint

se·ton (sí:t'n) *n.* (*vet.*) threads or horsehairs passed beneath a section of skin and left with the ends protruding to form an issue from, or to promote drainage of, a wound [fr. M.L. *seto* (*setonis*), silk]

Se·to Nai·kai (sétounáikái) *INLAND SEA

set·screw (sétskru:) *n.* a screw passed through one part of a machine into another part, or tightly against it, to prevent relative motion

set square a flat, triangular piece of wood, metal etc. with angles of 90°, 60° and 30° or 90°, 45° and 45°, for drawing lines at angles

set·tee (setí:) *n.* a long, usually padded seat or couch with a back and often with arms, for two people or for three

set·ter (sétər) *n.* a large long-haired gundog of any of various breeds trained to stand rigid on scenting game

set theory the division of mathematics or symbolic logic that treats the nature and relationships of groups

set·ting (sétiŋ) *n.* the act of someone who, or something which, sets || the frame in which a gem is set || the background against which a person or thing is seen, *she looks at home in that setting* || the local or historical background of a story || the music to which words are to be sung || the contrived or natural background against which actors play || the position at which the indicator is set on a scale || a clutch of eggs

set·tle (sét'l) *pres. part.* **set·tling** *past* and *past part.* **set·tled** *v.i.* to cease to move around and come quietly or gently to rest, *a bird settled on the bough* || take up permanent residence, *on retiring he settled in a village* || (often with 'out') to sink slowly and come to rest, *a sediment settled at the bottom of the bottle* || (of a turbid liquid) to become clear when the suspension sinks to the bottom || (of a building etc.) to sink very slowly || to come to a decision after hesitation between alternatives || to end a dispute or difference by dealing with one's opponents, *to settle out of court* || to adjust accounts, *we will settle with you later* || (of a fog etc.) to descend on the landscape || (of silence etc.) to descend on a group or person || (of a disease etc.) to become localized || to pay what is owing or agree on a sum of money to be paid out || (of the ground) to become firm, esp. after severe rain or frost || *v.t.* to cause to cease to move around || to cause to take up permanent residence || to provide (a region) with settlers || to take up residence in as settlers || to clarify (a liquid) by causing suspended matter to sink to the bottom || to pay (a debt) || to end (an argument, conflict, doubt etc.) by reaching a decision || to fix definitely (a price, hour etc.) by mutual agreement || to put in order, arrange || to make stable || (*old-fash.*) to establish in marriage, business etc. || to make (the nerves, stomach, mind etc.) calm || to decide (a legal dispute) out of court **to settle down** to adopt a quiet, regular way of life || to become quiet and peaceful || to apply oneself to **settle up** to arrange differences || to adjust accounts **to settle (something) upon** (or **on**) **someone** to make over (property etc.) to someone by legal means [O.E. *setlan*]

settle *n.* a long wooden seat with arms and a high, straight back [O.E. *setl*, a seat]

set·tle·ment (sét'lmənt) *n.* a settling or being settled || a choice or decision made to end a controversy || a region in which settlers live, esp. that small part of it in which they have their homes || a small, isolated hamlet or village || the conveyance of property etc. settled on a person, e.g. at marriage || the property etc. so conveyed || an institution established and maintained esp. in the poorer sections of a large city to provide e.g. educational and recreational facilities for those in the area

Settlement, Act of (*Eng. hist.*) a law passed (1701) by parliament, fixing the succession to the throne on the house of Hanover should William III and Anne die without heirs. George I owed his succession (1714) to this law

set·tler (sétlər) *n.* a colonist, esp. an early colonist in any area

settling day the fortnightly payday on the London Stock Exchange

set-to (séttu:) *pl.* **set-tos** *n.* (*pop.*) a verbal quarrel || a scuffle, a fight

Se·tú·bal (sitú:bɑl) a fishing port and agricultural market (pop. 64,531) in Portugal, 20 miles southeast of Lisbon. Gothic church, castle (16th c.)

set-up (sétʌp) *n.* (*pop.*) all the arrangements, installations etc. that enable some activity to be carried on || (*pop.*) the way in which the component parts make it possible for a mechanical etc. system to work

Seu·rat (sə:ræ), Georges (1859-91), French Post-impressionist painter. His consuming interest in theories of color was based on analysis of the mechanism of the eye's perception of the effects of light and led to his use of pointillism. He also developed equally brilliant methods of composition, based on the golden section ('le Chenal de Gravelines un soir'). His 'Baignade' (1884) and 'Un dimanche d'été à la Grande-Jatte' (1886) are generally considered his greatest works

Se·vas·to·pol (səvǽstəpoul, sevɑstɔ́pʌlj) a port, resort and naval base (pop. 328,000) in the Crimea, S. Ukraine, U.S.S.R., on the Black Sea. It withstood an Allied siege for 11 months (1854-5) during the Crimean War, and a German siege for eight months (1941-2) during the 2nd world war

se·ven (sévən) **1.** *adj.* being one more than six (*NUMBER TABLE) **2.** *n.* six plus one || the cardinal number representing this (7, VII) || seven o'clock || a playing card marked with seven spots [O.E. *seofon*]

Seven Days Battles a Confederate counteroffensive (1862) during the Civil War, led by General Robert E. Lee. For two years it saved Richmond, Va., from Union attack

seven deadly sins pride, covetousness, lust, gluttony, anger, envy, sloth

Sev·en·er (sévənər) *n.* an Isma'ili

Seven Sages, the the seven political philosophers and politicians of ancient Greece, usually taken as Bias, Chilon, Cleobulus, Periander, Pittaeus, Solon and Thales

seven seas, the (*rhet.*) the navigable waters of every part of the globe

Seven Sisters a group of long-established, distinguished colleges of the eastern U.S.A., comprising Vassar, Radcliffe, Sarah Lawrence, Wellesley, Mt Holyoke, Barnard, and Smith, all formerly exclusively for women || (*colloq.*) a nickname for the major oil producers Exxon, Royal Dutch-Shell, Texaco, Standard Oil Co. of California (Socol, marketed as Chevron), Mobil, Gulf, British Petroleum

sev·en·teen (sév'ntí:n) **1.** *adj.* being one more than 16 (*NUMBER TABLE) **2.** *n.* ten plus seven || the cardinal number representing this (17, XVII) [O.E. *seofontīene, seofontēne, seofontȳne*]

sev·en·teenth (sév'ntí:nθ) **1.** *adj.* being number 17 in a series (*NUMBER TABLE) || being one of the 17 equal parts of anything **2.** *n.* the person or thing next after the 16th || one of 17 equal parts of anything (1/17) || the 17th day of a month [O. E. *seofontēotha*]

Seventeenth Amendment (1913) an amendment to the U.S. Constitution that provides for the election of senators by popular vote. Vacancies can be filled by appointment, but only temporarily, until an election can take place

sev·enth (sév'nθ) **1.** *adj.* being number seven in a series (*NUMBER TABLE) || being one of the seven equal parts of anything || **2.** *n.* the person or thing next after the sixth || one of seven equal parts of anything(1/7) || the seventh day of a month || (*mus.*) the note seven steps above or below a given note in a diatonic scale, inclusive of both notes || (*mus.*) the interval between these notes || (*mus.*) a combination of these notes **3.** *adv.* in the seventh place || (followed by a superlative) except six, *the seventh biggest* [O.E. *seofunda, siofunda*]

Seventh Amendment (1791) an amendment to the U.S. Constitution that guarantees the right to trial by jury, part of the Bill of Rights. It has been defined by the Supreme Court as requiring twelve members of the jury (later (1973) six-member juries were made possible) before a judge. The verdict must be unanimous for acquittal or conviction

Seventh-Day Adventist a member of an Adventist sect, founded (1844) in the U.S.A., which keeps Saturday as the sabbath

seventh heaven a state of supreme bliss

sev·en·ti·eth (sévənti:iθ) **1.** *adj.* being number 70 in a series (*NUMBER TABLE) || being one of the 70 equal parts of anything **2.** *n.* the person or thing next after the 69th || one of 70 equal parts of anything (1/70) [SEVENTY]

sev·en·ty (sévənti:) **1.** *adj.* being ten more than 60 (*NUMBER TABLE) **2.** *pl.* **sev·en·ties** *n.* seven times ten || the cardinal number representing this (70, LXX) **the seventies** (of temperature, a person's age, a century etc.) the span 70-9 [O.E. *seofontig, hundseofontig*]

sev·en·ty-five (sévənti:fáiv) *n.* (*mil.*) a 75-mm. gun, esp. the famous French field gun of this caliber used in the 1st world war

Seven Weeks' War the Austro-Prussian war of 1866, provoked by Bismarck over the Schleswig-Holstein controversy. Prussia was supported by Italy, while Austria was allied with Saxony, Hanover and several S. German states. The Prussian army under von Moltke won rapid victories, ending with the decisive Battle of Sadowa (July 3, 1866) and the Treaty of Prague (Aug. 23, 1866)

Seven Wonders of the World seven monuments considered by the ancient world as remarkable for their size and splendor. They were usually listed as: the hanging gardens of Babylon, the pyramid of Khufu at Giza, the temple of Artemis at Ephesus, Phidias's statue of Zeus at Olympia, the Colossus of Rhodes, the tomb of Mausolus at Halicarnassus and the Pharos at Alexandria

Seven Years' War a war (1756-63) fought in Europe, North America and India between Prussia, with British financial support, and a coalition of Austria, Russia and France. It was provoked by Austrian attempts to regain Silesia after the War of the Austrian Succession (1740-8), and by colonial rivalry between France and Britain. The war was settled by the Treaty of Hubertusburg. In North America (*FRENCH AND INDIAN WAR), Britain gained Canada and other territories from France, and Florida from Spain (*PARIS, TREATY OF, 1763). French power in India was destroyed and Britain became the world's chief colonial power

sev·er (sévər) *v.t.* to cut completely through || to divide from the main part || to cut (esp. a part of the body) into two pieces, *to sever a nerve* || to break off, bring to an end, *to sever a friendship* || *v.i.* to become divided or ended in this way **sév·er·a·ble** *adj.* capable of being severed || (of a contract etc.) capable of being divided into distinct rights or obligations [A.F. *severer*, O.F. *sevrer*, to wean]

sev·er·al (sévərəl, sévrəl) **1.** *adj.* being more than two but not many, *we met several times* || separate, individual, *they went their several ways* **2.** *n.* (followed by 'of') a small number of persons or things, *several of the children were in the garden* **3.** *pron.* a small number of persons or things, *several were in the garden* **sév·er·al·ly** *adv.* each by itself, apart from others, separately [A.F.]

sev·er·al·ty (sévərəlti:, sévrəlti:) *pl.* **sev·er·al·ties** *n.* (*law*, usually with 'in') possession by a single individual only, *an estate held in severalty* || (*law*) land or property so possessed [A.F. *severalte, severaute*]

sev·er·ance (sévərəns, sévrəns) *n.* a severing or being severed [A.F.]

se·vere (sivíər) *adj.* having no sympathy for, and making no concessions to, what are regarded as human weaknesses, *a severe critic* || harsh, *severe punishment* || austere, *severe architecture* || difficult to endure, *a severe pain* || difficult and trying, *a severe test* [F. *sévère* or fr. L. *severus*]

se·ver·i·ty (sivériti:) *pl.* **se·ver·i·ties** *n.* the state or quality of being severe || an instance of being severe [F. *sévérité*]

Sev·ern (sévərn) a river (210 miles long, navigable for 178 miles) rising in central Wales and following in a semicircle through W. central England to a wide estuary forming the head of the Bristol Channel

Se·ver·na·ya Zem·lya (sjévərnɑjəzjəmljú) (North Land) an uninhabited archipelago (area 14,300 sq. miles) consisting of three large islands off the Taimyr Peninsula, U.S.S.R., discovered in 1913

Severus, Alexander *ALEXANDER SEVERUS

Se·ve·rus (sivíərəs), Lucius Septimius (146-211), Roman emperor (193-211). He was proclaimed emperor by his troops, and defeated two other usurpers (193 and 194). He took Byzantium (196), defeated another rival (197) and drove the Parthians from Mesopotamia (198)

Se·vier (sivíər), John (1745-1815), American frontiersman, Revolutionary War soldier, and first governor (1796-1801, 1803-9) of the state of Tennessee

Sé·vi·gné (seivi:njei), Marie de Rabutin-Chantal, marquise de (1626-96), French letter writer. Her letters to her daughter Madame de Grignan and to her friends were the literary work of an intelligent, devoted and witty woman, very human and generous. They tell of events and manners of the day, of court, city and country life and of the things of the heart

Se·ville (səvíl, sévil) (*Span.* Sevilla) a province (area 5,428 sq. miles, pop. 1,477,428) of S.W. Spain (*ANDALUSIA) || its capital (pop. 616,900), historic capital of Andalusia, a sea and river port on the Guadalquivir 50 miles from its mouth. Industries: textiles, chemicals, earthenware. Alcazar (Almohad palace, begun 1181), Gothic cathedral (15th c.), other Moorish, Renaissance and baroque monuments. University (1502). It has a famous Holy Week festival. Iberian in origin, Seville was a Roman city, and was a center of Arab culture before the Castilian reconquest in 1248. From 1503 to 1717 it had the monopoly of trade with Spanish America

Se·ville orange (sévil) a bitter orange, used for making marmalade || *Citrus aurantium*, the tree bearing this orange [after SEVILLE Spain]

Sè·vres (sevr) *n.* porcelain made at Sèvres, France, on the outskirts of Paris. The classic type of tableware is ornamented with painted designs and gilding (*POMPADOUR, MARQUISE DE)

Sèvres, Deux- *DEUX-SÈVRES

sew (sou) *pres. part.* **sew·ing** *past* **sewed** *past part.* **sewn** (soun), **sewed** *v.t.* to join or fasten by stitches made with a needle and thread || to make or repair (garments etc.) in this way || to bind (the sheets of a book) in this way (cf. STITCH) || *v.i.* to use a needle and thread || to earn one's living as a seamstress or tailor **to sew up** to close a gap in (a fabric) by sewing the edges together || to enclose by sewing || (*pop.*) to attend to all the detail of (something, e.g. a contract) and finish it [O.E. *siwan, siowan*]

sew·age (sú:idʒ) *n.* the waste matter that is carried away through sewers

sewage farm a farm where sewage is treated and used to fertilize and irrigate

Sew·all (sú:əl), Samuel (1652-1730), American colonial judge and diarist. He was one of the special commissioners presiding (1692) over the Salem witchcraft trials, which sentenced 19

CONCISE PRONUNCIATION KEY: (a) æ, *cat*; ɑ, *car*; ɔ *fawn*; ei, *snake*. (e) e, *hen*; i:, *sheep*; iə, *deer*; ɛə, *bear*. (i) i, *fish*; ai, *tiger*; ə:, *bird*. (o) ɒ, *ox*; au, *cow*; ou, *goat*; u, *poor*; ɔi, *royal*. (u) ʌ, *duck*; u, *bull*; u:, *goose*; ə, *bacillus*; ju:, *cube*. x, *loch*; θ, *think*; ð, *bother*; z, *Zen*; ʒ, *corsage*; dʒ, *savage*; ŋ, *orangutang*; j, *yak*; ʃ, *fish*; tʃ, *fetch*; 'l, *rabble*; 'n, *redden*. Complete pronunciation key appears inside front cover.

persons to death. He later (1697) acknowledged his mistake. His diary illustrates the mind and way of life of the American Puritan

Sew·ard (sú:wərd), William Henry (1801-72), U.S. secretary of state (1860-9) under Presidents Abraham Lincoln and Andrew Johnson. His purchase (1867) of Alaska from Russia for $7.2 million was dubbed at the time 'Seward's Folly'

Seward Peninsula a peninsula (c. 180 miles long, 130 miles wide) in W. Alaska, with Cape Prince of Wales, the most westerly point of the North American mainland, at its west tip. It contains rich gold deposits

sew·er (sú:ər) **1.** *n.* an underground tunnel that carries off the drainage and waste matter from a house or town **2.** *v.t.* to provide with sewers **séw·er·age** *n.* the system of sewers or drainage of a town ‖ sewage [A.F. fr. O.F. *seuwiere,* a canal for draining off excess water in a fishpond]

sew·ing (sóuiŋ) *n.* the act or method of someone who sews ‖ something sewn, being sewn, or waiting to be sewn

sew·ing machine (sóuiŋ) a machine for seaming and for making a variety of stitches. Its needle may be worked by an electric motor or be operated by hand or by treadle

sewing press an appliance used by bookbinders for stretching the cords of a book being sewn by hand

sewn alt. *past part.* of SEW

sex (seks) **1.** *n.* the sum of characteristic structures and functions by which an animal or plant is classed as male or female ‖ male or female as a classification, *which sex is the chicken?* ‖ the area of human behavior concerning sexual activity ‖ sexual desires and instincts and their expression **2.** *v.t.* to identify the sex of (e.g. day-old chicks) [fr. L. *sexus*]

sex·a·ge·nar·i·an (sęksədʒənέəri:ən) **1.** *adj.* in the age span 60-9 **2.** *n.* a sexagenarian person [fr. L. *sexagenarius,* of sixty]

sex·ag·e·nar·y (seksǽdʒəneri:) *adj.* of or relating to the number 60 ‖ advancing by units of 60 [fr. L. *sexagenarius*]

Sex·a·ges·i·ma (sęksədʒésəmə, sęksədʒéizəmə) *n.* the second Sunday before Lent [eccles. L.. fem. of *sexagesimus,* sixtieth]

sex·a·ges·i·mal (sęksədʒésəməl) *adj.* of or relating to the number 60 ‖ calculating or proceeding in units of 60, e.g. in spherical and time calculations ‖ (*math..* of a fraction) having a denominator of 60 or a multiple of 60 [fr. M.L. *sexagesimalis*]

sex appeal physical attractiveness to the opposite sex

sex·cen·te·nar·y (seksséntənęri:, sękssenténəri:) **1.** *adj.* related to 600, esp. 600 years **2.** *pl.* **sex·cen·te·nar·ies** *n.* a celebration of 600 years of existence or a 600th anniversary [fr. L. *sex,* six +CENTENARY]

sex chromosome a chromosome whose presence, absence or particular form may determine the sex of an organism. A fertilized egg containing two X chromosomes (one from each parent) develops into a female. One containing an X and a Y chromosome (male germ cells carry either one or the other) develops into a male

sex·de·cil·lion (sęksdisíljən) *n.* *NUMBER TABLE [fr. L. *sesdecim, sexdecim,* sixteen + MILLION]

sexed (sekst) *adj.* having sexuality in a specified degree, *highly sexed*

sex·en·ni·al (sekséni:əl) *adj.* enduring for six years ‖ happening every six years [fr. L. *sexennis* or *sexennium*]

sex·i·ly (séksili:) *adv.* in a sexy manner

sex·i·ness (séksi:nis) *n.* the state or quality of being sexy

sex·ism (séksizəm) *n.* **1.** attitudes and institutions, often unconscious, that judge human worth on the grounds of gender or sex roles **2.** prejudice or discrimination, usu. against women, based on their gender **—sexist** *n. Cf* MALE CHAUVINISM

sex·i·va·lent (sęksəvéilənt) *adj.* (*chem.*) having six valences (cf. HEXAVALENT) [fr. L. *sex,* six + *valens* (*valentis*) fr. *valere,* to be strong]

sex·less (séksliś) *adj.* without sex ‖ (*pop.*) lacking normal sexual desire or attractiveness

sex linkage a genetic determinant, esp. X chromosome, that is carried by members of only one sex, e.g., hemophilia through females

sex-linked (sékslįŋkt) *adj.* (*biol.*) of those factors which are due to the sex chromosomes

sex·ol·o·gy (seksɔ́lədʒi:) *n.* the study of sexual behavior in humans [fr. SEX+Gk *logos,* discourse]

sex·ones (séksounz) *n.* sex odors believed to affect human sexuality

sex·ploi·ta·tion (sęksplɔitéiʃən) *n.* (*slang*) promotion based on eroticism **—sexploiter** *n.*

sext (sekst) *n.* the fourth of the seven canonical hours, falling at noon or just before noon ‖ the service held at this time each day [fr. L. *sexta (hora),* sixth hour]

sex·tant (sékstənt) *n.* an instrument with a graduated arc of 60 degrees, used for measuring the angle subtended by two distant objects. It is used in navigation to measure the altitude of the sun, moon or a star above the horizon, so that, in conjunction with a chronometer and the nautical almanac, latitude and longitude can be determined [fr. L. *sestans (sextantis),* a sixth part]

sex·tet, sex·tette (sekstét) *n.* a musical composition for six instruments or voices ‖ a group of six players or singers performing together [altered fr. SESTET after L. *sex,* six]

sex therapy treatment of sexual dysfunction by psychological therapy and other means

sex·til·lion (sekstíljən) *n.* *NUMBER TABLE [fr. F. fr. L. *sex,* six + MILLION]

sex·to·dec·i·mo (sękstoudésəmou) *n.* (*abbr.* 16 mo) a book made of sheets each folded into 16 leaves ‖ this method of folding ‖ a sheet folded thus [L., abl. of *sextus decimus,* sixteenth]

sex·ton (sékstən) *n.* a person who acts as a caretaker of a church and its contents and often also acts as bell ringer, gravedigger etc. [A.F. *segerstaine*]

sex·tu·ple (sekstú:p'l, sekstjú:p'l, sékstup'l, sékstjup'l, sekstʌ́p'l) **1.** *adj.* six times as much or as many ‖ (*mus.*) having six beats in a bar **2.** *n.* the product of a number multiplied by six **3.** *v. pres. part.* **sex·tu·pling** *past* and *past part.* **sex·tu·pled** *v.t.* to multiply by six ‖ *v.i.* to increase by six times as much or as many [prob. fr. L.L. *sextuplus* fr. L. *sex,* six]

Sex·tus Em·pir·i·cus (sékstəsempírikəs) (2nd c. A.D.) Greek physician and philosopher. His works are valued chiefly because they contain the only full account of skeptical philosophy in antiquity

sex·u·al (sékʃu:əl) *adj.* pertaining to sex, to difference of sex or to the satisfaction of the sex instinct ‖ (*biol.*) having sex ‖ (*biol.*) of reproduction by the union of male and female germ cells **sex·u·al·i·ty** (sękʃu:ǽliti:) *n.* the quality of being sexual ‖ (*biol.*) the state of being either male or female ‖ sexual desires and their gratification [fr. L.L. *sexualis*]

sexual revolution loosening of social mores regarding sexual behavior

sex·y (séksi:) *comp.* **sex·i·er** *superl.* **sex·i·est** *adj.* exciting sexual desire

Sey·chelles (seiʃél, seiʃélz) republic consisting of an archipelago, comprising 85 islands and islets, in the W. Indian Ocean (area 87 sq. miles, pop. 64,000). Chief islands: Mahé, Praslin. Capital and chief port: Victoria (pop. 23,334), on Mahé. People: mulatto, with Chinese, Indian and European minorities. Languages: Creole (official). Highest point: 2,970 ft, on Mahé. Exports: copra, cinnamon and cinnamon oil, vanilla, salted fish. Monetary unit: rupee (100 cents). HISTORY. The islands were occupied by the French (mid-18th c.), were contested by the British during the Napoleonic Wars, and were ceded to Britain (1814). They were administered jointly with Mauritius until 1903, when the Seychelles became a separate Crown Colony. Certain atolls became (1965) part of the British Indian Ocean Territory. Seychelles became an independent republic (1976), but the government was overthrown and a one-party state was declared (1979)

Sey·fert (sí:fə:rt) *n.* (*astron.*) a group of galaxies of small stars with compact nuclei and high energy emissions discovered in 1940s; named for Carl K. Seyfert *Cf* N GALAXY

Seymour, Jane *JANE SEYMOUR

Sfax (sfɑks) the chief export port (pop. 171,297) of Tunisia, on the east coast

Sfor·za (sfórtsɑ) an Italian family which ruled Milan (15th and 16th cc.). Lodovico Sforza (1451-1508), duke of Milan (1494-9), was a patron of Leonardo da Vinci and Bramante

sfor·zan·do (sfɔrtsándou) **1.** *adv.* (*mus., abbr.* sf., sfz., *symbol* >, ^) with sudden energy or emphasis **2.** *adj.* to be played in this way [Ital.]

sfor·za·to (sfɔrtsátou) *adj.* and *adv.* sforzando [Ital.]

's Gra·ven·ha·ge (sxrɑvənhάxə) *HAGUE, THE

Sha·ba (ʃúbə) *KATANGA

shab·bi·ly (ʃǽbili:) *adv.* in a shabby manner

shab·bi·ness (ʃǽbi:nis) *n.* the state or quality of being shabby

shab·by (ʃǽbi:) *comp.* **shab·bi·er** *superl.* **shab·bi·est** (of clothing) looking badly worn ‖ wearing badly worn clothing ‖ shameful or mean in a petty way, *a shabby trick* ‖ poor in quality, *a shabby lot of recruits* [fr. older *shab,* a scab]

Sha·bu·oth (ʃɑbu:ɔ́t,ʃəvú:əs) *n.* the Jewish harvest festival, celebrated on the 50th day after the second day of Passover [Heb. *shābhū'ōth* pl. of *shābhūa',* week]

shack (ʃæk) *n.* a crudely made hut, esp. one to live in [etym. doubtful]

shack·le (ʃǽk'l) **1.** *n.* a chain or ring used to prevent the free movement of arms or legs ‖ any of certain fastening devices, e.g. the link that couples with the staple of a padlock or a U-shaped metal piece closed by a heavy pin ‖ (*pl.*) something considered to impede or prevent free movement, *matrimonial shackles* **2.** *v.t. pres. part.* **shack·ling** *past* and *past part.* **shack·led** to fasten with a shackle or shackles ‖ to impede the freedom of action or expression of [O.E. *sceacul*]

Shack·le·ton (ʃǽk'ltən), Sir Ernest Henry (1874-1922), British explorer in Antarctica. He was a member of Scott's expedition of 1901-4 and commanded his own expeditions (1907-9, 1914-17 and 1921-2). He located the south magnetic pole (1909)

shad (ʃæd)pl. **shad, shads** *n.* a member of *Alosa,* fam. *Clupeidae,* a genus of widely distributed marine food fishes that are closely related to herring and spawn in rivers, esp. *A. sapidissima,* the North American species [O.E. *sceadd*]

shad·ber·ry (ʃǽdbęri:) *pl.* **shad·ber·ries** *n.* the fruit of the shadbush ‖ the shadbush [after SHAD, because the bush flowers when the shad appear in U.S. rivers]

shad·bush (ʃǽdbuʃ) *n.* the Juneberry (plant)

shad·dock (ʃǽdək) *n.* a large pear-shaped citrus fruit, resembling coarse or spongy grapefruit, found in the East Indies and introduced to the West Indies ‖ *Citrus grandis,* fam. *Rutaceae,* the tree which bears this fruit [after Captain *Shaddock,* English naval officer who introduced it into Barbados (1696)]

shade (ʃeid) **1.** *n.* a color containing some black (*COLOR, cf. TINT) ‖ a place partly sheltered from the full light or heat of the sun ‖ this quality of sheltering, *the place lacks shade* ‖ an eyeshade ‖ a lampshade ‖ a window blind ‖ comparative darkness, *the light and shade of a picture* ‖ a variation of individual depth or brightness of a color, *a shade of pink* ‖ a slight variation, *a shade of meaning* ‖ a slight degree, *a shade to the left* ‖ (*rhet.*) a disembodied spirit ‖ (*pl., rhet.*) the dimming darkness of twilight, *shades of evening* ‖ (*pl., rhet.*) the place where the spirits of the dead are **to put someone** (or **something) in the shade** to be so much better than someone (or something) that attention is withdrawn from him (or it) **2.** *v. pres. part.* **shad·ing** *past* and *past part.* **shad·ed** *v.t.* to shelter from the full light or heat of the sun etc. ‖ to darken (parts of a drawing etc.) in order to suggest relief or differences of brightness etc. ‖ *v.i.* to change gradually, esp. in color [O.E. *sceadu, scead*]

shad·i·ly (ʃéidili:) *adv.* in a shady manner

shad·i·ness (ʃéidi:nis) *n.* the state or quality of being shady

shad·ing (ʃéidiŋ) *n.* a provision of shade ‖ the representation of degrees of light or dark in a drawing or painting or the strokes etc. used ‖ (*mus.*) a subtle dynamic modification for interpretive effect

sha·doof, sha·duf (ʃɑdú:f) *n.* a device consisting of a bucket and a pivoted pole with a balancing weight, used to raise water, esp. in Egypt [Arab. *shādūf*]

sha·dow (ʃǽdou) *n.* a region of relative darkness caused by the interception of the light of the sun etc. by an opaque or semiopaque body ‖ the image of an opaque body projected on a surface elsewhere illuminated ‖ a mere semblance, *a shadow of his former self* ‖ something insubstantial, *worn to a shadow* ‖ trace, hint, *not a shadow of doubt* ‖ an inseparable companion ‖ (*rhet.*) a foreshadowing, *shadows of events to come* ‖ (*rhet.*) protection, *under the shadow of his wings* ‖ the relatively dark or shaded portion of a painting etc. [O.E. *sceaduwe, sceadwe,* oblique case of *sceadu,* shade]

shadow *v.t.* to throw into shadow, darken, *the*

CONCISE PRONUNCIATION KEY: **(a)** æ, *cat*; ɑ, *car*; ɔ *fawn*; ei, *snake*. **(e)** e, *hen*; i:, *sheep*; iə, *deer*; εə, *bear*. **(i)** i, *fish*; ai, *tiger*; ə:, *bird*. **(o)** ɒ, *ox*; au, *cow*; ou, *goat*; u, *poor*; ɔi, *royal*. **(u)** ʌ, *duck*; u, *bull*; u:, *goose*; ə, *bacillus*; ju:, *cube*. x, *loch*; θ, *think*; ð, *bother*; z, *Zen*; ʒ, *corsage*; dʒ, *savage*; ŋ, *orangutang*; j, *yak*; ʃ, *fish*; tʃ, *fetch*; 'l, *rabble*; 'n, *redden*. Complete pronunciation key appears inside front cover.

canyon was shadowed by steep cliffs ‖ to follow and watch in secret ‖ (often with 'forth' and 'out') to suggest obscurely (what is to follow) [O.E. *sceadwian* fr. *sceadu,* shade]

sha·dow·box (ʃǽdoubɒks) *v.i.* to go through the movements of sparring with an imaginary boxing opponent as a method of training ‖ to deal warily with a person so as to cover up ignorance, avoid a decision, play for an advantage in argument etc.

shadow cabinet (esp. *Br.*) a group of parliamentary opposition leaders who constitute a prospective cabinet against the time when their party may be returned to power

shad·ow·graph (ʃǽdougræf, ʃǽdougrɑf) *n.* an image or a picture formed by shadows, e.g. as thrown on a wall by a hand lit from behind

shad·ow·i·ness (ʃǽdoui:nis) *n.* the state or quality of being shadowy

shadow play a play presented in images or pictures formed by shadows on a screen, e.g. of puppets lit from behind

shadow prices (*economics*) the maximum price level attainable if an extra unit of a resource were made available

shad·ow·y (ʃǽdoui:) *adj.* full of shadows ‖ like a shadow, indistinct or fleeting ‖ shaded

shaduf *SHADOOF

shad·y (ʃéidi:) *comp.* **shad·i·er** *superl.* **shad·i·est** *adj.* offering shade ‖ in shade ‖ (*pop.*) very probably dishonest, *a shady deal*

shaft (ʃæft,ʃɑft) *n.* a long, smooth-surfaced piece of wood or metal of roughly the same thickness throughout its length and usually of roughly circular cross section, e.g. the handle of an axe or golf club or the body of an arrow ‖ a long rod supporting a part of a machine or transmitting motion to a part of a machine ‖ (*archit.*) the part of a column separating the capital and the base ‖ a long, more or less vertical, hollow space, e.g. a mine shaft or ventilation shaft ‖ (*rhet.*) an arrow ‖ (*biol.*) the straight, cylindrical part of a long bone ‖ the distal part of a feather's stem ‖ a beam of light ‖ a bolt (of lightning) ‖ a remark or piece of verbal wit that scores off the person or thing to which it refers ‖ (*pl.* **shaves** ʃeivz) one of the bars between which a horse is harnessed when drawing a vehicle, a rotating axle etc. [O.E. *sceaft,* spear shaft]

Shaf·ter (ʃǽftər, ʃɑ́ftər), William Rufus (1835-1906), U.S. general during the Spanish-American War. After the destruction of the Spanish fleet, he captured (1898) Santiago de Cuba

Shaftes·bur·y (ʃǽftsbəri:, ʃɑ́ftsbəri:), Anthony Ashley Cooper, 3rd earl of (1671-1713), English philosopher. In his 'Characteristics of Men, Manners, Opinions and Times' (1711), he developed his view of moral sense as a harmony between the desires of society and those of the individual

Shaftesbury, Anthony Ashley Cooper, 7th earl of (1801-85), British Tory philanthropist and social reformer. He was responsible for much reforming legislation, including the prohibiting of the employment of women and children in mines (1842) and the limitation of the working day in factories to 10 hours (1847)

shag (ʃæg) *n.* coarse, rough-cut, shredded pipe tobacco ‖ thick, matted hair or wool ‖ the long nap on certain types of cloth or wool [O.E. *sceacga*]

shag *n. Phalacrocorax aristotelis,* a long-billed, shaggy-crested British cormorant (about 30 ins). Flocks fly in V formation like geese [perh. fr. *shag,* (*obs.*) mat of hair]

shag·bark (ʃǽgbɑrk) *n. Carya ovata,* fam. *Juglandaceae,* a white hickory tree found in the eastern and central U.S.A., yielding a sweet edible nut. Its light gray bark often peels back in rough strips ‖ the wood of this tree, used esp. for tool handles

shag·gi·ly (ʃǽgili:) *adv.* in a shaggy manner

shag·gi·ness (ʃǽgi:nis) *n.* the state or quality of being shaggy

shag·gy (ʃǽgi:) *comp.* **shag·gi·er** *superl.* **shag·gi·est** *adj.* rough-haired ‖ (of hair) thick, dense and (often) unkempt ‖ having a rough surface ‖ (of countryside) covered with a rough growth of shrubs and trees

shaggy-dog story a funny story with a calculatedly feeble ending. It is told at length with exasperating detail

sha·green (ʃəgrí:n) *n.* a type of leather prepared from the untanned hide of a horse, camel or ass, grained with rough raised spots and usually dyed green ‖ leather prepared from the rough skin of sharks and dogfish etc. and usually dyed green [var. of older *chagrin* fr. F.]

shah (ʃɑ) *n.* formerly the sovereign of Iran (Persia) or his title [Pers. *shāh,* king]

Sha·hap·ti·an (ʃɑhǽpti:ən) *n.* a member of an Indian people of the northwestern U.S.A. and British Columbia

Shah Ja·han, Shah Je·han (ʃɑ́dʒəhɑ́n) (c. 1592-1666), Mogul emperor (1627-58), son of Jahangir. His reign was especially noted for its magnificent architecture, incl. the Taj Mahal and Agra and Delhi mosques

shake (ʃeik) **1.** *v. pres. part.* **shak·ing** *past* **shook** (ʃuk) *past part.* **shak·en** (ʃéik'n) *v.t.* to cause to move rapidly up and down or from side to side of the normal position of rest ‖ to cause to vibrate or quiver ‖ to weaken (belief or confidence), *his lying shook my faith in him* ‖ to shock or jar the equilibrium of, *the fall shook me* ‖ to brandish (a weapon) etc., *to shake one's fist at someone* ‖ (*mus.*) to trill (a phrase) ‖ to agitate (dice) before casting them ‖ (*pop.*) to get rid of (someone or something), *to shake bad habits* ‖ *v.i.* to move rapidly to and fro about a normal position of rest ‖ to vibrate or quiver ‖ (*mus.*) to make a trill **to shake down** to cause to fall or descend by shaking ‖ (*pop.*) to extract money from ‖ to cause to settle by shaking ‖ to improvise a temporary bed or lodging ‖ to adjust to new conditions **to shake hands** to give someone a handshake ‖ to clasp hands in greeting, farewell etc. **to shake off** to get rid of (someone or something unwelcome) **to shake out** to shake in order to clean, open, restore to its proper shape or position etc. ‖ to cause to come out by shaking **to shake up** to mix by shaking ‖ to shock, agitate ‖ to destroy the complacency of **2.** *n.* a shaking or being shaken ‖ a tremble or quiver ‖ a crack in a tree parallel to the growth rings ‖ a shingle split by hand from a log ‖ (*pop.*) a milkshake ‖ (*mus.*) a trill **no great shakes** not of great quality or significance [O.E. *scacan*]

shake·down (ʃéikdaun) *n.* an improvised bed ‖ (*pop.*) an extorting of money ‖ a period of adjustment

shaken *past part.* of SHAKE

shak·er (ʃéikər) *n.* someone or something that shakes ‖ a container in which something is shaken, e.g. a cocktail shaker **Shak·er** a member of a sect (1747) the English founders of which emigrated to America after secession from the Quakers. They received their name because of their trembling when filled with religious ecstasy. The sect lives in celibate communities and by mid-20th c. had a few dozen remaining adherents

Shake·speare (ʃéikspiər), William (1564-1616), the greatest English poet and playwright. He was born and died at Stratford-upon-Avon. He was in London as actor, poet and playwright (with occasional visits to his home town) from about 1592 to about 1616, but there is a gap of 8 to 10 years before 1592 concerning which scarcely anything is known.

His greatest period was between 1600 and 1607, during which he produced the comedies 'As you Like It' and 'Twelfth Night' (1600-1), the tragedies 'Hamlet' (1602-3), 'Othello' (1604), 'King Lear' (1605-6), and 'Macbeth' (1606) as well as 'Antony and Cleopatra' (1607-8) and at least four other plays. The 'Sonnets' date from 1609.

Various ages have found various things in Shakespeare. The 18th c. saw in him 'just observation of general nature' (Johnson) or truth-to-life. The Romantics admired his freedom from literary convention, the sweep and grandeur of historical conflict, his parabolic insight into the extremes of the human predicament. The later 19th c. (e.g. Bradley) admired the delicate and complicated psychological insight of his characterization. All ages have admired his command of language, and our own age has presented a picture of Shakespeare as a conscious symphonic artist, producing in his greatest plays an elaborate structure in which theme answers theme and in which the whole, like music, is its own meaning, which any paraphrase denatures. He is presented by modern critics as deeply concerned with the moral basis of life. 'Nature', 'right', 'order', 'truth', the key concepts, are as it were both created and tested in the conflicts which form the plays

Shake·spear·e·an, Shake·spear·i·an (ʃeikspíəri:ən) **1.** *adj.* of or concerning Shakespeare **2.** *n.* a specialist in the works of Shakespeare

shake-up (féikʌp) *n.* a shaking up, esp. a jolting of someone's complacency or an administrative reorganization for greater efficiency

Shakh·ty (ʃɑ́xti:) a city (pop. 214,000) of the R.S.F.S.R., U.S.S.R., in the Donets Basin: anthracite mining, pig iron

shak·i·ly (ʃéikili:) *adv.* in a shaky manner

shak·i·ness (ʃéiki:nis) *n.* the state or quality of being shaky

shaking table a machine with a wide vibrating rubber belt used for dressing ores

shak·o (ʃǽkou, ʃéikou) *pl.* **shak·os, shak·oes** *n.* a stiff, high, cylindrical, peaked military headgear, with a plume [Hung. *csákó*]

sha·ku·ha·chi (ʃɑku:hɑtʃi:) *n.* (*music*) Japanese bamboo recorder

shak·y (ʃéiki:) *comp.* **shak·i·er** *superl.* **shak·i·est** *adj.* unsteady, apt to shake, *a shaky old table* ‖ trembling, infirm, *a shaky old man* ‖ shaking, not even or smooth, *a shaky voice* ‖ wavering, *shaky faith* ‖ weak, not firmly based, *a shaky argument* ‖ (of a tree) marked by shakes

shale (ʃeil) *n.* a fine-grained sedimentary rock readily splitting into thin plates or layers [perh. a use of older *shale,* a shell, fr. O. E. *scealu*]

shale oil an oil distilled from bituminous shale

shall (ʃæl) *past* **should** (ʃud) *auxiliary v.* used to express futurity, *we shall see,* or promise, intention or command, *you shall go to the theater tomorrow, I shall see to it, you shall do what I say* (cf. WILL, cf. SHOULD, cf. WOULD) [O.E. *sceal, sculon*]

shal·lop (ʃǽləp) *n.* a small open boat using oars or sail, for shallow waters [F. *chaloupe* prob. fr. Du.]

shal·lot (ʃəlɒ́t) *n. Allium ascalonicum,* fam. *Liliaceae,* a perennial producing clusters of small bulbs, resembling the common onion, used in cooking [fr. older *eschalot* fr. F.]

shal·low (ʃǽlou) **1.** *adj.* having relatively little distance between the top and bottom or front and back surfaces, *shallow streams, a shallow colonnade* ‖ superficial, *a shallow mind* **2.** *n.* (*pl.*) a shallow part of a body of water **3.** *v.t.* to make shallow ‖ *v.i.* to become shallow or shallower [M.E. *schalowe* prob. rel. to O. E. *sceald*]

Shal·ma·ne·ser III (ʃælmənί:zər) (*d.* c. 824 B.C.), king of Assyria (858–c. 824 B.C.). He made war on neighboring peoples, and fought an indecisive battle (c. 853 B.C.) against Ahab of Israel

Sha·lom A·lei·chem (ʃɑlóumɑléixəm) (Salomon Rabinowitz, 1859-1916), Ukrainian author of short stories, plays and novels written in Yiddish

shal·y (ʃéili:) *comp.* **shal·i·er** *superl.* **shal·i·est** *adj.* pertaining to or like shale

sham (ʃæm) **1.** *v. pres. part.* **sham·ming** *past* and *past part.* **shammed** *v.i.* to make pretense ‖ *v.t.* to simulate, *to sham death* **2.** *n.* someone who pretends to be what he is not ‖ something pretended to be other than it is ‖ a shamming **3.** *adj.* having the appearance of being what it is not, *a sham fight* [etym. doubtful]

sha·man (ʃɑ́mən, ʃéimən, ʃǽmən) *n.* a priest or witch doctor among some Ural-Altaic peoples. He uses magic to propitiate gods and spirits, foretell the future, heal etc. **Shá·man·ism** *n.* the religion practiced by a shaman ‖ a similar religion, e.g. among North American Indians [G. *schamane,* Russ. *shaman* fr. Tungus]

sham·ble (ʃǽmb'l) **1.** *v.i. pres. part.* **sham·bling** *past* and *past part.* **sham·bled** to walk awkwardly, with unorganized movements of the limbs and dragging the feet **2.** *n.* a shambling walk [etym. doubtful]

sham·bles (ʃǽmb'lz) *pl. n.* (*hist.*) a slaughterhouse ‖ a scene of great destruction ‖ (*pop.*) extreme disorder or a scene of this [O.E. *scamul. sceamul,* a bench]

shame (ʃeim) *n.* a painful emotion aroused by the recognition that one has failed to act, behave or think in accordance with the standards which one accepts as good ‖ the same feeling aroused by similar failure in others with whom one identifies oneself ‖ utter disgrace, *a life of shame* ‖ someone or something that causes disgrace ‖ (*pop.*) something unfair, *it's a shame that he got off scot-free* ‖ (*pop.*) something regrettable, *it was a shame that the rain spoiled your holiday* **for shame!** you ought to be ashamed! **to put (someone) to shame** to cause (someone) to feel shame by exposing his failures or misdeeds ‖ to cause (someone) to feel inadequate by surpassing him [O.E. *sceamu, scamu*]

shame *v.t. pres. part.* **sham·ing** *past* and *past part.* **shamed** to cause (someone) to feel shame ‖ to bring shame or disgrace on ‖ to impel (someone) to do something by making him feel shame, *to shame someone into doing something* || to put (someone) to shame by displaying superior ability, behavior etc. [O.E. *sceamian, scamian*]

shame·faced (ʃéimfeist) adj. exhibiting shame || painfully abashed **shame·fac·ed·ly** (ʃeimféisidli:, ʃéimféistli:) *adv.* **shame·fác·ed·ness** *n.*

shame·ful (ʃéimfəl) *adj.* causing shame || offending one's sense of what is right or just

shame·less (ʃéimlis) *adj.* lacking modesty || showing lack of modesty || imprudent

Sha·mir (ʃəmíər), Yitzhak (c. 1915-), Israeli statesman, prime minister (1983-4), born in Poland. He emigrated (1935) to Palestine and led a guerrilla group against the British. He was foreign minister (1980-3) before leading his Likud coalition into power in the elections of 1984. Under a power-sharing arrangement with the rival Labor party, it was agreed that he would resume the prime ministership in late 1986

sham·mash (ʃáməs, *Heb.* ʃamáʃ) *pl.* **sham·ma·shim** (ʃamɔ́sim, *Heb.* ʃamaʃí:m) *n.* the candle used for lighting the other candles of the menorah || the sexton of a synagogue [Yiddish *Shames* and *Heb. shāmmāsh* fr. Aram. *shemmāsh*, to serve]

sham·my (ʃǽmi:) *pl.* **sham·mies** *n.* (*pop.*) chamois (leather) [altered fr. CHAMOIS]

sham·poo (ʃæmpú:) **1.** *v.t. pres. part.* **sham·poo·ing** *past* and *past part.* **sham·pooed** to wash (the hair) **2.** *n.* a washing of the hair or an instance of this || a usually liquid or powder preparation for washing the hair [prob. Hind. *haček* imper. of *čāmpnā*, to press]

sham·rock (ʃǽmrɒk) *n.* any of several clovers commonly regarded as the national emblem of Ireland, esp. *Trifolium dubium*, which has small yellow flowers

Shamrock *n.* code name of one of two operations that permitted screening of overseas telegrams by the National Security Agency, a practice later discontinued

Shan (ʃɑn, ʃæn) a state (area 57,816 sq. miles, pop. 1,950,000) of E. Burma on a mountainous plateau, comprised of former Shan principalities and Wa states. Capital: Taunggyi. The Shans, a Thai people, ruled most of Burma (1287-1531), retained the best land in the east, and economically are advanced over other minorities

shan·dy (ʃǽndi:) *n.* beer mixed with lemonade or ginger beer [short for SHANDYGAFF]

shan·dy·gaff (ʃǽndi:gæf) *n.* shandy [origin unknown]

Shang·hai (ʃæŋhái, ʃɑ́ŋhái) the largest city (pop. 11,859,748) and chief industrial and commercial center of China, a port in the Yangtzekiang delta, Kiangsu. Industries: textiles, metallurgy, mechanical and electrical engineering, rolling stock, chemicals, rubber processing. Shanghai was the center of European trade in China (1842-1949). It consists of an old walled city with the former French concession and international settlement, surrounded by modern quarters. University (1905)

shanghai *v.t.* (*hist.*) to drug or otherwise stupefy and take aboard a ship to serve as a sailor || (*pop.*) to force (someone) by guile to do something [after SHANGHAI]

shank (ʃæŋk) **1.** *n.* the part of the leg in man between knee and ankle || the corresponding part in various animals || the leg in man || the straight connection between the handle and working part of a tool etc. || the long, roughly straight, portion of an object (e.g. a pin, nail, anchor) between its extremities || the back loop on a button || the narrow part of a shoe sole under the instep || (*printing*) the body of a type || the later part (of the afternoon or evening) **2.** *v.i.* (of a flower) to drop by reason of decay in the stalk || *v.t.* (*golf*) to strike with the heel of the club [O.E. *scanca, sceanca*]

Shan·non (ʃǽnən) the chief river (240 miles long) of Ireland, flowing from the central Irish Republic to a long estuary below Limerick, linked by canal to Dublin: hydroelectricity

shan·ny (ʃǽni:) *pl.* **shan·nies** *n. Blennius pholis*, fam. *Blennidae*, a smooth, spineless, olive-green European blenny [etym. doubtful]

Shan·si (ʃánsí:) a province (area 60,300 sq. miles, pop. 28,904,423) of E. Central China, with vast coal deposits. Capital: Taiyuan

shan't (ʃænt,ʃɑnt) *contr.* of SHALL NOT

Shan·tung (ʃǽntʌ́ŋ, ʃɑ́ndúŋ) a province (area 56,944 sq. miles, pop. 74,419,054) of E. China, partly formed by a large peninsula of the same name. Capital: Tsinan

shan·tung (ʃǽntʌŋ) *n.* a silk woven from coarse silk yarn and having a somewhat rough surface [after SHANTUNG]

shan·ty (ʃǽnti:) *pl.* **shan·ties** *n.* a chantey [perh. F. *chantez* imper. of *chanter*, to sing]

shanty *pl.* **shan·ties** *n.* a small shack of crude construction [Canad. F. *chantier*, workshop]

shan·ty·town (ʃǽnti:taun) *n.* a town, or part of a town, consisting of shanties

shape (ʃeip) *n.* the way in which an object is seen or felt to be extended as to its length, breadth and depth || this as conforming to an ideal or pattern or original, *it has lost its shape* || the outward appearance of a person's body as distinct from his facial appearance || a dimly perceived form, *weird shapes in the fog* || satisfactory arrangement, *to put a speech into shape* || state, condition, *his business was in bad shape* || a mold, e.g. for headcheese or jellies || a jelly, headcheese etc. made in such a mold || form, embodiment, *reward in the shape of an extra holiday* || false appearance, semblance, *a troublemaker in the shape of a friend* || nature, *the shape of things to come* **to take shape** to develop, esp. in an orderly or regular way [O.E. *gesceap*, creation, creature]

shape *pres. part.* **shap·ing** *past* and *past part.* **shaped** *v.t.* to cause to take on a certain shape, *to shape dough into loaves* || to produce by manipulating, *to shape figures out of clay* || to order, *to shape one's future* || to make suitable or fit, *to shape a boy for his career* || to cut (a garment) so as to fit the figure closely || *v.i.* to acquire a particular shape || to develop, *clouds shaping on the horizon* [O.E. *scieppan*]

shaped charge (*mil.*) a charge shaped so as to concentrate its explosive force in a particular direction

shape·less (ʃéiplis) *adj.* having no regular shape

shape·li·ness (ʃéipli:nis) *n.* the state or quality of being shapely

shape·ly (ʃéipli:) *comp.* **shape·li·er** *superl.* **shape·li·est** *adj.* well proportioned

shap·er (ʃéipər) *n.* someone or something that shapes, esp. a machine for producing a particular shape

shape up *v.* to get into proper condition; by extension, to conform

Sha·pi·ro (ʃəpíerou), Karl (1913-), U.S. poet and critic. His works, which present the poet as cultural spokesman, include 'Poems of a Jew' (1958) and 'In Defense of Ignorance' (1960)

Shap·ley (ʃǽpli:), Harlow (1885-1972), U.S. astronomer. As director (1921-52) of the Harvard College Observatory, he led pioneer research into the structure of the Milky Way and the universe beyond

shard (ʃɑrd) *n.* a broken piece of brittle material, esp. a potsherd || (*zool.*) the wing case of a beetle [O.E. *sceard*, a gap]

share (ʃɛər) **1.** *n.* a part shared, *he kept a share for the dog* || the part to which one is entitled, *he gave you your share*, or which is required of one, *he did her share of the work* || the part one receives or contributes || (*commerce*) one of the equal parts into which the capital of a corporation is divided **to go shares** to share equally **to have a share in** to be partly responsible for **2.** *v. pres. part.* **shar·ing** *past* and past part. **shared** *v.t.* (often with 'out') to distribute parts of (something) among others || (often with 'with') to retain one part of (something) and give the rest or part of the rest to another or others, *he will share the winnings with you* || to take or use a part of (something) with someone or something, *may she share your umbrella?* || to do or experience (something) with others || *v.i.* to join with others in doing or experiencing something, *he shared in the planning of it* [O.E. *scearu*, cutting, division]

share *n.* a plowshare [O.E. *scear, scær*]

share·crop (ʃéərkrɒp) *pres. part.* **share·crop·ping** *past* and *past part.* **share·cropped** *v.t.* to work (land) as a sharecropper || *v.i.* to work as a sharecropper

share·crop·per (ʃéərkrɒpər) *n.* a tenant farmer, esp. in the southern U.S.A., given certain credits and a share in crops and charged for certain incidentals of upkeep

shared appreciation mortgage (*banking*) loan secured by property made at a reduced interest rate with provision that lender share in price appreciation of property, usu. when sold

share·hold·er (ʃéərhouldər) *n.* someone who owns shares in a company or other shared property or business

Sha·ri (ʃári:) (*F.* Chari) a river (length excluding headstreams: 700 miles) flowing north from the S. Central African Republic through S.W. Chad to Lake Chad

sha·rif, she·rif (ʃərí:f) *n.* a descendant of Fatima and Ali || a title used by certain princes of Islam || the chief magistrate in Mecca [Arab *sharīf*, noble]

shark (ʃɑrk) *n.* any of several large, voracious, elasmobranch fishes, armed with several rows of serrated teeth and having tough, scaly skins. They are particularly abundant in the warmer oceans || a man who makes his living by swindles and trickery or by overcharging or otherwise exploiting in an antisocial way [etym. doubtful]

shark·skin (ʃárkskin) *n.* shagreen leather made from a shark's skin || smooth worsted material in twill or basket weave, with two-color or two-tone designs woven in || a rayon or cotton fabric with a smooth, sleek look, used esp. for sportswear

Sha·ron (ʃǽrən) the biblical name for the coastal plain of Israel from Jaffa to south of Haifa

Sharp (ʃɑrp), Granville (1735-1813), British philanthropist and pioneer in the struggle for the abolition of slavery. In 1772 he obtained the famous judgment making slavery illegal in Britain

sharp (ʃɑrp) **1.** *comp.* **sharp·er** *superl.* **sharp·est** *adj.* well adapted to cut or pierce || having a thin edge, *a sharp ridge*, or a pointed shape, *a sharp peak* || making an acute or sudden angle, *a sharp bend in the road* || as if cut with a knife, *a sharp outline, sharp features* || piercing suddenly, *a sharp pain* || (of a taste) acid || (of air) cold || (of a sound or voice) strong and shrill || alert, attentive, *a sharp lookout* || swiftly rebuking, *a sharp retort* || (*Br.*) quick, *we must be sharp if we are to catch the train* || brisk, energetic, *a sharp run* || hotly contested, *a sharp fight* || (of the senses, intelligence etc.) acute, keen, *sharp vision* || quick-witted || (*pop.*) clever, expert, *a sharp engineer* || quick to look after one's own interests, *a sharp man of business* || dishonest, *sharp practices* || (*mus.*, of a note or tone) raised a semitone in pitch || (*mus.*) above true pitch || (*mus.*, of a key) having a sharp or sharps in the signature **2.** *adv.* to a sharp point or edge || punctually, *at 3 o'clock sharp* || at a sudden angle, *turn sharp left* || (*mus.*) above true pitch **3.** *n.* (*mus.*) a note that is a semitone above a specified note || the sign for this (#) || a sharp piece of diamond used for cutting or for engraving gems **4.** *v.t.* (*mus., Am.* = *Br.* sharpen) to raise a semitone || *v.i.* (*mus., Am.*= *Br.* sharpen) to sing or play above true pitch **shárp·en** *v.t.* (*Br., mus.*) to sharp || to make sharp or sharper || *v.i.* (*Br., mus.*) to sharp || to become sharp or sharper **shárp·er** *n.* (*pop.*) a swindler, esp. at cards [O.E. *scearp*]

sharp-eyed (ʃárpaid) *adj.* having acute sight || quick to notice little details

sharp·ie (ʃárpi:) *n.* (*hist.*) a long, pointed, flat-bottomed boat with one or two masts each having a triangular sail || a sharper

sharp sand sand with angular, not rounded grains

Sharps·burg (ʃárpsbə:rg) *ANTIETAM

sharp-set (ʃárpset) adj. placed at a sharp angle || presenting sharp edges, *a sharp-set saw*

sharp·shoot·er (ʃárpʃu:tər) *n.* (*U.S.* army) a proficiency rating of marksmanship, above a marksman and below an expert || a soldier with this rating || a person who is a good shot

sharp-sight·ed (ʃárpsáitid) *adj.* sharp-eyed

sharp-wit·ted (ʃárpwítid) *adj.* having a quick, intelligent mind

Shas·tri (ʃástri:), Lal Bahadur (1904-66), Indian statesman, prime minister of India (1964-6)

Shatt-al-A·rab (ʃǽtælárab) a river (120 miles long) formed by the confluence of the Tigris and Euphrates in S.E. Iraq, flowing into the Persian Gulf

shat·ter (ʃǽtər) *v.t.* to cause to break suddenly into fragments || to destroy suddenly and totally, *to shatter one's hopes* || *v.i.* to break into fragments || to become suddenly and totally destroyed [etym. doubtful, rel. to SCATTER]

shatter cones (*geol.*) distinctive striated rock fragments shaped like cones believed produced by an intense force

shave (ʃeiv) **1.** *v. pres. part.* **shav·ing** *past* **shaved** *past. part.* **shaved, shav·en** (ʃéiv'n) *v.t.*

to remove using a sharp cutting edge, *to shave the bristles from a pig's back* || to remove hair from (the skin) with a razor || to remove thin slices from (leather, wood etc.) with a sharp tool || to pass very closely without touching || to graze, rub against lightly || *v.i.* to remove hair with a razor **2.** *n.* a shaving or being shaved || a thin slice || a tool used for shaving leather, wood etc. **sháv·er** *n.* an electric device for shaving || someone who shaves || (*pop.*) a young or small boy **sháv·ing** the act of one who shaves || a thin slice shaved off wood, metal etc. [O.E. *sceafan*]

Sha·vi·an (ʃéiviːən) **1.** *adj.* characteristic or imitative of the works of George Bernard Shaw **2.** *n.* a devotee of Shaw, his writings and opinions [fr. *Shavius*, Latinized form of SHAW]

Shaw (ʃɔ), George Bernard (1856-1950), Irish playwright and critic. His plays cover a wide range of modes: history ('Caesar and Cleopatra', 1901, 'Saint Joan', 1924), philosophy ('Man and Superman', 1903, 'Back to Methuselah', 1921), political fantasy ('The Apple Cart', 1929) etc. All his plays are linked by a uniform style of paradoxical volubility. They are entertaining and often acute. What Shaw stood for is hard to define, though he was a progressive in his own anarchic way (*FABIAN SOCIETY). Within his own style of verbal exchange he was a great theatrical craftsman. His best-made comedies include 'Arms and the Man' (1898), 'Major Barbara' (1905) and 'Pygmalion' (1913)

Shaw, Henry Wheeler *BILLINGS, JOSH

Shaw, Lemuel (1781-1861), chief justice (1830-60) of the supreme judicial court of Massachusetts. His decisions include 'Farwell v. Railroad' (in which he made the fellow-servant rule, that an employer is not liable for injuries caused by the negligence of a fellow servant, a principle of American law), 'Commonwealth v. Hunt' (in which he freed unions from the abusive application of the law of conspiracy), and 'Roberts v. Boston' (in which he ruled that racial segregation in public schools did not create unconstitutional inequalities)

shawl (ʃɔl) *n.* a square, oblong or triangular covering for the shoulders or head worn by women and girls || a woolen wrap for babies [Pers. *shāl*]

shawm (ʃɔm) *n.* an obsolete musical instrument akin to the oboe [M.E. *shallemelle* fr. O.F.]

Shaw·nee (ʃɔníː) *pl.* **Shaw·nee, Shaw·nees** *n.* a member of a North American Algonquian Indian tribe originally of the eastern U.S.A. and now living in Oklahoma

Shays (ʃaiz), Daniel (c. 1747-1825), American soldier. He led an unsuccessful rebellion (1786-7) against high land taxes, legal costs and officials' salaries

Shcher·ba·kov (ʃtʃerbɑkɔ́f) *RYBINSK

she (ʃiː) **1.** *pron., 3rd person sing., nominative case* a female person, animal or personified thing already mentioned **2.** *adj.* (*prefixed*) female, *a she-devil* **3.** *n.* a female, *is it a she or a he?* [prob. altered fr. O.E. *sīo*, sēo, *sīe*]

shea (ʃiː) *n. Butyrospermum parkii*, fam. *Sapotaceae*, a tropical African tree, whose large nuts yield shea butter [Mandingo *si, se, sye*]

shea butter the vegetable fat yielded by the crushed nuts of the shea tree

shead·ing (ʃíːdiŋ) *n.* any of the six administrative units of the Isle of Man [var. of *shedding*, pres. part. of SHED, (obs.) to divide]

sheaf (ʃiːf) **1.** *pl.* **sheaves** (ʃiːvz) *n.* cut stalks of grain bundled together in an orderly way || a quiverful of arrows, usually 24 || a collection of things put together, a *sheaf of papers* **2.** *v.t.* to make into a sheaf or sheaves [O.E. *sceāf*]

shear (ʃiər) **1.** *v. pres. part.* **shear·ing** *past* **sheared** *past part.* **sheared, shorn** (ʃɔrn) *v.t.* to cut or clip with shears, esp. to clip the wool from (a sheep) || (esp. *past part.*, with 'of') to deprive of, *shorn of his power* || (*mech.*) to deform by causing to undergo a shear || *v.i.* to use shears || (*mech.*) to suffer deformation through a shear **2.** *n.* a shearing or being sheared || (esp. *Br.*) this used in designating the age of a sheep, *a sheep of four shears* || something shorn off, esp. the wool cut off in one shearing || (*mech.*) a deformation within a body in which two adjacent planes tend to move in a parallel direction relative to one another while remaining parallel || (esp. *pl.*) a hoist of two or more poles joined at the top and steadied by guys, used e.g. for placing a ship's masts or engines in position || (*geol.*) a change in the direction of a stratum due to lateral pressure [O.E. *sceran*]

shear legs a shear (hoist)

shear·ling (ʃíərliŋ) *n.* (esp. *Br.*) a sheep shorn once only

shears (ʃíərz) *pl. n.* a pair of sharp cutting blades, larger than, but similar to, those of scissors, and often joined by a spring [O.E. *scērero* and O.E. *scēar*]

shear·wa·ter (ʃíərwɔtər, ʃíərwɒtər) *n.* any of several species of oceanic birds, esp. of genus *Puffinus*, fam. *Procellariidae*, that visit land only when breeding. They are blackish, with slender bills. They bank and glide and skim over the waves on long, narrow, stiff wings

sheat·fish (ʃíːtfiʃ) *pl.* **sheat·fish·es, sheat·fish** *n. Silurus glanis* fam. *Siluridae*, a large catfish (up to 10 ft) common in the Danube and some other European rivers [etym. doubtful]

sheath (ʃiːθ) *pl.* **sheaths** (ʃiːðz) *n.* a cover fitting closely over the blade of a weapon or tool || (*biol.*) a protective covering, e.g. a membrane covering a muscle || (*bot.*) a leaf base surrounding the stem || a close-fitting straight dress [O.E. *scǣth, scēath*]

sheath·bill (ʃíːθbil) *n.* a member of *Chionididae*, a family of sea birds found in the southern hemisphere. They have a horny sheath over the base of the upper mandible

sheathe (ʃiːð) *pres. part.* **sheath·ing** *past* and *past part.* **sheathed** *v.t.* to put into a sheath, scabbard etc. || to protect in a case || to retract (claws) || to provide (e.g. a roof, a ship's bottom) with sheathing **shéath·ing** *n.* a placing in a sheath || a protective covering, e.g. on the hull of a wooden ship or the waterproof layer on a wooden roof [SHEATH]

sheave (ʃiːv) *pres. part.* **sheav·ing** *past* and *past part.* **sheaved** *v.t.* to gather into sheaves

sheave (ʃiv, ʃiːv) *n.* a grooved wheel or pulley, or one of several, for running a rope through a pulley block or set of pulley blocks [M.E. *sheve, shive*, a sheave, slice]

sheaves *pl.* of SHEAF *n.*

She·ba (ʃíːbə) *SABA

she·bang (ʃəbǽŋ) *n.* (*pop.*, esp. with 'the whole') a thing, matter, affair, place etc., *he wrecked the whole shebang* [origin unknown]

She·chem (ʃíːkem, ʃékem) *NABLUS

Shechinah *SHEKINAH

shed (ʃed) **1.** *v. pres. part.* **shed·ding** *past* and *past part.* **shed** *v.t.* to throw off, *to shed one's wet clothes* || to throw off by repelling, *this cloth sheds water* || to become separated from, *some trees shed their leaves* || to pour forth, *to shed tears* || to cause (blood) to flow by injury || to cause (blood) to flow by violence || to spread around (e.g. favors, misery) [O.E. *scādan, scēadan*]

shed *n.* a small hut, lean-to or light shelter for boats, bicycles etc. || a large storage warehouse, e.g. in docks [var. of SHADE n.]

she'd (ʃiːd) *contr.* of SHE HAD, SHE WOULD

sheen (ʃiːn) *n.* brightness, shininess **shéen·y** *comp.* **sheen·i·er** *superl.* **sheen·i·est** *adj.* [O. E. *scīene*, beautiful]

sheep (ʃiːp) *pl.* **sheep** *n.* a member of *Ovis*, fam. *Bovidae*, a genus of gregarious, ruminant animals, many breeds of which have been domesticated for the sake of their wool, flesh (*LAMB, *MUTTON) and skin (*SHEEPSKIN) || a timid, easily led person **a wolf in sheep's clothing** someone who disguises his evil nature by appearing to be harmless and virtuous **to make sheep's eyes at** to keep making shy, amorous glances at [O.E. *scēap, scēp*]

—The three main classes of wool-bearing sheep are fine, coarse and medium. The very fine-wooled merino flourish in dry, warm climates (e.g. Australia, S. Africa and parts of South America). Very coarse-wooled sheep are found mainly in Asia and in mountainous regions, parts of the fleece being used for carpets. Medium-wooled breeds are subdivided into long wools and short wools, and their fleeces are used for cloth. Medium-wooled breeds also form the chief supply of mutton and lamb, either pure or crossed with other types. Mutton rams are mated with ewes of breeds kept on richer grassland, where the cost of production of fat lamb is cheaper. In the Mediterranean area, where grazing for cattle is in short supply, milking sheep are kept, mostly for making cheese

sheep·cot (ʃíːpkɒt) *n.* (esp. *Br.*) a sheepfold

sheep·cote (ʃíːpkout) *n.* (esp. *Br.*) a sheepfold

sheep-dip (ʃíːpdip) *n.* a liquid containing disinfectants, into a solution of which sheep are immersed for a few moments in order to cleanse and disinfect their wool and skin || the enclosure where sheep are dipped in this solution

sheep dog a dog, esp. a collie, trained to herd sheep and to guard them from other animals

sheep·fold (ʃíːpfould) *n.* an enclosure, bounded by hurdles or rough stone walls, for the protection of sheep in severe weather, in the lambing season etc.

sheep·herd·er (ʃíːphəːrdər) *n.* a shepherd

sheep·ish (ʃíːpiʃ) *adj.* shy and embarrassed, esp. through consciousness of being in the wrong and feeling a little foolish about it

sheep ked *Melophagus ovinus*, fam. *Hippoboscidae*, a wingless, dipteran fly that feeds on sheep and carries sheep trypanosomiasis

sheep·man (ʃíːpmən) *pl.* **sheep·men** (ʃíːpmən) *n.* a person whose business is raising sheep on a large scale

sheep·shank (ʃíːpʃæŋk) *n.* a knot or hitch tied to shorten a rope

sheep·shear·er (ʃíːpʃiərər) *n.* a person who shears sheep || a tool or machine used in shearing sheep

sheep·shear·ing (ʃíːpʃiəriŋ) *n.* the act of shearing sheep || the time for shearing sheep || a festival at this time

sheep·skin (ʃíːpskin) *n.* the skin of a sheep, esp. used, with the wool attached, as a rug or in a coat, slippers, gloves etc. || leather prepared from the skin itself, used for bookbinding etc. || parchment made from the skin of a sheep || (*pop.*) a diploma written on such parchment

sheep·walk (ʃiːpwɔk) *n.* (esp. *Br.*) a pasture for sheep

sheer (ʃiər) **1.** *adj.* complete, utter, *sheer nonsense* || perpendicular, without intervening ledges or slopes, *a sheer drop* || almost transparent, *sheer stockings* **2.** *adv.* perpendicularly, *it rises sheer out of the sea* [M.E. *schere*]

sheer *v.i.* to deviate from a course || *v.t.* to cause to turn aside from a course **to sheer off** (*Br.*) to go away abruptly so as to avoid work or avoid a person [perh. var. of SHEAR V.]

sheer *n.* (*naut.*) the fore-and-aft line of a ship curving upward to bow and stern [perh. var. of SHEAR n.]

sheer *n.* (*naut.*) a deviation from course || (*naut.*) the oblique position of a ship riding at a single anchor [SHEER v.]

sheer *n.* a shears (a hoist, *SHEAR)

sheer·legs (ʃíərlegz) *pl. n.* shears (a hoist, *SHEAR)

sheet (ʃiːt) **1.** *n.* a large rectangle of woven cotton, linen or silk etc. used esp. in pairs as bed linen between the mattress and the blankets || a rectangular or square piece of paper || a large, thin, flat piece of metal, glass etc. || a wide expanse of water, ice etc. || (*philately*) a complete page of stamps from one printing **in sheets** (of printed matter) not folded or bound **three sheets in the wind** drunk **2.** *v.t.* to cover with, or form into, a sheet || *v.i.* (*pop.*) to flow as if in a sheet, *the rain sheeted down* [O.E. *scīete, scēte*]

sheet **1.** *n.* (*naut.*) a rope fastened to the lower corner of a sail and used to control the sail || (*naut., pl.*) the spaces in an open boat fore or aft of the thwarts **2.** *v.t.* **to sheet home** (*naut.*) to haul upon (the topsail) so that it is fully extended against the wind [O.E. *scēata*]

sheet anchor a large anchor slung amidships and used in an emergency || something that in time of danger is a sure resource when other things have failed

sheet bend (*naut.*) a knot or hitch fastening one rope to the loop of another

sheet flow (*envir.*) water flowing in a thin layer over a land surface, usu. a storm runoff

sheet·ing (ʃíːtiŋ) *n.* the fabric in bulk from which sheets are made || a material, e.g. a plastic or metal, formed in sheets and used e.g. as a protective covering or lining

sheet lightning lightning which is a discharge from cloud to cloud, giving wide flashes of reflected light

sheet metal metal in the form of a thin sheet

sheet music music printed on unbound sheets of paper

Shef·field (ʃéfiːld) a town and county borough (pop. 547,400) in the West Riding of Yorkshire, England: cast iron, high-grade steel and steel manufactures, esp. cutlery, celebrated silver plate. University (1905)

sheikh, sheik (ʃiːk, ʃeik) *n.* a title of respect used by Arabs || an Arab chief, head of a family, or headman of a village **shéikh·dom, shéik·dom** *n.* [Arab. *shaikh*, old man]

shek·el (ʃék'l) *n.* any of several weight units used by the ancient Hebrews, Babylonians and Phoenicians ‖ an ancient coin of such a weight, esp. one used by the Hebrews ‖ (*pl., pop.*) money as riches ‖ unit of currency in Israel, equal to 10 pounds [Heb. *sheqel*]

She·ki·nah, She·chi·nah (ʃikí:nə, ʃikáinə) *n.* (*Heb. theol.*) the immanence of Jehovah as seen or felt or manifested [Heb.]

Shel·burne (ʃélbərn), William Petty Fitzmaurice, 2nd earl of (1737-1805), British statesman. He led a progressive but unpopular ministry (1782-3)

shel·drake (ʃéldreik) *pl.* **shel·drakes shel·drake** *n.* a member of *Tadorna,* fam. *Anatidae,* a genus of large wild duck found on coasts of Europe, Asia and N. Africa, esp. *T. tadorna,* the European species. It is about 24 ins long and is mainly black and white, with a green head and neck and a red bill having a prominent knob on it [prob. fr. older *sheld* adj., variegated+DRAKE]

shel·duck (ʃéldʌk) *pl.* **shel·ducks, shel·duck** *n.* the female sheldrake [prob. fr. older *sheld* adj., variegated+DUCK]

shelf (ʃelf) *pl.* **shelves** (ʃelvz) *n.* a horizontal board, stone slab etc. mounted against a perpendicular surface, to put things on ‖ such a support in a cabinet, bookcase etc. ‖ a projecting, roughly horizontal, layer of rock ‖ a roughly horizontal, narrow part of an otherwise steep cliff ‖ a ridge of rock or sand near the surface of a sea or other expanse of water [perh. fr. L.G. *schelf,* shelf or set of shelves]

shelf ice an extensive sheet of ice forming part of a land glacier or a frozen bay, stretching out to sea where it floats

shell (ʃel) **1.** *n.* the hard outer covering of an animal or fruit, or the calcareous, siliceous, bony, horny or chitinous covering of an organism, esp. the outer covering of a bird's egg ‖ a gutted building or one of which only the walls have been built ‖ (*mil.*) a cylindrical projectile containing an explosive within a metal container and exploded by impact or by a time fuse, or the container itself ‖ a cartridge or a cartridge case ‖ (*phys.* and *chem.*) a quantized energy level in an atom (*QUANTUM THEORY). In atoms the shells are denoted by the letters K, L, M,..., K representing the innermost and lowest energy level with quantum number (called the principal quantum number) 1, L with principal quantum number 2, M with 3 etc. In each shell except the K shell there are further subdivisions (orbitals). Each shell is associated with a region centered on the nucleus within which an electron of that shell spends most of its time, the effective diameter of the region getting larger with increasing principal quantum number. The number of atomic electrons that may exist in a given shell is equal to $2n^2$, where n is the principal quantum number ‖ (*rowing*) a light racing boat ‖ a baked unfilled pastry case, esp. the bottom crust of a pie **2.** *v.t.* to take out of the shell, *to shell peas* ‖ to separate the kernels of (wheat, corn etc.) from the ear ‖ (*mil.*) to fire shells at ‖ *v.i.* to become detached in scales ‖ to become free of the containing shell [O.E. *sciell, scill*]

she'll (ʃi:l) *contr.* of SHE SHALL, SHE WILL

shel·lac, shel·lack (ʃəlǽk) **1.** *n.* purified lac resin used in varnishes, stiffening agents, phonograph records, insulators etc. **2.** *v. pres. part.* **shel·lack·ing** *past* and *past part.* **shel·lacked** *v.t.* to coat with shellac ‖ (*pop.*) to defeat by a very large margin [trans. of F. *laque en écailles,* lac in fine plates]

Shel·ley (ʃéli:), Percy Bysshe (1792-1822), English poet. He was the most idealistic and uncompromising of Romantics. His works include longer poems, e.g. 'Queen Mab' (1813), 'The Revolt of Islam' (1818) and 'Prometheus Unbound' (1820), lyrics ('The Skylark', 'Ode to the West Wind', 'Ozymandias') and 'Adonais' (1821), a lament for Keats

shell·fire (ʃélfaiər) *n.* the firing of shells, e.g. at enemy positions, or the exploding shells

shell·fish (ʃélfiʃ) *pl.* **shell·fish, shell·fish·es** *n.* an aquatic invertebrate with a shell, e.g. a crab, lobster or oyster [O.E. *scilfisc*]

shell game a version of thimblerig, using walnut shells etc.

shell gland an organ from whose walls material for forming a shell is secreted

Shell Oil Company a U.S. petroleum industry company, one of the largest U.S. companies. It is connected with the Royal Dutch-Shell international group

shell·proof (ʃélpru:f) *adj.* not penetrable by shellfire or bombs

shell shock combat fatigue **shéll-shocked** *adj.*

shel·ly (ʃéli:) *comp.* **shell·i·er** *superl.* **shell·i·est** *adj.* covered with shells ‖ like or consisting of a shell or shells

shel·ter (ʃéltər) **1.** *n.* something providing protection from danger or injury, esp. from rain and wind ‖ protection, *to afford shelter* **to take shelter** to go to a place affording protection ‖ to go under cover so as not to be rained on **2.** *v.t.* to protect from danger, injury, rain or wind ‖ to protect as if by shelter, shield, *he sheltered her from gossip* ‖ *v.i.* to take refuge, esp. from bad weather [etym. doubtful]

sheltered workshop a place of work for persons not fully adjusted to private life, e.g., retarded, recently released mental patients *Cf* HALFWAY HOUSE

shelve (ʃelv) *pres. part.* **shelv·ing** *past* and *past part.* **shelved** *v.t.* to put on a shelf ‖ to supply or fit with shelves ‖ to defer for the moment, *to shelve a decision* ‖ to relegate as if to a shelf [fr. SHELVES (pl. of SHELF)]

shelve *pres. part.* **shelv·ing** *past* and *past part.* **shelved** *v.i.* (of a road surface etc.) to slope gradually [etym. doubtful]

shelves *pl.* of SHELF

shelv·ing (ʃélviŋ) *n.* shelves

Shen·an·do·ah (ʃenəndóuə) a river (170 miles long) rising in N. Virginia, flowing across the tip of West Virginia into the Potomac River. It was an important avenue for several Civil War campaigns

Shenandoah National Park a U.S. reservation (193,646 acres) in the Blue Ridge Mtns of Virginia. It was established in 1935

Shenandoah Valley Campaigns military operations in the Shenandoah Valley of Virginia during the Civil War. The valley served as the avenue for Confederate attempts to invade the North and as a chief supply source for General Robert E. Lee's army. The maneuvers included Stonewall Jackson's campaign (1862), the Gettysburg campaign (1863), and Jubal A. Early's raid (1864). Laying the region waste, General Philip Sheridan's troops drove out (1865) the Confederates

she·nan·i·gans (ʃənǽnigənz) *pl. n.* trickery ‖ spirited carryings-on, high jinks [origin unknown]

Shen·si (ʃénsi:) a province (area 75,580 sq. miles, pop. 26,000,000) of N. central China. Capital: Sian

Shen·yang (ʃʌ́njáŋ) (Mukden 17th c. -1911) the capital (pop. 4,400,000) of Liaoning, S. Manchuria, China, a communications and industrial center (mechanical engineering, textiles, paper, chemicals). Manchu palaces (17th c.). It was the Manchu capital (1625-44)

She·ol (ʃí:oul) *n.* (*Jewish theol.*) the subterranean place of the dead [Heb.]

Shep·ard (ʃépərd), Sam (1943-), U.S. playwright and actor whose plays fused the past with the future and myth with reality. His plays include 'Operation Sidewinder' (1970), 'The Tooth of Crime' (1972), 'Buried Child' (1978, Pulitzer Prize), and 'A Lie of the Mind' (1985). He appeared in several movies

shep·herd (ʃépərd) **1.** *n.* a man whose occupation is tending sheep and watching over their safety **2.** *v.t.* to act as shepherd to ‖ to conduct, guide (a group of people) and prevent them from lagging or straying [O. E. *scēaphirde, scēaphyrde*]

shepherd's pie a pie of already cooked chopped meat, covered with mashed potatoes and baked in an oven

shepherd's purse *Capsella bursapastoris,* fam. *Cruciferae,* an annual cosmopolitan weed. It has a basal rosette of leaves, a raceme of small white flowers and a quantity of seed in its purse-shaped seedpods

Sher·a·ton (ʃérətən), Thomas (c. 1751-1806), English furniture designer. He is esp. famous for his slender, graceful shapes and use of inlay, and for his ingenious construction of combination pieces. He wrote 'The Cabinet Maker's and Upholsterer's Drawing Book' (1791-4)

sher·bet (ʃə́:rbit) *n.* a cooling Oriental fruit drink ‖ a frozen dessert made of sugar, water, milk, egg white and fruit flavoring ‖ an effervescent drink made from a powder of sodium bicarbonate, tartaric acid, sugar and flavoring, or this powder [Turk., Pers. *sherbet* fr. Arab. *sharbah*]

Sher·brooke (ʃə́:rbruk) a town (pop. 74,075) in S.E. Quebec, Canada, market for a mining and logging region. University (1954)

sherd (ʃə:rd) *n.* a shard

Sher·i·dan (ʃéridən), Philip Henry (1831-88), Union cavalry general during the Civil War. He drove out (1865) the Confederate forces from the Shenandoah Valley and destroyed supply and communication sources, rendering the valley useless to the South

Sheridan, Richard Bridsley Butler (1751-1816), Irish dramatist and politician. He had written his best work for the stage, 'The Rivals' (1775) and 'The School for Scandal' (1777), by the age of 26. Thereafter he concerned himself mainly with the management of his Drury Lane Theater and with parliament, where he shone as an orator. His plays have both wit and humor and are among the few late-18th-c. plays to become classics

sherif *SHARIF

sher·iff (ʃérif) *n.* a usually elected officer responsible for law and order in his county ‖ (*Br.*) the chief administrative officer in charge of courts, elections etc. in a county [O.E. *scīrgerēfa,* shire reeve]

Sher·man (ʃə́:rmən), John (1823-1900), U.S. Senator (1861-77, 1881-97) from Ohio, secretary of the treasury (1877-81) under President Hayes, and secretary of state (1897-8) under President McKinley. Although both the Anti-Trust Act of 1890 and Silver Purchase Act (1890) bear his name, he gave them only qualified approval

Sherman, William Tecumseh (1820-91), Union general in the American Civil War. During his famous 'march to the sea' through Georgia (Nov.-Dec. 1864), he encouraged his troops to pillage and devastate

Sherman Anti-Trust Act a U.S. Congressional act (1890), named after Senator John Sherman. It declared illegal every contract, combination, or conspiracy in restraint of interstate and foreign trade. It was supplemented (1914) by the Clayton Anti-Trust Act

Sherman Silver Purchase Act a U.S. Congressional act (1890), named after Senator John Sherman, which required the U.S. government almost to double the amount of its silver purchases. When it threatened to undermine the U.S. treasury's gold reserves, it was repealed (1893) by the Grover Cleveland administration

Sher·pa (ʃérpə, ʃə́:rpə) *pl.* **Sher·pa, Sher·pas** *n.* a member of a Buddhist people of Mongolian origin living in N.E. Nepal, in the foothills of the Himalayas. They are noted as guides and porters on mountaineering expeditions (*TENZING NORKAY)

Sher·ring·ton (ʃériŋt'n), Sir Charles Scott (1861-1952), British physiologist whose work on reflexes, 'Integrative Action of the Nervous System' (1906), paved the way for modern understanding of the activity of the central nervous system. Nobel prize (1932)

sher·ry (ʃéri:) *pl.* **sher·ries** *n.* a fortified Spanish wine varying in color from light yellow to dark brown ‖ a wine of this type produced elsewhere [older *sherris* fr. *Xeres* (now Jerez), Spain]

Sher·wood (ʃə́:rwud), Robert Emmet (1896-1955), U.S. playwright. His plays include 'The Road to Rome' (1927), 'Abe Lincoln in Illinois' (1939) and 'There Shall Be No Night' (1941)

Sherwood Forest a former royal forest, of which little remains, in W. Nottinghamshire, England. It covered 150 sq. miles. It was the home of Robin Hood

she's (ʃi:z) *contr.* of SHE IS, SHE HAS

Shet·land Islands (ʃétlənd) an archipelago (some 100 islands and islets, 21 inhabited) 50 miles northeast of the Orkney Is, forming a Scottish county, Zetland (land area 550 sq. miles, pop. 20,400). Main islands: Mainland, Yell, Unst. County town: Lerwick, on Mainland. Industries: knitting, weaving, fishing, farming (oats, barley, root vegetables). Livestock: cattle, sheep, Shetland ponies

Shetland pony a member of a breed of small (32–46 ins), stocky ponies originating in the Shetland Is

shew·bread, show·bread (ʃóubred) *n.* twelve loaves of consecrated unleavened bread formerly displayed in the Jewish temple (one for each tribe) and renewed each sabbath. It symbolized gratitude to Yahweh as the giver of all things [after G. *schaubrot*]

CONCISE PRONUNCIATION KEY: **(a)** æ, *cat;* ɑ, *car;* ɔ *fawn;* ei, *snake.* **(e)** e, *hen;* i:, *sheep;* iə, *deer;* ɛə, *bear.* **(i)** i, *fish;* ai, *tiger;* ə:, *bird.* **(o)** o, *ox;* au, *cow;* ou, *goat;* u, *poor;* ɔi, *royal.* **(u)** ʌ, *duck;* u, *bull;* u:, *goose;* ə, *bacillus;* ju:, *cube.* x, *loch;* θ, *think;* ð, *bother;* z, *Zen;* ʒ, *corsage;* dʒ, *savage;* ŋ, *orangutang;* j, *yak;* ʃ, *fish;* tʃ, *fetch;* 'l, *rabble;* 'n, *redden.* Complete pronunciation key appears inside front cover.

Shi·'a (ʃí:ə) *n.* a member of the Shi'ite Moslem sect ‖ this sect [Arab.= sect]

Shi·at·su (ʃi:átsu:) *n.* Japanese massage technique using finger pressure at critical acupuncture points

shib·bo·leth (ʃíbəliθ, ʃíbəleθ) *n.* (*Bible*) a test word which betrayed the members of the tribe of Ephraim because it was hard for them to pronounce (Judges xii, 6) ‖ any such test word ‖ any word, formula etc. used by adherents to a cause and considered by them a distinguishing mark [Heb. = flood]

Shi·de·ha·ra (ʃi:dehɑrɑ), Kijūrō (1872-1951), Japanese statesman, prime minister (1945-6)

shied *past* and *past part.* of SHY

shield (ʃi:ld) **1.** *n.* (*hist.*) a broad piece of leather and metal, or metal only, gripped with the hand by a thong or handle at its back and held to protect the body from arrows, spear thrusts, blows etc. ‖ a plate, screen etc. which serves to protect, e.g. a gunner from blast or a worker from the moving parts of a machine ‖ (*zool.*) a protective body covering, e.g. one of the plates forming the shell of a turtle ‖ (*heraldry*) a flat, three-sided area or surface, most commonly horizontal at the top with curved sides tapering to a point, on which a coat of arms is displayed ‖ someone or something thought of as serving to defend **2.** *v.t.* to protect with or as if with a shield [O.E. *sceld*]

shield law 1. legislation or rules designed to protect a domestic market from imports, e.g., quality controls on imports, antidumping laws **2.** legislation protecting a journalist from disclosing information sources

shier alt. *comp.* of SHY

shiest alt. *superl.* of SHY

shift (ʃift) *n.* a change of position, place, direction or condition ‖ a substituting of one thing for another, *a shift of scenery* ‖ an ingenious expedient adopted in a time of need or emergency ‖ a tricky ruse, artifice or maneuver ‖ a group of workers who work in turn with another group or other groups ‖ the period during which such a group works, *the night shift* ‖ a woman's straight dress ‖ (*mining*) a fault, e.g. in a vein ‖ (*mus.*, esp. of a violin) a change in the position of the hand not holding the bow ‖ (*linguistics*) a phonetic change or system of changes **to make shift with** to do the best one can with (what is available) [M.E. *schift*]

shift *v.t.* to exchange for or replace by another similar thing or things, *to shift scenery* ‖ to alter the position, place, direction or condition of ‖ to alter (a place, position etc.), *to shift the location of a factory* ‖ to accomplish, get through (a job or task) ‖ to change (gears) from one speed to another ‖ (*linguistics*) to change phonetically ‖ *v.i.* to move from one position, place, direction or condition to another ‖ to change gears ‖ (*linguistics*) to undergo phonetic change **to shift for oneself** to get along as well as one can unaided [O.E. *sciftan*]

shift·i·ly (ʃíftili:) *adv.* in a shifty manner

shift·i·ness (ʃífti:nis) *n.* the state or quality of being shifty

shift·less (ʃíftlis) *adj.* lazy and inefficient ‖ incapable of using determination and ingenuity in order to surmount some difficulty or achieve some purpose ‖ showing such lack of determination and ingenuity [fr. SHIFT *n.*, (obs.) resourcefulness]

shift register (*computer*) a peripheral device for storing data in a form in which it may be manipulated

shift·y (ʃífti:) *comp.* **shift·i·er** *superl.* **shift·i·est** *adj.* mean and untrustworthy, deceitful [fr. SHIFT *n.*, (obs.) resourcefulness]

shift·y-eyed (ʃífti:aid) *adj.* having an air of dishonesty and low cunning

Shi·ga·tse (ʃi:gátse) a trade center (pop. 15,000) in S. central Tibet, China, on the Tsangpo (Brahmaputra), at 11,000 ft. Lamasery (1446)

Shih·kia·chwang (ʃə́:rdʒjádʒwɑ́ŋ) a textile industry center (pop. 598,000) of S.W. Hopei, China

Shi·'ism (ʃí:izəm) *n.* the doctrine and beliefs of the Shi'a sect

Shi·'ite (ʃí:ait) *n.* a member of a branch of Islam which separated from the orthodox Sunnites in 679. Shi'ites hold that the historical succession of the caliphate passes through Ali, Mohammed's son-in-law, and Ali's sons, Hasan and Husein, whom they revere as martyrs and imams. They differ from the Sunna. Splinter groups of Shi'ites later founded the Isma'ili, Twelvers, Fatimite and Assassin sects. The Shi'ites played a large part in the development of Sufism. They constitute about 15% of Moslems. They are found mainly in Iran, where Shi'ism is the state religion, and in Iraq, where half the Moslems are Shi'ites. Minorities exist in India, Syria, Lebanon, Egypt, Yemen and Oman [Arab. fr. *Shi'a*, a sect]

Shi·ko·ku (ʃi:kɔku:) the smallest island (area 7,246 sq. miles, pop. 4,097,000) of Japan's four main islands. Chief town: Matsuyama. Main industries: agriculture (rice, wheat, sugarcane, tea, mulberry trees), mining (*JAPAN)

Shillelagh (ʃiléili:) *n.* (*mil.*) a missile system (MBM-51) with infrared target guidance, mounted on the main battle tank and assault reconnaissance vehicle

shil·le·lagh, shil·la·lah (ʃəléili:) *n.* a cudgel of oak or blackthorn, cut from a sapling and left rough [after *Shillelagh*, a town in Wicklow, Ireland]

shil·ling (ʃíliŋ) *n.* a British nickel alloy coin worth £ .05 ‖ the basic monetary unit of Tanzania, Kenya and Uganda, divided into 100 cents [O.E. *scilling*]

Shil·long (ʃillɔ́ŋ) the capital (pop. 87,659) of Assam, India, an agricultural market and health resort at 4,980 ft

Shil·luk (ʃílʌk) *pl.* **Shil·luk, Shil·luks** *n.* a Nilotic people of Sudan living primarily on the west bank of the White Nile ‖ a member of this people ‖ their Nilotic language

shil·ly-shal·ly (ʃíli:ʃæli:) **1.** *v.i. pres. part* **shil·ly-shal·ly·ing** *past* and *past part.* **shil·ly-shal·lied** to waver continually between two opinions **2.** *pl.* **shil·ly-shal·lies** *n.* indecision, or an instance of it [originally *shill I, shall I*, alteration of 'shall I, shall I']

Shi·loh, Battle of (ʃáilou) a victory (Apr. 6-7, 1862) of the Union army under Grant, during the American Civil War

shim (ʃim) **1.** *n.* a sliver of wood, metal etc., often tapered, used in adjusting levels or to take up wear in machinery **2.** *v.t. pres. part.* **shim·ming** *past* and *past part.* **shimmed** to fit or pack with this [origin unknown]

shim·mer (ʃímər) **1.** *v.i.* to shine with glistening, tremulous light **2.** *n.* such a light **shím·mer·y** *adj.* [O.E. *scymrian*]

shim·my (ʃími:) **1.** *pl.* **shim·mies** *n.* a dance of the 1920s accompanied by a shaking of the body ‖ a wobble, e.g. in the front wheel of a car **2.** *v.i. pres. part.* **shim·my·ing** *past* and *past part.* **shim·mied** to dance a shimmy ‖ to oscillate abnormally [perh. fr. older *shimmy*, woman's undergarment]

Shi·mo·no·se·ki (ʃimənəséiki:) a port (pop. 269,000) at the southwest tip of Honshu, Japan: shipbuilding, building materials, fishing

Shin (ʃin, ʃi:n) a Japanese Buddhist sect, numbering about 13,000,000 adherents

shin (ʃin) **1.** *n.* the lower part of the front of the leg, above the ankle (in beef cattle) the lower part of the foreleg **2.** *v.i. pres. part.* **shin·ning** *past* and *past part.* **shinned** to climb by using the hands and legs [O.E. *scinu*]

Shi·na·no (ʃi:nɑnɔ) the longest river (230 miles) of Japan, flowing from central Honshu to the Sea of Japan at Niigata

shin·bone (ʃínboun) *n.* the tibia [O.E. *scinbān*]

shin·dig (ʃíndig) *n.* (*pop.*) a social gathering, esp. a very large one, on which no expense is spared [prob. alt. of SHINDY]

shin·dy (ʃíndi:) *pl.* **shin·dies** *n.* (*pop.*) an uproar, commotion [perh. alt. fr. *shinty*, an obsolete game like hockey]

shine (ʃain) **1.** *v. pres. part.* **shin·ing** *past* and *past part.* **shone** (ʃoun), **shined** *v.i.* to emit or reflect light ‖ to glow (e.g. with pleasure, happiness or rapture) ‖ to show great aptitude, *he doesn't shine in mathematics* ‖ *v.t.* to cause to shine, esp. by cleaning and polishing **to shine up to** (*pop.*) to lavish attentions on **2.** *n.* the quality of shining ‖ a finish given by polishing ‖ (*pop.*) a shoeshine **to take a shine to** (*pop.*) to take a liking to **shin·er** *n.* (*pop.*) a black eye ‖ any of various small, silvery, North American, freshwater fish ‖ something that shines or some one who shines [O.E. *scīnan*]

shin·gle (ʃíŋg'l) **1.** *n.* a wedge-shaped tile, esp. of wood, used esp. in roofing ‖ (*pop.*) a small signboard bearing the name esp. of a doctor or lawyer and hung outside his door ‖ a mannish style of women's hairdo, cut short esp. at the nape of the neck and tapering **to hang out one's shingle** (*pop.*, esp. of a doctor or lawyer) to start a professional practice **2.** *v.t. pres. part.* **shin·gling** *past* and *past part.* **shin·gled** to cover (e.g. a roof) with shingles ‖ to cut (a woman's hair) in a shingle [M.E. *scincle, shyngle*]

shingle *n.* an accumulation of rounded pebbles found on some seashores [etym. doubtful]

shin·gles (ʃíŋg'lz) *n. Herpes zoster*, a painful but transient virus infection of a nerve, resulting in blisters over a restricted part of the body [alt. fr. M.L. *cingulus*, var. of *cingulum*, a girdle]

shin·gly (ʃíŋgli:) *adj.* consisting of shingles (rounded pebbles)

Shin·gon (ʃíngɔn) a Japanese Buddhist sect, numbering about 8,000,000 adherents

shin·i·ly (ʃáinili:) *adv.* in a shiny manner

shin·i·ness (ʃáini:nis) *n.* the state or quality of being shiny

shin·ing (ʃáiniŋ) *adj.* gleaming, *shining silver* ‖ splendid, *a shining example*

shin·ny (ʃíni:) *pres. part.* **shin·ny·ing** *past* and *past part.* **shin·nied** to shin

Shin·to (ʃíntou) *n.* an ancient religion of Japan, without a historical founder or organized body of teachings. Its chief features are the worship of national heroes and family ancestors and belief in the divinity of the Emperor. Mingled with and superseded by Buddhism (6th c.), it was revived in the 17th c. and was the state religion (1867–1945) **Shín·to·ism, Shín·to·ist** *ns* [Jap. fr. Chin. *shin*, god+*tao*, way or law]

shin·y (ʃáini:) *comp.* **shin·i·er** *superl.* **shin·i·est** *adj.* emitting or reflecting light ‖ polished, *shiny shoes* ‖ so worn as to be smooth and glossy, *shiny trousers* [SHINE]

ship (ʃip) **1.** *n.* (*hist.*) a large seagoing sailing vessel with a bowsprit and three square-rigged masts, divided each into lower mast, topmast and topgallant mast, sometimes with higher masts ‖ any large seagoing vessel ‖ the crew of such a vessel ‖ (*pop.*) an aircraft **when one's ship comes home** (or **in**) when one comes to have plenty of money **2.** *v. pres. part.* **ship·ping** *past* and *past part.* **shipped** *v.t.* to put in a ship ‖ (*naut.*) to put in place ready to use ‖ to take on (crew) ‖ to send (goods) by sea or (*pop.*) by any means of transport ‖ to lift (oars) out of the water and lay them in the boat or let them rest in the oarlocks with the blades in the boat ‖ to have (water) enter over the side of the vessel ‖ *v.i.* to go by ship ‖ to join a ship's crew [O.E. scip]

-ship *suffix* indicating state or quality, as in 'friendship' ‖ indicating office, as in 'chancellorship' ‖ indicating ability, as in 'horsemanship' [O.E. *-sciepe, -scipe, -scype*]

ship biscuit hardtack

ship·board (ʃípbɔrd, ʃípbourd) *n.* (in the phrase) **on shipboard** on or in a ship

ship·break·er (ʃípbreikər) *n.* a person who breaks up obsolete ships to sell the scrap metal, fittings etc.

ship broker an agent who transacts a ship's business when the ship is in port ‖ someone who buys, sells, charters or insures ships

ship·build·er (ʃípbildər) *n.* someone whose business is to construct ships

ship·build·ing (ʃípbildiŋ) *n.* the construction of ships

ship canal a canal deep and broad enough for seagoing vessels

ship chandler a dealer in ships' canvas, cordage and other small equipment

ship·load (ʃíploud) *n.* the total quantity of goods, passengers etc. loaded or able to be loaded into a ship

ship·mas·ter (ʃípmæstər, ʃípmɑstər) *n.* the captain of a merchant ship

ship·mate (ʃípmeit) *n.* someone in relation to oneself or to a third person serving or traveling in the same ship

ship·ment (ʃípmənt) *n.* the loading of goods, esp. on a ship ‖ the goods so shipped

ship money (*Eng. hist.*) an ancient tax levied in coastal areas to provide ships, revived and extended by Charles I, and abolished in 1640

ship of the line (esp. *hist.*) a warship carrying heavy guns and forming part of the line of battle at sea

ship·own·er (ʃípounər) *n.* an owner or part owner of a ship or ships

ship·per (ʃípər) *n.* someone who ships goods, esp. as a profession

ship·ping (ʃípiŋ) *n.* the act of putting on board ship, going on board ship, or sending by ship or other means of transport ‖ (*collect.*) all the ships of a country or port ‖ ships in general

shipping articles the terms of contract signed by sailors on joining a ship's crew

CONCISE PRONUNCIATION KEY: **(a)** æ, *cat*; ɑ, *car*; ɔ *fawn*; ei, *snake*. **(e)** e, *hen*; i:, *sheep*; iə, *deer*; ɛə, *bear*. **(i)** i, *fish*; ai, *tiger*; ə:, *bird*. **(o)** o, *ox*; au, *cow*; ou, *goat*; u, *poor*; ɔi, *royal*. **(u)** ʌ, *duck*; u, *bull*; u:, *goose*; ə, *bacillus*; ju:, *cube*. x, *loch*; θ, *think*; ð, *bother*; z, *Zen*; ʒ, *corsage*; dʒ, *savage*; ŋ, *orangutang*; j, *yak*; ʃ, *fish*; tʃ, *fetch*; 'l, *rabble*; 'n, *redden*. Complete pronunciation key appears inside front cover.

shipping clerk (*Br.*) a clerk employed by a shipping line || a person employed in packing and sending goods
shipping commissioner (*Am.=Br.* shipping master) an official responsible for signing on and paying off a crew
shipping master (*Br.*) a shipping commissioner
shipping room a room, e.g. in a factory, from which goods are dispatched
ship's articles *SHIPPING ARTICLES
ship's biscuit hardtack
ship's chandler a ship chandler
ship's company the crew of a ship exclusive of the officers
ship·shape (ʃípʃeip) *adj.* tidy, orderly
ship's papers the documents relating to the nationality, ownership and cargo of a ship
ship·way (ʃípwei) *n.* a timber-built slope used for building and launching ships etc. || a ship canal
ship·worm (ʃípwə:rm) *n.* any of various long, thin marine clams, esp. of fam. *Teredinidae,* which bore into submerged wood and do heavy damage to piles, harbor installations, wooden ships etc.
ship·wreck (ʃíprek) **1.** *n.* destruction of a ship at sea by being sunk in stormy seas or being stranded, esp. by being driven on rocks || destruction as though by foundering at sea **2.** *v.t.* to cause to undergo shipwreck
ship·wright (ʃípraít) *n.* a carpenter who specializes in building and repairing ships || (*hist.*) a naval architect
ship·yard (ʃípjard) *n.* the premises where ships are built and repaired
Shi·raz (ʃi:rɑ́z) a communications center and agricultural market in S.W. Iran in the Zagros Mtns, producing wines, carpets, silks and mosaics. Mosques (notably 9th and 18th cc.), mausoleums (15th-16th cc.)
Shi·re (ʃí:rei) a river flowing 370 miles from Lake Malawi through Malawi and Mozambique to the Zambezi, navigable except at Murchison Falls
shire (ʃáiər) *n.* (*Eng. hist.*) an Anglo-Saxon administrative district coinciding with the modern county || (*Br.*) any of the British counties whose name ends in 'shire' **the Shires** Leicestershire, Northamptonshire and Rutland, noted for foxhunting [O.E. *scīr,* office, charge]
Shire Highlands an area of high ground in the south of Malawi, east of the Shire River, containing the capital, Zomba
shire horse a member of a breed of powerful draft horses, originally raised in the Midland counties of England
shirk (ʃə:rk) *v.t.* to avoid (e.g. work, responsibility or obligation), esp. out of indolence or selfishness || *v.i.* to avoid work, responsibility etc., esp. out of indolence or selfishness [perh. fr. G. *schurke,* rascal]
Shir·ley (ʃə́:rli:), William (1694-1771), colonial governor (1741-60) of Massachusetts. During King George's War he led the capture (1745) of Louisburg, but, as commander (1755-60) of the British forces in America, he failed in an expedition against Fort Niagara
shirr (ʃə:r) **1.** *n.* a gathering in a piece of cloth to create fullness and elasticity **2.** *v.t.* to make shirrs in || to bake (eggs) in a dish with cream **shirr·ing** (ʃə́:riŋ) *n.* [origin unknown]
shirt (ʃə:rt) *n.* a man's loose-fitting cloth garment covering the torso and usually having a collar and either long or short sleeves. It is often worn with a tie under a jacket || a woman's tailored blouse **to lose one's shirt** to lose virtually all one's money [O.E. *scyrte*]
shirt·front (ʃə́:rtfrʌnt) *n.* the starched part of a dress shirt covering the chest
shirt·ing (ʃə́:rtiŋ) *n.* fabric used for making shirts
shirt-sleeve (ʃə́:rtsli:v) *adj.* of down-to-earth (white-collar) work or worker
shirt·waist (ʃə́:rtweist) *n.* a woman's tailored blouse || a dress with this kind of top attached
Shiva *SIVA
shiv·er (ʃívər) **1.** *v.i.* to shake esp. with cold or fear **2.** *n.* the act or sensation of shivering [M.E. *chivere,* etym. doubtful]
shiver 1. *n.* a small fragment resulting from the breakage of a brittle substance **2.** *v.t.* to break (something) into shivers || *v.i.* to be smashed into shivers [M.E. *scifre*]
shiv·er·y (ʃívəri:) *adj.* feeling shivers || causing shivers
Shi·zu·o·ka (ʃi:zuɔ́kɑ) a city (pop. 329,000) and tea market of central E. Honshu, Japan: aluminum, textiles, food processing, handicrafts (lacquerware, bamboo)
Shko·dër (ʃkɔ́dər) (*Ital.* Scutari) a city (pop. 65,000) of Albania on Lake Shkodër. Manufactures: textiles, cement, cigarettes. Venetian citadel (15th c.) || (*Yugoslav* Skadarsko, *Ital.* Scutari) a lake (area varying between 150 and 200 sq. miles) in N.W. Albania and W. central Montenegro, Yugoslavia: fisheries
shoal (ʃoul) **1.** *n.* a part of a river, sea, lake etc. where the water is very shallow || a sandbank etc. causing such shallow water **2.** *adj.* (of water) shallow **3.** *v.i.* (of water) to become shallow || *v.t.* (of a ship etc.) to move into a shallower depth of (water) [earlier *shoal* adj., shallow fr. O.E. *sceald*]
shoal 1. *n.* a school of fish || (*pop.*) a large number or group, *a shoal of tourists* **2.** *v.i.* to gather together to form a shoal [perh. fr. M.Du. *schole*]
shoal·y (ʃouli:) *comp.* **shoal·i·er** *superl.* **shoal·i·est** *adj.* full of shoals (shallow areas of water)
shoat *n.* (*zool.*) hybrid sheep and goat *syn.* geep
shoat, shote (ʃout) *n.* a young pig, esp. one which has been weaned [M.E.]
shock (ʃɒk) *n.* a force of great magnitude applied suddenly, *the shock of a collision* || a sudden conduction of electric current through a person's body || a temporary but dangerous condition caused by pain, strong emotion or loss of blood and manifested by pallor, cold sweats and drowsiness which may pass into coma || a sudden arousing of emotion or disturbance of mental stability by something unexpected, offensive or unwelcome || something which causes this [F. *choc*]
shock *v.t.* to cause an emotional or mental shock to || to give painful offense to || to cause an electrical shock to || to affect with physical shock [F. *choquer*]
shock *n.* a thick, untidy mass of hair [etym. doubtful]
shock 1. *n.* a number of sheaves stood leaning against one another to dry **2.** *v.t.* to pile together in this way [M.E.]
shock absorber a device for protecting from shock by interposing something which converts the energy of the applied force into stresses within itself, e.g. into the stresses of a compressed spring or those of air or water compressed in a tube
shock·er (ʃɔ́kər) *n.* (*pop.*) a sensational novel or story, esp. one badly written || (*pop.*) someone or something that shocks
shock front (*mil.*) the boundary between the pressure disturbance created by an explosion (in air, water, or earth) and the ambient atmosphere, water, or earth
shock-head (ʃɔ́khed) *n.* a head of thick untidy hair **shóck-head·ed** *adj.*
shock·ing (ʃɔ́kiŋ) *adj.* causing shock, esp. to the emotions associated with what is thought to be morally right, *shocking behavior* || (*pop.*) very bad, *a shocking mistake*
Shock·ley (ʃɔ́kli:), William Bradford (1910-), U.S. physicist and co-winner (with John Bardeen and Walter H. Brattain) of the 1956 Nobel prize in physics for the invention and development of the junction transistor. From the late 1960s, Shockley became a controversial figure by supporting the view of Arthur Jensen and others that intelligence capacity is a genetic trait of races
shock rock rock'n'roll music accompanied by outrageous lyrics, costumes, lights, or other effects
shock therapy the treatment of mental disorder, esp. schizophrenia, by administering a shock (e.g. electrical shock or heavy insulin dosage)
shock treatment shock therapy
shock troops highly trained and disciplined troops used for offensive combat operations, esp. for leading attacks
shock wave a narrow region of high density, temperature, pressure and velocity formed in a medium around the leading surface of an object traveling through it at a speed greater than that of sound in that medium. The very high temperatures generated by shock waves have been used to study chemical reaction at extreme conditions of temperature and pressure
shod *past* and *past part.* of SHOE
shod·dy (ʃɔ́di:) **1.** *comp.* **shod·di·er** *superl.* **shod·di·est** *adj.* made of poor material || mean, shabby, *a shoddy trick* **2.** *pl.* **shod·dies** *n.,* fabric woven of yarn from the shredded fiber of other fabric which has already been worn or used || this yarn [origin unknown]
Shodop (*mil. acronym*) for short range doppler, system for measuring the trajectory of short-range missiles utilizing Doppler frequency shift as computed by ground stations
shoe (ʃu:) *n.* a foot covering of leather or other material which does not extend as far as the ankle, with a base or sole strong enough to be durable when worn out of doors, and giving some protection to the instep || a horseshoe || a wooden block placed under a wheel to prevent or retard its motion || something fitted to and placed at the bottom, foot or end of another object, or under it, e.g. a metal tip on the end of a cane, staff etc. or a metal band fastened to the bottom of the runner of a sled || the part of a bridge on which the superstructure rests || the part of a brake which presses on an upper part of a wheel to slow it down || the sliding contact which picks up current from a live rail || a metal plate between a moving and a stationary part of a machine || the outer cover of an automobile tire **if the shoe fits** (*Am.* =*Br.* if the cap fits) an expression used to indicate that a general remark is true for some particular person ('wear it' being understood) **in someone else's shoes** in the position or circumstances, or with the imaginative outlook, of someone else **where the shoe pinches** the cause of the trouble [O.E. *scōh*]
shoe *pres. part.* **shoe·ing** *past* and *past part.* **shod** (ʃɒd), **shoed** (ʃu:d) *v.t.* to supply or fit with shoes || to attach a protective cover to the bottom or end [O.E. *scōgan*]
shoe·black (ʃú:blæk) *n.* a bootblack
shoe·horn (ʃú:hɔrn) *n.* a narrow, curved instrument of e.g. horn or polished metal, inserted at the back of the shoe, to enable the foot to slide in easily
shoe·lace (ʃú:leis) *n.* a lace or cord used to fasten the uppers of a shoe together over the instep
shoe·mak·er (ʃú:meikər) *n.* someone whose business is to make or repair shoes **shóe·mak·ing** *n.* the trade of a shoemaker
shoe·shine (ʃú:ʃain) *n.* a shine or polish applied to the shoes
shoe·string (ʃú:striŋ) *n.* a shoelace **on a shoestring** on a very small budget, *living on a shoestring, making films on a shoestring*
shoe tree a metal or wooden device placed inside a shoe to help to keep it supple and preserve its shape
sho·far, sho·phar (ʃóufər, ʃoufár) *pl.* **sho·fars, sho·phars, sho·froth, sho·phroth** (ʃoufrɔ́t) *n.* a ram's horn formerly used by the ancient Hebrews as a battle signal and now blown in synagogues before and during Rosh Hashanah and at the end of Yom Kippur
sho·gun (ʃóugʌn,ʃóugu:n) *n.* (*hist.*) any of the hereditary military commanders who ruled Japan (1192–1867) **sho·gun·ate** (ʃóugʌnit, ʃóugu:nit) *n.* the rank or position of a shogun || government by a shogun or shoguns [Jap. fr. Chin. *chiang chiin,* to lead an army]
Sho·la·pur (ʃóuləpur) a commercial center (pop. 398,361) of S.E. Maharashtra, India: silk and cotton textiles
shone *past* and alt. *past part.* of SHINE
shoo (ʃu:) **1.** *interj.* a cry meaning 'move along!', used in driving esp. an animal away **2.** *v. pres. part.* **shoo·ing** *past* and *past part.* **shooed** *v.t.* to drive (an animal, child etc.) away, esp. by crying 'shoo!' || *v.i.* to make this cry in order to drive away animals etc.
shook (ʃuk) *n.* a set of staves and headings arranged ready for a cask to be built || a set of pieces of wood prepared for making into a box || a shock of sheaves [prob. var. of SHOCK]
shook *past* of SHAKE
shoot (ʃu:t) **1.** *v. pres. part.* **shoot·ing** *past* and *past part.* **shot** (ʃɒt) *v.t.* (of a person) to cause (a projectile) to be projected, *to shoot an arrow* || (of a gun etc.) to cause (a projectile) to be projected || to fire (a gun etc.) || to kill by doing this, *to shoot a rabbit* || to wound by doing this, *he shot him in the leg* || to put to death with a bullet as a punishment, *he was shot at dawn* || to hunt (game etc.) || to hunt the game on (land) || (usually with 'away', 'down', 'out' or 'off') to destroy or remove with a projectile from a gun etc., *to shoot down an airplane* || to go quickly through, under, over etc., *to shoot rapids* || to project (someone or something) forward, out, towards etc., *he shot them onto the back seat and drove off* || to direct (e.g. a reply question, glance etc.) with the rapidity of a moving bullet || (with 'through' or

'with') to streak with another color or colors ‖ to send (a letter, refuse etc.) down a chute or something resembling a chute ‖ (*games*) to drive (a ball etc.) in the direction of a goal ‖ (*basketball*) to score (a goal) ‖ to put (a marble) into action by a flick of the thumb ‖ to detonate (a blast) ‖ (esp. *movies*) to photograph ‖ (*naut.*) to take the altitude of (the sun etc.) ‖ to play (dice) ‖ *v.i.* to go, arrive or move with great speed like a moving projectile, *he shot past me on his bicycle* ‖ (with 'up') to grow quickly, *the boy has shot up during the last year* ‖ (of a plant) to begin to grow or put out young sprouts ‖ to hunt with a gun ‖ (of a person) to send forth a projectile, esp. from a gun or bow ‖ (of a gun etc.) to send forth a projectile ‖ to hunt with a gun ‖ (esp. *movies*) to photograph ‖ to jut out ‖ (*games*) to propel a ball, marble etc. toward the objective ‖ (*cricket*, of a ball) to increase in speed after hitting the ground ‖ (of a star, meteor etc.) to flash across the sky ‖ to dart painfully in or through a part or parts of the body **2.** *n.* a slope down which something can glide quickly, a chute ‖ a young outgrowth of a tree etc. ‖ land used for shooting over ‖ a number of persons engaged in shooting game ‖ the game shot ‖ the right to shoot ‖ a place where rubbish is thrown [O.E. *scēotan*]

shooting box (*Br.*) a shooting lodge

shooting brake (*Br.*) a station wagon

shooting gallery a place for target practice with firearms ‖ a booth at a fairground where persons pay to shoot at targets for prizes

shooting lodge a country lodge or cabin used as quarters by hunters during the shooting season

shooting star a meteor

shop (ʃɒp) **1.** *n.* (esp. *Br.*) a store (building where retail trade is carried on) ‖ a workshop or establishment where machines or goods are made or repaired **to set up shop** to open a shop, business etc., esp. for the first time in a particular place **to shut up shop** to cease to be in business ‖ **to talk shop** to discuss the techniques etc. of one's profession or trade **2.** *v.i. pres. part.* **shop·ping** *past* and *past part.* **shopped** to go to a shop or shops in order to buy goods [O.E. *sceoppa*, a place where goods are made and sold]

shop assistant (*Br.*) someone who serves in a retail store

Shope virus or **Shope papilloma** (*med.*) a virus causing warts (*papillomatosis*); named for Dr. R. E. Shope

shophar *SHOFAR

shop·keep·er (ʃɒ́pkiːpər) *n.* a person who owns and manages a store

shop·lift·er (ʃɒ́pliftər) *n.* someone who, pretending to be a customer, steals goods displayed for sale in a store **shop·lift·ing** *n.*

shop·per (ʃɒ́pər) *n.* a person who buys in a store ‖ a person hired by a store to do this for others ‖ a person hired by a store to check prices, quality of goods etc. in a rival store or stores

shop·ping (ʃɒ́piŋ) *n.* the action of someone who shops ‖ the goods bought

shopping center a complex consisting of food markets, stores of various kinds, parking facilities etc., designed to serve the needs of a local community

shop·soiled (ʃɒ́psɔild) *adj.* (*Br.*) shopworn

shop steward a person chosen by his fellow trade unionists in an industrial establishment to speak for them to the management and to watch over their interests

shop·talk (ʃɒ́ptɔk) *n.* chat or conversation narrowly limited to one's trade or profession

shop·walk·er (ʃɒ́pwɔkər) (*Br.*) a floorwalker

shop·worn (ʃɒ́pwɔrn) *adj.* (of goods) slightly damaged or dirty from long exposure for sale ‖ too familiar or overused to be stimulating or interesting, *shopworn ideas*

shor·an (shɔræn) *n.* (*mil. acronym*) for short-range electronic navigation system used in precision bombing

shore (ʃɔr,ʃour) *n.* the land forming the edge of a large expanse of water ‖ (*law*) the land between high and low water marks ‖ land as opposed to water [M.E. *schore* prob. fr. M.L.G. or M. Du.]

shore 1. *n.* a length of lumber or metal, resting firmly on the ground or other unyielding surface and adjusted usually at an angle with the vertical so as to support a structure above it **2.** *v.t. pres. part.* **shor·ing** *past* and *past part.* **shored** (with 'up') to support by using a shore [M.E. *schore* fr. M. Du. or M.L.G.]

shore·bird (ʃɔ́rbəːrd,ʃóurbəːrd) *n.* a member of *Charadrii*, a suborder of birds that live along the seashore, e.g. the plover, snipe and sandpiper

shore leave leave granted to members of a ship's crew for going ashore

shore·line (ʃɔ́rlain, ʃóurlain) *n.* where the shore ends and the water begins

shore patrol the U.S. Navy or Coast Guard military police on shore

shorn alt. *past part.* of SHEAR

short (ʃɔrt) **1.** *adj.* having a relatively smaller length, range, scope etc. than others of its kind, type etc. of or being the shorter or shortest in dimension, *the short side of the room* ‖ not lasting a long time ‖ not tall ‖ (of a mode of address, manner or treatment) less friendly or generous than true courtesy would require ‖ easily aroused, *a short temper* ‖ (of pastry) crumbly due to the high proportion of shortening used ‖ (*phon.*, of syllables, vowels etc.) comparatively brief in duration ‖ (*prosody*, of a syllable) not stressed ‖ (esp. *classical prosody*, of a syllable) of relatively little duration ‖ (*finance*) not in possession of the securities or commodities at the time of sale ‖ (*finance*) being or pertaining to a sale of securities or commodities not in possession of the seller ‖ (of memory) not retentive ‖ less than a correct or sufficient degree or amount, *short weight* ‖ (usually with 'of' or 'in') lacking the correct or sufficient amount of what is required, *short of funds* ‖ not extending to or reaching a particular point or objective ‖ (of an alcoholic beverage) served in a small glass ‖ (*pop.* with 'on') equipped with an inadequate amount of, *short on acceleration* **short for** being an abbreviation or contraction of **to make short work of** to dispose of very quickly **2.** *adv.* unexpectedly and suddenly, *to stop short* ‖ in a brusque, discourteous manner ‖ on the near side of a given point or objective ‖ without actually owning the securities etc. sold, *to sell short* **3.** *n.* (*movies*) a movie of one reel ‖ (*elec.*) a short circuit ‖ (*finance*) someone who sells short ‖ (*pl.*) short pants covering the body from the waist to above the knees ‖ (*pl.*) underpants ‖ (*pl.*) a byproduct of wheat milling consisting of wheat germ, bran and flour ‖ (*pl.*) the waste materials of various manufacturing processes ‖ (*prosody*) a short syllable ‖ (*baseball*) shortstop or a shortstop **for short** by way of abbreviation or contraction **in short** by way of summary **4.** *v.t.* and *i.* to short-circuit [O.E. *scort, sceort*]

short account the account of a person who sells short ‖ the total, at any time, of such accounts in a commodity or in the market

short·age (ʃɔ́rtidʒ) *n.* the fact that there is less of something than is required, or the amount by which what is available falls short

short·bread (ʃɔ́rtbred) *n.* a crisp, short, sweet cooky made with butter, flour, sugar etc.

short·cake (ʃɔ́rtkeik) *n.* a dessert consisting of a crisp, short biscuit which is split, filled with fresh fruit and topped with more fruit and often cream ‖ this biscuit ‖ (*Br.*) shortbread

short·change (ʃɔ́rttʃéindʒ) *pres. part.* **short·chang·ing** *past* and *past part.* **short·changed** *v.t.* (*pop.*) to give (a customer) less than the correct change

short circuit a connection, usually accidental, between two points at different potentials in an electric circuit of relatively low resistance **short-cír·cuit** *v.t.* to make a short circuit in ‖ *v.i.* to make a short circuit

short·com·ing (ʃɔ́rtkʌmiŋ) *n.* a failure to reach an expected or desired standard of conduct

short·cut (ʃɔ́rtkʌt) *n.* a shorter, quicker way to a place or objective than the customary road or course of action

short·en (ʃɔ́rt'n) *v.t.* to make shorter ‖ (*naut.*) to reduce the spread of (sail) by reefing or furling ‖ *v.i.* to become shorter ‖ (of odds) to decrease **shórt·en·ing** *n.* the act of making or becoming shorter ‖ butter, fat etc. used to make pastry or cake crisper or flakier

short·hand (ʃɔ́rthænd) **1.** *n.* a rapid way of writing by using symbols to represent syllables or complete words or phrases **2.** *adj.* of, relating to or consisting of shorthand

short·hand·ed (ʃɔ́rthǽndid) *adj.* having fewer persons available for work than is necessary or desirable

short head (*Br., racing*) a distance less than the length of a horse's head, separating two horses in a race

short·head (ʃɔ́rthed) *n.* a brachycephalic person **shórt·head·ed** *adj.*

Short·horn (ʃɔ́rthɔrn) *n.* one of a breed of beef or dairy cattle with short curving horns that originated in N. England and that are red, white or roan

short hundredweight the U.S. hundredweight of 100 lbs

short leg (*cricket*) a fielder occupying a position near to the batsman on the leg side ‖ this position

short list (*Br.*) the remaining list of candidates after a preliminary weeding out **shórt-list** *v.t.* (*Br.*) to place on a short list

short-lived (ʃɔ́rtláivd, ʃɔ́rtlívd) *adj.* not living or continuing long

short·ly (ʃɔ́rtliː) *adv.* in a few words ‖ soon ‖ discourteously, brusquely

short of *prep.* not quite up to, *short of the goal* ‖ without going as far as, *he would do anything short of murder that you asked*

short order an order for food that is quickly prepared after it has been ordered in a restaurant **in short order** with no delay **shórt-or·der** *adj.* preparing food in this way, *a short-order restaurant*

short-range (ʃɔ́rtréindʒ) *adj.* limited in range ‖ concerned only with the near future, not the long term

short ribs a cut of beef taken from the ends of the ribs

short shrift summary treatment through lack of sympathy etc., *to make short shrift of something, to give someone short shrift*

short-sight·ed (ʃɔ́rtsáitid) *adj.* myopic ‖ not taking into account the probable future results of one's behavior or actions

short slip (*cricket*) a position, or the fielder occupying it, in the slips but close to the batsman

short-spo·ken (ʃɔ́rtspoukən) *adj.* curt

short·stop (ʃɔ́rtstɒp) *n.* (*baseball*) the infielder between second and third base ‖ his position

short story a story in prose varying widely in length, but shorter than either a novel or a novelette, and concentrating on a single effect which the writer wants to achieve

short-tem·pered (ʃɔ́rttémpərd) *adj.* quick-tempered

short-term (ʃɔ́rttə́ːrm) *adj.* happening over or entailing only a brief period ‖ (*finance*) of or relating to a gain, loss, transaction etc. based on a relatively short period of time (usually less than a year)

short ton (*U.S.A., Canada* and *South Africa*) a unit of weight equal to 2,000 lbs, used for coal

short·wave (ʃɔ́rtwéiv) **1.** *n.* an electromagnetic wave having a 60-meter wavelength or less **2.** *adj.* of, pertaining to, or using shortwaves **3.** *v.t. pres. part.* **short·wav·ing** *past* and *past part.* **short·waved** to transmit by shortwaves

short-wind·ed (ʃɔ́rtwíndid) *adj.* out of breath or easily out of breath

Sho·sho·ne·an (ʃouʃóuniːən, ʃouʃəníːən) *pl.* **Sho·sho·ne·an, Sho·sho·ne·ans** *n.* a linguistic family of the Uto-Aztecan group ‖ a member of an Indian people speaking a Shoshonean language ‖ any such people

Sho·sho·ni, Sho·sho·ne (ʃouʃóuniː) *pl.* **Sho·sho·ni, Sho·sho·nis, Sho·sho·ne, Sho·sho·nes** *n.* a group of Shoshonean peoples of the western U.S.A. ‖ their language ‖ a member of this group

Sho·sta·ko·vich (ʃɒstəkóuvitʃ), Dmitri (1906-75), Russian composer. His style is eclectic and he has incurred the disapproval of Soviet critics at various times. His work includes symphonies, operas, ballets, songs, chamber music and music for the movies. The authenticity of his autobiography, 'Testimony: The Memoirs of Dmitri Shostakovich' (1979) was disputed by family members

shot (ʃɒt) **1.** *n.* an act of shooting ‖ a discharge of a firearm, cannon or gun ‖ the range or distance able to be passed over by a discharged missile, *within shot* ‖ (*collect.*) small spherical pieces of hardened lead packed into a cartridge ‖ a single piece of this ‖ (*hist.*) a solid, nonexplosive ball designed to be shot from a cannon ‖ an attempt to hit by shooting ‖ an attempt, *to have a shot at something* ‖ a guess ‖ an opportunity or chance to achieve or get something ‖ an obliquely critical remark, *that was a shot at you* ‖ a marksman ‖ (*movies*) a scene or portion of a scene photographed by one camera without stopping or cutting ‖ (*games*) a stroke, throw, drive etc., *a shot at a goal* ‖ a photograph ‖ an injection of a drug ‖ (*pop.*) a small quantity of whiskey or other liquor ‖ (*athletics*) a heavy metal ball, weighing up to 16 lbs, thrown by contestants in the shot put field event **like a shot** with great alacrity ‖ very willingly **to pay one's shot** (*Br.*) to pay one's share of the cost **2.** *v.t. pres. part.* **shot·ting** *past* and *past part.* **shot·ted** to load or weight with shot [O.E. *sceot, scot, gesceot, gescot*]

shot *past* and *past part.* of SHOOT *adj.* (of silk or other fabric) closely woven with a warp of one color and weft of another color so that it exhibits different colors and shades when viewed at different angles ‖ (*pop.*) worn out, broken, *this saucepan is shot* ‖ (*pop.*) ruined, in a useless state, *his nerves are shot*

shote *SHOAT

shot·gun (ʃótgʌn) *n.* a short-range, smooth-bore firearm, often with two barrels, from which shot is projected by the explosion of a cartridge, the shot spreading in a cone shape as it travels from the muzzle

shot put an athletic contest in which competitors put the shot ‖ a put of the shot in this contest

should (ʃud) *past* of SHALL *auxiliary v.* used to express moral obligation, necessity etc., *you should work harder,* or probability, *it should rain tonight if the wind drops,* futurity in indirect quotations to replace 'will' and 'shall' in direct quotations, *we said we should be happy to come,* futurity in polite requests or statements with implications of doubt, *I should think she will come,* or future condition, *if that should happen would you be able to go?* or past condition, *I should have been late if I hadn't taken a taxi* (cf. SHALL, cf. WOULD) [O.E. *sceolde, scolde*]

shoul·der (ʃóuldər) **1.** *n.* the joint connecting the arm or forelimb with the upper part of the body ‖ that part of the body to which is connected the arm of a person, the foreleg of a quadruped, or the wing of a bird ‖ (*pl.*) the upper part of a person's back and the two shoulders ‖ a cut of meat including the upper part of the foreleg and the part to which it is attached ‖ the part of a garment which covers the shoulder ‖ the part of a hide corresponding to an animal's shoulders ‖ a part of something thought of as like a shoulder, esp. in the way it projects, *the shoulder of a mountain* ‖ (*printing*) the flat top of the body of a type on which the bevel rises to the face ‖ either side of a road, off the roadway **shoulder to shoulder** standing side by side, close together ‖ acting closely together, helping one another to the utmost **straight from the shoulder** direct and frank, without qualification or reserve, esp. in expressing criticism **to put one's shoulder to the wheel** to make a great effort to further a project or piece of work **2.** *v.t.* to push with the shoulder ‖ to take or carry on the shoulder ‖ to accept (a burden of responsibility), *to shoulder the blame* ‖ *v.i.* to push with the shoulder **to shoulder arms** (*mil.*) to hold (a rifle) so that the barrel rests on the shoulder and the butt is supported in the palm of the hand [O.E. *sculdor*]

shoulder belt or **shoulder harness** across-the-chest restraint used in motor vehicles to hold back passengers in case of accidental impact

shoulder blade one of the two large flat bones of the upper back

shoulder loop a strap of cloth running from a button at the collar to the shoulder seam on Army, Air Force and Marine Corps uniforms. Commissioned and warrant officers' insignia of rank are attached to it

shoulder strap a band of ribbon etc. supporting a woman's dress or slip etc. across the shoulders ‖ a strap of cloth running from a button at the collar to the shoulder seam on a uniform

should·n't (ʃúd'nt) *contr.* of SHOULD NOT

shout (ʃaut) **1.** *n.* a loud, often wordless cry uttered in order to attract attention or to express some very strong emotion **2.** *v.i.* to utter this cry, *he shouted to warn me* ‖ to speak very loudly, *she had to shout because he was deaf* ‖ *v.t.* to express by a shout, *he shouted a warning* **to shout (someone) down** to silence (a speaker) by shouting [M.E. *shouten,* etym. doubtful]

shove (ʃʌv) **1.** *v. pres. part.* **shov·ing** *past* and *past part.* **shoved** *v.t.* to push (someone or something) hard ‖ *v.i.* to push **to shove off** to push (a boat) away from shore ‖ (*pop.*) to leave **2.** *n.* a hard push [O.E. *scūfan*]

shove-half·pen·ny (ʃʌvhéipəni, ʃʌvhéipni:) *n.* a game in which coins (halfpennies etc.) are made to slide across scoring lines on a marked board by resting them at the edge and striking with the ball of the thumb ‖ (*Br.*) shuffleboard (disk and cue game)

shov·el (ʃʌ́v'l) **1.** *n.* a tool consisting of a large shallow concave head attached to the end of a long handle, used for lifting loose material and moving it elsewhere ‖ the quantity it holds **2.** *v.t. pres. part.* **shov·el·ing,** esp. *Br.* **shov·el·ling** *past* and *past part.* **shov·eled,** esp. *Br.* **shov·elled** to lift and move with a shovel ‖ to dig out or clear (e.g. a path) with a shovel [O.E. *scofl*]

shov·el·board (ʃʌ́v'lbɔrd, ʃʌ́v'lbourd) *n.* shuffleboard (disk and cue game) ‖ (*Br.*) shove-halfpenny (coin game)

shov·el·er, esp. *Br.* **shov·el·ler** (ʃʌ́vələr, ʃʌ́vlər) *n. Anas clypeata,* fam. *Anatidae,* a freshwater duck with a huge spatulate beak

shovel hat a shallow black hat with a broad brim turned up at the sides, formerly worn by pastors and clergymen

shov·el·head (ʃʌ́vlhed) *n. Sphyrna tiburo,* fam. *Sphyrinidae,* a shark related to the hammerhead shark, but smaller

shoveller *SHOVELER

show (ʃou) **1.** *v. pres. part.* **show·ing** *past* **showed** *past part.* **shown** (ʃoun), **showed** *v.t.* to cause to be seen, *he showed his books to me* ‖ to guide, conduct, *she showed me to my seat* ‖ to offer for public view, *the firm showed its new designs* ‖ to put on view for entertainment, *they are showing a new movie* ‖ to indicate, give to understand, *his letter shows why he did not come* ‖ to point out, *he showed her why she ought to do it* ‖ to establish, prove, *the evidence showed that he was sane at the time, it showed him that he was right* ‖ (*law*) to plead, present in a court, *to show just cause* ‖ to give evidence of (feelings, character, disposition), *he showed no pity* ‖ to bestow (favor etc.) ‖ to register, *the farm showed a profit* ‖ to present (a message) to the eye or mind, *the signal showed all clear* ‖ to depict, *the account shows him as a scoundrel* ‖ *v.i.* to be visible ‖ to be seen, *to show to advantage* ‖ to have a specified appearance ‖ (*pop.*) to prove a point, *it just goes to show* ‖ (of a movie) to be on view ‖ (*pop.*) to finish third, esp. in a horse race **to show off** to make a show of one's virtues or skills ‖ to demonstrate so as to reveal the qualities of **to show up** to reveal the true character (usually unworthy) of ‖ to put in an appearance ‖ to appear in a specified way ‖ to be conspicuous **2.** *n.* a display, *a show of grief* ‖ a demonstration, *a show of strength* ‖ a public exhibition, *a flower show,* esp. one of paintings or sculpture, *a one-man show* ‖ a public presentation of entertainment, e.g. a play, a radio program ‖ a visible trace, *no show of fatigue* ‖ pretense, *he made a show of not hearing me* ‖ a chance to reveal quality, *it got no sort of show* ‖ performance, *to put up a good show* ‖ (*pop.*) an undertaking, business etc., *he wrecked the whole show* ‖ (*pop.*) third place, esp. in a horse race ‖ **for show** in order merely to attract attention [O.E. *scēawian,* to look at]

show bill an advertising poster

show·boat (ʃóubout) *n.* a river steamer with actors or entertainers on board giving a show ‖ (*colloq.*) a show-off

showbread *SHEWBREAD

show·case (ʃóukeis) *n.* a glass-fronted cupboard, fitted with shelves, in which goods are set out on view for sale or objects for exhibition

show·down (ʃóudaun) *n.* the last stage in a dispute immediately preceding a settlement ‖ (*poker*) a laying down of the cards face up

show·er (ʃáuər) **1.** *n.* a brief fall of rain, hail or sleet ‖ a thick but brief fall of objects, *a shower of confetti* ‖ a shower bath ‖ a festive gathering at which presents are given to a prospective bride or mother **showers of** a great many, *showers of compliments* **2.** *v.t.* to cover as if in a shower ‖ *v.i.* to fall in or as if in a shower ‖ to take a shower bath [O.E. *scūr*]

shower bath a bath taken standing up under a spray of water from an overhead nozzle ‖ the apparatus installed for such baths ‖ the room etc. where such baths are taken

show·er·y (ʃáuəri:) *adj.* with rain falling briefly and frequently ‖ like a shower, *showery pink blossoms*

show·i·ly (ʃóuəli:) *adv.* in a showy manner

show·i·ness (ʃóui:nis) *n.* the state or quality of being showy

show·ing (ʃóuiŋ) *n.* the act of offering for public view ‖ an exhibition for display, *a private showing of a film* ‖ performance in a competition, *to make a good showing* ‖ evidence, *on present showing we should finish next year*

show·man (ʃóumən) *pl.* **show·men** (ʃóumən) *n.* the owner or manager of a circus, menagerie or other lesser form of public entertainment ‖ someone who has a flair for putting something before the public effectively, esp. by using theatrical techniques, *the parson is something of a showman* **shów·man·ship** *n.*

shown *past* and alt. *past part.* of show

show-off (ʃóuɔf,ʃóupf) *n.* the act of showing off ‖ (*pop.*) a person who shows off for admiration

show of hands a raising of one hand by each member of a group as a method of voting, showing approval etc.

show·piece (ʃóupi:s) *n.* something being exhibited or that would exhibit well

show·room (ʃóuru:m,ʃóurum) *n.* a room set apart for showing samples of goods for sale

show window a store display window

show·y (ʃóui:) *comp.* **show·i·er** *superl.* **show·i·est** *adj.* ostentatious ‖ making attractive display, *showy blooms*

shrank *past* of SHRINK

shrap·nel (ʃrǽpn'l) *n.* bullets and jagged pieces of metal sprayed by a bursting shell ‖ a projectile fired for this effect [after Henry *Shrapnel* (1761-1842), British general]

shred (ʃred) *n.* a small piece torn or cut from something, usually in the form of a thin strip ‖ a small amount, *shreds of evidence* [O.E. *scrēade*]

shred *pres. part.* **shred·ding** *past* and *past part.* **shred·ded, shred** *v.t.* to tear or cut into shreds [O.E. *scrēadian*]

Shreve·port (ʃrí:vpɔrt, ʃrí:vpourt) a port and industrial town (pop. 205,815) of N.W. Louisiana: oil refining, chemicals, sawmilling

shrew (ʃru:) *n.* a member of *Soricidae,* a family of small, mouse-like, insectivorous, nocturnal animals with a long tail and a soft hairy coat ‖ a bad-tempered woman [O.E. *scrēawa, scrǣwa*]

shrewd (ʃru:d) *adj.* intelligent and worldly-wise, *a shrewd businessman* ‖ clever and true or very near the truth, *a shrewd guess* [M.E. *shrewede* fr. SHREW, (obs.) an evil person]

shrew·ish (ʃrú:iʃ) *adj.* (of a woman) bad-tempered, bullying

shriek (ʃri:k) **1.** *v.i.* to utter a shrill, sharp cry, esp. from pain, fear etc. ‖ to laugh in a shrill, high-pitched way ‖ *v.t.* to utter in a sharp, shrill way **2.** *n.* such a cry or laugh [etym. doubtful]

shriev·al·ty (ʃri:vəlti:) *pl.* **shriev·al·ties** *n.* (*Br.*) the office, tenure of office or jurisdiction of a sheriff

shrift (ʃrift) *n.* (*archaic*) confession to a priest in the sacrament of penance ‖ (*archaic*) the remission of sins pronounced by a priest to a penitent ‖ *SHORT SHRIFT [O.E. *scrift*]

shrike (ʃraik) *n.* any of various hook-billed songbirds of fam. *Lanidae,* esp. of genus *Lanius,* that feed mainly on insects which they impale on thorny bushes [O.E. *scrīc, scrēc,* a bird with a shrill cry]

Shrike *n.* (*mil.*) an air-launched antiradiation missile (AGM-45) designed to home on and destroy radar emitters

shrill (ʃril) **1.** *adj.* (of a voice or sound) high-pitched and piercing ‖ made in or accompanied by such sounds, *shrill demands* **2.** *v.t.* to utter in a shrill voice ‖ *v.i.* to make shrill cries [M.E. *shrille*]

shrimp (ʃrimp) **1.** *pl.* **shrimps, shrimp** *n.* any of various members of *Natantia,* a suborder of small, edible, chiefly marine crustaceans having 10 legs and a long slender body ‖ (*pop.*) a tiny or undersized person, esp. one who is unimposing **2.** *v.i.* to fish for shrimps [M.E. *schrimpe*]

shrimp boat a plastic chip placed on radarscope in air traffic control to track aircraft

shrine (ʃrain) *n.* a box of stone, metal or wood used to hold sacred relics ‖ a tomb, chapel or other place held sacred because of the presence of such relics ‖ a place which is hallowed because it has special associations [O.E. *scrin* fr. L.]

shrink (ʃriŋk) **1.** *pres. part.* **shrink·ing** *past* **shrank** (ʃræŋk), **shrunk** (ʃrʌŋk) *past part.* **shrunk,** (only in adj. uses) **shrunk·en** (ʃrʌ́ŋk'n) *v.i.* to become smaller, e.g. from heat, cold etc. ‖ (of cloth or clothing) to become smaller after being washed or thoroughly drenched ‖ to draw back in fear or unwillingness, *she shrank from the idea of meeting him* ‖ (e.g. of value) to lessen ‖ *v.t.* to cause to shrink **2.** *n.* the act of shrinking **shrink·age** *n.* the act, process or extent of shrinking [O.E. *scrincan*]

shrink-wrap (ʃríŋkræp) *n.* plastic film packaging that shrinks under heat to conform to shape of contents, e.g., a book —**shrink wrap** *v.*

shrive (ʃraiv) *pres. part.* **shriv·ing** *past* **shrove** (ʃrouv), **shrived** *past part.* **shriv·en** (ʃrív'n), **shrived** *v.i.* (*archaic*) to confess to a priest and receive absolution ‖ *v.t.* (*archaic*) to hear the confession of and absolve [O.E. *scrīfan*]

shriv·el (ʃrív'l) *pres. part.* **shriv·el·ing,** esp. *Br.* **shriv·el·ling** *past* and *past part.* **shriv·eled,** esp. *Br.* **shrivelled** *v.i.* (often with 'up') to become smaller, with the surface becoming wrinkled ‖ *v.t.* to cause to become smaller and wrinkled [origin unknown]

shriven alt. *past part.* of SHRIVE

Shrop·shire (ʃrɒ́pʃiər, ʃrɒ́pʃər) (*abbr.* Salop) a county (area 1,347 sq. miles, pop. 380,400) of England on the Welsh border. County town: Shrewsbury (pop. 58,826)

shroud (ʃraud) **1.** *n.* a long sheet wound around a corpse ‖ something which conceals or clouds, *a shroud of mist* ‖ (*naut.*) one of the ropes attached to the sides of a ship and the lower mastheads, to keep the mast in position **2.** *v.t.* to wind in a shroud ‖ to conceal or cloud, *her background was shrouded in mystery* [O.E. *scrūd,* garment]

shroud-laid (ʃráudleid) *adj.* (of a rope) having four strands and a core

shrove alt. *past* of SHRIVE

Shrove·tide (ʃróuvtaid) *n.* the three days before Ash Wednesday (Quinquagesima and the following Monday and Tuesday), when pre-Lent confessions are made and pre-Lent festivities are held [rel. to SHRIVE, origin unknown]

shrub (ʃrʌb) *n.* a plant with several branching woody stems and no main trunk, smaller than most trees **shrúb·ber·y** *pl.* **shrub·ber·ies** *n.* a number of shrubs growing close together ‖ (*collect.*) shrubs **shrúb·by** *comp.* **shrub·bi·er** *superl.* **shrub·bi·est** *adj.* composed of shrubs ‖ like a shrub [O.E. *scrybb,* shrubbery]

shrug (ʃrʌg) **1.** *v. pres. part.* **shrug·ging** *past* and *past part.* **shrugged** *v.t.* to lift (the shoulders) as a gesture expressing doubt, rejection of an idea, ignorance of the answer to a question etc. ‖ *v.i.* to lift the shoulders in this way **2.** *n.* this gesture [origin unknown]

shrunk alt. *past* and *past part.* of SHRINK

shrunken alt. *past part.* of SHRINK

shtetl or **shte·tel** (ʃtet'l) *n.* (*Yiddish*) small Jewish town or village in Eastern Europe during the 19th and 20th century until World War II

SH-3 *SEA KING

SH-2 *SEA SPRITE

shuck (ʃʌk) **1.** *n.* a shell or husk **2.** *v.t.* to extract (e.g. peas, fruit, nuts) from pods or shells ‖ to remove (oysters) from their shells **shucks** *interj.* an expression of disappointment, annoyance etc. [origin unknown]

shuck (*slang*) **1.** *n.* a sham **2.** *v.* to con or deceive verbally

shud·der (ʃʌ́dər) **1.** *v.i.* to experience a sudden and forceful muscular contraction throughout the body, arising from horror or disgust **2.** *n.* one of these muscular contractions ‖ the act of shuddering [M.E. *shodre, shoddre*]

shuf·fle (ʃʌ́f'l) **1.** *v. pres. part.* **shuf·fling** *past* and *past part.* **shuf·fled** *v.t.* to move (things) about, changing their positions relative to one another, *to shuffle cards* ‖ to slide (the feet) around continually on the ground ‖ to jumble together into a disordered state ‖ to change, shift, push, esp. in a clumsy way ‖ *v.i.* to move while dragging or sliding the feet instead of lifting them ‖ to dance in this way ‖ (with 'in', 'into' or 'out of') to get into or out of a position, state etc. by shifty or evasive means, *to shuffle out of a situation* ‖ to shift around from one position to another ‖ to shuffle cards **2.** *n.* the act of shuffling ‖ a shuffling of the feet ‖ a shuffling gait ‖ the rearranging of a pack of cards ‖ one's turn to do this [prob. L.G. *schüffeln,* to walk clumsily]

shuf·fle·board (ʃʌ́f'lbɔrd, ʃʌ́f'lbourd) *n.* a game in which players use a cue to push large disks into sections marked out on a flat, smooth surface ‖ (*Br.*) shove-halfpenny (coin game)

shuf·fler (ʃʌ́flər) *n.* (esp. in *cards*) a person who shuffles ‖ a scaup duck

Shu·fu (ʃú:fú:) *KASHGAR

shun (ʃʌn) *pres. part.* **shun·ning** *past* and *past part.* **shunned** *v.t.* to keep clear of, avoid, *to shun publicity* [O.E. *scunian*]

shun·pike (ʃʌ́npaik) *v.* to travel on secondary roads avoiding expressways —**shunpiker** *n.*

shunt (ʃʌnt) **1.** *v.t.* to move (a train etc.) to a different track ‖ (*elec.*) to divert (a current) to a different direction ‖ (*elec.*) to provide with a shunt ‖ to cause (someone) to divert his thoughts, interests, attention etc. in another direction ‖ *v.i.* (of trains) to move to a different track ‖ (*elec.,* of a current) to be diverted by a shunt **2.** *n.* a shunting ‖ (*elec.*) a conductor attached to a circuit at two points, reducing the amount of current flowing through the circuit (*rail.*) a switch ‖ (*auto racing*) an accident, esp. involving two or more cars [M.E. *shunten*]

shunt-wound (ʃʌ́ntwáund) *adj.* (*elec.*) designating a coil of an armature wound so that some of the current travels around the field magnet

shush (ʃʌʃ) **1.** *interj.* hush! be silent! **2.** *v.t.* to cause (someone) to be silent

shut (ʃʌt) *pres. part.* **shut·ting** *past* and *past part.* **shut** *v.t.* (sometimes with 'up' or 'down') to cause (something) to come together with another surface so that there is no space between them, *to shut a door* ‖ to fasten (a door etc.) with a catch, bolt etc. ‖ to prevent passage through by imposing a barrier, *to shut a road to all traffic* ‖ (sometimes with 'up') to bring together the parts of (the eye, mouth etc.) so that there is no space between them ‖ (often with 'up') to prevent exit from or entrance to *to shut a house for the winter* ‖ (sometimes with 'up') to confine, *shut the dog in the kitchen* ‖ (often with 'up') to stop or stop temporarily the business or operation of *he will have to shut the shop* ‖ (with 'up') to put away in a container, esp. in a safe place ‖ (with 'up') to cause (someone) to stop talking ‖ *v.i.* to be or become shut ‖ (often with 'up') to stop or stop temporarily the business or operation of a store, factory etc. ‖ (with 'up') to stop talking **to shut down** to cause (a factory etc.) to cease to work **to shut in** to prevent from coming out ‖ to surround, *the house is shut in by trees* **to shut off** to prevent (water, gas, steam etc.) from flowing ‖ to stop (machinery) from working by shutting off the power ‖ to keep from human contact, *he is shutting himself off from society* ‖ (of machinery) to stop working because the power has been cut off **to shut out** to prevent from entering ‖ to prevent the possibility of, *this shuts out any danger of fire* ‖ (*sports*) to keep (an opponent or opposing team) from scoring [O.E. *scyttan*]

shut-in (ʃʌ́tin) *n.* an invalid unable to leave his bed, room or house

shut·out (ʃʌ́taut) *n.* a lockout ‖ (*sports*) prevention from scoring in a game ‖ (*sports*) a game with no score on one side

shut·ter (ʃʌ́tər) **1.** *n.* a cover, often consisting of wooden boards or slats, used to secure a window against unlawful entry or to allow air but not sunlight to enter ‖ a mechanical device that acts to admit light into a camera or other optical instrument during a specified time interval. In cameras the shutter may be built into the lens system or may act in the focal plane. In motion-picture cameras it usually consists of a rotating device synchronized with the rate of passage of the film before the lenses ‖ a device for opening and closing the swell box of an organ **2.** *v.t.* to provide with a shutter or shutters ‖ to close the shutter or shutters of [SHUT]

shuttered fuse a fuse in which inadvertent initiation of the detonator will not initiate either the booster or the burst charge

shut·tle (ʃʌ́t'l) **1.** *n.* a device enclosing the bobbin which a weaver passes between the threads of the warp in order to make the weft ‖ the holder of the lower thread of a sewing machine ‖ a small device for holding the thread in tatting etc. ‖ a passenger train, plane or bus which travels back and forth over a short route between two places at scheduled intervals ‖ such a traveling back and forth **2.** *v. pres. part.* **shut·tling** *past* and *past part.* **shut·tled** *v.t.* to cause to move back and forth ‖ *v.i.* to move back and forth [O.E. *scytel,* a dart]

shuttle bombing (*mil.*) bombing of targets located between two friendly bases

shut·tle·cock (ʃʌ́t'lkɒk) *n.* a cork, winged with feathers, struck with a battledore in the game of battledore and shuttlecock, or with a racket in badminton ‖ the game of battledore and shuttlecock

shuttle diplomacy continuous travel between two disputing countries for the purpose of mediation

shuttle service a transport service consisting of vehicles which move back and forth between two places, esp. in short, scheduled trips ‖ regular air transport service, usu. hourly, between two centers, with guaranteed seating for all comers

shy (ʃai) **1.** *comp.* **shy·er, shi·er** *superl.* **shy·est, shi·est** *adj.* (of persons) finding it hard to overcome selfconsciousness and establish personal relations with others, and therefore seeking to avoid notice ‖ (of animals) easily frightened ‖ showing timidity or reserve, *a shy smile* ‖ (with 'about') wary of or reserved about doing something ‖ (*poker*) not having paid one's ante ‖ (with 'of') ‖ short, not having a sufficiency, *shy of money* ‖ short of money **to fight shy of** to try to avoid **2.** *v.i. pres. part.* **shy·ing** *past* and *past part.* **shied** (of a horse etc.) to move suddenly to one side when startled **3.** *pl.* **shies** *n.* an act of shying [O.E. *scēoh*]

shy (ʃai) **1.** *v.t. pres. part.* **shy·ing** *past* and *past part.* **shied** to throw (a stone, ball etc.) **2.** *pl.* **shies** *n.* a throw (*pop.*) a try, attempt [etym. doubtful]

shy·ster (ʃáistər) *n.* (*pop.*) a person, esp. a lawyer, who is unscrupulous in the practice of his profession [etym. doubtful]

si (si:) *n.* (*mus.*) the note B in the fixed-do system of solmization ‖ ti, the seventh note of the scale in movable-do solmization [*SOLMIZATION]

SI *SI UNITS

si·al·a·gog·ic (saiələgɒ́dʒik) **1.** *adj.* (*med.*) stimulating the flow of saliva **2.** *n.* (*med.*) a sialagogic agent [SIALAGOGUE]

si·al·a·gogue (saiǽləgɔg, saiǽləgɒg) *n.* (*med.*) an agent promoting the flow of saliva [F. fr. Gk *sialon,* saliva+*agōgos,* leading]

Si·al·kot (si:ɑ́lkout) a commercial center (pop. 185,000) in Pakistan in the N. Punjab. Manufactures: sporting goods, musical and surgical instruments. Ancient fortress, mausoleum of Nanak

Si·am (saiǽm, sáiæm) *THAILAND

si·a·mang (sí:əmæŋ) *n.* *Symphalangus syndactylus,* a large black gibbon of Sumatra [Malay *siāmang, siyāmang*]

Si·a·mese (saiəmí:z, saiəmí:s) **1.** *adj.* of or relating to Thailand, its people or language **2.** *pl.* **Si·a·mese** *n.* a native of Thailand ‖ the Sino-Tibetan language of Thailand

Siamese cat a cat of a short-haired, blue-eyed breed (*BLUE POINT, *SEAL POINT) noted for its sinewy elegance

Siamese twins twins born joined together at some point [from the twins In and Jun (1811–74), born in Siam, who were the first widely publicized instance of this condition]

Si·an (sí:ɑ́n, ʃí:ɑ́n) (medieval Changan or Singan and called Siking 1936-49) the capital (pop. 2,500,000) of Shensi, N. China. Industries: textiles, chemicals. Nestorian monument (c. 780), Ming dynasty walls. University

Siang·tan (sjɑ́ŋtɑ́n, ʃjɑ́ŋtɑ́n) an industrial center and river port (pop. 184,000) in E. Hunan, China: metallurgy, mechanical engineering, textiles

sib (sib) *n.* a blood relative, esp. a sibling ‖ kindred, relatives ‖ (*anthrop.*) a unilateral, usually exogamous kin group based on common descent whether matrilineal or patrilineal (cf. CLAN, cf. SEPT) [O.E. *sib, sibb,* kinship]

Si·be·li·us (sibéili:əs, sibéiljəs), Jean (1865-1957), Finnish composer. His work is fundamentally nationalistic. His symphonies seem to spring from a consciousness of the sternness of man's relation with nature in the far north. They have a considerable formal interest and a characteristic melodic style

Si·be·ri·a (saibíəri:ə) the Asiatic part (area c. 4,887,000 sq. miles) of the R.S.F.S.R., U.S.S.R. extending from the Urals to the Pacific. Geography: *R.S.F.S.R., *U.S.S.R. HISTORY. Siberia was the starting point for the Hun and Mongol invasions. It was annexed by Russia under Ivan IV in the 16th c. and became a place of political exile (17th c.). The building (1892-1905) of the Trans-Siberian Railroad led to colonization on a large scale, and the region is being industrialized rapidly

Si·be·ri·an (saibíəri:ən) **1.** *adj.* of or relating to Siberia **2.** *n.* a native or inhabitant of Siberia

sib·i·lance (síbələns) *n.* a sibilant quality ‖ a sibilant sound

sib·i·lan·cy (síbələnsi:) *n.* sibilance

sib·i·lant (síbələnt) **1.** *adj.* having or making a hissing sound ‖ uttered with a hissing sound **2.** *n.* a sibilant speech sound or the symbol for it (e.g. s, z, ʃ, ʒ) [fr. L. *sibilans* (*sibilantis*) fr. *sibilare,* to hiss]

sib·i·late (síbəleit) *pres. part.* **sib·i·lat·ing** *past* and *past part.* **sib·i·lat·ed** *v.t.* to pronounce with a hissing sound ‖ *v.i.* to make an initial hissing sound when pronouncing **sib·i·lá·tion** *n.* [fr. L. *sibilare* (*sibilatus*), to hiss]

Si·biu (si:bjú:) (*G.* Hermannstadt) a commercial center (pop. 156,854) of central Transylvania, Rumania

CONCISE PRONUNCIATION KEY: **(a)** æ, *cat;* ɑ, *car;* ɔ *fawn;* ei, *snake.* **(e)** e, *hen;* i:, *sheep;* iə, *deer;* ɛə, *bear.* **(i)** i, *fish;* ai, *tiger;* ə:, *bird.* **(o)** o, *ox;* au, *cow;* ou, *goat;* u, *poor;* ɔi, *royal.* **(u)** ʌ, *duck;* u, *bull;* u:, *goose;* ə, *bacillus;* ju:, *cube.* x, *loch;* θ, *think;* ð, *bother;* z, *Zen;* ʒ, *corsage;* dʒ, *savage;* ŋ, *orangutang;* j, *yak;* ʃ, *fish;* tʃ, *fetch;* 'l, *rabble;* 'n, *redden.* Complete pronunciation key appears inside front cover.

sib·ling (síbliŋ) *n.* a person in relation to someone having the same parents or having one parent in common
Sib·yl (síb'l) *n.* one of various women in antiquity (e.g. in Greece, Rome and Egypt) believed to possess prophetic powers through divine inspiration **sib·yl** a prophetess [O.F. *Sibile* or fr. M.L *Sibilla* fr. L. fr. Gk]
Sib·yl·line (síbəli:n, síbəlain, síbəlin) *adj.* of, relating to or uttered by a Sibyl **sib·yl·line** oracular, obscurely prophetic, *a sibylline utterance* [fr. L. *Sibyllinus*]
Sibylline books a collection of oracles bearing on the worship of the gods and the policy of Rome, fabled to have been bought from a Sibyl by Tarquinius Superbus, and used in ancient Rome for guidance in matters of law
sic (sik) *adv.* thus (added in brackets after a word or expression in a quotation which looks wrong or absurd, to show that it has been quoted correctly) [L.]
sic, sick (sik) *pres. part.* **sick·ing** *past* and *past part.* **sicked** *v.t.* (esp. of a dog, used esp. in imper.) to set upon, chase to incite (a dog) to attack [var. of SEEK]
sic·ca·tive (síkətiv) **1.** *adj.* promoting drying **2.** *n.* a substance promoting drying, esp. one mixed with oil paint, printing ink etc. [fr. L.L. *siccativus*]
Si·cil·ian (sisíljən) **1.** *adj.* relating to Sicily or its inhabitants ‖ relating to the Italian dialect of Sicily **2.** *n.* a native or inhabitant of Sicily ‖ the Italian dialect spoken in Sicily
Sicilian Vespers (*hist.*) a revolt (1282) against French rule in Sicily. It broke out at Palermo. The ringing of the vesper bell on Easter Monday was the signal for the people to kill or drive out the French. Sicily was joined to Aragon
Sic·i·lies, Kingdom of the Two (sísəli:z) (*Ital. hist.*) a former state consisting of Sicily and the southern portion of Italy. After the fall of Rome (476) this area was occupied by the Ostrogoths, and then by the Byzantines (535). The Saracens took Sicily (827-78), and Germans, Greeks and Arabs fought for the region until it was conquered (mid-11th c.) by Robert Guiscard and the Normans. The throne passed (1266) to the house of Anjou until the Sicilian Vespers (1282), when the house of Aragon took Sicily. The kingdom was reunited (1504) under the Spanish crown. After war with Austria, the Spanish Bourbons captured the kingdom (1734), and were restored (1815) after the Napoleonic Wars. Their despotic rule ended (1860) when Garibaldi invaded and joined (1861) the Two Sicilies to the kingdom of Italy
Sic·i·ly (sísəli:) (*Ital.* Sicilia) a mountainous, deforested island (area 9,815 sq. miles, pop. 4,884,000) off S.W. Italy, forming, with Pantelleria, the Lipari Is and other nearby islets, an autonomous region (area 9,928 sq. miles, pop. 4,936,200) of Italy. Capital: Palermo. Highest peak: 10,850 ft (*ETNA). The coasts are fertile, esp. in the north, and populous, the interior largely barren and sparsely inhabited. Main industries: agriculture (citrus fruit, bananas, olives, almonds, vines, cork, cotton), fishing, mining (sulfur), petroleum extraction (90% of Italian production) and refining, tourism. Universities: Catania (1434), Messina (1549), Palermo (1805). Part of the Mycenaean civilization of Crete, Sicily became a prosperous Greek colony (9th-5th cc. B.C.), was invaded by the Carthaginians, and fell (241 B.C.) to the Romans. After the fall of Rome (476) it became part of the Kingdom of the Two Sicilies
sick (sik) **1.** *adj.* not physically healthy ‖ not healthy mentally, morally or spiritually ‖ so consumed with passion as to have a feeling of illness, *sick with envy* ‖ likely to vomit, *to feel sick* ‖ suffering an attack of vomiting, *sick three times* ‖ betraying that a person is not in good health, *a sick look* ‖ of or for people not in good health, *sick leave,* ‖ (*pop.*) feeling disgusted, *his manners make me sick* ‖ feeling weak and depressed, *sick at heart* ‖ (with 'of') disgusted by having or being subjected to too much of something, *sick and tired of complaints* ‖ (*pop.*) weak, of relatively poor quality, *his painting looks pretty sick by comparison with yours* ‖ (of humor, jokes) sadistic or suggesting heartlessness ‖ (*rhet.*, with 'for') longing, *sick for home* ‖ forced, sickly, *a sick smile* **to go sick** (*mil.*) to report oneself as being ill **2.** *n.* **the sick** people not in good health [O.E. *sēoc*]
sick *v.t.* *SIC
sick bay quarters in a naval vessel, military establishment, or some institutions, where the sick are treated
sick·bed (síkbed) *n.* (*rhet.*) the bed where someone lies ill
sick·en (síkən) *v.i.* to become ill ‖ *v.t.* to cause to feel sick **sick·en·ing** *adj.* nauseating, revolting ‖ distressing
Sick·ert (síkərt), Walter Richard (1860-1942), English painter. He was greatly influenced by Degas in composition and subject matter, esp. theater interiors
sick headache a migraine ‖ a condition of headache accompanied by intermittent feelings of nausea
Sick·ing·en (zíkiŋən), Franz von (1481-1523), German knight and Protestant military leader
sick·le (sik'l) *n.* a tool with a curved blade and a short handle, used for cutting long grass or trimming rough hedges etc. **the Sickle** a sickle-shaped group of six stars in the constellation Leo [O.E. *sicol* perh. fr. L.]
sick leave leave of absence from duty granted because of illness
sick·li·ness (síkli:nis) *n.* the state or quality of being sickly
sick·ly (síkli:) *comp.* **sick·li·er** *superl.* **sick·li·est** *adj.* prone to illness, weak in health, *a sickly child* ‖ caused by, or suggestive of illness, *a sickly complexion* ‖ weak because forced, *a sickly smile* ‖ causing sickness, mildly nauseating, *the sickly smell of ether*
sick·ness (síknis) *n.* illness, being sick ‖ a disease ‖ (esp. *Br.*) vomiting or the desire to vomit
sick-out (síkaut) *n.* job action in which employees call in sick, esp. where a strike is not feasible
sick·room (síkru:m, síkrum) *n.* the room in which someone who is sick is being looked after
sid·dur (si:dú:r, sídər) *pl.* **sid·du·rim** (si:du:rí:m), **sid·durs** *n.* the Jewish daily prayer book, containing both Hebrew and Aramaic prayers [Heb. *siddūr*, order, arrangement]
side (said) **1.** *n.* any one of the flat or relatively flat surfaces of an object, *a cube has six sides* ‖ one of the vertical or relatively vertical surfaces of an object as distinguished from the top or bottom, *the side of a hill, the side of a box* ‖ such a surface, but also excluding front and back, *the side of a house* ‖ one of the two surfaces of something flat and thin, *write on both sides of the paper* ‖ (*math.*) one of the lines bounding a figure ‖ the right or left part of a person's body, esp. between armpit and hip ‖ the right or left part of an animal's body, esp. between foreleg and hindleg as cut for meat, *a side of bacon* ‖ one of the two halves of an object, place or space or one of the two directions to the right and left of a real line or a line in the mind of the observer, *the right side of the road, the debit side of an account book* ‖ a part of an object, place or space away from the central part, *the sides of the room* ‖ a space or direction in a certain relation to a person or thing, *arrows came at him from all sides* ‖ an aspect or view that is not complete, or that differs from other aspects, *he has many sides to his character* ‖ one of the contrasting aspects of something as it affects a person, *keep your side of the bargain* ‖ one of two teams or sets of opponents in sport, war politics etc. ‖ a position nearer than, or beyond, some dividing line, *stay on this side of the hedge* ‖ a line of descent traced through one parent, *a cousin on his father's side* ‖ (*billiards*) the spin imparted to a ball by striking it on the side ‖ (*Br., pop.*) conceit or snobbishness **on the side** as a secondary occupation ‖ in addition to the main course of a meal **side by side** close together, esp. for mutual support **to take sides** to support one of the sides in a dispute **2.** *adj.* of, on, by, from or towards a side, *side wind* ‖ subordinate, *side road, side issue* ‖ indirect, oblique, *a side glance* **3.** *v. pres. part.* **sid·ing** *past* and *past part.* **sid·ed** *v.t.* to furnish with sides *v.i.* (with 'with' or 'against') to give sympathy to or support one party in a dispute [O.E. *sīde*, the long part or view of something]
side arm a weapon (e.g. sword, pistol or bayonet) worn at the side
side·board (sáidbɔrd, sáidbourd) *n.* a piece of furniture, with cupboards and drawers, placed against the wall of a dining room or living room, and used to store dishes etc. or to put them on when meals are being served
side·burns (sáidbə:rnz) *pl. n.* the short hair growing on a man's face in front of the ears when the beard is shaved off [after Gen. A. E. *Burnside* (*d.* 1881), U.S. general]
side·car (sáidkɑr) *n.* a small one-wheeled car for a passenger, attached to the side of a motorcycle ‖ an iced cocktail consisting of a mixture of orange-flavored liqueur, brandy and lemon juice
side dish an extra dish at a meal, subsidiary to the main dish
side-dress (sáiddres) *v.i.* to apply fertilizer to plants by working it into the soil along one side of each row ‖ *v.t.* to apply fertilizer to (plants etc.) in this way (cf. TOP-DRESS) **side-dress·ing** *n.* the fertilizer so used
side drum a snare drum
side·head (sáidhed) *n.* a subheading placed to the side of the text, usually to the left of the first line of a paragraph
side·kick (sáidkik) *n.* (*pop.*) someone who associates with another as a partner, assistant or companion, esp. as a subordinate
side·light (sáidlait) *n.* a small lamp on the side of a ship or vehicle ‖ an anecdote or piece of information which indirectly reveals the nature of someone or something ‖ light from a side ‖ a window or opening at the side of a wall, door etc.
side·line (sáidlain) *n.* a kind of goods sold in addition to one's regular and more important stock ‖ a job done in addition to one's regular occupation ‖ (*sports*) a line marking the boundary at the side of a football field, tennis court etc. ‖ (*pl., sports*) the space along the outside of the lines at the side of an athletic field ‖ (*pl.*) the point of view of those not actually participating, *from the sidelines it looked like a complete accident*
side·long (sáidlɔŋ, sáidlɒŋ) **1.** *adv.* obliquely, to glance sidelong **2.** *adj.* oblique, directed sideways, *a sidelong glance*
side-look·ing airborne radar (saídlukiŋ) (*mil.*) airborne radar with reception from right and left, used to map a territory from its perimeter at altitudes up to 70,000 ft. (*acronym* SLAR)
side·piece (sáidpi:s) *n.* a piece forming the side of something
si·de·re·al (saidíəri:əl) *adj.* of or relating to the fixed stars or constellations, esp. as they are used in measures of time [fr. L. *sidereus*]
sidereal day the interval between successive transits of the March equinox over the upper meridian of a place: it is equal to 23 hours 56 minutes 4.09 seconds of mean solar time
sidereal time time based on the sidereal day consisting of 24 sidereal hours
sidereal year the period during which the earth makes a complete revolution in its orbit around the sun, with respect to the fixed stars: it is equal to 365 days 6 hours 9 minutes 9.54 seconds of mean solar time
sid·er·ite (sídərait) *n.* native ferrous carbonate, $FeCO_3$, a valuable ore of iron ‖ a meteorite largely consisting of iron **sid·er·it·ic** (sidərítik) *adj.* [F. *sidérite* or fr. *siderites* fr. Gk]
sid·er·o·lite (sídərəlait) *n.* a meteorite containing large proportions of metal and stone [fr. Gk *sidēros*, iron +*lithos*, stone]
sid·er·o·sis (sidəróusis) *pl.* **sid·er·o·ses** (sidəróusi:z) *n.* pneumoconiosis peculiar to iron workers resulting from the breathing in of iron particles ‖ iron pigment deposits in a tissue [Gk *sidēros*, iron]
side·sad·dle (sáidsæd'l) **1.** *n.* a saddle for a woman on which she sits with both legs on one side of the horse **2.** *adv.* mounted thus, *to ride sidesaddle*
side·show (sáidʃou) *n.* a small show or entertainment as part of a larger one ‖ an event or activity of less importance than the principal one
side·slip (sáidslip) **1.** *n.* a slip sideways, e.g. in a car or on skis ‖ (*aeron.*) a slip sideways, and broadside on, in a downward direction, usually caused by low air speed in a turn **2.** *v.i. pres. part.* **side·slip·ping** *past* and *past part.* **side·slipped** to make a sideslip
sides·man (sáidzmən) *pl.* **sides·men** (sáidzmən) *n.* an Anglican Church officer who shows members of the congregation to their seats, takes up the collection etc.
side·split·ting (sáidsplitiŋ) *adj.* hilariously funny
side·step (sáidstep) *pres. part.* **side·step·ping** *past* and *past part.* **side·stepped** *v.t.* to avoid by

stepping sideways ‖ to be evasive about (an issue)
side·stroke (sáidstrouk) *n.* a stroke made when swimming on one's side, both arms moving in alternate forward and backward strokes and the legs moving in a scissors kick. The sidestroke is esp. useful for long distances
side·swipe (sáidswạip) **1.** *v.t. pres. part.* **side·swip·ing** *past* and *past part.* **side·swiped** to strike with a glancing blow along the side **2.** *n.* a sideswiping or an instance of this ‖ (*pop.*) an oblique scathing remark
side·track (sáidtræk) **1.** *n.* a siding **2.** *v.t.* to shunt into siding ‖ to lead (someone) away from the proper subject ‖ to prevent action on (a matter) by diversionary tactics
side·walk (sáidwɔk) *n.* a hard-surfaced pedestrian way along the side of a street
sidewalk artist (*Am.*= *Br.* pavement artist) a person who chalks pictures on the sidewalk in the hope that passers-by will give him money
side·ward (sáidwərd) *adv.* and *adj.* toward one side **side·wards** *adv.* sideward
side·way (sáidwẹi) **1.** *adv.* and *adj.* sideways **2.** *n.* a byway
side·ways (sáidwẹiz) **1.** *adv.* to the side, *look sideways* ‖ from the side, *viewed sideways* ‖ on the side, with the side first, *carry it in sideways* **2.** *adj.* to one side, *a sideways look*
side-whisk·ers (sáidhwịskərs, sáidwịskərs) *pl. n.* long whiskers on the side of the face
Side·wind·er (sáidwáindər) *n.* (*mil.*) solid-propellant, air-to-air missile (AIM-9) with nonnuclear warhead, and infrared, heat-seeking homing with speed of Mach 2
side·wise (sáidwạiz) *adv.* and *adj.* sideways
Si·di-bel-Ab·bès (sí:di:beləbés) an agricultural market (pop. 151,148) of N.W. Algeria: cereals, vines, fruit, vegetables
sid·ing (sáidiŋ) *n.* a short railroad track beside and connected with the main line, used for shunting, loading and unloading goods, laying up rolling stock etc. ‖ (*collect.*) boards forming the exposed surface of the outside walls of a frame building
si·dle (sáid'l) **1.** *v.i. pres. part.* **si·dling** *past* and *past part.* **si·dled** to go forward with a sideways motion, *the fox sidled over the field* ‖ (with 'up to', 'over to' etc.) to make a rather furtive approach **2.** *n.* the act or movement of sidling [back-formation fr. obs. *sideling adv.*, sidelong]
Sid·mouth (sídməθ), Henry Addington, 1st Viscount (1757-1844), British Tory statesman, prime minister (1801-4). As home secretary (1812-21), he was responsible for much repressive legislation (1817-19)
Sid·ney (sídni:), Sir Philip (1554-86), English poet, critic, courtier and soldier. His works, published posthumously, include the pastoral prose romance 'Arcadia' (1590 and 1593), the sonnet sequence 'Astrophel and Stella' (1591) and a defense of poetry against utilitarian philistinism, 'The Defence of Poesie' (1595). He is often considered as the ideal Renaissance man
Sid·ney, Syd·ney, Algernon (1622-83), English statesman. A republican, he was one of the leaders of the Whig opposition, and was executed for alleged complicity in the Rye House Plot
Si·don (sáid'n) an ancient seaport (modern Saida, Lebanon, pop. 50,000) in Phoenicia, which flourished in the 2nd millennium B.C. as a center for Phoenician trade and colonization
SIDS *n.* (*med. abbr.*) for sudden infant death syndrome (which see)
siege (si:dʒ) *n.* the isolating of a fortified place by an attacking force in order to make it surrender ‖ a long, persistent attempt to force or persuade someone to do something ‖ a long, exhausting experience or period, esp. of ill health **to lay siege to** to begin the siege of **to raise a siege** to abandon a siege [O.F.]
Sieg·fried (sí:gfri:d, zí:kfri:t) a hero of Germanic legend, esp. of the 'Nibelungenlied'
sie·mens (sí:mənz) *n.* unit of conductance equal to 1 ampere per volt; named for Ernst Werner von Siemens, German electrical engineer
Sie·mens (sí:mənz, zí:məns), Ernst Werner von (1816-92), German electrical engineer and inventor. He invented an electroplating process (c. 1841) and the self-excited electric dynamo. With his brother, Sir William Siemens (1823-83), he was responsible for a process of steel-making (1866), which, with some adaptation, became the open-hearth process
Si·e·na (si:énə, sjénɑ) a walled city (pop. 61,888) of central Tuscany, Italy. Its shell-shaped piazza is dominated by the tower of the Gothic town hall (1297-1310). Romanesque-Gothic marble cathedral (mainly 12th-14th cc.), art museums. University (1300). Siena was a rich independent republic from the 12th c. until it was captured (1555) by Emperor Charles V
Si·en·ese (sí:əni:z, sí:əni:s) **1.** *adj.* of or pertaining to Siena or the people who live there **2.** *pl.* **Si·en·ese** *n.* an inhabitant of Siena
si·en·na (si:énə) *n.* earth, consisting of clay colored by iron and manganese, used as pigment (*BURNT SIENNA, *RAW SIENNA) [Ital. (*terra di) Siena,* (earth of) Siena]
si·er·ra (si:érə) *n.* a mountain chain with sharp peaks, esp. in Spain and the Americas [Span.]
Sier·ra de Gua·dar·ra·ma (sjérrάðegwɑðarrάmɑ) a mountain range in central Spain between Old and New Castile. Summit: Peñalara (7,900 ft)
Si·er·ra Le·o·ne (si:érəli:óuni:, si:érəli:óun) a republic (area 27,925 sq. miles, pop. 3,474,000), and member of the British Commonwealth, in W. Africa. Capital: Freetown. People: 26% Mende, 22% Temne, with Creole (descended from freed slaves) and Syrian-Lebanese minorities. Language: English (official), Krio, Mandingo, Mende, other local African languages. Religion: mainly local African, 20% Moslem, 4% Christian. The coastal plain is mainly deforested and cultivated, with mangrove swamps along the coast. The Sierra Leone peninsula, on the northern coast, rises to 2,912 ft and the northeastern plateau (mainly 1,000–3,000 ft) to 6,390 ft (Loma Mtns). Several navigable rivers flow southwest from the plateau to deep estuaries on the Gulf of Guinea. Average temperatures (F.): 75°-85° on the coast, 69°-95° inland. Rainfall: Freetown 150 ins, northeast 80 ins. Livestock: cattle, goats, sheep, poultry. Agricultural products: palm kernels and oil, piassava, rice and other cereals, cocoa, coffee, peanuts, ginger, kola nuts, cassava, coconuts, manioc, sweet potatoes. Mineral resources: diamonds, iron ore, bauxite, rutile. Manufactures and industries: fishing (esp. tuna), palm oil, rice milling, lumber, furniture, weaving. Exports: diamonds, iron ore, palm kernels, coffee, cocoa, piassava. Imports: cotton fabrics, oil, clothing and footwear, foodstuffs, vehicles, machinery, synthetic fibers, chemicals. University: University Colleges of Sierra Leone (1959) and of Njala (1964). Monetary unit: leone (100 cents). HISTORY. The area was inhabited by the Temne and other African peoples when the Portuguese explored the coast (c. 1462). The English raided it for slaves (16th c.), but a British abolitionist society founded Freetown (1787) as a settlement for freed American slaves. This became a British colony (1808) and the surrounding region became a British protectorate (1896). It gained independence within the Commonwealth (Apr. 27, 1961) and joined the U.N. (1961). Successful army coups d'état were mounted (1967 and 1968); the country's prime minister Siaka Stevens, although named premier in 1967, did not assume office until after the coups. Stevens became the country's first president (1971-85)
Sier·ra Ma·dre (sjérrɑmάðre) the principal mountain system of Mexico, running the length of the country. It comprises the Eastern Range (Orizaba, 18,700 ft) and the Western Range (over 10,000 ft in the south) enclosing the central plateau, and the Southern Range running along the southwestern coast (*ROCKY MTNS)
Sier·ra Ma·es·tra (sjérrɑmɑéstrɑ) a mountain range in E. Cuba, containing the highest point in Cuba: Pico Turquino (6,500 ft)
Sier·ra Mén·dez (sjérrɑméndes), Justo (1848-1912), Mexican romantic poet, author of 'Playeras', 'A Dios', and 'El funeral bucólico'. He is also known for his work in education
Sier·ra Mo·re·na (sjérrɑmɔrénɑ) a mountain range (summit 4,305 ft) in S.W. Spain between the Guadalquivir and Guadiana Rivers, separating Andalusia from central Spain. Chief pass: Despeñaperros
Sier·ra Ne·va·da (sjérrɑnevάðɑ) a snow-capped massif (60 miles long) of S.E. Andalusia, Spain, near Granada (Mulhacén, 11,420 ft)
Sier·ra Ne·vad·a (si:érənevǽdə, si:érənevάdə) a mountain range of E. California. Summit: Mt Whitney (14,495 ft). Chief pass: Donner (7,017 ft), linking San Francisco with Reno, Nevada
Sier·ra Ne·va·da de San·ta Mar·ta (sjérrɑnevάðɑðesάntɑmάrtɑ) a mountain range rising to 19,030 ft on the Caribbean coast in N. Colombia
si·es·ta (si:éstə) *n.* a short rest taken in the hottest part of the day, esp. by Latin peoples [Span.]
sieve (siv) **1.** *n.* a utensil with a fine wire-mesh bottom used for straining substances, for reducing substances to a finer consistency or for separating finer from coarser particles **2.** *v.t. pres. part.* **siev·ing** *past* and *past part.* **sieved** to put through a sieve ‖ to screen (candidates) [O.E. *sife*]
sieve cell (*bot.*) an elongate, tapering, thin-walled cell with a protoplast but without a nucleus when mature, and with areas of its walls closely perforated with minute openings. It is characteristic of the phloem and is variously modified to serve in sieve tubes and for storage and support
sieve tube a phloem vessel consisting of sugar-conducting sieve cells in vascular plants, sometimes associated with companion cells achieving protoplasmic continuity by sievelike perforated end walls
Sie·yès (sjejes), Emmanuel Joseph (1748-1836), French statesman. He emerged as a leader of the third estate with his pamphlet 'Qu'est-ce que le tiers état?' (1789). He was a member of the Directory and of the Consulate
sift (sift) *v.t.* (often with 'out') to separate or strain the finer from the coarser particles of (a material) by passing through a sieve, sifter or riddle ‖ to sprinkle through a sifter or other perforated utensil, *to sift sugar onto a cake* ‖ to examine and evaluate, *to sift evidence* ‖ *v.i.* to fall, or pass, as if through a sieve, *the sunlight sifted through the curtains* ‖ to use a sieve, sifter etc. **síft·er** *n.* a small cylindrical container with a fine wire mesh bottom through which flour, sugar etc. is passed to separate the finer particles from the coarser or to reduce the substance to a finer texture [O.E. *siftan, syftan*]
sig·a·to·ka (sịgətóukə) *n.* a disease of bananas, caused by *Cercospora musae*, a sooty mold
Si·ge·bert I (sígəbərt) (c. 535-75), king of Austrasia (561-75), son of Clotaire I. He overran Neustria, but was murdered by Fredegund
sigh (sai) **1.** *v.i.* to expel a deep audible breath, expressing relief, contentment, or sadness, weariness, resignation etc. (*rhet.*, with 'for') to think with regret of the loss or passing of something, *to sigh for the days of one's youth* ‖ to make a sound like sighing, *the wind sighed in the trees* ‖ *v.t.* to utter with a sigh or sighs **2.** *n.* a sighing ‖ the sound made in sighing [M.E. *sihen, sighen*]
sight (sait) **1.** *n.* the power of seeing ‖ the act of seeing ‖ a way of considering something in one's mind, *he can do no wrong in her sight* ‖ range of vision, *within sight* ‖ something seen or visible, *a beautiful sight* ‖ (*pl.*) something worth seeing, e.g. famous buildings, monuments etc., *the sights of London* ‖ a display, *poppies make a fine sight* ‖ something odd, absurd or ugly to look at, *what a sight you look in those slacks!* ‖ (*pop.*) a great deal, *you're a sight better off as you are* ‖ a device for guiding the eye when aiming a gun or directing a quadrant etc. ‖ aim, *take careful sight* ‖ observation with an instrument, *to take a sight* **at first sight** when first seen, before being examined closely **at** (or **on) sight** as soon as seen, *to shoot on sight* **at** (or **from) sight** (*mus.*) without previous study of the music **to catch sight of** to get (someone or something) suddenly within one's vision **to get sight of** to manage to see **to know by sight** to know (someone) by appearance only, not to talk to **to lose sight of** to cease to see **2.** *v.t.* to see, get a sight of, esp. by approaching, *to sight land* ‖ to observe with the aid of sights, *to sight a star* ‖ to provide with sights ‖ to adjust the sights of ‖ to aim by means of sights ‖ *v.i.* to take aim or an observation through a sight [O.E. *sihth* fr. *sih-*, stem of *sēon,* to see]
sight draft a draft ordering payment on presentation
sight·less (sáitlis) *adj.* not having vision
sight·li·ness (sái:tli:nis) *n.* the state or condition of being sightly
sight·ly (sáitli:) *comp.* **sight·li·er** *superl.* **sight·li·est** *adj.* of pleasing appearance
sight-read (sáitri̦:d) *pres. part.* **sight-read·ing** *past* and *past part* **sight-read** (sáitrẹd) *v.t.* to read (music, a passage for translation, etc.) without preparation ‖ *v.i.* to read music etc. in this way

CONCISE PRONUNCIATION KEY: (a) æ, cat; ɑ, car; ɔ fawn; ei, snake. (e) e, hen; i:, sheep; iə, deer; ɛə, bear. (i) i, fish; ai, tiger; ə:, bird. (o) o, ox; au, cow; ou, goat; u, poor; ɔi, royal. (u) ʌ, duck; u, bull; u:, goose; ə, bacillus; ju:, cube. x, loch; θ, think; ð, bother; z, Zen; ʒ, corsage; dʒ, savage; ŋ, orangutang; j, yak; ʃ, fish; tʃ, fetch; 'l, rabble; 'n, redden. Complete pronunciation key appears inside front cover.

sight-see·ing (sáitsi:iŋ) *n.* the act of going around looking at places of interest, famous buildings etc. **sight·se·er** (sáitsi:ər) *n.*
sight translation (*Am.=Br.* unseen) a passage, not previously seen, set for translation
sight unseen without previous inspection, *to buy something sight unseen*
sig·il·late (sídʒəleit, sídʒəlit) *adj.* (of pottery) with impressed patterns ‖ (*bot.*, of certain rhizomes and roots) having marks like those made with a seal or signet [fr. L.L. *sigillatus* fr. *sigillum*, seal, signet]
Sig·is·mund (sígismund) (1368-1437), Holy Roman Emperor and German king (1411-37), king of Hungary (1387-1437) and of Bohemia (1420-37), son of Charles IV. Having summoned the Council of Constance in an effort to end the Great Schism, he was responsible for the burning (1415) of Hus
Sigismund I (1467-1548), king of Poland (1506-48). His reign saw the development of the Renaissance in Poland
Sigismund II (1520-72), king of Poland (1548-72), son of Sigismund I. He transformed (1569) the personal union of Poland and Lithuania into a political union and was the last of the Jagiello dynasty to rule in Poland. His reign saw the spread of the Reformation in Poland
Sigismund III (1566-1632), king of Poland (1587-1632) and of Sweden (1592-9). Deposed from his Swedish throne on account of his refusal to tolerate Protestantism, he began a series of wars between Poland and Sweden (1621-9). He took advantage of Russia's weakness after the death of Boris Godunov, and invaded Moscow (1610-12)
sig·ma (sígmə) *n.* the eighteenth letter (Σ, σ, s = s) of the Greek alphabet **sig·mate** (sígmit, sígmeit) *adj.* curved like an S [L., Gk]
sigma factor (*genetics*) regulator of RNA polymerase *also* sigma protein *Cf* REPLICASE
sigma particle (*nuclear phys.*) a short-lived (10^{-10}sec) hyperon triplet with a rest mass of 1,189.5 MEV, an isotopic spin of 1, and a lifetime of 8.1×10^{-11} sec —**sigmic** *adj.*
sig·ma·tron (sígmətrɒn) *n.* (*phys.*) a cyclotron and a betatron operating in tandem, producing billion-volt rays
sig·moid (sígmɔid) *adj.* curved like a C ‖ sigmate ‖ of or relating to the sigmoid flexure of the large intestine [fr. Gk *sigmoeidēs*]
sigmoid flexure the part of the large intestine between the colon and the rectum ‖ (*zool.*) an S-shaped double curve such as characterizes e.g. the neck of some birds
sign (sain) *v.t.* to mark with a sign, esp. with one's name ‖ to accept as legally binding by doing this, *to sign an agreement* ‖ to write (one's name) ‖ to mark with the sign of the cross, e.g. in blessing or consecrating ‖ (often with 'up' or 'on') to engage (esp. an athlete) by written agreement ‖ to intimate (something) by gestures ‖ *v.i.* to write one's name **to sign away** (or **over**) to sign a written agreement to convey ownership of (something) to another **to sign off** (of a radio or television station) to stop broadcasting after making station identification **to sign on** to accept employment, esp. as a regular soldier ‖ to engage as an employee **to sign up** to enlist in some organization, esp. in military service ‖ to agree to some obligation by signing, e.g. a contract ‖ to cause (someone) to accept a commitment by getting his signature, e.g. to a contract [fr. F. *signer* or L. *signare*]
sign 1. *n.* a mark or gesture which conveys an idea or meaning, *plus and minus signs, deaf-mutes converse by signs, he nodded as a sign of agreement* ‖ something having symbolic character, *an outward and visible sign of an inward and spiritual grace* ‖ a mark or gesture adopted as a method of recognition ‖ (*med.*) an indication of a disease that is noted and interpreted by a doctor (cf. SYMPTOM) ‖ indication or evidence, *she saw no sign that he would change his mind* ‖ trace, vestige, *no sign of life anywhere* ‖ (*rhet.*) portent, *signs from heaven* ‖ a notice or device advertising, admonishing, identifying etc. ‖ a board, placard etc. bearing such a notice or device ‖ one of the divisions of the zodiac ‖ (*pl.* **sign**) the tracks of a wild animal or animals, *deer sign* [F. *signe*]
sig·nal (sígnəl) **1.** *n.* a usually prearranged or generally recognizable sign giving information, *distress signal*, or an order, *the signal to attack* **2.** *v. pres. part.* **sig·nal·ing**, esp. *Br.* **sig·nal·ling** *past* and *past part.* **sig·naled**, esp. *Br.* **sig·nalled** *v.t.* to order by signal, *he signaled the advance* ‖ to order (someone) by signal to do something, *he signaled them to advance* ‖ to give information of by using a sign, *to signal the surrender* ‖ *v.i.* to make a signal or signals ‖ (esp. *mil.*) to send a signal [F.]
signal *adj.* remarkable, noteworthy [fr. L. *signum*, sign, after F. *signalé*]
signal box (*Br.*) a signal tower
sig·nal·er, esp. *Br.* **sig·nal·ler** (sígnələr) *n.* someone who signals ‖ (*mil.*) someone responsible for communications in the field
sig·nal·ize (sígnəlaiz) *pres. part.* **sig·nal·iz·ing** *past* and *past part.* **sig·nal·ized** *v.t.* to treat as noteworthy or memorable, mark specially ‖ to point out
sig·nal·ler *SIGNALER
sig·nal·ly (sígnəli:) *adv.* notably, to a remarkable degree or in a remarkable way
sig·nal·man (sígnəlmən) *pl.* **sig·nal·men** (sígnəlmən) *n.* a man who operates railroad signals ‖ a military signaler
signal tower (*Am.=Br.* signal box) a building for men operating railroad signals
sig·na·to·ry (sígnətɔri:, sígnətouri:) **1.** *adj.* signing or having signed a document, *the signatory powers* **2.** *pl.* **sig·na·to·ries** *n.* a party signing a document, esp. a state which has signed a treaty [fr. L. *signatorius*, to do with sealing]
sig·na·ture (sígnətʃər) *n.* a person's name written by himself in signing a letter or document ‖ the act of signing one's name ‖ (*mus.*) the sign used to denote key or rhythm, placed to the right of the clef ‖ (*bookbinding*) a letter or number at the foot of the first page on an unfolded sheet of printed pages, used as a guide in folding, assembling and binding such a sheet ‖ the portion of a medical prescription instructing the patient how to take the prescribed medicine ‖ a signature tune [F. or fr. M.L. *signatura*]
signature tune a special, easily recognizable tune used by a performer or group of performers, or to identify a radio program etc.
sign·board (sáinbɔrd, sáinbourd) *n.* a board on which is printed an advertisement, directions, the name of an inn, an announcement etc.
sig·net (sígnit) *n.* a personal seal used to show the authenticity of documents, often in addition to the signature ‖ (*Br.*) a royal seal formerly used to authenticate letters patent, grants etc. ‖ the mark or impression made by a signet [O.F. or fr. M.L. *signetum*]
signet ring a finger ring set or engraved with the monogram, sign or initials of the owner, formerly used as a seal
sig·nif·i·cance (signífikəns) *n.* real or inner meaning, *the significance of your remark escaped me for the moment* ‖ importance, *a matter of no significance* [O.F. or fr. L. *significantia*]
sig·nif·i·cant (signífikənt) *adj.* having or conveying a meaning, *a word is a significant grouping of sounds* ‖ important and influential, *a significant contribution to knowledge* ‖ marked, *he placed significant emphasis on the word* ‖ expressive, heavy with implication, *a significant look* ‖ suggesting some specific cause, not due merely to chance, *a significant increase in population* [fr. L. *significans* (*significantis*) fr. *significare*, to signify]
significant figures the figures of a number, which are considered to give correct or sufficient information on its accuracy, that are read from the first non-zero digit on the left to the last non-zero digit on the right, unless a final zero expresses greater known accuracy
sig·ni·fi·ca·tion (signifikéiʃən) *n.* meaning or sense ‖ the act of signifying [O. F. or fr. L. *significatio* (*significationis*)]
sig·nif·i·ca·tive (signífikeitiv) *adj.* offering evidence, indicative, *significative of approval* having sense or meaning [O.F. fr. L.L. *significativus*]
sig·ni·fy (sígnifai) *pres. part.* **sig·ni·fy·ing** *past* and *past part.* **sig·ni·fied** *v.t.* to make known, communicate by some sign, *to signify assent* ‖ to be a sign of, indicate, *a nod signifies agreement* ‖ *v.i.* to be significant, have meaning [fr. F. *signifier*]
sign language a system of communication by gestures, e.g. that used by deaf and dumb people
sign manual *pl.* **signs manual** a personal signature, esp. the royal signature on grants, letters patent etc.
sign of the cross a sacramental movement of the hand outlining a cross to recall that of Christ, used in blessing, prayer or worship
sign on *v.* (*broadcasting*) to announce the beginning of the day's programming —**sign-on** *n.* the announcement
si·gnor (sí:njɔr, *Ital.* si:njɔ́r) *pl.* **signors**, *Ital.* **si·gno·ri** (si:njɔ́ri:) *n.* a courtesy title for an Italian man (the equivalent of 'Mr') and term of address (without the surname) [Ital., reduced form of *signore*, sir]
si·gno·ra (si:njɔ́rə, *Ital.* si:njɔ́rɑ) *pl.* **si·gno·ras**, *Ital.* **si·gno·re** (si:njɔ́re) *n.* a courtesy title for an Italian married woman (the equivalent of 'Mrs') and term of address (without the surname) [*Ital.*, fem. of *signore*, sir]
Si·gno·rel·li (si:njɔrélli:), Luca (c. 1450-1523), early Italian Renaissance painter, esp. noted for his fresco painting on a vast scale (Orvieto cathedral)
si·gno·ri·na (si:njərí:nə, *Ital.* si:njɔrí:nɑ) *pl.* **si·gno·ri·nas**, *Ital.* **si·gno·ri·ne** (si:njɔrí:ne) *n.* a courtesy title for an unmarried Italian girl or woman (the equivalent of 'Miss') and term of address (without the surname) [*Ital.*, dim. of *signora*]
sign·post (sáinpoust) *n.* a post at a crossroad or junction, with arms showing directions and sometimes distances to places
sign·writ·er (sáinraitər) *n.* a person who letters display signs for storekeepers, advertisers etc.
Sigs·bee (sígzbi:), Charles Dwight (1845-1923), U.S. admiral who commanded (1897-8) the 'Maine' at the time of her destruction in Havana harbor prior to the Spanish-American War
Si·ha·nouh (sí:ənuk), Prince Norodom (1922-), Cambodian statesman. He was king (1941-55), then prime minister (1955-60), and became (1960) chief of state. He was overthrown (Mar. 1970) by a right-wing coup d'état and set up, in Peking, a Government of National Union. He served again as nominal head of state (1975-6) then resigned and disappeared from public view until 1978, where he reappeared in China. He supported the Pol Pot regime against the Vietnamese invasion of Cambodia (1978) and appealed unsuccessfully to the U.N. Security Council for a halt to the invasion (1979)
Si·ha·nouk·ville (sí:ənukvil) *KOMPONG SOM
Si·kang (ʃí:kɑ́ŋ) a former province (1914-55) of S.W. China, partitioned (1955) between Szechwan and Tibet
Sikh (si:k) **1.** *n.* a member of the religion founded in the 16th c. by Nanak, a Punjabi Hindu strongly influenced by Islam. There are about eight million Sikhs in India and Pakistan. In the 17th c. the Sikhs were persecuted, and from this time springs the martial discipline which is still characteristic of them. Their sacred book, the Granth Sāhib, was compiled by Gobind Singh (1675–1708). Sikhs owe their monotheism to Islam, but hold such basic Hindu doctrines as karma and reincarnation **2.** *adj.* relating to the Sikhs or their religion **Sikh·ism** *n.*
Sikh War either of two wars in India between the Sikhs and the British. After the first (1845-6) the Sikhs were forced to cede Kashmir and pay an indemnity. After the second (1848-9), Britain annexed the Punjab
Si-kiang (ʃí:kjɑ́ŋ) (or Si) the longest river (1,200 miles) and major waterway of S. China. It rises in Yunnan as two streams which join in Kwansi-chuang, and flows across Kwangtung to the Yellow Sea. Its delta, around Kwangchow, is formed by three rivers (the Si, the Pei and the Tung) and is one of China's most densely populated regions
Sik·kim (síkim) a former principality and Indian protectorate, now a state of India (area 2,818 sq. miles, pop. 314,999) in the Himalayas. Capital: Gangtok (pop. 36,768). People: Nepalese (75%), Bhutia, Lepcha. Languages: Nepali, Lepcha. Religion: 30% Lamaist, 60% Hindu, small Jain, Sikh and Christian minorities. Elevation: 700 ft (southern border) to 28,146 ft (Kanchenjunga). The northern mountains are cut by deep river valleys. Intense cultivation up to 6,500 ft gives way to forest (9,000–12,000 ft) and permanent snow (15,000 ft). Strategic trade routes to Tibet cross at 13,000–15,000 ft. Rainfall: Gangtok 137 ins. Livestock: cattle, yak, sheep, goats. Agricultural products: rice and other cereals, cardamom, oranges, apples, lumber, pineapples, vegetables. Minerals: copper, graphite, gypsum, iron ore, gold, silver. Industries: foodstuffs, weaving, copper ware,

wooden goods. Exports: cardamom, oranges, apples, potatoes. Imports (from India): cotton goods, foodstuffs. Monetary unit: Indian rupee. HISTORY. Sikkim was established (1641) as a principality by a Tibetan family. British interest in the area dates from the early 19th c. A British protectorate over it was recognized (1890) by China and lasted until 1947, when Sikkim became independent. It signed a treaty (1950) giving India control of the country's defense, foreign relations and communications; India's role was extended after India's border war with China (1962) and strengthened (1974) after elections in Sikkim diminished the power of the Chogyal (ruler). Sikkim merged with India (1975) and became a state

Si·king (ʃíːdʒíŋ) *SIAN

Si·kor·ski (sikɔ́rskiː), Wladyslaw (1881-1943), Polish general and statesman. He was prime minister (1922-3) and war minister (1924-5), and was head of the exiled Polish government (1939-43) organizing Polish forces in the 2nd world war

si·lage (sáilidʒ) *n.* green fodder packed in a silo without drying and fermented by anaerobic lactic-acid bacteria often assisted by the addition of molasses, to preserve it for winter use [ENSILAGE]

si·lence (sáiləns) **1.** *n.* a not speaking or making any noise ‖ an abstaining from replying to a speech or letter, *his silence indicates disapproval* ‖ taciturnity ‖ a not betraying of some confidence, *can I rely on your silence?* ‖ deliberate or accidental failure to mention something ‖ stillness, quiet, *he can't work unless he has silence* ‖ (*rhet.*) oblivion **2.** *v.t. pres. part.* **si·lenc·ing** *past* and *past part.* **si·lenced** to cause to be quiet ‖ to quiet (fears, doubts, anxieties etc.) ‖ to compel to stop expressing an opinion ‖ to knock out (enemy guns) **si·lenc·er** *n.* (*Br.*) a muffler in the exhaust pipe of an engine ‖ a device for muffling the noise of a gun [O.F.]

si·lent (sáilənt) *adv.* making no sound, *a silent spectator* ‖ free from sound, *a silent house* ‖ not accompanied by audible speech or sound, *a silent prayer* ‖ taciturn, speaking little ‖ so smooth in action as to make scarcely any sound, *a silent car* ‖ (of a letter or group of letters) written but not pronounced, e.g. 'b' in doubt ‖ uninformative, *history is silent about what followed* ‖ witholding information, *he was silent about what he had seen* ‖ (of a motion picture) without any sound track ‖ (of a volcano) inactive but not extinct [fr. L. *silens* (*silentis*) fr. *silere*, to be silent]

silent butler a small metal receptacle, with a handle and hinged lid, for clearing away crumbs from the table and the contents of ash trays

silent majority the portion of the public not strongly committed to either side of a (right-left) controversy; citizens whose political opinions are seldom heard

silent partner a financial partner with no voice in the management of a business

silent spring hypothetical time when plant, bird, and insect life are destroyed by industrial pollutants; from *The Silent Spring*, by Rachel Carson, 1962

Si·le·nus (sailíːnəs) (*Gk mythol.*) an old, bearded, woodland satyr attendant upon Dionysus

Si·le·sia (silíːʒə, silíːʃə, sailíːʒə, sailíːʃə) a region around the upper and middle Oder in S.W. Poland. Colonized by Germans in the Middle Ages, it came under the Bohemian crown in the 14th c. and under the Hapsburgs in 1526. In 1742, Frederick the Great of Prussia took the whole of it except for a small part which in 1918 became Czech (*MORAVIA-SILESIA). In 1921, after a plebiscite, a large part of the economically important coal-mining and industrial area of Upper Silesia in the southeast was ceded to Poland. The latter annexed the whole of German Silesia after the 2nd world war

sil·hou·ette (siluːét) **1.** *n.* a portrait in profile, showing the outline only, and filled in with black, or cut out of black paper ‖ a similar representation of the outlines of any object ‖ a person or object seen against the light, with this effect **2.** *v.t. pres. part.* **sil·hou·et·ting** *past* and *past part.* **sil·hou·et·ted** to represent in silhouette ‖ to cause to show up thus against a background, *the cathedral was silhouetted against the sunset* [after Etienne de Silhouette (1709–67), French finance minister (1759) under Louis XV (in whose reign the silhouette became popular as a cheap kind of portrait), in satirical allusion to his extreme economy]

sil·i·ca (sílikə) *n.* silicon dioxide, SiO_2, one of the commonest minerals, occurring as quartz, agate, jasper, flint etc., and abundant in sandstone and other rocks. In the form of quartz sand, it is a main constituent of glass **sil·i·cate** (sílikit, sílikeit) *n.* a metal salt of a very large class, usually insoluble, containing silicon and oxygen in the anion. They constitute with silica the largest portion of the earth's crust, and are the principal constituent of cement, glass, bricks and other building materials ‖ a salt or ester of a silicic acid [Mod. L. fr. *silex* (*silicis*), flint]

silica gel (*chem.*) highly absorbent silica dehumidifier and dehydrating agent, used as a powder insecticide

si·li·ceous (silíʃəs) *adj.* of, pertaining to, like or containing silica growing in or needing soil containing silica [fr. L. *siliceus*]

si·lic·ic acid (silísik) any of several weak acids formed as solution or as gel-like masses by dissolving alkaline silicates in acids or obtained as salts or esters

si·lic·i·fy (silísifai) *pres. part.* **si·lic·i·fy·ing** *past* and *past part.* **si·lic·i·fied** *v.t.* to impregnate with silica ‖ to turn into silica ‖ *v.i.* to become impregnated with or turned into silica

sil·i·cle (sílik'l) *n.* (*bot.*) a short, flat silique [fr. F. *silicule* or L. *silicula*]

sil·i·con (sílikən, sílikɒn) *n.* a gray, brittle, tetravalent, nonmetallic element (symbol Si, at. no. 14, at. mass 28.086) occurring abundantly in nature, always in compounds. Next to oxygen it is the chief elementary constituent of the earth's crust. Silicon compounds are much used in industry (e.g. sand and glass making) and the element itself is used in the production of very hard alloys

silicon dioxide silica

sil·i·cone (sílikoun) *n.* any of a large class of polymers of R_2SiO where R is a hydrocarbon. Silicones are used as lubricants, as heatresisting resins and varnishes, as waterresisting films etc.

sil·i·co·sis (silikóusis) *n.* a disease of the lungs caused by inhaling silica dust over a long period of time [SILICA]

si·lic·u·la (silíkjulə) *n.* (*bot.*) a silicle [L., dim. of *siliqua*, pod]

si·lic·u·lose (silíkjulous) *adj.* (*bot.*) having silicles ‖ resembling a silicle [fr. Mod L. *siliculosus*]

si·lique (silíːk, sílik) *n.* a long cylindrical dry, dehiscent fruit (two carpels) divided into two by a false septum, and containing the seeds. It is characteristic of the fam. *Cruciferae*, e.g. mustard [F.]

silk (silk) **1.** *n.* a very fine, soft, lustrous fiber spun by the silkworm (*Bombyx mori*) as its cocoon ‖ a thread or fabric made of this fiber ‖ a garment made of this fiber ‖ a fiber spun by some arachnids ‖ (*Br., pop.*) a silk barrister's gown worn by a King's (or Queen's) Counsel ‖ corn silk ‖ (*pl., horse racing*) the distinctively colored cap and jacket worn by a jockey **to take silk** (*Br.*) to become a King's (or Queen's) Counsel **2.** *adj.* of, made of, or like silk **3.** *v.i.* (of corn) to blossom or be on the verge of blossoming [O.E. *sioloc*]

silk cotton a silky fiber, esp. kapok, obtained from the seeds of a silk-cotton tree

silk-cotton tree a member of *Bombaceae*, a family of tropical trees which produce silk cotton. They have palmate leaves and large fruit containing seeds which yield oil when crushed

silk·en (sílkən) *adj.* soft and lustrous, *silken skin* ‖ soft and delicate, *a silken touch* ‖ smooth, suave, *a silken voice* ‖ (*rhet.*) made of silk, *silken fabrics*

silk·i·ness (sílkiːnis) *n.* the state or quality of being silky

silk·ing (sílkiŋ) *n.* (*cosmetology*) technique of temporary hair straightening using pressing combs

silk-screen (sílkskriːn) **1.** *adj.* of or relating to the silk-screen process **2.** *v.t.* to reproduce or print by the silk-screen process **silk screen** the screen, esp. of silk or organdy, used in the silk-screen process

silk-screen process a stencil process in which coloring matter is forced through the meshes of a silk screen on which all the areas not to be printed have been blocked out by an impermeable substance

silk·worm (sílkwəːrm) *n.* the larva of any of various moths that spin cocoons of silk, esp. the larva of *Bombyx mori*, fam. *Bombycidae*. The female lays 300–500 eggs on the leaves of a mulberry, esp. *Morus alba*. The caterpillar feeds voraciously, molting several times. Then it spins its pupa case of silk thread, from which after three weeks it emerges as an adult moth. Silk thread from one cocoon may be from 400 to over 3,000 yards long

silk·y (sílkiː) *comp.* **silk·i·er** *superl.* **silk·i·est** *adj.* soft and glossy like silk

silky terrier a toy terrier with blue and tan silky coat, a cross bred from Yorkshire terrier and an Australian terrier

sill (sil) *n.* a ledge at the bottom of a window, outside or inside ‖ a stone or wooden threshold of a door ‖ (*geol.*) a layer of intrusive igneous rock [O.E. *syll, sylle*]

sillabub *SYLLABUB

sil·li·man·ite (síləmənait) *n.* an aluminum silicate, Al_2SiO_5, in orthorhombicrystals [after Benjamin *Silliman* (1779–1864), U.S. chemist]

sil·li·ness (síliːnis) *n.* the state or quality of being silly ‖ a silly act or series of such acts

Sil·li·toe (sílitou), Alan (1928-), British writer, one of the 'Angry Young Men' of the 1950s. His works, which exemplify the working class and show contempt for the middle class, include 'Saturday Night and Sunday Morning' (1958), 'The Loneliness of the Long-Distance Runner' (1959), 'This Foreign Field' (1970), 'The Widower's Son' (1977) and 'Her Victory' (1982)

Sills (silz), Beverly (1929-), U.S. soprano, born Belle Silverman. She made her opera debut in 1948 at the Philadelphia Civic Opera and joined the New York City Opera (1953), where she was made director upon her retirement from the stage (1980). She sang the heroine role in over 50 operas; one of her first and most well-known was Cleopatra in 'Julius Caesar'

sil·ly (síliː) *comp.* **sil·li·er** *superl.* **sil·li·est** **1.** *adj.* lacking or seeming to lack common sense (*pop.*, used post-positively) stunned, *to be knocked silly* **2.** *pl.* **sil·lies** *n.* (*pop.*) a foolish person [fr. older *seely*, lucky, happy, blessed]

silly point (*cricket*) a fielding position close to the batsman on the off side

si·lo (sáilou) **1.** *pl.* **si·los** *n.* a pit or tall cylindrical structure that can be made air-tight, used for making silage ‖ a tall cylindrical structure used for storing grain ‖ a subterranean shelter for guided missiles **2.** *v.t. pres. part.* **si·lo·ing** *past* and *past part.* **si·loed** to put or store in a silo [Span.]

Si·lo·ne (silóuniː, siːlɔ́ne), Ignazio (1900-78), Italian Socialist writer. He had a great influence on the realist writers of the 1930s. His best-known novels are 'Fontamara' (1933), 'Bread and Wine' (1936) and 'The Story of a Humble Christian' (1968)

silt (silt) **1.** *n.* mud, soil etc. deposited esp. by a river ‖ particles of minerals, soil etc. suspended in water, esp. in a river **2.** *v.t.* (with 'up') to block or choke with silt ‖ *v.i.* (with 'up') to become blocked or choked with silt [perh. of Scand. origin]

Sil·u·res (síljuriːz) *pl. n.* the ancient inhabitants of S.E. Wales conquered by the Romans, c. 80 A.D. **Si·lu·ri·an** (silúəriːən, sailúəriːən) *adj.* of the Silures or their territory ‖ (*geol.*) of the period or system of the Paleozoic era characterized by abundant marine invertebrates and coral reefs (*GEOLOGICAL TIME) **the Silurian** the Silurian period or system of rocks [L.]

Sil·va (síːlvɑ), José Asunción (1865-96), Colombian poet and precursor of modernism and symbolism, known esp. for his 'Nocturnos'. He influenced Rubén Darío and others

silvan *SYLVAN

Silva Xavier, Joaquim José de *TIRADENTES

sil·ver (sílvər) **1.** *n.* a white, stable, malleable, ductile, usually monovalent (rarely bivalent) metallic element (symbol Ag, at. no. 47, at. mass 107.870) that occurs naturally in an uncombined or combined state. It is the best-known conductor of heat and electricity and is resistant to oxidation. It is used for electrical contacts, for lining certain chemical equipment and for backing mirrors, in electroplating, coinage, photography and in jewelry and silverware ‖ coins minted from this metal or from an alloy resembling this ‖ silverware ‖ a somewhat shiny whitish-gray color **2.** *adj.* made of silver ‖ like silver, esp. in color ‖ of soft, clear tones ‖ (of a jubilee, wedding or other anniversary) twenty-

CONCISE PRONUNCIATION KEY: (a) æ, cat; ɑ, car; ɔ fawn; ei, snake. (e) e, hen; iː, sheep; iə, deer; ɛə, bear. (i) i, fish; ai, tiger; əː, bird. (o) o, ox; au, cow; ou, goat; u, poor; ɔi, royal. (u) ʌ, duck; u, bull; uː, goose; ə, bacillus; juː, cube. x, loch; θ, think; ð, bother; z, Zen; ʒ, corsage; dʒ, savage; ŋ, orangutang; j, yak; ʃ, fish; tʃ, fetch; 'l, rabble; 'n, redden. Complete pronunciation key appears inside front cover.

fifth **3.** *v.t.* to coat with silver, usually by electrolysis || to give (a surface) the appearance of silver, e.g. by using an amalgam of tinfoil and mercury || *v.i.* to take on the color of silver [O.E. *seolfor*]

silver age a period, esp. of literary history, thought of as inferior only to a preceding golden age

silver anniversary a 25th anniversary

silver birch *Betula alba,* a birch of cold and temperate Old World regions, with silvery or parchment-colored bark

sil·ver·fish (sílvərfiʃ) *pl.* **sil·ver·fish, sil·ver·fish·es** *n.* any of several members of *Thysanura,* an order of insects, esp. the small, silvery, primitive, wingless *Lepisma saccharina,* fam. *Lepismatidae.* They are omnivorous feeders and domestic pests || any of various silver fish, e.g. the tarpon

silver fox a fox valued for its black white-tipped fur. It is the American red fox in one color phase, but it can be bred stable

silver gilt silver covered with a thin coating of gold || a yellow-lacquered imitation of this

silver glance argentite

silver gray, silver grey *n.* a light, lustrous gray color **sil·ver-gráy, sil·ver-gréy** *adj.*

silver iodide a naturally occurring compound, AgI, which can also be synthetically produced, used in photography and medicine etc.

silver lining the ultimately hopeful aspect of a situation that causes gloom

silver maple *Acer saccharinum,* a maple of North America. Its leaves are light green above, silvery below || the hard wood of this tree

silver nitrate a colorless, crystalline salt, $AgNO_3$, obtained by dissolving silver in nitric acid and evaporating. It is used in photography as a chemical reagent, in medicine as an antiseptic, and in marking inks

silver paper tinfoil || a fine white tissue paper for wrapping silver

silver plate a thin coating of silver (*collect.*) articles having such a coating **sil·ver-pláte** *pres. part.* **sil·ver-plat·ing** *past* and *past part.* **sil·ver-plat·ed** *v.t.* to apply a thin coating of silver to, usually by electrolysis **sil·ver-plát·ed** *adj.*

sil·ver·point (sílvərpɔint) *n.* a process of drawing on prepared paper with a silver-tipped pencil || a drawing made by this process

silver side (*Br.*) the upper and best part of a round of beef

sil·ver·smith (sílvərsmiθ) *n.* a craftsman who works silver

silver-tongued (sílvərtʌŋd) *adj.* (*rhet.,* of an orator) wonderfully eloquent

sil·ver·ware (sílvərwɛər) *n.* tableware, esp. knives, forks and spoons, made of silver or silver plate

silver wedding the 25th anniversary of a wedding

sil·ver·y (sílvəri:) *adj.* of or like silver || soft and clear in tone || coated with or containing silver

Silvester *SYLVESTER I

sil·vex [$C_6H_7O_3Cl_3$] (sílveks) *n.* (*chem.*) herbicide used esp. against weeds in turf, aquatic plantings, and food crops

sil·vi·chem·i·cal (silvəkéməkəl) *n.* chemical derived from trees

sil·vi·cul·ture, syl·vi·cul·ture (sílvikʌltʃər) *n.* a branch of the science of forestry dealing with the development, cultivation and reproduction of forest trees [fr. L. *silva, sylva,* a wood + F. *culture,* cultivation]

si·ma·zine [$C_7H_{12}N_5Cl$] (sáiməzi:n) *n.* (*chem.*) moderately toxic herbicide used esp. to control weeds in farming, esp. for corn, alfalfa, and fruit

Sim·birsk (sjimbjí:rsk) *ULYANOVSK

Sim·e·on (sími:ən) Hebrew patriarch, son of Jacob || the Israelite tribe of which he was the ancestor

Sim·fe·ro·pol (simfjirɔ́pəl) a city (pop. 314,000) of the Ukraine, U.S.S.R., in the Crimea. Industries: food processing, mechanical engineering. Tatar mosque (16th c.)

sim·i·an (sími:ən) **1.** *adj.* like, or having the characteristics of, an ape or monkey **2.** *n.* an ape or monkey, esp. an anthropoid ape [fr. L. *simia,* ape]

sim·i·lar (símələr) *adj.* like, much the same, *the two rooms are of similar size* || (*geom.,* of figures) having the same shape **sim·i·lar·i·ty** (siməlǽriti:) *pl.* **sim·i·lar·i·ties** *n.* the state of being similar || a point of resemblance [fr. F. *similaire* or M.L. *similaris*]

sim·i·le (síməli:) *n.* a figure of speech in which one thing is likened to another in one respect by the use of 'like', 'as' etc., e.g. 'his explanation was as clear as crystal' (cf. METAPHOR) [L., neut. of *similis,* like]

si·mil·i·tude (simílitu:d, simílitju:d) *n.* resemblance, *similitude of character* || semblance, *in the similitude of an angel* [O.F.]

Sim·la (símlə) the capital (pop. 55,326) of Himachal Pradesh, India, a health resort in the Himalayas at 7,000 ft

sim·mer (símər) **1.** *v.i.* to be just below boiling point || (of liquids) to make a steady, low, bubbling sound while heated just to or just below boiling point || to be near an emotional explosion, *to simmer with rage* || *v.t.* to bring to, and cause to remain, just below boiling point **to simmer down** to become calm, esp. after anger **2.** *n.* a state of simmering [fr. earlier *simper,* prob. imit.]

Sim·nel (símn'l), Lambert (c. 1472-c. 1534), English pretender. Claiming to be Edward, earl of Warwick, the Yorkist heir, he led an unsuccessful rebellion (1687) against Henry VII. He was pardoned and given employment in the royal household

sim·nel cake (símn'l) (*Br.*) a rich fruit cake, associated with Easter and mid-Lent [O.F. *simenel, seminel*]

Si·mon (sáimən), St (1st c.), one of the 12 Apostles. Feast: Oct. 28

Si·mon (si:mɔ̃) Claude (1913-), French writer, winner of the Nobel prize for literature (1985). A proponent of the 'new novel', he usually disregarded chronology. His works include 'The Taut Rope' (1947), 'The Flanders Road' (1960) and 'The World About Us' (1975)

si·mo·ni·ac (simóuni:æk) *n.* someone who practices simony **si·mo·ni·a·cal** (saimənáiək'l, simənáiək'l) *adj.* of or relating to simony [fr. M.L. *simoniacus*]

Si·mon·i·des (saimɔ́nidi:z) (c. 556-468 B.C.), Greek lyric poet, celebrated for his epigrams, elegies and dirges

Si·mon Ma·gus (sáimənméigəs) a magician prominent in early Christian history and legend. The Apostle Philip (Acts viii, 9-24) converted him, but when Peter and John came to Samaria he offered them money (*SIMONY) in return for being taught what he believed was the magic of the gift of the Spirit through the laying on of hands. Rebuked by Peter, he begged him to intercede with God on his behalf, and appears no more in Acts. Later literature shows him reappearing in Rome in the time of Claudius in a new movement of his own, curiously combining Christian and pagan elements, and in which he figures as a god

Simon Peter *PETER, ST

Si·mons·town (sáimənztaun) a port and naval base (pop. 8,000) in Cape Province, South Africa, on the Cape of Good Hope

si·mo·ny (sáiməni:, síməni:) *n.* the offense of buying or selling positions in the Church (*SIMON MAGUS) [O.F. *simonie*]

si·moom (simú:m) *n.* a hot, dry, dust-laden wind, esp. in the Arabian desert [Arab. *semūm*]

si·moon (simú:n) *n.* a simoom

sim·per (símpər) **1.** *v.i.* to smile foolishly and self-consciously || *v.t.* to express with a simper **2.** *n.* an affected smile [origin unknown]

sim·ple (símp'l) **1.** *comp.* **sim·pler** *superl.* **sim·plest** *adj.* consisting of only one kind, part etc. || consisting of few parts, *a simple device* || easy to deal with, understand etc., *a simple problem* || (*chem.*) elementary || (*chem.*) composed of basically similar components || (*law*) unconditional || without any or much ornamentation, sophistication or complexity || bare, mere, *the simple truth* || of low rank or position, *a simple workman* || unpretentious, *he is a simple man and a great scholar* || possessed of little understanding, *he is simple about money matters* || guileless || half-witted **2.** *n.* (*archaic*) a medicine derived from only one plant || (*archaic*) a plant gathered for this [O.F.]

simple eye (*zool.*) an eye having only one lens

simple fraction a fraction containing an integer in the numerator and the denominator (cf. COMPLEX FRACTION)

simple harmonic motion a vibratory motion in which the acceleration of the object is proportional to and in a direction opposite to the displacement from a point of equilibrium, and that is characterized by a single frequency and amplitude. Thus, the projection of a point moving in uniform circular motion on the diameter of its trajectory moves with simple harmonic motion

sim·ple·heart·ed (símp'lhártid) *adj.* gladly accepting persons and things at their face value with sincerity, free of sophistication

simple interest (*finance*) interest calculated on principal only

simple leaf a lobed or unlobed leaf whose blade is not divided at the midrib

simple machine one of the elementary mechanisms, e.g. lever, pulley, wheel, inclined plane, screw, wedge, axle

sim·ple·mind·ed (símp'lmáindid) *adj.* simple-hearted || of subnormal intelligence

simple sentence a sentence having only one main clause and no subordinate clauses

sim·ple·ton (símp'ltən) *n.* a person who lacks common sense or is easily deceived

sim·plic·i·ty (simplísiti:) *pl.* **sim·plic·i·ties** *n.* the quality or state of being simple || a simple idea or fact [O.F. *simplicité* or fr. L. *simplicitas*]

sim·pli·fi·ca·tion (simplifikéiʃən) *n.* a simplifying or being simplified || a result of this [F.]

sim·pli·fy (símplifai) *pres. part.* **sim·pli·fy·ing** *past* and *past part.* **sim·pli·fied** *v.t.* to make less complex, *to simplify a structure* || to make easier to do or solve, *to simplify a problem* || to make easier to understand, *to simplify an explanation* [fr. F. *simplifier*]

Sim·plon (sɛ̃plɔ̃) a pass (summit 6,578 ft) in the Lepontine Alps connecting the upper Rhône valley, Switzerland, with Lake Maggiore, Italy. Its railroad tunnel (12.5 miles long) was opened in 1906

sim·ply (símpli:) *adv.* in a simple way || merely || (*pop.*) completely, utterly, *the play was simply awful* || (*pop.*) in point of fact, *there simply isn't anyone she can spare*

Simp·son (símps'n), Sir James Young (1811-70), Scottish physician. He was the first to use chloroform as an anesthetic

Sims (simz), William Sowden (1858-1936), U.S. admiral whose improvements in ship design, fleet tactics, and naval gunnery were a major contribution to modernizing the U.S. Navy

sim·u·la·crum (simjuléikrəm) *pl.* **sim·u·la·cra** (simjuléikrə), **sim·u·la·crums** *n.* something made to resemble some other thing || an inferior or deceptive likeness [L.]

Sim·u·la-In (símjulɑín) *n.* (*computer*) process-oriented, discrete simulation language based on Algol

sim·u·late (símjuleit) *pres. part.* **sim·u·lat·ing** *past* and *past part.* **sim·u·lat·ed** *v.t.* to assume the appearance of falsely, *to simulate death* (cf. DISSIMULATE) || to pretend to have, *to simulate a headache* || (*computer*) to reproduce a social or physical activity in computer terms to arrive at a solution [fr. L. *simulare* (*simulatus*)]

sim·u·la·tion (simjuléiʃən) a simulating || a superficial resemblance || a representation of a product, condition, or process in a different medium, e.g., computer, statistical chart, mock-up, esp. for the purpose of analysis [O.F.]

si·mul·cast (sáiməlkæst, sáiməlkɑst, síməlkæst, síməlkɑst) **1.** *v.t. pres. part.* **si·mul·cast·ing** *past* and *past part.* **si·mul·cast** to broadcast by radio and television at the same time **2.** *n.* a simultaneous broadcast by radio and television [SIMULTANEOUS+BROADCAST]

si·mul·ta·ne·i·ty (saiməltəní:iti:, siməltəní:iti:) *n.* the state or quality of being simultaneous

si·mul·ta·ne·ous (saiməltéini:əs, siməltéini:əs) *adj.* being or occurring at the same time [fr. L. *simul,* at the same time]

simultaneous equations (*math.*) a set of equations satisfied by the same values of the variables

sin (sin) *n.* an action contrary to the law of God || a state to be condemned in the light of God's law, *a life of sin* || (*loosely*) an offense against any widely accepted standard, *sins against propriety* || (*pop.*) an offense against good sense, *it's a sin to have a garden and then neglect it* [O. E. *syn, synn*]

sin *pres. part.* **sin·ning** *past* and *past part.* **sinned** *v.i.* to offend against a law of God || (*loosely*) to offend against any law, convention, standard of taste or reason [O.E. *syngian*]

Si·nai (sáinai, sáini:ai) a peninsula (area 11,055 sq. miles) at the head of the Red Sea between the gulfs of Suez and 'Aqaba, forming part of Egypt. It is mainly desert, with mountains in the south, incl. Mt Sinai (modern Gebel Musa, 7,363 ft), where God gave Moses the Ten Commandments (Exodus xix-xxxiv), and Gebel Katherina (*KATHERINA GEBEL). It is sparsely inhabited by nomadic Arab tribes

Si·na·lo·a (si:nalóa) a coastal state (area 22,582 sq. miles, pop. 1,882,200) of Mexico, on the Gulf of California and Pacific Ocean, with 400 miles of western coastline, and mountains on its eastern border. Capital and commercial center: Culiacán (pop. 302,229). Wheat, chickpeas, cotton, tobacco, sugarcane and fruits and vegetables are grown in the isolated valleys, mainly under irrigation. Industries: fishing (chiefly sharks), mining (salt, graphite, gold, silver), tourism

since (sins) **1.** *adv.* at some time between a point in the past and now, *he moved away three years ago but she has seen him since* ‖ (often preceded by 'ever') throughout the time between a point in the past and now, *he came in 1950 and has stayed ever since* ‖ ago, *he has married long since* **2.** *prep.* during the time between a point in the past and a more recent point or now, *they had not met since childhood* ‖ during the time between a point in the past and now, *they have been working since 10 o'clock* **3.** *conj.* during a period following a time when, *much has happened since they last met* ‖ continuously from some time in the past when, *he has not seen her since she was a child* ‖ because, *since you are so sure of it he will believe you* [fr. older *sithence* fr. *sithen* fr. O.E. *siththan,* subsequently to that, or fr. older *sith* adv., since]

sin·cere (sinsíər) *comp.* **sin·cer·er** *superl.* **sin·cer·est** *adj.* utterly honest and genuine, *a sincere friend* [fr. L. *sincerus,* clean, pure]

sin·cer·i·ty (sinsériti:) *pl.* **sin·cer·i·ties** *n.* the quality or state of being sincere [fr. L. *sinceritas*]

Sin·clair (sinkléər), Upton (1878-1968), U.S. social novelist. His 'The Jungle' (1906) fictionalizes his personal investigation into the Chicago stockyards. Later works include 'Dragon's Teeth' (1942)

Sind (sind) a region and former state of Pakistan, a flat, mainly arid region around the lower Indus Valley. Chief town: Hyderabad. Irrigated crops: cereals, hemp, cotton, indigo

Sin·dhi, Sin·di (síndi:) *pl.* **Sin·dhi, Sin·dhis, Sin·di, Sin·dis** *n.* a chiefly Islamic people inhabiting Sind ‖ a member of this people ‖ their Indic language

sine (sain) *n.* (*math., abbr.* sin) a measure of the magnitude of an angle expressed as the constant ratio of the side opposite the angle in a right-angled triangle to the hypotenuse [fr. L. *sinus,* curve, trans. Arab. *jaib*]

si·ne·cure (sáinəkjuər, sínəkjuər) *n.* a position offering profit or honor but carrying few or no duties ‖ (*hist.*) a benefice without cure of souls [fr. L. *sine cura,* without cure, care]

sin·ew (sínju:) *n.* a ligament ‖ (*rhet.*) physical strength ‖ (*pl., rhet.*) sources of strength, *sinews of war* **sin·ew·y** *adj.* of or like sinew ‖ having many or large sinews, muscular ‖ (of prose style) spare, strong and vigorous [O.E. *sinu, sionu*]

sin·fo·ni·a (sinfouní:ə) *pl.* **sin·fo·ni·e** (sinfouní:ei) *n.* a symphony [Ital.]

sin·ful (sínfəl) *adj.* marked by or full of sin ‖ (*pop.*) reprehensible, *a sinful waste*

sing (siŋ) **1.** *v. pres. part.* **sing·ing** *past* **sang** (sæŋ) *past part.* **sung** (sʌŋ) *v.i.* to utter musical sounds with the voice ‖ to utter words in a musical succession usually set to music ‖ to make a small shrill sound, *bullets sang past our ears* ‖ (*rhet.*) to celebrate something in verse ‖ (of birds, insects, brooks etc.) to produce sounds thought of as tuneful ‖ (of the ears) to be full of a whining noise ‖ *v.t.* to utter (a song, musical note etc.) ‖ (*rhet.*) to celebrate in verse, *poets sang her beauty* **to sing out** to answer, call out **to sing to sleep** to lull to sleep by singing **2.** *n.* (*pop.*) a singing in company ‖ a small shrill sound, esp. of a bullet in flight [O.E. *singan*]

Si·ngan (sí:ŋán) *SIAN

Sin·ga·pore (síŋgəpɔr, síŋgəpour) a republic (area 225 sq. miles, pop. 2,503,000), and member of the British Commonwealth, off the southern tip of the Malay peninsula, consisting of Singapore Is. (224 sq. miles) and nearby islets (15 sq. miles). People: 76% Chinese, 15% Malay and Indonesian, 8% Indian and Pakistani, small European and Eurasian minorities. Main languages: English, Chinese, Malay, Tamil. Religions: Buddhist, Taoist, Confucianist, Moslem, Christian, Hindu, Sikh. Average temperature (F.): 75°-87°. Rainfall: 95 ins. Crops: vegetables, fruit, rubber, tobacco. Tin, rubber, fruit, petroleum, tobacco, soybeans and palm oil are imported, processed and reexported. Other industries: fishing, engineering, textiles, building materials, light manufacturing. The island is a major air and naval base ‖ its capital (pop. 1,327,500), a great port, entrepôt and commercial center. University: National University of Singapore (1980). Monetary unit: Singapore dollar. HISTORY. Singapore was a prosperous commercial center (13th-14th cc.), and was destroyed (1377) by the Javanese. The British established a trading station (1819). Singapore was ceded (1824) to the British East India Company, and was administered (1826-1946) as part of Straits Settlements. After Japanese occupation (1942-5), it became a separate British colony (1946) and gained internal self-government (1959). It was part of Malaysia (1963-5) and became fully independent (Aug. 9, 1965). It became a republic within the Commonwealth (Dec. 22, 1965). Since independence Singapore has become an industrial and financial power with one of the highest standards of living in Asia

singe (sindʒ) **1.** *v.t. pres. part.* **singe·ing** *past* and *past part.* **singed** to burn slightly on the surface ‖ to burn off bristles or small feathers from (an animal carcass) ‖ to burn the ends of (hair) ‖ to burn off the excess fibers from (cloth) **2.** *n.* a slight burn ‖ the act of singeing [O.E. *sengan*]

Sing·er (siŋər), Isaac Bashevis (1904-), U.S.-Yiddish writer, born in Poland, winner of the Nobel prize for literature (1978). His stories concern the Jewish communities in eastern Europe before the 2nd world war. Novels include the trilogy 'The Family Moskat' (1950), 'The Manor' (1967) and 'The Estate' (1970). He is best known for his short stories, among them 'Gimpel the Fool' (1957) and 'The Spinoza of Market Street' (1961); they are collected in 'Passions and Other Stories' (1975), 'Collected Stories of Isaac Bashevis Singer' (1982) and 'The Image and Other Stories' (1985), among others. Autobiographical works are 'In My Father's Court' (1966) and 'Love and Exile' (1984)

Singer, Isaac Merrit (1811-75), U.S. inventor (1851) of the first practical domestic sewing machine. The Singer sewing machine company became (1860) the largest in the world

sing·er (síŋər) *n.* someone who sings, esp. as a professional ‖ a bird that sings

Sin·gha·lese (siŋgəlí:z, siŋgəlí:s) *SINHALESE

sing-in (síŋin) *n.* audience participation in a musical event

sin·gle (síŋg'l) **1.** *adj.* one and one only, *a single spectator remained* ‖ sole, only, *the single letter was found in the mailbox* ‖ individual, taken in isolation, *every single person present, the most important single influence* ‖ being or behaving as though one only, *we are single in our aim* ‖ (of a bed or room) for one person of the unmarried state ‖ unmarried ‖ being a complete whole, *three small towns became a single city* ‖ not double or compound, *a single plow* ‖ (*bot.,* of a flower) having only one row or set of floral leaves (cf. DOUBLE) ‖ (*bot.,* of a plant) bearing such flowers (cf. DOUBLE) ‖ (*Br.,* of a ticket) valid for a journey in one direction only **not a single (person or thing)** not even one (person or thing), *not a single mistake* **2.** *n.* one individual person or thing ‖ (*cricket*) one run scored ‖ (*baseball*) a hit by which the batter gets no farther than first base ‖ (*Br.*) a one-way ticket ‖ (*pl., golf*) a match between two players ‖ (*pl., tennis*) a game with only one player on each side ‖ (*slang*) an unmarried person **3.** *v. pres. part.* **sin·gling** *past* and *past part.* **sin·gled** *v.t.* (sometimes with 'out') to thin out (seedlings) ‖ (with 'out') to choose (one) from many, esp. for special treatment or as having special quality ‖ *v.i.* (*baseball*) to make a hit by which the batter gets no farther than first base [O.F.]

sin·gle-act·ing (síŋg'lǽktiŋ) *adj.* acting in one direction only, not reciprocating

sin·gle-ac·tion (síŋg'lǽkʃən) *adj.* of a firearm whose hammer must be cocked by hand before the weapon can be fired ‖ single-acting

sin·gle-bar·reled, esp. *Br.* **sin·gle-bar·relled** (síŋg'lbǽrəld) *adj.* (of a gun) having one barrel

single blind in an experimental situation, the condition in which only the one conducting the experiment understands the objectives —**single-blind** *adj.* *Cf* DOUBLE BLIND

sin·gle-breast·ed (síŋg'lbréstid) *adj.* (of a coat, waistcoat etc.) buttoned down the middle with a single row of buttons

single combat combat between two persons

single entry a method of bookkeeping by which debts owed to and by a firm are recorded once only in the ledger

single file a line of persons or animals arranged or moving one behind the other

sin·gle-foot (síŋg'lfut) **1.** *n.* the rack (horse's gait) **2.** *v.i.* (of a horse) to go at a rack

sin·gle-hand·ed (síŋg'lhǽndid) *adj.* done without assistance ‖ used with one hand only, *a single-handed sword* ‖ having only one hand

sin·gle-heart·ed (síŋg'lhártid) *adj.* devoted without reservation to one person, cause etc. ‖ marked by or resulting from such devotion

sin·gle-mind·ed (síŋg'lmáindid) *adj.* giving undivided effort to a single purpose ‖ without guile, utterly honest

single parents unmarried, divorced, or widowed mothers or fathers of nonadult children

sin·gle-phase (síŋg'lféiz) *adj.* (*elec.*) of a circuit having an alternating current in which the two conductors differ in phase by 180°

singles bar (*colloq.*) a dating bar

sin·gle-screw (síŋg'lskru:) *adj.* (of a ship) having one screw propeller (cf. TWIN-SCREW)

sin·gle·stick (síŋg'lstik) *n.* a stick of sword length used in a form of fencing ‖ the sport of fencing with singlesticks

sin·glet (síŋglit) *n.* (*Br.*) a man's sleeveless vest ‖ (*Br.*) an athletic jersey

sin·gle·ton (síŋg'ltən) *n.* (*cards*) the only card of its suit held in a hand [SINGLE]

sin·gle·tree (síŋg'ltri:) *n.* a whiffletree

sin·gly (síŋgli:) *adv.* separately, one at a time, *singly or in pairs*

sing·song (síŋsɔŋ, síŋsɒŋ) **1.** *n.* a monotonous chanting tone of voice ‖ (*Br.*) a sing (in company) **2.** *adj.* in or marked by a monotonous rising and falling tone **3.** *v.i.* to speak or sing in a singsong way ‖ *v.t.* to utter in a singsong

sin·gu·lar (síŋgjulər) **1.** *adj.* (*gram.*) of or denoting one person or thing (cf. PLURAL, cf. DUAL NUMBER) ‖ very remarkable, *singular beauty* ‖ eccentric, *singular behavior* ‖ extraordinary, *a singular experience* **2.** (*gram.*) the form of a word expressing one only ‖ (*gram.*) the singular number [O.F. *singuler* and *singulaire* or fr. L. *singularis*]

sin·gu·lar·i·ty (siŋgjulǽriti:) *pl.* **sin·gu·lar·i·ties** *n.* the state or quality of being very distinctive or unusual ‖ a peculiar characteristic [fr. F. *singularité* or L.L. *singularitas*]

Sin·hai (ʃínhái) *SINHAILIEN

Sin·hai·lien (ʃínháiljén) (or Sinhai, formerly Tunghai) a city (pop. 208,000) in N.W. Kiangsu, China, near the Yellow Sea: salt works

Sin·ha·lese, Sing·ha·lese (sinhəlí:z, sinhəlí:s) **1.** *n.* a member of the principal race of Ceylon ‖ its Indic language **2.** *adj.* of or belonging to this race, its language, culture etc.

sin·is·ter (sínistər) *adj.* evil or suggestive of evil, *a sinister face* ‖ (*rhet.*) disastrous or suggestive of misfortune, *sinister events* (*heraldry*) on the left of a shield (the viewer's right) [O.F. *sinistre* or L. *sinister,* left-hand]

sin·is·tral (sínistrəl) *adj.* (of spiral shells) having the whorls going from right to left ‖ (of flatfish) left side uppermost [O.F. or fr. M.L. *sinistralis*]

sin·is·tror·sal (sinistrɔ́rsəl) *adj.* sinistrorse

sin·is·trorse (sínistrɔrs, sínistrɔrs, sinistrɔ́rs) *adj.* (*bot.*) twining spirally upward from right to left ‖ (of spiral shells) sinistral [fr. L. *sinistrorsus*]

sink (siŋk) **1.** *v. pres. part.* **sink·ing** *past* **sank** (sæŋk) *past part.* **sunk** (sʌŋk), (only in adj. uses) **sunk·en** (sʌ́ŋkən) *v.i.* to move or settle slowly down, *to sink into a chair* ‖ (of a heavenly body) to disappear below the horizon ‖ to slope gradually downwards, *the hills sank to the sea's edge* ‖ to move down through or under water, snow etc. ‖ (of a ship etc.) to go to the bottom of the sea, a river etc. ‖ to become lower in level, *the city is steadily sinking* ‖ (usually with 'in' or 'into') to penetrate, esp. gradually, *the knife sank into his flesh, the facts don't seem to sink into his head* ‖ (with 'into') to drift into a specified condition, e.g. sleep, silence or despair ‖ to become lower according to some scale, *her opinion of him sank* ‖ (of the wind) to die down ‖ (of sound) to drop to a lower tone or pitch ‖ to lose courage or hope, *his heart sank* ‖ (with 'in' and 'into') to go down in social position, condition etc. ‖ to go down in value, amount etc. ‖ (of a sick person) to approach death ‖ (of the cheeks or eye sockets)

CONCISE PRONUNCIATION KEY: **(a)** æ, *cat;* ɑ, *car;* ɔ *fawn;* ei, *snake.* **(e)** e, *hen;* i:, *sheep;* iə, *deer;* ɛə, *bear.* **(i)** i, *fish;* ai, *tiger;* ə:, *bird.* **(o)** o, *ox;* au, *cow;* ou, *goat;* u, *poor;* ɔi, *royal.* **(u)** ʌ, *duck;* u, *bull;* u:, *goose;* ə, *bacillus;* ju:, *cube.* x, *loch;* θ, *think;* ð, *bother;* z, *Zen;* ʒ, *corsage;* dʒ, *savage;* ŋ, *orangutang;* j, *yak;* ʃ, *fish;* tʃ, *fetch;* 'l, *rabble;* 'n, *redden.* Complete pronunciation key appears inside front cover.

to become as if shrunken or hollow ‖ *v.t.* to cause (e.g. a ship) to go to the bottom ‖ to cause to go down to a lower level ‖ to countersink (a screw) ‖ to wreck, ruin (someone or a plan etc.) ‖ to fix in below ground level, *to sink a gatepost* ‖ to make (a well, mineshaft etc.) by digging, drilling etc. ‖ to reduce the intensity, volume etc. of, *she sank her voice to a whisper* ‖ to invest (capital) ‖ to pay off (a debt) ‖ (*billiards*) to pocket ‖ (*golf*) to putt (the ball) into the hole **2.** *n.* a fixed basin of stone, stoneware or metal with a water supply and a drainpipe, esp. one in a kitchen in which tableware is washed ‖ a place of vice or corruption ‖ a preliminary excavation for a shaft, pit etc. ‖ (*geog.*) an area of depressed land, esp. where water has collected to form a saline lake without an outlet ‖ a body or substance by which heat or liquid is dissipated in a thermodynamic or hydrodynamic process **sink·er** *n.* someone or something that causes a sinking ‖ a weight used to sink a fishing line or net etc. [O.E. *sincan*]

sink·hole (síŋkhoul) *n.* a place where drainage collects, esp. with an opening to an underground channel ‖ a place of filth, misery, vice etc.

Sin·kiang-Ui·ghur (ʃínkjáŋwí:gúr) an autonomous region (area 705,950 sq. miles, pop. 13,081,681) of China in central Asia, consisting mainly of the Dzungaria and Tarim basins, separated by the Tien Shan. Capital: Urumchi. People: mainly Turkic (Uighur, Kazak, Kirghiz), with Mongol, Tibetan and other minorities. Religion: mainly Sunni Moslem, with Shi'ite and Buddhist minorities. It is largely desert (*TURFAN, *TAKLA MAKAN), with large oases around Urumchi, Kashgar, Khotan and Yarkand. The inhabitants are nomadic herdsmen and oasis farmers. Livestock: camels, horses, sheep, goats. Crops: cereals, cotton, fruit. Formerly part of Turkestan, it became (1881) a Chinese province

Sin·king (ʃíndʒíŋ) *CHANGCHUN

sinking fund a sum of money formed by periodically setting aside revenue to accumulate at interest, used to reduce a debt

sin·ner (sínər) *n.* someone who sins

Sinn Fein (ʃínféin) an Irish nationalist movement organized (1905) as a political party by Arthur Griffith. It triumphed (1921) when the Irish Free State was set up [Ir. Gael. =we ourselves]

Si·no-Jap·a·nese (sáinoudʒæpəní:z, sínoudʒæpəní:z, sáinoudʒæpəní:s, sínoudʒæpəní:s) *adj.* relating to both China and Japan

Sino-Japanese War either of two wars between China and Japan. The first (1894-5) was fought for control of Korea, spread into Manchuria and resulted in the defeat of China (1895), which recognized the independence of Korea, paid an indemnity, and ceded Formosa, the Pescadores Is and the Liaotung peninsula to Japan. In the second (1931-45), Japan occupied Manchuria (1931), Peking and Tientsin (1937), and captured the eastern coastal region of China (1940). The Japanese bombing of Pearl Harbor (1941) merged the conflict in the 2nd world war

si·no·log·i·cal (sainəlɔ́dʒik'l, sinəlɔ́dʒik'l) *adj.* of sinology [SINOLOGUE]

si·nol·o·gist (sainɔ́lədʒist, sinɔ́lədʒist) *n.* a sinologue [prob. fr. F. *sinologie*, sinology]

si·no·logue (sáinəlɔg, sáinəlɒg, sínəlɔg, sínəlɒg) *n.* a specialist in sinology [F. fr. Gk *Sinai*, the Chinese+*logos*, discourse]

si·nol·o·gy (sainɔ́lədʒi:, sinɔ́lədʒi:) *n.* the study of the language, history and culture of China [prob. fr. F. *sinologie* fr. Gk *Sinai*, the Chinese+*logos*, discourse]

Si·no-Ti·bet·an (sáinoutibét'n, sinoutibét'n) *n.* a group of languages including Chinese, Tibetan and usually Thai

SINS *n.* (*acronym*) for ships inertial navigation system, sonar and guidance system for a submarine to determine a ship's position and speed in relation to the ocean bottom

sin·ta·ki (sintáki:) *n.* circular Greek folk dance with variations by individuals

sin·ter (síntər) **1.** *n.* (*geol.*) a deposit of calcareous or siliceous material precipitated from the water of a lake etc., which was previously held in solution ‖ the product of sintering **2.** *v.t.* to cause to form a fused mass by heating ‖ *v.i.* to become a fused mass from heating [G.]

sintering *n.* (*metallurgy*) process by which fine particles are held together when heated **—sinter** *v.* **—sintered conductor** *n.*

sin·u·ate (sínju:it, sínju:eit) *adj.* (esp. *bot.*, e.g. of the edges of some leaves) bending or winding in and out [fr. L. *sinuare* (*sinuatus*), to bend]

sin·u·a·tion (sinju:éiʃən) *n.* (esp. *bot.*) a bending or winding in and out [fr. L.L. *sinuatio* (*sinuationis*) fr. *sinuare*, to bend]

sin·u·os·i·ty (sinju:ɔ́siti:) *pl.* **sin·u·os·i·ties** *n.* the quality of winding or curving ‖ a curve, bend [F. *sinuosité*]

sin·u·ous (sínju:əs) *adj.* winding, *a sinuous road* ‖ having many curves ‖ (*bot.*) sinuate [fr. L. *sinuosus*]

si·nus (sáinəs) *pl.* **si·nus·es** *n.* one of the air-filled cavities within the bones of the face and skull, in communication with the nose and mouth ‖ (*med.*) a channel for drainage from a pus-filled cavity ‖ (*bot.*) an indentation between the lobes of a leaf [L.=fold, curve]

si·nus·i·tis (sainəsáitis) *n.* (*med.*) inflammation of a sinus, esp. of the skull

si·nus·oi·dal projection (sainəsɔ́id'l) an equal-area representation of the surface of the earth having a straight equator and a straight central meridian that is one half the equator's length. The other lines of longitude are curved. The lines of latitude are straight, and parallel to the equator [F. *sinusoïde*]

sinus ve·no·sus (vənóusəs) *n.* the main cavity of each auricle in the heart ‖ the posterior chamber of the tubular heart of an embryo ‖ (in lower vertebrates, e.g. the frog) a corresponding structure receiving venous blood and opening into the auricle

Siou·an (sú:ən) *n.* a group of North American Indian languages formerly spoken in West central U.S.A., central Canada and parts of Virginia and the Carolinas ‖ the Sioux ‖ a member of the Sioux

Sioux (su:) *pl.* **Sioux** (su:, su:z) *n.* the North American Indian peoples speaking Siouan, esp. the Dakotas ‖ a member of these peoples [F. contr. of *Nadowessioux* fr. Am. Ind. *Nadowessi*, little snake]

Sioux Falls a city (pop. 81,343) in southeastern S. Dakota, a commercial and industrial center and port. Livestock market, meat processing

sip (sip) **1.** *v. pres. part.* **sip·ping** *past* and *past part.* **sipped** *v.t.* to drink by taking in a very slight quantity with the lips, esp. repeatedly ‖ *v.i.* to drink in this way **2.** *n.* a small amount of liquid taken in by the lips ‖ the act of sipping [perh. alteration of SUP (to drink)]

si·phon, sy·phon (sáifən) **1.** *n.* a tube bent so that it has two roughly vertical and parallel legs of unequal length, used to transfer a liquid from a vessel placed at a higher level to a vessel at a lower level. The tube is filled with the liquid (e.g. by suction) and the shorter leg immersed in the liquid to be transferred. The longer leg is placed in or just above the lower vessel. The difference of the pressure in the shorter leg and at the lower end of the longer leg results in a continuous flow ‖ *SYPHON (bottle) ‖ (*zool.*) a tubular part in certain animals, e.g. clams, for drawing in or ejecting liquids **2.** *v.t.* to cause to flow out through a siphon ‖ *v.i.* to flow through a siphon **si·phon·age** *n.* [fr. L. *sipho* (*siphonis*), tube, pipe fr. Gk]

siphon bottle a syphon

si·pho·net (saifənét) *n.* (*zool.*) one of the abdominal tubes used by an aphid to exude honeydew [SIPHON]

si·pho·no·phore (sáifənəfɔr, sáifənəfour, saifɔ́nəfɔr, saifɔ́nəfour) *n.* a member of *Siphonophora*, an order of usually transparent, bright-colored, colonial, marine hydrozoans that float or swim [fr. Mod. L. *Siphonophora* fr. Gk *siphōn*, pipe, tube+*-phoros*, bearer]

si·pho·no·stele (saifɔ́nəsti:l, sáifənousti:l) *n.* (*bot.*) a hollow stele, e.g. in the stem of a fern (cf. PROTOSTELE)

si·phun·cle (sáifʌŋk'l) *n.* (*zool.*) a tube of skin, partly calcareous, connecting the compartments of a cephalopod shell [fr. L. *siphunculus* dim. of *sipho*, siphon]

sip·pet (sípit) *n.* a small piece of fried bread or toast for soaking in soup etc., or used for garnishing ‖ a morsel, *sippets of information* [prob. fr. SOP (piece of bread)]

SIPROS *n.* (*computer acronym*) for simultaneous processing operating system, used in management of computer equipment and programs selection; designed by Control Data Corp.

Si·quei·ros (si:kéirɔs), David Alfaro (1898-1974), Mexican painter. His striking murals and frescoes are violent social protests

sir (sə:r) **1.** *n.* a form of polite address to men ‖ a form of address used in writing to strangers or in business letters ‖ a title preceding the first name of a knight or baronet **2.** *v.t. pres. part.* **sir·ring** *past* and *part part.* **sirred** to address (someone) as sir [shortened from SIRE]

sire (saiər) **1.** *n.* the male parent of a quadruped, esp. a stallion ‖ (*archaic*) a form of address to a king **2.** *v.t. pres. part.* **sir·ing** *past* and *past part.* **sired** (esp. of quadrupeds) to beget [O.F.]

si·ren (sáirən) **1.** *n.* an instrument for producing a loud, penetrating sound as a warning, e.g. a signal for opening and closing a day's work at a factory etc., operated by revolving a perforated disk over a jet of compressed air or steam ‖ (*Gk* and *Roman mythol.*) a woman, or part-woman part-bird, who lured ships onto rocks by enchanting the sailors with her singing ‖ (*pop.*) an extremely seductive woman ‖ a member of *Sirenidae*, a family of eel-shaped amphibians with small forelimbs but without hind limbs or pelvis, having a compressed tail, and gills as well as lungs **2.** *adj.* of or relating to a siren [L.L. fr. L. fr. Gk *Seirēn*]

si·re·ni·an (sairí:ni:ən) **1.** *n.* a sea cow of order *Sirenia* **2.** *adj.* of or relating to such a sea cow [fr. Mod. L. *Sirenia* fr. L. *siren*, a siren]

Sir·i·o·no (síəri:ənou) *pl.* **Sir·i·o·no, Sir·i·o·nos** *n.* a Bolivian people inhabiting the tropical forests of E. Bolivia ‖ a member of this people ‖ their language

Sir·i·us (síri:əs) the brightest star in the sky. It is in *Canis Major*, a southern constellation

sir·loin (sə́:rlɔin) *n.* the upper part of a loin of beef including the meat above and under the bone [fr. O.F. fr. *sur*, over+*longe*, loin]

si·roc·co (sirɔ́kou) *pl.* **si·roc·cos** *n.* a hot, dust-laden wind from N. African deserts reaching S. Europe, esp. Italy, Malta and Sicily [Ital. *sirocco, scirocco* fr. Arab. *sharq*, east]

sirup *SYRUP

si·sal (sáisəl, sísəl) *n.* a strong fiber used for making twine, cordage etc., obtained from the leaves of *Agave sisalana*, fam. *Amaryllidaceae* ‖ this plant, widely cultivated e.g. in Java, E. Africa and Mexico ‖ a similar fiber obtained from various agaves, e.g. henequen

sis·kin (sískin) *n. Spinus spinus*, a small yellowish-green finch of temperate Europe and Asia related to the goldfinch. The male has a black crown and chin [fr. G. dial. *sisschen*]

Sis·ley (si:slei), Alfred (1839-99), French impressionist landscape painter, esp. of river scenes

sis·sy, *Br.* also **cis·sie, cis·sy** (sísi:) *pl.* **sis·sies**, *Br.* also **cis·sies** *n.* (*pop.*) an effeminate boy or man, esp. one who shows fear [shortened fr. SISTER]

sissy bar a support bar behind the rider or passenger of a two-wheeled vehicle

sis·ter (sístər) *n.* a daughter in her relationship to another child of the same parents ‖ (*Br.*) a senior hospital nurse, usually one in charge of a ward ‖ a member of a religious community of women [O.E. *sweoster, swuster*]

sis·ter-ger·man (sístərdʒə́:rmən) *pl.* **sis·ters-ger·man** *n.* one's sister born of the same two parents [SISTER+*german*, akin fr. O.F. *germain*]

sis·ter·hood (sístərhud) *n.* the state of being a sister ‖ the relationship between sisters ‖ a religious community of women

sis·ter-in-law (sístərinlɔ) *pl.* **sis·ters-in-law** *n.* the sister of one's husband or wife, or the wife of one's brother

sis·ter·ly (sístərli:) *adj.* of or like a sister

sister ship one of two or more ships having the same constructional characteristics and usually belonging to the same steamship line

Sis·tine Chapel (sísti:n, sístin, sístain) the pope's private chapel in the Vatican, Rome, built by Sixtus IV and famous for Michelangelo's frescoes

sis·trum (sístrəm) *pl.* **sis·trums, sis·tra** (sístrə) *n.* an ancient Egyptian percussion instrument of metal rings which rattled against a metal frame when jangled [L. fr. Gk *seistron*]

Sis·y·phus (sísəfəs) (*mythol.*) king of Corinth, feared for his cruelty and acts of brigandage. He was condemned in Hades eternally to push a rock to the top of a hill. It always rolled down again short of the top

sit (sit) **1.** *v. pres. part.* **sit·ting** *past* and *past part.* **sat** (sæt) *v.i.* to rest the body on the buttocks ‖ (of birds and many other animals) to rest with the legs huddled up to the body ‖ (of birds) to stay covering eggs so as to hatch them ‖ to be situated, *the cottage sits in a hollow* ‖ to take up,

CONCISE PRONUNCIATION KEY: (a) æ, *cat*; ɑ, *car*; ɔ *fawn*; ei, *snake*. (e) e, *hen*; i:, *sheep*; iə, *deer*; εə, *bear*. (i) i, *fish*; ai, *tiger*; ə:, *bird*. (o) o, *ox*; au, *cow*; ou, *goat*; u, *poor*; ɔi, *royal*. (u) ʌ, *duck*; u, *bull*; u:, *goose*; ə, *bacillus*; ju:, *cube*. x, *loch*; θ, *think*; ð, *bother*; z, *Zen*; ʒ, *corsage*; dʒ, *savage*; ŋ, *orangutang*; j, *yak*; ʃ, *fish*; tʃ, *fetch*; 'l, *rabble*; 'n, *redden*. Complete pronunciation key appears inside front cover.

or be in, a position to be painted, *to sit for a portrait* ‖ (of clothes) to fit (well or badly), esp. across the shoulders ‖ (*fig.*) to rest in a specified way, *his new authority sits heavily on him* ‖ (of courts, parliament, committees etc.) to be in session or to hold sessions ‖ to have a position as a member, *he sits on the board* ‖ (esp. *Br.*) to undergo an examination as candidate, *to sit for one's finals* ‖ to remain in the same condition, esp. idle or unused, *the scooter is sitting by the roadside* ‖ to look after a child, invalid etc. on behalf of a parent etc. ‖ (of the wind) to blow from a specified quarter ‖ *v.t.* to cause (someone) to take a seat, esp. to position (someone) at table, *sit him on her left* ‖ to place (oneself) in a sitting posture ‖ to ride (a horse), esp. with respect to carriage or capacity to stay in the saddle ‖ (*Br.*) to undergo (a written examination) ‖ to accommodate on chairs, *the table sits eight* ‖ **to sit down** to take a seat **to sit down under** (*Br.*) to accept without protest **to sit on** to consider (a case) with a view to deciding it ‖ (*pop.*) to cause to be less bumptious **to sit out** to choose not to dance (a dance) ‖ to stay until the end of ‖ to refrain from dancing **to sit up** to move from a lying to a sitting position ‖ to sit with one's back straight and shoulders held back ‖ to stay up late and not go to bed ‖ (of some animals, esp. a dog) to rest on its haunches with the body upright and front paws raised, esp. in order to beg for food [O.E. *sittan*]

si·tar (sitár) *n.* a lute-like instrument of India with a long fretted neck, two resonating gourds, and a set of sympathetic strings below the playing strings [Hindi *sitār*]

sit·com (sítkɒm) *n.* (*acronym*) for situation comedy, a television or radio series of usu. unconnected episodes with a continuing background and the same characters *Cf* SOAP OPERA

sit-down strike (sítdaun) a strike in which workers refuse to go away from their place of work

site (sait) **1.** *n.* the geographical situation in the past, present, or future of a town or building, *the site of ancient Carthage, a site for the new factory* ‖ the scene of a specified event, *the exact site of the battle* **2.** *v.t. pres. part.* **sit·ing** *past* and *past part.* **sit·ed** to fix in a location [A.F. or fr. L. *situs*]

sit-in (sítin) *n.* a group protest in which participants sit down in a public place, e.g. a racially segregated restaurant and stay there until their demands are considered or until they are removed by force

Sit·ka (sítkə) a town (pop. 7,803) on an island in the Alexander Archipelago off S.E. Alaska. In the 19th c. it was the headquarters of Russian America and the chief commercial center on the Pacific coast of North America. It was the capital of Alaska (1867-1900) after the U.S.A. purchased it

sit·ter (sítər) *n.* someone who poses for a portrait ‖ a baby-sitter ‖ a broody hen ‖ (esp. *Br., pop.*) an easy target

sit·ting (sítiŋ) **1.** *n.* the act of someone who sits ‖ a continuous period of time during which one sits over some occupation, *she read the novel at one sitting* ‖ the act of posing for a portrait, *the portrait required three sittings* ‖ a meeting, esp. of parliament or a court of law ‖ any of two or more consecutive eating sessions served in a canteen, dining room etc. too small to seat all the diners at one time ‖ a brooding of a hen on eggs ‖ the clutch of eggs on which a broody hen is sitting **2.** *adj.* being in office ‖ (of a target) very easy to hit ‖ (of a hen) on a clutch of eggs to hatch them ‖ (*Br.*, of a tenant) in occupancy

Sitting Bull (c. 1831-90), North American Indian warrior and principal chief of the Sioux nation. His refusal to be confined to a reservation led to many battles with the U.S. Army, notably Little Bighorn (1876). Starved into submission, he agreed to live (from 1883) on a reservation in S. Dakota. He was killed while being arrested for inciting the Sioux against the white man, in protest against expropriation of tribal lands

sitting room a living room in a house, furnished for sitting at leisure or sharing informal family activities

sit·u·ate (sítʃu:eit) *pres. part.* **sit·u·at·ing** *past* and *past part.* **sit·u·at·ed** *v.t.* to locate or site ‖ to fix in a particular set of circumstances or category, *she situates her characters in upper middle-class society* **sit·u·at·ed** *adj.* located or sited, *a house situated on a hill* ‖ placed in particular circumstances, *how are they situated financially?* [fr. M.L. *situare* (*situatus*), to place]

sit·u·a·tion (sitʃu:éiʃən) *n.* the manner in which something is situated, esp. with regard to aspect, view, accessibility etc., *the house has a fine situation* ‖ the circumstances in which someone is placed ‖ state of affairs, *the political situation*, esp. a crucial state of affairs, *what a situation to be in !* ‖ a paid occupation, esp. one in a household as maid, governess etc. (wider usage being restricted to journal advertisements) [F. or fr. M.L. *situatio* (*situationis*)]

situation ethics thesis that what is right in a moral problem is more dependent on the immediate situation than on a general code

situation room (*mil.*) a center where reports are received on a current operation

sit-up (sítʌp) *n.* an exercise in which a person lying on his back raises his torso until he is in a sitting position, without bending his knees

sitz bath (sits, zits) a bath tub in which one sits up and cannot recline, used esp. in medical therapy ‖ a bath so taken [part trans. fr. G. *Sitzbad* fr. *sitzen*, to sit]

sitz·fleisch (sítsflaiʃ) *n.* (*German;* usu. italics) ability to sit and wait

SI units (*phys. abbr.*) for Système International d' Unités, i.e., International System of Units, for length, time, mass, electric current, temperature, luminous intensity, and molecular weight; recommended by General Conference on Weights and Measures

Si·va, Shi·va (ʃí:və) the Hindu god of destruction and rebirth, the third god of the Hindu trinity (*VISHNU, *BRAHMA) [Skr.=the auspicious one]

Si·va·ji (sivádʒi:) (1627-80), Maratha leader. He established (1674) the Maratha empire

Si·vas (si:vás) a city (pop. 172,864) in N. central Turkey on the Kizil Irmak: textiles, copper mining. Mosque (12th c.)

Si·wa·lik Hills (si:wálik) a range (averaging 3,000 ft) of foothills of the Himalayas, running through N.W. India and S.W. Nepal, remarkable for their fossil beds

six (siks) **1.** *adj.* being one more than five (*NUMBER TABLE) **2.** *n.* twice three ‖ the cardinal number representing this (6, VI) ‖ six o'clock ‖ a playing card (domino etc.) marked with six symbols ‖ (*cricket*) a hit from which six runs are scored or made ‖ a team of six members, esp. in rowing or ice hockey **at sixes and sevens** in a state of confusion [O.E. *sex, six*]

Six-Day War (síksdei) the 1967 war between Egypt, Syria, Jordan and Israel

Six, les (leisi:s) a group of young musicians including Darius Milhaud, Arthur Honegger, Francis Poulenc, Georges Auric, Louis Durey and Germaine Tailleferre, who in 1918 in France banded together in reaction against the influence of Debussy and sought greater simplicity in music. They were influenced by Erik Satie

six·pence (síkspəns) *n.* (*Br.*) the sum represented by six pennies ‖ (*Br.*) a coin worth 2½ new pence

six-shoot·er (síksʃú:tər) *n.* a revolver that can be fired six times without reloading

sixte (sikst) *n.* (*fencing*) the sixth of eight parrying positions [F.]

six·teen (sikstí:n) **1.** *adj.* being one more than 15 (*NUMBER TABLE) **2.** *n.* ten plus six ‖ the cardinal number representing this (16, XVI) [O.E. *syxtine, sixtyne, sextyne*]

six·teen·mo (sikstí:nmou) *pl.* **six·teen·mos** *n.* a sextodecimo (*abbr.* 16mo)

six·teenth (sikstí:nθ) **1.** *adj.* being number 16 in a series (*NUMBER TABLE) ‖ being one of the 16 equal parts of anything **2.** *n.* the person or thing next after the 15th ‖ one of 16 equal parts of anything (1/16) ‖ the 16th day of a month

Sixteenth Amendment (1913) an amendment to the U.S. Constitution that established the federal income tax. The levying of taxes as provided in the Constitution (Article 1, Sections 2 and 9) was controversial and caused many disputes between the federal government and the states. The 16th Amendment accorded Congress the right to tax incomes without regard to state apportionment or census

sixteenth note (*mus., Am.=Br.* semiquaver) a note (symbol 𝅘𝅥𝅯) equal in duration to half an eighth note

sixth (siksθ) **1.** *adj.* being number six in a series (*NUMBER TABLE) ‖ being one of the six equal parts of anything **2.** *n.* the person or thing next after the fifth ‖ one of six equal parts of anything (1/6) ‖ the sixth day of a month ‖ (*mus.*) the note six steps above or below a given note in a diatonic scale, inclusive of both notes ‖ (*mus.*) the interval between these notes ‖ (*mus.*) a combination of these notes **3.** *adv.* in the sixth place ‖ (followed by a superlative) except five, *the sixth biggest* [O.E. *sixta*]

Sixth Amendment (1791) an amendment to the U.S. Constitution, part of the Bill of Rights, that guarantees a speedy trial, an impartial jury and other rights to those accused in a criminal proceeding

six·ti·eth (síksti:iθ) **1.** *adj.* being number 60 in a series (*NUMBER TABLE) ‖ being one of the 60 equal parts of anything **2.** *n.* the person or thing next after the 59th ‖ one of 60 equal parts of anything (1/60) [O.E. *sixteogotha*]

Six·tus IV (síkstəs) (Francesco della Rovere, 1414-84), pope (1471-84). A patron of letters and the arts, he sponsored the building of the Sistine Chapel. He consented to the establishment of the Inquisition in Spain

Sixtus V (Felice Peretti, 1521-90), pope (1585-90). He repressed civil disorder in the Papal States and was responsible for much new building in Rome

six·ty (síksti:) **1.** *adj.* being ten more than 50 (*NUMBER TABLE) **2.** *pl.* **six·ties** *n.* six times ten ‖ the cardinal number representing this (60, LX) **the sixties** (of temperature, a person's age, a century etc.) the span 60-9 [O.E. *siextig, syxtig, sextig*]

six·ty-fourth note (síksti:fɔ́rθ, síksti:fóurθ) (*mus., Am.=Br.* hemidemisemiquaver) a note equal in duration to half a thirty-second note

siz·a·ble, size·a·ble (sáizəb'l) *adj.* rather large, *a sizable majority*

siz·ar (sáizər) *n.* (*Br.*) the title of certain scholars in certain colleges at Cambridge University (England) and Trinity College (Dublin) [fr. SIZE n. (obs.) a portion of bread or ale]

size (saiz) **1.** *n.* the length, area, volume or dimensions of something or someone as compared with a specific or arbitrary standard, *this book is twice the size of that, a crowd of considerable size* ‖ one of a number of standards used for such comparison, *size 9 shoes* ‖ the total quantity, *the size of an order* ‖ magnitude, *bears of some size* ‖ (of things) scope, *defense projects of astounding size* ‖ intellectual capacity and force of character, *it is not a job for a man of his size* ‖ (*pop.*) true account, *that's about the size of it* **of a size** of equal size **2.** *v.t. pres. part.* **siz·ing** *past* and *past part.* **sized** to sort or arrange according to size, *to size potatoes* ‖ to make in a certain size or in a series of certain sizes **to size up** to estimate the size of ‖ to estimate the character or qualities of (someone) ‖ to estimate the importance or nature of (something) ‖ to compare in respect to size [O.F. *sise, cise* fr. *assise*, assize]

size **1.** *n.* a thin gelatinous liquid used in glazing or for stiffening paper, textiles etc. **2.** *v.t. pres. part.* **siz·ing** *past* and *past part.* **sized** to apply this liquid to **siz·ing** *n.* liquid size ‖ the process of applying it [perh. fr. SIZE n.]

sizeable *SIZABLE

siz·zle (síz'l) **1.** *v.i. pres. part.* **siz·zling** *past* and *past part.* **siz·zled** to make a hissing sound, esp. in being fried **2.** *n.* a noise so made **siz·zling** *adj.* very hot [imit.]

Sjael·land (ʃéllɑn) *ZEALAND

Ska·dar·sko (skádɑrskɔ) *SHKODËR

Skag·er·rak (skǽgəræk, skágərɑk) an arm (150 miles long, 80 miles wide) of the North Sea between Denmark, Norway and W. Sweden

skald, scald (skɔld, skɑld) *n.* a composer of elaborate courtly poetry in Old Norse, late 8th c. The poetry, notable for its metrical virtuosity, reached its highest point in Iceland (10th-11th cc.) **skáld·ic, scáld·ic** *adj.* [O.N., Icel. *skāld*, origin unknown]

skat (skɑt, skæt) *n.* a card game played by three people using 32 cards, bearing some resemblance to piquet [G.]

skate (skeit) *pl.* **skates, skate** *n.* a member of *Rajidae*, a family of cartilaginous fish related to rays, esp. genus *Raja*. Skates are peculiarly flattened, and rather rhomboidal in outline, having the mouth at one corner of a long snout and the anus at the opposite corner of the body [O.N. *skata*]

skate **1.** *n.* an ice skate ‖ a roller skate **2.** *v. pres. part.* **skat·ing** *past* and *past part.* **skat·ed** *v.i.* to move or glide along on skates ‖ *v.t.* to go (one's way or a distance) on skates [fr. Du. *schaats* fr. O.N.F. *escache*, stilt]

skate·board (skéitbɔrd, skéitbourd) *n.* a piece of wood mounted on skate wheels and used by children for riding on

skating rink an area of ice artificially produced and preserved for ice skating ‖ an area of other hard, smooth surface used for roller skating

ske·dad·dle (skidǽd'l) **1.** *v.i. pres. part.* **ske·dad·dling** *past* and *past part.* **ske·dad·dled** (*pop.*) to go away very quickly, run off **2.** *n.* (*pop.*) a hurried flight [etym. doubtful]

skeet (ski:t) *n.* trapshooting at targets which simulate the speed and angle of flight of birds

skein (skein) *n.* a length of yarn, thread, wool or silk, looped many times and then twisted ‖ a flock of wild geese in flight ‖ something thought of as full of coils and windings, *the skein of events* [fr. O.F. *escaigne*, origin unknown]

skel·e·tal (skélit'l) *adj.* of, relating to or being part of a skeleton ‖ like a skeleton

skeletal muscle a muscle attached to the skeleton (cf. SMOOTH MUSCLE, cf. CARDIAC MUSCLE, cf. STRIATED MUSCLE)

skel·e·ton (skélitən) *n.* a hard framework, internal or external, supporting or protecting the soft tissues and organs of a man, animal or plant. Vertebrates have an endoskeleton consisting mainly of cartilage at first, replaced by bone during growth. Invertebrates have an exoskeleton which is often calcareous or chitinous ‖ the dried bones of a dead man or animal, esp. assembled as in life ‖ a framework, e.g. of a building ‖ the essential nucleus of an organization, esp. what remains after the period of full activity is over ‖ an outline, *the skeleton of a novel* ‖ a very thin person or animal **a skeleton in the closet** (*Br.* **cupboard**) a secret of which a family is ashamed [Mod. L. *sceleton, skeleton* fr. Gk *skeleton* (*sōma*), dried up (body)]

skeleton key a key made so as to fit many locks

skeleton shrimp a member of *Caprella* or a related genus of amphipod crustaceans. They have a cylindrical body and swim by wriggling movements

Skel·ton (skéltən), John (c. 1460-1529), English poet and satirist, esp. of the clergy. He used an alliterative, shortlined, much-rhyming, tumbling verse (Skeltonics)

skep (skep) *n.* any of various kinds of farm basket ‖ any of these as a measure of quantity ‖ a straw or wicker beehive [O.N. *skeppa*]

skep·sis, esp. *Br.* **scep·sis** (sképsis) *n.* philosophical skepticism [Gk *skepsis*, inquiry, doubt]

skep·tic, esp. *Br.* **scep·tic** (sképtik) *n.* a person who doubts the truth of anything, esp. of that which others accept as true **Skep·tic,** esp. *Br.* **Scep·tic** (*hist.*) a member of the Greek philosophical school founded by Pyrrho **skép·ti·cal,** esp. *Br.* **scép·ti·cal** *adj.* [fr. F. *sceptique* or L.L. *scepticus* fr. Gk]

skep·ti·cism, esp. *Br.* **scep·ti·cism** (sképtisizəm) *n.* an attitude of doubt ‖ the philosophical view that nothing can be known with certainty [fr. Mod. L. *scepticismus* fr. L.L. *scepticus*, skeptic]

sketch (sketʃ) **1.** *n.* a quickly made drawing ‖ a drawing preliminary to more careful work ‖ a brief, slight story, account or description ‖ a preliminary outline of a literary work ‖ a slight, short (usually one-scene) comedy, often musical ‖ a descriptive musical composition of one movement ‖ (*pop., old-fash.*) someone who looks ridiculous or one whose jokes and antics cause general hilarity **2.** *v.t.* to make a sketch of ‖ *v.i.* to make a sketch or sketches [fr. Du. *schets* or G. *skizze* fr. Ital. fr. L. prob. fr. Gk]

sketch·book (skétʃbuk) *n.* leaves of drawing paper arranged in a book so as to be detachable ‖ a notebook of finished sketches ‖ a collection of short literary sketches

sketch·i·ly (skétʃili:) *adv.* in a sketchy manner

sketch·i·ness (skétʃi:nis) *n.* the state or quality of being sketchy

sketch·y (skétʃi:) *comp.* **sketch·i·er** *superl.* **sketch·i·est** *adj.* lacking detail, slight, *a sketchy account*

skeu·o·mor·phic (skju:oumɔ́rfik) *adj.* of an object copied in a form materially different from its original, e.g., a candy ax, a hammer reproduced in clay —**skeumorph** *n.* the object —**skeumorphism** *n.* the copying

skew (skju:) **1.** *v.t.* to cut or set slantingly ‖ to give a bias to, *the account was skewed in favor of the police* ‖ (*statistics*) to cause (a frequency distribution or its curve) to lack symmetry ‖ (*pop.*) to twist, *to skew one's head around* ‖ *v.i.* to twist around **2.** *adj.* running at an angle, oblique ‖ (*statistics*, of a frequency distribution or its curve) lacking symmetry **3.** *n.* a slant, oblique direction ‖ (in cloth) a deviation from the proper straight line of a weave [fr. O.N.F. *eskiuwer, eskiuer, escuer*]

skew·back (skjú:bæk) *n.* a sloping face of masonry taking the thrust of an arch

skew·bald (skjú:bɔld) **1.** *adj.* (of horses) having patches of white and another color, esp. other than black **2.** *n.* a skewbald horse (cf. PIEBALD)

skew·er (skjú:ər) **1.** *n.* a metal or wooden pin for holding meat together while cooking **2.** *v.t.* to pierce with, or as if with, a skewer [var. of SKIVER]

skew·eyed (skjú:aid) *adj.* (*Br.*) squinting

ski (ski:) **1.** *pl.* **skis, ski** *n.* one of a pair of long, narrow, wooden, metal or plastic strips which curve up and taper to a point at the front end. They are used for gliding downhill over snow at speeds up to 50 m.p.h. or more ‖ a similar device used in water-skiing **2.** *v.i. pres. part.* **ski·ing** *past* and *past part.* **skied** to move on skis [Norw.]

ski·bob (skí:bɒb) *n.* (*sports*) a bicyclelike sled mounted on two short skis, one behind the other, the forward ski maneuverable by handbars, an upholstered seat over the rear ski, with rider balanced by miniature skis —**skibob** *v.* —**skibobber** *n.*

skid (skid) **1.** *n.* a sideways slip or slide of a wheel through failure to grip the ground ‖ a block of wood or metal to prevent a wheel from turning, esp. on a slope ‖ one of a pair or set of bars etc. down which things can be slid or rolled ‖ (*aeron.*) a runner used as part of an airplane's landing gear ‖ (*naut.*, esp. *pl.*) a wooden bar hung over a ship's side to protect her when cargo is loaded or unloaded ‖ one of a number of timbers etc. used to shore up a boat, construction etc. **2.** *v. pres. part.* **skid·ding** *past* and *past part.* **skid·ded** *v.i.* (of a wheel) to slide without gripping, e.g. on slippery ground ‖ to slide sideways ‖ *v.t.* to use skids on for protecting, moving or checking movement ‖ to cause to slip sideways [etym. doubtful]

skid·board·ing (skídbɔrdiŋ) *n.* surfing on a coated plywood disk, introduced in England in 1960

ski-doo (skidú:) *n.* (*Br.*) ski-scooter, motorized snow-ice vehicle with endless tracks in rear and movable skis in front

skid pad a slick area of oiled asphalt used to test motor vehicles for skidding potential

ski·er (skí:ər) *n.* someone who skis

skiff (skif) *n.* a small rowing boat [fr. F. *esquif*, Span. or Port. *esquife* or Ital. *schifo*]

skif·fle (skíf'l) *n.* (*Br.*) mixture of rock 'n' roll and country music, with a blues rhythm, played on nonstandard, usu. homemade, instruments, e.g., washboards, combs, furniture; popular in English coffee shops during late 1950s

ski·jor·ing (skí:jɔriŋ) *n.* competitive skiing in which competitors are pulled by horses or motor vehicles

ski jump a jump made on skis ‖ a course prepared for jumping on skis and furnished with an elevated take-off platform or mound

skilful *SKILLFUL

ski lift a device consisting of a motordriven, overhead, endless cable with suspended seats for carrying skiers or sightseers up a mountain slope (cf. SKI TOW)

skill (skil) *n.* ability to do something well, esp. as the result of long practical experience ‖ a particular technique, *the work calls for various skills* ‖ tact, *to manage a person with skill* ‖ **skilled** *adj.* having skill ‖ requiring skilled workmen, *skilled trades* [O.N. *skil*, discernment]

skil·let (skílit) *n.* a frying pan ‖ (*Br.*) a small long-handled saucepan usually with short legs [origin unknown]

skill·ful, esp. *Br.* **skil·ful** (skílfəl) *adj.* having, showing or done with skill

skim (skim) **1.** *v. pres. part.* **skim·ming** *past* and *past part.* **skimmed** *v.t.* to remove floating matter from the surface of (a liquid) ‖ to throw (a stone) so that it skips across a surface of water ‖ to pass lightly over, *to skim the ground* ‖ to read superficially or hastily, *to skim the headlines* ‖ to form a thin covering over ‖ *v.i.* to go fast and smoothly on or just above some surface, *skimming along at treetop height* ‖ to make a hasty superficial reading, *to skim through an index* ‖ to become coated with a thin covering **2.** *n.* the act of skimming ‖ skim milk ‖ a thin covering ‖ the practice in health programs paid on a prepayment or capitation basis of seeking to enroll only the healthiest people as a way of controlling costs ‖ the practice in such of denying or delaying the provision of services to enrolled members as a way of controlling costs ‖ the practice of removing a portion of cash receipts from an accounting for tax evasion or cheating ‖ the use of a machine to remove oil or scum from the surface of bodies of water [fr. O.F. *escumer*]

skim·board (skímbɔrd) *n.* (*surfing*) a board, usu. circular, for skimming over shallow water

skim·mer (skímər) *n.* an implement, esp. a perforated, flat ladle, used for skimming liquids ‖ a member of *Rhynchops*, a genus of North American birds that skim over the water and scoop up small fish

skim milk milk from which the cream has been removed

skimp (skimp) **1.** *v.t.* to allow an inadequate or hardly adequate quantity of (something), *she skimped the material for the curtains* ‖ to keep (someone) in short supply, *they are skimped for pocket money* ‖ to do (a piece of work) without proper care and effort ‖ *v.i.* to economize, esp. by making do on short supplies **skimp·i·ly** *adv.* **skimp·i·ness** *n.* **skimp·y** *comp.* **skimp·i·er** *superl.* **skimp·i·est** *adj.* unsatisfactory because of insufficiency in some respect, e.g. short on material, *skimpy curtains* [origin unknown]

skim sweeping (*mil.*) in naval mine warfare, the technique of wire sweeping to a fixed depth above deep-laid mines to cut any mines shallow enough to endanger shipping

skin (skin) **1.** *n.* the membrane, of complex structure, which forms the outer covering of a human or animal body, or one of the layers of which it is composed (*EPIDERMIS, *DERMIS) ‖ such a membrane of an animal, esp. a small animal (cf. HIDE), when removed from the body, with or without the hair ‖ a container made of animal skin, e.g. a wine skin ‖ the outer covering of something, e.g. of a fruit, ship etc. ‖ an elastic film resembling skin, e.g. that forming on the surface of boiled milk **by the skin of one's teeth** with no margin to spare, *he escaped by the skin of his teeth* **to get under (someone's) skin** (*pop.*) to have an irritating effect on someone) **to save one's skin** to avoid capture, death, punishment or injury **2.** *v. pres. part.* **skin·ning** *past* and *past part.* **skinned** *v.t.* to provide with a covering of skin ‖ to remove the skin from, *to skin a rabbit* ‖ (with 'off') to strip off (close-fitting clothes) ‖ (*pop.*) to take all the money or other property from ‖ *v.i.* (e.g. of a wound when healing, or milk when boiled) to acquire a skin [O.N. *skinn*]

—The human skin is self-repairing, heat-resistant and water-resistant, and elastic. It serves as a protection for the flesh and bones. It has pores used for breathing and others used for perspiring, thus stabilizing bodily temperature. The inner skin, fed from small blood vessels, is the seat of nerve ends, through which the sense of touch operates. The hairs on the skin increase its heat-insulating and touch-sensitive properties

skin-deep (skíndí:p) *adj.* (of wounds) slight, affecting the skin only ‖ (of experiences, emotions etc.) not affecting a person at all deeply

skin diver someone who engages in skin diving

skin diving the sport of underwater swimming with a light, self-contained oxygen unit, goggles and rubber flippers

skin effect (*elec.*) the tendency of high-frequency alternating current to have greater density at the outer surface of a conductor than in the center, resulting in increased resistance

skin flick (*slang*) a motion picture containing much nudity; pornographic movie

skin·flint (skínflint) *n.* a mean, miserly person

skin game (*pop.*) a fraudulent trick or game of chance

skin·head (skínhed) *n.* (*Br.*) a young working-class street tough with cropped hair —**skinheadism** *n. also* agro-boy

skink (skiŋk) *n.* a member of *Scincidae*, a family of short-limbed lizards that creep or burrow. They are found in sandy desert areas [obs. F. *scinc* or fr. L. *scincus* fr. Gk]

Skin·ner (skínər), B(urrhus) F(rederick) (1904-), U.S. psychologist, developer of the Skinner Box for his use in the study of behaviorism. He developed the theory of conditioning of behavior by reinforcement with associative rewards.

His works include 'Science and Human Behavior' (1953), 'Verbal Behavior' (1957), 'Technology of Teaching' (1968) and 'Beyond Freedom and Dignity' (1971)

skinner *n.* someone who strips skins or prepares them for market ‖ (*pop.*) a swindler

Skinner box (*psych.*) a device used in training animals to press levers in order to gain a reward or avoid a punishment, developed by B. F. Skinner *Cf* SKINNERIAN

Skin·ner·i·an (skinéri:ən) *adj.* (*psych.*) of the behavior-modification theories (effected by means of rewards and reinforcements) developed by American psychologist B. F. Skinner *Cf* BEHAVIOR MODIFICATION, MOTIVATION HYGIENE, MOTIVATION RESEARCH, SKINNER BOX

skin·ni·ness (skíni:nis) *n.* the state or quality of being skinny

skin·ny (skíni:) *comp.* **skin·ni·er** *superl.* **skin·ni·est** *adj.* thin, with no superfluous fat

skin·ny-dip (skíni:dip) *v.* to swim in the nude —**skinny-dipping** *n.*

skin paint (*mil.*) a radar indication caused by the radar signal reflected by an object

skin-pop·ping or **skin-pop** (skínpɒpiŋ) *v.* (*slang*) a subcutaneous injection of a drug —**skin-pop** *v.* —**skin-popper** *n.* *Cf* MAINLINING

skin·tight (skintáit) *adj.* (of clothes) fitting closely to the body

skin tracking (*mil.*) the tracking of an object by means of a skin paint

skip (skip) **1.** *v. pres. part.* **skip·ping** *past* and *past part.* **skipped** *v.i.* (of a person) to move along with a series of short, quick hops, first on one foot then on the other ‖ (of a lamb) to cavort with tense, springy movements ‖ (*Br.*) to jump rope ‖ to go over the top of with a single hop, *to skip over a fence* ‖ to turn one's attention quickly, *to skip to another question* ‖ to read through a text hastily, omitting whole sections ‖ to omit whole sections, *the story skips to 20 years later* ‖ (of a missile) to skim along, grazing and jumping off a surface ‖ (*pop.*) to disappear quickly and secretly, *the bookie had skipped* ‖ *v.t.* to go up faster than is normal in a ladder of promotion by jumping (the grade next above one's own) and going straight to the one above that, *to skip a class in school* ‖ to omit deliberately to do (something normally done regularly), *they skipped the weekly visit this Sunday* ‖ to omit to attend, *to skip a lecture* ‖ to omit to read, notice or mention (something) ‖ to cause (a stone) to bounce on the surface of water by skimming it ‖ (*pop.*) to leave (town) quickly and secretly, esp. when wanted by the police or a creditor **2.** *n.* the act of skipping ‖ an omission (esp. in reading) [M.E. *skippen* prob. of Scand. origin]

skip *n.* the captain of a side in some games, e.g. lawn bowling or curling [shortened fr. SKIPPER]

skip *n.* a cage in which men or materials are raised or lowered in mines [VAR. of SKEP, (obs.) a skip]

skip bombing (*mil.*) a method of aerial bombing in which a bomb is released from such a low altitude that it slides or glances along the surface of the water or ground and strikes the target —**skip bomb** *v.*

skip distance (*radio*) the minimum distance at which waves from a transmitter, reflected from the Kennelly-Heaviside layer, can be received

skip·jack (skípdʒæk) *pl.* **skip·jacks, skip·jack** *n.* any of several kinds of tropical or subtropical fish which play near the surface of the water and often leap out of it ‖ an elater (beetle)

skip·per (skípər) **1.** *n.* the captain or master of any small vessel ‖ the chief pilot of an aircraft ‖ (*pop.*) someone who leads or directs, esp. in games **2.** *v.t.* to act as skipper of [fr. M.Du. or M.L.G. *schipper*]

skipping rope (*Br.*) a jump rope

skip rope a jump rope

skirl (skə:rl) **1.** *n.* the shrill, musical sound characteristic of bagpipes **2.** *v.i.* to make this sound [prob. of Scand. origin]

skir·mish (skə́:rmiʃ) *n.* a brief fight between small forces of soldiers ‖ a slight quarrel or argument [fr. O.F. *escaramuche*]

skirmish *v.i.* to take part in a skirmish [fr. O.F. *escaramucher* fr. Ital. and O. F. *eskirmir* (*eskirmiss*) fr. O.H.G.]

skirr (skə:r) **1.** *v.i.* to move, esp. to fly hastily, with a rushing sound **2.** *n.* the sound so made [etym. doubtful]

skir·ret (skírit) *n. Sium sisarum,* fam. *Umbelliferae,* an Asiatic plant, a perennial species of which is grown in Europe as an annual producing bunched, grayish, edible tuberous roots [M.E. *skirwhit* alt. of O.F. *eschervis*]

skirt (skə:rt) **1.** *n.* a woman's outer garment hanging from the waist ‖ the part of a coat, petticoat or dress that hangs from the waist ‖ anything hanging like a skirt, e.g. one of the flaps at the side of a saddle **2.** *v.i.* to be on or move around the edge, *the road skirts around the park* ‖ *v.t.* to surround or be situated along, *woods skirt the town on all sides* ‖ to move around or at a distance from, esp. to avoid danger or detection, *the soldiers skirted the town* [O.N. *skyrta,* shirt]

skirting board (*Br.*) a baseboard

skish (skiʃ) *n.* (*angling*) competition using a standard plug cast twice at each of 10 targets

skit (skit) *n.* a short burlesque or satirical story or theatrical sketch [fr. older *skit,* to taunt, prob. fr. O.N.]

ski touring *n.* cross-country touring on skis

ski tow a power-driven endless cable which skiers grasp to be hauled up a short mountain slope (cf. SKI LIFT)

skit·ter (skítər) *v.i.* (of small animals or children) to scurry ‖ (e.g. of ducks landing in water) to skim along the surface ‖ to draw bait along the surface of the water with twitches of the line [fr. older *skit,* to jump or dart around, of Scand. origin]

skit·tish (skítiʃ) *adj.* (of a person) playful, esp. in a coy way ‖ (of a horse) nervous, restive and easily frightened

skit·tle (skít'l) **1.** *n.* a bottle-shaped piece of wood bowled at in English ninepins or tenpins ‖ (*pl.,* construed as sing.) English ninepins **2.** *v.t. pres. part.* **skit·tling** *past* and *past part.* **skit·tled** to knock down (a skittle) ‖ (*cricket,* with 'out') to dismiss (batsmen) in quick succession [origin unknown]

skive (skaiv) *pres. part.* **skiv·ing** *past* and *past part.* **skived** *v.t.* to cut off (leather, rubber etc.) in thin layers **skiv·er** *n.* a knife or machine for skiving ‖ thin, soft, dressed leather from the grain side of a sheepskin, tanned in sumac and dyed [O.N. *skīfa*]

ski·wear (skí:wɛər) *n.* clothing designed to be worn while skiing

Skop·je (skɔ́pje) (or Skoplje, *Turk.* Üsküb) the capital (pop. 312,092) of Macedonia, Yugoslavia, a communications and commercial center. The old (medieval and Turkish) city was destroyed by earthquake (1963). University

sku·a (skjú:ə) *n.* a member of *Stercorariidae,* a family of large (18-24 ins), dark, hawklike seabirds of northern climates, with a white streak on the wing and central elongated tail feathers. They steal the prey of other birds [fr. Faroese *skūgvur*]

skul·dug·ger·y (skʌldʌ́gəri:) *n.* trickery, dishonest dealings [Scot. *sculdudrie*]

skulk (skʌlk) *v.i.* to hang around, under cover of doorways etc., in a sinister way or to avoid detection [M.E. *skulken* prob. of Scand. origin]

skull (skʌl) *n.* the bony covering of the head of a vertebrate that encloses the brain and the principal sense organs and consists of the cranium, jaws, and sockets for eyes, ears and nose ‖ (*pop.*) the mind of someone regarded as very obtuse [etym. doubtful]

skull and crossbones an emblem of death, having a skull surmounting crossed thighbones, formerly associated with pirate flags and now used in danger signs

skull·cap (skʌ́lkæp) *n.* a small, brimless, close-fitting cap

skunk (skʌŋk) **1.** *pl.* **skunks, skunk** *n.* any of various North American omnivorous mammals constituting a subfamily of *Mustelidae.* They are bushy-tailed, are striped black and white, and are about the size of a cat. They spray a stink from a secretion of the anal glands when they are attacked or fear attack. They are hunted for their fur ‖ the fur of any of these animals ‖ (*pop.*) a contemptible person **2.** *v.t.* (*pop.*) to defeat utterly (esp. an opponent at cards, so that he makes no score) [fr. Am. Indian *segankw* or *segongw*]

skunk cabbage *Symplocarpus foetidus,* fam. *Araceae,* a perennial plant growing in eastern North America and parts of Asia. Its early-flowering, purplish spathe emits a foul smell

skurfing *SKATEBOARDING

sky (skai) **1.** *pl.* **skies** *n.* (often *pl.*) the atmosphere above the earth, with or without clouds ‖ the apparent enclosing dome which this atmosphere forms ‖ (*rhet.*) heaven **to praise to the skies** to praise very highly **2.** *v.t. pres. part.* **sky·ing** *past* and *past part.* **skied, skyed** (*pop.*) to hit (a ball) up high ‖ to hang (a picture) high on the wall, esp. in an exhibition [O.N. *skȳ,* cloud]

sky blue the light to medium blue of the sky on a clear day **ský-blúe** *adj.*

sky·div·ing (skáidaiviŋ) *n.* (*sports*) jumping from a plane at a moderate altitude and delaying the opening of the parachute, while the jumper performs acrobatics —**sky diver** *n.* —**sky-dive** *v.*

Skye (skai) the largest island (area 670 sq. miles, pop. 7,372) of the Inner Hebrides, Scotland. Chief town: Portree

Skye terrier a terrier of a Scottish breed having a long body, short legs and a long, hard gray or fawn coat and bred originally for digging out foxes and badgers

Skyhawk *n.* (*mil.*) single-engine, turbojet reconnaissance/attack aircraft (A-4) designed to operate from aircraft carriers or short, unprepared fields, capable of being air refueled and of delivering nuclear and/or nonnuclear weapons; manufactured by McDonnell Douglas

sky-high (skáihái) **1.** *adv.* very, very high ‖ (*pop.*) to bits, *to blow someone's arguments sky-high* ‖ enthusiastically, *to praise someone sky-high* **2.** *adj.* very high or excessive, *sky-high prices*

sky·jack (skáijæk) *v.* to assume control of an aircraft by force or threat of force, usu. in order to divert it from its original destination —**sky·jacker** *n.* —**skyjacking** *n.* *Cf* HIJACK

Sky·lab (skáilæb) *n.* U.S. unmanned research space station orbiting earth, launched in 1973, lost upon falling to earth, July 12, 1979

sky·lark (skáilɑrk) **1.** *n. Alauda arvensis,* a European lark having brown, beige and white plumage and characterized by its high-pitched song uttered while soaring **2.** *v.i.* to be full of mischief and have fun

sky·light (skáilait) *n.* a window in a roof and level with it or one set into a flat roof as a dome etc.

sky·line (skáilain) *n.* the visible horizon ‖ objects seen against it, *a skyline of mountains*

Sky·loft (skáilɔft) *n.* a textured yarn created by passing the yarn through an air jet, causing its filaments to become wavy and intertwined; trade-name product of Arkzona Corporation

sky·lounge (skáilaunʒ) *n.* a vehicle that collects airline passengers and is then carried by helicopter to the airport

sky marshal an armed federal plainclothes security guard assigned to prevent skyjackings

sky·rock·et (skáirɒkit) **1.** *n.* a fire work that consists of a rocket which explodes high in the air in a dazzling cascade of colored sparks **2.** *v.i.* to rise very rapidly, rocket

Sky·ros (skáirɒs, skáirous, skí:rɔs) the largest island (area 81 sq. miles, pop. 2,352) of the N. Sporades, Greece: marble

sky·sail (skáiseil, skáis'l) *n.* (*naut.*) the sail above the royal of a square-rigged ship

sky·scrap·er (skáiskreipər) *n.* a very tall, narrow building with many stories

sky·ward (skáiwərd) **1.** *adv.* towards the sky **2.** *adj.* directed towards the sky **skȳ-wards** *adv.*

sky wave a radio wave transmitted by means of the ionosphere (cf. GROUND WAVE)

sky·writ·ing (skáiraitiŋ) *n.* the forming of words etc. in the air by smoke from an aircraft

SLA (*abbr.*) for Symbionese Liberation Army (which see)

slab (slæb) **1.** *n.* a thick, flat, oblong piece of something, *a slab of pie* ‖ the outside piece cut away when a log is squared **2.** *v.t. pres. part.* **slab·bing** *past* and *past part.* **slabbed** to put on thickly, *to slab paint on canvas* ‖ to remove a slab from (a log) [origin unknown]

slab·ber (slǽbər) **1.** *n.* slobber ‖ a machine for removing the outside slabs from lumber **2.** *v.t.* and *i.* to slobber [prob. fr. Du. or L.G. origin]

slack (slæk) *n.* minute particles of coal, coal dust [origin unknown]

slack 1. *adj.* not under any tension, *a slack rope* ‖ lacking in diligence, *a slack official* ‖ involving little work, *a slack job* ‖ inactive, *slack trade* ‖ (of tides, winds) slow-moving **2.** *v.i.* to be or become lazy ‖ to slacken ‖ *v.t.* to slacken ‖ to slake (lime) **to slack off** to slacken **to slack up** to become less diligent **3.** *n.* the loose part of a rope, *haul in the slack* ‖ (*commerce*) a period of little trade ‖ any interval of inactivity ‖ (*pl.*) men's or women's long pants for casual wear ‖ a period of slow movement in the tide when it is turning **slack·en** *v.t.* to make slower, *to slacken speed* ‖ to make looser, *to slacken a rope* ‖ to

CONCISE PRONUNCIATION KEY: **(a)** æ, *cat;* ɑ, *car;* ɔ *fawn;* ei, *snake.* **(e)** e, *hen;* i:, *sheep;* iə, *deer;* ɛə, *bear.* **(i)** i, *fish;* ai, *tiger;* ə:, *bird.* **(o)** o, *ox;* au, *cow;* ou, *goat;* u, *poor;* ɔi, *royal.* **(u)** ʌ, *duck;* u, *bull;* u:, *goose;* ə, *bacillus;* ju:, *cube.* x, *loch;* θ, *think;* ð, *bother;* z, *Zen;* ʒ, *corsage;* dʒ, *savage;* ŋ, *orangutang;* j, *yak;* ʃ, *fish;* tʃ, *fetch;* 'l, *rabble;* 'n, *redden.* Complete pronunciation key appears inside front cover.

slake (lime) ‖ *v.i.* to become less energetic or less diligent **sláck·er** *n.* (*pop.*) someone who is lazy, or shirks a duty [O.E. *sleac, slœc*]

slag (slæg) **1.** *n.* nonmetallic waste matter obtained when ore is smelted ‖ scoriaceous lava from a volcano **2.** *v.i. pres. part.* **slag·ging** *past* and *past part.* **slagged** to form as slag **slág·gy** *adj.* [M. L.G. *slagge*]

slain *past part.* of SLAY

slake (sleik) *pres. part.* **slak·ing** *past* and *past part.* **slaked** *v.t.* to quench (a thirst, fire) ‖ to satisfy (a passion) ‖ (*chem.*) to hydrate (lime) [O.E. *slacian*]

slaked lime calcium hydroxide, $Ca(OH)_2$

sla·lom (slάləm, slάloum) **1.** *n.* in skiing, a downhill race in which skiers zigzag between spaced markers **2.** *v.i.* to ski in such a race [Norw.]

slalom canoe (*sports*) canoe, usu. with a deck, designed for slalom racing

slam (slæm) **1.** *v. pres. part.* **slam·ming** *past* and *past part.* **slammed** *v.t.* to shut noisily and violently, *to slam a door* ‖ to cause (something) to strike against something violently and often frequently, *the wind slammed the shutters* ‖ to hit very hard, *to slam a ball* ‖ to bring into action violently, *to slam the brakes on* ‖ (*pop.*) to condemn in criticism ‖ *v.i.* to shut with a loud noise, *the door slammed* ‖ to move in a violent fashion, *he slammed down the hall* **to slam the door on** to dismiss (a proposal) outright **to slam through** to promote vigorously and secure agreement for (a proposal), *the committee slammed the new legislation through* **2.** *n.* a loud bang, esp. of something being shut, *the slam of a door* ‖ (*pop.*) a harshly critical notice ‖ (*cards*) the bidding and winning of all tricks in a hand of bridge (grand slam) or all but one (little slam) [etym. doubtful]

slam-bang (slǽmbǽŋ) **1.** *adv.* with noise and commotion **2.** *adj.* (*pop.*) done really well, giving carefree pleasure

slam dunk *DUNK SHOT

slam·mer (slǽmər) *n.* (*slang*) a jail, prison, or penitentiary

slan·der (slǽndər) *n.* (*pop.*) any false and insulting statement ‖ (*law*) an oral statement which without due cause has the result, or is intended to have the result, of bringing its subject into disrepute (cf. LIBEL) [fr. A.F. *esclaundre,* O.F. *esclandre*]

slander *v.t.* to write or say a slander against [fr. O.F. *esclondrer*]

slan·der·ous (slǽndərəs) *adj.* having the quality of slander ‖ given to speaking slander [late M.E.]

slang (slæŋ) **1.** *n.* currently widely used and understood language, consisting of new meanings attributed to existing words or of wholly new words, generally accepted as lying outside standard polite usage. Originating from the attempt to introduce fresh expression into a language, slang will either usually pass out of usage in time or be accepted into standard usage ‖ a conventional language that is peculiar to a group, profession or social class, *thieves' slang, schoolboy slang* **2.** *adj.* having the character of slang **3.** *v.t.* (esp. *Br., pop.*) to assail with coarse, slangy language ‖ *v.i.* to use slang or coarse language [origin unknown]

slang·i·ly (slǽŋili:) *adv.* in a slangy manner

slang·i·ness (slǽŋi:nis) *n.* the state or quality of being slangy

slang·y (slǽŋi:) *comp.* **slang·i·er** *superl.* **slang·i·est** *adj.* relating to, or being, slang ‖ fond of using slang

slant (slænt, slant) **1.** *v.t.* to be at an angle with a given line or surface, esp. horizontal or vertical, *the floor slants* ‖ *v.t.* to cause to slant **2.** *n.* the angle made with the given line ‖ the act or state of making such an angle, *the table is on a slant* ‖ an aspect, *the affair took on a new slant* **3.** *adj.* slanting, *slant eyes* **slánt-ways, slánt-wise** *advs* [fr. older *slent* v., to slope]

slant range (*mil.*) the line of sight distance between two points on different elevations

slap (slæp) **1.** *v. pres. part.* **slap·ping** *past* and *past part.* **slapped** *v.t.* to strike with the open hand, *she slapped his face* ‖ to put, place etc. with energetic force, *he slapped his hand on his thigh* ‖ *v.i.* to sound with the noise of such a striking, *the waves slapped against the boat* **2.** *n.* a blow thus given ‖ the sound of such a blow ‖ an insult, affront ‖ a piece of sharp criticism **a slap in the face** a remark or action that comes as a shock and that hurts one's pride **a slap on the back** congratulations, *the critics gave the author a slap on the back* **to have a slap at** (*pop.*) to make an attempt at (something one believes difficult) ‖ (*pop.*) to attack (someone or something) in criticism **3.** *adv.* suddenly and violently, like such a blow, *she ran slap into him* [L.G. *slapp,* imit.]

slap-bang (slæpbǽŋ) **1.** *adv.* with great force and suddenness, *to run slap-bang into someone* **2.** *adj.* characterized by rough, good-natured, blustering force in style, manner or method, *a slap-bang salesman*

slap·dash (slǽpdæʃ) **1.** *adj.* carelessly hasty, *slapdash work* **2.** *adv.* carelessly **3.** *n.* slapdash carelessness

slap·jack (slǽpdʒæk) *n.* a cake cooked on a griddle, a flapjack ‖ a card game

slap shot (*ice hockey*) a swinging shot at a puck that usually causes it to fly over the ice

slap·stick (slǽpstik) **1.** *n.* fast, farcical comedy dominated by physical boisterousness **2.** *adj.* of or relating to slapstick, *slapstick humor* [fr. Harlequin's cudgel in the commedia dell' arte, a slatted stick that made a loud noise when banged against someone's bottom]

SLAR *n.* (*mil. acronym*) for side-looking airborne radar

slash (slæʃ) **1.** *v.t.* to make a long cut in, esp. by striking violently and with wide sweeps ‖ to strike with a whip, or with the edge of a sword etc. ‖ to cut a slit in (a garment) so that the garment or lining beneath is partly revealed ‖ to criticize severely ‖ to reduce (prices etc.) greatly ‖ *v.i.* to use a whip, sword, scissors etc. in order to slash something **2.** *n.* the act of slashing ‖ a long cut made by slashing ‖ a slit in an article of clothing to show what lies beneath ‖ a great reduction in costs, prices, numbers etc. ‖ a clearing made in a forest by felling trees, before the branches etc. are removed from the site ‖ such debris [M.E. *slaschen* prob. fr. O.F.]

slash *n.* an area of soggy, esp. brush-covered swampland [origin unknown]

slat (slæt) *pres. part.* **slat·ting** *past* and *past part.* **slat·ted** *v.t.* (of sails etc.) to flap noisily against ‖ *v.i.* to move noisily with a flapping sound [M.E., origin unknown]

slat 1. *n.* a thin, narrow piece of wood, a lath **2.** *v.t. pres. part.* **slat·ting** *past* and *past part.* **slat·ted** to furnish with slats ‖ to construct with slats [fr. O.F. *esclat,* splinter]

slate (sleit) **1.** *n.* a laminated rock which is readily split along parallel planes of cleavage into large, thin, impervious pieces which, after trimming, are used to cover a timbered roof. Thicker masses, having a smooth, easily cleaned surface, are used as windowsills, doorsteps etc. ‖ a piece of split slate, used as a roofing tile or as a writing surface ‖ the blue-black or blue-gray color of slate ‖ a list of candidates drawn up by a political party **2.** *v.t. pres. part.* **slat·ing** *past* and *past part.* **slat·ed** to cover (a roof) with slates ‖ to list or designate for an appointment, appearance, activity etc., *the next man slated to appear* [fr. O.F. *esclate,* splinter]

slate *pres. part.* **slat·ing** *past* and *past part.* **slat·ed** *v.t.* (esp. *Br.*) to criticize severely [origin unknown]

slat·ing (sléitiŋ) *n.* (*Br.*) a severe reprimand ‖ (*Br.*) a harshly critical notice [fr. SLATE v., to criticize]

slating *n.* the work of a man who lays slates ‖ slates collectively or material for slates [fr. SLATE v., to cover with slates]

slat·tern (slǽtərn) *n.* a woman of unkempt appearance and sluttish habits [prob. fr. dial. *slatter,* to be wasteful]

slat·tern·li·ness (slǽtərnli:nis) *n.* the state or quality of being slatternly

slat·tern·ly (slǽtərnli:) **1.** *adj.* like a slattern, dirty, untidy **2.** *adv.* in a slatternly way

slat·y (sléiti:) *comp.* **slat·i·er** *superl.* **slat·i·est** *adj.* having the quality of slate ‖ slate-colored

slaugh·ter (slɔ́tər) **1.** *n.* the killing of animals for food ‖ a massacre **2.** *v.t.* to kill mercilessly ‖ to kill in large numbers ‖ to kill (animals) for food [M.E. *slahter* fr. O.N.]

slaugh·ter·house (slɔ́tərhaus) *pl.* **slaugh·ter·hous·es** (slɔ́tərhauziz) *n.* a place where animals are killed for market

slaugh·ter·ous (slɔ́tərəs) *adj.* of or characterized by slaughter

Slav (slɑv, slæv) **1.** *n.* a member of a group of Eastern European peoples, usually subdivided into Eastern Slavs (Great Russians, Ukrainians and Byelorussians), Western Slavs (e.g. Poles, Moravians, Czechs, Slovaks) and Southern Slavs (e.g. Serbs, Croats, Slovenes, Bulgars) **2.** *adj.* Slavic [older *sclave* fr. M. L. *sclavus*]

slave (sleiv) **1.** *n.* a person who is the property of, and completely subject to, another ‖ a person victimized by another ‖ a person dominated by some habit etc., *a slave to alcohol* **2.** *v.i. pres. part.* **slav·ing** *past* and *past part.* **slaved** to work like a slave [fr. O.F. *esclave*]

slave driver a hard taskmaster ‖ a person who directs the work of slaves

slave flash a photographic flash triggered by light from a master flash

slave·hold·er (sléivhouldər) *n.* a person who owns slaves

slave·hold·ing (sléivhouldiŋ) **1.** *n.* possession of slaves **2.** *adj.* having or owning slaves

slav·er (sléivər) *n.* a person trading in slaves ‖ a slave ship

slav·er (slǽvər, sléivər, slάvər) **1.** *v.i.* to let spittle drip from the mouth ‖ *v.t.* to cover with spittle **2.** *n.* spittle dripping from the mouth ‖ senseless talk, drivel [M.E. *slaveren* prob. of Scand. origin]

Slave River (sleiv) *MACKENZIE RIVER

slav·er·y (sléivəri:) *n.* the condition of a slave ‖ total subjection to a master ‖ slaveholding ‖ hard, grinding work ‖ addiction

slave ship (*hist.*) a ship engaged in the slave trade

slave state a totalitarian state ‖ (*hist.*) any of the 15 U.S. states south of the Mason-Dixon line, in which slavery was legal before the Civil War: Alabama, Arkansas, Delaware, Florida, Georgia, Kentucky, Louisiana, Maryland, Mississippi, Missouri, North Carolina, South Carolina, Tennessee, Texas, Virginia

slave trade the buying and selling of slaves, esp. the former transportation of Africans for sale in America

Slav·ic (slάvik, slǽvik) **1.** *adj.* of the Slavs, their languages etc. **2.** *n.* a major branch of the Indo-European family of languages. It includes East Slavic (Great Russian, Ukrainian, Byelorussian), West Slavic (Polish, Serbian, Czech, Slovak), and South Slavic (Old Church Slavonic, Bulgarian, Serbo-Croatian, Slovene)

slav·ish (sléiviʃ) *adj.* of, like or befitting a slave ‖ showing no independence or originality, *slavish imitation* ‖ grindingly meticulous, *slavish attention to detail*

Slav·ism (slάvizəm, slǽvizem) *n.* Slavic character, culture etc. ‖ a word characteristically Slavic occurring in some other language

Sla·vo·ni·a (sləvóuni:ə) a northeastern region of the Yugoslavian republic of Croatia, between the Drava and Sava valleys, largely forest and mountains: wine, lumber, cereals, cattle

Sla·vo·ni·an (sləvóuni:ən) **1.** *n.* an inhabitant of Slavonia ‖ the group of Slavic languages **2.** *adj.* belonging to Slavonia ‖ Slav

Sla·von·ic (sləvɔ́nik) **1.** *adj.* of the Slavs or their languages **2.** *n.* the group of Slavic languages [fr. M.L. *sclavonicus, slavonicus* fr. *Sclavonia, Slavonia,* land of the Slavs]

slaw (slɔ) *n.* coleslaw [fr. Du. *sla,* shortened form of *salade,* salad]

slay (slei) *pres. part.* **slay·ing** *past* **slew** (slu:) *past part.* **slain** (slein) *v.t.* (*rhet.*) to kill violently ‖ (*pop.*) to cause (someone) to be overcome by laughter, admiration etc. [O.E. *slēan*]

SLBM (*mil. abbr.*) for submarine-launched ballistic missile

SLCM (*mil. abbr.*) for sea-launched cruise missile

slea·zi·ly (slí:zili:, sléizili:) *adv.* in a sleazy way

slea·zi·ness (slí:zi:nis, sléizi:nis) *n.* the state or quality of being sleazy

slea·zy (slí:zi:, sléizi:) *comp.* **slea·zi·er** *superl.* **slea·zi·est** *adj.* (of materials) lacking substance, of poor texture ‖ tawdry, vulgar, of poor quality ‖ squalid, shabby [origin unknown]

sled (sled) **1.** *n.* a vehicle mounted on runners for use on snow or ice, esp. a small, light one used by children to slide down hills **2.** *v.i. pres. part.* **sled·ding** *past* and *past part.* **sled·ded** to ride on a sled [M. Flem. or M.L.G. *sledde*]

sledge (sledʒ) **1.** *n.* a low sled used to transport usually heavy loads ‖ (esp. *Br.*) a child's sled **2.** *v. pres. part.* **sledg·ing** *past* and *past part.* **sledged** *v.i.* to ride on a sledge ‖ *v.t.* to make (one's way) or convey by sledge [M. Du *sleedse*]

sledge 1. *n.* a sledgehammer **2.** *v.i. pres. part.* **sledg·ing** *past* and *past part.* **sledged** to use a sledgehammer [O.E. *slecg*]

sledge·ham·mer (slédʒhæmər) **1.** *n.* a large, heavy hammer usually swung with both hands

CONCISE PRONUNCIATION KEY: **(a)** æ, *cat*; ɑ, *car*; ɔ *fawn*; ei, *snake*. **(e)** e, *hen*; i:, *sheep*; iə, *deer*; ɛə, *bear*. **(i)** i, *fish*; ai, *tiger*; ə:, *bird*. **(o)** o, *ox*; au, *cow*; ou, *goat*; u, *poor*; ɔi, *royal*. **(u)** ʌ, *duck*; u, *bull*; u:, *goose*; ə, *bacillus*; ju:, *cube*. x, *loch*; θ, *think*; ð, *bother*; z, *Zen*; ʒ, *corsage*; dʒ, *savage*; ŋ, *orangutang*; j, *yak*; ʃ, *fish*; tʃ, *fetch*; 'l, *rabble*; 'n, *redden*. Complete pronunciation key appears inside front cover.

2. *v.t.* to strike with or as if with a sledgehammer ‖ *v.i.* to wield a sledgehammer 3. *adj.* very powerful, *a sledgehammer blow*
sleek (sli:k) 1. *adj.* smooth, soft and shiny, *sleek hair*, esp. this as evidence of good condition in animals ‖ very neat and polished, *a sleek appearance* ‖ stylish, elegant, *a sleek car* ‖ (*pop.*, of a person or his manners) smoothly polite in a way that displeases 2. *v.t.* to groom (hair) so that it is sleek [altered fr. M.E. *slike*, slick]
sleep (sli:p) *pres. part.* **sleep·ing** *past* and *past part.* **slept** (slept) *v.i.* to be in the natural and regular state of inactivity in which (in man and most other animals) consciousness ceases and the bodily functions slow down or cease, or (in plants) the normal processes of development cease or almost cease ‖ to be in a state resembling sleep (e.g. torpor, unconsciousness) ‖ *v.t.* to slumber in (a specified kind of sleep), *to sleep a deep sleep* ‖ to spend (time) sleeping, *she slept the night in the attic* ‖ to provide sleeping accommodation for, *this hotel sleeps 50 guests* **to sleep away** to get rid of by sleeping, *to sleep away one's cares* **to sleep in** (of a domestic servant) to sleep at the place of work **to sleep off** to recover from by resting in sleep, *to sleep off one's fatigue* [O.E. *slēpan, slǣpan*]
sleep *n.* the state of sleeping ‖ a period of sleeping ‖ (*bot.*) nyctitropism [O.E. *slēp, slǣp*]
sleep around *v.* (*colloq.*) to be sexually promiscuous
sleep·er (slí:pər) *n.* someone who sleeps ‖ a large horizontal beam used as a support, esp. (*Br.*) a railroad tie ‖ a railroad sleeping car ‖ a child's sleeping garment ‖ a book, racehorse etc. which achieves unexpected success ‖ an intelligence agent who remains inactive and undercover for many years before becoming involved in any activity or risk ‖ (*bowling*) a pin left hidden behind another
sleep·i·ly (slí:pili:) *adv.* in a sleepy manner
sleep-in (slí:pin) *n.* overnight occupation of a public place, esp. as a protest
sleep·i·ness (slí:pi:nis) *n.* the state or quality of being sleepy
sleeping bag a sack-shaped, padded bag, used for sleeping outdoors or where there is no bed available
sleeping car a railway coach with berths for sleeping
sleeping partner (*Br.*) a silent partner
sleeping pill a pill, esp. a barbiturate, for inducing sleep
sleeping sickness a chronic disease occurring in tropical Africa, caused by the parasites *Trypanosoma gambiense* and *T. rhodesiense* and carried by the tsetse fly. It causes fever, bodily and mental lethargy and, very often, death. It also occurs in Central America ‖ (*Am.=Br.* sleepy sickness) encephalitis lethargica (*ENCEPHALITIS)
sleep-learning (slí:plə:rniŋ) *n.* process of receiving instruction through recordings while asleep *also* hypnopedia *Cf* SLEEP-TEACHING
sleep·less (slí:plis) *adj.* without sleep, *a sleepless night* ‖ without cessation, *sleepless activity*
sleep-teaching (slí:pti:tʃiŋ) *n.* technique for instruction through recordings while learner is asleep *Cf* SLEEP-LEARNING
sleep·walk·er (slí:pwɔkər) *n.* someone who walks while asleep
sleep·walk·ing (slí:pwɔkiŋ) *n.* walking while asleep
sleep·y (slí:pi:) *comp.* **sleep·i·er** *superl.* **sleep·i·est** *adj.* feeling ready to go to sleep ‖ without much activity, *a sleepy countryside* ‖ lethargic, lacking alertness ‖ tending to cause sleep ‖ (of fruit, esp. a pear) overripe and beginning to rot
sleep·y·head (slí:pi:hed) *n.* a term of endearment for someone very sleepy, esp. a very sleepy child
sleepy sickness (*Br.*) sleeping sickness (encephalitis lethargica)
sleet (sli:t) 1. *n.* frozen or partly frozen rain ‖ hail or snow mixed with rain (*Am.=Br.* glaze) ice formed by rain falling on objects below freezing temperature 2. *v.i.* to shower in the form of sleet **sleet·y** *adj.* [M.E. *slete* prob. fr. O.E.]
sleeve (sli:v) 1. *n.* the part of a garment covering the arm ‖ a slipcase for a phonograph record ‖ a tube or part that fits over another part **to have something up one's sleeve** to keep something (e.g. an argument) secretly in reserve to be used to advantage at the right moment 2. *v.t. pres. part.* **sleev·ing** *past* and *past part.* **sleeved** to furnish or cover with a sleeve **sléeved** *adj.* (esp. in compounds) provided with sleeves, *short-sleeved* **sléeve·less** *adj.* [O.E. *slīefe, slyf*]
sleeve nut a long nut used for drawing together pipes or shafts, having screw threads in opposite directions at its ends
sleeve valve a valve in the form of a sleeve or sleeves fitting inside the cylinder and controlling the opening of the inlet and exhaust ports as it slides with the piston
sleigh (slei) 1. *n.* a sled, esp. a large one drawn by a horse or horses and carrying passengers 2. *v.i.* to ride on or in a sleigh [fr. Du. *slee*]
sleight of hand (slait) deft manual skill, esp. in performing conjuring tricks [fr. O. N. *slœgth*, dexterity]
slen·der (sléndər) *adj.* small in cross section as compared with length, *a slender stalk* ‖ gracefully slim, *a slender waist* ‖ slight, small, *a slender income* **slén·der·ize** *pres. part.* **slen·der·iz·ing** *past* and *past part.* **slen·der·ized** *v.t.* to make slender ‖ to cause to seem more slender [M.E. *slendre* prob. fr. A.F.]
slept *past* and *past part.* of SLEEP
Sles·vig (slésvix) *SCHLESWIG-HOLSTEIN
sleuth (slu:θ) 1. *n.* a detective 2. *v.i.* to act as a sleuth ‖ *v.t.* to investigate the doings of or track (someone) [O.N. *slōth*, track]
sleuth·hound (slú:θhaund) *n.* a bloodhound ‖ (*old-fash.*) a detective
slew (slu:) *n.* a slough (swamp) [variant spelling]
slew, slue *n.* (*pop.*) a large number or amount [Ir. Gael. *sluagh*, a host]
slew *past* of SLAY
slew *SLUE
slice (slais) *pres. part.* **slic·ing** *past* and *past part.* **sliced** *v.t.* to cut into slices, *to slice a loaf* ‖ to cut with a slicing movement, *to slice the air* ‖ (*golf*) to strike (the ball) across its center line so that it goes off to the right of a righthanded player or to the left of a lefthanded player (cf. HOOK) ‖ *v.i.* to make cutting movements as though cutting slices [fr. O.F. *esclicer*, to splinter]
slice *n.* a thin, flat piece, e.g. of bread or meat, cut from a larger piece ‖ a share of land, money etc. ‖ an instrument for lifting fish etc. from a frying pan ‖ (*golf*) a sliced stroke [fr. O.F. *esclice*, splinter]
slice of life (*advertising*) copy based on incidents from a life-style —**slice-of-life** *adj.*
slick (slik) 1. *adj.* admirably deft, *slick fielding* ‖ clever and suave, *a slick young lawyer* ‖ slippery, *a slick surface* 2. *adv.* smoothly ‖ smartly 3. *v.t.* (*pop.*) to sleek, *to slick one's hair* ‖ to smarten (oneself, one's appearance) ‖ to make smooth 4. *n.* a smooth or slippery surface ‖ an oil slick ‖ a tool for smoothing **slick·er** *n.* (*pop.*) a swindler ‖ an oilskin or raincoat ‖ a device for smoothing esp. leather ‖ (*pop.*) a natty city dweller [etym. doubtful]
slide (slaid) *pres. part.* **slid·ing** *past* and *past part.* **slid** (slid) *v.i.* to move with continuous contact and little friction over a smooth surface ‖ to slip so as to fall or nearly fall ‖ to move quietly and with great ease, *she slid across the stage* ‖ to move without attracting attention, *he slid into the room* ‖ to run up to a smooth flat surface and then let one's momentum carry one over it, keeping upright, or to slither down an inclined smooth surface on one's bottom ‖ to change slowly for the worse, *sliding into bad habits* ‖ *v.t.* to cause to slide, *he slid the book across the table* ‖ to add (a remark, clause, condition etc.) in a manner designed not to attract attention, *he slid a saving clause into the contract* **to let things slide** to make no effort to dominate a situation or keep up standards **to slide over** to gloss over, hardly mention (a topic) 2. *n.* the act of sliding ‖ a smooth surface, esp. ice, on which to slide ‖ a smooth slope down which things can be slid, or down which children can slide on their bottoms ‖ (*mus.*) a portamento ‖ (*photog.*) a transparency ‖ a glass plate, on which the specimen is mounted, to be slid onto a platform in front of the objective of a microscope ‖ the fall of a mass (e.g. of rock, snow) down a mountainside ‖ such a mass ‖ (*Br.*) a decorative clip for the hair ‖ (of instruments, esp. the trombone) that section of the tube which, when pushed in or out, alters the pitch of the notes [O.E. *slīdan*]
slide fastener a zipper
Slide Mountain (slaid) the highest peak (4,204 ft) in the Catskill Mountains, S.E. New York State
slide rule an instrument used in mathematical calculation comprising a ruler with a sliding bar along the middle, both graduated with similar logarithmic scales labeled with corresponding antilogarithms. Multiplication and division thus become addition and subtraction and can be performed rapidly by reading the scales
slide valve a machine part which slides to and fro, opening and closing apertures in a steam cylinder etc.
sliding scale a scale varying in accordance with variation in a scale or scales to which it is geared, *the tuition fees are on a sliding scale according to income*
sliding scale deductible an insurance policy deductible amount that varies according to income, e.g., 25% of income deductible before medical insurance takes effect
slight (slait) 1. *adj.* very little (in amount or importance), *a slight difference, a slight indisposition* ‖ (of a person) lightly built and not very tall 2. *v.t.* to treat as of very little importance, *he slighted my efforts* ‖ to treat with indifference or calculated rudeness ‖ to do in a careless or negligent way, *to slight one's work* 3. *n.* an instance of slighting something or someone **slight·ly** *adv.* [M.E. *slight, sleght* fr. O. Scand.]
Sli·go (sláigou) a county (area 693 sq. miles, pop. 55,474) of the N.W. Irish Republic (*CONNACHT) ‖ its county seat (pop. 17,232)
slily *SLYLY
Slim (slim), William Joseph, 1st Viscount Slim (1891-1970), British field marshal and statesman. He commanded British operations in Burma (1943-5), and was governor general of Australia (1953-60)
slim (slim) 1. *comp.* **slim·mer** *superl.* **slim·mest** *adj.* not thick, *a slim rod* ‖ not fat, *a slim figure* ‖ meager, *a slim chance* 2. *v. pres. part.* **slim·ming** *past* and *past part.* **slimmed** *v.i.* to make oneself thinner, by dieting, exercises, drugs etc. ‖ *v.t.* to make slim or to give an appearance of slimness, *lines that slim the waist* [Du. or L.G. *slim, bad*]
slime (slaim) 1. *n.* fine, moist mud or similar substance ‖ mucus exuded by slugs, snails etc. 2. *v. pres. part.* **slim·ing** *past* and *past part.* **slimed** *v.t.* to cover with slime ‖ *v.i.* to become slimy [O.E. *slīm*]
slime mold, *Br.* **slime mould** a saprophytic plant of the phylum *Myxomycophyta* having a complex variable life cycle, the vegetative phase of which is a motile plasmodium. After a period of feeding this produces characteristic fruiting bodies, which give rise to spores. Upon germination these produce one or two small cells that swim by means of flagella. Fusion of these cells results in the plasmodium, completing the cycle
slim·i·ly (sláimili:) *adv.* in a slimy manner
slim·i·ness (sláimi:nis) *n.* the state or quality of being slimy
slim·nas·tics (slimnǽstiks) *n.* a weight-reducing exercise regimen
slim·y (sláimi:) *comp.* **slim·i·er** *superl.* **slim·i·est** *adj.* of or like slime ‖ covered with slime ‖ (*Br.*) marked by despicable lack of candor, *a slimy trick* ‖ (*Br.*) of a person who seeks to insinuate himself into one's favor by obsequiousness and flattery ‖ filthy, disgusting
sling (sliŋ) *n.* a drink made of liquor, water, sugar, and sometimes lemon, served hot or iced [etym. doubtful]
sling 1. *v.t. pres. part.* **sling·ing** *past* and *past part.* **slung** (slʌŋ) to suspend by, or transport in, a sling ‖ to throw from, or as if from, a sling, *he slung a stone at it* 2. *n.* a loop of leather, rope, chain etc., used to suspend an object, *a rifle sling* ‖ (*naut., pl.*) the rope or chain supporting the middle part of a yard ‖ an instrument for casting missiles, consisting of a loop of leather with strings attached to each end, which when swung rapidly projects the missile by centrifugal force ‖ a large, triangular bandage hung around the neck to support an injured arm or hand [etym. doubtful]
sling·shot (slíŋʃɒt) *n.* (*Am.=Br.* catapult) a forked stick with elastics and a leather sling attached, used with small stones as ammunition
slingshot *n.* (*auto racing*) 1. a drag car in which its driver sits behind the rear wheels 2. a maneuver by a trailing car to take the lead by use of its reserve power
slink (sliŋk) *pres. part.* **slink·ing** *past* and *past part.* **slunk** (slʌŋk) *v.i.* to move stealthily in fear or shame **slínk·y** *comp.* **slink·i·er** *superl.*

slink·i·est *adj.* stealthy, *slinky as a fox* ‖ (of women's clothes) fitting the figure closely and attractively ‖ (of a woman's figure) slim and sinuous [O.E. *slincan*, to creep]

slip (slip) *pres. part.* **slip·ping** *past* and *past part.* **slipped** *v.i.* to move in a sliding motion, *his hand slipped over the windowsill* ‖ to lose one's balance by sliding on a slippery surface ‖ to slide from its or one's support or from one's grasp and fall, *the jug slipped to the floor* ‖ to move easily and rapidly, esp. without attracting attention, *he slipped from the room, the time slipped by* ‖ to sink a little from a previous standard of ability, health etc., *he used to be efficient but has been slipping lately* ‖ (often with 'up') to make a mistake, *he slipped up when he made that decision* ‖ to put a garment on quickly, *to slip into a jacket* ‖ to escape from one's consciousness or memory, *his name slipped from my mind* ‖ *v.t.* to cause (something) to slip or move quickly or easily, *she slipped a ring on her finger* ‖ to give in a manner which does not draw attention, *he slipped me a note* ‖ to escape from, *she slipped her pursuers, it had slipped his mind* ‖ to let loose, *to slip a hound* ‖ to release, *to slip a catch* ‖ to change (a stitch) from one needle to another without knitting it ‖ (of an animal) to give birth prematurely to ‖ to allow (the anchor) to run out too fast and so lose it ‖ to get rid of (an anchor) instead of hauling it in ‖ to dislocate, *to slip a disk* ‖ to molt, *the snake slipped its skin* **to slip it** (or **one**) **over on somebody** to cheat or deceive someone by catching him off his guard **2.** *n.* a slipping ‖ a small unintentional mistake ‖ a covering which is easily slipped on and off, *a pillow slip* ‖ a dress-length undergarment, usually having adjustable shoulder straps ‖ a galley proof ‖ a sloping surface down which a vessel is slipped into the water, or on which it is built, repaired or laid up ‖ (*cricket*) a fielder on the offside of and close behind the batsman ‖ (*pl., cricket*) the part of the field in which these fielders stand ‖ a dog's leash that can be slipped very quickly **to give someone the slip** to get away from someone without his noticing at the moment [perh. fr. M. L.G. *slippen*]

slip 1. *n.* (*hort.*) a plant cutting ‖ a long, narrow piece of wood, paper etc. ‖ a small person, esp. when not quite grown up, *a slip of a girl* **2.** *v.t. pres. part.* **slip·ping** *past* and *past part.* **slipped** to take cuttings from (a plant) [perh. M. Du. or M. L.G. *slippe*, cut, strip]

slip *n.* liquid clay used for coating partly dried ceramic ware in order to have more than one color, or for joining leather-hard clay components together, or for casting ‖ (*envir.*) downhill movement of a soil mass [O.E. *slipa, slype*]

slip·case (slípkeis) *n.* a stiff container into which a book can be inserted for protection with only its spine visible ‖ a record jacket

slip·cov·er (slípkʌvər) *n.* (*Am.=Br.* loose cover) a removable, usually fitted, decorative cover for an upholstered chair etc. ‖ a book slipcase

Sli·pher (sláifər), Vesto Melvin (1875-1969), U.S. astronomer whose research culminated in the first observational evidence for the expanding universe theory. He determined by spectroscopic methods the rotation periods of the planets, discovered molecular bands in the planetary spectrum and the existence in space of interstellar sodium and calcium, and demonstrated that many diffuse nebulae shine by the reflected light of adjacent stars

slip·knot (slípnɒt) *n.* a knot that can move along the string or rope around which it was made

slip law in Congress, the final version of an act and its first official publication, usu. with the legislative history of the act

slip·per (slípər) *n.* a light, comfortable item of indoor footwear ‖ a drag for a vehicle to break its speed

slip·per·i·ness (slípəri:nis) *n.* the state or quality of being slippery

slip·per·y (slípəri:, slípri:) *comp.* **slip·per·i·er** *superl.* **slip·per·i·est** *adj.* of a surface offering so little friction that slipping easily occurs on it ‖ difficult to hold in one's grasp, *a slippery eel* ‖ difficult to hold to an agreement or to a point in discussion, *a slippery customer* ‖ requiring very tactful and attentive handling, *a slippery problem* ‖ untrustworthy, deceitful [O.E. *slipor*]

slippery elm *Ulmus rubra*, fam. *Ulmaceae*, a species of North American elm ‖ the wood of this tree ‖ its fragrant, sticky bark, used medicinally

slip·py (slípi:) *adj.* (*Br., pop.*) quick, alert, *look slippy about it* ‖ (*pop.*) slippery

slip ring a conducting ring in a generator or motor used by the brushes to take or deliver electric current

slip·shod (slípʃɒd) *adj.* negligent, careless, *slipshod work* ‖ wearing heels trodden down on one side

slip·stream (slípstri:m) **1.** *n.* air or water recovering its normal volume after being compressed and displaced by some solid body (aircraft, ship, projectile etc.) which has passed through it ‖ (*auto racing*) the low-pressure area behind a speeding car **2.** *v.* to drive in another's slipstream

slip·up (slípʌp) *n.* (*pop.*) a slip, mistake

slip·ware (slípwεər) *n.* earthenware using colored slips and usually lead glazes

slip·way (slípwei) *n.* a launching slope on which a ship is built or repaired

slit (slit) **1.** *v.t. pres. part.* **slit·ting** *past* and *past part.* **slit** to cut or tear lengthwise ‖ to cut or tear into slips ‖ to make a long, thin opening in **2.** *n.* a long cut or tear ‖ a long, thin opening [rel. to O.E. *slītan*]

slith·er (slíðər) **1.** *v.i.* to slide, esp. with imperfect control of balance ‖ to move with a smooth and slightly sinuous motion ‖ *v.t.* to cause to slide or move in such a way **2.** *n.* a smooth, slightly sinuous motion ‖ the sound of something moving on a slippery surface **slith·er·y** *adj.* slippery [var. of older *slidder* fr. O.E. *sliderian*]

slit skirt woman's midlength skirt with side slit

slit trench a narrow trench, often quite shallow, which a soldier digs for protection from flying fragments

sliv·er (slívər) **1.** *n.* a splinter of wood ‖ a very thin piece cut or torn off something, *a sliver of bacon* ‖ a piece sliced off a fish for use as bait ‖ a strand of cotton fiber from a carding or combing machine ready for twisting ‖ wool from a carding machine **2.** *v.t.* to cut or tear into very thin pieces ‖ *v.i.* to slice or shred [fr. older *slive* v. fr. O.E. *slīfan*, to split]

sliv·o·vitz (slívəvits) *n.* a colorless plum brandy made in the Balkan countries [Serbo-Croation *sljivovica* fr. *sljva, sliva*, plum]

slob (slob) *n.* (*pop.*) a boorish, vulgar or slovenly person [Irish *slab*, mud]

slob·ber (slɒ́bər) **1.** *v.i.* to let saliva run from the mouth ‖ to gush sentimentally ‖ *v.t.* to wet or smear with dribbling saliva **2.** *n.* dribbling saliva ‖ feebly sentimental talk, writing or emotion **slób·ber·y** *adj.* [prob. fr. Du. *slobberen*]

sloe (slou) *n.* *Prunus spinosa*, fam. *Rosaceae*, a widely distributed, spiny shrub bearing white flowers and small dark blue, very astringent plums ‖ this fruit, used for making sloe gin

sloe-eyed (slóuaid) *adj.* having dark blue, or purplish-black, eyes ‖ having slant eyes

sloe gin liqueur made of gin flavored with sloes in place of juniper berries, and sweetened

slog (slɒg) **1.** *v. pres. part.* **slog·ging** *past* and *past part.* **slogged** *v.t.* to hit hard, slug, esp. (*Br.*) in boxing or cricket without care for style ‖ to make (one's way) through difficult country or a long, difficult or tedious job, by sheer determination ‖ *v.i.* to push one's way forward persistently, esp. on foot, through hard country ‖ to grind away at a long, hard or tedious job **2.** *n.* a hard blow lacking style, esp. in boxing, baseball or cricket ‖ something involving long hard effort, esp. at what is tedious [origin unknown]

slo·gan (slóugən) *n.* a catchword used by an advertiser in sales promotion ‖ a pithy phrase used by a political party or by any other group to indicate a party line on a topic [fr. Gael. *sluaghghairm* fr. *sluagh*, host + *gairm*, cry]

sloop (slu:p) *n.* a small fore-and-aft-rigged vessel with one mast ‖ a small armed vessel [fr. Du. *sloep* perh. fr. F.]

sloop of war a war vessel armed with guns only on the upper deck and larger than a gunboat

slop (slɒp) **1.** *n.* (*pl.*) dirty water, esp. that a person has washed in or that dishes have been washed in ‖ (*pl., Br.*) dregs of tea left in a cup ‖ (esp. *pl.*) liquid food as taken by invalids ‖ (esp. *pl.*) swill fed to hogs **2.** *v. pres. part.* **slop·ping** *past* and *past part.* **slopped** *v.i.* (of a liquid) to flow over the edge of a vessel ‖ to plod through mud, flood water etc. ‖ (of water) to make a slapping sound ‖ *v.t.* to pour or splash (liquid), *to slop some paint on a canvas* ‖ to splash (someone) with liquid ‖ to serve or take (food or drink) clumsily [O. E. *sloppe*]

slop basin (*Br.*) the little bowl in a tea service into which dregs are emptied before a cup is refilled

slope (sloup) **1.** *n.* a natural or artificial incline ‖ the degree or nature of such an incline, *a slope of 30°, a gentle slope* ‖ (*mil.*) the position of a rifle carried on the shoulder, *at the slope* **2.** *v. pres. part.* **slop·ing** *past* and *past part.* **sloped** *v.i.* to be inclined at an angle with the horizontal, *the roof slopes steeply* ‖ (*pop.*) to walk, esp. in a casual manner ‖ *v.t.* to cause to make an angle with the horizontal **to slope arms** (*formerly*) to bring the rifle as a drill movement so that it is held in the left hand with the barrel on one's left shoulder and the muzzle sloping to the back of the shoulder **to slope off** (*pop.*) to go away so as to avoid having to work, pay etc., or just without announcing one's departure [fr. *aslope* fr. O.E. *aslopen* past part. of *aslupan*, to slip away]

slop·pi·ly (slɒ́pili:) *adv.* in a sloppy way

slop·pi·ness (slɒ́pi:nis) *n.* the state or quality of being sloppy

slop·py (slɒ́pi:) *comp.* **slop·pi·er** *superl.* **slop·pi·est** *adj.* wet with slopped-over liquid ‖ excessively liquid, *sloppy porridge* ‖ weakly sentimental, *sloppy talk* ‖ slovenly, *a sloppy soldier* ‖ careless, *sloppy work*

sloppy joe a hot, open sandwich, usu. on a whole bread or bun, with seasoned chopped or smoked meat in a spicy sauce

slops (slɒps) *pl. n.* clothes etc. supplied to sailors from ship's stores [etym. doubtful]

slosh (slɒʃ) **1.** *v.i.* to move through water, mud etc. with splashing, sucking and gurgling noises ‖ to flow with splashing noises and movement ‖ *v.t.* to apply (paint) thickly and without care ‖ to splash (something) around energetically in liquid ‖ to splash (liquid) freely ‖ (*Br., pop.*) to strike (someone, a ball etc.) hard [imit.]

slot (slɒt) **1.** *n.* a groove or channel into which something fits or slides ‖ a narrow opening ‖ a slit in a machine for the insertion of a coin ‖ allocation in a program or budget, e.g., for a salaried position ‖ (*football*) a gap in the defense line, usu. between end and tackle **2.** *v.t. pres. part.* **slot·ting** *past* and *past part.* **slot·ted** to provide with openings ‖ to cut a groove in [fr. O.F. *esclot*, hollow of the breast]

slot *n.* the track of an animal [fr. O.F. *esclot*, hoofprint, prob. fr. O.N.]

slot·back (slɒ́tbæk) *n.* (*football*) the offensive halfback placed between end and tackle, but behind the line of scrimmage

slot car (*games*) a remote-controlled electric toy racing car operating on metal strips —**slot racer** *n.* —**slot racing** *n.*

sloth (slɔθ, *Br.* esp. slouθ) *n.* laziness, esp. habitual laziness ‖ spiritual apathy, failure to pursue virtue ‖ any of several tropical South and Central American edentate mammals, slowmoving and exclusively arboreal, which have gray or brown hairy bodies, long forelimbs with either two toes (in *Choloepus*) or three (in *Bradypus*), and only a rudimentary tail. They like hanging (face upwards) from branches [M.E. *slāwthe, slōwthe* fr. *slāw, slōw*, slow]

sloth bear *Melursus labiatus*, fam. *Ursidae*, a black, shaggy bear of India and Ceylon, feeding on fruit, honey and insects

sloth·ful (slɔ́θfəl, slóuθfəl) *adj.* lazy ‖ spiritually apathetic

slot machine (*Am.*= *Br.* fruit machine) a coin-operated gambling machine ‖ (*Br.*) a machine (esp. one selling candy, cigarettes etc., or one used for playing a mechanical game) set in operation by the insertion of a coin in a slot

slouch (slautʃ) **1.** *n.* a bad posture or manner of walking, with drooping back and shoulders and loose, lax muscles and limbs ‖ a lazy or incompetent person ‖ the downward bend of the brim of a hat **2.** *v.i.* to hold oneself or move with a drooping posture ‖ (of a hat brim) to droop downward ‖ *v.t.* to cause (one's shoulders) to droop ‖ to pull down (one's hat) so that it partly hides one's face [origin unknown]

slouch hat a soft felt hat with a wide drooping brim

slouch·i·ly (sláutʃili:) *adv.* in a slouchy manner

slouch·i·ness (sláutʃi:nis) *n.* the state or quality of being slouchy

slouch·y (sláutʃi:) *comp.* **slouch·i·er** *superl.* **slouch·i·est** *adj.* slouching, esp. in posture

slough (slʌf) **1.** *n.* any part that an animal casts or molts, esp. a snake's cast-off skin ‖ dead outer skin that comes away when a wound heals **2.**

CONCISE PRONUNCIATION KEY: **(a)** æ, *cat*; ɑ, *car*; ɔ *fawn*; ei, *snake*. **(e)** e, *hen*; i:, *sheep*; iə, *deer*; εə, *bear*. **(i)** i, *fish*; ai, *tiger*; ə:, *bird*. **(o)** ɒ, *ox*; au, *cow*; ou, *goat*; u, *poor*; ɔi, *royal*. **(u)** ʌ, *duck*; u, *bull*; u:, *goose*; ə, *bacillus*; ju:, *cube*. x, *loch*; θ, *think*; ð, *bother*; z, *Zen*; ʒ, *corsage*; dʒ, *savage*; ŋ, *orangutang*; j, *yak*; ʃ, *fish*; tʃ, *fetch*; 'l, *rabble*; 'n, *redden*. Complete pronunciation key appears inside front cover.

v.t. to throw off, shed ‖ *v.i.* to shed a skin etc. ‖ to be shed [M.E. *slouh*]
slough (slau, slu:) *n.* a marshy, muddy place or swamp ‖ a state of hopeless dejection [O.E. *slōh*]
Slo·vak (slóuvæk, slóuvɑk) **1.** *n.* a member of a Slavic people of Slovakia ‖ their W. Slavic language, related to Czech **2.** *adj.* of Slovakia, the Slovaks or their language
Slo·va·ki·a (slouvɑ́ki:ə, slouvǽkiə) the eastern region of Czechoslovakia, containing the western Carpathians (Gerlachovka, 8,737 ft). Chief town: Bratislava. Slovakia is chiefly agricultural (wheat, corn, wine and cattle raising in the mountains), but industry is being developed (textiles, lumber products, paper, hydroelectricity, metal working). Slovakia was settled (c. 6th c.) by Slavs and conquered by the Magyars (10th c.). It remained part of Hungary until 1918, when it became part of Czechoslovakia. It became a Nazi puppet state (1939), and was returned to Czechoslovakia (1945)
Slo·va·ki·an (slouvɑ́ki:ən, slouvǽki:ən) *n.* and *adj.* Slovak
slov·en (slʌ́vən) *n.* a person who is habitually untidy in appearance, slipshod or lazy in his work and mental outlook, and dirty in his habits [etym. doubtful]
Slo·vene (slóuvi:n, slouví:n) **1.** *n.* a member of a Slavic people in Slovenia ‖ their Slavic language **2.** *adj.* of Slovenia, the Slovenes, their language etc. [G.]
Slo·ve·ni·a (slouví:ni:ə) the northernmost constituent republic (area 7,837 sq. miles, pop. 1,792,000) of Yugoslavia. Capital: Ljubljana. It is largely mountainous, rising to 9,393 ft in the northwest (Julian Alps). Crops: cereals, potatoes, wine, fruit, hops and flax. Livestock: cattle. Minerals: coal, mercury, petroleum. Industries: iron and steel, textiles, wood industries, tourism. Slovenia was under Hapsburg domination from the 13th c. until the collapse of Austria-Hungary (1918), when it became part ot the kingdom later called Yugoslavia
Slo·ve·ni·an (slouví:ni:ən) *n.* and *adj.* Slovene
slov·en·li·ness (slʌ́vənli:nis) *n.* the state or quality of being slovenly
slov·en·ly (slʌ́vənli:) *comp.* **slov·en·li·er** *superl.* **slov·en·li·est** *adj.* of or like a sloven ‖ loose, undisciplined, *slovenly thinking*
slow (slou) **1.** *adj.* taking more time than is regarded as normal, *a slow response to a stimulus, slow combustion* ‖ acting, changing, moving etc. in such a way that more time is occupied than is usual, *a slow train, a slow worker* ‖ long drawn out, *a slow recovery* ‖ not easily roused, *a slow audience* ‖ not hasty, *slow to take offense* ‖ dilatory, in a way that shows lack of prudence, *slow to grasp an opportunity* ‖ (of business) not active, slack ‖ (of a timepiece) indicating a time behind the actual time ‖ needing more time than is usual to grasp, memorize or deal with ideas, *a rather slow boy* ‖ failing to amuse, interest or stimulate, *the party was a slow affair* ‖ (of a fire or oven) burning or heating very moderately ‖ (of a pitch, wicket, court, track etc.) soft and causing a slowing down **2.** *v.t.* (with 'down' or 'up') to reduce the speed or rate of production of, *to slow up a machine* ‖ *v.i.* (with 'down' or 'up') to move or act at a reduced speed, *he slowed down at the crossroads* **3.** *adv.* slowly **to go slow** (*Br.*) to work at less than full production as a way of enforcing a demand [O.E. *slāw*]
slow coach a person who thinks or acts slowly
slow·down (slóudaun) *n.* (*Am.*=*Br.* go-slow) a deliberate slowing down in production by workers, to put pressure on management
slow·ly (slóuli:) *adv.* in a slow way
slow match a match or fuse used for firing blasting charges, made to burn slowly and evenly at a given rate
slow-mo·tion (slóumóuʃən) **1.** *adj.* of a film taken at an accelerated rate of exposures per second, which produces very slow action when projected at normal speed ‖ of a film projected at a greatly reduced speed **2.** *n.* this action or speed
slow-mov·ing (slóumú:viŋ) *adj.* moving slowly ‖ (*commerce*, of stock) slow in selling
slow·ness (slóunis) *n.* the state or quality of being slow
slow·poke (slóupouk) *n.* (*pop.*) a person who thinks or acts with irritating slowness
slow virus (*med.*) a virus that remains latent for many years, believed to be causative agent in rheumatoid arthritis and in multiple sclerosis, kuru, and other nervous disorders
slow·worm (slóuwə:rm) *n.* a blindworm [O.E. *slāwyrm*]
slub (slʌb) **1.** *n.* a lump in yarn, either accidental or contrived ‖ (*slang*) a badly developed suburban area comprising cheap housing and commercial or industrial properties **2.** *v.t. pres. part.* **slub·bing** *past* and *past part.* **slubbed** to draw out (wool) and twist it slightly, in preparation for spinning [origin unknown]
sludge (slʌdʒ) *n.* a thick suspension of solid matter in a liquid, e.g. the mud on a riverbed, or carbonaceous mixture with oil as the waste product of an internal-combustion engine ‖ the treated solid matter of sewage after drying, used as a fertilizer ‖ floating (partly melted) ice or snow **slúdg·y** *adj.* [origin unknown]
slue *n.* *SLEW
slue (slu:) *n.* a slough, swamp
slue, slew 1. *v.i. pres. part.* **slu·ing, slew·ing** *past* and *past part.* **slued, slewed** to swing or turn in an arc, esp. about a point or axis ‖ *v.t.* to cause to swing around **2.** *n.* a movement of this kind [origin unknown]
slug (slʌg) *n.* any roughly shaped piece of metal, esp. the head of a bullet ‖ (*printing*) a line of linotype type ‖ (*printing*) a strip of metal for spacing between lines ‖ (*printing*) a short title of one line used by compositors, editors etc. to identify a piece in process of going to press ‖ a token for an automatic machine ‖ a piece of metal put fraudulently into an automatic machine instead of the proper coin [etym. doubtful]
slug *n.* a usually terrestrial gastropod mollusk, having a much reduced shell or the shell represented by calcareous granules only. The lower surface is a creeping organ. Slugs are herbivorous and are often destructive to cultivated plants. They are widely distributed in tropical and temperate regions [etym. doubtful]
slug 1. *v.t. pres. part.* **slug·ging** *past* and *past part.* **slugged** (*pop.*) to hit hard, esp. with the fist **2.** *n.* a heavy blow [etym. doubtful]
slug·gard (slʌ́gərd) *n.* a lazy, slow, inactive person
slug·ger (slʌ́gər) *n.* a hard-hitting boxer or baseball batter
slug·gish (slʌ́giʃ) *adj.* slow to act or move, *a sluggish engine, sluggish liver* ‖ (*commerce*) with few transactions taking place, *a sluggish market*
sluice (slu:s) **1.** *n.* an artificial waterway with a gate or other device to control the flow and level of the water ‖ the device itself ‖ the stream on either side of the device ‖ any channel which drains off surplus water ‖ an inclined trough for floating down logs or washing ores, esp. such a trough with a grooved bottom to hold quicksilver for catching gold **2.** *v. pres. part.* **sluic·ing** *past* and *past part.* **sluiced** *v.t.* to flood or cleanse with water from a sluice ‖ to wash thoroughly ‖ to transport (logs etc.) by the stream of a sluice ‖ to wash (ores) in a sluice ‖ *v.i.* to pour through, or as if through, a sluice [fr. O.F. *escluse*]
sluice·way (slú:swei) *n.* an artificial channel controlled by a sluice gate, a sluice
Sluis, Battle of (slɔis) a naval battle (1340) off the coast of the Low Countries, in which the fleet of Edward III of England defeated that of Philippe VI of France. It was the first important battle of the Hundred Years' War
slum (slʌm) **1.** *n.* a heavily populated urban area of dilapidated buildings characterized by poverty and filth **2.** *v.i. pres. part.* **slum·ming** *past* and *past part.* **slummed** to visit a poor neighborhood in search of amusement [cant origin]
slum·ber (slʌ́mbər) **1.** *n.* (*rhet.*) sleep ‖ a light sleep **2.** *v.i.* (*rhet.*) to sleep ‖ to sleep lightly ‖ *v.t.* (with 'away') to spend or waste (time) in sleep or as if in sleep **slum·ber·ous** (slʌ́mbərəs), **slum·brous** (slʌ́mbrəs) *adjs* [M.E. *slumeren*]
slum·lord (slʌ́mlɔrd) *n.* (pejorative) a landlord who neglects or abandons urban properties
slump (slʌmp) **1.** *v.i.* to fall suddenly, e.g. into a bog or water or through ice ‖ to fall bodily, *he slumped to the floor* ‖ (*commerce*) to fall suddenly in value or activity **2.** *n.* a sudden or continued drop in prices or stagnation in economic activity (cf. RECESSION) **in a slump** in a period of low spirits or flagging inspiration [prob. imit.]
slump·in·fla·tion (slʌmpinfléiʃən) *n.* (*economics*) a period of combined recession and inflation *Cf* STAGFLATION
slung *past* and *past part.* of SLING
slunk *past* and *past part.* of SLINK
slur (slə:r) **1.** *v. pres. part.* **slur·ring** *past* and *past part.* **slurred** *v.i.* to speak indistinctly by running sounds together ‖ (with 'over') to make deliberately unemphatic reference, *he slurred over the facts and figures in his argument* ‖ *v.t.* to utter (speech sounds) indistinctly by running them together ‖ to speak of someone in such a way as to throw doubt on (his reputation) ‖ (*mus.*) to sing or play legato, or mark (notes) for performance in this way **2.** *n.* the act of slurring ‖ a remark which throws doubt on a reputation ‖ (*mus.*) a sign showing that the notes should be sung or played legato ‖ (*printing*) an indistinct, blurred impression [fr. dial. *slur*, thin watery mud]
slurb (slə:rb) *n.* (*slang*) a poorly designed, constructed, and/or maintained suburb *Cf* SLUB
slur·ry (slə́:ri:) *pl.* **slur·ries** *n.* a thin mixture of water and insoluble matter, e.g. clay, lime or cement [M.E. *slory*]
slur·vi·ar (slə́:rvi:ə:r) *n.* slurred speech
slush (slʌʃ) *n.* watery mud ‖ melting snow ‖ a greasy mixture used to prevent rust or to lubricate machinery ‖ (*pop.*) sickly sentiment, gush [origin unknown]
slush fund a fund for use in bribery or other corrupt practices in favor of a private interest
slush·y (slʌ́ʃi:) *comp.* **slush·i·er** *superl.* **slush·i·est** *adj.* of or having the character of slush ‖ covered with or full of slush
slut (slʌt) *n.* a dirty, slovenly woman ‖ a loose woman, esp. a prostitute [origin unknown]
Slu·ter (slú:tər) Claus (c. 1350-1406), sculptor of the Burgundian school. He brought the Renaissance ideal of lifelikeness and natural expressiveness in pose into the sculpture of Gothic Europe. The 'Well of Moses' (Dijon) is his masterpiece
slut·tish (slʌ́tiʃ) *adj.* characteristic of a slut ‖ (of a woman) very dirtily and untidily dressed
sly (slai) *comp.* **sly·er, sli·er** *superl.* **sly·est, sli·est** *adj.* clever at concealing one's intention, artful, *a sly rogue* ‖ showing clever underhandedness, *a sly trick* ‖ crafty, mischievous, *sly wit* **on the sly** slyly, *he did it on the sly* **slý·ly, slí·ly** *adv.* [fr. O.N. *slœgr*]
slype (slaip) *n.* a covered passage between a transept in an English cathedral and the chapter house or deanery [perh. fr. W. Flem. *slipe, slijpe*, secret path]
smack (smæk) **1.** *n.* a slight characteristic taste or flavor, *a smack of cinnamon in the sauce* ‖ a very small quantity, *give each of them just a smack out of your glass* **2.** *v.i.* (with 'of') to have a taste or flavor, *this vegetable smacks of aniseed* ‖ to have a hint or suggestion, *his stories smacked of the sea* [O.E. *smæc*]
smack 1. *n.* a slap, a quick blow with the open hand or other flat surface ‖ the sound of such a blow ‖ the sharp noise made by compressing and suddenly opening the lips, expressing enjoyment or anticipation, esp. of food or drink ‖ a loud kiss **2.** *v.t.* to slap loudly ‖ to part (the lips) with a sharp sound, in anticipation or enjoyment, esp. of food or drink ‖ to put, throw or bring into contact with a smack, *he smacked his hand against the pillar* ‖ *v.i.* to strike against something with the noise of a smack **3.** *adv.* with sudden direct violence, *he drove smack into a tree* ‖ completely, directly, *each shot was smack on the bull's-eye* [prob. imit.]
smack *n.* a fishing boat rigged fore and aft and having a well for keeping the catch alive [prob. fr. Du. *smak*]
smack·er (smǽkər) *n.* (*pop.*) a loud kiss ‖ a heavy blow
small (smɔl) **1.** *adj.* restricted in size by comparison with most others of the same kind or class etc., *a small garden* ‖ more restricted in quality, amount, value, duration etc. than some standard of comparision, *a small spoonful* ‖ of little importance, *a small matter* ‖ of inferior rank or influence ‖ not prominent, modest, *in a small way* ‖ acting or doing business on a limited scale, *a small investor* ‖ small-minded, petty, (of sound or the voice) weak **to feel small** to feel humiliated **2.** *adv.* in small pieces **3.** *n.* the small, narrow part of something, *the small of the back* ‖ (*Br., pl.*) small articles of clothing or laundry, esp. underclothes [O.E. *smæl*]
small arms firearms which can be carried on one's person
small beer a beer weak or poor in quality ‖ someone or something of little importance
small bond a baby bond

CONCISE PRONUNCIATION KEY: **(a)** æ, *c*a*t*; ɑ, *c*a*r*; ɔ *f*aw*n*; ei, *sn*a*ke*. **(e)** e, *h*e*n*; i:, *sh*ee*p*; iə, *d*ee*r*; ɛə, *b*ea*r*. **(i)** i, *f*i*sh*; ai, *t*i*ger*; ə:, *b*i*rd*. **(o)** o, *o*x; au, *c*ow; ou, *g*oa*t*; u, *p*oo*r*; ɔi, *r*oy*al*. **(u)** ʌ, *d*u*ck*; u, *b*u*ll*; u:, *g*oo*se*; ə, *b*a*cill*u*s*; ju:, *c*u*be*. x, *lo*ch; θ, *th*ink; ð, *b*oth*er*; z, *Z*en; ʒ, *cors*age; dʒ, *sav*age; ŋ, *orangut*ang; j, *y*ak; ʃ, *f*ish; tʃ, *fe*tch; 'l, *rabb*le; 'n, *redd*en. Complete pronunciation key appears inside front cover.

small-bore (smɔ́lbɔr, smɔ́lbour) *adj.* of or involving firearms having a relatively small bore, esp. a caliber of .22 in.
small bower *BOWER (either of two anchors)
small business an enterprise eligible for special consideration in dealing with government agencies because of limitation in volume of business and number of employees, such limitation varying by industry
small change coins, esp. of low denomination
small fruit (*Am.*=*Br.* soft fruit) strawberries, raspberries and red, black or white currants, or similar fruit for the table growing on plants or low bushes
small fry children ‖ people of minor importance
small·hold·er (smɔ́lhouldər) *n.* (*Br.*) a person who works a small holding
small holding (*Br.*) a piece of land small enough to be farmed by one man and usually rented
small hours (with 'the') the hours from midnight to approximately 4 a.m.
small intestine the narrow upper part of the intestines lined with a glandular mucous membrane which secretes enzymes responsible for the digestion of food and through which digested nutrients pass into the blood and lymph. It is divided into three parts, the duodenum, jejunum and ileum
small-mind·ed (smɔ́lmáindid) *adj.* narrow in outlook and sympathies ‖ petty
small nettle *Urtica urens,* an annual stinging weed found in Europe and North America
small of the back the hollow part of the back just above the hips
small pica an old size of type (approx. 11 point)
small potatoes (*pop.*) a person or thing of trivial importance
small·pox (smɔ́lpɒks) *n.* a severe and contagious virus disease causing fever, prostration, skin pustules and in many cases death
small stuff (*naut.*) small rope, usually designated by the number of threads it contains
small·sword (smɔ́lsɔrd, smɔ́lsourd) *n.* a light tapering sword for thrusting only and used, esp. in the 18th c., for duels and fencing
small talk light conversation about insignificant matters
small-time (smɔ́ltáim) *adj.* (*pop.*) insignificant, petty ‖ (*pop.*) of amateur standing
small-town (smɔ́ltáun) *adj.* of or characteristic of a small town
smalt (smɔlt) *n.* blue glass made by the fusion of potash, cobalt oxide and silica ‖ the deep-blue pigment ground from this [F. fr. Ital.]
sma·rag·dite (smərǽgdait) *n.* a green variety of hornblende [F. fr. Gk]
smarm·y (smɑ́rmi:) *adj.* fulsomely flattering [etym. doubtful]
Smart (smɑrt), Christopher (1722-71), English poet. He is best known for his 'A Song to David' (1763)
smart (smɑrt) **1.** *adj.* sharp, severe, *a smart rebuke* ‖ brisk, lively, *a smart pace* ‖ clever in an impudent way, *don't get smart with me* ‖ intelligent, *a smart student* ‖ showing lively intelligence, *a smart piece of investigation* ‖ shrewd in a selfish or dishonest way, *a smart politician* ‖ well styled, *a smart car* ‖ fashionable, *a smart nightclub* ‖ well cut, *a smart suit* ‖ well groomed and carefully dressed **2.** *adv.* (*pop.*) smartly [O.E. *smeart*]
smart 1. *v.i.* to cause a sharp, stinging pain ‖ to feel such a pain ‖ (with 'under') to suffer mental pain, *smarting under a sense of injustice* **2.** *n.* a sharp, stinging pain ‖ mental pain, esp. because of hurt pride [O.E. *smeortan*]
smart al·eck, smart-al·ec (smɑ́rtælik) *n.* someone who shows off in an obnoxiously conceited way
smart bomb (*mil.*) an airborne missile capable of being directed to its target by laser beams, television, or other homing device
smart·en (smɑ́rt'n) *v.t.* to make smart ‖ *v.i.* (with 'up') to become smart, esp. in appearance
smart instrument (*mil.*) device equipped with infrared, radar, or similar guidance that makes possible automatic selection of objectives
smart·ly (smɑ́rtli:) *adv.* in a smart way
smart·ness (smɑ́rtnis) *n.* the quality of being smart
smash (smæʃ) **1.** *v.t.* to break violently to pieces, to shatter ‖ to hurt or damage very badly, *he smashed his hand in the door* ‖ to destroy or wreck ‖ to defeat, *to smash an attack* ‖ to ruin, esp. to cause to become bankrupt ‖ to hit or throw violently, *I smashed it on the head with a hammer, he smashed a brick through the window* ‖ (*tennis*) to hit (the ball) sharply downwards with a hard overhand stroke ‖ *v.i.* to come into violent collision, *my car smashed into the bridge* ‖ to break into many pieces ‖ to progress with violent effort so as to overcome obstacles, *they smashed through the jungle* ‖ to be ruined or go bankrupt **2.** *n.* the act or noise of breaking into pieces ‖ a heavy blow with the fist ‖ (*tennis*) a hard overhand hit ‖ (*Br.*) a collision with another car etc. ‖ ruin, complete financial failure **3.** *adv.* (*pop.*) smack, *we went smash into a tree* **smásh·ing** *adj.* crushing, *a smashing blow on the chin* ‖ (esp. *Br.*) very impressive, *a smashing victory* [imit.]
smash hit a play or film which has an enormous success
smash-up (smǽʃʌp) *n.* a violent collision between motor vehicles ‖ a sudden, disastrous collapse in health, business, national economy, human relationships etc.
smat·ter·ing (smǽtəriŋ) *n.* (with 'of') a slight, superficial knowledge, *a smattering of French* [origin unknown]
smear (smiər) *v.t.* to spread, daub (a greasy, oily or sticky substance) over an area, *to smear butter on bread* ‖ to spread (something) with a greasy, oily or sticky substance, *to smear bread with butter* ‖ to spread (e.g. wet ink or paint) beyond its proper outline by rubbing, *he smeared the paint with his hand* ‖ to soil or stain (something) in this manner ‖ to spoil the good reputation of (someone), esp. falsely ‖ to prepare as a smear for microscopic examination ‖ (*pop.*) to defeat overwhelmingly [O.E. *smerian*]
smear *n.* a mark on a surface made by smearing ‖ a preparation of a substance for microscopic examination ‖ something which casts a slur on someone's good reputation, esp. falsely [O.E. *smeoru, smeru*]
smell (smel) **1.** *v. pres. part.* **smel·ling** *past* and *past part.* **smelled, smelt** (smelt) *v.t.* to perceive or recognize by means of the nose and olfactory nerves ‖ to sniff the odor of (something) either to enjoy it or to identify it ‖ to detect or discover as if by smell ‖ *v.i.* to emit a smell, *the pastry smells good* ‖ (with 'of') to emit a characteristic smell, *the old man smelled of whiskey* ‖ to have a sense of smell **to smell out** to look for or discover as if by smell **to smell up** to fill up with a (usually bad) odor **2.** *n.* the sensation which results when the olfactory organs respond to the stimuli of some gases, vapors or very fine solid suspensions in the air ‖ the sense by which odor is perceived ‖ the act of smelling ‖ the characteristic odor of a substance ‖ an air or hint of something bad, *a smell of corruption lingers about the name* [M.E. *smellen* prob. fr. O.E.]
smelling salts ammonium carbonate mixed with ammonia water and various aromatic substances, whose fumes can be inhaled as a stimulant or restorative
smell·y (sméli:) *comp.* **smell·i·er** *superl.* **smell·i·est** *adj.* having an unpleasant smell
smelt (smelt) *pl.* **smelts, smelt** *n.* a member of *Osmerus,* fam. *Osmeridae,* a genus of small food fishes that resemble the salmon in structure. They are found in the northern hemisphere. They are a translucent greenish color above, are silvery on the sides, and average 8 to 10 ins in length [O.E.]
smelt alt. *past* and *past part.* of SMELL
smelt *v.t.* (*metall.*) to fuse (an ore), usually with chemical reducing agents (e.g. coke), in order to separate out the metal in a molten form **smélt·er** *n.* someone who smelts ‖ the owner or operator of a smelting works ‖ the works itself **smélt·er·y** *pl.* **smelt·er·ies** *n.* a smelting works [prob. fr. M.Du. or M.L.G. *smelten*]
Sme·ta·na (smét'nə, smétɑnɑ), Bedřich (1824-84), Czech composer. His best-known work is 'Ma Vlast' ('My Fatherland'), a set of six orchestral tone poems (1874-9). His successful operas include 'The Bartered Bride' (1866)
sme·tan·e sauce (smétənə) sauce with sour cream, white wine, and onions, and seasoned with salt and pepper, that is served with chicken, veal, or game
smew (smju:) *n. Mergus albellus,* fam. *Anatidae,* a N. European and Asian duck which is the smallest of the merganser group. The male is black and white with a white crest. The female is smaller and grayer. They frequent lakes, reservoirs, rivers and sometimes sea estuaries and are very expert at diving [etym. doubtful]
smid·gen (smídʒən) *n.* (*pop.*) a very small amount [origin unknown]
smi·lax (smáilæks) *n.* a member of *Smilax,* fam. *Liliaceae,* a genus of widely distributed climbing plants with tough, tuberous roots and evergreen leaves. Many species yield sarsaparilla and are cultivated in Mexico, Honduras, Costa Rica, Ecuador, Peru and Jamaica ‖ *Asparagus asparagoides,* fam. *Liliaceae,* a climbing South African plant, with ovate, bright green cladophylls, much cultivated in greenhouses and used by florists for bouquets [L. fr. Gk=bindweed]
smile (smail) **1.** *v. pres. part.* **smil·ing** *past* and *past part.* **smiled** *v.i.* to make a facial expression which may show amusement, satisfaction, affection, irony or derision etc. and which is characterized by a lateral and upward movement of the lips and cheeks and a bright sparkle in the eyes ‖ (with 'at', 'on' or 'upon') to look with this expression ‖ (*rhet.*) to look with favor, *fortune smiled on them* ‖ (*rhet.*) to look welcoming and delightful, *a smiling landscape* ‖ *v.t.* to express with a smile, *to smile a welcome* ‖ to affect or change by smiling, *to smile someone back into good spirits* **2.** *n.* the act of smiling ‖ the facial expression made in smiling ‖ (*rhet.*) favorable aspect, *smiles of fortune* [M.E. *smilen* perh. fr. M.L.G.]
smirch (smə:rtʃ) **1.** *v.t.* to smear (esp. a reputation) **2.** *n.* something which smears, esp. a reputation [prob. fr. O.F. *esmorcher,* to torment]
smirk (smə:rk) **1.** *v.t.* to smile in a conceited or affected way **2.** *n.* such a smile [O.E. *smearcian, smercian*]
smite (smait) **1.** *v.t. pres. part.* **smit·ing** *past* **smote** (smout) *past part.* **smit·ten** (smít'n) (*rhet.*) to deliver a powerful, sudden blow to ‖ (*rhet.*) to inflict a crushing defeat on ‖ (esp. *past part.*) to arouse an intense emotion in, *smitten with remorse* ‖ (esp. *past part.*) to afflict with, *smitten with arthritis* **2.** *n.* (*rhet.*) a tremendous blow [O.E. *smītan*]
Smith (smiθ), Adam (1723-90), Scottish economist. His 'Wealth of Nations' (1776), surveying the new world of industry and commerce, founded modern classical economics, substituting economic liberalism for mercantilist protection. He condemned unwarranted state control and monopoly and upheld private enterprise, competition, free trade and the laissez-faire state as the right and efficient way of producing maximum wealth and happiness. His ideas dominated the whole of industrial Europe and America until the revival of the opposing theories of state control and protection
Smith, Alfred Emanuel (1873-1944), U.S. politician and governor (1918-20, 1922-8) of New York. He was the first Roman Catholic to run (1928) for the U.S. presidency. He lost to Herbert Hoover, but polled the largest (c. 15 million) popular vote given to a Democrat up to that time
Smith, David (1906-65), U.S. painter and sculptor. He changed (c. 1933) from painting to sculpture, and was a pioneer in working with metal
Smith, Sir Francis Pettit (1808-74), English inventor. He devised and patented the screw-propelled boat (1836) adopted by the British Navy in 1844
Smith, Ian Douglas (1919-), Rhodesian politician, leader of a white supremacist party, prime minister of Southern Rhodesia (1964-5) and Rhodesia (1965-79). After leading his country in a unilateral declaration of independence from the United Kingdom (1965), he was forced to accept the formation of a multiracial coalition government (1978). Black majority rule was established (1980), and Rhodesia became Zimbabwe
Smith, John (1580-1631), English colonist. He was one of the original settlers of Jamestown (1607), and was the colony's leader (1608-9). He mapped the New England coast (1614)
Smith, Joseph (1805-44), American religious leader, founder (1830) of the Church of Jesus Christ of Latter-Day Saints (*MORMON)
Smith, Walter Bedell (1895-1961), U.S. general and diplomat. As chief of staff (1942-5) to Gen. Dwight D. Eisenhower, he negotiated for the Allies the surrender (1943) of Italy and (1945) that of Germany
smith (smiθ) *n.* someone, e.g. a blacksmith or silversmith, who works metal [O.E.]
Smith Act a U.S. Congressional act (1940) passed during the 2nd world war. It made it a crime to advocate, or belong to a group that

advocated, the violent overthrow of the U.S. government

Smith College the private women's college founded (1871) in Northampton, Mass., under the will of Sophia Smith (1796-1870) of Hatfield

smith·er·eens (smìðərí:nz) *pl. n.* (*pop.*) small fragments [SMITHERS+Ir. dim. ending]

smith·ers (smíθərz) *pl. n.* (*pop.*) smithereens [origin unknown]

smith·er·y (smíθəri:) *pl.* **smith·er·ies** *n.* the work of a smith ‖ a smithy

Smith·so·ni·an Institution (smiθsóuni:ən) an educational institution in Washington, D.C., founded (1846) by an act of Congress which accepted a trust bequeathed by James Smithson (1765-1829), a British scientist, providing for its establishment. Its governing board of regents includes the U.S. vice-president. The institution conducts activities in all branches of science

smith·son·ite (smíθsənait) *n.* natural zinc carbonate, $ZnCO_3$ ‖ (*Br.*) a former name for hemimorphite [after James *Smithson* (1765–1829), British chemist and mineralogist]

smith·y (smíθi:, smíði:) *pl.* **smith·ies** *n.* a blacksmith's workshop, forge [fr. O.N. *smithja*]

smitten *past part.* of SMITE

smock (smɒk) **1.** *n.* a loose outer garment, resembling a long shirt, worn esp. by children and artists to protect their clothes **2.** *v.t.* to ornament with smocking **smóck·ing** *n.* decorative needlework used to gather cloth and make it hang in folds [O.E. *smoc*]

smock·mill (smɒ́kmil) *n.* a windmill with revolving cap and stationary body

smog (smɒg, smɔg) *n.* heavy fog injurious to health because it contains smoke and gases produced by the partial combustion of fuels [SMOKE+FOG]

smog·out (smɒ́gaut) *n.* (*meteor*) a condition of nonvisibility because of smog

smoke (smouk) *n.* fine solid particles, usually carbon, resulting from incomplete combustion suspended in the air and carried by air currents ‖ (*phys. chem.*) a suspension of solid particles in a gas ‖ any vapor resembling smoke ‖ the act of smoking tobacco ‖ something to smoke, esp. a cigarette **to go up in smoke** to be pure waste ‖ to have no useful outcome [O.E. *smoca*]

smoke *pres. part.* **smok·ing** *past* and *past part.* **smoked** *v.i.* to draw smoke into the mouth or lungs and exhale it ‖ to emit smoke by virtue of being in action ‖ to emit smoke by reason of faulty burning or improper draft, *the fire is smoking badly* ‖ to emit any vapor resembling smoke ‖ *v.t.* to cover with carbon particles by exposing to smoke, *to smoke glass* ‖ to cure (meat etc.) by exposure to smoke ‖ to draw smoke from (tobacco, a pipe etc.) into the mouth or lungs and then exhale it ‖ to bring to a given condition by smoking, *to smoke oneself to death* ‖ to fumigate **to smoke out** to expose to smoke so as to be rid of (a nuisance), *to smoke out a wasps' nest* ‖ to force (someone) from concealment with, or as if with, smoke, *to smoke out the enemy* [O.E. *smocian*]

smoke bomb a missile which, when it explodes, frees canisters of chemical smoke to act as a screen or marker

smoke·house (smóukhaus) *pl.* **smoke·hous·es** (smóukhauziz) *n.* a room or building where meat or fish is cured by means of smoke ‖ a room in a tannery used for softening hides by smoke from spent tanbark

smoke-in *n.* a gathering in which participants publicly smoke marijuana to protest the drug's legal status

smoke·less (smóuklis) *adj.* making little or no smoke, *smokeless fuel* ‖ free from smoke

smok·er (smóukər) *n.* someone who or something which smokes ‖ a person who smokes tobacco habitually ‖ a railroad car in which passengers are permitted to smoke ‖ a social gathering for men only

smoke screen a dense cloud of smoke produced by chemicals, used to hide military or naval movements or positions from the enemy

smoke-shade *n.* **1.** standard for measuring air pollution **2.** air pollutants *Cf* COEFFICIENT OF HAZE, SOILING INDEX

smoke·stack (smóukstæk) *n.* a chimney or funnel which conveys the smoke from a fire to a high level before it escapes into the air

smok·i·ly (smóukili:) *adv.* in a smoky manner

smok·i·ness (smóuki:nis) *n.* the state or quality of being smoky

smok·y (smóuki:) *comp.* **smok·i·er** *superl.* **smok·i·est** *adj.* of or like smoke ‖ giving off smoke, esp. more than is desired or expected ‖ filled with smoke ‖ soiled by smoke ‖ of the color or smell of smoke

Smoky Mountains *GREAT SMOKY MOUNTAINS

smoky quartz cairngorm

smol·der, smoul·der (smóuldər) **1.** *v.i.* to burn slowly at a low heat without flames ‖ to betray feelings one is trying hard to suppress, *his eyes smoldered with indignation* ‖ to exist in a suppressed state, *smoldering resentment* **2.** *n.* the state of smoldering [origin unknown]

Smo·lensk (smoulénsk, smʌljénsk) a communications and industrial center (pop. 305,800) in the R.S.F.S.R., U.S.S.R., on the upper Dnieper. Industries: textiles, engineering, woodworking, food processing. Its famous kremlin (16th c.) and cathedral (17th c.) were largely destroyed in the 2nd world war

Smol·lett (smɒ́let), Tobias George (1721-71), Scottish novelist. His racy, picaresque novels include 'Roderick Random' (1748), 'Peregrine Pickle' (1751) and 'Humphry Clinker' (1771)

smolt (smoult) *n.* a two-year-old salmon, about 7 ins long, with newly acquired silvery scales, heading seaward from the river for the first time (cf. PARR, cf. GRILSE) [origin unknown]

SM-1 (*mil.*) U.S. surface-to-air solid-fuel missile

smooth (smu:ð) **1.** *adj.* having an even surface which is free from bumps, projections etc., not rough, *a smooth tabletop* ‖ having a surface which offers little frictional resistance when a body slides or rolls over it ‖ homogeneous, not granular, in structure, *a smooth paste* ‖ even in flow ‖ free from obstacles or difficulties ‖ free from hair, beard etc. ‖ suave, ingratiating, *smooth talk* ‖ marked by calm even progress ‖ not jolting, *a smooth crossing* ‖ having a surface leveled down by wear, *a smooth tire* ‖ (of sound) not grating, rasping or loud ‖ (*phon.*) not aspirated **2.** *v.t.* to make smooth ‖ to free from difficulty, *he smoothed the way for us* **to smooth over** to handle (e.g. a situation) in such a way as to reduce or avoid anger, ill will etc. **3.** *n.* an act of smoothing ‖ *ROUGH [O.E. *smōth*]

Smoot-Haw·ley Tariff Act (smú:thɔ́li:) a U.S. Congressional act (1930) of President Hoover's administration. Initiated by U.S. Senator Reed Smoot (1862-1941) from Utah, it provided for a U.S. tariff at the highest protective level in the nation's history. It provoked retaliatory tariff acts from foreign countries, causing a sharp decline in U.S. foreign trade

smooth·bore (smú:ðbɔr, smú:ðbour) **1.** *n.* a gun whose barrel is not rifled **2.** *adj.* (of a gun) having no rifling

smooth breathing *BREATHING

smooth·en (smú:ðən) *v.t.* to make smooth ‖ *v.i.* to become smooth

smooth-faced (smú:ðféist) *adj.* cleanshaven ‖ (*Br.*) smooth but insincere in manner ‖ having a smooth surface

smoothing plane a small, finely set carpenter's plane used in finishing

smooth muscle contractile tissue, lacking cross striations, associated with the walls of hollow viscera, e.g. the stomach and bladder, in the vertebrate body (cf. STRIATED MUSCLE, cf. CARDIAC MUSCLE, cf. SKELETAL MUSCLE)

smooth-spo·ken (smú:ðspóukən) *adj.* speaking in a pleasing, polished manner, sometimes with a hint of deception

smooth-tongued (smú:ðtʌ́ŋd) *adj.* smooth-spoken, esp. saying only what is accepted with pleasure and without question

smor·gas·bord (smɔ́rgəsbɔrd, smɔ́rgəsbourd) *n.* a buffet meal at which a great variety of dishes is offered [Swed. *smörgåsbord*]

smote *past* of SMITE

smoth·er (smʌ́ðər) **1.** *v.t.* to cover so completely, esp. with a mass of little density, that air or light is excluded, *to smother a fire with ash* ‖ to kill by depriving of air ‖ to suppress and hide (e.g. laughter, oaths, a yawn, rage etc.) by an effort of the will, *to smother a yawn* ‖ to give to in profusion, *to smother with kisses* ‖ to cover thickly, *to smother a steak in mushrooms* ‖ (*pop.*) to overcome (opponents) or win (a game) overwhelmingly ‖ *v.i.* to die for lack of air ‖ to be unable to breathe freely **2.** *n.* something which smothers, esp. a thick cloud of dust, gas, vapor etc. [M.E. *smorther* fr. O.E.]

smoul·der *SMOLDER

smudge (smʌdʒ) **1.** *v. pres. part.* **smudg·ing** *past* and *past part.* **smudged** *v.t.* to blur (ink, paint, a piece of writing or painting) ‖ to soil by touching with something dirty ‖ to smoke (an orchard) against frost or insects ‖ *v.i.* to become smudged ‖ to be susceptible to becoming smudged, *pastel smudges easily* **2.** *n.* a mark made by smudging ‖ heavy smoke used to protect an orchard against frost or repel insects etc. **smúdg·i·ly** *adv.* **smúdg·i·ness** *n.* **smúdg·y** *comp.* **smudg·i·er** *superl.* **smudg·i·est** *adj.* [origin unknown]

smudge pot a burner put in an orchard, for producing smudge

smug (smʌg) *comp.* **smug·ger** *superl.* **smug·gest** *adj.* very self-satisfied and showing this by manner or appearance [origin unknown]

smug·gle (smʌ́g'l) *pres. part.* **smug·gling** *past* and *past part.* **smug·gled** *v.t.* to import or export (goods liable to customs duty) without paying duty ‖ to convey secretly in defiance of the law or of prohibitions, *he smuggled the letter out of the country* ‖ *v.i.* to engage in smuggling **smúg·gler** *n.* someone who smuggles, esp. for gain [prob. of L.G. or Du. origin]

smut (smʌt) **1.** *n.* a small piece of solid, usually unburned carbon, carried off from burning fuel by the uprush of hot air and gases ‖ the black mark made by a smut ‖ a disease of cereal or other plants, affecting the seed-bearing stem and the seed itself and turning them black, caused by basidiomycete fungi ‖ such a fungus ‖ indecent talk, pictures etc. **2.** *v. pres. part.* **smut·ting** *past* and *past part.* **smut·ted** *v.t.* to mark with smuts ‖ to infect with smut ‖ to blacken ‖ *v.i.* to become infected by smut [akin to M.H.G. *smutzen*]

Smuts (smʌts), Jan Christiaan (1870-1950), South African statesman and field marshal. A Boer guerrilla leader in the Boer War (1899-1902), he supported Botha's postwar policy of Anglo-Boer cooperation and played a leading part in the establishment of the Union of South Africa (1910). He served as a general in the 1st world war and as a member of the British war cabinet (1917-18). He helped to found the League of Nations. He was prime minister of South Africa (1919-24 and 1939-48). Smuts commanded the South African army in the 2nd world war and became a British field marshal (1941). He drafted the preamble to the U.N. charter and had much influence on the development of the British Commonwealth. He is the author of 'Holism and Evolution' (1926), a philosophical study of evolution

smut·ti·ly (smʌ́tili:) *adv.* in a smutty way

smut·ti·ness (smʌ́ti:nis) *n.* the state or quality of being smutty

smut·ty (smʌ́ti:) *comp.* **smut·ti·er** *superl.* **smut·ti·est** *adj.* soiled with smut ‖ (of plants) affected with smut ‖ indecent

Smyr·na (smɔ́:rnə) *IZMIR

snack (snæk) *n.* a very slight, hurried meal, esp. between regular meals [prob. fr. M.Du.]

snaf·fle (snǽfəl) **1.** *n.* a bridle bit jointed in the middle and having no curb **2.** *v.t. pres. part.* **snaf·fling** *past* and *past part.* **snaf·fled** to fit with or control with a snaffle ‖ (*Br., pop.*) to filch [perh. akin to Du. or L.G. *snavel*, horse's muzzle]

snag (snæg) **1.** *n.* the roughly pointed piece left when a tree trunk, branch, tooth etc. is unevenly broken off ‖ a submerged tree or branch in a river etc. which may impede navigation or damage the hull of a boat ‖ a difficulty which at first is not seen to exist but which emerges ‖ any sharp projection ‖ a small tear, broken thread etc. made by such a projection **2.** *v.t. pres. part.* **snag·ging** *past* and *past part.* **snagged** to catch (a boat etc.) on a snag [prob. of Scand. origin]

snag·gle·tooth (snǽg'ltu:θ) *pl.* **snag·gle·teeth** (snǽg'lti:θ) *n.* the sharp, broken stump of a tooth ‖ a tooth that sticks out past the others **snag·gle·toothed** (snǽg'ltu:θt, snǽg'ltu:ðd) *adj.* [fr. dial. *snaggle*, irregularly shaped tooth +TOOTH]

snail (sneil) *n.* one of many species of gastropod mollusks with a spiral protective shell into which it can withdraw its body. The lower surface of the body is a creeping organ. Snails have a mantle cavity that acts as a type of lung. There are marine, freshwater and terrestrial forms. Some species are edible ‖ an irritatingly slow person [O.E. *snægel*]

snail darter (*biol.*) endangered species of small fish native to, and believed unique to, the Little Tennessee River

Snake (sneik) a river (1,038 miles long, navigable for 180 miles) rising in N.W. Wyoming, crossing Idaho, and flowing through Hell's Can-

CONCISE PRONUNCIATION KEY: **(a)** æ, *cat*; ɑ, *car*; ɔ *fawn*; ei, *snake*. **(e)** e, *hen*; i:, *sheep*; iə, *deer*; ɛə, *bear*. **(i)** i, *fish*; ai, *tiger*; ə:, *bird*. **(o)** o, *ox*; au, *cow*; ou, *goat*; u, *poor*; ɔi, *royal*. **(u)** ʌ, *duck*; u, *bull*; u:, *goose*; ə, *bacillus*; ju:, *cube*. x, *loch*; θ, *think*; ð, *bother*; z, *Zen*; ʒ, *corsage*; dʒ, *savage*; ŋ, *orangutang*; j, *yak*; ʃ, *fish*; tʃ, *fetch*; 'l, *rabble*; 'n, *redden*. Complete pronunciation key appears inside front cover.

yon (40 miles long, greatest depth 7,000 ft) in Oregon and Washington before entering the Columbia

snake (sneik) **1.** *n.* any member of the suborder *Ophidia* (or *Serpentes*), order *Squamata*, limbless reptiles with epidermal scales which move by alternately contracting and stretching the body segments ‖ a treacherous, malevolent person **2.** *v.i. pres. part.* **snak·ing** *past* and *past part.* **snaked** to move or twist and turn like a snake ‖ *v.t.* to haul (a log) by a chain or rope ‖ to skid (logs) [O.E. *snaca*]

—More than 2,000 varieties of snake are known. They abound esp. in tropical and subtropical regions. A few, e.g. the poisonous adder and the harmless grass snake, are common in temperate regions. The snake's eyelids are fused near the eye, forming a transparent membrane. Its wide jaws enable it to swallow prey much larger than its own diameter, its body being very extensile and the skin elastic. Some varieties have poisonous fangs, others kill their prey by constriction. Most snakes are oviparous and most are terrestrial, but there are aquatic and arboreal varieties. Snakes slough their skin whole. They are useful to man as destroyers of vermin

snake·bird (snéikbə:rd) *n.* a member of *Anhinga*, a genus of several fish-eating birds with small heads and sharp bills. They are esp. characterized by long slender necks, and are allied to the cormorant

snake·bite (snéikbait) *n.* the bite of a snake ‖ the poisoned condition resulting from the injection of venom by a snake

snake charmer a person who can control (usually poisonous) snakes chiefly by rhythmic movements while playing quiet music on a wind instrument

snake in the grass a secret, treacherous enemy, esp. a secretly faithless friend

snake mode (*mil.*) a control mode in which the pursuing aircraft flies a programmed weaving flight path to allow time to accomplish identification functions

snake muishond *Poecilogale albinucha*, a small, burrowing African muishond

snak·y (snéiki:) *comp.* **snak·i·er** *superl.* **snak·i·est** *adj.* resembling a snake ‖ infested with snakes, *snaky undergrowth* ‖ having the qualities of a snake in the grass

snap (snæp) **1.** *v. pres. part.* **snap·ping** *past* and *past part.* **snapped** *v.t.* to close or open with a sudden rapid movement or action, *to snap a lid on* ‖ to seize with the jaws or as if with the jaws ‖ to cause to make a snapping sound, *to snap one's fingers* ‖ to break with a sharp sound, *to snap a twig in two* ‖ (with 'out', 'back') to utter very fast, esp. in anger, *she snapped back a retort* ‖ to take a snapshot of ‖ (*football*) to put (the ball) in play by sending it back with a quick movement ‖ *v.i.* to break suddenly ‖ to speak sharply, *don't snap at the boy* ‖ to take sharp quick bites, *the fish snapped at the bait* ‖ (with 'at') to snatch eagerly, *he snapped at the chance to go* ‖ to make a sudden sharp sound ‖ to close sharply with such a sound ‖ to move suddenly and fast, *he snapped into action* **to snap one's fingers at** to take no heed of, defy (authority etc.) **to snap out of it** to make an effort of the will and dominate one's lethargy, self-pity etc. **to snap someone's head off** to speak crossly and impatiently to someone **to snap up** to seize (e.g. seats in a theater, bargains, offers etc.) by quick, decisive action **2.** *n.* the act or sound of snapping ‖ the act, or sound, of breaking suddenly ‖ a snap fastener ‖ a snapshot ‖ a short period of unpleasant weather, *a cold snap* ‖ a children's card game in which players simultaneously turn up cards in succession and when two alike are exposed the first to shout 'snap' takes all the exposed cards ‖ (*pop.*) vigor, *put plenty of snap into it* ‖ a kind of crisp, hard cooky, *a ginger snap* (*Am.=Br.* snip) ‖ an easy task giving sure promise of success **3.** *adj.* done quickly without deliberation, *a snap decision* ‖ done quickly, without preparation or warning, *a snap vote* ‖ of something which closes with a snap, *a snap fastener* ‖ (*pop.*) simple, easy **4.** *adv.* with a snap [prob. fr. M.Du. or M.L.G. *snappen*]

snap bean any bean of genus *Phaseolus* of which the entire young green pod is eaten

snap·drag·on (snǽpdrægən) *n.* a member of *Antirrhinum*, fam. *Scrophulariaceae*, a genus of flowering garden plants of Mediterranean origin. The lipped petals meet, and only bees are strong enough to force an entrance

snap fastener (*Am.=Br.* press stud) a fastening device for openings in garments etc. It is in two pieces, the one being a small knob and the other a socket into which this fits when the opening is to be closed

snap·per (snǽpər) *pl.* **snap·per, snap·pers** *n.* any of various carnivorous food or game fishes of fam. *Lutjanidae*, growing up to 2 or 3 ft in length and living in warm seas ‖ a snapping turtle ‖ a click beetle ‖ a snappish irritable person

snap·pi·ly (snǽpili:) *adv.* in a snappy manner

snap·pi·ness (snǽpi:nis) *n.* the state or quality of being snappy

snapping turtle any of several large, ferocious turtles, fam. *Chelydridae*, which inhabit freshwater streams of North America. They seize their prey with a snap of their powerful jaws. They are considered a food delicacy

snap·pish (snǽpiʃ) *adj.* frequently cross, testy ‖ (of dogs) liable to bite

snap·py (snǽpi:) *comp.* **snap·pi·er** *superl.* **snap·pi·est** *adj.* short-tempered ‖ lively, *snappy conversation* ‖ (*pop.*) fast and stylish, *a snappy sports car*

snap·shot (snǽpʃɒt) *n.* a photograph taken with a very short exposure, usually of unposed subjects

snap shot a quick shot with a rifle or other firearm without sighting

snare (snɛər) **1.** *n.* a device, usually a slip noose, used for catching birds and animals ‖ an artifice for deceiving somebody ‖ (*pl.*) twisted strings of gut, leather or wire, stretched inside a drumhead in order to make a rattling sound ‖ one of these ‖ a wire loop or noose used to remove tonsils, small tumors etc. **2.** *v.t. pres. part.* **snar·ing** *past* and *past part.* **snared** to catch in a snare ‖ to deceive (a person) into acting to his own disadvantage [O.N. *snara*]

snare drum a small drum hung with its head horizontal at the drummer's side in a military band, or used in an orchestra for martial music

snarl (snɑrl) **1.** *v.i.* (of a dog or some other animals) to growl fiercely, usually with bared teeth ‖ to show anger or resentment in a growling manner **2.** *n.* the act or sound of snarling [fr. older *snar*, prob. imit.]

snarl 1. *n.* a tangle of threads, hair etc. ‖ an entanglement **2.** *v.t.* to entangle ‖ to emboss the upper surface of (metal) by hammering with a snarling iron ‖ *v.i.* to become entangled [prob. fr. SNARE]

snarling iron a long-beaked tool used in embossing metal. Vibrations caused by hammering on it are transmitted to the working end of the tool, which is in contact with the inner surface of the ware being shaped

snarl-up (snɑ́rlʌp) *n.* delay caused by confusion —**snarl up** *v.*

snatch (snætʃ) **1.** *v.t.* to seize suddenly, esp. without permission ‖ to use an opportunity suddenly offered in order to enjoy, *to snatch an hour's sleep* ‖ to remove suddenly from or out of something, *they snatched the drowning man from the river* ‖ to put (a rope) in a snatch block **to snatch at** to try to grab ‖ to take quick advantage of **2.** *n.* a snatching, sudden grab ‖ a portion of talk, song etc. of short duration, *snatches of conversation* **in snatches** in short, sharp bursts, *to work in snatches* [origin unknown]

snatch block (*naut.*) a block of which one side can be opened to receive, and closed to grip, the bight of a rope

snatch squad (*Br.*) military unit assigned to defuse a disturbance by arresting its leaders

snatch·y (snǽtʃi:) *adj.* done in snatches

SNCC (*abbr.*) for Student Nonviolent Coordinating Committee, a predominantly black splinter group from Students for a Democratic Society (SDS) in the 1960s *Cf* NEW LEFT

sneak (sni:k) **1.** *v.i.* to move stealthily or furtively ‖ *v.t.* to transfer, carry, do etc. in a stealthy manner, *he sneaked the papers into his desk, to sneak a look* ‖ (*pop.*) to steal **2.** *n.* someone who sneaks ‖ an act of sneaking **3.** *adj.* happening without warning, *a sneak attack* [origin unknown]

sneak·ers (sní:kərz) *pl. n.* light, rubber-soled, canvas shoes worn for sports, esp. tennis

sneak·ing (sní:kiŋ) *adj.* of or characteristic of a sneak ‖ obstinately lurking in the mind, *a sneaking suspicion* ‖ sometimes entertained in thought but never openly declared, *a sneaking desire*

sneak path *PATH

sneak preview an unannounced film shown to the public before general release in order to get the reaction of the audience

sneak thief someone who steals what they can get without using violence or breaking into a place

sneak·y (sní:ki:) *comp.* **sneak·i·er** *superl.* **sneak·i·est** *adj.* of or like a sneak

sneer (sniər) **1.** *v.i.* to make a scornful or contemptuous grimace ‖ to express contempt or derision in writing etc. ‖ *v.t.* to utter in a scornfully derisive way **2.** *n.* the act of sneering ‖ an expression of scornful derision [prob. imit.]

sneeze (sni:z) **1.** *v.i. pres. part.* **sneez·ing** *past* and *past part.* **sneezed** to expel air from the nose and mouth suddenly (often with a loud noise) as a result of irritation of the inner nasal membrane **not to be sneezed at** worthy of serious consideration **2.** *n.* the act or sound of sneezing [prob. alteration of older *fnese* v.]

sneeze·wort (sní:zwə:rt) *n.* *Achillea ptarmica*, fam. *Compositae*, a perennial plant with creeping woody stock, white ray florets and greenish-white disk florets. Its leaves are used in snuff

snell (snel) *n.* a short line of gut, horsehair etc. used to attach hooks to a fishline [origin unknown]

Snell's law (snelz) (*phys.*) a law of refraction, which states that the ratio of the sines of the angles of incidence and of refraction is equal to the ratio of the velocities of the disturbance (at constant frequency) in the first and second media. It follows that the refractive index may be measured by a simple measurement of these angles [after Willebrord *Snell* (1591–1626), Du. mathematician]

SNG (*abbr.*) for **1.** synthetic natural gas; **2.** substitute natural gas

snick (snik) **1.** *v.t.* to make a small cut in ‖ (*cricket*) to strike (a ball) with a light, glancing blow **2.** *n.* a snicking ‖ a small cut made by snicking ‖ (*cricket*) a snicked ball [etym. doubtful]

snick·er (sníkər) **1.** *v.i.* to laugh in a sly, half-suppressed manner, esp. at an indecent joke **2.** *n.* this kind of laugh [imit.]

snide (snaid) *adj.* mean, cheap ‖ obliquely malicious, *snide remarks* [formerly=counterfeit, fr. thieves' cant]

sniff (snif) **1.** *v.i.* to inhale suddenly and so forcefully through the nose that the action is audible ‖ *v.t.* to draw forcibly into the nostrils ‖ to test the smell of by sniffing ‖ to become aware of (as if by sniffing), *to sniff danger in the air* **not to be sniffed at** not to be treated with contempt **2.** *n.* the sound or act of sniffing ‖ something sniffed, *a sniff of new-mown hay* [imit.]

snif·fle (snífəl) **1.** *v.i. pres. part.* **snif·fling** *past* and *past part.* **snif·fled** to sniff repeatedly because one's nose is blocked with catarrh or as a result of weeping **2.** *n.* the act or sound of sniffling **the sniffles** a slight head cold [imit.]

snif·fy (snífi:) *comp.* **snif·fi·er** *superl.* **snif·fi·est** *adj.* (*pop.*) disdainful

snif·ter (sníftər) *n.* a wide brandy glass on a short stem, tapered at the opening to facilitate inhaling the bouquet ‖ (*pop.*) a small drink of liquor [imit.]

snift·ing valve (sníftiŋ) a valve in the cylinder of a steam engine, permitting air and condensed moisture to escape

snig·ger (snígər) **1.** *v.i.* to snicker **2.** *n.* a snicker [imit.]

snip (snip) **1.** *v. pres. part.* **snip·ping** *past* and *past part.* **snipped** *v.t.* to cut with scissors or shears using quick short strokes in a snappy action **2.** *n.* one cut made with scissors or shears ‖ the act or sound of snipping ‖ a piece snipped off ‖ (*pop.*) an impertinent person ‖ (*Br., pop.*) a steal (real bargain) ‖ (*Br., pop.*) a snap (easy task) [prob. of Du. or L.G. origin]

snipe (snaip) **1.** *pl.* **snipe, snipes** *n.* a member of *Capella*, a genus of long-billed brown marsh birds, related to the woodcock. They have a characteristic swift zigzag flight and a hoarse rasping cry **2.** *v. pres. part.* **snip·ing** *past* and *past part.* **sniped** *v.i.* to shoot snipe ‖ to fire single shots from cover at an enemy ‖ *v.t.* to shoot at (the enemy) in this way **snip·er** *n.* [akin to O.N. *snípa*]

snip·er·scope (snáipə:rskoup) *n.* snooperscope attached to a rifle *Cf* SNOOPERSCOPE

snip·pet (snípit) *n.* a fragment cut off ‖ (*pl.*) scraps, fragments (of knowledge, news etc.)

snip·pet·y *adj.* made esp. of snippets ‖ snobbishly curt [dim. of SNIP]

snip·py (snípi:) *comp.* **snip·pi·er** *superl.* **snip·pi·est** *adj.* snappish ‖ sniffy, supercilious

CONCISE PRONUNCIATION KEY: **(a)** æ, *cat*; ɑ, *car*; ɔ *fawn*; ei, *snake*. **(e)** e, *hen*; i:, *sheep*; iə, *deer*; ɛə, *bear*. **(i)** i, *fish*; ai, *tiger*; ə:, *bird*. **(o)** o, *ox*; au, *cow*; ou, *goat*; u, *poor*; ɔi, *royal*. **(u)** ʌ, *duck*; u, *bull*; u:, *goose*; ə, *bacillus*; ju:, *cube*. x, *loch*; θ, *think*; ð, *bother*; z, *Zen*; ʒ, *corsage*; dʒ, *savage*; ŋ, *orangutang*; j, *yak*; ʃ, *fish*; tʃ, *fetch*; 'l, *rabble*; 'n, *redden*. Complete pronunciation key appears inside front cover.

snitch (snitʃ) **1.** *v.t.* (*pop.*) to steal (something of small value) ‖ *v.i.* (*pop.*, esp. with 'on') to give evidence against someone, inform **2.** *n.* (*pop.*) an informer [origin unknown]

sniv·el (snívəl) *pres. part.* **sniv·el·ing,** esp. *Br.* **sniv·el·ling** *past* and *past part.* **sniv·eled,** esp. *Br.* **sniv·elled 1.** *v.i.* to have mucus running from the nose ‖ to breathe audibly through nostrils made wet with mucus or with tears ‖ to whine and make a pretense of weeping, esp. as a sign of contrition **2.** *n.* the act of sniveling [fr. O.E. *snofl*, mucus]

snob (snɒb) *n.* a socially exclusive person ‖ someone deriving simple pleasure from being in the company of his social betters or who likes to think of himself as belonging to the social class next above his own ‖ a knowing person, e.g. about art or a branch of scholarship, who despises those less well informed, *an intellectual snob* **snób·ber·y** *n.* **snób·bish** *adj.* [origin unknown]

SNOBOL (*computer acronym*) for string oriented symbolic language, a programming language adapted for processing strings of symbols

snoek (snu:k) *n.* a member of *Thyrsites* (*BARRACOUTA) and other genera of large, edible S. African fish [Du.=pike]

sno·far·i (snoufári:) *n.* a hunting or other expedition into a snow-covered area

snood (snu:d) *n.* a ribbon or net bag worn to keep the hair at the back of a woman's head in place ‖ a part of a hat resembling this ‖ a snell [O.E. *snōd*]

snook (snuk, snu:k) *n.* (in the phrase) **to cock a snook at** (*Br.*) to thumb one's nose in derision at [origin unknown]

snook (snu:k, snuk) *pl.* **snook, snooks** *n.* *Centropomus undecimalis*, fam. *Centropomidae*, a large game and food fish, resembling the pike and inhabiting warm seas ‖ any of various other fishes of this family [fr. Du. *snoek*, pike]

snook·er (snúkər) **1.** *n.* a form of pool played with a number of colored billiard balls, of differing score value **2.** *v.t.* to leave (an opponent) with a ball between the cue ball and ball he is to aim at **snóok·ered** *adj.* unable to play a direct shot because of an intervening ball ‖ (*pop.*) in a difficult situation where one is thwarted [origin unknown]

snoop (snu:p) **1.** *v.i.* to pry in a sneaking or interfering way **2.** *n.* someone who snoops **snóop·er** *n.* a snoop [fr. Du. *snoepen*]

snoop·er·scope (snú:pə:rskoup) *n.* an infrared image converter that permits viewing in the dark *Cf* ELECTRON TELESCOPE, SNIPERSCOPE

snoot (snu:t) *n.* (*pop.*) the nose ‖ (*pop.*) a snob [var. of SNOUT]

snoot·i·ly (snú:tili:) *adv.* (*pop.*) in a snooty manner

snoot·i·ness (snú:ti:nis) *n.* (*pop.*) the state or quality of being snooty

snoot·y (snú:ti:) *comp.* **snoot·i·er** *superl.* **snoot·i·est** *adj.* (*pop.*) snobbish ‖ (*pop.*) supercilious

snooze (snu:z) **1.** *v.i. pres. part.* **snooz·ing** *past* and *past part.* **snoozed** to sleep lightly for a short time, esp. in the daytime **2.** *n.* a short, light sleep, esp. in the daytime [cant word]

snopes (snoups) *n.* unscrupulous politicians or businessmen in the southern U.S.; from characters created by American novelist William Faulkner

snore (snɔr, snour) **1.** *v.i. pres. part.* **snor·ing** *past* and *past part.* **snored** to breathe through the open mouth and the nose when asleep, producing a harsh noise by the vibration of the soft palate ‖ *v.t.* (esp. with 'away') to pass or waste (time) in this manner, *he snored away the afternoon* **2.** *n.* the sound made by snoring [prob. imit.]

snor·kel (snɔ́rk'l) *n.* a pair of intake and outlet tubes pushed above water level by a submerged submarine in order to obtain fresh air and discharge exhaust fumes etc. ‖ an air tube enabling a swimmer to breathe under the surface of the water [G. *schnörkel*, spiral]

Snor·ri Stur·lu·son (snɔ́ri:stə́:rləsən) (1179–1241), Icelandic poet and historian. His 'History of the Norwegian Kings' and his 'Prose Edda' are valuable sources for Norse mythology and history

snort (snɔrt) **1.** *v.i.* to expel air suddenly and loudly through the nostrils, expressing (in people) anger or contempt, (in a horse etc.) fear or excitement ‖ to make a similar noise (e.g. of a steam engine) ‖ *v.t.* to express by or with a snort ‖ (*slang*) to inhale drugs, esp. cocaine **2.** *n.* the sound or act of snorting ‖ (*Br.*) a submarine's snorkel ‖ (*Am., pop.*) a small drink of liquor, esp. swallowed in one gulp **snórt·er** *n.* a violent gale ‖ (*pop.*) something very powerful, impressive or remarkable [prob. imit.]

snot (snɒt) *n.* mucus in the nose [M.E. *snotte, snot*]

snot·ty (snɒ́ti:) **1.** *adj. comp.* **snot·ti·er** *superl.* **snot·ti·est** dirty with snot ‖ (*pop.*) contemptible ‖ (*pop.*) snooty **2.** *pl.* **snot·ties** *n.* (*Br., pop.*) a midshipman

snout (snaut) *n.* the nose of a hog or of various other animals ‖ (*pop.*) the human nose, esp. when large and ugly ‖ a projection resembling the snout of an animal [M.E. *snūt, snūte*]

snow (snou) **1.** *n.* frozen water vapor which falls to the earth in soft, white crystalline flakes ‖ a fall of snow ‖ a deposit of fallen snow, *tracks in the snow* ‖ (*slang*) cocaine ‖ (*slang*) heroine **2.** *v.i.* (*impers.*) to be forming a fall of snow, *it is snowing* ‖ *v.t.* (*impers.*) to be forming a mass of (something compared with snow), *to be snowing invitations* **snowed in** or **up** prevented from going outdoors or traveling etc. because of snow **snowed under** overwhelmed (by correspondence, things to do etc.) [O.E. *snāw*]

—A sufficiently large and sudden cooling of the air at some height above the ground can cause the water vapor to pass directly into the solid state in the form of small hexagonal ice crystals, without first liquefying. Since the vapor pressure of ice is low, these suspended crystals grow by accretion, in aggregates of small crystals which have regular geometrical patterns of structure (snowflakes), until their mass causes them to fall through the air and they are deposited on the ground. The air trapped between the small crystals of these aggregates causes internal reflection of light at the crystal surfaces, giving snow a sparkle and a pure white color. The air trapped in this way, and between the flakes themselves as they settle, makes the deposit of snow a very bad conductor of heat. The ground, and its animal and plant life, are thus protected from further loss of heat by radiation. The conversion of vapor into solid also releases latent heat, causing an appreciable rise of air temperature

snow·ball (snóubɔl) **1.** *n.* a handful of snow, pressed or rolled and shaped into a ball ‖ the guelder rose **2.** *v.i.* to grow rapidly larger, at an ever increasing rate, *the rumors snowballed into a major scandal* ‖ to throw snowballs ‖ *v.t.* to throw snowballs at

snow·bank (snóubæŋk) *n.* a great heap of snow

snow·ber·ry (snóuberi:, snóubəri:) *pl.* **snow·ber·ries** *n.* a member of *Symphoricarpos*, fam. *Caprifoliaceae*, a species of cultivated ornamental shrub, esp. the North American species, *S. albas*, bearing pink flowers in terminal racemes. The fruits are globose white berries

snow·bird (snóubə:rd) *n.* any of various North American finches of genus *Junco*

snowbirds 1. Northern residents who vacation in southern regions, esp. Florida **2.** (*slang*) cocaine users **3.** (*slang*) heroin users *Cf* SNOWFLAKES

snow·blind (snóublaind) *adj.* afflicted with snow blindness **snow blindness** temporary blindness caused by overstimulation of the retina through prolonged exposure to the white light reflected from expanses of snow or ice

snow·blink (snóubliŋk) *n.* glaring reflection from fields of ice in polar regions (*ICEBLINK)

snow·bound (snóubaund) *adj.* forced to stay where one is because of snow

snow bunting *Plectrophenax nivalis*, a small finch which breeds in the Arctic and migrates farther south in winter. It is largely of white plumage and common in Europe and North America

snow-capped (snóukæpt) *adj.* (of a mountain) having snow on its summit

Snow·don (snóud'n) a mountain in N. Wales with five peaks, rising to 3,560 ft

Snow·do·ni·a (snoudóuni:ə) the massif in Caernarvonshire and Merioneth, N. Wales, of which Snowdon is the highest mountain

snow·drift (snóudrift) *n.* a heaped mass of snow, driven by the wind from more exposed places

snow·drop (snóudrɒp) *n.* *Galanthus nivalis*, fam. *Amaryllidaceae*, a small, early blossoming, bulbous plant which bears one white, nodding flower early in the year

snow·fall (snóufɔl) *n.* a fall of snow ‖ the amount of snow falling during a stated period of time

snow·field (snóufi:ld) *n.* a smooth and fairly level expanse of snow, esp. such a mass at the head of a glacier

snow·flake (snóufleik) *n.* a single crystal of snow ‖ a member of *Leucojum*, fam. *Amaryllidaceae*, a genus of cultivated plants of Mediterranean origin growing from a large bulb and having one or several nodding flowers ‖ the snow bunting

snowflakes Northerners who commute to southern regions on weekends, esp. to Florida

snow goose *pl.* **snow geese** a small white goose of genus *Chen* with black-tipped wings, indigenous to the Arctic and migrating south

snow leopard the ounce

snow line the altitude on a mountain slope above which the snow never completely melts during the year

snow·mak·er (snóumeikə:r) *n.* device for making artificial snow

snow·man (snóumæn) *pl.* **snow·men** (snóumen) *n.* a rough likeness of a man made by rolling and heaping snow

snow·mo·bile (snóumoubi:l) *n.* motor vehicle for travel on snow —**snowmobile** *v.* —**snowmobiler** *n.* —**snowmobilist** *n.*

snow·plow, *Br.* **snow·plough** (snóuplau) *n.* any plowlike device used for cleaning snow from a road or railroad ‖ (*skiing*) a maneuver in which the tips of the skis are pointed inward, causing one to brake

snow·shoe (snóuʃu:) *n.* a light lattice, in a frame, worn under the shoes or boots, enabling a person to walk on soft snow without sinking

snow·slide (snóuslaid) *n.* an avalanche of snow

snow·storm (snóustɔrm) *n.* a heavy fall of snow, esp. when accompanied by a strong wind ‖ something resembling this, e.g. an electrical disturbance of a television screen image

snow-white (snóuhwáit, snóuwáit) *adj.* as white as snow, pure white

snow·y (snóui:) *comp.* **snow·i·er** *superl.* **snow·i·est** *adj.* covered by, or abounding in, snow, *a snowy landscape* ‖ as white as snow, *snowy hair*

Snowy Mountains the highest part of the Australian Alps, in New South Wales and Victoria: Mt Kosciusko (7,316 ft)

snub (snʌb) **1.** *v.t. pres. part.* **snub·bing** *past* and *past part.* **snubbed** to refuse to notice the presence of (someone) ‖ to stave (someone) off deliberately by refusing to respond to a friendly approach ‖ to check the movement of (e.g. a horse or boat) by a rope attached to a stationary object ‖ (*naut.*) to check suddenly (e.g. a rope or chain) that is running out **2.** *n.* the act or an instance of snubbing [O.N. *snubba*, to rebuke]

snub nose a short, slightly turned-up nose

snuff (snʌf) **1.** *v.t.* to inhale through the nose usually in order to smell, to sniff ‖ *v.i.* to inhale through the nostrils in a noisy fashion **2.** *n.* the act of snuffing ‖ powdered tobacco inhaled into the nose [prob. fr. M.Du. *snoffen, snuffen*, to snuffle]

snuff 1. *v.t.* to cut off the snuff of (a candle) ‖ (with 'out') to put out (a candle) ‖ (with 'out') to put an end to (a conspiracy etc.) **2.** *n.* the charred end of a candle wick [origin unknown]

snuff·box (snʌ́fbɒks) *n.* a small, usually ornamented box for holding snuff

snuf·fer (snʌ́fər) *n.* a device used for snuffing out candles, consisting of a hollow cone attached to a handle ‖ (*pl.*) a pair of scissors used for clipping the snuff off a candle

snuff film violent, illegal sex film in which the female participant is actually murdered

snuf·fle (snʌ́fəl) **1.** *v. pres. part.* **snuf·fling** *past* and *past part.* **snuf·fled** *v.i.* to breathe noisily through the nose when this is partly obstructed by mucus or moisture ‖ *v.t.* to say with such snuffling **2.** *n.* the sound or act of snuffling **the snuffles** a congestion of mucus in the nose causing difficulty in breathing or talking ‖ a respiratory disease in rats, pigs etc. [prob. fr. Du. and Flem. *snuffelen*]

snug (snʌg) **1.** *comp.* **snug·ger** *superl.* **snug·gest** *adj.* safe and comfortable (esp. warm) ‖ small but comfortably arranged ‖ close-fitting, *a snug jacket* ‖ (*naut.*) trim and seaworthy ‖ (of income) certain and sufficient to ensure comfort **2.** *v.t. pres. part.* **snug·ging** *past* and *past part.* **snugged** (*naut.*, with 'down') to prepare (a ship) for a storm by reducing sail, fastening down movables etc. **snúg·ger·y** *pl.* **snug·ger·ies** *n.* (*Br.*) a place where one can be undisturbed and at ease, esp. a small, warm room of one's own [origin unknown]

CONCISE PRONUNCIATION KEY: **(a)** æ, *cat*; ɑ, *car*; ɔ *fawn*; ei, *snake*. **(e)** e, *hen*; i:, *sheep*; iə, *deer*; εə, *bear*. **(i)** i, *fish*; ai, *tiger*; ə:, *bird*. **(o)** o, *ox*; au, *cow*; ou, *goat*; u, *poor*; ɔi, *royal*. **(u)** ʌ, *duck*; u, *bull*; u:, *goose*; ə, *bacillus*; ju:, *cube*. x, *loch*; θ, *think*; ð, *bother*; z, *Zen*; ʒ, *corsage*; dʒ, *savage*; ŋ, *orangutang*; j, *yak*; ʃ, *fish*; tʃ, *fetch*; 'l, *rabble*; 'n, *redden*. Complete pronunciation key appears inside front cover.

snug·gle (snʌ́g'l) *pres. part.* **snug·gling** *past and past part.* **snug·gled** *v.i.* to lie closely for warmth, protection, affection etc. || *v.t.* to move (oneself, one's head etc.) close to someone or something for warmth, protection etc. [fr. SNUG V., (obs.) to nestle closely]

so (sou) **1.** *adv.* in a certain way, *it must be done so* || to a certain degree, *you may only go so far* || to a large degree, *he was so angry* || as a result, *she wrapped up well and so was warm* || also, *she wants to leave and so do I* || then, *so that's what you think* || in a manner previously mentioned, *the wall is painted green and has been so for some time* || (in comparative constructions) as, *it won't be so bad as you think* **and so on** et cetera || and continuing in the same way **so as** in order to, *he left early so as not to be tired* **so . . . as** so great in quantity or number that a specified result follows, *cars so numerous as to block traffic for hours* **2.** *conj.* in order that, *I'll show you so you can see how it's done* || (*pop.*) with the result that, *I covered him so he kept warm* || therefore, *you aren't listening so I'll shut up* **3.** *pron.* approximately that much, *can you lend me a dollar or so?* || as has been described or as will be understood, *he was ill but did not seem so* **4.** *adj.* true, *is that so?* **5.** *interj.* used to express surprise, understanding or indifference [O.E. *swa, swā*]

soak (souk) *v.i.* to be or become thoroughly wet by lying immersed in fluid || (*pop.*) to penetrate the mind, *the idea hasn't soaked into his head* || (of a liquid) to enter through pores or interstices || *v.t.* to make very wet, *the rain soaked my clothes* || (esp. with 'up') to take in (liquid) by absorbing || to place (something) in a liquid in order to saturate it || (with 'out') to cleanse or drain (something) by soaking, *to soak out stains* || (*pop.*) to absorb mentally **sóak·age** *n.* the process of soaking || the liquid soaked up by a porous body or lost by leaking **sóak·ers** *pl. n.* a pair of light woolen pants put on over a baby's diaper [O.E. *socian*]

so-and-so (sóuənsou) *pl.* **so-and-sos** *n.* an unnamed or undetermined person or thing || (a euphemism for) a bastard (harsh or unjust person)

Soane (soun), Sir John (1753-1837), English architect. He was a leader of the classical revival with a highly imaginative personal style. His most important building is the Bank of England. The Soane Museum in London houses some of his designs as well as his collection of pictures, furniture and sculpture

soap (soup) **1.** *n.* a cleaning or emulsifying agent usually made from fats by saponification. It consists of a mixture of alkali metal salts of fatty acids, soluble in water, and various additions such as perfume or coloring agents, disinfectants etc. || a metallic salt of a fatty acid **2.** *v.t.* to treat with soap [O.E. *sāpe*]

soap·bark (sóupbɑrk) *n.* *Quillaja saponaria*, fam. *Rosaceae*, a Chilean tree whose bark contains saponin and gives a soapy lather when rubbed in water. It is used in cleaning and emulsifying fluids || any of several tropical shrubs of the genus *Pithecolobium*, fam. *Leguminosae*, which have saponaceous bark

soap·ber·ry (sóupbəri:, sóupberi:) *pl.* **soap·ber·ries** *n.* a tree of genus *Sapindus*, fam. *Sapindaceae*, whose fruit is used as a cleansing agent, and which yields gum as well as saponin || the fruit of this tree

soap·box (sóupbɒks) **1.** *n.* an improvised platform used by a free-lance open-air orator with a pet subject to expound to anyone he can persuade to listen **2.** *adj.* of or relating to such oratory or orators

soap bubble an iridescent bubble of soapy water

soap opera radio or television serial drama or dramas of ongoing romantic and domestic crises; from its original sponsorship by soap manufacturers *Cf* SITCOM

soap plant *Chlorogalum pomeridianum*, fam. *Liliaceae*, a California plant yielding saponin

soap·root (sóuprυ:t, sóuprυt) *n.* any of various S. European plants of genus *Gypsophilia*, fam. *Caryophyllaceae*, whose roots are used as soap

soap·stone (sóupstoun) *n.* steatite

soap·suds (sóupsʌdz) *pl. n.* the mass of soap bubbles in a solution of soap and water

soap·wort (sóupwə:rt) *n.* *Saponaria officinalis*, fam. *Carophyllaceae*, a plant whose leaves lather when rubbed with water

soap·y (sóupi:) *comp.* **soap·i·er** *superl.* **soap·i·est** *adj.* resembling, mixed or covered with soap || (of a person) ingratiating, smooth

soar (sɔr, sour) **1.** *v.i.* to rise high into the air || (of birds) to float high in the air while moving forward || (*aeron.*, of a glider) to fly gaining height using rising air currents || (of prices, profits etc.) to rise to a very high level || (of hopes, thoughts etc.) to become more spiritual **2.** *n.* the act of soaring || the height or distance attained in soaring [fr. F. *essorer*]

Soa·ve (swávei) *n.* a dry, white wine from the Soave area in Italy

sob (sɒb) **1.** *v. pres. part.* **sob·bing** *past and past part.* **sobbed** *v.i.* to weep violently with convulsive catches of the breath || to make a sound like sobbing || *v.t.* to utter thus || to bring (oneself) thus to a certain condition, *she sobbed herself to sleep* **2.** *n.* the sound of sobbing || the convulsive catch of the breath in sobbing [prob. imit.]

so·ber (sóubər) **1.** *adj.* not drunk || not given to drinking alcohol excessively || temperate in the use of all sources of pleasure || staid, sedate, *sober habits* || thought out with proper care, *a sober judgment* || showing discretion and moderation || serious, grave, *sober aldermen* || giving cause for gravity, *a sober thought* || not ornamented, not fanciful, a *sober style* || subdued, *sober colors* **2.** *v.t.* to make sober || *v.i.* to become sober [O.F. *sobre*]

so·ber·sides (sóubərsaidz) *n.* (*pop.*) a too earnest, serious-minded person

So·bies·ki (soubjéski:), John *JOHN III SOBIESKI

so·bri·e·ty (səbráiiti:, soubráiiti:) *n.* the quality or state of being sober [fr. F. *sobriété* or L. *sobrietas*]

so·bri·quet (sóubrəkei, sóubrəket, soubrəkéi, soubrəkét) *n.* an epithet || a nickname [F.]

sob sister (*pop.*) a journalist who writes sentimental human-interest stories

sob story (*pop.*) a sentimental story intended to arouse sympathy

soc·age, soc·cage (sɒ́kidʒ) *n.* (*hist.*) the holding and use of land under the feudal system in return for payment of rent or some service other than military service [A.F.]

so-called (sóukɔ́ld) *adj.* popularly named, esp. improperly or undeservedly so, *a so-called liberal*

soccage *SOCAGE

soc·cer (sɒ́kər) *n.* a game developed in Britain since 1863. It is played by two teams each of 11 men, with a round football, on a rectangular field (120 yds x 80 yds) having a goal 8 yds wide and 8 ft high at either end. Players kick, dribble and pass the ball with their feet, though the head and trunk may be brought into play as well. Only the goalkeeper may handle the ball. A goal is scored when the ball is sent between the opponent's goalposts

So·che (sɔ́tʃʌ́) *YARKAND

so·cia·bil·i·ty (souʃəbíliti:) *pl.* **so·cia·bil·i·ties** *n.* the quality or state of being sociable || an instance of being sociable

so·cia·ble (sóuʃəb'l) *adj.* fond of the company of others and apt to seek or welcome it || friendly, *a sociable gathering* [F. or fr. L. *sociabilis*]

so·cial (sóuʃəl) **1.** *adj.* relating to human society, *social legislation* || living in communities, *social insects* || enjoyed or taken in company || sociable || relating to or designed for social activities, *a social club* || relating to rank in the community, *social equals* || (*bot.*) growing in clumps **2.** *n.* an informal community gathering [F. or fr. L. *socialis*]

social anthropology the science which studies the culture and social structure of primitive peoples through their language, law, technical ability, religion etc. (*PHYSICAL ANTHROPOLOGY, *ANTHROPOLOGY)

social climber a person who tries to be accepted into a higher social milieu than the one to which he belongs

social compact a proposal by 1974 British Labour Government to trade unions, promising price subsidies, and price and dividend controls in exchange for restrained wage demands

Social Credit the theory that the profits of industry should be distributed to all consumers by a system of dividends so as to ensure a high level of consumption and allay the possibilities of economic depression. The theory was originated by C. H. Douglas

social democracy the political principles of those who hold that socialism should be achieved as an economic and political form of human society in place of capitalism, and that it should be done through the normal workings of democracy

social democrat an advocate of social democracy **Social Democrat** a member of a Social Democratic party

Social Democratic party any of several European political parties advocating gradual transition to a socialist society through the normal workings of democratic government || (*Am. hist.*) a U.S. political party (founded c. 1897) which merged with dissident members of the Socialist Labor party to become (1901) the Socialist party

Social Democratic Party British political party that splintered from the Labor Party in 1980; generally regarded as expounding middle-of-the-road policies

social disease venereal disease || a disease, e.g. tuberculosis, whose incidence is related directly to social conditions

so·cial·ism (sóuʃəlizəm) *n.* a political and economic theory advocating collective ownership of the means of production and control of distribution. It is based on the belief that all, while contributing to the good of the community, are equally entitled to the care and protection which the community can provide. The theory assumes different forms according to the relative stress laid on its social, economic and political corollaries. Thus Marxian socialism is concerned very largely with the economic issues, and postulates the communal ownership and control of the means of production, distribution and exchange. Christian socialism stresses the social aspect, making of the theory a way of life. Democratic socialism stresses the political aspect, accepting a compromise in the economic field between state and private enterprise. All forms of the theory agree in being opposed to uncontrolled capitalism and in seeking equality of opportunity for all members of the community [F. *socialisme* or fr. SOCIAL]

so·cial·ist (sóuʃəlist) **1.** *n.* a person who advocates socialism **So·cial·ist** a member of a socialist party **2.** *adj.* of, relating to, based on or favoring socialism **so·cial·ís·tic** *adj.*

socialist pluralism political socialism in its various manifestations, e.g., as practiced in the U.S.S.R., China, Yugoslavia

socialist realism 1. didactic use of the arts for the development of social consciousness and the enhancement of the socialist state **2.** official art of the Communist Party, esp. in U.S.S.R. *Cf* SOCIAL REALISM

socialist republic a title adopted by certain people's republics (e.g. Czechoslovakia, Yugoslavia, Rumania) denoting a more advanced stage in the transition from capitalism to communism

so·cial·ite (sóuʃəlait) *n.* (*pop.*) someone prominent in fashionable, affluent society

so·cial·i·za·tion (souʃəlaizéiʃən) *n.* a socializing or being socialized

so·cial·ize (sóuʃəlaiz) *pres. part.* **so·cial·iz·ing** *past and past part.* **so·cial·ized** *v.t.* to bring under public ownership and control, *to socialize an industry* || *v.i.* (*Am., pop.*) to be active in social affairs

socialized medicine medical and hospital care made available for all members of a community, district or nation through funds obtained by taxation, philanthropy assessments or other means

social learning (*psych.*) concept that cognitive, vicarious, and self-regulatory factors in human behavior can best be learned from observation of others, as contrasted with expected rewards and punishments; coined by A. Bandura *Cf* SKINNERIAN

so·cial·ly (sóuʃəli:) *adv.* in a social way || with respect to society

social mobility (*sociology*) movement of individuals from one social group to another social group, e.g., from the working class to the middle class, or vice versa

social promotion (*education*) automatic advancement in school without regard to grades or ability

social psychology that part of psychology which studies the relationships and reciprocal influences between individuals and between the individual and society

social realism realistic art works that depict contemporary social problems *Cf* SOCIALIST REALISM

social register a list of persons considered as belonging to the top ranks of society

social science the study of human society, esp. of its organization and of the relationship of individual members to it || any of several studies, e.g. history, political science, economics, which treat an aspect of human society

social security a system, or the theory and legislation behind it, whereby individual members of the community can count on some degree of care and protection provided by the community as a whole (e.g. health insurance or unemployment and retirement benefits)

social service welfare work

Social War a war fought (90-88 B.C.) between Rome and its allies of S. and central Italy. The war was caused by the allies' demands for the privileges of Roman citizenship and was ended by the promise that the privileges would be granted to all who had not borne arms against Rome

social work any of various professional services, kinds of material assistance and organized activities etc. concerned with the treatment of social problems, esp. in the underprivileged classes

social worker a person who does social work

so·ci·e·ty (səsáiiti:) *pl.* **so·ci·e·ties** *n.* the state of living in organized groups ‖ any number of people associated together geographically, racially or otherwise with collective interests ‖ any stage in the development of a community, *a primitive society, feudal society* ‖ an association of people with some interest in common and some central discipline, *a debating society* ‖ a civil or business association organized under law and endowed by it with a moral personality ‖ that part of a community considered to be the élite by birth, wealth or culture etc. ‖ personal association, companionship, *he enjoys the society of younger people* ‖ (*biol.*) a group of organisms forming a community ‖ (*bot.*) a community of plants other than dominants within an association [fr. O.F. *societe*]

Society Islands (*F.* Îles de la Société) the principal archipelago (land area 650 sq. miles, pop. 75,000) of French Polynesia, comprising the Windward Is (*F.* Îles du Vent), including Tahiti, Moorea and islets, and the Leeward Is (*F.* Îles Sousle-Vent), made up of Huahine, Raiatea, Bora Bora and islets. They are mountainous (of volcanic origin), wooded, and circled by reefs. Chief town and port: Papeete. People: Polynesian, French, Chinese. Religion: Protestant, Roman Catholic. Exports: copra, vanilla (*TAHITI). Tahiti was discovered (1767) by the British, and the group was named after the Royal Society. The French established a protectorate over Tahiti (1843) and annexed it (1880). The other islands were annexed in 1887

Society of Friends *FRIENDS, THE SOCIETY OF

Society of Jesus *JESUS, SOCIETY OF

So·cin·i·an (sousíni:ən) **1.** *n.* an adherent of Socinianism **2.** *adj.* of or to do with the doctrine of Socinus **So·cin·i·an·ism** *n.* the doctrine of Laelius and Faustus Socinus

So·ci·nus (sousáinəs), Laelius (Lelio Sozzini, 1525-62), Italian theologian. His anti-Trinitarian rationalistic teachings resemble those of modern Unitarians, and were spread into Poland, Hungary and the Netherlands by his nephew, Faustus Socinus (Fausto Sozzini, 1539-1604)

so·ci·o·bi·ol·o·gy (sousi:oubaiɒ́lədʒi:) *n.* **1.** study of social behavior in nonhuman animal life **2.** study of behavioral traits supposedly affected by hereditary factors

so·ci·o·ec·o·nom·ic (sousi:ouekənɒ́mik, souʃi:ouekənɒ́mik) *adj.* of or relating to combined social and economic conditions

so·ci·o·lin·guis·tics (sousi:ouliŋgwístiks) *n.* study of language as determined or affected by sociocultural factors, e.g., education —**sociolinguist** *n.* —**sociolinguistic** *adj.*

so·ci·o·log·i·cal (sousi:əlɒ́dʒik'l, souʃi:əlɒ́dʒik'l) *adj.* of sociology ‖ of human society and its development and organization [fr. F. *sociologique*]

sociological jurisprudence theory that laws alone cannot regulate the conflict between social interests and values, but that the courts must decide some issues

so·ci·ol·o·gist (sousi:ɒ́lədʒist:, souʃi:ɒ́lədʒist:) *n.* a specialist in sociology

so·ci·ol·o·gy (sousi:ɒ́lədʒi:, souʃi:ɒ́lədʒi:) *n.* the study of the origin, the history and the structure of human society and its institutions [fr. F. *sociologie*]

so·ci·o·re·li·gious (sousi:ouri:lídʒəs) *adj.* involving both religious and social influences

sock (sɒk) *n.* a wool, cotton or nylon etc. covering for the foot, ankle and lower part of the leg ‖ a light, removable inner sole worn in a shoe ‖ a wind sock ‖ (*Gk* and *Rom. hist.*) a shoe worn by comic actors **to pull up one's socks** (*Br.*) to try harder [O.E. *socc*]

sock 1. *v.t.* (*pop.*) to hit hard with the fist or a heavy object **2.** *n.* (*pop.*) such a blow [origin unknown]

sock·et (sɒ́kit) *n.* a hollow part or piece adapted or contrived to receive and hold something, *a bone socket, an electrical socket* ‖ *BALL AND SOCKET JOINT [A.F. *soket* dim. of *soc*, plowshare]

socket wrench (*Am.*=*Br.* box spanner) a hollow tubular wrench designed to fit over a nut and be turned by a tommy bar set into it at right angles (for getting at nuts inaccessible to an ordinary wrench)

sock·eye (sɒ́kai) *n.* *Oncorhynchus nerka*, fam. *Salmonidae*, a small N. Pacific salmon of economic importance. It reaches a weight of about 5 lbs

so·cle (sɒ́k'l, sóuk'l) *n.* (*archit.*) a simple, low, rectangular block of stone serving as a support for a pedestal, statue, wall etc. (*PLINTH) [F. fr. Ital. *zoccolo*]

So·co·tra, So·ko·tra (soukóutrə, sɒ́kətrə) (*Arab.* Suqutra) a mountainous island (area 1,400 sq. miles, pop. 15,000) in the Indian Ocean near the entrance to the Gulf of Aden. It is a dependency of the People's Democratic Republic of Yemen. Highest point: 4,686 ft. Chief town (residence of the sultan): Tamridah. Exports: dates, gum, incense, ghee

Soc·ra·tes (sɒ́krəti:z) (c. 470-399 B.C.), Greek philosopher of Athens. Most of his mature life was devoted to philosophy, although he developed no formal doctrine, founded no school and wrote nothing. His life, thought and method are known to us chiefly through Plato and Xenophon. He was familiar with the natural philosophers but they dissatisfied him by their lack of interest in human conduct. He studied the methods of the Sophists but attacked them for their indifference to virtue. He himself held that virtue is understanding and that no man knowingly does wrong. A strong patriot, he believed that a citizen is bound by conscience to obey the laws of the state. Thus, when (at the age of 70) he was imprisoned and condemned to death for irreligion and for corrupting the young men of Athens, he made no attempt to escape, despite the entreaties of his friends. More than any other philosopher, Socrates lived his philosophy. Several divergent schools of thought looked to him as their founder, and he has been widely regarded as the type and embodiment of the philosopher

So·crat·ic (səkrǽtik, soukrǽtik) **1.** *adj.* pertaining to Socrates or his philosophy **2.** *n.* a follower of Socrates **So·crát·i·cal·ly** *adv.*

Socratic irony the simulating of ignorance in argument in order to lead an opponent on to affirm something that reveals the absurdity of his position. This method was employed by Socrates in his teaching and plays an important part in Plato's earlier dialogues

sod (sɒd) **1.** *n.* surface soil with grass growing on it ‖ a piece of this, dug out or otherwise removed **2.** *v.t. pres. part.* **sod·ding** *past* and *past part.* **sod·ded** to lay sods on (an area) in order to make it a lawn [prob. fr. M.Du. *sode*]

sod *n.* (*pop.* used esp. as a general term of abuse or with a qualifying adjective) someone one considers peculiarly harsh, mean, silly etc. [abbr. of SODOMITE]

so·da (sóudə) *n.* crystalline sodium carbonate ‖ sodium bicarbonate ‖ sodium hydroxide ‖ soda water ‖ an ice-cream soda [M.L., origin unknown]

soda ash anhydrous sodium carbonate, Na_2CO_3, a product of the alkali industry

soda biscuit a biscuit made by baking a mixture of flour and buttermilk or sour milk, leavened with baking soda ‖ a soda cracker

soda cracker a crisp wafer leavened with bicarbonate of soda and cream of tartar

soda fountain a counter where sundaes, sodas, sandwiches, soft drinks etc. are served ‖ a device for delivering soda water into a drinking vessel

soda jerk (*pop.*) someone who serves at a soda fountain

soda lime a granular mixture prepared by slaking calcium oxide with sodium hydroxide and/or potassium hydroxide. It is used as an absorbent of moisture and acid gases

so·da·lite (sóud'lait) *n.* a compound of aluminum silicate, sodium silicate and sodium chloride, occurring in some igneous rocks as a transparent or translucent mineral

so·dal·i·ty (soudǽliti:, sədǽliti:) *pl.* **so·dal·i·ties** *n.* a fellowship, community or organized society ‖ (*Roman Catholicism*) a lay society formed for devotional or mutual aid purposes [F. *sodalité* or fr. L. *sodalitas*]

soda niter, *Br.* **soda nitre** sodium nitrate

soda water water charged under pressure with carbonic acid gas. It is used as a beverage, release of the excess pressure causing bubbles of gas to form, rise and burst ‖ a similar beverage consisting of sodium bicarbonate in a weak solution to which a little acid has been added to cause effervescence

sod·den (sɒ́d'n) *adj.* saturated with moisture ‖ (of bread etc.) too moist and doughy because not baked enough ‖ dulled and stupid from frequent drunkenness [old irregular past part. of SEETHE]

Sod·dy (sɒ́di:), Sir Frederick (1877-1956), English scientist who predicted (1902) the formation of helium as the end product of atomic degradation, verified this in 1904, and discovered the isotopes of lead (1913). He was awarded a Nobel prize (1921) for his discovery of the laws of radioactivity

so·di·um (sóudi:əm) *n.* a metallic element (symbol Na, at. no. 11, at. mass 22.9898), of small density (0.971), oxidizing rapidly when exposed to the air and reacting violently with water to liberate hydrogen and give a solution of sodium hydroxide. It is widely distributed in compounds, esp. common salt. It is essential to bodily health, the body needing a balance between potassium and sodium. Its salts are of great industrial importance [fr. SODA+Mod. L. *-ium*]

sodium bicarbonate a weakly basic salt, $NaHCO_3$, which liberates carbon dioxide on heating and when combined with acids. It is used in baking powder, effervescent salts, as an antacid and in fire extinguishers

sodium carbonate a white crystalline salt, $Na_2CO_3{\cdot}10H_2O$, used to give an alkaline solution with water, to soften water (by precipitating calcium carbonate) and in soapmaking etc. ‖ soda ash

sodium chloride salt (NaCl)

sodium fluoride the poisonous crystalline salt NaF produced by the reaction of hydrofluoric acid with soda ash and used in the fluoridation of water and in rat and insect poisons etc.

sodium hydroxide a brittle, white deliquescent solid, NaOH, with a soapy feel. It dissolves in water to form a strongly alkaline solution. It is widely used in the manufacture of soap, detergents, rayon and cellulose etc.

sodium lamp an electric discharge tube filled with sodium vapor under low pressure, emitting a powerful yellowish light and often used for street lighting

sodium nitrate the deliquescent salt, $NaNO_3$, occurring naturally as caliche, or made by the reaction of nitric acid and soda ash. It is used as a fertilizer, in explosives etc.

sodium palmitate [$NaC_{16}H_{31}O_2$] *SODIUM STEARATE

sodium potassium tartrate Rochelle salt

sodium pump or **sodium potassium pump** (*biochem.*) an intramembranous transport system that expels selected sodium through a membrane while concentrating potassium with a cell, utilizing energy from hydrolysis of adenosine triphosphate

sodium silicate any of various water-soluble substances obtained esp. by melting silica with a sodium compound. They are used e.g. in detergents

sodium stearate [$C_{17}H_{35}COONa$] (*chem.*) with sodium palmitate the basis of soap and detergent used for laundry, cosmetics, and toothpaste

sodium thiosulfate a salt, usually in the form of the hydrate $Na_2S_2{\cdot}5H_2O$, used in photography as a fixing agent

sodium-vapor lamp a sodium lamp

Sod·om (sɒdəm) a city of ancient Palestine in the lower Jordan valley, destroyed by God, with Gomorrah, because of the vices of its inhabitants (Genesis xviii-xix)

So·do·ma, Il (i:lsɔ́dɔmɑ) (Giovanni Antonio Bazzi, 1477-1549), Sienese painter. His work includes a series of frescoes at Monte Oliveto near Siena, and frescoes for the Villa Farnesina, Rome

sod·om·itc (sɒ́dəmait) *n.* a person who practices sodomy [O.F.]

CONCISE PRONUNCIATION KEY: **(a)** æ, *cat*; ɑ, *car*; ɔ *fawn*; ei, *snake*. **(e)** e, *hen*; i:, *sheep*; iə, *deer*; ɛə, *bear*. **(i)** i, *fish*; ai, *tiger*; ə:, *bird*. **(o)** o, *ox*; au, *cow*; ou, *goat*; u, *poor*; ɔi, *royal*. **(u)** ʌ, *duck*; u, *bull*; u:, *goose*; ə, *bacillus*; ju:, *cube*. x, *loch*; θ, *think*; ð, *bother*; z, *Zen*; ʒ, *corsage*; dʒ, *savage*; ŋ, *orangutang*; j, *yak*; ʃ, *fish*; tʃ, *fetch*; 'l, *rabble*; 'n, *redden*. Complete pronunciation key appears inside front cover.

sod·om·y (sɒ́dəmi:) *n.* sexual intercourse between males or (*law*) between members of the same sex or with animals, or unnatural sexual intercourse between a man and a woman [O.F. *sodomie* after SODOM]
Soerabaya *SURABAYA
Soerakarta *SURAKARTA
so·fa (sóufə) *n.* a long, upholstered seat, often with a raised back and raised arms or a raised end [F. fr. Arab.]
sofa bed a sofa that can be opened into a bed, e.g. by folding the back down
Sofala (soufála) (formerly Beira) a chief town (pop. 113,770) of Mozambique. A seaport on the Pungwe River estuary, it is connected by rail with Malawi, Zambia and Zimbabwe, for which it is the nearest port
so·far (sóufɑr) *n.* (*acronym*) for sound fixing and ranging, a system of determining a subsurface explosion at sea by triangulation
sof·fit (sɒ́fit) *n.* (*archit.*) the under surface of an arch, balcony, cornice etc. [F. *soffite* fr. Ital.]
So·fi·a (sóufi:ə, soufí:ə) the capital (pop. 1,047,920) and industrial center of Bulgaria, in the W. Balkan Mtns. Industries: mechanical and electrical engineering, automobile assembly, rolling stock, textiles, food processing. Roman baths (now a chapel), medieval churches, mosques, synagogue. Cathedral (late 19th c.). University (1880). Sofia was founded by the Romans (2nd c.) and was taken by the Bulgars (9th c.). It was under Turkish rule 1382-1878, and became the capital of Bulgaria in 1879.
soft (sɔft, sɒft) *adj.* offering little resistance to pressure, *a soft bed* (opp. HARD) ‖ not hard of its kind, *soft butter* ‖ mild, *a soft climate* ‖ (*pop.*, of jobs) not requiring much effort ‖ not providing a strong sense stimulus, *a soft light, soft colors* ‖ not loud ‖ not sharp in outline, *soft contours* ‖ (*pop.*) of weak intellect, feeble-minded, *soft in the head* ‖ (*pop.*) foolishly sentimental ‖ (*pop.*) easily put upon ‖ (of words) smooth, insinuating ‖ weak ‖ (*phon.*) sibilant, *c is soft in 'cement', g is soft in 'gelatin'* ‖ (*phon.*) lenis or lenis and voiced ‖ (of certain Slavic consonants) palatalized ‖ (of drinks) nonalcoholic ‖ (of diet) bland ‖ (of metal) malleable ‖ (*phys.*) of electromagnetic waves which have little penetrating power ‖ (of water) containing no dissolved bicarbonates or sulfates of calcium, magnesium or iron and therefore giving an immediate lather with soap without the formation of an insoluble curd ‖ (of securities etc.) weakening in price because of selling activity ‖ (of currency) that cannot be converted into gold and is not backed by gold reserves ‖ (of currency) freely available for borrowing at a low rate of interest ‖ (of currency) not easily convertible into foreign currency ‖ (*bookbinding*) using paper, not board ‖ (*photog.*) having very subtle tone gradations (cf. CONTRASTY) [O.E. *sōfte*]
soft answer an answer designed not to arouse anger
soft art **1.** art form considered psychologically or technically unfinished **2.** tentative art using pliable material *Cf* SOFT SCULPTURE
soft·ball (sɔ́ftbɔ̧l, sɒ́ftbɔ̧l) *n.* a variety of baseball, played with a softer, larger ball and on a smaller diamond ‖ the ball used in this game
soft-boiled (sɔ́ftbɔ́ild, sɒ́ftbɔ́ild) *adj.* (of an egg) boiled in its shell for not more than 3 minutes so that the yolk does not set
soft·bound (sɔ́ftbaund) *adj.* bound in paper, e.g., a paperback book *also* soft-cover *Cf* HARDBOUND
soft coal bituminous coal
soft copy (*computer*) output that leaves no permanent record, e.g., the display in a cathode-ray tube
soft-core (sɒ́ftcɔr) *adj.* of pornography, not as explicit or prurient as hard-core *Cf* HARDCORE, R-RATED, X-RATED
soft dollars the portion of an investment that can be taken as a income-tax deduction *Cf* TAX SHELTER
soft drink a nonalcoholic drink, esp. a carbonated one
soft drug a nonaddictive drug, e.g., marijuana *Cf* HARD DRUG
sof·ten (sɔ́fən, sɒ́fən) *v.t.* to make soft or softer, *to soften a blow* ‖ (with 'up') to wear down the opposition or resistance of (esp. an opponent) ‖ *v.i.* to become soft or softer
soft fruit (*Br.*) *SMALL FRUIT
soft furnishings (*Br., commerce*) materials for curtains, chair covers etc.
soft goods (*commerce*) textiles
soft-heart·ed (sɔ́fthɑ̧rtid, sɒ́fthɑ̧rtid) *adj.* very ready to sympathize with others and act accordingly
soft ice cream ice cream that has been aerated while in a semiviscous state, to approximately double its original volume, then refrigerated
soft iron iron almost free from carbon, unable to retain magnetism in the absence of a magnetizing agent and therefore used as the core of an electromagnet
soft landing the landing of a space vehicle on a celestial body without damage to the vehicle
soft lens porous-plastic contact lens said to be less irritating than a glass lens
soft line a flexible domestic or international political policy —**soft-line** *adj.* —**soft-line** *v.* —**soft-liner** *n. Cf* HARD LINE
soft loan a no-interest loan granted to a developing country, esp. by the International Development Association
soft news news without immediacy, e.g., feature stories *Cf* HARD NEWS
soft palate the soft, fleshy part of the palate located behind the hard palate
soft-paste porcelain a porcelain made of glass or grit and china clay, and used for making esp. household china. It is fired at a lower temperature than true porcelain
soft pedal a pedal on a piano, operated by the right foot, which lessens the volume by causing fewer strings to be hit (per note) or by bringing the hammers nearer the strings so they cannot hit so forcefully **sóft-ped·al** *pres. part.* **sóft-ped·al·ing,** esp. *Br.* **soft-ped·al·ling** *past* and *past part.* **soft-ped·aled,** esp. *Br.* **soft-ped·alled** *v.t.* to reduce emphasis on ‖ to soften the tone of by using a soft pedal
soft rock sophisticated, low-keyed rock 'n' roll with a less defined rhythm than hard rock *Cf* HARD ROCK
soft roe milt
soft science a science dealing with human behavior, e.g., psychology, economics, sociology *Cf* HARD SCIENCE, NATURAL SCIENCE
soft sculpture sculpture utilizing pliable materials, e.g., plastic, foam rubber, cloth, or papier-mâché *Cf* SOFT ART
soft sell a sales technique using persuasion and suggestion (cf. HARD SELL)
soft soap a soap in semiliquid form made by the action of potassium hydroxide on fats ‖ (*pop.*) flattery **sóft-sóap** *v.t.* (*pop.*) to flatter
soft solder an alloy of lead and tin, melting at a low temperature
soft-spo·ken (sɔ́ftspóukən, sɒ́ftspóukən) *adj.* suave in speech
soft spot (*pop.*) a sentimentally affectionate feeling towards another person
soft state an inefficient sovereign government unresponsive to its people's needs *Cf* HARD STATE
soft·ware (sɔ́ftwɛ̧ər, sɒ́ftwɛ̧ər) *n.* (*electronics*) the system of general programs which simplifies and links the work of computer and user ‖ (*computer*) nonhardware properties, e.g., programs, languages, routines, instructions etc., utilized in operations ‖ in other technologies, nondurable supplies and equipment, e.g., fuel, plans, housekeeping materials (cf. HARDWARE)
soft·wood (sɔ́ftwụd, sɒ́ftwụd) *n.* any soft, light-textured wood, esp. the wood of a coniferous tree (cf. HARDWOOD)
soft·y (sɔ́fti:, sɒ́fti:) *pl.* **soft·ies** *n.* (*pop.*) a sentimental, unintelligent or weak person
sog·gy (sɒ́gi:) *comp.* **sog·gi·er** *superl.* **sog·gi·est** *adj.* soft and heavy because impregnated with water, *soggy ground* [fr. dial. *sog*, a swamp]
Sog·ne (sɔ́ŋnə) the longest fiord (115 miles) of Norway, on the west coast, north of Bergen
soh (sou) *n.* (*Br., mus.*) sol
So·ho (sóuhou, souhóu) a cosmopolitan quarter of London, noted for its restaurants and bohemian life
So·ho (sóuhou) *n.* area in Manhattan between Houston and Canal Streets, where many factory buildings have been converted to artists' residences and studios, galleries, restaurants, and boutiques
soi·gné (swɑnjéi) *adj.* (of a woman) elegantly and carefully dressed ‖ showing evidence of great care and attention to detail [F.]
soil (sɔil) *n.* the uppermost stratum of the earth's crust, esp. the top few inches from which plants and ultimately man derive food ‖ (*rhet.*) land, country, *on native soil* [A.F.]
—Soils vary enormously in composition. Basically they consist of an inorganic portion, e.g. silicates of aluminum, iron, calcium, magnesium, silica etc., derived from the original rock by weathering and producing characteristic soil types (sands, silts, clays, loam), together with an organic portion produced by decomposed plants and animals as a result of the activity of innumerable microorganisms, particularly bacteria. Air and water are additional elements, the whole forming a biological entity whose proper balance is dependent on external environmental factors. Most soils belong to one of two great groups: the lime-rich pedocals or lime-poor pedalfers. Soils may also be classified as zonal, where climate and vegetation are the dominant influence on development, or azonal, where the influence of climate and vegetation is not dominant, or intrazonal, where the influence of local factors (relief, parent material, age) is more determinant than climate and vegetation
soil **1.** *v.t.* to make dirty, to stain ‖ to tarnish or harm (a reputation etc.) ‖ *v.i.* to become stained or dirty **2.** *n.* a dirty mark ‖ refuse, esp. excrement [fr. O.F. *soillier*]
soil *v.t.* to feed (cattle etc.) on freshly cut green fodder in order to fatten them [perh. fr. SOIL (dirty mark), (obs.) pool used by wild boar]
soil bank U.S. Government-sponsored program providing compensation to farmers for leaving portions of land fallow, designed to control overproduction and conserve soil fertility *also* land retirement
soil·borne (sɔ́ilbɔrn) *adj.* carried in or through soil, e.g., diseases, fungi
soiling index (*envir.*) measure of soiling properties of particles suspended in air, measured through a Whatman number 4 filter for a specified period, expressed as coefficient of haze [CoH] ÷ 1,000 linear ft *Cf* COEFFICIENT OF HAZE, SMOKE SHADE
soil pipe the pipe connecting a house etc. with a main sewer
soi·ree, soi·rée (swɑréi) *n.* a formal evening party or gathering [F.]
so·ja bean (sóiə) a soybean
so·journ **1.** (sóudʒɜ:rn, soudʒɜ́:rn) *v.i.* (*rhet.*) to stay or dwell for a time in a place or among certain people **2.** (sóudʒə:rn) *n.* (*rhet.*) a temporary stay [O.F. *sojorner*]
soke (souk) *n.* (*Br. hist.*) the right to hold a local court of justice and receive certain fees and fines ‖ the district over which this right extended [fr. M.L. *soca* fr. O.E. *sōcn*]
So·ko·to (sóukoutou, sọukoutóu, sɔkətú:) the capital (pop. 108,565) of North Western State, Nigeria, a trading center ‖ an ancient kingdom of W. central Africa, esp. powerful 16th-19th cc.
Sokotra *SOCOTRA
Sol (sɒl) the Roman Sun god, or (in rhetorical use) the Sun
sol (sɒl, soul) *n.* a fluid colloidal system (cf. GEL)
sol (soul, sɒl) *n.* (*mus.*) the note G in the fixed-do system of solmization ‖ the fifth note of any diatonic scale in movable-do solmization
sol (soul, sɒl, *Span.* sɔl) *pl.* **sols,** *Span.* **so·les** (sɔ́les) *n.* the basic monetary unit of Peru, divided into 100 centavos ‖ a coin or note worth one sol
sol·ace (sɒ́lis) **1.** *n.* that which lessens disappointment or grief or loneliness **2.** *v.t. pres. part.* **sol·ac·ing** *past* and *past part.* **sol·aced** to lessen the disappointment, grief or loneliness of [O.F. *solas*]
so·lan goose (sóulən) *n. Sula bassana* or *Moris bassana*, a large white gannet with black-tipped wings [older *soland* fr. O.N. *sūla*, gannet+*-ond, -and*, duck]
so·la·num (souléinəm) *n.* a member of *Solanum*, fam. *Solanaceae*, a large genus of plants, trees and shrubs. They include the eggplant and the potato [L.=nightshade]
so·lar (sóulər) *adj.* of or relating to the sun, *a solar eclipse* [fr. L. *solaris*]
solar battery a thermopile or photovoltaic pile that uses radiation from the sun or its heating effect to produce an electrical current
solar cell (*electr.*) a photoelectric cell capable of converting photons from the sun's energy into electrical energy; used as a power or heat source *Cf* SOLAR PANEL
solar coalition a group of members of U.S. Congress advocating development of solar energy, esp. as an inexpensive alternative energy source
solar flare a transient explosive brightening originating from special bright areas in the solar chromosphere. Solar flares often occur in

association with explosive activity of solar prominences and sunspots

so·lar·i·um (souléəri:əm, səléəri:əm) *pl.* **so·lar·i·ums, so·lar·i·a** (souléəri:ə, səléəri:ə) *n.* a room or building so constructed as to be exposed to the radiant energy of the sun and to trap much of this energy, esp. one used for therapeutic purposes [L.]

solar month one twelfth of a solar year

solar panel a group of solar cells used as a power source, e.g., in a spacecraft *Cf* SOLAR SAIL

solar plexus a group of ganglia situated behind the stomach ‖ (*pop.*) the upper front part of the abdomen just below the rib cage

solar pond body of water with a salted lower layer producing energy through tendency of denser bottom water to retain heat without rising to top. The water's heat is funneled into coiled tubes of a heat exchanger

solar prominence any of several types of incandescent gaseous mass containing hydrogen and metallic ions that circulate between the sun's chromosphere and corona along gently curved trajectories. Prominences occasionally erupt violently outward and are found esp. in regions containing sunspots

solar sail a flat sheet capable of receiving thrust from solar radiation, used as a power source e.g., in a spacecraft *Cf* SOLAR PANEL

solar system the sun, its nine planets (Mercury, Venus, Earth, Mars, Jupiter, Saturn, Uranus, Neptune, Pluto, in order of distance from the sun) and other celestial bodies (e.g. asteroids, comets and meteors) held to orbits around it by gravitation

solar wind (*meteor.*) a continuous stream of charged plasma protons emitted from the sun at 250 to 800 kms, causing distortion of earth's magnetic field and acceleration in comets *Cf* STELLAR WIND

solar year the average time taken by the earth to complete one orbit around the sun (=approx. 365¼ days)

sold *past* and *past part.* of SELL **to be sold on** to be thoroughly convinced about the excellence of (something)

sol·der (sɒ́dər, *Br.* esp. sóldə) **1.** *n.* a metallic alloy which, melted between clean metal surfaces, itself alloys with these and so bonds them together **2.** *v.t.* to join (metal surfaces) thus [M.E. *soudour* fr. O.F.]

soldering iron an iron tool, heated and used to melt solder

sol·dier (sóuldʒər) **1.** *n.* a man serving in an army ‖ such a man who is not an officer ‖ *ANT **2.** *v.i.* to serve as a soldier **sól·dier·ly** *adj.* of or befitting a good soldier, *a soldierly bearing* [M.E. *soldiour, soudiour* fr. O.F.]

soldier of fortune an adventurous person prepared to earn his livelihood as a soldier wherever he will be well paid ‖ a person who seeks an adventurous life in whatever circumstances chance offers

sol·dier·y (sóuldʒəri:) *n.* a specified body of soldiers ‖ (*collect.*) soldiers ‖ soldiering as a technique, *the art of soldiery*

sole (soul) *adj.* only, *the sole survivor* ‖ unshared, exclusive, *sole right* [O.F. *sol*]

sole *n.* any of several varieties of edible flatfish, fam. *Soleidae*, esp. the European *Solea solea* [O.F.]

sole 1. *n.* the undersurface of the foot ‖ the part of a shoe etc. which meets the ground, esp. forward from the heel ‖ the lower part or surface of something, e.g. of a golf club, plowshare etc. **2.** *v.t. pres. part.* **sol·ing** *past* and *past part.* **soled** to provide (a shoe, sock etc.) with a sole ‖ (*golf*) to place (the club) on its sole in preparation for a stroke [O.F.]

sol·e·cism (sɒ́lisizəm) *n.* a grammatical or syntactical deviation from what is conventionally regarded as correct speech ‖ a deviation from what are regarded as good social manners [fr. L. *solœcismus* fr. Gk]

sole·ly (sóulli:) *adv.* only, exclusively

sol·emn (sɒ́ləm) *adj.* arousing or expressing serious or profound thoughts and feelings of reverence, *solemn music* ‖ accompanied by or performed according to religious rites, *a solemn ceremony* ‖ (of an oath) made in a form and under circumstances such as to render it legally binding ‖ (*eccles.*) celebrated with full liturgy, *a solemn high mass* ‖ of grave significance, *solemn pronouncements* ‖ earnest and gloomy, *don't look so solemn!* ‖ pompous, *he's a solemn ass* [M.E. *solempne* fr. O.F.]

sol·em·ni·ty (səlémniti:) *pl.* **so·lem·ni·ties** *n.* solemn expression, behavior or character ‖ a solemn rite ‖ (*law*) a formality required to validate an act [M.E. *solempnite* fr. O.F.]

sol·em·ni·za·tion (sɒləmnizéiʃən) *n.* a solemnizing or being solemnized

sol·em·nize (sɒ́ləmnaiz) *pres. part.* **sol·em·niz·ing** *past* and *past part.* **sol·em·nized** *v.t.* to perform (a religious marriage ceremony) ‖ to perform, invest or honor with ceremony [fr. O.F. *solempniser*]

so·le·noid (sóulənɔid) *n.* a cylindrical coil of wire which creates a magnetic field within itself when an electric current is passed through it and so can draw a core of iron or steel into itself **so·le·nói·dal** *adj.* [F. *solénoïde* fr. Gk]

solenoid sweep (*mil.*) a magnetic mine sweep consisting of a horizontal axis coil wound on a floating iron tube

So·lent (sóulənt) the channel (15 miles long, ¾ mile–4 miles wide) between Hampshire and the Isle of Wight, England: yacht racing

sol-fa *TONIC SOL-FA, *SOLMIZATION

sol·fa·ta·ra (soulfətɑ́rə, sɒlfətɑ́rə) *n.* a vent from which issue volcanic gases rich in sulfur dioxide, indicating that the volcano is nearly extinct [name of a volcano near Naples fr. *solfo*, sulfur]

sol·fège (sɒlféʒ) *n.* solfeggio [F.]

sol·feg·gio (sɒlfédʒou, sɒlfédʒi:ou) *pl.* **sol·feg·gi** (sɒlfédʒi:), **sol·feg·gios** *n.* a vocal exercise in sol-fa syllables ‖ application of sol-fa syllables to notes [Ital.]

Sol·fe·ri·no, Battle of (sɒlferí:nɔ) a French and Sardinian victory (1859) over Austrian forces in northern Italy, after which Lombardy joined Sardinia

so·lic·it (səlísit) *v.t.* to beg for, canvass, appeal for (favor, help, a vote etc.) ‖ to importune, approach with appeals ‖ (of a prostitute) to propose sexual intercourse to in return for money ‖ *v.i.* (of a prostitute) to propose sexual intercourse to someone in return for money [fr. O.F. *soliciter, solliciter*]

so·lic·i·ta·tion (səlisitéiʃən) *n.* the practice, or an act, of soliciting [O.F. or fr. L. *sollicitatio* (*sollicitationis*)]

so·lic·i·tor (səlísitər) *n.* a lawyer who acts as official law officer for a city, department etc. ‖ (*Br., law*) a lawyer qualified to advise clients in all legal matters, to prepare wills and deeds etc., to instruct counsel in cases for the higher courts and to appear on behalf of clients in some lower courts ‖ a professional canvasser for money for a fund, trade, support etc. [fr. O.F. *solliciteur, soliciteur*]

solicitor general *pl.* **solicitors general** the federally appointed assistant to the attorney general or the chief law officer in certain states ‖ a chief legal adviser to any of certain governments

so·lic·i·tous (səlísitəs) *adj.* attentive, full of anxious concern ‖ (with *infin.*) eager [fr. L. *sollicitus, solicitus*]

so·lic·i·tude (səlísitu:d, səlísitju:d) *n.* anxious concern [O.F. or fr. L. *sollicitudo, solicitudo*]

sol·id (sɒ́lid) **1.** *adj.* having the properties of a solid, nonfluid ‖ having three dimensions ‖ unyielding, *solid conviction* ‖ continuous, *a solid line of houses* ‖ without openings, *solid jungle* ‖ (of time) unbroken, *he waited two solid hours* ‖ real, sound, *solid grounds for belief* ‖ homogeneous, *a solid mass of red* ‖ (of gold etc.) containing no more alloy than is specified by law to ensure hardness ‖ dense, thick, *a solid cloud of smoke* ‖ not hollow, not loosely packed, filled with matter, *a solid foot of snow* ‖ firm and compact, *solid ground* ‖ cubic, *a solid foot* ‖ (of structures, furniture etc.) firmly built, stout and strong ‖ (of compound words) written or printed without a hyphen ‖ sound, serious, but not inspired, *solid work* ‖ full, complete, *a solid day's work* ‖ unanimous, *a solid vote of approval* ‖ staunch, dependable, a *solid friend* ‖ (*printing*) having no leads separating the lines of type **2.** *n.* a substance which when acted upon by moderate forces tends to retain its shape and volume, i.e. a substance that has little or no tendency to flow (cf. FLUID) ‖ a figure having three spatial dimensions ‖ (*pl.*) food which is not liquid [O.F. *solide*]

solid angle the angular spread of the vertex of a cone, expressed as the area of its intercept on the surface of the sphere of unit radius described about the vertex, the total solid angle subtended by such a sphere being 4π. Unit solid angle subtends an area of r^2 on a sphere of radius r

sol·i·dar·i·ty (sɒlidǽriti:) *pl.* **sol·i·dar·i·ties** *n.* common interest and active loyalty within a group [fr. F. *solidarité*]

Solidarity *n.* a worker-run trade union, established in Poland in 1980

solid geometry the branch of geometry dealing with three-dimensional figures

so·lid·i·fi·ca·tion (səlidifikéiʃən) *n.* a solidifying or being solidified

so·lid·i·fy (səlídəfai) *pres. part.* **so·lid·i·fy·ing** *past* and *past part.* **so·lid·i·fied** *v.t.* to make hard and nonfluid ‖ (*fig.*) to make clear and compact, *to solidify conclusions* ‖ *v.i.* to become solid [fr. F. *solidifier*]

so·lid·i·ty (səlíditi:) *n.* the quality or state of being solid ‖ moral or financial soundness [fr. F. *solidité*]

solid laser a laser in which a solid (ruby, neodymium-doped yttrium-aluminum garnet) is excited by optical pumping to provide an intense, narrow beam

sol·id-state (sɒlidstéit) *adj.* (*electr.*) of semiconducting material connected to electrodes used to control flow of electricity, e.g., transistor, thrysistor *Cf* SEMICONDUCTOR, SOLID-STATE PHYSICS

solid-state memory (*computer*) a memory utilizing a metal-oxide semiconductor for storage

solid-state physics branch of physics dealing with the properties of crystal lattice in arrangement of atoms, dislocations and defects in this arrangement, esp. in connection with the conductance of heat and electricity, semiconductors, and the energy bands that insulate and conduct electricity —**solid-state** *adj.*

sol·i·dus (sɒ́lidəs) *pl.* **sol·i·di** (sɒ́lidai) *n.* a gold coin introduced by the Roman Emperor Constantine. The *s.* used to denote a shilling or shillings is an abbreviation of this word ‖ the diagonal stroke used sometimes to divide pounds, shillings and pence, as in £1/7/6, or the stroke e.g. in and/or ‖ a solidus curve [L.]

solidus curve a curve, usually expressing the temperature-composition relationship of a mixture, that corresponds with the liquidus, and which indicates the temperatures below which only the solid phase exists

so·lil·o·quist (səlíləkwist) *n.* a person who soliloquizes

so·lil·o·quize (səlíləkwaiz) *pres. part.* **so·lil·o·quiz·ing** *past* and *past part.* **so·lil·o·quized** *v.i.* to deliver a soliloquy ‖ *v.t.* to address in a soliloquy

so·lil·o·quy (səlíləkwi:) *pl.* **so·lil·o·quies** *n.* the act of speaking one's thoughts aloud in solitude ‖ a speech in a play through which a character reveals his thoughts to the audience, but not to any of the other characters, by voicing them aloud, usually in solitude [fr. L. *soliloquium*]

So·li·mões (sɒlimwẽs) *AMAZON

So·ling·en (zóuliŋən) a town (pop. 169,600) of North Rhine-Westphalia, West Germany, celebrated for its cutlery, metalwork and surgical instruments

sol·ip·sism (sɒ́ləpsizəm) *n.* (*philos.*) the view that only the self can be known to exist **sól·ip·sist** *n.* [fr. L. *solus*, alone+*ipse*, self]

So·lís (sɒlí:s), Juan Díaz de (*d.* 1516), Spanish explorer. With Vicente Yáñez Pinzón he explored (1508) the Yucatán and the Amazon and discovered (1516) the Rio de la Plata

sol·i·taire (sɒ́litɛər) *n.* a single gem, usually a diamond, set alone, e.g. in a ring ‖ a game played on a board by one person with marbles or pegs, which are moved by jumping. The object is to clear the board of all but one of the pieces ‖ (*Am.=Br.* patience) any of certain card games, generally for a single player, in which the cards are taken as they happen to fall and are arranged into set patterns for as long as this proves possible [F.]

sol·i·tar·i·ly (sɒliterili:) *adv.* in a solitary way

sol·i·tar·i·ness (sɒ́literi:nis) *n.* the state or quality of being solitary

sol·i·tar·y (sɒ́literi:) **1.** *adj.* one alone, without others, *a solitary straggler* ‖ preferring seclusion, not gregarious ‖ lonely, without company, *a solitary life* ‖ unfrequented, characterized by lack of human life ‖ (of insects) not social **2.** *pl.* **sol·i·tar·ies** *n.* a recluse, someone who prefers to live remote from human contacts ‖ (*pop.*) solitary confinement [fr. L. *solitarius*]

solitary confinement the confinement of a prisoner in a place where he is kept from contact with other prisoners

sol·i·tude (sɒlitu:d, sɒlitju:d) *n.* the state of being solitary ‖ loneliness ‖ isolation ‖ a lonely place, *Arctic solitudes* [O.F.]

sol·ler·et (sɒləret, sɒlərét) *n.* (*hist.*) a pliable steel shoe forming part of a 14th-c. or 15th-c. suit of armor [O.F.]

sol·mi·za·tion (sɒlmizéiʃən) *n.* (*mus.*) the application of syllabic names (*do, re, mi, fa, sol, la, si* or *ti*) to the notes of the C-major scale, to facilitate sight-singing (fixed-do system), developed from Guido d'Arezzo's 11th-c. system ‖ the application of these syllables to the tones of any scale, *do* always representing the tonic, *re* the second note etc. (movable-do system) (*TONIC SOL-FA) [fr. F.]

so·lo (sóulou) **1.** *n. pl.* **so·los, so·li** (sóuli:) a passage of music to be performed by one instrument or voice, with or without subordinate accompaniment ‖ any performance by one person ‖ a game of cards for four persons in which one player attempts to score a declared point on which he has wagered over the other three ‖ an airplane flight alone without passengers or instructor **2.** *adj.* alone, without accompaniment ‖ performed, made or done alone **3.** *v.i.* to fly an airplane alone, esp. for the first time without an instructor [Ital.]

So·logne (sɔlɔnj) a wooded, sandy region south of the Loire comprising parts of Loiret, Cher and Loir-et-Cher: hunting, forestry

so·lo·ist (sóulouist) *n.* a person who performs a solo

Sol·o·mon (sɒləmən) (c. 986–c. 932 B.C.), king of the Hebrews (c. 972–c. 932 B.C.), son of David and Bathsheba. Famous for his wisdom and his wealth, he established foreign alliances and made trading agreements, and built the first Temple in Jerusalem. The Books of Proverbs and Ecclesiastes, and the Song of Solomon, are attributed to him, though modern scholarship disputes this attribution

Solomon Islands an archipelago (land area 16,120 sq. miles, pop. 273,000) in the W. Pacific, comprising eight mountainous, volcanic, forested islands, with 40-odd islets and atolls. People: Melanesian, with Polynesian and Micronesian minorities. The westernmost islands (Bougainville, Buka and islets) belong to Papua New Guinea. The remainder (main islands: Guadalcanal, Malaita) form an independent state within the British Commonwealth (area 11,500 sq. miles, capital Honiara, on Guadalcanal). People: predominantly Melanesians. Religions: Anglican, Roman Catholic, Protestant. University of the Pacific (1977). Crops: cocoa, coconuts, yams, bananas, pineapples. Main exports: fish, lumber, copra, pine, shell. The archipelago was visited by a Spanish expedition (1568). The various islands were formed into a British protectorate (1893-1900). Self-government was achieved (1976) and full independence was granted (1978)

Solomon's seal *Polygonatum multiflorum,* fam. *Liliaceae,* a genus of perennial plants with terminal inflorescences of white, tubular, pendulous flowers. There are seal-like scars on the rhizome ‖ a magic figure composed of two triangles interlaced to form a star [trans. M.L. *sigillum Salomonis*]

So·lon (sóulən) (c. 640–c. 558 B.C.), Athenian statesman and lawgiver, one of the Seven Sages of Greece. As archon (594-3 B.C.) he issued a new humane code of laws and reformed the constitution, defining the rights of the people's assembly, and establishing a senate and popular courts

so long (*pop.*) goodbye

So·lo·thurn (zóulɔturn) a German-speaking, mainly Catholic canton (area 305 sq. miles, pop. 218,102) of N.W. Switzerland, in the Jura ‖ its capital (pop. 17,708)

sol·stice (sɒlstis, sóulstis) *n.* either of the two points in the sun's apparent annual orbit in relation to the fixed stars (the ecliptic) at which it is furthest from the equator (i.e. June 21–2, the summer solstice, Dec. 21–2, the winter solstice, which are correspondingly the longest and shortest days in the year, for the northern hemisphere) [O.F.]

sol·sti·tial point (sɒlstíʃəl, soulstíʃəl) the point in its ecliptic reached by the sun at the time of solstice

sol·u·bil·i·ty (sɒljubíliti:) *n.* the quality of being soluble ‖ the amount of a substance (the solute) that will dissolve in a given amount of another substance (the solvent) to give a saturated solution, usually expressed as the mass of solute per 100 parts by mass or volume of the solvent, at specified temperature and pressure

solubility product (*abbr.* S.P.) the product of the concentrations of the ions of a dissolved electrolyte when the latter is in physical equilibrium with its solid state

sol·u·ble (sɒljub'l) *adj.* capable of being dissolved ‖ capable of being solved or explained [O.F.]

sol·ute (sɒlju:t, sóulu:t) *n.* a substance which is dissolved, esp. the component in the lower concentration in a solution (cf. SOLVENT) [fr. L. *solvere (solutus),* to loosen]

so·lu·tion (səlú:ʃən) *n.* a homogeneous mixture of two (or more) substances in which a solid, liquid or gas forms a single phase with another liquid (or sometimes a gas or solid), and which has the same physical and chemical properties throughout at any given concentration up to its saturation point ‖ the act by which a substance is put into solution ‖ the state of being thus put into solution ‖ the answer to a problem ‖ the act, method or process by which such an answer is obtained [O.F. or fr. L. *solutio (solutionis)*]

solv·a·bil·i·ty (sɒlvəbíliti:) *n.* capability of being solved

solv·a·ble (sɒlvəb'l) *adj.* capable of being solved

Sol·vay process (sɒlvei) the manufacturing process by which carbon dioxide (from heated limestone) and ammonia precipitate sodium bicarbonate from a solution of common salt (sodium chloride), the bicarbonate is converted into carbonate (washing soda) by heat and the ammonia is recovered by the action of quicklime on the residual solution. The process is the basis of the alkali industry [after Ernest *Solvay* (1838–1922), Belgian chemist]

solve (sɒlv) *pres. part.* **solv·ing** *past* and *past part.* **solved** *v.t.* to find the answer to, work out (e.g. a problem) [fr. L. *solvere,* to loosen]

sol·ven·cy (sɒlvənsi:) *n.* the state or quality of being solvent (having enough money)

sol·vent (sɒlvənt) **1.** *adj.* having enough money to pay all debts ‖ able to dissolve **2.** *n.* a substance, usually a liquid, capable of dissolving other substances, esp. the component in the higher concentration in a solution (cf. SOLUTE) ‖ something that solves, *no solvent has been found for the problem of unemployment* [fr. L. *solvens (solventis)* fr. *solvere,* to loosen]

Sol·zhe·ni·tsyn (sʌlʒəní:tsin), Aleksandr (1918-), Soviet writer. In his novels, including 'One Day in the Life of Ivan Deniscovich' (1962), 'Cancer Ward' (1968) and 'The First Circle' (1968) he describes the injustice and degradation suffered by millions of Russians in the Stalinist concentration camps. He won the Nobel Prize (1970). Publication of the first volume of 'August 1914' (1971) and the first volume of 'The Gulag Archipelago' (1973) as well as his outspoken criticism of the Soviet treatment of writers, led to his exile to the West (1974), first to Switzerland and later to the U.S.A., where he completed 'The Gulag Archipelago' (1974-8) and wrote 'The Oak and the Calf' (1975) and other works

so·ma (sóumə) *pl.* **so·ma·ta** (sóumətə), **so·mas** *n.* an animal or plant body as a whole, with the exception of the germ cells [Gk *sōma,* body]

So·ma·li (soumáli:, səmáli:) *pl.* **So·ma·lis, So·ma·li** *n.* a member of the principal people of Somaliland ‖ the Cushitic language spoken by this race

So·ma·li·a (soumáli:ə, soumáljə) (or Somali Republic) a republic (area 246,135 sq. miles, pop. 3,640,000) in N.E. Africa. Capital: Mogadiscio. People: Somali (6 tribal confederacies), with minorities of related groups, small Bantu and other Negroid peoples, Arabs, Indians and Europeans. The population is 80% nomadic. Languages: Somali, Arabic (both official), minority languages. Religion: Sunni Moslem. The land is 28% potentially arable (with irrigation), 31% pasture and grazing and 17% desert. The north (except for a narrow coastal plain) and west belong to the central African plateau, with mountains in the north rising to 7,900 ft. The low-lying semidesert of the east and south includes the flood plains of the Webbe Shibeli and Juba Rivers. Average temperatures (F.): 70°-100° along the coast. Rainfall: Mogadiscio 15 ins, highlands 20 ins, elsewhere 0-15 ins. Livestock: cattle, sheep, goats, camels. Agricultural products: sugarcane, bananas, durra, corn, sorghum, sesame, oil seeds, cotton, tobacco, beans, fruit, gum arabic, myrrh. Minerals: salt, iron ore, gypsum, beryl, columbite. Industries: fishing, meat and fish canning, tanning, footwear, weaving, woodwork, textiles, sugar. Exports: fresh fruit and vegetables, livestock, hides and skins, wood and charcoal. Imports: manufactures, machinery, foodstuffs, vehicles, oil, chemicals. Ports: Berbera, Mogadiscio. University institute: Mogadiscio. Monetary unit: Somali shilling or Somalo (100 cents). HISTORY. The area was settled (13th and 14th cc.) by Somali tribes. A Moslem kingdom waged war on Ethiopia (15th and 16th cc.). Egypt occupied several places on the coast (1874-84). Britain established (1884) the protectorate of British Somaliland in the north. Italy established (1889) the protectorate of Italian Somaliland along the east coast, to which was added (1924) a region west of the Juba, ceded by Kenya. Italian Somaliland was incorporated (1936) in Italian East Africa. Italy invaded British Somaliland (1940), but the British conquered both protectorates (1941). Italian Somaliland was restored to Italian control (1950-60). British Somaliland became independent (June 26, 1960) and united with Italian Somaliland to form the independent republic of Somalia (July 1, 1960). By 1978, Somalia had regained most of the Ogaden region from Ethiopia, which had been given it by Britain although most of its inhabitants are Somalis; however Ethiopia retook it in 1978. Conflict continued, and famine and a serious refugee problem ensued

So·ma·li·land (soumáli:lænd, səmáli:lænd) a region of East Africa incl. Somalia, the Djibouti coast, E. Ethiopia and N.E. Kenya (to the Tana)

So·man (sóumən) *n.* (*mil.*) U.S.S.R. nerve gas that causes nausea, shortness of breath, blindness, paralysis, and death depending on the amount inhaled

so·mat·ic (soumǽtik, səmǽtik) *adj.* of or relating to the body or body cells as contrasted with the reproductive or germ cells ‖ relating to the body as distinguished from the soul or mind [fr. Gk *sōmatikos*]

somatic cell one of the cells composing the tissues, organs etc. of a body (*GAMETE)

so·ma·to·gen·ic (soumətədʒénik, səmætədʒénik) *adj.* developing from, affecting, or acting through the somatic cells (cf. PSYCHOGENIC) [fr. Gk *sōma (sōmatos),* body+*genes,* born]

so·ma·to·log·ic (soumət'lɒdʒik, səmæt'lɒdʒik) *adj.* of somatology **so·ma·to·lóg·i·cal** *adj.*

so·ma·tol·o·gy (soumətɒlədʒi:) *n.* physical anthropology [fr. Gk *sōma (sōmatos),* body+*logos,* word]

so·ma·tome (sóumətoum) *n.* a somite

so·ma·to·sén·so·ry (soumətousénsəri:) *adj.* of sensations received by the body proper, excluding the eyes, ears, tongue, and nose

so·ma·to·stat·in (soumətoustǽt'n) *n.* (*med.*) a brain hormone made synthetically by gene splicing that is used for the treatment of diabetes, gastric bleeding, and other body ailments

so·ma·to·ther·a·py (soumətouθérəpi:) *n.* treatment of mental and/or emotional disorders by physical means —**somatotherapist** *n.*

so·ma·to·tro·phic hormone (soumətoutróufik) pituitary hormone that regulates growth and influences metabolism, esp. of carbohydrates, fats, proteins (*abbr.* **STH**) *also* growth hormone

som·ber, esp. *Br.* **som·bre** (sɒmbər) *adj.* depressingly dark and shadowy ‖ conveying or giving rise to feelings of gloom or melancholy, or experiencing such feelings [F.]

som·bre·ro (sɒmbréərou) *pl.* **som·bre·ros** *n.* a large felt or straw hat with a wide and often upturned brim originally worn in Mexico, Spain and South America [Span.]

some (sʌm) **1.** *adj.* of a person or persons not known or specified, *some people can't make up their minds* ‖ being an unspecified amount or proportion of a whole or quantity, *leave us some oranges* ‖ of a person or persons only vaguely or implicitly determined, *some fool left the light on* ‖ (with 'other') one or several of a number of unspecified alternatives, *they must have found some other way* ‖ a considerable amount, *they had been waiting some time* ‖ (with 'only') a relatively small number or amount, *they finished only some of the food* ‖ (*pop.*) remarkable, notable, striking, *that was some game!* **2.** *pron.* an indefinite quantity or indefinite number of people or things, *the flowers are out, but some have died already* **3.** *adv.* (with a number) approximately, *some six months ago* [O.E. *sum*]

-some *suffix* used added to numbers to indicate a group, as in 'foursome'

CONCISE PRONUNCIATION KEY: **(a)** æ, cat; ɑ, car; ɔ fawn; ei, snake. **(e)** e, hen; i:, sheep; iə, deer; εə, bear. **(i)** i, fish; ai, tiger; ə:, bird. **(o)** o, ox; au, cow; ou, goat; u, poor; ɔi, royal. **(u)** ʌ, duck; u, bull; u:, goose; ə, bacillus; ju:, cube. x, loch; θ, think; ð, bother; z, Zen; ʒ, corsage; dʒ, savage; ŋ, orangutang; j, yak; ʃ, fish; tʃ, fetch; 'l, rabble; 'n, redden. Complete pronunciation key appears inside front cover.

-some *suffix* being or tending to be, as in 'loathsome'

some·bod·y (sʌ́mbɒdi:, sʌ́mbʌdi:, sʌ́mbədi:) **1.** *pron.* an unspecified or unknown person, *will somebody please light the lamp?* **2.** *pl.* **some·bod·ies** *n.* a person of importance, *he must be somebody to receive a welcome like that*

some·day (sʌ́mdei) *adv.* at some indefinite, usually distant, future time

some·how (sʌ́mhau) *adv.* (often with 'or other') by some means unknown or undefined, *we shall manage somehow* ‖ for some unknown cause or reason, *somehow it seems strange*

some·one (sʌ́mwʌn, sʌ́mwən) *pron.* somebody

some·place (sʌ́mpleis) *adv.* (*pop.*) somewhere

som·er·sault, sum·mer·sault (sʌ́mərsɔlt) **1.** *n.* a forward roll executed by putting the head on the ground in a tucked-in position and rolling forward so that the back of the neck, shoulders and back all touch the ground successively and the feet pass above them ‖ a leap in which this forward roll is performed in the air **2.** *v.i.* to perform a somersault [fr. O.F. *sombresaut*]

Som·er·set (sʌ́mərset, sʌ́mərsit), Edward Seymour, duke of (c. 1506-52), protector of England (1547-51) during the minority of Edward VI. The virtual ruler of England, he successfully invaded Scotland (1547), but was overthrown (1551) and executed (1552) by John Dudley, earl of Warwick

Somerset, Fitzroy James Henry *RAGLAN

Somerset a county (area 1,620 sq. miles, pop. 424,988) of S.W. England. County town: Taunton

some·thing (sʌ́mθiŋ) **1.** *pron.* (often with 'or other') a thing, act or quality undefined or unspecified, *there must be something we can do* ‖ (with 'like' and a number) some number near to the one stated, *something like six weeks* ‖ (often with 'quite' or 'really') a thing which can be regarded as a minor achievement, *it is quite something to have persuaded him to speak* ‖ somewhat **2.** *adv.* in a limited degree, *something more than pretense* **something like** something which nearly approximates an understood or specified ideal

some·time (sʌ́mtaim) **1.** *adv.* at some indefinite time in the future or past **2.** *adj.* former, *the sometime mayor*

some·times (sʌ́mtaimz) *adv.* occasionally, now and then

some·way (sʌ́mwei) *adv.* somehow, in some way

some·ways (sʌ́mweiz) *adv.* someway

some·what (sʌ́mhwɒt, sʌ́mhwʌt, sʌ́mwɒt, sʌ́mwʌt) **1.** *adv.* to a certain degree, rather, *the speech was somewhat pompous* **2.** *pron.* some previously mentioned person or thing having to some degree the nature of something specified, *it was somewhat of an ordeal*

some·where (sʌ́mhwɛər, sʌ́mwɛər) **1.** *adv.* in or to some place unknown or unspecified, *you will find her somewhere around* ‖ (with 'between' and numbers) approximately, *somewhere between two and three months*

so·mi·tal (sóumit'l) *adj.* of or having a somite or somites

so·mite (sóumait) *n.* a longitudinal segment of an animal body, esp. a primitive segment in the early developmental stage of higher segmented animals **so·mit·ic** (soumítik) *adj.* [fr. Gk *soma*, body]

Somme (sɔm) a river (147 miles long) of N. France, navigable past Amiens. It was the scene of heavy fighting in both world wars, esp. in July-Oct. 1916, when a French and British offensive pushed back the German lines at very heavy cost to both sides, but relieved the Verdun front. In June 1940 an attempt was made to halt the German drive south

Somme a department (area 2,443 sq. miles, pop. 538,500) of N. France (*PICARDY). Chief town: Amiens (pop. 110,000), the only town with a population over 30,000

som·nam·bu·late (sɒmnǽmbjuleit) *pres. part.* **som·nam·bu·lat·ing** *past* and *past part.* **som·nam·bu·lat·ed** *v.i.* to walk when asleep **som·nám·bu·lism, som·nám·bu·list** *ns* [fr. L. *somnus*, sleep+*ambulare* (*ambulatus*), to walk]

som·no·lence (sɒ́mnələns) *n.* the inclination or longing for sleep **sóm·no·len·cy** *n.* [O.F. *sompnolence* or fr. L. *somnolentia*]

som·no·lent (sɒ́mnələnt) *adj.* inclined to sleep, drowsy ‖ inducing sleep [O.F. *sompnolent* or fr. L. *somnolentus*]

So·mo·za (sɔmɔ́sɑ), Anastasio (1896-1956), Nicaraguan general and president (1937-47, 1950-6). After his assassination the presidency passed to his sons Anastasio Somoza Debayle and Luis Somoza Debayle or to a candidate approved by the Somoza family until 1979

So·mo·za De·bay·le (sɔmɔ́sɑðebáile), Anastasio (1925-80), Nicaraguan soldier and politician, son of Anastasio Somoza, and president (1967-74) and again from 1979 until his overthrow by the left-wing Sandinistas (1979)

Somoza Debayle, Luis Anastasio (1922-67), Nicaraguan politician, son of Anastasio Somoza, and president (1956-63) after the assassination of his father

son (sʌn) *n.* a male human being in relation to his parents ‖ (*pl., rhet.*) male descendants ‖ a form of address from an older man or woman to a young man or boy ‖ (*rhet.*) a male person considered as the product of his native land, his school etc. **the Son** (*theol.*) the second person of the Trinity ‖ Jesus Christ [O.E. *sunu*]

so·nance (sóunəns) *n.* the state or quality of being sonant [fr. L. *sonare*, to sound]

so·nant (sóunənt) **1.** *adj.* having sound ‖ (*phon.*, of speech sounds) voiced **2.** *n.* (*phon.*) a voiced speech sound (opp. SURD) ‖ a speech sound used as a syllabic ‖ (in Indo-European) a voiced syllabic consonant [fr. L. *sonans* (*sonantis*) fr. *sonare*, to sound]

so·nar (sóunɑr) *n.* an apparatus which locates a submerged object by emitting high-frequency sound waves and registering the vibrations reflected back from the object. It is used for detecting submarines, shoals of fish etc., and for finding ocean depths [fr. initial letters of *sound navigation ranging*]

so·na·ta (sənɑ́tə) *n.* a musical composition for piano, or solo instrument usually accompanied by piano, consisting of three or four movements of varying mood and speed but related in key. Pre-18th-c. sonatas were sometimes in one movement only. A double sonata is one written for two solo instruments [Ital.]

sonata form a pattern of musical composition derived from that of the first movement of a sonata. A work in sonata form opens with an exposition (a statement of the first and second subjects or themes) followed by a development (of the subjects) and ends with a recapitulation (of the subjects) and coda. Sonatas, quartets, concertos, symphonies etc. may all use sonata form

son·a·ti·na (sɒnətí:nə) *pl.* **son·a·ti·nas, son·a·ti·ne** (sɒnətí:nei) *n.* a shorter form of sonata, sometimes simpler to play [Ital.]

sonde (sɒnd) *n.* a device for testing atmospheric conditions at high altitudes [F.]

Son·der·bund (zɔ́ndərbunt) a league (1845-7) of seven Catholic cantons of Switzerland. It was formed to protect the interests of the cantons against the growing strength of the radicals. After the Sonderbund had been defeated in a short civil war (1847), Switzerland adopted a federal constitution

son et lu·mi·ère (sɔ̃n ei lu:myɛ́ər) *n.* (*Fr.*, often italics) sound-and-light spectacle including music and narration presented at some historic sites

song (sɔŋ, sɒŋ) *n.* the act or art of singing, *to burst into song* ‖ a short composition in which words and music together form a unity ‖ the utterance of some birds and certain other creatures ‖ (*rhet.*) a pleasing characteristic sound, *the song of the waves* ‖ (*rhet.*) poetry, verse **a song and dance** (*pop.*) an involved explanation, not necessarily true, designed to confuse or put someone off, *he gave me a song and dance about his absences* **for a song** (*pop.*) for a disproportionately small amount of money, *she sold the necklace for a song* **to make a song and dance** (*Br.*) to make a fuss [O.E. *sang*, *song*]

song·bird (sɔ́ŋbə:rd, sɒ́ŋbə:rd) *n.* a singing bird

song cycle a group or sequence of songs generally unified by theme or subject

Song·hai (sɔ́ŋhai) *n.* a people of the W. African middle Niger region ‖ a member of this people ‖ their language

—The kingdom of Songhai was a W. African state based on the middle Niger, founded c. 700. Islam became its official religion (c. 1000). It reached its greatest territorial extent in the late 15th and early 16th cc., but was destroyed (1591) by the Almohades

Song·koi (sɔ́ŋkɔ́i) *RED RIVER

Song of Solomon a Hebrew love poem (probably 5th-4th cc. B.C.) included among the sacred books of the Old Testament. Its imagery has been interpreted as an allegory of God's love for Israel or of Christ's love for his Church. It is also known as the Song of Songs and as Canticles

song·sce·na (sɔ́ŋʃeinə, sɒ́ŋʃeinə) *n.* (*mus.*) a scena (composition for solo voice)

song sparrow *Melospiza melodia*, a common brown and white North American sparrow

song·ster (sɔ́ŋstər, sɒ́ŋstər) *n.* a songbird **song·stress** (sɔ́ŋstris, sɒ́ŋstris) *n.* a woman singer of light popular music [O.E. *sangestre*]

song thrush *Turdus ericetorum*, a brown and white Old World thrush

song·writ·er (sɔ́ŋraitər, sɒ́ŋraiter) *n.* someone who composes either the words or the music of a song, or both

son·ic (sɒ́nik) *adj.* of sound waves which can be heard by the human ear ‖ of or relating to the speed of sound in air (about 1,087 feet per second, or about 738 m.p.h. at sea level) [fr. L. *sonus*, sound]

sonic alarm device that responds to disturbances of sonic field by emitting a loud noise or making an electrical contact with other devices used for security

son·i·ca·tion (sɒnikéiʃən) *n.* use of high-frequency sound waves for physical therapy, cleaning, separating solid materials, etc. —**sonicate** *v.* —**sonicator** *n.*

sonic bang (*Br.*) a sonic boom

sonic barrier the sound barrier

sonic boom a loud booming sound produced when the shock wave formed at the nose of a supersonic aircraft reaches the ground

so·nif·er·ous (sənífərəs, souníferəs) *adj.* making or carrying sound [fr. L. *sonus*, sound+*ferre*, to carry]

son-in-law (sʌ́ninlɔ) *pl.* **sons-in-law** *n.* a daughter's husband

son·net (sɒ́nit) *n.* a poem of 14 lines (the number varied in its early development) written to a regular rhyme scheme, of which there are many patterns. It was invented in Italy in the early 13th c. Dante was the first great poet to use it, Petrarch the first to write a great sonnet cycle. The form lends itself to the concise expression of contemplative thought and emotion. The Petrarchan (or Italian) sonnet, used also by Milton, has an octave rhyming *abba abba* and a sestet freely using 3 rhymes. The Shakespearean (or English or Elizabethan) sonnet consists of three quatrains, *abab cdcd efef* or *abba cddc effe*, and a couplet *gg*. English sonnets are normally in 10-syllable lines, Italian in 11 and French in 12 [F. or fr. Ital. *sonetto*]

son·net·eer (sɒnitíər) *n.* (*old-fash.*) someone who writes sonnets ‖ (*old-fash.*) someone dismissed contemptuously as a mere versifier, not a poet of quality [fr. Ital. *Sonettiere* or fr. SONNET+*-eer*, suffix denoting someone concerned with]

son·ny (sʌ́ni:) *n.* a friendly or patronizing form of address by an older person to a boy

son·o·chem·is·try (sɒnoukémәstri:) *n.* the study of the effects of ultrasonic waves on chemicals —**sonochemical** *adj.*

So·no·ra (sɔnɔ́rɑ) a northwest state (area 70,484 sq. miles, pop. 1,614,000) of Mexico, bounded on the north by the U.S.A. and on the west by Lower California and the Gulf of California. Capital: Hermosillo (pop. 264,073), situated within a flourishing cotton district. Winter vegetables, cereals, cotton, tobacco and corn are grown under irrigation. It was a famous colonial mining center, and still yields quantities of copper, gold, and silver. The Seri Indians live primitively on the offshore island of Tiburón

so·nor·i·ty (sənɔ́riti:, sənɒ́riti:) *pl.* **so·nor·i·ties** *n.* the state or quality of being sonorous [F. *sonorité* or fr. L. *sonoritas*]

so·no·rous (sənɔ́rəs, sənóurəs, sɒ́nərəs) *adj.* giving out sound, esp. ringing or resonant and full sound ‖ impressive, lofty (or intended to be so), *sonorous rhetoric* [fr. L. *sonorus*]

Sons of Liberty a secret organization formed (1765) in the American colonies to protest the Stamp Act. The organization evoked a colonial spirit of liberty, supported the nonimportation agreement, and helped to convoke the Continental Congress of 1774

Soo·chow (sú:tʃáu, sú:dʒóu) *WUHSIEN

soon (su:n) *adv.* in a short time from now, *it will soon begin* ‖ close after a stated time or event, *soon after 12, soon after the accident* ‖ quickly, *he will soon set things straight* ‖ willingly, *I would as soon do it by myself* ‖ early, *you needn't leave so soon* **as soon as** at the moment when, *as soon as she saw him she remembered him* ‖ as quickly or early as, *come as soon as you* can **no sooner . . . than** as soon as, *no sooner had he arrived than he began to complain* **no sooner said than done** it was put into effect as soon as it was decided or suggested **sooner or later** inevitably but with no certainty when, *sooner or later you will be glad of it* [O.E. *sōna*]

Soong (suŋ), Tse-ven (1894-1971), Chinese statesman. He was foreign minister of China (1941-5) and prime minister (1945-9)

soot (sut, su:t) **1.** *n.* black particles of carbon formed by the incomplete combustion of carbonaceous fuel (coal, oil etc.) which contains enough hydrocarbon gases to carry these particles upward by convection. Soot contains an admixture of other volatile elements, some of which are valuable trace elements in soil **2.** *v.t.* to cover or treat with soot [O.E. *sōt*]

soothe (su:ð) *pres. part.* **sooth·ing** *past* and *past part.* **soothed** *v.t.* to calm, reassure, *to soothe an anxious child* ‖ to smooth, *to soothe ruffled feelings* ‖ to alleviate (e.g. pain) **sóoth·ing** *adj.* [O.E. *sōthian,* to confirm]

sooth·say·er (sú:θseiər) *n.* (*hist.*) a person whose profession was telling the future [M.E. *sothseyer,* one who speaks the truth]

soot·y (súti:, sú:ti:) *comp.* **soot·i·er** *superl.* **soot·i·est** *adj.* having the color of soot ‖ covered with, or full of soot ‖ of or like soot

sop (sɒp) *n.* a piece of bread, cake etc. soaked in liquid before it is eaten ‖ something given to soothe or propitiate or as a concession, *a sop to one's pride* [O.E. *sopp*]

sop *pres. part.* **sop·ping** *past* and *past part.* **sopped** *v.t.* to soak (food) in soup, milk etc. ‖ (with 'up') to absorb [O.E. *soppian*]

soph·ism (sɒ́fizəm) *n.* a piece of plausible but false reasoning intended either to deceive or to display intellectual virtuosity [O.F. *sophisme* fr. L. fr. Gk]

Soph·ist (sɒ́fist) *n.* a paid itinerant professional teacher of logic, philosophy and rhetoric in ancient Greece. The most famous were Gorgias and Protagoras. The Sophists were the first to systematize the laws of thought, and were forerunners of the Socratic dialectic and of Aristotelian logic. Later Sophists emphasized material success and the ability to argue any case irrespective of its truth **soph·ist** someone who uses sophistry, e.g. to make the worse cause appear the better [fr. L. *sophista, sophistes* fr. Gk]

so·phis·tic (səfístik) *adj.* of or characteristic of sophists using sophistry **so·phís·ti·cal** *adj.* **so·phís·ti·cal·ly** *adv.* [fr. L. *sophisticus* fr. Gk]

so·phis·ti·cate (səfístikeit) *pres. part.* **so·phis·ti·cat·ing** *past* and *past part.* **so·phis·ti·cat·ed** *v.t.* to deprive of simplicity or sincerity by making artificial or affected ‖ to make complex ‖ to alter (a text) without authority **so·phís·ti·cat·ed** *adj.* having the worldly wisdom characteristic of fashionable life ‖ adapted to this way of life, *a sophisticated style* ‖ elaborated, made complex ‖ too affected or artificial, lacking in naiveté or naturalness ‖ (of peoples, societies) no longer primitive **so·phis·ti·cá·tion** *n.* [fr. M.L. *sophisticare* (*sophisticatus*) fr. *sophisticus,* sophistic]

soph·ist·ry (sɒ́fistri:) *pl.* **soph·ist·ries** *n.* a piece of plausible but false reasoning, sophism ‖ the use of sophisms **Soph·ist·ry** the methods of the ancient Greek Sophists

Soph·o·cles (sɒ́fəkli:z) (c. 496-406 B.C.) Greek poetic dramatist, author of about 123 plays of which seven complete tragedies survive: 'Antigone', 'Electra', 'Trachiniae', 'Oedipus Rex', 'Ajax', 'Philoctetes' and 'Oedipus at Colonus'. Sophocles modified contemporary dramatic form and extended the range of emotion that could be portrayed in plays, by introducing a part for a third actor and by cutting down the commenting role of the chorus, though he increased the size of the chorus. He made the destinies of his characters dependent on their faults rather than on the actions of the gods

soph·o·more (sɒfəmɔr, sɒfəmour, sɒ́fmɔr, sɒ́fmour) *n.* a second-year student at a college or secondary school **soph·o·mor·ic** (sɒfəmɔ́rik, sɒfəmɒ́rik) *adj.* of or relating to a sophomore ‖ immature, brash [prob. fr. Gk *sophom,* sophism]

sop·o·rif·ic (sɒpərífik, soupərífik) **1.** *adj.* inducing sleep ‖ showing or characterized by sleepiness **2.** *n.* something which induces sleep, esp. a drug [fr. L. *sopor,* sleep]

sop·ping (sɒ́piŋ) *adj.* soaked through, thoroughly wet

sop·py (sɒ́pi:) *comp.* **sop·pi·er** *superl.* **sop·pi·est** *adj.* soaked ‖ (*Br., pop.*) foolishly sentimental, *a soppy smile*

so·pran·o (səprǽnou, səprúnou) **1.** *n.* the highest singing voice in women, boys or castrati, ranging approx. from middle C to two octaves above it ‖ a singer with such a voice ‖ the musical part written for such a voice **2.** *adj.* of or relating to a soprano ‖ (of an instrument in a family of instruments) having roughly the range of the soprano voice, *a soprano saxophone* [Ital.]

So·pron (ʃɔ́prɔn) (*G.* Ödenburg) a town (pop. 43,000) in W. Hungary: Gothic churches

so·ra (sɔ́rə, sóurə) *n. Porzana carolina,* a small edible North American marsh bird of the rail family [perh. fr. Am. Ind.]

sora rail a sora

Sorb (sɔrb) *n.* a Wend ‖ Wendish [fr. G. *Sorbe*]

sorb (sɔrb) *n.* the service tree ‖ the rowan ‖ the fruit of either [F. *sorbe*]

sorb apple the fruit of the service tree or the rowan ‖ either of these trees

sor·bet (sɔ́rbət) *n.* a sherbet [F. fr. Ital. fr. Turk.]

Sor·bi·an (sɔ́rbi:ən) **1.** *adj.* of or relating to the Sorbs or their language **2.** *n.* a Sorb ‖ the language of the Sorbs ‖ Wendish

Sor·bonne (sɔrbɒ́n, sɔrbʌ́n, *F.* sɔrbɔn) the part of the University of Paris housing the faculties of science and letters. It was founded (1257) by Robert de Sorbon (1201-74), the chaplain and confessor of Louis IX, as a theological college, and became in effect the theological faculty of the university. In the 16th c. it was hostile to the Jesuits, in the 17th c. it condemned the Jansenists, in 1792 it was suppressed, and in 1808 given formally to the university. The present buildings (17th c.) were restored in the late 19th c.

sor·cer·er (sɔ́rsərər) *n.* a person who practices sorcery [earlier *sorcer* fr. O.F. *sorcier*]

sor·cer·ess (sɔ́rsəris) *n.* a female sorcerer [A.F. *sorceresse*]

sor·cer·y (sɔ́rsəri:) *pl.* **sor·cer·ies** *n.* the use of magic powers derived from evil spirits ‖ an instance of this [O.F. *sorcerie*]

sor·did (sɔ́rdid) *adj.* dirty, squalid, *sordid dwellings* ‖ dealing with squalor or moral degradation, *a sordid story* ‖ mean, contemptible, *sordid squabbles* [F. *sordide*]

sor·di·no (sɔrdí:nou) *pl.* **sor·di·ni** (sɔrdí:ni:) *n.* (*mus., abbr.* sord.) a mute [Ital.]

sore (sɔr, sour) **1.** *comp.* **sor·er** *superl.* **sor·est** *adj.* painful, *a sore finger* ‖ causing painful emotions, *a sore memory* ‖ (*pop.*) feeling wounded in one's pride, *he is sore about not being promoted* ‖ hard to bear, *a sore disappointment* ‖ (*rhet.*) grievous, *in sore need* **2.** *n.* a sore place on the body, esp. one where the skin has been broken **3.** *adv.* (*archaic*) sorely, *sore afraid* [O.E. *sār*]

sore·head (sɔ́rhed, sóurhed) *n.* (*pop.*) someone who is aggrieved or disgruntled, angry etc., or easily made so

So·rel (sɔrel), Georges (1847-1922), French syndicalist philosopher, author of 'Réflections sur la violence' (1908)

sore·ly (sɔ́rli:, sóurli:) *adv.* painfully ‖ in a great degree, *sorely wanted* [O.E. *sārlīce*]

sore·ness (sɔ́rnis, sóurnis) *n.* the quality or state of being sore ‖ something painful

Sör·en·sen (sə́:rənsən), Sören Peter Lauritz (1868-1939), Danish biochemist. He devised the pH scale of hydrogen ion concentration (1909)

sor·ghum (sɔ́rgəm) *n.* a member of *Sorghum,* fam. *Gramineae,* a genus of tropical grasses including several types used as cash crops, e.g. durra. Other species yield fiber, and some yield sugar ‖ the syrup obtained from a sorghum grown for sugar. Sorghum is most widely grown in Africa, but is also cultivated in India, China and the U.S.A. [Mod. L. fr. Ital. *sorgo*]

So·ria (sɔ́rjɑ) a province (area 3,983 sq. miles, pop. 98,803) in N. central Spain (*OLD CASTILE) ‖ its capital (pop. 19,000)

sor·i·tes (sɔráiti:z, souráiti:z) *pl.* **sor·ites** *n.* (*logic*) a series of syllogistical propositions in which the predicate of the first becomes the subject of the next, and so on, until it is concluded that the predicate of the last proposition can also be the predicate of the first [L. fr. Gk *sōreitēs* fr. *sōros,* heap]

so·ror·i·cide (sərɔ́risaid, sərɒ́risaid) *n.* the killing of one's sister ‖ someone who kills his sister [fr. L. *soror,* sister+*caedere,* to kill]

so·ror·i·ty (sərɔ́riti:, sərɒ́riti:) *pl.* **so·ror·i·ties** *n.* (esp. in U.S. colleges) a private, often residential social club of female students [fr. M.L. *sororitas* fr. *soror,* sister]

so·ro·sis (səróusis) *pl.* **so·ro·ses** (səróusi:z) *n.* (*bot.*) a compound fruit formed by the fusion of fleshy axis and flowers, e.g. the mulberry, pineapple [Mod. L. fr. Gk *sōros,* heap]

sorp·tion (sɔ́rpʃən) *n.* the process of taking up and holding a substance by absorption or adsorption

sor·rel (sɔ́rəl, sɒ́rəl) **1.** *adj.* of a reddish brown or chestnut color **2.** *n.* a reddish brown or chestnut color ‖ a sorrel-colored horse [O.F. *sorel*]

sorrel *n.* a member of *Rumex,* fam. *Polygonaceae,* a genus of plants with sour juice, of which 150 species are known in temperate regions. Some have rhizomes. They have whorled inflorescences with small inconspicuous flowers [O.F. *surele, sorele*]

sor·ri·ly (sɔ́rili:, sɒ́rili:) *adv.* in a sorry manner

sor·ri·ness (sɔ́ri:nis, sɒ́ri:nis) *n.* the state or quality of being sorry

sor·row (sɒ́rou, sɔ́rou) *v.i.* to grieve, to feel sorrow ‖ (*rhet.*) to express grief [O.E. *sorgian*]

sorrow *n.* grief, sadness ‖ a cause of grief, *he is a sorrow to his parents* **sór·row·ful** *adj.* [O.E. *sorh, sorg*]

sor·ry (sɒri:, sɔ́ri:) *comp.* **sor·ri·er** *superl.* **sor·ri·est** *adj.* feeling pity, *he was sorry for the poor man* ‖ feeling sympathy, *I am sorry that it hurts you* ‖ feeling regret, *I am sorry that I troubled you* ‖ (*rhet.*) arousing pity or contempt, *a sorry sight* [O.E. *sārig,* in pain fr. *sār,* sore]

sort (sɔrt) **1.** *n.* a group having its own special qualities, *different sorts of flowers* someone having the qualities characteristic of a group, *he is not the sort to complain* ‖ (*printing*) a letter, figure etc. of a particular font **of a sort, of sorts** of a not very good kind, *it unfolds into a bed of sorts* **out of sorts** a little unwell ‖ cross, in a bad humor **2.** *v.t.* to separate into groups having special qualities, *to sort apples according to size* ‖ (with 'out') to select (one, or some) of a particular kind ‖ to arrange (postal matter) in a suitable order for delivery ‖ (*computer*) to segregate into groups according to an instructed pattern [O.F. *sorte*]

sor·tie (sɔ́rti:) *n.* a sally of troops from a besieged position ‖ a mission or raiding flight by a single plane or ship [F.]

sor·ti·lege (sɔ́rt'lidʒ) *n.* divination by casting lots ‖ sorcery [O.F. or fr. M.L. *sortilegium*]

so·rus (sɔ́rəs, sóurəs) *pl.* **so·ri** (sɔ́rai, sóurai) *n.* a cluster of stalked sporangia on the undersurface of a fern frond ‖ a cluster of spores on lower plants [fr. Mod. L. fr. Gk *sōros,* heap]

SOS (ésouès) *n.* an internationally recognized signal (three dots, three dashes, three dots in Morse code) used in radiotelegraphy to call for help in distress ‖ (*pop.*) any call for help in need

so-so (sóusou) **1.** *adj.* neither good nor bad, middling, *his health is only so-so* **2.** *adv.* passably ‖ not very well

sos·te·nu·to (sɒstənú:tou, soustənú:tou) *adv.* (*mus.*) in a sustained, smooth manner [Ital.]

SOSUS (*mil. acronym*) for sound surveillance system, in which sonar devices are mounted on the ocean floor to sound an alert of submarine approach

sot (sɒt) *n.* a habitual drunkard [O.E.=fool]

so·te·ri·o·log·i·cal (sətiəri:əlɒ́dʒik'l) *adj.* of or relating to soteriology

so·te·ri·ol·o·gy (sətiəri:ɒ́lədʒi:) *n.* the branch of theology concerned with the doctrine of salvation through Christ [fr. Gk *sōtēria,* salvation]

So·thic (sóuθik, sɒ́θik) *adj.* (ancient Egypt) of a year of 365 ¼ days as compared with the ordinary Egyptian year of 365 days ‖ of a period of 1,460 Sothic years (=1,461 solar years) [fr. Gk *sōthis,* an Egyptian name for the dog star]

sot·tish (sɒ́tiʃ) *adj.* of or like a sot

sot·to vo·ce (sɒ́touvóutʃi:) **1.** *adv.* in a low or soft voice ‖ (*mus.,* of the voice or an instrument) very softly indeed, just audibly **2.** *adj.* very quietly spoken [Ital.]

sou (su:) *n.* a former French coin worth 5 centimes ‖ a former French coin worth 10 centimes ‖ (*pop.*) the least little bit of money, *they haven't a sou* [F.]

sou·a·ri (su:ɑ́ri:) *n.* a member of *Caryocar,* fam. *Caryocaraceae,* a genus of South American tropical trees, producing large, rich, thick-shelled nuts, resembling large Brazil nuts, and durable lumber. The woody capsule may weigh 25 lbs. The nuts yield an oil used in cooking [F. *saouari* fr. native name in Guiana]

sou·brette (su:brét) *n.* a maid or servant girl, usually frivolous or intriguing, in a play or opera || an actress or singer taking such a part [F.]

sou·bri·quet (sú:brikei, sú:briket) *n.* a sobriquet

Sou·dan (su:dǽn, *F.* su:dɑ̃) *MALI

souf·flé (su:fléi, sú:flei) **1.** *n.* a light, baked dish made by adding whipped egg whites to a sweet or savory mixture **2.** *adj.* (*cooking*) of a dish, or of pastry, in which beaten egg whites are incorporated || (of pottery) decorated with small spots of color that have been blown on [F.]

sough (sau, sʌf) **1.** *n.* a murmuring sighing sound, as of wind through trees **2.** *v.i.* to make such a sound [O.E. *swōgan*, to sound]

sought *past* and *past part.* of SEEK

sought·af·ter (sɔ́tæftər, sɔ́tɑftər) *adj.* much in demand or desired

souk, suq (su:k) *n.* (in Arab countries) a market [Arab. *sūq*]

soul (soul) **1.** *n.* the immortal part of man, as distinguished from his body || the moral and emotional nature of man, as distinguished from his mind || the vital principle which moves and animates all life || a human being, *not a soul in sight* || personification or embodiment, *he was the soul of honor* || (*pop.*) emotional expressiveness that appeals for emotional response in others, *his performance lacks soul* **like a lost soul** utterly forlorn **to be the life and soul of** (*Br.*) to make (a party) gay by one's own animation **2.** *adj.* (*pop.*) characteristic of or associated with blacks, *soul music* **sóul·ful** *adj.* expressing or appealing to the emotions, often with sentimentality **sóul·less** *adj.* having no soul || lacking nobility of mind || deadening, rousing no enthusiasm, *a soulless job* [O.E. *sāwol, sāwl*]

soul brother a fellow black person (male) *Cf* SOUL SISTER

soul food traditional food of American blacks in the South (now nationwide), e.g., chitterlings, ham hocks, pigs feet, collard greens

soul music traditional rhythm and blues-related music of American blacks based on gospel songs that is direct, immediate, and of immense vitality

Sou·louque (su:lu:k), Faustin (1782-1867), Haitian black, emperor of Haiti (1849-59) under the name of Faustin I. His despotism led to his being overthrown

soul sister a fellow black person (female) *Cf* SOUL BROTHER

Soult (su:lt), Nicolas Jean de Dieu (1769-1851), French marshal. He distinguished himself in the Napoleonic Wars, notably at Austerlitz (1805). He was minister of war (1830-4) and nominal head (1840-4) of the conservative government effectively led by Guizot

sound (saund) *v.t.* to cause to emit sound, *to sound a trumpet* || to signal or indicate with usually drum, trumpet, horn or bugle, *to sound the retreat* || to pronounce, give sound to, articulate, *sound your consonants clearly* || to test (something, e.g. the ground) by causing it to emit sounds || to test (e.g. the heart) by auscultation || *v.i.* to emit sound || to convey a specified impression, *it sounds silly* **to sound off** (*pop.*) to speak out openly in a somewhat pugnacious manner || (*mil.*) to count cadence while marching [fr. O.F. *suner, soner*]

sound *n.* the sensation experienced when the brain interprets vibrations within the structure of the ear caused by rapid variations of air pressure || such a sensation understood as due to a particular source, *the sound of wheels* || the distance over which something can be heard, *within sound of the sea* || mere noise, or noise as distinguished from sense || an impression gained from what one is told or learns about something, *I don't like the sound of it* [A.F. *soun*]

sound *n.* a narrow channel of water connecting two seas or a sea and a lake etc. || a long, rather broad ocean inlet || the air bladder of a fish || (*med.*) a probe for investigating esp. cavities in the body [O.E. or O.N. *sund*]

sound 1. *adj.* not diseased or injured || firm and solid || wise, reliable, *sound advice, a sound character* || financially satisfactory, *a sound investment* || thorough, *a sound thrashing* || deep, *a sound sleep* || valid, convincing, *a sound argument* || legally valid || (of religious or political tenets etc.) orthodox **2.** *adv.* (with 'sleep' or 'asleep' and used in combination) soundly [O.E. *sund*]

sound *v.t.* to measure the depth of (usually water) by using a rod or weighted line || to examine (the ocean floor etc.) with a lead that brings up samples || (sometimes with 'out') to ask (a person) discreet questions in order to discover how he feels or thinks || to investigate (feelings or ideas) in this way || (*med.*) to examine (a person's body) with a sound || *v.i.* to use a line etc. for measuring the depth of water || to examine the ocean floor etc. with a lead that brings up samples || (of a whale) to dive deeply and suddenly [fr. O.F. *sonder*]

sound and light *SON ET LUMIÈRE

sound barrier a sudden large increase in aerodynamic resistance to objects moving at speeds approaching that of sound

sound·board (sáundbɔrd, sáundbourd) *n.* the sounding board of a musical instrument

sound bow (bou) the thick part of a bell that the clapper strikes

sound box a mechanism in a nonelectric phonograph which converts into sounds the vibrating movements of the needle or stylus in the record grooves || the hollow boxlike part in a musical instrument (e.g. a violin) which augments its resonance

sound·ing (sáundiŋ) *adj.* resonant || making a sound || (*rhet.*) high-sounding

sounding *n.* the act of someone who sounds || a measurement or investigation made by sounding || a part of the bottom of the sea or of a river etc. which can be reached by sounding || (*pl.*) the depth of water in the sea or a river measured by sounding || (*pl.*) entries of these depths in a logbook

sounding balloon a balloon used in recording the temperature, pressure etc. of the atmosphere

sounding board a thin board or plate in a musical instrument which resonates to amplify the notes || a board placed above a pulpit etc. to reflect a speaker's voice to his audience || an agency which gives greater force, scope etc. to various opinions, *the government used the press as its sounding board*

sounding line (*naut.*) a rope, wire etc., with a lead sinker, used for sounding depths

sound·ly (sáundli:) *adv.* wisely, prudently, *she advised them soundly* || thoroughly, *he thrashed them soundly* || deeply, *she slept soundly all through the journey*

sound·ness (sáundnis) *n.* the state or quality of being sound

sound pollution *NOISE POLLUTION

sound post a small wooden peg in a violin etc. supporting the belly and transmitting vibrations to the back of the instrument

sound·proof (sáundpru:f) **1.** *adj.* impenetrable to sound waves **2.** *v.t.* to make soundproof **sóund·proof·ing** *n.* the material used in making something soundproof || the act or process of making something soundproof

sound ranging (*mil.*) the location of an enemy gun by taking bearings on a detonation and measuring how long it takes the sound to reach surveyed positions

sound·scape (sáundskeip) *n.* the overall feeling in music; a sound panorama

sound track the side strip of a motion-picture film on which sound is electrically recorded by tracks of variable density or variable width

sound wave (*phys.*) a periodic progression of alternations between high and low pressure through an elastic medium

soup (su:p) **1.** *n.* a liquid food, usually savory, made by stewing ingredients such as meat, vegetables, fish or game, often in a stock and with seasoning **from soup to nuts** (*pop.*) from beginning to end, everything included **in the soup** (*pop.*) in a difficult position || a chemical mixture, often a residual or waste product || the white water remaining after a wave **2.** *v.t.* **to soup up** (*pop.*) to increase the horsepower of (a car) [fr. F. *soupe*]

soup·çon (su:psɔ̃, sú:psɔ̃) *n.* a trace, suspicion, suggestion || a very small quantity of something [F.=suspicion]

soup kitchen a place where food (not only soup) is provided without charge to people in need through poverty, a natural disaster etc.

sour (sáuər) **1.** *adj.* tasting or smelling acid, sharp or biting, *sour fruit* || changed, e.g. by fermentation, to an acid, esp. spoiled in this way, *sour milk* || morosely angry or embittered, or expressing such a condition, *a sour look* || (of soil) acid in reaction **2.** *v.t.* to make sour || *v.i.* to become sour **3.** *n.* a cocktail of a specified liquor made acid with lemon or lime juice and a slice of orange, *a whiskey sour* [O.E. *sūr*]

source (sɔrs) *n.* the spring, or starting point, of a stream or river || the place or thing from which, or person because of whom, something begins or arises, *the source of the trouble* || a person, book, document etc. consulted for information or providing initial inspiration [O.F. *sors, source*]

source language (*computer*) the language in which a program is written before translation into a language that the processor can utilize *Cf* TARGET LANGUAGE

sour cream cream soured by lactic acid bacteria

sour·dine (suərdí:n) *n.* (*mus.*) a mute, sordino [F.]

sour·dough (sáuərdou) *n.* an old inhabitant of Alaska or N.W. Canada || fermented dough from one baking set aside to start the next [from the prospectors' practice of carrying fermented dough for breadmaking]

sour grapes the disparagement of something out of chagrin at not being able to get it [from a fable by Aesop]

sour·sop (sáuərsɒp) *n.* *Annona muricata*, fam. *Annonaceae*, a tree native to the West Indies which bears large, ovoid, pulpy, edible fruit, resembling the sweetsop but more acid in taste || the fruit of the soursop tree

Sou·sa (sú:zə), John Philip (1854-1932), American composer. Besides his famous marches, e.g. 'Stars and Stripes Forever', 'Washington Post', he composed comic operas, songs and suites

Sou·sa (sóuzə), Martim Affonso de (c. 1500-1564), Portuguese explorer. He led (1530) the first expedition to Brazil, organized (1531) the Portuguese settlement against the incursions of Spaniards, French and Dutch, and founded (1532) São Vicente

sou·sa·phone (sú:zəfoun, sú:səfoun) *n.* a large tubalike instrument used in American brass bands [after J. P. *Sousa*, the originator]

souse (saus) **1.** *n.* pickled food || a preparation used for pickling || a soaking || (*pop.*) a drunkard **2.** *v.t. pres. part.* **sous·ing** *past* and *past part.* **soused** to pickle || to soak or drench **soused** *adj.* pickled || (*pop.*) very drunk [O.F. *sous, souce*, pickle fr. O.H.G.]

Sousse (su:s) (*Arab.* Susa) a walled port (pop. 255,000) in N.E. Tunisia: fortified Moslem convent (9th c.), Christian catacombs (2nd-3rd cc.). It was a Phoenician city, was destroyed by the Vandals (434) and rebuilt by Justinian

sou·tache (su:tǽʃ) *n.* a narrow braid used for trimming or ornamenting fabric [F. fr. Hung. *szuszak*, a curl of hair]

sou·tane (sú:tɑ́n) *n.* a Roman Catholic priest's cassock [F. fr. Ital.]

south (sauθ) **1.** *adv.* toward the south **2.** *n.* (usually with 'the') one of the four cardinal points of the compass (*abbr.* S., *COMPASS POINT) || the direction to the right of a person facing east **the South** the southern part of a country, esp. the states of the U.S.A. south of the Mason-Dixon line which fought against the Union in the Civil War (*CONFEDERATE STATES OF AMERICA) **3.** *adj.* of, belonging to or situated toward the south || facing south, *a south window* || (of winds) blowing from the south [O.E. *sūth*]

South Africa a republic (area 471,445 sq. miles, pop. 32,465,000) occupying the southern tip of Africa. Administrative capital: Pretoria. Seat of legislature: Cape Town. Largest city: Johannesburg. People: 68% African, 19% European, 9% Coloured, 3% Asian (mainly Indian). Racial segregation (*APARTHEID) is enforced. Native reservations occupy 12% of the land. Language: Bantu languages (mainly Xhosa, Zulu, Sotho, Tswana, Ciskei), Afrikaans (spoken by 57% of Europeans and most Coloured), English (39% of Europeans and most Asians), Indian languages. Religion: 50% local African religions, 42% Protestant (incl. Dutch Reformed, Methodist, Anglican and Native Separatist Churches), with Roman Catholic, Hindu, Moslem and Jewish minorities. The land is 8% cultivated and 1% forest. Broad, flat plateaus, broken by *kopjes* (dry ridges and gulleys), cover most of the country, sloping from the High Veld (mainly 5,000-7,000 ft) in the S. Transvaal, E. Orange Free State and N.E. Cape Province, to under 2,000 ft in the west. Mountains in the east (*DRAKENSBERG) and south (with the Great and Little Karoos) separate the plateaus from the Indian Ocean coastal plain. The plateaus are savanna (veld) in the east, semidesert in the west and north (*KALAHARI). The coastal plain is desert in the west, Mediterranean in the south and tropical in the east. Average temperatures (F.) in Jan. and July: Durban 75° and 65°, Mozambique border 92° and 79°, Johannesburg 80° and 38°, Kimberley 91° and 66°, Cape

Town 70° and 55°. Rainfall: N. Natal 45-50 ins, Drakensberg 68 ins, High Veld 20-30 ins, Johannesburg and Port Elizabeth 33 ins, Kimberley 16 ins, Cape Town 25 ins, northwest coast 2 ins. Livestock: cattle, sheep, goats, hogs, poultry, horses, mules, donkeys. Agricultural products: corn, Kaffir corn, wheat, other cereals, sugarcane, peanuts, sunflower seed, fruit (esp. oranges, apples, grapes and pears), dairy products, tobacco, potatoes, cotton, wool. Fisheries: esp. pilchards, lobsters, whales. Mineral resources: gold, uranium, coal, diamonds, asbestos, copper, manganese ore, iron ore. Industries: mining, ranching, subsistence farming (native reserves), iron and steel, foodstuffs, metals, machinery, chemicals, clothing and footwear, textiles, wines and spirits, furniture, vehicles, transport equipment, bark extract, soap, cement, bricks, tires, tourism. Exports: minerals, wool, cereals, hides and skins, machinery, oils and paints, citrus fruits, textiles, sugar, wines and spirits, bark extract. Imports: vehicles, drugs and fertilizers, cotton goods, rough diamonds, wood products, fuels and oil, jewelry and fancy goods, tea, rubber. Ports: Durban, Cape Town, Port Elizabeth, East London. There are nine universities for Europeans, and five university colleges for non-Europeans. Monetary unit: rand (100 cents). HISTORY. South Africa was inhabited by Bushmen and Hottentots when Dias discovered the Cape of Good Hope (1487). After Vasco da Gama rounded the Cape (1497), South Africa became important as a supply station on the route to the East Indies. The Dutch East India Company established a settlement at Cape Town (1652). Settlement extended inland to form Cape Colony (18th c.), giving rise to many wars with Bantu tribes (18th-19th cc.). The colony prospered with slave labor, largely imported from the Dutch East Indies. Britain annexed the colony (1806) to protect its route to India, an act officially recognized by the Netherlands in 1814. Increasing numbers of British settlers arrived (1820s), and to escape British domination the Boers moved northward in the Great Trek (1835-6) to Natal, the Transvaal and the Orange Free State, defeating the Zulus (1838). Britain annexed Natal (1843) but recognized the independence of the Transvaal (1852) and the Orange Free State (1854). Relations between the British colony and the Boer republics deteriorated, esp. when Britain annexed (1871) Griqualand, an area of the Orange Free State where diamonds had been discovered (1867). An attempt to annex the Transvaal (1877) resulted in war between Britain and the Boers (1880-1) in which Britain was defeated, and the Transvaal's independence was recognized. But the discovery (1886) of gold at Witwatersrand brought many new immigrants, known as Uitlanders, to the Transvaal. Kruger's refusal to give them the franchise and the Jameson Raid (1895) provoked the Boer War (1899-1902). After the British victory, the Transvaal and the Orange Free State became British colonies (1902) and were united with Cape Province and Natal to form the Union of South Africa (1910). Led by Botha and Smuts, South Africa fought Germany in the lst world war and received German South West Africa as a mandate (1920). In opposition to Smuts's policy of promoting cooperation between the British and Boer elements, the Nationalist party was formed, advocating Boer supremacy and secession from the Commonwealth. Despite Nationalist opposition, South Africa took an active part in the 2nd world war. The Nationalists came to power (1948) under Malan, put apartheid into practice, and virtually annexed South West Africa (1949). European supremacy was enforced by government control of electoral districts and the judicature and by strict segregation of residential areas and educational establishments. Amid mounting pressure from other African states, the U.N. and the Commonwealth to abandon apartheid, South Africa withdrew from the Commonwealth, as a republic (May 31, 1961). The U.N. terminated (1966) the mandate over South West Africa (Namibia), but South Africa described this as illegal and continued its administration. Between 1964 and 1985 some 3.5 million blacks were resettled into ten African 'homelands,' four of which, Transkei (1976), Bophuthatswana (1977), Venda (1979) and Ciskei (1981), were granted independence by South Africa, although no other country recognized them as nations. Opposition to apartheid in South Africa grew, intensifying in 1976 when rioting broke out in several cities, including Soweto, a black township of Johannesburg. The death while in police custody of Stephen Biko, a young black detained in a government crackdown following the riots, caused international protests. Under pressure the government began to amend some apartheid laws from 1978, and in 1984 Coloureds and Asians were offered a limited role in the central government, although blacks were still excluded. Bishop Desmond Tutu, head of the South African Council of Churches, received the Nobel peace prize (1984) for his efforts to gain a nonviolent end to apartheid. Violence continued, however, leading the government to declare a state of emergency (1985-6) and to grant blacks a few concessions. Some of South Africa's trading partners imposed limited sanctions on South Africa to increase pressure on the government. South Africa continued to exert control over Namibia, despite continuous international pressure

South African 1. *adj.* of or relating to South Africa 2. *n.* a native or inhabitant of South Africa esp. one of European origin

South African Dutch *AFRIKAANS

South African Republic the name (1856-81) of the Transvaal

South African War *BOER WAR

South America the fourth largest continent (area 7,035,340 sq. miles) comprising Argentina, Bolivia, Brazil, Chile, Colombia, Ecuador, French Guiana, Guyana, Paraguay, Peru, Suriname, Uruguay and Venezuela and including Curaçao, the Falkland and Galapagos Is, Trinidad and Tobago, and adjacent smaller islands (*AMERICA). (For history see articles on separate countries)

South American Indians *LATIN AMERICAN INDIANS

South·amp·ton (sauθǽmptən, sauθhǽmptən) a passenger port and county borough (pop. 207,500) in Hampshire, England. Industries: shipbuilding, oil refining, chemicals, engineering. University (1952)

South Arabia, Federation of *YEMEN, PEOPLES DEMOCRATIC REPUBLIC OF

South Australia a state (area 380,070 sq. miles, pop. 1,302,400) in S. central Australia. Capital: Adelaide. It is low-lying and arid except in the south. Agriculture: wheat, barley, fruit (mainly in irrigated areas along the Murray), sheep, some cattle. Resources: iron ore, pyrites, gypsum, salt, coral. Industries: metallurgy, textiles, chemicals, food processing, engineering. University (1874), at Adelaide

south by east S. 11° 15′E., one point east of due south (*abbr.* S. b. E., *Br.* esp. S. by E., *COMPASS POINT)

south by west S. 11° 15′W., one point west of due south (*abbr.* S. b. W., *Br.* esp. S. by W., *COMPASS POINT)

South Canadian River *CANADIAN RIVER

South Car·o·li·na (kærəláinə) (*abbr.* S.C.) a state (area 31,055 sq. miles, pop. 3,203,000) on the S.E. Atlantic coast of the U.S.A. Capital: Columbia. It lies largely in the coastal plain and Appalachian piedmont plateau, rising to 3,548 ft in the northwest (Blue Ridge Mtns). It is primarily industrial. Agriculture: tobacco, cotton, soybeans, peaches, corn, hogs, cattle. Resources: building materials, timber. Industries: textiles, chemicals, forest products. State university (1801) at Columbia. South Carolina was colonized by the Spanish (16th c.) and the English (late 17th c.), was one of the Thirteen Colonies, and became (1788) the 8th state of the U.S.A.

South China Sea *CHINA SEA

South Dakota (*abbr.* S.D.) a state (area 77,047 sq. miles, pop. 691,000) of the N. central U.S.A. in the Great Plains, with the rugged Black Hills (summit 7,242 ft) and badlands in the southwest. Capital: Pierre. Agriculture: beef cattle, hogs, corn, fodder crops. Resources: gold (leading state producer), beryl, silver, sand, gravel. Industries: meat packing, butter making. State university (1882) at Vermillion. South Dakota was settled in the 19th c. and became (1889) the 40th state of the U.S.A.

South·down (sáuθdąun) *n.* a sheep of a hornless breed, with fine soft wool, valued chiefly for its meat [after the *South Downs* of Sussex and Hampshire, England, where the breed originated]

South Downs *DOWNS

south·east (sąuθí:st) 1. *adv.* toward the southeast 2. *n.* (usually with 'the') the compass point or direction midway between south and east (*abbr.* S.E., *COMPASS POINT) **the Southeast** the southeastern part of a country 3. *adj.* of, belonging to or situated toward the southeast ‖ (of winds) blowing from the southeast [O.E. *sūthēast*]

South East Asia Treaty Organization (*abbr.* SEATO) an organization set up (1954) by the U.S.A., Great Britain, Australia, France, New Zealand, Pakistan, the Philippines and Thailand, as a bulwark against Chinese Communism after the Korean War. It was dissolved in 1977

southeast by east S. 56° 15′E., one point east of due southeast (*abbr.* S.E. b. E., *Br.* esp. S.E. by E., *COMPASS POINT)

southeast by south S. 33° 45′ E., one point south of due southeast (*abbr.* S.E. b. S., *Br.* esp. S.E. by S., *COMPASS POINT)

south·east·er (sąuθí:stər) *n.* a strong wind or storm from the southeast

south·east·er·ly (sąuθí:stərli:) 1. *adj.* and *adv.* in or toward the southeast ‖ (of winds) from that direction 2. *pl.* **south·east·er·lies** *n.* a wind blowing from the southeast

south·east·ern (sąuθí:stə:rn) *adj.* situated, facing or moving toward the southeast ‖ of or relating to the southeast or the Southeast

south·east·ward (sąuθí:stwərd) *adv.* and *adj.* toward the southeast **south·éast·wards** *adv.*

South·end (sáuθénd) (or Southend-on-Sea) a resort and county borough (pop. 156,683) in Essex, England, on the Thames estuary, providing the nearest beach to London (43 miles away). Industries: electrical equipment, chemicals

south·er·ly (sʌ́ðərli:) 1. *adj.* and *adv.* in or toward the south ‖ (of winds) from that direction 2. *pl.* **south·er·lies** *n.* a wind blowing from the south

south·ern (sʌ́ðərn) *adj.* situated, facing, or moving toward the south **South·ern** of or relating to the South [O.E. *sūtherne*]

Southern Alps a mountain range along the west central coast of South Island, New Zealand (Mt Cook, 12,350 ft), with gorges and glaciers

Southern Bug (bu:g, *Russ.* bu:k) a river (520 miles long, mostly unnavigable) of the U.S.S.R., which flows through the S.W. Ukraine to the Black Sea (Dnieper estuary)

Southern Cross a cross-shaped constellation in the southern hemisphere with a bright star at each extremity

South·ern·er (sʌ́ðərnər) *n.* a native or inhabitant of the South, esp. of the Southern part of the U.S.A.

southern hemisphere the half of the earth south of the equator

south·ern·most (sʌ́θərnmǫust) *adj.* farthest south

southern pea black-eyed pea

Sou·they (sáuði:, sʌ́ði:), Robert (1774-1843), English poet and man of letters. From 1803 he lived in the Lake District, met Wordsworth, and himself became one of the Lake poets. He was poet laureate from 1813. With Coleridge he attempted to found a utopian community, but the idea failed for lack of funds. Of his poems, only the shorter ones are now read, though his early works are long narrative poems. Of his many prose works, his 'Life of Nelson' (1813) is the best known

South Georgia an island (area 1,600 sq. miles, pop. 400 in the whaling season) in the S.W. Atlantic, part of the Falkland Islands Dependencies. Highest point: 9,200 ft. Capt. Cook took possession of it in 1775

South Holland *HOLLAND

south·ing (sáuθiŋ) *n.* (*naut.*) a sailing towards the south ‖ (*naut.*) the distance thus sailed since the last point of reckoning ‖ (*astron.*) the distance, in degrees, of any heavenly body south of the celestial equator

South Island *NEW ZEALAND

South Korea *KOREA, REPUBLIC OF

South Orkney Islands an uninhabited archipelago (land area 240 sq. miles) in the S.W. Atlantic and Antarctic Oceans, part of the Falkland Islands Dependencies. They were claimed by the British in 1821

south·paw (sáuθpǫ) 1. *adj.* (*pop.*) left-handed 2. *n.* (*pop.*) a left-handed person, esp. a pitcher in baseball or a boxer

South Platte a river (424 miles long) rising in central Colorado, flowing across the Nebraska boundary to join the North Platte River in central Nebraska and form the Platte River

South Pole the southern end of the earth's axis, in Antarctica. The first man to reach this point was Amundsen (1911) **south pole** the zenith of the heavens as viewed from the south terrestrial pole ‖ the pole of a magnet that points to the south when the magnet is allowed to rotate freely in the earth's magnetic field (cf. NORTH POLE)

South·port (sáuθpɔrt, sáuθpourt) a town (pop. 89,745) and resort in Lancashire, England, on the Irish sea

South Sandwich Islands an uninhabited volcanic archipelago (land area 130 sq. miles) in the S. Atlantic, part of the Falkland Islands Dependencies

South Sea Islands Oceania

South Seas a name given to the oceans of the southern hemisphere (excluding the Antarctic Ocean), esp. the S. Pacific

South Shetland Islands a group of uninhabited islands (land area 1,800 sq. miles) off the Antarctic Peninsula, part of the Falkland Islands Dependencies. They were discovered (1819) by William Smith, an English mariner

South Shields a county borough and resort (pop. 87,203) in Durham, England, at the mouth of the Tyne: glass and chemical industries

south south·east (sáuθsauθí:st) **1.** *adv.* toward south-southeast **2.** *n.* S. 22° 30′ E., a compass point midway between south and southeast (*abbr.* S.S.E., *COMPASS POINT) **3.** *adj.* of or situated toward south-southeast ‖ (of winds) blowing from south-southeast

south-south·west (sáuθsauθwést) **1.** *adv.* toward south-southwest **2.** *n.* S. 22° 30′ W., a compass point midway between south and southwest (*abbr.* S.S.W., *COMPASS POINT) **3.** *adj.* of or situated toward south-southwest ‖ (of winds) blowing from south-southwest

South Tirol *TRENTINO-ALTO ADIGE

south·ward (sáuθwərd, sʌ́ðərd) **1.** *adv.* and *adj.* toward the south **2.** *n.* the southward direction or part **sóuth·wards** *adv.*

South·well (sáuθwəl), Robert (c. 1561-95), English Jesuit, religious tract writer and poet. He was imprisoned, tortured, tried and hanged for his faith. In 1929 he was beatified. His best-known poem is 'The Burning Babe'

south·west (sauθwést) **1.** *adv.* toward the southwest **2.** *n.* (usually with 'the') the compass point or direction midway between south and west (*abbr.* S.W., *COMPASS POINT) **the Southwest** the southwestern part of a country **3.** *adj.* of, belonging to or situated toward the southwest ‖ (of winds) blowing from the southwest [O.E. *sūthwest*]

South West Africa *NAMIBIA

southwest by south S. 33° 45′ W., one point south of due southwest (*abbr.* S.W. b. S., *Br.* esp. S.W. by S., *COMPASS POINT)

southwest by west S. 56° 15′ W., one point west of due southwest (*abbr.* S.W. b. W., *Br.* esp. S.W. by W., *COMPASS POINT)

south·west·er (sauθwéstər) *n.* a strong wind or storm from the southwest ‖ a sou'wester

south·west·er·ly (sauθwéstərli:) **1.** *adj.* and *adv.* in or toward the southwest ‖ (of winds) from that direction **2.** *n. pl.* **south·west·er·lies** a wind blowing from the southwest

south·west·ern (sauθwéstərn) *adj.* situated, facing or moving toward the southwest ‖ of or relating to the southwest or the Southwest

southwestern corn borer (*entomology*) a moth (*Diatraea grandiosella*) whose larva bore into corn stalks, thereby causing crop damage

south·west·ward (sauθwéstwərd) *adv.* and *adj.* toward the southwest **south·wést·wards** *adv.*

South Yemen, People's Republic of *YEMEN, PEOPLE'S DEMOCRATIC REPUBLIC OF

Sou·tine (su:ti:n), Chaïm (1894-1943), French painter born in Lithuania. His violently expressionist works include turbulent landscapes, studies of carcasses, and moody portraits charged with emotion

sou·ve·nir (su:vənír, sú:vəniər) *n.* something that serves to recall the past [F.]

sou'west·er (sauwéstər) *n.* a waterproof hat with a broad flap at the back to protect the neck, worn esp. by sailors, fishermen etc. [SOUTHWESTER]

Sou·za (su:sa), Tomé de (16th c.), Portuguese politician, first governor (1549-53) of Brazil. He founded Salvador, Bahia

sov·er·eign (sóvrin, sóvərin, sʌ́vrin, sʌ́vərin) **1.** *adj.* of or relating to a sovereign ‖ having undisputed right to make decisions and act accordingly, *a sovereign state* ‖ unlimited, absolute, *sovereign power* ‖ (of a remedy) very effective **2.** *n.* a person or body of persons supreme in a state ‖ a British gold coin worth 20 shillings, first struck in 1489 and last issued in 1931 ‖ a coin of Saudi Arabia worth 40 rials [O.F. *soverain, souverein*]

sov·er·eign·ty (sóvrinti:, sʌ́vrinti:) *pl.* **sov·er·eign·ties** *n.* undisputed political power ‖ the state or quality of being sovereign ‖ the status or authority of a sovereign ‖ a sovereign state [A.F. *sovereyneté*]

So·vetsk, So·vietsk (sʌvjétsk) (formerly Tilsit) a port (pop. 38,000) of the R.S.F.S.R. (Kaliningrad enclave), U.S.S.R., on the lower Niemen, on the Lithuanian border

so·vi·et (sóuvi:et, sóuvi:it, souvi:ét) *n.* an elected governing council in the U.S.S.R. ‖ any of the associated republics of the U.S.S.R. **So·vi·et** *adj.* of or relating to the U.S.S.R. **só·vi·et·ism** *n.* the soviet system of government **so·vi·et·i·zá·tion** *n.* **só·vi·et·ize** *pres. part.* **so·vi·et·iz·ing** *past* and *past part.* **so·vi·et·ized** *v.t.* to bring under the soviet system [Russ.=council]

—Soviets were originally revolutionary committees elected by factory workers after the revolution of 1905. At the time of the revolution of 1917, soviets were elected throughout Russia by workers, peasants and soldiers. The term was then applied to the primary units of government in the U.S.S.R., at local, provincial and national levels. The national soviet is called the Supreme Soviet, comprising delegates from all the Soviet Republics

So·vi·et·ol·o·gy (souvi:ətólədʒi:) *n.* the study of mores and politics of leadership in the U.S.S.R. —**Sovietologist** *n. also* Kremlinology

Soviet Russia the Union of Soviet Socialist Republics

Sovietsk *SOVETSK

Soviet Union the Union of Soviet Socialist Republics

sow (sau) *n.* an adult female hog ‖ the female of certain other animals, e.g. the badger ‖ a main trough into which molten iron is poured and from which it flows into subsidiary molds to form pigs ‖ the large block of iron that hardens in this main trough [O.E. *sugu*]

sow (sou) *pres. part.* **sow·ing** *past* **sowed** *past part.* **sown** (soun), **sowed** *v.t.* to scatter or bury (seed) on or in the soil, so that it may germinate and grow ‖ to scatter seed in (land), *to sow a field with barley* ‖ to implant or spread (unrest, discontent etc.) ‖ to introduce (anchovies, oysters etc.) into an environment for cultivation ‖ (*mil.*) to lay (mines) in a stretch of water or land ‖ *v.i.* to scatter seed [O.E. *sāwan*]

sow bug (sau) a wood louse

sown alt. *past part.* of sow

sow thistle (sau) a member of *Sonchus,* fam. *Compositae,* a genus of tall grasses with copious latex. They are like thistles but have no prickles

sox (sɒks) *pl. n.* socks (articles of clothing)

soy (sɔi) n. an Oriental piquant sauce made from soybeans fermented and then treated in brine ‖ the soybean [Jap. fr. *shōyū* fr. Chin.]

soy·a bean (sɔ́iə) *SOYBEAN

soy·bean (sɔ́ibi:n) *n.* (*Am.*=*Br.* soya bean) *Glycine max,* fam. *Papilionaceae,* a plant native to Asia, now cultivated in many parts of the world. The edible, highly nourishing seeds are used as a source of oil, flour and meal. The plant is used for fodder and for soil improvement

soybean cyst nematode (*entomology*) a long, thin worm (*Heterodera glycines*) that stunts and yellows soybeans

Soyinka (sɔiíŋkə), Wole (1934-), Nigerian playwright and poet, whose works, written in English, combine Western culture with African traditions. Plays include 'The Swamp Dwellers' (1958), 'Death and the King's Horseman' (1975), 'Opera Wonyosi' (1979) and 'A Play of Giants' (1984). 'A Shuttle in the Crypt' (1972) is a collection of poems written during a prison term (1967-9) for opposition to the war in Biafra. His autobiography 'Aké: The Years of Childhood' was published in 1982

soy·milk (sɔ́imilk) *n.* milklike substance derived from soybeans

soy sauce *SOY

So·yuz (soujú:s) *n.* (*aerospace*) U.S.S.R. spacecraft with 2–3 man crew for earth orbit, first launched in 1967 and modified in 1979

Soz·zi·ni (sɒttsí:ni:) *SOCINUS

spa (spɑ) *n.* a resort where there is a spring of mineral water ‖ a spring of mineral water ‖ a hotel that features weight-reducing diets, exercise, massage, and water therapy [after *Spa,* in Belgium]

Spaak (spɑk), Paul Henri (1899-1972), Belgian socialist statesman. He was Belgian foreign minister (1936-8, 1939-45, 1946-50, 1954-7 and 1961-6) and prime minister (1938-9, 1946 and 1947-50). He was the first president of the U.N. General Assembly (1946) and secretary-general of NATO (1957-61), and helped to plan the European Economic Community

space (speis) **1.** *n.* (without the article) that which contains and surrounds all material bodies ‖ the distance between two points, objects etc. ‖ a time interval, *within the space of half an hour* ‖ (without the article) the region outside the earth's atmosphere ‖ a limited extent or area for a specific purpose, *write your name in the blank space* ‖ (*printing*) a piece of metal used to separate words or letters, or lines of type ‖ (*mus.*) one of the degrees on the staff between lines **to gaze into space** to stare, normally for a long time and with the eyes unfocused on anything, as though into the infinite distance **2.** *v.t. pres. part.* **spac·ing** *past* and *past part.* **spaced** to arrange at regular or suitable distances or time intervals ‖ (*printing, typing* etc.) to separate (words, lines etc.) by spaces [fr. O.F. *espace*]

—Space is the idea which each person forms and develops, as the result of his sense perceptions, that there exist 'things' other than himself, and that his own body consists of 'parts', and that these bear an orderly relationship to one another which he describes in terms of position in space and distance from one another. Experience associates with this idea the quality of being the same always, and thus the idea of time is also involved. The interrelationship of space and time as a condition of being is treated mathematically in the study of the space-time continuum. The idea 'space', like the idea 'time', is a relative concept, since it is based solely upon sensory experience

space·borne (spéisbɔrn) *adj.* carried beyond the earth's atmosphere

space charge (*phys.*) the negative charge created by the stream of electrons from the filament of a thermionic valve, opposing the motion of the electrons

space·craft (spéiskræft, spéiskrɑft) *pl.* **space·craft** *n.* a vehicle designed to travel beyond the earth's atmosphere

spaced-out (speisdáut) *adj.* (*slang*) under the influence of a narcotic or nonnarcotic drug, as shown, e.g., in disorientation, inappropriate affect

space exploration the exploration of space by instrumented and manned spacecraft from 1957. When the Soviet Union's 'Sputnik I' with cosmonaut Yuri Gagarin aboard was successfully launched and orbited the earth (1957), the Space Age had begun and the U.S.A. formed the National Aeronautics and Space Administration (NASA) (1958). The Mercury program saw John Glenn rocket into space (1962) in 'Friendship 7'; the Gemini program produced the first walk in space (1965) by Edward H. White; and the Apollo program sent Neil Armstrong, Edwin Aldrin and Michael Collins to the Moon (1969). As a cooperative venture a Soviet Soyuz spacecraft and an American Apollo spacecraft docked in space in 1975. By 1981 the space shuttle was in operation, but flights were suspended temporarily when 'Challenger' exploded (1986) (*SPACE SHUTTLE). Unmanned space exploration saw Earth satellites, lunar probes and interplanetary probes studying the Earth's radiation belts, atmosphere and ionosphere, as well as other planets (1962-) including Mercury, Venus, Mars, Jupiter, Saturn and Uranus

spacelab laboratory and workshop built by 10 European countries, all but one members of the European Space Agency, for the U.S. space shuttle. Begun in 1973, it consists of two adaptable modules—one a laboratory, the other a flat platform on which equipment can be exposed directly to space. Spacelab is carried in the cargo bay of the shuttle and is used to conduct various experiments. Its first flight aboard a space shuttle was in 1983

space lattice the geometrical arrangement of atoms in a crystal, esp. as revealed by X-ray spectroscopy

space·man (spéismæn, spéismən) *pl.* **space·men** (spéismen, spéismən) *n.* (esp. *science fic-*

CONCISE PRONUNCIATION KEY: **(a)** æ, *cat*; ɑ, *car*; ɔ *fawn*; ei, *snake*. **(e)** e, *hen*; i:, *sheep*; iə, *deer*; ɛə, *bear*. **(i)** i, *fish*; ai, *tiger*; ə:, *bird*. **(o)** o, *ox*; au, *cow*; ou, *goat*; u, *poor*; ɔi, *royal*. **(u)** ʌ, *duck*; u, *bull*; u:, *goose*; ə, *bacillus*; ju:, *cube*. x, *loch*; θ, *think*; ð, *bother*; z, *Zen*; ʒ, *corsage*; dʒ, *savage*; ŋ, *orangutang*; j, *yak*; ʃ, *fish*; tʃ, *fetch*; 'l, *rabble*; 'n, *redden*. Complete pronunciation key appears inside front cover.

tion) a man who travels in space ‖ a visitor from outer space ‖ an astronaut

space plane prototype plane designed to serve as shuttle between space satellites and earth *Cf* SPACE SHUTTLE

space·ship (spéisʃip) *n.* a spacecraft

space shuttle reusable space launcher and carrier vehicle, consisting of the orbiter, external tank and solid rocket launch, that lands on a runway. U.S. astronauts John Young and Robert Crippen made the first orbit (1981) in 'Columbia.' 'Challenger' made 9 flights (1983-5) before exploding within 2 minutes of takeoff on its 10th mission (Jan. 28, 1986). All shuttle flights were cancelled pending investigation and reorganization of safety procedures. Four operational shuttles—'Challenger,' 'Columbia,' 'Discovery' and 'Atlantis'—made 24 flights before the 'Challenger' accident

space sickness physical maladjustment during space flight

space station a long-term earth-orbiting satellite, manned or unmanned, for observation or communication *also* space platform

space suit a pressurized suit worn by astronauts to protect them in outer space

Space Telescope U.S. satellite with optical instruments

space-time continuum (*phys.*) the concept of a space of four dimensions, arising from the theory of relativity. The presence of a body in space not being independent of time, a time axis must be added to the three axes of space dimensions in order to locate it

Spacetrack *n.* (*mil.*) a global system of radar, optical, and radiometric sensors linked to a computation and analysis center in the North American Air Defense Command complex *Cf* SPADATS

space walk *v.* to move beyond a craft in space as from one spaceship to another —**spacewalk** *n.* —**spacewalker** *n.* —**spacewalking** *n.*

spacial *SPATIAL

spac·ing (spéisiŋ) *n.* the arrangement of spaces ‖ the space between printed words in a line of type ‖ the act of someone who spaces

spa·cious (spéiʃəs) *adj.* roomy, giving or having ample space ‖ marked by ease, comfort, leisure, opportunity etc. [fr. L. *spatiosus*]

spa·cis·tor (speisístər) *n.* (*electr.*) a solid-state transistorlike device with several terminals, designed to generate an electron flow through layers in a germanium wafer

Spadats (*acronym*) a space detection and tracking system, for detecting and tracking space vehicles and reporting their orbital characteristics to a central control facility, designed as an early warning system of enemy ICBMs *Cf* SPACETRACK

spade (speid) **1.** *n.* a long-handled tool with a broad, flat blade, used for digging ‖ a tool of similar shape with a sharp edge to the blade, used for cutting turf, whale blubber etc. ‖ a spadelike part on the trail of a gun carriage. It is planted in the ground to check the recoil of the carriage **to call a spade a spade** to name bluntly what one might choose to refer to by a euphemism **2.** *v.t. pres. part.* **spad·ing** *past* and *past part.* **spad·ed** to dig or cut with a spade [O.E. *spadu*]

spade *n.* the mark of one of the four suits of playing cards (♤) ‖ (*pl.*) the suit of cards so marked ‖ a card of this suit [fr. Ital. *spade* pl. of *spada*, a sword]

spade·work (spéidwə:rk) *n.* laborious preparatory work

spa·di·ceous (speidíʃəs) *adj.* having a spadix ‖ being a spadix ‖ bright clear brown in color [fr. Mod. L. *spadiceus*]

spa·dix (spéidiks) *pl.* **spa·di·ces** (speidáisi:z) *n.* (*bot.*) a racemose inflorescence with sessile flowers, elongated axis and enveloping spathe, e.g. the arum lily [Mod. L. fr. L.=a leaf torn off a palm tree, fr. Gk]

spa·ghet·ti (spəgéti:) *n.* pasta in the form of very thin, long, solid rods, a little thicker than vermicelli, which are boiled and normally served with a sauce [Ital.]

spaghetti Western motion picture about the American West made in Italy

spa·hi (spɑ́hi:) *pl.* **spa·his** *n.* (*hist.*) a member of a largely irregular Turkish cavalry corps, organized on a more or less feudal basis and disbanded after 1826 ‖ (*hist.*) a member of an Algerian native cavalry corps serving under the French Government. The corps was disbanded after 1962 [fr. Turk. *sipāhi*]

Spain (spein) a state (area incl. the Balearic and Canary Is 194,945 sq. miles, pop. 37,746,260) of S.W. Europe, occupying most of the Iberian Peninsula. Capital: Madrid. Overseas possessions: Ceuta, Melilla and small offshore islands. Language: Spanish, with Catalan, Basque and Galician minorities. Religion: Roman Catholic, with 26,000 Protestants, 1,000 Jews. The land is 32% arable, 50% pasture and grazing, and 8% forest. The core of Spain is the dry, deforested central Iberian plateau, or Meseta (mainly 1,500-3,000 ft), divided into north (Old Castile and León) and south (New Castile and Estremadura) by the Sierra de Gredos (to 8,504 ft) and Sierra de Guadarrama, west and north of Madrid. The Meseta is bordered on the north, northeast and south by the Cantabrian Mtns, Iberian Mtns and Sierra Morena. Outside the Meseta lie the wooded hills of Galicia, the Pyrenees and Catalonian Mtns (separated from the Iberian Mtns by the Ebro basin) and the Andalusian ranges (Mulhacén, 11,420 ft), separated from the Sierra Morena by the Guadalquivir. Intensive agriculture is largely confined to the well-watered coastal strips (where industry is also concentrated) and the valleys of the Ebro, Douro, Tagus, Guadiana and Guadalquivir. The center (where large estates predominate) is mainly devoted to stock raising and cereals. Irrigation projects are under construction. Average temperatures (F.): (Jan.) south coast and Andalusia over 50°, other coasts 42°-50°, central Spain 36°-42°, mountains under 36°, (July) Alicante and Andalusia over 80°, S. Spain and Ebro basin 72°-80°, N. Spain and southern mountains 64°-72°, northern mountains, incl. Galicia, under 64°. Rainfall: N. Meseta, Ebro basin and Mureia under 16 ins, Galicia, Asturias and Basque coast over 30 ins. Livestock: sheep, goats, cattle, hogs, mules, donkeys, horses. Agricultural products: cereals, olives, oranges, potatoes, rice, vines, onions, lemons, almonds and raisins, esparto, flax, hemp, pulses, silk, tobacco, sugarcane, sugar beets, cotton. Forest products: cork, pine lumber, resin, eucalyptus. Mineral resources: coal, iron ore, iron pyrites, copper, lead, mercury, manganese, potash, salt, tin, zinc, wolfram, ilmenite, silver, gold, quartz, sulfur, titanium, cobalt, nickel, bismuth, antimony. Industries: mining, iron and steel, textiles, fishing, machinery and chemicals, fertilizers, explosives, paper, aluminum, shipbuilding, foodstuffs, wine, sugar, cork, oil refining, cement, vehicles, hydroelectricity, tobacco, footwear, pottery, glass, leather, tourism. Exports: vegetable products, foodstuffs, wine, tobacco, minerals, fats and oils, metals, textiles. Imports: minerals and metals, machinery, vehicles, cotton, foodstuffs, chemicals. Ports: Cádiz, Barcelona, Bilbao. There are 13 universities, the oldest being Salamanca (c. 1230). Monetary unit: peseta (100 céntimos). HISTORY. There is much evidence, notably the cave paintings at Altamira, of Stone Age habitation in Spain. Celts invaded (1st millennium B.C.) and mingled with the native Iberians. Colonies were established in Andalusia by the Phoenicians (11th c. B.C.) and on the east coast by the Greeks (6th c. B.C.). The Carthaginians under Hamilcar Barca conquered Spain (3rd c. B.C.) but were expelled by the Romans after the 2nd Punic War (218-201 B.C.). Roman control was established over the whole peninsula by the 1st c. A.D., the economy prospered, and Christianity was introduced. Spain was a center of Roman culture, and produced Seneca, Lucian, Trajan, Hadrian, Martial and Quintilian. It was overrun (5th c.) by the Vandals and the Visigoths, under whom a legal code was evolved and ecclesiastical learning flourished, notably with Orosius and Isidore of Seville. The Moors overran most of the peninsula (711) and Cordova became a splendid center of the Umayyad caliphate (756-1031). Irrigation works were constructed, new crops were introduced and crafts and trade flourished. Portugal became an independent kingdom (1143). Spain was gradually reconquered by the Christians, working first from Asturias, and then from the new kingdoms of León, Navarre, Castile and Aragon. These kingdoms merged by conquest and marriage, culminating in the union (1479) of Castile and Aragon. Ferdinand V and Isabella I completed the reconquest of Spain by driving the Moors from Granada, their last stronghold (1492). In the same year, Columbus claimed America for Spain, and Spaniards explored much of Mexico, Central America, the West Indies and South America (16th c.), building up a vast empire which yielded great quantities of gold. The Inquisition was introduced (1478), the Jews were expelled (1492), with severe consequences for Spanish commerce, and the Moors were forcibly converted to Christianity (16th c.) and expelled (1609). Spain was victorious in the Italian Wars (1494-1559) and reached the height of its power under its first Hapsburg ruler, Emperor Charles V. His son, Philip II, inherited the Kingdom of the Two Sicilies, the Netherlands, Sardinia, Milan and Franche-Comté as well as Spain and its colonies. Portugal was under Spanish rule (1580-1640). The northern provinces of the Netherlands rebelled successfully (1581), and Spain was involved in protracted warfare in the southern provinces until 1648 (*THIRTY YEARS' WAR). Spain defeated the Turkish fleet at Lepanto (1571) but failed in its attempt to invade England with the Armada (1588). The Treaties of Westphalia (1648) and the Pyrenees (1659) were unfavorable to Spain, and the Spanish decline was hastened by the War of Devolution and the War of the Grand Alliance. The death (1700) of Charles II without direct heir, and the rivalry of Austria and France, provoked the War of the Spanish Succession. The resultant Peace of Utrecht (1713) deprived Spain of its European possessions and transferred Gilbraltar to British rule. The attempts of Philip V and Alberoni to regain these losses were defeated by the Quadruple Alliance (1720). Under Bourbon rule (1700-1931), Spain entered the Family Compacts with France and regained (1734) the Two Sicilies in the War of the Polish Succession. By the Treaty of Paris (1763), Spain gained Louisiana and lost Florida. It regained the latter by the Treaty of Paris (1783), and sold it to the U.S.A. (1819). During the reign (1759-88) of Charles III, Floridablanca carried out much-needed economic reforms, but the expulsion (1767) of the Jesuits had an adverse effect on education. Spain was involved in the French Revolutionary Wars and the Napoleonic Wars, was forced to accept Joseph Bonaparte as king (1808), and was devastated during the Peninsular War. Ferdinand VII was restored (1814) under a constitutional regime, but his reactionary rule led to the loss of the Latin American colonies and an unsuccessful revolution (1820). His daughter, Isabella II, was deposed after a reactionary reign (1833-68), and disorder broke out, with fighting between Carlists and republicans. Under Alfonso XIII (1886-1931), the Spanish-American War resulted in the loss of Cuba, Puerto Rico and the Philippines (1898). Primo de Rivera brought off a coup d'état (1923) and established a military dictatorship (1923-30). The growth of republicanism resulted in the overthrow of the monarchy (1931). The ensuing republic was strongly anticlerical and hostile to the landowners, and was overthrown by the Falangists under Franco in the Spanish Civil War (1936-9). Franco established a Fascist dictatorship (1939) and kept Spain neutral in the 2nd world war though friendly to the Axis powers. The Falange was declared the only legal party, Church property and privileges were restored, and Spain was declared a monarchy (1947) with Franco as regent for life. The U.S.A. supplied much economic and technical aid (1950s). Spain joined the U.N. (1955) and the Organization for European Economic Cooperation (1959). The Spanish government renewed its claim to Gibraltar (1964) by imposing frontier restrictions. The Cortes approved (1969) General Franco's proposal that on his death or retirement Prince Juan Carlos of Bourbon should become king of Spain, which he did (1975). Under a 1978 constitution Spain became a hereditary, constitutional monarchy. An attempted military coup (1981) was suppressed. Although the election of regional parliaments gave the regions more autonomy, Basque separatist groups demanded greater self-rule

spake *archaic past* of SPEAK

Spa·la·to (spɑlɑ́tou) *SPLIT

spall (spɔl) **1.** *n.* a fragment split off stone, concrete etc. or one separated from a rock by weathering **2.** *v.t.* to chip or break up (ore) for sorting or crushing ‖ *v.i.* to split off in particles or chips [etym. doubtful]

Spal·lan·za·ni (spɑllɑntsɑ́ni:), Abbé Lazzaro (1729-99), Italian biologist who first advocated artificial insemination

CONCISE PRONUNCIATION KEY: (a) æ, *cat*; ɑ, *car*; ɔ *fawn*; ei, *snake*. (e) e, *hen*; i:, *sheep*; iə, *deer*; ɛə, *bear*. (i) i, *fish*; ai, *tiger*; ə:, *bird*. (o) o, *ox*; au, *cow*; ou, *goat*; u, *poor*; ɔi, *royal*. (u) ʌ, *duck*; u, *bull*; u:, *goose*; ə, *bacillus*; ju:, *cube*. x, *loch*; θ, *think*; ð, *bother*; z, *Zen*; ʒ, *corsage*; dʒ, *savage*; ŋ, *orangutang*; j, *yak*; ʃ, *fish*; tʃ, *fetch*; 'l, *rabble*; 'n, *redden*. Complete pronunciation key appears inside front cover.

span (spæn) **1.** *n.* (*naut.*) a rope with both ends fastened forming a loop ‖ a pair of animals used together, esp. a matched pair of horses **2.** *v.t. pres. part.* **span·ning** *past* and *past part.* **spanned** (*naut.*, sometimes with 'in') to make fast with ropes [Du. and L.G.]

span 1. *v. pres. part.* **span·ning** *past* and *past part.* **spanned** *v.t.* to extend from side to side of (a wide object) or over (a distance or period of time), esp. so as to be a link, *his life spanned three reigns* ‖ to form an arch across, *to span a river with a bridge* ‖ to measure, using the extended hand as a unit ‖ to encircle with the hand or hands in, or as if in, measuring ‖ *v.i.* to move by making successive stretching movements like a caterpillar ‖ (of whales) to swim under water, rising for breath at regular intervals **2.** *n.* the distance between two extremities, e.g. the piers of an arch, the ends of a bridge, the tips of wings etc. ‖ the interval between two points in time, *the normal span of human life* ‖ the distance between tips of the little finger and thumb (=approx. 9 ins) when the hand is extended [O.E. *spann*]

span dogs a pair of clawed iron bars for hoisting logs in lumbering

span·drel (spǽndrəl) *n.* (*archit.*) the space between the outer curve of an arch and the rectangular molding that frames it ‖ the space between the exterior curves of adjoining arches and the horizontal molding etc. above [prob. rel. to A.F. *spaundre*, to expand]

span·gle (spǽŋg'l) **1.** *n.* a tiny disk of glittering material, esp. one sewn onto a garment **2.** *v. pres. part.* **span·gling** *past* and *past part.* **span·gled** *v.t.* to adorn with spangles ‖ *v.i.* to glitter with or as if with spangles [M.E. *spangel* dim. of O.E. *spang*, buckle]

Span·glish (spǽŋgliʃ) *n.* mixture of Spanish and English, common in Latin America and Southwest U.S. *Cf* FRINGLISH, HINGLISH, JAPLISH

Span·iard (spǽnjərd) *n.* a native or inhabitant of Spain

span·iel (spǽnjəl) *n.* a dog of any of several breeds with large drooping ears and a silky coat, used as sporting dogs for flushing or retrieving game, or kept as pets [fr. O.F. *espaigneul*, Spanish dog]

Span·ish (spǽniʃ) **1.** *adj.* of or relating to Spain, its people or language **2.** *n.* the Romance language of Spain and Spanish America, including Aragonese, Asturian, Andalusian and Castilian dialects. In all, Spanish is spoken by over 100,000,000 people **the Spanish** the people of Spain

Spanish America the countries in Central and South America and the Caribbean islands where Spanish is the chief language

Spanish-American *adj.* of Spain and America ‖ of Spanish America or its people **Spanish American** *n.* a native or inhabitant of Spanish America

Spanish-American War a war fought (1898) in Cuba, the Philippines and Puerto Rico by the U.S.A. and Cuban revolutionaries against Spain to free Cuba from Spanish control. Spanish fleets were rapidly defeated, and by the Treaty of Paris (1898), the Philippines, Guam and Puerto Rico were ceded by Spain to the U.S.A. Cuba was placed provisionally under U.S. military occupation

Spanish Armada *ARMADA

Spanish bayonet a yucca with spiky swordlike leaves, found in the southern U.S.A. and tropical America

Spanish Civil War *CIVIL WAR, SPANISH

Spanish fly *Lytta vesicatoria*, fam. *Meloidae*, a bright golden-green blister beetle ‖ cantharides

Spanish Guinea *EQUATORIAL GUINEA

Spanish Inquisition *INQUISITION

Spanish Main the name given in the 16th and 17th cc. to the Spanish possessions along the coast of South America from the Isthmus of Panama to the Orinoco. The name was also applied to the Caribbean Sea

Spanish moss *Tillandsia usneoides*, fam. *Usneaceae*, a mossy plant which grows in long green-gray festoons on many trees in the southern U.S.A. and West Indies ‖ *Ramalina reticulata*, fam. *Usneaceae*, a lichen that grows in large laced nets on various trees in coastal areas of the western U.S.A.

Spanish onion a large, juicy, mild-flavored onion of any of a great many varieties

Spanish Sahara *WESTERN SAHARA

Spanish Succession, War of the the war (1701-14) fought between England, the Netherlands and most of the German states against France, Spain, Bavaria, Portugal and Savoy. It was precipitated by Louis XIV's proclamation (1700) of his grandson as Philip V of Spain, and by his invasion (1701) of the Spanish Netherlands. The victories of Marlborough and Eugene at Blenheim (1704), Ramillies, Turin (1706), Oudenarde, Lille (1708) and Malplaquet (1709) crushed French military supremacy. The war was ended by the Peace of Utrecht (1713) and subsidiary settlements at Rastatt and Baden (1714)

Spanish West Africa a former overseas territory of Spain divided (1958) into the overseas provinces of Ifni and Spanish Sahara (now Western Sahara)

spank (spæŋk) *v.i.* to move briskly when riding or driving [prob. back-formation fr. SPANKING]

spank 1. *v.t.* to smack or slap (someone) on the bottom **2.** *n.* a smack or slap on someone's bottom [imit.]

spank·er (spǽŋkər) *n.* a fast horse, esp. one that trots briskly and stylishly ‖ (*naut.*) a fore-and-aft sail set on the after side of the mizzenmast

spank·ing (spǽŋkiŋ) *adj.* of unusually fine quality or impressive for its size, freshness or vigor ‖ (of a breeze) strong ‖ (of pace) quick, brisk, lively [origin unknown]

spanking *n.* a series of slaps on the bottom with the open hand, to punish a child etc.

span·ner (spǽnər) *n.* (*Br.*) a wrench for tightening or loosening nuts etc. **to throw a spanner in the works** (*Br., pop.*) to spoil or thwart esp. the plans of others deliberately [G. fr. *spannen*, to fix, fasten, draw tight]

span roof a common form of roof, with two sides sloping downward from a central ridge

spansule (*pharm.*) *TIMED CAPSULE

span·worm (spǽnwə:rm) *n.* a looper

spar (spɑr) **1.** *n.* a pole used e.g. as a mast, yard or boom of a ship ‖ one of the longitudinal members of an aircraft wing into which the struts are set **2.** *v.t. pres. part.* **spar·ring** *past* and *past part.* **sparred** to supply with spars [M.E. *sperre, sparre*]

spar *n.* any of various lustrous, crystalline minerals, cleaving easily into flakes or chips [rel. to O.E. *spæren*, gypsum]

spar 1. *v.i. pres. part.* **spar·ring** *past* and *past part.* **sparred** (*boxing*) to make the motions of attack and defense without landing a blow, so as to draw the opponent or to seek protection or time ‖ (*boxing*) to fight practice rounds ‖ (of fighting cocks) to strike with the feet or spurs ‖ to try to score verbally in argument **2.** *n.* the act or a session of sparring [origin obscure]

spar·a·ble (spǽrəb'l) *n.* a small headless nail used in shoemaking [altered fr. *sparrow bill*, with reference to its shape]

spar deck the upper deck above the main deck of a ship

spare (spɛər) **1.** *v.t. pres. part.* **spar·ing** *past* and *past part.* **spared** to conserve (one's strength or energy) ‖ to leave unhurt or undamaged, let go free, let live, *the prisoner was spared* ‖ to refrain from injuring or distressing or punishing, *she spared his feelings* ‖ to omit, exclude, *spare the details, nothing was spared for his comfort* ‖ to part temporarily with, or give away, without inconvenience, *can you spare 5 dollars?* ‖ to relieve (a person) of the necessity of doing something, *he was spared answering* ‖ to make available, *can you spare the time to help me?* ‖ to refrain from making use of, to use frugally or economically, *don't spare the wine* ‖ to show consideration for by relieving of work, *he spares neither himself nor his employees* ‖ to have left over as a margin or surplus, *it fitted tightly with no room to spare, we arrived with no time to spare* **2.** *adj.* held in reserve for future use, *spare cash* ‖ left over, more than needed, *some of the food was spare* ‖ thin, esp. without excess flesh, *of spare build* ‖ meager, frugal, thin, *spare diet* **3.** *n.* a surplus, superfluous object ‖ a duplicate kept in reserve ‖ (*bowling*) the act of knocking down all the pins with two consecutive rolls of the ball ‖ the score so made ‖ a spare part, esp. of a machine [O.E. *sparian*]

spare part a duplicate part of a machine for use as a replacement

spare-part surgery (*med.*) popular term for the branch of surgery dealing with transplants of organs or with prosthetic devices

spare·ribs (spɛ́ərribz) *pl. n.* a cut of pork consisting of the ribs with little meat left on them because the fleshy part has been cut off for bacon

sparge (spɑrdʒ) *pres. part.* **sparg·ing** *past* and *past part.* **sparged** *v.t.* (*brewing*) to sprinkle (the mash) with water heated to about 180° F. after the sweetwort has been drained off ‖ to plaster, roughcast ‖ to sprinkle, splash (water etc.) ‖ *v.i.* to sprinkle water [prob. fr. O.F. *espargier*]

spar·ing (spɛ́əriŋ) *adj.* using or taking little, because of shortage, for economy, out of abstemiousness or out of meanness

Spark (spɑrk), Muriel (1918-), British writer. She wrote 'The Prime of Miss Jean Brodie' (1961), also a play (1964) and movie (1969). Other novels include 'Memento Mori' (1959), 'The Mandelbaum Gate' (1965), 'The Public Image' (1968), 'The Driver's Seat' (1970), 'The Takeover' (1976) and 'Territorial Rights' (1979). Her short stories are collected in 'The Stories of Muriel Spark' (1985)

spark (spɑrk) **1.** *n.* a particle e.g. thrown off from a burning log, which is so hot that it emits light as well as heat, or such a particle produced by the striking of flint or steel etc. on another hard substance ‖ (*elec.*) a discharge of static electricity which raises the air, gas or vapor to incandescence ‖ (*elec.*) the light produced by this discharge ‖ (*elec.*) such a discharge in the spark plug of an internal-combustion engine ‖ a small or momentary indication of something thought of as like this, esp. with respect to its latent possibilities, *a spark of humor* ‖ (*old-fash.*, usually with 'bright' or 'bright young') a quick-witted young fellow **2.** *v.i.* to emit sparks ‖ (of an internal-combustion engine) to produce sparks correctly ‖ *v.t.* (with 'off') to initiate (a process) as if by using a spark, *the trouble was sparked off by an apparently harmless phrase* [O.E. *spœrca, spearca*]

spark arrester a safety device to prevent sparks from escaping from a smokestack (e.g. of a steam locomotive) ‖ a device to prevent sparking where the continuity of a circuit is broken

spark chamber an instrument for defining the tracks of high-energy particles. It contains a gas and a series of metal plates that can be electrically charged to such a potential that a spark is almost caused to pass from one plate to an adjacent one. If a track of ions is formed by an ionizing particle the spark follows the track and can be photographed

spark coil (*elec.*) an induction force used to induce an electromotive force large enough to spark across a gap between conductors

spark gap (*elec.*) the gap between the electrodes (e.g. of an induction coil) across which a spark passes

sparking plug (*Br.*) a spark plug

spar·kle (spɑ́rk'l) **1.** *v.i. pres. part* **spar·kling** *past* and *past part.* **spar·kled** to give off flashes of reflected light ‖ to give off flashes of wit or gaiety ‖ (of eyes) to show animation, intelligence, wit, pleasure, mischief etc. by their brightness ‖ (of wine) to effervesce with bubbles of carbon dioxide ‖ (of a performer or a performance) to be brilliant **2.** *n.* a flash of reflected light ‖ brilliance of performance, conversation etc. ‖ animation **spár·kler** *n.* an indoor firework, consisting of a piece of wire (which can be held in the hand) having part of its length coated with a substance which produces a shower of tiny sparks when lit **spár·kling** *adj.* glittering ‖ lively, vivacious ‖ (of wine) effervescent

sparkling water soda water

spark plug (*Am.*=*Br.* sparking plug) a device fitted into the cylinder of an internalcombustion engine, consisting of two electrodes between which the battery passes a spark which ignites the mixture of gasoline vapor and air

sparring partner someone employed to fight with a boxer during training ‖ a partner with whom one can argue amicably to sharpen one's wits

spar·row (spǽrou) *n.* a member of *Passer*, fam. *Fringillidae* (*FINCH), esp. the house sparrow [O.E. *spearwa*]

Sparrow *n.* (*mil.*) an air-to-air, solid-propellant missile (AIM-7) with nonnuclear warhead, electronic-controlled homing, and a range of 25 km *Cf* SEA SPARROW

sparrow hawk *Accipiter nisus*, fam. *Accipitri-*

dae, a bird (11–15 ins) of N. Europe and Asia related to the buzzard, but with short rounded wings and long tail. It preys on small birds. In flight it alternates several rapid wingbeats with short glides || *Falco sparverius,* fam. *Falconidae,* a small North American falcon closely related to the kestrel. It feeds on insects, small birds and game

sparse (spɑrs) *adj.* occurring at widely separated places or times, without any regularity, *sparse vegetation* || not thickly grown, *a sparse beard* **spar·si·ty** (spɑ́rsiti:) *n.* [fr. L. *spargere* (*sparsus*), to scatter]

Spar·ta (spɑ́rtə) (Lacedaemon) ancient city of the S. central Peloponnesus, Greece, adjacent to the modern town (pop. 8,000) of the same name (*Gk* Sparti): remains of temples (9th, 6th and 2nd cc. B.C.). After 600 B.C. Sparta was governed by a stern military constitution attributed to Lycurgus, and it became the predominant power in the Peloponnesus. Sparta played a leading part (480-479 B.C.) in repulsing the Persian invasions during the Persian Wars, and defeated the growing empire of Athens in the Peloponnesian War (431-404 B.C.). Sparta was defeated by Thebes (4th c. B.C.) and its power declined

Spar·ta·cus (spɑ́rtəkəs) (*d.* 71 B.C.), Roman gladiator. He led an unsuccessful revolt of slaves against Rome (73-71 B.C.)

Spar·tan (spɑ́rt'n) **1.** *adj.* of or relating to Sparta || hardy, austere, *a Spartan character* || rigorous, offering no comfort, *Spartan living conditions* **2.** *n.* a native of Sparta || someone of Spartan endurance **Spár·tan·ism** *n.* [fr. L. *Spartanus*]

Spartan *n.* (*mil.*) a nuclear surface-to-air guided missile formerly deployed as part of the Safeguard ballistic missile defense weapon system, designed to intercept strategic ballistic reentry vehicles in the exoatmosphere

spasm (spǽzəm) *n.* a sudden, strong, involuntary muscular contraction, esp. one that is painful or convulsive || a short, violent effort, *he works in spasms* [O.F. *spasme* or fr. L. *spasmus* fr. Gk]

spas·mod·ic (spæzmɒ́dik) *adj.* of, affected or marked by, or relating to, spasms || intermittent, not sustained, *he takes a spasmodic interest in the child* **spas·mód·i·cal·ly** *adv.* [fr. M.L. or Mod. L. *spasmodicus* fr. Gk]

spas·tic (spǽstik) **1.** *adj.* of, relating to or characterized by a spasm or spasms tightly contracted as though by a prolonged spasm || of a long-standing paralysis of some or many muscles, esp. caused by injury at birth || suffering from such paralysis **2.** *n.* someone who suffers from such paralysis **spás·ti·cal·ly** *adv.* [fr. L. *spasticus* fr. Gk]

spat (spæt) *n.* a short gaiter covering the upper part of the foot and the ankle, and fastened under the shoe [short for SPATTERDASH]

spat alt. *past* and *past part.* of SPIT

spat 1. *pl.* **spat, spats** *n.* the spawn or young of bivalve mollusks, esp. of oysters **2.** *v.i. pres. part.* **spat·ting** *past* and *past part.* **spat·ted** to spawn [perh. rel. to SPIT]

spat 1. *n.* (*pop.*) a brief, trifling quarrel || a little splash, *a spat of rain* **2.** *v. pres. part.* **spat·ting** *past* and *past part.* **spat·ted** *v.t.* to strike with a sound like that made by a splash of rain || *v.i.* (*pop.*) to engage in a trifling quarrel [prob. imit.]

spatch·cock (spǽtʃkɒk) **1.** *n.* a fowl killed and dressed hastily and cooked at once split open on a grill **2.** *v.t.* to cook (a fowl) in this way || to fit (extra matter) into a text, esp. too hurriedly or inappropriately [etym. doubtful]

spate (speit) *n.* a river flood || a rapid flow, a gush, *a spate of words* || a large amount or number, *a spate of articles* **in spate** in flood [etym. doubtful]

spa·tha·ceous (spəθéiʃəs) *adj.* having a spathe || like a spathe [Mod. L. *spathaceus*]

spathe (speið, speiθ) *n.* (*bot.*) a large enveloping leaf, green or petaloid, enveloping a spadix [fr. L. *spatha* or Gk *spathē,* broad blade]

spath·ic (spǽθik) *adj.* of or like spar (mineral) [G. *spath, spat,* spar]

spath·ose (spǽθous) *adj.* spathic

spa·tial, spa·cial (spéiʃəl) *adj.* of or relating to space **spá·tial·ly, spá·cial·ly** *adv.* [fr. L. *spatium,* space]

spatial summation the total effect of stimuli from different sources converging simultaneously at a sensory receptor

spat·ter (spǽtər) **1.** *v.t.* to project (a fluid, e.g. water, mud etc.) in drops, *the wheels spattered the mud on all sides* || to project drops of a fluid onto, *the car spattered him with mud as it passed* || *v.i.* to fall in drops, *the rain spattered down* **2.** *n.* a short fall of rain etc. || the act or sound of spattering || a spot caused by this [prob. fr. Du. or L.G. *spatten,* to burst]

spat·ter·dash (spǽtərdæʃ) *n.* (*hist.*) a long legging or gaiter worn as a protection from mud || roughcast

spatter glass a glass of mixed colors resembling an amalgam of the day's scraps in a factory, used decoratively *also* end-of-day glass

spat·u·la (spǽtʃulə) *n.* an instrument with a broad, flexible, usually dull-edged blade, used for mixing, scooping or spreading soft substances such as paint etc. || (*med.*) an instrument used in the examination of certain parts of the body [L. dim. of *spatha,* broad blade fr. Gk]

spat·u·late (spǽtʃulit) *adj.* with a broad rounded end, *a spatulate table leg* || markedly broad at the tip, *spatulate fingers* || (*biol.*) spoon-shaped [fr. Mod. L. *spatulatus*]

spav·in (spǽvin) *n.* a disease of the hock in horses, marked by a bony enlargement caused by strain || this enlargement **spáv·ined** *adj.* [fr. O.F. *espavain*]

spawn (spɔn) **1.** *n.* the mass of eggs deposited by fish, bivalve mollusks, batrachians and some other aquatic animals || the mycelium of some fungi, esp. of cultivated mushrooms **2.** *v.t.* to produce (spawn) || (*pop.*) to produce (something, e.g. books) in great numbers || *v.i.* to deposit spawn || (*pop.*) to produce young in great numbers [fr. A.F. *espaundre*]

spay (spei) *v.t.* to remove the ovaries of (an animal) [fr. A.F. *espeier*]

speak (spi:k) *pres. part.* **speak·ing** *past* **spoke** (spouk), *archaic* **spake** (speik) *past part.* **spo·ken** (spóukən), *archaic* **spoke** *v.i.* to utter words with the ordinary voice, *he speaks clearly* || to talk, *she was too upset to speak* || to make a speech, *I am going to speak at the meeting* || (with 'about') to discuss, *we spoke about the need for economy* || (with 'about') to rebuke or reprimand, *will you speak to her about her laziness?* || (*rhet.*) to sound, *the organ spoke* || (*rhet.*) to be expressive of opinions, ideas, emotions etc., *his face spoke of suffering* || *v.t.* to express (an idea) by speaking, *she spoke the truth* || to use (a language) in speaking, *he can speak German* || to utter orally || to express (opinions, ideas, emotions etc.) without using words, *her eyes and smile spoke a warm welcome* || (*naut.*) to communicate with (a ship), *he spoke to S.S. Orontes* **so to speak** if the expression is admissible **to speak for** to recommend, *I hope you will speak for him* to reserve, *this table is spoken for* **to speak of** to mention, *he was speaking of you yesterday* || (usually in negative constructions) of any significance, *he has no problems to speak of* **to speak one's mind** to be completely frank **to speak out** (or **up**) to speak openly and with conviction, *she always speaks out against injustice* **to speak up** to speak rather loudly, to raise the voice, *you must speak up if you are to be heard* **to speak well of** (or **for**) to be favorable evidence of, *it speaks well of his good nature that he took no offense* [O.E. *sprecan,* later *specan*]

speak·eas·y (spí:ki:zi:) *pl.* **speak·eas·ies** *n.* (*pop. hist.*) a place where alcoholic drink was sold illegally (esp. associated with Prohibition)

speak·er (spí:kər) *n.* someone who speaks || someone who makes a speech, gives a talk etc. || a loudspeaker **Speak·er** the presiding officer of the U.S. House of Representatives, the British House of Commons, and of certain other legislative bodies

speak·er·phone (spí:kərfoun) *n.* device containing microphone and speaker often attached to a telephone, permitting all within range to listen and speak over the system to which it is attached

speak·ing (spí:kiŋ) **1.** *adj.* (of a likeness) close, immediately perceptible || seeming to speak, eloquent, vivid, *a speaking glance* || involving speaking or talking, esp. as opposed to singing, *his speaking voice is low-pitched, she took the only speaking part in the opera* **2.** *n.* the act of one who speaks **generally speaking** usually, in most cases **on speaking terms** on terms friendly enough to permit the exchange of conversation **strictly speaking** in the strict sense of the words

spear (spiər) **1.** *n.* a thrusting, hurling or stabbing weapon consisting of a long shaft with a pointed blade || a similar weapon for stabbing fish **2.** *v.t.* to pierce with a spear, or as if with one [O.E. *spere*]

spear *n.* a thin pointed shoot of grass or wheat etc. || a sapling [var. of SPIRE]

spear·head (spíərhed) **1.** *n.* the pointed head or blade of a spear || the foremost person, or body of troops, in an attack || the most forceful element, *the spearhead of the opposition* **2.** *v.t.* to be the vital thrusting force of, *he spearheaded the opposition* || (*mil.*) to precede in (an attack or advance)

spear·ing (spíəriŋ) *n.* (*hockey*) an illegal jab

spear·man (spíərmən) *pl.* **spear·men** (spíərmən) *n.* a warrior armed with a spear

spear·mint (spíərmint) *n.* *Mentha spicata,* fam. *Labiatae,* common garden mint. It yields the essential oil, carvone

spec (spek) *n.* (*Br., pop.*) a commercial speculation **on spec** (*Br., pop.*) in the hope that things will turn out as one wishes but without certainty that they will [short for SPECULATION]

spe·cial (spéʃəl) **1.** *adj.* particular in kind, *each spice imparts a special flavor* || superior, *a special brand* || serving a particular purpose, *a special tool* || specialized, *it requires special knowledge* || (of friends) intimate, close **2.** *n.* a train run in addition to the scheduled trains, for a special occasion || a special edition of a newspaper || a special offer for some regularly stocked item, e.g. of food || (*television*) a featured program that is not part of a series || something specially singled out and featured [fr. O.F. *especial*]

special constable (*Br.*) a man employed as a policeman on special occasions

special court-martial a military court for offenses less serious than those warranting a general court-martial. It is composed of three or more officers, the judge advocate and defense counsel, and can impose only certain limited fines or punishment

special delivery (*Am.=Br.* express post) the system of delivering mail for a special fee without waiting for the next regular delivery || (*Am.=Br.* express letter) a letter sent by this system

Special Drawing Rights international reserve units created by the International Monetary Fund in 1969 to supplement the limited supplies of gold and dollars, which had been the prime stable international monetary assets *abbr.* **SDRs** *also* paper gold

spe·cial·ism (spéʃəlizəm) *n.* a specializing in a particular branch of study or in a particular field of a profession || such a branch or field

spe·cial·ist (spéʃəlist) *n.* someone who devotes himself to a particular branch of study, or (esp. a doctor) to a particular branch of his profession

spe·ci·al·i·ty (speʃi:ǽliti:) *pl.* **spe·ci·al·i·ties** *n.* (*Br.*) a specialty || some particular distinguishing feature [fr. O.F. *specialite*]

spe·cial·i·za·tion (speʃəlizéiʃən) *n.* a specializing or being specialized

spe·cial·ize (spéʃəlaiz) *pres. part.* **spe·cial·iz·ing** *past* and *past part.* **spe·cial·ized** *v.i.* to become a specialist, to restrict one's studies, interests, activities etc. to a particular branch or field, *he specializes in modern languages* || to become specialized || (*biol.*) to adapt an organ for a particular purpose || *v.t.* to restrict, to limit, *to specialize one's interests* [fr. F. *spécialiser*]

special licence (*Br.*) a license giving permission to marry without the usual preliminaries of public notice and residence, and in a place or at a time other than those legally appointed

spe·cial·ly (spéʃəli:) *adv.* in a special manner for a special purpose, with a special intention

Special Mission Fleet U.S. Air Force unit assigned to transport government officials and visiting dignitaries

special pleading (*law*) the introduction of fresh matter into a plea, as opposed to the denial of allegations made by the other side, esp. to avoid damaging admissions || an argument used for persuasion rather than for truth's sake, one supporting an arguable point of view

special relativity *RELATIVITY

special revenue sharing *REVENUE SHARING

spe·cial·ty (spéʃəlti:) *pl.* **spe·cial·ties** *n.* something in which one has special skill or special interest || something for which a district, restaurant, store etc. is particularly well known || (*law*) a contract under seal

special verdict (*law*) a verdict which sets out the facts on the material issues of a case as found by the jury, but which leaves the court to reach the legal conclusions from the facts so found

spe·cie (spí:ʃi:) *n.* money in coin **in specie** in coin ‖ in kind [L. abl. of *species,* shape, kind]

spe·cies (spí:ʃi:z) *pl.* **spe·cies** *n.* (*biol.*) a group of individuals closely related in structure, capable of breeding within the group but not normally outside it ‖ (*biol.*) a systematic unit including geographical races and varieties and included within a structure of more comprehensive classification (e.g. a genus) ‖ (*logic*) a group having certain attributes in common and given a common name ‖ (*Roman Catholicism*) the outward form of the consecrated bread and wine ‖ (*pop.*) a sort, kind [L.=appearance, form, kind]

spe·ci·fi·a·ble (spésifaiəb'l) *adj.* that can be specified

spe·cif·ic (spisífik) **1.** *adj.* clearly distinguished, stated or understood, *he had no specific reason for coming* ‖ of a species, *specific name* ‖ characteristic of something, *specific properties* ‖ (*phys.*) being an arbitrary constant ‖ (of a disease) caused by a particular infection ‖ (of a remedy) having particular influence on a particular disease or particular part of the body **2.** *n.* (*med.*) a remedy for a particular ailment **spe·cíf·i·cal·ly** *adv.* [fr. M.L. *specificus*]

specific address (*computer*) permanent location of data in a computer storage *also* absolute address

spec·i·fi·ca·tion (spesifikéiʃən) *n.* the act of specifying ‖ a detailed item, something specified ‖ (often *pl.*) a list of materials supplied and work done by a builder, engineer etc. or required for a project to be carried out ‖ a detailed description of a person's invention submitted by an inventor when applying for a patent [fr. M.L. *specificatio* (*specificationis*)]

specific gravity (*phys.*) the numerical ratio between the weight, at any chosen place, of a given volume of a substance and the weight, at the same place, of an equal volume of water at 4°C., i.e. the ratio of the density of a substance to the density of water at 4°C. (or other standard)

specific heat (*phys.*) the amount of heat required to raise the temperature of 1 gram of a substance through 1°C.

specific inductive capacity (*abbr.* s.i.c.) *DIELECTRIC CONSTANT

spec·i·fic·i·ty (spesifísiti:) *n.* the quality or state of being specific

spec·i·fy (spésifai) *pres. part.* **spec·i·fy·ing** *past* and *past part.* **spec·i·fied** *v.t.* to name or mention explicitly ‖ to include in a specification [O.F. *specifier*]

spec·i·men (spésəmən) *n.* a part or individual taken to typify the whole or the class, esp. for the purpose of scientific investigation, a sample ‖ (*pop.,* used pejoratively) an individual of a specified sort, *he's a nasty specimen* [L. fr. *specere,* to look, look at]

specimen page a sample of a manuscript or other copy set up in type to establish the format, typeface, conventions etc. to be used when the complete work is printed

spe·ci·os·i·ty (spi:ʃi:ɒ́siti:) *n.* the state or quality of being specious [fr. L.L. *speciositas*]

spe·cious (spí:ʃəs) *adj.* apparently sound and reasonable, but fallacious [fr. L. *speciosus,* beautiful]

Speck (spek), Frank Gouldsmith (1881-1950), U.S. anthropologist and authority on Indian tribes of eastern North America, especially the Algonquian and Iroquois. His works include 'Ethnology of the Yuchi Indians' (1909) and 'Penobscot Man: the Life History of a Forest Tribe in Maine' (1940)

speck (spek) **1.** *n.* a small bit, a particle, *a speck of dust* ‖ a small spot or stain ‖ a spot indicating decay, e.g. in blemished fruit ‖ something made to appear very small by distance, *he was a speck on the horizon* **2.** *v.t.* to mark with specks [O.E. *specca*]

speck·le (spék'l) **1.** *n.* a small spot or mark, esp. a natural one on skin etc. **2.** *v.t. pres. part.* **speck·ling** *past* and *past part.* **speck·led** to mark with speckles

specs (speks) *pl. n.* (*pop.*) a pair of spectacles

spec·ta·cle (spéktək'l) *n.* a display, usually on a large scale, which attracts attention ‖ someone who, by his appearance or behavior, is seen to be ludicrous ‖ (*pl.*) a pair of lenses, mounted in a light frame which rests on the bridge of the nose and hooks or rests behind the ears, designed to correct certain defects of vision or to protect the eyes **spéc·ta·cled** *adj.* wearing spectacles ‖ (of animals) having a marking suggesting spectacles [O.F.]

spec·tac·u·lar (spektǽkjulər) **1.** *adj.* impressive to see, *a spectacular dive* ‖ of a kind to attract attention of or relating to a spectacle **2.** *n.* a long, lavish television show or movie [fr. L. *spectaculum,* a spectacle]

spec·ta·tor (spékteitər, spektéitər) *n.* an onlooker, someone who watches (a show, display etc.) [L.]

spec·ter, esp. *Br.* **spec·tre** (spéktər) *n.* the spirit of someone dead made visible, esp. with a terrifying appearance ‖ a threatening vision of something to come, *the specter of famine* [F. or fr. L. *spectrum*]

spectinomycin *ACTINOSPECTOCIN

spec·to·graph (spéktəgræf) *n.* a device for recording voiceprints *Cf* VOICEPRINT

spec·tral (spéktrəl) *adj.* of or resembling a specter ‖ of or relating to a spectrum or spectra

spectral type (*astron.*) the classification to which a star belongs on the basis of its spectrum. This system of classification comprises 10 categories which depend on the color, the observed relative prominence of spectral lines and bands, and the inferences obtained from these concerning surface temperature

spectre *SPECTER

spec·tro·graph (spéktrəgræf, spéktrəgrɑf) *n.* a spectroscope equipped with a device for photographing or otherwise recording the spectrum produced (*SPECTROMETER) [SPECTRUM+GRAPH]

spec·trom·e·ter (spektrɒ́mitər) *n.* a spectroscope equipped with some form of detector that measures the intensity of light falling on it and that is used to produce a record of the emission or absorption of radiation as a function of wavelength (cf. MASS SPECTROMETER) ‖ an instrument used to measure refractive indices [SPECTRUM+METER]

spec·tro·pho·tom·e·ter (spektroufoutɒ́mitər) *n.* a spectroscope equipped with a photometer for measuring the intensities of radiation in different parts of the spectrum, usually compared with a standard beam of the same frequency [SPECTRUM+PHOTOMETER]

spec·tro·scope (spéktrəskoup) *n.* any of various instruments used to disperse a beam of electromagnetic radiation into narrow wave bands (*RESOLVING POWER). A spectroscope consists of a source of radiation (in emission spectroscopy it is the material being studied), a collimator, a prism or diffraction grating for separating the narrow wave bands, and an optical system for bringing these to a focus. The optics and mechanics of spectroscopes vary widely, depending upon the kind of radiation employed (*SPECTROMETER, *SPECTROGRAPH, *SPECTROPHOTOMETER) **spec·tro·scop·ic** (spektrəskɒ́pik), **spec·tro·scóp·i·cal** *adjs* **spec·tro·scóp·i·cal·ly** *adv.* **spec·trós·co·pist** (spektrɒ́skəpist) *n.* **spec·trós·co·py** *n.* (*phys., chem.*) the study of the interaction of electromagnetic radiation with matter by means of the production and analysis of spectra. Modern models of matter picture the particles of which it is composed as being in a state of continuous vibrational, rotational and translational motion. Underlying most spectroscopic techniques is the fact that these atomic and subatomic particles are capable (since they bear charges) of absorbing and emitting energy in the form of electromagnetic radiation. Furthermore, depending upon the energy (and hence the frequency, *PLANCK RADIATION LAW) of this radiation, different portions of the atomic or molecular structure are involved (*INFRARED SPECTRUM, *ULTRAVIOLET SPECTRUM, *VISIBLE SPECTRUM, *MICROWAVE SPECTRUM). Quantum theory requires that e.g. a spinning molecule or circulating electron can possess energy only in certain definite, permitted amounts: it follows that in absorbing or emitting energy only those transitions that bring the system from one allowed state to another can occur, and therefore only certain wavelengths of electromagnetic radiation will be emitted or absorbed.

Generally there are two methods of studying these interactions: the production of emission spectra and of absorption spectra. Emission and absorption spectra are further subdivided according to the character of the radiation employed, different optical and mechanical systems being required for handling each band.

Spectroscopy finds increasingly wide use as an analytic tool in theoretical studies and is a potent means of identifying the components of complex mixtures and of unknown substances. Thus the infrared absorption spectrum of a pure substance is accepted as a proof that the substance is present, and it provides an extremely useful clue to the structure of the substance (cf. NUCLEAR MAGNETIC RESONANCE, *MASS SPECTROSCOPY) [G. *spektroskop*]

spec·trum (spéktrəm) *pl.* **spec·tra** (spéktrə), **spec·trums** *n.* an arrangement of the components of a beam, wave band or sound separated and displayed in order according to some varying factor, e.g. energy, charge-to-mass ratio, wavelength ‖ the band of colors (red, orange, yellow, green, blue, indigo, violet) into which a beam of light is decomposed by a prism ‖ the image retained on the retina when the eyes are turned away after staring at a bright colored object (*MASS SPECTRUM, *MOLECULAR SPECTRUM, *SPECTROSCOPY) [F. or fr. L. *spectrum* fr. *specere,* to look]

spectrum of war (*mil.*) **1.** the full range of a conflict **2.** cold, limited, and general war

spec·u·lar (spékjulər) *adj.* of, pertaining to or having the qualities of a mirror ‖ (of a surface) producing an image, i.e. reflecting coherently [fr. L. *specularis*]

spec·u·late (spékjuleit) *pres. part.* **spec·u·lat·ing** *past* and *past part.* **spec·u·lat·ed** *v.i.* to consider possibilities and probabilities, *it is idle to speculate about what might have happened* ‖ to undertake commercial transactions involving serious risk for the sake of possible large winnings, esp. to buy and sell in the hope of profiting from fluctuating prices, sometimes in an antisocial way [fr. L. *speculari* (*speculatus*), to watch]

spec·u·la·tion (spekjuléiʃən) *n.* theorizing, conjecture, *her departure gave rise to speculation* ‖ commercial activity involving serious risk in the hope of large profits ‖ an enterprise involving such activity [fr. L.L. *speculatio* (*speculationis*)]

spec·u·la·tive (spékjuleitiv, spékjulətiv) *adj.* of or concerning speculation ‖ given to speculating [O.F. *speculatif*]

spec·u·la·tor (spékjuleitər) *n.* someone who speculates [L. fr. *speculari,* to watch]

spec·u·lum (spékjuləm) *pl.* **spec·u·la** (spékjulə) **spec·u·lums** *n.* an instrument for examining body cavities ‖ a mirror of polished metal, used in telescopes etc. ‖ a colored patch on the wing of some birds [L. =mirror]

speculum metal an alloy, principally of copper and tin, which takes a very high polish and is used for making reflecting surfaces

sped alt. *past* and *past part.* of SPEED

speech (spi:tʃ) *n.* the ability to speak, *he lost his speech* ‖ the act of speaking, *she broke into speech* ‖ that which is spoken, esp. an address to an audience ‖ a group of lines given to a character in a play ‖ manner of speaking, *country speech* ‖ the theory of oral communication, e.g. as studied in some colleges ‖ (*mus.*) the sounding of an instrument, esp. of an organ pipe [O.E. *sprǣc,* later *spǣc*]

speech community all the people who speak a mutually intelligible language or dialect

speech day (*Br.*) the day when parents attend a school to witness the presentation of prizes to the pupils, and to hear speeches

speech·i·fy (spí:tʃifai) *pres. part.* **speech·i·fy·ing** *past* and *past part.* **speech·i·fied** *v.i.* to make unnecessary speeches, holding forth in a tedious or pompous manner

speech·less (spí:tʃlis) *adj.* without the ability to speak ‖ temporarily unable to speak because of some emotional shock or injury ‖ silent

speech pathology *SPEECH THERAPY

speech processing technique for changing characteristics of voice to improve intelligibility for transmission

speech synthesis artificial simulation of speech, e.g., electronically, by computer —**speech synthesizer** *n.*

speech therapy the study, examination, and treatment of defects and diseases of the voice, and of spoken and written language *also* speech pathology —**speech pathologist** *n.* —**speech therapist** *n.*

Speed (spi:d), John (c. 1552-1629), English antiquarian and cartographer. His 'Theatre of the Empire of Great Britaine' (1611) is a valuable collection of detailed maps of the English counties

speed (spi:d) *n.* rate of motion ‖ (*phys.*) the magnitude of a velocity vector irrespective of its direction ‖ a transmission gear ‖ the rate at which something proceeds or is done ‖ (*photog.*) the rapidity with which a sensitized surface is acted on by light, usually expressed by a number ‖ (*photog.*) the time during which the shutter of a camera is open [O.E. *spēd*]

speed *pres. part.* **speed·ing** *past* and *past part.* **sped** (sped), **speed·ed** *v.i.* to move, act, change, pass etc. at a high speed ‖ to drive a vehicle more rapidly than is safe or legal ‖ *v.t.* to cause to move at a high speed ‖ to set (an engine) to run at a certain speed **to speed up** to increase the speed of ‖ to go faster [O.E. *spēdan*]

speed (*slang*) a stimulant drug, esp. methamphetamine

speed·ball (spí:dbɔl) *n.* (*sports*) a field ballgame of 11 players on each team, combining elements of basketball and football, invented in 1921 by Elmer D. Mitchell

speed·boat (spí:dbout) *n.* a motorboat capable of traveling at high speed

speed freak (*slang*) a habitual speed user

speed·i·ly (spí:dili:) *adv.* with speed, quickly

speed·i·ness (spí:di:nis) *n.* the state or quality of being speedy

speed·om·e·ter (spidɒ́mitər) *n.* a device that shows the speed at which a vehicle is traveling

speed-read·ing (spi:drí:diŋ) *n.* technique and practice of rapid reading accomplished by extending sight and comprehension span to include several words or passages at one glance —**speed-read** *v.* —**speed-reader** *n.*

speed shop (*automobile*) a hot-rodders' supply store

speed·up (spí:dʌp) *n.* the act of speeding up ‖ (esp. in factories) an increase in speed and output not accompanied by an increase in salary

speed·way (spí:dwei) *n.* a racetrack, esp. for motorcycles ‖ a road on which fast driving is permitted

speed·well (spí:dwel) *n.* a member of *Veronica,* fam. *Scrophulariaceae,* a genus of plants native to the temperate regions of both hemispheres, many species of which are cultivated as garden flowers

speed·y (spí:di:) *comp.* **speed·i·er** *superl.* **speed·i·est** *adj.* swift, having a good capacity for speed ‖ prompt, *it gives speedy relief*

speiss (spais) *n.* a compound of arsenic, nickel, copper etc. produced in smelting certain lead ores [fr. G. *speise,* amalgam]

Speke (spi:k), John Hanning (1827-64), British explorer. He accompanied Sir Richard Burton to Somaliland (1854) and to E. Africa (1857-9). After they had discovered Lake Tanganyika (1858), Speke went on to discover Lake Victoria (1858), claiming it as the source of the Nile. In 1860-3 he traced the White Nile from its source, through the Sudan, to its mouth

spe·le·ol·o·gist (spi:li:ɒ́lədʒist) *n.* someone who specializes in speleology

spe·le·ol·o·gy, *Br.* also **spe·lae·ol·o·gy** (spi:li:ɒ́lədʒi:) *n.* the scientific study of caves ‖ spelunking [fr. L. *spelaeum,* cave+Gk *logos,* discourse]

spell (spel) **1.** *v.t.* (*pop.*) to relieve (a person) by taking a turn at work ‖ *v.i.* to rest from work for a period **2.** *n.* a turn at work, a shift ‖ a short period, *a spell in the country* ‖ (*Austral.*) a period of relaxation, rest from work ‖ a bout or period (of illness, depression etc.), *he's going through a bad spell* [etym. doubtful]

spell *pres. part.* **spell·ing** *past* and *past part.* **spelled,** esp. *Br.* **spelt** (spelt) *v.t.* to name or write the letters of (a word) in order ‖ (of specified letters) to make up (a word), *c-a-t spells cat* ‖ to signify, *the drought spells disaster for thousands* ‖ *v.i.* to form words by letters, *her typing is good, but she spells badly* **to spell out** to make out the meaning of (words, a written passage etc.) with difficulty ‖ to read out letter by letter ‖ to explain in full detail [fr. O.F. *espeller, espeler*]

spell *n.* an incantation, words which properly chanted or uttered are supposed to have magical effect ‖ the power to charm or fascinate, *the spell of Ireland* ‖ a state of enchantment, *putting on the light broke the spell* [O.E. *spel, spell,* a story]

spell·bind (spélbaind) *pres. part.* **spell·bind·ing** *past* and *past part.* **spéll·bound** (spélbaund) *v.t.* to put a spell upon ‖ to enchant, fascinate **spéll·bind·er** *n.* a speaker or entertainer who has strong power over an audience **spell·bound** *adj.* entranced ‖ bound as if by a spell, esp. rendered motionless or speechless

spell·ing (spéliŋ) *n.* the act of one who spells ‖ orthography

spelling bee a spelling competition

spelt (spelt) *n. Triticum spelta,* German wheat, a variety of wheat grown in Germany and Switzerland [O.E. fr. L.L. *spelta*]

spelt alt. *past* and *past part.* of SPELL

spel·ter (spéltər) *n.* commercial zinc, about 97% pure, lead being the main impurity [rel. to pewter]

spe·lunk·er (spilʌ́ŋkər) *n.* (*pop.*) a spelunking enthusiast

spe·lunk·ing (spilʌ́ŋkiŋ) *n.* (*Am.=Br.* potholing) the sport of exploring underground caves [fr. L. *spelunca,* cave]

Spen·cer (spénsər), Herbert (1820-1903), English philosopher. His chief work was 'Synthetic Philosophy' (1860-1900) in several volumes, each treating a different branch of knowledge. He was the founder of an evolutionist philosophy, and an exponent of laissez-faire social philosophy

Spencer, Sir Stanley (1891-1961), English painter. His works include landscapes, portraits and nudes, but he is best known for his paintings on religious themes, which are often on a very large scale and show much distortion and some private symbolism. His pictures often show Christ in a 20th-c. English setting

spen·cer (spénsər) *n.* a fore-and-aft sail that serves as a trysail [etym. doubtful]

spencer *n.* a woman's close-fitting jacket (waist-length) or bodice ‖ (*hist.*) a man's double-breasted tailless coat or jacket of the late 18th c. and early 19th c. [after the 2nd Earl *Spencer* (1758–1834)]

spend (spend) *pres. part.* **spend·ing** *past* and *past part.* **spent** (spent) *v.t.* to pay out (money) for purchases ‖ to exhaust, wear out (oneself or itself) ‖ to pass (time) ‖ *v.i.* to pay out money [O.E. *spendan* fr. L. *expendere*]

spend·thrift (spéndθrift) **1.** *n.* someone who spends too much and spends wastefully **2.** *adj.* spending too much, wasteful

Speng·ler (ʃpéŋglər), Oswald (1880-1936), German philosopher. In his chief work, 'The Decline of the West' (2 vols, 1918, 1922), he predicts the end of Western civilization by examining aspects of it (politics, mathematics, art etc.) and finding analogies with declining civilizations of the past

Spen·ser (spénsər), Edmund (c. 1552-99), English poet. His most celebrated poem is 'The Faerie Queene' (1589, 1596), an allegorical, chivalric, epic romance originally conceived in 12 books, of which only the first six and fragments of a seventh were written. Spenser's other works include 'The Shepheardes Calender' (1579), 'Epithalamion' (1595) and 'Prothalamion' (1596) and many sonnets. He enriched poetic diction by introducing into his own poetry foreign loanwords, archaisms, pseudo-archaisms and dialect words. He adapted contemporary sonnet form, writing three linked quatrains and a couplet, and in 'The Faerie Queene' perfected a new stanza form which became known as the Spenserian stanza. Many of his poems contain thinly disguised references to contemporary political figures: thus the faerie queene served by the knights in the poem is, at one level of the allegory, Queen Elizabeth. Spenser's poetry influenced Milton, Wordsworth and Keats, and cast a spell on those for whom poetry was the creation of another world, a dream world of romance and enchantment, largely insulated from the realities of human life

Spen·se·ri·an (spensíəri:ən) *adj.* of or characteristic of Edmund Spenser or his poetry

Spenserian stanza a nine-lined stanza perfected by Edmund Spenser, who used it in 'The Faerie Queene'. It was later employed by Byron, Shelley and Keats. It is suitable only for long narrative poems. Eight iambic pentameters are followed by an alexandrine and are rhymed a b a b b c b c c

spent *past part.* of SPEND ‖ *adj.* exhausted ‖ devoid of further energy ‖ (of shells, cartridges etc.) exploded ‖ having lost its elasticity, plasticity or other active principle

sperm (spə:rm) *n.* semen ‖ a spermatozoon [fr. O.F. *esperme* or L. *sperma* fr. Gk]

sper·ma·ce·ti (spə:rməséti:) *n.* a glistening white fatty, waxy substance, chiefly cetyl palmitate, $C_{15}H_{31}COOC_{16}H_{33}$, found in sperm oil and used in the preparation of textile finishes, cosmetics, candles etc. [M.L. fr. L.L. *sperma,* sperm (for which it was mistaken)+*ceti,* gen. of *cetus,* whale]

sper·mar·y (spə́:rməri:) *pl.* **sper·mar·ies** *n.* an organ in which spermatozoa are produced, e.g. a testis ‖ an antheridium

sper·mat·ic (spə:rmǽtik) *adj.* (*zool.*) relating to spermatozoa ‖ relating to a testis [fr. M.L. *spermaticus*]

spermatic cord a cord on which a testis hangs and which contains vessels and nerves

spermatic fluid semen

sper·ma·tid (spə́:rmətid) *n.* a nonmotile and otherwise immature male germ cell produced by the second meiotic division and leading to the mature spermatozoon by cytoplasmic differentiation (*SPERMATOGENESIS) [fr. Gk *sperma* (*spermatos*), seed]

sper·ma·ti·um (spə:rméiʃi:əm) *pl.* **sper·ma·ti·a** (spə:rméiʃi:ə) *n.* a nonmotile male gamete in red algae ‖ a cell functioning as a male gamete in various lichens and fungi [Mod. L. fr. Gk *spermation* dim. of *sperma,* seed]

sper·mat·o·cyte (spə:rmǽtəsait) *n.* an immature male germ cell (the primary spermatocyte) just prior to the first maturation division, or each cell (secondary spermatocyte) formed during that process and transformed into a spermatid by the second maturation division (*MEIOSIS, *SPERMATOGENESIS) [fr. Gk *sperma* (*spermatos*), seed+*kutos,* receptacle]

sper·ma·to·gen·e·sis (spə:rmətədʒénisis) *n.* the entire process of formation and maturation of the male gamete from spermatogonium through primary and secondary spermatocytes and spermatid to spermatozoon **sper·ma·to·ge·nét·ic** *adj.* [Mod. L. fr. Gk *sperma* (*spermatos*), seed+*genesis,* origin]

sper·ma·to·go·ni·um (spə:rmətəgóuni:əm) *pl.* **sper·ma·to·go·ni·a** (spə:rmətəgóuni:ə) *n.* a primordial male germ cell (*SPERMATOGENESIS) [Mod. L. fr. Gk *sperma* (*spermatos*), seed+*gonē,* offspring]

sperm·a·toph·o·ral (spə:rmətɒ́fərəl) *adj.* of or having to do with a spermatophore

sper·mat·o·phore (spə:rmǽtəfɔr, spə:rmǽtəfour) *n.* a capsule or mass containing spermatozoa ejaculated by male mollusks, annelids and other animals [fr. Gk *sperma* (*spermatos*), seed+-*phoros,* bearing]

sper·mat·o·phyte (spə:rmǽtəfait) *n.* a member of *Spermatophyta,* plants producing seeds **sper·ma·to·phyt·ic** (spə:rmətəfítik) *adj.* [fr. Gk *sperma* (*spermatos*), seed+*phuton,* plant]

spermatozoa *pl.* of SPERMATOZOON

sper·ma·to·zo·al (spə:rmətəzóuəl) *adj.* of or having to do with spermatozoa

sper·ma·to·zo·an (spə:rmətəzóuən) *adj.* spermatozoal

sper·ma·to·zo·ic (spə:rmətəzóuik) *adj.* spermatozoal

sper·ma·to·zo·id (spə:rmətəzóuid) *n.* the motile male gamete or sexual cell of a plant freed in the water from the antheridium in which it has developed

sper·ma·to·zo·on (spə:rmətəzóuɒn) *pl.* **sper·ma·to·zo·a** (spə:rmətəzóuə) *n.* a motile male reproductive haploid cell (*SPERMATOGENESIS, *FERTILIZATION) [Mod. L. fr. Gk *sperma* (*spermatos*), seed+*zōon,* animal]

sper·mo·go·ni·um (spə:rməgóuni:əm) *pl.* **sper·mo·go·ni·a** (spə:rməgóuni:ə) *n.* the receptacle or capsule of spermatia in certain lichens and fungi [Mod. L. fr. Gk *sperma,* seed+*gonē,* offspring]

sperm oil a liquid wax, not a true oil, light yellow in color and contained in the large head cavities of the sperm whale. When the spermaceti in it has been extracted, sperm oil is used as a lubricant and, in conjunction with other marine oils, as a leather dressing (cf. WHALE OIL)

sperm whale *Physeter catodon* or *P. macrocephalus,* fam. *Physeteridae,* a genus of toothed whales, measuring up to 60 ft in length, having a closed head cavity containing spermaceti and oil. A large sperm whale may yield up to 100 barrels of sperm oil and 24 barrels of spermaceti [short for *spermaceti whale*]

Sper·ry (spéri:), Elmer Ambrose (1860-1930), American inventor of the gyroscopic compass

sper·ry·lite (spérəlait) *n.* platinum arsenide, $PtAs_2$, the only natural compound of platinum. It occurs in white crystals and granular form [after Francis L. *Sperry,* 19th-c. Canadian chemist, its discoverer]

spew (spju:) **1.** *v.t.* (*rhet.*) to vomit ‖ (*rhet.,* usually with 'out') to pour out (curses etc.) with abhorrence or disgust ‖ *v.i.* to vomit **2.** *n.* vomit [O.E. *spīwan, spēowan*]

Spey (spei) a river of N.E. Scotland, flowing northeast 110 miles from Loch Spey, in the

CONCISE PRONUNCIATION KEY: **(a)** æ, *cat;* ɑ, *car;* ɔ *fawn;* ei, *snake.* **(e)** e, *hen;* i:, *sheep;* iə, *deer;* εə, *bear.* **(i)** i, *fish;* ai, *tiger;* ə:, *bird.* **(o)** ɒ, *ox;* au, *cow;* ou, *goat;* u, *poor;* ɔi, *royal.* **(u)** ʌ, *duck;* u, *bull;* u:, *goose;* ə, *bacillus;* ju:, *cube.* x, *loch;* θ, *think;* ð, *bother;* z, *Zen;* ʒ, *corsage;* dʒ, *savage;* ŋ, *orangutang;* j, *yak;* ʃ, *fish;* tʃ, *fetch;* 'l, *rabble;* 'n, *redden.* Complete pronunciation key appears inside front cover.

Inverness highlands, to the North Sea: salmon fishing

Spey·er, Diet of (ʃpáiər) the Imperial Diet (1529) at which toleration was refused to Lutherans in Catholic states and to Zwinglians and Anabaptists

sphag·num (sfǽgnəm) *pl.* **sphag·na** (sfǽgnə), **sphag·nums** *n.* a member of *Sphagnum,* a genus of soft mosses, the only representative of the order *Sphagnaceae.* The plants are colored by chlorophyll and brown, yellow or red pigments, but are pale on account of air-containing tissues. Their remains, with other plant debris, form peat [Mod. L. fr. Gk *sphagnos,* a kind of moss]

sphal·er·ite (sfǽlərait) *n.* zinc blende [fr. Gk *sphaleros,* deceptive]

sphene (sfi:n) *n.* titanite [F. *sphène* fr. Gk]

sphe·no·don (sfí:nədɒn) *n.* the tuatara [fr. Gk *sphēn,* a wedge+*odous* (*odontos*), tooth]

sphe·noid (sfí:nɔid) **1.** *adj.* (*anat.*) of the compound bone at the base of the cranium ‖ sphenoidal **2.** *n.* a wedge-shaped crystal with four equal isosceles triangles as faces ‖ the sphenoid bone **sphe·nói·dal** *adj.* wedge-shaped [fr. Mod. L. *sphenoides* fr. Gk fr. *sphēn,* a wedge+*eidēs,* form]

sphe·nop·sid (sfi:nɒ́psid) *n.* a member of *Sphenopsida,* a subphylum of chlorophyll-bearing, vascular plants (the horsetails) and many much larger fossil forms that flourished in the Carboniferous [fr. Mod. L. *Sphenopsida* fr. Gk *sphēn,* a wedge+*opsis,* vision, appearance]

sphere (sfiər) *n.* (*geom.*) the solid figure generated when a circle rotates about a diameter, every point on its surface being thus equidistant from the center of this circle (called the center of the sphere). The surface area of a sphere = 4π (radius)$_2$, the volume of a sphere = 4/3π (radius)$_3$ ‖ (*loosely*) anything of approximately this shape ‖ a limited domain within which something is effective, *sphere of influence* ‖ a range of knowledge, *it lies outside my sphere* ‖ a group of people in the social hierarchy (with respect to belonging or not belonging to it), *he moves in more exalted spheres than they do* ‖ (*hist.*) any of the hollow concentric transparent globes once conceived as moving around the earth and carrying in them the sun, planets and fixed stars and producing music by their vibrations ‖ (*hist.*) the path, within one of these concentric globes, followed by the sun, planets or fixed stars [O.F. *espere* fr. L.L. fr. Gk]

spher·ic (sférik) *adj.* spherical **sphér·i·cal** *adj.* shaped like a sphere ‖ relating to a sphere [fr. L.L. *sphericus, sphaericus* fr. Gk]

spherical aberration the distortion of an image produced by a spherical lens or mirror because of the different focal points for rays incident upon the central region and those incident upon the outer margins

spherical angle (*math.*) the angle between two intersecting arcs of great circles on a sphere measured between the tangents at the point of intersection

spherical polygon a figure formed by arcs of great circles on a sphere

spherical triangle the three-sided enclosed figure formed on the surface of a sphere which is bounded by the arcs of three great circles

sphe·ric·i·ty (sfirísiti:) *n.* the quality or state of being spherical [fr. Mod. L.]

spher·ics (sfériks) *n.* spherical geometry and spherical trigonometry

sphe·roid (sfíərɔid) *n.* a figure resembling a sphere, esp. an ellipsoid **sphe·roi·dal** (sfiərɔ́id'l) *adj.* **sphe·roi·dic·i·ty** (sfiərɔidísiti:) *n.* [fr. L. *sphaeroides* fr. Gk]

sphe·rom·e·ter (sfirɒ́mitər) *n.* an instrument used to measure the curvature of a spherical or cylindrical surface [fr. F. *sphéromètre*]

spher·o·plasts (sfíərəplæst) *n.* (*cytol.*) mitochondria or other cytoplasmic bodies, threadlike bodies in the protoplasm of cells, involved in the enzyme processes *also* chondriosomes

spher·u·lar (sférjulər) *adj.* having the form of a spherule

spher·ule (sférju:l) *n.* a small sphere [fr. L. sphœrula]

spher·u·lite (sférjulait) *n.* a spherical crystalline concretion, esp. of quartz and feldspar, found in some rocks **spher·u·lit·ic** (sferjulítik) *adj.* [L.]

sphinc·ter (sfíŋktər) *n.* (*anat.*) a ring-shaped muscle which, by its contraction, is able to close or narrow an orifice **sphínc·ter·al** *adj.* [L. fr. Gk *sphinktēr,* band]

sphing·o·lip·i·do·sis (sfiŋoulipədóusis) *n.* (*med.*) a metabolic disorder in which certain glycolipids and phospholipids accumulate in tissue, e.g, Tay-Sachs disease, Gaucher's disease, Nieman-Pick disease

sphinx (sfiŋks) *pl.* **sphinx·es, sphin·ges** (sfíndʒi:z) *n.* a compound creature having (in its most common form) a lion's body and a human head, either male or female. It originated in Egypt and the concept of the sphinx spread throughout the ancient world. Representations of the sphinx are found in Egyptian, Assyrian, Greek, Mayan and Roman art and sculpture. They are usually recumbent, may or may not be winged, and sometimes have a ram's or hawk's head. The heads of Egyptian sphinxes are usually royal portraits, and the lion bodies represent the pharaoh's strength. In Greek mythology, the Sphinx of Thebes had the head of a woman, the feet and tail of a lion and the wings of a bird. It devoured everyone who could not answer the riddle it asked, but when this was finally solved by Oedipus, the Sphinx killed itself ‖ an inscrutable person ‖ a member of *Sphinx,* a genus of hawkmoths **the Sphinx** the great sphinx of Giza, 187 ft long, the head and body of which are carved of living rock [L. fr. Gk prob. fr. *sphingein,* to bind together]

sphra·gis·tic (sfrədʒístik) *adj.* of or relating to engraved seals **sphra·gís·tics** *n.* the study of engraved seals or signet rings [fr. Gk *sphragistikos*]

sphyg·mo·graph (sfígməgræf, sfígməgrɑf) *n.* an instrument for recording the arterial pulse rate on a graph [fr. Gk *sphugmos,* the pulse+GRAPH]

sphyg·mo·ma·nom·e·ter (sfigmoumənɒ́mitər) *n.* an instrument for measuring blood pressure, esp. of the arteries [fr. Gk *sphugmos,* the pulse+MANOMETER]

sphyg·mom·e·ter (sfigmɒ́mitər) *n.* an instrument for measuring the strength of the pulse [fr. Gk *sphugmos,* the pulse+METER]

spi·cate (spáikeit) *adj.* (*bot.*) having spikes ‖ (*biol.,* e.g. of an inflorescence) arranged in the form of a spike or spikes [fr. L. *spicatus,* furnished with spikes]

spic·ca·to (spikɑ́tou) *adj.* (*mus.*) with springy bowing (the bow rebounding off the strings in the achieving of a series of rapid detached notes) [Ital.]

spice (spais) **1.** *n.* any of many vegetable substances, mostly plant parts from which the essential oils have not been extracted, used to impart their strong and aromatic flavors to food, and formerly to preserve foodstuffs from decay (e.g. cinnamon, cloves, nutmeg etc.) ‖ these substances collectively ‖ something which stimulates agreeably, *variety is the spice of life* **2.** *v.t. pres. part.* **spic·ing** *past* and *past part.* **spiced** to flavor by adding spice ‖ to make more interesting, *a description spiced with humor* [fr. O.F. *espicer*]

spice·bush (spáisbuʃ) *n. Lindera bezoin,* fam. *Lauraceae,* an aromatic shrub having yellow flowers and scarlet or yellow berries

Spice Islands *MOLUCCAS

spic·i·ly (spáisili:) *adv.* in a spicy manner

spic·i·ness (spáisi:nis) *n.* the quality of being spicy

spick-and-span (spíkənspǽn) *adj.* cleaned up or turned out to look extremely smart ‖ all fresh and new [fr. older *spick and span new* extension of *spannew* fr. O.N. *spānn,* chip+*nȳr,* new]

spic·u·late (spíkjulit) *adj.* (*biol.*) covered with, having or consisting of spicules ‖ needlelike [fr. L. *spiculatus*]

spic·ule (spíkju:l) *n.* (*zool.*) a minute needlelike body, siliceous or calcareous, found in some invertebrates, e.g. in sponges and radiolarians ‖ (*bot.*) a small spike ‖ any small needlelike formation, esp. of a hard material, e.g. ice [F.]

spic·y (spáisi:) *comp.* **spic·i·er** *superl.* **spic·i·est** *adj.* having the flavor of spices ‖ stimulating the imagination, *spicy adventures* ‖ stimulating erotically, *spicy stories*

spi·der (spáidər) *n.* an animal of the order *Araneida,* subclass *Arachnida,* having eight legs, a large unsegmented abdomen, jaws often equipped with poison glands for paralyzing insect prey, usually four pairs of compound eyes, and spinnerets from which a very fine thread is drawn and woven into a web. The web is used as a nest or, rendered sticky by a secretion, as a trap for flying insects, though some species catch their prey by running and capturing. There are at least 20,000 species ‖ any of several contrivances with long, thin structural parts ‖ a frying pan, originally one supported on three legs ‖ a light phaeton with big, thin wheels [O.E. *spīthra*]

spider hole (*mil.*) a disguised foxhole, esp. one used by a sniper

spider monkey one of many South American monkeys, esp. of genus *Ateles,* with long, slender, flexible limbs, prehensile tail and slender bodies (*MONKEY)

spider web a web made by a spider

spi·der·wort (spáidərwə:rt, spáidərwɔrt) *n.* a member of *Tradescantia,* fam. *Commelinaceae,* cultivated plants with usually blue or violet flowers. The six slender stamens are covered with hairs

spi·der·y (spáidəri:) *adj.* resembling or suggesting the appearance of a spider, esp. its long thin legs, *spidery handwriting* ‖ like a cobweb in formation, *spidery lace* ‖ infested with spiders

spie·gel·ei·sen (ʃpí:gəlaizən) *n.* pig iron containing manganese used in making steel by the Bessemer process [G. fr. *spiegel,* mirror+*eisen,* iron]

spiel (spi:l) **1.** *n.* (*pop.*) a speech or story, usually delivered volubly and with intent to persuade **2.** *v.t.* (*pop.,* with 'off') to recite or utter volubly, usually with intent to persuade ‖ (*pop.,* with 'off') to recite at length (something memorized) ‖ *v.i.* to talk volubly and often extravagantly [G. *spielen,* to play]

Spiel·berg (spí:lbə:rg), Steven (1947-), U.S. film director, known for his adventure and fantasy films. He directed 'Jaws' (1975), 'Close Encounters of the Third Kind' (1977), 'Raiders of the Lost Ark' (1981), 'E.T.: The Extraterrestrial' (1982), 'Indiana Jones and the Temple of Doom' (1984) and 'The Color Purple' (1985)

spig·ot (spígət) *n.* a device which controls the flow of a fluid from or through a pipe or from a container ‖ a peg or plug for the vent of a barrel or cask ‖ the end of one pipe fitting into the socket of another [prob. fr. Prov. *espigot*]

spike (spaik) **1.** *n.* a thin, sharp-pointed piece of metal, rock or other hard material ‖ a sharply pointed rod or shaft set with the point upward, e.g. on a wall, as an obstacle ‖ a pointed nail set (in small quantity) into the soles of climbing boots or running shoes to prevent slipping ‖ a large nail used to fasten a rail to a railroad tie ‖ a single antler of a young deer ‖ an ear of grain, e.g. wheat ‖ (*Br.*) a spindle (filing device) ‖ (*bot.*) an inflorescence with sessile flowers along the stem, the youngest towards the tip **2.** *v. pres. part.* **spik·ing** *past* and *past part.* **spiked** *v.t.* to furnish, fasten or pierce with a spike or with spikes ‖ to render (a gun) useless to an enemy who captures it ‖ to thwart, *to spike someone's plans* ‖ to put an end to (e.g. a rumor) ‖ (*baseball* etc.) to injure (a player) with the spikes of one's shoes ‖ (*pop.*) to add liquor to (a nonalcoholic drink) ‖ *v.i.* to form a spike, or project like one [fr. L. *spica,* ear of grain]

spike·let (spáiklit) *n.* (*bot.*) a small spike, bearing few flowers, esp. in certain sedges and grasses

spike·nard (spáiknɑrd) *n. Nardostachys jatamansi,* fam. *Valerianaceae,* an East Indian plant with fragrant rhizomes ‖ (*hist.*) a costly ointment prepared from these rhizomes ‖ *Aralia racemosa,* an American plant like sarsaparilla [fr. M.L. or L.L. *spica,* ear of grain+*nardi,* gen. of *nardus,* aromatic root]

spik·y (spáiki:) *comp.* **spik·i·er** *superl.* **spik·i·est** *adj.* having a spike or spikes ‖ having the shape of a spike ‖ (*Br.*) being touchy and aggressive

spile (spail) **1.** *n.* a small peg or plug to stop the vent in a barrel or cask ‖ a timber pile driven into the earth as a support ‖ a spout inserted in a sugar maple tree to drain off sap **2.** *v.t. pres. part.* **spil·ing** *past* and *past part.* **spiled** to make a vent in (a cask) ‖ to empty through a spile ‖ to furnish (a barrel etc.) with a spile or spiles ‖ to plug (a hole) with a spile [M.Du.=a splinter]

spill (spil) *n.* a thin wooden strip, or folded strip of paper, for lighting a pipe etc. ‖ a small peg or plug for stopping up holes, a spile ‖ a splinter [var. of SPILE]

spill 1. *v. pres. part.* **spill·ing** *past* and *past part.* **spilled, spilt** (spilt) *v.t.* to lose or waste (a fluid etc.) by causing or permitting it to fall out of or escape from its container ‖ (*naut.*) to empty (a sail) of wind ‖ (*rhet.*) to shed (blood) in violence ‖ (*pop.*) to divulge (information), *he spilled the whole story* ‖ (*pop.*) to cause (someone) to fall from a horse, vehicle etc. ‖ *v.i.* (of a liquid etc.) to fall out of or escape from a container and so be lost or wasted || (of waves, with 'onto') to break gently || to descend as though overflowing || (with 'out') to overflow **to spill the beans** (*pop.*) to divulge information **2.** *n.* a fall from a saddle, vehicle, wall etc. [O.E. *spillan,* to destroy]

spill·back (spílbæk) *n.* traffic condition in which motorists become trapped in an intersection when the light turns red, preventing drivers on cross streets from passing through

spil·li·kin (spílikin) *n.* a jackstraw **spil·li·kins** n. the game of jackstraws [dim. of SPILL *n.*, a splinter]

spill·way (spílwei) *n.* a passage for the overflow of water from a reservoir etc. || the part of a dam over which water flows

spi·lo·site (spáiləsait) *n.* greenish, schistose rock spotted with chlorite [G. *spilosit* fr. Gk *spilos,* spot]

spilt alt. *past* and *past part.* of SPILL

spin (spin) **1.** *v. pres. part.* **spin·ning** *past* and *past part.* **spun** (spʌn) *v.i.* to turn rapidly about an internal axis || (*aeron.*) to dive in a spiral || to engage in the process of drawing out and twisting cotton, silk etc. into a long, continuous thread || (of spiders and silkworms) to secrete a thread or threads || to move very fast || (of ideas, thoughts etc.) to become wildly confused || (*fishing*) to fish using a spinner || *v.t.* to cause to spin, *to spin a top* || to draw out and twist (cotton, silk etc.) into a long, continuous thread || to secrete threads to make (a cocoon, web etc.) || to give a round shape to, by using a lathe etc. || to tell (a story) at great length || (*fishing*) to fish for, using a spinner **to spin a yarn** to tell a rather long involved story, esp. in order to deceive **to spin out** to cause to last or seem to last for a long time, *to spin out a vacation* **2.** *n.* the act of spinning || a rapid rotating movement, *to put spin on a ball,* or such a motion downwards, *the aircraft went into a spin* || (*old-fash.*) a short, rapid journey for pleasure, *to go for a spin on a motorcycle* || a state of wild mental confusion || (*phys.*) the rotation of an electron or other fundamental particle about its own axis, producing a magnetic moment and associated with an angular momentum. Electron spin is mainly responsible for the magnetic properties of matter. In quantum theory an electron has an angular momentum whose space orientation is quantized taking on two values, designated by the spin quantum number (*abbr.* s, where s= ½±, the sign indicating the sense of the motion) (*BOHR MAGNETON) [O.E. *spinnan*]

spi·na bi·fi·da (spáinə báifədə) *n.* (*med.*) an inherited defect in the closure of the vertebral canal allowing the meninges to protrude

spin·ach (spínitʃ) *n.* *Spinacia oleracea,* fam. *Chenopodiaceae,* a herbaceous annual native to S.W. Asia, introduced to Europe after Roman times. Its dark green,crisp leaves are cooked as a vegetable [fr. O.F. *espinage, espinache, spinache*]

spinach beet *Beta vulgaris cicla,* a variety of beet, the leaves of which are eaten as a substitute for spinach

spi·nal (spáin'l) *adj.* in the region of, pertaining to, or like the spinal column, spinal cord or spinal canal [fr. L.L. *spinalis*]

spinal canal the canal, formed by the neural arches of the vertebrae, which encloses and protects the spinal cord

spinal column the series of vertebrae extending from the base of the skull through the median dorsal part of the body to the tail. It serves to protect the spinal cord and acts as a principal supporting structure in virtually all vertebrates. Flexible cartilaginous intervertebral disks allow the vertebrae to move with some degree of freedom with respect to one another. The vertebrae are joined by ligaments allowing for considerable flexibility (*NOTOCHORD)

spinal cord the dorsal cord of neural tissue continuous with the medulla oblongata that lies within the spinal canal in vertebrates. In man there are 31 pairs of nerves along the spinal cord, which acts as a pathway for sensory and motor impulses to and from the brain and as a system of reflex centers often independent of the brain

spin·ar (spínɑr) *n.* (*astron.*) a heavenly body spinning very rapidly

spin·dle (spínd'l) **1.** *n.* a thin cylindrical rod which serves as an axis of rotation or itself rotates || the thin rod in a spinning wheel serving to twist and wind the thread || the rod bearing a bobbin in a spinning machine || a measure of length for yarn (15,120 yds of cotton, 14,400 yds of linen) || (*naut.*) a long vertical iron rod set up on a rock as a navigational aid || (*biol.*) the thin rod-shaped portion of the nucleus formed during the prophase of meiosis and mitosis along which the chromosomes are distributed to daughter nuclei || a shaft in a lathe, capstan etc. || the fixed spike on a phonograph turntable over which the record fits || (*Am.=Br.* spike) a filing device consisting of a mounted nail or hook on which receipts, bills etc. are impaled **2.** *v.i. pres. part.* **spin·dling** *past* and *past part.* **spin·dled** (esp. of a plant which develops a stem rather than a flower or fruit) to grow long and thin || *v.t.* to impale on a spindle || to give the form of a spindle to [O.E. *spinel*]

spin·dle-leg·ged (spínd'llegid, spínd'llegd) *adj.* having thin or scrawny legs

spin·dle·legs (spínd'llegz) *n.* someone who has long scrawny legs || (*pl.*) long thin legs

spin·dle·shanks (spínd'lʃæŋks) *n.* (of a person or his legs) spindlelegs

spindle tree *Euonymus europaeus,* fam. *Celastraceae,* a small tree or shrub whose hard wood is used for skewers etc. The inconspicuous green flowers produce red four-valved capsules, enclosing seeds with orange arils

spin·dling (spíndliŋ) *adj.* spindly

spin·dly (spíndli:) *comp.* **spin·dli·er** *superl.* **spin·dli·est** *adj.* very long and thin, esp. (in a person) suggesting weakness or scrawniness from overgrowth

spin·drift (spíndrift) *n.* fine spray blown from the surface of water [alt. fr. *spoondrift,* etym. doubtful]

spine (spain) *n.* the spinal column || (*bot.*) a sharp-pointed outgrowth, e.g. from the stem or leaf of a thistle || (*zool.*) a similar protective outgrowth, e.g. one of the quills of a porcupine || (*anat.*) any of the thin, pointed processes of various bones || a ridge of land, rock etc. resembling a backbone || (*printing*) the back of a bound book, on which title and author are usually given **spined** *adj.* having a spine or spines [fr. O.F. *espine* or L. *spina,* thorn]

spi·nel (spinél) *n.* any one of a group of minerals of composition $MO{\cdot}M^{1}{}_{2}O_{3}$ where M is a divalent metal, M^{1} a trivalent metal [F. *spinelle*]

spine·less (spáinlis) *adj.* invertebrate || having no spines or thorns || without determination and strength of character

spi·nes·cent (spainésənt) *adj.* (*bot.*) tending to be spinous [fr. L. *spinescens* (*spinescentis*) fr. *spinescere,* to grow thorny]

spin·et (spínit) *n.* a small stringed musical instrument resembling a harpsichord || a small electronic organ || an upright piano of reduced dimensions, esp. for use in limited space [Ital. *spinetta* prob. after Giovanni *Spinetti,* the 16th-c. inventor]

spin·na·ker (spínəkər) *n.* (*naut.*) a large triangular sail, carried by a yacht on a long, light pole, on the side opposite the mainsail. It is used when running before the wind [etym. doubtful]

spin·ner (spínər) *n.* a person or machine which spins || a manufacturer engaged in spinning || (*fishing*) a bright metal vane which spins as the line is drawn through the water, used as a lure || (*fishing*) a kind of fly used in trout fishing || (*games*) a ball made to spin so that it rebounds obliquely when it hits the ground || (*football*) a feint, in which the ball carrier spins around when about to play the ball || a nightjar || (*surfing*) a stunt of making a complete turn while the board continues its forward movement

spin·ner·et (spinərét) *n.* a process or organ found on the abdomen of the larvae of certain silk-producing insects and on the abdomen of a spider. From this organ are exuded the secretions of the silk glands, which usually fuse to form a single thread used e.g. for making a web or cocoon [dim. of SPINNER]

spin·ney (spíni:) *n.* (*Br.*) a small group of trees with undergrowth [fr. O.F. *espinei,* a place full of thorns]

spin·ning (spíniŋ) *n.* the process of making thread or yarn from natural or man-made fibers || (in spiders and certain silk-producing insect larvae) the process of exuding a secretion through the spinnerets which hardens into a thread

spinning jenny a power-driven machine, fitted with many spindles, invented (1764) by James Hargreaves

spinning wheel a machine for domestic spinning fitted with a single spindle driven by a wheel worked by the hand or foot

spin-off (spínɔf, spínɒf) *n.* things derived as useful by-products from some larger and more or less unrelated whole, activity etc., *spin-off from space research includes many medical inventions* || an example of such derivations || divestment of a subsidiary company by a parent corporation

Spi·no·la (spi:nɔ́lɑ), Ambrosio, marquis of (1569-1630), Italian general. He distinguished himself in the service of Spain in capturing Ostend (1604) and in the Thirty Years' War

spi·nose (spáinous) *adj.* spinous (covered with spines)

spi·nous (spáinəs) *adj.* covered with or full of spines or thorns || having the form of a spine or thorn [fr. L. *spinosus*]

spin·out (spínaut) *n.* **1.** uncontrolled movement of an automobile, esp. at a turn, causing it to run off the highway **2.** a spin in a complete circle

Spi·no·za (spinóuzə), Baruch (1632-77), Dutch philosopher. In his 'Tractatus theologico-politicus' (1670) he develops a religious rationalism. In his 'Ethics' (1677), written in a strictly mathematical form, he expounds a theory of human salvation as knowledge of God, and also analyzes the human soul. His system is a pantheistic doctrine, according to which God is a substance constituted by an infinity of attributes, of which we know only two: thought and extension. The world is the sum of modes of these two attributes. Man is a collection of modes of thought and extension. The distinction between God and the created world can be reduced to a point of view ('Deus sive Natura'). He was a firm believer in political democracy as a reflection of reason

spin resonance *MAGNETIC RESONANCE

spin-scan (spínskæn) *n.* an infrared radiometer that provides a picture of cloud cover, day or night

spin·ster (spínstər) *n.* an unmarried woman || an old maid **spín·ster·hood** *n.* [fr. SPIN V.]

spin·to (spí:ntou) *n.* (usu. ital.) the capacity to both sing and act—said of an opera singer — **spinto** *adj.*

spi·nule (spáinju:l) *n.* a very small spine [fr. L. *spinula*]

spi·nu·lose (spáinjulous) *adj.* having or covered with spinules || shaped like a spinule [fr. Mod. L. *spinulosus*]

spin wave (*nuclear phys.*) a wave caused by change in direction of the spin of electrons *Cf* MAGNON

spin·y (spáini:) *comp.* **spin·i·er** *superl.* **spin·i·est** *adj.* covered with spines || shaped like a spine or thorn || difficult to overcome, troublesome, perplexing, *a spiny problem*

spiny anteater the echidna

spi·ra·cle (spáirək'l) *n.* (*zool.*) a breathing orifice, e.g. the lateral branchial opening in tadpoles or blowhole in cetaceans || a vent for lava etc. **spi·rac·u·lar** (spairǽkjulər) *adj.* having one or more spiracles [fr. L. *spiraculum,* breath]

spiraea *SPIREA

spi·ral (spáirəl) **1.** *adj.* of a curve which continuously changes its plane, and sometimes its curvature, in relation to a fixed axis || curving in this way, *a spiral staircase* || of a curve in a fixed plane which changes its curvature as it steadily increases or diminishes its distance from a fixed central point **2.** *n.* a curve of either of these forms || something having either of these forms || a tendency to decrease or esp. increase steadily, *the wage spiral* || a single coil or turn in something spiral || a descent or an ascent in a spiral path || (*football*) a kick or pass which makes the ball rotate on its long axis **3.** *v. pres. part.* **spi·ral·ing,** esp. *Br.* **spi·ral·ling** *past* and *past part.* **spi·raled,** esp. *Br.*, **spi·ralled** *v.i.* to move, esp. to ascend or descend, in a spiral || *v.i.* to cause to move or evolve in a spiral, *inflation spiraled prices* [fr. M.L. *spiralis*]

spiral galaxy a galaxy that can be seen, when viewed through a telescope, to possess a central nucleus with curved, radiating arms. The nucleus sometimes possesses a barred structure from which the arms extend

spiral nebula a spiral galaxy

spi·rant (spáirənt) *n.* (*phon.*) a consonantal sound which is articulated with the oral cavity partly closed and is not a stop, i.e. it can be prolonged (e.g. f, v, s, z) [L. *spirans* (*spirantis*) fr. *spirare,* to breathe]

spire (spáiər) *n.* (*archit.*) a tall thin structure

CONCISE PRONUNCIATION KEY: **(a)** æ, *c*a*t*; ɑ, *c*a*r*; ɔ *f*aw*n*; ei, *sn*a*ke*. **(e)** e, *h*e*n*; i:, *sh*ee*p*; iə, *d*ee*r*; ɛə, *b*ea*r*. **(i)** i, *f*i*sh*; ai, *t*i*ger*; ə:, *b*i*rd*. **(o)** o, *o*x; au, *c*ow; ou, *g*oa*t*; u, *p*oo*r*; ɔi, *r*oy*al*. **(u)** ʌ, *d*u*ck*; u, *b*u*ll*; u:, *g*oo*se*; ə, *bac*i*llus*; ju:, *c*u*be*. x, *lo*ch; θ, *th*ink; ð, *bo*th*er*; z, *Z*en; ʒ, *corsa*ge; dʒ, *sava*ge; ŋ, *orangutan*g; j, *y*ak; ʃ, *fi*sh; tʃ, *fe*tch; 'l, *rabb*le; 'n, *redd*en. Complete pronunciation key appears inside front cover.

surmounting a tower, esp. of a church, and being of conical or pyramidal form and of very small diameter in relation to its length || anything compared with this, esp. with regard to its tip only, *spires of young wheat* [O.E. *spīr*]

spire *n.* a spiral || a single turn in a coil || (*zool.*) the upper part of a spiral shell [F. fr. L. fr. Gk]

spi·re·a, spi·rae·a (spairíːə) *n.* a member of *Spiraea,* fam. *Rosaceae,* a genus of shrubs found in temperate regions bearing small pink or white flowers, e.g. the meadowsweet [L. fr. Gk *speiraia,* meadowsweet]

spi·ril·lum (spairíləm) *pl.* **spi·ril·la** (spairílə) *n.* a member of *Spirillum,* a genus of bacteria having the form of a spiral thread, sometimes with flagella || any of various other microorganisms with a similar form [Mod. L. dim. of *spira,* a coil]

spir·it (spírit) *n.* the intelligent or immaterial part of man as distinguished from the body || the animating or vital principle in living things || the moral nature of a man || a disembodied soul || a supernatural being, usually regarded as invisible but as having the power to become visible at will || a specified mental or emotional attitude characterizing words, actions, opinions etc., *she said it in a forgiving spirit* || a person animated by a specified quality, *he was one of the braver spirits* || the emotional attitude or frame of mind characteristic of a group of people, *team spirit,* or of people at a particular time, *the spirit of the age* || the essential character of something, *he considered the spirit of the law as more important than the letter of the law* || cheerful or assertive liveliness, *full of spirit* || (often *pl.*) mood or temperamental state, *in high spirits, in poor spirits* || (esp. *pl.*) liquor of high alcoholic content || (esp. *pl.*) a volatile distillate || (*pharm.*) the alcoholic solution of a volatile ingredient **the Spirit,** the Holy Ghost **2.** *adj.* of spirits or spiritualism, *the spirit world* || (of lamps, engines etc.) using alcohol as a fuel **3.** *v.t.* (with 'off', 'away') to cause (something) to be removed unseen, with mysterious rapidity **spir·it·ed** *adj.* lively, *a spirited argument* || showing creative energy, *spirited brushwork* || (of a horse) keen, eager, full of energy and courage || having a strong, assertive personality || (in hyphenated compounds) having a specified character, quality etc., *public-spirited* [A.F. or fr. L. *spiritus,* breath]

spir·it·ism (spíritizəm) *n.* spiritualism || the belief that natural objects have indwelling spirits **spír·it·ist** *n.*

spir·it·less (spíritlis) *adj.* having little or no animation || lacking boldness and resolution

spirit level a short glass tube of alcohol containing a bubble, usually enclosed in a wooden or metal casing, used in testing whether a surface is horizontal. The bubble rests midway in the tube if the surface is accurately horizontal (cf. PLUMB LINE)

spi·ri·to·so (spiritóusou) *adj.* (*mus.*) played, sung etc. with animation [Ital.]

spirit rapping alleged communication with spirits of the dead by the interpretation of rapping noises allegedly made by them in answer to questions

spirits of salt (commercial name of) hydrochloric acid

spirits of wine alcohol obtained by distilling wine

spir·it·u·al (spíritʃuːəl) **1.** *adj.* of, relating to, or concerned with the soul or spirit (opp. TEMPORAL) || relating to religious or sacred matters, *spiritual counsel* || full of spirituality || having a relationship based on sympathy of thought or feeling, *she considered him as her spiritual father* || (*Br.*) of the archbishops and bishops with seats in the House of Lords, *the Lords spiritual* **2.** *n.* a religious song, asserting a strong simple faith, sung originally by blacks of the Southern U.S.A. Spirituals are characterized by strong rhythm and vivid narrative [O.F. *spirituel* or fr. L. *spiritualis*]

spiritual home the place where a person feels the fullest sympathy with his surroundings

spir·it·u·al·ism (spíritʃuːəlizəm) *n.* the doctrine that the spirit, surviving after the death of the body, can communicate with persons still living, esp. through the agency of a medium || spiritualistic practices || (*philos.*) the doctrine that spirit exists independently of matter (opp. MATERIALISM) || spiritual quality **spír·it·u·al·ist** *n.* a person who believes in or practices spiritualism || a person who believes in philosophical spiritualism

spir·it·u·al·i·ty (spiritʃuːǽlitiː) *pl.* **spir·it·u·al·i·ties** *n.* attachment to all that concerns the life of the soul || the quality of being spiritual || (*eccles. law*) something which belongs to the Church or to a priest of the Church [O.F. *spiritualite*]

spir·it·u·al·i·za·tion (spiritʃuːəlizéiʃən) *n.* a spiritualizing or being spiritualized

spir·it·u·al·ize (spíritʃuːəlaiz) *pres. part.* **spir·it·u·al·iz·ing** *past* and *past part.* **spir·it·u·al·ized** *v.t.* to make spiritual || to give a spiritual meaning to

spir·it·u·ous (spíritʃuːəs) *adj.* containing alcohol derived from distillation [fr. L. *spiritus,* spirit]

spir·i·tus as·per (spíritəsǽspər) (*Gk gram.*) rough breathing [L.]

spir·i·tus le·nis (spíritəslíːnəs, spíritəsléinəs) (*Gk gram.*) smooth breathing

spi·ro·chete, spi·ro·chaete (spáirəkiːt) *n.* a bacterium of the order *Spirochaetales.* Many are important pathogenic species (causing e.g. syphilis and relapsing fever). Spirochetes are slender spiral organisms, many of which are normally aquatic [fr. L. *spira,* coil+Gk *chaitē,* long, flowing hair]

spi·ro·gy·ra (spairədʒáirə) *n.* any plant of *Spirogyra,* fam. *Zygnemataceae,* a genus of filamentous green freshwater algae, with spiral chloroplasts containing large starch-storage bodies [Mod. L. fr. Gk *speira,* coil+*guros,* ring]

spi·ro·no·lac·tone [$C_{21}H_{32}O_4S$] (spairounoulǽktoun) *n.* (*pharm.*) steroid diuretic drug that counteracts sodium, retaining action of aldosterone; marketed as Aldactazide and Aldactone

spirt *SPURT

spit (spit) **1.** *v. pres. part.* **spit·ting** *past* and *past part.* **spit, spat** (spæt) *v.t.* to get rid of (saliva etc.) from the mouth by a forceful muscular action of the tongue and lips || to emit or eject as though spitting, *the guns spat fire* || to express anger, scorn, hatred or malice by uttering (words) vehemently and explosively and sometimes with a sound imitative of the action of spitting || *v.i* to eject saliva from the mouth || to do this as a means of expressing anger, scorn, hatred or malice || to make sounds imitative of this or to imitate this action, *the fire was spitting* || (of angry or threatened cats etc.) to make a hissing sound || (esp. *Br.*) to rain in scattered, infrequent drops || (of a pen point) to catch in the paper and throw off spatters of ink **to spit it out** to divulge some piece of information that one has been slow to give **2.** *n.* saliva || the act or an instance of spitting || the frothy secretion of some insects || (*pop.,* esp. in **spit and image**) exact physical resemblance of somebody else, *he's the spit and image of his grandfather at that age* [O.E. *spittan*]

spit 1. *n.* a metal skewer on which meat to be roasted is impaled and slowly turned over an open fire, or an electric device based on this principle || a thin projection of land into the sea, lake or river || a shoal or reef extending from the shore **2.** *v.t. pres. part.* **spit·ting** *past* and *past part.* **spit·ted** to fix (meat) on a spit [O.E. *spitu*]

spit *n.* (*Br.*) the depth of the blade of a spade || (*Br.*) the quantity of earth lifted by a spade [M.Du., M.L.G.]

spit and polish extreme cleanliness and order || (*mil.*) irksome preparation for ceremonial parades

spit·ball (spítbɔl) *n.* a missile consisting of a piece of moist paper crushed into a ball || (*baseball, hist.*) a pitch in which the ball is made to curve after being moistened on one side

spitch·cock (spítʃkɒk) **1.** *v.t.* to split and broil, fry or grill (an eel) **2.** *n.* an eel split and cooked in one of these ways [etym. doubtful]

spite (spait) **1.** *n.* animosity towards a person which results in a desire to do him petty injury || a spiteful feeling of resentment, a grudge, *a spite against intellectuals* **in spite of,** regardless of, notwithstanding, *he did it in spite of our efforts to stop him* **2.** *v.t. pres. part.* **spit·ing** *past* and *past part.* **spit·ed** to injure out of spite, *he did it to spite me* **to cut off one's nose to spite one's face** to injure one's own interests knowingly in seeking to injure another's **spíte·ful** *adj.* [fr. DESPITE]

spit·fire (spítfaiər) *n.* someone, esp. a woman or girl, very quick to become angry

Spit·head (spíthéd) the eastern entrance (4-5 miles wide) of the Solent, England, an anchorage used for naval displays

Spits·ber·gen (spítsbərːgən) *SVALBARD

spit·ting (spítiŋ) *n.* (*mil.*) in air intercept, a code meaning *I am about to lay, or am laying, sonobuoys. I may be out of radio contact for a few minutes.* If transmitted from a submarine, it indicates that the submarine has launched a sonobuoy

spitting image someone who exactly resembles someone else addressed or referred to (*SPIT *n.*)

spit·tle (spít'l) *n.* saliva, esp. when spit out || the frothy secretion of some insects [O.E. *spittan*]

spit·toon (spitúːn) *n.* a round, flat vessel of earthenware, brass etc. on the floor to receive spit

spitz (spits) *n.* a dog of a medium-sized breed with a pointed muzzle and pointed ears and very thick double coat, usually white, and having the tail curved back over the body || a pomeranian || a chow chow || a samoyed [G. *spitz,* pointed]

spitz dog a spitz

spiv (spiv) *n.* (*Br.*) a man who lives by trading in ways of doubtful honesty, does no hard work, and dresses flashily [etym. doubtful]

splash (splæʃ) **1.** *v.t.* to cause to receive the impact of drops of liquid and so be made wet or stained, *a car splashed her with mud as it passed* || to cause (liquid) to move through the air in separate drops, *the car splashed mud on his clothes* || to cause (something) to agitate and scatter a liquid, *to splash one's toes in the water* || to make (one's way) by splashing thus || to apply (paint etc.) in a careless or lavish way || to decorate (e.g. a canvas) thus || to drive (logs) by releasing water from a dam || to make a display of (money, news) || *v.i.* to agitate a liquid and scatter it or cause it to fly around in drops || (of a liquid) to be suddenly and violently thrown up or off in drops || to move through or into a liquid so that it is thrown around in this way, *we splashed through the waves* **2.** *n.* the act or sound of splashing || the liquid which is splashed || a spot made by splashing || a bright patch of color || (*Br.*) a small quantity of soda water squirted from a siphon || the act of driving logs by releasing water from a dam || **to make a splash** to make an ostentatious display [etym. doubtful]

splash·board (splǽʃbɔrd, splǽʃbourd) *n.* a fender || a board or panel behind a sink to receive the splashes made in the sink || a device for closing a dam

splash·down (splǽʃdaun) *n.* the landing of a spacecraft or missile on a body of water || the moment of this landing

splashed *n.* (*mil.*) in air intercept, a code meaning *Enemy aircraft shot down* (followed by number and type)

splash·y (splǽʃiː) *comp.* **splash·i·er** *superl.* **splash·i·est** *adj.* causing splashes || very showy, *a splashy front page* || marked by splashes of color

splat (splæt) *n.* a single, broad, flat piece of wood forming the central upright of a chair back, e.g. in a Queen Anne dining chair || a piece of wood performing the same function placed horizontally [etym. doubtful]

splat·ter (splǽtər) **1.** *v.t.* to spatter || *v.i.* to become spattered **2.** *n.* a spatter [perh. fr. SPLASH+SPATTER]

splay (splei) **1.** *n.* (*archit.*) a sloping surface or bevel, e.g. at the side of a lancet window || a spreading **2.** *adj.* turned outwards, broad and flat, *splay feet* **3.** *v.t.* to spread, *to splay one's elbows* || to bevel, set oblique || *v.i.* to be or become splayed [fr. DISPLAY]

splay·foot (spléifut) *pl.* **splay·feet** (spléifiːt) *n.* a flattened foot turned outwards **spláy·fóot·ed** *adj.*

spleen (spliːn) *n.* a soft fleshy organ in the upper left abdomen, chiefly concerned with the formation and purification of blood. It becomes enlarged and hard in certain blood diseases such as malaria, kala-azar and leukemia || (*old-fash.*) ill temper, *a fit of spleen* **spléen·ful** *adj.* [fr. O.F. *esplen* or L. *splen* fr. Gk]

spleen·wort (splíːnwəːrt, splíːnwɔrt) *n.* a fern of the genus *Asplenium* || a fern of the genus *Athyrium*

splen·dent (spléndənt) *adj.* (*mineral.*) having a bright metallic luster [fr. L. *splendens* (*splendentis*) fr. *splendere,* to shine]

splen·did (spléndid) *adj.* magnificent, gorgeous, sumptuous, *splendid palaces* || exciting admiration by its fine or noble quality, *a splendid performance* [fr. L. *splendidus* fr. *splendere,* to be bright]

splen·dor, *Br.* **splen·dour** (spléndər) *n.* the quality of being splendid ‖ great brilliance ‖ display of wealth or magnificence **the sun in splendor** (*heraldry*) a sun represented as having a human face and emitting golden rays [fr. A.F. *esplendour, splendor* or fr. L. *splendor*]

sple·net·ic (splinétik) **1.** *adj.* (*med.*) of or relating to the spleen ‖ apt to be peevishly or morosely ill-tempered **2.** *n.* a person apt to be peevishly or morosely ill-tempered **sple·nét·i·cal·ly** *adv.* [fr. L.L. *spleneticus*]

splen·ic (splénik, splí:nik) *adj.* (*med.*) splenetic [fr. L. *splenicus* fr. Gk]

splice (splais) **1.** *v.t. pres. part.* **splic·ing** *past* and *past part.* **spliced** to join together (two rope ends) by first unraveling both a little way and then twisting the strands of each around those of the other to form one continuous length ‖ to unite two parts of the same rope (forming a loop) by interweaving the partially unraveled strands of one end into those of another part ‖ to join together the ends of (two pieces of wood) by thinning them, making them overlap and fastening the overlaps together ‖ to join (film, tape etc.) at the ends ‖ to make (the handle of a tennis racket etc.) a better shock absorber by laminating it with layers treated in this way **to get spliced** (*pop.*) to get married **to splice the main brace** (*naut.*) to serve out an extra ration of rum **2.** *n.* a join made by splicing ‖ the part of a cricket-bat handle which fits into the blade [fr. M.Du. *splissen*]

spline (splain) **1.** *n.* a thin, narrow strip of wood, plastic or metal ‖ a flexible lath, or strip of rubber, used by draftsmen to trace arcs of large radius ‖ (*mech.*) a rectangular key fitting permanently into slots in two parts of a mechanism, e.g. a shaft and wheel, ensuring that these revolve together and giving maximum strength ‖ either of these slots **2.** *v.t. pres. part.* **splin·ing** *past* and *past part.* **splined** to fit with a spline ‖ to provide with a groove for a spline [perh. rel. to SPLINTER]

splint (splint) **1.** *n.* a strip of wood etc. which, bound to a limb, keeps broken bones from moving apart ‖ a strip of wood used in the same way in grafting fruit trees etc. ‖ a thin flexible strip of wood or cane woven with others to make a chair seat, basket etc. ‖ (esp. of a horse) a morbid bony growth on the splint bone ‖ (*armor*) one of the flexibly overlapping metallic plates for protecting esp. the elbows **2.** *v.t.* to secure with a splint [M.Du. *splinte*]

splint bone one of two small metacarpal bones in the foreleg of a horse (and related animals), lying behind and in close contact with the cannon bone or shank

splin·ter (splíntər) **1.** *n.* a thin, sharp piece of wood etc. broken or split off, esp. as the result of violent impact **2.** *v.i.* to break off in thin, sharp pieces, esp. as the result of violent impact ‖ *v.t.* to break or split into thin, sharp pieces, esp. by violent impact **3.** *adj.* (of a political or religious group) broken off from and independent of a larger or primary organization, esp. because of violent disagreement [M.Du.]

splin·ter·y (splíntəri:) *adj.* of or like a splinter

Split (spli:t) a port (pop. 193,600) on the Dalmatian coast, Croatia, Yugoslavia. It dates from the 7th c. and is built within the ruined 4th-c. palace of Diocletian, incorporating its walls, gates, mausoleum and temples. Industries: shipbuilding, plastics, building materials, tourism, fishing

split (split) **1.** *v. pres. part.* **split·ting** *past* and *past part.* **split** *v.t.* to divide, separate, cleave, burst or force apart the layers of (a solid), esp. along its grain or length and esp. with force or violence, *the lightning split the tree* ‖ to divide into parts, *they split the profit between them* ‖ to cause division in (a group of people) so that those holding one view are opposed to those holding another, *the abdication split the country* ‖ (*gram.*) to separate the two parts of (an infinitive) by an adverb, as in 'to carelessly write' ‖ (*chem.*) to decompose (a compound) ‖ (*phys.*) to break (a molecule) into atoms ‖ (*phys.*) to produce nuclear fission in (an atom) **to split one's vote** (or **ticket**) to vote for candidates of more than one party at the same election ‖ *v.i.* to become divided, separated, cleft or forced apart, esp. along a grain or seam, or lengthwise ‖ to separate into groups holding opposing views ‖ to part, break asunder ‖ (*Br., pop.*) to divulge information (sometimes unintentionally) **2.** *n.* the act or result of splitting ‖ a separation into groups holding different views ‖ something that has been split, e.g. a split osier used in basket-making or a single thickness of split leather ‖ (*Br.*) a bun opened up to be filled with jam and cream ‖ a dessert made of sliced fruit, ice cream and syrup with nuts added, *a banana split* ‖ (also *pl.*) the acrobatic feat of sitting down with the legs straight and in the same line either right and left of the body or in front and behind ‖ (*bowling*) an arrangement of the pins after the first bowl, esp. one that makes a spare almost impossible ‖ a small bottle of some drink, usually about half the normal size for such a drink **3.** *adj.* that has undergone the process of splitting ‖ divided into layers ‖ separated ‖ torn by bursting ‖ (of a stock exchange quotation) given in sixteenths, not in eighths [M.Du. *splitten*]

split-brain (splitbréin) *n.* (*neuropsychology*) concept of separation of right and left hemispheres of the brain, each functioning independently, in which the left is dominant in language and verbal recognition, the right in spatial recognition and motor activity

split end (*football*) an end position at some distance from an interior linesman *also* spread end

split-lev·el (splítlévəl) **1.** *adj.* of a building so constructed that the floor level of one part is roughly midway between those of adjoining parts **2.** *n.* a house constructed in this way

split personality a schizophrenic condition in which a person appears to be inhabited by two internally consistent but irreconcilable characters

split pin a securing pin split at one end for some distance along its length so that it may be spread open to keep it in position after insertion

split ring a metal ring consisting of two complete turns of a spiral pressed flat together. A metal loop (esp. of a key) can be forced between them and worked around till the ring and loop are freely but securely linked

split screen (*cinematography*) the presentation of two scenes on the screen at the same time, each having a different portion of the screen

split second an almost imperceptible moment of time

split·ting (splítiŋ) *adj.* that splits ‖ (of pain) very severe, causing one to feel as though being split, a *splitting headache* ‖ very funny, producing violent laughter

split vertical photography the process of taking photographs simultaneously by two cameras mounted at an angle from the vertical, one tilted to the left and one to the right, to obtain a small side overlap —**split cameras** *n. pl.* an assembly of two cameras disposed at a fixed overlapping angle relative to each other *Cf* FAN CAMERA

splodge (splɒdʒ) (*Br.*) **1.** *n.* a splotch of some thick heavy material, e.g. mud, which is not usually absorbed **2.** *v.t. pres. part.* **splodg·ing** *past* and *past part.* **splodged** to mark with a splodge or splodges **splódg·y** *comp.* **splodg·i·er** *superl.* **splodg·i·est** *adj.* [imit.]

splotch (splɒtʃ) **1.** *n.* an irregular, usually unintentional, displeasing patch of paint, stain etc. **2.** *v.t.* to mark with a splotch or splotches **splótch·y** *comp.* **splotch·i·er** *superl.* **splotch·i·est** *adj.* marked with such patches [imit.]

splurge (splə:rdʒ) **1.** *n.* (*pop.*) a showy effect, esp. as the result of lavish spending **2.** *v.i. pres. part.* **splurg·ing** *past* and *past part.* **splurged** to make a splurge [imit.]

splut·ter (splʌ́tər) **1.** *v.i.* to speak rapidly with bad articulation, sometimes spitting particles of saliva while doing so ‖ (e.g. of a car engine) to make a sound resembling this manner of speaking ‖ to splash, spatter, *the rain spluttered against the window* ‖ *v.t.* to express in this way, *he spluttered a hasty apology* ‖ to cause to spatter **2.** *n.* the sound of spluttering [imit.]

Spock (spɒk), Benjamin (1903-), U.S. pediatrician and a leader of the anti-war movement during the Vietnam War

Spode (spoud), Josiah (1754-1827), English potter. In 1799 he first produced the fine bone china which bears his name

spod·u·mene (spɒ́dʒumi:n, spɒ́djumi:n) *n.* (*mineral.*) $LiAlSi_2O_6$, a monoclinic aluminum and lithium silicate occurring in various colors, often in very large crystals, e.g. kunzite [F. ult. fr. Gk *spodousthai*, to be burned to ashes]

spoil (spɔil) *pres. part.* **spoil·ing** *past* and *past part.* **spoiled, spoilt** (spɔilt) *v.t.* to take away the pleasure from, *quarreling spoiled the picnic* ‖ to fail to make as good as possible, *she spoiled the curtains by skimping the material* ‖ to damage or ruin, *spilled ink spoiled the cloth* ‖ to impair, detract from, *her ridiculous gestures spoiled her singing* ‖ to injure (esp. a child or domestic animal) with respect to character during the formative period by overindulgence or too much leniency ‖ to pamper and make much of ‖ *v.i.* to become less good, valuable, enjoyable or useful ‖ to become unfit for use ‖ (*pop.*) to be eager for aggressive action, *spoiling for a fight* [fr. O.F. *espoillier*]

spoil *n.* (esp. *pl.*) goods taken from a defeated enemy, *spoils of war* ‖ goods acquired by theft ‖ (*pl.*) special privileges and rewards resulting from success in winning political office ‖ waste material resulting from mining etc. [fr. O.F. *espoille*]

spoil·age (spɔ́ilidʒ) *n.* unavoidable waste, e.g. of raw material in the initial stage of using a machine ‖ waste through decay, e.g. of fruit and vegetables ‖ goods spoiled ‖ the process of decay in foods through bacteria or fungi

spoil·er (spɔ́ilə:r) *n.* **1.** (*politics*) a candidate who enters a race principally for the purpose of splitting the votes of the opposition **2.** (*automobile*) a device on a motor vehicle to deflect air upward in order to provide additional stability at high speeds

spoils·man (spɔ́ilzmən) *pl.* **spoils·men** (spɔ́ilzmən) *n.* a politician actuated by desire to share in the spoils

spoil·sport (spɔ́ilspɔrt spɔ́ilspourt) *n.* someone who willfully prevents others from having fun

spoils system the system whereby offices, incomes and privileges once belonging to a defeated party are considered to be rightly distributed among members of the political party come to power

spoilt alt. *past* and *past part.* of SPOIL

Spo·kane (spoukǽn) an agricultural market town (pop. 171,300) in E. Washington: wood industries, flour mills, metallurgy, meat packing

spoke (spouk) **1.** *n.* a radial rod transmitting stress from the rim to the hub of a wheel ‖ something resembling this ‖ a rung of a ladder ‖ (*naut.*) a radial handle of a steering wheel **2.** *v.t. pres. part.* **spok·ing** *past* and *past part.* **spoked** to furnish with spokes **to put a spoke in someone's wheel** to prevent the success of his plan [O.E. *spāca*]

spoke *past* of SPEAK

spo·ken (spóukən) *past part.* of SPEAK ‖ *adj.* oral as opposed to written ‖ (in compounds) having a specified kind of voice or manner of speaking, *softspoken, plainspoken*

spoke·shave (spóukʃeiv) *n.* a plane with a handle on each side of a small blade, drawn or pushed along wood to give a curved surface

spokes·per·son (spóukspə:rsən) *n.* one who speaks for another person, a group, or a cause, esp. for public consumption

spokes·wom·an (spóukswumən) *pl.* **spokes·wom·en** (spóukswimən) *n.* a female spokesman

spok·ing (spóukiŋ) *n.* (*radar*) periodic flashes on a radial display for abnormal periods due to radar malfunction, sometimes caused by mutual interference

Spo·le·to (spɔlétɔ) a walled town (pop. 37,396) in Umbria, Italy: Roman basilica, arch, theaters, Romanesque cathedral (12th c., restored 15th and 17th cc.)

spo·li·a·tion (spouli:éiʃən) *n.* the seizing of goods belonging to others, esp. the goods of neutrals in wartime ‖ (*law*) the alteration or mutilation of a document to prevent its use in evidence ‖ (*eccles.*) the taking of the emoluments of a benefice without legal entitlement to do so [fr. L. *spoliatio* (*spoliationis*)]

spon·da·ic (spɒndéiik) *adj.* of or characterized by a spondee ‖ constituting a spondee [fr. F. *spondaïque* or L. *spondaicus*]

spon·dee (spɒ́ndi:) *n.* a metrical foot consisting of two long or stressed syllables [F. *spondée* or fr. L. *spondeus* fr. Gk]

spon·dy·li·tis (spɒnd'láitis) *n.* inflammation of a vertebra or vertebrae [fr. Gk *spondulos*, a vertebra]

sponge (spʌndʒ) **1.** *n.* a parazoan and member of the phylum *Porifera*. Sponges vary greatly in shape, size and color and live permanently attached (e.g. to a rock) either alone or in colonies. They consist of two layers of cells surrounding a central cavity and have skeletons of a calcareous or siliceous substance or of spongin. These skeletons are traversed by a system of canals through which food-bearing water is circulated by flagellated cells lining the canal walls. Sponges reproduce either sexually or asexually ‖ the macerated, highly porous, elastic, spongin skeleton of a sponge of genera *Spongia* or *Hippospongia,* used commercially, esp. for its ability to absorb fluids and yield them again on pressure ‖ (without article) the material of which this is composed ‖ a synthetic substitute for this material ‖ (*Br.*) a sponge cake or sponge pudding ‖ a sterile cotton gauze used for sponging and wiping in surgical operations ‖ raised bread dough ‖ (*pop.*) a heavy drinker ‖ someone who tries to live parasitically ‖ a wash or rubdown with a sponge **to throw up** (or **in**) **the sponge** to admit defeat or failure **2.** *v. pres. part.* **spong·ing** *past* and *past part.* **sponged** *v.t.* to moisten, clean or wipe with a wet sponge ‖ (with 'out') to efface with, or as if with, a sponge ‖ (with 'up') to absorb with, or as if with, a sponge ‖ (*pop.*) to get without cost by imposing oneself on someone, *to sponge a meal* ‖ *v.i.* (with 'on') to prey on other people's good nature parasitically, *he is always sponging on her for meals* ‖ to harvest sponges [O.E. *sponge, spunge* fr. L. fr. G]

sponge bag (*Br.*) a waterproof bag used to carry toilet accessories, esp. when one is traveling

sponge cake a light, sweet cake, made without fat, and spongy in texture, in which eggs are the leavening agent

sponge iron (*metallurgy*) high-grade ore, usu. from scrap, necessary for use with electric arc furnace

sponge pudding a pudding made of sponge-cake mixture

spong·er (spʌ́ndʒər) *n.* a person who harvests sponges or a boat used for this ‖ someone who lives or tries to live parasitically

sponge rubber rubber given a very porous structure and used as a soft but elastic cushioning material

sponges *n.* temporary employees of a nuclear energy plant hired especially to perform a small task where exposure to radiation is involved *also* steam generator jumpers, jumpers

sponge·ware (spʌ́ndʒwɛər) *n.* ceramics produced by applying glaze with a sponge to create a mottled surface, common in early American ware

spon·gin (spʌ́ndʒin) *n.* the scleroprotein which chiefly forms the skeleton of commercial sponges

spong·i·ness (spʌ́ndʒi:nis) *n.* the state or quality of being spongy

spon·gy (spʌ́ndʒi:) *comp.* **spong·i·er** *superl.* **spong·i·est** *adj.* having the porous, absorbent, elastic properties of a sponge ‖ (of a metal) in a finely porous, absorbent condition, *spongy lead* (in a storage battery), *spongy platinum* (used as an adsorber of gases)

spongy parenchyma a tissue of the mesophyll, usually on the lower side of the leaf blade. It consists of a meshwork of cellular strands with large intercellular spaces. The spongy parenchyma also contains very many chloroplasts (*PALISADE PARENCHYMA)

spon·sion (spɒ́nʃən) *n.* the act of going surety ‖ (*internat. law*) an undertaking given on behalf of a state by an agent who is not directly authorized to do so [fr. L. *sponsio* (*sponsionis*) fr. *spondere,* to promise solemnly]

spon·son (spɒ́nsən) *n.* a projection of the side of a warship or tank to give a gun a greater arc of fire ‖ (*aeron.*) a projection from the wing of a hydroplane enabling it to rest steadily on water ‖ an air chamber along the gunwale of a canoe giving it greater stability [etym. doubtful]

spon·sor (spɒ́nsər) **1.** *n.* someone who accepts personal responsibility for another ‖ a godparent ‖ (*radio, television*) a person or firm paying for a broadcast during which time will be allowed to advertise his or its wares **2.** *vt.* to act as sponsor for **spon·so·ri·al** (spɒnsɔ́ri:əl, spɒnsóuri:əl) *adj.* **spón·sor·ship** *n.* [L.=surety]

spon·ta·ne·i·ty (spɒntəní:iti: spɒntənéiiti:) *n.* the state or quality of being spontaneous [fr. L. *spontaneus* adj.]

spon·ta·ne·ous (spɒntéini:əs) *adj.* arising from impulse, not suggested by another and not premeditated, *a spontaneous offer to help* ‖ happening without external cause or control, *the movements of the heart are spontaneous* ‖ growing without human intervention, in the wild state [fr. L. *spontaneus*]

spontaneous combustion combustion arising with no direct application of spark or flame. It is due to an internal rise of temperature to the ignition point, usually caused by a slow oxidation process

spontaneous generation abiogenesis

spoof (spu:f) **1.** *v.i.* (*old-fash., pop.*) to fool, pretend ‖ *v.t.* (*old-fash., pop.*) to deceive (someone) **2.** *n.* (*old-fash., pop.*) a hoax ‖ a humorous, light, but telling parody [name of a game, invented (c. 1889) by Arthur Roberts, Eng. comedian]

spoof·er (spú:fə:r) *n.* (*mil.*) in air intercept, a contact employing electronic or tactical deception measures

spook (spu:k) *n.* (a seriocomic word, meeting the supernatural with joking awe) a specter ‖ (*slang*) an intelligence agent **spóok·y** *comp.* **spook·i·er** *superl.* **spook·i·est** *adj.* [Du.]

spool (spu:l) **1.** *n.* a short cylinder, with a rim or head at each end and usually a hole up the middle for a spindle, on which thread or yarn is wound ‖ a reel on which e.g. a photographic film or an angler's line is wound **2.** *v.t.* to wind on a spool [fr. M. Du. *spoele*]

spoon (spu:n) **1.** *n.* a domestic utensil consisting of a shallow, oval or round bowl at the end of a handle, used for eating liquid or semiliquid food, and for mixing, stirring etc. ‖ something shaped like this utensil, esp. a spinner (fishing lure) ‖ (*golf*) a wood with a lofted face, used for long, high shots **2.** *v.t.* to gather up with a spoon (domestic utensil) ‖ (*cricket, golf* etc.) to loft (a ball) with the bat, club etc. ‖ *v.i.* to fish with a spinner ‖ (*old-fash., pop.*) (of lovers) to hug and kiss [O.E. *spōn*]

spoon·bill (spú:nbil) *n. Platalea leucorodia,* fam. *Plataleidae,* a wading bird of S. Europe, N. Africa and Asia, resembling a small stork or heron. It is crested, has snow-white plumage and a long spatulate bill, and breeds colonially in reed beds

spoo·ner·ism (spú:nərizəm) *n.* the transposition with bizarre effect of (usually) the initial sounds of words adjacent in a phrase, e.g. 'a half-warmed fish' for 'a half-formed wish' [after the Rev. W.A. *Spooner* (1844–1930), Warden of New College, Oxford]

spoon-fed (spú:nfed) *adj.* indulged by being given all that is needed without having to make any effort to get it ‖ fed with a spoon

spoon·ful (spú:nful) *pl.* **spoon·fuls** *n.* the amount a spoon will hold

spoor (spuər) **1.** *n.* the footprints and other signs of the passage of an animal, esp. a game animal **2.** *v.i.* to follow a spoor ‖ *v.t.* to track (an animal) by its spoor [Du.]

Spor·a·des (spɔ́rədi:z, spɔ́rədi:z) two groups of Greek islands in the Aegean: the N. Sporades, off Thessaly, and the S. Sporades (consisting largely of the Dodecanese), off S.W. Asia Minor

spo·rad·ic (spərǽdik) *adj.* occurring at infrequent and irregular intervals in time or space, *sporadic outbursts of plague* ‖ occurring in isolated or single instances **spo·rád·i·cal·ly** *adv.* [fr. M.L. *sporadicus* fr. Gk]

sporan *SPORRAN

spo·ran·gi·al (spɔrǽndʒi:əl, spourǽndʒi:əl) *adj.* of or like a sporangium ‖ characterized by sporangia

spo·ran·gi·um (spɔrǽndʒi:əm, spourǽndʒi:əm) *pl.* **spo·ran·gi·a** (spɔrǽndʒi:ə, spourǽndʒi:ə) *n.* a capsule in which spores are produced or carried in algae, fungi, bacteria, ferns and mosses [Mod. L. fr. Gk *spora,* seed+*angeion,* vessel]

spore (spɔr, spour) **1.** *n.* a minute one-celled reproductive or resistant resting body produced usually by lower forms of plant and animal life and often adapted to withstand unfavorable environmental conditions. When these conditions improve the spore can produce a new vegetative individual **2.** *v.i. pres. part.* **spor·ing** *past* and *past part.* **spored** to bear or develop spores [fr. Mod. L. *spora* fr. Gk]

spore case a sporangium

spo·ro·carp (spɔ́rəkɑrp, spóurəkɑrp) *n.* a structure in which or on which spores are reproduced [fr. Gk *spora,* seed+*karpos,* fruit]

spo·ro·cyst (spɔ́rəsist, spóurəsist) *n.* a stage in spore formation prior to sporogony ‖ the encysted sporozoan [fr. Gk *spora,* seed+*kustis,* sac]

spo·ro·gen·e·sis (spɔrədʒénisis, spourədʒénisis) *n.* reproduction by spores ‖ spore formation [Mod. L. fr. Gk *spora,* seed+L. *genesis,* origin]

spo·rog·e·nous (spɔrɒ́dʒənəs, spourɒ́dʒənəs) *adj.* producing or able to produce spores ‖ reproducing by spores [fr. SPORE+Gk *-genes,* born of]

spo·rog·e·ny (spɔrɒ́dʒəni:, spourɒ́dʒəni:) *n.* sporogenesis

spo·ro·go·ni·um (spɔrəgóuni:əm, spourəgóuni:əm) *pl.* **spo·ro·go·ni·a** (spɔrəgóuni:ə, spourəgóuni:ə) *n.* the sporophyte of a moss or liverwort consisting typically of a stalk bearing a sporangium [Mod. L. fr. Gk *spora,* seed+*gonos,* offspring]

spo·rog·o·ny (spɔrɒ́gəni:, spourɒ́dʒəni:) *n.* sporogenesis ‖ spore formation in a sporozoan by encystment and subsequent division of a zygote [fr. Gk *spora,* seed+*-gonia,* product]

spo·ro·phore (spɔ́rəfɔr, spóurəfour) *n.* a spore-bearing structure, esp. in fungi [fr. Gk *spora,* seed+*-phoros,* bearing]

spo·ro·phyll, spo·ro·phyl (spɔ́rəfil, spóurəfil) *n.* a sporangium-bearing leaf [fr. Gk *spora,* seed+*phullos,* leaf]

spo·ro·phyte (spɔ́rəfait, spóurəfait) *n.* (in plants which exhibit alternation of generations) the individual or generation that bears asexual spores [fr. Gk *spora,* seed+*phuton,* plant]

spo·ro·pol·len·in (spɔropɑlenin) *n.* the outer covering of pollen or spores

spo·ro·zo·an (spɔrəzóuən, spourəzóuən) **1.** *n.* a parasitic protozoan, of the class *Sporozoa.* They are usually without locomotory structures, and pass through a complicated life cycle often (as with the malaria parasites) involving two dissimilar hosts **2.** *adj.* of or belonging to this class [fr. Mod. L. fr. Gk *spora,* seed+*zōon,* animal]

spo·ro·zo·ite (spɔrəzóuait, spourəzóuait) *n.* a small, elongate, usually motile, infective stage of some sporozoans

spor·ran, spor·an (spɔ́rən) *n.* a large pouch made of skin, usually with the hair left on, used as a purse and worn by Scottish Highlanders with the kilt. It is slung around the waist to hang down in front [Scot. Gael. *sporan,* Ir. Gael. *sparān,* purse]

sport (spɔrt, spourt) **1.** *n.* the playing of games or participation in competitive pastimes involving physical exertion and skill, esp. those played outdoors ‖ any such game or pastime ‖ (esp. *Br.*) such games collectively ‖ the pleasure and satisfaction derived from such games or pastimes or from hunting etc., *it was good sport* ‖ an activity pursued for pleasure involving the hunting, taking or killing of wild animals, game or fish, *blood sports* ‖ (*pl.*) athletics (track events, jumping etc.) ‖ (*Br., pl.*) an organized meeting for these ‖ a person who has the qualities of sportsmanship ‖ (*biol.*) an animal or plant differing greatly from the normal ‖ (*bot.*) a bud variation **in sport** as a joke or for fun, not in earnest **to make sport of** to cause to look silly **2.** *v.i.* (*rhet.*) to play ‖ (*rhet.*) to joke ‖ (*rhet.*) to gambol, frolic ‖ (*biol.*) to differ greatly from the normal ‖ (*bot.*) to show bud variation ‖ *v.t.* to wear esp. in order to show off, *to sport a new tie* ‖ (*biol.*) to produce as a sport **to sport one's oak** (*Oxford* and *Cambridge Universities*) to shut one's door as an indication that one is out or does not wish to be disturbed **3.** *adj.* sports [shortened fr. M.E. *desport, disport*]

sport·ing (spɔ́rtiŋ, spóurtiŋ) *adj.* pertaining to sport ‖ involving risk but offering some possibility of success, *a sporting chance* ‖ sportsmanlike in conduct

spor·tive (spɔ́rtiv, spóurtiv) *adj.* (*old-fash.*) playful

sports (spɔrts, spourts) *adj.* concerned with, suitable for or devoted to sports, *sports page, sports instructor* ‖ (of clothes) comfortable and casual, for informal wear

sports car an automobile for traveling fast on public roads. Sports cars are usually open or convertible and seat two

sports·man (spɔ́rtsmən, spóurtsmən) *pl.* **sports·men** (spɔ́rtsmən, spóurtsmən) *n.* a person who practices a sport ‖ a person who behaves generously in defeat or victory **spórts·man·ly** *adj.*

sports·man·like (spɔ́rtsmənlaik, spóurtsmənlaik) *adj.* showing the moral qualities of a good sportsman

sports·man·ship (spɔ́rtsmənʃip, spóurtsmənʃip) *n.* generous behavior befitting a good sportsman

sports·wear (spɔ́rtswɛər, spóurtswɛər) *n.* (*commerce*) clothes for outdoor sports ‖ (*commerce*) casual, comfortable clothes for informal wear

sports·wom·an (spɔ́rtswumən, spóurtswumən) *pl.* **sports·wom·en** (spɔ́rtswimin, spóurtswimin) *n.* a woman who takes part in sports

sports·writ·er (spɔ́rtsraitər, spóurtsraitər) *n.* a journalist who writes about sports

sport·y (spɔ́rti:, spóurti:) *comp.* **sport·i·er** *superl.* **sport·i·est** *adj.* (*old-fash.*) sportsmanlike ‖

CONCISE PRONUNCIATION KEY: **(a)** æ, *cat;* ɑ, *car;* ɔ *fawn;* ei, *snake.* **(e)** e, *hen;* i:, *sheep;* iə, *deer;* ɛə, *bear.* **(i)** i, *fish;* ai, *tiger;* ə:, *bird.* **(o)** o, *ox;* au, *cow;* ou, *goat;* u, *poor;* ɔi, *royal.* **(u)** ʌ, *duck;* u, *bull;* u:, *goose;* ə, *bacillus;* ju:, *cube.* x, *loch;* θ, *think;* ð, *bother;* z, *Zen;* ʒ, *corsage;* dʒ, *savage;* ŋ, *orangutang;* j, *yak;* ʃ, *fish;* tʃ, *fetch;* 'l, *rabble;* 'n, *redden.* Complete pronunciation key appears inside front cover.

suitable for, or affording good sport, *a sporty little model* || (of a girl or woman) too fond of sports to be very feminine, but with strong sportsmanlike qualities

spor·u·late (spɔ́rjuleit, spóurjuleit) *pres. part.* **spor·u·lat·ing** *past* and *past part.* **spor·u·lat·ed** *v.i.* to undergo sporulation

spor·u·la·tion (spɔrjuléiʃən, spourjuléiʃən) *n.* (*biol.*) the formation of spores

spor·ule (spɔ́rju:l, spóurju:l) *n.* a very small or secondary spore [Mod. L. *sporula*, dim. of *spora*, seed]

spot (spɒt) **1.** *n.* a small disfiguring mark of dirt etc. || a small, usually round, decorative mark of different color or texture from its background, *the leopard's spots* || (on human skin) a pimple || a dark area on the face of the sun, moon or a planet || (*rhet.*) a blemish on a good reputation, character, name etc. || a place, *the spot where the crash occurred, good in spots* || (esp *Br.*) a drop of a liquid, esp. water, *spots of rain* || (*Br., pop.*) a small amount, *a spot of supper* || (*billiards*) the mark on the upper end of the table where the red ball is placed or one of two other marked places on the table || *Leiostomus xanthurus*, a fish found off the northeast coast of the U.S.A., with a black spot behind the shoulders || (*bot.*) a mark on a leaf etc. produced by a fungus || a small, usually round mark used as a distinguishing device || (*pop.*) a spotlight || (*radio, television*) a short interval set aside in a broadcast for announcements or advertisements, or the announcement or advertisement itself || a situation **in a spot** in a difficult situation **on the spot** at once || on the site where something happened, is happening or is expected to happen || alert, quick to grasp a situation **to put on the spot** (*pop.*, esp. of gangsters) to threaten with real intent to murder (a person or persons) || to force to justify oneself, give information or an answer etc. **2.** *v. pres. part.* **spot·ting** *past* and *past part.* **spot·ted** *v.t.* to look out for with the purpose of recording information, *the boys were spotting trains* || to mark or discolor with spots || to blemish || to pick out beforehand, *spot the winner* || to catch sight of, *she spotted him across the room* || to notice, *did you spot the errors?* || (*mil.*) to discover the exact position of || to place (things or people) in scattered strategic positions || (*pop.*) to allow as a handicap, *I'll spot you three points* || *v.i.* to become stained or soiled || to cause a spot or spots **3.** *adj.* involving immediate payment, *spot cash* || made at random, *a spot check* || (of a broadcast or broadcasting) done from a local station || (*radio*) of an announcement made between programs || (*commerce*) ready for delivery, *spot wheat* [prob. M.Du. *spotte*]

spot ball (*billiards*) the cue ball, having a black spot on it

spot·less (spɒ́tlis) *adj.* (*rhet.*, of character) irreproachable || (of a thing) perfectly clean

spot·light (spɒ́tlait) *n.* a bright, narrow beam of light used e.g. to illuminate a small part of a theater stage || a lamp used to project such a beam || public attention **2.** *v.t.* to throw the beam of a spotlight upon || to draw attention to, *to spotlight a social problem*

Spots·wood (spɒ́tswud), Alexander (1676-1740), American colonial governor (1710-22) of Virginia. He established and promoted the state's iron industry at Germanna, a German settlement in Spotsylvania County, which is named after him

spot·ted (spɒ́tid) *adj.* marked with spots

spotted alfalfa aphid a destructive aphid (*Therioaphis maculata*), established in southern and southwestern U.S., that stunts and yellows plants, esp. alfalfa

spotted fever any of various febrile diseases, resulting in spots on the skin, esp. Rocky Mountain spotted fever or typhus

spotted sandpiper *Actitis macularia*, a common North American sandpiper whose underparts, in the adult, have black spots in the summer

spot·ter (spɒ́tər) *n.* someone who watches out for esp. airplanes or trains, in order to record information about their identification and movements etc. || a pilot, or the airplane he uses, sent up to locate enemy positions || (*mil.*) someone who finds the position of a military objective || a device attached to a train to enable defects in the track to be discovered

spot·ti·ness (spɒ́ti:nis) *n.* the state or quality of being spotty

spot·ty (spɒ́ti:) *comp.* **spot·ti·er** *superl.* **spot·ti·est** *adj.* marked with spots || occurring in spots || irregular, uneven in quality, *a spotty performance*

spouse (spaus) *n.* (*old-fash. except in legal contexts*) a husband or wife [O.F. *spous*]

spout (spaut) **1.** *v.t.* to force (a fluid) out of an aperture under pressure, *the volcano spouted lava* || (*pop.*) to utter (esp. something declamatory) volubly and at some length and esp. without subtleties of expression || *v.i.* to gush (as if under pressure) || to talk or recite, esp. at length in a voluble and declamatory manner **2.** *n.* a tubular projection for conducting e.g. rain off a roof, or pouring e.g. tea from a teapot || a column of fluid ejected by pressure || a column of water raised by a whirlwind || the spiracle of a whale || that which the whale ejects from its spiracle || a trough for carrying and discharging grain, flour etc. **up the spout** (*pop.*) in an irremediable situation, beyond help [etym. doubtful]

sprag (spræg) **1.** *n.* a length of wood or metal used to support the roof of a mine gallery, or to lock the wheel of a vehicle || a projection that prevents the movement of platforms or pallets in the side guidance rails in an aircraft cabin **2.** *v.t. pres. part.* **sprag·ging** *past* and *past part.* **spragged** to support with sprags || to check the motion of with a sprag [etym. doubtful]

sprain (sprein) **1.** *v.t.* to injure (a muscle or joint) by a sudden violent twist **2.** *n.* the injury thus caused [etym. doubtful]

sprang alt. *past* of SPRING

sprat (spræt) *n. Clupea sprattus*, fam. *Clupeidae*, a small sea fish allied to the herring but much smaller, found in the Atlantic and the Mediterranean || a young herring [O.E. *sprot*]

sprawl (sprɔl) **1.** *v.i.* to slump with the limbs stretched out in an ungainly way || to spread out in a disorderly way, *London sprawls over miles of suburbs* || *v.t.* to stretch out (the limbs) in an ungainly and relaxed way || to cause to spread out in an irregular straggling way **2.** *n.* the posture of sprawling || unplanned development of open land, e.g., urban sprawl [O.E. *spreawlian*]

spray (sprei) **1.** *n.* liquid moving in the air in the form of fine drops that have been thrown, blown or projected under pressure || the stream of fine drops ejected by an atomizer || a device for ejecting such a stream || the liquid used in this device **2.** *v.t.* to shoot out or apply in the form of spray, *to spray lacquer on hair* || to treat or cover with a spray, *to spray hair with lacquer* || *v.i.* to shoot out a spray || to shoot out in a spray [M. Du. *sprayen* prob. fr. L.G.]

spray *n.* a small branch with attached leaves, flowers etc., used as a decoration || a bouquet in a linear, trailing arrangement || an ornament resembling either of these, *a spray of diamonds* [etym. doubtful]

spray dome the mount of water spray thrown into the air when the shock wave from an underwater nuclear detonation reaches the surface

sprayed printed circuit an electrical circuit applied by spraying metal particles on a base

spray gun a device using air pressure for spraying paint, insecticides etc.

spray steel steel treated with oxygen sprays to remove impurities, while the molten metal is being poured

spread (spred) **1.** *v. pres. part.* **spread·ing** *past* and *past part.* **spread** *v.t.* to open out more or less fully, *she spread the clothes to dry* || to display for sale, *the potter spread his wares* || (esp. with 'out') to cause to occupy more space by unfurling or smoothing out, *he spread out the newspaper* || to distribute in a layer, *he spread varnish on the wood* || to overlay (something) esp. extensively, *she spread the floor with rugs* || to distribute so as to cover, *to spread papers on a desk* || to prepare (a table) for a meal || to put (food) on a table || to extend, stretch (esp. limbs), *the eagle spread its wings* || to allow (e.g. energies, interests etc.) to range widely || to disseminate or cause to extend, esp. over a wide area or among many people, *to spread happiness* || to make known (news etc.) to many people || to cause or allow (e.g. work) to occupy longer time than normal || to share (something burdensome) || to push apart, esp. by bearing down with weight or force, to distend || (*printing*) to display (matter) widely across two columns or two pages || to fan out a hand of (cards) || to display (cards) face upwards || (*naut.*) to expand, unfurl or set (sails) || *v.i.* to become widely distributed or scattered, *the dust spread over the books* || (esp. with 'out') to extend in length and breadth, *the woods spread out as far as the eye could see* || (with a preposition) to flow outwards and cover, swamp, saturate etc., *the syrup spread over the table, the damp spread into the next room* || (of news, disease, emotion etc.) to become widely or more widely shared, known, suffered etc. || to increase esp. in growth or numbers, *weeds spread all over the garden* || to admit of being distributed in a layer, *it will spread better if it is warmed* || to move apart under the effect of force, *the chair legs spread under his weight* || (*pop.*) to grow stout **to spread oneself** to make a great display || to busy oneself with a variety of activities **2.** *n.* the act of spreading or being spread, *the spread of disease* || the quality of being spread out, *the spread of the city* || the distance, area or time over which something is spread || a soft food for spreading on bread etc. || a bedspread || (*pop.*) increase in girth, *middle-age spread* || (*pop.*) a lavish, sumptuous meal or feast || (*aeron.*) wingspan || (*printing*) two facing pages used for display || printed matter running across more than one column or across two pages || (*stock exchange*) an option in which put and call price differ || the difference between these prices [O.E. *sprǣdan*]

spread city a large urban-suburban area with uncontrolled, random zoning

spread eagle the representation of an eagle with legs and wings outspread, e.g. the emblem of the U.S.A.

spread-ea·gle (sprédi:g'l) **1.** *adj.* like a spread eagle || of exaggerated, aggressive patriotic sentiment for the U.S.A. **2.** *v.t. pres. part.* **spread-ea·gling** *past* and *past part.* **spread-ea·gled** to straddle or extend over or across (something) so as to have the arms and legs stretched out or sprawling

spread end (*football*) *SPLIT END

Sprech·stim·me (ʃpréxstime) *n.* (*German*) the portion of a musical presentation that is recited instead of sung

spree (spri:) *n.* an outing in pursuit of pleasure or fun and usually involving lavish spending or drinking, *a shopping spree* [etym. doubtful]

sprig (sprig) **1.** *n.* a short or pretty little spray from a shrub or tree, *a sprig of rosemary* || an ornament resembling this || a small headless nail **2.** *v.t. pres. part.* **sprig·ging** *past* and *past part.* **sprigged** to adorn with sprigs || to drive brads into [etym. doubtful]

spright·li·ness (spráitli:nis) *n.* the state or quality of being sprightly

spright·ly (spráitli:) *comp.* **spright·li·er** *superl.* **spright·li·est** *adj.* brisk and lively in movement or manner, often unexpectedly so [var. of SPRITE]

spring (spriŋ) **1.** *n.* the action of springing || the ability to spring || an instance of springing || in latitudes where the climate is seasonal, the season of the year following winter and preceding summer || a place where water or natural oil is forced out of the ground by its own pressure || resilience || a device of bent or coiled metal etc. e.g. in watches, cars or mattresses, which, because of its elasticity, can store and release energy when bent or twisted || an origin or cause of action || (*rhet.*) a beginning period characterized by growth and abundant life, *the spring of life* || a crack, split, warp etc., e.g. in a ship's mast or spar || (*archit.*) the point at which an arch or vault rises from its support **2.** *adj.* of, appearing in or planted in the spring of the year || supported on springs || coming from a spring [O.E.]

spring *pres. part.* **spring·ing** *past* **sprang** (spræŋ), **sprung** (sprʌŋ) *past part.* **sprung** *v.i.* to make a bound upwards or in a curve || to rise suddenly and rapidly from a sitting or lying position || to come, appear or arise suddenly and quickly || to move as a result of elasticity, *to spring back into position* || (*rhet.*) to be descended, *his family sprang from northern stock* || to originate, *the quarrel sprang from a casual remark* || to begin to grow or put out leaves etc., *the winter wheat is springing* || (of winds, storms etc., with 'up') to begin to blow, be felt or have effect || (of wood) to warp or split || (of a mine) to explode || to appear to have a strong upward movement, *the arch springs from that slender pillar* || *v.t.* to jump over or across, *the dog sprang the gate* || to release the spring of, *to spring a trap* || to produce unexpectedly, *to spring a surprise* || to cause (a mine) to explode || to develop (a leak) suddenly || to cause (wood) to warp or split || to cause (game) to leave cover [O.E. *springan*]

spring balance an instrument for measuring

weight in terms of the compression or extension of a coiled spring

spring·board (spríŋbɔrd, spríŋbourd) *n.* a resilient board which, by releasing the energy which has bent it, assists a jumper, diver etc. to gain height. The board is fixed at one end and acts about a fulcrum ‖ something used as a starting point for further progress, *the job was a springboard to one with more scope*

spring·bok (spríŋbɒk) *n. Antidorcas euchore,* fam. *Boridae,* a S. African antelope closely allied to the gazelle, and noted for its high perpendicular leaps in play or when alarmed. The horns are lyre-shaped [Af. fr. *springen,* to spring+*bok,* antelope]

spring bolt a bolt released by pressure and closed by a spring when the pressure is removed

spring-clean (spríŋklí:n) **1.** *n.* (*Br.*) a spring-cleaning **2.** *v.t.* to do a spring-cleaning of ‖ *v.i.* to do a spring-cleaning

spring-clean·ing (spríŋklí:niŋ) *n.* a particularly thorough cleaning given to a house or room to remove the accumulation of winter dirt

springe (sprindʒ) **1.** *n.* a noose or other snare used to catch small animals **2.** *v. pres. part.* **spring·ing** (sprínd͡ʒiŋ) *past* and *past part.* **springed** *v.t.* to catch in this way ‖ *v.i.* to set springes [M.E., etym. doubtful]

spring·er (spríŋər) *n.* a springer spaniel ‖ (*archit.*) the first stone (voussoir) of an arch at the point where it springs

springer spaniel a medium-sized gundog of a breed used for flushing game. They are usually black and white

Spring·field (spríŋfi:ld) the capital (pop. 99,637) of Illinois. An important agricultural, wholesale and industrial center. Home and burial place of Abraham Lincoln

Springfield a city (pop. 152,319) in S.W. Massachusetts: electric equipment, arms, tools, gasoline pumps, pack machinery, magnetos, plastics. Springfield College (1885), American International College (1855)

spring·head (spríŋhed) *n.* a source, fountain

spring·i·ly (spríŋili:) *adv.* in a springy manner

spring·i·ness (spríŋi:nis) *n.* the state or quality of being springy

spring·like (spríŋlaik) *adj.* having the qualities of or associated with spring ‖ resembling a spring or its action

spring lock a lock which fastens automatically with a spring bolt

Springs (spriŋz) a market town (pop. 153,974) of S. central Transvaal, South Africa, in Witwatersrand: gold and coal mines

spring·tail (spríŋteil) *n.* a member of *Collembola,* an order of primitive, wingless arthropods, which leap by suddenly straightening the penultimate segment of their bodies

spring tide a tide, with a range greater than that of ordinary tides, occurring a day or two after the new and full moon in each month (cf. NEAP TIDE)

spring·tide (spríŋtaid) *n.* (*rhet.*) springtime

spring·time (spríŋtaim) *n.* the season of spring ‖ (*rhet.*) the early stage of something, having the qualities associated with this season, e.g. new life, strong growth etc.

spring washer (*engin.*) a washer constructed of spiral coils, used to absorb vibrations which might otherwise loosen a nut

spring·y (spríŋi:) *comp.* **spring·i·er** *superl.* **spring·i·est** *adj.* resilient esp. under pressure, e.g. of feet etc. ‖ having many springs

sprin·kle (spríŋk'l) **1.** *v. pres. part.* **sprin·kling** *past* and *past part.* **sprin·kled** *v.t.* to scatter in separate drops or particles, *to sprinkle water on clothes for ironing* ‖ to cover with drops or particles, *to sprinkle a floor with sand* ‖ to place (esp. small quantities of something) at wide intervals ‖ (with 'with') to vary or intersperse (e.g. talk or a text), *his book is sprinkled with anecdotes* ‖ *v.i.* to scatter or fly about in small drops or particles ‖ to rain lightly **2.** *n.* the act or result of sprinkling [late M.E.]

sprinkler system a system of pipes designed to sprinkle water e.g. on a lawn, or on flying dust ‖ a fire protection device consisting of a system of pipes carrying water or some other extinguishing fluid. The pipes are designed to discharge automatically under the effect of the heat of fire

sprin·kling (spríŋkliŋ) *n.* a small quantity or number distributed here and there ‖ a small quantity falling, or made to fall, in little drops or scatterings

sprint (sprint) **1.** *v.i.* to run for a short distance at the greatest speed of which one is capable ‖ *v.t.* to traverse in this way **2.** *n.* a run of this kind, e.g. at the end of a distance race ‖ a short-distance race ‖ a horse race under one mile ‖ a short period of intensive activity [early Scand.]

Sprint *n.* (*mil.*) a high-acceleration, U.S. nuclear surface-to-air guided missile formerly deployed as part of the Safeguard ballistic missile system

sprint car (*sports*) a medium-size car with a large-car engine run in dirt track races

sprit (sprit) *n.* (*naut.*) a short pole set from the mast to the further and upper corner of a sail for extending and raising it ‖ a bowsprit [O.E. *sprēot,* a spear or pole]

sprite (sprait) *n.* a fairy, an elf [fr. O.F. *esprit* or *esperit,* spirit]

sprit·sail (sprítś'l) *n.* a sail extended by a sprit

sprock·et (sprɒ́kit) *n.* a tooth on a wheel's rim, engaging with the links of a chain ‖ a sprocket wheel ‖ a triangular piece of wood fastened to the upper surface of a rafter to change the angle of the eaves [etym. doubtful]

sprocket wheel a wheel with sprockets on it, such as that which engages with the chain of a bicycle

sprout (spraut) **1.** *v.i.* (of a plant, shrub etc.) to put out young growth, *after the rain the trees sprouted* ‖ (of a person) to begin to be noticeably tall ‖ to germinate ‖ *v.t.* to grow (something new), *the tree sprouted leaves* ‖ to let (e.g. a moustache) grow ‖ to support (something that could be likened to a sprout), *every roof now sprouts an antenna* **2.** *n.* a shoot on a plant ‖ (*pl.*) Brussels sprouts ‖ a new growth from a bud, seed etc. [O.E. *sprūtan*]

sprouting broccoli *Brassica oleracea italica,* fam. *Cruciferae,* a cauliflower bearing florets at the ends of branches which are cut for food while still tight and purplish or green

Spru·ance (sprú:əns), Raymond Ames (1886-1969), the youngest full admiral (at age 57) in U.S. naval history and probably the greatest U.S. naval tactician in the 2nd world war. As commander of a U.S. Navy task force, he secured the U.S. victory at Midway (1942)

spruce (spru:s) **1.** *adj.* very neat, clean, tidy ‖ (of dress and appearance) trim **2.** *v.t. pres. part.* **spruc·ing** *past* and *past part.* **spruced** (with 'up') to make very neat, tidy or trim ‖ *v.i.* (with 'up') to make oneself neat and trim [altered fr. *Pruce,* Prussia in the phrase *spruce leather*]

spruce *n.* a member of *Picea,* fam. *Pinaceae,* a genus of quick-growing conifers, with the branches close together and forming a conical head ‖ their light but strong wood [altered fr. *Pruce,* Prussia]

spruce beer a beverage made by fermenting with yeast a mixture of water, spruce leaves, spruce twigs and sugar

sprue (spru:) *n.* a channel or hole through which molten metal etc. is poured into a mold ‖ the waste metal filling this hole [etym. doubtful]

sprue *n.* a chronic disease of the digestive system occurring chiefly in visitors to certain tropical or subtropical areas. It is manifested by diarrhea, loss of weight, appetite and energy, and changes in the tongue and skin [fr. Du. *spruw*]

sprung alt. *past* and the *past part.* of SPRING

sprung rhythm a poetic rhythm (*HOPKINS) with origins traceable to Old English verse and nursery rhymes. Each metrical foot consists of a single stress, which can stand either alone or be placed before a number of unstressed syllables. Usually the feet contain from one to four syllables. They are assumed to be equal in strength and length, their seeming inequality being compensated by pause or emphasis. Scansion runs without break from beginning to end of the stanza [invented by G. M. HOPKINS]

spry (sprai) *comp.* **spry·er, spri·er** *superl.* **spry·est, spri·est** *adj.* (esp. of old people) quick in movement and in thought [etym. doubtful]

spud (spʌd) **1.** *n.* a spade with a small blade, or sometimes with prongs, used for digging up big-rooted weeds ‖ (*pop.*) a potato **2.** *v.t. pres. part.* **spud·ding** *past* and *past part.* **spud·ded** to dig up with a spud [prob. fr. O.N.]

spume (spju:m) **1.** *n.* a mass of bubbles formed from a liquid **2.** *v. pres. part.* **spum·ing** *past* and *past part.* **spumed** *v.i.* to foam or discharge bubbles ‖ *v.t.* (esp. with 'out') to discharge (something) like foam [fr. O.F. *espume* or L. *spuma,* foam]

spu·mes·cence (spju:més'ns) *n.* the state or quality of being spumous

spu·mes·cent (spju:més'nt) *adj.* spumous

spu·mous (spjú:məs) *adj.* of, like or covered with spume

spum·y (spjú:mi:) *comp.* **spum·i·er** *superl.* **spum·i·est** *adj.* spumous

spun *past* and *past part.* of SPIN

spun glass fiber glass

spunk (spʌŋk) *n.* (*pop.*) spirited courage ‖ punk [etym. doubtful]

spunk·i·ly (spʌ́ŋkili:) *adv.* (*pop.*) in a spunky manner

spunk·i·ness (spʌ́ŋki:nis) *n.* the state or quality of being spunky

spunk·y (spʌ́ŋki:) *comp.* **spunk·i·er** *superl.* **spunk·i·est** *adj.* (*pop.*) courageous, having spirit

spun silk yarn or cloth made from waste silk sometimes mixed with cotton

spun yarn (*naut.*) a line or rope made of two or more twisted rope yarns

spur (spə:r) **1.** *n.* a device sometimes worn on the heel of a riding boot, with a point or spiked wheel (rowel) for pressing into a horse's flanks to force its pace ‖ a projection bearing some resemblance to this, e.g. a process on the legs of a cock ‖ a ridge projecting from a mountain ‖ the largest root of a tree ‖ a wall connecting a rampart with an interior work ‖ a climbing iron ‖ (*bot.*) a tubelike structure formed by the extension of a petal or sepal, e.g. in larkspur ‖ a metal device fastened to the leg of a gamecock for fighting ‖ a mental stimulus which results in a greater effort being made, *the spur of ambition* ‖ a spur track **on the spur of the moment** impulsively, without previous thought or plans **to win one's spurs** (*rhet.*) to secure recognition of one's work **2.** *v. pres. part.* **spur·ring** *past* and *past part.* **spurred** *v.t.* to use a spur on (a horse) ‖ to furnish with spurs ‖ to cause to make a great effort, *ambition spurred him on* ‖ *v.i.* to spur a horse [O.E. *spora, spura*]

spurge (spə:rdʒ) *n.* a member of *Euphorbia,* fam. *Euphorbiaceae,* a genus of some 1,600 species of plants or bushes of tropical or temperate regions, yielding a bitter, milky juice. The flowers are very small, with one male and several females within a cup-shaped involucre [fr. O.F. *espurge*]

spur gear a wheel with teeth parallel to the axle

spurge laurel a member of *Daphne,* fam. *Thymelaeaceae,* a genus of Eurasian shrubs bearing yellow flowers before leafing

spu·ri·ous (spjúəri:əs) *adj.* having the appearance of being genuine, but without being so ‖ (*biol.*) like in appearance but morphologically or pathologically false ‖ (*law*) illegitimate, bastard [fr. L. *spurius*]

spurn (spə:rn) *v.t.* to reject with contempt [O.E. *spurnan*]

spur·ri·er (spə́:ri:ər, spʌ́ri:ər) *n.* a person who makes spurs

Spurs, Battle of the a battle (1302) in which a Flemish army defeated the French army of Philippe IV ‖ a battle (1513) in which an army under Henry VIII of England and the Emperor Maximilian I defeated the army of Louis XII of France

spurt, spirt (spə:rt) **1.** *v.i.* (of a fluid) to shoot out suddenly in a jet, but not in great volume ‖ (of a person) to make a sudden, violent effort, esp. in a race ‖ *v.t.* to cause to rush out suddenly in a jet **2.** *n.* a sudden shooting out of liquid in a jet ‖ a sudden short burst of activity or energy [etym. doubtful]

spur track a railroad track, or branch line, over which there is only irregular traffic

spur wheel a spur gear

sput·nik (spútnik) *n.* the first of the artificial satellites put in orbit by the U.S.S.R. [Russ.]

sput·ter (spʌ́tər) **1.** *v.i.* to splutter ‖ *v.t.* to splutter ‖ (*phys.*) to deposit a very thin film of metal on (a surface) **2.** *n.* a sputtering ‖ the sound of sputtering ‖ rapid, confused speech [imit.]

spu·tum (spjú:təm) *pl.* **spu·ta** (spjú:tə), **spu·tums** *n.* material expelled from the respiratory passages by clearing the throat, or by coughing [L.=spit]

spy (spai) *pl.* **spies** *n.* a person instructed to act secretly in gathering information, by observation or otherwise, about the actions, circumstances and intentions of an enemy, a potential enemy or rival, or a criminal, *a police spy* ‖ someone who keeps secret, close watch on others [fr. O.F. *espie*]

spy *pres. part.* **spy·ing** *past* and *past part.* **spied**

v.t. to see, catch sight of ‖ (with 'out') to make a secret investigation of, *to spy out the terrain* ‖ (with 'on') to watch the activities of in the manner of a spy, *to spy on one's neighbors* ‖ *v.i.* to act as a spy [fr. O.F. *espier*]

spy·glass (spáiglæs, spáiglɑs) *n.* a portable terrestrial telescope

sq. square

squab (skwɒb) **1.** *adj.* fat and dumpy ‖ unfledged **2.** *n.* a short, fat person ‖ an unfledged pigeon ‖ a thick cushion [etym. doubtful]

squab·ble (skwɒ́b'l) **1.** *v. pres. part.* **squab·bling** *past* and *past part.* **squab·bled** *v.i.* to engage in a noisy but not very serious argument or quarrel ‖ *v.t.* (*printing*) to disarrange (type that has been set) **2.** *n.* a noisy but not serious quarrel or argument [imit.]

squab·by (skwɒ́bi:) *comp.* **squab·bi·er** *superl.* **squab·bi·est** *adj.* short and fat, squab

squad (skwɒd) *n.* a small number of men organized to act together in work or in a military maneuver ‖ a number of men organized to act together, e.g. an athletic team [fr. F. *escouade*]

squad car a police patrol car equipped with radio communication

squad·ron (skwɒ́drən) *n.* an air force unit between group and flight ‖ a unit of cavalry or of mechanized troops, tanks etc. ‖ a unit of battleships, varying in size and composition [fr. Ital. *squadrone*]

squadron leader an officer in the British Royal Air Force ranking below a wing commander and above a flight lieutenant

squal·id (skwɒ́lid) *adj.* repellently filthy, esp. because of neglect, *a squalid slum* ‖ wretched and often morally degrading, *squalid poverty* [fr. L. *squalidus*]

squall (skwɔl) **1.** *v.i.* (esp. of babies or young children) to cry loudly and discordantly ‖ to blow in a squall ‖ *v.t.* to utter in this way **2.** *n.* a sudden high wind, esp. when accompanied by rain, snow, hail etc. ‖ a noisy bout of temper, tearful screaming etc. **squál·ly** *adj.* characterized by squalls ‖ stormy [prob. imit.]

squal·or (skwɒ́lər) *n.* the state or quality of being squalid [L. fr. *squalere*, to be dry, rough, dirty]

squa·ma (skwéimə) *pl.* **squa·mae** (skwéimi:) *n.* (*biol.*) a scale, or feather or bony structure resembling a scale [L.=scale]

squa·mate (skwéimeit) *adj.* scaly, covered with scales [fr. L. *squamatus*]

squa·ma·tion (skwəméiʃən) *n.* the condition of being squamate ‖ arrangement of scales [fr. SQUAMA]

squa·mo·sal (skwəmóus'l) **1.** *n.* a membrane bone forming part of the posterior sidewall of the skull of many vertebrates **2.** *adj.* of this membrane bone ‖ squamous

squa·mose (skwéimous) *adj.* squamous

squa·mous (skwéiməs) *adj.* covered with scales ‖ like scales ‖ (*anat.*) of the thin upper anterior portion of the temporal bone [fr. L. *squamosus*]

squan·der (skwɒ́ndər) *v.t.* to use up unwisely and to no useful purpose, *to squander wealth* [etym. doubtful]

square (skwɛər) *pres. part.* **squar·ing** *past* and *past part.* **squared** *v.t.* to make square ‖ to cause to be at right angles ‖ to check for evenness or straightness ‖ to bring near the form of a right angle, *square your shoulders* ‖ to cause to conform, make consistent ‖ (esp. with 'off') to mark out in squares ‖ to bring into a state of even balance, *to square accounts* ‖ to pay (a bill) ‖ (*pop.*) to bribe ‖ (*math.*) to multiply (a number or quantity) by itself ‖ (*golf* etc.) to make the score in (a match) equal ‖ *v.i.* (with 'with') to agree or conform exactly, *his version does not square with theirs* ‖ (*golf* etc.) to even scores **to square the circle** to find a square equal in area to a given circle (an impossible geometrical calculation) ‖ to try to do the impossible **to square up** to move up (to someone) in a fighting posture ‖ to pay debts or bills [fr. O.F. *esquarrer*]

square 1. *adj.* having the shape of a square ‖ being at right angles or at a right angle ‖ broad in relation to height, *a square build* ‖ straight rather than curved, *a square jaw* ‖ unequivocal, *a square statement* ‖ leaving no balance ‖ in perfect adjustment, arranged in good order ‖ converted from linear to area measurement, *a square inch* ‖ being of a specified length in each of two directions at right angles, *10 meters square* ‖ (*naut.*) at right angles to the keel and mast **all square** having scored the same number of points in a game or completed a bargain of equal value to both parties **2.** *adv.* frankly, honestly, *he came square out with the facts* ‖ directly, *square in the middle of the town* ‖ so as to be in a square form, *fold the tea towels square* [fr. O.F. *esquarre*]

square *n.* a plane figure having four equal rectilinear sides, each adjacent pair forming a right angle ‖ anything approximating to this shape ‖ an instrument for determining and testing right angles ‖ a number which is the product of another number multiplied by itself, *9 is the square of 3* ‖ an open space surrounded by houses, esp. at the intersection of several streets, roughly square in shape and often laid out ornamentally ‖ (*hist.*) a body of troops drawn up in the form of a rectangle ‖ the unopened flower of the cotton plant and the bracts which enclose it ‖ (*pop.*) a person who is ignorant of the latest in slang, styles, fads etc. [fr. O.F. *esquire, esquare*]

square bracket (esp. *Br.*) one of a pair of punctuation marks [ ] very often used in texts to enclose either direct quotation or matter supplementary or extraneous to the text, as in U[nited] N[ations]

square dance a dance typically for four couples in which the dancers arrange themselves in a given form, e.g. a square, as in a quadrille

square deal (*pop.*) a transaction or treatment that is fair and honest

square knot a knot comprising opposite loops, each enclosing the parallel sides of the other

square leg (*cricket*) a position along a direction at right angles to the pitch and to the left of a right-handed batsman or right of one who is left-handed ‖ the fielder who has this position

square meal a satisfying meal

square measure a system of units of area (*MEASURES AND WEIGHTS)

square one the starting point

square out (*football*) a forward-pass play in which the receiver makes a short right angle after his initial run down the field

square piano an early oblong form of piano, like a box in shape, strung horizontally

square-rigged (skwɛ́ərrĭg'd) *adj.* of a sailing vessel the chief sails of which extend by horizontal yards suspended from the middle (cf. FORE-AND-AFT)

square root (*math.*) a quantity which, multiplied by itself, is equal to a given number, *3 is the square root of 9*

square sail (*naut.*) a rectangular sail set on a yard slung across the vessel

square shooter (*pop.*) a person who can be relied upon to be fair and honest

squar·rose (skwǽrous, skwɒ́rous) *adj.* (*biol.*) rough-surfaced with scales or processes ‖ (of leaves) stiff and crowded together [fr. L. *squarrosus*, scurfy, scabby]

squash (skwɒʃ, skwɔʃ) *n.* a member of *Cucurbita*, fam. *Cucurbitaceae*, a genus of gourd plants grown for their fruit. This is eaten baked, boiled or mashed as a vegetable, or fed to livestock ‖ one of these fruits [abbr. of Narragansett *asquutasquash*]

squash 1. *v.t.* to press into a shapeless state ‖ (with 'in') to force by pressure into too small a space, *we might squash five people into the back seat* ‖ (*pop.*) to suppress, *to squash a rebellion* ‖ (*pop.*) to reduce (a person) to silence by making a remark which belittles him or to which there is no possible answer ‖ *v.i.* to become pressed into a shapeless state ‖ (with 'into') to push and make oneself small enough to enter, *she squashed into the crowded train* **2.** *n.* (*Br.*) a beverage partly composed of fruit juice ‖ a closely packed crowd ‖ a game for two or four players played in a four-walled court with a special racket and soft ball. The ball is made to rebound off the front wall against any of the others. It is in play so long as it hits the front wall above the line drawn on this and does not hit the floor ‖ a squashing or the fact of being squashed ‖ the sound made by a soft body which collapses into a shapeless mass when it hits a hard surface **3.** *adv.* with the sound of a squash ‖ so as to squash [fr. O.F. *esquasser, esquacer*]

squash·i·ly (skwɒ́ʃili:, skwɔ́ʃili:) *adv.* in a squashy way

squash·i·ness (skwɒ́ʃi:nis, skwɔ́ʃi:nis) *n.* the state or quality of being squashy

squash racquets, squash rackets the game of squash, developed from the game of racquets

squash·y (skwɒ́ʃi:, skwɔ́ʃi:) *comp.* **squash·i·er** *superl.* **squash·i·est** *adj.* easily squashed ‖ looking squashed ‖ mushy

squat (skwɒt) **1.** *v. pres. part.* **squat·ting** *past* and *past part.* **squat·ted** *v.i.* to lower the body into a sitting posture, or sustain this posture, supporting it by the thigh muscles only ‖ (of animals) to keep as close to the ground as possible so as to escape observation ‖ to settle on land or in premises without any legal right to do so ‖ to settle on public land under government regulation in order to get a title to it ‖ *v.t. refl.* to cause (oneself) to assume a squatting position **2.** *adj.* short and thick ‖ being in a squatting position **3.** *n.* the posture of squatting [fr. O.F. *esquatir, esquater*, to beat or press down]

squat·ter (skwɒ́tər) *n.* a settler occupying government land in order to acquire legal title to it ‖ a person who occupies (esp. premises) without legal title ‖ (*Austral.*) a large-scale sheep farmer ‖ (*Austral.*) someone occupying an area of grazing land as a crown tenant

squat·ty (skwɒ́ti:) *comp.* **squat·ti·er** *superl.* **squat·ti·est** *adj.* dumpy

squaw (skwɔ) *n.* a North American Indian woman or wife [Narragansett *squaws*, Massachusetts *squa*, woman]

squawk (skwɔk) **1.** *v.i.* (esp. of birds) to utter a short, harsh, loud cry or cries, usually expressing angry complaint **2.** *n.* the sound of squawking ‖ *Nycticorax nycticorax hoactli*, a North American heron [imit.]

squawk standby (*mil.*) a code meaning *Switch identification friend or foe master control to 'standby' position. Cf* STOP SQUAWK

squeak (skwi:k) **1.** *v.i.* (of mice etc.) to utter a squeak or squeaks ‖ to make a sound like this, *the door squeaked on its hinges* ‖ (with 'past', 'by', 'through', 'into' etc.) to get by with a narrow margin, *he squeaked past with an inch to spare* ‖ (*pop.*) to tell the secrets one knows under fear of punishment ‖ *v.t.* to utter with a squeak **2.** *n.* a high-pitched, short cry of little volume *NARROW SQUEAK **squéak·i·ly** *adv.* **squéak·i·ness** *n.* **squéak·y** *comp.* **squeak·i·er** *superl.* **squeak·i·est** *adj.* squeaking [imit.]

squeal (skwi:l) **1.** *n.* a prolonged, very shrill cry, uttered under intense emotional stress or excitement, fear etc. **2.** *v.i.* to utter this cry ‖ (*pop.*) to become an informer [imit.]

squeam·ish (skwí:miʃ) *adj.* affected with nausea ‖ a little too easily disgusted or shocked ‖ excessively scrupulous [var. of older *squaymes, squemes, squeamous*, squeamish]

squee·gee (skwí:dʒi:) **1.** *n.* a strip of rubber mounted transversely at the end of a long handle, like a blade, used to sweep a surface clear of water ‖ (*photog.*) a rubber roller used to press a print flat on a mount **2.** *v.t. pres. part.* **squee·gee·ing** *past* and *past part.* **squee·geed** to sweep, smooth out etc. with a squeegee [etym. doubtful]

squeeze (skwi:z) **1.** *v. pres. part.* **squeez·ing** *past* and *past part.* **squeezed** *v.t.* to exert pressure on, esp. with opposite pressures, *to squeeze someone's hand* ‖ to force into a place by pressing, *she squeezed an extra shirt into his suitcase* ‖ to cause (people) to occupy less space than is comfortable, *we squeezed 20 people into our tiny room* ‖ to provide time or space for (something or someone) that cannot easily be fitted in, *the doctor squeezed him in before a patient who arrived late* ‖ to press (a fruit) so as to expel the juice ‖ to force (the juice) out of a fruit by pressing ‖ to exert financial or other pressure on (a person) in order to make him act in a certain way ‖ to get by force or unfair means ‖ to take an impression of (something) by pressing between waxed or wetted sheets of paper ‖ (*bridge*) to make (a player) unguard a suit as a result of discarding ‖ to hug ‖ *v.i.* to exert pressure (esp. two opposite pressures) ‖ to force one's way by compressing oneself, *he squeezed through the narrow gap* **2.** *n.* a squeezing or being squeezed ‖ a hug ‖ (*pop.*) enforced payment, or the force used to secure payment, *to put the squeeze on somebody* ‖ (*politics*) a financial policy designed to reduce the volume of personal or corporate expenditure ‖ a small quantity of something (e.g. juice) obtained by pressing ‖ (*bridge*) a technique of play which forces an opponent to give up a valuable card ‖ a papier mâché or wax mold [perh. an intensive of obs. *quease*, to press]

squelch (skweltʃ) **1.** *v.i.* to make a sucking sound with one's boots or shoes as one walks through mud, wet snow etc. or as one walks in wet boots or shoes ‖ *v.t.* to tread heavily on (mud, wet snow etc.) and make this sound ‖ to crush with a very firm refusal or rebuke etc. **2.** *n.* the sucking sound made when one walks over soft wet ground or in wet boots etc. ‖ a silencing remark [imit.]

squib (skwib) *n.* a small firework that burns with a hissing noise before exploding ‖ a witty attack in writing or speech **a damp squib** (*Br.*) such an attack which falls flat [prob. imit.]

squid (skwid) *pl.* **squid, squids** *n.* a member of various genera of marine cephalopod mollusks having a long, tapered body, two caudal fins, ten arms and an internal shell. Squids range greatly in size, are widely distributed and are used for food and as fish bait [etym. doubtful]

SQUID (*electr. acronym*) for superconducting quantum interference device, a superconductor ring connecting two or several junctions used in measuring small electric currents and magnetic fields

squig·gle (skwíg'l) **1.** *v.i. pres. part.* **squig·gling** *past* and *past part.* **squig·gled** to writhe and squirm ‖ to progress in a confined area by making writhing, squirming movements **2.** *n.* a mark resembling the shape of a squiggling worm [imit. or fr. SQUIRM+WRIGGLE]

squill (skwil) *n. Urginea maritima,* fam. *Liliaceae,* a bulbous plant found in the Mediterranean area. The bulb of the white variety is used as a diuretic and heart stimulant, and that of the red variety as a raticide [fr. L. *squilla* fr. Gk]

squinch (skwintʃ) *n.* an arch across the internal angle of a square tower, serving to support an octagonal spire etc. [fr. earlier *scunch* fr. O.F.]

squint (skwint) **1.** *v.i.* to be crosseyed ‖ to look out of the corner of the eye ‖ to look through almost closed eyelids ‖ *v.t.* to narrow (one's eyes), e.g. in a look of suspicion **2.** *n.* strabismus, the condition causing squinting ‖ a look out of the corner of the eye ‖ (*pop.*) a rapid glance, *to have a squint at something* ‖ a hole in the wall or pillar of a church giving an oblique view of the altar **3.** *adj.* (of the eyes) affected with strabismus ‖ (of a look) out of the corner of the eye, oblique [shortened fr. ASQUINT]

squire (skwáiər) **1.** *n.* (in England) a title of respect for a country gentleman, esp. the principal, local, resident landowner ‖ (*hist.*) the wellborn personal attendant of a knight **2.** *v. pres. part.* **squir·ing** *past* and *past part.* **squired** to accompany (a girl), esp. to a dance ‖ (*hist.*) to be squire to [fr. O.F. *esquier*]

squire·ar·chy (skwáiərɑrki:) *pl.* **squire·ar·chies** *n.* (esp. *Br. hist.*) rule by the landed gentry or the landed gentry themselves, esp. with respect to their political influence

squirm (skwə:rm) **1.** *v.i.* to contort the body in little writhing movements ‖ (with 'along') to proceed in this manner ‖ to have feelings of shame and discomfort **2.** *n.* the act of squirming ‖ (*naut.*) a twist in a rope **squírm·y** *comp.* **squirm·i·er** *superl.* **squirm·i·est** *adj.* [prob. imit.]

squir·rel (skwə́:rəl, skwʌ́rəl, esp. *Br.* skwírəl) *n.* a widely distributed rodent mammal of fam. *Sciuridae,* esp. *Sciurus vulgaris,* the red squirrel, and *S. carolinensis,* the gray squirrel. They live in trees, have lithe bodies, strong hind limbs and bushy tails. They feed mainly on nuts and seeds, and make stores of food. Their average size is around 10-12 ins, excluding the tail (*GROUND SQUIRREL, *FLYING SQUIRREL) [fr. A.F. *esquirel,* O.F. *esquireul* fr. L. fr. Gk]

squirt (skwə:rt) **1.** *v.t.* to shoot a thin stream of (fluid) from a small orifice, *the pipe squirted water* ‖ to wet with a liquid or cover or hit with a fluid shot in this way, *the pipe squirted him as he passed* ‖ *v.i.* to be forced out in this way, *the beer squirted from the barrel* ‖ to eject liquid in a thin stream from a small orifice, *the barrel squirted in his face* **2.** *n.* the act or an instance of squirting ‖ a thin stream of fluid forced out under pressure ‖ a device for squirting out a liquid ‖ (*pop.*) a pretentious boy or man whom one considers insignificant [prob. imit.]

squirting cucumber *Ecballium elaterium,* fam. *Cucurbitaceae,* a Mediterranean plant. When ripe, the long fruit ejects its seeds mixed in watery fluid from one end

SRAM (*mil. acronym*) for short-range, solid-propellant, air-to-surface attack missile

Sri Lanka, formerly Ceylon, an independent state (area 25,332 sq. miles, pop. 12,240,000) in S. Asia, an island in the Indian Ocean. Capital: Colombo. Race: 74% Sinhalese, and minorities of Tamils and Tamil-speaking Muslims or Moors. Languages: Sinhalese (official) and Tamil. Religion: 78% Hinayana Buddhist, 18% Hindu, smaller Christian and Moslem minorities. The land is 20% forest. The north is flat, with a swampy coast. The south is mountainous (highest point Mt Pidurutalagala, 8,297 ft). The climate is tropical with southwest monsoons in summer and northeast monsoons in winter. Rainfall: 25-50 ins in the north and east, 75-200 ins in the center and southwest. Average temperatures (F.): 80° in the lowlands (with little seasonal variation), 54° (Jan.) and 62° (May) in the highlands. Livestock: cattle, water buffaloes, goats. Agricultural products: rice, tea, coconuts, rubber. Mineral resources: graphite, iron. Exports: tea, rubber, coconuts. Imports: rice, textiles, petroleum products, machinery, vehicles, sugar. University of Ceylon (1942) and two other universities. Monetary unit: rupee (100 cents). HISTORY. The Sinhalese migrated from S. India to Ceylon about the 5th c. B.C. Ceylon became the center of Buddhist civilization (3rd c. B.C.). Arabs introduced Mohammedanism (8th c. A.D.) and controlled trade until the arrival of the Portuguese (1505). The Dutch superseded the Portuguese (1638) but were overthrown by the British (1796). Ceylon was annexed to the East India Co. (1796-1802), became a British Crown Colony (1802) and an independent member of the Commonwealth (1948). In 1972 it was renamed Sri Lanka (beautiful island). Conflict between the majority Sinhalese, who controlled the government after independence and the Tamils, who had held most civil service and professional positions under the British, turned increasingly violent after 1983. Militant Tamils demanded a separate Tamil state in the north and east, where Tamils predominate. The continuing conflict disrupted the country's economy, and efforts to end the violence by granting the Tamils greater autonomy made little progress

Srin·a·gar (sri̯nəgɑ́r) the summer capital (pop. 531,094) of Jammu and Kashmir (*KASHMIR), on both sides of the Jhelum in the Vale of Kashmir. Handicraft products: carpets, silver, copperware. Industry: textiles

sRNA transfer (*physiol.*) a ribonucleic acid that combines with some amino acids and messenger RNA in protein synthesis *also* (soluble) RNA *Cf* MESSENGER RNA

SR-71 (*mil.*) U.S. strategic reconnaissance plane (succeeding U-2) for long-range (3,000-mi) high-altitude (80,000 feet) flight, with speed of Mach 3; operative in 1981

SS-8 *GECKO

SS-18 U.S.S.R. ICBM, capable of delivering ten warheads

SS-15 *SCROOGE

SS-5 *GAMMON, KELT

SS-4 *GANEF, KITCHEN

SS-14 *SCAPEGOAT

SSN-18 U.S.S.R. submarine-launched, liquid-propellant, ballistic missile with a 7,500-km range; operational since 1975

SSN-4 (*mil.*) U.S.S.R. surface-to-surface and surface-to-air missile

SS-9 (*mil.*) *GASKIN

SS-19 (*mil.*) U.S.S.R. intercontinental MIRV missile

SSN-X-17 (*mil.*) U.S.S.R. submarine-launched, solid-propellant ballistic missile with postboost vehicle, MIRV capability; operational in mid-1970s

SSPE (*med. abbr.*) for subacute sclerosis panencephalitis, a fatal brain disorder caused by dormant measles virus

SS-7 (*mil.*) *GRAIL, KERRY

SS-17 (*mil.*) U.S.S.R. missile with a 5-mi range

SS-6 (*mil.*) *GAINFUL, KINGFISH

SS-16 (*mil.*) U.S.S.R. ICBM that the U.S.S.R. agreed not to deploy during the life of the SALT I treaty

SST (*abbr.*) for supersonic transport

SS-10 (*mil.*) U.S.S.R. low-level air-defense weapon

SS-20 (*mil.*) U.S.S.R. 2 stage, solid-fuel ballistic missile launched from a tracked transport, in any of three versions: 1, a 1.5 megaton bomb with range of 3,500 mi., 2, a 50-kiloton warhead with range of 4,500, 3, with three individually targeted warheads

SS-22 (*mil.*) U.S.S.R. strategic solid-fuel, nuclear missile under development with 5,000-mi range

St *common nouns, proper names and place-names beginning thus are listed at* 'Saint'. (*The saints themselves are listed at 'John', 'Peter' etc.*)

stab (stæb) **1.** *v. pres. part.* **stab·bing** *past* and *past part.* **stabbed** *v.t.* to wound by piercing with a knife or other pointed weapon held in the hand ‖ to thrust (a knife etc.) in a specified way, direction etc. ‖ to inflict sharp emotional pain on ‖ *v.i.* to make a thrust or wound with or as if with a dagger, knife etc. **2.** *n.* a thrust made with or as if with a pointed weapon ‖ a wound inflicted in this way ‖ (*pop.,* usually with 'at') an attempt to do something, *a stab at finding the answer* ‖ a sudden sensation of pain, anguish, envy etc. **a stab in the back** a treacherous attack **a stab in the dark** a random guess [of Scot. origin]

stab·al·loy (stǽbælɔi) *n.* (*mil.*) a metal alloy made from high-density depleted uranium with titanium and molybdenum for use in kinetic energy penetrators for armor-piercing munitions

Sta·bat Ma·ter (stɑ́bɑtmɑ́tər) a 13th-c. Latin hymn describing the sorrows of the mother of Christ at the Crucifixion ‖ a musical setting of this hymn [L. *stabat mater dolorosa,* the mother stood sorrowing (the opening words)]

Stabex export stabilization scheme created by the 1975 Rome Convention and signed by the Common Market and the 46 developing countries, to compensate a developing country when its export earnings in 18 specific commodities for one year fall below its average earnings of the previous five years, with funds contributed by Common Market members

sta·bile 1. (stéibil, *Br.* esp. stéibail) *adj.* stationary ‖ not fluctuating ‖ (*chem.*) resisting decomposition **2.** (stéibi:l, *Br.* esp. stéibail) *n.* an abstract sculpture e.g. of metal (*CALDER, cf. MOBILE), none of the parts being articulated [fr. L. *stabilis*]

sta·bil·i·ty (stəbíliti:) *pl.* **sta·bil·i·ties** *n.* the quality or state of being stable ‖ a vow, made by certain monks, to remain in the same monastery for life [M.E. *stablete* fr. O.F. *stableté, estableté*]

stability analysis (*economics*) study of economic equilibrium between supply and demand

sta·bi·li·za·tion (steibəlizéiʃən) *n.* a stabilizing or being stabilized

sta·bi·lize (stéibəlaiz) *pres. part.* **sta·bi·liz·ing** *past* and *past part.* **sta·bi·lized** *v.t.* to render stable ‖ to prevent from changing, *to stabilize the cost of living* ‖ to equip (a vessel, aircraft etc.) with a stabilizer **stá·bi·liz·er** *n.* something that stabilizes, esp. a gyroscopic device to maintain steadiness in a vessel at sea [fr. F. *stabiliser* fr. L. *stabilis*]

sta·ble (stéib'l) **1.** *n.* (often *pl.*) a building in which horses are housed, or a similar building for cattle ‖ a group of horses kept in such a building ‖ a group of racehorses belonging to a particular owner ‖ an establishment for the training of racehorses, or the owners and personnel of such an establishment **2.** *v.t. pres. part.* **sta·bling** *past* and *past part.* **sta·bled** to put or keep (a horse etc.) in a stable [O.F. *estable*]

stable *adj.* remaining or able to remain unchanged in form, structure, character etc. under conditions tending to cause such change ‖ able to return to its original condition or recover its equilibrium after being slightly displaced ‖ permanent, enduring ‖ firm of purpose ‖ not easily thrown off balance ‖ (*chem.*) not readily decomposing or changing [O.F. *stable, estable*]

sta·ble·boy (stéib'lbɔi) *n.* a boy who works in a stable

sta·ble·man (stéib'lmən) *pl.* **sta·ble·men** (stéib'lmən) *n.* a man who works in a stable

sta·bling (stéibliŋ) *n.* accommodation for keeping and tending horses ‖ buildings used for this

Sta·broek (stɑ́bru:k) the original Dutch name for Georgetown, Guyana

stac·ca·to (stəkɑ́tou) **1.** *adj.* (*mus.,* of a note) cut short and sharply detached from the other notes ‖ (*mus.,* of a passage) consisting of such notes (cf. LEGATO) **2.** *adv.* in a staccato manner **3.** *pl.* **stac·ca·tos, stac·ca·ti** (stəkɑ́ti:) *n.* a staccato manner of playing ‖ a series of abrupt disconnected sounds, *she spoke in a rapid staccato* [Ital.]

stack (staek) **1.** *n.* a man-made pile, usually conical or rectangular, of hay, straw etc., frequently capped with a thatch ‖ a more or less orderly pile of things, *a stack of dishes* ‖ a pile of poker chips, sold to or won by a player ‖ (*pl.*) a structure filled with bookshelves separated by narrow aisles ‖ (*pl.*) the part of a library consist-

CONCISE PRONUNCIATION KEY: **(a)** æ, *cat;* ɑ, *car;* ɔ *fawn;* ei, *snake.* **(e)** e, *hen;* i:, *sheep;* iə, *deer;* ɛə, *bear.* **(i)** i, *fish;* ai, *tiger;* ə:, *bird.* **(o)** o, *ox;* au, *cow;* ou, *goat;* u, *poor;* ɔi, *royal.* **(u)** ʌ, *duck;* u, *bull;* u:, *goose;* ə, *bacillus;* ju:, *cube.* x, *loch;* θ, *think;* ð, *bother;* z, *Zen;* ʒ, *corsage;* dʒ, *savage;* ŋ, *orangutang;* j, *yak;* ʃ, *fish;* tʃ, *fetch;* 'l, *rabble;* 'n, *redden.* Complete pronunciation key appears inside front cover.

ing of such bookshelves || (*Br.*) a measure of volume for fuel (wood or coal) equaling 108 cu. ft || a tall vertical pipe or chimmey, e.g. on a ship || a chimney stack || (*pop.*, often *pl.*) a large quantity, *stacks of money* || (*mil.*) three rifles standing upright and leaning against each other with their butt ends resting on the ground **2.** *v.t.* to make a stack of || to load with stacks of something || *v.i.* (often with 'up') to form a stack **to stack the cards** to cheat by arranging the cards so that they will be dealt in a certain way || to prearrange a situation unfairly or dishonestly so that it will work to one's advantage [O.N. *stakkr*]

stacked heel a shoe heel built by laminating slices of leather

stack·yard (stǽkjɑrd) *n.* the area near farm buildings where the hay, straw, etc. is stacked

stad·dle (stǽd'l) *n.* a young forest tree, esp. one left to grow when others around it are felled || the base or supporting framework of a stack [O.E. *stathol*, foundation, tree trunk]

stadholder *STADTHOLDER

sta·di·a (stéidi:ə) *n.* a stadia rod || a method of surveying involving the use of a stadia rod [etym. doubtful]

stadia alt. *pl.* of STADIUM

stadia rod (*surveying*) a graduated rod used, with a theodolite or other instrument having a telescope and cross hairs, to measure distances

sta·di·um (stéidi:əm) *pl.* **sta·di·ums** *n.* an athletic field surrounded wholly or in part by a tiered structure seating spectators, usually having no roof || (*Gk hist.*, *pl.* **sta·di·a,** stéidi:ə) a unit of length, usually about 200 yds long, or a running track of this length, usually semicircular with tiered seats for spectators || (*pl.* **sta·di·a,** stéidi:ə) a stage in development, esp. the period between molts of an insect [L. fr. Gk *stadion*]

stadt·hold·er, stad·hold·er (stǽthouldər) *n.* (*hist.*) a governor or viceroy of a province or town in the Netherlands || (*hist.*) the chief magistrate in the United Provinces [Du. *stadhouder* fr. *stad*, a place+*houder*, holder]

Staël (stɑl), Madame de (Anne Louise Germaine Necker, baronne de Staël-Holstein, 1766-1817), French woman of letters, who held one of the most brilliant political and intellectual salons of her time. Her most famous work was 'De l'Allemagne' (1810). She lived mainly in exile because of her opposition to Napoleon I

Staël, Nicolas de (1914-55), French painter born in Russia. His freely geometric abstractions, in rich colors and textures, derive remotely from nature

staff (stæf, stɑf) **1.** *pl.* **staffs, staves** (steivz) *n.* a stick, pole etc. used as support in walking or climbing, or as a weapon || a rod carried as a symbol of authority or of pastoral care || (*mil.*, *pl.* **staffs**) a body of officers subordinate to the commanding officer and responsible to him for the administration and planning of his command || (*pl.* **staffs**) a body of people working for a chief authority || (*pl.* **staffs**) the personnel of an organization, *the school staff* || a tall pole supporting a flag || (*surveying*) a stick used in measuring altitudes || (*mus.*) a set of five horizontal lines on or between which symbols of notes are written or printed, pitch being indicated by the position of the symbol (the top line representing the highest pitch) **2.** *adj.* of or relating to a staff of people **3.** *v.t.* to furnish with a staff of people [O.E. *stæf*]

staff *n.* a building material consisting of a mixture of cement, plaster of paris etc., used esp. in exterior work on temporary structures [etym. doubtful]

Staf·fa (stǽfə) an uninhabited islet of the Inner Hebrides, Scotland, comprised of basaltic pillars and caves (*FINGAL'S CAVE)

Staf·ford (stǽfərd), Henry, 2nd duke of Buckingham (c. 1454-83), English nobleman. He helped to place Richard III on the throne, but later revolted unsuccessfully and was beheaded

Staf·ford·shire (stǽfərdʃiər) (*abbr.* Staffs.) a county (area 1,153 sq. miles, pop. 994,000) of W. central England. County town: Stafford (pop. 54,900). University of Keele (1950)

staff sergeant a noncommissioned officer ranking just above a sergeant in the U.S. Army or the Marine Corps

stag (stæg) **1.** *n.* the adult male of certain deer, esp. of the red deer and other members of genus *Cervus* (cf. HIND) || a male animal castrated when nearly mature || a young gamecock before its first molt || (*Br.*, *stock exchange*) someone who applies for shares before their issue, in the hope that he can sell them at a premium when the issue is made || (*pop.*) a man who attends a social gathering unaccompanied by a woman **2.** *adj.* (*pop.*) for men only, *a stag party* **3.** *v.i. pres. part.* **stag·ging** *past* and *past part.* **stagged** (*Br.*) to act as a stag on the stock exchange **4.** *adv.* (*pop.*) as a stag (unaccompanied man), *to go stag* [prob. fr. O.E. *stagga*]

stag beetle any of several large beetles of fam. *Lucanidae*, esp. *Lucanus capreolus,* the males of which have long branched mandibles resembling antlers

stage (steidʒ) **1.** *n.* a large, raised platform on which plays etc. are performed before an audience || the entire part of a theater that lies behind the proscenium || (*rhet.*) the scene of an event || a platform for landing passengers and goods from a vessel || a building scaffold || a platform for holding the objects to be observed through a microscope || a tier of shelves for potted plants, esp. in a greenhouse || a stopping place in a journey || a point, period or level in a progressive change or development || a section of a regularly traveled route || the distance between two stopping places as a division of a journey, *to travel by easy stages* || (*geol.*) a division of stratified rocks, corresponding to an age and ranking below series || a section of a rocket containing a rocket engine or engines. It is usually detached and jettisoned when its propellant is used up || a stagecoach **the stage** drama or the theater as a profession **to go on the stage** to become an actor or actress **2.** *v. pres. part.* **stag·ing** *past* and *past part.* **staged** *v.t.* to put (a play) on the stage or organize (a similar entertainment) || to conceive and carry out (something) in a surprising, dramatic way, *to stage a comeback* || *v.i.* (of a play) to lend itself to theatrical performance, *the play stages well* [fr. O.F. *estage*]

stage·coach (stéidʒkoutʃ) *n.* (*hist.*) a horse-drawn coach carrying passengers and goods and running regularly over a set route divided into stages

stage·craft (stéidʒkræft, stéidʒkrɑft) *n.* the art of writing, acting or producing a play

stage direction a notation in the text of a play directing the action, movement etc. of the players

stage door the door by which players, stage personnel etc. enter and leave a theater

stage fright nervous tension or fear sometimes experienced by a person about to perform or speak in public

stage·hand (stéidʒhænd) *n.* a person employed to move scenery and stage properties

stage-man·age (stéidʒmænidʒ) *pres. part.* **stage-man·ag·ing** *past* and *past part.* **stage-man·aged** *v.t.* to act as stage manager of (a production) || to rig (something apparently taking its proper course, e.g. a trial, committee meeting etc.) so as to produce a certain outcome or effect

stage manager the person responsible for the technical efficiency (curtains, stage, scenery, properties etc.) of a stage production (cf. HOUSE MANAGER)

stage·struck (stéidʒstrʌk) *adj.* fascinated with the stage, esp. passionately set on becoming an actor or actress

stage whisper any loud whisper that is (usually by intention) audible to others than the person addressed

stagey *STAGY

stag·fla·tion (stægfléiʃən) *n.* (*economics*) period of economic stagnation with substantial increases in prices —**stagflationary** *adj.* *Cf* SLUMPINFLATION

stag·ger (stǽgər) **1.** *v.i.* to walk with uncertain, uneven steps, continually veering in direction and keeping a precarious balance || *v.t.* to cause to reel under a blow || to shock or astonish as if with a blow || to arrange (things) in oblique or zigzag fashion, e.g. so as not to interrupt a view || (*aeron.*) to set (a wing) so that its forward edge projects beyond the forward edge of another wing || to arrange (holidays, periods of activity, attendance etc.) so that different groups of people are away, active, present etc. at different times, *staff lunch hours have been staggered* **2.** *n.* a staggering movement || a zigzag or oblique arrangement || (*aeron.*) the staggering of a wing, or resulting distance by which a forward edge projects beyond another || (*pl.*) a disease of domestic animals, esp. horses, affecting the central nervous system and causing a staggering gait [altered fr. dial. *stacker*, to reel fr. O.N. *stakra*]

staggered hours system of staff assignments beginning and ending at various hours to avoid overcrowding of facilities *Cf* FLEXTIME

stag·ing (stéidʒiŋ) *n.* the act or manner of putting on a play on the stage || scaffolding || (*hist.*) travel by stagecoach or the running of a stagecoach as a business || in-flight separation of the first stage of a missile with more than one propulsion stage

staging post (*mil.*) troop assembly area for a military operation *also* staging area

stag·nan·cy (stǽgnənsi:) *n.* the quality or state of being stagnant

stag·nant (stǽgnənt) *adj.* (of a fluid or a body of water) not in motion or flowing || foul from lack of motion || dull through lack of variety of activity [fr. L. *stagnans* (*stagnantis*)]

stag·nate (stǽgneit) *pres. part.* **stag·nat·ing** *past* and *past part.* **stag·nat·ed** *v.i.* (of a liquid or gas) to be motionless or cease to flow || to become foul because of lack of motion || to become dull, e.g. by staying too long in the same place **stag·ná·tion** *n.* a stagnating or being stagnant [fr. L. *stagnare* (*stagnatus*)]

stag party a social gathering for men only

stag·y, stage·y (stéidʒi:) *comp.* **stag·i·er** *superl.* **stag·i·est** *adj.* showily exaggerated, e.g. in dress, manner or speech

staid (steid) *adj.* set in steady habits, well balanced and rather dull [var. of *stayed*, past part. of STAY]

stain (stein) **1.** *v.t.* to make an unwanted spot on the surface of, *ink stained the cloth* || to color by using a pigment which soaks in, *to stain a section for microscope examination* || to spoil, taint (a reputation etc.) || *v.i.* to become stained in any of these ways, *this material stains easily* **2.** *n.* the colored area resulting from staining || the material with which one stains, esp. in staining wood or sections to be examined through the microscope || a moral taint etc. [fr. O.F. *desteindre*, to cause to lose color]

stained glass glass given a color by the presence of a metal or metallic oxide in its composition, or by having a pigment burned into its surface. It is used for decorative windows, esp. in churches. The earliest extant stained glass dates from the 11th c. (Augsburg)

Stai·ner (stéinər), Sir John (1840-1901), English composer and organist. He wrote much church music and is best known for his oratorio 'The Crucifixion' (1887)

stain·less (stéinlis) *adj.* not blemished || not susceptible to discoloration

stainless steel steel that is highly resistant to stain or rust because its principal alloying constituent is chromium (12% to 20%)

stair (stɛər) *n.* a constructed step or one of a set of such steps by which one can ascend or descend from one level or floor to another, esp. indoors || (*pl.*) such a set of steps [O.E. *stǣger*]

stair·case (stɛ́ərkeis) *n.* a flight of stairs together with its supporting and protecting structures || the part of a building occupied by this

stair rod a rod of wood, metal etc. serving to hold a stair carpet in place where it turns upward from one tread to the next

stair·way (stɛ́ərwei) *n.* a flight or several flights of stairs

stair·well (stɛ́ərwel) *n.* the vertical shaft enclosing the stairs in a building

stake (steik) **1.** *n.* a length of esp. wood, pointed at one end so that it can be driven into the ground and used as a marker, support etc. || (*hist.*) the post to which a person was bound for burning to death || a share or interest in something jointly owned, or in something affecting many, *a stake in the country's welfare* || money deposited as a wager || (*pl.*) money competed for, e.g. in a horse race || a horse race etc. in which a prize is offered || (*hist.*) a grubstake **at stake** being risked, *he has a lot at stake in this venture* **the stake** (*hist.*) execution by burning **2.** *v.t. pres. part.* **stak·ing** *past* and *past part.* **staked** to support, protect, mark out, secure etc. with a stake or stakes || to wager (money etc.) on the success or failure of an event || (*pop.*) to back (someone or something) financially in hope of future profit || to assert (a claim) (*hist.*) to grubstake [O.E. *staca*]

Staked Plain *LLANO ESTACADO

stake·hold·er (stéikhouldər) *n.* someone with

whom money stakes are deposited until it is known who has won the wager

Sta·kha·nov·ism (stəkɑ́nəvizəm) *n.* (*Russ. hist.*) a collective effort at increasing production by a simplification and reorganization of methods of work, the initiative coming from the workers themselves, and special privileges and bonuses being accorded for superior performance. The term is associated particularly with a movement of the mid-1930s [after Aleksei G. *Stakhanov* (*b.* 1906), Russ. miner of the Donbas]

sta·lac·tite (stəlǽktait, stǽləktait) *n.* a deposit of calcium carbonate resembling an icicle, formed cumulatively when water containing calcium bicarbonate has dripped very slowly from the roof of a limestone cave **stal·ac·tit·ic** (stæləktítik) *adj.* [fr. Mod. L. *stalactites* fr. Gk *stalaktos*, dropping, dripping]

sta·lag·mite (stəlǽgmait, stǽləgmait) *n.* a deposit of calcium carbonate somewhat like an inverted stalactite, standing on the floor of a limestone cave. It is formed cumulatively when water containing calcium bicarbonate has dripped from the roof **stal·ag·mit·ic** (stæləgmítik) *adj.* [fr. Mod. L. *stalagmites* fr. Gk *stalagma*, drop, drip]

stale (steil) **1.** *adj.* (of food or drink) impaired in texture, taste etc. through age ‖ (of a smell) suggesting the presence of something impaired in this way ‖ (of an atmosphere) no longer fresh ‖ (of bread) being a day or more old ‖ (of information, a joke etc.) having lost novelty and interest through being already well known ‖ (of an athlete etc.) in a deteriorated condition through too much or too little activity ‖ (*law*, esp. of a claim) impaired in force through having been allowed to be dormant too long **2.** *v. pres. part.* **stal·ing** *past* and *past part.* **staled** *v.i.* to become stale ‖ *v.t.* to make stale [M.E., etym. doubtful]

stale 1. *n.* the urine of horses, cattle etc. **2.** *v.i. pres. part.* **stal·ing** *past* and *past part.* **staled** (of horses, cattle etc.) to urinate [etym. doubtful]

stale·mate (stéilmeit) **1.** *n.* (*chess*) a position in which one player not in check cannot move without putting his king in check. It results in a draw ‖ a set of circumstances in which no progress can be made, *a stalemate in negotiations* **2.** *v.t. pres. part.* **stale·mat·ing** *past* and *past part.* **stale·mat·ed** to bring into the position of stalemate [fr. obs. *stale* fr. A.F.+MATE (checkmate)]

Sta·lin (stɑ́lin) (Joseph Vissarionovich Dzhugashvili, 1879-1953), Russian Communist statesman. The son of a Georgian shoemaker, he studied for the priesthood, but became a Marxist and was expelled (1899) from his seminary. He became a leading member of the Bolshevik party and, after several periods of imprisonment, joined the Soviet cabinet as people's commissar for nationalities (1917). He was elected general secretary of the central committee of the party (1922) and, after Lenin's death (1924), established himself as the virtual ruler of the U.S.S.R., ousting opponents and potential rivals in a series of purges in the 1930s. He departed from Lenin's economic policy (1928) and forced through a program of agricultural collectivization, liquidating the kulaks and attempting rapid industrialization through five-year plans. Army reforms were carried out, and a police state was set up, dominated by the OGPU. He formed a nonaggression pact with Nazi Germany (1939). When Germany attacked the U.S.S.R. (1941) he assumed full military and political leadership. He took part in the conferences at Tehran (1943), Yalta (1945) and Potsdam (1945). He retained most of his offices until his death. His rule was denounced officially in the U.S.S.R. from 1956 onwards

Sta·lin·a·bad (stɑ́linəbɑd) *DYUSHAMBE

Sta·lin·grad (stɑ́lingræd) *VOLGOGRAD

Sta·li·no (stɑlí:nou) *DONETSK

Sta·lin·o·grod (stɑlinougróud) *KATOWICE

Stalin Peak *COMMUNISM, MT

Sta·linsk (stɑ́linsk) *NOVOKUZNETSK

stalk (stɔk) *n.* the main stem of a herbaceous plant ‖ a slender supporting or connecting part, e.g. (*biol.*) a pedicel, peduncle or petiole [M.E. *stalke*, etym. doubtful]

stalk 1. *v.i.* to walk stiffly, as wading birds do ‖ to walk with exaggerated haughtiness, usually in anger ‖ to pursue e.g. deer in such a way as not to be seen, heard or scented by them ‖ (*rhet.*) to progress in an ominous, silent manner, *plague stalked through the streets* ‖ *v.t.* to pursue (deer etc.) by stalking ‖ (*rhet.*) to move through in an ominous, silent manner, *famine stalked the land* **2.** *n.* a stiff gait ‖ the act of stalking deer etc. [M.E. *stalke* fr. O.E.]

stalk·ing-horse (stɔ́kiŋhɔrs) *n.* a real or dummy horse used as cover by a hunter ‖ something used as a mask to conceal one's real intentions etc. ‖ (*politics*) a candidate put forward to cause division in the opposition or to conceal someone else's candidacy

stalk·y (stɔ́ki:) *comp.* **stalk·i·er** *superl.* **stalk·i·est** *adj.* long and slender, like a stalk ‖ having stalks

stall (stɔl) **1.** *n.* a compartment in a barn or stable, housing one animal ‖ a booth or table used elsewhere than in a store for displaying goods on sale (e.g. in a market, at a charity bazaar etc.) ‖ a fixed seat in the choir of a church used by a member of the clergy, or one used by a member of the choir ‖ (*Br.*) any of the theater seats in the rows nearest to the stage (*Br.*, *pl.*) the occupants of these seats ‖ a cover to protect a sore finger, toe etc. ‖ (*aeron.*) the condition resulting from stalling, marked by loss of altitude and failure of the controls to respond normally **2.** *v.t.* to put or keep (an animal) in a stall ‖ to cause (an engine) to stop because of overloading or insufficient fuel ‖ to cause (a motor vehicle) to stop, by stopping its engine in this way ‖ to cause (an aircraft) to lose the forward speed necessary to maintain its altitude and respond to the controls ‖ to cause to stick fast, e.g. in mud or snow ‖ *v.i.* of (an engine or vehicle) to stop by being stalled ‖ to stick fast, e.g. in mud or snow ‖ (of an aircraft) to become stalled [O.E. *steall*]

stall 1. *v.i.* (*pop.*) to talk or act evasively in the hope of delaying something or putting someone off ‖ *v.t.* (*pop.*, esp. with 'off') to get rid of or delay by evasion, *stall off the insurance man* **2.** *n.* (*pop.*) a trick used to get out of making a decision, giving a straight answer etc. [A.F. *estal*, *estale*, decoy bird]

stall-feed (stɔ́lfi:d) *pres. part.* **stall-feed·ing** *past* and *past part.* **stall-fed** (stɔ́lfed) *v.t.* to fatten (an animal) by keeping it in its stall and feeding it well

stal·lion (stǽljən) *n.* an uncastrated male horse, esp. one kept for breeding purposes [O.F. *estalon*]

stal·wart (stɔ́lwərt) **1.** *adj.* (*rhet.*) unshaken in determination or loyalty by risks or difficulties ‖ (*rhet.*, esp. of a man) of strong, sturdy build **2.** *n.* (*rhet.*) a stalwart person ‖ (*rhet.*) a zealous supporter of a cause, esp. a political one [fr. obs. *stalworth* fr. O.E. *stǣlwierthe*]

sta·men (stéimən) *n.* the male organ of a flower, consisting of a filament bearing an anther containing pollen [L.=thread]

Stam·ford Bridge, Battle of (stǽmfərd) a battle fought (Sept. 25, 1066) in Yorkshire, England, in which Harold II of England defeated an invasion by his brother Tostig and Harald III of Norway

stam·i·na (stǽminə) *n.* capacity for resisting fatigue or disease [L. pl. of *stamen*, thread]

stam·i·nal (stǽmin'l) *adj.* (*bot.*) of or having a stamen or stamens ‖ of, relating to or having stamina [fr. L. *stamen* (*staminis*), thread and STAMINA]

stam·i·nate (stǽminit) *adj.* having or producing stamens ‖ having stamens but no pistils [fr. L. *staminatus*, consisting of threads]

stam·i·node (stǽminoud) *n.* a staminodium

stam·i·no·di·um (stæminóudi:əm) *pl.* **stam·i·no·di·a** (stæminóudi:ə) *n.* a rudimentary, imperfect or sterile stamen [Mod. L. fr. L. *stamen* (*staminis*), a thread]

stam·mer (stǽmər) **1.** *v.i.* to speak with difficulty, repeating sounds and syllables and making frequent pauses in which no sound can be made ‖ *v.t.* (often with 'out') to utter in this way, *to stammer out an excuse* **2.** *n.* the affliction or habit of stammering [O.E. *stamerian*]

stamp (stæmp) **1.** *v.t.* to make (a mark) by pressure, *to stamp a design in clay* ‖ to print or affix a mark by pressure on, *to stamp a dish with a design* ‖ to affix postage or revenue stamps to (an envelope, document etc.) ‖ to bring (one's foot or feet) down heavily, *to stamp one's foot with impatience* ‖ to bring one's foot down heavily on, *to stamp the floor* ‖ to mark out, identify, *his tastes stamp him as a reactionary* ‖ to affect so deeply as to change permanently, *stamped by his experiences as a prisoner* ‖ (with 'out') to crush, put an end to, extinguish etc. by or as if by a heavy downward pressure of the foot, *to stamp out a cigarette*, *to stamp out a rebellion*, *to stamp out malaria* ‖ to crush (ore etc.) into powder ‖ *v.i.* to bring the feet or a foot down heavily **2.** *n.* the act of stamping, esp. with the foot ‖ a device used to impress a mark ‖ the mark made by such a device, *the document bears the regimental stamp* ‖ an official mark, seal etc. set on goods or documents as proof that duty or taxes have been paid, or that other legal obligations have been fulfilled ‖ a postage stamp ‖ a machine or machine part used to crush ore etc. ‖ a distinguishing quality or sign, *he has the stamp of a soldier about him* [M.E. *stampen* fr. Gmc]

Stamp Act (*hist.*) a British act of parliament (1765) extending the stamp duty on various documents to the colonies. It aroused much hostility in America, and was repealed (1766)

stam·pede (stæmpí:d) **1.** *n.* a sudden flight or rush of a number of frightened animals ‖ an impulsive concerted rush, *a stampede for the doors* ‖ any spontaneous mass action, *a stampede for reform of tax laws* **2.** *v. pres. part.* **stam·ped·ing** *past* and *past part.* **stam·ped·ed** *v.i.* to move or take part in a stampede ‖ *v.t.* to cause to stampede [fr. Span. *estampida*, a crash]

stamping ground (*pop.*) a favorite place of resort

stamp mill a mill in which ore is crushed to powder

stance (stæns) *n.* a way of standing, esp. the way one places one's feet in certain sports, e.g. fencing and golf [F. fr. Ital. *stanza*, station, stopping place]

stanch (stɑntʃ, stɔntʃ) *adj.* staunch

stanch (stɔntʃ, stɑntʃ) *v.t.* to prevent or stop the flow of (blood) from a wound ‖ to treat (a wound) so that the blood ceases to flow from it [fr. O.F. *estanchier*]

stan·chion (stǽnʃən, stɑ́nʃən) **1.** *n.* an upright bar, post etc. used as a support, esp. for a roof, deck etc. ‖ a yoke consisting of two linked uprights for confining cattle in a stall **2.** *v.t.* to provide or secure with a stanchion [O.F. *estanchon*, *estançon*]

stand (stænd) **1.** *v. pres. part.* **stand·ing** *past* and *past part.* **stood** (stud) *v.i.* to be or remain in a position in which the body is motionless and more or less vertical, supported by one or both feet ‖ to rise to such a position, *will volunteers please stand* ‖ to be or remain erect and supported on its base, *the house still stood after the earthquake* ‖ to be of a specified height, *he stands six feet* ‖ to remain in the same position or place, *let the dough stand for an hour before baking it* ‖ to be or remain in a specified position, condition etc., *stand at attention*, *stand aloof* ‖ to maintain a position, resolve etc., *stand firm*, *how does he stand on this question?* ‖ to cease walking, halt, *stand where you are* ‖ to be in a certain place, *his house stands at the corner* ‖ to have a certain position or be at a certain point on a scale, *the temperature stands at 25°C* ‖ to remain unchanged, *the dividend stands at 5%* ‖ (with *infin.* 'to gain', 'to lose' etc.) to be in a position to gain, lose etc., *he stands to win a fortune on this race* ‖ (*Br.*, with 'for') to be a political candidate, *he is standing for the council* ‖ to remain valid or effective, *old as they are, these rules still stand* ‖ (*naut.*) to move in a specified direction or in a specified course, *they stood into harbor* ‖ *v.t.* to place in an erect position, *he stood it on end* ‖ to place in a certain position, *stand the table in the corner* ‖ to support without deformation, *it will stand firing up to 1,300°*, ‖ to undergo, *to stand trial* ‖ to endure, *she cannot stand noise* ‖ (*pop.*) to meet the expense of (e.g. a drink) when treating **to stand a chance** to have a possibility of succeeding, winning etc., *he doesn't stand a chance against the others* **to stand by** to be a passive spectator ‖ to be present and ready to take action, *stand by in case of trouble* ‖ (*naut.*) to be prepared to operate, *stand by the lifeboat* ‖ to back up with support ‖ to adhere to (a promise etc.) **to stand down** to withdraw (from a competition or an official position) ‖ to leave the witness stand **to stand for** to represent, *the symbol % stands for percent* ‖ (*pop.*) to tolerate, *he won't stand for such nonsense* ‖ to advocate, *to stand for free trade* **to stand off** to remain at a distance ‖ to keep (someone or something) at a distance ‖ (*Br.*) to suspend for a time from employment ‖ (*naut.*) to stand out **to stand on** (or **upon**) to insist on the observing or respecting of, *to stand on ceremony* ‖ (*naut.*, only with 'on') to keep on the same course **to stand one's ground** to maintain one's position against opposition **to stand out** to be prominent, attract special attention ‖ to be persistent, *he stands out for his rights* ‖ (*naut.*) to hold a course away from shore **to stand over** to be postponed, *payment can stand over until next month* ‖ to supervise (someone) very closely in some activity, esp. disagreeably closely **to stand pat** to refuse to contemplate changes **to stand to** (*mil.*) to take up action positions at, or positions for inspection at **to stand up** to rise into, or be in, a standing posture ‖ to prove valid or durable **to stand up for** to defend against opposition or from censure **to stand up to** to resist successfully, *to stand up to an ordeal* ‖ to face with courage, *you must stand up to him* **2.** *n.* a stopping of motion or progress ‖ (*mil.*) an action fought on the defensive ‖ (*fig.*) a position, maintained with regard to some issue, *to take a stand in favor of something* ‖ a place where one stands or is placed ‖ a piece of furniture for holding something specified, *umbrella stand, music stand* ‖ a raised structure used to accommodate spectators, members of a band etc. ‖ a temporary stall for exhibiting wares to be sold or looked at (e.g. at a fair or beside a road) ‖ a standing growth esp. of trees, *a stand of white pines* ‖ a place where a touring theatrical or other company gives a performance ‖ the stop made by such a company, *a one-night stand* ‖ a place where public vehicles, taxis etc. are parked while waiting for passengers ‖ a witness stand **to make a stand** to express one's support for a position or opinion and make no concessions ‖ to fight a defensive battle, *they fled instead of making a stand* [O.E. *standan*]

stand·a·lone (stǽndəloun) *adj.* of equipment that stands alone, i.e., not on a desk or other furniture

stand·ard (stǽndərd) **1.** *n.* a model to be followed or imitated, established by custom and consent ‖ a degree of quality, level of achievement etc. regarded as desirable and necessary for some purpose, *his performance was not up to our standards* ‖ an established unit of weight or other measurement, *standard of length* ‖ the legally established proportion of pure gold or silver in a coin ‖ the basis of value in a monetary system, *gold standard* (*heraldry*) the long, tapering flag of a king, lord, city etc. ‖ (*mil.*) the flag of a cavalry regiment ‖ a vertical supporting pillar, post etc. ‖ (*bot.*) a vexillum ‖ (*bot.*) a shrub or tree grafted on one upright stem, not dwarfed or espaliered ‖ (*Br.*) one of the classes in a primary school **2.** *adj.* accepted as a model to be followed or imitated ‖ meeting the required standard ‖ regarded as having authoritative quality, *the standard work on the subject* ‖ of the ordinary type, without extra or unusual features, *the standard model of a washing machine* ‖ (*bot.*) of a shrub or tree grafted on one upright stem [O.F. *estendard*]

Standard (MR) *n.* (*mil.*) solid-fuel surface-to-air missile weighing 1,200 lbs, with 12-mi range, and radar detection

Standard Arm (*mil.*) an air-launched antiradiation missile (AGM-78) designed to home on and destroy radar emitters

stand·ard-bear·er (stǽndərdbɛərər) *n.* a soldier etc. carrying a standard (flag) ‖ (*rhet.*) a leader or representative of a movement, political party etc.

Stan·dard·bred (stǽndərdbréd) *n.* a trotting horse of an American breed used in harness racing

standard industrial classification U.S. Government method of classifying business and public establishments according to their primary activity *also* SIC codes

stand·ard·i·za·tion (stændərdizéiʃən) *n.* a standardizing or being standardized

stand·ard·ize (stǽndərdaiz) *pres. part.* **stand·ard·iz·ing** *past* and *past part.* **stand·ard·ized** *v.t.* to make conform to a standard, *to standardize educational methods* ‖ to test against a standard

Standard Metropolitan Statistical Area geographic region designated by U.S. Government for allocation of grants, etc.

Standard Missile (*mil.*) a shipboard, surface-to-surface or surface-to-air missile [RIM 66; RIM 67 (extended range)] with a solid-propellant rocket engine, equipped with nonnuclear warhead and semiactive or passive homing

standard of living the level of material well-being, esp. of a community, nation etc.

Standard Oil Companies major units of the U.S. oil industry incorporated (1870) in Ohio by John D. Rockefeller, who became the first president. As a result of U.S. antitrust legislation, the organization was broken up (1911) into more than 30 companies, including Standard Oil Company (New Jersey), Socony Mobil Oil Company, the Standard Oil Company of California, and the Standard Oil Company (Indiana)

Standards, National Bureau of the chief U.S. government agency established (1901) to conduct basic research in physics, chemistry, metallurgy, and engineering sciences. It is responsible for maintaining and developing standards of measurement for the U.S.A.

standard time the time in a country or locality, usually established by legislation or local custom, expressed in relation to a selected meridian

stand·by (stǽndbai) **1.** *n.* someone who or something that can be relied on in an emergency **2.** *adj.* ready to utilize time or space that may become available due to cancellations by others

stand·ee (stændí:) *n.* (*pop.*) a person standing in standing room, *this bus takes 25 standees*

stand-in (stǽndin) *n.* someone who takes up the position of a film actor until the cameras are ready ‖ any person who is a substitute

stand·ing (stǽndiŋ) **1.** *n.* reputation or status, esp. when high, *a man of standing* ‖ duration, *a feud of long standing* ‖ (*law*) qualification to initiate a law suit, esp. a class action suit **2.** *adj.* upright ‖ established, *a standing joke* ‖ permanent, not occasional, changing or temporary, *a standing arrangement* ‖ (of crops) not yet cut ‖ (of water) stagnant ‖ done from an erect position, *a standing jump* [STAND]

standing army a permanent army of regular soldiers

standing committee a permanent committee, esp. of a legislative body

standing-on-nines carry *HIGH-SPEED CARRY

standing order a standard procedural instruction constantly in force, *regimental standing orders* ‖ (*pl.*) standard rules of parliamentary procedure ‖ (*Br.*) a banker's order for the regular payment of a fixed amount on behalf of a customer

standing room space to stand ‖ accommodation available for standing when all seats in a theater, bus etc. are taken

standing wave a single-frequency mode of vibration of a body or physical system (e.g. an organ pipe or vibrating string) in which the amplitude varies from point to point, being constantly zero at certain points

Stan·dish (stǽndiʃ), Miles (or Myles, c. 1584-1656), American colonist born in England, the military leader of Plymouth Colony

stand-off bomb (*mil.*) a pilotless homing mini-aircraft with a 100-mi range, launched from a bomber, capable of carrying a nuclear warhead

stand·off half (stǽndɔf, stǽndɒf) (*rugby*) the halfback having a position between the scrum half and the three-quarter backs, during a scrum

stand·off·ish (stændɔ́fiʃ, stændɒ́fiʃ) *adj.* reserved, aloof

stand·out (stǽndaut) *n.* a person or thing of conspicuous excellence

stand·pat (stǽndpæt) *adj.* (*pop.*) opposing change, conservative **stánd·pát·ter** *n.* (*pop.*) a conservative person

stand·pipe (stǽndpaip) *n.* a vertical pipe or tank in which water is stored at a certain level, esp. in order to secure uniform pressure in a water-supply system

stand·point (stǽndpɔint) *n.* a point of view from which something is considered or judged

stand·still (stǽndstil) *n.* a ceasing of movement or activity

stand-up (stǽndʌp) *adj.* done or taken while standing, *a stand-up lunch* ‖ (of a fight) characterized by hard hitting, without any attempts to disengage ‖ (of a collar) stiffened so as to stay upright ‖ (of a comedian) performing a monologue alone on stage without the help of a straight man or props or decor

Stan·ford Research Institute (stǽnfərd) (*abbr.* SRI) an organization founded (1946) under the auspices of Stanford University, Calif., as a nonprofit establishment providing specialized research services under contract to business, industry, foundations, and the U.S. government

Stanford University (Leland Stanford Junior University), a private U.S. institution of higher learning founded (1885) near Palo Alto, Calif., by Senator Leland Stanford (1824-93) and his wife Jane Lathrop (1825-1905) as a memorial to their son. The campus covers about 9,000 acres. The Hoover Institution of War, Revolution and Peace, founded during the 1st world war by Herbert Hoover, houses more than one million documents dealing with the 1st and 2nd world wars, 20th-c. revolutionary movements, and international relations

Stan·hope (stǽnəp), Philip Dormer *CHESTERFIELD, 4th earl of

Stanhope, Lady Hester Lucy (1776-1839), British traveler. She settled (1814) among the Druses in Syria, adopted a religion which combined elements of Islam and Christianity, and was venerated as a prophetess by the Beduin tribes

Stanhope, James, 1st Earl Stanhope (1673-1721), English statesman. A Whig, he was in charge of foreign affairs (1714-17, 1718-21) and was first lord of the treasury (1717-18)

Stan·is·laus I Leszczyński (stǽnislɔs) (1677-1766), king of Poland (1704-9, 1733-5) and duke of Lorraine (1736-66). He gained the throne as a result of Charles XII of Sweden's victories in the Northern War, but went into exile when Charles was defeated (1709). His election as king (1733) precipitated the War of the Polish Succession. He was defeated and, although he retained the title of king, was forced to give up his royal power. In exile in France, he became a patron of science and the arts

Stanislaus II Augustus (1732-98), last king of Poland (1764-95). He gained the throne through the influence of his mistress, Catherine II of Russia. The country remained under Russian influence throughout his reign, and was gradually reduced in size by the partitions of Poland, disappearing altogether in 1795

Stan·i·slav·sky (stænislάvski:), Konstantin (Konstantin Sergeyevich Alekseyev, 1863-1938), Russian theatrical producer. A founder of the Moscow Art Theater (1898), he developed a new approach to acting and production based on realism, ensemble acting and the actor's complete identification with his character

stank alt. *past* of STINK

Stan·ley (stǽnli:), Edward George Geoffrey Smith *DERBY, 14th earl of

Stanley, Sir Henry Morton (1841-1904), British explorer. He found Livingstone near Lake Tanganyika (1871) and explored equatorial Africa (1874-7). He founded the Congo Free State (1879) in the service of King Leopold II of the Belgians

Stanley, Wendell Meredith (1904-71), U.S. biochemist and co-winner (with John H. Northrop and James B. Sumner) of the 1946 Nobel prize in chemistry, for preparation of enzymes and virus proteins in a pure form

Stanley Falls a series of waterfalls (dropping about 200 ft in 60 miles) in the upper Congo River above Kisangani, offering enormous hydroelectric potential

Stanley Pool an expanded section of the middle Congo River. Ports: Kinshasa, Brazzaville

Stanley v. Georgia a landmark decision (1969) of the U.S. Supreme Court, which ruled that to make private possession of obscene material a crime was unconstitutional

Stan·ley·ville (stǽnli:vil) *KISANGANI

stan·na·ry (stǽnəri:) *pl.* **stan·na·ries** *n.* (*Br.*) a tin mine or tin works **the Stannaries** (*Br. hist.*) a tin-mining district of Devon and Cornwall under the jurisdiction of special courts [fr. M.L. *stannaria*]

stan·nate (stǽneit) *n.* a salt of a stannic acid

stan·nic (stǽnik) *adj.* of, relating to or containing tin, esp. of a compound in which tin has a valence of 4 [fr. L.L. *stannum,* tin]

stan·nite (stǽnait) *n.* a natural sulfide of tin, copper and iron having a gray to black metallic luster [fr. L.L. *stannum,* tin]

stan·nous (stǽnəs) *adj.* of, relating to or containing tin, esp. of a compound in which tin has a valence of 2 [fr. L.L. *stannum,* tin]

stannous fluoride [SnF_2] (*chem.*) a fluoride compound used in toothpaste

Stan·ton (stǽntən), Edwin McMasters (1814-69), U.S. lawyer and secretary of war (1862-8) under Abraham Lincoln and Andrew Johnson. When President Johnson attempted to remove him from office for his harsh reconstruction measures, Stanton claimed protection under the Tenure of Office Act. He finally resigned after President Johnson survived impeachment by the Senate

CONCISE PRONUNCIATION KEY: **(a)** æ, *cat;* ɑ, *car;* ɔ *fawn;* ei, *snake.* **(e)** e, *hen;* i:, *sheep;* iə, *deer;* ɛə, *bear.* **(i)** i, *fish;* ai, *tiger;* ə:, *bird.* **(o)** o, *ox;* au, *cow;* ou, *goat;* u, *poor;* ɔi, *royal.* **(u)** ʌ, *duck;* u, *bull;* u:, *goose;* ə, *bacillus;* ju:, *cube.* x, *loch;* θ, *think;* ð, *bother;* z, *Zen;* ʒ, *corsage;* dʒ, *savage;* ŋ, *orangutang;* j, *yak;* ʃ, *fish;* tʃ, *fetch;* 'l, *rabble;* 'n, *redden.* Complete pronunciation key appears inside front cover.

Stanton, Elizabeth Cady (1815-1902), U.S. leader of women's rights. With Lucretia Mott she organized (1848) in New York the first U.S. women's rights convention, drafted a women's bill of rights, and drew up the first formal demand in the U.S.A. for women's suffrage

stan·za (stǽnzə) *n.* a group of lines of verse forming a structural division of a poem, usually in a recurring metrical pattern **stan·za·ic** (stænzéiik) *adj.* [Ital.=room, stanza]

sta·pe·dec·to·my (steipdéktəmi:) *(med.)* surgical removal (and replacement) of the stapes, innermost of three middle-ear bones —**stape·dectomized** *adj.*

stapedes alt. *pl.* of STAPES

sta·pe·di·al (stəpí:di:əl) *adj.* of the stapes ‖ near the stapes [fr. Mod. L. *stupedius* fr. *stapes (stapedis)*, stapes]

sta·pes (stéipi:z) *pl.* **sta·pes, sta·pe·des** (stéipi:dí:z) *n.* the innermost of the three bones of the middle ear [Mod. L. fr. M. L. =stirrup]

staph·y·lo·coc·cic (stæfələkɔ́ksik) *adj.* relating to or caused by a staphylococcus

staph·y·lo·coc·cus (stæfələkɔ́kəs) *pl.* **staph·y·lo·coc·ci** (stæfələkɔ́ksai) *n.* a member of *Staphylococcus,* fam. *Micrococcaceae,* a genus of nonmotile bacteria living on the skin and mucous membranes, that are gram-positive and cause inflammation [Mod. L. *Staphylococcus* fr. Gk *staphulē,* bunch of grapes+*kokkos,* berry]

sta·ple (stéip'l) **1.** *n.* the principal commodity produced, grown or sold in a particular place, *coffee is the staple of the country* ‖ a chief ingredient or constituent, *potatoes are the staple of their diet* ‖ a commodity for which the demand is constant and which is regularly kept in stock, e.g. flour, sugar and salt ‖ a raw material ‖ fiber of wool, cotton etc. with reference to its length or quality **the Staple** (*Eng. hist.*) a place royally appointed as a market for certain English goods intended for export in the 14th and 15th cc. ‖ (*hist.*) the merchant group having exclusive purchase rights at these markets **2.** *adj.* of, relating to or having the nature of a staple (commodity) **3.** *v.t. pres. part.* **sta·pling** *past* and *past part.* **sta·pled** to grade (wool, cotton etc.) according to the quality of its fiber [O.F. *estaple,* emporium]

staple 1. *n.* a U-shaped metal bar with pointed ends, designed to be driven into a post or wall to form a holder for a hook etc. ‖ a small piece of wire in the form of a square bracket, used to fasten sheets of paper etc. together by pushing both ends through the sheets and bending them back so that they cannot slip out **2.** *v.t. pres. part.* **sta·pling** *past* and *past part.* **sta·pled** to fasten with a staple or staples [O.E. *stapol,* a post]

Staple Act a British act of parliament (1663) under which all trade, whether English or foreign, to English colonies had to be shipped from an English port

sta·pler (stéiplər) *n.* a person whose job is grading wool

stapler *n.* a hand-operated device for stapling together sheets of paper etc.

star (stɑr) **1.** *n.* any of a vast number of hot, usually luminous celestial bodies, consisting of matter comprising most of the known elements in varying percentages in a highly ionized state, and found distributed in galaxies throughout the known universe ‖ a conventional symbol for such a body, often having five projecting points or several lines radiating from a central point ‖ this as a sign of excellence, rank etc. ‖ a mark thought of as resembling this, e.g. a white mark on a horse's forehead ‖ a person preeminent in some activity, esp. in the entertainment world or in sports, *stars of screen and stage* ‖ a leading performer in a play, film etc. ‖ an asterisk ‖ (*pl.*) heavenly bodies supposed to exert an influence on a person's life **to see stars** (*pop.*) to see bright points of light as a result of a blow on the head **2.** *v. pres. part.* **star·ring** *past* and *past part.* **starred** *v.i.* to be the most prominent person in a collective activity ‖ to be the star in a film, play etc. ‖ *v.t.* to furnish or mark with the symbol of a star or with an asterisk ‖ to introduce or publicize (an actor or actress) as a star [O.E. *steorra*]

—In the Milky Way galaxy alone it is estimated that there are about 200 billion stars. Stars are classified and catalogued according to size (*DWARF STAR, *GIANT STAR), temperature and spectrum, positions and motions, luminosity (*MAGNITUDE) and other special characteristics (e.g. periodic or sudden variations in brightness or spectrum, *VARIABLE STAR, *DOUBLE STAR). While magnitudes, densities and diameters vary widely, the masses of stars are limited: almost all star masses measured vary between one-tenth and 10 times the mass of our sun. The principal energy-producing reaction is thought to be the same for most stars: the thermonuclear conversion of hydrogen to helium (*CARBON CYCLE)

star anise *Illicium verum,* fam. *Magnoliaceae,* a small tree native to E. Asia, cultivated in China ‖ the dried fruit of this tree, used as a spice

star aniseed the dried fruit of the star anise, used as a spice

star apple a tree of genus *Chrysophyllum,* fam. *Sapotaceae,* esp. *C. cainito,* a tropical American evergreen bearing an apple-shaped purplish edible fruit, whose carpels in section present a starlike figure ‖ this fruit

star·board (stɑ́rbərd) **1.** *n.* the side of a ship or aircraft that is on the right of someone aboard facing forward (opp. PORT) **2.** *v.t.* to turn or put (the helm) over to starboard [O.E. *stēorbord*]

starch (stɑrtʃ) **1.** *n.* a white granular polysaccharide ($C_6H_{10}O_5$)n, synthesized by green plants and stored by them as a food reserve, and which upon hydrolysis yields an indeterminate number of dextrose molecules. Starch is obtained industrially from corn and potatoes, is an important foodstuff, and is used also as an adhesive in the paper and textile industries, in laundering and in pharmacy and medicine ‖ starchy foods ‖ stiffness of manner **2.** *v.t.* to stiffen (cloth etc.) with starch [M.E. *sterche* fr. O.E. fr. *stearc,* stiff]

Star Chamber (*Eng. hist.*) a court which developed (14th and 15th cc.) out of the king's council, and was used by the Tudors as a tribunal to deal with powerful nobles. The court was used by James I and Charles I as a tool of arbitrary government, and became notorious for summary procedure, torture and extortion. It was abolished (1641) by the Long Parliament

starch·i·ness (stɑ́rtʃi:nis) *n.* the quality or state of being starchy

starch·y (stɑ́rtʃi:) *comp.* **starch·i·er** *superl.* **starch·i·est** *adj.* of or like starch ‖ containing starch ‖ stiff and unbending in manner or attitude ‖ stiffened with starch

star·dom (stɑ́rdəm) *n.* the status of being a star in the entertainment or sports world

star·dust (stɑ́rdʌst) *n.* a great number of small stars in the night sky, appearing to the observer like a scattering of dust ‖ a mood of dreamy or romantic enchantment

stare (stɛər) **1.** *v. pres. part.* **star·ing** *past* and *past part.* **stared** *v.i.* to look fixedly with wide eyes, *to stare in amazement* ‖ to be vividly conspicuous, *the staring white houses of Greece* ‖ to have a blank, unseeing look, *staring factory windows* ‖ *v.t.* to affect (a person) in a specified way by a stare, *she stared him into silence* **to stare (someone) down** to meet the stare of (someone) by staring back at him till he looks away **to stare (someone) in the face** to be seen by (someone) to be obvious or inevitable, *ruin stared him in the face* **to stare (someone) up and down** to stare at (someone), as if inspecting him, in a rude manner **2.** *n.* a fixed gaze [O.E. *starian*]

Star·fight·er *n.* (*mil.*) a U.S. supersonic, single-engine, turbojet (F-104) with a nuclear and nonnuclear weapon capable of carrying 450 lbs. It is used by non-U.S. nations as a prime air interceptor; manufactured by Lockheed

star·fish (stɑ́rfiʃ) *pl.* **star·fish·es, star·fish** *n.* a member of *Asteroidea,* a class of echinoderms possessing five radially symmetric arms, and a mouth on the under surface of a central disk. The under surface of the arms bears rows of tube feet by which the animal crawls and grasps its prey

star·gaze (stɑ́rgeiz) *pres. part.* **star·gaz·ing** *past* and *past part.* **star·gazed** *v.i.* to contemplate the stars ‖ to be lost in abstract contemplation [back-formation fr. older *stargazer,* astrologer or astronomer]

stark (stɑrk) **1.** *adj.* bare, bleak, *a stark landscape* ‖ sheer, utter, *stark lunacy* **2.** *adv.* absolutely, *stark mad* [O.E. *stearc,* hard, unyielding]

stark-nak·ed (stɑ́rknéikid) *adj.* completely naked [older *start-naked* fr. obs. *start,* tail of an animal+NAKED]

star·let (stɑ́rlit) *n.* (*pop.*) a young film actress who is being prepared for a career as a star

Star·lift·er (stɑ́rliftə:r) *n.* (*mil.*) a large cargo transport (C-141) powered by four turbofan engines, capable of intercontinental range with heavy payloads and airdrops

star·light (stɑ́rlait) *n.* the light emitted by the stars

star·like (stɑ́rlaik) *adj.* resembling a star in brilliance or in having the shape of a conventional star symbol

star·ling (stɑ́rliŋ) *n.* a bird of genus *Sturnus,* fam. *Sturnidae,* esp. *S. vulgaris,* a very active, gregarious bird, about 8 ins long, with a short tail, sharp-pointed bill, and dark brown or black iridescent plumage. Starlings live near human habitations in Europe, the U.S.A., Australia and New Zealand ‖ any bird of fam. *Sturnidae* [O.E. *stærlinc*]

starling *n.* a protective structure of piles around the piers of a bridge [perh. corrup. of obs. *staddling* fr. O.E. *stathol,* foundation]

star·lit (stɑ́rlit) *adj.* illuminated by the light from stars

star-of-Beth·le·hem (stɑ́rəvbéθlihem) *pl.* **stars-of-Beth·le·hem, star-of-Beth·le·hem** *n.* a plant of genus *Ornithogalum,* fam. *Liliaceae,* esp. *O. umbellatum,* an Old World plant now also found in the eastern U.S.A., having small, greenish, star-shaped blossoms

Star of David a six-pointed star consisting of two equilateral triangles, a symbol of Judaism and of the Republic of Israel [trans. Heb. *mogēn dovid,* shield of David]

star·quake (stɑ́rkweik) *n.* (*astron.*) a major eruption or change in the shape, size, energy output, etc., in a celestial body

starred (stɑrd) *adj.* marked with stars ‖ influenced by the stars

starred form (*linguistics*) a form marked to indicate a historical reconstruction or deviation from the normal use of a term

star route a surface route in the U.S. postal service not accessible by railroad or steamship. Before rural free delivery was established, private contracts were made with bonded bidders to carry the mail over these routes. A Second Assistant Postmaster General was indicted during President Garfield's administration for fraudulently increasing the compensation of star-route contractors, but was cleared of such charges by President Arthur's administration. The scandal led to civil service reform

star·ry (stɑ́ri:) *comp.* **star·ri·er** *superl.* **star·ri·est** *adj.* full of stars ‖ shining like stars ‖ coming from the stars

star·ry-eyed (stɑ́ri:aid) *adj.* bemused with enchantment or wonder ‖ filled with or characterized by foolish, blindly enthusiastic idealism

STARS (*acronym*) proposed solar thermal aerostat research station, a rigid, spherical envelope up to one mile in diameter, designed to collect solar energy sufficient to supply some to earth and to modify weather, esp. fog dispersal

Stars and Bars (*Am. hist.*) the original flag of the Confederate States of America, consisting of three bars of red, white, red, and in the upper left-hand corner a blue field containing seven stars representing the seven states that had seceded at the time that the flag was adopted

Stars and Stripes the flag of the U.S.A., consisting of 13 horizontal stripes alternately red (7) and white (6), and 50 white stars (one for each state) on a blue field in the upper left-hand corner

star sapphire a sapphire that, when cut with a convex surface and polished, exhibits asterism

star shell (*mil.*) an explosive shell which upon bursting releases a shower of brilliant lights and is used esp. for signaling

star-span·gled (stɑ́rspæŋg'ld) *adj.* scattered or dusted with stars

Star-Spangled Banner the flag of the U.S.A. ‖ the name of the national anthem of the U.S.A., from a poem by Francis Scott Key

start (stɑrt) **1.** *v.t.* to cause (something) to come into existence, operation or activity, *who started that rumor?, start the car, they started the meeting with cocktails* ‖ to experience the first stage of (something) for the first time or after a period of not experiencing it, *he started life in poverty, she started feeling sick just after dessert* ‖ to perform or do the first stages of (an action, course etc.) for the first time or after a period of not performing or doing it, *to start reading a book* ‖ to cause (someone) to become engaged in a specified course of action or to experience something for the first time, *start him learning Latin next year, to start a baby on solid food* ‖ to establish, *to start a millinery shop*

‖ to drive (an animal) from its lair, nest, hiding place etc. ‖ to cause (nails, mechanical parts etc.) to loosen and become displaced ‖ to give the signal for the beginning of (a race) ‖ to give (runners in a race) the signal to run ‖ *v.i.* to come into existence, operation or activity, *the party starts at 9:00, the train started with a jolt* ‖ (of a person, vehicle, ship etc.) to set forth on a journey ‖ to spring up or out suddenly from or as if from shock ‖ (of mechanical parts etc.) to become displaced or loosened, *some timbers in the hull have started* ‖ (of the eyes) to bulge out or seem to bulge out, as an effect of shock etc. **to start in** to begin the preliminary work of an undertaking **to start off** to begin a program, undertaking etc. ‖ (of a program, undertaking etc.) to start, *the evening started off badly* **to start out** to start a journey or a course of action etc., *she started out to make a cake but it ended up as fudge* **to start up** to begin to function, *the Japanese course starts up next week* ‖ to give a little jump in fear ‖ to cause to begin to function, *to start up a generator* **2.** *n.* the starting of an action, journey, race or course of events ‖ an opportunity, advantage etc. assisting the starting of something, *a rich uncle gave him a start in life* ‖ a position in advance of others in a race etc. ‖ the point where a race etc. starts ‖ a nervous jerk or jump due to surprise or shock **stárt·er** *n.* someone who gives the signal for the start of a race ‖ a person or animal that starts in a race ‖ the self-starter of a motor [O.E. *styrtan,* to leap]

starting gate (*horse racing*) a barrier behind which the horses line up for a race. The barrier lifts automatically when the starting bell is rung

starting post a post at the starting point of a race

starting price the final odds offered on a horse before a race

star·tle (stɑ́rt'l) *v. pres. part.* **star·tling** *past* and *past part.* **star·tled** *v.t.* to cause to jump in alarm or surprise ‖ *v.i.* to become alarmed **stár·tling** [O.E. *steartlian,* to kick, struggle]

star·va·tion (stɑrvéiʃən) *n.* a starving or being starved

starve (stɑrv) *pres. part.* **starv·ing** *past* and *past part.* **starved** *v.i.* to die for lack of food ‖ to suffer acutely from lack of food ‖ (*pop.*) to feel very hungry ‖ (with 'for') to suffer from mental or spiritual deprivation, *starving for affection* ‖ *v.t.* to cause to die of hunger ‖ to deprive of food ‖ to compel by depriving of food, *starve the city into submission* ‖ (with 'for' or 'of') to cause to suffer from mental or spiritual privation, *starved for affection* **stárve·ling** *n.* (*rhet.*) a badly undernourished person or animal [O.E. *steorfan,* to die]

stash (stæʃ) *v.t.* (*pop.*) to hide or put (something) away for future use [prob. a blend of STORE+CACHE]

sta·sis (stéisis, stǽsis) *pl.* **sta·ses** (stéisi:z, stǽsi:z) *n.* a stoppage or slowing of the normal flow of fluids or semifluids in a bodily organ or vessel, esp. a slowing of e.g. circulating blood or of movement of the intestines [Mod. L. fr. Gk *stasis,* a standing still]

stat·cou·lomb (stætkú:lɒm) *n.* (*phys.*) a unit of charge in the cgs system of electrostatic units, equal to 33 x 10^{-10} coulomb [fr. ELECTROSTATIC+COULOMB]

state (steit) **1.** *n.* a form or mode of being, a condition, *what is the state of your health?* ‖ such a condition with respect to the mind or emotions, or to growth or development, *a state of great happiness, the larval state* ‖ a condition of emotional agitation, *to work oneself up into a state* ‖ a self-governing political community occupying its own territory ‖ a partly autonomous member of a political federation, *the 50th state of the U.S.A.* ‖ luxury and splendor, *to live in state* ‖ (*chem., phys.*) the condition of aggregation or arrangement of matter, *the gaseous state* (cf. PHASE) ‖ the condition of a physical system separate from all other conditions of that system and specified by definite quantities of energy, entropy, momentum etc. **State** the political organism as an abstract concept, *Church and State* **the States** (*pop.*) the U.S.A. **to lie in state** (of a dead person, esp. a public figure) to be laid in a draped coffin in a public place so that mourners can pay the last respects **2.** *adj.* pertaining to a state ‖ involving or calling for some display of ceremony, *a state occasion* **3.** *v.t. pres. part.* **stat·ing** *past* and *past part.* **stat·ed** to utter (a fact, opinion, principle etc.) or put it in writing etc., esp. in a way that is formal [fr. ESTATE and fr. L. *status*]

State attorney a legal officer appointed to represent a state in the courts

state bank a bank owned, chartered or controlled by a government **State bank** a bank chartered by a state of the U.S.A. and operating under its laws

state capitalism an economic system under which the State owns a very large part of the means of production

state chicken (*mil.*) in air intercept, a code meaning *I am at a fuel state requiring recovery, tanker service, or diversion to an airfield.*

state·craft (stéitkræft, stéitkrɑft) *n.* the art of managing state affairs

stat·ed (stéitid) *adj.* fixed, declared, *the stated price* ‖ officially recognized ‖ explicitly announced, *his stated opinion*

State Department the department of the executive branch of the U.S. government in charge of foreign relations

state·house (stéithaus) *pl.* **state·hous·es** (stéithauziz) *n.* a state capitol

state lamb (*mil.*) in air intercept, a code meaning *I do not have enough fuel for an intercept plus reserve required for carrier recovery.*

state·less (stéitlis) *adj.* being without a registered or recognized nationality or citizenship

state·li·ness (stéitli:nis) *n.* the quality of being stately

state·ly (stéitli:) *comp.* **state·li·er** *superl.* **state·li·est** *adj.* of dignified and impressive appearance or manner

state·ment (stéitmənt) *n.* the act of stating in speech, writing etc. ‖ that which is stated ‖ (*mus.*) the stating of a theme or the theme itself ‖ a financial accounting sheet setting out liabilities and assets

Stat·en Island (stǽt'n) an island (area 57 sq. miles) in New York harbor, part of New York City (*RICHMOND, New York)

Staten Island (*Span.* Isla de los Estados) an island (c. 45 miles long) of Argentina, off the eastern tip of Tierra del Fuego

state of grace (*theol.*) the condition of being in receipt of divine favor

state of nature (*theol.*) the normal moral condition of man

state of the art the highest level of technology in a field at any given time —**state-of-the-art** *adj.*

state-registered nurse (*Br., abbr.* S.R.N.) a nurse who is fully qualified, having passed the national examination

state·room (stéitru:m, stéitrum) *n.* a private cabin on a ship ‖ a private room on a train

State's attorney a State attorney

States General the bicameral legislative body in the Netherlands ‖ (*hist.*) the assembly of the three estates (clergy, nobles and commons) in the Netherlands (15th c.-1796) or in France (14th c.-1789) [trans. of F. *Etats Généraux*]

states·man (stéitsmən) *pl.* **states·men** (stéitsmən) *n.* a person having a large degree of responsibility in the government of a state ‖ such a person when characterized by wisdom and broadmindedness **státes·man·like** *adj.* characteristic of a wise statesman **státes·man·ly** *adj.* **státes·man·ship** *n.*

state socialism a theory that equalization of income and opportunity should be achieved through legislation by the existing state power, rather than through revolution

states' rights rights allowed (i.e. not denied) by the U.S. Constitution to individual states, as opposed to those vested in the federal government. A strong states' rights doctrine was expounded (1861–5) by the Confederate states. Any conflict between state and federal authority is settled by the supreme court of the U.S.A.

state tiger (*mil.*) in air intercept, a code meaning *I have sufficient fuel to complete my mission as assigned.*

stat·ic (stǽtik) **1.** *adj.* having no motion relative to the earth ‖ being in equilibrium while subject to two or more forces ‖ not changing, *static economy* **2.** *n.* atmospherics **stát·i·cal** *adj.* of statics [fr. Mod. L. *staticus,* acting by weight only fr. Gk *statikos,* causing to stand]

static electricity the charge possessed by stationary electric particles

static friction the force resisting the starting of sliding friction (cf. DYNAMIC FRICTION)

stat·ics (stǽtiks) *n.* a branch of science dealing with the relations among the forces that produce equilibrium

sta·tion (stéiʃən) **1.** *n.* a place where someone or something stands, either habitually or for a specified time, *the policeman took up his station near the door* ‖ a building, post etc. where a body of people work together, *a police station* ‖ a place along a route where trains or buses stop to take on or discharge passengers, merchandise etc. ‖ the building or buildings connected with this place ‖ an installation for the transmission and/or receipt of radio or television communication ‖ (*Austral.*) a sheep or cattle run with its buildings ‖ a place or region to which a ship, fleet etc. is assigned ‖ a position on a ship assigned to each member of the crew in case of emergency or battle ‖ rank, status in society ‖ (*biol.*) the characteristic habitat of a plant or animal **2.** *v.t.* to assign a position or post to [F.]

sta·tion·ar·y (stéiʃəneri:) *adj.* not moving ‖ not changing, *the temperature is stationary* ‖ not migratory or itinerant [fr. L. *stationarius,* having a fixed station]

stationary state (*phys.*) a stable or metastable quantum state associated with a wave (*QUANTUM THEORY), an integral number of whose wavelengths may be accommodated by the dimensions of the system

stationary wave (*phys.*) a standing wave

sta·tion·er (stéiʃənər) *n.* a seller of writing materials **sta·tion·er·y** (stéiʃəneri:) *n.* writing materials, esp. writing paper and envelopes [fr. L. *stationarius,* a tradesman with a fixed shop (not itinerant)]

sta·tion·mas·ter (stéiʃənmæstər, stéiʃənmɑstər) *n.* the official in charge of a railroad station

Stations of the Cross a series of 14 symbols, pictures or bas-reliefs, recalling episodes of the Passion of Jesus Christ, before which special devotions are performed, usually in a church

station wagon a car having a door at the rear end, and one row or two rows of rear seats which can be folded or removed to make room for extra luggage, equipment etc.

stat·ism (stéitizəm) *n.* economic control and planning by a highly centralized state government

stat·ist (stǽtist) *n.* a statistician [fr. L. *status,* state]

stat·ist (stéitist) **1.** *n.* an advocate of statism **2.** *adj.* of or advocating statism

sta·tis·tic (stətístik) *n.* a statistical item [back-formation fr. STATISTICS]

sta·tis·ti·cal (stətístik'l) *adj.* of, concerning, based on or consisting of statistics [fr. older *statistic* fr. G. *statistisch* fr. Mod. L. *statisticus*]

statistical mechanics the study and description of physicochemical phenomena from the point of view of the statistical behavior of large ensembles of parts comprising a system, or of their mechanical motions (*KINETIC THEORY, *MAXWELL-BOLTZMAN DISTRIBUTION)

stat·is·ti·cian (stætistíʃən) *n.* an expert in collecting, compiling and interpreting statistics [fr. obs. *statistic,* statistics]

sta·tis·tics (stətístiks) *n.* the collection and study of numerical data, esp. as a branch of mathematics in which deductions are made on the assumption that the relationships between a sufficient sample of numerical data are characteristic of those between all such data ‖ (*pl.*) these data [pl. of obs. *statistic,* statistics fr. G. *statistik* fr. Mod. L. *statisticus* adj., of the state, statistical]

Sta·ti·us (stéiʃi:əs) Latin epic poet (c. 40-c. 96), author of the 'Thebaid' and the 'Achilleid'

stat·o·cyst (stǽtəsist) *n.* a vesicle containing a statolith, found in certain invertebrates. It functions as an organ of equilibrium [fr. Gk *statos,* stationary+CYST]

stat·o·lith (stǽtəliθ) *n.* the body contained in a statocyst. It is composed mainly of calcium carbonate ‖ a similar body in a fish or amphibian ‖ (*bot.*) a solid body in the cytoplasm, e.g. a starch grain, thought to be responsible for variations in orientation of an organ or part [fr. Gk *statos,* stationary+*lithos,* stone]

sta·tor (stéitər) *n.* the fixed part of an electrical machine, within which or around which the rotor revolves [L. fr. *stare,* to stand]

stat·o·scope (stǽtəskoup) *n.* an aneroid barometer for recording small variations in atmospheric pressure ‖ an instrument which registers small changes in the rise and fall of an aircraft [fr. Gk *statos,* stationary+*skopein,* to observe]

stat·u·ar·y (stǽtʃu:eri:) **1.** *n.* statues collectively ‖ the art of making statues **2.** *adj.* of or relating to statues or the making of statues ‖ (of a mate-

rial) suitable for making statues [fr. L. *statuarius* adj.]
stat·ue (stǽtʃu:) *n.* a three-dimensional representation of a person or animal, carved in stone, wood etc., or cast in bronze or plaster, or modeled in some plastic material [F. fr. L. *statua* fr. *stare (status)*, to stand]
Statue of Liberty a bronze figure (almost 150 ft high) of a woman holding up a torch, on Liberty Island in New York harbor, designed by Bartholdi. It was completely refurbished for the celebration of its centennial in 1986
stat·u·esque (stætʃu:ésk) *adj.* (esp. of a woman) strikingly tall and well proportioned ‖ having the stateliness and grace associated with statues
stat·u·ette (stætʃu:ét) *n.* a very small statue [F.]
stat·ure (stǽtʃər) *n.* the height of a person ‖ moral or intellectual worth, esp. when impressively high [O.F.]
sta·tus (stéitəs, stǽtəs) *n.* position, rank or social standing ‖ prestige, *to confer status on someone* ‖ the legal position of a person, *marital status, the status of an alien* [L.]
status quo (kwou) *n.* the existing state of affairs [L.=state in which]
stat·ut·a·ble (stǽtʃutəb'l) *adj.* statutory
stat·ute (stǽtʃu:t) *n.* a law passed by a legislative body and formally placed on record in a written or printed form ‖ the written or printed record of this law ‖ an ordinance of some chartered body, corporation etc. [F. *statut*]
statute book the written or printed record of the statutes of a state or nation
statute law the written law to be used in given circumstances as established by legislative acts (cf. COMMON LAW, cf. EQUITY)
statute mile a mile (1,760 yds) as a fixed unit of distance in the U.S.A. and Great Britain
statute of limitations (*law*) a statute stipulating a period of time after the elapsing of which civil or criminal proceedings cannot be undertaken in cases of specified kinds
Statute of Westminster *WESTMINSTER, STATUTE OF
stat·u·to·ry (stǽtʃutɔri:, stǽtʃutouri:) *adj.* of or relating to or having the nature of a statute or statutes ‖ conforming to a statute ‖ established by statute ‖ (of an offense) declared by statute to be an offense and therefore legally punishable
statutory rape sexual intercourse with a girl below the age of consent (even when she is willing)
staunch (stɔntʃ, stantʃ) *v.t.* to stanch
staunch *adj.* firmly loyal, *a staunch friend* ‖ (esp. of a ship) watertight ‖ strongly made [fr. O.F. *estanche*, watertight]
Sta·vang·er (stəvάŋər) a port (pop. 52,000) in S.W. Norway. Industries: fishing, shipbuilding, metallurgy, mechanical engineering. Romanesque-Gothic cathedral (12th-13th cc.)
stave (steiv) **1.** *n.* one of the strips of wood set edge to edge to form the sides of a barrel, tub etc. ‖ (*mus.*) a staff ‖ the rung of a ladder ‖ a stanza of a poem or song **2.** *v. pres. part.* **stav·ing** *past* and *past part.* **staved,** (esp. *naut.*) **stove** (stouv) *v.t.* (esp. with 'in') to break a hole in (a boat, cask etc.) ‖ to supply with staves ‖ *v.i.* (e.g. of a boat) to become stove in **to stave off** to keep at a distance, ward off, *to stave off a disaster* [fr. STAVES, alt. pl. of STAFF]
staves alt. *pl.* of STAFF
Stav·ro·pol (stάvrʌpʌl) (called Voroshilovsk 1935-43) a city (pop. 271,000) in the R.S.F.S.R., U.S.S.R., in the N. Caucasus: food processing, mechanical engineering, natural gas extraction
stay (stei) **1.** *v.i.* to be in the same place or condition over a period, rather than change place or condition, *to stay indoors, stay calm* ‖ to reside for a while, *to stay at a hotel* ‖ to stop, halt, *stay where you are* ‖ to wait, *won't you stay till he comes?* ‖ to go on without flagging, *the favorite is staying well* ‖ *v.t.* (*rhet.*) to prevent or slow the progress of ‖ to postpone ‖ to appease (hunger, thirst etc.) temporarily ‖ to be in the same place or condition during (a period of time) ‖ (esp. with 'out') to be in the same place or condition until the end of, *he decided to stay the month out* ‖ to have unflagging endurance in (a race, course etc.) **2.** *n.* a remaining in one place or residing, *a stay of one week* ‖ (*law*) a postponement, *a stay of execution* [A.F. *estaier*]
stay 1. *v.t.* to support, prop up **2.** *n.* a prop, buttress etc. ‖ someone who or something that provides support and aid ‖ a strip of stiffening material used in corsets, shirt collars etc. ‖ (*pl., old-fash.*) a corset [O.F. *estayer*]
stay 1. *n.* (*naut.*) a strong rope or cable supporting a mast or spar **in stays** (of a ship) tacking **to miss stays** (of a ship) to fail to make a tack **2.** *v.t.* (*naut.*) to support or secure by means of stays ‖ (*naut.*) to put (a ship) on the other tack ‖ *v.i.* (*naut.*) to tack [O.E. *stæg*]
stay-at-home (stéiəthoum) **1.** *n.* a person who prefers remaining in or near his own home to traveling around **2.** *adj.* of, designating or characteristic of such a person
stay·be·hind (stéibi:haind) *n.* (*mil.*) agent, or group of agents established in a given country to be activated in the event of overrun by hostile forces or other circumstances under which normal access would be denied —**staybehind force** *n.*
staying power stamina
stay-in strike a strike in which employees stay at their place of work but refuse to perform their duties
stay·sail (stéis'l, stéiseil) *n.* (*naut.*) a sail spread on a stay
stead (sted) *n.* (in phrases) **in someone's** (or **something's**) **stead** in someone's (or something's) place as a substitute **to stand** (**someone**) **in good stead** to be of service to (someone), esp. in a difficulty [O.E *stede*]
stead·fast (stédfæst, stédfɑst, stédfəst) *adj.* adhering firmly and faithfully to a principle, cause etc. ‖ firm, unchanging, fixed, *a steadfast gaze* [O.E. *stedefæst*]
stead·i·ly (stédili:) *adv.* in a steady manner
stead·i·ness (stédi:nis) *n.* the quality or state of being steady
stead·y (stédi:) **1.** *comp.* **stead·i·er** *superl.* **stead·i·est** *adj.* not changing, constant, regular, *a steady speed* ‖ maintaining an unchanging position, posture or quality ‖ well balanced and serious, not frivolous ‖ (of a ship) keeping almost upright or keeping to the same course ‖ not easily excited or upset ‖ not given to sudden changes of behavior etc. **to go steady** (*pop.*) to go out regularly with the same person of the opposite sex, and only with that person ‖ (*pop.*, of two persons of the opposite sex) to go out together in this way **2.** *v. pres. part.* **stead·y·ing** *past* and *past part.* **stead·ied** *v.t.* to make steady ‖ *v.i.* to become steady [prob. fr. STEAD]
steady state theory (*meteor.*) hypothesis that the universe had no beginning but was formed and continues to grow through the spontaneous creation of hydrogen, replenishing matter from all that is destroyed *Cf* BIG BANG THEORY
steak (steik) *n.* a beefsteak ‖ any thick slice of meat or fish [O.N. *steik*]
steak Diane a sirloin steak pounded thin, cooked in sherry and cognac
steal (sti:l) **1.** *v. pres. part.* **steal·ing** *past* **stole** (stoul) *past part.* **sto·len** (stóulən) *v.t.* to take (something not rightfully belonging to one) without its owner's consent, esp. secretly ‖ to obtain without asking permission, *to steal a kiss* ‖ to secure, accomplish etc. without being seen, *she stole a glance at him* ‖ (*games*) to secure (a point, run etc.) by surprising the opponents' defense ‖ (*baseball*) to gain (another base) without the help of a hit or error ‖ *v.i.* to engage in stealing to go, come etc. without being noticed, *he stole silently away* ‖ (*baseball*) to get to a base without the help of a hit or error **to steal a march on** to get an advantage over by craftiness **2.** *n.* (*Am.=Br.* snip) something bought or for sale at an unexpectedly low price, a real bargain ‖ (*baseball*) the act of stealing a base ‖ an instance of this [O.E. *stelan*]
stealth (stelθ) *n.* a way of taking action designed to escape notice, *they came upon him by stealth* [M.E. *stalthe, stelthe* fr. *stelan*, to steal]
Stealth (*mil.*) an aircraft coated with radar-absorbent material making it virtually invisible to radar. It was announced August 1980 *also* stealthy aircraft
stealth·i·ly (stélθili:) *adv.* in a stealthy way
stealth·i·ness (stélθi:nis) *n.* the quality or state of being stealthy
stealth·y (stélθi:) *comp.* **stealth·i·er** *superl.* **stealth·i·est** *adj.* characterized by stealth
steam (sti:m) *n.* the invisible vapor into which water is converted when it boils ‖ the cloud of water droplets formed by the partial condensation of this vapor as it is cooled ‖ (*pop.*) energy, drive **to let** (or **blow**) **off steam** to get rid of surplus energy by activity or of emotional tension by expressing oneself strongly [O.E. *stēam*]
steam *v.i.* to emit steam or vapor ‖ to be converted into steam ‖ to escape into the air as steam, esp. as a cloud of steam ‖ to move as the result of propulsion by steam, *the train steamed out of the station* ‖ (of a surface) to become covered with condensed vapor ‖ *v.t.* to subject to the action of steam, in cooking, cleaning etc. ‖ to emit (steam or vapor) [O.E. *stēman, stȳman*]
steam·boat (stí:mbout) *n.* a steamship
steam boiler a boiler in which water is converted into steam
steam box the steam chest of a steam engine
steam chest a chamber where steam is stored before it enters the cylinder of a steam engine
steam coal hard coal used esp. for steam boilers
steam engine an engine, esp. a locomotive, driven by steam pressure
—The invention of the coal-burning steam engine revolutionized industrial production in the 18th c. and opened the way to the development of mechanized transport by rail and sea. The modern steam engine, using high-pressure superheated steam, remains a major source of electrical power and means of marine propulsion, though oil has replaced coal as the fuel in many installations and the reciprocating engine has given way to the steam turbine
steam·er (stí:mər) *n.* something driven by steam, e.g. a steamship or a steam engine ‖ a container, esp. a cooking utensil, in which things are steamed
steamer chair a deck chair
steam fitter a person who installs and repairs steam pipes and similar equipment
steam generator jumpers *SPONGES
steam hammer a forging hammer worked by steam power
steam·i·ly (stí:mili:) *adv.* in a steamy manner
steam·i·ness (stí:mi:nis) *n.* the quality or state of being steamy
steam navvy (*Br.*) a steam shovel
steam·roll·er (stí:mroulər) **1.** *n.* a steam-driven vehicle with a very heavy roller used for flattening freshly laid road surfaces ‖ (*pop.*) a person who or force that ruthlessly overrides any opposition **2.** *v.t.* to flatten with a steamroller ‖ to impose (a policy, idea etc.) by overriding all opposition ‖ to force (a group etc.) to accept or approve a policy etc. ‖ *v.i.* to move ahead in the manner of a steamroller
steam·ship (stí:mʃip) *n.* a ship driven by steam
steam shovel (*Am.=Br.* steam navvy) a large, steam-operated digging machine
steam·y (stí:mi:) *comp.* **steam·i·er** *superl.* **steam·i·est** *adj.* full of steam ‖ giving off steam ‖ of or like steam ‖ covered with steam
steamy (*golf*) a short shot or putt that goes beyond the hole
ste·ar·ic (sti:ǽrik:, stíərik) *adj.* of, relating to, like or obtained from stearin ‖ of or relating to stearic acid [fr. F. *stéarique* fr. Gk *stear*, fat, tallow]
stearic acid a white, crystalline fatty acid, $CH_3(CH_2)_{16}COOH$, obtained esp. by saponification from animal and hard vegetable fats, and used in making candles, soap etc.
ste·a·rin (stí:ərin) *n.* an ester of glycerol and stearic acid, found in many vegetable and animal fats **ste·a·rine** (stí:ər:n) *n.* the solid part of a fat (cf. OLEIN) [F. *stéarine* fr. Gk *stear*, fat, tallow]
ste·a·tite (stí:ətait) *n.* a gray-green or brown talc ‖ a porcelain made mainly from this, and used for insulators **ste·a·tit·ic** (sti:ətítik) *adj.* [fr. L. *steatitis* fr. Gk fr. *stear*, tallow]
steed (sti:d) *n.* (*rhet.*) a horse, esp. one full of mettle and ridden in battle [O.E. *stēda*, stallion]
steel (sti:l) **1.** *n.* any of numerous alloys of iron and 0.1–1.5% carbon in the form of iron carbide (esp. cementite), often with other metals (e.g. chromium, manganese, nickel etc.) alloyed to impart special physical properties. Steel can be cast, rolled, drawn etc. In the solid state it is hard and possesses great tensile strength. It is used in construction work, in cutting tools, in wire cables etc. It is formed by reducing the carbon content of cast iron, or by the diffusion of carbon into wrought iron ‖ a rod of steel with a rough surface, for sharpening knives ‖ (*rhet.*) a sword ‖ firm resolution, *a man of steel* ‖ a narrow, thin piece of steel used for stiffening, e.g. in a corset **2.** *v.t.* to make (esp. oneself) resolute, *he steeled himself to undergo the pain* **3.** *adj.*

CONCISE PRONUNCIATION KEY: (a) æ, cat; ɑ, car; ɔ fawn; ei, snake. (e) e, hen; i:, sheep; iə, deer; εə, bear. (i) i, fish; ai, tiger; ə:, bird. (o) o, ox; au, cow; ou, goat; u, poor; ɔi, royal. (u) ʌ, duck; u, bull; u:, goose; ə, bacillus; ju:, cube. x, loch; θ, think; ð, bother; z, Zen; ʒ, corsage; dʒ, savage; ŋ, orangutang; j, yak; ʃ, fish; tʃ, fetch; 'l, rabble; 'n, redden. Complete pronunciation key appears inside front cover.

made of, pertaining to, or like steel || having the color of steel [O.E. *stȳle*]
Steele (sti:l), Sir Richard (1672-1729), English man of letters, born in Dublin. He is best known for his essays in 'The Tatler' and 'The Spectator', the periodicals he edited, and largely wrote, in collaboration with Addison. He also wrote several comedies
steel engraving the process of engraving a design in steel || an impression taken from the steel plate
steel·i·ness (stí:li:nis) *n.* the quality or state of being steely
steel wool a material made of intricately meshed fine steel shavings used for cleaning metal surfaces and smoothing wood surfaces
steel·work (stí:lwə:rk) *n.* the steel part of a construction || articles in steel
steel·work·er (stí:lwə:rkər) *n.* someone employed in manufacturing steel
steel·works (stí:lwərks) *pl.* **steelworks** *n., sing.* or *pl.* a plant where steel in manufactured
steel·y (stí:li:) *comp.* **steel·i·er** *superl.* **steel·i·est** *adj.* made of steel || having great strength and hardness || severe, cold and penetrating, *a steely stare* || of the gray-blue color of tempered steel
Steel·yard (stíljərd, stí:ljɑrd) (*Eng. hist.*) the headquarters (13th c.-1597) in London of the Hanseatic League
steel·yard (stí:ljɑrd, stíljərd) *n.* a horizontal bar with its pivot near one end, having a short arm from which an object to be weighed is suspended, and a long graduated arm along which a counterweight is moved to produce equilibrium and give a reading from the graduations. Known masses suspended from the free end of the long arm enable greater loads to be weighed [fr. STEEL+YARD, (*obs.*) a rod]
Steen (stein), Jan (1626-79), Dutch painter. He specialized in domestic and tavern scenes
steen·bok (stí:nbɒk, stéinbɒk) *n.* a member of *Raphicerus,* a genus of small antelopes of E. and S. Africa, esp. *R. campestris* [Du. fr. *steen,* stone+*bok,* buck (male goat)]
steep (sti:p) **1.** *adj.* making a large angle, approaching 90° with the horizontal, *a steep hillside* || (*pop.,* of a demand, price etc.) excessive || (of an account, tale etc.) exaggerated or incredible **2.** *n.* a steep slope, esp. of a hill [O.E. *stēap,* high]
steep 1. *v.t.* to soak (something) thoroughly in a liquid || to cause (tea etc.) to infuse || (often *fig.*) to immerse, saturate || *v.i.* to soak in a liquid to infuse **2.** *n.* a steeping or being steeped || the liquid in which something is steeped [M.E. *stepe, stipa*]
steep·en (stí:pən) *v.t.* to make (a slope etc.) steeper || *v.i.* to become steeper
stee·ple (stí:p'l) *n.* a church tower together with a spire || a spire [O.E. *stȳpel, stēpel*]
stee·ple·chase (stí:p'ltʃeis) *n.* a horse race with jumps, either across country or on a special course || a cross-country foot race with obstacles
stée·ple·chas·er *n.* a horse or rider, or a runner, in a steeplechase [orig.=a cross-country race towards a church steeple]
stee·ple·jack (sti:p'ldʒæk) *n.* a man who professionally repairs or paints lofty structures, e.g. spires or tall chimneys
Steer (stiər), Philip Wilson (1860-1942), English landscape painter. He was greatly influenced by the French Impressionists
steer (stiər) *n.* a young castrated bull [O.E. *stēor*]
steer 1. *v.t.* to direct the course of, *to steer a ship, to steer the conversation around to a certain topic* || to direct (a course) || *v.i.* to direct the course of a ship, car etc. || to respond to such directing, *this car steers easily* **to steer clear of** to avoid **2.** *n.* (*pop.*) a friendly hint or suggestion [O.E. *stīeran*]
steer·age (stíəridʒ) *n.* the part of some passenger ships allotted to passengers paying the smallest fare, and providing the barest accommodation || the effectiveness of the helm in steering a ship
steer·age·way (stíəridʒwei) *n.* (*naut.*) a forward speed sufficient to enable a ship to answer the helm
steering committee a committee in a legislative or other body concerned with controlling the order of business
steering wheel the wheel which controls the direction of a vehicle or vessel
steers·man (stíərzmən) *pl.* **steers·men** (stíərzmən) *n.* (*naut.*) a helmsman
steeve (sti:v) **1.** *v.t. pres. part.* **steev·ing** *past* and *past part.* **steeved** to stow (cargo) in the hold of a ship **2.** *n.* a long spar used for stowing cargo [F. *estiver*]
steeve 1. *v. pres. part.* **steev·ing** *past* and *past part.* **steeved** *v.i.* (of a bowsprit) to have an upward angle from the horizontal || *v.t.* to cause (a bowsprit) to have such an angle **2.** *n.* this angle [etym. doubtful]
Stef·an's law (stéfɑnz) (*phys.*) the statement that the total amount of thermal radiation emitted per second per square centimeter of a black body is proportional to the fourth power of the body's absolute temperature [after Josef *Stefan* (1835–93), Austrian physicist]
Stef·fens (stéfənz), (Joseph) Lincoln I (18661936), U.S. journalist, political philosopher, and leader in the muckraker movement. His articles, collected in 'The Shame of the Cities' (1904), reveal with wit and irony the shortcomings of the Horatio Alger success story. His visit (1919) to Petrograd occasioned his remark, 'I have been over into the future, and it works'
steg·o·saur (stégəsɔr) *n.* a member of *Stegosaurus,* suborder *Stegosauria,* a genus of large herbivorous dinosaurs of the Upper Jurassic of North America, esp. *S. ungulatus,* which had a small head and rows of bony plates projecting up from the backbone [fr. Mod. L. *Stegosaurus* fr. Gk *stegos,* roof+*sauros,* lizard]
Stei·chen (stáikən), Edward (1879-1973), U.S. photographer. During the 1st world war he helped to introduce aerial photography
Stein (stain), Gertrude (1874-1946), American writer who lived chiefly in Paris from 1903. Her best-known book is 'The Autobiography of Alice B. Toklas' (1933). Her prose style was marked by syntactical experiment, and she had some influence on American writers of the 1920s
Stein (ʃtain), Baron Heinrich Friedrich Karl von and zum (1757-1813), Prussian statesman. As Prussian prime minister (1807-9) he abolished serfdom, made military service obligatory for all classes, and rearranged financial and administrative affairs. He was instrumental in forming the final coalition against Napoleon
stein (stain) *n.* an earthenware beer mug, usually with an attached lid || the quantity of beer held in this [G., prob. fr. *steingut,* stoneware]
Stein·beck (stáinbek), John Ernst (1902-68), American novelist whose works include 'Of Mice and Men' (1937), 'The Grapes of Wrath' (1939), 'Cannery Row' (1945), 'East of Eden' (1952; film, 1955), 'The Winter of Our Discontent' (1961), and 'Travels with Charley' (1962). He won the Nobel prize for literature (1962)
stein·bock (stáinbɒk) *n.* an ibex [G.=wild goat]
steinbock *n.* a steenbok
Stei·ner (stáinər, ʃtáinər), Rudolf (1861-1925), German teacher and philosopher, born in Austria. He founded anthroposophy, a system of thought which attempted to deduce the nature of the world from the nature of humanity. His system of education is followed in a number of schools named after him
Stein·metz (stáinmets), Charles Proteus (1865-1923), American engineer and inventor, born in Germany. His work in electricity did much to advance the progress of applied industrial chemistry. The magnetic arc lamp was one of his many inventions
Stein·way (stáinwei), Henry (Heinrich Engelhard Steinweg, 1797-1871), German-U.S. piano manufacturer. who completed the first Steinway piano in New York City in the 1820s
ste·le (stí:li:, sti:l) *n.* an upright inscribed slab or pillar serving as a monument, grave marker etc. || (*bot.*) the central cylinder of vascular tissue in the roots and stems of plants, surrounding the pith and consisting of the xylem, phloem and pericycle, and enclosed in turn by the cortex [fr. Gk *stēlē*]
stel·lar (stélər) *adj.* of or relating to a star || like or having the nature of a star || made of stars || principal, *a stellar role* [fr. L.L. *stellaris* fr. L. *stella,* star]
stellar guidance (*mil.*) a system in which a guided missile may follow a predetermined course with reference primarily to the relative position of certain preselected celestial bodies
stellar wind (*meteor.*) charged particles (plasma) emitted from the corona of stars *Cf* SOLAR WIND
stel·late (stéleit) *adj.* shaped like a conventional star || (of leaves, cells, ganglia etc.) coming out from a center in rays or points **stél·lat·ed** *adj.* [fr. L. *stellatus,* covered with stars]
Stel·len·bosch (stélənbuʃ) an agricultural market (pop. 18,000) in S.W. Cape Province, South Africa, founded in 1681. Afrikaans University (1916)
stel·li·form (stélifɔrm) *adj.* having the shape of a star [fr. Mod. L. *stelliformis* fr. L. *stella,* star]
stel·lite (stélait) *n.* (*metall.*) any of several alloys composed mainly of cobalt with a smaller proportion of chromium, sometimes with other metals. Stellite is used in making surgical instruments, cutting tools etc. [*Stellite,* a trademark]
stel·lu·lar (stéljulər) *adj.* shaped like a small conventional star || radiating like a star [fr. L.L. *stellula* dim. of *stella,* star]
stem (stem) **1.** *n.* the roughly cylindrical main aerial axis of a tree or plant which serves as its support and as the channel for conveying plant foods from the roots to the leaves, fruits etc. || the slender connection between a flower, fruit or leaf and the branch, main stem or twig || the shaft projecting from a watch, having a knob at the end for winding the spring || the slender rod or tube supporting a wineglass or other vessel on its base || the tube of a tobacco pipe || the thick stroke of a printed or written letter || (*mus.*) the vertical line extending up or down from the rounded part of a note || (*gram.*) the part of a word which remains unchanged by inflectional additions || the chief line of descent of a family || (*naut.*) the vertical piece of iron or timber at the bow of a ship, to which the sides are fastened || (*naut.*) the bow **from stem to stern** from one end to the other **2.** *v. pres. part.* **stem·ming** *past* and *past part.* **stemmed** *v.t.* to remove the stem of || (of a ship or navigator) to make headway against (a current, tide etc.) || (*rhet.*) to make progress against (a difficulty etc.) || *v.i.* to be derived, *his recklessness stems from vanity* [O.E. *stefn, stemn*]
stem 1. *v. pres. part.* **stem·ming** *past* and *past part.* **stemmed** *v.t.* to dam up (a stream etc.) || to hold back, *to stem an attack* || *v.i.* (*skiing*) to slow down or stop by forcing outward the heel of one ski (single stemming) or both skis (double stemming) **2.** *n.* (*skiing*) an act of stemming [O.N. *stemma*]
stem-wind·ing (stémwaindiŋ) *adj.* very good; stirring; firstrate —**stem-winder** *n.*
sten (sten) *n.* a Sten gun
stench (stentʃ) *n.* a powerful, offensive smell [O.E. *stenc*]
sten·cil (sténsəl) **1.** *n.* a thin sheet of metal, waxed paper etc., perforated with lettering or a design which is reproduced on a paper or fabric, on which the sheet is laid, when ink or paint is forced through the apertures || the pattern or lettering so produced **2.** *v.t. pres. part.* **sten·cil·ing,** esp. *Br.* **sten·cil·ling** *past* and *past part.* **sten·ciled** esp. *Br.* **sten·cilled** to make (an impression) from a stencil || to make an impression on (a paper or fabric) using a stencil [older *stanesile* prob. fr. M.E. *stansel* v., to ornament with varied colors]
Sten·dhal (stɛ̃dæl) (Marie Henri Beyle, 1783-1842), French writer. His deep psychological insight and the irony underlying his romanticism put him far in advance of his time, and his two greatest novels, 'le Rouge et le Noir' (1830) and 'la Chartreuse de Parme' (1839), became famous only long after his death. Each of these novels revolves around the unsuccessful struggle of a sensitive, intelligent young man to make a career or find happiness in the bigoted, reactionary society of the period following Napoleon's downfall. Stendhal also wrote short stories, accounts of travels and several autobiographical studies
Sten gun a British small, light submachine gun [fr. the initials of Sheppard and Turpin, its inventors+ENGLAND]
ste·nog·ra·pher (stənɒ́grəfər) *n.* a person employed, e.g. in an office, to take down and transcribe shorthand [STENOGRAPHY]
sten·o·graph·ic (stenəgræ̃fik) *adj.* of or relating to stenography || written in shorthand **sten·o·gráph·i·cal** *adj.*
ste·nog·ra·phy (stənɒ́grəfi:) *n.* the process or skill of making and transcribing shorthand notes [fr. Gk *stenos,* narrow+*graphia,* writing]
sten·o·type (sténətaip) *n.* a letter or letter combination that represents a phonogram in stenotypy || a machine that reproduces such symbols
sten·o·typ·y (sténətaipi:) *n.* a type of shorthand using ordinary letters to represent sounds,

words and phrases [fr. Gk *stenos*, narrow+*tupē*, impression]
sten·tor (sténtɔr) *n.* a member of *Stentor*, a genus of trumpet-shaped protozoans, often brightly colored [Mod. L., after *Stentor*, Gk herald in the Iliad who had a powerful voice]
sten·to·ri·an (stentɔ́ri:ən, stentóuri:ən) *adj.* (of the voice, spoken sounds etc.) very loud [after *Stentor*, Gk herald in the Iliad who had a powerful voice]
step- (step) *prefix* a combining element used with kinship terms to specify degree of affinity as a result of parental remarriage [O.E. *stēop-*]
step (step) *n.* a single movement made by lifting up one foot and setting it down in a different position ‖ the distance covered by such a movement ‖ a manner of moving on foot, *a heavy step* ‖ a mark or sound made by the foot in walking etc. ‖ one of a series of movements in dancing ‖ a set sequence of movements in dancing ‖ (*pl.*) a course followed in walking, *to retrace one's steps* ‖ pace, esp. in marching ‖ something on which the foot is placed in ascending or descending ‖ one unit in a flight of stairs or (*pl.*) a flight of esp. outdoor stairs or a series of these ‖ the rung of a ladder ‖ (*Br., pl.*) a stepladder ‖ a very short distance, *a step away* ‖ a degree in a scale, *to go up a step in someone's estimation* ‖ one of a series of stages in a process, activity etc. ‖ (*mus.*) a degree of the staff or scale ‖ (*mus.*) the interval between two such consecutive degrees ‖ (*naut.*) the socket holding a mast ‖ (of a quarry or mine) a shelf or ledge cut in the vertical surface ‖ (*mech.*) the lower bearing on which a vertical shaft rotates **in step** synchronizing the movements of one's feet with those of others with whom one is walking, marching or dancing **out of step** not in step **step by step** gradually **to keep step** to stay in step **to take steps** to begin to do what is necessary in order to achieve a certain purpose [O.E. *stæpe, stepi*]
step *pres. part.* **step·ping** *past* and *past part.* **stepped** *v.i.* to move by performing a step or steps, *please step forward* ‖ to execute a step with the foot ‖ to put or press the foot on something specified, *to step on someone's foot* ‖ (*pop.*) to walk a little way, *step down to the drug store* ‖ to enter into a position, condition etc. as if with a step, *to step into a fortune* ‖ *v.t.* to take (a stride etc.), *step three paces* ‖ to execute the steps of (a dance) ‖ (*naut.*) to fit (a mast) into its socket ‖ to provide with steps **to step down** to give up a position of authority, retire ‖ to decrease the voltage of (an electric current) using a transformer **to step in** to intervene **to step off** to pace (a distance) **to step on it** (*pop.*) to hurry **to step out** to begin to walk faster ‖ to go out to have a good time ‖ to leave a room, house etc. for a short time ‖ (*Br.*) to pace (a distance) **to step up** to increase, *to step up production* ‖ to increase the voltage of (an electric current) using a transformer [O.E. *stepan, stæpan*]
step·broth·er (stépbrʌðər) *n.* one's stepparent's son by a former marriage
step-by-step (stépbaistép) *adj.* gradual
step-by-step diplomacy the techniques of the Nixon-Ford administrations' efforts from 1973 to 1975 to settle the Arab-Israeli conflict
step·child (stéptʃaild) *pl.* **step·chil·dren** (stéptʃildrin) *n.* the child of one's husband or wife by a former marriage [O.E. *stēopcild*]
step·daugh·ter (stépdɔtər) *n.* a female stepchild [O.E. *stēopdohtor*]
step-down (stépdaun) *n.* a decrease in amount, size, power, importance etc.
step·fath·er (stépfɑðər) *n.* a male stepparent [O.E. *stēopfæder*]
Ste·phen (stí:vən) (c. 1097-1154), king of England (1135-54). Ignoring the oath he had sworn to his uncle Henry I that he would support the claim of Henry's daughter Matilda to the English throne, he invaded England on Henry's death (1135) and had himself proclaimed king. Matilda waged a civil war (1139-53) against him, in the course of which Stephen was imprisoned for six months (1141). The war ended when Stephen recognized Matilda's son Henry (later Henry II) as his heir
Stephen I, St (c. 969-1038), duke (997-1001) and first king (1001-38) of Hungary. He introduced Christianity into his kingdom, and is the patron saint of Hungary. Feast: Sept. 2
Stephen, St (*d.* c. 35 A.D.). the first Christian martyr, whose death by stoning prepared the eyewitness Saul (later St Paul) for his conversion. Feast: Dec. 26
Stephen Harding, St (*d.* 1134), English monastic reformer. As abbot of Cîteaux (c. 1109–c. 1134) he did much to strengthen the newly formed Cistercian order. Feast: Apr. 17
Ste·phens (stí:vənz), Alexander Hamilton (1812-83), vice-president of the Confederate States during the Civil War. As a champion of states' rights and civil liberty, he opposed the grant of extraconstitutional war powers to President Jefferson Davis. He urged (1864) the unconditional discharge of Federal prisoners in the South
Ste·phen·son (stí:vənsən), George (1781-1848), British engineer. He constructed the first successful steam locomotive (1814) and built the Stockton and Darlington line (1825), the first British passenger railroad. His 'Rocket' won an open competition for locomotives (1829), covering 12 miles in 53 minutes. He and his son Robert (1803-59) engineered many of the earliest railroads, in Britain and abroad
step·lad·der (stéplædər) *n.* a folding ladder having broad flat steps and a frame hinged to the back
step·moth·er (stépmʌðər) *n.* a female stepparent [O.E. *stēopmōdor*]
step·par·ent (stéppɛərənt, stéppærənt) *n.* the husband or wife of one's mother or father by a remarriage
steppe (step) *n.* a vast, treeless, usually level plain in S.E. Europe or Asia [fr. Russ. *stepĭ*]
step·ping-stone (stépiŋstoun) *n.* a stone, usually one of a series, projecting above the water of a stream, firmly placed in a marsh etc., enabling a crossing to be made by stepping from one stone to the next ‖ a means of advancement
step·sis·ter (stépsistər) *n.* one's stepparent's daughter by a former marriage
step·son (stépsʌn) *n.* a male stepchild [O.E. *stēopsunu*]
step-up (stépʌp) *n.* an increase in amount, size, power, importance etc.
ste·ra·di·an (stəréidi:ən) *n.* unit solid angle, being the solid angle subtended at the center of a sphere by an area of its surface equal to the square of the radius [fr. Gk *stereos*, solid+RADIAN]
ster·co·ra·ceous (stə:rkəréiʃəs) *adj.* of, relating to or containing dung [fr. L. *stercus* (*stercoris*), dung]
ster·e·o (stéri:ou, stíəri:ou) **1.** *n.* (*printing*) a stereotype ‖ a stereoscopic method, effect or system, e.g. a stereoscopic photograph or a stereophonic sound system **2.** *adj.* of or relating to space ‖ stereoscopic ‖ stereophonic [by shortening]
ster·e·o·bate (stéri:əbeit, stíəri:əbeit) *n.* (*archit.*) a solid foundation of a building, pillar etc. as visible above ground [F. or L.]
ster·e·o·chem·is·try (steri:oukémistri:, stiəri:oukémistri:) *n.* the study of the space arrangement of the atoms in a molecule and their effect on chemical properties [fr. Gk *stereos*, solid+CHEMISTRY]
ster·e·o·gram (stéri:əgræm, stíəri:əgræm) *n.* a stereographic diagram or stereograph [fr. Gk *stereos*, solid+*gramma*, a letter]
ster·e·o·graph (stéri:əgræf, stíəri:əgræf, stéri:əgrɑf, stíəri:əgrɑf) *n.* a design or picture viewed stereoscopically, or made to represent solid figures in three dimensions **ster·e·og·ra·phy** (steri:ɒgrəfi:, stiəri:ɒgrəfi:) *n.* the technique of drawing solid bodies on a plane surface ‖ stereoscopic photography [fr. Gk *stereos*, solid+*graphos*, written]
ster·e·o·i·so·mer·ic (steri:ouaisəmérik, stiəri:ouaisəmérik) *adj.* of, pertaining to or exhibiting stereoisomerism
ster·e·o·i·som·er·ism (steri:ouaisɒ́mərizəm, stiəri:ouaisɒ́mərizəm) *n.* isomerism which results from different space arrangements of atoms in molecules of the same composition and structural formula (*STRUCTURAL ISOMERISM, cf. OPTICAL ISOMERISM, cf. GEOMETRICAL ISOMERISM) [fr. Gk *stereos*, solid+ISOMERISM]
ster·e·ol·o·gy (steri:ɒ́lədʒi:) *n.* the study of three-dimensional objects seen in two dimensions, e.g., in brain studies —**stereological** *adj.* —**stereologically** *adv.*
ster·e·o·met·ric (steri:əmétrik, stiəri:əmétrik) *adj.* of or produced by stereometry **ster·e·o·mét·ri·cal** *adj.* **ster·e·o·mét·ri·cal·ly** *adv.*
ster·e·om·e·try (steri:ɒ́mitri:, stiəri:ɒ́mitri:) *n.* the science of determining the volumes of solid figures [fr. Gk *stereos*, solid+*-metria*, measurement]
ster·e·o·phon·ic (steri:əfɒ́nik, stiəri:əfɒ́nik) *adj.* of sounds which appear to have their sources distributed in space, even when they are emitted by e.g. two loudspeakers [fr. Gk *stereos*, solid+*phōnē*, voice]
ster·e·op·ti·con (steri:ɒ́ptikɒn, stiəri:ɒ́ptikɒn) *n.* a pair of projectors used in conjunction so that one view seems to dissolve while the next forms [Mod. L. fr. Gk *stereos*, solid+*optikos*, optic]
ster·e·o·scope (stéri:əskoup, stíəri:əskoup) *n.* a device by which each of two photographs, taken from slightly different angles, is viewed by one eye only, giving the impression of a three-dimensional view **ster·e·o·scop·ic** (steri:əskɒ́pik, stiəri:əskɒ́pik), **ster·e·o·scóp·i·cal** *adjs* **ster·e·o·scóp·i·cal·ly** *adv.* **ster·eos·co·py** (steri:ɒ́skəpi:, stiəri:ɒ́skəpi:) *n.* [fr. Gk *stereos*, solid+*skopein*, to observe]
ster·e·o·tape (stéri:əteip) *n.* magnetic tape that records sound stereophonically —**stereotape** *adj.*
ster·e·o·tax·is (steri:ətæksis) *n.* (*med.*) three-dimensional location of a point in the nervous system from coordinates guiding an electrode or needle —**stereotaxic** *adj.* —**stereotaxically** *adv.*
ster·e·o·type (stéri:ətaip, stíəri:ətaip) **1.** *n.* a plate providing a solid printing surface cast from a mold taken from a body of movable type ‖ a rigidly conventional expression, idea, character etc. **2.** *v.t. pres. part.* **ster·e·o·typ·ing** *past* and *past part.* **ster·e·o·typed** to make (a plate) from movable type ‖ to print (an impression) from a stereotype **stér·e·o·typed** *adj.* lacking originality [F. *stéréotype*]
ster·e·o·typ·y (stéri:ətaipi:, stíəri:ətaipi:) *n.* (*printing*) the process of making, and printing from, stereotype plates ‖ (*med.*) frequent, almost mechanical, repetition of the same action or formulas of speech, as in some cases of schizophrenia [F. *stéréotypie*]
ster·ic (stérik) *adj.* pertaining to the spatial arrangement of atoms [fr. Gk *stereos*, solid]
ste·rig·ma (stərígmə) *pl.* **ste·rig·ma·ta** (stərígmətə), **ste·rig·mas** *n.* a filament (esp. growing from the basidium of some fungi) from the top of which conidia are produced [Mod. L.]
ster·ile (stérəl, *Br.* esp. stérail) *adj.* lacking the ability to produce offspring ‖ lacking the ability to bear fruit, spores etc. ‖ (of land) unproductive ‖ (*bacteriol.*) free from living microorganisms ‖ lacking in inspiration, ideas etc., *a sterile writer* ‖ leading to no conclusion, *a sterile argument* [fr. L. *sterilis*]
ste·ril·i·ty (stərɪ́liti:) *n.* the state or quality of being sterile [fr. L. *sterilitas*]
ster·i·li·za·tion (sterəlizéiʃən) *n.* a sterilizing or being sterilized
ster·i·lize (stérəlaiz) *pres. part.* **ster·i·liz·ing** *past* and *past part.* **ster·i·lized** *v.t.* to render incapable of producing offspring ‖ to cause (soil) to become unfruitful by the deliberate use of a herbicide, or as the result of natural exhaustion of fertility ‖ to rid (instruments, surgical dressings etc.) of living microorganisms [fr. STERILE]
ster·let (stə́:rlit) *n.* *Acipenser ruthenus*, fam. *Acipenseridae*, a small variety of sturgeon prized for its flavor and its caviar [fr. Russ. *sterlyadĭ*]
ster·ling (stə́:rliŋ) **1.** *n.* the legal currency of England ‖ the legal currency (1707) of Great Britain ‖ (*hist.*) the English silver penny ‖ sterling silver ‖ articles made from sterling silver **2.** *adj.* of or relating to British sterling ‖ calculated in terms of British sterling ‖ (of silver) having an accepted standard of purity, usually 925 parts of silver alloyed with 75 parts of copper ‖ made of sterling silver ‖ of excellent quality, *sterling character* [prob. O.E. perh. fr. supposed *steorling*, coin with a star (some Norman coins bore a star)]
stern (stə:rn) *adj.* severe, *stern discipline* ‖ uncompromising, *a stern judge* ‖ cold and forbidding in appearance, *a stern landscape, a stern face* ‖ (*rhet.*) determined, *stern resolve* [O.E. *styrne*]
stern *n.* the rear end of a ship [prob. fr. O.N. *stjōrn*, steering]
sterna alt. *pl.* of STERNUM
ster·nal (stə́:rn'l) *adj.* of, relating to or situated near the sternum
stern chase (*naut.*) a chase in which the pursuing vessel follows in the wake of the vessel being pursued
stern drive (*motorboating*) motor with an inboard engine on an outboard drive *also* inboard-outboard

Sterne (stə:rn), Laurence (1713-68), British writer, born in Ireland. His works include 'The Life and Opinions of Tristram Shandy, Gentleman' (1759-67) and 'A Sentimental Journey through France and Italy' (1768). These are an extraordinary mixture of prurience, robustness and sentimentality. Their sentimental element is a part of the 18th-c. cult of sensibility. The enormous rambling structure is all Sterne's own

stern·fore·most (stə́:rnfɔ̃rmǫust, stə́:rnfóurmǫust) *adv.* (of a ship) with the stern foremost

stern·most (stə́:rnmǫust) *adj.* farthest astern

stern·post (stə́:rnpǫust) *n.* (*naut.*) a post, usually now of metal, joining the keel to the stern deck and usually having the rudder attached

stern sheets (*naut.*) the space between the stern of an open boat and the thwart nearest to it

stern·son (stə́:rnsən) *n.* (*naut.*) the end of a keelson to which the sternpost is fastened

ster·num (stə́:rnəm) *pl.* **ster·nums, ster·na** (stə́:rnə) *n.* the broad vertical bone to which the ribs are attached in front [Mod. L. fr. Gk *sternon,* chest]

stern·way (stə́:rnwęi) *n.* (*naut.*) progress stern foremost

ster·oid (stérɔid) *n.* (*chem.*) any of a class of compounds having a complex structure like the sterols, and that usually includes the sterols and numerous naturally occurring compounds, e.g. vitamin D, certain hormones and glucosides [fr. STEROL+Gk *eidos,* form]

ster·ol (stéroul, stérɔl) *n.* (*chem.*) any of a large class of complex alcohols, some of which (e.g. cholesterol, ergosterol) are highly active physiologically. They are characterized by a complex four-ring molecular system [fr. CHOLESTEROL, ERGOSTEROL]

ster·tor (stə́:rtər) *n.* (*med.*) the act of making a heavy sound like snoring while breathing, or an instance of this **ster·tor·ous** (stə́:rtərəs) *adj.* [Mod. L. fr. *stertere,* to snore]

Ste·sich·o·rus (stesíkərəs) (6th c. B.C.), Greek poet, author of choral lyrics on epic subjects. Only fragments survive

stet (stet) **1.** *n.* the word used as an indication to a printer that an instruction to delete is to be ignored. (Dots are also put under the matter concerned.) **2.** *v.t. pres. part.* **stet·ting** *past* and *past part.* **stet·ted** to write 'stet' against [L.=let it stand]

steth·o·scope (stéθəskǫup) *n.* (*med.*) an instrument which, placed on the thorax, conveys amplified sounds of the heartbeat or lung action, through earphones, to a doctor examining a patient **steth·o·scop·ic** (steθəskɒ́pik), **steth·o·scóp·i·cal** *adj* **steth·o·scóp·i·cal·ly** *adv.* **ste·thos·co·py** (steθɒ́skəpi:) *n.* [F. *stéthoscope* fr. Gk *stethos,* chest+*skopein,* to observe]

Stet·son (stétsən) *n.* a wide-brimmed felt hat with a high crown, worn esp. by cowboys [Trademark, after John Batterson *Stetson* (1830–1906), U.S. hat manufacturer]

Stet·tin (ʃtetí:n) *SZCZECIN

Stet·tin·i·us (stətíni:əs), Edward Reilly, Jr (1900-49), U.S. industrialist and statesman. He strongly influenced the formation of the United Nations, and served (1945-9) as the first U.S. delegate to that body

Steuart *STUART

Steu·ben (stú:bən, stjú:bən, ʃtɔ́ibən), Frederick William Augustus, Baron von (1730-94), Prussian officer who trained American soldiers during the Revolutionary War. His Regulations for the Order and Discipline of the Troops of the United States (1779) served until 1812 as the official U.S. military manual

Ste·van Du·šan (stévɑndu:ʃɑn) (c. 1308-55), king (1331-46) and czar (1346-55) of Serbia. He subjugated Albania, Thessaly, Epirus and all of Macedonia except Salonica, and dominated much of the Byzantine Empire. He died while marching on Constantinople

Stevan Ne·man·ja (nimɑ́njɑ) (1114-1200), ruler of Serbia (1168-96). He founded the first effective Serbian state, which was ruled by his descendants until 1371

ste·ve·dore (stí:vədɔr, stí:vədour) *n.* a man employed to store goods in a ship's hold, or to unload such goods [fr. Span. *estivador* fr. *estivar,* to stow cargo]

Ste·vens (stí:vənz), Alfred (1817-75), British sculptor, painter and draftsman best known for his equestrian statue of Wellington in St Paul's Cathedral

Stevens, John (1749-1838), U.S. inventor of marine and rail conveyances. His petition to Congress secured the Patent Law of 1790, the basis for the present U.S. patent system. He was the first to use steam power for screw propulsion in navigation. His 'Phoenix' made (1807) the first voyage of a steamboat in ocean waters. He introduced (1811) the world's first steam-ferry service. He obtained (1815) the first U.S. charter for a railway ever granted, and designed (1825) the first U.S. steam locomotive

Stevens, Thaddeus (1792-1868), U.S. politician. A Whig (1849-53) and then a Republican (1859-68) member of the House of Representatives from Pennsylvania, he became chairman of the House Ways and Means committee in 1861 and was instrumental in developing Reconstruction policy. At odds with Pres. Andrew Johnson over the Reconstruction issue, he was unable to get his own rigid schedule passed, but he did establish one of political and legal equality for blacks. He served as a House prosecutor during the impeachment trial of Pres. Johnson (1868)

Stevens, Wallace (1879-1955), American poet. His themes are the related ones of the relativity (and sensuousness) of sense perception, the nature of art and the order it creates, the relations of subject and object, the problem of belief, the possibility of the meeting of minds in art. All this is expressed in colorful, whimsical, light-toned verse, full of neologisms, words borrowed from other languages, and curious turns of phrase. His ideas are well expressed in his earliest work 'Harmonium' (1923). Other works include 'Ideas of Order' (1936), 'The Man with the Blue Guitar' (1937), 'Transport to Summer' (1947)

Ste·ven·son (stí:vənsən), Adlai Ewing (1900-65), U.S. political leader, twice defeated (1952, 1956) as Democratic contender for the U.S. presidency by Dwight D. Eisenhower. He became (1961) U.S. Ambassador to the United Nations

Stevenson, Robert (1772-1850), Scottish engineer, famous as a builder of lighthouses

Stevenson, Robert Louis (1850-94), British novelist, essayist and poet. Among his novels are 'Kidnapped' (1886), 'The Strange Case of Dr Jekyll and Mr Hyde' (1886) and 'The Master of Ballantrae' (1889). Some of his essays were collected in 'Virginibus Puerisque' (1881) and he also wrote travel accounts, e.g. 'Travels with a Donkey in the Cévennes' (1879). He was a meticulous craftsman and a rare storyteller. His adventure story 'Treasure Island' (1883) is one of the immortal children's books, and 'A Child's Garden of Verses' (1885) remains a classic

stew (stu:, stju:) **1.** *v.t.* to cook slowly and for a long time in a relatively small amount of liquid in a closed vessel, just below boiling point ‖ *v.i.* to be cooked in this way ‖ (of a person) to feel as if being slowly cooked because of heat or lack of oxygen ‖ (*pop.*) to fret, be anxious, *to stew about the weather* **to stew in one's own juice** to suffer the consequences of one's actions **2.** *n.* stewed meat and vegetables or a dish of this ‖ (*pop.*) a condition of anxious turmoil, *to be in a stew* [O.F. *estuver*]

stew·ard (stú:ərd, stjú:ərd) **1.** *n.* a ship's officer in charge of stores and arrangements about meals ‖ a male attendant who looks after the personal needs of passengers aboard ship ‖ an employee on an airplane, train etc. in charge of preparing and serving meals etc. (*Br.*) someone who shows people to their seats and maintains order at a public meeting, dance, public performance etc. ‖ someone who is responsible for the conduct of a race, athletic meet etc. ‖ a manager, acting for the owner, of a large landed estate, its mansion, tenants etc. ‖ an official responsible for provisioning a club, college etc. **2.** *v.t.* to act as a steward for **stéw·ard·ess** *n.* a woman steward, e.g. on an airplane (Am.= *Br.* air hostess) or one who attends female passengers on a ship **stéw·ard·ship** *n.* [O.E. *stīweard*]

Stew·art (stú:ərt, stjú:ərt), Potter (1915-85), U.S. Supreme Court associate justice (1956-81). A judge of the 6th circuit U.S. Court of Appeals, he was appointed to the Supreme Court by Pres. Dwight Eisenhower. He was a moderate and often responsible for casting the 'swing vote' when the court was split. He wrote the majority opinion in 'Elkins v. United States' (1960), concerning illegally obtained evidence; 'Katz v. United States' (1967), prohibiting unauthorized wiretaps; and 'Jones v. Alfred H. Mayer Co.' (1968) and 'Hills v. Gautreaux' (1976), both civil rights cases

Stewart, Robert, Viscount Castlereagh *CASTLEREAGH

Stewart *STUART

Stewart, Dugald (1753-1828), British moral philosopher. He expounded the philosophy of Reid, i.e. a belief in the existence of the external world and in the application of common sense to philosophical problems. His principal work is 'Elements of the Philosophy of the Human Mind' (3 vols, 1792-1827)

Stewart Island an island (area 670 sq. miles, pop. 500) south of South Island, New Zealand: fish, granite

stew·pan (stú:pæn, stjú:pæn) *n.* a pan with a lid, used for stewing

S-3 (*mil.*) *VIKING

stib·ine (stíbi:n, stíbain) *n.* a poisonous, gaseous compound, SbH_3, of antimony and hydrogen [STIBIUM]

stib·i·um (stíbi:əm) *n.* antimony [L.]

stib·nite (stíbnait) *n.* a mineral, Sb_2S_3, occurring in prismatic crystals and providing one of the main sources of antimony [STIBINE]

stick (stik) **1.** *n.* a piece of wood cut or broken from a tree ‖ such a piece of wood shaped and smoothed for a particular use, e.g. a walking stick, a drumstick ‖ something resembling a thin, shaped piece of wood, *a stick of sealing wax* ‖ a number of bombs released from an aircraft to explode at regularly spaced points along a straight line ‖ (*naut.*) a mast ‖ (*sports*) any of the various implements used to propel a ball etc., e.g. a hockey stick ‖ (*aeron.*) a vertical lever by which certain controls are operated ‖ (*printing*) a composing stick ‖ (*printing*) type which, when set, occupies 2 ins of one column, esp. in a newspaper ‖ a piece or part of something, *not a stick of furniture remained* ‖ (*pop.*, with 'the') a beating ‖ (*pop.*) a stiff, formal person, *a dull old stick* **the sticks** (*pop.*) the remote countryside, backwoods **2.** *v.t.* to furnish (a plant) with sticks as climbing supports [O.E. *sticca*]

stick *pres. part.* **stick·ing** *past* and *past part.* **stuck** (stʌk) *v.t.* to cause to adhere, *to stick a stamp on an envelope* ‖ to paste or otherwise fasten (a notice, poster etc.) to a board, wall etc. for public attention ‖ (with 'in', 'into' or 'through') to thrust (a pointed object) so as to penetrate or pierce something or someone, *she stuck a pin into the cloth* ‖ to penetrate or pierce with a pointed thing or things, *to stick a pincushion with pins* ‖ to place (various objects) here and there, *to stick knickknacks all over a room* ‖ to put casually, *he stuck the letter in his pocket* ‖ (*pop.*) to force to do an unpleasant chore or to pay a bill, by some kind of ruse, *they stuck him for the entire dinner* ‖ *v.i.* to become embedded in something by means of a sharp point ‖ to adhere ‖ to become fixed, *the car stuck in the mud* ‖ to become or remain motionless, *the car stuck on the hill* ‖ to continue one's efforts in spite of a desire to let them slack off, *he never sticks to anything for very long* ‖ to scruple, draw the line, *he sticks at nothing* ‖ to remain, *he stuck close to my heels* ‖ (with 'out', 'up', 'down' etc.) to protrude **to stick by** to remain loyal to **to stick out** to be insistent and not give in ‖ to endure **to stick up** to commit armed robbery upon **to stick up for** to support in argument, take the part of **stick·er** *n.* someone who pastes up notices ‖ someone whose job is to sever the jugular vein of an animal in a slaughterhouse ‖ an adhesive label ‖ a rod connecting two reciprocating levers of an organ ‖ a person, racehorse etc. showing powers of endurance ‖ (*pop.*) a puzzling problem [O.E. *stician*]

stick·com·mand·er (stíkəmændər) *n.* (*mil.*) individual who is in charge of parachutists from the time they enter an aircraft until the time of their exit

stick·i·ly (stíkili:) *adv.* in a sticky way

stick·i·ness (stíki:nis) *n.* the state or quality of being sticky

sticking plaster adhesive tape used to cover wounds

stick insect any of various insects of *Phasmatidae* and related families of suborder *Phasmatodea,* having a long, thin, sticklike body

stick lac the natural lac that covers small twigs and lac insects, used in dyes, polishes etc.

stick·le (stík'l) *pres. part.* **stick·ling,** *past* and *past part.* **stick·led** *v.i.* to be obstinate about a trifling matter ‖ (with 'at') to refrain from action because of scruples, *to stickle at signing a petition* [M.E. *stightle* fr. O.E. *stihtan,* to rule, set in order]

stick·le·back (stík'lbæk) *n.* any of various small scaleless fishes of fam. *Gasterosteidae* found in both fresh and salt water and having sharp spines in front of the dorsal fin. The male builds the nest and guards it during the breeding season [fr. O.E. *sticel,* a prick]

stick·ler (stíklər) *n.* a person who exaggerates the importance and insists on the observance of regulations etc. ‖ (*pop.*) a puzzling problem, question etc.

stick·pin (stíkpin) *n.* an ornamental pin worn in a necktie

stick shift (*automobile*) a manually operated gearshift mechanism on the floor or steering column of a motor vehicle

stick·up (stíkʌp) *n.* an armed robbery

stick·y (stíki:) *comp.* **stick·i·er** *superl.* **stick·i·est** *adj.* tending to stick ‖ covered with something adhesive or gummy, *sticky fingers* ‖ (*cricket,* of a wicket) having a yielding surface after rain ‖ (*pop.*) difficult, *a sticky problem* ‖ apt to be hard to please or persuade ‖ (of climate) very humid

Stieg·litz (stí:glits), Alfred (1864-1946), U.S. photographer whose photographic prints, notably the portrait of Georgia O'Keeffe and the 'Equivalents', were the first to be displayed in U.S. museums

stiff (stif) **1.** *adj.* resistant to bending or change of shape, *stiff bristles* ‖ (of muscles, joints etc.) sore and lacking in suppleness ‖ (of a semifluid substance) resisting the relative motion of its parts, *a stiff paste* ‖ (of machinery) hard to move ‖ resolute and unyielding ‖ lacking ease or grace ‖ formidable, *stiff competition* ‖ difficult, *a stiff examination* ‖ (of winds, currents) blowing or moving with strong, steady force ‖ (*pop.*) of high alcoholic content, *a stiff drink* ‖ (*pop.,* of prices) very high ‖ (*pop.*) severe, harsh, *a stiff fine* **2.** *n.* (*pop.*) a person, *he's a lucky stiff* ‖ (*pop.*) a corpse **3.** *adv.* exceedingly, *scared stiff* **stíf·fen** *v.t.* to make stiff ‖ *v.i.* to become stiff [O.E. *stīf*]

stiff·necked (stífnekt) *adj.* (*rhet.*) obstinate in an arrogant way

sti·fle (stáifəl) *pres. part.* **sti·fling** *past* and *past part.* **sti·fled** *v.t.* to keep (someone) from breathing by preventing the access of enough air ‖ to repress, *to stifle a yawn* ‖ to suppress, *to stifle a revolt* ‖ to silence, *the noise of the machine stifled his cries* ‖ *v.i.* to be or become stifled [M.E. *stufle, stuffle* cf. O.F. *estouffer,* to smother]

stifle *n.* the joint between the femur and tibia in the hind leg of a horse, dog and some other quadrupeds, corresponding to the knee in man [origin unknown]

sti·fling (stáifliŋ) *adj.* almost unbearably hot and stuffy

Stif·ter (ʃtíftər), Adalbert (1805-68), Austrian novelist. 'Der Nachsommer' (1857) and 'Witiko' (1865-7) were his best-known works, characterized by poetic realism. His 'Studien' (6 vols, 1844-50) is a collection of tales of the Bohemian forest

stig·ma (stígmə) *pl.* **stig·ma·ta** (stígmətə), **stig·mas** *n.* (*bot.*) that part of the pistil or gynoecium which receives the pollen ‖ (*zool.*) a body in some algae and protozoans that is sensitive to red light ‖ (*zool.*) an arthropod spiracle ‖ (*zool.*) the aperture of the trachea of insects ‖ (*zool.*) a colored wing spot of certain butterflies and other insects ‖ a mark of social disgrace, *the stigma attached to going bankrupt* **stig·ma·ta** *pl. n.* marks appearing on the body, sometimes accompanied by bleeding, which resemble the wounds of the crucified Christ [L. fr. Gk *stigma,* a prick]

stig·mat·ic (stigmǽtik) **1.** *adj.* of or relating to a social stigma ‖ of or relating to stigmata ‖ (*phys.*) anastigmatic **2.** *n.* someone who has stigmata [fr. M.L. *stigmaticus*]

stig·ma·tism (stígmətizəm) *n.* (*optics*) the condition of coming to a true focal point [prob. fr. Gk *stigmatismos*]

stig·ma·ti·za·tion (stigmətizéiʃən) *n.* a stigmatizing or being stigmatized

stig·ma·tize (stígmətaiz) *pres. part.* **stig·ma·tiz·ing** *past* and *past part.* **stig·ma·tized** *v.t.* to attach a label of disgrace to, *he stigmatized it as an act of cowardice* ‖ to mark with stigmata [M.L. *stigmatizare*]

Stijl, De (dəstáil) a Dutch movement advocating the synthesis of art and architecture, originated in 1917 by Theo van Doesburg and based on the neoplasticism of Mondrian. It stressed the exclusive use of horizontal and vertical lines and of primary colors. It influenced the Bauhaus

stil·bite (stílbait) *n.* a crystalline hydrous silicate of aluminum, calcium and sodium [F. fr. Gk *stilbein,* to shine]

stile (stail) *n.* an arrangement of steps on either side of a fence, for people to climb over. It eliminates the need for people to open a gate and so reduces the risk of cattle etc. escaping

stile *n.* one of the vertical boards in the frame of a paneled door etc. [perh. fr. Du. *stijl,* doorpost]

sti·let·to (stilétou) *pl.* **sti·let·tos, sti·let·toes** *n.* a small, thin dagger ‖ a pointed tool used to pierce holes in leather or cloth [Ital. dim. of *stilo,* dagger]

stiletto heel a very thin high heel on a woman's shoe

Stil·i·cho (stílikou), Flavius (c. 360-408), Roman general. As guardian of Honorius and regent of the Western Roman Empire (395-408), he fought several battles against the Visigoths under Alaric. He was arrested on the orders of Honorius, and executed for high treason after he had been accused of collusion with Alaric

Still (stil), Andrew Taylor (1828-1917), U.S. physician who founded (1892) at Kirksville, Mo., the first American School of Osteopathy

still (stil) *n.* an apparatus used for distilling alcoholic liquors or preparing distilled water

still 1. *adj.* having no motion, *still water* ‖ (of a beverage) not effervescing, *still cider* ‖ making or having no sound, *a still night* **2.** *n.* complete silence, *the still of the night* ‖ a static photograph, esp. one taken from a motion picture and used in publicity **3.** *adv.* at a given time just as before it, *he was still expecting to be asked, I am still wondering what to do, they will still be here tomorrow* ‖ even now (even then), *I still don't (didn't) understand* ‖ (with *comp.*) even, *this is still hotter* ‖ without sound or movement, *sit still* ‖ (used intensively) yet, *still another example* **4.** *conj.* nevertheless [O.E. *stille*]

still *v.t.* to quiet, *to still one's fears* ‖ to make silent, *he stilled the crowd* ‖ to satisfy or appease (a desire etc.) ‖ *v.i.* (*rhet.*) to become motionless or silent, the *music stilled and they began to chatter* [O.E. *stillan*]

still·age (stílidʒ) *n.* a stand on which e.g. a cask is placed to keep it off the ground

still bank nonmechanical bank with slot for inserting coins

still·birth (stílbə:rθ) *n.* the birth of a dead fetus

still·born (stílbɔrn) *adj.* dead when born

still life *pl.* **still lifes, still lives** a painting or photograph of inanimate objects ‖ painting or photography of such objects, as a genre

still·room (stílru:m, stílrum) *n.* (*Br.*) a room in a large house in which preserves, liqueurs etc. are kept

still·son wrench (stílsən) a wrench with an adjustable, milled jaw loosely bolted to a fixed milled jaw in such a way that pressure on the handle tightens the grip of the jaws. It is used for gripping and turning round objects (pipes etc.)

stilt (stilt) *n.* one of a pair of long poles, each of which has a footrest at some distance from its lower end, used to elevate the wearer and permit him to walk with long strides ‖ one of a number of posts on which a house is supported to raise it above ground or water level ‖ (*pottery*) a support which holds a pot above a shelf or sagger base in a kiln, so that the glaze will not unite with shelf or sagger ‖ a member of *Himantopus* or of *Cladorhynchus,* genera of long-legged, three-toed, limicoline birds inhabiting marshy places **stílt·ed** *adj.* raised on or supported by stilts ‖ (of speech, manner, style etc.) stiff and artificial ‖ (*archit.*) supported by vertical masonry set on the imposts of an arch [M.E.]

Stil·ton cheese (stíltən) a rich cow's milk cheese made in Leicestershire, England [fr. *Stilton,* England, where it was first sold]

Stil·well (stílwel, stílwəl), Joseph Warren ('Vinegar Joe') (1883-1946), U.S. general, commander of U.S. Army forces in the China-Burma-India (CBI) theater during the 2nd world war. He fought vigorously but unsuccessfully to preserve the Burma Road supply line and to persuade China to break the Japanese blockade. A U.S. proposal that he be given command of all Chinese forces was rejected by the Chiang Kai-shek regime, which forced his recall

Stim·son (stímsən), Henry Lewis (1867-1950), U.S. lawyer and political leader. Appointed special commissioner to Nicaragua (then occupied by U.S. Marines) by President Calvin Coolidge, he arranged (1927) an armistice between President Adolfo Díaz and rebel leader José María Moncada, under which the U.S.A. would supervise the 1928 elections. As governor general of the Philippine Is, he strove to convert them into 'self-governing possessions or colonies whose citizens did not participate in our citizenship'. As Secretary of State (1929-33) under President Herbert Hoover, he set forth, in the wake of Japanese aggression in Manchuria, the Stimson Doctrine, whereby the U.S. government would not formally recognize any situation, treaty, or agreement violating U.S. treaty rights or the Pact of Paris. As secretary of war under President Franklin Roosevelt, he helped to expand the U.S. Army during the 2nd world war, and as chief atomic policy adviser to President Harry Truman, he recommended the bombing of Hiroshima and Nagasaki and later justified this on humanitarian grounds

stim·u·lant (stímjulənt) *n.* something which stimulates ‖ a drug or other agent which temporarily increases the activity of an organ or some vital process [fr. L. *stimulans (stimulantis)* fr. *stimulare,* to goad]

stim·u·late (stímjuleit) *pres. part.* **stim·u·lat·ing** *past* and *past part.* **stim·u·lat·ed** *v.t.* to rouse (a person), e.g. to greater effort ‖ to act as a spur to (intelligence, application etc.) ‖ to arouse (appetite) ‖ (*med.*) to activate the functioning of (an organ) ‖ *v.i.* to act as a stimulant [fr. L. *stimulare (stimulatus)*]

stim·u·la·tion (stímjuléiʃən) *n.* a stimulating or being stimulated [fr. L. *stimulatio (stimulationis)*]

stim·u·la·tive (stímjuleitiv) **1.** *adj.* tending to stimulate **2.** *n.* something which stimulates

stim·u·lose (stímjulous) *adj.* (*bot.*) having stinging hairs or cells [fr. Mod. L. *stimulosus*]

sti·mu·lus (stímjuləs) *pl.* **stim·u·li** (stímjulai) *n.* something (e.g. an environmental change) that stimulates physiological activity ‖ something that acts as a spur to mental processes [L.=goad]

sting (stiŋ) **1.** *v. pres. part.* **sting·ing** *past* and *past part.* **stung** (stʌŋ) *v.t.* to wound with a sting, esp. so as to produce a swelling or inflammation on the skin ‖ to affect with pain like that caused by a sting, *stung by sleet and wind* ‖ (*fig.*) to goad, *he was stung into action* ‖ to cause emotional pain to, *to be stung by a remark* ‖ (*pop.*) to overcharge or extract money from, *he stung me for ten dollars* ‖ *v.i.* to cause or feel the pain of a sting, *stinging icy water, his face stung in the wind* **2.** *n.* the wound or pain caused by a stinger ‖ a sudden, sharp pain like that caused by a stinger ‖ a stinger ‖ something which causes an emotional pain ‖ the act of stinging ‖ stinging quality or capacity, *the sting of his words* ‖ (*slang*) a successful confidence game; a rigged chance to fleece someone; a simulated criminal operation set up to entrap criminals [O.E. *stingan*]

sting·er (stíŋər) *n.* a small sharp organ in some animals and plants, able to pierce the skin of a victim and often to inject poison or an irritant from a connected gland, thus causing pain or paralysis ‖ (*pop.*) a painful blow or remark ‖ a cocktail made of brandy and liqueur

Stinger *n.* (*mil.*) an 11-lb, shoulder-fired, artillery missile weapon with infrared homing; manufactured by General Dynamics Co.

stin·gi·ly (stíndʒili:) *adv.* in a stingy manner

stin·gi·ness (stíndʒi:nis) *n.* the state or quality of being stingy

stinging cell a nematocyst

stinging nettle a plant of fam. *Urticaceae,* esp. *Urtica dioica,* a perennial stinging weed of Eurasia and North America

sting·ray (stíŋrei) *n.* a member of fam. *Dasyatidae,* rays having sharp spines near the end of their whiplike tail which are capable of inflicting great pain

stin·gy (stíndʒi:) *comp.* **stin·gi·er** *superl.* **stin·gi·est** *adj.* refusing, or being extremely unwilling to give any more than a very small amount ‖ meager, inadequate, *a stingy helping of meat*

stink (stiŋk) **1.** *v. pres. part.* **stink·ing** *past* **stank** (stæŋk), **stunk** (stʌŋk) *past part.* **stunk** *v.i.* to emit a strong and very unpleasant smell ‖ to offend one's moral sense extremely, *the deal stinks of corruption* ‖ (*pop.*) to be very low in quality, *his performance stank* ‖ *v.t.* (esp. with 'up') to cause to stink **to stink out** to drive out with an offensive smell **2.** *n.* a strong, foul smell **to make** (or **raise** or **cause**) **a stink** to cause trouble, esp. in public over something offensive or supposedly offensive [O.E. *stincan*]

stink bomb a small bomb which emits an evil smell when made to explode

stink·bug (stíŋkbʌg) *n.* any of several insects, esp. of fam. *Pentatomidae,* which emit a foul smell

stink·horn (stíŋkhɔrn) *n.* any of several foul-smelling fungi of the order *Phallales*

stink·ing (stíŋkiŋ) **1.** *adj.* foul-smelling ‖ (*pop.*) very objectionable **2.** *adv.* (*pop.*) to an extreme degree, *stinking rich*

stink·pot (stíŋkpɒt) *n.* (*hist.*) a pot of burning sulfur hurled on the deck of an enemy vessel

stint (stint) **1.** *v.t.* to be parsimonious with (something), *don't stint the paint* ‖ to limit (someone) parsimoniously or with frugality, *they stint themselves to buy books* ‖ *v.i.* to be sparing in giving **2.** *n.* limitation, *he gives without stint* ‖ an allotment or period of work, *he has done his stint for today, he did his stint in the army* [O.E. *styntan,* to blunt]

stipe (staip) *n.* (*biol.*) a short stalk, stem or stemlike support, e.g. the stem-bearing pileus in agaric fungi, the stalk of seaweeds etc. [F.]

sti·pel (stáip'l) *n.* (*bot.*) the stipule of a leaflet [Mod. L. *stipella* dim. of *stipula,* a stalk]

sti·pend (stáipend) *n.* a fixed, usually moderate sum of money paid, e.g. to a clergyman, at regular intervals for services rendered [O.F. *stipende, stipendie* fr. L.]

sti·pen·da·ry magistrate (staipéndəri:) (*Br.*) a paid magistrate who is a qualified lawyer and who exercises duties similar to those of a justice of the peace

sti·pen·di·ar·y (staipéndi:ɛri:) **1.** *adj.* working for, or receiving, a stipend ‖ (of services) paid for by a stipend **2.** *pl.* **sti·pen·di·ar·ies** *n.* (*Br.*) a stipendary magistrate [fr. L. *stipendiarius*]

sti·pes (stáipi:z) *pl.* **stip·i·tes** (stípiti:z) *n.* (*zool.*) a stemlike part, esp. the second segment of a maxilla in insects and crustaceans [L.]

stip·ple (stip'l) **1.** *v.t. pres. part.* **stip·pling** *past* and *past part.* **stip·pled** to cover with dots (in drawing, engraving, painting etc.) in order to shade or make gradations of tone **2.** *n.* this method of work ‖ the effect produced in this work ‖ a thin layer of paint applied over another color, allowing the ground color to show through in many places [Du. *stippelen* fr. *stippen,* to speckle]

stip·u·late (stípjuleit) *pres. part.* **stip·u·lat·ing** *past* and *past part.* **stip·u·lat·ed** *v.t.* to state as a condition for reaching an agreement ‖ to specify, *to stipulate a date* ‖ *v.i.* (with 'for') to state a demand or requirement, *we stipulated for the use of marble* [fr. L. *stipulari (stipulatus)*]

stip·u·late (stípjulit) *adj.* having stipules [fr. Mod. L. *stipulatus*]

stip·u·la·tion (stipjuléiʃən) *n.* a stipulating ‖ something stipulated [L. *stipulatio (stipulationis)*]

stip·u·la·tor (stípjuleitər) *n.* someone who stipulates [L.]

stip·ule (stípju:l) *n.* one of two leaflike or membranous processes developed at the base of a leaf, sometimes modified into a tendril or spine [F.]

stir (stə:r) **1.** *v. pres. part.* **stir·ring** *past* and *past part.* **stirred** *v.t.* to give relative motion to the parts of (a fluid or semifluid), usually by moving an implement through it with a continued rotary motion in order to make the composition homogeneous ‖ to cause (something added) to form a uniform mixture with that to which it is added, *to stir pigment into paint* ‖ (esp. with 'up') to cause to rise by stirring or as if by stirring, *his dive stirred up some mud, to stir up trouble* ‖ to cause to move, esp. to change the position of very slightly, *the breeze stirred the leaves* ‖ to cause to act, feel or think, *the news stirred him to action, to stir the imagination* ‖ to arouse strong emotions of an idealistic kind in ‖ *v.i.* to begin to move, *nobody stirred before daybreak* ‖ to move a little, *he stirred slightly in his sleep* ‖ to move, *he did not stir while you were gone* ‖ to be able to be stirred, *the glaze does not stir easily* ‖ to begin to develop, *discontent is stirring among the farmers* **2.** *n.* the act of stirring ‖ a slight movement among things, persons etc., *a stir in the audience* ‖ a state of excitement, *he created a stir by his behavior* [O.E. *styrian*]

Stir·ling (stə́:rliŋ) a county (area 451 sq. miles, pop. 195,000) in central Scotland ‖ its county town (pop. 38,638), with a medieval castle, residence of many Scottish monarchs (12th c.-1603)

stir·ring (stə́:riŋ) *adj.* arousing strong emotions of an idealistic kind

stir·rup (stírəp, stə́:rəp) *n.* a footrest for a horseman, usually a loop of iron, suspended by a strap from the saddle ‖ a clamp or support having a similar U-shape [O.E. *stigrāp*]

stirrup bone the stapes

stirrup cup a drink handed as a farewell gesture to a mounted horseman before he rides away

stirrup iron the iron part of a riding stirrup

stirrup leather the adjustable leather strap of a stirrup

stirrup pump a small hand pump with a stirrup support and a short hose attached. The pump is placed e.g. in a bucket of water and is used to put out small fires

stish·o·vite [SiO_2] (stíʃəvait) a dense polymorph of quartz created under pressure believed of extraterrestrial origin; named for S. M. Stishov, Russian mineralogist. It was discovered by Edward Ching Te-Cha and others in 1962

stitch (stitʃ) **1.** *n.* one in-and-out passage of a thread through a fabric in sewing or embroidering ‖ the piece or loop of thread left in the material by this action ‖ one turn of the wool etc. around the needle or hook in knitting, crocheting etc. ‖ the resulting loop in the knitted or crocheted fabric ‖ a particular style of making such loops in sewing, embroidering, knitting or crocheting ‖ (*pop.,* always neg., or quasi-neg.) a bit, the least bit, *he hasn't done a stitch of work, hardly a stitch of clothing on* ‖ one in-and-out passage of a needle threaded with catgut, wire etc. used by a surgeon in closing a wound ‖ one of the loops of catgut, wire etc. so made ‖ a sudden sharp pain in the side **in stitches** in helpless laughter **2.** *v.t.* (often with 'up') to fasten, repair, make or ornament with stitches ‖ to staple (folded printed sheets) for binding ‖ *v.i.* to sew [O.E. *stice*]

sto·a (stóuə) *pl.* **sto·ae** (stóui:), **sto·as** *n.* (*archit.*) an ancient Greek portico [Gk]

stoat (stout) *pl.* **stoats, stoat** *n.* the European ermine, esp. in its brown, summer coat [etym. doubtful]

sto·chas·tic (stəkǽstik) *adj.* pertaining to chance or conjecture ‖ (*math.*) random [fr. Gk *stochastikos* fr. *stochazesthai,* to aim at a target, guess]

stochastic process (*math.*) in probability theory a system involving time parameters used to define a process utilizing random variables, e.g., of the economy, ecosystem, etc. *also* random process

stock (stɒk) **1.** *n.* an accumulation of things which is maintained as a constant source of supply, esp. as the basis of a storekeeper's or manufacturer's business ‖ an accumulation of goods for future use, *a stock of provisions* ‖ ancestors, family ‖ a group of animals or plants having the same line of descent ‖ a major racial division of mankind ‖ a group of related languages ‖ shares of corporate capital or their certificates of ownership ‖ the material necessary for running an enterprise, e.g. the tractors, tools, hen houses etc. of a farm ‖ livestock ‖ the raw material from which a manufactured article, e.g. paper, is made ‖ the fixed base or holding part of a tool, weapon, anchor etc. ‖ the wooden part of a rifle by which the barrel is held ‖ the butt of a whip ‖ the estimation in which a thing or person is held, *his stock has gone up* ‖ (*pl., naut.*) a wooden framework supporting the hull of a ship being built or repaired on land ‖ (*pl., hist.*) a wooden frame with holes for confining the ankles (and sometimes the wrists) of a wrongdoer sentenced to be exposed in this way to public view and ridicule ‖ liquid in which bones, meat, fish or vegetables have been simmered, used as a basis for soups, sauces etc. ‖ a theatrical stock company ‖ the plays presented by a stock company ‖ a piece of cotton or silk material worn over the chest with a stiff white collar by some priests and clergymen ‖ (*hist.*) a wide cravat wrapped twice around the neck and looped in front in a loose knot ‖ a similar cravat worn as part of a riding outfit ‖ a member of *Matthiola,* fam. *Cruciferae,* a genus of plants bearing fragrant, four-petaled flowers on long stalks ‖ (*zool.*) a colony of zooids connected to form a compound organism ‖ a hive of bees ‖ the stem of a tree or bush into which a graft is inserted ‖ a plant from which cuttings are prepared ‖ the trunk of a tree or stem of a plant **in stock** manufactured and available for purchase **off the stocks** (of a ship) launched ‖ completed **on the stocks** (of a ship) being built ‖ in progress, *he has two novels on the stocks* **out of stock** not available for purchase because current stocks are exhausted **to take stock** to check the number, condition etc. of what is in supply ‖ to make an inspection so as to assess resources etc. **2.** *v.t.* to furnish with a supply, *he stocked his shop with canned foods* ‖ to have and be able to supply, *he does not stock that kind of food* ‖ to furnish (a tool, weapon etc.) with a stock ‖ to furnish (a farm) with stock ‖ to accumulate a supply of ‖ *v.i.* (esp. with 'up') to take in stocks esp. of manufactured goods **3.** *adj.* always maintained in stock ‖ pertaining to the recording or handling of a stock, *stock clerk* ‖ (of an argument, answer etc.) usually used, not original ‖ relating to a theatrical stock company ‖ (of an animal) used to breed a strain ‖ (of a farm) devoted to breeding [O.E. *stoc, stocc*]

stock·ade (stɒkéid) **1.** *n.* a fortification consisting of a fence of posts set firmly and close together ‖ any strong enclosure fenced in by posts in this way **2.** *v.t. pres. part.* **stock·ad·ing** *past* and *past part.* **stock·ad·ed** to furnish with a stockade [F. *estacade* fr. Span.]

stock·brok·er (stɒ́kbroukər) *n.* someone who deals in stocks and shares **stock·brok·er·age** (stɒ́kbroukəridʒ) *n.* stockbroking **stóck·brok·ing** *n.* the business of a stockbroker

stock·car (stɒ́kkɑr) *n.* (*rail.*) a car for transporting livestock

stock car a standard make of car with a supercharged engine used for racing in competition with similar cars

stock company a company the capital of which is subscribed by, or owned by, stockholders or shareholders ‖ a permanent company of repertory actors usually having its own theater

stock exchange a place where stocks are bought and sold ‖ a regulated association of stockbrokers for the business of buying and selling stocks

stock·fish (stɒ́kfiʃ) *pl.* **stock·fish, stock·fish·es** *n.* a fish cured in the open air without salt [prob. fr. Du. *stokvisch*]

Stock·hau·sen (stɒ́khauz'n), Karlheinz (1928-), German composer, a leading exponent of serial music

stock·hold·er (stɒ́khouldər) *n.* a person who owns stock (shares of corporate capital)

Stock·holm (stɒ́khoum) the capital (pop. 1,512,200 with agglom. 1,145,000) and commercial and industrial center of Sweden, on a cluster of islands and peninsulas where Lake Mälar joins the Baltic. Industries: iron and steel, mechanical and electrical engineering, chemicals, oil refining, metalwork, textiles, printing and publishing. The old city (13th-c. churches, 18th-c. royal palace) is on the central islands, surrounded by modern quarters cut by canals and gardens. University (1877), national museums. Stockholm was founded in the 13th c. and became the capital in the 17th c.

stock·i·ly (stɒ́kili:) *adv.* in a stocky manner

stock·i·ness (stɒ́ki:nis) *n.* the state or quality of being stocky

stock·i·net, stock·i·nette (stɒkinét) *n.* a machine-knitted cotton fabric with some elasticity, used esp. for underwear

stock·ing (stɒ́kiŋ) *n.* a close-fitting covering for the foot and leg knit in nylon, silk, wool, cotton or other fiber **in one's stocking feet** wearing stockings, but no shoes

stocking cap a long knitted cap tapering at the end and finished off with a pom-pom

stocking mask a nylon stocking worn over the face to conceal identity, e.g., for use in a robbery

stock-in-trade (stɒ́kintréid) *n.* the goods, equipment etc. of a shop or business

stock·ist (stɒ́kist) *n.* (*Br.*) someone who keeps a supply of specified goods for sale

stock·job·ber (stɒ́kdʒɒbər) *n.* a stockbroker, esp. an unscrupulous one ‖ (*Br.*) someone who acts as an intermediary between a broker selling and a broker buying. He often speculates by buying on the rise

stock·man (stɒ́kmən) *pl.* **stock·men** (stɒ́kmən) *n.* a man who owns or raises livestock ‖ (stɒ́kmæn) a man who keeps records of stock or gives out supplies, e.g. in a warehouse ‖ (*Br.* and *Austral.*) someone who herds livestock, esp. sheep or cattle

stock market a stock exchange ‖ the buying and selling of stocks and shares

stock·pile (stɒ́kpail) **1.** *n.* a reserve, esp. of essential matériel accumulated for use when the normal sources of supply are cut off **2.** *v. pres. part.* **stock·pil·ing** *past* and *past part.* **stock·piled** *v.t.* to accumulate a stockpile of ‖ *v.i.* to accumulate a stockpile

Stock·port (stɒ́kpɔrt, stɒ́kpourt) a port and county borough (pop. 136,496) in Cheshire and Lancashire, England, on the Mersey: cotton textiles, metalware, machinery

stock·pot (stɒ́kpɒt) *n.* a pot in which stock (e.g. for soup) is prepared and kept

stock raising the breeding and raising of livestock

stock saddle a cowboy's saddle with a high pommel and horn for the lariat

stock-still (stɒ́kstíl) *adj.* completely motionless

stock·tak·ing (stɒ́ktеikiŋ) *n.* the periodic checking and valuing of a business's stock

stock·whip (stɒ́khwip, stɒ́kwip) *n.* (*Br.*) a short-handled whip with a long lash, used by stockmen in herding cattle

stock·y (stɒ́ki:) *comp.* **stock·i·er** *superl.* **stock·i·est** *adj.* short, sturdy and thickly built ‖ (of plants) having sturdy, thick stems

stock·yard (stɒ́kjɑrd) *n.* a place where livestock, esp. cattle and hogs, are penned, usually prior to slaughter or shipment

Stod·dert (stɒ́dərt), Benjamin (1751-1813), the first U.S. secretary of the navy (1798-1801). He expanded the navy from a complement of three frigates to a total of more than 50 vessels

stodge (stɒdʒ) **1.** *v.t. pres. part.* **stodg·ing** *past* and *past part.* **stodged** to cram with food, facts etc. ‖ *v.i.* to eat to excess **2.** *n.* (*pop.*) dull, heavy, filling food **stódg·i·ly** *adv.* in a stodgy way **stodg·i·ness** *n.* the state or quality of being stodgy **stódg·y** *comp.* **stodg·i·er** *superl.* **stódg·i·est** *adj.* (of food) heavy and filling ‖ dull, tedious, *a stodgy person* [etym. doubtful]

sto·gie, sto·gy (stóugi:) *pl.* **sto·gies** *n.* a thin, cylindrical cigar with a strong flavor

sto·ic (stóuik) **1.** *n.* a person who endures hardship and adversity with fortitude **Sto·ic** an adherent of Stoicism **2.** *adj.* able to bear hardship and adversity with fortitude, or manifesting this ability, *stoic calm* **Sto·ic** of or relating to the Stoics and their doctrines **stó·i·cal** *adj.* **sto·i·cism** (stóuisizəm) *n.* stoical behavior **Sto·i·cism** the philosophical doctrine of the Stoics. As first conceived by Zeno, Stoicism was a metaphysical system which stressed the correspondence between man and nature as a whole. Wisdom was held to consist in the knowledge of the whole, but to pursue it man had to hold his passions in check. In later Stoicism, represented by Seneca, Epictetus and Marcus Aurelius, the emphasis shifted to the ethical aspect: a Stoic was taught to endure hardship and adversity with fortitude [fr. L. *stoicus* fr. Gk fr. *stoa,* porch (from which Zeno taught)]

stoi·chi·om·e·try (stɔikaiɒ́mitri:) *n.* the study of the laws of chemical combination by weight and volume [fr. Gk *stoicheion,* element+*metron,* measure]

stoke (stouk) *pres. part.* **stok·ing** *past* and *past part.* **stoked** *v.t.* to look after (a fire, furnace etc.) by adding fresh fuel and spreading it around, regulating the air supply etc. ‖ to add fuel to (a fire, furnace etc.) ‖ *v.i.* to be a stoker [backformation fr. STOKER]

stoke·hold (stóukhould) *n.* (*naut.*) the hold containing the furnaces, where the ship's stokers work

stoke·hole (stóukhoul) *n.* the mouth of a furnace, into which fuel is fed ‖ the place in front of a furnace where the stoker or stokers stand [fr. and partly trans. of Du. *stookgat*]

Stoke-on-Trent (stóukɒntrént, stóukɒntrént) a county borough (pop. 257,800) in N. Staffordshire, England, center of the English pottery industry. Other industries: coal mining, brickmaking

stok·er (stóukər) *n.* a man who feeds and tends a fire, furnace etc. ‖ a device which automatically feeds a furnace etc. [Du.]

Stokes' law (stouks) (*phys.*) a law stating that a small sphere falling through a viscous medium acquires a uniform velocity given by

$$\frac{2}{9} \cdot \frac{r^2 g}{\eta} \cdot (d_1 - d_2)$$

where r is its radius, g the acceleration due to gravity, η the coefficient of viscosity, d_1 and d_2 the densities of the sphere and the medium respectively ‖ (*phys.*) a law stating that the frequency of luminescence excited by radiation cannot be in excess of the luminescence of the radiation which excites it [after Sir George *Stokes* (1819–1903), Br. physicist]

STOL (*aerospace acronym*) short takeoff and landing —**stolport** *n.* the airfield *Cf* CTOL, VTOL, V/STOL

stole (stoul) *n.* a long, wide length of material, fur etc. worn by women, draped over the shoulders ‖ (*eccles.*) a long, narrow length of silk worn by bishops and priests around the neck and hanging in front from the shoulders ‖ (*hist.*) the outer robe of a Roman matron [fr. L. *stola* fr. Gk]

stole *past* of STEAL

stolen *past part.* of STEAL

stol·id (stɒ́lid) *adj.* difficult to arouse, either emotionally or mentally [fr. L. *stolidus*]

sto·lid·i·ty (stəlíditi:) *n.* the state or quality of being stolid [fr. L. *stoliditas*]

sto·lon (stóulən) *n.* (*bot.*) a trailing stem, either above or below ground, which roots at intervals along its length to develop new plants ‖ (*zool.*) a creeping growth which gives rise to new individuals or colonies, e.g. coral [fr. L. *stolo* (*stolonis*), sucker of a plant]

Sto·ly·pin (stɒlí:pin), PiotrArkadevich (1863-1911), Russian statesman. As minister of the interior and prime minister (1906-11), he sought to suppress the revolutionary movement by mass exiles and executions. His agrarian reforms (1906) created a landowning kulak class, and freed labor for industry

sto·ma (stóumə) *pl.* **sto·ma·ta** (stóumətə), **sto·mas** *n.* (*bot.*) a minute epidermal pore on a leaf through which gaseous exchange takes place, together with the two bean-shaped guard cells which surround it ‖ (*zool.*) a mouth or mouthlike orifice, esp. an ingestive opening in lower animals [Mod. L. fr. Gk *stoma* (*stomatos*), mouth]

stom·ach (stʌ́mək) **1.** *n.* an enlarged portion of the alimentary canal of a vertebrate between the esophagus and the small intestine. It has a strong muscular wall which contracts rhythmically, thoroughly grinding and mixing food, and a lining that contains glands which secrete digestive enzymes ‖ any of the separate parts of such an organ, e.g. in ruminants ‖ a digestive cavity, e.g. in invertebrates ‖ the soft part of the body which contains the stomach ‖ (*rhet.*) appetite, liking, to *have no stomach for* (*something*) **2.** *v.t.* to find palatable or digestible, *to be unable to stomach rich food* ‖ to accept without revulsion or protest, *nobody could stomach such insolence* [O.F. *estomac, stomaque* fr. L. fr. Gk]

stom·ach·ache (stʌ́məkeik) *n.* a pain in the stomach or in the area of the body surrounding the stomach

stom·ach·er (stʌ́məkər) *n.* (*hist.*) a woman's ornamental garment worn in the 15th–17th cc. under or over a laced bodice and covering the breast and abdomen, ending downwards in a point

sto·mach·ic (stəmǽkik) **1.** *adj.* of or pertaining to the stomach ‖ aiding the digestive processes **2.** *n.* a medicine for aiding digestion [fr. L. *stomachicus* fr. Gk]

stomach pump a type of suction pump used to withdraw the contents of the stomach, esp. when these include a poison

stomach tooth (*pop.*) either of the first canine teeth in the lower jaw, the appearance of which is often accompanied by stomach disorders

stomata alt. *pl.* of STOMA

stom·a·tal (stɒ́mət'l, stóumət'l) *adj.* of, relating to, or being a stoma [fr. Gk *stoma* (*stomatos*), mouth]

sto·mat·ic (stoumǽtik) *adj.* relating to or being a stoma [fr. Mod. L. *stomaticus* fr. Gk]

stom·a·ti·tis (stɒmətáitis, stoumətáitis) *n.* inflammation of the inside of the mouth [Mod. L. fr. Gk *stoma* (*stomatos*), mouth+*-itis,* inflammation]

sto·ma·tol·o·gy (stoumətɒ́lədʒi:) *n.* the branch of medicine dealing with the mouth and its diseases [fr. Gk *stoma* (*stomatos*), mouth+*logos,* discourse]

sto·mo·dae·um, sto·mo·de·um (stoumədi:əm) *pl.* **sto·mo·dae·a, sto·mo·de·a** (stoumədí:ə), **sto·mo·dae·ums, sto·mo·de·ums** *n.* the anterior ectoderm-lined portion of the alimentary canal [Mod. L. fr. Gk *stoma,* mouth+*hodaios,* on the way]

stomp (stɒmp) **1.** *v.t.* to bring (one's feet) down heavily ‖ to bring one's feet heavily down on, *stomping the platform impatiently* ‖ *v.i.* to put one's feet down heavily, *to stomp up and down in a rage* ‖ to dance a stomp **2.** *n.* a jazz dance involving heavy stamping, or the music for this

Stone (stoun), Harlan Fiske (1872-1946), U.S. Supreme Court associate justice (1925-41) and chief justice (1941-6). He was dean of Columbia Law School (1910-23) and U.S. attorney general (1924-5) before being appointed to the Court by Pres. Calvin Coolidge. He was esp. concerned with individual liberty and social justice. As an associate justice he wrote the majority opinion in such cases as 'United States v. Classic' (1941) and 'United States v. Darby Lumber Co.' (1941). As chief justice he spoke for the Court in 'Ex parte Quirin' (1942), 'Hirabayashi v. United States' (1943), 'In re Yamachita' (1946) and 'Girouard v. United States' (1946)

Stone, Lucy Blackwell (1818-93), U.S. social reformer and lecturer. She campaigned (1848) throughout Canada and the U.S.A. against slavery. She helped to organize (1869) the American Woman's Suffrage Association, and served (1869-72) as its first president

stone (stoun) **1.** *n.* rock (an aggregate of particles) ‖ a piece of rock, esp. larger than a grain or particle but smaller than a boulder ‖ a piece of rock shaped and used for a particular purpose, e.g. a grindstone, a tombstone ‖ a small piece of an ornamental and rare mineral, cut and polished to show its color or refraction and reflection of light to the best advantage (*med.*) a calculus ‖ something hard, and usually rounded, e.g. the hard case of the kernel in a drupaceous fruit or the seed in some other fruits ‖ a piece of prepared limestone upon which a lithographic design is drawn ‖ (*pl.* **stone**) a British unit of weight equal to 14 lbs avoirdupois ‖ (*printing*) the smooth, flat surface upon which type is imposed ‖ (*backgammon*) a playing piece **a stone's throw** a short distance **to leave no stone unturned** to use every possible means to achieve a purpose **2.** *v.t. pres. part.* **ston·ing** *past* and *past part.* **stoned** to throw stones at ‖ to take the stones out of (fruit) ‖ to pave or face with stone **3.** *adj.* made of stone or of a hard substance resembling stone [O.E. *stān*]

Stone Age the earliest prehistoric period, when stone implements and weapons were used (preceding the Bronze Age). It is divided into the Eolithic, Paleolithic, Mesolithic and Neolithic periods

stone-broke (stóunbróuk) *adj.* completely without funds

stone cell a sclereid

stone·chat (stóuntʃæt) *n.* *Saxicola torquata,* a European songbird. The male has a predominantly black head, wings and tail, with a white collar and white upper tail coverts

stone-cold (stóunkóuld) *adj.* very cold

stone·crop (stóunkrɒp) *n.* a member of *Sedum,* fam. *Crassulaceae,* esp. *S. acre,* a European creeping evergreen plant having pungent leaves and yellow flowers [O.E. *stāncrop* fr. *stān,* stone+crop, a sprout]

stone·cut·ter (stóunkʌtər) *n.* someone who cuts and shapes stone ‖ a machine which does this

stone-deaf (stóundéf) *adj.* completely deaf

stone fly a member of *Plecoptera,* an order of insects whose aquatic, carnivorous larvae are used as bait in trout fishing

stone fruit a drupe

Stone·henge (stóunhendʒ) the remains of a large group of standing stones on Salisbury Plain, England, probably erected between 1800 B.C. and 1400 B.C. When complete, Stonehenge consisted of two concentric circles of tooled stones, surrounding two concentric horseshoe-shaped groups, the whole surrounded by a circular ditch 300 ft in diameter. The uprights of the outer circle were connected by lintels, the fitting of which required great technical skill. There are many theories about the purpose of Stonehenge, emphasis being placed on the marking of sunrise and sunset at particular points of the calendar by the alignment of the stones. It seems to have been a sanctuary for the worship of the sun, perhaps also an observatory. The monument is surrounded by Bronze Age barrows, and may well have been connected with burial ceremonies

stone marten *Martes foina,* a S. European and Asian marten with a white mark on its breast and throat ‖ its fur

stone·ma·son (stóunmeis'n) *n.* a mason who builds with or works stone

Stones River, Battle of (stóunz) a major Civil War engagement (Dec. 31, 1862 – Jan. 2, 1863)

in central Tennessee, part of a Union campaign to split the Confederate forces into three parts. U.S. troops led by Gen. William Rosecrans routed Confederate forces under Gen. Braxton Bragg and captured Murfreesboro, a city (pop. 13,000) nine miles to the south. Both sides suffered heavy losses

stone·wall (stóunwɔ́l) *v.i.* (*cricket*, of a batsman) to play defensive strokes only and not attempt to score

stonewalling *v. pres. part.* (*slang or colloq.*) **1.** obstructing or permanently stopping something, e.g., an investigation, a vote **2.** refusing to move from a position —**stonewall** *v.*

stone·ware (stóunwɛ̧ər) *n.* a nonporous, well-vitrified pottery made of high-fired siliceous clay or a mixture of clay and crushed flint

stone·work (stóunwə̧:rk) *n.* stone construction ‖ the part of a construction that is made of stone

ston·i·ly (stóunili:) *adv.* in a stony way

ston·i·ness (stóuni:nis) *n.* the state or quality of being stony

ston·y (stóuni:) *comp.* **ston·i·er** *superl.* **ston·i·est** *adj.* containing many stones, *stony ground* ‖ as hard as stone ‖ lacking pity, *stony hearts* ‖ without human warmth, *a stony silence, stony glance*

ston·y-broke (stóuni:bróuk) *adj.* (*Br.*) stone-broke

stood *past* and *past part.* of STAND

stooge (stu:dʒ) **1.** *n.* someone who acts as a butt for a comedian ‖ (*pop.*) a stool pigeon (informer) ‖ any underling with no say of his own **2.** *v.i. pres. part.* **stoog·ing** *past* and *past part.* **stooged** to act as a stooge [origin unknown]

stook (stuk, stu:k) **1.** *n.* (*Br.*) a shock of sheaves **2.** *v.t.* (*Br.*) to pile (sheaves of grain) in this way [M.E. *stouk* prob. fr. M.L.G. *stûke*]

stool (stu:l) **1.** *n.* a backless and armless seat ‖ a footstool ‖ a decoy bird ‖ the stump of a tree, or a group of stumps capable of putting out new shoots ‖ one of these shoots ‖ the evacuation of waste matter from the bowels ‖ the waste matter so evacuated ‖ (*pop.*) a stool pigeon **2.** *v.i.* to send up shoots from a root or stump [O.E. *stōl*, seat]

stool pigeon a pigeon used as a decoy ‖ (*pop.*) a person who informs to the police

stoop (stu:p) *n.* a small porch at the entrance of a house

stoop 1. *v.i.* to bend the body forward and downward, *he stooped to write in the dust* ‖ to walk or stand habitually with the head, neck and shoulders bent forward and downward ‖ (of a bird of prey) to fly or drop swiftly downwards ‖ to lower one's dignity or moral standards, *to stoop to spying* ‖ *v.t.* to bend (part of the body) forward and downward **2.** *n.* a stooping ‖ a posture in which the head, neck and shoulders are permanently bent forward and downward ‖ the swoop of a bird towards its prey [O.E. *stūpian*]

stoop *STOUP

stop (stɒp) **1.** *v. pres. part.* **stop·ping** *past* and *past part.* **stopped** *v.t.* to discontinue, cease (doing something), *to stop running* ‖ to cause to cease to move or to act, *he stopped his car at the crossroads, she stopped him in the middle of his speech* ‖ to prevent from moving or acting, *he won't stop me from going* ‖ to cut off, withhold, *to stop supplies* ‖ (often with 'up') to fill (a hole, crack etc.) in order to prevent passage through or into it, or to prevent it from becoming larger ‖ (often with 'up') to close, obstruct (a passageway, opening etc.), *leaves stopped up the drain* ‖ to close, plug (a body orifice), *to stop one's ears* ‖ (*securities*) to buy or sell at a specified price should the market reach such a price ‖ (*Br.*) to fill (a tooth) in order to arrest decay ‖ to instruct one's bank to withhold payment of (a check etc.) ‖ (*pop.*) to receive (a blow), *he stopped a fast one* ‖ (*bridge*) to constitute a stop for (a suit) ‖ (*mus.*) to alter the vibrating length of (the string of a violin etc.) by the pressure of a finger ‖ (*mus.*) to close one or more finger holes of (a wind instrument) in order to produce a particular note ‖ (*mus.*) to produce (a note) thus ‖ *v.i.* to cease to do something ‖ to cease operating ‖ to come to an end ‖ to leave off, discontinue an activity, journey etc. permanently or temporarily ‖ (often with 'up') to become obstructed ‖ (*Br.*) to stay, *to stop at home* **to stop down** (*photog.*) to narrow the opening of (a lens) by means of a diaphragm **to stop off** to make a brief stay at a place while on a journey **to stop out** to cover part or parts of (a surface to be printed) with a substance which prevents printing **2.** *n.* a stopping or being stopped, *to put a stop to something* ‖ a place where a bus, streetcar etc. picks up or deposits passengers ‖ (*Br.*) a punctuation mark in printing or writing indicating a pause, esp. a full stop ‖ a stopper (plug) ‖ (*Br., bridge*) a stopper ‖ (*mus.*) the act of closing a finger hole of a wind instrument to alter the pitch of its tone, or the finger hole itself, or a key closing it ‖ (*mus.*) the act of pressing a string of a stringed instrument in order to alter the pitch, or the place on the string where this pressure is applied ‖ (*mus.*) a set of organ pipes of like tone and quality ‖ (*mus.*) a device for admitting, or preventing the access of, air to such a set of pipes ‖ (*phon.*) a consonant formed by completely stopping the outgoing breath, e.g. with the lips, tongue or velum ‖ (*photog.*) the aperture of a lens camera ‖ the depression between and in front of the eyes that is present in most dogs, where the nose ends and the forehead begins [O.E. *stoppian*]

stop·cock (stɒ́pkɒ̧k) *n.* a device for permitting or preventing the flow of a fluid through a pipe

stope (stoup) *n.* (*mining*) the underground excavation formed as layers of ore are mined [perh. rel. to STEP]

stop·gap (stɒ́pgæp) *n.* a person or thing serving as a substitute or temporary expedient

stop·light (stɒ́plạit) *n.* a traffic signal ‖ a red light on the back of a motor vehicle which goes on when the brake pedal is pressed

stop·out (stɒ́paut) *n.* one who interrupts an education for a short period

stop·o·ver (stɒ́pọuvər) *n.* a short stop at a place breaking a journey

stop·page (stɒ́pidʒ) *n.* a stopping or being stopped

stop·per (stɒ́pər) **1.** *n.* a plug or other device which closes an opening, e.g. of a decanter ‖ (*naut.*) a rope or other means of checking the run of a cable etc. ‖ (*bridge, Am.*=*Br.* stop) a card or group of cards in a suit which prevents an opponent from scoring **2.** *v.t.* to close or fit with a stopper

stop press (*Br.*) a late news bulletin added to a newspaper after it has been put on the machines ready for printing **stóp-press** *adj.* done or inserted while a printing press is stopped during its run

stop squawk (*mil.*) in air intercept, a code meaning *Turn identification friend or foe master control to 'off.'* *Cf* SQUAWK STANDBY

stop·watch (stɒpwɒtʃ) *n.* a watch with a dial reading up to fractions of a second. It can be started and stopped by a control and is used in timing races etc.

stor·age (stɔ́ridʒ, stóuridʒ) *n.* a storing or being stored ‖ space for storing ‖ the charge for storing

storage battery a storage cell

storage cell a device for storing electricity as chemical energy. It is charged by passing an electric current between two plates (electrodes) in an ionizing liquid (the electrolyte.) This current causes chemical changes in the electrolyte and plates. When electrical energy is required the plates are joined via an electrical circuit and the stored chemical energy is released as electrical energy until the charges have been completely reversed, the storage cell then being discharged

stor·age-ring (stɔ́ridʒriŋ) *n.* (*nuclear phys.*) a circular tract on which a beam of accelerated particles moves to collide with a beam moving in a counter direction, for the creation of new particles

sto·rax (stɔ́ræks, stóuræks) *n.* a resin obtained from the bark of *Liquidambar orientalis*, fam. *Hamamelidaceae*, an Asiatic tree, used as an expectorant (*FRIAR'S BALSAM) and in perfumery ‖ a sweet-smelling resin obtained from various trees of genus *Styrax*, esp. *S. officinalis* [L. fr. Gk *sturax*]

store (stɔr, stour) *n.* a number of things, or an amount of something, put aside for future use, *a store of food* ‖ a place where a store of something is kept, *ammunition store* ‖ a room, set of rooms or building where retail sale is carried on ‖ any shop ‖ (*pl.*) supplies kept for use when needed, *ship's stores* **in store** kept for future use ‖ in waiting, *a surprise in store for them* **to set store by** to value greatly [M.E. *stor* fr. O.F. *estor*, storing]

store *pres. part.* **stor·ing** *past* and *past part.* **stored** *v.t.* to accumulate and keep for future use ‖ (esp. passive) to furnish or supply ‖ to put into storage ‖ to provide storage room for ‖ *v.i.* to bear storing, *some foods won't store* [M.E. *storen* fr. O.F.]

store·house (stɔ́rhạus, stóurhạus) *pl.* **store·hous·es** (stɔ́rhạuziz, stóurhạuziz) *n.* a place where things are stored ‖ a rich source, *a storehouse of information*

store·keep·er (stɔ́rkị:pər, stóurkị:pər) *n.* a person who is in charge of stores ‖ someone who owns and manages a store

store·room (stɔ́rrụ:m, stóurrụ:m, stɔ́rrụm, stóurrụm) *n.* a room in which goods are stored

store·ship (stɔ́rʃịp, stóurʃịp) *n.* (*naut.*) a ship which carries supplies

sto·ry, sto·rey, *pl.* **sto·ries, sto·reys** *n.* one of the floor-to-ceiling portions of a building above ground level ‖ (*collect.*) all the rooms on the same level of a building [prob. same word as STORY (oral or written account)]

storey *STORY (portion of a building)

sto·ried (stɔ́ri:d, stóuri:d) *adj.* (*rhet.*) celebrated in legend or history ‖ (*rhet.*) decorated with legendary or historical scenes

storied, storeyed *adj.* (in compounds, of a building) having a specified number of stories, *two-storied*

stork (stɔrk) *pl.* **storks, stork** *n.* a member of *Ciconiidae*, a family of large Old World wading birds with a long bill and long legs, related to the herons [O.E. *storc*]

Storm (ʃtɔrm), Theodor (1817-88), German lyric poet and novelist, known esp. for his story 'Immensee' (1852)

storm (stɔrm) **1.** *n.* a very strong wind (64–72 m.p.h. on the Beaufort scale) ‖ a heavy fall of rain, snow, hail or sleet ‖ any violent atmospheric disturbance in the air, e.g. a thunderstorm ‖ a cloud of dust or sand driven by the wind ‖ a thick fall of missiles ‖ a violent access of passion, esp. of jealousy or rage ‖ any domestic commotion or public agitation, *a storm in parliament* ‖ a loud and vigorous expression, *a storm of protests* ‖ (*mil.*) an attack in force on a fortified place, *to take by storm* **2.** *v.i.* to rain, snow, hail etc. ‖ with violence to be in a passion of rage ‖ to rush angrily and violently, *to storm out of the house* ‖ *v.t.* to capture or attempt to capture by attack, *to storm a citadel* [O.E.]

storm·bound (stɔ́rmbạund) *adj.* unable to proceed because of a storm

storm cellar a cyclone cellar

storm center, *Br.* **storm centre** the center of an atmospheric storm ‖ the center or focus of a disturbance

storm cone (*Br.*) a cone-shaped device hoisted as a signal that a storm is imminent

storm door an additional door placed outside an entrance door for protection against winter weather

storm·i·ly (stɔ́:rmili:) *adv.* in a stormy way

storm·i·ness (stɔ́rmi:nis) *n.* the state or quality of being stormy

storm petrel *Hydrobates pelagicus*, fam. *Hydrobatidae*, a small (6 ins) black petrel, having white wing and tail markings and frequenting the coasts of the N. Atlantic and Mediterranean. It is popularly thought to presage storms

storm surge (*meteor.*) a large rise of the water level during a gale

storm window an additional window placed outside a regular one for protection against winter weather

storm·y (stɔ́rmi:) *comp.* **storm·i·er** *superl.* **storm·i·est** *adj.* having the characteristics of a storm ‖ characterized by storms ‖ characterized by violence or passion, *a stormy meeting*

stormy petrel a storm petrel ‖ a person regarded as a herald of trouble, strife or violence or someone who delights in such trouble etc.

Sto·ry (stɔ́ri:, stóuri:), Joseph (1779-1845), U.S. jurist and associate justice (1812-45) of the U.S. Supreme Court. The decisions he wrote include 'Martin v. Hunter's Lessee' (1816), which assured Supreme Court supremacy over State courts in all civil cases involving the U.S. constitution and laws. He wrote several concurring opinions in support of John Marshall. He usually dissented from the opinions of the Taney court

sto·ry (stɔ́ri:, stóuri:) *pl.* **sto·ries** *n.* an oral or written account of a real or imagined event or events, *the story of one's life, adventure stories* ‖ the plot of a literary work ‖ a news item in a newspaper ‖ a particular, esp. a biased, account of an event etc. ‖ an amusing anecdote ‖ a rumor circulating ‖ (*pop.*) a lie [A.F. *estoire*]

sto·ry·book (stɔ́ri:bụk, stóuri:bụk) **1.** *n.* a book consisting of a story or stories for children **2.**

adj. tenderly romantic and idealistic, *a story book romance*

sto·ry·tell·er (stɔ́ri:tɛlər, stóuri:tɛlər) *n.* someone who writes or tells stories ‖ (*pop.*) a liar

Stoss (ʃtɔs), Veit (c. 1440-1533), German sculptor and wood-carver, known esp. for his altarpiece at Krakow

sto·tin·ka (stoutíŋkə) *n.* unit of currency in Bulgaria, equal to 1/100th lev

stoup, stoop (stu:p) *n.* (*Roman Catholicism*) a basin for holy water ‖ (*hist.*) a large drinking mug or bowl or its contents [O.N. *staup*]

stout (staut) *adj.* having a heavy and rotund body ‖ strong, *stout timbers* ‖ brave, *a stout fellow* ‖ (*rhet.*) resolute, firm, *stout resistance* [O.F. *estout*, brave fr. Gmc]

stout *n.* a dark brown beer, brewed from black malt in the grist and strongly flavored with hops [prob.=*stout beer, stout ale* fr. (obs.) *stout* adj., having body]

stout·heart·ed (stáuthártid) *adj.* (*rhet.*) courageous

stove (stouv) *n.* a largely enclosed apparatus in which fuel is burned to provide heat for comfort or cooking ‖ any heated chamber, used e.g. for drying manufactured articles [prob. M.L.G. or M.Du.=a heated room]

stove alt. *past* and *past part.* of STAVE

stove·pipe (stóuvpaip) *n.* an iron or steel tube conveying the gaseous products of combustion from a stove to a flue or to the open air ‖ a stovepipe hat

stovepipe hat a man's tall silk hat

stow (stou) *v.t.* to pack away in an enclosed space, *to stow books in a cupboard* ‖ to fill (a hold etc.) with cargo ‖ to hold, have enough space for, *the attic will stow all the apples you grow* ‖ (*naut.*) to furl **to stow away** to store (something) where it will not be in the way ‖ to hide on board a ship, train etc. in order to travel without paying the fare [fr. older *stow*, a place, fr. O.E. *stōw*]

stow·age (stóuidʒ) *n.* a stowing or being stowed ‖ the manner of being stowed ‖ the goods stowed ‖ storage capacity

stow·a·way (stóuəwei) *n.* a person who hides on board a ship, train etc. in order to avoid paying the fare

Stowe (stou), Harriet Elizabeth Beecher (1811-96), American writer, who wrote 'Uncle Tom's Cabin' (1852), an antislavery novel which had great political influence

S.T.P. (*phys.*) standard temperature and pressure, i.e. normal temperature and pressure (*N.T.P.) ‖ (*abbr.*) for a psychedelic drug named for the serenity, tranquility, and peace it purports to bring about

stra·bis·mal (strəbízməl) *adj.* of or relating to strabismus

stra·bis·mic (strəbízmik) *adj.* strabismal **stra·bís·mi·cal** *adj.*

stra·bis·mus (strəbízməs) *n.* (*med.*) a disorder of vision in which both eyes cannot be focused on the same spot at the same time [Mod. L. fr. Gk]

Stra·chey (stréitʃi:), Giles Lytton (1880-1932), English author, known for his ironic biographies 'Eminent Victorians' (1918) and 'Queen Victoria' (1921). His 'Landmarks in French Literature' (1912) is a minor classic of literary criticism

strad·dle (strǽd'l) 1. *v. pres. part.* **strad·dling** *past* and *past part.* **strad·dled** *v.i.* to walk, or stand, with the legs wide apart ‖ to sprawl ‖ to sit on a fence, wall etc. with one leg on either side of it ‖ (*pop.*) to favor or seem to favor both sides of an issue ‖ *v.t.* to stand over or sit on (something) with one leg on either side of it ‖ to spread (the legs) wide apart ‖ (*pop.*) to be or seem to be in favor of both sides of (an issue) ‖ (*gunnery*) to put down shots beyond and short of (a target) 2. *n.* the act or position of straddling ‖ (*stock exchange*) an option enabling the holder to deliver or call for a certain number of shares at a certain price within a certain time [rel. to STRIDE]

Stra·del·la (strədélə), Allessandro (1645-82), Italian composer. His work included operas, cantatas, oratorios and motets

Stra·di·va·ri (strɑdivɑ́ri:, strædivéəri:) a famous family of Italian violin makers of Cremona. The most famous is Antonio (1644-1737). He produced at least 1,116 instruments, many of which are still in existence

strad·i·var·i·us (strædivéəri:əs) *n.* a violin made by the Stradivari family, esp. by Antonio Stradivari

strafe (streif, *Br.* esp. strɑf) 1. *v.t. pres. part.* **straf·ing** *past* and *past part.* **strafed** to sweep (e.g. a ground area) with machine-gun fire, esp. from low-flying aircraft 2. *n.* such an attack [fr. G. *Gott strafe England*, God punish England (a 1st World War phrase)]

Straf·ford (strǽfərd), Thomas Wentworth, 1st earl of (1593-1641), English statesman entrusted by Charles I with the task of bringing the north of England (1629-33) and Ireland (1633-40) into subjugation. The ruthless methods he employed led to his impeachment. The Long Parliament brought in a bill of attainder. Strafford was executed with the king's consent, the royal authority being thus greatly diminished

strag·gle (strǽg'l) *pres. part.* **strag·gling** *past* and *past part.* **strag·gled** *v.i.* to lag behind, or stray away from, the main body, esp. from a line of march ‖ to grow or be untidily separated from the rest **strág·gly** *comp.* **strag·gli·er** *superl.* **strag·gli·est** *adj.* [etym. doubtful]

straight (streit) 1. *adj.* having an unchanging direction, like a thread pulled tight between two points on a plane surface ‖ of something approximately thus, *a straight back* ‖ showing no deviation from the vertical or horizontal ‖ (of character) honest, trustworthy ‖ frank, esp. acknowledging unpleasant truths, *a straight answer* ‖ tidy and in proper order, *put the room straight* ‖ correctly stated or understood, *let's get the facts straight* ‖ unmixed, *it was straight farce* ‖ (of alcoholic liquor) undiluted ‖ (of hair) not curly ‖ (of racing tips) coming direct from a supposedly reliable source ‖ (of actors and parts in plays) portraying individuals and not types (cf. CHARACTER) ‖ (of an engine) having its cylinders arranged in line ‖ (of a cricket bat) held (for play) at right angles to the ground ‖ (*slang*) of one who is conventional, e.g., esp. not homosexual, a drug user, or a hippie 2. *adv.* in a straight line ‖ vertically and/or horizontally, not at an angle ‖ in a morally upright way ‖ directly, unequivocally 3. *n.* a straight part of something, esp. the final stretch of a racetrack between the last bend and the winning post ‖ (*poker*) a sequence of five cards not all of one suit [M.E. *streght, straght*, originally an adjectival use of the past part. of *strecchen*, to stretch]

straight and narrow (with 'to keep to the' or 'to follow the') a morally and legally irreproachable way of living or behaving [adaptation of Matthew vii, 14]

straight angle an angle of 180°

straight-arm (stréitɑrm) *v.t.* (esp. *football*) to ward off (a would-be tackler) by keeping an arm extended straight from the shoulder and by placing the palm of the hand anywhere on the tackler's body

straight·a·way (stréitəwei) 1. *adj.* extending in a straight course ahead 2. *n.* the straight part of a racecourse 3. *adv.* immediately, at once

straight·bred (stréitbred) *adj.* (of animals) having the blood of only one single breed or strain (*CROSSBRED)

straight-cut (stréitkʌt) *adj.* (of tobacco prepared for smoking) cut lengthwise from the leaf

straight·edge (stréitedʒ) *n.* a length of metal or wood etc. having a straight edge, used in carpentry, metalwork etc. to rule a straight line or to check the straightness of something

straight·en (stréit'n) *v.t.* to make straight ‖ *v.i.* to become straight

straight-faced (stréitféist) *adj.* betraying no facial sign of amusement

straight fight (*Br., politics*) an election contest between the candidates of two parties only

straight flush (*poker*) a hand consisting of five cards in sequence and of the same suit

straight·for·ward (streitfɔ́rwərd) 1. *adj.* honest and direct without hiding anything, frank ‖ presenting no hidden difficulties ‖ clear-cut, unequivocal 2. *adv.* straight ahead ‖ in a straightforward way **straight·for·wards** *adv.*

straightjacket *STRAITJACKET

straightlaced *STRAITLACED

straight man (*Am.*=*Br.* feed) an actor who supplies a comedian with cue lines for jokes

straight-out (stréitaut) *adj.* (*pop.*) straightforward, frank **straight out** *adv.* frankly, directly

straight razor (*Am.*=*Br.* cutthroat) a razor with a rigid blade, the case of which forms a handle when the razor is in use

straight ticket a ballot cast for all the candidates of a single party (cf. SPLIT TICKET)

straight·way (stréitwei) *adv.* (*rhet.*) straightaway

strain (strein) *n.* a group of organisms possessing a particular physiological quality (e.g. high mortality in microorganisms, good wool yield in sheep or strong scent in roses) though lacking clear structural distinctions from related forms ‖ (*rhet.*) a line of descendants, *the royal strain* ‖ an inherited but not dominant quality ‖ a persistent trait of character, *a strain of selfishness* [O.E. *strēon, strīon*]

strain 1. *v.t.* to exert such a force on (a body) that it ceases to be elastic and is damaged or suffers injury, *to strain a muscle* ‖ to injure by overuse or misuse, *to strain one's eyes* ‖ to force (oneself) to the utmost, *she strained herself to finish in time* ‖ to injure (oneself) either mentally or physically by too much effort, *she strained herself getting the work finished in time* ‖ to cause mental tension in ‖ to make excessive demands on, *to strain a person's generosity* ‖ to subject (a relationship) to a considerable degree of tension ‖ (esp. past participle) to introduce such tension into (an atmosphere) ‖ to force from words (a meaning not intended by the author or speaker) ‖ to change the dimensions of (an elastic body) by the application of external force ‖ to force (a body) to its elastic limit ‖ to pass (a liquid) through a filter or sieve ‖ to remove (solid particles) from a liquid by filtering ‖ *v.i.* to make or exert great physical or mental effort ‖ to be subjected to great physical or mental stress ‖ to filter or sieve **to strain at** to try to move (e.g. a stone) or pull etc. on (e.g. a rope) with a great effort **to strain one's ears** to listen very carefully, esp. for something barely audible 2. *n.* a straining or being strained ‖ a deformation of an elastic body under an applied force (*HOOKE'S LAW, cf. STRESS) ‖ the resistance offered by an elastic body to the straining force ‖ a straining force which exceeds the elastic limit of a body ‖ mental tension causing distress ‖ injury or damage caused by straining ‖ a great demand imposing hardship, *a strain on one's resources* ‖ the tenor or tone of something written or uttered, *to speak in lofty strains* ‖ a tune or part of one ‖ (esp. *pl.*) sounds, esp. heard from a distance [M.E. *streyne* fr. O.F.]

strain·er (stréinər) *n.* a sieve or filter

straining piece a short, thick timber which takes the strain of joists or rafters

strait (streit) *n.* (often *pl.*) a narrow stretch of water between two land masses ‖ (often *pl.*) severely restricting difficulties, *financial straits* [M.E. *streit*, O.F. *estreit*]

straitened circumstances lack of money, poverty (usually in connection with someone not used to this condition)

strait·jack·et, straight·jack·et (stréitdʒækit) *n.* a garment of very strong material used to bind the arms against the body and so restrain the movements of a violent, usually insane, person who could harm himself or others

strait·laced, straight·laced (stréitleist) *adj.* exceedingly strict about matters of propriety, often in conjunction with an apparently joyless observance of religion

Straits Question (streits) (*hist.*) an international dispute over the right of passage through the Dardanelles and the Bosporus. By the Treaty of Unkiar Skelessi (1833), the Turks undertook to close the Straits to foreign warships, except those of Russia. A new international agreement (1841) closed the Straits to all foreign warships in peacetime. This remained in force until 1923, when the Straits were demilitarized by the Treaty of Lausanne. They were again militarized by Turkey after an international convention (1936), but were reopened to Allied shipping in 1945 (*EASTERN QUESTION)

Straits Settlements a former British colony in the Malay Peninsula, comprising Malacca, Penang, Singapore and dependencies, established (1826) by the British East India Company. It became a Crown colony (1867) and was dissolved (1946)

strait waistcoat (*Br.*) a straitjacket

strake (streik) *n.* (*naut.*) an unbroken line of planks or plates running along the side of a vessel from stem to stern [O.E. *streccan*, stretch]

stra·mo·ni·um (strəmóuni:əm) *n.* the thorn apple ‖ the dried leaf of a thorn apple, used esp. in the treatment of asthma

strand (strænd) 1. *n.* (*rhet.* and *Ir.*) the shore of a body of water (esp. of a sea or lake) 2. *v.t.* to drive onto the shore ‖ to run (a boat) aground ‖ to cause (someone) to find himself accidentally

CONCISE PRONUNCIATION KEY: **(a)** æ, *cat*; ɑ, *car*; ɔ *fawn*; ei, *snake*. **(e)** e, *hen*; i:, *sheep*; iə, *deer*; εə, *bear*. **(i)** i, *fish*; ai, *tiger*; ə:, *bird*. **(o)** o, *ox*; au, *cow*; ou, *goat*; u, *poor*; ɔi, *royal*. **(u)** ʌ, *duck*; u, *bull*; u:, *goose*; ə, *bacillus*; ju:, *cube*. x, *loch*; θ, *think*; ð, *bother*; z, *Zen*; ʒ, *corsage*; dʒ, *savage*; ŋ, *orangutang*; j, *yak*; ʃ, *fish*; tʃ, *fetch*; 'l, *rabble*; 'n, *redden*. Complete pronunciation key appears inside front cover.

and unwillingly held up on a journey or left suddenly somewhere without resources, *the fog stranded passengers at the airport* (esp. *pass.*) to leave ashore when the tide goes out or water level sinks, *the whale was stranded* [O.E.]

strand 1. *n.* any of the threads, strings, wires etc. which, when twisted together, form a rope, cord, cable etc. ‖ a tress or single long hair ‖ a single string of beads or pearls etc. **2.** *v.t.* to form (e.g. a rope) from strands ‖ to insert strands into (e.g. cloth) ‖ to break one or more of the strands of (a rope) ‖ *v.i.* (of a rope) to break one or more of its strands [etym. doubtful]

Strang (stræŋ), James Jesse (1813-56), U.S. Mormon leader. He established (1847) at Beaver Is. in Lake Michigan a colony for Mormons unwilling to accept the leadership of Brigham Young. His despotic rule led to his assassination

strange (streindʒ) *adj.* not within one's previous experience, *the town was strange to him* ‖ not expected, *a strange result* ‖ unusual, outlandish, *strange clothes* ‖ (*rhet.*) not accustomed, *to be strange to desert life* ‖ odd, unaccountable, *strange behavior* ‖ arousing wonder or astonishment, *strange shapes* [O.F. *estrange*]

strangeness number (*particle phys.*) a quantum number (0, a negative or positive integral) representing an unexplained delay in interactions between elementary particles —**strange particle** *n.* —**symbol S**

stran·ger (stréindʒər) *n.* a person who has not been in a place before, a newcomer, *a stranger to the town* ‖ a person who is not known to one ‖ (*rhet.*) a person who has had no experience of some specified thing, *a stranger to fear* ‖ (*law*) a person who is not a party to an agreement, title etc. ‖ (*Br., parliament*) a person not a member of the British House of Commons [fr. O.F. *estrangier*]

stran·gle (strǽŋg'l) *pres. part.* **stran·gling** *past* and *past part.* **stran·gled** *v.t.* to kill by compressing the windpipe and so preventing breathing ‖ to make breathing very difficult for ‖ to crowd out (a plant) so that it cannot develop ‖ to suppress (e.g. criticism) ‖ *v.i.* to be strangled [O.F. *estrangler*]

stran·gle·hold (strǽŋg'lhould) *n.* an illegal hold in wrestling which prevents free breathing ‖ any force or influence which prevents freedom of action

stran·gles (strǽŋg'lz) *n.* an infectious catarrh of horses and other equines, caused by a bacterium

stran·gu·late (strǽŋgjuleit) *pres. part.* **stran·gu·lat·ing** *past* and *past part.* **stran·gu·lat·ed** *v.t.* to stop the circulation of fluid or blood supply in (a tissue), e.g. in hernia ‖ *v.i.* to become constricted in this way **stran·gu·lá·tion** *n.* the action or process of strangling ‖ the state of being strangled ‖ the state of being strangulated [fr. L. *strangulare* (*strangulatus*), to choke]

stran·gu·ry (strǽŋgjuri:) *pl.* **stran·gu·ries** *n.* a disease causing the urine to be passed painfully and in drops ‖ slow and painful urination [fr. L. *stranguria*]

strap (stræp) **1.** *n.* a long strip of leather etc. of uniform width, and usually pierced with holes for the insertion of the pin of a buckle, used to fasten or bind ‖ a strip of metal used similarly ‖ a razor strop ‖ a shoulder strap ‖ a leather loop fastened to the top of a boot to help in pulling it on ‖ a similar loop suspended from the ceiling of public vehicles for a standing passenger to hold as a support **2.** *v.t. pres. part.* **strap·ping** *past* and *past part.* **strapped** to fasten or bind with a strap ‖ to beat with a leather strap ‖ to strop (a razor) [dial. var. of STROP]

strap·hang·er (strǽphæŋər) *n.* (*pop.*) a standing passenger who clings for support to one of the straps suspended for this purpose in a public vehicle

strap·pa·do (strəpéidou, strəpɑ́dou) **1.** *n.* (*hist.*) a torture consisting of hoisting the victim on a rope by his wrists (usually tied behind his back) and then allowing him to drop part of the way to the ground ‖ the apparatus for inflicting this torture **2.** *v.t.* to torture in this way [fr. F. *strapade, estrapade* fr. Ital.]

strap·per (strǽpər) *n.* (*pop.*) someone very big and strong in build

strap·ping (strǽpiŋ) *adj.* (*pop.*) very big and strong in build

strap·work (strǽpwə:rk) *n.* an ornamental design (inlaid, cut into stone etc.) resembling endless, intertwined straps, in regular geometrical pattern

Stras·bourg (strǽzbu:r, strǽsbə:rg) a port and industrial center (pop. 248,712) in Bas-Rhin, E. France, on the Ill River, near the Rhine. Industries: metallurgy, food and drink processing, woodworking, chemicals, oil refining. Cathedral (12th-16th cc.), palaces (18th c.), churches, half-timbered houses. University (1621)

Strasbourg, Oath of an oath of alliance sworn (842) by Louis the German and Charles the Bald, in revolt against Lothair I. The Romance text of the oath is the earliest known specimen of French in its oldest form

strass (stræs) *n.* a glass of high lead content used in making artificial gems [G. after Joseph *Strasser,* a German jeweler]

strata alt. *pl.* of STRATUM

strat·a·gem (strǽtədʒəm) *n.* a subtle piece of planning designed to trick or gain an end ‖ a ruse, esp. (*hist.*) one to deceive the enemy in warfare [F. *stratagème* fr. L.]

stra·tal (stréit'l, strǽt'l, strɑ́t'l) *adj.* of or relating to a stratum or strata

stra·te·gic (strətí:dʒik) *adj.* of or relating to strategy ‖ of material needed for war but not available in sufficient quantity in the country needing it **stra·té·gi·cal** *adj.* **stra·té·gi·cal·ly** *adv.* **stra·té·gics** *n.* the science of strategy [fr. Gk *stratēgikos*]

strategic capability (*mil.*) the capacity to destroy an enemy under specified circumstances

strat·e·gist (strǽtidʒist) *n.* a person skilled in strategy [F. *stratégiste*]

strat·e·gy (strǽtidʒi:) *pl.* **strat·e·gies** *n.* the science and art of conducting a military campaign in its large-scale and long-term aspects (cf. TACTICS) ‖ an instance of the application of this ‖ skill in using stratagems ‖ the use of such skill in achieving a purpose [F. *stratégie* fr. Gk]

Strat·ford de Red·cliffe (strǽtfərddərédklif), 1st Viscount *CANNING, Stratford

Strat·ford-u·pon-A·von (strǽtfərdəpənéivən, strǽtfərdəpɒnéivən) a town (pop. 20,100) in Warwickshire, England, Shakespeare's birthplace: annual Shakespeare festival

Strath·clyde (stræθkláid) (*hist.*) a British kingdom in S.W. Scotland and N.W. England (c. 7th-10th cc.)

Strath·co·na and Mount Royal (stræθkóunə), Donald Alexander Smith, 1st Baron (1820-1914), Canadian statesman. He was largely responsible for the success of the Canadian Pacific Railway. He donated several million dollars to educational, religious, and financial institutions

Strath·more (stræθmɔ́r, stræθmóur) a fertile, populous valley (100 miles long, 5-10 miles wide) in E. Scotland on the southeast side of the Grampians, where the Highlands end

strath·spey (stræθspéi) *n.* a Scottish dance of slower tempo than the reel ‖ the music for this dance [after *Strathspey,* in Scotland]

strati *pl.* of STRATUS

stra·tic·u·late (strətíkjulit) *adj.* (*geol.*) having thin parallel strata [fr. Mod. L. *straticulum* fr. L. *stratum,* layer]

strat·i·fi·ca·tion (strætifikéiʃən) *n.* (*geol.*) the formation of strata ‖ (*geol.*) the condition of being stratified ‖ (*geol.*) the manner in which something is stratified ‖ arrangement in strata [fr. M.L. *stratificatio* (*stratificationis*) fr. *stratificare,* to stratify]

stratificational grammar (*linguistics*) a form of grammar conceiving of language as a series of levels linked by certain rules: developed by S. M. Lamb

stratified charge engine a dual-fed internal combustion engine in which one richer fuel sparks the engine and a less concentrated fuel sustains the motion

strat·i·form (strǽtifɔrm) *adj.* having a stratified formation ‖ having the form of a stratus

strat·i·fy (strǽtifai) *pres. part.* **strat·i·fy·ing** *past* and *past part.* **strat·i·fied** *v.t.* to arrange or form in strata ‖ *v.i.* to become arranged in strata

stra·tig·ra·phy (strətígrəfi:) *n.* the branch of geology dealing with the study of stratified rocks, in order to trace the historical changes in the geography of the earth [fr. L. *stratum,* something spread or laid down + Gk *-graphia,* writing]

stra·to·cu·mu·lus (streitoukjú:mjuləs, strætoukjú:mjuləs) *n.* a cloud formation having the appearance of dark mounds piled on top of one another. Clouds in this formation are usually seen in the northern hemisphere in winter and do not bring rain

Strat·o·for·tress (strǽtoufɔrtrəs) *n.* (*mil.*) an all-weather, intercontinental, strategic heavy bomber (B-52), powered by eight turbojet engines, with range extended by in-flight refueling

Strat·o·freight·er (strǽtoufreitə:r) *n.* (*mil.*) a strategic aerial tanker-freighter (KC-97), powered by four reciprocating engines, equipped for in-flight refueling of bombers and fighters

strat·o·pause (strǽtoupɔz) *n.* the level separating the stratosphere and mesosphere, occurring between 18 miles and 30 miles. It is the level at which the temperature begins to increase rapidly with altitude

strat·o·scope (strǽtouskoup) *n.* an astronomical telescope to take celestial photographs sent to earth, carried by a balloon

strat·o·sphere (strǽtəsfiər) *n.* a division of the earth's atmosphere extending about 30 miles (depending upon season, latitude and weather conditions in the troposphere) from the tropopause. In the stratosphere the temperature changes only little with increasing altitude. Because of its low moisture content and the absence of large convection currents the stratosphere is an excellent region for air travel (*STRATOPAUSE) [fr. STRATUM + ATMOSPHERE]

Strat·o·tank·er (strǽtoutæŋkər) *n.* (*mil.*) a multipurpose aerial tanker-transport (KC-135) powered by four turbojet engines, equipped for high-speed, high-altitude refueling of bombers and fighters

strat·o·vol·can·o (strǽtouvɒlkéinou) *n.* (*geol.*) a volcano made up of alternating layers of lava flows, volcanic ash, and cinders *also* composite volcano

stra·tum (stréitəm, strǽtəm, strɑ́təm) *pl.* **stra·ta** (stréitə, strǽtə, strɑ́tə), **stra·tums** *n.* a roughly horizontal layer of homogeneous material with its surfaces parallel to those of layers of material of different kinds on either side ‖ (*biol.*) a thin layer of tissue ‖ (*geol.*) a layer of rock composed of one material, e.g. shale or limestone, lying between rock beds of other materials ‖ a level or division, *social stratum* [L.=something spread or laid down]

stra·tus (stréitəs, strǽtəs) *pl.* **stra·ti** (stréitai, strǽtai) *n.* an unbroken sheet of low-altitude clouds [fr. L. *sternere* (*stratus*), to spread out]

Strauss (straus, *G.* ʃtraus), Johann (1825-99), Austrian composer. He is best known for his waltzes, esp. 'The Blue Danube' (1866). He also wrote popular operettas, 'Die Fledermaus' (1873) being the most successful. Johann was one of three sons of Johann the Elder (1804-49), himself a master of the waltz

Strauss, Richard (1864-1949), German composer. He is known chiefly for his symphonic poems and operas but his output includes works for string orchestra, horn concerti, songs and ballet music. His early compositions are symphonic poems, of which the best known are 'Don Juan' (1889), 'Death and Transfiguration' (1890), 'Till Eulenspiegel' (1895) and 'A Hero's Life' (1889). His operas begin with 'Salome' (1905), a setting of Oscar Wilde's play. Most of his other operas, which include 'Elektra' (1908), 'Der Rosenkavalier' (1909-11), 'Ariadne auf Naxos' (1912) and 'Arabella' (1933), have librettos by Hugo von Hofmannsthal

Stra·vin·sky (strəvínski:), Igor (1882-1971), Russian composer, naturalized French (1934), then American (1945). His first success was with the music for the ballet 'The Fire Bird' (1910). His collaboration with Diaghilev led to 'Petrouchka' (1911) and 'The Rite of Spring' (1913). The early works, scored for enormous orchestras, were strongly Russian in character and show the influence of Rimsky-Korsakov, his teacher, yet they were so novel and disturbing that there was a riot at the first performance of 'The Rite of Spring'. Stravinsky then went through a neoclassical period, modified in the 1930s, when he employed small forces and compact forms. He was a rhythmic and harmonic innovator and almost without exception kept to tonality, though in some later works he used a serialist technique allied to twelve-tone music. Stravinsky's was perhaps one of the most penetrating intelligences ever applied to music, yet this analytic search has produced the most 'primitive' or rhythmically exciting music of the century. Other works of his include 'Oedipus Rex' (1926-7), 'Symphony of Psalms' (1930), 'Persephone' (1934) and 'The Rake's Progress' (1951), an opera in neo-Mozartian style

straw (strɔ) **1.** *n.* the stems of any of several cereals after cutting and threshing. Straw is used esp. for bedding in stables and for thatching, stuffing and insulating etc. || one of these stems || a tube of plastic or paper used for drawing liquids into the mouth || used to indicate something of little or no worth, *she doesn't care a straw what happens* **a straw in the wind** a small sign indicative of some coming event, an omen **the last straw** the very last in a series of humiliations, misfortunes, blows of fate etc., after which nothing seems possible or bearable **to catch** (or **clutch** or **grasp**) **at a straw** to make use of anything, however small, that might possibly be of help in a desperate situation **2.** *adj.* made of straw, *straw matting* || resembling straw, straw-colored [O.E. *strēaw*]

straw·ber·ry (strɔ́beri:, strɔ́bəri:) *pl.* **straw·ber·ries** *n.* a member of *Fragaria*, fam. *Rosaceae*, a genus of plants widely cultivated for their edible, juicy, sweet, red fruit || the fruit of any of these plants || the vivid pinkish red of this fruit [O.E. *strēawberige, strēowberige*]

strawberry blonde a woman who has reddish blonde hair and a fair complexion

strawberry jar a ceramic plantholder resembling a strawberry, with openings on the sides through which additional plants may be grown

strawberry tree *ARBUTUS

straw·board (strɔ́bɔrd, strɔ́bourd) *n.* coarse cardboard made of straw pulp and used in making boxes, in bookbinding etc.

straw man a man of straw

straw vote an unofficial poll taken by letters of inquiry, group questioning etc. in order e.g. to determine the chances of a candidate

stray (strei) **1.** *v.i.* (with 'from') to leave a proper place or course, *they strayed from the path and were soon lost* || (*rhet.*) to deviate morally || to move lingeringly and absently, *her hand strayed over its fur* || (*rhet.*) to roam **2.** *n.* something (esp. a domestic animal) which has strayed || (*pl., radio*) static electrical effects which disturb reception **3.** *adj.* having strayed, *a stray dog* || out of place, *stray hairs* || random, *stray shots were heard* [var. of older *astray* v., *estray* v., fr. O.F. *estraier*]

streak (stri:k) **1.** *n.* a linear, usually irregular, mark differing in color and/or texture from the background it appears on || a trace, *a streak of cruelty* || a sudden temporary manifestation, *a streak of good luck, a streak of genius* || the color shown when a mineral is scratched (for identification) || (of lightning) a flash **2.** *v.t.* to mark with a streak or streaks || *v.i.* to become streaky || (*pop.*) to move very fast [O.E. *strica*]

streak·er (strí:kə:r) *n.* one who runs nude in public, usu. in a sprint or slightly longer run for the purpose of attracting attention in order to make some sort of statement, or for diversion — **streak** *v.* —**streaking** *n.*

streak·i·ly (strí:kili:) *adv.* in a streaky manner

streak·i·ness (strí:ki:nis) *n.* the state or quality of being streaky

streak·ing (strí:kiŋ) *n.* hair-coloring style in which some strands are bleached —**streaked** *adj.*

streak·y (strí:ki:) *comp.* **streak·i·er** *superl.* **streak·i·est** *adj.* marked with streaks || occurring in streaks

stream (stri:m) **1.** *n.* a small body of fresh water flowing either permanently or seasonally in a channel on or under the earth || a quantity of something fluid in motion, *a stream of sand trickled out* || a continuous procession of people or animals moving in one direction || a linked succession of events, *the stream of history* || a continuous emission, *a stream of words* || the flow or current of a fluid || the direction of this flow || a swift oceanic current, e.g. the Gulf Stream || (*Br. education*) a group (of pupils) who have been classed according to academic performance, *C-stream students* **2.** *v.i.* to flow in, or as if in, a stream, *the rain streamed down* || to emit fluid in a stream, *her eyes were streaming* || to be moved and esp. extended by, or as if by, a stream or current, *the flag streamed in the wind* || (of many people or things) to move in one direction, *workmen streamed from the factory* || (of something static, e.g. a road) to appear to have a fast current because of one's own speed of moving along or beside it || *v.t.* to emit (fluid) in a stream, *her eyes streamed tears* || to cause (e.g. a flag) to move and extend as if carried by a stream or current || (*naut.*) to throw (the anchor buoy) overboard before casting anchor || (*mining*) to wash (a surface) with a stream of water in order to see if it contains ore || (*Br. education*) to class (pupils) into streams according to their academic performance **stréam·er** *n.* a long, narrow piece of fabric attached at one end and put to stream out in the wind || a festive decoration for a room made of a long thin ribbon of colored paper || (*pl.*) the aurora borealis || a banner headline [O.E. *strēam*]

stream·let (strí:mlit) *n.* a small stream (body of fresh water)

stream·line (strí:mlạin) **1.** *n.* a direction of smooth flow within a liquid or gas past a solid body or a line drawn to indicate this || the contour given to a solid body so that it can move through a fluid with the minimum resistance **2.** *v.t. pres. part.* **stream·lin·ing** *past* and *past part.* **stream·lined** to shape (a solid body) in this way || to render more efficient by modernizing, *the new director soon streamlined the business* **stréam·lined** *adj.* shaped so as to be able to move through a fluid with minimum resistance || planned in such a way that progress is made as easy and rapid as possible || modernized and speeded up

streamline flow a manner of flow such that continuous streamlines can be drawn through the whole length of the course

stream of consciousness (*psychol.*) individual conscious experience regarded as continuously moving forward in time in an uneven flow. In creative writing the interior monologue makes use of this to reveal character and comment on life [originated by William JAMES]

street (stri:t) *n.* a road in a town or village, usually hard-surfaced and provided with drainage and artificial lighting and having buildings on one or both sides || this road together with the houses etc. abutting it || (*collect.*) the people who live or work in the houses etc. of this road, *the whole street knew about it* [O. E. *strǣt*]

street book (*trading*) a daily record kept by futures commission merchants and clearing members showing details of each futures transaction

street·car (strí:tkɑr) *n.* (*Am.=Br.* tram) a passenger car for public transport running on rails laid in the street or roadway and driven by electric current from a conduit or from overhead wires

street·cor·ner conservative (strí:tkɔrnər) one who calls him- or herself a conservative, without understanding the term

street-lev·el propulsion (strí:tlevəl) the force of opinions held by uninformed and unorganized masses of people

street·light (strí:tlạit) *n.* one of a series of lamps, each mounted on a lamppost, placed at intervals along a street or road

street people those who are habitually active in or present on the street or parks, e.g., hippies, hustlers, and, esp. in ethnic or ghetto neighborhoods, usu. older people who spend their day and early evening hours seated in chairs on the sidewalk or before their doors or watching from their windows

street·scape (strí:tskeip) *n.* an urban landscape or view of a street or streets

street theater short plays or pantomime, usu. antiestablishment, presented on the street or in a park, usu. by a volunteer company *also* GUERILLA THEATER

street·walk·er (strí:twɔ̣kər) *n.* a prostitute who solicits in the street

street·wise (strí:twaiz) *adj.* aware of the mores of street people and skilled in dealing with them *syn* streetsmart

street·work·er (strí:twə:rkər) *n.* social worker active with neighborhood youth

strength (streŋθ) *n.* capacity to exert force || ability to resist attack || capacity to resist strain, stress etc. || physical, emotional or mental resources || the potency of a drug or beverage || the effectiveness of something in stimulating the senses or influencing the mind || (*mil.*) fighting capacity, reckoned in numbers and equipment (of arguments, legal cases etc.) soundness || (*commerce*) the tendency of prices on the stock exchange or in the commodity market etc. to remain high **on the strength of** relying on **stréngth·en** *v.t.* to make stronger || *v.i.* to become stronger [O.E. *strengthu*]

stren·u·ous (strénju:əs) *adj.* involving a great effort, *strenuous attempts* || requiring a great effort, *a strenuous occupation* [fr. L. *strenuus*, vigorous]

strep·to·coc·cal (strẹptəkɔ́k'l) *adj.* of or caused by streptococci

strep·to·coc·cic (strẹptəkɔ́ksik) *adj.* streptococcal

strep·to·coc·cus (strẹptəkɔ́kəs) *pl.* **strep·to·coc·ci** (strẹptəkɔ́ksai) *n.* a member of *Streptococcus*, a genus of nonmotile, gram-positive bacteria, usually occurring in chains of coccoid cells. Many produce infections (e.g. erysipelas, impetigo) in man [Mod. L. fr. Gk *streptos*, twisted+*kokkos*, berry]

strep·to·my·cin (strẹptoumáisin) *n.* an antibiotic produced by the South American soil fungus *Streptomyces griseus* and used in the treatment of various bacterial infections (e.g. tuberculosis) [fr. Gk *streptos*, twisted+*mukēs*, fungus]

strep·to·ni·grin (streptounáigrin) [$C_{25}H_{22}N_4O_8$] *n.* (*pharm.*) toxic antibiotic used in cancer treatment

Stre·se·mann (ʃtréizəmɑn), Gustav (1878-1929), German liberal statesman. As foreign minister (1923-9), he signed the Locarno Pact (1925) and the Kellogg-Briand Pact (1928). Nobel peace prize (1926)

stress (stres) **1.** *n.* (*phys.*) the state of an elastic body under conditions of strain expressed quantitatively as force applied per unit area (*HOOKE'S LAW) || a state in which a strong demand is made on the nervous system || special emphasis given to something || the relative intensity with which a syllable is uttered || a strong syllable (*mus., prosody*) accent **2.** *v.t.* to give emphasis to || to accent, *stress the first syllable* || to impart mechanical stress to, *prestressed concrete* [prob. a form of DISTRESS n.]

stretch (stretʃ) **1.** *v.t.* to pull or otherwise exert force on (an elastic body), causing it to assume its full potential dimensions or dimensions greater than those it has when not thus pulled etc. || to pull or spread out fully || to cause (something) to occupy a given amount of space or given distance, *stretch the wires across the valley* || to strain (a tendon) || to make (something) permanently larger by exerting forces beyond the elastic limit, *to stretch a shoe* || (often with 'out') to cause (a limb etc.) to reach out to full length, *to stretch one's arms* || (*refl.*, often with 'out on') to cause (oneself) to lie full length || (*refl.*) to ease (oneself) from a cramped or curled position by straightening the body || to make (food etc.) appear to go further || to try to make (the law, the truth etc.) go beyond their proper limits || to lay (someone) flat || (*pop.*) to knock (someone) flat || to cause (e.g. the intelligence or imagination) to exceed previous limits || *v.i.* (of an elastic body) to become enlarged in length and/or breadth || to become permanently enlarged || to be able to endure strain, *will your generosity stretch that far?* || to ease oneself from a cramped or curled position by straightening the body || to occupy a given amount of time or space, *the war stretched over four years* || (often with 'out') to lie full length || to become stretched or capable of being stretched || to reach out, esp. one's hand, *can you stretch for it?* **to stretch a point** to make a special concession || to go beyond what is justified, e.g. in reaching a conclusion, interpreting a text etc. **to stretch one's legs** to take a short walk **2.** *n.* a stretching or being stretched || capacity for being stretched || the extent to which something can be stretched without damage || a length or area, *a stretch of rope, a stretch of grass* || a continuous period, *a stretch in the army* || (*pop.*) a period of imprisonment || a short walk for relaxation or mild exercise || a usually straight section of racetrack **strétch·er** *n.* a length of canvas etc. stretched between parallel poles and used for carrying, esp. the sick or dead in a prone position || a brick or stone laid lengthwise, parallel to the face of the wall of which it forms part || any of various frames upon which cloth, canvas etc. is stretched or shaped || (*rowing*) a cross-piece against which a rower can brace his feet [O.E. *streccan*]

stretch·er-bear·er (strétʃərbẹərər) *n.* a person carrying one end of a stretcher

stretch-out (strétʃaut) *n.* (*pop.*) a reorganization within an industry which results in more work being done by the same number of employees for little or no additional pay

stretch receptor a muscle end sensitive to stretch, e.g., in the lung *also* muscle spindle

stretch·y (strétʃi:) *comp.* **stretch·i·er** *superl.* **stretch·i·est** *adj.* elastic || apt to stretch too far

stret·to (strétou) *pl.* **stret·ti** (stréti:), **stret·tos** *n.* (*mus.*) a direction that the pace of a piece of music should quicken || (*mus.*) a term used of the overlapping of entries in fugal compositions. The second voice enters with the subject before the first voice has finished uttering it [Ital.]

strew (stru:) *pres. part.* **strew·ing** *past* **strewed** *past part.* **strewed, strewn** (stru:n) *v.t.* to scatter in separate particles or drops over a surface, *to strew sand* || to drop or throw about in a disorderly way || to cover (a surface) in this way, *the ground was strewn with leaves* [O.E. *streowian, streawian, strewian*]

strewn field a location where tektites (small meteorites) have fallen

stri·a (stráiə) *pl.* **stri·ae** (stráii:) *n.* a narrow groove || one of the thin, parallel bands of color marking some rocks, shells etc. || (*archit.*) a fillet, esp. one separating the flutes of a column || a stripe or line distinguished from its surroundings by color, relief or texture etc. [L.]

stri·ate 1. (stráieit) *v.t. pres. part.* **stri·at·ing** *past* and *past part.* **stri·at·ed** to mark with or as if with striae **2.** (stráiit) *adj.* marked with parallel striae **strí·at·ed** *adj.* [fr. L. *striare (striatus)*, to groove]

striated muscle contractile tissue with marked transverse striations, forming the skeletal muscle of the vertebrate body (cf. SMOOTH MUSCLE, cf. CARDIAC MUSCLE, cf. SKELETAL MUSCLE)

stri·a·tion (straiéiʃən) *n.* the condition of being striated || the way striae are arranged || a stria

strick·en (stríkən) alt. *past part.* of STRIKE || *adj.* afflicted by some overwhelming disaster, grief, disease etc. || (*rhet.*, of a hunted animal) wounded || (in compounds) suddenly possessed by a specified emotion etc., *panic-stricken, terror-stricken* || (of a measure) having its contents leveled with a strickle [alt. *past part.* of STRIKE]

strick·le (strík'l) **1.** *n.* an instrument for removing surplus grain from a measure above the level of the rim || a straightedge of stone or roughened steel used to sharpen the curved blade of a scythe etc. || a template with a beveled edge used to shape a mold in a foundry **2.** *v.t. pres. part.* **strick·ling** *past* and *past part.* **strick·led** to shape with a strickle [O.E. *stricel*]

strict (strikt) *adj.* rigorous and often severe in imposing discipline, *a strict schoolmaster* || adhering rigorously to rules or standards, *a strict teetotaler* || requiring unswerving obedience, *strict rules* || precise, exact, rigorously adhered to, *strict tempo* || (*bot.*, of stems etc.) not drooping **strict·ly** *adv.* **strictly speaking** according to the rules when interpreted without latitude, *strictly speaking I should not be here* || literally, in every respect corresponding with the facts, *it's not, strictly speaking, true* [fr. L. *stringere (strictus)*, to draw or bind tight]

stric·ture (stríktʃər) *n.* an adverse criticism || (*med.*) an abnormal contraction of a duct or channel of the body, esp. of the male urethra [fr. L. *strictura*, contraction]

stride (straid) **1.** *v. pres. part.* **strid·ing** *past* **strode** (stroud) *past part.* **strid·den** (stríd'n) *v.i.* to walk with long steps || *v.t.* to pass over (e.g. a ditch) in one step || to go over, through, along, up and down etc. with long steps, *to stride the deck* **2.** *n.* a long walking step || the distance covered by such a step || a striding gait || (*pl.*) rapid advances, *strides to recovery* **to hit one's stride** (*Am.*=*Br.* **to get into one's stride**) to become adjusted so that one works or plays with full efficiency **to take in one's stride** to do (something), or adjust oneself to (something) easily or without fuss [O.E. *stridan*]

stri·dence (stráid'ns) *n.* stridency

stri·den·cy (stráid'nsi:) *n.* the state or quality of being strident

stri·dent (stráid'nt) *adj.* (of a sound) loud, grating and harsh [fr. L. *stridens (stridentis)* fr. *stridere*, to creak]

stride piano jazz form of piano playing in which the right hand plays the melody while the left hand plays a chord or a note at a higher octave

strid·u·lant (strídʒulənt) *adj.* stridulating || stridulous

strid·u·late (strídʒuleit) *pres. part.* **strid·u·lat·ing** *past* and *past part.* **strid·u·lat·ed** *v.i.* (of cicadas, grasshoppers etc.) to make a shrill, strident sound by rubbing together certain hard parts of the body **strid·u·lá·tion** *n.* [fr. Mod. L. *stridulare (stridulatus)*]

strid·u·lous (strídʒuləs) *adj.* making a shrill chirping sound [fr. L. *stridulus*]

stri·é (stri:jéi) *n.* a cloth that has irregular stripes or streaks of similar color in the background, producing a mottled effect

strife (straif) *n.* a condition of enmity often arising out of rivalry || (*rhet.*) a prolonged struggle for power or superiority || discord, *domestic strife* [O.F. *estrif*]

stri·ga (stráigə) *pl.* **stri·gae** (stráigi:), **stri·gas** *n.* (*bot.*, esp. *pl.*) a stiff bristle [L.]

strig·il (strídʒəl) *n.* (*Gk* and *Rom. hist.*) a scraper for removing sweat from the skin || one of a group of curved or undulating flutings adorning esp. Roman architecture || (*zool.*) a comblike mechanism, situated on the junction of the tibia and the tarsus on the first legs of bees and other insects, and used for cleaning the antennae [fr. L. *strigilis*]

stri·gose (stráigous) *adj.* (*bot.*) having strigae || (*biol.*) marked by small furrows [fr. Mod. L. *strigosus* fr. *striga*, a furrow]

strike (straik) **1.** *v. pres. part.* **strik·ing** *past* **struck** (strʌk) *past part.* **struck, strick·en** (strikən) *v.t.* to deal (someone) a blow || to deliver (a blow) || to hit (e.g. a ball) || to collide forcibly with || (with 'together') to cause to collide or come into contact forcibly, *she struck their heads together* || to touch (e.g. keys), esp. so as to produce a musical note or sound || to touch e.g. keys so as to produce (a musical note or sound), *to strike a chord* || (of a clock) to chime (the hour) || to cause (a match) to ignite by friction || to remove with a sharp blow (*rhet.*, of disaster, illness, death) to come suddenly and esp. violently upon, *the plague struck the town yesterday* || (esp. used passively with 'down') to afflict suddenly and violently || (of lightning) to damage or destroy || (*rhet.*) to wound or affect the feelings of, *the news struck him to the quick* || to make (a medal) by stamping || (of sound) to become audible to || (of light) to fall on and illuminate brightly, *the sun struck the weathercock* || to make an impression or impact on, *they were struck by its speed* || (of an idea or thought) to occur suddenly to || to seem to (someone), *it strikes me as impossible* || to make a discovery of (e.g. oil) || to produce (sparks) to assume (an attitude or pose) to arrive at (a bargain, balance, average etc.) || to level off (a measure of grain) with a strickle || to cause (a plant) to take root || to lower, take down (sails, tents, flags etc.) || to vacate the site of (a camp) || to hook (a fish) by a sudden sharp pull || to dismantle (theater scenery) || (with 'on') to arrive at (a solution) || to come across unexpectedly, *he struck the main road* || to come up against, *they struck various difficulties* || to cause (someone) to become blind, dumb etc. || (*naut.*, with 'down') to lower (cargo) into the hold || to harpoon (a whale) || (of a snake) to sink the fangs into || to cease (work) in order to put pressure on an employer || (*mil.*) to attack (an enemy or target) || (with 'out') to cancel or erase || *v.i.* to deal a blow or blows || to attack || to proceed in a specified direction, *he struck south* || to chime, *one o'clock struck* || (of a match) to become ignited || (of a fish) to grab at the bait || (of a snake) to sink or try to sink its fangs into its prey || (of a ship) to run aground || (*naut.*) to lower the flag, esp. as a sign of surrender || (*geol.*) to extend in a certain direction || (of a plant) to take root || (of a seed) to germinate || (with 'for') to go in the direction of || to stop working in order to put pressure on an employer **to strike home** (of a punch, blow etc.) to be very effective || (of a remark) to produce a very pronounced effect to **strike off** to sever || to remove (the name of) someone from a register and thus debar him of specified privileges **to strike out** (*baseball*) to be put out as a result of three strikes || (*baseball*) to put (a batter) out by pitching three strikes **to strike out for** to begin to swim or row vigorously in the direction of **to strike out on one's own** to start a new enterprise alone **to strike up** to begin to make music, *the band struck up* || to begin to play (something), *the band struck up a waltz* || to begin (a friendship, a conversation) with someone met casually **2.** *n.* a blow || a ceasing to work in order to put pressure on an employer || the number of coins minted or medals struck at one time || a fish's bite at the bait || the discovery of a deposit of oil etc. || a strickle || (*geol.*) the horizontal direction of a stratum || (*baseball*) a pitched ball which is struck at but missed, or which is fairly delivered but not struck at, or which is hit foul but not caught, or which is, on a third strike, hit as a foul tip caught by the catcher, or which is, on a third strike, bunted foul || (*bowling*) the act of knocking down all the pins with the first bowl || the score made in this way [O.E. *strican*]

strike·break·er (stráikbrẹikər) *n.* a person engaged to do a striker's work || someone who supplies workers to an employer during a strike

strike·break·ing (stráikbrẹikiŋ) *n.* the breaking up of a workers' strike

strike cruiser (*mil.*) warship designed to operate with carrier strike forces or surface action groups

strike·out (stráikąut) *n.* (*baseball*) the out made by a batter when he has been charged with three strikes

strike pay an allowance paid out by a trade union to those on official strike

strik·er (stráikər) *n.* a person who strikes || a worker on strike || something that strikes, e.g. the hammer in a chiming clock || an enlisted man in the army employed as orderly to an officer

strik·ing (stráikiŋ) *adj.* remarkable, impressive, attracting attention || on strike || of or relating to a device that strikes

Strind·berg (stríndbə:rg, strínbə:rg, strínbærjə), August (1849-1912), Swedish writer best known for his plays. He also wrote poems, short stories, two volumes of autobiography, and novels, of which the best-known is 'The Red Room' (1879). He inaugurated a new movement in European drama with the dramatic naturalism of his two best-known plays, 'The Father' (1887) and 'Miss Julie' (1888). There are mystical, symbolic and supernatural elements in the later plays, of which the best-known are 'The Dance of Death' (1901) and 'The Ghost Sonata' (1907). Themes of social satire and criticism and of sexual and class conflict occur throughout his writings, which are also colored by his own conceptions of psychology

string (striŋ) **1.** *n.* a thin length of twisted fiber, thinner than cord, used for tying etc. || a length of e.g. silk or twine on which e.g. beads or fish can be threaded || a length of tape etc. used for tying or fastening || (*pl.*) the cords pulled to actuate a puppet || a natural fiber, e.g. that along one edge of a bean pod || a row of beads or other objects threaded on or as if on a string, *a string of onions* || a number of things of any kind arranged or ranging one behind the other, *a string of cars, a string of events* || a number of things linked or tied together, *a string of sausages, a string of mules* || several homogeneous business concerns owned by one person or company, *a string of hotels* || a length of wire, gut etc. which produces sound when under tension and when made to vibrate by striking, plucking or bowing || (*pl.*) the stringed instruments of an orchestra collectively || (*pl.*) the players of these instruments || a bowstring || the horses from one racing stable || a group of players rated according to ability || (*archit.*) a stringcourse || that part of the side of a stair supporting the treads and risers || (*billiards*) a balkline || (*billiards*) the score or device used to record this || (*pop.*) a condition attached to something || a source that can be used to promote the interests of someone **to have two strings to one's bow** to have two alternative courses of action at one's disposal **to pull strings** to exert one's personal influence, or ask someone else to do this for one **2.** *v. pres. part.* **string·ing** *past* and *past part.* **strung** (strʌŋ) *v.t.* to furnish with a string or strings || (*archery*) to fit a bowstring to (a bow) || to thread on a string || to fasten with a string || to remove the stringy fibers from, *to string beans* || to connect or put in an unbroken series, *to string ideas together* || (with 'out') to arrange in a long line || to cause (something) to extend along a given distance, *string the wire around the room* || *v.i.* (*billiards*) to determine the order of playing by causing the cue ball to rebound off the foot cushion and stop as close to the head cushion (or sometimes to the head string) as possible || to form stringy fibers || to stretch out in a long line **to string (someone) along** (*pop.*) to fool (someone) **to string along with** to stay with, follow or go along with (someone), esp. rather long-sufferingly **to string out** to prolong **to string up** (*pop.*) to hang (execute) || to bring into a state of nervous tension [O.E. *streng*]

string bean (*Am.*=*Br.* runner bean) a bean of which the unripe pod is eaten as food, the fiber down the side of the pod having first been removed

string·board (stríŋbɔrd, stríŋbɒurd) *n.* (*archit.*) a facing used to cover the ends of the steps in a staircase

string·course (stríŋkɔrs, stríŋkɒurs) *n.* (*archit.*) a projecting horizontal band stretching around the outside of a building

stringed (striŋd) *adj.* (of musical instruments) having strings

strin·gen·cy (stríndʒənsi:) *pl.* **strin·gen·cies** *n.* the state or quality, or an instance, of being stringent

strin·gen·do (strindʒéndou) *n.* (*mus.*) a direction to play at an accelerating speed [Ital.]

strin·gent (stríndʒənt) *adj.* strict, rigid, *stringent rules* ‖ tight, limiting, *stringent financial conditions* ‖ (of reasoning) convincing, closely argued [fr. L. *stringens* (*stringentis*) fr. *stringere,* to draw tight]

strin·ger (stríŋər) *n.* a long horizontal member of a structural framework, e.g. for supporting the floorboards of a building or the sections of a bridge ‖ (*aeron.*) a longitudinal member used for strengthening a fuselage or wing in certain types of aircraft ‖ a railroad tie

string·i·ness (stríŋi:nis) *n.* the state or quality of being stringy

string·piece (stríŋpi:s) *n.* a long heavy piece of timber laid horizontally and used to support and strengthen various sorts of framework

string tie a necktie made of a very narrow width of material and usually tied in a bow

string·y (stríŋi:) *comp.* **string·i·er** *superl.* **string·i·est** *adj.* consisting of fibers or strings ‖ like a string, long and thin ‖ (of meat) fibrous, tough ‖ (of liquid) viscid ‖ (of people) thin and wiry or scrawny

strip (strip) *pres. part.* **strip·ping** *past* and *past part.* **stripped** *v.t.* to remove (clothing) ‖ to remove the clothing of (someone) ‖ to remove (a covering), *to strip the bark from a tree* ‖ to deprive (something) of its covering, *to strip a tree of its bark* ‖ to deprive (someone) of a possession etc. ‖ to take (a possession etc.) from someone ‖ to divest (a person) of medals, decorations, honors etc. ‖ to remove (medals, decorations, honors etc.) from someone ‖ to remove or pull back the bedclothes from (a bed) ‖ to remove or pull back (the bedclothes) from a bed ‖ to squeeze the last drop of milk from (a cow) ‖ to dismantle (a gun) ‖ to pluck the old hair from (a rough-coated dog) ‖ to break the thread of (a screw) or the teeth of (a cog) ‖ to empty (e.g. a room) of furniture etc. ‖ to remove (furniture etc.) from a room ‖ to make (something) bare by taking away removable parts ‖ to take away (removable parts) from something ‖ (*pop.*) to make (an automobile) lighter, for extra speed, by removing nonessential parts ‖ to remove the central rib from (tobacco leaves) ‖ to pick the cured leaves from the stalks of (tobacco) ‖ to tear off ‖ *v.i.* to undress ‖ to come off in strips **to strip down** to prepare (a surface) for painting etc. by cleaning off old paint etc. ‖ to take to pieces (an engine) in order to clean and service it [M.E. *stripe, strepe, strupe,* O.E. *strīpan, strȳpan,* to plunder]

strip *n.* a long narrow piece of more or less uniform width, *a strip of land* ‖ a comic strip ‖ an airstrip ‖ (*Br.*) a trough in which ores are washed and separated **to tear a strip off** (*Br., pop.*) to rebuke (someone) very severely [prob. M.L.G. *strippe*]

strip cartoon (*Br.*) a comic strip

strip chart graph presented on a long, continuous strip, e.g., a patient's fever chart

strip city an urban area connecting two separate cities, e.g., between New York and Newark

strip cropping the planting of separate crops in contiguous strips along the contours of hillsides to combat erosion

stripe (straip) *n.* a stroke or lash with a whip (*rhet.*) the mark left on the body by such a stroke or lash [prob. fr. L.G. or Du.]

stripe 1. *n.* a long narrow band usually of uniform width, distinguished by color or texture from its surroundings ‖ a short band or one of a number sewn on a uniform to denote rank, service, good conduct etc. ‖ a particular kind of character, opinion etc., *scholars of a different stripe* **2.** *v.t. pres. part.* **strip·ing** *past* and *past part.* **striped** to mark with a stripe or stripes **striped** (straipt, stráipid) *adj.* [prob. fr. M.L.G. or Du. *strīpe*]

striped bass *Roccus saxatilis,* fam. *Serranidae,* a game and food fish having longitudinal black stripes and ranging from 20 lbs to (rarely) 100 lbs in weight

striped muishond *Ictonyx striata,* a ferretlike muishond

strip farming the allotment of land to individual farmers in separated strips so that good and bad land may be fairly distributed ‖ strip cropping

strip lighting the lighting of a room with one or more tubular, fluorescent lamps

strip·ling (stripliŋ) *n.* (*rhet.*) a youth

strip mining process of stripping the land of its surface rock and soil to make available underlying mineral deposits

strip·tease (strípti:z) *n.* a theatrical or cabaret act in which a person removes his/her clothes in front of the audience item by item usually to music

strip·y (stráipi:) *comp.* **strip·i·er** *superl.* **strip·i·est** *adj.* marked with stripes

strive (straiv) *pres. part.* **striv·ing** *past* **strove** (strouv) *past part.* **striv·en** (strívən) *v.i.* to make great efforts, *to strive to convince someone* ‖ (with 'towards') to struggle or endeavor to attain some end ‖ (with 'with') to vie or contend [M.E. *strīven*]

strobil *STROBILE

strob·i·la·ceous (strɒbəléiʃəs) *adj.* relating to a strobilus ‖ resembling a strobilus ‖ having strobili

strob·ile, strob·il (strɒ́bəl) *n.* a strobilus [F.]

strob·i·lus (strɒ́bələs) *pl.* **strob·i·li** (strɒ́bəlai) *n.* (*bot.*) a conelike aggregation of sporophylls, e.g. in club mosses ‖ a flower of imbricated scales, e.g. in hops ‖ the cone of a gymnosperm [L.]

stro·bo·scope (stróubəskoup, strɒ́bəskoup) *n.* (*phys.*) a device by which small differences of frequency between two simple periodic or simple oscillatory motions can be measured, depending on the principle that if they are viewed together, they will appear to coincide at regular intervals of time which can be measured. Thus if there are *n* coincidences per second, the difference in frequency is *n* **stro·bo·scop·ic** (stroubəskɒ́pik, strɒbəskɒ́pik), **stro·bo·scop·i·cal** *adjs.* [fr. Gk *strobos,* a twisting or whirling around+*skopein,* to observe]

strode *past* of STRIDE

Stroess·ner (strésnər), Alfredo (1912-), Paraguayan general and dictator (1954-). He had himself reelected president for the sixth time in 1983

stroke (strouk) **1.** *n.* a blow ‖ (in various ball games) the act of striking the ball ‖ an attempt to strike the ball ‖ a sudden manifestation (of e.g. genius, luck etc.) ‖ the sound of a bell or a striking clock ‖ a heartbeat ‖ an attack of apoplexy ‖ a single, combined movement of the limbs propelling a swimmer through the water ‖ a stylized set of such movements, e.g. breaststroke or crawl ‖ a single movement of a piston or similar thing ‖ the distance covered in this movement ‖ a single movement of the hand in painting, drawing, writing etc. ‖ a single mark made by a brush, pencil, pen etc. ‖ (in negative constructions) a minimum of work, *not a stroke was done* ‖ a movement made in keeping time ‖ an oblique or vertical line used in printing, esp. to divide alternatives, as in 'and/or' ‖ (*rowing*) the oarsman who sits nearest the stern of the boat and sets the pace ‖ the position he occupies ‖ (*rowing*) a single pull on the oar ‖ style of rowing in respect to length, speed and frequency of these pulls **2.** *v.t. pres. part.* **strok·ing** *past* and *past part.* **stroked** to be stroke for (a crew or boat) ‖ to draw the horizontal line across the upright in (the letter t) [M.E. *strōk* prob. fr. O.E.]

stroke 1. *v.t. pres. part.* **strok·ing** *past* and *past part.* **stroked** to pass esp. the hand gently over once or repeatedly, esp. in the same single direction ‖ to strip the last drop of milk from (a cow) **2.** *n.* a stroking movement [O.E. *strācian*]

stroll (stroul) **1.** *v.i.* to walk leisurely ‖ *v.t.* to walk leisurely along or through, *strolling the boulevard* **2.** *n.* a short leisurely walk **stróll·er** *n.* (*Am.=Br.* pushchair) a light wheeled chair for pushing a young child out in ‖ someone out for a stroll [etym. doubtful]

strolling player (*old-fash.*) one of a band of actors, acting on improvised stages etc. and going from place to place off the established theater circuits

stro·ma (stróumə) *pl.* **stro·ma·ta** (stróumətə) *n.* (*anat.*) the connective tissue binding and supporting an organ ‖ the transparent, filmy framework of some cells ‖ the soft, vascular framework in the meshes of which the ovarian follicles are embedded ‖ the protoplasmic body of a plastid [L.=bed covering fr. Gk]

stro·mat·o·lite (stroumǽtəlait) *n.* (*geol.*) fossil of blue-green, self-forming algae found in sedimentary layers of rock *also* callenia —**stromatolitic** *adj.*

Strom·bo·li (strɔ́mbəli:) the northern-most island (area 5 sq. miles, pop. 100) of the Lipari Is, Italy. It is an active volcano (3,040 ft), but is inhabited: Malmsey, capers

strong (strɔŋ) **1.** *adj.* having great physical strength ‖ performed with great physical strength ‖ able to resist considerable force ‖ morally powerful ‖ intellectually powerful ‖ (of appearance) indicative of strength of character ‖ (of personality, character) making an impact, tending to dominate or control ‖ especially proficient or well informed, *strong in history* ‖ powerful because of esp. physical resources (e.g. numbers, wealth, supplies), *a strong contingent of men, a strong economy* ‖ having the force of a specified number, *a contingent 100 strong* ‖ (of a course of action) efficacious but extreme, *strong measures* ‖ firmly grounded, *strong faith, a strong suspicion* ‖ exerting great effect on one of the senses, *strong light* ‖ (of things affecting the sense of smell) unpleasantly powerful ‖ loyal and enthusiastic, *strong supporters* ‖ (of language, words etc.) forceful sometimes to the point of abuse ‖ intense in degree or quality, *strong devotion, strong colors* ‖ concentrated or having a high content of some specified or understood ingredient, *strong tobacco, strong coffee* ‖ having a high alcohol content ‖ unaffected by alcohol, *a strong head* ‖ not squeamish, *a strong stomach* ‖ marked, *a strong resemblance* ‖ (of wind) blowing forcefully ‖ (of lenses) having a high magnifying power ‖ (*chem.,* of an acid or base) ionizing to a high degree in solution ‖ (*gram.,* in Germanic languages) designating a verb that changes its tense by an internal vowel variation (e.g. 'sing, sang, sung') ‖ (*commerce*) characterized by stable or rising prices **2.** *adv.* in a strong way, *at 80 he's still going strong* [O.E. *strang, strong*]

strong-arm (strɔ́ŋɑrm) **1.** *adj.* (*pop.*) using physical force, often without warrant **2.** *v.t.* (*pop.*) to use physical force upon

Strong·bow (strɔ́ŋbou), Richard *PEMBROKE, 2nd earl of

strong·box (strɔ́ŋbɒks) *n.* a small safe or chest for money and valuables

strong force (*nuclear phys.*) short (10^{-23}) elemental force in mesons and baryons that holds protons and neutrons together in the atomic nucleus, and that when released provides nuclear power *also* strong interaction

strong·hold (strɔ́ŋhould) *n.* a fortress ‖ a center of support for a cause or faction, *a stronghold of Catholicism*

strong man a man e.g. in a circus who performs feats of muscular strength ‖ (*pop.*) a dictator

strong-mind·ed (strɔŋmáindid) *adj.* having firm and independent convictions ‖ able to resist temptation, resolute

strong·room (strɔ́ŋru:m, strɔ́ŋrum) *n.* a special fireproof and burglarproof room for storing money or valuables

stron·gyl (strɒ́ndʒil) *n.* a strongyle

stron·gyle (strɒ́ndʒil, strɒ́ndʒail) *n.* any of various roundworms of fam. *Strongylus* parasitic in the digestive tract and tissues of horses and causing extreme debility [fr. Mod. L. *strongylus* fr. Gk *strongulos,* round]

stron·gy·lo·sis (strɒndʒəlóusis) *n.* infestation by strongyles [Mod. L.]

stron·ti·a (strɒ́nʃi:ə, strɒ́nti:ə) *n.* strontium oxide [Mod. L.]

stron·ti·an (strɒ́nʃi:ən, strɒ́nti:ən) *n.* strontium [after *Strontian,* Argyllshire, Scotland, where it was first discovered]

stron·ti·an·ite (strɒ́nʃi:ənait, strɒ́nti:ənait) *n.* strontium carbonate, $SrCO_3$, found in various natural forms

stron·ti·um (strɒ́nʃi:əm, strɒ́nti:əm) *n.* a metallic element (symbol Sr, at. no. 38, at. mass 87.63), chemically similar to calcium. Its compounds, which give a crimson flame coloration, are used in fireworks, and its oxide is used in sugar refining. Its radioactive isotope, strontium 90, released by the explosion of a hydrogen bomb, is dangerous to health [fr. STRONTIA]

strontium 90 (*nuclear phys.*) radioisotope with a half-life of 28 yrs, created by reactor-fusion, used in radiation therapy, atomic batteries, and measuring devices *also* radiostrontium

strontium oxide SrO, an oxide, esp. the crystalline monoxide, of strontium, resembling lime

strop (strɒp) **1.** *n.* a leather strip on which a razor can be sharpened **2.** *v.t. pres. part.* **strop·ping** *past* and *past part.* **stropped** to sharpen with a strop [O.E.]

stro·phan·thin-K (strəfǽnθinkéi) *n.* a bitter,

poisonous glycoside obtained from the seeds and bark of *Strophanthus kombé*, an E. African vine. It is used as a heart stimulant and as an arrow poison [fr. Mod. L. fr. Gk *strophos*, a twisted cord+*anthos*, flower]

stro·phe (stróufi:) the lines sung by the chorus as it moved from right to left in an ancient Greek choral drama ‖ the stanza answered by the antistrophe in a Pindaric ode ‖ a stanza, esp. one of the divisions of an ode **stroph·ic** (strófik) *adj.* [Gk *strophē*, a turning]

stro·phoid (stróufɔid) *n.* (*math.*) a curve in a plane that is made by a point moving on variable line *A* and passing through point *B*, where *A* to *B* is equal to the *B* intercept value

strove *past* of STRIVE

struck *past* and alt. *past part.* of STRIKE

struck jury (*law*) a jury of 12 members specially selected from an original panel of 48 special jurymen by various processes of elimination

struc·tur·al (strʌ́ktʃərəl) *adj.* of or relating to structure

structural engineering the branch of civil engineering dealing with the design and building of dams, bridges and other large structures

structural formula a chemical formula consisting of an arrangement of chemical symbols (e.g. lines for bonds, dots for nonbonding valence electrons and the usual abbreviations for the chemical elements) showing two-dimensionally the arrangement of atoms in a molecule (cf. EMPIRICAL FORMULA, cf. MOLECULAR FORMULA)

struc·tur·al-func·tion·al theory (strʌ́ktʃərəl-fʌ́ŋkʃənəl) the basis for analysis of a system deduced from analysis of intended and unintended effects in a smaller similar system *also* structural functionalism

struc·tur·al·ism (strʌ́ktʃərəlizm) *n.* a school of thought common to several of the human sciences (psychology, ethnology etc.) tending to define phenomena as elements of organized totalities that can be formulated in mathematical terms

structural isomerism isomerism in which the atoms are linked in different ways in each form (cf. STEREOISOMERISM, cf. OPTICAL ISOMERISM)

struc·tur·al·ly (strʌ́ktʃərəli:) *adv.* with regard to structure

structural reform (*agriculture*) process of improving elements of an agricultural industry by changing farm size, skills, and access

structural steel steel prepared in various shapes for use in the construction of bridges, buildings etc.

struc·ture (strʌ́ktʃər) **1.** *n.* something (e.g. a building or an organism) made of parts fitted or joined together ‖ the essential supporting portion of this (e.g. the framework of steel girders supporting a building) ‖ the way in which constituent parts are fitted or joined together, or arranged to give something its peculiar nature or character, *plant structure, the structure of society* **2.** *v.t. pres. part.* **struc·tur·ing** *past* and *past part.* **struc·tured** to give a structure to [fr. L. *structura* fr. *struere* (*structus*), to build]

struc·tur·ism (strʌ́ktə:rizəm) *n.* art form that has three dimensions of sculpture, uses color of painting, emphasizes basic geometric forms — **structurist** *n.*

struc·tur·iz·a·tion (strʌktə:rəzéiʃən) *n.* process of organizing any complex intellectual material into a cohesive form —**structurize** *v.*

strug·gle (strʌ́g'l) **1.** *v.i. pres. part.* **strug·gling** *past* and *past part.* **strug·gled** to make strenuous efforts, *to struggle to survive* ‖ to move the limbs or body violently to free oneself, *he struggled out of the car* ‖ (with 'with' or 'against') to contend physically with someone, or mentally with a problem etc. ‖ to make one's way with difficulty, *to struggle to the end of a book* **2.** *n.* the act of struggling ‖ a great effort ‖ a strenuous contending with someone or something [etym. doubtful]

strum (strʌm) **1.** *v. pres. part.* **strum·ming** *past* and *past part.* **strummed** *v.i.* to play a stringed musical instrument casually or without ability ‖ *v.t.* to play (a tune, or an instrument) in this way **2.** *n.* the act or sound of strumming [imit.]

stru·ma (strú:mə) *pl.* **stru·mae** (strú:mi:) *n.* (*bot.*) a cushionlike swelling on a plant organ, e.g. a moss capsule ‖ (*med.*) a goiter [L. = a scrofulous tumor]

stru·mose (strú:mous) *adj.* (*bot.*) having a struma [fr. L. *strumosus*]

strum·pet (strʌ́mpit) *n.* (*old-fash., rhet.*) a prostitute

strung *past* and *past part.* of STRING

strung out *adj.* (*slang or colloq.*) **1.** addicted to a drug **2.** debilitated from drug use

strut (strʌt) **1.** *v.i. pres. part.* **strut·ting** *past* and *past part.* **strut·ted** to walk esp. slowly, stiffly and with head erect, with an air of self-importance **2.** *n.* the characteristic walk of cocks, peacocks etc. or of a self-important person [O.E. *strūtian* (meaning obscure)]

strut 1. *n.* a piece or member of wood, metal etc. designed to resist stress **2.** *v.t. pres. part.* **strut·ting** *past* and *past part.* **strut·ted** to support with struts ‖ to fit struts to [etym. doubtful]

stru·thi·ous (strú:θi:əs) *adj.* of or relating to flightless birds, e.g. ostriches [fr. L. *struthio*, ostrich fr. Gk]

Stru·ve (ʃtrú:və), Friedrich Georg Wilhelm von (1793-1864), German-Russian astronomer born in Germany, noted for his discovery and study of double stars. His son Otto Wilhelm (1819-1905) discovered about 500 double stars and a satellite of Uranus. A grandson of Otto Wilhelm, Otto Struve (1897-1963), born in Russia, naturalized American (1927), was an outstanding U.S. astronomer, who discovered the existence of interstellar gas

strych·nine (stríknin, stríkni:n, stríknain) *n.* a highly poisonous crystalline alkaloid, $C_{21}H_{22}N_2O_2$, obtained from nux vomica. It is used in minute doses as a stimulant [F. fr. L. fr. Gk]

Stu·art, Stew·art, Steu·art (stú:ərt, stjú:ərt) a member of the Scottish dynasty which ruled Scotland (1371-1714) and England (1603-49, 1660-1714). Their claim to the English throne derived from the marriage of James IV of Scotland and Margaret Tudor, daughter of Henry VII of England. Their great-grandson ruled Scotland as James VI and England as James I. After the deposition (1688) of James II and the death without surviving issue of his daughters Mary II and Anne, the British throne passed to the house of Hanover. Thereafter the Jacobites upheld without success the claims of James Francis Edward Stuart, Charles Edward Stuart and Henry Stuart

Stuart, Charles Edward (1720-88), known as the 'Young Chevalier', 'Bonnie Prince Charlie' and the 'Young Pretender', son of James Francis Edward Stuart, 'the Old Pretender'. The center of Jacobite hopes for the restoration of the Stuart monarchy in Britain, he led (1745) the rebellion known as 'the 45' in favor of his father's claim to the throne, but was defeated at the Battle of Culloden (1746) by the army of George I

Stuart, Gilbert (1755-1828), American portrait painter, most famous for his portraits of George Washington

Stuart, Henry *DARNLEY

Stuart, Henry Benedict Maria Clement (1725-1807), Cardinal York, younger brother of Charles Edward Stuart, the last Jacobite pretender to the British throne

Stuart, James, 1st earl of Murray *MURRAY

Stuart, James Ewell Brown ('Jeb') (1833-64), Confederate cavalry commander in the American Civil War noted for his daring raids

Stuart, James Francis Edward (1688-1766), known as the 'Old Pretender', son of James II. The Jacobite claimant to the English throne after his father's death (1701), he made several unsuccessful attempts to incite rebellion in Scotland (1708, 1715, 1719, 1745)

Stuart, John *BUTE, 3rd earl of

Stuart, Mary *MARY QUEEN OF SCOTS

stub (stʌb) **1.** *n.* a stump of a tree ‖ the short piece left when a pencil, crayon, candle etc. is almost all used ‖ the butt of a cigarette ‖ the counterfoil of a check, a ticket or receipt etc. **2.** *v.t. pres. part.* **stub·bing** *past* and *past part.* **stubbed** to pull up (a stump) by the roots ‖ to clear (land) of stumps, roots etc. ‖ to strike and hurt (a toe) against a hard obstacle ‖ (with 'up') to dig or pull up (weeds) ‖ (often with 'out') to put out (a cigarette) by crushing the lit end [O.E.]

stub axle the axle of a single wheel, one end being attached by a swivel pin to the framework or chassis, allowing the wheel to be steered

stub·bi·ness (stʌ́bi:nis) *n.* the state or quality of being stubby

stub·ble (stʌ́b'l) *n.* the short stalk of wheat, barley etc. left standing in the field after reaping ‖ a rough, short growth, e.g. of beard **stúb·bly** *adj.* [O.F. *estuble, stuble*]

stub·born (stʌ́bərn) *adj.* (of people) inflexibly declining to change a chosen position, line of behavior, opinion etc., esp. when this attitude is unreasonable ‖ hard to get rid of, not responding to treatment, *a stubborn stain, a stubborn illness* ‖ (of animals) refusing obedience, difficult to handle ‖ (of wood or stone) hard to work ‖ (of problems etc.) hard to work out [etym. doubtful]

Stubbs (stʌbz), George (1724-1806), English painter. He is best known for his paintings of horses

Stubbs, William (1825-1901), British historian and bishop. He is best known for his 'Constitutional History of England' (1874-8) and his learned editions of medieval chronicles

stub·by (stʌ́bi:) *comp.* **stub·bi·er** *superl.* **stub·bi·est** *adj.* short and thick, *stubby fingers*

stuc·co (stʌ́kou) **1.** *n.* fine plaster used for covering interior walls and ceilings and for molding decorative work on them ‖ a mixture of cement, sand and lime applied to outside walls to form a hard covering ‖ work done in stucco **2.** *v.t.* to cover with stucco [Ital.]

stuck *past* and *past part.* of STICK **to be stuck with** to be unable to free oneself of (a bore, an unpleasant job etc.)

stuck-up (stʌ́kʌp) *adj.* (*pop.*) assuming an unwarranted attitude of superiority

stud (stʌd) **1.** *n.* a collection of horses kept for breeding, racing etc. ‖ the place where these horses are kept ‖ any male animal kept for breeding ‖ a studhorse **at** (or **in**) **stud** for breeding **2.** *adj.* of or pertaining to a stud ‖ kept for breeding [O.E. *stōd*]

stud 1. *n.* a short, thick nail or rivet with a large head often made in ornamental shapes and used mainly for decoration ‖ a shirt fastening consisting of a detached button, sometimes ornamental, joined by a short shank to a broader base ‖ a short, thick stump of leather or metal nailed to the bottom of a boot to give a better grip ‖ a crosspiece in a link of chain cable ‖ a post to which the laths of a partition are nailed ‖ a dowel, pin or spindle in a mechanism, e.g. a lathe or watch ‖ the stub of a tree ‖ a stud bolt **2.** *v.t. pres. part.* **stud·ding** *past* and *past part.* **stud·ded** to furnish with studs ‖ to set objects thickly on or as if on, *the piano was studded with ornaments* [O.E. *studu, stuthu*]

stud bolt a threaded bolt furnished with a nut

stud·book (stʌ́dbuk) *n.* an official register of pedigrees of horses and other purebred animals

stud·ding sail (stʌ́diŋseil, *naut.* stʌ́ns'l) (*naut.*) a light sail set at the side of a square sail in fair winds [etym. doubtful]

Stu·de·ba·ker (stú:dəbeikər, stjú:dəbeikər), Clement (1831-1901), U.S. wagon manufacturer. He founded (1868) with his brother John (1833-1917) the Studebaker Brothers Manufacturing Company, one of the world's largest producers of wagons and carriages. In the early 20th c. they began the manufacture of electric and gasoline automobiles

stu·dent (stú:d'nt, stjú:d'nt) *n.* a person who attends a university, college or school for study ‖ anyone making a serious study of a subject [Late M.E. *studiant, studient* fr. O.F. *estudiant*]

Student Nonviolent Coordinating Committee *SNCC

student power the influence of a student body in school administration

Students for a Democratic Society (*abbr.* SDS), a loosely organized U.S. political movement of the extreme left. It was founded (1962) and led campus demonstrations against U.S. policies during the 1960s and early 1970s. Its most militant members, the Weathermen, carried out violent attacks against the U.S. capitalist and police systems

student union 1. student activity group on a college campus **2.** the headquarters of such a group

stud farm a place where horses are bred

stud·horse (stʌ́dhɔrs) *n.* a stallion kept chiefly for breeding

stud·ied (stʌ́di:d) *adj.* thought-out, *a well studied plot* ‖ premeditated, calculated, *studied rudeness*

stu·di·o (stú:di:ou, stjú:di:ou) *pl.* **stu·di·os** *n.* the workroom of an artist, musician, photographer etc. a place from which radio or television programs are transmitted ‖ a building or group of buildings in which movies are made [Ital.]

studio couch an upholstered couch, usually with loose bolsters for the back. It converts into a bed, typically by means of a sliding bed frame stored away under the seat

stu·di·ous (stú:di:əs, stjú:di:əs) *adj.* devoted or given to study ‖ carefully meditated, painstaking, *a studious effort to appear unbiased* [fr. L. *studiosus*]

stud poker (*cards*) a variety of poker in which each player is dealt certain of his cards face up

stud·y (stʌ́di:) *pl.* **stud·ies** *n.* the acquiring of knowledge, esp. from books, *a life devoted to study* ‖ a close and prolonged process of observation, inquiry and thought, *Darwin made a study of certain finches* ‖ the subject thus inquired or thought about ‖ (*pl.*) institutional education, *to stop one's studies* ‖ a preliminary painting or drawing for a work of art or a comparable painting or drawing made as an exercise ‖ (*mus.*) a composition designed to give practice in a technique ‖ a literary work in which some theme or subject is explored, *'Macbeth' is a study of evil* ‖ an actor with respect to his capacity for learning a part, *a slow study* ‖ the learning of a part in a play ‖ something that can be scrutinized as though it were a book or a picture, *his face was a study* ‖ a room set apart for studying in [O.F. *estudie*]

study *pres. part.* **stud·y·ing** *past* and *past part.* **stud·ied** *v.t.* to seek knowledge of by study ‖ to observe very closely ‖ to pay careful attention to, *to study one's answer* ‖ to memorize (a part in a play) ‖ *v.i.* to be a student ‖ to apply the mind in order to get knowledge [O.F. *estudier*]

study hall a period for students to do homework in ‖ a room used for school students to study in

stuff (stʌf) *n.* the material of which something is made ‖ material or things used for some purpose, *the plumber went to collect his stuff* ‖ cloth, esp. woolen cloth ‖ the essence or basic quality of some esp. abstract thing, *the stuff of freedom* ‖ personal belongings, *leave your stuff in the hall* ‖ some thing or things not specified but usually identifiable from the context, *we eat a lot of stuff from our own garden, the publishers have produced a lot of new stuff this year* ‖ worthless ideas, opinions, writings etc. **to do one's stuff** (*pop.*) to do what one can be relied upon to do, esp. when this excites admiration **to know one's stuff** (*pop.*) to have thorough knowledge of a particular field [M.E. *stoffe, stof,* O.F. *estoffe*]

stuff *v.t.* to force (something or things) into a limited space by pressure, *to stuff onions into a jar* ‖ (with 'with') to fill (a limited space) with something or with things, *to stuff a jar with onions* ‖ to fill (a cushion, mattress etc.) with padding ‖ (of a padding) to distend (something) ‖ (*taxidermy*) to fill the skin of (a dead animal, bird, fish etc.) in order to restore its natural shape ‖ (*toymaking*) to give (e.g. a rag doll) a naturalistic shape by distending it fully ‖ to put a bill, circular etc. in (an envelope) for dispatching ‖ to put (a bill, circular etc.) into an envelope for dispatching ‖ (*cookery*) to fill (something to be eaten) with esp. a savory mixture ‖ to gorge (food) ‖ to fill with food, to give too much to eat to ‖ (*refl.*) to eat too much, to gorge ‖ to plug or stop up (e.g. a crack) ‖ (with 'up') to block, stop up (nasal passages) etc. ‖ to cram (something) esp. hastily and surreptitiously, *they stuffed the body under the bed* ‖ (with 'with') to fill or clutter (the mind) ‖ to force or cram (e.g. facts or notions) into the mind ‖ to put fraudulent votes into (a ballot box) ‖ to treat (leather) with oil, tallow etc. to soften and preserve it ‖ *v.i.* to eat too much, gorge oneself [O.F. *estoffer* or etym. doubtful]

stuff and nonsense worthless opinions, ideas, words etc.

stuffed shirt (*pop.*) a person, often pompous and self-satisfied, who is set in his ways and ideas

stuff·i·ly (stʌ́fili:) *adv.* in a stuffy manner

stuff·i·ness (stʌ́fi:nis) *n.* the state or quality of being stuffy

stuff·ing (stʌ́fiŋ) *n.* the material with which something is stuffed ‖ a preparation, esp. savory, used for filling food ‖ the act or process of someone who stuffs ‖ the result of this process **to knock the stuffing out of (someone)** to knock (someone) around until he has no fight left in him, or to shock (someone) into such a condition

stuffing box a container which holds packing firmly against a moving mechanical part, e.g. a piston rod, to prevent leakage of steam etc. along the part

stuffing drum a closed container in which leather is impregnated with softeners (oil, tallow) under heat and pressure

stuff shot (*basketball*) basket throw made from above the basket *also* dunk shot

stuff·y (stʌ́fi:) *comp.* **stuff·i·er** *superl.* **stuff·i·est** *adj.* close and ill-ventilated and usually hot ‖ (of the nasal passages) congested ‖ (*pop.*) prim ‖ (*pop.*) pompous and dull

stul·ti·fi·ca·tion (stʌltifikéiʃən) *n.* a stultifying or being stultified

stul·ti·fy (stʌ́ltifai) *pres. part.* **stul·ti·fy·ing** *past* and *past part.* **stul·ti·fied** *v.t.* to render futile or useless ‖ to cause to be ridiculous ‖ (*law*) to declare (someone) to be of unsound mind and therefore not legally responsible [fr. L.L. *stultificare,* to make foolish]

stum (stʌm) *n.* unfermented grape juice [Du. *stom,* must]

stum·ble (stʌ́mb'l) **1.** *v.i. pres. part.* **stum·bling** *past* and *past part.* **stum·bled** to have a partial fall or to lurch forward as a result of missing one's footing or hitting one's foot against an obstacle, *to stumble downstairs* ‖ (esp. of people) to progress unsteadily or lurchingly, *to stumble along the road* ‖ to hesitate and make a mistake or mistakes in speaking, reading aloud or playing a musical instrument etc. ‖ (*rhet.*) to err (with 'on', 'upon') to find, come upon by accident or chance **2.** *n.* the act of stumbling ‖ a slip (mistake) [M.E. *stomble, stumble*]

stumbling block (*fig.*) an obstacle esp. to the understanding

stump (stʌmp) **1.** *n.* a short piece of the trunk of a felled or fallen tree projecting from the ground ‖ the stalk of esp. a cabbage or related plant when the leaves have been removed ‖ the remaining part of an amputated limb or organ ‖ a rudimentary limb or vestigial organ ‖ a wooden leg ‖ the stub of a pencil or cigarette or check ‖ the part of a broken, ground down or badly decayed tooth remaining in the gum ‖ a heavy, clumsy step ‖ the sound of such a step ‖ (*cricket*) one of the three wooden sticks forming the uprights of a wicket ‖ a place where a political speech is made **to draw stumps** (*cricket*) to pull up the stumps to show play is discontinued or a game over **to go on the stump** to go around the country canvassing for political election **2.** *v.i.* to walk stiffly and heavily ‖ to make speeches in a political cause ‖ *v.t.* to remove stumps from (land) ‖ (*cricket*) to cause (a batsman not in his crease) to be out, by knocking a bail or the bails off, holding the ball in the hand which does this ‖ to tour (a district) in canvassing for political election ‖ (*pop.*) to baffle **to stump up** (*Br.*) to pay up money ‖ (*Br.*) to pay (a sum of money) [late M.E. *stompe*]

stump 1. *n.* (*Br.*) paper, soft leather or india rubber rolled or shaped into a cylinder and used to blur or soften lines drawn in pencil or crayon **2.** *v.t.* to blur, shade, soften or treat (a line, drawing etc.) with a stump [perh. fr. F. *estompe*]

stump·i·ness (stʌ́mpi:nis) *n.* the state or quality of being stumpy

stump·y (stʌ́mpi:) *comp.* **stump·i·er** *superl.* **stump·i·est** *adj.* (of people) stocky, thickset ‖ (of things) short and thick, *a stumpy tail*

stun (stʌn) **1.** *v.t. pres. part.* **stun·ning** *past* and *past part.* **stunned** (of a person) to render unconscious or semiconscious, esp. by a blow on the head, *to stun an ox* ‖ (of a blow) to render unconscious or semiconscious, *the blow stunned the ox* ‖ to cause (someone) to be mentally or emotionally numbed, esp. suddenly **2.** *n.* the act or effect of stunning ‖ the condition of being stunned [fr. O. F. *estoner,* to astonish]

stung *past* and *past part.* of STING

stun gas an antiriot gas that incapacitates by causing disorientation

stun gun antiriot gun that fires sand, bird shot, and similar nondeadly missiles *Cf* BATON GUN

stunk alt. *past* and *past part.* of STINK

stun·ning (stʌ́niŋ) *adj.* (*pop.*) very attractive ‖ that stuns, *a stunning blow* or profoundly shocks, *stunning news* ‖ causing admiring astonishment, *stunning workmanship*

stun·sail, stun·s'l (stʌ́ns'l) *n.* a studding sail

stunt (stʌnt) *v.t.* to check the growth or development of ‖ to check (growth or development) [O.E.=foolish]

stunt 1. *n.* something done to show off skill or daring or ingenuity, for publicity, to attract custom etc. **2.** *v.i.* to do stunts [etym. doubtful]

stunt man a man who doubles professionally for an actor when it is necessary for the part for dangerous feats to be performed

stu·pa (stú:pə) *n.* a domed monumental shrine to the Buddha [Skr. *stūpa*]

stu·pe·fa·cient (stu:piféiʃənt, stju:piféiʃənt) **1.** *adj.* causing profound drowsiness or stupor **2.** *n.* a medicine or narcotic causing either of these conditions [fr. L. *stupefaciens* (*stupefacientis*) fr. *stupefacere,* to make stupid]

stu·pe·fac·tion (stu:pifǽkʃən, stju:pifǽkʃən) *n.* utter astonishment ‖ a state of profound drowsiness or stupor [F. *stupéfaction*]

stu·pe·fy (stú:pifai, stjú:pifai) *pres. part.* **stu·pe·fy·ing** *past* and *past part.* **stu·pe·fied** *v.t.* to put into a state of profound lethargy ‖ to make dull-witted or stupid ‖ to cause utter consternation in [F. *stupéfier*]

stu·pen·dous (stu:péndəs, stju:péndəs) *adj.* amazing, esp. because of size or intensity, *a stupendous effort* [fr. L. *stupendus* gerundive of *stupere,* to be struck senseless, or be amazed at]

stu·pid (stú:pid, stjú:pid) **1.** *adj.* (of persons) lacking intelligence ‖ (of actions) resulting from lack of intelligence ‖ (of persons or animals) foolish in speech or behavior ‖ in a state of stupor **2.** *n.* a stupid person [fr. L. *stupidus*]

stu·pid·i·ty (stu:píditi:, stju:píditi:) *pl.* **stu·pid·i·ties** *n.* the quality or condition of being stupid ‖ a stupid act, remark etc. [fr. L. *stupiditas*]

stu·por (stú:pər, stjú:pər) *n.* a state of drowsiness or profound lethargy caused by drink, drugs etc. ‖ mental apathy often resulting from severe shock **stú·por·ous** *adj.* [L.]

stur·di·ly (stə́:rdili:) *adv.* in a sturdy way

stur·di·ness (stə́:rdi:nis) *n.* the state or quality of being sturdy

stur·dy (stə́:rdi:) **1.** *comp.* **stur·di·er** *superl.* **stur·di·est** *adj.* strongly built ‖ healthy and hardy, *a sturdy plant* ‖ resolute, *a sturdy fighter* **2.** *n.* gid [O.F. *estourdi,* stunned, dazed, reckless, violent]

Stur·geon (stə́:rdʒən), William (1783-1850), British scientist. He constructed the first useful electromagnet (1823), and devised the moving-coil galvanometer (1836)

stur·geon (stə́:rdʒən) *n.* a member of *Acipenser,* fam. *Acipenseridae,* a genus of ganoid fishes widely distributed in fresh and salt waters of the northern temperate regions, and highly valued for their roe, which is made into caviar, and for their flesh, esp. when smoked (*ISINGLASS) [A. F. *sturgeon, esturgeoun*]

Sturluson, Snorri *SNORRI STURLUSON

Sturm und Drang (ʃtúrmuntdráŋ) a late 18th-c. German literary movement in reaction to the Enlightenment, foreshadowing Romanticism. The main representatives were Goethe and Schiller as young men and Herder [G.=storm and stress]

stut·ter (stʌ́tər) **1.** *v.i.* to keep repeating sounds or syllables in an effort to speak, usually as the result of nervous tension ‖ *v.t.* to speak in this way **2.** *n.* an act or instance of stuttering ‖ the affliction of having to stutter [M.E. *stutten*]

Stutt·gart (stútgɑrt, ʃtútgɑrt) the capital (pop. 584,600) of Baden-Württemberg, West Germany: mechanical engineering, precision and optical instruments, automobiles, textiles chemicals, furniture, printing and publishing. University

Stuy·ve·sant (stáivəsənt), Peter (1592-1672), Dutch colonial administrator. As governor general of New Netherland (1647-64), he ruled autocratically but efficiently. He was forced to cede the colony to the English (1664)

sty (stai) **1.** *pl.* **sties** *n.* a pigsty **2.** *v.t. pres. part.* **sty·ing** *past* and *past part.* **stied** to keep in a sty [O.E. *stī*]

sty, stye *pl.* **sties, styes** *n.* a small, inflamed swelling at the base of an eyelash [etym. doubtful]

Styg·i·an (stídʒi:ən) *adj.* of or pertaining to the River Styx ‖ (*rhet.*) utterly black, *Stygian gloom* [fr. L. *Stygius* fr. Gk]

style (stail) **1.** *n.* the distinguishing way in which something is done, said, written, made, executed etc. ‖ the distinctive character of a particular school or type of music, painting, architecture or writing etc., or of the work of a particular person ‖ the way in which literary or musical content is expressed ‖ manner or tone assumed in speech or oratory ‖ sort, *a new style of lampshade* ‖ (*pop.*) preferred type, *not my style of film* ‖ the fashion, pattern and cut of

CONCISE PRONUNCIATION KEY: **(a)** æ, *c*a*t*; ɑ, *c*a*r*; ɔ *f*a*wn*; ei, *sn*a*ke*. **(e)** e, *h*e*n*; i:, *sh*ee*p*; iə, *d*ee*r*; ɛə, *b*ea*r*. **(i)** i, *f*i*sh*; ai, *t*i*ger*; ə:, *b*i*rd*. **(o)** o, *o*x; au, *c*o*w*; ou, *g*oa*t*; u, *p*oo*r*; ɔi, *r*oy*al*. **(u)** ʌ, *d*u*ck*; u, *b*u*ll*; u:, *g*oo*se*; ə, *b*a*cillus*; ju:, *c*u*be*. x, *lo*ch; θ, *th*ink; ð, *bo*th*er*; z, *Z*en; ʒ, *cor*sa*ge*; dʒ, *sa*v*age*; ŋ, *oran*gu*tan*g; j, *y*ak; ʃ, *f*i*sh*; tʃ, *fe*tch; 'l, *rabb*le; 'n, *redd*en. Complete pronunciation key appears inside front cover.

clothing ‖ a person's full title ‖ correct mode of address, *what is the correct style for addressing a dean?* ‖ (without article) a mode of living or way of acting judged elegant or distinguished ‖ (*hist.*) a writing instrument for use on wax tablets ‖ the conventions followed by a printer or publisher in using capital letters, hyphens, certain spellings etc. ‖ (*bot.*) the slender stalklike portion of the pistil connecting the stigma to the ovary ‖ (*zool.*) an abdominal bristlelike process on male insects **2.** *v.t. pres. part.* **styl·ing** *past* and *past part.* **styled** to give (someone) his proper designation ‖ to fashion (e.g. clothes or furniture) according to the current mode ‖ to cause to accord with a customary style [O.F. *style, stile* fr. L.]

sty·let (stáilit) *n.* a surgeon's probe ‖ a stiletto ‖ (*zool.*) a style ‖ a graver [F. fr. Ital.]

styl·ish (stáiliʃ) *adj.* in current fashion, esp. when this is fine or elegant ‖ showing marked elegance in dress, bearing, execution of a movement etc.

styl·ist (stáilist) *n.* a writer who cultivates a fine literary style ‖ an athlete or game player with good style ‖ a person who creates or advises on style in any commercial enterprise **sty·lís·tic, sty·lís·ti·cal** *adjs.* of or relating to style, esp. literary style **sty·lís·ti·cal·ly** *adv.*

stylistics *n.* (*linguistics*) study and art of the selection of language characteristics created by a situation, esp. a literary situation *Cf* FIRTHIAN

sty·lite (stáilait) *n.* one of a class of solitary ascetics who lived on platforms on top of pillars or columns in the 5th c., esp. in Syria

styl·ize (stáilaiz) *v.t. pres. part.* **styl·iz·ing** *past* and *past part.* **styl·ized** to use convention for calculated aesthetic effect in the rendering of (a subject) [fr. STYLE]

sty·lo·bate (stáiləbeit) *n.* (*archit.*) a length of raised, flat-topped stonework supporting a row of columns [fr. L. *stylobata* fr. Gk]

sty·loid (stáilɔid) *adj.* (*anat.*) of any of several long slender processes, esp. of the long, thin projection from the temporal bone of man [fr. Mod. L. *styloides* fr. Gk]

sty·lom·e·try (stailómətri:) *n.* (*stylistics*) study of the development of a work by analysis (usu. with computers) of the number of parts of speech, imagery, thoughts, and similar factors

sty·lus (stáiləs) *pl.* **sty·li** (stáilai), **sty·lus·es** *n.* a pointed instrument for writing on waxed surfaces or for making carbon copies ‖ a needle point, often of sapphire or diamond, for cutting recordings or playing records ‖ (*zool.*) a style ‖ (*bot.*) a style ‖ the gnomon on a sundial ‖ an ancient instrument used for writing on parchment or papyrus ‖ a device for punching dots in preparing Braille [L.]

sty·mie (stáimi:) **1.** *n.* (esp. *golf*) a lie of a player's ball on a green which prevents his opponent from making the shot he wants to make **2.** *v.t. pres. part.* **sty·mie·ing** *past* and *past part.* **sty·mied** to impede (one's opponent) thus ‖ to impede or hinder [etym. doubtful]

Stym·pha·lis (stimféilis) a lake of Arcadia where Hercules killed the iron-beaked birds (*HERACLES)

styp·tic (stíptik) **1.** *adj.* having an astringent effect ‖ tending to check bleeding **2.** *n.* a styptic substance [fr. L.L. *stypticus*]

sty·rax (stáiræks) *n.* a member of *Styrax*, fam. *Styracaceae*, a genus of shrubs and trees found in Java and Thailand, some of which yield benzoin ‖ a balm yielded by some species, storax

sty·rene (stáiri:n) *n.* liquid hydrocarbon $C_6H_5CH{=}CH_2$ obtained esp. from ethylbenzene and serving as the raw material for many plastics [fr. L. *styrax*, styrax]

Styr·i·a (stíri:ə) (*G.* Steiermark) a province (area 6,326 sq. miles, pop. 1,191,400) of S.E. Austria. Capital: Graz

Sty·ron (stáirən), William (1924-), U.S. writer, whose novel 'The Confessions of Nat Turner' (1967) won the Pulitzer Prize (1968). Other novels include 'Lie Down in Darkness' (1951), 'The Long March' (1956), 'Set This House on Fire' (1960) and 'Sophie's Choice' (1979). Some of his essays are collected in 'This Quiet Dust' (1982)

Styx (stiks) (*Gk mythol.*) one of the principal rivers of Hades across which Charon ferried the souls of the dead

su·a·bil·i·ty (su:əbíliti:) *n.* the state or quality of being suable

su·a·ble (sú:əb'l) *adj.* capable of being or liable to be sued in court

Suá·rez (swárez), Francisco de (1548-1617), Spanish Jesuit theologian. His most notable work was in political philosophy and international law, the 'De legibus ac Deo legislatore' (1612). He rejected the doctrine of the divine right of kings in 'Defensio fidei catholicae' (1613), and vested political authority in the sovereign people, this authority being ultimately from God. He placed spiritual authority above temporal authority

sua·sion (swéiʒən) *n.* (*rhet.*) persuasion, *moral suasion* [fr. L. *suasio (suasionis)*]

suave (swɑv) *adj.* bland, smooth and unctuous (when applied to people, suggesting also superficiality or lack of sincerity) **suáv·i·ty** *pl.* **suav·i·ties** *n.* the state or quality of being suave ‖ (*pl.*) delights, pleasures and amenities, *the suavities of civilized living* [F.]

sub (sʌb) **1.** *n.* (*pop.*) an abbreviation for various words beginning 'sub-', e.g. submarine, substitute **2.** *v.i. pres. part.* **sub·bing** *past* and *past part.* **subbed** (*pop.*) to be a substitute for another

sub- (sʌb) *prefix* under (e.g. subterranean) ‖ lower than or inferior to (e.g. sublieutenant) ‖ to a lesser degree than, not completely (e.g. subarctic) a smaller division or less important part (e.g. subarea) ‖ (*chem.*) with less than the normal amount of a specified substance (e.g. subalkaline) ‖ (*chem.*) basic [L. *sub*, under, close to, up to, towards]

sub·ac·id (sʌbæsid) *adj.* slightly acid to the taste ‖ (of remarks) rather sarcastic ‖ (*chem.*) having less than the normal amount of acid [fr. L. *subacidus*]

sub·a·cute (sʌbəkjú:t) *adj.* (*med.*) between acute and chronic

sub·a·gent (sʌbéidʒənt) *n.* an agent's agent

sub·al·pine (sʌbælpain) *adj.* of or relating to the lower slopes of the Alps ‖ of or relating to the higher upland slopes of mountains just below the tree line [fr. L. *subalpinus*]

sub·al·tern (slvbóltə:rn, *Br.* sʌ́bəltən) **1.** *n.* (*Br., mil.*) a commissioned officer below the rank of captain ‖ a person holding a subordinate position ‖ (*logic*) a subaltern proposition **2.** *adj.* subordinate ‖ (*logic*) particular, with reference to a related universal [fr. L.L. *subalternus*]

sub·ant·arc·tic (sʌbæntárktik, sʌbæntártik) *adj.* of, relating to or designating a region near or just north of the Antarctic Circle

sub·a·quat·ic (sʌbəkwǽtik, sʌbəkwɔ́tik) *adj.* (*biol.*) partly aquatic ‖ (*bot.*) of or relating to plants growing under water

sub·a·que·ous (sʌbéikwi:əs) *adj.* existing under the surface of water, esp. of the sea ‖ (*geol.*) formed under the water ‖ (of equipment etc.) made to be used under the water

sub·arc·tic (sʌbárktik, sʌbártik) *adj.* of, relating to or designating a region near or just south of the Arctic Circle

sub·a·tom·ic (sʌbətɔ́mik) *adj.* (*phys.*) of, relating to, or being any of the particles smaller than an atom

sub·ax·il·la·ry (sʌbǽksəleri:) *adj.* (*bot.*) situated beneath an axil

sub·base·ment (sʌ́bbeismənt) *n.* a basement or story, or a series of these, located beneath the true basement of a building

sub-Carpathian Russia *TRANSCARPATHIA

sub·class (sʌ́bklæs, sʌ́bklɑs) *n.* (*taxonomy*) the primary division of a class, esp. that between a class and an order

sub·cla·vi·an (sʌbkléivi:ən) **1.** *adj.* under the clavicle **2.** *n.* the subclavian artery, vein or muscle [fr. Mod. L. *subclavius*]

sub·clin·i·cal (sʌbklínik'l) *adj.* (*med.*) of an illness before it has manifested itself

sub·com·mit·tee (sʌ́bkəmiti:) *n.* a small committee formed from a larger one, appointed usually to consider or deal with some particular aspect of the latter's work

sub·com·pact (sʌ́bcɔ́mpækt) *n.* an automobile smaller than a compact car *Cf* INTERMEDIATE

sub·con·scious (sʌbkɔ́nʃəs) **1.** *adj.* (of memories, emotions etc.) not normally admitted to consciousness, or apparently forgotten **2.** *n.* the sum of such mental activity. The content of the subconscious may emerge into consciousness through dreams, psychotherapy etc.

sub·con·ti·nent (sʌbkɔ́ntinənt) *n.* a very large landmass smaller than those usually called continents, e.g. Greenland ‖ a very large landmass forming part of a continent and having a certain geographical or political independence, e.g. India

sub·con·tract **1.** (sʌbkɔ́ntrækt) *n.* a contract to do a specified part of the work for which someone else has made a prime contract **2.** (sʌ́bkəntrækt) *v.t.* to put out (part of the work for which one has contracted) as a subcontract **sub·con·trác·tor** *n.*

sub·cor·ti·cal (sʌbkɔ́rtik'l) *adj.* situated beneath a cortex, esp. the cerebral cortex ‖ (of insects) living and feeding under the bark of a tree

sub·cos·tal (sʌbkɔ́stəl, sʌbkɒ́stəl) **1.** *adj.* (*anat.*) situated below a rib **2.** *n.* (*anat.*) a subcostal part [fr. Mod. L. *subcostalis*]

sub·cul·ture (sʌ́bkʌltʃər) *n.* a religious, economic or regional etc. group identified by shared patterns of behavior which differ from those of the surrounding culture

sub·cu·ta·ne·ous (sʌbkju:téini:əs) *adj.* used, introduced, situated or occurring beneath the skin ‖ (of parasites) living beneath the skin of the host [L.L. *subcutaneus*]

sub·dea·con (sʌbdí:kən) *n.* (*Roman Catholic and Orthodox Church*) a priest in holy orders, below a deacon ‖ (*Anglican Church*) the epistoler, who may be either a priest or a layman [A.F., O.F. *soudiakene, subdiacne*]

sub·del·e·ga·tion (sʌbdeləgéiʃən) *n.* transference of one's responsibility and authority as a delegate to another person —**subdelegate** *n.* —**subdelegate** *v.*

sub·di·ac·o·nate (sʌbdaiǽkənit) *n.* the office or rank of a subdeacon

sub·di·vide (sʌbdiváid, sʌ́bdivaid) *pres. part.* **sub·di·vid·ing** *past* and *past part.* **sub·di·vid·ed** *v.t.* to divide again (a part resulting from a previous division) ‖ to divide up (a piece of land) into lots for selling ‖ *v.i.* to become subdivided [fr. L.L. *subdividere*]

sub·di·vi·sion (sʌ́bdiviʒən) *n.* one of the parts resulting when something is subdivided ‖ a subdividing or being subdivided ‖ a piece of land resulting from this [fr. L.L. *subdivisio (subdivisionis)*]

sub·dom·i·nant (sʌbdɒ́minənt) *n.* (*mus.*) the fourth degree in a major or minor scale, immediately below the dominant, or fifth

sub·duc·tion (sʌbdʌ́kʃən) *n.* process of moving under a base, e.g., a tectonic plate from the earth's crust —**subduct** *v.*

sub·due (səbdú:, səbdjú:) *pres. part.* **sub·du·ing** *past* and *past part.* **sub·dued** *v.t.* to control, discipline or bring into subjection ‖ to make (sound, color etc.) less intense ‖ to reduce the vivacity of (someone's, one's own, spirits) [late M.E. *sodewe, subdewe*]

sub·ed·it (sʌbédit) *v.t.* to act as subeditor of

sub·ed·i·tor (sʌbéditər) *n.* an assistant editor ‖ (*Br.*) someone who prepares copy for the editor's or publisher's approval

sub·em·ploy·ment (sʌbemplɔ́imənt) *n.* part-time or full-time employment at subsistence level *Cf* UNDEREMPLOYMENT

su·ber·ic acid (su:bérik) a crystalline acid $HOOC(CH_2)_6{\cdot}COOH$ obtained from alkaline hydrolysis of suberin or by oxidation of cork, castor oil etc. with nitric acid

su·ber·in (sú:bərin) *n.* a complex mixture of fatty substances which constitutes the basic part of the cell walls of cork and yields suberic acid among other acid products [F. *subérine*]

su·ber·i·za·tion (su:bərizéiʃən) *n.* (*bot.*) the conversion of the cell walls of plants into corklike tissue, impervious to water, through infiltration with suberin

su·ber·ize (sú:bəraiz) *pres. part.* **su·ber·iz·ing** *past* and *past part.* **su·ber·ized** *v.t.* (*bot.*) to cause the suberization of [fr. L. *suber*, cork, cork oak]

su·ber·ose (sú:bərous) *adj.* being, or having the physical properties of, cork [fr. Mod. L. *suberosus* fr. *suber*, cork]

su·ber·ous (sú:bərəs) *adj.* suberose

sub·fam·i·ly (sʌ́bfæməli:, sʌ́bfæmli:) *pl.* **sub·fam·i·lies** *n.* (*taxonomy*) the category between genus and family

sub·fusc (sʌbfʌ́sk) **1.** *adj.* drab **2.** *n.* (*Br.*, in some universities) dark clothes worn on formal occasions

sub·ge·nus (sʌbdʒí:nəs) *pl.* **sub·gen·er·a** (sʌbdʒénərə) *n.* (*taxonomy*) the category between genus and species

sub·gla·cial (sʌbgléiʃəl) *adj.* of, relating to, or formed in or by the bottom of a glacier

sub·head (sʌ́bhed) *n.* a subheading **súb·head·ing** *n.* the title or heading of part of a chapter, essay etc. ‖ a subordinate heading of a title, e.g. of a newspaper article

sub·hu·man (sʌbhjú:mən) *adj.* less than human, esp. failing to reach standards expected by or of humans || unfit or unsuitable for humans, *subhuman conditions* || (of taxonomic classifications) excluding man

sub·in·dex (sʌbíndeks) *pl.* **sub·in·dex·es, sub·in·di·ces** (sʌbíndisi:z) *n.* (*math.*) an inferior index, written on the right of the symbol

sub·ja·cent (sʌbdʒéisənt) *adj.* underlying, *subjacent causes* || situated lower down, *subjacent levels* [fr. L. *subjacens* (*subjacentis*) fr. *subjacere*]

sub·ject (səbdʒékt) *v.t.* (with 'to') to cause to submit || (with 'to') to cause to undergo, *to subject a person to cross-examination* || (with 'to') to expose or lay open, *to subject someone to ridicule* [O.F. *subjecter, subgetter* or L. *subjectare*]

sub·ject (sʌ́bdʒikt) *adj.* (esp. with 'to') owing allegiance, *subject to the crown* || under external government or rule, *a subject nation* || (with 'to') apt to suffer frequently, prone, *subject to fits* || (with 'to') exposed, *subject to typhoons* || falling under the control or authority of someone || (with 'to') depending, conditional, *subject to approval* [O.F. *suget, subject*]

subject (sʌ́bdʒikt) *n.* a member of a state in relation to his government, or owing allegiance to a sovereign or other ruler, or any member of a state except the sovereign himself || something constituting or chosen as a matter for thought, discussion, action or study etc. || that which is pictured or represented by an artist, sculptor, photographer etc. || the theme, argument or matter of a literary composition || one of the branches of learning taught in a school, college etc. || someone or something experimented on || a body used for anatomical demonstration or dissection || a person suffering from a specified physical or mental complaint, *an asthma subject* || (*gram.*) the noun, or its equivalent, governing a verb (cf. OBJECT) || (*logic*) the term of a proposition about which something is stated || (*philos.*) the thinking mind as opposed to the object thought about || (*philos.*) a substance as distinct from its attributes || (*mus.*) a group of notes forming the basis of esp. a formal composition, e.g. a fugue or sonata, usually prominently stated and repeated or developed [O.F. *suget, soget, subject* fr. L.]

sub·jec·tion (səbdʒékʃən) *n.* a subjecting or being subjected [O.F.]

sub·jec·tive (səbdʒéktiv) *adj.* seen from the point of view of the thinking subject and conditioned by his personal characteristics (opp. OBJECTIVE), *subjective opinion, a subjective poem* || (*gram.*) nominative || (*philos.*) determined by the thinking subject as opposed to universally accepted reality (*OBJECTIVE) **sub·jéc·tiv·ism** *n.* (*philos.*) an idealist system which admits no other reality than that of the thinking subject **sub·jec·tív·i·ty** *n.* [fr. L. L. *subjectivus*]

subject matter the matter, theme or argument of something written, often as opposed to the way in which it is treated or expressed || (*law*) a matter in dispute

sub·join (sʌbdʒɔ́in) *v.t.* to add (something) to the end of something stated or written [fr. obs. F. *subjoindre* fr. L.]

sub·ju·di·ce (sʌbdʒú:disi:, subjú:diki:) (*law*) before the judge or court, i.e. not decided [L.]

sub·ju·gate (sʌ́bdʒugeit) *pres. part.* **sub·ju·gat·ing** *past* and *past part.* **sub·ju·gat·ed** *v.t.* to conquer and hold in subjection [fr. L. *subjugare* (*subjugatus*)]

sub·ju·ga·tion (sʌbdʒugéiʃən) *n.* a subjugating or being subjugated [fr. L.L. *subjugatio* (*subjugationis*)]

sub·junc·tive (səbdʒʌ́ŋktiv) **1.** *adj.* (*gram.*) of or relating to a verbal mood denoting possibility, probability, desire etc. rather than actual fact (cf. INDICATIVE, cf. IMPERATIVE) **2.** *n.* a verb in this mood || the subjunctive mood [fr. L.L. *subjunctivus*]

sub·kil·o·ton weapon (sʌbkílətʌn) (*mil.*) less than 1 kiloton, having the effect of less than 1,000 tons of TNT, e.g., of a nuclear weapon *Cf* KILOTON WEAPON

sub·lan·guage (sʌ́blæŋgwidʒ) *n.* (*linguistics*) the language of a subculture (e.g., dialect) or special group (e.g., jargon) within a culture

sub·lease 1. (sʌ́bli:s) *n.* the lease granted by a tenant to a subtenant of part or all of a property **2.** (sʌbli:s) *v.t. pres. part.* **sub·leas·ing** *past* and *past part.* **sub·leased** to grant a sublease on || to receive or hold a sublease on

sub·let 1. (sʌblét) *v.t. pres. part.* **sub·let·ting** *past* and *past part.* **sub·let** to rent out part or all of (a property rented or leased from the owner) **2.** (sʌ́blet, sʌblét) *n.* a property obtained by or available for subletting

sub·lieu·ten·ant (sʌblu:ténənt, *Br.* sʌbleftónənt) *n.* (*Br.*) a Royal Navy officer ranking immediately below a lieutenant

sub·li·mate (sʌ́bləmeit) **1.** *v.t. pres. part.* **sub·li·mat·ing** *past* and *past part.* **sub·li·mat·ed** to purify (a solid) by heating it under such a pressure that it sublimes and then cooling the vapor until it passes directly into the solid state || (*psychol.*) to redirect (a primitive impulse) towards a higher aim more compatible with civilized man's tastes and aspirations || *v.i.* to become sublimated **2.** *n.* a substance obtained by sublimating [fr. L. *sublimare* (*sublimatus*)]

sub·li·ma·tion (sʌbləméiʃən) *n.* a sublimating or being sublimated || the process of sublimating || a product of sublimating [F. or fr. L.L. *sublimatio* (*sublimationis*)]

Sublimaze *FENTANYL

sub·lime (səbláim) **1.** *adj.* arousing the sensation of awe, esp. by reason of perfection, nobility etc. || lofty, exalted || outstanding with respect to spiritual, moral or intellectual qualities || (*anat.*, of muscles) lying near the surface **2.** *n.* **the sublime** that which is sublime, sublime quality [fr. L. *sublimis*]

sublime *pres. part.* **sub·lim·ing** *past* and *past part.* **sub·limed** *v.i.* to pass directly from the solid to the vapor state, usually by the action of heat || *v.t.* to cause to undergo this process, sometimes in both directions, e.g. in the purification of certain chemicals such as iodine, naphthalene etc. [O.F. *sublimer*, to make sublime]

sub·lim·i·nal (sʌblímin'l) *adj.* not rising above the threshold of consciousness (cf. SUPRALIMINAL) || (esp. of advertising) designed to act on the mind at a subconscious level [SUB-+L. *limen* (*liminis*), threshold]

sub·lim·i·ty (səblímiti:) *n.* the state or quality of being sublime [fr. L. *sublimitas*]

sub·lu·nar (sʌblú:nər) *adj.* sublunary

sub·lu·na·ry (sʌblú:nəri:) *adj.* (*astron.*) situated or existing beneath the moon [fr. Mod. L. *sublunaris*]

sub·lux·a·tion (sʌbləkséiʃən) *n.* an incomplete or partial dislocation (as of two vertebrae squarely situated atop one another) —**sublux** *v.* —**subluxed** *adj.*

sub·ma·chine gun (sʌbməʃí:n) a light machine gun designed to be fired from the shoulder or waist

sub·mar·gin·al (sʌbmárdʒin'l) *adj.* below the minimum necessary for e.g. economic exploitation or for living a normal life, *a submarginal salary* || (*biol.*) placed nearly at the margin

sub·ma·rine (sʌ́bməri:n, sʌbmərí:n) **1.** *adj.* existing, operating etc. under water, esp. the sea **2.** *n.* a vessel, esp. a warship, designed to operate submerged || (*surfing*) board too small for proper use

submarine launched ballistic missile (*mil.*) missile capable of being launched underwater, e.g., Polaris, Poseidon, Trident *abbr.* **SLBM**

submarine rocket (*mil.*) submarine-launched, surface-to-surface rocket (UUM-44A), primarily antisubmarine, with nuclear depth charge or homing torpedo payload, and a 50-mi range *acronym* subroc

sub·max·il·la (sʌbmæksílə) *pl.* **sub·max·il·lae** (sʌbmæksíli:) **sub·max·il·las** *n.* the lower jaw or jawbone, esp. the mandible of man **sub·max·il·lar·y** (sʌbmǽksəleri:, *Br.* esp. sʌbmæksíləri) *adj.* [Mod. L.]

submaxillary gland either of the two salivary glands located on each side of the lower jaw

sub·me·di·ant (sʌbmí:di:ənt) *n.* (*mus.*) the sixth degree of the major or minor scale halfway between the subdominant and upper tonic

sub·merge (səbmə́:rdʒ) *pres. part.* **sub·merg·ing** *past* and *past part.* **sub·merged** *v.t.* to place beneath or as if beneath the surface of a liquid, *the river submerged large tracts of land, submerged in debt* || *v.i.* to plunge beneath the surface of the water etc. || to become as though covered by water **sub·mér·gence** *n.* [fr. L. *submergere*]

sub·merse (səbmə́:rs) *pres. part.* **sub·mers·ing** *past* and *past part.* **sub·mersed** *v.t.* to submerge **sub·mérsed** *adj.* (*bot.*) growing entirely under water **sub·mers·i·ble** (səbmə́:rsəb'l) *adj.* capable of being submerged and of operating under water [fr. L. *submergere* (*submersus*)]

sub·mer·sion (səbmə́:rʒən, səbmə́:rʃən) *n.* a submerging or being submerged [fr. L. *submersio* (*submersionis*)]

sub·mi·cro·scop·ic (sʌbmaikrəskɒ́pik) *adj.* of things too small to be seen through an ordinary, light microscope

sub·mil·li·me·ter (sʌbmíləmi:tər) *adj.* of less than one mm in size

sub·min·i·a·ture (sʌbmíni:ətʃə:r) *adj.* smaller than miniature, e.g., microcircuits on small silicon chips *also* microminiature

sub·mis·sion (səbmíʃən) *n.* the act of submitting || the state of being willing to submit || something offered for consideration || (*law*) an agreement in which parties undertake to abide by a decision or obey an authority || (*law*) the act of referring a matter to arbitration [fr. O.F. or fr. L. *submissio* (*submissionis*)]

sub·mis·sive (səbmísiv) *adj.* willing to submit, humbly obedient [fr. L. *submittere* (*submissus*), to submit]

sub·mit (səbmít) *pres. part.* **sub·mit·ting** *past* and *past part.* **sub·mit·ted** *v.t.* to cause to undergo || to offer (oneself) of one's free will, *to submit oneself to an ordeal* || to offer for consideration, examination, a decision etc., *to submit a case for judgment* || to offer as an opinion, *I submit that there is another point of view* || *v.i.* to cease to offer resistance || to defer to another's wishes, opinions etc. [fr. L. *submittere*]

sub·mul·ti·ple (sʌbmʌ́ltəp'l) *n.* a number or quantity exactly dividing another number or quantity [fr. L.L. *submultiplus*]

sub·nor·mal (sʌbnɔ́rməl) **1.** *adj.* below, lower than, less than or smaller than normal || having less than normal intelligence **2.** *n.* a person of subnormal intelligence **sub·nor·mál·i·ty** *n.*

sub·nu·clear (sʌbnú:kli:ə:r) *adj.* of particles of the nucleus of the atom

sub·nu·cle·on (sʌbnú:kli:ɒn) *n.* hypothetical portion of a nuclear particle

sub·or·der (sʌ́bɔrdər) *n.* (*taxonomy*) the category between an order and a family

sub·or·di·nate 1. (səbɔ́rd'nit) *adj.* inferior in order, rank, importance etc., *a subordinate officer* || (with 'to') subject, subsidiary or subservient, *subordinate to one's superiors* **2.** (səbɔ́rd'nit) *n.* a person working under someone else or inferior in the official hierarchy **3.** (səbɔ́rd'neit) *v.t. pres. part.* **sub·or·di·nat·ing** *past* and *past part.* **sub·or·di·nat·ed** to treat or consider as of secondary importance, *you must subordinate your private interests* || (with 'to') to make subject or subservient, to *subordinate personal profit to the good of the community* [fr. M.L. *subordinare* (*subordinatus*)]

subordinate clause (*gram.*) a clause dependent upon another clause and not itself a formal sentence (cf. MAIN CLAUSE)

subordinate conjunction (*gram.*) a conjunction used to introduce a subordinate clause

sub·or·di·na·tion (səbɔrd'néiʃən) *n.* a subordinating or being subordinated [fr. L.L. *subordinatio* (*subordinationis*)]

sub·or·di·na·tive (səbɔ́rd'neitiv) *adj.* (*gram.*) containing or introducing a subordinate clause || involving subordination

sub·orn (səbɔ́rn) *v.t.* to incite (a person), usually by bribery, to commit perjury or other unlawful acts || to obtain (e.g. evidence) by bribery or other corrupt means [fr. L. *subornare*]

sub·or·na·tion (sʌbɔrnéiʃən) *n.* the act of suborning, esp. the crime of inciting someone to commit perjury || the testimony thus procured [fr. L. *subordinatio* (*subordinationis*)]

Su·bo·ti·ca (su:bɔ́titsə) a market town (pop. 75,000) in Vojvodina, Yugoslavia, near the Hungarian frontier: metallurgy, food processing

sub·phy·lum (sʌbfáiləm) *pl.* **sub·phy·la** (sʌbfáilə) *n.* (*taxonomy*) the main division of a phylum

sub·plot (sʌ́bplɒt) *n.* a secondary plot in a play, novel, film etc.

sub·poe·na (səpí:nə) **1.** *n.* (*law*) a written order commanding a person to appear in a court of justice under penalty **2.** *v.t. pres. part.* **sub·poe·na·ing** *past* and *past part.* **sub·poe·naed** (*law*) to serve with such an order [L.=under a penalty]

sub·pro·fes·sion·al (sʌbproufέʃənəl) *n.* paraprofessional

sub·re·gion (sʌbrí:dʒən) *n.* one of the principal divisions of a region, e.g. for administration or with regard to distribution of animals or plants **sub·ré·gion·al** *adj.*

sub·rep·tion (səbrépʃən) *n.* (*eccles. law*) the obtaining of a dispensation by concealing the

truth **sub·rep·ti·tious** (sʌbreptíʃəs) *adj.* [fr. L. *subreptio (subreptionis)*]
subroc (*mil. acronym*) for submarine rocket
sub·ro·ga·tion (sʌbrəgéiʃən) *n.* (*law*) the substitution of one party for another as creditor so that the new creditor succeeds to the first creditor's rights in law and equity [fr. L. *subrogatio (subrogationis)*]
sub·sat·el·lite (sʌbsǽtəlait) *n.* a satellite launched by an orbiting satellite
sub·scribe (səbskráib) *pres. part.* **sub·scrib·ing** *past* and *past part.* **sub·scribed** *v.t.* to contribute or agree to contribute, *to subscribe large sums to charity* ‖ to write (one's name) at the foot of a document ‖ to add one's signature to (a document, letter to the press etc.), esp. to do this so as to show agreement or solidarity ‖ (of a bookseller or publisher) to take prepublication orders for (new books etc.) ‖ *v.i.* to make a subscription ‖ to promise a subscription **to subscribe to** to take in regularly (a periodical, newspaper etc.) ‖ to express agreement with ‖ to sign one's name, esp. to an official document [fr. L. *subscribere,* to write underneath]
sub·script (sʌ́bskript) **1.** *adj.* of, relating to, or being a character printed or written directly below another character, e.g. the cedilla under the letter 'c' in 'Besançon', or below and to the side of it, e.g. the '2' in H_2O (cf. SUPERSCRIPT) **2.** *n.* a subscript sign, letter etc., e.g. a mathematical subindex [fr. L. *subscribere (subscriptus),* to write underneath]
sub·scrip·tion (səbskrípʃən) *n.* the act of subscribing ‖ a sum subscribed ‖ the amount raised through subscribed sums ‖ matter subscribed at the end of a document ‖ a signifying of assent or the assent itself, *subscription to the doctrine of infallibility* ‖ a method of selling a new publication by giving a price concession to those who order before publication ‖ (*Br.*) membership fees paid at regular intervals to a club, society etc. ‖ the prepayment made to secure future issues of e.g. a periodical [fr. L. *subscriptio (subscriptionis)*]
sub·sec·tion (sʌ́bsekʃən) *n.* a subdivision of a section ‖ a subordinate part
sub·se·quence (sʌ́bsikwəns) *n.* the act or state of being subsequent ‖ that which is subsequent
sub·se·quent (sʌ́bsikwənt) *adj.* following (in time or order), later **subsequent to** following [F. *subséquent* or fr. L. *subsequens (subsequentis)*]
sub·serve (səbsə́:rv) *pres. part.* **sub·serv·ing** *past* and *past part.* **sub·served** *v.t.* to serve as a means of promoting, *to subserve one's ends* [fr. L. *subservire*]
sub·ser·vi·ence (səbsə́:rvi:əns) *n.* the state or quality of being subservient ‖ subservient behavior
sub·ser·vi·en·cy (səbsə́:rvi:ənsi:) *pl.* **sub·ser·vi·en·cies** *n.* subservience
sub·ser·vi·ent (səbsə́:rvi:ənt) *adj.* servile, obsequious ‖ useful as a means or instrument [fr. L. *subserviens (subservientis)* fr. *subservire,* to serve below]
sub·shell (sʌ́bʃel) *n.* (*nuclear phys.*) a segment of an electron's orbit
sub·side (səbsáid) *pres. part.* **sub·sid·ing** *past* and *past part.* **sub·sid·ed** *v.i.* (of ground, a building etc.) to sink in level or settle down into a lower position ‖ (of water) to return to a normal level, *the flood soon subsided* ‖ (of the sea) to fall into a calmer state ‖ (of a storm, excitement, fever etc.) to abate ‖ to sink down exhaustedly, *to subside into a chair* [fr. L. *subsidere*]
sub·sid·ence (səbsáid'ns, sʌ́bsidəns) *n.* the act or process of subsiding [fr. L. *subsidentia*]
sub·sid·i·ar·y (səbsídi:eri:) **1.** *adj.* auxiliary, supplementary, *to serve in a subsidiary capacity* ‖ (of a company) controlled by another company which owns a majority of its shares ‖ pertaining to or of the nature of a subsidy, *a subsidiary payment* **2.** *pl.* **sub·sid·i·ar·ies** *n.* an assistant ‖ a subsidiary company [fr. L. *subsidiarius*]
sub·si·dize (sʌ́bsidaiz) *pres. part.* **sub·si·diz·ing** *past* and *past part.* **sub·si·dized** *v.t.* to pay a subsidy to ‖ to aid with public money
sub·si·dy (sʌ́bsidi:) *pl.* **sub·si·dies** *n.* a nonreturnable grant of money to an individual, group or subsection of the economy, by the state or by a public or private body, to secure some beneficial result, e.g. to help out of financial difficulty, to lower prices, to encourage development etc. ‖ (*Br. hist.*) money granted to the sovereign by parliament to meet special needs [A.F. *subsidie*]
sub·sist (səbsíst) *v.i.* to keep oneself alive esp. on means that provide only the barest necessities, *to subsist on a pension* ‖ to exist or continue to exist, *specimens still subsist in the forests of Peru* ‖ (*philos.*) to be logically true and sound [fr. L. *subsistere,* to stand still, stand firm, cease]
sub·sist·ence (səbsístəns) *n.* a means of providing oneself with the necessities of life, esp. the bare necessities ‖ (*philos.*) real existence ‖ (*philos.*) the quality of being logically true and sound [fr. L.L. *subsistentia*]
subsistence agriculture farming that produces all or almost all the necessities for a farm family, e.g., in low-income countries *also* subsistence farming
subsistence economy an economy not based on money and in which there is little or no buying and selling, though there may be bartering
subsistence farming a primitive system of farming, in which each farm provides only for the needs of the individual farm family and makes no surplus to sell
sub·soil (sʌ́bsɔil) *n.* the layer of material immediately beneath the soil, in process of being broken up through the agency of water, plant roots, worms etc., but as yet not enriched by humus or by the products of soil bacteria (cf. TOPSOIL)
sub·son·ic (sʌbsɔ́nik) *adj.* pertaining to speeds less than that of sound (opp. SUPERSONIC)
sub·spe·cies (sʌ́bspi:ʃi:z) *pl.* **sub·spe·cies** *n.* (*taxonomy*) the category below a species [Mod. L.]
sub·stance (sʌ́bstəns) *n.* the matter, stuff, material of which a thing is made ‖ the main content, *the substance of an argument* ‖ (*philos.*) the essential, underlying reality of something, in which accidents, qualities, attributes and phenomena inhere ‖ solidity, correspondence with reality, *there is no substance in his beliefs* ‖ (*rhet.*) wealth, *a man of substance* ‖ the quality in cloth etc. that makes for durability **in substance** essentially, details apart [O.F. fr. L.]
sub·stand·ard (sʌbstǽndərd) *adj.* falling short of a legally required or generally accepted standard
sub·stan·tial (səbstǽnʃəl) *adj.* having real existence, not imaginary ‖ firmly based, *a substantial argument* ‖ relatively great in size, value or importance, *a substantial income, substantial agreement* ‖ (of meals) large and filling ‖ (of food or drink) very nutritive ‖ strong, made to last, *substantial toys* ‖ well-off, financially sound ‖ (*philos.*) of the nature of substance [fr. L.L. *substantialis*]
sub·stan·tial·ism (səbstǽnʃəlizəm) *n.* (*philos.*) the doctrine that there are substantial realities underlying phenomena
sub·stan·ti·al·i·ty (səbstænʃi:ǽliti:) *n.* the quality or state of being substantial ‖ solidity ‖ genuineness [fr. L.L. *substantialitas*]
sub·stan·tial·ly (səbstǽnʃəli:) *adv.* in a substantial manner ‖ essentially, to a large degree
sub·stan·ti·ate (səbstǽnʃi:eit) *pres. part.* **sub·stan·ti·at·ing** *past* and *past part.* **sub·stan·ti·at·ed** *v.t.* to establish, prove or make good (a statement, claim, charge etc.) **sub·stan·ti·á·tion** *n.* [fr. Mod. L. *substantiare (substantiatus)* fr. *substantia,* substance]
sub·stan·ti·val (sʌbstəntáivəl) *adj.* (*gram.*) of, relating to or having the nature of a substantive **sub·stan·tí·val·ly** *adv.*
sub·stan·tive (sʌ́bstəntiv) **1.** *adj.* (*gram.*) expressing existence, *the substantive verb* (i.e. 'to be') ‖ (*gram.*) of or used as a substantive ‖ having a separate and independent existence, not inferred, derived etc. ‖ (of dyes) not requiring a mordant ‖ (*mil.,* of a person) appointed definitely to a specified rank ‖ (*mil.,* of a rank) definite (as distinct from 'acting', 'temporary' etc.) ‖ (*law*) of or pertaining to the rules of right administered by a court, as distinguished from the forms of procedure **2.** *n.* (*gram.*) a noun or group of words used as the grammatical equivalent of a noun [O.F. *substantif* fr. L.L.]
sub·state (sʌ́bsteit) *n.* a region within a state but less than a state, established for administration, e.g., West Berlin
sub·sta·tion (sʌ́bsteiʃən) *n.* a subsidiary or branch station
sub·sti·tute (sʌ́bstitu:t, sʌ́bstitju:t) **1.** *n.* a person or thing taking the place of another person or thing **2.** *v. pres. part.* **sub·sti·tut·ing** *past* and *past part.* **sub·sti·tut·ed** *v.t.* to put in the place of another person or thing, *to substitute nylon for cotton* ‖ *v.i.* to take the place of another person or thing, *he is substituting for his brother* **sub·sti·tú·tion·al, súb·sti·tu·tive,** *adjs.* [fr. L. *substituere (substitutus),* to set up]
sub·strate (sʌ́bstreit) *n.* a substratum ‖ (*biochem.*) a substance acted upon, e.g. by an enzyme [fr. Mod. L. *substratum*]
sub·strat·o·sphere (sʌbstrǽtəsfiər) *n.* the part of the atmosphere just below the stratosphere
sub·stra·tum (sʌbstréitəm, sʌbstrǽtəm, sʌbstrɑ́təm) *pl.* **sub·stra·ta** (sʌbstréitə, sʌbstrǽtə, sʌbstrɑ́tə), **sub·stra·tums** *n.* a layer underneath, esp. constituting a supporting layer for that which is above it, e.g. the subsoil under surface soil, or an element of truth in a rumor which deforms the truth [Mod. L. fr. *substernere,* to spread underneath]
sub·struc·ture (sʌ́bstrʌktʃər) *n.* the part of a building which serves as the foundation ‖ the earth track prepared to support the ties and rails of a railroad
sub·sume (səbsú:m) *pres. part.* **sub·sum·ing** *past* and *past part.* **sub·sumed** *v.t.* (*logic*) to include under a category or principle ‖ to include in a larger schema, class etc. [fr. Mod. L. *subsumere*]
sub·sump·tion (səbsʌ́mpʃən) *n.* a subsuming or being subsumed ‖ something subsumed [fr. Mod. L. *subsumptio (subsumptionis)* fr. *subsumere,* to subsume]
sub·tem·per·ate (sʌbtémpərit) *adj.* of or pertaining to the colder regions of the temperate zones
sub·ten·an·cy (sʌbténənsi:) *n.* the holding of a property as subtenant
sub·ten·ant (sʌbténənt) *n.* a person who rents a house, flat etc. from a tenant
sub·tend (səbténd) *v.t.* (*geom.*) to lie opposite to, *the arc of a circle subtends an angle at the center* ‖ (*bot.*) to surround so as to enclose [fr. L. *subtendere* fr. *sub,* under+*tendere,* to stretch]
sub·ter·fuge (sʌ́btərfju:dʒ) *n.* the use of stratagems as a means of avoiding or evading ‖ a deceptive stratagem enabling one to get out of a situation etc. [fr. L. *subterfugium* fr. *subterfugere,* to flee secretly]
sub·ter·ra·ne·an (sʌbtəréini:ən) *adj.* situated, existing, operating or functioning underground [fr. L. *subterraneus*]
sub·ther·a·peu·tic (sʌbθɛərəpjú:tik) *adj.* of a preventive drug dosage esp. in the feed of chickens and other animals
sub·til·i·sin (sʌbtíləsən) (*biochem.*) an enzyme involved in breaking down proteins produced by a soil bacillus
sub·til·i·za·tion (sʌt'lizéiʃən) *n.* a subtilizing or being subtilized [fr. M.L. *subtilizatio (subtilizationis)*]
sub·til·ize (sʌt'laiz) *pres. part.* **sub·til·iz·ing** *past* and *past part.* **sub·til·ized** *v.t.* to make subtle ‖ *v.i.* to use subtlety [fr. M.L. *subtilizare* fr. *subtilis,* subtle]
sub·ti·tle (sʌ́btait'l) **1.** *n.* a subsidiary title to a book ‖ (*esp. pl.*) words projected on the screen to explain the action in a silent movie or translate the dialogue of a foreign movie **2.** *v.t. pres. part.* **sub·ti·tling** *past* and *past part.* **sub·ti·tled** to give a subtitle or subtitles to
sub·tle (sʌ́t'l) *adj.* hard to grasp, difficult to define or distinguish, elusive, *a subtle distinction* ‖ making fine distinctions, acute, *a subtle mind* ‖ ingenious, cunning, clever, *a subtle argument* ‖ working insidiously, secretly or imperceptibly, *a subtle technique of extracting money* [O.F. *soutil, sotil, sutil*]
sub·tle·ty (sʌt'lti:) *pl.* **sub·tle·ties** *n.* the quality or state of being subtle, esp. the making of fine distinctions ‖ a subtle distinction [O.F. *sutilte, soutilte*]
sub·tly (sʌ́t'li:) *adv.* in a subtle manner
sub·ton·ic (sʌbtɔ́nik) *n.* (*mus.*) the seventh degree of a major or minor scale
sub·to·pi·a (sʌbtóupi:ə) (*Br., ironic*) a paradise consisting of endless suburbia ‖ an expanse of suburbs, esp. small houses, over the countryside [SUB+UTOPIA]
sub·tract (səbtrǽkt) *v.t.* (esp. with 'from') to take away (a number or quantity) from another number or quantity ‖ *v.i.* (with 'from') to cause an unwelcome lessening, *does it subtract from your enjoyment?* ‖ (*math.*) to do subtraction or a subtraction [fr. L. *subtrahere (subtractus)*]
sub·trac·tion (səbtrǽkʃən) *n.* (*math.*) the act or process of subtracting [fr. L.L. *subtractio (subtractionis)*]
sub·trac·tive (səbtrǽktiv) *adj.* involving sub-

traction || that is to be subtracted || tending to subtract [fr. M.L. *subtractivus*]
sub·tra·hend (sʌ́btrəhend) *n.* (*math.*) the number to be subtracted (from the minuend) [fr. L. *subtrahendus*]
sub·trop·ic (sʌbtrɔ́pik) *adj.* subtropical
sub·trop·i·cal (sʌbtrɔ́pik'l) *adj.* almost tropical || of or pertaining to regions near the Tropics || (of a plant) needing a subtropical climate
subtropical climate a warm climate which, unlike the tropical climate, has distinct seasons. Two types are distinguished: dry subtropical (or Mediterranean climate), characterized by long dry summers and usually found on the west side of continents, and wet subtropical, with higher rainfall and wet summers, found on the east of continents
sub·trop·ics (sʌbtrɔ́piks) *pl. n.* subtropical regions
su·bu·late (sú:bjulit) *adj.* (*biol.*, esp. of leaves) narrow and tapering from the base to a fine point [fr. Mod. L. *subulatus* fr. *subula*, awl]
sub·urb (sʌ́bə:rb) *n.* one of the residential or industrial districts on the edge of a big town or city **sub·úr·ban** *adj.* pertaining to the suburbs || having the qualities considered characteristic of the suburbs || having the qualities considered characteristic of the people who live in the suburbs, e.g. dreariness, narrowness of outlook, conformity etc. [O.F. *suburbe*]
sub·ur·ban·i·za·tion (sʌbə:rbənəzéiʃən) *n.* creation of suburbs —**suburbanize** *v.*
sub·ur·bi·a (səbə́:rbi:ə) *n.* the suburbs of a city and their inhabitants
sub·ven·tion (səbvénʃən) *n.* a grant of money from a government, charitable foundation etc. to further some undertaking [O.F. *subvencion, subvention*]
sub·ver·sion (səbvə́:rʒən, səbvə́:rʃən) *n.* a subverting or being subverted [O.F. fr. L.L. *subversio* (*subversionis*)]
sub·ver·sive (səbvə́:rsiv) **1.** *adj* tending to subvert **2.** *n.* a subversive person [fr. L. *subvertere* (*subversus*), to subvert]
sub·vert (səbvə́:rt) *v.t.* to cause the downfall or ruin of (e.g. the government of a country) || to corrupt (a person) by undermining his faith or morals etc. [O.F. *subvertir*]
sub·vi·ral (sʌbváir'l) *adj.* of a part of a virus
sub·way (sʌ́bwei) *n.* an underground passage or tunnel for pedestrians, esp. under a street or railroad || an underground conduit for gas mains, water supply, telephone wires etc. || (*Am.*=*Br.* underground) a city railroad system running entirely or mainly in tunnels under the ground
suc·ceed (səksí:d) *v.i.* to be successful, to have success, to attain a desired end || to be the successor, *to succeed to a throne* || to ensue, to follow (in order or time), a *long peace succeeded* || *v.t.* to take the place previously occupied by, be the successor to, *he succeeded his father as head of the firm* || to come after, to follow in order or time, *night succeeds day* **to succeed to** to inherit [O.F. *succeder* or fr. L. *succedere*]
suc·cess (səksés) *n.* the accomplishment of what is desired or aimed at, achievement, *military success, academic success* || attainment of wealth, fame, prosperity etc. || a person who or thing which succeeds **suc·céss·ful** *adj.* [fr. L. *succedere* (*successus*)]
suc·ces·sion (səkséʃən) *n.* a following in order, *shots in rapid succession* || a series of things in order, *a succession of disasters* || the act or right of following one's predecessor in a post, position or title || the order in which persons succeed each other (to thrones, titles etc.) || a geological, ecological or seasonal sequence of species || the process of development of plant communities **in succession** one after another **in succession to** as successor of **suc·cés·sion·al** *adj.* [fr. L. *successio* (*successionis*)]
suc·ces·sive (səksésiv) *adj.* following one immediately after another, consecutive, *six successive victories* [fr. M.L. *successivus*]
suc·ces·sor (səksésər) *n.* a person or thing that succeeds another [O.F. *successour* fr. L.]
suc·cinct (səksíŋkt) *adj.* clearly expressed in few words [fr. L. *succingere* (*succinctus*), to gird up]
suc·cin·ic acid (səksínik) white, crystalline acid ($(CH_2COOH)_2$) used in the preparation of dyes, lacquers etc. [fr. F. *succinique*]
suc·cor, *Br.* **suc·cour** (sʌ́kər) **1.** *v.t.* (*rhet.*) to relieve the difficulty or distress of, *to succor the homeless* **2.** *n.* (*rhet.*) help given in time of need [O.F. *socorre, sucurre, succurre, secourre*]
suc·cor·ance (sʌ́kərəns) *n.* the need for sustaining care —**succorant** *adj.*
suc·co·tash (sʌ́kətæf) *n.* a side dish consisting of lima beans and corn kernels cooked together [Narragansett *msiquatash*, fragments]
suc·cu·bus (sʌ́kjubəs) *pl.* **suc·cu·bi** (sʌ́kjubai) *n.* a demon in female form supposed to have sexual intercourse with men in their sleep (cf. INCUBUS) [M.L.]
suc·cu·lence (sʌ́kjuləns) *n.* the state or quality of being succulent
suc·cu·len·cy (sʌ́kjulənsi:) *n.* succulence
suc·cu·lent (sʌ́kjulənt) **1.** *adj.* juicy || (*bot.*) having tissues full of juice or sap **2.** *n.* a plant with fleshy leaves or fleshy stems or both [fr. L. *succulentus*]
suc·cumb (səkʌ́m) *v.i.* (with 'to') to yield to superior strength, *to succumb to a temptation* || to cease to offer resistance || (*rhet.*) to die [O.F. *succomber*]
suc·cur·sal (səkə́:rs'l) **1.** *adj.* (esp. *eccles.*) subsidiary, auxiliary, *succursal chapels* **2.** *n.* a succursal institution [fr. F. *succursale*]
suc·cus·sion (səkʌ́ʃən) *n.* the action or condition of shaking violently || (*med.*) a method of diagnosing if fluid is present in a body cavity, esp. the thorax, by shaking the body [fr. L. *succussio* (*succussionis*)]
such (sʌtʃ) **1.** *adj.* of a kind previously or about to be mentioned or implied, *such people are dangerous, such action as may be necessary* || so great, I *cannot afford such a price* || of the same quality as something just mentioned (used to avoid the repetition of one word twice in a sentence), *never accept a thing as factual unless you can prove it such* || of a degree or quantity stated or implicit, *such luxury is unfamiliar to me* || similar, comparable, *is there such a book in English?* || poor, inconspicuous, slight of its kind, *the crowd, such as it was, soon dispersed* **2.** *pron.* (with 'as') those people who, *such as heard the news came* || the same as something just mentioned (used to avoid repetition of one word twice in a sentence), *never call a man a thief till you can prove him such* || that part of something just stated or about to be stated, *the turkey, such of it as remained, fed the unexpected visitors* || this thing, these circumstances etc., *if such is the case we will go* || this or that kind of person or thing, *such is my considered opinion* **3.** *adv.* this or that degree of, *such bad spelling is intolerable* [O.E. *swelc, swilc, swylc*]
such and such (with 'a' or 'an') not specifically designated, *they went to such and such a place*
such·like (sʌ́tʃlaik) **1.** *adj.* of a similar kind, *he plays tennis and squash and such-like games* **2.** *pron.* persons or things of a similar kind
Su·chow (sú:dʒóu) (or Tungshan) a communications center (pop. 700,000) in N.W. Kiangsu, China, on the Grand Canal: textiles (esp. silk)
Suchow *KIUCHAN
suck (sʌk) **1.** *v.t.* to draw (liquid) into the mouth by producing a partial vacuum as a result of contracting the muscles of the lips, tongue and cheeks || to draw (air) into the lungs by inflating them || to draw up (moisture etc.) by or as if by suction, *roots suck water from the earth* || to draw liquid from (e.g. an orange) by the action of the tongue, lips and cheeks || to hold (e.g. the thumb) in the mouth || to allow (e.g. candy) to dissolve slowly in the mouth || *v.i.* to draw something by or as if by producing a vacuum || to draw milk from a breast or udder or bottle with the mouth || to make the sound of sucking || (of waves, with 'at') to cause erosion by their action || (of a defective water pump) to draw up air instead of water **to suck in** (or **down**) (of quicksand or a whirlpool) to swallow up, engulf **to suck up** to absorb by capillarity || to cause (a liquid) to rise by making the pressure above it less than atmospheric pressure **to suck up to** (esp. *Br., pop.*) to toady to (someone) in order to gain favor **2.** *n.* the act of sucking || the sound of sucking **súck·er** *n.* someone who, or something which, sucks || (*zool.*) an organ used to suck blood or to assist in attachment (e.g. on a fly's foot etc.) || (*bot.*) a shoot from a root or the underground part of a stem || (*pop.*) someone who is easily taken in and gotten the better of || (*pop.*) a lollipop [O.E. *sūcan*]
suck·le (sʌ́k'l) *pres. part.* **suck·ling** *past* and *past part.* **suck·led** *v.t.* (of mammals) to give (the newly born) milk from the teat
Suck·ling (sʌ́kliŋ), Sir John (1609-42), English Cavalier lyric poet
suck·ling (sʌ́kliŋ) *n.* an infant or a young animal still getting milk from the teat
Su·cre (sú:kre), Antonio José de (1795-1830), South American revolutionist. He helped Bolívar in the revolt of the Spanish-American colonies and was the first president of Bolivia (1826-8)
Sucre the constitutional capital (pop. 63,259) of Bolivia (*LA PAZ) on the central plateau at 9,331 ft. Spanish cathedral (17th c.). University (1624). Founded by the Spanish in 1538, Sucre was the first city in South America to revolt against Spain (1809)
su·cre (sú:kre) *n.* the monetary unit of Ecuador, or a coin of this amount
su·crose (sú:krous) *n.* a sweet, crystalline, dextrorotatory sugar, $C_{12}H_{22}O_{11}$, which occurs widely in the fluids of plants and upon hydrolysis yields a molecule of dextrose and one of fructose
suc·tion (sʌ́kʃən) **1.** *n.* the process of raising a fluid by reducing the pressure above it and so causing it to be forced upwards by the atmospheric pressure beneath it || the act of causing one body to adhere to another by making the pressure between them less than the external atmospheric pressure **2.** *adj.* causing suction || operating by suction [O.F.]
suction pump a pump which operates by causing a partial vacuum in a tube immersed in a fluid, by raising a close-fitting piston in the tube (cf. FORCE PUMP)
suction stop (*phon.*) a click
suc·to·ri·al (sʌktɔ́ri:əl, sʌktóuri:əl) *adj.* (*zool.*, of organs) adapted for sucking, either for feeding or for adhering || (*zool.*) having such organs || (*zool.*) of or relating to *Suctoria*, subphylum *Ciliophora*, a class of protozoans which suck up food through specialized tentacles [fr. Mod. L. *suctorius* fr. *sugere* (*suctus*), to suck]
Su·dan (su:dǽn) a republic (area 967,000 sq. miles, pop. 19,900,000) in N.E. Africa. Capital: Khartoum. People: mainly Arab-Nubian in the north, Nilotic (Dinka, Nuer, Shilluk, Bari) and Azande in the south. Languages: Arabic (official), African languages, English. Religion: 54% Moslem (north), 20% local African (south), 2% Christian. Universities: Khartoum (1956), Khartoum branch of Cairo University (1955), Islamic University (1965). The land is 3% arable, 10% pasture and grazing and 18% forest. It is mainly a plateau (1,000–3,000 ft), with mountains in the west (the Marra, rising to 10,130 ft), the south (to 10,456 ft), and near the Red Sea coast (to 9,000 ft). The south is mainly rain forest (White Nile valley) and savanna, the center semidesert except close to the Nile, and the north desert. South of Khartoum, between the White and the Blue Nile, is the fertile Gezira plain, the economic heart of the country. Average temperatures (F.) at Khartoum: Jan. 70°, July 80°. Extremes: 40°-115°. Rainfall: Khartoum 6 ins, S. White Nile valley 37 ins, southwest 43 ins. Livestock: cattle, sheep, goats, camels, donkeys, horses. Agricultural products: cotton, peanuts, sesame, dates, hides and skins, melon seeds, oil cake, durra, pulses, seed oil, castor seed, beans, wheat, corn, citrus and tropical fruits. Forestry products: gum arabic (95% of world supply), railroad ties. Mineral resources (largely unexploited): gold, iron, copper, manganese, white mica, vermiculites, salt, chromite, quartz and marble. Manufactures and industries: cement, food processing, rolling stock. Exports: cotton, gum arabic, peanuts, sesame, cottonseed, durra, oil cake, camels, hides and skins, cattle, sheep. Imports: cotton goods, machinery, metals, petroleum products, sugar, vehicles, tea, textiles, fertilizers, jute sacks. wheat flour, coffee, tires. cigarettes and tobacco. Port: Port Sudan. Monetary unit: Sudanese pound (100 piasters). HISTORY. The north of the Sudan formed the ancient country of Nubia, which was colonized by Egypt (2nd millennium B.C.). It was converted to Coptic Christianity (6th c. A.D.), but became part of Islam when conquered by the Arabs (15th c.). It was overrun (1820-2) by Mohammed Ali of Egypt. In Egyptian service, Baker and Gordon completed the conquest of the south and began to suppress the slave trade. The Mahdi led a revolt (1883-5), but his power was broken (1898) by an Anglo-Egyptian force under Kitchener. The Sudan was under an Anglo-Egyptian condominium (1899-1953), after which it was self-governing until Jan. 1, 1956, when it became an independent republic. It joined the Arab League and the U.N. (1956). A coup d'état

(1958) was followed by the establishment of military rule (1958-64). Parliamentary government was reestablished (1965). A revolt of the South against northern domination erupted (1962). A new army coup d'état (1969) introduced a degree of Arab socialism, and renamed the country the Sudan Democratic Republic. A certain autonomy was granted (1972) to the south. Civil war erupted again (1983) when the southern region was divided into three provinces and strict Islamic law was imposed throughout the country. Gen. Gaafar al Nimiery, in power since 1969 except for a brief period in 1971, was overthrown (1985) after nationwide riots protesting his imposition of economic austerity measures demanded by the U.S.A. and the International Monetary Fund. A transition government tried to improve the economy and to end foreign support for the southern rebels by attempting to improve relations with Libya and Ethiopia

Sudan an imprecisely delineated geographical region of Africa generally considered to include northern and central Chad, northern and central Sudan, and Eritrea ‖ the name given by the Arab invaders of N. Africa to the belt of sahel country south of the Sahara from the Atlantic to the Red Sea

Su·da·nese (su:d'ní:z, su:d'ní:s) **1.** *adj.* of or relating to the Sudan or its people **2.** *pl.* **Su·da·nese** *n.* a native or inhabitant of the Sadan

Su·dan·ic (su:dǽnik) **1.** *adj.* Sudanese **2.** *n.* a large group of languages spoken in an area of west and central Africa from S. Sudan to Senegal (*AFRICAN LANGUAGES)

Sudanic civilization a civilization, based on divine kingship and an elaborate bureaucracy, which flourished in west and central Africa from the 4th c. onward. The most famous Sudanic states were Ghana, Kanem, Songhai and Hausa. They were converted to Islam in the Middle Ages and fell into decay at various dates between the 16th and 19th cc.

su·dar·i·um (su:déəriəm) *pl.* **su·dar·i·a** (su:déəriə) *n.* a veronica (cloth) [L.]

su·da·to·ri·um (su:dətɔ́riəm, su:dətóuriəm) *pl.* **su·da·to·ri·a** (su:dətɔ́ri:ə, su:dətóuriə) *n.* (esp. *Rom. hist.*) the heated room in which sweat baths are taken [L.]

Sud·bur·y (sʌ́dbəri:, sʌ́dbəri:) a town (pop. 91,829) in central Ontario, Canada, center of a mining area producing nickel. University (1957)

sudd (sʌd) *n.* vegetable matter consisting mainly of papyrus stems and a type of aquatic grass (*Vossia procera*), floating on and congesting parts of the upper White Nile [Arab.=an obstructing]

sud·den (sʌ́d'n) **1.** *adj.* of a change or event which occurs without noticeable preparation, *a sudden fall of temperature* ‖ unexpected, *a sudden bend in the road* **2.** *n.* (only in the phrase) **all of a sudden** suddenly, unexpectedly [A.F. *sodein, sudein*]

sudden infant death syndrome (*med.*) unexpected infant (1 to 4 months) mortality that occurs during sleep, the cause of which is presently unknown *abbr.* SIDS *also* crib death, sleep apnea syndrome

Su·der·mann (zú:dərmɑn), Hermann (1857-1928), German dramatist and author of novels and short stories. These last include 'The Excursion to Tilsit' (1917). His play 'Heimat' (1893) was translated into English as 'Magda' (1896)

Su·de·ten·land (su:déit'nlænd, zu:déit'nlɑnt) the northern border region of Czechoslovakia, along the Erzgebirge and the Sudeten Mtns. It had a largely German-speaking population and was annexed (1938) by Hitler. It was returned (1945) to Czechoslovakia and most of the German population was expelled

Su·de·ten Mountains (su:déit'n, zu:déit'n) a mountain system separating Silesia, Poland from Bohemia, Czechoslovakia. Highest peak: Schneekoppe (5,259 ft)

su·dor·if·er·ous (su:dəríførəs) *adj.* (of glands) producing or carrying sweat [fr. Mod. L. *sudoriferus*]

su·dor·if·ic (su:dərífik) **1.** *adj.* inducing sweat **2.** *n.* a sweat-producing drug [fr. Mod. L. *sudorificus*]

Su·dra (sú:drə) *n.* a Hindu of the fourth and lowest of the chief castes, comprising manual workers (*BRAHMIN, *KSHATRIYA, *VAISYA) [fr. Skr. *śūdra*]

suds (sʌdz) *pl. n.* frothy, soapy water or the froth itself **súds·y** *comp.* **suds·i·er** *superl.* **suds·i·est** *adj.* frothy [etym. doubtful]

Sue (sy), Eugène (1804-57), French novelist, author of 'les Mystères de Paris' (1842-3) and 'le Juif errant' (1844-5)

sue (su:) *pres. part.* **su·ing** *past* and *past part.* **sued** *v.t.* to bring a legal action against, *to sue someone for damages* ‖ (*law*) to carry (an action) through to decision ‖ (*law*) to appeal to (a court) ‖ *v.i.* (*law*) to bring an action with a view to securing redress ‖ (*rhet.*) to make a petition or entreaty, *to sue for mercy* [A.F. *suer, siwer*]

suede, *Br.* esp. **suède** (sweid) *n.* leather having the flesh side napped by buffing. It is used for shoes, gloves etc. [F. *Suède,* Sweden in *gants de suède,* Swedish gloves]

sued·et·ta (sweidétə) *n.* synthetic suede

Su-11 *MAIDEN

su·et (sú:it) *n.* the hard fat surrounding the kidneys and loins of cattle and sheep, used in cooking or in making tallow [dim. of A.F. *sue, seu* fr. L. *sebum,* tallow]

Sue·to·ni·us (switóuni:əs) (Gaius Suetonius Tranquillus, c. 69–c. 140), Roman historian, author of the 'De vita Caesarum', historical biographies of the Roman emperors from Julius Caesar to Domitian

Su·ez (su:éz, *Br.* sú:iz) a port (pop. 368,000) in Egypt at the head of the Gulf of Suez (the northwestern arm of the Red Sea) and entrance to the Suez Canal: oil refining, fertilizers

Suez Canal a ship canal (100 miles long) in E. Egypt linking, by way of several lakes and without any locks, the Red Sea (Gulf of Suez) with the Mediterranean at Port Saïd. It enables vessels to sail between Europe and the East without rounding Africa (almost halving the distance between London and Bombay, for example). The canal was planned and built (1854-69) by de Lesseps with French and Egyptian capital. On Disraeli's initiative, Britain bought a major interest in the company controlling the canal (1875). It was nationalized (1956) by Egypt, and the resultant military intervention by Britain, France and Israel was stopped by the U.N. The canal, which had been blocked by Egypt, was reopened (1957) but was again blocked (June 1967) after the third Arab-Israeli war. It remained closed for eight years. Plans were announced to widen and deepen the canal (1975)

suf·fer (sʌ́fər) *v.t.* to be made to bear, *to suffer punishment, suffer discomfort* ‖ to be the victim of, *to suffer loss* ‖ to put up with, *to suffer fools gladly* ‖ to undergo, be subjected to, *to suffer damage in transport* ‖ (*old-fash.*) to allow ‖ *v.i.* to experience pain or injury ‖ to experience loss, damage, deterioration etc., *carpets suffer from damp* [A.F. *suffrir*]

suf·fer·ance (sʌ́fərəns) *n.* tacit consent **on sufferance** under conditions of being permitted but not welcomed [O.F. *suffrance, soffrance*]

suf·fer·ing (sʌ́fəriŋ) *n.* mental or physical pain ‖ the bearing of pain, distress, loss, damage etc.

suf·fice (səfáis) *pres. part.* **suf·fic·ing** *past* and *part.* **suf·ficed** *v.i.* to be enough ‖ *v.t.* to be enough for [fr. O.F. *suffire* (*suffis*)]

suf·fi·cien·cy (səfíʃənsi:) *pl.* **suf·fi·cien·cies** *n.* an adequate amount ‖ the state or quality of being sufficient [fr. L. *sufficientia*]

suf·fi·cient (səfíʃənt) *adj.* enough, as much as is needed [O.F.]

suf·fix (sʌ́fiks) *n.* a sound, syllable or syllables added to the end of a word or to a word base to change its meaning or give it grammatical function or to form a new word (e.g. '-ly', '-ness', '-ed' etc.) ‖ (*math.*) a subindex **2.** (sʌ́fiks, səfíks) *v.t.* to add as a suffix [fr. Mod. L. *suffixum* fr. *suffigere,* to fasten on beneath]

suf·fo·cate (sʌ́fəkeit) *pres. part.* **suf·fo·cat·ing** *past* and *past part.* **suf·fo·cat·ed** *v.t.* to kill by stopping respiration ‖ to hinder the respiration of ‖ to oppress, smother ‖ *v.i.* to die by being suffocated ‖ to have too little air to breathe [fr. L. *suffocare* (*suffocatus*), to choke]

suf·fo·ca·tion (sʌfəkéiʃən) *n.* a suffocating or being suffocated [fr. L. *suffocatio* (*suffocationis*)]

Suf·folk (sʌ́fək), Thomas Howard, 1st earl of (1561-1626), lord chamberlain of England (1603-14), lord high treasurer (1614-18). He was removed from office when found guilty of embezzlement

Suffolk a county (area 1,482 sq. miles, pop. 588,400) in E. central England. It is divided administratively into East Suffolk (area 871 sq. miles, pop. 343,000, county town: Ipswich) and West Suffolk (area 611 sq. miles, pop. 130,000, county town: Bury St Edmunds)

Suffolk Resolves resolutions adopted (1774) by the colonial assembly of Massachusetts which declared the Intolerable Acts void and recommended the establishment of a colonial militia

suf·fra·gan (sʌ́frəgən) **1.** *n.* a bishop who has no cathedral of his own, but serves as assistant to the bishop of a diocese **2.** *adj.* of such an assistant bishop [O.E.]

suf·frage (sʌ́fridʒ) *n.* the right to vote in political elections ‖ (esp. *pl.*) a vote of assent **suf·fra·gette** (sʌfrədʒét) *n.* a female agitator for women's suffrage **súf·fra·gist** *n.* an advocate of extension of political suffrage, esp. to women [O.F.]

suf·fuse (səfjú:z) *pres. part.* **suf·fus·ing** *past* and *past part.* **suf·fused** *v.t.* to spread or cover completely, to permeate with light, a liquid, a color etc. [fr. L. *suffundere* (*suffusus*)]

suf·fu·sion (səfjú:ʒən) *n.* a suffusing or being suffused ‖ something that suffuses, esp. a flush or a blush [fr. L. *suffusio* (*suffusionis*)]

Su·fi (sú:fi:) **1.** *n.* an adherent of Sufism **2.** *adj.* relating to Sufism or to Sufis **Sú·fism** *n.* a system of mainly heterodox, mystical groups within Islam. Developing in Persia and Iraq (9th–13th cc.) Sufism advocated asceticism and meditation as a means of achieving rapturous union with the Divine: among the dervish orders certain forms of dancing were used to induce ecstasy. It also encouraged the worship of saints, and it formed communities and orders, both practices being quite against orthodox teaching. The work of al-Ghazzali (1058–1111, *GHAZZALI) caused Sufism to be accepted in orthodox circles, however, and it then reinvigorated an Islam too much governed by arid scholasticism **Su·fís·tic** *adj.* [Arab. *çūfī,* man of wool]

Su-15 *FLAGON

sug·ar (ʃúgər) **1.** *n.* sucrose, esp. in the white crystallized form obtained chiefly by processing the juice expressed from sugarcane or from sliced sugar beets, and refining and evaporating it. Sugar is an important flavoring and preservative for other foods ‖ one of a class of simple carbohydrates soluble in water (e.g. fructose, maltose, sucrose, glucose) including oligosaccharides and monosaccharides, that vary widely in sweetness ‖ a spoonful or lump of sugar **2.** *v.t.* to sweeten with sugar ‖ to sprinkle with sugar ‖ (esp. *Br.*) to make (something unpleasant) more agreeable by flattery, cajolery etc. ‖ *v.i.* to form sugar ‖ to become granular like sugar **to sugar off** to finish the boiling down of maple syrup until it is thick enough to crystallize **to sugar the pill** to make something unpleasant acceptable [O.F. *çucre* fr. M.L. fr. Arab.]

Sugar Act of 1764 a British act of Parliament passed to raise revenue and offset colonial administrative costs. It gave customs officials more power, freed them from damage suits in colonial courts, and elaborated the bonds, bills of lading, and other papers used in colonial commerce in order to prevent fraud. It lowered the duty on foreign molasses, but this duty was henceforth to be collected (the contraband trade having being tolerated until then). It thus directly threatened the rum trade, which depended on molasses

sugar almond (*Br.*) a Jordan almond

sugar beet a beet having white roots grown for its sugar. After the root is crushed and the sugar extracted, the residue is used as fodder and as a fertilizer. The leaves are converted into silage

Sugar Bowl New Orleans stadium where post-season college football games have been played since 1935

sug·ar·cane (ʃúgərkein) *n. Saccharum officinarum,* a species of tall, coarse perennial grass (8–20 ft in height), having jointed stems and a terminal flower cluster. It is one of the chief sources of sugar

sug·ar·coat (ʃúgərkout) *v.t.* to coat something with sugar ‖ to make (something difficult or unpleasant) seem easier or more attractive than it really is ‖ to conceal (something unpalatable) under a pleasing surface **súg·ar·coat·ed** *adj.* **súg·ar·coat·ing** *n.*

sugar daddy (*pop.*) an elderly man who provides luxuries for the young woman he keeps as mistress

CONCISE PRONUNCIATION KEY: **(a)** æ, *cat;* ɑ, *car;* ɔ *fawn;* ei, *snake.* **(e)** e, *hen;* i:, *sheep;* iə, *deer;* ɛə, *bear.* **(i)** i, *fish;* ai, *tiger;* ə:, *bird.* **(o)** o, *ox;* au, *cow;* ou, *goat;* u, *poor;* ɔi, *royal.* **(u)** ʌ, *duck;* u, *bull;* u:, *goose;* ə, *bacillus;* ju:, *cube.* x, *loch;* θ, *think;* ð, *bother;* z, *Zen;* ʒ, *corsage;* dʒ, *savage;* ŋ, *orangutang;* j, *yak;* ʃ, *fish;* tʃ, *fetch;* 'l, *rabble;* 'n, *redden.* Complete pronunciation key appears inside front cover.

sug·ar·house (ʃúgərhaus) *pl.* **sug·ar·hous·es** (ʃúgərhauziz) *n.* a building where sugar is processed, esp. where maple sugar and maple syrup are made

sug·ar·i·ness (ʃúgəri:nis) *n.* the state or quality of being sugary

sug·ar·loaf (ʃúgərlouf) *pl.* **sug·ar·loaves** (ʃúgərlouvz) *n.* a conical mass of refined sugar ‖ a hill or mountain shaped like a sugarloaf **súg·ar·loaf** *adj.* shaped like a cone of sugar

sugar maple any of various North American maples, esp. *Acer saccharum,* from whose sap maple syrup and maple sugar are made. Sugar maples are also highly valued for their hardwood

sug·ar·y (ʃúgəri:) *adj.* of or containing sugar ‖ very sweet ‖ granular, like refined sugar ‖ sentimental and cloying ‖ (of a person's manner, voice etc.) excessively and usually insincerely sweet

Su·ger (syʒer) (c. 1081-1151), French cleric and statesman, abbot of Saint-Denis. He was the chief minister of Louis VI and Louis VII, and was regent of France (1147-9) during Louis VII's absence on crusade. He wrote a life of Louis VI

sug·gest (səgdʒést, sədʒést) *v.t.* to put forward for consideration, *to suggest an alternative route* ‖ to make one think of, bring to mind, esp. by free association, *the symphony suggests a sunrise* ‖ to propose (someone or something) as a possibility ‖ to intimate ‖ to serve as an inspiration for, prompt the doing of, *a drama suggested by Harlem race riots* [fr. L. *suggerere (suggestus),* to bring under]

sug·gest·i·bil·i·ty (səgdʒestəbíliti:, sədʒestəbíliti:) *n.* the state or quality of being suggestible

sug·gest·i·ble (səgdʒéstəb'l, sədʒéstəb'l) *adj.* (of a person) readily able to be influenced by suggestion, esp. hypnotic suggestion ‖ being mentally susceptible to the influence and opinions of persons other than oneself ‖ able to be suggested

sug·ges·tion (səgdʒéstʃən, sədʒéstʃən) *n.* a suggesting or being suggested ‖ that which is suggested ‖ a partly formed idea which, if developed, would be the basis of a judgment ‖ a very slight amount, *a suggestion of mockery in his tone* ‖ the process whereby one thought leads to another, a part evokes a whole etc. ‖ (*psychol.*) a mental process which results in the acceptance of beliefs arising from a source considered expert or authoritative. The technique of advertising often rests on it ‖ hypnosis [O.F. *suggestioun* fr. L.]

sug·ges·tive (səgdʒéstiv, sədʒéstiv) *adj.* stimulating ideas, emotions etc. ‖ tending to suggest something indecent

Su·har·to (su:hártou) (1921-), Indonesian general and statesman. When President Sukarno was deprived (1967) of his presidential powers Suharto had them temporarily ascribed (Mar. 1967) to himself, and set about rebuilding the economy. He adopted a peaceful policy toward Malaysia, and sought to counter the influence of Communist China. He was reelected in 1973, 1978, and 1983

Suhl (zu:l) a district (area 1,492 sq. miles, pop. 575,000) of East Germany (*THURINGIA)

Sui (swi:) a dynasty which ruled China (590-618). Under it the Chinese empire was greatly extended

su·i·cid·al (su:isáid'l) *adj.* having an inclination towards suicide ‖ involving or leading to suicide ‖ involving esp. willful destruction of one's own interests, career etc.

su·i·cide (sú:isaid) *n.* the act of killing oneself intentionally ‖ an action for which one is responsible and which damages one's career or reputation irreparably, *political suicide* [fr. Mod. L. *suicidum* fr. *sui,* of oneself+*caedere,* to kill]

suicide *n.* a person who intentionally takes his own life, or attempts to do so [Mod. L. *suicida* fr. *sui,* of oneself+*caedere,* to kill]

suicide connection technique for reversing rotation of a large electric motor (from full speed ahead to reverse) by so wiring the field and armature circuits to make it a generator, feeding energy to field coils to negate stored magnetism quickly

suicide seat seat next to the driver of a motor vehicle

suicide squad (*football*) team group that defends the player kicking off

su·i·cid·ol·o·gy (sú:isaidɒlədʒi:) *n.* the study of suicides —**suicidologist** *n.*

suit (su:t) **1.** *n.* a jacket and pants of the same material, sometimes with a vest as well ‖ a jacket and skirt of the same material ‖ the act of suing in a court of law ‖ an action taken to a court of law ‖ an act of petitioning or requesting ‖ (*old-fash.*) courtship, *to press one's suit* ‖ one of the four sets of cards (clubs, diamonds, spades, hearts) in a deck ‖ (*naut.*) a set of sails ‖ (*hist.*) a set of armor ‖ an outfit adapted to a particular activity or circumstance, *a space suit* ‖ a bathing suit **to follow suit** (*cards*) to play a card of the suit led ‖ to follow an example, *watch what he does and follow suit* **2.** *v.t.* to meet the needs or wishes of, be convenient for, *would it suit you to come tomorrow?* ‖ to fit in with, *that suits my plans* ‖ (esp. used passively) to fit for, *he isn't suited for salesmanship* ‖ to look well on, *green suits you* ‖ to be good for the health of, *the climate does not suit her* **to suit oneself** to satisfy one's own needs, convenience or wishes [A.F. *siute*]

suit·a·bil·i·ty (su:təbíliti:) *n.* the quality of being suitable

suit·a·ble (sú:təb'l) *adj.* meeting the requirements of a situation, purpose etc. ‖ unobjectionable as regards propriety **súit·a·bly** *adv.*

suit·case (sú:tkeis) *n.* a flat, rectangular container, with a hinged lid and a handle, used for carrying clothes etc. on a journey

suite (swi:t) *n.* a set of matching furniture ‖ a set of rooms, e.g. in a hotel ‖ a retinue, personal staff ‖ (*mus.*) an instrumental composition consisting of a set of movements, esp. (*hist.*) consisting of an allemande, courante, saraband, gigue, sometimes with additions, in related keys [F.]

suit·ing (sú:tiŋ) *n.* cloth of which men's and women's suits are made

suit·or (sú:tər) *n.* (*law*) a petitioner or plaintiff in a lawsuit ‖ a petitioner ‖ (*old-fash.*) a man who courts a woman with a view to marriage [A.F. *seutor, suitour*]

Sui·yüan (swí:jyán) a former province of N. China, part of Inner Mongolia since 1954

Su·kar·na·pu·ra (su:kɑrnəpúərə) *DJAJAPURA

Su·kar·no (su:kárnou), Achmed (1901-70), Indonesian statesman, first president of Indonesia (1945-67). He assumed dictatorial powers (1960) and became head of state for life (1963), but was forced to give up power in 1967

Su·khu·mi (sú:xumi:) the capital (pop. 114,000) of the Abkhazian A.S.S.R., U.S.S.R., a port and resort on the E. Black Sea

su·ki·ya·ki (su:ki:jáki:, ski:jáki:) *n.* a Japanese dish of thin slices of meat fried with bean sprouts, mushrooms, onions and other vegetables, served with soy sauce [Jap.]

Suk·koth (súkout, súkəs) *n.* a Jewish harvest festival commemorating the temporary shelter granted the Jews in the wilderness. It lasts 7–9 days, beginning the 15th of Tishri (cf. JEWISH CALENDAR) [Heb. *Sukkōth,* pl. of *sukkāh,* a thicket, arbor]

Suk·kur (súkkur) a town (pop. 158,876) in N. Sind, Pakistan, on the Indus, at the center of a great irrigation system (the Sukku and Lloyd barrage, 1928-32)

Su·lai·man Range (sulaimán) a mountain range 250 miles long in Pakistan, west of the middle Indus (Takht-i-Sulaiman, 11,100 ft)

Su·la·we·si (su:ləwéisi:) (Celebes) a mountainous fertile island (area 72,976 sq. miles, pop. 9,263,700) in the Greater Sundas, since 1950 one of the ten provinces of Indonesia. Chief town: Makassar. Products: rice, coffee, tobacco, cocoa, copra, nickel. The Dutch occupied the Makassar area in the south in the 17th c. but did not pacify all the tribes of the island, mainly Malay, until the early 20th c. (*INDONESIA)

sul·cate (sʌ́lkeit) *adj.* (*biol.*) grooved, furrowed **súl·cat·ed** *adj.* [fr. L. *sulcare (sulcatus),* to furrow]

sul·cus (sʌ́lkəs) *pl.* **sul·ci** (sʌ́lsai) *n.* a groove, furrow, esp. (*anat.*) a shallow furrow or fissure on the surface of the brain separating one convolution from another [L.]

Su·lei·man I (su:leimán) 'the Magnificent' (1494-1566), Ottoman sultan (1520-66). He expanded the Ottoman Empire to its greatest extent, capturing Belgrade (1521) and Rhodes (1522) and unsuccessfully besieging Vienna (1529). He defeated the Hungarians at Mohacs (1526) and annexed Hungary (1540). His fleet dominated the Mediterranean and he conquered the Red Sea coast of Arabia. He was a great legislator and patron of the arts, and built many famous mosques

sul·fa·di·a·zine, sul·pha·di·a·zine (sʌlfədáiəzi:n) *n.* $C_{10}H_{10}N_4O_2S$, a sulfa drug

sul·fa drug (sʌ́lfə) any of a class of therapeutic agents that are sulfonamides, chemically related to sulfanilamide. These bacteriostatic drugs are particularly effective against diseases caused by streptococci, pneumococci and meningococci. The most prominent of these drugs are, in addition to sulfanilamide: sulfapyridine, sulfathiazole and sulfadiazine

sul·fa·nil·a·mide, sul·pha·nil·a·mide (sʌlfəníləmaid) *n.* $H_2NC_6H_4SO_2NH_2$, the parent compound of most of the sulfa drugs

sul·fa·pyr·i·dine, sul·pha·pyr·i·dine (sʌlfəpíərədi:n) *n.* $C_{11}H_{11}N_3O_2S$, a sulfa drug

sul·fate, sul·phate (sʌ́lfeit) **1.** *n.* a salt or ester of sulfuric acid **2.** *v.t. pres. part.* **sul·fat·ing, sul·phat·ing** *past* and *past part.* **sul·fat·ed, sul·phat·ed** to treat with a sulfate, or sulfuric acid ‖ (*elec.*) to form a whitish deposit of lead sulfate on (the plates of a battery) ‖ *v.i.* to become sulfated

sul·fa·thi·a·zole, sul·pha·thi·a·zole (sʌlfəθáiəzoul) *n.* $C_9H_9N_3O_3S_2$, a sulfa drug

sul·fide, sul·phide (sʌ́lfaid) *n.* a binary compound of sulfur with another element ‖ a compound of sulfur with an organic radical

sul·fin·py·ra·zone [$C_{23}H_{20}N_2O_3S$] (sʌlfinpáirəzoun) *n.* (*pharm.*) drug that stimulates excretion of uric acid, used in treatment of gout and heart infarction; marketed as Anturane

sul·fite, sul·phite (sʌ́lfait) *n.* a salt or ester of sulfurous acid **sul·fit·ic, sul·phit·ic** (sʌlfítik) *adj.*

sul·fon·a·mide, sul·phon·a·mide (sʌlfónəmaid) *n.* any of the compounds of the group SO_2NH_2 or of its derivatives, many of which are used in destroying harmful bacteria. The first sulfonamide, known as 'M and B' (1933) was used in treating pneumonia. More recent members of the group are used to treat infections of the intestinal, urinary and respiratory tracts

sul·fo·nate, sul·pho·nate (sʌ́lfəneit) **1.** *n.* a salt or ester of a sulfonic acid **2.** *v.t. pres. part.* **sul·fo·nat·ing, sul·pho·nat·ing** *past* and *past part.* **sul·fo·nat·ed, sul·pho·nat·ed** to convert into a sulfonic acid, salt or halide

sul·fo·na·tion, sul·pho·na·tion (sʌlfənéiʃən) *n.* the process of sulfonating

sul·fone, sul·phone (sʌ́lfoun) *n.* any of a group of organic compounds containing the radical SO_2 in which the sulfur atom is linked doubly with carbon in various combinations ‖ a product of sulfur compound oxidation used in treatment of leprosy

sul·fon·ic acid, sul·phon·ic acid (sʌlfónik) any of several acids that contain the SO_3H group and are derived from sulfuric acid by the replacement of an OH group

sul·fo·nyl, sul·pho·nyl (sʌ́lfənil) *n.* the bivalent radical SO_2 occurring in sulfones, sulfonic acids etc.

sul·fo·nyl·u·re·a (sʌlfəniljurí:ə) *n.* (*pharm.*) any of a number of drugs that lessen blood sugar by increasing secretion of endogenous insulin, used in treating diabetes

sul·fur, sul·phur (sʌ́lfər) **1.** *n.* a multivalent nonmetallic element (symbol S, at. no. 16, at. mass 32,064) found in crystalline or amorphous form. It occurs abundantly and widely in nature, in the free state and combined as sulfides and sulfates. It is used in the making of sulfuric acid, vulcanizing rubber, gunpowder, matches, dyes, fungicides, insecticides and in medicines [L. *sulphur, sulfur*]

sul·fu·rate, sul·phu·rate (sʌ́lfjureit) *pres. part.* **sul·fu·rat·ing, sul·phu·rat·ing** *past* and *past part.* **sul·fu·rat·ed, sul·phu·rat·ed** *v.t.* to sulfurize **sul·fu·rá·tion, sul·phu·rá·tion** *n.*

sul·fur-bot·tom, sul·phur-bot·tom (sʌ́lfərbɒtəm) *n.* the blue whale

sulfur dioxide, sulphur dioxide the stable oxide of sulfur, SO_2. It is gaseous at ordinary atmospheric pressure, with a choking and penetrating smell, but is easily liquefied by pressure. It is used in making sulfuric acid, as a reducing and bleaching agent in refining, as a preservative, as an insecticide, as a disinfectant, in refrigerating circuits etc.

sul·fu·re·ous, sul·phu·re·ous (sʌlfjúəri:əs) *adj.* of, consisting of, or like sulfur ‖ sulfur yellow in color ‖ having the qualities of sulfur when burning

sul·fu·ret·ed hydrogen, sul·phu·ret·ted hydrogen, sul·fu·ret·ted hydrogen (sʌ́lfjuretid) hydrogen sulfide

sul·fu·ric, sul·phu·ric (sʌlfjúərik) *adj.* of, relating to, or containing sulfur

CONCISE PRONUNCIATION KEY: **(a)** æ, *cat*; ɑ, *car*; ɔ *fawn*; ei, *snake*. **(e)** e, *hen*; i:, *sheep*; iə, *deer*; ɛə, *bear*. **(i)** i, *fish*; ai, *tiger*; ə:, *bird*. **(o)** o, *ox*; au, *cow*; ou, *goat*; u, *poor*; ɔi, *royal*. **(u)** ʌ, *duck*; u, *bull*; u:, *goose*; ə, *bacillus*; ju:, *cube*. x, *loch*; θ, *think*; ð, *bother*; z, *Zen*; ʒ, *corsage*; dʒ, *savage*; ŋ, *orangutang*; j, *yak*; ʃ, *fish*; tʃ, *fetch*; 'l, *rabble*; 'n, *redden*. Complete pronunciation key appears inside front cover.

sulfuric acid, sulphuric acid the dibasic acid H_2SO_4, a dense, oily, colorless liquid (oil of vitriol) which very readily dissolves and ionizes in water, with the evolution of much heat. It is used extensively in the chemical industry, in oil refining, and in manufacturing fertilizers, detergents, explosives, dyes, rayon etc.
sul·fu·rize, sul·phu·rize (sʌ́lfjuraiz) *pres. part.* **sul·fu·riz·ing, sul·phu·riz·ing** *past* and *past part.* **sul·fu·rized, sul·phu·rized** *v.t.* to combine or impregnate with sulfur ‖ to fumigate or bleach with sulfur dioxide fumes
sul·fur·ous, sul·phur·ous (sʌlfjúərəs, sʌ́lfərəs) *adj.* of, pertaining to or containing sulfur
sulfurous acid, sulphurous acid an unstable, weak acid, H_2SO_3, known in its aqueous solution, that is a good reducing and bleaching agent
sulfur trioxide, sulphur trioxide the oxide SO_3, which readily combines with water to form sulfuric acid
sul·fur·y, sul·phur·y (sʌ́lfəri:) *adj.* of, relating to or resembling sulfur
sul·in·dac [$C_{20}H_{17}FO_3S$] (sʌ́lindɑk) *n.* (*pharm.*) analgesic anti-inflammatory drug used in treating arthritis; marketed as Clinoril
sulk (sʌlk) **1.** *v.i.* to make one's resentment or vexation felt by others by not talking to them, not cooperating etc. **2.** *n.* the state of sulking, *in a sulk* ‖ (*pl.*) a fit of sulking **súlk·i·ly** *adv.* **súlk·i·ness** *n.* the state of being sulky **súlk·y 1.** *comp.* **sulk·i·er** *superl.* **sulk·i·est** *adj.* sulking or inclined to sulk ‖ suggesting sulkiness **2.** *pl.* **sulk·ies** *n.* a light two-wheeled cart having one seat only and no body, esp. used for trotting races [origin unknown]
Sul·la (sʌ́lə), Lucius Cornelius (138 B.C.-78 B.C.), Roman soldier and statesman. Consul in 88 B.C., he defeated (85 B.C.) Mithridates VI of Pontus, overthrew his political opponents at Rome, and was made dictator with extraordinary powers. He proscribed his enemies and reinstated the power of the senate, establishing a moderately aristocratic constitution. This pattern of autocratic rule, followed by other military commanders, eventually overthrew the Roman republic
sul·lage (sʌ́lidʒ) *n.* a deposit of mud ‖ refuse or sewage ‖ molten metal scoria [origin unknown]
sul·len (sʌ́lən) *adj.* gloomy, ill-humored and unsociable, *a sullen mood* ‖ dull, heavy, *a sullen sky, sullen tones* ‖ sluggish, *a sullen pace* [M.E. *soleine* fr. O.F. *solain,* alone fr. L.]
Sul·li·van (sʌ́livən), Sir Arthur Seymour (1842-1900), English composer. The combination of W. S. Gilbert's witty and topical words and Sullivan's music gave the theater 'H.M.S. Pinafore' (1878), 'The Pirates of Penzance' (1880), 'The Mikado' (1885), 'The Gondoliers' (1889) and other highly skillful light operas. Sullivan was also the composer of sacred cantatas, anthems and hymn tunes which are still sung
Sullivan, Harry Stack (1892-1949), U.S. psychiatrist. Rejecting Sigmund Freud's libidinal theory of personality development, he believed that the development of human peculiarities was governed by interpersonal phenomena
Sullivan, Louis Henri (1856-1924), American architect. His functional approach to design made for organic unity in his steel-frame commercial buildings. His work was of great importance in the evolution of American architecture
Sul·ly (syli:), Maximilien de Béthune, baron de Rosny, duc de (1560-1641), French statesman. A Protestant, he served under the future Henri IV in the Wars of Religion, becoming that king's minister (1598-1610). He proved a brilliant administrator, restoring the country's finances, encouraging agriculture and industry, and building roads and canals
Sul·ly (sʌ́li:), Thomas (1783-1872), U.S. portrait painter. His works include 'Washington Crossing the Delaware' (1818) and portraits of the Marquis de Lafayette (1824-5) and of Queen Victoria (1837)
sul·ly (sʌ́li:) *pres. part.* **sul·ly·ing** *past* and *past part.* **sul·lied** *v.t.* to soil (a reputation etc.) [prob. fr. F. *souiller,* to soil]
sul·phur *SULFUR (and for other derived words beginning 'sulph-' *SULF-)
sul·tan (sʌ́ltən) *n.* a Moslem ruler, esp. a former emperor of Turkey [F. fr. Arab.]
sul·tan·a (sʌltǽnə, sʌltɑ́nə) *n.* the wife of a sultan or any female member of his family ‖ a small, seedless yellow grape grown esp. in the Mediterranean area, e.g. at Izmir, used to make a white wine or dried (*RAISIN) for use in cakes, puddings etc. ‖ this raisin ‖ a member of *Porphyrio,* a genus of purple gallinules [Ital.]
sul·tan·ate (sʌ́ltəneit, sʌ́ltənit) *n.* the rank, office or reign of a sultan ‖ the territory governed by a sultan
sul·tan·ship (sʌ́ltənʃip) *n.* the rank, office or reign of a sultan
sul·tri·ly (sʌ́ltrili:) *adv.* in a sultry manner
sul·tri·ness (sʌ́ltri:nis) *n.* the state or quality of being sultry
sul·try (sʌ́ltri:) *comp.* **sul·tri·er** *superl.* **sul·tri·est** *adj.* (of weather) hot and oppressive ‖ (of people) passionately sensual [fr. obs. *sulter* v., perh. fr. obs. *swulter,* var. of SWELTER]
Su·lu Archipelago (sú:lu:) a group of 870 islands (area 1,087 sq. miles, pop. 317,876) in the Philippines, southwest of Mindanao. Largest island: Jolo. Chief town and port: Jolo (pop. 18,000). Religion: 95% Moslem. Products: rice, coconuts, fruit, fish, pearls, lumber. A sultanate established in the 16th c., it resisted Spanish domination. It came under U.S. control (1899). It became (1940) part of the Commonwealth of the Philippines
Sulu Sea the part of the Pacific between the Philippine Is and Sabah
sum (sʌm) **1.** *n.* an amount of money either specified or indefinite, *he paid a big sum for it* ‖ the whole amount of something ‖ gist, summary ‖ the result obtained by adding ‖ numbers to be added together ‖ (*pop.*) a problem in arithmetic **in sum** in short **2.** *v.t. pres. part.* **sum·ming** *past* and *past part.* **summed** (often with 'up') to add together **to sum up** to gather together the important parts of (a speech, lecture etc.) in a brief statement ‖ to arrive at a considered opinion concerning the character, qualities etc. of (a person) [O.F. *summe, somme* fr. L. *summus,* highest]
su·mac, su·mach (ʃú:mæk, sú:mæk) *n.* any of various members of *Rhus,* fam. *Anacardiaceae,* a genus of shrubs native to warm and temperate regions, having simple or pinnate leaves ‖ a shrub of this genus ‖ a substance used in tanning and dyeing made from the dried and powdered leaves of certain of these shrubs ‖ the wood of one of these shrubs (*POISON SUMAC) [O.F. or M.L. fr. Arab. *summāq*].
Su·ma·tra (sumɑ́trə) an island (area 166,789 sq. miles, pop. 28,016,160) of the Greater Sundas, Indonesia. Chief town: Palembang. A volcanic range (Kerintji, 12,467 ft) runs along the west coast. The east is an alluvial plain, largely rain forest. At present undeveloped, Sumatra has great economic potential. Products: rice, spices, tobacco, coffee, palm kernels, lumber, petroleum, coal, tin, gold. HISTORY. Sumatra was the center of a Hindu empire (8th c.). Arab traders visited the island (13th c.) and, after a period of Javanese rule, Sumatra adopted Islam as its religion (late 16th c.). The Portuguese began to trade with Sumatra (early 16th c.) but were driven out by the Dutch, whose position was challenged in turn by the English. The Dutch gained control of the whole island, subjugating the last native state in 1905. It became part of Indonesia (1945)
Sum·ba (sú:mbə) an island (area 4,305 sq. miles, pop. 182,000) in the Lesser Sundas, Indonesia. Chief town and port: Waingapoe (pop. 3,000). Products: sandalwood (now largely depleted), horses, cattle, cereals, tobacco, copra, coffee
Sum·ba·wa (su:mbúwə) an island (area 5,693 sq. miles, pop. 320,000) of the Lesser Sundas, Indonesia. Chief town and port: Raba (pop. 7,000). Products: cattle and horses, cereals, tobacco, cotton, copra, coffee
Su·mer (sú:mər) an ancient region in S. Mesopotamia. Its non-Semitic people developed a flourishing civilization by c. 3500 B.C. They were masters of metalworking and pottery, and developed a cuneiform system of writing. Sumer became merged (c. 2200 B.C.) with Babylonia
Su·me·ri·an (sumíəri:ən, suméri:ən) **1.** *adj.* of, relating to or characteristic of Sumer ‖ of, relating to, or characteristic of the people of Sumer **2.** *n.* an inhabitant of Sumer ‖ the ancient language of Sumer, surviving in cuneiform inscriptions. It seems to be related to no other language, either living or dead
sum·mar·i·ly (səmérili:, sʌ́mərili:) *adv.* in a summary way
sum·ma·rist (sʌ́mərist) *n.* a person who makes a summary
sum·ma·ri·za·tion (sʌmərizéiʃən) *n.* a summarizing or being summarized
sum·ma·rize (sʌ́məraiz) *pres. part.* **sum·ma·riz·ing** *past* and *past part.* **sum·ma·rized** *v.t.* to sum up, make a summary of, *to summarize an argument* ‖ to be a summary of
sum·ma·ry (sʌ́məri:) *adj.* giving the essentials briefly, summarizing, *a summary report* ‖ done quickly without formality, *summary punishment* ‖ of or using procedure which omits much of the formality required by common law, *summary courts* (opp. PLENARY) ‖ marked by less than proper consideration, *summary treatment* [fr. L. *summarius*]
sum·ma·ry *pl.* **sum·ma·ries** *n.* a short statement of the essential points of a matter [fr. L. *summarium*]
summary court-martial a military court for offenses less serious than those warranting a special court-martial, with one commissioned officer presiding who can impose only certain limited fines or punishments
sum·ma·tion (səméiʃən) *n.* the act of adding ‖ an aggregate ‖ a cumulation, esp. (*biol.*) of small stimuli which together are able to induce a nerve impulse ‖ a final summing up **sum·má·tion·al** *adj.* [fr. Mod. L. *summatio* (*summationis*) fr. *summare,* to sum]
sum·mer (sʌ́mər) **1.** *n.* the warmest season of the year, when a region faces the sun most directly (from the June solstice to the September equinox in the northern hemisphere or from the December solstice to the March equinox in the southern hemisphere) **2.** *adj.* of summer ‖ done in the summer **3.** *v.i.* to pass the summer ‖ *v.t.* to provide (sheep, cattle etc.) with pasture during the summer [O.E. *sumor*]
summer *n.* a large, horizontal beam carrying a dead load in building, esp. a main beam supporting girders or the joists of a floor ‖ a stone or wooden lintel of a door or window [A.F. *sumer, somer*]
Sum·mer·all (sʌ́mərəl), Charles Pelot (1867-1955), U.S. general. As commander of U.S. forces in France during the 1st world war, he proved the value of coordinating artillery action with infantry operations
sum·mer·house (sʌ́mərhaus) *pl.* **sum·mer·hous·es** (sʌ́mərhauziz) *n.* a lightly constructed, covered building in a garden or park, for shade in summer
summer lightning heat lightning
summersault *SOMERSAULT
summer solstice the time when the sun reaches the June solstice for the northern hemisphere or the December solstice for the southern hemisphere
summer squash any of a number of small squashes grown in the summer. They are eaten when not quite ripe, before the seeds and rind become hard
summer stock plays put on during the summer season by a repertory company in a resort or small town
sum·mer·time (sʌ́mərtaim) *n.* the summer season
sum·mer·y (sʌ́məri:) *adj.* of, relating to, or like summer
sum·ming-up (sʌ́miŋʌ́p) *pl.* **sum·mings-up** *n.* a summary
sum·mit (sʌ́mit) *n.* the highest point, esp. of hills and mountains ‖ the top, the highest point e.g. of ambitions or achievements ‖ a conference held by heads of state [O.F. *sommette, somete* dim. of *some, sum,* sum]
summit diplomacy personal, face-to-face negotiation between heads of state, of the world's leading countries —**summit conference** *n.*
summit meeting a summit (conference)
sum·mon (sʌ́mən) *v.t.* to order to appear ‖ to cite (a jury) ‖ to cite (an accused person or witness) to appear in court ‖ to call a meeting of (e.g. a committee) ‖ to call upon for support for some action, *to summon all one's strength* ‖ to adjure, *he summoned them to surrender* [fr. O.F. *somondre,* to warn]
sum·mons (sʌ́mənz) **1.** *pl.* **sum·mons·es** *n.* a request or order to appear, attend, perform some action etc., esp. (*law*) an official written order to appear in court ‖ a signal which summons **2.** *v.t.* to serve with a summons [O.F. *sumunse, somunse*]
Sum·ner (sʌ́mnər), Charles (1811-74), American statesman, a leader of the antislavery movement
Sumner, James Batcheller (1887-1955), U.S. biochemist and co-winner (with J. H. Northrop

CONCISE PRONUNCIATION KEY: **(a)** æ, *cat*; ɑ, *car*; ɔ *fawn*; ei, *snake*. **(e)** e, *hen*; i:, *sheep*; iə, *deer*; εə, *bear*. **(i)** i, *fish*; ai, *tiger*; ə:, *bird*. **(o)** o, *ox*; au, *cow*; ou, *goat*; u, *poor*; ɔi, *royal*. **(u)** ʌ, *duck*; u, *bull*; u:, *goose*; ə, *bacillus*; ju:, *cube*. x, *loch*; θ, *think*; ð, *bother*; z, *Zen*; ʒ, *corsage*; dʒ, *savage*; ŋ, *orangutang*; j, *yak*; ʃ, *fish*; tʃ, *fetch*; 'l, *rabble*; 'n, *redden*. Complete pronunciation key appears inside front cover.

and W. M. Stanley) of the 1946 Nobel prize in chemistry, for research in enzymes
Sumner, William Graham (1840-1910), U.S. sociologist and economist. Advocating an extreme laissez-faire policy, he opposed any government measures which interfered with the natural intercourse of trade
sump (sʌmp) *n.* an oil container at the base of the crankcase of an internal-combustion engine ‖ a drainage pit ‖ a cesspool [M.L.G. *sump* or M.Du. *somp, sump* or fr. G. *sumpt,* swamp]
sump·tion (sʌ́mpʃən) *n.* (*logic*) a major premiss
sump·tu·ar·y (sʌ́mptʃu:eri:) *adj.* pertaining to or controlling expenditure [fr. L. *sumptuarius*]
sumptuary law a law limiting private expenditure, esp. (*hist.*) on religious or moral grounds
sump·tu·ous (sʌ́mptʃu:əs) *adj.* of very great splendor ‖ lavish, luxurious [O.F. *somptueux, sumptueux*]
Sumter *FORT SUMTER
sun (sʌn) **1.** *n.* the central controlling body of the solar system, lying at the principal focus of all the planetary orbits. In the galactic frame of reference, the sun is a typical dwarf yellow star located in a spiral arm near the outer edge of the Milky Way ‖ the light or heat received from the sun ‖ any heavenly body that is the center of a solar system ‖ (*rhet.*) a source of splendor **a place in the sun** an opportunity to expand and thrive **under the sun** in the world **2.** *v. pres. part.* **sun·ning** *past* and *past part.* **sunned** *v.t.* to expose to direct radiation from the sun ‖ *v.i.* to sit or lie in direct sunlight [O.E. *sunne*]
—The sun is a spherical body (diameter 865,400 miles) of mass 4.39 × 10^{27} tons (being 3.33 × 10^5 times more massive than the earth and 740 times more massive than the sum of the masses of the nine planets it controls) and density 1.44 times that of water. Its composition, spectroscopically determined (*FRAUNHOFER LINES), is approx. 90% hydrogen and approx. 10% helium, with small amounts of all the other known elements. Its structure includes a core whose center is at a temperature of 15 million degrees C. and at a pressure of billions of atmospheres: under such conditions matter is limited to an extremely dense gaseous state. The solar interior is surrounded by the photosphere. The extremely extended atmosphere of the sun consists of two regions: the chromosphere and the corona.
The energy of the sun is derived from the thermonuclear conversion of hydrogen into helium, which is thought to occur continuously in the extreme conditions found in the solar interior. This energy (in the form of heat and electromagnetic radiation) forces its way to the solar surface, the solar integrity being maintained by an oppositely directed intense gravitation (28 times greater at the surface of the sun than at the earth's surface). Only a small fraction of the total solar energy output (2.40 × 10^{14} horsepower distributed over its surface) reaches the earth, but it is responsible directly or indirectly for innumerable energy-requiring processes (e.g. growth of all plant and animal life, the winds, the production of power from natural fuels etc.) (*SUNSPOT CYCLE)
sun arc a sun lamp
sun·bath (sʌ́nbæθ, sʌ́nbɑθ) *n.* a period of exposure of the body to the sun or to a sun lamp
sun·bathe (sʌ́nbeið) *pres. part.* **sun·bath·ing** *past* and *past part.* **sun·bathed** *v.i.* to take a sunbath
sun·beam (sʌ́nbi:m) *n.* a ray of sunlight
sun bear *Helarctos malayanus* (or *Ursus malayanus*), fam. *Ursidae,* a small, mainly black bear with a short, fine coat, inhabiting the forests of the Malay Peninsula and islands east of Borneo
Sun·belt (sʌ́nbelt) *n.* the area of the southern U.S. from Virginia to California
sun·bird (sʌ́nbə:rd) *n.* any of a number of small songbirds of fam. *Nectariniidae,* with brilliant glossy plumage, resembling hummingbirds. They are found in Africa, S. Asia, Australia and the East Indies
sun·bon·net (sʌ́nbɒnit) *n.* a bonnet for women and girls with a front brim to shade the face and a back flap to shield the neck from the sun
sun·burn (sʌ́nbə:rn) **1.** *n.* reddening and blistering with consequent peeling of the skin through too sudden and too long exposure to the sun ‖ tanning of the skin through exposure to the sun **2.** *v. pres. part.* **sun·burn·ing** *past* and *past part.* **sun·burned, sun·burnt** (sʌ́nbə:rnt) *v.t.* to cause to be bronzed or blistered by the sun ‖ *v.i.* to become bronzed or blistered by exposure to the sun
sun·dae (sʌ́ndei) *n.* a portion of ice cream served with sauce, fruit, nuts, whipped cream etc. [etym. doubtful]
Sun·da Islands (sʌ́ndə) a group of mountainous, volcanic islands in the Malay Archipelago, divided into the Greater and the Lesser Sundas. The Greater Sundas consist of Java, Sumatra, Borneo, Sulawesi and adjacent islands. The Lesser Sundas (Nusa Tenggara) comprise the chain running from Bali to Timor
sun dance a ceremonial dance of North and South American Indians in honor of the sun at the summer solstice
Sun·dar·bans (sʌ́ndərbənz) a region (about 6,000 sq. miles) of swampy islets formed by the Ganges delta in Bengal, India and Bangladesh
Sun·day (sʌ́ndi:, sʌ́ndei) *n.* the first day of the week, the Christian sabbath **a month of Sundays** a very long time [O.E. *sunnandæg,* day of the sun]
Sunday best one's best clothes, kept esp. for wearing on Sundays
Sunday school a voluntary school held usually in a parish on Sunday for the religious instruction of children ‖ the teachers and pupils of such a school
sun·der (sʌ́ndər) *v.t.* (*rhet.*) to break or tear apart ‖ (*rhet.*) to keep apart ‖ *v.i.* (*rhet.*) to break apart, to separate **in sunder** (*rhet.*) asunder [Late O.E. *syndrian, sundrian*]
Sun·der·land (sʌ́ndərlənd), Robert Spencer, 2nd earl of (1640-1702), English statesman. An opportunist, he was in the pay of Louis XIV while also intriguing to put William of Orange on the English throne
Sunderland a port and county borough (pop. 196,152) in Durham, England: coal mining, shipbuilding, mechanical engineering
sun·dew (sʌ́ndu:, sʌ́ndju:) *n.* a member of *Drosera,* fam. *Droseraceae,* a genus of low-growing perennial insectivorous plants, with a rosette of broad, hairy leaves, found in swamps and other damp places
sun·di·al (sʌ́ndaiəl) *n.* a device which during hours of sunlight indicates the time by a shadow cast by a stationary arm (gnomon) on a dial marked in hours. The shadow is cast at different points of the dial because of changes in the position of the earth in relation to the sun
sun disk (*archaeol.*) a winged disk, symbol of Ra and other ancient Middle Eastern sun gods
sun dog a parhelion ‖ a small halo on the parhelic circle
sun·down (sʌ́ndaun) *n.* the part of day when the sun is setting
sun·dries (sʌ́ndri:z) *pl. n.* miscellaneous items, esp. items individually of small importance
sun·dry (sʌ́ndri:) *adj.* various ‖ miscellaneous, *sundry items* [O.E. *syndrig,* separate]
sun·fast (sʌ́nfæst, sʌ́nfɑst) *adj.* not fading when exposed to sunlight
sun·fish (sʌ́nfiʃ) *pl.* **sun·fish, sun·fish·es** *n.* any of several related forms of saltwater fishes of genus *Ranzania* ‖ any of several American freshwater fishes of fam. *Centrarchidae,* usually brilliantly colored
sun·flow·er (sʌ́nflauər) *n.* a member of *Helianthus,* fam. *Compositae,* a genus of tall-growing plants, esp. *H. annuus,* with large, often very large, yellow-rayed flowers which turn to face the sun. They are cultivated esp. for the oil extracted from the seeds
Sung (suŋ) a Chinese dynasty (960-1279) under whose rule Chinese culture was in one of its most creative periods
sung *past part.* of SING
Sun·ga·ri (súŋgɑ́ri) the chief river (800 miles long) of Manchuria, China, rising near the North Korean border and flowing north, by way of a large lake (Sungari Reservoir) below Yungki, the head of navigation, to the Amur. It is frozen Nov.-Apr.
sun·glass·es (sʌ́nglæsiz, sʌ́nglɑsiz) *pl. n.* spectacles with lenses which are tinted to protect the eyes from glare
sun-god (sʌ́ngɒd) *n.* a god, e.g. Mithras, identified with the sun
Su-9 *FISHPOT
Su-19 *FENCER
sunk *past* and alt. *past part.* of SINK
sunk·en (sʌ́ŋkən) alt. *past part.* of SINK ‖ *adj.* below the surrounding level, *a sunken garden* ‖ lying at the bottom of an ocean, river etc., *a sunken ship* ‖ appearing as if hollow, *sunken cheeks*
sun·lamp (sʌ́nlæmp) *n.* an electric lamp which produces ultraviolet radiation used as a substitute for sunlight for therapeutic purposes, or for acquiring a suntan at home
sun lamp a large lamp reflecting light by a parabolic mirror, used on film sets
sun·light (sʌ́nlait) *n.* the light emanating from the sun
sun·lit (sʌ́nlit) *adj.* shining in the light of the sun
sunn (sʌn) *n.* sunn hemp [Urdu, Hindi, *san*]
Sun·na, Sun·nah (súnə) *n.* the official tradition of the sayings and deeds of Mohammed held in reverence by most Moslems as supplementary to the Koran [Arab.= way, manner of life]
sunn hemp *Crotalaria iuncea,* fam. *Papilionaceae,* a plant with yellow flowers, grown in the East Indies ‖ the hemplike fiber of this plant, lighter and stronger than jute, and used for ropes, bags etc.
Sun·ni (súni:) *n.* a Sunnite [Arab. *sunnī,* lawful]
sun·ni·ly (sʌ́nili:) *adv.* in a sunny manner
sun·ni·ness (sʌ́ni:nis) *n.* the state or quality of being sunny
Sun·nite (súnait) *n.* one of the great majority of Moslems who accept the full Sunna
sun·ny (sʌ́ni:) *comp.* **sun·ni·er** *superl.* **sun·ni·est** *adj.* made bright or warm by the sun ‖ cheerful, *a sunny disposition*
sun parlor, *Br.* **sun parlour** a room or large porch having glass walls to keep the wind out and let the sunshine in
sun porch a sun parlor
sun-pumped laser (sʌ́npʌ́mpt) crystal laser utilizing solar energy concentrated by a parabolic mirror for pumping into a laser
sun·rise (sʌ́nraiz) *n.* the appearance of the sun above the horizon in the morning ‖ the time when this happens
sun·room (sʌ́nru:m, sʌ́nrum) *n.* a sun parlor
sun·set (sʌ́nset) *n.* the disappearance of the sun below the horizon at the end of the day ‖ the time when this happens ‖ the visually impressive effects of light, clouds etc. which accompany the disappearance of the sun
sunset laws legislation providing for lifetime limitation on new government agencies, established to curb growth of a bureaucratic establishment
sun·shade (sʌ́nʃeid) *n.* a parasol ‖ an awning
sun·shine (sʌ́nʃain) *n.* the light received directly from the sun ‖ the shining of the sun ‖ cheerfulness ‖ a cause of cheerfulness **sún·shin·y** *adj.*
—The three main components of sunshine are: visible radiation or light, ultraviolet radiation, which is a germicidal agent and producer of vitamin D, and infrared radiation, which is a heat-producing element forming half of all solar radiation reaching the earth's surface
sun·spot (sʌ́nspɒt) *n.* a dark area on the sun consisting of a gray region surrounding a darker central one. Sunspots occur singly and in groups (often pairs), are transient, appear to move steadily, vary widely in size, and are associated with strong magnetic fields (*SUNSPOT CYCLE)
sunspot cycle the roughly periodic variation in the number of sunspots, reaching a maximum, on an average, every 11 years, and accompanied by a reversal of magnetic polarity for the spots in the northern and southern hemispheres, which has not yet been satisfactorily explained. Sunspots are only one form of solar activity (*SOLAR FLARE, *SOLAR PROMINENCE)
sun·stone (sʌ́nstoun) *n.* aventurine feldspar
sun·stroke (sʌ́nstrouk) *n.* heatstroke brought about by excessive exposure to the heat of the sun
sun·tan (sʌ́ntæn) **1.** *n.* a tan color of the skin acquired by exposure to the sun or to a sunlamp **2.** *v.i. pres. part.* **sun·tan·ning** *past* and *past part.* **sun·tanned** to acquire such a tan
sun·up (sʌ́nʌp) *n.* sunrise
Sun Yat-sen (súnjátsén) (1866-1925), Chinese revolutionary. He united all the Chinese revolutionary parties under the Kuomintang (1911) and was appointed provisional president of the republic (1911-12) after the fall of the Manchus
sup (sʌp) **1.** *v.t. pres. part.* **sup·ping** *past* and *past part.* **supped** (*old-fash.*) to drink in small mouthfuls **2.** *n.* (*old-fash.*) a small mouthful of liquid [O.E. *sūpan*]
sup *pres. part.* **sup·ping** *past* and *past part.* **sup-**

ped *v.i.* to have supper [O.F. *soper, super, souper*]

su·per (sú:pər) **1.** *n.* (*theater*) a supernumerary actor ‖ (*pop.* and *commerce*) a product of extra quality, size etc. ‖ (*bookbinding*) mull ‖ (*pop.*) a superintendent ‖ a removable upper story of a beehive, where the bees store honey **2.** *v.t.* (*bookbinding*) to reinforce (books) with mull **3.** *adj.* (*pop.*) of high quality [L. *super*, above]

super- (sú:pər) *prefix* over, above (as in 'superstructure') ‖ higher in rank or position (as in 'supervisor') ‖ greater in quality, amount or degree (as in 'superabundance') ‖ surpassing all or most others of its kind (as in 'superbomber') ‖ extra, additional (as in 'supertax') ‖ (*biol.*) constituting a category more inclusive than is usual (as in 'superfamily') ‖ (*chem.*) having an unusually large amount of a specified ingredient (as in 'superphosphate') [fr. L. *super* adv. and prep., above, on top of, beyond etc.]

su·per·a·ble (sú:pərəb'l) *adj.* surmountable, conquerable [fr. L. *superabilis*]

su·per·a·bound (su:pərəbáund) *v.i.* to be very or too abundant [fr. L.L. *superabundare*]

su·per·a·bun·dance (su:pərəbʌ́ndəns) *n.* the quality or state of being superabundant ‖ an excess [fr. L.L. *superabundantia*]

su·per·a·bun·dant (su:pərəbʌ́ndənt) *adj.* abounding in great or too great quantity [fr. L.L. *superabundans* (*superabundantis*), to superabound]

su·per·ac·ti·nide series (sú:pərǽktənaid) *n.* hypothetical heavy elements 122 to 153

su·per·add (su:pərǽd) *v.t.* to add (something) to something that has already been added to [fr. L. *superaddere*]

su·per·al·loy (sú:pərǽlɔi) *n.* a metal alloy with the capacity to resist high stresses, temperatures, etc.

su·per·an·nu·ate (su:pərǽnju:eit) *v. pres. part.* **su·per·an·nu·at·ing** *past and past part.* **su·per·an·nu·at·ed** *v.t.* to cause to retire on pension, esp. because of old age ‖ *v.i.* to become retired, esp. because of old age [back-formation fr. SUPERANNUATED]

su·per·an·nu·at·ed (su:pərǽnju:eitid) *adj.* out-of-date ‖ disqualified from work, usually on a pension, esp. because of old age [fr. Mod. L. *superannuatus*]

su·per·an·nu·a·tion (su:pərænju:éiʃən) *n.* a superannuating or being superannuated ‖ a pension received by a superannuated person [fr. SUPERANNUATE or SUPERANNUATED]

su·perb (supə́:rb) *adj.* of the highest quality ‖ magnificent to behold ‖ majestic in size, proportions etc. [fr. L. *superbus*, proud]

Super Bowl annual championship game of winners of American and National Football Leagues; played in January since 1967

su·per·cal·en·der (su:pərkǽləndər) **1.** *n.* a calender consisting of highly polished rollers which impart a smooth, glazed finish to paper etc. **2.** *v.t.* to process with a supercalender

su·per·car·go (sú:pərkɑrgou) *pl.* **su·per·car·gos, su·per·car·goes** *n.* an officer in a merchant ship in charge of cargo and all commercial affairs [alt. of earlier *supracargo* fr. Span. *sobrecargo*]

su·per·charge (sú:pərtʃɑrdʒ) *pres. part.* **su·per·charg·ing** *past* and *past part.* **su·per·charged** *v.t.* to force air and/or fuel under pressure into (an internal-combustion engine) to increase its power **sú·per·charg·er** *n.* a mechanism (e.g. a pump or compressor) used to supply an internal-combustion engine with a greater volume of air than is possible at ambient pressures. It is used on most aircraft engines, for high-performance automotive engines etc.

su·per·cil·i·ar·y (su:pərsíli:eri:) *adj.* of, relating to, or in the region of the eyebrow [fr. Mod. L. *superciliaris* fr. *supercilium*, eyebrow]

su·per·cil·i·ous (su:pərsíli:əs) *adj.* showing patronizing disdain [fr. L. *superciliosus* fr. *supercilium*, eyebrow]

su·per·class (sú:pərklæs, sú:pərklɑs) *n.* (*taxonomy*) a classification ranking between a phylum and a class

su·per·clus·ter (sú:pərklʌstər) *n.* (*astron.*) a large group of galaxies

su·per·con·duc·tiv·i·ty (su:pərkɒndʌktiviti:) *n.* (*phys.*) the property in certain metals (lead, tin, vanadium etc.) and alloys of losing virtually all electrical resistance when cooled below a transition temperature near absolute zero. Practical use of this phenomenon is made esp. in magnetic-computer memory stores **su·per·con·dúc·tor** *n.*

supercontinent *PROTOCONTINENT

su·per·cool (sú:pərkú:l) *v.t.* (*chem.*) to bring to a temperature below the normal transition point for a change of state without this change occurring

supercountry *SUPERPOWER

su·per·cur·rent (sú:pərkʌrənt) *n.* (*electr.*) electrical current running without resistance, as through a metal at or near absolute zero

su·per·dense (sú:pərdens) *adj.* (*astron.*) extremely compacted, e.g., a quasar, a black hole

su·per·e·go (sú:pəri:gou, sú:pəregou) *n.* (*psychoanal.*) the idealized image that a person builds up of himself in response to authority and social pressures. Fundamentally unconscious, it rises to consciousness on critical occasions and serves as a kind of policeman of the personality

su·per·er·o·ga·tion (su:pərerəgéiʃən) *n.* the act or process of doing more than is required by duty or obligation ‖ an instance of this **works of supererogation** (*Roman Catholicism*) the good deeds done, e.g. by saints, over and above those required by God [fr. L.L. *supererogatio* (*supererogationis*)]

su·per·e·rog·a·to·ry (su:pərərɒ́gətɔri:, su:pərərɒ́gətouri:) *adj.* of, relating to, or characterized by supererogation ‖ performed to a degree beyond what is required or promised ‖ (*loosely*) superfluous [fr. M.L. *supererogatorius*]

su·per·fam·i·ly (sú:pərfæməli:, sú:pərfæmli:) *n.* (*taxonomy*) a classification ranking above a family and regarded as being equivalent to a suborder

su·per·fec·ta (sú:pərfektə) *n.* (*wagering*) a wager in which the first four finishers in a race must be selected in proper order *Cf* PERFECTA, TRIFECTA

su·per·fec·un·da·tion (su:pərfekəndéiʃən, su:pərfi:kəndéiʃən) *n.* the successive fertilization of two or more ova during the same ovulation period

su·per·fe·ta·tion, *Br.* also **su·per·foe·ta·tion** (su:pərfitéiʃən) *n.* (*biol.*) the successive fertilization of two or more ova of different ovulations in the same uterus, occurring normally in some viviparous fishes ‖ (*bot.*) the fertilization of an ovule by more than one type of pollen [Mod. L. *superfetatio*]

su·per·fi·cial (su:pərfíʃəl) *adj.* of or relating to a surface ‖ not penetrating further than the surface, *superficial cuts* ‖ apparent rather than real, *a superficial resemblance* ‖ without depth of mind, feeling or imagination ‖ (of a unit of measure) square **su·per·fi·ci·al·i·ty** (su:pərfiʃi:ǽliti:) *n.* **su·per·fí·cial·ly** *adv.* [fr. L. *superficialis*]

su·per·fi·cies (su:pərfíʃi:z, su:pərfíʃi:i:z) *pl.* **su·per·fi·cies** *n.* a surface [L. fr. *super*, above+*facies*, the face]

su·per·fine (su:pərfáin) *adj.* extremely fine

su·per·flu·i·ty (su:pərflú:iti:) *pl.* **su·per·flu·i·ties** *n.* the quality or state of being superfluous ‖ a copious oversupply ‖ (esp. *pl.*) something superfluous [O.F. *superfluité*]

su·per·flu·ous (supə́:rflu:əs) *adj.* being more than is needed, *superfluous words* ‖ not needed, unnecessary, *a superfluous remark* [fr. L. *superfluus*]

superfoetation *SUPERFETATION

su·per·grade (sú:pərgreid) *n.* U.S. Government employment status higher than the highest basic status

su·per·heat 1. (su:pərhí:t) *v.t.* (*chem.*) to bring to a temperature above the normal transition point for a change of state without this change occurring, esp. to heat above boiling point without boiling taking place ‖ to heat (esp. a vapor) not in contact with its liquid to keep it free from suspended liquid droplets, *superheated steam* **2.** (sú:pərhi:t) *n.* the amount of extra heat imparted to a vapor in superheating **su·per·héat·er** *n.* an apparatus for superheating steam

su·per·heav·y (sú:pərhévi:) *adj.* (*phys.*) of elements with a mass greater than known elements, sometimes prefixed by eka-, e.g., ekahafnium

su·per·het·er·o·dyne (su:pərhétərədain) **1.** *adj.* (*radio*) of a widely employed system of radio reception in which the heterodyne principle is used to produce a modulated beat signal of intermediate frequency. Substitution of the intermediate carrier signal for a radio frequency carrier signal permits more efficient amplification and precise tuning of the amplifier circuit to the locally produced beat frequency, the system resulting in a sensitive and selective radio receiver **2.** *n.* (*radio*) such a receiver [fr. SUPERSONIC+HETERODYNE]

su·per·high·way (su:pərháiwei) *n.* an expressway, freeway, turnpike or other main road for high-speed driving

su·per·hu·man (su:pərhjú:mən) *adj.* beyond normal human capacity or power, *superhuman strength* ‖ supernatural, *superhuman intervention* [fr. M.L. *superhumanus*]

su·per·im·pose (su:pərimpóuz) *pres. part.* **su·per·im·pos·ing** *past* and *past part.* **su·per·im·posed** *v.t.* to lay (one thing) on or upon another, *to superimpose speech on recorded music* **su·per·im·po·si·tion** (su:pərimpəzíʃən) *n.* a superimposing or being superimposed

su·per·in·cum·bent (su:pərinkʌ́mbənt) *adj.* lying on something else ‖ (of pressure) exerted from above [fr. L. *superincumbens* (*superincumbentis*) fr. *superincumbere*, to lie on]

su·per·in·tend (su:pərinténd) *v.t.* to direct the execution of (e.g. a job of work) ‖ to have charge of (a group of people) [fr. eccles. L. *superintendere*]

su·per·in·tend·ence (su:pərinténdəns) *n.* the act or function of superintending **su·per·in·ténd·en·cy** *n.* the office, rank or jurisdiction of a superintendent ‖ superintendence [fr. M.L. *superintendentia*]

su·per·in·tend·ent (su:pərinténdənt) *n.* a person who superintends ‖ the head of a police department ‖ the custodian of a building ‖ (*Br.*) a police officer ranking just above an inspector [eccles. L. *superintendens* (*superintendentis*) fr. *superintendere*]

su·pe·ri·or (supíəri:ər) **1.** *adj.* high or higher in position, rank, status etc. ‖ better in quality, worth, ability etc. ‖ greater in value, amount, power etc. ‖ showing that one thinks oneself better than others, *a superior smile* ‖ (*astron.*) farther from the sun than the earth, *a superior planet* ‖ (*bot.*) growing or arising from another part or organ ‖ (*anat.*) situated above a like part or organ, or above the normal position ‖ (*printing*, of a character) placed above the line of type, e.g. '3' in 'a³' **2.** *n.* a person who is superior in rank or authority ‖ a person who controls a religious community ‖ (*printing*) a superior character **su·pe·ri·or·i·ty** (supiəri:ɔ́riti:, supiəri:ɒ́riti:) *n.* [O.F.]

superiority complex a neurotic condition resulting from subconscious belief in one's superiority to others

Superior, Lake the most northwesterly of the Great Lakes of North America, and one of the world's largest sheets of fresh water (area 31,820 sq. miles, maximum depth 1,180 ft). It is bounded by the U.S.A. and Canada and is joined to Lakes Michigan and Huron by the St Mary River. Part of the St Lawrence Seaway system, it carries a large volume of grain and iron ore shipments. Main ports: Port Arthur and Thunder Bay, Ontario, and Duluth, Minnesota

su·per·jet (sú:pərdʒet) *n.* a supersonic jet aircraft

su·per·la·tive (supə́:rlətiv) **1.** *adj.* of the highest quality, kind, degree etc. ‖ excessive ‖ (*gram.*) expressing the highest degree of comparison of the quality indicated by the adjective or adverb (usually shown in English by the addition of '-est' or by the use of 'most' with the positive form) **2.** *n.* the highest degree of something ‖ someone or something superlative ‖ (*gram.*) the superlative degree of comparison ‖ (*gram.*) a word or form in this degree (esp. *pl.*) highly exaggerated language [O.F. *superlatif*]

su·per·lu·na·ry (su:pərlú:nəri:) *adj.* situated above the moon [fr. SUPER-+ L. *luna*, moon]

su·per·man (sú:pərmæn) *pl.* **su·per·men** (sú:pərmen) *n.* an idealized man, regarded by Nietzsche as the next stage in the evolution of man: a being with greatly superior physical and mental qualities ‖ (*loosely*) a person who possesses greatly developed physical or mental qualities

su·per·mar·ket (sú:pərmɑrkit) *n.* a large self-service food and household goods store, the articles being arranged in open-shelf display

su·per·min·i·com·put·er (sú:pərmíni:cʌmpjú:tər) *n.* (*computer*) processing unit with a 32-bit capacity

su·per·mol·e·cule (sú:pərmɒ́ləkju:l) *n.* (*phys.*) a molecule composed of more than one molecule, e.g., anomalous water, a polymer, a protein —

CONCISE PRONUNCIATION KEY: **(a)** æ, *cat*; ɑ, *car*; ɔ *fawn*; ei, *snake*. **(e)** e, *hen*; i:, *sheep*; iə, *deer*; εə, *bear*. **(i)** i, *fish*; ai, *tiger*; ə:, *bird*. **(o)** o, *ox*; au, *cow*; ou, *goat*; u, *poor*; ɔi, *royal*. **(u)** ʌ, *duck*; u, *bull*; u:, *goose*; ə, *bacillus*; ju:, *cube*. x, *loch*; θ, *think*; ð, *bother*; z, *Zen*; ʒ, *corsage*; dʒ, *savage*; ŋ, *orangutang*; j, *yak*; ʃ, *fish*; tʃ, *fetch*; 'l, *rabble*; 'n, *redden*. Complete pronunciation key appears inside front cover.

supermolecular *adj.* —**supramolecular** *adj.*
su·per·mul·ti·plet (sú:pərmʌltəplet) *n.* (*nuclear phys.*) a group consisting of smaller groups of nuclear particles
su·per·nal (supə́:rn'l) *adj.* (*rhet.*) pertaining to a celestial realm [O.F.]
su·per·na·tant (sụ:pərnéit'nt) *adj.* floating on the surface (e.g. of a clear liquid above a precipitate) [fr. L. *supernatans* (*supernatantis*) fr. *supernatare,* to float]
su·per·nat·u·ral (sụ:pərnǽtʃərəl) **1.** *adj.* not able to be explained in terms of the known laws which govern the material universe, *a supernatural phenomenon* **2.** *n.* (with 'the') that realm of experience which is inexplicable in terms of the known laws of nature ‖ a supernatural ‖ being, force etc. **su·per·nát·u·ral·ism** *n.* the quality or state of being supernatural belief in the supernatural **su·per·nát·u·ral·ist** *n.* **su·per·nat·u·ral·is·tic** *adj.* **su·per·nát·u·ral·ize** *v.t. pres. part.* **su·per·nat·u·ral·iz·ing** *past* and *past part.* **su·per·nát·u·ral·ized** to make supernatural ‖ to treat as supernatural [fr. M.L. *supernaturalis*]
su·per·no·va (sụ:pərnóuvə) *n.* (*astron.*) a nova with the brightness of many millions of suns, occurring very rarely ‖ a star that has exhausted its nuclear fuel, collapsed into a superdense state, and exploded with a final burst of enormous energy, releasing in one second an energy equivalent to that released by the sun in 60 years [Mod. L. fr. *super-*, above+NOVA]
su·per·nuke (sú:pərnu:k) *n.* (*slang*) a technical adviser in a nuclear energy plant
su·per·nu·mer·ar·y (sụ:pərnú:mərẹri:, su:pərnjú:mərẹri:) **1.** *adj.* above the prescribed number, extra ‖ superfluous **2.** *pl.* **su·per·nu·mer·ar·ies** *n.* a supernumerary person or thing ‖ a person employed for use as need directs rather than for regular service ‖ (*theater*) an actor having a small part, e.g. in a crowd scene [fr. L.L. *supernumerarius*]
su·per·or·der (sụ:pərɔ́rdər) *n.* (*taxonomy*) a classification ranking between an order and a class or subclass
su·per·o·vu·late (sú:pərɒ́vju:leit) *v.* to produce more eggs at one time than is normal —**superovulation** *n.*
su·per·phos·phate (sụ:pərfɒ́sfeit) *n.* any of various commercial phosphate fertilizers obtained by acidulating ground, insoluble phosphate rock
su·per·plas·tic (sú:pərplæstik) *adj.* of the ability to change form easily under heat or other treatment —**superplasticity** *n.*
su·per·pose (sụ:pərpóuz) *pres. part.* **su·per·pos·ing** *past* and *past part.* **su·per·posed** *v.t.* to place over, or upon, something else ‖ (*geom.*) to place (a figure) over another so that like parts of each coincide [F. *superposer*]
su·per·po·si·tion (sụ:pərpəzíʃən) *n.* a superposing or being superposed (*PRINCIPLE OF SUPERPOSITION) [F.]
su·per·po·tent (sú:pərpóutənt) *adj.* having excessive power
su·per·pow·er (sú:pərpauər) *n.* a nation which, by reason of its economic, political and military strength, influences the polices of less powerful nations
Super Sabre (*mil.*) a supersonic, single-engine, turbojet, tactical fighter/bomber (F-100), capable of employing nuclear and nonnuclear weapons
su·per·sat·u·rate (sụ:pərsǽtʃəreit) *pres. part.* **su·per·sat·u·rat·ing** *past* and *past part.* **su·per·sat·u·rat·ed** *v.t.* (*chem.*) to produce a solution of (something) or to produce (a solution) having a higher concentration of solute than at saturation, e.g. by the heating and slow undisturbed cooling or very rapid cooling of a saturated solution **su·per·sat·u·rá·tion** *n.*
su·per·scribe (sú:pərskraib, sụ:pərskráib) *pres. part.* **su·per·scrib·ing** *past* and *past part.* **su·per·scribed** *v.t.* to write (something) upon, put (an inscription) on or over something ‖ to write an inscription on the top or surface or outside of (something) [fr. L.L. *superscribere*]
su·per·script (sú:pərskript) **1.** *adj.* of, relating to, or being a character printed or written directly above, or above and to the side of another character, e.g. the acute accent on the final 'a' of 'Paraná' or the '3' in 'p^3' (cf. SUBSCRIPT) **2.** *n.* a superscript character [fr. L. *superscriptus*]
su·per·scrip·tion (sụ:pərskrípʃən) *n.* the act of superscribing ‖ that which is superscribed ‖ (*pharm.*) the Latin word 'recipe' or its symbol ℞ on a prescription [fr. L.L. *superscriptio* (*superscriptionis*)]
su·per·sede (sụ:pərsí:d) *pres. part.* **su·per·sed·ing** *past* and *past part.* **su·per·sed·ed** *v.t.* to outmode and take the place of, *buses superseded streetcars* ‖ to take the position, office etc. of, *to supersede someone as treasurer* ‖ to replace, to *supersede a written test by an oral* **su·per·se·dure** (sụ:pərsí:dʒər) *n.* supersession, esp. the superseding of an old or inferior queen bee by a better one [O.F. *superseder*]
su·per·sen·si·ble (sụ:pərsénsəb'l) *adj.* beyond the grasp of the senses **su·per·sén·si·bly** *adv.*
su·per·sen·so·ry (sụ:pərsénsəri:) *adj.* supersensible
su·per·sen·su·al (sụ:pərsénʃu:əl) *adj.* supersensible
su·per·ses·sion (sụ:pərséʃən) *n.* a superseding or being superseded [fr. M. L. *supersessio* (*supersessionis*)]
super set (*weight lifting*) exercises for a set of muscles, followed by exercises for an opposing set of muscles
super ship a large cargo ship capable of sailing around South America
su·per·son·ic (sụ:pərsɒ́nik) *adj.* of waves of greater frequency than those to which the human ear responds (above about 20,000 cycles per second, esp. in electronics) ‖ of motion faster than the speed of sound waves in air (above about 738 m.p.h.) ‖ moving at this speed **su·per·són·ics** *n.* the science dealing with supersonic phenomena (*SONIC, *SUBSONIC)
su·per·star (sú:pərstɑr) *n.* **1.** (*astron.*) a celestial body, emitting great energy, e.g., quasar **2.** a widely known personality of superior talent in the entertainment field or, by extension, in another field —**superstardom** *n.*
su·per·sta·tion (sú:pərstẹiʃən) *n.* a television station with national satellite connections
su·per·sti·tion (sụ:pərstíʃən) *n.* a belief or beliefs justified neither by reason nor evidence nor by any religious canon [O.F.]
su·per·sti·tious (sụ:pərstíʃəs) *adj.* of or relating to superstition ‖ manifesting superstition [O.F. *superstitieux*]
su·per·stra·tum (sú:pərstrẹitəm, sú:pərstrætəm, sú:pərstrɑtəm) *pl.* **su·per·stra·ta** (sú:pərstrẹitə, sú:pərstrætə, sú:pərstrɑtə), **su·per·stra·tums** *n.* a stratum overlying another
su·per·struc·ture (sú:pərstrʌktʃər) *n.* a structure built upon another structure ‖ (*archit.*) the entire building above the main supporting level ‖ (*naut.*) the structure of a ship above the main deck
su·per·tax (sú:pərtæks) *n.* (*Br. hist.*) tax at above the normal rate, on income over a certain level, replaced by surtax
su·per·ton·ic (sụ:pərtɒ́nik) *n.* (*mus.*) the second degree of the major or minor scale, next above the tonic
su·per·vene (sụ:pərví:n) *pres. part.* **su·per·ven·ing** *past* and *past part.* **su·per·vened** *v.i.* to happen unexpectedly and in a way which has the effect of preventing or radically changing some planned course of action ‖ to follow closely after some event or set of circumstances [fr. L. *supervenire*]
su·per·ven·ient (sụ:pərví:njənt) *adj.* supervening as something added, *supervenient grace* [fr. L. *superveniens* (*supervenientis*) fr. *supervenire,* to supervene]
su·per·ven·tion (sụ:pərvénʃən) *n.* the act or process of supervening ‖ a supervening event [fr. L.L. *superventio* (*superventionis*)]
Su·per·vielle (sypərvjel), Jules (1884–1960), French poet. He was born in Montevideo and lived in Uruguay for many years. His most famous poems are 'Gravitations' (1925), 'Naissances' (1951) and 'le Corps tragique' (1959). He also wrote short stories and plays
su·per·vise (sú:pərvaiz) *pres. part.* **su·per·vis·ing** *past* and *past part.* **su·per·vised** *v.t.* to superintend (work or the person doing it) [fr. M.L. *supervidere* (*supervisus*)]
su·per·vi·sion (sụ:pərvíʒən) *n.* a supervising or being supervised [fr. M.L. *supervisio* (*supervisionis*)]
su·per·vi·sor (sú:pərvạizər) *n.* a person who supervises ‖ (*education*) a person in some school systems who supervises teachers in planning, method etc. or in the teaching of special courses **su·per·vi·so·ry** *adj.* of or relating to supervision, *supervisory duties* [M.L.]
su·pi·nate (sú:pineit) *pres. part.* **su·pi·nat·ing** *past* and *past part.* **su·pi·nat·ed** *v.t.* to turn (a hand or hand and arm) so that the palm is upward (cf. PRONATE) [fr. L. *supinare* (*supinatus*), to lay backward]
su·pi·na·tion (sụ:pinéiʃən) *n.* a supinating or being supinated ‖ the position resulting from this [fr. L. *supinatio* (*supinationis*)]
su·pi·na·tor (sú:pinẹitər) *n.* a muscle in the forearm which causes supination [Mod. L. fr. *supinare,* supinate]
su·pine (su:páin) **1.** *adj.* lying flat on the back (opp. PRONE) ‖ (of a hand) with the palm upward or away from the body ‖ listless through laziness or indifference or both **2.** *n.* (*Latin gram.*) a verbal noun formed from the past participle and having only two forms, accusative and ablative [fr. L. *supinus*]
sup·per (sʌ́pər) *n.* a light meal taken in the evening ‖ the evening meal eaten by those who have dinner at midday [O.F. *soper, super, souper*]
sup·plant (səplǽnt, səplɑ́nt) *v.t.* to supersede (another) esp. by force, cunning etc. ‖ to take the place of, *why should tea supplant coffee as a national drink?* [O. F. *supplanter*]
sup·ple (sʌ́p'l) **1.** *adj.* easily bent, *a supple bow of yew* ‖ (of the body, limbs etc.) able to bend without effort, *supple fingers* ‖ (of a person or his mind) readily changing to meet new situations **2.** *pres. part.* **sup·pling** *past* and *past part.* **sup·pled** *v.t.* to make supple [O.F. fr. L. *supplex,* bending under]
sup·ple·ly (sʌ́p'li:) *adv.* in a supple manner
sup·ple·ment 1. (sʌ́pləmənt) *n.* something added ‖ a section added to a book etc., or a separate volume, giving additional information etc. ‖ a separate section issued with a newspaper containing feature articles etc. ‖ (*math.*) the amount to be added to a given angle or arc to make 180° or a semicircle **2.** *v.t.* to add to, *to supplement one's pay* ‖ to supply a déficiency in **sup·ple·men·tal** (sʌpləmént'l), **sup·ple·mén·ta·ry** *adjs.* [fr. L. *supplementum*]
supplementary angles two angles whose sum is 180°
sup·ple·men·ta·tion (sʌpləmentéiʃən) *n.* the act or process of supplementing ‖ an instance of supplementing
sup·pli·ant (sʌ́pli:ənt) **1.** *adj.* (*rhet.*) asking humbly ‖ (*rhet.*) expressing supplication, *a suppliant prayer* **2.** *n.* (*rhet.*) a person who supplicates [F.]
sup·pli·cant (sʌ́plikənt) **1.** *n.* a suppliant **2.** *adj.* supplicating [fr. L. *supplicans* fr. *supplicare,* to supplicate]
sup·pli·cate (sʌ́plikeit) *pres. part.* **sup·pli·cat·ing** *past* and *past part.* **sup·pli·cat·ed** *v.t.* to ask for in humble petition ‖ to entreat (God, a person) for something ‖ *v.i.* to make humble entreaty [fr. L. *supplicare* (*supplicatus*)]
sup·pli·ca·tion (sʌplikéiʃən) *n.* the act or process of supplicating ‖ a humble request, prayer etc. [O.F.]
sup·pli·ca·to·ry (sʌ́plikətɔri:, sʌ́plikətouri:) *adj.* supplicating [fr. M.L. *supplicatorius*]
sup·pli·er (səpláiər) *n.* someone who, or something which, supplies
sup·ply (səplái) **1.** *v. pres. part.* **sup·ply·ing** *past* and *past part.* **sup·plied** *v.t.* to give (something needed or wanted), *to supply necessary tools* ‖ to fill the needs of, *to supply a town with electricity* ‖ to satisfy (a need), *to supply proof* ‖ to furnish (something that was missing), to *supply a deficiency* ‖ to serve as a substitute for (a clergyman), or occupy (his church or pulpit) for him ‖ *v.i.* to act as substitute for a clergyman **2.** *pl.* **sup·plies** *n.* the act of supplying ‖ (often *pl.*) stock or stores available for use ‖ (*pl.*) stores for the armed forces ‖ (*pl.*) money granted for the expenses of a government ‖ (*econ.*) the amount or quantity of goods available on the market for purchase ‖ a clergyman who temporarily fills another clergyman's place [fr. O.F. *sopleer, soupleer*]
sup·ply (sʌ́pli:) *adv.* supplely
sup·ply-side (sʌpláisaid) *n.* (*economics*) approach to solution of economic problems with emphasis on increasing (or decreasing) the total supply of products, e.g., to reduce (or increase) prices
sup·ply teacher (səplái) (*Br.*) a teacher unassigned to a particular school but available to fill a temporary vacancy
sup·port (səpɔ́rt) **1.** *v.t.* to carry the weight of ‖ to prevent from falling, sinking etc., *to support a roof by struts* ‖ to be actively in favor of, *to support a cause* ‖ to assist or strengthen morally, *she supported him in his struggle* ‖ to be or provide an argument in favor of or additional

evidence for, *this supports his theory* || to bear, endure, *to support extremes of climate* || to bear the cost of providing for, *to support a family* || to give assistance to (troops already engaged) || to act with (a principal actor or actors) in a secondary role || to second (a resolution in committee) || (*heraldry*, only in passive) to flank as supporter **2.** *n.* a supporting or being supported || someone who or something which supports || a means of sustenance **sup·pórt·a·ble** *adj.* **sup·pórt·er** *n.* a person who supports a cause, team etc. || a partisan || (*heraldry*) one of a pair of figures standing beside or supporting the shield **sup·port·ive** (səpɔ́rtiv, səpóurtiv) *adj.* providing support [fr. O.F. or F. *supporter*]

support hose stockings with elastic threads

support level (*securities*) a price level at which customers customarily enter the market to buy

sup·pos·a·ble (səpóuzəb'l) *adj.* able to be supposed

sup·pose (səpóuz) *pres. part.* **sup·pos·ing** *past* and *past part.* **sup·posed** *v.t.* to think likely, *I suppose he may come today* || to presume, believe without firm cause, *I supposed him to be away from home* || to admit as a possibility or probability, *I suppose you know what to do* || (used in the imperative) to imagine (something) so as to consider an effect, *suppose you miss your train*, or as the basis, or illustration, of an argument, *suppose this grain of sand to be the universe* || (of a theory etc.) to postulate, presuppose || (used in passive) to expect, require, as being desired, *I'm supposed to tell you about it* **sup·posed** (səpóuzd, səpóuzid) *adj.* thought, but not known, to be true, *his supposed death by drowning* || imagined, *supposed profits* **sup·pos·ed·ly** (səpóuzidli:) *adv.* **sup·pos·ing** *conj.* on the supposition that, in the event that [O.F. *supposer*]

sup·po·si·tion (sʌpəzíʃən) *n.* the act of supposing || that which is supposed || **sup·po·sí·tion·al** *adj.* [O.F.]

sup·pos·i·to·ry (səpɒ́zitɔri:, səpɒ́zitouri:) *pl.* **sup·pos·i·to·ries** *n.* a cylinder, cone or oval made of cacao butter etc. which is inserted into the rectum or vagina, where it dissolves and releases the medicament it contains [fr. L.L. *suppositorium*]

sup·press (səprés) *v.t.* to subdue, put down by force, *to suppress a revolt* || to withhold (facts etc.) || to hold back, *to suppress laughter* || to prevent the publication or revelation of || to check the flow of, stop || to dismiss from the conscious mind [fr. L. *supprimere* (*suppressus*)]

sup·pres·sion (səpréʃən) *n.* a suppressing or being suppressed || the conscious dismissing of an unacceptable idea, desire, painful memory etc. from the mind (cf. REPRESSION) [fr. L. *suppressio* (*suppressionis*)]

sup·pu·rate (sʌ́pjureit) *pres. part.* **sup·pu·rat·ing** *past* and *past part.* **sup·pu·rat·ed** *v.i.* to discharge pus [fr. L. *suppurare* (*suppuratus*)]

sup·pu·ra·tion (sʌpjuréiʃən) *n.* the formation or discharging of pus

sup·pu·ra·tive (sʌ́pjureitiv) *adj.* characterized by suppuration [fr. Mod. L. *supperativus*]

su·pra·cel·lu·lar (su:prəséljuːlər) *adj.* having more than a single cell

su·pra·lap·sar·i·an (su:prəlæpséəri:ən) **1.** *n.* a believer in the Calvinist doctrine that predestination preceded man's creation and fall (cf. INFRALAPSARIAN) **2.** *adj.* of or relating to this doctrine or to someone holding it **su·pra·lap·sár·i·an·ism** *n.* [fr. Mod. L. *supralapsarius*]

su·pra·lim·i·nal (su:prəlímin'l) *adj.* conscious, rising above the threshold of consciousness (cf. SUBLIMINAL) [fr. L. *supra*, above, over+*limen* (*liminis*), threshold]

su·pra·re·nal (su:prərí:n'l) **1.** *adj.* adrenal **2.** *n.* an adrenal gland [fr. Mod. L. *suprarenalis*]

suprarenal gland an adrenal gland

su·pra·ther·mal ion detector (sú:prəθə:rm'l) a device for recording information about ions on lunar surfaces

su·prem·a·cy (suprémǝsi:) *n.* the quality or state of being supreme || the position of being superior to all others in something, *naval supremacy*

Supremacy, Act of (*Eng. hist.*) an act of parliament (1559) proclaiming the sovereign supreme head of the Church of England

su·preme (suprí:m) *adj.* being the highest authority || highest in quality || highest in degree [fr. L. *supremus* superl. of *superus*, that is above]

Supreme Being God

Supreme Court the highest judicial body in the U.S.A., consisting of nine members appointed for life by the President with the Senate's approval || its equivalent in some other countries || the highest judicial body in some states of the U.S.A.

Supreme Court of Judicature the high court system of England and Wales, established by acts of parliament (1873, 1875), which incorporates several former courts. It includes the Court of Appeal and the High Court of Justice, which has divisions of Chancery, King's Bench, probate, divorce and admiralty

supreme sacrifice the sacrifice of one's life, esp. as an act of heroism

Supreme Soviet the highest legislative body of the U.S.S.R., consisting of two elected chambers of equal status, the Soviet of the Union and the Soviet of Nationalities (1,443 members in all). It appoints the presidium of the Supreme Soviet, which acts as the supreme authority between sessions, and the Council of Ministers, the highest executive and administrative body

su·pre·mo (səprí:mou) *n.* (*Br.*) **1.** person in charge **2.** the head of an organization

Suppression of Communism Act in Republic of South Africa, law restricting the speech, writing, or gathering of nonwhites

suq *SOUK

Sur (suər) *TYRE

su·ra (súərə) *n.* any of the sections or chapters in the Koran [Arab. *sūrah*, step]

Su·ra·ba·ya, Soe·ra·ba·ya (suərəbájə) a port (pop. 2,289,000) in N. Java, Indonesia, at the west end of Madura Strait. Industries: mechanical and electrical engineering, chemicals, oil refining, textiles. University

su·rah (súərə) *n.* soft twilled silk or rayon used in clothing [perh. after SURAT in India]

Su·ra·kar·ta, Soe·ra·kar·ta (suərəkúrtə) a commercial center (pop. 368,000) in central S. Java, Indonesia. Industries: textiles, food processing, machinery

su·ral (súərəl) *adj.* (*anat.*) of or relating to the calf of the leg [fr. Mod. L. *suralis* fr. *sura*, calf of the leg]

Su·rat (sú:rət, surǽt) a port (pop. 471,656) in Gujarat, India, on the Tapti near its mouth: silk and cotton textiles, brocades, carpets, inlaid work

sur·charge (sə́:rtʃɑrdʒ) **1.** *v.t. pres. part.* **sur·charg·ing** *past* and *past part.* **sur·charged** to overcharge (a person or an amount) || to overprint (a stamp) with a surcharge || to overload || to overfill || (*law*) to make as an additional charge, *to surcharge legal fees involved in collecting an account* **2.** *n.* a charge or tax over and above what is standard || an overprint on a stamp (esp. to change its value), or the stamp bearing this || (*Br.*) a charge made for delivering an unstamped or understamped letter etc. || an additional burden || (*law*) a surcharging || (*law*) a statement showing this [O.F. *surcharger*]

sur·cin·gle (sə́:rsiŋg'l) *n.* a belt passing under a horse's belly to keep its blanket or pack in place [O.F. *surcengle*]

sur·coat (sə́:rkout) *n.* (*hist.*) a loose tunic worn over armor || (*hist.*) a long or short fitted robe worn in the late Middle Ages by men and women [O.F. *surcot, sorcot, sircot*]

surd (sə:rd) **1.** *adj.* (*math.*, of a quantity) irrational || (*phon.*) voiceless **2.** *n.* an irrational number || a voiceless speech sound (opp. SONANT) [fr. L. *surdus*, deaf, trans. Gk *alogos*, without reason]

sure (ʃuər) **1.** *adj.* accepted as the truth, *a sure sign of rain* || accepting something as true, I *am sure it will rain* || that can be relied upon, *a sure friend, a sure winner, a sure profit* || safe, *to make a rope sure* **2.** *adv.* (*pop.*) certainly **for sure** certainly, *we leave tomorrow for sure* **sure enough** just as expected or promised, *we cleaned the spark plugs and sure enough it started* **to be sure** certainly || admittedly to **make sure** to make certain [O.F. *sure, seure*]

sure·fire (ʃúərfaiər) *adj.* that can be relied on to be successful, do as is expected etc.

sure·foot·ed (ʃúərfútid) *adj.* placing the feet with certainty in difficult terrain

sure·ly (ʃúərli:) *adv.* in a sure manner || without a doubt

sure·ty (ʃúəriti:, ʃúərti:) *pl.* **sure·ties** *n.* the condition of being sure || a person who makes himself a guarantor for another's actions || something pledged as security **to stand surety** to pledge a sum of money for a person's appearance in court or for his payment of a debt [O.F. *surte, seurte*]

surf (sə:rf) **1.** *n.* the foam of waves breaking on the shore || the swell of the sea breaking on the shore **2.** *v.i.* to ride a wave to shore on a surfboard [etym. doubtful]

sur·face (sə́:rfis) **1.** *n.* the two-dimensional boundary of a material body, having zero or constant or variable curvature, *the surface of the earth* || (*geom.*) that which has length and breadth but no depth || the outward aspect of something, *a mere surface of sophistication* || (*aeron.*) an airfoil **on the surface** so far as the eye can judge **2.** *v. pres. part.* **sur·fac·ing** *past* and *past part.* **sur·faced** *v.t.* to smooth the surface of, to polish || to bring (e.g. a submarine) to the surface of the water || *v.i.* to come to the surface of the water || (*mining*) to work at or near the surface **3.** *adj.* of or at the surface || (*mining*) working at or near the surface || superficial [F.]

sur·face-ac·tive (sə́:rfisǽktiv) *adj.* of or pertaining to a substance that modifies the behavior of a liquid at its surfaces and interfaces (but not in the interior of the liquid), usually by changing the surface tension or interfacial tension of the liquid

sur·face-ef·fect ship (sə́:rfisifekt) an air-cushion vehicle that operates over water; e.g., a Hovercraft *Cf* GROUND-EFFECT MACHINE

surface plate (*mech.*) a steel plate used as a standard of flatness in precision work

surface structure (*linguistics*) in transformational grammar, the sentence structure expressed phonetically *Cf* DEEP STRUCTURE

surface tension a condition of (usually) liquid surfaces that causes liquids to tend to assume shapes of minimum surface and is the result of unbalanced intermolecular forces acting near the surfaces. It may be treated quantitatively as if the surface of a liquid were a thin elastic membrane under tension (*CAPILLARITY)

sur·face-to-air-missile (sə:rfistu:ɛərmís'l) *n.* (*mil.*) an earth-launched guided missile with an airborne target *acronym* SAM

surface-to-air missile envelope (*mil.*) the air space within the kill capabilities of a surface-to-air missile system

sur·fac·tant (sə:rfǽktənt) *n.* (*chem.*) **1.** a substance that facilitates the spreading of another substance, e.g., a detergent *also* surface-active agent **2.** an oil-water compound for application on skin or hair

surf and turf seafood and beef, e.g., in a restaurant, lobster and steak

surf·board (sə́:rfbɔrd, sə:rfbourd) *n.* a long narrow board used in riding in to shore on the surf

surf·boat (sə́:rfbout) *n.* a boat specially adapted to travel through the surf

sur·feit (sə́:rfit) **1.** *n.* an oversupply, excess, *a surfeit of apples* || overindulgence in eating and drinking || the feeling resulting from this **2.** *v.t.* to oversupply, *to surfeit a market* || to overfeed || to satiate [A.F., O.F. *sorfait*]

surfer's knot (*surfing*) a friction bump at knee or instep characteristic of active surfers

surf roof a removable ceiling panel in a motor vehicle

surge (sə:rdʒ) **1.** *v. pres. part.* **surg·ing** *past* and *past part.* **surged** *v.i.* (of the sea) to heave and swell in great force and agitation || to move through, or as if through, heavy seas, *a surging ship, surging crowds, surging emotions* || (*naut.*, of a rope or chain) to slip around the windlass etc. with a jerk || (*elec.*, of current) to make a sudden short rise followed by a drop || *v.t.* (*naut.*) to slip (a rope or chain) around the windlass etc. **2.** *n.* the heaving of waves || a great billow || a sudden access of interest, enthusiasm, pity etc. || (*naut.*) the tapered part of a windlass etc. on which the rope or chain slips || (*naut.*) the slipping movement of the rope or chain || (*elec.*) a sudden abnormal rise of current followed by a drop [fr. L. *surgere*, to rise]

sur·geon (sə́:rdʒən) *n.* a medical practitioner who performs surgery || a surgeonfish [A.F. *surgien*, O.F. *cirurgien*]

sur·geon·fish (sə́:rdʒənfiʃ) *pl.* **sur·geon·fish, sur·geon·fish·es** *n.* any of various fishes of fam. *Teuthididae*, having one or more movable lance-shaped spines on each side of the end of the tail

surgeon's knot a reef knot in which the first loop has two turns, used esp. in tying ligatures and surgical stitches

sur·ger·y (sə́:rdʒəri:) *pl.* **sur·ger·ies** *n.* the work of a surgeon in operating manually or instrumentally upon injuries, defects etc. || the branch of medicine dealing with this || the operating theater of a surgeon or hospital || (*Br.*) a doctor's, dentist's or veterinary surgeon's consulting room or dispensary [fr. O.F. *surgerie*]

sur·gi·cal (sə́:rdʒik'l) *adj.* of or relating to surgeons or surgery || used in surgery || resulting from surgery

su·ri·cate (súərikeit) *n. Suricata tetradactyla,* fam. *Viverridae,* a four-toed gray and black S. African mammal related to the mongoose [F. *surikate* fr. Afrik. prob. fr. native name]

Su·ri·name (sµərənǽm) (formerly Dutch or Netherlands Guiana) a republic (area 55,143 sq. miles, pop. 377,000) in N.E. South America. Capital: Paramaribo. People: 30% mulatto, 37% Asian Indian, 15% Indonesian, 10% Bush Negro, 1% Indian, 1% European, 1% Chinese. Religion: 20% Moslem, 20% Hindu, 20% Protestant, 16% Roman Catholic, 1% Confucian. Languages: Dutch (official), English, local patois. The land is mainly forest (gum and dyewoods, tropical hardwoods). Under 3% is cultivated. Hills in the center and south rise to 4,200 ft. Average temperature (F.): 75°-85°. Rainfall: over 100 ins along the coast, lower inland. Agricultural products (coastal belt only): rice, sugarcane, cocoa, coffee, corn, rum, tropical fruits. Forestry products: balata rubber, railroad ties, fuel, lumber. Mineral resources: bauxite. Exports: bauxite, lumber and plywood, rice, fruit. Imports: machinery, fuels and oil, textiles, food, vehicles. Monetary unit: Suriname guilder. HISTORY. Suriname was colonized by the English (17th c.) and was captured by the Dutch (1667). The colony was developed by slave labor (18th c.). It was again held by Britain (1799-1802 and 1804-14). Indian and Javanese laborers immigrated (19th c.). Suriname was integrated into the Netherlands (1922), gained self-government (1955) and full independence as a parliamentary republic (1975). The government was overthrown (1980) and a national military council assumed power

Su·ri·na·me (sµərinúmə) a river (c. 300 miles long) in N. Suriname, flowing into the Atlantic at Paramaribo

sur·li·ly (sə́:rlili:) *adv.* in a surly manner

sur·li·ness (sə́:rli:nis) *n.* the state or quality of being surly

sur·ly (sə́:rli:) *comp.* **sur·li·er** *superl.* **sur·li·est** *adj.* uncivil, bad-tempered [earlier *sirly,* masterful fr. SIR]

sur·mise 1. (sərmáiz, sə́:rmaiz) *n.* a supposition based on very slight evidence **2.** (sərmáiz) *v. pres. part.* **sur·mis·ing** *past* and *past part.* **sur·mised** *v.t.* to guess || *v.i.* to make a guess, suppose [O. F. *surmise,* accusation]

sur·mount (sə:rmáunt) *v.t.* to overcome, *to surmount a difficulty* || to place on the top of || to climb over || to surpass in height || to lie at the top of [A.F., O.F. *surmunter*]

sur·name (sə́:rneim) **1.** *n.* a family name || (*hist.*) a name attached to a person, e.g. by reason of his occupation or place of birth or residence, later developing into such a family name **2.** *v.t. pres. part.* **sur·nam·ing** *past* and *past part.* **sur·named** (*hist.*) to give a surname to [after A.F., O.F. *surnum, sornom*]

sur·pass (sərpǽs, sərpús) *v.t.* to excel || to exceed, *to surpass all expectations* **sur·páss·ing** *adj.* [F. *surpasser*]

sur·plice (sə́:rplis) *n.* (*eccles.*) a white, loose, linen vestment having wide sleeves, worn by officiating clergy and choristers [A.F. *surpliz,* O.F. *sourpeliz*]

sur·plus (sə́:rplʌs, sə́:rpləs) **1.** *n.* excess in receipts over expenditure, *budget surplus* || something left over and not required, *a surplus of stock* **2.** *adj.* in excess of requirements, *surplus stock* [A.F., O.F.]

sur·plus·age (sə́:rplʌsidʒ) *n.* surplus || unnecessary words, esp. (*law*) superfluous matter in a plea or indictment [fr. M.L. *surplusagium*]

surplus value (in Marxist theory) the difference between the value of a worker's labor and the wages paid him by his employer

sur·prise (sərpráiz) **1.** *n.* the emotion excited by something, e.g. an act or event, totally unexpected || the cause of this emotion **to take by surprise** to come upon suddenly or unexpectedly || to catch unprepared || to astonish || to capture by a sudden, unexpected attack **2.** *v.t. pres. part.* **sur·pris·ing** *past* and *past part.* **sur·prised** to cause to experience unexpected emotion, *his generosity surprised me* || to catch, come upon or attack suddenly and unexpectedly, *to surprise a thief, to surprise an enemy* || to cause to feel sudden, unexpected disapproval, *his behavior surprised me* || to bring (something) to light by some sudden, unexpected action, *to surprise a secret out of someone* **sur·prís·ing** *adj.* [fr. A.F., O.F. *surprise,* past part. of *surprendre*]

sur·re·al·ism (sərí:əlizəm) *n.* a movement in art and literature originated in Paris (1924) by Breton. Formulated at a time when psychoanalysis was gaining ground, surrealism aimed to liberate into the creative act the image-forming powers of the unconscious and so transcend reality as it is conceived by the day-to-day intelligence. Surrealism emerged out of dada, and it claimed writers, including de Quincey, Rimbaud and Lautréamont, as its precursors. It found direction and method in Breton's manifestos and his development of automatism, and it was furthered in the writings esp. of Eluard, Aragon and Prévert. Painters inspired by de Chirico portrayed unconscious or dream images. Masson, Ernst, Arp and Miró developed abstract forms symbolizing unconscious thought, Duchamp produced objects with symbolic significance, and Picabia, Chagall, Picasso and Giacometti all participated in surrealist exhibitions. Dali and Buñuel produced a surrealist film, 'Le Chien Andalou' (1928). Surrealism, which also became philosophical and political, ceased to be a formal group or school, but has been influential as a liberating force. Surrealist elements can be recognized in much contemporary art **sur·ré·al·ist 1.** *n.* a painter, writer etc. who practices surrealism **2.** *adj.* of, relating to, practicing or characterized by surrealism **sur·re·al·ís·tic** *adj.* [fr. F. *surréalisme*]

sur·re·but·tal (sə:ribʌ́t'l, sʌribʌ́t'l) *n.* (*law*) a surrebutter [fr. O.F. *sur,* over+ REBUTTAL]

sur·re·but·ter (sə:ribʌ́tər, sʌribʌ́tər) *n.* (*law*) a plaintiff's reply to a defendant's rebutter

sur·re·join·der (sə:ridʒɔ́indər, sʌridʒɔ́indər) *n.* (*law*) a plaintiff's reply to a defendant's rejoinder

sur·ren·der (səréndər) **1.** *v.t.* to give up (something) to someone or something, esp. under compulsion, *to surrender one's watch to a robber, to surrender one's army to the enemy* || to give (oneself) up to e.g. emotion || to sign away one's rights under (an insurance policy) in return for an agreed sum || *v.i.* to acknowledge defeat and by so doing put oneself into the power of an adversary, *the Germans surrendered to the Allies* **to surrender to bail** (*Br.*) to appear in court in discharge of bail **2.** *n.* the act of surrendering || the giving up of an insurance policy by the owner in return for a cash payment **in surrender** as an indication that defeat is accepted [A.F.]

sur·rep·ti·tious (sə:rəptíʃəs, sʌrəptíʃəs) *adj.* secretive, stealthy || acting in a secretive, stealthy way || obtained in a secretive, stealthy way [fr. L. *surrepticius*]

Sur·rey (sə́:ri:, sʌ́ri:), Henry Howard, earl of (c. 1517-47), English poet. With Wyatt, he introduced into English verse French and Italian forms. He employed the first English blank verse in his translation 'Certain Bokes of Virgiles Aenaeis' (1557)

Surrey a county (area 722 sq. miles, pop. 995,800) in S.E. England. County town: Kingston-upon-Thames

sur·rey (sə́:ri:, sʌ́ri:) a late 19th-c. fourwheeled, two-seated carriage [after SURREY in England]

sur·ro·gate 1. (sə́:rəgeit, sʌ́rəgeit) *v.t. pres. part.* **sur·ro·gat·ing** and *past part.* **sur·ro·gat·ed** to appoint as a substitute for oneself or another **2.** (sə́:rəgit, sʌ́rəgit) *n.* a substitute, esp. (*Church of England*) a deputy for a bishop or chancellor || (in certain states of the U.S.A.) a judicial officer who presides over the probate of wills and testaments, settlement of estates etc. [fr. L. *surrogare (surrogatus),* to elect in place of another]

surrogate mother a woman who bears a child for the convenience of another woman, conceiving such child by artificial insemination

sur·round (səráund) **1.** *v.t.* to encircle, *the ocean surrounds the land* || to cause to become encircled, *to surround a house with trees* || to cut off (a military unit etc.) by enclosing with troops || to form the entourage or setting of, *surrounded by sycophants, surrounded by luxury* **2.** *n.* (*Br.*) a floor covering between carpet and wall or any border or edging of a particular material **sur·róund·ing 1.** *adj.* which surrounds **2.** *n.* (*pl.*) environment || environs [O.F. *suronder, souronder,* to overflow]

sur·tax (sə́:rtæks) **1.** *n.* an extra tax, esp. a graduated tax on income above a certain sum in addition to the basic tax **2.** *v.t.* to levy such an extra tax on [F. fr. *surtaxe*]

Sur·tees (sə́:rti:z), Robert Smith (1803-64), English novelist. He created Jorrocks, a sporting grocer who appears in 'Jorrocks' Jaunts and Jollities' (1838) and 'Handley Cross' (1843). Hunting life provides much of the rollicking humor and satire

sur·veil·lance (sərvéiləns) *n.* a close watch, esp. one kept over a prisoner || supervisor, e.g. of a prison [F. fr. *surveiller,* to supervise]

sur·veil·lant (sərvéilənt) *n.* a person who keeps a close watch over another || a supervisor, e.g. of a prison [fr. F. *surveilter,* to supervise]

sur·veille (sə:rvéil) *v.* to keep under observation

sur·vey 1. (sərvéi) *v.t.* to measure the extent, contours etc. of (a land area) with a view to making an accurate and detailed map || to examine (a building) in detail in order to discover any defects in its structure etc. || to examine the whole extent of (something), noting details, *they sadly surveyed the scene before them* || to consider (a problem, state of affairs etc.) in general and in detail, *the last chapters survey the closing years of her reign* **2.** (sə́:rvei) *n.* a general inspection || a careful examination, as a whole and in detail || the process of surveying an area of land || an area that has been surveyed || a department or group of people engaged in such work || the result of surveying in the form of a map, report etc. [A.F. *surveier,* to look over]

sur·vey·or (sərvéiər) *n.* a person whose profession is surveying land etc. || a customs official who ascertains the amount, value etc. of imported goods || a person who inspects, e.g. a building, in detail for the purpose of ascertaining its value, condition etc. || (*Br.*) an official inspector of weights and measures etc. [A.F., O.F. *surveour, surveiour*]

surveyor's chain a Gunter's chain

sur·vey·or·ship (sərvéiərʃip) *n.* the office of surveyor

surveyor's level an instrument consisting of a revolving telescope fitted with a spirit level, used for testing horizontality

sur·viv·al (sərváivəl) *n.* the act, state or fact of surviving || something that survives, e.g. a custom, belief etc.

survival of the fittest *NATURAL SELECTION

sur·vive (sərváiv) *pres. part.* **sur·viv·ing** *past* and *past part.* **sur·vived** *v.t.* to live or exist longer than, *to survive one's husband* || to continue to live or exist in spite of (an experience, condition etc.), *to survive an earthquake* || *v.i.* to continue to live or exist **sur·ví·vor** *n.* a person who or thing which survives **sur·ví·vor·ship** *n.* (*law*) the right of any survivor of a small group sharing a joint inheritance or other property interest to take the share of any member of the group who dies [A.F. *survivre*]

survivor *n.* one who will not accept defeat

Su·sa (sú:sə) an ancient city of Persia in the lower Karun basin. It was the capital of Elam (c. 4000 B.C.) and was the residence of the Achaemenid kings of Persia: remains of the palace

Susa *SOUSSE

Su·šak (sú:ʃɑk) *RIJEKA

sus·cep·ti·bil·i·ty (səseptəbíliti:) *pl.* **sus·cep·ti·bil·i·ties** *n.* the state or quality of being susceptible || (*pl.*) sensibilities || the quality of being liable or exposed or prone, *susceptibility to attack* || (*elec.*) the ratio of the intensity of magnetization of a substance to the strength of the magnetizing force [SUSCEPTIBLE]

sus·cep·ti·ble (səséptəb'l) *adj.* affected or influenced particularly easily || (*Br.*) easily offended || responding easily to the attractions of women **susceptible of** admitting, allowing, *susceptible of proof* **susceptible to** liable to, *susceptible to disease* || able to be influenced by, *susceptible to flattery* **sus·cép·ti·bly** *adv.* [fr. M.L. *susceptibilis*]

sus·cep·tive (səséptiv) *adj.* emotionally susceptible [fr. M.L. *susceptivus*]

Su-7B *SUKHPI

Su-17 *FITTER

su·shi (sú:ʃi:) *n.* Japanese dish of raw fish served in thin slices

Su·si·an (sú:zi:ən) *n.* a native or inhabitant of Susa || the Iranian language spoken in Elam [fr. L. *Susiani,* inhabitants of Susa or of Susiana province of the ancient Persian empire, roughly coextensive with Elam]

sus·pect 1. (səspékt) *v.t.* to believe (someone) guilty of something to his discredit without conclusive proof ‖ to form a notion of (someone) not necessarily based on fact, *we suspect he is a genius* ‖ to presume (something) to be not what it seems, *to suspect a picture of being a fake* ‖ to mistrust, *to suspect a generalization on principle* ‖ *v.i.* to be suspicious **2.** (sʌ́spekt) *adj.* suspected **3.** (sʌ́spekt) *n.* someone suspected, esp. of a crime [fr. L. *suspicere (suspectus)*, to look up to, admire, mistrust]

sus·pend (səspénd) *v.t.* to attach to some elevated point without support from below, *to suspend a lamp from the ceiling* ‖ to hold floating on or in a fluid, or as if on or in a fluid, *a pall of smoke was suspended over the city* ‖ to debar, usually for a time, from the exercise of an office or function or the enjoyment of a privilege ‖ to hold or keep undetermined, *to suspend judgment* ‖ (*Am.=Br.* rusticate) to send (a student) away for a time from a university or college as punishment [O.F. *suspendre, sospendre*]

suspended animation temporary cessation of normal physical functions

sus·pend·er (səspéndər) *n.* (*pl., Am.=Br.* braces) shoulder supports for keeping trousers up ‖ (*Br.*) a garter (elastic device for keeping a sock or stocking up)

suspender belt (*Br.*) a garter belt

sus·pense (səspéns) *n.* the state of anxious expectancy or uncertainty that usually develops while waiting for a decision, outcome etc. ‖ (in drama, fiction and the movies) an effect of intense and prolonged expectancy ‖ (*law*) temporary suspension of a right etc. **to keep** (or **hold) in suspense** to keep in a state of uncertainty or indecision [O.F. *suspens, suspense,* delay]

suspense account (*bookkeeping*) an account for temporary entries before they are assigned to their proper places

sus·pen·sion (səspénʃən) *n.* a suspending or being suspended ‖ the method by which something is suspended ‖ the device by which something is suspended ‖ an imposed temporary withdrawal of a right or privilege ‖ the stoppage of payment of debts because of financial failure ‖ (*mus.*) the holding over and merging of a note or notes of a chord with the chord that follows, or a note or notes thus held and merged ‖ (*phys., chem.*) a two-phase system in which a finely divided solid is dispersed in a solid, liquid or gas [fr. L.L. *suspensio (suspensionis)*]

suspension bridge a bridge suspended from cables which pass over supporting towers and are firmly anchored at each end

sus·pen·sor (səspénsər) *n.* a suspensory (*bot.*) a mass of cells serving to force the developing plant embryo into contact with the food supply of the megaspore [M.L.]

sus·pen·so·ry (səspénsəri:) **1.** *adj.* serving to suspend, *a suspensory muscle* ‖ leaving undetermined or incomplete for the time being **2.** *pl.* **sus·pen·so·ries** *n.* a suspensory muscle, bandage etc. [fr. L. *suspendere (suspensus)*, to suspend]

sus·pi·cion (səspíʃən) *n.* the act or an instance of suspecting ‖ the state of mind of one who suspects ‖ the merest inkling, *he hadn't a suspicion of the truth* ‖ a barely noticeable amount, a *suspicion of garlic* **above suspicion** not to be suspected because held in such high reputation **on suspicion** because of being suspected **under suspicion** suspected [A.F. *suspecioun*]

sus·pi·cious (səspíʃəs) *adj.* suspecting or having a tendency to suspect ‖ arousing suspicion ‖ showing suspicion [O.F. *suspecious, suspicious*]

sus·pi·ra·tion (sʌspəréiʃən) *n.* (*rhet.*) a profound sigh [fr. L. *suspiratio (suspirationis)*]

sus·pire (səspáiər) *pres. part.* **sus·pir·ing** *past* and *past part.* **sus·pired** *v.i.* (*rhet.*, esp. with 'for') to sigh profoundly, esp. with longing [fr. L. *suspirare*, to breathe out]

Sus·que·han·na (sʌskwəhǽnə) a river (444 miles long) flowing from the Catskill Mtns, New York State, through E. Pennsylvania and N.E. Maryland to the Chesapeake Bay. A second headstream, the West Branch (200 miles long) flows from the Allegheniies through central Pennsylvania before joining the main stream

Sus·sex (sʌ́siks) a county (area 1,457 sq. miles, pop. 1,278,000) in S. England. University (1959, at Brighton). Sussex is divided administratively into East Sussex (area 829 sq. miles, pop. 652,900, county town: Lewes) and West Sussex (area 628 sq. miles, pop. 625,100, county town: Chichester) ‖ (*hist.*) the kingdom of the South Saxons, founded in the late 5th c. It became part of Wessex (825)

'Sussex' a French unarmed cross-Channel ship which was sunk (1916) by the Germans during the 1st world war. The casualties included several Americans, and the action led to a deterioration in U.S.-German relations

sus·tain (səstéin) *v.t.* to prevent from falling, collapsing or giving way, esp. for a time, *to sustain tension* ‖ to keep going, *to sustain a conversation* ‖ to provide with nourishment etc. ‖ to support, bear (a weight etc.) ‖ to endure (criticism etc.) ‖ to support the validity or truth of ‖ to experience (a loss or injury) ‖ to act (a role) [A. F., O.F. *sustenir, soustenir*]

sustained yield *adj.* of a requirement that trees cut down in a forest area be replaced by new plantings to ensure future lumber supplies — **sustained yield** *n.*

sus·tain·ment (səstéinmənt) *n.* a sustaining or being sustained

sus·te·nance (sʌ́stənəns) *n.* nourishment ‖ a means of livelihood ‖ a sustaining or being sustained [fr. A.F. *sustenaunce*, O. F. *sostenance*]

sus·ten·ta·tion (sʌstentéiʃən) *n.* a sustaining or being sustained, maintenance ‖ sustenance [A.F., O.F. *sustentacion*]

Su·su (sú:su:) *pl.* **Su·su, Su·sus** *n.* a member of a W. African people living in the Sudan, Guinea and N. Sierra Leone ‖ this people ‖ the Mande language of this people

Su·ther·land (sʌ́ðərlənd), Graham (1903-80), British artist. He is best-known for his war paintings of desolate landscapes, his portraits (including Maugham and Churchill), his 'Crucifixion' in St Matthew's Church, Northampton, England, and his tapestry of 'Christ in Majesty' at Coventry Cathedral, England

Sutherland a county (area 2,028 sq. miles, pop. 13,000) of northernmost Scotland. County town: Dornoch (pop. 900)

Sut·lej (sʌ́tlidʒ) a tributary (900 miles long) of the Indus flowing from S.W. Tibet through the Punjab, forming part of the India-Pakistan border. It joins the Chenab, forming the Panjnad, 50 miles above the junction with the Indus

sut·ler (sʌ́tlər) *n.* (*hist.*) a person who followed an army for the purpose of selling provisions [M. Du. *soeteler* fr. *soetelen,* to do menial work]

su·tra (sú:trə) *n.* (*Brahminism*) an aphorism or a collection of short rules ‖ (*Buddhism*) one of the narrative scriptures, esp. the dialogues of the Buddha ‖ (*Jainism*) any of various scriptures, esp. one recounting the life of the founder of Jainism [Skr. *sūtra*, a thread]

sut·tee (sʌtí:, sʌ́ti:) *n.* the act or custom by which a Hindu widow willingly immolates herself on her husband's funeral pyre. Suttee has been a statutory offense since 1829 ‖ a Hindu widow committing this act **sut·tée·ism** *n.* [Skr. *satī*, a virtuous wife]

Sut·ter (sʌ́tər), John Augustus (1803-80), U.S. frontiersman. He founded (1839) New Helvetia in the Sacramento Valley of California. It became a large, rich colony and the nucleus of the 1849 gold rush after gold was first discovered at his farm, 'Sutter's Mill', by his partner

Sut·ton Hoo (sʌ́t'nhú:) the site in Suffolk, England, of a burial mound (c. 650) of an Anglo-Saxon warrior, probably a king. It was remarkable for the fine cloisonné jewelry and the ornamental gold and silver goods from many parts of W. Europe, esp. from Scandinavia, which it contained

su·tu·ral (sú:tʃərəl) *adj.* of, relating to or near a suture [F. or fr. Mod. L. *suturalis*]

su·ture (sú:tʃər) **1.** *n.* (*anat.*) a line of union between bones, esp. in the skull ‖ (*surg.*) the stitching up of a wound ‖ the thread or wire used in this operation ‖ a line or seam along which two things or parts have been united ‖ (*bot.*) a line of dehiscence ‖ (*zool.*) a line of juncture between two structures, e.g. the cusps of bivalve mollusks **2.** *v.t. pres. part.* **su·tur·ing** *past* and *past part.* **su·tured** to stitch (a wound) [F.]

Su·va (sú:və) the chief port and capital (pop. 66,018) of Fiji, on Viti Levu

Su·vo·rov (su:vɔ́rəf), Aleksandr Vasilyevich (1729-1800), Russian field marshal. He distinguished himself in the Russo-Turkish Wars of 1768-74 and 1787-92, crushed Kosciusko's rebellion in Poland (1794), and led the Austrian and Russian forces in Italy (1798-9)

Su·wan·nee (səwɔ́ni:, səwɒni:, swɔ́ni:, swɔ́ni:) a river (240 miles long) rising in S.W. Georgia and flowing to the Gulf of Mexico. Its name was used by Stephen Foster in his popular ballad, 'Old Folks at Home' or 'Swanee River'

su·ze·rain (sú:zərein) *n.* (*hist.*) a feudal overlord ‖ a state with political control over another [F.]

su·ze·rain·ty (sú:zəreinti:) *n.* the position or power of a suzerain [F. *suzeraineté*]

Sval·bard (svɑ́lbɑr) (Spitsbergen) a mountainous, partly ice-covered archipelago (land area 24,295 sq. miles, pop. 3,600, mainly Russian) in the Arctic Ocean, belonging to Norway. Main islands: Vestspitsbergen (area 15,000 sq. miles), Nordaustlandet, Barentsöya, Edgeöya (*Eng.* West Spitsbergen, Northeast Land, Barents Is. and Edge I.). Highest point: 5,445 ft, on Vestspitsbergen. Products: coal, furs. There is oil on Vestspitsbergen

S-val·ue (ésvælju:) *n.* (*nuclear phys.*) increase in value of nuclear fuel after 1% burn up *Cf* R-VALUE

Sve·a·land (svéiələnd) *SWEDEN

svelte (svelt, sfelt) *adj.* slender, graceful [F.]

Sverd·lovsk (svɛərdlɔ́fsk) (formerly Ekaterinburg) a communications center (pop. 1,211,000) in the R.S.F.S.R., U.S.S.R., in the E. Urals. Industries: iron and steel, heavy machinery, chemicals, food processing. University, two cathedrals (18th c.), opera house. Czar Nicholas II and his family were shot here in 1918 by the Bolsheviks

Sve·vo (zvévɔ), Italo (Ettore Schmitz, 1861-1928), Italian novelist. He is best known for 'La coscienza di Zeno' (1923, trans. 'The Confessions of Zeno', 1930). James Joyce did much to make him widely known

SW, S.W. Southwest, southwestern

swab (swɒb) **1.** *n.* a floor mop, esp. one used for cleaning the decks of a ship ‖ a twist of cotton etc. attached to a thin stick and used for treating a wound, cleaning out the mouth, nose etc. ‖ a specimen collected on such a twist for examination ‖ (*pop.*) an unpleasant or contemptible man or boy **2.** *v.t. pres. part.* **swab·bing** *past* and *past part.* **swabbed** to clean (e.g. a deck) with a swab ‖ to medicate or clean with a swab [fr. Du. *zwabber* fr. *zwabben,* to splash, sway]

Swa·bi·a (swéibi:ə) German medieval duchy, seat of the Hohenstaufens in the 12th and 13th cc. Today it is a part of S.W. Bavaria

Swa·bi·an (swéibi:ən) **1.** *n.* a native or inhabitant of Swabia ‖ the High German dialect of the Swabians **2.** *adj.* of or relating to Swabia, its people, language etc.

swad·dle (swɔ́d'l) *pres. part.* **swad·dling** *past* and *past part.* **swad·dled** *v.t.* to wrap (a baby) in swaddling clothes [M.E. *swathel-* fr. *swathel-bond,* swaddling clothes]

swaddling clothes (esp. *hist.*) narrow bands of cloth wrapped around newborn and young infants to prevent free movement of the limbs

swag (swæg) **1.** *n.* (*pop.*) booty stolen by thieves ‖ (*pop.*) any ill-gotten gains ‖ (*Austral.*) a bundle carried by a miner, itinerant laborer etc. ‖ a festoon used as an ornamental motive ‖ a hanging fold of material ‖ a large hanging cluster of flowers **2.** *v.i. pres. part.* **swag·ging** *past* and *past part.* **swagged** (*Austral.*) to travel with a swag [prob. fr. O.N.]

swage (sweidʒ) **1.** *n.* a smith's die for working metal cold by hammering **2.** *v.t. pres. part.* **swag·ing** *past* and *past part.* **swaged** to shape with a swage [O.F. *souage, souaige*]

swage block a heavy block of iron with grooves or perforations, used for shaping metals by hammering

swag·ger (swǽgər) **1.** *v.i.* to walk in a way that betrays great conceit **2.** *n.* a swaggering gait [SWAG v.]

swagger stick a short light cane or stick carried in the hand by army officers

swag·ging (swǽgiŋ) *n.* appropriation of government property —**swag** *n.* —**swag** *v.*

swag·man (swǽgmən) *pl.* **swag·men** (swǽgmən) *n.* (*Austral.*) a worker traveling the countryside with a swag

Swa·hi·li (swɑhí:li:) *pl.* **Swa·hi·li, Swa·hi·lis** *n.* a member of a Bantu-speaking people living in and near Zanzibar ‖ this people ‖ a Bantu language spoken by them and used as a lingua franca in parts of E. Africa

swain (swein) *n.* (*old-fash.*) a male suitor [O.N. *sveinn,* boy, attendant]

swale (sweil) *n.* a marshy depression in a stretch of land [perh. fr. older *swale,* shade, a shady place, prob. of Scand. origin]

swal·low (swɒlou) *n.* a member of *Hirundini-*

dae, a family of small (7 ins) migratory birds, flying with great speed and occurring in almost all parts of the world [O.E. *swealwe*]

swallow 1. *v.t.* to cause (food, drink etc.) to pass down the throat and into the stomach ‖ (often with 'up') to engulf, envelop, *swallowed up by the shadows* ‖ to accept (e.g. a statement) without testing it for truth, *he swallowed the tale without hesitation* ‖ to accept (an insult etc.) in a submissive way ‖ to hold back (pride, tears, laughter etc.) ‖ to retract (e.g. words said) ‖ *v.i.* to take food etc. through the throat into the stomach ‖ to make the throat movement characteristic of this, esp. under stress of emotion **2.** *n.* the act of swallowing ‖ the amount swallowed in one gulp ‖ (*naut.*) an aperture in a block through which the rope reeves [O.E. *swelgan*]

swallow dive (*Br.*) a swan dive

swal·low·tail (swólouteil) *n.* a deeply forked tail ‖ a butterfly with such a tail ‖ any of several hummingbirds ‖ a swallow-tailed kite ‖ (*naut.*) a double-pointed pennant ‖ a tailcoat

swal·low-tailed kite (swóloutеild) *Elanoides forficatus*, fam. *Accipitridae*, a kite of central and southern U.S.A., white with black wings, black back and black forked tail

swam *past* of SWIM

swa·mi (swámi:) *pl.* **swa·mies** *n.* a title of respect for a Hindu religious teacher [Hindī *swāmi*, master, prince, fr. Skr. *svāmin*]

Swam·mer·dam (svúmərdɑm), Jan (1637-80), Dutch naturalist who founded the science of entomology. He was a pioneer in the use of the microscope, and is said to be the first to have observed red blood corpuscles

swamp (swɒmp) **1.** *n.* spongy ground largely covered by standing water of little depth **2.** *v.t.* to fill (a boat) with water ‖ (*loosely*) to make very wet ‖ to submerge under too many or too great demands, *swamped with orders* ‖ to overwhelm, *swamped by a crowd of admirers* ‖ *v.i.* to become submerged and sink **swámp·y** *comp.* **swamp·i·er** *superl.* **swamp·i·est** *adj.* [prob. fr. Du. *zwamp*, sponge]

Swan (swɒn), Sir Joseph Wilson (1828-1914), British physicist, electrician and inventor. He invented the photographic dry plate and bromide paper. He also devised a form of incandescent electric lamp and an electric safety lamp for miners

swan (swɒn) *n.* any of various large, stately, usually white, long-necked aquatic birds of fam. *Anatidae*, esp. *Cygnus olor*. They occur wild in many parts of the world, and are kept semidomesticated in ponds, lakes etc. in Europe and America. In the wild state they migrate south each winter in V-shaped flocks [O.E. *swan, swon*]

swan dive (*Am.=Br.* swallow dive) a forward dive in which the arms are spread sideways until the swimmer is about to enter the water

swank (swæŋk) **1.** *n.* (*pop.*) ostentatious display, e.g. in manner, dress or speech **2.** *v.i.* (*pop.*) to show off arrogantly **3.** *adj.* (*pop.*) swanky **swánk·y** *comp.* **swank·i·er** *superl.* **swank·i·est** *adj.* (*pop.*) ostentatious, showy ‖ elegant, stylish [etym. doubtful]

swan·ner·y (swɒ́nəri:) *pl.* **swan·ner·ies** *n.* a place where swans are bred or kept

swans·down (swɒ́nzdaun) *n.* the down of the swan, used for powder puffs, dress trimmings etc. ‖ a soft cotton flannel having a nap on the right side, used for making infants' apparel etc.

Swan·sea (swɒ́nzi:, swɒ́nsi:) a port (pop. 186,199) in Glamorganshire, S.E. Wales. Industries: metallurgy, shipbuilding, mechanical engineering. University College (1920), part of the University of Wales

swan song (in legend) the beautiful song of a dying swan ‖ a final pronouncement, or act, esp. the last work of a writer or musician

swan-up·ping (swɒ́nʌpiŋ) *n.* the process or practice of nicking young swans on the beak as a mark of ownership ‖ an annual English ceremony on the Thames in which swans belonging to the Crown or some corporation are so marked

swap maternity (*insurance*) provision in group health-insurance plans providing immediate maternity benefits to a newly covered woman but terminating coverage on a pregnancy in progress upon termination of a woman's coverage *Cf* FLAT MATERNITY, SWITCH AND FLAT MATERNITY

SWAPO (*acronym*) for South-West Africa Peoples Organization, native political and military movement in Namibia

swap, swop (swɒp) *pres. part.* **swap·ping, swop·ping** *past* and *past part.* **swapped, swopped 1.** *v.t.* (*pop.*) to exchange by barter **2.** *n.* (*pop.*) the act of bartering ‖ (*pop.*) something bartered [M.E. *swappen*, to strike, prob. imit.]

sward (swɔrd) *n.* (*rhet.*) an expanse of grass-covered soil [O.E. *sweard*, a skin]

swarm (swɔrm) **1.** *n.* a large number of honeybees emigrating from a hive with their queen to establish a new colony ‖ a colony of honeybees settled in a hive ‖ any great moving throng, *a swarm of pilgrims, a swarm of mosquitoes* ‖ (*biol.*) a collection of single-celled independent organisms, esp. zoospores **2.** *v.i.* (of bees) to emigrate in a body from a hive to form a new colony ‖ to move around in large numbers, *sightseers swarmed over the park* ‖ (of a place) to be crowded ‖ (*biol.*, e.g. of zoospores from a sporangium) to escape in a swarm with a characteristic oscillating movement [O.E. *swearm*]

swarm *v.i.* (esp. with 'up') to climb by gripping alternately with the hands and legs ‖ *v.t.* to climb up (a pole etc.) in this manner [etym. doubtful]

swarm cell a swarm spore

swarm spore (*biol.*) any of various motile sexual or asexual spores, e.g. a zoospore

swart (swɔrt) *adj.* (*rhet.*) swarthy [O.E. *sweart*]

swarth·i·ness (swɔ́rði:nis) *n.* the state or quality of being swarthy

swarth·y (swɔ́rði:, swɔ́rθi:) *comp.* **swarth·i·er** *superl.* **swarth·i·est** *adj.* dark-colored, *a swarthy complexion* [var. of SWART]

swash (swɔʃ, swɒʃ) *adj.* (*printing*, of capital letters) having ornamental strokes at top and bottom [prob. derived fr. obs. *aswash, aslant*]

swash 1. *v.i.* (of liquid) to move with a splash ‖ to act in a blustering, arrogant way ‖ *v.t.* to cause (water etc.) to splash about **2.** *n.* a body of water splashing forcefully against something ‖ the sound or motion of swashing water [imit.]

swash·buck·ler (swɔ́ʃbʌklər, swɒ́ʃbʌklər) *n.* (*hist.*) a swaggering, blustering, fighting man out for romantic adventure **swásh·buck·ling** *adj.* characterized by swagger and bluster

swas·ti·ka (swɒ́stikə) *n.* an ancient symbol or ornament in the form of a Greek cross having the ends of the arms bent to form right angles arranged clockwise or counterclockwise. The clockwise swastika was adopted (1933) as the emblem of the National Socialist German Workers' Party

swat, swot (swɒt) **1.** *v.t. pres part.* **swat·ting, swot·ting** *past* and *past part.* **swat·ted, swot·ted** to hit with a quick sharp blow, *to swat a fly* **2.** *n.* a quick sharp blow [variant of SQUAT]

SWAT 1. (*acronym*) Special Weapons and Tactics Team **2.** (*mil. acronym*) for Sidewinder (which see) angle tracking

swatch (swɒtʃ) *n.* a sample piece of fabric, leather etc. [etym. doubtful]

swath (swɔθ, swɒθ) *n.* a line of grass or grain after it has been scythed or reaped ‖ the width of the path so cut [O.E. *swæth, swathu*, track]

swathe (sweið, swɒð) **1.** *v.t. pres. part.* **swath·ing** *past* and *past part.* **swathed** to wrap, bind etc. with a swathe or swathes, *swathed in bandages* ‖ to enwrap deeply, so as partially to obscure, *swathed in furs, hills swathed in mist* **2.** *n.* a wrapping or bandage [O.E. *swarthian*]

Swa·tow (swátáu) a port and industrial center (pop. 280,400) in Kwangtung, China, at the mouth of the Han on the South China Sea

sway (swei) **1.** *v.i.* to swing rhythmically from side to side from or as if from a fixed base ‖ to go forward while moving in this way, *to sway down the road* ‖ to incline to one side as a result of some force, e.g. wind, *the bus swayed to the right* ‖ to fluctuate in one's attitude or opinions ‖ *v.t.* to cause to swing from side to side ‖ to cause to incline to one side as a result of some force ‖ to change the opinions of by eloquence, demagogy etc., *to sway a crowd in one's favor* ‖ to exert an influence upon ‖ (*naut.*, esp. with 'up') to hoist (a mast etc.) **2.** *n.* a swaying or being swayed ‖ control, *to hold sway* [prob. fr. L.G. *swájen*, to be moved hither and thither by the wind]

sway·back (swéibæk) *n.* (esp. of horses) a hollow sagging of the back **swáy·backed** *adj.*

swayed (sweid) *adj.* swaybacked

Swa·zi (swázi:) *pl.* **Swa·zi, Swa·zis** *n.* a member of a Bantu people inhabiting Swaziland ‖ this people ‖ the language spoken by this people

Swa·zi·land (swázi:lænd) (Ngwane) a state (area 6,704 sq. miles, pop. 601,200) in S.E. Africa, a member of the Commonwealth and of the U.N. Capital: Mbabane (pop. 29,875). People: 96% Swazi (Bantu), small European and mulatto minorities. Languages: Swazi, English. Religion: mainly local African, 30% Christian. The land is 6% cultivated. It lies on the east side of the S. African plateau, descending from the rugged, forested High Veld (over 5,000 ft), through a mixed farming and ranching region (averaging 3,000 ft), to a low, fertile plateau (1,000 ft), with hills (2,000 ft) along the Mozambique border. Average temperatures (F.): (Jan.) 60° in the west, 70° in the east, (July) 50° in the west, 60° in the east. Rainfall: 55 ins (west), 26 ins (east). Livestock: cattle, goats. Agricultural products: cotton, tobacco, corn, sugar, bananas, lumber, pineapples, rice, tomatoes, peanuts, beans, sweet potatoes. Mineral resources: asbestos, iron ore, tin, barytes, gold, silver, coal, beryl, diaspore, pyrophyllite, kaolin and alunite. Manufacturing industries (food processing, forestry products) are being developed. Exports: asbestos, sugar, cattle, seed cotton, rice, gum, lumber, hides and skins, citrus fruit, canned pineapples, tobacco. Monetary unit: lilangeni (100 cents). HISTORY. The Swazis migrated south to Swaziland (mid-18th c.) and came into conflict with the Zulus. Britain intervened to stop tribal warfare (1840s) and made Swaziland a protectorate of the Transvaal (1894). Its administration was transferred to the governor of the Transvaal (1903) and to a high commissioner (1907). It acquired internal self-government (1967) King Sobhuza II, who ruled 1921-82, was succeeded by his son Makhosetive, whose mother became queen regent (1983)

swear (swεər) **1.** *v. pres. part.* **swear·ing** *past* **swore** (swɔr, swour) *past part.* **sworn** (swɔrn, swourn) *v.i.* to make a solemn oath ‖ to use sacred words irreverently ‖ (*loosely*) to use obscene language ‖ *v.t.* to affirm by solemn oath ‖ to take (an oath) to declare forcefully to be true, *he swore he didn't know the man* ‖ to promise solemnly, *she swore not to be late* ‖ (*law*) to administer an oath to ‖ to bind by solemn oath **to swear by** to have or express complete confidence in, *he swears by that firm* **to swear in** to induct into office by administering an oath to **to swear off** to pledge oneself to renounce, *to swear off smoking* **to swear to** (in negative or interrogative constructions) to be positively sure of, *I couldn't swear to the color of his hair* **2.** *n.* a swearword ‖ a spell of swearing [O.E. *swerian*]

swear·word (swέərwə:rd) *n.* a blasphemous or obscene word

sweat (swet) *n.* the usually colorless saline fluid secreted by the sweat glands ‖ a sweating or being sweated, esp. sweating induced by a sudorific ‖ moisture exuded from, and forming beadlike drops on, a surface ‖ exercise, esp. a hard gallop, given a horse to make it sweat ‖ hard work ‖ the fermentation that occurs during the aging of tobacco ‖ a state of anxiety, impatience etc., *in a sweat to learn the results* [M.E. *swet, swete*]

sweat *v.i.* to excrete moisture through the openings of the sweat glands ‖ (of green plants, cheese etc.) to exude moisture in the form of beadlike drops ‖ (of rocks, glass etc.) to collect surface moisture from the air by condensation ‖ (of tobacco leaves) to ferment ‖ (of hides) to become putrid ‖ to toil laboriously, to *sweat to get a job done* ‖ *v.t.* to cause to excrete sweat from the skin, *to sweat a horse* (with 'away', 'off', 'out' etc.) to get rid of by excreting sweat, *to sweat out a fever* ‖ to make wet with sweat, to *sweat one's socks* ‖ to exact an unjustly large amount of labor from (employees etc.) at low wages and under bad conditions ‖ to ferment (e.g. tobacco leaves) ‖ to putrefy (e.g. hides) ‖ to heat (a metal) in order to extract a fusible component ‖ to join (a metal) to another metal by partial melting ‖ to cause (melted solder) to run between two contiguous surfaces in order to join them **to sweat blood** to slave away at some task ‖ to be in a fearful state of apprehension, anxiety etc. [O.E. *swǣtan*]

sweat·band (swétbænd) *n.* a leather band inside a hat serving to prevent sweat from the brow from seeping through and damaging the exterior of the hat

sweat·er (swétər) *n.* a knitted garment, with or without sleeves, for the upper part of the body. It can be in pullover or jacket style

sweat gland a tubular gland that excretes sweat through a duct connecting with a minute pore on the surface of the skin. In man these

CONCISE PRONUNCIATION KEY: **(a)** æ, *cat*; ɑ, *car*; ɔ *fawn*; ei, *snake*. **(e)** e, *hen*; i:, *sheep*; iə, *deer*; εə, *bear*. **(i)** i, *fish*; ai, *tiger*; ə:, *bird*. **(o)** o, *ox*; au, *cow*; ou, *goat*; u, *poor*; ɔi, *royal*. **(u)** ʌ, *duck*; u, *bull*; u:, *goose*; ə, *bacillus*; ju:, *cube*. x, *loch*; θ, *think*; ð, *bother*; z, *Zen*; ʒ, *corsage*; dʒ, *savage*; ŋ, *orangutang*; j, *yak*; ʃ, *fish*; tʃ, *fetch*; 'l, *rabble*; 'n, *redden*. Complete pronunciation key appears inside front cover.

glands are distributed in nearly all parts of the skin

sweat·i·ly (swétili:) *adv.* in a sweaty manner

sweat·i·ness (swéti:nis) *n.* the state or quality of being sweaty

sweat pants loose cotton jersey pants with a thick nap on the inner side, close-fitting cuffs, and a drawstring at the waist. They are worn esp. by athletes before and after exercising

sweat shirt a long-sleeved pullover of cotton jersey having a thick nap on the inner side, worn esp. by athletes before and after exercising

sweat-shop (swétʃɒp) *n.* a small factory where workers work long hours for low wages under unwholesome conditions

sweat suit an athlete's sweat pants and sweat shirt

sweat·y (swéti:) *comp.* **sweat·i·er** *superl.* **sweat·i·est** *adj.* running with sweat ‖ smelling of sweat ‖ causing sweat

Swede (swi:d) *n.* a native or inhabitant of Sweden [fr. M.L.G. or M. Du.]

swede (swi:d) *n.* (*Br.*) a rutabaga

Swe·den (swí:d'n) a kingdom (area 173,620 sq. miles, pop. 8,327,500) of N.W. Europe (Scandinavia). People and language: Swedish, small Lapp and Finnish minorities. Religion: 95% Evangelical Lutheran (established Church), small Nonconformist, Roman Catholic and Jewish minorities. The land is 9% cultivated, 2% pasture, 50% forest and 9% lakes. Sweden is divided into three geographical regions: Norrland (the northern 60%, incl. Lapland, mountainous except for a narrow coastal plain), Svealand (the central lake plain), and Götaland (the fertile southern plateau and plain, incl. Scania, the chief agricultural district, in the far south). The chief mountain range is the Kjölen, along the Norwegian border, highest in the north (Kebnekaise, 6,963 ft), and cut by many lakes, from which rivers flow to the Gulf of Bothnia. Average temperatures (F.) in Feb. and July: Stockholm 26° and 62°, Gothenburg 30° and 62°, Lapland 5° and 54°. Snow lasts an average of 47 days in Scania, 190 days in Lapland. Rainfall: N. Norrland under 20 ins, Stockholm 23 ins, W. Svealand 35 ins. Livestock: cattle, hogs, horses, sheep, reindeer, poultry. Agricultural products: cereals, vegetables, sugar beets, potatoes, hay, dairy products, furs. Forestry products: lumber, pulpwood, fuel, pitch, tar. Mineral resources: iron ore, silver, lead, copper, zinc, manganese, arsenic, sulfur, coal, uranium. Industries: mining, pig iron, steel and steel products, fishing, pulp and paper, chemicals, electrical and electronic machinery, aluminum, textiles, agricultural machinery, shipbuilding, porcelain, glass, vehicles, aircraft, hydroelectricity, tobacco, furniture, matches, armaments, cutlery, rayon, plastics, tourism, cement, bricks. Exports: machinery, raw materials, manufactures, pulp and paper, transport equipment, metals, wood, cork, iron and steel, hydroelectricity (to Denmark by submarine cable). Imports: machinery, raw materials, manufactures, oil and fuels, foodstuffs and livestock, transport equipment, chemicals. Ports: Stockholm, Gothenburg (ice-free). Stockholm and Gothenburg are connected by the Göta canal (360 miles). Sweden has rail access to Narvik and Murmansk. Universities: Uppsala (1477), Lund (1668), Gothenburg (1889), Stockholm (1877). Monetary unit: krona (100 öre). HISTORY. The inhabitants of Sweden, probably of Germanic origin, established trading links with the rest of Europe in the Iron Age. The chief tribes were the Svear in central Sweden and the Goths in the south. They took part in Viking raids (8th-10th cc.), esp. those toward Russia. Christianity was introduced (9th c.) by St Ansgar, but did not spread widely until the reign (1150-60) of Eric IX. Finland was conquered and Christianized (mid-12th c.). Many Swedish towns gained wealth and power under the influence of the Hanseatic League (13th c.). Stockholm emerged as the capital (mid-13th c.). Margaret, elected queen of Sweden in 1389, united the kingdom with Denmark and Norway by the Union of Kalmar (1397). Denmark proved unable to impose its rule on Sweden, and after many rebellions, Sweden broke away (1523) under Gustavus I. He established his rule over the whole country except the south, which remained under Danish rule, encouraged industry and trade, organized an army and navy, and made Lutheranism the state religion. His successor, Eric XIV, continued the struggle with Denmark and conquered Estonia (1561). Sweden was briefly united with Poland under Sigismund III before he was deposed (1599). Gustavus II and his minister Oxenstièrna made Sweden a dominant European power and leader of the Protestant cause in the Thirty Years' War, at the end of which Sweden gained Pomerania and Bremen (1648). Denmark was forced to cede the south of Sweden (1660). Under Charles XII, Sweden was involved in the Northern War (1700-21), in which, despite early victories, it lost all its German and Baltic territories except Finland. Sweden abandoned its ambition of dominating the Baltic, the nobility increased its power at the expense of the monarchy, and the cultural revival (which included the work of Celsius, Swedenborg and Linnaeus) ensued (18th c.). Gustavus III restored royal authority (1771-92). Under Charles XIII Sweden was involved in the Napoleonic Wars, in which it lost Finland (1809), but this was compensated by a union with Norway (1814). Bernadotte succeeded to the throne (1818) as Charles XIV. The 19th c. saw the growth of parliamentary government and of industrialization. Hostility toward Norway grew, and the two countries were separated (1905). During the long reign (1907-50) of Gustavus V, Sweden remained neutral in both world wars. Socialist governments carried out much social legislation. Sweden joined the U.N. (1946) and maintained its strictly neutral foreign policy. A new constitution was adopted (1975). Charles XVI Gustav became king (1973) on the death of Gustav VI Adolf. Prime Minister Olof Palme was assassinated (1986)

Swe·den·borg (swí:d'nbɔrg), Emmanuel (1688-1772), Swedish scientist and mystical thinker. He wrote on algebra, mining, metallurgy, physiology and psychology. He interpreted his mystical revelations of the spiritual world in 'Arcana coelestia' (1749-56)

Swe·den·bor·gi·an (swi:d'nbɔ́rdʒi:ən) **1.** *adj.* of a member of a Protestant sect, the Church of the New Jerusalem, founded (1788) by Robert Hindmarsh, a London printer, and based on Swedenborg's doctrines **2.** *n.* a member of this sect

Swed·ish (swí:diʃ) **1.** *adj.* of or relating to the country, language or inhabitants of Sweden **2.** *n.* the N. Germanic language spoken in Sweden and a section of Finland **the Swedish** the Swedish people

—The Swedish language is spoken by about 6,500,000 persons in Sweden and by the coastal population of a section of Finland. It is also spoken on most of the islands of the Baltic, including some off the coast of Estonia. It is spoken as a second language by many Finns. Swedish forms with Danish an E. Norse group. Runic inscriptions in Sweden date from the 5th c. The oldest manuscripts date from c. 1250

Swedish syndrome a psychological bonding between captors and usu. political captives, resulting from the absolute dependence of the latter

sweep (swi:p) **1.** *v. pres. part.* **sweep·ing** *past* and *past part.* **swept** (swept) *v.i.* (of news, disease, emotion etc.) to spread rapidly ‖ to move with proud or dignified grace, *she swept off the stage* ‖ (of a long dress or train) to trail with a rustling sound ‖ to move so that a long dress or train trails with a rustling sound ‖ to extend in a wide or long curve, *the hills sweep down to the sea* ‖ to move in a wide curve ‖ to use a broom or something resembling a broom in cleaning, clearing etc. ‖ *v.t.* to pass swiftly across, along, over or through, *plague swept the country* ‖ to have a large arc of fire command over, or to fire over, *the guns swept the landing beach* ‖ to move or remove with a continuous pushing force, *he swept the litter off his desk with his hand* ‖ to clean of dust, debris etc. by using a broom or brush or something resembling this ‖ to make (a path, way etc.) with or as if with a broom ‖ to direct the gaze over in a wide arc, *he swept the valley with his binoculars* ‖ to drag (e.g. the bottom of a river) ‖ to cause to move lightly over, *she swept her fingers over the strings* ‖ to touch lightly in passing over (e.g. the keys or strings of a musical instrument) **2.** *n.* the action or an act of sweeping ‖ someone whose work is sweeping, esp. a chimney sweep ‖ a long sweeping line or contour, *the sweep of a skirt* ‖ a long sweeping movement, *the sweep of an oar, the sweep of a scythe* ‖ the range of extent of a sweeping movement, *within the sweep of the telescope* ‖ a wide expanse, *a sweep of meadow* ‖ (*mil.*) a reconnaissance, attack etc. ranging over a specific area ‖ a device consisting of a pole pivoted to an upright, used to draw up a bucket of well water ‖ the sail of a windmill ‖ (*naut.*) a long pole used to propel a barge ‖ a length of cable used in dragging for obstructions, e.g. mines, in the sea ‖ (*pop.*) a sweepstake **swéep·er** *n.* [etym. doubtful]

sweep·ing (swí:piŋ) **1.** *n.* the action of a sweeper ‖ (*pl.*) things swept up, refuse **2.** *adj.* on a very large scale, *a sweeping victory* ‖ too comprehensive to allow of distinctions, *a sweeping statement* ‖ moving in a wide curve or having the shape of a wide curve, *a sweeping gesture*

sweep net a large seine let down from a boat in a wide curve and then hauled ashore

sweep·stake (swí:psteik) *n.* a horse race in which the total stakes put up by competitors go to the winner ‖ a method of gambling on a race in which the money put on by those taking part is shared among those who draw the horses running first, second and third **swéep·stakes** *n.* a sweepstake

sweet (swi:t) **1.** *adj.* having the characteristic taste of sugar ‖ containing sugar ‖ pleasing to the senses, *a sweet sound* ‖ not salted or salty, *sweet butter* ‖ (of milk) not sour ‖ (of wine) retaining some of its natural sugar ‖ (of soil) good for growing crops, not acid ‖ smooth-running, *a sweet engine* ‖ showing kindness or the desire to please, *that is very sweet of you* ‖ characterized by gentleness, kindliness etc., *a sweet nature* ‖ (*jazz*) characterized by suavity of rhythm, harmonies and tempo, not improvised **2.** *n.* (*pl.*) sweet edible things ‖ (*Br.*) the dessert course of a meal ‖ (*Br.*) a piece of candy ‖ (*pl., rhet.*) pleasures, delights, *the sweets of victory* ‖ (*rhet.*, in addressing someone) a beloved person **sweet on** (*old-fash.*) in love with, or beginning to be in love with, someone [O.E. *swēte*]

sweet basil *BASIL

sweet·bread (swí:tbred) *n.* the pancreas or thymus gland of a calf or other young animal prepared as a cooked dish

sweet·bri·er, sweet·bri·ar (swí:tbraiər) *n.* eglantine

sweet cicely *Myrrhis odorata*, fam. *Umbelliferae*, a white-flowered European aromatic herb ‖ any of several North American plants of genus *Osmorhiza*

sweet cider *CIDER (nonalcoholic)

sweet corn any of several varieties of corn grown for the table

sweet·en (swí:t'n) **1.** *v.t.* to make sweet to the taste, e.g. by adding sugar ‖ to make more agreeable to hear or to smell ‖ to put into a kinder mood ‖ (*rhet.*) to make more attractive or more enjoyable ‖ to make (soil) less acid by applying lime ‖ to neutralize (an acid) by means of an alkali ‖ to divest (e.g. seawater) of salt ‖ *v.i.* to become sweet **sweet·en·ing** (swí:t'niŋ, swí:tniŋ) *n.* that which sweetens ‖ the act or process of making sweet

sweet flag calamus (*Acorus calamus*)

sweet gale *Myrica gale*, fam. *Myricaceae*, a bog shrub of the north temperate zone having bitter-tasting, fragrant leaves

sweet·heart (swí:thɑrt) *n.* a girl or woman in relation to the boy or man in love with her, or a boy or man in relation to the girl or woman in love with him ‖ a term of endearment

sweet·meat (swí:tmi:t) *n.* (esp. *pl.*) a piece of confectionery

sweet pea *Lathyrus odoratus*, fam. *Papilionaceae*, an ornamental climbing plant having pinnate leaves and large, sweetly scented, blue, purple, red, pink, salmon or white flowers

sweet pepper any of certain plants of genus *Capsicum*, bearing a pepper of large size and mild flavor ‖ the fruit itself

sweet potato *Ipomoea batatas*, fam. *Convolvulaceae*, a trailing vine grown in warm regions for its sweet tubers ‖ the tuber, cooked and eaten as a vegetable

sweet-scent·ed (swí:tsentid) *adj.* having a sweet scent

sweet·sop (swí:tsɒp) *n. Annona squamosa*, fam. *Annonaceae*, a tropical American tree bearing sweet cone-shaped fruit ‖ the fruit itself

sweet-tem·pered (swí:ttémpərd) *adj.* possessing a loving, equable, patient disposition

sweet tooth fondness for sweet foods

sweet william *Dianthus barbatus*, fam. *Caryophyllaceae*, a biennial plant having bracteate heads of brightly colored flowers

Swein (svein) 'Forkbeard' (c. 960-1014), king of

Denmark (986-1014). He led a series of raids on England (1002-14) and exacted large sums as Danegeld from Ethelred II. His son Cnut succeeded (1016) to the English throne

swell (swel) **1.** *v. pres. part.* **swell·ing** *past* **swelled** *past part.* **swol·len** (swóul'n), **swelled** *v.i.* to increase in volume, esp. as a result of internal pressure, *the boil began to swell* ‖ to increase in number, degree, quantity etc., *the population has swollen to over a million* ‖ (of sound and of some musical instruments) to become louder ‖ (esp. of a body of water) to rise above the normal level, *the river is swelling* ‖ to curve outward or upward, *the cask swells in the middle* ‖ to seem to be puffed up (with conceit, pride etc.) ‖ (*rhet.*, of the heart) to become charged with emotion, *her heart swelled with grief* ‖ *v.t.* to cause (a body of water) to rise above the normal level ‖ to cause to increase in volume, size etc. ‖ to affect with pride etc. **2.** *n.* the act of swelling ‖ the state or quality of being swollen, *the swell of a belly, the swell of a pot* ‖ (*mus.*) an increase followed by a decrease in loudness ‖ (*mus.*) the symbol (<>) indicating this ‖ a device in some harpsichords for regulating volume ‖ a swell box ‖ (of the sea, or other large body of water) a succession of long, unbroken waves ‖ a rounded elevation, esp. on the floor of the sea ‖ (*pop.*) a person of high social standing **3.** *adj.* (*pop.*) excellent, marvelous etc., *a swell party* [O.E. *swellan*]

swell box a compartment in an organ containing the reeds or a set of pipes and fitted with shutters that open or close in order to regulate the volume

swell·ing (swéliŋ) *n.* an increase or being increased in size, volume etc. ‖ a swollen part of something, esp. an abnormal bodily protuberance or distension

swel·ter (swéltər) **1.** *v.i.* to be oppressively hot **2.** *n.* a sweltering condition ‖ oppressive heat **swél·ter·ing** *adj.* sweltry **swél·try** *comp.* **swel·tri·er** *superl.* **swel·tri·est** *adj.* oppressively hot [O.E. *sweltan*, to die]

swept *past* and *past part.* of SWEEP

swept·back (swéptbæk) *adj.* (of aircraft wings) set so that the leading edge is at an obtuse angle with the fuselage ‖ (of an aircraft) having such wings

swerve (swə:rv) **1.** *v. pres. part.* **swerv·ing** *past* and *past part.* **swerved** *v.i.* to change direction suddenly, *he swerved in order to avoid a collision* ‖ (of a ball) to curve in flight ‖ to deviate from an acceptable or right course of conduct, action etc. ‖ *v.t.* to cause to change direction, curve in flight, or deviate from an acceptable or right course of conduct etc. **2.** *n.* the act of swerving ‖ a sudden change of direction ‖ a curve in flight of a ball [O.E. *sweorfan*, to scour]

Swift (swift), Gustavus Franklin (1839-1903), U.S. merchant who founded (1885) Swift and Company, the first corporation to develop international markets for American beef. He was the first to ship dressed beef from Chicago to the east coast, to sponsor the creation of a refrigerator car, and to develop beef by-products (incl. margarine, soap, glue and fertilizer)

Swift, Jonathan (1667-1745), Irish satirist. He was dean of St Patrick's Cathedral, Dublin. 'Gulliver's Travels' (1726) is a universal satire, with the particular themes of courtly life, politics, academicism and mankind in general, but the public took it as fiction, and it has become a children's classic. His other works include 'A Tale of a Tub' (1704), a brilliant satire on the history of the Christian religion, 'The Battle of the Books' (1704), and the pathetic 'Journal to Stella'. In his own time Swift was an active though embittered politician, and his 'Drapier's Letters' (1724) had an immediate and decisive political effect. Swift's genius is flawed by a basic horror of human life: a horror that tends to impart a sense of terror and disequilibrium to his greatest works, as in 'The Modest Proposal' (1729) or the conclusion of 'Gulliver's Travels'

swift (swift) **1.** *adj.* moving or capable of moving with great speed, or characterized by great speed, *a swift horse, a swift gallop* ‖ rapid, made or done without hesitation, *a swift reply* **2.** *n.* any of numerous small birds of fam. *Apodidae*, resembling swallows but having narrower wings and shorter tails, esp. *Apus apus* ‖ a member of *Sceloporus*, a genus of fast-running lizards ‖ an adjustable reel for winding yarn, silk etc. ‖ one of the cylinders in a carding machine [O.E.]

Swift and Company *SWIFT, Gustavus Franklin

swig (swig) **1.** *v. pres. part.* **swig·ging** *past* and *past part.* **swigged** *v.t.* (*pop.*) to drink in large gulps ‖ *v.i.* (*pop.*) to drink large gulps or quantities **2.** *n.* (*pop.*) a drink taken in a long steady gulp or series of gulps [origin unknown]

swill (swil) **1.** *v.t.* (esp. with 'down' or 'out') to pour quantities of water in, on or over, so as to flush out ‖ to wash roughly, *to swill one's body under the pump* ‖ to cause (some liquid) to lap around inside a vessel by rotating it ‖ to drink greedily, to *swill beer* ‖ *v.i.* to drink something greedily **2.** *n.* hogs' liquid food ‖ garbage ‖ (*pop.*) a swig [O.E. *swillan, swilian*, to wash]

swim (swim) **1.** *v. pres. part.* **swim·ming** *past* **swam** (swæm) *past part.* **swum** (swʌm) *v.i.* to move through or under the surface of water by movements of the limbs, strokes of fins, flippers, tail etc. ‖ to move as if through water ‖ to be immersed in or surrounded by a liquid, or as if so immersed or surrounded, *swimming in chocolate sauce* ‖ to appear to whirl around one, *the room swam as I stood there* ‖ (of the head) to experience dizziness ‖ *v.t.* to cross by propelling oneself through water, *to swim a stream* ‖ to use (a specified stroke) for such propelling ‖ to force to swim, *to swim a mule across a pond* ‖ to compete in (a race for swimmers) **to swim against the stream** to go counter to the majority in one's ideas, policies etc. **2.** *n.* an act or a period of swimming ‖ a state of dizziness ‖ that part of a river etc. in which fish abound **in the swim** following currently fashionable modes [O.E. *swimman*]

swim bladder an air-filled bladder in fish, developed as a diverticulum of the alimentary canal, which makes swimming at varying depths possible

swim·mer·et (swímərét) *n.* (*zool.*) one of the small paired abdominal appendages of some crustaceans either for use in swimming or for carrying eggs

swimming (swímiŋ) **1.** *n.* the act or sport of swimming **2.** *adj.* used in, involving, or adapted to swimming ‖ overflowing with or as if with *water, swimming eyes* ‖ afflicted with dizziness, *a swimming head*

swim·ming·ly (swímiŋli:) *adv.* going along rapidly and easily with no hitches, *everything went swimmingly*

Swin·burne (swínbərn), Algernon Charles (1837-1909), English poet and critic. Swinburne's early verse, esp. 'Poems and Ballads' (1866), burst upon a Victorian public, used to Tennyson's melodies and didacticism, with the force of beating rhythm, contrived alliteration, an unconcealed pagan hedonism, an element of perversion, and an excess of imagery. His best poems have survived moral disapproval, and as a critic he led the way to a revaluation of the Jacobean dramatists

swin·dle (swínd'l) **1.** *v. pres. part.* **swin·dling** *past* and *past part.* **swin·dled** *v.t.* to trick (a victim) ‖ to get (e.g. money) by fraud or trickery ‖ *v.i.* to get money etc. by fraud or trickery **2.** *n.* the act or process or an instance of swindling [back-formation fr. SWINDLER]

swin·dler (swíndlər) *n.* a person who practices swindling [fr. G. *schwindler*, a fantastic schemer]

swine (swain) *pl.* **swine** *n.* a hog

swine fever (*Br.*) hog cholera

swine flu (swainflu:) a strain of influenza—an infectious disease of the respiratory tract—caused by the influenza virus similar to that that caused the worldwide epidemic in 1918-9, first researched by virologist Richard Slope in 1928. In 1976, fearful of another epidemic, U.S. health officials sponsored mass inoculation of the American public. Serious side effects in some recipients, however, suspended the vaccination program after a few months

swine·herd (swáinhə:rd) *n.* (*rhet.*) a person who tends swine

swing (swiŋ) **1.** *v. pres. part.* **swing·ing** *past* and *past part.* **swung** (swʌŋ) *v.i.* (of an object suspended from an overhead support) to sway freely to and fro, *a pendulum swings* ‖ to turn on or as if on a hinge, pivot etc., *she swung around on her heel* ‖ to move in a curved path, *he swung around the bend in the road* ‖ to go back and forth in a swing or hammock ‖ to turn as if in a certain direction, *opinion swung in his favor* ‖ to move along in a rhythmic, swaying motion, *to swing down a road* ‖ (*pop.*) to be executed by hanging ‖ to dance to swing music ‖ to use a sweeping arm movement in hitting or aiming at someone or something, *he swung at the man, but missed* ‖ (*naut.*, of a ship) to turn with the wind or tide while riding a single anchor ‖ to get oneself to a point or from point to point by grasping a fixed support and pulling, or by leaping from one fixed support to another, *to swing aboard a bus, to swing through the trees* ‖ *v.t.* to cause (something grasped) to move through the air with a sweeping motion, *to swing a bat* ‖ to cause (something suspended) to move back and forth, to *swing a censer* ‖ to cause (a person) to go back and forth in a swing or hammock ‖ to cause to turn on or as if on an axis, to *swing someone around to one's point of view* ‖ to cause to hang, *to swing a hammock* ‖ to convey (a suspended object) from one point to another, e.g. with a crane ‖ to exert an influence on in a way showing bias, *to swing a jury* ‖ (*pop.*) to manage (something) satisfactorily, *will he be able to swing the job?* ‖ to play (music) in the style of swing **2.** *n.* the arc or length of arc of a swinging object, *the swing of a pendulum* ‖ the act or an instance of swinging, *give it a swing* ‖ the manner of swinging, *with a steady swing* ‖ the rhythmic beat of poetry or music ‖ a seat suspended by ropes from a fixed support, in which one can swing to and fro ‖ the act of moving thus, *my turn for a swing* ‖ a free, easy motion, esp. in marching or walking ‖ the force behind a swinging or throwing motion (*commerce*) a shift markedly upwards or downwards in the price of stocks or in the trend of some business activity ‖ the course or development of some activity ‖ freedom of action, *let him have full swing in the management* ‖ the characteristic style of jazz music, esp. after 1935, depending on a distribution of accent that produces a lively but relaxed effect, the basic material being continuously taken up in free solo variations **in full swing** operating with full vigor [O.E. *swingan*]

swing bridge a type of drawbridge that can turn about a vertical axis to permit vessels to pass

swing-by (swíŋbai) *n.* (*aerospace*) **1.** the passing of celestial body by a spacecraft, usu. taking advantage of its gravitational force **2.** orbital deviation caused by gravitational pull, making possible a change in course of a passing body **3.** used attributively, the use of such force

swinge·ing (swíndʒiŋ) *adj.* (*Br., pop.*, e.g. of a fine or judicial sentence) enormous [O.E. *swengan*, to make swing]

swing·er (swíŋə:r) *n.* (*slang*) **1.** one who has many sexual partners **2.** one who is up-to-date in modern fashions and activities **3.** one who is active on the contemporary social scene —**swing** *v.* —**swinging** *n.*

swin·gle (swíŋg'l) *n.* a wooden instrument for beating and cleaning flax ‖ the swipple of a flail [M. Du. *swinghel*]

swingle *pres. part.* **swin·gling** *past* and *past part.* **swin·gled** *v.t.* to clean (flax) by beating with a swingle [M. Du. *swinghelen*]

swin·gle·tree (swíŋg'ltri:) *n.* a whiffletree

swing shift a shift normally from 4 p.m to midnight in a factory which operates 24 hours a day ‖ the workers working this shift

swing-wing (swíŋwiŋ) *n.* (*aerospace*) an aircraft in which retractable wings can be adjusted for various speeds, retreating toward the fuselage to minimize wind resistance —**swing wing** *n.* the wing itself —**swing-wing** *adj.*

swin·ish (swáiniʃ) *adj.* of, like or fit for swine

swipe (swaip) **1.** *v. pres. part.* **swip·ing** *past* and *past part.* **swiped** *v.i.* to make a powerful swinging blow, *to swipe at a ball* ‖ *v.t.* (*pop.*) to steal ‖ to hit with a swinging blow **2.** *n.* a powerful blow [var. of SWEEP]

swip·ple (swíp'l) *n.* that part of a flail that strikes the grain in threshing

swirl (swə:rl) **1.** *v.i.* (esp. of water) to move in eddies and whirls ‖ (of birds etc.) to move fast in a circular course ‖ (of the head) to have a whirling, dizzy sensation ‖ *v.t.* to cause to whirl **2.** *n.* a whirling movement ‖ an act or instance of swirling ‖ a swirling mass of water etc. ‖ a twist, curl, *a swirl of lace* [etym. doubtful]

swish (swiʃ) **1.** *v.i.* to cut through the air, e.g. with a whip, causing a sharp hissing or whistling sound ‖ (esp. of silk garments) to rustle ‖ *v.t.* to cause (e.g. a whip) to swish **2.** *n.* the sharp, hissing sound of a whip etc. cutting through the air, or the rustling sound of esp. silk garments brushing against the ground ‖ a movement accompanying the sound of swishing, *the swish of a lion's tail* **swish·y** *adj.* [imit.]

Swiss (swis) **1.** *adj.* of or relating to Switzerland or to a native or inhabitant of Switzerland **2.** *n.* a native or inhabitant of Switzerland

Swiss chard (tʃɑrd) *n. Beta vulgaris cicla,* a variety of beet having large, yellow-green leaves and thick, juicy stalks, both of which are eaten cooked or in salads [older *card* fr. F. *carde,* edible leafstalk of the artichoke]

Swiss cheese a hard, pale yellow cheese originating in Switzerland. Large holes form in it as it ripens

Swiss Guard (*hist.*) a member of any of various companies of Swiss mercenary soldiers ‖ a member of the papal guard of the Vatican

switch (switʃ) **1.** *n.* a device for diverting a train from one line to another ‖ a device for diverting an electric current from one wire to another, or for making or breaking an electric circuit ‖ the act of switching ‖ a thin, flexible stick, twig etc. ‖ a quick, lashing blow with a stick, twig etc. ‖ a tress of hair which a woman can add to her own to enhance her hairdo ‖ a wiry tuft of hairs at the end of the tail of some animals, e.g. a cow ‖ a complete change, *a switch in one's political opinions* **2.** *v.t.* to divert (something) to, or as if to, another track ‖ to beat with, or as if with, a switch ‖ to move with a jerk, *the horse switched its tail* ‖ *v.i.* to move from, or as if from, one set of railroad tracks to another **to switch on (off)** to turn on (off) by using an electric switch ‖ to start up (turn off) a radio or television set [prob. L.G.]

switch and flat maternity (*insurance*) provision in a group health-insurance plan providing maternity benefits to female employees only as dependents, i.e., when their husbands are covered, thereby denying maternity benefits to single women *Cf* FLAT MATERNITY, SWAP MATERNITY

switch·back (swítʃbæk) *n.* a zigzag railroad or road on a steep hill or mountain face ‖ (*Br.*) a roller coaster

switch·blade (swítʃbleid) *n.* a switchblade knife

switchblade knife a pocket knife with a spring-operated blade that is released by pressure on a button on the handle

switch·board (swítʃbɔrd, swítʃbourd) *n.* (*elec.*) a board or panel fitted with switches which control a number of electrical circuits, *a telephone switchboard*

switched-on (switʃdɔ́n) *adj.* (*slang*) in contact with events; alert to what is happening

switch foot (*surfing*) surfer who is comfortable on either foot

switch-hit·ter (swítʃhítər) *n.* (*baseball*) a player who can bat either right-handed or left-handed

switch horn (*mil.*) in naval mine warfare, a switch in a mine operated by a projecting spike *Cf* HORN

switch·man (swítʃmən) *pl.* **switch·men** (swítʃmən) *n.* a person who operates railroad switches

switch sale the unethical sale of a more expensive item by a store that advertised a bargain in order to attract customers *also* bait-and-switch, bait-and-switch sale —**switch selling** *n.* the practice

Swith·in, Swith·un (swíðin), St (*d.* 862), bishop of Winchester (852-62). Tradition has it that when his body was removed from its original burial place to Winchester Cathedral (July 15, 971), the saint expressed his disapproval by causing a 40-day rainfall. The superstition thus arose in Britain that rain on July 15 means rain for the next 40 days

Switz·er·land (swítsərlənd) a federal republic (area 15,941 sq. miles, pop. 6,384,300) of W. central Europe. Capital: Bern. Largest town: Zurich. Languages: German (72%), French (20%), Italian (6%), Romansh (1%, mainly in Graubünden). Religion: 53% Protestant, 46% Roman Catholic, small Old Catholic and Jewish minorities. The land is 6% arable, 46% meadow and pasture, 24% forest. The Bernese, Pennine, Lepontine and Rhaetian Alps, cut by deep valleys, cover the southern 60% of the country. Highest peak: Matterhorn, 14,780 ft. The Jura, on the French border, rise to over 5,000 ft. The rest of the country is a hilly plateau (1,000-3,000 ft), with several large lakes. Average temperatures (F.) in Jan. and July: Basel 32° and 66°, Davos 19° and 54°, St Gotthard 18° and 46°. Rainfall: Valais valley under 25 ins, upper Rhine valley 50 ins, northeastern mountains 96 ins. Livestock: cattle, hogs, sheep, poultry. Agricultural products: cereals, dairy products, fruit, vegetables, potatoes, sugar beets, wine, tobacco. Mineral resources: salt, coal, manganese, graphite, iron ore, lignite, marble, gneiss, granite. Industries: food processing, brewing, textiles, iron and steel, machinery, metals, scientific instruments, watches and clocks, aluminum, tourism, musical instruments, hydroelectricity, rolling stock, forestry, woodwork, pottery, jewelry, chemicals, tobacco, footwear, building materials. Exports: machinery, instruments, watches and clocks, chemicals, silk goods. cotton goods, cheese, iron and steel goods, embroidery, chocolate. Imports: machinery, iron and steel, vehicles, chemicals, coal and coke, cotton, wool, wheat. River port: Basle. There are seven universities, the oldest being Basle (1460), Lausanne (1537) and Geneva (1559). Monetary unit: Swiss franc (100 rappen or centimes). HISTORY. The region was inhabited by the Helvetii, a Celtic tribe, when it was conquered (58 B.C.) by the Romans. It was overrun by the Alemanni, the Burgundians and the Franks (5th-6th cc. A.D.). It was Christianized (7th-8th cc.). It was divided (9th c.) between Swabia and Burgundy, but was reunited (1032) as part of the Holy Roman Empire. By the 13th c. it had become split into a number of feudal principalities, many of them dominated by the houses of Hapsburg and Savoy. To meet the threat of Hapsburg domination the cantons of Schwyz, Unterwalden and Uri formed a defensive league (1291), defeated an Austrian army (1315), and were joined by Lucerne (1332), Zurich (1351), Glarus and Zug (1352) and Bern (1353). This Swiss Confederation defeated Charles the Bold of Burgundy and Emperor Maximilian I, and was recognized as independent (1499). More cantons joined the confederation, raising the number to 13 by 1513. After being defeated by the French (1515) in the Italian Wars, the cantons adopted a policy of permanent neutrality (1516), though many Swiss mercenaries continued to serve other countries. The Reformation, preached by Zwingli and Calvin, was widely adopted by the urban areas (16th c.), which were intermittently at war with the rural cantons until 1712. Swiss independence was formally recognized by the Treaties of Westphalia (1648). Switzerland lost political importance (18th c.) but prospered as a financial and intellectual center. The French established the Helvetic Republic (1798-1803), but Napoleon reestablished the confederation of cantons. The Congress of Vienna (1814-15) guaranteed Swiss independence and neutrality. After a short civil war (1847) between radicals and the Sonderbund, a new constitution made Switzerland a federal state (1848). Industry and communications were developed (late 19th c.). Switzerland gained importance as the headquarters of various international organizations (11% of the population are non-Swiss) and as an international financial center. It remained neutral in both world wars and after World War II it concentrated on maintaining its neutrality, improving education and welfare programs and developing its economy into one of the world's richest

swiv·el (swívəl) **1.** *n.* a mechanical device consisting of a pivot mounted in a ring so that the two parts of the device can revolve independently **2.** *v.i. pres. part.* **swiv·el·ing,** esp. *Br.* **swiv·el·ling** *past* and *past part.* **swiv·eled,** esp. *Br.* **swiv·elled** to turn on or as if on a swivel [rel. to O.E. *swīfan,* to move in a sweeping course]

swivel chair a chair having one pillar support which screws into a base so that the height of the seat can be altered and the user can swing around on it to face in any direction

swiz·zle stick (swíz'l) a thin rod, with or without prongs, for stirring drinks

swollen alt. *past part.* of SWELL

swoon (swu:n) **1.** *v.i.* (*rhet.*) to faint **2.** *n.* (*rhet.*) the action of fainting [M.E. *swounen* prob. fr. O.E. *geswōgen,* unconscious]

swoop (swu:p) **1.** *v.i.* (esp. of birds) to descend swiftly and suddenly, often in a wide, sweeping arc ‖ (esp. with 'down') to make a sudden attack, esp. from a great distance **2.** *n.* a swooping movement ‖ a sudden attack **at one fell swoop** by a single act of attack or a single effort [O.E. *swāpan,* to sweep]

swop *SWAP

sword (sɔrd, sourd) *n.* a weapon having a long, thin cutting blade fitted into a hilt which incorporates a guard **to cross swords** to disagree, argue violently [O.E. *sweord*]

sword dance a folk dance involving the use of swords ‖ a dance, esp. a solo dance, performed around swords laid on the ground

sword·fish (sɔ́rdfiʃ, sóurdfiʃ) *pl.* **sword·fish, sword·fish·es** *n. Xiphias gladius,* fam. *Iphiidae,* an enormous (200–600 lbs) game and food fish found in the Mediterranean and the Atlantic, having a long, rigid, swordlike upper jaw

sword grass any of several grasses or sedges of which the leaves have sharp or toothed edges

sword·play (sɔ́rdplei, sóurdplei) *n.* the art of fencing with the saber etc.

swords·man (sɔ́rdzmən, sóurdzmən) *pl.* **swords·men** (sɔ́rdzmən, sóurdzmən) *n.* a man skilled in fencing with the saber etc.

sword stick a hollow walking stick in which a sword blade is concealed

swore *past* of SWEAR

sworn (swɔrn, swourn) *past part.* of SWEAR ‖ *adj.* bound by oath or as if by oath, *sworn enemies*

swot *SWAT

swum *past part.* of SWIM

swung *past* and *past part.* of SWING

syb·a·rite (síbərait) *n.* a person inordinately attached to comfort, pleasure and luxury **syb·a·rít·ic** (sibəritik), **syb·a·rit·i·cal** *adjs.* **syb·a·rit·ism** (síbəraitizəm) *n.* [fr. L. *Sybarita* fr. Gk fr. *Sybaris,* an ancient Greek town in S. Italy famous as a center of luxury]

syc·a·more (síkəmɔr, síkəmour) *n. Platanus occidentalis,* a large, spreading plane tree of eastern and northern U.S.A. ‖ *Acer pseudoplatanus,* a genus of Eurasian maple trees, having striking yellow flowers. Sycamores are widely planted as shade trees ‖ the wood of either of these trees [O.F. *sicamor, sichamor* fr. L. fr. Gk]

sycamore fig *Ficus sycomorus,* fam. *Moraceae,* a genus of sycamore trees of Egypt and Asia Minor, having sweet, edible fruit resembling a fig

sy·co·ni·um (sikóuni:əm) *pl.* **sy·co·ni·a** (sikóuni:ə) *n.* a multiple fruit developed from many flowers enclosed in a fleshy receptacle, e.g. the fig [Mod. L. fr. Gk *sukon,* fig]

syc·o·phan·cy (síkəfənsi:) *n.* servile flattery [fr. L. *sycophantia* fr. Gk]

syc·o·phant (síkəfənt) *n.* a person who habitually uses flattery to gain personal advantage **syc·o·phan·tic** (sikəfǽntik) *adj.* [fr. L. *sycophanta* fr. Gk]

sy·co·sis (sikóusis) *pl.* **sy·co·ses** (sikóusi:z) *n.* an infection of the scalp or shaved area of the face [Mod. L. fr. Gk *sukōsis* fr. *sukon,* fig]

Sydney, Algernon *SIDNEY, ALGERNON

Syd·ney (sídni:) the chief city and port (pop. 3,231,700) of Australia, capital of New South Wales on Port Jackson, an inlet (½–1½ miles wide, 8 miles long) of the Pacific. Industries: textiles, food processing, foundries, automobiles, machinery, plastics, oil refining. Port Jackson is crossed by a single-span arch bridge (1932). Sydney University (1850) and University of New South Wales (1958)

sy·e·nite (sáiənait) *n.* an igneous rock, chiefly of orthoclase, with hornblende and other minerals **sy·e·nit·ic** (saiənitik) *adj.* [F. *syénite* fr. L. fr. Gk]

sy·li (sí:li:) *n.* unit of currency in Guinea, equal to 100 cauries

syl·la·bar·y (síləberi:) *pl.* **syl·la·bar·ies** *n.* a set or table or system of written characters representing syllables rather than individual sounds [fr. Mod. L. *syllabarium* fr. *syllaba,* syllable]

syl·lab·ic (silǽbik) **1.** *adj.* relating to a syllable or syllables ‖ of a consonant which by itself forms a syllable without a vowel sound (e.g. the 'l' in 'battle') ‖ pronounced distinctly with stress on each syllable ‖ of a verse form arranged according to syllables per line rather than according to rhythm or accent **2.** *n.* (*phon.*) a vocal speech sound capable by itself of forming a syllable **syl·láb·i·cal·ly** *adv.* [fr. Mod. L. *syllabicus* fr. Gk]

syl·lab·i·cate (silǽbikeit) *pres. part.* **syl·lab·i·cat·ing** *past* and *past part.* **syl·lab·i·cat·ed** *v.t.* to syllabify [fr. SYLLABICATION]

syl·lab·i·ca·tion (silæbikéiʃən) *n.* syllabification [fr. M.L. *syllabicatio* (*syllabicationis*) fr. *syllabicare,* to form into syllables]

syl·lab·i·fi·ca·tion (silæbifikéiʃən) *n.* formation of or division into syllables, or the method of such division [fr. M.L. *syllabificare* fr. *syllaba,* syllable]

syl·lab·ify (silǽbifai) *pres. part.* **syl·lab·i·fy·ing** *past* and *past part.* **syl·lab·i·fied** *v.t.* to form or divide into syllables [fr. L. *syllaba*, syllable]

syl·la·bize (síləbaiz) *pres. part.* **syl·la·biz·ing** *past* and *past part.* **syl·la·bized** *v.t.* to syllabify [fr. M.L. *syllabizare* fr. Gk]

syl·la·ble (síləb'l) *n.* a word or part of a word pronounced with a single sounding of the voice. It is usually composed of one vowel sound of great sonority and one or more consonants of less sonority ‖ the letter or letters (or symbols) written to represent a spoken syllable ‖ the least bit, *not a syllable of truth in it* [A.F. *sillable* fr. L. fr. Gk]

syllabub *SILLABUB

syl·la·bus (síləbəs) *pl.* **syl·la·bus·es, syl·la·bi** (síləbai) *n.* a brief outline of the ground to be covered in a course of lessons, lectures etc. [Mod. L. fr. Gk]

syl·lep·sis (silépsis) *pl.* **syl·lep·ses** (silépsi:z) *n.* (*gram.*) the application of one word to govern or modify two others in different senses though it agrees grammatically with only one of them **syl·lep·tic** (siléptik) *adj.* [L. fr. Gk *sullēpsis*, a putting together]

syl·lo·gism (síləd3izəm) *n.* a logically consistent argument consisting of two propositions (major and minor premises), and a conclusion deduced from them ‖ a branch of logic concerned with syllogisms **syl·lo·gis·tic, syl·lo·gís·ti·cal** *adjs.* [O.F. *sillogisme* or fr. L. fr. Gk]

syl·lo·gize (síləd3aiz) *pres. part.* **syl·lo·giz·ing** *past* and *past part.* **syl·lo·gized** *v.i.* to reason by syllogism ‖ *v.t.* to put (an argument) into syllogistic form [O.F. *silogiser, sillogiser* or fr. M.L.]

sylph (silf) *n.* (in the Paracelsian system) a spirit inhabiting the air, mortal and soulless, and generally female ‖ a slender, graceful woman or girl [fr. M.L. *sylphes pl. n.*, G. *sylphen*]

sylph·id (sílfid) *n.* a young or small sylph [F. *sylphide*]

Sylt (zilt) *SCHLESWIG-HOLSTEIN

syl·van, sil·van (sílvən) *adj.* of, relating to, characteristic of or situated in a wood ‖ wooded [fr. F. *sylvain* or fr. L. *silvanus, sylvanus*]

syl·van·ite (sílvənait) *n.* an ore of gold or silver combined with tellurium [after TRANSYLVANIA, place of earliest discovery]

Syl·ves·ter I, Sil·ves·ter I (silvéstər), St (*d.* 335), pope (314-35). Feast: Dec. 31

Sylvester II (c. 940-1003), pope (999-1003). He was a distinguished teacher and was the first French pope

sylviculture *SILVICULTURE

syl·vine (sílvin) *n.* sylvite

syl·vite (sílvait) *n.* a mineral, KCl, consisting of natural potassium chloride, found in colorless cubes or masses. It is an important source of potassium [fr. Mod. L. *sal digestivus sylvii* (old name)]

Symbionese Liberation Army terrorist anti-establishment organization, founded in California (1971), noted for kidnapping Patricia Hearst (1974) *abbr.* **SLA**

sym·bi·ont (símbaiɒnt, símbi:ɒnt) *n.* (*biol.*) an organism living in symbiosis [prob. fr. G. fr. Gk *sumbiountos* fr. *sumbioun*, to live together]

sym·bi·o·sis (sịmbaióusis, simbi:óusis) *n.* (*biol.*) the intimate association of two dissimilar organisms from which each organism benefits [Mod. L. fr. Gk *sumbiōsis*, a living together]

sym·bi·o·tic (sịmbaiɒ́tik, sịmbi:ɒ́tik) *adj.* of or characterized by symbiosis **sym·bi·ót·i·cal·ly** *adv.* [fr. Gk *sumbiōtikos*]

sym·bol (símb'l) *n.* a sign or object accepted as recalling, typifying or representing a thing, quality or idea ‖ a character, mark or sign standing for some process, idea, quality etc., e.g. as used in science, mathematics and music ‖ (*psychoanal.*) an act or object that represents a repressed unconscious drive, memory etc. **sym·bol·ic** (simbɒ́lik), **sym·ból·i·cal** *adjs.* **sym·ból·i·cal·ly** *adv.* [fr. L.L. *symbolum* fr. Gk]

symbolic logic a method of reasoning which operates with symbols rather than words

symbolic racism covert racism made legal by tokenism

sym·bol·ism (símb'lịzəm) *n.* representation by symbols ‖ a system of symbols symbolic meaning **Sym·bol·ism** the theories and practices of the Symbolists

—Symbolism came into being in the literature of Europe in the late 19th and early 20th cc. in reaction to naturalism and realism. Complex and deliberately planned, a Symbolist work was to express perfectly an intention on the part of the artist and create in the mind of the reader the exact equivalent. Mallarmé defined it as the recovering for poetry of the power of music, which communicated more subtly and precisely than any language could. Hence Symbolist poetry made use of the nonliteral, figurative powers of language: tone, association and metaphor. It became an art of elaborate structure, developing an image or network of images which caused the dislocation of normal syntax. Though this 'pure' symbolism is peculiar to Mallarmé and Valéry, it was prefigured by Laforgue and others and there are elements of it in such diverse writers as Hopkins, Eliot, Proust and Joyce. In music Symbolism is typified by Debussy, in drama by Maeterlinck, and its impact is felt in many Impressionist paintings

sym·bol·ist (símb'list) *n.* a person who uses symbols ‖ a writer or artist who uses symbolism **Sym·bol·ist** (*theol.*) a person who denies transubstantiation and regards the Eucharist as symbolic ‖ an exponent of Symbolism in literature, art or music

sym·bol·ize (símb'laiz) *pres. part.* **sym·bol·iz·ing** *past* and *past part.* **sym·bol·ized** *v.t.* to be a symbol of ‖ to represent by a symbol or symbols ‖ *v.i.* to use symbols [fr. F. *symboliser*]

sym·met·ric (simétrik) *adj.* symmetrical

sym·met·ri·cal (simétrik'l) *adj.* exhibiting symmetry

sym·me·trize (símitraiz) *pres. part.* **sym·me·triz·ing** *past* and *past part.* **sym·me·trized** *v.t.* to make symmetrical [fr. F. *symétriser*]

sym·me·try (símitri:) *pl.* **sym·me·tries** *n.* the quality of possessing exactly corresponding parts on either side of an axis (thus a circle has symmetry about any chosen diameter) ‖ a formal correspondence between two sets of mathematical symbols ‖ (*loosely*) the quality of being well balanced or well proportioned ‖ (*biol.*) regularity in form or similarity of structure [F. or fr. L.L. *symmetria* fr. Gk]

sym·mog·ra·phy (simɒ́grəfi:) *n.* art form of linear thread design, e.g., string craft, nail craft

sym·pa·thet·ic (sịmpəθétik) *adj.* of, relating to or possessing sympathy ‖ exactly fitting in with one's mood or attitude ‖ favorably disposed, *sympathetic towards contemporary design* ‖ (*physiol.*) of or relating to the sympathetic nervous system ‖ (*phys.*, of vibrations, sound etc.) caused by vibrations from a neighboring body ‖ (*literary criticism*) likable, attractive to the reader **sym·pa·thét·i·cal·ly** *adv.* [fr. Mod. L. *sympatheticus* fr. Gk]

sympathetic nervous system the part of the autonomic nervous system which has motor nerve fibers originating in the cervical, thoracic and lumbar regions of the spinal cord and that generally depresses glandular secretion, decreases muscle tone and induces blood-vessel contraction (cf. PARASYMPATHETIC NERVOUS SYSTEM)

sympathetic strike a strike in which workers not themselves involved in an industrial dispute go on strike to demonstrate their solidarity with those directly concerned

sym·pa·thize (símpəθaiz) *pres. part.* **sym·pa·thiz·ing** *past* and *past part.* **sym·pa·thized** *v.i.* to feel or communicate sympathy ‖ (esp. with 'with') to feel or express compassion for the sufferings, sorrows etc. of others ‖ to be in intellectual agreement ‖ (with 'with') to be favorably disposed [F. *sympathiser*]

sym·pa·tho·lyt·ic (sịmpəθoulítək) *adj.* (*chem.*) antagonistic to the sympathetic nervous system —**sympatholytic** *n.*

sym·pa·thy (símpəθi:) *pl.* **sym·pa·thies** *n.* a sharing in the emotions of others, esp. the sharing of grief, pain etc. ‖ a feeling for the ills, difficulties etc. of others ‖ a mutual liking resulting from an affinity of feeling ‖ (*physiol.*) the relation between bodily parts or organs whereby a disorder, pain etc. in one part or organ induces a similar effect in another **to be in sympathy with** to be favorably disposed towards (a cause, opinion etc.) ‖ to identify oneself with the opinion of (someone) [fr. L.L. *sympathia* fr. Gk]

sympathy strike a sympathetic strike

sym·pat·ric (simpǽtrək) *adj.* (*envir.*) occupying an area in common with another species

sym·pet·al·ous (simpét'ləs) *adj.* (*bot.*) having a tubular corolla formed by the union of a number of petals (opp. POLYPETALOUS) [fr. Gk *sun*, with+PETALOUS]

sym·phon·ic (simfɒ́nik) *adj.* of, relating to, or having the form or nature of a symphony ‖ of or relating to harmony of sound

symphonic poem a term introduced by Liszt to describe an orchestral work of symphonic dimensions which interprets something nonmusical, e.g. a legend

sym·pho·ny (símfəni:) *pl.* **sym·pho·nies** *n.* (*mus.*) an extended musical composition in sonata form for full orchestra ‖ a symphony orchestra [O.F. *simphonie* fr. L. fr. Gk]

symphony orchestra a large orchestra which performs symphonies and other large-scale orchestral works

sym·phy·sis (símfisis) *pl.* **sym·phy·ses** (símfisi:z) *n.* (*anat., zool.*) the union of certain bones, e.g. the halves of the lower jaw meeting at the chin ‖ the union of bones by fibrocartilage without a synovial membrane [Mod. L. fr. Gk *sumphusis*, a growing together]

sym·po·di·al (simpóudi:əl) *adj.* of, designating or characterized by a sympodium

sym·po·di·um (simpóudi:əm) *pl.* **sym·po·di·a** (simpóudi:ə) *n.* (*bot.*) a system of branches in which the main axis stops growing and the process of elongation is carried on by lateral branches (cf. MONOPODIUM) [Mod. L. fr. Gk *sun*, with+*podion*, a little foot]

sym·po·si·um (simpóuzi:əm) *pl.* **sym·po·si·a** (simpóuzi:ə), **sym·po·si·ums** *n.* a group discussion or a collection of published articles on a single theme ‖ a set of spoken or written contributions to a discussion of a single subject ‖ (*ancient Greece*) a banquet followed by drinking, music and intellectual discussion [L. fr. Gk *sun*, with+*potēs*, a drinker]

symp·tom (símptəm) *n.* a condition in the body or in its behavior, noted by the patient, suggesting the presence of injury or disease (cf. SIGN)

symp·to·mat·ic (sịmptəmǽtik) *adj.* of or relating to symptoms ‖ constituting a symptom ‖ in accordance with symptoms **symp·to·mát·i·cal·ly** *adv.* [F. *symptomatique*]

symp·tom·a·tol·o·gy (sịmptəmətɒ́ləd3i:) *n.* the branch of medicine dealing with the symptoms of disease [fr. Mod. L. *symptomatologia*]

syn- (sin) *prefix* with, together with, at the same time, by means of [Gk *sun*, with]

synaeresis *SYNERESIS

synaesthesia *SYNESTHESIA

syn·a·gog·i·cal (sịnəgɒ́d3ik'l) *adj.* of a synagogue

syn·a·gogue (sínəgɔg, sínəgɒg) *n.* a Jewish community meeting for religious observances or instruction ‖ the building or assembly place used by Jewish communities for this [O.F. *sinagoge* or fr. L.L. fr. Gk]

syn·a·loe·pha, syn·a·le·pha (sịnəlí:fə) *n.* (*gram.*) the blending of two syllables into one, esp. by suppressing the final vowel of the first, e.g. 'th' unknown' for 'the unknown' [L.L. fr. Gk fr. *sunaleiphein*, to coalesce, melt together]

syn·an·thro·py (sinǽnθroupi:) *n.* of the ecology in which human beings exist —**synanthropic** *adj.*

syn·apse (sinǽps, sínæps) *n.* (*physiol.*) the region at which a nervous impulse passes from one nerve cell to another, formed by the contact of processes of the two cells and responsible for the selection and propagation of nerve impulses characteristic of developed central nervous systems (*ACETYLCHOLINE) [fr. Gk *sunapsis*, junction]

syn·ap·sis (sinǽpsis) *pl.* **syn·ap·ses** (sinǽpsi:z) *n.* (*biol.*) the process characteristic of the prophase of the first meiotic division in which the chromosomes, without prior splitting, join in pairs, corresponding chromosomes from each parent being associated ‖ synapse [Mod. L. fr. Gk *sunapsis*, junction]

syn·ap·to·ne·mal (sinæptəní:məl) *n.* (*genetics*) ribbon-shaped structures in pairing of chromosomes, believed to take part in the genetic process *also* synaptinemal complex

syn·ar·thro·sis (sịnɑrθróusis) *pl.* **syn·ar·thro·ses** (sịnɑrθróusi:z) *n.* (*anat.*) a joining of bones by a fibrous tissue which does not permit movement between them [Mod. L. fr. Gk *sunarthrōsis*, a linking together]

syn·carp (sínkɑrp) *n.* (*bot.*) a multiple fleshy fruit **syn·cár·pous** *adj.* (*bot.*) possessing carpels joined in a compound ovary (e.g. in the tulip) ‖ referring to a syncarp [fr. SYN-+Gk *karpos*, fruit]

synch·ing (síŋkiŋ) *n.* synchronization of an onstage entertainer's lip movements to a tape played off-stage *also* lip-synching —**lip-synch** *v.* —**synch** *v.*

CONCISE PRONUNCIATION KEY: **(a)** æ, *cat*; ɑ, *car*; ɔ *fawn*; ei, *snake*. **(e)** e, *hen*; i:, *sheep*; iə, *deer*; εə, *bear*. **(i)** i, *fish*; ai, *tiger*; ə:, *bird*. **(o)** o, *ox*; au, *cow*; ou, *goat*; u, *poor*; ɔi, *royal*. **(u)** ʌ, *duck*; u, *bull*; u:, *goose*; ə, *bacillus*; ju:, *cube*. x, *loch*; θ, *think*; ð, *bother*; z, *Zen*; 3, *corsage*; d3, *savage*; ŋ, *orangutang*; j, *yak*; ʃ, *fish*; tʃ, *fetch*; 'l, *rabble*; 'n, *redden*. Complete pronunciation key appears inside front cover.

syn·chro·cy·clo·tron (siŋkrousáiklətrɒn) *n.* (*phys.*) a device similar to a cyclotron but having an alternating electric field whose frequency may be adjusted to compensate relativistic mass changes. The synchrocyclotron produces particles having energies in the range 10^5–10^7 eV [fr. *synchro-*, synchronous, synchronized+CYCLOTRON]

syn·chro·mesh (síŋkrəmeʃ) *n.* an arrangement of gears which synchronizes the driving and driven parts before they engage, eliminating shock and noise when the engagement is made [fr. *synchro-*, synchronous, synchronized+MESH]

syn·chron·ic (siŋkrɒ́nik, sinkrɒ́nik) *adj.* synchronous ‖ (*linguistics*) of or describing the structure of a language at one particular time (opp. DIACHRONIC) [fr. L.L. *synchronus*]

syn·chro·nism (síŋkrənizəm) *n.* the fact or quality of being synchronous ‖ the chronological arrangement of contemporary events, trends, leading figures etc. in different parts of the world or in different aspects of history ‖ a table setting this out [fr. Mod. L. *synchronismus* fr. Gk]

syn·chro·nis·tic (siŋkrənístik) *adj.* synchronous

syn·chro·ni·za·tion (siŋkrənizéiʃən) *n.* a synchronizing or being synchronized

syn·chro·nize (síŋkrənaiz) *pres. part.* **syn·chro·niz·ing** *past and past part.* **syn·chro·nized** *v.i.* to occur at the same time ‖ to proceed at the same rate ‖ *v.t.* to cause to occur at the same time or to proceed at the same rate ‖ to regulate so as to agree in time, *to synchronize watches* ‖ to put (events) at the same date or time ‖ (*movies*) to adjust (sounds) with the action ‖ to adjust (the shutter of a camera) so that the flashbulb goes off when the shutter opens [fr. Mod. L. *synchronismus* fr. Gk *sunchronizein* fr. *sunchronos*, contemporary]

synchronized swimming sport in which competitors perform gymnastic maneuvers, ballet, circular swimming, underwater somersaults *also* water ballet

syn·chro·nous (síŋkrənəs) *adj.* existing or occurring at the same time ‖ exactly coinciding in time, rate etc. ‖ (*phys.*) having the same phase and period [fr. L.L. *synchronus* fr. Gk]

synchronous orbit (*aerospace*) path of a communications relay station satellite that is traveling at the same speed as the earth, the satellite thus appearing to remain over one point on earth —**synchronous satellite** *n.*

syn·chro·tron (síŋkrətrɒn) *n.* (*phys.*) any of several particle accelerators utilizing some combination of frequency modulated alternating electric fields (as in the synchrocyclotron) for accelerating the particles and using specially designed focusing magnetic fields (as in the betatron) for maintaining stable orbits. Synchrotrons can be used to accelerate positively charged or negatively charged particles and produce particles with energies in the range 10^{10}–10^{12} eV [fr. *synchro-*, synchronous, synchronized+Gk *-tron*, instrument]

synchrotron radiation (*phys.*) radiation emitted by celestial bodies conceived as orbiting in and accelerated by a magnetic field similar to a vast synchrotron

syn·clas·tic (sinklǽstik) *adj.* (of a surface, e.g. the surface of a sphere) having the same curvature in all directions around any given point (opp. ANTICLASTIC) [fr. SYN-+Gk *klastos*, broken]

syn·cli·nal (sinkláin'l) *adj.* (*geol.*) of strata which dip towards a common point or line (opp. ANTICLINAL) **sýn·cline** *n.* (*geol.*) such an arrangement of strata (opp. ANTICLINE) [fr. Gk *sun*, syn+*klinein*, to incline together]

Syncom *n.* any of several U.S. communications relay satellite placed in synchronous equatorial orbit

syn·co·pate (síŋkəpeit, sínkəpeit) *pres. part.* **syn·co·pat·ing** *past and past part.* **syn·co·pat·ed** *v.t.* to shorten (a word) by syncope ‖ (*mus.*) to shift the regular accent in (a composition) to a normally unaccented beat **syn·co·pá·tion** (siŋkəpéiʃən) *n.* a syncopating or being syncopated ‖ (*gram.*) syncope ‖ syncopated rhythm [fr. L.L. *syncopare* (*syncopatus*), to affect with syncope]

syn·co·pe (síŋkəpi:, sínkəpi:) *n.* (*gram.*) the shortening of a word by dropping sounds or syllables from the middle of it ‖ loss of consciousness due to a sudden transient failure of blood supply to the brain [fr. L.L. fr. Gk fr. *sun*, together+*koptein*, to cut off, cut short]

syn·cret·ic (siŋkrétik, sinkrétik) *adj.* syncretistic

syn·cre·tism (síŋkrətizəm, sínkrətizəm) *n.* attempted reconciliation of conflicting or opposite beliefs, e.g. in philosophy or religion, esp. uncritically ‖ the development of a religion by the subsuming of older forms ‖ perception in which incompatible elements are fused, e.g., in dreams ‖ (*gram.*) the fusion into one of two or more differently inflected grammatical forms of a word **sýn·cre·tist** *n.* **syn·cre·tís·tic** *adj.* of or relating to syncretism or to a syncretist [fr. Mod. L. *syncretismus* fr. Gk]

syn·cre·tize (síŋkritaiz, sínkritaiz) *pres. part.* **syn·cre·tiz·ing** *past and past part.* **syn·cre·tized** *v.t.* to unite or attempt to unite (conflicting tenets), esp. without critical understanding ‖ *v.i.* to become fused or united ‖ to practice syncretism [fr. Mod. L. *syncretizare* fr. Gk]

syn·dac·tyl, syn·dac·tyle (sindǽktil) **1.** *adj.* (of some birds and some mammals) having two or more digits wholly or partly united **2.** *n.* a bird or mammal having syndactyl digits **syn·dác·tyl·ism** *n.* [fr. SYN-+Gk *daktulos*, finger]

syn·des·mo·sis (sindesmóusis) *pl.* **syn·des·mo·ses** (sindesmóusi:z) *n.* (*anat.*) an articulation of joints in which the bones are united by a ligament **syn·des·mot·ic** (sindesmɒ́tik) *adj.* [Mod. L. fr. Gk *sundesmos*, ligament]

syn·det·ic (sindétik) *adj.* (*gram.*) serving to connect [fr. Gk *sundetikos* fr. *sundein*, to bind together]

syn·dic (síndik) *n.* an official, esp. one who manages the business matters of a university or other corporation **sýn·di·cal** *adj.* [fr. F. fr. L.L. fr. Gk]

syn·di·cal·ism (síndik'lizəm) *n.* a political and economic theory advocating the use of general strikes and force by the workers to enable them to overthrow parliamentary government and establish a dictatorship of the proletariat, in which the means of production would be controlled by the trade unions. The theory, allied to anarchism, originated in France in the 19th c. **sýn·di·cal·ist** *adj.* and *n.* [fr. F. *syndicalisme*]

syn·di·cate 1. (síndikit) *n.* a body of syndics ‖ a group of persons or firms authorized jointly to promote some common interest ‖ a chain of newspapers ‖ an organization selling feature stories, cartoons etc. to several newspapers or magazines for simultaneous publication **2.** (síndikeit) *v. pres. part.* **syn·di·cat·ing** *past and past part.* **syn·di·cat·ed** *v.i.* to join together to form a syndicate ‖ *v.t.* to control as or form into a syndicate ‖ to sell (feature stories etc.) to several newspapers or magazines for simultaneous publication **syn·di·cá·tion** *n.* [fr. F. *syndicat* fr. M.L.]

syn·drome (síndroum) *n.* a group of disease symptoms commonly found in association with one another ‖ a number of disparate things regarded as an associated group [Mod. L. fr. Gk *sundromē*, a running together]

syn·ec·do·che (sinékdəki:) *n.* the rhetorical device by which the part is taken for the whole ('so much a head' instead of 'so much per person'), the whole for the part, the genus for the species, the species for the genus, the matter for the thing made of it etc. [L.L. fr. Gk *sunekdochē*, a receiving together]

syn·ec·tics (sinéktiks) *n.* method of stating and solving problems through analogy by brain storming, utilizing persons of diverse backgrounds —**synectic** *adj.* —**synectically** *adv.*

syn·er·e·sis, syn·aer·e·sis (siníərisis, sinérisis) *n.* (*prosody*) the contraction of two like vowels into a single syllable, esp. so as to form a diphthong (opp. DIAERESIS) ‖ synizesis [Mod. L. fr. Gk *sunairesis*, a taking together]

syn·erg·a·my (sinə́:rgəmi:) *n.* group marriage —**synergamous** *adj.*

syn·er·get·ic (sinərdʒétik) *adj.* synergic [fr. Gk *sunergētikos* fr. *sunergein*, to work with, cooperate]

syn·er·gic (sinə́:rdʒik) *adj.* of or characterized by synergy [fr. Mod. L. *synergicus* fr. Gk]

syn·er·gism (sínərdʒizəm) *n.* (*theol.*) the doctrine that divine grace and human activity cooperate in the work of regeneration ‖ (esp. of drugs) the combined action of two or more which have a greater total effect than the sum of their individual effects **sýn·er·gist** *n.* (*theol.*) a person who holds the doctrine of synergism ‖ (*med.*) a muscle, organ or drug acting in synergy with another or others **syn·er·gis·tic** *adj.* (*theol.*) of or relating to synergism ‖ (*med.*) able to act in synergism [fr. Mod. L. *synergismus* fr. Gk]

syn·er·gy (sínərdʒi:) *pl.* **syn·er·gies** *n.* (*med.*) the working together of two or more muscles, organs or drugs [fr. Mod. L. *synergia*, joint work fr. Gk]

syn·e·sis (sínisis) *n.* (*gram.*) a construction which conforms to the general sense rather than to syntax (e.g. use of a plural verb with a collective singular noun) [Mod. L. fr. Gk *sunesis*, understanding]

syn·es·the·sia, syn·aes·the·sia (sinisθí:ʒi:ə, sinisθí:ʒə) *n.* (*psychol.*) the spontaneous association of sensations of different kinds, e.g. the suggestion of a certain color by certain sounds [Mod. L. fr. Gk *sun*, with+*aisthēsia*, sensation]

syn·fuel (sínfju:l) *n.* synthetic fuel

syn·gam·ic (siŋgǽmik, singǽmik) *adj.* of or characteristic of syngamy

syn·ga·my (síŋgəmi:) *n.* (*biol.*) sexual: reproduction by the fusion of gametes [fr. SYN-+Gk *gamos*, marriage]

Synge (siŋ), John Millington (1871-1909), Irish playwright. His works include 'Riders to the Sea' (1905), 'The Playboy of the Western World' (1907) and 'Deirdre of the Sorrows' (1910). In these plays he makes use of the vigorous and vivid dialect of the fishermen and peasants of W. Ireland

syn·ge·ne·ic (sindʒəní:ik) *adj.* (*genetics*) of a similar or identical genotype *Cf* ALLOGENEIC

syn·gen·e·sis (sindʒénisis) *n.* (*biol.*) derivation of the zygote in sexual reproduction from both the paternal and the maternal substance ‖ (*geol.*) the formation of sediments in place **syn·ge·net·ic** (sindʒənétik) *adj.* [Mod. L.]

syn·graph (síngræf) *n.* a written agreement signed by all parties involved

syn·i·ze·sis (sinizí:sis) *n.* the contraction of two syllables into a single syllable by the pronunciation of two adjacent vowels as though they were a single vowel [L.L. fr. Gk *sunizēsis*, collapse]

syn·met·al (sínmet'l) *n.* synthetic nonmetallic material that conducts electricity

syn·od (sínəd) *n.* (*eccles.*) a consultative council of clergy ‖ a Presbyterian ecclesiastical court which acts as an administrative body intermediate between the General Assembly and the presbyteries ‖ a council [fr. L.L. *synodus* fr. Gk]

syn·od·al (sínəd'l) *adj.* of, relating to, or constituting a synod [fr. L.L. *synodalis*]

syn·od·ic (sinɒ́dik) *adj.* synodical **syn·ód·i·cal** *adj.* synodal ‖ (*astron.*) of or relating to conjunction, exp. of the interval between two successive conjunctions of the same bodies [fr. L.L. *synodicus* fr. Gk]

syn·oe·cism (siní:sizəm) *n.* a joining together of villages or small towns to form one administrative complex, e.g. a Greek city-state ‖ (*bot.*) the state of being synoicous [fr. Gk *sunoikismos*, wedlock, act of combining into one city-state]

syn·oi·cous (sinɔ́ikəs) *adj.* (*bot.*) having stamens and pistils in the same flower or on the same flower head or, in certain mosses, having archegonia and antheridia in the same involucre or on the same receptacle [Gk *sunoikos*, dwelling together]

syn·o·nym (sínənim) *n.* a word having the same meaning as another word in the same language in one or more of its senses, *'car'* and *'automobile'* are synonyms (opp. ANTONYM) ‖ a metonym ‖ (*biol.*) a rejected taxonomic name **syn·o·ným·ic** *adj.* **syn·o·nym·i·ty** (sinənímiti:) *n.* **syn·on·y·mous** (sinɒ́nəməs) *adj.* [fr. L.L. *synonymum*, *synonymon* fr. Gk *sunōnumos* fr. *sun*, together+*onum*, name]

syn·on·y·my (sinɒ́nəmi:) *pl.* **syn·on·y·mies** *n.* the quality or fact of being synonymous ‖ a collection of synonyms ‖ the study of synonyms [fr. L.L. *synonymia* fr. Gk]

syn·op·sis (sinɒ́psis) *pl.* **syn·op·ses** (sinɒ́psi:z) *n.* an outline, summary [L.L. fr. Gk *sunopsis*, a general view]

syn·op·tic (sinɒ́ptik) **1.** *adj.* providing a general summary **Syn·op·tic** of or relating to the first three books (Matthew, Mark, Luke) of the New Testament, which agree frequently in subject, order and language **2.** *n.* one of the Synoptic Gospels **syn·óp·ti·cal** *adj.* **syn·óp·ti·cal·ly** *adv.* [fr. Mod. L. *synopticus* fr. Gk]

synoptic (*meteor.*) of data collected at many points simultaneously to present overview of weather conditions

synoptic chart a meteorological map presenting data and analyses which describe weather conditions over a large area at a given moment in time

Syn·op·tist (sinóptist) *n.* an author of one of the Synoptic Gospels

syn·o·vi·a (sinóuvi:ə) *n.* the fluid produced by the transparent internal lining membrane of joints, acting as a lubricant **syn·ó·vi·al** *adj.* of or secreting synovia **syn·o·vi·tis** (sinəváitis) *n.* inflammation in a synovial membrane [Mod. L.]

syn·tac·tic (sintǽktik) *adj.* syntactical **syn·tác·ti·cal** *adj.* of or relating to syntax or in accordance with the rules of syntax [fr. Mod. L. *syntacticus* fr. Gk]

syn·tax (síntæks) *n.* the arrangement of words in a sentence showing their constructional relationship ‖ the branch of grammar concerned with this [fr. F. *syntaxe* fr. L.L. fr. Gk]

syn·thase (sínθeis) *n.* (*biochem.*) any synthetic enzyme used in catalysis

syn·the·sis (sínθisis) *pl.* **syn·the·ses** (sínθisi:z) *n.* (*logic*) a method of demonstration which consists in reasoning from self-evident propositions, laws or principles to arrive by a series of deductions at what one seeks to establish ‖ an exposition assembling the various parts into a whole, *a historical synthesis* ‖ (*chem.*) the formation of a compound from elements or simpler compounds **sýn·the·sist** *n.* **sýn·the·size** (sínθisaiz) *v.t. pres. part.* **syn·the·siz·ing** *past* and *past part.* **syn·the·sized** to form into a whole by synthesis ‖ (*chem.*) to produce (e.g. an organic compound) by synthesis [L. fr. Gk *sunthesis*, a putting together, composition]

syn·the·tase (sínθəteis) *n.* (*biochem.*) a catalytic enzyme that causes the formation of nucleoside monophosphate or diphosphate from nucleoside triphosphate *also* ligase

syn·the·siz·er (sínθəsaizər) *n.* (*electr.*) a device that creates complex entities of simple sound or frequency elements, e.g., a voice synthesizer in a computer

syn·thet·ic (sinθétik) **1.** *adj.* relating to or involving synthesis produced by synthesis ‖ artificial, man-made, *synthetic fibers* ‖ using inflections or affixes to express syntactical relationships **2.** *n.* a synthetic product, e.g. nylon **syn·thét·i·cal·ly** *adv.* [fr. F. *synthétique* or Mod. L. *syntheticus* fr. Gk]

synthetic foam a strong, pressure-resistant plastic containing air cells to reduce weight in packing

synthetic fur fun fur (which see)

syn·the·tize (sínθitaiz) *pres. part.* **syn·the·tiz·ing** *past* and *past part.* **syn·the·tized** *v.t.* to synthesize

syph·i·lis (sífəlis) *n.* a chronic, often congenital venereal disease, caused by the spirochete *Treponema pallidum.* If untreated the disease may result in the degeneration of many organs and tissues of the body **syph·i·lit·ic** (sifəlitik) *n.* and *adj.* [Mod. L. after 'Syphilis sive Morbus Gallicus', a poem by Girolamo Fracastoro (1483–1553)]

sy·phon, si·phon (sáifən) *n.* a bottle holding a tube fitted at the top with a valve which when opened allows the carbonated water in the bottle to be ejected [fr. L. *sipho* (*siphonis*), tube, pipe fr. Gk]

Syr·a·cuse (sírəkju:s) a city (pop. 170,105) in central New York State: chemicals, car parts, electrical appliances, mechanical engineering. University (1870)

Syr·a·cuse (*Ital.* Siracusa) a port (pop. 89,000) in S.E. Sicily: Greek theater (5th c. B.C.) and temples, Roman amphitheater. Castle (13th c.), baroque cathedral (17th-18th cc.), palaces. Syracuse was founded as a Greek colony (8th c. B.C.), defeated an attack by Athens (415-413 B.C.) and was sacked (212 B.C.) by the Romans

Syr-Dar·ya (si:rdárjɑ) (ancient Jaxartes) a river (1,370 miles long, navigable along its middle course) formed in the Ferghana Valley by streams from the Tien Shan and Altai Mtns, and flowing north through Uzbekistan, Tadzhikistan and Kazakhstan, U.S.S.R., to the Aral Sea

Syr·i·a (síri:ə) a republic (area 71,210 sq. miles, pop. 8,979,000) in W. Asia. Capital: Damascus. People: 90% Arab, small Turkish, Turkoman, Kurdish, Circassian, Armenian and other minorities. Language: Arabic, minority languages. Religion: 72% Sunnites, 11% Shi'ites, 2% Druze, 3% Greek Orthodox, 2% Armenian Orthodox, 2% Roman Catholic, smaller Christian sects, some Jews. The population is 10% nomadic (Beduins). The land is 30% arable, 34% pasture and grazing, and 2% forest. It is largely a plateau (1,000-3,000 ft), with the Ansariyeh Mtns (rising to 5,194 ft) near the northwest coast, the Anti-Lebanon Mtns (*HERMON) on the Lebanon border, Gebel Druse (5,900 ft) in the south, and isolated massifs in the center. The Euphrates basin (1,000-3,000 ft) crosses the northeast. East of the Anti-Lebanon Mtns, the Syrian Desert covers the south. The north is semiarid grassland (livestock, dry cereal culture). Average temperatures (F.) for Jan. and July: Latakia 56° and 81°, Palmyra 46° and 110°, E. Euphrates valley 43° and 90°. Rainfall: Aleppo 15 ins, Damascus 9 ins, coast 20-40 ins, desert under 5 ins. Livestock: sheep, goats, cattle, donkeys, mules, camels. Agricultural products: wheat, rice, other cereals, sugar beets, pulses, fruit, olives, tomatoes, figs, cotton, tobacco, almonds, dairy products. Mineral resources: asphalt, natural gas, bitumen, basalt, building stone, salt. Industries: food processing, soap, cement, tobacco, tanning, textiles, glass, footwear, metalware, wine. Exports: cotton, cereals, silk fabrics, wool, cottonseed, lentils, sheep. Imports: iron and steel, machinery, fuel and oils, silk, wool, wood, vehicles, chemicals. Chief port: Latakia. Universities: Damascus (1924) and Aleppo (1961). Monetary unit: Syrian pound (100 piasters). HISTORY. Situated on trade routes between the Mediterranean and Mesopotamia, Syria was settled (3rd millennium B.C.) by Semitic Amorites. Canaanites settled on the coast (2nd millennium B.C.) and the Aramaeans established their capital at Damascus (11th c. B.C.). Parts of Syria were overrun by the Egyptians and the Hittites (18th-10th cc. B.C.), the Assyrians (8th c. B.C.), the Babylonians or Chaldeans (7th c. B.C.) and the Persians (6th c. B.C.). Control passed (333 B.C.) to Alexander the Great, and after his death (323 B.C.) to the Seleucids, under whom Hellenistic culture was introduced. Syria was conquered (63 B.C.) by the Romans under Pompey. It flourished under Roman rule and the south of the country saw the rise of Christianity. Syria passed to the Byzantine Empire (395 A.D.) and was fully converted to Christianity, but was overrun (633-6) by the Arabs and was gradually converted to Islam. Damascus prospered as the capital of the Umayyad caliphate (651-750), but Syria declined when the Abbasids moved the caliphate to Baghdad. The Seljuk Turks and the Mamelukes repelled the Crusades (11th-13th cc.), and the Ottoman Turks established their rule (1516). Syria was invaded by the French (1799), and by the Egyptians (1832) under Ibrahim Pasha, who ruled as governor (1833-9). Arab nationalism began in Lebanon and Syria about the turn of the century, and separatist movements against the Turks were encouraged by Britain and France during the 1st world war. With Lebanon, Syria became a French mandate (1920). The French put down a rebellion (1925-7) with severity. Syria was occupied (1941) by the British and the Free French, and was declared independent (Jan. 1, 1944), but sporadic fighting continued between French and Syrian forces until 1945. Syria joined the Arab League and the U.N. (1945). After a series of coups d'état, Syria joined the United Arab Republic (1958), but seceded (1961). After further revolts, it sought closer links with the United Arab Republic (1963). A further military coup took place in 1966. Syria joined (1971) the Union of Arab Republics (with Egypt and Lebanon). Syria lost territory on the Golan Heights to Israel during wars (1967, 1973). Syrian troops occupied most of Lebanon (1976) in an effort to end civil war in that country. A military coup (1970) brought Gen. Hafiz al-Assad to power. He was elected president by public referendum (1971) and reelected (1978, 1985)

Syr·i·ac (síri:æk) **1.** *adj.* of, relating to or written in Syriac **2.** *n.* Aramaic ‖ a form of Aramaic spoken by Eastern Christian communities ‖ the liturgical language used by some Eastern Christian Churches (cf. PESHITTA, cf. NESTORIAN CHURCH)

Syr·i·an (síri:ən) **1.** *n.* a native or inhabitant of Syria ‖ a member of a Syrian Church **2.** *adj.* of or relating to Syria, its peoples, language, culture etc. ‖ of, relating to or being one of the Eastern Churches using Syriac liturgies, e.g. the Nestorian-Church

Syrian Desert (*Arab.* Hamad) a desert region covering most of S. Syria and S.W. Iraq, and adjoining regions of Jordan and Saudi Arabia

sy·rin·ga (siríŋgə) *n.* a member of *Philadelphus*, fam. *Saxifragaceae*, a genus of shrubs of temperate regions having strong-scented white flowers [Mod. L. fr. Gk *surinx* (*suringos*), shepherd's pipe]

sy·ringe (sirínd3, sirínd3) **1.** *n.* a piston-fitted hand cylinder, or a rubber bulb with a nozzle, into which a liquid is sucked and then ejected in a stream for cleansing, spraying or injecting **2.** *v.t. pres. part.* **sy·ring·ing** *past* and *past part.* **sy·ringed** to inject, cleanse etc. with a syringe [fr. M.L. *siringa, syrynga*]

sy·rin·ge·al (sirínd3i:əl) *adj.* of or relating to the syrinx

syr·inx (síriŋks) *pl.* **sy·rin·ges** (sirínd3i:z), **syr·inx·es** *n.* a panpipe ‖ the vocal organ of birds [L. fr. Gk *surinx*, a pipe]

Syro- (sírou) *combining form* Syrian and ‖ Syriac and

Sy·ros (sáirɒs) (or Syra) an island (area 31 sq. miles, pop. 18,642) of the N. Cyclades, containing their chief port, Hermoupolis (pop. 14,000)

syr·up, sir·up (sírəp, sə́:rəp) *n.* a thick liquid consisting of a concentrated solution of sugar and water ‖ such a thick liquid with flavoring or some medicinal substance added, *cough syrup* ‖ evaporated juice of sugarcane before crystallization of the sugar, in the process of manufacturing cane sugar ‖ cloying sentimentality **sýr·up·y, sír·up·y** *adj.* [O. F. *sirop, cyrop*]

sys·tal·tic (sistǽltik, sistóltik) *adj.* (*physiol.*, of the heart) characterized by regular contraction and dilatation [fr. L.L. *systalticus* fr. Gk]

sys·tem (sístəm) *n.* an orderly, interconnected, complex arrangement of parts, *the nervous system* ‖ a set of principles linked to form a coherent doctrine, *a philosophical system* ‖ a method of organization, administration or procedure ‖ (*geol.*) a major division of rocks, formed during a period or era, *the Devonian system* ‖ (*astron.*) a group of orbiting heavenly bodies moving about a central body ‖ (*biol.*) a group of bodily organs having the same or similar structure and which act as a unit in performing a vital bodily function, *the circulatory system* ‖ (*biol.*) a method of classification ‖ a set of units permitting the basic measurements to be clearly and simply stated, *the metric system* ‖ calculated orderliness, *to work with system* [fr. L.L. *systema* fr. Gk]

system approach a mathematical approach to the study of the components of a system to define how the system will behave under various circumstances *Cf* SYSTEMS ANALYSIS

sys·tem·at·ic (sistəmǽtik) *adj.* constituting a system, *a systematic philosophy* ‖ working in accordance with a system, methodical ‖ relating to classification in biology **sys·tem·át·i·cal·ly** *adv.* **sys·tem·at·ics** *n.* the science of classification [fr. L.L. *systematicus* fr. late Gk]

sys·tem·a·tist (sístəmətist) *n.* a taxonomist

sys·tem·a·ti·za·tion (sistəmətizéiʃən) *n.* a systematizing or being systematized

sys·tem·a·tize (sístəmətaiz) *pres. part.* **sys·tem·a·tiz·ing** *past* and *past part.* **sys·tem·a·tized** *v.t.* to make into a system

sys·tem·ic (sistémik) *adj.* of or relating to a system, esp. (*physiol.*) of or relating to the entire bodily system

sys·tem·i·za·tion (sistəmizéiʃən) *n.* systematization

sys·tem·ize (sístəmaiz) *pres. part.* **sys·tem·iz·ing** *past* and *past part.* **sys·tem·ized** *v.t.* to systematize

system levels a set of criteria used to analyze political systems, their efficiency, benefits, problems, etc.

systems analysis the study of an activity to determine objectives and how to accomplish them most efficiently, e.g., procedures for collecting, manipulating, and evaluating computer data to improve control over an operation —**systems analyst** *n.*

systems engineering a technique of management theory involving rationalistic models of business organizations, based on the interrelation of components and on the input and output of the total system under consideration

sys·to·le (sístəli:) *n.* (*physiol.*) the regular contraction of an organ (e.g. the heart or an artery) by which the blood is driven forward (opp. DIAS-

CONCISE PRONUNCIATION KEY: **(a)** æ, *cat*; ɑ, *car*; ɔ *fawn*; ei, *snake*. **(e)** e, *hen*; i:, *sheep*; iə, *deer*; ɛə, *bear*. **(i)** i, *fish*; ai, *tiger*; ə:, *bird*. **(o)** o, *ox*; au, *cow*; ou, *goat*; u, *poor*; ɔi, *royal*. **(u)** ʌ, *duck*; u, *bull*; u:, *goose*; ə, *bacillus*; ju:, *cube*. x, *loch*; θ, *think*; ð, *bother*; z, *Zen*; ʒ, *corsage*; dʒ, *savage*; ŋ, *orangutang*; j, *yak*; ʃ, *fish*; tʃ, *fetch*; 'l, *rabble*; 'n, *redden*. Complete pronunciation key appears inside front cover.

TOLE) **sys·tol·ic** (sistólik) *adj.* [Mod. L. fr. Gk *sustolē*, contraction]

syz·y·gy (sízidʒi:) *pl.* **syz·y·gies** *n.* (*astron.*) a point of conjunction or opposition of a planet, esp. the moon, with the sun [fr. L.L. *syzygia* fr. Gk]

Szcze·cin (ʃtʃetsí:n) (*G.* Stettin) a port and naval base (pop. 381,000) in Poland on the Oder near its mouth, with shipbuilding, machinery, paper, chemical and metallurgical industries.

It includes a free port. Churches (12th and 14th cc.)

Sze·chwan (sʌtʃwán) a province (pop. 90,000,000) of western and central China, around the middle Yang-tze-kiang. Capital: Chengtu. It is the largest and most populous province, at the heart of which lies the Red Basin, a rich agricultural region with extensive mineral resources

Sze·ged (séged) a town (pop. 175,700) in S. Hun-

gary on the Tisza. Industries: textiles, food processing. University

Szek·ler (séklər) *n.* the Transylvanian branch of the Magyar people ‖ their dialect of Hungarian, written in its own runic alphabet

Sze·ming (súːmíŋ) *AMOY

Szent-Györ·gyi (sentdjéardji:), Albert von Nagyrapolt (1893–), Hungarian biochemist. He isolated vitamin C and prepared it in bulk from Hungarian paprika (Nobel prize, 1937)

CONCISE PRONUNCIATION KEY: **(a)** æ, c*a*t; ɑ, c*a*r; ɔ f*aw*n; ei, sn*a*ke. **(e)** e, h*e*n; iː, sh*ee*p; iə, d*ee*r; ɛə, b*ea*r. **(i)** i, f*i*sh; ai, t*i*ger; əː, b*i*rd. **(o)** o, *o*x; au, c*ow*; ou, g*oa*t; u, p*oo*r; ɔi, r*o*yal. **(u)** ʌ, d*u*ck; u, b*u*ll; uː, g*oo*se; ə, b*a*cill*u*s; juː, c*u*be. x, lo*ch*; θ, *th*ink; ð, bo*th*er; z, *Z*en; ʒ, cor*s*age; dʒ, *s*avage; ŋ, ora*n*guta*ng*; j, *y*ak; ʃ, *fi*sh; tʃ, fe*tch*; 'l, rab*ble*; 'n, red*den*. Complete pronunciation key appears inside front cover.

	EARLY NORTH SEMITIC	PHOENICIAN	EARLY HEBREW (GEZER)	EARLY GREEK	CLASSICAL GREEK	ETRUSCAN Early Classical	EARLY LATIN	CLASSICAL LATIN

CURSIVE MAJUSCULE (ROMAN)	CURSIVE MINUSCULE (ROMAN)	ANGLO-IRISH MAJUSCULE	CAROLINE MINUSCULE	VENETIAN MINUSCULE (ITALIC)	N. ITALIAN MINUSCULE (ROMAN)

A. C. SYLVESTER, CAMBRIDGE, ENGLAND

Development of the letter T, beginning with the early North Semitic letter. Evolution of both the majuscule, or capital, letter T and the minuscule, or lowercase, letter t are shown.

T,t (ti:) the twentieth letter of the English alphabet **to a T** exactly

T (*electr. symbol*) for **1.** tera (10^{12}) **2.** (*symbol*) for testa, high-frequency current with moderate voltage

TA (*abbr.*) for **1.** teaching assistant **2.** (*abbr.*) for transactional analysis

Taal (tɑl) (with 'the') Afrikaans [Du.=language, speech]

tab (tæb) *n.* a small loop or flap attached to or forming an extension of something, having a special use or ornamental value, e.g. the lettered projection of a filing card or a point of lace or other trimming ‖ an unpaid bill, *pick up the tab*, or the price that has to be paid for something, *what will the tab be?* ‖ (*Br., mil.*) a collar mark denoting the rank of a staff officer **to keep tab** (or **tabs**) **on** (*Br.* **to keep tab of**) to keep a check on [etym. doubtful]

tab·a·nid (tǽbənid) *n.* a member of *Tabanidae*, a family of flies comprising the horseflies etc., whose females suck blood [fr. L. *tabanus*, gadfly]

tab·ard (tǽbərd) *n.* (*hist.*) a tunic worn by a knight over his armor and emblazoned with his arms ‖ a herald's cloak emblazoned with his sovereign's arms [O.F. *tabart, tabar*]

Ta·bas·co (təbǽskou, tɑbɑ́skɔ) a gulf state (area 9,783 sq. miles, pop. 1,101,300) of S.E. Mexico, covered by lagoons, swamps, and dense forests (Tabasco means 'damp earth'). Capital: Villahermosa (pop. 34,000). Main agricultural products: bananas, cocoa, coffee, rice, sugarcane, corn and tropical fruits. Forest products: valuable fine woods and dyewoods. Potential oil wealth

ta·bas·co (təbǽskou) *n.* a pungent sauce made from the fruit of the capsicum [after *Tabasco*, a river and state in Mexico]

tab·by (tǽbi:) *pl.* **tab·bies** *n.* a cat with brownish-gray fur marked with dark, wavy stripes ‖ a female cat (opp. TOM) ‖ (*old-fash.*) a sour scandalmongering woman, esp. if she is unmarried [etym. doubtful]

tab·er·nac·le (tǽbərnæk'l) *n.* (*eccles.*) an ornamental repository for the pyx or consecrated elements ‖ (*archit.*) a niche or recess having a canopy ‖ a Nonconformist place of worship ‖ (*naut.*) a socket or hinged post enabling the mast of a vessel to be lowered in order to pass under a low bridge **the Tabernacle** the portable sanctuary containing the Ark of the Covenant serving as a place of worship for the Jews in their wanderings in the desert when they came out of Egypt [O.F.]

tabernacle work (*archit.*) pierced tracery or other carved ornamental work, e.g. over niches, choir stalls etc. in churches

ta·bes (téibi:z) *pl.* **ta·bes** *n.* (*med.*) the process of wasting that sometimes accompanies a chronic disease, e.g. tuberculosis ‖ (*med.*) tabes dorsalis [L.= a wasting away]

tabes dor·sa·lis (dɔrséilis) (*med.*) a form of syphilis marked by wasting, lack of coordination of movement and disturbances of digestive and sensory organs

ta·bet·ic (təbétik) **1.** *adj.* of, resembling, or having tabes dorsalis **2.** *n.* a person having tabes dorsalis [fr. L. *tabes*, a wasting away]

ta·bla (tǽblə) *n.* Indian tuned drum, usu. in a pair, of two sizes

ta·ble (téib'l) **1.** *n.* a piece of furniture having a flat, horizontal, usually smooth surface of wood or other material. It is supported by legs or a pedestal or pedestals, and is used to sit at for meals, for working, for playing games etc. ‖ a group of people sitting around this, esp. for eating ‖ a flat, often movable part of a machine tool on which material to be worked is fastened ‖ a stringcourse ‖ a tableland ‖ the upper flat facet of a gem (cf. CULET) ‖ (*anat.*) the internal or external layer of the bony tissue of the skull ‖ (*backgammon*) one of the two leaves of the board or either half of a leaf ‖ an orderly arrangement of facts set out for easy reference, *a table of contents* ‖ an arrangement of numerical values etc. in vertical columns, *logarithmic tables* **to keep** (or **set**) **a good** (**poor** etc.) **table** to serve good (poor etc.) food at one's table **to turn the tables on** (someone) to put (someone) who had the advantage over one at a disadvantage **under the table** into a state of unconsciousness or near unconsciousness, *to drink someone under the table* **2.** *v.t. pres. part.* **ta·bling** *past* and *past part.* **ta·bled** (*Br.*) to put forward (a proposal etc.) for consideration by an assembly ‖ to postpone a decision on (e.g. a proposal) indefinitely ‖ to tabulate ‖ (*naut.*) to reinforce the edge of (a sail) by making a wide hem [O.E. *tabule, tabele*]

tab·leau (tǽblou, tæblóu) *pl.* **tab·leaus**, **tab·leaux** (tǽblouz, tæblóu) *n.* a group of people so posed (e.g. in a pageant) as to seem to the beholder to have a significant unity [F.]

ta·bleau vi·vant (tæblouvi:vɑ̃) *pl.* **ta·bleaux vivants** (tæblouvi:vɑ̃) *n.* a static, wordless representation of a scene, esp. a historical scene, famous picture etc. by one or more persons [F.]

ta·ble·cloth (téib'lklɔθ, téib'lklɔθ) *pl.* **ta·blecloths** (téib'lklɔθs, téib'lklɔθs, téib'lklɔðz, téib'lklɔ̃ðz) *n.* a cloth used to cover a dining table

ta·ble-cut (téib'lkʌt) *adj.* (of a gem) cut with a flat upper surface larger than the culet, with facets linking the table to the girdle

ta·ble d'hôte (tɑbldout) *n.* a fixed list of dishes for a fixed price, in a restaurant etc. (cf. A LA CARTE) [F.=the host's table]

ta·ble·land (téib'llænd) *n.* (*geol.*) a plateau

table linen tablecloths, napkins etc.

Table Mountain a flat-topped mountain (3,550 ft) rising steeply above Cape Town, South Africa

table rapping spirit rapping

ta·ble·spoon (téib'lspu:n) *n.* a large spoon used for serving food from a dish to a plate. It holds about four teaspoonfuls ‖ a tablespoonful **ta·ble·spoon·ful** (téib'lspu:nful) *pl.* **ta·ble·spoon·fuls** *n.* as much as a tablespoon will hold

tab·let (tǽblit) *n.* a flat piece of stone or metal inscribed as a memorial ‖ a medical pastille ‖ a pad of writing paper ‖ a small flat block of soap, chocolate etc. ‖ (*hist.*) a small thin, flat piece of clay, wax etc. used to write on a table-cut gem [O.F. *tablete*]

table talk informal conversation, e.g. at a dinner table, esp. such discursive matter in published form

table tennis a game distantly related to tennis, played usually indoors on a table with round wooden bats and a small plastic ball

table turning spirit rapping

ta·ble·ware (téib'lwɛər) *n.* dishes, plates, glasses, cutlery etc. used in setting a table and for serving food and drink

tab·loid (tǽblɔid) *n.* a small-format, heavily illustrated newspaper featuring news items of a sensational nature ‖ any publication adopting a similar format or size of page [*Tabloid*, a trademark applied to certain chemicals used in concentrated form in pharmacy and medicine]

ta·boo, ta·bu (təbú:) **1.** *n.* the prohibition of certain contacts, words, actions etc. on religious grounds among many primitive peoples ‖ the state or quality of being thus prohibited ‖ anything which is prohibited by tradition or social usage **2.** *adj.* placed under taboo ‖ forbidden on grounds of tradition or social usage **3.** *v.t.* to place under taboo ‖ to condemn as not proper because of convention etc. [Tongan *tabu*]

ta·bor (téibər) *n.* (*hist.*) a small drum played with the hand by a musician to accompany his own playing of a threeholed pipe [O.F. *tabur, tabour* fr. Pers.]

Ta·bo·ra (təbɔ́rə, təbóurə) a commercial center and rail junction (pop. 67,392) in W. Tanganyika, Tanzania

tab·o·ret, tab·ou·ret (tǽbərit) *n.* a low stool [fr. F. *tabouret*, small drum]

Ta·bor, Mount (téibər) a domelike hill (929 ft) near Nazareth, traditionally regarded as the mountain of the Transfiguration

tabouret *TABORET

Ta·briz (tɑbríːz) the chief city (pop. 598,576) of Azerbaijan, Iran, a trade center: dried fruit, rugs, silks. University
tabu *TABOO
tab·u·la (tǽbjulə) *pl.* **tab·u·lae** (tǽbjuliː) *n.* one of the transverse septa of various corals and hydroids [L.=table]
tab·u·lar (tǽbjulər) *adj.* set out in the form of a table, *a tabular statement* ‖ used in setting out such a table ‖ computed from a table ‖ having a flat, tablelike surface, laminated ‖ composed of broad, flat crystals, *a tabular mineral* ‖ (of a crystal) having a flat parallel base and top [fr. L. *tabularis*]
tab·u·la ra·sa (tǽbjulərɑ́sə) *pl.* **tab·u·lae ra·sae** (tǽbjuliːrɑ́siː) the human mind thought of as being a perfect blank at birth, before it begins to receive impressions ‖ a clean sweep, complete obliteration (e.g. of awkward or painful memories) [L. =cleaned tablet]
tab·u·late (tǽbjuleit) **1.** *v.t. pres. part.* **tab·u·lat·ing** *past* and *past part.* **tab·u·lated** to arrange in tabular form **2.** *adj.* having tabulae ‖ (of rocks, crystals etc.) having a flat, tablelike surface **tab·u·lá·tion** *n.* **táb·u·la·tor** *n.* an arrangement of stops for the carriage of a typewriter so that columns of figures etc. can be set out in vertical lines ‖ an office worker who makes tabulations ‖ a business machine for tabulating data [fr. L.L. *tabulari* (*tabulatus*)]
tac·a·ma·hac (tǽkəməhæk) *n.* a pungent oleoresin obtained from any of several tropical trees of the genera *Protium* (esp. *P. heptaphyllum* and *P. altissimum*) and *Bursera*, used as incense and in ointments ‖ the resin exuded by the North American balsam poplar [fr. obs. Span. *tacamahaca*, fr. Aztec]
tacan (*mil. acronym*) for tactical air navigation, an ultrahigh frequency electronic air navigation system that provides a single continuous indication of bearing and distance (slant range) to the tacan station
Ta·ca·ri·gua, Lake (tɑkɑríːgwɑ) *VALENCIA, LAKE
tach (tæk) *n.* short for tachometer, a rotation speed-measuring device
tach·e·om·e·ter (tækiːɔ́mitər) *n.* a tachymeter [F. *tachéomètre*]
tach·i·na fly (tǽkinə) any of numerous dark gray or black dipterous flies of fam. *Tachinidae*, whose larvae are parasitic in caterpillars and other harmful insects
tachism (French, *tâche*, 'spot, blot') abstract painting utilizing improvised techniques, e.g., splattering, dribbling, pouring, as works of Jackson Pollock *also* tachist *adj, n. Cf* ACTION PAINTING
tach·isme (tǽʃizəm) *n.* *ABSTRACT EXPRESSIONISM [F.]
ta·chom·e·ter (tækɔ́mitər) *n.* an instrument for measuring the speed of rotation of a revolving shaft etc. **ta·chóm·e·try** *n.* [fr. Gk *tachos*, speed+METER]
tach·y·car·di·a (tækikɑ́rdiːə) *n.* (*med.*) an abnormally fast heartbeat [fr. Gk *tachus*, swift+*kardia*, heart]
tach·y·lyte (tǽkəlait) *n.* a black, glassy form of basalt **tach·y·lyt·ic** (tækəlítik) *adj.* [G. *tachylit* fr. Gk *tachus*, swift+*lutos*, soluble]
ta·chym·e·ter (tækímitər) *n.* (*survey.*) an instrument used to locate distant points quickly ‖ an instrument for measuring speed [fr. Gk *tachus*, swift+METER]
tach·y·on (tǽkiːɒn) *n.* (*particle phys.*) hypothetical elementary particle characterized by speed greater than light, with energy decreasing in proportion to speed, named by American physicist Gerald Feinberg (1933–) based on Einstein's theories
tac·it (tǽsit) *adj.* existing or implied but not stated, *tacit agreement* ‖ (*law*) arising by operation of law [fr. L. *tacere* (*tacitus*), to be silent]
tac·i·turn (tǽsitəːrn) *adj.* not given to saying much [fr. L. *taciturnus*]
tac·i·tur·ni·ty (tæsitə́ːrnitiː) *n.* the state or quality of being taciturn [M.F. *taciturnité* or fr. L.]
Tac·i·tus (tǽsitəs), Marcus Claudius (c. 200-76), Roman emperor (275-6). An austere and honest ruler, he was assassinated after a reign of 10 months
Tacitus, Publius Cornelius (c. 55–c. 120), Roman historian. His works include 'Dialogue on Orators' (c. 79-81), 'Agricola' (c. 98), 'Germania' (c. 98) and two fragments of longer histories: the 'Histories' (104-10, covering the years 68-70) and the 'Annals' (115-17, covering most of the years 14-68). His style is exceedingly terse and polished

tack (tæk) **1.** *n.* a short, sharp nail having a broad, usually flat, head ‖ a long stitch, esp. a basting stitch ‖ a stitch used to hold down a pleat etc. temporarily ‖ (*naut.*) a rope used to fasten the corner of any of certain sails ‖ the corner so fastened ‖ the direction in which a vessel sails as the result of the position of her sails and helm ‖ the act of changing this direction by shifting the sails and helm ‖ the distance sailed after such a change and before the course is altered ‖ an act of tacking ‖ a course of action, *to try a new tack* **2.** *v.t.* to fasten with a tack or tacks ‖ to baste (stitch temporarily) ‖ to hold down (a pleat etc.) temporarily by a stitch ‖ to append as an addition, *to tack a postscript on a letter* ‖ (*naut.*) to change the course of (a ship or boat) when sailing against the wind by putting the helm over and shifting the sails ‖ to navigate (a sailing ship or boat) by a series of tacks ‖ *v.i.* (*naut.*) to change the direction of a sailing ship or boat ‖ (*naut.*, of a sailing ship or boat) to change direction by making a tack ‖ to change one's course of action [fr. O.F. *tache*, fibula, large nail]
tack·i·ness (tǽkiːnis) *n.* the state or quality of being tacky
tack·le (tǽk'l) **1.** *n.* (*naut.*) a ship's rigging ‖ a mechanism for lifting weights by ropes and pulleys ‖ equipment, *fishing tackle* ‖ (*football* and *rugby*) the act of tackling an opponent ‖ an instance of this ‖ (*football*) either of two players between the guard and the end on either side of the line of scrimmage ‖ the harness for a horse **2.** *v. pres. part.* **tack·ling** *past* and *past part.* **tack·led** *v.t.* to come to grips with, esp. in order to subdue, *to tackle an opponent* ‖ (*pop.*) to apply oneself to (a problem or a hard piece of work) ‖ (often with 'up') to harness (a horse) ‖ (*football* and *rugby*) to seize and stop or pull down (an opposing player with the ball) ‖ (*soccer*) to intercept or obstruct (an opponent with the ball) ‖ *v.i.* (*football* and *rugby*) to seize and stop or pull down an opponent with the ball ‖ (*soccer*) to intercept or obstruct an opponent with the ball [M.L.G., L.G. *takel*]
tack·y (tǽkiː) *comp.* **tack·i·er** *superl.* **tack·i·est** *adj.* (of glue, paint etc.) not quite set and still sticky to the touch [fr. older *tack* n., adhesiveness]
tacky *comp.* **tack·i·er** *superl.* **tack·i·est** *adj.* (*pop.*) shabby, dowdy [etym. doubtful]
tac-log group (tǽklɔg) (*mil.*) representatives designated by army troop commanders to assist Navy control officers aboard control ships in the ship-to-shore movements of troops, equipment, and supplies
Ta·co·ma (təkóumə) a port (pop. 158,501) in the state of Washington, on Puget Sound: wood and metallurgical industries, food processing
Ta·con·ic (təkɔ́nik) *adj.* (*geol.*) of a North American mountain-making episode during the late Ordovician period [fr. *Taconic* Mtns in northeastern U.S.A.]
tact (tækt) *n.* an understanding of how to avoid giving offense and of how to keep or win goodwill **tact·ful** (tǽktfəl) *adj.* [fr. L. *tactus*, touch]
tac·tic (tǽktik) *n.* tactics ‖ a detail of tactics [fr. Mod. L. *tactica* fr. Gk]
tactic *adj.* of, relating to, or showing biological taxis [fr. Mod. L. *tacticus* fr. Gk]
tac·ti·cal (tǽktik'l) *adj.* of or pertaining to tactics ‖ (of a plan of action etc.) astutely thought out so as to advance a purpose or gain an advantage ‖ (*mil.*) of relatively short-range U.S. and U.S.S.R. nuclear weapons stationed in Europe [fr. Gk *taktikos*]
tactical warning (*mil.*) **1.** a notification that the enemy has initiated hostilities **2.** in satellite and missile surveillance, a notification to operational command centers that a specific threat is occurring
tactical weapon (*mil.*) weapon used in the battlefield
tac·ti·cian (tæktíʃən) *n.* a person with a sound knowledge of tactics ‖ a person who maneuvers cleverly in any situation
tac·tics (tǽktiks) *n.* (construed as *sing.*) the science and art of using a fighting force to the best advantage having regard to the immediate situation of combat (cf. STRATEGY) ‖ (construed as *pl.*) carefully worked-out steps taken to achieve a purpose [TACTIC]
tac·tile (tǽktəl, tǽktail) *adj.* of, relating to or perceived by the sense of touch ‖ (*physiol.*) of capsular corpuscles in the skin and some mucous membranes believed to constitute special organs of touch **tac·til·i·ty** (tæktíliti:) *n.* [fr. L. *tactilis*, tangible]

tact·less (tǽktlis) *adj.* lacking tact
tac·tu·al (tǽktʃuːəl) *adj.* of or relating to the sense or the organs of touch [fr. L. *tactus*, touch]
Tadjikistan *TADZHIKISTAN
tad·pole (tǽdpoul) *n.* the tailed, legless, aquatic larva of the frog, toad or certain other amphibians after emerging from the egg and while still possessing external or internal gills [M.E. *tāde*, *tadde*, toad +*poll*, head]
Ta·dzhik (tɑ́dʒik) *n.* a member of a people of old Iranian stock scattered among the populations of Afghanistan and Turkestan
Ta·dzhik·i·stan (tɑdʒikistɑ́n) (or Tadjikistan) a constituent republic (area 55,240 sq. miles, pop. 3,801,000) of the U.S.S.R., in central Asia. Capital: Dyushambe. Religion: mainly Moslem. The country is mountainous, rising to the Pamirs in the east. Resources (largely unexploited): brown coal, lead, zinc, oil, uranium, arsenic. Industries: agriculture (cattle and sheep raising, fruit, cotton, cereals), engineering, food processing, hydroelectricity, cotton and silk textiles. It became a constituent republic in 1929
Tae·gu (táigúː) a city (pop. 1,311,078) in central South Korea, the market for a cereal and tobacco-growing region: textiles, foodstuffs
Tae·jon (táidʒɔ́n) a rail center (pop. 506,703) in S.E. South Korea: railroad stock, silk, leather
tae·ni·a, te·ni·a (tíːniːə) *n.* (*archit.*, Doric order) a band separating the frieze from the architrave ‖ (*anat.*) a ribbonlike band of muscle or nerve tissue ‖ (*zool.*) the tapeworm [L. fr. Gk *tainia*, ribbon]
taf·fe·ta (tǽfitə) *n.* a thin, rather stiff glossy fabric of natural or artificial silk [O.F. *taffetas*, *taphetas* fr. Pers.]
taff·rail (tǽfreil) *n.* (*naut.*) the rail around the stern of a ship [fr. Du. *tafereel*, a panel]
taf·fy (tǽfiː) *n.* candy made by boiling down brown sugar or molasses, then pulling it until it is supple and light in color [etym. doubtful]
ta·fi·a (tǽfiːə) *n.* a variety of inferior rum distilled from sugarcane juice [Creole F. or Malay]
Taft (tæft), Robert Alphonso (1889-1953), U.S. political leader. As U.S. senator (1938-53) from Ohio, he led opposition to President Franklin Roosevelt's New Deal and vigorously fought U.S. participation in the United Nations Organization, the European Recovery Program, and the Atlantic Pact. He drafted (1947) the Taft-Hartley Labor Act. He lost (1952) the Republican presidential nomination to Dwight D. Eisenhower
Taft, William Howard (1857-1930), 27th president (1909-13) of the U.S.A., a Republican. As the first civil governor (1900-4) of the Philippine Is, he improved U.S.-Filipino relations. He worked closely with President Theodore Roosevelt as his secretary of war (1904-8), and succeeded him. As president he continued Roosevelt's policy of dollar diplomacy in Latin America, introduced (1910) the postal savings bank and (1912) the parcel-post system, and created (1911) the Department of Labor. He was nevertheless criticized by progressives for his conservatism. He served (1921-30) as chief justice of the Supreme Court
Taft-Hartley Labor Act (Labor-Management Relations Act) a U.S. Congressional act (1947) sponsored by Senator Robert A. Taft and Representative Fred A. Hartley, which was passed over President Harry Truman's veto. It declared that the union or the employer must, before ending a collective-bargaining agreement, notify the other party and a government mediation service. It authorized the government to obtain an 80-day injunction against any strike that endangered national health or safety. Other provisions prohibited jurisdictional strikes and secondary boycotts, denied protection to workers on wildcat strikes, and outlawed the closed shop. It bound unions to file evidence with the U.S. Department of Labor that their union officers were not Communists before they could use the facilities of the National Labor Relations Board
tag (tæg) **1.** *n.* a label of plastic, metal etc. for fastening to something for identification, classification etc. ‖ the hard tip on each end of a shoelace to facilitate insertion through eyelets ‖ the tip of the tail of an animal, esp. of a fox ‖ a cliché or hackneyed quotation ‖ a lock of dirty, matted sheep's wool ‖ a hanging, tattered bit of cloth **2.** *v. pres. part.* **tag·ging** *past* and *past part.* **tagged** *v.t.* to attach a tag to ‖ (with 'on') to

attach as an addition, esp. rather clumsily and awkwardly, *to tag a few notes on to a new edition* ‖ to rid (a sheep) of tags ‖ (*pop.*) to follow closely and with persistence ‖ *v.i.* (with 'along') to join up temporarily with someone else, esp. without previous arrangement or invitation ‖ to drag oneself (itself) along a little to the rear [etym. doubtful]

tag 1. *n.* a children's game in which a player (called 'it') chases other players until he manages to touch one, who in turn becomes 'it' **2.** *v.t. pres. part.* **tag·ging** *past* and *past part.* **tagged** to touch (a player) in this game ‖ (*baseball*) to hit (the ball) with the bat **to tag out** (*baseball*) to put out (a runner) by touching him with the ball [etym. doubtful]

Ta·ga·log (təgúlɒg) *pl.* **Ta·ga·log, Ta·ga·logs** *n.* a people of central Luzon in the Philippines ‖ a member of this people ‖ an Austronesian language of this people that is the official national language of the Republic of the Philippines

Ta·gan·rog (tɑ́gənrɒg) a port (pop. 277,000) in the R.S.F.S.R., U.S.S.R., on the Sea of Azov: iron and steel, machinery, leather, food processing

tag day (*Am.=Br.* flag day) a day on which small emblems are permitted to be sold on the streets by volunteers in aid of charity

tag end the very last part of something, *the tag end of the day* ‖ (*pl.*) bits or fragments

tag·ma (tǽgmə) *pl.* **tag·ma·ta** (tǽgmətə) *n.* a body segment of an arthropod, e.g. the thorax of an insect or a compound body section formed by the embryonic fusion of two or more somites, e.g. the cephalothorax of a spider [Mod. L. fr. Gk *tagma*, arrangement]

tag·meme (tǽgmi:m) *n.* (*linguistics*) in tagmemic grammar, a unit of arrangement at a substitution point or a correlation shot (including the class of words found or to be substituted at that point), any part of a sentence where other words could be substituted within the same structure

tagmemic grammar (*linguistics*) theory of grammar involving concept of a tagmeme to convey formal and functional information developed by American grammarian K. L. Pike (1930–) *Cf* EMICETIC

tag·mene (tǽgmi:n) *n.* (*linguistics*) the smallest meaningful unit of grammatical form —**tagmentist** *n.*

Ta·gore (təgɔ́r), Rabindranath (1861-1941), Indian author. He wrote in Bengali, but translated much of his work into English. 'Gitanjali' is his best-known work. His 'Collected Poems and Plays' appeared in 1936

tag sale sale of personal property from one's home or immediately outside one's home *also* garage sale, yard sale

Ta·gus (téigəs) (*Span.* Tajo, *Port.* Tejo) the longest river (566 miles) of Iberia, flowing from E. New Castile, Spain, across Estremadura and central Portugal to a wide estuary at Lisbon, navigable only in W. Portugal

Ta·hi·ti (təhí:ti:) the main island (area 402 sq. miles, pop. 95,604) of French Polynesia, in the Society Is. Chief town: Papeete. People: mainly mixed Polynesian-European, 10% Chinese. Highest point: 7,339 ft. Industries: agriculture (taro, breadfruit, yams, coconuts, vanilla), fishing, tourism

Ta·hi·tian (təhí:ʃən) **1.** *adj.* pertaining to Tahiti, its inhabitants, language etc. **2.** *n.* a native or inhabitant of Tahiti, esp. one of the native Polynesian people ‖ the Polynesian language of Tahiti

Tai *THAI

tai chi or **tai chi chuan** (tai dʒi: tʃu:ɑn) *n.* Chinese system of calisthenics, self-defense, and mediation that produces bodily flexibility and peace of mind

Tai·chung (táidʒúŋ) a commercial center (pop. 330,000) in W. Taiwan

Ta·if (tɑ́:if) the summer capital (pop. 30,000) of Hejaz, Saudi Arabia, 50 miles east of Mecca, a resort (on the edge of an oasis) at 5,200 ft

tai·ga (táigə) *n.* the coniferous forests of Siberia separating the tundra from the steppe [Russ.]

Taigeytos *TAYGETUS MOUNTAINS

tail (teil) **1.** *n.* the part of the body posterior to the anus in many vertebrates, *peacock's tail*, or this as a caudal appendage in prolongation of the vertebral column, *monkey's tail* ‖ something resembling this in form or position, e.g. the long bright trail behind a comet or meteor ‖ the last part of something, *the tail of a procession* ‖ (also *pl.*) the reverse side of a coin ‖ (*cricket*) the weaker members of the team ‖ the unit at the rear of an aircraft combining horizontal and vertical stabilizing surfaces with movable surfaces for controlling flight direction ‖ the bottom of a printed page ‖ the part of a man's coat which hangs at the back ‖ (*pl.*) a tailcoat ‖ (*pl.*) full evening dress ‖ (*mus.*) the stem of a written note ‖ the string of paper weights or rags which stabilize a kite ‖ a long braid or switch of hair ‖ the rear end of a vehicle or implement, e.g. a cart or plow **to turn tail** to cease facing someone or something because of fear **with the tail between the legs** in a defeated or dejected way **2.** *v.t.* to remove the ends or stalks from, *to tail gooseberries* ‖ to furnish with a tail, *to tail a kite* ‖ (*pop.*) to follow (someone) so as to observe his actions ‖ to form the tail of (e.g. a procession) ‖ to add on at the end, esp. with excessive length, *to tail on strings of dependent clauses* ‖ (esp. with 'in' or 'into') to fasten the end of (a beam, brick etc.) into a wall etc. ‖ *v.i.* (with 'along' or 'behind') to tag along behind someone or something ‖ (with 'off' or 'away') to subside, *her voice tailed off* ‖ (with 'off') to become gradually poorer in quality towards the end ‖ (with 'out' or 'away') to spread out so as to form a straggling line ‖ (of a timber, brick etc., with 'in' or 'into') to be fastened by an end into a wall etc. **to tail aground** (*naut.*) to ground stern first [O.E. *tægel*]

tail 1. *n.* (*law*) the state or condition of entailment **2.** *adj.* (*law*) limited as to tenure [A.F. *taylé, tailé* fr. O.F. *taillier*, to cut, shape]

tail·board (téilbɔrd, téilbourd) a tail gate

tail·coat (téilkout) *n.* a man's coat, worn on formal occasions, having a long, divided skirt at the back

tail end the concluding part of anything

tail gate the hinged or sliding board or platform at the rear of a van, station wagon etc., which can be raised or lowered to facilitate loading and unloading ‖ the lower gate of a canal lock

tail·gate (téilgeit) *v. pres. part.* **tail·gat·ing** *past* and *past part.* **tail·gat·ed** *v.i.* to drive dangerously close behind another vehicle ‖ *v.t.* to drive dangerously close behind (another vehicle)

tail·ing (téiliŋ) *n.* (*pl.*) the refuse material separated out in processing, e.g. in milling, mining etc. ‖ (*archit.*, of a projecting stone or brick) the part embedded in the wall

tail lamp a taillight

taille (taij) *n.* (*F. hist.*) a feudal tax levied on commoners under the ancient regime [F.]

tail·light (téillait) *n.* a red warning light at the back of a vehicle

tai·lor (téilər) **1.** *n.* a person whose occupation is making men's and women's coats, suits etc. **2.** *v.i.* to work as a tailor ‖ *v.t.* to make (garments) to measure ‖ to fashion to suit a particular need, *the play was tailored for a special audience* ‖ to style (women's garments) with the trim, simple lines characteristic of men's clothes [O.F. *tailleor, tailleur*]

tai·lor·bird (téilərbə:rd) *n.* any of several varieties of Asiatic and African birds of fam. *Sylviidae*, esp. *Orthotomus sutorius*, that sew leaves together to support and hide their nests

tai·lor-made (téilərméid) *adj.* made and fitted by a tailor, *a tailor-made suit* ‖ fashioned specially for the occasion or conditions

tail·piece (téilpi:s) *n.* a part forming the end of something ‖ an ornamental design at the end of a chapter or page of a book ‖ the triangular block to which the strings of a violin etc. are fastened ‖ a short beam or rafter tailed in a wall and supported by a header

tail plane the horizontal surfaces of an aircraft tail, including the elevator and stabilizer

tail·race (téilreis) *n.* the part of a millrace just beyond the millwheel ‖ a channel in which the tailings from treated ore are floated away

tail skid a device on an aircraft to take the weight at the rear end of the fuselage when the aircraft is at rest or taxiing

tail·spin (téilspin) *n.* a spiral dive, nose-foremost, by an aircraft

tail·stock (téilstɒk) *n.* the movable head of a lathe

tail·wa·ter (téilwɑtər) *n.* (*envir.*) water immediately downstream from a structure, e.g., a dam, hydroelectric plant

tail wind a wind blowing in the same general direction as the course of an aircraft or a boat in motion

Tai·myr Peninsula, Tay·myr Peninsula (taimí:r) the northernmost part of Siberia, U.S.S.R., on the central Arctic coast, inhabited by nomads. Products: uranium, cobalt, nickel, lead

Tai·nan (táinɑ́n) a port (pop. 474,835) of S.W. Taiwan, formerly the capital: ironworks, food processing

Taine (ten), Hippolyte Adolphe (1828-93), French critic and historian. He applied theories of determinism to literary criticism, aesthetics and psychology. His best-known work is 'Origines de la France contemporaine' (1875-93). He wrote a lively and unorthodox 'Histoire de la littérature anglaise' (1864-72)

Tai·no (táinou) *n.* an Amerind of the Arawak group living at the time of discovery in Puerto Rico, Haiti and E. Cuba. They were decimated by the Spanish conquistadores

taint (teint) **1.** *v.t.* to cause to rot, putrefy, *tainted meat* ‖ to corrupt morally ‖ to cause to be slightly spoiled by some undesirable quality, *tainted with suspicion* **2.** *n.* a trace of infection or corruption [fr. ATTAINT]

Tai·pei (taipéi) the capital (pop. 2,238,840 and economic center of Taiwan, near the northern coast. Industries: metalworking, food processing, glass, chemicals. University

Tai·ping Rebellion (táipíŋ) a rebellion in China (1850-65), led by Hung Hsiu-ch'uan, which attempted to overthrow the Manchu government. The rising was suppressed with the aid of American and British troops under Gordon, leaving China bankrupt and chaotic

Tai·ta·o Peninsula (taitɑ́ɔ) a peninsula on the southwest coast of Chile, north of the Gulf of Peñas

Tai·wan (táiwɑ́n) (Formosa) a republic (area 13,890 sq. miles, pop. 19,157,407) in E. Asia. It is a Pacific island, 90 miles off S.E. China. It includes the Pescadores (Penghu) Islands, and 13 scattered offshore islands, incl. Quemoy and Matsu. Capital: Taipei. People: 98% Chinese, with Japanese and aboriginal minorities. Language: Chinese (Amoy dialect). Japanese is widely spoken. The land is 50% forest and 24% arable. The mud flats and sandbanks of the west coast give way to lowlands, while on the east coast steep cliffs rise to the densely wooded peaks of the Taitung and Chungyang Mtns (highest point 14,000 ft). The monsoons bring up to 290 ins of rain to the northern and southern tips but only 40–60 ins in the west. There are frequent typhoons. Average temperatures (F.): 50°-60° in winter, 80°-90° in summer. Pigs are raised. Taiwan is the world's chief source of camphor. Timber: hardwoods, pine. Minerals: silver, copper, coal, oil. Industries: flour milling, sugar refining, tobacco. Exports: camphor, sugar, bananas and pineapples, coal, tea, rice, gold. Other products: sweet potatoes, tobacco. Imports: vegetables, iron, opium, textiles. Ports: Kaohsiung, Keelung. National Taiwan university. Monetary unit: new Taiwan yuan. HISTORY. Chinese immigrants settled the island extensively (15th-17th cc.) and Spanish, Dutch and Portuguese traders visited it (16th and 17th cc.). China annexed the island (1683). It was ceded to Japan (1895) and restored to China (1945). Chiang Kai-shek retreated to the island after his expulsion from the mainland by the Communists (1949) and controls it as president of the National Republic of China. The People's Republic of China considers Taiwan as one of its 22 provinces and the Communists are determined to 'liberate' the island. The Kuomintang government and the U.S.A. signed a pact (1954) under which the U.S.A agreed to protect the republic. After its expulsion from the mainland, the Taiwan government continued to represent China, a founding member, at the U.N., until it was unseated in 1971. In 1975 Chiang Kai-Shek died and vice-president Yen Chia-kan took office as president, although leadership of the Kuomintang passed to Chiang's son Chiang Ching-Kuo. In 1978 the U.S.A. unilaterally terminated its security pact with Taiwan, and U.S.-Taiwan relations have continued to be ambiguous

Tai·yuan (táijyɑ́n) (formerly Yangku) the capital (pop. 1,020,000) of Shansi, N. China. Industries: iron and steel, heavy engineering, textiles. Institute of Technology

Ta·ja·mul·co, Ta·ju·mul·co (tɑhɑmú:lkɔ, tɑhu:mú:lkɔ) a volcanic mountain (13,816 ft) in W. Guatemala. It is the highest point in Central America

Taj Ma·hal (tɑ́ʒməhɑ́l, tɑ́dʒməhɑ́l) the magnificent white marble mausoleum built (c. 1632–c. 1643) in Agra, Uttar Pradesh, India, by the Mogul emperor Shah Jahan in memory of his favorite wife Mumtaz Mahal. It is in a garden with pools and fountains. The sun filters rest-

CONCISE PRONUNCIATION KEY: **(a)** æ, *cat*; ɑ, *car*; ɔ *fawn*; ei, *snake*. **(e)** e, *hen*; i:, *sheep*; iə, *deer*; ɛə, *bear*. **(i)** i, *fish*; ai, *tiger*; ə:, *bird*. **(o)** o, *ox*; au, *cow*; ou, *goat*; u, *poor*; ɔi, *royal*. **(u)** ʌ, *duck*; u, *bull*; u:, *goose*; ə, *bacillus*; ju:, *cube*. x, *loch*; θ, *think*; ð, *bother*; z, *Zen*; ʒ, *corsage*; dʒ, *savage*; ŋ, *orangutang*; j, *yak*; ʃ, *fish*; tʃ, *fetch*; 'l, *rabble*; 'n, *redden*. Complete pronunciation key appears inside front cover.

fully into the building through fretted marble screens

Tajumulco *TAJAMULCO

ta·ka (tɑ́kə) *n.* currency unit of Bangladesh since 1977 *abbr.*, Tk

Ta·ka·ma·tsu (tɑkɑmɑtsu:) a port (pop. 228,000) of N. Shikoku, Japan, on the Inland Sea. Industries: textiles, lacquerware. Ruins of Takamatsu castle (built 1588), gardens

Ta·kao (tɑ́kɑ́ou) *KAOHSIUNG

take (teik) **1.** *v. pres. part.* **tak·ing** *past* **took** (tuk) *past part.* **tak·en** (téikən) *v.t.* to get possession of by using force or superior strength, *the army took the town* ‖ to capture, *the thief was taken by the police* ‖ (*cards*) to win (a trick) or capture (an opponent's card) ‖ (*chess*) to put out of play, *bishop takes pawn* ‖ (*cricket*) to cause (a wicket) to fall ‖ to put the hand on or in so as to give or receive guidance, *take my hand while we cross the road* ‖ to guide (somebody) in this way, *to take a child by the hand* ‖ to grip, grasp or seize etc. with the fingers, hands, arms, teeth or an instrument ‖ to surprise, attack, catch or overcome, esp. suddenly, *we took them unawares* ‖ (with 'with', in passive constructions) to have as a sudden illness or indisposition, *to be taken with a violent pain* ‖ (with 'with', in passive constructions) to captivate, charm, *she was taken with the house on sight* ‖ to eat, drink or receive into the body in some other way, *to take snuff, take sedatives* ‖ to expose oneself to the benefits of (the air and the sun) ‖ to enter into a relationship with (someone), *to take a lover, to take pupils* ‖ to steal or remove without right, *who has taken the dictionary from the library?* ‖ to assume (office, control etc.) ‖ to hire or rent, *to take a house by the sea* ‖ to pay for (something) to be regularly delivered, *the family takes one newspaper and two pints of milk daily* ‖ to bind oneself by (e.g. an oath, vow) ‖ to win in competition, *to take third place in a race* ‖ to proceed along, *we took a different road home* ‖ to select, *take any example you wish* ‖ to make use of, *he took every opportunity to insult us* ‖ to make use of as a means of transport, *to take a bus across Paris* ‖ to convey or cause to go, *the blue bus takes you past the door, that road takes you a longer way around* ‖ to write down (notes, dictation) ‖ to write down esp. as a record, *to take someone's measurements* ‖ to read as a measurement *to take someone's temperature, take soundings* ‖ to require, *it took two men to lift the bed* ‖ to need with respect to size, *to take size 11 shoes* ‖ to derive (nourishment, comfort, satisfaction etc.) ‖ to provide room for, *the car takes six people comfortably* ‖ to photograph ‖ to allow oneself to be given, *don't take lifts from strangers* ‖ to supervise (e.g. a rehearsal) ‖ to give a lesson to (a class) ‖ (esp. *Br.*) to give as a lesson, *to take French with seven-year-olds* ‖ to study or have as a course of study, *to take French at the university* ‖ to allow oneself to adopt (a specified attitude), *to take a serious view of a situation* ‖ to decide to have or be in the process of having (something) for one's pleasure or benefit, *to take exercise, take a holiday* ‖ to conduct (someone or something) somewhere in one's company, *to take a dog for a walk* ‖ to carry (something) to someone, *take the eggs to your grandmother* ‖ (with 'with') to carry (something) and keep it, *take it with you* ‖ to keep (something) for a specified time or purpose, *take the book to read in bed* ‖ to remove, *to take a bone from a hungry dog* ‖ to subtract, *take 13 from 20* ‖ to capture the attention of, *it takes the eye* ‖ to react to, *to take news badly* ‖ to react well to (punishment, criticism, a joke etc.) ‖ to occupy (a chair, a place in line etc.) ‖ (*gram.*) to be constructed with, *a transitive verb takes a direct object* ‖ *v.i.* to get or gain possession ‖ (of an inoculation) to be effective ‖ (of a graft, cutting etc.) ‖ to begin to thrive ‖ to be liked by an audience, *the play did not take well in the provinces* ‖ to be a subject of a specified quality or sort for photography, *she never takes well* ‖ (with 'from') to detract, *it takes from her enjoyment* **to take aback** to cause to feel a small unpleasant shock of surprise **to take away** to carry off in one's possession ‖ to subtract **to take down** to lower ‖ to pull down piece by piece (e.g. a building) ‖ to make a written record of **to take for** to identify (someone) wrongly as someone or something, *what do you take me for?* ‖ (*pop.*) to cheat (a person), *he took me for $5* **to take in** to receive into one's home for money, *to take in lodgers* or out of kindness, *to take in stray cats* ‖ to undertake to do at home, *to take in washing* ‖ to carry inside ‖ to make narrower or smaller, esp. by sewing, *to take in a skirt* ‖ to furl (a sail) ‖ to deceive, *he was taken in by their apparent kindness* ‖ to seize the meaning of, *we could hardly take in what was being said* ‖ to include in a visit, *we took in the Louvre on our weekend in Paris* **to take it** to submit to criticism, ridicule etc. with composure **to take it easy** to rest, work less hard **to take it hard** to be intensely hurt emotionally **to take it lying down** to be submissive **to take it on the chin** to endure punishment, suffering etc. bravely **to take it out of (someone)** to make (someone) exhausted **to take it out on (someone)** to vent one's bad temper etc. on (someone) **to take off** to remove (clothes etc.) ‖ to begin to move, esp. of an aircraft as it becomes airborne ‖ to deduct ‖ (*pop.*) to mimic ‖ to conduct away (also used reflexively) **to take on** to agree to do, *to take on a job* ‖ to accept a fight or contest with ‖ to engage (an employee) ‖ (*pop.*) to express sorrow or vexation with a painful display of emotion ‖ to assume (e.g. a quality) **to take out** to remove ‖ to acquire (insurance, a patent, a license) by making the necessary payment ‖ to pay the first installment of (a subscription) ‖ (*pop.*) to escort to places of entertainment etc. ‖ (*bridge*) to counter a call by (one's partner) in a suit by bidding higher in a different suit **to take over** to assume responsibility for (e.g. a debt, lease) ‖ to assume control of ‖ to relieve someone of a responsibility by assuming it **to take to** to develop a fondness or aptitude for ‖ to betake oneself to, begin to walk etc. in, on etc. ‖ to develop the habit of using, *to take to a cane* **to take up** to pick up ‖ to make shorter, esp. by sewing ‖ to absorb ‖ to adopt as a pastime or pursuit ‖ to resume, to pursue further, *to take up a story* ‖ to challenge on a matter of argument, *I'll take you up on that point* ‖ to occupy (time) ‖ to make a protégé of (someone) ‖ to subscribe to (a loan etc.) **to take upon oneself** to begin (to do something) without invitation, instruction or prompting **to take up with** (*pop.*) to become friendly with **2.** *n.* the act of taking ‖ an amount taken or received in payment ‖ the act of capturing an animal or the number of animals caught at one time ‖ the portion of one scene in the making of a film that is photographed at one time ‖ an instance of photographing this [O.E. *tacan*]

take·a·way (téikəwei) *n.* **1.** *GIVEBACK **2.** (*Br.*) takeout

take-home pay pay after all deductions (income tax, social security etc.) have been made

taken *past part.* of TAKE

take·off (téikɔf, téikɒf) *n.* the act of leaving the ground, e.g. in jumping or in beginning a flight in an aircraft ‖ the point at which this takes place ‖ the act of mimicking someone or something, esp. in order to ridicule

take·out (téikaut) *adj.* of food prepared to be eaten off-premises

take·o·ver (téikouvər) *n.* the assuming of control, ownership or management of e.g. a corporation, or an instance of this

tak·ing (téikiŋ) **1.** *adj.* attractive, *very taking ways* **2.** *n.* (*pl.*) money received for the sale of goods, tickets etc.

Ta·kla Ma·kan (tɑ́klɑmɑkɑ́n) a sandy desert (area 125,000 sq. miles) in the Tarim Basin, Sinkiang, China, between the Kunlun and Tien Shan. Chief oases: Yarkand, Khotan

Takoradi *SEKONDI-TAKORADI

tal·a·poin (tǽləpɔin) *n. Cercopithecus talapoin*, fam. *Cercopithecidae*, a small, white and olive-colored W. African monkey [Port. *talapão*, Buddhist monk]

Tal·bot (tǽlbət), William Henry Fox (1800-77), English scientist. He developed an early system of photography (1839), independently of Daguerre

talc (tælk) *n.* a basic silicate of magnesium, $Mg_3Si_4O_{10}(OH)_2$, occurring in nature and having a soapy feel (varieties are soapstone and French chalk), used as a solid lubricant, toilet powder etc. ‖ (*pop.*) talcum powder ‖ mica, or a thin sheet of it [F. fr. M.L. fr. Arab. fr. Pers.]

tal·cum (tǽlkəm) *n.* talc [M.L.]

talcum powder powdered talc, usually perfumed, used as a powder for the body

tale (teil) *n.* an account of a real or imagined event ‖ a piece of gossip ‖ a lie **to tell tales** to make known things which another person would prefer kept secret, and which do not concern the teller [O.E. *talu*=Du. *taal*, speech]

tale·bear·er (téilbɛərər) *n.* someone who reports privately out of malice or officiousness, esp. to someone in authority, the doings of a third person likely to meet with disapproval or punishment

tale·bear·ing (téilbɛəriŋ) *n.* the activity of a talebearer

tal·ent (tǽlənt) *n.* innate mental or artistic aptitude (as opposed to acquired ability) less than genius, *his work shows talent* ‖ (*hist.*) any of several units of weight or money of account used in Greece, Syria, Palestine and Babylon **tál·ent·ed** *adj.* having talent [O.E. fr. L. fr. Gk *talanton*, pair of scales, unit of weight or money]

ta·ler, tha·ler (tɑ́lər) *pl.* **ta·ler, tha·ler** *n.* (*hist.*) any of various large silver coins used in certain German states from the 15th to the late 19th cc. [G.]

ta·les (téili:z) *pl.* **ta·les** *n.* (*law, pl.*) persons summoned from among bystanders for jury service in order to make up the full number ‖ (*law*) the writ summoning such jurors to attend **to pray a tales** to plead that a jury be completed in number [L., pl. of *talis*, such]

ta·les·man (téili:zmən, téilzmən) *pl.* **ta·les·men** (téili:zmən, téilzmən) *n.* a person summoned to serve on a jury in order to complete its number

tale-tell·er (téiltɛlər) *n.* a talebearer ‖ someone who tells stories

Ta·lien (dɑ́ljén) (*Jap.* Dairen) the northernmost year-round port of China, in S.W. Liaoning (Manchuria), with Lushun forming the agglomeration of Luta (pop. 1,508,000). Industries: heavy and precision engineering, shipbuilding, food processing (esp. soybeans), textiles, chemicals, building materials. A former treaty port, it was modernized (1899) as the terminus of the Trans-Siberian railroad. It was the capital of Kwantung (1905-45), when the territory was leased to the Japanese

Tal·i·es·in (tæli:ésin) (late 6th c.) Welsh bard, the author of about a dozen heroic odes or lays in 'The Book of Taliesin'

tal·i·pes (tǽləpi:z) *n.* (*med.*) clubfoot [Mod. L. fr. *talus*, ankle+*pes*, foot]

tal·i·pot (tǽləpɒt) *n. Corypha umbroculifera*, fam. *Palmae*, the lofty fan palm (60–100 ft) of Ceylon, the Malabar Coast and the Philippines. The fanlike leaves are used for umbrellas, fans and, cut into strips, as a substitute for writing paper ‖ a starch obtained from this tree [fr. Sinhalese *talapata*]

tal·is·man (tǽlizmən, tǽlismən) *n.* an object, esp. a figure carved or cut at a time regarded as astrologically favorable, supposed to have magical protective qualities **tal·is·man·ic** (tælizmǽnik, tælismǽnik), **tal·is·mán·i·cal** *adj.* [fr. Span. fr. Ital. fr. Gk]

talk (tɔk) **1.** *v.i.* to express ideas, thoughts etc. in speech ‖ to chatter idly to gossip ‖ to hold consultation ‖ to convey ideas by manual signs ‖ to make sounds resembling those of speech ‖ *v.t.* to express in speech, *to talk sense* ‖ to make use of in speaking, *to talk French* ‖ to bring into a specified condition by talking, *to talk oneself hoarse, talk someone into agreement* ‖ to discuss, *to talk business* ‖ to talk about one's prowess in (something) without matching one's words with one's performance, *he talks a good game of tennis* **to talk (someone) around** to persuade by talking **to talk at** to say something critical of (a person) in his hearing, to a third person **to talk back** to answer rudely or impertinently **to talk big** to boast **to talk down** to reduce (a person) to silence by speaking loudly **to talk down to** to talk patronizingly to **to talk of** to take as a topic of conversation **to talk out** (*Br.*) to prevent a vote from being taken in parliament on (a bill) by speaking until the closure is moved **to talk (someone) over** to persuade (a person) to change his mind by talking to him **to talk (something) over** to discuss (a subject) at length and in detail **to talk (someone) round** (*Br.*) to persuade by talking **to talk shop** to talk about one's occupation, to the exclusion of matters of more general interest **2.** *n.* the act of talking ‖ a speech ‖ a formal conference ‖ gossip ‖ idle chatter ‖ empty phrases ‖ the subject of conversation, *the talk of the town* [M.E. *talkien, talken*]

talk·a·tive (tɔ́kətiv) *adj.* inclined to talk

talk·ie (tɔ́ki:) *n.* (*pop.*) an early film equipped with a sound track

talk·ing-to (tɔ́kiŋtu:) *n.* a carefully argued rebuke at some length

talk show (*broadcasting*) a program in which celebrities or other persons discuss or are interviewed on subjects of interest

tall (tɔl) *adj.* above average height, *he is tall for his age* ‖ of a specified height, *four feet tall* ‖ (of things) rising high in the air, *a tall oak* ‖ (*pop.*) difficult to believe, exaggerated, *a tall story* ‖ (of a drink) served in a long, narrow glass ‖ (*pop.*, of talk) high-flown ‖ (*pop.*) great or large in amount, *a tall price* ‖ (*pop.*) formidable, *a tall order* [etym. doubtful]

tal·lage (tǽlidʒ) *n.* (*hist.*) a feudal fee paid by a tenant to his lord ‖ (*hist.*) a feudal due levied by a lord, esp. one levied arbitrarily by Norman kings on their demesne lands and royal boroughs [O. F. *taillage*]

Tal·la·has·see (tæləhǽsi:) the capital (pop. 81,548) of Florida

tall·boy (tɔ́lbɔi) *n.* a high chest of drawers composed of two sections, one on top of the other

Tall·chief (tɔ́ltʃi:f), Maria (1925-), U.S. ballet dancer, notable as prima ballerina in the New York City ballet for her dancing in e.g. 'The Firebird', 'Orpheus', and 'Nutcracker'

Tal·ley·rand-Pé·ri·gord (tælrãpeiri:gɔr), Charles Maurice de, prince of Benevento (1754-1838), French diplomat. As bishop of Autun, Talleyrand supported the cause of the French Revolution, and resigned his see (1791). He was minister of foreign affairs (1797-1807), surviving the political changes of Directory, Consulate and Empire. He began (1808) to intrigue against Napoleon, and supported (1814) the Bourbon restoration. He represented France with great skill at the Congress of Vienna (1815), and helped Louis-Philippe to overthrow the Bourbon monarchy (1830), after which he was ambassador in London (1830-5). He claimed in his 'Mémoires' (published 1891-2) that his frequent changes of policy were dictated by the interests of France, but he has often been considered a mere opportunist

Tal·linn (tǽlin) (formerly Revel, Reval) the capital (pop. 430,000) and chief port of Estonia, U.S.S.R., on the Gulf of Finland. Industries: shipbuilding, woodworking, metalworking, textiles, food processing. Castle (14th c.), Gothic churches (13th-15th cc.) and town hall (14th c.), baroque palace (18th c.)

Tal·lis (tǽlis), Thomas (c. 1515-85), English composer. His skill is shown as much in his simple motets (still sung as anthems) as in his stupendous 'Spem in alium' for 40 voices, i.e. 8 five-part choirs. He was the father of English choral church music

tal·lith (tɑ́lis) *n.* a scarf worn during prayer by orthodox Jewish males over the age of 13 [Rabbinical Heb. *ṭallīth* fr. *ṭālal,* to cover]

tal·low (tǽlou) *n.* a mixture of hard animal fats obtained by rendering esp. beef or mutton fat. It is composed of glycerides, and is used in making candles, soap etc. ‖ any of various fats resembling this obtained from plants **tál·low·y** *adj.* [M.E. *talz, talgh* prob. fr. M.L.G.]

tal·ly (tǽli:) **1.** *pl.* **tal·lies** *n.* (*hist.*) a piece of wood in which notches were cut as a method of recording number. When it was used as a record of payment, the stick was split across the notches, each party to the transaction keeping one of the matching sections ‖ a recorded score or recorded count of objects ‖ something complementary to or completing something else ‖ an identifying tag or label ‖ a card for recording a bridge player's score **2.** *v. pres. part.* **tal·ly·ing** *past* and *past part.* **tal·lied** *v.t.* (often with 'up') to count, *to tally up the election returns* ‖ to furnish (e.g. a bale of goods) with a tag or label ‖ to record (e.g. a number) on or as if on a tally ‖ *v.i.* to match or be consistent, *their stories did not tally* [fr. L. *talea,* stick]

tal·ly·ho (tæli:hóu) **1.** *n.* and *interj.* the cry of a huntsman upon sighting a fox **2.** *v.i.* to make this cry [prob. alt. of F. *taïaut, tayaut,* used in hunting deer]

Tal·mud (tɑ́lmud, tǽlmud) *n.* the body of oral Jewish law, comprising the Mishnah and the Gemara, additional to the Torah, compiled (6th c.) in Babylonia **Tal·múd·ic, Tal·múd·i·cal** *adjs.* **Tál·mud·ist** *n.* [Heb. *talmūdh,* instruction]

tal·on (tǽlən) *n.* a pointed, curved claw, esp. the claw of a bird of prey ‖ the back heel of a molar tooth ‖ the projection of the bolt of a lock which the key bears on in turning ‖ the stock of cards left after dealing in certain games, e.g. solitaire ‖ (*archit.*) an ogee molding [O.F.]

Talos (*mil.*) a 7,000-lb shipborne, surface-to-air missile (RIM-8) with solidpropellant rocket ramjet engine, with a speed of Mach 3.25, a 50-mi range, nuclear or nonnuclear warhead capability, and command, beam-rider homing guidance

ta·lus (téiləs) *pl.* **ta·lus·es, ta·li** (téilai) *n.* (*anat.*) the astragalus, which, with the tibia and fibula, forms the ankle joint ‖ (*anat.*) the entire ankle ‖ (*zool.*, esp. of birds and insects) a part corresponding to the ankle [L.]

talus *n.* (*fortification*) the slope of a wall which tapers or is built against an inclined bank ‖ (*geol.*) a slope of fragments of rock formed by the weathering of a cliff face ‖ (*geol.*) a mass of rock debris at the foot of a cliff [F.]

tam (tæm) *n.* a tam-o'-shanter

tam·a·ble, tame·a·ble (téiməb'l) *adj.* able to be tamed

Ta·ma·le (tæmɑ́li:) the main commercial center (pop. 120,000) and airport of N. Ghana. Cotton ginning

ta·ma·le (təmɑ́li:) *n.* a Mexican dish consisting of ground meat seasoned with chile pepper and rolled in cornmeal pastry, wrapped in corn husks and steamed [Span. *tamal,* pl. *tamales*]

ta·man·du·a (təmǽndu:ə) *n.* *Tamandua tetradactyla,* fam. *Myrmecophagidae,* a Central and South American tree-dwelling anteater having a long, prehensile tail [Port. fr. Tupi]

tam·a·rack (tǽməræk) *n.* any of several North American larches, esp. *Larix larieina,* fam. *Pinaceae* ‖ the wood of this tree [etym. doubtful]

tam·a·rin (tǽmərin) *n.* a member of *Leontocebus,* fam. *Callithricidae,* a genus of small South American marmosets, having silky fur and long, canine teeth [F. fr. Carib.]

tam·a·rind (tǽmərind) *n.* *Tamarindus indica,* fam. *Papilionaceae,* a widely cultivated tropical tree having hard yellowish wood used in work done on the lathe ‖ its fruit, the acid pulp of which is used in cooking and as a laxative drink [fr. Arab. *tamr-hindi,* date of India]

tam·a·risk (tǽmərisk) *n.* a member of *Tamarix,* fam. *Tamaricaceae,* a genus of evergreen shrubs (16–20 ft), having feathery clusters of pink or white flowers and small leaves [fr. L. *tamariscus* fr. Arab. *tamir,* a date]

Ta·ma·tave (tɑmɑtɑ́v) the chief port (pop. 59,100) of Madagascar, linked to Antananarino by rail: meat packing

Ta·mau·li·pas (tɑmaulí:pɑs) a northern state (area 30,822 sq. miles, pop. 1,968,800) of Mexico. The land ranges from the sparsely inhabited sandy coast to the wooded mountains and fertile plains of the interior. Capital: Ciudad Victoria (pop. 62,551). Agriculture: sugar, cereals, tobacco, cotton, fruit and coffee. Other important industries: stock raising and mining (primarily copper). Important cities: Tampico, Nuevo Laredo, Matamoros

Ta·ma·yo (tamɑ́jɔ), Franz (1880-1956), Bolivian poet and defender of the Indians. He was elected president in 1935, but the Army refused to allow him to take office

Tamayo, Rufino (1899-), Mexican painter. Influenced by cubism and esp. by Picasso, he paints richly colored expressionist compositions of figures, animals and birds, incorporating elements of Mexican folklore

tam·ba·la *pl.,* **-la** or **-las** (tɑmbɑ́lə) *n.* currency unit of Malawai, equal to 1/100 kwacha

tam·bour (tǽmbuər) **1.** *n.* (*mus.*) a drum ‖ a person playing a drum ‖ a frame consisting of two closely fitting hoops between which a fabric is stretched when it is being embroidered ‖ the embroidery made on such a frame ‖ (*archit.*) one of the cylindrical courses of a column ‖ (*archit.*) the circular wall supporting a dome etc. ‖ the sloping buttress or projection in a court tennis or fives court for deflecting the ball **2.** *v.t.* to embroider, using a tambour ‖ *v.i.* to work this type of embroidery [F. fr. Ital. fr. Arab. fr. Pers.]

tam·bou·rine (tæmbərí:n) *n.* a small drum consisting of a wooden hoop with skin or parchment stretched across it at one end and loose metal disks set around the circumference. It is rattled and struck with the hand or knuckles [fr. F. *tambourin* dim. of *tambour,* drum]

tame (teim) **1.** *adj.* (of animals) domesticated ‖ (of undomesticated animals) unafraid of man ‖ lacking liveliness, mild and dull ‖ (of plants or land) cultivated **2.** *v.t. pres. part.* **tam·ing** *past* and *past part.* **tamed** to make tame ‖ to bring under control, make submissive [O.E. *tam*]

tameable *TAMABLE

Tam·er·lane (tǽmərlein) *TIMUR

Tam·il (tǽməl) *pl.* **Tam·il, Tam·ils** *n.* a member of a Dravidian people living in S. India and N. Ceylon ‖ the Dravidian language of the Tamils ‖ the script used in writing this language

Ta·mil Na·du (tǽməlnɑ́du:) (formerly Madras) a state (area 50,331 sq. miles, pop. 48,297,456) on the Coromandel Coast of India, sloping down from the Eastern Ghats. Crops (mainly under irrigation): cereals, peanuts, coffee, tea, cotton. Minerals (largely unexploited): iron ore, bauxite, gypsum ‖ its capital (pop. 1,729,000), a port (artificial harbor) and commercial center. Industries: textiles, tanning, pottery, dyemaking. University (1857)

Tam·ma·ny (tǽməni:) a political organization founded in Manhattan, New York, after the Revolutionary War. It exercised great influence over the Democratic party in New York. It became notorious for corruption in the 19th c., notably (1865-71) when, under Tweed, it gained control of New York and defrauded it of many millions of dollars. The organization declined in the 1930s. The name comes from a 17th-c. Delaware Indian chief, Tamanend

Tammany Hall Tammany ‖ the Tammany headquarters

tam-o'-shan·ter (tǽməʃǽntər) *n.* a woolen cap having a close-fitting headband and flat, round, very full crown, usually decorated with a pompon [after the hero of Burns's poem 'Tam o' Shanter']

tam·ox·i·fen [$C_{26}H_{29}NO$] (tæmɔ́ksifen) *n.* (*pharm.*) nonsteroidal drug used to counter estrogenic properties, tested on animals; marketed as Nolvade

tamp (tæmp) *v.t.* (*mining*) to pack (a drill hole) with clay, sand etc. above the charge, to obtain a full directed blast ‖ to ram down (the charge) in a drill hole ‖ to pack down tightly (e.g. tobacco in a pipe) [perh. back-formation fr. *tampin* var. of TAMPION]

Tam·pa (tǽmpə) a port and resort (pop. 271,523) in central W. Florida: tobacco and chemical industries, food processing, shipbuilding. University (1931)

tam·per (tǽmpər) *v.i.* (only in) **to tamper with** to bribe or intimidate, *to tamper with a witness* to meddle with, so as to alter for the worse, *do not tamper with old traditions* [var. of TEMPER]

Tam·pe·re (tɑ́mperə) an industrial and commercial center (pop. 165,807) in S.W. Finland: textile, chemical, wood and metal industries

Tam·pi·co (tæmpí:kou, tɑmpí:kɔ) a sea and river port (pop. 123,000) in central E. Mexico near the chief oil fields: oil refining, chemicals

Tampico Incident a U.S.-Mexican incident (1914) in Tampico, Mexico. When some of Admiral Henry Mayo's sailors were arrested without warrant, he demanded an immediate apology from the Mexican government. The latter's failure to acquiesce led to the U.S. naval occupation of the port of Veracruz

tam·pi·on (tǽmpi:ən) *n.* a plug or canvas cover for the muzzle of a gun to keep out dirt and damp ‖ a plug for the end of an organ pipe [fr. F. *tampon*]

tam·pon (tǽmpɒn) **1.** *n.* a plug of cotton etc. put into an orifice or wound in order to stop bleeding or to absorb secretions **2.** *v.t.* to plug with a tampon [F.]

tam·tam (tǽmtæm) *n.* a tom-tom ‖ a large disk-shaped gong [Hindi]

tan (tæn) **1.** *n.* the bark of oak or other trees containing tannic acid, used in tanning hides ‖ any tanning substance ‖ a color of the skin acquired by exposure to the sun and wind ‖ a light brown color **2.** *comp.* **tan·ner** *superl.* **tan·nest** *adj.* of or for tan or tanning ‖ light brown [F., prob. of Celtic origin]

tan *pres. part.* **tan·ning** *past* and *past part.* **tanned** *v.t.* to convert (hide) into leather. Heavy and medium-weight hides are usually treated with vegetable tanning agents and lighter hides and skins with liquors containing chromium salts ‖ to treat (nets, sails etc.) with a hardening mixture of oak bark etc. ‖ to make brown by exposure to the sun or wind ‖ (*pop.*) to thrash (someone) severely ‖ *v.i.* to become brown by exposure to the sun etc. **to tan (someone's) hide** to thrash (someone) severely [O.E. *tannian* fr. M.L.]

tan *abbr.* of TANGENT

Ta·na (tɑ́nɑ) a river (500 miles long) rising in the Aberdare Mtns, Kenya, and curving northeast and south to the Indian Ocean

Tana a marshy lake (area 1,100 sq. miles) in N. Ethiopia, south of Gondar, considered as the main source of the Blue Nile

tan·a·ger (tǽnədʒər) *n.* any of various North and South American passerine birds of fam. *Thraupidae.* They are 6–8 ins long and the males are brilliantly colored (*SCARLET TANAGER) [fr. Mod. L. *Tanagra* fr. Tupi]

CONCISE PRONUNCIATION KEY: **(a)** æ, *c*a*t*; ɑ, *c*a*r*; ɔ *f*aw*n*; ei, *sn*a*ke*. **(e)** e, *h*e*n*; i:, *sh*ee*p*; iə, *d*ee*r*; ɛə, *b*ea*r*. **(i)** i, *f*i*sh*; ai, *t*i*ger*; ə:, *b*i*rd*. **(o)** o, *o*x; au, *c*ow; ou, *g*oa*t*; u, *p*oo*r*; ɔi, *r*oy*al*. **(u)** ʌ, *d*u*ck*; u, *b*u*ll*; u:, *g*oo*se*; ə, *bac*i*llus*; ju:, *c*u*be*. x, *lo*ch; θ, *th*ink; ð, *bo*th*er*; z, *Z*en; ʒ, *cor*s*age*; dʒ, *sa*v*age*; ŋ, *orangu*tang; j, *y*ak; ʃ, *f*ish; tʃ, *f*etch; 'l, *rabb*le; 'n, *redd*en. Complete pronunciation key appears inside front cover.

Tan·a·gra (tǽnəgrə) an ancient town of Boeotia famous for the delicate terra-cotta figurines discovered in ancient tombs
Ta·na·na·rive *ANTANANARIVO
tan·bark (tǽnbɑrk) *n.* a bark used in tanning or (when spent) as a covering for a circus ring, racetrack etc.
Tan·cred (tǽŋkrid) (*d.* 1112), Norman, Sicilian prince, one of the leaders of the 1st Crusade. He took part in the capture of Jerusalem (1099) and was prince of Galilee (1099-1112) and prince of Antioch (1111-12)
tan·dem (tǽndəm) **1.** *n.* a bicycle with two seats, one behind the other ‖ a carriage drawn by two horses harnessed one behind the other ‖ the team of horses so harnessed **2.** *adv.* one behind another [L.= at length (of time)]
Ta·ney (tɔ́ni:), Roger Brooke (1777-1864), U.S. lawyer and jurist. As attorney general (1831-3) under President Andrew Jackson, he opposed renewing the charter of the Bank of the United States and was chiefly responsible for Jackson's veto of the renewal. As secretary of the treasury (1833-5) under Jackson, he removed all federal funds from the bank. He was appointed (1836) chief justice of the Supreme Court where he wrote, notably, the Dred Scott decision
T'ang (tæŋ) a Chinese dynasty (618-906) during which internal organization and diplomacy were extensively developed. Peace and prosperity were accompanied by great achievements in the arts
tang (tæŋ) **1.** *n.* a sharp taste or smell ‖ a characteristic quality ‖ (with 'of') a trace, *a tang of autumn in the air* ‖ a projecting piece, e.g. the shank of a chisel or knife, which joins the blade of the tool to the haft ‖ a surgeonfish ‖ a projecting finger rest on the handle of a scissors **2.** *v.t.* to furnish (a knife etc.) with a tang [O.N. *tange,* point]
tang *n.* any of several coarse seaweeds, esp. of the genus *Fucus,* fam. *Fucaceae* [of Scand. origin]
Tan·ga (tǽŋgə) a port and rail terminus (pop. 21,000) in N.E. Tanganyika, Tanzania
Tan·gan·yi·ka *TANZANIA
Tanganyika a long narrow lake (area 12,700 sq. miles), part of the Great Rift Valley, separating Burundi and Tanzania from the Democratic Republic of the Congo and Zambia
Tan·ge (tæŋge), Kenzo (1913-), Japanese architect. His works integrate Japanese architectural traditions with modern needs, materials and functional concepts. His buildings include Kagawa Prefectural Office (1955-8)
tan·gen·cy (tǽndʒənsi:) *n.* the quality or state of being tangent
tan·gent (tǽndʒənt) **1.** *n.* a line or plane which meets a curve or curved surface at a single point without intersecting it, even if further extended ‖ (*math., abbr.* tan) a measure of the magnitude of an angle expressed as the constant ratio of the opposite to the adjacent side (not the hypotenuse) of the angle in a right-angled triangle **to go** (or **fly**) **off on** (or **at**) **a tangent** to change abruptly from the subject under consideration **2.** *adj.* touching without intersecting **tan·gen·tial** (tændʒénʃəl) *adj.* of, relating to or of the nature of a tangent [fr. L. *tangens* (*tangentis*) fr. *tangere,* to touch]
tangential motion (*astron.*) the motion through space of a star, corrected for distance, i.e. its velocity component perpendicular to the observer (cf. PROPER MOTION)
tan·ge·rine (tændʒərí:n) *n.* a variety of mandarin orange grown in the U.S.A. and southern Africa [fr. F. *Tanger,* Tangier]
tan·gi·bil·i·ty (tændʒəbíliti:) *n.* the state or quality of being tangible
tan·gi·ble (tǽndʒəb'l) *adj.* able to be perceived by the sense of touch ‖ objective, definite, *tangible proof of crime* ‖ (*law*) being a corporeal item able to be valued, *tangible assets* **tán·gi·bly** *adv.* [fr. L. *tangibilis* fr. *tangere,* to touch]
Tan·gier (tændʒíər) (*F.* Tanger, *Arab.* Tanja) a port of entry (pop. 187,894) and former free port in Morocco on the Strait of Gibraltar. Ceded to Britain by Portugal (1662), abandoned to the Moors (1684), it became an international zone (1924), was under Spain (1939-45) and again had its international status restored (1945), finally becoming part of Morocco (1956) as a free zone. It was fully integrated (1962) into the country
tan·gle (tǽŋg'l) **1.** *n.* an interweaving of fibers or of stems, branches etc. so caught up and confused as to be almost inextricable, *a tangle of undergrowth* ‖ a state of confusion, *his business affairs are in a tangle* ‖ a device, consisting of a bar to which are attached pieces of rope etc., used for sweeping over the sea bottom in order to entangle and catch delicate sea animals **2.** *v. pres. part.* **tan·gling** *past* and *past part.* **tan·gled** *v.t.* to form into a tangle ‖ to catch in or as if in a net ‖ *v.i.* to become tangled **to tangle with** (*pop.*) to become involved in an argument or a fight with (someone) **tán·gly** *comp.* **tan·gli·er** *superl.* **tan·gli·est** *adj.* [prob. var. of older *tagle,* of Scand. origin]
tan·go (tǽŋgou) **1.** *n.* a ballroom dance of Argentinian provenance ‖ the music for this dance **2.** *v.i.* to dance the tango [Span.]
tan·gram (tǽŋgrəm) *n.* a square Chinese puzzle in seven pieces, from which many figures can be made [etym. doubtful]
Tang·shan (tɑ́ŋʃɑ́n) a coal-mining center (pop. 800,000) in N.E. Hopei, China: steel, glass, cement
Tan·guy (tãgi:), Yves (1900-55), American painter born in France. An adherent of surrealism, he created works in which vast, realistic settings are filled with dreamlike images
tang·y (tǽŋi:) *comp.* **tang·i·er** *superl.* **tang·i·est** *adj.* having a tang
Tan·jore (tændʒɔ́r, tændʒóur) (or Thanjavur) a former princely capital (pop. 140,547) in E. Madras, India, on the River Cauvery. Handicrafts: silks, carpets, inlaid metalwork. Hindu temple (11th c.)
tank (tæŋk) **1.** *n.* a large container for liquids or gases ‖ (*mil.*) a tracked vehicle, armor-plated and carrying a gun and automatic weapons, capable of rapid movement over difficult country **2.** *v.t.* to put, process or store in a tank [fr. Port. *tanque,* pond. The military vehicle was so named during production (1915) as a security measure]
tan·ka (tǽŋkə) *n.* a Japanese verse form consisting of five lines, the first and third of which have five syllables and the others seven [Jap.]
tank·age (tǽŋkidʒ) *n.* the act of putting into tanks ‖ the capacity or contents of a tank ‖ the charge for storage in tanks ‖ the dried animal residues of slaughterhouses used as a fertilizer or coarse feed
tank·ard (tǽŋkərd) *n.* a large beer mug or other drinking vessel with a handle, sometimes having a lid [M.E.]
tank car a truck or railroad car used for transporting liquids or gases in a tank or tanks
tank·er (tǽŋkər) *n.* a ship built to carry liquids, esp. mineral oil in bulk ‖ a heavy road or rail vehicle which is essentially a large tank on wheels, for transporting gasoline, milk, wine etc.
tank suit a one-piece swim suit with shoulder straps
tank top informal outer shirt with wide shoulder straps
tan·nage (tǽnidʒ) *n.* the act, process or result of tanning hides to make leather
Tan·nen·berg, Battle of (tǽnənbə:rg) a battle (1410) in E. Prussia in which Ladislaus II of Poland defeated the Teutonic Knights, stopping their advance eastward ‖ a battle (Aug. 26-30, 1914) in which a German army under Hindenburg and Ludendorff heavily defeated a Russian army and took over 100,000 prisoners. With the ensuing German victory at the Masurian Lakes (Sept. 6-15, 1914), Russia's invasion of Germany was totally crushed
tan·ner (tǽnər) *n.* a craftsman who tans hides to make leather [TAN V.]
tanner *n.* (*Br., pop.*) the former sixpenny bit, a coin of the value of six pennies that ceased to be minted when the British money was decimalized (1971) [etym. doubtful]
tan·ner·y (tǽnəri:) *pl.* **tan·ner·ies** *n.* a place where hides are tanned ‖ tannage
tan·nic (tǽnik) *adj.* of, relating to, derived from or resembling tan or tannin
tannic acid tannin
tan·nin (tǽnin) *n.* any of various astringent, complex phenolic substances, obtained from barks, woods, leaves, roots and fruits of plants and variously used in tanning, medicine, dyeing, ink manufacture etc. [F. *tanin* fr. *tan,* tan]
tan·rec (tǽnrek) *n.* a tenrec
tan·sy (tǽnzi:) *pl.* **tan·sies** *n.* a member of *Tanacetum,* fam. *Compositae,* a genus of herbaceous, strong-smelling plants, esp. *T. vulgare,* having yellow flowers and bitter leaves [O.F. *tanesie* fr. M.L. fr. Gk *athanasia,* immortality]
Tan·ta (tɑ́ntə) a town (pop. 285,000) in the Nile delta, Egypt, site of annual fairs and Moslem festivals
tan·ta·li·za·tion (tænt'lizéiʃən) *n.* a tantalizing or being tantalized
tan·ta·lize (tǽnt'laiz) *pres. part.* **tan·ta·liz·ing** *past* and *past part.* **tan·ta·lized** *v.t.* to tease by arousing expectations that are repeatedly disappointed [after TANTALUS]
tan·ta·lum (tǽnt'ləm) *n.* a metallic element (symbol Ta, at. no. 73, at. mass 180.948) that is very unreactive and has a high melting point. It is used in heat resistant and corrosion-resistant alloys and in surgical instruments. The carbide is used as an abrasive and in tools [Mod. L. after TANTALUS (because of the difficulties resulting from its unreactiveness)]
Tan·ta·lus (tǽnt'ləs) (*mythol.*) a king of Lydia, who served the flesh of his son Pelops to the gods at a banquet. He was punished in Hades with eternal thirst and hunger: he had to stand up to his neck in water which disappeared when he tried to drink, and under branches of fruit which constantly eluded his grasp
tan·ta·mount (tǽntəmaunt) *adj.* (with 'to') equivalent in effect or value, *the tax was tantamount to robbery* [fr. A.F. *tant amunter,* to amount to as much]
Tan·tra (tʌ́ntrə) *n.* any of several Hindu religious writings (8th–13th cc.) of a kind which opposed the religious and social sanctions of Brahmanism **Tán·trism** *n.* a form of Mahayana Buddhism which arose in N. India and incorporated the teachings of the Hindu Tantras and traditional mystical beliefs. It encourages theurgic practices in the attainment of enlightenment [Skr.=loom, warp, system]
tan·trum (tǽntrəm) *n.* a fit of bad temper indulged in before another person or persons [origin unknown]
Tan·za·ni·a (tænzéini:ə, tænzəní:ə) a republic (area 364,900 sq. miles, pop. 19,112,000) and member of the Commonwealth in E. Africa, formed (Apr. 27, 1964) by the union of Tanganyika and Zanzibar, with Julius Nyerere as its first president (1961-85). A 1977 constitution calls for a president, vice-president, and national assembly. Zanzibar has controlled its own internal affairs since 1965. The breakup of the East African Community, a growing trade deficit, and a costly invasion of Uganda in 1979 to help overthrow Idi Amin all contributed to a 30% decline in per capita income between 1978 and 1984. A secessionist movement on Zanzibar led to the resignation of Zanzibar President Aboud Jumbe, and his successor, Ali Hassan Mwinyi, became president of Tanzania in 1985 (*TANGANYIKA, *ZANZIBAR)
Tao·ism (táuizəm, dáuizəm) *n.* a Chinese religion founded (6th c. B.C.) by Lao-tzu. Classic Taoism is based on the concept of Tao, the universal force harmonizing nature. To achieve harmony, man should identify himself with the basic spirit of nature by contemplation. This philosophic Taoism, influenced by Buddhism and Confucianism, evolved (c. 5th c.) into a pantheistic religion of hero worship and magical and mystical rites, with monastic orders. Taoism has about 30 million adherents in China
Ta·or·mi·na (tɑɔrmí:nə) a resort (pop. 10,085) in E. Sicily at the foot of Etna: Greek theater (restored)
T'ao Yuan-ming (táujwánmíŋ) (c. 365-427), Chinese poet, who wrote in praise of the simple life
tap (tæp) *n.* a device which controls the flow of a fluid from or through a pipe or from a container ‖ a tool for cutting the thread of an internal screw ‖ (*elec.*) a point where a connection can be made in a circuit **on tap** available when required ‖ on draft [O.E. *tæppa*]
tap 1. *v. pres. part.* **tap·ping** *past* and *past part.* **tapped** *v.t.* to cause (something) to rap on something else, *to tap a stick on a table* ‖ to strike lightly with a rapping sound, *to tap a table with a stick* ‖ (with 'out') to type or keyboard (literary copy) ‖ (esp. with 'out') to produce by light little raps, *to tap out a message on a wall* ‖ to reinforce the heel or toe of (a shoe) with a thickness of leather or metal ‖ *v.i.* to make a light impact or series of little raps on something, *to tap impatiently with one's fingers* ‖ to walk lightly, making clicking sounds with the heels **2.** *n.* a light rap or blow ‖ the sound of this ‖ a leather or metal reinforcement of the sole or heel of a shoe [O.F. *taper*]
tap *pres. part.* **tap·ping** *past* and *past part.* **tapped** *v.t.* to furnish (a cask etc.) with a tap ‖

to permit (liquid) to flow from a cask, tree etc. by opening a hole or vent ‖ to open a hole in (a cask, tree etc.) so that liquid can flow out ‖ to draw off a fluid from (an abscess etc.) ‖ to make a connection with (a service pipe or cable) ‖ to connect a listening device to (an electric wire, cable etc.) in order to intercept telephonic etc. communications ‖ to steal (electricity) by connecting up with another circuit ‖ to make a female screw thread on (a nut) ‖ to draw on (resources) [O. E. *tæppian*]

ta·pa (tɑ́pə) *n.* the bark of the paper mulberry ‖ a rough cloth made in Polynesia from the pounded bark of the paper mulberry and other plants. It is decorated and used for ceremonial clothing, house decoration etc. [Polynesian]

Ta·pa·jós (tɑpɑʒɔ́s) (or Tapajóz) a navigable tributary (500 miles long) of the Amazon in central Brazil

tap dance an exhibition dance in which the rhythm of the music is tapped out by the feet of the dancer, who wears specially made shoes **tap-dance** (tǽpdæns) *pres. part.* **tap-danc·ing** *past* and *past part.* **tap-danced** *v.i.* to perform a tap dance

tape (teip) **1.** *n.* a narrow strip of cotton, silk, rayon etc. used in dressmaking, for tying bundles etc. ‖ a narrow roll of thin adhesive paper or plastic ‖ a long, narrow flexible strip of metal used by surveyors for measuring ‖ a narrow roll of paper on which a teleprinter prints a message ‖ a narrow band of plastic covered with magnetic oxide on which tape recordings are made ‖ (*pop.*) a tape recording ‖ (*bookbinding*) one of the bands to which the signatures are sewn and which help to attach the sewn pages to the cover ‖ a length of narrow material stretched breast-high across the finishing line of a race track ‖ a tape measure **2.** *v.t. pres. part.* **tap·ing** *past* and *past part.* **taped** to furnish with tape ‖ to fasten with tape ‖ to record on magnetic tape ‖ to join the sections of (a book) with tape [perh. fr. O.E. *tæppan*]

tape deck device for recording and playing magnetic tapes (or tape cassettes) of words, music, or other sounds *also* tape player

tape eraser *BULK ERASER

tape measure a tape or strip of strong fabric or flexible metal, marked in inches, feet, meters etc., used for measuring

tape music electronic music recorded on magnetic tape for commercial distribution

ta·per (téipər) **1.** *n.* (*hist.*) a small, slender wax candle ‖ a long, wax-covered wick used for lighting candles etc. ‖ a gradual narrowing **2.** *v.i.* to narrow gradually ‖ *v.t.* to make gradually narrower **to taper off** to become gradually less in number, amount etc. **3.** *adj.* regularly narrowing down to a point, *a chair with taper legs* [O.E. *tapur, tapor, taper*]

tape-re·cord (téiprikɔrd) *v.t.* to record on a magnetic tape [back-formation fr. TAPE RECORDING]

tape recorder a magnetic recorder using magnetic tape

tape recording the act of recording on magnetic tape (*MAGNETIC RECORDER) ‖ the recording produced

tap·es·tried (tǽpistri:d) *adj.* covered with or as if with tapestry ‖ worked in tapestry

tap·es·try (tǽpistri:) *pl.* **tap·es·tries** *n.* a heavy, hand-worked fabric with pictures or designs formed by threads inserted over and under the warp according to the requirements of color (not worked from selvage to selvage as in weaving) and used for hangings, chair seats etc. ‖ a machine-made fabric imitating this [O.F. *tapisserie*]

ta·pe·tum (təpí:təm) *pl.* **ta·pe·ta** (təpí:tə) *n.* (*biol.*) any of various membranous layers of the retina or choroid of the eye, esp. a reflecting layer in the choroid of nocturnal animals ‖ (*bot.*) the special nutritive layer investing the sporogenous tissue of a sporangium [L.L.=carpet]

tape·worm (téipwə:rm) *n.* a member of *Cestoda*, a subclass of long, ribbonshaped parasitic worms which as adults infest the intestines of man and other vertebrates and, in the larval stage, infest great numbers of vertebrates and invertebrates

tap·i·o·ca (tæpi:óukə) *n.* cassava starch processed into grains, flakes etc. and used in milk puddings, for thickening soups etc. and commercially as a size or adhesive [fr. Tupi-Guarani *tipioca*]

ta·pir (téipər) *pl.* **ta·pir, ta·pirs** *n.* any of several nonruminant, chiefly nocturnal ungulates of fam. *Tapiridae,* native to South and Central America, Malaya and Sumatra. They are about 3 ft tall, are clumsily and heavily built, and have four front and three hind toes, a short but flexible proboscis, and a brownish, almost hairless body [fr. Tupi *tapira* or *tapura*]

tap·pet (tǽpit) *n.* (*mach.*) an arm or lever moved by a cam etc. to cause intermittent motion, as in the valve gear of an internal-combustion engine etc.

tap·room (tǽpru:m, tǽprum) *n.* a bar where esp. beer is kept on tap

tap·root (tǽpru:t, tǽprut) *n.* a primary root growing vertically downward and giving off small subsidiary roots in succession

taps (tæps) *pl. n.* (*mil.*) lights-out sounded by a bugle ‖ the bugle call sounded at a military funeral [prob. alt. of obs. *taptoo,* tattoo]

Tap·ti (tɑ́pti:) a river (436 miles long) of Madhya Pradesh and Gujarat, India, flowing from the central Satpura Range to the Arabian Sea

tar (tar) **1.** *n.* a thick, black or dark brown viscous liquid obtained by the destructive distillation of wood, coal etc. It is used in road making, to preserve wood and iron, and as the source of many dyes, antiseptics etc. **2.** *v.t. pres. part.* **tar·ring** *past* and *past part.* **tarred** to cover with tar ‖ to attach a moral stigma to **tarred with the same brush** (or **stick**) having the same faults or having committed the same misdemeanors **to tar and feather** to cover (a person) with tar and feathers as a punishment or humiliation [O.E. *teru, teoru*]

tar *n.* (*pop.*) a sailor [shortened fr. TARPAULIN]

Tar·a (tǽrə) a low hill in County Meath, Ireland, the seat of Irish kings from prehistoric times to the 6th c. St Patrick preached here

Tar·a·na·ki (tærənɑ́ki) a region (area 3,750 sq. miles, pop. 103,000) of W. North Island, New Zealand: dairy products, lumber. Chief town: New Plymouth (pop. 31,000)

tar·an·tel·la (tærəntélə) *n.* a whirling S. Italian folk dance in 6/8 time for couples with tambourines ‖ the music for this dance [Ital., dim. of *Taranto,* Italy]

Ta·ran·to (tɑ́rɑntɔ) (ancient Tarentum) a port and naval base (pop. 243,800) in Apulia, Italy, on the Gulf of Taranto, which separates the heel and the toe of Italy: shipbuilding, engineering, textiles, chemicals, fishing

ta·ran·tu·la (tərǽntʃulə) *n.* any of various hairy, big spiders of fam. *Theraphosidae,* found in hot countries. The bite of the tarantula is painful but not dangerous to man ‖ *Lycosa tarantula,* fam. *Lycosidae,* a very large brown European spider [M.L. after *Taranto,* Italy]

Ta·ra·wa Island (tərɑ́wə, tǽrəwə) an atoll (area 7.7 sq. miles) of the Gilbert Is in the western central Pacific. Occupied (1941) by the Japanese during the 2nd world war, it was recaptured (1943) by the U.S. Marines

ta·rax·a·cum (tərǽksəkəm) *n.* the dried rhizome and roots of the dandelion used medicinally [M.L. fr. Arab.]

Tar Baby policy action undertaken by President Richard M. Nixon of nonsupport for colonial powers in Africa, verbal encouragement to emerging African nations, and continuation of good relations with Rhodesia (now Zimbabwe) and Republic of South Africa

Tar·be·la (tɑrbélə) the site of a great dam project, on the Indus in Pakistan, northwest of Rawalpindi (*INDUS)

Tar·bell (tɑ́rbel, tɑ́rbəl), Ida Minerva (1857-1944), U.S. journalist, known for 'muckraking' exposés of political and corporate corruption, and biographer, notably of Abraham Lincoln

tar·boosh (tɑrbú:ʃ) *n.* a brimless red felt cap resembling a fez, worn alone or as part of a turban by Moslem men in E. Mediterranean countries [Arab. *tarbūsh*]

tar·di·grade (tɑ́rdigreid) *n.* a member of *Tardigrada,* a division of *Arthropoda,* comprising minute, aquatic, spiderlike animals having four pairs of legs and no mouth appendages [F. or fr. L. *tardigradus,* walking slowly]

tar·di·ly (tɑ́rdili:) *adv.* in a tardy manner

tar·di·ness (tɑ́rdi:nis) *n.* the quality or state of being tardy

tar·dy (tɑ́rdi:) *comp.* **tar·di·er** *superl.* **tar·di·est** *adj.* coming late, *a tardy apology* ‖ happening later than is desirable or expected, *a tardy departure* [F. *tardif*]

tare (tɛər) **1.** *n.* the weight of the container or vehicle in which goods are packed and weighed, deducted from the gross weight in order to arrive at the net weight ‖ this deduction **2.** *v.t. pres. part.* **tar·ing** *past* and *past part.* **tared** to ascertain the weight of (a container, vehicle etc.) or to allow for this [F. fr. Arab. *tarhah,* that which is thrown away]

tare *n.* any of several vetches, esp. *Vicia sativa,* fam. *Papilionaceae* ‖ the seed of any of these ‖ (*pl., Bible*) choking weeds [etym. doubtful]

tar·get (tɑ́rgit) *n.* a circular straw mat having a canvas cover painted with five concentric circles, shot at in archery ‖ a sheet of cardboard or thin wood, similarly marked, aimed at in rifle shooting etc. ‖ the score made in target shooting ‖ any object at which a missile is aimed ‖ an object of attack, criticism etc. ‖ an end which it is hoped to reach by an effort, or any planning objective, *his target was the saving of $1000* ‖ (of an X-ray tube) the metallic surface upon which the stream of cathode rays is focused ‖ a small railroad switch signal ‖ (*surveying*) a sliding sight on a leveling staff ‖ (*hist.*) a small, round shield [dim. of *targe,* a shield]

target language (*computer*) the language into which the language of a program is to be translated for the ongoing operation *also Cf* SOURCE LANGUAGE

tar·get·a·ble (tɑ́rgətəb'l) *adj.* capable of being hit or accomplished **—on target** in the right direction; correct

target marketing (*business*) strategy or strategies designed for a single market segment

Tar·gum (tɑ́rgəm) *pl.* **Tar·gums, Tar·gu·mim** (tɑrgumí:m) *n.* an Aramaic translation or paraphrase of part of the Old Testament [fr. Chaldean *targūm*]

tar·iff (tǽrif) *n.* a scale of duties imposed by a government on goods imported or exported ‖ the duty imposed ‖ any scale of rates or charges, e.g. for accommodation in a hotel [fr. Ital. *tariffa* fr. Arab.]

Ta·ri·ja (tɑrí:hɑ) a city and the commercial center (pop. 24,000, altitude 6,400 ft) of S. Bolivia

Ta·rim (tɑrí:m) a river (1,250 miles long) rising (as the Khotan) in the Kunlun and curving in a marshy course through S. Sinkiang-Uighor, China, to end in a sink ‖ its basin (350,000 sq. miles), enclosed by the Kunlun, Pamirs and Tien Shan

Tar·king·ton (tɑ́rkiŋtən), (Newton) Booth (1869-1946), U.S. novelist and playwright. His novels, notably 'Seventeen' (1916) and 'The Magnificent Ambersons' (1918) explore the adolescent and adult life of the middle class in midwest towns

tar·la·tan (tɑ́rlətən) *n.* a thin muslin, stiffened with size and used esp. as a dress material [F. *tarlatane* prob. of Indian origin]

tar·mac (tɑ́rmæk) *n.* the hard, level surface of a road, airfield runway etc. [short for *tarmacadam* fr. TAR+MACADAM]

Tarn (tærn) a department (area 2,231 sq. miles, pop. 338,000) of S. France (*LANGUEDOC). Chief town: Albi (pop. 49,456)

tarn (tɑrn) *n.* a small lake surrounded by mountains [M.E. *terne* fr. O.N.]

Tarn-et-Ga·ronne (tærneigærɔn) a department (area 1,440 sq. miles, pop. 183,300) of S. France (*GUYENNE, *LANGUEDOC). Chief town: Montauban (pop. 50,420)

tar·nish (tɑ́rniʃ) **1.** *v.t.* to dull the brightness of (a metallic surface) by covering it with a film of sulfide, oxide etc. ‖ to sully ‖ *v.i.* to become tarnished **2.** *n.* the condition of being tarnished ‖ the film causing this ‖ (of honor or reputation) the condition of being sullied [fr. F. *ternir* (*terniss-*)]

ta·ro (tɑ́rou) *n. Colocasia esculenta,* fam. *Araceoe,* a plant grown throughout the tropics for its starchy, edible rhizome ‖ this rhizome [native Polynesian name]

ta·rot (tǽrou) *n.* one of a set of playing cards first used in Italy in the 14th c. The figured cards are used in fortune-telling and as trumps in the game played with the entire set ‖ the game played [F. fr. Ital., origin unknown]

tar·pan (tɑrpǽn) *n.* a small grayish-brown wild horse of central Asia [Tatar]

tar·pau·lin (tɑrpɔ́lin, tɑ́rpəlin) *n.* waterproof canvas or a sheet of this [etym. doubtful]

tar·pon (tɑ́rpən) *pl.* **tar·pon, tar·pons** *n. Tarpon atlanticus* or *Megalops atlanticus,* a large (up to 200 lbs) marine game fish common in the Gulf of Mexico off the coast of Florida [etym. doubtful]

Tar·quin·i·us Pris·cus (tɑrkwíni:əspriskəs), Lucius, fifth king of Rome (616-579 B.C.)

Tarquinius Su·per·bus (supə́:rbəs), Lucius, seventh and last king of Rome (534-510 B.C.), expelled by Brutus (*LUCRETIA)

CONCISE PRONUNCIATION KEY: **(a)** æ, *cat;* ɑ, *car;* ɔ *fawn;* ei, *snake.* **(e)** e, *hen;* i:, *sheep;* iə, *deer;* ɛə, *bear.* **(i)** i, *fish;* ai, *tiger;* ə:, *bird.* **(o)** o, *ox;* au, *cow;* ou, *goat;* u, *poor;* ɔi, *royal.* **(u)** ʌ, *duck;* u, *bull;* u:, *goose;* ə, *bacillus;* ju:, *cube.* x, *loch;* θ, *think;* ð, *bother;* z, *Zen;* ʒ, *corsage;* dʒ, *savage;* ŋ, *orangutang;* j, *yak;* ʃ, *fish;* tʃ, *fetch;* 'l, *rabble;* 'n, *redden.* Complete pronunciation key appears inside front cover.

tar·ra·gon (tǽrəgən, tǽrəgɒn) *n. Artemisia dracunculus,* fam. *Compositae,* a European perennial wormwood, grown for its aromatic leaves [fr. Span. *taragona* fr. Arab. fr. Gk]

Tar·ra·go·na (tærəgóunə) a province (area 2,505 sq. miles, pop. 516,078) of E. Spain (*CATALONIA) || its capital (pop. 138,705), a walled port. Roman walls, aqueduct, theater etc., Romanesque-Gothic cathedral (12th-13th cc.)

tar·ry (tɑ́ri:) *comp.* **tar·ri·er** *superl.* **tar·ri·est** *adj.* covered with tar of or resembling tar

tar·ry (tǽri:) *pres. part.* **tar·ry·ing** *past* and *past part.* **tar·ried** *v.i.* (*rhet.*) to linger behind, delay [origin unknown]

tar·sal (tɑ́rs'l) **1.** *adj.* of or relating to the tarsus || being or relating to the tarsi of the eyelids **2.** *n.* a tarsal bone or plate [fr. Mod. L. *tarsalis* fr. *tarsus,* tarsus]

tar sands oil-rich sands, principally in Canada

tar·si·a (tɑ́rsi:ə) *n.* intarsia [Ital.]

tar·si·er (tɑ́rsi:ər) *n.* any of several members of *Tarsius,* fam. *Tarsiidae,* a genus of nocturnal, arboreal mammals of the East Indies, related to the lemurs, and having elongated tarsal bones in the hands and feet. Of a grayish-brown color, they are about the size of a squirrel, and have large ears, large eyes and a long tufted tail [F. fr. *tarse,* tarsus]

Tar·sus (tɑ́rsəs) a trade center (pop. 102,186) in S.W. central Turkey. In ancient times it was the capital of Cilicia. It prospered under Roman rule and was the birthplace of St Paul

tar·sus (tɑ́rsəs) *pl.* **tar·si** (tɑ́rsai) *n.* (*anat.*) the ankle || (*anat.*) the small bones supporting the ankle || the shank of a bird's leg || the end segment of an insect's or crustacean's leg || a plate of fibrous connective tissue serving to support the eyelid [Mod. L. fr. Gk *tarsos,* the flat part of the foot or rim of the eyelid]

tart (tɑrt) *n.* a piece of baked pastry containing jam, fruit etc. || (*Br.*) fruit covered with pastry and baked [O.F. *tarte*]

tart *adj.* having an acid taste || (*fig.*) sharp, cutting, *a tart reply* [O.E. *teart*]

tart *n.* a girl or woman of loose morals, esp. a prostitute [shortened fr. SWEETHEART]

tar·tan (tɑ́rt'n) *n.* a closely woven woolen fabric, cross-barred with stripes in various widths and colors which form distinctive patterns. The fabric is used mainly by the Highlanders of Scotland, almost every clan having its own individual pattern || any such pattern [etym. doubtful]

tartan *n.* a single-masted Mediterranean vessel, carrying a large lateen sail and a jib [F. *tartane* fr. Ital. perh. fr. Arab.]

tar·tar (tɑ́rtər) *n.* a brownish-red deposit, chiefly of acid potassium tartrate, found in the juice of grapes and deposited in wine barrels (*CREAM OF TARTAR) || a deposit on the teeth consisting mainly of calcium phosphate [O.F. *tartre,* perh. of Arab. origin]

Tar·tar (tɑ́rtər) Tatar

Tartar (*mil.*) a 1,500-lb shipborne, surface-to-air missile (RIM-24) with solid-propellant rocket engine, 10-mi range, semiactive radar direction, and a nonnuclear warhead capability

Tartar A.S.S.R. Tatar A.S.S.R.

Tar·tar·e·an (tɑrtɛ́əri:ən) *adj.* of or relating to Tartarus

tartar emetic a poisonous crystalline salt, $2K(SbO)C_4H_4O_6 \cdot H_2O$, used in medicine and as a mordant in dyeing

tar·tar·ic (tɑrtǽrik) *adj.* of, relating to, containing or derived from tartar or tartaric acid

tartaric acid $HOOC(CHOH)_2 \cdot COOH$, an acid, having four stereoisomeric forms, occurring widely in plants and used in dyeing, calico printing, in making effervescent laxatives etc.

Tar·ta·rus (tɑ́rtərəs) (*Gk mythol.*) a region of the underworld where the wicked were punished, and the place where Zeus confined the Titans

Tar·ta·ry (tɑ́rtəri:) Tatary

tart·let (tɑ́rtlit) *n.* a small pastry tart

tar·trate (tɑ́rtreit) *n.* a salt or ester of tartaric acid [F.]

Tar·tu (tɑ́rtu:) (*G.* Dorpat, *Russ.* formerly Yurev) a city (pop. 104,000) of E. Estonia, U.S.S.R. Industries: mechanical engineering, wood and food processing. University (1632 and 1802)

tart up or **tart** *v.* (*Br.*) to dress up or overadorn

Tar·zan (tɑ́rzən, tɑ́rzæn) a fictional character created by Edgar Rice Burroughs and popularized in many movies. Tarzan was the child of parents who died in the African jungle. He was brought up by an ape, became immensely strong and agile and the friend of all the jungle creatures, and had fabulous adventures

Ta·shi La·ma (tɑ́ʃi:lɑ́mə) *LAMA

Tash·kent (tɑʃként) the capital (pop. 1,779,000) of Uzbekistan, U.S.S.R., an ancient oasis trading city, now economic and cultural center of Soviet central Asia. Industries: heavy machinery, cotton textiles, food processing, paper, chemicals. Arab mausoleum (9th c.). University

TASI (*acronym*) for time assignment speech interpolation, a technique for using intervals of silence on transatlantic telephone cables to transmit information, involving complex switching, enabling a doubling of capacity

task (tæsk, task) **1.** *n.* a definite amount of work set or undertaken || any piece of work that has to be done **to take to task** to blame or censure for neglecting to do a task or for committing a fault **2.** *v.t.* (*rhet.*) to burden with a task [O.N.F. *tasque*]

task force (*mil.*) a temporary grouping of men or units under one commander, formed for carrying out a special mission || a group of people formed temporarily to solve a particular problem

task·mas·ter (tǽskmæstər, tɑ́skmɑstər) *n.* (esp. in phrase) **a hard taskmaster** a person who demands hard work from others, and who is difficult to satisfy

Tas·man (tǽzmən), Abel Janszoon (c. 1603-59), Dutch navigator. Under the patronage of Van Diemen, he led an expedition (1642-3) which discovered Tasmania and New Zealand, and visited some of the islands of Tonga and Fiji. On a later expedition he explored the north coast of Australia (1644)

Tas·ma·ni·a (tæzméini:ə) an island (area 24,450 sq. miles) and state (area, including the Macquarie Is, 26,215 sq. miles, pop. 414,000) of Australia, 268 miles off the southeast coast, between the Indian Ocean and the Tasman Sea. Capital: Hobart. Chief port: Launceston. It is mountainous (Ben Lomond, 5,160 ft) and largely forested. Exports: metals, newsprint, lumber, fruit, wool, cereals, dairy produce. State university (1890). Tasmania was discovered (1642) by Tasman, and called Van Diemen's Land until 1855

Tas·ma·ni·an (tæzméini:ən) **1.** *n.* a native or inhabitant of Tasmania, esp. one of the extinct aborigines || any of various languages of the Tasmanian aborigines **2.** *adj.* pertaining to Tasmania or its inhabitants

Tasmanian devil *Sarcophilus Harrisii,* a fierce, carnivorous, burrowing marsupial of Tasmania. It is about the size of a large cat and has a black coat and white chest markings

Tasmanian wolf *Thylacinus cynocephalus,* fam. *Dasyuridae,* a carnivorous doglike marsupial of Tasmania. It is about 40 ins long and has a smooth grayish-brown coat striped with black towards the back

Tasman Sea the part of the Pacific between Australia and New Zealand

tas·sel (tǽs'l) **1.** *n.* a tuft of threads or cords fastened at one end to form a pendant ornament || a tuft of loose threads, occurring as the inflorescence of some plants (e.g. corn) **2.** *v. pres. part.* **tas·sel·ing,** esp. *Br.* **tas·sel·ling** *past* and *past part.* **tas·seled,** esp. *Br.* **tas·selled** *v.i.* (often with 'out') to put forth tassels || *v.t.* to furnish with or as if with tassels [O.F. *tasel, tassel,* a clasp]

tas·ses (tǽsiz) *pl. n.* (*hist.,* of armor) a series of overlapping metal plates suspended from the waist to form a short skirt for protecting the thighs [fr. F. *tassette,* a small pocket or pouch]

tas·sets (tǽsits) *pl. n.* tasses [fr. F. *tassette,* a small pocket or pouch]

Tas·so (tɑ́sɔ), Torquato (1544-95), Italian epic poet. His 'Aminta' (1573) is a lyrical and pastoral drama. His masterpiece, 'Jerusalem Delivered' (1581), is an epic celebrating the 1st Crusade. He inspired many poets, esp. Spenser and Byron

taste (teist) *n.* the sense which perceives and distinguishes between salt, bitter, sour and sweet substances through the stimulation of the taste buds in the mouth by a solution of the substance in the saliva || the flavor detected through this sense || the sensation resulting from this stimulation || a tasting || a small amount of a substance examined for its taste || discernment where beauty is concerned || a brief experiencing of something, *a taste of night life* || a liking, predilection, *a taste for adventure* **in good (poor, bad** etc.) **taste** pleasing (not pleasing) aesthetically, morally etc. **to leave a nasty taste in the mouth** to make one feel slightly disgusted in the aftermath by what seemed momentarily enjoyable [O.F. *tast*]

taste *pres. part.* **tast·ing** *past* and *past part.* **tast·ed** *v.t.* to examine (a substance) for its taste by putting some in one's mouth || to distinguish the taste of, *you could taste the rum in the cake* || to experience, *to taste the rigors of an Arctic winter* || to eat or drink a small amount of || (esp. *hist.*) to sample (food or drink prepared for another) to discover if it is poisoned || *v.i.* to have the sense of taste || to have a specified flavor, *the ice cream tasted of rum* [O.F. *taster*]

taste bud a cluster of cells at the base of the papillae of the tongue constituting the sense organ of taste

taste·ful (téistfəl) *adj.* being in or showing good taste

taste·less (téistlis) *adj.* failing to excite the sensation of taste || lacking artistic taste || being in bad taste

tast·er (téistər) *n.* a person who tests quality by tasting || any of several devices used by tasters || (esp. *hist.*) a person who tastes food or drink prepared for another to discover if poison is present || an instrument for taking a sample of butter or cheese [A.F. *tastour*]

tast·i·ly (téistili:) *adv.* in a tasty way

tast·i·ness (téisti:nis) *n.* the state or quality of being tasty

tast·y (téisti:) *comp.* **tast·i·er** *superl.* **tast·i·est** *adj.* having a very pleasant taste

tat (tæt) *n.* *TIT FOR TAT

tat *pres. part.* **tat·ting** *past* and *past part.* **tat·ted** *v.i.* to do tatting || *v.t.* to make by tatting [etym. doubtful]

TAT (*psych.*) thematic apperception test (which see)

Ta·tar (tɑ́tər) **1.** *n.* (*hist.*) a member of the Mongolian horde which overran Asia and part of Europe in the Middle Ages (*MONGOL) || a member of a people of Turkish origin, chiefly Moslem, living in the U.S.S.R. They number 5 million and are divided into three groups: Kazan or Volga Tatars, living mainly in the Volga region and the Urals, Siberian Tatars, living in scattered groups in W. Siberia, and Crimean Tatars. These last lived in the Crimea until 1945, formerly a Tatar autonomous republic, when they were all deported to Uzbekistan and Kazakhstan for alleged collaboration with the Germans. They have not since been rehabilitated **2.** *adj.* of Tatary or the Tatars || of the language of the Tatars [Pers. *Tātār*]

Tatar A.S.S.R. an autonomous republic (area 26,200 sq. miles, pop. 3,453,000) of the R.S.F.S.R., U.S.S.R., on the middle Volga. Capital: Kazan. People: Tatar

Ta·ta·ry (tɑ́təri:) (*hist.*) the area ruled by the Tatars

Ta·tra Mountains (tɑ́trə) a pair of rugged massifs: the High Tatra (summit: 8,737 ft), on the Polish-Czechoslovakian frontier, and the Low Tatra, entirely in Czechoslovakia, containing the highest peaks of the Carpathians

tat·ter (tǽtər) *n.* a torn piece of fabric, paper etc., usually hanging loosely || (*pl.*) ragged clothing, *dressed in tatters* [of Scand. origin]

tatter *v.t.* to tear into shreds, make ragged || *v.i.* to become ragged [prob. back-formation fr. TATTERED]

tat·tered (tǽtərd) *adj.* in tatters || wearing torn, ragged clothing

tat·ter·de·mal·ion (tætərdəméiljən) *n.* a person clothed in rags [TATTER+*demalion,* origin unknown]

tat·ting (tǽtiŋ) *n.* narrow lace made by knotting each loop of thread, using a small shuttle || the act or process of making this lace [origin unknown]

tat·tle (tǽt'l) **1.** *v.i. pres. part.* **tat·tling** *past* and *past part.* **tat·tled** to engage in idle talk || to tell other people's secrets **2.** *n.* idle talk, gossip **tát·tler** (*old-fash.*) a gossip [imit.]

tat·tle·tale (tǽt'lteil) *n.* a talebearer

tat·too (tætú:, esp. *Br.* tətú:) *pl.* **tat·toos** *n.* a signal sounded on a drum or bugle to call troops to quarters || a rapid succession of light taps, *the rain beat a tattoo on the roof* || (*mil.*) an outdoor entertainment given at night, consisting of military exercises accompanied by music [earlier *taptoo* fr. Du. *tap toe,* shut the tap (a signal for closing bars)]

tattoo 1. *v.t.* to mark (the skin) with a permanent pattern by puncturing it and inserting a pigment ‖ to make (patterns) in this way **2.** *n.* the marks thus made [fr. Polynesian *tatau*]

tat·ty (tǽti:) *comp.* **tat·ti·er** *superl.* **tat·ti·est** *adj.* of an inferior sort or quality or in an inferior condition, shabby [perh. rel. to O.E. *tœtteca,* rag, tatter]

tau (tau) *n.* the 19th letter (T, τ = t) of the Greek alphabet

taught *past* and *past part.* of TEACH

tau meson *K MESON

taunt (tɔnt) *adj.* (*naut.,* of a mast) very tall [etym. doubtful]

taunt 1. *v.t.* to jeer at ‖ to accuse (someone) in a jeering way of some contemptible crime or failing (e.g. cowardice) ‖ to provoke by a taunt **2.** *n.* a jibe, a jeering accusation [etym. doubtful]

Tau·nus Mountains (táunus) a wooded range (rising to 2,886 ft) on the E. Rhine plateau in Hesse, West Germany: tourism

taupe (toup) *n.* a soft, brownish-gray color

Tau·po (táupou) the largest lake (area 238 sq. miles) in New Zealand, in central North Island

tau·rine (tɔ́ri:n) *n.* a crystalline compound, $H_2NCH_2CH_2HSO_3$, occurring esp. in the muscle juices of invertebrates etc. [fr. L. *taurus,* bull (because it was first found in the bile of an ox)]

taurine *adj.* of or relating to a bull [fr. L. *taurinus*]

tau·rom·a·chy (tɔrɔ́məki:) *n.* the art or practice of bullfighting [Span. *tauromaquia*]

Tau·rus (tɔ́rəs) a northern constellation ‖ the second sign of the zodiac, represented as a bull [L.=bull]

Taurus Mountains (*Turk.* Toros) a mountain chain of central S.W. Turkey running parallel to the Mediterranean coast, with several peaks over 11,000 ft. Chief pass: the Cilician Gates, above Tarsus

Taus·sig (tóusig), Frank William (1859-1940), U.S. economist. His 'Wages and Capital' (1896) and 'International Trade' (1927) modernized the classical school of economics as formulated by John Stuart Mill. He helped to draft the tariff and commercial policy clauses of the Treaty of Versailles (1919)

taut (tɔt) *adj.* (of a rope, wire, muscle etc.) under longitudinal tension, *a taut string* ‖ tense, *taut nerves* ‖ (esp. *naut.*) trim and tidy **táut·en** *v.t.* to make taut ‖ *v.i.* to become taut [M.E. *toght*]

tau·tog (tɔtɔ́g, tɔtɒ́g) *n. Tautoga onitis,* fam. *Labridae,* an edible marine fish of the Atlantic coast of the U.S.A. [fr. Algonquian *tautauog* pl. of *tautau,* a blackfish]

tau·to·log·i·cal (tɔ̧t'lɒ́dʒik'l) *adj.* of, relating to or using tautology

tau·tol·o·gism (tɔtɒ́lədʒizəm) *n.* the use or an instance of tautology

tau·tol·o·gist (tɔtɒ́lədʒist) *n.* a person who uses tautology

tau·tol·o·gize (tɔtɒ́lədʒaiz) *pres. part.* **tau·tol·o·giz·ing** *past* and *past part.* **tau·tol·o·gized** *v.i.* to use tautology

tau·tol·o·gy (tɔtɒ́lədʒi:) *pl.* **tau·tol·o·gies** *n.* the useless repetition of an identical meaning in different terms ‖ an example of this [fr. L.L. *tautologia* fr. Gk]

tau·to·mer (tɔ́təmər) *n.* one form of a tautomeric compound

tau·to·mer·ic (tɔ̧təmérik) *adj.* of, relating to or characterized by tautomerism

tau·tom·er·ism (tɔtɒ́mərizəm) *n.* (*chem.*) the existence of two isomers in a mixture in stable equilibrium, this equilibrium being preserved by their interconvertibility [fr. Gk *to auto,* the same+*meros,* a part]

tav·ern (tǽvərn) *n.* (*old-fash.*) an inn or bar [O.F. *taverne*]

Tav·er·ner (tǽvərnər), John (c. 1495-1545), English composer of church music (masses, motets etc.). He also wrote songs and madrigals

taw (tɔ) *n.* the large, usually glass, marble which a marble player shoots with ‖ the mark from which a marble is played ‖ one of the games played with marbles [etym. doubtful]

taw *v.t.* to convert (a skin) into leather by treating it with alum, salt etc. [O.E. *tawian,* to make]

taw·dri·ly (tɔ́drili:) *adv.* in a tawdry manner

taw·dri·ness (tɔ́dri:nis) *n.* the state or quality of being tawdry

taw·dry (tɔ́dri:) *comp.* **taw·dri·er** *superl.* **taw·dri·est** *adj.* showy but of very poor quality [after the old *St Audrey's* fair at Ely, England]

taw·ni·ness (tɔ́ni:nis) *n.* the quality of being tawny

taw·ny (tɔ́ni:) *comp.* **taw·ni·er** *superl.* **taw·ni·est** *adj.* of a light reddish-yellow brown color [A.F. *taune,* O.F. *tané* fr. *tan,* tan]

tax (tæks) **1.** *n.* a charge on a person's income or property, *direct tax* or on the price of goods sold, *indirect tax* made by a government to collect revenue ‖ a heavy demand made upon one's strength, patience etc. **2.** *v.t.* to impose a tax on (a person) or upon (goods) ‖ to make a heavy demand on, *his persistence taxed my patience* ‖ to accuse in a challenging way, *to tax someone with being idle* ‖ (*law*) to fix the amount of (costs etc.) **tax·a·bíl·i·ty** *n.* **táx·a·ble** *adj.* [O.F. *taxer*]

tax·a·tion (tækséiʃən) *n.* the imposition of a tax ‖ the system by which taxes are imposed ‖ the revenue obtained by imposing taxes

tax-based income policy *TIP

tax-de·ferred income (tæksdifə́:rd) cash received by an investor on which tax is not presently payable, but which may have to be paid at a later date, e.g., deduction for depreciation

tax-ex·empt (tǽksigzempt) *adj.* of dividends distributed to shareholders after taxes have been paid by the corporation ‖ exempt from tax

tax exile one who leaves a country to avoid paying taxes

tax farmer (*hist.,* esp. in France) someone who bought from the government the right to collect taxes

tax-free (tǽksfrí:) *adj.* tax-exempt

tax haven a country that has a low rate of or no business, income, or inheritance taxes

tax·i (tǽksi:) **1.** *n.* an automobile carrying passengers for a charge **2.** *v. pres. part.* **tax·i·ing, tax·y·ing** *past* and *past part.* **tax·ied** *v.i.* to ride in a taxi ‖ (of an aircraft) to move over the surface of the ground or water e.g. in parking or in taking off ‖ *v.t.* to transport by or as if by taxi ‖ to cause (an aircraft) to taxi [short for TAXIMETER]

tax·i·cab (tǽksi:kæb) *n.* a taxi

taxi dancer a girl employed in a dance hall to dance with patrons for a fee

tax·i·der·mal (tæksidə́:rməl) *adj.* of or pertaining to taxidermy

tax·i·der·mic (tæksidə́:rmik) *adj.* taxidermal

tax·i·der·mist (tǽksidə:rmist) *n.* a person skilled in taxidermy

tax·i·der·my (tǽksidə:rmi:) *n.* the art of preparing and mounting the skins of animals to give a lifelike effect [fr. Gk *taxis,* arrangement+*derma,* skin]

Tax·il·a (tæksílə) an ancient city near Peshawar, Pakistan, where excavations have revealed extensive remains of civilizations which flourished from the 7th c. B.C. to the 7th c. A.D. and numerous Gandharan sculptures showing strong Hellenistic influences

tax·i·me·ter (tǽksi:mi:tər) *n.* a device fitted to a taxi which registers the distance traveled and the fare due [F. *taximètre* fr. *taxe,* a tariff+*mètre,* a meter]

tax·is (tǽksis) *pl.* **tax·es** (tǽksi:z) *n.* (*biol.*) the movement (sometimes orientation) of a small mobile organism towards the source of a stimulus (positive taxis), or away from it (negative taxis) (cf. KINESIS, cf. TROPISM) ‖ (*med.*) manual pressure used to adjust displaced organs ‖ (*Gk hist.*) an army subunit of varying size [Gk=arrangement]

taxi squad 1. (*sports*) a group of professional football players who practice with a team but are not eligible to play **2.** (*politics*) a group of political partisans who drive voters to the polls

tax loss 1. of a business loss used to offset federal income tax **2.** (*Br.*) lossmaker

tax·o·di·um (tæksóudi:əm) *n.* a member of *Taxodium,* fam. *Taxodiaceae,* a genus of deciduous conifers common in North American swamps. The hard red wood of some species is used for roof shingles [Mod. L. fr. *taxus,* yew]

tax·o·nom·ic (tæksənɒ́mik) *adj.* of or pertaining to taxonomy **tax·o·nóm·i·cal** *adj.* **tax·o·nóm·i·cal·ly** *adv.*

tax·on·o·my (tæksɒ́nəmi:) *n.* the science of classification ‖ the principles and method of classification of living organisms into phyla, species etc. [fr. F. *taxonomie* fr. Gk]

tax·pay·er (tǽkspeiər) *n.* a person who pays or is liable to pay a tax

tax selling (*securities*) sales made near the end of the year to establish gains or losses in order to minimize income taxes

tax shelter an investment that enables the taxpayer to have substantial deductions from income tax, e.g., for depletion, depreciation — **tax-sheltered** *adj.*

Tay (tei) the longest river (120 miles) of Scotland, rising in W. Perth and flowing southeast through its estuary, the Firth of Tay, to the North Sea. Ports: Dundee, Perth. The lake Loch Tay (15 miles long, up to 1 mile wide) lies on its upper course

Tay·ge·tus Mountains (teiídʒitəs) (*Gk* Taigeytos) a range (summit 7,904 ft) of the S. central Peloponnesus, Greece

Tay·lor (téilər), Edward (c. 1645-1729), American Puritan minister and poet. His 'Poetical Works' (published 1939), characterized by elaborate images of heaven and hell, are in the metaphysical tradition

Taylor, Jeremy (1613-67), English bishop and writer. He is known for his sermons and for his 'Holy Living' (1650) and 'Holy Dying' (1651)

Taylor, Maxwell Davenport (1901-), U.S. general. During the 2nd world war he helped to organize (1942) the U.S. Army's first airborne units and commanded them in the invasions of North Africa, Sicily, and Italy. He served (1955-9) as chief of staff of the U.S. Army and (1962-4) as chairman of the Joint Chiefs of Staff. He was Ambassador (1964-5) to the Republic of Vietnam

Taylor, Zachary (1784-1850), 12th president (1849-50) of the U.S.A., a Whig. His election was due to his successful command of a U.S. force in the Mexican War (1846-8). He died before he could implement his policies: the exclusion of slavery from newly acquired lands and opposition to what became the Compromise of 1850

Taymyr Peninsula *TAIMYR PENINSULA

Tay-Sachs disease (téisæks) *n.* (*med.*) an inherited (esp. among Jews) neurological disease of infants leading to brain degeneration, blindness, paralysis, and death by age 2; named for British physician Warren Tay and American neurologist Bernard P. Sachs

Tbi·li·si (tpílisi) (formerly Tiflis) the capital (pop. 1,066,000) of Georgia, U.S.S.R., on the Kura, an ancient trading center. Industries: mechanical engineering, textiles (esp. silk), food processing, wood, tourism. Byzantine cathedral (6th c.), churches, hot springs, university

T-Bond (tí:bond) *n.* U.S. treasury bond; T-Bond futures market is the purchase and sale of government bonds for future delivery

TCE (*abbr.*) for trichlorethylene chloroformate diphogene, a toxic waste substance with a safe level of 2–4 parts per billion. It was used as poison gas in World War I

T cell *n.* (*cytol.*) a lymph antibody freely circulating in blood that attaches to and destroys viruses, fungi, and certain bacterial infections, and rejects foreign tissue and tumors *also* T lymphocyte *Cf* B CELL

Tchai·kov·sky (tʃaikɔ́fski:), Piotr Ilyich (1840-93), Russian composer. His symphonies, e.g. No. 4 (1877) and No. 6, the 'Pathetic' (1893), and his piano and violin concertos express the lonely, romantic and striving aspects of Tchaikovsky. His 'light' music, esp. the ballet music, shows an immense melodic and rhythmical fertility. He also wrote songs and operas

TDR (*abbr.*) for transferable development rights, a device that enables the owner of a property to transfer the privilege of construction to another property owner suitably situated

te (ti:) *n.* (*Br., mus.*) ti

tea (ti:) *n. Thea sinensis* or *Camellia sinensis,* fam. *Theaceae,* a shrub cultivated from antiquity in China, and now grown in Japan, India, Ceylon etc. ‖ its dried and prepared leaves, used to make a beverage ‖ this beverage ‖ any of a number of plants used like tea ‖ a beverage made like tea by infusion ‖ a light meal towards late afternoon ‖ a social gathering at which tea is served ‖ (*Br.*) high tea [prob. fr. Du. *thee* fr. Malay fr. Chin.]

—Tea is a hardy evergreen bush, having whitish, mildly fragrant flowers. The fruit is a capsule containing three hard-shelled nuts. Most commercial propagation is from seed. Cultivation is in plantations, often terraces. The plants thrive best in protected, well-drained, near-tropical localities. The leaves can be picked two or three years after the seeds have been planted, and the shrub may yield for 25 to 50 years. There are three main types of tea:

CONCISE PRONUNCIATION KEY: (a) æ, cat; ɑ, car; ɔ fawn; ei, snake. (e) e, hen; i:, sheep; iə, deer; ɛə, bear. (i) i, fish; ai, tiger; ə:, bird. (o) o, ox; au, cow; ou, goat; u, poor; ɔi, royal. (u) ʌ, duck; u, bull; u:, goose; ə, bacillus; ju:, cube. x, loch; θ, think; ð, bother; z, Zen; ʒ, corsage; dʒ, savage; ŋ, orangutang; j, yak; ʃ, fish; tʃ, fetch; 'l, rabble; 'n, redden. Complete pronunciation key appears inside front cover.

green, oolong and black. Green tea is unfermented, its leaves being put immediately into firing machines. Oolong tea is partially fermented and black tea is fermented for 12 to 24 hrs. The leading tea-producing country is India, though it began to be cultivated there as late as 1836

Tea Act a British act of parliament (1773) which repealed all the Townshend acts except that which placed a tax on tea imported into the American colonies. It led to the Boston Tea Party

tea bag a cloth or filter paper bag holding enough tea for one serving, for infusion in boiling water

tea ball a small perforated metal ball-shaped container used esp. for making an individual cup of tea

tea break (*Br.*) a short rest period during the working day, equivalent to U.S. coffee break

tea cart a tea wagon

tea ceremony a semireligious social custom of Zen origin introduced into Japan from China in the 15th c. It is marked by extreme refinement of gesture

teach (ti:tʃ) *pres. part.* **teach·ing** *past* and *past part.* **taught** (tɔt) *v.t.* to give instruction to, to train, *to teach a class of nurses* ‖ to give to another (knowledge or skill which one has oneself), *to teach someone how to drive* ‖ to give instruction in for a living, *he teaches the violin* ‖ to cause to understand, *that will teach him not to interfere* ‖ *v.i.* to be a teacher **to teach school** to be a schoolteacher **téach·a·ble** *adj.* capable of being taught **téach·er** *n.* a person who teaches, esp. for a living **téach·ing** *n.* the act of someone who teaches ‖ the profession of a teacher ‖ (often *pl.*) something that is taught, *the teachings of religion* [O.E. *tǣcean*]

teach-in (tí:tʃin) *n.* long, often unauthorized, meeting, debate, or lecture on a controversial issue

teaching hospital a large hospital to which a medical school is attached

teaching machine (*education*) device to provide instruction, esp. one programmed to ask questions and respond to answers on a one-to-one basis

tea·cup (tí:kʌp) *n.* a cup for drinking esp. tea **a storm in a teacup** much fuss and excitement about something of small importance

tea·cup·ful (tí:kʌpful) *pl.* **tea·cup·fuls** *n.* as much as a teacup can hold

tea·house (tí:haus) *pl.* **tea·hous·es** (tí:hauziz) *n.* a place where tea is served in the Orient

teak (ti:k) *n. Tectona grandis,* fam. *Verbenaceae,* a large East Indian tree now also grown in W. Africa and tropical America for its wood ‖ this hard, close-grained wood, used esp. for shipbuilding and furniture [Port. *teca* fr. Malayalam]

tea·ket·tle (tí:ket'l) *n.* a utensil having a lid, spout and handle, used to boil water in

teal (ti:l) *pl.* **teal, teals** *n.* a member of *Anas,* fam. *Anatidae,* a genus of small freshwater ducks of Europe and North America, esp. the green-winged *A. carolinensis* [M.E. *tele*]

tea leaf *pl.* **tea leaves** a leaf of tea, esp. after it has infused

team (ti:m) **1.** *n.* two or more draft animals harnessed together ‖ two or more draft animals and the vehicle they draw ‖ a single draft animal and the vehicle it draws ‖ a number of people working together on a common task ‖ a group forming one side in a game **2.** *v.i.* (often with 'up') to join in a common task, *the farmers teamed up to get the crops in* ‖ *v.t.* to cause to work in a team ‖ to haul with a team [O.E. *tēam*]

team foul (*sports*) one of the maximum personal fouls allowed at the beginning of a basketball game before free throws are given to the opposing team

team handball (*sports*) a soccerlike game of two seven-player teams involving a large ball that is thrown, dribbled, and caught

team·ster (tí:mstər) *n.* the driver of a team of animals ‖ a person who drives a truck for a living

team teaching (*education*) instruction by a group of teachers for a small group of students, directed by a leading teacher, usu. under an open plan (which see) usu. associated with a special project

team·work (tí:mwə:rk) *n.* the quality whereby individuals unselfishly subordinate their own part to the general effort of the group with whom they are working or playing

tea·pot (tí:pɒt) *n.* a pot in which tea is brewed and which has a spout for pouring out the brew **a tempest in a teapot** a storm in a teacup (*TEACUP)

'Teapot Dome' Scandal *OIL RESERVES SCANDAL

tear (tiər) **1.** *n.* a drop of the saline fluid secreted by the lachrymal gland and serving normally to moisten, lubricate and cleanse the eye ‖ (*pl.*) drops of this secretion that overflow the eyelids and stream down the face when certain strong emotions, e.g. sadness, pity, joy or great amusement, are aroused, or when the eye is irritated by dust, soap etc. ‖ (*pl.*) the visible expression of grief ‖ something resembling a tear, e.g. a defect in glass caused by a bit of vitrified clay **in tears** weeping **2.** *v.i.* (of the eyes) to fill with tears [O.E. *tēar*]

tear (tεər) **1.** *v. pres. part.* **tear·ing** *past* **tore** (tɔr) *past part.* **torn** (tɔrn) *v.t.* to break the fiber of (a fabric, paper etc.) by exerting a strong pull, *to tear a piece of cloth* ‖ to make (e.g. a hole) in this way ‖ to remove by making an opening in this way, *to tear a letter from its envelope* ‖ to injure by lacerating, *the teeth of the saw tore his leg* ‖ to subject to intense or conflicting emotions, *she was torn as to what she ought to do* ‖ to divide into opposing groups, *the nation was torn by dissension* ‖ *v.i.* to give way under a strong pull, *the paper tore when the parcel fell* ‖ (*pop.*) to move rapidly, *he tore down the road* ‖ **to tear at** to pull wildly at, *he tore at the rope which bound him* ‖ **to tear down** to pull down violently ‖ to demolish ‖ to denigrate **to tear into** to attack critically or physically with wild violence **to tear oneself away** to overcome a strong desire to stay by an effort of will **to tear to pieces** to criticize devastatingly **to tear up** to destroy by tearing into pieces ‖ to cause to cease to be operative, *to tear up a treaty* **2.** *n.* the act of tearing ‖ the line of break resulting from tearing [O.E. *teran*]

tear bomb (tiər) a bomb containing tear gas

tear·drop (tíərdrɒp) *n.* a tear ‖ a pendant gem on an earring or necklace shaped like a tear

tear·ful (tíərfəl) *adj.* shedding tears ‖ accompanied by tears ‖ causing tears

tear gas (tiər) any one of several substances, used in the form of vapor or smoke, that irritate the eyes and often cause chemical burns on the skin. Tear gas is used mainly for dispersing crowds

tear·ing (tέəriŋ) *adj.* violent, *a tearing rage*

tear·jerk·er (tíərdʒə:rkər) *n.* a sentimental story, play etc. with a sad ending

tea·room (tí:ru:m, tí:rum) *n.* a restaurant serving light meals

tea rose any of various half-hardy hybrid shrub roses derived mainly from *Rosa odorata,* a Chinese rose, the flowers of which have a scent resembling tea

tear sheet (tεər) a part of a publication torn out and sent to the advertiser etc. whom it concerns, as evidence that his copy was duly printed

Teas·dale (tí:zdeil), Sara (1884-1933), U.S. poet. Her works include 'Sonnets to Duse and Other Poems' (1907) and 'Love Songs' (1917)

tease (ti:z) **1.** *v. pres. part.* **teas·ing** *past* and *past part.* **teased** *v.t.* to annoy (a person or animal) by making him or it the victim of irritating remarks or actions repeated time and time again ‖ to attempt to do this ‖ (esp. of children) to importune persistently, *they teased their father for more candies* ‖ to separate or pull apart the fibers of (wool, flax etc.) by using a comb or tease ‖ to raise a nap on (cloth) with a teasel ‖ *v.i.* to indulge in teasing **2.** *n.* a teasing or being teased ‖ a person who teases [O.E. *tǣsan,* to tear or pull to pieces]

tea·sel, tea·zel (tí:z'l) *n.* a member of *Dipsacus,* fam. *Dipsacaceae,* a genus of thistlelike plants, esp. *D. fullonum,* having a prickly stem and hooked bracts surrounding the flower heads ‖ this flower head when dried, used to separate the surface fibers of a fabric and raise a nap ‖ a wire device used in place of this [O.E. *tǣsel, tǣsl*]

tea·spoon (tí:spu:n) *n.* a small spoon for stirring tea etc. and for eating certain foods ‖ a teaspoonful **tea·spoon·ful** (tí:spu:nful) *pl.* **tea·spoon·fuls** *n.* as much as a teaspoon will hold

teat (ti:t) *n.* the protrusion of a mammal's breast or udder through which milk is drawn ‖ (*Br.*) a rubber nipple through which milk can be sucked from a nursing bottle [O. F. *tete*]

tea towel (*Br.*) a dish towel

tea tree *Lycium afrum,* fam. *Solanaceae,* an African spiny shrub bearing solitary purple flowers ‖ any of various members of *Leptospermum* or *Melaleuca,* genera of Australian shrubs or trees

tea wagon a small table on casters or wheels used to transport food etc. within a room or building

teazel *TEASEL

Teb·el·ized (tebélaizd) *adj.* application of a finish to fabrics that resists creasing and crushing and recovers from wrinkling; trademark of Tootal, Broadhurst & Lee Company, Ltd.

tech·ne·ti·um (tekní:ʃi:əm) *n.* a very rare radioactive metallic element (symbol Tc, at. no. 43, mass of isotope of longest known half-life 97) [Mod. L. fr. Gk *technētos,* artificial]

tech·nic (téknik) **1.** *adj.* (*rare*) technical **2.** *n.* (*pl., rare*) technique ‖ (*pl.*) technology **téch·ni·cal** *adj.* pertaining to the mechanical, industrial or applied sciences of, used in or pertaining to a particular science, art, skill etc., *technical terms* ‖ showing technique, *technical skill* ‖ pertaining to the law as this is stated, *a technical right* ‖ arising from mechanical causes, *a technical difficulty* **tech·ni·cál·i·ty** *pl.* **tech·ni·cal·i·ties** *n.* the use of technical terms ‖ a detail of no particular importance arising merely from the way in which a regulation etc. is worded ‖ the state or quality of being technical ‖ a point of detail etc. in a given science or skill which only a specialist would be aware of [fr. Gk *technikos* fr. *techne,* an art]

technical knockout (*boxing*) a knockout occurring when the referee rules that a boxer is unable to continue fighting because of injury

technical sergeant a non-commissioned officer in the air force ranking above a staff sergeant and below a master sergeant

tech·ni·cian (tekníʃən) *n.* a person skilled in the technical details and techniques of a subject ‖ a painter, musician etc. whose mastery of the technique of his art may or may not serve the quality of his expression [TECHNIC]

Tech·ni·col·or (téknikʌlər) *n.* a color process used in making some movies [Trademark]

tech·nique (tekní:k) *n.* the entire body of procedures and methods of a science, art or craft ‖ skill in these procedures and methods ‖ (*loosely*) a way of achieving a purpose, *a technique for getting money out of the country* [F.]

tech·noc·ra·cy (teknókrəsi:) *pl.* **tech·noc·ra·cies** *n.* government by technical experts **tech·no·crat** (téknəkræt) *n.* **tech·no·crát·ic** *adj.* [fr. Gk *technē,* art+*-kratia,* rule]

tech·no·log·ic (teknəlódʒik) *adj.* technological

tech·no·log·i·cal (teknəlódʒik'l) *adj.* of, relating to or characterized by technology ‖ due to developments in technology

tech·nol·o·gist (teknɒlədʒist) *n.* someone who specializes in some branch of technology [fr. TECHNOLOGY]

tech·nol·o·gize (teknólədʒaiz) *v.* to change by introducing new technology

tech·nol·o·gy (teknólədʒi:) *pl.* **tech·nol·o·gies** *n.* the science of technical processes in a wide, though related, field of knowledge. Thus industrial technology embraces the chemical, mechanical and physical sciences as these are applied in industrial processes ‖ technical terminology [fr. Gk *technologia,* systematic treatment]

technology transfer transfer of technical knowledge generated and developed in one place to another in order to achieve some practical end

tech·nop·o·lis (teknópələs) *n.* a large community in which technology plays a dominant role —**technopolitan** *adj.*

tech·no·struc·ture (téknəstrʌktʃə:r) *n.* **1.** in a society, the personnel, equipment, and facilities for high-technology industry **2.** the hierarchy of technology management

techy *TETCHY

tec·ton·ic (tektónik) *adj.* of or relating to tectonics

tec·tón·ics *n.* the art and science of constructing buildings ‖ a branch of geology dealing with land structure, esp. folding and faulting [fr. L.L. *tectonicus* fr. Gk fr. *tektōn,* builder]

tec·tri·ces (téktrisi:z) *pl. n.* the coverts of a bird [L.]

Te·cum·seh (tikʌ́msə) (c. 1768-1813), chief of the Shawnee Indians. He sided with the British in the War of 1812

ted (ted) *pres. part.* **ted·ding** *past* and *past part.* **ted·ded** *v.t.* to turn over and spread (grass) to dry in the air **téd·der** *n.* [M.E., akin to O.N. *tethja,* to manure]

Ted·der (tédər), Arthur William, 1st Baron Tedder (1890-1967), marshal of the Royal Air Force. As commander of the Allied air forces in the Middle East (1941-3), he helped to drive the German army from N. Africa. He was deputy supreme commander of the Allied invasion of Europe (1944-5)

teddy bear a child's stuffed toy bear [after Theodore (*Teddy*) Roosevelt]

Te De·um (ti:dí:əm, teidéium) *n.* an ancient Latin hymn beginning 'Te Deum laudamus' ('We praise Thee, O God') sung at Matins ‖ a special thanksgiving service in which this hymn is sung ‖ the musical setting for this hymn [L.]

te·di·ous (tí:di:əs) *adj.* boring, causing psychological fatigue, usually because of needless repetition and lengthiness [fr. L.L. *taediosus*]

te·di·um (tí:di:əm) *n.* the state or quality of being tedious [fr. L. *taedium*]

Ted·lar (tédlɑr) *n.* trademark for insulation using alternating layers of aluminum, nylon, and nylon net used to retain heat in a space vehicle

tee (ti:) *n.* the letter T, t in the alphabet ‖ anything shaped like a T **to a tee, to a T** exactly

tee 1. *n.* (*golf*) the area from which a person drives at the beginning of a hole ‖ (*golf*) a wooden or plastic peg, or conical elevation of earth etc., on which the ball is placed for driving **2.** *v.t. pres. part.* **tee·ing** *past* and *past part.* **teed** (*golf*, often with 'up') to place (the ball) on a tee ‖ to tee off ‖ (*golf*) to drive [etym. doubtful]

teed-off (tí:dɒf) *adj.* (*colloq.*) angry; irritated

teem (ti:m) *v.i.* (of rain etc.) to come down in torrents ‖ *v.t.* to pour (molten metal) into a mold [M.E. *tēmen* fr. O.N. *tœma,* to empty]

teem *v.i.* to be full, *the river teems with fish* ‖ to pullulate, *ideas teemed in his mind* [O.E. *tīeman,* to produce]

-teen *suffix* used to form cardinal numbers from thirteen through nineteen

teen-age (tí:neidʒ) *adj.* of or relating to teenagers or to adolescence

teen-ag·er (tí:neidʒər) *n.* a person in his teens

teens (ti:nz) *pl. n.* the years 13–19 in a person's life

tee·ny (tí:ni:) *comp.* **tee·ni·er** *superl.* **tee·ni·est** *adj.* (*pop.*) very small [var. of TINY]

teen·y·bop·per (tí:ni:bɒpə:r) *n.* (*slang or colloq.*) (pejorative) a teenager devoted to adolescent fads in dress, rock 'n' roll music, star worship *Cf* GROUPIES

teepee *TEPEE

Tees (ti:z) a river (70 miles long) rising in Cumberland, N. England. It forms the Yorkshire-Durham border as far as the North Sea

tee·ter (tí:tər) **1.** *v.i.* to move along in a wobbly manner ‖ to show doubt, indecision etc. ‖ (of children) to seesaw **2.** *n.* the act of teetering

tee·ter-tot·ter (tí:tərtɒtər) **1.** *n.* a seesaw **2.** *v.i.* to play on a seesaw

teeth *pl.* of TOOTH

teethe (ti:ð) *pres. part.* **teeth·ing** *past* and *past part.* **teethed** *v.i.* to develop teeth [M.E. prob. representing supposed O.E. *tēthan* fr. *tōth,* tooth]

teething ring a bone, rubber or plastic ring on which a teething infant can bite

tee·to·tal (ti:tóut'l) *adj.* of or pertaining to complete abstinence from alcoholic drinks ‖ completely abstaining from alcoholic drinks ‖ (*pop.*) complete, *a teetotal failure* **tee·tó·tal·ism** *n.* **tee·tó·tal·er,** esp. *Br.* **tee·tó·tal·ler** *n.* a person who never drinks alcohol

teff (tef) *n. Eragrostis abyssinica,* fam. *Gramineae,* an African cereal grass, the grain of which yields a fine, white flour

Tef·lon (téflɒn) *n.* (*chem.*) trade name of the Du Pont Corp. for its tetrafluoroethylene polymer fiber, Teflon is chemical-resistant, does not absorb moisture, and is the most nonwettable fiber known

teg (teg) *n.* (*Br.*) a sheep in its second year [perh. of Scand. origin]

Te·ge·a (ti:dʒí:ə) an ancient Greek city in S.E. Arcadia: ruins of the temple of Athene

teg·men (tégmən) *pl.* **teg·mi·na** (tégminə) *n.* (*biol.*) the covering of an organ or part of a living organism, esp. the integument, e.g. endopleura **teg·men·tal** (tegmént'l) *adj.* [L. fr. *tegere,* to cover]

Teg·ner (teŋnéir), Esaias (1782-1846), Swedish poet. His most famous work is 'Frithjof's Saga' (1825), based on an Old Icelandic saga

Te·gu·ci·gal·pa (tegu:si:gálpɑ) the capital (pop: 316,800) and commercial center of Honduras, on the S. central plateau. Industries: textiles, food processing. Spanish cathedral (18th c.). National university and theater

teg·u·lar (tégjulər) *adj.* (*archit.*) made of, resembling or pertaining to tiles [fr. L. *tegula,* a tile]

teg·u·ment (tégjumənt) *n.* (*biol.*) an integument **teg·u·men·tal** (tegjumént'l), **teg·u·mén·ta·ry** *adjs* [fr. L. *tegumentum* fr. *tegere,* to cover]

Teh·ran, Te·he·ran (teərǽn, teərán) the capital (pop. 3,774,000) of Iran, near the S. Elburz foothills. Industries: metallurgy, mechanical engineering, textiles, glass, tobacco, chemicals. Palace (18th c.). National university (1935), museums. Founded in the 12th c., Tehran became the capital in 1788

Tehran Conference the meeting (Nov. 28–Dec. 1, 1943) of Stalin, Roosevelt and Churchill, at which plans for an Allied invasion of France were coordinated with a Russian offensive against Germany

Te·huan·te·pec, Gulf of (təwántəpek) a wide-mouthed gulf bounded by the states of Chiapas and Oaxaca in S.E. Mexico

Tehuantepec, Isthmus of an isthmus (130 miles wide) between the Bay of Campeche and the Gulf of Tehuantepec in S. Mexico

T-80 tank (*mil.*) U.S.S.R. tank with an automatic loading, 125-mm gun, laser rangefinder, and night-vision equipment

Teil·hard de Char·din (teijærdəʃærdɛ̃), Pierre (1881-1955), French Jesuit priest, paleontologist, theologian and philosopher. In his principal work 'The Phenomenon of Man' (1938-40) he attempts to unfold the mystery of the evolution of man and to correlate religious experience with the findings of natural science

Teil·hard·i·an (ti:lhárdi:ən) *adj.* of the social evolutionary theories formulated by French theologian Pierre Teilhard de Chardin (1881–1955)

tek·tite (téktait) *n.* a rounded glassy body, probably of meteoritic origin, found in several parts of the world [fr. Gk *tēktos,* molten]

telaesthesia *TELESTHESIA

tel·a·mon (téləmɒn) *pl.* **tel·a·mo·nes** (teləmóuni:z) *n.* (*archit.*) a male figure used as a supporting pillar or column (cf. CARYATID) [L. fr. Gk *telamōn,* bearer]

tel·au·to·gram (telɔ́təgræm) *n.* the image transmitted by telautograph [TELAUTOGRAPH+Gk *gramma,* a letter]

tel·au·to·graph (telɔ́təgræf, telɔ́təgrɑf) *n.* a telegraph which transmits facsimile half-tone images by a reception process of electrolysis or of scanning with a modulated light beam [fr. Gk *tēle,* far off+ AUTOGRAPH]

Tel A·viv (teləví:v) the main industrial center (pop. with Jaffa 334,900) of Israel, on the Mediterranean. Industries: metallurgy, textiles, chemicals, leatherwork, diamond cutting, food processing, printing and publishing. University. Ashdod replaced Tel Aviv-Jaffa as a port (1965)

tele- (téli) *prefix* far off, covering a distance ‖ television [fr. Gk *tēle-* fr. *tēle,* far off]

tel·e·cast (télikæst, télikɑst) **1.** *pres. part.* **tel·e·cast·ing** *past* and *past part.* **tel·e·cast, tel·e·cast·ed** *v.t.* and *i.* to televise **2.** *n.* a television broadcast [TELE-+ BROADCAST]

tel·e·com·mu·ni·ca·tion (telikəmju:nikéiʃən) *n.* any process of communication over a considerable distance (by telegraph, telephone, radio etc.) ‖ (*pl.*) the science that deals with these processes

tel·e·con·fer·ence (téləkɒnf'rəns) *n.* a conference held telecommunicationally

tel·e·di·ag·no·sis (telədaiəgnóusəs) *n.* (*med.*) diagnosis of an illness through closed-circuit electronic equipment, principally television, e.g., to shipboard or a region without medical facilities

tel·e·du (télidu:) *n. Mydaus meliceps,* fam. *Viverridae,* a small carnivorous mammal of Java and Sumatra which ejects a stinking fluid when alarmed [Malay]

tel·e·fac·sim·i·le (teləfæksíməli:) *n.* technique for transmitting letters, photographs, and other graphic material over telephone lines *also* facsimile transmission

tel·e·gram (téligræm) *n.* a message transmitted, or received, by telegraphy [fr. TELE+Gk *gramma,* a letter]

tel·e·graph (téligræf, téligrɑf) **1.** *n.* a method of transmitting messages over long distances by sending electrical impulses along a conducting wire or, in wireless telegraphy, in the form of electromagnetic waves. The timing of the impulses transmitted is controlled according to an agreed system, e.g. the Morse code, and the impulses received are deciphered by the same code ‖ a telegram **2.** *v.t.* to send (a message) by telegraphy ‖ to send a message to by telegraphy ‖ *v.i.* to send a telegram **tel·e·graph·ic** (teligrǽfik) *adj.* **tel·e·gráph·i·cal·ly** *adv.* **te·leg·ra·phy** (təlégrəfi:) *n.* the act or process of sending by telegraph [F. *télégraphe* fr. Gk *tēle,* far off+*graphos,* written]

Telegu *TELUGU

tel·e·ki·ne·sis (telikiní:sis, telikainí:sis) *n.* the movement of a body without any apparent physical agency (as reported in psychic research) **tel·e·ki·net·ic** (telikinétik) *adj.* [fr. TELE-+Gk *kinēsis,* motion]

tel·e·mail (téləmeil) *n.* subscription network with video display terminals that provides instant communication with subscribers and nonsubscribers via Western Union Telex and Mailgram

Tel·e·mann (téləmɑn), Georg Philipp (1681-1767), German composer. He wrote 600 overtures, 40 operas, over 160 church services and many sonatas and suites

tel·e·mark (téləmɑrk) *n.* (*skiing*) a swinging turn, the ski on the outer curve being advanced and then turned gradually inward [after *Telemark,* a region in S. Norway]

tel·e·me·chan·ics (téləməkǽniks) *pl. n.* the science of controlling the moving parts of a machine by remote control

te·lem·e·ter (təlémitər, téləmi:tər) **1.** *n.* an apparatus for recording physical changes which occur at a distance **2.** *v.t.* to transmit (data) from a distant source, e.g. a spacecraft, to a receiving station for recording **tel·e·met·ric** (telәmétrik) *adj.* **te·lém·e·try** *n.*

tel·en·ce·phal·ic (telənsəfǽlik) *adj.* of the telencephalon

tel·en·ceph·a·lon (telenséfəlɒn) *n.* (*anat.*) the cerebral hemispheres of a vertebrate's forebrain [Mod. L. fr. Gk *telos,* end+ ENCEPHALON]

tel·e·o·log·ic (teli:əlɒ́dʒik, ti:li:əlɒ́dʒik) *adj.* of or relating to teleology **te·le·o·lóg·i·cal** *adj.*

tel·e·ol·o·gist (teli:ɒ́lədʒist, ti:li:ɒ́lədʒist) *n.* someone who subscribes to teleology

tel·e·ol·o·gy (teli:ɒ́lədʒi:, ti:li:ɒ́lədʒi:) *n.* the doctrine of final causes, esp. that natural and historic processes are determined not only by causality but also by their ultimate purposes, e.g. attainment of the kingdom of heaven, human welfare etc. [fr. Mod. L. *teleologia* fr. Gk *telos,* end+ *logos,* word]

tel·e·on·o·my (teli:ɒ́nəmi:) *n.* government policy dominated by a single purpose or project

tel·e·op·er·a·tor (teli:ɒ́pə:reitə:r) *n.* mechanical device that is operated from a distance *Cf* AUGMENTOR

tel·e·o·saur (téli:əsɔr, tí:li:əsɔr) *n.* a member of *Teleosaurus,* fam. *Teleosauridae,* a genus of extinct crocodiles, whose fossils occur in the Jurassic strata [fr. Mod. L. *Teleosaurus* fr. Gk *teleos,* end+*sauros,* lizard]

tel·e·ost (téli:ɒst, tí:li:ɒst) **1.** *n.* a member of *Teleostei,* a class or subclass of true bony fishes, incl. the majority of all present-day fishes **2.** *adj.* of or belonging to the teleosts **tel·e·os·te·an** (teli:ɒ́sti:ən, ti:li:ɒ́sti:ən) *n.* and *adj.* [fr. Gk *teleos,* complete+*osteon,* bone]

tel·e·path·ic (teləpǽθik) *adj.* of or communicated through telepathy **tel·e·páth·i·cal·ly** *adv.*

te·lep·a·thist (təlépəθist) *n.* a believer in telepathy ‖ a supposed possessor of telepathic power

te·lep·a·thy (təlépəθi:) *n.* communication, apparently without the use of sight, sound etc., between the minds of different persons [fr. TELE-+Gk *pathos,* suffering]

tel·e·phone (téləfoun) **1.** *n.* a device for converting sounds into electrical impulses, transmitting these through a conducting wire and reconverting them into sounds at the receiving end of the wire. The transmitter is usually a carbon microphone. The receiver is an iron diaphragm which vibrates as the impulses affect an electromagnet, between the poles of which the impulses pass around a solenoid **2.** *v. pres. part.* **tel·e·phon·ing** *past* and *past part.* **tel·e·phoned** *v.t.* to transmit (a message) by means of a telephone ‖ to speak to on the telephone. esp. to initiate a call to ‖ *v.i.* to use the telephone

tel·e·phon·ic (tɛləfɒnik) *adj.* of or relating to the telephone ‖ transmitted by telephone **tel·e·phón·i·cal·ly** *adv.* [fr. Gk *tele,* far off+*phone,* sound]

telephone book a book containing the names, addresses and telephone numbers of telephone subscribers

telephone diplomacy the practice of conducting international negotiations by telephone *Cf* HOT LINE

telephone directory a telephone book

te·leph·o·ny (təléfəni:) *n.* the system of transmitting and receiving sounds by telephone [fr. Gk *tēle,* far off+*-phonia,* sounding]

tel·e·pho·to (tɛləfóutou) *adj.* of a narrow-angle lens system of long focal length which gives a magnified image of a distant object, used esp. in cameras [abbr. of TELEPHOTOGRAPHIC]

tel·e·pho·to·graph (tɛləfóutəgræf, tɛləfóutəgrɒf) *n.* a photograph taken with a telephoto lens [fr. Gk *tēle,* far off+PHOTOGRAPH or back-formation fr. TELEPHOTOGRAPHIC]

tel·e·pho·to·graph·ic (tɛləfoutəgrǽfik) *adj.* of or relating to telephotography [fr. Gk *tēle,* far off+PHOTOGRAPHIC]

tel·e·pho·tog·ra·phy (tɛləfətɒ́grəfi:) *n.* phototelegraphy (transmission of photographs by telegraphy) ‖ the photographing of distant objects using a telephoto lens [TELEPHOTOGRAPH]

tel·e·print·er (téləprɪntər) *n.* a teletypewriter

tel·e·pro·cess·ing (tɛləprɒ́sesiŋ) *n.* (*computer*) processing systems that use data from remote points

tel·e·prompt·er (téləprɒmptər) *n.* a prompting device for a speaker or actor on television

tel·e·ran (télərən) *n.* (*air traffic control acronym*) for television-radar navigation, a navigational system that employs television and radar to locate and guide in-flight aircraft

tel·e·scope (téliskoup) **1.** *n.* an optical device that focuses light (*OBJECTIVE) from distant objects so that the image formed may be observed (*EYEPIECE). Telescopes are usually tubular in form and vary in size from easily portable to very large instruments mounted so that they can be focused and turned on several axes by means of electric motors and fine gears. They are classified according to function (*TERRESTRIAL TELESCOPE, *ASTRONOMICAL TELESCOPE) or according to the nature of the objective (*REFLECTING TELESCOPE, *REFRACTING TELESCOPE) **2.** *v. pres. part.* **tel·e·scop·ing** *past* and *past part.* **tel·e·scoped** *v.t.* to cause to close up in such a way that the parts are thrust one into another like sections of a hand telescope, *the collision telescoped four coaches of the train* ‖ to shorten (a plan, speech, form of organization etc.) by condensing the important parts and omitting the less important ‖ *v.i.* to close up like a hand telescope **tel·e·scop·ic** (tɛliskɒ́pik) *adj.* **tel·e·scóp·i·cal·ly** *adv.* **te·les·co·py** (təléskəpi:) *n.* the science of the construction and use of telescopes [fr. Ital. *telescopio* or Mod. L. *telescopium* fr. Gk *teleskopos,* far-seeing fr. *tēle,* far off+ *skopein,* to observe]

tel·es·the·sia, tel·aes·the·sia (tɛlesθí:ʒə) *n.* perception of a distant object or event which cannot be due to any of the normal senses receiving a stimulus **tel·es·thet·ic, tel·aes·thet·ic** (tɛlesθétik) *adj.* [Mod. L. fr. Gk *tēle,* far off+*aisthēsis,* perception]

tel·e·thon (téləθɒn) *n.* an hours-long television program designed to promote a cause or raise funds for a charity

Tel·e·type (télitaip) *n.* a teletypewriter ‖ a message sent by this [Trademark]

tel·e·type·writ·er (tɛlitáipraitər, télitaipraitər) *n.* a device, similar to a typewriter, by which electrical impulses are transmitted telegraphically by a keyboard, and typed by an attachment to the receiving apparatus

tel·e·vise (télәvaiz) *pres. part.* **tel·e·vis·ing** *past* and *past. part.* **tel·e·vised** *v.t.* and *i.* to broadcast by television

tel·e·vi·sion (télivɪʒən) *n.* the transmission of visual images by means of electromagnetic waves. The television camera scans the field of view and activates a photoelectric cell, the impulses from which, propagated as electromagnetic waves, cause the electron beam of a cathode-ray tube in the receiver (television set) to scan the viewing screen in steps identical with those of the scanning camera, thus reproducing the field of view on the screen ‖ a television receiving set

television diplomacy the use of television to affect public opinion in international relations

Tel·ex (téleks) *n.* (*acronym*) for teleprinter and exchange, a system for communication by teletypewriters wire-connected through automatic exchanges —**telex** *n.* the message; *v.* to send messages by Telex

telfer *TELPHER

Tel·ford (télfərd), Thomas (1757-1834), Scottish engineer, famous for the roads, bridges, canals, docks, harbors and buildings which he constructed. They include the London-to-Holyhead road, the Menai Strait suspension bridge and the Caledonian Canal

Tell (tel), Wilhelm (early 14th c.), legendary Swiss hero who, refusing to do homage to a symbol of the German emperor, was sentenced to shoot an apple from his son's head, using bow and arrow. He did it successfully. He is looked on as a hero of the Swiss struggle for independence, and is the subject of a drama by Schiller and an opera by Rossini

tell (tel) *pres. part.* **tell·ing** *past* and *past part.* **told** (tould) *v.t.* to make (something) known esp. by saying or writing it, *to tell the facts* ‖ to give an account of (something) esp. by saying or writing it, esp. in a detailed and orderly manner, *to tell a story* ‖ to inform (someone) of something ‖ to supply information about ‖ to command, order (someone) to do something ‖ to reveal by gestures, glances, change of color etc. ‖ to divulge ‖ to decide, choose, *she can't tell which is best* ‖ to discern, differentiate, *she could not tell him by his voice, it is difficult to tell them apart* ‖ *v.i.* (with 'of') to give a description, account, report etc. ‖ (with 'of') to give or be an indication ‖ to be a determining factor, *the boxer's experience told in his favor* ‖ (*pop.*) to make known something which ought to be kept secret **to tell off** to count off a number of (persons) from a larger total, e.g. so as to assign a task to them ‖ (*pop.*) to rebuke **to tell on** to make a demand on, produce strain or fatigue in, *the pace began to tell on them* ‖ (*pop.*) to report the misdeeds of [O.E. *tellan*]

Tell-el-A·mar·na (téléləmɑ́rnə) an ancient city of upper Egypt in the Nile valley with impressive remains of the palace of Amenhotep IV. Many cuneiform tablets have been recovered from its archives

Tel·ler (télər), Edward (1908-), Hungarian-U.S. physicist. His research into the development, application, and control of nuclear energy made possible (1952) the first successful U.S. hydrogen bomb explosion

tell·er (télər) *n.* a person who tells a story etc. ‖ a bank employee who receives or pays out money ‖ a person who counts the votes cast e.g. in a legislative assembly

Teller Amendment a U.S. amendment (1898) to the declaration of war against Spain. It was sponsored by Senator Henry Moore Teller (1830-1914). It pledged the U.S.A. to the creation of an independent Cuba

tell·ing (téliŋ) *adj.* effective, impressive, *a telling argument* ‖ making a big demand, *a telling climb*

tell·tale (télteil) **1.** *n.* a person who informs, esp. about the small misdeeds of others ‖ any of many mechanical devices serving to record or warn, esp. (*naut.*) a device attached to a ship's steering wheel showing the position of the tiller or rudder **2.** *adj.* revealing, *a telltale blush*

tel·lu·ri·an (telúəri:ən) **1.** *adj.* of, pertaining to, or characteristic of the earth **2.** *n.* (*rhet.*) an inhabitant of the earth [fr. L. *tellus (telluris),* the earth]

tel·lu·ric (telúərik) *adj.* of or pertaining to the earth [fr. L. *tellus (telluris),* the earth]

telluric *adj.* of or containing tellurium, esp. tellurium of high valence [TELLURIUM]

tel·lu·ride (téljuraid) *n.* a compound of tellurium with one other element or radical, esp. one more highly electropositive

tel·lu·rite (téljurait) a mineral, TeO_2, found as small yellow or white crystals in the earth's crust ‖ a salt of tellurous acid

tel·lu·ri·um (telúəri:əm) *n.* a semimetallic chemical element (symbol Te, at. no. 52, at. mass 127.60) occurring in a white brittle crystalline form and a brown-to-black amorphous form. It resembles sulfur in its chemical behavior. It is used chiefly as a secondary vulcanizing agent in heavy-duty rubbers. It is also used as an alloying element with lead and in steels **tél·lu·rized** *adj.* combined with tellurium **tél·lu·rous** *adj.* of or containing tellurium, esp. tellurium of low valence [Mod. L. fr. *tellus (telluris),* the earth]

Tel·lus (téləs) (*Rom. mythol.*) the goddess of the earth

tel·o·dy·nam·ic (tɛloudainǽmik) *adj.* of or pertaining to the transmission of machine power to a distant place, esp. by means of ropes, pulleys etc. [fr. Gk *tēle,* far off+ DYNAMIC]

tel·o·phase (téləfeiz) *n.* (*biol.*) the fourth and final stage of mitosis and meiosis, during which the chromosome material disperses, forming two new nuclei. Cytoplasmic division follows (*PROPHASE, *METAPHASE, *ANAPHASE) [fr. Gk *telos,* end+PHASE]

Te·los (tí:lɒs) (*Gk* Tilos) an island (area 25 sq. miles, pop. 1,100) of the Dodecanese, Greece

Tel·pak (télpæk) *n.* a Bell System service that leases wide-band communication channels

tel·pher, tel·fer (télfər) *n.* a container or passenger car slung from an overhead cable and propelled by electric power **tél·pher·age, tél·fer·age** *n.* a system of conveyance using telphers [fr. Gk *tēle,* far off+*pherein,* to bear]

tel·son (télsən) *n.* (*zool.*) the unpaired terminal abdominal segment of many arthropods, e.g. the middle lobe of a lobster's tail [Gk=limit]

Tel·star (télstɑr) *n.* (*communications*) a transatlantic communication satellite, launched in 1962

Tel·u·gu, Tel·e·gu (téləgu:) *pl.* **Tel·u·gu, Tel·u·gus, Tel·e·gu, Tel·e·gus 1.** *n.* a Dravidian people living in Andhra Pradesh, India ‖ a member of this people ‖ their Dravidian language **2.** *adj.* of Telugu or the Telugus

Te·ma (téimə) a deepwater port in S.E. Ghana, opened in 1962

Tem·bi (témbi:) *TEMPE, VALE OF

tem·blor (témblər) *n.* an earthquake [Span.]

Tem·bu·land (témbu:lænd) *TRANSKEIAN TERRITORIES

tem·er·ar·i·ous (tɛmərɛ́əri:əs) *adj.* (*rhet.*) taking no account of probable consequences, reckless [fr. L. *temerarius*]

te·mer·i·ty (təmériti:) *n.* recklessness [fr. L. *temeritas*]

Tem·ne (témni:) *n.* a people of central and E. Sierra Leone ‖ a member of this people ‖ the language of this people

tem·peh (témpei) *n.* a high-protein Asian food or condiment prepared by fermenting soybeans with a mold fungus

tem·per (témpər) **1.** *v.t.* to bring (glass, steel etc.) to a desired state of consistency, hardness etc. by heating and then cooling rapidly ‖ to bring (clay) to a desired consistency by adding water and kneading ‖ to prepare (pigment) for use by adding oil ‖ to make less harsh, *to temper justice with mercy* ‖ (*mus.*) to modify the pitch of (an instrument, note or chord) to a temperament ‖ *v.i.* to be or become tempered **2.** *n.* the state of a metal, alloy, clay etc. as regards its hardness, consistency etc. ‖ anger, *a fit of temper* or the tendency to become angry, *she has a temper* ‖ the emotional state of a person or community, *in a good temper* **to get** (or **fly**) **into a temper** to become suddenly angry **to keep (lose) one's temper** to control (fail to control) the impulse to be angry [O.E. *temprian* fr. L. *temperare* and O.F. *temprer*]

tem·per·a (témpərə) *n.* a method of painting pictures using pigments suspended in an albuminous or colloidal substance (e.g. white of egg) [Ital.]

tem·per·a·ment (témprəmənt) *n.* the characteristic physiological and emotional state of an individual, which tends to condition his responses to the various situations of life, *a gloomy temperament* ‖ hypersensitivity common in artists, actors, musicians etc. and frequently displayed in fits of temper ‖ (*mus.*) the method or act of adjusting the relationship between the fragments of successive semitones on the piano, organ and other fixed-pitch instruments, or the system of relationships adopted (*EQUAL TEMPERAMENT, *MEANTONE TEMPERAMENT) **tem·per·a·men·tal** (tɛmprəméntʼl) *adj.* (of a person) liable to rapid and intense changes of mood [fr. L. *temperamentum,* proper mixing]

tem·per·ance (témpərəns) *n.* the quality or state of being temperate ‖ the virtue which moderates desires and passions (*CARDINAL VIRTUES) ‖ moderation in eating and drinking, esp. in drinking alcoholic drinks ‖ total abstinence from alcoholic drinks [A.F. *temperaunce*]

tem·per·ate (témpərit) *adj.* moderate, avoiding both of two extremes ‖ (of climate) never very hot or very cold ‖ of the regions between the Tropic of Cancer and the Arctic Circle or between the Tropic of Capricorn and the Antarctic

Circle ‖ (*mus.*) tempered (esp. to equal temperament) [fr. L. *temperare (temperatus)*, to mix in due proportions]

tem·per·a·ture (témprətʃər) *n.* (*phys.*) a quantitative measure of the tendency of heat to flow in a given direction using one of a number of arbitrary scales based on an observable phenomenon, such as the volume change of mercury ‖ the internal heat of the body, *his temperature was above normal* ‖ the excess of this above normal (98.4°F. or 98.6°F.) [fr. L. *temperatura*]

temperature-humidity index *COMFORT INDEX

tem·pered (témpərd) *adj.* (used in combination) having a specified disposition, *bad-tempered, even-tempered* ‖ modified by the admixture of another quality or substance, *justice tempered with mercy* ‖ (*mus.*) tuned to temperament ‖ (of a metal) brought to the proper degree of hardness or elasticity

tem·pest (témpist) *n.* a very violent wind, esp. when accompanied by hail, heavy rain or snow ‖ a very violent upsurge or expression of emotion [O.F. *tempeste*]

tem·pes·tu·ous (tempéstʃu:əs) *adj.* of or marked by raging storms or gales ‖ violent, turbulent [fr. L. *tempestuosus*]

Tem·pe, Vale of (témpi:) (*Gk* Tembi) a narrow wooded valley (5 miles long) in N.E. Thessaly, Greece, between Mt Ossa and Mt Olympus, opening on to the Gulf of Salonica

Tem·plar (témplər) *n.* (*hist.*) a Knight Templar ‖ (*Br.*) a barrister having chambers in the Temple, London [O.F. *templier* after the Temple in Jerusalem, near which the Templars had their headquarters]

tem·plate, tem·plet (témplit) *n.* a pattern, usually of thin sheet metal or wood, used when cutting, shaping etc. ‖ a block of wood or metal inserted in a wall to distribute vertical pressures ‖ (*genetics*) a macro-molecule (DNA or RNA) on which an enzyme creates a complementary strand [etym. doubtful]

Temple (témp'l), Sir William (1628-99), English diplomat and author. He negotiated an alliance with the Netherlands and Sweden (1668) and the marriage of the future William III and Mary II (*OSBORNE)

Temple, William (1881-1944), archbishop of Canterbury (1942-4). His works include 'Readings in St John's Gospel' (1939-40), 'Nature, Man and God' (1934) and 'Christianity and the Social Order' (1942). He exercised powerful leadership in reform movements within the Anglican Church, and in the formation of the World Council of Churches

tem·ple (témp'l) *n.* a device in a loom for keeping the cloth stretched transversely [F.]

temple *n.* (esp. in ancient Greece, Rome or Egypt) a building used for the worship of a god **Temple** (*hist.*) one of three successive religious buildings of the Jews in ancient Jerusalem **The Temple** the Inner Temple and Middle Temple of the Inns of Court [O.E. *tempel, templ* fr. L. *templum* and O.F. *temple*]

temple *n.* either of the flat portions of the head between the ear and the forehead [O.F.]

Temple of Jerusalem Solomon's temple to God, built by Phoenician craftsmen. It had a unifying influence in Judaism as it was its only center of sacrificial worship. The fortunes of Judaism were involved in its destruction in 586 B.C. and reconstruction in 516 B.C. A third Temple built by Herod c. 20 B.C., still standing in the time of Christ, was destroyed in 70 A.D. The site is now occupied by the Moslem shrines of the Dome of the Rock and the Mosque of Omar

templet *TEMPLATE

tem·po (témpou) *pl.* **tem·pi** (témpi:), **tem·pos** *n.* (*mus.*) the speed at which a piece of music is played or is meant to be played ‖ rate of movement or of some activity (e.g. at which a play is performed) [Ital.]

tem·po·ral (témpərəl) *adj.* of or situated near a temple or the temples of the head [fr. L. *temporalis* fr. *tempora*, the temples of the head]

temporal *adj.* concerned with life on earth, in contrast to life after death (opp. SPIRITUAL) ‖ of or relating to secular, worldly matters (cf. ECCLESIASTICAL) ‖ of or relating to life in time (cf. ETERNAL) ‖ of time (cf. SPATIAL) ‖ (*gram.*) expressing time or tense ‖ (*Br.*) of peers of the realm as distinguished from archbishops or bishops in the House of Lords, *Lords temporal* **tém·po·ral·ism** *n.* (*philos.*) a doctrine stressing the ultimate reality of time **tém·po·ral·ist** *n.* **tém·po·ral·is·tic** *adj.* [fr. L. L. *temporalis*]

tem·po·ral·i·ty (tempərǽliti:) *pl.* **tem·po·ral·i·ties** *n.* secular property, esp. (*pl.*) the revenues of a church or an ecclesiastic [fr. L. *temporalitas*]

tem·po·rar·i·ly (tempəréərili:) *adv.* for a time only [TEMPORARY]

tem·po·rar·i·ness (témpərəri:nis) *n.* the state or quality of being temporary

tem·po·rar·y (témpərəri:) *adj.* lasting, or intended to last, only for a short time [fr. L. *temporarius*]

tem·po·ri·za·tion (tempərizéiʃən) *n.* the practice or act of temporizing

tem·po·rize (témpəraiz) *pres. part.* **tem·po·riz·ing** *past* and *past part.* **tem·po·rized** *v.i.* to act so as to gain time in a difficult situation, esp. by making a policy of avoiding decisions or of agreeing only to what does not commit one very far ‖ (with 'with') to come to terms [F. *temporiser*]

tempt (tempt) *v.t.* to try to persuade (someone) to do something, esp. something which will involve him in a sinful or wrongful act ‖ to be attractive, enticing etc. to, *the publicity tempts me* ‖ (*rhet.*) to run the risk of provoking, *to tempt fate* [O.F. and A.F. *tempter*]

temp·ta·tion (temptéiʃən) *n.* a tempting or being tempted ‖ something which tempts [O.F. *temptaciun, tentation*]

tempt·er (témptər) *n.* someone who tempts **tempt·ress** (témptris) *n.* a woman who tempts [M.E. *temptour*]

Te·mu·co (temú:kɔ) a city and trade center (pop. 150,560) in S. central Chile: grains, fruit, lumber

ten (ten) **1.** *adj.* being one more than nine (*NUMBER TABLE) **2.** *n.* twice five ‖ the cardinal number representing this (10, X) ‖ 10 o'clock ‖ a playing card marked with 10 spots ‖ (*pl.*) in mathematical calculations, the column of figures two places to the left of the decimal point [O.E. *tien, tēn*]

ten·a·bil·i·ty (tenəbíliti:) *n.* the state or quality of being tenable

ten·a·ble (ténəb'l) *adj.* able to be held, *the office is tenable for one year* ‖ able to be held against attack ‖ able to be maintained, *an opinion no longer tenable* [F]

ten·ace (téneis) *n.* (*cards*) a combination in one hand of the best and third-best cards of a suit, the second-best card being held by an opponent [fr. Span. *tenaza*, pincers]

te·na·cious (tənéiʃəs) *adj.* holding fast, *a tenacious grasp* ‖ firmly held, *tenacious beliefs* ‖ adhesive ‖ retentive, *a tenacious memory* ‖ persistent, *a tenacious bore* [fr. L. *tenax (tenacis)*]

te·nac·i·ty (tənǽsiti:) *n.* the state or quality of being tenacious ‖ (*phys.*) tensile strength [fr. L. *tenacitas*]

te·nac·u·lum (tinǽkjuləm) *pl.* **te·nac·u·la** (tinǽkjulə), **te·nac·u·lums** *n.* a surgical instrument with a sharp hook for picking up arteries etc. in the course of an operation [L.=holder]

te·nail, te·naille (tinéil) *n.* (*fortification*) a low outwork between two bastions in the main defense ditch [F. *tenaille*, pincers]

ten·an·cy (ténənsi:) *pl.* **ten·an·cies** *n.* tenure as tenant ‖ property held by a tenant

ten·ant (ténənt) **1.** *n.* someone paying rent to the owner for the use of land or a building ‖ (*law*) someone holding real estate by any kind of right **2.** *v.t.* (esp. *past part.*) to occupy as a tenant **tén·ant·a·ble** *adj.* fit to be occupied by a tenant [O.F.]

tenant farmer a farmer cultivating land owned by another and paying a rent in money or produce

ten·ant·ry (ténəntri:) *pl.* **ten·ant·ries** *n.* tenants collectively ‖ the state or condition of being a tenant

Te·nas·ser·im (tənǽsərim) the southernmost coastal region of Burma: rubber plantations, rice

tench (tenʃ) *pl.* **tench, tench·es** *n. Tinca tinca*, fam. *Cyprinidae*, a teleostean fish (10–12 ins) inhabiting European and Asiatic lakes and rivers. The flesh is coarse and insipid [O.F. *tenche*]

Ten Commandments *DECALOGUE

tend (tend) *v.t.* to take care of, look after (people, animals, machines etc.) ‖ (*naut.*) to stand by (a cable) in order to prevent fouling ‖ *v.i.* (*pop.*, with 'to') to give attention, *you tend to the baby* [shortened fr. ATTEND]

tend *v.i.* to have a prevailing direction, *the wind is tending to the south* ‖ to be prone to act or think in a certain way, *he tends to drive too fast* ‖ to lead or be directed towards a condition or result, *a political situation tending towards anarchy* [F. *tendre*]

ten·den·cy (téndənsi:) *pl.* **ten·den·cies** *n.* the quality of tending towards something or of tending to do something [fr. M. L. *tendentia*]

ten·den·tious, ten·den·cious (tendénʃəs) *adj.* (of thought, writing etc.) having deliberate bias [as if fr. M.L. *tendentia*, tendency, after G. *tendenziös*]

ten·der (téndər) *n.* someone who tends ‖ a small vessel used to transport passengers, goods, fuel etc. from or to a larger ship ‖ a small vessel for passing communications between shore and a larger ship ‖ a vehicle attached to a locomotive, carrying its fuel and water supply

tender 1. *v.t.* to offer (services etc.), offer for acceptance, *to tender one's resignation* ‖ (*law*) to offer (money or services) to meet an obligation and avoid prosecution ‖ *v.i.* (often with 'for') to put in a competitive estimate for work to be done **2.** *n.* an offer of a formal nature, esp. a competitive offer for a contract for work to be done ‖ (*law*) an offer of money or services made to meet an obligation and avoid prosecution ‖ *LEGAL TENDER [A. F. *tender*, F. *tendre*]

tender *adj.* easily damaged, *a tender plant* ‖ (of food) easily chewed ‖ sore to the touch, *tender gums* ‖ sensitive to emotional pain ‖ young and readily impressionable, *of a tender age* ‖ quick to feel compassion or affection etc. ‖ expressing or resulting from such emotions, *a tender smile* ‖ (of a subject of talk) apt or able to cause emotional pain [O.F. *tendre*]

ten·der·foot (téndərfut) *pl.* **ten·der·foots** *n.* a newcomer to a place or situation ‖ a Scout or Girl Scout in the beginners' group

ten·der·heart·ed (téndərhártid) *adj.* easily aroused to pity, sorrow etc.

ten·der·ize (téndəraiz) *v.t. pres. part.* **ten·der·iz·ing** *past* and *past part.* **ten·der·ized** to subject (meat) to a process or machine which makes it tender

ten·der·loin (téndərlɔin) *n.* the most tender undercut of the loin of pork or beef

ten·der·om·e·ter (tendə:rómətə:r) *n.* a device for testing the maturity and tenderness of vegetables and fruit

ten·di·nous (téndinəs) *adj.* of or like a tendon or tendons ‖ consisting of tendons [fr. F. *tendineux* fr. Mod. L.]

ten·don (téndən) *n.* a strong band of connective tissue joining a muscle to some other part [fr. M.L. *tendo (tendonis, tendinis)*]

ten·dril (téndrəl) *n.* a leafless organ in climbing plants, resembling a thin coil of wire and serving as a means of attachment to a support [perh. fr. L. *tendere*, F. *tendre*]

Ten·e·brae (ténəbri:) *pl. n.* (*Roman Catholicism*) Matins and Lauds during the last three days of Holy Week, at which the candles are progressively extinguished [L.=shadows]

ten·e·bres·cence (tenəbrésəns) *n.* process of darkening by exposure to X-rays, cathode rays, heat, or some forms of light

ten·e·brous (ténəbrəs) *adj.* (*rhet.*) mysterious, full of obscurities ‖ (*rhet.*) dark, gloomy [O.F. *tenebrus* fr. L.]

Tène, La (læten) a locality of Neuchâtel, Switzerland which has given its name to the civilization of the second Iron Age, the Gallic period preceding the Roman occupation. Archaeological finds at La Tène include remains of vehicles and harness, weapons and many tools

ten·e·ment (ténəmənt) *n.* (*law*) any kind of permanent property, e.g. land or titles or rents, held by one person ‖ a tenement house ‖ an apartment in a tenement house [A.F. fr. M.L. *tenementum*, a holding]

tenement house a building divided into rented apartments, esp. in the poor, crowded, squalid section of a city

Ten·e·rife (tenərí:f) the largest island (area 795 sq. miles, pop. 473,971) of the Canary Is, Spain. Capital: Santa Cruz de Tenerife. Highest point: 12,192 ft (an active volcano). Exports: wine, oranges and bananas, market produce

te·nes·mus (tinézməs) *n.* (*med.*) a continual desire to evacuate the bowels and bladder, characterized by painful straining without effect [M.L. fr. Gk]

ten·et (ténit, *Br.* also tí:net) *n.* a principle, belief or doctrine held by a person or a group [L.=he holds]

Teng H'saio-ping (Deng Xiaoping) (duŋʃi:áupiŋ) (1904-), Chinese Communist revolutionary and political leader. An early Communist leader, he became China's vice-premier (1952) and then Communist party general secretary

CONCISE PRONUNCIATION KEY: **(a)** æ, *cat*; ɑ, *car*; ɔ *fawn*; ei, *snake*. **(e)** e, *hen*; i:, *sheep*; iə, *deer*; ɛə, *bear*. **(i)** i, *fish*; ai, *tiger*; ə:, *bird*. **(o)** o, *ox*; au, *cow*; ou, *goat*; u, *poor*; ɔi, *royal*. **(u)** ʌ, *duck*; u, *bull*; u:, *goose*; ə, *bacillus*; ju:, *cube*. x, *loch*; θ, *think*; ð, *bother*; z, *Zen*; ʒ, *corsage*; dʒ, *savage*; ŋ, *orangutang*; j, *yak*; ʃ, *fish*; tʃ, *fetch*; 'l, *rabble*; 'n, *redden*. Complete pronunciation key appears inside front cover.

(1956). He was purged during the Cultural Revolution and again in 1976 but was reinstated (1977) and as the party's senior vice-chairman became China's most powerful leader. In 1982, Teng was named chairman of the newly created Central Advisory Commission after resigning as party vice-chairman. He remained the most influential member of the Politburo and chairman of the party's Military Commission. He sought more foreign participation in Chinese enterprise and attempted to reform China's economy

tenia *TAENIA

Ten·iers (ténjərz), David (1610-90), Flemish painter, son of David Teniers the Elder (1582-1649). The son, the more famous of the two, is noted esp. for his genre scenes of peasant life

Tenn. Tennessee

Ten·nent (ténənt), Gilbert (1703-64), Presbyterian leader of the Great Awakening religious revival. While a minister in New Brunswick, N.J. (from 1726) he was influenced by Theodore Frelinghuysen, who taught that religion should be a matter of the heart as well as the mind. Tennent traveled on evangelistic missions (1740-1) and a sermon he preached (1740) contributed to the breach between New Side (pro-revival) and Old Side (traditionalist) Presbyterians. Later he modified his views and was influential in reuniting the Presbyterians (1758)

Ten·nes·see (tẹnəsí:) (*abbr.* Tenn.) a state (area 42,244 sq. miles, pop. 4,651,000) of the south-east central U.S.A. Capital: Nashville. Chief city: Memphis. Its rolling uplands lie between the Appalachians in the east and the Mississippi valley in the west. Agriculture: cotton, tobacco, corn, fodder crops, dairy and beef cattle. Resources: coal, zinc (leading state producer), phosphates, copper, building stone. Industries: chemicals (esp. synthetic fibers), metal refining and products, food processing, textiles. State university (1794) at Knoxville. Tennessee was ceded (1783) by Britain to the U.S.A. It became (1796) the 16th state

Tennessee the chief tributary (652 miles long) of the Ohio River, rising near Knoxville, Tennessee, and flowing first south, then north, through Alabama, Tennessee and S.W. Kentucky (*TENNESSEE VALLEY AUTHORITY)

Tennessee Valley Authority (*abbr.* T.V.A.) a federal agency of the U.S.A. founded in 1933 for developing the resources of the natural economic unit formed by the Tennessee valley states: Tennessee, Kentucky, Mississippi, Alabama, North Carolina, Georgia and Virginia. Its chief duties are flood control, maintenance of navigation, provision of electric power, afforestation and development and production of fertilizers and munitions

ten·nis (ténis) *n.* lawn tennis ‖ court tennis [M.E. *tenetz* prob. fr. A.F. *tenetz*=F. *tenez*, take, catch]

Tennis-Court Oath (*F. hist.*, Serment du Jeu de Paume) the oath taken (June 20, 1789) by the third estate that they would not separate until they had given France a constitution. The king having closed the assembly's usual meeting place, the deputies had assembled in a nearby tennis court

tennis elbow pain and inflammation of the elbow, caused by violent or suddenly frequent use of certain muscles in a twisting movement of the hand

ten·nist (ténist) *n.* tennis player

Ten·ny·son (ténis'n), Alfred, Lord (1809-92), English poet. His collections 'Poems Chiefly Lyrical' (1832) and 'Poems' (2 vols, 1842) established his reputation. In 1850 he published 'In Memoriam', a series of lyric elegies in which his art reaches full expression. His later work never consistently reached these heights, although there were occasional lyric triumphs, e.g. 'Ode on the Death of the Duke of Wellington' (1852), 'Maud' (1855), and 'The Idylls of the King' (1859). He had a very fine ear for the melody and movement of verse

Te·noch·ti·tlán (tenọutʃti:tlán) the capital of the Aztecs, today Mexico City. Founded c. 1325, it was an impressive city of canals and floating gardens, with more than 300 temples and 146 shrines. The principal temple (teocali) stood on the site of the present cathedral. The city was destroyed by the Spaniards in 1521

ten·on (ténən) **1.** *n.* the end of a piece of wood shaped to fit into a corresponding mortise in a second piece **2.** *v.t.* to shape to fit into a mortise ‖ to join (two pieces of wood) with a mortise ‖ to join (two pieces of wood) with a mortise and tenon [F.]

ten·or (ténər) **1.** *n.* the general, little varying course or overall direction, *the even tenor of events* ‖ the general drift of spoken or written remarks etc. ‖ (*law*) intent or purpose ‖ (*law*) an exact copy ‖ (*mus.*) a male voice between baritone and alto, ranging approx. from one octave below middle C to one octave above it ‖ someone who sings with this voice ‖ a musical part written for such a singer ‖ the lowest bell of a peal used for change ringing **2.** *adj.* (*mus.*) of or relating to a tenor ‖ (of an instrument in a family of instruments) having approx. the range of a tenor voice, *a tenor saxophone* [O.F.]

Te·nos (tí:nɒs) (*Gk* Tinos) an island (area 79 sq. miles, pop. 10,000) of the N. Cyclades, Greece

ten·pence (ténpəns) *n.* (*Br., hist.*) the sum of ten pennies

ten·pin (ténpịn) *n.* a pin used in tenpins ‖ (*pl.*, construed as sing.) a game of American origin, in which a large heavy ball is bowled along a long wooden alley at 10 pins set up in a triangular pattern

ten·rec (ténrek) *n.* any of several small insectivorous mammals of fam. *Tenrecidae* native to Madagascar, esp. *Tenrec ecaudatus*, a common tailless species [fr. Malagasy *tàndraka*]

tense (tens) **1.** *adj.* showing or undergoing emotional strain ‖ characterized by or causing emotional stress ‖ stretched tight ‖ (*phon.*) spoken with tensed muscles esp. of the tongue **2.** *v. pres. part.* **tens·ing** *past* and *past part.* **tensed** *v.t.* to make tense ‖ *v.i.* (often with 'up') to be or become tense [fr. L. *tendere* (*tensus*), to stretch]

tense *n.* (*gram.*) any of the forms of a verb expressing the time of the action or the state of being, *present tense, future perfect tense* ‖ (*gram.*) a set of forms for the various persons for a given time, *recite the present tense of 'amare'* [O.F. *tens*, time]

ten·si·bil·i·ty (tẹnsəbíliti:) *n.* the state or quality of being tensible

ten·si·ble (ténsəb'l) *adj.* able to be extended or stretched [fr. L. *tendere* (*tensus*), to stretch]

ten·sile (ténsəl, esp. *Br.* ténsail) *adj.* able to be extended in length ‖ pertaining to tension [fr. Mod. L. *tensilis* fr. *tendere* (*tensus*), to stretch]

tensile strength (*phys.*) the maximum force of tension to which a material can respond without breaking

ten·sil·i·ty (tensíliti:) *n.* the state or quality of being tensile

ten·si·om·e·try (tẹnsi:ɒ́mətri:) *n.* (*phys.*) the study of tensile stength —**tensiometric** *adj.*

ten·sion (ténʃən) *n.* a tensing or being tensed ‖ a force tending to cause extension of a body, or the force tending to restore the shape of an extended elastic object ‖ the force tending to minimize the surface of a fluid (*SURFACE TENSION) ‖ the state of a conductor carrying an electric current ‖ a state of emotional stress ‖ a state of repressed hostility ‖ the dynamic relationship between parts of a work of art set off one against another **tén·sion·al** *adj.* [prob. F. fr. L.L. *tensio* (*tensionis*)]

tension lag platform floating structure moored by steel pipe tether at deepwater sea bottom that resists natural weather forces; developed by Conoco *abbr.* TLP

ten·sor (ténsər) *n.* (*anat.*) a muscle which stretches or tightens ‖ (*math.*) a magnitude by which components of a system may be transformed linearly and of which the notion of vector is a special case [Mod. L. fr. *tendere* (*tensus*), to stretch]

tent (tent) **1.** *n.* a shelter made of canvas, skins etc., supported by a pole or poles and secured by ropes **2.** *v.i.* to live in a tent ‖ *v.t.* to equip with a tent or tents ‖ to lodge in a tent or tents [O.F. *tente*]

tent 1. *n.* (*med.*) a roll of absorbent material used to keep a wound open **2.** *v.t.* (*med.*) to keep open with a tent [F. *tente*, a probe (surgical instrument)]

ten·ta·cle (téntək'l) *n.* a slender flexible organ on the head of many invertebrate animals, used for feeding, exploration, prehension or attachment ‖ a hairlike outgrowth on the leaves of some insectivorous plants (e.g. sundew) ‖ something that seems to reach out and have a grasp hard to evade, *the tentacles of the law* **ten·tac·u·lar** (tentǽkjulər), **ten·tac·u·late** (tentǽkjulit) *adjs* [fr. Mod. L. *tentaculum* fr. *tentare*, to touch]

ten·ta·tive (téntətiv) *adj.* provisional, subject to modification if unsatisfactory, *a tentative arrangement* ‖ hesitating, *a tentative smile* [fr. M.L. *tentativus*]

ten·ter (téntər) *n.* a frame for stretching cloth to keep its shape when drying [etym. doubtful]

ten·ter·hook (téntərhụk) *n.* a hook used to hold cloth on a tenter **on tenterhooks** in a state of acutely anxious expectancy

tenth (tenθ) **1.** *adj.* being number ten in a series ‖ being one of the ten equal parts of anything **2.** *n.* the person or thing next after the ninth ‖ one of ten equal parts of anything (1/10) ‖ the tenth day of a month **3.** *adv.* in the tenth place ‖ (followed by a superlative) except nine, *the tenth biggest* [O.E. *tēotha*]

Tenth Amendment (1791) final amendment in the Bill of Rights of the U.S. Constitution. It provides that powers not delegated to the federal government by the Constitution nor prohibited to the states are reserved to the states or to the people. The amendment was intended to prevent the new national government from usurping the authority of the states. Although the reserved powers are not enumerated in the amendment, they have been understood to include internal matters such as local government, education and regulation of intrastate commerce, labor and business, as well as family concerns such as marriage, divorce and inheritance. Although today the 10th Amendment is not seen as limiting the authority of the federal government, it was cited to curtail powers of Congress in such landmark Supreme Court cases as *Hammer* v. *Dagenhart* (1918) and *Schecter Poultry Corporation* v. *United States* (1935)

tent stitch a diagonal stitch used in embroidery

tent-trail·er (ténttrẹilər) *n.* a flat trailer drawn by a motor vehicle carrying a deployable canvas ceiling and sides that can provide tent shelter

ten·u·is (ténju:is) *pl.* **ten·u·es** (ténju:i:z) *n.* (*phon.*) a voiceless stop (e.g. k, p, t) [L.=thin, narrow]

ten·u·i·ty (tenú:iti:, tenjú:iti:) *n.* slenderness ‖ (of air or a fluid) thinness, lack of density ‖ (*fig.*) poverty, meagerness [fr. L. *tenuitas*]

ten·u·ous (ténju:əs) *adj.* flimsy, thin, *a tenuous web* ‖ (of air, fluid) not dense ‖ so subtle as to be only vaguely apprehensible, *a tenuous distinction* [fr. L. *tenuis*, thin]

ten·ure (ténjər) *n.* the act, manner or right of holding office or property, esp. real estate ‖ the period of holding this [A.F., O.F.]

Tenure of Office Act a U.S. Congressional act (1867) sponsored by Congressmen who opposed the policies of President Andrew Johnson. It denied the president authority to dismiss any official whose appointment had been confirmed by the Senate, unless the Senate approved the dismissal. Johnson's subsequent removal of Secretary of War Edwin Stanton led to the president's trial for impeachment. In 1926 the Supreme Court ruled the act unconstitutional

te·nu·to (tənú:tou, tənjú:tou) **1.** *adj.* (*mus.*) sustained to its full time value **2.** *adv.* to be sustained in this way (opp. STACCATO) [Ital.=held]

Ten Years' War the war fought (1866-78) in Cuba in the east between the Spanish authorities and the guerrillas (*mambises*) led by Carlos Manuel de Céspedes. Spanish domination continued

Ten·zing Norkay (ténziŋ) (c. 1913-86), the Sherpa who, with Sir Edmund Hillary, climbed Mount Everest for the first time (May 29, 1953)

Te·o·a·mox·tli (tẹiouamɒ́stli:) the ancient chronicle of the Toltecs, written (pictographically) by the patriarch Hueman, who led the Toltecs south from California. The book is now in the Historische Kunstmuseum, Vienna

te·o·nan·a·catl (ti:ounánəcætl) *n.* any of several American mushrooms (e.g., *Psilocybe*) that is hallucinogenic when ingested

Te·o·ti·hua·can (tẹioutị:wakán) a religious center of a pre-Toltec and Toltec civilization (300 B.C.–900 A.D.) on a site 34 miles northeast of Mexico City. With a population of 250,000 at its zenith, and with an area larger than that of Athens or Rome, it was the largest city in pre-Columbian America, and was America's first real urban center. Among its monuments are the pyramids of the sun (216 ft. high) and the moon, built between the 1st and 2nd cc. A.D. (In the absence of the wheel, domestic animals and metal tools, they required the labor of 10,000 men for 20 years.) Their purpose was religious and scientific, a temple on the top of the larger pyramid serving as an observatory. The temple of Quetzalcóatl is adorned with alternating figures of Quetzalcóatl and Tlaloc

te·pa [$C_6H_{12}N_3OP$] (tí:pə) *n.* (*chem.*) a compound related to ethylenimine, used as an insecticide, in flame-proofing textiles, and in the treatment of some forms of cancer

te·pee, tee·pee (tí:pi:) *n.* a conical tent made esp. of skins stretched over a framework of poles, used by North American Indians [fr. Siouan or Dakota *tīpi*]

tep·id (tépid) *adj.* slightly warm ‖ unenthusiastic, without warmth, *a tepid reception* **te·pid·i·ty** (tepíditi:) *n.* the state or quality of being tepid [fr. L. *tepidus*]

te·qui·la (tikí:lə) *n.* a fiery Mexican drink distilled from several species of agave, esp. *Agave tequilana* ‖ this plant [Span.]

ter- (tər) *prefix* three ‖ (*chem.*) having three atoms, radicals etc. [L.]

tera- combining form meaning a trillion

ter·a·bit (tέərəbit) *n.* (*computer*) one million million bits (binary digits) of information *Cf* GIGABIT, KILOBIT, MEGABIT

ter·a·to·gen (tərǽtədʒən) *n.* (*med.*) an agent that causes fetal malformation during the first three months of pregnancy, e.g., rubella —**teratogenesis** *n.* production of such malformations —**teratogenic** *adj.* —**teratogenicity** the tendency to cause such malformation

ter·a·toid (térətɔid) *adj.* (*biol.*) abnormally formed [fr. Gk *teras* (*terat-*), monster]

ter·a·tol·o·gy (tęrətɔ́lədʒi:) *n.* (*biol.*) the study of malformations and monstrosities [fr. Gk *teras* (*teratos*), monster+*logos*, discourse]

ter·bi·um (tə́:rbi:əm) *n.* (*chem.*) a usually trivalent and rarely tetravalent rare-earth element (symbol Tb, at. no. 65, at. mass 158.924) [Mod. L. after *Ytterby*, Sweden]

Ter Borch, Ter·borch (tərbɔ́rʃ), Gerard (1617-81), Dutch painter. He excelled in portraits and in genre painting. His interiors faithfully reflect the life of the rich burgher class of his day

ter·bu·ta·line [$C_{12}H_{19}NO_3$] (terbjú:təli:n) *n.* (*pharm.*) bronchodilator used to relieve acute bronchospasm in pulmonary disease; marketed as Brethine and Bricanyl

terce (tə:rs) *n.* (*eccles.*) the third of the canonical hours (9 a.m.) ‖ the office for this [O.F.]

ter·cel (tə́:rs'l) *n.* a tiercel

terce·let (tə́:rslit) *n.* a tiercel

ter·cen·te·nar·y (tə:rséntənęri: tə:rsenténəri:) **1.** *pl.* **ter·cen·te·nar·ies** *n.* a 300th anniversary ‖ a period of 300 years **2.** *adj.* of a 300-year period [fr. L. *ter*, three times+CENTENARY]

ter·cen·ten·ni·al (tə:rsenténi:əl) **1.** *n.* a tercentenary **2.** *adj.* tercentenary

ter·cet (tə́:rsit) *n.* (*prosody*) three successive lines, e.g. a stanza esp. in terza rima or a triplet [F. fr. Ital.]

-tere combining form meaning a chromosome filament in the process of cell division in the formation of germ cells

ter·e·binth (térəbinθ) *n.* *Pistacia terebinthus*, fam. *Anacaraiaceae*, a small European tree yielding a kind of turpentine [fr. L. *terebinthus* fr. Gk]

ter·e·bin·thine (tęrəbínθin, tęrəbínθain) *adj.* of turpentine [fr. L. *terebinthinus*]

te·re·bra (tərí:brə) *pl.* **te·re·bras, te·re·brae** (tərí:bri:) *n.* an ovipositor modified for boring in certain hymenopterans [L.=borer]

te·re·do (tərí:dou) *pl.* **te·re·dos, te·re·di·nes** (tərí:d'ni:z) *n.* a shipworm [L. fr. Gk *teredon*, a boring worm]

Ter·ence (térəns) Latin dramatist (c. 190-159 B.C.), author of six surviving plays based on Greek comedies: the 'Andria', 'Hecyra', 'Heautontimorumenos', 'Eunuchus', 'Phormio' and 'Adelphi'. They are polished and humanitarian, and have more psychological interest than the comedies of Plautus

Te·re·sa (təri:sə, teréisə), **Mother** (1910-), Albanian nun, known for her humanitarian work in the slums of Calcutta, India. She began as a teacher in the Calcutta school run by her order but in 1946 received permission to leave the convent and establish a home for the dying poor. She also founded an orphanage and in 1950 established a new Roman Catholic order of sisters, the Missionaries of Charity. The order now comprises 700 women who work with the very poor on five continents. She received the Nobel peace prize (1979)

Teresa (Theresa) of Avila St (1515-82), Spanish reformer of the Carmelite order, and Doctor of the Church. She founded 17 houses for nuns and, with St John of the Cross, nearly as many houses for monks. Her writings, which are among the greatest in Christian mysticism, include 'The Way of Perfection' (c. 1565). Feast: Oct. 15

Teresa (Theresa) of Li·sieux (li:zjə:), St (1873-97), French Carmelite nun, also known as St Teresa of the Child Jesus and the Little Flower of Jesus. She wrote 'The Story of a Soul' (1897), her spiritual autobiography. Feast: Oct. 3

te·rete (tərí:t) *adj.* (*biol.*) cylindrical, usually tapering at the ends [fr. L. *teres* (*teretis*), round]

ter·gal (tə́:rg'l) *adj.* (*zool.*) of the tergum, dorsal [fr. L. *tergum*, the back]

ter·gi·ver·sate (tə́:rdʒivərseit) *pres. part.* **ter·gi·ver·sat·ing** *past* and *past part.* **ter·gi·ver·sat·ed** *v.i.* to practice tergiversation [fr. L. *tergiversari* (*tergiversatus*), to turn one's back]

ter·gi·ver·sa·tion (tə:rdʒivərséiʃən) *n.* change of principles or allegiance, esp. involving a desertion ‖ avoidance of decisions or firm action by roundabout ways [fr. L. *tergiversatio* (*tergiversationis*)]

ter·gum (tə́:rgəm) *pl.* **ter·ga** (tə́:rgə) *n.* (*zool.*) the back [L.]

ter·i·ya·ki (teri:jáki:) *n.* Japanese dish of steak, fish, chicken, or shellfish with garlic, and/or ginger and then broiled or grilled over charcoal

term (tə:rm) **1.** *n.* a period of time, measured between its beginning and end, *a term of 10 years, term of office* ‖ a subdivision of the academic year ‖ (*law*) one of the periods of the year during which the courts are in session ‖ the end of a period, *to come to its term* ‖ (*law*) an estate the enjoyment of which is fixed to end on a certain date ‖ (*law*) the period for which an estate is granted ‖ one of a set of words having exact limited meanings in cetrain uses, *a technical term* ‖ one of the words peculiar in certain meanings to a particular subject, *a medical term* ‖ (*math.*) each of the quantities composing a ratio, a sum, or an algebraic expression ‖ (*math.*) the numerator or denominator of a fraction ‖ (*logic*) a word or phrase which is the subject or predicate of a proposition ‖ the normal time for the end of pregnancy, *born before term* ‖ (*pl.*) requirements as to conditions, price etc., *terms of surrender, terms of an agreement* ‖ (*pl.*) language of a specified sort, *vague terms* ‖ (*archit.*) an armless statue the lower part of which ends in a pedestal **in terms of** as expressed by, *it is not to be considered in terms of money* **on good (bad) terms with** having good (bad) personal relations with **to bring (someone) to terms** to persuade (someone) to enter into an agreement **to come to terms** to arrive at an agreement **2.** *v.t.* to name or define by a term [F. *terme*]

ter·ma·gant (tə́:rməgənt) *n.* a woman who is a terrible scold [early M.E. *tervagant*, a character in the mystery plays]

Ter·man (tə́:rmən), Lewis Madison (1877-1956), U.S. psychologist, best known for his application of intelligence tests to schoolchildren. His chief contribution was the Stanford Revision of the Binet-Simon Intelligence Tests (1916, 1937)

ter·mi·na·bil·i·ty (tə:rminəbíliti:) *n.* the state or quality of being terminable

ter·mi·na·ble (tə́:rminəb'l) *adj.* (of an agreement) able to be terminated [fr. (obs.) *terminen*, to terminate]

ter·mi·nal (tə́:rmin'l) **1.** *adj.* of or forming the end ‖ occurring each term, *terminal examinations* ‖ (of a disease) considered likely to be fatal ‖ (*bot.*) growing at the end of a branch or stem ‖ ending a series, *terminal joints* ‖ of or relating to a terminus **2.** *n.* an end, extremity ‖ a terminus (end of route, station, town or building) ‖ a device at the end of an electric wire etc. for facilitating connections ‖ (*archit.*) a carving, ornament etc. at the end of a pillar, column etc. ‖ (*computer*) the instrument, usu. a keyboard, enabling data to enter or leave a system [fr. L. *terminalis*]

ter·mi·nate (tə́:rmineit) *pres. part.* **ter·mi·nat·ing** *past* and *past part.* **ter·mi·nat·ed** *v.t.* to bring to an end, to close, *to terminate an agreement* ‖ *v.i.* to come to an end [fr. L. *terminare* (*terminatus*)]

ter·mi·na·tion (tə:rminéiʃən) *n.* a terminating or being terminated ‖ the end of something in space or time, *at the termination of the examination* ‖ (*gram.*) the final sound, letters or syllable of a word [fr. L. *terminatio* (*terminationis*)]

ter·mi·na·tive (tə́:rminęitiv) *adj.* tending to terminate

ter·mi·na·tor (tə́:rminęitər) *n.* someone or something that terminates ‖ (*astron.*) the line dividing the light from the dark part of the moon or a planet [L.L.]

terminer *OYER AND TERMINER

ter·mi·no·log·i·cal (tə:rmin'lɔ́dʒik'l) *adj.* having to do with terminology

ter·mi·nol·o·gy (tə:rminɔ́lədʒi:) *pl.* **ter·mi·nol·o·gies** *n.* the terms proper to an art, science, profession etc. [fr. L. *terminus*, term+*logos*, discourse]

ter·mi·nus (tə́:rminəs) *pl.* **ter·mi·ni** (tə́:rminai), **ter·mi·nus·es** *n.* either end of a rail, air or bus route ‖ the station, buildings, town etc. at such an end ‖ (*archit.*) a term [L.=end, limit, boundary]

ter·mi·tar·i·um (tə:rmitέəri:əm) *pl.* **ter·mi·tar·i·a** (tə:rmitέəri:ə) *n.* an elaborate, chambered earth mound, often 10–12 ft high, built as a nest by a termite colony [L.]

ter·mite (tə́:rmait) *n.* a member of *Isoptera*, an order of very small, white, soft-bodied, social insects living esp. in the tropics. Each colony has a large, winged king and queen, with multitudes of wingless, sterile workers and soldiers. The many species do very great damage to wood [fr. L. *termes* (*termitis*), woodeating worm]

term·or (tə́:rmər) *n.* (*law*) someone who holds land etc. for a term of years, or for life [A.F. *termer*]

terms of reference (*Br.*) instructions given to define the limits within which an inquiry, report etc. must be kept and up to which it must go

terms of trade the ratio between prices of two trading countries, a factor in the balance of payments of each one

tern (tə:rn) *n.* a member of various genera of *Laridae*, esp. *Sterna*, a genus of slender, gull-like sea birds, 9–21 ins in length. They have sharply pointed bills which they point downwards while diving. The tail is deeply forked. Most terns are pearly-white with black caps. They are found in many parts of the world, esp. along the North Atlantic coasts [of Norse origin]

tern *n.* something consisting of a set of three, e.g. three numbers drawn to win a big lottery prize [F. *terne*]

ter·na·ry (tə́:rnəri:) *adj.* consisting of three ‖ arranged in groups of three ‖ third in a series ‖ (*chem.*) containing three different parts, e.g. elements, atoms or components ‖ (*metall.*) of an alloy of three elements ‖ (*math.*) having three variables ‖ of a scale of numbers using three as the base [fr. L.L. *ternarius*]

ternary alloy an alloy of iron, silicon, and aluminum with high magnetic properties

ternary form (*mus.*) a form in which a movement consists of three sections, the third being a repetition or near-repetition of the first

ter·nate (tə́:rneit) *adj.* being or arranged in a group of three ‖ (*bot.*) having three leaflets

ter·pene (tə́:rpi:n) *n.* (*chem.*) one of a series of isomeric hydrocarbons, $C_{10}H_{16}$, obtained by distillation from certain plants, esp. conifers. They include pinene (in oil of turpentine) and limonene (in citrus oils) ‖ any of a large class of hydrocarbons (C_5H_8), that are generally regarded as constituted from a linking up of branched fragments containing five carbon atoms and that are found in plants, esp. as constituents of resins or essential oils (*ISOPRENE) [fr. obs. *terpentin* fr. TURPENTINE]

Terp·sich·o·re (tə:rpsíkəri:) (*Gk mythol.*) the Muse of dancing

terp·si·cho·re·an (tę:rpsikərí:ən) *adj.* (*rhet.*) of or pertaining to dancing [TERPSICHORE]

Ter·ra (térrɑ), Gabriel (1873-1942), Uruguayan jurist, politician, and president of the Republic (1931-8). In 1933 he suspended congress, dissolved the council of administration which served as a check on the power of the executive, and abolished the constitution. In 1934 he promulgated a new constitution, but ruled largely by decree

ter·ra *pl.* **-rae** (térə) *n.* (*astron.*) surface area of the moon as distinguished from its *marias*, or seas

ter·race (térəs) *n.* a raised level cut into the side of a hill ‖ a level space, often paved, adjoining a house etc. and used e.g. for sitting in the sun or enjoying a view ‖ (*geol.*) a raised bench ‖ a row of houses joined together ‖ a row of houses built on a raised level or on the side of a hill [F. *terrasse*]

terrace *v.t. pres. part.* **ter·rac·ing** *past* and *past*

CONCISE PRONUNCIATION KEY: **(a)** æ, *cat*; ɑ, *car*; ɔ *fawn*; ei, *snake*. **(e)** e, *hen*; i:, *sheep*; iə, *deer*; εə, *bear*. **(i)** i, *fish*; ai, *tiger*; ə:, *bird*. **(o)** o, *ox*; au, *cow*; ou, *goat*; u, *poor*; ɔi, *royal*. **(u)** ʌ, *duck*; u, *bull*; u:, *goose*; ə, *bacillus*; ju:, *cube*. x, *loch*; θ, *think*; ð, *bother*; z, *Zen*; ʒ, *corsage*; dʒ, *savage*; ŋ, *orangutang*; j, *yak*; ʃ, *fish*; tʃ, *fetch*; 'l, *rabble*; 'n, *redden*. Complete pronunciation key appears inside front cover.

part. **ter·raced** to form into a terrace or terraces || to add a terrace to [TERRACE n. or F. *terrasser*]

terrace house (*Br.*) a town house (which see)

ter·ra-cot·ta (terəkótə) **1.** *n.* hard, brownish-red pottery (of which statues etc. are made) fired unglazed || a statue made of this || the brownish-red color of terra-cotta **2.** *adj.* brownish-red || made of terra-cotta [Ital.=baked earth]

ter·ra fir·ma (térəfə́:rmə) *n.* the solid land we walk securely on (as opposed to water or space) [L.=firm land]

ter·rain (təréin) *n.* a stretch of land with respect to its features or condition considered from a particular (e.g. tactical) point of view || (*geol.*) a terrane [F.]

ter·rane (təréin) *n.* (*geol.*) a rock formation or series of formations [TERRAIN]

ter·ra·pin (térəpin) *n.* a freshwater, edible turtle of fam. *Testudinidae* found mainly in North America [of Algonquian origin]

ter·raz·zo (tərǽzou, tərázou, tərǽtsou, tarátsou) *n.* a flooring consisting of broken bits of marble or stone set in cement and rubbed to a high polish [Ital.=terrace, balcony]

ter·re·plein (térəplein) *n.* (*fortification*) the platform of a rampart behind the parapet, where the guns are mounted [F.]

ter·res·tri·al (təréstri:əl) **1.** *adj.* earthly (opp. CELESTIAL) || of the earth, *terrestrial motion* || consisting of land, not water || (*zool.*) living on land || (*bot.*) growing on land **2.** *n.* an inhabitant of the earth [fr. L. *terrestris*]

terrestrial magnetism the weak, natural magnetic field of the earth as a whole. Its origin is unknown. It would result at points external to the earth's surface if there were a short bar magnet at the center of the earth, with its south pole pointing to the north magnetic pole of the earth. The intensity and direction of this field varies irregularly over the surface of the earth, both diurnally and over long periods of time, the variations being attributed to the source within the earth and the electric currents in the atmosphere, in space, and flowing between the earth and space (*MAGNETIC MERIDIAN, *DIP, *SUNSPOT CYCLE, *MAGNETIC STORM, *DECLINATION)

terrestrial telescope a refracting telescope with an erecting lens system, used for viewing terrestrial objects

ter·ret (térit) *n.* a ring on a harness pad through which the driving reins pass [O.F. *toret, touret* dim. of *tor, tour,* tour]

ter·ri·ble (térəb'l) *adj.* arousing terror || (*pop.*) excessive, hard to bear, *terrible heat* || (*pop.*) very bad, *a terrible reception* **tér·ri·bly** *adv.* very || in a terrible manner [F.]

ter·ric·o·lous (teríkələs) *adj.* (*biol.*) living in or on the earth [fr. L. *terricola,* earth dweller]

ter·ri·er (téri:ər) *n.* any of various small, exceedingly active dogs which dig into the burrow of the creature they are hunting. There are many breeds, mainly short-haired or rough-haired [F. (*chien*) *terrier*]

Terrier *n.* (*mil.*) a 3,000-lb surface-to-air missile (RIM-2) with solid-fuel rocket engine, equipped with beam-rider homing guidance and a nuclear or nonnuclear warhead capability

ter·rif·ic (təríflk) *adj.* (*pop.*) extreme, very great, very large, or in any way extraordinary, *terrific haste, a terrific success* || (*pop.*) very good indeed, *a terrific welcome* **ter·rif·i·cal·ly** *adv.* [fr. L. *terrificus* fr. *terrere,* to frighten]

ter·ri·fy (térifai) *pres. part.* **ter·ri·fy·ing** *past* and *past part.* **ter·ri·fied** *v.t.* to fill with terror [fr. L. *terrificare*]

ter·rig·e·nous (terídʒənəs) *adj.* (esp. of an ocean floor) produced by erosion from the earth [fr. L. *terrigenus,* born of earth]

ter·ri·to·ri·al (teritɔ́ri:əl, teritóuri:əl) **1.** *adj.* of territory or a territory, *territorial possessions* || of or limited to a specific territory, *territorial waters* **2.** *n.* (*Br.*) a member of the Territorial Army [fr. L.L. *territorialis*]

Territorial Army (*Br.*) a standing, reserve army organized in 1908 on a county basis. It was disbanded (Jan. 1968) on grounds of economy

territorial imperative (*zool.*) possible innate characteristic of animals to define and regard areas as their own; title of book by American writer Robert Ardrey (1908–)

ter·ri·to·ry (téritɔri:, téritouri:) *pl.* **ter·ri·to·ries** *n.* the area ruled by a sovereign or other authority || (*games*) either half of the playing area (e.g. in hockey) with respect to its defense by a team || (*zool.*) an area defended by a male bird or mammal as breeding and feeding ground || a region depending on a foreign government but having some degree of autonomy, *overseas territories* || (*U.S., Canadian* and *Austral. hist.*) an area not admitted to full rights as a state or province || an administrative division || an area allotted to a traveling salesman etc. to cover || a very large tract of country || a sphere or field of scholarship etc. [fr. L. *territorium*]

ter·ror (térər) *n.* great fear || a person or thing that causes great fear || (*pop.*) a person who is a dreadful nuisance **the Terror** the period of the French Revolution from the fall of the Girondists (June 2, 1793) to the fall of Robespierre (July 27, 1794), dominated by the Committee of Public Safety. Its mass executions were intended to galvanize national resistance in the face of foreign invasion [O. F. *terreur*]

ter·ror·ism (térərizəm) *n.* the policy of using acts inspiring terror as a method of ruling or of conducting political opposition [F. *terrorisme*]

ter·ror·ist (térərist) *n.* a person who favors or practices terrorism [F. *terroriste*]

ter·ror·ize (térəraiz) *pres. part.* **ter·ror·iz·ing** *past* and *past part.* **ter·ror·ized** *v.t.* to fill with terror || to dominate by inducing terror

ter·ry (téri:) *pl.* **ter·ries** *n.* one of the uncut loops forming the pile of a pile fabric || terry cloth [origin unknown]

terry cloth a cotton pile fabric made of uncut loops, used e.g. for toweling

terse (tə:rs) *adj.* concise, succinct [fr. L. *tergere* (*tersus*), to wipe]

ter·tial (tə́:rʃəl) **1.** *adj.* (*zool.*) of the flight feathers of a bird's wing **2.** *n.* a tertial feather [fr. L. *tertius,* third]

ter·tian (tə́:rʃən) **1.** *adj.* (*med.,* of a fever) occurring every 48 hours **2.** *n.* (*med.*) a tertian fever [M.E. *fever terciane* or *terciane*]

ter·ti·ar·y (tə́:rʃi:eri:, tə́:rʃəri:) **1.** *adj.* third in order or rank || (*chem.*) characterized by replacement in the third degree or by a carbon atom united by three bonds to chain members || (*eccles.*) of a monastic third (lay) order **Ter·ti·ar·y** of the period of geological time before the Quaternary, marked by the dominance of mammals and by the formation of high mountains such as the Alps and Himalayas (*GEOLOGICAL TIME) **2.** *pl.* **ter·ti·ar·ies** *n.* a tertial feather || (*eccles.*) a member of a monastic third order **the Tertiary** the Tertiary period or system of rocks [fr. L. *tertiarius*]

tertiary care (*med.*) services provided by highly specialized providers, e.g., neurologists, neurosurgeons, thoracic surgeons, intensive care units

tertiary education (*Br.*) education beyond the secondary level, universities, and technical training

tertiary treatment (*envir.*) cleaning of waste water that goes beyond the second or biological state, to remove nutrients, e.g., phosphorous, nitrogen, and most suspended solids

Ter·tul·li·an (tə:rtʌ́li:ən) (Quintus Septimius Florens Tertullianus, c. 160-c. 220), theologian and apologist, born in Carthage. One of the first Christian theologians to write in Latin, he gave the Western Church its terminology. In his 'De praescriptione haereticorum' (197-8) he championed orthodox Trinitarianism and Christology. He was later (c. 210) an influential adherent of Montanism

Ter·uell (terwél) a province (area 5,720 sq. miles, pop. 150,900) of E. Spain (*ARAGON) || its capital (pop. 19,000)

ter·va·lent (tə:rvéilənt) *adj.* (*chem.*) having three valences (cf. TRIVALENT) [fr. L. *ter,* thrice+*valens* (*valentis*) fr. *valere,* to be strong]

ter·za ri·ma (tértsərí:mə) *n.* a verse form consisting of hendecasyllable tercets, rhyming aba, bcb, cdc and so on. It was used by Dante in the 'Divine Comedy' [Ital.=third rhyme]

TESL (*education abbr.*) for teaching English as a second language *Cf* TFL

Tes·la (téslə), Nikola (1856-1943), Croatian-American electrician and inventor who made practical the use of alternating current. He emigrated to the U.S.A. (1884) and worked briefly for Thomas Edison. His demonstration (1888) of how a magnetic field could be made to rotate by supplying two coils at right angles with alternating current of different phases led to his patenting of the alternating-current motor and its sale to George Westinghouse, who made it the basis for the Westinghouse power system. Tesla also did noteworthy research on high-voltage electricity, transformers, telephone and telegraph systems, and plants for wireless power transmission

tes·la (téslə) *n.* a unit of magnetic flue density in the mks system equal to one weber per sq meter; named for Austrian-born electrician Nikola Tesla (1856–1943) *abbr.* T

tes·se·late, tes·sel·late (tésəleit) *pres. part.* **tes·se·lat·ing, tes·sel·lat·ing** *past* and *past part.* **tes·se·lat·ed, tes·sel·lat·ed** *v.t.* to form into mosaic || to decorate with mosaic **tés·se·lat·ed, tés·sel·lat·ed** *adj.* made into a mosaic || (*biol.*) reticulate **tes·se·lá·tion, tes·sel·lá·tion** *n.* [fr. M.L. *tessellare* (*tessellatus*) fr. L. *tessella,* tessera]

tes·ser·a (tésərə) *pl.* **tes·ser·ae** (tésəri:) *n.* a small usually square piece of marble, glass etc. used in mosaic **tés·ser·al** *adj.* [L. fr. Gk]

test (test) **1.** *n.* an examination of the nature or value of anything || the method used in making such an examination || a standard by which a thing's qualities are tried || a set of problems, questions etc. by which a person's knowledge, abilities, aptitudes or character are assessed || a set of circumstances, occurring naturally or deliberately contrived, in which the nature or qualities of a person or thing are revealed, *the race was an endurance test for both driver and car* || (*chem.*) a method or reaction for identifying a substance || the reagent used for this || (*Br., hist.*) a cupel (cup) || (*Br.*) such a cup and its support, which form the hearth of a reverberatory furnace **2.** *v.t.* to submit to a test || (*chem.*) to examine by means of a reagent or reagents [O.F. *test,* pot]

test *n.* (*zool.*) the external shell or hard covering of many invertebrates [fr. L. *testa,* tile, pot]

tes·ta (téstə) *pl.* **tes·tae** (tésti:), **tes·ta** *n.* (*bot.*) the outer coat of a seed [L.]

tes·ta·ceous (testéiʃəs) *adj.* of or of the nature of a shell or shells || having a shell || (*biol.*) of the reddish-brown color of unglazed earthenware [fr. L. *testaceus,* consisting of shell, brick or tile]

Test Act (*Br. hist.*) any of several acts of parliament, in force 1672-1828, requiring a person holding office under the Crown to take oaths of allegiance and supremacy, renounce belief in transubstantiation etc.

tes·ta·cy (téstəsi:) *n.* (*law*) the state of being testate

tes·ta·ment (téstəmənt) *n.* (*law*) a will || (*Bible*) a solemn covenant, esp. the covenant between God and man, *Old Testament* **Tes·ta·ment** a copy of the New Testament books of the Bible [fr. L. *testamentum,* will]

tes·ta·men·ta·ry (testəméntəri:) *adj.* (*law*) of a will or its administration || (*law*) bequeathed by will || (*law*) in accordance with a will [fr. L. *testamentarius*]

tes·tate (téstit) **1.** *adj.* (*law*) having left a legally valid will **2.** *n.* (*law*) a deceased person who left such a will [fr. L. *testari* (*testatus*), to testify]

tes·ta·tor (tésteitər, testéitər) *n.* (*law*) a testate [A.F. *testatour*]

tes·ta·trix (testéitriks) *pl.* **tes·ta·tri·ces** (testéitrisi:z) *n.* (*law*) a female testator [L.L.]

test ban an international agreement not to hold atmospheric tests of nuclear weapons

test case (*law*) a matter submitted for a legal decision in order that a general principle may be established which will govern similar matters

test drive a short trial run of a motor vehicle, esp. in order to determine whether to purchase it **—test-drive** *v.*

tes·ter (téstər) *n.* the frame on which the canopy of a four-poster bed rests, or the canopy and frame together || a baldacain over an altar or pulpit [prob. fr. O.F.]

tes·ti·cle (téstik'l) *n.* one of the two male gonads, the site of production both of male gametes (spermatozoa) and of the male sex hormone (*TESTOSTERONE). In most mammals the testicles are formed inside the developing embryo and descend into the scrotum before the attainment of sexual maturity (*ENDOCRINE GLAND) [fr. L. *testiculus*]

tes·tic·u·late (testíkjulit) *adj.* (*bot.,* of some orchids) having two tubercles shaped like testicles [fr. L.L. *testiculatus*]

tes·ti·fy (téstifai) *pres. part.* **tes·ti·fy·ing** *past* and *past part.* **tes·ti·fied** *v.i.* to bear witness || (*law*) to give evidence || to be evidence || *v.t.* to be evidence of, *his look testified his guilt* || to affirm, esp. under oath [fr. L.L. or M.L. *testificare*]

tes·ti·ly (téstili:) *adv.* in a testy manner

CONCISE PRONUNCIATION KEY: **(a)** æ, *cat*; ɑ, *car*; ɔ *fawn*; ei, *snake*. **(e)** e, *hen*; i:, *sheep*; iə, *deer*; εə, *bear*. **(i)** i, *fish*; ai, *tiger*; ə:, *bird*. **(o)** o, *ox*; au, *cow*; ou, *goat*; u, *poor*; ɔi, *royal*. **(u)** ʌ, *duck*; u, *bull*; u:, *goose*; ə, *bacillus*; ju:, *cube*. x, *loch*; θ, *think*; ð, *bother*; z, *Zen*; ʒ, *corsage*; dʒ, *savage*; ŋ, *orangutang*; j, *yak*; ʃ, *fish*; tʃ, *fetch*; 'l, *rabble*; 'n, *redden*. Complete pronunciation key appears inside front cover.

tes·ti·mo·ni·al (tęstəmóuni:əl) **1.** *n.* a written statement concerning the character of a person or value of a thing ‖ a gift made to show corporate appreciation of services rendered by an individual **2.** *adj.* pertaining to or constituting a testimonial or testimony [O.F.]

tes·ti·mo·ny (téstəmǫuni:) *pl.* **tes·ti·mo·nies** *n.* evidence ‖ something which is evidence ‖ (*law*) an oral or written statement made under oath, esp. by a witness in a legal proceeding [fr. L. *testimonium*]

tes·ti·ness (tésti:nis) *n.* the state or quality of being testy

tes·tis (téstis) *pl.* **tes·tes** (ésti:z) *n.* a testicle [L.]

test match (*cricket*) one of a short series of international cricket matches

tes·tos·ter·one (testóstəroun) *n.* a male sex hormone produced by the testicles that promotes the development of the genital glands and male secondary sexual characteristics, as well as having an influence on the overall growth and vigor of the organism [TESTIS+STEROL]

test pilot a pilot employed to fly and test new aircraft, esp. prototypes

Tes·tra Ben·a·zine [$C_{19}H_{27}NO_3$] (téstrəbénəzi:n) *n.* (*pharm.*) trademark for tranquilizer drug used in treating depression and psychoses

test tube (*chem.*) a glass tube, closed at one end, used in making chemical tests

test-tube baby (test tju:b) **1.** embryo resulting from an egg that is removed from the mother's ovary, fertilized in a test tube with the father's sperm, then inserted into the mother's uterus for term of pregnancy **2.** a baby conceived by this process *Cf* EMBRYO TRANSFER

tes·tu·di·nal (testú:d'n'l, testjú:d'n'l) *adj.* (*zool.*) of or like a tortoise or tortoiseshell **tes·tu·di·nar·i·ous** (testụ:d'néəri:əs, testjụ:d'néəri:əs) *adj.* [fr. L. *testudo* (*testudinis*), tortoise]

tes·tu·di·nate (testú:d'nit, testjú:d'nit) **1.** *n.* a member of *Testudinata* (or *Chelonia*), an order of reptiles comprising turtles and tortoises. Their vertebrae, ribs and dermal bones are fused with a bony box having horny scales **2.** *adj.* of or relating to such a reptile [fr. L.L. *testudinatus*]

tes·tu·do (testú:dou, testjú:dou) *pl.* **tes·tu·dos, tes·tu·di·nes** (testú:d'ni:z, testjú:d'ni:z) *n.* (*Rom. hist.*) a formation of soldiers with their shields held over their heads in close order, used to screen other troops, or to attack the walls of a building or town under siege [L.=tortoise, tortoiseshell]

tes·ty (tésti:) *comp.* **tes·ti·er** *superl.* **tes·ti·est** *adj.* irritable, given to petty fits of ill temper [A.F. *testif*]

te·tan·ic (tətǽnik) *adj.* of, producing or tending to produce tetanus ‖ of, producing or tending to produce tetany [fr. L. *tetanicus* fr. Gk]

tet·a·nus (tét'nəs) *n.* a disease, marked by painful, tonic spasms of the voluntary muscles esp. of the jaw, caused by the bacterial infection of wounds, esp. by bacteria in mud or dust. The disease does not readily answer to treatment, but may be prevented by inoculation ‖ (*physiol.*) a muscular contraction of long duration due to rapid, successive stimuli [L. fr. Gk *tetanos*, spasm]

tet·a·ny (tét'ni:) *n.* (*med.*) a disorder characterized by periodic tonic spasms of the involuntary muscles, caused by deficiency of calcium in the blood due to malfunction of the parathyroid glands [fr. F. *tétanie*, periodic tetanus]

tetch·y, tech·y (tétʃi:) *comp.* **tetch·i·er, tech·i·er** *superl.* **tetch·i·est, tech·i·est** *adj.* irritable, peevish [etym. doubtful]

tête-á-tête (téitətéit, tétətét) **1.** *adv.* between two people, privately **2.** *adj.* confidential, private **3.** *pl.* **tête-á-têtes** *n.* a private conversation between two people [F.]

tête-bêche (tétbéʃ) *adj.* (*philately*, of a pair of stamps) printed so that one stamp is inverted in relation to the other [F. *n.*=pair of inverted stamps fr. *tête*, head+*bêche* fr. obs. *bechevet*, double bed-head]

teth·er (téðər) **1.** *n.* a rope, chain etc. preventing an animal from moving away from a restricted locality **at the end of one's tether** having borne as much as one can bear ‖ at the end of one's financial resources **2.** *v.t.* to attach a tether to [prob. fr. O.N. *tjōthr*]

Tetouan *TETUAN

tetra- (tétrə) *prefix* four, consisting of four ‖ (*chem.*) having four atoms, radicals etc. [Gk fr. *tettares, tettara*, four]

tet·ra·ba·sic (tętrəbéisik) *adj.* (*chem.*) of an acid containing four hydrogen atoms replaceable by basic atoms or radicals

tet·ra·chord (tétrəkǫrd) *n.* (*mus.*) a diatonic series of four notes with an interval of a perfect fourth between the first and last notes, the basic unit of ancient Greek music **tet·ra·chór·dal** *adj.* [fr. Gk *tetrachordon*, a musical instrument fr. *tetra-*, four+*chorde*, string]

tet·rad (tétræd) *n.* a set of four ‖ (*chem.*) a tetravalent element, atom or radical ‖ (*biol.*) a group of four cells produced by the successive divisions of a mother cell ‖ (*biol.*) a temporary grouping of chromosomes by fours formed by the first meiotic division [fr. Gk *tetras* (*tetrad-*), group of four]

tet·ra·dac·tyl (tętrədǽktəl) **1.** *adj.* (of an animal) having four digits **2.** *n.* a tetradactyl animal

tet·ra·dy·na·mous (tętrədáinəməs) *adj.* (*bot.*) having four long stamens and two shorter ones, e.g. in *Cruciferae* [fr. Mod. L. *tetradynamia* fr. Gk *tetra-*, four+*dunamis*, power]

tet·ra·eth·yl lead (tętrəéθəl) a heavy, colorless, poisonous liquid, $Pb(C_2H_5)_4$, added to gasoline to prevent knocking in an internal-combustion engine

tet·ra·gon (tétrəgɒn) *n.* (*geom.*) a four-angled plane figure **te·trag·o·nal** (tetrǽgən'l) *adj.* (*geom.*) having four angles ‖ of a crystal system in which there are three axes at right angles, the two lateral axes being equal [fr. Gk *tetragonon*]

Tet·ra·gram·ma·ton (tętrəgrǽmətɒn) *n.* the word composed of four letters which is the Hebrew name for Jehovah (written JHVH, IHVH, JHWH, YHVH, YHWH, considered too sacred to pronounce) [Gk fr. *tetragrammatos* adj., having four letters]

tet·ra·he·dral (tętrəhí:drəl) *adj.* of, pertaining to or like a tetrahedron [fr. late Gk *tetraëdros*]

tet·ra·he·drite (tętrəhí:drait) *n.* a gray mineral, $(CuFe)_{12}B_4S_{13}$, usually consisting of tetrahedral crystals, worked esp. for the silver and copper which it often contains [G. *tetraëdrit*]

tet·ra·he·dron (tętrəhí:drən) *pl.* **tet·ra·he·drons, tet·ra·he·dra** (tętrəhí:drə) *n.* (*geom.*) a solid figure with four faces, esp. four triangular faces [fr. late Gk *tetraedron*]

tet·ra·hy·dro·can·nab·i·nol [$C_{21}H_{30}O_2$] (tętrəhąidroukənǽbinɔl) *n.* (*chem.*) **1.** a phenol derived from hemp resin that provides the chief intoxicant in marijuana **2.** a synthetic preparation with the same qualities *abbr.* THC

tet·ra·hy·droz·o·line [$C_{13}H_{16}N_2$] (tetrəhaidrɒ́zouli:n) *n.* (*pharm.*) a nasal decongestant; marketed as Tyzine and Visine

tet·ra·hy·men·a (tetrəháimenə) *n.* (*biol.*) a ciliate protozoan commonly used in biochemical (esp. genetic) research

te·tral·o·gy (tetrǽlədʒi:) *pl.* **te·tral·o·gies** *n.* a series of four connected dramatic works, esp. three ancient Greek tragedies followed by a satyric play given at the festival of Dionysus [fr. Gk *tetralogia*]

te·tram·er·al (tetrǽmərəl) *adj.* tetramerous

te·tram·er·ous (tetrǽmərəs) *adj.* (*bot.*) arranged in sets of four ‖ (*zool.*) having four joints in each tarsus [fr. Mod. L. *tetramerus* fr. Gk]

te·tram·e·ter (tetrǽmitər) *n.* (*prosody*) a line of four feet [fr. L. *tetrametrus* fr. Gk]

tet·ra·ploid (tétrəplɔid) **1.** *adj.* having or being four times the haploid number of chromosomes **2.** *n.* a tetraploid organism [TETRA-+-*ploid* fr. DIPLOID and HAPLOID]

tet·ra·pod (tétrəpɒd) **1.** *adj.* having four feet or four limbs **2.** *n.* a four-footed animal, esp. one of the higher vertebrates [fr. Mod. L. *tetrapodus* fr. Gk]

te·trap·ter·ous (tetrǽptərəs) *adj.* (*biol.*) having four wings [Mod. L. *tetrapterus*]

tet·ra·py·rrole or tetrapyrrol (tetrəpáiroul) *n.* (*chem.*) a group of compounds with four pyrole rings connected in a ring, e.g., in chlorophyll, or in a chain, e.g., phycobilins

te·trarch (tí:trɑrk, tétrɑrk) *n.* (*hist.*) a governor of the fourth part of a province of the Roman Empire **té·trarch·ate** *n.* the office of a tetrarch [fr. L.L. *tetrarcha*, L. *tetrarches* fr. Gk]

te·trar·chy (tí:trɑrki: tétrɑrki:) *pl.* **te·trar·chies** *n.* the area governed by a tetrarch ‖ the jurisdiction of a tetrarch [fr. L. L. *tetrarchia*]

tet·ra·spore (tétrəspǫr, tétrəspǫur) *n.* (*bot.*) a group of four asexual nonmotile spores produced by the sporangium of certain algae

tet·ra·stich (tétrəstįk) *n.* a poem or stanza of four lines [fr. L. *tetrastichon* fr. Gk]

te·tras·ti·chous (tetrǽstikəs) *adj.* (*bot.*, e.g. of the flowers on some spikes) arranged in four rows [L.L. *tetrastichus*, of four rows]

tet·ra·syl·lab·ic (tętrəsilǽbik) *adj.* having four syllables [TETRASYLLABLE]

tet·ra·syl·la·ble (tétrəsįləb'l) *n.* a four-syllable word

tet·ra·va·lent (tętrəvéilənt) *adj.* (*chem.*) having a valence of four (cf. QUADRIVALENT) [fr. Gk *tetra-*, four+L. *valens* (*valentis*) fr. *valere*, to be strong]

tet·rode (tétroud) *n.* (*elec.*) a four-electrode electron tube containing an anode, a cathode, a control grid and a screen grid [TETRA-+Gk *hodos*, way]

te·trox·ide (tetrɒ́ksaid) *n.* an oxide containing four oxygen atoms

Te·tuan (tetwɑ́n) (*F.* Tetouan) a city (pop. 137,080) in N. Morocco: food processing, tobacco

Tet·zel (tétsəl), Johann (c. 1465-1519), German Dominican monk. His preaching on indulgences provoked Luther to publish his Wittenberg theses (1517)

Teu·co *BERMEJO

Teu·to·bur·ger Wald, Battle of (tɔ́itoubųərgərvɑ́lt) a battle (9 A.D.) in Westphalia, Germany, in which a group of German tribes annihilated a Roman army, ending Rome's attempts to conquer Germany

Teu·ton (tú:t'n, tjú:t'n) *n.* a member of the Teutonic people, esp. a German ‖ (*hist.*) a member of an ancient German tribe which invaded Gaul and was wiped out by Marius at Aix-en-Provence (102 B.C.) [fr. L. *Teutones, Teutoni* pl. ns.]

Teu·ton·ic (tu:tɒ́nik, tju:tɒ́nik) *adj.* pertaining to the peoples of N. Europe who speak a Germanic language, esp. the Germans ‖ (*hist.*) pertaining to the ancient Teutons [fr. L. *Teutonicus*]

Teutonic Knight a member of a military and religious order founded at Acre (1190-1) by German merchant crusaders during the third Crusade, to care for the sick. It became (1198) an order of knights, confined to Germans of noble birth, and increasingly military. The Teutonic Knights embarked (1229) on a crusade against Prussia, which they ruled during the 13th and 14th cc. The order was secularized in 1525, suppressed by Napoleon in 1809, and revived in Austria in 1840. It became a mendicant order in 1929. A Protestant branch, the bailiwick of Utrecht, exists as a corporation of noblemen

Tew·fik Pasha (tú:fik, tjú:fik) (Mohammed Tewfik, 1852-92), khedive of Egypt (1879-92), son of Ismail Pasha. He was ruler in little more than name, the real power being exercised by Britain and France during his reign

Tewkes·bur·y, Battle of (tú:ksbəri:, tjú:ksbəri:, tú:ksbęri:, tjú:ksbęri:) a battle (1471) in which Edward IV of England defeated Henry VI and Margaret of Anjou during the Wars of the Roses

Tex. Texas

Tex·as (téksəs) (*abbr.* Tex.) a state (area 267,399 sq. miles, pop. 15,280,000) of the southwest U.S.A., on the Gulf of Mexico. Capital: Austin. Chief cities: Houston, Dallas. It is largely a plain, with a wide flat coastal belt and semiarid mountains and plateaus in the extreme west. Agriculture: cotton, sorghums, beef cattle, pecans (first state producer of all these), cereals (incl. rice), vegetables, citrus fruits, dairy and poultry products. Resources: oil and natural gas (first state producer), salt, sulfur, limestone. Industries: chemicals, oil refining, food processing, transport equipment, machinery. State university (1883) at Austin. Texas was explored (16th and 17th cc.) by the Spanish, and was part of Mexico (1821-36). It became an independent republic (1836) and the 28th state of the U.S.A. (1845)

Texas citrus mite a red spider (*Eutetrarychus banksi*) that attacks leaves of citrus trees

'Texas v. White' a ruling (1869) of the U.S. Supreme Court after the Civil War. Invoking the Constitution, the Court declared that secession from the Union was inadmissible, as the United States was 'an indissoluble Union of indissoluble states'

Tex·co·co de Mo·ra (teskɔ́koðemɔ́rɑ) a town in central Mexico, in the state of Mexico. Originally it was the city-state of the kingdom of the Chichimecas, whose most famous monarch was Netzahualcoyotl

text (tekst) *n.* the sustained narrative, train of thought or argument etc. in a written or printed

CONCISE PRONUNCIATION KEY: **(a)** æ, *cat*; ɑ, *car*; ɔ *fawn*; ei, *snake*. **(e)** e, *hen*; i:, *sheep*; iə, *deer*; εə, *bear*. **(i)** i, *fish*; ai, *tiger*; ə:, *bird*. **(o)** o, *ox*; au, *cow*; ou, *goat*; u, *poor*; ɔi, *royal*. **(u)** ʌ, *duck*; u, *bull*; u:, *goose*; ə, *bacillus*; ju:, *cube*. x, *loch*; θ, *think*; ð, *bother*; z, *Zen*; ʒ, *corsage*; dʒ, *savage*; ŋ, *orangutang*; j, *yak*; ʃ, *fish*; tʃ, *fetch*; 'l, *rabble*; 'n, *redden*. Complete pronunciation key appears inside front cover.

work, as distinguished from footnotes, commentaries etc. ‖ the subject matter of a speech etc., esp. as written down ‖ a short extract from the Scriptures, often used as the theme of a sermon ‖ an author's original writing, as compared with e.g. a translation of it ‖ a particular version of a writing, *the First Folio text* ‖ the wording used in something written, engraved etc. ‖ (*mus.*) a printed score ‖ (*mus.*) the words of a song, libretto etc. or the words of a poem etc. set to music ‖ a textbook [F. *texte*]

text·book (tékstbu̦k) *n.* a book written and published for use by students as a basis for their studies

text hand a large style of handwriting (from the custom of writing the text in a larger hand than the notes etc.)

tex·tile (tékstil, tékstail, tékstəl) **1.** *adj.* woven ‖ suitable for weaving ‖ pertaining to weaving **2.** *n.* a woven fabric ‖ a fiber suitable for weaving [fr. L. *textilis,* woven and *textile opus,* woven fabric]

textile finishing the final treatment of a fabric, after it has been woven, dyed or printed, designed to give it special qualities (impermeability etc.), esp. surface qualities of glossiness (*CALENDERING), fleeciness etc.

textile printing a process of imprinting colored patterns on a fabric by means of a roller or press, in contrast to interweaving or dyeing

tex·tu·al (tékstʃu:əl) *adj.* pertaining to a literary text, *textual criticism* ‖ contained in the text, *textual errors* [O.F. *textuel*]

textual criticism the close study and analysis of a literary text, esp. to determine the best reading ‖ a method of literary criticism based on close study of the text itself rather than on sources, biography etc.

tex·tu·al·ly (tékstʃu:əli:) *adv.* as regards the text ‖ verbatim

text·ure (tékstʃər) *n.* the distinctive character of a textile fabric which results from the quality of its threads and the way these are woven ‖ the parts of a whole thought of as woven like a textile fabric ‖ the structure of a rock, tissue etc. ‖ (*arts*) the quality produced by the arrangement, treatment or handling of a medium, material etc., *the rich texture of the orchestration* [fr. L. *textura,* a weaving]

T-50 *n.* (*mil.*) Chinese main battle tank, with 85-mm guns

T-55 *n.* (*mil.*) U.S.S.R. main battle tank, with 100-mm gun, eight machine guns; considered obsolescent

TFL (*education abbr.*) for teaching English as a foreign language *Cf* TESL

TG (*linguistics abbr.*) for **1.** transformational generative **2.** transformational grammar

T-group (tí:gru:p) *n.* (*psych.*) short for training group, a form of psychotherapy depending on the process of feedback from interactions within the group in a psychologically unthreatening environment *Cf* ENCOUNTER GROUP, SENSITIVITY TRAINING

-th *suffix* used to denote a state or condition, as in 'warmth' [part O. Gmc., part O.E. or O.N.]

-th *suffix* used to indicate ordinal numbers after three, as in 'fourth' [fr. O.E. *-pa, -pe* or *-opa, -ope*]

Th (*chem.*) thorium

Thack·er·ay (θǽkəri:), William Makepeace (1811-83), English novelist. He wrote the 'History of Henry Esmond' (1852), 'Vanity Fair' (1847-8), 'Pendennis' (1848-50), 'The Newcomes' (1853-5), 'The Virginians' (1857-9) and books of lectures and essays. Like his near contemporary Dickens, Thackeray was a popular writer, working for the enlarged reading public of his day and esp. for serial publication. Both authors were humorists, sentimentalists and social satirists. But instead of writing about the lower classes and social abuses, Thackeray satirized romantic sentimentality and the snobbishness and futility of upper-class life

Thad·dae·us (θǽdi:əs), St *JUDE, St

Thai·land (táilænd) (formerly Siam) a kingdom (area 198,250 sq. miles, pop. 52,700,000) in S.E. Asia. Capital: Bangkok. People: 94% Thai, with Chinese, Malay, and smaller Cambodian, Annamese, Shan and Burmese minorities. Language: Thai, some Chinese and English. Religion: 90% Hinayana Buddhism, 4% Moslem, with small Confucianist and Christian minorities. 60% of the land is forest. 16% is cultivated in the central basin and 7% elsewhere. The central alluvial plain (under 150 ft) of the Chao Phraya is surrounded by mountains, highest in the northwest (Doi Inthanon 8,514 ft). N. Thailand, between the Salween and the Mekong, is a region of deep valleys (1,000 ft) and mountain ranges (5,000-8,000 ft) covered with hardwood forest, running north-south. The east is a shallow, sparsely populated sandstone basin. Mountains running the length of the southern peninsula (rain forest) rise to 3,000 ft. Average temperatures (F.): Bangkok 77° (Dec.) and 86° (Apr.). Rainfall: north and center 50 ins, Chao Phraya delta 40-50 ins, Bangkok 77 ins, eastern basin 15 ins, Isthmus of Kra 130 ins. Livestock: water buffaloes, cattle, hogs, horses, elephants. Agricultural products: rice, corn, sugarcane, copra, peanuts, cotton, kenaf, tobacco, sesame, coconuts, beans, rubber, fruit. Forestry products: teak and other hardwoods, gurjun, charcoal. Mineral resources (mainly in the peninsula): tin, lead, coal, copper, lignite, wolfram, antimony, manganese, iron ore, fluorite, gypsum, silver, gold, tungsten, semiprecious stones, salt. Industries: textiles, paper, cement, sugar refining, fishing, furniture, tourism. Exports: rice, rubber, corn, tin, tapioca, jute, teak. Imports: manufactures, machinery, fuels and oil, chemicals, foodstuffs. Chief port: Bangkok. There are six universities, the oldest being Chulalongkorn, Bangkok (1917). Monetary unit: baht (100 satang). HISTORY. Asian tribes settled in Thailand (c. 1st c. A.D.). Thais from the mountains of Yunnan moved down into the valley and set up several independent kingdoms. The country came under the influence of the Khmer kingdom (c. 10th c.), but asserted its independence (14th c.) under a new line of kings with their capital at Ayudhya. Wars followed with the Burmese and the Cambodians until the 19th c. The Portuguese began trading with Thailand (1511) and were replaced by the British, the Dutch and the French (17th c.). A coup d'état (1688) largely cut Siam off from foreign influence. Ayudhya was destroyed (1767) by the Burmese, and the capital was moved to Bangkok (late 18th c.) by the founder of the present ruling dynasty. Thailand was again opened to Western influence (mid-19th c.) and many Western reforms were introduced. France forced Thailand to surrender its claims to Cambodia (1867) and Laos (1893). Kedah, Kelantan, Trengganu and Perlis were ceded to Britain (1909). Thailand joined the Allies (1917) in the 1st world war. A coup d'état (1932) resulted in a constitutional monarchy. After attempting to seize back the regions it had lost to French Indochina, Thailand was invaded by the Japanese (1941-4). It joined the U.N. (1946) and SEATO (1954). A coup d'état (1951) restored the 1932 constitution. Britain, Australia and the U.S.A. contributed to Thailand's defense against Communist infiltration from Laos (1960s)

Thai, Tai (tai) *pl.* **Thais, Thai, Tais, Tai** *n.* a native or inhabitant or a descendant of a native or inhabitant of Thailand ‖ the language of Thailand ‖ a race of people living in parts of Thailand, Laos, North Vietnam, S. China and Burma ‖ a group of languages usually considered as belonging to the Sino-Tibetan language group

thal·a·men·ceph·a·lon (θæləmenséfəlɒn) *n.* the diencephalon [fr. Gk *thalamos,* thalamus+ENCEPHALON]

thal·a·mus (θǽləməs) *pl.* **thal·a·mi** (θǽləmai) *n.* the receptacle of a flower ‖ the larger portion of the diencephalon (*BRAIN) that is a major sensory coordinating area, sending sensory impulses to the cerebral cortex [L.]

thal·as·se·m·ia (θæləsí:mi:ə) *n.* (*med.*) a congenital form of anemia, esp. among Mediterranean peoples, due to impaired synthesis of a polypeptide chain —**thalassemic** *adj.*

tha·las·sic (θəlǽsik) *adj.* of or relating to the sea ‖ of or relating to bays, gulfs and small bodies of water or inland seas [F. *thalassique* fr. Gk]

tha·las·so chemistry (θəlǽsou) chemistry of sea water

tha·las·so·pho·bi·a (θəlæsəfóubi:ə) *n.* abnormal fear of the sea —**thalassophobe** *n.* —**thalassophobic** *adj.*

tha·las·so·ther·a·py (θəlæsəθérəpi:) *n.* treatment of illness by sea voyages —**thalassotherapeutic** *adj.*

thaler *TALER

Tha·les (θéili:z) (c. 640–c. 547 B.C.), philosopher of Miletus, one of the Seven Sages of Greece. He was also renowned as a mathematician, statesman and astronomer. He predicted the total eclipse of the sun which occurred on May 25, 585 B.C. He believed that water was the origin of the world

Tha·li·a (θəláiə, θéili:ə) (*Gk mythol.*) the Muse of comedy ‖ one of the three Graces, patroness of festivities

tha·lid·o·mide [$C_{13}H_{10}N_2O_4$] (θəlídəmaid) *n.* (*pharm.*) a sedative and hypnotic drug that was found to be responsible for malformed offspring when used during pregnancy —**thalidomide embryopathy** *n.* the malformation

thal·lic (θǽlik) *adj.* of, relating to or containing thallium, esp. of compounds in which it is trivalent

thal·li·um (θǽli:əm) *n.* a bluish-white, usually monovalent but sometimes trivalent, metallic element (symbol Tl, at. no. 81, at. mass 204.37), resembling soft lead. Thallium compounds are very poisonous and are used esp. in pesticides [fr. Gk *thallos,* green shoot (because of the bright green line of the thallium spectrum)]

thal·loid (θǽlɔid) *adj.* (*bot.*) of, resembling or consisting of a thallus

thal·lo·phyte (θǽləfait) *n.* a member of *Thallophyta,* a primary division or subkingdom of the plant kingdom including algae, fungi and bacteria (cf. EMBRYOPHYTE) [fr. Mod. L. *Thallophyta* pl. n. fr. Gk *thallos,* green shoot+*phuton,* plant]

thal·lous (θǽləs) *adj.* of or relating to thallium, esp. of compounds in which the element is monovalent

thal·lus (θǽləs) *pl.* **thal·li** (θǽlai), **thal·lus·es** *n.* the plant body of a thallophyte that does not possess any organs or tissues homologous with those of higher plants but is composed of parts performing the same functions as the root, stem, leaves and vascular system of higher plants. There is wide variation in size and form of thalli, from microscopic one-celled plants to complex treelike marine algae [L. fr. Gk *thallos,* green shoot]

thal·weg (túlveg, túlveik) *n.* the principle of law widely adopted in the Americas to establish the exact territorial limit where a border runs along a river. The limit is taken as the deepest point of the river, as against the principle adopted in Europe of taking the midpoint [G., fr. *Thal,* valley+*weg,* way]

Thames (temz) a river (209 miles long) rising in the Cotswolds, S. England, and flowing east to the North Sea, navigable by large ships to London

Thames, Battle of the an engagement (1813) on the Thames River near Chatham, Ont., during the War of 1812. A U.S. force commanded by Gen. William H. Harrison defeated the British and their Indian supporters. The victory restored U.S. supremacy in the Northwest

than (ðæn, *unstressed* ðən) **1.** *conj.* used after a comparative adjective or adverb to connect the first to the second part of a comparison, *he runs faster than you, we finished sooner than we expected* ‖ used to express difference of kind, manner etc., *nothing other than a two-year contract would satisfy him* ‖ when, *hardly were the words uttered than he began to regret them* **2.** *prep.* (only in phrases) **than whom, than which** compared to whom, compared to which, *than which there is nothing better* [O.E. *thanne, thonne, thænne*]

than·age (θéinidʒ) *n.* the land held by a thane ‖ the tenure of this land ‖ the office of a thane

thane, thegn (θein) *n.* (*Eng. hist.*) a freeman (in Anglo-Saxon England) holding land in return for military service to a noble [O.E. *thegen, thegn, thēn*]

thank (θæŋk) **1.** *v.t.* to express gratitude to ‖ to hold responsible for, *we can thank him for our loss* **to have oneself to thank** to be oneself to blame for one's loss, failure etc., *if you get into trouble you'll have only yourself to thank* [O.E. *thancian, thoncian*]

thank·ful (θǽŋkfəl) *adj.* feeling or expressing gratitude [fr. obs. *thank,* thanks]

thank·less (θǽŋklis) *adj.* (of a person) ungrateful ‖ (of a task or occupation) unproductive, unprofitable, unrewarding [fr. obs. *thank,* thanks]

thank offering something offered as an expression of gratitude, esp. to God

thanks (θæŋks) *pl. n.* gratitude or an expression of gratitude ‖ a formula usually without a following verb for expressing gratitude, *thanks for telling me* ‖ grace before or after a meal, *to return thanks* **thanks to** owing to ‖ with the help of **no** (esp. *Br.* **small**) **thanks to** without any help from ‖ in spite of [O.E. *thanc, thonc*]

CONCISE PRONUNCIATION KEY: **(a)** æ, *cat;* ɑ, *car;* ɔ *fawn;* ei, *snake.* **(e)** e, *hen;* i:, *sheep;* iə, *deer;* εə, *bear.* **(i)** i, *fish;* ai, *tiger;* ə:, *bird.* **(o)** o, *ox;* au, *cow;* ou, *goat;* u, *poor;* ɔi, *royal.* **(u)** ʌ, *duck;* u, *bull;* u:, *goose;* ə, *bacillus;* ju:, *cube.* x, *loch;* θ, *think;* ð, *bother;* z, *Zen;* ʒ, *corsage;* dʒ, *savage;* ŋ, *orangutang;* j, *yak;* ʃ, *fish;* tʃ, *fetch;* 'l, *rabble;* 'n, *redden.* Complete pronunciation key appears inside front cover.

thanks·giv·ing (θæŋksgívịŋ) *n.* the act of expressing thanks, esp. to God **Thanksgiving** *n.* Thanksgiving Day

Thanksgiving Day a day, the fourth Thursday in November, set apart in the U.S.A. for recalling the goodness of God in blessing the Pilgrims with their first good harvest (1621) and, by association, for thanking God for all his bounty ‖ (in Canada) the second Monday in October, similarly kept as a national holiday

Thant (tɑnt, θɑnt), U (1909-74), Burmese diplomat, secretary-general of the U.N. (1962-72)

Thar (tɑr) (or Indian Desert) a sandy desert (about 100,000 sq. miles) in Rajasthan, India, and West Pakistan

Tha·sos (θéisɒs) a wooded, mountainous Greek island (area 152 sq. miles, pop. 15,000) off the Macedonian coast: olives, wine, marble

that (ðæt) **1.** *pl.* **those** (ðouz) *adj.* designating the person to whom or thing to which attention is drawn, *he will like that one, take that road* ‖ designating one of two things which are compared or contrasted, *this hat is cheaper than that one* ‖ designating the person or thing further away than another, *she can reach this shelf but not that one* ‖ designating some well-known person or thing not described, *oh, that laugh of his!* **2.** *pl.* those *pron.* (demonstrative) the person or thing indicated or understood, *that will be enough, those who agree are in the majority* ‖ the thing farther away, *she can reach this but not that* ‖ one of two things which are compared or contrasted, *this is cheaper than that* ‖ (relative, used in restrictive clauses, or often omitted) who, whom or which, *the play that we saw together* or when, *the day that he was born* **3.** *adv.* (*pop.*) to such a degree, *he isn't that blind and is sure to notice* ‖ to an extent previously designated or about to be designated, *you shouldn't spend that much* **4.** *conj.* introducing a noun clause, *she saw that he was ill* ‖ introducing a causal clause, *he regrets that he was too ill to come* ‖ (*rhet.*) introducing a clause expressing purpose, *she did it that he might go free* ‖ introducing a clause expressing a result, *he drove so fast that he had an accident* ‖ (*rhet.*) introducing an elliptical sentence expressing surprise, indignation, a wish etc., *would that the end might never come!* **at that** even so, what is more ‖ at that point **in that** because, insofar as, *he was right in that the name had not changed, but...* **that is, that is to say** used to introduce a further explanation of something previously stated, explained, discussed etc. **that's that** that's settled, finished [O.E. *thæt*]

thatch (θætʃ) **1.** *v.t.* to cover with thatch **2.** *n.* a covering, esp. for a roof, made of straw, reeds, leaves, rushes etc. ‖ this material [O.E. *theccan, theccean*]

Thatch·er (θǽtʃər), Margaret Hilda (1925-), Britain's first woman prime minister (1979-). A member of the House of Commons from 1959, she became secretary of state for education and science when the Conservatives returned to power (1970). She replaced Edward Heath as Conservative party leader (1975) and when her party won a decisive victory in a general election (1979) she became the first woman prime minister in European history. Her popularity eroded (1981) when cuts in government spending and strict control of the money supply contributed to Britain's worst recession since the 1930s. The Falkland Islands War (1982), which restored British sovereignty in the Falklands through military force to expel Argentina, was extremely popular. Her government was reelected (1983), winning a substantial majority in Parliament. Her decision to allow British-based U.S. jets to attack Libya and her stand opposing economic sanctions against South Africa caused controversy in 1986

Thau·mas (θɔ́məs) (*Gk mythol.*) father of the Harpies

thau·ma·turge (θɔ́mətə:rdʒ) *n.* someone who works or supposedly works miracles **thau·ma·túr·gic, thau·ma·tur·gi·cal** *adjs* [fr. M.L. *thaumaturgus* fr. Gk]

thau·ma·tur·gy (θɔ́mətə:rdʒi:) *n.* the working of miracles or supposed miracles [fr. Gk *thaumatourgia*]

thaw (θɔ) **1.** *v.i.* (esp. of ice, snow or frozen food) to become liquid or soft due to the temperature rising above freezing point ‖ (of weather) to become warm enough to melt ice or snow ‖ to become less hard, less numb, less icy etc. as a result of being warmed ‖ to become more friendly, less stiff in manner ‖ *v.t.* to cause to thaw ‖ to cause to become more friendly **2.** *n.* a thawing ‖ (of weather) warmth which will cause a thaw ‖ a becoming less stiff in manner [O.E. *thawian*]

THC *TETRAHYDROCANNABINOL

the (ðə *before consonants,* ði: *before vowels and when used emphatically*) **1.** *adj.* the definite article used to denote a person or thing or persons or things being spoken of or already mentioned, *the paint is dry* ‖ used to denote that which is present, near at hand etc., *the soup is good* ‖ used before the names of things which are unique or designated or identified by a title, *the Irrawaddy, the Prince of Wales* ‖ used emphatically to denote best, best-known, most valued etc., *he is the best composer for me* ‖ (equivalent to a possessive pronoun) used of something belonging to a person already mentioned, *take her by the elbow* or of someone in an understood family relationship, *how are the children?* ‖ (*commerce*) for every, per, each, *potatoes at 2 dollars the sack* ‖ used to denote the particular person or thing or particular kind out of many, identified by a modifier, *the next house, the man who lives there, the car of the year, the duty to vote, the spoken word* ‖ used to denote a person, animal etc. considered generically, *the rose is my favorite flower* ‖ preceding an adjective used substantivally, *the young, the occult* **2.** *adv.* (used before a comparative adjective or adverb) to that extent, in that degree, *it is the more precious because of its association* ‖ **the... the** to what extent... to that extent, *the sooner the better* [O.E. *se* masc. nom. (with 'th-' from other genders and cases)]

the·an·throp·ic (θi:ənθrɒ́pik) *adj.* being both God and man **the·an·thro·pism** (θi:ǽnθrəpizəm) *n.* the theological doctrine of the union of divine and human nature in the incarnate Christ ‖ the attributing of human characteristics to the divine ‖ belief in a theanthropic being [fr. eccles. Gk *theanthrōpos* fr. *theos*, god+*anthrōpos*, man]

the·ar·chy (θí:ɑrki:) *pl.* **the·ar·chies** *n.* a political system under which men are governed by God or gods ‖ a class or body of ruling gods [fr. eccles. *Gk thearchia* fr. *theos*, god+*-archia*, a ruling]

theater of cruelty dramatic art form designed to convey sense of suffering and evil by creating a nonverbal atmosphere and utilizing various shock techniques, originated in the 1930s by French surrealist actor and writer Antonin Artaud (1896–1948), who saw such drama as a ceremonial act of purgation

theater of fact dramatic presentations based on current events, often utilizing involved personalities and actual public statements and words from the news

theater of involvement dramatic presentations designed to shock and upset middle-class standards and so to create social change

theater of panic (*Fr., théâtre panique*) theater characterized by a contrasting blend of rustic vitality (Pan), tragedy and fun, refinement and bad taste; coined by Fernando Arrabal (1932–)

theater of protest dramatic presentations, e.g., street theater, designed to influence public opinion in favor of social change

theater of the absurd dramatic presentations that depict the absurdity of the human condition in an incomprehensible universe by abandoning realistic form and utilizing fantastic or other eccentric means

theater of the mind dramatic presentations designed to simulate a psychedelic milieu, e.g., with flashing lights, hallucinogenic background

theater of the streets *STREET THEATER

the·a·ter, the·a·tre (θí:ətər) *n.* a building or open space where dramatic performances are given, furnished with a stage for the actors and seats for the audience ‖ dramatic art, *it makes good theater* ‖ the written dramatic literature of a country, period or person, *the theater of Elizabethan England* ‖ a place where dramatic events occur, *a theater of war* ‖ a room furnished with a demonstration bench and tiers of seats, used for teaching and demonstrating ‖ (*Br.*) an operating theater [fr. L. *theatrum* fr. Gk]

the·a·ter·go·er, the·a·tre·go·er (θi:ətərgouər) *n.* a person who attends the theater frequently

the·at·ri·cal (θi:ǽtrik'l) *adj.* of or pertaining to the theater, *a theatrical entertainment* ‖ suggesting the theater, *theatrical gestures* **the·at·ri·cal·ism, the·at·ri·cál·i·ty** *ns* **the·at·ri·cals** *pl. n.* dramatic performances (esp. amateur and private) [fr. L.L. *theatricus* fr. Gk]

the·at·rics (θi:ǽtriks) *n.* theatrical performances ‖ theatrical behavior or effects [fr. L.L. *theatricus*, of the theater, fr. Gk]

Thebes (θi:bz) an ancient city of Upper Egypt on the Nile, the site of two modern villages, Luxor and Karnak. It was the capital of the Middle Kingdom. Restored by the Ptolemies and the Romans, it was destroyed by an earthquake (27 B.C.). Principal ruins: tombs of the Kings (in the Valley of the Kings, across the Nile from Luxor and Karnak) and several temples of Ammon, esp. the Great Temple (begun in the 12th dynasty) at Karnak

Thebes (modern Thiva, pop. 15,899) an ancient city of Boeotia which became for a short period (mid-4th c. B.C.) the leading power in Greece, under Epaminondas

the·ca (θí:kə) *pl.* **the·cae** (θí:si:) *n.* (*bot.*) a spore case, sac or capsule ‖ (*anat., zool.*) a structure serving as a protective covering for an organ or for a whole organism, e.g. the spinal cord, follicle or pupa [L. fr. Gk *thēkē*, a case]

thee (ði:) pron. objective case of THOU [O.E. *thec, theh*, accusative of *thu, thū*, thou and *the*, dative of *thu, thū*]

theft (θeft) *n.* the act of stealing something ‖ an instance of this

thegn *THANE

the·ine (θí:i:n, θí:ain) *n.* (*chem.*) caffeine [fr. Mod. L. *thea*, tea]

their (ðεər) *possessive adj.* of, belonging to or done by them [fr. O.N. *theira, theirra* genitive pl. of demonstrative *sā, sū*, that, the]

theirs (ðεərz) *possessive pron.* that or those belonging to them, *the fault is theirs* [THEIR]

the·ism (θí:izəm) *n.* the belief in a god or gods, esp. belief in the one God who created and rules the universe (cf. ATHEISM, cf. DEISM) [fr. Gk *theos*, god]

the·ist (θí:ist) *n.* someone who believes in theism **the·ís·tic** *adj.* [fr. Gk *theos*, god]

them (ðem) *pron.* objective case of THEY, *we caught them* [M.E. *theim, theym* fr. O.N. *theim*]

the·mat·ic (θi:mǽtik) *adj.* of or constituting a theme **the·mát·i·cal·ly** *adv.* [fr. Gk *thematikos*]

thematic apperception test (*psych.*) projective psychological test in which the subject describes or otherwise responds to a series of black-and-white pictures, developed by American psychometrist Henry Murray (1892–) *abbr.* TAT

theme (θi:m) *n.* the matter with which a speech, essay etc. is chiefly concerned ‖ (*gram.*) a stem ‖ (*mus.*) a structurally important element of a composition developed, repeated, inverted etc. ‖ an entire musical passage on which variations are based ‖ a short composition set by a schoolteacher ‖ a signature tune [M.E. *teme* fr. O.F.]

theme song a recurrent song in a musical, movie etc. ‖ a signature tune

The·mis (θí:mis) (*Gk mythol.*) the goddess of justice or law

The·mis·to·cles (θimístəkli:z) (c. 525-c. 460 B.C.), Athenian statesman and general. As leader of the democratic party during the Persian Wars he determined the strategy which led to the decisive Greek naval victory at Salamis (480 B.C.) and the retreat of Xerxes I. Accused of treason and corruption, he was ostracized (c. 471 B.C.) and fled to Persia, where he was well received by Artaxerxes I

them·selves (ðəmsélvz) *pl. pron.* refl. form of THEY, *they hurt themselves* ‖ emphatic form of THEY, *they themselves escaped unhurt*

then (ðen) **1.** *adv.* at that time, *he was not there then* ‖ at the time immediately following, *he shut the door and then locked it* ‖ at another time, *if you are going to be in this neighborhood I will see you then* ‖ next in sequence, order etc., *first come the girls and then the boys* ‖ in addition, *and then there's the problem of finding capable nurses* ‖ consequently, as a logical result, *if you didn't bring it then you must be very forgetful* **2.** *adj.* being at an understood past time, *the then headmaster ordered these books* ‖ **3.** *n.* that time, *since then I have not seen him* [O.E. *thanne, thænne, thonne*]

then and there at once, immediately

the·nar (θí:nɑr) **1.** *n.* the palm of the hand or the sole of the foot ‖ the muscular ball at the base of the thumb **2.** *adj.* of a thenar [Mod. L. fr. Gk]

thence (ðens) *adv.* (*rhet.*) from that place or that time ‖ for that reason ‖ (*rhet.*) from that source [M.E. *thennes, thannes* fr. earlier *thenne*]

thence·forth (ðénsfɔ́rθ, ðénsfóurθ) *adv.* from that time onward

thence·for·ward (ðénsfɔ́rwərd) *adv.* thenceforth

thence·for·wards (ðénsfɔ́rwərdz) *adv.* thenceforth

the·o·bro·mine (θi:əbróumi:n) *n.* (*chem.*) a bitter crystalline alkaloid, resembling caffeine, contained in cacao beans, and to a less extent in kola nuts and tea, used as a heart stimulant and diuretic [fr. Mod. L. *Theobroma*, a genus of trees including cacao fr. Gk *theos*, god+*broma*, food]

the·o·cen·tric (θi:əséntrik) *adj.* centered in God [fr. Gk *theos*, god+ *kentrikos*, in or at the center]

the·oc·ra·cy (θi:ɒ́krəsi:) *pl.* **the·oc·ra·cies** *n.* government by priests or men claiming to know the will of God ‖ a state thus governed [fr. Gk *theokratia*]

the·oc·ra·sy (θi:ɒ́krəsi:) *n.* a mixing of several gods in one in the minds of worshipers ‖ the identification of one god with another in worship ‖ an act of union of the soul with the supreme spirit resulting from contemplation [fr. Gk *theokrasia*]

the·o·crat (θí:əkræt) *n.* a ruler in a theocracy ‖ someone who advocates theocracy [THEOCRATIC]

the·o·crat·ic (θi:əkrǽtik) *adj.* of or pertaining to a theocracy [fr. Gk *theokratia*, theocracy]

The·oc·ri·tus (θi:ɒ́kritəs) (3rd-2nd cc. B.C.), Greek poet born at Syracuse, author of the 'Idylls'. He was the first to write bucolic poems

the·od·i·cy (θi:ɒ́disi:) *pl.* **the·od·i·cies** *n.* vindication of the justice and goodness of God in spite of the existence of evil in the world ‖ natural theology [fr. F. *'Théodicée'*, a work by Leibniz fr. Gk *theos*, god+*dikē*, justice]

the·od·o·lite (θi:ɒ́d'lait) *n.* an instrument used by surveyors to measure vertical and horizontal angles, consisting of a small telescope moving along a graduated scale [origin unknown]

The·o·do·ra (θi:ədɔ́rə, θi:ədóurə) (c. 508-48), Byzantine empress (527-48), consort of Justinian I, over whom she exercised great influence

The·od·o·ric (θi:ɒ́dərik) 'the Great' (c. 454-526), king of the Ostrogoths (c. 474-526). Encouraged by the Byzantine emperor Zeno, he invaded Italy (488) and defeated (489-93) Odoacer, the Gothic king. He had Odoacer murdered (493). He took the title 'king of Italy', and he ruled well, preserving Roman laws and institutions, repairing roads and public buildings, and showing toleration toward the Roman Catholic Church

The·o·do·si·us I (θi:ədóuʃi:əs, θi:ədóuʃəs) 'the Great' (c. 346-95), Roman emperor (379-95). He was appointed by Gratian to rule the eastern part of the empire after the death of Valens. He also administered the western part in the name of Valentinian II after the death (388) of Maximus. A Christian, he established Catholicism as the official religion (380), condemned both Arianism and paganism, and convened the Council of Constantinople (381). On his death, the division of the Roman Empire became final, Arcadius inheriting the east and Honorius the west

Theodosius II (401-50), Byzantine emperor (408-50), son of Arcadius. He was forced to pay increasing amounts of tribute to the Huns under Attila. The Council of Ephesus (431) was held during his reign, and the Codex Theodosianus, a summary of imperial legislation since Constantine I, was compiled (438)

the·o·gon·ic (θi:əgɒ́nik) *adj.* of or relating to theogony

the·og·o·ny (θi:ɒ́gəni:) *pl.* **the·og·o·nies** *n.* the origin, generation or descent of the gods, as told in myths [fr. Gk *theogonia*]

the·o·lo·gian (θi:əlóudʒən) *n.* a person who is learned in theology [F. *théologien*]

the·o·log·i·cal (θi:əlɒ́dʒik'l) *adj.* of or relating to theology

theological virtues the three virtues: faith, hope and charity

the·ol·o·gize (θi:ɒ́lədʒaiz) *pres. part.* **the·ol·o·giz·ing** *past* and *past part.* **the·ol·o·gized** *v.i.* to write or speculate about theology ‖ *v.t.* to treat from the point of view of theology, to fit into a theological scheme [fr. M.L. *theologizare* and prob. THEOLOGY]

the·ol·o·gy (θi:ɒ́lədʒi:) *pl.* **the·ol·o·gies** *n.* the science which studies God and all that relates to him, including religion and morals. Christian theology has many branches, e.g. ascetical (dealing with training in virtue), dogmatic (the formulation of doctrine), moral (the behavior of man in the light of his final destiny), mystical (contemplation of union with God), natural (in which God is known by the light of human reason alone), pastoral (dealing with the care of souls) and positive (dealing with revealed truth) ‖ a particular system of religious teaching and practice [F. *théologie* fr. L. fr. Gk]

the·om·a·chy (θi:ɒ́məki:) *pl.* **the·om·a·chies** *n.* war or a battle among the gods [fr. Gk *theomachia*]

the·o·mor·phic (θi:əmɔ́rfik) *adj.* made in the image of a deity [fr. Gk *theomorphos*]

the·oph·a·ny (θi:ɒ́fəni:) *pl.* **the·oph·a·nies** *n.* the appearance of God or a deity in a form visible to man [fr. L.L. *theophania* fr. Gk]

The·oph·i·lus (θi:ɒ́fələs), St (2nd c.), bishop of Antioch, a Father of the Christian Church, author of the 'Apologia'. Feast: Dec. 20

The·o·phras·tus (θi:əfrǽstəs) (c. 372–c. 287 B.C.), Greek philosopher. He succeeded Aristotle as head of the Lyceum. He wrote scientific and philosophical treatises, but is best known for 'Characters', a collection of vivid sketches depicting various ethical types. The book was widely imitated by later writers

the·or·bo (θi:ɔ́rbou) *n.* (*hist.*) a musical instrument, a lute with a double neck to accommodate extra bass strings, played esp. in the 17th c. [fr. F. *théorbe, téorbe* fr. Ital.]

the·o·rem (θí:ərəm, θíərəm) *n.* (*math.*) a statement susceptible of logical proof when certain facts are accepted as true ‖ (*math.*) an expression of a rule or relationship in terms of a formula or symbols, *binomial theorem* [F. *théorème* or fr. L.L. *theorema* fr. Gk]

the·o·ret·ic (θi:ərétik) *adj.* theoretical [fr. L. L. *theoreticus* fr. Gk]

the·o·ret·i·cal (θi:ərétik'l) *adj.* based on theory, not on factual knowledge ‖ of, pertaining to or being theory ‖ tending to theorize **the·o·re·ti·cian** (θi:əretíʃən) *n.* a theorist [fr. L.L. *theoreticus* fr. Gk]

the·o·ret·ics (θi:ərétiks) *pl. n.* the speculative parts of a science or art [THEORETIC]

the·o·rist (θí:ərist) *n.* someone who theorizes [THEORY]

the·o·rize (θí:əraiz) *pres. part.* **the·o·riz·ing** *past* and *past part.* **the·o·rized** *v.i.* to engage in constructing a theory or theories ‖ *v.t.* to construct a theory or theories about

the·o·ry (θí:əri:, θíəri:) *pl.* **the·o·ries** *n.* an organized body of ideas as to the truth of something, usually derived from the study of a number of facts relating to it, but sometimes entirely a result of exercising the speculative imagination ‖ knowledge of a science or art derived from such study and speculation (cf. PRACTICE) ‖ a general body of assumptions and principles, *the theory of democracy* ‖ a group of mathematical theorems presenting a comprehensive and systematic view of a subject, *the theory of probability* ‖ a conjecture, *have you any theory as to who could have done it?* [fr. L.L. *theoria* fr. Gk]

theory of games the application of mathematical logic to the strategy, tactical moves and fluctuating odds of situations involving conflict and where several lines of action are possible for the opponents, e.g. in competitive business and in war

theory of knowledge *EPISTEMOLOGY

theory of numbers number theory

Theory Z (*business*) management technique in which employees are enlisted to assume responsibility for greater productivity and in meeting problems, usu. in order to meet or surpass competition

the·o·soph·ic (θi:əsɒ́fik) *adj.* of or relating to theosophy **the·o·sóph·i·cal** *adj.*

the·os·o·phist (θi:ɒ́səfist) *n.* a believer in theosophy **The·os·o·phist** an adherent of Theosophy [fr. M.L. *theosophus* fr. late Gk]

the·os·o·phy (θi:ɒ́səfi:) *n.* any philosophical and religious system based on intuitive knowledge of the divine

The·os·o·phy a system of thought and practice derived from esp. Buddhist and Brahminical religious mysticism by Madame Blavatsky in 1875 in the U.S.A., and propagated by the Theosophical Society which she founded. It claims to be a synthesis of those elements in all religions which result from divine revelation, and to enable its followers to establish personal communion with God [fr. M.L. *theosophia* fr. late Gk]

The·ra (θíərə) *SANTORIN

ther·a·peu·tic (θerəpjú:tik) *adj.* curative **ther·a·péu·ti·cal** *adj.* [fr. Mod. L. *therapeuticus* fr. Gk]

therapeutic community (*psych.*) a social organization within a structured therapeutic setting, integrating responsibility between patients and staff, overcoming patient dependency, that is esp. effective in rehabilitating drug addicts and alcoholics

therapeutic index (*pharm.*) a measure of drug effectiveness based on the ratio of the largest dose producing no side effects to the lowest dose therapeutically effective

ther·a·peu·tics (θerəpjú:tiks) *n.* the branch of medical practice concerned with curing or treating diseases, injuries etc. [fr. Mod. L. *therapeutica* adj. fr. Gk *therapeutikē* (*technē*), (the art of) healing]

ther·a·pist (θérəpist) *n.* someone skilled in a particular therapy, *an occupational therapist*

ther·a·py (θérəpi:) *n.* the treating of the physically or mentally ill by therapeutic means [fr. Mod. L. *therapia* fr. Gk]

Ther·a·va·da (θerəvúdə) *BUDDHISM

there (ðɛər) **1.** *adv.* in or at that place, *she saw him there* ‖ to or towards that place, *he went there yesterday* ‖ then, at that point, *there he interrupted* ‖ in those circumstances, *there was his chance of escape* ‖ right now, *there goes the bell* **2.** *pron.* used as an introductory word in impersonal constructions, esp. when the verb has no complement, *there were only two left* **3.** *n.* that place, *from there they went south* **4.** *interj.* used to express confirmation, *there, I told you so!* or comfort, *there, you will soon be better* or triumph, *there, it's finished* [O.E. *thǣr, thēr*]

there·at (ðɛərǽt) *adv.* (*archaic*) on account of that ‖ (*archaic*) at that place or time

there·a·bout (ðɛ́ərəbaut) *adv.* thereabouts

there·a·bouts (ðɛ́ərəbauts) *adv.* near that place ‖ near to that number, amount etc., *ten pounds or thereabouts* [O.E. *thǣr, abūtan*]

there·af·ter (ðɛərǽftər,ðɛərúftər) *adv.* after that time or place [O.E. *thǣrǣfter*]

there·by (ðɛərbái) *adv.* thus, by this or that means **thereby hangs a tale** there is an interesting story in this connection [O.E. *thǣrbī*]

there·fore (ðɛ́ərfɔr, ðɛ́ərfour) *adv.* for that reason [M.E. *therfore, therefore*]

there·from (ðɛərfrʌ́m, ðɛərfrɒ́m) *adv.* (*rhet.*) from that, from it [M.E.]

there·in (ðɛərin) *adv.* (*legal contexts*) in that thing, place etc. ‖ (*rhet.*) in that respect, *we don't know all the facts and therein lies our difficulty* [O.E. *thǣrin*]

there·in·af·ter (ðɛərinǽftər, ðɛərinúftər) *adv.* (*legal contexts*) later in the same document

there·in·be·fore (ðɛərinbifɔ́r, ðɛərinbifóur) *adv.* (*legal contexts*) earlier in the same document

there·of (ðɛərʌ́v, ðɛərɒ́v) *adv.* (*legal contexts*) of the place, thing, event etc. just mentioned [O.E. *thǣr of*]

there·on (ðɛərɔ́n, ðɛərɒ́n) *adv.* (*rhet.*) on that thing just mentioned ‖ (*rhet.*) thereupon [O.E. *thǣron*]

Theresa *TERESA

there·to (ðɛərtú:) *adv.* (*legal contexts*) to it, to that, *the condition applying thereto* [O.E. *thǣr tō, thǣrtō*]

there·un·der (ðɛərʌ́ndər) *adv.* (*legal contexts*) under that heading or under the conditions just set out ‖ (*rhet.*) under that thing, place etc. just specified [O.E. *thǣrunder*]

there·u·pon (ðɛ́ərəpɔ́n, ðɛ́ərəpɒ́n) *adv.* immediately after that ‖ (*legal contexts*) as a result of that [M.E. *ther upon, ther up on*]

there·with (ðɛərwiθ, ðɛərwið) *adv.* (*archaic*) immediately after that ‖ (*archaic*) with this, that or it ‖ (*archaic*) in addition to that

the·ri·an·throp·ic (θiəri:ænθrɒ́pik) *adj.* (e.g. of a sphinx or a mermaid) half human and half animal ‖ relating to belief in or worship of such beings [fr. Gk *thērion*, beast+*anthrōpos*, man]

the·ri·o·mor·phic (θiəri:əmɔ́rfik) *adj.* (esp. of a god) having the form of an animal [fr. Gk *thērion*, beast+*morphē*, shape]

therm (θə:rm) *n.* any of several practical units of heat energy, e.g. one equal to 100,000 British thermal units [fr. Gk *thermos*, hot, *thermē*, heat]

ther·mal (θə́:rməl) *adj.* pertaining to heat, *thermal capacity* or to a source of heat, *thermal spring* or to something caused by heat, *thermal dissociation* [fr. Gk *thermē*, heat]

thermal breeder (*nuclear phys.*) atomic power plant using slow neutrons, producing small amounts of fissionable material fuel as a by-product *also* thermal reactor

thermal capacity (*phys.*) heat capacity

thermal conductivity (*phys.*) ability to conduct heat ‖ (of a substance) the amount of heat transmitted across a cube of unit volume in unit time when the temperature difference between the faces of the cube is 1° C. (cf. ELECTRICAL CONDUCTIVITY)

thermal diffusion (*phys.*) the separation of the heavy from the light components of a fluid mixture under the influence of a temperature gradient

thermal energy analyzer device used to pinpoint nitrosome concentrations in chemicals; developed by Thermo Electron Corp. *abbr.* TEA

thermal neutron (*phys.*) a neutron of low energy, emitted in the disintegration of some radioactive nuclei, e.g. U^{235}

thermal pollution (*envir.*) industrial disposal of heated liquid into rivers or other natural waters, causing undesirable ecosystemic changes *also* heat pollution

thermal volt *KELVIN

ther·mic (θə́:rmik) *adj.* thermal [fr. Gk *thermē,* heat]

Ther·mi·dor (θə́:rmidɔr, termi:dɔr) *n.* (*F. hist.*) the 11th month of the French Revolutionary calendar ‖ the coup d'etat of 9 Thermidor (July 27, 1794) in which Robespierre and his supporters were overthrown and the Terror was ended [F. fr. Gk *thermē,* heat+*dōron,* gift]

therm·i·on (θə́:rmaiən) *n.* (*phys.*) an ion produced by heating a substance (usually to incandescence) **therm·i·on·ic** (θə:rmaiɔ́nik) *adj.* of or operating by means of thermions [fr. Gk *thermos,* hot, *thermē,* heat+ION]

thermionic tube (*electr.*) device that emits electrons from a hot metal cathode, e.g., electron gun in a cathode-ray tube, precursor of the transistor

ther·mis·tor (θə:rmístər) *n.* an electrical resistor whose resistance is a known, rapidly varying function of temperature. Thermistors are made usually of rare-earth and certain other metallic oxides, and are used esp. as thermometers and in katharometers [fr. THERMAL+RESISTOR]

ther·mit (θə́:rmit) *n.* thermite

ther·mite (θə́:rmait) *n.* a mixture of aluminum powder and a metallic oxide (usually iron oxide), which yields molten iron, alumina and large quantities of heat when ignited by a magnesium fuse. It is used in welding and in incendiary bombs [fr. *Thermit,* a trademark]

thermo- (θə́:rmou) *prefix* heat ‖ thermoelectric [Gk fr. *thermos,* hot, *thermē,* heat]

ther·mo·chem·is·try (θə:rmoukémistri:) *n.* the study of the heat relations in chemical changes

ther·mo·cou·ple (θə́:rmoukʌp'l) *n.* (*phys.*) a device, consisting of two dissimilar metallic conductors in contact, that produces an electrical current whose magnitude depends on the temperature of the junction. It is used to measure temperature and in thermopiles (*SEEBECK EFFECT)

ther·mo·dy·nam·ic (θə:rmoudainǽmik) *adj.* pertaining to thermodynamics **ther·mo·dy·nám·ics** *n.* the branch of physics dealing with the relation between heat and other forms of energy (*LAW OF THERMODYNAMICS)

ther·mo·e·lec·tric (θə:rmouiléktrik) *adj.* of or relating to thermoelectricity **ther·mo·e·léc·tri·cal** *adj.*

thermoelectric effects *JOULE EFFECT, *PELTIER EFFECT, *SEEBECK EFFECT, *THOMSON EFFECT

ther·mo·e·lec·tric·i·ty (θə:rmouilektrísiti:, θə:rmoui:lektrísiti:) *n.* electrical energy produced by the action of heat, e.g. in the Seebeck and other thermoelectric effects

ther·mo·form (θə́:rməfɔrm) *n.* process of molding plastics (for packaging) by using heat — **thermoform** *v.* —**thermoformable** *adj.*

ther·mo·gen·e·sis (θə:rmoudʒénisis) *n.* (*biol.*) the production of heat by the oxidation of foodstuffs in the body, or by other physical or chemical changes within the body

ther·mo·ge·net·ic (θə:rmoudʒənétik) *adj.* of thermogenesis [fr. Gk *thermē,* heat+GENETIC]

ther·mo·gen·ic (θə:rmoudʒénik) *adj.* of or relating to thermogenesis [fr. THERMO-+ Gk *-genēs,* born of]

ther·mo·graph (θə́:rməgræf, θə́:rməgrɑf) *n.* a recording thermometer, used chiefly by meteorologists

ther·mog·ra·phy (θərmɔ́grəfi:) *n.* **1.** raised-printing process in which resin dusts are used to raise lettering, imitating copperplate engraving **2.** (*med.*) technique of body-heat measurement used for early detection of cancer cells, which tend to have an elevated temperature **3.** technique for measuring temperatures of distant surfaces —**thermogram** *n.* the product —**thermograph** *n.* the apparatus —**thermograph** *v.*

ther·mo·gra·vim·e·try (θə:rməgrəvímətri:) *n.* the measurement of changes in weight due to temperature change —**thermogravimetric** *adj.*

ther·mo·la·bile (θə:rmouléibil) *adj.* (*biochem.*) unstable, i.e. losing its characteristic properties, when heated (opp. THERMOSTABLE)

ther·mom·e·ter (θərmɔ́mitər) *n.* any of several types of instrument used to measure temperature on any of several temperature scales **ther·mo·met·ric** (θə:r·məmétrik), **ther·mo·mét·ri·cal** *adjs.* **ther·mom·e·try** (θərmɔ́mitri:) *n.* (*THERMISTOR, *RESISTANCE THERMOMETER, *THERMOCOUPLE, *PYROMETER, *GAS THERMOMETER) [fr. Gk *thermē,* heat, *thermos,* hot +mētron, measure]

ther·mo·nu·cle·ar (θə:rmounú:kli:ər, θə:rmounjú:kli:ər) *adj.* relating to nuclear fusion

ther·mo·phil (θə́:rməfil) **1.** *n.* a thermophile **2.** *adj.* thermophile **ther·mo·phile** (θə́:rməfail) **1.** *n.* (*biol.,* e.g. of certain bacteria) an organism which thrives at relatively high temperatures (e.g. 50–55° C.) **2.** *adj.* (*Br.*) of or relating to a thermophile [THERMO-+Gk *philos,* dear, loving]

ther·mo·phys·i·cal *adj.* of the physical properties of materials at various temperatures

ther·mo·pile (θə́:rməpail) *n.* an instrument, consisting of a number of thermocouples arranged in series, used for measuring incident radiant energy by the heating effect it produces, or as a portable generator of electric current (*SOLAR BATTERY)

ther·mo·plas·tic (θə:rmouplǽstik) **1.** *adj.* becoming soft or plastic when heated and rigid again when cool **2.** *n.* a thermoplastic substance, e.g. polystyrene

Ther·mop·y·lae (θərmɔ́pəli:) a passage (wider now than in ancient times) between the Oeta Mtns and the marshy shore of Thessaly, Greece, 9 miles southeast of Lamia. Leonidas and 300 Spartans fought a rearguard action here to the death (480 B.C.) to delay the Persian army of Xerxes I during the Persian War

Ther·mos (θə́:rməs) *n.* a doublewalled vessel used to keep substances at a temperature other than that of the surroundings. The space between the walls is evacuated to prevent heat transfer by conduction and convection, and the walls are silvered to reduce radiation [Trademark]

Thermos bottle a Thermos

ther·mo·set·ting (θə:rmousétiŋ) *adj.* of plastics and resins, which when once heated and compressed, resist further heat treatment

Thermos flask (esp. *Br.*) a Thermos

ther·mo·sol (θə́:rməsɔl) *n.* process for dyeing synthetic fibers by utilizing heat for dispersal and penetration of dyestuffs

ther·mo·sphere (θə́:rməsfiər) *n.* (*meteor.*) the region of the earth's atmosphere above the mesosphere about 50 mi. from the surface, including exosphere and part of ionosphere, at which temperature increases with height —**thermospheric** *adj. Cf* MESOSPHERE

ther·mo·sta·ble (θə:rmoustéib'l) *adj.* (*biochem.*) not losing its characteristic properties when heated (opp. THERMOLABILE)

ther·mo·stat (θə́:rməstæt) *n.* a device used to maintain a constant temperature by cutting off the heat supply when this temperature is reached and restoring it when the temperature begins to fall as a result of cooling **ther·mo·stát·ic** *adj.* **ther·mo·stát·i·cal·ly** *adv.* [fr. THERMO-+Gk *statos,* standing]

ther·mo·tax·is (θə:rmoutǽksis) *n.* (*biol.*) a reaction, esp. a locomotor reaction, of an organism to heat stimuli ‖ the regulation of body temperature [Mod. L. fr. Gk *thermē,* heat+*taxis,* arrangement]

ther·mo·trop·ic (θə:rmoutrɔ́pik) *adj.* of or showing thermotropism [fr. THERMO-+Gk *tropos,* a turning]

ther·mot·ro·pism (θə:rmɔ́trəpizəm) *n.* (*bot.*) a tropism in plants in response to heat stimuli

the·sau·rus (θisɔ́rəs) *pl.* **the·sau·ri** (θisɔ́rai), **the·sau·rus·es** *n.* a useful literary collection or selection, esp. a book of synonyms and antonyms [L. fr. Gk *thēsauros,* treasure]

these *pl.* of THIS

The·se·us (θí:si:əs, θí:sju:s) (*Gk mythol.*) hero and king of Athens. He is associated with Heracles and his campaign against the Amazons. Helped by Ariadne, daughter of King Minos, he killed the Minotaur in the labyrinth of Crete. He married Ariadne, but deserted her in Naxos

the·sis (θí:sis) *pl.* **the·ses** (θí:si:z) *n.* a proposition ‖ a reasoned argument, esp. in a written dissertation on a theme connected with the specialty by a candidate for any of certain academic degrees ‖ (*logic*) an affirmation (cf. ANTITHESIS, cf. HYPOTHESIS) ‖ (*prosody*) the unaccented part of a metrical foot (opp. ARSIS) [Gk =a placing]

Thes·pi·an (θéspi:ən) **1.** *adj.* of dramatic art ‖ of Thespis **2.** *n.* (*rhet.*) an actor ‖ (*hist.*) a native or inhabitant of Thespiae, a town of ancient Greece [after THESPIS]

Thes·pis (θéspis) (6th c. B.C.) Greek poet who won a prize for tragedy at Athens (534 B.C.). He is considered the founder of Greek tragedy

Thes·sa·lo·ni·ans, Epistles to the (θesəlóuni:ənz) the 13th and 14th books of the New Testament, almost certainly written (c. 51) by St Paul to the Church at Thessaloniki. They condemn false ideas that the second coming of Christ is at hand

Thes·sa·lon·i·ki (θesəlɔ́nikai) *SALONICA

Thes·sa·ly (θésəli:) a region of N. Greece consisting of plains surrounded by mountains: Ossa and Pelion on the Aegean coast (east), Olympus (north), Pindus (west), Oeta (south). It includes the Vale of Tempe. It was famous in antiquity for its cavalry. It was conquered by Macedon (4th c. B.C.) and became part of the Roman Empire (146 B.C.), of Turkey (1393) and of Greece (1881)

the·ta (θéitə, θí:tə) *n.* the eighth letter (Θ, θ=th) of the Greek alphabet [Gk *thēta*]

theta pinch quick-pulsed compression of a magnetic field around ionized gas (plasma), used to control fusion

theta wave (*physiol.*) a brain wave pattern of 4 to 8 Hz with voltage greater than in alpha waves, which occurs in many brain regions, esp. the hippocampus *Cf* ALPHA WAVE, DELTA WAVE

the·ur·gic (θi:ə́:rdʒik) *adj.* of or relating to theurgy **the·ur·gi·cal** *adj.*

the·ur·gist (θí:ə:rdʒist) *n.* a person who practices theurgy

the·ur·gy (θí:ərdʒi:) *n.* divine intervention in nature or in human affairs, e.g. in a miracle ‖ the power possessed by a human being to secure or prevent such divine action, esp. the magical power which certain Neoplatonists believed might be acquired by long training, self-purification and esoteric learning and practices [fr. L. *theurgia* fr. Gk]

thew (θju:) *n.* (*rhet.,* esp. *pl.*) muscle, strength [fr. O.E. *thēaw,* custom]

they (ðei) *pron., 3rd person pl., nominative case* two or more persons, animals or things already mentioned ‖ (*pop.*) people or a group of people generally, *they say it will be a hard winter* [M.E. *thei* fr. O.N. *their*]

they'd (ðeid) *contr.* of THEY HAD, THEY WOULD

they'll (ðeil) *contr.* of THEY WILL, THEY SHALL

they're (ðɛər, ðéiər) *contr.* of THEY ARE

they've (ðeiv) *contr.* of THEY HAVE

thi·a·min (θáiəmin) *n.* thiamine

thi·a·mine (θáiəmi:n, θáiəmin) *n.* vitamin B_1 (*DIET), the antineuritic member of the vitamin B complex [fr. Gk *theion,* sulfur+AMINE]

thi·a·zine (θáiəzi:n) *n.* any of a class of compounds having a ring comprised of an atom of sulfur, an atom of nitrogen and four atoms of carbon ‖ a derivative of one of these compounds [fr. Gk *theion,* sulfur+AZINE]

thi·a·zole (θáiəzoul) *n.* a colorless liquid, C_3H_3NS, resembling pyridine ‖ any of its derivatives, used in dyes [fr. Gk *theion,* sulfur+AZOLE]

thick (θik) **1.** *adj.* of relatively great depth from one surface to its opposite surface ‖ large in diameter, *a thick log* ‖ broad, *a thick line* ‖ dense, closely massed together, *thick underbrush* ‖ (of the atmosphere in a room) stuffy ‖ viscous, *a thick syrup* ‖ measured between opposite surfaces, *three inches thick* ‖ (of speech) hoarse and indistinct because the words are run together ‖ (of regional or foreign accent) strongly marked ‖ (*pop.*) slow to understand ‖ (*pop.*) intimately friendly **a bit thick** (*Br., pop.*) unreasonable, *he thought it a bit thick that he was not allowed to speak* **2.** *adv.* thickly ‖ in close succession, *the questions came thick on one another* **to lay it on thick** to exaggerate ‖ to flatter grossly **3.** *n.* the most intense, crowded part, *the thick of the fray*

through thick and thin through all circumstances, favorable and unfavorable **thick·en** *v.t.* to make thick, *to thicken a sauce* ‖ *v.i.* to become thick or thicker, *the fog has thickened* ‖ to become more involved, *the plot thickens* **thick·en·ing** *n.* the act of making or becoming thick ‖ an ingredient, e.g. flour, used to thicken ‖ the part where something becomes thicker [O.E. *thicce*]

thick·et (θíkit) *n.* a thick growth of small trees and undergrowth [O.E. *thiccet*]

thick film (*electr.*) a multimolecular film of ink used to cover and insulate circuit wiring

thick·head (θíkhed) *n.* (*pop.*) a stupid person **thíck·héad·ed** *adj.*

thick·ness (θíknis) *n.* the state or quality of being thick ‖ the smallest of the three linear dimensions (cf. LENGTH, cf. WIDTH) [O.E. *thicness*]

thick·set (θiksét) *adj.* (of a person) short, but strong and compact in build ‖ planted or set close together

thick-skinned (θikskínd) *adj.* having a thick skin ‖ insensitive to insults, criticisms, reproaches etc.

thick-wit·ted (θikwítid) *adj.* stupid, slow to understand

thief (θi:f) *pl.* **thieves** (θi:vz) *n.* a person who steals [O.E. *thēof*]

Thiers (tjer), Adolphe (1797-1877) French statesman and historian. A moderate liberal, he helped to bring about the revolution of 1830. He was prime minister in 1836 and 1840, but later became an opponent of the July Monarchy. His opposition to Napoleon III's coup d'état (1851) sent him into temporary exile. Thiers warned of the disastrous consequences of war with Prussia (1870). After the Franco-Prussian War he negotiated peace, suppressed the Commune and became president of France (1871-3). He is the author of 'History of the French Revolution' and 'History of the Consulate and the Empire'

Thiès (tjes) a commercial center (pop. 69,000) in W. Senegal, on the lower Niger: aluminum phosphates

thieve (θi:v) *pres. part.* **thiev·ing** *past* and *past part.* **thieved** *v.t.* to take by theft ‖ *v.i.* to practice theft **thiev·er·y** *n.* theft [O. E. *thēofian*]

thiev·ish (θí:viʃ) *adj.* characteristic of, or like, a thief

thigh (θai) *n.* the part of the human leg between the hip and the knee ‖ the corresponding part in the leg of a bird or quadruped ‖ the third section of the leg of an insect [O.E. *thēoh*]

thigh·bone (θáibоun) *n.* the bone of the leg extending from the hip to the knee. In man it is the longest and largest bone

thill (θil) *n.* the shaft of a cart or wagon, esp. one of a pair between which a draft animal is hitched [origin unknown]

thim·ble (θímb'l) *n.* a cap of metal etc. worn on the fingertip in sewing so that the needle can be pushed through a fabric without hurting the finger ‖ a short metal tube or sleeve ‖ (*naut.*) an iron ring with a grooved rim around which a rope is spliced to prevent it from chafing [O.E. *thȳmel*, thumbstall]

thim·ble·ber·ry (θímb'lberi:) *pl.* **thim·ble·ber·ries** *n.* any of several American blackberries or raspberries bearing soft fruits shaped like sewing thimbles

thim·ble·ful (θímb'lful) *pl.* **thim·ble·fuls** *n.* a very small quantity of a liquid, generally alcoholic liquor

thim·ble·rig (θímb'lrig) **1.** *n.* a swindling game in which the operator has three thimble-shaped cups and a pea. He passes the cups over the pea and the victim bets that the pea will be found under a particular cup **2.** *v.t. pres. part.* **thim·ble·rig·ging** *past* and *past part.* **thim·ble·rigged** to cheat or swindle by this game **thim·ble·rig·ger** *n.* someone who operates the game

thin (θin) **1.** *adj. comp.* **thin·ner** *superl.* **thin·nest** having little extent between opposite surfaces, *a thin sheet of paper* ‖ small in diameter, *a thin rope* ‖ (of a person or animal) of slender build, or noticeably lacking fat ‖ not closely massed together, *his hair is thin on top* ‖ of little density, *a thin oil, a thin mist* ‖ of little strength or substance, *a thin voice, thin tea, a thin plot* ‖ lacking plausibility or persuasion, *a thin excuse* ‖ (*photog.*) not contrasty, lacking density **a thin time** a time of hardship or great discomfort, tedium, trouble etc. **2.** *adv.* thinly, *spread the butter thin* [O.E. *thynne*]

thin *pres. part.* **thin·ning** *past* and *past part.* **thinned** *v.t.* to make thin ‖ (esp. with 'out') to reduce in number or mass ‖ *v.i.* to become thin, or thinner [O.E. *thynnian*]

thine (ðain) **1.** *possessive pron.* that or those belonging to thee **2.** *possessive adj.* (used in place of 'thy' before a noun beginning with a vowel or mute 'h'), *thine honor* [O.E. *thīn*]

thin-film solar cells (θinfílm) (*electr.*) inexpensive solar cells consisting of a thin, flexible metal or plastic material in which a thin film of a semiconductor material has been evaporated, used as a power source in spacecraft

thing (θiŋ) *n.* that which consists of matter, a body, or object, esp. that which is no more than matter, i.e. not a living person or animal ‖ used in reference to a person, esp. in often condescending expressions of affection, pity etc., *she's a sweet thing, he's a wicked old thing* ‖ an action, *what would be the best thing to do next?* ‖ something not specifically named, *what's that thing he's carrying?* ‖ (*colloq.*) a uniquely personal activity, *he's doing his thing* ‖ something uttered or thought, *the president said some good things in his speech* ‖ (*pl.*) affairs or concerns, *the things of the mind* ‖ (*pl.*) belongings, clothes, utensils etc., *he left his things at the station* ‖ (*pl.*) circumstances in general, *things will get better* **a thing** (in negative expressions) anything, *he wouldn't do a thing to help us* **a thing or two** (with 'know' or 'tell') facts derived from thorough familiarity with a subject, *he knows a thing or two about economics* **first thing** at the earliest possible moment, *do it first thing in the morning* **to make a good thing of** to profit financially by **to see things** to have hallucinations **the thing** that which is appropriate or correct, *the thing to do in that case is rush to the hospital* ‖ that which is polite, *it is hardly the thing to leave an invitation unanswered* ‖ that which is fashionable, *stripes are the thing this season* [O.E.]

thing·um·a·bob (θíŋəməbɒb) *n.* a thingumajig

thing·um·a·jig (θíŋəmədʒig) *n.* (*pop.*) a substitute used when one doesn't know, or has momentarily forgotten, the proper name of something or (*Br.*) someone

think (θiŋk) *pres. part.* **think·ing** *past* and *past part.* **thought** (θɔt) *v.i.* to engage in the process of arranging ideas in a pattern of relationships or of adding new ideas soon to be related to such a pattern ‖ to turn something over in the mind, e.g. to consider advantages and disadvantages ‖ (with 'of') to have a specified opinion, *he doesn't think much of that play* ‖ (with 'of') to have consideration or concern, *think of your family first* ‖ (with 'of') to make provision, *you must think of the future* ‖ (with 'of' or 'about') to have in mind as a provisional plan, *we're thinking of going to the beach* ‖ to consider as a possible candidate, *we are thinking of John for that position* ‖ to remember, *can you think of his name?* ‖ *v.t.* to conceive in the mind, *to think strange thoughts* ‖ to have as a firm conviction, *I think she is lying* ‖ to have as a tentative opinion, *I think she might refuse* ‖ to work out by reasoning, *I can't think how the story will end* ‖ to determine by reflection, *I can't think what is best to do* ‖ to bring to a specified condition by mental activity, *to think oneself into a state of depression* ‖ (with 'to'+infinitive) to remember, or have the idea of doing etc. (something) when one could reasonably be expected to have it, *he didn't think to lock the door* ‖ to be obsessed with the idea of, *he thinks and dreams flying* **to think aloud** to speak one's ideas as they occur **to think better of** to change (e.g. an opinion or decision) on further reflection, *he was going to tell us the story but thought better of it* ‖ **to think nothing of** to take for granted (what would seem odd, hard etc., to others), *he thinks nothing of walking 20 miles a day* **to think out** (or **through**) to examine carefully (a problem) so as to reach a conclusion **to think over** to consider or reconsider, ponder at length **to think twice** to reflect with special care before taking action **to think up** to make up (a plan, answer etc.) in the mind [O.E. *thencan, thencean*]

thin·ka·ble (θíŋkəb'l) *adj.* able to be thought ‖ able to be entertained as an idea or possibility

think·ing (θíŋkiŋ) **1.** *n.* the mental process of one who thinks ‖ an opinion or judgment, *to my thinking they will be outmoded in four years* ‖ a body of thought, *modern thinking* **2.** that thinks or can think

think tank an institution or group involved in researching and solving difficult, interdisciplinary problems, the solutions to which often affect public policy *also* think factory

thin-lay·er chromatography (θinléiər) (*chem.*) an accurate, rapid process of color photography in which the absorbent medium is a thin layer of silica gel, aluminum, or cellulose on a glass plate *abbr.* TLC —**thin-layer chromatographic** *adj. Cf* GAS-LIQUID CHROMATOGRAPHY

thin·ner (θínər) **1.** *adj.* more thin **2.** *n.* a liquid used to make something (e.g. paint or printing ink) more thin

thin-skinned (θínskínd) *adj.* having a thin skin ‖ unusually sensitive to criticism

thi·o acid (θáiou) an acid in which sulfur wholly or partly replaces oxygen [fr. Gk *theion*, sulfur]

thi·o·al·de·hyde (θaiouǽldəhaid) *n.* an aldehyde in which oxygen is replaced by sulfur

thi·o·ben·da·zol [$C_{10}H_7N_3S$] (θaioubéndəzɒl) *n.* (*pharm.*) a drug used to treat fungus or roundworm infection

thi·o·cy·a·nate (θaiousáiəneit) *n.* a salt or ester of thiocyanic acid

thi·o·cy·an·ic acid (θaiousaiǽnik) a strong-smelling, unstable liquid acid, HSCN or HNCS, obtained by distilling a thiocyanate salt with dilute sulfuric acid

Thi·o·kol (θáiəkɔl) *n.* (*chem.*) any of a number of rubberlike polymers (RSXN), where R is a divalent organic radical and X varies usually between 2 and 4. They are very resistant to the swelling effect of oils [Trademark]

thi·on·ic (θaiɒ́nik) *adj.* relating to or containing sulfur [fr. Gk *theion*, sulfur]

Thi·o·nine (θáiəni:n, θáiənin) *n.* a violet dye, $C_{12}H_9N_3S$, used in microscopy to stain objects [Trademark]

thi·o·rid·a·zine [$C_{21}H_{26}N_2S_2HCl$] (thaiouríd-əzi:n) *n.* (*pharm.*) a phenothiazine tranquilizer and antidepressant used in treating schizophrenia; marketed as Mellaril

thi·o·sul·fate, thi·o·sul·phate (θaiousʌ́lfeit) *n.* a salt or ester of thiosulfuric acid, used in photography, dyeing etc.

thi·o·sul·fu·ric acid, thi·o·sul·phu·ric acid (θaiousʌlfjúərik) an unstable acid, $H_2S_2O_3$, derived from sulfuric acid. It exists in solution or in the form of salts and esters

thi·o·u·re·a (θaioujurí:ə) *n.* a crystalline substance, $CS(NH_2)_2$, used in organic syntheses [Mod. L. fr. Gk *theion*, sulfur +*ouron*, urine]

third (θə:rd) **1.** *adj.* being number three in a series (*NUMBER TABLE) ‖ next after the second in importance, quality, rank etc. ‖ being one of the three equal parts of anything ‖ of or pertaining to the gear immediately above second in a vehicle **2.** *n.* the person or thing next after the second ‖ one of three equal parts of anything (1/3) ‖ (*Br.*) a grading in the third class of an examination ‖ a third prize in a race or other contest ‖ the gear immediately above second in a vehicle ‖ the third day of a month ‖ (*mus.*) the note three steps above or below a given note in a diatonic scale, inclusive of both notes ‖ (*mus.*) the interval between these notes ‖ (*mus.*) a combination of these notes **3.** *adv.* in the third place ‖ (followed by a superlative) except two, *the third biggest* [O.E. *thridda, thridde*]

Third Amendment (1791) part of the Bill of Rights in the U.S. Constitution that requires permission of the owner for the peacetime quartering of soldiers in a private home; in wartime the matter must be resolved 'in a manner to be prescribed by law.' Arising from the American colonists' resentment over the housing of British soldiers, the amendment is not relevant in modern times, nor has it ever been the subject of a judicial decision. The amendment's underlying principle remains significant, however, because of its implication that civilian authority has precedence over that of the military

third base (*baseball*) the base to be touched third by a base runner ‖ the player placed here

third-class (θə́:rdklǽs, θə́:rdklás) **1.** *adj.* of or relating to a class, grade etc. below second **2.** *adv.* at third-class rate, in third-class accommodation

third degree a severe, sometimes brutal, questioning of a criminal suspect to try to force a confession ‖ (*freemasonry*) a mastermason

third-degree burn a burn in which the skin is destroyed through the depth of the derma and possibly into the underlying tissues. It may be accompanied by shock

third estate the commons, as distinguished

CONCISE PRONUNCIATION KEY: **(a)** æ, *cat*; ɑ, *car*; ɔ *fawn*; ei, *snake*. **(e)** e, *hen*; i:, *sheep*; iə, *deer*; ɛə, *bear*. **(i)** i, *fish*; ai, *tiger*; ə:, *bird*. **(o)** o, *ox*; au, *cow*; ou, *goat*; u, *poor*; ɔi, *royal*. **(u)** ʌ, *duck*; u, *bull*; u:, *goose*; ə, *bacillus*; ju:, *cube*. x, *loch*; θ, *think*; ð, *bother*; z, *Zen*; ʒ, *corsage*; dʒ, *savage*; ŋ, *orangutang*; j, *yak*; ʃ, *fish*; tʃ, *fetch*; 'l, *rabble*; 'n, *redden*. Complete pronunciation key appears inside front cover.

from the nobles and clergy, in a States General or parliament
Third International the Comintern
third man (*cricket*) a fielder, or his position, further from the wicket than point and in the same straight line
third market (*securities*) the over-the-counter market *Cf* FOURTH MARKET
third order a body of Christian lay men and women either living in the world and affiliated to a religious order as seculars or living in community as regulars
third party (*law*) a person other than the two principals involved in a case
third person (*gram.*) the person or thing spoken of, as distinguished from the person speaking and the person spoken to
third-rate (θə́:rdréit) *adj.* of poor quality, *a third-rate hotel*
Third Reich the Nazi regime in Germany (1933-45). The First Reich was the Holy Roman Empire (962-1806) and the Second was the German Empire (1871-1918)
third-stream (θə:rdstrí:m) *adj.* of music combining jazz and classical music
Third World the countries in which economic development still has far to go, and which belong neither to the group of industrial states having a liberal economy nor to the socialist-type group of states
thirst (θə:rst) *n.* a desire for drink ‖ any keen desire, *a thirst for knowledge* [O.E. *thurst*]
thirst *v.i.* to feel thirsty ‖ (*rhet.*) to have a keen desire, *thirsting for revenge* [O.E. *thyrstan*]
thirst·i·ly (θə́:rstili:) *adv.* in a thirsty manner
thirst·i·ness (θə́:rsti:nis) *n.* the state or quality of being thirsty
thirst·y (θə́:rsti:) *comp.* **thirst·i·er** *superl.* **thirst·i·est** *adj.* feeling thirst ‖ dry, *thirsty soil* ‖ (*rhet.*) having a strong desire, *thirsty for adventure* [O.E. *thurstig, thyrstig*]
thir·teen (θə́:rtí:n) **1.** *adj.* being one more than 12 (*NUMBER TABLE) **2.** *n.* ten plus three ‖ the cardinal number representing this (13, XIII) [O.E. *thrēotīene, thrēotēne*]
Thirteen Colonies, the (*Am. hist.*) the colonies of British North America which adopted (1776) the Declaration of Independence, and became the original United States. They were Connecticut, Delaware, Georgia, Maryland, Massachusetts, New Hampshire, New Jersey, New York, North Carolina, Pennsylvania, Rhode Island, South Carolina and Virginia
thir·teenth (θə́:rtí:nθ) **1.** *adj.* being number 13 in a series (*NUMBER TABLE) ‖ being one of the 13 equal parts of anything **2.** *n.* the person or thing next after the 12th ‖ one of 13 equal parts of anything (1/13) ‖ the 13th day of a month [O.E. *thrīetēotha, thrēotēotha*]
Thirteenth Amendment (1865) an amendment to the U.S. Constitution providing that 'neither slavery nor involuntary servitude' will exist in the United States and giving Congress the power to enforce this article by legislation. The amendment was the first unconditional constitutional action against the institution of slavery and the first of four amendments (others are the 14th, 15th and 24th) protecting the equal status of black Americans. Recent Supreme Court decisions have interpreted the amendment to include prohibition of racial discrimination in the disposal of property, in the making and enforcement of contracts, and in private employment
thir·ti·eth (θə́:rti:iθ) **1.** *adj.* being number 30 in a series (*NUMBER TABLE) ‖ being one of the 30 equal parts of anything **2.** *n.* the person or thing next after the 29th ‖ one of 30 equal parts of anything (1/30) ‖ the 30th day of a month [O.E. *thrītigotha*]
thir·ty (θə́:rti:) **1.** *adj.* being 10 more than 20 (*NUMBER TABLE) **2.** *pl.* **thir·ties** *n.* three times 10 ‖ the cardinal number representing this (30, XXX) **the thirties** (of temperature, a person's age, a century etc.) the span 30-9 [O.E. *thrītig*]
Thirty-nine Articles the statements of belief to which Anglican clergymen give general assent at their ordination. They broadly define the doctrinal position of the Church of England in terms of the Reformation controversies. They were ratified by Convocation (1571)
30-pull *n.* (*football*) a play in which the quarterback spins and fakes a pass to the fullback but throws the ball to a linesman
thir·ty-sec·ond note (θə́:rti:sékənd) *n.* (*mus., Am.=Br.* demisemiquaver) a note equal to half a sixteenth note
Thirty Years' War a series of political and religious wars (1618-48) caused mainly by the political rivalry between Catholic and Protestant princes in Germany and the interest of foreign powers in German affairs. The chief phases of the war were: (a) The BOHEMIAN WAR (1618-23), in which a Protestant revolt in Bohemia was crushed by the Catholic League at the White Mountain (1620) and Spain conquered the Palatinate (1621-3). (b) The DANISH WAR (1624-9), in which Christian IV of Denmark was defeated by the Hapsburgs (1626) and signed the Treaty of Lübeck (1629). (c) The SWEDISH WAR (1630-5), in which Gustavus II of Sweden invaded Germany (1630) and defeated the Hapsburg army at Breitenfeld (1631). The Hapsburg victory of Nordlingen (1634) was followed by the Treaty of Prague (1635). (d) The FRENCH WAR (1635-48), in which France under Richelieu entered the war against the Hapsburgs, winning the victories of Rocroi (1643) and Lens (1648). The Thirty Years' War, which devastated Germany and increased French power at the expense of Spain, was ended by the Treaties of Westphalia (1648)
this (ðis) **1.** *pl.* **these** (ði:z) *adj.* of that which is here (compared with that which is there), or near (in space or time), or just mentioned **2.** *pl.* **these** *pron.* the person or thing here, or near (in space or time), or just mentioned **3.** *adv.* to this extent or degree, *this long* [O.E. *thes* masc., *thēos* fem., *this* neut.]
this·tle (θísəl) *n.* any of several genera of tall, prickly plants of fam. *Compositae*, esp. of genera *Carduus, Circium* and *Onopordon*. Many are troublesome weeds [O. E. *thistil*]
this·tle·down (θísəldaun) *n.* the pappus attached to the seeds of a thistle, by which they are carried by the wind
this·tly (θísli:) *adj.* full of thistles
thith·er (θíðər,ðiðər) **1.** *adv.* (*rhet.*) to or towards that place **2.** *adj.* (*rhet.*) on the more distant side, *the thither shore of the lake* [O.E. *thider*]
Thi·va (θí:və) *THEBES
thix·ot·ro·py (θiksɔ́trəpi:) *n.* the property exhibited by certain gels of becoming liquefied on being shaken, stirred etc. and of settling into a gel again when left standing [fr. Gk *thixis*, action of touching+*tropos*, turning]
tho, tho' (ðou) *conj., adv.* (*pop.*) though
thole (θoul) *n.* one of two pegs in the gunwale of a boat used as an oarlock [O.E. *thol, tholl*]
tho·lei·ite (θóuləait) *n.* (*geol.*) a basalt generated in the upper mantle of the earth's crust under the oceans —**tholeiitic** *adj.* containing tholeiite
thole·pin (θoulpin) *n.* a thole
Thom·as (tɔ́məs), St, one of the 12 Apostles. He doubted the Resurrection until he saw and touched the wounds of Christ. According to tradition he went to India as a missionary (*CHRISTIANS OF ST THOMAS). Feast: Dec. 21
Thomas Becket, St *BECKET
Thomas, Christians of St *CHRISTIANS OF ST THOMAS
Thomas, Dylan (1914-53), British poet, born in Wales. His books include '18 Poems' (1934) and 'Twenty-five Poems' (1936), in which the symbolism owes much to Freud and to the Bible, but where much is also highly personal and obscure, and 'Deaths and Entrances' (1946) on which his greatness ultimately rests: a handful of passionate lyrics, with love and death, childhood and the beauty of the world for their themes, and a diction, imagery and metrical skill which make many of them memorable. He also published various prose works among which are the 10 autobiographical stories, 'Portrait of the Artist as a Young Dog' (1940), and the radio script 'Under Milk Wood' (a poetic play, 1954). He also made a reputation as a reader of poetry, his own and others
Thomas, George Henry (1816-70), U.S. Union general during the Civil War. His stand at the Battle of Chattanooga (1863) saved the Union army from complete rout. He defeated (1864) Gen. J. B. Hood at Nashville
Thomas à Kem·pis (kémpis) (c. 1379-1471), German monk, author of devotional works. He is generally supposed to have written 'The Imitation of Christ'. He lived most of his adult life in the Augustinian convent of Mount St Agnes near Zwolle (Netherlands)
Thomas A·qui·nas (əkwáinəs), St (c. 1225-74), Italian theologian and scholastic philosopher. He is the author of 'Summa contra Gentiles' (1259-64), a defense of Christianity in the light of the attacks made by Averroes and his followers in their interpretations of Aristotle, and 'Summa Theologica' (1267-73), his greatest work, which he intended to be a sum of all learning. He also wrote several commentaries on Aristotle, who greatly influenced his thinking. The teachings of St Thomas have had an enormous influence on the Roman Catholic Church and have been officially declared the basis of theological studies
Thomas More, St *MORE
Tho·mism (tóumizəm) *n.* the philosophy and theology of Thomas Aquinas. Thomism distinguishes sharply between faith and reason: while reason cannot establish doctrines, which are a matter of faith, it can show that they are not contrary to reason **Thó·mist** *adj.* and *n.* **Tho·mis·tic** *adj.*
Thomp·son (tɔ́mpsən), Sir Benjamin (Count von Rumford, 1753-1814), British-U.S. scientist. His 'Enquiry Concerning the Source of Heat Which is Excited by Friction', a study which he presented (1798) to the British Royal Society, defined heat as a mode of motion rather than a material substance
Thompson, Francis (1859-1907), British poet. He is best known for his long mystical poem 'The Hound of Heaven' (included in 'Poems', 1893)
Thompson, Sir John Sparrow David (1844-94), Canadian statesman. His term as minister of justice in the Sir John Macdonald administration was marked by his masterly exposition of the government position on the execution (1885) of Louis Riel and the Jesuit Estates Act (1885). He became (1892) prime minister of Canada
Thompson submachine gun (*abbr.* tommy gun) a light automatic weapon with a pistol grip, which may be fired from the shoulder or hip [after John Taliaferro *Thompson* (1860–1940), American general, one of its two inventors]
Thom·son (tɔ́msən), Elihu (1853-1937), U.S. electrical engineer and inventor. He demonstrated (1875) the transmission of signals without wires
Thomson, Sir George Paget (1892-1975), British physicist, son of Sir J. J. Thomson. He is known for his work on the diffraction of electrons by crystals. Nobel prize (1937)
Thomson, James (1700-48), British poet, born in Scotland. He is best known for 'The Seasons' (1726-30), four long meditative and descriptive poems which foreshadowed the Romantics' interest in nature
Thomson, Sir Joseph John (1856-1940), British physicist. He discovered the electron (1897) and added to the development of the electrical theory of atomic structure. Nobel prize (1906)
Thomson, Virgil (1896-), U.S. composer and critic. He created two operas, 'Four Saints in Three Acts' (1928) and 'The Mother of Us All' (1947), and wrote songs, piano sonatas, a cello concerto, stage and film music etc.
Thomson, William *KELVIN
Thomson effect (*phys.*) the redistribution of the temperature differential along an otherwise homogenous conductor due to the passage of a current [after William *Thomson*, Lord Kelvin]
thong (θɔŋ, θɒŋ) *n.* a leather strip used for fastening e.g. heavy boots ‖ the leather lash of a whip [O.E. *thwang, thwong*]
Thor (θɔr) (*Norse mythol.*) the god of thunder, the son of Odin. He was represented as being armed with a remarkable hammer, which returned to his hand after he had thrown it. Thursday is named after Thor
tho·rac·ic (θɔrǽsik, θourǽsik) *adj.* of, in or near the thorax or of, in or near the vertebra between the lumbar and cervical vertebrae [fr. Mod. L. *thoracicus* fr. Gk]
thoracic duct the trunk of the system of lymphatic vessels emptying into the subclavian vein and receiving lymph and intestinal fluids from the abdomen, lower limbs and the entire left side of the body
thoracic gland (*entomology*) the gland in some insects that controls moulting *also* prothoracic gland
tho·rax (θɔ́ræks, θóuræks) *pl.* **tho·rax·es, tho·ra·ces** (θɔ́rəsi:z, θóurəsi:z) *n.* that part of the body in higher vertebrates which contains the heart and lungs and a number of structures passing between the neck and the abdomen. It is supported by the ribs and sternum. Movement of these and the diaphragm causes a partial vacuum within the thorax, as a result of

CONCISE PRONUNCIATION KEY: (a) æ, cat; ɑ, car; ɔ fawn; ei, snake. (e) e, hen; i:, sheep; iə, deer; ɛə, bear. (i) i, fish; ai, tiger; ə:, bird. (o) o, ox; au, cow; ou, goat; u, poor; ɔi, royal. (u) ʌ, duck; u, bull; u:, goose; ə, bacillus; ju:, cube. x, loch; θ, think; ð, bother; z, Zen; ʒ, corsage; dʒ, savage; ŋ, orangutang; j, yak; ʃ, fish; tʃ, fetch; 'l, rabble; 'n, redden. Complete pronunciation key appears inside front cover.

which air is drawn into the lungs (*RESPIRATION) || the body region behind the head in insects and some other animals [L. fr. Gk *thōrax*, the chest]

Tho·reau (θəróu), Henry David (1817-62), American naturalist and writer. He is best known for 'Walden' (1854), an account of his experiment in living alone at Walden Pond, near Concord, Massachusetts, to observe the life of the woods. Thoreau was a friend of Emerson and the transcendentalists. A powerful social critic, he was disturbed by the trend of Western civilization toward a fully industrial urban society dominated by the profit motive. His essay 'On the Duty of Civil Disobedience' (1849) has inspired such men as Gandhi

tho·ri·a (θɔ́ri:ə, θóuri:ə) *n.* thorium oxide, ThO_2, a white powder

tho·rite (θɔ́rait, θóurait) *n.* the naturally occurring silicate of thorium, $ThSiO_4$ [Swed. *thorit*]

tho·ri·um (θɔ́ri:əm, θóuri:əm) *n.* a heavy, radioactive metallic chemical element (symbol Th, at. no. 90, at. mass 232.038). Its compounds occur in the minerals monazite and thorite, and its oxide is used for coating incandescent mantles [Mod. L. after THOR]

Thorn (θɔrn) *TORUN

thorn (θɔrn) *n.* the woody part of a leaf or stem modified to a stiff, sharp point || a hawthorn or other plant or tree bearing thorns || the wood of any of these || any of various sharply pointed protuberances on an animal, e.g. on a sea urchin || a source of sharp irritation || (in Old English and Old Norse) the name of the runic symbol for the 'th' sounds e.g. in 'thin' and 'this' **a thorn in one's side** a continual or frequent cause of annoyance or trouble [O.E.]

thorn apple a member of *Datura*, fam. *Solanaceae*, a genus of plants, shrubs etc. bearing prickly fruit and large trumpet-shaped flowers, esp. the jimson weed || the fruit of the hawthorn

Thorn·dike (θɔ́rndaik), Edward Lee (1874-1949), U.S. educator and psychologist. He developed a method of testing and measuring intelligence and learning ability

Thorn·hill (θɔ́rnhil), Sir James (c. 1676-1734), English baroque painter. He is best known for decorative works, e.g. the dome at St Paul's Cathedral, London and the Painted Hall of the Royal Naval College, Greenwich

thorn·i·ness (θɔ́rni:nis) *n.* the quality or state of being thorny

Thorn·ton (θɔ́rntən), William (1759-1828), U.S. architect. He designed most of the central portion of the Capitol exterior at Washington, D.C., and many Washington residences

thorn·y (θɔ́rni:) *comp.* **thorn·i·er** *superl.* **thorn·i·est** *adj.* full of thorns or spines || beset with difficulties or controversy, *a thorny question*

thor·ough (θə́:rou, θʌ́rou) *adj.* proceeding or done with great care or attention to detail, completeness etc., *a thorough worker, thorough knowledge* || complete in all respects, *a thorough gentleman* [Later O.E. *thuruh*]

thorough bass (*mus.*) continuo

thor·ough·bred (θə́:rəbred, θʌ́rəbred) **1.** *adj.* of or pertaining to any horse, dog etc. of pure breed **Thor·ough·bred** of or pertaining to a Thoroughbred **2.** *n.* any horse, dog etc. of pure breed **Thoroughbred** an English breed of horse, raced or used for hunting or riding, bred from English mares crossed with Arab stallions

thor·ough·fare (θə́:rəfɛər, θʌ́rəfɛər) *n.* a road or passage available to traffic and not closed at either end, esp. a main highway

thor·ough·go·ing (θə́:rəgouiŋ, θʌ́rəgouiŋ) *adj.* very thorough

Thorpe (θɔrp), James Francis 'Jim' (1888-1953), U.S. athlete, selected by sportswriters as the greatest athlete of the first half of the 20th century. Of American Indian, Irish and French descent, he competed in track and field, lacrosse, baseball and football (All-American 1911, 1912), at Carlisle (Pa.) Indian School. In the 1912 Olympic Games he won the decathlon and pentathlon, setting records in both events, but he was stripped of his gold medals (1913) when it was learned that he had earned money playing baseball. He played professional football (from 1915) and professional baseball (1913-9). He became a charter member (1963) of the Pro Football Hall of Fame, and in 1982 the Olympic Committee voted to restore his gold medals

those *pl.* of THAT

Thoth (θouθ, tout) (*Egyptian mythol.*) the god of wisdom and magic, identified with the Greek Hermes. He is the inventor of speech and writing, the arts and sciences. He is usually represented as having the body of a man and the head of an ibis

thou (ðau) (objective THEE, possessive THY or THINE) 2nd *pers. sing. personal pron.* now almost only used in prayer to God [O.E. *thu, thū*]

thou (θau) *n.* (*pop.*) a thousand

though (ðou) **1.** *conj.* used to introduce a statement of fact or a possibility which might prevent a second statement from being true but does not in fact do so (drawing attention to the opposition involved in the two statements), *he is still active though very old* **as though** as if, *he spoke as though he meant it* **2.** *adv.* nevertheless, *the ground was muddy, it was a good game though* [of Scand. origin]

thought (θɔt) *n.* the action or process of thinking || the capacity to think || an idea or pattern of ideas || the patterns of ideas characteristic of a period, a person, social group or field of activity, *modern thought, political thought* || consideration, *don't give it a moment's thought* || intention, *he once had the thought of selling the house* || meditation, *engrossed in thought* [O.E. *thoht*]

thought *past* and *past part.* of THINK

thought·ful (θɔ́tfəl) *adj.* absorbed in the process of thinking, *you look very thoughtful* || characterized by or resulting from a long or careful process of thought, *a thoughtful speech* || showing consideration for others, *a thoughtful act*

thought·less (θɔ́tlis) *adj.* said or done without having given thought to a probable result || showing lack of consideration for others

thou·sand (θáuzənd) **1.** *n.* 10 times 100 (*NUMBER TABLE) || the cardinal number representing this (1,000, M) || (*pl.*) in mathematical calculations, the column of figures four places to the left of the decimal point **thousands of** a great many **2.** *adj.* being 10 times 100 **thou·sandth** (θáuzəndθ) **1.** *adj.* being number 1,000 in a series (*NUMBER TABLE) || being one of the 1,000 equal parts of anything **2.** *n.* the person or thing next after the 999th || one of 1,000 equal parts of anything (1/1,000) [O.E. *thūsend*]

Thousand Days' War a civil war fought (1899-1902) in Colombia between conservative and liberal forces. It resulted in 100,000 deaths, and this left Colombia unable to resist (1903) the U.S.-backed, secession of Panama

Thrace (θreis) (*Gk* Thraki) the southeastern part of the Balkan peninsula shared by Greece, Turkey and Bulgaria since 1878. Historically the region has varied greatly in extent. Its coast was settled by the Greeks (8th-1st cc. B.C.). The rest of the region remained independent until conquered by Persia (512-479 B.C.), Macedon (342-281 and 211-196 B.C.), and Rome (46 A.D.). The Ottoman Turks took Adrianople (1361) and Constantinople (1453) and the region became part of the Ottoman Empire

Thra·cian (θréiʃən) **1.** *adj.* pertaining to Thrace, its people, culture etc. 2. a native or inhabitant of Thrace || (*hist.*) an Indo-European language spoken by the early inhabitants of Thrace

thraldom *THRALLDOM

thrall (θrɔl) *n.* (*hist.*) a slave or person held in bondage **to hold in thrall** (*rhet.*) to enchant, enthrall [O.E. *thrǣl*]

thrall·dom, thral·dom (θrɔ́ldəm) *n.* (*hist.*) the condition of a thrall || (*rhet.*) servitude

thrash (θræʃ) **1.** *v.t.* to strike repeatedly with a cane or whip || to thresh (wheat etc.) || to defeat soundly || *v.i.* to move the limbs or body violently || (*naut.*) to sail against contrary winds **to thrash over** (or **out**) to discuss (a matter) in detail in order to discover the truth or a solution **2.** *n.* the act of thrashing || a leg movement used by swimmers in the crawl and backstroke [O.E. *therscan*]

thrash·er (θrǽʃər) *n.* any of several American songbirds of fam. *Mimidae* [perh. fr. Br. dial. *thrusher, thresher*, thrush]

thread (θred) **1.** *n.* a fine cord made by twisting two or more strands of cotton, silk etc. together, used in sewing || such cords collectively || any of the fibers used in weaving a material || a natural or manufactured threadlike filament || that which gives continuity to, or is continuous in, an argument, speech, story etc. || the spiral grooves of a screw, bolt etc. **2.** *v.t.* to pass a thread through the eye of (a needle) || to put (beads etc.) together by passing a thread through each || to furnish (e.g. a screw or tube) with a thread || to feed film into (a movie camera or projector) || to interweave with or as if with threads, *hair threaded with silver* || to make (a way) between a number of obstacles, or in a maze of streets, by changes of direction || *v.i.* (esp. with 'through') to make a way [O.E. *thrǣd*]

thread·bare (θrédbɛər) *adj.* of a fabric from which the nap has been worn away || wearing shabby clothes || (of an argument, expressed opinion, joke etc.) so familiar as to have lost its interest || (of an excuse, plot etc.) obviously inadequate

thread·worm (θrédwə:rm) *n.* a threadlike nematode, esp. one infesting the human rectum

thread·y (θrédi:) *comp.* **thread·i·er** *superl.* **thread·i·est** *adj.* of or resembling a thread || (of the pulse) thin and feeble (of the voice) weak

threat (θret) *n.* a statement or other indication of intention to hurt, punish, destroy etc. || an indication that an undesirable event or catastrophe may occur, *a threat of rain, a threat to party unity* [O.E. *thrēat*]

threat·en (θrét'n) *v.t.* to utter or otherwise indicate a threat to (someone) || to promise (something harmful, evil etc.) as a threat || to indicate the approach of (something unpleasant, harmful etc.), *the clouds threaten rain* [O.E. *thrēatnian*]

threatened species (*biol.*) a species that might become endangered within a short period of time *Cf* ENDANGERED SPECIES

three (θri:) **1.** *adj.* being one more than two (*NUMBER TABLE) **2.** *n.* two plus one || the cardinal number representing this (3, III) || three o'clock || a playing card (domino etc.) marked with three symbols (spots etc.) [O.E. *thrī, thrīo, thrēo*]

three-base hit (*baseball*) a triple

three-color process (*printing*) a color-printing process in which three inks of different primary colors are superimposed in separate printings, sometimes with a fourth printing, in black

three-cor·nered (θrí:kɔ́rnərd) *adj.* having three corners or angles || (of a contest) having three contestants, each competing with the other two, *a three-cornered election fight*

three-di·men·sion·al (θrí:diménʃən'l) *adj.* (*abbr.* 3-D) having, or appearing to have, length, breadth and depth in space || (*math.*) able to be represented by reference to three axes at right angles to one another

three·fold (θrí:fould) **1.** *adj.* triple **2.** *adv.* to three times as much or as many || by three times [O.E. *thrīfeald, thrȳfeald*]

Three Mile Island 1. site near Harrisburg, PA, of 1979 nuclear accident **2.** by extension, prototype of risk of nuclear energy

three-mile limit (*internat. law*) the strip of coastal waters three miles wide over which a state has national sovereignty

three·pence (θrépəns, θrʌ́pəns, θrí pəns) *n.* (*Br.*) a value, expressed in terms of money, equal to that of three pence (*Br., hist.*) a threepenny bit

three·pen·ny (θrépəni:, θrʌ́pəni:, θrípəni:) *adj.* (*Br.*) costing or worth threepence

threepenny bit (*Br., hist.*) a coin worth three pennies. It ceased to be minted when the British currency was decimalized (1971)

three-phase (θrí:feiz) *adj.* (*elec.*) of, relating to, or operating by a combination of three circuits actuated by superimposed electromotive currents that differ in phase by 120°.

three-piece (θrí:pi:s) **1.** *adj.* made or consisting of three pieces, e.g. a costume of separate coat, skirt and jacket **2.** *n.* such a costume

three-ply (θrí:plai) *adj.* having three strands, layers etc.

three-quar·ter (θrí:kwɔ́rtər) *n.* (*rugby*) a back whose position lies between that of halfback and fullback

three-quarter *adj.* of or relating to three quarters of the full length or size

three-quarter binding a book binding in which the spine and corners are covered in one material and the sides in another, the material on the spine extending over one third of the width of the sides (cf. FULL BINDING, cf. HALF BINDING, cf. QUARTER BINDING)

three-quar·ter-bound (θrí:kwɔ́rtərbaund) *adj.* (of a book) having a threequarter binding

Three Rivers *TROIS RIVIÈRES

three·score (θrí:skɔ́r, θrí:skóur) *adj.* sixty, three times twenty

three·some (θrí:səm) *n.* a group of three persons

‖ (*golf*) a game in which three players compete

Three-Tier Agreement (θrí:tíər) an arms limitation proposal advanced by the U.S. at the Geneva SALT talks in May 1977, including a treaty limiting strategic weapons for eight years, a protocol limiting certain other weapons for three years, and a statement of principles for future arms reduction

thre·node (θrí:noud, θrénoud) *n.* a threnody

thre·no·di·al (θrinóudi:əl) *adj.* threnodic

thre·nod·ic (θrinódik) *adj.* of or like a threnody

thren·o·dist (θrénədist) *n.* a singer or composer of threnodies

thren·o·dy (θrénədi:) *pl.* **thren·o·dies** *n.* (*rhet.*) a song of lamentation, esp. a funeral song, dirge [fr. Gk *thrēnōdia*]

thresh (θreʃ, *Br.* also θræʃ) *v.t.* to separate the grain from the ear of (wheat etc.) *v.i.* to thresh grain ‖ to toss about, thrash **to thresh out** to go over (a problem) repeatedly until it is clarified and solved **thrésh·er** *n.* a threshing machine [O.E. *threscan, therscan*]

thresher shark *Alopias vulpinus,* fam. *Lamnidae,* a large, long-tailed shark measuring up to 20 ft in length, found in all oceans. It is an excellent game fish, but not highly regarded as food

threshing machine a power-driven machine for threshing out grain

thresh·old (θréʃhould, θréʃould) *n.* the plank or stone at the bottom of a doorway ‖ a beginning, *the threshold of a career* ‖ the point at which a stimulus of increasing strength is first perceived or produces its specific response, *auditory threshold* [O.E. *therscold, therscwold*]

threw *past* of THROW

thrice (θrais) *adv.* (*rhet.*) three times [M.E. *thries,* three times]

thrift (θrift) *n.* the practice of avoiding wasteful or avoidable expenditure ‖ a member of *Armeria,* fam. *Plumbaginaceae,* a genus of low-growing plants, esp. *A. maritima,* bearing pink or white flowers and found in coastal and mountainous regions of the north temperate zone [O.N.]

thrift·i·ly (θríftili:) *adv.* in a thrifty manner

thrift·i·ness (θrífti:nis) *n.* the quality or state of being thrifty

thrift shop 1. a shop that sells secondhand merchandise contributed to a charity **2.** by extension a shop dealing in secondhand merchandise

thrift·y (θrífti:) *comp.* **thrift·i·er** *superl.* **thrift·i·est** *adj.* practicing thrift ‖ (esp. of plants and animals) thriving, growing well

thrill (θril) **1.** *v.t.* to cause tense emotional excitement (of joy, horror etc.) in ‖ *v.i.* to feel tense emotional excitement **2.** *n.* a moment of excitement or intense emotion ‖ (*med.*) an unnatural vibration in the respiratory or circulatory systems

thrill·er *n.* a fictional work designed to thrill the audience or reader [M.E.]

thrips (θrips) *n.* a member of *Thrips,* fam. *Thripidae,* a genus of minute hemipterons having thin, fringed wings and sucking mouthparts. They feed mainly on plant juices and are regarded as pests [L. fr. Gk *thrips,* woodworm]

thrive (θraiv) *pres. part.* **thriv·ing** *past* **throve** (θrouv), **thrived** *past part.* **thrived, thriv·en** (θrívən) *v.i.* to grow and function well ‖ to have good health ‖ to do well financially [M.E. fr. O.N.]

throat (θrout) *n.* the front part of the neck ‖ the upper part of the passage leading from the mouth to the stomach and lungs and including the larynx, pharynx, trachea and esophagus ‖ a narrow passage, esp. one serving as an entrance **to cut one's own throat** to act to one's own disadvantage **to ram something down somebody's throat** to compel someone to listen to something he does not want to hear **to stick in one's throat** to fail to be uttered through pressure of emotion [O.E. *throte, throtul*]

throat·i·ly (θróutili:) *adv.* in a throaty manner

throat·i·ness (θróuti:nis) *n.* the state or quality of being throaty

throat·y (θróuti:) *comp.* **throat·i·er** *superl.* **throat·i·est** *adj.* (of a sound) produced chiefly in the throat ‖ (of the voice) rather deep and rough, as though coming from low down in the throat ‖ (of an animal) having a large, loose-skinned throat

throb (θrɒb) **1.** *v.i. pres. part.* **throb·bing** *past* and *past part.* **throbbed** to vibrate ‖ (of the pulse etc.) to beat strongly ‖ to show emotional excitement **2.** *n.* a pulsation of low frequency but large amplitude, esp. of the heart or arteries ‖ the sound produced by throbbing, *the throb of the drums* [M.E. perh. imit.]

throe (θrou) *n.* (*rhet.*) a spasm of pain or anguish ‖ (*pl.*) a painful struggle, esp. of childbirth or of death [M.E. *throw, throwe* prob. fr. O.E. *thrāwu,* pain]

throm·bin (θrómbin) *n.* (*biochem.*) an enzyme which enables fibrinogen to form fibrin, causing blood clots (*PROTHROMBIN) [fr. Gk *thrŏmbos,* a clot of blood]

throm·bo·gen (θrómbədʒin) *n.* prothrombin [fr. Gk *thrŏmbos,* a clot of blood, lump+*-genēs,* born of]

throm·bo·sis (θrɒmbóusis) *n.* the formation of a clot inside a blood vessel, esp. in the coronary or cerebral arteries [Mod. L. fr. Gk *thrŏmbosis,* curdling]

throm·bus (θrómbəs) *pl.* **throm·bi** (θrómbai) *n.* a fibrinous clot formed in a blood vessel, which remains where it formed (cf. EMBOLUS) [Mod. L. fr. Gk *thrŏmbos,* a clot of blood]

throne (θroun) **1.** *n.* a chair (usually decorated with carving, inlaid woods or jewels etc.) reserved for the use of a sovereign, bishop etc. when he is exercising his authority, and placed on a dais in order to symbolize this authority ‖ sovereignty ‖ the sovereign ruler ‖ a raised seat for a painter's model ‖ (*pl.*) an order of angels (*ANGEL) **2.** *v.t. pres. part.* **thron·ing** *past* and *past part.* **throned** to place on a throne ‖ to vest with the powers of sovereignty [O.F. *trone* fr. L. fr. Gk]

throng (θrɔŋ, θrɒŋ) **1.** *n.* a great many people assembled together, esp. crowded together ‖ a great number of things crowded together, *a throng of ants* **2.** *v.i.* to move in a throng or assemble so as to form a throng ‖ *v.t.* to occupy (a space) by crowding into it [M.E. *thrang, throng* prob. shortened fr. O.E. *gethrang,* a crowd]

thros·tle (θrós'l) *n.* a song thrush ‖ (*Br.*) a worsted spinning frame [O.E. *throstle*]

throt·tle (θrót'l) **1.** *v.t. pres. part.* **throt·tling** *past* and *past part.* **throt·tled** to choke ‖ to reduce the supply of steam, air, gasoline etc. in (an engine) and so reduce its rate of working **2.** *n.* a valve which regulates the supply of gasoline vapor and air to an engine ‖ the hand lever or foot pedal controlling this valve [perh. dim. of THROAT]

throttle valve a throttle

through (θru:) **1.** *prep.* from one end to the other end of, *to walk through a room* ‖ in one side and out the other side of, *to climb through a window* ‖ from the beginning to the end of, during, *to sleep through the night* ‖ in the state of being or having finished, esp. successfully, *to be through one's finals* ‖ among, *the news spread through the crowd* ‖ by way of, *we came through Rome* ‖ by means of, *he got the job through her influence* ‖ by reason of, *they stopped through fear of reprisal* ‖ (with a preceding specified time) up to and including, *Monday through Friday* **2.** *adv.* in one side and out the other ‖ from end to end ‖ from the beginning to the end ‖ all the way, *this train goes through to Chicago* ‖ to a conclusion, *to see a thing through* ‖ completely, *wet through* **3.** *adj.* not involving a change of e.g. train, *a through ticket* ‖ not involving a passenger in a change, *a through train* ‖ at the end of one's abilities or resources, *he's through as a tennis player* ‖ finished, *are you through with that book?* ‖ allowing free passage, *no through way* ‖ having no further dealings, *he's through with her forever* [O.E. *thurh*]

through and through utterly, *he is a scholar through and through*

through·out (θru:áut) **1.** *adv.* continuously, from beginning to end of a distance or period of time **2.** *prep.* in or during every part of

through·put (θrú:put) *n.* (*computer*) the total product of all facets of a unit's operations

throughway *THRUWAY

throve alt. *past* of THRIVE

throw (θrou) **1.** *v. pres. part.* **throw·ing** *past* **threw** (θru:) *past part.* **thrown** (θroun) *v.t.* to cause suddenly to move through the air by a muscular effort and fling of the arm ‖ to propel through the air, *the hose throws a 20-foot jet* ‖ to cause to fall to the floor or ground ‖ to cause to move rapidly, *he threw his reserves into the battle* ‖ to project, *that lamp throws a poor light* ‖ (with 'on') to put hurriedly, *he threw a log on the fire, throw some clothes on the boy* ‖ to construct (something) quickly, *to throw a bridge across a river* ‖ to cause a sudden change in the circumstances of, *he was thrown out of work* ‖ to shed, *the horse threw a shoe, a snake throws its skin* ‖ (of animals) to give birth to ‖ (*card games*) to play or discard ‖ to cast (dice) ‖ to make (a specified cast) at dice ‖ (*pop.*) to lose (a contest) by choice ‖ (*pop.*) to give (a party) ‖ to twist strands of (silk) into thread ‖ to shape on a potter's wheel ‖ to activate (the lever) of a machine, engine etc. or (the switch) of an electric circuit etc. ‖ to cause (the blame) to fall on someone or something ‖ to place (an obstacle) in the way of someone ‖ to put (an automobile etc.) into a specified gear ‖ *v.i.* to cast or hurl something **to throw away** to discard as of no value ‖ to be wasteful of ‖ to fail to use (a chance) **to throw back** to reflect (light, heat etc.) ‖ to cause to fall back ‖ to revert to ancestral type **to throw in** to add as an extra, esp. without charge ‖ to interject (e.g. a remark) ‖ to engage (the clutch of a motorcar etc.) **to throw in one's lot with** to choose (one party or group) and accept its fate **to throw off** to elude (a pursuer) ‖ to cast off ‖ to emit ‖ to write or say in a casual manner ‖ to cause (hounds) to lose the scent ‖ to mislead, *his air of innocence threw them off* **to throw oneself at** to try to win the friendship or love of in too blatant a fashion **to throw oneself into** to become wholeheartedly engaged in **to throw oneself on** (or **upon**) to abandon oneself to (e.g. the mercy of someone) **to throw open** to open suddenly and completely ‖ to permit unrestricted access to ‖ **to throw out** to remove forcibly from a place ‖ to dismiss ‖ to reject ‖ to throw away ‖ to utter (e.g. a suggestion) ‖ to disengage (a clutch) ‖ (*baseball*) to put out (a runner) by throwing the ball to a baseman ‖ to upset the calculations of, disconcert ‖ to cause to stand out **to throw over** to have no more to do with ‖ to abandon **to throw together** to construct or make hastily and carelessly **to throw up** to vomit ‖ to construct very quickly ‖ to abandon (a job etc.) ‖ to remind someone uncharitably of (something) as a reproach or criticism **2.** *n.* the action of one who throws ‖ an instance of throwing ‖ the distance something is or can be thrown, *a throw of 100 yards* ‖ a cast of dice or the number cast ‖ (*geol.*) the vertical displacement of strata due to faulting ‖ (*pottery*) a period of using the wheel ‖ (*pottery*) one complete movement of the hands up the wall of a pot in throwing ‖ a light spread for a bed etc. ‖ (*mach.*) the motion of a moving part, e.g. a cam, or the extent of its motion ‖ (*wrestling*) the act of throwing an opponent or a particular method of doing this [O.E. *thrāwan*]

throw·a·way (θróuəwei) *n.* a handbill

throwaway *adj.* **1.** designed to be discarded after use **2.** (*theater*) of dialogue delivered so to be hardly heard

throwaway children children (usu. ages 1–13 yrs) whose parents do not want them at home

throw·back (θróubæk) *n.* a reversion to ancestral type ‖ an instance of this ‖ someone or something exhibiting this

throw·off (θróuɔf, θróuɒf) *n.* (printing) a device that stops impression but allows the press to keep running

throw·ster (θroustər) *n.* a person who throws silk

throw-weight (θróuweit) *n.* (*mil.*) a measure of the warhead-carrying capacity of an ICBM

thru (θru:) *prep., adv.* and *adj.* (*pop.*) through

thrum (θrʌm) **1.** *n.* the loose fringe on a loom when the web has been cut ‖ one of the warp threads of which this consists ‖ a thread of a tassel ‖ (*pl.*) waste yarn ‖ (*naut.,* esp. *pl.*) short pieces of rope or spun yarn used e.g. to wrap around rigging to prevent chafing **2.** *v.t. pres. part.* **thrum·ming** *past* and *past part.* **thrummed** to cover with thrum ‖ (*naut.*) to sew thrums on (a sail) [O.E.=ligament]

thrum 1. *v. pres. part.* **thrum·ming** *past* and *past part.* **thrummed** *v.i.* to make a drumming sound with the fingers ‖ to play idly on a stringed instrument ‖ *v.t.* to drum on (something) with the fingers ‖ to play idly on (a stringed instrument) **2.** *n.* the act or sound of thrumming [imit.]

thrum-eyed (θrʌ́maid) *adj.* (of a flower, esp. of fam. *Primulaceae*) having a short style and long stamens extending to the mouth of the tubular corolla (cf. PIN-EYED)

thrush (θrʌʃ) *n.* any of various small or medium-sized songbirds of fam. *Turdidae* incl. the song thrush and the American robin [O.E. *thrȳsce*]

thrush *n.* a disease of the mouth and throat caused by infection with a fungus. It appears in the form of slightly raised white patches on the membranes of the mouth, tongue and throat, and occurs esp. in emaciated children ‖ a suppurative and inflammatory disease of the frog of a horse's hoof [origin unknown]

thrust (θrʌst) **1.** *v. pres. part.* **thrust·ing** *past* and *past part.* **thrust** *v.t.* to push suddenly and with force, *he thrust his weight against the crowd* ‖ to cause (a weapon or sharp body) to pierce, *he thrust the dagger into his side* ‖ to force (a person) into a situation against his own or someone else's wishes ‖ to impose, *the obligation was thrust upon him* ‖ to interpose (a question etc.), esp. aggressively ‖ to force (a way) by pushing ‖ to extend (a limb, branch etc.) in some direction or into some place ‖ *v.i.* to make a sudden push ‖ to force one's way, *he thrust through the crowd* ‖ to make a stab ‖ (*rhet.*) to surge powerfully upwards or press outwards, *a great oak thrusting upwards towards the sky* **2.** *n.* a sudden violent push, e.g. with a pointed weapon ‖ the strong pressure of one part of a structure against another, e.g. of an arch on its abutments ‖ the driving force exerted through a propeller shaft, e.g. in an airplane ‖ the forward reaction to the jet exhaust of an engine ‖ (*geol.*) an almost horizontal fault [M.E. *thrusten, thrysten*]

thrust chamber (*aerospace*) the area in a propulsion rocket in which force accumulates before ejection, e.g., the reaction chamber

thrust·er or **thrust·or** (θrʌ́stə:r) *n.* (*eng.*) **1.** an engine including motor hydraulic pump and piston that produces a thrust by expelling a jet of gas, fluid, or particles **2.** (initial capitals) trade name for a device used to apply force to a brake

thrust stage (*theater*) stage sometimes including an extending runway in which audience surrounds the performing area on three sides

thru·way, through·way (θrú:wei) *n.* an expressway

Thu·cyd·i·des (θu:sídidi:z)(c. 460–c. 395 B.C.), Athenian historian. The failure of an expedition led by him during the Peloponnesian War led to his exile (424-404 B.C.). His 'History of the Peloponnesian War' (to 411 B.C.) is an impartial, concise and scientific work which sets him among the greatest ancient historians

thud (θʌd) **1.** *v.i. pres. part.* **thud·ding** *past* and *past part.* **thud·ded** to fall with or make a dull heavy sound **2.** *n.* a dull sound of short duration caused by an impact without vibration [prob. imit.]

thug (θʌg) *n.* any person who uses violence or brutality, esp. a criminal **Thug** (*hist.*) a member of an Indian religious organization of murderers and robbers (c. 13th–19th cc.) put down (1828–35) by the British under Bentinck [Hindi *ṭhag*, swindler]

thug·gee (θʌ́gi:) *n.* (*hist.*) the practice of murder and robbery by the Thugs of India [Hindi *ṭhagī*]

Thu·le (θú:li:) the name given by the Greeks and Romans to an island (Iceland, Norway, or most probably one of the Shetlands) which was the most northerly part of the then known world

Thule a former trading center in N.W. Greenland, now a U.S. strategic base

thu·li·um (θú:li:əm) *n.* a chemical element (symbol Tm, at. no. 69, at. mass 168.934) belonging to the rare-earth group [Mod. L. fr. THULE]

thumb (θʌm) **1.** *n.* the short thick digit of the hand which is opposable to the fingers and is also distinguished from them by having only two phalanges ‖ the part of a glove or mitten which covers this digit ‖ the corresponding digit in an animal **all thumbs** clumsy in handling something **under someone's thumb** completely dominated by someone **2.** *v.t.* to handle or manipulate with the thumb, *to thumb the pages of a book* ‖ to try to stop (a driver or his car) in order to get a ride ‖ to make (one's way) by this method **to thumb a ride, thumb a lift** to hitchhike **to thumb through** to turn over the pages of (a book etc.) in a quick reading or search [O.E. *thūma*]

thumb index an index in which the initial letters or titles are made visible by grooves or tabs **thúmb-in·dex** *v.t.* to supply with a thumb index

thumb·nail (θʌ́mneil) **1·** *n.* the nail of the thumb **2.** *adj.* very small or concise, *a thumbnail sketch*

thumb piano *MBIRA

thumb·print (θʌ́mprint) *n.* an impression made by the inside top joint of the thumb

thumb·screw (θʌ́mskru:) *n.* a screw with a flattened head that may be turned with the thumb and finger ‖ (*hist.*) an instrument of torture in which the thumb was crushed

thumbs-down (θʌ́mzdáun) *n.* a signal of rejection or disapproval

thumb·stall (θʌ́mstɔl) *n.* a leather sheath worn to protect the thumb ‖ a rubber device worn on the thumb, e.g. to help one in sorting mail

thumbs-up (θʌ́mzʌ́p) *n.* a signal of acceptance or approval **thumbs up!** good luck!

thumb·tack (θʌ́mtæk) *n.* (*Am.*=*Br.* drawing pin) a tack or pin with a round, flat head, used esp. for fastening paper to a drawing board or bulletin board

thump (θʌmp) **1.** *v.t.* to strike with a thump ‖ to defeat heavily ‖ (with 'out') to play (a tune) in a loud, unmusical way, esp. on the piano ‖ *v.i.* to deliver thumps ‖ to fall with a thump ‖ to make the noise of a thump or thumps, *his heart thumped in his chest* **2.** *n.* a dull, heavy blow, or the sound of it **thúmp·ing** *adj.* (*pop.*) very big, *a thumping price* [imit.]

thun·der (θʌ́ndər) **1.** *n.* the sound accompanying an atmospheric electrical discharge (i.e. lightning) due to the explosive expansion of suddenly heated air ‖ loud sounds compared with this, *the thunder of horses' hoofs* ‖ vehement rhetoric **to steal someone's thunder** to use the ideas, arguments etc. of someone before he can use and get credit for them himself **2.** *v.i.* (*impers.*) to produce the sound of thunder ‖ to produce a very loud sound ‖ to utter violent denunciations ‖ *v.t.* to utter in a thundering voice [O.E. *thunor*]

Thunder Bay, a city (pop. 112,486) and port in Ontario, Canada, on Lake Superior. Formerly Fort William, it handles enormous outgoing shipments of grain, newsprint and furs and incoming freights of coal

thun·der·bolt (θʌ́ndərboult) *n.* a single, intense discharge of electricity, accompanied by the sound of thunder ‖ an imaginary missile hurled to earth when a great clap of thunder bursts ‖ a conventional representation of this ‖ something or someone destructive or violent

Thunderbolt II *n.* (*mil.*) a twin-engine, subsonic, turbofan, STOL tactical fighter/bomber (A-110), equipped with a 30-mm cannon, capable of employing a variety of air-to-surface launched weapons in the close air support role, and is supplemented by air refueling; manufactured by Fairchild and Republic

Thunderchief *n.* (*mil.*) a supersonic, single-engine, turbojet-powered tactical, all-weather fighter (F-105), capable of delivering nuclear or nonnuclear weapons and rockets, equipped with the Sidewinder weapon and an in-flight refueling capacity

thun·der·clap (θʌ́ndərklæp) *n.* a loud crash of thunder ‖ anything that is profoundly shocking because of its suddenness, violence etc.

thun·der·cloud (θʌ́ndərklaud) *n.* a dense cloud of water drops which, by coalescing, have acquired electric charges equal to, and likely to exceed, their capacities

thun·der·head (θʌ́ndərhed) *n.* a round mass of cumulus cloud with shining white edges that often appears before a thunderstorm

thun·der·ing (θʌ́ndəriŋ) *adj.* that thunders ‖ (*pop.*) extremely big or impressive, *a thundering lie*

thun·der·ous (θʌ́ndərəs) *adj.* like thunder, esp. in its loudness

thun·der·show·er (θʌ́ndərʃauər) *n.* a rain shower accompanied by thunder and lightning

thun·der·storm (θʌ́ndərstɔrm) *n.* a storm of rain and wind accompanied by lightning and thunder

thun·der·strick·en (θʌ́ndərstrikən) *adj.* thunderstruck

thun·der·struck (θʌ́ndərstrʌk) *adj.* temporarily deprived of the power to speak or think by a sudden access of emotion, esp. astonishment

thun·der·y (θʌ́ndəri:) *adj.* thundering or threatening to thunder

Thur. Thursday

Thur·ber (θə́:rbər), James (1894-1961), U.S. humorist and cartoonist, author of 'The Owl in the Attic' (1931), 'Thurber Country' (1953) etc.

Thur·gau (tú:rgau) a German-speaking, largely Protestant canton (area 397 sq. miles, pop. 183,795) of N. Switzerland, on Lake Constance. Capital: Frauenfeld (pop. 11,000)

Thü·ring·er Wald (týriŋərvɑlt) a wooded mountain range (rising to 3,225 ft) on the southwest border of East Germany, with scattered industries (glassmaking, light engineering)

Thu·rin·gi·a (θuríndʒi:ə) (*G.* Thüringen) a former state of East Germany in the central German highland, now included in the districts of Suhl, Erfurt and Gera. (Other centers: Weimar, Eisenach.) The wooded Harz Mtns in the north, and Thüringer Wald in the south, descend to the fertile Thuringian basin on the upper Saale. Agriculture: cereals, root vegetables, market produce, fruit, flowers, wine. Industries: engineering, light manufacturing. An old tribal land conquered by the Franks (6th–8th cc.), it passed (14th c.) to the ruling house of Saxony and split into several duchies, which joined the German Empire (1871) and were united in 1920

Thur·mond (θə́:rmənd), (James) Strom (1902-), U.S. political leader, Senator (South Carolina). He ran (1948) as the presidential candidate for the States' Rights Democratic party ('Dixiecrats'), comprising Southerners who bolted the Democratic party in opposition to President Harry Truman's civil rights program. Elected to the Senate as a Democrat in 1954, he became a Republican in 1964; chairman of the Judiciary Committee from 1981

Thurs. Thursday

thu·ri·ble (θúərəb'l) *n.* a censer [fr. L. *thuribulum*]

thu·ri·fer (θúərəfər) *n.* an acolyte who carries and swings a censer [Mod. L. fr. *thus* (*thuris*), incense + *-fer*, bearing]

Thu·rin·gi·an (θurínd ʒi:ən) *adj.* of or relating to Thuringia

Thurs·day (θə́:rzdi:, θə́:rzdei) *n.* the fifth day of the week [O.E. *Thunres-dæg, thursdæg, thuresdæg*, Thor's day]

thus (ðʌs) *adv.* in this way, *do it thus* ‖ for this reason, *he was not there and thus you could not have seen him* ‖ to this extent or degree, *thus far* ‖ as an example of what immediately precedes [O.E.]

Thut·mo·se I (θʌtmóusə) (*d.* c. 1508 B.C.), Egyptian pharaoh (c. 1525–c. 1508 B.C.) of the 18th dynasty. He conquered Nubia as far as the third cataract of the Nile and Syria as far as the Euphrates

Thutmose III (*d.* c. 1436 B.C.), Egyptian pharaoh (c. 1490–c. 1436 B.C.) of the 18th dynasty, son of Thutmose I. He ruled jointly until c. 1469 B.C. with his wife and half sister Hatshepsut. He firmly established Egyptian rule in Syria and built up an empire stretching to the Euphrates

thwack (θwæk) **1.** *v.t.* to whack **2.** *n.* a flat heavy blow [prob. imit.]

thwart (θwɔrt) **1.** *v.t.* to prevent (a plan) from being carried out ‖ to prevent (someone) from carrying out a plan **2.** *adj.* transverse **3.** *adv.* transversely **4.** *n.* (*naut.*) an oarsman's seat at right angles to the length of the boat [Early M.E. *thwert* fr. O.N. *thvert*, transverse]

thy (ðai) *possessive adj.* (THINE before an initial vowel and in the absolute) of or pertaining to or done by thee [Early M.E. *thī*]

Thy·es·tes (θaiésti:z) *ATREUS

thyme (taim) *n.* a member of *Thymus*, fam. *Labiatae*, a genus of plants found chiefly in Mediterranean regions. They are low aromatic shrubs with tiny leaves and small bilabiate purple flowers. Oil used in thymol is obtained from the foliage. *T. vulgaris*, the common garden thyme, is used for seasoning in cooking [fr. F. *thym* fr. L. fr. Gk]

thy·mine (θáimi:n) *n.* a crystalline pyrimidine base ($C_5H_6N_2O_2$) obtained by hydrolysis from deoxyribonucleic acid [fr. G. *thymin*]

thy·mol (θáimɔl) *n.* an aromatic phenol, $CH_3C_6H_3(C_3H_7)OH$, derived from the natural oil of thyme and used as an antiseptic

thy·mus (θáiməs) *n.* a ductless glandular structure of undetermined function behind the breastbone, which degenerates with the onset of puberty [Mod. L. fr. Gk]

thy·ra·tron (θáirətrɒn) *n.* (*electr.*) a triode filled with argon, neon, helium, or other gas, in which ionization takes place when sufficient positive swing of the negative grid potential exists and the anode and grid potentials lose control *abbr.* TN

thy·ris·tor (θairístə:r) *n.* (*electr.*) solid-state switching device, similar to a thyratron, for semiconductors to convert alternating current in one or two directions controlled by an electrode, e.g., a silicon-controlled rectifier, gate turn-off switch

thyrocalcitonin *CALCITONIN

thy·roid (θáirɔid) **1.** *n.* an endocrine gland of many vertebrates in the pharyngeal area secreting thyroxine, which principally increases the rate of oxidative reactions in metabolism, thus greatly influencing growth and development ‖ thyroid extract **2.** *adj.* of or pertaining to the thyroid [fr. Gk *thureoeidēs*, shield-shaped]

thyroid cartilage a large cartilage in the larynx

thy·rox·in (θairɔ́ksin) *n.* thyroxine

thy·rox·ine (θairɔ́ksi:n, θairɔ́ksin) *n.* (*biochem.*) a hormone secreted by the thyroid that stimulates the rate of metabolism of the entire organism

thyr·sus (θə́:rsəs) *pl.* **thyr·si** (θə́:rsai) *n.* a long shaft or spear, tipped with a pine cone and wrapped with vine leaves or ivy carried by Dionysus, the satyrs etc. ‖ (*bot.*) an inflorescence in which the main axis is racemose and the secondary axes are cymose (e.g. in the lilac) [L. fr. Gk]

thy·sa·nu·ran (θaisənúərən, θaisənjúərən) **1.** *adj.* of *Thysanura*, an order of wingless insects having bristle-like caudal appendages **2.** *n.* a member of this order **thy·sa·nú·rous** *adj.* [fr. Mod. L. fr. Gk *thusanos*, tassel+*oura*, a tail]

thy·self (ðaisélf) *pron.* reflexive or emphatic form of THOU

ti, *Br.* also **te** (ti:) *n.* (*mus.*) the seventh note of any diatonic scale in movable-do solmization

ti (ti:) *n.* any of many varieties of Asiatic and Pacific woody plants of genus *Cordyline*, fam. *Liliaceae* [Tahitian, Marquesan, Samoan and Maori]

Ti·a·hua·na·co (ti:ɑwɑnɑ́kou, tjɑwɑnɑ́kou) the center in W. Bolivia of a pre-Inca civilization which dominated Peru and Bolivia. The stone structures at Tiahuanaco are particularly fine. Construction began prior to 600 A.D., and additional building took place c. 1100

ti·ar·a (ti:ǽrə, ti:ɑ́rə) *n.* a coronet of usually precious metal and precious stones worn by women ‖ the triple crown worn by the pope ‖ (*hist.*) a headdress worn by ancient Persians [L. fr. Gk]

Tib·bu (tíbu:) *pl.* **Tib·bus, Tib·bu** *n.* a Negroid people living in the Tibesti Mtns area of Central Africa ‖ a member of this people

Ti·ber (táibər) (*Ital.* Tevere) a river 244 miles long, rising in the Apennines in Tuscany and flowing through Umbria and Latium to the Tyrrhenian Sea, navigable by small boats 30 miles past Rome

Ti·be·ri·as (taibíəri:əs) a town (pop. 26,000) of N. Israel on the Sea of Galilee (or Sea of Tiberias)

Ti·be·ri·us (taibíəri:əs) (Tiberius Julius Caesar Augustus, 42 B.C.-37 A.D.), second Roman emperor (14-37), adopted son of Augustus. He won military distinction in many parts of Europe, and was an efficient if austere and unpopular emperor. After 26 A.D. he lived in seclusion on Capri

Ti·bes·ti Mtns (tibésti:) a range in N. Chad, the highest part (Emi Koussi, 11,204 ft) of the central Saharan mountain system

Ti·bet (tibét) an autonomous region (area 470,000 sq. miles, pop. 1,750,000) of China. Capital: Lhasa. Language: Tibetan. Religion: Lamaism. Tibet consists largely of a plateau (averaging 13,000 ft) between the Himalayas and the Kunlun Mtns. In the south are the forested valleys of the Sutlej and Tsangpo (Brahmaputra). Livestock: yaks, goats, sheep, camels. Agriculture (barley, fruit, vegetables) is confined to the Tsangpo valley. Minerals: salt, gold, uranium, iron, coal. Manufactures: cloth, carpets, leather. A modern road (1957) links Tibet with the rest of China. HISTORY. Tibet emerged as an independent kingdom in the 7th c. It came under the influence of the Chinese T'ang dynasty and Buddhism was introduced from India (8th c.). It was conquered by the Mongols under Kublai Khan (13th c.), and by the Chinese Manchu dynasty (1720). With British encouragement, Tibet declared its independence from China (1913). It was invaded by China (1950) and a Communist administration was set up. A revolt broke out (1959) against Communist rule, and the Dalai Lama took refuge in India. The Panchen Lama took over as head of government (1959-64). In 1965, Tibet became an autonomous region of China and since 1980 has been ruled by the head of the Tibetan Communist party. In 1980, Tibetan pilgrims were once again allowed to visit holy sites and Tibetan language and culture were no longer suppressed. In 1985 tourists were allowed to pass between Tibet and Nepal

Ti·bet·an (tibét'n) **1.** *n.* a member of the native race of Tibet. Tibetans are mixed in the west and south with Indian peoples and in the east with Chinese ‖ a native or inhabitant of Tibet ‖ the Tibeto-Burman language of the Tibetans **2.** *adj.* of or relating to Tibet, its people, language, culture etc.

Ti·bet·o-Bur·man (tibétoubə́:rmən) **1.** *n.* a family of languages including Tibetan and Burmese ‖ a member of a people speaking a Tibeto-Burman language **2.** *adj.* of or relating to any of these languages or peoples

Ti·bet·o-Bur·mese (tibétoubə:rmí:z, tibétoubə:rmí:s) *n.* and *adj.* Tibeto-Burman

tib·i·a (tíbi:ə) *pl.* **tib·i·ae** (tíbi:i:), **tib·i·as** *n.* the inner and usually larger of the two bones between the knee and ankle of the vertebrate leg ‖ the fourth joint (from the base) of the leg of an insect [L.]

tib·i·al (tíbi:əl) *adj.* of the tibia [fr. L. *tibialis*]

Ti·bul·lus (tibʌ́ləs) (c. 50–19 B.C.), Roman lyric poet. He wrote elegies on love and nature

tic (tik) *n.* a sudden or recurrent twitch usually of the facial muscles [etym. doubtful]

ti·cal (təkɑ́l, tíkəl) *n.* (*pop. abbr.* tic) the baht, the basic monetary unit of Thailand [Thai fr. Malay *tikal*, a monetary unit]

tic dou·lou·reux (ti:kdu:lu:rə:) *n.* trigeminal neuralgia [F.=painful tic]

ti·car·cil·lin [$C_{15}H_{16}N_2O_6S_2$] (tɑicɑrsílin) *n.* (*pharm.*) semisynthetic penicillin used in septicemia and in respiratory, genito-urinary, skin, and soft tissue infections; marketed as Ticar

Ti·ci·no (titʃí:nou) an Italian-speaking Catholic canton (area 1,088 sq. miles, pop. 265,899) in S. Switzerland. Capital: Bellinzona (pop. 12,000)

tick (tik) **1.** *n.* one of the light sounds made by the escapement of a clock etc. ‖ any similar noise ‖ (*Br., pop.*) a short interval of time ‖ a small distinguishing mark usually signifying agreement and used e.g. by someone checking for correctness **2.** *v.i.* to make the sound of a tick or of a series of ticks ‖ *v.t.* to mark with a tick ‖ (with 'off' or 'out') to register or announce with a ticking sound ‖ (*Br., pop.*, with 'off') to rebuke **to tick along** to move forward, go by or progress at an even, reasonably satisfactory rate **to tick over** (*Br.*, of an engine) to idle ‖ (*Br.*) to keep on working smoothly on minimum effort [prob. imit.]

tick *n.* any of various arachnids of the superfamily *Ixododae*, related to mites but larger than these. An adult tick has an oval nonsegmented body with a movable head through which it draws blood from man and other animals after burrowing under the skin. Ticks transmit various infectious diseases, e.g. Rocky Mountain spotted fever ‖ any of various parasitic dipterous insects, e.g. the sheep ked [M.E. *teke, tyke* prob. fr. O.E.]

tick *n.* a case or covering containing feathers, hair etc., used to form a mattress, pillow etc. ‖ ticking [fr. L. *teca, theca* fr. Gk]

tick *n.* (*Br., pop.*) credit, *to buy on tick* ‖ (*securities*) a change in price up or down [shortened fr. TICKET]

tick·er (tíkər) *n.* a telegraphic instrument that prints news, stock quotations etc. on a paper ribbon

ticker tape the paper ribbon used in a ticker

tick·et (tíkit) **1.** *n.* a tag (label) showing the price, material etc. of an article ‖ a piece of paper or cardboard authorizing the bearer to use a specified service, *a train ticket* or to be admitted to a concert, meeting, theater etc. ‖ a document serving as a license, *captain's ticket* ‖ the candidates of a particular political party ‖ the principles and program of a political party ‖ (*pop.*) a means of getting something desirable, *a car is the ticket to happiness* ‖ a notice issued to someone who has violated a traffic regulation **2.** *v.t.* to attach a ticket to ‖ to provide a ticket for [F. *étiquette*]

ticket inspector (*Br.*) the conductor on a train

ticket-of-leave man (*Br. hist.*) a convict released from prison but required to report regularly to the police and behave well

tick·ing (tíkiŋ) *n.* a strong heavy cotton material of which mattress or pillow covers are made

tick·le (tík'l) **1.** *v.t. pres. part.* **tick·ling** *past* and *past part.* **tick·led** *v.t.* to touch (someone, or a part of the body) where the nerve ends are numerous and sensitive, and by so doing to cause laughter, spasmodic movement etc. ‖ to capture (trout etc.) with bare hands ‖ to excite agreeably ‖ to amuse ‖ *v.i.* to have a tingling sensation **to tickle (someone) pink** (or **to death**) to make (someone) very pleased indeed or amuse (someone) intensely **2.** *n.* a tickling or being tickled ‖ a tickling sensation **tick·lish** (tíkliʃ) *adj.* sensitive to tickling ‖ needing very careful handling, difficult, *a ticklish situation* ‖ sensitive, touchy, *he is ticklish on points of protocol* [etym. doubtful]

Tick·nor (tíknər, tíknɔr), William Davis (1810-64), U.S. publisher, the first to pay foreign authors for rights in their works. He became (1832) a founder of Ticknor and Fields, a firm which published the works of famous contemporaries

tick off *v.* (*colloq.*) to make irate

tick-tack (tíktæk) *n.* (*Br.*) a code of signaling with hands and arms used by men employed at a race track by bookmakers to keep them informed about the trends in the betting

tick·tack·toe (tíktǽktóu) *n.* (*Am.=Br.* naughts-and-crosses) a game of skill in which two players take turns marking Xs and Os, respectively, on a nine-spaced figure formed by two pairs of parallel lines intersecting at right angles. The first to complete a diagonal or row with his marks is the winner

tick·y-tack·y (tíki:tǽki:) *adj.* (*slang or colloq.*) undistinguished, shoddy —**ticky-tack** *n.*

Ti·con·der·o·ga, Fort (tɑikɒndəróugə) a British fort in N.E. New York, captured (1775) during the Revolutionary War by American troops under Benedict Arnold and Ethan Allen

tid·al (táid'l) *adj.* pertaining to, due to or affected by the tides

tidal barrage a barrier in a watercourse which utilizes the natural movements of the tide, usually to generate electricity (*TIDAL POWER STATION)

tidal dock a dock within which the depth of water varies with the tides, i.e. is at the same level as the water outside it

tidal power station a construction by means of which the inrush and outrush of seawater, during the flow and ebb of the tides, into and out of an enclosed reservoir, operate turbines which generate electricity

tidal wave an unusually large wave or very high water, esp. one caused by an earthquake ‖ a sudden spread of intense emotion throughout a community or some other reaction on a big scale, e.g. as manifest in a very large majority vote

tid·bit (tídbit) *n.* a dainty or delicate morsel of food ‖ an interesting bit of information, gossip etc.

tid·dly·wink (tídli:wiŋk) *n.* a piece used in tiddlywinks **tíd·dly·winks** *pl. n.* a game in which small disks are flicked by the downward and backward slipping pressure of a larger disk into a small container [origin unknown]

tide (taid) **1.** *n.* the alternate rising and falling of the seas, usually twice a day, in response to the gravitational attractions of the moon and sun ‖ (in compounds only) a period of time, esp. the season of one of the great Christian festivals, *Christmas-tide* ‖ something thought of as ebbing and flowing like the tide, *the tide of public opinion* **2.** *v. pres. part.* **tid·ing** *past* and *past part.* **tid·ed** *v.i.* (*naut.*) to use the tide in entering or leaving an estuary, harbor etc. ‖ to flow like the tide ‖ *v.t.* to carry with the tide **to tide over** to see (someone) safely through a temporary difficulty [O.E. *tīd*, time]

tide·land (táidlænd) *n.* land that is exposed at low tide and covered at high tide

tide rip rough water caused by opposing tides or currents

tide·wa·ter (táidwɔtər, táidwɒtər) *n.* the water that overflows a land surface at flood tide ‖ low coastal land affected by the tide

tide·way (táidwei) *n.* the channel, part of a river etc. in which tidal currents flow

ti·di·ly (táidili:) *adv.* in a tidy manner

ti·di·ness (táidi:nis) *n.* the state or quality of being tidy

ti·dings (táidiŋz) *pl. n.* (rhet.) news [O.E. *tīdung*, an event]

ti·dy (táidi:) **1.** *comp.* **ti·di·er** *superl.* **ti·di·est** *adj.* in place, in order, *tidy hair* ‖ in the habit of arranging things in their proper places, *a tidy housekeeper* ‖ (*pop.*) substantial, large, *a tidy sum* **2.** *v.t. pres. part.* **ti·dy·ing** *past* and *past part.* **ti·died** (esp. with 'up') to make tidy, *to tidy up a room* **3.** *n. pl.* **ti·dies** a lace or other cover for the arms or headrest of a chair etc. to protect it from dirt or wear [M.E. fr. *tīd*, tide]

tie (tai) **1.** *v. pres. part.* **ty·ing** *past* and *past part.* **tied** *v.t.* to secure (a cord etc.) by a knot or bow ‖ to make (a knot or bow) in a cord etc. ‖ to prevent from moving by means of a knotted cord etc. ‖ to fasten together or connect firmly ‖ to prevent the freedom of action of, *tied to one's bed by illness* ‖ to be equal with in a competition ‖ (*mus.*) to join (notes) by a line ‖ to put under some conditional relationship, *the house is tied to the job* ‖ *v.i.* to be closed or fastened by means of a tie ‖ to be equal in a competition, *they tied for third place* **to tie down** to fasten down (e.g. a hatch) ‖ to commit (e.g. capital) so as to leave one without freedom of action **to tie in** to link (an additional part) with a whole ‖ to arrange so as to be coordinated and not to conflict with something else, *tie in your holiday plans with theirs* ‖ to be in agreement, *the statements do not tie in* **to tie up** to fasten (someone or something) by tying ‖ to restrict the freedom of, esp. to cause to be so busy that invitations or engagements cannot be accepted ‖ to cause to be not readily available, *capital tied up in property* ‖ to fasten (a boat) by a hawser **2.** *n.* a cord, string etc. used for tying something ‖ something which restricts freedom of movement, e.g. a beam holding together a structure ‖ something which restricts personal freedom ‖ a linking force between two or more things, *religious ties* ‖ a competition or election that ends in a draw ‖ (*mus.*) a curved line indicating notes of the same pitch which are to have their time values run together and not be sounded separately ‖ (*Am.*=*Br.* sleeper) a beam of wood resting in loose stones (to allow for small lateral movement), to the surface of which are fastened the steel rails of a railroad track ‖ a necktie [O.E. *tīgan*]

tie·back (táibæk) *n.* a strip of material used for tying back a curtain ‖ (*pl.*) curtains with tie-backs

tie beam a horizontal beam holding rafters in position ‖ any beam serving as a tie

Tieck (ti:k), Ludwig (1773-1853), German Romantic poet, dramatist and novelist. One of his most successful books was 'Volksmärchen von Peter Lebrecht' (1795-6, 3 vols), a collection of fairy tales, poetry and satiric dramas. He was also a literary scholar, critic and translator

tied cottage (*Br.*) a cottage which a farm worker can live in only so long as he is employed by its owner

tied house (*Br.*) a public house whose manager is free to sell the beer etc. only of the brewer to whom the place belongs (cf. FREE HOUSE)

tie-dye (táidai) *v.* to create designs in fabrics by knotting them before immersion in a dye so that some areas are not colored **—tie-dyed** *adj. Cf* BANDHIA

Tien Shan (tjénʃán) a mountain range running along the Kirghizia-China border through central Sinkiang-Uighur, with several peaks over 15,000 ft (summit: 23,260 ft, in the center), and caravan passes over 12,000 ft. Three glaciers around the central peaks are 48, 44 and 31 miles long

Tien·tsin (tjéntsín) a port (pop. 4,250,000) in Hopei, N. China, on the Grand Canal, commercial center of the N. China plain. Industries: metallurgy, chemicals, textiles, food processing. University (1919). A treaty signed here (1858) opened China to European trade. The city was governed by an international commission (1900-7) after the Boxer Rebellion

Tie·po·lo (tjépɔlɔ), Giovanni Battista (1696-1770), Italian painter. The influence of Veronese is seen in his frescoes, with their splendid figures in elaborate colorful costume seen from a characteristically low viewpoint against a cloudless bright sky. He decorated numerous palaces in Würzburg and in Madrid. He is also known as a draftsman and etcher

tier (tiər) **1.** *n.* one of two or more parallel rows of seats at different levels, e.g. in a Greek theater ‖ one of any comparable series of rows, e.g. of shelves in a greenhouse or layers of a wedding cake **2.** *v.t.* to pile or arrange in tiers [fr. older *tire* fr. F. *tire* fr. *tirer*, to elongate]

tierce (tiərs) *n.* (*fencing*) the third position for guard, parry or thrust ‖ (*heraldry*) a field of three differently colored parts ‖ (*hist.*) a liquid measure, a third of a pipe or 42 gallons ‖ (*hist.*) a cask holding this amount ‖ (*eccles.*) terce ‖ (*card games*, təːrs) a sequence of three cards of the same suit [O.F.]

tier·cel (tíərs'l) *n.* the male of certain hawks, e.g. the peregrine [O.F. *tercel*]

Tier·ra del Fue·go (tjérrαðelfwégɔ) a mountainous, sparsely inhabited archipelago (area 27,595 sq. miles) at the southern tip of South America. The eastern half plus Staten Is. (area 8,095 sq. miles) belongs to Argentina, the western half (area 19,500 sq. miles) to Chile. Industries: sheep farming, fishing, trapping, petroleum extraction ‖ the main island (area 18,530 sq. miles) of this archipelago

Tier·ra y Li·ber·tad (tjérrαi:li:bertáð) the Mexican crusade against oppression led by Emiliano Zapata [Span.=land and liberty]

tie·up (táiʌp) *n.* a close connection, *is there any tie-up between the firms?* ‖ a cessation of movement or action, e.g. a traffic jam

tiff (tif) **1.** *n.* an emotional mood of mild anger or indignation ‖ a slight quarrel **2.** *v.i.* to be in a tiff ‖ (with 'with') to quarrel slightly [origin unknown]

Tif·fa·ny (tífəni:), Charles Lewis 1812-1902), U.S. merchant. He founded the jewelry firm of Tiffany and Company, New York City. He introduced (1851) the English standard of sterling silver into the U.S.A.

Tiffany, Lewis Comfort (1848-1923), U.S. artist. He established the interior decorating firm known as Tiffany Studios in New York, which specialized in iridescent and Art Nouveau glass work

Tif·lis (tíflis) *TBILISI

ti·ger (táigər) *pl.* **ti·gers, ti·ger** *n. Felis tigris,* fam. *Felidae,* a large (8-10 ft long), ferocious, carnivorous mammal native to Asia. It has an orange-fawn coat irregularly crossed with black stripes, a white belly and no mane ‖ any of several related animals, e.g. the American jaguar and the S. African leopard ‖ a fiercely aggressive person in a position of authority ‖ (*Br., hist.*) a groom standing at the back of a light vehicle driven by his master [O.F. *tigre*]

tiger beetle any of several voracious carnivorous beetles of fam. *Cicindelidae* with striped or spotted wing cases

ti·ger·flow·er (táigərflαuər) *n.* a member of *Tigridia,* fam. *Iridaceae,* a genus of tropical American bulbous plants with brilliant yellow, purple, white or orange flowers

Tiger II *n.* (*mil.*) aircraft (F-5E) carrying two 30-mm guns, missiles, etc.; made by Northrop for export

tiger lily *Lilium tigrinum,* fam. *Liliaceae,* a lily native to China, widely cultivated for its black-spotted, pendent, orange flowers

tiger moth any of various richly colored, long-winged moths of fam. *Arctiidae*

tight (tait) **1.** *adj.* closely packed, *a tight arrangement* ‖ allowing too little freedom of movement, *a tight coat* ‖ rigidly set, *a tight smile* ‖ (esp. in compounds) so constructed that air, water etc. cannot pass through, *an airtight can, watertight shoes* ‖ (of money) hard to borrow, at high interest rates ‖ (of a commodity) in short supply ‖ (of a market) characterized by scarcity ‖ strict, *tight control* ‖ (*pop.*) drunk ‖ (*pop.*) stingy ‖ (of a contest) in which the opponents are evenly matched, *a tight game* ‖ (of a situation) difficult or dangerous to deal with ‖ (*printing,* of a page) too full of matter ‖ (*printing,* of setting) characterized by having very little space between words **2.** *adv.* in a tight way **to sit tight** to avoid action and bide one's time **tíght·en** *v.t.* to make tight ‖ *v.i.* to become tight [of Scand. origin]

tight end (*football*) an offensive end who places himself within two yds of the tackle

tight·fist·ed (táitfístid) *adj.* loath to part with money

tight-lipped (táitlípt) *adj.* making a strong effort of the will so as to surmount a difficulty and esp. so as not to betray emotion ‖ giving no secrets away

tight·rope (táitroup) *n.* a tautly stretched rope or wire, some height above the ground, on which an acrobat performs

tights (taits) *pl. n.* a skintight garment covering the body usually from the waist down

tight·wad (táitwɒd) *n.* a tightfisted person

Tig·lath-pi·le·ser I (tíglæθpailí:zər) (*d.* 1078 B.C.), king of Assyria (c.1116–1078 B.C.). A great soldier, he conquered Armenia, Cappadocia and Lebanon

Tiglath-pileser III (*d.* 728 B.C.), king of Assyria (746-728 B.C.), having usurped the throne. He conquered N. Syria

ti·gress (táigris) *n.* a female tiger ‖ a fiercetempered woman

Ti·gris (táigris) one of the two great rivers of Mesopotamia. It flows 1,150 miles from the mountains of E. Turkey through Iraq (navigable to Baghdad), joining the Euphrates to form the Shatt-al-Arab. Its middle course is liable to flood disastrously

Tih·wa (tí:wə) *URUMCHI

Ti·jua·na (ti:hwánα, ti:əwánə) a town (pop. 461,257) in N.W. Mexico near the U.S. border. Industries: tourism, gambling

Ti·kal (ti:kál) the largest of the ancient Mayan cities, in N. Guatemala, noted for the number of its monuments, pyramids and temples and the quality of its wood carvings

tik·chung (tiktʃú:ŋ) *n.* silver currency of Bhutan *Cf* NGULTRUM

tike *TYKE

Til·burg (tílbəːrg) a town (pop. 153,117) in North Brabant, Netherlands: textiles, railroad cars etc.

til·bur·y (tílberi:, tílbəri:) *pl.* **til·bur·ies** *n.* (*hist.*) a light, springy, two-wheeled open carriage for two persons [after a 19th-c. British coach builder]

til·de (tíldə) *n.* a sign (˜) placed e.g. over the letter 'n' in Spanish to denote that it is pronounced as a palatal nasal sound (nj), e.g. in 'señor' ‖ this sign used in Portuguese to denote nasalization of a vowel [Span.]

Til·den (tíldən), Samuel Jones (1814-86), U.S. statesman. A leading New York Democrat, he played an important role in the destruction of the Tweed Ring. He ran as the Democratic presidential nominee in the disputed 1876 election, in which a new Electoral Commission voted in favor of the Republican candidate (*COMPROMISE OF 1877)

tile (tail) **1.** *pl.* **tiles, tile** *n.* a thin, usually rectangular piece of fired, unglazed clay, sometimes ogee-shaped when used on roofs or walls ‖ a square or shaped piece of fired clay or other material (e.g. vinyl) used for flooring ‖ a similar piece of porcelain or other glazed ware, used ornamentally ‖ an earthenware or concrete drainpipe ‖ a small flat piece of baked earthenware used in covering vessels in which metals are fused ‖ tiling **2.** *v.t. pres. part.* **til·ing** *past* and *past part.* **tiled** to cover with tiles **tíl·ing** *n.* the process of covering with tiles ‖ tiles collectively ‖ a surface covered with tiles [O.E. *tigule, tigele*]

till (til) *n.* (*geol.*) boulder clay [origin unknown]

till *n.* a money drawer or tray, e.g. in a bank ‖ a cash register ‖ the money contained in any of these [origin unknown]

till 1. *prep.* up to the time of, *he waited till 10 p.m.* **2.** *conj.* up to the time when, until, *wait till he comes* [Old Northumbrian *til* fr. O.N.]

till *v.t.* (*rhet.*) to work (the soil) for cultivation **tíll·age** *n.* the tilling of the soil ‖ land that has been tilled ‖ the crops on such land [O.E. *tilian,* to strive]

til·ler (tílər) *n.* (*naut.*) the lever arm by means of which the rudder is turned [O.F. *telier, tellier*]

tiller 1. *n.* one of the side shoots of a plant, esp. of grasses and cereals, sprouting from the base of the axils of the lower leaves ‖ a sapling or young tree, esp. a shoot sprouting from the stump of a felled tree **2.** *v.i.* to put forth tillers [prob. fr. O.E. *telgor*]

Til·ley (tíli:), Sir Samuel Leonard (1818-96), Canadian statesman. As minister of finance (1878-85) in the 2nd Sir John Alexander Macdonald administration, he introduced (1878) the protective tariff plan which became the basis of Canadian financial policy

Til·lich (tílix), Paul Johannes (1886-1965), U.S. theologian. He incorporated depth psychology into Christian doctrine, postulating that faith is 'ultimate concern', that God is the 'ground of being' or 'being-itself', and that man should strive for 'new being', rather than salvation

Til·ly (tíli:), Johann Tserklaes, count of (1559-1632), general of the Catholic League during the Thirty Years' War, in which he won the battles of the White Mountain (1620), Magdeburg (1631) and Breitenfeld (1631). He was defeated (1632) by Gustavus II of Sweden, and mortally wounded

Tilos *TELOS

Til·sit (tílzit) *SOVETSK

Tilsit, Treaty of a treaty signed July 1807, by France, Russia and Prussia. Part of Prussia became the Grand Duchy of Warsaw, part went to Russia and part to Saxony. The Prussian army was limited to 42,000 men. The Confederation of the Rhine was recognized

tilt (tilt) **1.** *v.i.* to slant from the horizontal or the vertical ‖ (*hist.*) to joust ‖ *v.t.* to cause to slant from the horizontal or the vertical ‖ (*hist.*) to poise (a lance) for a thrust ‖ (*hist.*) to charge (one's opponent) in a tilt ‖ to hammer or forge (metal) with a tilt hammer **2.** *n.* a tilting or being tilted ‖ (*hist.*) a joust ‖ a tilt hammer **at full tilt** at full speed [M.E. *tilten* fr. O.E. *tealt,* shaky]
tilt *n.* a covering, esp. of canvas, stretched on a frame and mounted over a wagon, a market stall, or a boat etc. [M.E. *tild* perh. influenced by 'tent']
tilth (tilθ) *n.* (*rhet.*) cultivation of the soil ‖ (*rhet.*) cultivated land [O.E. *tilth, tilthe* fr. *tilian,* to till]
tilt hammer a heavy hammer used in forging which is tilted up and then allowed to drop
tilt wheel (*automobile*) steering wheel of a motor vehicle capable of angle adjustment by the driver
tilt·yard (tíltjɑrd) *n.* (*hist.*) a place used for tilts and tournaments
tim·bal, tym·bal (tímb'l) *n.* (*hist.*) a kettledrum [F. *timbale*]
tim·bale (tímb'l, tɛ̃bɑl) *n.* a dish of creamed chicken, lobster or fish etc., seasoned and cooked in a pastry mold [F.]
tim·ber (tímbər) **1.** *n.* trees yielding wood suitable for construction ‖ timberland ‖ (*Br.*) lumber (wood for construction) ‖ a thick piece of wood forming, or ready to form, part of a structure, *roof timbers* ‖ (*naut.*) one of the curved beams of wood forming the ribs of a ship **2.** *interj.* a shouted warning that a tree is falling
timber *v.t.* to cover, supply, support etc. with timbers [O.E. *timbran* and *timbrian*]
tim·bered (tímbərd) *adj.* made of or furnished with timbers ‖ covered with growing timber [O.E.]
tim·ber·head (tímbərhed) *n.* (*naut.*) the upper end of a ship's timber, esp. such a timber used as a bollard
timber hitch a looped knot in a rope used in tying a rope to a spar or log
tim·ber·ing (tímbəriŋ) *n.* a construction, esp. the support network of a mineshaft, made of timbers
tim·ber·land (tímbərlænd) *n.* an expanse of trees, esp. of trees used for lumber
tim·ber·line (tímbərlain) *n.* the tree line
timber wolf *Canis lupus lycaon,* a large brownish-gray wolf of northern North America, now largely extinct
tim·bre (tǽmbər, tɛ̃br) *n.* the quality of a musical sound, depending on what overtones are present and their respective amplitudes [F.]
tim·brel (tímbrəl) *n.* an ancient tambourine [dim. of M.E. *timbre,* kettledrum fr. O.F.]
Tim·buk·tu, Tim·buc·too (timbʌktú:) (*F.* Tombouctou) an ancient caravan trading center (pop. 20,483) in central Mali near the Niger on the edge of the Sahara. It flourished in the 14th-16th cc. as a center of Moslem culture and commerce
Tim·by (tímbi:), Theodore Ruggles (1819-1909), U.S. inventor of the revolving turret (1843), which was the main feature of the Civil War armored vessel the 'Merrimack'
time (taim) **1.** *n.* the physical quantity measured by clocks. In classical physics time was regarded as extending infinitely into the past and future and was considered independent of the events which defined it. This implied that the simultaneity of events was absolute, i.e. independent of the situation of the observer. The special theory and general theory of relativity radically changed this concept of time, linking it to the position and relative motion of the clock and its observer ‖ finite duration as distinguished from infinity ‖ earthly duration as distinguished from eternity ‖ a duration, *it lasted a long time* ‖ a point in progress, *at that time he was away from home* ‖ (often *pl.*) a period of history with reference to a region, person etc., *the time of Persia's supremacy* ‖ (esp. *pl.*) a period of history having certain characteristics, customs etc., *in biblical times* ‖ a specific period of a year, *harvest time,* or of a day, *dinner time* ‖ a period of duration available for certain action to be taken, *I will do it if I have the time* ‖ a period during which certain action is taken, *he served his time in the navy* ‖ the point or period appropriate to the beginning, performance or ending of a course of action, *it is time we went, it's time to make a change* ‖ a favorable period, *now is the time to buy* ‖ (*mus.*) the duration of a note or pause ‖ (*mus.*) the rhythm of a composition in terms of the grouping of beats into bars of equal duration, indicated by the time signature ‖ (*mus.*) the tempo at which a composition is to be performed or is performed ‖ (esp. *pl.*) general conditions, *exciting times* ‖ a period characterized by a general condition or event, *a time of struggle* ‖ a period or occasion with reference to a personal reaction to it, *to have a good time* ‖ rate of speed in driving, marching, working etc. ‖ the period worked or to be worked by an employee ‖ rate of pay, esp. reckoned by the hour, *time and a half for overtime* ‖ lifetime ‖ the end of life, *his time had come* ‖ (*Br.*) closing time in a public house as fixed by law, *'Time, gentlemen, please'* ‖ end of play in a game or match formally declared by the umpire, referee etc. ‖ a period of imprisonment ‖ a term of apprenticeship ‖ the usual, allotted or shortest period during which something is done, *what is the cooking time for a boiled egg?* ‖ a repeated occasion, recurrence of the same thing, *that's the third time you've told me* ‖ (*pl.*) following a number and used with a comparative adjective or adverb to indicate magnitude, *five times higher* **against time** before a certain time and with barely enough time for what must be done **ahead of time** before the required, proper or expected moment **all the time** during all the specified period ‖ continuously ‖ very often, *he says it all the time* **at a time** in one operation, *it does six pairs at a time* **at the same time** occurring at the same point in the progress of time ‖ nevertheless, though it is so, *I like it but at the same time it frightens me* **at times** sometimes **behind time** late, in arrears **behind the times** old-fashioned, not up-to-date **for the time being** for the present, provisionally **from time to time** occasionally **in time** before a specified point in the progress of time has passed, *were you in time for the train?* ‖ after the passage of sufficient time, *we will find out in time* ‖ in the right tempo **in good time** with an ample margin of time, *he got there in good time for his train* ‖ as a happy end to a period of waiting, *and in good time they were married* **in no time** very quickly, *he did it in no time* **many a time** on many occasions **on time** at the appointed hour, on schedule ‖ (*pop.*) on the installment plan **out of time** (*mus.*) failing to sound notes at the same time as others in a choir, orchestra etc. or to keep step in marching **to gain time** to play for time, delay action until a more favorable time ‖ (of a timepiece) to go too fast **to pass the time of day** to stop for a little chat **to take one's time** to take all the time one needs to do something ‖ to be slow doing something **2.** *v.t. pres. part.* **tim·ing** *past* and *past part.* **timed** to cause to occur at a particular point in the progress of time, *he timed his arrival for nightfall* ‖ to measure the duration of ‖ to adjust the performance of (something) so that it occupies a particular portion of time, *he timed his speech to last 20 minutes* ‖ to set the rhythm or tempo of **3.** *adj.* having to do with time ‖ regulated to open, explode etc. at a given time ‖ payable at a future date ‖ having to do with payment of goods over a period of time [O.E. *tīma*]
time after time repeatedly
time and again repeatedly
time and motion study a study of the time taken, and the energy used, in doing work, with a view to securing greater efficiency and establishing standards
time and time again repeatedly, esp. tiresomely often
time bomb a bomb fitted with a clockwork device which detonates it at a predetermined time
time card a card recording the time of arrival at and departure from one's place of work
time clock a clock which records on a card the time of arrival and departure of an employee
timed capsule (*pharm.*) encapsulated drug that is effective at a time later than ingestion *also* spansule
time dilation (*phys.*) the slowing of time in a speeding object as its velocity increases relative to another moving body, as hypothesized in the theory of relativity
time-ef·fec·tive (táimifektiv) *adj.* sufficiently rewarding to warrant the time spent
time exposure exposure of a film for a fixed time, usually more than half a second ‖ a photograph taken in this way
time frame a period of time
time fuse a fuse so contrived that it will burn for a known time before detonating an explosive
time-hon·ored, *Br.* **time-hon·oured** (táimɒnərd) *adj.* having the authority that goes with long custom
time·keep·er (táimki:pər) *n.* (*Br.*) a clock or watch, esp. with regard to its efficiency, *a good timekeeper* ‖ someone whose job is to observe and record the time or duration of a game, race etc., e.g. of a round in a boxing match ‖ someone who records the hours worked by employees
time lag a period of time which passes before a cause produces its effect ‖ a delay
time·less (táimlis) *adj.* not limited by time ‖ unaffected by the passing of time
time·li·ness (táimli:nis) *n.* the state or quality of being timely
time·ly (táimli:) *comp.* **time·li·er** *superl.* **time·li·est** *adj.* at a very suitable time, opportune
time out a pause in work or other activity ‖ (*football, basketball* etc.) any time requested, e.g. to make substitutions, discuss strategy etc., during play and not counted in the playing time
time·piece (táimpi:s) *n.* any instrument used for measuring time
time reversal (*phys.*) the principle that a sequence of operations will occur in reverse order if the time sequence is reversed
times (taimz) *prep.* multiplied by
time·sav·ing (táimseiviŋ) *adj.* enabling work etc. to be done in less time
time·serv·er (táimsə:rvər) *n.* a person who adapts his actions to please someone in authority instead of acting according to his convictions **time·serv·ing** *adj.*
time sharing **1.** (*computer*) arrangement for use of equipment on an hourly basis **2.** (*real estate*) purchase of a property for use at a specified time only, e.g., for vacations
time signal a broadcast to announce the exact time of day so that clocks and watches can be synchronized
time signature a sign denoting the tempo of a piece of music, placed after the key signature. It is usually a fraction, the denominator of which indicates the kind of note taken as the unit, the numerator indicating the number of these to a bar
time·ta·ble (táimteib'l) *n.* a tabulated list of the times at which certain events or activities are required to occur, or the order of occurrence ‖ a schedule of arrival and departure times of regular services of buses, trains, aircraft etc.
time-test·ed (táimtéstəd) *adj.* not disproved over a long period
time trial (*sports*) a competition in which the recorded time is used as the basis of judging the winner
time·work (táimwə:rk) *n.* work paid for by the day or by the hour (cf. PIECEWORK)
time·worn (táimwɔrn) *adj.* hackneyed ‖ showing signs of wear because of age
time zone any of the 24 zones, each approx. 15° of longitude in width, into which the globe is divided successively from the Greenwich meridian, for maintaining a regular sequence of time changes, each 1 hour earlier than in the zone immediately east of it
tim·id (tímid) *adj.* very sensitive to real or imagined causes of fear ‖ lacking self-confidence [fr. L. *timidus*]
ti·mid·i·ty (timíditi:) *n.* the state or quality of being timid [fr. L. *timiditas*]
tim·ing (táimiŋ) *n.* the regulation of the speed of e.g. an engine or a theatrical production so as to give the most effective result
Ti·mi·şoa·ra (ti:mi:ʃwárɑ) a communications center (pop. 288,237) in Banat, W. Rumania. Industries: textiles, food processing. Castle (16th c.). University (1945)
Ti·mor (tí:mɔr) a mountainous island (area 13,071 sq. miles) of the Lesser Sundas, part of Indonesia. The Indonesian province East Nusa Tenggara occupies the western half with its capital at Kupang (pop. 7,000). People: Malay-Papuan, with small Negrito (interior) and Chinese minorities. Religion: Christian and Moslem. The north is savanna, while the center and south are largely covered with rain forest. Highest point: 9,678 ft, in the east. Exports: sandalwood, copra, trepang, some coffee, meat and fish. HISTORY. The island was visited by the Portuguese (16th c.), but their control over it was challenged after 1613 by the Dutch. Timor was partitioned between them (1859). After Japanese occupation of the island (1942-5), Dutch

CONCISE PRONUNCIATION KEY: **(a)** æ, *c*a*t*; ɑ, *car*; ɔ *fawn*; ei, *snake*. **(e)** e, *hen*; i:, *sheep*; iə, *deer*; ɛə, *bear*. **(i)** i, *fish*; ai, *tiger*; ə:, *bird*. **(o)** o, *ox*; au, *cow*; ou, *goat*; u, *poor*; ɔi, *royal*. **(u)** ʌ, *duck*; u, *bull*; u:, *goose*; ə, *bacillus*; ju:, *cube*. x, *loch*; θ, *think*; ð, *bother*; z, *Zen*; ʒ, *corsage*; dʒ, *savage*; ŋ, *orangutang*; j, *yak*; ʃ, *fish*; tʃ, *fetch*; 'l, *rabble*; 'n, *redden*. Complete pronunciation key appears inside front cover.

Timor became part of Indonesia. Divided between Portuguese Timor (E half) and Ambeno (W half) until the Portuguese left in 1975, Timor now consists of two provinces, West and East, with Kupang and Dili as respective provincial capitals. An independence movement, Fretelin, was suppressed by Indonesia following the Portuguese departure and East Timor was formally incorporated as Indonesia's 27th province in 1976

tim·o·rous (tímərəs) *adj.* timid, easily frightened ‖ indicating or marked by timidity, *a timorous voice* [O.F. *temeros, temerous*]

Timor Sea the part of the Indian Ocean between N. Australia and Timor

Tim·o·thy (tíməθi:), St (*d.* c. 97), first bishop of Ephesus, companion and helper of St Paul. Feast: Jan. 24

tim·o·thy (tíməθi:) *n. Phleum pratense,* a long, spiked European grass introduced into North America and grown chiefly for hay [prob. after *Timothy* Hanson, who introduced it c. 1720 into the U.S.A.]

Timothy and Titus, Epistles to the 15th, 16th and 17th books of the New Testament, three encyclical letters of doubtful authorship, written in the late 1st c. or early 2nd c., warning against heresies. They are known as the Pastoral Epistles

timothy grass timothy

tim·pa·ni, tym·pa·ni (tímpəni:) *pl. n.* a set of two or more kettledrums played by one man in an orchestra or band **tímpanist** *TYMPANIST [Ital., pl. of *timpano,* kettledrum]

Tim·rod (tímrɒd), Henry (1828-67), U.S. poet, known as the 'laureate of the Confederacy'. His works include 'The Cotton Boll' and 'Ethnogenesis'

Ti·mur (timúər) (Tamerlane, c. 1336-1405), Mongol conqueror. Having gained the throne of Samarkand, he tried to reunite the empire of Genghis Khan, conquering the Tatars (1392) and the Turks (1402). He died during an invasion of China

tin (tin) **1.** *n.* a lustrous, silvery metallic element (symbol Sn, at. no. 50, at. mass 118.70) which is soft, malleable, ductile and resistant to the chemical action of air and water at ordinary temperatures ‖ (*Br.*) a can (container for preserving foodstuffs) ‖ tinplate **2.** *v.t. pres. part.* **tin·ning** *past* and *past part.* **tinned** to coat with tin ‖ (*Br.*) to can (preserve by packing in an airtight can) **3.** *adj.* made of tin [O.E.]

—Tin occurs mainly as the oxide, cassiterite, the principal sources being Malaya, Indonesia, Bolivia and the Congo. It is extracted by reducing the concentrated ore with carbon at 1,200–1,300° C. Refined tin is used in the manufacture of tinplate and as an alloy in solder, bronze, Babbitt metal etc. Lesser uses include the manufacture of tinfoil and of collapsible tubes for packaging

tin·a·mou (tínəmu:) *n.* any of various members of *Tinamidae,* a family of South American birds which resemble partridges. They are heavily built and measure from 9–15 ins long. Their eggs have a curious metallic luster [F. fr. Galibi (Carib) *tinamu*]

Tin·ber·gen (tínbεərgən), Jan (1903-69), Dutch economist, who shared the first Nobel prize for economics (1969) with Ragnar Frisch. He won the award for constructing econometric systems—developing and using mathematical models to analyze and structure economic behavior. His books include 'Shaping the World Economy' (1962) and 'Development Planning' (1967)

Tinbergen, Nikolaas (1907-   ), Dutch zoologist and ethologist, who shared the Nobel prize for physiology or medicine (1973) with Konrad Lorenz and Karl von Frisch. A pioneer in the study of animal behavior under natural conditions, Tinbergen analyzed specific stimuli that elicit specific responses in animals. His works include 'The Study of Instinct' (1951), 'Social Behavior in Animals' (1953), 'The Herring Gull's World' (1960) and 'Animal Behavior' (1965)

tin·cal (tíŋk'l) *n.* a crude, commercial, hydrated borax [Malay *tingkal*]

Tin·che·brai, Battle of (tε̃ʃbrei) a battle in Normandy (1106) in which Henry I of England defeated his brother Robert II of Normandy

tinc·to·ri·al (tiŋktɔ́ri:əl, tiŋktóuri:əl) *adj.* pertaining to color, esp. that of a dye [fr. L. *tinctorius*]

tinc·ture (tíŋktʃər) **1.** *n.* a solution, usually in alcohol, of a medicinal substance, *tincture of iodine* ‖ a slight coloration ‖ an imbued quality, *a tincture of liberalism* ‖ (*heraldry*) any of the colors, metals or furs used in emblazoning **2.** *v.t. pres. part.* **tinc·tur·ing** *past* and *past part.* **tinc·tured** to add a trace of color to ‖ to imbue slightly with a specified quality [fr. L. *tinctura* a dyeing]

Tindal, Tindale *TYNDALE

tin·der (tíndər) *n.* a dry substance with a low ignition temperature, readily ignited by a spark [O.E. *tynder, tyndre*]

tin·der·box (tíndərbɒks) *n.* (*hist.*) a small metal box containing charred linen as tinder and equipped with a flint and steel for making a spark

tine (tain) *n.* one of the thin, pointed parts of an antler, fork, harrow etc. [O.E. *tind*]

tin·e·a (tíni:ə) *n.* (*med.*) any of several fungus skin infections, esp. ringworm [L.=worm, moth]

tin·foil (tínfɔil) *n.* an alloy of lead and tin or aluminum beaten into thin sheets and used for wrapping

ting (tiŋ) **1.** *n.* a light ringing sound produced by a single tap e.g. on a small bell **2.** *v.i.* to make this sound ‖ *v.t.* to cause to make this sound [imit.]

tinge (tindʒ) **1.** *v.t. pres. part.* **tinge·ing, ting·ing** *past* and *past part.* **tinged** to impart a little color or flavor to ‖ to impart a certain slight quality to, *thanks tinged with envy* **2.** *n.* the color, flavor, quality etc. imparted [fr. L. *tingere,* to stain]

tin·gle (tíŋg'l) **1.** *v. pres. part.* **tin·gling** *past* and *past part.* **tin·gled** *v.i.* to have a sensation as if the skin were being gently pricked or stung at innumerable points ‖ *v.t.* to cause to have this sensation **2.** *n.* this sensation [var. of TINKLE]

ti·ni·ly (táinili:) *adv.* in a tiny way

ti·ni·ness (táini:nis) *n.* the state or quality of being tiny

tink·er (tíŋkər) **1.** *n.* an itinerant tinsmith who mends metal kitchen utensils ‖ (in Ireland and Scotland) a gipsy or wandering beggar **2.** *v.t.* to mend (metal utensils) ‖ *v.i.* to make an amateurish attempt to repair or adjust something [M.E. *tinkere*]

tin·kle (tíŋk'l) **1.** *v. pres. part.* **tin·kling** *past* and *past part.* **tin·kled** *v.i.* to make a succession of light metallic tings ‖ *v.t.* to cause to make these sounds **2.** *n.* a tinkling sound [prob. frequentative of older *tink,* to emit a metallic sound]

tin·man (tínmən) *pl.* **tin·men** (tínmən) *n.* a tinsmith

tin·ni·ly (tínili:) *adv.* in a tinny manner

tin·ni·ness (tíni:nis) *n.* the quality or state of being tinny

tin·ni·tus (tináitəs) *n.* a ringing sound in the ears not caused by any external stimulation [L. fr. *tinnire,* to tinkle]

tin·ny (tíni:) *comp.* **tin·ni·er** *superl.* **tin·ni·est** *adj.* of or containing tin ‖ like tin, esp. in sound, taste or material

Tinos *TENOS

Tin Pan Alley the commercial world of popular music publishers and composers

tin·plate (tínpleit) *n.* thin sheet steel or iron coated with tin **tín-plate** *pres. part.* **tin-plat·ing** *past* and *past part.* **tin-plat·ed** *v.t.* to coat with tin

tin-pot (tínpɒt) *adj.* (*pop.*) poor in conception, execution or quality

tin pyrites stannite

tin·sel (tínsəl) **1.** *n.* tin, brass or an alloy with a bright luster, beaten into very thin sheets and used in thin strips, threads etc. to give glittering decorative effects ‖ that which is brilliant but worthless **2.** *adj.* made of, or adorned with, tinsel ‖ superficially brilliant but worthless **3.** *v.t. pres. part.* **tin·sel·ing,** esp. *Br.* **tin·sel·ling** *past* and *past part.* **tin·seled,** esp. *Br.* **tin·selled** to adorn with or as if with tinsel **tín·sel·ly** *adj.* [fr. O. F. *estincelle*]

tin·smith (tínsmiθ) *n.* someone who works tin

tin·stone (tínstoun) *n.* cassiterite

tint (tint) **1.** *n.* a color containing some white (*COLOR, cf. SHADE) ‖ any lighter or darker hue of the same color ‖ a small quantity of one color present in another ‖ any slight modifying element in something ‖ (*engraving*) an effect of shadow or texture produced by a series of close parallel lines ‖ (*printing*) a background of light color, e.g. one on which a halftone block can be printed ‖ a hair dye **2.** *v.t.* to furnish with a tint [prob. fr. earlier *tinct,* perh. influenced by Ital. *tinta*]

tin·tin·nab·u·la·tion (tintinæbjuléiʃən) *n.* the ringing, jingling or tinkling sound of bells [fr. L. *tintinnabulum,* bell]

Tin·to·ret·to (tintərétou) (Jacopo Robusti, 1518-94), Venetian painter. He painted a vast number of magnificently conceived works, full of a sense of drama and very rich in color. They are executed with an impressionistic brushwork, unconventional and even violent contrasts of perspective, and with extreme contrasts of light and shade. The Scuola di S. Rocco in Venice was entirely decorated by him, with scenes from the life of the Virgin, the life of Christ, and Christ's Passion

tin·type (tíntaip) *n.* a positive photograph made directly on an iron plate that has been coated with a sensitized film

tin·ware (tínwεər) *n.* articles made of tinplate

ti·ny (táini:) *comp.* **ti·ni·er** *superl.* **ti·ni·est** *adj.* exceedingly small [etym. doubtful]

tip (tip) **1.** *v.t. pres. part.* **tip·ping** *past* and *past part.* **tipped** (*baseball, cricket*) to strike (the ball) lightly with a glancing blow **2.** *n.* a light, glancing stroke [origin unknown]

tip 1. *n.* the pointed or tapering end of a long slim object ‖ a small object attached to the end of something thin, e.g. the ferrule of an umbrella, the filter of a cigarette etc. ‖ a thin brush of camel's hair etc. used for laying gold leaf in bookbinding **2.** *v.t. pres. part.* **tip·ping** *past* and *past part.* **tipped** to furnish with a tip ‖ to form the tip of [origin unknown]

tip 1. *v. pres. part.* **tip·ping** *past* and *past part.* **tipped** *v.t.* to cause to incline ‖ (often with 'over') to cause to overturn ‖ (*Br.*) to empty by tilting ‖ to raise slightly or touch (one's hat) in deference ‖ *v.i.* to become inclined ‖ (often with 'over') to become overturned **2.** *n.* a tipping or being tipped ‖ (*Br.*) a tipple (place where trucks are emptied) ‖ (*Br.*) a place where something is tipped, *a rubbish tip* [origin unknown]

tip 1. *v.t. pres. part.* **tip·ping** *past* and *past part.* **tipped** (*pop.,* often with 'off') to impart information to, or give useful advance warning of, in a confidential manner ‖ to forecast (something) as a winner or likely to bring in money ‖ to give a small gift of money to, esp. in recognition of services rendered **2.** *n.* a suggestion, or piece of information, privately given, esp. the probable winner of a race etc., or the best way to do something ‖ a small gift of money, esp. in recognition of services rendered [etym. doubtful]

TIP (*acronym*) for tax-based income policy, a system of rewarding price and wage stability and penalizing wage increases

tip·cart (típkɑrt) *n.* a vehicle with a body so pivoted that its contents may be tipped out

tip lorry *pl.* **tip lorries** (*Br.*) a dump truck

tip-off (típɔf, típɒf) *n.* a useful warning or hint conveyed privately

Tip·pe·ca·noe, Battle of (tipikənú:) an engagement (1811) in Indiana, in which William Henry Harrison led U.S. troops to victory against an Indian force headed by Tecumseh

Tip·per·ar·y (tipərέəri:) an inland county (area 1,643 sq. miles, pop. 123,565) of the Irish Republic (*MUNSTER). County seat: Clonmel (pop. 11,622)

tip·pet (típit) *n.* (*hist.*) a long hanging piece of material attached to a sleeve, hood or cape ‖ (*hist.*) a short cape, esp. of fur, having loose, dangling ends ‖ an ecclesiastical vestment [origin unknown]

Tip·pett (típit), Michael Kemp (1905-   ), English composer. He first became known with his oratorio 'A Child of our Time' (1941), written on a political theme. He has also written operas, orchestral and chamber music, and songs

tip·ple (típ'l) **1.** *v. pres. part.* **tip·pling** *past* and *past part.* **tip·pled** *v.i.* to tend to be a drunkard ‖ *v.t.* to drink (intoxicating liquor) in small quantities at a time but persistently **2.** *n.* (*rhet.*) an alcoholic drink [rel. to Norw. dial. *tipla,* to drip slowly]

tipple *n.* (*Am.=Br.* tip) a place where loaded trucks etc. are emptied ‖ the place where tipping from wagons etc. is done

tip·si·ly (típsili:) *adv.* in a tipsy way

tip·si·ness (típsi:nis) *n.* the state or quality of being tipsy

tip·staff (típstæf, típstɑf) *n.* a lawcourt official [contr. of 'tipped staff' from his former badge of office]

tip·ster (típstər) *n.* a person who supplies racing tips or other information, usually for a fee

tip·sy (típsi:) *comp.* **tip·si·er** *superl.* **tip·si·est** *adj.* somewhat intoxicated ‖ not steady, shaky [perh. fr. TIP V. (to cause to incline)]

tip·toe (típtou) **1.** *adv.* on the tips of one's toes **2.** *v.i.* to proceed on the tips of one's toes **3.** *n.* (in the phrase) **on tiptoe** on the tips of one's toes ‖ in a state of alert expectancy

tip-top (típtɒp) **1.** *adj.* (*pop.*) of the highest quality **2.** *n.* the highest point or part ‖ the best of all

Ti·pu Sa·hib, Tip·poo Sa·hib (tí:pu:sáhib) (c. 1751-99), sultan of Mysore (1782-99), son of Hyder Ali. He continued (1782-4, 1790-9) his father's wars against the British

ti·rade (tairéid) *n.* a long, rhetorical harangue or written passage full of vehement criticism or invective [F. fr. Ital.]

Ti·ra·den·tes (ti:rɑdénti:s) (né Joaquim José de Silva Xavier, 1748-92), leader of a Brazilian independence movement centered in a conspiracy (1789) in the state of Minas Gerais. He was executed and his rebellion aborted by the Portuguese authorities. He was considered a national hero after Brazil became independent (1822)

Ti·ra·na (ti:rúnɑ) the capital (pop. 175,000) of Albania, 18 miles east of Durres at the foot of the central mountains. Industries: textiles, lignite mining. University (1957)

tire (tair) *pres. part.* **tir·ing** *past* and *past part.* **tired** *v.t.* to use up the strength of ‖ to use up the patience or interest of ‖ *v.i.* to lose strength by exertion etc. ‖ to lose patience or interest **to tire of** to lose patience with or interest in **to tire out** to make very tired [O.E. *tīorian, tēorian*]

tire 1. *n.* a band of elastic steel etc. around the rim of e.g. a wagon wheel, holding its sections together or reducing rolling friction ‖ (*Am.*=*Br.* tyre) a solid rubber band, or a rubber casing making an airtight fit with a wheel rim (the whole being treated as a tube and filled with air, no inner tube being used), or a heavy rubber casing to contain an inner tube filled with air, placed around the wheel of a vehicle to absorb shock **2.** *v.t. pres. part.* **tir·ing** *past* and *past part.* **tired** to fit with a tire [perh. short for M.E. *atir,* attire]

tired (táiərd) *adj.* weary ‖ hackneyed, *a tired joke* **tired of** having endured as much as one is willing to stand of (something)

tire·less (táiərlis) *adj.* seemingly incapable of becoming tired

Ti·re·si·as (tairí:si:əs) (*Gk mythol:*) a blind prophet of Thebes mentioned frequently in Greek literature, esp. in connection with the family of Oedipus

tire·some (táiərsəm) *adj.* tending to exhaust one's patience

Ti·ro·le·an (tiróuli:ən) *adj.* Tirolese

Tir·o·lese (tirəlí:z, tirəlí:s) **1.** *adj.* pertaining to the Tirol or its people **2.** *n.* a native of the Tirol

Tir·ol, Tyr·ol (tírəl, tiróul) an alpine province (area 4,884 sq. miles, pop. 586,297) of W. Austria. Capital: Innsbruck ‖ (*hist.*) a former province of Austria, divided (1919) between Austria (modern Tirol) and Italy (Trentino-Alto Adige)

TIROS (*meteor. acronym*) for television infrared observation satellite, a satellite with infrared cameras used to obtain and transmit weather information, esp. about clouds, ice floes

Tir·pitz (tírpits), Alfred von (1849-1930), German admiral. After being state secretary of the navy (1896) and minister of state for Prussia (1898), he became lord high admiral (1911). He organized and planned the submarine blockade of the British Isles (1915-16)

Tir·so de Mo·li·na (tí:rsɔðeməlí:nɑ) (Gabriel Tellez, c. 1571-1648), Spanish dramatist. 'El burlador de Sevilla' established the popular Don Juan theme in drama

Ti·ru·chi·ra·pal·li (tirutʃirəpʌli:, tirutʃirúpəli:) (formerly Trichinopoly) a town (pop. 307,400) in Madras, India, at the head of the Cauvery delta. Industries: railroad engineering, silk textiles, cigars, goldwork

Tir·yns (tírinz) an ancient Achaean city in Argolis, Greece, near modern Nauplia: remains of palaces (c. 1600-900 B.C.)

Tisa (River) *TISZA

tis·sue (tíʃu:, *Br.* tísju:) *n.* (*biol.*) an aggregate of like cells and intercellular material, of which animal and plant organs are composed ‖ a thin, semitransparent woven fabric ‖ an intricately interwoven group of ideas etc., *a tissue of lies* ‖ a piece of tissue paper [O.F. *tissu*]

tissue committee (*med.*) a committee that evaluates surgery performed in a hospital on the basis of the extent of agreement among the preoperative, postoperative, and pathological diagnoses, and on the acceptability of the procedures undertaken for the diagnosis —**tissue review** *n.* the review and evaluation

tissue culture the process or technique of growing tissues in an artificial medium ‖ a culture of tissue

tissue paper very thin, soft, translucent paper used in gift wrapping etc.

tissue typing (*med.*) technique for analyzing and selecting human tissues for compatibility on a transplant

tis·su·lar (tíʃələ:r) *adj.* of organic tissue

Ti·sza (tísɒ), István (1861-1918), Hungarian statesman, son of Kálmán Tisza. As prime minister (1903-5, 1913-17), he sought to make Magyar influence dominant in Austria-Hungary, esp. over the Serbs

Tisza, Kálmán (1830-1902), Hungarian statesman, prime minister (1875-90). He rehabilitated Hungary financially and politically, and introduced compulsory education

Tisza (*Serb.* and *Russ.* Tisa) the chief tributary (610 miles long) of the Danube, flowing from the Carpathians in the S.W. Ukraine, U.S.S.R., across E. Hungary and N.E. Yugoslavia

tit (tit) *n.* a titmouse [prob. onomatopoeic]

tit *n.* (*pop.,* not in polite usage) a woman's breast or the nipple of this [O.E. *titt*]

Ti·tan (táit'n) (*mythol.*) any of the 12 children of Heaven and Earth, ancient gods of Greece, probably of the pre-Hellenic population. They were Oceanus, Coeus, Crius, Hyperion, Iapetus, Cronus, Theia, Rhea, Themis, Mnemosyne, Phoebe, Tethys. They were crushed by their descendants, the Olympian gods, led by Zeus

Ti·tan·ic (taitǽnik) *adj.* of or like the Titans **ti·tan·ic** having great size or strength ‖ calling for very great effort [fr. Gk *Titanikos*]

ti·tan·ite (táit'nait) *n.* a silicate of calcium and titanium, $CaTiSiO_5$ [G. *titanit*]

ti·ta·ni·um (taitéini:əm) *n.* a silvery-gray metallic element (symbol Ti, at. no. 22, at. mass 47.90) resembling iron. It is widely distributed as compounds but difficult to extract. It is often added to various steel alloys and used as a structural material in jet engines, missiles etc. because of its heat-resistant qualities [fr. Gk *Titanes,* the Titans]

titanium dioxide the compound TiO_2, occurring naturally in various crystalline forms (e.g. rutile, anatase). It is used commercially in the form of a white amorphous powder as a pigment or to improve the covering or light-reflecting properties of paints, plastics, rubber etc. Certain of the crystalline forms are valued as gems

Titan II *n.* (*mil.*) a liquid-propellant, two-stage, rocket-powered ICBM (LGM-25C) that is guided to its target by an all-inertial guidance and control system. It is equipped with a nuclear warhead and deployed in underground silos

tit·bit (títbit) *n.* a tidbit

Titch·e·ner (títʃənər), Edward Bradford (1867-1927), English-U.S. experimental and systematic psychologist and head of the structural school. His chief contribution is the encyclopedic handbook 'Experimental Psychology' (1901-5)

ti·ter, esp. *Br.* **ti·tre** (táitər) *n.* the concentration of a substance in a solution as determined by titration [F. *titre*]

tit for tat a blow delivered in return for a blow ‖ a reply in kind

tithe (taið) *n.* a tenth part of agricultural produce etc. paid as tax or as an offering, esp. (*hist.*) such a tax levied to support a church [early M.E. *tigthe, tigethe*]

tithe *pres. part.* **tith·ing** *past* and *past part.* **tithed** *v.t.* (*hist.*) to subject to a tithe [O.E. *teogothian*]

tith·ing (táiðiŋ) *n.* the act of levying or collecting a tithe ‖ (*Eng. hist.*) an administrative division of 10 householders (*FRANKPLEDGE) [O.E. *tēothung*]

Ti·tian (tíʃən) (Tiziano Vecelli) (c. 1490-1576), Venetian painter. His most famous works include 'The Assumption of the Virgin' (1518, in Venice), 'Sacred and Profane Love' (1510-12, in Rome), 'Holy Family with Adoring Shepherd' and 'Noli me tangere' (both c. 1516 and both in the National Gallery, London), and many noble portraits. Besides the great religious masterpieces he also painted classical figures and historical scenes. He communicated directly through paint, and his color sense and mastery of light as a unifying factor allowed him to infringe the classical rules of composition with safety. His dynamic compositions, asymmetrical, rising and receding, helped to establish the canons of baroque art. His portraits were the first in European art which by painterly means fixed a personality, as distinct from merely recording a set of features by draftsmanship

ti·tian (tíʃən) *adj.* of a reddish-brown color [after Titian, who often painted hair this color]

Ti·ti·ca·ca (ti:ti:kúkɑ) a navigable lake (area 3,500 sq. miles) in Bolivia and Peru, in the Andes at 12,500 ft

tit·il·late (tít'leit) *pres. part.* **tit·il·lat·ing** *past* and *past part.* **tit·il·lat·ed** *v.t.* to stimulate pleasantly by or as if by tickling [fr. L. *titillare* (*titillatus*), to tickle]

tit·i·vate, tit·ti·vate (títiveit) *pres. part.* **tit·i·vat·ing, tit·ti·vat·ing** *past* and *past part.* **tit·i·vat·ed, tit·ti·vat·ed** *v.t.* to make (esp. oneself) smart or neat in appearance **tit·i·vá·tion, tit·ti·vá·tion** *n.* [earlier *tiddivate* fr. TIDY]

tit·lark (títlɑrk) *n.* the pipit

ti·tle (táit'l) **1.** *n.* a word, phrase or sentence used to designate a book, chapter, poem etc., thus distinguishing it from others and often indicating the nature of its contents ‖ a similar indication for a painting, statue etc. ‖ a title page ‖ a division of a law book, statute etc. ‖ the form of words at the beginning of a legal document or statute, indicating its nature ‖ a word or phrase attached, usually as a prefix, to the name of a person in order to denote his office, social dignity or status, esp. a status of nobility ‖ an epithet ‖ a ground for a claim, *he has lost all title to our esteem* ‖ (*law*) the legal right to the ownership of property, or the evidence of this right ‖ (*Anglican Communion*) a source of income and fixed sphere of work required of a candidate for ordination ‖ (*Roman Catholicism*) a parish or church, esp. in or near Rome, in the charge of a cardinal ‖ (*sports*) that which affords recognition as the best athlete, team etc. in a particular sport, *world heavyweight title* **2.** *v.t. pres. part.* **ti·tling** *past* and *past part.* **ti·tled** to furnish with a title **tí·tled** *adj.* having a title of nobility [O.F.]

title deed a deed containing the evidence of someone's legal ownership

title page a page at the beginning of a book, treatise etc. giving the name of the book, its author and its publisher etc.

title role the character in a play etc. after whom the play is titled

ti·tling (táitliŋ) *n.* the act of impressing a title on a book or the title thus impressed ‖ (*printing*) type used for display

tit·mouse (títmaus) *pl.* **tit·mice** (títmais) *n.* any of various small (4–6 ins), short-billed birds of fam. *Paridae.* They generally roam in mixed bands, and nest in holes in summer [M.E. *titmose*]

Ti·to (tí:tou) (Josip Broz, 1892-1980), Yugoslav statesman and marshal. He led the Communist guerrilla resistance against the German Occupation of Yugoslavia (1941-5), and became (1945) the head of state of the federal people's republic. At first dominated by the U.S.S.R., he broke with the Cominform (1948) and established his own version of communism in Yugoslavia. He was elected president in 1953 and president for life in 1974. He adopted a foreign policy independent of the Soviet bloc, maintaining sound relations with East European socialist states as well as with Western and nonaligned nations

ti·trate (táitreit) *pres. part.* **ti·trat·ing** *past* and *past part.* **ti·trat·ed** *v.t.* to subject to titration ‖ *v.i.* to perform titration **ti·trá·tion** *n.* an analytical procedure for the determination of reactive capacity, usually of a solution. It consists of adding a reagent in small portions of known volume (e.g. from a burette) to a known volume or mass of a solution or substance until a desired end point (e.g. a color change in an indicator or in the reactants) indicating a known degree of reaction is obtained. It is widely used in quantitative analysis [fr. F. *titrer* fr. *titre,* title]

titre *TITER

tit·ter (títər) **1.** *v.i.* to laugh in a halfhearted or half-suppressed way, often suggesting affectation or nervousness **2.** *n.* such a laugh [imit.]

tittivate *TITIVATE

tit·tle (tít'l) *n.* (only in) **not one jot or tittle** absolutely none at all [M.E. *titel, titil,* a small mark over a letter or word]

tit·tle-tat·tle (tít'ltæt'l) 1. *n.* idle gossip 2. *v.i. pres. part.* **tit·tle-tat·tling** *past* and *past part.* **tit·tle-tat·tled** to engage in idle gossip

tit·tup (títʌp) *pres. part.* **tit·tup·ing,** esp. *Br.* **tit·tup·ping** *past* and *past part.* **tit·tuped,** esp. *Br.* **tit·tupped** *v.i.* to prance and caper along in a way designed to attract attention ‖ (of a horse) to gallop or canter easily **tít·tup·py** *adj.* inclined to tittup ‖ wobbly [prob. imit.]

tit·u·ba·tion (titʃubéiʃən) *n.* an unsteady, staggering gait, esp. caused by certain nervous disorders

tit·u·lar (títʃulər) 1. *adj.* being as specified in title only, *titular head of state* ‖ of or relating to a title, *titular privileges* ‖ (of a bishop or abbot) holding his title from a defunct administration 2. *n.* a person having the title of an office, esp. without its duties or obligations ‖ (*Roman Catholicism*) the person or thing after which a church is named [fr. L. *titulus,* title]

Ti·tus (táitəs) (*New Testament*) the convert and assistant to whom St Paul addressed one of the Pastoral Epistles

Titus (Titus Flavius Sabinus Vespasianus, c. 40-81), Roman emperor (79-81), son of Vespasian. He succeeded his father as Roman commander in the war against the Jews and sacked Jerusalem (70). He was a popular emperor and helped the victims of the eruption of Vesuvius (79), which destroyed Pompeii and Herculaneum, and those of the great fire at Rome (80)

tiz·zy (tízi:) *pl.* **tiz·zies** *n.* (*pop.*) a state of foolish excitement or temporary emotional disturbance [origin unknown]

Tlá·loc (tlɑlóuk), the Otomí god of rain (and hence among the highest in the pantheon)

Tlax·ca·la (tlɑskúlɑ) the smallest state (area 1,555 sq. miles, pop: 556,597) in Mexico, with the highest density (183 persons per sq. mile) among the states. It lies at a mean altitude of 7,000 ft on the central plateau. Capital: Tlaxcala (pop. 35,384). Agriculture (cereals) and handicrafts (weaving) are the main occupations. After being conquered (1519) it was Hernán Cortés' principal ally in the conquest of Mexico (1519-21), its loyalty to Spain bringing it many privileges and relative prosperity. It contains the oldest church (1521) in the Americas

Tlem·cen (tlemsén) an ancient commercial center (pop. 115,054) in N.W. Algeria. Mosques (11th and 14th cc.)

Tlin·git (tlíŋgit) *pl.* **Tlin·git, Tlin·gits** *n.* a group of Indian peoples of the southeastern coast of Alaska. They have declined from about 10,000 (18th c.) to about 4,000 ‖ a member of one of this group of peoples ‖ their language

TLP (*astron. abbr.*) for transient lunar phenomena

T lymphocyte (*cytol.*) T cell (which see)

TM (*abbr.*) for Transcendental Meditation

tme·sis (tmí:sis) *pl.* **tme·ses** (tmí:si:z) *n.* the interposition of one or more words between the parts of a compound word, e.g. 'what man soever' for 'whatsoever man' [L. fr. Gk *tmēsis,* a cutting]

TM-65 (*mil.*) U.S.S.R. main tank with turbojet aircraft engine mounted on a turnable truck used to expel chemicals with engine exhaust

TNT *TRINITROTOLUENE

TNT equivalent (*mil.*) a measure of the energy release, esp. from the detonation of a nuclear weapon, in terms of the amount of TNT that would release the same amount of energy when exploded

to (tu:, *unstressed* tə) 1. *prep.* in the direction of, *to the left* ‖ used to indicate someone or something reached, *he ran to his father's arms* ‖ used to indicate position or contact, *perpendicular to the base, his hands to the wall* ‖ into a condition of, *ground to powder* ‖ used to indicate a result, *they fought to a standstill, to our surprise they arrived on time* ‖ for the purpose of, *they came to our aid* ‖ used to indicate the object of a right or claim, *pretensions to learning* ‖ in accompaniment with, *marching to the band* ‖ with respect to, *subject to criticism* ‖ used to indicate degree or extent, *stirred to the depths* ‖ in conformity with, *made to his specifications* ‖ in comparison with, *the score was 6 to 4* ‖ used to indicate possession or attribution, *the key to the door* ‖ used to indicate attachment, *he held to his opinion* ‖ (in time expressions) used to indicate the period before the hour, *5 to 7* ‖ until, *from 2 to 6* ‖ constituting, *4 quarts to a gallon* ‖ introducing the subject of a toast, *here's to your health* ‖ used after a verb to indicate the receiver of the action, *give the book to her* ‖ used to define the scope of an adjective, *it looks easy to me* or a noun, *a threat to society* ‖ used as a sign of the verbal noun, *no objection to his coming* ‖ as a sign of the infinitive, *he wants to go* ‖ used elliptically for the infinitive, *don't work harder than you have to* 2. *adv.* fixed or fastened, *the window was fast to* ‖ to consciousness, *he came to after* 5 *minutes* ‖ (*naut.*) close to the wind [O.E. *tō*]

toad (toud) *n.* a member of *Bufonidae,* a family of small, tailless, leaping amphibians with a warty skin having poison glands. They are terrestrial except when breeding, and feed primarily on insects ‖ a contemptible, repulsive person [O.E. *tādige,* origin unknown]

toad·flax (tóudflæks) *n.* a European and North American perennial plant, *Linaria vulgaris,* with small yellow or orange flowers

toad spit cuckoo spit

toad·stool (tóudstu:l) *n.* a fungus with an umbrella-shaped pileus ‖ (*pop.*) a poisonous mushroom

toad·y (tóudi:) 1. *pl.* **toad·ies** *n.* someone who grossly and servilely flatters people from whom he hopes to get advantages 2. *v.i. pres. part.* **toad·y·ing** *past* and *past part.* **toad·ied** (with 'to') to behave in this way (toward someone) **tóad·y·ism** *n.* [fr. older *toadeater,* charlatan's assistant, toady]

to and fro in one direction and then in the opposite one, repeatedly

toast (toust) 1. *v.t.* to brown the surface of by exposure to heat ‖ to make hot or very hot ‖ to propose or drink a toast to ‖ *v.i.* to become toasted or as if toasted ‖ to drink a toast 2. *n.* bread browned by exposure to heat and served hot or cold with butter etc. ‖ a drink in honor of a person or thing ‖ a proposal to drink to someone or something ‖ the person or thing drunk to ‖ someone who is the subject of public admiration [O.F. *toster,* to roast or grill]

toasting fork a long-handled fork for toasting bread etc. over a fire

toast·mas·ter (tóustmæstər, tóustmɑstər) *n.* a person appointed to propose toasts, introduce speakers etc., e.g. at a banquet

to·bac·co (təbǽkou) *n.* a member of *Nicotiana,* fam. *Solanaceae,* a genus of plants with large ovate leaves and white or pink flowers, native to tropical America but now cultivated in many parts of the world ‖ the dried and cured leaves of *N. tabacum* smoked, chewed or used as snuff ‖ manufactured products made from these leaves (*NICOTINE) [Span. *tabaco* fr. Carib]

to·bac·co·nist (təbǽkənist) *n.* a retailer in tobacco

To·bey (tóubi:), Mark (1890-1976), American painter. His works, which have a close relation to abstract expressionism, reveal the influence of Oriental calligraphy

To·bi·as (təbáiəs) (*Bible*) the son of Tobit in the book Tobit

To·bit (tóubit) a book included in the Roman Catholic canon but placed in the Apocrypha in the King James Version, telling the story of Tobit, a devout Jew. It is a story of family life and filial devotion

to·bog·gan (təbɒ́gən) 1. *n.* a long, narrow sled of flat boards which curve upward at the front, used for coasting downhill or for travel or transport on ice or snow 2. *v.i.* to ride on a toboggan ‖ to fall rapidly in value [Canadian F. *tabagan* fr. Algonquian]

to·bra·my·cin [$C_{18}H_{37}N_5O_9$] (tọubrəmáisin) *n.* (*pharm.*) antibiotic used against pseudomonic aeruginosa, *E coli,* klebsiella, staphylococcus, etc.; marketed as Nebcin

To·bruk (tóubruk) a port (pop. 58,869) in E. Libya, the scene of much fighting (Jan. 1941-Nov. 1942) in the 2nd world war. It was evacuated by the Germans after the Battle of Alamein

To·by (tóubi:) *pl.* **To·bies** *n.* a jug or mug for beer or ale in the shape of a heavy old man with a three-cornered hat [fr. *Toby,* dim. of Tobias]

To·can·tins (tọkɑntí:ns) a river (1,700 miles long) in Brazil flowing from the central highlands to the Amazon delta above Belém

toc·ca·ta (təkɑ́tə) *n.* (*mus.*) a fast single movement for a keyboard instrument originally designed to exhibit a performer's technique. The term is also used for other compositions, not necessarily of a single movement [Ital.]

To·char·i·an, To·khar·i·an (toukέəri:ən) 1. *n.* a member of a people of European origin living in central Asia (lst millennium A.D.) ‖ their IndoEuropean language 2. *adj.* of this people or their language

Tocque·ville (tóukvil, tɔkví:l), Charles Alexis Henri Clérel de (1805-59), French liberal statesman and political writer. His 'Democracy in America' (1835) is a penetrating study of American society and politics and an indirect lesson to nations striving for democracy. His 'The Ancien Régime and the Revolution' (1856) stressed the continuity of prerevolutionary trends in the French Revolution

toc·sin (tɒ́ksin) *n.* a warning bell ‖ the ringing of a warning bell ‖ something thought of as a signal of disaster [F.]

to·day (tədéi) 1. *adv.* in or during this present day ‖ in the present time, nowadays 2. *n.* the present time or period [O.E. *tō dæg*]

tod·dle (tɒ́d'l) 1. *v.i. pres. part.* **tod·dling** *past* and *past part.* **tod·dled** (esp. of a small child) to walk with short, uncertain steps 2. *n.* a toddling **tód·dler** *n.* a child beginning to learn to walk [origin obscure]

tod·dy (tɒ́di:) *pl.* **tod·dies** *n.* sap obtained from several E. Indian palms ‖ a drink consisting of whiskey, brandy etc., mixed with hot water, sugar and spices [Hind. *tārī* fr. *tār,* palm tree]

Tod·le·ben, Tot·le·ben (tóutlẹibən), Franz Eduard Ivanovich (1818-84), Russian general. He distinguished himself in the Crimean War by his brilliant defense of Sevastopol (1854-5)

to-do (tədú:) *n.* a fuss, commotion

to·dy (tóudi:) *pl.* **to·dies** *n.* a member of *Todus,* fam. *Todidae,* a genus of small West Indian insectivorous birds, allied to the kingfisher [fr. F. *todier*]

toe (tou) 1. *n.* any of the five digits of the human foot ‖ any of the digits of an animal's foot ‖ the forepart of the foot (opp. HEEL) ‖ that part of a shoe, sock or other foot covering which covers the forepart of the foot ‖ anything suggesting a toe in location, shape etc., e.g. the forepart of the hitting surface of a golf club **on one's toes** alert **to step on someone's toes** to offend someone, esp. by stealing his prerogatives 2. *v.t. pres. part.* **toe·ing** *past* and *past part.* **toed** to equip (a stocking etc.) with a toe ‖ to drive (a nail) in slantwise for greater security ‖ (*golf*) to hit (the ball) with the toe of the club [O.E. *tā*]

toe cap an extra piece of leather which covers the toe of a shoe or boot

toed (toud) *adj.* (in compounds) furnished with a specified number or kind of toes ‖ (of a nail) driven in slantwise ‖ (of wood) held firmly by nails driven in slantwise

toe·hold (tóuhọuld) *n.* a niche, crevice etc. just large enough to support the toes in climbing ‖ a means of access, *the inheritance gave him a toehold in society* ‖ a hold in which a wrestler wrenches his opponent's foot

toe-in (tóuịn) *n.* an adjustment of the front wheels of a car so that they make a slight angle with one another, being closer together at the front than at the back. This reduces the wear and makes steering more accurate

toe·nail (tóunẹil) *n.* the nail growing on a toe ‖ a nail driven in obliquely

toe pick (*ice skating*) a short serration of front of the skate blade *also* toe rake

toff (tɒf) *n.* (*Br., pop.*) a man who by dress and manner shows himself to be of superior social status [perh. fr. TUFT, tassel]

tof·fee, tof·fy (tɔ́fi:, tɒ́fi:) *pl.* **tof·fees, tof·fies** *n.* a hard or chewy candy made by boiling sugar with butter, sometimes mixed with nuts etc. [origin unknown]

tog (tɒg) 1. *n.* (*pl., pop.*) clothes, *football togs* 2. *v.t. pres. part.* **tog·ging** *past* and *past part.* **togged** (*Br., pop.,* with 'up' or 'out') to dress for some special occasion, activity etc. [prob. fr. cant *togeman, togman* fr. L. *toga,* cloak]

to·ga (tóugə) *n.* (*hist.*) a man's loose outer garment hanging from a shoulder, worn in public by a Roman citizen ‖ a similar garment worn e.g. by Africans **to·gaed** (tóugəd) *adj.* wearing a toga [L.]

to·geth·er (təgéðər) *adv.* in or into contact or union, *the pages are stuck together* ‖ in or into the same place, group etc., *put them all together so that you can find them again* ‖ at the same time, *the two things happened together* ‖ with each other ‖ in succession, *it rained for days together* ‖ in a body, *all the workers together* ‖ into agreement, *try to bring the two firms together* ‖ by combined action, *together they pushed the stalled car* **together with** including, with in addition, *the house together with its grounds* **to get together** to meet in order to engage in a joint activity **to go together** to accompany one another ‖ to be sweethearts, *they have been going together for 2 years* ‖ to harmonize, *these colors don't go together* **to hang together** to be consistent, be logical, *his story doesn't hang together* **to·geth·er·ness** *n.* (*pop.*) warm fellowship [O.E. *togœdere, tōgadore*]

together *adj.* (*colloq.*) **1.** in control **2.** well organized or integrated *get yourself together*

tog·gle (tɒ́g'l) **1.** *n.* a wooden or metal pin or bolt passed through a loop, staple, eye of a rope etc., esp. as a fastening ‖ a toggle joint or a device having one **2.** *v.t. pres. part.* **tog·gling** *past* and *past part.* **tog·gled** to fasten with, or fit with, a toggle [etym. doubtful]

toggle joint two rods or plates joined together at their ends and at an angle by a hinge, enabling the direction of the resistance to an applied force to be varied

toggle switch the common electric light switch, in which pressure on the lever operates a toggle joint

To·go (tóugou) a republic (area 19,000 sq. miles, pop. 2,872,000) in W. Africa. Capital and port: Lomé. People: Ewe and other groups in the south, smaller Negro and Hamitic groups in the north. Language: French, African languages. Religion: 75% local African, 20% Christian, 5% Moslem. The land is 41% cultivated and 9% forest. Behind the coastal lagoons and swampy plain it rises to an undulating plateau (largely savanna in the north and south, deciduous forest in the center), crossed diagonally by the Togo Mtns (rising to 3,346 ft). Average temperatures (F.): north of the Togo Mtns 72°-92°, south of them 70°-85°. Rainfall: north 45 ins, Togo Mtns 60 ins, south 30 ins. Livestock: goats, cattle, sheep, hogs. Agricultural products: corn, yams, cassava, plantains, peanuts, coffee, cocoa, palm oil and kernels, copra, cotton, manioc, millet, sorghum, rice, meat, hides and skins. Fish is plentiful. Minerals: phosphates, bauxite, iron. Exports: cocoa, coffee, palm kernels, copra, cotton. Imports: cotton cloth, machinery, vehicles, oil, wines and spirits, sugar, cement. Monetary unit: franc CFA. Togo was created an independent republic (Apr. 27, 1960) from the former French Togoland. Sylvanus Olympio served as the first president until his assassination in 1963. A second coup in 1967 forced his successor, Nicolas Grunitzy, to flee the country and established Gnassingbe Eyadema as military chief. Eyadema founded the Togolese People's Assembly, Togo's only political party, in 1969, and appointed a civilian cabinet. A new constitution established in 1979 a directly elected legislature and Eyadema was elected to a second 7-year term as president

To·go·land (tóugoulænd) a former German protectorate in W. Africa, on the Gulf of Guinea. The area was settled by the Ewe people from the Niger (12th c. onwards). The Portuguese began trading in slaves (15th c.) and the French established trading posts (17th c.). The Germans united the area (1880s) as a protectorate, recognized by France (1897) and Britain (1899). Britain occupied the western third and France the rest (1914), and this partition was confirmed (1922) in the League of Nations mandates of British Togoland and French Togoland. These became U.N. trusteeships (1946). After an election (1956), British Togoland joined Ghana (1957). French Togoland became an autonomous republic (1956) and became fully independent (Apr. 27, 1960) as Togo

toil (tɔil) *n.* long, hard effort ‖ (*rhet.*) a task performed with such effort [A.F.=dispute]

toil *v.i.* to work very hard and for a long time ‖ to move slowly and with great effort, *to toil up a hill* [A.F. *toiler*, to strive]

toi·let (tɔ́ilit) *n.* the process of dressing, washing, shaving, making up the face, doing one's hair etc. ‖ (*rhet.*) all the clothes and accessories which a woman dressed with style is wearing, *an elaborate toilet* ‖ a lavatory ‖ a plumbing fixture for receiving human urine and feces, consisting of a hopper into which water is released usually by a system of weights and plungers, and a device for flushing away the contents of the hopper ‖ the room containing this fixture [F. *toilette*, dim. of *toile*, cloth]

toi·let·ries (tɔ́ilitri:z) *pl. n.* articles used in making one's toilet, e.g. soap

toilet water a scented liquid containing alcohol, used after washing or bathing

toils (tɔilz) *pl. n.* circumstances from which it is difficult to escape, entanglements, *in the toils of the moneylender* [O.F. *teile, toile*, a cloth, a net]

toil·some (tɔ́ilsəm) *adj.* laborious

toil·worn (tɔ́ilwɔrn) *adj.* worn out by toil ‖ showing signs of being so worn, *toilworn features*

To·jo (toudʒou), Hideki (1884-1948), Japanese general. As Japanese premier (1941-4), he attacked Pearl Harbor and led operations against the Allies, and was executed as a war criminal

toka unit of currency in Bangladesh

to·ka·mak (tóukəmæk) (*nuclear phys.*) a doughnut-shaped endless-tube device in which ionized gas (plasma) is contained by magnetic fields, used in attempts to produce thermonuclear fusion *Cf* STELLARATOR

To·kay (toukéi) *n.* a sweet, golden Hungarian dessert wine [after *Tokaj* in Hungary]

To·ke·lau Islands (toukəláu) a group of three atolls (area 4 sq. miles, pop. 1,554) in the central Pacific (Polynesia), formerly part of the Gilbert and Ellice Is colony but administered by New Zealand since 1926

to·ken (tóukən) **1.** *n.* an act or object serving as a symbol or evidence of something, *accept this book as a token of our friendship* ‖ a keepsake ‖ a disk (usually metal) exchangeable under some systems for goods, transportation etc. ‖ (*Br.*) a paper voucher, *a book token* **by the same token** on the same grounds, following from this **in token of** as evidence of **2.** *adj.* serving as a token ‖ merely symbolic, *they put up a token resistance* [O.E. *tācn, tācen*]

to·ken·ism (tóukənizəm) *n.* policy or practice of fulfilling legal and/or moral obligations by a nominal conformity, e.g., in hiring practices as by hiring a single black person —**tokenistic** *adj.*

token payment a small sum paid as evidence that the total debt is acknowledged

token strike (*Br.*) a labor strike which lasts only a few hours

Tokharian *TOCHARIAN

To·ku·ga·wa (tɔku:gɑwɑ) a family of shoguns founded by Ieyasu, which controlled Japan (1603-1867)

To·ku·shi·ma (tɔku:ʃi:mɑ) a port (pop. 171,000) in N.E. Shikoku, Japan: cotton textiles, mechanical engineering

To·ky·o (tóuki:ou, tóukjou) the capital (pop. 11,634,927) and the financial and commercial center of Japan, a port on Tokyo Bay (area approx. 600 sq. miles), on central E. Honshu. Industries: mechanical engineering, chemicals, textiles, food processing, light manufacturing printing and publishing. Built on a river plain and cut by canals, it centers on the imperial palace (19th c.) and park, surrounded by moats. The city was rebuilt in Occidental style after an earthquake (1923) and heavy bombing (1945). Principal cultural institutions: university (1877), imperial museums, National Diet library, Kabuki theater. Tokyo was founded in 1456. It became a provincial capital in 1590 and the imperial capital in 1868

Tokyo Round the seventh of the major multilateral trade negotiations held under the auspices of GATT in Geneva in October 1973, placing special emphasis on the export needs of developing countries, and discussions on nontariff barriers to trade, trade in agricultural goods, and trade protectionism

Tol·bert (tóulbərt), William Richard (1913-80), president of Liberia (1971-80). He was killed during a military coup

told *past* and *past part.* of TELL **all told** in total

To·le·do (təlí:dou) a port and rail center (pop. 354,635) in Ohio, on Lake Erie: glass, mechanical engineering, automobiles, coal shipment. University (1872)

To·le·do (təlí:dou, tɔléðɔ) a province (area 5,919 sq. miles, pop. 471,806) of central Spain (*NEW CASTILE) ‖ its capital (pop. 51,400), also the historic capital of New Castile. Visigothic-Moorish-Spanish city walls, medieval bridges, alcazar (16th-c. fortress, restored after near destruction in 1936), Gothic cathedral (13th-15th cc.) and churches. Conquered by the Romans in 192 B.C., Toledo became a Church center very early, and later (534-712) became the capital of Visigothic Spain. It remained important under the Moslems and, after reconquest (1085) by Castile, was the Castilian capital until 1560. Its sword blades have been famous since Roman times

tol·er·a·ble (tɒ́lərəb'l) *adj.* able to be tolerated ‖ adequate or fairly good, *a tolerable knowledge of French* **tól·er·a·bly** *adv.* [F. *tolérable*]

tol·er·ance (tɒ́lərəns) *n.* readiness to allow others to believe or act as they judge best ‖ (*biol.*) the ability of an organism to survive in difficult conditions (of heat, cold, drought etc.) ‖ (*mech.*) the permissible error in size etc. of a machine part or manufactured article, *a tolerance of a thousandth of an inch* ‖ (*med.*) the natural or developed ability to take in drugs etc. without suffering harmful effects ‖ (*coinage*) remedy [F. *tolérance*]

tol·er·ant (tɒ́lərənt) *adj.* willing to tolerate the beliefs, way of living etc. of others ‖ (*med.*) of or having a tolerance F. *tolérant*]

tol·er·ate (tɒ́ləreit) *pres. part.* **tol·er·at·ing** *past* and *past part.* **tol·er·at·ed** *v.t.* to support (pain) with fortitude or (a nuisance) with forbearance ‖ to permit, *you should not tolerate such rudeness* ‖ to respect (the conduct, opinions, beliefs etc. of others) without sitting in judgment on them ‖ (*med.*) to be able to take (a drug etc.) without suffering harmful effects [fr. F. *tolérer*]

tol·er·a·tion (tɒləréiʃən) *n.* the act of tolerating something ‖ freedom to practice a particular religious cult without incurring civil disabilities [F. *tolération*]

Toleration, Act of (*Eng. hist.*) an act of parliament (1689) granting limited religious freedom to Protestant dissenters

Toleration Act of 1649 (Maryland's Act Concerning Religion), a pioneer act passed by the assembly of Maryland which granted freedom of conscience to all Christian denominations

Tol·kien (tóulki:n, tɒ́lki:n), John Ronald Reuel (1892-1973), British writer and medievalist. His best-known works include 'The Hobbit' (1937), the trilogy 'The Lord of the Rings' (1954-5), and 'The Silmarillion' (1977)

toll (toul) *n.* a tax or charge levied on those who use a particular service (e.g. a bridge, road etc.) ‖ (*rhet.*) a cost in life or limb or in suffering, damage etc., *the war took a terrible toll of the youth of the nation* [O.E.]

toll **1.** *v.t.* to ring (a bell) with strokes separated by long, equal intervals, usually as a solemn signal of death, disaster etc. ‖ *v.i.* (of a bell) to sound thus **2.** *n.* a tolling ‖ the sound made thus [perh. fr. M.E. *tollen*, to pull, prob. fr. O.E.]

toll bar an obstruction on a road, bridge etc. where a toll must be paid

toll·booth (tóulbu:θ) *n.* a booth where tolls are paid

toll bridge a bridge at which a toll is charged for passage

toll-free number (tóulfrí:) a Bell System telephone number preceded by 800 permitting calls to be made from certain areas and charged at wholesale rate to the receiver of the calls

toll·gate (tóulgeit) *n.* a gate on a road, bridge etc. where a toll is to be paid

toll·house (tóulhaus) *pl.* **toll·hous·es** (tóulhauziz) *n.* a booth etc. where a toll is taken ‖ a tollkeeper's house

toll·keep·er (tóulki:pər) *n.* (*Br.*) a person who collects tolls

Tol·man (tóulmən), Richard Chace (1881-1948), U.S. physical chemist and physicist. His major contributions were in chemical kinetics, statistical mechanics, relativity and relativistic cosmology

tol·met·in [$C_{15}H_{15}NO_3$] (tóulmetin) *n.* (*pharm.*) nonsteroidal anti-inflammatory drug used in treating rheumatoid arthritis; marketed as Tolectin

Tol·pud·dle Martyrs (tɒ́lpʌd'l) a group of six farm workers sentenced (1834) to transportation for seven years for having formed a trade-union branch at the village of Tolpuddle, Dorset, England. The affair showed the hostility of the Whig government to the growing trade-union movement, and led to the dissolution of the Grand National Consolidated Trades Union

Tol·stoy (tóulstɔi, tɒ́lstɔi), Alexy Nikolayevich (1882-1945), Russian novelist. His best-known work was 'Peter the Great' (1929-34, Eng. trans. 1936), a fictionalized biography

Tolstoy, Count Leo (Lev) Nikolayevich (1828-1910), Russian novelist and moral philosopher. He came of a rich and noble family. Toward the end of his life he rejected the institutions of society, including personal property and the state itself, together with corrupted art, in a kind of saintly anarchism. Before this crisis he had written his two masterpieces: 'War and Peace' (1864-9) and 'Anna Karenina' (1875-7). Few novelists can approach Tolstoy either in scope (the whole movement of European soci-

CONCISE PRONUNCIATION KEY: **(a)** æ, *cat*; ɑ, *car*; ɔ *fawn*; ei, *snake*. **(e)** e, *hen*; i:, *sheep*; iə, *deer*; εə, *bear*. **(i)** i, *fish*; ai, *tiger*; ə:, *bird*. **(o)** o, *ox*; au, *cow*; ou, *goat*; u, *poor*; ɔi, *royal*. **(u)** ʌ, *duck*; u, *bull*; u:, *goose*; ə, *bacillus*; ju:, *cube*. x, *loch*; θ, *think*; ð, *bother*; z, *Zen*; ʒ, *corsage*; dʒ, *savage*; ŋ, *orangutang*; j, *yak*; ʃ, *fish*; tʃ, *fetch*; 'l, *rabble*; 'n, *redden*. Complete pronunciation key appears inside front cover.

ety, the nature and conduct of a continental war) or in the depth of his analysis of man as a social being

Tol·tec (tóltek) *n.* (*hist.*) a member of a Nahuatlan people who flourished in Mexico (c. 7th–12th cc.). The Toltecs smelted metal, built massive pyramids and practiced sun worship and human sacrifice. Their culture was assimilated by the Aztecs **Tól·tec·an** *adj.* [Span. *tolteca*]

to·lu (təlú:) *n.* balsam of Tolu [Span. *tolú* after Santiago de Tolú, in Colombia]

tol·u·ene (tólju:i:n) *n.* a colorless liquid hydrocarbon, $C_6H_5CH_3$, distilled esp. from coal tar and used in the manufacture of dyes, drugs and trinitrotoluene [fr. *tolu,* balsam of Tolu+Gk *-ēnē,* fem. patronymic suffix]

to·lu·i·dene (təlú:idi:n) *n.* an isomeric amine, $CH_3C_6H_4NH_2$, derived from toluene and used in the manufacture of dyes

tol·u·ol (tólju:oul) *n.* toluene, esp. when referring to commercial grades [fr. *tolu,* balsam of Tolu+ALCOHOL]

tom (tɒm) *n.* the male of some animals, esp. the cat [dim. of *Thomas*]

Tom (*slang*) (pejorative) a black person who humbles himself to white people or advocates a white position in a black-white controversy; from the character in *Uncle Tom's Cabin,* by Harriet Beecher Stowe *also* Uncle Tom —**Tom** *v.* —**Tomism, Uncle Tomism** *n.* the response or practice

tom·a·hawk (tóməhɔ̨k) *n.* a light ax used by North American Indians [of Algonquian origin]

Tomahawk *n.* (*mil.*) a pilotless, turbojet, solid-fuel missile (BGM-109), 18 ft. long, weighing 3,200 lbs, fired from a submarine, with nuclear capability and a 1,200-mi range

tom·al·ley (tómæli:) *n.* a fatty substance (often called liver) in the North American lobster, considered a delicacy [prob. fr. Carib]

to·ma·to (təméitou, təmátou) *pl.* **to·ma·toes** *n.* *Lycopersicon esculentum,* fam. *Solanaceae,* a trailing herbaceous annual originating in South America and widely cultivated for its fruit ‖ this fruit, red or yellow when ripe, fleshy, juicy and rich in vitamins, eaten fresh, cooked, or canned, and also processed into juice [Span. *tomate* fr. Nahuatl *tomatl*]

tomb (tu:m) *n.* a burial chamber ‖ a stone construction within or under which a person lies buried [Early M.E. *toumbe, tumbe* fr. A.F. *tumbe,* O.F. *tombe*]

tom·bac, tom·bak (tómbæk) *n.* an alloy of copper and zinc used for cheap jewelry etc. [F. fr. Malay *tambâga,* copper]

tom·bo·la (tɒmbóulə) *n.* ‖ (*Br.*) bingo ‖ (*Br.*) a lottery, esp. one organized for charity [F. or Ital. fr. *tombolare,* tumble]

Tom·bouc·tou (tɔ̨mbu:ktú:) *TIMBUKTU

tom·boy (tómbɔ̨i) *n.* a girl who likes boyish sports and activities

tomb·stone (tú:mstɔ̨un) *n.* a gravestone

tom·cat (tómkæt) *n.* a male cat

Tomcat *n.* (*mil.*) a twin-turbofan, dual-crew, supersonic, long-range interceptor (F-14) designed to operate from aircraft carriers, with air-to-air and air-to-ground missiles and conventional ordnance

Tom, Dick and Harry (tɒm, dik, hǽri:) (often preceded by 'any' or 'every') anybody or everybody, people of no particular importance

tome (toum) *n.* a book, esp. one that is large, heavy and scholarly [F. fr. L. fr. Gk]

to·men·tose (təméntous) *adj.* covered with short woolly hairs [fr. Mod. L. *tomentosus* fr. L. *tomentum,* stuffing for cushions]

to·men·tum (təméntəm) *pl.* **to·men·ta** (təméntə) *n.* (*bot.*) a close covering or felting of downy, cottony or woolly hairs on leaves or stems ‖ (*anat.*) the mass of wool-like blood vessels comprising the inner surface of the pia mater [Mod. L. fr. L.=cushion stuffing]

tom·fool (tómfú:l) **1.** *n.* a silly fool, esp. someone who acts with stupid thoughtlessness **2.** *adj.* silly, senseless **3.** *v.i.* to play the tomfool **tom·fool·er·y** (tómfú:ləri:) *pl.* **tom·fool·er·ies** *n.* silly behavior

tom·my (tómi:) *pl.* **tom·mies** *n.* (*Br.*) a rod used e.g. to give purchase on a socket wrench [fr. *Tommy,* nickname for Thomas]

tommy *pl.* **tommies** *n.* (*Br.*) a private in the army ‖ any British soldier [fr. *Thomas* Atkins, made-up name on model army forms showing soldiers how to fill them in]

tommy gun a Thompson submachine gun ‖ a similar automatic weapon

tom·my·rot (tómi:rɒt) *n.* utter nonsense

to·mog·ra·phy (toumógrəfi:) *n.* (*med.*) system of X-rays that photographs a body layer by layer through movement of the apparatus *also* body-section radiography, laminography, planigraphy, sectional radiography

to·mor·row (təmórou) **1.** *n.* the day following today **2.** *adv.* on or during the day following today [M.E. fr. *to morgen, to morwen*]

tom·pi·on (tómpi:ən) *n.* a tampion

Tomp·kins (tómpkənz), Daniel D. (1774-1825), U.S. vice-president under James Monroe (1817-25). His vice-presidency was marked by a long controversy over charges that he had mishandled funds while serving as governor of New York (1807-17)

Tomsk (tɒmsk) a city (pop. 439,000) in the R.S.F.S.R., U.S.S.R., in W. Siberia: engineering, chemical and wood industries and nuclear research. University (1888)

tom·tit (tómtít) *n.* (*Br.*) *Parus caeruleus,* the blue tit ‖ one of various small birds, e.t. a nuthatch

tom-tom (tómtɒm) *n.* an Oriental or African drum with a small head, played with the hands or sticks [Hind. *tam-tam,* imit.]

ton (tʌn) *n.* a register ton ‖ a unit of volume for a ship's cargo, usually equal to 40 cu. ft ‖ a unit of volume for measuring the displacement of a ship equal to 35 cu. ft ‖ a European measure of capacity for lumber, usually equal to 40 cu. ft ‖ any of various units of weight, e.g. for wheat, lime, plaster, gravel, stone etc. ‖ (*pop.,* esp. *pl.*) a great deal, *tons of money* (*LONG TON, *SHORT TON, *METRIC TON) [O.E. *tunne*]

ton *n.* (*Br.*) **1.** a century **2.** a score of 100% **3.** a speed of 100 mph **4.** (*cricket*) 100 runs

ton·al (tóun'l) *adj.* pertaining to tone or to tonality ‖ (*mus.*) having the internal intervals of a musical phrase modified when it is repeated at an interval on grounds of key (instead of being exactly reproduced), *a tonal fugue* **to·nál·i·ty** *pl.* **to·nal·i·ties** *n.* (*mus.*) the quality of having key (cf. ATONALITY) ‖ (*painting*) the color relationships in a painting [fr. M.L. *tonalis*]

Tone (toun), Theobald Wolfe (1763-98), Irish revolutionary. He negotiated with the French for an invasion of Ireland to assist the Irish rebels, but was captured by the English and convicted of treason. He committed suicide

tone (toun) **1.** *n.* the quality of a sound, *the mellow tone of a cello* ‖ (*mus.*) a pure sound which is vibrating as a whole with its minimum frequency (the fundamental note) ‖ (*mus.*) an interval of two semitones ‖ (*mus.*) any of the eight Gregorian modes used in singing the Psalms ‖ (*mus.*) a note ‖ an inflection or modulation of the voice denoting an emotion etc., *a cross tone of voice* ‖ a way of speaking or writing which denotes the person's sentiments, purpose etc., *the tone of a letter* ‖ (*painting*) the general effect of a painting in relation to its color, light and shade ‖ (of color) degree of luminosity ‖ (*linguistics*) the musical pitch of a sound, word etc. ‖ (*linguistics*) a rising, falling or other pitch by which words are distinguished, e.g. in ancient Greek or in Pekingese Chinese ‖ (*photog.*) the color or shade of a print ‖ (*physiol.*) the proper condition of organs or tissues for healthy functioning ‖ the general moral or social condition of a city, community etc. **2.** *v. pres. part.* **ton·ing** *past* and *past part.* **toned** *v.t.* to give a certain tone of color or sound to ‖ (*photog.*) to change the silver color of (a print) into a colored image ‖ *v.i.* to be harmonious ‖ (*photog.,* of a print) to change in color through a chemical reaction **to tone down** to reduce the loudness, pitch, contrast, luminosity etc. of ‖ to reduce (demands) or soften (remarks etc.) ‖ to become reduced or modified thus **to tone up** to impart tone to (muscles, the system etc.) [O.F. *ton*]

tone color, *Br.* **tone colour** (*mus.*) timbre

toned (tound) *adj.* (of paper) slightly off-white ‖ characterizing a tone language

tone-deaf (tóundéf) *adj.* unable to distinguish differences of pitch in music

tone language a language, e.g. Pekingese Chinese, in which variations in tones are utilized to distinguish words of different meanings which ordinarily would sound alike

tone·less (tóunlis) *adj.* without any expressive quality, *a toneless voice*

tone poem an orchestral composition, usually in one movement, based on a literary theme and tending to evoke images

to·net·ic (tounétik) *adj.* (*linguistics*) of or relating to tones ‖ of or relating to tone languages **to·nét·ics** *n.* (*linguistics*) the study of tones

tong (tɔŋ, tɒŋ) *n.* a Chinese secret society in the U.S.A., Singapore etc., esp. one involved in vice or racketeering [Chin. *t'ang,* meeting place]

Ton·ga (tóŋgə) (or Friendly Islands) an independent sovereign state (land area 270 sq. miles, pop. 104,000) in the S. Pacific (Polynesia), consisting of some 150 volcanic and coral islands. The three main groups (north-south) are Vava'u, Ha'apai and Tongatapu. Capital and chief port: Nukualofa (pop. 20,357), on Tongatapu, the main island. People: Polynesian. Language: Tongan. Religion: mainly Methodist. Highest point: 3,380 ft. Average temperatures (F.): 70°-80°. Rainfall: Vava'u 110 ins, Tongatapu 70 ins. Exports: copra, bananas, watermelons, pineapples. Other products: cereals, vegetables. fish. Imports: textiles, processed foods, hardware, fuels, tobacco. Monetary unit: Tongan pound. HISTORY. The islands were peopled by Polynesians from Samoa when discovered (1616) by the Dutch. They were explored (1773, 1777) by Cook, and named the Friendly Islands. A successful Wesleyan mission was established (1826). Tonga became a constitutional monarchy (1862) and a British protectorate (1900). It became independent (June 4, 1970), and a member of the Commonwealth. King Taufa'ahau Tupou IV succeeded his mother, Queen Salote, in 1965

ton·ga (tóŋgə) *n.* a light, horse-drawn, two-wheeled carriage used in India [Hind. *tāngā*]

Tong·hak (tóŋgək) a syncretist religion founded (1859) in Korea, based on Shamanism, Confucianism and Buddhism, with a ritual based on Roman Catholic usage. It has about 2,000,000 adherents

tongs (tɔŋz, tɒŋz) *pl. n.* (sometimes construed as sing.) an implement constructed of two rods, often with clawed working ends, pivoted together at or near the handle end, used to grasp and lift (coal lumps in a hearth etc.) [O.E. *tang, tange*]

tongue (tʌŋ) **1.** *n.* a mobile, extensible structure of muscles of most vertebrates which is attached to the floor of the mouth and to the hyoid bone. It is an important organ of taste, ingestion of food and, in man, of articulation in speech ‖ a similar organ, e.g. a lingula or radula, found in various invertebrates ‖ an animal's tongue prepared for the table ‖ manner of speech with regard to the way something is said or what is said, *a smooth tongue, a lying tongue* ‖ a language or dialect, *a foreign tongue* ‖ the leather flap under the laces of a shoe ‖ a projecting part of a piece of wood, as in matchboard, for fitting into a groove ‖ the clapper of a bell ‖ the pin of a buckle ‖ a tapering rail forming part of a railroad switch ‖ a long, thin promontory of land or inlet of water ‖ a vibrating part in the reed of some wind instruments **on the tip of one's tongue** one's immediate intention (to say something specified), *it was on the tip of my tongue to ask the same question* ‖ almost, but not quite, remembered, *his name is on the tip of my tongue* **to find one's tongue** to be able to speak again after shock or embarrassment **to give tongue** (of hounds) to bay, esp. when in sight of game **to hold one's tongue** to remain silent **2.** *v. pres. part.* **tongu·ing** *past* and *past part.* **tongued** *v.i.* (*mus.*) to use tonguing ‖ to project like a tongue ‖ *v.t.* (*mus.*) to play by tonguing ‖ to cut a tongue on (a piece of wood etc.) ‖ to fit together by means of a tongue-and-groove joint [O.E. *tunge*]

tongue-and-groove joint (tʌ́ŋəngrú:v) a joint in which a tongue on the edge of one board fits into a groove on the edge of another

tongue in cheek *adv.* with irony or insincerity

tongue-lash·ing (tʌ́ŋlæʃiŋ) *n.* a very severe reproof

tongue-tie (tʌ́ŋtai) *n.* the inability to move the tongue normally, owing to excessive shortness of the frenum **tóngue-tied** *adj.* suffering from this disability ‖ speechless through shyness etc.

tongue twister a word or phrase which is difficult to pronounce because of similarity of sounds, alliteration etc.

tongu·ing (tʌ́ŋiŋ) *n.* (*mus.*) the use of the tongue on a wind instrument to obtain a rapid staccato effect or to modulate the intonation

ton·ic (tónik) **1.** *adj.* inducing tonicity ‖ (*med.*) characterized by prolonged muscular contraction, *tonic spasm* ‖ mentally or morally invigorating ‖ (*mus.*) pertaining to or based on a keynote ‖ relating to tone in painting or photography ‖ (*phon.*) stressed ‖ (*linguistics*) tonetic **2.**

n. an invigorating medicine, meant to tone up the system ‖ anything which has a similar effect on the nerves or mind ‖ (*mus.*) the keynote of the scale ‖ (*phon.*) an accented syllable [fr. Gk *tonikos*]

tonic accent stress placed on a syllable, esp. by raising the pitch

to·nic·i·ty (tounísiti:) *n.* (*physiol.*) a normal healthy elasticity in the tissues or muscles

tonic sol-fa (*mus.*) an English system of notation for a diatonic scale based not on fixed pitch but on tonality or relation to the keynote. The notes are named *do* (keynote), *re, mi, fa, sol, la, ti.* The system is used to train singers in sight-reading (*SOLMIZATION)

to·night (tənáit) **1.** *adv.* on or during the present night, *you are tired tonight* ‖ on the coming night of the present day, *I'll see you tonight* **2.** *n.* the night that has begun but not ended ‖ the coming night, *tonight is the play's first night* [O.E. *tō niht*]

to·nite (tóunait) *n.* a high explosive prepared from guncotton [fr. L. *tonare,* to thunder]

ton·ka bean (tɒ́ŋkə) any of various members of *Dipteryx,* fam. *Leguminosae,* a South American plant, esp. *D. odorata* ‖ the pleasant-smelling seed of *D. odorata,* containing coumarin, and used in perfumes and as flavoring for tobacco etc.

Ton·kin (tɒ́nkín) (*hist.*) the former name of the northern provinces of Vietnam, established (1883) as a protectorate by the French. It was administered (1887-1945) as part of French Indochina, became (1945) a province of the independent republic of Vietnam, and then formed (1954) the northern and central region of North Vietnam

Tonkin Gulf resolution an authorization requested (1964) by U.S. President Lyndon B. Johnson of Congress, following the alleged attack by North Vietnamese warships on U.S. Navy vessels in international waters in the Gulf of Tonkin. The resolution gave Congressional support for 'all necessary action to protect our armed forces and to assist nations covered by the SEATO treaty'. In effect this was a blank check for the president, as Congress had not declared war. The resolution was repealed (Jan. 12, 1971)

Ton·le·Sap (tɒ́nleisáp) a lake (area 1,000-2,500 sq. miles, depending on season, esp. on the effect of the S.W. monsoon) in W. Cambodia: fisheries

ton·nage, tun·nage (tʌ́nidʒ) *n.* the carrying capacity of a vessel measured in tons ‖ the total carrying capacity of a fleet, esp. of a merchant fleet ‖ a duty based on the cargo capacity of a vessel ‖ a charge per ton on cargo carried on canals or in ports

to·nom·e·ter (tounɒ́mitər) *n.* (*mus.*) an instrument, esp. a tuning fork, for determining pitch ‖ (*med.*) an instrument for measuring pressure (e.g. blood pressure) or tension (e.g. of the eyeball) ‖ an instrument for measuring vapor pressure **to·no·met·ric** (tɒunəmétrik) *adj.* **to·nóm·e·try** *n.* [fr. Gk *tonos,* stretching, pitch+METER]

ton·sil (tɒ́nsəl) *n.* one of a pair of lymphatic organs situated on either side of the throat at the entrance to the pharynx [fr. L. *tonsillae* pl. n.]

ton·sil·lar (tɒ́nsələr) *adj.* of, pertaining to or affected by the tonsils [fr. M.L. or Mod. L. *tonsillaris*]

ton·sil·lec·to·my (tɒnsəléktəmi:) *pl.* **ton·sil·lec·to·mies** *n.* removal of the tonsils by surgery [fr. L. *tonsillae,* tonsils +Gk *-ektomē,* a cutting out]

ton·sil·li·tis (tɒnsəláitis) *n.* inflammation of the tonsils [Mod. L. fr. L. *tonsillae,* tonsils]

ton·sil·lot·o·my (tɒnsəlɒ́təmi:) *pl.* **ton·sil·lot·o·mies** *n.* the incision of a tonsil [fr. L, *tonsillae,* tonsils+Gk *-tome-,* a cutting]

ton·so·ri·al (tɒnsɔ́ri:əl, tɒnsóuri:əl) *adj.* (esp. *jocular*) of or relating to barbers or their trade [fr. L. *tonsorius*]

ton·sure (tɒ́nʃər) **1.** *n.* the shaving of the head or of a portion of the head on admission to the priesthood or to some monastic orders ‖ the part of the head left bare by such shaving **2.** *v.t. pres. part.* **ton·sur·ing** *past* and *past part.* **ton·sured** to shave the head or crown of [F. or fr. L. *tonsura*]

ton·tine (tɒntí:n) *n.* an annuity system in which the share of a subscriber who dies is divided among the surviving subscribers until ultimately the whole income is enjoyed by the last survivor ‖ the share of each subscriber [after Lorenzo *Tonti* (*c.* 1630–*c.* 1695), Italian banker who originated the system]

Ton·ton Ma·coute (tɔ̃tɔ̃mæku:t) *DUVALIER

to·nus (tóunəs) *n.* (*physiol.*) tonicity [L. fr. Gk *tonos*]

too (tu:) *adv.* excessively, more than is sufficient, necessary or desirable, *the cup is too big* ‖ (intensively) very, *you are too kind* ‖ also, *they are coming tomorrow and I hope you will come too* ‖ to a regrettable degree, *it's too bad* [stressed form of TO]

took *past* of TAKE

tool (tu:l) **1.** *n.* anything which, held in the hand or hands, assists a person to do manual work ‖ the working part of a machine ‖ a machine tool ‖ anything used in the performance of nonmanual work, *a dictionary is a useful tool for a translator* ‖ a person who is made use of by another, e.g. for committing a crime ‖ (*bookbinding*) a hand stamp used to impress a letter or design on the cover of a book **2.** *v.t.* to shape with a tool ‖ to impress letters or designs on (a book cover) with a tool ‖ (often with 'up') to equip (a factory etc.) with tools, machines etc. ‖ *v.i.* to use a tool or tools [O.E. *tōl*]

tool·bar (tú:lbɑr) *n.* a bar at the rear of a tractor to which different implements (harrow, roller etc.) can be attached

tool·box (tú:lbɒks) *n.* a box for tools ‖ a box in which the cutting tool of a planing or other machine is clamped

tool·ing (tú:liŋ) *n.* decorative work or designs done with a tool ‖ the set of tools used in a factory

tool·mak·er (tú:lmeikər) *n.* a machinist who makes and repairs the tools, instruments etc. used in a machine shop

toon (tu:n) *n. Cedrela toona,* fam. *Meliaceae,* a large East Indian and Australian tree yielding a reddish wood used esp. for cabinetmaking, and whose flowers yield a dye ‖ the wood of this tree [Hind. *tun, tün,* Skr. *tunna*]

toot (tu:t) **1.** *v.t.* to cause (a horn etc.) to produce a short sharp note ‖ to blow a short note on (a horn or trumpet) ‖ *v.i.* to sound a short note on a whistle, horn or trumpet **2.** *n.* such a sound [prob. imit.]

tooth (tu:θ) **1.** *pl.* **teeth** (ti:θ) *n.* one of the hard, bonelike processes set in the jaws of most vertebrates and some invertebrates, used in man for masticating food and in forming speech sounds, and in animals for tearing, grinding and holding food, and for defense (cf. CANINE TOOTH, cf. INCISOR, cf. MOLAR). An adult human normally has 32 teeth, each one rooted in a socket in the jaw, developing around a central bundle of nerves and coated with a hard white enamel ‖ a toothlike projection e.g. on the edge of a leaf or the rim of a cogwheel **armed to the teeth** very heavily armed **in the teeth of** facing, fully esposed to, *in the teeth of the wind* ‖ in direct opposition to, in spite of, *in the teeth of the hostile critics* **to get one's teeth into** (something) to begin to cope effectively with (a difficulty) or to begin to grasp or master (something) **to put teeth into** to provide (esp. a law) with effective means of enforcement **to set one's teeth** to bring the upper and lower teeth tightly together ‖ to adopt a determined attitude, show oneself ready to suffer or endure or master **to show one's teeth** to put on a threatening attitude **2.** *v.t.* to furnish with teeth ‖ *v.i.* to interlock as cogged wheels [O.E. *tōth*]

tooth·ache (tú:θeik) *n.* a pain in or near the nerve of a tooth

tooth and nail with all one's energy and every resource (in a fight, argument etc.)

tooth·brush (tú:θbrʌʃ) *n.* a small brush for cleaning the teeth

tooth·comb (tú:θkoum) *n.* (*Br.*) a comb with very close-set teeth **to go through something with a fine-tooth comb** (*Br.* **with a toothcomb**) to search or examine something with minute care

toothed (tu:θt) *adj.* having teeth ‖ (in compounds) having a specified number or kind of teeth, *saber-toothed tiger*

toothed whale one of the two main divisions of whales, constituting the suborder *Odontoceti,* e.g. the sperm whale

tooth·ing (tú:θiŋ) *n.* (generally *pl.*) alternate gaps and projections left at the end of a brick or stone wall to allow bonding in a later extension

tooth·less (tú:θlis) *adj.* having no teeth

tooth·paste (tú:θpeist) *n.* a paste dentifrice

tooth·pick (tú:θpik) *n.* a small pointed stick of wood, metal or plastic for removing fragments of food lodged in or between the teeth

tooth powder a powdered dentifrice

tooth·some (tú:θsəm) *adj.* (*old-fash.*) with an appetizing taste, tasty

tooth·wort (tú:θwə:rt, tú:θwɔrt) *n. Lathraea squamaria,* fam. *Orobanchaceae,* a herbaceous parasite on the hazel and beech with creeping rhizomes covered with broad fleshy scales ‖ a member of *Dentaria,* fam. *Cruciferae,* a genus of perennial creeping plants cultivated for their big white, rose or purple flowers

tooth·y (tú:θi:) *comp.* **tooth·i·er** *superl.* **tooth·i·est** *adj.* having large teeth or showing lots of teeth, *a toothy grin*

too·tle (tú:t'l) **1.** *v. pres. part.* **too·tling** *past* and *past part.* **too·tled** *v.i.* to make fluty noises, esp. on a musical instrument **2.** *n.* the act or sound of tootling [frequentative of TOOT]

top (tɒp) **1.** *n.* the highest peak of something, *the top of the hill* ‖ the highest or best attainable position, rank, status, degree, pitch etc., *there is room at the top in his profession, at the top of one's voice* ‖ a cover, esp. a lid ‖ the upper part of a garment ‖ (*chem.*) the most volatile part of a mixture ‖ (*naut.*) a small platform near the top of a lower mast to which are fastened the shrouds of the topmast ‖ the part of a plant (esp. one with an edible root) that grows above the ground ‖ (*Br.*) high (the highest-ratio gear of a vehicle) ‖ the folding roof of a car or baby carriage **on top** successful **on top of** in addition to **on top of the world** in a state of great elation **over the top** over the front of a trench in order to attack ‖ above a specified goal or limit **2.** *v.t. pres. part.* **top·ping** *past* and *past part.* **topped** to be higher or more than, *he tops his companions by six inches* ‖ to go over the top of ‖ to constitute the top of ‖ to do better than, *he topped his previous performance* ‖ to be at the top of ‖ to furnish with a top ‖ (*Br.,* with 'up') to add fresh liquid to so as to bring the contents to a higher level, *let me top up your glass* ‖ to remove the top or tops of, *top the bean plants* ‖ (*naut.*) to tilt (a yard) so that one end is higher than the other ‖ (*chem.*) to remove the most volatile parts from ‖ (*games*) to hit (a ball) above the center **to top off** to finish by adding a final touch **3.** *adj.* on or at the top, *the top sheet* ‖ highest, *top prices* ‖ in the greatest degree, *top priority* ‖ (*pop.*) first in some understood scale, *top performance* [O.E.]

top *n.* a toy shaped to spin on its tapered point [O.E.]

to·paz (tóupæz) *n.* a mineral, $Al_2SiO_4(F,OH)_2$, consisting of a compound of aluminum and silica. It may be transparent, white, pale blue, pale green or yellow. Topazes are used mainly as gem stones, the yellow topaz being the most precious ‖ either of two large, brilliant South American hummingbirds, *Topaza pella* and *T. pyra* [M.E. fr. O.F. *topaze, topace* fr. L. fr. Gk]

to·paz·o·lite (toupǽzəlait) *n.* a yellow or greenish variety of garnet, esp. andradite

top boot a high boot reaching to just below the knee, worn by jockeys, hunters etc.

top·coat (tɒ́pkout) *n.* an overcoat ‖ a final coat of paint etc.

top dog (*pop.*) a person who is recognized as boss, esp. after having to fight for power

top dollar (*colloq.*) the highest possible price *ant.* bottom dollar

top drawer (esp. in the phrase) **out of the top drawer** (*Br., pop.*) born to the high social position actually occupied

top·dress (tɒ́pdres) *v.t.* to apply a topdressing to (cf. SIDE-DRESS) **tóp·dress·ing** *n.* a dressing of fertilizer spread on the surface of a field or garden

tope (toup) *n.* a dome-shaped Buddhist shrine [Hindi *tōp* prob. fr. Skr. *stūpa*]

tope (toup) *pres. part.* **top·ing** *past* and *past part.* **toped** *v.i.* (*rhet.*) to drink alcohol frequently and heavily [origin unknown]

to·pee, to·pi (tóupi:) *n.* a pith helmet, worn for protection against the sun [Hind. *topī*]

To·pe·ka (təpí:kə) the capital (pop. 115,266) of Kansas: meat packing, mechanical engineering, flour milling. University (1944)

Topeka (Free State) Constitution a constitution drafted (1854) by antislavery elements in the territory of Kansas. Opposing the proslavery territorial government, it outlawed slavery in Kansas, but nevertheless prohibited all blacks from entering the state. It was finally passed (1856) by Congress after bitter debate.

Kansas joined the Union as a free state only in 1861, however

top·flight (tópfláit) *adj.* (*pop.*) of the highest rank, ability etc.

top·gal·lant (təgǽlənt, tɒpgǽlənt) **1.** *adj.* (*naut.*, of a mast or sail) above the topmast and below the royal mast ‖ (of weather) allowing top gallant sails to be set **2.** *n.* a topgallant mast or sail

top-ham·per (tɒ́phæmpər) *n.* (*naut.*) all the weight carried on or above a ship's deck, including masts, rigging, bridge etc. ‖ needlessly encumbering matter, e.g. superfluous possessions

top hat a man's tall cylindrical hat that is black or gray in color and usually made of silk. It is worn on certain formal occasions or as part of certain civilian uniforms

top-heav·i·ness (tɒ́phevi:nis) *n.* the quality or state of being top-heavy

top-heav·y (tɒ́phevi:) *adj.* unstable because the center of mass is high above the base ‖ (of an organization) having an unstable structure due to too great a concentration of highly paid top personnel ‖ overcapitalized

to·phus (tóufəs) *pl.* **to·phi** (tóufai) *n.* tufa ‖ (*med.*) a hard crystalline deposit in the tissues of sufferers from gout, causing great pain [L.=sandy stone]

topi *TOPEE

to·pi·ar·y (tóupi:eri:) **1.** *adj.* relating to the art of clipping or training shrubs, trees, hedges etc., into ornamental shapes **2.** *n.* bushes clipped thus ‖ the art of clipping bushes thus [fr. L. *topiarius*, of or relating to ornamental gardening]

top·ic (tɒ́pik) *n.* a subject of discussion, argument or writing **tóp·i·cal** *adj.* dealing with or referring to what is happening currently ‖ arranged by topics ‖ (*med.*) local, affecting or applied to a particular part of the body, *topical application* [fr. L. *topica* fr. Gk]

top·knot (tɒ́pnɒt) *n.* an arrangement of hair gathered into a knot high on the head, esp. arranged with flowers or ribbons ‖ a little crest of feathers ‖ a little tuft of hair on the top of the head ‖ *Zeugopterus punctatus*, an edible European flatfish with a tapering filament on its head

top·less (tóplәs) *adj.* without covering the breasts *topless dancing*

top·mast (tɒ́pmæst, tɒ́pmɑst) *n.* the section of mast immediately above the lower mast and below the topgallant

top·most (tɒ́pmoust) *adj.* highest

top·notch (tɒpnɒ́tʃ) *adj.* (*pop.*) first-rate, of the highest skill or quality

top·o·cen·tric (tɒpəséntrik) *adj.* of perception from a specific point on earth

to·pog·ra·pher (təpɒ́grəfər) *n.* a specialist in topography

top·o·graph·ic (tɒpəgrǽfik) *adj.* topographical (of or relating to topography)

top·o·graph·i·cal (tɒpəgrǽfik'l) *adj.* of or relating to topography ‖ relating to the representation or mention of a locality in a poem, painting etc.

to·pog·ra·phy (təpɒ́grəfi:) *pl.* **to·pog·ra·phies** *n.* a description of all the surface features, natural and artificial, of a particular region ‖ all such surface features of a region ‖ the science of drawing maps and/or diagrams which represent these features ‖ topographic surveying [fr. L.L. *topographia* fr. Gk]

top·o·log·i·cal (tɒpəlɒ́dʒik'l) *adj.* of properties that do not change in structure or form

topological equivalent an object similar to another in that it could be a copy of the other made on a stretched elastic plate

to·pol·o·gy (təpɒ́lədʒi:) *n.* (*math.*) the study of the properties of a geometrical figure that are unaffected when it is subjected to any continuous transformation or deformation [fr. Gk *topos*, place + *logos*, word]

to·pon·y·my (təpɒ́nəmi:) *n.* the study, esp. etymological, of place-names [fr. Gk *topos*, a place+*onoma*, a name]

top·per (tɒ́pər) *n.* (*pop.*) a top hat

top·ple (tɒ́p'l) *pres. part.* **top·pling** *past* and *past part.* **top·pled** *v.i.* to cease to be stable on a base and fall ‖ to be, or seem to be, on the point of falling over because of top-heaviness ‖ *v.t.* to cause to topple ‖ to cause to fall from a position of power or privilege

tops (tɒps) **1.** *adj.* (*pop.*) first-rate in quality, performance etc. **2.** *n.* **the tops** a person or thing one heartily approves of

TOPS (*acronym*) for **1.** (*aerospace*) thermoelectric outer planet spacecraft, used in exploration of planets **2.** teletype optical projection system, a system for plotting radar data received by teletype on the projection of a target with a grease pencil *Cf* DOPS, POPS

top·sail (tɒ́ps'l, tɒ́pseil) *n.* (in a square-rigged ship) the square sail immediately above the mainsail or course (sometimes divided into the upper and lower topsails) ‖ (in a fore-and-aft-rigged ship) the sail above or on the gaff

topsail schooner a two-masted schooner with a square topsail or topsails on the foremast

top sawyer the man who works in the upper position when using a saw in a sawpit ‖ (*Br., pop.*) the dominating person in an activity or situation

top secret (of military or governmental documentary information) of the highest category of secrecy **tóp-sé·cret** *adj.*

top sergeant (*pop.*) a first sergeant

top·side (tɒ́psaid) **1.** *n.* (*naut.*, esp. in *pl.*) the side of a ship above the waterline ‖ (*Br.*) a cut of beef, the outer part of a round of beef, cut from the middle of a hind leg **2.** *adv.* (*naut.*) on deck **tóp·sides** *adv.*

top·soil (tɒ́psɔil) *n.* the upper few inches of the soil in which worms, beneficial bacteria and naturally accumulating humus are to be found (cf. SUBSOIL)

top·sy-tur·vi·ly (tɒ́psi:tə́:rvili:) *adv.* in a topsy-turvy manner

top·sy-tur·vi·ness (tɒ́psi:tə́:rvi:nis) *n.* the state or quality of being topsy-turvy

top·sy-tur·vy (tɒ́psi:tə́:rvi:) **1.** *adv.* upside down ‖ in or into a disorderly or muddled state **2.** *adj.* in this condition [prob. fr. TOP +earlier *terve*, to turn, turn over or overturn]

toque (touk) *n.* a woman's close-fitting hat usually with no brim ‖ (*hist.*) a man's hat of the 16th c., with a small narrow brim and pleated fullness on top, decorated with a plume ‖ *Macaca sinica*, a small brown or reddish-brown macaque [F.]

tor (tɔr) *n.* a steep rocky hill or an outcrop of rock, standing up steeply from its surroundings [O.E.]

To·rah, To·ra (tɔ́rə, tóurə) *n.* the Hebrew name for the Mosaic Law (Pentateuch) ‖ the scroll of the Pentateuch used liturgically in a synagogue [Heb.]

torc *TORQUE (necklace)

torch (tɔrtʃ) *n.* a portable light made of resinous wood or tow impregnated with e.g. tallow to make it inflammable ‖ (*Br.*) a flashlight ‖ (*Roman Catholicism*) a candle in a tall candlestick with no foot or base, carried esp. by some of the servers at Benediction ‖ a very hot flame device, e.g. an oxyacetylene lamp for welding ‖ (*rhet.*) a source of enlightenment, *the torch of learning* **to carry a** (or **the**) **torch for** (*pop.*) to be in love with (esp. someone who doesn't reciprocate) [O.F. *torche*]

torch·bear·er (tɔ́rtʃbeərər) *n.* a person who carries a flaming torch ‖ (*rhet.*) a person who hands on knowledge, enlightenment etc.

torch·light (tɔ́rtʃlait) **1.** *n.* the light of a torch or torches **2.** *adj.* of, pertaining to or done by torchlight

tor·chon lace (tɔ́rʃɒn) a coarse single-thread bobbin or machine-made lace [F. *torchon*, duster, dishcloth]

torch singer a person who sings torch songs

torch song a popular song of sentimental character, usually about unrequited love [fr. the phrase *to carry a torch for someone* (*TORCH)]

torch·wood (tɔ́rtʃwud) *n.* a member of *Amyris*, fam. *Rutaceae*, a genus of tropical American shrubs and trees the wood of which is resinous and burns very readily

Tor·de·si·llas, Treaty of (tɔrdeisí:ljɑs) an agreement (1494) between Spain and Portugal, dividing the non-Christian world into two zones of influence, the division passing 370 leagues west of the Cape Verde Islands. This gave the New World to Spain, except for part of Brazil, which fell within Portugal's share. Portugal was also to have Africa and India (*LONDON, TREATY OF (1604))

tore (tɔr) *n.* (*archit.* and *geom.*) a torus

tore *past* of TEAR

tor·e·a·dor (tɔ́ri:ədɔr) *n.* (not used by Spaniards) a bullfighter (*TORERO) [Span.]

to·re·ro (tɔrérɔ) *n.* a bullfighter [Span.]

tor·ic (tɔ́rik, tórik) *adj.* of or shaped like a torus

toric lens a lens of which one surface has different curvatures in its two main meridians, and is used for correcting astigmatic vision

to·ri·i (tɔ́ri:i:, tóuri:i:) *pl.* **to·ri·i** *n.* a gateway to a Shinto shrine, consisting of two uprights supporting an upward-curving lintel with a straight crosspiece below it [Jap.]

tor·ment (tɔ́rment) *n.* great and usually protracted pain of mind or body ‖ a source or cause of this [O.F. *tourment*]

tor·ment (tɔrmént) *v.t.* to cause torment to ‖ to vex, worry or annoy excessively [O.F. *tourmenter, tormenter*]

tor·men·til (tɔ́rməntəl) *n.* *Potentilla tormentilla*, fam. *Rosaceae*, a yellow-flowered, low-growing Eurasian plant, the astringent root of which is used esp. in dyeing and in tanning [F. *tormentille*]

tor·men·tor (tɔrméntər) *n.* someone who torments ‖ (*theater*) either of the flats or curtains projecting into the wings on each side of the stage ‖ (*movies*) a covered screen on a set for absorbing echoes [O.F. *tormenteour*]

torn *past part.* of TEAR

tor·na·do (tɔrnéidou) *pl.* **tor·na·does, tor·na·dos** *n.* a violent, whirling wind accompanied by a funnel-shaped cloud, small in diameter and appearing to grow down from dark cumulonimbus clouds. Tornadoes of this kind, which are terribly destructive, occur most frequently in the central Mississippi valley. Their average width is 300-400 yds. Their paths may extend up to 50 miles and their speeds vary between 10 and 50 m.p.h. The wind speed in the vortex has been estimated as between 100 and 500 m.p.h., but in the very center, because of centrifugal effects, there is an area of near calm ‖ a violent storm consisting of a squall accompanying a thunderstorm, sudden in origin and short in duration, occurring in W. Africa. With this kind of tornado, which is caused by the meeting of warm, damp, monsoon air with dry air from the Sahara, there is usually torrential rain. The front of such a tornado can extend up to 200 miles [perh. fr. Span. *tronada*, thunderstorm]

Tornado *n.* U.S.S.R. mechanized infantry combat vehicle armed with 25-millimeter automatic gun and 7.2-millimeter machine guns

to·roid (tɔ́rɔid, tóurɔid) **1.** *n.* the surface generated by the rotation of a plane closed curve about an axis lying in its plane which does not intersect it **2.** *adj.* of or pertaining to a toroid **to·rói·dal** *adj.*

To·ron·to (tərɒ́ntou) the second largest city (pop. 599,217, with agglom. 2,137,395) in Canada and capital of Ontario, a port on Lake Ontario. Industries: mechanical and electrical engineering, automobiles, shipbuilding, textiles, food processing, publishing, banking. University (1827)

Toronto, University of a Canadian educational institution founded (1827) in Toronto. It blends the English college system with the U.S. faculty system

to·rose (tɔ́rous, tóurous) *adj.* (*zool.*) knobbed ‖ (*bot.*, of a stem etc.) swollen or bulging here and there [fr. L. *torosus*, brawny]

To·ros Mountains (tɔrɔ́s) *TAURUS MOUNTAINS

tor·pe·do (tɔrpí:dou) **1.** *pl.* **tor·pe·does** *n.* a long, self-propelled, cigar-shaped missile, charged with an explosive warhead and fired underwater or from an aircraft to blow up ships ‖ (*rail.*) a detonator, fastened to the top of a rail, which explodes when a locomotive goes over it, warning the crew of impending danger ‖ an explosive cartridge lowered into an oil well to clear it ‖ (*zool.*) the electric ray ‖ a small firework which when thrown against a hard surface explodes loudly ‖ a large sandwich on a long roll, usu. of cheese, cold cuts, and condiments **2.** *v.t.* to destroy or attack with a torpedo ‖ to clear (an oil well or its shaft) with a torpedo [L.— stiffness, numbness, the electric ray]

torpedo net a heavy steel net suspended in the water, e.g. across a harbor entrance, to protect warships from attack by torpedoes

torpedo tube a tube from which a warship fires torpedoes

tor·pid (tɔ́rpid) *adj.* having ceased to move or feel for a period, e.g. in hibernation ‖ lethargic **tor·pid·i·ty** *n.* [fr. L. *torpidus*]

tor·por (tɔ́rpər) *n.* suspended animation ‖ a state of mental inactivity ‖ mental or spiritual listlessness or apathy **tor·por·íf·ic** *adj.* [L.]

tor·quate (tɔ́rkweit) *adj.* (*zool.*) collared, having a ring of distinctive color around the neck [fr. L. *torquatus*, wearing a necklace]

torque (tɔrk) *n.* (*phys.*) the agency that produces or tends to produce torsion: a vector quantity defined as the product of the tangential force and the perpendicular distance from

CONCISE PRONUNCIATION KEY: **(a)** æ, *cat*; ɑ, *car*; ɔ *fawn*; ei, *snake*. **(e)** e, *hen*; i:, *sheep*; iə, *deer*; εə, *bear*. **(i)** i, *fish*; ai, *tiger*; ə:, *bird*. **(o)** o, *ox*; au, *cow*; ou, *goat*; u, *poor*; ɔi, *royal*. **(u)** ʌ, *duck*; u, *bull*; u:, *goose*; ə, *bacillus*; ju:, *cube*. x, *loch*; θ, *think*; ð, *bother*; z, *Zen*; ʒ, *corsage*; dʒ, *savage*; ŋ, *orangutang*; j, *yak*; ʃ, *fish*; tʃ, *fetch*; 'l, *rabble*; 'n, *redden*. Complete pronunciation key appears inside front cover.

the line of action of the force of the axis of rotation || (*Br.* also **torc**, *hist.*) a necklace of twisted metal, esp. gold, worn e.g. by the ancient Celts [fr. L. *torques*, a twisted necklace]
torque arm a rod running from the axle housing to the torque tube in an automobile etc. for taking up the torque reactions of driving and braking
torque converter a hydraulic device for providing the torque required at the driven shaft by transmitting and multiplying the torque from the driving shaft
Tor·que·ma·da (tɔrkimádə, tɔrkemáðɑ) Tomás de) (1420-98), Spanish inquisitor-general notorious for his cruelty (*INQUISITION). He was largely responsible for the expulsion of the Jews from Spain (1492)
torque·me·ter (tɔ́rkmi:tər) *n.* an instrument that measures torque
torque tube a hollow tube surrounding the propeller shaft of an automotive vehicle designed to take up the torque reactions of braking and driving
torr (tɔr) *n.* a unit of pressure equal to the pressure of 1 mm. of mercury at standard temperature and gravity [after TORRICELLI]
tor·re·fac·tion (tɔrifǽkʃən, tɒrifǽkʃən) *n.* a torrefying or being torrefied
tor·re·fy, tor·ri·fy (tɔ́rifai, tɒ́rifai) *pres. part.* **tor·re·fy·ing, tor·ri·fy·ing** *past* and *past part.* **tor·re·fied, tor·ri·fied** *v.t.* to dry up or parch with heat (esp. drugs and ores, so that they may be powdered) [F. *torréfier*]
Tor·rens (tɔ́renz, tɒ́renz) a salt lake (area approx. 2,500 sq. miles) in E. South Australia, 25 ft below sea level. In the dry season it becomes a salt marsh
tor·rent (tɔ́rənt, tɒ́rənt) *n.* a violently rushing stream || a great downpour of rain or great flow of a fluid || a flood of violent language, tears etc. **tor·ren·tial** (tərénʃəl) *adj.* [F. fr. L. fr. *torrere*, to burn, boil, rush]
Tor·re·ón (tɔreɔ́n) a commercial center (pop. 262,744) in N.E. Mexico: cotton textiles, metallurgy
Tor·res Strait (tɔ́ris) the shallow strait (average width: 90 miles) separating Queensland, Australia and New Guinea, containing many shoals and reefs
Tor·res Ve·dras (tɔ́risvéidrəs) (*hist.*) three lines of fortification built by Wellington to defend Lisbon against the French (1810-11)
Tor·ri·cel·li (tɔritʃéli:), Evangelista (1608-47), Italian mathematician and physicist. He discovered the principle of the mercury barometer (1643) and showed that Aristotle was in error in stating that a vacuum is an impossibility. He also improved the microscope and the telescope
Tor·ri·cel·li·an vacuum (tɔritʃéli:ən) the near-vacuum above the mercury in a barometer. This space contains mercury vapor of vapor pressure not greater than 0.004 mm.
tor·rid (tɔ́rid, tɒ́rid) *adj.* (of land areas) very hot and dry or exposed to great heat || of the zone between the Tropic of Cancer and the Tropic of Capricorn, where the sun is vertically overhead at some point of the year [fr. L. *toridus*]
torrify *TORREFY
Tor·ri·gia·no (tɔrri:dʒɑ́nɔ), Pietro (1472-1522), Florentine sculptor. He was invited to England, where his main work is Henry VII's tomb in Westminster Abbey
Tor·ri·jos (tɔrrí:hɔs), Omar (1929-81), Panamanian general, and president (1968-81) following a coup d'état which ousted President Arnulfo Arias. He survived (1969) a conspiracy by National Guard officers and José Pinilla to remove him and remained a powerful political figure until his death in a plane crash in 1981. He and U.S. President Jimmy Carter negotiated the Panama Canal treaties of 1978
tor·sade (tɔrsɑ́d) *n.* (*cosmetology*) small hairpiece of coils or curls used in creating a hairstyle
tor·sel (tɔ́rs'l) *n.* a piece of iron or wood or stone in a wall, on which the end of a floor joist rests [fr. O.F. *tassel*, a bit of stone or wood to stop a hole]
tor·si·bil·i·ty (tɔrsəbíliti:) *n.* the ability to resist torsion
tor·sion (tɔ́rʃən) *n.* the act of turning one end of an object about a longitudinal axis while the other is fixed or turned in the opposite direction || the state of being so twisted || the force tending to restore an elastic object so twisted || (*math.*) the rate of change of the curvature with arc length **tór·sion·al** *adj.* [F. fr. L.L.]
torsion balance (*phys.*) an instrument that can measure small forces by allowing them to twist a calibrated fiber measuring the deflection by means of a mirror fixed to the fiber and a lamp and scale
torsion bar a rod in an automobile etc. that restricts sideways movement of the rear axle relative to the frame
tor·so (tɔ́rsou) *pl.* **tor·sos** *n.* the trunk of the human body || a carved, modeled, painted or drawn representation of this, whether as a complete work of art, or as a fragment, or as part of a complete figure [Ital.=stump]
Tor·stens·son (tɔ́rstensən), Lennart, count of Ortala (1603-51), Swedish general. He led the Swedish invasion of Germany (1641-6) during the Thirty Years' War, distinguishing himself at Breitenfeld (1642)
tort (tɔrt) *n.* (*law*) a breach of duty, other than a breach of contract, for which the offender will be subject to legal responsibility [O.F.]
tor·ti·col·lis (tɔrtikɒ́lis) *n.* (*med.*) a persistent muscular spasm which causes the head and neck to be held at an unnatural angle [Mod. L. fr. *tortus*, twisted+*collum*, neck]
tor·til·la (tɔrtí:ə) *n.* a pancake, made of corn flour, cooked on a hot iron plate or stone, and eaten in Mexico as the equivalent of bread || an omelet originating in Spain and containing potatoes and onions [Span dim. of *torta*, a cake]
tor·tious (tɔ́rʃəs) *adj.* (*law*) of or involving a tort
tor·toise (tɔ́rtəs) *n.* any terrestrial species of turtle, esp. of genera *Testudo* and *Gopherus* [fr. L.L. *tortuca*]
tortoise beetle a member of *Chrysomelidae*, a family of tortoise-shaped beetles whose larvae feed on leaves
tor·toise·shell (tɔ́rtəsʃel) **1.** *n.* the material forming the shell of the turtle, esp. the semi-transparent material forming the carapace of the hawksbill turtle. It is of a rich mottled reddish or golden brown color and can be molded when heat is applied to it. It is used for inlaying and for making combs and small decorative boxes etc. **2.** *adj.* made of tortoiseshell || colored like tortoiseshell
tortoiseshell butterfly a member of *Nymphalis*, fam. *Nymphalidae*, a genus of widely distributed butterflies with wings patterned like tortoiseshell
Tor·to·la (tɔrtóulə) the largest island (area 24 sq. miles, pop. 6,800) of the Virgin Is and chief island of the British group, in the Leeward Is, West Indies. Capital: Road Town (pop. 2,000), a port of entry
Tor·tu·ga, La (lɑtɔrtú:gə) an island (area 85 sq. miles) in the Caribbean Sea off the north central coast of Venezuela. It became (early 17th c.) the chief pirate stronghold in the West Indies
tor·tu·os·i·ty (tɔrtʃu:ɒ́siti:) *pl.* **tor·tu·os·i·ties** *n.* the state or quality of being tortuous || an instance or example of this [fr. L. *tortuositas*]
tor·tu·ous (tɔ́rtʃu:əs) *adj.* having many twists and turns || not open, frank or straightforward || hard to follow because involved [A.F.]
tor·ture (tɔ́rtʃər) **1.** *n.* intense pain or suffering of body or mind || the infliction of such pain or suffering. Physical torture was once employed on a worldwide scale as part of the ordinary process of judicial procedure || a method of inflicting intense pain or suffering || a cause of such pain or suffering **2.** *v.t. pres. part.* **tor·tur·ing** *past* and *past part.* **tor·tured** to subject to torture || to misuse (words) so as to distort their meaning || to wrench out of shape [F. fr. L.]
tor·tur·ous (tɔ́rtʃərəs) *adj.* causing torture || accompanied by torture [A.F.=O. F. *torturens, tortureux* fr. L. *tortura*, torture]
To·run (tɔ́ru:nj) (*G.* Thorn) a port (pop. 170,000) in N. central Poland on the Vistula. Industries: chemicals, food processing. University (1945)
to·rus (tɔ́rəs, tóurəs) *pl.* **to·ri** (tɔ́rai, tóurai) *n.* (*archit.*) a semicircular molding, esp. at the base of a column || (*bot.*) a receptacle of a flower || (*bot.*) a swollen stalk bearing flowers || (*bot.*) a thickened membrane between plant cells || (*anat.*) any smooth, rounded, esp. bony projection on a part of the body || (*geom.*) a surface or solid generated by the revolution of a circle about an axis in its plane which does not intersect it [L.]
To·ry (tɔri:), Geoffroy (c. 1480-1533), French typographer, engraver and writer. He was influential in introducing Roman type into France as well as in standardizing spelling, punctuation and the use of accent marks. In 1530 he became the king's printer
To·ry (tɔ́ri:, tóuri) **1.** *pl.* **To·ries** *n.* (*Am. hist.*) a person who opposed the breach with Britain in the Revolutionary War (1775–83) || (*Br.*) a member or supporter of the Conservative party || (*Ir. hist.*) any of the dispossessed Irish outlaws (17th c.) who plundered and killed English settlers || (*Eng. hist.*) a member of the political group who opposed (1679) Whig attempts to exclude the future James II from the succession to the throne. After 1688, most Tories supported the Anglican Church and the hereditary right to the throne. Briefly in power (1710–14) under Harley and Bolingbroke, they were discredited for their Jacobite leanings, and were out of office until the accession (1760) of George III, when many of them joined the 'king's friends'. The French Revolution brought many Whigs to support the Tories in the defense of the landed classes, and made the party more reactionary. The Tory party was ousted (1830) by the Whigs, and was remodeled in the 1830s by Peel to form the Conservative party **2.** *adj.* of, being or holding the beliefs of a Tory **Tó·ry·ism** *n.* [Anglicized spelling of Ir. Gael. assumed *tōraidhe, tōraighe*, pursuer]
Tos·ca·ni·ni (tɔskəní:ni:), Arturo (1867-1957), Italian conductor, considered one of the greatest of his time. He began his conducting career when he stepped in at short notice and conducted Verdi's 'Aida' without a score (1886). By 1898 he had become chief conductor at La Scala, Milan. He served with the Metropolitan Opera, New York (1908-15) and was principal conductor of the New York Philharmonic (1928-36) before the NBC Symphony was created for him (1937). He led this group until his retirement (1954). Known for his fidelity to composers' scores, he was also noted for his ability to elicit virtuoso performances from his musicians
tosh (tɒʃ) *n.* stupid nonsense [origin unknown]
toss (tɔs, tɒs) **1.** *v.t.* to throw casually or without force, esp. over a short distance || (of horned animals) to throw up into the air with the horns || (of a horse etc.) to unseat (its rider) || (*Br.*) to flip (a pancake) || to cause to move up and down or to and fro jerkily or restlessly, *waves tossed the boat* || to allow to move in this way, *the flowers tossed their heads in the wind* || to flick (a coin) into the air and let it fall heads or tails, as a method of letting fate decide whether the course of action previously agreed on if the coin falls heads is to be put into operation or that agreed on if it falls tails || to agree with (someone) to let a matter be settled in this way, *I'll toss you for who goes first* || to jerk (the head) quickly upwards and backwards, esp. in people as a willful gesture of defiance and in horses as a sign of restiveness || to mix (food) gently so as to coat e.g. with a dressing, *to toss a salad, to toss carrots in butter* || to put (clothes) on carelessly and hurriedly || (with 'down') to swallow quickly, esp. in a single draft || to turn (hay) over with a pitchfork in order to dry it || *v.i.* to move violently, jerkily and restlessly or as if restlessly up and down or to and fro, *the clothes on the line tossed in the wind* || (of people unable to sleep properly) to roll around restlessly in bed || to flip a coin **to toss aside** to reject casually or summarily **to toss for it** to decide between alternatives by flipping a coin **to toss off** to swallow (a drink) in a single draft || to compose without apparent effort, *to toss off a sonnet* || to enumerate casually, *to toss off a few names* **to toss out of** to leave with a flounce **to toss up** to flip a coin in order to decide between two alternatives **2.** *n.* a tossing or being tossed or an instance of being tossed || a toss-up **to argue the toss** (*Br.*) to continue to object or argue etc. after a decision has been given in a dispute etc. **to take a toss** to be thrown by a horse [origin unknown]
toss-up (tɔ́sʌp, tɒ́sʌp) *n.* an even chance or a matter in which an even chance is involved, *it's a toss-up whether or not he'll come* || the tossing of a coin
Tos·tig (tɒ́stig) (*d.* 1066), earl of Northumbria, son of Earl Godwin. With Harald III of Norway, he invaded England (1066) and was defeated and killed at Stamford Bridge by the army of his brother Harold II
tot (tɒt) *n.* a toddler || (esp. *Br.*) a small measure of drink, esp. of spirits, *a tot of rum* [etym. doubtful]
tot *pres. part.* **tot·ting** *past* and *past part.* **tot·ted** *v.t.* (with 'up') to add up || *v.i.* (with 'up') to total

CONCISE PRONUNCIATION KEY: (a) æ, cat; ɑ, car; ɔ fawn; ei, snake. (e) e, hen; i:, sheep; iə, deer; ɛə, bear. (i) i, fish; ai, tiger; ə:, bird. (o) o, ox; au, cow; ou, goat; u, poor; ɔi, royal. (u) ʌ, duck; u, bull; u:, goose; ə, bacillus; ju:, cube. x, loch; θ, think; ð, bother; z, Zen; ʒ, corsage; dʒ, savage; ŋ, orangutang; j, yak; ʃ, fish; tʃ, fetch; 'l, rabble; 'n, redden. Complete pronunciation key appears inside front cover.

up, *the mileage soon tots up if you drive in town* [shortened fr. TOTAL]

to·tal (tóut'l) **1.** *adj.* entire, constituting the whole, *the total sum* || utter, complete, *a total failure* **2.** *n.* the sum of a number of items || a total wreck **3.** *v. pres. part.* **to·tal·ing** esp. *Br.* **to·tal·ling** *past* and *past part.* **to·taled**, esp. *Br.* **to·talled** *v.t.* to calculate the total of || to amount to as a total, *the damages totaled $50* || (*slang or colloq.*) to wreck a motor vehicle beyond repair || *v.i.* (with 'up') to begin to be considerable in amount, number etc., *incidental expenses soon total up* || (with 'up to') to add up to, amount to, *the bill totals up to $100* [F.]

total eclipse an eclipse in which a celestial body is wholly obscured

to·tal·i·tar·i·an (toutælitέəri:ən) *adj.* of a form of government or state in which the lives and actions of every individual, and every enterprise, are controlled by a dictator or dictatorial caucus **to·tal·i·tár·i·an·ism** *n.*

to·tal·i·ty (toutǽliti:) *pl.* **to·tal·i·ties** *n.* the condition of being total || a whole || (*astron.*) the phase during which an eclipse is total [fr. M.L. *totalitas*]

to·tal·i·za·tor (tóut'lizeitər) *n.* a parimutuel machine

to·tal·ize (tóut'laiz) *pres. part.* **to·tal·iz·ing** *past* and *past part.* **to·tal·ized** *v.t.* to combine into a total **tó·tal·iz·er** *n.* a totalizator

to·tal·i·zer, totalisator, tote (tóut'laizə:r) *n.* device that lists sums bet on each horse race and the odds on each competitor

to·tal·ly (tóut'li:) *adv.* completely

total war war in which the whole population of a country is involved, and to which all its resources are devoted, waged against the whole population and resources of the enemy, civilian as well as military

tote (tout) **1.** *pres. part.* **tot·ing** *past* and *past part.* **tot·ed** *v.t.* (*pop.*) to carry, esp. in the arms or on the back, *to tote a gun* **2.** *n.* (*pop.*) a carrying || (*pop.*) something carried [etym. doubtful]

tote *n.* a pari-mutuel machine

to·tem (tóutəm) *n.* something, esp. an animal, which members of a totem group have as their sign. In many cases the members believe it shares some sort of kinship with them, e.g. descent from a common ancestor. Animals make the most common totems, but parts of animals, plants, objects, abstract qualities and colors can also serve || a fabricated, esp. a carved, image of this [fr. Ojibwa or some kindred Algonquian language]

totem group a group of people united by their relationship to a common totem

to·tem·ic (toutémik) *adj.* of, like or relating to a totem || having the nature of a totem || characterized by totemism

to·tem·ism (tóutəmizəm) *n.* religious beliefs and practices based on totems || social organization by totem groups

to·tem·ist (tóutəmist) *n.* a person who practices totemism || a specialist in the study of totemism **to·tem·ís·tic** *adj.*

totem pole (only of Indians of N.W. America) a column of cedarwood carved with totemic symbols

To·ti·la (tɒtílə) (*d.* 552), last king of the Ostrogoths (541-52). After conquering central and S. Italy, Sicily, Corsica and Sardinia he was defeated and killed by Narses

to·ti·pal·mate (toutəpǽlmit) *adj.* (of certain swimming birds) having the four toes completely joined by a web **to·ti·pal·ma·tion** (toutəpælméiʃən) *n.*

Totleben *TODLEBEN

tot lot a small recreation area for children

tot·ter (tɒ́tər) **1.** *v.i.* to walk, or stand shakily, as if about to overbalance || to be so weak as to be about to lose authority, power etc. **2.** *n.* an unsteady gait **tót·ter·y** *adj.* [perh. fr. Norse]

tou·can (tú:kən) *n.* any of various members of *Ramphastidae,* a family of tropical American birds having a lightly constructed, brilliantly colored bill about 8 ins long, roughly as long as the body itself. They feed on fruit, seeds, insects etc. The plumage is yellow, black and red [F. fr. Port. fr. Tupi]

touch (tʌtʃ) **1.** *v.t.* to perceive, experience or explore the nature of (something) by e.g. putting a finger into or onto it, i.e. by letting the nerve ends in and under the skin register its presence and nature, *do not touch the poison cactus* || to be or become so close to (something) that there is no intervening space, *the wheels of the car touched the curb* || to seem to do this, *the sun touched the horizon* || to exert very slight force on, *touch the ball with your cue* || to go as high or as low or as far as, *the temperature touched* 40° || to operate (an electric switch etc.) || (in negative constructions) to compare in quality with, *she can't touch him as a pianist* || (in negative or interrogative constructions) to interfere with or disarrange, *don't touch the papers on my desk* || (in negative or interrogative constructions) to injure slightly, *he was hardly touched by the fall* || to get possession of, *you can't touch trust money* || to do physical harm to, esp. by violence, *don't you dare touch that child* || to relate to, *anything touching that subject interests me* || to begin to deal with, *we didn't touch the last item on the agenda* || (in negative or interrogative constructions) to eat a bite of or consume a drop of, *he did not touch his lunch* || to arouse a tender or sympathetic response in, *the story touched us all* || (in negative or interrogative constructions) to cause pain or anger in, *her husband's rages no longer touch her* || (*pop.*) to obtain a loan, subscription or gift of money from, *he touched us for 50 dollars* || (in negative or interrogative constructions) to be efficacious in removing, curing or dealing with, *water won't touch that stain* || (*hist.*) to test (gold etc.) by a touchstone || to mark (metal) with an official stamp after it has been tested || to press (the keys) of or pluck or bow (the strings) of a musical instrument in order to make it sound || to cause (a musical instrument) to sound by pressing its keys or plucking or bowing its strings || to cause (a chord) to sound || (in negative or interrogative constructions) to leave a mark or impression on, *his years in prison appear not to have touched him* || (*geom.*) to be tangential to || to misappropriate or use without right, *he would never have touched your bicycle* || (of a ship) to touch at || (*hist.*, of English or French sovereigns) to lay the hand on (a scrofulous person) in order to cure him || (in negative constructions) to concern oneself with, handle, *don't touch the project* || to put the fingers briefly to (the hat or forelock) as a polite salutation || (in negative or interrogative constructions) to make use of, *she never touches the typewriter now* || to apply (something) lightly and briefly to something else, *touch a match to the fire* || to apply something lightly and briefly to, *he just touched the horse with the whip* || *v.i.* (of two or more things) to be or become so close to one another that there is no intervening space || (*math.*) to be tangential **to touch at** (of a ship) to call at (a port) **to touch down** (of an aircraft) to land || (*rugby*) to score a try by touching the ground with the ball behind the opponents' goal line **to touch in** to draw or paint in (a detail) very lightly **to touch off** to start off, get going, *to touch off a revolution* || to ignite or cause to explode || to describe briefly with pleasing subtlety **to touch on** (or **upon**) to relate to, pertain to || to make brief reference to || to verge on **to touch up** to work on (e.g. a painting) by adding some corrective strokes to treat (a photograph) so that it will reproduce well || to rouse with or as if with a flick of the whip **2.** *n.* a touching or being touched || the manner of playing the keys or strings of a musical instrument or of tapping the keys of a keyboard machine, usually in relation to lightness or heaviness || the manner in which the keys of an instrument or machine respond to being touched || a distinctive manner, trait, quality etc., *the touch of a master* || the well-contrived introduction of a detail for special effect, *his referring to the social aspect of the problem was a clever touch* || a gentle stroke, tap etc. || a small quantity, *a touch of red* || a slight degree, *he fired a touch too high* || (of a disease or illness) a mild attack, *a touch of lumbago* || a light mark made with a brush, pen or pencil || (*physiol.*) the sense by which nerve ends in and under the skin give the perception that something is in contact with the skin || the sensation conveyed by this sense, *she revels in the touch of fur* || (*change ringing*) a set of changes amounting to less than a full peal || (*pop.*) the act of borrowing money or getting a subscription or money gift out of someone || (*pop.*) the person the money is obtained from, *an easy touch* || (*pop.*) the money obtained || (*hist.*) the act of testing the quality of gold and silver by rubbing it on a touchstone || the official stamp or mark put upon gold or silver to show that it has been tested || the stamp or punch used || (*fencing*) a hit that scores a point || (*rugby* and *soccer*) the area outside the touchlines, *to kick the ball into touch* **in (out of) touch** in (not in) communication by correspondence, radio etc. or informed (not informed) about events etc. **to lose touch** to fail to maintain communication or keep oneself informed [O.F. *tochier, tuchier*]

Touch-A-Mat·ic (tʌtʃəmǽtik) *n.* Bell System telephone automatic dialer that remembers and dials up to 31 numbers at the touch of a button

touch and go a highly precarious situation which could prove disastrous, *it was touch and go whether he would survive*

touch·back (tʌ́tʃbæk) *n.* (*football*) a grounding of the ball behind one's own goal line, when the ball has been passed over the goal line by an opponent (cf. SAFETY)

touch·down (tʌ́tʃdaun) *n.* (*football*) a play in which a player grounds the ball on or past the opponent's goal line, or the score so made (6 points) || (*rugby*) the scoring of a try (3 points) || the moment when the landing gear of an aircraft touches the ground as it comes in to land

tou·ché (tu:ʃéi) **1.** *interj.* (*fencing*) used to to acknowledge a touch || used to acknowledge that one has been scored off by a clever remark etc. **2.** *n.* (*fencing*) a touch [F.]

touched (tʌtʃt) *adj.* moved by feelings of pity or gratitude || showing slight traces of esp. some color, *the sky in the west was touched with pink* || (*pop.*) slightly crazy

touch football a form of football in which tackling is replaced by touching

touch·i·ly (tʌ́tʃili:) *adv.* in a touchy manner

touch·i·ness (tʌ́tʃi:nis) *n.* the quality or state of being touchy

touch·ing (tʌ́tʃiŋ) **1.** *adj.* arousing tender or grateful feeling **2.** *prep.* (*rhet.*) concerning

touch·line (tʌ́tʃlain) *n.* either of two lines marking the side limits of the playing field in various games (hockey, rugby and soccer etc.)

touch paper paper impregnated with potassium nitrate, used as a slow-burning fuse in fireworks etc.

touch·stone (tʌ́tʃstoun) *n.* a black flintlike stone, e.g. jasper or schist, formerly used in assaying gold or silver || a criterion or test of quality, ability etc.

Touch-Tone telephone (tʌ́tʃtoun) touch-button telephone that produce tones to control automatic dialing; trademark of the Bell System

touch-type (tʌ́tʃtaip) *pres. part.* **touch-typ·ing** *past* and *past part.* **touch-typed** *v.i.* to type on a typewriter without needing to look at the keys

touch·wood (tʌ́tʃwud) *n.* punk

touch·y (tʌ́tʃi:) *comp.* **touch·i·er** *superl.* **touch·i·est** *adj.* apt to be easily offended || apt to cause offense, *a touchy subject*

Tou·cou·leur (tu:ku:lǝ́:r) *n.* a Moslem people of W. Africa, esp. the Senegal River valley

Toug·gourt (tu:gú:rt) an oasis trading center (pop. 84,000) in E. Algeria in the N. Sahara

tough (tʌf) **1.** *adj.* hard to break but not necessarily hard to bend || (of food) difficult to cut, bite into or chew (opp. TENDER) || strong, difficult to tear or wear through, *a tough fabric* || able to resist disease, endure hardship etc., *a tough constitution* || difficult to get the better of, *a tough bargainer* || challenging because difficult to do or perform, *a tough job* || requiring endurance, *a tough fight* || hard to bear, harsh, *tough sanctions* || (of people) apt to be aggressive and lawless || (of districts) frequented by such people and therefore hard to supervise and potentially dangerous || hard to impress or win around, *a tough audience* || hard to learn, understand, solve etc., *a tough problem* **to get tough with** to change one's attitude and begin to be aggressive towards **2.** *n.* someone, esp. a man or boy, apt to be aggressive and lawless **3.** *adv.* **to act tough** (*pop.*) to behave in a menacing, aggressive manner, esp. as a bluff **tóugh·en** *v.t.* to make tough or tougher || *v.i.* to become tough or tougher [O.E. *tōh*]

Tou·lon (tu:lɔ̃) a port (pop. 180,508) and naval base in Var, France, 42 miles east of Marseilles. Industries: shipbuilding, engineering, chemicals

Tou·louse (tu:lu:z) the chief town (pop. 371,143) of Haute-Garonne, France, and historical capital of Languedoc, on the Garonne. Industries: metalworking, textiles, paper, chemicals and fertilizers, aircraft. Gothic cathedral (12th-13th cc.), Romanesque (11th c.) and Gothic churches, mansions in pink brick (16th c.), neoclassical town hall (18th c.). University (1230)

Tou·louse-Lau·trec (tu:lu:zloutrek), Henri de (1864-1901), French painter and lithographer.

CONCISE PRONUNCIATION KEY: **(a)** æ, *cat*; ɑ, *car*; ɔ *fawn*; ei, *snake*. **(e)** e, *hen*; i:, *sheep*; iə, *deer*; εə, *bear*. **(i)** i, *fish*; ai, *tiger*; ə:, *bird*. **(o)** ɒ, *ox*; au, *cow*; ou, *goat*; u, *poor*; ɔi, *royal*. **(u)** ʌ, *duck*; u, *bull*; u:, *goose*; ə, *bacillus*; ju:, *cube*. x, *loch*; θ, *think*; ð, *bother*; z, *Zen*; ʒ, *corsage*; dʒ, *savage*; ŋ, *orangutang*; j, *yak*; ʃ, *fish*; tʃ, *fetch*; 'l, *rabble*; 'n, *redden*. Complete pronunciation key appears inside front cover.

Much of his work, which included many brilliant poster designs, was a sardonic comment on the life of the Parisian demimonde

tou·pee (tu:péi) *n.* (*hist.*) a topknot of hair usually forming the crowning feature of an 18th–c. wig ‖ (*hist.*) an 18th–c. wig with such a topknot ‖ a small wig or a patch of false hair used to hide baldness [prob. fr. F. *toupet*, a tuft of hair]

tour (tuər) **1.** *n.* a journey made for sightseeing, business or education, ending at the place from which one started out ‖ a walk around a garden, house etc. for purposes of inspection ‖ a series of performances by a theatrical or similar company in a succession of theaters ‖ a tour of duty **2.** *v.i.* to make a tour, be on tour ‖ *v.t.* to make a tour through or of ‖ to present (a play etc.) in a circuit of theaters [F.]

tou·ra·co (túərəkou) *n.* a member of *Turacus*, fam. *Musophagidae*, a genus of African birds (1–2 ft long) having brilliant red wing feathers which yield turacin [F. fr. a W. African name]

Tou·raine (tu:ren) a former province of France in the S. Paris basin, comprising most of Indre-et-Loire and small parts of Loir-et-Cher and Indre. It consists largely of wooded plateaus and fertile valleys, with famous châteaus, esp. along the Loire. Industries: agriculture (wine, fruit, market produce), tourism. Historic capital: Tours. Formed in Merovingian times as the countship of Tours, it passed to Anjou (11th c.) and England before the French crown annexed it (1259). It was a duchy-apanage until 1584

Tou·rane (tu:réin) *DA NANG

Tour·coing (tur:kwɛ̃) a textile-manufacturing town (pop. 102,543) in Nord, France, near the Belgian frontier

tour de force (túərdəfɔ́rs, túərdəfóurs) *pl.* **tours de force** (túərdəfɔ́rs, túərdəfóurs) *n.* a feat of strength or skill [F.]

tour·ism (túərizəm) *n.* the practice of touring for pleasure ‖ the industry of attracting tourists and catering to them

tour·ist (túərist) *n.* a person visiting or staying at a place on holiday ‖ tourist class

tourist class a type of accommodation on ocean liners etc. cheaper and less comfortable than first or second class but more comfortable than steerage

tourist trap (pejorative) a site designed to attract tourists, esp. for the purpose of exploiting them

tour·ma·line, tur·ma·line (túərməlin) *n.* any of several complex silicates, containing boron, the crystals of which polarize light and exhibit pyroelectric and piezoelectric properties. Some varieties are cut as gems [F. fr. Sinhalese]

Tour·nai (tu:rnei) a town (pop. 67,291) in Hainault, Belgium, on the Scheldt. Romanesque-Gothic cathedral (12th-13th cc.)

tour·na·ment (túərnəmənt, tə́:rnəmənt) *n.* (*hist.*) a contest in which mounted knights in armor fought with blunted weapons ‖ (*hist.*) a meeting for knights to practice their sports and exercises ‖ a meeting at which a number of individual competitors or teams of competitors compete for championship in some particular game by a series of elimination contests, *a chess tournament* [O.F. *torneiement, tornoiement*]

Tour·neur (tə́:rnər), Cyril (c. 1575-1626), English playwright. His reputation rests on two tragedies, 'The Revenger's Tragedy' (1607) and 'The Atheist's Tragedy' (1611)

tour·ney (túərni:, tə́:rni:) **1.** *pl.* **tour·neys** *n.* a tournament **2.** *v.i.* to contend in a tournament [M. E. fr. O.F. *tornei, torneier*]

tour·ni·quet (tə́:rnikit, túərnikit) *n.* a bandage or cloth for temporarily stopping bleeding or for arresting the circulation of the blood by compression. It is twisted tightly around a limb, finger or toe above the wound, sting etc. by threading a stick or other similar thing through the cloth and winding it around [F. fr. *tourner*, to turn]

tour of duty a period spent doing military or administrative duty, esp. in a foreign country

Tours (tu:r) the chief town (pop. 132,209) of Indre-et-Loire, France, historic capital of Touraine, on the Loire. Gothic cathedral (13th-16th cc.), medieval and Renaissance quarters

tou·sle (táuz'l) **1.** *v.t. pres. part.* **tou·sling** *past* and *past part.* **tou·sled** to make (hair, bedclothes, garments etc.) wildly untidy and out of place, esp. by rough handling **2.** *n.* the state of being tousled ‖ a tousled mass (of hair etc.) [frequentative of M.E. *tusen*, to handle roughly]

Tous·saint Lou·ver·ture (tu:sɛ̃lu:vertyr) (1743-1803), Haitian general and statesman. An African slave, he joined the slave revolt against the French (1791) and made himself the ruler of Haiti (1801), but was taken prisoner and died in France

tout (taut) **1.** *v.i.* (*pop.*, often with 'for') to solicit custom with often annoying persistence, or appeal to individuals for votes, donations etc. ‖ (esp. *Br.*) to watch racehorses in training so as to get information for betting ‖ *v.t.* to hawk (something) with annoying persistence ‖ to get information on (racehorses) for betting purposes **2.** *n.* a person who touts [M.E. *tuten*]

tow (tou) **1.** *n.* coarse and broken fibers removed from flax, hemp or jute during scutching or hackling and used for twine etc. [perh. rel. to O.N. *tō*, uncleaned flax or wool]

TOW (*mil. acronym*) for tube-launched, optically tracked, wire-guided antitank-missile weapon system (BGM-71A), with a 23-mi range; manufactured by Hughes Aircraft Co.

tow 1. *v.t.* to pull along with a rope or hawser **2.** *n.* a towing or being towed ‖ a towline ‖ something towed **in tow** attached by a rope and pulled along ‖ in or under one's care, guidance etc. [O.E. *togian*]

to·wage (tóuidʒ) *n.* a towing or being towed ‖ the fee for being towed

to·ward (tɔrd, tourd, təwɔ́rd) *prep.* in the direction of, *walk toward the sea* ‖ with regard to, in relation to, *to feel angry toward someone* ‖ for the purpose of helping, augmenting or making possible etc., *the money will go toward a holiday* ‖ (of time) approaching, near, *toward midnight* ‖ facing, *the handle toward my hand* [O.E. *tōweard*]

to·wards (tɔrdz, tourdz, təwɔ́rdz) *prep.* toward [O.E. *tōweardes*]

tow·a·way zone (tóuəwei zoun) *n.* zone from which illegally parked vehicles may be towed away by the police

tow·boat (tóubǫut) *n.* a tugboat with squared bows

tow car (*Am.*=*Br.* breakdown lorry) a tow truck

tow·el (táuəl) **1.** *n.* a piece of absorbent material used to dry something **to throw in the towel** to admit defeat or failure **2.** *v. pres. part.* **tow·el·ing**, esp. *Br.* **tow·el·ling** *past* and *past part.* **tow·eled**, esp. *Br.* **tow·elled** *v.t.* to dry or rub down with a towel ‖ *v.i.* to use a towel **tów·el·ing**, esp. *Br.*, **tów·el·ling** *n.* the absorbent material of which towels are made [O.F. *toaille*]

towel horse a rack for drying or airing towels on

tow·er (táuər) **1.** *n.* a tall structure, high in proportion to its lateral dimensions, either standing independently or forming part of another edifice. Towers may be used e.g. as reservoirs, for hanging bells, or may contain rooms, usually one above the other. When used e.g. for transmission or observation, they are very often mere skeleton steel frameworks ‖ a tower and its surrounding edifices used as a fortress or prison ‖ a vertical structure, not necessarily particularly tall, through which gases or liquids are passed to be cooled or purified etc. **2.** *v.i.* to rise high in the air ‖ (of birds of prey) to soar high in the air in order to be able to swoop on prey ‖ (of wounded game birds) to rise vertically in the air before falling ‖ (with 'above' or 'over') to be extremely tall, esp. to rise to dominating height **tów·er·ing** *adj.* very high, esp. from the point of view of someone looking up from below ‖ (of emotions) very intense, *a towering rage* [O.E. *torr* fr. L. *turris*]

Tower Hill rising ground on the north bank of the Thames by the Tower of London, once a place of execution

Tower of Babel a tower intended to reach heaven but which stopped short when God caused the builders to speak a multitude of different languages (Genesis xi, 1-9)

Tower of London a group of buildings east of the City of London on the north bank of the Thames. The central keep was begun in 1078. For centuries the Tower was the main state prison. Today it is a historical museum containing the Crown jewels, a collection of armor, and other historical objects

tower of strength a person who provides in valuable encouragement and practical support

tow·head (tóuhęd) *n.* a person who has a head of very light blond hair ‖ such a head of hair **tow·head·ed** *adj.*

tow·hee (təhwí:, təwí:) *n.* the North American chewink [imit.]

tow·line (tóulạin) *n.* a rope etc. used for towing

town (taun) *n.* a place consisting of an agglomeration of houses, shops and other buildings, bigger than a village but usually smaller than a city. Most towns have paved roads, street lighting and public systems of drainage, water supply, power supply and transport and an organized local government. The inhabitants are mostly engaged in trade, industry or administration ‖ the people who live in this place, *the whole town was discussing the news* ‖ the way of life of such people, *to prefer the town to the country* ‖ a municipal corporation, simpler than a city, having powers of rural administration ‖ (*pop.*) a city ‖ (without article) a particular town clearly understood from the context, *to be out of town* ‖ (without article) the business or shopping center of a town, *to go into town* ‖ (*Br.*, without article and always with 'in' or 'up to') the capital, *to go up to town* (i.e. to go to London) ‖ a piece of ground having a great many prairie dog burrows ‖ a piece of ground having many penguin nests **on the town** seeking the pleasures of town, esp. its night life **to go to town** (*pop.*) to do something (made clear by the context) very intensely, often to the point of excess, *the organist went to town in the last movement* **to go to town on** (*pop.*) to work on (something) fast and efficiently, esp. in short bursts [O.E. *tūn*]

town clerk (*Am.*) an official who keeps a town's records and writes up its official proceedings ‖ (*Br.*) an official, usually a lawyer, appointed to administer a town's affairs and act as secretary to the town council

town council (*Br.*) the elected administrative body of a town **town councillor** a member of such a body

town crier (esp. *hist.*) a town official who makes public announcements by word of mouth

town hall the main public building of a town, used for transacting official business etc.

town house a single-family house that is attached to a similar house on one side *Cf* TERRACE HOUSE

town meeting a general meeting of the taxpaying inhabitants of a town

town·scape (táunskeip) *n.* overall view of an urban area involving plan, lighting, street surfaces, etc.; coined by Camillo Sette (1920–)

towns·folk (táunzfǫuk) *n.* townspeople

Town·shend (táunzend), Charles, 2nd viscount ('Turnip Townshend', 1674-1738), English statesman and agriculturist. After an active life in politics, he resigned (1730) over disagreements with his brother-in-law, Sir Robert Walpole. He made experiments in four-course crop rotation and the cultivation of turnips which are important in the history of agriculture

Townshend, Charles (1725-67), British statesman, grandson of the 2nd Viscount Townshend. As chancellor of the exchequer (1766-7) he promoted the Townshend Acts (1767), a series of measures taxing the American colonies, notably by imposing duties on glass, lead, paints, paper and tea. The duties aroused bitter opposition, and all except the one on tea were repealed (1770). They helped to precipitate the Revolutionary War

town·ship (táunʃip) *n.* (*U.S.A., Canada*) a division of a county with some administrative powers ‖ (*public land surveying*) a district containing 36 sq. miles [O.E. *tūnscipe*]

towns·man (táunzmən) *pl.* **towns·men** (táunzmən) *n.* (esp. *Br.*) a person who lives in a town, esp. a man born and bred in a town

towns·peo·ple (táunzpị:p'l) *n.* the inhabitants of a town

Towns·ville (táunzvil) a port (pop. 59,000) in Queensland, Australia

tow·path (tóupæθ, tóupǫθ) *pl.* **tow·paths** (tóupæðz, tóupǫðz, tóupæθs, tóupǫθs) *n.* a path, esp. along a canal, used by men or animals for towing boats

tow·rope (tóurǫup) *n.* a rope used for towing

tow truck (*Am.*=*Br.* breakdown lorry) a truck for towing disabled cars or cars immobilized by snow etc.

tox·ae·mi·a *TOXEMIA

toxaemia of pregnancy *TOXEMIA OF PREGNANCY

tox·e·mi·a, tox·ae·mi·a (tɒksí:mi:ə) *n.* the presence in the blood of poisonous substances usually of bacterial origin [Mod. L.]

toxemia of pregnancy a condition of unknown origin, peculiar to pregnant women, characterized by hypertension, visual disturbances, and the presence of albumin in the urine etc.

CONCISE PRONUNCIATION KEY: **(a)** æ, *cat*; ɑ, *car*; ɔ *fawn*; ei, *snake*. **(e)** e, *hen*; i:, *sheep*; iə, *deer*; ɛə, *bear*. **(i)** i, *fish*; ai, *tiger*; ə:, *bird*. **(o)** ɒ, *ox*; au, *cow*; ou, *goat*; u, *poor*; ɔi, *royal*. **(u)** ʌ, *duck*; u, *bull*; u:, *goose*; ə, *bacillus*; ju:, *cube*. x, *loch*; θ, *think*; ð, *bother*; z, *Zen*; ʒ, *corsage*; dʒ, *savage*; ŋ, *orangutang*; j, *yak*; ʃ, *fish*; tʃ, *fetch*; 'l, *rabble*; 'n, *redden*. Complete pronunciation key appears inside front cover.

tox·ic (tɒ́ksik) *adj.* of or pertaining to or caused by poison, *a toxic symptom* ‖ poisonous, *toxic gas* [fr. M.L. *toxicus,* poisoned]

tox·i·cant (tɒ́ksikənt) **1.** *adj.* poisonous **2.** *n.* a pest control which kills by poisoning (as distinct from one which repels) [fr. M.L. *toxicans (toxicantis)* fr. *toxicare,* to poison]

tox·ic·i·ty (tɒksísiti:) *n.* the state, quality or degree of being poisonous

tox·i·co·log·i·cal (tɒksikəlɒ́dʒik'l) *adj.* of or pertaining to toxicology

tox·i·col·o·gy (tɒksikɒ́lədʒi:) *n.* the study of poisons [F. *toxicologie*]

tox·i·co·sis (tɒksikóusis) *pl.* **tox·i·co·ses** (tɒksikóusi:z) *n.* a diseased condition caused by a poison [Mod. L.]

toxic shock syndrome (*med.*) vaginal infection (*bacterium staphylococcus aureus*) sometimes fatal, characterized by drop in blood pressure, kidney malfunction, vomiting, and diarrhea. It is associated with use of tampons *abbr.* TSS

tox·in (tɒ́ksin) *n.* any of several intensely poisonous substances produced by certain bacteria

tox·oid (tɒ́ksɔid) *n.* a toxin rendered nonpoisonous, capable of inducing the formation of powerful antibodies. Toxoids are used in immunization e.g. against diphtheria

tox·oph·i·lite (tɒksɒ́fəlait) **1.** *n.* a person skilled in archery **2.** *adj.* relating to archers or archery **tox·óph·i·ly** *n.* the sport of archery ‖ love of archery [fr. *Toxophilus,* a book by Ascham fr. Gk *toxon,* bow+ *-philos,* loving]

toy (tɔi) **1.** *n.* a child's plaything **2.** *adj.* made as a toy, *toy soldiers* ‖ of or like a toy ‖ (of some breeds of animal, esp. dogs) bred so as to be very small, *a toy bull terrier* **3.** *v.i.* (with 'with') to give something not very serious consideration, *to toy with an idea* ‖ (with 'with') to make halfhearted attempts at eating something because one has no appetite, *to toy with one's food* [origin unknown]

To·ya·ma (tɔjɑmɑ) a commercial center (pop. 305,000) in central W. Honshu, Japan: pharmaceuticals, aluminum, textiles

Toyn·bee (tɔ́inbi:), Arnold (1852-83), British economist and social reformer. His most important work is 'Lectures on the Industrial Revolution of the 18th Century in England' (1884)

Toynbee, Arnold Joseph (1889-1975), British historian, nephew of Arnold Toynbee. His 'A Study of History' (1934-54) is an attempt to analyze history in terms of the growth and decline of civilizations. His thesis is that a civilization's survival depends on its ability to respond successfully to challenges, both spiritual and material

To·yo·ha·shi (tɔjɔhɑʃi:) an industrial town (pop. 215,000) in central E. Honshu, Japan: textiles, metallurgy, food processing

TQC (*acronym*) for total quality control, system for building "perfection" into all aspects of manufacturing and business administration, with zero allowable defects, developed in Japan 1970's

tra·be·at·ed (tréibi:eitid) *adj.* (*archit.*) constructed with horizontal beams, not arched **tra·be·a·tion** *n.* (*archit.*) an entablature [fr. L. *trabs (trabis),* a beam]

tra·bec·u·la (trəbékjulə) *pl.* **tra·bec·u·lae** (trəbékjuli:), **tra·bec·u·las** *n.* (*anat.*) a row of cells bridging a cavity, e.g. a cartilage ‖ (*bot.*) a row of sterile cells extending across the sporangium of a pteridophyte **tra·béc·u·lar** *adj.* [L. dim. of *trabs,* a beam]

Trab·zon (trɑbzɔ́n) *TREBIZOND

trace (treis) *n.* (esp. *pl.*) a sign (e.g. a footprint, or slime) left by something moving over a surface ‖ an indication left behind, *there was no trace of his having been there* ‖ a survival from the past, vestige, *that great empire left few traces* ‖ a very small amount, the merest indication, *no trace of embarrassment* ‖ (*phys.*) the bright spot on the screen of a cathode ray tube, or the path it follows ‖ (*psychol.*) a neural or mental change resulting from the learning process ‖ the marking made by certain instruments, e.g. a seismograph ‖ something traced or drawn [F.]

trace *pres. part.* **trac·ing** *past* and *past part.* **traced** *v.t.* to follow (a path, track etc.) ‖ to follow the traces of ‖ to follow back the course or line of, *to trace a river to its source* ‖ to follow back the history or development of, *to trace one's ancestry* ‖ to discern (esp. by touch) by following the outlines of ‖ to discover by inquiry, investigation etc. (esp. something lost etc.), *to trace a missing person* ‖ to mark out (a sketch, plan etc.) ‖ to copy (esp. an outline drawing) by marking the lines on a transparent paper etc. laid over the original ‖ (of a machine) to record (e.g. heartbeats) in linear form ‖ to write, form (characters or outlines) laboriously ‖ *v.i.* (of e.g. a family) to have a traceable history, go back in time [O.F. *tracier*]

trace *n.* one of the two side straps, chains etc. by which a horse etc. pulls a vehicle. It is attached at one end to the animal's collar and at the other to the whiffletree **to kick over the traces** to cease to accept authority, restraints etc. and act as one pleases [M.E. *traice, trais* fr. O.F.]

trace element a chemical element involved in the physiological processes of plants and animals, essential to them although present only in very small quantities (e.g. copper, iodine etc.)

trace element micronutrients chemicals required in minute quantities for healthy animal or plant life

trac·er (tréisər) *n.* a bullet or shell which reveals its trajectory by illuminating it, usually with a phosphorescent light ‖ a device for tracing designs ‖ a substance (e.g. an element, atom or compound) that is introduced into a biological, chemical or physical process and can be followed along its path by its radioactivity, unusual isotopic mass, color etc. ‖ a person who traces missing articles, esp. in transportation services ‖ the official form sent out to expedite the tracing of a missing article

Tracer *n.* (*mil.*) a twin-reciprocating engine, airborne radar platform (E–1) designed to operate from aircraft carriers for the detection and interception control of airborne targets

tracers *n.* (*med.*) conditions or diseases chosen for inclusion in programs that seek to assess the quality of medical care as representative of the quality of care given generally

trac·er·y (tréisəri:) *pl.* **trac·er·ies** *n.* graceful and decorative interlacing of lines, esp. open stonework in the head of Gothic windows or vaulting, or natural phenomena (e.g. frost flowers on windowpanes) recalling these

tra·che·a (tréiki:ə) *pl.* **tra·che·ae** (tréiki:i:), **tra·che·as** *n.* (in vertebrates) a tube through which air passes to and from the lungs, extending from the larynx to the lungs. In man it is about 4 ins long and about 1 in. in diameter ‖ (in insects and other arthropods) an air tube of the respiratory system ‖ (*bot.*) a xylem element or series of elements resembling an animal trachea (*VESSEL) **trá·che·al** *adj.* [M.L.]

tra·che·id (tréiki:id) *pl.* **tra·che·ids, tra·che·i·des** (trəkí:idi:z) *n.* an elongate, tapering firm-walled cell characteristic of the xylem. When mature it lacks protoplasm. Variously modified, it serves in water conduction, storage and support (*VESSEL) [fr. M.L. *trachea,* trachea]

tra·che·o·phyte (tréiki:əfait) *n.* a member of *Tracheophyta,* a phylum of *Embryophyta,* including green plants with a vascular support and water-transport system. The phylum includes lycopsids, pteropsids, psilopsids and sphenopsids [fr. Mod. L. *Tracheophyta* fr. M.L. *trachea,* trachea+Gk *phuton,* plant]

tra·che·ot·o·my (treiki:ɒ́təmi:) *pl.* **tra·che·ot·o·mies** *n.* a surgical incision of the trachea [fr. TRACHEA+Gk *-tomē,* a cutting]

tra·cho·ma (trəkóumə) *n.* a chronic contagious disease of the eye, with roughening of the inner surface of the lids, often causing blindness if not treated. It is common in many tropical countries **tra·chom·a·tous** (trəkɒ́mətəs) *adj.* [Mod. L. fr. Gk *trachōma,* roughness]

trac·ing (tréisiŋ) *n.* the act of someone who traces ‖ the copy of a design, map, drawing etc. traced on transparent paper or cloth ‖ a record made by a cardiograph, seismograph etc.

track (træk) **1.** *n.* a path worn by the passage of men or animals ‖ a narrow, unpaved road ‖ something, e.g. the ruts left by wheels, the scent of an animal or the wake of a ship, which shows that a person or thing has passed ‖ (*Br., education*) system of grouping students according to intelligence, ability, or aptitude ‖ (*pl.*) footprints ‖ the course followed by something, *the track of a meteor* ‖ any of various prepared courses (e.g. of grass or cinder) on which athletic contests or races are held ‖ the width between a pair of wheels on a vehicle ‖ one of the jointed metal caterpillar treads of e.g. a tank ‖ the road with rails and ties on which a train or similar thing runs **in one's tracks** just where one is, *to stop in one's tracks* **on the right (wrong) track** pursuing the line of investigation likely (unlikely) to lead to the solution **on the track of** actively and successfully occupied in finding or pursuing (a person, solution or thing) **to cover (or cover up) one's tracks** deliberately to conceal what one has been doing or leave no evidence of where one has been **to follow in someone's tracks** to mirror in one's own career the earlier career of someone else **to keep (lose) track of** to keep (fail to keep) an up-to-date record of (e.g. expenses) ‖ to have (no longer to have) up-to-date information, news etc. about (e.g. friends or current events) **to make tracks** to take one's leave **to make tracks for** to go, esp. make a departure, hurriedly and purposefully toward **2.** *v.t.* to hunt or pursue by following the tracks of ‖ to follow the course of (someone or something) by the traces left behind ‖ to keep up with (something) on its course, *to track an airplane with a searchlight* ‖ (with 'down') to follow the traces of and find ‖ (Am.=*Br.* tread) to bring (e.g. mud) on the feet into a room etc. and leave marks where one walks ‖ to equip with caterpillar treads ‖ *v.i.* to have a specified width between a pair of wheels or runners, *this car tracks 4 ft* ‖ (of wheels) to be in alignment ‖ to leave tracks all over a surface ‖ (*movies,* of the camera) to move toward or away from a static subject or along beside a moving subject while photographing it **track·age** (trǽkidʒ) *n.* rails of railroad track ‖ (of a railroad company) the right to use the tracks of another company ‖ the charge for this right [O.F. *trac, traq*]

tracker action the mechanical action joining the pipes and keyboards in older types of organ

track event an athletic contest, carried out on a track prepared for racing (cf. FIELD EVENT)

track·lay·er (trǽkleiər) *n.* (*Am.*=*Br.* platelayer) someone who places or maintains railroad tracks

track·man (trǽkmən) *pl.* **track·men** (trǽkmən) *n.* (*Am.*=*Br.* linesman) someone who checks railroad tracks for safety

track record (*colloq.*) any record of successes or failures

track suit warm-up suit used by athletes

track telling (*mil.*) communication between command and operations during and after surveillance *Cf* BACK TELL

tract (trækt) *n.* a short pamphlet or treatise, usually on a religious or political subject, intended for distribution or propaganda purposes [M.E. *tracte* fr. L.]

tract *n.* a wide expanse of land etc. without precise boundaries ‖ (*anat.*) a structure through or along which something passes, *respiratory tract* ‖ (*anat.*) a bundle of nerve fibers having the same origin, termination and function ‖ (*eccles.*) verses of Scripture sung or recited at Mass before the reading of the Gospel, at special times, e.g. Lent, requiems etc. [fr. L. *trahere (tractus),* to draw]

trac·ta·bil·i·ty (træktəbíliti:) *n.* the, quality or state of being tractable

trac·ta·ble (trǽktəb'l) *adj.* (of persons or animals) easily handled or controlled, pliant ‖ (of materials) malleable, easily worked **trác·ta·bly** *adv.* [fr. L. *tractabilis*]

Trac·tar·i·an (træktéəri:ən) **1.** *adj.* pertaining to the Oxford movement **2.** *n.* a founder or supporter of the Oxford movement **Trac·tár·i·an·ism** *n.* the Oxford movement [after the 'Tracts for the Times' published 1833–41 by the Oxford movement]

trac·tate (trǽkteit) *n.* a treatise [fr. L. *tractatus,* a handling]

tract house a house similar in style to all others in a development area

trac·tile (trǽktəl, *Br.* trǽktail) *adj.* that can be physically drawn out in length [fr. L. *trahere (tractus),* to draw]

trac·tion (trǽkʃən) *n.* the act of hauling, or power used in hauling, a vehicle ‖ pulling force ‖ the force of adhesive friction exerted by a body on the surface on which it moves ‖ a pulling force exerted, esp. on a limb containing a fractured bone, by an apparatus consisting of weights and pulleys ‖ the state of tension created by this force, *three months in traction* **trác·tion·al** *adj.* [fr. M.L. *tractio (tractionis)*]

traction engine a steam or diesel engine used for hauling heavy vehicles on roads or over difficult terrain

trac·tive (trǽktiv) *adj.* used for pulling or hauling

CONCISE PRONUNCIATION KEY: **(a)** æ, cat; ɑ, car; ɔ fawn; ei, snake. **(e)** e, hen; i:, sheep; iə, deer; ɛə, bear. **(i)** i, fish; ai, tiger; ə:, bird. **(o)** o, ox; au, cow; ou, goat; u, poor; ɔi, royal. **(u)** ʌ, duck; u, bull; u:, goose; ə, bacillus; ju:, cube. x, loch; θ, think; ð, bother; z, Zen; ʒ, corsage; dʒ, savage; ŋ, orangutang; j, yak; ʃ, fish; tʃ, fetch; 'l, rabble; 'n, redden. Complete pronunciation key appears inside front cover.

trac·tor (trǽktər) *n.* a vehicle, either wheeled or fitted with tank tracks, used for hauling or propelling, esp. on farms, or as a source of power, e.g. for threshing machines ‖ a truck with a driver's cab and no body, used for hauling a large trailer or trailers etc. ‖ a traction engine ‖ an airplane with a propeller or propellers forward of the main supporting surfaces ‖ (*med.*) an instrument used to exert traction [Mod. L. fr. *trahere (tractus)*, to draw]

trac·tor·cade (trǽktərkeid) *n.* an organized demonstration by farmers driving their tractors to the site of protest (U.S., 1977–1978)

trade (treid) **1.** *n.* the business of distribution, selling and exchange ‖ any branch of such business, *the grocery trade* ‖ persons engaged in a field of commerce ‖ a deal, a purchase and sale ‖ an exchange ‖ a craft (cf. PROFESSION, cf. OCCUPATION) ‖ (*pl.*) trade winds **2.** *v. pres. part.* **trad·ing** *past* and *past part.* **trad·ed** *v.i.* to engage in trade, buy and sell as a business ‖ to have business dealings (with someone) ‖ to make an exchange (with someone) ‖ to be a customer (at a specified store) ‖ *v.t.* to exchange or barter, *they traded rum for gold dust* **to trade in** to hand over (a discarded article) as part payment for its replacement, *to trade in an old car for a new one* **to trade on** to take unfair advantage of [M.L.G. *trade*, a track]

Trade Agreements Act a U.S. Congressional act (1934) of President Franklin Roosevelt's New Deal. It created reciprocal trade treaties with several foreign countries, to encourage foreign trade

trade cycle (*Br.*) business cycle

trade discount a deduction from the retail price of goods made by the manufacturer in favor of the retailer

Trade Expansion Act a U.S. Congressional act (1962) under the John Kennedy administration. It empowered the President to cut tariffs, to give him leverage if needed in getting tariff concessions from Europe and so meet the competition of the European Common Market

trade gap the amount by which a country's imports have exceeded its exports over a period

trade-in (tréidịn) *n.* an article taken by a dealer from a purchaser as part payment for some other article, usually of the same kind

trade·mark (tréidmɑrk) **1.** *n.* the name or distinctive symbol or device attached to goods for sale, and usually legally registered, as a warrant of their production by a particular firm or individual **2.** *v.t.* to affix a trademark to ‖ to register (a symbol etc.) as a trademark

trade name the name by which an article is known to the trade that deals in it ‖ the name under which a firm does business ‖ a name used as a trademark, esp. one that is registered and legally protected

trade-off (tréidɔf) *n.* **1.** in decision-making, selecting the choice from analysis of advantages and disadvantages of two or more alternatives **2.** an offset in a bargain —**trade off** *v.*

trade price the price at which goods are sold between members of the same trade, or by wholesale dealers or manufacturers to retailers

trad·er (tréidər) *n.* a person engaged in some form of commerce ‖ a ship chartered for carrying goods for trade

trade school a secondary school specializing in courses in skilled trades

trades·folk (tréidzfouk) *n.* (*old-fash.*) tradespeople

trades·man (tréidzmən) *pl.* **trades·men** (tréidzmən) *n.* a storekeeper ‖ (*Br., mil.*) a soldier with special technical qualifications, e.g. a radio operator, who receives pay over and above that due to his military rank

trades·peo·ple (tréidzpi:p'l) *n.* people engaged in trade

trades union a trade union

Trades Union Congress (*abbr.* T.U.C.) the central body representing all British trade unions affiliated to it, founded 1868

trades unionism trade unionism

trades unionist trade unionist

trade union a labor union ‖ (*hist.*) a voluntary association of wage earners in any craft or trade organized to protect their interests, i.e. wages, conditions and hours of work etc., against the employers **trade unionism** the system or principles of collective bargaining through trade unions **trade unionist** a member of a trade union

trade wind a wind blowing from the tropical high-pressure belts toward the equatorial region of low pressure, from the northeast in the northern hemisphere and southeast in the southern hemisphere. In many areas trade winds blow with regularity throughout the year, though there are variations with season and location [fr. naut. phrase *to blow trade*, to blow a regular course]

trading post the station of a trader or trading company established in a remote undeveloped region for purposes of trade with the local population

trading stamp a paper stamp handed by a tradesman to a customer making a purchase. Devised to encourage business, trading stamps represent a small percentage of the value of each purchase and can be redeemed for merchandise or cash

tra·di·tion (trədíʃən) *n.* a cultural continuity transmitted in the form of social attitudes, beliefs, principles and conventions of behavior etc. deriving from past experience and helping to shape the present ‖ a convention established by constant practice ‖ a belief, legend etc. based on oral report, usually accepted as historically true though not verifiable ‖ the transmitting of cultural continuity, beliefs, legends etc. ‖ a religious law or teaching, or a body of these, held to have been received originally by oral transmission. In the Jewish religion these are the laws given to Moses on Sinai and later embodied in the Mishnah. In the Christian religion they are a body of extra-biblical teachings handed down orally within the Christian community. In the Moslem religion they are an account of the sayings and doings of Mohammed later embodied in the Sunna **tra·dí·tion·al** *adj.* **tra·dí·tion·al·ism** *n.* exaggerated respect for tradition ‖ fundamentalism **tra·dí·tion·al·ist** *n.* **tra·di·tion·al·ís·tic** *adj.* **tra·dí·tion·al·ly** *adv.* [O.F. *tradicion*, a handing over]

trad·i·tor (trǽditər) *pl.* **trad·i·to·res** (trædıtɔ́ri:z, trædıtóuri:z) *n.* (*hist.*) a traitor or informer among early Christians at the time of the Roman persecutions [L.]

tra·duce (trədú:s, trədjú:s) *pres. part.* **tra·duc·ing** *past* and *past part.* **tra·duced** *v.t.* to speak evil of or misrepresent [fr. L. *traducere*, to lead across, lead along as a spectacle, bring into disgrace]

tra·du·cian·ism (trədú:ʃənịzəm, trədjú:ʃənịzəm) *n.* (*theol.*) the doctrine that the soul of a child, with its attribute of original sin, derives from its parents at the moment of conception [fr. L.L. *traducianus* fr. *tradux (traducis)*, a propagated shoot]

Tra·fal·gar, Battle of (trəfǽlgər) a decisive sea battle (Oct. 21, 1805) off S.W. Spain. The British fleet under Nelson broke the line of the French and Spanish fleets, capturing 20 vessels. The battle established British naval supremacy in the Napoleonic Wars and forced Napoleon to abandon his plan of invading Britain. Nelson was killed in the battle

traf·fic (trǽfik) *n.* the passage to and fro of people and esp. of vehicles on a road or street, or of ships, aircraft etc. on their routes ‖ the volume of passengers or freight carried, e.g. by a particular transport company, within a given period ‖ the passage of calls, signals etc. through a communications system or the volume of calls, signals etc. passed ‖ illicit or shady business dealings ‖ (*rhet.*) exchange by barter or by buying and selling ‖ (*rhet.*) any dealings, e.g. intellectual ones, involving exchange [F. *trafique*]

traffic *pres. part.* **traf·fick·ing** *past* and *past part.* **traf·ficked** *v.i.* to conduct traffic, esp. illicit traffic (in a commodity) [fr. O.F. *trafiquer*]

traffic circle (*Am.=Br.* roundabout) a round plot of ground at the intersection of crossroads, around which all traffic must go in the direction indicated

traffic light a system of colored lights, usually automatically controlled, at road crossings or points of traffic concentration, to regulate traffic

trag·a·canth (trǽgəkænθ) *n.* a member of *Astragalus*, fam. *Papilionaceae*, a genus of low perennial shrubs native to S.E. Europe and W. Asia (Iran) ‖ the gum which exudes from this shrub, used esp. in preparing pills, emulsions and creams and as an adhesive [F. *tragacante* fr. L. fr. Gk]

tra·ge·di·an (trədʒí:di:ən) *n.* an actor specializing in tragic roles ‖ an author of tragedies [prob. fr. O.F. *tragediane*]

tra·ge·di·enne (trədʒi:di:én) *n.* an actress specializing in tragic roles [F. *tragédienne*]

trag·e·dy (trǽdʒidi:) *pl.* **trag·e·dies** *n.* a drama portraying the conflict between the individual human will and fate or necessity, traditionally depicting a hero or heroine transcending, or succumbing to, a series of catastrophic events ‖ the theoretical principles of this kind of drama ‖ a calamity, an event causing distress, sadness, anguish, shock etc. in varying degrees ‖ tragic quality [O.F. *tragedie* fr. L. fr. Gk]

—Aristotle, basing his theory on the practice of the great Athenian tragedians, said that tragedy should move the reader or spectator to pity and terror, performing a catharsis, or purification by purging, of the emotions. The tragic hero evoked sympathy for his greatness of character but alienated it also—and caused his own downfall—by some personal flaw, esp. arrogant pride (*HUBRIS). Later writers on tragedy also tend to concentrate on these two features: the spectator's involvement—part identification, part repudiation—in the nature of the central figure, and the conflict and final balance of emotion which the greatest tragedy calls forth. It is curiously allied to the greatest comedy: there is the same complexity in the hero (e.g. Moliére's Alceste in 'le Misanthrope'), though in comedy the spectator feels a smaller degree of involvement in his fate. But in both comedy and tragedy the spectator is finally reconciled to the hero's fate. The degree to which the dramatist can invoke sympathy and understanding, the bitterness of the fate which overtakes the hero, and yet the ultimate rightness of the result: these three produce the most serious, the most painful, the most inward, and yet the most liberating moments in literature

trag·ic (trǽdʒik) *adj.* causing grief, disappointment or horror and shock, *a tragic accident* ‖ appropriate to, or pertaining to, tragic drama ‖ expressing tragedy, *a tragic expression* **trág·i·cal·ly** *adv.* [fr. L. *tragicus*]

trag·i·com·e·dy (trædʒikɔ́midi:) *pl.* **trag·i·com·e·dies** *n.* a drama in which the currents of tragedy and comedy are (usually ironically) blended ‖ an event or situation in which the elements of tragedy and comedy are intermixed [F. *tragicomédie* fr. L. fr. Gk]

trag·i·com·ic (trædʒikɔ́mik) *adj.* having the nature of tragicomedy [fr. *tragi-* (combining form of 'tragic')+COMIC]

trag·o·pan (trǽgəpæn) *n.* a member of *Tragopan*, a genus of brilliantly colored Asiatic pheasants, having the back and breast covered with white or buff ocelli. The male has two brightly colored wattles and a pair of fleshy erectile horns on its head [L.=a fabulous Ethiopian bird fr. Gk *tragos*, goat+PAN (the God)]

Tra·herne (trəhə́:rn), Thomas (1637-74), English mystical writer. His poems were not published till 1903 and his prose work, 'Centuries of Meditations', till 1908. The latter were written to provide instruction in 'the way of felicity'

trail (treil) **1.** *v.t.* to pull (something) along behind one, esp. over the ground or another surface ‖ to pursue (a person) by following up information about his movements ‖ to hunt (an animal) by following its tracks ‖ to trace the whereabouts of by esp. long investigation, *they trailed the stolen jewels to an alley in Rome* ‖ to shadow, keep secret watch on (someone) ‖ to allow to hang loosely or float behind one, *to trail one's fingers in the water* ‖ (*mil.*) to carry (e.g. a rifle) at the trail arms ‖ to lag behind (another or others) e.g. in a race ‖ to leave traces of (something), *to trail sand all over the floor* ‖ *v.i.* to hang down or float loosely ‖ to walk or progress slowly because of weariness or unwillingness ‖ (with 'behind') to fail to keep up with others ‖ (of a plant) to grow to a considerable length along the ground or over a surface ‖ to leave haphazard tracks or traces, *she could see where the water had trailed all over the clean floor* **to trail off** (of a sound) to dwindle gradually into silence, *her voice trailed off* **to trail one's coat** to try to provoke a calculated reaction in someone **2.** *n.* the track or traces left by the passage of an animal or person ‖ a blazed or trodden path through a wild region ‖ something left behind by or following in the wake of a moving object, *the car raised a trail of dust* ‖ a long, thin wisp, *trails of smoke were coming from the factories* ‖ (*Br., mil.*) a horizontal position for carrying a rifle in the right hand, with the right arm fully extended downward, *at the trail* ‖ the part of the stock of a towed field gun which rests

CONCISE PRONUNCIATION KEY: **(a)** æ, *cat*; ɑ, *car*; ɔ *fawn*; ei, *snake*. **(e)** e, *hen*; i:, *sheep*; iə, *deer*; ɛə, *bear*. **(i)** i, *fish*; ai, *tiger*; ə:, *bird*. **(o)** o, *ox*; au, *cow*; ou, *goat*; u, *poor*; ɔi, *royal*. **(u)** ʌ, *duck*; u, *bull*; u:, *goose*; ə, *bacillus*; ju:, *cube*. x, *loch*; θ, *think*; ð, *bother*; z, *Zen*; ʒ, *corsage*; dʒ, *savage*; ŋ, *orangutang*; j, *yak*; ʃ, *fish*; tʃ, *fetch*; 'l, *rabble*; 'n, *redden*. Complete pronunciation key appears inside front cover.

on the ground when the gun is unlimbered and put into action [prob. fr. O.N.F. *trailler*]

trail arms (*mil.*) a position in drilling in which the rifle is held in the right hand with the butt end raised just above the ground and the muzzle inclined forward

trail bike a lightweight motorcycle designed for rough terrain

trail·blaz·er (tréilblẹizər) *n.* the first person to mark out a path for others to follow ‖ a pioneer in some enterprise

trail·er (tréilər) *n.* someone who or something which trails ‖ a short extract from a new film exhibited as advance publicity ‖ a wheeled vehicle designed to be towed by a car or truck, esp. (*Am.*= *Br.* caravan) one containing sleeping quarters and arrangements for cooking and eating

trailer park area licensed to permit the parking of recreational vehicles, i.e., campers and trailers, and usu. providing water and electricity *also* trailer camp, trailer court

trailing arbutus *Epigaea repens,* fam. *Ericaceae,* a creeping, evergreen plant, having fragrant pink and white flowers and oblong, hairy leaves. It blossoms in early spring mainly in the northeastern U.S.A.

trailing edge (*aeron.*) the rear edge of an airfoil (cf. LEADING EDGE)

train (trein) *n.* a line of railroad cars coupled together with or without the engine that draws them ‖ (*old-fash.*) a retinue, body of habitual followers ‖ a series of persons or things following or linked to one another, *a mule train, train of events* ‖ (*mil., hist.*) a group of men, vehicles and animals carrying supplies, ammunition etc. at the rear of an army ‖ an elongation of a robe or the skirt of a woman's dress made to trail along the ground or to be carried ‖ a bird's long tail, esp. a peacock's ‖ a line of inflammable material, usually gunpowder, laid over a distance to an explosive charge, for safe firing of the charge ‖ a series of connected wheels or parts in machinery, for transmitting or modifying motion, esp. in a watch or clock ‖ a series of physical oscillations, *a train of sound waves* ‖ an orderly linked sequence, *a train of thought, train of reactions* **in the train of** following (something) as a result, *the tornado brought havoc in its train* **to set in train** to cause (events) to happen which will lead to other desired effects [F. *traîne* fem. and *train* masc.]

train *v.t.* to cause (a person or animal) to respond to discipline and instruction ‖ to make (a person or animal) efficient in some activity by instruction and repeated practice ‖ to make (a plant) grow in a desired direction by pruning and tying it ‖ (with 'on') to direct (a gun, camera etc.) ‖ *v.i.* to make one's own body more efficient by exercise and diet, or one's intelligence and memory by application ‖ to go by rail [M.E. fr. O.F. *traïner, trahiner*]

train·band (tréinbænd) *n.* a 16th-c., 17th-c. or 18th-c. militia [shortened fr. trained band]

train·bear·er (tréinbẹərər) *n.* a person appointed to carry the train of another's robe or gown on ceremonial occasions

train·ee (treiníː) *n.* a person undergoing training ‖ someone undergoing military training

train·ee·ship (treiníːʃip) *n.* the period of status of being a trainee

train·er (tréinər) *n.* a person who trains, esp. someone who trains athletes, horses etc. for racing or sport, or someone who trains circus animals ‖ a machine used in training

train·ing (tréiniŋ) *n.* preparatory discipline for participants in athletics etc. ‖ the instructing and directing of such participants ‖ instruction and practice in a particular skill, *first-aid training* **in training** undergoing a course of instruction or direction ‖ at full pitch of physical condition and expertise for sport or athletics **out of training** not at the pitch of physical fitness and expertise needed for sport or athletics

training ship a ship for training boys in seamanship ‖ a ship equipped to train men for the merchant marine or the navy

train·man (tréinmən) *pl.* **train·men** (tréinmən) *n.* a subordinate member of a train crew

train oil whale oil

traipse, *Br.* also **trapes** (treips) **1.** *v.i. pres. part.* **traips·ing,** *Br.* also **trapes·ing** *past* and *past part.* **traipsed,** *Br.* also **trapesed** to trudge for a long distance without a fixed route, *we traipsed all over town looking for a room* **2.** *n.* a long, tiring walk [earlier *trapass* prob. fr. O.F. *trapasser,* to pass beyond]

trait (treit, esp. *Br.* trei) *n.* a distinguishing characteristic, quality or feature [F.]

trai·tor (tréitər) *n.* a person who betrays a trust or acts against a sworn loyalty, esp. someone guilty of the crime of treason [O.F. *traitre*]

trai·tor·ous (tréitərəs) *adj.* characteristic of or having the character of a traitor ‖ having the nature of treason

trai·tress (tréitris) *n.* a female traitor [O.F. *traitresse*]

Tra·jan (tréidʒən) (Marcus Ulpius Trajanus, 53-117), Roman emperor (98-117). His conquest of Dacia (c. 106) is commemorated in the sculptures of Trajan's Column in Rome. His military and civil administration was firm and efficient

tra·jec·to·ry (trədʒéktəriː) *pl.* **tra·jec·to·ries** *n.* the path of a body in space, esp. of a projectile ‖ (*geom.*) a curve or surface cutting at a constant angle a system of curves or surfaces [fr. M.L. *trajectorius*]

tram (træm) *n.* (*Br.*) a streetcar ‖ a four-wheeled wagon running on rails for transporting coal from the face to the loading base in a mine [prob.=L.G. *traam,* a beam]

tram *n.* yarn made of lightly twisted silk strands, used esp. for the weft of the best velvets and silks [F. *trame*]

tram·car (trǽmkɑr) *n.* (*Br.*) a streetcar

tram·line (trǽmlạin) *n.* (*Br.*) a route served by streetcars ‖ (*Br., pl.*) the rails on which a streetcar runs ‖ (*pl., Br., pop.*) a pair of parallel lines bounding the sides of a lawn-tennis court, of which the inner marks the boundary of the singles court

tram·mel (trǽməl) **1.** *n.* a net used for fowling or fishing, esp. a triple dragnet made with three layers of different sized mesh ‖ a shackle used to teach a horse to amble ‖ an adjustable pothook set in the chimney of an open fireplace ‖ (*pl.*) impediments to free movement or action, *the trammels of legal procedure* ‖ (*mech.*) an instrument for drawing ellipses ‖ a gauge for aligning or adjusting machine parts ‖ (*pl.,* often with 'pair of') a beam compass **2.** *v.t. pres. part.* **tram·mel·ing,** esp. *Br.* **tram·mel·ling** *past* and *past part.* **tram·meled,** esp. *Br.* **tram·melled** to catch in a trammel ‖ to hamper, prevent the free play of [O.F. *tramail*]

tra·mon·tane (trəmɒ́ntein) *n.* the cold, dry, northerly wind in Italy and the Mediterranean blowing from the Alps [fr. Ital. *tramontana,* north wind]

tramp (træmp) **1.** *v.i.* to march or walk with a heavy tread ‖ to travel on foot or go for long walks, *to spend a week tramping across the hills* ‖ *v.t.* to trample ‖ to make (one's way or a specified distance) by tramping ‖ to walk purposefully across, down, over etc., esp. wearily or reluctantly, *to tramp the streets looking for work* **2.** *n.* the sound of heavy footsteps ‖ a cargo boat not traveling on a regular line but picking up cargo wherever it offers ‖ a long walk usually for pleasure ‖ a person without work and with no fixed home who tramps the country living by begging and sometimes by casual labor ‖ a woman of loose morals [M.E. *trampen*]

tram·ple (trǽmp'l) **1.** *v. pres. part.* **tram·pling** *past* and *past part.* **tram·pled** *v.t.* to crush or pack down by treading on, *to trample grapes* ‖ (with 'out') to extinguish (a fire) by stamping it out with one's feet ‖ to bring (e.g. mud) on the feet somewhere where it is not wanted, *to trample mud into a carpet* ‖ *v.i.* to tread heavily ‖ (with 'on', 'upon' or 'over') to tread heavily and crush, bruise, injure or spoil something, *to trample over flowerbeds* **2.** *n.* the sound of trampling [M.E. *trampelen* frequentative of *trampen,* to tramp]

tram·po·lin (trǽmpəlin) *n.* a trampoline

tram·po·line (trǽmpəliːn) *n.* a large canvas sheet stretched in a frame by springs, providing a platform of extreme elasticity for acrobats, tumblers, clowns etc. or for exercising on [Span. *trampolin* fr. Ital. *trampoli,* stilts]

tram·way (trǽmwẹi) *n.* (*Br.*) the rails along which streetcars run

trance (træns, trɑns) *n.* a state of insensibility to external surroundings with partial, but unconscious, retention of function. It may be either self-induced or brought on by hypnosis ‖ a state of profound abstraction due to intense concentration of mind, as in religious contemplation, which may be accompanied by ecstasy, exaltation or (sometimes) hallucination [O.F. *transe*]

tran·dem (trǽndəm) *n.* (*surfing*) a surfboard holding three surfers

tran·quil (trǽŋkwil) *adj.* free from agitation or perturbation, peaceful [fr. L. *tranquillus*]

tran·quil·ite (trǽŋkwilait) *n.* compound of titanium, iron, and magnesium found in rock recovered from the moon's Sea of Tranquility

tran·quil·i·za·tion, tran·quil·li·za·tion (træŋkwilizéiʃən) *n.* a tranquilizing or being tranquilized

tran·quil·ize, tran·quil·lize (trǽŋkwilaiz) *pres. part.* **tran·quil·iz·ing, tran·quil·liz·ing** *past* and *past part.* **tran·quil·ized, tran·quil·lized** *v.t.* to make tranquil ‖ (*med.*) to reduce tension in by drugs **tran·quil·iz·er, tran·quil·liz·er** (trǽŋkwilaizər) *n.* something that tranquilizes, esp. a sedative drug

tran·quil·li·ty, tran·quil·i·ty (træŋkwíliti:) *n.* the stage or quality of being tranquil [O.F. *tranquillité*]

trans- (trænz, træns) *prefix* on or to the other side of, beyond, over, across ‖ from one state to another, as in 'transliterate'

trans·act (trænsǽkt, trænzǽkt) *v.t.* to perform, carry through (e.g. a business affair) ‖ *v.i.* to conduct business [fr. L. *transigere* (*transactus*), to carry through, accomplish]

trans·ac·ti·nide series (trænsǽktənaid) hypothetical elements following element 103 (lawrencium) in the periodic table *Cf* SUPERACTINIDE SERIES

trans·ac·tion (trænsǽkʃən, trænzǽkʃən) *n.* the performance or management of business etc. ‖ something transacted, a business deal ‖ (*pl.*) records, esp. published, of the proceedings of a learned society [fr. L. *transactio* (*transactionis*)]

trans·ac·tion·al analysis (trænsǽkʃənəl) (*psych.*) a form of group therapy based on three positions or roles (child, adult, parent), and six types of transactions (work, intimacy, etc.) carried on as 'games' in which subjects alternately assumes roles in order to provide verbal outlets for undesired responses; developed by American psychologist Eric Berne (1910–1970) *abbr.* TA

trans·ac·tor (trænsǽktər, trænzǽktər) *n.* a person who transacts

Trans A·lai (trǽnsɑlái, trǽnzɑlái) a mountain range extending west from the Chinese border between Kirghizia and Tadzhikistan, U.S.S.R. (Lenin, 23,386 ft)

Trans-Alaska Pipeline (trænzəlǽskə) an oil pipeline that runs from Prudhoe Bay, an arm of the Arctic Ocean, to Valdez, an ice-free port on the Gulf of Alaska, a distance of 800 miles. The 48-inch-diameter pipeline can carry over 2 million barrels of crude oil per day from Alaska's North Slope fields. The pipeline, built by a consortium of 8 oil companies, was completed in 1977 at a cost of nearly $8 billion, making it the costliest private construction project in history

trans·al·pine (trænsǽlpain, trænzǽlpain) *adj.* on the north side of the Alps (cf. CISALPINE) [fr. L. *transalpinus,* across the Alps (i.e. from Italy)]

Transalpine Gaul *GAUL

trans·am·i·na·tion (trænsæmənéiʃən) *n.* (*biochem.*) change of amino acids from one molecule to another, promoted by an enzyme —**transaminase** or **aminotransferase** *n.* the enzyme

trans·at·lan·tic (trænsətlǽntik, trænzətlǽntik) *adj.* on the other side of the Atlantic Ocean, esp. from the European point of view ‖ crossing or extending across the Atlantic Ocean ‖ pertaining to, characteristic of or coming from the region or people on the other side of the Atlantic, *transatlantic cultural influences*

trans·bus (trǽnsbʌs) *n.* bus designed to accommodate the handicapped, esp. in urban transit

Trans·cau·ca·sia (trænskɔkéiʒə, trænzkɔkéiʒə) a region of the U.S.S.R. south of the Caucasus comprising the Armenian, Azerbaijan and Georgian Soviet Socialist Republics. Products: oil, manganese, tea, citrus fruits and wine. A Transcaucasian republic existed until 1936, when it was split up into its present divisions

tran·scend (trænsénd) *v.t.* to be or go beyond the limits or powers of, *to transcend belief* ‖ to surpass, excel, *it transcended all our hopes* ‖ (*philos., theol.,* of God or a god) to be above, separate from or independent of (experience, the material universe) [fr. L. *transcendere*]

tran·scend·ence (trænséndəns) *n.* the fact, state or act of being transcendent **tran·scénd·en·cy** *n.* [fr. M.L. *transcendentia*]

tran·scend·ent (trænséndənt) *adj.* beyond normal limits, surpassing, *of transcendent beauty* ‖ being outside or going beyond the limits of possible human experience ‖ (in Kant) going beyond the limits of possible knowledge (cf. TRANSCENDENTAL) ‖ being above and independent of the limitations of the material universe (cf. IMMANENT) [fr. L. *transcendens* (*transcendentis*) fr. *transcendere*, to transcend]

tran·scen·den·tal (trænsendént'l) *adj.* belonging to pure reason, prior to all experience and a necessary condition of that experience, *according to Kant space and time are transcendental concepts* (cf. TRANSCENDENT) **tran·scen·dén·tal·ism** *n.* any philosophical system which attributes *a priori* reality to what exists outside the bounds of human experience ‖ an American philosophical school represented by Emerson and characterized by a certain pantheistic mysticism **tran·scen·dén·tal·ist** *n.* [fr. M.L. *transcendentalis*]

transcendental meditation a meditation technique in which mind is released from tension through use of a mantra, creating a feeling of calm and spiritual well-being *abbr.* TM

trans·con·ti·nen·tal (trænskɒntinént'l, trænzkɒntinént'l) *adj.* extending or going across a continent

tran·scribe (trænskráib) *pres. part.* **tran·scrib·ing** *past* and *past part.* **tran·scribed** *v.t.* to copy out in manuscript or type (notes, shorthand etc.) ‖ to arrange or adapt (a piece of music) for an instrument, voice etc. other than that for which it was originally written ‖ (*radio*) to record (material) for broadcast at a later time ‖ (*genetics*) to carry a message from DNA to RNA through the synthesis of an enzyme ‖ *v.i.* to make a transcription [fr. L. *transcribere*]

tran·script (trǽnskript) *n.* a copy written or typed [O.F. *transcrit*]

transcriptase *REVERSE TRANSCRIPTASE

tran·scrip·tion (trænskrípʃən) *n.* something transcribed ‖ a transcribing or being transcribed [F.]

trans·duce (trænsdú:s) *v.* (*biol.*) to cause the transfer of molecules between microorganisms by means of a viral agent

trans·duc·er (trænsdú:sər, trænzdú:sər, trænsdjú:sər, trænzdjú:sər) *n.* (*phys.*) a device for transferring power, generated in one system, to another system, in the same or another form ‖ (*biol.*) a virus that causes a change in the genetic character of a microorganism through action of nucleic acid [fr. L. *transducere*, to lead across]

trans·earth (trænsə́:rθ) *adj.* (*astronautics*) of the path of a spacecraft between the earth and a celestial body

tran·sect 1. (trǽnsekt) *n.* (*bot.*) a line or strip of vegetation chosen for study **2.** (trænsékt) *v.t.* to cut across **tran·séc·tion** *n.* [fr. L. *trans*, across+*secare* (*sectus*), to cut]

tran·sept (trǽnsept) *n.* either of the two transverse wings of a cruciform church built at right angles to the nave ‖ the entire transverse section crossing between nave and choir in a cruciform church **tran·sép·tal** *adj.* [fr. M.L. or Mod. L. *transseptum* fr. *trans*, across+*septum*, hedge]

trans·fer 1. (trænsfə́:r, trænzfə́:r, trǽnsfər, trǽnzfər) *v. pres. part.* **trans·fer·ring** *past* and *past part.* **trans·ferred** *v.t.* to move from one place or position to another, *the manager was transferred to a different branch* ‖ to redirect from one person or object to another, *to transfer one's affection to someone else* ‖ to pass legal ownership or control of to another person, *he transferred the shares to a nephew* ‖ (*sports*) to trade (a professional player) to another club etc. ‖ (*arts*) to convey (a design etc.) from one surface to another, esp. by transfer paper to a lithograph stone ‖ *v.i.* to get out of one bus, train etc. and into another so as to continue a journey ‖ to change one's work or position, esp. within an organization, *he transferred from sales to advertising* **2.** (trǽnsfər, trǽnzfər) *n.* a transferring or being transferred ‖ something or someone transferred ‖ a design on paper etc. which can be transferred to another surface ‖ (*law*) an act of conveyance of property from one person to another or the deed drawn up for it ‖ a ticket entitling the bearer to change from one bus or streetcar to another within a specified period **trans·fer·ence** (trǽnsfərəns, trǽnzfərəns, trænsfə́:rəns, trænzfə́:rəns) *n.* a transferring or being transferred ‖ (*psychoanal.*) the transfer of desires or sentiments, esp. those retained in the unconscious from childhood, to another object, e.g. the redirection of a girl's feelings for her father to a male figure usually much older than herself [fr. L. *transferre*, to carry across]

transfer cell (*botany*) the cell in a plant that exchanges dissolved substances with the outside environment

trans·fer·en·tial (trænsfərénʃəl, trænzfərénʃəl) *adj.* of or relating to transference or to a transfer

transfer factor (*med.*) the immunity protein stored in white blood cells that recognizes a disease and prevents its recurrence; discovered by American biochemist H. Sherwood Lawrence (1916–)

transfer paper a specially prepared coated paper that allows a design on it to be transferred to another surface. Some papers need moisture for this, some need heat, some need pressure

transfer payments public funds distributed to persons for a special purpose in accordance to a legal formula, e.g., social security, unemployment compensation, veterans' benefits

transfer RNA (*genetics*) a form of RNA that combines with amino acids and messenger RNA to cause remaining amino acids to combine in a certain sequence in protein synthesis *abbr.* tRNA *Cf* MESSENGER RNA, RIBOSOMAL RNA

trans·fig·u·ra·tion (trænsfigjuréiʃən, trænzfigjuréiʃən, trænsfigjuréiʃən, trænzfigjuréiʃən) *n.* a transfiguring or being transfigured **the Transfiguration** the change in Christ's appearance described in Matthew xvii and celebrated by the Christian Church on Aug. 6 [fr. L. *transfiguratio* (*transfigurationis*)]

trans·fig·ure (trænsfígjər, trænzfígjər) *pres. part.* **trans·fig·ur·ing** *past* and *past part.* **trans·fig·ured** *v.t.* to change the appearance of in a very great degree, usually in a pleasing way, *the architect had transfigured the old barns, joy transfigured her face* [fr. L. *transfigurare*, to change the shape of]

trans·fix (trænsfíks, trænzfíks) *v.t.* to impale upon or pierce with a pointed instrument ‖ to pierce through or to make as if paralyzed by a strong emotion etc., *transfixed with horror* **trans·fix·ion** *n.* [fr. L. *transfigere* (*transfixus*), to fix through]

trans·form (trænsfɔ́rm, trænzfɔ́rm) *v.t.* to change the form or appearance of, esp. (with 'into') to metamorphose ‖ to change the character or nature of radically ‖ (*phys.*) to change (energy) from one kind to another ‖ (*elec.*) to change (an electric current) into one of different voltage [fr. L. *transformare*]

trans·for·ma·tion (trænsfərméiʃən, trænzfərméiʃən) *n.* a transforming or being transformed ‖ (*old-fash.*) false hair worn to supplement a woman's natural hair, or as a wig ‖ (*genetics*) the taking up of free DNA to acquire genetic properties ‖ (*computer*) the change in composition or structure of data without any change in values or meanings [fr. L.L. *transformatio* (*transformationis*)]

trans·for·ma·tion·al grammar (trænsfərméiʃən'l) a generative grammar with a transformational component, i.e. a section of rules for the transformation and transposition of elements of a sentence to make a different sentence

transformation scene (*pantomime*) an elaborate scene in which the actors and scenery gradually change their appearance in full view of the audience for the lavish finale

trans·form·er (trænsfɔ́rmər, trænzfɔ́rmər) *n.* (*elec.*) a device for converting a varying current from one voltage to another. In a step-up transformer the low-voltage current is passed through a primary coil of a few thick turns, wound on an iron core. An alternating magnetic field is thus created, and this produces, by mutual induction, a high-voltage current in a secondary coil consisting of a large number of turns of thin wire, the ratio of the voltages being roughly equal to that of the number of turns in the two coils. A step-down transformer operates in the reverse sense

transform fault (*geol.*) a crack in the earth's crust in a steplike pattern that is believed to indicate direction of plate movements

trans·fuse (trænsfjú:z, trænzfjú:z) *pres. part.* **trans·fus·ing** *past* and *past part.* **trans·fused** *v.t.* to communicate (a quality) to, *to transfuse one's enthusiasm into a class* ‖ to permeate, *his enthusiasm transfused the class* ‖ to transfer (blood) from one person into the vein of another or from one animal into another ‖ to inject (a saline solution) into a vein ‖ to subject (a patient) to a transfusion [fr. L. *transfundere* (*transfusus*), to pour across]

trans·fu·sion (trænsfjú:ʒən, trænzfjú:ʒən) *n.* a transfusing, esp. of fluids (blood, plasma, solutions containing various foods, minerals or drugs) into the veins of a patient [fr. L. *transfusio* (*transfusionis*)]

trans·gress (trænsgrés, trænzgrés) *v.t.* to break (a rule, law etc.) ‖ to go beyond (a limit etc.) ‖ *v.i.* (*rhet.*) to sin [F. *transgresser*]

trans·gres·sion (trænsgréʃən, trænzgréʃən) *n.* a sin ‖ a transgressing [F.]

trans·gres·sor (trænsgrésər, trænzgrésər) *n.* a person who transgresses

tran·ship (trænʃíp) *pres. part.* **tran·ship·ping** *past* and *past part.* **tran·shipped** *v.t.* and *i.* to transship **tran·shíp·ment** *n.*

trans·hu·mance (trænshjú:məns, trænzhjú:məns) *n.* the seasonal transfer of livestock to mountain or lowland pastures [F.]

tran·sience (trǽnʃəns, trǽnʒəns) *n.* the state or quality of being transient **trán·sien·cy** *n.*

tran·sient (trǽnʃənt, trǽnʒənt) **1.** *adj.* brief, short-lived, impermanent ‖ staying for only a short time, esp. of hotel guests **2.** *n.* a person who stays in a hotel etc. for only a short time ‖ a person who has no fixed abode or employment and who wanders about looking for temporary work [fr. L. *transiens* (*transientis*) fr. *transire*, to go across]

trans·il·lu·mi·nate (trænsilú:mineit, trænzilú:mineit) *pres. part.* **trans·il·lu·mi·nat·ing** *past* and *past part.* **trans·il·lu·mi·nat·ed** *v.t.* (*med.*) to pass a strong light through (tissue or an organ) for examination

tran·sis·tor (trænzístər) *n.* any of several types of device incorporating an arrangement of semiconductor material (esp. germanium with controlled low concentrations of arsenic, indium, antimony etc.) and suitable contacts capable of performing many of the functions of thermionic and photoemissive tubes (such as power, voltage or current amplification) with low power requirements and large saving of space ‖ a radio set using transistors instead of tubes [TRANSFER+RESISTOR]

trans·it (trǽnsit, trǽnzit) **1.** *n.* a moving or being moved across, over, or from one place to another ‖ the movement of one heavenly body across the disk of a larger one, or its apparent movement across a meridian ‖ a transit instrument ‖ the transport or conveyance of goods or persons from one place to another **in transit** in the process of being moved ‖ (*aerospace*) navigation satellite that utilizes the Doppler effect for fixing position of ships and aircraft **2.** *v.t.* (*astron.*) to move across the disk of (a larger heavenly body) ‖ (*astron.*) to cross (a meridian) ‖ to turn (a telescope etc.) about its horizonal transverse axis ‖ *v.i.* to make a transit [fr. L. *transire* (*transitus*), to go across]

transit compass a variety of theodolite used to measure horizontal angles

transit instrument an instrument furnished with a rotating telescope and a circular scale, used to observe the transit of a heavenly body across a meridian ‖ a transit compass

tran·si·tion (trænzíʃən, trænsíʃən, *Br.* trænsíʒən) *n.* a change or passage from one place, action, mood, topic etc. to another ‖ a development that forms part of an ordered progression, *a transition from limited autonomy to full independence* ‖ (*mus.*) a passage which joins two others more important than itself ‖ (*mus.*) a sudden change of key not effected by modulation ‖ (*genetics*) a mutation in RNA or DNA in which a purine or a pyrimidine base is substituted for another **tran·sí·tion·al** *adj.* [fr. L. *transitio* (*transitionis*)]

transition point (*phys.*) the temperature at which two physical states of the same substance are in equilibrium ‖ (*loosely*) the temperature at which a substance changes its physical state

transition temperature (*phys.*) a transition point

tran·si·tive (trǽnsitiv, trǽnzitiv) **1.** *adj.* (*gram.*, of certain verbs) expressing an action directed toward or performed on some person or thing (*DIRECT OBJECT) **2.** *n.* a verb or construction which is transitive [fr. L.L. *transitivus*]

tran·si·to·ri·ly (trǽnsitɔrili:, trǽnzitɔrili:, trǽnsitourili:, trǽnzitourili:) *adv.* in a transitory manner

tran·si·to·ri·ness (trǽnsitɔri:nis, trǽnzitɔri:nis, trǽnsitouri:nis, trǽnzitouri:nis) *n.* the state or quality of being transitory

tran·si·to·ry (trǽnsitɔri:, trǽnzitɔri:, trǽnsitouri:, trǽnzitouri:) *adj.* passing, temporary, not lasting [O.F. *transitoire*]

Trans·jor·dan (trænsdʒɔ́rd'n, trænzdʒɔ́rd'n) the former name of the Hashimite Kingdom of Jordan (*JORDAN)

CONCISE PRONUNCIATION KEY: **(a)** æ, *cat*; ɑ, *car*; ɔ *fawn*; ei, *snake*. **(e)** e, *hen*; i:, *sheep*; iə, *deer*; εə, *bear*. **(i)** i, *fish*; ai, *tiger*; ə:, *bird*. **(o)** o, *ox*; au, *cow*; ou, *goat*; u, *poor*; ɔi, *royal*. **(u)** ʌ, *duck*; u, *bull*; u:, *goose*; ə, *bacillus*; ju:, *cube*. x, *loch*; θ, *think*; ð, *bother*; z, *Zen*; ʒ, *corsage*; dʒ, *savage*; ŋ, *orangutang*; j, *yak*; ʃ, *fish*; tʃ, *fetch*; 'l, *rabble*; 'n, *redden*. Complete pronunciation key appears inside front cover.

Trans·kei (trǽnskai) *n.* enclave nation in the Republic of South Africa whose 'independence' since October 15, 1976 has been largely unrecognized by other nations. It is the home of the Xhosa people

Trans·kei·an Territories (trænskéiən, trænzkéiən) an African reserve (area 16,554 sq. miles, pop. 2,238,000), mainly pasture and grazing land, in N.E. Cape Province, South Africa. It comprises Transkei and Tembuland (inhabited by Kaffirs), Griqualand East (inhabited by people of mixed Bushman and Hottentot origin) and Pondoland (inhabited by a Bantu people related to the Zulus). Capital: Umtata (pop. 7,000)

trans·late (trænzléit, trænsléit) *pres. part.* **trans·lat·ing** *past* and *past part.* **trans·lat·ed** *v.t.* to put (a word, text or language) into another language retaining the sense ‖ to put in different words of the same language, esp. in order to make clearer, *to translate scientific language for the layman* ‖ to convert into another form, *to translate words into deeds* ‖ (*eccles.*) to transfer (a bishop) to another see ‖ to retransmit (a telegraphic message) ‖ (*phys.*) to subject (a body) to simple displacement, without any other mode of motion ‖ to convey (someone) straight to heaven or paradise without death's intervention ‖ (*genetics*) to form an amino acid molecule from codon material provided by messenger RNA ‖ *v.i.* to make a translation or translations ‖ to be able to be translated [prob. fr. L. *transferre* (*translatus*)]

trans·la·tion (trænzléiʃən, trænsléiʃən) *n.* a translating or being translated ‖ something translated, either the original or the new version ‖ (*phys.*) motion by displacement only **trans·lá·tion·al** *adj.* [O.F. or fr. L. *translatio* (*translationis*)]

trans·la·tor (trænzléitər, trænsléitər, trǽnzleitər, trǽnsleitər) *n.* a person who makes linguistic translations [O.F. or L.]

trans·lit·er·ate (trænzlítəreit, trænslítəreit) *pres. part.* **trans·lit·er·at·ing** *past* and *past part.* **trans·lit·er·at·ed** *v.t.* to replace (letters of one alphabet) by letters of another with the same phonetic sounds ‖ to write (a word or words) in the letters of another alphabet **trans·lit·er·a·tion** *n.* [fr. L. *trans*, across+*littera*, letter]

trans·lo·cate (trænzlóukeit, trænslóukeit) *pres. part.* **trans·lo·cat·ing** *past* and *past part.* **trans·lo·cat·ed** *v.t.* to cause to change location, esp. to transfer (dissolved food materials) from one position in a plant body to another **trans·lo·ca·tion** *n.* the passage of food material in solution inside the body of a plant ‖ the transfer of part of a chromosome to another part of the same chromosome or to a different chromosome

trans·lu·cence (trænzlú:s'ns, trænslú:s'ns) *n.* the state or quality of being translucent **trans·lú·cen·cy** *n.*

trans·lu·cent (trænzlú:s'nt, trænslú:s'nt) *adj.* of a medium through which light passes, but in such a way that a clear image cannot be formed of the object viewed through it (cf. TRANSPARENT, cf. OPAQUE) [fr. *translucens* (*translucentis*) fr. *translucere*, to shine through]

trans·lu·cid (trænzlú:sid, trænslú:sid) *adj.* translucent [fr. L. *translucidus*]

trans·lu·nar (trænslú:nə:r) *adj.* (*astronautics*) of the travel of a spacecraft from earth toward the moon

trans·mem·brane (trænsmémbrein) *adj.* of the transfer from one side of a membrane to an other

trans·mi·grant (trænzmáigrənt, trænsmáigrənt) *n.* a person passing through a country on his way to a new country in which he is to settle

trans·mi·grate (trænzmáigreit, trænsmáigreit) *pres. part.* **trans·mi·grat·ing** *past* and *past part.* **trans·mi·grat·ed** *v.i.* to migrate from one place or country to another ‖ (of the soul) to pass at death from one body to another [fr. L. *transmigrare* (*transmigratus*)]

trans·mi·gra·tion (trænzmaigréiʃən, trænsmaigréiʃən) *n.* the act or an instance of transmigrating ‖ the transmigration of souls [fr. L.L. *transmigratio* (*transmigrationis*)]

transmigration of souls the passing of individual souls at death into new bodies or different forms of life

trans·mi·gra·to·ry (trænzmáigrətɔri:, trænsmáigrətɔri:, trænzmáigrətouri:, trænsmáigrətouri:) *adj.* of transmigration ‖ tending to or in the habit of transmigrating

trans·mis·si·bil·i·ty (trænzmisəbíliti:, trænsmisəbíliti:) *n.* the state or quality of being transmissible

trans·mis·si·ble (trænzmísəb'l, trænsmísəb'l) *adj.* able to be transmitted [fr. L. *transmittere* (*transmissus*)]

trans·mis·sion (trænzmíʃən, trænsmíʃən) *n.* a transmitting or being transmitted ‖ something transmitted, esp. a radio or television program ‖ the passage of radio waves in the space between the transmitting and receiving stations ‖ the mechanism (e.g. clutch, gearbox, transmission shaft) by which power is transmitted from the engine to the axle of a car etc. [fr. L. *transmissio* (*transmissionis*)]

transmission electron microscope microscope that illuminates an image by transmitted electrons passing through the specimen

trans·mit (trænzmít, trænsmít) *pres. part.* **trans·mit·ting** *past* and *past part.* **trans·mit·ted** *v.t.* to send, or cause or permit to pass, from one place or person to another ‖ to be a medium for, or serve to communicate (light, heat, sound etc.) ‖ to communicate ‖ to pass on to others by inheritance or heredity ‖ to pass on (an infection or disease) to a person, animal or organism ‖ to convey (drive) from one mechanical part to another ‖ to send (a signal) by radio waves or over a wire ‖ *v.i.* to send out a signal by radio waves or over a wire **trans·mít·ter** *n.* a person who or thing which transmits [fr. L. *transmittere*, to send across]

trans·mog·ri·fy (trænzmógrifai, trænsmógrifai) *v.t. pres. part.* **trans·mog·ri·fy·ing** *past* and *past part.* **trans·mog·ri·fied** to change or alter utterly in form or appearance, esp. with grotesque or humorous effect [origin unknown]

trans·mut·a·bil·i·ty (trænzmju:təbíliti:, trænsmju:təbíliti:) *n.* the state or quality of being transmutable

trans·mut·a·ble (trænzmjú:təb'l, trænsmjú:təb'l) *adj.* capable of being transmuted **trans·mút·a·bly** *adv.* [fr. M.L. *transmutabilis*]

trans·mu·ta·tion (trænzmju:téiʃən, trænsmju:téiʃən) *n.* a transmuting or being transmuted ‖ (*chem.*) the change of one element into another ‖ (*biol.*) the change of one species into another [fr. L.L. *transmutatio* (*transmutationis*)]

trans·mute (trænzmjú:t, trænsmjú:t) *pres. part.* **trans·mut·ing** *past* and *past part.* **trans·mut·ed** *v.t.* to cause to change in form, nature or substance ‖ *v.i.* to be transmuted [fr. L. *transmutare*, to change]

tran·som (trǽnsəm) *n.* a lintel ‖ a horizontal bar in a window (cf. MULLION) or between the top of a door and a window directly over it ‖ a window above the lintel of esp. a door ‖ the horizontal bar of a cross or a gallows ‖ any of various horizontal beams, esp. one supporting the afterdeck of a vessel [M.E. *traunsum* prob. fr. L. *transtrum*, crossbeam]

tran·son·ic (trænsónik) *adj.* (*aeron.*) of, relating to or moving at a speed close to the speed of sound

trans·pa·cif·ic (trænspəsífik, trænzpəsífik) *adj.* on the other side of the Pacific Ocean ‖ crossing the Pacific Ocean

trans·par·en·cy (trænspéərənsi:, trænzpéərənsi:, trænspǽrənsi:, trænzpǽrənsi:) *pl.* **trans·par·en·cies** *n.* the state or quality of being transparent ‖ something transparent, esp. a color photograph, picture or design imprinted on a thin transparent piece of film, glass etc. and viewed by transmitted light [fr. M.L. *transparentia*]

tran·spar·ent (trænspéərənt, trænzpéərənt, trænspǽrənt, trænzpǽrənt) *adj.* of a medium through which light can travel with minimal scattering, so that objects can be viewed clearly through it (cf. TRANSLUCENT, cf. OPAQUE) ‖ easy to detect or perceive, *a transparent lie* ‖ of a medium through which radiation of any sort can travel without deformation [fr. M.L. *transparens* (*transparentis*) fr. *transparere*, to appear through]

trans·pierce (trænspíərs, trænzpíərs) *v.t. pres. part.* **trans·pierc·ing** *past* and *past part.* **trans·pierced** to pierce through [F. *transpercer*]

tran·spi·ra·tion (trænspəréiʃən) *n.* the giving off of water vapor through the pores or stomata ‖ the passage of gas through a capillary tube or porous substance because of pressure or temperature differences [fr. M.L. or Mod. L. *transpiratio* (*transpirationis*)]

tran·spire (trænspáiər) *pres. part.* **tran·spir·ing** *past* and *past part.* **tran·spired** *v.i.* to become known or apparent ‖ (*pop.*) to come about, happen, *it transpired that he could come after all* ‖ to emit a gas or liquid through tissues or pores, e.g. (of plants) to give off watery vapor ‖ to be emitted as a gas or liquid ‖ *v.t.* to give off (water vapor, perspiration) through pores or stomata [F. *transpirer*]

trans·plant 1. (trænsplǽnt, trænzplǽnt, trænsplɑ́nt, trænzplɑ́nt) *v.t.* to remove and plant in another place ‖ to settle (people or animals) in another area ‖ (*surgery*) to graft (living tissue or an organ) from one part of the body to another or from one person to another ‖ *v.i.* to bear being transplanted **2.** (trǽnsplænt, trǽnzplænt, trǽnsplɑnt, trǽnzplɑnt) *n.* a transplanting ‖ something transplanted, e.g. body tissue **trans·plan·tá·tion** *n.* [fr. L. *transplantare*]

trans·plan·tate (trænsplǽntət) *n.* (*med.*) tissue that has been used in a transplant

tran·spon·der (trænspóndə:r) *n.* device capable of receiving a signal and responding immediately, e.g., in a satellite

trans·port 1. (trænspɔ́rt, trænzpɔ́rt, trænspóurt, trænzpóurt) *v.t.* to carry (goods, people or animals) from one place to another ‖ (*hist.*) to ship (a convict) to a penal colony overseas ‖ to cause (a person) to be carried away with strong emotion **2.** (trǽnspɔrt, trǽnzpɔrt, trǽnspourt, trǽnzpourt) *n.* the act or process of transporting ‖ a vessel or vehicle, esp. a ship or large aircraft, used to transport ‖ (*hist.*) a convict sentenced to be transported ‖ the state of being very strongly moved by an emotion, *in a transport of rage* ‖ (*computer*) the mechanism that carries disk, tape, or paper past the sensing and recording heads **trans·por·tá·tion** *n.* a transporting or being transported ‖ a means of transporting ‖ the cost of transporting ‖ (*hist.*) the punishment of shipping a convict to a penal colony [fr. F. *transporter*]

Transportation, U.S. Department of (*abbr.* DOT) a cabinet-level department of the U.S. government. Established in 1966, it is headed by the secretary of transportation. Major divisions are U.S. Coast Guard, Federal Aviation Administration, Federal Highway Administration, Federal Railroad Administration, Urban Mass Transportation Administration, Maritime Administration, St. Lawrence Seaway Development Corp. and National Highway Traffic Safety Administration

transporter bridge a bridge with a high span from which a movable platform is suspended on which loads can be conveyed across a navigable waterway without disturbing shipping

trans·pose (trænspóuz, trænzpóuz) *pres. part.* **trans·pos·ing** *past* and *past part.* **trans·posed** *v.t.* to cause (two things) to change places, each being made to occupy the position previously occupied by the other (esp. words in a sentence, sentences in a paragraph etc.) ‖ (*algebra*) to move (a term) from one side to the other of an equation sign (involving a change of sign) ‖ to write or play (a musical composition) in a key other than the original ‖ *v.i.* to write or play music in a key other than the original ‖ to admit of transposing [F. *transposer*]

transposing instrument a musical instrument, e.g. the clarinet, that sounds at a fixed interval above or below the note written

trans·po·si·tion (trænspəzíʃən, trænzpəzíʃən) *n.* a transposing or being transposed ‖ something transposed [prob. F. or fr. M.L. *transpositio* (*transpositionis*) fr. L. *transponere*, to place across]

trans·sex·u·al (trænsékʃu:əl) *n.* a person of one sex who undergoes surgery to modify his or her sex organs to become physically like the opposite sex, commonly because of psychological identity with the other sex —**transsexual** *adj.* —**transsexualism** *n.*

trans·ship (trænsʃíp, trænzʃíp) *pres. part.* **trans·ship·ping** *past* and *past part.* **trans·shipped** *v.t.* to transfer (men or cargo) from one ship or vehicle to another ‖ *v.i.* to leave one ship or vehicle and board another **trans·shíp·ment** *n.*

Trans-Si·be·ri·an Railroad (trænssaibíəri:ən, trænzsaibíəri:ən) the world's longest railroad, in the U.S.S.R., from Chelyabinsk in the Urals to Vladivostok on the Pacific (4,388 miles). Built 1891-1915, it greatly speeded up the colonization of Siberia and the development of industrially important mineral deposits (*KUZNETZ, *KARAGANDA)

tran·sub·stan·ti·ate (trænsəbstǽnʃi:eit) *pres. part.* **tran·sub·stan·ti·at·ing** *past* and *past part.* **tran·sub·stan·ti·at·ed** *v.t.* to change from one substance to another ‖ (*Roman Catholicism*) to effect transubstantiation in (the sacramental elements) **tran·sub·stan·ti·á·tion** *n.* (*Roman Catholicism*) the doctrine that the sacramental elements of bread and wine, when consecrated in the Mass, are changed into the body and blood of the risen Christ (cf. CONSUBSTANTIATION, cf. IMPANATION) [fr. M.L. *transubstantiare (transubstantiatus)*]

tran·su·date (trǽnsudeit) *n.* a fluid which has passed through a membrane or other permeable substance [fr. Mod. L. *transudare (transudatus)*, to transude]

tran·su·da·tion (trænsudéiʃən) *n.* a transuding or being transuded ‖ a transudate [F. *transudation*]

tran·sude (trænsú:d) *pres. part.* **tran·sud·ing** *past* and *past part.* **tran·sud·ed** *v.i.* to pass through a membrane or other permeable substance ‖ *v.t.* to cause to pass through a membrane etc., to exude [F. *transuder*]

trans·u·ran·ic (trænsjurǽnik, trænzjurǽnik) *adj.* pertaining to the artificial, radioactive elements having atomic numbers greater than that of uranium (92) (*PERIODIC TABLE)

Trans·vaal, the (trǽnzvɑl, trǽnsvɑl) the northern province (area 109,621 sq. miles, pop. 8,351,000) of South Africa. Capital: Pretoria. Chief city: Johannesburg. It is largely veld (3,000–6,000 ft), sloping down from the Drakensberg Mtns to the Vaal and Limpopo Rivers. Agriculture: stock raising, corn and other cereals, potatoes, citrus fruits. Resources: gold (leading world producer), coal, diamonds, copper, tin, asbestos, chrome. Industries: metallurgy, iron and steel, electrical products, chemicals, textiles, food processing, engineering. There are three universities: Witwatersrand, Pretoria and Potchefstroom. HISTORY. The indigenous Matabele were defeated (1836-8) by Boers of the Great Trek, and an independent Boer republic was established (1856). It was annexed by Britain (1877) but rebelled successfully (1881). The discovery (1886) of gold at Witwatersrand brought many new immigrants, known as Uitlanders, to the Transvaal. After the Boer War (1899-1902), the Transvaal became a British colony (1902). It joined the Union of South Africa (1910)

trans·ver·sal (trænzvə́:rs'l, trænsvə́:rs'l) **1.** *adj.* transverse **2.** *n.* (*geom.*) a straight line intersecting other lines [fr. M.L. *transversalis*]

trans·verse 1. (trænzvə́:rs, trænsvə́:rs, trǽnzvə:rs, trǽnsvə:rs) *adj.* crossing from side to side or lying across or crosswise **2.** (trænzvə́:rs, trænsvə́:rs) *v.t. pres. part.* **trans·vers·ing** *past* and *past part.* **trans·versed** to lie across or pass across **3.** (trænzvə́:rs, trænsvə́:rs, trǽnzvə:rs, trǽnsvə:rs) *n.* something transverse, esp. a muscle which is transverse to other parts of the body [fr. L. *transvertere (transversus)*, to turn across]

transverse wave a wave (e.g. a water wave or an electromagnetic wave) in which the vibrating element (e.g. the particles of the medium or field vector) oscillates in a direction perpendicular to the direction of propagation of the wave

trans·ves·tism (trænzvéstizəm, trænsvéstizəm) *n.* (*psychol.*) the practice of dressing in the clothes of the opposite sex as a form of sexual inversion [fr. G. *transvestismus*]

trans·ves·tite (trænzvéstait, trænsvéstait) *n.* (*psychol.*) someone who practices transvestism [G. *transvestit*]

Tran·syl·va·ni·a (trænsilvéini:ə) the northwestern region of Rumania, a fertile, wooded plateau surrounded north, east and south by the Carpathians: cereals, fruit, cattle raising. Natural gas and lignite are exploited. Chief town: Cluj

Tran·syl·va·ni·an Alps (trænsilvéini:ən) the southern range of the Carpathians in S.W. Rumania between Transylvania and Walachia. Highest point: Negoi (8,346 ft)

tran·yl·cy·pro·mine [$C_9H_{11}N$] (trænilsaipróumi:n) *n.* (*pharm.*) a monoamine oxidase inhibitor used as an antidepressant; marketed as Parnate

trap (træp) **1.** *n.* a man-made device into which an animal may enter unawares, or be driven or lured, and in which it is captured and sometimes killed ‖ something devised to put an unsuspecting person in a situation which is to his disadvantage and from which it is hard or impossible for him to escape ‖ any hidden hazard, *a linguistic trap* ‖ a device, e.g. a water-filled bend, in a pipe, to prevent noxious gases from passing (e.g. in the outflow pipe of a sink, toilet etc.) ‖ a light, horse-drawn, two or four-wheeled passenger vehicle, the body of which is supported on springs ‖ (*sports*) a compartment or other device from which e.g. a racing greyhound or clay pigeons can be suddenly released ‖ (*golf*) a bunker ‖ a trapdoor ‖ (*mus., pl.*) the percussion instruments of a dance band **2.** *v. pres. part.* **trap·ping** *past* and *past part.* **trapped** *v.t.* to catch in a trap or as if in a trap ‖ to furnish with a trap, *to trap a pipe* ‖ to prevent (a gas, liquid etc.) from passing or proceeding further ‖ *v.i.* to set traps for game [O.E. *treppe, trœppe*]

trap *n.* (*geol.*) any of various dark igneous rocks, e.g. basalt, which have a structure resembling a flight of steps [Swed. *trapp*]

trap·door (trǽpdɔ́r, trǽpdóur) *n.* a small, sliding, lifting or hinged door in a floor, roof or ceiling

trapdoor spider a member of *Ctenizidae,* a family of large spiders living in warm, dry climates, which construct subterranean dwellings lined with silk and closed by a hinged door. The spider sits behind this and waits for prey

tra·peze (trəpí:z) *n.* a short horizontal bar suspended by two parallel ropes or wires, used by gymnasts and acrobats [F. *trapèze*]

tra·pe·zi·um (trəpí:zi:əm) *pl.* **tra·pe·zi·ums, tra·pe·zi·a** (trəpí:zi:ə) *n.* (*Am.=Br.* trapezoid) a quadrilateral having no two sides parallel ‖ (*Br.=Am.* trapezoid) a quadrilateral with two sides parallel ‖ (*anat.*) a small bone of the wrist near the base of the thumb [Mod. L. fr. Gk]

tra·pe·zi·us (trəpí:zi:əs) *n.* one of a pair of large, flat triangular muscles of the back serving to rotate the scapula [Mod. L. *trapezius*]

tra·pe·zo·he·dron (trəpi:zouhí:drən, træpizouhí:drən) *pl.* **tra·pe·zo·he·drons, tra·pe·zo·he·dra** (trəpi:zouhí:drə, træpizouhí:drə) *n.* a solid figure, the faces of which are trapezoids [Mod. L. fr. *trapezium*+Gk *hedra*, a seat]

trap·e·zoid (trǽpizɔid) **1.** *n.* (*Am.=Br.* trapezium) an irregular four-sided figure with two sides parallel ‖ (*Br.=Am.* trapezium) a quadrilateral having no two sides parallel ‖ (*anat.*) a small bone of the wrist near the base of the index finger **2.** *adj.* of, or in the form of, a trapezoid **trap·e·zói·dal** *adj.* [Mod. L. fr. Gk]

trap·per (trǽpər) *n.* a person who traps wild animals, esp. for their furs

trap·pings (trǽpiŋz) *pl. n.* ornamental equipment or embellishments, esp. those associated with an official position ‖ a horse's ornamented cloth covering, caparison

Trap·pist (trǽpist) **1.** *adj.* of or pertaining to the austere reform of the Cistercian order carried out (c. 1664) by de Rancé, on the principles of strict seclusion from the world, silence and liturgical worship for seven hours daily **2.** *n.* a Cistercian monk under the Trappist rule [fr. F. *trappiste* after *La Trappe,* an abbey in Normandy where the reform began]

traps (træps) *pl. n.* (Br., pop.) personal effects [prob. fr. TRAPPINGS]

trap·shoot·ing (trǽpʃu:tiŋ) *n.* the sport of shooting at clay pigeons catapulted into the air from traps

trash (træʃ) **1.** *n.* shoddily made articles ‖ rubbish ‖ meaningless talk or writing, nonsense ‖ worthless books etc. ‖ (without article) people considered as of no account ‖ loppings off trees, hedges etc. ‖ bagasse **2.** *v.t.* to lop (trees) ‖ to strip the outer leaves from (immature sugarcane) [origin unknown] ‖ (*slang*) to turn something into trash by vandalism, spoilation, or (figuratively) disparagement

trash·i·ly (trǽʃili:) *adv.* in a trashy manner

trash·i·ness (trǽʃi:nis) *n.* the state or quality of being trashy

trash·y (trǽʃi:) *comp.* **trash·i·er** *superl.* **trash·i·est** *adj.* of or like trash (shoddily made articles, nonsense)

Tras·i·mene (trǽzəmi:n) (*Ital.* Trasimeno) a lake (area 50 sq. miles) near Perugia in the Central Apennines, Italy, the scene of Hannibal's ambush of the Roman consul Flaminius (217 B.C.)

Trasop (*acronym*) for investment tax credit employee stock ownership plan, from the Technical Corrections Act of 1979

trass (træs) *n.* (*geol.*) a volcanic rock rich in fragments of pumice, used in making hydraulic cement [Du. *tras*]

trau·ma (tráumə, trɔ́mə) *pl.* **trau·ma·ta** (tráumətə, trɔ́mətə), **trau·mas** *n.* a physical wound or injury ‖ a violent emotional blow, esp. one which has a lasting psychic effect ‖ a neurotic condition resulting from physical or emotional injury [Gk]

trau·mat·ic (trəmǽtik) *adj.* concerning, producing or resulting from trauma [fr. L.L. *traumaticus* fr. Gk]

trau·ma·tism (tráumətizəm, trɔ́mətizəm) *n.* the neurotic condition caused by a trauma ‖ a trauma [fr. Gk *trauma (traumatos)*, a wound]

tra·vail (trəvéil, trǽveil) **1.** *n.* (*rhet.*) the pains of childbirth ‖ (*rhet.*) any intense mental or physical pain or laborious work **2.** *v.i.* (*rhet.*) to suffer the pains of childbirth (*rhet.*) to work hard or painfully [O.F.]

Trav·an·core (trǽvənkɔr) a former princely state in S. India, included since 1956 in Kerala. Chief town: Trivandrum

trav·el (trǽvəl) **1.** *v. pres. part.* **trav·el·ing,** esp. *Br.* **trav·el·ling** *past* and *past part.* **trav·eled,** esp. *Br.*, **trav·elled** *v.i.* to make a journey, esp. one of considerable length ‖ to make journeys abroad ‖ to proceed in a given direction or pass from one point to another, *the pain traveled down his arm* ‖ to be transmitted, *sound waves will not travel through a vacuum* ‖ to seem to move or journey, *thoughts travel fast, her glance traveled over the crowd* ‖ (sometimes with 'in') to work as a traveling salesman, *to travel in encyclopedias* ‖ to bear transporting, *some wines will not travel* ‖ (of a piece of machinery) to move in a set path ‖ *v.t.* to journey over or through (a region etc.) ‖ to cover (a distance) ‖ (of a traveling salesman) to have (a region) as the territory to be covered **to travel light** to travel with the minimum of baggage **2.** *n.* the act or process of traveling ‖ the movement of a piece of machinery in a set path or the extent of this, *the piston has a travel of nine inches* ‖ (also *pl.*) journeys, esp. those made abroad ‖ a branch of literature describing such journeys ‖ the number of people or vehicles traveling on a route, traffic [var. of TRAVAIL]

trav·el·a·tor or **trav·el·la·tor** (trǽvəleit'r) *n.* a moving walkway, e.g., in some airports

trav·eled, esp. *Br.* **trav·elled** (trǽv'ld) *adj.* having experience of traveling, *a much traveled man* ‖ used by travelers, *a much traveled route* ‖ (*geol.*) erratic

trav·el·er, esp. *Br.* **trav·el·ler** (trǽvələr) *n.* a person who travels ‖ (*Br.*) a commercial traveler ‖ a piece of machinery, e.g. a type of crane, constructed to slide laterally along a support ‖ (*naut.*) an iron ring that slides up and down a rope or spar

traveler's check, *Br.* **traveller's cheque** a check, purchased from a banking concern, which can be cashed when presented at any of the bank's correspondents anywhere, or can be used for purchases

trav·el·er's-joy, esp. Br. **trav·el·ler's-joy** (trǽvələrzdʒɔi) *n. Clematis vitalba,* the wild clematis

trav·el·er's-tree, esp. *Br.* **trav·el·ler's-tree** (trǽvələrztri:) *n. Ravenala madagascariensis,* fam. *Musaceae,* a subtropical or tropical tree having leaf petioles which contain a clear, watery, drinkable sap

traveling salesman (*Am.=Br.* commercial traveller) a manufacturer's representative who goes from retailer to retailer to secure orders

trav·e·logue, trav·e·log (trǽvəlɔg, trǽvəlɒg) *n.* a documentary film describing a foreign country ‖ a lecture on a journey, illustrated by slides etc.

trav·erse (trǽvə:rs) **1.** *n.* the action or instance of traversing ‖ something which lies or goes across, e.g. a section of a road, cut in diagonals up a steep hillside ‖ a bar, line etc. placed across something ‖ a sideways course, e.g. of a climber negotiating an obstacle to upward movement ‖ a place where it is necessary to follow such a course ‖ a zigzag course followed, e.g. by a ship at sea or by a skier ‖ a survey made in a series of legs, the end of one being the start of the next ‖ one of the legs of such a survey ‖ a curtain divided vertically and running on a rail, wire etc. as part of stage scenery ‖ (*geom.*) a transversal line ‖ (*mach.*) the sideways movement of a part ‖ (*mach.*) a device for imparting this movement ‖ the horizontal sweep of a gun ‖ (*law*) the formal denial of an allegation etc. ‖ (*manège*) the movement of a horse forward and sideways, with the head turned to one side and the tail to the other ‖ (*fencing*) the act of traversing **2.** *adj.* transverse [O.F. *travers* and *traverse*]

tra·verse (trəvə́:rs, trǽvə:rs) *pres. part.* **tra·vers·ing** *past* and *past part.* **tra·versed** *v.t.* to move across or through ‖ to move back and forth along ‖ to extend across ‖ to turn (a gun) and direct it on its target ‖ to make a survey of by means of a traverse ‖ (*law*) to deny the truth of (an allegation etc.) ‖ (*law*) to deny or take issue upon (an indictment) ‖ *v.i.* to go across, along, up and down etc. ‖ to pivot laterally ‖ (*climbing, skiing, survey.* etc.) to make a traverse ‖ (*manège*) to execute a traverse ‖ (*fencing*) to slide one's blade toward the opponent's hilt while applying pressure to his blade [O.F. *traverser*]

trav·er·tin (trǽvərtin) *n.* travertine

trav·er·tine (trǽvərti:n) *n.* a buff-colored porous mineral, formed in streams and esp. hot springs by the deposition of calcium carbonate. It hardens on exposure to the air and is used as a building stone in warm climates, esp. Italy [Ital. *travertino*]

trav·es·ty (trǽvisti:) **1.** *pl.* **trav·es·ties** *n.* a grotesque or crude imitation intended to make a thing imitated appear ridiculous ‖ a ridiculously inferior imitation **2.** *v.t. pres. part.* **trav·es·ty·ing** *past* and *past part.* **trav·es·tied** to make a travesty of [F. *travesti,* disguised]

Trav·is (trǽvɔs), William B. (1809-36), U.S. lawyer and soldier, a hero of the Texas Revolution. He participated in the capture of San Antonio (1835) and led the defense against Mexican siege (Feb. 23–March 6, 1836) of the Alamo, where he died

trawl (trɔl) **1.** *n.* a large, wide-mouthed bag net which is dragged along the bottom of the sea for fish by a boat ‖ a trot (for fishing) **2.** *v.i.* to fish with a trawl ‖ *v.t.* to catch (fish) with a trawl **tráwl·er** *n.* a boat used to catch fish by using trawl nets [etym. doubtful]

tray (trei) *n.* a flat piece of wood, metal, plastic etc., usually rimmed, for carrying or holding small, light objects ‖ the contents of a tray ‖ a shallow lidless compartment in a traveling trunk etc. [O.E. *trīg*]

treach·er·ous (trétʃərəs) *adj.* of the character or actions of a traitor ‖ unreliable, full of hazards, *treacherous ice* [O.F. *trecheros*]

treach·er·y (trétʃəri:) *pl.* **treach·er·ies** *n.* disloyalty, perfidy ‖ treason ‖ an act of disloyalty or treason [O.F. *tricherie, trecherie* fr. *tricher,* to cheat]

trea·cle (trí:k'l) *n.* (*Br.*) molasses **tréa·cly** *adj.* thick and sticky [M.E. *tryacle, triacle*]

tread (tred) **1.** *v. pres. part.* **tread·ing** *past* **trod** (trɒd) *past part.* **trod·den** (trɒ́d'n), **trod** *v.i.* to move on foot, to walk, *to tread lightly across the room* ‖ to set the foot down, *to tread on a cigarette stub, tread in a puddle* ‖ to put down the foot so as to exert pressure, *to tread on the accelerator* ‖ (of a male bird) to copulate ‖ to proceed, *tread cautiously in your dealings with him* ‖ *v.t.* to beat down or wear away by walking on, *to tread a path, to tread a hole in a carpet* ‖ to pack down by pressing with a foot or feet, *to tread soil around newly planted seedlings* ‖ to crush with the foot or feet, *to tread grapes* ‖ (*rhet.*) to walk on, *to tread dry land* ‖ (of a male bird) to copulate with (a female bird) ‖ (*Br.*) to track (mud etc.) **to tread down** to oppress ‖ to wear down **to tread on** (*Br.*) to dismiss (a suggestion, idea) summarily **to tread on someone's toes** to offend someone esp. by usurping his prerogatives **to tread water** to keep oneself upright and one's head above water level in water where one is out of one's depth, by moving one's feet up and down with treading movements **2.** *n.* the action, sound or way of treading, *we heard his tread on the stairs, a heavy tread* ‖ the horizontal part of a step in a staircase (cf. RISER) ‖ the width of this from front to back ‖ a piece of e.g. rubber put on a step to protect the step from becoming worn ‖ the undersurface of a shoe or the thickened, scored face of a tire which makes contact with the ground ‖ a chalaza of a bird's egg [O.E. *tredan*]

trea·dle (tréd'l) **1.** *n.* a foot-operated lever on a machine etc. **2.** *v.i. pres. part.* **trea·dling** *past* and *past part.* **trea·dled** to operate a treadle [O.E. fr. *tredan*]

tread·mill (trédmil) *n.* (*hist.*) a mill worked by people constantly treading on steps set in the circumference of the great mill wheel. The work was formerly a punishment for prisoners ‖ a mill driven by an animal treading on an endless belt ‖ any wearyingly monotonous activity

trea·son (trí:z'n) *n.* an attempt to overthrow by illegal means the government to which a person owes allegiance ‖ the act or attempted act of working for the enemies of the state ‖ (*Br.*) an attempt to kill or injure the sovereign ‖ betrayal of trust, disloyalty (to a cause, friend etc.) **tréa·son·a·ble, tréa·son·ous** *adjs* [F. *tresun*]

treas·ure (tréʒər) **1.** *n.* anything very valuable ‖ (*hist.*) a store of money, jewels etc. ‖ a person whom one thinks of as being of rare excellence **2.** *v.t. pres. part.* **treas·ur·ing** *past* and *past part.* **treas·ured** to value highly ‖ to keep in the memory with special pleasure, *to treasure someone's words* [O.F. *tresor*]

treas·ur·er (tréʒərər) *n.* an official in charge of the finances of a government, society etc. ‖ a governmental officer in charge of the receipt, care and paying out of public money [A.F. *tresorer*]

treasure trove money, jewels etc., of unknown ownership, found hidden [A.F. *tresor trové*]

treas·ur·y (tréʒəri:) *pl.* **treas·ur·ies** *n.* a building used to store money, valuables etc. ‖ (esp. in book titles) a collection of things prized, *a treasury of poetry* ‖ the funds of a society, corporation, state etc. **Treas·ur·y** a government department responsible for the public revenue and expenditure or the buildings in which the business of this department is transacted [O.F. *tresorie*]

treasury bill a government obligation bearing no interest but issued at a discount and payable at par when it matures (usually in 90 days)

treasury bond a government promissory note, valid for not more than five years and bearing a fixed rate of interest

treasury note a currency note issued by the U.S. Treasury Department ‖ (*Br., hist.*) a £1 or 10-shilling currency note issued by the Treasury 1914–28

Treasury, U.S. Department of the a cabinet-level department of the U.S. government that oversees the nation's finances. Established in 1789, its first secretary was Alexander Hamilton. The secretary of the treasury ranks second in the president's cabinet, is the president's chief adviser on fiscal affairs, and is required by law to report to Congress each year on the government's fiscal operations and its financial condition. The secretary must also manage the public debt and conduct financial dealings with other nations. Operating bureaus of the Treasury Department include Comptroller of the Currency, U.S. Customs Service, Bureau of Engraving and Printing, Internal Revenue Service, U.S. Mint, Bureau of Alcohol, Tobacco and Firearms, and the Secret Service

Treasury Bench (*Br.*) the front bench occupied by British government ministers in the House of Commons

treat (tri:t) **1.** *v.t.* to behave toward (someone or something), *I don't like the way he treats his dog* ‖ to regard in a specified way, *to treat something as a joke* ‖ to pay for the food, drink or entertainment etc. of (another person) ‖ to give medical attention to (a patient) ‖ to try to cure or alleviate (a disease) ‖ to subject to chemical action ‖ to cover or coat with some preparation ‖ (sometimes with 'of') to expound or be an exposition of (something) in words or writing, *the book treats two main topics* ‖ *v.i.* (sometimes with 'with') to negotiate ‖ to pay for another's food, drink or entertainment etc. ‖ (with 'of') to offer an exposition or discussion **2.** *n.* something that gives special delight, pleasure or satisfaction ‖ one's turn to pay for the food, drinks or entertainment of another or others [O.F. *tretier, traitier*]

treat-and-re·lease (trí:tændrilí:s) *n.* hospital policy of providing only emergency out-patient treatment and refusing to admit patients when a hospital has few available beds

trea·tise (trí:tis) *n.* a written study of a particular subject, dealt with systematically and thoroughly [A.F. *tretiz*]

treat·ment (trí:tmənt) *n.* the act or a method or manner of treating someone or something ‖ medical or surgical care ‖ an instance of this ‖ a detailed outline of the plot of a proposed screenplay or television script

trea·ty (trí:ti:) *pl.* **trea·ties** *n.* a formal, signed and ratified agreement between states [A.F. *treté*]

treaty port (*hist.*) a port opened by treaty to foreign trade, esp. in 19th-c. China

Treb·i·zond (trébizɒnd) (*Turk.* Trabzon) a port (pop. 107,412 of Turkey on the Black Sea. Founded as a Greek colony (8th c. B.C.) on the trade route from central Europe to Asia, it became famous as the center of an empire founded (1204) by the Comnenus family. It fell (1461) to the Turks. Byzantine churches

tre·ble (tréb'l) **1.** *adj.* three times as much, as many or as great ‖ consisting of or existing in three parts ‖ (*mus.*, of a voice or instrument) singing or playing the upper part in musical harmony ‖ (*mus.*) of or for a soprano, esp. (*Br.*) a boy soprano, or of the upper part in instrumental music ‖ high-pitched **2.** *n.* the highest singing voice ‖ (*Br.*) a boy soprano or boy soprano voice ‖ the upper part of a musical composition ‖ an instrument playing this part ‖ (*old-fash.*) a highpitched voice or sound ‖ (*change ringing*) the highest bell of a ring [O.F.]

treble *pres. part.* **tre·bling** *past* and *past part.* **tre·bled** *v.t.* to make three times as much, as many or as great ‖ *v.i.* to become three times as much, as many or as great

treble clef (*mus.*) the symbol (𝄞) placing G above middle C on the second line of the staff from the bottom. Parts for high-pitched instruments and voices and right-hand piano parts are written in the treble clef

treble staff *pl.* **treble staves** (*mus.*) the staff carrying the treble clef

tre·cen·to (tretʃéntou) *n.* the 14th c. in Italy with respect to its art, architecture etc. [Ital. short for *mil trecento,* 1300]

tre·de·cil·lion (treidisíljən) *n.* *NUMBER TABLE [fr. L. *tres,* three+DECILLION]

tree (tri:) **1.** *n.* any tall, perennial, woody plant usually with a single elongated stem (trunk) and having a head of branches and foliage, or foliage only ‖ anything resembling this, or thought of as resembling this, esp. as having branches spreading from a single stem, *family tree* ‖ (in compounds) part of a structure or implement, *axletree* ‖ a shoe tree ‖ (*chem.*) a tree-shaped mass of crystals **the Tree** the cross on which Christ died **up a tree** in a tight or difficult situation ‖ (*computer*) a directed graph in which each node has one or more predecessors (parents), used in logic **2.** *v.t.* to chase up a tree ‖ to stretch (a shoe) on a shoe tree ‖ to place in a difficult situation [O.E. *trēow*]

tree bark a rippled or wavy effect caused by bias tensions that sometimes appears on a bonded fabric when it is stretched horizontally

tree creeper *Certhia familiaris,* fam. *Certhiidae,* a small brown and buff European bird with a silvery underside. It climbs trees spirally searching for food in the bark ‖ *Certhia familiaris americana,* also called 'brown creeper'

tree diagram (*linguistics*) in transformational grammar, a diagram of components as branches of the sentence structure

tree fern a member of *Cyatheaceae* or *Marattiaceae,* families of tropical treelike ferns

tree frog any of various arboreal frogs of fam. *Polypedatidae.* They have adhesive suckers on the toes

tree line the limit above which trees do not grow on mountains or in high latitudes

tree·nail, tre·nail (trí:neil) *n.* a wooden peg which swells in its hole when moistened and is used to fasten timbers together, esp. in shipbuilding

tree of heaven a member of *Ailanthus,* fam. *Simaroubaceae,* a genus of ornamental trees grown esp. for shade

tree toad a tree frog

tree·top (trí:tɒp) *n.* the top branches of a tree

tre·foil (trí:fɔil) *n.* a clover ‖ (*archit.*) an ornament with three lobes or cusps in window tracery etc. [A.F. *trifoil*]

Treitsch·ke (tráitʃkə), Heinrich von (1834-96), German historian. His strongly nationalist views had a considerable influence on Germany in the 20th c. His main work was his 'History of Germany in the Nineteenth Century' (1874-94)

trek (trek) **1.** *v.i. pres. part.* **trek·king** *past* and *past part.* **trekked** (*hist.*) to travel by ox wagon ‖ to make a long, hard or tedious journey **2.** *n.* (*hist.*) a long journey by ox wagon or a stage on the journey ‖ a long, hard or tedious journey or leg of a journey (*GREAT TREK) [Afrik. fr. Du. *trekken*]

trel·lis (trélis) **1.** *n.* a flat, light frame consisting of wooden or metal latticelike strips crossing one another in various patterns, used as a screen or for plants to climb on **2.** *v.t.* to furnish with a trellis ‖ to train on a trellis [O.F. *treliz, trelis, trelice*]

trel·lis·work (tréliswə:rk) *n.* latticework of wooden or metal strips

trem·a·tode (trémətoud) *n.* a member of *Trematoda,* a class of *Platyhelminthes,* including flukes and parasitic flatworms. Most of these move by muscular action and have organs of attachment consisting of suckers and hooks. The life history of some trematodes (e.g. liver fluke) is completed in two hosts [fr. Mod. L. *Trematoda* fr. Gk fr. *trēma* (*trēmatos*), hole]

trem·blant (trémblənt) *adj.* constructed with springs to create a vibrating motion, e.g., in jewelry

trem·ble (trémb'l) **1.** *v.i. pres. part.* **trem·bling** *past* and *past part.* **trem·bled** to shake involuntarily from fear, excitement etc. ‖ to vibrate with light, rapid movements **2.** *n.* a trembling or fit of trembling **trém·bler** *n.* (*elec.*) the automatic vibrator which makes and breaks an electric circuit, e.g. in a type of electric bell ‖ any of various birds of genera *Cinclocerthia* and *Rhamphocinclus*, fam. *Mimidae*, found in the West Indies **trém·bles** *pl. n.* the poisoning of livestock, esp. cattle, by an alcohol present in *Eupatorium rugosum* and some other plants. It can be fatal **trém·bly** *comp.* **trem·bli·er** *superl.* **trem·bli·est** *adj.* trembling, shaky [O.F. *trembler*]

tre·men·dous (triméndəs) *adj.* enormous ‖ arousing awe or wonder because of extreme size, power, majesty etc. [fr. L. *tremendus*]

trem·o·lan·do (trɛməlǽndou) *adv.* (*mus.*) with a tremolo effect [Ital.]

trem·o·lant (tréməlǝnt) **1.** *adj.* (esp. of certain organ pipes) having a vibrating note **2.** *n.* an organ pipe whose notes have a vibrating quality ‖ a device in a musical instrument which causes a note to have vibrating quality

trem·o·lite (tréməlait) *n.* a calcium magnesium silicate [after *Tremola*, in Switzerland, where it was discovered]

trem·o·lo (tréməlou) *pl.* **trem·o·los** *n.* the quick repetition of a single note on a stringed instrument produced by rapid bowing up and down ‖ the quick alternation between two notes on an instrument ‖ an organ stop which produces a vibrating effect ‖ a rapid variation of pitch in the singing voice, esp. as a fault [Ital.]

trem·or (trémər) *n.* a trembling, e.g. in poplar leaves ‖ a vibration such as accompanies an earthquake ‖ a quavering sound in speaking ‖ an involuntary quivering of the limbs etc. from weakness, disease or age ‖ a shudder such as marks the onset of fever ‖ a state of tremulous excitement [O.F. *tremor, tremour*]

trem·u·lant (trémjulənt) **1.** *adj.* tremulous **2.** *n.* (*mus.*) a tremolo (organ stop) [fr. L. *tremulans* (*tremulantis*) fr. *tremulare*, to tremble]

trem·u·lous (trémjuləs) *adj.* trembling ‖ apprehensive ‖ betraying apprehension ‖ quivering, e.g. with excitement [fr. L. *tremulus*]

trenail *TREENAIL

trench (trentʃ) *n.* a long, narrow and usually deep hollow cut in the ground ‖ (*mil.*) such a hollow with parapets formed of the earth dug out of it, often strengthened with sandbags, for protecting soldiers from enemy fire [O.F. *trenche*]

trench *v.t.* to dig (ground) in order to make a trench ‖ to dig (ground) in successive trenches so that the soil well below the surface is brought to the top ‖ *v.i.* to dig a trench or trenches ‖ (with 'on' or 'upon') to encroach [O.F. *trenchier*]

trench·an·cy (tréntʃənsi:) *n.* the state or quality of being trenchant

trench·ant (tréntʃənt) *adj.* keen and effective, vigorous, *trenchant measures* ‖ penetrating, incisive, *trenchant criticisms* ‖ (*biol.*) adapted for cutting [O.F.]

trench coat a thick, usually lined, double-breasted, belted, waterproof coat having deep pockets and sleeves with buckled straps on them

trench·er (tréntʃər) *n.* (*hist.*) a wooden board on which meat used to be carved [A.F. *trenchour*]

trench·er·man (tréntʃərmən) *pl.* **trench·er·men** (tréntʃərmən) *n.* (*rhet.*, used with the epithets 'good', 'stout' etc.) a hearty eater

trench fever an intermittent fever, thought to be transmitted by body lice. It affected soldiers living for long periods in the trenches in the lst world war

trench foot a condition of the feet characterized by chilblains, swelling and sharp pain, sometimes leading to gangrene, caused by prolonged standing under cold, wet conditions

trench mortar a light mortar which lobs a small bomb or grenade from a trench

trench mouth Vincent's infection

trend (trend) **1.** *n.* a tendency, general direction, *the trend of public opinion* ‖ a dominant movement revealed by a statistical process, *decennial price trends* **2.** *v.i.* to have a tendency or general direction [O.E. *trendan*]

tren·dy (tréndi:) *adj.* (*slang or colloq.*) fashion-following —**trendily** *adv.* —**trendiness** *n.* —**trendsetter** *n.* —**trendsetting** *adj.*

Treng·ga·nu (treŋgánu:) a state (area 5,027 sq. miles, pop. 542,280) of Malaysia in E. Malaya. Capital: Kuala Trengganu (pop. 29,000). Transferred (1909) from Siam to Britain, it joined the Federation of Malaya (1948)

Trent (trent) a river (170 miles long, navigable for 95) flowing from N. Staffordshire, England, to the Humber

Trent *TRENTO

Trent Affair an Anglo-U.S. incident (1861) during the Civil War. The U.S. warship 'San Jacinto' detained the British vessel 'Trent' and seized two Confederate commissioners on board. Great Britain, outraged by this violation of its neutrality, deliberated a declaration of war against the Union. War was averted (1862) when the U.S.A. disavowed the act and released the Confederate prisoners

Trent, Council of the 19th ecumenical council, held at Trento (1545-7, 1551-2, 1562-3). Certain Catholic doctrines were freshly formulated in the spirit of the Counter-Reformation, in an attempt to strengthen the Roman Catholic Church doctrinally and administratively against Protestantism

trente-et-qua·rante (trɑnteikærɑnt) *n.* rouge et noir [F.]

Tren·ti·no-Al·to A·di·ge (trentí:nɔáltɔádi:dʒe) an autonomous region (area 5,256 sq. miles, pop. 876,249) of Italy in the Alps, comprised of the semiautonomous provinces of Alto Adige or South Tirol (language: 65% German, 32% Italian, 3% Ladin) and Trentino (Italian-speaking). Alternating capitals: Bolzano (*G.* Bozen), Trento. Industries: cattle-raising, fruit, tourism. HISTORY. The whole area was given to Austria (1815), but Trentino passed to Italy (1866). Austria attempted to Germanize Alto Adige, provoking the Irredentist movement, but this and Trentino were given to Italy (1919), and Austrian agitation increased. Despite a large degree of automony granted in 1947, the problem continued to cause tension between Italy and Austria

Tren·to (tréntɔ) a communications center (pop. 91,767) and capital (alternating with Bolzano) of Trentino-Alto Adige, Italy, in Trentino on the River Adige. Byzantine cathedral (13th-14th cc.) (*TRENT, COUNCIL OF)

Tren·ton (tréntən) the capital city (pop. 92,124) of New Jersey, on the Delaware: textiles, mechanical engineering, light manufacturing. Washington crossed the Delaware near Trenton and decisively defeated the British here (1776)

Trenton and Princeton, Battles of the first engagements (1776-7) of the American Revolution won by Gen. George Washington in the open field. American forces under Washington crossed the Delaware River and surprised and captured (1776) 918 Hessians around Trenton, N.J. The patriots, avoiding a British relief force led by Cornwallis, then struck at Princeton. The battles greatly raised American morale

tre·pan (tripǽn) **1.** *n.* a tool used in boring shafts etc. ‖ a trephine **2.** *v.t. pres. part.* **tre·pan·ning** *past* and *past part.* **tre·panned** to cut out or bore with such a tool ‖ to trephine [fr. M.L. *trepanum* fr. Gk]

tre·pang (tripǽŋ) *n.* any of several holothurians, dried and smoked for use in soup in China [Malay *trīpang*]

tre·phine (trifí:n) **1.** *n.* a small cylindrical saw used in surgery for removing circular disks of bone from the skull **2.** *v. pres. part.* **tre·phin·ing** *past* and *past part.* **tre·phined** *v.t.* to operate on with a trephine ‖ *v.i.* to perform this operation [older *trafine* fr. L. *tres fines*, three ends]

trep·i·da·tion (trɛpidéiʃən) *n.* a state of fear, excitement or apprehension [fr. L. *trepidatio* (*trepidationis*) fr. *trepidare*, to tremble]

tres·pass (tréspəs) **1.** *n.* a trespassing ‖ (*Bible*) a sin ‖ (*law*) an actionable wrong against another's person, property or rights, or an action for damages arising from this **2.** *v.i.* to enter someone's property unlawfully ‖ to encroach or make an undue claim, *to trespass on someone's hospitality* ‖ (*Bible*) to sin ‖ (*law*) to commit a trespass [O.F. fr. *trespasser*]

Tres Pun·tas, Cape (trɛspú:ntɑs) a cape in S. Argentina, at the south entrance to the Gulf of San Jorge

tress (tres) *n.* (*rhet.*) a lock of hair ‖ (*pl.*, *rhet.*) a woman's hair, esp. when long and loose [O.F. *tresce*]

tres·sure (tréʃər) *n.* (*heraldry*) a narrow orle

tres·tle (trés'l) *n.* a pair of hinged or jointed splayed legs used as one of two or more supports on which planks, a tabletop etc. are laid ‖ a braced framework of wood or metal for carrying a road or railroad over a gully or other depression [O.F. *trestel*]

tres·tle·tree (trés'ltri:) *n.* (*naut.*) one of a pair of horizontal fore-and-aft timbers on a mast supporting the crosstrees, topmast etc.

tret·i·noin (trétinɔin) *n.* vitamin A medication used to cause light peeling of the skin in treating acne

Trèves (trev) *TRIER

Tre·vi·so (treví:zɔ) a walled town (pop. 75,000) in Veneto, Italy: Romanesque-Renaissance cathedral, 13th-c. palaces, churches

Trev·i·thick (trévəθik, trəvíθik), Richard (1771-1833), British engineer. He invented the high-pressure steam engine (1800)

trews (tru:z) *pl. n.* the close-fitting tartan pants worn by certain Scottish regiments [Ir. Gael. *trius*]

trey (trei) *n.* a playing card, die or domino having three spots [A.F., O.F. *trei, treis*]

tri- (trai) *prefix* three, consisting of three ‖ three times or into three ‖ occurring every three ‖ (*chem.*) having three atoms, radicals etc. [Gk]

tri·a·ble (tráiəb'l) *adj.* (*law*) that can be tried

tri·ac·id (traiǽsid) **1.** *n.* (*chem.*) an acid having three acid hydrogen atoms **2.** *adj.* (*chem.*) capable of combining with three molecules of a monoacid or one of a triacid ‖ (*chem.*, of acid salts) containing three replaceable hydrogen atoms

tri·ad (tráiæd) *n.* a group of three ‖ (*chem.*) an element, atom or radical with a valence of three ‖ (*mus.*) a chord of three notes, esp. a common chord ‖ a Welsh literary form consisting of short prose aphorisms grouped in threes [F. *triade* fr. L. fr. Gk]

triad *n.* (*computer*) research tool that permits work on microcomputer full development system (FDS) and target system used in minicomputer research

triad concept (*mil.*) U.S. defense strategy based on fixed intercontinental missiles, submarine-launched missiles, and bombers

Triad 1 U.S. three-part strategic defense system based on submarine-launched missiles, MX land-based missiles, and bombers

tri·age (trí:ɑʒ) *n.* (*med.*) **1.** the sorting or screening of patients seeking hospital care, to determine which service (e.g., medical, surgical, or nonphysician) is initially required and with what priority **2.** originally, the sorting of battle or disaster casualties for those requiring immediate help, those who can wait, and those beyond help

tri·al (tráiəl) **1.** *n.* a test or testing by examination or experiment ‖ (*loosely*) a trying out ‖ a test of character, powers of endurance etc. ‖ a hardship ‖ a person who or thing which is a source of annoyance or trouble ‖ the state or fact of being proved by suffering or endurance, *hour of trial* ‖ a judicial examination of inquiry and determination of a cause in a court of law **on trial** in the state of being tested for a period ‖ in the midst of judicial examination by a court ‖ provisionally accepted, that is to be rejected or sent back if not satisfactory **2.** *adj.* relating to, serving as or used as a trial, *a trial period* [A.F. *trial, tried*]

trial and error the process of finding the solution to a problem by making random tests instead of by applying first principles

trial balance a comparison of the totals on the credit and debit side of a record of accounts at a given date

trial balloon a project, statement etc. tentatively advanced in order to test public reaction

trial jury a petty jury

trial run an initial testing of something (e.g. a mechanism or a play) under normal working conditions

tri·am·cin·o·lone [$C_{21}H_{27}FO_6$] (traiæmsínəloun) *n.* (*pharm.*) a corti-drug used in treating psoriasis and other allergies marketed as Aristocort, Kenacort, and Kenalog

tri·an·gle (tráiæŋg'l) *n.* (*geom.*) a plane figure bounded by three straight lines ‖ part of a spherical surface bounded by three arcs of great circles ‖ anything of this shape, or any three things which, if joined by straight lines, would result in this shape being formed ‖ a set square ‖

CONCISE PRONUNCIATION KEY: **(a)** æ, *cat*; ɑ, *car*; ɔ *fawn*; ei, *snake*. **(e)** e, *hen*; i:, *sheep*; iə, *deer*; ɛə, *bear*. **(i)** i, *fish*; ai, *tiger*; ə:, *bird*. **(o)** o, *ox*; au, *cow*; ou, *goat*; u, *poor*; ɔi, *royal*. **(u)** ʌ, *duck*; u, *bull*; u:, *goose*; ə, *bacillus*; ju:, *cube*. x, *loch*; θ, *think*; ð, *bother*; z, *Zen*; ʒ, *corsage*; dʒ, *savage*; ŋ, *orangutang*; j, *yak*; ʃ, *fish*; tʃ, *fetch*; 'l, *rabble*; 'n, *redden*. Complete pronunciation key appears inside front cover.

(*mus.*) a percussion instrument consisting of a triangular steel rod with one angle open. It emits a clear note when struck with another steel rod ‖ a person who plays this instrument in a band or orchestra ‖ a group of three people involved in some situation, esp. an eternal triangle ‖ this situation [F. or fr. L. *triangulum*]

triangle of forces the polygon law of vectors applied to three vectors. It was discovered by Stevinus

tri·an·gu·lar (traiǽŋgjulər) *adj.* of or shaped like a triangle ‖ involving three things, parts, persons etc. ‖ (e.g. of a prism) having a triangle for its base **tri·an·gu·lár·i·ty** *n.* [fr. L.L. *triangularis*]

tri·an·gu·late (traiǽŋgjuleit) **1.** *v.t. pres. part.* **tri·an·gu·lat·ing** *past* and *past part.* **tri·an·gu·lat·ed** to make triangular ‖ to divide into triangles ‖ (*survey.*) to measure or map (a region) by dividing it into triangles, working from a fixed base **2.** *adj.* consisting of or marked with triangles **tri·an·gu·lá·tion** *n.*

Tri·a·non (tri:ænɔ̃) either of two small palaces in the park of Versailles, France. The Grand Trianon was built (1687) by J. H. Mansart for Louis XIV. The Petit Trianon was built (1762-8) by J. A. Gabriel for Louis XV

Tri·as (tráiæs) *adj.* (*geol.*) Triassic **the Trias** the Triassic [L.L. fr. Gk *trias,* three]

Tri·as·sic (traiǽsik) *adj.* of or relating to the earliest period or system of the Mesozoic era, marked by the dominance of reptiles and the appearance of gymnosperm plants (*GEOLOGICAL TIME) **the Triassic** the Triassic period or system of rocks [fr. TRIAS]

tri·ath·lon (traiǽθlɒn) *n.* competitive sporting event for women including 100-meter sprint, shotput, and high jump, sometimes including trap-shooting and fly-casting

tri·at·ic stay (traiǽtik) (*naut.*) a rope attached at one end to the foremast and at the other to the mainmast and used for hoisting boats etc. [etym. doubtful]

tri·a·tom·ic (traiətɒ́mik) *adj.* of a molecule having three atoms ‖ of a molecule having three replaceable atoms or radicals

trib·al (tráib'l) *adj.* of, relating to, or like a tribe or tribes ‖ organized by tribes, *a tribal society* **tríb·al·ism** *n.* organization by tribes ‖ strong feeling for the tribe

tri·ba·sic (traibéisik) *adj.* (*chem.*) of an acid containing three hydrogen atoms replaceable by basic atoms or radicals, e.g. phosphoric acid [fr. Gk *tri-,* three+BASIC]

tribe (traib) *n.* a human community developed by an association of, and interbreeding between, a number of families, opposed in principle to crossbreeding with other communities, and preserving its own customs, beliefs and organization ‖ (*Gk. hist.*) a phyle ‖ (*Rom. hist.*) one of the three original divisions of the Roman people or one of the 35 divisions into which these were later subdivided ‖ a subdivision in some taxonomic classifications between genus and order or genus and family ‖ (*pop.*) a number of people associated by family relationship or by common interests etc, a *dislike for journalists as a tribe* [M.E. *tribu* fr. O.F.]

Tri·bec·a (traibékə) *n.* area in Manhattan between Canal and Barclay Sts., west of Church St., where lofts have been converted into artists' studios

tribes·man (tráibzmən) *pl.* **tribes·men** (tráibzmən) *n.* a member of a tribe

tri·bol·o·gy (traibɒ́lədʒi:) *n.* the science of lubrication [fr. Gk. *tribein,* to rub+*logos,* discourse]

tri·brach (tráibræk) *n.* a metrical foot of three short syllables [fr. L. *tribrachys* fr. Gk]

trib·u·la·tion (tribjuléiʃən) *n.* suffering caused by adversity ‖ an instance of this ‖ a cause of such suffering or distress [O.F.]

tri·bu·nal (traibjú:n'l) *n.* a group of persons empowered to decide a specific issue according to the law, arbitrate in a dispute etc. ‖ a bench or seat for judges, magistrates etc. [L.]

trib·u·nate (tríbjunit) *n.* (*hist.*) the office or function of a tribune ‖ (*hist.*) the term of office of a tribune [fr. L. *tribunatus*]

trib·une (tríbju:n) *n.* (*Rom. hist.*) an official originally elected to protect plebeians' rights against the patricians ‖ (*Rom. hist.*) an officer who had two months a year in command of a legion **tríb·une·ship** *n.* tribunate [fr. L. *tribunus,* head of a tribe]

tribune *n.* a dais for speakers confronting an assembly ‖ (in a basilica) the bishop's throne ‖ the apselike structure containing this [F. fr. Ital.]

trib·u·tar·y (tríbjuteri:) **1.** *pl.* **trib·u·tar·ies** *n.* a stream flowing into a larger stream or a lake **2.** *adj.* contributory ‖ in the nature of tribute ‖ paying tribute, as an acknowledgment of subjection [fr. L. *tributarius*]

trib·ute (tríbju:t) *n.* a payment in money or kind exacted from a city or state by a more powerful state, by right of conquest or in return for protection ‖ the obligation or liability to make such a payment ‖ (*loosely*) any forced payment ‖ a grateful, affectionate or admiring acknowledgment made to a person ‖ a gift or offering expressing admiration, gratitude or affection [fr. L. *tributum*]

trice (trais) **1.** *v.t. pres. part.* **tric·ing** *past* and *past part.* **triced** (*naut.*, with 'up') to haul up and secure (a sail) **2.** *n.* (only in) **in a trice** in an instant [M.Du. *trîsen,* Du. *trijsen*]

tri·ceps (tráiseps) *pl.* **tri·cep·ses** (tráisepsiz), **tri·ceps** *n.* a muscle with three points of origin, esp. the muscle situated at the back of the upper arm [Mod. L. fr. *triceps,* triple-headed]

tri·cha·tro·phi·a (traikætətróufi:ə) *n.* hair brittleness due to atrophy of hair bulbs

tri·chi·a·sis (trikáiəsis) *n.* (*med.*) the turning inward of the eyelashes so that they rub against the eye [Mod. L. fr. Gk fr. *thrix* (*trichos*), hair]

tri·chi·na (trikáinə) *pl.* **tri·chi·nae** (trikáini:), **tri·chi·nas** *n.* *Trichinella spiralis,* fam. *Trichinellidae,* a hairlike, parasitic nematode infesting the intestine and (in larval form) the muscle or muscle fibers esp. of hogs. Eating insufficiently cooked pork from a hog infested with trichinae can communicate trichinosis to man **trich·i·nized** (tríkinaizd) *adj.* infested with trichinae [Mod. L. fr. Gk *trichinos* adj., of hair]

trich·i·ni·a·sis (trikináiəsis) *n.* trichinosis

Trich·i·nop·o·ly (trikinɒ́pəli:) *TIRUCHIRAPALLI

trich·i·no·sis (trikinóusis) *n.* a disease, characterized by fever, diarrhea and muscular pains, caused by infestation with trichinae [Mod. L.]

trich·i·nous (tríkinəs) *adj.* infested with trichinae ‖ relating to trichinae or trichinosis

tri·chlor·fon [$C_4H_8Cl_3O_4P$] (traiklɔ́rfɒn) *n.* (*organic chem.*) a compound used as an agricultural insecticide and vermicide

tri·chlo·ride (traiklɔ́raid, traiklóuraid) *n.* a compound having three atoms of chlorine in combination with an element or radical

tri·chlor·o·phe·nol [$C_6H_2Cl_3OH$] (traiklɔrəfí:nɔl) *n.* (*chem.*) a toxic bactericide and fungicide used as a defoliant *syn.* 2,4,6-T

trich·o·cyst (tríkəsist) *n.* a hairlike process in the ectoderm of certain ciliate protozoans, thought to serve as an organ of attachment [fr. Gk *thrix* (*trichos*), hair+ *kustis,* sac]

trich·oid (tríkɔid) *adj.* like hair, capillary [fr. Gk *trichoeidēs* fr. *thrix* (*trichos*), hair]

tri·cho·lo·gi·a (traikəlóudʒi:ə) *n.* the plucking out of one's hair

tri·chol·o·gy (trikɒ́lədʒi:) *n.* the study of hair and its diseases **tri·chól·o·gist** *n.* [fr. Gk *thrix* (*trichos*), hair+*logos,* discourse]

tri·chome (tráikoum, tríkoum) *n.* (*bot.*) an outgrowth from the epidermis of a plant, e.g. a hair, scale etc. ‖ a filamentous thallus ‖ a hair tuft on a myrmecophilous insect [fr. Gk *trichōma,* growth of hair]

tri·chot·o·mous (traikɒ́təməs) *adj.* divided into three parts ‖ dividing into three parts

tri·chot·o·my (traikɒ́təmi:) *n.* a division into three parts [fr. Gk *tricha,* in three+*-tomē,* a cutting]

tri·chro·ic (traikróuik) *adj.* exhibiting trichroism

tri·chro·ism (traikróuizəm) *n.* the property in some crystals of showing different colors when viewed from three different points

tri·chro·mat·ic (traikrəmǽtik) *adj.* of, pertaining to, having or using three colors

tri·chro·ma·tism (traikróumətizəm) *n.* the quality or state of being trichromatic

trick (trik) **1.** *n.* an act or action designed to deceive ‖ a dextrous feat intended to puzzle or cause wondering admiration, *a conjuring trick* ‖ a practical joke ‖ an act of mischief or meanness ‖ an inexplicable process, *by some trick of memory* ‖ a knack, *to learn the trick of flipping a pancake* ‖ a mannerism or habitual peculiarity, *she had a trick of half closing her eyes* ‖ (*cards*) the cards played and taken in one round ‖ (*cards*) a scoring unit ‖ (*naut.*) a turn at the helm usually lasting two hours **the tricks of the trade** the special techniques that constitute the expertise of an experienced craftsman **to do the trick** to produce the desired effect **up to tricks** resorting to mischievous or deceptive behavior **2.** *adj.* of or relating to or intended as a trick **3.** *v.t.* to deceive by a trick ‖ (esp. with 'out of') to defraud, cheat, *tricked out of his winnings* **to trick out** (or **up**) to dress in finery ‖ to put pretty things on, deck **tríck·er·y** *n.* [O.N.F. *trique*]

trick·i·ly (tríkili:) *adv.* in a tricky manner

trick·i·ness (tríki:nis) *n.* the state or quality of being tricky

trick·le (trík'l) **1.** *v. pres. part.* **trick·ling** *past* and *past part.* **trickled** *v.i.* (of a liquid) barely to flow, to come in a succession of drops ‖ (of an object) to emit or have dripping over it a thin stream of liquid, *the cave roof trickled with moisture* ‖ to come or go as if in a thin, intermittent stream, *news came trickling in, the guests trickled away* ‖ to move very slowly and as if hesitantly ‖ *v.t.* to give forth or cause to flow in a thin stream or in drops **2.** *n.* a series of drops, a thin stream, or something compared to this, *a trickle of information* [M.E. *triklen*]

trickle *v.t.* (*golf*) to cause (a ball) to move forward very slowly as if creeping forward ‖ *v.i.* (of a golf ball) to move in this way [prob. fr. E. Anglian var. of TRUCKLE]

trick·ster (tríkstər) *n.* a person who plays dishonest tricks

trick·y (tríki:) *comp.* **trick·i·er** *superl.* **trick·i·est** *adj.* difficult to understand or deal with, calling for careful handling, *a tricky situation* ‖ deft, adroit, *some tricky driving*

tri·clin·ic (traiklínik) *adj.* (of a crystal) having or characterized by three unequal axes which are obliquely inclined

tri·col·or, *Br.* **tri·col·our** (tráikʌlər, *Br.* tríkələ) **1.** *adj.* having three colors **2.** *n.* a three-colored flag, esp. the French flag of three vertical colors (blue, white, red) [fr. L.L. *tricolor* and F. *tricolore*]

tri·con (tráikɒn) *n.* a navigation system in which three ground stations send radio signals arranged so that pulses arrive at the same time from different distances

tri·corn (tráikɔrn) *n.* a cocked hat

tri·cot (trí:kou) *n.* a warp-knitted run-resistant fabric used in underwear etc. ‖ a soft ribbed fabric of wool or wool blend used in dresses etc. [F. fr. *tricoter,* to knit]

tri·cus·pid (traikʌ́spid) **1.** *adj.* (e.g. of a tooth) having three cups ‖ of or relating to the tricuspid valve **2.** *n.* the tricuspid valve ‖ a tricuspid tooth **tri·cus·pi·date** (traikʌ́spideit) *adj.* [fr. L. *tricuspis* (*tricuspidis*)]

tricuspid valve a valve in the heart of higher vertebrates that consists of three triangular overlapping flaps permitting the flow of blood in a single direction, from the right auricle to the right ventricle

tri·cy·cle (tráisik'l) **1.** *n.* a light vehicle like a bicycle, but having a pair of wheels arranged side by side behind a single front wheel **2.** *v.i. pres. part.* **tri·cy·cling** *past* and *past part.* **tri·cy·cled** to ride a tricycle [F.]

tri·dent (tráid'nt) **1.** *n.* a fish spear with three prongs, esp. as associated with Neptune and Britannia, who are portrayed carrying one as a scepter ‖ a three-pronged spear used in gladiatorial fights **2.** *adj.* having three prongs **tri·dént·al** *adj.* [fr. L. *tridens* (*tridentis*)]

Trident *n.* (*mil.*) the sea-based strategic weapons system consisting of the nuclear-powered Trident submarine and Trident ballistic missiles; manufactured by Lockheed as part of the CONUS support complex designed to replace Polaris and Poseidon in 1982 *Cf* TRIAD

Trident I *n.* (*mil.*) a three-stage, solid-propellant ballistic missile (UGM-96) capable of being launched from a Trident submarine, sized to permit backfit into Poseidon submarines, equipped with advanced guidance and MIRV nuclear warheads

Trident II *n.* (*mil.*) a solid-propellant 18,700-lb ballistic missile (UGM-93A) with 4,500 nautical mi range, capable of being launched from a Trident submarine, larger than and replacing the Trident I, Poseidon, and Polaris

Tri·den·tine (traidénti:n) *adj.* of or relating to the Council of Trent [fr. M.L. *Tridentinus* fr. *Tridentum,* Trent]

tri·duc·tor (traidʌ́ktə:r) *n.* a device utilizing iron-core transformers and capacitors to increase power line frequency

triecious *TRIOECIOUS

tried (traid) *past* and *past part.* of TRY *adj.* proved, tested reliable

CONCISE PRONUNCIATION KEY: **(a)** æ, *cat;* ɑ, *car;* ɔ *fawn;* ei, *snake.* **(e)** e, *hen;* i:, *sheep;* iə, *deer;* εə, *bear.* **(i)** i, *fish;* ai, *tiger;* ə:, *bird.* **(o)** o, *ox;* au, *cow;* ou, *goat;* u, *poor;* ɔi, *royal.* **(u)** ʌ, *duck;* u, *bull;* u:, *goose;* ə, *bacillus;* ju:, *cube.* x, *loch;* θ, *think;* ð, *bother;* z, *Zen;* ʒ, *corsage;* dʒ, *savage;* ŋ, *orangutang;* j, *yak;* ʃ, *fish;* tʃ, *fetch;* 'l, *rabble;* 'n, *redden.* Complete pronunciation key appears inside front cover.

tri·en·ni·al (traiéni:əl) **1.** *adj.* happening every three years ‖ lasting three years **2.** *n.* an event that occurs every three years ‖ a third anniversary [fr. L. *triennium*, a period of three years]

tri·en·ni·um (traiéni:əm) *pl.* **tri·en·ni·ums, tri·en·ni·a** (traiéni:ə) *n.* a period of three years [L.]

Trier (tríər) (*F.* Trèves) a communications center (pop. 100,338) and wine market in Rhineland-Palatinate, West Germany, on the Moselle. Roman ruins, Romanesque cathedral (4th-12th cc.)

tri·er (tráiər) *n.* a person or animal who tries hard (makes great efforts) ‖ a person who tests something ‖ an implement used in testing something, *a seed trier*

Tri·este (tri:ést) a port (pop. 265,500) in Friuli-Venezia Giulia, Italy, at the head of the Adriatic. Industries: shipbuilding, mechanical engineering, oil refining. It includes a free port. Cathedral (12th-14th cc.). Under the Hapsburgs from 1382, it prospered in the 18th and 19th cc. and became a great trading, shipping and financial center. It became Italian in 1920. From 1945 the Trieste region was divided into two zones, under British-American and Yugoslav military administrations. In 1954, the northern zone, with a mainly Italian population and including the city, went to Italy, and the southern zone (N.W. Istria) became Yugoslav. University (1924)

tri·fec·ta (traifékta) *n.* (*horse racing*) method of betting in which the winner must select the first three finishers of a race in proper order to win *also* triple *Cf* PERFECTA, QUINIELA

tri·fid (tráifid) *adj.* (*biol.*) divided, or partially cleft, into three lobes [fr. L. *trifidus*]

tri·fle (tráifəl) *n.* a valueless, insignificant fact or thing ‖ a small amount of money, *it cost a mere trifle* ‖ a dessert made of sponge cake, cream, fruit etc. ‖ a common type of pewter used in small utensils ‖ (*pl.*) utensils made from this **a trifle** (used adverbially) a little, *a trifle too old for the part* [M.E. *trufle*]

trifle *pres. part.* **tri·fling** *past* and *past part.* **tri·fled** *v.i.* (with 'with') to talk or act lightly or insincerely, *to trifle with someone's affections* ‖ *v.t.* (with 'away') to pass (time) idly or wastefully ‖ to spend (money) frivolously **not to be trifled with** to be treated with proper respect **tri·fling** *adj.* slight, insignificant [O.F. *truffler, truiffler*]

tri·flu·o·per·a·zine [$C_{21}H_{24}F_3N_3S$] (traiflu:oupεárəzin) *n.* (*pharm.*) a tranquilizer used in treating severe anxiety and some forms of mental illness; marketed as Stelazine

tri·flu·ra·lin [$C_{13}H_{16}F_3N_3O_4$] (traiflú:rəlin) *n.* (*organic chem.*) a weed killer used to protect cotton, beans, and vegetables

tri·fo·li·ate (traifóuli:it) *adj.* (*bot.*) having three leaves growing from the same point ‖ trifoliolate **tri·fo·li·at·ed** (traifóuli:eitid) *adj.* [fr. Gk *tri-*, three+L. *foliatus* fr. *folium*, leaf]

tri·fo·li·o·late (traifóuli:əleit) *adj.* (*bot.*) having three leaflets growing from the same point [fr. Gk *tri-*, three+Mod. L. *foliolum* dim. of *folium*, leaf]

tri·fo·ri·um (traifɔ́ri:əm, traifóuri:əm) *pl.* **tri·fo·ri·a** (traifɔ́ri:ə, traifóuri:ə) *n.* (*archit.*) a gallery or arcade in the wall above the arches of the nave and sometimes those of the choir of a church [M.L.]

tri·form (tráifɔrm) *adj.* existing in three forms ‖ formed in three parts [fr. L. *triformis*]

tri·func·tion·al (traifʌ́ŋkʃən'l) *adj.* (*chem.*) of a compound containing a molecule with three highly reactive sites capable of combining with other molecules, e.g., in polymerization

trig (trig) *adj.* (*old-fash.*) trim and neat in appearance [O.N. *tryggr*]

trig 1. *n.* trigonometry **2.** *adj.* trigonometrical [by shortening]

Tri·ga·ran·te (tri:garánte) the name (=Three Guarantees) given to the Mexican army formed (1821) by Iturbide and to the Plan of Iguala which it proclaimed. It guaranteed for Mexico independence from Spain, the Catholic religion as the sole religion, and racial equality in that anyone could hold office

tri·gem·i·nal (traidʒémin'l) **1.** *adj.* (*anat.*) relating to a trigeminal nerve **2.** *n.* (*anat.*) a trigeminal nerve [fr. L. *trigeminus*, born three together]

trigeminal nerve either nerve of the fifth pair of cranial nerves

trigeminal neuralgia neuralgia affecting the trigeminal nerves, characterized by painful muscular spasms

trig·ger (trígər) **1.** *n.* the steel catch which is pulled to fire a firearm, or similar catch used to actuate some other mechanism **quick on the trigger** apt to shoot (or take other action) imprudently quickly **2.** *v.t.* (sometimes with 'off') to start, get going, esp. to be the immediate, relatively unimportant cause of (some event or series of events) ‖ to release the trigger of (a gun etc.) [earlier *tricker* fr. Du. *trekker* fr. *trekken*, to pull]

trig·ger·fish (trígərfiʃ) *pl.* **trig·ger·fish, trig·ger·fish·es** *n.* a member of *Balistidae*, a family of fish inhabiting warm seas, having up to three sturdy erectile spines on the anterior dorsal fin. There are both edible and poisonous varieties

trig·ger-hap·py (trígərhæpi:) *adj.* too ready to take action by shooting

trigger price a minimum fair price for imported goods. Products sold below this price 'trigger' an immediate investigation of presumed 'dumping'

trig list (*mil.*) a list published by some Army units that includes essential survey-point information for triangulation in determining position

tri·glyph (tráiglif) *n.* (*archit.*) a tablet with three vertical grooves projecting from a Doric frieze and alternating with the metopes **tri·glýph·ic** *adj.* [fr. L. *triglyphus* fr. Gk]

tri·gon (tráigɒn) *n.* a triangle ‖ an ancient triangular Oriental harp with four strings ‖ (*astrology*) one of the groups of three signs of the zodiac 120° distant from each other into which the zodiac is divided ‖ the cutting edge of an upper molar [fr. L. *trigonum* fr. Gk]

trig·o·nal (trígən'l) *adj.* triangular, esp. in section ‖ (*math.*) of a system of trilinear coordinates ‖ (of a crystal) characterized by a vertical axis of threefold symmetry [fr. L. *trigonalis*]

trig·o·no·met·ric (trigənəmétrik) *adj.* of, relating to or done by trigonometry **trig·o·no·mét·ri·cal** *adj.*

trig·o·nom·e·try (trigənɒ́mitri:) *n.* the branch of mathematics concerned with the sides and angles of triangles, their measurement and the relations between them [fr. Mod. L. *trigonometria* fr. Gk *trigōnon*, triangle+*-metria*, measurement]

tri·graph (tráigræf, tráigraf) *n.* (*phon.*) a combination of three letters which represent one sound [fr. Gk *tri-*, three+*graphē*, writing]

tri·he·dral (traihí:drəl) *adj.* of or relating to a trihedron

tri·he·dron (traihí:drən) *pl.* **tri·he·drons, tri·he·dra** (traihí:drə) *n.* a figure formed by three plane surfaces meeting at a point [Mod. L. fr. Gk *tri-* three+*hedra*, a seat]

tri·jet (tráidʒet) *n.* a vehicle powered by three jet engines —**trijet** *adj.*

tri·ju·gate (traidʒú:git, tráidʒugeit) *adj.* (*bot.*, of a leaf) having three pairs of leaflets [fr. L. *trijugus*, threefold]

tri·lat·er·al (trailǽtərəl) **1.** *adj.* having three sides ‖ involving three parties **2.** *n.* a figure having three sides, triangle [fr. L. *trilaterus*]

tri·lat·er·al·ism (trailǽtərəlizəm) *n.* the relationship based on economic and military cooperation among the U.S., Western Europe, and Japan in the 1970s (in contrast to the unilateralism of the Nixon-Kissinger era)

tril·by (trílbi:) *pl.* **tril·bies** *n.* (*Br.*) a fedora [worn in the stage version (1895) of G. du Maurier's novel *Trilby*]

tri·lin·e·ar (trailíni:ər) *adj.* consisting of, involving or enclosed by three lines [fr. TRI-+L. *linearis*, linear]

tri·lin·gual (trailíŋgwəl) *adj.* knowing and able to use three languages ‖ consisting of or expressed in three languages [fr. L. *trilinguis*]

tri·lit·er·al (trailítərəl) **1.** *adj.* consisting of three letters, esp. three consonants **2.** *n.* a triliteral root or word [fr. TRI-+L. *littera*, a letter]

trill (tril) **1.** *n.* a musical ornament consisting of the alternation of a note and the note a whole step or half step above it ‖ a similar sound, e.g. the warble of a bird ‖ (*phon.*) a quick vibration of the tongue or uvula, e.g. in pronouncing the 'r' of some languages ‖ (*phon.*) the sound made ‖ (*phon.*) the letter or word pronounced in this way **2.** *v.t.* to sing, say or produce (a sound) with a trill ‖ *v.i.* to make trills with the voice [fr. Ital. *trillare*]

Tril·ling (tríliŋ), Lionel (1905-75), U.S. critic and author. His socio-psychological essays include 'The Liberal Imagination' (1950), 'The Opposing Self' (1955), and 'A Gathering of Fugitives' (1956). His novel 'The Middle of the Journey' (1947) explores the moral and political structure of the U.S.A. during the 1930s and 1940s

tril·lion (tríljən) *n.* *NUMBER TABLE **tríl·lionth** *n.* and *adj.* [F.]

tri·lo·bate (trailóubeit) *adj.* (*bot.*) having three lobes

tri·lo·bite (tráiləbait) *n.* a member of the class or subclass *Trilobita*, extinct aquatic arthropods found widely in Paleozoic deposits. The body is divided into three lobes. The central lobe bears biramous appendages [fr. Mod. L. *Trilobites* fr. Gk *tri-*, three+*lobos*, lobe]

tril·o·gy (trílədʒi:) *pl.* **tril·o·gies** *n.* (*Gk drama*) a group of three tragedies each complete in itself but each connected in subject with the other two. The three plays of such a group were performed in succession in Athens at the festival of Dionysus ‖ any set of three novels, musical compositions etc. so related [fr. Gk *trilogia*]

trim (trim) **1.** *v. pres. part.* **trim·ming** *past* and *past part.* **trimmed** *v.t.* to cut away unnecessary or unwanted parts from, *to trim a moustache, to trim meat of fat* ‖ to shorten by cutting, *to trim one's nails* ‖ (often with 'up') to make tidy ‖ to decorate (e.g. a garment) with ornamental additions ‖ (*bookbinding*) to guillotine folded sheets ‖ to clean and cut (the wick of a lamp) ‖ (*carpentry*) to shape and smooth ‖ (*naut.*) to adjust the cargo, ballast etc. of (a ship) to make her float on an even keel ‖ (*aeron.*) to adjust for up-and-down or horizontal movement ‖ (*naut.*) to adjust (the sails or a sail) according to the direction of the wind ‖ to decorate (a shop window) with goods ‖ (*pop.*) to thrash soundly ‖ *v.i.* to adjust one's opinion to fall in with the party in power or the majority ‖ (*naut.*, of a vessel) to assume a position in the water on an even keel **2.** *n.* a state of proper fitness for work or action, *in fighting trim* ‖ (*naut.*) the position of a ship or boat etc. in the water with respect to balance fore-and-aft ‖ (*aeron.*) the angle of flight of an aircraft with respect to balance fore-and-aft ‖ a light haircut ‖ (*bookbinding*) the amount to be cut away from folded sheets at the edges ‖ material cut away in order to trim something ‖ a decorative addition to e.g. a garment ‖ the interior furnishings of a car ‖ the lighter woodwork used in the finishing of a building, esp. the frames around windows and doors ‖ (*Am.*=*Br.* window dressing) the displaying of goods attractively in a shop window **3.** *comp.* **trim·mer** *superl.* **trim·mest** *adj.* neat, compact ‖ in good order, well arranged and well cared for, *trim lawns* [O.E. *trymian, trymman*, to put in order]

tri·mar·an (tráiməræn) *n.* a pleasure sailboat with three parallel hulls *Cf* CATAMARAN

trim·er·ous (trímərəs) *adj.* (*bot.*, of flowers) composed of three similar parts ‖ (*zool.*) possessing or seeming to possess three joints in each tarsus [Mod. L. *trimerus*]

trim·e·ter (trímitər) **1.** *n.* a line of verse consisting of three metrical feet **2.** *adj.* having three metrical feet **tri·met·ri·cal** (traimétrik'l) *adj.* [fr. L. *trimetrus* fr. Gk]

tri·meth·o·prim [$C_{14}H_{18}N_4O_3$] (traiméθəprim) *n.* (*pharm.*) synthetic antibacterial drug; marketed as Proloprim

trimetrogen (*photography*) *FAN CAMERAS

tri·mip·ra·mine (traimíprəmi:n) *n.* (*pharm.*) antidepressant, sedative drug; marketed as Surmontil

trim·mer (trímər) *n.* a person who or thing which trims, e.g. in various manufacturing processes ‖ a person who changes his political beliefs or fluctuates between one political party and another out of self-interest ‖ a person who stores coal or cargo in a ship so as to keep her correct balance ‖ (*pl.*) shears for clipping etc. ‖ a transverse beam holding the ends of joists truncated so as to leave a well for a staircase or passage for a chimney etc. ‖ a person responsible for window displays in a shop

trim·ming (trímiŋ) *n.* the act of trimming ‖ ornamental material sewn on to clothes ‖ (*pl.*, *pop.*) the usual garnishes (esp. supplementary dishes) that accompany roast meat ‖ (*pl.*) things trimmed away ‖ (*pop.*) a sound thrashing

tri·morph (tráimɔrf) *n.* any of the three crystalline forms of a trimorphic substance [back-formation fr. TRIMORPHISM]

tri·mor·phic (traimɔ́rfik) *adj.* exhibiting trimorphism

tri·mor·phism (traimɔ́rfizəm) *n.* (*zool.*) the existence of one species in three different forms ‖ (*bot.*) the existence of three different forms (of leaves, flowers etc.) upon specimens of the same species ‖ (*crystall.*) the property in certain sub-

CONCISE PRONUNCIATION KEY: **(a)** æ, *cat*; ɑ, *car*; ɔ *fawn*; ei, *snake*. **(e)** e, *hen*; i:, *sheep*; iə, *deer*; εə, *bear*. **(i)** i, *fish*; ai, *tiger*; ə:, *bird*. **(o)** ɒ, *ox*; au, *cow*; ou, *goat*; u, *poor*; ɔi, *royal*. **(u)** ʌ, *duck*; u, *bull*; u:, *goose*; ə, *bacillus*; ju:, *cube*. x, *loch*; θ, *think*; ð, *bother*; z, *Zen*; ʒ, *corsage*; dʒ, *savage*; ŋ, *orangutang*; j, *yak*; ʃ, *fish*; tʃ, *fetch*; 'l, *rabble*; 'n, *redden*. Complete pronunciation key appears inside front cover.

stances of crystallizing in three different forms [fr. Gk *trimorphos* fr. *tri-*, three+*morphē*, form]

tri·mor·phous (traimɔ́rfəs) *adj.* trimorphic

tri·nal (tráin'l) *adj.* triple [fr. L.L. *trinalis*]

tri·na·ry (tráinəri:) *adj.* triple [fr. L.L. *trinarius*]

Trin·co·ma·lee (triŋkouməlí:) a port (pop. 44,000) in N.E. Sri Lanka

trine (train) **1.** *adj.* triple ‖ (*astrology*) favorable **2.** *n.* (*astrology*) the aspect of two signs of the zodiac 120° apart, considered as favorable ‖ a set of three **the Trine** the Trinity [O.F.]

trine immersion a form of baptism in which the person being baptized is immersed three times, in the names of the Trinity

Trin·i·dad and To·ba·go (trínidæd, təbéigou) a state in the lesser Antilles off the Orinoco estuary, composed of Trinidad (area 1,980 sq. miles, pop. 1,168,000) and Tobago (area 116 sq. miles) islands. Capital: Port-of-Spain. People: mainly African and East Indian, with mulatto, European, and Chinese minorities. The islands are mountainous and wooded. Main industries: oil extraction and refining, asphalt (both on Trinidad), agriculture (copra, cacao, sugar, fruit and vegetables, livestock raising), tourism. HISTORY. Inhabited by Arawak and Carib Indians, Trinidad was visited and Tobago sighted by Columbus (1498). Trinidad was settled by the Spanish from 1532, but remained subject to raids by the Dutch and French until ceded to Britain (1802). Possession of Tobago was disputed between the Dutch and French (17th-18th cc.), and the island was ceded to Britain (1814). Trinidad and Tobago were amalgamated (1888). Jointly they became a member of the Federation of the West Indies (1958-62) and an independent state within the Commonwealth (Aug. 31, 1962), and a member of the Organization of American States (1967). Despite a prosperous tourist industry, unemployment remains high. The economic advantage held by the white minorities has increased black militancy, which erupted (1970) into widespread violence

Trinidad asphalt a natural asphalt found in a pitch lake in Trinidad

Trin·i·tar·i·an (triniteéəri:ən) **1.** *adj.* of or relating to the Roman Catholic order of the Holy Trinity formally founded in Rome (1198), having as its principal purpose the ransoming of Christians held captive by the Moslems. Today the order is devoted mainly to teaching and nursing ‖ of or relating to the Trinity ‖ of or relating to the doctrine of the Trinity or to the adherents of this doctrine **2.** *n.* a member of the Order of the Holy Trinity ‖ someone who adheres to the doctrine of the Trinity **Trin·i·tar·i·an·ism** *n.* the doctrine of the Trinity ‖ adherence to this doctrine [16th-c. L. *trinitarius*]

tri·ni·tro·tol·u·ene (trainaitroutóljuːiːn) *n.* (*abbr.* TNT) a flammable toxic derivative of toluene ($C_7H_5N_3O_6$) obtained by the nitration of toluene. Though moderately stable to heat and friction, it is a powerful explosive used for shells, bombs etc., either alone or in conjunction with other explosive or stabilizing substances (e.g. cordite) [fr. TRI-+Gk *nitron*, niter+TOLUENE]

tri·ni·tro·tol·u·ol (trainaitroutóljuːɔl, trainaitroutóljuːɒl) *n.* trinitrotoluene

trin·i·ty (tríniti:) *pl.* **trin·i·ties** *n.* a group of three **the Trin·i·ty** (*Christian theology*) the union in one Godhead of three persons: Father, Son and Holy Ghost [O.F. *trinite*]

Trinity Brethren members of Trinity House

Trinity House a corporation, providing navigational aids (pilots, lighthouses, buoys etc.) in British coastal waters, founded by Henry VIII in 1514

trin·ket (tríŋkit) *n.* a small ornament worn on the dress or person ‖ a small ornamental object [origin unknown]

tri·no·mi·al (trainóumi:əl) **1.** *adj.* (*math.*) consisting of three terms ‖ (*taxonomy*) of a name comprising three terms (genus, species and subspecies) **2.** *n.* (*math.*) a trinomial expression ‖ (*biol.*) a trinomial name [fr. TRI-+BINOMIAL]

trin·o·scope (trínəskoup) *n.* a color-television projection system utilizing three color-filtered picture tubes

tri·o (tríːou) *pl.* **tri·os** *n.* a group of three, *a trio of friends* ‖ a musical composition written for three performers ‖ the performers of such a piece ‖ the middle section of a minuet (or march or scherzo written in minuet form) [Ital.]

tri·ode (tráioud) *n.* a thermionic vacuum tube, possessing three electrodes: anode, cathode and control grid [fr. TRI-+ELECTRODE]

tri·oe·cious, tri·e·cious (traiíːʃəs) *adj.* (*bot.*) having staminate, pistillate and hermaphrodite flowers on different plants of the same species [fr. Mod. L. *Triœcia* fr. Gk *tri-*, three+*oikos*, house]

tri·o·let (tráiəlit) *n.* an eight-lined stanza rhyming a b a a a b a b, the first line being repeated at the 4th and 7th and the second line at the 8th [F.]

tri·ox·ide (traiɒ́ksaid) *n.* an oxide containing three oxygen atoms

trip (trip) **1.** *v. pres. part.* **trip·ping** *past* and *past part.* **tripped** *v.i.* (often with 'up') to lose one's balance by e.g. catching one's toe on something ‖ (often with 'up') to make a mistake, blunder ‖ to make a mistake in speaking, *to trip over a word* ‖ (*rhet.*) to move with light, rapid steps or (of a meter) as if with such steps ‖ (*horology*, of the tooth of an escape wheel) to run past the pallet without locking ‖ to become actuated by the operating of a switch ‖ *v.t.* (often with 'up') to cause (someone) to lose his balance by e.g. impeding the movement of his feet ‖ (often with 'up') to cause to make a mistake ‖ to expose (someone) as having told a lie by e.g. asking him a catch question ‖ (*naut.*) to raise (an anchor) so that it hangs clear of the bottom ‖ (*naut.*) to tilt (a yard or topmast) preparatory to lowering it ‖ to operate (a switch or other mechanism) by releasing a catch **2.** *n.* a tripping up ‖ a short journey over a set route, *regular trips between the islands* ‖ a journey ‖ (*Br.*) a group outing, excursion ‖ (*mech.*) the action of tripping ‖ (*naut.*) a tack to windward ‖ (*slang or colloq.*) a hallucinatory experience induced by a psychedelic drug, esp. LSD; by extension, an intensely interesting experience or hobby [O.F. *treper, triper, tripper*]

tri·par·tite (traipɑ́rtait) *adj.* divided into or having three parts ‖ (*biol.*) divided into three parts extending nearly to the base, *a tripartite leaf* ‖ of an action or agreement made by three persons or groups [fr. L. *tripartitus*]

tripe (traip) *n.* part of the first or second stomach of a ruminant used for food ‖ (*pop.*) worthless matter, e.g. poor entertainment or foolish talk [O.F. *tripe, trippe*]

trip-ham·mer (tríphæmər) *n.* a heavy power hammer operated by the tripping action of a cam or lever

tri·phen·yl·meth·ane (traifen'lméθein) *n.* a crystalline hydrocarbon, $CH(C_6H_5)_3$, used as a base in synthetic dyes

triph·thong (trífθəŋ, trífθɒŋ) *n.* a combination of three vowel sounds together in a single utterance of the voice [fr. TRI-+DIPHTHONG]

tri·pin·nate (traipíneit) *adj.* (*bot.*) trebly pinnate **tri·pín·nat·ed** *adj.*

tri·ple (tríp'l) **1.** *adj.* having three parts ‖ repeated three times ‖ three times as much, as many or as great ‖ (of musical time) having three beats to the bar **2.** *n.* (*baseball*) a hit which enables the batter to reach third base ‖ a group of three ‖ an amount three times as much, as many or as great ‖ (*pl., change ringing*) a peal rung on seven bells ‖ combining form meaning sets with ordered elements, e.g., sextriple [F. or fr. L. *triplus*]

triple *pres. part.* **tri·pling** *past* and *past part.* **tri·pled** *v.t.* to make three times as much, as many or as great ‖ *v.i.* to become three times as much, as many or as great [fr. M. L. *triplare*]

Triple Alliance an alliance (1668) of England, the Netherlands and Sweden against France ‖ an alliance (1717) of Britain, the Netherlands and France against Spain ‖ an alliance (1865) of Argentina, Brazil and Uruguay against Paraguay ‖ an alliance (1882) of Germany, Austria and Italy against France and Russia, which survived until 1915

Triple Alliance, War of the the conflict (1865-70) that pitted Paraguay against the combined forces of Argentina, Brazil and Uruguay. Paraguay suffered enormous losses (305,000 out of a population of 525,000, incl. all but 28,000 of its menfolk)

triple blind a research method, esp. for evaluating drugs in which subjects, those carrying out the experiment, and those analyzing the data, are unaware of the treatment used *Cf* DOUBLE BLIND

Triple Entente an informal alliance (c. 1907-17) between Great Britain, France and Russia, in opposition to the Triple Alliance of 1882

tri·ple-ex·pan·sion (tríp'likspænʃən) *adj.* of an engine in which the steam expands successively in three cylinders at different, decreasing pressures while working the same crankshaft

triple jump (*sports*) a track-and-field event combining a hop, a step, and a jump in succession

triple play (*baseball*) a play by which three players are put out

triple point (*phys.*) the temperature and pressure at which three phases of a substance (i.e. solid, liquid, vapor) can exist in equilibrium

triple sheer a tightly woven, opaque, flat-surfaced cloth that appears to be almost sheer

trip·let (tríplit) *n.* a set of three ‖ one of a set of three offspring born at one birth ‖ three rhyming lines of verse as a stanza or subunit of a sonnet etc. ‖ (*mus.*) three notes equal in value performed in the place of the two or four etc. which the key signature would suggest as normal ‖ (*pl., naut.*) three links of chain between cable and anchor ring ‖ (*chem.*) a state in which two unpaired electrons are present ‖ (*navigation*) a system for determining position utilizing signals from three stations ‖ (*optics*) a trifocal lens

triple time (*mus.*) a time with three beats to the bar

tri·plex (tráipleks) *adj.* triple, esp. having three constituent parts [L.]

trip·li·cate 1. (tríplikit) *adj.* made in three identical copies ‖ of one of these copies **2.** (tríplikit) *n.* one of three such copies **in triplicate** in three identical copies **3.** (triplikeit) *v.t. pres. part.* **trip·li·cat·ing** *past* and *past part.* **trip·li·cat·ed** to reproduce so as to have three identical copies **trip·li·cá·tion** *n.* [fr. L. *triplicare* (*triplicatus*), to treble]

tri·plic·i·ty (triplísiti:) *pl.* **tri·plic·i·ties** *n.* the state or quality of being triple ‖ a group of three ‖ (*astrology*) a trigon [fr. L.L. *triplicitas* (*triplicitatis*)]

trip·lo·blas·tic (triploublǽstik) *adj.* having three primary germ layers

trip·loid (tríplɔid) **1.** *adj.* having or being three times the haploid number of chromosomes **2.** *n.* a triploid organism (Cf. TETRAPLOID) [TRI-+-*ploid* fr. DIPLOID and HAPLOID]

tri·ply (trípli:) *adv.* in a triple degree or amount

tri·pod (tráipɒd) *n.* a seat, table, stool etc. having three legs ‖ a stand with three legs for setting up a camera, theodolite etc. ‖ a cauldron etc. resting on three legs ‖ (*Gk hist.*) the altar at Delphi from which the priestess delivered her oracles **trip·o·dal** (trípəd'l), **tri·pod·ic** (traipɒ́dik) *adjs* [fr. L. *tripus* (*tripodis*) fr. Gk]

Trip·o·li (trípəli:) a port (pop. 551,477) and former capital of Libya, in W. Tripolitania, an ancient trading center. Industries: light manufacturing, food processing

Tripoli a port (pop. 175,000) and agricultural market in N. Lebanon. Industries: oil refining, tanning, soap making, spinning

Tri·pol·i·ta·ni·a (tripɒlitéini:ə) the northwestern province (area 110,000 sq. miles, pop. 800,000) of Libya, extending from the Mediterranean into the Sahara. Chief town: Tripoli. It was taken by the Turks (1551). Italy conquered it (1912), colonized it, and held it until the 2nd world war. Products: olives, cereals, fruit, cattle, oil

Tri·pol·i·tan War (tripɒ́litən) a U.S. war (1803) initiated by President Thomas Jefferson against the Barbary pirates of North Africa. He sent a naval force to Tripoli and so put an end to the harassing of U.S. ships in that area

tri·pos (tráipɒs) *n.* (*Cambridge University*) the final examination for the honors degree ‖ an honours course [prob. fr. L. *tripus*, tripod]

trip·per (trípər) *n.* (*Br.*) a person visiting a holiday or pleasure resort ‖ (*Br.*) a person going on a group excursion ‖ a mechanical device that trips something

trip·ping (trípiŋ) *adj.* moving or as if moving with a light and nimble step, *a tripping rhythm* ‖ (*heraldry*) passant

trip·tych, trip·tich (tríptik) *n.* a painting or carving on three adjacent and usually hinged panels. The lateral panels are usually half the width of the central one and made to fold across it [fr. TRI-+DIPTYCH]

Tri·pu·ra (tripúərə) a former princely state (area 4,036 sq. miles, pop. 1,699,000) in the hilly jungle region between Assam and Bangladesh, forming a territory of India. Capital:

CONCISE PRONUNCIATION KEY: **(a)** æ, *cat*; ɑ, *car*; ɔ *fawn*; ei, *snake*. **(e)** e, *hen*; iː, *sheep*; iə, *deer*; ɛə, *bear*. **(i)** i, *fish*; ai, *tiger*; əː, *bird*. **(o)** ɒ, *ox*; au, *cow*; ou, *goat*; u, *poor*; ɔi, *royal*. **(u)** ʌ, *duck*; u, *bull*; uː, *goose*; ə, *bacillus*; juː, *cube*. x, *loch*; θ, *think*; ð, *bother*; z, *Zen*; ʒ, *corsage*; dʒ, *savage*; ŋ, *orangutang*; j, *yak*; ʃ, *fish*; tʃ, *fetch*; 'l, *rabble*; 'n, *redden*. Complete pronunciation key appears inside front cover.

Agartala (pop. 59,625). Products: rice, tea, tobacco, jute
tri·que·tra (traikwí:trə) *n.* a triangular ornament constructed of three intersecting loops or lobes [L.]
tri·que·trous (traikwí:trəs) *adj.* triangular ‖ (*bot.*) of a stem which has three sharp angles on its surface [fr. L. *triquetrus*]
tri·reme (tráiri:m) *n.* an ancient Roman or Greek galley with three banks of oars [fr. L. *triremis*]
tri·sect (traisékt) *v.t.* to divide into three equal parts **tri·séc·tion, tri·séc·tor** *ns.* [fr. TRI-+L. *secare (sectus)*, to cut]
tris·kele (tríski:l) *n.* a triskelion
tris·kel·i·on (triskéli:ɒn) *n.* a figure or device whose central part bears three bent legs or branches radiating outwards [fr. Gk *tri-*, three+*skelos*, a leg]
tris·mus (trízməs) *n.* lockjaw [Mod. L. fr. Gk *trismos*, a scream, a grinding or rasping]
tri·so·mic (traisóumik) *adj.* (*genetics*, of a nucleus or organism) triploid, having one chromosome present in triplicate and the others in duplicate [fr. *Gk tri-*, three+*sōma*, body]
Trist (trist), Nicholas Philip (1800-74), U.S. diplomat who negotiated (1848) the Treaty of Guadalupe Hidalgo, ending the Mexican War
Tris·tan (trístæn, trístɑn, trístən) the hero of a medieval legend, the oldest known version of which comes from Scotland, though the most familiar version is of 12th-c. French origin remodeled on Celtic material. Tristan (or Tristram), accompanying Iseult (or Isolde) to Cornwall from Brittany for her marriage with King Mark, accidentally drinks with her a magic love potion. It binds them inextricably together in a love which ultimately brings about both their deaths. The story has been retold in English by Malory, Matthew Arnold and Swinburne and in German by Gottfried von Strassburg, whose version was used by Wagner in his opera (1865)
Tris·tan da Cu·nha (trístəndəkú:njə) a group of four small islands in the S. Atlantic, forming a dependency (pop. 300) of St Helena. Only Tristan (a volcano 6,750 ft high, with a habitable plateau of 12 sq. miles) is inhabited. Products: potatoes, fruit, livestock, fish. The islands were discovered by the Portuguese (1506), were settled from 1810, and were annexed by Britain (1816). The inhabitants were evacuated to Britain after volcanic eruptions (1961) but most of them returned to the island (1963). Some of these emigrated to Britain (1966)
tris·tich·ous (trístikəs) *adj.* arranged in three rows, esp. (*bot.*) three vertical rows [Late Gk *tristichos*]
Tris·tram (trístrəm) *TRISTAN
tri·sul·fide, tri·sul·phide (traisʌ́lfaid) *n.* (*chem.*) a compound consisting of three atoms of sulfur combined with either an element or a radical
tri·syl·lab·ic (traisilǽbik) *adj.* having three syllables **tri·syl·láb·i·cal·ly** *adv.*
tri·syl·la·ble (tráisiləb'l) *n.* a word of three syllables
trite (trait) *adj.* stale through too frequent repetition, and boringly obvious [fr. L. *terere (tritus)*, to rub]
tri·ter·pene [$C_{30}H_{48}C_5H_{86}$] (traitə́:rpi:n) *n.* (*chem.*) a group of hydrocarbons related to terpene that occurs in plants and volatile oils
trit·i·um (tríti:əm, tríʃəm) *n.* a radioactive isotope of hydrogen (at. mass 3, symbol H^3, ^3H or T) having a half-life of 12.5 years [Mod. L. fr. Gk *tritos*, third]
Tri·ton (tráit'n) (*Gk mythol.*) the sea god, son of Poseidon and Amphitrite ‖ (*Gk mythol.*) any of a race of inferior sea gods having a fish's tail but the head and torso of a man
tri·ton (tráit'n) *n.* (*zool.*) any of various gastropod mollusks, esp. of fam. *Cymatiidae*, measuring up to 1 ft in length. They have a rough, wrinkly conical shell and are found in tropical seas [after TRITON (sea god)]
triton *n.* (*chem.*) the nucleus of the tritium atom [Gk neuter of *tritos*, third]
trit·u·ra·ble (trítʃərəb'l) *adj.* that can be triturated
trit·u·rate (trítʃəreit) **1.** *v.t. pres. part.* **trit·u·rat·ing** *past* and *past part.* **trit·u·rat·ed** to grind to fine powder, esp. under a liquid **2.** *n.* (*pharm.*) a triturated preparation **trit·u·rá·tion, trít·u·ra·tor** *ns* [fr. L.L. *triturare (trituratus)*]
tri·umph (tráiəmf) *n.* a complete and thoroughly decisive victory ‖ the feeling of pride and joy associated with the winning of such a victory ‖ (*Rom. hist.*) a pageant in which a victorious general, on his return to Rome, paraded through the city and displayed his prisoners and spoils of war [O.F. *triumphe, triomphe*]
triumph *v.i.* to exult in victory ‖ (with 'over') to boast at the expense of the vanquished ‖ (with 'over') to get the better of after a hard struggle, *to triumph over one's difficulties* ‖ (*Rom. hist.*) to celebrate a military triumph [O.F. *triumpher*]
tri·um·phal (traiʌ́mfəl) *adj.* pertaining to or commemorating a triumph [fr. L. *triumphalis*]
tri·um·phal·ism (traiʌ́mfəlizəm) *n.* belief that a particular set of dogma is universal and eternal —**triumphalist** *n.*
tri·um·phant (traiʌ́mfənt) *adj.* victorious ‖ exultant [fr. L. *triumphans (triumphantis)* fr. *triumphare*, to triumph]
tri·um·vir (traiʌ́mvər) *pl.* **tri·um·virs, tri·um·vi·ri** (traiʌ́mvərai) *n.* (*Rom. hist.*) a magistrate jointly charged with two colleagues to administer a branch of government **tri·úm·vi·ral** *adj.* [L.]
tri·um·vi·rate (traiʌ́mvərit) *n.* (*Rom. hist.*) government by triumvirs, or the term of office of a triumvir ‖ any group of three men in authority [fr. L. *triumviratus*]
—The word is esp. applied to the political association of Pompey, Julius Caesar and Crassus (60 B.C.) to seize power (the 1st Triumvirate) and to that of Mark Antony, Octavius and Lepidus (43 B.C.) after the murder of Caesar (the 2nd Triumvirate)
tri·une (tráiju:n) *adj.* three in one, the *triune God* **tri·ú·ni·ty** *n.* [fr. TRI-+L. *unus*, one]
tri·va·lent (traivéilənt) *adj.* (*chem.*) having a valence of three (cf. TERVALENT) [fr. TRI-+L. *valens (valentis)* fr. *valere*, to be strong]
Tri·van·drum (trivǽndrəm) the capital (pop. 409,672) of Kerala, India. Industries: rubber, fisheries, textiles, pharmaceuticals. Crafts: wood and ivory carving. University of Kerala (1937)
triv·et (trívit) *n.* a three-legged iron stand or a bracket hooking on to a grate to put a kettle etc. on by the fire ‖ a metal plate mounted on three short legs to hold a hot dish in order to protect the top of a table [M.E. *trefet* prob. fr. L. *tripes (tripedis)*, three-footed]
triv·i·a (trívi:ə) *pl. n.* insignificant, unimportant matters or things [L.]
triv·i·al (trívi:əl) *adj.* of very little importance or value, trifling [fr. L. *trivialis*, of a place where three ways meet]
triv·i·al·i·ty (trivi:ǽliti:) *pl.* **triv·i·al·i·ties** *n.* the state or quality of being trivial ‖ a trifle (a valueless, insignificant fact or thing) [fr. L. *trivialitas*]
trivial name (*biol.*) the Latin species name, following the genus name and agreeing with it grammatically ‖ the vernacular name for an organism or chemical substance (as compared with its scientific name)
triv·i·um (trívi:əm) *pl.* **triv·i·a** (trívi:ə) *n.* (in medieval education) grammar, rhetoric and logic, the elementary division of the seven liberal arts (*QUADRIVIUM), being the required studies for the bachelor's degree [L.=a place where three roads meet]
tRNA (*genetics abbr.*) for transfer RNA (which see)
Tro·ad (tróuæd) the region in northwestern Asia Minor which surrounded ancient Troy
troat (trout) *v.i.* to make the cry of a buck in rut [prob. fr. O.F. *trout*, a cry to urge on hounds etc.]
tro·car (tróukər) *n.* a triangular surgical instrument used to pierce body cavities in order to withdraw fluid [fr. F. *troquart, trois-quarts* fr. *trois*, three+*carre*, side]
tro·cha·ic (troukéiik) **1.** *adj.* of or made up of trochees **2.** *n.* (*pl.*) a trochaic foot or verse [F. *trochaïque* or fr. L. *trochaicus* fr. Gk]
tro·chan·ter (troukǽntər) *n.* a bony prominence serving for the attachment of muscles located on the upper part of the femur in many vertebrates including man ‖ the second segment from the base of the leg of an insect [F. fr. Gk *trechein*, to run]
tro·chee (tróuki:) *n.* a prosodic foot consisting of a long or stressed syllable followed by a short or unstressed one [fr. L. *trochaeus* fr. Gk *trochaios (pous)*, running (foot)]
troch·i·lus (trɒ́kələs) *pl.* **troch·i·li** (trɒ́kəlai) *n.* *Trochilus polytmus*, a Jamaican long-tailed hummingbird ‖ the North American hummingbird ‖ the crocodile bird ‖ any of several European warblers [L. fr. Gk *trochilos*, a runner]
troch·le·a (trɒklí:ə) *n.* (*anat.*) a bone structure resembling a pulley, e.g. the surface of the inner condyle of the humerus, with which the ulna articulates **troch·lé·ar** *adj.* of or connected with a trochlea [L.=pulley]
trochlear muscle the superior oblique muscle of the eye, which controls its downward and lateral motion
trochlear nerve either one of the fourth pair of cranial nerves, which are motor nerves for trochlear muscles
tro·choid (tróukɔid) **1.** *adj.* (*anat.*, of a joint) rotating on a longitudinal axis ‖ (*geom.*) of a curve generated by a point in the plane of one curve rolling on another **2.** *n.* (*anat.*) a trochoid joint ‖ (*geom.*) a trochoidal curve **tro·chói·dal** *adj.* [fr. Gk *trochoeidēs*, wheel-like]
troch·o·phore (trɒ́kəfɔr, trɒ́kəfour) *n.* (*zool.*) the free-swimming ciliated larval stage of many annelid worms, mollusks, rotifers and other aquatic invertebrates [fr. Gk *trochos*, wheel+*-phoros*, bearing]
trod *past* and alt. *past part.* of TREAD
trodden alt. *past part.* of TREAD
trog·lo·dyte (trɒ́glədait) *n.* a prehistoric cave dweller ‖ a person who lives in a house built in the living rock ‖ an anthropoid ape **trog·lo·dyt·ic** (trɒglədítik), **trog·lo·dýt·i·cal** *adjs* [fr. L. *troglodyta* fr. Gk]
troi·ka (trɔ́ikə) *n.* a Russian carriage drawn by three horses abreast ‖ such a team of horses ‖ a group of three, esp. of rulers [Russ.]
Trois-Ri·vières (trwæri:vjer) (*Eng.* Three Rivers) a port (pop. 50,466) in Quebec, Canada, on the St Lawrence, founded in 1634
Tro·jan (tróudʒən) **1.** *adj.* of ancient Troy, its people or culture **2.** *n.* a native of ancient Troy **to work like a Trojan** to work intensely hard [fr. L. *Troianus*]
Trojan War (*Gk mythol.*) the 10-year siege of Troy by the Greeks, provoked by Paris' abduction of Helen, wife of Menelaus of Sparta. Agamemnon attacked Troy with an army which included Achilles, Patroclus, Odysseus, Nestor and two warriors called Ajax. The Trojans under Hector kept up their resistance until they were tricked (despite the warnings of Cassandra and Laocoön) into hauling inside the walls a huge wooden horse which the Greeks had apparently abandoned, but which in fact was full of Greek soldiers who, once inside, were able to sack the city. The story of the war, which is thought to reflect a real siege of Troy c. 1200 B.C., is the subject of Homer's 'Iliad'. It has been the greatest single pagan influence on later art, being a repository of allusion, metaphor and situation
troll (troul) **1.** *v.t.* to sing (a song) in a loud, jolly, carefree way ‖ to fish in (a lake etc.), or to fish for, by drawing a line with a spoon attached behind a boat ‖ *v.i.* to fish in this way ‖ to sing away loudly and merrily **2.** *n.* the act of trolling ‖ the spoon or spoon and line used in trolling ‖ (*Br.*) the reel of a fishing rod [etym. doubtful]
troll *n.* (*Scand. mythol.*) one of the supernatural beings, formerly thought of as giants, but later as dwarfs, inhabiting caves, hills etc. [O.N.]
trol·ley, trol·ly (trɒ́li:) *pl.* **trol·leys, trol·lies** *n.* (*Br.*) a small, low, four-wheeled vehicle used for transporting goods ‖ (*Br., rail.*) a handcar ‖ a grooved wheel, at the end of a pole, running along an overhead wire from which electric power is conducted to the motor of a vehicle ‖ a wheeled basket or carriage etc. that runs suspended from an overhead track ‖ a trolleybus ‖ a streetcar ‖ (*Br.*) a tea wagon [etym. doubtful]
trol·ley·bus (trɒ́li:bʌs) *n.* an electric bus powered from overhead wires but running on tires (not on a laid track)
trolley car a streetcar
trol·lop (trɒ́ləp) *n.* a slattern [etym. doubtful]
Trol·lope (trɒ́ləp), Anthony (1815-82), English novelist. His most successful novels center in the imaginary cathedral town of Barchester and portray clerical life and provincial society with realism, a touch of satire, and neat character drawing. They include 'The Warden' (1855), 'Barchester Towers' (1857), 'Doctor Thorne' (1858) and 'The Last Chronicle of Barset' (1867)
trolly *TROLLEY
trom·bone (trɒmbóun) *n.* (*mus.*) a brass wind instrument consisting of a metal U-shaped tube bent twice upon itself and ending in a trumpet-shaped mouth, with a slide for controlling the length of vibrating column of air, or (rarely) valves, like a trumpet ‖ (*mus.*) an organ stop having a comparable tone **trom·bón·ist** *n.* [fr. Ital. fr. *tromba*, trumpet]

trom·mel (trɒ́məl) *n.* (*mining*) a revolving sieve used for sizing crushed ore or rock [G.=drum]

tro·mom·e·ter (troumɒ́mitər) *n.* an instrument for detecting and recording slight earth tremors [fr. Gk *tromos,* trembling+METER]

Tromp (trɒmp), Maarten Harpertszoon (1597-1653), Dutch admiral. His victory over a Spanish fleet (1639) marked the end of Spain's naval power. He won control (Nov. 1652) of the English Channel from England in the 1st Dutch War, but was twice defeated in 1653 and killed in the final battle

trompe (trɒmp) *n.* an apparatus for producing a blast in a forge or furnace by means of a column of water descending in a tube to suck air down [F.]

trompe l'œil (trɒ́mplɔ̀i, trɔ̃plə:j) *n.* (*painting*) an illusory effect of reality produced e.g. by shading and perspective [F.=trick the eye]

Trom·sö (trɒ́msou) a fishing port (pop. 46,454) in N. Norway: polar research stations

Trond·heim (trɒ́nheim) a port (pop. 135,100) and former capital (pre-14th c.) of Norway, on the central west coast. Industries: fishing, shipbuilding, mechanical engineering, hydroelectricity. Gothic cathedral (12th-13th cc.)

troop (tru:p) **1.** *n.* (*pl.*) soldiers, armed forces ‖ a body of soldiers, esp. a unit of cavalry under a captain, a unit of artillery within a battery or a unit of armored vehicles ‖ a scout unit ‖ a lot of people, *troops of summer visitors* ‖ a herd or flock **2.** *v.i.* (often with 'off') to go in groups or crowds, *they went trooping off to the movies* ‖ to go in a more or less orderly file, *they trooped into the canteen* [O.F. *trope,* F. *troupe*]

troop carrier an armored vehicle for cross-country transport of infantry ‖ an aircraft for carrying troops with their equipment to an operational zone

troop·er (trú:pər) *n.* a cavalry soldier with the rank of private ‖ a private in a state police, esp. one using a motorcycle ‖ a mounted policeman ‖ (*Br.*) a troopship

Trooping the Color a ceremonial mounting of the guard on the British sovereign's official birthday, in the presence of the sovereign, the regimental colors being carried along the ranks of the Brigade of Guards

troop·ship (trú:pʃip) *n.* a ship for transporting troops

tro·pae·o·lin, tro·pe·o·lin (troupí:əlin) *n.* any of various orange and orange-yellow azo dyes, some of which are used for staining in biological work [TROPAEOLUM]

tro·pae·o·lum (troupí:ələm) *n.* a member of *Tropaeolum,* fam. *Tropaeolaceae,* a genus of mainly climbing, flowering plants native to South America, esp. *T. majus,* the nasturtium [Mod. L. dim. of Gk *tropaion,* trophy]

trope (troup) *n.* (*rhet.*) a word or expression used figuratively ‖ a medieval liturgical interpolation, melodic or textual [fr. L. *tropus* fr. Gk]

tropeolin *TROPAEOLIN

troph·ic (trɒ́fik) *adj.* relating to nutrition, *trophic ulcers* [fr. Gk *trophikos* fr. *trophē,* nourishment]

troph·o·blast (trɒ́fəblæst) *n.* (*embry.*) a specialized ectodermic layer on the outside of the blastula in many mammal embryos. It is believed to attach the egg to the wall of the uterus and to supply food to the embryo **troph·o·blás·tic** *adj.* [fr. Gk *trophē,* nourishment+*blastos,* germ]

troph·o·plasm (trɒ́fəplæzəm) *n.* the nutritive or vegetative part of a cell (cf. IDIOPLASM, cf. KINOPLASM) [fr. Gk *trophē,* nourishment+PLASM]

tro·phy (tróufi:) *pl.* **tro·phies** *n.* a silver cup or other object won in a sporting contest ‖ a mounted hunting memorial, e.g. a fox's mask ‖ any object cherished as a memento of a success won ‖ (in ancient Greece and Rome) a memorial consisting of armor, weapons etc. taken from an enemy and set up in honor of a god ‖ an architectural or decorative motif grouping a shield, spear, plumed helmet, standard etc. [F. *trophée* fr. L. fr. Gk]

trop·ic (trɒ́pik) **1.** *n.* either of two parallels of latitude on the globe passing through the most northerly and southerly points on the earth's surface (approx. 23½° N. and S.) at which the sun can be vertically overhead at noon (*TROPIC OF CANCER, *TROPIC OF CAPRICORN) ‖ either of the two corresponding circles of the celestial sphere which the sun just reaches at the point of its greatest declination **the Tropics** the region between the Tropics of Cancer and Capricorn **2.** *adj.* pertaining to the Tropics **tróp·i·cal** *adj.* of or as if of the Tropics ‖ of or like a trope [fr. L. *tropicus* fr. Gk]

tropical climate a climatic regime characterized by high temperatures (minimum average 64° F.) and heavy rainfall (yearly minimum about 60 ins) throughout the year, except on the tropical margins, where there is a distinct dry season

tropical fish any of various exotic fish kept in aquariums

tropical year a solar year

tropic bird a member of *Phaëthon,* fam. *Phaëthontidae,* a genus of tropical seabirds. They have white plumage with black markings, and the central pair of tail feathers is greatly elongated

Tropic of Cancer the parallel of latitude 23½° north of the equator (*TORRID)

Tropic of Capricorn the parallel of latitude 23½° south of the equator (*TORRID)

tro·pism (tróupizəm) *n.* the involuntary movement or orientation toward (positive tropism) or away from (negative tropism) a source of stimulus, e.g. a response of plants to light (*TAXIS) [fr. Gk *tropos,* a turning]

tro·po·col·la·gen (trɒpəkɒ́lədʒən) *n.* (*biochem.*) a fundamental precursor of connective tissue (bone and cartilage of animals) containing similar elongated molecules

trop·o·log·i·cal (trɒpəlɒ́dʒik'l) *adj.* of or involving tropology

tro·pol·o·gy (trəpɒ́lədʒi:) *pl.* **tro·pol·o·gies** *n.* the use of metaphors in speaking or writing ‖ figurative exegesis of the Bible, stressing moral meaning ‖ a collection of tropes or a treatise on figurative language [fr. L.L. *tropologia* fr. Gk]

trop·o·pause (trɒ́pəpɔz) *n.* the level separating the troposphere and the stratosphere, occurring at an altitude of 5-10 miles [fr. *tropos,* a turning+PAUSE]

trop·o·phyte (trɒ́pəfait) *n.* a plant which is mesophytic in summer and xerophytic in winter [fr. Gk *tropos,* a turning+*phuton,* a plant]

trop·o·sphere (trɒ́pəsfiər) *n.* a division of the earth's atmosphere extending from ground level to altitudes ranging 5-10 miles (depending on season and where it is measured on the earth). It is the region in which the temperature declines rapidly with altitude and which contains most of the moisture in the atmosphere, and is therefore the region where convection currents (winds) and clouds are found (*TROPOPAUSE) [fr. Gk *tropos,* a turning+SPHERE]

tropospheric scatter 1. the scatter propagation of radio waves by a result of irregularities in the physical properties of the troposphere **2.** an over-the-horizon ground-to-ground multichannel radio system that utilizes the reflective properties of the troposphere

Tros·sachs, the (trɒ́sæks) a romantic wooded mountain valley in Perth, Scotland

trot (trɒt) *n.* a setline ‖ one of the short attached lines

trot *pres. part.* **trot·ting** *past* and *past part.* **trot·ted** *v.i.* (of a horse etc.) to move at a steady pace, the action of the feet being in diagonal pairs and the rhythm duple (not quadruple) ‖ (of bipeds) to move at a pace between walking and running ‖ *v.t.* to make (a horse) trot ‖ to go (a specified distance) at this gait **to trot out** (*pop.*) to produce or introduce (an often repeated joke, superior knowledge etc.) for admiration or consideration or approval [O.F. *troter*]

trot *n.* the action of trotting ‖ the sound of a horse trotting ‖ (*pop.*) a crib (translation used by students) [F.]

Trot *n.* (*slang*) a Trotskyist; one who subscribes to the socialist doctrine of Leon Trotsky (1879–1940)

troth (trəθ, trouθ) *n.* (*rhet.*) one's plighted word **to plight one's troth** (*rhet.*) to pledge one's loyalty in betrothal [O.E. *trēowth,* truth]

trot·line (trɒ́tlain) *n.* a setline

Trot·sky (trɒ́tski:), Leon (Lev Davidovich Bronstein, 1879-1940), Russian revolutionist. Returning to Russia (1917) after long periods of imprisonment and exile, he played a leading part in bringing the Bolsheviks to power. He was minister of war (1918-25), but, after Lenin's death (1924), came into conflict with Stalin's policy of abandoning the aim of world revolution. He was exiled from the U.S.S.R. (1929) and was murdered in Mexico (possibly at the instigation of Stalin)

Trot·sky·ist (trɒ́tski:ist) **1.** *n.* a follower of Trotsky, believing like him in the necessity for armed revolution in every country **2.** *adj.* of or pertaining to Trotsky or his ideas or followers

Trot·sky·ite (trɒ́tski:ait) **1.** *n.* a Trotskyist **2.** *adj.* Trotskyist

trot·ter (trɒ́tər) *n.* a horse bred and trained for trotting races ‖ the foot of a pig or other animal, esp. as food

trotting race a form of horse racing. Specially bred horses race at a trot, pulling a sulky on which the driver sits

trou·ba·dour (trú:bədɔr, trú:bədour, trú:bəduər) *n.* one of a class of poets and poet-musicians, often of noble birth or knightly rank, and sometimes itinerant, living in S. France, N. Spain and Italy in the 11th, 12th and 13th cc. (cf. TROUVÈRE). They wrote mainly in the langue d'oc, on courtly love and deeds of chivalry, and are responsible for many set forms of verse (*BERTRAN DE BORN) ‖ a strolling minstrel [F. fr. Prov.]

trou·ble (trʌ́b'l) **1.** *v. pres. part.* **trou·bling** *past* and *past part.* **trou·bled** *v.t.* to cause to worry or grieve ‖ to disturb mentally ‖ to afflict, *troubled by rheumatism* ‖ to put to inconvenience ‖ to make turbid ‖ *v.i.* to put oneself to some inconvenience, *don't trouble to fetch it* **2.** *n.* worry ‖ misfortune ‖ a difficult situation ‖ a person or thing that causes difficulty ‖ effort, pains, *he takes trouble with his work* ‖ (*pop.*) that which is wrong, *the trouble with you is that you don't try* ‖ (*pl.*) social disturbances ‖ a physical weakness or ailment not specifically named, *stomach trouble* **to take trouble** to exert oneself and be painstaking [O.F. *troubler*]

troubled waters a situation involving difficulties for somebody which someone not concerned may be tempted to turn to his own profit

trou·ble·mak·er (trʌ́b'lmeikər) *n.* a person who sets up discord between others

trou·ble·shoot·er (trʌ́b'lʃu:tər) *n.* a person employed to locate faults in power circuits etc. ‖ a mediator in social disputes ‖ an expert at detecting and dissolving an obstruction to business, political or military affairs

trou·ble·some (trʌ́b'lsəm) *adj.* giving trouble

trou·blous (trʌ́bləs) *adj.* (*rhet.*) disturbed or disturbing [O.F. *troubleus*]

trough (trɔf, trɒf) *n.* a long open receptacle for animal food etc. ‖ a similar receptacle for washing ore, kneading dough etc. ‖ a depression, esp. between ocean waves ‖ (*meteorol.*) a long, narrow area of low atmospheric pressure between areas of higher pressure ‖ a water conduit, esp. a rainwater gutter under the eaves of a roof ‖ the low point in a business cycle ‖ (*statistics*) the low point in a curve between higher points ‖ (*geol.*) a valley that is longer than it is wide [O.E. *trog*]

trounce (trauns) *pres. part.* **trounc·ing** *past* and *past part.* **trounced** *v.t.* to defeat overwhelmingly [etym. doubtful]

troupe (tru:p) *n.* a company of entertainers, acrobats etc. **tróup·er** *n.* a member of a troupe, esp. one on tour **a real trouper** a person who can be relied on to show team spirit in all circumstances [F. = a troop]

trou·sers (tráuzərz) *pl. n.* an outer garment (often called a 'pair of trousers') extending from the waist to the ankles and divided so that the wearer's legs are separately covered ‖ (*Br.*) a boy's short pants [older *trouse* perh. fr. Ir. Gael. *triubhas*]

trouser suit (*Br.*) a pantsuit

trous·seau (trú:sou) *pl.* **trous·seaux** (tru:sóu, trú:souz), **trous·seaus** *n.* a bride's personal clothing, together with the linen etc. for the household [F.]

trout (traut) *pl.* **trout, trouts** *n.* any of several food and game fishes of fam. *Salmonidae,* esp. genera *Salmo* and *Salvelinus,* closely related to, but smaller than, the salmon. Most are freshwater species [O.E. *truht*]

trou·vère (trú:vεər) *n.* one of a class of poets living in N. France (cf. TROUBADOUR) in the 11th-14th cc., writing in the langue d'oïl, and famous esp. for their chansons de geste and chivalric romances, including those drawn from the Arthurian legend (*CHRÉTIEN DE TROYES) [O.F.]

trove (trouv) *TREASURE TROVE

tro·ver (tróuvər) *n.* (*law*) a gaining possession of goods by finding and keeping ‖ an action in common law to recover the value of goods stolen or wrongfully detained [O.F. *trover,* to find]

trow·el (tráuəl) **1.** *n.* a short, flat-bladed tool for spreading mortar etc. ‖ a scoop for lifting or planting small plants, bulbs etc. **to lay it on with a trowel** to praise, flatter, apologize etc. fulsomely **2.** *v.t. pres. part.* **trow·el·ing,** esp. *Br.*

trow·el·ling *past* and *past part.* **trow·eled**, esp. *Br.* **trow·elled** to spread, smooth, shape etc. with a trowel [M.E. *truel* fr. O.F. *truele*]

Troy (trɔi) an ancient city (*TROJAN WAR) near the western entrance to the Dardanelles, in modern Turkey. Excavations, begun (1871) by Schliemann, revealed nine successive cities on the site, dating from Neolithic to Roman times

troy *adj.* in or by troy weight

Troyes (trwæ) the chief town (pop. 72,167) in Aube, France, and historic capital of Champagne, on the upper Seine, center of the hosiery industry. Gothic cathedral (13th-14th cc.), churches (12th-16th cc.)

Troyes, Treaty of an agreement (1420) between Henry V of England and Charles VI of France during the Hundred Years' War. Henry was to marry Charles's daughter and was to succeed to the French throne after Charles's death. The treaty was repudiated (1429) by Charles VII

troy weight a system of weight units used esp. for precious metals (*MEASURES AND WEIGHTS) [after TROYES, France, where it was first used]

tru·an·cy (trúːənsiː) *pl.* **tru·an·cies** *n.* an act or instance of playing truant ‖ the state of being truant

tru·ant (trúːənt) **1.** *n.* a pupil who stays away from school without permission ‖ anyone who absents himself from work or duty without good reason **to play truant** to absent oneself in this manner **2.** *adj.* of or pertaining to a truant ‖ (*rhet.*) idle, wandering, *truant thoughts* [O.F. = beggar, prob. fr. Celt.]

truce (truːs) *n.* a temporary peace arranged between enemies or opponents [M.E. *trewes, triewes* pl. of *trewe, triewe,* truth to a promise]

tru·cial (trúːʃəl) *adj.* denoting or relating to any of the Trucial States, or their rulers, or to the coast of the Persian Gulf where the Trucial States are situated [fr. TRUCE]

Trucial States or **Trucial Oman** *UNITED ARAB EMIRATES

truck (trʌk) **1.** *n.* commodities suitable for exchange, barter or sale in small quantities ‖ barter as a practice ‖ vegetables raised to sell ‖ (*pop.*) dealings, *she won't have any truck with him* ‖ odds and ends of little value ‖ (*Br. hist.*) goods supplied in lieu of money wages, a method of payment suppressed by the Truck Acts of the 19th c. **2.** *v.t.* to exchange, barter or trade ‖ (*Br. hist.*) to pay on the truck system ‖ *v.i.* to exchange or barter goods [O.F. *troquer,* to exchange]

truck 1. *n.* a strong, usually four-wheeled vehicle used for road transport of heavy loads ‖ a wheeled vehicle, often with a flat top, for moving loads e.g. in a warehouse ‖ (*Br., rail.*) an open freight car ‖ (*rail.*) a revolving undercarriage on wheels ‖ (*naut.*) a wooden disk at a masthead, with holes for fastening halyards ‖ a handcart for moving loads on a railroad platform etc. ‖ shelved framework mounted on wheels **2.** *v.t.* to transport in or on a truck [prob. fr. L. *trochus,* a hoop]

truck·age (trʌ́kidʒ) *n.* transportation by truck ‖ the charge for this

truck·er (trʌ́kər) *n.* a truck farmer

trucker *n.* a person in the business of transporting goods by truck ‖ a truck driver

truck farm a market garden **truck farmer** a market gardener

truck·le (trʌ́k'l) *pres. part* **truck·ling** *past* and *past part.* **truck·led** *v.i.* (with 'to') to cringe, be servile [A.F. *trocle,* a pulley]

truckle bed a low bed mounted on small wheels that can be stowed away easily under a higher bed

truc·u·lent (trʌ́kjulənt) *adj.* (of a person or behavior) sharply self-assertive ‖ (of criticisms etc.) harsh and scathing [fr. L. *truculentus,* wild, fierce]

Tru·deau (truːdóu), Pierre Elliot (1921-), Canadian statesman. He was appointed minister of justice and attorney-general of Canada (Apr. 1967), succeeded Lester Pearson as leader of the Liberal party and was elected prime minister (Apr. 1968). He invoked (1970) emergency police powers to counter the terrorist acts of the separatist Front de Libération du Québec. His party lost its majority in parliament in 1972 and Trudeau formed a coalition with the New Democratic Party. Although the Liberals regained a parliamentary majority in 1974, they were defeated in May 1979, and Trudeau resigned as prime minister. He was returned to office in Feb. 1980 and oversaw the rewriting of the federal constitution, which became law in 1982. Trudeau resigned as prime minister in June 1984

trudge (trʌdʒ) **1.** *v. pres. part.* **trudg·ing** *past* and *past part.* **trudged** *v.i.* to walk doggedly under fatiguing conditions ‖ *v.t.* to cover (a distance) in this way **2.** *n.* a long walk in such conditions [etym. doubtful]

trudg·en, trudg·eon (trʌ́dʒən) *n.* the trudgen stroke

trudgen stroke a stroke in swimming combining a scissors kick and alternate overarm movement [after John *Trudgen,* 19th-c. English swimmer]

true (truː) **1.** *adj.* in agreement with fact ‖ faithful to another or others, or to a cause or allegiance, *a true friend, true to his principles* ‖ rightful, *the true heir* ‖ genuine, sincere, *a true Christian* ‖ accurate, correct, *true to a thousandth of an inch* ‖ correctly and accurately shaped, fitted, placed etc., *these boards are not true* ‖ properly so called, *true statesmanship, the whale is a true mammal* **to come true** to turn out in reality as desired, expected or prophesied **2.** *adv.* accurately, *to aim true* ‖ (*biol.*) in conformity with the characteristics of the stock, *to breed true* **3.** *v.t. pres. part.* **true·ing, tru·ing** *past* and *past part.* **trued** (often with 'up') to make accurate, straight, level etc. or adjust so as to conform to a standard **4.** *n.* **in (out of) true** correctly (not correctly) aligned or adjusted [O.E. *trēowe*]

true bill a legal indictment found by a grand jury to be justified by the evidence

true-blue (trúːblúː) *adj.* utterly loyal ‖ (*Br.*) staunchly Conservative in politics

true·bred (trúːbréd) *adj.* of unmixed breed, purebred

true north the direction determined by the geographic north pole of the earth (cf. MAGNETIC NORTH)

truf·fle (trʌ́fəl) *n.* the very dark brown, edible fruiting body of *Tuber,* a genus of fungi (class *Ascomycetes*) growing underground in parts of Europe. Truffles are esteemed as a delicacy [prob. fr. O.F. *trufe, truffe*]

trug (trʌg) *n.* (*Br.*) a rounded oblong shallow basket of wood strips or plastic, with a handle, for garden produce [perh. var. of TROUGH]

tru·ism (trúːizəm) *n.* a statement the truth of which is self-evident

Tru·ji·llo (truːhíːjou) a coastal city and commercial center (pop. 240,322) in N.W. Peru. The ruins of the pre-Incan city of Chan-Chan lie four miles to the east

Tru·ji·llo Mo·li·na (truːhíːjɔməlíːnɑ), Rafael Leonidas (1891-1961), president of the Dominican Republic (1930-8, 1942-52). His absolute dictatorship achieved some economic progress but aroused widespread opposition. He was assassinated

tru·ly (trúːliː) *adv.* truthfully, in accordance with the truth ‖ (*intensive*) utterly, really, *a truly lamentable performance* ‖ accurately, *foundations laid truly* **yours truly** a formal ending for an impersonal letter, followed by the signature [O.E. *trēowlīce*]

Tru·man (trúːmən), Harry S (1884-1972), 33rd president (1945-53) of the U.S.A., a Democrat, who succeeded on the death of President Franklin Roosevelt. After Germany's surrender (1945) he attended the Potsdam Conference, and ordered the dropping of the atomic bomb on Japan. He unified (1947) the army, navy, and air force under the U.S. Department of Defense. In the cold war which followed the 2nd world war he formulated the Truman Doctrine. Military and economic aid was given to Greece and Turkey to counter Soviet influence in that area. The policy of resisting Soviet expansion was strengthened by the Marshall Plan and the Point Four Program. Plagued by the Republican-controlled 80th Congress (1946-8), Truman had difficulty in implementing his Fair Deal. He promoted the formation (1949) of NATO. He ordered (1950) U.S. troops to the defense of South Korea, placing them under the aegis of the United Nations but assuming the leadership of the Allied cause in the Korean War. His administration was marked by the 'Red Scare' of the early 1950s

Truman Doctrine a U.S. foreign policy doctrine (1947) formulated by President Harry S Truman, which declared that 'whenever aggression, direct or indirect, threatened the peace and security of the United States, action would be taken to stop that aggression'. The doctrine was applied esp. in Greece and Turkey

Trum·bull (trʌ́mb'l), Jonathan (1710-85), American political leader and governor (1769-84) of the colony of Connecticut. During the Revolutionary War he was a chief counselor of George Washington

trump (trʌmp) **1.** *n.* (*card games*) any card of a suit designated as having temporarily a higher rank than the other suits ‖ (*pl.*) this suit of cards ‖ (*pop.*) a person who gives one great help in a crisis **to turn up trumps** (*Br.,* of a person) to show an excellent side to one's character, esp. by giving help in some crisis **2.** *v.t.* to take (a card) with a trump card, play a trump card on ‖ *v.i.* to play a card from the trump suit **to trump up** to concoct fraudulently (an excuse, charge etc.) [alt. fr. TRIUMPH]

trump card a trump ‖ an ultimate course of action which one believes cannot fail

trump·er·y (trʌ́mpəriː) **1.** *pl.* **trump·er·ies** *n.* worthless articles ‖ nonsense **2.** *adj.* worthless, paltry (though often showy) [F. *tromperie,* deceit]

trum·pet (trʌ́mpit) **1.** *n.* (*mus.*) a wind instrument fashioned from a long metal tube, with a small cup-shaped mouthpiece and a wide, curved, funnel-shaped free end. The type used in the orchestra and in dance bands has three valves ‖ something resembling this in shape, *an ear trumpet* ‖ an organ stop with a tone like a trumpet's ‖ the sound made by a trumpet ‖ a similar sound, esp. that of an elephant **to blow one's own trumpet** to praise oneself to others **2.** *v.t.* to announce by, or as if by, sounding a trumpet ‖ *v.i.* to play the trumpet ‖ to make a sound like that of a trumpet [F. *trompette*]

trumpet creeper *Campsis radicans,* fam. *Bignoniaceae,* a North American creeper having large, red, trumpet-shaped flowers

trum·pet·er (trʌ́mpitər) *n.* a person who plays a trumpet ‖ a soldier, herald etc. who signals on a trumpet ‖ a trumpeter swan ‖ a member of *Psophia,* fam. *Psophidae,* esp. *P. crepitans,* a long-legged, long-necked South American bird with a loud cry ‖ a member of *Latris,* fam. *Latrididae,* esp. *L. lineata,* a food fish of New Zealand and Australia ‖ any of various other fishes that make a trumpetlike sound when taken from the water ‖ a pigeon of an Asiatic breed with a crested crown and feathered feet

trumpeter swan *Olor buccinator,* a North American wild swan

Trum·pler (trʌ́mplər), Robert Julius (1886-1956), Swiss-U.S. astronomer, noted for his research into galactic star clusters, observational tests of relativity theory, and the study of Mars

trun·cate (trʌ́ŋkeit) **1.** *v.t. pres. part.* **trun·cat·ing** *past* and *past part.* **trun·cat·ed** to shorten by cutting off the top or end ‖ (*crystall.*) to replace (an angle, edge, corner) by a plane, esp. a plane inclined equally to adjacent faces **2.** *adj.* (*biol.*) ending as though cut off at the tip **trún·cat·ed** *adj.* [fr. L. *truncare (truncatus)*]

trun·ca·tion (trʌŋkéiʃən) *n.* a truncating or being truncated ‖ (*banking*) a system of storing customers' cancelled checks in lieu of returning them with monthly statements [fr. L.L. *truncatio (truncationis)*]

trun·cheon (trʌ́ntʃən) *n.* a policeman's nightstick [O.F. *tronchon*]

trun·dle (trʌ́nd'l) **1.** *n.* a small wheel or roller ‖ the act of trundling ‖ a lantern pinion or one of its bars ‖ a mechanism for transmitting motion in an organ-stop action **2.** *v. pres. part.* **trun·dling** *past* and *past part.* **trun·dled** *v.t.* to cause (esp. a heavy, awkward object) to roll along ‖ *v.i.* to roll awkwardly on or as if on wheels [O.E. *trendel,* a circle, ring]

trundle bed a truckle bed

trunk (trʌŋk) **1.** *n.* the main stem of a tree, excluding branches and roots ‖ the human or animal body excluding the head and limbs ‖ a proboscis, esp. of an elephant ‖ the thorax of an insect ‖ the main stem of a blood vessel or nerve ‖ a trunk line ‖ (*archit.*) the central shaft of a column ‖ a large piece of heavy luggage with a hinged lid, used for transporting a quantity of clothes etc. on a journey ‖ the covered luggage container of an automobile ‖ a perforated box for keeping fish alive in after they have been caught ‖ the pipe piston of a trunk engine ‖ (*naut.*) the part of a cabin rising above deck level, or the superstructure above the hatches ‖ (*naut.*) a watertight housing for a centerboard or rudder ‖ (*pl.*) a man's bathing suit ‖ (*pl.*) light

CONCISE PRONUNCIATION KEY: **(a)** æ, *cat;* ɑ, *car;* ɔ *fawn;* ei, *snake.* **(e)** e, *hen;* iː, *sheep;* iə, *deer;* ɛə, *bear.* **(i)** i, *fish;* ai, *tiger;* əː, *bird.* **(o)** o, *ox;* au, *cow;* ou, *goat;* u, *poor;* ɔi, *royal.* **(u)** ʌ, *duck;* u, *bull;* uː, *goose;* ə, *bacillus;* juː, *cube.* x, *loch;* θ, *think;* ð, *bother;* z, *Zen;* ʒ, *corsage;* dʒ, *savage;* ŋ, *orangutang;* j, *yak;* ʃ, *fish;* tʃ, *fetch;* 'l, *rabble;* 'n, *redden.* Complete pronunciation key appears inside front cover.

shorts worn for sports **2.** *adj.* of a main line in a rail, road, telephone etc. system [O.F. *tronc*]

trunk call a long-distance telephone call

trunk engine a steam engine having a pipe piston (trunk), wide enough for one end of the connecting rod to be attached to the crank and the other to pass through the trunk and be pivoted to the piston ‖ an engine with a trunk piston to the open end of which the connecting rod is pivoted. Most internal-combustion engines are of this type

trunk hose (*hist.*) short, puffed-out breeches reaching halfway down the thigh, worn esp. in the late 16th c.

trunk line the main telephone connection between exchanges at a considerable distance from one another ‖ a main line in a rail or other transport system

trun·nion (trʌ́njən) *n.* (*mech.*) a cylindrical pivot around which a piece may turn ‖ each of the two fixed projecting gudgeons on the side of a cannon which rest on the carriage and allow movement in the vertical plane [fr. F. *trognon*, stump]

truss (trʌs) *n.* a padded belt or other device used to support a hernia ‖ a supporting framework e.g. for a bridge, roof etc. ‖ (*Br.*) a bundle of hay or straw of standard weight ‖ (*archit.*) a projection of stone, wood etc. like a large corbel, to support a structure ‖ (*naut.*) a heavy iron fitting for securing the lower yards to the mast, esp. a ring around the lower mast with a pivot attachment to a lower yard at the center ‖ a compact terminal flower or fruit cluster [F. *trousse*]

truss *v.t.* to tie up by binding fast ‖ to secure the limbs of (a chicken etc.) with skewers in preparation for cooking ‖ to support with a truss or trusses [fr. F. *trousser*]

trust (trʌst) *n.* confidence in a person or thing because of the qualities one perceives or seems to perceive in him or it ‖ the person in whom or thing in which one has confidence ‖ acceptance of something as true or reliable without being able to verify it, *on trust* ‖ a responsibility, charge or duty involving the confidence of others, *a position of trust* ‖ a person or thing committed to one as a charge, duty etc. ‖ faith in the future ‖ the responsibility resulting from having others' confidence placed in one, *he considered his office a sacred trust* ‖ (*law*) an equitable right or interest in a property held by one person on behalf of another ‖ the property so administered ‖ a body of trustees ‖ an association of companies organized for defeating competition, obliging the shareholders in each to transfer their stock to a central committee and to surrender voting rights while retaining rights to profit shares [O.N. *traust*]

trust *v.t.* to have faith or trust in, *she trusts him implicitly* ‖ to rely on (someone) to do something or permit (someone) to use something in the proper way ‖ to believe, *if one can trust the report in the papers* ‖ to confide (someone or something) to a person's responsible care ‖ to commit someone or something to the responsible care of (a person) ‖ *v.i.* to have faith, *to trust in God* ‖ (with 'to') to resign hopefully one's chances of success, *to trust to luck* [O.N. *treysta*]

trust company any corporation formed in order to function as a trustee ‖ a bank formed under state laws for handling trusts as well as performing ordinary bank duties except the issuing of bank notes

trus·tee (trʌstí:) *n.* a person legally invested with property rights in the interests of another ‖ each of a body of people, often elected, managing the affairs of an institution ‖ a country responsible for a trust territory ‖ a garnishee

trustee process the process of attachment by garnishment

trus·tee·ship (trʌstí:ʃip) *n.* a position as a trustee ‖ the work of a trustee ‖ the administrative control exerted by a country over a trust territory placed under its authority

trust·ful (trʌ́stfəl) *adj.* ready to trust, not suspicious

trust fund a fund established (esp. by testament) for the benefit of a person or institution under provisions over which the beneficiary has no control and which a trustee has the duty of applying

trust·i·ly (trʌ́stili:) *adv.* in a trusty manner

trust·i·ness (trʌ́sti:nis) *n.* the quality of being trusty

trust·ing (trʌ́stiŋ) *adj.* disposed to trust

trust territory a non-self-governing territory placed under the authority of the United Nations or a deputed authority by the U.N. Trusteeship Council. Such a territory may be a former mandate under the League of Nations, a territory taken from an ex-enemy state after the 2nd world war, or one placed under such authority by the state responsible for its government

trust·wor·thi·ly (trʌ́stwə:rðili:) *adv.* in a trustworthy manner

trust·wor·thi·ness (trʌ́stwə:rði:nis) *n.* the quality of being trustworthy

trust·wor·thy (trʌ́stwə:rði:) *adj.* deserving trust

trust·y (trʌ́sti:) **1.** *adj. comp.* **trust·i·er** *superl.* **trust·i·est** (*rhet.*) trustworthy **2.** *pl.* **trust·ies** *n.* a convict who is considered trustworthy and who is given special privileges

Truth (tru:θ), Sojourner (1797–1883), U.S. preacher, abolitionist and feminist. Born a slave and named Isabella Baumfree, she ran away (1827) and settled in New York City, where she joined a religious cult. Disillusioned, she broke with it (1843) and adopted the name Sojourner Truth as a symbol of her spiritual mission. She campaigned for black emancipation and women's suffrage, becoming the leading black woman orator. After the U.S. Civil War she helped in the resettlement of emancipated slaves and continued her work on behalf of women and blacks

truth (tru:θ) *pl.* **truths** (tru:ðz, tru:θs) *n.* the state or quality of being true ‖ something which is true ‖ accuracy ‖ sincerity, integrity, *he argued thus in all truth* ‖ agreement with fact, *how can you test the truth of what he says?* **trúth·ful** *adj.* telling the truth ‖ habitually telling the truth ‖ (of a story, account, evidence etc.) true [O.E. *trīewth, trȳwth, trēowth*]

truth-in-lend·ing (trú:θinléndiŋ) *n.* (*banking*) 1968 requirement that full disclosure of credit terms be made to consumers

Truth Squad a team of propagandists devoted to denying (false) statements made by the opposition, esp. regarding controversial political issues

truth table (*computer*) a compilation of switching function to follow a logical path in which the all configurations of input and output are presented, showing the truth or falsity of each configuration; used as the basis for a logical integrated circuit

try (trai) **1.** *v. pres. part.* **try·ing** *past* and *past part.* **tried** *v.t.* to attempt to do, *he tried skiing but never liked it* ‖ to test the operation of, *try the brakes* ‖ to test experimentally, *try twice the quantity* ‖ to submit (someone) to judicial inquiry ‖ to submit (a case) to judicial examination ‖ to bore, irritate ‖ to fatigue ‖ to strain (the eyes, someone's patience etc.) ‖ to attempt to open (a door, window etc.) in order to see if it is fastened ‖ to submit (something) to a testing experience ‖ *v.i.* (often with 'to' or 'and' and a coordinate verb) to make an effort to do something, *try and be patient* ‖ to make an experiment **to try it on** (*Br.*) to see how far one can go in some attempt to deceive or wheedle, well knowing there is little chance of succeeding **to try on** to put (a garment) on to test it for fit or see if one likes it **to try one's hand** to see if one has an aptitude for something by attempting it **to try out** to use in order to test the efficiency or quality of ‖ to test the ability of (someone) to perform a given job etc. ‖ to render down (blubber or fat) **to try out for** to submit oneself to a test or audition in order to gain a place e.g. on a team or in the cast of a play **2.** *pl.* **tries** *n.* an effort ‖ (*rugby*) a score of 3 points made by touching down the ball in the opponents' in-goal, entitling the scoring side to attempt to convert the try into a goal [O.F. *trier*]

try·ing (tráiiŋ) *adj.* causing impatience and annoyance ‖ causing worry or affliction

try·ma (tráimə) *n.* (*bot.*) a nutlike drupe, e.g. the fruit of the walnut, in which the epicarp and mesocarp separate from the hard two-valved endocarp [Mod. L. fr. Gk *truma, trumē*, a hole]

Try·on (tráiən), William (1729-88), British colonial governor. As governor (1765-71) of North Carolina, he suppressed colonial agitation against British taxation and refused the colonial assembly permission to meet. As governor (1771-80) of New York, he vigorously supported the Loyalist cause

try-on (tráiən, tráiɒn) *n.* (*Br., pop.*) an attempt to deceive or get something not likely to be given etc., without expecting to succeed

try·out (tráiaut) *n.* a practical test of efficiency ‖ an opportunity to demonstrate qualifications, e.g. for a role in a play etc. ‖ a performance or series of performances of a play before its official opening, to test the reaction of the audience, make improvements etc.

tryp·a·no·some (trípənəsoum) *n.* a member of *Trypanosoma*, fam. *Trypanosomatidae*, a genus of parasitic infusorian flagellate protozoans which live in the blood of man and other vertebrates and are the cause of sleeping sickness and other serious diseases [Mod. L. fr. Gk *trupanon*, borer+*soma*, body]

tryp·a·no·so·mi·a·sis (tripənousoumáiəsis) *n.* any disease caused by a trypanosome, esp. sleeping sickness

tryp·sin (trípsin) *n.* a pancreatic enzyme, splitting proteins into amino acids **tryp·tic** (tríptik) *adj.* of or relating to trypsin [perh. fr. Gk *truein*, to rub down, digest]

tryp·sin·i·za·tion (tripsinəzéiʃən) *n.* (*physiol.*) the process of digestion

tryp·to·phan (tríptəfæn) *n.* a crystalline amino acid, $(C_8H_6N)CH_2CH(NH_2)COOH$, resulting e.g. from tryptic digestion, and necessary in the nutrition of humans and animals [fr. TRYPTIC+Gk *phainein*, to appear]

tryp·to·phane (tríptəfein) *n.* tryptophan

try·sail (tráis'l) *n.* (*naut.*) a small triangular sail bent to a gaff and hoisted on a small mast behind a lower mast, esp. as a storm sail

try square an instrument having a flat metal blade at right angles to the handle, used for measuring right angles

tryst (trist, traist) *n.* (*rhet.*) an agreement between lovers to meet at a certain time and place ‖ (*rhet.*) that meeting [fr. M.E. *triste*, trust]

Tsam·kong (tsámkɔ́ŋ) a port (pop. 269,000) in S. Kwangtung, China, on Kwangchow Bay, under extensive development since 1955

Tsang·po (tsáŋpɔ́) *BRAHMAPUTRA

tsar *CZAR

tsarina *CZARINA

tset·se, tzet·ze (tsétsi:, tsí:tsi:) *n.* the tsetse fly [Tswana (Bantu language of Botswana)]

tsetse fly, tzetze fly a member of *Glossina*, fam. *Glossinidae*, a genus of central and S. African bloodsucking flies which transmit sleeping sickness and other diseases to man and cause a highly fatal disease in domestic animals, esp. cattle and horses

T-72 *n.* (*mil.*) U.S.S.R. tank with 120-mm smooth-bore gun, panoramic day-night sight, and infrared searchlight or laser range finder

T-shirt (tí:ʃə:rt) *n.* a collarless, short-sleeved, pullover shirt, usually in cotton

Tshom·be (tʃɒ́mbei), Moise (1919-69), Congolese statesman. He led his province of Katanga in secession from the Congo (1960-3), and was prime minister of the provisional government of the Congo (1964-5). He was condemned to death (Mar. 1967) in absentia by a Kinshasa military tribunal. An airplane in which he was flying (July 1967) to the Balearic Is was forced down in Algeria, where he died in captivity, untried

Tsi·nan (dʒí:nán) the ancient capital (pop. 867,379) of Shantung, China, a canal port near the Hwang-ho. Industries: textiles, food processing, mechanical engineering, light manufactures

Tsing·hai (tʃíŋhái) a province (area 278,300 sq. miles, pop. 3,897,706) of N.W. China. Capital: Sining (pop. 72,000)

Tsing Hai (tʃíŋhái) (*Mongol* Koko Nor) a shallow lake (area 2,300 sq. miles) with no outlet, in N.E. Tsinghai, China, at 10,500 ft

Tsing·tao (tsíŋtáu, tʃíŋdáu) a port and industrial center (pop. 1,500,000) in E. Shantung, China. Industries: textiles, food processing, paper, building materials, railroad stock. University (1926)

Tsing·yuan (tʃíŋjyán) *PAOTING

Tsinling Shan *CHINLING SHAN

Tsi·tsi·har (tsí:tsi:hɑr) *LUNGKIANG

T-64 *n.* (*mil.*) U.S.S.R. tank, similar to T-62, with missile firing capacity

T-62 *n.* (*mil.*) U.S.S.R. tank with 115-mm main gun, with telescopic device, produced since 1964

T square a drawing instrument shaped like a T for drawing parallel lines or used to support a set square

TSS (*abbr.*) for toxic shock syndrome

tsu·nam·i (tsu:námi:) *n.* a large destructive sea wave generated by an earthquake or volcanic eruption

CONCISE PRONUNCIATION KEY: **(a)** æ, *cat*; ɑ, *car*; ɔ *fawn*; ei, *snake*. **(e)** e, *hen*; i:, *sheep*; iə, *deer*; ɛə, *bear*. **(i)** i, *fish*; ai, *tiger*; ə:, *bird*. **(o)** o, *ox*; au, *cow*; ou, *goat*; u, *poor*; ɔi, *royal*. **(u)** ʌ, *duck*; u, *bull*; u:, *goose*; ə, *bacillus*; ju:, *cube*. x, *loch*; θ, *think*; ð, *bother*; z, *Zen*; ʒ, *corsage*; dʒ, *savage*; ŋ, *orangutang*; j, *yak*; ʃ, *fish*; tʃ, *fetch*; 'l, *rabble*; 'n, *redden*. Complete pronunciation key appears inside front cover.

Tsu·shi·ma Islands (tsú:ʃi:mɑ) two islands (area 269 sq. miles, pop. 59,000) of Japan, between Kyushu and Korea: fishing. They are separate only at high tide

TTBT (*abbr.*) for Threshold Test Ban Treaty, signed by the U.S. and the U.S.S.R. on July 3, 1974, prohibiting underground nuclear tests in excess of 150 kiloton limit

T-time (tí:taim) *n.* (*aerospace*) the take-off or firing time

Tu·a·mo·tu Archipelago (tu:əmóutu:) (*F.* Tuamotu) a coral archipelago (area 330 sq. miles, pop. 8,537) comprising some 60 atolls and islets, in French Polynesia. Main islands: Rangiroa, Fakarava. Religion: mainly Roman Catholic. Exports: copra, phosphates, mother-of-pearl

Tua·reg (twɑ́reg) *n.* a member of a nomadic Berber people of the central and Western Sahara, Hamitic in speech and Moslem in religion. The men wear indigo-dyed veils over the lower part of the face, while the women go unveiled

tu·a·ta·ra (tu:ətɑ́rə) *n. Sphenodon punctatum,* a reptile (about two and a half feet in length) found only in little islands off the New Zealand coast

tub (tʌb) **1.** *n.* an open circular wooden vessel with a flat bottom, made of staves held together by hoops ‖ a similar vessel of metal, plastic etc. ‖ (*mining*) a bucket used for carrying ore etc. ‖ a boat used for practice rowing ‖ a tub and its contents or the contents of a tub, esp. this as a measure, *a tub of butter* ‖ (*pop.*) a slow or clumsy ship ‖ (*pop.*) a bathtub ‖ (*old-fash.*) the act of taking a bath **2.** *v. pres. part.* **tub·bing** *past* and *past part.* **tubbed** *v.t.* to wash in a tub ‖ to put or plant in a tub ‖ to train (a rower) in a tub ‖ *v.i.* (*old-fash.*) to take a bath ‖ to practice rowing in a tub [late M.E. *tubbe*]

tu·ba (tú:bə, tjú:bə) *n.* one of several low-pitched musical instruments, having valves and a cupped mouthpiece. The largest often encircle the body of the musician. The bass tuba is normally the lowest bass brass instrument in an orchestra ‖ a powerful organ stop of 8-ft pitch ‖ *pl.* **tu·bae** (tú:bi:, tjú:bi:) (*Rom. hist.*) a straight bronze war trumpet [L. = a trumpet]

tu·bal (tú:b'l, tjú:b'l) *adj.* like or of a tube, esp. a Fallopian tube

tu·bate (tú:beit, tjú:beit) *adj.* having or forming a tube

tub·by (tʌ́bi:) *comp.* **tub·bi·er** *superl.* **tub·bi·est** *adj.* (esp. of a person) very fat and usually short ‖ tub-shaped

tube (tu:b, tju:b) **1.** *n.* a long, narrow, hollow cylinder for holding or passing liquids, gases etc. ‖ a small, flexible cylinder with a screw cap for holding toothpaste, mustard etc. ‖ a thin, hollow channel in a plant or animal, *bronchial tubes* ‖ (*Br.*) the subway ‖ a tunnel for motor or rail traffic ‖ an electron tube ‖ (with "the") (*slang*) television **2.** *v.t. pres. part.* **tub·ing** *past* and *past part.* **tubed** to provide with tubes ‖ to enclose in tubes [F.]

tu·ber (tú:bər, tjú:bər) *n.* a modified underground stem (e.g. the potato), shortened, thickened and fleshy, with buds which may become new plants (cf. TUBEROUS ROOT) ‖ (*anat.*) a swelling ‖ a member of *Tuber,* a genus of underground fungi (*TRUFFLE) [L.=swelling]

tu·ber·cle (tú:bə:rk'l, tjú:bə:rk'l) *n.* (*anat., zool.*) a small, round elevation, esp. of a bone ‖ (*med.*) a nodular lesion, esp. of a tuberculous infection ‖ (*bot.*) a small swelling or nodule, esp. one on the roots of leguminous plants ‖ a rib knob articulating with the transverse process of a vertebra ‖ a prominence marking the nuclei of various nerves of the central nervous system [fr. L. *tuberculum* dim. of *tuber,* a swelling]

tubercle bacillus *Mycobacterium tuberculosis,* the microorganism causing tuberculosis

tu·ber·cu·lar (tubə́:rkjulər, tjubə́:rkjulər) *adj.* of, having or like tubercles ‖ tuberculous [fr. L. *tuberculum,* tubercle]

tu·ber·cu·late (tubə́:rkjuleit, tjubə́:rkjuleit) *adj.* (*bot.*) having tubercles **tu·bér·cu·lat·ed** *adj.* **tu·ber·cu·lá·tion** *n.* [fr. Mod. L. *tuberculatus* fr. *tuberculum,* tubercle]

tu·ber·cu·lin (tu:bə́:rkjulin, tjubə́:rkjulin) *n.* an extract of tuberculosis bacilli used in diagnosing tuberculosis [fr. L. *tuberculum,* tubercle]

tuberculin test a diagnostic test of tuberculosis: the presence of past or present infection is indicated by the appearance of inflammation at the site of a subcutaneous injection of tuberculin

tu·ber·cu·lo·sis (tubə:rkjulóusis, tjubə:rkjulóusis) *n.* a highly variable infectious disease of man and some other vertebrates caused by the tubercle bacillus. The disease may be acute or chronic and generally attacks the respiratory tract, although any tissue may be affected. The symptoms (fever, loss of weight etc.) are caused by the toxins produced by the infecting organism, which also cause the formation of characteristic nodes consisting of a packed mass of cells and disintegration products surrounding a knot of dead tissue [Mod. L. fr. *tuberculum,* tubercle]

tu·ber·cu·lous (tubə́:rkjuləs, tjubə́:rkjuləs) *adj.* having or pertaining to tuberculosis ‖ tubercular

tu·be·rose (tú:bərouz, tjú:bərouz) *n. Polianthes tuberosa,* fam. *Amaryllidaceae,* a bulbous, low-growing plant, bearing fragrant white, lilylike flowers [fr. Mod. L. *tuberosa* fr. *tuberosus,* knobby]

tu·ber·ose (tú:bərous, tjú:bərous) *adj.* tuberous

tu·ber·os·i·ty (tu:bərɒ́siti:, tju:bərɒ́siti:) *pl.* **tu·ber·os·i·ties** *n.* a rounded eminence, e.g. on a bone for the attachment of a muscle or tendon [F. *tubérosité*]

tu·ber·ous (tú:bərəs, tjú:bərəs) *adj.* (*bot.*) of, like, having or being a tuber or tubers ‖ reproducing by tubers [F. *tubéreux*]

tuberous root a thick root, e.g. the dahlia, like a tuber but bearing no buds to scale leaves

tu·bic·o·lous (tubíkələs, tjubíkələs) *adj.* (e.g. of certain annelids) living in a self-made tube ‖ (of certain spiders) weaving a tubelike web [fr. L. *tubus,* a rube+*colere,* to dwell]

tub·ing (tú:biŋ, tjú:biŋ) *n.* tubes collectively ‖ a set of tubes ‖ a piece of tube ‖ material for tubes

Tü·bin·gen (týbiŋən) a town (pop. 67,800) in Baden-Württemberg, West Germany, on the Neckar. University (1477)

Tub·man (tʌ́bmən), Harriet (c. 1820-1913), U.S. black abolitionist leader. A Maryland slave, she escaped (1849) to Philadelphia. She returned to the South almost every year, leading over 300 slaves to freedom in the North

Tubman, William Vacanarat Shadrach (1895-1971), Liberian statesman, president of Liberia (1944-71)

tub-thump·er (tʌ́bθʌmpər) *n.* someone who is often guilty of tub-thumping

tub-thump·ing (tʌ́bθʌmpiŋ) *n.* the use of ranting, extravagant language in speeches, sermons etc.

tu·bu·lar (tú:bjulər, tjú:bjulər) *adj.* of, shaped like, made of or provided with a tube or tubes ‖ sounding like air passing through tubes [fr. L. *tubulus*]

tu·bule (tú:bju:l, tjú:bju:l) *n.* a small tube or (esp. *anat.*) tubular structure [fr. L. *tubulus*]

Tu·ca·pel (tu:kɑpél) a Spanish fort in Arauco, Chile, site of a battle (1554) between the Spaniards under Valdivia and the Indians under Lautaro, in which Valdivia was killed

tuck (tʌk) **1.** *v.t.* to push (something) into a little space, pocket etc., or under something, where it will be neatly held or conveniently hidden ‖ to thrust the edges of (a sheet, napkin, shirt etc.) in or under something which will keep it secured ‖ to make tucks in (a garment or fabric) ‖ to draw up in, or as if in, a folded manner, *to tuck one's legs under a chair* ‖ (with 'up') to push up or back into folds so as to hold in position, *tuck your sleeves up* ‖ (with 'in') to cover (a person) with bedclothes, *tuck the baby in* ‖ *v.i.* to make tucks ‖ to be disposed of by tucking, *the ends tuck in under the mattress* **to tuck in** (*Br., pop.*) to eat with a hearty appetite **2.** *n.* the act or an instance of tucking ‖ a fold sewn into a garment so as to shorten it or take it in, or for decoration ‖ (*naut.*) the after part of the hull where the bottom planks meet ‖ (*Br., pop.*) candy, cookies etc. for children **túck·er 1.** *v.t.* (*pop.,* often with 'out') to exhaust **2.** *n.* **best bib and tucker** one's smartest set of clothes [O.E. *tūcian*]

tuck-in (tʌ́kin) *n.* (*Br., pop.*) a big meal eaten with appetite

tuck-point (tʌ́kpɔint) *v.t.* to finish (brickwork or stonework) with projecting lines of putty or fine lime mortar

tuck-shop (tʌ́kʃɒp) *n.* (*Br.*) a shop at a school, selling eatables, esp. candy

Tuc·son (tú:sɒn) an agricultural market town (pop. 330,537) in S. Arizona. Industries: food processing, electronic engineering, tourism. Spanish mission church (18th c.). University (1891)

Tu·cu·mán (tu:ku:mɑ́n) a city (pop. 366,392) in N. Argentina at the foot of the Andes, founded in 1565. Industries: food processing (esp. sugar), railroad stock. University (1914)

Tucumán, Declaration of the declaration of Argentina's independence from Spain, signed (July 9, 1816) in the name of the United Provinces of La Plata at the Constituent General Congress held in Tucumán

Tu·dor (tú:dər, tjú:dər) **1.** *n.* a member of the dynasty ruling England 1485-1603 (Henry VII, Henry VIII, Edward VI, Mary I, Elizabeth I) **2.** *adj.* of or relating to a Tudor or his times ‖ (*archit.*) of the late perpendicular Gothic style, marked by a characteristic flattened arch, shallow moldings, and much wall paneling

Tues. Tuesday

Tues·day (tú:zdi:, tjú:zdi:, tú:zdei, tjú:zdei) *n.* the third day of the week [O.E. *Tīwes dæg,* Tīw's day after Tīw, god of war]

tu·fa (tú:fə, tjú:fə) *n.* a soft porous rock (calcium carbonate) formed as a deposit around springs ‖ tuff **tu·fa·ceous** (tu:féiʃəs, tju:féiʃəs) *adj.* [Ital. *tufo, tufa,* a kind of porous stone]

tuff (tʌf) *n.* a rock formed of compacted volcanic fragments of varied composition **tuff·a·ceous** (tʌféiʃəs) *adj.* [fr. F. *tufe, tuffe, tuf* fr. Ital.]

tuft (tʌft) **1.** *n.* a bunch or cluster of feathers, hairs etc. growing together at the base ‖ a small clump of plants or trees ‖ a beard on the tip of a man's chin ‖ (*hist.*) a gold tassel worn by titled undergraduates at Oxford and Cambridge ‖ a buttonlike cluster of loops serving to finish off the threads drawn tightly through a mattress or quilt to secure the padding, or a covered button serving this purpose **2.** *v.t.* to arrange in tufts ‖ to provide with a tuft, esp. to pass tufts of thread through depressions in (mattresses etc.) to hold the stuffing in place ‖ *v.i.* to grow in or take the form of tufts **túft·ed** *adj.* (of birds) having a crest ‖ (of plants) growing in tufts ‖ (of plants) bearing flowers in dense clusters **túft·y** *comp.* **tuft·i·er** *superl.* **tuft·i·est** *adj.* [perh. fr. O. F. *touffe*]

tug (tʌg) **1.** *v. pres. part.* **tug·ging** *past* and *past part.* **tugged** *v.t.* to pull with force, *to tug a heavy cart* ‖ to make a sudden vigorous pull at ‖ (*shipping*) to pull by means of a tugboat, *to tug a liner out of port* ‖ *v.i.* to use force or violence in pulling **2.** *n.* a strong, violent pull ‖ a pulling force ‖ a struggle, esp. a struggle between conflicting emotions, desires etc. ‖ the trace of a harness ‖ a tugboat [M.E. *toggen* fr. O.E. *tēon,* to draw, pull, tug]

tug·boat (tʌ́gbout) *n.* a small powerful steamer for towing e.g. larger ships, logs etc.

tu·ghrik (tú:gri:k) *n.* the basic monetary unit of the Mongolian People's Republic ‖ a note or coin of the value of one tughrik [Mongol *dughurik,* a round thing, a wheel]

tug-of-war (tʌ́gəvwɔ́r) *pl.* **tugs-of-war** *n.* a contest in which a team of men at one end of a rope tries to pull a team at the other end of the rope across a line between them ‖ a close, hard struggle between two parties etc.

Tug·well (tʌ́gwəl), Rexford Guy (1891-1979), the last U.S. governor of Puerto Rico (1941-6), sent by Pres. Franklin Roosevelt to prepare the island for conversion to commonwealth status. Part of Roosevelt's 'brain trust' group of advisers, he served as assistant and under-secretary of agriculture, where he headed the Rural Resettlement Administration, which sought to relocate farmers to more productive land. He also served as director of the University of Chicago's Institute of Planning (1946-52)

tui (tú:i:) *n. Prosthemadera novaeseelandiae,* a New Zealand glossy black honey eater with white markings [Maori]

Tui·le·ries (twi:ləri:) a former royal palace in Paris, begun in 1564 and destroyed (1871) by the Commune. Its vast formal gardens are now a public park

tu·i·tion (tu:íʃən, tju:íʃən) *n.* the price charged for instruction ‖ teaching **tu·i·tion·al, tu·i·tion·ar·y** *adjs* [A.F. fr. L. *tuitio,* guard, guardianship]

Tu·la (tú:lə) a city (pop. 521,000) in the R.S.F.S.R., U.S.S.R., in the Moscow basin. Industries: iron and steel, mechanical engineering, metalworking. Medieval kremlin

Tu·la (tú:lə) a town (pop. 2,000) in central Mexico, 45 miles north of Mexico City. It is the site of the impressive ruins of what is believed to have been the capital of the Toltec kingdom, founded in 677 and destroyed by the Chichimecas in 1116

tu·la·re·mi·a (tu:ləri:mi:ə) *n.* an infectious disease of rodents, some domestic animals and man. It is caused by a bacterium and is transmitted by the bite of bloodsucking insects, or (in man) by the handling of infected animals. It occurs chiefly in North America, Scandinavia and parts of Asia Minor. It causes an ulcer at the site bitten, with inflamed lymph glands and fever [Mod. L. after *Tulare* County, California+Gk *haima*, blood]

tu·lip (tú:lip, tjú:lip) *n.* a member of *Tulipa*, fam. *Liliaceae*, a genus of bulbous herbaceous plants bearing a large, showy, bell-shaped flower on a single tall stem. About 50 species are known, and innumerable varieties of *T. gesneriana*, the garden tulip, have been developed. It was introduced into W. Europe from Turkey in the 16th c. || the flower or the bulb of this plant [F. *tulipe* fr. Turk. fr. Pers.]

tulip tree *Liriodendron tulipifera*, fam. *Magnoliaceae*, a tall North American timber tree with flowers resembling the tulip. It yields a light, fine-grained white wood used for making furniture

tu·lip·wood (tú:lipwụd, tjú:lipwụd) *n.* the wood of the tulip tree || any of various colored or striped woods yielded by certain Brazilian and Australian trees

Tull (tʌl), Jethro (1674-1741), English agriculturist. The seed drill which he invented (c. 1701), and his advocacy of thorough tilling with plow and hoe, were important in the history of English agriculture

tulle (tu:l, tju:l, tyl) *n.* a sheer, sometimes stiffened, machine-made net, of silk or nylon, used for veils, dresses etc. [after *Tulle*, a city in France]

Tul·sa (tʌ́lsə) a city (pop. 360,919) in N.E. Oklahoma, on the Arkansas River, center of a great oil field. Industries: oil refining, metallurgy, mechanical engineering, cotton textiles. University (1921)

Tul·si Das (tú:lsi:dɑ́s) (c. 1532-1623), Indian poet. His poetry, devoted almost exclusively to the praise of Rama, includes the epic 'Ramacarit-manas' (1575)

tum·ble (tʌ́mb'l) **1.** *v. pres. part.* **tum·bling** *past* and *past part.* **tum·bled** *v.i.* to fall to the ground through tripping up or losing one's balance or no longer having support || to move hurriedly and without restraint, control or grace, *they came tumbling into the study* || (with 'down') to fall into ruin || to drop in price at a rapidly increasing pace || to fall suddenly from power || to toss or roll about || (of words) to issue in a spate without proper control || to perform feats of acrobatic agility such as handsprings and somersaults || (*pop.*, with 'to') to understand something suddenly, or become aware of a situation || *v.t.* to cause to fall || to rumple, put in disorder by rough handling || to spin (metal objects etc.) in a tumbling barrel **2.** *n.* a fall || the state of being rumpled or disorderly, *in a tumble* || a confused pile or litter, *a tumble of books and papers covered the desk* || a handspring, somersault etc. [M.E. *tumbel* frequentative or dim. of O.E. *tumbian* to dance, to fall]

tum·ble·bug (tʌ́mb'lbʌg) *n.* a dung beetle

tum·ble·down (tʌ́mb'ldaun) *adj.* dilapidated, beginning to fall into ruin

tumble home 1. *n.* a curving of the sides of a ship inwards above the point of greatest breadth **2.** *v.i.* (of the sides of a ship) to curve in this way

tum·bler (tʌ́mblər) *n.* an acrobat || someone who tumbles || an ordinary drinking glass without a foot or stem || the quantity it holds || a tumbling barrel || a person who operates a tumbling barrel || a domestic pigeon of a breed which somersaults in flight || (*mach.*) a projecting piece on a revolving shaft or rockshaft, setting in motion another piece || the movable part of a reversing or speed-changing gear || a moving part of the mechanism of a lock that must be moved to a certain position (e.g. by a key) for the bolt to be thrown || the part of the hammer in a gunlock on which the mainspring acts || a roly-poly (weighted toy)

tum·ble·weed (tʌ́mb'lwi:d) *n.* any of various plants that break away from their roots at maturity and are blown by the wind over the prairies, scattering seed

tumbling barrel a revolving box containing emery powder in which castings etc. are cleaned by friction || a similar device in which plastics, leather, clothes etc. are whirled as part of a finishing process

tumbling bay a weir

tumbling box a tumbling barrel for small articles

tum·brel, tum·bril (tʌ́mbrəl) *n.* a heavy two-wheeled farm tipcart for carting manure etc. || an open cart used in the French Revolution to carry victims to the guillotine [fr. M.L. *tumbrellum, tumberellum*, a ducking stool fr. O.F.]

tu·me·fac·tion (tu:mifǽkʃən, tju:mifǽkʃən) *n.* a tumefying or being tumefied || a swollen part

tu·me·fy (tú:mifai, tjú:mifai) *pres. part.* **tu·me·fy·ing** *past* and *past part.* **tu·me·fied** *v.t.* to cause to swell, inflate || *v.i.* to become swollen || to become tumid [F. *tuméfier*]

tu·mes·cence (tu:més'ns, tju:més'ns) *n.* a swelling up or the state of swelling up || a swollen part [TUMESCENT]

tu·mes·cent (tu:més'nt, tju:més'nt) *adj.* becoming swollen || somewhat tumid [fr. L. *tumescens (tumescentis)* fr. *tumescere*, to swell up]

tu·mid (tú:mid, tjú:mid) *adj.* swollen || (of language) bombastic, inflated **tu·mid·i·ty** *n.* [fr. L. *tumidus*]

tum·my (tʌ́mi:) *pl.* **tum·mies** *n.* (a child's word, or euphemism) the stomach or belly

tu·mor, *Br.* **tu·mour** (tú:mər, tjú:mər) *n.* a body swelling, esp. an abnormal growth of tissue, either benign or malignant [L. *tumor*=a swelling]

tu·mor·gen·ic or **tum·or·i·gen·ic** (tú:mərdʒénik) *adj.* (*med.*) causing or tending to cause tumors —**tumorigenesis** *n.* the creation of tumors

tu·mor·ous (tú:mərəs, tjú:mərəs) *adj.* of, like or relating to a tumor || having tumors or a tumor [fr. L. *tumorosus*]

tumour *TUMOR

Tu·muc-Hu·mac Mtns (tu:mú:ku:mɑ́k) a range (2,000-3,000 ft) in N. Brazil, extending west to east along the boundary between Suriname and French Guiana on the north and Brazil on the south

tu·mult (tú:məlt, tjú:məlt) *n.* an uproar made by a crowd of people, esp. when rioting || any noisy and violent, usually confused, disturbance || a confused and excited state of mind or of the emotions || a jumble of objects, words etc. **tu·mul·tu·ous** (tu:mʌ́ltʃu:əs, tju:mʌ́ltʃu:əs) *adj.* [fr. L. *tumultus*]

tu·mu·lus (tú:mjuləs, tjú:mjuləs) *pl.* **tu·mu·li** (tú:mjulai, tjú:mjulai) *n.* an ancient burial mound [L.=a mound]

tun (tʌn) *n.* a large cask for beer, wine etc. || a measure of liquid capacity (esp. one equivalent to 252 wine gallons) || a brewer's fermenting vat [O.E. *tunne*]

tu·na (tú:nə, tjú:nə) *n.* a member of *Thunnus*, fam. *Scombroidea*, a genus of large marine fishes, esp. *T. thynnus*, a highly prized game and food fish, living in shoals in temperate seas and sometimes growing up to 10 ft in length || the flesh of this fish [Am. Span., perh. rel. to L. *tunnus, thunnus*, tunny]

tuna *n.* a member of *Opuntia*, a genus of prickly pears, esp. *O. tuna* of Central America and the West Indies || the edible fruit of these plants [Span., of West Indian origin]

tun·a·ble laser (tú:nəb'l) a laser that can be adjusted to cover the light spectrum used in holography, plasma physics, and spectroscopy

Tuna War prohibition of tuna fishing by Peru for an area 200 mi off its coast (1972–1977), resulting in ship seizures and other incidents *Cf* COD WAR

tun·dra (tʌ́ndrə) *n.* an often flat, treeless plain largely covered with mosses and lichens, having a marshy soil with a permanently frozen subsoil, found in Arctic and subarctic regions [Russ.]

tune (tu:n, tju:n) **1.** *n.* a succession of notes so related that they constitute a musical structure, with a sequence and rhythm which are relatively simple, esp. the melody in the upper part of a simple composition || correct musical pitch, *to sing out of tune* || harmonious relationship, *in tune with current ideas* **to change one's tune** to adopt a radically different attitude towards something or someone **to the tune of** to the amount of **2.** *v. pres. part.* **tun·ing** *past* and *past part.* **tuned** *v.t.* to adjust (an instrument) to correct musical pitch || (*radio*) to adjust (a circuit) with respect to resonant frequency || (*radio*) to adjust (a receiving apparatus) to the wavelength of a particular transmitter || to adjust (a motor) so that it runs perfectly || *v.i.* (*radio*, with 'in') to adjust a radio receiver to the wavelength of a particular transmitter || (of an orchestra, with 'up') to check instruments for pitch in readiness to play **túne·ful** *adj.* melodious || full of catchy airs **tún·er** *n.* a person whose job is to tune pianos, organs etc. || (*radio*) a resonant circuit, or more than one, in a receiving set [perh. var. of TONE]

tune out *v.* **1.** to cease watching a television broadcast or listening to radio broadcast by turning to another channel or turning off the receiver **2.** (*colloq.*) by extension, to refuse to notice

Tung·hai (túŋhái) *SINHAILEN

tung oil (tʌŋ) an oil extracted from the seeds of any of several Chinese trees of genus *Aleurites*, fam. *Euphorbiaceae*, esp. *A. fordii*, and used mainly in the manufacture of hard-drying paints, varnishes etc. [fr. Chin. *yu t'ung* fr. *yu*, oil+ *t'ung*, name of the tree]

Tung·shan (tʌ́ŋʃán) *SUCHOW

tung·sten (tʌ́ŋstən) *n.* a metallic element akin to chromium (symbol W, at. no. 74, at. mass 183.85) having the highest melting point of all metals. It is used esp. in electric light filaments and for alloying steel **túng·stic** *adj.* [Swed. fr. *tung*, heavy +*sten*, stone]

Tung·ting Hu (túŋtíŋhú:) a lake (area 4,000 sq. miles in the rainy season) in N.E. Hunan, China, fed by many rivers, and connected by canal to the Yangtze, for which it serves as overflow during the summer rains

Tun·gus (tuŋgú:z) *pl.* **Tun·gus, Tun·gus·es** *n.* a member of a people of esp. Siberia speaking Tungusic languages. They number about 45,000. They are mainly reindeer herdsmen and fishermen, and practice Shamanism || their Tungusic language **Tun·gú·sic 1.** *n.* a subfamily of Altaic languages of central and E. Siberia and Manchuria, including Manchu **2.** *adj.* of the Tungus people || of Tungusic

Tun·gus·ka (tʌŋgú:skə) the name of three tributaries of the Yenisei in central Siberia, U.S.S.R.: the Lower Tunguska (2,550 miles long), rising north of L. Baikal, the Stony Tunguska (980 miles), further south, and the Upper Tunguska (another name for the Lower Angara)

tu·nic (tú:nik, tjú:nik) *n.* (*hist.*) a loose, knee-length or longer, usually sleeveless, slip-on garment belted at the waist and worn by men and women in ancient Greece and Rome || (*Br.*) a jumper (sleeveless slip-on garment) || (esp. *Br.*) a short, close-fitting jacket worn e.g. by policemen || a short garment worn by girls and women for dancing classes, sports etc. || (*eccles.*) a tunicle || a tunica [fr. L. *tunica*]

tu·ni·ca (tú:nikə, tjú:nikə) *pl.* **tu·ni·cae** (tú:niki:, tjú:niki:) *n.* (*anat., zool.*) a membrane or tissue encasing or covering an organ [Mod. L.=coat]

tu·ni·cate (tú:nikit, tjú:nikit) **1.** *adj.* (*biol.*) covered with a tunica || of or relating to a tunicate || (*bot.*) having many concentric layers, e.g. a bulb || (esp. of insects) having each joint buried in the preceding one **2.** *n.* any member of the subphylum *Urochorda*, degenerate sessile marine animals, the larvae of which show typical chordate features, but which lack most chordate characteristics in the adult form (e.g. the sea squirt) **tu·ni·cat·ed** (tú:nikẹitid, tjú:nikẹitid) *adj.* [fr. L. *tunicare (tunicatus)*, to clothe with a tunic]

tu·ni·cle (tú:nik'l, tjú:nik'l) *n.* (*eccles.*) a short vestment worn by a subdeacon over the alb at Mass || a close-fitting vestment worn under the dalmatic by a bishop at pontifical Mass || (*anat.*) a tunica [fr. L. *tunicula*, a little tunic]

TU-95 *TU-20

tuning fork a two-pronged steel instrument which gives a tone of constant pitch when struck, thus serving as a standard for tuning instruments or for indicating pitch to voices

Tu·nis (tú:nis, tjú:nis) the capital (pop. 550,404), commercial center and (with its outport La Goulette) chief port of Tunisia, on the northeast coast. Industries: superphosphates and other chemical products, metallurgy, building materials, food processing, fishing, handicrafts. Great Mosque (8th-9th cc.), casbah (13th c.), medieval quarters

Tu·ni·sia (tu:ní:ʒə, tu:ní:ʃə) a republic (area 63,362 sq. miles, pop. 6,629,600) in N. Africa. Capital: Tunis. People: Arab (94%), with small European and Berber minorities. Language: Arabic, French, small Berber and Italian minorities. Religion: Sunni Moslem (state religion), 4% Roman Catholic, small Orthodox, Jewish and Protestant minorities. The land is 13% arable, 23% pasture and grazing, and 6% forest (cork, oak, pine). The wooded E. Atlas Mtns (highest peak 5,065 ft) cross the north, cut by wide, fertile plains (cereals), which with the eastern coastal zone (citrus fruit in the north, olives in the south) and Djerba constitute the

CONCISE PRONUNCIATION KEY: **(a)** æ, *cat*; ɑ, *car*; ɔ *fawn*; ei, *snake*. **(e)** e, *hen*; i:, *sheep*; iə, *deer*; ɛə, *bear*. **(i)** i, *fish*; ai, *tiger*; ə:, *bird*. **(o)** o, *ox*; au, *cow*; ou, *goat*; u, *poor*; ɔi, *royal*. **(u)** ʌ, *duck*; u, *bull*; u:, *goose*; ə, *bacillus*; ju:, *cube*. x, *loch*; θ, *think*; ð, *bother*; z, *Zen*; ʒ, *corsage*; dʒ, *savage*; ŋ, *orangutang*; j, *yak*; ʃ, *fish*; tʃ, *fetch*; 'l, *rabble*; 'n, *redden*. Complete pronunciation key appears inside front cover.

agricultural region. The center is dry steppe (livestock), merging with the Sahara in the south. Average temperatures (F.): Tunis 53° (Jan.), 79° (July). Rainfall: northern mountains over 24 ins, northeast and center 16-24 ins, Tunis 16 ins, Sfax 8 ins, Gafsa 4 ins. Livestock: sheep, goats, cattle, donkeys, camels, horses. Agricultural products: cereals, olives, citrus fruit, dates (Saharan oases), vines, esparto, tobacco, vegetables. Forestry products: lumber, cork. Minerals: phosphates, iron ore, lead and zinc, natural gas, silver. Manufactures and industries: textiles, carpets, leather goods, footwear, pottery, copperware, olive oil refining, wines and liquors, fishing, food processing, cement. Exports: olive oil, phosphates, wines, iron ore, fruit, wheat, lead, dates. Imports: foodstuffs, machinery, fuels and oil, iron and steel, textiles, clothing, vehicles, paper, chemicals. Main ports: Tunis, Bizerta. University (in Tunis). Monetary unit: Tunisian dinar (1,000 millièmes). HISTORY. Tunisia was colonized by the Phoenicians, who founded (c. 814 B.C.) the city of Carthage. This was destroyed (146 B.C.) by the Romans. The area was conquered by the Vandals (5th c. A.D.), became part of the Byzantine Empire (6th c.) and was conquered by the Arabs (7th c.). The native Berbers were converted to Islam. Tunisia became part of the Ottoman Empire (16th c.) and a center of Barbary pirates. The beys of Tunisia gained virtual independence, but were heavily in debt by the 19th c. and submitted to Italian and French intervention. Tunisia became a French protectorate (1881), though this was contested by Italy until the 2nd world war, when Tunisia was a center of the N. African campaign. A nationalist movement developed under Bourguiba, and Tunisia became independent (Sept. 1, 1955) and a republic (July 25, 1957) with Bourguiba as president. The country joined the United Nations (1956) and the Arab League (1958). Palestinian Liberation Organization headquarters moved to Tunis in 1982. In 1983, Tunisia, Algeria and Mauritania signed a cooperation treaty

tunnage *TONNAGE

tun·nel (tʌ́n'l) **1.** *n.* a passageway of wide section cut through a hill or cliff side or under the ground, sea or a river, and made permanent with masonry, for a road or railroad to go through ‖ (*mining*) an underground gallery ‖ a passage dug underground by an animal ‖ a wind tunnel **2.** *v. pres. part.* **tun·nel·ing,** esp. *Br.* **tun·nel·ling** *past* and *past part.* **tun·neled,** esp. *Br.* **tun·nelled** *v.t.* to pass through or under (something) with or as if with a tunnel ‖ *v.i.* to make or use a tunnel [O.F. *tonel*]

tunnel curl tube (*surfing*) the arch of an ocean wave just before it breaks

tunnel diode (*electr.*) a junction diode containing a thin depletion layer, permitting electrons to bypass a negative-resistant barrier, used for amplification at low levels, switching, and computer data storage *also* Esaki diode

tunnel vision **1.** straight-ahead vision without periphery **2.** (*colloq.*) by extension, narrow-mindedness

tun·ny (tʌ́ni:) *pl.* **tun·nies** *n.* tuna [prob. fr. F. *thon* fr. Prov. or Ital. fr. L. fr. Gk]

TU-154A *n.* (*mil.*) NATO code name 'Careless,' U.S.S.R. transport aircraft with 87,630-lb capacity, 3,727-mi range, capable of carrying 120 passengers

TU-144 *n.* (*mil.*) U.S.S.R. transport with a speed of Mach 2.35, capable of carrying 140 passengers, competitive with Concorde

TU-134 *n.* (*mil.*) U.S.S.R. short-to-medium-range bomber with turbofan engines, 18,000-lb capacity, range of 500 mi.

tup (tʌp) **1.** *n.* (*Br.*) a ram (male sheep) ‖ the striking face of a steam hammer ‖ any of various devices acting as hammers, e.g. a pile driver **2.** v. *pres. part.* **tup·ping** *past* and *past part.* **tupped** *v.t.* (*Br.*, of a ram) to cover (a ewe) ‖ *v.i.* (*Br.*, of a ewe) to accept the ram [etym. doubtful]

Tú·pac A·ma·ru (tú:pɑkɑmɑ́ru:) (*d.* 1579), Peruvian Inca who rebelled against Spanish rule and was executed by order of Francisco de Toledo (viceroy 1569-81, *d.* c. 1582)

Túpac Amaru (né José Gabriel Condorcanqui, 1742-81), Peruvian cacique and descendant of the Incas. He rebelled (1780) against Spanish rule. He was defeated (1781) by the forces under viceroy Agustín de Jáuregui y Aldecoa, and he and his family were tortured and executed

Tu·pa·ma·ros (tu:pəmɑ́rous) an extreme left-wing organization in Uruguay which is also known as the National Liberation Movement. It is named after Túpac Amaru and specializes in urban guerrilla warfare

tu·pe·lo gum (tú:pəlou, tjú:pəlou) *Nyssa aquatica,* fam. *Cornaceae,* a swamp tree of the southern U.S.A. ‖ its wood, used for cheap construction work and inexpensive furniture [Creek]

Tu·pi (tú:pi:) *pl.* **Tu·pi, Tu·pis** *n.* a member of a group of Tupi-Guaranian peoples inhabiting parts of Brazil, esp. the valleys of the Amazon ‖ their language, serving as a lingua franca in the Amazon valley **Tú·pi·an** *adj.* of or relating to the Tupi or other Tupi Guaranian peoples or the Tupi language

Tu·pi-Gua·ra·ni (tú:pi:gwɑruni:) *n.* a South American people living in an area extending from eastern Brazil to the Peruvian Andes, and from Guiana to Uruguay ‖ a member of this people ‖ Tupi-Guaranian **Tú·pi-Gua·rá·ni·an** **1.** *adj.* of or relating to the Tupi-Guarani **2.** *n.* a group of languages widely distributed in tropical South America and including Tupi and Guarani

tuppence *TWOPENCE

tuppenny *TWOPENNY

Tu·pun·ga·to (tu:pu:ŋgɑ́tɔ) a peak (22,300 ft) in the Andes Mtns on the Chile-Argentina border, about 40 miles northeast of Santiago, Chile

Tu·ra (tú:ra), Cosimo (c. 1430–c. 1498), Italian painter of Ferrara, much influenced by Mantegna

tu·ra·cin (túərəsin, tjúərəsin) *n.* a red pigment containing copper, obtained from the touraco

Tu·ra·ni·an (turéini:ən, tjuréini:ən) **1.** *n.* the Ural-Altaic family of languages ‖ a member of any of the peoples who speak them **2.** *adj.* of these languages or the people who speak them [fr. Pers. *Turān,* region north of the oxus]

tur·ban (tə́:rbən) *n.* a headdress, formed of a long piece of cloth wound around the head or sometimes around a cap, worn by men, esp. in eastern Mediterranean and southern Asian countries ‖ a hat for women resembling this **túr·baned** *adj.* [fr. Pers. *dulband, dōlband*]

tur·ba·ry (tə́:rbəri:) *pl.* **tur·ba·ries** *n.* a place where turf or peat is dug ‖ (*Br. law*) the right to dig turf on another person's land [A.F. *turberie* fr. O.F.]

tur·bel·lar·i·an (tə:rbəléəri:ən) *n.* a member of *Turbellaria,* a class of free-living, soft-bodied flatworms of the phylum *Platyhelminthes,* living in fresh or salt water or occasionally on land. Some are parasitic [fr. Mod. L. *Turbellaria* fr. L. *turbella,* a little crowd]

tur·bid (tə́:rbid) *adj.* having the sediment stirred up ‖ thick, dense, e.g. with smoke ‖ not clear, muddled in thought or feeling **tur·bid·i·ty** *n.* [fr. L. *turbidus,* disturbed]

tur·bid·im·e·ter (tə:rbədímətə:r) *n.* a device that measures the amount of suspended solids in a liquid

turbidity **1.** haziness in the atmosphere due to pollution **2.** murkiness in water due to suspended materials

tur·bi·nal (tə́:rbin'l) **1.** *adj.* turbinate **2.** *n.* a turbinate bone or cartilage

tur·bi·nate (tə́:rbinit) **1.** *adj.* (*anat.*) of the thin, scroll-like, bony or cartilaginous plates on the walls of the nasal chambers ‖ (*zool.*, of a shell) rolled in sharply decreasing spiral whorls ‖ (*bot.*) shaped like a cone resting on its apex **2.** *n.* a turbinate bone ‖ a turbinate shell **tur·bi·nat·ed** (tə́:rbineitid) *adj.* **tur·bi·na·tion** *n.* [fr. L. *turbinatus* fr. *turbo,* a whirlwind]

tur·bine (tə́:rbain, tə́:rbin) *n.* an engine, usually consisting of curved vanes on a central rotating spindle, actuated by the reaction, impulse, or both, of a current (water, steam or gas) subjected to pressure. Turbines are more economical, mechanically simpler, and at higher speed provide more regular rotation than reciprocating engines [F. fr. L. *turbo (turbinis),* a whirlwind]

tur·bo·car (tə́:rboukɑr) *n.* (*automobile*) fuel-efficient motor vehicle powered by a turbine engine

tur·bo·charg·er (tə́:rboutʃɑrdʒə:r) *n.* (*automobile*) a device for motor vehicles using exhaust gases to force the air-fuel mixture into cylinders, causing a bigger detonation than in normally aspirated motors

tur·bo·cop·ter (tə́:rboukɒptə:r) *n.* a helicopter deriving its power from gas turbine engines

tur·bo·e·lec·tric (tə́:rbouiléktrik) *adj.* of a turbine generator used as a power source

tur·bo·fan (tə́:rboufæn) *n.* (*aerospace*) gas turbine engine that shares its power with a multi-bladed propeller, used esp. for ventilation *also* ducted fan

turbojet a jet engine with air supplied by a turbine-driven compressor, the turbine being activated by exhaust gases

tur·bo·jet engine (tə́:rboudʒet) (*aeron.*) a jet engine having a compressor, driven by the power developed from a turbine, which supplies compressed air to the combustion chamber, and having a discharge nozzle directing heated air and gases rearward

tur·bo·prop (tə́:rbouprɒp) *n.* a jet engine having a turbine-driven propeller, usually with additional thrust from the expulsion of hot exhaust gases ‖ an aircraft powered by such an engine [short for *turbo-propeller engine*]

tur·bo·pump (tə́:rboupʌmp) *n.* a pump that is powered by a ram-air turbine and full or hydraulic pump, used for guided missiles and as emergency equipment for aircraft, e.g., in a nuclear rocket

tur·bo·shaft (tə́:rbouʃæft) *n.* a turbine engine used through a transmission system to power helicopter rotors, pumps, etc.

tur·bot (tə́:rbət) *pl.* **tur·bot, tur·bots** *n. Psetta maxima,* a European flatfish weighing up to 30 or 40 lbs, highly valued as food [O.F. *tourbout*]

tur·bo·train (tə́:rboutrein) *n.* turbine engine-powered train

tur·bu·lence (tə́:rbjuləns) *n.* the state or quality of being turbulent **túr·bu·len·cy** *n.*

tur·bu·lent (tə́:rbjulənt) *adj.* in a state of commotion or stormy agitation ‖ violent by nature and hard to control ‖ (*phys.*, of flow) erratic in velocity [fr. L. *turbulentus* fr. *turbare,* to disturb (*turba,* a crowd)]

tu·reen (turí:n, tjurí:n) *n.* a deep, covered dish for holding soup etc. [F. *terrine*]

Tu·renne (tyren), Henri de la Tour d'Auvergne, vicomte de (1611-75), French marshal. He displayed his genius for strategy in the Thirty Years' War, the wars of the Fronde, the War of Devolution and the 3rd Dutch War

turf (tə:rf) **1.** *pl.* **turves** (tə:rvz), **turfs** *n.* grass and the earth in which its matted roots are mingled ‖ a piece of this peat used as fuel ‖ (*pop.*) the grass-grown surface of a piece of land ‖ (with 'the') horseracing **2.** *v.t.* to cover with turf **to turf out** (*Br.*) to throw out or away **túrf·y** *adj.* [O.E.]

Tur·fan (túrfɑ́n) a depression (about 5,000 sq. miles) in the Tarim basin, E. Sinkiang, China, south of the Tien Shan, containing the lowest point (425 ft below sea level) in Asia. An Indo-Persian civilization flourished here (c. 300 A.D.) ‖ an oasis trading town (pop. 20,000) at its northern edge: Buddhist temples, sculptures, Nestorian and Manichaean manuscripts

Tur·ge·nev (tə:rgéinjev), Ivan Sergeyevich (1818-83), Russian writer. His work was unpopular in official circles, partly because of his liberal Western tendencies. 'A Sportsman's Sketches' (1852), a collection of stories of peasant life, was an impassioned plea for the abolition of serfdom. His other works include the play 'A Month in the Country' (1850) and the novel 'Fathers and Sons' (1862). He influenced Chekhov and, through him, European literature as a whole

tur·ges·cence (tə:rdʒés'ns) *n.* the condition of being swollen ‖ a swelling ‖ (*rhet.*) bombast

tur·ges·cent (tə:rdʒés'nt) *adj.* becoming turgid or swollen [fr. L. *turgescens* (*turgescentis*) fr. *turgescere,* to swell up]

tur·gid (tə́:rdʒid) *adj.* unhealthily or abnormally swollen ‖ bombastic, inflated, *a turgid literary style* **tur·gid·i·ty** *n.* [fr. L. *turgidus* fr. *turgere,* to swell]

tur·gor (tə́:rgər) *n.* (esp. *bot.*) normal turgidity in living cells or tissues, esp. due to the taking up of fluid [L.L. fr. L. *turgere,* to swell]

Tur·got (tyrgou), Anne Robert Jacques, Baron de l'Aulne (1727-81), French economist, controller general of finances (1774-6). Influenced by the teachings of the physiocrats, he attempted a radical reform of the French economy, freeing trade, encouraging industry and attacking monopolies. The privileged classes rallied against him, and brought about his fall

Tu·rin (túərin, tjúərin, turín, tjurín) (*Ital.* Torino) an industrial center (pop. 1,143,263) in Piedmont, Italy, on the Po. Industries: automobiles, mechanical engineering, chemical industries, textiles, food processing, vermouth.

Cathedral (15th c.), palaces (12th-14th and 17th cc.), museums (celebrated Egyptian and Renaissance art collections), libraries, university (1404). Of pre-Roman origin, Turin was ruled by the house of Savoy (13th-18th cc.) and became the capital of the kingdom of Sardinia in 1720. It was the capital of Italy 1861-5

Tu·ring machine (túːriŋ) *(computer)* a mathematical model of a computer with a potentially infinite storage capacity; named for A. M. Turing, English mathematician (1912–1954)

tu·ri·on (túəriːən, tjúəriːən) *n. (bot.)* a young, scaly shoot, e.g. an asparagus shoot, rising from a bud on an underground stem [F. fr. L. *turio (turionis)*, shoot]

Turk (təːrk) *n.* a native or inhabitant of Turkey, esp. one of the Moslem people of Turkey ‖ a member of any of numerous Asiatic peoples speaking a Turkic language

Tur·ke·stan (təːrkistǽn, təːrkistán) a historical region of central Asia, now comprising W. Sinkiang-Uighur (China) and Kazakhstan, Kirghizia, Tadzhikistan, Uzbekistan and Turkmenistan (U.S.S.R.). It was chiefly under Persian and Chinese influence until conquered by the Arabs (8th c.). It was invaded by Genghis Khan (13th c.) and Timur (14th c.). Bukhara and Samarkand became centers of culture and trade. The east remained under Chinese control, and the west was annexed by Russia (1853-76)

Tur·key (tə́ːrkiː) a republic (area 301,302 sq. miles, pop. 49,155,000) in W. Asia and S.E. Europe. Capital: Ankara. Chief city: Istanbul. People: 84% Turks, 12% Kurds, 1% Arabs, small Circassian, Greek, Georgian, Armenian and Bulgarian minorities. Language: 90% Turkish, 6% Kurdish, minority languages. Religion: 98% Moslem, 1% Christian (mainly Greek Orthodox and Gregorian), small Jewish minority. The land is 32% arable, 37% pasture and 13% forest. Trakya or Thrace (European Turkey) is a rolling, cultivated plain with mountains on the north and south. Asian Turkey (Anatolia, Armenia and Kurdistan), except for coastal plains, is an elevated plateau (mainly 6,000–10,000 ft), crossed by many high ranges, esp. east of the Mediterranean, and cut by river valleys. Highest peaks: Buyak Agri or Ararat (16,946 ft), Suphan (13,697 ft). The plateau, partly cultivated (esp. in the west), is largely semidesert, with alpine pasture and evergreen forest on higher slopes and in the east. The Black Sea slopes are fertile. Average temperatures (F.) in Jan. and July: Istanbul 42° and 74°, central Black Sea coast 45° and 74°, Ankara 30° and 75°, Erzurum 15° and 66°, E. Syrian border 65° and 85°. Rainfall: Lake Tuz basin 1-8 ins, Istanbul 24 ins, central Black Sea coast 28 ins, E. Black Sea coast 92 ins, Ankara 13 ins, Erzurum 20 ins. Livestock: sheep, goats, cattle, donkeys, mules, horses, water buffalo, camels. Agricultural products: cotton, tobacco, cereals (esp. wheat), olives and olive oil, silk, dried fruits, dairy products, rice, hemp, flax, sugar beets, grapes, figs, citrus fruit, nuts, licorice root, almonds, mohair, skins and hides, furs, wool, gums, canary seed, linseed, sesame, vegetables, sultana raisins, opium. Forestry products: pine, fir, beech, cedar, oak. Mineral resources: coal, petroleum, iron ore, uranium, chrome, sulfur, copper, antimony, manganese, salt, tungsten, lignite. Manufactures and industries: mining, textiles, iron and steel, fishing, cement, paper and pulp, carpets, glass, pottery, hydroelectricity, tourism, silk, sugar, leather, chemicals, fertilizers, canned goods, wines and liquor, vegetable oils, soap, oil refining. Exports: tobacco, fruit and nuts, cotton, mohair, livestock, minerals, sugar, hides and skins. Imports: machinery, cereals, vehicles, oil and petroleum products, iron and steel, chemicals, fabrics and yarns, rubber, paper. Chief ports: Istanbul, Izmir. Universities: Istanbul (2), Ankara (2), Izmir and Erzurum. Monetary unit: Turkish pound or lira (100 piasters or kurus). HISTORY. (For early history *ASIA MINOR, *THRACE, *OTTOMAN EMPIRE.) The overthrow (1922) of the Ottoman Empire by Atatürk was followed by the Treaty of Lausanne (1923) and the proclamation of a republic (Oct. 29, 1923). Under Atatürk's dictatorial presidency (1923-38), many Western reforms were introduced and economic problems were tackled. Turkey joined he Balkan Entente (1934) but remained neutral in the 2nd world war until 1945, when it declared war on Germany and Japan. It joined the U.N. (1945), NATO (1952), the Balkan Pact (1954) and the Central Treaty Organization (1955). The government was overthrown (1960) by a coup d'état, and a new constitution was introduced (1961). Greek and Turkish sections of the population on Cyprus erupted in fighting in 1964. In 1974, Cypriot President Makarios had been overthrown and Greece seemed about to annex the island, prompting Turkish troops to invade and occupy almost half of the island. U.S.-Turkey relations suffered from the continuing Turkish presence in Cyprus: in 1975 the U.S.A. cut off military aid to Turkey and Turkey promptly closed U.S. military bases in Turkey. Some bases were reopened following negotiations the following year. Aegean Sea oil exploration further exacerbated tensions between Greece and Turkey, and political and economic conditions in Turkey worsened as oil prices rose and terrorism became more of a problem. In 1980 the military took control of the government

tur·key (tə́ːrkiː) *pl.* **tur·keys** *n. Meleagris gallopavo*, fam. *Meleagrididae*, a large (up to 4 ft long and up to 35 lbs in weight) gallinaceous American bird domesticated in many parts of the world, raised mainly for its excellent flesh **to talk turkey** to be realistic in commercial bargaining, esp. by making proposals likely to be acceptable [short for TURKEYCOCK, applied in the 16th c. to the guinea fowl]

turkey *(slang)* **1.** a failure; a flop **2.** an inpatient whom a hospital believes does not need hospital admission, not usu. a malingerer

turkey buzzard *Cathartes aura*, fam. *Cathartidae*, a vulture of South and Central America and the southern U.S.A.

tur·key-cock (tə́ːrkiːkɒk) *n.* a male turkey

Tur·ki (tə́ːrkiː) **1.** *adj.* of any of the central Asian Turkic languages ‖ of the peoples who speak these languages **2.** *n.* these languages ‖ any of the peoples who speak them

Tur·kic (tə́ːrkik) **1.** *adj.* of or relating to a subfamily of the Altaic language group ‖ of or relating to any of the people who speak these languages ‖ *(loosely)* Turkish **2.** *n.* the Turkic subfamily of languages

Turk·ish (tə́ːrkiʃ) **1.** *adj.* of Turkey or the Turks ‖ of the Turkic languages, esp. of Osmanli **2.** *n.* the Turkic language of Turkey, esp. Osmanli

Turkish bath a bath in which a person is surrounded by hot steam and made to perspire heavily and is then given a massage and a cold shower ‖ the place where such a bath is given

Turkish delight a jellylike candy, cut in cubes and dusted with sugar

Turkish Empire the Ottoman Empire

Turkish tobacco a highly aromatic tobacco used chiefly in cigarettes, and grown esp. in Turkey and Greece

Turkish towel a towel made of terry cloth

Turk·man (tə́ːrkmən) *pl.* **Turk·men** (tə́ːrkmən) *n.* a native of Turkmenistan ‖ a Turkoman

Turk·men (tə́ːrkmən) *n.* the Turkic language of the Turkomans, Turkoman

Turk·me·ni·an (təːrkmíːniːən) *adj.* of or relating to Turkmenistan or its people

Turk·me·ni·stan (təːrkmenistǽn, təːrkmenistán) a constituent republic (area 188,400 sq. miles, pop. 2,759,000) of the U.S.S.R. in central Asia. Capital: Ashkhabad. The Kara Kum desert occupies most of the region. Agriculture (dependent on irrigation): cotton, cereals, fruit, vines, vegetables. Livestock: camels, goats, sheep (esp. for astrakhan fur). Resources: oil, coal, sulfur, salt, magnesium. Industries: chemical manufactures, cotton, light engineering, oil refining. Part of Turkestan, it was conquered by Russia (1869-95) and became a constituent republic in 1924

Tur·ko·man (tə́ːrkəmən) *pl.* **Tur·ko·mans** *n.* a member of any of a group of chiefly Moslem Turkic tribes inhabiting Turkmenistan, Uzbekistan and Kazakhstan, U.S.S.R. ‖ the language of the Turkomans

Tur·ko·men (tə́ːrkəmən) Turkmenistan

Turks and Cai·cos Islands (təːrks, káikɒs) two groups of islands (land area 166 sq. miles, pop. 7,436), nine being inhabited, at the east end of the Bahamas, geographically part of the latter but forming a distinct British Crown Colony. Main islands: Grand Caicos, Cockburn Town. Capital: Grand Turk (pop. 2,300). People: Afro-West Indian and mullatto. Exports: salt, fish, conch shell, sisal. The islands were discovered by the Spanish (1512), came under British control (18th c.) and were administered as a dependency of Jamaica (1874-1959). They were part of the Federation of the West Indies (1959-62) and became a Crown Colony

Tur·ku (túrkuː) *(Swed.* Abo) a port (pop. 163,665) in S.W. Finland. Industries: shipbuilding, textiles, food processing. Cathedral, castle (both 13th c.). Finnish (1922) and Swedish (1919) universities

turmaline *TOURMALINE

tur·mer·ic (tə́ːrmərik) *n. Curcuma longa*, fam. *Zingiberaceae*, a perennial low-growing East Indian plant ‖ its yellow rhizome, dried and powdered and used esp. in curry powder, for coloring foods, as a stimulant and as a chemical indicator of alkalis, which turn the color reddish brown ‖ an orange or reddish-brown dye obtained from the rhizome [etym. doubtful]

tur·moil (tə́ːrmɔil) *n.* violent agitation or great confusion, *mental turmoil* [etym. doubtful]

turn (təːrn) **1.** *v.t.* to cause to move through an arc of a circle or about an axis or central point, *to turn a wheel* ‖ to cause to move in this way as part of a process of opening or shutting, *to turn a door handle* ‖ to perform (a cartwheel, somersault or handspring) ‖ to shape (something) on a lathe ‖ to trim superfluous clay from (a pot) on a potter's wheel ‖ to cause (a lathe) to work ‖ *(knitting)* to form (a heel) by increasing and decreasing ‖ (sometimes with 'over') to put the other side of (a page) uppermost in order to read or write on it ‖ to dig or plow (soil) so as to bring to the surface the parts formerly lying underneath ‖ (with 'out') to expel, drive out ‖ (with 'out') to cause (something) to come out of its mold, *to turn out a jelly* ‖ to unpick (a garment or part of a garment) and sew it together again wholly or partially inside out so that the worn side is hidden, *to turn a collar* ‖ (with 'up') to make (a folded collar) stand up ‖ to alter the course of (something), *he turned the conversation to more cheerful topics* ‖ to proceed around (a corner) ‖ to cause to go away, or to send away, *to turn someone from one's door* ‖ (with 'on') to direct, aim, *turn the hose on the fire* ‖ to cause to change opinion or attitude, *the speech turned the crowd in our favor* ‖ to get beyond (a certain age), *he has turned 40* ‖ (with 'into') to drive, cause to enter, *to turn sheep into a pen* ‖ to affect (a person) in a specified way, *prison turned him bitter* ‖ to twist (an ankle) ‖ to make sour, rancid, bad, curdled, *the heat turned the milk*, or to seem to cause curdling in, *it turns one's stomach* ‖ to form or construct neatly or gracefully, *to turn a phrase* ‖ (with 'to') to cause (the mind, attention, thoughts) to concentrate on ‖ to cause to change color, *frost turned the leaves early* ‖ to cause to take on a specified color, *cold turned their ears pink* ‖ to cause (something) to change the direction in which it is facing, *turn your chair to the table* ‖ (with 'down') to fold back the sheets of (a bed) to make it ready to occupy ‖ *(mil.)* to go around, *to turn the enemy's flank* ‖ *(cricket)* to cause (a ball) to break ‖ (with 'into') to paraphrase, translate or express in different words, *can you turn the text into good English?* ‖ (with 'into' or 'to') to cause to be regarded in a specified way, *he turned the play into a farce* ‖ *v.i.* to move through an arc of a circle or about an axis or central point, *the wheel turned slowly* ‖ to use a lathe ‖ to become altered in form, outlook, attitude etc., *the wine turned to vinegar, the man turned nasty, the leaf turned yellow* ‖ to change direction, *turn right here, they turned and ran* ‖ (of leaves) to change color ‖ to become sour or rancid ‖ to be dependent for its development on something specified, *the plot turns on a lost bracelet* ‖ (esp. with 'toss and') to move about restlessly in bed ‖ (of the wind) to change quarter ‖ (of the tide) to start to ebb or flow ‖ (of the mind) to become deranged ‖ (of the eye, gaze etc.) to look ‖ (with 'from') to glance aside ‖ (with 'from') to face about so as not to see something, *she turned from the sight* ‖ to seem to go in a certain direction, *his thoughts turned homeward* ‖ (of the stomach) to be upset ‖ (of the head) to seem to reel ‖ (with 'to') to take up something as a new interest, hobby etc., *to turn to gardening* ‖ (with 'to') to change in nature, *sorrow turned to joy* ‖ *(impers.*, of the weather) to change in character in a specified way, *it turned to rain* **not to know which way to turn** not to know how to start dealing with harassing circumstances **to turn against** to become hostile towards or prejudiced against someone or something one formerly liked ‖ to cause (someone) to become hostile or prejudiced in this way **to turn away** to change the direction in which one is going or looking, from horror etc. or from indifference ‖ to send away (someone seeking

CONCISE PRONUNCIATION KEY: **(a)** æ, *cat*; ɑ, *car*; ɔ *fawn*; ei, *snake*. **(e)** e, *hen*; iː, *sheep*; iə, *deer*; ɛə, *bear*. **(i)** i, *fish*; ai, *tiger*; əː, *bird*. **(o)** ɒ, *ox*; au, *cow*; ou, *goat*; uː, *poor*; ɔi, *royal*. **(u)** ʌ, *duck*; u, *bull*; uː, *goose*; ə, *bacillus*; juː, *cube*. x, *loch*; θ, *think*; ð, *bother*; z, *Zen*; ʒ, *corsage*; dʒ, *savage*; ŋ, *orangutang*; j, *yak*; ʃ, *fish*; tʃ, *fetch*; 'l, *rabble*; 'n, *redden*. Complete pronunciation key appears inside front cover.

admittance, work etc.) unsatisfied **to turn back** to abandon progress and return by the way one has come ‖ to cause (someone or something) to do this **to turn down** to reject (an offer, application, person proposing marriage or a proposal of marriage) ‖ to lessen the output of heat, light or sound of (something) by manipulating controls ‖ to manipulate controls to lessen (sound, heat, brightness) ‖ (of the mouth or of eyes at the corners) to point downwards **to turn in** (of feet, toes, eyes) to point inwards, *his toes turn in* ‖ to submit, hand in, *to turn in a report* ‖ to relinquish, give up to an authority, *he turned in his revolver to the police* ‖ (*Br.*) to trade (e.g. a car) in ‖ (*pop.*) to go to bed to sleep **to turn into** to change form and become, *tadpoles turn into frogs* ‖ to change in character and become, *it turned into a nice day* ‖ to transform, *to turn ideas into deeds* **to turn loose** to put (esp. domestic animals) to roam free e.g. in a field ‖ to leave complete liberty to, *you can turn him loose in the library* **to turn low** to decrease the flow of (sound, light, heat) by operating a control ‖ to decrease the flow of sound, light, heat in (something) by operating a control **to turn off** to stop the flow of (water, gas, oil, electric current, or sound, light or heat) by operating a control ‖ to stop the flow of water, gas, oil, electric current etc. by operating (a tap or switch) **to turn on** to make a sudden unexpected attack on, *the dog turned on its master* ‖ to start (water, gas, oil, electric current, or sound, light or heat) flowing by operating a control ‖ to start the flow of water, gas, oil, electric current etc. by operating (a tap or switch) **to turn out** (of feet) to point outwards ‖ to cause to have a specified quality with respect to dress or appearance, *a well turned-out regiment* ‖ to cause to assemble or parade, *turn out the guard* ‖ to empty, esp. for search or inspection, *to turn out one's pockets* ‖ to turn off (a light etc.) ‖ to produce, *the factory turns out 5,000 cars a week* ‖ (*Br.*) to clean (e.g. a room) thoroughly ‖ to prove to be, *it turned out a disaster* ‖ to leave one's home to assemble, *the whole town turned out to welcome them* or (*Br.*) leave the house and face bad weather, *do we have to turn out on such a night?* ‖ (*pop.*) to get out of bed **to turn over** to transfer ownership of or responsibility for, *he turned over the business to his son* ‖ to think about, consider the different aspects of (something), *to turn over a problem* ‖ to buy and then sell (a stock of goods) in the course of business ‖ to trade to the value of, *they turn over a small fortune each month* ‖ to read cursorily or glance at (the pages of a book) **to turn to** to apply to, call on, for help ‖ to consult for reference ‖ (*pop.*) to begin to work in earnest **to turn up** (of eyes, noses, mouths, toes or shoes) to point slightly upward ‖ to shorten (a dress etc.) at the hem ‖ to fold (a hem) and stitch it, esp. so as to shorten a garment ‖ to expose (a playing card) ‖ to bring to the surface by digging etc. ‖ to increase the output of heat, light or sound of (something) by manipulating controls ‖ to manipulate controls in order to increase (sound, heat, brightness) ‖ to arrive, esp. unexpectedly ‖ to be found after being missing ‖ to happen in an unplanned way, *something will turn up to get you out of the difficulty* **2.** *n.* a turning through an arc of a circle or about an axis or central point ‖ the act of taking or changing a direction, *to make a turn to the right* ‖ a bend or curve where a change of direction occurs ‖ a single coil ‖ a winding of rope or wire etc. around something ‖ a twisted condition ‖ one of alternating or successive opportunities or obligations, *my turn to start, your turn to pay* ‖ (*Br.*) an act in a variety show, circus etc. ‖ a small unpleasant shock, *it gave him a turn to hear her voice* ‖ a sudden attack of feeling unwell or ill ‖ (*mus.*) an ornament around a written note, consisting of the notes above and below the written note and played in the order E D C D where the written note is D ‖ (*mus.*) the symbol (∞) indicating this ‖ a deed of a specified character done to someone, *a good turn* ‖ a development in the progress of something, *a new turn of affairs* ‖ (*Br., stock exchange*) the mean between a stock-jobber's buying and selling price ‖ a short walk or drive, *a turn around the town* ‖ a period of duty or activity, *a turn at the helm* ‖ a specific period in which a person or group of people is at work ‖ (*mil.*) a drill maneuver in which marching troops change direction by turning through 90° (cf. WHEEL) so as to advance in ranks not files ‖ a bent (mental inclination), *to be of a scientific turn* ‖ a form thought of as molded, *the turn of her neck, an ugly turn of phrase* ‖ (of a year or century) the period when the date changes **at every turn** constantly and in all directions, *held up at every turn* **by turns** in succession **in turn** in proper sequence **on the turn** (of the tide) about to begin ebbing or flowing ‖ (of milk, butter etc.) beginning to go sour, rancid or bad **out of turn** not in proper sequence ‖ tactlessly, without prudence, *I'm afraid I spoke out of turn* **to a turn** to just the right degree **to serve someone's turn** to suffice for someone's particular need **to take turns** to do something one after another in regular order **turn and turn about** in turn [O.E. *tyrnan* and *turnian* fr. L. *tornare*, to turn in a lathe, round off]

turn·a·round (tə́:rnəraund) *adj.* of the time required to complete an operation and begin the next one

turn·buck·le (tə́:rnbʌk'l) *n.* a tubular link commonly having a right-hand thread on one end and a left-hand thread on the other, used for tightening a rod or wire

turn·coat (tə́:rnkout) *n.* a renegade

turn·down (tə́:rndaun) *adj.* made to be worn folded downwards, or able to be worn in this way

Tur·ner (tə́:rnər), Joseph Mallord William (1775-1851), English landscape painter. At first he worked exclusively in watercolor, but later he worked in oil as well. He began as an emulator of Claude's calm, static, visionary landscapes bathed in clear liquid light, but evolved steadily toward another vision: of the broken light and prismatic colors of an atmosphere which partly revealed, partly concealed the accidents of an actual scene. After Turner's first trip to Italy (1819) his works became remarkable for their color and luminosity and the swirling movement of his brushwork. Rushing wind, tossing water, broken and reflected light, a world of reflections and movement, a rainbow of pure colors: such things characterize his later art. He incorporated the iron ships, the trains and bridges of the industrial age, but they seem as visionary and phantasmal as all else in his universe. As a firm adherent of the direct vision in the open air, and as a keen analyst of the effects of light, Turner led to the French Impressionists

Turner, Nat (1800-31), black leader of the Southampton slave insurrection (1831) in Virginia. He believed himself to be prompted by divine inspiration, and he and his band of 60 murdered 55 whites before being captured and convicted. The incident led to stricter slave codes

turn·er (tə́:rnər) *n.* a person who works a lathe **túrn·er·y** *pl.* **turn·er·ies** *n.* the craft of lathe work ‖ the products of a turner ‖ a turner's workshop

Turner's syndrome *n.* (*med.*) an inherited sex aberration in which only one sex chromosome (*X*) is included in the chromosomes, named for American physician Henry Herbert Turner (1892–) *also* gonadial dysgenesis

turn·ing (tə́:rniŋ) *n.* a point where a road turns or where it diverges from another ‖ the act of a person or thing making a turn ‖ the process of shaping things on a lathe, turnery ‖ (*pl.*) scraps that become detached from material turned

turning point a point in any process or situation at which a decisive change occurs

tur·nip (tə́:rnip) *n.* *Brassica rapa*, fam. *Cruciferae*, a rough hairy-leaved biennial plant with a large fleshy taproot ‖ the rutabaga ‖ the root of either plant, used for stock and human food [earlier *turnepe, turnep* rel. to O.E. *nǣp*, a turnip fr. L.]

turn·key (tə́:rnki:) *pl.* **turn·keys** *n.* (*hist.*) a prison warder having charge of the keys

turnkey *adj.* complete and ready for use

turn·off (tə́:rnɔf, tə́:rnɒf) *n.* a side road ‖ a ramp leading from an express highway

turn off *v.* (*slang*) **1.** to cause a lack of interest in **2.** to become disinterested *ant.* turn on —**turn-off** *n.* —**turn-off, turned-off** *adj.*

turn on *v.* (*slang*) **1.** to awaken a strong interest in, *she turns me on.* **2.** to become interested in *ant.* turn off —**turn-on, turned-on** *adj.* —**turn-on** *n.*

turn·out (tə́:rnaut) *n.* a turning out ‖ a gathering of people for a demonstration, parade, meeting etc. ‖ personal appearance as regards dress and equipment ‖ a coach or carriage with its horse or horses, harness and attendants ‖ a clearing out of drawers and cupboards etc., usually with a view to cleaning ‖ the output of a product over a specified period

turn·o·ver (tə́:rnouvər) *n.* the total money received by a business from sales over a specified period or for a particular transaction ‖ the cycle of purchase, sale and replacement of stock in a business ‖ the rate at which this process is completed ‖ the rate of production of a machine ‖ the movement of people or things into and out of an establishment, *the depot's turnover of recruits doubled* ‖ the number of workers leaving employment and being replaced within a given period ‖ the ratio of this number to the average labor force maintained ‖ a pie or pastry made by folding one half of the crust upon the other half to contain meat, fruit or jam ‖ something that is turned over, e.g. the flap on an envelope ‖ (*Br.*) a newspaper article in essay style given a prominent position ‖ (*sports*) an error or violation that causes loss of the ball

turn·pike (tə́rnpaik) *n.* (*hist.*) a tollgate ‖ a fast highway on which a toll is levied ‖ (*loosely*) any main road [TURN+older *pike*, pickaxe. A turnpike was originally a spiked road barrier]

turn·plate (tə́:rnpleit) *n.* (*rail.*) a turntable

turn·stile (tə́:rnstail) *n.* a gate, with four arms set at right angles, revolving on a central post, allowing the passage of only one person at a time, and used at entrances to ball parks etc.

turn·ta·ble (tə́:rnteib'l) *n.* (*rail.*) a circular revolving platform for reversing engines ‖ the revolving disk which carries the record in a record player ‖ any revolving disk or platform like these, e.g. one used for theatrical scenery

turn·up (tə́:rnʌp) **1.** *n.* (*Br.*) a trouser cuff **2.** *adj.* made to be turned or folded upwards

tur·pen·tine (tə́:rpəntain) *n.* an essential oil, chiefly pinene, derived by distilling the oleoresin secreted by several coniferous trees, esp. the terebinth [older *terebentyne, terbentyne* fr. O.F. fr. L.]

Tur·pin (tə́:rpin), Dick (1706-39), English highwayman who, according to legend, rode his horse Black Bess without a stop from London to York, in an effort to escape capture. He was hanged

tur·pi·tude (tə́:rpitu:d, tə́:rpitju:d) *n.* inherent wickedness ‖ a particular example of such wickedness [F.]

Tur·qui·no, Pico (tu:rkí:nɔ) *SIERRA MAESTRA

tur·quoise (tə́:rkwɔiz, tə́:rkɔiz) **1.** *n.* an opaque sky-blue or blue-green precious stone, consisting of basic aluminum phosphate colored by traces of copper. It occurs in rock deposits, esp. in Iran, Arizona and New Mexico ‖ this blue-green color **2.** *adj.* of this blue-green color [M.E. *turkeis* fr. O.F. *turqueise*, Turkish (because it was first introduced into Europe from Turkey)]

tur·ret (tə́:rit, tʌ́rit) *n.* a small tower projecting from the wall or a corner of a larger structure ‖ a revolving armored covering for a gun on a fort, ship or tank or mounted on a heavily armored aircraft ‖ a holder for cutting tools etc. in a machine tool ‖ (*hist.*) a very tall square structure on wheels used for assaulting a fortified place **túr·ret·ed** *adj.* having a turret or turrets ‖ (of a shell) having whorls that form a high turretlike spiral [O.F. *torete, tourete*]

turret lathe (*Am.*=*Br.* capstan lathe) a lathe with cutting tools held in a special head

tur·ric·u·late (təríkjulit) *adj.* having a small turret or shaped like one

tur·tle (tə́:rt'l) **1.** *pl.* **tur·tles, tur·tle** *n.* a reptile of the order *Testudinata* (or *Chelonia*), including both marine and terrestrial species (*TORTOISE), but (esp. *Br.*) popularly limited to the marine genera. 'Turtle' properly designates all reptiles with a shell. Turtles are characterized by having soft scaly-skinned bodies, strong, horny-edged, toothless jaws and retractile heads, limbs and tails. The turtle's characteristic shell is a case of bone, covered by horny shields. In some marine species the shell is more leathery than horny. Turtles may be herbivorous and/or carnivorous. They lay eggs which they bury in sand and leave to hatch by the heat of the sun. Their size can vary from a few inches to several feet. Turtles are longer-lived than other animals ‖ (*loosely*) a tortoise esp. a small one **to turn turtle** to turn upside down or capsize **2.** *v.i. pres. part.* **tur·tling** *past* and *past part.* **tur·tled** to hunt for turtles [O.E. *turtla, turtle* fr. L. *turtur*, a turtledove]

tur·tle·dove (tə́:rt'ldʌv) *n.* *Streptopelia turtur*, a small variety (11 ins) of lightbrown dove found throughout temperate areas of Europe and Asia. It is known for its plaintive cooing and the affection it shows for its mate [fr. obs. *turtle* fr. O.E. *turtla, turtle* fr. L. *turtur*+DOVE]

tur·tle·neck (tə́:rt'lnęk) *n.* (*Am.=Br.* poloneck) a turnover collar fitting the neck closely, mainly used for sweaters, or a sweater having such a collar ‖ (*Br.*) a high, close-fitting collar on a knitted garment, worn not turned down, or a sweater with such a collar

turves alt. *pl.* of TURF

Tus·can (tʌ́skən) **1.** *adj.* of or referring to Tuscany or its inhabitants ‖ of or relating to or resembling one of the classical orders of Roman architecture characterized by the angular plainness of its capitals **2.** *n.* an inhabitant or native of Tuscany ‖ any of the dialects spoken in Tuscany, esp. the one accepted as standard literary Italian [F. fr. L.L. *Tuscanus*]

Tus·ca·ny (tʌ́skəni:) (*Ital.* Toscana) a region (area 8,876 sq. miles, pop. 3,600,233) of N.W. central Italy. Chief towns: Florence, Leghorn. The mountains of the north and east, and the hills of the center, are cut by broad river valleys opening on to a wide marshy coastal plain. Industries: agriculture (vines, wheat and other cereals, sugarcane, olives), mining (lignite, iron, sulfur, marble), textiles, wine, tourism. Its small medieval states (Pisa, Siena etc.) were united in the 15th and 16th cc. under Florence, which became (1569) the capital of the grand duchy of Tuscany and was incorporated (1860) into Sardinia

Tus·ca·ro·ra (tʌskərɔ́rə, tʌskəróurə) *pl.* **Tus·ca·ro·ra, Tus·ca·ro·ras** *n.* an Iroquois Indian people originally of North Carolina. War (1711–13) with the white settlers forced them to join the Iroquois League as a sixth nation ‖ a member of this people. In the 1960s they numbered about 700, in Canada and New York ‖ their language

tush (tʌʃ) *n.* a long pointed tooth, esp. the canine tooth of a horse ‖ a small or dwarfed tusk in some Indian elephants [var. of TUSK]

tusk (tʌsk) **1.** *n.* a long, sharp tooth, often curved, which projects beyond the closed mouth of certain animals (e.g. the elephant, wild boar and walrus) and is used for digging up food or for defense ‖ (*carpentry*) an additional, strengthening tenon below a principal tenon **2.** *v.t.* to gore, tear up etc. with tusks ‖ to provide with tusks **túsk·er** *n.* an elephant or wild boar with strongly developed tusks [O.E. *tusc, tux*]

tus·sah (tʌ́sə) *n.* a strong, coarse, light-brown silk obtained from the undomesticated silkworm which is the larva of the moth *Antheraea paphia* (or *A. mylitta*) ‖ a fabric (e.g. shantung) made of this silk ‖ the silkworm producing this silk [Hindi and Urdu *tasar*]

Tus·saud (tysou), Marie (1760-1850), Swiss founder of the famous 'Madame Tussaud's' (təsódz) permanent exhibition in London of some 500 life-size wax models of historical and contemporary figures

tus·sive (tʌ́siv) *adj.* (*med.*) pertaining to or caused by a cough [fr. L. *tussis,* a cough]

tus·sle (tʌ́s'l) **1.** *v.i. pres. part.* **tus·sling** *past* and *past part.* **tus·sled** to struggle in fight, sport or controversy **2.** *n.* a struggle, scuffle or controversy [prob. rel. to TOUSLE]

tus·sock (tʌ́sək) *n.* a thick bunch of grass or sedge forming a little hillock [prob. alt. fr. obs. *tusk,* a tuft]

tus·sore (tʌ́sɔr) *n.* (esp. *Br.*) tussah

tut (tʌt) *interj.* an exclamation of remonstrance, impatience etc.

Tut·ankh·a·men (tu̧:taŋkámən) Egyptian king (1352-1343 B.C.) of the 18th dynasty. His tomb, discovered (1922) almost intact near Thebes, yielded furniture and other funerary objects of great splendor, throwing new light on the art and life of ancient Egypt

tu·te·lage (tú:t'lidʒ, tjú:t'lidʒ) *n.* guardianship, protection ‖ instruction ‖ the state of being under a guardian or tutor [fr. L. *tutela,* guardianship]

tu·te·lar (tú:t'lər, tjú:t'lər) *adj.* tutelary

tu·te·lar·y (tú:t'lęri:, tjú:t'lęri:) **1.** *adj.* pertaining to a guardian or to guardianship ‖ serving as a guardian **2.** *pl.* **tu·te·lar·ies** *n.* a tutelary deity or saint [fr. L. *tutelarius* fr. *tutela,* protection]

Tu·ti·co·rin (tu̧tikɔrín) a port (pop. 124,000) in S. Madras, India: cotton spinning, salt, pearl fishing

tu·tor (tú:tər, tjú:tər) **1.** *n.* a private teacher ‖ (in some American universities) a teacher below the rank of instructor ‖ (*Br.*) an official responsible in some universities and colleges for the studies and in others for the welfare of a number of students ‖ (*Br.*) a book of instructions, *a guitar tutor* **2.** *v.t.* to teach privately or on an individual basis ‖ *v.i.* to earn a living by private or individual teaching **tú·tor·age** *n.* [O.F.]

tu·to·ri·al (tu:tɔ́ri:əl, tju:tɔ́r:i:əl, tu:tóuri:əl, tju:tóuri:əl) **1.** *n.* a session of personal instruction with a college tutor **2.** *adj.* of a tutor or tutors

tu·tor·ship (tú:tərʃip, tjú:tərʃip) *n.* the position or duties of a tutor

tut·ti (tú:ti:) **1.** *adj.* (*mus.*) for all voices or instruments **2.** *n.* (*mus.*) a passage for chorus or orchestra without soloists [Ital. pl. of *tutto,* all]

tut·ti-frut·ti (tú:ti:frú:ti:) *n.* a confection or an ice cream dish containing mixed (usually candied) fruits [Ital.=all fruits]

tut·ty (tʌ́ti:) *n.* an impure zinc oxide obtained from zinc-smelting furnace flues and used as a polishing powder [F. *tutie* fr. Arab.]

Tu·tu (tú:tu:), Desmond Mpilo (1931-), African Anglican clergyman, who received the Nobel peace prize (1984) for his efforts to end apartheid in South Africa. Ordained in 1960, he became Anglican dean of Johannesburg (1975-6), bishop of Lesotho (1976-8) and the first black general secretary of the South African Council of Churches (1979) before being elected the first black bishop of Johannesburg (1984-86). From 1986 he was archbishop of Cape Town. An advocate of nonviolence, he has called for outside economic pressure to force South Africa's white-dominated government to end apartheid

tu·tu (tú:tu:) *n.* a ballet dancer's very short skirt of gauze frills [F.]

Tu·tu·ola (tu:tu:óulə), Amos (1920-), Nigerian writer, who writes in English. His novels include 'The Palm-Wine Drinkard' (1952), 'Simbi and the Satyr of the Dark Jungle' (1955), 'Feather Woman of the Jungle' (1962), 'Ajaiyi and His Inherited Poverty' (1967) and 'The Witch Herbalist of the Remote Town' (1980)

TU-20 *n.* (*mil.*) NATO code name 'Bear,' U.S.S.R. maritime reconnaissance plane with range of 7,800 mi, ceiling of 41,000 ft, speed of 500 mph (805 km) equipped with radar scanner, streamlined blisters for refueling (Formerly TU-95)

TU-28 *n.* (*mil.*) NATO code name 'Fiddler,' U.S.S.R. twin-jet interceptor with range of 3,100 mi speed of 1,150 mph, ceiling of 65,620 ft.

Tu·va A.S.S.R. (tú:və) an autonomous republic (area 65,810 sq. miles, pop. 274,000) of the R.S.F.S.R., U.S.S.R., in S. Siberia bordering the Mongolian People's Republic. People: Turkic. Capital: Kyzyl (pop. 42,000)

Tu·va·lu (tu:vəlú:) (formerly Ellice Islands) an independent state (area 10 sq. mi, pop. 8,000) of the Commonwealth of Nations, comprising nine islands in the Pacific Ocean just south of Kiribati (formerly Gilbert Islands) and near the intersection of the equator and the international date line. Capital: Funafuti atoll. Industry: fishing. Remittances from Tuvaluans living abroad, foreign aid and the sale of postage stamps are important sources of income. A British protectorate (from 1892), part of the Gilbert and Ellice Islands Colony (from 1916) and a separate self-governing colony (from 1975), Tuvalu gained independence in 1978

tux·e·do (tʌksí:dou) *pl.* **tux·e·dos** *n.* a tailless, usually dark-colored, dress coat [after a country club at *Tuxedo* Park, N.Y.]

tu·yere (twi:jέər) *n.* a nozzle or pipe used to blow air with force into a blast furnace, forge etc. [F.=nozzle]

Tuz (tu:z) a salt lake (area 770 sq. miles) in central Anatolia, Turkey. In summer it becomes a salt marsh

TV television

TV dinner a packaged, precooked, usu. quick-frozen, dish, requiring only heating before serving

twad·dell (twɔ́d'l) *n.* a hydrometer for measuring the specific gravity of liquids heavier than water [after W. *Twaddell,* its 19th-c. Scottish inventor]

twad·dle (twɔ́d'l) **1.** *n.* silly, meaningless talk or writing **2.** *v.i. pres. part.* **twad·dling** *past* and *past part.* **twad·dled** to talk or write foolishly [origin unknown]

Twain (twein), Mark (Samuel Langhorne Clemens, 1835-1910), American writer. His fame rests on his brilliant books based on the Mississippi River: 'The Adventures of Tom Sawyer' (1876) and 'The Adventures of Huckleberry Finn' (1883). The two great children's books, with 'The Tragedy of Pudd'nhead Wilson' (1894), are really an effective comment on Southern life, full of deft irony. His many other books, which vary in quality, include 'Life on the Mississippi' (1883), based on his adventures as a riverboat pilot, and 'Roughing It' (1872), drawn from his experiences as a young man in the Far West. He was a great storyteller. His powerful presence in his writing, and the relationship he establishes with his readers, have helped to make him perhaps the most widely read of all American authors

twain (twein) *adj.* and *n.* (*archaic*) two [O.E. *twēgen*]

twang (twæŋ) **1.** *n.* the harsh, vibrating sound made by a string under tension when it is plucked ‖ a sharp, nasal quality in the speaking voice **2.** *v.t.* to pluck (a stretched string) so that it makes this sound ‖ to play (an instrument or a tune) in this way ‖ to pronounce with a twang ‖ *v.i.* to make the sound of a taut, plucked string ‖ to speak with a twang [imit.]

tweak (twi:k) **1.** *v.t.* to pinch and pull with a quick twisting jerk, *to tweak someone's nose* **2.** *n.* a sharp pinch or pull [origin unknown]

Tweed (twi:d), 'Boss' William Marcy (1823-78), American politician. As head of Tammany, he gained effective control of New York (1865-71) and, with his corrupt subordinates, defrauded the city of many millions of dollars

Tweed a river (97 miles long) in S.E. Scotland, flowing from S. Peebles to the North Sea, forming part of the English border: salmon fishing

tweed (twi:d) *n.* a strong twilled woolen or wool and cotton cloth, originating in S. Scotland, usually woven with different colored yarns, and used esp. for suits and coats ‖ (*pl.*) clothes made from this material **twéed·y** *adj.* [a trade name originally based on a misreading of Scottish *tweel,* twill and associations with R. *Tweed*]

Tweed Ring a corrupt political machine which controlled city government in New York in the latter 19th c., headed by William Marcy 'Boss' Tweed

tweet (twi:t) **1.** *n.* the chirping note of a bird **2.** *v.i.* to make this sound [imit.]

tweez·ers (twí:zərz) *pl. n.* a small two-pronged instrument used to pick up or grip small objects, pull out hairs etc. [fr. earlier *tweeze,* a case for small instruments fr. F. *étuys, étuis,* cases]

twelfth (twelfθ) **1.** *adj.* being number 12 in a series (*NUMBER TABLE) ‖ being one of the 12 equal parts of anything **2.** *n.* the person or thing next after the 11th ‖ one of 12 equal parts of anything (1/12) ‖ the 12th day of a month [O.E. *twelfta*]

Twelfth Amendment (1804) an amendment to the U.S. Constitution reforming the method by which the Electoral College elects the president and vice-president. Under Article II, Section 1 of the Constitution, each elector was to cast a single ballot for both offices, not specifying a preference as to which of the two candidates was for which of the two offices. The candidate receiving the most votes would become president and the runner-up vice-president. The unforeseen formation of political parties, however, resulted in the electors' choosing (1796) a president and vice-president from different parties. In the 1800 election party-pledged electors were chosen. The casting of two ballots for the same ticket resulted in a tie between presidential candidate Thomas Jefferson, who was chosen by the House of Representatives, and his running-mate, Aaron Burr. The situation led to a call for reform and to the 12th Amendment. The amendment specifies: 1) separate ballots for each office; 2) whoever has the most votes (if a majority) for each office will be elected to that office; 3) if a majority is lacking, the House of Representatives will vote for the president among the three leading candidates, and the Senate will elect the vice-president from between the two highest candidates; 4) no person legally ineligible to be president can be vice-president

Twelfth Day Epiphany, formerly marking the close of the Christmas festival

Twelfth Night the eve of Epiphany, kept as the last night of Christmas festivities

twelve (twelv) **1.** *adj.* being one more than 11 (*NUMBER TABLE) **2.** *n.* 10 plus two ‖ the cardinal number representing this (12, XII) ‖ 12 o'clock **the Twelve** the 12 Apostles [O.E. *twelf*]

twelve·mo (twélvmou) *adj.* and *n.* duodecimo

twelve·month (twélvmʌnθ) *n.* a year

twelve-note (twélvnǫut) *adj.* twelve-tone

Twelv·er (twélvər) *n.* a member of a Shi'ite sect which recognizes 12 Imams and awaits the reappearance of the last as the Mahdi on the Last Day. The beliefs of this sect have been the official religion of Persia since 1502

twelve-tone (twélvtoun) *adj.* (*mus.*) based on a system of composition developed esp. by Schönberg in which the 12 notes of the octave are treated as equal, i.e. as having relation only to one another (cf. KEY), all parts of a composition being constructed from these 12 separate tones in conformity with the series or row in which the composer has chosen to place them

Twelve Tribes of Israel, the *ISRAEL (Jacob)

twen·ti·eth (twéntiːiθ) **1.** *adj.* being number 20 in a series (*NUMBER TABLE) ‖ being one of the 20 equal parts of anything **2.** *n.* the person or thing next after the 19th ‖ one of 20 equal parts of anything (1/20) ‖ the 20th day of a month [O.E. *twentigotha*]

Twentieth Amendment (1933) an amendment to the U.S. Constitution providing for the orderly installation of the president, vice-president and members of Congress, shortening their 'lame duck' status, and clarifying the status of the president-elect and vice-president-elect with respect to presidential succession. The major provisions are: 1) the terms of the president and vice-president will end and new terms will begin on January 20 following an election, and members of Congress will end and begin their terms on January 3; 2) Congress will convene at least once a year, beginning on January 3 unless Congress selects another day; 3) if the president-elect dies, the vice-president-elect becomes president; or, if the president has not been chosen (under the Twelfth Amendment) or if the president-elect does not qualify, the vice-president-elect serves as president until the president-elect does qualify; or, if neither qualifies, Congress will declare how to appoint an acting president until a president or vice-president is qualified; 4) if Congress must choose a president or vice-president, Congress will also provide by law for the orderly succession to these offices in the event the designated person dies or is disqualified

twen·ty (twéntiː) **1.** *adj.* being one more than 19 (*NUMBER TABLE) **2.** *pl.* **twen·ties** *n.* twice 10 ‖ the cardinal number representing this (20, XX) **the twenties** (of temperature, a person's age, a century etc.) the span 20 to 29 [O.E. *twentig*]

Twenty-fifth Amendment (1967) an amendment to the U.S. Constitution that provides procedures for fulfilling the duties of the presidency in the event of a president's death, resignation or removal as well as the prompt filling of a vice-presidential vacancy. The amendment's four provisions are: 1) in the event of removal, death or resignation of a president, the vice-president becomes president; 2) in the event of a vacancy in the vice-presidency, the president nominates a vice-president, who must be confirmed by a majority vote in both houses of Congress; 3) when a president declares an inability to serve in office, the president's duties will be assumed by the vice-president as acting president until the president declares his or her ability to resume them; 4) when the vice-president and either a majority of the heads of the executive departments or a specific congressionally determined body consider a president unable to fulfill his or her duties, the vice-president becomes acting president

Twenty-first Amendment (1933) an amendment to the U.S. Constitution that repeals the 18th Amendment, which prohibited the manufacture of and trafficking in intoxicating liquors. The 21st Amendment thus became the first amendment adopted to repeal another amendment

twen·ty-five (twéntiːfáiv) *n.* (*rugby, hockey*) the line 25 yards in front of the goal line or the space between this line and the goal line

Twenty-fourth Amendment (1964) an amendment to the U.S. Constitution that bans the use of poll taxes in federal elections and gives Congress the power to enforce the amendment. It states that in any presidential or congressional election, no citizen can be denied, by the state or federal government, the right to vote because of failure to pay a poll tax or any other tax. Although only 5 states (Alabama, Arkansas, Mississippi, Texas and Virginia) required payment of a poll tax as a prerequisite to vote, an amendment was needed to eliminate the practice completely

Twenty-second Amendment (1951) an amendment to the U.S. Constitution that limits the presidential tenure to two terms of office. It further states that if a vice-president succeeds to the presidency with 2 years or less of the former president's remaining term, the new president may be elected to 2 more terms; otherwise the new president may be elected to only 1 more term. This amendment was proposed by a Republican Congress in reaction to the 4-term presidency of Franklin D. Roosevelt, who broke the 2-term tradition begun by George Washington

Twenty-sixth Amendment (1971) an amendment to the U.S. Constitution providing that citizens who are 18 years old or older may vote. This amendment is the 4th of the amendments to clarify voting rights (others are the 15th, 19th and 23rd). Its passage was occasioned by the massive protests in the 1960s by students and other young people against the Vietnam war and by their argument that 'if we're old enough to fight, we're old enough to vote.' The amendment reduced the voting age from 21 to 18

Twenty-third Amendment (1961) an amendment to the U.S. Constitution granting the right of citizens in the District of Columbia to vote in presidential elections, a right denied since 1802, when the district was established. The amendment states that the number of electors, appointed by the district government, for president and vice-president cannot exceed those of the least-populous state—or 3 votes in the electoral college

twice (twais) *adv.* two times ‖ on two occasions ‖ doubly **to think twice** to reflect carefully, hesitate out of prudence [O.E. *twiges*]

twice-laid (twáisléid) *adj.* made from strands of old rope or ends of rope

twid·dle (twíd'l) **1.** *v. pres. part.* **twid·dling** *past* and *past part.* **twid·dled** *v.t.* to twirl idly ‖ *v.i.* to toy fussily, *to twiddle with the radio* **to twiddle one's thumbs** to have nothing better to do than turn one's thumbs around each other **2.** *n.* a slight twisting motion [prob. onomatopoeic]

twig (twig) *n.* a small shoot from a branch of a tree, often one without leaves ‖ a very small branch of a nerve or artery ‖ a divining rod

twig·gy *comp.* **twig·gi·er** *superl.* **twig·gi·est** *adj.* long and thin like a twig ‖ full of twigs [Northern O.E. *twigge*]

twi·light (twáilait) **1.** *n.* the dim light between total darkness and sunrise, or esp. between sunset and darkness ‖ the period when this light appears ‖ any dim light ‖ a period or range of existence just beyond the illumination of human knowledge ‖ the period that follows full development, glory etc. **2.** *adj.* of, pertaining to, like or appearing at twilight [Late M.E. fr. *twi-*, two+*lēoht*, light]

twill (twil) **1.** *n.* a textile fabric patterned with diagonal lines, produced by passing the weft threads over one and under two (or more) warp threads ‖ this pattern **2.** *v.t.* to weave so as to produce this pattern [O.E. *twili*]

twin (twin) **1.** *adj.* related as one of a pair of twins, *a twin sister* or (e.g. of ideas) as if one of a pair of twins ‖ having identical characteristics with another thing and functioning as the complement to it, *twin propellers* ‖ (*biol.*) occurring in pairs ‖ (*crystall.*) formed by twinning **2.** *n.* either one of a pair of offspring produced in a single birth. Twins are conceived from the fertilization and subsequent splitting of a single ovum, *identical twins* or from separate ova, *fraternal twins* ‖ a person or thing very closely resembling another ‖ a compound crystal composed of crystals which have grown together in a relation of symmetry **the Twins** Gemini **3.** *v. pres. part.* **twin·ning** *past* and *past part.* **twinned** *v.i.* to give birth to twins ‖ to be paired (with another) ‖ (*crystall.*) to grow together in a relation of symmetry ‖ *v.t.* to associate as a pair, *the projects are twinned in the chairman's plan* [O.E. *twinn*]

twin double (*wagering*) a contract in which the bettor must pick the winners of four consecutive events to win

twine (twain) **1.** *n.* strong cord composed of two or more strands of e.g. Manila hemp twisted together ‖ a vine or plant stem which curves and twists ‖ a coil, twist **2.** *v. pres. part.* **twin·ing** *past* and *past part.* **twined** *v.t.* to form (something) by twisting strands together ‖ to twist (strands) so as to form something ‖ to interweave flowers into (a garland) ‖ to cause to wind around and clasp someone or something ‖ to interlace, *she twined her fingers in his* ‖ *v.i.* to coil ‖ to grow in coils, wind so as to clasp a branch etc. ‖ to be winding in form, *the road twines through narrow valleys* [O.E. *twīn*]

twinge (twindʒ) **1.** *v. pres. part.* **twing·ing** *past* and *past part.* **twinged** *v.t.* to affect with a sudden sharp pain ‖ *v.i.* to be affected in this way **2.** *n.* a sudden sharp physical pain ‖ a stab of mental pain [O.E. *twengan*, etym. doubtful]

twink (twink) **1.** *v.i.* to wink or blink ‖ to twinkle **2.** *n.* (*pop.*) an instant, *in a twink* [Late M.E. *twinken*]

twin·kle (twíŋk'l) **1.** *v. pres. part.* **twin·kling** *past* and *past part.* **twin·kled** *v.i.* (e.g. of the stars viewed through the earth's atmosphere) to emit intermittent gleams of light in rapid succession ‖ (of the eyes) to sparkle with fun, malice etc. ‖ *v.t.* to emit (light) in intermittent gleams in rapid succession **2.** *n.* a twinkling

twin·kling *n.* a quick sparkling or flashing, esp. of a star or of eyes ‖ an instant, *in a twinkling* [O.E. *twinclian*]

twin-screw (twínskrúː) *adj.* (of a ship) having two screw propellers, twisted in opposite directions

twirl (twəːrl) **1.** *v.t.* to cause to rotate rapidly, esp. with the fingers ‖ to whirl with a flourish, *to twirl drumsticks* ‖ to twiddle ‖ to twist so as to curl (esp. moustache ends) ‖ *v.i.* to rotate rapidly ‖ (with 'around') to turn around with a very quick movement **2.** *n.* a rapid rotation ‖ a curl, esp. a curling flourish made with the pen [etym. doubtful]

twist (twist) **1.** *v.t.* to alter the shape of (an object) by applying equal, parallel but oppositely directed forces ‖ to cause to rotate ‖ to cause to spiral ‖ to distort or warp ‖ to cause (two or more threads, strands etc.) to wind around one another, e.g. in making a rope ‖ to make (e.g. a rope) by this action ‖ to wrench so as to cause to be out of shape or place, *to twist an ankle* ‖ (*games*) to cause (a ball) to move with a rotary or spinning motion ‖ to distort the meaning of, *to twist someone's words* ‖ to contort (the facial muscles) ‖ (*Br., pop.*) to cheat (someone) ‖ *v.i.* to turn, or be distorted, about an axis ‖ to change direction sharply and repeatedly ‖ to writhe, squirm, *he twisted free of the rope which tied him* **2.** *n.* a twisting or being twisted ‖ a personal tendency, esp. an eccentric one, thought of as deforming the personality ‖ an unexpected development in a situation or story ‖ a deliberate distortion or perversion of meaning ‖ a bad wrench, *he gave his ankle a twist* ‖ a loaf of bread made in a twisted form ‖ tobacco leaves twisted into a roll ‖ strong cotton or silk yarn made by twisting, *a twist of silk* ‖ (*phys.*) a torque ‖ (of rifling) the degree of slope of the grooves ‖ (*games*) spin imparted to a ball ‖ (*Br.*) a spiral of paper serving as a packet or carrier, e.g. for groceries ‖ a type of front or back dive

twist·er *n.* (*pop.*) a tornado or cyclone ‖ (*games*) a ball that twists ‖ a baffling problem etc.

twist·y *comp.* **twist·i·er** *superl.* **twist·i·est** *adj.* having many twists and turns, *a twisty path* ‖ not straightforward, dishonest, *a twisty politician* [M.E.]

twist·or (twístər) *n.* (*computer*) a storage device utilizing a helical magnetic wire enwrapped by a nonmagnetic wire to send the signals

twit (twit) *pres. part.* **twit·ting** *past* and *past part.* **twit·ted** *v.t.* to tease, mock, esp. in order to comment on some fault or weakness [O.E. *ætwītan*]

twitch (twitʃ) **1.** *v.i.* to move involuntarily with slight spasmodic jerks ‖ (with 'at') to make a light, jerking pull or pulls ‖ *v.t.* to pull with a light jerk or jerks ‖ to move (a body part) nervously and jerkily **2.** *n.* a sudden involuntary jerk or contraction, e.g. of a muscle ‖ a quick light pull or tug ‖ a device for restraining a horse, e.g. during an operation. It consists of a loop of cord or leather fastened around its lip or muzzle and tightened with an attached stick [O.E. *twiccian*]

twitch grass couch grass

twit·ter (twítər) **1.** *v.i.* (of small birds) to utter a succession of thin chirps ‖ (of people) to be in a flurry and make agitated little noises or say silly things ‖ to tremble and be very agitated, *twittering with fear* ‖ *v.t.* to express in an agitated manner **2.** *n.* the succession of chirping sounds made by birds ‖ a state of nervous agitation in people **twit·ter·y** *adj.* [M.E. *twiteren*, imit.]

two (tuː) **1.** *adj.* being one more than one (*NUMBER TABLE) **2.** *n.* one plus one ‖ the cardinal number representing this (2, II) ‖ two o'clock ‖ a playing card (domino etc.) marked with two symbols (spots etc.) **in two** into two parts **or two** (with 'a' + singular noun) used as an imprecise plural, *they walked a mile or two* **to put two and two together** to guess correctly from separate incomplete pieces of information [O.E. *twā, tū*]

two-base hit (*baseball*) a double

two-bit (tú:bit) *adj.* (*pop.*) cheap, worthless ‖ petty, of little importance [=worth two bits (*BIT)]

two-by-four (tú:bəfɔr, tú:bəfour) **1.** *adj.* (*pop.*) small, petty, of little importance ‖ (*pop.*) cramped, narrow **2.** *n.* a piece of lumber of cross-section two inches by four inches

two-edged (tú:édʒd) *adj.* having two cutting edges ‖ ambiguous, esp. able to be understood as a compliment or the reverse

two-faced (tú:feist) *adj.* having two surfaces ‖ hypocritically deceitful **two-fac·ed·ly** (tú:feisidli:) *adv.*

two-fist·ed (tú:fistid) *adj.* virile, vigorous

two·fold (tú:fould) **1.** *adj.* dual **2.** *adv.* two times as much or as many ‖ by two times [M.E. fr. older *twifold*]

two-hand·ed (tú:hǽndid) *adj.* needing two hands for use, used with both hands, *a two-handed sword* ‖ ambidextrous ‖ (of a card game) for two people ‖ needing two people to operate (e.g. a saw)

two-man rule (tú:mǽn) **1.** (*mil.*) system prohibiting individual access to nuclear weapons and their components by requiring the presence of at least two authorized persons, each capable of detecting incorrect or unauthorized procedures with respect to the task to be performed **2.** (*Br. education*) system of schooling with a common program from ages 11 to 13 or 14 and an upper school with selective training thereafter *also* two-man concept, two-man policy

two-mast·er (tú:mǽstər, tú:mɑ́stər) *n.* a sailing ship having two masts

two·pence, tup·pence (tʌ́pəns) *n.* (*hist.*) the sum of two British pennies before decimalization (1971)

two·pen·ny, tup·pen·ny (tʌ́pni:) *adj.* worth or costing twopence

two·pen·ny-half·pen·ny (tʌ́pni:héipni:) *adj.* (*Br.*) unimportant, worthless

two-piece (tú:pi:s) *adj.* (of a garment) consisting of two separate matching pieces

two-ply (tú:plai) *adj.* (of wood) having two layers ‖ (of wool, wire etc.) having two strands ‖ woven double, *a two-ply carpet*

Two Sicilies, Kingdom of the *SICILIES, KINGDOM OF THE TWO

two·some (tú:səm) *n.* (*golf*) a game or match between two players ‖ (*pop.*) a couple, two people together

two-step (tú:step) *n.* a ballroom dance in 2/4 time ‖ a piece of music for this

two-time (tú:taim) *pres part.* **two-tim·ing** *past* and *past part.* **two-timed** *v.t.* (*pop.*) to deceive (a mistress, lover, wife or husband) with someone else ‖ (*pop.*) to double-cross (someone)

two-way (tú:wei) *adj.* moving or permitting movement, transmission etc. in each of two directions ‖ (*math.*) varying in two ways ‖ (*mech.*, of a cock or valve) arranged to permit the flow to be in either of two channels ‖ mutual ‖ involving two persons or groups

-ty *suffix* indicating a state or quality, as in 'enmity' [M.E. *-tie, -tee, -te* fr. O.F. *-te*, earlier *-tet* (*-ted*) fr. L. *-itas*]

-ty *suffix* indicating a multiple of ten, as in 'forty' [O.E. *-tig*]

ty·coon (taikú:n) *n.* a business magnate, powerful financier [fr. Jap. *taikun*, great prince fr. Chin.]

Ty·dings-Mc·Duf·fie Independence Act (táidiŋzməkdʌ́fi:) a U.S. Congressional act (1934) under President Franklin Roosevelt's administration. It granted independence to the Philippines after a ten-year probationary period, which was interrupted by the 2nd world war. In 1946 the Philippines achieved an independent commonwealth status

Tye (tai), Christopher (c. 1500-73), English composer. His style influenced the church music of the Elizabethan composers

tying *pres. part.* of TIE

tyke, tike (taik) *n.* a mongrel dog ‖ a mischievous child ‖ (*Br.*) a rascal [O.N. *tík*, bitch]

Ty·ler (táilər), John (1790-1862), 10th president (1841-5) of the U.S.A., following the death of President William Harrison. He was a Whig, and was the first vice-president to assume the presidency. His opposition to many Whig policies and his staunch states' rights policy aroused the vigorous opposition of his cabinet which resigned (1841) in block, except for secretary of state Daniel Webster, who remained to complete negotiations on the Webster-Ashburton Treaty (1843). President Tyler advanced the annexation of Texas

Tyler, Wat *PEASANTS' REVOLT

ty·lo·sin [$C_{45}H_{77}NO_{17}$] (táiləsin) *n.* (*pharm.*) an antibiotic derived from an actinomycete, used as a food additive and in veterinary medicine; marketed as Tylan

tymbal *TIMBAL

tym·pan (tímpən) *n.* a frame across which paper, cloth or parchment is stretched for equalizing the type pressure of a hand printing press ‖ a membranous part of an apparatus which functions like the eardrum ‖ (*archit.*) a tympanum [fr. L. *tympanum*, drum or O.F. *tympan, timpan*, drum]

tympani *TIMPANI

tym·pan·ic (timpǽnik) *adj.* of or like a drum ‖ of the tympanum or eardrum [fr. TYMPANUM]

tympanic bone the bone which supports the eardrum and partly encloses the tympanum in a mammal's skull

tympanic membrane the eardrum

tym·pa·nist, tim·pa·nist (tímpənist) *n.* a musician who plays the timpani [fr. L. *tympanista* fr. Gk]

tym·pa·ni·tes (timpənáiti:z) *n.* (*med.*) a swelling of the abdomen caused by accumulation of gas or air, esp. in the intestine **tym·pa·nít·ic** (timpənítik) *adj.* [fr. Gk *tumpanitēs*, of a drum]

tym·pa·num (tímpənəm) *pl.* **tym·pa·na** (tímpənə), **tym·pa·nums** *n.* the eardrum ‖ the middle ear ‖ a drum ‖ the diaphragm of a telephone ‖ (*archit.*) the triangular recessed face of a pediment, or triangular space in a door between the lintel and the arch [L.=drum fr. Gk]

Tyn·dale, Tin·dal, Tin·dale (tínd'l), William (c. 1494-1536), English Protestant reformer. Forced into exile in 1524, he made a translation of the Bible into English of exceptional literary quality. He was burned as a heretic

Tyn·dall (tínd'l), John (1820-93), British physicist, noted for his work on the conductivity of heat by gases, on the audibility of sound, and on the qualities of atmospheric light

Tyne (tain) a river (30 miles long) flowing across E. Northumberland, England, to the North Sea, navigable to Newcastle

Tyn·wald, Tyne·wald (tínwɔld, tínwəld) the legislature of the Isle of Man

typ·al (táip'l) *adj.* of or serving as a type

type (taip) **1.** *n.* a kind or sort, *music of a type we enjoy* ‖ (*biol.*) the individual regarded as most fully exemplifying the characteristics of a genus etc. and which gives its name to that genus etc. ‖ (*biol.*) the sum of the characteristics of a large number of individuals, used in arriving at a classification and providing the norm against which variants are assessed and classified ‖ the combination of characteristics in a breed of animal that make it suitable for a specific use, *dairy type* ‖ a person, thing or event regarded as symbolic, esp. (*Bible*) one prefiguring the antitype that was to follow ‖ a piece of esp. metal having on its upper surface a character in relief which when inked and brought under pressure against paper leaves an impression of the character ‖ such pieces collectively, *is the book in type yet?* ‖ the design and size of the impressions printed from such pieces, *what type is the book printed in?* ‖ the central device on either side of a medal or coin etc. 2. *v. pres. part.* **typ·ing** *past* and *past part.* **typed** *v.t.* to write (matter) using a typewriter ‖ to classify according to type ‖ to prefigure as a type ‖ to cast (an actor) over and over in the same kind of role until he becomes identified in the mind of the public with it ‖ *v.i.* to use a typewriter [fr. F. *type* or L. *typus* fr. Gk *tupos*, impression]

type·face (táipfeis) *n.* (*printing*) a face (surface or set of characters)

type·found·er (táipfaundər) *n.* someone who makes printers' type for setting by hand

type·found·ry (táipfaundri:) *pl.* **type·found·ries** *n.* a factory or workshop where type is made by a typefounder

type genus (*biol.*) the genus regarded as most typical of a family and which gives the family its name

type-high (táiphái) *adj.* having the same height as printing type (0.9186 in. in English-speaking countries)

type metal the alloy used esp. to cast printers' type and plates. It consists mainly of lead, with antimony, tin and sometimes copper

type·script (táipskript) *n.* a piece of typewritten matter

type·set (táipset) *v.t. pres. part.* **type·set·ting** *past* and *past part.* **type·set** (*printing*) to set in type, compose **týpe·set·ter** *n.* a compositor ‖ a machine for setting type

type species (*biol.*) the species regarded as most typical of a genus and which gives the genus its name

type specimen (*biol.*) an individual plant or animal serving as the type of a species or a smaller group ‖ (*printing*) a printed sample of a font or series of types displayed to show content, form and capacities

type·write (táiprait) *pres. part.* **type·writ·ing** *past* **type·wrote** (táiprout) *past part.* **type·writ·ten** (táiprit'n) *v.t.* to write (something) with a typewriter ‖ *v.i.* to use a typewriter [back-formation fr. TYPEWRITER]

type·writ·er (táipraitər) *n.* a machine operated by a keyboard which causes metal characters to strike paper through an inked ribbon and so leave an impression on the paper

type·writ·ing (táipraitiŋ) *n.* the act or process of using a typewriter ‖ typewriter work

type·writ·ten (táiprit'n) *adj.* typed on a typewriter [fr. older *typewrite*, to type]

ty·phoid (táifɔid) **1.** *n.* typhoid fever **2.** *adj.* of or relating to typhus ‖ of or relating to typhoid fever [fr. TYPHUS]

typhoid fever an acute infectious disease caused by a bacterium in impure food or water, producing a prolonged, debilitating fever and diarrhea

Typhon *n.* (*mil.*) Navy surface-to-air missile with a short range and nuclear capability

ty·phoon (taifú:n) *n.* a violent cyclone in the China Sea and around the Philippines occurring most frequently in late summer and early autumn [fr. Chin. dial. *tai fung*, big wind]

Typhoon *n.* (*mil.*) NATO term for U.S.S.R. 30,000-ton, nuclear-powered submarine with an estimated speed of 45 knots. Diving capability of 4,000 ft, and carrying 20 ballistic missiles, it was first launched in 1980

ty·phous (táifəs) *adj.* of or of the nature of typhus

ty·phus (táifəs) *n.* any of several human infectious diseases conveyed by the bite of lice, fleas and other biting arthropods whose cells are inhabited by rickettsiae. The louse-borne variety occurs in explosive epidemics, often as a result of wars, earthquakes and other disasters which cause large numbers of people to be herded together in insanitary conditions. The other varieties are endemic in parts of Asia, Africa and America. Symptoms include a rash, high fever lasting about a fortnight, with vomiting, prostration, delirium and sometimes pneumonia [Mod. L. fr. Gk *tuphos*, stupor]

typ·ic (típik) *adj.* (*biol.*) of or conforming to a type [F. *typique* fr. L. fr. Gk]

typ·i·cal (típik'l) *adj.* characteristic of an individual, *one of his typical scathing remarks* ‖ characteristic of a class, *a typical sample of what we produce* ‖ (*biol.*) displaying the essential characteristics of a group ‖ relating to a symbolic type or types, *typical interpretations are characteristic of medieval criticism* [fr. M.L. *typicalis*]

typ·i·fi·ca·tion (tipifikéiʃən) *n.* a typifying or being typified ‖ something which typifies

typ·i·fy (típifai) *pres. part.* **typ·i·fy·ing** *past* and *past part.* **typ·i·fied** *v.t.* to be the representative symbol of, *the dove typifies peace* ‖ to embody the essential characteristics of, *love of the poor and oppressed typified the man* ‖ (*biol.*) to be the type of (a genus, species etc.)

typ·ist (táipist) *n.* a person who operates a typewriter, esp. for a living

ty·pog·ra·pher (taipógrəfər) *n.* someone who lays out copy and sees to all the elements of printing design [fr. M.L. *typographus*, printer]

ty·po·graph·ic (taipəgrǽfik) *adj.* typographical **ty·po·gráph·i·cal** *adj.* of or relating to typography ‖ of or relating to printing by letterpress **ty·po·gráph·i·cal·ly** *adv.*

ty·pog·ra·phy (taipógrəfi:) *n.* the art and practice of the typographer ‖ printed matter with respect to the way in which it is set out [F. *typographie*]

ty·pol·o·gy (taipólədʒi:) *n.* the doctrine or study of symbols or types, esp. those of Scripture ‖ a study based on the comparison or classification of types, e.g. of social groups, of archaeological remains etc. [fr. Gk *tupos*, type+*logos*, discourse]

ty·ran·nic (tirǽnik) *adj.* tyrannical **ty·rán·ni·cal** *adj.* acting like or characteristic of a tyrant, esp. unjustly severe in the use of power or authority **ty·rán·ni·cal·ly** *adv.* [fr. L. *tyrannicus* fr. Gk]

ty·ran·ni·cide (tirǽnisaid) *n.* someone who kills a tyrant ‖ the act of killing a tyrant [F. fr. L. *tyrannicida* (1st definition) and *tyrannicidium* (2nd definition) fr. *tyrannus*, tyrant+*caedere*, to kill]

tyr·an·nize (tirənaiz) *pres. part.* **tyr·an·niz·ing** *past* and *past part.* **tyr·an·nized** *v.i.* to behave like a tyrant ‖ *v.t.* to treat tyrannically [F. *tyranniser*]

ty·ran·no·saur (tirǽnəsɔr) *n.* *Tyrannosaurus rex*, an enormous two-footed carnivorous dinosaur of the Upper Cretaceous in North America [Mod. L. *tyrannosaurus*]

tyr·an·nous (tírənəs) *adj.* characterized by tyranny [fr. L. *tyrannus*, tyrant]

tyr·an·ny (tírəni:) *pl.* **tyr·an·nies** *n.* despotic rule ‖ the unjust and cruel exercise of power of any sort ‖ a tyrannical act [O.F. *tyrannie* fr. L. fr. Gk]

tyr·ant (táirənt) *n.* an oppressive or cruel ruler or master, a despot ‖ someone behaving like a despot ‖ (*Gk hist.*) an arbitrary and absolute ruler who took power by force [O.F. fr. L. fr. Gk]

Tyre (taiər) an ancient seaport (modern Sur, Lebanon, pop. 14,000) of Phoenicia, which flourished (12th-8th cc. B.C.) as a trading center, esp. for the export of Tyrian purple dye and silk

tyre (taiər) **1.** *n.* (*Br.*) a tire (solid rubber tube or casing) **2.** *v.t. pres. part.* **tyr·ing** *past* and *past part.* **tyred** (*Br.*) to fit with a tire

Tyr·i·an purple (tíri:ən) a crimson or purple dye prepared by the ancient Greeks and Romans from the glands of various gastropod mollusks and used in the robes of emperors, nobles etc. (*TYRE) ‖ a strong purplish red

ty·ro (táirou) *pl.* **ty·ros** *n.* a beginner, someone learning a craft etc. [L. *tiro*, a newly enlisted soldier]

Tyrol *TIROL

Ty·rone (tiróun) an inland county (area 1,261 sq. miles, pop. 139,073) of Northern Ireland. County town: Omagh (pop. 8,000)

Tyr·rhe·ni·an Sea (tiri:ni:ən) the part of the Mediterranean between the Italian mainland and Corsica, Sardinia and Sicily

Tyr·tae·us (tərtíːəs) (7th c. B.C.), Greek poet, leader of the Spartans in one of their wars against Messenia. A few fragments survive of his patriotic and war songs, said to have been sung by Spartans on the march

Tyu·men (tju:mén) a communications center (pop. 378,000) in the R.S.F.S.R.. U.S.S.R., on a tributary of the Irtysh, the oldest (1586) Russian town in Siberia: shipbuilding, wood industries

tzar *CZAR

Tza·ra (tsúrə), Tristan (1896-1963), Rumanian poet. As editor of the magazine 'Dada' (1916-20) he was a pioneer of surrealism (*DADA)

tzarina *CZARINA

Tze·po (dzépɔ́) (formerly Poshan) a coal-mining center (pop. 184,000) in central Shantung Province, China

tzetze *TSETSE

tzi·gane (tsigán) *n.* a gypsy, esp. a Hungarian gypsy [F. fr. Hung.]

				CLASSICAL GREEK	ETRUSCAN		EARLY LATIN	MODERN ROMAN
					Early	Classical		
				Y	Y	V	V	U

| CURSIVE MAJUSCULE (ROMAN) | CURSIVE MINUSCULE (ROMAN) | ANGLO-IRISH MAJUSCULE | CAROLINE MINUSCULE | VENETIAN MINUSCULE (ITALIC) | N. ITALIAN MINUSCULE (ROMAN) |
| u | 4 | u | u | u | u |

A. C. SYLVESTER, CAMBRIDGE, ENGLAND

Development of the letter U, beginning with the classical Greek letter. Evolution of both the majuscule, or capital, letter U and the minuscule, or lowercase, letter u are shown.

U, u (ju:) the 21st letter of the English alphabet

U (ju:) *adj.* upper-class *ant.* non-U

U·ban·gi (ju:bǽŋgi:) (*F.* Oubangui) a tributary (660 miles long, navigable by steamer for 350) of the Congo, rising in N.E. Zaïre and forming part of the country's frontiers with the Central African Republic and the Republic of the Congo

U·ban·gi-Sha·ri (ju:bæŋgi:ʃári:) *CENTRAL AFRICAN REPUBLIC

U·be (ú:bi:) a port (pop. 160,000) in S.W. Honshu, Japan: coal mines, textile and chemical industries

U·bi·co (u:bí:kou), Jorge (1878-1946), Guatemalan general and president (1931-44), who made liberal concessions to U.S. enterprises and twice changed the constitution in order to prolong his term of office. He was overthrown by a popular movement

u·biq·ui·none (ju:bəkwínoun) *n.* (*chem.*) a yellow compound that carries electrons through filaments in the cell's energy supply system *also* coenzyme

u·biq·ui·tous (ju:bíkwitəs) *adj.* present everywhere, esp. present everywhere at the same time [fr. Mod. L. *ubiquitarius* fr. L. *ubique*, everywhere]

u·biq·ui·ty (ju:bíkwiti:) *n.* the state of being everywhere at the same time [fr. Mod. L. *ubiquitas* fr. L. *ubique*, everywhere]

U-boat (jú:bout) *n.* a German submarine [fr. G. *U-boot*, short for *Unterseeboot*, undersea boat]

U·ca·ya·li (u:kəjúli:) the chief tributary (1,200 miles long, navigable for 600) of the Amazon, in E. and N. Peru

Uc·cel·lo (u:tʃélou, *Ital.* u:ttʃèllɔ), Paolo (1397-1475), Florentine painter, important in the history of painting for his intensive study of linear perspective and foreshortening. He is esp. famous for his three paintings of 'The Battle of San Romano, 1432' (1456-60) in the Uffizi, Florence, the National Gallery, London and the Louvre, Paris

u·dal (jú:d'l) *n.* an ancient system of land tenure which survives in Orkney and the Shetlands [O.N. *ōthal*]

U·dall (jú:d'l), Nicholas (1505-56), English playwright. He is best known for his posthumous 'Ralph Roister Doister' (c. 1577), a 'comic interlude' based on classical models, e.g. Plautus and Terence, and generally considered to be the first complete English comedy

ud·der (ʌ́dər) *n.* in cattle etc. the pendulous baggy organ containing two or more mammary glands, each having one teat or nipple [O.E. *ūder*]

U·di·ne (ú:di:ne) a city (pop. 103,600) in Friuli-Venezia Giulia, Italy, at the foot of the Alps. Castle (11th c.), Romanesque cathedral, 15th-c. town hall

Ud·murt A.S.S.R. (údmʌərt) an autonomous republic (area 16,250 sq. miles, pop. 1,516,000) of the E. European R.S.F.S.R., U.S.S.R. People: Finnic. Capital: Izhevsk

u·dom·e·ter (ju:dómitər) *n.* a rain gauge **u·do·met·ric** (ju:dəmétrik) *adj.* [fr. F. *udomètre*]

Ue·le (wélei) a headstream (700 miles long) of the Ubangi, crossing northeastern Zaïre

U·fa (u:fú) the capital (pop. 1,009,000) of the Bashkirian A.S.S.R., U.S.S.R., in the W. Urals: engineering, oil refining, lumber, food processing, metallurgy

Uf·fi·zi (u:fí:tsi:) *FLORENCE

UFO, U.F.O. unidentified flying object

u·fol·o·gy (ju:fólədʒi:) *n.* the study of unidentified flying objects (UFOs) —**ufological** *adj.* —**ufologist** *n.*

U·gan·da (ju:gǽndə) a republic (area 93,981 sq. miles, pop. 13,651,000), comprised of 18 administrative districts, and a member of the British Commonwealth, in E. central Africa. Capital: Kampala. People: about half belong to Bantu groups, while non-African minorities include Indians (1%), Europeans and Arabs. Language: English (official), Luganda, Swahili, local and minority languages. Religion: mainly traditional African, with Christian (20%) and Moslem minorities. The country is 8% forest, and predominantly agricultural. It is a plateau (3,000-5,000 ft), mainly savanna, between the Great Rift Valley and Lake Victoria, with high massifs (*RUWENZORI, *ELGON) on the southwestern and eastern borders, and with many lakes and rivers. Average temperatures (F.) in Kampala 69° (July), 74° (Jan.). Rainfall: Kampala 46 ins, interior under 40 ins. Livestock: cattle, goats, sheep. Agricultural products: cotton, coffee, tea, tobacco, peanuts, corn, castor-oil plant seeds, sisal, sugar, millet, plantains, beans, sweet potatoes. Mineral resources: copper, cobalt, limestone, phosphates, tungsten, tin, beryl. Industries: fishing, lumber (hardwoods), hydroelectricity, fertilizers, cement, chemicals, bicycles. Exports: cotton, coffee, copper, tea, animal foodstuffs, hides and skins, peanuts, electricity. Imports: machinery, textiles, clothing, metals, vehicles, rubber, gasoline. University College of the University of East Africa at Kampala (1939). Monetary unit: shilling (100 cents). HISTORY. Various tribes migrated to Uganda before the 18th c., forming clans in the northeast and kingdoms in the southwest, notably that of Buganda. Arab slave and ivory traders reached Uganda from Zanzibar (mid-19th c.). The first European to reach it

was Speke (1862). Baker discovered Lake Albert (1864) and Stanley explored Buganda (1875). Britain proclaimed a protectorate over Buganda (1894), extended (1896) to most of the rest of Uganda. Executive and legislative councils were established (1921), and Uganda became an independent member of the Commonwealth (Oct. 9, 1962). The constitution proclaiming the republic, and the creation of a unitary state in place of the federal state, was approved (Sept. 8, 1968). President Obote was overthrown (Jan. 25, 1971) by an army coup d'état. Gen. Amin formed a new government, which rapidly took the shape of a dictatorship. Amin's erratic and ruthless behavior alienated many other countries and led to his overthrow in April 1979 by exiled Tanzanian-supported Ugandan troops. Political conditions continued unstable and in May 1980 new President Binaisa was deposed by a military commission. Obote returned from exile and was elected president but he was overthrown in July 1985. New President Lt. Gen. Tito Okello promised an early return to civilian rule

U·ga·rit (u:gərí:t) an ancient city excavated at Ras-Shamra, near Latakia, N. Syria. It flourished as a cultural and trading center (4th millennium-2nd millennium B.C.). Excavations yielded cuneiform tablets of the 14th c. B.C.

ugh (ʌg, ʌx, ux) *interj.* used to express disgust or extreme repugnance

ug·li·fi·ca·tion (ʌglifikéiʃən) *n.* an uglifying or being uglified

ug·li·fy (ʌ́glifai) *pres. part.* **ug·li·fy·ing** *past* and *past part.* **ug·li·fied** *v.t.* to make ugly

ug·li·ness (ʌ́gli:nis) *n.* the state or quality of being ugly

ug·ly (ʌ́gli:) *comp.* **ug·li·er** *superl.* **ug·li·est** *adj.* unpleasant to look at, unsightly ‖ morally offensive ‖ (*pop.*) surly, quarrelsome, *an ugly mood* ‖ fraught with danger, *an ugly situation* [O.N. *uggligr*, to be dreaded]

ugly American an American abroad who is unappreciative of the native culture: from the 1955 book, *The Ugly American*, by Eugene Burdick (1918–1965) and William Lederer (1912–)

ugly duckling someone who after an unpromising start turns out to have fine qualities or personal beauty [fr. a story by Hans ANDERSEN]

UGM-84A (*mil.*) *HARPOON

UGM-96 (*mil.*) *TRIDENT I

UGM-73A (*mil.*) *POSEIDON

UGM-27 (*mil.*) *POLARIS

U·gri·an (ú:gri:ən, jú:gri:ən) **1.** *n.* a member of the eastern division of the Finno-Ugrian peoples **2.** *adj.* of or relating to the Ugrians ‖ Ugric

U·gric (ú:grik, jú:grik) *adj.* of, relating to or characteristic of the Finno-Ugric languages of the Ugrians

UH-1 (*mil.*) *IROQUOIS

Uh·land (ú:lɑnt), Johann Ludwig (1787-1862), German Romantic poet, playwright and essayist, famous mainly for his ballads and patriotic songs

Ui·ghur (wí:guər) *n.* a member of a Turkic people found primarily in the Tarim Basin ‖ their Turkic language

Uit·land·er (éitlændər) *n.* (*hist.*) a foreign immigrant, esp. a British one, in the Transvaal and the Orange Free State as referred to by the Boers before the Boer War (1899–1902) [Afrik. fr. *uit,* out+*land,* land]

Uj·jain (ú:dʒain) a Hindu holy city (pop. 203,278) in N.W. Madhya Pradesh, India. Industries: textiles. Temples

u·kase (ju:kéiz, jú:keis) *n.* an edict, esp. an edict of czarist Russia having the force of law [Russ *ukazŭ,* edict]

ukelele *UKULELE

U·kraine (ju:kréin) an E. European constituent republic (area 231,990 sq. miles, pop. 49,757,000) of the U.S.S.R., occupying most of the southwest and consisting mainly of fertile steppe. Capital: Kiev. Other centers: Kharkov, Donetsk, Odessa. People: 77% Ukrainian, 17% Russian, Polish and other minorities. Agriculture: wheat, corn (25% of Soviet grain production), sugar beets (50% of Soviet production), sunflower seed, cotton, flax, vegetables, fruit, tobacco, cattle, hogs, sheep. Resources: coal (36% of Soviet production), iron ore, oil, salt, fish. Industries: mining (esp. coal, iron, manganese), iron and steel, chemical and mechanical engineering, food processing, textiles. HISTORY. The Ukraine was divided between Russia and Austria (18th c.), was briefly independent (1917-20), and became a constituent republic of the U.S.S.R. (1923). It joined the United Nations (1945)

U·krain·i·an (ju:kréini:ən) **1.** *adj.* of or relating to the Ukraine, its people or language **2.** *n.* a native or inhabitant of the Ukraine ‖ the Slavic language of the Ukrainians

u·ku·le·le, u·ke·le·le (ju̦:kəléili:) *n.* a small four-stringed musical instrument resembling the guitar [Hawaiian]

U·lad·is·laus I (ju:lǽdislɔs) (*Hung.* Ulászló) king of Hungary *LADISLAUS III king of Poland

Uladislaus II king of Hungary *LADISLAUS II, king of Bohemia

U·lagh Muz·tagh (u:lɑ́:mu:stɑ́) *KUNLUN

u·la·ma, u·le·ma (ú:ləmɑ) *pl.* **u·la·ma, u·la·mas, u·le·ma, u·le·mas** *n.* the body of professional theologians and legalists of Islam. The ulama provides the teachers and leaders of worship in the mosques, as there is no ordained priesthood within Islam ‖ a member of an ulama [fr. Arab. *'ulamā* pl. of *'alim,* learned]

U·lan Ba·tor (ú:lɑnbɑ́tɔr) (formerly Urga) the capital (pop. 457,000) of the Mongolian People's Republic, at the northern edge of the Gobi Desert, formerly a lamasery and caravan station, now a rail and industrial center (meat packing, tanning, felt and fur industries). University

U·lan U·de (ú:lɑnu:déi) the capital (pop. 310,000) of the Buriat A.S.S.R., R.S.F.S.R., U.S.S.R.: railroad stock, building materials, textiles, food processing, glass

U·lász·ló (u:lɑ́ʒlou) kings of Hungary *LADISLAUS III, king of Poland, *LADISLAUS II, king of Bohemia

Ul·bricht (ú:lbrixt), Walter (1893–1973), East German political leader. He joined the communist party (1918) when it was established and was a member of the German Reichstag (1928-33) but left Germany when Hitler came to power. He worked with the Republicans during the Spanish Civil War and the Russians during the 2nd world war. Ulbricht became East Germany's deputy prime minister (1949) and secretary of the Socialist Unity (Communist) party (1950). His harsh regime led to open rebellion (1953) and to a stream of refugees to West Germany until the Berlin Wall was built (1961). During the last decade of Ulbricht's regime, his economic reforms resulted in East Germany's attaining the Communist world's highest standard of living. He resigned as party secretary (1971) but remained chairman of the Council of State until his death

ul·cer (ʌ́lsər) *n.* an inflamed discontinuity in the skin or mucous membranes of the body. It may be due to injury, infection or the action of corrosive fluids (*PEPTIC ULCER) ‖ (*rhet.*) a source or condition of corruption [fr. L. *ulcus* (*ulceris*), a sore]

ul·cer·ate (ʌ́lsəreit) *pres. part.* **ul·cer·at·ing** *past* and *past part.* **ul·cer·at·ed** *v.t.* to make ulcerous ‖ *v.i.* to become ulcerous [fr. L. *ulcerare* (*ulceratus*)]

ul·cer·a·tion (ʌlsəréiʃən) *n.* a becoming ulcerated or state of being ulcerated ‖ an ulcer or several ulcers in a group [fr. L. *ulceratio* (*ulcerationis*)]

ul·cer·a·tive (ʌ́lsərətiv, ʌ́lsəreitiv) *adj.* of, relating to, characterized by or causing an ulcer or ulcers [fr. M.L. *ulcerativus*]

ul·cer·ous (ʌ́lsərəs) *adj.* having an ulcer or ulcers ‖ having the nature of an ulcer [fr. L. *ulcerosus*]

U·le·å·borg (ú:leoubɔrj) *OULU

ulema *ULAMA

Ul·fi·las (úlfilæs) *WULFILA

ul·lage (ʌ́lidʒ) *n.* the amount by which a barrel or similar vessel falls short of being full ‖ loss of contents by evaporation, oozing etc. [A.F. *ulliage*]

Ulls·wa·ter (ʌ́lzwɔtər, ʌ́lzwɒtər) a lake (8 miles long) in Cumberland and Westmorland, England (*LAKE DISTRICT)

Ulm (ulm) a town (pop. 93,800) in Baden-Württemberg, West Germany, on the Danube. Gothic cathedral (14th c.-19th c.)

Ulm, Battle of, a battle (Oct. 20, 1805) in which the Austrian army surrendered to Napoleon early in the Napoleonic Wars

ul·na (ʌ́lnə) *pl.* **ul·nae** (ʌ́lni:), **ul·nas** *n.* the inner of the two bones of the forearm of man or corresponding part of the forelimb of vertebrates higher than fishes **úl·nar** *adj.* [L.= elbow]

u·lot·ri·chous (ju:lɒ́trikəs) *adj.* (*anthrop.*) belonging to a race having crisp, crinkled hair [fr. Mod. L. *ulotrichi* fr. Gk *oulos,* crisp+*thrix* (*trichos*), hair]

Ul·ster (ʌ́lstər) the northernmost province (area 3,094 sq. miles, pop. 226,037) of Ireland, comprising Cavan, Donegal and Monaghan counties ‖ (*hist.*) an ancient kingdom of N. Ireland, now comprising modern Ulster and Northern Ireland ‖ (*pop.*) Northern Ireland

ul·ster (ʌ́lstər) *n.* a long loose overcoat, often belted [after ULSTER, Ireland, where such coats were originally made]

ul·te·ri·or (ʌltíəri:ər) *adj.* further, more distant ‖ beyond what is evident or professed, *ulterior motives* [L. comp. adj.=further]

ul·ti·mate (ʌ́ltəmit) **1.** *adj.* farthest away in space or time ‖ eventual, *their ultimate victory is not in question* ‖ final, *the ultimate test* ‖ that cannot be analyzed, separated out etc. in any greater detail, *in the ultimate analysis* **2.** *n.* that which is ultimate [fr. L.L. *ultimare* (*ultimatus*), to come to an end]

ultimate frisbee team field game with 7 competitors on each side, with objective of placing frisbee across opponent's goal line

ul·tim·a·tist (ʌltəméitist) *n.* an uncompromising extremist **—ultimatism** *n.* **—ultimatistic** *adj.*

ul·ti·ma·tum (ʌltəméitəm, ʌltəmɑ́təm) *pl.* **ul·ti·ma·tums, ul·ti·ma·ta** (ʌltəméitə, ʌltəmɑ́tə) *n.* the final terms offered or demanded by one of the parties in diplomatic negotiations, the rejection of which usually leads to complete rupture, or war [fr. L.L. neut. of *ultimatus,* ultimate]

ul·ti·mo (ʌ́ltəmou) *adv.* (*commerce, abbr.* ult., ulto.) in the month preceding the present one [L. *ultimo* (*mense*), in the last (month)]

ul·tra (ʌ́ltrə) **1.** *adj.* extreme, sometimes to the point of being fanatical **2.** *n.* an extremist [L.= beyond]

ultra- *prefix* beyond, as in 'ultraviolet' ‖ to an extreme degree, as in 'ultramodernism' ‖ beyond the range of, as in 'ultramicroscopic' [fr. L. *ultra,* beyond]

ul·tra·cen·tri·fuge (ʌltrəséntrifju:dʒ) *n.* a high-speed centrifuge for effecting the sedimentation of submicroscopic particles

ul·tra·fax (ʌ́ltrəfæks) *n.* (*electr.*) trademark of RCA Corporation incorporating television, radio, facsimile, and film recording

ul·tra·fiche (ʌ́ltrəfi:ʃ) *n.* (*optics*) a microfilm of documents reduced for filing to 1/90 or less normal size **—ultrafiche** *adj.*

ul·tra·ís·mo (u̦:ltrɑí:smɔ) *n.* a literary movement created (1919) by Spanish and Spanish-American poets, notably Jorge Luis Borges and Eugenio Montes. The movement called for a total renewal of the spirit and technique of poetry. Its poems are characterized by vivid images and striking metaphors [Span.]

ul·tra·ma·rine (ʌltrəmərí:n) **1.** *n.* a vivid blue pigment originally obtained by reducing lapis lazuli to powder ‖ a blue pigment prepared by heating a mixture of soda ash, sulfur, charcoal etc. It is used in paints, printing inks etc. ‖ the blue color of this pigment **2.** *adj.* ultramarine-colored [fr. M.L. *ultramarinus* fr. L. *ultra,* beyond+*mare,* sea (because lapis lazuli came from beyond the sea)]

ul·tra·mi·cro·scope (ʌltrəmáikrəskoup) *n.* a microscope employing a beam of intense light projected through the sample perpendicularly to the axis of the objective, permitting the observation of submicroscopic, colloidal particles by the light they scatter against a dark field **ul·tra·mi·cro·scop·ic** (ʌltrəmaikrəskɒ́pik) *adj.*

ul·tra·mi·cro·tome (ʌ́ltrəmáikrətoum) *n.* (*electr.*) a device designed to cut very thin tissue sections for use in an electron microscope — **ultramicrotomy** *n.*

ul·tra·mon·tane (ʌltrəmɒ́ntein) **1.** *adj.* of the principles or practices of ultramontanism **2.** *n.* an advocate of ultramontanism [fr. M.L. *ultramontanus* fr. *ultra,* beyond+*mons* (*montis*), mountain]

ul·tra·mon·ta·nism (ʌltrəmɒ́ntənizəm) *n.* (*hist.*) the advocacy, within the Roman Catholic Church, of the increase of papal authority, as opposed to such theories as Gallicanism. It was firmly established by the declaration of papal infallibility (1870) **ul·tra·món·ta·nist** *n.* [F. *ultramontanisme*]

ul·tra·mun·dane (ʌltrəmʌ́ndein, ʌltrəmʌndéin) *adj.* being beyond the limits of the known universe [fr. L.L. *ultramundanus* fr. *ultra,* beyond+*mundus,* the world]

ul·tra·son·ic (ʌltrəsɒ́nik) *adj.* supersonic **ul·tra·són·ics** *n.* supersonics [fr. L. *ultra,* beyond+ *sonus,* sound]

ultrasonic bonding technique of bonding metals by utilizing ultrasonic vibration, mechanical pressure, and a wiping motion *Cf* ULTRASONIC SOLDERING, ULTRASONIC WELDING

ultrasonic cleaning technique creating ultrasonic waves in a liquid in which objects are washed

ultrasonic coagulation technique using ultrasonic waves to bond small particles into larger ones

ultrasonic holography technique for reproducing an interior or exterior three-dimensional image of a solid through the interference pattern of ultrasonic waves *Cf* HOLOGRAPHY

ultrasonics *n.* (*acoustics*) study of source waves beyond the range of human hearing (20 kHz) used for nondestructive testing of metals, medical examination of a fetus, and, in very high intensity, for scaling boilers and in dentist's drilling **—ultrasonic** *adj.* **—ultrasonically** *adv.*

ultrasonic scanner (*med.*) device that utilizes echoes from ultrasonic waves for body tissue diagnosis *Cf* ULTRASONOGRAPH

ultrasonic sealing technique for sealing plastic packages by heat, utilizing the pressure of ultrasonic vibrations

ultrasonic soldering technique utilizing heat and high-frequency vibrations for creating bubbles in soldering, avoiding the use of a flue to remove oxide films on metal *Cf* ULTRASONIC BONDING, ULTRASONIC WELDING

ultrasonic stroboscope device utilizing an ultrasonic beam to interrupt a light beam

ultrasonic therapy (*med.*) therapeutic use of ultrasonic (0.7 to 1.0 MHz) pulse converted to heat *also* ultrasound diathermy

ultrasonic welding technique that utilizes ultrasonic waves to bond metal without heat *Cf* ULTRASONIC BONDING, ULTRASONIC SOLDERING

ul·tra·son·o·graph (ʌltrəsɒ́nəgræf) *n.* (*acoustics*) diagnostic device utilizing ultrasonic (15–20 MHz) waves to penetrate tissue *Cf* ULTRASONIC SCANNER **—ultrasonogram** *n.* the resulting record **—ultrasonography** *n.* the use **—ultrasonologist** *n.* the user **—ultrasound diagnosis** *n.*

ul·tra·sound (ʌ́ltrəsaund) *n.* produce of ultrasonic waves, widely used in diathermy, medical diagnosis, cleaning, etc.

Ul·tra·suede (ʌ́ltrəsweid) *n.* trademark for washable, suedelike fabric that is 60% polyester and 40% nonpolyurethane

ul·tra·vi·o·let (ʌltrəváiəlit) **1.** *adj.* (*abbr.* UV) relating to, producing or using ultraviolet radiation **2.** *n.* ultraviolet radiation

ultraviolet imagery (*electromagnetics*) imagery produced from the sensing of ultraviolet radiations reflected from a surface
ultraviolet microscope a microscope that employs ultraviolet light to stimulate fluorescence in the sample
ultraviolet radiation electromagnetic waves of wavelength between the violet end of the visible band and X rays (3,800 Å–100 Å). It is present in sunlight and has an important role as a photochemical agent in certain life processes (*FLUORESCENCE, *VITAMIN D, *SPECTROSCOPY)
ul·u·late (jú:ljuleit, ʌ́ljuleit) *pres. part.* **ul·u·lat·ing** *past* and *past part.* **ul·u·lat·ed** *v.i.* (*rhet.*) to howl ‖ (*rhet.*) to wail and lament **ul·u·lá·tion** *n.* [fr. L. *ululare* (*ululatus*), imit.]
Ul·ya·novsk (uljánɔfsk) (formerly Simbirsk) a city (pop. 485,000) in the R.S.F.S.R., U.S.S.R., on the middle Volga: engineering, wood industries, food processing
U·lys·ses (ju:lísi:z) Latin name for Odysseus
U·may·yad (u:máijæd) a member of a Moslem caliphate which ruled Islam (661-750). The Umayyads also ruled in Spain (756-1031)
um·bel (ʌ́mb'l) *n.* an inflorescence in which all the pedicels arise from the top of the main stem and form a flat or rounded cluster ‖ an arrangement of parts resembling this [fr. L. *umbella*, parasol]
um·bel·late (ʌ́mbəleit, ʌ́mbəlit) *adj.* having, consisting of, resembling or forming an umbel or umbels **úm·bel·lat·ed** *adj.* [fr. Mod. L. *umbellatus*]
um·bel·lif·er·ous (ʌmbəlífərəs) *adj.* having an umbel or umbels [fr. UMBEL+L. *ferre*, to bear]
um·ber (ʌ́mbər) **1.** *n.* a dark brown earth rich in manganese and ferric oxides and used as a permanent pigment (cf BURNT UMBER, cf. RAW UMBER) **2.** *adj.* of the color of umber [fr. F. (*terre d'*) *ombre* or Ital. (*terra di*) *ombra*, (earth of) shade]
Um·ber·to I (umbértou) (1844-1900), king of Italy (1878-1900)
Umberto II (1904-83), last king of Italy (1946). On the abdication of his father, Victor Emmanuel III, he was made king, but a month later a referendum established a republic, and he went into exile
um·bil·i·cal (ʌmbílik'l) *adj.* of or relating to the navel [fr. M.L. *umbilicalis*]
umbilical cord a cordlike structure joining the fetus to the placenta of the mother ‖ the cable connecting an outside astronaut or aquanaut to his or her ship ‖ a power supply line to a rocket or spacecraft preceding takeoff
um·bil·i·cate (ʌmbílikeit, ʌmbílikit) *adj.* shaped like a navel, having a central depression ‖ (of some spiral shells) having an open umbilicus [fr. L. *umbilicatus*]
um·bil·i·cus (ʌmbílikəs, ʌmbiláikəs) *pl.* **um·bil·i·ci** (ʌmbílisai, ʌmbəláisai) *n.* the navel ‖ the hilum of a seed ‖ the basal depression of certain spiral shells [L.]
um·bo (ʌ́mbou) *pl.* **um·bo·nes** (ʌmbóuni:z), **um·bos** *n.* the boss of a shield ‖ (*anat.*) the rounded elevation in the tympanic membrane of the ear ‖ the swollen point of a cone scale of a pine tree ‖ the rounded elevation above the hinge of a bivalve shell **um·bo·nal** (ʌ́mbən'l), **um·bo·nate** (ʌ́mbəneit) *adjs* [L.=boss of a shield]
um·bra (ʌ́mbrə) *pl.* **um·brae** (ʌ́mbri:) *n.* the shadow from which all light from a given source is excluded by an object, e.g. a planet, esp. by the earth or moon in an eclipse (cf. PENUMBRA) ‖ the darker central part of a sunspot [L.=shade]
um·brage (ʌ́mbridʒ) *n.* resentment **to take (give) umbrage** to feel (cause to feel) pique [O.F. fr. L. *umbra*, shadow]
um·bra·geous (ʌmbréidʒəs) *adj.* (*rhet.*) shady ‖ (*rhet.*) quick to feel suspicious and resentful [F. *ombrageux*]
um·brel·la (ʌmbrélə) *n.* a portable device which, when opened, is used to keep rain off a person or to protect him from the sun, or in some Asian and African countries serves as a symbol of dignity. It consists of a circular canopy of cotton, silk etc. stretched across collapsible steel etc. ribs radiating from a center pole, the end of the pole forming a handle ‖ a larger version of this used to provide shade ‖ a protective force of fighter aircraft ‖ the contractile dome-shaped disk of a jellyfish, serving as a swimming organ [fr. Ital. *ombrella*, sunshade]
umbrella 1. *adj.* of a general covering of many things, groups, or subjects *an umbrella organization* **2.** (*business*) a contract or protective arrangement covering many or all risks
umbrella bird a member of *Cephalopterus*, fam. *Cotingidae*, a genus of South and Central American birds allied to the crow, remarkable for their crest of blueblack feathers rising from the head and curving forward over the beak
umbrella pine *Sciadopitys verticillata*, fam. *Pinaceae*, a Japanese evergreen tree having needle-shaped leaves in whorls like umbrellas, and a flat-domed crown
umbrella tree *Magnolia tripetala*, a North American magnolia having thin, oval leaves clustered at the ends of the branches ‖ any of various trees having leaves shaped or arranged in an umbrellalike fashion
Um·bri·a (ʌ́mbri:ə) a mountainous region (area 3,377 sq. miles, pop. 802,400) of central Italy, cut by the upper Tiber. Chief town: Perugia. Industries: agriculture (olives, vines), livestock raising (cattle, hogs), metalworking
Um·bri·an (ʌ́mbri:ən) **1.** *adj.* of, relating to or characteristic of the province of Umbria or the people inhabiting Umbria ‖ of, relating to or characteristic of the Italian language of ancient Umbria **2.** *n.* a native or inhabitant of Umbria ‖ the Italic language of ancient Umbria
Umbrian school the school of painting (15th-16th cc.) which included Perugino
u·mi·ak (ú:mi:æk) *n.* an open Eskimo boat made by stretching skins over a wooden frame, paddled esp. by women and children [Eskimo]
um·laut (úmlaut) *n.* a vowel modification caused by assimilation to a vowel or semivowel (now generally lost) in the following syllable ‖ a vowel resulting from such assimilation ‖ a mark (¨) placed over the affected vowel, esp. in modern German [G. fr. *um*, about+*laut*, sound]
um·pir·age (ʌ́mpaiəridʒ) *n.* the authority or position of an umpire ‖ an instance of umpiring
um·pire (ʌ́mpaiər) **1.** *n.* someone chosen to enforce the rules of play and decide disputes in certain games, e.g. cricket or baseball (cf. REFEREE) ‖ an arbitrator ‖ (*law*) a third person appointed to make a decision in a disagreement between arbitrators **2.** *v. pres. part.* **um·pir·ing** *past* and *past part.* **um·pired** *v.i.* to act as umpire ‖ *v.t.* to act as umpire in or of [older *a numpire* taken as *an umpire* fr. O.F. *nonper*, uneven (i.e. a third party)]
ump·teen (ʌ́mptí:n) *adj.* (*pop.*) very many [facetious extension of words in *-teen*]
ump·ti·eth (ʌ́mpti:əθ) *adj.* numberless
Um·ta·li (u:mtáli:) an agricultural and gold-mining center (pop. 30,000) in Zimbabwe near the Mozambique border, linked by rail with the coast
U.N., UN *UNITED NATIONS
un- (ʌn) *prefix* not, lack of, opposite, as in 'unemployment' [O.E. *un-*]
un- *prefix* added to verbs to indicate a reversal of the action of the verb, as in 'untie' ‖ added to nouns to indicate a release from the state expressed by the noun, as in 'undress' [O.E. *un-*, *on*]
un·a·ble (ʌnéib'l) *adj.* not able
un·a·bridged (ʌnəbrídʒd) *adj.* not abridged
un·ac·com·pa·nied (ʌnəkʌ́mpəni:d) *adj.* not accompanied ‖ (*mus.*) with no accompaniment
un·ac·com·plished (ʌnəkómpliʃt) *adj.* not finished or achieved ‖ having no accomplishments
un·ac·count·a·ble (ʌnəkáuntəb'l) *adj.* inexplicable ‖ not accountable, not responsible **un·ac·cóunt·a·bly** *adv.*
un·ac·count·ed for (ʌnəkáuntid) unexplained, not accounted for
un·ac·cus·tomed (ʌnəkʌ́stəmd) *adj.* unusual ‖ (with 'to') not accustomed, *unaccustomed to this sort of thing*
un·a·dopt·ed (ʌnədóptid) *adj.* (*Br.*, of roads) not made up or maintained by the local authority
un·ad·vised (ʌnædváizd) *adj.* ill-considered, rash ‖ without advice **un·ad·vis·ed·ly** (ʌnædváizidli:) *adv.*
un·af·fect·ed (ʌnəféktid) *adj.* without affectation ‖ not affected or influenced
un·al·ien·a·ble (ʌnéiljənəb'l, ʌnéili:ənəb'l) *adj.* inalienable
U·na·mu·no (u:nəmú:nou), Miguel de (1864-1936), Spanish philosopher and essayist. In 'The Tragic Sense of Life in Men and in Peoples' (1913) he made a profound and highly individualistic analysis of modern man
u·na·nim·i·ty (ju:nənímiti:) *n.* the state or quality of being unanimous [fr. O.F. *unanimite*]
u·nan·i·mous (ju:nǽnəməs) *adj.* being of one mind, being in complete agreement ‖ arrived at with complete agreement, *a unanimous decision*
un·an·swer·a·ble (ʌnǽnsərəb'l) *adj.* that cannot be refuted or answered
un·ap·proach·a·ble (ʌnəpróutʃəb'l) *adj.* not able to be approached ‖ unrivaled
un·armed (ʌnɑ́rmd) *adj.* having no weapons ‖ (of plants or animals) having no scales, claws, spines etc.
u·na·ry (jú:nəri:) *adj.* made up of only one component *also* monadic
un·as·sum·ing (ʌnəsú:miŋ) *adj.* modest, not pretentious
un·at·tached (ʌnətǽtʃt) *adj.* not attached ‖ not belonging to a particular group, organization etc. ‖ (*old-fash.*) not married or engaged
un·at·tend·ed (ʌnəténdid) *adj.* alone, not accompanied ‖ not looked after, not attended to
un·a·vail·ing (ʌnəvéiliŋ) *adj.* having no useful effect
un·a·void·a·ble (ʌnəvɔ́idəb'l) *adj.* inevitable, not avoidable **un·a·vóid·a·bly** *adv.*
un·a·ware (ʌnəwɛ́ər) **1.** *adj.* not aware **2.** *adv.* unawares
un·a·wares (ʌnəwɛ́ərz) *adv.* by surprise, *we caught him unawares* ‖ unintentionally, without noticing
un·bal·anced (ʌnbǽlənst) *adj.* lacking balance ‖ mentally unstable ‖ (*accounting*) not balanced
un·beat·en (ʌnbí:t'n) *adj.* not defeated ‖ (*rhet.*) untrodden, *unbeaten paths* ‖ not whipped
un·be·com·ing (ʌnbikʌ́miŋ) *adj.* not becoming, *unbecoming clothes* ‖ unseemly, not decent
un·be·known (ʌnbinóun) **1.** *adj.* unknown **2.** *adv.* **unbeknown to** without the knowledge of, unknown to
un·be·lief (ʌnbilí:f) *n.* disbelief, incredulity ‖ lack of belief, esp. of religious belief
un·be·liev·a·ble (ʌnbilí:vəb'l) *adj.* true but astounding ‖ unacceptable as being true
un·be·liev·er (ʌnbilí:vər) *n.* someone who questions the truth of something ‖ a person who has no belief in matters of religion
un·be·liev·ing (ʌnbilí:viŋ) *adj.* incredulous ‖ not believing
un·bend (ʌnbénd) *pres. part.* **un·bend·ing** *past* and *past part.* **un·bent** (ʌnbént) *v.t.* to make straight ‖ (*naut.*) to unfasten (sails, ropes etc.) ‖ *v.i.* to become straight ‖ to become less distant or less stiff in manner
un·bend·ing (ʌnbéndiŋ) *adj.* inflexible in decision ‖ stiff and distant in manner
unbent *past* and *past part.* of UNBEND
un·bid·den (ʌnbíd'n) *adj.* not invited ‖ not commanded
un·bind (ʌnbáind) *pres. part.* **un·bind·ing** *past* and *past part.* **un·bound** (ʌnbáund) *v.t.* to untie, unfasten ‖ to remove restraints or restrictions from ‖ to undo the binding of (a book) [O.E. *unbindan*]
un·blessed (ʌnblést) *adj.* without something considered a blessing, *a house unblessed with modern comforts* ‖ unholy, wicked
un·blush·ing (ʌnblʌ́ʃiŋ) *adj.* shameless ‖ not blushing
un·born (ʌnbɔ́rn) *adj.* not yet born ‖ not brought into being
un·bos·om (ʌnbúzəm, ʌnbú:zəm) *v.t.* to reveal (one's feelings, thoughts etc.) ‖ *v.i.* to reveal one's feelings, thoughts etc. **to unbosom oneself** to relieve (oneself) of the strain of hidden feelings, thoughts etc. by revealing them
un·bound (ʌnbáund) *past* and *past part.* of UNBIND ‖ *adj.* not bound ‖ (of a book) not having a binding
un·bound·ed (ʌnbáundid) *adj.* without restraint, *unbounded joy* ‖ without limits in extent, quantity etc.
un·bowed (ʌnbáud) *adj.* (*rhet.*) undefeated ‖ not bowed
un·bri·dled (ʌnbráid'ld) *adj.* unrestrained ‖ having no bridle on
un·bro·ken (ʌnbróukən) *adj.* intact, whole ‖ not disordered, *despite the casualties their ranks remained unbroken* ‖ uninterrupted ‖ (of a horse) not broken in
un·bun·dle (ʌnbʌ́nd'l) *v.* to separate the elements of combined cost price, etc., from a package figure
un·bur·den (ʌnbə́:rd'n) *v.t.* to remove a burden from ‖ to relieve (oneself, one's conscience or one's mind) of worry or anxiety ‖ to rid oneself of the burden of (guilt, remorse etc.) e.g. by confiding in someone
un·called-for (ʌnkɔ́ldfɔr) *adj.* unnecessary ‖ impertinent, *an uncalled-for remark*

CONCISE PRONUNCIATION KEY: **(a)** æ, *cat*; ɑ, *car*; ɔ *fawn*; ei, *snake*. **(e)** e, *hen*; i:, *sheep*; iə, *deer*; ɛə, *bear*. **(i)** i, *fish*; ai, *tiger*; ə:, *bird*. **(o)** o, *ox*; au, *cow*; ou, *goat*; u, *poor*; ɔi, *royal*. **(u)** ʌ, *duck*; u, *bull*; u:, *goose*; ə, *bacillus*; ju:, *cube*. x, *loch*; θ, *think*; ð, *bother*; z, *Zen*; ʒ, *corsage*; dʒ, *savage*; ŋ, *orangutang*; j, *yak*; ʃ, *fish*; tʃ, *fetch*; 'l, *rabble*; 'n, *redden*. Complete pronunciation key appears inside front cover.

un·can·ni·ly (ʌnkǽnili:) *adv.* in an uncanny way or to an uncanny degree
un·can·ni·ness (ʌnkǽni:nis) *n.* the quality of being uncanny
un·can·ny (ʌnkǽni:) *comp.* **un·can·ni·er** *superl.* **un·can·ni·est** *adj.* inspiring feelings of apprehension ‖ almost superhuman, *uncanny powers of observation*
un·cap (ʌnkǽp) *v.* to uncover; to reveal
un·cer·e·mo·ni·ous (ʌnserəmóuni:əs) *adj.* brusque, curt, abrupt ‖ without ceremony or formality
un·cer·tain (ʌnsə́:rt'n) *adj.* not certainly known ‖ not having certain knowledge ‖ not certain to occur ‖ not reliable variable
un·cer·tain·ty (ʌnsə́:rt'nti:) *pl.* **un·cer·tain·ties** *n.* the quality or state of being uncertain ‖ something uncertain
uncertainty principle a principle, derived by Heisenberg as a logical consequence of quantum mechanics, according to which it is impossible to specify simultaneously the values of position and momentum or energy and time for a particle in a quantized system. The more precisely one of these quantities is known the less precise becomes our knowledge of the other
un·chris·tian (ʌnkrístʃən) *adj.* not of the Christian religion ‖ not befitting a Christian ‖ not according to principles of Christian behavior
un·ci·al (ʌ́nʃi:əl, ʌ́nʃəl) **1.** *adj.* of, relating to, or written in, the rounded unlinked letters used esp. in Greek and Latin manuscripts 300–900 A.D. **2.** *n.* an uncial letter ‖ a manuscript written in uncials [fr. L. *uncialis,* of an inch fr. *uncia,* twelfth part (of a pound or foot)]
un·ci·form (ʌ́nsifɔrm) **1.** *adj.* of a bone in the distal row of the wrist, on the same side as the ulna ‖ of a hook-shaped process on the unciform bone or a similar process on the ethmoid bone **2.** *n.* an unciform bone [fr. L. *uncus,* a hook]
un·ci·nate (ʌ́nsinit, ʌ́nsineit) *adj.* (*biol.*) hooked [fr. L. *uncinatus* fr. *uncinus,* a hook-shaped part]
un·cir·cum·cised (ʌnsə́:rkəmsaizd) *adj.* not circumcised ‖ (*Bible*) heathen ‖ (*Bible*) gentile, not Jewish
unclad alt. *past* and *past part.* of UNCLOTHE
un·clasp (ʌnklǽsp, ʌnklɑ́sp) *v.t.* to loosen or release the clasp of ‖ to release from a clasp ‖ *v.i.* to loosen a grasp or grip
un·cle (ʌ́ŋk'l) *n.* the brother of one's mother or father ‖ the husband of one's aunt ‖ (*pop.*) a cry meaning 'Stop, I've had enough!' [A.F.]
un·clean (ʌnklí:n) *adj.* morally impure ‖ ceremonially impure ‖ not clean, dirty
Uncle Sam (*pop.*) the government of the U.S.A. personified ‖ (*pop.*) the U.S.A. as a nation [prob. a jocular expansion of U.S.]
Uncle Tom *n.* a servile black person, esp. in relation to white people, from *Uncle Tom's Cabin,* by Harriet Beecher Stowe —**Uncle Tom** *adj.* —**Uncle Tomish** *adj.* —**Uncle Tomism** *n.*
un·cloak (ʌnklóuk) *v.t.* to remove a cloak from ‖ to expose (a plot etc. or a criminal) ‖ *v.i.* to take off a cloak
un·clothe (ʌnklóuð) *pres. part.* **un·cloth·ing** *past* and *past part.* **un·clothed, un·clad** (ʌnklǽd) *v.t.* to undress (someone)
un·com·fort·a·ble (ʌnkʌ́mfərtəb'l) *adj.* causing discomfort ‖ feeling discomfort ‖ uneasy **un·cóm·fort·a·bly** *adv.*
un·com·mit·ted (ʌnkəmítid) *adj.* not committed ‖ not bound to do something
un·com·mon (ʌnkɔ́mən) *adj.* unusual
un·com·mu·ni·ca·tive (ʌnkəmjú:nikətiv, ʌnkəmjú:nikeitiv) *adj.* reticent, disinclined to talk or to give information
un·com·pro·mis·ing (ʌnkɔ́mprəmaiziŋ) *adj.* making no concessions in negotiation, bargaining etc. ‖ free of compromise, *uncompromising integrity*
un·con·cern (ʌnkənsə́:rn) *n.* lack of concern, indifference
un·con·cerned (ʌnkənsə́:rnd) *adj.* not troubled, worried etc. ‖ not concerned, *unconcerned with the merits or demerits of the case* **un·con·cern·ed·ly** (ʌnkənsə́:rnidli:) *adv.*
un·con·di·tion·al (ʌnkəndíʃən'l) *adj.* absolute, without qualifying conditions
un·con·di·tioned (ʌnkəndíʃənd) *adj.* (*psychol.*) not conditioned ‖ (*philos.*) absolute, not subject to conditions
un·con·form·i·ty (ʌnkənfɔ́rmiti:) *pl.* **un·con·form·i·ties** *n.* (*geol.*) a rock formation in which the strata are not arranged in the order in which they were formed, usually because intermediate strata were completely eroded before the later strata were formed
un·con·scion·a·ble (ʌnkɔ́nʃənəb'l) *adj.* unscrupulous, unaffected by conscience ‖ immoderate, inordinate **un·cón·scion·a·bly** *adv.*
un·con·scious (ʌnkɔ́nʃəs) **1.** *adj.* not endowed with consciousness ‖ temporarily without consciousness ‖ (with 'of') not conscious ‖ not intended, *an unconscious insult* ‖ of or relating to the unconscious **2.** *n.* the area of mental activity which escapes mental awareness. It contains images, ideas etc. which have been repressed, but which emerge in dreams, pathological states etc., and may motivate behavior
un·con·scious·ness (ʌnkɔ́nʃəsnis) *n.* lack of consciousness
un·con·sti·tu·tion·al (ʌnkɒnstitú:ʃən'l, ʌnkɒnstitjú:ʃən'l) *adj.* not in accordance with the constitution **un·con·sti·tu·tion·ál·i·ty** *n.*
un·cor·rect·a·ble (ʌnkəréktəb'l) *adj.* not capable of being corrected —**uncorrectably** *adv.*
un·count·ed (ʌnkáuntid) *adj.* not counted ‖ innumerable
un·cou·ple (ʌnkʌ́p'l) *pres. part.* **un·cou·pling** *past* and *past part.* **un·cou·pled** *v.t.* to disconnect ‖ to set (hounds) free from a leash
un·couth (ʌnkú:θ) *adj.* (of a person or his manners, bearing etc.) awkward, rough ‖ (of style, language etc.) not polished [O.E. *uncūth,* unknown]
un·cov·er (ʌnkʌ́vər) *v.t.* to remove the cover or covering from ‖ to reveal, disclose ‖ *v.i.* (*old-fash.*) to take one's hat off one's head
un·cov·ered (ʌnkʌ́vərd) *adj.* without a cover or covering ‖ not covered by insurance etc. ‖ wearing no protection against the rain, wind or cold, esp. bareheaded
un·crowned (ʌnkráund) *adj.* reigning but not having gone through the coronation rite, *Edward VIII was uncrowned king of England*
unc·tion (ʌ́ŋkʃən) *n.* an anointing with oil as an act of religious significance ‖ the oil used ‖ an anointing with an ointment etc. for healing purposes ‖ religious fervor ‖ effusiveness in speech or manner [fr. L. *unctio* (*unctionis*)]
unc·tu·ous (ʌ́ŋktʃu:əs) *adj.* (esp. of speech or manner) effusive ‖ made of or containing oil or fat ‖ (of soil) soft and rich ‖ (of clay) plastic [fr. M.L. *unctuosus,* greasy]
un·cut (ʌnkʌ́t) *adj.* not cut ‖ (of a gem) not cut to shape ‖ (of a book) not having the pages trimmed ‖ (of a play etc.) not abridged
un·daunt·ed (ʌndɔ́ntid) *adj.* fearless, not daunted
un·de·ceive (ʌndisí:v) *pres. part.* **un·de·ceiv·ing** *past* and *past part.* **un·de·ceived** *v.t.* to free from false beliefs, ideas or impressions
un·de·cid·ed (ʌndisáidid) *adj.* that is not decided ‖ not having reached a decision
un·de·cil·lion (ʌndisíljən) *n.* *NUMBER TABLE [fr. L. *undecim,* eleven+MILLION]
un·dee, un·dé, un·dée (ʌ́ndei) *adj.* (*heraldry*) wavy [O.F. *unde* fr. L. *unda,* wave]
un·de·mon·stra·tive (ʌndəmɔ́nstrətiv) *adj.* not showing one's feelings
un·de·ni·a·ble (ʌndináiəb'l) *adj.* indisputable, certain, that cannot be denied **un·de·ní·a·bly** *adv.*
un·der (ʌ́ndər) **1.** *prep.* in, at, or to a position lower than, *to put felt under a carpet* ‖ in a position lower than the surface of, *under the ground* ‖ covered by, *under heavy blankets* ‖ lower in amount, quality, rank etc. than, *under average in weight* ‖ according to, *under the terms of the new contract* ‖ taking into account, *under the circumstances* ‖ indicated or represented by, *under a new name* ‖ suffering the action or effect of, *under ether* ‖ concealed by, sheltered by, *under a false name, under cover of darkness* ‖ within the designation of, *classify the entry under 'music'* ‖ bound by, *under an oath of secrecy* ‖ subject to (a specified penalty, threat etc.), *under pain of dismissal* ‖ subject to the guidance, authority, instruction etc. of, *Raphael studied under Perugino* ‖ during the reign of, *the monasteries were destroyed under Henry VIII* ‖ (of a piece of ground) planted or sown with, *under clover* **2.** *adv.* in or to a lower position, beneath ‖ in or to a position of subordination, subjection etc. ‖ so as to be covered, concealed etc. ‖ less than the required amount etc. ‖ less than a certain age, weight, length etc., *forbidden to children of 10 and under* **3.** *adj.* located or moving at a lower position than something or on the lower surface of something ‖ lower in amount, degree etc. ‖ lower in authority, rank etc. [O.E.]
under- *prefix* in, at, to or from a lower position ‖ in a subordinate position, as in 'understudy' ‖ to a degree, amount etc. considered below standard [M.E.]
un·der·a·chiev·er (ʌ́ndərətʃí:və:r) *n.* one who performs below his or her capacity —**underachieve** *v.* —**underachievement** *n.*
un·der·act (ʌndərǽkt) *v.t.* to act (a part) with less than full dramatic feeling ‖ *v.i.* to perform with less than full dramatic feeling
un·der·age (ʌndəréidʒ) *adj.* below the legal or required age
un·der·arm (ʌ́ndərɑrm) **1.** *adj.* performed with the arm swinging below the level of the shoulder **2.** *adv.* with an underarm movement **3.** *n.* the armpit
un·der·bid (ʌndərbíd) **1.** *v.t. pres. part.* **un·der·bid·ding** *past* and *past part.* **un·der·bid** to bid less than (a competing bidder) ‖ (*cards*) to bid less on (a hand) than its strength warrants **2.** *n.* an instance of underbidding
un·der·brush (ʌ́ndərbrʌʃ) *n.* undergrowth
un·der·car·riage (ʌ́ndərkæridʒ) *n.* the landing gear of an aircraft ‖ a supporting framework
un·der·char·ac·ter·i·za·tion (ʌ́ndərkærəktə:rəzéiʃən) *n.* insufficient development of the characters in a play, novel, or story
un·der·charge 1. (ʌndərtʃɑ́rdʒ) *v.t. pres. part.* **un·der·charg·ing** *past* and *past part.* **un·der·charged** to charge (someone) too little ‖ to charge (goods) at a lower price than is usual or permissible ‖ to load (a gun) with an insufficient charge **2.** (ʌ́ndərtʃɑrdʒ) *n.* an instance of undercharging for goods or the amount of this
un·der·class (ʌ́ndərklæs) *n.* those on a lower economic, social, or educational level than those of the middle class
un·der·class·man (ʌndərklǽsmən, ʌndərklɑ́smən) *pl.* **un·der·class·men** (ʌndərklǽsmən, ʌndərklɑ́smən) *n.* a freshman or sophomore
un·der·clothes (ʌ́ndərklouðz, ʌ́ndərklouz) *pl. n.* clothes worn next to the body, under the outer garments
un·der·cloth·ing (ʌ́ndərklouðiŋ) *n.* underclothes
un·der·coat (ʌ́ndərkout) *n.* (of longhaired animals) a growth of hair under and partly concealed by the main growth of hair ‖ a layer of paint etc. applied as base for a top coat
undercoating *n.* (*motor vehicle*) a rustproofing placed on the under surface of a chassis —**undercoat** *v.*
un·der·cov·er (ʌ́ndərkʌvər, ʌndərkʌ́vər) *adj.* acting or carried out secretly
un·der·croft (ʌ́ndərkrɔft, ʌ́ndərkrɒft) *n.* a crypt [fr. UNDER+obs. *croft,* crypt fr. L.]
un·der·cur·rent (ʌ́ndərkə:rənt, ʌ́ndərkʌrənt) *n.* a current below the upper surface of water or air ‖ an underlying tendency running counter to openly expressed opinion or feeling
un·der·cut 1. (ʌndərkʌ́t) *v.t. pres. part.* **un·der·cut·ting** *past* and *past part.* **un·der·cut** to cut away from the undersurface of ‖ to make an undercut in (a tree) ‖ to undersell ‖ to work for lower wages than ‖ (*golf, tennis etc.*) to hit (the ball) so as to give it backspin **2.** (ʌ́ndərkʌt) *n.* an underhand stroke, e.g. in tennis, to impart backspin ‖ a notch cut in a tree below the level of the major cut, on the side where the tree is to fall ‖ (*Br.*) a joint of meat cut from the lower side of a sirloin ‖ a cut made below or beneath another cut **3.** (ʌ́ndərkʌt) *adj.* cut away so as to stand out in relief
un·der·de·vel·oped (ʌndərdivéləpt) *adj.* less developed than is normal ‖ (*photog.*) not developed enough to give a good image ‖ (of a country or region) not industrially or economically reaching the level that could be reached if the necessary capital, technicians etc. were available
un·der·do (ʌndərdú:) *pres. part.* **un·der·do·ing** *past* **un·der·did** (ʌndərdíd) *past part.* **un·der·done** (ʌndərdʌ́n) *v.t.* to cook (meat) very lightly ‖ to cook (food) for insufficient time
un·der·dog (ʌ́ndərdɔg, ʌ́ndərdɒg) *n.* someone who gets the worst of a struggle ‖ a victim of social injustice
un·der·done (ʌndərdʌ́n) *past part.* of UNDERDO ‖ *adj.* (of meat) very lightly cooked, rare ‖ (of food) insufficiently cooked
un·der·em·ploy·ment (ʌndərimplɔ́imənt) *n.* **1.** employment that does not utilize one's best skills **2.** part-time employment *Cf* SUBEMPLOYMENT
un·der·es·ti·mate 1. (ʌndəréstəmeit) *v.t. pres. part.* **un·der·es·ti·mat·ing** *past* and *past part.* **un·der·es·ti·mat·ed** to rate (something or someone) below true worth ‖ to quote too low a

figure in giving an estimate for 2. (ʌndəréstəmit) *n.* too low a rating or estimate **un·der·es·ti·má·tion** *n.*

un·der·ex·pose (ʌndərikspóuz) *pres. part.* **un·der·ex·pos·ing** *past* and *past part.* **un·der·ex·posed** *v.t.* (*photog.*) to expose (*film*) for too short a time **un·der·ex·po·sure** (ʌndərikspóuʒər) *n.*

un·der·feed (ʌndərfíːd) *pres. part.* **un·der·feed·ing** *past* and *past part.* **un·der·fed** (ʌndərféd) *v.t.* to give insufficient food to ‖ to stoke (a fire) from below

un·der·foot (ʌndərfút) *adv.* under the foot or feet ‖ (*pop.*) in the way

un·der·gar·ment (ʌ́ndərgɑrmənt) *n.* a garment, e.g. a petticoat, meant to be worn under another garment

un·der·glaze (ʌ́ndərglẹiz) **1.** *adj.* (*ceramics*) applied before glazing **2.** *n.* a pigment for application before glazing

un·der·go (ʌndərgóu) *pres. part.* **un·der·go·ing** *past* **un·der·went** (ʌndərwént) *past part.* **un·der·gone** (ʌndərgɔ́n, ʌndərgɔ́n) *v.t.* to endure, experience

un·der·grad·u·ate (ʌndərgrǽdʒuːit) **1.** *n.* a university student who has not yet obtained his first (or bachelor's) degree **2.** *adj.* of, for or consisting of undergraduates ‖ having the status of an undergraduate

un·der·ground 1. (ʌ́ndərgraund) *adj.* being below the surface of the ground ‖ not public, secret **2.** *n.* (ʌ́ndərgraund) (*Br.=Am.* subway) an underground railroad **the underground** a secret resistance movement, esp. in an occupied or totalitarian country **3.** (ʌndərgráund) *adv.* beneath the earth's surface ‖ in or into hiding

underground railroad a city railroad running in tunnels under the ground **Underground Railroad** (*Am. hist.*) a chain of sympathizers who provided a system of escape before the Civil War for slaves who ran away from the South to the free states and Canada

underground railway an underground railroad

un·der·grown (ʌndərgróun, ʌ́ndərgroun) *adj.* not grown to full or normal size or development

un·der·growth (ʌ́ndərgrouθ) *n.* shrubs, saplings etc. growing on the forest floor

un·der·hand (ʌ́ndərhænd) **1.** *adj.* deceitful, sly ‖ performed with the hand below the level of the shoulder **2.** *adv.* in an underhand manner ‖ with an underhand arm action

un·der·hand·ed (ʌndərhǽndid) *adj.* secret, sly ‖ shorthanded

un·der·hung (ʌndərhʌ́ŋ) *adj.* (of the lower jaw) projecting beyond the upper jaw ‖ having such a jaw ‖ resting and moving on a track or rail underneath, not suspended

un·der·kill (ʌ́ndərkil) *n.* **1.** use of force inadequate to accomplish the task **2.** by extension, use of restraint in the exercise of power

un·der·laid (ʌndərléid) *past* and *past part.* of UNDERLAY ‖ *adj.* laid underneath ‖ supported or strengthened by having something laid underneath

underlain *past part.* of UNDERLIE

un·der·lay 1. (ʌndərléi) *v. pres. part.* **un·der·lay·ing** *past* and *past part.* **un·der·laid** (ʌndərléid) *v.t.* to lay under, to support or line with something placed underneath ‖ to adjust with an underlay ‖ *v.i.* (*Br., mining,* of a vein) to incline from the vertical **2.** (ʌ́ndərlẹi) *n.* something laid under, esp. a varying thickness of paper placed under type to raise it to the right level for printing ‖ (*Br., mining*) an inclination of a vein from the vertical

underlay *past* of UNDERLIE

un·der·lie (ʌndərlái) *pres. part.* **un·der·ly·ing** *past* **un·der·lay** (ʌndərléi) *past part.* **un·der·lain** (ʌndərléin) *v.t.* to lie or be under ‖ to be the basis or foundation of ‖ to lie hidden under (external appearances) ‖ (*finance,* of a right, security etc.) to be prior to (another right etc.) ‖ (*Br., mining*) to underlay

un·der·line 1. (ʌndərláin, ʌ́ndərlɑin) *v.t. pres. part.* **un·der·lin·ing** *past* and *past part.* **un·der·lined** to draw a line under (e.g. a word) esp. for emphasis ‖ to emphasize **2.** (ʌ́ndərlɑin) *n.* a line drawn underneath a printed or written word

un·der·ling (ʌ́ndərliŋ) *n.* (used contemptuously) a subordinate

un·der·lip (ʌ́ndərlip) *n.* the lower lip

un·der·ly·ing (ʌ́ndərlɑiiŋ) *adj.* lying or placed underneath ‖ being at the basis but not immediately obvious

underlying structure *DEEP STRUCTURE

un·der·mine (ʌndərmáin) *pres. part.* **un·der·min·ing** *past* and *past part.* **un·der·mined** *v.t.* to dig under so as to cause a fall ‖ (of water) to wash away the foundations of ‖ (*fig.*) to weaken or injure by crafty, indirect methods ‖ to weaken or ruin gradually, *drugs undermined his health*

un·der·most (ʌ́ndərmoust) **1.** *adj.* lowest in position, rank etc. **2.** *adv.* lowest

un·der·neath (ʌndərníːθ) **1.** *adv.* beneath, below **2.** *prep.* beneath, below **3.** *adj.* lower, under **4.** *n.* the bottom surface

un·der·nour·ished (ʌndərnə́ːriʃt, ʌndərnʌ́riʃt) *adj.* not provided with enough food

un·der·nour·ish·ment (ʌndərnə́ːriʃmənt, ʌndərnʌ́riʃmənt) *n.* lack of adequate food

un·der·oc·cu·pied (ʌndərɒ́kjuːpaid) *adj.* of not utilizing space, skill, or a facility to its capacity

underpaid *past* and *past part.* of UNDERPAY

un·der·pants (ʌ́ndərpænts) *pl. n.* an undergarment covering the lower torso and sometimes the upper thigh, with a separate division for each leg

un·der·pass (ʌ́ndərpæs, ʌ́ndərpɑs) *n.* a tunnel or passageway for traffic or pedestrians or both, passing under a railroad or highway

un·der·pay (ʌndərpéi) *pres. part.* **un·der·pay·ing** *past* and *past part.* **un·der·paid** (ʌndərpéid) *v.t.* and *i.* to pay less than is just or adequate

un·der·pin (ʌndərpín) *pres. part.* **un·der·pin·ning** *past* and *past part.* **under·pinned** *v.t.* to support by placing masonry, woodwork etc. underneath **ún·der·pin·ning** *n.* materials or a structure that gives support e.g. for a wall

un·der·play (ʌndərpléi) *v.t.* to play (a role) in an intentionally restrained manner ‖ to fail to give (a role) its full dramatic emphasis ‖ to minimize the importance of ‖ (*cards*) to play (one's hand) for less than its full value

un·der·plot (ʌ́ndərplɒt) *n.* a subordinate plot in a story, play etc.

un·der·pop·u·la·tion (ʌndərpɒpjuːléiʃən) *n.* a state of having less population than would be acceptable, esp. with consideration of available resources

un·der·priv·i·leged (ʌndərprívəlidʒd, ʌndərprívlidʒd) *adj.* living under social and economic conditions below an acceptable level

un·der·pro·duc·tion (ʌndərprədʌ́kʃən) *n.* the production of an amount that is too small to satisfy demand, less than the norm, or less than full capacity

un·der·proof (ʌndərprúːf) *adj.* lower in alcohol content than proof spirit

un·der·rate (ʌndərréit) *pres. part.* **un·der·rat·ing** *past* and *past part.* **un·der·rat·ed** *v.t.* to attribute less than full worth or importance to

un·der·score (ʌndərskɔ́r, ʌndərskóur) *pres. part.* **un·der·scor·ing** *past* and *past part.* **un·der·scored** *v.t.* to underline

un·der·sea 1. (ʌ́ndərsịː) *adj.* being, happening, or meant for use below the surface of the sea **2.** (ʌndərsíː) *adv.* under the sea

un·der·seas (ʌndərsiːz) *adv.* undersea

un·der·sec·re·tar·y (ʌndərsékritẹriː) *pl.* **un·der·sec·re·tar·ies** *n.* an assistant secretary, esp. in a department of state

un·der·sell (ʌndərsél) *pres. part.* **un·der·sell·ing** *past* and *past part.* **un·der·sold** (ʌndərsóuld) *v.t.* to sell at a lower price than ‖ to sell at a price lower than the value of

un·der·set (ʌ́ndərsẹt) *n.* an underlying vein of ore ‖ an undercurrent

un·der·shap·er (ʌ́ndərʃeipəːr) *n.* women's elastic undergarment

un·der·shirt (ʌ́ndərʃəːrt) *n.* (*Am.=Br.* vest) an undergarment covering the upper part of the body

un·der·shoot (ʌ́ndərʃuːt, ʌndərʃúːt) *pres. part.* **un·der·shoot·ing** *past* and *past part.* **un·der·shot** (ʌ́ndərʃɒt, ʌndərʃɒ́t) *v.t.* to shoot or fire short of (the target) ‖ (of an aircraft) to fail to get onto (the runway or flight deck) in coming into land ‖ *v.i.* to shoot or fire short of the target

un·der·shorts (ʌ́ndərʃɔrts) *pl. n.* underpants

un·der·shot (ʌ́ndərʃɒt) *adj.* (of the lower jaw) underhung ‖ (of a wheel) driven by water passing beneath it

un·der·side (ʌ́ndərsaid) *n.* the underneath, the side or surface facing downwards

un·der·signed 1. (ʌndərsáind) *adj.* signed below ‖ whose name is signed below **2.** (ʌ́ndərsaind) *n.* (with 'the') the person or persons having signed below

un·der·size (ʌndərsáiz) *adj.* undersized

un·der·sized (ʌndərsáizd) *adj.* smaller than average or normal

un·der·skirt (ʌ́ndərskəːrt) *n.* a skirt worn under another skirt, esp. a waistlength petticoat

un·der·slung (ʌ́ndərslʌŋ) *adj.* (of a chassis) with the frame slung below the axles

undersold *past part.* of UNDERSELL

un·der·stand (ʌndərstǽnd) *pres. part.* **un·der·stand·ing** *past* and *past part.* **un·der·stood** (ʌndərstúd) *v.t.* to seize the meaning of ‖ to be thoroughly acquainted with, expert in the use or practice of, *to understand machinery* ‖ (*philos.*) to form a reasoned judgment concerning (something) ‖ to possess a passive knowledge of (a language) ‖ to appreciate and sympathize with ‖ to gather, infer, *what do you understand will happen?* ‖ to interpret, attribute a specified meaning to, *I understand the message to mean they aren't coming* ‖ to accept as a fact, believe, *I understand that I shall be repaid* ‖ (used in the passive) to supply mentally (a word, idea etc.) ‖ *v.i.* to have the power of seizing meanings, forming reasoned judgments etc. ‖ to feel and show sympathy, tolerance etc. [O.E. *understandan,* to stand under]

un·der·stand·ing (ʌndərstǽndiŋ) **1.** *n.* the ability to understand ‖ the act of one who understands ‖ (*philos.*) the power to form reasoned judgments ‖ an informal agreement that is only morally binding ‖ a resolution of differences **2.** *adj.* feeling and showing sympathy, tolerance etc.

un·der·state (ʌndərstéit) *pres. part.* **un·der·stat·ing** *past* and *past part.* **under·stat·ed** *v.t.* to represent as being less or less important etc. than is in fact the case, often as a trick of style for effect **un·der·state·ment** *n.*

un·der·steer (ʌndərstíər) *v.* (*motor vehicle*) to turn a vehicle less than intended

un·der·stood (ʌndərstúd) *past* and *past part.* of UNDERSTAND ‖ *adj.* agreed upon ‖ (esp. *gram.*) implied, not specified

un·der·stud·y (ʌ́ndərstʌdiː) **1.** *pl.* **un·der·stud·ies** *n.* an actor who learns another actor's part in order to be able to replace him if necessary **2.** *v. pres. part.* **un·der·stud·y·ing** *past* and *past part.* **un·der·stud·ied** *v.t.* to be the understudy of ‖ to study (someone else's part) ‖ *v.i.* to be an understudy

un·der·sur·face (ʌ́ndərsəːrfis) *n.* the surface lying underneath

un·der·take (ʌndərtéik) *pres. part.* **un·der·tak·ing** *past* **un·der·took** (ʌndərtúk) *past part.* **un·der·tak·en** (ʌndərtéikən) *v.t.* to embark on, *to undertake a journey* ‖ to assume responsibility for (something) ‖ to promise (to do something) **ún·der·tak·er** *n.* a person whose trade is preparing the dead for burial and managing funerals **un·der·ták·ing** *n.* something undertaken, e.g. a heavy task ‖ a promise, esp. one required by law ‖ (ʌ́ndərtẹikiŋ) the business of an undertaker

un·der·tone (ʌ́ndərtoun) *n.* a low sound ‖ a barely audible tone of voice ‖ a subdued color, esp. one which softens or transmutes another

undertook *past* of UNDERTAKE

un·der·tow (ʌ́ndərtou) *n.* the undercurrent pulling strongly seaward or parallel with the coastline when waves are breaking on the shore

un·der·trick (ʌ́ndərtrịk) *n.* (*bridge*) a trick falling short of contract

un·der·val·u·a·tion (ʌndərvæljuːéiʃən) *n.* an undervaluing ‖ a valuation that is too low

un·der·val·ue (ʌndərvǽljuː) *pres. part.* **un·der·val·u·ing** *past* and *past part.* **un·der·val·ued** *v.t.* to set too low a value on ‖ to underestimate

un·der·wa·ter (ʌ́ndərwɔtər, ʌ́ndərwɒtər) **1.** *adj.* placed, growing, happening etc. under water used or to be used under water below a ship's waterline **2.** *adv.* under the water

underwater hockey form of stick hockey played underwater by skin divers in a deep swimming pool

un·der·wear (ʌ́ndərwɛər) *n.* underclothes

un·der·weight 1. (ʌndərwéit) *adj.* weighing less than the weight normal for an age or height ‖ weighing less than the legally required weight **2.** (ʌ́ndərwẹit) *n.* the condition of weighing less than is normal or legally required

underwent *past* of UNDERGO

un·der·whelm (ʌndərwélm) *v.* to fail to impress —**underwhelming** *adj. ant.* overwhelm

un·der·wing (ʌ́ndərwịŋ) *n.* one of the posterior wings of some insects, esp. moths

un·der·wood (ʌ́ndərwụd) *n.* undergrowth

Underwood Tariff Act a U.S. Congressional act (1913) introduced by Representative Oscar Wilder Underwood (1862-1929). It drastically

CONCISE PRONUNCIATION KEY: **(a)** æ, *cat*; ɑ, *car*; ɔ *fawn*; ei, *snake*. **(e)** e, *hen*; iː, *sheep*; iə, *deer*; ɛə, *bear*. **(i)** i, *fish*; ai, *tiger*; əː, *bird*. **(o)** o, *ox*; au, *cow*; ou, *goat*; u, *poor*; ɔi, *royal*. **(u)** ʌ, *duck*; u, *bull*; uː, *goose*; ə, *bacillus*; juː, *cube*. x, *loch*; θ, *think*; ð, *bother*; z, *Zen*; ʒ, *corsage*; dʒ, *savage*; ŋ, *orangutang*; j, *yak*; ʃ, *fish*; tʃ, *fetch*; ˈl, *rabble*; ˈn, *redden*. Complete pronunciation key appears inside front cover.

reduced tariff schedules and transferred many articles to the free list. It provided for free trade between the Philippine Is and the U.S.A. Its enforcement was interrupted (1914) by the outbreak of the 1st world war

un·der·world (ʌ́ndərwə:rld) *n.* (*rhet.*) the home of departed spirits ‖ the criminal section of society

un·der·write (ʌ́ndərrait, ʌndərráit) *pres. part.* **un·der·writ·ing** *past* **un·der·wrote** (ʌ́ndərrout, ʌndərróut) *past part.* **un·der·writ·ten** (ʌ́ndərrít'n, ʌndərrít'n) *v.t.* to execute (an insurance policy, esp. a marine policy) ‖ to undertake to meet the financial losses of ‖ to purchase (an issue of bonds etc.) on a fixed date and at a fixed price ‖ to guarantee the purchase of (stocks, bonds etc.) issued for public subscription ‖ to affix one's signature to (an insurance policy) thereby assuming liability in case of specified loss or damage ‖ to assume liability to the sum of ‖ *v.i.* to be an underwriter in the insurance business **ún·der·writ·er** *n.*

un·de·sign·ing (ʌndizáiniŋ) *adj.* having no hidden, self-seeking purpose

un·de·sir·a·ble (ʌndizáiərəb'l) **1.** *adj.* objectionable ‖ not wanted, not to be encouraged **2.** *n.* an objectionable person

un·did *past* of UNDO

un·dies (ʌ́ndi:z) *pl. n.* (*pop.*) women's or children's underclothes

un·dine (ʌ́ndi:n, ʌndí:n) *n.* a female water sprite who, according to some legends, could acquire a soul if she married a mortal and had a child [fr. Gk fr. Mod. L. *Undina* fr. L. *unda*, wave]

un·di·rect·ed (ʌndiréktid, ʌndairéktid) *adj.* not directed ‖ (e.g. of a letter) not addressed

un·do (ʌndú:) *pres. part.* **un·do·ing** *past* **un·did** (ʌndíd) *past part.* **un·done** (ʌndʌ́n) *v.t.* to open by untying etc. ‖ to unfasten (a button, garment etc.) ‖ to destroy (what has been done or accomplished) ‖ (*rhet.*) to bring to ruin or destruction **un·dó·ing** *n.* the act of unfastening ‖ (*rhet.*) a bringing to ruin or destruction ‖ (*rhet.*) a cause of this ‖ the destruction of something done or accomplished **un·dóne** *adj.* unfastened ‖ (*rhet.*) brought to ruin [O.E. *undōn*]

un·dock (ʌndɔ́k) *v.* (*aerospace*) to disconnect or uncouple from another spacecraft

undone *adj.* not done

un·doubt·ed (ʌndáutid) *adj.* not doubted or disputed, regarded as certain **un·dóubt·ed·ly** *adv.* certainly

UNDP (*abbr.*) for United Nations Development Program, agency to assist in technical training and technology transfer to developing nations

un·draw (ʌndrɔ́) *pres. part.* **un·draw·ing** *past* **un·drew** (ʌndrú:) *past part.* **un·drawn** (ʌndrɔ́n) *v.t.* to draw or pull back or aside (e.g. a curtain)

un·dreamed (ʌndrí:md) *adj.* (usually with 'of') beyond what one would have thought to be possible, *splendors undreamed of*

un·dreamt (ʌndrémt) *adj.* undreamed

un·dress 1. (ʌndrés) *v.t.* to take off the clothes of ‖ *v.i.* to take off one's clothes **2.** (ʌndrés) *n.* comfortable, informal dress ‖ ordinary clothes as opposed to uniform ‖ a state of being only partly dressed **3.** (ʌ́ndres) *adj.* of or relating to informal clothes, esp. uniform

un·dressed (ʌndrést) *adj.* not dressed ‖ without a dressing

undrew *past* of UNDRAW

UNDRO (*acronym*) for United Nations Disaster Relief Organization

Und·set (únset), Sigrid (1882-1949), Norwegian novelist. Her best-known work is the trilogy 'Kristin Lavransdatter' (1920-2), the story of a woman's life in medieval Norway

un·due (ʌndú:,ʌndjú:) *adj.* excessive, beyond what is expected or required ‖ improper, inappropriate

undue influence (*law*) influence over another person which prevents him from exercising his own will

un·du·lant (ʌ́ndʒulənt, ʌ́ndjulənt) *adj.* wavelike in form or movement

undulant fever a disease caused by bacteria of the genus *Brucella*, fam. *Brucellaceae*, contracted by human beings, esp. from infected milk or dairy products. It is characterized by remittent fever and general exhaustion, and can last for months

un·du·late (ʌ́ndʒuleit, ʌ́ndjuleit) *pres. part,* **un·du·lat·ing** *past* and *past part.* **un·du·lat·ed** *v.i.* to have a wavelike motion or form ‖ *v.t.* to cause to move in a wavy, sinuous manner ‖ to give a wavelike form to **ún·du·lat·ed** *adj.* having a wavelike surface, edge or marking **un·du·lá·tion** *n.* a wavelike motion ‖ a wavy form ‖ a pulsation ‖ (*phys.*) wave motion or a wave or vibration **un·du·la·to·ry** (ʌ́ndʒulətɔri:, ʌ́ndjulətɔri:, ʌ́ndʒulətouri:, ʌ́ndjulətouri:) *adj.* [fr. L. *undulatus* fr. *unda*, a wave]

undulatory theory *WAVE THEORY

un·du·ly (ʌndú:li:, ʌndjú:li:) *adv.* excessively

un·dy·ing (ʌndáiiŋ) *adj.* (of fame, devotion etc.) perpetual

un·earned (ʌnə́:rnd) *adj.* undeserved ‖ derived from investments etc., *unearned income*

unearned increment an increase of value of land etc. due to increased demand, rather than to any labor or expenditure by the owner

un·earth (ʌnə́:rθ) *v.t.* to dig up ‖ to bring to light, *to unearth new facts*

un·earth·li·ness (ʌnə́:rθli:nis) *n.* the state or quality of being unearthly

un·earth·ly (ʌnə́:rθli:) *adj.* not belonging to the earth ‖ celestial, supernatural ‖ (*pop.*) preposterous, *an unearthly time to get up*

un·eas·i·ly (ʌní:zili:) *adv.* in an uneasy manner

un·eas·i·ness (ʌní:zi:nis) *n.* the state or quality of being uneasy

un·eas·y (ʌní:zi:) *comp.* **un·eas·i·er** *superl.* **un·eas·i·est** *adj.* uncomfortable, restless ‖ disturbed, troubled, *he fell into an uneasy sleep* ‖ anxious, rather frightened ‖ ill at ease

un·em·ploy·a·ble (ʌnimplɔ́iəb'l) **1.** *adj.* not employable, esp. not fit for paid employment, because of age, physical incapacity etc. **2.** *n.* a person not fit for paid employment

un·em·ployed (ʌnimplɔ́id) **1.** *adj.* not in paid employment ‖ not being used ‖ not invested **2.** *n.* (only in) **the unemployed** that part of the working population not in paid employment

un·em·ploy·ment (ʌnimplɔ́imənt) *n.* the state of being unable to secure paid employment ‖ lack of employment

unemployment benefit a weekly sum paid from public funds to an unemployed worker under a state security scheme ‖ a payment by a trade union or by an employer to an employee unable to work

unemployment compensation unemployment benefit paid under state laws

un·en·closed (ʌninklóuzd) *adj.* not fenced in ‖ (of nuns) not restricted to the convent

un·e·qual (ʌní:kwəl) *adj.* not of the same dimensions, *unequal lengths* ‖ not uniform in quality, degree etc., *unequal abilities, unequal vibrations* ‖ (esp. with 'to') not fit or adequate, *unequal to hard work*

un·e·qualed, esp. *Br.* **un·e·qualled** (ʌní:kwəld) *adj.* without equal, *unequaled beauty*

un·e·quiv·o·cal (ʌnikwívək'l) *adj.* admitting of no doubt or question as to meaning or intention, not ambiguous

un·err·ing (ʌnə́:riŋ, ʌnériŋ) *adj.* certain, sure ‖ free from error

UNESCO (ju:néskou) *UNITED NATIONS EDUCATIONAL, SCIENTIFIC AND CULTURAL ORGANIZATION

un·es·sen·tial (ʌnisénʃəl) **1.** *adj.* not of basic importance **2.** *n.* something not of basic importance

un·e·ven (ʌní:vən) *adi.* not smooth, *an uneven road surface* ‖ not of the same size, length or quantity, *uneven rates of pay* ‖ not of the same quality or capacity, *uneven competitors* ‖ not consistently good or bad, *uneven progress* ‖ (of numbers) odd

un·ex·am·pled (ʌnigzǽmp'ld, ʌnigzámp'ld) *adj.* without precedent

un·ex·cep·tion·a·ble (ʌniksépʃənəb'l) *adj.* beyond the reach of criticism, above reproach **un·ex·cép·tion·a·bly** *adv.*

un·ex·cep·tion·al (ʌniksépʃən'l) *adj.* not exceptional, ordinary ‖ unexceptionable ‖ not admitting of any exception

un·fail·ing (ʌnféiliŋ) *adj.* not failing ‖ inexhaustible ‖ certain, reliable

un·fair (ʌnféər) *adj.* not just ‖ not according to business ethics, *unfair practices*

un·faith·ful (ʌnféiθfəl) *adj.* failing one's trust, disloyal ‖ adulterous ‖ not accurate

un·fa·mil·iar (ʌnfəmíljər) *adj.* not well known, strange ‖ (with 'with') having little or no experience, *unfamiliar with firearms* **un·fa·mil·i·ar·i·ty** (ʌnfəmili:ǽriti:) *n.*

un·fa·vor·a·ble, *Br.* **un·fa·vour·a·ble** (ʌnféivərəb'l) *adj.* not favorable, adverse, *unfavorable criticisms* ‖ (*rhet.*, of the wind) contrary

Unfederated Malay States *MALAYA

un·feel·ing (ʌnfí:liŋ) *adj.* unsympathetic, hardhearted ‖ without feeling

un·fin·ished (ʌnfíniʃt) *adj.* not finished, incomplete ‖ rough, unpolished ‖ (of woolen cloth) not bleached or dyed etc. after weaving

un·fit (ʌnfít) **1.** *adj.* not fit, not suitable ‖ not fitted, not suitably adapted for a given purpose ‖ not well, in poor physical condition **2.** *v.t. pres. part.* **un·fit·ting** *past* and *past part.* **un·fit·ted** to render unsuitable

un·fix (ʌnfíks) *v.t.* to undo the fixing of, disengage ‖ to unsettle ‖ (*chem.*) to make (a compound) soluble

un·flap·pa·ble (ʌnflǽpəb'l) *adj.* (*colloq.*) not easily ruffled —**unflappability** *n.* —**unflappably** *adj. ant.* flappable

un·fledged (ʌnflédʒd) *adj.* not fledged ‖ immature, undeveloped ‖ (of an arrow) not having vanes

un·flinch·ing (ʌnflíntʃiŋ) *adj.* resolute, not wavering

un·fold (ʌnfóuld) *v.t.* to open from its folds ‖ to cause to reveal itself gradually to the vision or mind ‖ *v.i.* to open out ‖ to reveal itself gradually to the vision or mind [O.E. *unfealdan*]

un·formed (ʌnfɔ́rmd) *adj.* not having a definite shape or structure ‖ immature

un·for·tu·nate (ʌnfɔ́rtʃənit) **1.** *adj.* not favored by chance, fortune etc., unlucky ‖ much to be regretted, *an unfortunate incident* **2.** *n.* an unfortunate person

un·found·ed (ʌnfáundid) *adj.* having no foundation of reason or fact

un·friend·li·ness (ʌnfréndli:nis) *n.* the state or quality of being unfriendly

un·friend·ly (ʌnfréndli:) **1.** *adj.* (of relations between people) not friendly ‖ (of people, nations, animals etc.) hostile ‖ (*rhet.*) unfavorable, *a regime unfriendly towards artists* **2.** *adv.* in an unfriendly manner

un·frock (ʌnfrɔ́k) *v.t.* to deprive (a priest) of his priest's orders

un·fruit·ful (ʌnfrú:tfəl) *adj.* not producing offspring ‖ not bearing fruit ‖ (of soil) bad for producing crops ‖ unprofitable

un·furl (ʌnfə́:rl) *v.t.* to unfold, to loose from a state of being furled ‖ *v.i.* to become unfurled

un·gain·li·ness (ʌngéinli:nis) *n.* the state or quality of being ungainly

un·gain·ly (ʌngéinli:) *adj.* clumsy, awkward [M.E. *ungeinliche* fr. *ungein*, perilous fr. *un-*, not+ O.N. *gegn*, ready]

Un·ga·ret·ti (u:ŋgarétti:), Giuseppe (1888-1970), Italian poet, author of 'Allegria' (1931), 'Sentimento del Tempore' (1933), 'Il Dolore' (1947), 'La Terra Promessa' (1950), 'Un grido e paesaggi' (1952)

Un·ga·va Bay (ʌŋgéivə) a large inlet (200 miles long, 160 miles wide at the mouth) between the northern tip of Labrador and the Ungava Peninsula, Canada

Ungava Peninsula a hilly, lake-studded peninsula (400 miles long, 350 miles wide) between the Hudson Bay and Ungava Bay, Quebec, Canada

un·god·li·ness (ʌngɔ́dli:nis) *n.* the state or quality of being ungodly

un·god·ly (ʌngɔ́dli:) *adj.* wicked ‖ (*pop.*) unreasonable, *what an ungodly hour to call*

un·gov·ern·a·ble (ʌngʌ́vərnəb'l) *adj.* that will not submit to control

un·gra·cious (ʌngréiʃəs) *adj.* lacking courtesy or good manners ‖ not attractive

un·gram·mat·i·cal (ʌngrəmǽtik'l) *adj.* not according to the rules of grammar

un·grate·ful (ʌngréitfəl) *adj.* without gratitude ‖ of an unpleasant nature, *ungrateful chores*

un·gual (ʌ́ŋgwəl) **1.** *adj* of, relating to or resemble a claw, nail or hoof **2.** *n.* a claw, nail or hoof [fr. L. *unguis*, claw, nail]

un·guard (ʌngárd) *v.t.* to expose to attack ‖ (*bridge*) to expose (a high card) to the risk of loss by discarding a lower card **un·gúard·ed** *adj.* without a guard ‖ marked by lack of caution, *an unguarded moment*

un·guent (ʌ́ŋgwənt) *n.* an ointment [fr. L. *unguens* (*unguentis*) fr. *unguere*, to anoint]

un·guic·u·late (ʌŋgwíkjulit) **1.** *adj.* (*zool.*, of mammals) having claws or nails as distinct from hoofs ‖ (*bot.*) having an unguis **2.** *n.* a mammal having claws or nails **un·guíc·u·lat·ed** *adj.* [fr. L. *unguiculus* dim. of *unguis*, nail, claw]

un·guis (ʌ́ŋgwis) *pl.* **un·gues** (ʌ́ŋgwi:z) *n.* (*zool.*, of vertebrates) a claw, nail or hoof ‖ (*zool.*) the chitinous hook on the foot of an insect ‖ (*bot.*) a clawshaped petal base [L.]

un·gu·la (ʌ́ngjulə) *pl.* **un·gu·lae** (ʌ́ŋgjuli:) *n.* an ungual **ún·gu·lar** *adj.* [L.=a hoof]

un·gu·late (ʌ́ŋgjulit) 1. *adj.* hoofed ‖ of or relating to hoofed mammals 2. *n.* a hoofed mammal [fr. L. *ungulatus* fr. *ungula*, hoof]

un·hal·lowed (ʌnhǽloud) *adj.* not consecrated, *unhallowed ground* ‖ wicked, impious

un·hap·pi·ness (ʌnhǽpi:nis) *n.* the state or quality of being unhappy

un·hap·py (ʌnhǽpi:) *comp.* **un·hap·pi·er** *superl.* **un·hap·pi·est** *adj.* sad, in low spirits ‖ unlucky, *it was an unhappy day for me when they met* ‖ not appropriate, *an unhappy combination of colors*

un·har·ness (ʌnhɑ́rnis) *v.t.* to remove the harness from ‖ to liberate (e.g. a source of energy)

un·health·i·ness (ʌnhélθi:nis) *n.* the state or quality of being unhealthy

un·health·y (ʌnhélθi:) *comp.* **un·health·i·er** *superl.* **un·health·i·est** *adj.* not in good health ‖ not evincing good health, *an unhealthy complexion* ‖ not conducive to good health, *an unhealthy diet* ‖ not sound morally ‖ (*pop.*) risky

un·heard (ʌnhə́:rd)*adj.* not heard ‖ not given a hearing

un·heard-of (ʌnhə́:rdɒv, ʌnhə́:rdʌv) *adj.* never met with until now, unprecedented

un·hinge (ʌnhíndʒ) *pres. part.* **un·hing·ing** *past* and *past part.* **un·hinged** *v.t.* to remove from its hinges ‖ to upset the balance of (the mind)

un·ho·ly (ʌnhóuli:) *comp.* **un·ho·li·er** *superl.* **un·ho·li·est** *adj.* not holy, impious ‖ used intensively) very bad, *an unholy mess*

un·hook (ʌnhúk) *v.t.* to unfasten the hook or hooks of ‖ to remove from a hook

un·hoped-for (ʌnhóuptfɔr) *adj.* not expected

un·horse (ʌnhɔ́rs) *pres. part.* **un·hors·ing** *past* and *past part.* **un·horsed** *v.t.* to throw from a horse ‖ to take a horse away from (a vehicle)

uni- (jú:ni:) *combining form* having or consisting of one only, as in 'uniparous' [L. *unus*, one]

U·ni·ate, U·ni·at (jú:ni:æt) *n.* a member of an Eastern Christian church which acknowledges the pope's supremacy but preserves its own rites, liturgy and canon law, and has its own patriarch [Russ. *uniyatu* fr. *uniya*, a union fr. L. *unus*, one]

u·ni·ax·i·al (ju:ni:ǽksi:əl) *adj.* (esp. of a crystal) having only one optic axis ‖ (*biol.*) monaxial

u·ni·cam·er·al (ju:nikǽmərəl) *adj.* (of a parliament etc.) having only one chamber [fr. UNI-+L. *camera*, chamber]

UNICEF the agency established (1946) by the United Nations General Assembly for dealing with malnutrition, diseases etc. of children all over the world [*U*nited *N*ations *I*nternational *C*hildren's *E*mergency *F*und]

u·ni·cel·lu·lar (ju:niséljulər) *adj.* (*biol.*) consisting of only one cell

u·ni·corn (jú:nikɔrn) *n.* a legendary animal generally depicted as having the head and body of a horse, the hind legs of a stag, the tail of a lion, and having a long tapering horn growing from the middle of its forehead. In the Middle Ages the unicorn was a symbol of strength and virginity. Its powdered horn would safeguard one from poison, and sweeten the foulest or most bitter waters ‖ a representation of this animal, e.g. in heraldry or as a supporter of the royal arms in Britain or Scotland [A.F., O.F. *unicorne* or fr. L. *unicornis* fr. *unus, one+cornu*, horn]

u·ni·cy·cle (jú:nisaik'l) *n.* a singlewheeled, pedal-propelled vehicle used esp. by clowns or other entertainers

unidentified flying object (*abbr.* UFO, U.F.O.) a flying saucer or other mysterious, apparently man-made thing seen flying through the air

u·ni·fi·a·ble (jú:nifaiəb'l) *adj.* that can be unified

u·ni·fi·ca·tion (ju:nifikéiʃən) *n.* a unifying or being unified

u·ni·fied tax (jú:nifaid) *n.* (*Br.*) progressive individual tax (replacing income tax and surtax), established in 1973

u·ni·fo·li·ate (ju:nifóuli:it) *adj.* (*bot.*) having only one leaf ‖ unifoliolate

u·ni·fo·li·o·late (ju:nifóuli:əleit) *adj.* (*bot.*) compound in structure but having only one leaflet

u·ni·form (jú:nifɔrm) 1. *adj.* being the same in form, character, degree etc. without variation, *a rod of uniform thickness* ‖ conforming to a rule, pattern or norm ‖ consistent throughout a state, country etc. **uniform with** having the same form, appearance etc. as 2. *n.* a military costume ‖ a costume worn by all of a certain category (prisoners, airline stewardesses etc.) **ú·ni·formed** *adj.* wearing a uniform [F. *uniforme* or fr. L. *uniformis*]

u·ni·form·i·ty (ju:nifɔ́rmiti:) *n.* the state or quality of being uniform [F. *uniformité* or fr. L. *uniformitas*]

Uniformity, Act of (*Eng. hist.*) any of four acts of parliament (1549, 1552, 1559, 1662) prescribing the use of the Book of Common Prayer in the services of the Church of England

u·ni·fy (jú:nifai) *pres. part.* **u·ni·fy·ing** *past* and *past part.* **u·ni·fied** *v.t.* to make one ‖ *v.i.* to become one [fr. M.L. *unificare*]

u·ni·lat·er·al (ju:nəlǽtərəl) *adj.* done or undertaken etc. by one side or party only, *unilateral disarmament* ‖ (*biol.*) arranged or produced on one side only ‖ (*med.*) affecting only one side of the body, *unilateral paralysis* ‖ (*law*) binding or affecting one party only ‖ (*sociology*) indicating or tracing descent through either the maternal or paternal line only (cf. BILATERAL) ‖ (*phon.*) pronounced with the breath passing along one side of the tongue only [fr. Mod. L. *unilateralis*]

un·im·peach·a·ble (ʌnimpí:tʃəb'l) *adj.* not open to question, beyond reproach

un·im·proved (ʌnimprú:vd) *adj.* (of land) not improved, e.g. not cultivated, built upon etc. ‖ not bred selectively ‖ (of a road) not paved

un·ion (jú:njən) *n.* a uniting or being united ‖ something united ‖ a combination (esp. of qualities), *the union of strength and beauty* ‖ unity, harmony ‖ a marriage ‖ a grouping of states, political groups etc. for some specific purpose ‖ an emblem symbolizing the unification of states, sovereignties etc., used esp. on the upper inner corner of a national flag ‖ this part of the flag ‖ (*Eng. hist.*) a 19th-c. governmental unit comprising two or more parishes united for administration of poor relief ‖ a device for joining parts together, esp. a kind of joint for coupling pipes ‖ a trade union **the Union** the United States of America ‖ (*Am. hist.*) the 23 Northern states which opposed the Confederate states in the Civil War (1861-5). They were: Maine, New Hampshire, Vermont, Massachusetts, Rhode Island, Connecticut, New York, New Jersey, Delaware, Maryland, Pennsylvania, Ohio, Michigan, Indiana, Kentucky, Illinois, Wisconsin, Minnesota, Iowa, Missouri, Kansas, Oregon and California [F.]

Union, Act of the Act (1707) unifying Scotland and England in the United Kingdom of Great Britain under a single government, each retaining its own legal system and national Church. Scotland thus recognized the Hanoverian succession, and acquired a share of English trade

Union Islands the Tokelau Islands

un·ion·ism (jú:njənizəm) *n.* the tradeunion movement **Un·ion·ism** (*Am. hist.*) loyalty to the Union during the Civil War

un·ion·ist (jú:njənist) *n.* a member of a trade union ‖ a supporter of trade unionism **Un·ion·ist** (*Am. hist.*) a supporter of the Union during the Civil War

un·ion·i·za·tion (ju:njənizéiʃən) *n.* a unionizing or being unionized

un·ion·ize (jú:njənaiz) *pres. part.* **un·ion·iz·ing** *past* and *past part.* **un·ion·ized** *v.t.* to organize into a trade union or unions ‖ to cause to conform with the rules etc. of a trade union

Union Jack the national flag of the United Kingdom, combining the crosses of St George, St Andrew and St Patrick ‖ any flag consisting only of a national union

Union League of America, the a U.S. organization of clubs formed in the North (1862) by Ohio Republicans to inspire 'uncompromising and unconditional loyalty to the Union' and to revitalize the enervated Republican party. At its peak of influence after the Civil War, it worked in the cause of Negro enfranchisement, seeking the resultant vote for the Republican party. Membership came to consist mainly of blacks, directed by white politicians who introduced elaborate secret ceremonies with a politico-mystical tenor. As a result of discord between blacks and whites, it rapidly declined after 1869, while giving rise to reactionary movements, notably the Ku Klux Klan

Union of South Africa *SOUTH AFRICA

Union of Soviet Socialist Republics (U.S.S.R.) a federal republic (area 8,650,000 sq. miles, pop. 277,930,000) in E. Europe and Northern and Central Asia. Capital: Moscow. It consists of 15 constituent republics, each inhabited by a major national group: the Russian Soviet Federal Socialist Republic (R.S.F.S.R.), Ukraine, Kazakhstan, Uzbekistan, Byelorussia, Georgia, Azerbaijan, Moldavia, Lithuania, Kirghizia, Tadzhikstan, Latvia, Armenia, Turkmenistan and Estonia. (For physical geography see separate entries.) These constituent republics include a number of national autonomous republics and autonomous regions. People: 77% Slavic (incl. 55% Russian, 18% Ukrainian, 4% Byelorussian), with Baltic, Armenian, Jewish and various Caucasian, Turkic, Iranian and Mongol minorities. Religion (the majority profess none): 24% Russian Orthodox, 11% Moslem (esp. Central Asia and Caucasia), 2% Protestant (esp. Latvia and Estonia), 2% Roman Catholic (esp. Lithuania and W. Ukraine), 1% Armenian, 1% Jewish, small Buddhist minority (esp. Buriat and Kalmyk A.S.S.R.s). The land is 32% forest, 20% pasture, 18% arable or cultivated. Average temperatures (F.): Kaliningrad 25° (Jan.) and 64° (July), Lvov 25°-66°, Riga 25°-64°, Leningrad 18°-64°, Archangel 9°-59°, Moscow 12°-64°, Kiev 21°-67°, Batumi 43°-73°, Tbilisi 20°-75°, Samarkand 32°-77°, Sverdlovsk 3°-63°, Irkutsk −6°-63°, Dikson (Yenisei estuary) −13°-41°, Vladivostok 5°-65°, Delen (Bering Strait) −10°-41°, Verkhoyansk (E. Siberia) −58°-60°. Rainfall: Kaliningrad 28 ins, Riga 24 ins, Leningrad 21 ins, Archangel 19 ins, Moscow 25 ins, Batumi 95 ins, Baku 10 ins, Samarkand 13 ins, Sverdlovsk 18 ins, Irkutsk 15 ins, Vladivostok 15 ins, Verkhoyansk 4 ins. Livestock: cattle, sheep, hogs, goats, horses. Agricultural products: cereals (esp. Ukraine, Central European R.S.F.S.R., W. Siberia, N. Kazakhstan, Urals, Volga region, N. Caucasus), cotton, sugar beets, potatoes, vegetables, meat, wool, dairy produce, fruit, tea, flax, hemp, sunflower seed, beans, furs, lumber, fish. Mineral resources: coal, petroleum, iron ore, copper, titanium, manganese, chromites, lead, zinc, bauxite, gold, uranium, asbestos, mica, phosphates, wolframite and molybdenite, potash and deposits of most other minerals. Manufactures and industries: mining, iron and steel, oil refining, aluminum, chemicals and fertilizers, textiles, machinery, vehicles, locomotives, tractors, hydroelectricity, lumber, paper, woodwork and furniture, atomic energy, footwear, clocks and watches, armaments, aircraft, foodstuffs, radio and television sets, refrigerators, sewing machines, bicycles, rubber, sugar, soap, cement, bricks. The world's longest pipeline links the Ural-Volga oil fields with Poland, East Germany, Czechoslovakia and Hungary. Exports: fuels and raw materials including grain (47%), machinery and equipment (10%), consumer goods (9%). Imports: fuels and raw materials (29%), machinery and equipment (35%), consumer goods (24%). Main ports: Leningrad, Archangel, Murmansk, Odessa, Baku, Vladivostok, Riga, Tallinn. There is an extensive network of canals. There are about 750 institutes for higher education, the oldest universities being Vilnius (1578), Tartu (1632) and Moscow (1755). Monetary unit: ruble (100 kopeks). HISTORY. (For previous history *RUSSIA.) The Bolsheviks having seized power (Nov. 7, 1917) under Lenin, the country was faced with a civil war (1918-21), in which anti-Communist forces unsuccessfully opposed the new regime, and a war with Poland (1920), in which Pilsudski unsuccessfully invaded the Ukraine. Lenin regained control (1921), but in the face of a severe economic crisis was forced to modify his Marxian socialist policy as a temporary concession to capitalism (1921-8). The U.S.S.R. was officially established (1922), and the 1924 constitution, based upon public ownership of the land and of the means of production, put legislative power in the hands of the soviets, under the leadership of the Supreme Soviet. After Lenin's death (1924), a struggle for leadership developed, notably between Trotsky and Stalin, resulting in the victory of Stalin. Lenin's economic policy was abandoned in favor of the first five-year plan (1928), under which heavy industry was greatly expanded and a collectivization of agriculture was carried out. Opposition from kulaks and private tradesmen was ruthlessly stamped out. State control over culture and education was increased, and a series of political purges was carried out (1930s) by the secret police. The U.S.S.R. signed (1939) a mutual nonaggression pact with Germany, and shared in the annexation of Poland (1939). Estonia, Latvia and Lithuania were annexed (1939), and Bessarabia and N. Bukovina were occupied (1940). The U.S.S.R. invaded Finland (1939) and annexed the Karelian Isthmus (1940). Germany invaded the U.S.S.R. (1941) and besieged Leningrad, but was repulsed from Moscow. The German attack on Stalingrad (1942-3) was one of the decisive battles of the 2nd world war. The Russian counteroffensive (1943-5) drove the Germans back through E. Europe, reaching Berlin (1945). The U.S.S.R. declared war on Japan (1945) and rapidly conquered much of Manchuria and Korea. It took part in the conferences at Tehran (1943), Yalta (1945) and Potsdam (1945), joined the U.N. (1945) and emerged as a major world power. The Russian policy of Communist expansion, abandoned officially (1943) with the dissolution of the Comintern, was resumed (1947) with the establishment of the Cominform. Nonaggression and mutual assistance pacts were made with the neighboring countries of E. Europe, which now became people's republics. Relations between the U.S.S.R. and the West deteriorated in the cold war, and worsened further with the outbreak of the Korean War (1950-3). After Stalin's death (1953), the regime showed more liberal tendencies. The post of prime minister was held by Malenkov (1953-5), Bulganin (1955-8), Khrushchev (1958-64) and Kosygin (1964-80). Soviet economic planning placed more emphasis on consumer goods, in a seven-year plan (1959-65) which was incorporated (1960) in a 20-year plan. Khrushchev's government found increasing difficulty in increasing agricultural output at the desired rate. The U.S.S.R. launched the first artificial satellite into space (1957), sent the first rocket to the moon (1959), sent the first man into space (1961), landed the first probe on the moon (1966) and landed the first probe on Venus (1967). Tension with the West was maintained over the question of German reunification, the building of the Berlin wall (1961), the Cuba crisis (1962) and the war in Vietnam (1964-75). Ideological disagreements with China appeared (1959), and the rift widened progressively, involving other Communist countries. Relations with European socialist countries were marked by difficulties with Rumania and, esp., by the intervention (1968) of Warsaw Pact troops in Czechoslovakia to end the liberalization of the regime. Khrushchev was ousted from power in 1964 by a group led by Leonid Brezhnev, who pursued a policy of détente with the West. In 1982 leadership passed to Yuri Andropov, who died two years later, and then to Konstantin Chernenko, who died in 1985. Mikhail Gorbachev assumed power in 1985

Union Pacific Railroad the first transcontinental railroad in the U.S.A., chartered (1862) by Congress. The Union Pacific joined (1869) the Central Pacific near Ogden, Utah, and a golden spike marks the juncture. The railroad was involved in the Crédit Mobilier of America scandal. Greatly expanded under the direction of Edward H. Harriman, it lost (1904-13) its monopolistic control through the action of the U.S. Supreme Court

union shop an establishment where workers are employed even if they do not belong to a trade union, provided they become members within a specified time (*CLOSED SHOP)

union suit long underwear with the shirt and drawers cut as a single garment

u·nip·ar·ous (ju:nípərəs) *adj.* producing one egg or offspring at a birth ‖ (*bot.*) having a cymose inflorescence with only one axis at each branching [fr. Mod. L. *uniparus* fr. *unus,* one+*parere,* to bear]

u·ni·po·lar (ju:nəpóulər) *adj.* (*biol.,* of a nerve cell) having one process only ‖ (*elec.*) having or acting by one magnetic or electrical pole

u·ni·pol·i·tics (jú:nipɒlətiks) *n.* concept of a global authority to protect humankind, offered at the World Habitat Conference, Canada, 1972

u·nique (ju:ní:k) *adj.* being the only one of its kind ‖ not like anything else of its kind, incomparable ‖ (*loosely*) rare, unusual [F.]

unique species (*envir.*) species of special scientific, local, or national interest

u·ni·sex (jú:niseks) *adj.* **1.** suitable for both men and women, e.g., clothes, hairstyles **2.** indistinguishable as to sex —**unisex** *n.* the trend *Cf* INTERSEX, UNISEXUAL

u·ni·sex·u·al (ju:nisékʃu:əl) *adj.* of one sex only, esp. (*zool.*) male only or female only, not hermaphroditic ‖ (*bot.*) diclinous

u·ni·son (jú:niz'n, jú:nis'n) *n.* coincidence in pitch of two or more notes, voices etc. **in unison** with identity of note and pitch ‖ in complete agreement [O.F. or fr. L.L. *unisonus*]

u·nit (jú:nit) *n.* a fixed quantity adopted as a standard of measurement for other quantities of the same kind, *the centimeter is a unit of length* ‖ a single thing, person or group that is a distinguishable element of a larger whole, *the family is the basic unit of society* ‖ (*math.*) the element which divides every other of a set of elements ‖ (*pl.*) in mathematical calculations, the column of figures immediately to the left of the decimal point ‖ any subdivision (regiment, battalion etc.) of an army whose strength is laid down by regulations ‖ an element of furniture manufactured in such a way that it can be fitted with others like it, or with complementary elements, to form an ensemble (bookcase, kitchen cabinet etc.) [fr. L. *unus,* one]

U·ni·tar·i·an (ju:nitέəri:ən) **1.** *n.* a member of a Protestant denomination believing in the unity of God as opposed to the doctrine of the Trinity. The Unitarian denomination developed in Poland and Transylvania (late 16th c.) and in England and North America (17th-18th cc.) and has come to be undogmatic, advocating tolerance and stressing reason as a guide to belief **2.** *adj.* of or relating to the Unitarians **U·ni·tár·i·an·ism** *n.*

Unitarian Universalist Association *UNIVERSALIST CHURCH

u·ni·ta·rio (u:ni:tári:ɔ) *n.* (*Argentinian hist.*) a supporter of strong central government in a close federation of the provinces. The conflict between unitarios and federalistas was the cause of civil war in Argentina in the 19th c. [Span.]

u·ni·tar·y (jú:niteri:) *adj.* of or relating to a unit or units ‖ having the character of a unit ‖ based on or characterized by unity

unit car a freight train that operates with little or no uncoupling, usu. in a shuttle run

unit character (*biol.*) a trait dependent on a single gene, inherited according to Mendel's laws

u·nite (ju:náit) *pres. part.* **u·nit·ing** *past* and *past part.* **u·nit·ed** *v.t.* to bring together so as to make one ‖ to have or show (qualities etc.) in common ‖ to bring together in common cause ‖ to cause to become attached ‖ to bring together by a legal or moral bond ‖ *v.i.* to become one or as if one ‖ to cooperate ‖ to become combined **u·nít·ed** *adj.* made one, brought together ‖ resulting from being brought together or made one, *a united effort* ‖ getting on together well, harmonious, *a united staff*

United Arab Emirates (formerly Trucial States) seven Arab sheikhdoms (total area approx. 32,000 sq. miles, pop. 1,121,800) on the Persian Gulf coast of Arabia between Qatar and the Musandam peninsula (formerly known as the Pirate Coast): Abu Dhabi, Dubai, Sharjah and Kalba, Ajman, Umm al Qaiwain, Ras al Khaimah, Fujairah. Capital, chief town and port: Abu Dhabi (pop. 243,000), in Abu Dhabi. The land is flat desert, except for mountains on the east (Gulf of Oman) coast, rising to 4,000 ft. Main export: petroleum (esp. from Abu Dhabi). Other products: fish, vegetables, dates, pearls. Monetary unit: the Bahrain dinar in Abu Dhabi, elsewhere the Saudi rial (100 paise). HISTORY. The sheikhdoms, Moslem since the 7th c., entered into a series of treaties with Britain (1820, 1853 and 1892), suppressing piracy and slavery and establishing British protection. Independence was declared in Dec. 1971. A flood of foreign workers came into the country because of the oil boom; almost half the population is South Asian. The native Arabs are nearly all Moslems. Authority remains with the seven hereditary sheiks, who choose a president from among themselves. Since 1971 Zaid bin Sultan al-Nahayan of Abu Dhabi has been president

United Arab Republic a union (1958-61) of Egypt and Syria. Yemen entered (Feb. 1958) into a Federal Union with the United Arab Republic. Syria seceded (1961) and the union was dissolved, but Egypt maintained the name as its official title until 1971. Attempts were made to revive the union with the addition of Iraq (1963), and to form a common market with Iraq, Kuawit and Jordan (1964)

United Church of Canada a Protestant denomination formed (1925) by the union of the Methodist, Congregationalist, and Presbyterian Churches in Canada

United Church of Christ a U.S. Protestant denomination formed (1957) by the union of the Congregational Christian Churches and the Evangelical and Reformed Church

United Fruit Company a U.S. corporation formed (1899) in New Jersey that soon monopolized the cultivation, transportation, and marketing of bananas in the West Indies and Central America. It came to dominate the communications and transportation facilities in Central America and became deeply involved in Caribbean politics

United Kingdom of Great Britain and Northern Ireland *GREAT BRITAIN

United Nations (*abbr.* U.N., UN) an international organization to maintain world peace and security and to promote economic, social and cultural cooperation among nations, set up (1945) as a successor to the League of Nations. Its charter was signed by 50 nations and there are now more than 150 members meeting annually in the General Assembly. Problems of world peace are dealt with by the Security Council, and the U.N.'s main judicial organ is the International Court of Justice. The U.N.'s specialized agencies include the Food and Agriculture Organization, the General Agreement on Tariffs and Trade, the International Atomic Energy Agency, the International Civil Aviation Organization, the International Finance Corporation, the International Labor Organization, the International Monetary Fund, the International Telecommunication Union, the United Nations Educational, Scientific and Cultural Organization, the Universal Postal Union, the World Bank, the World Health Organization and the World Meteorological Organization. Headquarters: New York

United Nations Children's Fund *UNICEF

United Nations Educational, Scientific and Cultural Organization (*abbr.* UNESCO) an agency of the U.N. set up in 1946 to contribute to peace and security by promoting international collaboration in education, science and culture

United Provinces the name given to the independent republic of the Netherlands (1648-1795)

United States Air Force Academy a military institution in Colorado Springs, Colo., authorized (1958) by Congress to train cadets to be U.S. Air Force officers

United States Coast Guard Academy an institution established (1876) in New London, Conn., to train officers for the U.S. Coast Guard

United States Information Agency (*abbr.* USIA) an agency of the U.S. government, established (1953) to promote, through communications media, a better understanding abroad of the U.S.A. and its foreign policies. Its best-known activity is the Voice of America radio program, which transmits information overseas in more than 36 languages

United States Marine Corps an armed service (originally within the U.S. Naval Department) established (1798) by Act of Congress. It is trained for integrated land-sea-air action. In 1834 the president was authorized to order marines to duty with the army. Since its creation it has made over 300 landings on foreign shores

United States Merchant Marine Academy an institution established (1936) at Kings Point, N.Y., to train officers for the U.S. Merchant Marine

United States Military Academy an institution established (1802) at West Point, N.Y., to train cadets to be U.S. Army officers

United States Naval Academy an institution for training U.S. Navy officers founded (1845) at Annapolis, Md.

United States of America (*abbr.* U.S.A., USA) a federal republic (area 13,618,770 sq. miles, pop. 231,534,000) in North America, incl. Hawaii and Alaska. Capital: Washington. Largest city: New York. Overseas territories: Puerto Rico, Virgin Is, American Samoa, Guam, Wake and Midway. The U.S.A. also controls the Trust Territory of the Pacific Islands (the Caroline Is, Marshall Is and Marianas Is). People: white, Afro-American and mulatto, small American Indian, Japanese, Chinese, Southeast Asian and Filipino minorities. Language: English, minority and immigrant languages. Religion: 51% Protestant (30 principal denominations), 22% Roman Catholic, 3% Jewish, 2% Orthodox. The land (excluding

Hawaii and Alaska) is 25% forest, 36% pasture and 24% arable. Main industrial zone: the Great Lakes-North Atlantic coast region. The Atlantic coast is greatly indented. The cultivated (increasingly industrialized) coastal plain, narrow between Maine and Cape Cod, widens toward the Gulf of Mexico to merge with the lower Mississippi basin and E. Texas plains. Behind it the wooded Appalachian system stretches from New England to central Alabama, incl. wide fertile valleys between New York State and Tennessee, and poor, eroded hills in Kentucky and West Virginia. The Mississippi-Missouri basin (cereals, cotton, petroleum) stretches from the Gulf of Mexico to the Great Lakes, broken only by the Ozarks and by the lower Canadian Shield around Lake Superior. West of it to the Rockies (Mt Elbert, 14,431 ft) lie the Great Plains (cereals, grazing land), rising to 5,000 ft in the west. Between the Rockies (*ROCKY MTNS) and the Cascade (Mt Rainier, 14,410 ft) and Sierra Nevada (Mt Whitney, 14,495 ft) ranges lies an arid plateau region (mining, cattle raising, cereals) divided into the Columbia and Colorado plateaus and the Great Basin, with a large desert in S. Nevada, S.E. California and W. Arizona. Fertile valleys in Washington, most of Oregon, and central California and desert valleys elsewhere separate the Cascades and Sierra Nevada from the wooded coast ranges (1,000-5,000 ft). The Pacific coast has few harbors. Average temperatures (F.) in Jan. and July: New York City 32°-75°, Chicago 26°-74°, Nashville 39°-79°, New Orleans 54°-80°, Denver 30°-71°, S.W. Arizona 55°-91°, Los Angeles 52°-71°, Seattle 39°-63°. Rainfall: New York City 42 ins, Chicago 33 ins, Nashville 47 ins, New Orleans 60 ins, Denver 14 ins, Arizona desert 3 ins, Los Angeles 15 ins, Seattle 32 ins. Livestock: cattle, hogs, sheep, horses, mules, poultry. Agricultural products: corn, cotton, hay, wheat, soybeans, tobacco, rice, oats and other cereals, potatoes, sugar beets, beans, cottonseed, sugarcane, sweet potatoes, apples, peaches, pears, citrus fruit, linseed, peanuts, meat, dairy products and market produce. Forestry products: Douglas fir, yellow pine, hardwood, resin, turpentine. It is the world's fourth producer of fish. Mineral resources: copper (leading world producer), iron ore (2nd world producer), coal and anthracite (2nd world producer), petroleum (leading world producer), uranium, silver, lead, zinc, bauxite, gold, natural gas, gypsum, chromite, molybdenum, phosphates, sulfur, salt. Manufactures and industries: iron and steel, mining, heavy engineering, hydroelectricity, food processing, textiles, vehicles, flour milling, meat packing, chemicals, locomotives and rolling stock, aircraft, electrical machinery, metallurgy, leather, tires, atomic energy, precision and optical instruments, tobacco, clothing, furniture, paper and pulp, printing, light manufactures, ships, aluminum, plastics, armaments, electronics. Exports: machinery, chemicals, wheat, vehicles, metals, textiles, foodstuffs, aircraft, tobacco, oil, coal, wood, pulp and paper, rubber, oilseeds and oils, raw cotton, radio and television sets, fruit, meat, military equipment, vegetables, iron and steel. Imports: oil, machinery and vehicles, metals, coffee, textiles, wood and paper, cane sugar, iron and steel, iron ore, meat, fish, rubber, chemicals, fruit, whiskey and other liquor, raw wool, diamonds, animals, cocoa. There are over 300 universities, the oldest being Harvard (1636). Chief ports: New York City, Philadelphia, Baltimore, New Orleans, San Francisco. Main fishing ports: Boston, Portland (Maine), Monterey, Los Angeles. Monetary unit: U.S. dollar (100 cents). HISTORY. The North American continent is thought to have been discovered (c. 1000 A.D.) by Vikings under Leif Ericson, but the existence of the New World was not known for certain in Europe until the voyage (1492) of Columbus. There were probably about 1,500,000 American Indians at this time in what is now the U.S.A. Spain began to colonize Florida (1565) and extended its control over much of Texas and the West. France explored from the Great Lakes, down the Mississippi, to Louisiana. After Sir Walter Raleigh had failed in his attempt to found a colony in Virginia (1584-9), the first permanent English settlement in North America was established there (1607) by a chartered company. Effective colonization in New England began when the Pilgrim Fathers settled at Plymouth (1620). Maine and New Hampshire were settled (1622) by a chartered company. The Puritans of Massachusetts founded Connecticut (1635) and Rhode Island (1636). The Dutch founded a colony along the Hudson and the Delaware (1620s), which was conquered by the English (1664), together with a former Swedish colony which had been founded on the Delaware (1638) and taken by the Dutch (1655). Maryland was founded by English Roman Catholics (1634). The Carolinas were settled (1670) by a company chartered by Charles II. New Jersey was detached (1664) from the former Dutch colony now renamed New York, and was colonized by Quakers (1670s). Quakers also founded Pennsylvania (1682), granted by Charles II to Penn, who also received Delaware (1682). Georgia was founded (1733) as an English military post against French and Spanish rivalry and as a refuge for imprisoned debtors. Most of these Thirteen Colonies eventually passed to royal control. The colonies attracted increasing numbers of settlers from Europe, many of them fleeing from religious or political persecution, until by 1775 the population was over two and a half million. The economy was based on agriculture, notably in the Southern states, where tobacco and cotton plantations were worked by imported African slaves. The Indians were driven back westward. Colonial and maritime rivalry with France led to King William's War (1689-97), Queen Anne's War (1701-13). King George's War (1745-8) and the French and Indian War (1754-63). The colonies increased their powers of self-government during these wars, and the British triumph in the Treaty of Paris (1763), by removing the French and Indian threat, lessened the colonies' dependence on Britain. British attempts to prevent westward migration (1763), to tax the colonies in accordance with mercantilist theory and to enforce the Navigation Acts caused widespread resentment. The Stamp Act was withdrawn (1766) but an attempt to allow the British East India Company a tax exemption to dispose of a tea surplus on the American market provoked the Boston Tea Party (1773). Britain retaliated with the Intolerable Acts (1774). The Revolutionary War broke out (1775-83), and the Thirteen Colonies adopted the Declaration of Independence (July 4, 1776). The colonies united as the U.S.A. under the Articles of Confederation (1781), superseded by the U.S. Constitution (1789), which gave the federal government greatly increased powers. Washington, the leader of the American colonies during the war, became the first president of the U.S.A. (1789-97) under the Constitution. Out of the disagreement between Hamilton and Jefferson as to states' rights arose a two-party system. In foreign policy, the Federalists tended to be pro-English and the Antifederalists pro-French. During Jefferson's administration (1801-9), the Louisiana Purchase (1803) greatly increased U.S. territory. As the frontier was pushed back westwards, the U.S.A. came into conflict with the British in the north, and the Spanish in the south. The invention (1793) of the cotton gin rapidly made cotton the dominant crop in the South, and encouraged the spread of plantations and slave labor. Maritime rivalry with Britain led to the War of 1812, after which the U.S.A. recognized Canada as a British possession, and obtained full access to the northwest. During Monroe's administration (1817-25), Florida was bought from Spain (1819), and the Monroe Doctrine was proclaimed (1823). As more settlers moved west and southwest, and new states were set up, a sharp division arose between states in which slavery was legal and those in which it was not. The issue was postponed by the Missouri Compromise (1820-1). The frontier made its mark on U.S. democracy during the presidency (1829-37) of Jackson, under whom the Democratic party took shape, the spoils system was developed and the nullification issue was raised. As a result of Jackson's financial measures, Van Buren had to face an economic crisis during his administration (1837-41). As the Industrial Revolution made its influence felt, communications and industry were developed. By the 1840s, the population had risen to 17,000,000. Settlement in Texas led the U.S.A. to annex it (1845), provoking the Mexican War (1846-8). The U.S.A. gained new territory by the settlement (1846) of the Oregon Question, the Treaty of Guadalupe Hidalgo (1848) and the Gadsden Purchase (1854). The California gold rush (1849) raised the question of whether California should be a slave or free-soil state. The attempt to settle this by the Compromise of 1850 created more bitterness, which was increased by the Kansas-Nebraska Act (1854) and the Dred Scott Decision (1857). After Lincoln's election as president (1860) the Civil War broke out (1861-5). The Emancipation Proclamation abolished slavery (1863) and the war ended in victory for the North. In the Reconstruction period which followed, war damage in the South was slowly repaired and industrialization begun. Mineral wealth was exploited, industrial progress continued rapidly in the North and, at a time when speculation and business combinations were unchecked by legislation, vast fortunes were made by Rockefeller, Carnegie and Morgan among others. Labor began to organize. The West was fully opened up for mining, cattle ranching and grain production. The Indians were virtually confined to reservations. Settlement rapidly followed the building of railroads across the continent. Alaska was bought from Russia (1867), Hawaii was annexed (1898) and, after the Spanish-American War (1898), American influence was extended to Puerto Rico, Cuba and the Philippines. With the opening (1914) of the Panama Canal, the U.S.A. had become a major world power, with a population of 92,000,000. After McKinley's assassination, Theodore Roosevelt held the presidency (1901-9), attacking trusts and encouraging the conservation of national resources. Under his successor, Taft, the Republican party was weakened by the secession of the Progressive party, and Woodrow Wilson, a Democrat, became president (1913-21). This administration established the Federal Reserve System (1913) and carried out social reform. Wilson attempted to keep the U.S.A. neutral in the 1st world war, but the German use of unrestricted submarine warfare brought the U.S.A. into the war on the side of the Allies (1917). Wilson took a leading part in peace negotiations (1918) and in setting up the League of Nations, but the Senate refused to ratify the treaty. Apart from promoting the Kellogg-Briand Pact (1928), the U.S.A. adopted an isolationist foreign policy. Prohibition was in force (1919-33). National prosperity rapidly increased in a speculative boom during the administrations of Harding (1921-3) and Coolidge (1923-9). Hoover's administration (1929-33) faced the ensuing economic depression without great success. F. D. Roosevelt's New Deal was more successful. U.S. isolationism came to an end with Roosevelt's good-neighbor policy toward Latin America. When the 2nd world war broke out, the U.S.A. remained neutral, but supplied lend-lease help to Britain (1941). After the Japanese attack on Pearl Harbor (1941), the U.S.A. declared war on the Axis (1941). Industry was organized for war production and a huge war effort was made. The U.S.A. developed the atomic bomb, and used it on Japan, bringing the war to a close (1945). The U.S.A. took a leading part in the organization of the U.N. (1945), supplied aid to Europe under the Marshall Plan (1948-52) and, as the cold war developed, proposed the formation of NATO (1949). Truman's administration (1945-53) brought in a program of social reform. The U.S.A. gave massive support to South Korea in the Korean War (1950-3). McCarthy went to extreme lengths to root out communist sympathizers in government office. The presidency passed to the Republicans under Eisenhower (1953-61). His administration saw the end of the Korean War and the formation (1954) of SEATO. Under the guidance of Dulles, the U.S.A. built up a defense system capable of meeting any aggression by immediate retaliation. Technological rivalry with the U.S.S.R. gave rise to competition in the exploration of space, and the U.S.A. launched its first artificial satellite (1958). Alaska and Hawaii became states of the U.S.A. (1959). The question of civil rights for blacks flared up and became the major domestic issue during Kennedy's presidency (1961-3). His prestige suffered from U.S. collusion in the abortive attempt by Cuban exiles to oust Castro by a landing at the Bay of Pigs (Apr. 1961). The presence of Soviet missiles on Cuba brought (Oct. 1962) the U.S.A. and the U.S.S.R. to the brink of war before Khrushchev backed down. Following Kennedy's assassination (Nov. 1963), the presidency passed to Vice-President

Lyndon B. Johnson, who gradually increased U.S. military support for South Vietnam, without achieving the military victory he sought. He intervened (Apr. 1965) in the Dominican Republic, reviving Latin American distrust of U.S. motives. Despite his unprecedented success in legislation, esp. in the field of civil rights and in his 'unconditional war on poverty', he decided (Apr. 1968) not to seek reelection. The eight-year Democratic run was ended by the election of Republican Richard Nixon, whose platform was based on an end to the war, the return to law and order, and the control of inflation. The first manned circumnavigation of the moon (Dec. 1968) and the first landing of a man (Neil Armstrong) on the moon (July 1969) enhanced U.S. prestige, somewhat offset by unprecedented disaffection in the U.S. academic community and esp. among youth over the continuing war and domestic racism. U.S. and South Vietnamese forces were sent (Apr. 1970) into Cambodia in search of North Vietnam's sanctuaries, and the operation aroused massive protest at home. U.S. land forces were withdrawn (by July 1, 1970) from Cambodia. President Nixon paid official visits (1972) to China and to the U.S.S.R. The Watergate crisis (1973-4) resulted in the resignations of several high government officials and culminated in the threat of impeachment and subsequent resignation of Pres. Nixon in Aug. 1974. Gerald Ford, who had replaced Spiro Agnew as vice president, served as president until 1977, when Democrat Jimmy Carter assumed office. Pres. Carter was instrumental in negotiating an Egyptian-Israeli peace treaty and the Panama Canal treaty; he also dealt with oil shortages, high inflation rates, and international crises caused by the Soviet invasion of Afghanistan and the taking of U.S. embassy personnel as hostages by Iranian students. The 1980 elections provided a landslide victory for Republican challenger Ronald Reagan, who survived an assassination attempt in 1981 and a serious recession early in his administration. A very large federal budget deficit continued to be a problem but unemployment and inflation rates dropped and Reagan was reelected in 1984 over opponent Walter Mondale. Civil strife in Central America, the growing budget deficit, tax reform, and long-term defense planning, esp. of the 'star wars' program, were among the chief issues of Reagan's second term

United States Steel Corporation steel producer. Incorporated (1901) by J.P. Morgan and Company, it became the first billion-dollar corporation in the U.S.A. It represented an early example of the domination of industry by investment bankers

United States Trust Territory of the Pacific former Japanese-mandated islands (area 700 sq. miles, pop. 91,000) of the Caroline, Marshall, and Mariana groups, administered by the U.S.A. as a Trusteeship for the United Nations. The area contains 2,141 atolls and islands (only 96 are inhabited). Administrative center: Saipan (pop. 6,700), Mariana Is

United States v. Roth (rɔθ, rɒθ) a landmark decision (1957) of the U.S. Supreme Court which confirmed that 'obscenity is not within the area of constitutionally protected speech or press'

'United States v. Seeger' (síːgər) a landmark decision (1965) of the U.S. Supreme Court, which held that it was not necessary to believe in a 'Supreme Being' in order to register as a conscientious objector

'United States v. Welsh' a landmark decision (1970) of the U.S. Supreme Court which extended the rights guaranteed by the 'U.S. v. Seeger' decision (1965). It held that exemption from military service could be solely on moral and ethical grounds, provided only that the dissentients' conscience 'would give them no rest or peace if they allowed themselves to become a part of an instrument of war'

unit factor (*biol.*) a gene on which a unit character depends

u·nit·hold·er (júːnithouldəːr) *n.* (*Br.*) (*securities*) a stockholder

u·ni·tive (júːnitiv) *adj.* having unity ‖ tending to unite

unit magnetic pole a unit of magnetic pole strength equal to the strength of a magnetic pole that would exert a force of 1 dyne on an identical pole 1 centimeter away

unit train a train that provides pickup from sender and delivery to consumer

unit trust (*securities*) a share in an inflexible portfolio of securities, (especially bonds not to be sold) deposited with a trustee until underlying securities mature or the trust is dissolved; designed to lower trust-management fees

u·ni·ty (júːnitiː) *pl.* **u·ni·ties** *n.* the state of being one, singleness ‖ the state of being made one, unification ‖ a whole made up of separate elements ‖ full agreement, harmony ‖ (*math.*) the numeral or unit 1 ‖ (*math.*) any quantity considered as a unit or 1 ‖ continuity of purpose, action etc. ‖ an arrangement of parts capable of producing a concentrated total effect in an artistic work, or the effect so produced ‖ any of the three principles laid down by Aristotle (and observed esp. in French classical drama) affirming that the action must occur within 24 hours, in one place and with no comic relief or subplot, so as to produce the desired heightening and concentration [F. *unité*]

u·ni·va·lent (jʊːnivéilənt) *adj.* (*biol.*) of a single, unpaired chromosome separating in the first meiotic division ‖ (*chem.*) having one valence (cf. MONOVALENT) [fr. UNI- + L. *valens* (*valentis*) fr. *valere*, to be strong]

u·ni·valve (júːnivælv) **1.** *adj.* (of a shell) having only one valve ‖ (of a mollusk) having such a shell **2.** *n.* a mollusk having a univalve shell ‖ this shell

u·ni·ver·sal (jʊːnivə́ːrs'l) **1.** *adj.* general, for everything or everybody, *a universal remedy* ‖ involving all of a kind, e.g. everybody concerned or present, *by universal request* ‖ of widest scope, *a universal genius* ‖ present everywhere ‖ (of a machine tool) able to perform all the operations on a piece without being taken down and set up again ‖ (*logic*) of every member of a class (opp. PARTICULAR) **2.** *n.* (*philos.*) a general proposition, concept or idea [O.F. *universel* or fr. L. *universalis*]

universal coupling a universal joint

U·ni·ver·sal·ism (jʊːnivə́ːrsl'izəm) *n.* the theological doctrine that ultimately all men will be saved by God's grace **U·ni·vér·sal·ist** *n.*

Universalist Church a liberal Protestant denomination of the U.S.A. and Canada, founded (late 18th c.) in the U.S.A. Under the leadership of Hosea Ballou, it established colleges, seminaries, and newspapers. Its basic tenet posits that the love and goodness of God assure triumph over all evil. In 1960 its members numbered over 70,000, in about 400 churches. In 1961 it merged with the American Unitarian Association to form the Unitarian Universalist Association

u·ni·ver·sal·i·ty (jʊːnivərsǽliti:) *n.* the state or quality of being universal [F *universalité* or fr. L.L. *universalitas*]

u·ni·ver·sal·ize (jʊːnivə́ːrsəlaiz) *pres. part.* **u·ni·ver·sal·iz·ing** *past* and *past part.* **u·ni·ver·sal·ized** *v.t.* to make universal

universal joint a joint or coupling allowing freedom of movement in all directions

u·ni·ver·sal·ly (jʊːnivə́ːrsəliː) *adv.* in a universal manner, in every instance or in every part or place

Universal Postal Union (*abbr.* U.P.U.) an international organization regulating postage agreements between countries. Founded in 1874, it became (1947) a specialized agency of the U.N.

universal product code a 10-digit code based on ratio of printed bars to adjacent space, affixed to a package and readable electronically or by laser beam. It is used by retail stores for inventory control and checkout *abbr.* UPC

universal suffrage suffrage for all adult citizens except the insane, aliens and criminals

u·ni·verse (júːnivəːrs) *n.* the cosmos ‖ the earth and its inhabitants ‖ one's environment or field of interest regarded as a distinct world [F. *univers*]

U·ni·ver·si·dad de Bue·nos Ai·res (ʊːniːvɛrsiː-ðáðőebwénɔsáires) the leading university of Argentina, founded in 1821

U·ni·ver·si·dad de Chi·le (ʊːniːvɛrsiːðáðőetʃíː-le) the leading university of Chile, founded (1737) in Santiago and reorganized by Andrés Bello

U·ni·ver·si·dad de Cór·do·ba (ʊːniːvɛrsiːðáð-ðekɔ́rðɔbɑ) the oldest university (1621) in Argentina

U·ni·ver·si·dad Na·cio·nal Au·tón·o·ma de Mé·xi·co (ʊːniːvɛrsiːðáðnɑsjɔnálautɔ́nɔmaðe-méhiːkɔ) (*abbr.* UNAM) the second oldest university in the Americas, founded (1551) in Mexico City. Its university city was built by President Miguel Alemán. Its buildings, esp. the Central Library, are famous for their murals

U·ni·ver·si·dad de San Cris·tó·bal de Hua·man·ga (ʊːniːvɛrsíːdáðőesánkriːstɔ́bɑlðewɑ-máŋgɑ) a Peruvian university in Ayacucho. In opening (1960) its doors to Quechua Indians, it became the first Latin American university to offer higher education in an Indian language

U·ni·ver·si·dad de San Mar·cos (ʊːniːvɛrsiː-ðáðőesánmárkɔs) the oldest surviving university in the Americas, founded (1551) in Lima, Peru

U·ni·ver·si·da·de do Bra·sil (ʊːniːvɛrsiːdádedɔ-brɑzíːl) the first university in Brazil, founded (1920) in Rio de Janeiro by the federal government as a prototype for twenty others

u·ni·ver·si·ty (jʊːnivə́ːrsitiː) *pl.* **u·ni·ver·si·ties** *n.* a group of faculties providing higher education and empowered to grant academic degrees ‖ the teachers and the persons taught in such an institution ‖ the buildings and grounds of such an institution [A.F. *université*]

—All universities can trace their spiritual origin (and many their actual origin) to the 'studia generalia' of the Middle Ages, centers of study licensed and privileged by secular or ecclesiastical authority, open to students of all classes and nationalities. The earliest universities (apart from the 10th-c. medical school of Salerno) were in Paris, Bologna, Oxford and Cambridge

university extension the making available by a university of its lecturers, and the running of courses of instruction, for the benefit of people who are not members of that university

University of Puerto Rico the leading university of Puerto Rico, at Río Piedras outside San Juan, with other campuses at San Juan, Mayagüez and Humacao

un·kempt (ʌnkémpt) *adj.* (of hair) uncombed ‖ very untidy because of neglect, *an unkempt garden* [fr. UN-+older *kempt* fr. *kemb*, to comb]

Un·ki·ar Ske·les·si, Treaty of (uŋkjárskelesíː) a treaty (1833) between Russia and Turkey, closing the Dardanelles to foreign warships except those of Russia

un·kind (ʌnkáind) *adj.* not kind ‖ (of climate or weather) harsh **un·kínd·ly** *adv.*

un·kind·ly (ʌnkáindliː) *adj.* unkind [M.E.]

un·known (ʌnnóun) **1.** *adj.* not known **2.** *n.* an unknown quantity

unknown quantity (*math.*) an undetermined quantity figuring in a mathematical formulation and usually designated by a symbol, e.g. 'x' or 'y'

un·lead·ed (ʌnlédid) *adj.* (*printing*) without leads between the lines, set solid ‖ of a gasoline containing no lead

un·learn (ʌnlə́ːrn) *pres. part.* **un·learn·ing** *past* and *past part.* **un·learned, un·learnt** (ʌnlə́ːrnt) *v.t.* to rid one's mind of (something already learned)

un·learn·ed (ʌnlə́ːrnid, ʌnlə́ːrnd) *adj.* possessing no learning ‖ characterized by a lack of learning *unlearned speech* ‖ not acquired by study ‖ known without being learned

un·leash (ʌnlíːʃ) *v.t.* to release from, or as if from, a leash

un·leav·ened (ʌnlévənd) *adj.* made without leaven

un·less (ʌnlés) **1.** *conj.* if... not, *we have met before, unless I am mistaken* ‖ except when, except that, *unless he is hungry he will not touch it* **2.** *prep.* except, *nothing, unless rain, could prevent us from coming* [fr. on+less, 'on' assimilated to ,un-,]

un·let·tered (ʌnlétərd) *adj.* lacking education ‖ illiterate

un·like (ʌnláik) **1.** *adj.* not alike, dissimilar **2.** *prep.* not like, *such behavior is unlike him* [M.E. *unliche, unlike*]

un·like·li·hood (ʌnláikliːhud) *n.* improbability ‖ something improbable

un·like·li·ness (ʌnláikliːnis) *n.* improbability

un·like·ly (ʌnláikliː) **1.** *adj.* improbable, not likely ‖ unpromising, not likely to succeed **2.** *adv.* improbably

un·lim·ber (ʌnlímbər) *v.t.* to make (a gun) ready for action by detaching the limber

un·lim·it·ed (ʌnlímitid) *adj.* without limits ‖ boundless, vast

un·linked (ʌnlínkt) *adj.* (*genetics*) of a different linkage group

un·list·ed (ʌnlístid) *adj.* not listed ‖ (of securities) not listed among the ones admitted for trading on the stock market

unlisted number a telephone number not recorded in the published directory and not available from Information; (*Br.*) exdirectory number
un·load (ʌnlóud) *v.t.* to remove the goods from (a vehicle, vessel etc.) ‖ to remove (a cargo, load etc.) ‖ to remove the burden from ‖ to remove the charge from (a gun) ‖ (*pop.*) to sell (stock holdings etc.) in quantity and at a low price ‖ *v.i.* to discharge something, esp. a cargo
un·lock (ʌnlɒ́k) *v.t.* to open the lock of (a door) ‖ to free (a lock) with a key ‖ to tell the secrets of, *to unlock one's heart* ‖ (*rhet.*) to solve, *to unlock a mystery* ‖ *v.i.* to become unlocked
un·looked-for (ʌnlúkt-fɔr) *adj.* not anticipated, not expected
un·loose (ʌnlú:s) *pres. part.* **un·loos·ing** *past* and *past part.* **un·loosed** *v.t.* to loosen ‖ to set free
un·loos·en (ʌnlú:s'n) *v.t.* to unloose
un·love·ly (ʌnlʌ́vli:) *adj.* unsightly
un·luck·i·ly (ʌnlʌ́kili:) *adv.* in an unlucky way, by a misfortune
un·luck·i·ness (ʌnlʌ́ki:nis) *n.* the state or quality of being unlucky
un·luck·y (ʌnlʌ́ki:) *comp.* **un·luck·i·er** *superl.* **un·luck·i·est** *adj.* not lucky ‖ (*rhet.*) ill-omened
un·make (ʌnméik) *pres. part.* **un·mak·ing** *past* and *past part.* **un·made** (ʌnméid) *v.t.* to ruin, destroy ‖ to depose from a position of authority, rank etc.
un·man (ʌnmǽn) *pres. part.* **un·man·ning** *past* and *past part.* **un·manned** *v.t.* to deprive of manly qualities **un·mánned** *adj.* lacking a crew of men, *guns left unmanned*
un·man·ner·li·ness (ʌnmǽnərli:nis) *n.* the state or quality of being unmannerly
un·man·ner·ly (ʌnmǽnərli:) *adj.* impolite
un·mask (ʌnmǽsk, ʌnmúsk) *v.t.* to remove the mask from ‖ to expose the true nature or identity of, *to unmask a criminal* ‖ *v.i.* to take off one's mask
un·mean·ing (ʌnmí:niŋ) *adj.* without meaning
un·men·tion·a·ble (ʌnménʃənəb'l) *adj.* not fit to be mentioned, esp. because indecent
un·mis·tak·a·ble (ʌnmistéikəb'l) *adj.* that cannot be mistaken, clear, obvious **un·mis·ták·a·bly** *adv.*
un·mit·i·gat·ed (ʌnmítigeitid) *adj.* not lessened in intensity etc., *unmitigated grief* ‖ absolute, unqualified, *an unmitigated ass*
un·mor·al (ʌnmɔ́rəl, ʌnmɒ́rəl) *adj.* amoral
un·nat·u·ral (ʌnnǽtʃərəl) *adj.* not natural ‖ lacking or counter to behavior, feelings etc. that are considered natural or normal
un·nec·es·sar·y (ʌnnésiseri:) *adj.* not necessary, needless
un·nerve (ʌnnə́:rv) *pres. part.* **un·nerv·ing** *past* and *past part.* **un·nerved** *v.t.* to destroy the self-control of, cause to be nervous
un·num·bered (ʌnnʌ́mbərd) *adj.* (*rhet.*) innumerable ‖ bearing no number
un·oc·cu·pied (ʌnɒ́kupaid) *adj.* empty, not occupied ‖ without occupation, idle ‖ not occupied by troops
un·or·gan·ized (ʌnɔ́rgənaizd) *adj.* not organized ‖ not having organic structure ‖ not belonging to a trade union
un·pack (ʌnpǽk) *v.t.* to remove from its packaging ‖ to empty (a trunk, case etc.) of its contents ‖ *v.i.* to unpack a trunk, case etc.
un·par·al·leled (ʌnpǽrəleld) *adj.* having no equal
un·par·lia·men·ta·ry (ʌnpɑrləméntəri:) *adj.* not in accordance with parliamentary practice
un·per·son (ʌnpə́:rsən) *n.* an individual the memory of whom has been erased from all records and who is otherwise not recognized (based on practice in U.S.S.R., 1936–1938); coined by English author George Orwell
un·pick (ʌnpík) *adj.* to remove stitches from (sewing, knitting etc.), *to unpick a seam*
un·pleas·ant (ʌnpléz'nt) *adj.* disagreeable, not pleasant **un·pléas·ant·ness** *n.* the quality or state of being unpleasant ‖ an unpleasant situation etc., esp. a quarrel
un·plumbed (ʌnplʌ́md) *adj.* not fully investigated
un·polled (ʌnpóuld) *adj.* (of a vote) not cast ‖ not included in a poll
un·pop·u·lar (ʌnpɒ́pjulər) *adj.* not popular, viewed with disfavor by the majority
un·prac·ticed, *Br.* **un·prac·tised** (ʌnprǽktist) *adj.* not skilled
un·prec·e·dent·ed (ʌnprésidəntid) *adj.* without precedent
un·pre·pared (ʌnpripéərd) *adj.* not worked out ahead ‖ not ready ‖ not emotionally adjusted in advance, esp. for a shock
un·prin·ci·pled (ʌnprínsəpəld) *adj.* without moral principles
un·print·a·ble (ʌnpríntəb'l) *adj.* not suitable for printing (because blasphemous, obscene, slanderous etc.)
un·pro·fes·sion·al (ʌnprəféʃən'l) *adj.* not professional ‖ not in accordance with professional etiquette
un·qual·i·fied (ʌnkwɒ́lifaid) *adj.* lacking the necessary qualifications ‖ without reservation, *unqualified praise*
un·quan·ti·fi·a·ble (ʌnkwɒntəfáiəb'l) *adj.* not capable of being measured
un·ques·tion·a·ble (ʌnkwéstʃənəb'l) *adj.* not open to question **un·qués·tion·a·bly** *adv.*
un·quote (ʌnkwóut) *pres. part.* **un·quot·ing** *past* and *past part.* **un·quot·ed** (used in the imperative, esp. in dictating) to close a quotation
un·rav·el (ʌnrǽvəl) *pres. part.* **un·rav·el·ing,** esp. *Br.* **un·rav·el·ling** *past* and *past part.* **un·rav·eled,** esp. *Br.* **un·rav·elled** *v.t.* to untangle ‖ to undo (a knitted garment) ‖ to solve (a complex problem) ‖ *v.i.* to become unraveled
un·read (ʌnréd) *adj.* not read ‖ not well-read
un·read·a·ble (ʌnrí:dəb'l) *adj.* too turgid, dull, precious etc. to be read with pleasure ‖ illegible
un·read·y (ʌnrédi:) *adj.* not ready ‖ slow to learn, *an unready pupil*
un·re·al (ʌnríəl) *adj.* not real ‖ existing only in the mind
un·re·al·i·ty (ʌnri:ǽliti:) *pl.* **un·re·al·i·ties** *n.* the state or quality of being unreal ‖ something unreal
un·rea·son (ʌnrí:z'n) *n.* absence of reason
un·rea·son·a·ble (ʌnrí:z'nəb'l) *adj.* not reasonable ‖ beyond the bounds of reason, immoderate **un·réa·son·a·bly** *adv.*
un·rea·son·ing (ʌnrí:z,niŋ) *adj.* not reasoning ‖ not controlled by reason
un·reeve (ʌnrí:v) *pres. part.* **un·reev·ing** *past* and *past part.* **un·rove** (ʌnróuv), **un·reeved** *v.t.* (*naut.*) to withdraw (a rope) from a block or other opening
un·re·gen·er·ate (ʌnridʒénərit) *adj.* not made spiritually regenerate ‖ persisting obstinately in an opinion or outlook, *an unregenerate philistine* **un·re·gen·er·at·ed** (ʌnridʒénəreitid) *adj.* unregenerate
un·re·lent·ing (ʌnriléntiŋ) *adj.* not weakening in determination ‖ not becoming compassionate ‖ not slackening in intensity, speed etc.
un·re·mit·ting (ʌnrimítiŋ) *adj.* persevering ‖ kept up without interruption
un·re·served (ʌnrizə́:rvd) *adj.* unqualified, without modification, *unreserved praise* ‖ frank in speech or behavior **un·re·serv·ed·ly** (ʌnrizə́:rvidli:) *adv.*
un·rest (ʌnrést) *n.* restlessness, uneasiness ‖ collective discontent
un·re·strained (ʌnristréind) *adj.* not reticent or reserved ‖ not kept in check
un·rip (ʌnríp) *pres. part.* **un·rip·ping** *past* and *past part.* **un·ripped** *v.t.* and *i.* to rip open
un·ripe (ʌnráip) *adj.* (of fruit etc.) not ripe
un·ri·valed, esp. *Br.* **un·ri·valled** (ʌnráivəld) *adj.* without a rival or equal
un·roll (ʌnróul) *v.t.* to open from a rolled position ‖ to unfold to the view ‖ *v.i.* to become unrolled
un·round (ʌnráund) *v.t.* to pronounce (a normally rounded vowel) without rounding the lips ‖ to make (the lips) not rounded, e.g. in pronouncing a normally rounded vowel
unrove alt. *past* and *past part.* of UNREEVE
un·ruf·fled (ʌnrʌ́fəld) *adj.* not ruffled emotionally serene
un·ru·li·ness (ʌnrú:li:nis) *n.* the state or quality of being unruly
un·ru·ly (ʌnrú:li:) *comp.* **un·ru·li·er** *superl.* **un·ru·li·est** *adj.* refusing to submit to rule, undisciplined and causing trouble
un·sad·dle (ʌnsǽd'l) *pres. part.* **un·sad·dling** *past* and *past part.* **un·sad·dled** *v.t.* to remove the saddle from ‖ to throw from the saddle
un·said (ʌnséd) *past part.* of UNSAY ‖ *adj.* thought but not uttered, kept suppressed in the mind ‖ *UNSAY
un·sat·u·rat·ed (ʌnsǽtʃəreitid) *adj.* not saturated ‖ (*chem.*, of a compound, esp. of carbon) containing double or triple bonds and hence capable of forming other compounds by addition ‖ (*chem.*, of a solution) capable of absorbing or dissolving further solute at a given temperature and pressure
un·sa·vor·y, *Br.* **un·sa·vour·y** (ʌnséivəri:) *adj.* unpleasant in taste or smell ‖ tasteless, insipid ‖ morally offensive, disgusting
un·say (ʌnséi) *pres. part.* **un·say·ing** *past* and *past part.* **un·said** (ʌnséd) *v.t.* to withdraw (what one has said)
un·scathed (ʌnskéiðd) *adj.* without being physically or morally hurt
un·sci·en·tif·ic (ʌnsaiəntífik) *adj.* not in accordance with scientific method ‖ not acting from knowledge of scientific method
un·scram·ble (ʌnskrǽmb'l) *pres. part.* **un·scram·bling** *past* and *past part.* **un·scram·bled** *v.t.* to put (a scrambled message) into clear form
un·screw (ʌnskrú:) *v.t.* to remove or loosen (a screw, lid etc.) by turning ‖ to remove a screw-on lid from ‖ to remove the screws from ‖ *v.i.* to admit of unscrewing ‖ to become unscrewed
un·scru·pu·lous (ʌnskrú:pjuləs) *adj.* unprincipled ‖ dishonest
un·seal (ʌnsí:l) *v.i.* to break the seal on or undo the sealing of ‖ to end the imposed constraint on, open, *drink unsealed his lips*
un·sea·son·a·ble (ʌnsí:zənəb'l) *adj.* not usual for the time of year, *unseasonable weather* ‖ (*rhet.*) badly timed, inopportune, *an unseasonable remark*
un·seat (ʌnsí:t) *v.t.* to throw or remove from a seat, esp. from the saddle ‖ to remove from office, e.g. from a seat in Parliament
un·seem·ly (ʌnsí:mli:) **1.** *adj.* not seemly, indecorous, unbecoming **2.** *adv.* in an unseemly way
un·seen (ʌnsí:n) **1.** *adj.* not seen ‖ not able to be seen ‖ (*Br.*, esp. of a passage set for translation) sight **2.** *n.* (*Br.*) a sight translation
un·set·tle (ʌnsét'l) *pres. part.* **un·set·tling** *past* and *past part.* **un·set·tled** *v.t.* to cause to be no longer stable ‖ to cause to be no longer sure or determined ‖ to cause to lose one's mental or emotional composure ‖ to cause (the stomach) to be slightly upset **un·sét·tled** *adj.* (of an account) not paid ‖ not stable ‖ not orderly ‖ not decided ‖ not populated or cultivated ‖ not settled in one place ‖ not legally disposed of, *unsettled property* ‖ (of weather) changeable ‖ mentally or emotionally discomposed
un·ship (ʌnʃíp) *pres. part.* **un·ship·ping** *past* and *past part.* **un·shipped** *v.t.* (*naut.*) to unload (cargo etc.) from a ship ‖ (*naut.*) to remove (e.g. oars or the mast) from position
un·sight·ly (ʌnsáitli:) *adj.* unpleasant to see
un·skilled (ʌnskíld) *adj.* not skilled ‖ not requiring skill
un·skill·ful, esp. *Br.* **un·skil·ful** (ʌnskílfəl) *adj.* not skillful ‖ betraying lack of skill
un·sling (ʌnslíŋ) *pres. part.* **un·sling·ing** *past* and *past part.* **un·slung** (ʌnslʌ́ŋ) *v.t.* to take from a slung position ‖ (*naut.*) to remove from slings
un·so·cia·bil·i·ty (ʌnsouʃəbíliti:) *n.* the state or quality of being unsociable
un·so·cia·ble (ʌnsóuʃəb'l) *adj.* not sociable, by nature solitary, shunning society ‖ not conducive to sociability **un·só·cia·bly** *adv.*
un·so·cial (ʌnsóuʃəl) *adj.* not willingly associating with others ‖ antisocial
un·sound (ʌnsáund) *adj.* not physically, mentally or morally sound ‖ (esp. of market produce) not in good condition ‖ open to logical attack ‖ (of a thing) liable to collapse, *an unsound chair* ‖ (of sleep) uneasy, fitful
un·spar·ing (ʌnspéəriŋ) *adj.* without reserve in giving, striving etc. ‖ without mercy
un·speak·a·ble (ʌnspí:kəb'l) *adj.* indescribably bad ‖ inexpressibly delightful **un·spéak·a·bly** *adv.*
un·sta·ble (ʌnstéib'l) *adj.* in a condition which may very easily change or be changed ‖ not to be depended on ‖ characterized by emotional instability (*chem.*) readily decomposing
un·stead·y (ʌnstédi:) *comp.* **un·stead·i·er** *superl.* **un·stead·i·est** *adj.* not firm or firmly under control ‖ emotionally changeable ‖ lacking regularity, *an unsteady pulse*
un·stop (ʌnstɒ́p) *pres. part.* **un·stopping** *past* and *past part.* **un·stopped** *v.t.* to take the stopper from ‖ to free from obstruction
un·strik·a·ble (ʌnstráikəb'l) *adj.* of a job on which a strike is illegal
un·string (ʌnstríŋ) *pres. part.* **un·string·ing** *past* and *past part.* **un·strung** (ʌnstrʌ́ŋ) *v.t.* to loosen or remove the strings of (a violin etc.) ‖ to take (beads etc.) from a string ‖ (esp. in passive)

CONCISE PRONUNCIATION KEY: **(a)** æ, *cat*; ɑ, *car*; ɔ *fawn*; ei, *snake*. **(e)** e, *hen*; i:, *sheep*; iə, *deer*; ɛə, *bear*. **(i)** i, *fish*; ai, *tiger*; ə:, *bird*. **(o)** o, *ox*; au, *cow*; ou, *goat*; u, *poor*; ɔi, *royal*. **(u)** ʌ, *duck*; u, *bull*; u:, *goose*; ə, *bacillus*; ju:, *cube*. x, *loch*; θ, *think*; ð, *bother*; z, *Zen*; ʒ, *corsage*; dʒ, *savage*; ŋ, *orangutang*; j, *yak*; ʃ, *fish*; tʃ, *fetch*; 'l, *rabble*; 'n, *redden*. Complete pronunciation key appears inside front cover.

to cause (a person or his nerves) to become disordered

un·strung (ʌnstrʌ́ŋ) *adj.* having the strings removed or loosened ‖ emotionally distressed

un·stud·ied (ʌnstʌ́di:d) *adj.* unaffected, not artificial

un·sub·stan·tial (ʌnsəbstǽnʃəl) *adj.* not having material substance ‖ not very solid ‖ having no real basis of fact

un·sung (ʌnsʌ́ŋ) *adj.* not sung ‖ not praised in verse or song, not given recognition, *unsung heroes*

un·sus·pect·ed (ʌnsəspéktid) *adj.* not suspected ‖ not known or thought to exist

un·taught (ʌntɔ́t) *adj.* without formal education ‖ not learned from teachers

un·teach (ʌntí:tʃ) *pres. part.* **un·teach·ing** *past* and *past part.* **un·taught** (ʌntɔ́t) *v.t.* to cause (someone) to forget something learned ‖ to teach the opposite of (something previously taught)

Un·ter·mensch (úntɛərmenʃ) *pl.* **-en** (*German*) an alleged lower species or type of human being *ant.* Übermensch

Un·ter·wal·den (úntərvɑldən) a German-speaking and mainly Catholic canton in central Switzerland. It is divided into Nidwalden (area 106 sq. miles, pop. 28,617) and Obwalden (area 189 sq. miles, pop. 25,865). It formed (1291) part of the original league with Schwyz and Uri which was the nucleus of the Swiss Confederation

un·thank·ful (ʌnθǽŋkfəl) *adj.* not thankful ‖ not pleasant and not appreciated, *an unthankful task*

un·think·a·ble (ʌnθíŋkəb'l) *adj.* so extraordinary as not to be conceivable to the mind ‖ out of the question, not to be considered as a possibility

un·think·ing (ʌnθíŋkiŋ) *adj.* thoughtless or showing lack of thought ‖ lacking the power of thought

un·ti·dy (ʌntáidi:) *adj.* not neat or orderly in dress, appearance, habit etc. ‖ not kept in proper order, *untidy account books*

un·tie (ʌntái) *pres. part.* **un·ty·ing, un·tie·ing** *past* and *past part.* **un·tied** *v.t.* to undo (something tied, fastened or knotted) ‖ *v.i.* (of something tied, fastened or knotted) to become undone

un·til (ʌntíl) **1.** *prep.* till, to the time of, *we waited until nightfall* (in negative constructions) before (some specified time), *don't come until after dark* **2.** *conj.* to the time when ‖ to the degree, place or point that, *he pleaded until he got it* ‖ (in negative constructions) before, *he didn't come until the show began* [M.E. *untill* fr. O.N.]

un·time·li·ness (ʌntáimli:nis) *n.* the state or quality of being untimely

un·time·ly (ʌntáimli:) **1.** *adj. comp.* **un·time·li·er** *superl.* **un·time·li·est** done or occurring before the proper time, premature ‖ inopportune **2.** *adv.* too soon ‖ inopportunely

un·to (ʌ́ntu:) *prep.* (*rhet.* or *archaic*) to, *render unto Caesar...* ‖ (*rhet.* or *archaic*) till, until, *unto this day*

un·told (ʌntóuld) *adj.* not told ‖ too much or too many to count or measure

un·touch·a·ble (ʌntʌ́tʃəb'l) **1.** *adj.* not to be touched ‖ immune from criticism or attack **2.** *n.* a member of a large group in India belonging to the lowest caste or regarded as having no caste, and formerly excluded from the social and religious privileges of Hinduism. The persecution of untouchables was made illegal by the Indian constituent assembly (1949) and the Pakistan constituent assembly (1950)

un·to·ward (ʌntɔ́rd, ʌntóurd, ʌntəwɔ́rd) *adj.* fractious, difficult to manage ‖ not favorable or lucky, *untoward circumstances* ‖ unseemly

un·trav·eled, esp. *Br.* **un·trav·elled** (ʌntrǽvəld) *adj.* (of a road etc.) not used by travelers ‖ (of a person) not having traveled much

un·tried (ʌntráid) *adj.* not tested, inexperienced ‖ not tried in court

un·true (ʌntrú:) *adj.* not true, false ‖ (*rhet.*) unfaithful or disloyal ‖ not perfectly flat, level etc., not forming a perfect right angle etc. **un·trú·ly** *adv.*

un·truth (ʌntrú:θ) *pl.* **un·truths** (ʌntrú:θs, ʌntrú:ðz) *n.* lack of truthfulness a falsehood

un·truth·ful (ʌntrú:θfəl) *adj.* untrue, false ‖ inclined to tell lies

un·tu·tored (ʌntú:tərd, ʌntjú:tərd) *adj.* untaught, owing nothing to formal instruction

un·used (ʌnjú:zd) *adj.* not currently in use ‖ never having been used ‖ (ʌnjú:st) (with 'to') unaccustomed

un·u·su·al (ʌnjú:ʒu:əl) *adj.* rare, different from others ‖ being of or showing a greater or stronger degree than usual, *to work with unusual speed*

un·ut·ter·a·ble (ʌnʌ́tərəb'l) *adj.* inexpressibly delightful ‖ unspeakably horrid

un·var·nished (ʌnvárniʃt) *adj.* not varnished ‖ plain, unembellished, *the unvarnished truth*

Un·ver·dor·ben (únferdɔrbən), Otto (1806-73), German chemist who was the first to prepare aniline (1826)

un·voice (ʌnvɔ́is) *pres. part.* **un·voic·ing** *past* and *past part.* **un·voiced** *v.t.* (*phon.*) to pronounce without voicing

un·voiced (ʌnvɔ́ist) *adj.* not expressed, not spoken ‖ (*phon.*) not voiced

un·wea·ried (ʌnwíəri:d) *adj.* doggedly persistent in effort ‖ showing dogged persistence

un·wept (ʌnwépt) *adj.* (*rhet.*, of tears) not shed ‖ (*rhet.*) not wept for

un·whole·some (ʌnhóulsəm) *adj.* not wholesome, not conducive to physical or mental health ‖ morally harmful

un·wield·i·ly (ʌnwí:ldili:) *adv.* in an unwieldy way

un·wield·i·ness (ʌnwí:ldi:nis) *n.* the state or quality of being unwieldy

un·wield·y (ʌnwí:ldi:) *comp.* **un·wield·i·er** *superl* **un·wield·i·est** *adj.* difficult to handle or manage because of bulk or size ‖ clumsy, ungainly

un·wil·ling (ʌnwíliŋ) *adj.* not willing, reluctant ‖ done, said etc. reluctantly

un·wind (ʌnwáind) *pres. part.* **un·wind·ing** *past* and *past part.* **un·wound** (ʌnwáund) *v.t.* to undo, unroll (what is wound) ‖ (*rhet.*) to sort out or straighten (something muddled or involved) ‖ *v.i.* to become unwound

un·wise (ʌnwáiz) *adj.* ill-considered ‖ foolish

un·wit·ting (ʌnwítiŋ) *adj.* unaware, not knowing ‖ not intentional [O.E. *unwitende*]

un·wont·ed (ʌnwɔ́ntid, ʌnwóuntid, ʌnwʌ́ntid) *adj.* unaccustomed ‖ uncommon, rarely met with

un·world·li·ness (ʌnwɔ́:rldli:nis) *n.* the state or quality of being unworldly

un·world·ly (ʌnwɔ́:rldli:) *comp.* **un·world·li·er** *superl.* **un·world·li·est** *adj.* not concerned with worldly matters ‖ not of this world, spiritual

un·wor·thi·ly (ʌnwɔ́:rðili:) *adv.* in an unworthy manner

un·wor·thi·ness (ʌnwɔ́:rði:nis) *n.* the state or quality of being unworthy

un·wor·thy (ʌnwɔ́:rði:) *comp.* **un·wor·thi·er** *superl.* **un·wor·thi·est** *adj.* falling short of what is required, lamentably below standard ‖ (esp. with 'of') not deserving ‖ mean, contemptible

unwound *past* and *past part.* of UNWIND

un·writ·ten (ʌnrít'n) *adj.* not written ‖ (of laws) not included in the statutes but based on long custom or strong general feeling ‖ not written on

up (ʌp) **1.** *adv.* from a lower towards a higher location ‖ towards a greater degree of intensity, *warming up* ‖ towards a higher rank or social condition ‖ to a higher amount, value, degree etc., *the property has gone up since he bought it* ‖ from an earlier to a later period, *from youth up* ‖ from below the horizon ‖ (*Br.*) to the capital ‖ in the direction thought of as higher, *going up north* ‖ in or to a standing position ‖ out of bed ‖ in reserve, *to lay up stores* ‖ into view, consideration, action etc. ‖ into a state of excitement, *don't get worked up* ‖ (*baseball*) to a turn at bat, *who is coming up next?* ‖ so as to be even with in space, time, condition etc., *keeping up with the neighbors* ‖ (*naut.*) towards the point from which the wind blows ‖ (*sports, games*) ahead of an opponent with respect to points, strokes etc. (*sports, games*) for each side, *the score is 2 up* ‖ (in combination with verbs) used as an intensive, *burn up, eat up, dry up* ‖ (used in combination with verbs without effecting a change in meaning), *to light up one's pipe* **2.** *prep.* to, toward or at a higher point on or in, *climb up the stairs* ‖ to or towards a higher condition in or on, *up the social scale* ‖ at a point farther along, *she lives up the road* ‖ toward the source of (a river) **up to** as far as (a designated part or point), *up to her knees in mud* ‖ as much as, *the elevator will hold up to three people* ‖ until, *up to this time* **3.** *adj.* directed toward a position that is higher or that is thought of as higher ‖ in a higher position or condition showing above the ground, *the corn is up* ‖ above the horizon, *the moon is up* ‖ advanced in amount, degree etc. ‖ in a standing position ‖ out of bed ‖ (e.g. of the wind) in an active or agitated state ‖ in an inner or elevated part of a country or territory ‖ (*Br.*) resident at a university etc. ‖ at an end, *our time is up* ‖ happening, being planned etc. ‖ (*baseball*) at bat ‖ (*sports, games*) ahead of one's opponent **it's all up with** there is no hope for **up against** faced with, confronted with, *up against a difficult problem* **up against it** in difficulty **up and doing** actively busy **up for** before court for (trial) ‖ being considered for (an office etc.) **up on** (or **in**) informed about, *she is always well up on the latest fashions* **up to** doing, *what are they up to?* ‖ equal to (a task etc.) ‖ incumbent upon ‖ dependent on the decision or action of ‖ well aware of, *she's up to his tricks* **4.** *n.* (in the phrase) **on the up and up** getting better and better or more and more successful ‖ straightforward, honest **ups and downs** periods of good and bad fortune **5.** *v. pres. part.* **up·ping** *past* and *past part.* **upped** *v.i.* (with 'and' and a verb) to take decisive action with regard to some specified matter, *she upped and slapped him on the cheek* ‖ *v.t.* (*Br.*) to collect together (swans) for their annual marking (cf. SWAN-UPPING) ‖ to increase, *to up taxes* ‖ to bet more than ‖ to move to a higher position, *to up sails* **to up with** to raise (the arm, a weapon etc.), esp. in a threatening way, *he upped with an ax* [O.E. *up, uppe*]

up- (ʌp) the combining form of UP [O.E.]

up·an·chor (ʌ́pǽŋkər) *v.i.* (*naut.*) to draw up the anchor before getting under way

up-and-com·ing (ʌ́pənkʌ́miŋ) *adj.* able and energetic and on the way to being successful

up-and-down (ʌ́pəndáun) *adj.* rising and falling alternately

U·pan·i·shads (u:pǽniʃædz, u:pániʃadz) the main body of the sacred writings of Hinduism. There are over 100 separate books, most of them consisting of a mixture of stories, dialogues, aphorisms and allegorizings of ideas from the Vedas. The books were written c. 600–c. 300 B.C. Their most characteristic doctrine is that of monism [Skr.=secret teachings]

u·pas (jú:pəs) *n. Antiaris toxicaria*, fam. *Moraceae*, a tall evergreen tree of S.E. Asia yielding a latex used in concocting an arrow poison ‖ this poison [fr. Malay *ūpas*, poison (*pōhun ūpas*, poison tree)]

up·beat (ʌ́pbi:t) *n.* (*mus.*) the beat before the main accented note, or the conductor's gesture indicating this

up·bow (ʌ́pbou) *n.* (in playing a bowed instrument) a stroke from the tip to the heel of the bow (cf. DOWN-BOW)

up·braid (ʌpbréid) *v.t.* to scold, reproach [O.E. *upbregdan*]

up·bring·ing (ʌ́pbriŋiŋ) *n.* the process of training and education in childhood and youth

up·cast (ʌ́pkæst, ʌ́pkɑst) **1.** *adj.* directed or inclined upwards, *upcast eyes* **2.** *n.* (*mining*) a shaft provided for the upward passage of air ‖ (*mining*) the material cast up in digging

up·con·vert·er (ʌ́pkənvɔ́:rtə:r) *n.* (*electr.*) **1.** device that converts radiant energy to another form, e.g., using a laser beam to produce a three-dimensional image **2.** an amplifier that converts input frequency to a greater output frequency —**upconvert** *v.t.*

up·coun·try 1. (ʌ́pkʌntri:) *adj.* of, relating to or situated in the interior of a country or region **2.** (ʌ́pkʌntri) *n.* the interior of a country or region **3.** (ʌpkʌ́ntri:) *adv.* in or toward the interior of a country or region

up·date (ʌpdéit) *pres. part.* **up·dat·ing** *past* and *past part.* **up·dat·ed** *v.t.* to bring (e.g. matter in a book) up to date by adding or correcting

Up·dike (ʌ́pdaik), John (1932-), U.S. writer of short stories, notably 'Same Door' (1959), and of novels, notably 'Rabbit, Run' (1961), 'The Centaur' (1962), 'Couples' (1968), 'Bech: A Book' (1970), 'A Month of Sundays' (1975), 'Rabbit is Rich' (1981, Pulitzer Prize), 'Bech is Back' (1982) and 'The Witches of Eastwick' (1984)

up·draft (ʌ́pdræft, ʌ́pdrɑft) **1.** *adj.* (of a kiln) in which the heated air passes upward, to an outlet at the top **2.** *n.* an upward movement of air or other gas

up·end (ʌpénd) *v.t.* to set on end or as if on end ‖ *v.i.* to rise on end

up·field (ʌpfí:ld) *n.* (*football*) area toward the goal post —**upfield** *adj.* —**upfield** *adv.*

up·front (ʌpfrʌ́nt) *adj.* **1.** paid in advance **2.** straightforward and honest

up·grade 1. (ʌ́pgreid) *n.* a rising slope **on the upgrade** improving ‖ increasing **2.** (ʌ́pgréid) *adv.* uphill **3.** (ʌ́pgreid) *v.t. pres. part.* **up·grad-**

ing *past* and *past part.* **up·grad·ed** to promote, advance to a higher grade || (*commerce*) to raise the quality of (a product)
up·heav·al (ʌphíːvəl) *n.* an upheaving or a being upheaved, esp. by volcanic action || a violent social commotion
up·heave (ʌphíːv) *pres. part.* **up·heav·ing** *past* and *past part.* **up·heaved** *v.t.* (esp. *geol.*) to lift up with violent effort or force || *v.i.* to rise upward with great force
upheld *past* and *past part.* of UPHOLD
up·hill 1. (ʌphíl) *adv.* in an ascending direction **2.** (ʌ́phil) *adj.* ascending || (of a task, struggle etc.) slow and difficult
up·hold (ʌphóuld) *pres. part.* **up·hold·ing** *past* and *past part.* **up·held** (ʌphéld) *v.t.* to maintain or support morally or spiritually || to give physical support to || to confirm, decide in favor of, *the court upheld his claim* || to lift up to a higher position, *with arms upheld*
up·hol·ster (ʌphóulstər, əpóulstər) *v.t.* to provide (furniture) with padding, springs, textile covering etc. [backformation fr. UPHOLSTERER or UPHOLSTERY]
up·hol·ster·er (ʌphóulstərər, əpóulstərər) *n.* a person whose trade is upholstery [fr. earlier *upholdster* fr. M.E. *upholder,* auctioneer, tradesman]
up·hol·ster·y (ʌphóulstəriː, əpóulstəriː) *n.* the craft and trade of upholstering || the materials used in upholstering [fr. earlier *upholdster*]
up·keep (ʌ́pkiːp) *n.* the maintenance of buildings, roads, equipment etc. || the cost of such maintenance || the state of a building etc. with regard to such maintenance, *in good upkeep*
up·land (ʌ́plənd,ʌ́plænd) **1.** *n.* the area of land high above sea level **2.** *adj.* situated on high land || living or growing on high ground
up·lift 1. (ʌplíft) *v.t.* to sing out, utter loudly, *voices uplifted in praise* || to give spiritual or moral encouragement to || (*geol.*) to push up (part of the earth's surface) above the surrounding land **2.** (ʌ́plift) *n.* (*Br., pop.*) morally elevating talk of a vaguely benevolent nature || spiritual encouragement || (*geol.*) the raising of a part of the earth's surface above the surrounding land || (*geol.*) the mass raised
up·man·ship (ʌ́pmənʃip) *n.* the practice of scoring an advantage in status *syn.* one-upmanship
up·most (ʌ́pmoust) *adj.* uppermost
up·on (əpɔ́n,əpɒ́n) *prep.* on || up and on
up·per (ʌ́pər) **1.** *adj.* higher in position or place, *an upper story* || (of notes, voices etc.) higher in pitch || higher in status, *the upper classes* || farther north or higher up or farther from the sea, *the upper Amazon* || pertaining to or being the northern part of an area, *upper Manhattan* || (*geol.,* of strata) nearer the surface of the earth **Upper** (*geol.,* of a division of a period etc.) later, more recent, *Upper Cambrian* **2.** *n.* the part of a shoe or boot above the sole || (*pop.*) an upper berth **on one's uppers** in dire need, penniless or almost so || (*slang or colloq.*) a stimulant drug, esp. amphetamine
Upper Austria (*G.* Oberösterreich) a province (area 4,625 sq. miles, pop. 1,132,000) of N. Austria. Capital: Linz
Upper Canada (*hist.*) a province of Canada (1791-1840) which was predominantly English in population. It was equivalent to the southern part of modern Ontario
up·per·case (ʌ́pərkéis) **1.** *n.* (*printing, abbr.* u.c.) capital letters **2.** *adj.* (of a letter) capital (cf. LOWERCASE)
upper class the class of people generally considered to rank above the middle class. The usual criteria are wealth, cultivation and ancestry **úp·per-cláss** *adj.*
upper crust (*pop.*) the best or most prominent of a social class, esp. the upper class
up·per·cut 1. (ʌ́pərkʌt) *n.* a blow delivered at close quarters from below to the point of the chin, with the arm bent at the elbow **2.** (ʌ́pərkʌ́t) *v. pres. part.* **up·per·cut·ting** *past* and *past part.* **up·per·cut** *v.t.* to hit with such a blow || *v.i.* to deliver such a blow
upper house the higher chamber in a legislative body having two chambers (cf. LOWER HOUSE)
up·per·most (ʌ́pərmoust) **1.** *adj.* highest in place, rank, power, position etc., *the uppermost layers* || being in the most prominent position, *the uppermost thoughts in his mind* **2.** *adv.* in or into the highest position || in or into the most prominent position
Upper Volta *BURKINA FASO
up·ping (ʌ́piŋ) *n.* *SWAN-UPPING
up·pish (ʌ́piʃ) *adj.* (*pop.*) uppity
up·pi·ty (ʌ́pitiː) *adj.* (*pop.*) aggressively conceited, arrogant
Upp·sa·la (ʌ́psɑlə) a city (pop. 146,192) in E. central Sweden. Gothic cathedral (13th-15th cc.). University (1477) and library with fine collection of manuscripts
up·raise (ʌpréiz) *pres. part.* **up·rais·ing** *past* and *past part.* **up·raised** *v.t.* to lift up, *with upraised eyebrows*
up·rak·en (uːprɑkən) *n.* (*karate*) an inverted fist with the roof of the middle finger forming the contact point
up·rate (ʌ́preit) *v.* to improve on a rating scale
up·right (ʌ́prait) **1.** *adj.* being in a vertical or erect position || morally honorable || greater in height than in width **2.** *adv.* in a vertical position **3.** *n.* a vertical support for a structure, e.g. a stake || (*pl.*) a goalpost on e.g. a football field || an upright piano [O.E. *upriht, uppriht*]
upright piano a piano with vertical strings (cf. GRAND PIANO)
up·ris·ing (ʌ́praiziŋ) *n.* an insurrection
up·roar (ʌ́prɔr, ʌ́prour) *n.* a noisy tumult **up·roar·i·ous** (ʌprɔ́riːəs, ʌpróuriːəs) *adj.* very noisy, usually as a result of, or provoking, convulsive laughter [fr. Du. *oproer,* confusion]
up·root (ʌprúːt,ʌprút) *v.t.* to tear up by the roots || to remove from a settled residence or occupation || to eradicate
up·rush (ʌ́prʌʃ) *n.* a powerful upward movement || a sudden rising of emotion, *an uprush of pity*
up·set 1. (ʌ́pset) *n.* an upsetting or being upset || a slight physical ailment || an emotional disturbance || a totally unexpected defeat, e.g. in an athletic contest || (*mech.*) that part of a bar etc. that is upset || (*mech.*) a tool used in upsetting **2.** *v.* (ʌpsét) *pres. part.* **up·set·ting** *past* and *past part.* **up·set** *v.t.* to tip over or capsize || to cause physical or mental distress to || to disarrange, cause confusion in, *to upset plans* || *mech.*) to shorten or thicken (a bar of heated metal) by hammering the end || to defeat unexpectedly, e.g. in an athletic contest || *v.i.* to be tipped over, capsize **3.** (ʌpsét) *adj.* emotionally or physically distressed
upset price the fixed minimum price for property put up for auction
up·shot (ʌ́pʃɒt) *n.* outcome, final result
up·side down (ʌ́psaid) in an inverted position or condition, with the top part underneath || in great disorder, *thieves left the place upside down* **to turn upside down** to reduce (e.g. a room) to a state of great disorder, e.g. in searching for a lost article **úp·side-dówn** *adj.* in an inverted position, with the top part underneath [M.E. *up so doun,* up as if down]
up·si·lon (júːpsəlɒn, ʌ́psəlɒn, *Br.* esp. juːpsáilən) *n.* the 20th letter (Υ, υ=y, u) of the Greek alphabet
up·stage (ʌ́pstéidʒ) **1.** *adv.* toward the back of the stage, away from the footlights **2.** *adj.* of or relating to the rear part of the stage || (*pop.*) affecting superiority, distant and condescending **3.** *v.t. pres. part.* **up·stag·ing** *past* and *past part.* **up·staged** to treat with condescension and superiority || to put (a fellow actor) at a disadvantage by maneuvering to keep him in an upstage position
up·stairs (ʌ́pstέərz) **1.** *adv.* on or towards an upper floor of a house etc. **2.** *adj.* of or relating to an upper floor || situated above the ground floor **3.** *n.* that part of a house etc. that is above the ground floor
up·stand·ing (ʌpstǽndiŋ) *adj.* (of a youth or man) independent in spirit and morally upright || standing up straight
up·start (ʌ́pstɑrt) *n.* a person who has risen swiftly from a humble position to wealth or power, and presumes on it by arrogant behavior
up·state (ʌ́pstéit) **1.** *adj.* of or from that part of a state outside some large city, esp. to the north **2.** *n.* an upstate region, esp. northern New York State **úp·stát·er** *n.*
up·stream (ʌ́pstríːm) **1.** *adv.* in a direction towards the source of a stream **2.** *adj.* located or directed upstream
up·stroke (ʌ́pstrouk) *n.* an upward stroke of the pen in writing
up·swing (ʌ́pswiŋ) *n.* the upward arc of a swinging movement || an upward trend, improvement
up·take (ʌ́pteik) *n.* a ventilating shaft || a pipe for carrying gases and smoke from a furnace etc. to a chimney **quick (slow) on** (*Br.* **in**) **the uptake** quick (slow) in understanding
up·thrust (ʌ́pθrʌst) *n.* (*geol.*) an upheaval of part of the earth's crust, commonly occurring with faulting
up·tick (ʌ́ptik) *n.* (*securities*) a small price rise
up·tight (ʌ́ptáit) *adj.* (*pop.*) not relaxed, showing nervous tension || (*pop.*) rigidly conservative, *uptight about the race problem*
up·time (ʌ́ptaim) *n.* time in which equipment is in operation *Cf* DOWNTIME
up-to-date (ʌ́ptədéit) *adj.* including all information available up to the present moment||(of a person) informed about current events || currently fashionable || dealt with up to the present, *all my correspondence is up-to-date* || (of a person) having left nothing undone, *he is up-to-date as regards his cataloguing*
up-to-the-min·ute (ʌ́ptuːðəmínit) *adj.* (*pop.*) including or taking into account the latest information, *an up-to-the-minute weather report* || in the very latest style
up·town (ʌ́ptáun) **1.** *adv.* in or toward the upper residential area of a city, esp. that removed from the main business section **2.** *adj.* belonging to, or situated in, this area **3.** *n.* this area
up·turn 1. (ʌptə́ːrn) *v.t.* to turn over, *to upturn a boat* || to direct upward, *upturned eyes* **2.** (ʌ́ptəːrn) *n.* an upward trend
up·val·ue (ʌ́pvæljuː) *v.* to revalue upward — **upvaluation** *n. Cf* DEVALUE
up·ward (ʌ́pwərd) **1.** *adv.* to or toward a higher position || toward the head, *from the waist upward* || toward a higher rank, degree, price etc. || toward a higher or better condition || turned toward the sky, *palms upward* || indefinitely more, *50 francs and upward* || toward or into later life, *from boyhood upward* || toward the top of the paper, *a stroke made with the pen traveling upward* **upward** (or **upwards**) **of** more than || rather less than **2.** *adj.* directed or moving toward or situated in a higher position || showing improvement, *an upward trend* [O.E. *upweard*]
upward mobility 1. the condition in which persons of lower economic and social status may rise to higher levels **2.** that movement upward —**upwardly mobile** *adj. ant.* downward mobility
up·wards (ʌ́pwərdz) *adv.* upward
up·well·ing (ʌ́pweliŋ) *n.* (*biol.*) movement of nutrient life from the bottom of the sea toward the surface
Ur (əːr, uər) an ancient city of Chaldaea in Babylonia, the original home of Abraham. It had developed a flourishing civilization by c. 3500 B.C., and had extended its power over Sumer, Akkad, Elam and N. Mesopotamia by the 2nd millennium B.C. It was destroyed (c. 2009 B.C.) by the Elamites and Amorites, although its ziggurat remained
Ur- (*prefix*) meaning original; original form, e.g., Ur-text, Ur-instrument, Ur-racialism
U·ra·bá, Gulf of (uːrɑbɑ́) a bay on the northwest coast of Colombia, the inner section of the Gulf of Darien
uraemia *UREMIA
u·rae·us (juəríːəs) *pl.* **u·rae·i** (juəríːai) *n.* a representation of the sacred asp on the headdress of ancient Egyptian divinities and rulers, symbolizing supreme power [Mod. L. fr. Gk *ouraios,* trans. of Egyptian word for 'cobra']
U·ral (júərəl) a river (1,580 miles long) in the R.S.F.S.R. and Kazakhstan, U.S.S.R., flowing from the S. Urals to the Caspian, navigable by steamer to Orenburg: sturgeon fisheries
U·ral-Al·ta·ic (júərəlæltéiik) **1.** *adj.* pertaining to the Ural and Altai mountain regions || belonging to a large group of languages of N. Europe and Asia, including the Uralic and Altaic families || of the people speaking these languages **2.** *n.* this group of languages
U·ra·li·an (juəréiliːən) *adj.* Uralic
U·ral·ic (jurǽlik) **1.** *adj.* of a family of languages, with two main subfamilies: Finno-Ugric, which includes Hungarian, Finnish and a number of languages spoken by small groups in Russia, and Samoyed, spoken by less than 20,000 people, mostly nomads in the N.W. Russian tundra **2.** *n.* this family of languages
U·rals (júərəlz) a chain of mountains (highest peak 6,184 ft) in the U.S.S.R., running from the Arctic Ocean nearly to the Aral Sea, generally considered to form the boundary between Europe and Asia. The central area, rich in minerals (coal, oil, iron ore, manganese, platinum, nickel, gold etc.), has become a leading industrial center: iron and steel, other metal prod-

CONCISE PRONUNCIATION KEY: **(a)** æ, *cat*; ɑ, *car*; ɔ *fawn*; ei, *snake*. **(e)** e, *hen*; iː, *sheep*; iə, *deer*; εə, *bear*. **(i)** i, *fish*; ai, *tiger*; əː, *bird*. **(o)** o, *ox*; au, *cow*; ou, *goat*; u, *poor*; ɔi, *royal*. **(u)** ʌ, *duck*; u, *bull*; uː, *goose*; ə, *bacillus*; juː, *cube*. x, *loch*; θ, *think*; ð, *bother*; z, *Zen*; ʒ, *corsage*; dʒ, *savage*; ŋ, *orangutang*; j, *yak*; ʃ, *fish*; tʃ, *fetch*; 'l, *rabble*; 'n, *redden*. Complete pronunciation key appears inside front cover.

ucts, nitrates, heavy machinery. Chief city: Magnitogorsk

u·ra·nal·y·sis (jʊərənǽlisis) *n.* urinalysis

U·ra·ni·a (juəréini:ə) the Muse of astronomy ‖ an epithet of Aphrodite

u·ran·ic (juərǽnik) *adj.* of, relating to or containing uranium, esp. in its higher valence

u·ran·i·nite (juərǽnənait) *n.* a mineral, UO_2, consisting largely of an oxide of uranium, and containing thorium, certain rare-earth metals and lead. When heated it often yields a gas consisting chiefly of helium (*PITCHBLENDE)

u·ra·ni·um (juəréini:əm) *n.* a radioactive white metallic element of the chromium group (symbol U, at. no. 92, at. mass 238.03), the heaviest of the elements found in nature, occurring in combination in pitchblende and certain other minerals. Natural uranium consists of the isotopes U238 (which can be converted into plutonium) 99.28%, U235 0.71%, and U234 in a minute amount. U235 and plutonium are used as a source of atomic energy [Mod. L. fr. *Uranus*, the planet]

uranium dioxide (*chem.*) toxic, flammable, radioactive crystals derived from uranium trioxide by heating in ceramic glazing and packing nuclear fuel rods *symbol* UO_2

uranium trioxide [UO_3] (*chem.*) an orange-colored radioactive compound used in ceramics, pigments, and in the uranium refining process, used for coloring ceramics *syn.* orange oxide, uranium oxide

u·ra·nous (júərənəs) *adj.* of, relating to, or containing uranium, esp. in its tower valence

U·ra·nus (júərənəs, juəréinəs) (*Rom. mythol.*) the god of the heavens, father of Saturn ‖ the seventh planet from the sun (mean orbital diameter=1.783 billion miles) and the third largest in the solar system (mass approx. 14.63 times that of Earth), having a linear diameter of 32,320 miles. Uranus revolves around the sun with a sidereal period of 84 earth years and rotates on its own axis with a period of 10.1 hrs. Its physical condition and atmosphere resemble that of Jupiter, Saturn and Neptune. It has five known satellites. Voyager 2 spacecraft visited Uranus in Jan. 1986

u·ra·ra·te (ju:rɑrɑtei) *n.* (*judo*) a rear throw

urb (ə:rb) *n.* an urban area

Ur·bain (yrbɛ̃), Georges (1872-1938), French chemist known for his studies of rare earths

ur·ban (ə́:rbən) *adj.* of, relating to, belonging to or characteristic of a city or town or of people living in a city or town (opp. RURAL) [fr. L. *urbanus*, of the city]

ur·bane (ə:rbéin) *adj.* having the sophisticated manners or polish associated with life in urban society [F. *urbain*]

urban enterprise zones program of tax incentives for small businesses to locate in rundown areas and so provide local employment, proposed in 1980 by Congressman Jack Kemp and Robert Garcia

urban guerrilla a revolutionary who conducts guerrilla tactics in a metropolitan area

Ur·ban II (ə́:rbən) (c. 1042-99), pope (1088-99). He proclaimed the 1st Crusade

ur·ban·i·ty (ə:rbǽniti:) *pl.* **ur·ban·i·ties** *n.* the quality of being urbane ‖ polished manners ‖ (*pl.*) sophisticated remarks [F. *urbanité*]

ur·ban·i·za·tion (ə̜:rbənizéiʃən) *n.* an urbanizing or being urbanized

ur·ban·ize (ə́:rbənaiz) *pres. part.* **ur·ban·iz·ing** *past* and *past part.* **ur·ban·ized** *v.t.* to render (a rural area) more urban by adding features characteristic of city life

ur·ban·oid (ə́:rbənɔid) *adj.* similar to a city

ur·ban·ol·o·gy (ə:rbənɒ́lədʒi:) *n.* the study of cities and their social and economic problems —**urbanologist** *n.*

urban renewal 1. a program to replace city slums with habitable for usable buildings **2.** rehabilitation (and rebuilding) of a decaying urban area with or without government aid

urban sprawl the erratic growth of a city

Urban VI (Bartolomeo Prignano, 1318-89), pope (1378-89). His election provoked the Great Schism

Ur·bi·no (u:rbí:nɔ) an agricultural market (pop. 16,296) in the N. Marches, Italy: ducal palace (mainly 15th c.), Renaissance churches. University (1564)

ur·ce·o·late (ə́:rsi:əlit, ə́:rsi:əleit) *adj.* (*bot.*) urn-shaped [fr. Mod. L. *urceolatus* fr. *urceolus* dim. of *urceus*, pitcher]

ur·chin (ə́:rtʃin) *n.* a mischievous young boy ‖ a sea urchin [var. of older *hurcheon* fr. O.N.F. *herichon*, a hedgehog]

Ur·du (úərdu:, ə́:rdu:) *n.* an Indic language of India and the official literary language of Pakistan. It is closely related to Hindi but is usually written in Persian script and shows a strong Persian influence [Hind. *urdū*=camp, fr. Turki]

-ure *sufix* indicating act, process or result, as in 'exposure', or function or office, as in 'prefecture' [fr. F. *-ure* and L. *-ura*]

u·re·a (jurí:ə, júəri:ə) *n.* a soluble crystalline compound, $CO(NH_2)_2$, formed in the body of man and other mammals by the decomposition of protein. It is passed into the urine by the kidneys. Urea is also present in small quantities in blood, perspiration and other body fluids. Synthesized urea is used in fertilizers etc. [Mod. L. fr. F. *urée* fr. Gk]

urea-formaldehyde resin a thermosetting resin produced by condensing urea with formaldehyde and used in plastics, adhesives and finishes

u·re·di·o·spore (jurí:di:əspɔ̜r, jurí:di:əspour) *n.* (*bot.*) one of the reddish summer spores borne on the sporophore of rust fungi [alt. fr. UREDOSPORE]

u·re·do·spore (jurí:dəspɔ̜r, jurí:dəspour) *n.* a urediospore [fr. L. *uredo*, blight+SPORE]

u·re·mi·a, u·rae·mi·a (juərí:mi:ə) *n.* a serious toxic condition caused by an accumulation in the blood of waste products normally eliminated in the urine. It is characterized by violent headache, vomiting and, in its acute form, by convulsions and coma [Mod. L.]

u·re·o·tel·ic (jʊ:ri:ətélik) or **u·re·o·co·tel·ic** *adj.* of the excretion of urea containing nitrogen, e.g., in mammals —**ureotelism** *n.*

u·re·ter (jurí:tər) *n.* one of the paired ducts which convey urine from the kidneys to the bladder in man or other mammals or from the cloaca in lower vertebrates [Med. L. fr. Gk]

u·re·thra (jurí:θrə) *pl.* **u·re·thras, u·re·thrae** (juərí:θri:) *n.* the canal which in most mammals discharges urine from the bladder, and in the male serves also as the genital duct **u·ré·thral** *adj.* [L.L. fr. Gk]

U·rey (júəri:), Harold Clayton (1893-1981), American chemist. He is known for his work on the various methods of separating uranium isotopes. Nobel prize (1934)

Ur·fa (uərfú) (*anc.* Edessa) a commercial center (pop. 147,488) in S. Turkey. The rise of its theological school (4th-5th cc.), refuting the heresies of Manes and Arius, made it a religious center in the Byzantine Empire. Under Arab rule from 639, it was occupied by the Crusaders from 1098 to 1144 when it fell to the Turks

Ur·fé (yrfei), Honoré d', marquis de Valbromey, comte de Châteauneuf (1567-1625), French author of the pastoral romance 'l'Astrée' (1607-19), which influenced French taste until the mid-17th c.

Ur·ga (ú:rgə) *ULAN BATOR

urge (ə:rdʒ) **1.** *v. pres. part.* **urg·ing** *past* and *past part.* **urged** *v.t.* to compel to go in a specified direction ‖ to attempt earnestly to persuade or encourage ‖ to bring (a need) to notice or to advocate (an action) in a persistent way, *to urge reform* ‖ to force to greater speed ‖ *v.i.* to make earnest recommendations, entreaties etc. **2.** *n.* the act or process of urging ‖ a strong, instinctive desire, *an urge to travel* [fr. L. *urgere*, to press, drive]

ur·gen·cy (ə́:rdʒənsi:) *pl.* **ur·gen·cies** *n.* the state or quality of being urgent

ur·gent (ə́:rdʒənt) *adj.* requiring immediate attention, of pressing importance importunate, *urgent entreaties* [F.]

U·ri (úəri:) a German-speaking, mainly Catholic canton (area 415 sq. miles, pop. 33,883) in central Switzerland. With Schwyz and Unterwalden it formed the 13th-c. league which was the nucleus of the Swiss Confederation

U·ri·bu·ru (ʊ:ri:bú:ru:), José Evaristo (1831-1914), Argentinian politician and president of the Republic (1895-8), and interim president (1903)

Uriburu, José Félix (1868-1933), Argentinian general and provisional president of the Republic (1930-2), after leading a military coup d'état against President Hipólito Yrigoyen. His administration (dominated mainly by the rich and conservative classes) ruled by decree

u·ric (júərik) *adj.* of or relating to urine, occurring in or derived from urine [F. *urique*]

uric acid a white, odorless, tasteless, nearly insoluble, dibasic acid, $C_5H_4N_4O_3$. It is found in small quantities in the urine of man and other mammals and is the chief constituent in the excrement of birds, reptiles and invertebrates

u·ri·nal (júərin'l) *n.* a fixture into which men or boys urinate ‖ a building, room or enclosure containing one or more of these ‖ a receptacle into which a bedridden male can pass urine [O.F.]

u·ri·nal·y·sis (jʊərinǽlisis) *pl* **u·ri·nal·y·ses** (jʊərinǽlisi:z) *n.* a chemical analysis of the urine [Mod. L.]

u·ri·nar·y (júərinęri:) **1.** *adj.* of or relating to urine ‖ of or relating to, or occurring in, the organs concerned with the formation and discharge of urine **2.** *pl.* **u·ri·nar·ies** *n.* a urinal (fixture or building) [fr. L. *urina*, urine]

urinary system a system in man and most mammals consisting essentially of the kidneys, ureters, bladder and urethra

u·ri·nate (júərineit) *pres. part.* **u·ri·nat·ing** *past* and *past part.* **u·ri·nat·ed** *v.i.* to discharge urine [fr. M.L. *urinare (urinatus)*]

u·ri·na·tion (jʊərinéiʃən) *n.* the act or process of urinating

u·rine (júərin) *n.* in mammals, a fluid formed in the kidneys and excreted through the urinary organs [O.F.]

u·ri·nif·er·ous (jʊəriníf ərəs) *adj.* (*anat.*) conveying urine

u·ri·nous (júərinəs) *adj.* of, pertaining to, resembling or containing urine

Uris (júərəs), Leon (1924), U.S. novelist and screenwriter. He achieved fame with his massive adventure novels that placed fictional protagonists in semifactual historical contexts such as the founding of the state of Israel ('Exodus,' 1959; film, 1961), the Berlin airlift ('Armaggedon,' 1964), the Cuban missile crisis ('Topaz,' 1967; film, 1969) and the Easter Rising in Ireland ('Trinity,' 1976). Earlier novels included 'Battle Cry' (1953) and 'Mila 18' (1960). He has also written screenplays, such as 'Gunfight at the OK Corral' (1957)

Ur·mi·a (úərmi:ə) *REZAYEH

urn (ə:rn) *n.* a closed metal vessel fitted with a tap and sometimes equipped with a heating device, used for making and dispensing a large supply of tea, coffee etc. ‖ a vase or jar with a pedestal, esp. as used in ancient times for preserving the ashes of the dead after cremation [fr. L. *urna*]

uro- (júərou) *combining form* urine, urination [fr. Gk *ouron*, urine]

uro- *combining form* tail [fr. Gk *oura*, tail]

u·ro·chord (júərəkɔ̜rd) *n.* (*zool.*) the notochord of larval ascidians and some adult tunicates

u·ro·gen·i·tal (jʊəroudʒénit'l) *adj.* relating to the urinary and genital organs

u·ro·ki·nase (ju:roukáineis) *n.* (*biochem.*) kidney-produced enzyme that increases fibrinolytic activity and is used to disintegrate blood clots

u·ro·log·ic (juərəlɒ́dʒik) *adj.* urological

u·ro·log·i·cal (jʊərəlɒ́dʒik'l) *adj.* of or relating to urology

u·rol·o·gist (juərɒ́lədʒist) *n.* a specialist in urology

u·rol·o·gy (juərɒ́lədʒi:) *n.* a branch of medicine dealing with the urogenital tract in the male and the urinary tract of the female

u·ro·pod (júərəpɒd) *n.* any of the abdominal appendages of a crustacean, esp. either of the flat appendages of the last abdominal segment of the lobster [fr. URO-+Gk *pous (podos)*, a foot]

u·ro·pyg·i·al (jʊərəpídʒi:əl) *adj.* of or relating to the uropygium

u·ro·pyg·i·um (jʊərəpídʒi:əm) *n.* that part of the termination of a bird's body that supports the tail feathers [M.L. fr. Gk]

Ur·quhart (ə́:rkərt), Sir Thomas (1611-60), Scottish translator of three books of Rabelais (1653, 1693)

Ur·qui·za (u:rkí:sɑ), Justo José de (1801-70), Argentinian general and caudillo, and victor over Rosas at Monte Caseros (1852). He served (1852-4) as director of the confederation and (1854-60) as president. During the civil war which followed his forces were defeated (1861) by Mitre at Pavón. While governor of Entre Ríos he was assassinated

Ur·sa Ma·jor (ə́:rsəméidʒər) the most conspicuous constellation of the northern hemisphere. It contains the seven bright stars called the Big Dipper

Ur·sa Mi·nor (ə́:rsəmáinər) the northern constellation which contains the polestar

ur·sine (ə́:rsain) *adj.* of, relating to or characteristic of a bear ‖ resembling a bear [fr. L. *ursinus*]

Ur·su·la (ə́:rsulə, ə́:rsjulə), St (c. 4th c.), British princess martyred by the Huns at Cologne, together with other virgins numbering, according to medieval legend, 11,000. Feast: Oct. 21

Ur·su·line (ə́:rsulain, ə́:rsjulain, ə́:rsulin, ə́:rsjulin) *n.* a member of a teaching and nursing order of nuns, founded 1535 at Brescia [after St URSULA]

ur·ti·car·i·a (ə̧:rtikέəri:ə) *n.* hives [Mod. L. fr. *urtica*, a nettle]

ur·ti·ca·ri·a·gen·ic (ə:rtikεəri:ɑdʒénik) *adj.* (*med.*) causing a temporary nettle rash, welts, or hives on the skin —**urtica** *n.* a wheal on the skin —**urticant** *n.* a substance causing a skin wheal —**urticaria** *n.* the allergic disorder —**urticate** *v.*

U·ru·guay (júərugwai, u:ru:gwái) a republic (area 72,172 sq. miles, pop. 2,967,000) on the southeast coast of South America. Capital: Montevideo. People: mostly of European stock, some mestizos. Language: Spanish. Religion: mainly Roman Catholic. The land is 66% pasture and grazing, 12% cultivated, and 3% forest. It is mainly a rolling, grassland plain, crossed by two chains of hills, and rising to tablelands (2,000 ft) on the Brazilian border. Average temperatures (F.) in Montevideo: Jan. 72°, July 50°. Rainfall: 38 ins along the Río de la Plata, 50 ins in the north. Livestock: sheep, cattle, horses, hogs. Agricultural products: wheat, rice, other cereals, linseed, sunflower seed, peanuts, cotton, sugar beets, sugarcane, fruit, wine. Mineral resources: gold, copper. Manufactures and industries: meat packing, oil refining, cement, steel, aluminum, textiles, chemicals, engineering, wool processing, hydroelectricity. Exports: wool, meat, leather and hides, combed wool, wheat flour, linseed and linseed oil. Imports: machinery, vehicles, fuels and oil, lumber, raw cotton. University at Montevideo (1949). Monetary unit: peso (100 centésimos). HISTORY. Uruguay was inhabited by Indian tribes when the Río de la Plata was explored (1516) by a Spanish expedition. Settlements were established by the Spanish (1624) and the Portuguese (1680). The Spanish drove the Portuguese out (18th c.). After a military revolt (1810-20) led by Artigas against Spanish rule, the Portuguese annexed Uruguay to Brazil (1820) but it again revolted (1825) and joined Argentina in war against Brazil. After British intervention, Uruguay was recognized as an independent republic (1828). It was weakened by civil war (1836-52), sporadic rebellions and war against Paraguay (1865-70). Great economic progress was made in the early 20th c. President Batlle y Ordóñez introduced (1903-7, 1911-15) a New Deal of radical social reform and dominated Uruguayan politics until his death in 1929. The vacuum he left, and the Depression of the early 1930s, allowed Gabriel Terra to establish (1933-8) a dictatorship. Despite fissions, Batlle's Colorado party retained power until it was ousted in the elections of 1958 by the opposition Blanco (Nationalist) party. During that time Uruguay developed its welfare state, joined (Feb. 15, 1945) the Allies in the 2nd world war, and became (1945) a member of the U.N. The presidency was replaced (1951) by a succession of Swiss-style National Councils, composed of six members drawn from the majority party and three from the minority, and operating by majority vote. Four members of the majority party took turns as the nation's nominal president. After the inauguration (1965) of Washington Beltrán, the Blanco party leader, inflation was such (38% in 1965) that a referendum was held in the 1966 elections. The executive council was scrapped and Uruguay, in a new constitution, reverted to government by a single chief executive. Gen. Oscar Gestido was elected president. On his death (1967), he was succeeded by Vice-President Jorge Pacheco Areco. Growing inflation (135% in 1967) fanned economic and political discontent, symbolized in the activities of the Tupamaros, who engage in daring, well planned robbery and kidnapping which earn popular sympathy by their exposure of corruption. Despite this, Uruguay's democratic stability and noninvolvement in Latin American rivalries have made it the natural choice of locale for several Western Hemisphere diplomatic conferences. At Punta del Este the Alliance for Progress was launched (1961), and Montevideo became (1961) the headquarters of the Latin American Free Trade Association (LAFTA). Strikes and urban terrorism disrupted political life in the mid-1960s, and between 1973-6 elected government officials were ousted by the military. Civil rights violations became widespread and thousands of political dissenters were jailed. Following elections in 1984, Julio Sanguinetti took office as president

Uruguay a river (980 miles long, navigable most of its length) flowing from S.E. Brazil to the Río de la Plata, forming the borders of S. Brazil and Uruguay with Argentina

U·rum·chi (u:rú:mtʃi:) (*Chin.* Tihwa) the walled capital (pop. 275,000) of Sinkiang-Uighur, W. China, an oasis trading center: iron and steel, textiles, chemical industries

u·rus (júərəs) *n. Bos primigenus*, fam. *Bovidae*, an extinct wild ox thought to be the ancestor of domestic cattle [L.]

U.S., US *UNITED STATES OF AMERICA

us (ʌs) *pron., objective case of* WE, *send it to us, he gave us a lecture* [O.E. *ūs*]

U.S.A., USA *UNITED STATES OF AMERICA

us·a·bil·i·ty (jų:zəbiliti:) *n.* the quality or state of being usable

us·a·ble, use·a·ble (jú:zəb'l) *adj.* fit to be used

U.S.A.F. United States Air Force

us·age (jú:sidʒ, jú:zidʒ) *n.* the way in which someone or something is used or treated, or an instance of this ‖ long established use or custom ‖ the way of using language in speech or writing, or an instance of this, *a usage borrowed from the french* [O.F.]

us·ance (jú:zəns) *n.* (*commerce*) the time allowed (not counting a period of grace) for payment of bills of exchange [O.F.]

use (ju:z) *pres. part.* **us·ing** *past* and *past part.* **used** *v.t.* to make (something) perform its function for a specified or understood end, *they used bulldozers to clear the forest, use your intelligence* ‖ to deal with, *he considers himself unfairly used* ‖ (often with 'up') to consume completely, *they use half a ton of coal every week* ‖ (*old-fash.*) to smoke or chew (tobacco) or to take (narcotics) habitually ‖ to exploit for some end, esp. a selfish one ‖ (in the passive (ju:st) with 'to') to accustom, *he was used to her way of working* ‖ *v.i.* (in the past (ju:st) with an infinitive) to be accustomed, *I used to see a lot of him* [O.F. *user*]

use (ju:s) *n.* the act, state or custom of using or being used ‖ the power to use, *to lose the use of an eye* ‖ a way of using, *to put to an unaccustomed use* ‖ usefulness, *what use is there in attempting to do it?* ‖ the right, permission or privilege to use, *the firm gave us the use of its name* ‖ the opportunity to use ‖ function, the purpose for which something is used ‖ custom, habit, practice ‖ (*law*) the enjoyment of the benefits deriving from property either by the occupier or by someone to whom it is delegated under a trust ‖ (*eccles.*) a body of ritual, *the Sarum use* **in use** being used **to have no use for** to have no need of ‖ to dislike strongly ‖ to be impatient with **to make use of** to use ‖ to turn to advantage **to put to use** to find a use for **to turn** (or **put**) **to good use** to do something useful with (something or someone) [O.F. *us*]

useable *USABLE

used (ju:zd) *adj.* secondhand, *a used-car market* **used up** fully consumed

use·ful (jú:sfəl) *adj.* likely to be of some practical value, *useful advice*

use·less (jú:slis) *adj.* of no practical value ‖ (of a person) rendering no service whatsoever

us·er (jú:zər) *n.* (*law*) the enjoyment of a right of use, esp. a presumptive right arising from long-continued use [prob. fr. F. *user*, to use]

Usher *USSHER

ush·er (ʌ́ʃər) **1.** *n.* someone who escorts people to seats, e.g. in a church, theater etc. ‖ (esp. *Br.*) an official whose function is to walk ahead of a person or persons of rank ‖ (*Br. hist.*) an assistant teacher in a private school **2.** *v.t.* to conduct to a seat or into someone's presence ‖ *v.i.* to act as an usher **to usher in** to mark the beginning of, *a series of reforms ushered in the new regime* **ush·er·ette** (ʌʃərét) *n.* a woman employed to show people to seats in a cinema, theater etc. [A.F. *usser*, O.F. *ussier, uissier* var. of *huissier*]

Us·hua·ia (u:swájɑ) an Argentine town (pop. 10,998) at the southern tip of Tierra del Fuego, the most southerly agglomeration in the world

Üs·küb (uskúb) *SKOPJE

Us·ku·dar (úsku:dɑr) Turkish name for Scutari (*ISTANBUL)

Us·pa·lla·ta Pass (ų:spɑjátɑ) (or La Cumbre) a pass in the Andes Mtns between Mendoza, Argentina, and Santiago, Chile

Ussh·er, Ush·er (ʌ́ʃər), James (1581-1656), Irish bishop and scholar. His 'Annales Veteris et Novi Testamenti' (1650-4), ascribing the creation of the world to 4004 B.C., was for long the basis of biblical chronology

U.S.S.R. *UNION OF SOVIET SOCIALIST REPUBLICS

Us·turt Plateau (ú:sturt) a rocky desert (area 92,000 sq. miles) in the southern R.S.F.S.R. and Uzbekistan, U.S.S.R., between the Caspian and Aral Seas

u·su·al (jú:ʒu:əl, jú:ʒwəl) *adj.* normal in practice **as usual** in his or its habitual way, *as usual he overate* **ú·su·al·ly** *adv.* on most occasions, customarily [O.F. or fr. L. *usualis*]

u·su·fruct (jú:sufrʌkt, jú:zufrʌkt) *n.* (*law*) the right to use and enjoy the profits of another person's property, without diminishing, impairing or wasting the substance of it [fr. L.L. *usufructus* fr. *usus*, use + *fructus*, fruit]

u·su·fruc·tu·ar·y (jų:zufrʌ́ktʃu:ęri:) **1.** *adj.* of or relating to the right of usufruct **2.** *pl.* **u·su·fruc·tu·ar·ies** *n.* someone who enjoys the right of usufruct [fr. L.L. *usufructuarius*]

U·sum·bu·ra (ų:sumbúra) *BUJUMBURA

u·su·rer (jú:ʒərər) *n.* someone who lends money at interest, esp. at exorbitant interest [A.F.]

u·su·ri·ous (ju:ʒúəri:əs) *adj.* practicing usury involving usury, *usurious transactions*

u·surp (ju:sə́:rp, ju:zə́:rp) *v.t.* to seize and hold (a position, function, prerogative) rightly belonging to another ‖ *v.i.* (with 'on' or 'upon') to encroach upon a right, privilege, office etc. **u·sur·pá·tion** *n.* [O.F. *usurper*]

u·su·ry (jú:zəri:) *n.* the practice of lending money at interest, esp. at an exorbitant or illegal rate of interest [A.F. *usurie* fr. M.L. *usuria*]

U·tah (jú:tɔ, jú:tɑ) (*abbr.* Ut.) a state (area 84,916 sq. miles, pop. 1,554,000) of the western U.S.A. in the Great Basin and the Rocky Mtns. Capital: Salt Lake City. Agriculture: beef cattle, dairy and poultry products, sheep, wheat and fodder crops (dependent upon irrigation). Resources: copper, gold, oil, coal, iron ore, uranium, lead, silver, zinc and salt. Industries: metal and oil refining, food processing. State university (1850) at Salt Lake City. Utah was settled by Mormons (1847) and was ceded (1848) by Mexico to the U.S.A. After the Mormons, under their president Wilford Woodruff (1807-98), agreed (1890) to abandon polygamy, Utah was admitted (1896) into the Union as the 45th state

U·ta·ma·ro (u:tɑmɑrɔ) (1753-1806), Japanese master of the colored woodcut. The freshness of his vision, the precision yet freedom of his compositional devices and his unconventionality of theme had some influence on French Impressionist painting

Ute (ju:t, jú:ti) *pl.* **Ute, Utes** *n.* a group of Shoshonean peoples of Colorado, Utah and New Mexico ‖ a member of any of these peoples ‖ their language

u·ten·sil (ju:ténsəl) *n.* any of various vessels or devices used in a kitchen, e.g. a cooking pot or eggbeater ‖ any of various tools used by artisans, farmers etc. ‖ a vessel, ornament etc. used in church services [O.F. *utensile*]

u·ter·ine (jú:tərain, jú:tərin) *adj.* of, relating to or situated in the uterus ‖ having the same mother but a different father, *uterine brothers* [O.F. *uterin, uterine* or fr. L.L. *uterinus*]

u·ter·us (jú:tərəs) *pl.* **u·ter·i** (jú:tərai) *n.* the organ in female mammals in which the embryo (fetus) develops and is nourished before birth ‖ an enlarged portion of the oviduct of various vertebrate and invertebrate animals, e.g. monotremes, modified into a place where the young or eggs can develop [L.]

U Thant *THANT, U

U·ther Pen·drag·on (jú:θərpendrǽgən) king of the Britons in the Arthurian legend, father of King Arthur

U·ti·ca (jú:tikə) a manufacturing city and port of entry (pop. 75,632) in central New York, within an agricultural and dairying region. Manufactures: textiles, firearms, machinery, beds. Utica college (1946)

u·tile (jú:t'l) *adj.* practical, useful (as opposed to purely ornamental or aesthetic) [F.]

u·til·i·tar·i·an (ju:tįlitέəri:ən) **1.** *adj.* of or relating to utility ‖ stressing utility (as opposed to beauty) ‖ of or relating to utilitarianism ‖ advocating utilitarianism **2.** *n.* a supporter of the doctrine of utilitarianism

u·til·i·tar·i·an·ism (ju:tįlitέəri:ənįzəm) *n.* the

CONCISE PRONUNCIATION KEY: **(a)** æ, *cat*; ɑ, *car*; ɔ *fawn*; ei, *snake*. **(e)** e, *hen*; i:, *sheep*; iə, *deer*; εə, *bear*. **(i)** i, *fish*; ai, *tiger*; ə:, *bird*. **(o)** o, *ox*; au, *cow*; ou, *goat*; u, *poor*; ɔi, *royal*. **(u)** ʌ, *duck*; u, *bull*; u:, *goose*; ə, *bacillus*; ju:, *cube*. x, *loch*; θ, *think*; ð, *bother*; z, *Zen*; ʒ, *corsage*; dʒ, *savage*; ŋ, *orangutang*; j, *yak*; ʃ, *fish*; tʃ, *fetch*; 'l, *rabble*; 'n, *redden*. Complete pronunciation key appears inside front cover.

doctrine, expounded by Jeremy Bentham, that the moral and political rightness of an action is determined by its utility, defined as its contribution to the greatest good of the greatest number

u·til·i·ty (ju:tíliti:) *pl.* **u·til·i·ties** *n.* the quality or state of being useful ‖ (*econ.*) the ability to satisfy human wants ‖ a public utility ‖ a service provided by one of these ‖ (*pl.*) stock shares in public utility companies [O.F. *utilite*]

utility player (*sports*) a team member capable of playing several different positions

u·til·iz·a·ble (jú:t'l̩aizəb'l) *adj.* able to be utilized

u·ti·li·za·tion (ju:tilizéiʃən) *n.* a utilizing or being utilize'd

u·ti·lize (jú:t'laiz) *pres. part.* **u·ti·liz·ing** past and past part. **u·ti·lized** *v.t.* to make use of [fr. F. *utiliser*]

u·ti pos·si·de·tis (jú:taippsidí:tis) a principle of international law, widely applied in treaties in the Americas, whereby at the end of a war belligerents' territorial rights are determined according to the territory they occupy or control

ut·most (ʌtmoust) **1.** *adj.* of the greatest degree, *one's utmost efforts* ‖ situated at the most remote point **2.** *n.* the best of one's ability or power, *to do one's utmost* ‖ the highest attainable point or degree [O.E. *ūtemest,* double superl. of *ūt,* out]

U·to-Az·tec·an (ju:touǽztekən) *n.* an American Indian linguistic group of the western U.S.A., including the Shoshonean, Piman and Nahuatlan families ‖ a member of a people speaking a Uto-Aztecan language

u·to·pi·a (ju:tóupi:ə) *n.* any imaginary political and social system in which relationships between individuals and the State are perfectly adjusted **u·tó·pi·an 1.** *adj.* ideal but impractical **2.** *n.* someone who believes in the immediate perfectibility of human society by the application of some idealistic scheme **u·tó·pi·an·ism** *n.* [Mod. L. fr. Gk *ou,* not + *topos,* place (after 'Utopia' by Sir Thomas More (1516), describing an island in which such conditions existed)]

U·trecht (jú:trekt, jú:trext) a province (area 535 sq. miles, pop. 922,800) of the central Netherlands ‖ its capital (pop. 264,000). Industries:

metalwork, mechanical and chemical engineering, textiles, ceramics. Gothic cathedral (14th c.) and churches, moat, canals. University (1636)

Utrecht, Peace of a series of treaties (1713) concluding the War of the Spanish Succession. Philip V kept Spain and abandoned his claims to the French throne and Emperor Charles VI obtained Milan, Naples, Sardinia and the Spanish Netherlands. Britain gained Gibraltar, Minorca, Newfoundland and Acadia, as well as the monopoly of the slave trade with Spanish America. French expansion was halted, and Louis XIV recognized the Protestant succession in Britain

u·tri·cle (jú:trik'l) *n.* the pouchlike part of the labyrinth of the ear into which the semicircular canals open ‖ (*anar.*) any of several other pouchlike parts ‖ an air cell or bladder in some aquatic plants [fr. F. *utricule* or L. *utriculus*]

u·tric·u·lar (ju:tríkjulər) *adj.* of or relating to a utricle ‖ containing or resembling a utricle [fr. L. *utriculus,* small bag]

U·tril·lo (ytri:jou), Maurice (1883-1955), French painter. He is best known for his Paris street scenes

Ut·tar Pra·desh (ʊtərpradéʃ) a state (area 113,410 sq. miles, pop. 94,775,000) of India bordering Tibet and Nepal, consisting largely of the Ganges-Jumna basin. Capital: Lucknow. Largest town: Kanpur. Industries: intensive agriculture (rice, other cereals, cotton, sugarcane, pulses), textiles, chemicals, paper, food processing

ut·ter (ʌtər) *v.t.* to express vocally, esp. in speech ‖ to emit (sounds) as if speaking ‖ to fabricate and put into circulation (false coins etc.) [fr. M.Du. *uteren,* to speak, make known, drive away and fr. OUT]

utter *adj.* with no qualification whatsoever, *utter ruin* [O.E. *ūtera, ūttera* comp. *Ofūt,* out]

ut·ter·ance (ʌtərəns) *n.* the act, power or manner of expressing vocally ‖ something uttered ‖ (*rhet.*) power of speech, *to be robbed of utterance* **to give utterance to** to express verbally [fr. UTTER v.]

ut·ter·ly (ʌtərli:) *adv.* fully [fr. UTTER adj.]

ut·ter·most (ʌtərmoust) *adj.* and *n.* (used as an intensive) utmost

U-2 Incident an international incident (1960) precipitated when the Soviet Union shot down a

U.S. U-2 high-altitude intelligence plane. The U.N. Security Council refused to censure the U.S.A. The pilot was sentenced in the Soviet Union to ten years' imprisonment for espionage, but was exchanged (1962) for two Soviet Union spies who had been imprisoned in the U.S.A.

UUM-44A (*mil.*) *SUBMARINE ROCKET

u·ve·a (jú:vi:ə) *n.* (*anat.,* of the eye) the posterior pigmented layer of the iris ‖ (*anat.,* of the eye) the iris, choroid and ciliary body, taken collectively [M.L. fr. L. *uva,* a grape]

U·vi·con (jú:vəkɒn) *n.* a special television camera that includes an ultraviolet-sensitive cathode-ray tube, an electron accelerator, and other features

u·vu·la (jú:vjulə) *pl.* **u·vu·las, u·vu·lae** (jú:vjuli:) *n.* a fleshy conical body suspended from the soft palate over the back of the tongue [M.L. dim. of *uva,* a grape]

u·vu·lar (jú:vjulər) **1.** *adj.* of or pertaining to the uvula ‖ (*phon.*) pronounced with the aid of the uvula **2.** *n.* (*phon.*) a uvular sound [fr. Mod. L. *uvularis*]

Ux·mal (u:zmál) a town in Mexico, in N. Yucatán. Built in stone, c. 1000 A.D., it was an important center of Mayan civilization

ux·o·ri·ous (ʌksóri:əs, ʌksóuri:əs, ʌgzóri:əs, ʌgzóuri:əs) *adj.* excessively fond of one's wife ‖ showing such excessive fondness [fr. L. *uxorius*]

U·yu·ni, Sa·lar de (sɑlɑrðeu:jú:ni:) a salt marsh (90 miles long, 75 miles wide) in S.W. Bolivia, near the Chilean border

Uz·bek, Uz·beg (úzbek) *n.* a Turkic people of Turkestan ‖ a member of this people ‖ their Turkic language

Uz·bek·i·stan (úzbekistæn, úzbekistɑn) a constituent republic (area 173,546 sq. miles, pop. 15,391,000) of the U.S.S.R. in central Asia. Capital: Tashkent. It is a plateau, mainly desert in the west, rising to high mountains in the east. Agriculture: cereals on the highest plains, sheep breeding in the desert regions, with cotton (third largest world producer), fruit and silk dependent on intensive irrigation. Resources: coal, oil, copper, building materials. Industries: mining, oil refining, iron and steel, mineral fertilizers, cotton. Part of Turkestan, Uzbekistan was conquered by Russia (1865-76), and became a constituent republic in 1925

CONCISE PRONUNCIATION KEY: (a) æ, c*a*t; ɑ, c*a*r; ɔ f*aw*n; ei, sn*a*ke. **(e)** e, h*e*n; i:, sh*ee*p; iə, d*ee*r; ɛə, b*ea*r. **(i)** i, f*i*sh; ai, t*i*ger; ə:, b*i*rd. **(o)** o, *o*x; au, c*ow*; ou, g*oa*t; u, p*oo*r; ɔi, r*oy*al. **(u)** ʌ, d*u*ck; u, b*u*ll; u:, g*oo*se; ə, b*a*cillus; ju:, c*u*be. x, lo*ch*; θ, *th*ink; ð, bo*th*er; z, *Z*en; ʒ, corsa*g*e; dʒ, sava*g*e; ŋ, ora*ng*uta*ng*; j, *y*ak; ʃ, *f*ish; tʃ, fe*tch*; 'l, rabb*le*; 'n, redd*en*. Complete pronunciation key appears inside front cover.

				CLASSICAL GREEK	ETRUSCAN Early	ETRUSCAN Classical	EARLY LATIN	CLASSICAL LATIN
V				Y	Y	V	V	V
		ROMAN UNCIAL	ANGLO-IRISH MAJUSCULE	CAROLINE MINUSCULE	MODERN ITALIC		MODERN ROMAN	
		V	U	U	*v*		V	

A. C. SYLVESTER, CAMBRIDGE, ENGLAND

Development of the letter V, beginning with the classical Greek letter. Evolution of both the majuscule, or capital, letter V and the minuscule, or lowercase, letter v are shown.

V, v (viː) the 22nd letter of the English alphabet ‖ the roman numeral for 5

Va. Virginia

Vaal (vɑl) a river (700 miles long) rising in the High Veld, Transvaal, South Africa, and forming the Transvaal-Orange Free State border. It joins the Orange River near Kimberley. Its dams furnish vast irrigation systems

va·can·cy (véikənsi:) *pl.* **va·can·cies** *n.* the state of being vacant ‖ an empty place or space ‖ a room in a hotel etc. available for occupation ‖ a post in employment which is not occupied ‖ vacuity of mind [fr. M.L. *vacantia*]

va·cant (véikənt) *adj.* empty, not filled ‖ (of a post or seat etc.) unoccupied ‖ untenanted ‖ not mentally active ‖ showing empty-headedness, *a vacant grin* ‖ (*law*, of land) unused or unoccupied ‖ (*law*) having no claimant [O.F.]

vacant possession (*Br., law*) availability for immediate occupation

va·cate (veikéit, véikeit) *pres. part.* **va·cat·ing** *past* and *past part.* **va·cat·ed** *v.t.* to go away and leave unoccupied, *to vacate a house* ‖ to make vacant (a position or occupation) ‖ (*law*) to annul, to make void [fr. *vacare* (*vacatus*), to be empty]

va·ca·tion (veikéiʃən, vəkéiʃən) **1.** *n.* a holiday ‖ a fixed and regular period of holiday (esp. in courts of law and universities) ‖ the act of going away and leaving a place or position empty **on vacation** away from work, school etc. for a period of leisure **2.** *v.i.* to take a vacation **va·ca·tion·er, va·ca·tion·ist** *ns* a holidaymaker [O.F.]

vac·ci·nal (væksin'l) *adj.* of vaccine or vaccination

vac·ci·nate (væksineit) *pres. part.* **vac·ci·nat·ing** *past* and *past part.* **vac·ci·nat·ed** *v.t.* to inoculate with a vaccine **vac·ci·ná·tion** *n.* a vaccinating or the practice of vaccinating

vac·cine (væksiːn, væksíːn) **1.** *n.* a preparation consisting of the living viruses of cowpox, used in vaccination ‖ a preparation of microorganisms, either dead, or virulent and living, or attenuated and living, that are administered so as to produce (or increase) immunity to a particular disease **2.** *adj.* of or pertaining to vaccinia or vaccination [fr. L. *vaccinus* fr. *vacca*, a cow]

vac·cin·i·a (væksíniːə) *n.* (*med.*) cowpox (esp. when produced by inoculation) [Mod. L.]

vac·il·late (væsəleit) *pres. part.* **vac·il·lat·ing** *past* and *past part.* **vac·il·lat·ed** *v.i.* to change repeatedly from one opinion or intention to another ‖ to sway to and fro **vac·il·lá·tion** *n.* **vac·il·la·to·ry** (væsələtɔri:, væsələtóuri:) *adj.* [fr. L. *vacillare* (*vacillatus*), to waver]

va·cu·i·ty (vækjúːiti:) *pl.* **va·cu·i·ties** *n.* the state or quality of being vacuous ‖ something pointless [fr. L. *vacuitas*]

vac·u·o·late (vækjuːoleit) *adj.* vacuolated **vác·u·o·lat·ed** *adj.* containing vacuoles

vac·u·ole (vækjuːoul) *n.* (*biol.*) a minute cavity in cell protoplasm containing air, sap or partly digested food ‖ a small cavity in organic tissue [F.]

vac·u·ous (vækjuːəs) *adj.* having or showing a lack of understanding or intelligence or serious purpose ‖ emptied of content (e.g. of air or gas) [fr. L. *vacuus*, empty]

vac·u·um (vækjuːəm, vækjuːm) **1.** *pl.* **vac·u·ums, vac·u·a** (vækjuːə) *n.* a part of space in which no matter exists ‖ a space largely exhausted of air ‖ space containing air or gas at a pressure below that of the atmosphere ‖ (*pl.* **vacuums**) a void, *her departure left a vacuum* ‖ (*pl.* **vacuums**) a vacuum cleaner **2.** *v.t.* to clean with a vacuum cleaner [L. neut. of *vacuus*, empty]

—Aristotle insisted that a vacuum was an impossibility, using this argument to explain the cohesion of a solid, and this dogma persisted for 2,000 years. Galileo, Torricelli, Otto von Guericke, Pascal and Boyle showed that it was possible to create a close approximation to a vacuum, the only limitation being the vapor emitted by the container. The possibility of a perfect-vacuum in nature is now not excluded

vacuum bottle a Thermos

vacuum brake a continuous series of brakes applied to the wheels of a train etc. when a brake rod, held in position by a bellows exhausted of air, is released by admitting air to the bellows. The brakes are released when an air pump again exhausts the bellows

vacuum cleaner a machine which removes dirt and dust from carpets etc. by the suction produced by a motordriven air pump

vacuum flask (*Br.*) a Thermos

va·cu·um-packed (vækjuːəmpækt, vækjuːmpækt) *adj.* packed in a can, jar etc. from which most of the air has been removed before it was sealed

vacuum pump an air pump which exhausts the air from a container ‖ a pulsometer

vacuum tube an electron tube containing an almost perfect vacuum

va·de me·cum (véidiːmiːkəm, vɑ́diːmíːkəm) *n.* a handbook or manual [L.=go with me]

vag·a·bond (vǽgəbɒnd) **1.** *adj.* wandering, not settled in a fixed home ‖ characteristic of a wandering way of life **2.** *n.* a person who wanders around from place to place rather than settle down in one place or to one job ‖ a tramp **vag·a·bond·age** (vǽgəbɒndidʒ) *n.* [O.F. or fr. L. *vagabundus*]

va·gar·y (véigəri:, vəgɛ́əri:) *pl.* **va·gar·ies** *n.* an irrational idea, passing fancy ‖ an odd or irrational action [prob. fr. L. *vagari*, to wander]

V-agent (víːeidʒənt) *n.* a toxic chemical nerve gas, e.g., Vx, GB

va·gi·na (vədʒáinə) *pl.* **va·gi·nae** (vədʒáini:), **va·gi·nas** *n.* a sheath or sheathlike tube, esp. the canal leading from the uterus to the vulva in female mammals ‖ (*bot.*) the expanded sheathlike portion of a leaf base **vag·i·nal** (vədʒáin'l, vædʒín'l) *adj.* [L.=sheath]

vaginal ring (*med.*) intrauterine contraceptive device that releases hormones over a three-year period, approved for use in Western Europe

vag·i·nate (vædʒineit) *adj.* having or in the form of a sheath or vagina [fr. Mod. L. *vaginatus*]

va·gran·cy (véigrənsi:) *n.* vagabondage ‖ the offense of being a vagrant

va·grant (véigrənt) **1.** *adj.* wandering, esp. having no settled home ‖ living the life of a tramp ‖ random, stray, *vagrant thoughts* ‖ of or characteristic of a vagrant ‖ (of plants) growing in a straggly way **2.** *n.* someone who has no settled home, a vagabond ‖ (*law*) a tramp, beggar, prostitute etc. whose way of life makes him or her liable to arrest [M.E. *vagraunt, vagaraunt* perh. fr. A.F.]

vague (veig) *adj.* not clearly grasped in the mind, *vague ideas* ‖ not precise in expression, *vague language* ‖ not firmly determined, *vague plans* ‖ hazy, not clearly perceived, *a vague figure in the background* ‖ (of a person) not clearly formulating or expressing ideas [F.]

va·gus nerve (véigəs) (*anat.*) either one of the tenth pair of cranial nerves arising from the medulla

vain (vein) *adj.* thinking too highly of one's appearance, attainments etc. ‖ failing to produce the desired result, *a vain attempt to escape* ‖ empty, *vain boasts* **in vain** without success ‖ to no purpose **to take someone's name in vain** to speak about someone without proper respect [O.F.]

vain·glo·ri·ous (veinglóri:əs, veinglóuri:əs) *adj.* full of vainglory ‖ boastful

vain·glo·ry (veinglóri:, veinglóuri:) *n.* excessive show of vanity ‖ extreme conceit [fr. M.L. *vana gloria*]

vair (vɛər) *n.* (*hist.*) the fur of a squirrel used for lining and trimming clothes in the 13th and 14th cc. ‖ (*heraldry*) a fur represented by rows of small bell-shaped figures of two alternate tinctures, usually azure and argent [O.F. *vair, veir*]

Vai·she·shi·ka, Vai·se·si·ka (vaiʃéiʃikə, vaiʃeʃíːkə) *n.* a system of Hindu philosophy involving an atomic theory of cosmology, founded c. 500 B.C. [Skr.]

Vaish·na·va, Vais·na·va (váiʃnəvə) *n.* a worshipper of Vishnu **Váish·na·vism, Váis·na·vism** *ns*

Vais·ya (váisjə, váiʃə) *n.* a Hindu of the third of the four chief castes, comprising farmers and merchants (*BRAHMIN, *SUDRA, *KSHATRIYA) [Skr.=peasant]

Va·la·don (vælædɔ̃), Marie-Clémentine, called Suzanne (1867-1938), French painter, mother of Utrillo

Va·lais (vælei) a mainly French-speaking and Catholic canton (area 2,026 sq. miles, pop. 218,707) of S.W. Switzerland. Capital: Sion (pop. 16,000)

val·ance (vǽləns, véiləns) *n.* a length of curtain hung decoratively across the top of a window ‖ a length of cloth draped along the sides and bottom of a bed, or under a shelf etc. [prob. fr. O.F.]

Val·dai Hills (vɑldái) a range of hills (rising to 1,050 ft) between Moscow and Leningrad, U.S.S.R., forming the Volga-Dnieper watershed

Val-de-Marne (vældəmarn) a department (area 94 sq. miles, pop. 1,215,700) of N. central France, southeast of Paris (*ILE-DE-FRANCE). Chief town: Créteil (pop. 31,000)

Val·di·via (vɑldí:vjɑ), Pedro de (c. 1500-54), Spanish conquistador. At the head of 150 Spaniards he conquered Chile and founded Santiago (1541), Valdivia (1552) etc. He died at Tucapel in a battle with the Araucanian Indians under Lautaro

Valdivia the chief town (pop. 103,600) of S. Chile, founded in 1552

Val-d'Oise (vældwæz) a department (area 482 sq. miles, pop. 840,900) of N. central France, north of Paris (*ILE-DE-FRANCE). Chief town: Pontoise (pop. 14,000)

vale (veil) *n.* (*rhet.*, and in place names) valley [O.F. *val*]

val·e·dic·tion (vælidíkʃən) *n.* a farewell [fr. L. *valedicere (valedictus),* to say farewell]

val·e·dic·to·ri·an (vælidiktɔ́ri:ən, vælidiktóu-ri:ən) *n.* a student, usually the one with the highest marks, who delivers a valedictory

val·e·dic·to·ry (vælidíktəri:) **1.** *adj.* spoken or done as a valediction **2.** *pl.* **val·e·dic·to·ries** *n.* a parting speech, a farewell oration, esp. at graduation in high schools, universities etc. [fr. L. *valedicere (valedictus),* to say farewell]

va·lence (véiləns) *n.* the combining power of an element or radical, which may be defined as the number of atoms of hydrogen (or its equivalent) that one atom of the element or one radical will combine with or displace. The Latin prefixes (uni-, bi-, ter-, quadri- etc.) are preferred when indicating the number of valences exhibited and the Greek ones (mono-, di-, tri-, tetra- etc.) are preferred for the specific valence of an atom or radical (*OXIDATION STATE) [fr. L. *valentia,* vigor, capacity]

Va·len·cia (vɑlénsjɑ), Guillermo (1873-1943), Colombian poet, politician, orator and diplomat. He wrote 'Ritos' (1898) and 'Catay' (1928)

Valencia, Guillermo León (1909-71), Colombian politician and president (1962-6), son of the poet Guillermo Valencia

Va·len·ci·a (vəlénʃi:ə, vəlénsi:ə, vɑlénθi:ɑ) a region of S. Spain on the Mediterranean, forming Castellón, Valencia, and Alicante provinces. The coastal plain, much of it intensely irrigated, rises to mountains in the east. Agricultural products: citrus fruits, olives, vines, vegetables, rice, silk. Industries: textiles, food processing, chemicals, tourism. Historic capital: Valencia. Colonized by Greeks and Carthaginians before the Romans, it was conquered from the Moors (1238) by Aragon

Valencia a province (area 4,150 sq. miles, pop. 3,487,200) of E. Spain ‖ its capital (pop. 750,994), also the historic capital of the region of Valencia, a port. Industries: ceramics, food processing, automobile assembly, mechanical engineering, plastics, steel. Gothic cathedral (restored 18th c.), fortifications, public buildings (15th c.) and baroque churches. University (1500)

Valencia a city (pop. 455,000) in N. Venezuela, founded in 1555: textiles, food processing, tanning

Va·len·ci·a, Lake (vəlénʃi:ə, vɑlénsja) or Tacarigua, a lake (area 125 sq. miles) in N. Venezuela, southwest of Caracas

Va·len·ci·ennes (vælɑ̃sjen) *n.* a fine bobbin lace of wide net and very clear pattern, the net background and the pattern being made from the same threads [after *valenciennes,* a city in N. France]

va·len·cy (véilənsi:) *pl.* **va·len·cies** *n.*, (esp. *Br.*) valence [fr. L. *valentia,* vigor, capacity]

Va·lens (véilənz) (c. 328-78), Roman emperor (364-78). The younger brother of Valentinian I, he was appointed to rule the eastern part of the empire

Val·en·tine (vǽləntain), St, bishop of Terni in Umbria, martyred c. 273. Feast: Feb. 14

val·en·tine (vǽləntain) *n.* a sweetheart chosen on St Valentine's Day (Feb. 14), the day when birds were believed to begin mating ‖ a sentimental or satiric letter or greeting card sent to someone of the opposite sex on this day [O.F.]

Val·en·tin·i·an I (væləntíni:ən) (321-75), Roman emperor (364-75). He ruled the western part of the empire and appointed his brother Valens to rule the east

Valentinian II (c. 371-92), Roman emperor (375-92). He ruled jointly with his half brother Gratian

Valentinian III (419-55), Roman emperor (425-55). He was driven by the Vandals from Africa

Val·en·ti·no (væləntí:nou), Rudolph (Rodolpho d'Antonguolla, 1895-1926), U.S. movie star, the screen's first 'Latin lover'. His roles in 'The Four Horsemen of the Apocalypse', 'The Sheik', 'Blood and Sand', and 'Monsieur Beaucaire' made him the idol of millions of women

Valera *DE VALERA

Va·le·ri·an (vəlíəri:ən) (Publius Licinius Valerianus, c. 190–c. 260), Roman emperor (253-60). He left the government in the hands of his son Gallienus, while he led the army against the Goths and the Persians. He was captured (260) by the Persians, and died in captivity

va·le·ri·an (vəlíəri:ən) *n.* any species of *valeriana,* fam. *valerianaceae,* a genus of herbaceous plants with clusters of small, strong-smelling, pink or white flowers. The rhizomes and roots of *v. officinalis* yield a carminative and antispasmodic preparation [fr. O.F. *valeriane* or M.L. *valeriana*]

Va·le·ri·us Flac·cus (vəlíəri:əsflǽkəs), Gaius (*d.* c. 90 A.D.), Latin epic poet, author of the 'Argonautica'

Va·le·ri·us Max·i·mus (vəlíəri:əs mǽksəməs) (early 1st c. A.D.), Roman historian, author of an unreliable historical work in nine volumes dedicated to Tiberius

Va·lé·ry (væleiri:), Paul Ambroise (1871-1945), French poet and critic. He was strongly influenced by Mallarmé, and his poetry is in many ways a continuation of Mallarmé's work. It is extremely deliberate, though striving toward the status of magic or music, syntactically original, oblique, and calculatingly metaphorical. With Valéry art became so much a matter of deliberation that not surprisingly it became hard for him to write at all, and much of his art is 'about' the process of creating art. His poem 'le Cimetière marin' (1922) rises to a moment of anguished directness, and awareness of the quality of being alive, and of being dead. His criticism sums up a whole French tradition of writing about the nature of art, and the relationships between the art-object, the artist and the world of experience

val·et (vǽlit, vǽlei, væléi) **1.** *n.* a personal manservant ‖ a hotel attendant who looks after the clothes of patrons **2.** *v.t.* to act as valet to [F.]

Valetta *VALLETTA

val·e·tu·di·nar·i·an (vælitu̧:d'nέəri:ən, vælitju̧:-d'nέəri:ən) **1.** *n.* an invalid, esp. one who is morbidly interested in or anxious about his state of health **2.** *adj.* relating to or characteristic of a valetudinarian **val·e·tu·di·nár·i·an·ism** *n.* **va·le·tu·di·nar·y** (vælitú:d'nȩri:, vælitjú:d'nȩri:) *adj.* [fr. L. *valetudinarius* fr. *valetudo (valetudinis),* state of health]

val·gus (vǽlgəs) *n.* (*med.*) a position of abnormal outward turn of a joint or joints (cf. VARUS) [L.=bandy-legged]

Val·hal·la (vælhǽlə) (*Norse mythol.*) the hall of the heroes into which Odin receives those who have fallen bravely in battle

val·iance (vǽljəns) *n.* (*rhet.*) bravery **vál·ian·cy** *n.* (*rhet.*) valiance [A.F. or fr. O.F. *vaillance*]

val·iant (vǽljənt) *adj.* (*rhet.*) stouthearted, brave, heroic [fr. O.F. *vailant, vaillant*]

val·id (vǽlid) *adj.* seen to be in agreement with the facts or to be logically sound, *valid arguments* ‖ (*law*) in conformity with the law, and therefore binding ‖ based on sound principle, *a valid method* [fr. F. *valide* or L. *validus,* strong]

val·i·date (vǽlideit) *pres. part.* **val·i·dat·ing** *past* and *past part.* **val·i·dat·ed** *v.t.* to make valid or binding ‖ to confirm the validity of [fr. M.L. *validare (validatus)*]

val·i·da·tion (vælidéiʃən) *n.* a making or being made valid

va·lid·i·ty (vəliditi:) *pl.* **va·lid·i·ties** *n.* the state, fact or quality of being valid legally or in argument [fr. L.L. *validitas*]

val·in·o·my·cin (vælinəmáisin) *n.* an antibiotic that makes cell walls permeable to ions of some chemicals (e.g., potassium), useful in ion transport experiments

va·lise (vəlí:s, vəlí:z) *n.* a small traveling case ‖ (*Br.*) an officer's bedding roll [F. fr. Ital.]

Val·kyr·ie (vælkíəri:, vǽlkiəri:) *n.* (*Norse mythol.*) one of the virgin goddesses, riding in the air over the field of battle, who escort to valhalla the heroes who fall

Va·lla·do·lid (vɑljɑðɔlí:ð) a province (area 2,922 sq. miles, pop. 489,636) of N. central Spain (*OLD CASTILE, *LEÓN) ‖ its capital (pop. 297,255). Industries: mechanical engineering, automobile assembly, aluminum, chemicals. Cathedral (16th c.), Gothic and baroque churches. University

Valladolid (Mexico) *MORELIA

Val·lan·di·gham (vəlǽndigəm), Clement Laird (1820-71), U.S. politician, advocate of states' rights. He was banished (1863) behind Confederate lines for voicing pro-Southern sympathies. Upon his return (1864) into national politics he was leader of the Knights of the Golden Circle, a copperhead secret society

Va·lle (vάje), José Cecilio del (1780-1834), Honduran writer and leader in the struggle for Central American independence. He drafted the declaration (1821) proclaiming it

val·lec·u·la (vəlékjulə) *pl.* **va·lec·u·lae** (vəlékjuli:) *n.* (*anat., bot.*) a groove or furrow **val·léc·u·lar, val·lec·u·late** (vəlékjuleit) *adjs* [L.L. var. of L. *vallicula* dim. of *valles (vallis),* valley]

Val·le d'A·o·sta (vάlledɑɔ́stɑ) an autonomous region (area 1,260 sq. miles, pop. 114,591) of N.W. Italy in the Alps, bordering France and Switzerland. Capital: Aosta. Language: French dialect. Agriculture: cereals, wine, fruit, livestock. Resources: coal, iron ore, copper, hydroelectricity. It became a duchy (1238) and was allied to Savoy until 1814, when it was made part of the kingdom of Sardinia

Va·lle-In·clán (vάljei:ŋklάn), Ramón María Del (1869-1936), Spanish poet, novelist and dramatist. His best-known work is perhaps 'Sonatas' (1902-5), four novels with a Don Juan-type hero

Val·le·jo (vɑjéhɔ), César (1895-1938), Peruvian poet and novelist, spokesman for the underprivileged, esp. the Andean Indian, and champion of social reform. His works include the poems 'Heraldos negros' (1918) and the novels 'Trilce' (1922) and 'El tungsteno' (1931)

Val·let·ta, Va·let·ta (vəlétə) the capital (pop. 14,042) and chief port of Malta, founded (1566) by the Knights Hospitalers. University (1769). Dockyards

val·ley (vǽli:) *pl.* **val·leys** *n.* a long depression in the earth's surface resulting either from its folding or from erosion by a river or glacier ‖ (*archit.*) the internal angle at the junction of two roof slopes ‖ any dip or hollow ‖ the land drained or watered by a great river system [O.F. *valee, vallee*]

Valley Forge the winter quarters (1777-8) near Philadelphia of Washington and his army of 11,000 during a critical period of the Revolutionary War. About 3,000 died of cold, malnutrition and sickness

vallonia *VALONIA

Val·my, Battle of (vǽlmi:) the first battle (Sept. 20, 1792) of the French Revolutionary Wars. The Prussian army was repulsed by the French, and forced to withdraw beyond the Rhine

Va·lois (vælwæ) the royal house of France (1328-1589), a younger branch of the Capetian line. It was succeeded by the Bourbons

Va·lo·na (vɑlóunɑ) *VLONA

va·lo·ni·a, val·lo·ni·a (vəlóuni:ə) *n.* large dried acorn cups of *Quercus aegilops,* the valonia oak of S.W. Europe and Asia Minor, used in tanning, dyeing and making ink [Ital. *vallonía, vallonéa* fr. Mod. Gk]

val·or, *Br.* **val·our** (vǽlər) *n.* (*rhet.*) personal courage, esp. in battle [O.F.]

val·or·i·za·tion (vælərizéiʃən) *n.* an attempt, usually by a government, to fix or stabilize artificially the price of an article **val·or·ize** (vǽləraiz) *pres. part.* **val·or·iz·ing** *past* and *past*

part. **val·or·ized** *v.t.* to determine and stabilize the price of (an article) [fr. VALOR, (obs.) value]
val·or·ous (vǽlərəs) *adj.* (*rhet.*, of people) courageous ‖ (*rhet.*, of actions) showing valor [fr. O.F. *valeureux*]
valour *VALOR
Val·pa·rai·so (vælpəráizou) the chief port (pop. 249,000) of Chile and of W. South America. Industries: oil refining, food processing, light manufactures, chemical products. University (1949), Catholic University (1929)
val·pro·ic acid [$C_8H_{16}O_2$] (vælpróuik) (*pharm.*) a carboxylic derivative used as an anticonvulsive, marketed as Depakene
val·u·a·ble (vǽljuːəb'l, vǽljub'l) **1.** *adj.* of great value, *a valuable property* ‖ very useful, *his help was most valuable* **2.** *n.* (*pl.*) precious possessions, small personal objects of value such as jewelry etc. **vál·u·a·bly** *adv.*
val·u·a·tion (vælјuːéiʃən) *n.* an estimation of a thing's worth, esp. by a professional appraiser ‖ the value, cost or price estimated ‖ a personal view of one's own or somebody else's character or merits [O.F. *valuacion*]
val·u·a·tor (vǽljuːeitər) *n.* an appraiser
val·ue (vǽljuː) **1.** *n.* the measure of how strongly something is desired for its physical or moral beauty, usefulness, rarity etc., esp. expressed in terms of the effort, money etc. one is willing to expend in acquiring, retaining possession of, or preserving it ‖ a principle, quality etc. that arouses such desire, *moral values* ‖ fair return, *to get good value for one's money* ‖ purchasing power, *the value of the pound* ‖ the monetary equivalent of something, *property to the value of $5,000* ‖ (*math.*) the amount represented by an expression or symbol ‖ (*mus.*) the duration of a tone as indicated by its note ‖ (*phon.*) the quality of a sound ‖ (*painting*) the relationship between the parts of a painting in terms of light and shade ‖ the importance or rank accorded to a playing card, chessman etc. **2.** *v.t. pres. part.* **val·u·ing** *past* and *past part.* **val·ued** to estimate the value of, *he valued the property at $10,000* ‖ to regard as having a high value, *to value someone's friendship* **vál·u·er** *n.* (*Br.*) an appraiser [O.F. fem. of *valu* past part. of *valoir*, to be worth]
value added by manufacture (*business*) value measure derived by subtracting the cost of materials from the value of shipments. *abbr.* VAM. *Cf* VALUE-ADDED TAX
value-added tax (*business*) a tax based on the value added at each stage of production from raw-material processing to consumer. It is designed to fall ultimately on the consumer. *abbr.* VAT. *Cf* VALUE ADDED BY MANUFACTURE
va·lu·ta (vəlúːtə) *n.* the exchange value of a currency in terms of another currency [Ital.= value]
val·vate (vǽlveit) *adj.* like a valve ‖ (*bot.*) of, or having, petals or sepals which meet at their edges but do not overlap ‖ (*bot.*) opening as if by valves, e.g. of anthers which release pollen, or of fruits which release seeds by means of valve-like structures [fr. L. *valvatus*, having folding doors]
valve (vælv) *n.* any of innumerable natural or man-made devices which control the direction or volume of flow of a fluid or (*Br.*=*Am.* tube) of electricity ‖ (*bot.*) the lidlike structure of certain anthers ‖ (*bot.*) one of the segments into which a capsule dehisces ‖ (*zool.*) one of the separate parts of the shell of a diatom or of any of certain mollusks ‖ (*mus.*, of the trumpet etc.) a device for varying the tube length to alter the pitch of a tone [fr. L. *valva*, leaf of a door]
valve chest the steam chest of a steam engine
val·vu·lar (vǽlvjulər) *adj.* of or relating to a valve or valves, esp. the cardiac valves, *valvular disease*
val·vule (vǽlvjuːl) *n.* a small valve [F.]
vamp (væmp) **1.** *n.* the upper part of a boot or shoe in front of the ankle seam ‖ (*mus.*) an improvised accompaniment or introduction or fill-in between verses **2.** *v.t.* to repair the vamp of (a boot or shoe) ‖ to patch ‖ (*mus.*) to improvise (an accompaniment, introduction etc.) ‖ *v.i.* (*mus.*) to improvise an accompaniment etc. [O.F. *avanpié* fr. *avant*, before+*pié*, foot]
vamp 1. *n.* a woman who uses her physical allure to attract and exploit men ‖ an actress who plays the part of such a woman **2.** *v.t.* to attract and exploit (a man) by playing the vamp ‖ *v.i.* to act the vamp [shortened fr. VAMPIRE]
vam·pire (vǽmpaiər) *n.* (in popular superstition) a ghost or evil spirit which leaves a grave at night to suck the blood of people asleep ‖ a person who exploits others ruthlessly ‖ a vampire bat ‖ a stage trapdoor used in theaters to effect sudden disappearances [F. fr. Magyar *vampir* fr. Slavic]
vampire bat a member of *Desmodus* or of *Diphylla*, fam. *Desmodontidae*, genera of South and Central American bats which live on the fresh blood of animals and are often carriers of disease ‖ any of several large South and Central American bats once reputed to suck blood, but which actually feed on insects
vam·pir·ism (vǽmpaiərizəm) *n.* belief in vampires ‖ the habits or actions of vampires
Van (vɑn) a salt lake (area 1,450 sq. miles) in E. Turkey (Armenia)
van (væn) *n.* the leading section of an army, fleet, or procession ‖ the people who take the lead in some movement [shortened fr. VANGUARD]
van *n.* a large covered vehicle for carrying furniture and other goods by road ‖ (*Br.*) a small covered truck, e.g. for delivery of groceries, parcels etc. ‖ (*Br., rail.*) a baggage car [shortened fr. CARAVAN]
van *n.* a shovel for dressing ores ‖ (*rhet.*) a bird's wing [var. of FAN]
va·na·di·um (vənéidiːəm) *n.* (*chem.*) a malleable, white metallic element (symbol V, at. no. 23, at. mass 50.942) occurring in a few rare minerals. It is used in alloying, esp. to make a very hard steel, and in the form of vanadic acid, HVO_3, as a catalyst in oxidizing aniline (using sodium chlorate as the oxidizer) [Mod. L. fr. O.N. *Vanadis*, a Scandinavian goddess]
Van Al·len radiation belt (vænǽlən) either of two layers of intense ionizing radiation that surround the earth in its outer atmosphere, ranging from approx. 1,500 to approx. 12,000 miles above its surface. They have particles charged with high energies [after James A. *van Allen* (*b.* 1914), U.S. physicist]
Van·brugh (vǽnbrə), Sir John (1664-1726), English playwright and architect. His plays, notably 'The Relapse' (1697) and 'The Provok'd Wife' (1697), are comedies of manners. His country mansions, e.g. Castle Howard and Blenheim Palace, are in an impressive baroque style
Van Bur·en (vænbjúərən), Martin (1782-1862), eighth president (1837-41) of the U.S.A., a Democrat. He organized the Albany Regency. He served as secretary of state (1829-31) and as vice-president (1832-6) under President Andrew Jackson. As president he responded to the economic crisis of 1837 by endorsing a federal Treasury independent of the nation's banking and financial system, ultimately established in 1840 by an act of Congress. Later he became (1840) the Democratic presidential candidate and (1848) candidate of the Freesoil party, and was both times defeated
van·co·my·cin (vænkəmáisin) *n.* (*pharm.*) antibiotic used to combat gram-positive staphylococcic infections; marketed as Vancocin
Van·cou·ver (vænkúːvər), George (1758-98), English navigator and explorer. After mapping the coasts of Australia and New Zealand (1791) he made a thorough survey of the northwest coast of America (1792-4)
Vancouver the chief Pacific port (pop. 414,281, with agglom. 1,169,831) of Canada, in British Columbia, on the Inside Passage and the Fraser River. Industries: oil refining, sawmilling, pulp and paper, food processing, shipbuilding. University of British Columbia (1915)
Vancouver Island a mountainous, wooded island (area 13,408 sq. miles, pop. 437,802) off S.W. Canada, part of British Columbia. Chief town: Victoria. Products: lumber, coal
Van·dal (vǽnd'l) *n.* a member of an E. Germanic tribe originally from the southern shores of the Baltic. They overran Gaul and Spain (406-29) and N.W. Africa (429-42), sacked Rome (455) and commanded the Mediterranean until their kingdom was overthrown (534) by Belisarius **vandal** someone who wantonly or ignorantly destroys or disfigures natural or human works of beauty **ván·dal·ism** *n.* wanton destruction or spoiling of what should be preserved [fr. L. *vandalus*]
Van de Graaff generator (vǽndəgræf) (*phys.*) a device for separating electrostatic charges by a continuous process, thus building up extremely high electrostatic potential (e.g. up to 15 million volts). It is used to accelerate the charged particles of the atom (e.g. protons) to high energies [after R. *van de Graaff* (1901-67), U.S. physicist]
Van·der·bilt (vǽndərbilt), Cornelius (1794-1877), U.S. railroad magnate. He gained control (1867) of the New York Central Railroad and connected (1873) Chicago with New York by rail. He donated $1 million to found Vanderbilt University in Nashville, Tenn.
van der Goes (vǽndərgouz), Hugo (c. 1440-82), Flemish painter. Only one authenticated painting of his has survived, a triptych of the Adoration in the Uffizi gallery at Florence, other attributions being based on this
van der Helst (vǽndərhelst), Bartholomaeus (c. 1611-70), Dutch painter. He was a masterly draftsman and is esp. known for his collective portraits
van der Waals equation (vǽndərwɔlz) (*phys.*) an equation of state for gases and vapors that is related to the ideal gas law but which takes into account the actual volume of the gas molecules and the effect of intermolecular attractions between them. It is written

$$\left(P + \frac{a}{V_2}\right)\left(V - b\right) = nRT$$

(where P = pressure, V = volume, T = temperature on the Kelvin scale, R = the gas constant, n = the number of moles and a and b are constants which depend on the gas). It describes the behavior of gases over a considerably wider range of pressure than the ideal gas law [after Johannes D. *van der Waals* (*d.* 1923), Du. physicist]
van der Wey·den (vǽndərváid'n), Roger (c. 1400-64), Flemish painter. His religious works, e.g. 'The Descent from the Cross' (c. 1435) in the Prado, Madrid, show a deep spirituality combined with great dramatic power, and a profound understanding of human suffering. He also painted fine portraits
Van De·van·ter (vændəvǽntər), Willis (1859-1941), associate justice of the U.S. Supreme Court (1911-37). He practiced law before becoming (1890) chief justice of the Wyoming Supreme Court. He served (1903-10) on the U.S. Circuit Court until appointed to the U.S. Supreme Court by Pres. William Howard Taft. A conservative, he was one of the Court majority that struck down much of Pres. Franklin D. Roosevelt's New Deal legislation
van de Vel·de (vǽndəveld), Adriaen (1636-72), Dutch painter. He specialized in landscapes and animal paintings
van de Velde, Henry (1863-1957), Belgian architect and decorator. From an early art nouveau style, he developed theories of pure form and functional aesthetics which influenced the development of modern design, esp. in Germany
van de Velde, Willem (1633-1707), Dutch painter, brother of Adriaen. He painted at the courts of Charles II and James II of England and excelled in seascapes and naval battles
Van Die·men (vændíːmən), Anton (1593-1645), Dutch colonial administrator. An expedition sent by him to Australia discovered (1642) Van Diemen's Land, now Tasmania
van Don·gen (vændɔ́ŋən), Kees (1877-1968), French painter of Dutch origin. He was one of the early protagonists of Fauvism but is best known for his later society portraits
Vandyke beard a neatly trimmed, pointed beard
Van·dyke, van Dyck (vændáik), Sir Anthony (1599-1641), Flemish painter. After six years in Italy (1621-7) he became, jointly with Rubens, court painter at Antwerp. His technique owes much to Rubens' swift, very sensitive painting. From about 1630 to his death he lived mainly in London. He is famous for his portraits, esp. those of the patricians and courtiers of Caroline England. He was one of the first society painters: his subjects are made to represent an ideal of arrogant refinement
vane (vein) *n.* a broad, thin, often curved surface fastened to a pivoted or rotating body. Vanes are used under a current of air or water to make a pivoted body (e.g. a weather vane, sail of a windmill etc.) rotate, or to drive a body forward or to give a bomb etc. a steady direction ‖ the barbs of a feather ‖ (*archery*) a feather on an arrow shaft ‖ (*surveying*) a movable disk on a surveying staff which can be brought into line with the telescope ‖ one of the sights on a com-

pass etc. [var. of older *fane* fr. O.E. *fana,* a flag]

Vä·nern (vénərn) a lake (area 2,141 sq. miles) in S.W. Sweden

van Eyck (vænáik), Jan (*d.* 1441), the founder with his brother Hubert (*d.* c. 1426; some art historians have doubted that Hubert existed) of the Flemish school of painting. Their work survives in an altarpiece, 'The Adoration of the Lamb' in the church of St Bavon, at Ghent (inaugurated 1432), in other religious paintings, and in portraits. The van Eycks mark the moment in N. Europe when medieval art is left behind and 'modern' modeling, perspective and lighting based on close observation take its place

vang (væŋ) *n.* (*naut.*) either of the two guy ropes extending from the top of the gaff to the deck [var. of O.E. *fang*]

van Gogh (vænxɔ́x, *Eng.* væŋgóu), Vincent (1853-90), Dutch Postimpressionist painter, one of the first expressionists. His early work, inspired by Millet's paintings and by religious missionary zeal, portrayed Dutch peasant life in dark, somber colors. In 1886 he went to live in France. In Paris, where he came in contact with the Impressionists, and esp. when he moved to Provence, he began to use pure, bright color, and his brush strokes themselves, in their very shapes and rhythms, convey the pressure of a joyous perception of life, of growth, goodness and love, as well as agonized premonitions of madness and death. His paintings convey the reality of landscapes, still life and people, transfigured by his intensity of feeling about them. His painting career was concentrated in some ten years of feverish work. His last years were spent in asylums, and finally he shot himself

van Goy·en (væŋgɔ́ijən), Jan Josephszoon (1596-1656), Dutch painter. He is noted for his landscapes and seascapes

van·guard (vǽngɑrd) *n.* the soldiers who march at the front of an army, or this section of an army ‖ the forefront of a movement [fr. O.F. *avangarde*]

va·nil·la (vənílə) *n.* a member of *vanilla,* fam. *Orchidaceae,* a genus of climbing, epiphytic orchids, native to tropical America and the West Indies ‖ a food and tobacco flavoring extracted from the pods of *V. planifolia* (now synthesized on a large scale) [fr. early Span. *vainilla,* little sheath]

van·ish (vǽniʃ) *v.i.* to become no longer able to be seen or felt, *he vanished in the mist, the pain suddenly vanished* ‖ to pass out of existence, *all hope of recovery finally vanished* ‖ (*math.,* of a number or quantity) to become zero [aphetic fr. O.F. *evanir* (*evaniss-*)]

vanishing cream a cosmetic cream, used as a foundation, which is absorbed by the skin

vanishing point the point at which receding parallels, drawn in perspective, would meet

van·i·ty (vǽniti:) *pl.* **van·i·ties** *n.* the fact or quality of being vain ‖ something of no real worth ‖ a source of self-satisfaction ‖ a vanity case ‖ a dressing table [O.F. *vanite*]

vanity case a small case fitted with lipstick, compact, mirror etc.

vanity plate a motor vehicle license plate carrying a word, name, and/or numbers selected by the owner

vanity surgery (*med.*) cosmetic surgery

van·ner (vǽnər) *n.* a machine with a wide shaking rubber belt used for dressing ores ‖ a man who separates ore with a van

van Os·ta·de (vænɔ́stɑdə), Adriaen (1610-85), Dutch painter and etcher, pupil of Franz Hals. He painted scenes of village life and tranquil Dutch exteriors

van Ostade, Isaac (1621-49), brother and pupil of Adriaen van Ostade, known for his brilliant wintry landscapes

van·quish (vǽŋkwiʃ, vǽnkwiʃ) *v.t.* (*rhet.*) to overcome in battle or conflict, to conquer ‖ (*rhet.*) to overcome (a feeling) [M.E. fr. O.F. *vencus* past part. and *venquis* past tense of *veintre,* to conquer]

van·tage (vǽntidʒ, vɑ́ntidʒ) *n.* a condition or position conferring superiority ‖ (*Br., tennis*) advantage [fr. A.F., var. of O.F. *avantage*]

vantage point a place or condition particularly favorable for viewing or understanding something

Va·nu·atu (vanu:átu:) formerly New Hebrides, an island republic, part of a volcanic archipelago (total area 5,700 sq. miles, pop. 112,596, incl. some 3,000 Europeans) in the S.W. Pacific (Melanesia). Main islands: Espiritu Santo, Malekula, Epi, Efate. Capital: Vila (pop. 14,000, on Efate). Main exports: copra, cocoa. The islands were visited by the Portuguese (1606), the French (1768) and the British (1774). They were placed under an Anglo-French naval commission (1887), and were administered (1906-80) as an Anglo-French condominium until independence on July 30, 1980

vap·id (vǽpid) *adj.* lacking zest or interest **va·píd·i·ty,** *n.* [fr. L. *vapidus,* savorless]

va·por, *Br.* **va·pour** (véipər) **1.** *n.* (*chem.* and *phys.*) a substance in a gaseous state but below its critical temperature, and so liquefiable by pressure alone ‖ a liquid, esp. water, dispersed and suspended in the air in the form of very small drops ‖ a combination of vaporized matter and air, e.g. the explosive mixture in an internal-combustion engine ‖ (*pl., old-fash.*) nervous depression **2.** *v.t.* to emit as vapor ‖ to reduce to vapor ‖ *v.i.* to rise as vapor [A.F.]

vapor density, *Br.* **vapour density** the density of a vapor or gas by comparison with that of some standard (e.g. hydrogen)

va·por·if·ic (veipərífik) *adj.* vaporous [fr. Mod. L. *vaporificus*]

va·por·i·za·tion (veipərizéiʃən) *n.* a vaporizing or being vaporized

va·por·ize (véipəraiz) *pres. part.* **va·por·iz·ing** *past* and *past part.* **va·por·ized** *v.t.* to change into vapor ‖ *v.i.* to be changed into vapor

va·por·iz·er (véipəraizər) *n.* a device for converting a liquid into a vapor or fine droplets, usually by the application of heat or by spraying (cf. ATOMIZER)

va·por·ous (véipərəs) *adj.* forming vapor ‖ giving off vapor ‖ like vapor

vapor plumes emissions of visible droplets in fine gas

vapor pressure, *Br.* **vapour pressure** the pressure exerted by the vapor of a substance

vapour *VAPOR

va·que·ro (vɑkéərou) *n.* a Spanish-American or southwest U.S. cowboy [Span.]

Var (vær) a department (area 2,333 sq. miles, pop. 626,100) of S. France (*PROVENCE). Chief towns: Draguignan, Toulon

var·ac·tor or **varactor diode** (værǽktə:r) *n.* (*electr.*) a semiconductor diode on which the capacitance varies with the voltage applied, used as a tuning element in amplifier and oscillator circuits

Va·ra·na·si (vɑrɑnázi:) (or Banaras, *Eng.* Benares) a trade center (pop. 583,856) in S.E. Uttar Pradesh, India, on the Ganges. It is a holy city to Hindus, Buddhists and Jains, receiving a million pilgrims annually. Handicrafts and manufactures: silks, shawls, brocades, brass, jewelry, textiles, chemicals. There are some 1,500 temples. Mosque of Aurangzeb (1669), observatory (1693), Hindu university (1916)

Va·rang·i·an (vərǽndʒi:ən) *n.* (*hist.*) one of the viking warriors who raided the Baltic coast, founded states in Russia (9th c.), and attacked Constantinople (10th c.). The Russ, a Varangian tribe, gave their name to Russia

Var·dha·ma·na (vɑrdhəméinə) *JAINISM

var·ec, var·ech (vǽrek) *n.* kelp [F. *varech*]

Va·re·la (bɑrélɑ), Juan Cruz (1794-1839), Argentinian neoclassical poet

Va·rèse (vɑréz), Edgar (1883-1965), U.S. composer (born French). His experiments in sonority (incl. the use of electronic instruments) were 30 years ahead of his time. He was a pupil of Roussel, d'Indy and Widor

Var·gas (vɑ́rgəs), Getúlio Dornelles (1883-1954), Brazilian politician and dictator (1930-45, 1951-4), following a coup d'état. He established (1937) a corporative state, the Estado Novo, modeled after Salazar's Portugal. He was ousted (1945) by the military but was nevertheless reelected (1950) by the masses. Pressure by the military again forced his resignation (1954). He committed suicide in the same year

var·i·a·bil·i·ty (vɛəri:əbíliti:) *n.* the state or quality of being variable ‖ a tendency to vary

var·i·a·ble (vɛ́əri:əb'l) **1.** *adj.* apt to change, *variable winds* ‖ able to be changed ‖ (*biol.,* of a structure, species, function etc.) not true to type ‖ (*math.*) characteristic of a quantity which may have different values **2.** *n.* something variable ‖ (*pl.*) the latitudes between the trade-wind zones ‖ (*math.*) a term representing a quantity which may have any value, or any of the values within certain limits ‖ (*math.*) a symbol for such a quantity (cf. CONSTANT) [O.F.]

variable annuity a contract in which annual payments fluctuate with the return on stocks or other income sources that change with economic conditions

variable condenser (*elec.*) a condenser of which the capacity can readily be varied

variable geometry aircraft (*aeronautics*) a retractable wing that can be adjusted inflight for speed changes. *also* variable sweep wing, swing wing

variable levy a formula applied to agricultural imports providing a rise in tariff levies as international prices drop

variable rate mortgage (*banking*) a mortgage in which the interest is adjusted periodically in accordance with prevailing interest rates

variable star a star displaying varying magnitude either cyclically or without any discernible period (*CEPHEID, *NOVA, *DOUBLE STAR)

variable time fuze, esp. *Br.* **variable time fuse** a proximity fuze

var·i·a·bly (vɛ́əri:əbli:) *adv.* in a variable manner

var·i·ance (vɛ́əri:əns) *n.* a sharp disagreement or difference of opinion ‖ a variation, difference, change, *a marked variance in temperature* ‖ (*law*) a difference or disagreement between two documents, statements etc. which should agree **at variance** in disagreement, *at variance with the known facts* ‖ antagonistic, at loggerheads, *husband and wife were often at variance* [O.F.]

var·i·ant (vɛ́əri:ənt) **1.** *adj.* differing and alternative, *variant spellings of 'Shakespeare'* **2.** *n.* one of two or more alternatives of a form, reading, spelling etc. [O.F.]

var·i·a·tion (vɛəri:éiʃən) *n.* change as a process, condition or fact ‖ departure from a standard or norm, or an instance of this ‖ the measure of this departure, the extent to which a thing varies ‖ (*mus.*) one of a number of repetitions of a theme in a variety of elaborate, developed or disguised forms ‖ (*biol.*) the structural or functional difference between closely related individuals within a species ‖ (*astron.*) a change in the normal movement of a heavenly body, esp. in the orbit of a planet ‖ (*phys.*) *DECLINATION **var·i·á·tion·al** *adj.* [O.F.]

var·i·cel·la (værisélə) *n.* (*med.*) chicken pox **var·i·cél·loid** *adj.* resembling chicken pox [Mod. L. dim. of *variola*]

varices *pl.* of VARIX

var·i·co·cele (vǽrikousi:l) *n.* (*med.*) a swelling formed by varicose veins of the spermatic cord in the scrotum [Mod. L. fr. L. *varix,* an enlarged vein+Gk *kēlē,* tumor]

var·i·col·ored, *Br.* **var·i·col·oured** (vɛ́ərikʌlərd) *adj.* having various colors [fr. L. *varius,* varied+COLORED]

var·i·cose (vǽrikous) *adj.* swollen, distended, esp. of veins (*VARIX) ‖ of or having varicose veins **var·i·co·sis, var·i·cos·i·ty** (værikɔ́siti:) *ns* the condition of being varicose [fr. L. *varicosus* fr. *varix,* an enlarged vein]

var·ied (vɛ́əri:d) *adj.* of different kinds, not all the same ‖ variegated ‖ varying

var·ie·gate (vɛ́ərigeit, vɛ́əri:əgeit) *pres. part.* **var·ie·gat·ing** *past* and *past part.* **var·ie·gat·ed** *v.t.* to supply with various colors ‖ to diversify, to give variety to **vár·ie·gat·ed** *adj.* (*bot.*) dappled or streaked with various colors ‖ varied, full of variety **var·ie·gá·tion** *n.* [fr. L. *variegare* (*variegatus*), to make varied]

vari·e·tal (vəráiit'l) *adj.* of or pertaining to a variety ‖ constituting a variety (as opposed to an individual or species)

va·ri·e·ty (vəráiiti:) *pl.* **va·ri·e·ties** *n.* the state or quality of not being always or everywhere the same ‖ a number or collection of things differing in character, *a variety of reasons* ‖ (*biol.*) a group having certain qualities in common which distinguish it from a larger class to which it belongs, and which may or may not be inherited, *a variety of strawberry noted for its late fruiting* ‖ one of a number of different forms or kinds of the same thing, *a thousand varieties of selfishness* ‖ entertainment as given in variety shows [F. *variété* or fr. L. *varietas,* diversity]

variety show a presentation of different forms of light entertainment (e.g. acrobatics, conjuring, dancing, singing etc.)

var·i·form (vɛ́əri:fɔrm) *adj.* having various forms

va·ri·o·la (vəráiələ) *n.* smallpox **va·ri·o·lar** *adj.* [M.L. fr. L. *varius,* varied]

var·i·ole (vɛ́əri:oul) *n.* (*biol.*) a small shallow

CONCISE PRONUNCIATION KEY: **(a)** æ, *cat;* ɑ, *car;* ɔ *fawn;* ei, *snake.* **(e)** e, *hen;* i:, *sheep;* iə, *deer;* ɛə, *bear.* **(i)** i, *fish;* ai, *tiger;* ə:, *bird.* **(o)** o, *ox;* au, *cow;* ou, *goat;* u, *poor;* ɔi, *royal.* **(u)** ʌ, *duck;* u, *bull;* u:, *goose;* ə, *bacillus;* ju:, *cube.* x, *loch;* θ, *think;* ð, *bother;* z, *Zen;* ʒ, *corsage;* dʒ, *savage;* ŋ, *orangutang;* j, *yak;* ʃ, *fish;* tʃ, *fetch;* 'l, *rabble;* 'n, *redden.* Complete pronunciation key appears inside front cover.

pitlike depression resembling a pockmark || a spherule of a variolite [M.L. *variola,* pustule]

var·i·o·lite (vέəriːəlait) *n.* (*geol.*) a spherulitic basalt the surface of which resembles pockmarked skin **var·i·o·lit·ic** (vɛəriːəlítik) *adj.* of or like variolite || pockmarked [fr. M.L. *variola*]

va·ri·o·lous (vəráiələs) *adj.* of, resembling or having variola

var·i·om·e·ter (vɛəriːómitər) *n.* (*radio*) a variable inductance of two coils connected in series, one inside the other, the inner coil rotating [fr. L. *varius,* various+METER]

var·i·o·rum edition (vɛəriːórəm, vɛəriːóurəm) an edition containing textual variants with notes by various commentators [L.=of various (persons)]

var·i·ous (vέəriːəs) *adj.* of different kinds, *various crops* || characterized by variety, *his reasons are many and various* || (*loosely*) several [fr. L. *varius,* diverse]

var·ix (vέəriks) *pl.* **var·i·ces** (vέərisiːz) *n.* (*med.*) a permanent abnormal swelling of a vein, artery or lymph vessel || a vein, artery or lymph vessel swollen thus || a ridge on the whorl of some univalves [L.]

var·let (várlit) *n.* a medieval page || (*hist.*) a knight's attendant training to become a squire || (*archaic*) a knave [O.F.]

var·mint (vármint) *n.* (*pop.*) an animal classed as vermin || (*pop.*) a lowdown, troublesome pest of a person

Var·na (várnə) (called Stalin 1949-56) the chief port (pop. 124,000) of Bulgaria. Industries: mechanical engineering, shipbuilding. University (1920)

var·nish (várniʃ) **1.** *n.* a liquid solution of resin, prepared in spirits or oil, applied to wood and metal surfaces to give a hard glossy transparent coating || the gloss or shine of any polished surface, natural or man-made || a superficial polish of manners and outward behavior **2.** *v.t.* to put a coat of varnish on || to improve superficially, *to varnish a reputation* [fr. O.F. *vernis*]

Var·ro (vǽrou), Marcus Terentius (116-27 B.C.), Roman scholar. Of his many works, only his treatise on agriculture and parts of 'De lingua latina' survive

var·si·ty (vársitiː) *pl.* **var·si·ties** *n.* (*Br., pop.*) university || (*sports*) a team that represents a university, college, school or club, in a game [shortened fr. 18th-c. pronunciation of UNIVERSITY]

var·us (vέərəs, vǽrəs) *n.* (*med.*) a position of abnormal inward turn of a joint or joints (cf. VALGUS) [L.=knockkneed]

varve dating (vɑrv) (*archaeology*) use of sequence of sedimentary layers formed by melting ice as a means of establishing the time of an archeological deposit

var·y (vέəriː) *pres. part.* **var·y·ing** *past* and *past part.* **var·ied** *v.t.* to introduce variety into || *v.i.* to undergo change, *the temperature varies greatly* || to differ, *opinions on the matter vary* || (with 'from') to deviate from e.g. a standard, *this varies from the normal practice* || (*biol.*) to display variation **to vary as** to change in value, amount or quality in direct or indirect proportion to [fr. O.F. *varier*]

VAS (*meteor. acronym*) for visible-infrared spin, a scan radiometer sonde sensor that provides three-dimensional analysis of weather conditions; produced for NASA by Hughes Aircraft Co.

Va·sa (vázə) a royal dynasty which ruled in Sweden (1523-1654) and in Poland (1587-1668)

Va·sa·ri (vɑzáriː), Giorgio (1511-74), Italian artist and architect, chiefly famous for his book 'Lives of the Most Eminent Painters, Sculptors and Architects' (1550, 2nd enlarged edition 1568), known as Vasari's 'Lives'

Vasco da Gama *GAMA, VASCO DA

Vas·con·ce·los (vɑskɔnsélɔs), José (1882-1959), Mexican educator, philosopher, writer and politician. As director (1920-4) of the National University of Mexico and minister of education in Obregón's administration, he constructed schools and raised the literacy level. As teacher and philosopher he led the movement which asserted the uniqueness of Latin American culture as a product of a particular racial mixture in a particular physical setting. He lost the presidential election (1929) to Calles and went into exile. His autobiographical work 'Ulises Criollo' (trans. 'Mexican Ulysses') is in four volumes (1935-9). Other works are 'La Raza cósmica' (1925) and 'Indología' (1927)

vas·cu·lar (vǽskjulər) *adj.* of, consisting of or containing vessels or ducts adapted for the transmission or circulation of blood, sap etc. [fr. Mod. L. *vascularis* fr. *vasculum,* small vessel]

vascular bundle a group of special plant cells, consisting of vessels and sieve tubes, often in association with parenchyma and sclerenchyma, which may be separated by a band of cambial cells forming a strand of the vascular system

vascular cylinder (*bot.*) the stele

vas·cu·lar·i·ty (væskjulǽriti:) *n.* the quality or state of being vascular

vascular ray (*bot.*) a ribbonlike band of parenchyma cells stretching radially through tissues of the vascular cylinder from the xylem to the phloem, serving to store synthesized food material

vascular system the system of a body made up of vascular tissue and, in humans, comprising the heart, arteries, veins etc.

vascular tissue (*bot.*) tissue involved mainly in fluid transport, esp. the tissue of plants including xylem and phloem, through which the sap flows

vas·cu·li·tus (væskju:láitis) *n.* (*med.*) inflammation of a vessel, esp. blood, lymph

vas de·fe·rens (væsdéfərenz) *pl.* **va·sa de·fe·ren·ti·a** (véisədefərénʃiːə) *n.* (*anat.*) the duct that carries sperm from the testicle to the ejaculatory duct of the penis [Mod. L.=the vessel which carries down]

vase (veis, veiz, vɑz) *n.* a glass, pottery or metal vessel used as a container for cut flowers or as an ornament [F.]

vas·e·line (vǽsiliːn, væsəlíːn) *n.* petrolatum [fr. vaseline, a trademark, fr. G. *wasser,* water+Gk *elaion,* oil]

va·si·form (véisifɔrm, véizifɔrm) *adj.* shaped like a hollow tube or vase || consisting of a duct [fr. Mod. L. *vasiformis*]

va·so·ac·tive (vɛizouǽktəv) *adj.* (*med.*) affecting the expansion or contraction of blood vessels —**vasoactivity** *n.*

vas·o·con·stric·tor (væsoukənstríktər) **1.** *adj.* (*physiol.*) causing constriction of a blood vessel **2.** *n.* a nerve or drug causing such constriction [fr. L. *vas,* vessel+CONSTRICTOR]

vas·o·di·la·tor (væsoudailéitər, væsoudiléitər) **1.** *adj.* (*physiol.*) causing dilatation of a blood vessel **2.** *n.* a nerve or drug causing such dilatation [fr. L. *vas,* vessel+DILATOR]

vas·o·mo·tor (væsoumóutər) *adj.* (*physiol.*) pertaining to the nerves or nerve centers which control the size of the blood vessels, e.g. sympathetic and parasympathetic nerves [fr. L. *vas,* vessel+MOTOR]

vas·sal (vǽs'l) **1.** *n.* (*hist.*) a feudal tenant who vowed obedience to his lord and in return held land under him || (*hist.*) a servant, bondman, slave **2.** *adj.* (*hist.*) of or relating to a vassal || (*rhet.*) subject, *vassal states* [O.F. fr. M.L. fr. Celt.]

vas·sal·age (vǽsəlidʒ) *n.* (*hist.*) the state of being a vassal || (*rhet.*) servitude, esp. political servitude [O.F.]

Vas·sar College (vǽsər) a U.S. private educational institution formerly for women only, now coeducational. It was founded (1861) by Matthew Vassar (1792-1868) near Poughkeepsie, N.Y., as Vassar Female College, and renamed (1867)

vast (væst, vast) *adj.* immensely large in area || very great, *a vast improvement* [fr. L. *vastus,* immense]

Väs·ter·ås (vɛstəróus) a city (pop. 118,100) in Sweden on Lake Mälar. Gothic cathedral (13th c.)

vat (væt) **1.** *n.* a large open tub, tank etc., used usually to hold liquids in bulk or in which to dye or steep **2.** *v.t. pres. part.* **vat·ting** *past* and *past part.* **vat·ted** to place or treat in a vat [var. of FAT fr. O.E. *fæt*]

VAT (*abbr.*) for value-added tax

vat dye a dye of a large class rendered soluble in alkalis by reducing them to leuco compounds, and becoming insoluble again by oxidation after fabrics have been steeped in the solution in a vat (e.g. indigo)

Vat·i·can (vǽtikən) the pope's palace on the Vatican hill in Rome. Its many buildings, of different dates and styles, begun in 1277 but mainly mid-15th-late 16th cc., include the Sistine Chapel (1473-81, *MICHELANGELO), the Nicholas V chapel decorated by Fra Angelico (1477), great rooms decorated by Raphael (1508-17), galleries of painting, sculpture and archaeology, and the library of about 67,000 manuscripts and half a million books

Vatican City the only surviving Papal State (area 108 acres, pop. 1,000) surrounding the Vatican in Rome, recognized as an independent state by the Lateran Treaty (1929). It has full sovereign rights and powers (army, police force, currency, diplomatic service etc.), under the sovereignty of the pope. It contains the Basilica of St Peter (1506-1629)

Vatican Council the 20th ecumenical council, held in Rome (1869-70), which affirmed papal infallibility (1870) || the 21st ecumenical council, held in Rome (1962-5). It discussed liturgical reform and Christian unity

Vät·tern (vétərn) a lake (area 733 sq. miles) in S. Sweden, linked to Lake Vänern and hence to the Baltic by the Göta Canal

Vau·ban (voubã), Sébastien Le Prestre, seigneur de (1633-1707), French military engineer. He fortified France's frontiers, strengthening over 300 old fortresses and building 33 new ones. He developed a devastating siege method based on a system of parallel trenches, and conducted 53 sieges

Vau·cluse (vouklyz) a department in S.E. France (area 1,381 sq. miles, pop. 390,400) (*PROVENCE, *COMTAT-VENAISSIN). Chief town: Avignon

Vaud (vou) a French-speaking, largely Protestant canton (area 1,256 sq. miles, pop. 528,747) of W. Switzerland. Capital: Lausanne

vaud·e·ville (vɔ́dəvil, vóudəvil, vɔ́dvil, vóudvil) *n.* music-hall variety entertainment [fr. L. *vadere,* to go+*virer* to turn]

Vau·dreuil de Ca·va·gnal (voudrəːjdəkævænjæl), Pierre François de Rigaud, marquis de (1698-1778), the last governor (1755-60) of New France. In 1760 he surrendered all French Canada to the British

Vaughan (vɔn), Henry (1622-95), Welsh metaphysical poet. His output was small and has more of Herbert's quiet simplicity than of Donne's energy and complexity in it. His collections include 'Silex scintillans' (1650) and 'Thalia rediviva' (1678)

Vaughan Wil·liams (vɔnwíljəmz), Ralph (1872-1958), British composer. His work springs from his interest in the traditional folk music of Britain, and esp. its characteristic modes, which give his music its tonality. He wrote 9 symphonies, operas, much choral music, orchestral works, hymns, songs and chamber music. He was also a scholar and an arranger of genius, and was active in the publication of much English folk music and the republishing of much English church music

vault (vɔlt) **1.** *v.i.* to project oneself through the air, often over an object or barrier, esp. using one's hands or a pole as a lever to provide the necessary impetus || *v.t.* to project oneself over in this way, *to vault a gate* **2.** *n.* a leap or jump made with the help of the hands or a pole || *POLE VAULT [fr. O.F. *vouter* fr. *voute,* vault]

vault 1. *n.* (*archit.*) an arched construction in masonry forming a roof or decorating or supporting the true roof || a usually arched room, usually underground, esp. a cellar or burial chamber || the fireproof, burglarproof room of a bank (*rhet.*) a vaultlike space or covering, the *vault of heaven* || (*anat.*) the arched roof of a cavity **2.** *v.t.* to cover with a vault or arched roof structure || to construct as a vault, *a vaulted roof* || *v.i.* to curve in the shape of a vault **váult·ing** *n.* (*archit.*) vaulted work || the art of building vaults [Late M.E. *voute* fr. O.F. *voute, vaulte, vaute*]

vaulting horse a wooden horse or frame used for agility exercises in gymnastics

vaunt (vɔnt, vɑnt) **1.** *v.t.* (*rhet.*) to boast of, to brag about || *v.i.* (*rhet.*) to boast, to brag **2.** *n.* (*rhet.*) a boast [O.F. *vanter*]

Vau·que·lin (vouklɛ̃), Louis Nicolas (1763-1829), French chemist who discovered chromium (1798) and many compounds of beryllium

Vau·ve·nargues (vouvənærg), Luc de Clapiers, marquis de (1715-47), French writer and moralist best known for his 'Introduction à la connaissance de l'esprit humaine' (1746), characterized by a confident optimism in the human heart and its passions

vav·a·sor, vav·a·sour (vǽvəsɔr, vǽvəsour) *n.* a feudal lord of intermediary rank having vassals under him but holding his land under a superior lord or knight [O.F. *vavasour, vavassour* or M.L. *vavassor*]

vav·a·so·ry (vǽvəsɔriː, vǽvəsouriː) *pl.* **vav·a·so·ries** *n.* (*hist.*) the lands held by a vavasor || tenure of land by a vavasor

vavasour *VAVASOR
Vá·quez (vάskes), Horacio (1860-1936), Dominican general and president of the Republic (1902-3, 1924-30), his second term dating from the departure of the U.S. Marines
Vâz·quez de Co·ro·na·do (vάθkeθðekɔrɔnάðɔ), Juan (c. 1523-65), Spanish colonial administrator, son of the conquistador Francisco Vázquez de Coronado (1510-50). He was Spain's first governor (adelantado) in that country
V-beam radar (ví:bi:m) (*electr. mil.*) a system for measuring height, distance, and bearing of a target, using two beams of radar, one vertical, the other inclined
VC (*abbr.*) for Vietcong, term for the Communist and insurgent forces in South Vietnam during Vietnam War, 1965–1975
veal (vi:l) *n.* calf's flesh as food [A.F. *vel,* O.F. *veel, veal*]
Veb·len (véblən), Thorstein (1857-1929), U.S. economist and social scientist. He was one of the first to analyze the psychological bases of social institutions. His two most important works are 'The Theory of the Leisure Class' (1899) and 'The Theory of Business Enterprise' (1904)
vec·tor (véktər) *n.* (*math.*) a quantity that is specified by magnitude, direction and sense, that may be represented in some reference systems by an orientated arrowed line segment whose length is a simple function of the magnitude. The displacement, acceleration or velocity of a particle, or the force on a body, are examples of vectors (cf. SCALAR) ‖ (*biol.*) an agent that transmits a pathogen from one organism to another either mechanically as a carrier (e.g. the housefly for typhoid) or biologically, with a role in a life cycle (e.g. the mosquito for the malaria parasite) **vec·to·ri·al** (vektɔ́ri:əl, vektóuri:əl) *adj.* [L.=carrier]
vector *v.* (*aeronautics*) to direct
vector meson (*particle phys.*) a class of unstable elementary particles (including omega, phi, and rho mesons) with a mass of more than 1,200 million electron volts
vector quantity a vector
vectors, law of *POLYGON LAW OF VECTORS
Ve·da (véidə) any of the four books of the ancient Hindu scripture [fr. Skr. *vēda,* knowledge, sacred book]
Ve·dan·ta (vədάntə, vədǽntə) *n.* the orthodox Hindu school of philosophy concerned chiefly with the latter part of the Vedas [Skr. *vēdânta*]
Vedanta Society the Ramakrishna Mission
Ve·dan·tic (vədάntik, vədǽntik) *adj.* of or relating to Vedanta
Ve·dan·tism (vədάntizəm, vədǽntizəm) *n.* the philosophy of Vedanta
Ve·dan·tist (vədάntist, vədǽntist) **1.** *n.* someone who professes vedantism **2.** *adj.* Vedantic
V. E. Day May 8, 1945, the date of the Allied victory in Europe in the 2nd world war
Ved·da, Ved·dah (védə) *n.* a member of an aboriginal people living in the forests of Ceylon. They are hunters and cave dwellers and practice ancestor worship
ve·dette (vidét) *n.* (*navy*) a small armed vessel used for scouting or escorting ‖ (*mil., hist.*) a mounted sentry in the advance of an army for observing enemy activities [F. fr. Ital.]
Ve·dic (véidik) **1.** *n.* the Indic language of the Vedas, Vedic Sanskrit **2.** *adj.* of or relating to the Vedas, the language in which they are written etc.
ve·du·tis·ta (veidu:tístɑ) *n.* (*Italian, veduta,* 'view') cityscape artist, e.g., Piranesi, Panini
veer (viər) **1.** *v.i.* (of the wind) to change direction clockwise (opp. BACK) ‖ (of a ship) to turn with the head away from the direction of the wind ‖ to turn gradually or change direction, *then the road veers to the right* ‖ (esp. of a mental attitude, opinion etc.) to change in direction ‖ *v.t.* (*naut.*) to change the course of (a vessel) away from the direction of the wind **2.** *n.* a change of direction [fr. F. *virer,* to turn]
veer *v.t.* (*naut.,* usually with 'out') to let out (a rope, chain etc.) [M.Du. *vieren*]
veer·y (víəri:) *pl.* **veer·ies** *n. Hylocichla fuscescens,* a very small tawny thrush of E. North America [perh. imit.]
Ve·ga (véigɑ) the brightest star in the constellation Lyra
Vega, Lope de *LOPE DE VEGA
veg·an (védʒ'n) *n.* a vegetarian who eats no dairy products. —**veganism** *n.*
veg·e·ta·ble (védʒitəb'l, védʒtəb'l) **1.** *n.* a plant (as distinguished from an animal or mineral), esp. an edible plant or an edible part of a plant (e.g. cabbage, lettuce, bean, potato etc.) ‖ a human being who is nonfunctional, either figuratively or literally **2.** *adj.* pertaining to, having the nature of, or made from, a plant [O.F.]
vegetable butter any vegetable oil which is solid at ordinary temperatures, e.g. cacao butter
vegetable ivory the endosperm of the ivory nut. It has the appearance of ivory, takes a high polish, and is used esp. for buttons
vegetable marrow the large, tender fruit of *Cucurbita pepo,* fam. *Cucurbitaceae,* cultivated and eaten as a vegetable. It is one of several varieties of summer squash
veg·e·tal (védʒit'l) *adj.* of or relating to vegetation ‖ consisting of or extracted from vegetables ‖ of or relating to growth (e.g. in plants) [fr. L. *vegetare*]
veg·e·tar·i·an (vedʒitέəri:ən) **1.** *n.* a person who abstains from eating meat, either keeping strictly to a vegetable and fruit diet, or also eating eggs, milk and butter **2.** *adj.* relating to vegetarians or vegetarianism ‖ consisting of vegetables **veg·e·tár·i·an·ism** *n.*
veg·e·tate (védʒiteit) *pres. part.* **veg·e·tat·ing** *past* and *past part.* **veg·e·tat·ed** *v.i.* to grow in the manner of a plant ‖ to live an inactive life without much intellectual stimulus or physical exertion [fr. L. *vegetare* (*vegetatus*), to enliven]
veg·e·ta·tion (vedʒitéiʃən) *n.* plant life in general, with respect to geographical variation or scenery ‖ the act or process of vegetating ‖ (*med.*) a morbid bodily plantlike or spongelike growth [fr. L.L. and M.L. *vegetatio* (*vegetationis*)]
veg·e·ta·tive (védʒiteitiv) *adj.* of or concerned with vegetation ‖ of growth in plants, as opposed to the reproductive period ‖ having the power to stimulate growth in plants ‖ (*biol.*) of reproduction by bud formation, or by other asexual methods in plants or animals ‖ of a life lived without intellectual stimulus or physical exertion [fr. M.L. *vegetativus*]
veg out (vedʒ) *v.* (*slang*) to become a vegetable
ve·he·mence (ví:əməns) *n.* the state or quality of being vehement **vé·he·men·cy** *n.* vehemence [fr. late O.F. or fr. L. *vehementia*]
ve·he·ment (ví:əmənt) *adj.* violent ‖ showing or arousing intense feeling [fr. O.F. or fr. L. *vehemens* (*vehementis*), violent]
ve·hi·cle (ví:ik'l) *n.* any kind of contrivance, on wheels or runners, used to carry people or goods from one place to another over land (e.g. a carriage, bicycle, sleigh etc.) ‖ a means of transmission, *matter is the vehicle of energy* ‖ a fluid used as a medium for a suspension of a pigment ‖ a substance with which the active agent of a medicine is compounded ‖ any person or thing used as a medium to convey ideas, emotions etc., *a newspaper is a powerful propaganda vehicle* [fr. F. *véhicule* or L. *vehiculum*]
ve·hic·u·lar (vi:híkjulər) *adj.* of or for vehicles ‖ serving as a vehicle [fr. L.L. *vehicularis*]
veil (veil) **1.** *n.* a piece of light material draped over the face, worn esp. by many oriental women for modesty and protection from sun and dust ‖ a piece of transparent material used as a hat trimming, sometimes covering the eyes or face ‖ the headdress of a nun, usually covering the head and shoulders ‖ a cover or curtain to hide or protect something (e.g. a veil on a statue or plaque) ‖ a covering ‖ (*fig.*) a cloak, disguise, mask etc., *interference under the veil of friendship* ‖ the calyptra of a moss ‖ a velum **to take the veil** to become a nun **2.** *v.t.* to cover or hide with a veil, *mist veiled the valley* ‖ to conceal, disguise etc., *to veil one's intentions* **véil·ing** *n.* material used for veils ‖ an act or instance of covering with a veil or as if with a veil ‖ a veil [A.F. and O.N.F. *veile* and *veil*]
veiling luminance the phenomenon of diffusion of light by water
vein (vein) *n.* one of the tubular vessels with moderately thin walls that carry blood in a steady stream from the capillaries to the heart in vertebrates. The pressure of the blood in the veins is low and because of this they are equipped on the inner walls with cuplike valves to keep the blood from flowing back ‖ (*geol.*) a fissure in rock filled with ore (in most cases deposited there by water) ‖ (*geol.*) a mineral deposit ‖ a specified attitude or mood expressed in speech or writing, *in a jocular vein* ‖ a streak or stripe in wood, marble etc. of a different shade or color or texture from the rest ‖ (*biol.*) a rib in a leaf or insect's wing **veined** *adj.* having veins ‖ marked with veins **véin·ing** *n.* a pattern of veins, e.g. in marble [O.F. *veine*]
ve·la·men (vəléimən) *pl.* **ve·lam·i·na** (vəlǽminə) *n.* (*anat.*) a membrane, esp. one covering parts of the brain ‖ (*bot.*) a specialized moisture-absorbing tissue at the apex of the aerial roots of epiphytic orchids [L.=a covering]
ve·lar (ví:lər) *adj.* of a velum, esp. of the soft palate of the mouth ‖ (*phon.,* of a sound) formed with the back of the tongue against the soft palate [fr. L. *velaris* fr. *velum,* a sail]
Ve·las·co I·bar·ra (velάskɔi:bάrra), José María (1893-1979), five times (1934-5, 1944-7, 1952-6, 1960-1, 1968-72) the elected president of Ecuador. A demagogue without party or program, he was three times deposed as a result of political and economic chaos and his unpopular austerity measures. He resigned (1970) for the fourth time, but the military persuaded him to accept dictatorial powers. He shut down the universities, dissolved Congress, and ranged himself against the Supreme Court. He was overthrown (1972) by an army coup d'état and replaced by Brig. Gen. Guillermo Rodriguez Lara
ve·late (ví:lit, ví:leit) *adj.* (*biol.*) having a veil or velum [fr. L. *velum* or fr. L. *velare* (*velatus*), to cover]
Ve·laz·quez (vəlǽskiz, veldάθkeθ), Diego Rodriguez de Silva y (1599-1660), Spanish painter. Philip IV was his patron and many of his finest portraits were of the royal family and the court, including dwarfs and jesters. Velazquez was early influenced by Caravaggio's 'realism' and chiaroscuro. A whole range of paintings is devoted to Spanish domestic life, in subtle color schemes of warm brown, gray and cream. They are pictures of acceptance, dignity and harmony. In contrast with them are the court portraits, where cardinal red and royal purple take the place of brown sackcloth, and the character of the noble sitter is rendered with sometimes terrifying perception. The speed and economy of Velazquez's brushwork, and his ability to capture surface and light with techniques which seem to disappear on close inspection, made him a powerful influence on French Impressionism
Ve·láz·quez de Cué·llar (velάθkeθðekwéjar), Diego de (1465-1524), Spanish conquistador. With Pánfilo de Narváez he led (1511) an expedition to Cuba and by 1514 the island was conquered. As Cuba's first governor (1514-21, 1523-4), he founded (1514) Santiago and (1519) Havana. He organized four expeditions to Mexico
Vel·cro (vélkrou) *n.* trade name for fabric created with hooked surface to adhere to other fabrics, sometimes in lieu of fasteners
veld, veldt (velt) *n.* open grassland in S. Africa, esp. the flat, treeless country of the Transvaal plateau [Du. *veld,* a field]
vel·le·i·ty (velí:iti:) *pl.* **vel·le·i·ties** *n.* a weak desire or resolution, esp. one so weak that it does not lead to action [fr. F. *velléité* or M.L. *velleitas*]
Vel·lore (velɔ́r, velóur) an agricultural center (pop. 114,000) in N. Madras, India: temple (14th c.), fortress (17th c.)
vel·lum (véləm) *n.* a fine parchment made from specially treated calfskin etc. and used for writing on or for binding books ‖ a manuscript written on this [O. F. *velin*]
vellum paper imitation vellum, esp. for letter writing
ve·loc·im·e·ter (vi:lousímətə:r) *n.* a device that uses the Doppler effect and its echo to measure sound velocity in water, e.g., sound, machinery
ve·loc·i·pede (vəlɔ́səpi:d) *n.* (*hist.*) an early form of bicycle or tricycle propelled by thrusts of the feet against pedals [fr. F. *vélocipède*]
ve·loc·i·ty (vəlɔ́siti:) *pl.* **ve·loc·i·ties** *n.* rate of motion ‖ (*phys.*) the time rate of change of a displacement vector, being a vector parallel to the displacement vector ‖ (*chem.*) the rate of disappearance of the reactants or of the appearance of products in a chemical reaction [fr. F. *vélocité* or fr. L. *velocitas*]
velocity of escape *ESCAPE VELOCITY
velocity ratio the ratio of the displacement of any part of a machine to that of the driving part in the same time
vel·o·drome (vélə"droum) *n.* a building or sta-

CONCISE PRONUNCIATION KEY: **(a)** æ, *cat;* ɑ, *car;* ɔ *fawn;* ei, *snake.* **(e)** e, *hen;* i:, *sheep;* iə, *deer;* εə, *bear.* **(i)** i, *fish;* ai, *tiger;* ə:, *bird.* **(o)** o, *ox;* au, *cow;* ou, *goat;* u, *poor;* ɔi, *royal.* **(u)** ʌ, *duck;* u, *bull;* u:, *goose;* ə, *bacillus;* ju:, *cube.* x, *loch;* θ, *think;* ð, *bother;* z, *Zen;* ʒ, *corsage;* dʒ, *savage;* ŋ, *orangutang;* j, *yak;* ʃ, *fish;* tʃ, *fetch;* 'l, *rabble;* 'n, *redden.* Complete pronunciation key appears inside front cover.

dium with a specially designed track for cycle racing [F. *vélodrome*]

ve·lour, ve·lours (vəlúər) *pl.* **ve·lours** (vəlúərz) *n.* a velvetlike woven fabric ‖ a fur felt used for hats [F.+velvet]

ve·lum (ví:ləm) *pl.* **ve·la** (ví:lə) *n.* (*biol.*) a membrane, esp. the soft palate of the mouth [L.=sail, covering]

ve·lu·ti·nous (vəlú:t'nəs) *adj.* (*biol.*) velvety, covered with very fine, short, upright hairs [fr. Mod. L. *velutiniis* fr. M.L. *velutum,* velvet]

vel·vet (vélvit) **1.** *n.* a closely woven fabric, esp. one wholly or partly of silk, with a short, soft nap or pile on one side ‖ something resembling this, e.g. in softness ‖ the furry skin covering the growing antlers of deer **2.** *adj.* made of or covered with velvet ‖ like velvet [fr. M.L. *velvetum*]

vel·vet·een (vẹlvití:n) *n.* cotton material woven with a short pile

vel·vet·y (vélviti:) *adj.* soft and smooth to the touch, the palate or the ear etc.

ve·nal (ví:n'l) *adj.* mercenary, esp. open to bribery and corruption ‖ involving mercenary motives or corruption [fr. L. *venalis*]

ve·nal·i·ty (vi:nǽliti:) *n.* the state or quality of being venal [fr. F. *vénalité* or L. L. *venalitas*]

ve·na·tion (vi:néiʃən, vənéiʃən) *n.* the system or arrangement of veins on leaves and insects' wings [fr. L. *vena,* vein]

vend (vend) *v.t.* (esp. *law*) to sell, offer for sale

vend·ee (vendí:) *n.* (*law*) the person to whom an object is sold [fr. F. *vendre* or L. *vendere,* to sell]

Ven·dée (vɑ̃dei) a department (area 2,690 sq. miles, pop. 450,600) in W. France (*POITOU). Chief town: La Roche-sur-Yon (pop. 48,053). The Vendée was the center of a royalist uprising (1793-6) against the 1st French republic

Ven·dé·miaire (vɑ̃deimjɛər) *n.* (*F. hist.*) the 1st month of the French Revolutionary calendar ‖ the Paris royalist insurrection of 13 Vendémiaire (Oct. 5, 1795), crushed by Barras and Napoleon with a 'whiff of grapeshot'

ven·det·ta (vendétə) *n.* a blood feud, laying an obligation of honor on the members of a family to take revenge upon the killer or injurer of one of them, or upon a member of his family, thus instigating a chain of vengeance from generation to generation [Ital.]

vending machine an automatic coin-operated machine from which goods (candies, cigarettes etc.) can be obtained

ven·dor (véndər, vendɔ́r) *n.* a person who sells, esp. one who hawks his goods in a public place

ve·neer (vəníər) **1.** *v.t.* to cover (a surface of wood) with a thin coating of a finer wood ‖ to bond together (layers of wood) to form plywood **2.** *n.* a thin layer of fine wood laid over the surface of a cheaper wood and used in cabinetmaking ‖ any of the thin layers bonded together to form plywood ‖ any refined outer covering concealing a coarse structure ‖ a superficial show, *a veneer of charm* **ve·neer·ing** (vəníəriŋ) *n.* a thin layer of material for plywood etc. ‖ the process of applying a veneer to wood [fr. G. *furnieren* fr. F.]

venepuncture *VENIPUNCTURE

ven·er·a·bil·i·ty (vẹnərəbíliti:) *n.* the state or quality of being venerable

ven·er·a·ble (vénərəb'l) *adj.* deserving or evoking profound respect and veneration on account of age, probity, intellectual power, or (of objects and places) historical or religious associations ‖ (*Anglican Communion*) used as a courtesy title of an archdeacon ‖ (*Roman Catholicism*) used as a title given to those judged to have attained the first of three degrees of sanctity (cf. BLESSED, cf. SAINT) **vén·er·a·bly** *adv.* [fr. L. *venerabilis*]

ven·er·ate (vénəreit) *pres. part.* **ven·er·at·ing** *past* and *past part.* **ven·er·at·ed** *v.t.* to regard with the deepest respect or reverence ‖ to worship as holy **ven·er·á·tion, vén·er·a·tor** *ns* [fr. L. *venerari* (*veneratus*), to worship]

ve·ne·re·al (vəníəri:əl) *adj.* (of disease) contracted by sexual intercourse (*GONORRHEA, *SYPHILIS) ‖ having or relating to venereal disease ‖ (*rhet.*) of or relating to sexual activity [fr. L. *venereus* fr. *Venus* (veneris), goddess of love]

ven·er·y (vénəri:) *n.* (*hist.*) the sport of hunting with hounds [O.F. *venerie*]

venery *n.* (*rhet.*) the practice or pursuit of sexual pleasure [fr. L. *Venus* (Veneris), the goddess of love]

Ve·ne·tian (vəní:ʃən) **1.** *n.* a native or inhabitant of Venice **2.** *adj.* of or relating to Venice

Venetian blind a window covering constructed of thin horizontal slats of wood, plastic etc. held together by vertical tapes in such a way that they can be turned, lowered or raised to admit or exclude light

Venetian glass decorative glassware made at Murano in the Venice lagoon (since the 13th c.)

Venetian School a school of painters in Venice in the 15th and 16th cc. including notably the Bellini brothers, Carpaccio, Giorgione, Titian, Tintoretto and Veronese

Ve·ne·to (vénetɔ) a region (area 9,858 sq. miles, pop. 4,355,049) of N.E. Italy in the Dolomites and the N. Italian plain. Chief towns: Venice, Verona. Agriculture: (30% irrigated) cereals, sugar beets, fruit, vines, silk. Industries: sugar refining, oil refining, metallurgy, textiles. It formed part of Lombardy-Venetia (1815-66)

Ven·e·zue·la (vẹnəzwéilə) a republic (area 352,143 sq. miles, pop. 17,993,000) in N. South America. Capital: Caracas. People: 70% mestizo, 20% European stock, small Indian, African and mulatto minorities. Language: Spanish. Religion: Roman Catholic. The land is 3% arable, 16% pasture and 20% forest. In the West, separated by the Maracaibo basin (the country's great oil field) are the northernmost chains of the Andes, the Sierra de Perija on the Colombian border and the Sierra de Merida (to 16,000 ft) extended in the coast ranges. The lengthwise valley, which divides the latter (and in which Caracas lies), is the chief agricultural region. The lower Andean slopes and, progressively, the savanna lowlands (traditionally grazing land) of the Orinoco basin are also cultivated. The southeast is occupied by the largely unexplored Guiana highlands (rain forest), rising to 8,260 ft. Venezuela includes 72 islands in the Caribbean. Average temperatures (F.): Caracas 69°, coast and interior 80°. Rainfall: coast and coast ranges 20-40 ins, interior 40-80 ins (rainy season: Apr.-Dec.). Livestock: cattle, hogs. Agricultural products: coffee, corn, rice, cotton, cocoa, sugarcane, wheat, tobacco, beans, sisal, rubber, divi-divi, copaiba, vanilla, dairy products, potatoes, bananas. Mineral resources: petroleum (second world producer), iron ore, coal, gold, natural gas, diamonds, manganese, phosphate, sulfur, nickel, salt, asbestos, copper. Manufactures and industries: petroleum products, steel, foodstuffs, textiles, cement, tires, clothing, footwear, lumber, leather, hydroelectricity, fishing. Exports: petroleum and petroleum products, iron ore, coffee, cocoa. Imports: chemicals, machinery, manufactured goods, vehicles, foodstuffs, metals. Chief ports: La Guaira (for Caracas), Maracaibo. Universities: Caracas (3), Mérida, Maracaibo, Carabobo, Oriente. Monetary unit: bolívar (100 centimos). HISTORY. Columbus discovered the mouth of the Orinoco (1498), and Ojeda and Vespucci explored the coast (1499). Despite attacks by the native Carib Indians, Spanish settlements were made (1520s). Emperor Charles V leased the colony to a German merchant family until 1546. The coast formed part of the Spanish Main and was a center of piracy and smuggling (16th and 17th cc.). Venezuela was joined to the Spanish viceroyalty of New Granada (*COLOMBIA), revolted (1810) under Miranda and declared itself independent (July 5, 1811). Fighting continued until Bolívar incorporated Venezuela in Greater Colombia (1819). It became a separate state (1830). A boundary dispute with British Guiana (1895-6) provoked considerable tension between Britain and the U.S.A. Venezuela's political history has been punctuated by civil wars, revolts and military coups. The state was almost bankrupt in the late 19th c. but the exploitation of oil helped to restore solvency (early 20th c.) and the bolívar had become (late 1960s) South America's most stable currency. Modern Venezuela may be said to date from 1936, following the death (1935) of the patriarchal dictator Juan Vicente Gómez. The military junta under Rómulo Betancourt (1945-7) was followed by the first constitutionally elected president, Rómulo Gallegos (1948). A military coup d'état overthrew his government and installed the dictatorship (1953-8) of Marcos Pérez Jiménez. In the elections of 1958, Betancourt, founder of the Democratic Action (AD) party, was constitutionally elected. He supported friendly U.S.-Venezuelan relations and American investments and he implemented moderate agrarian reform and industrial development. The elections of 1963 were won by his AD lieutenant Raúl Leoni, who continued his programs. As a result of three fissions in the AD, the party lost the elections of 1968 to the Social Christian party (COPEI) under Rafael Caldera. Succeeding elections put Carlos Andrés Pérez (AD), Louis Herrera Campíns (COPEI), and Jaime Lusinchi (AD) into the presidency

Venezuela, Gulf of a gulf in N.W. Venezuela, between the Guajira peninsula in Colombia and the Paraguaná peninsula in Venezuela

Ven·e·zue·lan (vẹnəzwéilən) **1.** *n.* a native or inhabitant of Venezuela **2.** *adj.* of or relating to Venezuela

venge·ance (véndʒəns) *n.* damage or harm done to another in retaliation for damage or harm to oneself or an associate **with a vengeance** intensively, to a degree much greater than might be expected, *he has cleaned up the organization with a vengeance* [O.F.]

venge·ful (véndʒfəl) *adj.* disposed to acts of vengeance ‖ vindictive [fr. older *venge,* to avenge]

ve·nial (ví:njəl, ví:ni:əl) *adj.* pardonable, *a venial offense* ‖ (*Roman Catholicism,* of a sin) minor in gravity or committed heedlessly (cf. MORTAL) **ve·nial·i·ty** (vi:njǽliti:, vị:ni:ǽliti:) *n.* [O.F. or fr. L. *venialis*]

Ven·ice (vénis) (*Ital.* Venezia) a port (pop. 360,300) in Veneto, Italy, built on islands (cut by over 100 canals and linked by some 400 bridges) in a lagoon of the Adriatic. Industries (confined to the suburbs): oil refining, metallurgical and chemical industries, shipbuilding, glass and jewelry manufacture. The Grand Canal, lined with palaces (mainly 15th c.) and crossed by the Rialto bridge (1590), divides the city. The eastern, older part centers on San Marco Basilica (Byzantine, 11th c.) and the Doges' Palace (Gothic, 14th-15th cc.). There are Gothic, Renaissance and baroque churches, a university (1868), and museums (works of the Venetian School etc.). The town grew during the barbarian and Lombard invasions of Italy, and was united (697) under one leader, the doge. It became an independent republic, gained control of the Adriatic, and prospered under a merchant aristocracy. Venice used the Crusades to extend its trade through the Levant and into the Black Sea, defeating (1380) Genoa, its main commercial rival. By the mid-15th c. it had conquered the Dalmatian coast, Euboea, Crete and Cyprus, as well as a wide area of N.E. Italy, but its prosperity suffered from Turkish competition (late 15th c.) in the eastern Mediterranean, and the discovery (end of the 16th c.) of the Cape route to India. Venice remained important for its schools of painting (15th and 16th cc.) and music (17th and 18th cc.). After the Napoleonic Wars, Venice was placed (1815) under Austrian rule, which a revolution (1848) failed to shake off. Venice joined Italy (1866) after the Seven Weeks' War

ven·i·punc·ture, ven·e·punc·ture (ví:nəpʌŋktʃər, vénəpʌŋktʃər) *n.* (*med.*) insertion of a hollow needle into a vein, either to take a blood test or to give an injection [fr. L. *vena,* vein+PUNCTURE]

ven·i·son (vénis,n, véniz,n, *Br.* vénzən) *n.* the flesh of deer as food [A.F. and O.F.]

Ve·ni·zé·los (vẹnəzéilɔs), Eleuthérios (1864-1936), Greek politician, prime minister (1910-15, 1917-20, 1924, 1928-32). Born on the island of Crete, he worked for the union of Crete with Greece, a union proclaimed in 1905 but not realized until 1913. He went to Greece (1909) and became the Liberal party leader, then prime minister (1910). During the Bakan Wars (1912-13) he helped defeat the Turks and almost doubled Greece's territory. He favored Britain and France in the 1st world war and resigned as prime minister (1915) because Greece's pro-German King Constantine advocated continuing neutrality. He returned to Athens (1917) as prime minister on the abdication of Constantine. Greece then entered the war on the Allied side. Venizélos acquired considerable territory for Greece, principally at Turkey's expense, following the war. He fled Greece (1935) after being implicated in an antimonarchist revolt and died in exile in Paris

ven·om (vénəm) *n.* the poisonous fluid secreted by certain snakes, spiders, insects etc. and transmitted by bite or sting ‖ spite, malice, in character, speech or behavior [A.F. and O.F. *venim,* var. of *venin*]

ven·om·ous (vénəməs) *adj.* poisonous, containing venom ‖ malicious, spiteful ‖ having a poison gland or glands [O.F. *venimeux*]
ve·nose (vi:nous) *adj.* (*bot.*) venous
ve·nos·i·ty (vi:nɒsiti:) *n.* the state or quality of being venous or venose
ve·nous (ví:nəs) *adj.* (*physiol.*) of a vein or veins ‖ (*bot.*) having veins ‖ (*physiol.*, of blood) being carried in the veins back to the heart after circulating in the body [fr. L. *venosus*]
vent (vent) **1.** *n.* a small aperture designed to provide an outlet from a confined space or an inlet into it, e.g. the bunghole of a barrel ‖ a channel of release e.g. for energy etc. ‖ the anus, esp. the anal aperture of lower vertebrates **2.** *v.t.* to make an aperture in ‖ to relieve (one's feelings) in words or actions, *to vent one's anger on someone* [fr. F. *vent*, wind and F. *évent*, a vent]
vent *n.* a tailored slit, esp. one in the back of a coat [var. of older *fent* fr. F. *fente*, slit]
ven·ter (véntər) *n.* (*bot.*) the swollen base of an archegonium ‖ (*zool.*, of vertebrates) the abdomen ‖ a protuberance, e.g. of muscle, or shallow concavity in a bone ‖ (*law*) the womb ‖ (*law*) a wife as the mother of a man's children [A.F. *ventre, venter* or L. *venter*, womb]
ven·ti·late (véntəleit) *pres. part.* **ven·ti·lat·ing** *past* and *past part.* **ven·ti·lat·ed** *v.t.* to cause the passage of air into or through ‖ to expose to the air so as to freshen ‖ to furnish with an opening for the escape of air, gas etc. ‖ to give full and free expression to (a grievance, controversy etc.) [fr. L. *ventilare* (*ventilatus*), to fan]
ven·ti·la·tion (vȩntəléiʃən) *n.* a ventilating or being ventilated ‖ a system for ensuring the circulation of fresh air in a room, building or other confined space [fr. L. *ventilatio* (*ventilationis*)]
ven·ti·la·tor (véntəlȩitər) *n.* a contrivance for ensuring the free passage of air in an enclosed space
ven·tral (véntrəl) *adj.* (*anat.*) of or relating to the lower or abdominal surfaces, in human anatomy sometimes anterior (opp. DORSAL) ‖ (*bot.*) of or relating to the lower surface [F. or fr. L. *ventralis*]
ven·tri·cle (véntrik'l) *n.* a cavity or chamber of the body, esp. in the heart ‖ the main contractile chamber or either of the two chambers connecting the auricles and the arteries ‖ a cavity in the brain's system of communicating cavities [F. *ventricule* or fr. L. *ventriculus*]
ven·tri·cose (véntrikous) *adj.* (*biol.*) swelling out in the middle or to one side [fr. Mod. L. *ventricosus*]
ven·tric·u·lar (ventríkjulər) *adj.* of or like a ventricle ‖ abdominal [fr. L. *ventriculus*]
ven·tri·lo·qui·al (vȩntrəlóukwi:əl) *adj.* of, belonging to, or using ventriloquism
ven·tril·o·quism (ventríləkwizəm) *n.* utterance which makes hearers think that the sound comes from a source other than the actual speaker
ven·tril·o·quist (ventríləkwist) *n.* someone who practices the art of ventriloquism, esp. an entertainer **ven·tril·o·quis·tic** *adj.*
ven·tril·o·quize (ventríləkwaiz) *pres. part.* **ven·tril·o·quiz·ing** *past* and *past part.* **ven·tril·o·quized** *v.i.* to act as a ventriloquist ‖ *v.t.* to utter (sounds) as a ventriloquist
ven·tril·o·quy (ventríləkwi:) *n.* ventriloquism [fr. M.L. or Mod. L. *ventriloquium*]
Ven·tris (véntris), Michael George Francis (1922-56), British architect. He deciphered (1953) the Linear B script of Minoan civilization, showing it to be an early form of Greek
ven·ture (véntʃər) **1.** *n.* something involving a risk which one decides to attempt **at a venture** as a guess, without real calculation **2.** *v. pres. part.* **ven·tur·ing** *past* and *past part.* **ven·tured** *v.t.* to risk, dare, *to venture an opinion* ‖ *v.i.* to take a risk **vén·ture·some** *adj.* [fr. older *aventure*, adventure]
Ven·tu·ri (ventú:ri:) *n.* a Venturi meter
Venturi meter a device to determine fluid flow, e.g. in a pipeline, or in measuring airspeed, that measures the pressure drop at a constriction in a tube [after G. B. *Venturi* (1746–1822), Ital. physicist]
Venturi tube a Venturi meter
ven·tur·ous (véntʃərəs) *adj.* prepared to face danger, take risks etc. ‖ attended with risk or danger [aphetic var. of ADVENTUROUS]
ven·ue (vénju:, vénu:) *n.* the scene or area of an action, esp. of a crime ‖ (*law*) the area within which the original proceedings in a trial are held, and the jury is gathered **to change the venue** (*law*) to remove the legal proceedings from the area where originally brought (so as to avoid prejudice, riot etc. or for the convenience of the parties or witnesses) ‖ (*Br.*) an appointed meeting place, point of assembly [O.F.=a coming]
Ve·nus (ví:nəs) (*Rom. mythol.*) the goddess of beauty and love, identified with the Greek Aphrodite ‖ the second planet from the sun (mean orbital diameter=67 million miles), roughly comparable to the earth in mass and size (mass=4.81 x 10^{21} tons, diameter=7,550 miles). Venus revolves around the sun with a sidereal period of 224.7 earth days and appears to have a rotation period of 117 earth days (the planet's atmosphere turning with an independent retrograde motion in only 4 earth days). Its atmosphere, containing a yellowish cloud blanket, is composed of carbon dioxide with 4% nitrogen, 0.5% oxygen and traces of water vapor. Temperature in the ground is about 890°F. and pressure about 90 atmospheres. Pioneer Venus I has been orbiting the planet since 1978, and other spacecraft observations have been made by U.S. Mariner and Soviet Venera landers
Venus probe *n.* (*aerospace*) 1978 mission to explore Venus, made by U.S. Pioneer and Mariner and U.S.S.R. Venera
Ve·nus's-flow·er-bas·ket (ví:nəsəsfláuərbæskit, ví:nəsəsfláuərbɒskit) *n.* a member of *Euplectella*, a glass sponge inhabiting deep waters off the Philippines. The dried skeletons, made of lacy siliceous spicules, are of great beauty
Ve·nus's-fly·trap (ví:nəsəsfláitræp) *n. Dionaea muscipula*, fam. *Droseraceae*, an insectivorous plant native to North and South Carolina
Venus's looking-glass a plant of the genus *Specularia*, esp. *S. speculum-veneris*
ve·ra·cious (vəréiʃəs) *adj.* truthful, speaking the truth as a matter of course ‖ true, accurate [fr. L. *verax* (*veracis*), truthful]
ve·rac·i·ty (vərǽsiti:) *pl.* **ve·rac·i·ties** *n.* the quality of telling the truth ‖ the quality of being true ‖ something true [F. *véracité* or M.L. *veracitas*]
Ver·a·cruz (vȩrəkrú:z) a central gulf state (area 27,759 sq. miles, pop. 5,091,000) of Mexico. Capital: Jalapa (pop. 72,000). The land varies from the tropical lowlands of its 50-mile coastline to the central plateau region of the interior, cut into rich forested valleys. Its wealth is based on commerce (over 40 rivers cross the state), agriculture (cotton, sugar, rum, pineapples, tobacco, cacao, vanilla, and various fruits), and manufacturing (cotton and other textiles). Under a massive reclamation project (1950s) three dams were built to provide hydroelectric power, and modern farm methods were introduced. There are important archaeological remains
Veracruz a port (pop. 340,500) in E. Mexico. Industries: food and tobacco processing, tanning. Colonial fortresses and church. Founded (1519) by Cortes, the city prospered as the chief link between New Spain and Cádiz, though vulnerable to piracy. It was captured by the French in 1838, by the Americans under Winfield Scott in 1847, by the French in 1861, and by a U.S. force under Admiral Mayo in 1914, when President Wilson intervened to prevent foreign supplies from reaching Gen. Victoriano Huerta during the Mexican revolution
Ver·a Cruz (vérəkrú:s) the original name given to Brazil by the Portuguese
ve·ran·da, ve·ran·dah (vərǽndə) *n.* an open, roofed portico or gallery extending along a side of a house [fr. Port. *varanda* fr. Hind.] .
verb (və:rb) *n.* (*gram.*) any of a class of words expressing an action performed or state suffered or experienced by a subject [O.F. *verbe* or fr. L. *verbum*, word, verb]
ver·bal (vǝ́:rb'l) *adj.* relating to or consisting of words, *verbal dexterity* ‖ oral, spoken, not written, *a verbal message* ‖ (of translation) literal, word for word ‖ (*gram.*) relating to or derived from a verb ‖ (*gram.*) used to form verbs **vér·bal·ism** *n.* a verbal expression ‖ the use of words which sound well but have little content in reality, or an instance of this [O.F. or fr. L. *verbalis*, consisting of words]
ver·bal·ize (vǝ́:rb'laiz) *pres. part.* **ver·bal·iz·ing** *past* and *past part.* **ver·bal·ized** *v.i.* to be verbose ‖ *v.t.* to express in words ‖ to convert (another part of speech) into the form of a verb [F. *verbaliser*]
ver·bal·ly (vǝ́:rb'li:) *adv.* in words, esp. in spoken words
verbal noun a noun derived from a verb and having some of the characteristics of a verb. In English it is either a noun ending in '-ing' or an infinitive (e.g. 'reading' in 'reading is fun', or 'to read' in 'to read is fun')
ver·bas·cum (vərbǽskəm) *n.* mullein [L.]
ver·ba·tim (vərbéitim) **1.** *adv.* word for word, exactly as spoken or written **2.** *adj.* copied exactly from the original word-for-word [M.L.]
ver·be·na (vərbí:nə) *n.* a member of *Verbena*, fam. *Verbenaceae*, a genus of plants mainly of tropical America. Several varieties are widely cultivated as garden plants for their showy, sweet-smelling flowers (*VERVAIN) [M.L. and Mod. L.]
ver·bi·age (vǝ́:rbi:idʒ) *n.* the use of more words than are needed [F.]
verb·i·cide (vǝ́:rbəsaid) *n.* inflation of word meanings with use of large-scale modifiers and avoidance in precision, e.g., excessive use of 'very,' 'really,' 'unbelievable,' etc.
ver·bose (vərbóus) *adj.* employing or containing more words than are necessary [fr. L. *verbosus*]
ver·bos·i·ty (vərbɒ́siti:) *n.* the state or quality of being verbose [F. *verbosité* or fr. postclassical L. *verbositas*]
Ver·cin·get·o·rix (vȩ:rsindʒétəriks) (*d.* 46 B.C.), Gallic chieftain. He was the leader of an unsuccessful Gallic revolt (52 B.C.) against the Romans under Caesar. He graced Caesar's triumph in Rome and was then put to death
Ver·da·guer (vȩrdɑgér), Mosen Jacinto (1845-1902), Catalan poet. One of his most intensely patriotic epics, 'La Atlántida' (1877), was set to music, in part, by Falla
ver·dan·cy (vǝ́:rd'nsi:) *n.* the state or quality of being verdant
ver·dant (vǝ́:rd'nt) *adj.* (esp. of vegetation) very green or fresh ‖ (*rhet.*) immature, inexperienced, *verdant youth* [prob. fr. VERDURE]
Ver·di (vɛ́ərdi:), Giuseppi Fortunino Francesco (1813-1901), Italian composer. 'Nabucodonosor' (1842) was his first popular opera but he reached his peak with 'Rigoletto' (1851), 'Il Trovatore' (1853) and 'La Traviata' (1853). In his last period, ushered in by 'Aïda' (1871), Verdi forsook melodrama and his noblest operas, e.g. 'Otello' (1887), and his comic opera 'Falstaff' (1893), contain few set arias. The seamless vocal line is intensely dramatic and expressive. His whole gift issued in sounds uniquely adapted to the open-throated Italian voice, expressing through this, with orchestral and dramatic genius, a passionate involvement in human conflicts. In addition to the operas Verdi wrote a dramatic 'Requiem' (1874)
ver·dict (vǝ́:rdikt) *n.* (*law*) the decision of a jury after hearing evidence in a case of civil or criminal law ‖ a considered judgment after examination of evidence [A. F. *verdit*]
ver·di·gris (vǝ́:rdigris, vǝ́:rdigri:s) *n.* a green or greenish-blue crystalline substance formed on copper, brass or bronze, consisting of basic copper carbonate or copper sulfate or both ‖ a green or greenish-blue poisonous substance obtained from treating copper with acetic acid and used as a pigment [A.F. and O.F. *vert de Grece, vert-de-gris*, green of Greece]
Ver·dun (verdœ̃, ve:rdʌ́n) a town (pop. 23,621) in Meuse department, France, on the Meuse. Romanesque-Gothic cathedral (11th-13th cc.). In the 1st world war, Pétain held it against a massive German offensive in a battle (Feb. 21-Dec. 15, 1916) in which more than a million men were killed
Verdun, Treaty of a treaty (843) among the three sons of Emperor Louis I, dividing up Charlemagne's empire. Louis II 'the German' received the eastern part, Charles II 'the Bald' the western part and Lothair I the center and the Imperial crown
ver·dure (vǝ́:rdʒər) *n.* the greenness of fresh vegetation ‖ green vegetation [O.F.]
Ve·ree·ni·ging (fərí:niŋiŋ) a coal-mining center (pop. 79,000) in Transvaal, South Africa, on the Vaal. The treaty ending the Boer War was signed here (1902)
verge (və:rdʒ) *pres. part.* **verg·ing** *past* and *past part.* **verged** *v.i.* to tend towards a certain direction, *the road verges eastward, his policies verge increasingiy to the Left* [fr. L. *vergere*, to bend, turn]
verge 1. *n.* a border, edge ‖ the imaginary line at which a new condition or action starts, *on the verge of madness, on the verge of jumping* ‖ the grass border of a road, flower bed, path etc. ‖ a rod or staff carried before a dignitary as a sym-

CONCISE PRONUNCIATION KEY: **(a)** æ, *cat*; ɑ, *car*; ɔ *fawn*; ei, *snake*. **(e)** e, *hen*; i:, *sheep*; iə, *deer*; ɛə, *bear*. **(i)** i, *fish*; ai, *tiger*; ə:, *bird*. **(o)** o, *ox*; au, *cow*; ou, *goat*; u, *poor*; ɔi, *royal*. **(u)** ʌ, *duck*; u, *bull*; u:, *goose*; ə, *bacillus*; ju:, *cube*. x, *loch*; θ, *think*; ð, *bother*; z, *Zen*; ʒ, *corsage*; dʒ, *savage*; ŋ, *orangutang*; j, *yak*; ʃ, *fish*; tʃ, *fetch*; 'l, *rabble*; 'n, *redden*. Complete pronunciation key appears inside front cover.

bol of authority ‖ (*archit.*) the shaft of a column ‖ (*archit.*) an edge of tiling projecting over a gable ‖ (*horology*) the spindle of a watch balance ‖ (*Br. hist.*) the 12-mile area around the king's court delimited as subject to the Lord High Steward's jurisdiction **2.** *v.i. pres. part.* **verg·ing** *past* and *past part.* **verged** (with 'on') to come near to being something specified, *this remark verges on libel* [O.F.]

Ver·gennes (vɑːrʒen), Charles Gravier, comte de (1717-87), French statesman. As foreign minister (1774-86) he supported the American colonies in their revolt against British rule

ver·ger (vɜ́ːrdʒər) *n.* a church official who directs the congregation to their seats in a church, and has the general care of the church's interior ‖ (*Br.*) a beadle employed to carry a verge before certain dignitaries [prob. fr. A.F.]

Vergilian *VIRGILIAN

Ver·gil, Vir·gil (vɜ́ːrdʒil), Polydore (c. 1475-1555), English historian and humanist, born in Italy. Under the patronage of Henry VII he wrote 'Historiae Anglicae libri XXVI' (1534), a history of England based on a critical study of documents and much used by later writers

Vergil (Publius Vergilius Maro) *VIRGIL

Ver·gniaud (vernjou), Pierre Victurnien (1753-93), French revolutionist. He was a leader of the Girondists, and one of the greatest orators of the French Revolution

Ver·hae·ren (vereiren), Emile (1855-1916), Belgian lyric poet writing in French. He belonged to the Symbolist school

ver·i·fi·a·ble (vérifaiəb'l) *adj.* able to be verified

ver·i·fi·ca·tion (verifikéiʃən) *n.* a verifying or being verified [O.F. *verificacion*]

ver·i·fy (vérifai) *pres. part.* **ver·i·fy·ing** *past* and *past part.* **ver·i·fied** *v.t.* to confirm, or test, the truth or accuracy of ‖ to cause the truth of (something) to be perceived (usually in passive constructions) ‖ (*law*) to affirm, at the end of a pleading, the truth of (matters alleged in the pleading) ‖ (*law*) to substantiate by proofs [fr. O.F. *verifier*]

ver·i·ly (vérili:) *adv.* (*archaic*) in truth

ver·i·si·mil·i·tude (verisimílitu:d, verisimílitju:d) *n.* the quality, in a work of the imagination, of seeming to be true, either by reference to the external world of reality or by reference solely to the artist's canons of truth for his imagined world ‖ an apparent truth [fr. L. *verisimilitudo*]

ve·ris·mo (veirí:zmou) *n.* use of ordinary material in the arts in preference to classic or historic material, esp. in opera —**verist** *adj.* —**verist** *n.* —**veristic** *adj.*

Ver·ís·si·mo (verí:si:mɔ), Erico Lopes (1905-75), Brazilian novelist, author of 'Gato prêto em campo de neve' (1941) and 'O senhor embaixador' (1965)

ver·i·ta·ble (véritəb'l) *adj.* real, genuine, authentic (often loosely and merely as an intensive), *a veritable mountain of a man* **vér·i·ta·bly** *adv.* [fr. O.F. and A.F.]

ver·i·ty (vériti:) *pl.* **ver·i·ties** *n.* truth ‖ a basic truth of religion or ethics etc. [A.F. and O.F. *verite, veritet*]

ver·juice (vɜ́ːrdʒu:s) *n.* the sour juice extracted from unripe fruit (esp. grapes and crab apples), formerly used in cooking [O.F. *verjus*]

Ver·kho·yansk (vɑːrkoujǽnsk, *Russ.* verxʌjɔ́nsk) a mining town (pop. 10,000) in the Yakut A.S.S.R., U.S.S.R., in E. Siberia, reputed to have the lowest recorded temperature (-94°F.) in the northern hemisphere

ver·kramp·te (fɛərkrúmptə) *n.* (narrow-minded ones) member of right-wing faction of the Republic of South Africa's National Party

Ver·laine (verlen), Paul (1844-96), French poet. He is generally considered a Symbolist, but he was rather a lyric poet with an intensely refined musical and rhythmic sense. His poems are highly sophisticated, yet cultivate a simplicity akin to folk poetry. His verse attracted French composers, especially Fauré, and the combination of Verlaine's and Fauré's gifts is exquisite

ver·lig·tes (fɛərlixtes) *n.* (enlightened ones) liberal faction of the Republic of South Africa's National Party

Ver·meer (vərmíər) (Jan Vermeer van Delft, 1632-75), Dutch painter. Only 40 of his pictures are known. His favorite subjects are interiors and domestic scenes, where, often, the calm, silent figure of a woman is surrounded by a softly diffused light that echoes from surface to surface. Vermeer's subtle composition, his exceptional handling of light and his cool, delicate colors place him among the greatest of the Dutch masters

ver·meil (vɜ́ːrmeil, vɜ́ːrməl) *n.* silver gilt ‖ a transparent varnish used to give a luster to gilt [A.F. and O.F.]

ver·mi·cel·li (vɜːrmiséli:, vɜːrmitʃéli:) *n.* very thin threads or tubes of rolled and dried pasta used esp. to give substance to soups [Ital.=little worms]

ver·mi·cide (vɜ́ːrmisaid) *n.* (*med.*) a chemical compound used for destroying intestinal worms [fr. L. *vermis*, worm+*caedere*, to kill]

ver·mic·u·lar (vɑːrmíkjulər) *adj.* wormlike in appearance or movement ‖ marked with wavy lines like worm tracks ‖ caused by worms [fr. M.L. *vermicularis*]

ver·mic·u·late (vɑːrmíkjuleit) *adj.* decorated with coiling, wormlike patterns **ver·mic·u·lat·ed** *adj.* vermiculate [fr. L. *vermiculari* (*vermiculatus*)]

ver·mic·u·la·tion (vɑːrmikjuléiʃən) *n.* motion like that of a worm ‖ the state of being worm-eaten ‖ decoration, e.g. in stonework, resembling a tight coiling pattern of worm tracks [fr. L. *vermiculatio* (*vermiculationis*)]

ver·mic·u·lite (vɑːrmíkjulait) *n.* a silicate mineral of the mica family which expands greatly on heating and yields a lightweight product used as a heat and sound insulator and as a mulch in seedbeds [fr. L. *vermiculari*, to be wormy]

ver·mi·form (vɜ́ːrmifɔrm) *adj.* in the shape of a worm [fr. M.L. *vermiformis*]

vermiform appendix *APPENDIX

ver·mi·fuge (vɜ́ːrmifju:dʒ) **1.** *adj.* intended to eliminate intestinal worms **2.** *n.* a vermifuge medicine [F. or fr. Mod. L. *vermifugus*]

ver·mil·ion, ver·mil·lion (vərmíljən) **1.** *n.* mercuric sulfide, HgS, used as a pigment ‖ the brilliant red color produced by this pigment **2.** *adj.* of this color [A.F. and O.F. *vermeillon*]

ver·min (vɜ́ːrmin) *n.* (*collect.*) animals (e.g. rats), insects (e.g. lice) or certain birds (e.g. jays) harmful to crops, plants, human health or hygiene ‖ people thought of as resembling such creatures [A.F. and O.F. *vermin, vermine*]

ver·min·ous (vɜ́ːrminəs) *adj.* infested with lice, rats, or other vermin ‖ of or consisting of vermin ‖ caused or carried by vermin [fr. L. *verminosus*]

Ver·mont (vərmɔ́nt) (*abbr.* Vt.) a state (area 9,609 sq. miles, pop. 516,000) in the northeast U.S.A., in New England, crossed by the Green Mtns. Capital: Montpelier. Agriculture: maple sugar, dairy and poultry farming, hay and fodder crops. Resources: timber, asbestos, granite, marble. Industries: forest products, food processing, machinery and machine tools, tourism. State university (1791) at Burlington. Vermont was explored by the French (17th c.) and settled (18th c.) by the English. It declared itself an independent republic (1777) and became (1791) the 14th state of the U.S.A.

ver·mouth (vərmú:θ) *n.* a liquor used chiefly as an appetizer. It is produced from a blend of white wine with aromatic herbs (French vermouth) and sometimes sweetening (Italian vermouth) [F. fr. G. *wermuth*, wormwood]

ver·nac·u·lar (vərnǽkjulər) **1.** *adj.* of, using, or relating to the speech of a region or ethnic group (not one introduced from outside, not a dead language of learning) **2.** *n.* the indigenous language or dialect of a region [fr. L. *vernaculus*, domestic]

ver·nal (vɜ́ːrn'l) *adj.* belonging to, occurring in or associated with, the season of spring ‖ *EQUINOX [fr. L. *vernalis*]

ver·nal·i·za·tion (vɜːrn'lizéiʃən) *n.* the act or process of vernalizing

ver·nal·ize (vɜ́ːrn'laiz) *pres. part.* **ver·nal·iz·ing** *past* and *past part.* **ver·nal·ized** *v.t.* to induce the premature flowering and fruiting of (a plant) by artificial treatment of the seed or bulb, e.g. by exposure to moisture at low temperature in darkness, so that the plant embryo completes part of its development independently of its rate of growth [VERNAL]

ver·na·tion (vərnéiʃən) *n.* (*bot.*) the arrangement of leaves within a bud [fr. Mod. L. *vernatio* (*vernationis*) fr. *vernare*, to flourish]

Verne (vɑːrn, *F.* vern), Jules (1828-1905), French novelist. His classic science-fiction novels include 'Five Weeks in a Balloon' (1863), 'Twenty Thousand Leagues under the Sea' (1870), and 'Around the World in 80 Days' (1873), and anticipate many later inventions. He also wrote romances equally popular with children, e.g. 'Michael Strogoff' (1876)

Ver·net (verne), Claude Joseph (1714-89), French painter of seascapes and landscapes. His son Carle (1758-1835) painted horses and battles. Carle's son Horace (1789-1863) also painted battles, notably for Louis-Philippe

ver·ni·er (vɜ́ːrni:ər) *n.* a small auxiliary scale made to slide along the main, fixed scale of an instrument to enable smaller intervals of the main scale to be measured ‖ a small auxiliary device used with a main device to obtain finer adjustment, e.g. a small-capacity variable condenser connected in parallel with a main condenser [after Pierre *Vernier* (1580–1637), F. mathematician]

vernier rocket (*aerospace*) an auxiliary rocket used for fine adjustments in speed or direction

Ver·non (vɜ́ːrnən), Edward (1684-1757), British admiral. Commanding an expedition against the Spanish West Indies colonists, he sacked (1739) Portobelo (Porto Bello). He was called 'Old Grog', from his wearing of grogram cloth-ing. He diluted his seamen's rum ration to reduce drunkenness, and the drink came to be known as 'grog', from his nickname. Mt Vernon, George Washington's half brother's estate, is named after him

Ve·ro·na (vəróunə) an agricultural market (pop. 118,600) in Veneto, Italy, on the Adige. Industries: food processing, fertilizers, paper. Roman amphitheater, Romanesque churches, Romanesque-Gothic cathedral (12th-16th cc.), Renaissance piazzas and palaces

Ver·o·nal (vérən'l) *n.* barbital [trademark fr. G.]

Ve·ro·ne·se (verɔnéze) (Paolo Cagliari, 1528-88), Italian painter of the Venetian school. Apart from frescoes, his masterpieces are huge and magnificent pageant paintings often treating religious subjects, e.g. 'The Marriage of Cana' (1563) and 'The Feast of Levi' (1573). Many of his paintings are crowded with graceful courtly figures, sumptuously dressed and dignified in gesture, and very often seen from a viewpoint low down which emphasizes their grandeur

Ve·ron·i·ca (vərɔ́nikə), St, a woman who, according to tradition, met Jesus on his way to Calvary and wiped the sweat and blood from his face with a piece of white linen. The imprint of his face was miraculously preserved on it. The act is commemorated in the devotions of the Stations of the Cross. Feast: July 12

veronica *n.* speedwell

veronica *n.* a bullfighter's pass with the cape to swing the charging bull to the side of his body as he stands without moving his feet [Span.]

vé·ron·ique (veirouní:k) *adj.* of a dish garnished with grapes

Ver·ra·za·no (verəzánou, *Ital.* verratsánɔ), Giovanni da (c. 1480–c. 1527), Italian explorer. Commissioned by François I of France, he sailed along the North American coast from North Carolina to Maine, penetrated the Hudson estuary, and reached Newfoundland

Ver·roc·chio (verɔ́kjɔ), Andrea del (1435-88), Florentine sculptor, painter and goldsmith. His most famous surviving work is the equestrian statue in bronze of Bartolommeo Colleoni at Venice

ver·ru·ca (vərú:kə) *pl.* **ver·ru·cae** (verú:si:) *n.* a wart ‖ (*biol.*) a wartlike elevation or projection on a plant or animal [L.=wart]

ver·ru·cose (vərú:kous) *adj.* covered with verrucae [fr. L. *verrucosus*]

ver·ru·cous (vərú:kəs) *adj.* of, like or pertaining to a wart [fr. L. *verruca*]

Ver·sailles (versaij) the chief town (pop. 94,145) of Yvelines, France, 12 miles southwest of Paris. The palace of Versailles, long the model of royal and princely magnificence throughout Europe, was built (1661-86) for Louis XIV, as residence, court, and seat of government, chiefly by Le Vau and Jules Mansart, in French classical style. In the park, laid out by Le Nôtre, are the Great Trianon (1687), and the Little Trianon (1762) and other separate buildings

Versailles, Treaty of the treaty (June 28, 1919) between Germany and the Allies at the end of the 1st world war. Its most notable features were the establishment of the League of Nations and its penal treatment of Germany. Germany was forced to pay heavy reparations and to yield Alsace-Lorraine to France as well as other possessions to Poland, Belgium, Denmark and Japan. Danzig was to be a free city, the Saar was to be occupied by the French for 15 years and the Rhineland by the Allies for the same period. Germany renounced its overseas colonies, which were placed under League of Nations mandate. The U.S. Senate refused to ratify the treaty and many of its armament clauses remained a dead letter

ver·sant (vɔ́:rsənt) *n.* (*geog.*) the slope of the side of a range of hills or mountains ‖ the general inclination of mountainous country [F.]

ver·sa·tile (vɔ́:rsət'l, *Br.* vɔ́:rsətail) *adj.* possessing various skills ‖ easily adapted to different activities ‖ (*zool.*) capable of turning forward or backward or up and down ‖ (*bot.*, of an anther) swinging freely [F. or fr. L. *versatilis*]

ver·sa·til·i·ty (vɔ:rsətíliti:) *n.* the state or quality of being versatile [F. *versatilité*]

verse (vɔ:rs) *n.* poetry, esp. metrical poetry ‖ a stanza of a poem ‖ (in classical prosody) one metrical line ‖ the solo part of a song having a chorus ‖ a numbered section of a chapter in the Bible [O.E. *fers* fr. L.]

versed (vɔ:rst) *adj.* (with 'in') skilled or knowledgeable from study, experience etc., *a man versed in the arts of navigation* [fr. L. *versari* (*versatus*), to be experienced]

versed sine the remainder after subtracting the cosine of an angle from unity

ver·si·cle (vɔ́:rsik'l) *n.* a short verse, esp. as said or sung by the priest liturgically and followed by a response from the congregation [fr. L. *versiculus*]

ver·si·fi·ca·tion (vɔ:rsifikéiʃən) *n.* a versifying ‖ metrical structure ‖ a metrical version of something [fr. L. *versificatio* (*versificationis*)]

ver·si·fy (vɔ́:rsifai) *pres. part.* **ver·si·fy·ing** *past* and *past part.* **ver·si·fied** *v.t.* to turn into verse ‖ *v.i.* to compose verses [O.F. *versifier*]

ver·sion (vɔ́:rʒən, vɔ́:rʃən) *n.* a passage or work translated from one language into another ‖ an account or description of something from a particular point of view ‖ one stage in the evolution of a developing form, *she preferred the first version of the portrait to the final one* ‖ (*med.*) the manual turning of a fetus in the uterus [F. or fr. L. *versio* (*versionis*)]

ver·so (vɔ́:rsou) *pl.* **ver·sos** *n.* the lefthand page of a book or folded sheet ‖ (*printing*) the back of a leaf (opp. RECTO) ‖ the reverse side of a coin, medal etc. [fr. L. *verso* (*folio*), on the left (leaf)]

verst (vɔ:rst) *n.* a Russian measure of length equal to 3,500 feet (1,067 meters) [fr. Russ. *versta*]

ver·sus (vɔ́:rsəs) *prep.* (*law, sports, abbr.* v. or vs.) against, opposed to ‖ as contrasted with, *town v. country* [L.]

ver·te·bra (vɔ́:rtəbrə) *pl.* **ver·te·brae** (vɔ́:rtəbri:), **ver·te·bras** *n.* one of the bony or cartilaginous segments composing the spinal column of a vertebrate, consisting of a cylindrical mass of bone with a dorsal arch arising from it enclosing the spinal cord. Vertebrae are jointed to each other, and in higher vertebrates bear various appendages by which the spinal column is strengthened and attached to muscles and other bones, e.g. ribs [L.=joint]

ver·te·bral (vɔ́:rtəbrəl) *adj.* of or referring to a vertebra, the vertebrae or the spinal column ‖ having, or composed of, vertebrae [fr. M.L. or Mod. L. *vertebralis*]

ver·te·brate (vɔ́:rtəbrit, vɔ́:rtəbreit) **1.** *adj.* having a spinal column, furnished with a jointed backbone **2.** *n.* (*zool.*) a member of *Vertebrata*, a subphylum of animals including all those with a segmented spinal column, together with a few primitive forms in which the backbone is represented by a persistent notochord [fr. L. *vertebratus*, jointed]

ver·te·bra·tion (vɔ:rtəbréiʃən) *n.* the formation of or division into vertebrae or similar segments [VERTEBRA]

ver·tex (vɔ́:rteks) *pl.* **ver·tex·es, ver·ti·ces** (vɔ́:rtisi:z) *n.* the top, highest point ‖ (*geom.*) the point opposite a base ‖ (*geom.*) the meeting point of an axis and a curve ‖ (*astron.*) the zenith ‖ (*anat.*) the apex of the skull [L.=whirl, whirlpool]

ver·ti·cal (vɔ́:rtik'l) **1.** *adj.* having a direction in line with the earth's center, perpendicular ‖ of or at the highest point or zenith ‖ (*anat.*) of or at the crown of the head ‖ (*econ.*) of an organization combining every stage of the production and distribution of manufactured goods **2.** *n.* a perpendicular line, plane or circle [F. or fr. L.L. *verticalis*]

vertical angle (*astron.*) an angle measured vertically upwards or downwards from the horizon ‖ a vertically opposite angle

vertical circle an azimuth circle

vertical grouping placement of children of ages 5–7 into a familylike group in which older children help teach the younger, e.g., in kibbutzim

ver·ti·cal·i·ty (vɔ:rtikǽliti:) *n.* the state or quality of being vertical

ver·ti·cal·ly (vɔ́:rtikli:) *adv.* in a vertical manner ‖ straight up and down or straight overhead

vertically opposite angle (*math.*) either of the two opposed angles resulting from the intersection of two lines or planes

vertical thinking problem-solving technique involving overcoming obstacles in the path chosen, said to be characteristic of 'convergers.' *Cf* LATERAL THINKING

vertices alt. *pl.* of VERTEX

ver·ti·cil (vɔ́:rtis'l) *n.* (*bot.*) a set of similar parts, e.g. leaves or flowers, radiating from the same point on an axis, a whorl **ver·ti·cil·late** (vɔ:rtisílit, vɔ:rtisíleit), **ver·tic·il·lát·ed** *adjs.* **ver·tic·il·lá·tion** *n.* [fr. L. *verticillus*, a whorl]

ver·tig·i·nous (vɔ:rtídʒinəs) *adj.* of or having vertigo ‖ causing vertigo [fr. L. *vertiginosus*, someone suffering from giddiness]

ver·ti·go (vɔ́:rtigou) *n.* (*med.*) a sensation of whirling caused e.g. by heights, in which one tends to lose one's equilibrium. The sensation is also associated with certain diseases [L.]

ver·ti·port (vɔ́:rtəpɔrt) *n.* pad for takeoff and landing of VTOLs. *also* VTOL port. *Cf* STOLPORT

vertu *VIRTU

ver·vain (vɔ́:rvein) *n.* a verbena, esp. the European *Verbena officinalis* [A.F. and O.F. *verveine*]

verve (vɔ:rv) *n.* vivacity, liveliness, energy, esp. in conversation, works of imagination etc. [F.]

ver·vet (vɔ́:rvit) *n. Cercopithecus pygerythrus*, the S. and E. African guenon, a small monkey with black chin, hands and feet [F.]

Ver·woerd (fərvúərd), Hendrik Frensch (1901-66), South African statesman, Nationalist prime minister of South Africa (1958-66). He pursued a policy of apartheid. He was assassinated

Ve·ry (víəri:), Frank Washington (1852-1927), U.S. astronomer and physicist. He estimated the temperature of the moon's surface, studied the radiation of the firefly, showed that the white nebulae are galaxies, and verified the presence of oxygen and hydrogen in the atmosphere of Mars

ver·y (véri:) **1.** *comp.* **ver·i·er** *superl.* **ver·i·est** *adj.* same, precise, *the very man we want to see* ‖ actual, *caught in the very act* ‖ complete, absolute, *that's the very opposite of what I said* ‖ (used as an intensive) even, *they tax the very air you breathe* **2.** *adv.* (used as an intensifier) absolutely, *that is the very same one* ‖ in a high degree, extremely, *a very steep cliff* [A.F. *verrey, verai*, O.F. *verai, vrai*]

Ve·ry light (víəri:, véri:) a flare fired from a pistol as a signal [after Edward W. *Very* (1852–1910), U.S. naval officer]

Ve·sa·li·us (viséili:əs), Andreas (1514-64), Flemish anatomist who questioned the medical doctrines of Aristotle and Galen, which had held sway for centuries, and whose 'De humani corporis fabrica' (1543) formed the basis from which modern research was developed

Ve·sey (ví:zi:), Denmark (1767-1822), leader of a U.S. slave revolt (1822). Born in Africa, he purchased his freedom from a slave-ship captain (1800) with $600 won in a lottery. He plotted a slave uprising in Charleston, S.C. (1822), but was executed along with 34 other blacks when the plot was discovered

ve·si·ca (vəsáikə) *pl.* **ve·si·cae** (vəsáisi:t:) *n.* (*anat.*) a bladder **ves·i·cal** (vésəkəl) *adj.* [L.]

ves·i·cant (vésikənt) **1.** *adj.* producing or tending to produce blisters **2.** *n.* a drug etc. that produces blisters [fr. Mod. L. *vesicans* (*vesicantis*)]

ves·i·ca pis·cis (vésikəpísis, vésikəpískis) *n.* an upright, pointed oval, often used in Christian art to surround a sacred figure

ves·i·cate (vésikeit) *pres. part.* **ves·i·cat·ing** *past* and *past part.* **ves·i·cat·ed** *v.t.* to raise a blister or blisters on ‖ *v.i.* to become blistered [fr. Mod. L. *vesicare*]

ves·i·ca·to·ry (vésikətɔ̀ri:, vésikətouri:) **1.** *pl.* **ves·i·ca·to·ries** *n.* a vesicant **2.** *adj.* vesicant [fr. M.L. or early Mod. L. *vesicatorius*]

ves·i·cle (vésik'l) *n.* (*bot.*) a globular swelling containing air ‖ (*zool.*) a small globular or bladderlike air space in tissue ‖ (*zool.*) a small cavity or sac, usually containing fluid ‖ (*geol.*) a small cavity in a mineral or rock [fr. F. *vésicule* or L. *vesicula*]

ve·sic·u·lar (vəsíkjulər) *adj.* covered with vesicles ‖ resembling a vesicle in form or structure [fr. early Mod. L. *vesicularis*]

ve·sic·u·late (vəsíkjuleit) *adj.* vesicular **ve·síc·u·lat·ed** *adj.* vesiculate [fr. Mod. L. *vesiculatus*]

Ves·pa·si·an (vespéiʒən, vespéiʒi:ən) (Titus Flavius Sabinus Vespasianus, 9-79), Roman emperor (69-79). Commander in the war against the Jews, he was proclaimed emperor by his troops and overthrew Vitellius. He reestablished the economic and political stability of the empire after the civil wars of 68-9

Ves·per (véspər) the evening star (Venus)

ves·per·al (véspərəl) *n.* (*eccles.*) a book of prayers and music used at vespers ‖ a covering for the white linen altar cloths when no service is being held [fr. L.L. *vesperalis*]

ves·pers (véspərz) *pl. n.* (*eccles.*) the sixth of the seven canonical hours, marked in a monastic community by an act of worship ‖ a public act of worship at this hour, evensong ‖ *SICILIAN VESPERS [O.F. *vespres*]

ves·per·tine (véspərtain) *adj.* of, occurring, or active in the evening, e.g. of the opening of a flower or the flying of an insect [fr. L. *vespertinus*]

ves·pi·ar·y (véspi:əri:) *pl.* **ves·pi·ar·ies** *n.* a nest of social wasps [irreg. fr. L. *vespa*, wasp, after 'apiary']

ves·pid (véspid) **1.** *n.* (*zool.*) a member of the insect family *Vespidae*, which includes wasps, hornets etc. **2.** *adj.* of these insects [fr. Mod. L. *Vespidae* fr. *vespa*, wasp]

ves·pine (véspain) *adj.* of or pertaining to a wasp or wasps [fr. L. *vespa*, wasp]

Ves·puc·ci (vespú:tʃi:), Amerigo (1454-1512), Italian navigator. He made two journeys to the New World, for Spain (1499-1500) and for Portugal (1501-2), exploring the northeast coast of South America. His account of these discoveries spread over Europe, and a German cartographer named the American continent after him

ves·sel (vés'l) *n.* a container for liquids ‖ a boat or ship (excluding boats propelled by oars or poles and excluding small sailboats) ‖ (*biol.*) a tube or canal through which a fluid can pass ‖ (*bot.*) a continuous tube formed by the superposition of numerous specially adapted tracheids, that serves in water conduction [O.F.]

vest (vest) *v.t.* (usually of a priest) to clothe with a ceremonial garment ‖ to grant authority, property, rights or privileges to (someone) ‖ (with 'in') to put (a right or privilege) in the control of someone ‖ *v.i.* to put on robes or vestments ‖ (of a right etc.) to be vested [fr. O.F. *vestir*]

vest *n.* a man's short, close-fitting, sleeveless garment covering the chest and belly, worn over the trouser top and under the jacket ‖ (*Br.*) an undershirt [fr. F. *veste*]

Ves·ta (véstə) (*Rom. mythol.*) goddess of the hearth, identified with the Greek Hestia. Her temple in Rome was served by six priestesses, the Vestal virgins, vowed to chastity

vested interest a personal interest or right to derive or share a benefit, protected by law, custom etc. ‖ (*pl.*) persons who derive or stand to derive financial benefit or power from a situation, esp. who derive benefits which they are unwilling to forgo even if these benefits conflict with public welfare or social morality

ves·tib·u·lar (vestíbjulər) *adj.* of or like a vestibule

ves·ti·bule (véstibju:l) *n.* an enclosed space between the outer and inner door or doors of a building, through which one must pass in order to enter the building proper ‖ (*Gk* and *Rom. hist.*) an enclosed or partially enclosed courtyard before the entrance of a house etc. ‖ the partly enclosed porch of a church etc. ‖ (*anat., zool.*) a cavity which forms an entrance to another cavity ‖ the enclosed entrance to a railroad car on a passenger train or the covered passage between two cars [fr. L. *vestibulum*, entrance hall]

ves·tige (véstidʒ) *n.* faintly visible or otherwise discernible evidence of the former presence or existence of something which is no longer present || (usually in negative constructions) a very small amount, *not a vestige of truth in his statement* || (*biol.*) a small degenerate or imperfectly developed structure, e.g. the vermiform appendix, which may have been complete and functional in some ancestor **ves·tig·i·al** (vestídʒi:əl) *adj.* [F. fr. L. *vestigium*, footprint, trace]

ves·ti·ture (véstitʃər) *n.* (*zool.*) a natural body covering, e.g. of feathers, hairs, scales etc. [fr. M.L. *vestitura*]

vest·ment (véstmənt) *n.* (*eccles.*) a liturgical garment worn by a priest, deacon, acolyte etc. during an act of worship || a ceremonial robe [A.F. and O.F. *vestement*]

ves·try (véstri:) *pl.* **ves·tries** *n.* a sacristy, a room in a church used to contain the vestments and sacred vessels, the official records etc. The clergy and the choir robe and disrobe in it, and it serves as the official office of the parish || (*Anglican* and *Episcopal Churches*) a body of church members which administers the secular affairs of the parish [prob. fr. A.F. *vestrie, vesterie*]

ves·try·man (véstri:mən) *pl.* **ves·try·men** (véstri:mən) *n.* a member of a vestry

ves·ture (véstʃər) *n.* (*archaic*) garments collectively || (*law*) everything that grows on a piece of land except trees [A.F. and O.F.]

ve·su·vi·an·ite (vəsú:vi:ənait) *n.* a brown or green double silicate of aluminum and calcium, colored by traces of iron, first found in the ejections of Vesuvius

Ve·su·vi·us (vəsú:vi:əs) an active volcano (4,000 ft) 5 miles southeast of Naples, Italy. Its first known eruption (79 A.D.) destroyed the towns of Pompeii and Herculaneum at its foot

vet (vet) **1.** *n.* (*pop.*) a veterinarian **2.** *v.t. pres. part.* **vet·ting** *past* and *past part.* **vet·ted** (*pop.*) to make a veterinary examination of or give treatment to (an animal) || (*Br., pop.*) to examine and check, esp. for accuracy

vet. a veteran

vetch (vetʃ) *n.* a member of *Vicia*, fam. *Papilionaceae*, a genus of scrambling annual or perennial plants, found in many parts of the world. Some species are cultivated as fodder plants [O.N.F. *veche, vecche*]

vetch·ling (vétʃliŋ) *n.* a member of *Lathyrus*, fam. *Papilionaceae*, a genus of small plants closely allied to vetch

vet·er·an (vétərən, vétrən) **1.** *adj.* of or pertaining to long service or experience in some form of activity, esp. in soldiering **2.** *n.* (*abbr.* vet.) someone who has had long service or experience in some form of activity, esp. in soldiering || an ex-serviceman qualified to receive benefits according to status [fr. early Mod. F. or fr. L. *veteranus* fr. *vetus* (*veteris*), old]

Veterans Day an annual U.S. holiday held every Nov. 11th, originally (1919) celebrated as Armistice Day to commemorate the end of the 1st World war. President Dwight Eisenhower changed (1954) its name and dedicated it to the sacrifices made by all U.S. servicemen

Veterans of Foreign Wars (*abbr.* V.F.W.) a U.S. organization created (1899) at Columbus, Ohio, by veterans of the Spanish-American War, and chartered (1936) by Congress to promote the welfare of all veterans

vet·er·i·nar·i·an (vetərinéəri:ən, vetrinéəri:ən) *n.* (*Am.=Br.* veterinary surgeon) a person who practices veterinary medicine or surgery [fr. L. *veterinarius*]

vet·er·i·nar·y (vétərineri:, vétrineri:) **1.** *adj.* of the science of treating and preventing diseases of animals, esp. of domestic animals **2.** *pl.* **vet·er·i·nar·ies** *n.* a veterinarian [fr. L. *veterinarius* fr. *veterinus*, of or pertaining to (draft) cattle]

veterinary surgeon (*Br.*) a veterinarian

vet·i·ver (vétivər) *n.* *Andropogon zizamoides*, cuscus [fr. F. *vétyver* fr. Tamil *vettvēru*]

ve·to (ví:tou) **1.** *n. pl.* **ve·toes** a right, vested by law in a person or constitutional body, to declare inoperative a decision made by others || the exercise of this right || a veto message **2.** *v.t.* to refuse consent to by using the right of veto || (*pop.*) to forbid flatly [L.=I forbid]

veto message a document in which the executive power sets out its reasons for not approving a proposed law

vex (veks) *v.t.* to annoy (someone) [O.F. *vexer*]

vex·a·tion (vekséiʃən) *n.* a vexing or being vexed || something which annoys one **vex·á·tious** *adj.* causing vexation || (*law*, of actions) instituted without real grounds and meant to cause trouble or annoyance [O.F. or fr. L. *vexatio* (*vexationis*)]

vexed question a matter about which people have argued, or do argue, hotly

vex·il·lar·y (véksəleri:) **1.** *adj.* of a standard or ensign **2.** *n.* (*Rom. hist.*) one of a class of veteran soldiers || a standard-bearer [fr. L. *vexillarius*, standard-bearer]

vex·il·late (véksəleit) *adj.* having a vexillum or vexilla

vex·il·lol·o·gy (veksəlólədʒi:) *n.* the study of flags, their design and manufacture **—vexillologic** *adj.* **—vexillological** *adj.* **—vexillologist** *n.*

vex·il·lum (veksíləm) *pl.* **vex·il·la** (veksilə) *n.* (*Rom. hist.*) a square flag carried by a Roman standard-bearer || (*Rom. hist.*) a body of troops under one banner || (*bot.*) the large upper petal of a papilionaceous flower || the vane of a feather || (*eccles.*) a linen or silk pennant or flag partly wound around a bishop's staff [L.]

Vé·ze·lay (veizəlei) a town (pop. 500) in Yonne, France, where St Bernard preached (1146) the 2nd Crusade. Romanesque-Gothic abbey (11th-12th cc.)

VFW-Fokker F-28 *n.* 85-seat passenger jet with range of 1,000 nautical mi.

vi·a (váiə, vi:ə) *prep.* by way or means of, *he went to Rome via Paris* [L.]

vi·a·bil·i·ty (vaiəbíliti:) *n.* the state or quality of being viable [F. *viabilité*]

vi·a·ble (váiəb'l) *adj.* (of a fetus) able to maintain an independent life || (of seeds etc.) capable of growth and development || (of a state) economically, politically or socially able to be independent || (of ideas, propositions, theories) sound, workable if translated into action [F.=able to live]

vi·a·duct (váiədʌkt) *n.* a bridge supported by many pillared arches, over which road or rail transport can pass [fr. L. *via*, a way (after 'aqueduct')]

vi·al (váiəl) *n.* a small cylindrical container of glass etc., used to contain liquids [M.E. *viole, fiole*]

vi·and (váiənd) *n.* (usually *pl.*, *rhet.*) food [A.F., O.F. *viande*]

vi·at·i·cum (vaiǽtikəm) *pl.* **vi·at·i·cums, vi·at·i·ca** (vaiǽtikə) *n.* (*eccles.*) the Eucharist administered to a dying person || (*Rom. hist.*) provisions or money granted to an envoy about to make a journey [L.=traveling money]

Viau (vjou), Théophile de (1590-1626), French poet, author of the tragedy 'Pyrame et Thisbé' (1617) and of the scurrilous satire 'le Parnasse satyrique' (1622)

vibes or **vibrations** (vaibs) *n.* **1.** an aura or spirit emanating from a person or situation. **2.** an instinctive sense of the nature of a person or a situation

Viborg *VYBORG

vi·brac·u·lar (vaibrǽkjulər) *adj.* of or like vibracula || having vibracula

vi·brac·u·loid (vaibrǽkjulɔid) *adj.* of or like a vibraculum or vibracula

vi·brac·u·lum (vaibrǽkjuləm) *pl.* **vi·brac·u·la** (vaibrǽkjulə) *n.* (*zool.*) one of the threads by which bryozoans lash the water so as to bring food within reach, or in order to defend themselves [Mod. L. fr. L. *vibrare*, to shake]

vi·bra·harp or **vi·bra·phone** (váibrəhɑrp, váibrəfoun) *n.* a percussion instrument containing electrically operated valves **—vibraharpist** *n.* **—vibraphonist** *n.*

vi·bran·cy (váibrənsi:) *n.* the state or quality of being vibrant

vi·brant (váibrənt) *adj.* vibrating || full of life and energy || (of sound) resonant [fr. L. *vibrans* (*vibraniis*) fr. *vibrare*, to vibrate]

vi·bra·phone (váibrəfoun) *n.* a percussion instrument like a xylophone but having electrically operated resonators under the bars which give a vibrating effect

vi·brate (váibreit) *pres. part.* **vi·brat·ing** *past* and *past part.* **vi·brat·ed** *v.i.* to move to and fro with simple periodic motion || (of sounds) to seem to quiver || to respond sympathetically || *v.t.* to cause to vibrate [fr. L. *vibrare* (*vibratus*), to shake]

vi·bra·tile (váibrət'l, váibrətail) *adj.* able to vibrate or be vibrated || of, like, or characterized by vibration **vi·bra·til·i·ty** (vaibrətíliti:) *n.* [fr. Mod. L. *vibratilis* fr. L., *vibrare* (*vibratus*), to vibrate]

vi·bra·tion (vaibréiʃən) *n.* a vibrating or being vibrated || (*phys.*) the simple periodic to-and-fro motion of a body etc., e.g. the vibrating string of a violin || a single instance of this [fr. L. *vibratio* (*vibrationis*)]

vibration syndrome *n.* (*med.*) Raynaud's Phenomenon

vi·bra·tive (váibrətiv) *adj.* vibratory

vi·bra·to (vibrɑ́tou) *n.* (*mus.*) an effect produced by rapid changes in the loudness of a single note [Ital.]

vi·bra·tor (váibreitər) *n.* a device which vibrates or causes vibration

vi·bra·to·ry (váibrətɔri:, váibrətouri:) *adj.* of, like, or consisting of vibration causing vibration || vibrating or capable of vibrating || vibrant

vi·bris·sa (vaibrísə) *pl.* **vi·bris·sae** (vaibrísi:) *n.* (*zool.*) one of the stiff facial hairs in some mammals often serving as a tactile organ, esp. near the mouth, e.g. a cat's whisker || one of the stiff feathers near the beak or around the eye of a bird || one of a pair of bristles near the upper angles of the mouth cavity in some dipterans || a hair in the nostril [L. *vibrissae* pl. fr. *vibrare*, to vibrate]

vi·bro·graph (váibrəgræf, váibrəgrɑf) *n.* an instrument used to measure and record vibrations

vi·bron·ic (vaibrónik) *adj.* of electronic vibrations

Vi·bro·sis (vaibróusis) *n.* trade name by Conoco for vibrators used to create seismic signals for geological exploration

vi·bur·num (vaibə́:rnəm) *n.* a member of *Viburnum*, fam. *Caprifoliaceae*, a genus of shrubs and small trees native to northern temperate and subtropical regions, including *V. lantana*, the wayfaring tree, and *V. opulus*, the guelder rose. Many species are cultivated for their ornamental white or pink flowers [L.=the wayfaring tree]

vic·ar (víkər) *n.* (*Br.*) the priest in charge of a parish in which formerly all or the greater part of the tithes were paid to another recipient and the vicar received a stipend (cf. RECTOR) || (*Roman Catholicism*) a priest acting as the representative of another || (*Episcopal Church*) a priest in charge of a church dependent on a larger church || a representative, *the pope is called 'the Vicar of Christ'* [A.F. *vicare, vicaire* fr. L. *vicarius*, substitute]

vic·ar·age (víkəridʒ) *n.* the residence of a vicar || his benefice

vicar apostolic *pl.* **vicars apostolic** (*Roman Catholicism*) a titular bishop acting as the papal delegate in administering a missionary area

vic·ar-gen·er·al (víkərdʒénərəl) *pl.* **vic·ars-gen·er·al** (*Church of England*) a lay legal official assisting a bishop or archbishop || a representative of a bishop in matters of jurisdiction in a diocese

vi·car·i·al (vaikéəri:əl, vikéəri:əl) *adj.* of or pertaining to a vicar or to his office || delegated [fr. L. *vicarius*]

vi·car·i·ous (vaikéəri:əs, vikéəri:əs) *adj.* acting, or done, on behalf of someone else or in his place, *vicarious suffering* || of someone else's experiences which one shares imaginatively, *vicarious pleasure* || (*physiol.*) of the performing by one organ of the function normally performed by another organ [fr. L. *vicarius*]

vice (vais) *n.* a habitual disposition to choose evil || an evil practice || (in animals) a fault, e.g. (in a horse) tossing back the head [A.F., O.F.]

vice *VISE

vi·ce (váisi:) *prep.* (*rhet.*) in place of [L.]

vice- (vais) *prefix* someone acting in the place of someone else

vice admiral a naval officer ranking above a rear admiral and below an admiral **vice admiralty**

vice-chan·cel·lor (váistʃǽnsələr, váistʃɑ́nsələr) *n.* the assistant to a chancellor, esp. the administrative head of a university, acting for the chancellor **více-chan·cel·lor·ship** *n.*

vice-con·sul (váiskónsəl) *n.* a consular representative appointed to serve where the duties are too light to warrant the appointment of a consul || an assistant to a consul general **více-cón·su·late** *n.*

vice·ge·ren·cy (vaisdʒíərənsi:) *pl.* **vice·ge·ren·cies** *n.* the office or jurisdiction of a vicegerent

vice·ge·rent (vaisdʒíərənt) *n.* someone appointed to act for a superior, esp. a ruler [fr. M.L. *vicegerens* (*vicegerentis*)]

vi·cen·ni·al (vaiséni:əl) *adj.* occurring at intervals of 20 years || lasting for 20 years [fr. L.L. *vicennium*, period of 20 years]

CONCISE PRONUNCIATION KEY: **(a)** æ, *cat*; ɑ, *car*; ɔ *fawn*; ei, *snake*. **(e)** e, *hen*; i:, *sheep*; iə, *deer*; ɛə, *bear*. **(i)** i, *fish*; ai, *tiger*; ə:, *bird*. **(o)** o, *ox*; au, *cow*; ou, *goat*; u, *poor*; ɔi, *royal*. **(u)** ʌ, *duck*; u, *bull*; u:, *goose*; ə, *bacillus*; ju:, *cube*. x, *loch*; θ, *think*; ð, *bother*; z, *Zen*; ʒ, *corsage*; dʒ, *savage*; ŋ, *orangutang*; j, *yak*; ʃ, *fish*; tʃ, *fetch*; 'l, *rabble*; 'n, *redden*. Complete pronunciation key appears inside front cover.

Vi·cen·te (vi:sénti:), Gil (c. 1465-1536), Portuguese dramatist. His 44 plays, some of which are written in Portuguese and some in Spanish, include religious dramas ('Trilogia de las Barcas') and comedies ('Don Duardos'). He was also a goldsmith
Vi·cen·za (vi:tʃénzɑ) a city (pop. 117,571) in Veneto, Italy. Gothic cathedral (13th c.), many buildings designed by Palladio, notably the Teatro Olimpico (1580-5)
vice-pres·i·den·cy (váisprézidənsi:) *n.* the office or term of office of a vicepresident
vice-pres·i·dent (váisprézidənt) *n.* someone empowered to act for, or in the absence of, a president ‖ someone serving as a president's assistant, e.g. in a corporation **vice-pres·i·dén·tial** *adj.*
vice·re·gal (váisrí:g'l) *adj.* pertaining to a viceroy
vice-re·gent (váisrí:dʒənt) *n.* the assistant or deputy of a regent
vice·roy (váisrɔi) *n.* a man appointed by a sovereign to rule in his stead over one of his dominions ‖ *Limenitis archippus,* a red and black American butterfly [F. *viceroi*]
vi·ce ver·sa (váisivə́:rsə, váisvə́:rsə) *adv.* similarly when the terms are reversed, *green enhances yellow and vice versa* [L.]
Vi·chy (vi:ʃi:) a spa (pop. 32,117) in Allier, central France. It was the seat of Pétain's government of France (1940-4)
vic·i·nage (vísinidʒ) *n.* (*rhet.*) a neighboring area, vicinity [fr. O.F. *visenage, voisinage*]
vic·i·nal (vísin'l) *adj.* (*rhet.*) of a locality, local, *a vicinal road* ‖ (*crystall.*) of a subordinate facet [fr. L. *vicinalis*]
vi·cin·i·ty (visíniti:) *pl.* **vi·cin·i·ties** *n.* the immediate neighborhood **in the vicinity of** close to, *accidents in the vicinity of 10,000 a year* [fr. L. *vicinitas* fr. *vicinus,* neighbor]
vi·cious (víʃəs) *adj.* characterized by vice ‖ given over to vice, *a vicious neighborhood* ‖ seeking to injure, *a vicious kick* ‖ (esp. of a horse) having a vice or vices ‖ spiteful, vindictive ‖ faulty, not valid, *a vicious argument* [A.F. or fr. L. *vitiosus* fr. *vitium,* vice]
vicious circle a course of action in which the result achieved defeats the purpose of the act, e.g. making a wage demand because of the cost of living when to secure the demand raises the cost of living ‖ a combination of problems or disorders which aggravate one another, *a vicious circle of poverty-ignorance-poverty* ‖ (*logic*) a faulty reasoning which consists of drawing a conclusion from a proposition which itself assumes the conclusion ‖ (*economics*) in currency markets, events leading to the decline in the value of a currency
vi·cis·si·tude (visísitu:d, visísitju:d) *n.* (esp. *pl.*) a change in fortune or in a situation, esp. for the worse **vi·cis·si·tú·di·nous** *adj.* [O.F. and F. or fr. L. *vicissitudo*]
Vick·er·y (víkəri:), Howard Leroy (1892-1946), U.S. admiral. During the 2nd world war he directed a shipbuilding program which produced over 5,500 oceangoing ships, greatly contributing to the Allied victory
Vicks·burg Campaign (víksbə:rg) a Civil War campaign (1862-3) launched by U.S. Gen. Ulysses S. Grant to gain control of the section of the Mississippi River, between Port Hudson, La., and Vicksburg, Miss., still held by the Confederates. After an initial failure, Grant captured many Confederate-held towns, including Vicksburg after a six months' siege. The Union subsequently held full control of the Mississippi River
Vi·co (ví:kɔ), Giambattista (1668-1744), Italian philosopher and historian. He was the first to write history in terms of the rise and fall of human societies and to make use of myths, legends, poetry and the study of linguistics as historical evidence. His philosophical work 'The New Science' (1725) has had a wide influence
vic·tim (víktim) *n.* a person or thing made to suffer by a cause which is stated or implied, *a victim of circumstances* ‖ (*hist.*) a living creature offered up as a sacrifice ‖ someone who is cheated or made a dupe **vic·tim·i·zá·tion** *n.*
vic·tim·ize *pres. part.* **vic·tim·iz·ing** *past* and *past part.* **vic·tim·ized** *v.t.* to cause to be a victim [fr. L. *victima*]
vic·tim·less crime (víktimləs) an illegal act that hurts no one but the person who commits it, e.g., drug taking
vic·tim·ol·ogy (vi̥ktəmɒ́lədʒi:) *n.* the study of victims of crimes and their behavior, esp. that leading to their becoming victims —**victimologist** *n.*
vic·tor (víktər) *n.* the winner of a contest [A.F. or L. fr. *vincere* (*victus*), to overcome]
Vic·tor Em·man·u·el I (víktərimǽnju:əl) (*Ital.* Vittorio Emanuele) (1759-1824), king of Sardinia (1802-21). A reactionary, he abdicated (1821) rather than accede to demands for a constitution
Victor Emmanuel II (1820-78), last king of Sardinia (1849-61) and first king of Italy (1861-78), son of Charles Albert. With the aid of Cavour, he carried out many liberal reforms, and obtained French support in driving the Austrians from northern Italy (1859)
Victor Emmanuel III (1869-1947), king of Italy (1900-46). After the defeat and death of Mussolini, with whose policies he had concurred, he was forced to abdicate (1946). Italy became a republic one month later
Vic·to·ri·a (viktɔ́ri:ə, viktóuri:ə) (1819-1901), queen of Great Britain (1837-1901) and empress of India (1876-1901), niece of William IV. Her accession marked the end of the connection between the British and Hanoverian thrones. Victoria took an active interest in the policy of her ministers, and was soundly advised and supported by her husband, Albert of Saxe-Coburg Gotha. Her relations with Melbourne, Peel and Disraeli were excellent but she was not on good terms with Palmerston and Gladstone. Her conscientious approach to her duties did much to raise the reputation of the monarchy. Her long retirement after Albert's death was unpopular, but the diamond jubilee of her reign was celebrated (1897) with universal enthusiasm. Victoria's reign saw the rapid industrialization of Britain, and a vast growth of national wealth, reflected in the imperialism of the late 19th c.
Vic·to·ria (vi:ktɔ́rjɑ), Manuel Félix Fernández (called Guadelupe, 1786-1843), Mexican soldier, politician, and the first federalist president of Mexico (1824-9), following the overthrow of Iturbide. He introduced (1824) the first liberal constitution
Vic·to·ri·a (viktɔ́ri:ə, viktóuri:ə) a state (area 87,884 sq. miles, pop. 3,907,900) at the southeast tip of Australia. Capital: Melbourne. The Great Dividing Range occupies the east and center. The northwest is semiarid. Agriculture: wheat, oats, barley, hay, potatoes, fruit and vines, sheep and cattle farming, dairying. Resources: timber, lignite, antimony, silver, tin, hydroelectric power. Industries: food processing, agricultural machinery, textiles, chemicals, iron and steel. University of Melbourne (1853), Monash University (1958), Latrobe University (1967)
Victoria the capital (pop. 64,379) of British Columbia, Canada, a port on S.E. Vancouver I.: fishing, tourism. University (1961)
Victoria *HONG KONG
Victoria a lake (area 26,828 sq. miles, altitude 3,720 ft) in Kenya, Tanzania and Uganda. Its outlet is the White Nile. It was discovered (1858) by Speke, and explored (1875) by Stanley
Vic·to·ri·a (viktɔ́ri:ə, viktóuri:ə, vi:ktɔ́ri:ɑ), Tomás Luis de (Tommasso Ludovico da Vittoria, c. 1540-1611), Spanish composer. He was a contemporary of Palestrina, and worked in Rome for much of his life. He was a master of polyphonic church music (masses, motets, psalms, hymns)
vic·to·ri·a (viktɔ́ri:ə, viktóuri:ə) *n.* (*hist.*) a four-wheeled horse-drawn carriage, with a low seat for two persons, a raised seat for the driver, and a folding top ‖ *Victoria regia,* the royal or giant water lily of the Amazon [after Queen VICTORIA]
Victoria Cross (*abbr.* V.C.) the highest British award for valor, instituted (1856) by Queen Victoria during the Crimean War
Victoria Falls a waterfall (5,580 ft wide, 350-400 ft high), broken by islands into four parts, in the Zambezi on the Zimbabwe-Zambia border: hydroelectricity. The falls were discovered by Livingstone (1855)
Victoria Island an island (area 82,000 sq. miles, pop. about 612, Eskimos) in the Arctic Ocean, forming part of the Northwest Territories of Canada
Vic·to·ri·an (viktɔ́ri:ən, viktóuri:ən) **1.** *n.* someone living during, or born in, the reign of Queen Victoria (1837–1901) **2.** *adj.* characteristic of, or pertaining to, the British way of life during the reign of Queen Victoria ‖ having stiff or prim habits of thought and manner **vic·tó·ri·an·ism** *n.*
Vic·tor·i·an·a (viktɔri:ánə) *n.* **1.** artifacts of the Victorian era **2.** a collection of such artifacts
Victoria Ny·an·za (naiǽnzə) the former name of Lake Victoria
Vic·to·ri·o (viktóuri:ou) (1825-80), American Apache Indian chief and military leader. After leading sporadic raids during the 1870s, he broke out of the San Carlos reservation (1879) and led the Warm Springs Apache to the Black Mountains, where he held off U.S. and Mexican troops for 15 months by using strategically placed encampments to limit the enemy attackers to a number comparable to his own 35 to 50 warriors. Surprised by the Mexicans at Tres Castillos, on the Plains of Chihuahua, he fought until his ammunition gave out, then killed himself
vic·to·ri·ous (viktɔ́ri:əs, viktóuri:əs) *adj.* having won a victory ‖ of or pertaining to victory [A.F. or fr. L. *victoriosus*]
vic·to·ry (víktəri:) *pl.* **vic·to·ries** *n.* the winning of a contest, esp. final success in battle or war ‖ a military engagement fought and won ‖ a contest won [A.F. and O.F. *victorie*]
vict·ual (vít'l) *n.* (*pl., old-fash.*) food and, more rarely, other provisions [A.F. and O.F. *vitaile, vitaille*]
victual *pres. part.* **vict·ual·ing,** esp. *Br.* **vict·ual·ling** *past* and *past part.* **vict·ualed,** esp. *Br.,* **vict·ualled** *v.t.* to provision (e.g. a ship) ‖ *v.i.* to take on provisions [fr. A.F. and O.F. *vitailler*]
vict·ual·ler, vic·tual·er (vít'lər) *n.* (*Br.*) a publican holding a license to sell food and alcoholic drinks on his premises ‖ a provisioning ship ‖ (*hist.*) a person who provisioned an army or navy [A.F. and O.F. *vitailler, vitaillier*]
vi·cu·ña, vi·cu·gna (vikú:nə, vikjú:nə, vikú:njə) *n.* *Lama vicugna,* a mammal of the Andes related to the llama and alpaca, but smaller. Its coat produces very soft, highly valued wool ‖ this wool ‖ a cloth woven from this wool [Span. fr. Quechuan]
Vi·dal (vidɑ́l), Gore (1925-), U.S. author, known for his cynical humor and literary eclecticism. His first 3 novels, 'Williwaw' (1946), 'The City and the Pillar' (1948) and 'The Judgment of Paris' (1952), were critical successes, but he gained wider fame with his Hollywood spoof 'Myra Breckinridge' (1968) and with such later works as 'Burr' (1973), '1876' (1976), 'Creation' (1981) and 'Lincoln' (1984). He also wrote 2 successful plays, 'Visit to a Small Planet' (1957) and 'The Best Man' (1960; film, 1964), and published collections of literary and political essays including 'The Second American Revolution' (1982)
vi·dar·a·bine [$C_5H_5N_5$] (vaidɑ́rəbi:n) *n.* (*pharm.*) an antiviral ointment used to treat inflammation of the cornea and the conjunctiva; marketed as Vira-A. *also* adenine, arabinoside
vi·de (váidi:) *v. imper.* (*abbr.* v.) see (directing a reader to some other page or passage in a book etc.) [L. imper. sing. of *videre,* to see]
vi·de·li·cet (vidéliset) *adv.* (*abbr.* viz.) that is to say, namely [L. fr. *videre licet,* it is permitted to see]
vid·e·o (vídi:ou) **1.** *n.* the visual element of television (cf.. AUDIO) ‖ television **2.** *adj.* of or pertaining to television
video cassette or **video cartridge** a videotape encased in a cartridge that can be played on a video cassette recorder
video cassette recorder device for recording a television program from a television set for later playback. *abbr.* VCR
vid·eo·disc (vídi:oudisk) *n.* a plastic disc containing a television recording
vid·e·o·ize (vídi:ouaiz) *v.* to adapt for television
vid·e·o·phone or **vid·e·o·tel·e·phone** (vídi:oufoun) *n.* a telephone that transmits a view of the speaker. *also* viewphone. *Cf* PICTUREPHONE
vid·e·o·play·er (vídi:oupleijər) *n.* a device attached to a television set, that can record and replay a television program
video tape a magnetic tape used to record a television program or part of a program to be broadcast at a later time
vid·e·o·tex (vídi:outeks) *n.* system of information retrieval through home television sets
vid·i·con (vídəkɒn) *n.* (*electr.*) camera tube ca-

pable of receiving photoconduction that is scanned by electrons to transmit images

vie (vai) *pres. part.* **vy·ing** *past* and *past part.* **vied** *v.i.* to compete, *they vied for first place* [aphetic fr. O.F. *envier*, to increase the stake]

Vied·ma, Lake (vjédmɑ) a lake (53 miles long) north of Lake Argentino, in S. central Argentina

Vi·en·na (vi:énə) (*G.* Wien) the capital (pop. 1,515,666) and economic center of Austria, on a branch of the Danube, constituting a province (area 250 sq. miles). Industries: machinery, metalworking, food processing, textiles, light manufactures. The ancient and medieval site, now circled by the 'Ring' boulevard, remains the center of the city. The principal monuments, apart from the Gothic cathedral (14th c.), are of the 18th and 19th cc. Examples of Viennese baroque architecture include Belvedere and Schönbrunn palaces, the winter palace and Karlskirche. Main cultural institutions: opera (Staatsoper, 1861), theater (Burgtheater), university (1365), national library, museums (celebrated Renaissance and baroque collections). A Celtic settlement and Roman garrison town, it became (1278) the residence of the Hapsburgs. It withstood sieges by the Turks in 1529 and 1683. At the end of the Napoleonic Wars it was the political center of Europe and was a flourishing cultural center (18th-19th cc.)

Vienna, Congress of the conference (1814-15) of European powers at the end of the Napoleonic Wars. Statesmen present included Metternich, Castlereagh and Talleyrand. By the Treaty of Vienna (June 8, 1815), Austria lost Belgium to Holland, but gained interests in Italy. Prussia gained territory notably along the Rhine. Russia gained Finland from Sweden, and much of Poland. Denmark lost Norway to Sweden. Great Britain gained many colonies, notably Cape Colony, Heligoland and Malta. The German Confederation was set up. France, by the Second Treaty of Paris (Nov. 20, 1815), was deprived of her imperial conquests, and made to pay a war indemnity

Vienne (vjen) a department (area 2,711 sq. miles, pop. 357,400) in W. central France (*POITOU, *TOURAINE). Chief town: Poitiers

Vienne, Council of an ecumenical council (1311-12) at which the Knights Templars were suppressed at the instigation of Philippe IV of France

Vienne (Haute-) *HAUTE-VIENNE

Vi·en·nese (vi:əni:s, vi:əní:z) **1.** *adj.* of or pertaining to Vienna **2.** *n.* a native or inhabitant of Vienna

Vien·tiane (vjəntjɑ́n) the administrative capital (pop. 176,637) and commercial center of Laos, a port on the Mekong River (cf. LUANG PRABANG)

Vie·ques (vjékes) (or Crab Island) a fertile island and municipality (area 51 sq. miles, pop. 7,000), ten miles east of Puerto Rico. The U.S. Navy leases the east half of the island from Puerto Rico

Vier·wald·stät·ter See (fíərvɑltʃtetərzéi) *LUCERNE

Vi·et·cong (vi:etkɔ́ŋ, vjetkɔ́ŋ, vi:étkɒŋ) **1.** *n.* the name given by their adversaries to the National Liberation Front, the Communist-led political and military organization operating against the U.S.-supported South Vietnamese government ‖ a member of this organization **2.** *adj.* of or pertaining to this organization [short for Vietnamese *Viet Nam Cong Sam,* Vietnamese Communist]

Vi·et·minh (vjetmín, vi:etmín, vi:étmin) *HÔ-CHIMINH

Vi·et·nam·ese (vjetnəmí:z, vi:etnəmí:z, vjetnəmí:s, vi:etnəmí:s) *pl.* **Vi·et·nam·ese** **1.** *adj.* of or pertaining to Vietnam ‖ of or pertaining to the language of Vietnam **2.** *n.* a native or inhabitant of Vietnam ‖ the language of Vietnam

Vietnam, Socialist Republic of, a country in S.E. Asia, bordered by the South China Sea (S), Gulf of Tonkin (E), People's Republic of China (N), Laos (W), and Cambodia (SW) (area: 127,242 sq. miles, pop. 55,503,000). Capital: Hanoi. People: Vietnamese, highland tribes, some Chinese. Language: Vietnamese, minority languages. Religion: mainly Buddhist and Taoist, with animist minorities. Mountains, mainly wooded and cut by deep river valleys, cover most of the country. Highest peak: Fan Si Pan (11,191 ft). The coast is largely muddy. Average temperatures (F.) in Hanoi: (Jan.) 63°, (June) 80°. Rainfall: 70-100 ins. Agricultural products: rice, sugarcane, rubber, peanuts, copra, corn, cotton, tea, vegetables, coffee, tobacco, castor oil, shellac, silk, fruit. Minerals: coal, apatite, gold, phosphates, salt, tin, chromite, iron, zinc, tungsten, antimony, manganese. Industries: steel, building materials, textiles, hydroelectricity, fishing, food processing and brewing, paper. Exports: minerals, rice, rubber, salt, tea, cinnamon, bamboo, hardwoods, manufactures, foodstuffs. Ports: Haiphong, Da Nang, Ho Chi Minh City. University: Hanoi. Monetary unit: dong (10 hao, 100 xu). HISTORY. After Chinese rule for more than 1,000 years, Vietnam achieved independence 939 A.D. The conflict between the Vietnamese monarchy and Catholic missionaries from Europe (18th c.) allowed the French to conquer the region (1858-83). It was administered first as Annam, Chochin-China, and Tonkin, and later (after 1887) as part of French Indochina. After the Japanese occupation (1940-5), Vietnamese nationalists declared the country an independent republic (1945). Despite war (1946-54) the French were unable to regain control and ended with French defeat at Dien Bien Phu (1954). A Geneva conference (1954) divided the country at the 17th parallel into North and South Vietnam. Under the presidency of Ho Chi Minh, guerrilla troops from North Vietnam began in 1958 to invade South Vietnam and fierce fighting developed, gradually involving the U.S.A. The U.S.A. steadily increased its military commitment in South Vietnam to a high (July 1969) of 550,000. Yet North Vietnam's Tet offensive (Feb. 1968), though costly to the North, disabused the American people of the hope of a military solution to the conflict. Discouraged by the growing anti-war movement at home, Johnson decided (Apr. 1968) not to seek reelection. Richard Nixon's electoral promise to end the war was based on three premises: success in the peace negotiations in Paris initiated by Johnson, success in the 'Vietnamization' program of steadily turning the military operations over to the South Vietnamese themselves, and a deescalation of North Vietnamese and Viet Cong operations in South Vietnam. On Apr. 30, 1970, President Nixon announced an attack on the North's sanctuaries and arms stockpiles in Cambodia, by U.S. and South Vietnamese forces. The invasion was limited to 21.7 miles and U.S. forces were withdrawn by July 1, 1970. South Vietnamese forces remained in Cambodia and retained the support of U.S. air power. A new North Vietnamese offensive was launched (1972) in South Vietnam. U.S. troops were finally withdrawn in 1973 and two years later the South Vietnam govenment, under Nguyen Van Thieu, collapsed. The country was officially reunited on July 2, 1976, and has since developed closer ties with the Soviet Union, joining COMECON in 1978. Also in 1978, Vietnam invaded neighboring Cambodia (Kampuchea), managing the 1979 overthrow of the ruling regime and establishing a pro-Vietnamese government in its place. A guerrilla war continued between the two forces, however. China, allied with Cambodia, briefly invaded Vietnam in Feb. 1979

Vi·et·nam syndrome (vi:etnɑ́m) (*psych.*) sense of guilt and other complexes over the Vietnam war inhibiting similar overt foreign involvement by U.S.

view (vju:) **1.** *n.* what one can see from where one is, *a truck blocked the view* ‖ a wide spread of country as seen from a commanding position, *fine views to north and west* ‖ a painting or photograph of a scene ‖ visual inspection, *they asked for a view of the house and grounds,* esp. an inspection by a jury of the scene of a crime ‖ range of vision, *she disappeared from view* ‖ a mental survey, *a critical view of postwar literature* ‖ an opinion or set of opinions, *differing views* **in full view** completely visible **in view of** in sight of ‖ having regard to, considering **on view** displayed for public inspection **to have in view** to have as a possible option, opportunity, employment etc. ‖ to keep in mind the possibility of, *we must have in view the danger of a surprise attack* **with a view to** in order to arrive at or secure **2.** *v.t.* to inspect, *permission to view the house* ‖ to regard attentively ‖ to consider, take up a mental attitude towards, *he views the situation with alarm* **view·er** *n.* member of a television audience ‖ a device for looking at color slides [A. F. *veiwe, viewe*]

view·find·er (vjú:faindər) *n.* (*photog.*) a camera attachment which shows in miniature the field of view

view·phone (vjú:foun) *n.* videophone

view·point (vjú:pɔint) *n.* a point of view

vig·il (vídʒəl) *n.* the act of remaining awake at night, esp. in order to keep watch, or to pray ‖ the period of such wakefulness ‖ (*eccles.*) the eve of a festival, esp. when observed as a fast ‖ (*pl.*) evening prayers [A.F. and O.F. *vigile*]

vig·i·lance (vídʒələns) *n.* watchfulness, a being on the alert, esp. in order to guard against possible harm or error [F. or fr. L. *vigilantia*]

vigilance committee a group of citizens who agree voluntarily to watch for any infringement of a law or of their rights and privileges, esp. with a view to taking the law into their own hands where the law appears to be ineffective. Such groups were formed in U.S. frontier communities, esp. mining towns, to maintain law and order until a regularly constituted government force could be created (*VIGILANTE)

vig·i·lant (vídʒələnt) *adj.* of someone who is tirelessly on the alert [F. or fr. L. *vigilans (vigilantis)*]

vig·i·lan·te (vidʒəlǽnti:) *n.* a member of a vigilance committee [Span.]

vi·gin·til·lion (vaidʒintíljən) *n.* *NUMBER TABLE [fr. L. *viginti,* twenty+MILLION]

vi·gnette (vinjét) **1.** *n.* a portrait (engraving, photograph etc.) of head and shoulders which shades off into the background ‖ an ornament, esp. of vine leaves and tendrils to decorate a chapter head or chapter end of a book or the title page or half title ‖ a flourish around a capital letter in a manuscript or on a title page ‖ a brief but clear verbal description, esp. of a person **2.** *v.t. pres. part.* **vi·gnet·ting** *past* and *past part.* **vi·gnet·ted** to make a vignette portrait of ‖ to shade off the background of (a portrait) [F.]

Vi·gno·la (vi:njɔ́lɑ), Giacomo Barozzi da (1507-73), Italian architect. He built many fine churches and palaces, esp. in Rome, and is famous for his 'Treatise on the Five Orders of Architecture' (1562)

Vi·gny (vi:nji:), Alfred de (1797-1863), French poet. His romanticism was of a stoical and elevated sort which sets larger-than-life figures face-to-face with an impressive destiny. Besides lyric poetry ('Poèmes antiques et modernes', 1826 and 'les Destinées', 1864) he wrote novels, including 'Cinq-Mars' (1826) and dramas, including 'Chatterton' (1835)

Vi·go (vi:gou) a port (pop. 230,611) in Galicia, Spain: sardine fishing, canning

vig·or *Br.* **vig·our** (vígər) *n.* physical or intellectual power ‖ vitality, strength **in vigor** (*law*) in force or enforceable [A. F., O.F. *vigor*]

vig·or·ous (vígərəs) *adj.* of, having, calling for or done with vigor [A.F., O.F.]

vigour *VIGOR

Vii·pu·ri (vi:puəri:) *VYBORG

Vi·ja·ya·wa·da (vidʒəjəwɑ́də) (formerly Bezwada) a rail center (pop. 317,258) in Andhra Pradesh, India, on the Kistna, headquarters of the Kistna canal system. Industries: steel, chemicals. Hindu and Buddhist shrines

vi·king (váikiŋ) *n.* (*hist.*) one of the Scandinavian warriors who raided (8th–10th cc.) the coasts of Europe, the British Isles, Iceland and Greenland. One group, the Varangians, pillaged the Baltic, settled in Russia (9th c.) and reached Constantinople (10th c.). Others harried the north coast of Europe (9th c.), sacking Paris (845 and 856) and giving their name of Norsemen or Northmen to Normandy. In England (9th and 10th cc.), where they were known as the Danes, they settled in the Danelaw, took the English throne (11th c.) and built up a vast empire under Cnut. Other vikings, under such leaders as Eric the Red and Leif Ericson, reached Greenland and are thought to have landed in North America (c. 1000) [fr. O.N. *vikingr* perh. fr. O.N. *vik,* creek, inlet]

Viking *n.* (*mil.*) a twin-turbofan-engine, multicrew aircraft (S-3) capable of operating from aircraft carriers

Viking I *n.* U.S. rocket to Mars, touched down July 20, 1976

vi·la·yet (vi:lɑ́jet) *n.* a Turkish province or main administrative division [Turk. fr. Arab.]

Vil·ca·bam·ba (vi:lkɑbɑ́mbɑ) the last great capital of the Incas, located by 16th-c. chronicles in the southern Peruvian Andes. For about 40 years after the Conquest (1530), some 4,000 Indians continued to resist the Spaniards from their last redoubt, which they embellished with palaces, temples, fountains, gardens and courtyards. After the Spaniards killed (1572) the last Inca ruler, Vilcabamba was apparently abandoned and became the 'lost city of the Incas'. An expedition (1959-64) discovered (1964) 6-10 sq. miles of ruins, on three succeeding plateaus between 4,500 ft and 12,000 ft, to the northwest of Machu Picchu

vile (vail) *comp.* **vil·er** *superl.* **vil·est** *adj.* morally hateful ‖ foul, *a vile stench* [A.F. and O.F. *vil*]

vil·i·fi·ca·tion (vılifikéiʃən) *n.* a vilifying or being vilified

vil·i·fy (vílifai) *pres. part.* **vil·i·fy·ing** *past* and *past part.* **vil·i·fied** *v.t.* to impute scandalous behavior to, say abusive things about [fr. L.L. *vilificare*]

vil·i·pend (víləpend) *v.t.* (*rhet.*) to speak of with contempt [O.F. *vilipender* or fr. L. *vilipendere*]

Vi·lla (víːjɑ), Francisco ('Pancho', né Doroteo Arango, 1887-1923), Mexican bandit and revolutionist, and one of the most popular figures of the Mexican Revolution. His contribution in the initial stage of 1910-11 helped to overthrow Porfirio Díaz and secure the presidency for Francisco Madero. When Madero was overthrown (1913) by Victoriano Huerta, Villa joined the opposing constitutionalist forces of Venustiano Carranza. At the head of his cavalry, Los Dorados, he gained control of N. Mexico and was instrumental in forcing (1914) Huerta's resignation. Breaking with Carranza, he and Emiliano Zapata occupied (1914-15) Mexico City. Angered by U.S. President Wilson's recognition of Carranza, his followers attacked (1917) Columbus, N.M. It is not known if Villa took part, but he was held responsible. He was unsuccessfully pursued for 11 months (1916-17) by a U.S. punitive expedition led by Gen. Pershing. He was assassinated at Parral (Chihuahua). His life is retold in numerous stories and songs

vil·la (vílə) *n.* a holiday house, esp. by the sea or in mountains ‖ a country house, esp. an imposing one ‖ (*Br.*) a small suburban house with its own garden ‖ (*Rom. hist.*) a luxurious residence, usually with extensive grounds and often with an agricultural estate attached [L. and Ital.]

Vi·lla Cis·ne·ros (víːjɑθiːsnérɔs, víːjɑsiːsnérɔs) *SPANISH SAHARA

vil·lage (vílidʒ) *n.* the houses and other buildings of a community of between about a hundred and a few thousand people ‖ the community occupying a village **vil·lag·er** *n.* someone who lives and works in a village [O.F.]

vil·lag·i·za·tion (vıləd3əzéiʃən) *n.* placing land rights in the hands of the village. *ant.* nationalization

vil·lain (vílən) *n.* someone guilty or capable of vile deeds or wickedness ‖ the character in a play or novel opposed to the hero and motivating much of the action ‖ *VILLEIN **víl·lain·ous** *adj.* [A.F. and O.F. *vilein, villain*]

vil·lain·y (víləniː) *pl.* **vil·lain·ies** *n.* villainous conduct ‖ a villainous act ‖ the state or quality of being villainous [A.F. and O.F. *vilenie, vileinie, vilanie*]

Vil·la-Lo·bos (víləlóubɔs), Heitor (1887-1959), prolific Brazilian composer. His compositions (instrumental, chamber, vocal, operatic and symphonic) include many which echo or exploit African and Indian themes in local Brazilian music

vil·la·nelle (vılənél) *n.* a poem of five tercets and a final quatrain with two rhymes [F. fr. Ital.]

Vil·lard (vilár, vilárd), Henry (1835-1900), U.S. journalist and financier, of German origin. He reported the Lincoln-Douglas debates (1858), the discovery (1859-60) of gold in Colorado, and some of the major engagements of the Civil War. He purchased (1881) and combined the 'New York Evening Post' and the weekly 'Nation', and organized (1890) the Edison General Electric Company

Vi·lla·ro·el (viːjɑrɔ́el), Gualberto (1908-46), Bolivian army officer and dictator (1943-6). He was assassinated

Vi·llar·ri·ca (vıːjɑrríːkɑ) an industrial city (pop. 35,000) in S. central Paraguay: sugar refineries, distilleries, sawmills, flour mills, brick and tile works

-ville (*colloq.*) combining form usu. used with an adjective to indicate the character of a thing or place, e.g., dullsville, weirdsville

Vi·lle·da Mo·ra·les (viːjéðɑmɔrάles), Ramón (1909-71), Honduran liberal politician and president of the Republic (1957-63). He was deposed by the army

Ville·har·douin (viːlærdwɛ̃), Geoffroi de (c. 1150–c. 1213), French chronicler, author of 'la Conquête de Constantinople' (c. 1212), a main source for the history of the 4th Crusade, in which he took part

vil·lein, vil·lain (vílən) *n.* (*hist.*) a workman bound in service to his feudal lord or to a feudal estate [A.F. *villein, villain*]

vil·lein·age (víləniḍʒ) *n.* the status of a villein ‖ a villein's tenure [A.F. *vilenage, villenage*]

Ville·neuve (viːlnəːv), Pierre Charles Jean Baptiste Sylvestre de (1763-1806), French admiral. He was defeated by Nelson at Trafalgar (1805) and committed suicide

Vil·liers (vílərz, víljərz), George, dukes of Buckingham *BUCKINGHAM

vil·li·form (vílifɔrm) *adj.* resembling villi (*VILLUS) ‖ set densely together like the pile of velvet

Vil·lon (viːjɔ̃), François (1431–c. 1465), French poet. His name was probably François de Montcorbier, but he took the name of his patron, Guillaume de Villon. His 'Petit testament' (c. 1456), 'Grand testament' (1461) and 'Epitaphe Villon' ('Ballade des Pendus', 1462-3) show him as at once sardonic and humane, earthy and impassioned

Villon (viːlɔ̃), Jacques (Gaston Duchamp, 1875-1956), French cubist painter and engraver. His works, comprising still lifes, landscapes and figure studies, combine cubism and representation of nature, suggesting a continuation of the researches of Cézanne

vil·lose (vílous) *adj.* villous

vil·los·i·ty (vilɔ́sitiː) *n.* the state of being villous ‖ a villus ‖ a coating of villi

vil·lous (víləs) *adj.* of, like, or covered with, villi

vil·lus (víləs) *pl.* **vil·li** (vílai) *n.* one of the minute vascular processes on the inner lining of the small intestine. They project into the lumen and help the absorption of digested food ‖ one of the processes on the chorion through which nourishment passes to the embryo [L.=tuft of hair]

Vil·ni·us (vílniːəs) (*Russ.* Vilna, *Pol.* Wilno) the capital (pop. 492,000) of Lithuania, U.S.S.R. Industries: mechanical engineering, food processing, textiles, woodworking, light manufactures. University (1578)

Vil·yu·i (vjıljuːíː, vıljuːíː) (Viljny) a tributary (1,500 miles long, navigable for 750) of the Lena in central Siberia, U.S.S.R.

vim (vim) *n.* vigor, energy [L. acc. of *vis*, strength]

Vi·my Ridge, Battle of (viːmiː) the site of a very costly Allied attack (1917) on a German position, mainly by Canadian troops, during the 1st world war

vi·na (víːnə) *n.* an Indian musical instrument, usually with four strings, with a fingerboard of bamboo, and two gourd resonators [Skr. and Hindi *vīṇā*]

vi·na·ceous (vainéiʃəs) *adj.* wine-colored [fr. L. *vinaceus*]

Vi·ña del Mar (víːnjɑðelmάr) a residential suburb and seaside resort (pop. 262,100) of Valparaíso, Chile

vin·ai·grette (vınəgrét) *n.* an ornamental vessel containing aromatic vinegar or smelling salts etc. ‖ a vinaigrette sauce [F. fr. *vinaigre*, vinegar]

vinaigrette sauce a sauce of chopped parsley, shallots etc., in vinegar and oil, served cold with artichokes, asparagus, cold meat, fish etc.

vi·nasse (vinǽs) *n.* the liquor remaining when alcoholic liquor is fermented and distilled, used as a source of potassium carbonate [F.]

vin·blas·tine [$C_{46}H_{58}O_9N_4$] (vınblǽstiːn) *n.* (*pharm.*) an alkaloid drug used in treating leukemia and lymphoma; marketed as Velban. *also* vincaleukoblastine

Vin·cent de Paul (vínsəntdəpɔ́l, vɛ̃sɑ̃dəpɔl), St (c. 1581-1660), French priest. He worked to help foundlings, galley slaves, war wounded and all sick and suffering, and to send out missionaries. He founded the Lazarists (1625) and the Sisters of Charity (1633). Feast: July 19

Vin·cent of Beau·vais (vɛ̃sɑ̃əvbouvei) (c. 1190–c. 1264), French friar. He wrote most of the 'Speculum majus (c. 1244), an encyclopedia summarizing the knowledge of his time

Vin·cent's infection (vínsənts) infection of the respiratory tract and the mouth, marked by painful ulceration, esp. of the mucous membranes [after Jean H. *Vincent* (*d.* 1950), F. bacteriologist]

Vinci, Leonardo da *LEONARDO DA VINCI

vin·cris·tine [$C_{46}H_{56}N_4O$] (vıŋkrístiːn) *n.* (*pharm.*) an anticarcinogenic made from the Madagascar periwinkle; marketed as Oncovin

vin·cu·lum (víŋkjuləm) *pl.* **vin·cu·lums, vin·cu·la** (víŋkjulə) *n.* (*math.*) a line drawn above two or more terms to indicate that these are to be treated as a unit ‖ (*anat.*) a ligament [L.]

Vin·dhya Range (víndjə) a range of hills (mainly 1,500-2,000 ft) crossing India from Gujarat to Bihar, forming the Ganges-Narbada watershed

vin·di·cate (víndikeit) *pres. part.* **vin·di·cat·ing** *past* and *past part.* **vin·di·cat·ed** *v.t* to prove the truth or virtue of, after this has been questioned or denied [fr. L. *vindicare* (*vindicatus*), to claim]

vin·di·ca·tion (vındikéiʃən) *n.* a vindicating or being vindicated ‖ a fact which vindicates [O.F. or fr. L. *vindicatio* (*vindicationis*)]

vin·di·ca·to·ry (víndiketɔriː, víndikətouriː) *adj.* serving to vindicate ‖ (*law*) punitive, *vindicatory legislation*

vin·dic·tive (vindíktiv) *adj.* having the motive of revenge [fr. L. *vindicta*, revenge]

vine (vain) *n.* a member of *Vitis*, fam. *Vitaceae*, a genus of slender, woody, climbing plants, with alternate, palmate-veined leaves, esp. *V. vinifera*, the grapevine, cultivated in Mediterranean-type climates since very early civilizations ‖ any plant having a long, slender, flexible stem that supports itself by creeping along the ground or by climbing over some object [O.F. *vine, vigne*]

vin·e·gar (vínigər) *n.* a liquid containing up to 6% acetic acid, obtained by the oxidation of the ethyl alcohol in wine, beer etc. by bacteria, and used as a preservative in pickling and as a condiment **vín·e·gar·y** *adj.* [O.F. *vynegre, vinaigre*]

vin·er·y (váinəriː) *pl.* **vin·er·ies** *n.* a greenhouse in which vines are cultivated for dessert grapes [fr. M.L. *vinarium*]

vine·yard (vínjərd) *n.* a plot of land where grapevines are growing

vingt·et·un (vɛ̃teiœ̃) *n.* blackjack

vin·i·fy (vínəfai) *v.* to ferment grape juice into wine

vi·nos·i·ty (vainɔ́sitiː) *n.* the state or quality of being vinous [fr. L. *vinositas*, the flavor of wine]

vi·nous (váinəs) *adj.* pertaining to, caused by, made from or addicted to wine [fr. L. *vinosus*]

Vin·son (vínsən), Frederick Moore (1890-1953), U.S. lawyer, Congressman, and chief justice (1946-53) of the U.S. Supreme Court. As secretary of the treasury (1945-6) under President Harry Truman, he helped to establish the International Monetary Fund. As chief justice he believed in a broad interpretation of federal governmental powers, as is shown in his dissenting opinion in 'Youngstown Sheet and Tube Co. v. Sawyer' (1952), in which he supported President Wilson's seizure of the steel industry. In 'Shelley v. Kraemer' (1948) he upheld the rights of racial minorities under the equal protection clause of the 14th amendment

vin·tage (víntidʒ) **1.** *n.* the picking and pressing of grapes for wine ‖ the season for this ‖ the yield of wine or grapes gathered in a particular season or district ‖ a wine of a particular year, *a prewar vintage* **2.** *adj.* venerable, having an excellence that has survived the passing of time, *a vintage car* ‖ not in style any more, outmoded [A.F. altered fr. *vindage, vendage*]

vintage wine a wine of superior quality of a particular year and place put aside for full maturing

vintage year a year productive of vintage wines ‖ a year productive of some specified thing of good quality in good numbers

vint·ner (víntnər) *n.* a wine merchant [alteration of older *vinter*, A.F. fr. L. *vinum*, vine]

vi·nyl (váin'l) *n.* the monovalent, unsaturated group $CH_2{=}\,CH$ derived from ethylene ‖ a polymer of a vinyl compound ‖ a resin, plastic or synthetic fiber made from a vinyl compound [fr. L. *vinum*, vine]

vi·nyl·i·dene (vainilidiːn) *n.* the divalent, unsaturated group $CH_2{=}C$, the polymerized compounds of which form useful resins [fr. VINYL]

vi·ol (váiəl) *n.* a medieval stringed instrument

CONCISE PRONUNCIATION KEY: **(a)** æ, *cat*; ɑ, *car*; ɔ *fawn*; ei, *snake*. **(e)** e, *hen*; iː, *sheep*; iə, *deer*; ɛə, *bear*. **(i)** i, *fish*; ai, *tiger*; əː, *bird*. **(o)** o, *ox*; au, *cow*; ou, *goat*; u, *poor*; ɔi, *royal*. **(u)** ʌ, *duck*; u, *bull*; uː, *goose*; ə, *bacillus*; juː, *cube*. x, *loch*; θ, *think*; ð, *bother*; z, *Zen*; ʒ, *corsage*; dʒ, *savage*; ŋ, *orangutang*; j, *yak*; ʃ, *fish*; tʃ, *fetch*; 'l, *rabble*; 'n, *redden*. Complete pronunciation key appears inside front cover.

made chiefly in treble, tenor and bass sizes, having frets, and bowed in a style differing from that used for the violin, viola etc., to which they gave place at about the end of the 17th c. [fr. A.F., O.F. *viele, vielle* altered after F. *viole*]

vi·o·la (vi:óulə) *n.* a stringed instrument larger than a violin, tuned one-fifth lower than a violin, and having a range of more than three octaves above C below middle C ‖ a member of the orchestra who plays this instrument [Ital. and Span.]

vi·o·la (váiələ, vaióulə) *n.* a member of *Viola*, fam. *Violaceae*, a genus of lowgrowing plants bearing large, solitary flowers of various colors (cf. PANSY, cf. VIOLET). About 400 species are known ‖ a hybrid derived from the garden pansy [L.=a violet]

vi·o·la·ceous (vạiəléiʃəs) *adj.* of violet color ‖ belonging to fam. *Violaceae*, the violet family [fr. L. *violaceus*, violet-colored]

vi·o·la da gam·ba (vi:óulədəgǽmbə, vi:óulədəgúmbə) *n.* a bass instrument of the viol family, having a range roughly equal to that of the cello. It remained in use as a solo instrument until the late 18th c. [Ital.+leg viol]

vi·o·la d'a·mo·re (vi:óulədɑmɔ́rei, vi:óulədɑmóurei) *n.* a stringed instrument related to the viols, but without frets. When one of the seven main strings is bowed a sympathetic resonance is set up in the under string of a secondary set [Ital.=viol of love]

vi·o·late (váiəleit) *pres. part.* **vi·o·lat·ing** *past* and *past part.* **vi·o·lat·ed** *v.t.* to break (a promise, law, principle etc.) by forceful opposition to it ‖ to rape ‖ to fail conspicuously to show respect for, *to violate a person's privacy* ‖ to desecrate (something sacred) [fr. L. *violare* (*violatus*)]

vi·o·la·tion (vạiəléiʃən) *n.* a violating or being violated [O.F. *violacion* or fr. L. *violatio* (*violationis*)]

vi·o·la·tor (váiəlẹitər) *n.* a person who violates

vi·o·lence (váiələns) *n.* a use of physical force so as to damage or injure ‖ intense natural force or energy ‖ an abusive use of force ‖ passion, fury ‖ distortion of meaning ‖ desecration **to do violence to** to offend, outrage, *to do violence to someone's sense of justice* [A.F. and O.F.]

vi·o·lent (váiələnt) *adj.* characterized by the exercise or production of very great force, *a violent storm* ‖ markedly intense, *violent colors* ‖ furious, *violent language* ‖ caused by violence ‖ tending to pervert meaning [O.F. or fr. L. *violentus*]

vi·o·let (váiəlit) **1.** *n.* a small-flowered plant of the genus *Viola*, esp. the fragrant *V. odorata* ‖ the bluish-purple color of the flowers of *V. odorata* ‖ a pigment, fabric etc. of the color of these flowers ‖ any of various similar plants of different genera **2.** *adj.* having a violet color [dim. of O.F. *viole*]

vi·o·lin (vạiəlín) *n.* a four-stringed treble musical instrument played with a bow and having a compass of three and a half octaves or more above G below middle C ‖ the member of an orchestra who plays this instrument, *first violin* [fr. Ital. *violino*]

vi·o·lin·ist (vạiəlínist) *n.* a violin player [fr. Ital. *violinista*]

Viol·let-le-Duc (vjɔleilədyk), Eugene Emmanuel (1814-79), French architect. He led the Gothic revival, and his two dictionaries of medieval architecture and furniture are standard works. He also restored many medieval buildings and monuments, including Notre-Dame de Paris and Carcassonne

vi·o·lon·cel·lo (vạiələntʃélou) *n.* a cello [Ital.]

VIP (vị:aipí:) *n.* a person of eminence or importance, esp. a high government official [very important person]

VIP (*computer abbr.*) for variable information processing, an extensive general information storage system used by Naval Ordnance Laboratory

vi·per (váipər) *n.* an adder ‖ (*rhet.*) a person who behaves with great malice, or who shows rank ingratitude **vi·per·ous** (váipərəs) *adj.* of, relating to or characteristic of a viper or vipers ‖ (*rhet*) malicious [O.F. *vipere, vipre* or fr. L. *vipera*, snake]

viper's bugloss *n. Echium vulgare*, fam. *Borraginaceae*, a rough hairy biennial, with short dense cymose inflorescenses of flowers, pink in bud and bright blue in bloom

Vi·ra·co·cha (vi:rɑkóutʃɑ) the Inca creator god and god of rain. He dwelt in Lake Titicaca. The name was given (16th c.) by the ancient Peruvians and Chileans to the Spanish conquistadores

vi·ra·go (virɑ́gou) *pl.* **vi·ra·goes, vi·ra·gos** *n.* a shrewish, noisy woman, esp. one who is big and strong [L.=manlike woman]

vir·e·lay (vírəlei) *n.* a Provençal verse form of short lines, either composed in stanzas each of which have two rhymes only, the last rhyme in a stanza becoming the main rhyme of the succeeding stanza, or else composed entirely on two rhymes, lines 1 and 2 ending alternate stanzas and closing the poem together but reversed in order [O.F. *virelai*]

vir·e·o (víri:ou) *pl.* **vir·e·os** *n.* any of various small New World insectivorous birds of fam. *vireonidae*, having gray or olive-green plumage

vi·res·cence (virés,ns, vairés,ns) *n.* (*bot.*) greenness, esp. abnormal greenness in a petal usually colored otherwise

vi·res·cent (virés'nt, vairés'nt) *adj.* turning green ‖ greenish [fr. L. *virescens* (*virescentis*) fr. *virescere*, to become green]

vir·gate (və́:rgit, və́:rgeit) *adj.* (*bot.*) long, straight and slim as a rod ‖ (*bot.*) having many twigs [fr. L. *virgatus*]

Vir·gil·i·an (və:rdʒíli:ən) *adj.* in the style of Virgil [fr. L. *Vergilianus*]

Vir·gil, Ver·gil (və́:rdʒəl), (Publius Vergilius Maro, 70-19 B.C.), Latin poet. Patronized by Maecenas and Augustus, he was able to devote his entire life to poetry. The 'Eclogues' (43-37 B.C.), a collection of pastoral poems, and the 'Georgics' (37-30 B.C.), a series of didactic poems on the art of farming, established him as the foremost poet of his age. The remaining 11 years of his life were devoted to the composition of 'Aeneid', his masterpiece. In this epic he employed Homeric hexameters to glorify the legendary past of Rome. Throughout the Latin Middle Ages Virgil was looked upon as the model of the poet, and widely imitated. Dante takes him as his guide in the first two books of the 'Divine Comedy'

vir·gin (və́:rdʒin) **1.** *n.* a person who has not had sexual intercourse, esp. a girl or woman ‖ (in the early Christian Church) a chaste woman or girl noted for her piety and faith and so accorded a special place in the community **the Virgin** *MARY, THE VIRGIN ‖ (*astron.*) the constellation Virgo **2.** *adj.* of or being a virgin ‖ not yet cultivated or otherwise brought into use, *virgin forest* ‖ (of elements) occurring uncombined in the earth's crust, *virgin sulfur* ‖ (of metals) obtained by simple smelting of an ore ‖ (of oils) obtained from the first pressing of a fruit or nut [A.F. and O.F. *virgine*]

vir·gin·al (və́:rdʒin'l) *n.* a small keyboard musical instrument in a frame without legs. of the 16th and 17th cc. The strings are plucked, as in a harpsichord [prob. O.F. or fr. L. *virginalis*]

virginal *adj.* of or appropriate to a virgin [O.F. or fr. L. *virginalis*]

virgin birth (*theol.*) the doctrine that Jesus was born to a virgin mother, Mary. According to Christian theology Jesus was begotten by the Holy Ghost ‖ (*zool.*) parthenogenesis

Vir·gin·ia (vərdʒínjə) (*abbr.* Va.) a state (area 40,815 sq. miles, pop. 5,550,000) on the southern Atlantic coast of the U.S.A. Capital: Richmond. It is largely a hilly plateau extending from the Appalachians to the coastal plain. Agriculture: tobacco, cereals, peanuts, apples, dairying, poultry, beef cattle. Resources: coal, building materials, lead, zinc. Industries: chemicals, tobacco products, textiles, shipbuilding, food processing. State university (1819) at Charlottesville. Virginia, named after Elizabeth I, 'the Virgin Queen', was the first permanent English settlement in North America (1607). It was one of the Thirteen Colonies, and became (1788) the 10th state of the U.S.A.

Virginia and Kentucky Resolutions three resolutions passed by state legislatures during the administration of President John Adams. The first (1798) was authored by James Madison and the other two (1798, 1799) by Vice-President Thomas Jefferson. They advocated the repeal of the Alien and Sedition Acts (1798) and held that the Federal government possessed only limited and delegated powers. Jefferson further contended that the states, and not the national government, should be the arbiter of whether the latter had exceeded its mandate. This authority to determine the constitutionality of federal laws eventually passed to the U.S. Supreme Court. The resolutions were invoked (1860) by the seceding Southern states

Virginia Company *LONDON COMPANY

Virginia creeper *Parthenocissus quinquefolia*, fam. *Vitaceae*, a vine which climbs by attaching tendrils to its host

Virginia deer *Odocoileus virginianus*, the most abundant North American deer, also called white-tailed deer because its long tail has a white underside

Virginia Plan a plan proposed by the Virginia delegation at the Constitutional Convention of 1787. It advocated the creation of strong national government rather than the strengthening of the confederation of states, and it provided for a federal judiciary and a power of amendment to be lodged outside the legislature. The plan was opposed by the less populous states because its distribution of the legislative seats favored the more populous states

Virginia reel a spirited American country dance in which couples form a long set opposite one another and execute lively steps in a pattern including a reel, to the music of a fiddle

Virginia, University of a U.S. educational institution founded (1819) near Charlottesville, Va., by Thomas Jefferson

Virginia, West *WEST VIRGINIA

Virgin Islands a cluster of small islands in the Leeward group, West Indies, divided between the British Virgin Islands and the Virgin Islands of the U.S.A. Population: mainly Afro-West Indian and mulatto. The islands were discovered (1493) by Columbus, and were settled (17th c.) by England and Denmark

Virgin Islands, British a British colony (land area 59 sq. miles, pop. 10,030) occupying the 36 eastern islands (11 inhabited) of the Virgin Is. Capital: Road Town (pop. 2,000) on Tortola Is. Industries: truck farming, fruit, fishing. The islands were taken by English pirates (1666) and were administered (1871-1956) as part of the Leeward Is colony

Virgin Islands of the United States an overseas territory (land area 133 sq. miles, pop. 95,591) of the U.S.A. occupying the 52 western islands (3 inhabited) of the Virgin Is. Main islands: St Thomas (area 32 sq. miles) and St Croix (area 82 sq. miles). Capital: Charlotte Amalie on St Thomas. Industries: agriculture (cattle raising, sugarcane, truck farming), fuel bunkering, rum, fishing, tourism. The islands were bought from Denmark by the U.S.A. (1917)

vir·gin·i·ty (və:rdʒíniti:) *n.* the state or quality of being a virgin [A.F. and O.F. *virginite*]

vir·gin·i·um (vərdʒíni:əm) *n.* the old name for francium [Mod. L. after the state of VIRGINIA]

Virgin Mary *MARY, THE VIRGIN

Vir·go (və́:rgou) an equatorial constellation ‖ the sixth sign of the zodiac

vir·gu·late (və́:rgjulit, və́:rgjuleit) *adj.* (*bot.*) rod-shaped [fr. L. *virgulatus* fr. *virgula* dim. of *virga*, rod]

vir·i·des·cence (vịridés'ns) *n.* greenishness

vir·i·des·cent (vịridés'nt) *adj.* greenish [fr. L.L. *viridescens* (*viridescentis*) fr. *viridescere*, to become green]

vi·rid·i·an (virídi:ən) *n.* a deep green pigment with blue overtones [fr. L. *viridis*]

vi·rid·i·ty (viríditi:) *n.* greenness, e.g. of the color of young leaves ‖ (*rhet.*) freshness, innocence [fr. L. *viriditas*]

vir·ile (vírəl, *Br.* vírail) *adj.* having in marked degree the characteristics of a man as a male being ‖ capable of procreating ‖ forceful and vigorous as befits a man [O.F. *viril* or fr. L. *virilis*]

vi·ril·i·ty (viríliti:) *n.* the state or quality of being virile [fr. F. *virilité* or L. *virilitas*]

vi·ri·on (váiri:ɒn) *n.* (*genetics*) a complete infective viral particle made up of RNA in a protein shell that controls the form of viral replicating. *Cf* INTERFERON

vi·rol·o·gy (vairólədʒi:) *n.* the study of viruses [fr. Mod. L. *virus*, virus+Gk *logos*, discourse]

virtual literacy the capacity to understand the world

virtual memory (*computer*) a peripheral look ahead, look behind notational memory. *also* virtual storage

virtual process (*quantum mech.*) a process used in creating a hypothetical model, where a real model is not realizable

virtual storage (*computer*) virtual memory (which see)

virtuous cycle (*economics*) proposed procedure that a government would set in motion automatically to prevent currency devaluation, e.g., increase in interest rates, price stabilization, import restriction. *Cf* VICIOUS CYCLE

vir·tu, ver·tu (vərtú:) *n.* a liking for, or knowledge of, curios, antiques etc. curios, antiques etc. collectively [Ital. *virtù*]

vir·tu·al (və́:rtʃu:əl) *adj.* being something specified in essence or effect though not in name [fr. M.L. *virtualis*]

virtual focus the point from which light appears to diverge but does not in fact do so, or the point to which convergent rays are directed but which they do not reach

virtual image an image formed of virtual foci

vir·tu·al·i·ty (və:rtʃu:ǽliti:) *n.* the state or quality of being virtual

vir·tu·al·ly (və́:rtʃu:əli:) *adv.* almost entirely

vir·tue (və́:rtʃu:) *n.* a quality held to be of great moral value (*CARDINAL VIRTUES, *THEOLOGICAL VIRTUES) ‖ moral excellence, goodness ‖ female chastity ‖ (of a remedy) power to do good ‖ (*pl.*) an order of angels (*ANGEL) **by** (or **in**) **virtue of** on the strength or authority of, *he was able to do it by virtue of his office* [A.F., O.F. *vertu*]

vir·tu·os·i·ty (və:rtʃu:ɒ́siti:) *n.* great technical ability in a fine art, esp. in the playing of a musical instrument

vir·tu·o·so (və:rtʃu:óusou) *pl.* **vir·tu·o·sos, vir·tu·o·si** (və:rtʃu:óusi:) *n.* someone very highly skilled in the technique of a fine art, esp. in the playing of a musical instrument [Ital.=skilled, learned]

vir·tu·ous (və́:rtʃu:əs) *adj.* showing or having moral virtue ‖ chaste [A.F. and O.F. *vertuous*]

vir·u·lence (vírulǝns, vírjulǝns) *n.* the quality of being virulent **vir·u·len·cy** *n.* virulence [fr. L. *virulentia*]

vir·u·lent (vírulǝnt, vírjulǝnt) *adj.* (of a disease) characterized by severity, rapidity of course and malignancy ‖ (of a microorganism) extremely toxic or poisonous ‖ malignant, bitterly hostile, *virulent enmity* [fr. L. *virulentus*, poisonous]

vi·rus (váirəs) *pl.* **vi·rus·es** *n.* a submicroscopic entity consisting principally of nucleoprotein and able to pass through bacteria-retaining filters. Viruses have many characteristics of living organisms (e.g. they are capable of growth and multiplication in living cells) and are recognized by their toxic or pathogenic effects in plants and animal cells (e.g. they are the agents which cause mumps, rabies or mosaic) [L.=a slimy liquid]

vi·sa (ví:zə) **1.** *n.* an official endorsement of a passport denoting that the owner has permission either to enter or cross a particular country **2.** *v.t.* to endorse (a passport) in this way [F.]

vis·age (vízidʒ) *n.* (*rhet.*) the face [A.F. and O.F.]

vis·a·giste (vi:zɑʒí:st) *n.* a makeup artist

Vi·sa·kha·pat·nam (visɑ́kəpʌ́tnəm) (formerly Vizagapatam) a port (pop. 352,504) in N. Andhra Pradesh, India: shipbuilding

vis·à·vis (vi:zɑví:) **1.** *adv.* face to face, *they talked vis-à-vis* **2.** *n.* the person facing one **3.** *prep.* as compared with ‖ with respect to ‖ facing [F.]

Vi·sa·yas (visáiəz) the central group of islands in the Philippines: Panay, Samar, Leyte, Negros, Bohol, Masbate, and about 480 adjacent smaller islands

viscacha *VIZCACHA

vis·cer·a (vísərə) *pl. n.* the bodily organs occupying the great cavities, esp. the stomach, intestines etc. which occupy the trunk [L.=inner organs]

vis·cer·al (vísərəl) *adj.* of, like, or felt in the viscera [fr. M.L. *visceralis*]

vis·cid (vísid) *adj.* viscous ‖ (of leaves) covered with a sticky substance **vis·cíd·i·ty** *n.* [fr. L.L. *viscidus*]

vis·cin (vísin) *n.* a sticky substance, $C_{10}H_{24}O_4$, obtained from various plants, esp. from mistletoe berries [F.]

Vis·con·ti (vi:skɔ́nti:) the ruling family of Milan (1277-1447)

vis·cose (vískous) *n.* a thick, brownish liquid prepared by the interaction of cellulose with sodium hydroxide and carbon disulfide. The liquid, which is largely a solution of cellulose xanthate, is forced through small holes into a solution (*CUPRAMMONIUM SOLUTION) which decomposes the xanthate and gives threads of cellulose (viscose rayon). The liquid is also used for the manufacture of cellulose film from which transparent wrappings are made [fr. L. *viscosus*, viscous]

vis·cos·i·ty (viskɒ́siti:) *pl.* **vis·cos·i·ties** *n.* the quality or property of a fluid that causes it to resist flow (*VISCOSITY, COEFFICIENT OF) [O.E. *viscosite* or fr. M.L. *viscositas*]

viscosity, coefficient of the ratio in a fluid flow of the shearing stress to the rate of shear strain. With increasing temperature the coefficient falls for a liquid (e.g. molasses) and rises for a gas (e.g. steam)

vis·count (váikaunt) *n.* a British peer of lower rank than an earl but of higher rank than a baron ‖ the courtesy title of the eldest son of an earl before he succeeds to the title **vís·count·cy** *n.* the rank of a viscount [A.F. *vescounte, viscounte*, O.F. *visconte, viconte*]

vis·count·ess (váikauntis) *n.* the wife of a viscount, or sometimes the title held in the holder's own right

vis·count·y (váikaunti:) *pl.* **vis·count·ies** *n.* a viscountcy ‖ (*hist.*) the land or jurisdiction of a viscount

vis·cous (vískəs) *adj.* having viscosity ‖ (of leaves) viscid ‖ sticky, slow-flowing [A.F. *viscous* or fr. L. *viscosus*]

vise, *Br.* **vice** (vais) *n.* a tool by which an object being worked is gripped between two jaws, which are brought together by a screw [O.F. *vis*]

Vi·shin·sky, Vy·shin·sky (viʃínski:), Andrei Yanuarievich (1883-1954), Russian diplomat. As foreign minister (1949-53) and as the chief U.S.S.R. delegate to the U.N. he attacked Western rearmament policy

Vish·nu (víʃnu:) one of the chief gods of Hinduism. Originally a member of the pantheon worshipped in the Vedic hymns, he came to be identified with the divine principle of grace. Brahma (the creator), Vishnu (the preserver) and Siva (the dissolver) form the threefold manifestation of divine activity. Vishnu is believed to have been incarnated on nine occasions in order to save the world. The last of these incarnations (avatars) was as Krishna, and there is to be a tenth, as Kalkin, whose coming will herald the end of the world as we know it

vis·i·bil·i·ty (vizəbíliti:) *n.* the fact or state of being visible ‖ range of vision, esp. with respect to weather conditions (mist, fog etc.) [fr. L.L. *visibilitas*]

vis·i·ble (vízəb'l) *adj.* able to be seen ‖ apparent to the mind, *without visible means of support* **vís·i·bly** *adv.* [O.F. or fr. L. *visibilis*]

vis·i·ble-in·fra·red spin-scan radiometer (vízəb'línfrəred) device that takes pictures during day or night by sensing reflected sunlight or surface heat radiation

visible spectrum the part of the electromagnetic spectrum that may be perceived by the human eye. It extends from a wavelength of almost 3800Å (violet light) to almost 7600Å (red light)

Vis·i·goth (vízigɒθ) *n.* a member of the western division of the Goths, who, under their leader Alaric, invaded Italy and sacked Rome (410). They established a kingdom covering most of S. Gaul and Spain (5th c.), but they lost Gaul to Clovis (507), while the Spanish kingdom survived until the Moorish conquest (711)

vi·sion (víʒən) **1.** *n.* the act of seeing or the ability to see, *range of vision* ‖ a picture formed in the mind, *visions of future greatness* ‖ imaginative foresight, *a man of vision* ‖ a supernatural apparition ‖ something seen, esp. something very beautiful **2.** *v.t.* to see as if in a vision **ví·sion·al** *adj.* **vi·sion·ar·y 1.** *pl.* **vi·sion·ar·ies** *n.* someone who imagines how things should be and pays little regard to how they actually are or are likely in fact to be **2.** *adj.* conjured up in the imagination without being related to facts ‖ inclined to be a visionary ‖ of the nature of a vision [A.F. *visiun, visioun*, O.F. *vision* or fr. L. *visio* (*visionis*)]

—Vision occurs when light, entering the eye and focused on the retina, causes chemical changes in the cells of the retina. Impulses travel from these cells by way of the optic nerve to the brain, where they are interpreted in the conscious mind. The brain is therefore an active partner with the eye, and its misinterpretation can result in an optical illusion. Thus judgments of color and of the speed of a moving object may easily be subject to error

vi·sion-mix (víʒənmiks) *v.* (*cinematography*) to integrate current shots or stills with motion pictures or video pictures

vis·it (vízit) **1.** *v.t.* to go or come to see (someone) socially, often for a short vacation, *to visit relatives* ‖ to inspect as a sightseer, *to visit a monument* ‖ to inspect with authority, *an archdeacon visits the parishes of a diocese* ‖ to call on in charity, *to visit the sick* ‖ to pay a professional call on, *to visit a patient* ‖ to call on for professional advice, *to visit one's doctor* ‖ to go to (a holy place) as an act of devotion ‖ (*Bible*) to bless, comfort (someone) ‖ (*Bible*, with 'on' or 'upon') to take vengeance for (sin) ‖ (*Bible*) to avenge sin on (a person) ‖ (*rhet.*, with 'with') to afflict with injury or trouble ‖ to migrate for part of the year to ‖ *v.i.* to make a visit **2.** *n.* a visiting or being visited ‖ a period of time spent in visiting ‖ (*naut.*) the boarding of a neutral state by an officer of a state at war, for reasons of search [O.F. *visiter* or fr. L. *visitare*, to go to see]

vis·i·tant (vízitənt) *n.* a migratory bird coming to a district for a certain time ‖ a fantastic visitor, *visitants from Mars* ‖ a phantom **Vis·i·tant** a member of the order of Sisters of the Visitation [F. or fr. L. *visitans* (*visitantis*) fr. *visitare*, to visit]

vis·it·a·tion (vizitéiʃən) *n.* an official visit for inspection, e.g. by an archdeacon ‖ an instance of affliction or of blessing regarded as divine punishment or reward ‖ (*zool.*) an abnormal invasion of a district by animals, *a visitation of rats* ‖ (*naut.*) a visit **the Vis·it·a·tion,** the visit of the virgin Mary to S. Elizabeth (Luke i, 39) ‖ the feast commemorating this (July 2) [A.F. *visitacioun* or fr. L. *visitatio* (*visitationis*)]

Visitation, Sisters of the a contemplative order of nuns (Visitants) founded (1610) by St Francis of Sales for the care of the sick

vis·it·a·to·ri·al (vizitətɔ́ri:əl, vizitətóuri:əl) *adj.* of or pertaining to visitation ‖ having the power of inspection

visiting card (*Br.*) a calling card

vis·i·tor (vízitər) *n.* someone who makes a visit [A.F. *visitour*, O.F. *visiteor, visiteur*]

vis·i·to·ri·al (vizitɔ́ri:əl, vizitóuri:əl) *adj.* visitatorial

vi·sor, vi·zor (váizər) *n.* (*armor*) a movable, perforated part of a helmet, covering the face but permitting sight and speech through the perforations ‖ the peak of a cap, shielding the eyes from direct sunlight ‖ any of various similar devices used to shade the eyes, e.g. one on a car windshield [A.F. *viser* fr. F. *vis*, face]

VISTA *VOLUNTEERS IN SERVICE TO AMERICA

vis·ta (vístə) *n.* a view extending into the distance but bounded, e.g. by headlands or rows of trees ‖ a mental view into the distant past or future [Ital.]

Vis·tu·la (vístʃu:lə) (*Pol.* Wisla) the chief river (680 miles long) of Poland, flowing from the Carpathians to the Baltic, navigable to Torun

vis·u·al (víʒu:əl) *adj.* of, pertaining to, or used in, seeing ‖ obtained by or arising from seeing, *visual proof* ‖ relying on sight, *visual control* ‖ visible ‖ of or producing a mental image ‖ (*optics*) optical [O.F. or fr. L.L. *visualis*]

visual aids devices to assist understanding or memory by displaying what is to be understood or memorized in a visible form (picture, chart etc.)

visual instrument a keyboard device that projects colored visual patterns on a screen, often to accompany music

vis·u·al·i·za·tion (viʒu:əlizéiʃən) *n.* a visualizing or being visualized ‖ a mental picture

vis·u·al·ize (víʒú:əlaiz) *pres. part.* **vis·u·al·iz·ing** *past* and *past part.* **vis·u·al·ized** *v.t.* to form a mental picture of

visual pollution the unsightly products of industry, advertisements, waste disposal, graffiti, etc.

visual purple rhodopsin

vi·tal (váit'l) **1.** *adj.* of, concerned with or necessary to life ‖ full of life ‖ essential, *of vital importance* **2.** *n.* (*pl.*) those parts of the body without which life cannot continue (e.g. the heart or brain, in contrast to a limb) [O.F. or fr. L. *vitalis*]

vi·tal·ism (váit'lizəm) *n.* the doctrine that life has its origin elsewhere than in physical or chemical causation (opp. MECHANISM) **vi·tal·ist** *n.* **vi·tal·ís·tic** *adj.* [F. *vitalisme*]

vi·tal·i·ty (vaitǽliti:) *pl.* **vi·tal·i·ties** *n.* the quality of being alive, esp. the strength of this quality, *his vitality was lowered by his long illness* ‖ animation, energy, liveliness [fr. L. *vitalitas*]

vi·tal·ize (váit'laiz) *pres. part.* **vi·tal·iz·ing** *past* and *past part.* **vi·tal·ized** *v.t.* to give energy or vigor to, to animate

CONCISE PRONUNCIATION KEY: **(a)** æ, *cat*; ɑ, *car*; ɔ *fawn*; ei, *snake*. **(e)** e, *hen*; i:, *sheep*; iə, *deer*; ɛə, *bear*. **(i)** i, *fish*; ai, *tiger*; ə:, *bird*. **(o)** o, *ox*; au, *cow*; ou, *goat*; u, *poor*; ɔi, *royal*. **(u)** ʌ, *duck*; u, *bull*; u:, *goose*; ə, *bacillus*; ju:, *cube*. x, *loch*; θ, *think*; ð, *bother*; z, *Zen*; ʒ, *corsage*; dʒ, *savage*; ŋ, *orangutang*; j, *yak*; ʃ, *fish*; tʃ, *fetch*; 'l, *rabble*; 'n, *redden*. Complete pronunciation key appears inside front cover.

vital signs (*med.*) basic diagnostic elements, e.g., pulse rate, respiratory rate, body temperature, blood pressure
vital statistics a record of births, marriages and deaths ‖ (*pop.*, of a woman) measurements around the bosom, the waist and the hips
vi·ta·min (váitəmin) *n.* any of a number of organic chemical substances, present in various foods and essential in very small quantities (less than 25 mg. per day) to health (*DIET) [fr. L. *vita*, life+AMINE]
vi·ta·mi·za·tion (váitəməzéiʃən) *n.* process of taking or giving vitamins —**vitamize** *v.*
vi·tel·lar·i·um (vitelέəri:əm) *pl.* **vi·tel·lar·i·a** (vitelέəri:ə) *n.* a yolk gland [Mod. L. fr. *vitellus*]
vi·tel·lin (vitélin, vaitélin) *n.* a protein in the yolk of an egg [fr. L. *vitellus*, the yolk of an egg]
vi·tel·line (vitélin, vaitélin) *adj.* of the yolk of an egg ‖ of the color of an egg yolk [fr. M.L. *vitellinus*]
vitelline duct (*med.*) in an embryo, the part of the yolk sac that opens into the midgut or the lower portion of the future ileum. *also* umbilical duct, yolk stalk
vitelline membrane the transparent membrane surrounding an egg yolk
Vi·tel·li·us (vitéli:əs), Aulus (15-69), Roman emperor (69). Commander of the legions on the Rhine, he was proclaimed emperor by his troops but was defeated by Vespasian later in the year
vi·tel·lus (vitéləs, vaitéləs) *pl.* **vi·tel·lus·es** *n.* (*embry.*) the yolk of an egg [L.]
Vi·ter·bo (vitérbou) an agricultural market (pop. 58,618) in Latium, Italy. Romanesque-Gothic cathedral (12th-16th cc.), Romanesque and Gothic churches, papal palace (13th c.), Farnese palace (15th c.)
vi·ti·ate (víʃi:eit) *pres. part.* **vi·ti·at·ing** *past* and *past part.* **vi·ti·at·ed** *v.t.* to spoil, make defective, lessen the quality of ‖ to corrupt (morals or taste) ‖ (*law*) to invalidate or make wholly or partly ineffective **vi·ti·á·tion, ví·ti·a·tor** *ns* [fr. L. *vitiare* (*vitiatus*)]
vit·i·cul·ture (vítikʌltʃər, váitikʌltʃər) *n.* the science of growing grapes ‖ the cultivation of grapevines [fr. L. *vitis*, VINE+CULTURE]
Vi·ti Le·vu (ví:ti:lévu:) *FIJI
Vit·im (vítəm) a tributary (1,190 miles long) of the Lena in southern Siberia, U.S.S.R., rising east of Lake Baikal
Vi·to·ri·a (vitɔ́ri:ə, vitóuri:ə) the capital (pop. 175,000) of Álava, Spain: Gothic cathedral (14th c.). Wellington defeated the French here (1813)
vit·re·ous (vítri:əs) *adj.* of, pertaining to or made of glass ‖ like glass, glassy [fr. L. *vitreus* fr. *vitrum*, glass]
vitreous body vitreous humor
vitreous electricity positive electricity generated by rubbing glass with silk
vitreous humor, *Br.* **vitreous humour** (*anat.*) the transparent jellylike content of the back chamber of the eyeball
vi·tres·cence (vitrés'ns) *n.* the state of becoming or being vitreous
vi·tres·cent (vitrés'nt) *adj.* tending to become glass [fr. L. *vitrum*, glass]
vit·ri·fac·tion (vitrifǽkʃən) *n.* vitrification
vit·ri·fi·a·ble (vítrifaiəb'l) *adj* capable of being vitrified
vit·ri·fi·ca·tion (vitrifikéiʃən) *n.* a vitrifying or being vitrified ‖ something vitrified [fr. M.L. or Mod. L. *vitrificatio* (*vitrificationis*)]
vit·ri·form (vítrifɔrm) *adj.* having the form or appearance of glass
vit·ri·fy (vítrifai) *pres. part.* **vit·ri·fy·ing** *past* and *past part.* **vit·ri·fied** *v.i.* to become glass or glasslike ‖ *v.t.* to change into glass or a glasslike substance by heat and fusion [fr. F. *vitrifier* or M.L. *vitrificare*]
vit·ri·ol (vítri:əl) *n.* any of several metallic sulfates, esp. sulfate of iron ‖ oil of vitriol ‖ savage criticism or invective [O.F. or fr. M.L. *vitriolum*]
vit·ri·ol·ic (vitri:ɔ́lik) *adj.* of, like or made from vitriol ‖ (of criticism or invective) savage [F. *vitriolique*]
Vi·tru·vi·us (vitrú:vi:əs) (Marcus Vitruvius Pollio, 1st c. B.C.), Roman architect, author of the celebrated treatise 'De architectura', based on earlier Greek works and his own experience. It had great influence on the Renaissance
vit·ta (vítə) *pl.* **vit·tae** (víti:), **vit·tas** *n.* (*Rom. hist.*) a headband, fillet or garland ‖ (*eccles.*) the lappet of a miter ‖ (*bot.*) one of the oil receptacles in the pericarp of plants of fam. *Umbelliferae* ‖ (*zool.*) a band or stripe of color ‖ (*zool.*) a longitudinal ridge in diatoms **vit·tate** (víteit) *adj.* [L.]
vi·tu·per·ate (vitú:pəreit, vaitú:pəreit, vitjú:pəreit, vaitjú:pəreit) *pres. part.* **vi·tu·per·at·ing** *past* and *past part.* **vi·tu·per·at·ed** *v.t.* to hurl abuse at [fr. L. *vituperare* (*vituperatus*)]
vi·tu·per·a·tion (vitu:pəréiʃən, vaitu:pəréiʃən, vitju:pəréiʃən, vaitju:pəréiʃen) *n.* the act of vituperating ‖ wordy and vehement abuse [O.F. or fr. L. *vituperatio* (*vituperationis*), blaming]
vi·tu·per·a·tive (vitú:pərətiv, vaitú:pərətiv, vitjú:pərətiv, vaitjú:pərətiv) *adj.* characterized by or having the nature of vituperation [fr. L. *vituperativus* or fr. VITUPERATE]
Vi·tus (váitəs), St, Sicilian martyr (c. 303) of the Diocletian persecution, one of the saints invoked for the cure of convulsive disorders (*CHOREA). Feast: June 15
vi·va·ce (vivátʃei) *adv.* (*mus.*) in a lively, brisk manner [Ital.]
vi·va·cious (vivéiʃəs, vaivéiʃəs) *adj.* full of life, high-spirited, animated [fr. L. *vivax* (*vivacis*), tenacious of life]
vi·vac·i·ty (vivǽsiti:, vaivǽsiti:) *n.* the state or quality of being vivacious ‖ mental liveliness [O.F. *vivacite* or fr. L. *vivacitas*]
Vi·val·di (vivúldi:), Antonio (c. 1675-1741), Italian composer of suites and concertos, mainly for strings, e.g. 'The Four Seasons'. He also wrote church music and over 40 operas, and was a violin virtuoso
vi·var·i·um (vaivέəri:əm) *pl.* **vi·var·i·a** (vaivέəri:ə), **vi·var·i·ums** *n.* a glass tank or enclosure for keeping animals or plants as nearly as possible in their natural state, esp. for observation [L.]
vi·va vo·ce (váivəvóusi:) **1.** *adv.* by word of mouth, orally **2.** *adj.* oral, *a viva voce examination* [M.L.=with the living voice]
vi·ver·rine (vivérin, váivərain) *adj.* of or relating to *Viverridae*, a family of small, catlike, carnivorous mammals that includes the civet [fr. Mod. L. *viverrinus*]
Vi·ves (ví:ves), Juan Luis (1492-1540), Spanish humanist philosopher and educationalist. His 'De anima et vita' (1538) was one of the first works on psychology
viv·id (vivid) *adj.* providing a very strong stimulus to the eye, *vivid colors* or to the imagination or memory, *a vivid recollection* [fr. L. *vividus*]
viv·i·fi·ca·tion (vivifikéiʃən) *n.* a vivifying or being vivified [fr. L. *vivificatio* (*vivificationis*)]
viv·i·fy (vívifai) *pres. part.* **viv·i·fy·ing** *past* and *past part.* **viv·i·fied** *v.t.* to enliven, animate [fr. F. *vivifier*]
viv·i·par·i·ty (vivəpǽriti:) *n.* the state or quality of being viviparous
vi·vip·ar·ous (vivípərəs, vaivípərəs) *adj.* (*zool.*) bringing forth young alive (cf. OVIPAROUS) ‖ (*bot.*) producing bulbs or seeds that germinate while still attached to the parent plant **vi·víp·a·ry** *n.* reproduction by means of shoots and bulbils [fr. L. *viviparus*]
viv·i·sect (vivisékt, vívisekt) *v.t.* to perform vivisection on ‖ *v.i.* to practice vivisection [back-formation fr. VIVISECTION]
viv·i·sec·tion (vivisékʃən) *n.* the performance of scientific experiments involving surgical operation on living animals for the furtherance of medical or other research **viv·i·séc·tion·al** *adj.* **viv·i·séc·tion·ist** *n.* someone who approves of or practices vivisection **vív·i·sec·tor** *n.* someone who vivisects [fr. L. *vivus*, alive+*sectio* (*sectionis*), a cutting]
vix·en (víksən) *n.* a she-fox ‖ a badtempered, spiteful or quarrelsome woman **víx·en·ish** *adj.* [Late M.E. *fixen* fr. O.E.]
vi·yel·la (vaijélə) *n.* twill-weave cloth of 50% cotton, 50% wool, designed to look like all-wool flannel
viz. *VIDELICET
Vi·za·ga·pat·am (vizɑgəpʌ́təm) *VISAKHAPATNAM
viz·ca·cha, vis·ca·cha (vizkɑ́tʃə) *n.* a member of *Lagostomus*, a genus of South American burrowing rodents, resembling the chinchilla, but larger (about 2 ft long) [Span. fr. Quechuan]
Viz·ca·ya (viskɑ́jɑ) a province (area 836 sq. miles, pop. 1,181,401) in N. Spain. Capital: Bilbao (*BASQUE PROVINCES)
vi·zier, vi·zir (vizíər, víziər) *n.* a highranking government official in Moslem countries [fr. Turk. *vezir* fr. Arab.]
vizor *VISOR
V.J. Day Sept. 2, 1945, the date of the victory over Japan and the end of the 2nd world war
Vlach (vlɑx) *n.* a member of a people living in parts of S.E. Europe who speak a Rumanian dialect [Bulg. and Serbian]
Vlad·i·mir (vlǽdəmiər), St (c. 955-1015), prince of Kiev, grandson of St Olga. He accepted Christianity (c. 989) and established the Greek Orthodox faith in Kiev. Feast: July 15
Vladimir a town (pop. 296,000) in the R.S.F.S.R., U.S.S.R., in the Moscow industrial region. Industries: mechanical engineering, textiles and food processing. 12th-c. cathedrals, churches. Vladimir was the capital of Russia (c. 1150-1238)
Vladimir II Mo·nom·a·chus (mounɔ́məkəs) (1053-1125), grand duke of Kiev (1113-25). He was the author of a humane code of laws
Vla·di·vos·tok (vlædivɔ́stɒk) the chief Pacific port (pop. 550,000) of the U.S.S.R., in S.E. Siberia, terminus of the Trans-Siberian Railroad, and a naval base. Industries: shipbuilding, engineering and food processing. University
Vla·minck (vlæmɛ̃k), Maurice de (1876-1958), French painter of the Fauve school, best known for his landscapes
Vlis·sing·en (vlísiŋən) *FLUSHING
Vlo·na, Vlo·në (vlóunɑ) (or Vlorë, *Ital.* Valona) a port and naval base (pop. 55,500) in S.W. Albania
Vl·ta·va (vʌ́ltɑvɑ) *MOLDAU
vo·ca·ble (vóukəb'l) *n.* a word, esp. one regarded phonologically (i.e. with regard to its sound rather than to its meaning) [F. or fr. L. *vocabulum*]
vo·cab·u·lar·y (voukǽbjuleri:) *pl.* **vo·cab·u·lar·ies** *n.* a list of words, usually arranged alphabetically and defined, explained or translated ‖ the range of language, the stock of words at a person's command, or used in a particular work, branch of a subject, language etc. [fr. M.L. *vocabularius*]
vo·cal (vóuk'l) **1.** *adj.* of or pertaining to the voice, *vocal organs* ‖ made or uttered by the voice, spoken or sung composed for the voice ‖ having a voice ‖ inclined to express oneself or one's opinions freely ‖ (*phon.*) voiced ‖ vocalic **2.** *n.* (*phon.*) a voiced sound ‖ what the singer sings in a popular song [fr. L. *vocalis*]
vocal cords elastic folds of membrane inside the larynx which vibrate to produce voice sounds
vo·cal·ic (voukǽlik) *adj.* of or containing vowel sounds ‖ being a vowel, or functioning as one
vo·cal·ism (vóuk'lizəm) *n.* the use of the voice in speech or song ‖ the art of singing a vowel system
vo·cal·ist (vóuk'list) *n.* a singer
vo·cal·i·ty (voukǽliti:) *n.* the quality of having voice ‖ the quality of being vocal
vo·cal·ize (vóuk'laiz) *pres. part.* **vo·cal·iz·ing** *past* and *past part.* **vo·cal·ized** *v.t.* to form or utter with the voice, esp. to sing ‖ to insert the vowel marks in (Hebrew or Arabic texts) ‖ (*phon.*) to voice ‖ (*phon.*) to change into or use as a vowel ‖ *v.i.* to utter sounds, esp. to sing or exercise the voice with runs of vowel sounds ‖ (*phon.*) to be changed into a vowel
vo·cal·ly (vóuk'li:) *adv.* in a vocal manner by singing ‖ in regard to vowels
vo·ca·tion (voukéiʃən) *n.* a conviction that one is called by God to do a particular kind of work, that one is fitted for it and has a duty to do it ‖ the work about which one has this conviction ‖ any trade, profession or occupation (cf. AVOCATION) **vo·cá·tion·al** *adj.* [O.F. or fr. L. *vocatio* (*vocationis*)]
voc·a·tive (vɒ́kətiv) **1.** *adj.* (*gram.*, in certain inflected languages) of the case used in addressing a person or thing directly **2.** *n.* the vocative case ‖ a word in the vocative case [O.F. *vocatif*, *vocative* or fr. L. *vocativus*]
vo·cif·er·ance (vousífərəns) *n.* the quality of being vociferous
vo·cif·er·ant (vousífərənt) *adj.* vociferous [fr. L. *vociferans* (*vociferantis*)]
vo·cif·er·ate (vousífəreit) *pres. part.* **vo·cif·er·at·ing** *past* and *past part.* **vo·cif·er·at·ed** *v.t.* to utter in a loud voice ‖ *v.i.* to shout or cry out in a loud voice [fr. L. *vociferari* (*vociferatus*)]
vo·cif·er·a·tion (vousifəréiʃən) *n.* a vociferating, clamor [O.F. *vociferacion* or fr. L. *vociferatio* (*vociferationis*)]
vo·cif·er·ous (vousífərəs) *adj.* noisily clamorous, making an outcry [fr. L. *vociferari*, to cry out]

vodas 1. (*acronym*) for voice-operated switching device to cut out singing, used to improve communications in oceanic radio telephone by suppressing echoes **2.** an echo-suppressing device that automatically switches a subscriber's line on to a transmitting station

vod·ka (vɔ́dkə) *n.* liquor with a high percentage of alcohol, distilled from rye, wheat or potatoes etc. [Russ.]

Vo·gel (fóug'l), Hermann Karl (1841-1907), German astronomer who discovered spectroscopic binaries

Vo·gels·berg (fóugəlsberx, vóugəlzbə:rg) *HESSEN

vogue (voug) *n.* a prevalent or current fashion popularity or a period of popularity **in vogue** in fashion [F.=rowing fr. Ital.]

Vo·gul (vóug'l) *n.* a member of an Asiatic people now chiefly located in the N. Urals ‖ their Finno-Ugric language

voice (vɔis) **1.** *n.* the sound uttered from the mouth, esp. from the human mouth in speaking or singing etc. ‖ the faculty or power of human utterance ‖ the vocal organs, *he strained his voice* ‖ expression, utterance, *to give voice to one's misgivings* ‖ a vote or opinion ‖ the medium by which something is expressed or represented, *the voice of party policy* ‖ (*phon.*) a sound uttered when the breath vibrates the vocal cords, producing a resonance absent in breath alone ‖ (*gram.*) one of the verb forms which express the relation of subject to action in a sentence, *active voice, passive voice* ‖ (*mus.*, in harmony or counterpoint) one of the threads running through a composition, esp. a fugue **in voice** in good condition for talking or singing **to have a voice in** to have the right to express an opinion about (a matter) **to raise one's voice** to give expression to one's disapproval or disagreement **with one voice** unanimously **2.** *v.t. pres. part.* **voic·ing** *past* and *past part.* **voiced** to express, give utterance to, *he voiced the general feeling of the meeting* ‖ (*mus.*) to regulate the tones of (an organ pipe or wind instrument under construction) ‖ (*phon.*) to give voice to [A.F. *voiz, voice,* O.F. *voiz, vois*]

voice box the larynx

voiced (vɔist) *adj.* having a specified kind of voice, *a loud-voiced man* ‖ (*phon.*) uttered with the vocal cords vibrating, '*b*' and '*v*' are voiced consonants

voice·less (vɔ́islis) *adj.* having no voice ‖ (*phon.*, e.g. of 'k', 'p' and 't') not voiced ‖ (*rhet.*) having no vote

voice multiplexing technique for compressing two to four voices into a single channel for simultaneous transmission

Voice of America *UNITED STATES INFORMATION AGENCY

voice-o·ver (vɔ́isouvər) *n.* the voice of an unseen narrator in a television or motion picture

voice·print (vɔ́isprint) *n.* a distinctive spectographic pattern of a person's voice, developed by Dr. Lawrence G. Kersla —**voiceprinter** *n.* —**voiceprinting** *n.*

voice recognition unit (*computer*) a peripheral computer device that responds to spoken words

voice response (*computer*) a device that stores sounds and plays them back on signal, e.g., bank records that are voiced when authorized signal is presented

voice synthesizer (*computer*) a computer programmed to simulate speech in response to queries or signals. *also* speech synthesizer

voice warning system device that issues prerecorded vocal warnings under conditions that warrant them, e.g., failure of an aircraft operational system

void (vɔid) **1.** *adj.* containing nothing ‖ (of an office or position) vacant, unfilled ‖ (*law*) invalid, null ‖ (with 'of') lacking, without, *void of good taste* **2.** *n.* an empty space, vacuum ‖ a feeling of emptiness or great loss ‖ (*archit.*) an opening left in a wall etc., e.g. for a window [A.F., O.F. *voide*]

void *v.t.* (*law*) to annul, to invalidate ‖ to discharge (the contents of something) **vóid·a·ble** *adj.* [partly fr. A.F. and O.F. *voider, vuider,* partly an aphetic form of AVOID]

void·ance (vɔ́id'ns) *n.* (*eccles.*, of a benefice) the state of being vacant ‖ the act of voiding [A.F. *voidaunce,* O.F. *vuidance*]

void·ed (vɔ́idid) *adj.* made void ‖ having an opening ‖ (*heraldry*, of a charge or bearing) having the central part cut away so as to show the field

voile (vɔil) *n.* a thin, semi-transparent dress material in cotton, wool or silk [F.= veil]

Voi·ture (vwætyr), Vincent (1579-1648), French poet. He was an original member of the Académie, and one of the most distinguished wits of the Rambouillet salon

voix ce·leste (vwáseilést) *n.* an organ stop of 8-foot pitch with a soft, tremulous effect, produced by the combination of two pipes to each note, tuned with a slight interval [F.=heavenly voice]

Voj·vo·di·na, Voi·vo·di·na (vɔ́ivədi:nɑ) an autonomous province (area 8,407 sq. miles, pop. 1,935,115) of Serbia, Yugoslavia. Capital: Novi Sad. Hungarian from the 11th c., it was devastated under Turkish rule (16th c.), passed to the Hapsburgs (1699) and to Yugoslavia (1918)

vol. volume

vo·lant (vóulənt) *adj.* flying, able to fly ‖ (*heraldry*) represented in flying posture [F.]

Vol·a·pük (vɔ́ləpyk, vóuləpyk) *n.* an artificial international language derived mostly from German, English and Latin, invented (1879) by Johann M. Schleyer (1831–1912), a German priest [fr. *vol,* world (alteration of Eng. 'world')+*a,* connecting vowel+*pük,* speech (alteration of Eng. 'speak')]

vo·lar (vóulər) *adj.* (*anat.*) of the palm of the hand or of the sole of the foot [fr. L. *vola*]

volar (*abbr.*) for volunteer army (which see)

vol·a·tile (vɔ́lət'l, *Br.* vɔ́lətail) *adj.* evaporating quickly and easily at ordinary temperature ‖ changeable, fickle, *volatile behavior* **vol·a·til·i·ty** (vɒlətíliti:) *n.* [O.F. and F. *volatil, volatile* or fr. L. *volatilis*]

volatile oil an essential oil

volatile storage (*computer*) storage where data are lost when power is turned off

vol·a·til·i·za·tion (vɒlətilizéiʃən) *n.* a volatilizing or being volatilized

vol·a·til·ize (vɔ́lət'laiz) *pres. part.* **vol·a·til·iz·ing** *past* and *past part.* **vol·a·til·ized** *v.t.* to cause to evaporate ‖ *v.i.* to evaporate

vol-au-vent (voulouvɑ̃) *n.* a baked casing of puff pastry with a filling of meat, chicken or fish etc. [F.]

vol·can·ic (vɒlkǽnik) *adj.* of, like, or produced by, a volcano **vol·cán·i·cal·ly** *adv.* [F. *volcanique* fr. Ital.]

volcanic glass glass formed naturally by molten lava which has cooled too rapidly to crystallize

vol·can·ic·i·ty (vɒlkənísiti:) *n.* the state or quality of being volcanic [F. *volcanicité*]

vol·can·ism (vɔ́lkənizəm) *n.* volcanic power or activity [F. *volcanisme*]

vol·can·ist (vɔ́lkənist) *n.* a person who specializes in volcanos [fr. VOLCANO or F. *volcaniste*]

vol·can·ize (vɔ́lkənaiz) *pres. part.* **vol·can·iz·ing** *past* and *past part.* **vol·can·ized** *v.t.* to treat with, or subject to, volcanic heat [fr. F. *volcaniser*]

vol·ca·no (vɒlkéinou) *pl.* **vol·ca·noes, vol·ca·nos** *n.* a rift or vent in the earth's crust through which molten material from the depths of the earth is erupted at the surface as flows of lava or clouds of gas and ashes. Characteristically a conical hill is formed, but the appearance of a volcano may vary with such factors as the fluidity of the lava, position of the orifices etc. Active volcanoes include Cotopaxi, Mauna Loa, Vesuvius, Etna and Stromboli. Among those dormant are Pelée and Popocatepetl. Believed extinct are Aconcagua, Kilimanjaro, Orizaba and Fujiyama [Ital. *volcano, vulcano*]

vol·ca·no·gen·ic (vɒlkænoudʒénik) *adj.* created by a volcano

vol·ca·nol·o·gist or **vulcanologist** (vɒlkənɔ́lədʒist) *n.* an expert on volcanic phenomenona

vol·can·ol·o·gy (vɒlkənɔ́lədʒi:) *n.* the science of volcanic phenomena [VOLCANO + Gk *logos,* discourse]

vole (voul) *n.* a member of *Microtus,* fam. *Cricetidae,* a genus of rodents widely distributed in the northern hemisphere. They are closely related to the lemmings and muskrats and resemble rats and mice physically [orig. *vole mouse* fr. Norw. *vollmus* fr. *voll,* field+*mus,* mouse]

vol·et (vɔ́lei) *n.* a wing or panel of a triptych [F.=shutter]

Vol·ga (vɔ́lgə) a river (2,300 miles long) in the western R.S.F.S.R., the longest in Europe, flowing from the Valdai Hills east to Kazan, then south to a great delta on the Caspian, navigable past Rybinsk. Though frozen five months a year in the north, it is the country's chief waterway (linked by canal to the Baltic, the White Sea, the Don and Moscow). It drains 530,000 sq. miles. Hydroelectricity

Vol·go·grad (vɔ́lgəgræd) (Stalingrad 1925-61, previously Tsaritsyn), a communications and industrial center (pop. 929,000) in the R.S.F.S.R., U.S.S.R., on the lower Volga and the Volga-Don canal: metallurgical industries, metalworking, heavy machinery, hydroelectricity, oil refining, sawmilling, food processing. It was the scene of a heavy German defeat (Sept. 1942–Feb. 1943) which was one of the turning points of the 2nd world war. The town was completely destroyed

vol·i·tant (vɔ́litənt) *adj.* (*rhet.*) flying or capable of flying [fr. L. *volitans* (*volitantis*) fr. *volitare,* to fly about]

vol·i·ta·tion (vɒlitéiʃən) *n.* (*rhet.*) flight [fr. M.L. *volitatio* (*volitationis*)]

vo·li·tion (voulíʃən) *n.* the exercise of one's will ‖ the ability to use one's will **vo·lí·tion·al** *adj.* [F.]

vol·ley (vɔ́li:) **1.** *pl.* **vol·leys** *n.* (of a firearm etc.) a discharge of many missiles at the same time ‖ the missiles thus discharged ‖ a loud, rapid outburst of noise, oaths, cheers etc. ‖ (*cricket*) a full toss ‖ (*tennis*) the flight of a ball in play before it bounces ‖ (*tennis*) a return of the ball before it bounces, or a series of returns of this kind **2.** *v. pres. part.* **vol·ley·ing** *past* and *past part.* **vol·leyed, vol·lied** *v.t.* to discharge, return, bowl, throw etc. in a volley ‖ *v.i.* to make a volley [fr. F. *volée*]

vol·ley·ball (vɔ́li:bɔl) *n.* a game played by volleying a large inflated ball between players' hands over a net 8 ft high. Teams are six to a side. The court measures 60 ft × 30 ft maximum

Vo·los, Bo·los (vóulɔs) a port (pop. 49,000) in E. Thessaly, Greece, at the head of the gulf of the same name (the ancient Gulf of Pagasae)

Vol·sci (vɔ́lski:, vɔ́lsi:) *n.* an ancient people of pre-Roman Italy living in Latium **Vol·sci·an** (vɔ́lski:ən, vɔ́lʃən) **1.** *n.* one of the Volsci **2.** *adj.* of the Volsci [L.]

Vol·stead Act (vɔ́lsted) a law passed by the U.S. Congress (1919) defining alcoholic liquor and providing for the enforcement of Prohibition [after Andrew Joseph *Volstead* (1860-1947), U.S. legislator, who promoted the law]

Vol·sun·ga Saga (vɔ́lsuŋə) an Icelandic saga of a family of heroic warriors, descended from Volsung (or Walsung), grandson of Odin, chief of the gods. Volsung's son Siegfried (or Sigurd, or Sigemund) is the hero of the 'Nibelungenlied' and of Wagner's romanticized operatic cycle 'The Ring'

volt (voult) *n.* the practical unit of electromotive force, being the force necessary to transmit 1 ampere of current against 1 ohm resistance [after Alessandro VOLTA]

volt, volte (vɒlt, voult) *n.* (*manège*) the gait of a horse moving sideways in a circle ‖ (*fencing*) a sudden movement or leap back to avoid a thrust [F. *volte* fr. Ital.]

Vol·ta (vɔ́ltɑ), Count Alessandro (1745-1872), Italian physicist. He developed a theory of current electricity, devised the voltaic pile, the electrophorus and electroscope, and hydrolyzed water. The volt is named after him.

Vol·ta (vóultə) a river system of W. Africa whose main streams, the Black Volta (540 miles long), flowing from western Burkina Faso (formerly Upper Volta) and forming the northwest frontier of Ghana, and the White Volta (450 miles long), flowing from central Burkina Faso, join in central Ghana to form the Volta proper (250 miles long), which continues across Ghana to a delta east of Accra. The smaller Red Volta, rising between the Black and White, joins the latter in N.E. Ghana. The system is navigable only between rapids but supports a vast hydroelectric scheme in Ghana

volt·age (vóultidʒ) *n.* potential difference, expressed in volts

vol·ta·ic (vɒltéiik) *adj.* pertaining to electricity produced by chemical action or by surface contact and friction [after Alessandro VOLTA]

voltaic cell a primary cell

Vol·taire (voultéər, vɔlter) (François Marie Arouet, 1694-1778), French man of letters, historian and philosopher. His plays include 'Zaïre' (1732) and 'Mérope' (1743). His prose tales, notably 'Zadig' (1747) and 'Candide' (1759), were vehicles for social and political satire. His philosophical work, e.g. 'Lettres philosophiques' (1734) and 'Essai sur les mœurs et l'esprit des nations' (1756), influenced European thought for generations. His historical work 'Le siècle de Louis XIV' (1751) is readable and reasonably accurate. Voltaire has been accepted as one of the world's great men partly because of the force of his personality. Endowed with enormous wit, he was the foremost propagandist for the leading ideas of the 18th c.: free inquiry, the dignity of man, equality (despite his own aristocratic attitudes) and freedom of conscience. It has been said that he fostered not a revolutionary proletariat but an ungovernable middle class

vol·tam·e·ter (vɒltǽmitər) *n.* an instrument for measuring the amount of an electric current by the gas generated or by the amount of metal (usually copper or silver) deposited by electrolysis

volt-am·me·ter (vóultǽmmi:tər) *n.* an instrument for indicating the range or ranges of volts and amperes

volt-am·pere (vóultǽmpiər) *n.* an electrical unit equal to the product of 1 volt and 1 ampere which for direct current is equivalent to 1 watt

Vol·ta Re·don·da (vɔ́ltərəðɔ́ndə) a city (pop. 147,261) in E. Brazil, near Rio de Janeiro. It is the largest iron and steel center in Latin America

volte *VOLT

volte-face (vɒltfɑ́s) *n.* a sudden, total change of opinion, line of conduct etc. [F.]

volt·me·ter (vóultmi:tər) *n.* (*elec.*) an instrument used to measure potential difference (in volts or millivolts). It is similar in structure to an ammeter, but has a high resistance in series, little current passing through the instrument

vol·u·bil·i·ty (vɒljubíliti:) *n.* the quality or state of being voluble [fr. F. *volubilité* or fr. L. *volubilitas*]

vol·u·ble (vɒ́ljub'l) *adj.* characterized by or producing an unhesitating flow of words ‖ (*bot.*) twisting, twining **vól·u·bly** *adv.* [F. or fr. L. *volubilis*]

vol·ume (vɒ́lju:m, vɒ́ljum) *n.* the amount of space occupied by, or contained in, something measured by the number of cubes each with an edge 1 unit long that it can contain, or measured in any other standard manner appropriate to the shape (sphere, cone etc.) concerned ‖ an amount, quantity etc., *the volume of turnover* ‖ (*mus.*) loudness or fullness of sound ‖ a bound assemblage of printed sheets, forming a book or one of several separately bound parts of a book ‖ (*archit., sculpture*) a defined mass ‖ (*hist.*) a roll or scroll (of papyrus etc.) **to speak volumes for** to be abundant evidence of, *it speaks volumes for his kindness of heart* [O.F. *volum, volume*]

vo·lu·me·ter (vɒlú:mitər, vɒljú:mitər) *n.* an instrument for measuring the volumes of gases, liquids and solids [VOLUME+METER]

vol·u·met·ric (vɒljumétrik) *adj.* of or pertaining to the measurement of volume, esp. pertaining to a system of quantitative chemical analysis based on measurements of concentrations by volume (cf. GRAVIMETRIC) **vol·u·mét·ri·cal** *adj.* **vol·u·mét·ri·cal·ly** *adv.* [VOLUME+METRIC]

vo·lu·mi·nos·i·ty (vəlu:minɒ́siti:) *n.* the state or quality of being voluminous

vo·lu·mi·nous (vəlú:minəs) *adj.* (of a work) consisting of many volumes ‖ (of a writer) producing many books ‖ writing or speaking at length, *a voluminous critic* ‖ written or spoken at great length, *voluminous correspondence* ‖ of great size, bulky ‖ loose, ample, *voluminous folds of drapery* [fr. L.L. *voluminosus*, full of folds]

vol·un·tar·i·ly (vɒ́ləntẹrili:, vɒləntéərili:) *adv.* in a voluntary manner

vol·un·tar·i·ness (vɒ́lənteri:nis) *n.* the state or quality of being voluntary

vol·un·tar·y (vɒ́lənteri:) **1.** *adj.* acting, made or done freely, not under constraint or compulsion, *a voluntary contribution* ‖ brought about, established or supported by voluntary action ‖ (of body parts or movements) controlled by or subject to the will, *a voluntary muscle* ‖ able to act of one's own free will, having free will, *man is a voluntary agent* ‖ (*law*) done or made by consent without consideration in the form of money or services **2.** *pl.* **vol·un·tar·ies** *n.* an organ solo, esp. one played in church before, during or after a service ‖ the music written for this [fr. O.F. *voluntaire, volontaire* or fr. L. *voluntarius*]

vol·un·teer (vɒləntíər) **1.** *n.* a person who undertakes some task or service of his own free will, esp. one who chooses to serve in the armed forces ‖ (*law*) a person to whom a voluntary transfer of property is made **2.** *adj.* voluntary ‖ made up of volunteers, *a volunteer army* ‖ (of crops) self-sown **3.** *v.i.* to offer oneself willingly, esp. for service in the armed forces ‖ *v.t.* to offer willingly (one's services, a remark, an explanation etc.) [fr. F. *volontaire*]

volunteer army an army made up of volunteers, without resort to a draft. *abbr.* volar

Volunteers in Service to America (*abbr.* VISTA), a U.S. government agency introduced (1964) by President Lyndon Johnson under the Economic Opportunity Act. Akin to a domestic Peace Corps, it provided for men and women to serve as teachers and social workers among American Indians, migratory workers, the mentally ill, and other disadvantaged groups

Volunteers of America a religious and philanthropic organization, akin to the Salvation Army, founded in 1896

vo·lup·tu·ar·y (vəlʌ́ptʃu:eri:) **1.** *pl.* **vo·lup·tu·ar·ies** *n.* someone who loves sensual pleasures inordinately (cf. ASCETIC) **2.** *adj.* of, concerned with, or given up to, sensual pleasure [fr. L. *voluptuarius*, postclassical form of *voluptarius* fr. *voluptas*, pleasure]

vo·lup·tu·ous (vəlʌ́ptʃu:əs) *adj.* full of sensual delight ‖ enjoying sensual pleasures to the full ‖ suggesting sensual pleasure [fr. O.F. *voluptueux* or L. *voluptuosus*]

vo·lute (vəlú:t) **1.** *n.* (*archit.*) a spiral scroll used esp. to decorate Ionic, Corinthian and Composite capitals ‖ a spiralshaped form ‖ (*zool.*) a member of *Voluta*, a genus of chiefly tropical gastropods with a spiral shell ‖ a volution of a spiral shell **2.** *adj.* having a spiral shape **vo·lút·ed** *adj.* twisted spirally ‖ (*archit.*) ornamented with volutes [fr. L. *voluta* or fr. F.]

vo·lu·tion (vəlú:ʃən) *n.* a revolving or rolling movement ‖ a spiral ‖ a whorl of a spiral shell [fr. L. *volere* (*volutus*), to roll]

vol·va (vɒ́lvə) *n.* (*bot.*) the cup-shaped membranous structure around the base of the stem of some mushrooms (e.g. agarics and stinkhorns), or enveloping the sporophore [L. fr. *volvere*, to roll]

vo·mer (vóumər) *n.* (*anat.*) the small thin bone which in man and most vertebrates forms part of the separation of the nostrils [L.=plowshare]

vom·it (vɒ́mit) *v.t.* to throw up from the stomach through the mouth ‖ (*rhet.*) to pour out violently or in quantity, *to vomit obscenities* ‖ *v.i.* to throw up the contents of the stomach through the mouth [fr. L. *vomere* (*vomitus*) or fr. *vomitare* (frequentative of *vomere*)]

vomit *n.* that which is vomited ‖ the act of vomiting [A.F. *vomit, vomite,* O.F. *vomite* or fr. L. *vomitus*]

vom·i·tive (vɒ́mitiv) *adj.* vomitory [F. *vomitif, vomitive*]

vom·i·to·ry (vɒ́mitəri:, vɒ́mitouri:) *adj.* of or pertaining to vomiting ‖ inducing vomiting [fr. L. *vomitorius*]

vomitory *pl* **vom·i·to·ries** *n.* (*Rom. hist.*) one of the passages for entrance and exit in a theater or amphitheater [fr. L. *vomitorium*]

Von·ne·gut (vɑ́nəgət), Kurt, Jr. (1922-), U.S. writer. One of the country's most popular authors from the 1960s, he combines science fiction, social satire and black comedy in his novels, which include 'Player Piano' (1951), 'Cat's Cradle' (1963), 'Slaughterhouse-Five' (1969; film, 1972), 'Breakfast of Champions' (1973), 'Slapstick' (1976), 'Jailbird' (1979) and 'Galápagos' (1985). His play, 'Happy Birthday, Wanda June,' was successfully produced in 1971

voo·doo (vú:du:) **1.** *pl.* **voo·doos** *n.* an Animist religion accompanied by black magic. It was originally African, and is still practiced by some Creoles and Afro-West Indians in the West Indies (esp. Haiti) and southern U.S.A. ‖ a sorcerer skilled in this ‖ the spell cast by such a sorcerer ‖ a person or thing bringing bad luck **2.** *v.t.* to bewitch with voodoo **vóo·doo·ism, vóo·doo·ist** *ns* [Dahomey *vodu*]

Voodoo *n.* (*mil.*) a supersonic, twin-engine turbojet (F-101B) carrying both nuclear and nonnuclear air-to-air missiles

vor (*acronym*) for very-high-frequency omni ranges, an air navigational radio aid that uses phase comparison of a ground-transmitted signal to determine bearing

vo·ra·cious (vəréiʃəs, vɔréiʃəs, vouréiʃəs) *adj.* greedy for food, gluttonous, *a voracious eater* ‖ characterized by insatiable eagerness, *a voracious reader* [fr. L. *vorax* (*voracis*)]

vo·rac·i·ty (vərǽsiti:, vɔrǽsiti:, vourǽsiti:) *n.* the state or quality of being voracious [F. *voracité* or fr. L. *voracitas*]

Vor·arl·berg (fɔ́rɑrlberx) the western-most province (area 1,005 sq. miles, pop. 226,000) of Austria. Capital: Bregenz (21,000)

vor·lage (fɔ́rlɑgə) *n.* (*skiing*) a forward leaning position with skis flat on the ground

Vo·ro·nezh (vʌrɔ́nəʃ) an industrial center (pop. 820,000) in the S.W. European R.S.F.S.R., U.S.S.R., the market for the black earth region. Industries: synthetic rubber, food processing, agricultural and nuclear engineering. University (1918)

Vo·ro·shi·lov (vɔrʌʃí:lʌf), Kliment Yefremovich (1881-1969), Russian general and statesman. He was defense minister (1925-40), helped to organize the defense of Leningrad (1941-3) and was president in the U.S.S.R. (1953-60)

Vo·ro·shi·lov·grad (vɔrʌʃí:lʌfgrɑt) (formerly Lugansk) a city (pop. 474,000) of the Ukraine, U.S.S.R., in the Donbas: railroad engineering, metallurgy, coal mining

Vo·ro·shi·lovsk (vɔrʌʃí:lʌfsk) *STAVROPOL

Vor·ster (fɔ́rstər), Balthazar Johannes (1915-83), South African Nationalist statesman, minister of justice (1961-6), prime minister (1966-78), and president (1978-79)

vortac (*acronym*) for very-high-frequency omnirange tacan, an air navigation system in heavily trafficked air routes, utilizing civilian-operated facilities for guidance and military tacan for distance

vor·tex (vɔ́rteks) *pl.* **vor·ti·ces** (vɔ́rtisi:z), **vor·tex·es** *n.* a mass of whirling fluid, esp. a whirlpool ‖ a whirlwind ‖ (*phys.*) a volume of matter the particles of which rotate rapidly around an axis ‖ a social situation thought of as tending to engulf **vor·ti·cal** (vɔ́rtik'l) *adj.* [L. *vortex* (*vorticis*)]

vor·ti·cel·la (vɔrtisélə) *pl.* **vor·ti·cel·lae** (vɔrtiséli:), **vor·ti·cel·las** *n.* (*biol.*) a member of *Vorticella*, a genus of unicellular protozoans having a bell-shaped, ciliated body, the protoplasm being extended as a stalk which can be spirally contracted. They usually inhabit fresh water, attached to plants [Mod. L. dim. fr. *vortex* (*vorticis*)]

vor·ti·cism (vɔ́rtisizəm) *n.* an English art movement related to cubism and futurism, dating from 1912, founded by Wyndham Lewis **vór·ti·cist** *n.* [fr. L. *vortex* (*vorticis*)]

Vos (vous), Cornelis de (1585-1651), Flemish painter, esp. of portraits

Vosges (vouʒ) a wooded mountain range (Ballon de Guebwiller, 4,672 ft) in N.E. France, rising from the Rhine plain parallel with the Black Forest: dairy farming, forestry, hydroelectricity, textiles, wine, paper

Vosges a department (area 2,303 sq. miles, pop. 398,000) of N.E. France in the Vosges Mtns (*LORRAINE). Chief town: Épinal (pop. 42,810)

vo·ta·ress (vóutəris) *n.* a woman votary

vo·ta·ry (vóutəri:) *pl.* **vo·ta·ries** *n.* (*hist.*) someone who devoted himself to the service and worship of a pagan god ‖ (*rhet.*) a devotee [fr. L. *vovere* (*votus*), to vow]

vote (vout) *n.* a formal expression of opinion, or of a decision to elect someone or to pass a law or resolution, usually signified in response to a proposal by voice, gesture or ballot ‖ an opinion expressed by a majority, *a vote of censure* ‖ the act of voting ‖ votes collectively, *the vote was 18,000* ‖ the collective votes of a group or party, *the Irish vote* ‖ the right to vote ‖ (*Br.*) money granted for a specific purpose, *the army vote* [fr. L. *votum*, a vow]

vote *pres. part.* **vot·ing** *past* and *past part.* **vot·ed** *v.i.* to use one's vote ‖ *v.t.* to decide, accept or establish etc. by a vote ‖ to grant (e.g. a sum of money) by vote ‖ to declare by general consent, *the picnic was voted a success* ‖ (*pop.*) to suggest, *I vote we stop for lunch* **to vote down** to defeat by a vote **to vote in** to elect or establish by a vote **to vote out** to defeat (and esp. so remove from office) by a vote [fr. L. *vovere* (*votus*), to vow]

vote of confidence (*Br.*) a vote demanded for a proposed bill or measure which the government considers essential to its policy and is prepared to resign over

voting booth (*Am.*=*Br.* polling booth) a partitioned-off compartment set up temporarily at the polls to allow privacy in voting

vo·tive (vóutiv) *adj.* offered, consecrated etc. in fulfillment of a vow or promise [fr. L. *votivus*]

votive Mass (*Roman Catholicism*) a mass celebrated in place of that appointed for the day, e.g. one for a private intention

vouch (vautʃ) *v.i.* (with 'for') to be guaranteed ‖ *v.t.* to testify, *she vouched that he was with her at the time* ‖ (*law*) to summon (a person) into court to give warranty of title [A.F. and O.F. *vocher, voucher*]

vouch·er (váutʃər) *n.* (*law*) a document, receipt etc. certifying that a sum of money has been paid or that accounts are correct ‖ (*law*) the calling to court of a person to give warranty of title ‖ (*Br., commerce*) a coupon that entitles a buyer or customer to goods at reduced prices, or to articles given away by a manufacturer to stimulate sales. ‖ (*Br.*) a coupon serving in lieu of cash payment, *a luncheon voucher* [A.F. *voicher*]

vouch·safe (vautʃséif) *pres. part.* **vouch·safing** *past* and *past part.* **vouch·safed** *v.t.* to condescend to grant, to give as a favor

Vou·et (vu:ei), Simon (1590-1649), French painter. He worked as court painter for Louis XIII on the decoration of the Louvre and the Luxembourg palaces, in the baroque style

vous·soir (vu:swár) *n.* one of the wedge-shaped stones forming an arch or vault [O.F. *vausoir, vaussoir*]

vow (vau) *n.* a solemn promise or pledge, esp. one made to a deity **to take vows** to join a religious community [A.F. *vu, vou, vo*]

vow *v.t.* to promise solemnly, esp. to God, *to vow obedience* ‖ to resolve emphatically ‖ *v.i.* to make a vow [fr. O.F. *vouer, vower*]

vow·el (váuəl) *n.* a voiced speech sound where the breath is not stopped (cf. CONSONANT) ‖ a letter in the alphabet representing a vowel sound (a, e, i, o, u) **vów·el·ize** *pres. part.* **vow·el·iz·ing** *past* and *past part.* **vow·el·ized** *v.t.* to insert the vowel points or signs in (e.g. a Hebrew text) [O.F. *vouel*]

vowel point a mark above, below or attached to a consonant to indicate the vowels, e.g. in Hebrew

vox an·gel·i·ca (vóksændʒélikə) *n.* an organ stop of 8-foot pitch producing a delicate tone [L. = angelic voice]

vox hu·ma·na (vókshju:mánə) *n.* an organ stop of 8-foot pitch producing a sound akin to the human voice [L.=human voice]

voy·age (vɔ́iidʒ) *n.* a long journey, esp. by sea [M.E. *veage, vayage, voiage* fr. O.F., A.F.]

voyage *pres. part.* **voy·ag·ing** *past* and *past part.* **voy·aged** *v.i.* to make or go on a voyage ‖ *v.t.* to travel over (a distance) on a voyage [fr. F. *voyager*]

Voyager I *n.* U.S. spacecraft launched in 1977 to explore Jupiter

Voyager II *n.* spacecraft launched in 1977 to explore Saturn

vo·ya·geur (vɔ́iidʒər) *n.* a man employed by Ca-nadian fur companies to carry goods and passengers mainly by boat between remote trading posts in the Hudson Bay territory [F.]

vo·yeur (vwajé:r, vɔijé:r) *n.* someone who finds sexual pleasure in looking at sex acts, genital organs etc. **vo·yéur·ism** *n.* [F.]

Voy·sey (vɔ́isi:), Charles Francis Annesley (1857-1941), British architect whose work strongly influenced art nouveau. He designed town and country houses with attention to the logical and tasteful fulfillment of living requirements

VP (*abbr.*) for verb phrase.

VP, V.P. Vice-President

vs. versus

VSO (*abbr.*) for liquor, *very superior old*, 12–17 yrs old

VSOP (*abbr.*) for liquor, *very superior old pale*, 18–25 yrs old

V/STOL (*abbr.*) for vertical short take-off and landing, an aircraft that only requires a short runway. *Cf* CTOL, Q/STOL, STOL, VTOL

Vt. Vermont

VTOL (*abbr.*) for vertical take-off and landing aircraft capable of vertical ascent

VTOLport *See* VERTIPORT

Vuil·lard (vwi:jær), Édouard (1868-1940), French painter, known esp. for his quiet domestic scenes

Vul·can (válkən) (*Rom. mythol.*) *HEPHAESTUS

vul·ca·nist (válkənist) *n.* one who believes that volcanoes exist on the moon. *Cf* HOT MOONER

vul·can·ite (válkənait) *n.* ebonite

vul·can·i·za·tion (vʌlkənizéiʃən) *n.* the act or process of vulcanizing

vul·can·ize (válkənaiz) *pres. part.* **vul·can·iz·ing** *past* and *past part.* **vul·can·ized** *v.t.* to treat (rubber) with sulfur at a high temperature so as to increase its strength and elasticity ‖ *v.i.* to undergo this process [fr. VULCAN]

vul·can·ol·o·gy (vʌlkənólədʒi:) *n.* volcanology [fr. VULCAN+Gk *logos*, discourse]

Vulcan Phalanx (*mil.*) an Army sixbarrelled, 20-mm rotary-fired artillery gun that provides low-altitude air defense

vul·gar (válgər) *adj.* indecent, *a vulgar joke* ‖ offensive to one's finer feelings, *a vulgar display of riches* ‖ of or characteristic of the common people, *a vulgar superstition* ‖ normally accepted, most common, *take the word in its vulgar connotation* ‖ (of speech) vernacular [fr. L. *vulgaris* fr. *vulgus*, the common people]

vulgar fraction (*math.*) a common fraction

vul·gar·i·an (vʌlgéəri:ən) *n.* a vulgar person, esp. a rich person of low tastes and manners

vul·gar·ism (válgərizəm) *n.* a word, phrase or expression considered vulgar ‖ vulgarity

vul·gar·i·ty (vʌlgǽriti:) *pl.* **vul·gar·i·ties** *n.* the state or quality of being vulgar ‖ a vulgar act, habit etc. [fr. L. *vulgaritas*]

vul·gar·i·za·tion (vʌlgərizéiʃən) *n.* a vulgarizing or being vulgarized

vul·gar·ize (válgəraiz) *pres. part.* **vul·gar·iz·ing** *past* and *past part.* **vul·gar·ized** *v.t.* to popularize ‖ to make coarse

vulgar Latin a form of Latin spoken by the people of ancient Rome (as distinguished from classical Latin). It is the chief source of the Romance languages

Vul·gate (válgit, válgeit) the Latin version of the Scriptures made largely by St Jerome directly from Hebrew, and in use in the Roman Catholic Church. The Council of Trent chose it (recension of 1592) as the authentic text to which reference must be made in matters of theology

vul·ner·a·bil·i·ty (vʌlnərəbíliti:) *n.* the state or quality of being vulnerable

vul·ner·a·ble (válnərəb'l) *adj.* open to attack, hurt or injury, *a vulnerable position* ‖ capable of being hurt or wounded (either because insufficiently protected or because sensitive and tender) ‖ (*bridge*, of the side that has won one game) liable to greater penalties than the opponents **vul·ner·a·bly** *adv.* [fr. L.L. *vulnerabilis*]

vul·ner·ar·y (válnərǝri:) **1.** *adj.* used in healing, *a vulnerary herb* **2.** *pl.* **vul·ner·ar·ies** *n.* a plant, ointment, drug etc. for healing wounds [fr. L. *vulnerarius*]

vul·pine (válpain) *adj.* of or like a fox ‖ crafty, cunning [fr. L. *vulpinus*]

vul·ture (váltʃər) *n.* one of a group of large birds of prey of tropical and temperate regions, characterized by a strong elongated ripping beak and a featherless neck and head. They often feed on carrion. Examples include the griffon vulture, the turkey buzzard, the lammergeyer and the condor ‖ a rapacious person [A.F. *vultur* and *voutre*, O.F. *voltour, voutour* or L. *vultur* or fr. L. *vulturius*]

vul·tur·ine (váltʃərain) *adj.* of or like a vulture [fr. L. *vulturinus*]

vul·tur·ous (váltʃərəs) *adj.* like a vulture

vul·va (válvə) *n.* (*anat.*) the orifice or external parts of the female genitals **vúl·var, vúl·vate** *adjs* [L.]

VVSOP (*abbr.*) for liquor, *very, very superior old pale liquor*, 25–40 yrs old

VX (*mil.*) symbol for a very lethal secret nerve gas believed to be ethyl. S-diementhylaminoethyl methylphosphonothiolate; responsible for death of 6,000 sheep in Utah, March 1960. *Cf* BZ, CS, GB

Vyat·ka (vjátkɑ) *KIROV

Vy·borg, Vi·borg (ví:bɔrg) (*Finn.* Viipuri) a lumber port (pop. 65,000) in the northwestern R.S.F.S.R., U.S.S.R., near the Finnish border, blocked by ice four months a year. Swedish castle (1293), town hall (15th c.)

vying *pres. part.* of VIE

Vyshinsky *VISHINSKY

CONCISE PRONUNCIATION KEY: **(a)** æ, c*a*t; ɑ, c*a*r; ɔ f*aw*n; ei, sn*a*ke. **(e)** e, h*e*n; i:, sh*ee*p; iə, d*ee*r; ɛə, b*ea*r. **(i)** i, f*i*sh; ai, t*i*ger; ə:, b*i*rd. **(o)** o, *o*x; au, c*ow*; ou, g*oa*t; u, p*oo*r; ɔi, r*oy*al. **(u)** ʌ, d*u*ck; u, b*u*ll; u:, g*oo*se; ə, b*a*cillus; ju:, c*u*be. x, lo*ch*; θ, *th*ink; δ, bo*th*er; z, *Z*en; ʒ, corsa*g*e; dʒ, sava*g*e; ŋ, ora*ng*utang; j, *y*ak; ʃ, *f*ish; tʃ, fe*tch*; 'l, rabb*le*; 'n, redd*en*. Complete pronunciation key appears inside front cover.

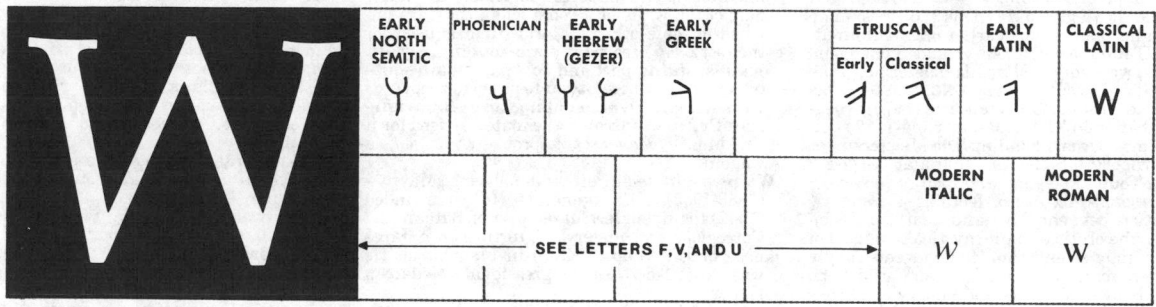

	EARLY NORTH SEMITIC	PHOENICIAN	EARLY HEBREW (GEZER)	EARLY GREEK	ETRUSCAN		EARLY LATIN	CLASSICAL LATIN
					Early	Classical		
	Y	Ч	ΥΥ	7	ᓮ	7	7	W

					MODERN ITALIC	MODERN ROMAN
SEE LETTERS F, V, AND U					*W*	W

Development of the letter W, beginning with the early North Semitic letter. Evolution of both the majuscule, or capital, letter W and the minuscule, or lowercase, letter w are shown.

A. C. SYLVESTER, CAMBRIDGE, ENGLAND

W, w (dʌb'lju:) the 23rd letter of the English alphabet

W, W. West, Western

Wa (wæ) *n.* a tribal people living in the mountains of N.E. Burma and Yunnan, China ‖ a member of this people ‖ their Mon-Khmer language

Waal, Arm of the (vɑl) the southern branch of the Rhine delta

Waals (vɑls), Johannes Diderik Van der (1837-1923), Dutch physicist who worked on molecular forces of attraction. He derived the equation expressing the pressure, volume and temperature relations for a substance in both the gaseous and liquid states. Nobel prize (1910)

WAAM program *n.* U.S. 3-weapon tactical anti-tank defense, including Cyclops, cruise-type missile; ERAM, extended range anti-armor mines; and WASP, multiple miniature missiles

Wa·bash (wɔ́bæʃ) a river (475 miles long) rising in W. Ohio, flowing southwesterly across Indiana to form the S. Indiana-Illinois boundary, and emptying into the Ohio River in S.W. Indiana

wack·e (wǽkə) *n.* (*geol.*) a chiefly dark gray rock, like sandstone, produced by decomposition of igneous rock [G.]

wack·y (wǽki:) *comp.* **wack·i·er** *superl.* **wack·i·est** *adj.* (*pop.*) crazy, absurdly silly [etym. doubtful]

wad (wɒd) **1.** *n.* a handy, compact lump of soft material (paper, cotton wool, rag etc.), esp. when used to stop an opening or to stuff between things to keep them apart ‖ (*pop.*) a roll, esp. of paper money ‖ (*pop.*) a great deal of money ‖ a felt disk used to keep powder and shot in position in a cartridge **2.** *v.t. pres. part.* **wad·ding** *past* and *past part.* **wad·ded** to stuff, pack, plug or stop with a wad or wads ‖ to pad or line with soft material ‖ to press into a wad [etym. doubtful]

wad·cut·ter (wɑ́dkʌtər) *n.* (*shooting*) a flat-topped target bullet

Wad·den·zee (vɑ́d'nzei) part of the North Sea between the Frisian Is and the Dutch mainland, forming the inlet to the Ijsselmeer

wad·ding (wɒ́diŋ) *n.* (*collect.*) wads (lumps of soft material) ‖ the material used in making wads or for packing fragile objects, lining garments, stuffing cushions etc.

Wad·ding·ton, Mt (wɔ́diŋtən) the highest point (13,260 ft) in British Columbia, Canada, in the Coast Range

wad·dle (wɒ́d'l) **1.** *v.i. pres. part.* **wad·dling** *past* and *past part.* **wad·dled** to walk like a duck with short, ungainly steps and the body moving slightly from side to side **2.** *n.* such a gait [rel. to WADE]

Wade (weid), Benjamin Franklin (1800-78), U.S. Senator (1851-69) from Ohio. With Representative Henry W. Davis he drafted the Wade-Davis bill and, when President Lincoln rejected it by pocket veto, they wrote the Wade-Davis Manifesto (1864) attacking Lincoln. As president pro tempore (1865) of the Senate and therefore next in line for the presidency, Wade vigorously sought the impeachment of President Andrew Johnson

wade (weid) **1.** *v. pres. part.* **wad·ing** *past* and *past part.* **wad·ed** *v.i.* to walk through some depth of water, mud, snow or sand etc. ‖ *v.t.* to cross (a stream etc.) on foot **to wade in** to make an energetic start **to wade into** to attack (someone) or set to work on (something) vigorously **to wade through** to get through with effort and difficulty, e.g. to read (a difficult or verbose book) with perseverance **2.** *n.* an act of wading ‖ (*pl.*) a wading bird **wad·er** *n.* a wading bird ‖ (*pl.*) thigh-high or waist-high waterproof boots or pants and boots for wading, worn by anglers etc. [O.E. *wadan*, to go, wade]

Wade-Davis Bill a U.S. Congressional bill (1864) of the Civil War, initiated by Senator Benjamin F. Wade and Representative Henry W. Davis, who held that reconstruction of the Southern states was a matter for the legislature, and not for the executive branch of the government. It was rejected by President Abraham Lincoln by pocket veto

Wa·di Hal·fa (wɑ́di:hɑ́lfə) a port (pop. 10,000) in the N. Sudan on the Nile, whose original site is flooded by the Aswan High Dam reservoir

wa·di, wa·dy (wɑ́di:) *pl.* **wa·dis, wa·dies** *n.* (in N. Africa and S.W. Asia) a riverbed through which water flows only in the rainy reason [Arab. *wādī*]

wading bird a long-legged bird (e.g. a stork or heron) which wades in shallow water after food

Wad Me·da·ni (wɑ́dmédɑni:) an agricultural market (pop. 57,000) in the central Sudan on the lower Blue Nile

wa·fer (wéifər) **1.** *n.* a very thin, crisp cake, e.g. as eaten with ice cream ‖ a thin, papery disk of unleavened bread consecrated in the Eucharist ‖ a disk of red gummed paper or dried paste stuck on documents instead of a seal ‖ (*electr.*) a thin polished piece of semiconductor crystal material, usu. silicon, on which circuits are fabricated, etched, or printed **2.** *v.t.* to seal or fasten with a wafer ‖ (*agriculture*) to compress agricultural products, e.g., alfalfa, into cookie-size cakes [M.E. *wafre* fr. A.F. fr. M.L.G.]

waf·fle (wɒ́fəl) *n.* a soft, crisp batter cake baked on a waffle iron [fr. Du. *wafel*, wafer]

waffle 1. *n.* (*Br., pop.*) imprecise verbosity **2.** *v.i. pres. part.* **waf·fling** *past* and *past part.* **waf·fled** (*Br., pop.*) to talk or write verbosely and imprecisely [origin unknown]

waffle iron a utensil with studded, sometimes folding pans in which batter is baked to make a waffle

waft (wɑft, wæft) **1.** *v.t.* to carry (e.g. a small boat, balloon, feathers, seeds, sounds, scents etc.) gently across water by wave or wind, or through the air ‖ *v.i.* to move floating or as if floating on water or in the air **2.** *n.* a puff, whiff, gentle gust or breath (of scent, wind, smoke etc.) ‖ (*naut.*) a usually knotted flag or pennant used e.g. as a signal ‖ (*rhet.*) a wafting motion [back-formation fr. older *wafter*, a convoy prob. fr. Du. or L.G. *wachter*, a guard]

wag (wæg) **1.** *v. pres. part.* **wag·ging** *past* and *past part.* **wagged** *v.t.* to shake quickly to and fro or up and down a number of times ‖ *v.i.* to move in this way ‖ (*pop.*, of the tongue) to move busily in idle chattering **2.** *n.* an instance of wagging [M.E. *wagge* fr. O.E. *wagian*, to shake, oscillate]

wag *n.* someone with a reputation for making witticisms [prob. fr. WAG *v.*]

wage (weidʒ) *n.* a reward received by nonprofessional workers, usually in the form of a weekly payment of an agreed sum (cf. SALARY), calculated either according to the hours worked (including overtime) or according to the work done (piecework) ‖ (*econ., pl.*) the share of the total product of industry that goes to labor ‖ (*archaic,* usually *pl.* construed as *sing.*) reward, *the wages of sin is death* [A.F.]

wage *pres. part.* **wag·ing** *past* and *past part.* **waged** *v.t.* to engage in, carry on (a war, conflict, campaign) [O.N.F. *wagier*, to pledge]

wage differential an agreed ratio or sum by which a skilled worker's wages are to exceed an unskilled worker's wages

wage drift tendency of wages to move upward from an agreed-upon base

wage-push inflation (wéidʒpuʃ) the rise in prices induced by increased wages. *Cf* DEMAND-PULL INFLATION

wa·ger (wéidʒər) **1.** *n.* something, esp. money, staked on the outcome of an uncertain event ‖ an act of wagering ‖ something on which such an act is made **2.** *v.t.* to stake (money etc.) on the outcome of an uncertain event [A.F. *wageure* fr. *wager*, to wage]

wag·ger·y (wǽgəri:) *pl.* **wag·ger·ies** *n.* waggish humor or an instance of this

wag·gish (wǽgiʃ) *adj.* involving practical joking or witticisms ‖ of or like a wag (joker)

wag·gle (wǽg'l) **1.** *v. pres. part.* **wag·gling** *past* and *past part.* **wag·gled** *v.i.* to wag frequently and rapidly ‖ to move with quick little undulations ‖ *v.t.* to cause to waggle ‖ (*golf*) to swing (a club) over a ball as a preparation for the stroke proper **2.** *n.* a short rapid wag or undulating movement ‖ (*golf*) a waggling **wág·gly** *adj.* swaying, unsteady, twisting [WAG]

waggon *WAGON

waggonette *WAGONETTE

Wag·ner (vágnər), Wilhelm Richard (1813-83), German operatic composer. Apart from an early symphony (1832), a few marches and songs, and 'Siegfried Idyll' (1870), his fame rests on his operas. The earlier ones, culminating in 'Tannhäuser' (1843-4) and 'Lohengrin' (1846-8), were followed by his masterpiece, the great 'Ring' cycle (*NIBELUNGENLIED): 'Das Rheingold' (1869), 'Die Walküre' (1870), 'Siegfried' (1876) and 'Götterdämmerung' (1874). In most of his operas, including 'Die Meistersinger von Nürnberg' (1862-7) and 'Parsifal' (1877-82) he used Teutonic legend and history to serve a very personal mixture of feelings: a romantic association between love and death, a fusion between the erotic and the mystical, an ideal of heroism and nationalism. He believed strongly that opera must be a unified work of art; he wrote his own librettos and supervised every detail of production to achieve a carefully calculated impact on the beholder. His operas are structurally indivisible units. He used leitmotifs to identify his characters, or to allude to symbolic themes, and these leitmotifs could be transformed, blended, or carried on from one work to another. The whole structure and procedure of his operas, esp. his continuous but varied melodic line and his orchestration and characteristic harmony, were new in European music. Through Mahler, Berg and Schönberg, Wagner leads to 20th-c. music

Wagner Act (wǽgnər) a law passed (1935) by the U.S. Congress setting up the National Labor Relations Board, and affirming the right of employees to organize themselves in trade unions and to bargain collectively

wag·on, *Br.* also **wag·gon** (wǽgən) *n.* a four-wheeled vehicle for transporting heavy loads ‖ a dinner wagon ‖ a patrol wagon ‖ (*Br.*) an open railroad car ‖ **on (off) the wagon** (*pop.*) no longer (again) drinking alcoholic beverages **wág·on·er,** *Br.* also **wág·gon·er** *n.* the driver of a wagon [Du. *wagen*]

wag·on·ette, *Br.* also **wag·gon·ette** (wægənét) *n.* (*hist.*) a four-wheeled, horse-drawn pleasure carriage (open or with a removable cover) with facing seats along each side, behind a transverse seat

wa·gon-lit (vægɔ̃li:, wǽgənli:) *pl.* **wa·gons-lits** (vægɔ̃li:, wǽgənzli:z) *n.* (in Europe) a railroad sleeping car divided into individual compartments ‖ one such compartment [F.]

Wa·gram, Battle of (vágrɑm) a battle fought (July 6, 1809) northeast of Vienna in which Napoleon defeated Austria during the Napoleonic Wars

wag·tail (wǽgteil) *n.* any of several small, slim, mainly European birds of fam. *Motacillidae,* related to the pipits. They jerk their long tails up and down when they are running or perching ‖ any of various similar American and Australian birds

Wah·ha·bi, Wa·ha·bi (wəhɑ́bi:) *n.* a member of a puritanical sect of Islam founded (c. 1744) by Muhammad ibn Abd-el-Wahhab (1703–92) in Nejd, Saudi Arabia. The Wahhabis conquered Arabia (1803), were beaten by the Ottoman Turks (1819) and acquired political power under King ibn Saud (early 20th c.) **Wah·há·bism, Wa·há·bism** *n.*

wa·hi·ne (wɑhí:ni:) *n.* (*surfing*) a woman surfer, from a Polynesian word for woman

wa·hoo (wɑ́hu:) *pl.* **wa·hoos** *n.* a North American shrub of fam. *Celastraceae,* esp. *Euonymus atropurpureus,* bearing purple capsules and scarlet seeds [Am. Indian *úhawhu,* cork elm]

waif (weif) *n.* a stray, helpless person, esp. an abandoned or neglected child ‖ a stray animal ‖ (*law*) any ownerless property found by chance [A.F., O.F. *gaif,* prob. of Scand. origin]

Wai·ka·to (waikɑ́tou) the longest river (220 miles) of New Zealand, flowing from Lake Taupo across N. North Island to the Pacific

wail (weil) **1.** *n.* a long drawn-out cry of pain or grief ‖ the act of making such cries ‖ a sound like such a cry, *the wail of the sirens* **2.** *v.i.* to utter a wail ‖ (*pop.*) to complain, esp. with self-pity [prob. O.N. *vei,* woe]

Wailing Wall a wall in Jerusalem, reputed to contain some of the stones from Solomon's Temple. Jews traditionally bewail at it the destruction (70 A.D.) of the Temple by the Romans

wain (wein) *n.* (*archaic*) a four-wheeled large farm wagon **the Wain** the Big Dipper, the seven bright stars in Ursa Major [O.E. *wægen, wǣn,* wheeled vehicle]

wain·scot (wéinskət, wéinskɒt) **1.** *n.* wooden paneling or boarding covering the walls of a room, esp. the lower part of them ‖ (*Br. hist.*) fine-quality oak imported for this ‖ the lower part of the walls of a room when they are finished in some other material than is used for the rest **2.** *v.t. pres. part.* **wain·scot·ing,** esp. *Br.* **wain·scot·ting** *past* and *past part.* **wain·scot·ed,** esp. *Br.* **wain·scot·ted** to panel (a room etc.) with wainscot **wáin·scot·ing,** esp. *Br.* **wáin·scot·ting** *n.* wainscot or the material used for it [fr. M.L.G. *wagenschot* prob. fr. *wagen,* a wagon]

Wain·wright (wéinrait), Jonathan Mayhew (1883-1953), U.S. general. He commanded (1942) the unsuccessful defense of Bataan and Corregidor and underwent torture in a Japanese prison camp (1942-5) in Manchuria. He was awarded the Congressional Medal of Honor

wain·wright (wéinrait) *n.* a craftsman who makes and repairs wagons

waist (weist) *n.* the narrow part of the human body between ribs and hips ‖ that part of a garment which covers the waist ‖ (*old-fash.*) the bodice or upper part of a woman's dress ‖ (*old-fash.*) a blouse ‖ the waistline ‖ the narrow part of the abdomen of some insects, e.g. the wasp ‖ (*naut.*) the middle part of a ship between quarterdeck and forecastle ‖ the narrow middle part of an object, *the waist of a violin* [M.E. *wast* prob. rel. to O.E. *weaxan,* to grow]

waist·band (wéistbænd) *n.* a band or belt around the waist attached to a garment, e.g. the top part of a skirt, trousers etc. or the lower part of a jacket, blouse etc., often serving to keep the garment in position

waist·cloth (wéistklɔθ, wéistklɒθ) *pl.* **waist·cloths** (wéistklɔðz, wéistklɒðz, wéistklɔθs, wéistklɒθs) *n.* a loincloth

waist·coat (wéskət, wéistkout) *n.* (*Br.*) a vest (man's garment worn over the trouser top and under the jacket)

waist·line (wéistlain) *n.* the waist of the human body, considered with respect to position or size ‖ the line at which the bodice and skirt of a dress meet

wait (weit) **1.** *v.i.* (often with 'for') to remain in a place or in a state of inactivity, indecision, delay or anticipation because of some event expected to happen or a person expected to arrive etc. ‖ to be in readiness, *your dinner is waiting for you* ‖ to be set aside for later action, to remain undone for the time being, *that decision can't wait* ‖ to act as a waiter ‖ *v.t.* to await, wait for, *to wait one's opportunity* ‖ to delay, *to wait dinner for someone* **to wait on** to attend or serve (someone), esp. at table **to wait out** to endure something distressing, e.g. a storm or a setback, hoping that it will change for the better or stop **to wait up** (with 'for') to refrain from going to bed at one's normal bedtime in expectation of someone's arrival or of news etc. **2.** *n.* an act or period of waiting, *a long wait at the station* ‖ (*pl.,* esp. *Br.*) street singers of Christmas carols **to lie in wait** to be on the watch, in hiding, ready to make an attack etc. [early M.E. *waite, waiten* fr. A.F., O.N.F. *waitier* fr. O.H.G.]

Wai·tan·gi Day (waitǽŋi:) New Zealand's national day, Feb. 6, a public holiday

Waitangi, Treaty of a treaty (1840) between Britain and the Maori chiefs of New Zealand, by which the Maoris ceded all rights and powers of sovereignty to the British monarch while retaining all territorial rights, in return for British protection

Waite (weit), Morrison Remick (1816-88), U.S. jurist, Chief Justice (1874-88) of the U.S. Supreme Court. He represented the U.S.A. as prosecutor in the Alabama Arbitration. As Chief Justice he broadly interpreted the 'due process' clause of the 14th amendment in favor of private businesses, a position maintained by the Court until the 1930s

wait·er (wéitər) *n.* a man employed to serve food or drink, esp. one who waits on tables in a restaurant ‖ a salver or tray for dishes etc.

wait·ing (wéitiŋ) **1.** *adj.* that waits ‖ of or for a wait ‖ that is in attendance **2.** *n.* the act of someone who waits **in waiting** in attendance (e.g. on a king or queen) ‖ (*Br., mil.*) next in turn for some duty etc.

waiting game a deliberate reserving of action so as to allow a situation to develop, in the hope of having better opportunities later on

waiting room a room provided for those who have to wait, esp. for a train or to see a doctor, dentist etc.

wait·ress (wéitris) *n.* a woman or girl who waits on tables in a restaurant etc.

waive (weiv) *pres. part.* **waiv·ing** *past* and *past part.* **waived** *v.t.* to agree to forgo or prefer not to insist on (a claim, right or privilege) **wáiv·er** *n.* (*law*) the act of waiving or giving up some established claim, right or privilege ‖ a document, or clause in an agreement, making this effective [fr. A.F. *weyver,* to allow to become a waif]

Wa·ka·ya·ma (wɑkɑjɑ́mɑ) a port (pop. 285,000) in S.E. Honshu, Japan: cotton textiles, woodworking

wake (weik) *pres. part.* **wak·ing** *past* **woke** (wouk), **waked** *past part.* **waked, wok·en** (wóukən) *v.i.* (often with 'up') to become conscious after sleep or after being in a semiconscious state ‖ (often with 'up') to return to alertness, pay attention again ‖ to become imaginatively aware of something, *he woke to the beauty of his surroundings* ‖ (among the Irish) to hold a wake ‖ *v.t.* (often with 'up') to rouse (someone) from sleep ‖ to rouse, revive, *the music wakes sad memories* ‖ (often with 'to') to cause to become aware of something, *he woke his audience to the need for concerted action* ‖ (among the Irish) to hold a wake over [O.E. *wæcnan,* to arise, be born and *wacian,* to wake, watch]

wake *n.* (among the Irish) a vigil over a corpse before burial, often accompanied by drinking and festivity ‖ (*Br., hist.*) a parish festival held annually in commemoration of the patron saint of the church ‖ (*pl.,* in some parts of England) an annual holiday [M.E. prob. representative of supposed O.E. *wacu,* and partly a new formation of WAKE v.]

wake *n.* the track in the water behind a moving ship, or something thought of as like this **in the wake of** behind, following in the tracks of, *traders came in the wake of explorers and missionaries* [fr. O.N. *vaku, vök,* hole, opening in ice]

wake·ful (wéikfəl) *adj.* watchful, alert ‖ unable to sleep ‖ marked by lack of sleep

Wake Island (weik) an atoll comprising three islets (area 3 sq. miles, pop. 150) in the N. Pacific between the Marianas and Hawaii, annexed by the U.S.A. (1900) and used as a calling place for transpacific aircraft. It was occupied (1941-5) by the Japanese

Wake·field (wéikfi:ld), Edward Gibbon (1796-1862), British colonial statesman. He contributed to the drawing up of the Durham Report (1839) and promoted the colonization of New Zealand

wak·en (wéikən) *v.t.* to rouse from sleep or lethargy ‖ to stir into awareness, activity etc. ‖ to cause to realize or remember ‖ *v.i.* to become awake [O.E. *wæcnan*]

wake-surf·ing (wéiksə:rfiŋ) *n.* surfing behind a motor boat

wak·ing (wéikiŋ) *adj.* marked by a condition of wakefulness, *waking hours*

Waks·man (wɑ́ksmən), Selman Abraham (1888-1973), U.S. microbiologist who received the 1952 Nobel prize in physiology and medicine for his discovery of streptomycin and its value in treating tuberculosis

Wa·la·chi·a, Wal·la·chi·a (wɒléiki:ə) the southern region of Rumania, consisting largely of the fertile plain (wheat, corn) of the lower Danube basin. Chief towns: Bucharest, Ploesti. Historically, it was comprised of Oltenia, or Lesser Walachia, in the west and Muntenia, or Greater Walachia, in the east. There are rich oil fields in the north, in the foothills of the S. Carpathians. It united with Moldavia to form Rumania (1859)

Wa·la·chi·an, Wal·la·chi·an (wɒléiki:ən) **1.** *adj.* of Walachia, its people or language **2.** *n.* the Rumanian language of the Walachians ‖ a native or inhabitant of Walachia ‖ a Vlach

Wal·bur·ga (wɔlbə́:rgə, vɑlbúərgə), St (c. 710–c. 779), English abbess. Feast: Feb. 25

Wal·che·ren (wɑ́lxərən) a former island (area 82 sq. miles) at the mouth of the Scheldt in Zeeland, Netherlands, now attached to the mainland. Chief towns: Flushing, Middelburg

Wal·deck-Rous·seau (vældekru:sou), Pierre Marie René (1846-1904), French statesman. During his term of office (1899-1902) as prime minister, a law was passed (1901) which suppressed some secular powers of the Church and resulted in the separation (1905) of Church and State in France

Wal·den·ses (wɒldénsi:z) *pl. n.* the members of a reforming Christian sect founded (c. 1175) by Peter Waldo (Pierre Waldo, c. 1140–c. 1217), French religious reformer. He preached in the valleys of Dauphiné, Provence and Piedmont. He taught from the Scriptures in the vernacular and was vowed to poverty and simplicity. The Waldenses were excommunicated (1184) and suffered persecution (16th c.) and were not officially tolerated until 1848 **Wal·den·si·an** (wɒldénsi:ən, wɒldénʃən) *adj.* [M.L.]

Wal·den·ström's mac·ro·glo·bu·lin·e·me·a (vɑ́ldenstremz mækrəglɒbju:liní:mi:ə) *n.* (*med.*) disease of proteins in antibodies that fight infection, resulting in excess production of plasma cells and lymphocytes; discovered in 1914 by Dr. Jan G. Waldenstrom, Swedish physician

Wald·heim (vɑ́lthaim), Kurt (1918-), Austrian statesman, foreign minister (1968-70), Secretary-General of the United Nations (1972-81). Controversy over his having been in Hitler's army during World War II and his possible involvement in sending Jews to their deaths marked his successful campaign for election as president of Austria (1986)

Wald·see·mül·ler (vɑ́ltzeimylər), Martin (c. 1475–c.1521), German geographer. He gave to the American continent the first name of his friend Amerigo Vespucci, on the grounds that Vespucci was the first to call America a 'new world'

wale (weil) **1.** *n.* a weal on the skin left by a whip, cane etc. ‖ a ridge on the surface of cloth, e.g. in corduroy ‖ (*naut.*, esp. *pl.*) one of the extra thick planks in the sides of a wooden ship ‖ a wooden or steel brace on a row of piles on a dam or trench ‖ (*basketry*) a strong band formed by weaving three or four rods one after the other into a single course **2.** *v.t. pres. part.* **wal·ing** *past* and *past part.* **waled** to mark (the flesh) with a wale or wales ‖ to supply with a wale or wales [O.E. *walu*]

Wales (weilz) a country (area, including Monmouthshire, 8,016 sq. miles, pop. 2,790,462) in the west of Great Britain. It is a division of the United Kingdom. Chief town: Cardiff. Language: English, Welsh (1% Welsh only, 25% bilingual). The land is 12% arable, 6% forest, largely pasture and grazing. Wales forms a rugged massif, partly covered with forest and moorland, with a lowland fringe widest along the English border and south coast. The massif is largely between 600 and 2,000 ft, rocky in the north and coal-bearing (esp. anthracite) in the south. It is highest in the northwest, rising to 3,560 ft (Snowdon). Average temperatures (F.): 42° (Jan.) and 60° (July). Rainfall: less than 50 ins in the lowlands, 50-80 ins in the moorland massif, well over 80 ins in the mountains. Chief ports: Cardiff, Swansea, Newport. The University of Wales is made up of colleges in Aberystwyth (1872), Bangor (1884), Cardiff (1883) and Swansea (1920). HISTORY. Wales is thought to have been originally inhabited by Iberians and to have been overrun (c. 6th c. B.C.) by Celts. The Romans conquered the north and south (1st c. A.D.), but had little influence on most of the country. After the Roman withdrawal (early 5th c.), the Celts of Wales maintained their independence against the Anglo-Saxon invaders of England, challenging the authority of Offa of Mercia (8th c.). Wales was converted to Christianity (c. 6th c.) by Celtic missionaries, notably St David. William I of England, unable to subdue Wales, appointed earls to control the Welsh marches. The Welsh, notably under Llewelyn ap Iorwerth and Llewelyn ap Gruffydd, successfully opposed English attempts to invade until the late 13th c., when Edward I conquered the country, his son, the future Edward II, becoming prince of Wales (1301).. Revolts against English rule continued, notably (1400-9) under Owen Glendower. The Tudors, a Welsh dynasty, fought in the Wars of the Roses as representatives of the Lancastrian claim, and one of them ascended (1485) the English throne as Henry VII. Under Henry VIII, Wales and the marches were brought into a legal union with England (1534-6). (For subsequent history *ENGLAND, *GREAT BRITAIN)

Walesa (vawénsə), Lech (1943-) Polish labor leader, chairman of the Solidarity labor organization (1980-2), winner of the Nobel peace prize (1983). An electrician, he was leader of his factory's strike coordination committee and was named chairman of Solidarity soon after the government granted the right to form independent trade unions. He was jailed after martial law was imposed (1981) and was released when Solidarity was dissolved by the government (1982). He continued to work for labor's rights

walk (wɔk) **1.** *v.i.* to move in such a way that the legs support the body, one foot (in two-legged creatures) or two feet (in four-legged creatures) being always on the ground (cf. RUN) ‖ to travel on foot ‖ (of a ghost) to show itself ‖ (*baseball*) to advance to first base as a result of having been pitched four balls ‖ (*basketball*) to foul by moving more than two steps with the ball without either passing or dribbling ‖ *v.t.* to pass over, through etc. by walking, *to walk the Lake District* ‖ to cause to walk, *he walked his horse through the village* ‖ to walk beside and push (a bicycle or motorcycle) ‖ to accompany on foot, *I'll walk you home* ‖ (*baseball*) to advance (a batter) to first base by pitching four balls ‖ (*basketball*) to foul by advancing more than two steps with (the ball) without either passing or dribbling **to walk away from** to outdistance (one's opponents or rivals) easily ‖ to emerge from (an accident) without serious injury **to walk away with** to win (something) by a large margin ‖ to steal ‖ (of an actor, singer etc.) to win far the most attention and applause from the audience in (a show) **to walk off** to leave, esp. without saying good-bye ‖ to rid oneself of (e.g. excess fat) by walking ‖ to measure (a distance, boundary etc.) by walking **to walk off with** to win (something) by a large margin ‖ to steal ‖ (of an actor, singer etc.) to win by far the most attention and applause from the audience in (a show) **to walk out** to leave, esp. in such a way as to show disapproval, disappointment etc. ‖ to go on strike **to walk out on** to abandon or desert without warning **to walk over** (or **all over**) to show complete disregard for the rights, wishes etc. of (someone) ‖ (*pop.*) to defeat (one's opponent) overwhelmingly **to walk over the course** (of a horse) to be the only competitor in a race and win it by going over (the course) at a walk **to walk (someone) off his feet** to tire (someone) out by making him walk a long way **to walk the streets** to walk aimlessly in the streets ‖ to be a prostitute **2.** *n.* the act of walking ‖ the route taken when walking ‖ a route pleasant to walk over ‖ a path designed to be walked along ‖ a stroll taken or journey made on foot for pleasure or exercise ‖ a distance walked ‖ a manner of walking ‖ a slow pace, *to go at a walk* ‖ (*Br.*) the circuit taken by a hawker etc. ‖ (*athletics*) a race in which one walks over the course ‖ (*baseball*) an advance to first base as a result of four balls ‖ a sheepwalk ‖ a ropewalk ‖ (*Br.*) a section of forest under the charge of a keeper ‖ (in the West Indies) a plantation of trees [O.E. *wealcan*, to roll, toss and *wealcian*, to muffle up, curl]

walk·a·way (wɔ́kəwei) *n.* an easily won contest

Walk·er (wɔ́kər), David (1785-1830), U.S. black leader, one of the first militants to protest against the repression of blacks. His pamphlet 'Walker's Appeal in four articles together with a preamble to the Colored Citizens of the World, but in particular and very expressly to those of the United States of America' was an argument against slavery. He himself had the status of a free man

Walker, Francis Amasa (1840-97), U.S. economist and statistician, known for his theories on wages and profits in 'The Wages Question' (1876) and for his advocacy of international bimetallism

Walker, Robert John (1801-69), U.S. statesman. As secretary of the treasury (1845-9) under President James Polk, he made it independent of the U.S. banking and financial system, and he helped to improve Anglo-U.S. relations by the Walker Tariff (1846), a revenue as opposed to a protective tariff. He served (1857) as governor of Kansas during the critical period when proslavery and antislavery forces vied for supremacy

Walker, William (1824-60), U.S. adventurer. Leading a small band of filibusters, he seized (1856) Nicaragua and proclaimed himself president. He planned to establish slave labor to develop the economy, build a canal that would attract world trade, and create a military empire of Central American states. He was deposed (1857) largely through the efforts of Cornelius Vanderbilt. After a final seizure of Nicaragua (1860) he was executed by a British firing squad in Honduras

walk·ie-talk·ie, walk·y-talk·y (wɔ́ki:tɔ́ki:) *n.* a portable battery-operated radio transmitter and receiver used out of doors and when on the move over short distances

walking catfish a catfish (*Clarias batrachas*) capable of moving about on dry land

walking papers (*Am.=Br.* marching orders) dismissal from employment

walking stick a stick carried when walking, often as a support **walk·ing·stick** (wɔ́:kiŋstik) *n.* a stick insect

walk-off (wɔ́kɔf) *n.* **1.** a departure marking the end of an incident **2.** a desire not to be associated with a person or event; a walkout

walk of life calling, profession ‖ social status

walk-on (wɔ́kɒn, wɔ́kɒn) *n.* (*theater, movies* etc.) a minor role that involves only a brief appearance, usually without spoken lines ‖ the actor who plays this

walk·out (wɔ́kaut) *n.* a strike ‖ the act of leaving as a sign of disapproval etc.

walk·o·ver (wɔ́kouvər) *n.* a horse race in which the only starter has merely to walk over the course in order to win ‖ an easy win

walk·up (wɔ́kʌp) *n.* an apartment house without an elevator ‖ an apartment above the ground floor in such a building

walk-up *adj.* open to the street for doing business without customers having to enter a building, esp. of a bank

walk·way (wɔ́kwei) *n.* a passage for walking

Walkyrie *VALKYRIE

walky-talky *WALKIE-TALKIE

wall (wɔl) *n.* a usually vertical structure, esp. in masonry, large in surface area as compared with thickness, built to enclose, support, divide, protect, retain etc. ‖ the surface of such a structure, *hang it up on the wall* ‖ something which resembles a man-made wall, *a wall of mountains*, esp. with regard to surface, *paintings on the walls of a cave* ‖ the upright part of the structure of a hollow vessel, *the wall of a pot* ‖ (*anat., biol.*) a layer of structural material bounding an organ, cavity, cell etc. ‖ something seen as a barrier to understanding or social intercourse, *a wall of silence* **to drive** (or **push**) **to the wall** to force (someone) into a desperate or difficult position **to go to the wall** to experience defeat ‖ to fail in business **to have one's back to the wall** to be hard pressed, be in a very difficult situation **with one's back to the wall** in a desperate or very difficult situation [O.E.]

wall *v.t.* to furnish with a wall (with 'in') to enclose within a wall ‖ (with 'up') to shut with a wall ‖ (with 'off') to divide, separate etc. with a wall [O.E. *weallan*]

wal·la·by (wɔ́ləbi:) *pl.* **wal·la·bies** *n.* any of several small kangaroos of *Macropus* and related genera [native Austral. *wolabā*]

Wal·lace (wɔ́lis), Alfred Russel (1823-1913), British naturalist. He spent many years in South America and the East Indies. He developed, independently, a theory of evolution similar to Darwin's. The theories were published simultaneously in 1858

Wallace, George Corley (1919-), U.S. politician and 5-time governor of Alabama, a conservative Democrat. The champion of states' rights and 'segregation forever', he polled 13.5% of the popular vote as 3rd party candidate in the 1968 presidential election. With 46 electoral votes, he almost put the election into the House of Representatives. He was a candidate (1972) for the Democratic presidential nomination. An attempt on his life (1972) left him as a paraplegic. He retired from public life (1986), citing ill health

Wallace, Henry Agard (1888-1965), American politician, Democratic vice-president of the U.S.A. (1941-5). He founded the Progressive party (1948)

Wallace, Lewis (1827-1905), U.S. general, politician and author of three historical romances: 'The Fair God' (1873), a tale of the Mexican conquest; 'Ben Hur' (1880), a story of the coming of Christ, made into a successful play and two motion pictures; and 'Prince of India' (1893), a narrative concerning the Wandering Jew and the Byzantine empire

Wallace, Sir Richard (1818-90), British art collector and philanthropist. His collection of pictures (esp. French 18th-c.), sculpture and furniture, bequeathed to Britain (1897), forms the national Wallace Collection, London

Wallace, Sir William (c. 1272-1305), Scottish patriot. He led the resistance to Edward I, whom he defeated at Stirling (1297). He was routed at Falkirk (1298), betrayed (1305) and executed in London

Wal·lace·ism (wɔ́ləsizəm) *n.* a principle supporting states rights and espousing anti-integration policies; from George C. Wallace, former governor of Alabama

Wallachia *WALACHIA

Wallachian *WALACHIAN

wall·board (wɔ́lbɔrd, wɔ́lbourd) *n.* a large sheet of boarding made from wood pulp, gypsum etc. and used to line walls or ceilings

wall cloud eyewall (*meteor.*) the high wall surrounding the eye of a hurricane

Wal·len·stein (válenʃtain, wɒ́lənstain), Albrecht Wenzel Eusebius von, duke of Friedland and Mecklenburg, prince of Sagan (1583-1634), German soldier and statesman. He commanded the Hapsburg armies in the Thirty Years' War, winning many victories until his defeat at Lützen (1632). He was assassinated on the orders of Ferdinand II

Wal·ler (wɔ́lər, wɒ́lər), Edmund (1606-87), English poet and politician. He is remembered esp. for two poems, 'Go, Lovely Rose' and 'On a Girdle'

wal·let (wɔ́lit, wɒ́lit) *n.* a pocketbook or small flat, folding case for carrying papers, paper money etc. ‖ (*hist.*) a beggar's or pilgrim's bag in which he carried his provisions [origin unknown]

wall·eye (wɔ́lai) *pl.* **wall·eyes** *n.* an eye in which the iris is streaked or whitish or different from the other eye, or which has a divergent squint ‖ opaqueness and whiteness of the cornea of the eye due to injury or disease [back-formation fr. *walleyed*]

Walleye *n. (mil.)* U.S. air-to-surface glide bomb (AGM-62X A) for the stand-off destruction of large, semihard targets, incorporating a contrast tracking television system for guidance

wall·eyed (wɔ́laid) *adj.* having walleye ‖ having glaring eyes [Late M.E. *wawileghed,* O.N. *vagleygr*]

walleyed pike *Stizostedion vitreum,* fam. *Percidae,* a large pike perch of North America valued as a food and game fish

wall·flow·er (wɔ́lflauər) *n.* a perennial plant of genus *Cheiranthus,* fam. *Cruciferae,* esp. *C. cheiri,* native to S. Europe and widely cultivated for its fragrant yellow, brown, red or purplish flowers ‖ (*pop.*) a girl sitting out at a dance because she has not been asked to dance

wall game a kind of football played only at Eton College, England

Wal·lis (wɔ́lis, wɒ́lis), John (1616-1703), English mathematician, one of the founders of the Royal Society. He was the first to deal mathematically with the concept of infinity, and his 'Arithmetica Infinitorum' (1657) paved the way for the development of the calculus and of the binomial theorem

Wallis and Futuna two groups of volcanic and coral islands (area 119 sq. miles, pop. 9,192) in the Pacific between Fiji and Samoa, forming an overseas territory of France. It is ruled by native kings. People: Polynesian. Main islands: Futuna, Uvea. The islands became a French protectorate (1842) and an overseas territory (1961) of France

Wal·loon (wɒlú:n) **1.** *n.* a member of the French-speaking population of Belgium occupying the southern part of the country (cf. FLEMING) ‖ the French dialect of the Walloons **2.** *adj.* of the Walloons or their French dialect [F. *Wallon* fr. Gmc]

wal·lop (wɒ́ləp) **1.** *v.t.* (*pop.*) to hit hard ‖ (*pop.*) to thrash ‖ (*pop.*) to defeat soundly **2.** *n.* (*pop.*) a heavy blow **wál·lop·ing 1.** *adj.* (*pop.*) huge, thumping, whopping **2.** *n.* (*pop.*) a severe thrashing [M.E. *walopen,* to gallop fr. O.N.F.]

wal·low (wɒ́lou) **1.** *v.i.* (esp. of some animals) to roll about with pleasure (e.g. in mud) ‖ (of a ship) to roll in rough water ‖ to revel with self-indulgence (e.g. in sentiment or luxury) **2.** *n.* a mudhole or other place where animals (esp. buffaloes and hippopotamuses) wallow [O.E. *wealwian*]

wall·pa·per (wɔ́lpeipər) **1.** *n.* paper, usually decorative, for covering the walls of a room **2.** *v.t.* to cover with such paper

wallpaper music (*Br.*) piped background music in a public place

Wall Street the stock exchange and money market of the U.S.A. [after a street in Manhattan, New York City]

wall-to-wall (wɔ́ltu:wɔ́l) *adj.* completely covering a floor

wal·nut (wɔ́lnʌt, wɔ́lnət) *n.* a member of *Juglans,* fam. *Juglandaceae,* a genus of tall-growing trees of temperate regions ‖ the edible fruit (a two-lobed seed in a shell, enclosed by a husk) of these trees ‖ the wood of these trees, esp. of the black walnut, which takes a high polish and is used in cabinetmaking, for gunstocks etc. [O.E. *walhhnutu*]

Wal·pole (wɔ́lpoul, wɒ́lpoul), Horace, 4th earl of Orford (1717-97), English man of letters. He is famous for his Gothic novel. 'The Castle of Otranto' (1765) and for his 3,000 letters. He was one of the men responsible for the growing pre-Romantic taste for the Gothic, as a reaction to 18th–c. classicism in the arts

Walpole, Sir Robert, 1st earl of Orford (1676-1745), English statesman. As first lord of the treasury and chancellor of the exchequer, he led the Whig administration (1721-42) and was effectively prime minister. His encouragement of trade and his cautious domestic policy did much to increase national wealth and to strengthen the Hanoverian dynasty. He reduced the national debt, land tax and customs duties. He avoided involving Britain in war, until he was forced to participate in the War of Jenkins' Ear (1739-41) and the War of the Austrian Succession (1740-8). He helped to establish the collective responsibility of prime minister and cabinet to parliament

Wal·pur·gis Night (valpúərgis) the night of April 30/May 1, when a witches' sabbath (particularly associated with the Brocken peak in the Harz Mtns.) was said to take place. St Walburga was accidentally connected with this ancient superstition (her bodily remains were transferred from her monastery to Eichstätt in Germany on May 1)

wal·rus (wɔ́lrəs, wɒ́lrəs) *n.* either of two species of Arctic, marine, seal-like, carnivorous mammals of fam. *Odobenidae: Odobenus rosmarus,* which inhabits the N.W. Atlantic Arctic, and *O. divergens,* which inhabits the Bering Sea and the Siberian and Alaskan coasts. Males weigh up to 2,000 lbs and are up to 12 ft long; females are smaller. Walruses are hunted for their blubber (which yields an excellent oil), skins (leather) and canine tusks (ivory) [prob. fr. Du. *walrus, walros*]

Wal·sall (wɔ́lsɔl) a county borough (pop. 178,900) in Staffordshire, England: coal mining, tanning, mechanical engineering

Walsh (wɔlʃ), Thomas James (1859-1933), U.S. lawyer and senator (1912-33) from Montana. He prosecuted with vigor the investigations into the oil reserves scandals of the Harding administration. He helped write the 18th and 19th amendments to the Constitution

Wal·sing·ham (wɔ́lsiŋəm), Sir Francis (c. 1530-90), English statesman. He was secretary of state (1573-90) to Elizabeth I

Wal·ter (wɔ́ltər), Hubert (*d.* 1205), English prelate and statesman, archbishop of Canterbury (1193-1205). As chief justiciar of England (1193-8), he was the effective ruler when Richard I was at the Crusades. He was chancellor (1199-1205) under King John

Wal·ther von der Vo·gel·wei·de (váltərfɔnderfóugəlvaidə) (c. 1170-1230), German lyric poet. After service at the court of Vienna he became a minnesinger. His love poetry and his treatment of social and political themes in verse and maxims make him the most celebrated of the German medieval lyric poets

Wal·ton (wɔ́ltən), Izaak (1593-1683), English writer. 'The Compleat Angler' (1653, enlarged in 1655 and subsequently) is his most popular work. He also wrote lives of John Donne (1640), Richard Hooker (1665), George Herbert (1670) and others

Walton, Sir William (1902-83), British composer. His works include 'Façade', a suite for 'declamation' and chamber orchestra (1923, 1926), 'Sinfonia Concertante for piano and orchestra' (1929), the cantata 'Belshazzar's Feast' (1931) and 'Symphony' (1935)

waltz (wɔlts) **1.** *n.* a smooth, graceful dance in triple time to a flowing melody ‖ the music for this dance ‖ a composition in this rhythm **2.** *v.i.* to dance a waltz ‖ *v.t.* to dance a waltz with **to waltz off with** to win (a race, prize etc.) with great ease [fr. G. *walzer*]

waltzing Matilda (*Austral.*) traveling on foot carrying a pack [prob. fr. WALTZ (*slang*), to carry+*matilda,* a tramp's roll]

Wal·vis Bay (wɔ́lvis) an enclave (area 374 sq. miles, pop. 25,000) of Cape Province, South Africa, on the coast of Namibia, administered as part of the latter territory ‖ the deep-water port which gives it its importance: whaling, refueling

wam·pum (wɔ́mpəm, wómpəm) *n.* beads made of shells strung together and used by North American Indians as money or ornaments [shortened fr. *wampumpeag* fr. Narragansett *wampompeag* fr. *wampan,* white+*api,* string +*-ag,* pl. suffix]

wan (wɒn) *comp.* **wan·ner** *superl.* **wan·nest** *adj.* (of a person's complexion) unhealthily pale ‖ (of the light or stars etc.) barely perceptible ‖ (of a smile) faint, feeble [O.E. *wann,* dark]

Wan·a·ma·ker (wɒ́nəmeikər), John (1838-1922), U.S. merchant who established (1869) John Wanamaker and Company, one of the first large department stores in the U.S.A. He was a pioneer in the use of advertising

Wan·chu·an (wántʃyán) *CHANGKIAKOW

wand (wɒnd) *n.* a slender stick or rod, esp. one carried by a fairy, magician, conjurer etc. ‖ a wooden or metal staff carried as a symbol of authority ‖ (*archery*) a slat 6 ft by 2 ins used as a target, placed at 100 yds for men, 60 yds for women [O.N. *vǫndr*]

wan·der (wɒ́ndər) *v.i.* (of a person) to travel or move around with no set route or goal ‖ (often with 'off') to stray away without set purpose from one's home, companions etc. ‖ (of the mind or a person) to be confused, incoherent or delirious ‖ to digress, *to wander from the subject* ‖ (of a river, road etc.) to follow an intricate course **wán·der·ing** *n.* a leisurely traveling around ‖ (*pl.*) leisurely journeys ‖ (*pl.*) incoherent speech or thoughts [O.E. *wandrian*]

Wandering Jew a Jew who, according to a legend first recorded in the 13th c., insulted Christ on the way to Calvary and was condemned to wander from place to place knowing no rest until the Day of Judgment

wan·der·lust (wɒ́ndərlʌst) *n.* a strong desire to travel, esp. an obsessive desire to get away from a settled way of living [G.]

wan·der·oo (wɒndərú:) *pl.* **wan·der·oos** *n.* *Presbytis senex,* fam. *Colobidae,* a purple-faced langur of eastern Asia ‖ *Macaca silenus,* a black macaque of India having a tufted tail and a gray ruff [Sinhalese *wanderu,* monkey]

wane (wein) **1.** *v.i. pres. part.* **wan·ing** *past* and *past part.* **waned** (of the moon) to diminish in size and brilliance after being at the full (cf. WAX) ‖ (of the tide) to ebb ‖ to decline or decrease in power, strength, importance, reputation, influence etc. **2.** *n.* the act or process of waning ‖ the period from the full moon to the new moon **on the wane** on the decline [O.E. *wanian*]

Wang·a·nu·i (wɒŋənú:i:) a port (pop. 37,000) in Wellington, North Island, New Zealand

wan·gle (wǽŋg'l) **1.** *v.t. pres. part.* **wan·gling** *past* and *past part.* **wan·gled** (*pop.*) to get by cunning, *to wangle a free ticket* ‖ (*pop.*) to falsify, *to wangle the accounts* **2.** *n.* (*pop.*) a wangling [etym. doubtful]

Wan·kel engine (váŋkəl) *n.* (*motor vehicle*) a small, light, rotary engine that utilizes a rounded triangular rotor-piston and that has only two major moving parts. It was named for Felix Wankel, German engineer. *also* epitrochoidal engine

want (wɒnt, wɒnt) *n.* the state or fact of having too little of something desirable or needed ‖ an insufficiency through personal failing, *a want of tact* ‖ need, *in want of a haircut* ‖ privation because of poverty, *freedom from want* ‖ (esp. *pl.*) desires, requirements, *a man of few wants* [fr. O.N. *vant* neut. of *vanr,* lacking, wanting]

want *v.t.* (with the infinitive) to wish fervently, *they want to go to America* ‖ to wish for, *I want some coffee* ‖ (esp. *Br.*) to need, *the house wants a cleaning* ‖ to possess less than the usual or required amount of, *he wants the stamina of a long-distance runner* ‖ to wish to see or speak to (someone), *your father wants you* ‖ *v.i.* (esp. with 'for') to suffer need, *he never wanted for affection as a child* **to want for nothing** to have everything one needs (even though poor, or because rich) [O.N. *vanta*]

want ad a classified advertisement (esp. in a newspaper) for employment or an employee etc.

want·ed (wɔ́ntid, wɒ́ntid) *adj.* being searched for so as to be brought to trial

want·ing (wɔ́ntiŋ, wɒ́ntiŋ) **1.** *adj.* not present when it should be, *mustard was wanting in the salad* ‖ deficient, *wanting in initiative* **2.** *prep.* without, short of, *a watch wanting only its spring*

wan·ton (wɒ́ntən) **1.** *adj.* lewd, licentious, *wanton thoughts* ‖ showing utter lack of moderation or justification, *wanton destruction* ‖ luxuriant, uncontrolled, *roses in wanton profusion* ‖ (*rhet.*) sportive, playful, *in wanton mood* **2.** *n.* (*old-fash.*) a sexually promiscuous woman [M.E. *wantowen* fr. O.E. *wan-*, wanting+ *togen*, past part. of *tēon*, to discipline]

wap·en·take (wǽpəntəik, wɒ́pəntəik) *n.* (*hist.*) a division corresponding to the hundred in certain English shires [fr. O.N. *vāpnatak*, weapon-taking fr. the showing of weapons as a form of voting]

wap·i·ti (wɒ́piti:) *pl.* **wap·i·ti, wap·i·tis** *n. Cervus canadensis*, fam. *Cervidae*, a North American elk related to, but larger than, the European and Asian red deer [fr. Am. Ind. name]

war (wɔr) **1.** *n.* armed conflict between nations, tribes or other groups or an instance of this, *civil war, a war of conquest, the wars of religion* ‖ a concerted effort to put down, reduce or exterminate *a war on locusts* ‖ a state of hostility without resort to arms, *the cold war* ‖ the theory of conducting a war **at war** engaged in a war **to declare war** to declare officially that a state of war exists **to go to war** to enter into a war **2.** *v.i. pres. part.* **war·ring** *past* and *past part.* **warred** to be at war ‖ to engage in an effort to reduce or exterminate something [O.N.F. *werre* fr. O.H.G.]

Wa·ran·gal (wʌ́rəŋg'l) a town (pop. 156,000) in N. Andhra Pradesh, India: cotton spinning, carpets

War·beck (wɔ́rbek), Perkin (c. 1474-99), Flemish pretender to the English throne who led an unsuccessful rising against Henry VII (1497)

War between the States the American Civil War (*CIVIL WAR, AMERICAN)

war·ble (wɔ́rb'l) **1.** *v. pres. part.* **war·bling** *past* and *past part.* **war·bled** *v.i.* (of birds) to sing with long trills ‖ to produce a continuous trilling sound ‖ *v.t.* to sing (a song) thus **2.** *n.* the sound, or act, of warbling [O.F. *werbler, werbloier*]

warble *n.* a small tumor or swelling produced on the back of cattle, deer etc. by the larva of a botfly or a warble fly ‖ the larva of a warble fly [etym. doubtful]

warble fly any of various dipterous flies of fam. *Oestridae*, the larvae of which live under the skin of certain animals (cattle, deer, rabbits etc.)

war·bler (wɔ́rblər) *n.* any of various small, vividly marked North American songbirds of fam. *Parulidae* ‖ any of various small Old World songbirds of fam. *Sylviidae*, related to the thrushes [fr. WARBLE *n.*]

war·bon·net (wɔ́rbɒnit) *n.* a headdress worn by certain Plains Indians consisting of a band with a long extension of eagle feathers attached to it at the back

war correspondent a journalist reporting news from a war zone

war cry *pl.* **war cries** (*hist.*) a name or phrase shouted by soldiers when charging, to encourage each other or to intimidate the enemy ‖ a party slogan, catchword

Ward (wɔrd), Lester Frank (1841-1913), U.S. sociologist, a founder of systematic American sociology. He postulated a 'sociocracy', a society which could be scientifically planned, and he emphasized the need for the study of function rather than of structure

ward (wɔrd) *v.t.* (with 'off') to turn aside (a blow) ‖ (with 'off') to avert (a danger) [O.E. *weardian*]

ward *n.* a person, esp. a minor, under the care of a court or a legal guardian ‖ the state of being under the care of a court or guardian, *a child in ward* ‖ the guardianship of a person in this state ‖ an administrative district in a borough or city, esp. an electoral district ‖ a division of a prison or hospital ‖ a large room containing several beds or a set of such rooms in a hospital, *a children's ward* ‖ the inner court of a castle ‖ one of the projections in a lock case that resists the turning of a key other than the right one ‖ one of the corresponding key notches [O.E. *weard*, a watching]

-ward *suffix* toward a specified point, position, area etc., as in 'northward', 'skyward' [O.E. *-weard*]

ward·en (wɔ́rd'n) *n.* an official having special supervisory duties and who sees that regulations or laws are observed, *game warden, air-raid warden* ‖ (*eccles.*) a churchwarden ‖ the official in charge of a prison ‖ (*Br.*) the title of the principal of some colleges or other institutions **wárd·en·cy, wárd·en·ship** *ns* [fr. O.F. *wardein*]

ward·er (wɔ́rdər) *n.* (*Br.*) a prison guard **wárd·ress** *n.* (*Br.*) a woman warder [A. F. *wardour*]

ward·robe (wɔ́rdroub) *n.* a tall piece of furniture to keep clothes in, usually fitted with racks, hangers, shelves etc. ‖ a person's clothes ‖ (*theater*) a room where costumes are kept ‖ (in titles) the department of a royal household in charge of the royal clothes, jewels etc. [A.F. *warderobe*]

ward·room (wɔ́rdru:m, wɔ́rdrum) *n.* the living quarters, esp. the mess, for the officers of a warship ‖ a ship's officers collectively

-wards *suffix* -ward [O.E. *-weardes* fr. *-weard*, toward+*-es*, gen. ending]

ward·ship (wɔ́rdʃip) *n.* guardianship

ware (wɛər) *n.* (*pl.*) goods for sale ‖ (in compounds) manufactured articles, *silverware, ironware* ‖ pottery classified according to its nature, *earthenware* or provenance, *Chelsea ware* [O.E. *waru*, merchandise]

ware *v.t.* (imperative only, esp. in hunting) to beware of, avoid [O.E. *warian*, fr. *wær* adj., cautious]

ware·house (wɛ́ərhaus) **1.** *pl.* **ware·hous·es** (wɛ́ərhauziz) *n.* a building, or room in a building, where goods are stored ‖ a repository for furniture etc. ‖ a customs storehouse where dutiable goods are kept until duty is paid **2.** *v.t. pres. part.* **ware·hous·ing** *past* and *past. part.* **ware·housed** to put (goods etc.) in a warehouse for safekeeping ‖ to put (goods etc.) in a warehouse under bond

war·fare (wɔ́rfɛər) *n.* a state of war ‖ (*fig.*) strife

war game a training exercise for military staffs carried out without the participation of troops

war·head (wɔ́rhed) *n.* the explosive head of a missile (detached when not needed)

Warhol (wɔ́rhɔl), Andy (1931-) U.S. artist, founder of the Pop-Art movement of the 1960s. He was known for his paintings of enlarged comic strip and mass media images, the latter usually repeated across and up and down the canvas. He pioneered a unique silk-screening process to produce such images as Popeye, Superman, Coca Cola cans, Campbell's soup cans, and the face of Elizabeth Taylor (1964). He also made some experimental films, including 'Sleep' (1963), 'Empire' (1964) and 'The Chelsea Girls' (1966)

war-horse (wɔ́rhɔrs) *n.* a cavalry officer's mount ‖ a veteran soldier or old political campaigner

war·i·ly (wɛ́ərili:) *adv.* in a wary manner

war·i·ness (wɛ́əri:nis) *n.* the state or quality of being wary

war·like (wɔ́rlaik) *adj.* favoring or inclined to favor war or strife ‖ (*mil.*) of, relating to or for war ‖ (*rhet.*) befitting a soldier

War·lock (wɔ́rlɒk), Peter (Philip Heseltine, 1894-1930), British composer. His work was slight but filled with grace, wit and energy. His songs (many in the Elizabethan style) and his 'Capriol' suite for strings (1926) are best known

war·lock (wɔ́rlɒk) *n.* a man who practices witchcraft, sorcery etc. [O.E. *wǣrloga*, traitor, enemy, devil]

war·lord (wɔ́rlɔrd) *n.* a military commander who has seized effective power over the civilians of an area

warm (wɔrm) **1.** *adj.* having roughly the same temperature as the human body, *warm water* ‖ serving to keep the body at this temperature, *warm clothes* ‖ emitting heat, esp. in a comforting degree, *a warm fire* ‖ (of a person) slightly overheated, esp. after strenuous work or exercise ‖ affectionate, *warm friends* ‖ very cordial, *a warm welcome* ‖ emotionally excited, esp. slightly angry ‖ (of color) in the range yellow through orange to red ‖ (of an animal's scent or trail) fresh, strong ‖ (of a player in a game involving a search for a hidden object) near to the object being looked for ‖ (*pop.*) not very pleasant, *he left when things began to get warm* **2.** *v.i.* (often with 'up') to become warm ‖ *v.t.* (often with 'up') to make warm ‖ to fill with pleasant emotions, *the crackling of the fire warmed her heart* **to warm over** to reheat (cooked food) **to warm up** to make or become more animated ‖ (*sports*) to exercise before going into a game, race etc. ‖ to reheat (cooked food) [O.E. *wearm*]

warm-blood·ed (wɔ́rmblʌ́did) *adj.* (of a bird or mammal) having a constant blood temperature considerably above that of the surrounding medium

warm front (*meteor.*) the edge of a warm air mass advancing against a colder air mass

warm·heart·ed (wɔ́rmhártid) *adj.* affectionate, readily sympathetic etc.

warming pan a closed brass or copper pan to hold hot embers, with a long handle, formerly used to warm beds

war·mon·ger (wɔ́rmʌŋgər, wɔ́rmɒŋgər) *n.* a person who advocates war, esp. under the guise of patriotism

warmth (wɔrmθ) *n.* the state or quality of being warm [M.E. *wermthe* prob. fr. O.E.]

warm-up (wɔ́rmʌp) *n.* an act or period of exercising before a game, race etc.

warn (wɔrn) *v.t.* to draw the attention of (someone) to the probable results of an act, or to an impending danger ‖ to inform beforehand, *he warned them that he intended to leave in two weeks* ‖ to rebuke (someone) mildly for misbehavior, breaking a rule etc., *this time I'm just warning you* ‖ *v.i.* to give warning **to warn off the course** (*Br.*) to prohibit (a jockey) from riding or (an owner) from running a horse in races **to warn off the premises** to order or advise (someone) to refrain from trespassing ‖ to order (someone) to leave the premises **wárn·ing 1.** *adj.* that warns **2.** *n.* the act of someone who warns ‖ the fact of being warned ‖ something which warns [O.E. *warenian, wearnian*]

warning path or **warning track** (*baseball*) a cleared area near the outside fence designed to alert an outfielder that he is approaching an obstacle

War of 1812 a war (1812-15) between Britain and the U.S.A. It arose from American resentment at the trade embargo imposed by France in the Continental System and by Britain in the orders-in-council of 1807 and 1809 during the Napoleonic Wars. Other causes were the British claim to search American ships for British deserters, and Anglo-American rivalry in the American northwest. During the war an American invasion of Canada failed (1812), a British force sacked Washington (1814), and several sea battles failed to produce a decisive result. New England remained hostile to the war. The war was settled by an agreement that both sides should give up territory captured, and appoint a commission to settle the Canadian boundary. After the signing of the treaty (Dec. 24, 1814) the British were defeated at New Orleans (Jan. 8, 1815). The war strengthened American nationalism and encouraged the growth of American industry

War of American Independence *REVOLUTIONARY WAR

War of Independence the Revolutionary war

war of nerves warfare designed to undermine the morale of the enemy, esp. by psychological means

War of Secession the American Civil War

War on Poverty *OFFICE OF ECONOMIC OPPORTUNITY

War on Poverty a series of long- and short-range plans designed to help the U.S. poor, proposed by President Lyndon Johnson (1964)

warp (wɔrp) *n.* the lengthwise threads in a fabric or on a loom, crossed by the weft or woof ‖ a twist or distortion in wood, esp. due to improper drying ‖ the state or fact of being so distorted ‖ a twist or distortion in the mind or character often resulting in perverse or irrational behavior ‖ (*naut.*) a towline attached to a fixed object, e.g. an anchor, and used for hauling a boat toward the object ‖ sediment deposited by water [O.E. *wearp*]

warp *v.t.* to cause (wood) to become twisted ‖ to cause (the mind, character etc.) to become as though twisted ‖ to give a false account or interpretation of ‖ to arrange (yarn etc.) so as to form a warp ‖ (*naut.*) to haul (a ship) with a warp ‖ to let water flood (land) so as to leave a deposit of warp ‖ to choke (a passage) with warp ‖ *v.i.* to become twisted or distorted ‖ to warp a ship ‖ (of a ship) to be warped ‖ to wind the yarn off bobbins in order to form the warp [O.E. *weorpan*, to throw]

CONCISE PRONUNCIATION KEY: **(a)** æ, *cat*; ɑ, *car*; ɔ *fawn*; ei, *snake*. **(e)** e, *hen*; i:, *sheep*; iə, *deer*; ɛə, *bear*. **(i)** i, *fish*; ai, *tiger*; ə:, *bird*. **(o)** o, *ox*; au, *cow*; ou, *goat*; u, *poor*; ɔi, *royal*. **(u)** ʌ, *duck*; u, *bull*; u:, *goose*; ə, *bacillus*; ju:, *cube*. x, *loch*; θ, *think*; ð, *bother*; z, *Zen*; ʒ, *corsage*; dʒ, *savage*; ŋ, *orangutang*; j, *yak*; ʃ, *fish*; tʃ, *fetch*; 'l, *rabble*; 'n, *redden*. Complete pronunciation key appears inside front cover.

war paint paint applied to the face and body esp. by American Indians preparing to make war

war·path (wɔ́rpæθ, wɔ́rpɑθ) *pl.* **war·paths** (wɔ́rpæðz, wɔ́rpɑðz, wɔ́rpæθs, wɔ́rpɑθs) *n.* the route taken by North American Indians when moving to attack an enemy **on the warpath** bearing down to punish, on the lookout for offenders

warp beam (*weaving*) a roller in a loom, on which the warp threads are wound

war·plane (wɔ́rplein) *n.* an airplane used for warfare

war·rant (wɔ́rənt, wɒ́rənt) *n.* legal authorization ‖ moral justification ‖ a document authorizing the arrest of a person, the search of premises etc. ‖ a voucher authorizing the payment of a sum of money, *a pension warrant* ‖ the authorizing certificate of rank granted to a warrant officer ‖ a royal or official authorization or license ‖ (*Br.*) a receipt for goods stored in a warehouse [O.F. *warant, warand*]

warrant *v.t.* to justify, *the circumstances warrant these measures* ‖ to guarantee, *warranted 22-carat gold* ‖ (*law*) to secure the title of (e.g. an estate) **wár·rant·a·ble** *adj.* **wár·rant·a·bly** *adv.* **war·ran·tee** (wɔrəntí:, wɒrəntí:) *n.* (*law*) the person to whom a warranty is made **wár·rant·er, wár·rant·or** *ns* (*law*) someone who gives a warrant or warranty [O.F. *warantir*]

warrant officer an officer in the armed forces, between a commissioned officer and a noncommissioned officer in rank

warrantor *WARRANTER

war·ran·ty (wɔ́rənti:, wɒ́rənti:) *pl.* **war·ran·ties** *n.* (*law*) an assurance given by the seller that the thing sold is exactly as represented in the sale agreement ‖ (*insurance*) an undertaking by the person insured that a statement of risk is a true statement, or that a condition of the contract as stated has been or will be exactly fulfilled ‖ a justification or authorization ‖ a guarantee [fr. A.F. *warantie*]

War·rau (wəráu) *pl.* **War·rau, War·raus** *n.* a South American Indian people chiefly inhabiting the delta of the Orinoco River, but also scattered along the coasts of Guyana and Suriname ‖ a member of this people ‖ their language

War·ren (wɔ́rən, wɒ́rən), Earl (1891-1974), U.S. jurist, chief justice (1953-69) of the U.S. Supreme Court. A defender of civil liberties against government encroachment, his notable decisions include 'Brown v. Board of Education of Topeka, Kansas' (1954). In the economic realm he supported federal anti-trust laws

Warren, Robert Penn (1905-), U.S. novelist, poet and critic. His novels include 'At Heaven's Gate' (1943), 'All the King's Men' (1946, Pulitzer prize), 'Band of Angels' (1955) and 'A Place to Come To' (1977). Two of his poetry collections also won Pulitzer Prizes: 'Promises' (1957) and 'Now and Then' (1979). He had a distinguished teaching career at several universities, notably Louisiana State (1934-42) and Yale (1950-6, 1961-73). He was named the U.S.A.'s first poet laureate (1986)

war·ren (wɔ́rən, wɒ́rən) *n.* a piece of uncultivated ground containing many rabbit burrows ‖ the rabbits inhabiting this area ‖ a cramped and overcrowded district, tenement house etc. ‖ any network of narrow roads or passages [fr. A.F. *warenne*]

Warren Commission (1963-4) committee charged with the investigation of the assassination of Pres. John F. Kennedy. Pres. Lyndon B. Johnson chose Chief Justice Earl Warren as chairman and Senators Richard Russell and John Sherman Cooper, Representatives Hale Boggs and Gerald R. Ford, Allen Dulles and John J. McCloy as members. In Sept. 1964, when the committee issued its findings, its conclusion that no conspiracy existed became a controversial issue

war·ri·or (wɔ́ri:ər, wɔ́rjər, wɒ́ri:ər, wɒ́rjər) *n.* (*rhet.* and *hist.*) a man experienced in warfare ‖ a fighting man in a tribe [A.F. *werreieor*]

War·saw (wɔ́rsɔ) (*Pol.* Warszawa) the capital and economic center (pop. 1,611,600) of Poland, on the middle Vistula. Industries: iron and steel, motor vehicles, mechanical and electrical engineering, printing and publishing, light manufactures. The central old city, on the high left bank, was restored to its 18th-c. appearance after the 2nd world war. Principal monuments: Gothic cathedral (14th c.), 15th-c. and 17th-c. churches, 18th-c. neoclassical palaces (now government buildings). Modern quarters, with the Soviet-style Palace of Culture, stadium etc., surround it on both banks. Main cultural institutions: university (1818), national libraries, academies and museums, celebrated national theaters. Warsaw became the capital in the 16th c. It was conquered by the Swedes (1655-6, 1702-5), the Russians (1794, 1813, 1831), the French (1806) and the Germans (1915-18). In the 2nd world war, it was bombarded by the Germans (1939), the Jewish ghetto was exterminated (1943) by Nazi troops, and a revolt by the Polish underground was put down (1944). The city was systematically destroyed and 600,000 people were killed

Warsaw, Grand Duchy of a state (1807-15) formed by Napoleon, including most of the land gained by Prussia in the partitions of Poland

Warsaw Pact a treaty (1955) of defense and mutual assistance signed by Albania, Bulgaria, Czechoslovakia, East Germany, Hungary, Poland, Rumania and the U.S.S.R. in response to the formation of NATO. Albania withdrew (1968) when Czechoslovakia was invaded

war·ship (wɔ́rʃip) *n.* a heavily armed ship used in naval combat

wart (wɔrt) *n.* a small hard excrescence on the skin, esp. of the hands or face, resulting from abnormal proliferation of the papillae ‖ (*bot.*) a small protuberance or lump on the surface of plants [O.E. *wearte*]

War·ta (vártə) the chief tributary (474 miles long, navigable for 250) of the Oder, flowing north and west through W. Poland

wart·hog (wɔ́rthɒg, wɔ́rthɔg) *n.* a member of *Phacochoerus,* fam. *Suidae,* a genus of large-headed wild hogs of N.E. and S. Africa having warty excrescences on the face and large protruding tusks

war·time (wɔ́rtaim) *n.* the period during which a war is being fought

wart·y (wɔ́rti:) *comp.* **wart·i·er** *superl.* **wart·i·est** *adj.* having warts or lumps like warts ‖ resembling a wart

War·wick (wɔ́rik, wɒ́rik), John Dudley, earl of, and duke of Northumberland (c. 1502-53), English soldier and conspirator. He was executed after having persuaded Edward VI to alter the succession in favor of his daughter-in-law, Lady Jane Grey

Warwick, Richard Neville, earl of, 'the Kingmaker' (1428-71), English nobleman who fought for the Yorkists in the Wars of the Roses, securing the throne (1461) for Edward IV, but restoring (1470-1) the Lancastrian Henry VI. He was killed in battle (1471) at Barnet when Edward IV regained the throne

War·wick·shire (wɔ́rikʃiər, wɒ́rikʃiər) (*abbr.* Warwick) a county (area 976 sq. miles, pop. 473,620) in central England. County town: Warwick. University of Warwick, near Coventry (1965)

war·y (wέəri:) *comp.* **war·i·er** *superl.* **war·i·est** *adj.* on one's guard, on the lookout for danger, trickery etc.

was *past* (1st and 3rd person sing.) of BE

Wash. Washington

wash (wɔʃ, wɒʃ) **1.** *v.t.* to make (clothes etc.) clean with soap and water ‖ to remove (dirt, stains etc.) from clothes etc. by soaping and scrubbing these in water ‖ to cleanse (esp. the face and hands) with soap and water ‖ to be suitable as a washing agent for, *this powder will not wash woolens* ‖ (*chem.*) to pass (a gas) through a liquid in order to remove soluble elements ‖ (*chem.*) to pass distilled water through (a precipitate in a filter) ‖ to pass water through or over (earth etc.) in order to separate ore etc. ‖ to sift (ore etc.) by the action of water ‖ (of the sea, a river, waves etc.) to flow over, against or past, *the waves washed the decks, heavy seas washed the lighthouse* ‖ to make (a gulley etc.) by the action of water ‖ to sweep along or away in a rush of water, *several crates were washed overboard* ‖ to purify (the soul) ‖ to brush a thin coat of color on in a continuous movement with a fully charged brush ‖ to cover (a metal) with a thin coat of gold, silver etc. ‖ (esp. of a cat) to cleanse (the body or fur) by licking a paw and rubbing its body or fur repeatedly with the wet paw ‖ *v.i.* to cleanse oneself, one's hands, face etc. with soap and water ‖ to clean clothes etc. by soaping, rubbing etc. in water ‖ to bear or stand up to the operation of being laundered ‖ to serve as a cleansing agent ‖ (*Br., pop.,* in negative constructions) to bear investigation, *that excuse won't wash* ‖ (of water) to move with a gentle, splashing sound ‖ to be eroded by the action of rain, a river etc. ‖ (*stock exchange*) to make a wash sale **to wash away** to remove or be removed by washing or by a rush of water **to wash down** to clean with quantities of water ‖ to follow (food, a pill etc.) with a drink of water or other liquid **to wash off** to remove or be removed by washing **to wash one's hands of** to disclaim responsibility for ‖ to refuse to have anything more to do with **to wash out** to wash (clothes etc.) ‖ to remove (stains etc.) by soaping and rubbing in water ‖ (of a stain) to be removed by washing **to wash up** (*Br.*) to wash the dishes and cutlery after a meal **2.** *n.* the action or process of washing ‖ a quantity of linen, clothes etc. washed or waiting to be washed ‖ an eddy or swirl of agitated water, esp. that made by a ship, or the sound of this debris (soil, mud etc.) accumulated and deposited by the tide, running rivers etc. ‖ soil yielding gold or other precious metals or gems under washing ‖ kitchen slops and waste scraps given to hogs ‖ any thin, tasteless beverage (e.g. weak tea), or something compared with this, e.g. vapid speech or writing ‖ a liquid used for a thin coat of color, esp. watercolor, applied in a continuous movement with a fully charged brush ‖ a wash drawing ‖ a thin coat of gold, silver etc. laid on something ‖ the disturbance behind the passing of an aircraft or its propeller ‖ (*stock exchange*) a wash sale [O.E. *wœscan*]

wash·a·ble (wɔ́ʃəb'l, wɒ́ʃəb'l) *adj.* capable of being washed without fading, shrinking etc. ‖ soluble in water

wash·ba·sin (wɔ́ʃbeisin, wɒ́ʃbeisin) *n.* a shallow bowl for washing the hands and face, or this as a bathroom fixture

wash·board (wɔ́ʃbɔrd, wɔ́ʃbourd, wɒ́ʃbɔrd, wɒ́ʃbourd) *n.* a wooden board having a ribbed section of metal or glass set into it for scrubbing clothes ‖ (*naut.*) a plank fixed along the gunwale or lower deck port to keep out the sea

wash·bowl (wɔ́ʃboul, wɒ́ʃboul) *n.* a washbasin

wash·cloth (wɔʃklɔθ, wɔ́ʃklɒθ, wɒ́ʃklɔθ, wɒ́ʃklɒθ) *pl.* **wash·cloths** (wɔ́ʃklɔðz, wɔ́ʃklɒðz, wɒ́ʃklɔðz, wɒ́ʃklɒðz, wɔ́ʃklɔθs, wɔ́ʃklɒθs, wɒ́ʃklɔθs, wɒ́ʃklɒθs) *n.* a cloth for washing oneself

wash drawing a drawing done mainly in washes of ink or watercolor

washed-out (wɔ́ʃtáut, wɒ́ʃtáut) *adj.* faded in color ‖ (*pop.*) tired out, played out

washed-up (wɔ́ʃtʌ́p, wɒ́ʃtʌ́p) *adj.* (*pop.,* of a person) done for, that is to be accounted a failure ‖ (*pop.,* of a thing, e.g. a marriage) come to grief

wash·er (wɔ́ʃər, wɒ́ʃər) *n.* a flat ring or perforated disk of leather, rubber, metal etc. used to tighten a joint, screw etc. ‖ a machine for washing something (e.g. clothes) ‖ an apparatus in which gases are washed

wash·er·wom·an (wɔ́ʃərwumən, wɒ́ʃərwumən) *pl.* **wash·er·wom·en** (wɔ́ʃərwimin, wɒ́ʃərwimin) *n.* a woman who earns her living by washing clothes

wash·e·te·ri·a (wɑʃətíəri:ə) *n.* (*Br.*) **1.** a self-service laundry **2.** a self-service car wash

wash·house (wɔ́ʃhaus, wɒ́ʃhaus) *pl.* **wash·hous·es** (wɔ́ʃhauziz, wɒ́ʃhauziz) *n.* an outbuilding used as a laundry

wash·i·ness (wɔ́ʃi:nis, wɒ́ʃi:nis) *n.* the state or quality of being washy

wash·ing (wɔ́ʃiŋ, wɒ́ʃiŋ) *n.* the act of a person who or thing which washes ‖ clothes, linen etc. washed or to be washed, esp. at one time ‖ (*pl.*) the metal etc. obtained by washing ore etc.

washing machine a power-driven machine for washing clothes, linen etc.

washing soda crystalline sodium carbonate

Wash·ing·ton (wɔ́ʃiŋtən, wɒ́ʃiŋtən), Booker Taliaferro (1856-1915), American educator, author and black leader

Washington, George (1732-99), first president (1789-97) of the U.S.A. under the Constitution, called the 'Father of His Country'. He gained military experience in the French and Indian War (1754-63) and as a Virginian landowner, was a leader of the opposition to British colonial policy. With the outbreak of the Revolutionary War, he was appointed (1775) commander-in-chief of the Continental army. After his victory at Yorktown (1781), he presided over the Federal Constitutional Convention of 1787 and was largely responsible for its adoption of the U.S. Constitution. Unanimously elected president, he established a nonpartisan government which was respected at home and abroad. His Federalist policy, however, and his neutrality policy in the French Revolutionary Wars aroused the opposition of the Jeffersonians,

CONCISE PRONUNCIATION KEY: **(a)** æ, *cat;* ɑ, *car;* ɔ *fawn;* ei, *snake.* **(e)** e, *hen;* i:, *sheep;* iə, *deer;* εə, *bear.* **(i)** i, *fish;* ai, *tiger;* ə:, *bird.* **(o)** o, *ox;* au, *cow;* ou, *goat;* u, *poor;* ɔi, *royal.* **(u)** ʌ, *duck;* u, *bull;* u:, *goose;* ə, *bacillus;* ju:, *cube.* x, *loch;* θ, *think;* ð, *bother;* z, *Zen;* ʒ, *corsage;* dʒ, *savage;* ŋ, *orangutang;* j, *yak;* ʃ, *fish;* tʃ, *fetch;* 'l, *rabble;* 'n, *redden.* Complete pronunciation key appears inside front cover.

which led to the organization of the Republican party (later the Democratic party)

Washington (*abbr.* Wash.) a state (area 68,192 sq. miles, pop. 4,245,000) in the northwest U.S.A. Capital: Olympia. Chief city: Seattle. The Cascade and Coast ranges cross the west. The east is an elevated plateau cut by the Columbia. Agriculture: fruit (esp. apples), vegetables, flower bulbs, wheat and other cereals, dairying. Resources: timber, building materials, uranium, lead and zinc. Industries: wood, pulp, paper, aircraft, shipbuilding, metal products, food processing, fishing. State university (1861) at Seattle. The coast was explored (late 18th c.) by the British, and the area was occupied jointly (1818-46) by Britain and the U.S.A. Washington became (1889) the 42nd state of the U.S.A.

Washington 2000 plan 1960–1980 development program for Washington, D.C., including renewal of surrounding communities

Washington, D.C. the capital (pop. 637,651) of the U.S.A., constituting the District of Columbia. The center was built on a radial plan (1793). The government buildings (White House, Capitol, Supreme Court etc.) are mainly neoclassical in style. Principal cultural institutions: National Gallery of Art, Smithsonian Institution (natural history museum), Library of Congress, Georgetown University (Catholic, 1815), George Washington University (1821), Howard University

Washington Conference (1921-2), an international meeting called by U.S. President Warren G. Harding in Washington, D.C., to negotiate a naval arms limitation program and reduce naval rivalries among the five powers. The U.S.A., Great Britain, Japan, France, Italy, China, Belgium, the Netherlands, and Portugal attended. The U.S.S.R. was excluded. In a Five-Power Treaty, the Conference agreed to limit the total capital ship tonnage of Great Britain, the U.S.A., and Japan to a ratio of 5:5:3 respectively and of France and Italy to 1.67 each. The conference produced the Four-Power Pact and an agreement to respect the military status quo in the territories and possessions of the powers in the North Pacific between Singapore and Pearl Harbor. It improved Japanese-American relations for a decade, and enhanced China's position by reaffirming the open door policy

wash·ing·to·ni·a (wɔʃiŋtóuniːə, wɒʃiŋtóuniːə) *n.* the sequoia [after George WASHINGTON]

Washington, Mount the highest peak (6,288 ft) in the White Mountains, New Hampshire, a part of the Appalachians

Washington's Birthday Feb. 22, a legal holiday in the majority of the states of the U.S.A. [after George WASHINGTON - (b. Feb. 22, 1732)]

Washington, Treaties of international agreements (1921-2) drawn up at the Washington Conference, namely the Four-Power Pact, the Naval Limitation Treaty, and the Nine-Power Treaty

Washington, Treaty of an international treaty (1871) drawn up in Washington, D.C., by an Anglo-U.S. commission. It provided notably for international arbitration in Geneva of the 'Alabama' incident. It improved relations among Great Britain, Canada and the U.S.A.

washing-up bowl (*Br.*) a dishpan

wash·leath·er (wɔ́ʃleðər, wɒ́ʃleðər) *n.* (*Br.*) a piece of soft sheepskin leather used for cleaning cars, windows etc. || this leather

wash·out (wɔ́ʃaut, wɒ́ʃaut) *n.* the washing away of earth in the bed of a road, railroad etc. by a rainstorm, flood etc. || the place where earth has been washed away || (*pop.*) someone or something which is a complete failure

wash·rag (wɔ́ʃræg, wɒ́ʃræg) *n.* a cloth for washing oneself

wash·room (wɔ́ʃruːm, wɔ́ʃrum, wɒ́ʃruːm, wɒ́ʃrum) *n.* a lavatory in a public building, store, restaurant etc.

wash sale (*stock exchange*) a pretended sale of securities to make the market appear active

wash·stand (wɔ́ʃstænd, wɒ́ʃstænd) *n.* a piece of furniture designed to hold a washbasin and toilet requisites

Wash, the a bay of the North Sea between the coasts of Lincolnshire and N. Norfolk, England

wash·tub (wɔ́ʃtʌb, wɒ́ʃtʌb) *n.* a tub in which clothes are washed

wash·y (wɔ́ʃiː, wɒ́ʃiː) *comp.* **wash·i·er** *superl.* **wash·i·est** *adj.* weak and watery, *washy soup* || (of style, emotions etc.) feeble and diffuse, *washy sentiments* || (of color) too pale

was·n't (wɒ́zənt, wʌ́zənt) *contr.* of WAS NOT

wasp (wɒsp) *n.* any of numerous winged hymenopterous insects of many different families, esp. fam. *Vespidae.* They are universally distributed and include both social and solitary forms. The wasp is characterized by its well-developed wings, slender body (the abdomen of which is attached to the thorax by a narrow stalk) and its biting mouthparts. The sting of the female and worker wasps is mortal or paralyzing to other insects, spiders etc., and very painful to man **wásp·ish** *adj.* maliciously critical or apt to be so **wásp·y** *comp.* **wasp·i·er** *superl.* **wasp·i·est** *adj.* waspish || full of wasps [O.E. *wæfs, wæps, wæsp*]

WASP or **Wasp** (*acronym*) for white Anglo-Saxon Protestant, esp a descendant of early settlers in U.S. —**Waspish** *adj.* —**Waspishness** *n.* —**Waspdom** *n.* the milieu

was·sail (wɒ́səl, wɒ́seil, wǽsəl, wǽseil, wɒséil) **1.** *n.* (*Eng. hist.*) the toast offered when presenting a person with a cup of spiced wine or ale at a festivity, or the drink itself || (*Eng hist.*) festivity with heavy drinking **2.** *v.t.* (*Eng. hist.*) to drink to the health of || *v.i.* (*Eng. hist.*) to drink a wassail [M.E. *wæs hail* fr. O.N. *ves heill* rel. to O.E. *weshál*=be in good health, be fortunate]

Was·ser·mann test (wɑ́sərmən) (*med.*) a test used to diagnose certain infectious diseases, esp. syphilis [after A. von *Wassermann* (1866–1925), G. bacteriologist].

Wast (vɑst), Hugo (Gustavo Martínez Zuviría, 1883-1962), Argentinian novelist. His novels depict rural life and tradition, notably 'Flor de Durazno' (1922),'Valle negro' (1918), and 'Desierto de piedra' (1925)

wast·age (wéistidʒ) *n.* loss by use, decay etc. || the quantity or amount so lost || avoidable loss due to wastefulness

waste (weist) **1.** *n.* expenditure of goods, materials etc. without proportionate result, *a waste of fuel, a waste of time* || needless and excessive consumption || deterioration or decay by use, misuse or lack of use || useless or damaged material produced during or left over from a manufacturing process || a region naturally barren and desolate, or made so by man || remnants of cotton fiber rejected during the process of manufacturing textiles and used to wipe machinery, absorb oil etc. || superfluous matter, e.g. garbage, rubbish, ashes, human or animal excrement || (*geog.*) the material resulting from land erosion, e.g. disintegrated rock, carried by streams to the sea **to go to waste** to be wasted, to become spoiled and useless **2.** *adj.* (of land) desolate, uncultivated, or made barren by natural catastrophe or man || (of land) not able to be cultivated || of or pertaining to refuse, *waste matter* || serving to hold or convey refuse, *a waste bin* || discarded as useless or in excess of requirements **to lay waste to** ravage [A.F. *wast*]

waste *pres. part.* **wast·ing** *past* and *past part.* **wast·ed** *v.t.* to consume or spend to no purpose, or excessively, *to waste effort* || to enfeeble and emaciate || (*rhet.*) to lay waste, to devastate **to waste away** to be in process of being used up || to destroy || to dwindle in health and vitality [A.F. *waster*]

waste·bas·ket (wéistbæskit, wéistbɑskit) *n.* a receptacle for wastepaper

waste·ful (wéistfəl) *adj.* (of a person) spending money, or using materials extravagantly || showing such extravagance, *wasteful spending* **wasteful of** causing the waste of

waste·land (wéistlænd) *n.* a tract of desolate, uncultivated country || a devastated area || a period in life or history thought of as spiritually barren

waste·pa·per (wéistpeipər) *n.* paper thrown away as being no longer useful

wastepaper basket a wastebasket

waste pipe a pipe connecting with a sewer etc. to carry away bath water, sink water etc.

waste products refuse produced during or left over from a manufacturing process || material, e.g. feces, excreted from a living human or animal body

wast·er (wéistər) *n.* a ruinously extravagant, self-centered person without moral strength

wast·rel (wéistrəl) *n.* (*old-fash.*) a waster

watch (wɒtʃ) *n.* a small portable timepiece worked by a coiled spring, and designed to be worn on the wrist or carried in a pocket etc. || (*naut.*) a period of time (usually 4 hours) during which part of a ship's company is required to be on duty || (*naut.*) that part of a ship's company on duty for a specified period || (*naut.*) a sailor's period of duty || a person or group of persons on duty, esp. at night, for purposes of guarding, protecting etc. || (*hist.*) a guard, esp. a watchman or watchmen patrolling the streets at night || (*hist.*) a division of the night (into three watches by the Jews and four watches by the Romans) **on the watch** on the lookout **to keep watch** to keep awake and alert for purposes of observing, discovering etc. || (with 'over') to do this for the purpose of protecting or guarding [O.E. *wæcce*]

watch *v.t.* to observe (someone or something) attentively, *to watch someone's reaction* || to be a spectator at, *to watch a play on television* || to look after, *to watch sheep* || to take a professional or private interest in, *to watch a patient's progress* || to be careful about, pay attention to, *watch your manners* || (*Br.*) to sit in on the trial of (a case) on behalf of a client who may be indirectly concerned || *v.i.* to be closely observant, *to watch while an experiment is being performed* || to stay awake, esp. at night, in order to attend a sick person, guard a prisoner etc. || to be a spectator (as distinct from a participant) || (with 'for') to keep a lookout, *watch for the postman* **to watch one's step** to act cautiously, proceed with care **to watch out** to keep a lookout || to be careful **to watch over** to keep protective watch over (esp. a sick person) [fr. stem of O.E. *wacian,* to wake]

watch·case (wɒ́tʃkeis) *n.* the metal case enclosing the mechanism of a watch

Watch Committee (*Br.*) a special body of a county or borough council dealing with police discipline and matters of public order

watch crystal a cover of glass or plastic protecting the face of a watch

watch·dog (wɒ́tʃdɔg, wɒ́tʃdɒg) *n.* a dog kept to guard property

Watchdog Committee *n.* **1.** originally, a Congressional Intelligence Oversight Board created to oversee activities of CIA by Executive Officers **2.** by extension, any oversight committee

watch fire a fire lighted at night in a camp

watch·ful (wɒ́tʃfəl) *adj.* keenly observant or vigilant

watch glass (*Br.*) a crystal (cover of glass or plastic over the face of a watch)

watching brief (*Br.*) the brief of a barrister who watches a case for an indirectly concerned client

watch·mak·er (wɒ́tʃmeikər) *n.* a person who makes or repairs watches

watch·mak·ing (wɒ́tʃmeikiŋ) *n.* the business of making or repairing watches

watch·man (wɒ́tʃmən) *pl.* **watch·men** (wɒ́tʃmən) *n.* a guard, esp. of a large building at night

watch night a religious service lasting until after midnight on New Year's Eve (a practice begun by the Methodists in the 18th c.)

watch·tow·er (wɒ́tʃtauər) *n.* an observation tower from which a guard keeps lookout

watch·word (wɒ́tʃwəːrd) *n.* a motto or slogan, esp. one used as a rallying cry

wa·ter (wɔ́tər, wɒ́tər) **1.** *n.* the transparent, colorless liquid, H_2O, which falls from the sky as rain, issues from the ground in springs, and composes three-quarters of the earth's surface in the form of seas, rivers, lakes etc. || a body of this liquid || this liquid with reference to its level (*HIGH WATER, *LOW WATER) || the depth of this liquid, esp. with reference to displacement, *the boat draws 6 ft of water* || a solution of some substance in this liquid, *ammonia water* || any of various bodily fluids or secretions, e.g. tears, saliva, urine, amniotic fluid || a shiny, wavy pattern imparted to some fabrics, e.g. silk, or some metals || (*pl.*) natural mineral water || (*jewelry*) the luster or transparency of a diamond or a pearl || (*commerce*) nominal capital created by the issue of shares without a corresponding increase of paid-up capital or assets **by water** by ship or boat **in deep water** in great difficulties **in smooth water** in the state of no longer having difficulties **of the first water** (of a diamond or pearl) of first quality || (of a person in a specified category) of the finest quality, *a pianist of the first water* **on** (or **upon**) **the water** (of a person) on a ship at sea || (of a ship) at sea **to keep one's head above water** to manage to stay out of esp. financial difficulties, but only with a great struggle **to make one's mouth water** to excite a strong desire in one by looking or smelling appetizing **to make water** to urinate ||

(of a ship or boat) to leak or ship water **to take** (or **take in**) **water** (of a ship or boat) to leak or ship water **to throw** (or **dash** or **pour**) **cold water on** to take a discouraging attitude towards (a plan etc.) **2.** *v.i.* (of the eyes) to run or fill with tears ‖ (of the mouth) to fill with saliva ‖ (esp. of a ship) to take on a supply of water ‖ (of animals) to drink water, *the cattle water at the creek* ‖ *v.t.* to soak or wet with water, *to water a garden* ‖ to give water to (an animal) to drink, *have the horses been watered?* ‖ to furnish (e.g. an army or a ship) with a supply of water ‖ to dilute by adding water to ‖ (*commerce*) to dilute (stock) by issuing shares uncovered by any increase of assets ‖ to impart a shiny, wavy pattern to (a fabric) by calendering ‖ (of a river etc.) to supply water to (land) ‖ to sprinkle (a road etc.) with water in order to lay dust **to water down** to dilute with or as if with water ‖ to make (criticism) less forceful by adding remarks intended to mollify [O.E. *wæter*]

—Pure water is odorless, tasteless, transparent (although bluish in bulk) and relatively incompressible. It has a high specific heat and poor electrical conductivity. Under standard pressure it freezes (with slight expansion) to ice at 0°C, and boils at 100°C giving steam. The density is a maximum at 4°C, where it is taken as exactly 1 gm/cm^3. Water has the chemical composition H_2O, ionizing as $H_2O=H^++OH^-$. It is neutral, a good ionizing agent and a good solvent

water bear a tardigrade

water bed a bed whose mattress is a vinyl bag filled with water, sometimes temperature controlled

water beetle any of numerous aquatic beetles, esp. of fam. *Dytiscidae,* having fringed hind legs that function like oars

water bird a swimming or wading bird

water biscuit a thin hard biscuit usually made of flour and water

water boatman *pl.* **water boatmen** a hemipteran insect of fam. *Notonectidae,* living in still water. They move about the surface of water upside down, and are also good swimmers, propelling themselves with their long, thin, hairy hind legs

wa·ter·buck (wɔ́tərbʌk, wɒ́tərbʌk) *n.* any of various antelopes that live close to rivers and swim with ease, esp. either of two species of *kobus* of E. Africa [Du. *waterbok*]

water buffalo *pl.* **water buffalo, water buffaloes** *Bubalus bubalis* (or *Bos bubalis),* fam. *Bovidae,* the common domesticated Indian buffalo, used in most of the warm countries of Asia as a draft and milch animal

water butt a large open barrel for catching and storing rainwater

water cannon a large hose, usu. mounted on a truck, used to discharge pressurized water for riot control

water cart (*Br.*) a watering cart

water clock (*hist.*) a device for measuring time by the flow of a certain quantity of water

water closet (*abbr.* W.C.) a toilet (plumbing fixture) or the room containing it

wa·ter·col·or, *Br.* **wa·ter·col·our** (wɔ́tərkʌlər, wɒ́tərkʌlər) *n.* paint in solid or semisolid form for which water, rather than oil, is the solvent ‖ a picture executed with this paint ‖ the art of painting with this paint **wá·ter·col·or·ist,** *Br.* **wá·ter·col·our·ist** *n.*

wa·ter-cool (wɔ́tərkuːl, wɒ́tərkuːl) *v.t.* to cool (e.g. an engine) by means of circulating water

water cooler a device for dispensing cold drinking water in some public place

wa·ter·course (wɔ́tərkɔrs, wɔ́tərkours, wɒ́tərkɔrs, wɒ́tərkours) *n.* a stream of water, e.g. a river or brook ‖ the bed of such a stream, whether this flows permanently or seasonally ‖ a natural or artificial channel (e.g. a canal) for carrying water

wa·ter·craft (wɔ́tərkræft, wɔ́tərkrɑft, wɒ́tərkræft, wɒ́tərkrɑft) *n.* ships, boats etc. collectively ‖ skill in managing boats etc.

wa·ter·cress (wɔ́tərkres, wɒ́tərkres) *n. Nasturtium officinale,* fam. *Cruciferae,* a perennial cress living in running streams. Its pungent leaves are eaten as salad, cooked in soup etc.

wa·ter·fall (wɔ́tərfɔl, wɒ́tərfɔl) *n.* a steep or perpendicular descent of a stream or river

water flea any of various small, active aquatic crustaceans of genera *Cyclops* and *Daphnia*

wa·ter·flood (wɔ́tərflʌd) *n.* a process for pumping steam or water into a seemingly depleted oil well to force out residual oil. —**waterflood** *v.*

Wa·ter·ford (wɔ́tərfərd, wɒ́tərfərd) a southern county (area 710 sq. miles, pop. 77,315) of Munster province, Irish Republic ‖ its county seat (pop. 31,968), a port

wa·ter·fowl (wɔ́tərfaul, wɒ́tərfaul) *pl.* **wa·ter·fowl** *n.* any bird that frequents rivers and lakes, esp. a swimming bird ‖ (*pl.*) swimming game birds

water fowling the hunting of water fowl —**water fowl** *v.* —**water fowler** *n.*

wa·ter·front (wɔ́tərfrʌnt, wɒ́tərfrʌnt) *n.* the land or land and buildings or a section of a town abutting on a body of water

water gage, *Br.* **water gauge** an instrument attached to a steam boiler etc. for indicating the height of water inside ‖ water pressure expressed as a height in inches

water gap a pass in mountains with a stream running through it

water gas a mixture of carbon monoxide and hydrogen, obtained by passing steam over or through glowing coke kept at a high temperature by intermittent blasts of hot air. It is used chiefly as a source of hydrogen and in the manufacture of liquid fuels

water gate a floodgate for controlling the flow of water ‖ a gate giving access from a property to a river etc.

water gauge *WATER GAGE

water glass a tube or box with a glass bottom for examining objects under water ‖ (*chem.*) a viscous solution of sodium or potassium silicate, used for preserving eggs and in the manufacture of soaps and detergents, and in industry as a protective cement

water hammer the loud thumping noise in a water pipe caused by an air pocket interrupting the flow of water or by the entrance of water into a steam pipe

water hen the European moorhen ‖ the American coot ‖ any of several Australian birds of the genus *Tribonyx*

water hole a cavity or depression where water gathers, esp. a pool in a dry river bed ‖ a hole in the surface of ice

water hyacinth *Eichhornia crassipes,* fam. *Pontederiaceae,* a tropical floating aquatic plant troublesome as a river weed, esp. in Florida

water ice a dessert of frozen water, sweetened and flavored with fruit juice

wa·ter·i·ness (wɔ́tәriːnis, wɒ́tәriːnis) *n.* the state or quality of being watery

watering can a metal or plastic container having a spout with (usually) a perforated nozzle, for watering plants

watering cart (*Am.=Br.* water cart) a tank on wheels carrying water or for sprinkling roads etc.

watering place a place where animals resort to drink ‖ a place where water can be obtained ‖ (*old-fash.*) a resort for swimming, boating etc. ‖ (*old-fash.*) a resort having mineral springs

water jacket a casing, through which water is circulated, surrounding a piece of machinery, esp. in the cooling system of many internal-combustion engines

water jump a water obstacle for a horse or runner in a steeplechase

water level the surface level of a body of water ‖ the waterline of a ship ‖ an instrument for showing the level of a body of water

water lily *pl.* **water lilies** any of several aquatic plants of fam. *Nymphaeaceae,* having large floating leaves and white or brightly colored (esp. yellow) flowers, found in warm and tropical fresh water

wa·ter·line (wɔ́tərlain, wɒ́tərlain) *n.* any of various lines on a ship up to which she may be submerged in the water, esp. when fully loaded (*PLIMSOLL LINE) ‖ (*papermaking*) a linear watermark ‖ the surface level of a body of water ‖ the mark left e.g. on a building by water which has subsided

wa·ter·logged (wɔ́tərlɔgd, wɔ́tərlɒgd, wɒ́tərlɔgd, wɒ́tərlɒgd) *adj.* (of ground) soaked with water, saturated ‖ (of a ship or boat) so full of water that she hardly floats and can barely be managed ‖ (of wood) so saturated with water that it has lost its buoyancy

Wa·ter·loo, Battle of (wɔtərlúː, wɒtərlúː) the final action (June 18, 1815) of the Napoleonic Wars, fought near the Belgian village of Waterloo. Napoleon was defeated by the British and Prussian armies under Wellington and Blücher

water main the main pipe in a water supply system

wa·ter·man (wɔ́tərmən, wɒ́tərmən) *pl.* **wa·ter·men** (wɔ́tərmən, wɒ́tərmən) *n.* a boatman, esp. one who makes a living by hiring out boats

wa·ter·mark (wɔ́tərmɑrk, wɒ́tərmɑrk) **1.** *n.* a mark showing the level to which water has risen or is expected to rise ‖ a faint translucent design impressed on certain kinds of paper at the moment of manufacture and visible only against the light, serving as a trademark or indication of type, size, category etc., and important in philately for the classification of stamps **2.** *v.t.* to stamp (paper) with a watermark ‖ to impress (a certain design) as a watermark

water meadow a meadow that is flooded at certain seasons

wa·ter·mel·on (wɔ́tərmelən, wɒ́tərmelən) *n. Citrullus vulgaris,* fam. *Cucurbitaceae,* a trailing vine native to tropical Africa but widely cultivated, esp. in warm climates ‖ its large round or elongated fruit, having a green or white rind and a pink, red or yellow, edible, very juicy, sweet pulp

water mill a mill powered by water

water moccasin *Agkistrodon piscivorus,* a pit viper of esp. the southern U.S.A. It is semi-aquatic and lives mainly in marshes and ditches

water nymph (*Gk* and *Rom. mythol.*) a goddess, e.g. a naiad, who lives in—or (in some cases) presides over—a body of water

water of constitution (*chem.*) water combined in a molecule in such a way that it cannot be expelled without destroying the unity of the entire molecule

water of crystallization (*chem.*) water of hydration found in many crystallized substances

water of hydration (*chem.*) water combined with some substance to form a hydrate. It can be expelled without fundamentally altering the composition of the substance

water on the brain hydrocephalus

water on the knee inflamed material exuded from the blood cells in the area of the knee joint following an injury to this part

water ouzel a member of *Cinclus,* fam. *Cinclidae,* a genus of birds related to the thrushes. They are able to walk on the bottom of streams in search of food

Water Pik a trademarked device designed to clean teeth by directing forceful streams of water onto and between teeth. *also* water toothpick, water pulse

water polo a game played in water by two teams of seven swimmers who pass a ball resembling a soccer ball to each other and try to throw it into the opponents' goal

wa·ter·pow·er (wɔ́tərpauər, wɒ́tərpauər) *n.* the energy of moving water converted into mechanical energy

wa·ter·proof (wɔ́tərpruːf, wɒ́tərpruːf) **1.** *adj.* that will not let water in or through **2.** *n.* (*Br.*) a waterproof garment, esp. a raincoat **3.** *v.t.* to make waterproof (e.g. by applying a silicone to a fabric)

water rail *Rallus aquaticus,* a European rail that lives in marshes

water rat a member of *Arvicola,* a genus of large aquatic voles ‖ a muskrat

water rate the charge for supply of water filtered, purified and piped to the consumer

wa·ter-re·pel·lent (wɔ́tərripelənt, wɒ́tərripelənt) *adj.* having a finish that minimizes absorption of water

water sail a sail set below a lower studding sail and close to the water, used when the breeze is extremely slight

water scorpion any of numerous aquatic insects of fam. *Nepidae,* having a long breathing tube extending from the abdomen

water seal a body of water in the bend of a pipe to prevent the passage of gas

wa·ter·shed (wɔ́tərʃed, wɒ́tərʃed) *n.* a ridge, or other line of separation, between two river systems or drainage areas ‖ the catchment area of a river system

wa·ter·side (wɔ́tərsaid, wɒ́tərsaid) **1.** *n.* the land on the edge of a river, lake or sea **2.** *adj.* of or on the waterside ‖ living or employed on the waterside

wa·ter-ski (wɔ́tərskiː, wɒ́tərskiː) *v.i.* to skim across water on short, broad skis (water skis) while being towed by a motorboat

water snake a member of *Natrix,* a genus of harmless freshwater snakes widely distributed in eastern U.S.A.

wa·ter-sol·u·ble (wɔ́tərsɒljub'l, wɒ́tərsɒljub'l) *adj.* (esp. of certain vitamins) soluble in water

water spider *Argyroneta aquatica*, a European aquatic spider that spins a balloon-shaped web beneath the surface of the water

wa·ter·spout (wɔ́tərspaut, wɒ́tərspaut) *n.* a pipe etc. for clearing water off a roof ‖ a column or spout of mist, spray and water caused by the meeting of a funnel-shaped cloud (extending from a heavy cumulonimbus cloud) and a mass of spray thrown up from the sea by a whirling wind. Waterspouts are most common in tropical or subtropical regions

water sprite a water nymph

water suit (*mil.*) a g-suit in which water is used in the interlining, automatically approximating the required hydrostatic pressure-gradient under G forces. *Cf* PRESSURE SUIT

water supply a system of storing water in reservoirs and piping it for use in houses, factories etc. ‖ the water thus stored

water table (*archit.*) a projecting, horizontal ledge set along the side of a wall for throwing off rainwater ‖ the surface below which the ground is saturated with water ‖ a gutter at the side of a road to take away water

wa·ter·tight (wɔ́tərtait, wɒ́tərtait) *adj.* constructed so as to be impermeable to water ‖ not liable to doubt, thoroughly sound, *a watertight alibi, a watertight project*

watertight compartment one of the compartments in a large ship, equipped with watertight doors or partitions which enable it to be sealed off completely in case of an emergency

water tower an elevated tank or reservoir into which water is pumped, thus furnishing a steady pressure to the system it feeds ‖ a fire-fighting apparatus capable of projecting water at a considerable height

water vapor, *Br.* **water vapour** water in the vapor state and below the critical temperature for water, in the earth's atmosphere (cf. STEAM)

wa·ter·way (wɔ́tərwei, wɒ́tərwei) *n.* a navigable channel, esp. a dredged river or canal ‖ a wooden channel hollowed out of thick planks along the edge of a ship's deck to drain away water into the scuppers ‖ a traffic route by water

wa·ter·wheel (wɔ́tərhwi:l, wɔ́tərwi:l, wɒ́tərhwi:l, wɒ́tərwi:l) *n.* a wheel rotated by the flow of water and used to work machinery, esp. in a mill ‖ a contrivance for raising water in buckets worked by a wheel

water wings inflated supports for a person learning to swim

wa·ter·works (wɔ́tərwə:rks, wɒ́tərwə:rks) *pl. n.* (usually construed as *sing.*) a system of reservoirs, mains, pumping stations etc. for the conservation and distribution of a water supply

wa·ter·y (wɔ́təri:, wɒ́təri:) *adj.* containing too much water, overdiluted, *watery soup* ‖ soggy, *watery cabbage* ‖ soaked in or running with liquid, moist, *watery eyes* ‖ suggesting rain, rainy looking, *a watery sky* ‖ (of color) washy, *a watery green* ‖ (of blisters, pustules etc.) exuding a liquid resembling water

Wat·kin Mtns (wɒ́tkin) mountains in S.E. Greenland containing the highest peak (12,200 ft) in the country

Wat·lings Island (wɒ́tliŋz) *SAN SALVADOR

WATS (*acronym*) for Wide Area Telecommunication Service (which see)

Wat·son (wɒ́tsən), James Dewey (1928-), U.S. biologist. He researched into the molecular structure of deoxyribonucleic acid (DNA). In 1962 he shared the Nobel prize for physiology or medicine

Watson, John Broadus (1878-1958), American psychologist. He originated the school of psychology known as behaviorism

Wat·son-Watt (wɒ́tsənwɒ́t), Sir Robert Alexander (1892-1973), Scottish physicist. His proposals for locating aircraft by radio-pulse echo detection led to the development of radar

Watt (wɒt), James (1736-1819), Scottish engineer who made (1765) fundamental improvements to the Newcomen steam engine, leading to the widespread use of steam power in mines, factories etc. In partnership with Matthew Boulton, Watt built many engines at their foundry in Birmingham. The unit of power is named after him

watt (wɒt) *n.* the mks unit of power, equal to 1 joule/sec (1/746 horsepower) [after James WATT]

watt·age (wɒ́tidʒ) *n.* amount of electrical power expressed in watts

Wat·teau (vætou, wɒ́tou, wɒtóu), Jean Antoine (1684-1721), French painter. His work expresses the 18th-c. ideal of courtly grace and elegance beneath which one discerns a keen intelligence and an underlying melancholy. His favorite scenes are leafy parks in which satin-clad aristocrats pay court in a shimmer of approaching twilight, and of country festivals in which burly peasants and robust working people wear the costumes and masks of the commedia dell' arte. Watteau was a superb draftsman (e.g. his chalk studies) and colorist

Wat·ter·son (wɒ́tərs'n), Henry (1840-1921), U.S. journalist and newspaper editor. With Walter N. Haldeman he became (1868) founding-editor of the Louisville Courier-Journal, one of the South's most influential newspapers. He was largely responsible for the nomination of Samuel J. Tilden as the Democratic candidate in the 1876 presidential election

watt-hour (wɒ́tauər) *n.* a unit of energy equivalent to the power of one watt operating for one hour, and equivalent to 3,600 joules

wat·tle (wɒ́t'l) **1.** *n.* a framework of interwoven sticks and twigs used to make walls, fences and roofs ‖ (*sing.* or *pl.*) rods and twigs so used, esp. to support a thatched roof ‖ any of various trees and shrubs of the genus *Acacia* ‖ wattle bark **2.** *v.t. pres. part.* **wat·tling** *past* and *past part.* **wat·tled** to weave (twigs etc.) into wattle ‖ to make (walls etc.) of wattle ‖ to use (fence posts etc.) to make a barrier by interweaving flexible twigs and branches [O.E. *watul*]

wattle *n.* a wrinkled, usually brightly colored flap of skin hanging from the throat of some birds, e.g. the turkey, and some reptiles ‖ a barbel of a fish [origin unknown]

wattle bark the bark obtained from various Australian acacias and used in tanning

watt·me·ter (wɒ́tmi:tər) *n.* an instrument for measuring electrical power, esp. in watts

Watts (wɒts), Isaac (1674-1748), English hymn writer

Wa·tu·si (watú:tsi:) *pl.* **Wa·tu·si, Wa·tu·sis** *n.* a tribe of tall, cattle-raising people inhabiting Burundi and Rwanda ‖ a member of this tribe

Waugh (wɔ), Evelyn (1903-66), British novelist. Hilarious satirical early novels include 'Decline and Fall' (1929) and 'Vile Bodies' (1930). Later works include 'Brideshead Revisited' (1944) and the war trilogy 'Men at Arms' (1952), 'Officers and Gentlemen' (1955) and 'Unconditional Surrender' (1961), brought together in 'The Sword of Honour'

wave (weiv) **1.** *n.* (*phys.*) an energy-bearing, self-propagating disturbance in a medium or in space, that may be in the form of an elastic displacement of the particles of the medium, or of a cyclical change in its temperature or pressure, or a variation in the electric, magnetic or electric potential field of space ‖ a wave form ‖ a forward-moving swell on the surface of a liquid (e.g. of the ocean). The particles that make it up have an oscillatory motion, perpendicular to the direction of its motion. Its size depends on its cause, e.g. the friction between the water and the wind ‖ something which has the shape of a wave, e.g. an undulation in hair or in a rippling flag ‖ a gesture of the hand or arm in a sweeping movement ‖ a sudden temporary surge of strong feeling, *a wave of disgust* ‖ a natural or social phenomenon resulting in a sudden increase, *a crime wave* ‖ a movement having the impetus of an ocean wave, e.g. an advance of soldiers or a great influx of migrating people or animals ‖ (*pl., rhet.*) the ocean **2.** *v. pres. part.* **wav·ing** *past* and *past part.* **waved** *v.t.* to cause to move to and fro with a motion resembling that of a wave, *to wave a handkerchief* ‖ to make a threatening gesture with, *he waved his fist in my face* ‖ to call, order, express etc. with a waving motion of the hand or arm, *to wave good-bye* ‖ to give the form of waves to, *to wave one's hair* ‖ *v.i.* to move to and fro or up and down with the motion of a wave ‖ to have the form of a wave or waves, *her hair waves naturally* ‖ to make a signal of farewell, welcome etc. by moving something to and fro etc. with a wavelike motion **to wave aside** to dismiss (objections etc.) airily [O.E. *wafian*]

wave band a range of radio frequencies within which a radio or television transmission is permitted

wave cloud a lens-shaped cloud indicating a high point in air motion, an important phenomenon in glider aeronautics

wave equation the fundamental equation of wave mechanics. It is a partial differential equation whose physically admissible solutions (wave functions) describe states in which the system may exist. These states possess certain characteristic values of energy and angular momentum (*QUANTUM NUMBER). The square of the modulus of the wave function is proportional to the probability that the particle may be found in a given region at any given time when it is in a state represented by that wave function

wave form (*phys.*) a curve that represents graphically the state of a wave-propagating medium at an instant in time or the condition at a single point in the medium during the passage of a disturbance. Wave forms are usually constructed on rectangular coordinates whose ordinates represent the values of the propagated variation, corresponding to distance or time of propagation on the other axis

wave front (*phys.*) the surface comprising at some given moment the positions just reached by the waves proceeding from a given source ‖ a surface that is the locus of all points of a wave producing equal distortion in a wave-propagating medium

wave function (*phys., abbr. Q*, ψ) a solution of the wave equation (*ORBITAL)

wave guide (*phys.*) a hollow metal conductor or cylindrical dielectric through which electromagnetic waves of length approx. 1 cm. (radar and television range) are transmitted with low energy loss by radiation and attenuation

wave·length (wéivleŋθ) *n.* (*phys.*, symbol λ) the distance, measured parallel to the path of propagation of a wave, between any point and the next successive point in phase at the same instant (e.g. the distance between successive points of maximum or minimum amplitude on the wave form)

wave·let (wéivlit) *n.* a tiny wave, a ripple ‖ (*phys.*) an elementary wave considered as a point source of a continuing disturbance

Wa·vell (wéivəl), Archibald Percival, 1st Earl Wavell (1883-1950), British field marshal. As commander in chief of the Middle East (1939-41) he distinguished himself in N. Africa. He was commander in chief in India (1941-3) and viceroy of India (1943-7)

wave mechanics a branch of quantum mechanics which represents the state of a physical system by means of an equation (*WAVE EQUATION) that attributes to the particle a wave character (*WAVE-PARTICLE DUALITY). This equation may be solved to provide meaningful values which accord with the wave character of the particle (*QUANTUM NUMBER), for the energy, momentum and position (e.g. an electron moving in the potential field of a nucleus). Such solutions are of an essentially statistical character, giving the probability that the particle will be in a given region at a given time rather than giving definite positions etc. Although wave-mechanics procedures lead in principle to exact solutions for any physical problem, they are of such great mathematical complexity that in practice only the simplest (2-body) systems (e.g. the hydrogen atom) can at present be solved exactly

wave motion (*phys.*) the motion of the particles of a medium in mechanically propagated waves (e.g. in water waves or sound waves)

wave number (*phys.*, used only of electromagnetic waves) the number of waves per centimeter of radiation of a given wavelength, being the reciprocal of the wavelength in centimeters (cf. FREQUENCY, cf. PERIOD)

wave-particle duality the concept in modern physics that associates a wavelength with a material particle, or a momentum of energy with a wave, in order to explain certain phenomena. Thus, electrons may be diffracted as if they were waves of wavelength $\lambda = h/mv$, where h is the Planck constant, m is the mass and v the velocity of the electron. Similarly electromagnetic radiation may behave as a beam of particles (e.g. photons in photoemission). It is found that electrons, photons, neutrons etc. have the properties of both waves and particles, and it may be appropriate to employ either wave mechanics or particle mechanics in their study

wa·ver (wéivər) **1.** *v.i.* to hesitate between a choice of opinions or courses of action, *she wavered between going and staying* ‖ to begin to give way, to falter, *his confidence wavered under cross-examination* ‖ to move about unsteadily, *a wavering flame* ‖ (of the voice or a

glance) to be unsteady **2.** *n.* a wavering [M.E. *waveren* fr. *waven,* to wave]
wave theory a theory in physics that light is transmitted by a wave motion (cf. CORPUSCULAR THEORY, *WAVE MECHANICS)
wave train (*phys.*) a uniform periodic wave of finite duration
wav·i·ly (wéivili:) *adv.* in a wavy manner
wav·i·ness (wéivi:nis) *n.* the state or quality of being wavy
wav·y (wéivi:) *comp.* **wav·i·er** *superl.* **wav·i·est** *adj.* (of a line or surface) having a form consisting of a succession of many little waves ‖ moving back and forth in a wavelike way, *fields of wavy corn*
wax (wæks) **1.** *n.* any of numerous mixtures that differ from fats in being harder and less greasy and that are principally constituted from higher fatty acids in the form of esters, e.g. beeswax, carnauba wax ‖ cerumen ‖ any of various natural or synthetic substances resembling wax in physical or chemical properties or both, e.g. paraffin wax ‖ a resinous preparation used by shoemakers for rubbing thread ‖ sealing wax **2.** *v.t.* to apply wax to [O.E. *weax*]
wax *v.i.* (esp. of the moon) to increase in size and brilliance until full (cf. WANE) ‖ (*rhet.*) to grow, to become (as specified), *to wax eloquent* [O.E. *weaxan*]
wax bean any of various kidney beans having long, yellow edible pods
wax·ber·ry (wǽksberi:) *pl.* **wax·ber·ries** *n.* the waxy fruit of the wax myrtle ‖ the snowberry
wax·bill (wǽksbil) *n.* a member of *Estrilda,* fam. *Ploceidae,* a genus of small seed-eating birds, having bright bills resembling red, pink or white sealing wax, commonly kept as cage birds
waxed paper paper coated with white wax to make it waterproof and greaseproof
wax·en (wǽksən) *adj.* resembling wax ‖ covered with wax ‖ made of wax
wax·i·ness (wǽksi:nis) *n.* the state or quality of being waxy
wax insect any of various wax-secreting scale insects of fam. *Coccidae,* esp. *Ericerus pe-la,* a Chinese variety
wax myrtle any of various shrubs or trees of fam. *Myricideae,* esp. *Myrica cerifera,* a shrub of eastern North America having aromatic foliage and small hard berries coated with a grayish-white wax that is used for making candles
wax palm *Ceroxylon andicolum,* a South American palm, the stem of which secretes a resinous wax ‖ the carnauba
wax paper paper coated with white wax to make it waterproof and greaseproof
wax·wing (wǽkswiŋ) *n.* a member of *Bombycilla,* fam. *Bombycillidae,* a genus of American and European passerine birds having a showy crest, brown, velvety plumage and secondary quills with tips resembling scarlet sealing wax
wax·work (wǽkswə:rk) *n.* a figure modeled in wax, usually representing a famous or notorious person, living or dead ‖ (*pl.*) an exhibition of such wax figures (*TUSSAUD)
wax·y (wǽksi:) *comp.* **wax·i·er** *superl.* **wax·i·est** *adj.* made of or resembling wax ‖ covered with or as if with wax ‖ (of tissue) affected with amyloid degeneration
way (wei) *n.* the course taken, or to be taken, in getting from one place to another, or the ground traveled over in taking such a course, *the way to the beach is rocky, clear the way* ‖ the distance to be moved through in going from one place to another, *a long way to Rome* ‖ direction of movement, *come this way* ‖ (with 'in') an aspect, respect, *in some ways you are mistaken* ‖ a characteristic trait of behavior, *winning ways* ‖ (with 'with') the ability to please, *a way with girls* ‖ (with 'with') the ability to handle or manipulate, *a way with motors* ‖ the procedures etc. involved in an activity, *the way to tie a reef knot* ‖ (*naut.*) the motion or rate of progress of a vessel through water ‖ (*naut., pl.*) the wooden structure over which a ship moves when being launched ‖ (*pl.*) the parallel guides on the bed of a machine, e.g. a lathe, along which a carriage moves ‖ (*pop.*) one's physical, mental, moral or economic condition, *in a poor way* ‖ (*pop.*) a district, area, *down our way* **by the way** along or near the side of the road ‖ incidentally **by way of** by a route passing through, *to Hong Kong by way of the Suez Canal* ‖ (followed by a gerund) in the state of, *she is by way of being a fine actress* **each way** (*Br.,* of a bet) laid for a win or a place **in a way** despite certain reservations, *I like the work in a way* **in the family way** (*old-fash.*) pregnant **in the way of** in the course of **once in a way** (*Br.*) occasionally **on the** (or **its** etc.) **way** in transit, *the package is on the way* ‖ in the course of the journey, *it happened on the way to Quebec* **out of harm's way** stored away safely **the way of the world** the way people do behave (rather than the way they should behave) **to come one's way** to come into one's experience or possession **to feel one's way** to proceed with great caution **to gather way** (*naut.*) to increase in speed from being stationary, or nearly so, until the engines or sails control movement **to give way** to yield ‖ to break, collapse **to go one's own way** to act independently **to go on one's way** to resume a journey **to go out of one's way** to put oneself to some trouble, *he went out of his way to amuse the children* **to have it both ways** to benefit by each of two contrary possibilities **to have** (or **get**) **one's way** to do (or be allowed to do) what one wishes **to know one's way around** to be experienced enough to be able to protect one's interests or achieve one's purposes in circumstances where the ignorant would find it hard to do so **to lead the way** to go first and lead others **to make one's own way** to prosper by one's own resources **to make one's way** to advance, esp. in a leisurely manner **to pave the way for** to take the preliminary actions which will cause or permit (something) to happen **to pay its way** (esp. of a business) to be self-supporting **to pay one's own way** to meet one's own expenses **to see one's way clear** to feel that one can and should do something, *I can't see my way clear to taking that trip* **to stand in the way of** to be an obstacle to **under way** (*naut.,* of a ship or boat) making headway ‖ making progress [O.E. *weg*]
way *adv.* to a great degree, *way too deep* ‖ at a great distance, *way over there* [aphetic var. of AWAY]
way·bill (wéibil) *n.* a document containing information as to the nature of a shipment of goods in transit and instructions for delivery
way·far·er (wéifɛərər) *n.* (*rhet.*) a traveler, esp. on foot
way·far·ing (wéifɛəriŋ) *adj.* (*rhet.*) traveling, esp. on foot
wayfaring tree *Viburnum lantana,* fam. *Caprifoliaceae,* a Eurasian shrub related to the guelder rose, and bearing dense white flowers and black berries. It is frequently found growing along the roadside ‖ *V. alnifolium,* a North American shrub
way·lay (weiléi) *pres. part.* **way·lay·ing** *past* and *past part.* **way·laid** (weiléid) *v.t.* to wait for and attack in order to rob etc. ‖ to catch (someone) on his way somewhere in order to engage him in conversation
Wayne (wein), Anthony (1745-96), American general. He distinguished himself by his courage and daring tactics in the Revolutionary War
way-out (wéiaut) *adj.* (*slang*) **1.** extreme **2.** unreal. *syn.* far-out
-ways *suffix* used to indicate direction, manner etc., as in 'sideways' [orig. gen. of WAY n.]
ways and means methods by which money can be raised or made available
way·side (wéisaid) **1.** *n.* the side of a road etc. **2.** *adj.* situated on, at or near the side of a road etc.
way station (*Am.=Br.* halt) a minor stopping place without a siding or facilities for handling goods other than passengers' luggage
way train a local train
way·ward (wéiwərd) *adj.* willfully turning away from what is right and proper, and heedless of the counsel of others, or showing willfulness and heedlessness [shortened fr. older *awayward*]
wayz·goose (wéizgu:s) *n.* the annual festivity (esp. an outing) of the employees in a printing establishment [etym. doubtful]
Wa·zir·i·stan (wəziristán) a mountainous, arid, border region of Pakistan, inhabited by unsubdued nomadic Pathan tribes, and disputed by Afghanistan
we (wi:) *pron., 1st person pl., nominative case* oneself and others, as named by oneself ‖ (used formally, esp. by a sovereign, an author or a judge) I [O.E. *we, wē*]
weak (wi:k) *adj.* having little physical strength, *too weak to climb higher* ‖ lacking force, *a weak blow* ‖ able to resist only small strains, *a weak link* ‖ low in intensity, *weak sight* ‖ having a desired quality in only a slight degree, *a weak joke, weak tea* ‖ morally feeble, *weak will* ‖ ineffective in the use of authority, *a weak government* ‖ lacking logical or persuasive force, *a weak argument* ‖ deficient in mental power, *a weak mind* ‖ having or showing a lack of knowledge or skill, *weak in history, a weak set of answers* ‖ (of bodily organs) liable to collapse or not performing well, *a weak bladder* ‖ (*gram.*) of a verb which is inflected by adding a suffix to the stem, not by an internal vowel change ‖ (*gram.*) of Germanic nouns and adjectives inflected by the addition of a suffix formerly belonging to a stem in -n ‖ (*prosody,* of a verse ending) not stressed ‖ (*commerce*) tending toward lower prices, *a weak market* ‖ (*chem.,* of an acid or base) only slightly ionized in solution **wéak·en** *v.t.* to make weak ‖ *v.i.* to become weak [O.N. *veikr*]
weak·fish (wí:kfiʃ) *pl.* **weak·fish, weak·fish·es** *n.* a member of *Cynoscion,* fam. *Sciaenidae,* a genus of North American marine food fishes, esp. *C. regalis*
weak force (*particle phys.*) a force with a hypothetical quantum of W particle, that governs the interactions of neutrinos, modifies the forces of gravity and electromagnetism, and causes radioactive decay. **also** weak interaction. *Cf* STRONG FORCE
weak-kneed (wí:kni:d) *adj.* lacking moral resolution
weak·ling (wí:kliŋ) *n.* a physically weak person or animal ‖ a person without strength of character
weak·ly (wí:kli:) **1.** *comp.* **weak·li·er** *superl.* **weak·li·est** *adj.* delicate in health, lacking a strong constitution **2.** *adv.* in a weak manner
weak-mind·ed (wí:kmáindid) *adj.* lacking in resolution ‖ foolish ‖ indicating foolishness or lack of resolution
weak·ness (wí:knis) *n.* the state of being weak ‖ a defect ‖ a self-indulgent fondness, *a weakness for olives*
weal (wi:l) *n.* (*rhet.*) well-being [O.E. *wela,* wealth]
weal *n.* the stinging, red mark on the skin left by the lash of a whip etc. [var. of WALE]
Weald (wi:ld) a region of open country, formerly forested, lying between the chalk hills of the North and South Downs in Kent, Sussex, Surrey and Hampshire, England
wealth (welθ) *n.* abundant worldly possessions ‖ an abundance of possessions or an abundance of anything, *a wealth of illustrations* ‖ (*econ.*) the natural resources of a country, whether or not exploited ‖ (*econ.*) the products of the economic activity of a nation ‖ (*econ.*) anything which can be exchanged for money or barter **wéalth·i·ly** *adv.* **wéalth·i·ness** *n.* **wéalth·y** *comp.* **wealth·i·er** *superl.* **wealth·i·est** *adj.* having an abundance of worldly possessions ‖ characterized by abundance [M.E. *welthe* perh. rel. to WEAL]
wean (wi:n) *v.t.* to train (an infant or young animal that has been suckled) to accept food other than its mother's milk ‖ (with 'from') to induce (a person) to give up (undesirable associates or habits etc.) [O.E. *wenian,* to accustom]
wea·pon (wépən) *n.* any instrument used for fighting ‖ (*zool.*) any part used in attacking, fighting or defending, esp. the spur of a gamecock ‖ any means of attack or defense, e.g. tears, strike action, irony [O.E. *wǣpen*]
wear (weər) **1.** *v. pres. part.* **wear·ing** *past* **wore** (wɔr) *past part.* **worn** (wɔrn) *v.t.* to have (garments, ornaments) on the body, *to wear a coat, to wear a necklace* ‖ to have on one's person habitually, *to wear spectacles, to wear a beard* ‖ to arrange (one's hair, clothes etc.) in a specified way, *to wear one's hair short* ‖ to have (an expression) on the face, *to wear a smile* ‖ to diminish or impair by prolonged use, abrasion etc. ‖ to bring to a specified state by use, *to wear one's shirt to tatters* ‖ to make by scraping, rubbing, using etc., *to wear a hole in the carpet* ‖ (*naut.,* of a ship or boat) to fly (her flag) ‖ *v.i.* to diminish or deteriorate through use, friction etc. ‖ to resist damage or loss of quality by use etc., *material which wears well* ‖ to come to a specified state, *their hopes wore thin* **to wear down** to make or become worn ‖ to diminish the resistance of (a person) by nagging ‖ to exhaust (a person) **to wear off** to diminish gradually, *the effects of the ether wore off* **to wear on** (of a specified period) to undergo the passage of time, *the day wore on* **to wear out** to make or become unfit for further use as a result of being worn ‖ to exhaust (a person) **2.** *n.* a wearing by friction, abrasion etc. or being so worn ‖ damage due to

CONCISE PRONUNCIATION KEY: **(a)** æ, *cat;* ɑ, *car;* ɔ *fawn;* ei, *snake.* **(e)** e, *hen;* i:, *sheep;* iə, *deer;* ɛə, *bear.* **(i)** i, *fish;* ai, *tiger;* ə:, *bird.* **(o)** o, *ox;* au, *cow;* ou, *goat;* u, *poor;* ɔi, *royal.* **(u)** ʌ, *duck;* u, *bull;* u:, *goose;* ə, *bacillus;* ju:, *cube.* x, *loch;* θ, *think;* ð, *bother;* z, *Zen;* ʒ, *corsage;* dʒ, *savage;* ŋ, *orangutang;* j, *yak;* ʃ, *fish;* tʃ, *fetch;* 'l, *rabble;* 'n, *redden.* Complete pronunciation key appears inside front cover.

use || the amount of such damage || the ability to resist damage due to use || (*commerce*) garments, ornaments etc. worn on the body, *beach wear* [O.E. *werian*]

wear *v.t.* (*naut.*) to bring (a ship) about by putting up the helm || *v.i.* (*naut.*, of a ship) to come about by turning the stern to the wind [etym. doubtful]

wear·a·ble (wέərəb'l) *adj.* suitable for wearing || able to be worn

wear and tear loss of quality due to use over a passage of time

wea·ri·ly (wíərili:) *adv.* in a weary manner

wea·ri·ness (wíəri:nis) *n.* the state or quality of being weary

wear·ing (wέəriŋ) *adj.* of or pertaining to clothing, *wearing apparel* || very tiring, *a wearing day*

wea·ri·some (wíəri:səm) *adj.* causing physical or mental fatigue || causing boredom

wea·ry (wíəri:) **1.** *comp.* **wea·ri·er** *superl.* **wea·ri·est** *adj.* tired and dispirited || at the end of one's patience || causing or showing tiredness or dispiritedness, *weary work, a weary sigh* || (with 'of') bored or tired, *weary of studying* **2.** *v. pres. part.* **wea·ry·ing** *past* and *past part.* **wea·ried** *v.t.* to cause to be weary || *v.i.* to become weary [O.E. *wērig*]

wea·sel (wí:z'l) **1.** *n.* a member of *Mustela,* fam. *Mustelidae,* a genus of small carnivorous mammals, native to almost all temperate and cold regions of the northern hemisphere. The weasel has a slender body, flattened head, long neck and short legs || the fur or pelt of such an animal || a tracked (land or amphibious) motor vehicle capable of going over snow or ice, traversing rivers etc. **2.** *v.i.* (*pop.*, esp. with 'out') to get out of a bad situation, evade an obligation etc. in a cunning, equivocal manner [O.E. *wesule*]

weath·er (wéðər) **1.** *n.* the atmospheric conditions (heat, cold, wetness, dryness, clearness, cloudiness etc.) prevailing at a given place and time || adverse atmospheric conditions, e.g. rain, sleet etc., *the weather kept us in* **to make good (bad) weather** (*naut.*, of a vessel) to behave well (badly) in bad weather **to make heavy weather of** (*Br.*) to exaggerate the difficulty of (some task one is busy with) **under the weather** feeling slightly ill **2.** *v.t.* to expose (e.g. wood, stone) to changing atmospheric conditions || to discolor, disintegrate, wear away etc. by such exposure, *the stone facing was badly weathered* || to pass safely through a storm, a dangerous or difficult time etc., *to weather a crisis* || (*naut.*) to get to the windward of (a cape etc.) || to slope (e.g. a roof) so that it will shed rain || *v.i.* to resist the bad effects of weather, *the paint has weathered well* || to undergo some change, e.g. discoloration or disintegration due to exposure to the weather **3.** *adj.* (*naut.*) windward, *the weather beam* **to keep one's weather eye open** to be on the lookout [O.E. *weder*]

weath·er-beat·en (wéðərbi:t'n) *adj.* showing permanent signs of exposure to weather || roughened, hardened, sunburned etc., *a weather-beaten face*

weath·er·board (wéðərbɔrd, wéðərbourd) **1.** *n.* a board adapted to shedding water easily by overlapping the one beneath || (*naut.*) the windward side of a ship **2.** *v.t.* to equip with weatherboards **wéath·er·board·ing** *n.* weatherboards collectively

weath·er-bound (wéðərbaund) *adj.* (esp. of a ship) delayed or kept back by bad weather

weath·er·cock (wéðərkɒk) *n.* a flat device often shaped like a cock and free to pivot in the wind so as to show wind direction || a person whose opinions and line of conduct change rapidly, according to what is fashionable or likely to be advantageous

weather gauge (*naut.*) the position of a sailing boat on the windward side of another, giving her an advantage in handling **to get the weather gauge of someone** to get an advantage over someone

weath·er·glass (wéðərglæs, wéðərglɑs) *n.* a barometer

weath·er·ing (wéðəriŋ) *n.* the action of the weather over a long period on the appearance of exposed objects, esp. (*geol.*) the erosive effects of weather on the earth's crust

weath·er·ly (wéðərli:) *adj.* (*naut.*) exerting so much lateral pressure (on the water) as to make little leeway

weath·er·man (wéðərmæn) *pl.* **weath·er·men** (wéðərmen) *n.* a person who forecasts or reports on weather conditions

Weatherman *n.* member of the militant underground radical splinter group of Students for a Democratic Society. Weathermen (and Weatherwomen) advocated revolution and practiced frequent demonstrations most actively in the early 1970s. The group was named for a line in Bob Dylan's 'Subterranean Homesick Blues,' *You don't need a weatherman / to know which way the wind blows*

weather map a map showing the state of the weather conditions at a given time, and over an extended area, by indicating the temperatures, wind directions and wind forces, areas of low and high pressures etc.

weath·er·om·e·ter (wéðərɒmətə:r) *n.* (*meteor.*) an all-purpose machine that can simulate in a few days the cumulative effects of years of heavy dew, rain, sunlight, and thermal shock

weath·er·proof (wéðərpru:f) **1.** *adj.* able to resist exposure to the weather without suffering serious damage **2.** *v.t.* to treat (a material) so as to make it thus

weather strip a strip of material used to cover cracks, joints etc. so as to exclude rain or drafts

weather stripping a weather strip

weather vane a vane pivoted so that it turns in the direction of the wind

weave (wi:v) **1.** *v. pres. part.* **weav·ing** *past* **wove** (wouv) *past part.* **wo·ven** (wóuvən), **wove** *v.t.* to form (thread etc.) into a fabric by interlacing (the weft and warp) || to make (a fabric) thus || to make something by interlacing (rushes etc.) || to make (something) thus || to connect (a number of details, facts, ideas etc.) into a narrative, theory etc. || to construct (a narrative, plot, scheme etc.) thus || to direct in a winding course, *to weave one's way through a crowd* || *v.i.* to engage in weaving || to move this way and that in order to avoid obstacles, *to weave through traffic* **2.** *n.* a manner or style of weaving, *a close weave* **wéav·er** *n.* a person who weaves, esp. for a living || a weaverbird || (*basketball, lacrosse*) a series of movements in the form of an 8 involving several players to confuse opponents [O.E. *wefan*]

weav·er·bird (wí:vərbə:rd) *n.* any of various members of *Ploceidae,* a family of Asiatic, East Indian and African birds resembling finches. Their elaborate nests are woven of grasses, reeds etc. and very often hang from the branches of trees

web (web) **1.** *n.* a piece of cloth in the process of being woven on a loom or just taken off the loom || the fine network of threads spun by a spider or some other insects, e.g. the silkworm || something intended to create mystery, entangle etc., *a web of conspiracy* || (*biol.*) a tissue or membrane || (*zool.*) a membrane uniting the digits of certain aquatic birds, frogs etc. || (*zool.*) the vane of a feather || a thin flat piece connecting the more solid parts in a girder etc. || the arm of a crank || a large reel of paper used on a rotary press, esp. in printing newspapers **2.** *v.t. pres. part.* **web·bing** *past* and *past part.* **webbed** to cover or join with or as if with a web || to snare with or as if with a web [O.E. *webb*]

Webb (web), Sidney James, 1st Baron Passfield (1859-1947), English social historian and Fabian socialist. He and his wife Beatrice (1858-1943) helped to found the London School of Economics (1895) and published the minority report of the Poor Law Commission (1909), 'History of Trade Unionism' (1894), 'English Local Government' (1906-29), and 'Soviet Communism: a New Civilization' (1935)

webbed (webd) *adj.* (e.g. of the feet of certain water birds) having the toes connected by a web or membrane

Web·be She·be·li (wébeiʃibéili:) a river (700 miles long) flowing from south central Ethiopia across S. Somalia to the Juba

web·bing (wébiŋ) *n.* a strong, woven fabric in the form of a narrow strip used for straps, upholstery tapes etc. || (*Br., mil.*) a soldier's belt and equipment made mainly of hemp or jute fiber

We·ber (véibər), Carl Maria Friedrich Ernst von (1786-1828), German composer. His three operatic masterpieces are 'Der Freischütz' (1821), 'Euryanthe' (1823) and 'Oberon' (1826)

Weber, Max (1864-1920), German sociologist and economist. He was the first to view sociology as an empirical science. In 'The Protestant Ethic and the Spirit of Capitalism' (trans. 1930), he advanced the theory that there is a connection between Protestantism, esp. Calvinism, and the development of capitalism

Weber, Wilhelm Eduard (1804-91), German physicist who rationalized the system of electrical units by relating them to mass, length and time, and carried out many researches in electricity and magnetism

we·ber (véibər, wébər) *n.* the mks unit of magnetic flux equal to 10^8 maxwells [after Wilhelm E. WEBER]

We·bern (véibərn), Anton von (1883-1945), Austrian composer. He was a pupil of Schönberg (1904-8), and moved from early atonality to a later music in which there is no relation to tonal structure at all. His works include 'Five Pieces for Orchestra' (1911), songs, cantatas and string quartets

web·foot (wébfut) *pl.* **web·feet** (wébfi:t) *n.* (*zool.*) a foot having digits joined by webs **wéb-fóot·ed** *adj.* having digits joined thus

Web·ster (wébstər), Daniel (1782-1852), American statesman, orator and lawyer. He supported nullification and the supremacy of the Union, and became a leader of the Whig party. He defended (1819) his alma mater in the Dartmouth College case, and the Bank of the U.S.A. in 'McCulloch v. Maryland'

Webster, John (c. 1580–c. 1625), English Jacobean dramatist. His tragedies 'The White Devil' (1612) and 'The Duchess of Malfi' (1623) are remarkable for their intense passion and their poetry

Webster, Noah (1758-1843), American lexicographer. His 'Compendious Dictionary of the English Language' (1806) preceded his crowning work, 'An American Dictionary of the English Language' (1828), revisions and abridgments of which have appeared from c. 1850 to the present day

Webster-Ashburton Treaty an Anglo-U.S. treaty (1842) negotiated in Washington, D.C., by Daniel Webster, the U.S. Secretary of State, and Lord Ashburton, the British representative. It settled the boundary dispute of the northeastern U.S.A. by granting over 7,000 sq. miles to the U.S.A. and opening to free navigation several waterways to both countries. It also settled the disputed U.S.-Canadian border along the Great Lakes. It was a precedent for peaceful settlement of disputes between Great Britain and the U.S.A.

Webster-Hayne Debate (hein), a debate (1830) between U.S. Senators Robert Hayne, a states' rights Southerner, and Daniel Webster, the defender of the supremacy of the Union

we'd (wi:d) *contr.* of WE HAD, WE SHOULD, WE WOULD

wed (wed) *pres. part.* **wed·ding** *past* and *past part.* **wed·ded, wed** *v.t.* to marry || to unite, *to wed charm and efficiency* || *v.i.* to get married **wéd·ded** *adj.* married || of marriage [O.E. *weddian,* to pledge]

Wed. Wednesday

wed·ding (wédiŋ) *n.* the ceremony of marriage with its accompanying festivities || (used in combinations) the anniversary of a marriage or the celebration of this, *silver wedding* [O.E. *weddung*]

We·de·kind (véidəkint), Frank (1864-1918), German dramatist. His plays were sharply critical of the bourgeoisie

we·deln (véid'ln) *n.* (*skiing;* German *wedeln,* 'to wag a tail'). a quick, short, rhythmic, fluid, parallel swiveling, by moving the rear of the skis sidewise —**wedel** *v.*

wedge (wedʒ) **1.** *n.* a piece of wood or metal, thick at one end and narrowing down to a thin edge at the other, used for splitting wood, rock etc., for forcing something open, or for fixing into a crack to keep something in place etc. || something shaped like a wedge, *a wedge of cake* || an arrangement of troops, tanks etc. moving in the form of a wedge || a formation of flying geese etc. || a stroke resembling a wedge in cuneiform characters || a golf club used for lofting **the thin end of the wedge** (*Br.*) a seemingly trifling demand etc. which sooner or later entails larger concession **2.** *v.t. pres. part.* **wedg·ing** *past* and *past. part.* **wedged** (with 'in', 'up' etc.) to fix tightly with a wedge or wedges || to split open, force apart etc. by driving in a wedge || to drive (an object) into a narrow area where it is held fast || to cram into a small space, *wedged into the bus like sardines* [O.E. *wecg*]

wedge *pres. part.* **wedg·ing** *past* and *past part.* **wedged** *v.t.* to make (potter's clay) homogeneous and free of air bubbles by cutting it into wedges and slamming one wedge on top of another [origin unknown]

Wedg·wood (wédʒwụd), Josiah (1730-95), English potter. He applied artistic standards to utilitarian objects (using Flaxman, among others, for his designs) and perfected the soft porcelain which bears his name

wed·lock (wédlɒk) *n.* (*rhet.*) the state of being married **born in (out of) wedlock** having parents legally (not legally) married [O.E. *wedlāc*]

Wednes·day (wénzdi:, wénzdẹi) *n.* the fourth day of the week [O.E. *Wōdnes dæg,* day of Woden]

wee (wi:) *comp.* **we·er** (wi:ər) *superl.* **we·est** (wí:əst) *adj.* very small [M.E. *we, wei*]

weed (wi:d) **1.** *n.* any plant growing where it is not desired, esp. a wild plant growing in ground that is under cultivation ‖ seaweed ‖ a weak animal considered unfit for breeding ‖ (*old-fash.*) tobacco, esp. a cigarette or cigar **2.** *v.t.* to remove weeds from ‖ to remove (weeds) esp. by pulling or forking up ‖ (with 'out') to get rid of undesirable elements ‖ *v.i.* to remove weeds **wéed·i·ness** *n.* the state or quality of being weedy **wéed·y** *comp.* **weed·i·er** *superl.* **weed·i·est** *adj.* full of weeds ‖ of, relating to or consisting of weeds ‖ thin and lanky, *a weedy youth* [O.E. *wēod*]

weeds (wi:dz) *pl. n.* mourning clothes ‖ (*archaic*) clothes [M.E. *wede* fr. O.E. *wǣd, wǣde*]

week (wi:k) *n.* a period of seven days, beginning (in the Christian calendar) with Sunday ‖ this period containing a specified holiday, *Easter week* ‖ the working days or hours of a seven-day period, *a 40-hour week* ‖ seven days before or after a specified day, *last Monday week, next Tuesday week* **a week of Sundays** a very long time **week after week** every week over a long period **week by week** each week **week in, week out** week after week without respite [O.E. *wice*]

week·day (wí:kdẹi) *n.* any day of the week except the sabbath

week·end (wí:kẹnd) **1.** *n.* the end of the week, esp. the period from Friday night or Saturday until Monday morning **2.** *adj.* of or on a weekend **3.** *v.i.* to pass the weekend

week·end-use zone (wí:kendjụ:s) recreation area one to three hrs travel time from an urban center

week·ly (wí:kli:) **1.** *adj.* happening, produced, done every week, *a weekly newspaper* ‖ lasting or continuing for a week ‖ reckoned by the week, *weekly pay* **2.** *adv.* every week ‖ once a week ‖ by the week **3.** *pl.* **week·lies** *n.* a publication produced every week

Weelkes (wi:lks), Thomas (c. 1575-1623), English composer, esp. of madrigals and anthems

weep (wi:p) *pres. part.* **weep·ing** *past* and *past part.* **wept** (wept) *v.i.* to shed tears, esp. in grief ‖ (with 'for') to mourn ‖ to exude or let fall water or some watery fluid ‖ *v.t.* (*rhet.*) to lament or cry for ‖ to shed (tears) ‖ to exude (a watery fluid) ‖ to bring to a specified condition by weeping, *to weep oneself to sleep* **wéep·er** *n.* someone who weeps ‖ a statue of a mourning figure found in some funerary sculptures ‖ a capuchin monkey **wéep·ing** *adj.* that weeps ‖ oozing moisture ‖ (of some trees) having slender, drooping branches [O.E. *wēpan*]

wee·ver (wí:vər) *n.* any of various members of *Trachinidae,* a family of edible marine fishes having a spinose head, upward-looking eyes and sharp, poisonous dorsal fins capable of causing serious wounds [O.F. *wivre,* serpent, dragon]

wee·vil (wí:vəl) *n.* any of various members of *Rhynchophora,* a group of small beetles widely distributed in Europe, Asia and North America, having a long head prolonged into a snout. The larvae of most of these do great damage to fruit, nuts, grain etc. [O.E. *wifel*]

weft (weft) *n.* (*weaving*) the thread crossing and woven into the warp to make the web [O.E. *wefta, weft*]

weigh (wei) *v.t.* to determine the weight of ‖ to hold (an object) in the hand in order to estimate its weight ‖ to consider the importance, relative truth or advantage of, *to weigh evidence* ‖ (*naut.*) to hoist or lift (an anchor) ‖ (esp. with 'out') to serve out (a quantity of something) by weight ‖ *v.i.* to have a certain weight, *it weighs 30 lbs* ‖ (with 'on' or 'upon') to be a burden, *the problem weighed on his mind* ‖ (often with 'with') to have importance, *his argument does not weigh with me* ‖ (*naut.*) to hoist anchor **to weigh down** to burden, cause to stoop or bend under a load ‖ to bring under emotional stress, *weighed down by grief* **to weigh in** to weigh (a boxer, jockey etc.) before a contest or race in order to verify his weight ‖ to be so weighed ‖ to take strong physical action, or attack verbally, in order to deal with a situation etc. ‖ to have oneself and one's luggage etc. weighed before an airplane flight **to weigh one's words** to consider well the full implication of a statement before making it **to weigh out** to weigh (a jockey) after a race ‖ (of a jockey) to be weighed after a race [O.E. *wegan,* to carry]

weigh·beam (wéibị:m) *n.* a big steelyard

weigh·bridge (wéibrịdʒ) *n.* a scale, at road-surface level, onto which vehicles etc. can be driven to be weighed

weight (weit) **1.** *n.* the force acting on a body in a gravitational field, equal to the product of its mass and the acceleration of the body produced by the field. Strictly speaking, the value for the acceleration due to gravity depends upon position in the gravitational field and thus weight depends on where it is measured. However, since the value of the acceleration due to gravity is approximately equal (9.8 m/sec^2) everywhere on the surface of the earth, and exactly the same when measured at different times but in the same place, this factor is often neglected. The value of the mass (with mass units) is often used instead, to mean the force (weight) on an object of given mass measured at the surface of the earth ‖ a known mass of metal used for comparing other weights ‖ a unit of mass or weight ‖ a system of units of weight, *Troy weight* ‖ the amount something or someone weighs ‖ a mass of metal used in a grandfather clock etc. to drive the mechanism ‖ an amount of matter, *can the floor support such a weight of furniture?* ‖ importance, *a matter of great weight to discuss* ‖ preponderance, *the weight of evidence is in his favor* ‖ (*sports*) a heavy metal ball that is put ‖ one of the various categories by which boxers and wrestlers are classified ‖ (*horse racing*) a number of pounds weight which a horse must carry in a handicap race ‖ (*statistics*) the importance of a value, usually related to its frequency ‖ (of clothing) heaviness or lightness according to season, *winter weight* ‖ the rhythm and stress value of sounds and syllables in verse **to carry weight** to be given serious consideration in the making of a decision, *his argument will carry weight* **to pull one's weight** to do one's share of work **2.** *v.t.* to add weight to ‖ to lay a specified stress on, *to weight an argument unfairly* ‖ to add size etc. to (paper or a textile) ‖ to assign a weight to (a horse in a handicap race) ‖ (*statistics*) to give a value to (some item in a frequency distribution) [O.E. *wiht*]

weight·less (wéitlis) *adj.* apparently without gravitational pull ‖ having little or no weight **wéight·less·ness**

weight-lift·ing (wéitlịftiŋ) *n.* a sport in which weights attached to a long bar are lifted competitively according to prescribed rules, or as an exercise

weight-watch·er (wéitwɑtʃər) *n.* **1.** one who diets to lose weight **2.** Weight-Watcher, member of Weight-Watchers, Inc., a group organized to assist those who wish to lose weight; trademark

weight·y (wéiti:) *comp.* **weight·i·er** *superl.* **weight·i·est** *adj.* heavy, *a weighty load* ‖ burdensome, oppressive ‖ (*rhet.*) important, worthy of consideration, *weighty matters*

Wei·hai·wei (wéiháiwéi) (or Weihaï) a port (pop. 222,000) near the tip of the Shantung peninsula, N.E. China: textiles, fishing. It was leased to Britain as a naval base (1898-1930)

Weill (vail), Kurt (1900-50), German-American composer. He is best known for his collaborations with Brecht on the satirical operas 'Aufstieg und Fall der Stadt Mahogonny' (1927) and 'Die Dreigroschenoper' (1929). He was eminent in America as a composer of musical comedies, e.g. 'One Touch of Venus' (1943). He also wrote a musical version of Elmer Rice's 'Street Scene' (1947)

Wei·mar (váimɑr) a town (pop. 63,326) in Thuringia, East Germany. Under Grand Duke Charles Augustus (1775-1828) it was one of Germany's leading cultural centers and was the home of Goethe, Schiller, Herder and Wieland. The republican constitution under which Germany was governed (1919-33) was drawn up and adopted here

Weir (wiər), Robert Walter (1803-89), U.S. portrait and landscape painter. His 'The Embarkation of the Pilgrims' hangs in the rotunda of the Capitol in Washington, D.C.

weir (wiər) *n.* an obstruction built across a river to raise the water level or to divert the flow of water ‖ a row of stakes set in a stream, river etc. to catch fish [O.E. *wer*]

weird (wiərd) *adj.* uncanny, supernatural ‖ (*pop.*) queer, odd, *a weird notion* [O.E. *wyrd*]

weird·o (wíərdou) *n.* (*slang*) a queer person

Weis·mann (váismɑn), August (1834-1914), German biologist. He demonstrated that acquired characteristics are not inherited by the progeny

Weiz·mann (váitsmɑn), Chaim (1874-1952), Israeli statesman and scientist. A leading Zionist, he was largely responsible for the Balfour Declaration (1917). He was the first president of Israel (1949-52)

Welch *WELSH (relating to Wales)

welch *WELSH (of bookmakers)

wel·come (wélkəm) **1.** *v.t. pres. part.* **wel·com·ing** *past* and *past part.* **wel·comed** to receive or greet (a person) with signs of pleasure ‖ to be glad about, *to welcome someone's return* ‖ to receive gladly, *to welcome suggestions* **2.** *n.* a welcoming or being welcomed ‖ a manner of welcoming, *a hearty welcome* **3.** *adj.* giving pleasure or received gladly, *welcome news, a welcome guest* ‖ permitted gladly, *you are welcome to use my car* **4.** *interj.* a conventional expression of pleasure in greeting a guest or visitor [O.E. *wilcuma,* a welcome guest]

Weld (weld), Theodore Dwight (1803-95), U.S. abolitionist leader. He was editor (1836-40) of the American Anti-Slavery Society's newspaper, 'The Emancipator.' He led the national campaign to petition Congress against slavery, and wrote 'American Slavery As it Is' (1839), which influenced Harriet Beecher Stowe and many others

weld (weld) **1.** *v.t.* to unite (metal surfaces) by heating the parts to be joined sufficiently for them to melt and mix before cooling (usually with an oxyacetylene or oxyhydrogen flame) ‖ to unite (surfaces) by softening them with heat and then hammering them together (as in wrought-iron work) ‖ to cause to become a unified whole, *he welded their stories into a single coherent account* ‖ *v.i.* to become welded **2.** *n.* a welding or being welded ‖ a welded joint [altered fr. WELL, (obs.) to boil]

Welf (welf) *n.* a member of the German Guelph family

wel·fare (wélfẹər) *n.* the state of being healthy, happy and free from want ‖ organized work to promote this state in the members of a community who need to be helped [M.E. fr. *welfaren,* to fare well]

welfare mother a woman with dependent children, usu. with no husband, receiving government support via welfare benefits

welfare state a state based on the principle that the welfare of every individual is the collective responsibility of the community (cf. LAISSEZ-FAIRE)

welfare work *WELFARE (organized work)

well (wel) **1.** *comp.* **bet·ter** (bétər) *superl.* **best** (best) *adv.* in a manner which gives satisfaction, *to work well* or which others would approve, *he treats his staff well but they still complain* ‖ proficiently, *to speak Urdu well* ‖ thoroughly, *soak the roots well* ‖ fully, quite, *well up to the knees in mud* ‖ by a large amount, *well over 50* ‖ very likely, *it may well be true* ‖ properly, correctly, *he can't very well refuse* ‖ intimately, *I know him well* ‖ satisfactorily from a material point of view, *do the boys eat well at school?* ‖ more than moderately or merely adequately, *do the brothers get on well?* ‖ easily, *he can well spare the money* **as well** also ‖ in the circumstances, *you might as well agree* **as well as** in addition to **to do well** to succeed materially **to do well to** to be wise to, *he would do well to see a dentist* **2.** *adj.* in good health ‖ satisfactory, *is all well with him?* ‖ pleasing, *they look well against that wall* **very well** expressing agreement, approval etc. **3.** *inten.* expressing surprise, resignation, satisfaction etc., *well! I never expected to see you here* [O.E. *wel, well*]

well *n.* a deep hole, usually cylindrical in shape and lined with bricks, stone etc., dug into the earth to such a depth as to reach a supply of water ‖ a shaft sunk into the earth to obtain oil, gas etc. ‖ the space running vertically through the floors of a building and containing the stairs or elevator ‖ any of various small cylindrical receptacles for holding a liquid, e.g. the reservoir of a fountain pen ‖ a spring of water, or a pool fed by a spring ‖ (*Br., pl.,* used esp. in place names) a place having mineral springs ‖ a rich source of supply, *a well of knowledge* || (*naut.*) the enclosure containing and protecting the pumps of a vessel || a compartment, having a perforated bottom, in the hold of a fishing boat, where the catch can be kept alive || a space in the body of a vehicle designed to hold luggage || (*Br.*) the space in a law court reserved for counsel [Anglian form of O.E. *wielle* and fr. *weallan*, to boil]

well *v.i.* (of a liquid or tears) to rise up and pour out copiously, *oil welled from the ground* || to seem to rise up and pour forth copiously, *anger welled in his heart* [O.E. *wiellan*, to make boil]

we'll (wi:l) *contr.* of WE SHALL, WE WILL

well-ad·vised (wélədváizd) *adj.* sensible, wise

Wel·land Ship Canal (wélənd) a ship waterway (28 miles long) opened by the Canadian government (1932), connecting Lakes Erie and Ontario, in S.E. Ontario. It has eight locks and a minimum depth of 25 ft

well-ap·point·ed (wéləpɔ́intid) *adj.* well-furnished

well-bal·anced (wélbǽlənst) *adj.* (of a person) possessing a fortunate mixture of character traits || (of a diet, meal etc.) composed of different foodstuffs in the right nutritive proportions

well-be·ing (wélbí:iŋ) *n.* the state of being healthy, happy and free from want

well-born (wélbɔ́rn) *adj.* born of a socially privileged family

well-bred (wélbréd) *adj.* educated for polite society, or displaying such education || of good stock, *a well-bred terrier*

well-built (wélbílt) *adj.* (of a person) having pleasing proportions

well-dis·posed (wéldispóuzd) *adj.* feeling kindly or sympathetic

well-done (wéldʌ́n) *adj.* performed or executed well || (esp. of meat) thoroughly cooked

Wel·ler (wélər), Thomas Huckle (1915-), U.S. physician and parasitologist who shared (with J.F. Enders and F.C. Robbins) the 1954 Nobel prize in physiology and medicine, for cultivation of the poliomyelitis viruses in tissue culture

Welles (welz), (George) Orson (1915-85) U.S. actor and director, principally known for his radio adaptation of 'The War of the Worlds' (1938) and the Academy Award-winning movie 'Citizen Kane' (1941), based on the life of William Randolph Hearst. He cofounded the Mercury Theatre on radio in 1937 on which the presentation of 'The War of the Worlds' created panic nationwide when some listeners thought the invasion from outer space was real. Other films include 'The Magnificent Ambersons' (1942), 'The Lady from Shanghai' (1948), 'Touch of Evil' (1958) and 'Chimes at Midnight' (1966)

Welles Gideon (1802-78), U.S. secretary of the navy (1861-9) under Presidents Abraham Lincoln and Andrew Johnson in the first Republican cabinet. He increased over sevenfold the number of ships and over sixfold the number of officers and seamen. He stressed the value of blockade against the Confederacy and supported the development of ironclads. He returned (1868) to the Democratic party

Welles, Sumner (1892-1961), U.S. diplomat. An expert in Latin American affairs, he was appointed (1922) commissioner to the Dominican Republic and was entrusted with the evacuation of U.S. troops from that country. He also served in Honduras and Cuba, and was undersecretary of state (1937-42)

Welles·ley (wélzli:), Richard Colley, Marquis Wellesley (1760-1842), British administrator. As governor general of India (1797-1805) he extended and strengthened British rule, and crushed the revolt of Tipu Sahib

Wellesley College a U.S. private educational institution for women in Wellesley, Mass., chartered (1870) as Wellesley Female Seminary

well-fa·vored, *Br.* **well-fa·voured** (wélféivərd) *adj.* (*rhet.*, of women) attractive in appearance

well-found (wélfáund) *adj.* furnished and equipped, *a well-found ship*

well-found·ed (wélfáundid) *adj.* firmly based on fact

well-groomed (wélgrú:md) *adj.* (of a person) impeccable in dress and appearance || (of a horse etc.) well tended

well-ground·ed (wélgráundid) *adj.* well-founded || well instructed in the initial stages or fundamental principles of some discipline

well-han·dled (wélhǽnd'ld) *adj.* adroitly managed || much handled, *well-handled stock*

well·head (wélhed) *n.* the top of a well shaft, or the structure built over it || the source of a spring or stream

well-heeled (wélhí:ld) *adj.* (*pop.*) quite wealthy

Wel·ling·ton (wéliŋtən), Arthur Wellesley, 1st duke of (1769-1852), British soldier and statesman, prime minister (1828-30). He distinguished himself in the Indian army (1797-1805), and commanded the British army in the Peninsular War (1808-14) and at Waterloo (1815), gaining the nickname 'the Iron Duke'. He attended the Congress of Vienna (1815). He became (1819) a member of the reactionary Tory cabinet. As prime minister (1828-30), he was persuaded to repeal the Test and Corporation Acts and to pass the Catholic Emancipation Act, but became unpopular for his opposition to parliamentary reform

Wellington a region (area 10,870 sq. miles, pop. 495,000) at the south end of North Island, New Zealand: dairy products, lumber, sheep. Chief town: Wellington

Wellington the capital (pop. 343,982), of New Zealand, a port at the south end of North Island. Industries: woolen textiles, meat packing, motor vehicle assembly. University (1897), National Art Gallery, national library

wel·ling·ton (wéliŋtən) *n.* a knee-length rubber boot [after the Duke of WELLINGTON]

wel·ling·to·ni·a (weliŋtóuni:ə) *n.* (*Br., pop.*) a sequoia [after the Duke of WELLINGTON]

well-in·ten·tioned (wélinténʃənd) *adj.* having or showing good intentions, but often misguided

well-knit (wélnít) *adj.* compact, *a well-knit frame* || well-constructed, *a well-knit essay*

well-known (wélnóun) *adj.* widely known || intimately known

well-mean·ing (wélmi:niŋ) *adj.* well-intentioned

well-meant (wélmént) *adj.* well-intentioned

well-nigh (wélnái) *adv.* (*rhet.*) almost

well-off (wélɔ́f, wélɒ́f) *adj.* well-to-do || (with 'for') well provided

well-pre·served (wélprizə́:rvd) *adj.* (of an elderly person) carrying his or her age noticeably well

well-read (wélréd) *adj.* having read a great deal

Wells (welz), Henry (1805-78), U.S. pioneer expressman. He founded (1852, with William Fargo) Wells, Fargo & Company, an express firm which served the growing West

Wells, Herbert George (1866-1946), English author. Certain of his works, e.g. 'The Time Machine' (1895), 'The Invisible Man' (1897), 'The Shape of Things to Come' (1933), explore the effect of modern science and technology on men's lives and thought. His humorous, often satirical novels of realistic contemporary life include 'Kipps' (1908), 'Tono Bungay' (1909), 'The History of Mr Polly' (1910), 'Mr Britling Sees It Through' (1916). He also wrote many short stories and a popular 'Outline of History' (1920)

well-spo·ken (wélspóukən) *adj.* having a pleasant speaking voice and accent || (*old-fash.*) courteous in speech

well·spring (wélspriŋ) *n.* (*rhet.*) a source of supply or inspiration etc.

well-thought-of (wélθɔ́tʌv, wélθɔ́tɒv) *adj.* of good reputation, esteemed highly

well-timed (wéltáimd) *adj.* arranged to occur at just the right moment, *a well-timed remark*

well-to-do (wéltədú:) *adj.* having a comfortably large income

well-wish·er (wélwiʃər) *n.* someone who wishes well to someone or something

well-worn (wélwɔ́rn, wélwóurn) *adj.* so often used as to be ineffective, *well-worn excuses*

wels (welz) *n.* a variety of large (up to 200-lbs) catfish

Wels·bach (vélsbɑx), Carl Auer, Baron von (1858-1929), Austrian chemist who used rare earths in constructing incandescent gas mantles (1886)

Wel·ser (vélsər) a German banking family from Augsburg, known from the 14th c. The company it formed set itself up (1509) in the Canaries and later in Santo Domingo. Between 1528 and 1546 it was authorized by Charles V to colonize Venezuela as a hereditary fief

Welsh (welʃ) **1.** *adj.* of or relating to Wales, its inhabitants or their language (the old spelling 'Welch' is preferred in some names, *Royal Welch Fusiliers*) **2.** *n.* the Brythonic Celtic language spoken in Wales **the Welsh** the people of Wales [O.E. *Welisc, Wœlisc*]

—Welsh was the language spoken in Britain before the coming of the Romans, and it survived and developed in the comparative isolation of Wales until the later Middle Ages. It is still spoken and written (with some difference between the spoken and literary languages) by a quarter of the Welsh population, and is taught in Welsh schools and colleges. A literary tradition has persisted

welsh, welch (welʃ, weltʃ) *v.i.* (of bookmakers) to leave the race track secretly and fail to pay winning bets || to swindle by failing to pay one's debts [origin unknown]

Welsh corgi a cattle dog of a breed having short legs, an elongated body and a foxlike muzzle. Two distinct varieties (the Cardiganshire and the Pembrokeshire) are bred [Welsh *corgi* fr. *cor*, dwarf+*ci*, dog]

Welsh rabbit a dish consisting of seasoned cheese, melted and poured over toast

Welsh rarebit Welsh rabbit

Welsh terrier a terrier of a wire-haired black and tan breed (about 15 ins in height) resembling, though smaller than, an Airedale

welt (welt) **1.** *n.* a narrow strip of leather sometimes stitched between the upper of a shoe or boot and the sole || an inflamed ridge raised on the skin by the lash of a whip etc. || a narrow strip of material sewn along the edge or over the seam etc. of a garment as a trimming or reinforcement **2.** *v.t.* to provide (e.g. a shoe or boot) with a welt [origin unknown]

Welt·an·schau·ung (véltɑ́nʃauuŋ) *n.* a general view of life || a cosmological philosophy [G.]

wel·ter (wéltər) **1.** *v.i.* to wallow **2.** *n.* turmoil, *a welter of blood and destruction* [M.Du. *welteren* or M.L.G. *weltern*]

welter 1. *adj.* (*horse racing*) of or relating to a race in which welterweights are carried **2.** *n.* (*pop.*) a welterweight [origin unknown]

wel·ter·weight (wéltərweit) *n.* (*horse racing*) a heavyweight rider || (*horse racing*) a weight of 28 lbs sometimes carried as a handicap || a professional or amateur boxer whose weight does not exceed 147 lbs

Welt·po·li·tik (véltpoulití:k) *n.* participation in international affairs, world politics [G.]

Welty (wélti:), Eudora (1909-) U.S. writer whose novels and stories usually depicted life in the South, esp. Mississippi. She won the Pulitzer Prize for 'The Optimist's Daughter' (1972). Other works include the novels 'The Robber Bridegroom' (1942), 'Delta Wedding' (1946), 'The Ponder Heart' (1954) and 'Losing Battles' (1970); short stories collected in 'The Golden Apples' (1949), 'The Bride of the Innisfallen' (1955), 'A Sweet Devouring' (1969) and 'The Collected Stories of Eudora Welty' (1980). Her autobiography 'One Writer's Beginnings' was published in 1984

wen (wen) *n.* a rune corresponding in Old English and early Middle English to 'w' in the modern English alphabet [O.E.]

wen *n.* a cyst filled with sebaceous matter, generally located on the scalp [O.E. *wenn*]

Wen·ces·las (wénsisləs), St (*Czech* Václav, *G.* Wenzel, c. 907-29), duke of Bohemia (921-9) and patron saint of Czechoslovakia. Feast: Sept. 28

Wenceslas IV (1361-1419), king of Bohemia and uncrowned Emperor (1378-1419), son of Emperor Charles IV. He failed to impose his authority on the Czechs and Germans. The Hussites defenestrated (1419) his Catholic counselors

wench (wentʃ) *n.* (*jocular*) a young woman [O.E. *wencel*, a child]

Wen·chow (wʌ́ndʒóu) (or Yungkia) a port (pop. 325,000) in Chekiang, E. China, founded in the 4th c. It was opened to international trade in 1876

Wend (wend) *n.* a member of a Slavic people of Saxony and East Prussia [fr. G. *Wende, Winde*]

wend (wend) *v.t.* (only in the phrase) **to wend one's way** to go unhurriedly along one's path [O.E. *wendan*, to turn]

Wend·ish (wéndiʃ) **1.** *adj.* of or relating to the Wends or to their West Slavic language **2.** *n.* the West Slavic language of the Wends

went *past* of GO

wen·tle·trap (wént'ltræp) *n.* any of various spirally coiled, usually white, mollusk shells much sought after by collectors || any of various mollusks of fam. *Epitoniidae,* having this sort of shell [Du. *wenteltrap,* a spiral staircase]

Went·worth (wéntwəːrθ), Thomas *STRAFFORD

wept *past* and *past part.* of WEEP

were (wəːr) *pl.* and *2nd pers. sing. past indicative* and *past subjunctive* of BE

we're (wiər) *contr.* of WE ARE

weren't (wəːrnt, wə́ːrənt) *contr.* of WERE NOT

were·wolf (wə́ːrwulf, wíərwulf, wέərwulf) *pl.* **were·wolves** (wə́ːrwulvz, wíərwulvz, wέərwulvz) *n.* (in superstitious belief) a human being changed, or capable of changing, into a wolf [O.E. *werewulf*]

wer·geld (wə́ːrgeld) *n.* (*hist.*) the money value set on a man, based on his rank, possessions etc., and exacted as a fine in cases of serious crime in Anglo-Saxon and Germanic law [fr. O.E. *wer,* man and *geld,* yield, payment]

Wer·ner (vέərnər), Alfred (1866-1919), Swiss chemist who formulated the coordination theory of valence. Nobel prize (1913)

We·ser (véizər) a navigable river (300 miles long) flowing from Hesse through lower Saxony, West Germany, to the Baltic. Chief port: Bremen

Wes·ley (wésliː, wézliː), Charles (1707-88), English Methodist and writer of hymns, brother of John Wesley. His son, Samuel (1766-1837), and grandson, Samuel Sebastian (1810-76), were both distinguished organists and composers

Wesley, John (1703-91), English Anglican clergyman, evangelist, founder of Methodism, and writer of hymns. He rode yearly on horseback through Britain, preaching in the open air and organizing Methodist Societies. He inaugurated lay preachers and he ordained Dr Thomas Coke (1760) for evangelism in America

Wes·ley·an (wésliːən, wézliːən) **1.** *adj.* of or relating to the Methodist denomination founded by John Wesley **2.** *n.* a member of this denomination, a Wesleyan Methodist **Wés·ley·an·ism** *n.*

Wes·sex (wésiks) (*Eng. hist.*) an AngloSaxon kingdom, settled in the late 5th c., and originally centered on the upper Thames valley. It expanded in S. and W. England and became (early 9th c.) the dominant English kingdom. Under Alfred it resisted the Danes, and under Edward the Elder extended its power over the Danelaw (10th c.). The successors of these kings became the English royal house

West (west), Benjamin (1738-1820), Anglo-American painter. He excelled in historical subjects, e.g. 'The Death of General Wolfe' (1771), and portraits, and succeeded Reynolds as president of the Royal Academy (1792-1805, 1807-20)

west (west) **1.** *adv.* toward the west **2.** *n.* (usually with 'the') one of the four cardinal points of the compass (*abbr.* W., *COMPASS POINT) || the direction of the setting sun at the equinox **the West** the western part of a country, esp. the states of the U.S.A. west of the Mississippi || western Europe and America as opposed to the communist countries of eastern Europe and Asia **3.** *adj.* of, belonging to or situated toward the west || facing west, *a west window* || (of winds) blowing from the west [O.E.]

Wes·tar satellite (wéstɑr) Western Union's communication satellite for transmission of facsimile material, including color TV pictures

West Bengal *BENGAL

West Berlin *BERLIN

west by north N. 78° 45′ W., one point north of due west (*abbr.* W. b. N., W. by N., *COMPASS POINT)

west by south S. 78° 45′ W., one point south of due west (*abbr.* W. b. S., W. by S., *COMPASS POINT)

West End the western part of London, containing the smart shopping, entertainment and residential districts

west·er (wéstər) *v.i.* (*rhet.,* esp. of the sun) to move towards the west

west·er·ly (wéstərliː) **1.** *adj.* and *adv.* in or toward the west || (of winds) from the west **2.** *pl.* **west·er·lies** *n.* a wind blowing from the west

west·ern (wéstərn) *adj.* situated, facing, coming from or moving toward the west **West·ern 1.** *adj.* of or relating to the West **2.** *n.* a story, film etc. of life in the West of the U.S.A. during the 2nd half of the 19th c. [O.E. *westerne*]

Western Australia the western state (area 975,920 sq. miles, pop. 1,673,200) of Australia. Capital: Perth. It is largely an arid, gently undulating plateau with vast desert areas in the interior. Population is concentrated in the southwest. Agriculture: cattle and sheep ranching, and (southwest) cereals, fruit, dairying. Resources: gold, some coal, asbestos, iron ore and other minerals, timber. Industries: agricultural processing, forestry. University of Western Australia (1912) near Perth

Western Bug a river (470 miles long) flowing from the W. Ukraine, U.S.S.R., forming part of the Soviet-Polish border, and across E. Poland to the Vistula

Western Church that part of the Catholic Church which continued to recognize the Roman pope after the schism of the 9th c. || (*loosely*) the Christian Churches of Western Europe and America (*ORTHODOX EASTERN CHURCH, *ROMAN CATHOLIC CHURCH)

Western Empire the Western Roman Empire

West·ern·er (wéstərnər) *n.* a native or inhabitant of the West, esp. of the Western part of the U.S.A.

Western Ghats *GHATS

western hemisphere the part of the earth west of the Atlantic Ocean, comprising North and South America

Western Isles the Hebrides

west·ern·ize (wéstərnaiz) *pres. part.* **west·ern·iz·ing** *past* and *past part.* **west·ern·ized** *v.t.* to cause to become Western in outlook, dress, character etc.

west·ern·most (wéstərnmoust) *adj.* furthest west

Western Nigeria *NIGERIA

Western Roman Empire the western part of the Roman Empire after the Byzantine Empire had separated from it (395)

Western saddle a stock saddle

Western Sahara (formerly Spanish Sahara) an area (area 102,680 sq. miles) on the N.W. African coast, with important fisheries. Chief port: Villa Cisneros (pop. 2,000). Livestock: camels, sheep, goats. Spanish settlement began in the 15th c. The area was taken under Spanish protection (1884) and became a Spanish province (1958). After discovery of high-grade phosphate in Western Sahara (1963), Morocco and Mauritania pressured Spain to relinquish the area; Algeria and later Libya backed a pro-independence group called the Polisario Front. The World Court ruled (1975) that Western Sahara should be given self-determination. Morocco sent 350,000 civilians into the area and Spain withdrew (1976, ceding the northern two thirds to Morocco and the remainder to Mauritania. Mauritania signed a treaty with Polisario renouncing its claims (1979) and Morocco annexed the entire area. Refusing to negotiate directly with the Polisario, Morocco built a fortified wall around the northwestern corner of Western Sahara, which contained most of the population and mineral resources as well as the coastal fisheries. Drought drove many nomadic Saharans into towns behind the wall, where Moroccan investment and settlement, designed to gain local support, caused an economic boom. Libya halted aid to the Polisario when it signed a treaty of union with Morocco (1984)

West Frisian Islands *FRISIAN ISLANDS

West Germany *GERMANY, FEDERAL REPUBLIC OF

West Indian 1. *n.* a native or inhabitant of the West Indies **2.** *adj.* of or relating to the West Indies

West Indies an archipelago of E. North America, divided into the Bahamas, in the Atlantic, and the Antilles, which curve east, south, and west from Florida to western Venezuela, separating the Atlantic from the Caribbean. The islands are mainly wooded, mountainous, and of volcanic origin, with some small coral atolls. The economy is everywhere based upon tropical agriculture. HISTORY. Columbus landed in the Bahamas (1492) and discovered many of the larger islands (1492-1504). The English settled Bermuda (1609), Barbados (1627) and the Bahamas (1629). Curaçao was settled by the Dutch (1634) and Guadeloupe and Martinique by the French (1635). England took Jamaica from Spain (1655), Dominica (1783), Grenada (1783), St Lucia (1803) and Tobago (1814) from France, and Trinidad (1802) from Spain. The Dominican Republic and Haiti became independent in the 19th c. After the Spanish-American War (1898), Puerto Rico and Cuba came under American control. Sugar-growing, based on slavery, prospered in the late 17th c. and 18th c., but declined in the 19th c. The Virgin Islands were purchased by the U.S.A. from Denmark (1917). A trend toward self-government in the 20th c. culminated in the independence of most of the islands

West Indies, Federation of the a federation (1958-62) of Caribbean islands within the Commonwealth, comprising Jamaica, Barbados, Trinidad and the colonies of the Windward Islands and of the Leeward Islands. It was dissolved after the withdrawal of Jamaica and Trinidad

west·ing (wéstiŋ) *n.* (*naut.*) a sailing towards the west || (*naut.*) the distance thus sailed

West·ing·house (wéstiŋhaus), George (1846-1914), American engineer. He invented (1869) the automatic compressedair brake used on railroads

West·land (wéstlənd) a region (area 6,010 sq. miles, pop. 25,000) of S.W. South Island, New Zealand. Industries: mining (coal, gold), lumber, tourism. Chief town: Greymouth (pop. 9,000)

West·ma·cott (wéstməkɒt), Sir Richard (1775-1856), British sculptor. His best-known work is probably 'Achilles' in Hyde Park, London, the memorial to Wellington (1822)

West·meath (westmíːð) a northern county (area 681 sq. miles, pop. 61,300) in Leinster province, Irish Republic. County seat: Mullingar (pop. 6,000)

West·min·ster Abbey (wéstminstər) the ancient church in Westminster, London, developed from a Benedictine monastery (1050-65) and rebuilt in the 13th to 15th cc. Henry VII's chapel dates from 1503-19. The Abbey has been the coronation church of almost all English monarchs since William I and until 1760 most of them were also buried there. It is also the burial place of many distinguished citizens

Westminster Assembly an assembly of divines and some laity summoned (1643-9) by the Long Parliament to advise on ways of bringing the Church of England into line with Calvinist theology

Westminster, City of a borough (pop. 214,000) of London, site of the Houses of Parliament

Westminster Confession the Calvinist creed drawn up (1646) by the Westminster Assembly. It was adopted officially by the Church of Scotland and forms the basis of Congregationalism

Westminster, Palace of the neo-Gothic parliament building designed by Sir Charles Barry and built (1840-67) on the site of the old royal palace, of which the Hall (1097-9) remains

Westminster, Statute of the statute (1931) under which the full independence of the Dominions of the British Empire was recognized, including their responsibility for foreign affairs || any of three statutes promulgated (1275, 1285 and 1290) during the reign of Edward II, establishing many of the bases of English law

West·more·land (westmɔ́rlənd, westmóurlənd), William Childs (1914-), U.S. general, commander (1964-8) of U.S. forces in Vietnam. His over-optimistic reports from the field contributed to the growing disillusionment at home among wide sections of the nation

West·mor·land (wéstmərlənd) a former county of N.W. England, now part of Cumbria

west-north·west (wéstnɔrθwést) **1.** *adv.* towards west-northwest **2.** *n.* N. 67° 30′ W., a compass point midway between west and northwest (*abbr.* W.N.W., *COMPASS POINT) **3.** *adj.* of or situated towards west-northwest || (of winds) blowing from west-northwest

Wes·ton cell (wéstən) (*elec.*) a cadmium-mercury primary cell, used as giving a standard, uniform emf [after its inventor Edward *Weston* (1850–1936), Anglo-American manufacturer]

West·pha·li·a (westféiljə, westféiliːə) *NORTH RHINE-WESTPHALIA

Westphalia, Treaties of treaties signed (Oct. 24, 1648) by the Holy Roman Empire, France, Sweden, and the Protestant states of the Empire, ending the Thirty Years' War. The Holy Roman Empire was greatly weakened by the recognition of the German states. France gained Alsace, and emerged as the dominant power in Europe. Sweden gained the western part of Pomerania. Switzerland and the United Netherlands were recognized as independent. Religious toleration was extended to the Calvinists

West Point a military post on the Hudson River in New York State, site of the U.S. Military Academy (1802)

CONCISE PRONUNCIATION KEY: **(a)** æ, *cat;* ɑ, *car;* ɔ *fawn;* ei, *snake.* **(e)** e, *hen;* iː, *sheep;* iə, *deer;* εə, *bear.* **(i)** i, *fish;* ai, *tiger;* əː, *bird.* **(o)** o, *ox;* au, *cow;* ou, *goat;* u, *poor;* ɔi, *royal.* **(u)** ʌ, *duck;* u, *bull;* uː, *goose;* ə, *bacillus;* juː, *cube.* x, *loch;* θ, *think;* ð, *bother;* z, *Zen;* ʒ, *corsage;* dʒ, *savage;* ŋ, *orangutang;* j, *yak;* ʃ, *fish;* tʃ, *fetch;* 'l, *rabble;* 'n, *redden.* Complete pronunciation key appears inside front cover.

West·pol·i·tik (wẹstpólitik) *n.* Communist nations' policy of maintaining trade relations with the West. *Cf* OSTPOLITIK.
West Quod·dy Head (kwódi:) a cape off S.E. Maine, the easternmost point of continental U.S.A.
West Saxon (*hist.*) a native of the kingdom of Wessex ‖ (*hist.*) the dialect spoken in Wessex, the main literary dialect of Anglo-Saxon
west-south·west (wéstsauθwést) **1.** *adv.* towards west-southwest **2.** *n.* S. 67° 30′ W., a compass point midway between west and southwest (*abbr.* W.S.W., *COMPASS POINT) **3.** *adj.* of or situated towards west-southwest ‖ (of winds) blowing from west-southwest
West Virginia (*abbr.* W.Va.) a state (area 24,282 sq. miles, pop. 1,948,000) in the central eastern U.S.A. Capital: Charleston. It is crossed by the Appalachians in the east, and the remainder is an elevated hilly plateau. Agriculture: beef cattle, dairying, poultry, fruit (esp. apples, peaches), corn. Resources: coal (first state producer), oil and natural gas, building materials. Industries: chemicals, iron and steel, metal products, glass and pottery. State university (1867) at Morgantown. West Virginia split (1861) from Virginia during the Civil War, and became (1863) the 35th state of the U.S.A.
west·ward (wéstwərd) **1.** *adv.* and *adj.* towards the west **2.** *n.* the westward direction or part **wést·wards** *adv.*
wet (wet) *comp.* **wet·ter** *superl.* **wet·test** *adj.* imbued with, covered with or soaked in water or some other liquid ‖ characterized by much rain, *a wet climate* ‖ (of paint, ink etc.) not yet dried ‖ (of a baby) having urinated in his diaper ‖ (*naut.*, of a boat) apt to ship water over the bows or sides ‖ involving the use of water or some other liquid, *a wet process* ‖ preserved in a liquid ‖ permitting or favoring the sale of alcoholic liquors, *a wet state* [O.E. *wǣt*]
wet *pres. part.* **wet·ting** *past* and *past part.* **wet, wet·ted** *v.t.* to make wet ‖ to urinate in or on ‖ *v.i.* to become wet to wet down to damp with water or some other liquid [O.E. *wǣtan*]
wet *n.* water or some other liquid substance ‖ (with 'the') rain, rainy weather, *don't go out in the wet* ‖ someone in favor of the sale of alcoholic liquors [partly O.E. *wǣt, wǣta*, partly fr. WET adj.]
wet-and-dry-bulb thermometer (*phys.*) two similar thermometers mounted side by side, the bulb of one being kept wet and therefore cooled by evaporation. The difference between the two thermometer readings can be used to determine the relative humidity of the air
wet blanket a person who discourages fun or conversation by his sober mood
weth·er (wéðər) *n.* a castrated male sheep [O.E.]
wet lab entrance and egress compartment in an artificial underwater habitat
wet·look (wétluk) *n.* a shiny finish on fabric created by a urethane coating
wet nurse a nurse who suckles another woman's baby **wét-nurse** *pres. part.* **wet-nurs·ing** *past* and *past part.* **wet-nursed** *v.t.* to be a wet nurse to ‖ to pamper
we've (wi:v) *contr.* of WE HAVE
Wex·ford (wéksfərd) a southeastern county (area 908 sq. miles, pop. 86,351) of Leinster province, Irish Republic. County seat: Wexford (pop. 11,849)
Weyden *VAN DER WEYDEN
Wey·gand (veigã), Maxime (1867-1965), French general. Foch's chief of staff (1914-23), and army chief of staff (1930), Weygand was appointed French supreme commander (May 1940). He was Pétain's delegate-general in N. Africa (1940-1) but was relieved of his post and was imprisoned by the Germans (1942-5)
WF (*abbr.*) for 'withdrawn failing,' a grade given to a failing student who withdraws from a course. *Cf* WP.
whack (hwæk, wæk) **1.** *v.t.* to strike, esp. with a resounding blow ‖ (*Br., pop.*) to defeat **2.** *n.* a resounding blow ‖ the sound of such a blow **out of whack** not in proper working order or condition **to take** (or **have**) **a whack at** to attempt **whacked** *adj.* (*Br., pop.*) tired out [prob. imit.]
whack·ing (hwǽkiŋ, wǽkiŋ) **1.** *adj.* (*pop.*) very large, *a whacking success* **2.** *adv.* (*pop.*) extremely, *a whacking big elephant*
whack·y (hwǽki:, wǽki:) *comp.* **whack·i·er** *superl.* **whack·i·est** *adj.* (*pop.*) wacky
whale (hweil, weil) **1.** *n.* a member of any of many species of immense, fishlike marine mammals of the order *Cetacea*. They measure up to 100 ft in length and can weigh as much as 150 tons. Whales are hunted for their flesh, for the oil extracted from their blubber, for their very elastic whalebone, and for ambergris and spermaceti. Whales form two groups: toothed whales and whalebone whales **a whale of a** (*pop.*) exceptionally good in quality, *a whale of a game* ‖ (*pop.*) very large, *a whale of a difference* **2.** *v.i. pres. part.* **whal·ing** *past* and *past part.* **whaled** to hunt whales [O.E. hwœl]
whale *pres. part.* **whal·ing** *past* and *past part.* **whaled** *v.t.* (*pop.*) to beat (a person, animal etc.) severely, *he whaled his dog for chasing sheep* ‖ (*pop.*) to defeat thoroughly [origin unknown]
whale·boat (hwéilbọut, wéilbọut) *n.* (*hist.*) a long narrow rowboat pointed at both ends and used in whaling
whale·bone (hwéilbọun, wéilbọun) *n.* a horny substance growing in fringed plates in the palate of whalebone whales. It is exploited for use as a stiffening e.g. in corsets
whalebone whale one of the two main divisions of whales, constituting the suborder *Mysticeti* and including the rorqual, humpback, right whale etc.
whale oil a true fat, obtained from whales, consisting almost entirely of one molecule of glycerol in combination with three of fatty acids. By a process in which molecules of hydrogen are added to molecules of fatty matter in the presence of a nickel catalyst, whale oil is converted into high-grade soapmaking material and an edible fat used in the manufacture of margarine and other cooking fats (cf. SPERM OIL)
whal·er (hwéilər, wéilər) *n.* a boat used in hunting whales ‖ a person who hunts whales
wham (hwæm, wæm) **1.** *v. pres. part.* **wham·ming** *past* and *past part.* **whammed** *v.t.* to hit, propel etc. with a hard blow, *he whammed the ball 250 yards down the fairway* ‖ *v.i.* to make a loud, heavy impact, *his car whammed into the tree* **2.** *n.* this noisy impact [imit.]
wham·my (wǽmi:) *n.* (*colloq.*) a shocking or lethal blow
whang (hwæŋ, wæŋ) **1.** *n.* a blow that makes a loud noise **2.** *v.i.* to make this noise ‖ to make a very energetic attack, *he whanged into him* ‖ *v.t.* to hit with a whang [imit.]
wharf (hworf, worf) **1.** *pl.* **wharves,** (hwɔrvz, wɔrvz), **wharfs** *n.* a landing stage to which barges and ships can be moored for loading and unloading **2.** *v.t.* to moor (a ship) beside a wharf ‖ to place (goods) on a wharf **whárf·age** *n.* the fee for using a wharf ‖ accommodation at a wharf [Late O.E. *hwearf*]
wharf·in·ger (hwɔ́rfindʒər, wɔ́rfindʒər) *n.* the owner or manager of a wharf [apparently altered fr. earlier *wharfager* fr. WHARFAGE]
Whar·ton (hwɔ́rt'n, wɔ́rt'n), Edith (1862-1937), American writer. Her works include the novels 'Ethan Frome' (1911) and 'The Age of Innocence' (1920). She also wrote many short stories.
what (hwɒt, hwʌt, wɒt, wʌt, *unstressed* hwət, wət) **1.** *pron.* used interrogatively, requiring something to be identified, *what is the time?*, (often used also elliptically) *did what?* ‖ that which, *he heard what I said* ‖ how much, *he told me what it would cost* **no matter what** despite anything that **to have what it takes** (*pop.*) to have the necessary qualities, *he has what it takes to make an officer* **what about** an expression used to introduce a suggestion, *what about having dinner together?* ‖ what is the state of affairs regarding, *what about your homework?* **what for?** for what reason or purpose? **what have you** et cetera **what if** what is (or will be or would be) the result if, *what if he can't come after all?* **what's what** the true state of affairs ‖ good quality, *he knows what's what in wines* **2.** *adj.* used interrogatively, referring to the nature, identity etc. of a person or thing, *what kind of person is he?* ‖ whatever, *invent what stories you will* ‖ (in exclamations) how great, ridiculous etc., *what a pity!* **3.** *adv.* to what extent, to what degree, *what do you care?* ‖ used to introduce 'with' in phrases suggesting 'because of', *what with the noise and the dogs we could hardly listen* ‖ (in exclamations) used as an intensive, *what cold weather!* **4.** *interj.* an exclamation of surprise, anger etc., *what! he really jumped?* [O.E. hwœt]
what·ev·er (hwɒtévər, hwʌtévər, hwətévər, wɒtévər, wʌtévər, wətévər **1.** *pron.* anything that, *eat whatever you like* ‖ no matter what, *I'll do it, whatever he says* ‖ used as an intensive form of the interrogative 'what', usually expressing astonishment, surprise etc., *whatever are you doing?* ‖ something of the sort, *he has a cottage, shack or whatever* **2.** *adj.* all the, *they gave him whatever clothes he possesses* ‖ (in negative constructions) at all, *he has no clothes whatever*
Whatman-number *SOILING INDEX
what·not (hwɒ́tnɒt, hwʌ́tnɒt, wɒ́tnɒt, wʌ́tnɒt) *n.* a piece of furniture standing on legs and consisting of a set of open shelves, one above another, for displaying or storing away miscellaneous objects ‖ any of various other miscellaneous items, *pockets full of string, worms and whatnot* ‖ something of that sort, *use a rope or chain or whatnot*
what·so·ev·er (hwɒtsouévər, hwʌtsouévər, wɒtsouévər, wʌtsouévər) *pron.* and *adj.* whatever
wheal (hwi:l, wi:l) *n.* a weal [misspelled form of WEAL]
wheat (hwi:t, wi:t) *n.* any of various grasses of the genus *Triticum* cultivated widely in temperate regions, esp. *T. aestivum*, an annual cereal grass ‖ the grain yielded from these, which is processed into flour or meal and used as the major breadstuff in temperate areas and for animal feeding [O.E. *hwǣte*]
wheat·ear (hwí:tiər, wí:tiər) *n.* *Oenanthe oenanthe*, a small bluish-gray, black and white passerine bird of N. Europe, Asia and Alaska, related to the stonechat [older *wheatears*=white ass]
wheat·en (hwí:t'n, wí:t'n) *adj.* of or made of wheat or wheat flour ‖ of the fawn or pale yellow color of wheat [O.E. *hwǣten*]
wheat germ the embryo of the wheat seed rich in vitamins, esp. vitamin E, and linoleic acid oil
wheat·meal (hwi:tmi:l, wi:tmi:l) *n.* (*Br.*) the pure meal of wheat, the whole berry being ground (*WHOLE WHEAT) [O.E. *hwǣtemelu*]
Wheat·on (hwí:t'n, wí:t'n), Henry (1785-1848), U.S. jurist and diplomat. His works include 'Elements of International Law' (1836) and 'A History of the Law of Nations' (1845)
Wheat·stone (hwí:tstọun, wí:tstọun, *Br.* esp. hwí:tstən, wí:tstən), Sir Charles (1802-75), British physicist. With William Cooke, he patented a successful electric telegraph. He also invented the concertina
Wheatstone bridge a device for comparing and measuring electrical resistances. It consists of two parallel branches of conductors containing the resistances to be compared and a device (usually a galvanometer) to indicate the voltage or current flowing in each branch [after Sir Charles WHEATSTONE]
whee·dle (hwí:d'l, wí:d'l) *pres. part.* **whee·dling** *past* and *past part.* **whee·dled** *v.t.* to persuade by flattery, coaxing etc., *she wheedled him into giving her a new coat* ‖ to obtain in this way, *she wheedled a new coat out of him* [origin unknown]
wheel (hwi:l, wi:l) **1.** *n.* a circular device, thin in relation to its face area, usually able to rotate about a central axle or pivot, with a durable but elastic rim or with regular teeth cut on the rim, and for lightness often supported by spokes joined to the hub instead of being left solid. The invention of the wheel enabled loads to be transported with relative ease, rolling friction being always much less than sliding friction. The use of cogged wheels also enabled power to be transmitted, e.g. in a clockwork mechanism, and to be varied at will (*GEAR) ‖ something resembling this device in shape, movement etc., e.g. a roulette wheel ‖ a large wheel formerly used as an instrument of torture ‖ the control of a car, ship etc., *the ship's captain had the wheel* ‖ a cycle of events, *the wheel has come full circle* ‖ a circular motion e.g. of marching soldiers, warships in line etc. turning around a pivot point ‖ (*pl.*) the functioning of something likened to a wheel mechanism, *the wheels of government* **to put one's shoulder to the wheel** to begin to use one's energies with determination in accomplishing some purpose or task **to take the wheel** to assume control of a ship, car etc. **2.** *v.i.* to turn around on or as if on an axis, *he wheeled around when he heard her voice* ‖ to move on or as if on wheels ‖ to turn in a circular motion ‖ to change one's course of action, opinion etc. ‖ (*mil.*) to execute a wheel ‖ *v.t.* to cause to move on wheels ‖ to carry on wheels or in a wheeled vehicle ‖ to walk beside and push (a bicycle or motorcycle) ‖ to drive (a car, truck etc.) ‖ to

cause to revolve or rotate ‖ (*mil.*) to cause to execute a wheel [O.E. *hweogol, hwēol*]

wheel and axle a wheel fixed to an axle of smaller diameter, arranged so that a rope unwinds and winds on each respectively, the effort being applied to the wheel rope and the load hauled by the axle rope. A mechanical advantage is thus derived from the difference in turning moments

wheel animal a rotifer

wheel animalcule a rotifer

wheel·bar·row (hwí:lbærou, wí:lbærou) *n.* a shallow vehicle with one wheel in front and two legs and handles at the back, pushed by hand to transport earth, bricks etc.

wheel·base (hwí:lbeis, wí:lbeis) *n.* the distance between a vehicle's front and back axles

wheel·chair (hwí:ltʃεər, wí:ltʃεər) *n.* a chair on wheels in which an invalid can propel himself along, or be pushed by someone else

Whee·ler (hwí:lər, wí:lər), Benjamin Ide (1854-1927), U.S. classical scholar, philologist, and president (1899-1919) of the University of California during the period of its greatest development

wheel·er (hwí:lər, wí:lər) *n.* a wheelhorse ‖ (used in hyphenated compounds) a vehicle having a specified number of wheels, *a two-wheeler*

wheel·er-deal·er (wí:lərdí:lər) *n.* a shrewd negotiator, businessperson, politician, or operator who specializes in fast purchases and sales —**wheeler-dealer** *adj.* —**wheeler-dealing** *v.*

wheel·horse (hwí:lhɔrs, wí:lhɔrs) *pl.* **wheel·hors·es** *n.* the horse or one of the horses nearest to the wheels of a vehicle (cf. LEADER) ‖ (*pop.*) a hardworking and effective employee of an enterprise

wheel·house (hwí:lhaus, wí:lhaus) *pl.* **wheel·hous·es** (hwí:lhauziz, wí:lhauziz) *n.* the structure on a ship containing the wheel and navigating equipment

wheel·ie (wí:li:) *n.* (*sports*) a stunt of momentarily standing a vehicle, esp. a motorcycle, on its back wheel or wheels

wheel lock an obsolete type of gunlock in which the charge was ignited by sparks from a wheel spinning against a flint

Whee·lock (hwí:lɒk, wí:lɒk), Eleazar (1711-79), U.S. educator, founder (1770) and first president of Dartmouth College

wheel·race (hwí:lreis, wí:lreis) *n.* the place in a millrace where the mill wheel is set

wheel·wright (hwí:lrait, wí:lrait) *n.* someone who makes and repairs wheels, carts etc.

wheeze (hwi:z, wi:z) **1.** *v.i. pres. part.* **wheez·ing** *past* and *past part.* **wheezed** to breathe with difficulty, making a whistling sound ‖ *v.t.* to utter wheezily **2.** *n.* a wheezing sound **whéez·i·ly** *adv.* **whéez·i·ness** *n.* **whéez·y** *comp.* **wheez·i·er** *superl.* **wheez·i·est** *adj.* [prob. O.N. *hvœsa*, to hiss]

whelk (hwelk, welk) *n.* a member of *Buccinum* and other genera of carnivorous gastropod mollusks, fam. *Buccinidae* and related families, esp. *B. undatum* of the Atlantic coasts, esteemed as food in Europe [O.E. *wioloc, weoloc*]

whelp (hwelp, welp) **1.** *n.* a young lion, tiger, bear, wolf etc. ‖ a puppy ‖ a naughty, insupportable child or youth ‖ a tooth on a sprocket wheel ‖ (*naut.*, esp. *pl.*) one of the ribs or ridges on the barrel of a capstan or windlass **2.** *v.t.* (of animals) to give birth to ‖ *v.i.* (of animals) to give birth [O.E. *hwelp*]

when (hwen, wen) **1.** *adv.* at what time, *when does the train leave?* ‖ on which occasion, *when did you last eat?* **2.** *conj.* at, during or after the time that, *that was when we missed you most, stop the machine when the whistle is blown* ‖ every time that, *she gets a rash when she eats strawberries* ‖ in view of the fact that, *why does he live like a miser when he is so rich?* ‖ if, in the event that, *when three balls are missed the player is out* **3.** *pron.* what or which time, *when is the contract effective from?, when will you wait until?* **4.** *n.* the time of an event or an action, *I can't remember the when or the why of it* [O.E. *hwanne, hwonne, hwenne*]

whence (hwens, wens) **1.** *adv.* (*rhet.*) from where ‖ (*rhet.*) from what source or origin **2.** *conj.* (*rhet.*) from what place or source [M.E. *whannes, whennes* fr. *whanne* fr. O.E. *hwanone*]

when·ev·er (hwenévər, wenévər) *adv.* and *conj.* at whatever time, as often as, *come whenever you like* ‖ (used emphatically) when, *whenever will you grow up?*

when·so·ev·er (hwensouévər, wensouévər) *adv.* and *conj.* (*rhet.*, used emphatically) at whatever time

where (hwεər, wεər) **1.** *adv.* in or at what place, *where are you?* ‖ to or toward what place, *where are you going?* ‖ in what respect, *where does this argument break down?* ‖ in what circumstances, *without friends where are you?* ‖ from what place or source, *where do you get your money?* **2.** *conj.* in or at what or which place, *they have gone where the police can't get them* ‖ to or toward the place to which, *I'll drive you where you're going* ‖ in the or a case, situation, respect in which, *where some are weak and old others must shoulder the burden* ‖ insofar as, *there can be no problem where you are concerned* **3.** *n.* a place, esp. a place in which something is or occurs, *I only know it happened, but not the where or how* [O.E. *hwǣr, hwār*]

where·a·bouts (hwέərəbauts, wέərəbauts) **1.** *adv.* (used interrogatively) near or at what place, *whereabouts is your home?* **2.** *conj.* in what place, *tell us roughly whereabouts you put them* **3.** *n.* the place where someone or something is, *he's hiding his whereabouts*

where·as (hwεəræz, wεəræz) *conj.* while on the contrary, *some praise him, whereas others condemn him* ‖ (in legal documents) since, considering that

where·at (hwεərǽt, wεərǽt) **1.** *adv.* (*archaic*) at which, at what **2.** *conj.* (*archaic*) upon which event

where·by (hwεərbái, wεərbái) **1.** *adv.* by which, *the ruse whereby they succeeded* **2.** *conj.* by which

where·fore (hwέərfɔr, hwέərfour, wέərfɔr, wέərfour) **1.** *adv.* (*rhet.*) why, for what reason or purpose **2.** *conj.* (*rhet.*) for which reason **3.** *n.* (esp. *pl.*) the reason, *the whys and the wherefores*

where·in (hwεərín, wεərín) **1.** *adv.* (*rhet.*) in which place ‖ in what respect, *wherein did they transgress?* ‖ (*rhet.*) in which, *armor wherein he trusted* **2.** *conj.* in what or in which

where·of (hwεərʌ́v, hwεərɒ́v, wεərʌ́v, wεərɒ́v) *adv.* and *conj.* (*rhet.*) of which, of what or of whom

where·on (hwεərɒ́n, hwεərɒ́n, wεərɒ́n, wεərɒ́n) **1.** *conj.* (*rhet.*) on what, on which **2.** *adv.* (*archaic*) on what?

where·so·ev·er (hwεərsouévər, wεərsouévər) *adv.* and *conj.* (*archaic*, emphatic for) wherever ‖ (*archaic*) in or to whatever place

where·to (hwεərtú:, wεərtú:) *adv.* (*archaic*) to what place, purpose etc. ‖ (*archaic*) to which

where·up·on (hwεərəpɒ́n, hwεərəpɒ́n, wεərəpɒ́n, wεərəpɒ́n) **1.** *conj.* (*rhet.*) after which, in consequence of which, *we disagreed, whereupon he left me* **2.** *adv.* upon which

wher·ev·er (hwεərévər, wεərévər) **1.** *conj.* at, in or to whatever place, *wherever you go you will find people much the same* **2.** *adv.* (used to express astonishment or incredulity) where, *wherever are you taking me?* ‖ in any circumstance in which, *wherever it is possible*

where·with (hwεərwíθ, hwεərwíð, wεərwíθ, wεərwíð) *adv.* (*rhet.*) with which, *the means wherewith to travel* ‖ (*archaic*) with what?

where·with·al (hwέərwiðɔl, wέərwiðɔl) *n.* the means, what is necessary, *how can he do that if he lacks the wherewithal?*

wher·ry (hwéri:, wéri:) *pl.* **wher·ries** *n.* a light shallow rowboat, pointed at both ends, used for carrying passengers and freight on rivers ‖ a large lighter or barge used in Great Britain to transport freight **whér·ry·man** *pl.* **wher·ry·men** *n.* (*Br.*) someone who works on a wherry [origin unknown]

whet (hwet, wet) **1.** *v.t. pres. part.* **whet·ting** *past* and *past part.* **whet·ted** to sharpen by rubbing against a whetstone etc. ‖ to stimulate, arouse, *to whet one's appetite* **2.** *n.* (*rhet.*) something that whets, *a whet to the appetite* [O.E. *hwettan*]

wheth·er (hwéðər, wéðər) *conj.* (followed by 'or', 'or whether') introducing the first of two or more possibilities, *I wonder whether it will rain or snow, I wonder whether it will rain or whether it will be fine* ‖ (introducing an indirect question) if, *he asked me whether I would sing* ‖ either, *we'll take the next offer, whether good or bad* [O.E. *hwæther, hwether*]

whet·stone (hwétstoun, wétstoun) *n.* a stone used for sharpening the blades of cutting tools [O.E. *hwetstān*]

whey (hwei, wei) *n.* the watery part of milk left when curds have formed and separated [O.E. *hwæg, hweg*]

which (hwitʃ, witʃ) **1.** *pron.* what one or ones of several things, persons etc. pointed out, denoted, described etc., *which do you prefer?* ‖ whichever one or ones, *you may select which you like* ‖ used as a relative in a subordinate clause representing a noun or noun phrase in the principal sentence, *he read the book which you lent him* ‖ (used as a connective) a fact that, *he left—which in itself isn't important—abruptly* **2.** *adj.* what one or ones, *which road should I take?* ‖ whatever, *run which way you will, you won't escape* ‖ used as an introductory word, modifying a noun, and referring to an antecedent noun, clause etc., *he is studying economics, which knowledge is very important today* [O.E. *hwelc, hwilc, hwylc*]

which·ev·er, (hwitʃévər, witʃévər) **1.** *pron.* any one or ones of several, *buy whichever is cheapest* **2.** *adj.* no matter which, *it's a nuisance whichever way you look at it*

which·so·ev·er (hwitʃsouévər, witʃsouévər) *pron.* and *adj.* (*archaic*, emphatic form of) whichever

whid·ah, whyd·ah (hwídə, wídə) *n.* the widow bird [alt. fr. *widow bird* after *Whidah* (now Ouidah), a town in Benin]

whiff (hwif, wif) **1.** *n.* a small volume of smoke, air etc., esp. one having a smell, suddenly expelled ‖ the smell of this, *a whiff of perfume* ‖ an inhalation of tobacco smoke, odor etc. **2.** *v.t.* to emit a small amount of (smoke, scent etc.) ‖ *v.i.* to blow lightly [imit.]

whif·fle (hwífəl, wífəl) **1.** *v. pres. part.* **whif·fling** *past* and *past part.* **whif·fled** *v.i.* (of the wind) to blow in little gusts ‖ to make a light whistling sound ‖ (*Am.*) to change one's mind frequently ‖ *v.t.* to blow, drive etc. with or as if with a gust of wind **2.** *n.* the act or a sound of whiffling [WHIFF]

whif·fle·ball (hwífəlbɔl) *n.* (*sports*) a plastic ball with openings to increase air resistance, used for golf, softball, or baseball practice

whif·fle·tree (hwífəltri:, wífəltri:) *n.* the pivoted crossbar of a cart, or of a plow or other implement, to which a horse's traces are fastened

Whig (hwig, wig) **1.** *n.* (*Scot. hist.*) someone supporting the Covenanters' cause (17th c.) ‖ (*Eng. hist.*) someone belonging to the political group, led by Shaftesbury, which opposed (1679) the succession of the future James II on account of his Catholic sympathies. The Whigs were among the organizers of the Glorious Revolution (1688–9), and ruled Britain (1714–60), notably in the ministry (1721–42) of Walpole. They were again briefly in power (1782) under Rockingham, but were ousted by the Tories until 1830. They secured the passage of the Reform Act (1832) and other measures of reform. By 1868 the Whig party had merged with the new Liberal party ‖ (*Am. hist.*) a colonist who supported the Revolutionary War (1775–83) ‖ (*Am. hist.*) a member of the party which opposed (1834–56) the Democratic party. It was succeeded by the Republican party **2.** *adj.* of, being or holding the beliefs of a Whig **Whíg·ger·y** *n.* **Whíg·gish** *adj.* of or like Whigs or their doctrines **Whíg·gism** *n.* the doctrines and principles of Whigs, esp. of English Whigs [etym. doubtful]

while (hwail, wail) **1.** *n.* a period of time, *he stayed only for a short while* **once in a while** on infrequent occasions, *he comes once in a while* **the while** (*old-fash.*) during that time, *he kept his eyes on her the while* **2.** *v.t. pres. part.* **whil·ing** *past* and *past part.* **whiled** (with 'away') to make (time) pass pleasantly in order esp. to escape boredom, *she whiled away the hours of waiting by looking at the shops* [O.E. *hwīl*, time]

while *conj.* during the time that, *she saw him only twice while he was staying there* ‖ at the same time that, *he came to the door while I was ringing the bell* ‖ although, *while we don't agree we continue to be friends* [O.E. *hwīle*]

whilst (hwailst, wailst) *conj.* (esp. *Br.*) while

whim (hwim, wim) *n.* a freakish pattern of ideas and their associated emotions as a motive of action ‖ (*mining*) a device for hoisting ore or water, with extending arms to which a horse or horses may be tied to do the turning [fr. older *whim-wham*, a trinket, origin unknown]

whim·brel (hwímbrəl, wímbrəl) *n.* *Numenius phaeopus*, a small European curlew [prob. imit.]

whim·per (hwímpər, wímpər) **1.** *v.i.* to utter feeble little cries of fear or complaint or discontent continued over a period almost nonstop ‖ *v.t.* to

CONCISE PRONUNCIATION KEY: **(a)** æ, *cat*; ɑ, *car*; ɔ *fawn*; ei, *snake*. **(e)** e, *hen*; i:, *sheep*; iə, *deer*; εə, *bear*. **(i)** i, *fish*; ai, *tiger*; ə:, *bird*. **(o)** o, *ox*; au, *cow*; ou, *goat*; u, *poor*; ɔi, *royal*. **(u)** ʌ, *duck*; u, *bull*; u:, *goose*; ə, *bacillus*; ju:, *cube*. x, *loch*; θ, *think*; ð, *bother*; z, *Zen*; ʒ, *corsage*; dʒ, *savage*; ŋ, *orangutang*; j, *yak*; ʃ, *fish*; tʃ, *fetch*; 'l, *rabble*; 'n, *redden*. Complete pronunciation key appears inside front cover.

utter whimperingly **2.** *n.* a whimpering sound [imit.]
whimsey *WHIMSY
whim·si·cal (hwímzik'l, wímzik'l) *adj.* full of whims ‖ subject to whims **whim·si·cal·i·ty** (hwimzikǽliti:, wimzikǽliti:) *pl.* **whim·si·cal·i·ties** *n.*
whim·sy, whim·sey (hwímzi:, wímzi:) *n.* feeble or sentimental fancy, esp. as a degenerate element in a work of art
whin (hwin, win) *n.* gorse [prob. of Scand. origin]
whin (hwin, win) *n.* whinstone [origin unknown]
whin·chat (hwíntʃæt, wíntʃæt) *n.* *Saxicola rubetra,* a small European songbird
whine (hwain, wain) **1.** *v. pres. part.* **whin·ing** *past* and *past part.* **whined** *v.i.* to cry in or utter a high-pitched, long drawn-out, plaintive sound ‖ to complain in a querulous or childish way ‖ *v.t.* to utter whiningly **2.** *n.* a whining sound ‖ a complaint, esp. one that causes mild contempt [O.E. *hwīnan*]
whin·ny (hwíni:, wíni:) **1.** *v. pres. part.* **whin·ny·ing** *past* and *past part.* **whin·nied** *v.i.* (of a horse) to neigh, esp. in a soft, gentle way ‖ *v.t.* to express by whinnying **2.** *pl.* **whin·nies** *n.* a whinnying sound [imit.]
whin·stone (hwínstoun, wínstoun) *n.* any of various hard, dark, esp. basaltic rocks
whin·y (hwáini:, wáini:) *comp.* **whin·i·er** *superl.* **whin·i·est** *adj.* of, characterized by or given to whining
whip (hwip, wip) *n.* a lash with a handle used for driving a horse or urging one on, or for punishing ‖ something resembling a whip, e.g. a flexible rod ‖ a whipping or thrashing motion ‖ the sail arm of a windmill ‖ a light dessert made with whipped ingredients ‖ a hoisting apparatus consisting of a single rope and pulley ‖ a hunt official responsible for whipping in the hounds ‖ (*politics*) an official appointed to maintain party discipline and esp. to enforce attendance in Congress etc. ‖ a written notice sent around by this official in the House of Commons requesting members' attendance [partly fr. WHIP v. partly M.L.G., L.G. *wippe, wip,* quick movement]
whip *pres. part.* **whip·ping** *past* and *past part.* **whipped** *v.t.* to strike with a lash, rod etc. ‖ to beat to a froth, *to whip cream* ‖ to strike stingingly, *rain whipped our faces* ‖ to move, take, jerk etc. quickly, *he whipped the knife out of her hand* ‖ (*pop.*) to defeat by a good margin ‖ to fish (a river etc.) with a rod and line, casting with a whiplike action ‖ to bind (a rope etc.) with cord or twine to prevent fraying ‖ to wrap (a cord, twine etc.) around something, e.g. a handle ‖ to oversew (a seam) ‖ (esp. *naut.*) to hoist by rope and pulley ‖ *v.i.* to move quickly, to dart, *he whipped across the road* ‖ to flap with the noise made by the lash of a whip, *the flags whipped in the breeze* ‖ (*fishing*) to cast with a whiplike action **to whip in** to force (hounds) to form a close pack at a hunt ‖ to gather together (members of a political party) for a particular occasion **to whip out** to take out (something) with a sudden, quick movement, *he whipped out his pistol* **to whip up** to arouse, esp. by oratory or forceful persuasion, *to whip up enthusiasm* ‖ (*pop.*) to improvise (e.g. a meal) hurriedly [rel. to M.L.G., L.G. or Du. *wippen,* to swing]
whip·cord (hwípkɔrd, wípkɔrd) **1.** *n.* tightly twisted cord, esp. that used for making whips ‖ a durable corded fabric, used for coats, riding breeches etc., made from worsted yarns **2.** *adj.* tough, strong, and tightly knit, like the cord of a whip
whip hand control, position of advantage, *to have the whip hand over a person* [lit.=the hand used for holding the whip when driving a carriage]
whip·lash (hwíplæʃ, wíplæʃ) *n.* the lash of a whip ‖ a whiplash injury
whiplash injury a neck injury, common in automobile accidents, suffered when the head jerks suddenly backward or forward
whip·per-in (hwípərin, wípərin) *pl.* **whip·pers-in** *n.* a hunt official who whips in the hounds ‖ (*politics*) a party whip
whip·per·snap·per (hwípərsnæpər, wípərsnæpər) *n.* a young, esp. undersized boy who behaves with more self-importance than is proper [prob. an extension of obs. 'whip snapper', a cracker of whips]
whip·pet (hwípit, wípit) *n.* a dog of a fast-running breed resembling a small greyhound and used in coursing
whip·ping (hwípiŋ, wípiŋ) *n.* the act of someone who whips ‖ a beating or flogging ‖ stitching used in overcasting ‖ twine etc. used for whipping or binding, or the binding itself
whipping boy (*hist.*) a boy who shared a prince's education and was whipped in his stead for the prince's faults ‖ a person made to bear the blame which should fall on others
whipping post (*hist.*) a post to which a person was tied for a public whipping
Whip·ple (hwíp'l, wíp'l), George Hoyt (1878-1976), U.S. pathologist and educator, co-winner (with George R.Minot and William P. Murphy) of the 1934 Nobel prize in physiology and medicine for discovering that liver is essential to blood formation and is curative in the treatment of pernicious anemia
whip·ple·tree (hwíp'ltri:, wíp'ltri:) *n.* a whiffletree [perh. rel. to WHIP]
whip·poor·will (hwípərwil, wípərwil, hwipərwíl, wipərwíl) *n.* *Caprimulgus vociferus,* a North American goatsucker active at night, when it repeats its call over and over [imit. of its cry]
whip-round (hwípraund, wípraund) *n.* (*Br.*) a collection or appeal for contributions, esp. towards a collective gift or to help someone in an emergency
whip·saw (hwípsɔ, wípsɔ) *n.* a long, narrow saw blade with its ends fixed in an elastic metal frame
whir, whirr (hwəːr, wəːr) **1.** *v.i. pres. part.* **whir·ring, whirr·ing** *past* and *past part.* **whirred** to move, esp. through the air, with a sound resembling that of a bird's wings in rapid flight **2.** *n.* the sound itself [prob. of Scand. origin]
whirl (hwəːrl, wəːrl) **1.** *v.i.* to revolve rapidly, *an unknown mass whirling through space* or seem to do so, *his brain was whirling* ‖ to rush with a great commotion, *to come whirling into a room* ‖ *v.t.* to cause to whirl **2.** *n.* the act of whirling ‖ a whirling motion ‖ something that whirls ‖ a feeling of giddiness or confusion ‖ a continuous series of hectic activities, *a whirl of parties* [O.N. *hvirfla*]
whirl·i·gig (hwə́ːrligig, wə́ːrligig) *n.* (*Br.*) a pinwheel (child's toy)
whirligig beetle any of various members of *Gyrinidae,* a family of beetles which whirl on the surface of ponds, lakes etc.
whirling dervish *DERVISH
whirl·pool (hwə́ːrlpuːl, wə́ːrlpuːl) *n.* a circular eddy or current in a river or the sea caused by the shape of the channel, the effect of wind on tides, or by the meeting of currents
whirl·wind (hwə́ːrlwind, wə́ːrlwind) *n.* a rotating windstorm produced by a column of air moving rapidly in an upward spiral course and moving progressively over the surface of land or water
whirr *WHIR
whisk (hwisk, wisk) **1.** *n.* an instrument for beating eggs, cream etc. ‖ a hairlike appendage, e.g. on the tail of some insects ‖ a quick, light movement **2.** *v.t.* to beat (eggs, cream etc.) into a froth ‖ to transport with speed, *he whisked them off to the station in his car* ‖ to remove (something) with a quick, light motion, *she whisked the crumbs from the table* ‖ *v.i.* to move quickly **to whisk away** to remove (something) with a swift motion ‖ to go darting off [prob. fr. O.N.]
whisk broom a small, short-handled broom used esp. to brush clothes
whisk·er (hwískər, wískər) *n.* one of the long stiff bristles growing at either side of the mouth of some animals ‖ (*pl.*) the hairs growing in a beard or down the side of a man's cheeks ‖ (*naut.*) either of two spars extending on each side of the bowsprit for spreading the guys of the jibboom **whísk·ered, whísk·er·y** *adjs.* [WHISK v.]
whiskers *n.* (*chem.*) a monocrystalline fiber composite, used for reinforcing cement, resin, and silver amalgam
whis·key, *Br.* **whis·ky** (hwíski:, wíski:) *pl.* **whis·keys, whis·kies** *n.* a strong alcoholic liquor distilled from various grains (esp. malted barley, rye, wheat, corn) or from potatoes. 'Whisky' is (*Br.*) the preferred spelling for Scotch, 'whiskey' for Irish or bourbon ‖ a drink of whiskey [shortened fr. *usquebaugh* fr. Ir. Gael. *uisgebeatha,* water of life]
Whiskey insurrection an uprising (1794) of farmers in W. Pennsylvania against the U.S. government's efforts to enforce an excise tax on distilled liquors. About 500 armed men burned down the home of the regional inspector and others tarred and feathered revenue officers. The uprising was suppressed without violence after President George Washington dispatched 13,000 troops to Pennsylvania. The Federalists considered that federal authority had triumphed over local defiance, but antifederalist feelings persisted in the region long afterwards
whis·per (hwíspər, wíspər) **1.** *v.i.* to speak quietly without vibrating the vocal cords, esp. so as to be heard only by the person addressed ‖ to rustle, to make a soft sibilant sound, *the leaves whispered in the breeze* ‖ *v.t.* to utter in a whisper ‖ to mention secretly, spread as a rumor **2.** *n.* a low soft utterance ‖ a soft sibilant sound ‖ a rumor [O.E. *hwisprian*]
whispering campaign a deliberate and systematic attempt to besmear someone (esp. in political contests) by spreading vicious rumors
whist (hwist, wist) *n.* a card game for four players paired as partners, each player having 13 cards. The game has many variations, and contract bridge was developed from it [earlier *whisk* prob. fr. whisking the cards from the table]
whis·tle (hwís'l, wís'l) **1.** *v. pres. part.* **whis·tling** *past* and *past part.* **whis·tled** *v.i.* to make a shrill, piping sound by forcing the breath through pursed lips, or through a special instrument ‖ (of a bird) to make a sound resembling this ‖ to produce such a sound, esp. by swift movement, *the wind whistled through the trees* ‖ *v.t.* to utter by whistling ‖ to give an order to by whistling **to whistle for** to ask for or wish for in vain **2.** *n.* a small instrument of wood, metal etc. blown to produce a shrill, piping sound ‖ a device used as a signal etc. through which air or steam is forced to produce a loud, piercing sound, *a factory whistle* ‖ the sound produced by either of these ‖ the sound produced when the breath is forced through pursed lips ‖ the piercing note of a bird ‖ something resembling this, *the whistle of bullets* ‖ an act of whistling **to wet one's whistle** (*old-fash.*) to take a drink, esp. a drink, of beer or liquor **whis·tler** *n.* someone who or something that whistles ‖ any of various Australian and Polynesian birds related to the shrikes, having a whistling call ‖ *Marmota caligata,* a large marmot of North America ‖ a horse with the heaves [O.E. *hwistiian*]
whistle blower one who informs authorities of malfeasance in government or business
Whis·tler (hwíslər, wíslər), James Abbott McNeill (1834-1903), American painter and etcher. In his portraits and genre paintings he concentrated on subtle composition and refined color harmony
whis·tle-stop (hwís'lstɒp, wís'lstɒp) **1.** *n.* an insignificant station where a train stops only by prearrangement or at a signal ‖ a brief stop at a small station in order that a political candidate on tour may stop to make a speech **2.** *v.i. pres. part.* **whis·tle-stop·ping** *past* and *past part.* **whis·tle-stopped** (of a political candidate) to stop at whistle-stops in order to make speeches
Whit (hwit, wit) *adj.* of or relating to Pentecost (Whitsuntide)
whit (hwit, wit) *n.* the smallest possible amount, *not one whit the wiser* [O.E. *wiht,* a person]
Whit·by, synod of (hwítbi:, wítbi:) a meeting summoned at Whitby, N.E. England (664) by King Oswy of Northumbria to decide between Roman and Celtic ecclesiastical usages. The decision in favor of the Roman usage determined that the English Church was to be linked with continental Christendom (*WILFRID)
White (hwait, wait), Byron Raymond (1917-) U.S. associate justice of the Supreme Court (1962-). He played professional football (1938-9), was a Rhodes scholar (1939-40) and, after serving in the Navy, took his law degree at Yale. He was appointed to the Court by Pres. John F. Kennedy. Relatively conservative, he wrote the majority opinion in 'Duncan v. Louisiana' (1968), 'Williams v. Florida' (1970) and 'Taylor v. Louisiana' (1975), all concerning jury selection and trials. He also spoke for the Court in 'Washington v. Davis' (1976) and 'Columbus Board of Education v. Penick' (1979)
White, Edward Douglass, Jr. (1845-1921) U.S. Supreme Court associate justice (1894-1911) and chief justice (1911-21). A U.S. senator

CONCISE PRONUNCIATION KEY: **(a)** æ, *cat;* ɑ, *car;* ɔ *fawn;* ei, *snake.* **(e)** e, *hen;* iː, *sheep;* iə, *deer;* ɛə, *bear.* **(i)** i, *fish;* ai, *tiger;* əː, *bird.* **(o)** o, *ox;* au, *cow;* ou, *goat;* u, *poor;* ɔi, *royal.* **(u)** ʌ, *duck;* u, *bull;* uː, *goose;* ə, *bacillus;* juː, *cube.* x, *loch;* θ, *think;* ð, *bother;* z, *Zen;* ʒ, *corsage;* dʒ, *savage;* ŋ, *orangutang;* j, *yak;* ʃ, *fish;* tʃ, *fetch;* 'l, *rabble;* 'n, *redden.* Complete pronunciation key appears inside front cover.

(1890-94) he was appointed to the Court by Pres. Grover Cleveland. He wrote the majority opinion in 'Standard Oil Co. v. United States' (1911), which established the definition of a trust, and 'United States v. American Tobacco Co.' (1911). He spoke for the Court in 'Brushaber v. Union Pacific Railroad' (1916), which upheld the income tax; 'Guinn v. United States' (1915), which abolished the 'grandfather clause' in voting laws; and 'Selective Draft Law Cases' (1918)

White Gilbert (1720-93), English naturalist, author of 'The Natural History and Antiquities of Selborne' (1789)

White, Patrick (1912-) Australian writer, Nobel prize for literature (1973), born in England. His novels, usually of a search for truth, love and reality, include 'Happy Valley' (1939), 'The Tree of Man' (1955), 'Voss' (1957), 'Riders in the Chariot' (1961) and 'The Twyborn Affair' (1980). Short stories are collected in 'The Cockatoo' (1974) and poems in 'Thirteen Poems' (1929) and 'The Ploughman and Other Poems' (1935). He wrote 'Four Plays' (1965) and his autobiography 'Flaws in the Glass' (1982)

White a river (690 miles long) rising in the mountains of N.W. Arkansas, bending north into Missouri and returning southeast across Arkansas into the Mississippi River on the east boundary of Arkansas

white (hwait, wait) **1.** *adj.* of the color sensation stimulated by a combination of all the wavelengths of visible light, or resulting from combinations of certain pairs of wavelengths, being the color of e.g. milk ‖ (of hair) gray or silver ‖ (of hair) very blond ‖ (of wines) very pale yellow ‖ free from sin, pure ‖ pale, *white with terror* ‖ of or relating to the Caucasian division of mankind ‖ covered with snow ‖ blank, not printed upon, *leave the rest of the page white* ‖ (of silver and other metals) unburnished ‖ (of the members of a religious order) wearing white **to bleed (someone) white** to get money from (someone) until there is no more to be had **2.** *n.* a white pigment, fabric etc. ‖ a member of the Caucasian division of mankind ‖ the white part of something ‖ the albuminous matter surrounding the yolk of an egg ‖ the white part of the eye surrounding the cornea ‖ any of various breeds or species of white hog, white horse, white butterfly etc. ‖ (*printing*) a blank space between words or lines ‖ (*archery*) the outermost ring of a target ‖ (*archery*) the shot that hits this ring ‖ (*board games*) the light-colored men or pieces, or the player having these ‖ (*pl., pop.*) leukorrhea [O.E. *hwit*]

White Alice *ALICE

white ant a termite

white arsenic (*chem.*) an intensely poisonous arsenious oxide, As_2O_3

white·bait (hwáitbeit, wáitbeit) *n.* the young of various fishes used as food, esp. the young of any of various European herrings, or of the sprat

white·beam (hwáitbi:m, wáitbi:m) *n. Sorbus aria* (or *Pyrus aria*), fam. *Rosaceae,* a European ornamental tree bearing white flowers and red fruits

white bear polar bear

white blood cell a leucocyte

white book a book bound in white, containing an official government report or reports (in certain countries)

white bread light-colored bread made from refined wheat flour

white·cap (hwáitkæp, wáitkæp) *n.* the foam on the crest of a wave ‖ the male of the European redstart

white-col·lar (hwáitkɒlər, wáitkɒlər) *adj.* of, relating to or designating the salaried section of the working population (e.g. teachers, civil servants) whose duties call for the wearing of neat, conventional clothes

white corpuscle a leukocyte

white currant a shrub of genus *Ribes,* bearing white, edible berries ‖ its fruit

white damp a poisonous gas occurring in mines, formed by incomplete combustion of coal and composed mainly of carbon monoxide

whited sepulcher, *Br.* **whited sepulchre** a hypocrite, a corrupt person who makes a show of righteousness (Matthew xxiii, 27)

white dwarf (*astron.*) a whitish star of approximately the same size as the sun but with a greater density

white elephant a rare, pale-colored elephant of India, Ceylon, Thailand and Burma ‖ (*pop.*) any unwanted possession, esp. a property that is troublesome or expensive to keep

white ensign a white flag with the union in the upper quarter, flown by British warships and a few other, privileged vessels

white feather a symbol of cowardice (a white feather in a gamecock's tail supposedly being a sign of degeneracy)

White·field (hwáitfi:ld, wáitfi:ld, hwítfi:ld, wítfi:ld), George (1714-70), English Methodist preacher. He was associated with the Wesleys in the early days of Methodism, but separated from them (c. 1741) when he adopted Calvinistic views. He became chaplain to the Countess of Huntingdon's Connexion. He preached widely in North America

white·fish (hwáitfiʃ, wáitfiʃ) *pl.* **white·fish, white·fish·es** *n.* (*Br.*) any of various food fishes having white, dry flesh, e.g. cod, sole, whiting ‖ a member of *Coregonus,* fam. *Salmonidae,* a genus of food fishes resembling the salmon or trout and inhabiting freshwater lakes etc. of North America, Europe and Asia

white flag (*mil.*) a flag or white piece of cloth generally recognized as a signal of truce, or as a token of surrender or of some peaceful intention

White Friar a Carmelite friar

white frost hoarfrost

white gold gold alloyed usually with nickel and sometimes with zinc, tin or copper

White·hall (hwáithɔl, wáithɔl) a London street in which there are many government offices ‖ the British government, esp. in its administrative capacity

White·head (hwáithed, wáithed), Alfred North (1861-1947), British mathematician and philosopher. With Bertrand Russell he wrote 'Principia Mathematica' (1910-13), in which the fundamental propositions of logic and mathematics are derived from a few basic assumptions. In 'Concept of Nature' (1920) and 'Principle of Relativity' (1922) he developed an alternative to Einstein in physics, and in 'Process and Reality' (1927-9) a 'philosophy of organism'. Opposing positive and antireligious science, he sought to establish a modern philosophy which would take account of religious experience as well as of 20th-c. physics and sociology

white heat the temperature at which a body emits the whole range of wavelengths of the visible spectrum ‖ a state of extreme emotion or febrile activity

White·horse (hwáithɔrs, wáithɔrs) the capital (pop. 14,814) of Yukon Territory, Canada, on the upper Yukon River, a distributing and communications center

white horses waves crested with foam

white-hot (hwáithɒ́t, wáithɒ́t) *adj.* at white heat ‖ very excited, angry etc. ‖ working at intense pressure of activity

White House the official residence of the U.S. president, in Washington. It was built in the late 18th c. ‖ the executive government of the U.S.A.

white knight champion of a good cause

white lead basic lead carbonate, $2(PbCO_3) \cdot Pb(OH)_2$, used on account of its good covering power as a pigment

white lie a lie told for unmalicious reasons and therefore regarded as excusable

White·locke (hwítlɒk, wítlɒk), John (1757-1835), British general who led (1807) the unsuccessful British attack on Buenos Aires. He surrendered (July 6, 1807) to Liniers

white magic magic used in the service of good

white matter (*anat.*) the light-colored neural tissue, esp. of the central nervous system, mainly composed of cell processes (cf. GRAY MATTER)

white metal any of various tin-based alloys, used for bearings, castings etc. ‖ any of various lead-based alloys

White Monk a Cistercian monk

White Mountain, Battle of the a battle (Nov. 8, 1620) during the Thirty Years' War. The forces of the Catholic League, under Tilly, overwhelmed the Bavarian army, ending the Bavarian revolt and suppressing Protestantism in Bavaria

White Mountains a range in N. New Hampshire, part of the Appalachians: Mt Washington, 6,288 ft

whit·en (hwáit'n, wáit'n) *v.t.* to make white ‖ *v.i.* to become white

White Nile the main headstream (2,200 miles long) of the Nile (cf. BLUE NILE). It emerges from Lake Victoria at Ripon Falls and flows north through Lake Kyoga and the Murchison Falls into Lake Albert, then through N.W. Uganda and (as the Bahr-el-Jebel) into the Sudan, becoming the Bahr-el-Abiad ('white river'). It joins the Blue Nile at Khartoum. Its most distant source (the chief affluent of Lake Victoria) is the River Kagera (430 miles long) rising in W. Uganda

whit·en·ing (hwáit'niŋ, wáit'niŋ) *n.* whiting (powdered chalk) ‖ the act or process of making or becoming white

white noise (*acoustics*) nondescript, undefinable static sound used to mask annoying or distracting sound. *also* white sound

white oak *Quercus alba* a large, slow-maturing oak of the eastern U.S.A., yielding a hard wood ‖ this wood

white paper (esp. *Br.*) an informative government report issued on a matter which has received official investigation (cf. BLUE BOOK)

white pepper a powdered condiment obtained by grinding the husked seeds of the peppercorn

white pine *Pinus strobus,* a tall, graceful pine of eastern North America yielding a soft, light-colored wood of great commercial value ‖ this wood

white room *CLEAN ROOM

White Russia Byelorussia

white sauce a sauce made by blending butter and flour with milk, cream or stock

White Sea a gulf (area 36,000 sq. miles) of the Barents Sea on the northern coast of the U.S.S.R., in Europe. It receives the Northern Dvina and Onega Rivers. It is connected to the Baltic via Lakes Ladoga and Onega. Ice is a menace to shipping in winter. Chief port: Archangel

white slave a female held against her will and transported esp. from one state or country to another for purposes of prostitution **white slavery** such prostitution

white·smith (hwáitsmiθ, wáitsmiθ) **1.** *n.* a tinsmith ‖ a finisher of metal goods **2.** *v.i.* to work as a whitesmith

white sound (*acoustics*) white noise (which see).

white spirit (esp. *pl.*) a mixture of petroleum hydrocarbons, boiling at less than 200°C., used as a solvent and in paints and varnishes

white·throat (hwáitθrout, wáitθrout) *n. Sylvia communis,* an Old World warbler ‖ *Zonotrichia albicollis,* a common brown North American sparrow

white vitriol hydrated zinc sulfate, $ZnSO_4 \cdot 7H_4O$

white·wash (hwáitwɔʃ, wáitwɔʃ, hwáitwɒʃ, wáitwɒʃ) **1.** *n.* a liquid mixture of powdered lime or chalk and water, used for whitening walls, ceilings etc. ‖ an act or instance of covering up someone's faults, defects of character etc. ‖ (esp. *Br., law*) the act or instance of clearing a bankrupt ‖ (*pop.*) a total defeat in a game (i.e. when the loser fails to score) **2.** *v.t.* to cover with whitewash ‖ to gloss over or cover up (a person's faults etc.) ‖ (esp. *Br., law*) to clear (a bankrupt) of liabilities ‖ (*pop.*) to prevent (an opponent) from scoring in a game

white whale *Delphinapterus leucas,* a beluga

whit·ey (hwáiti:) *n.* (*slang*) perjorative term for a white person, esp. as representative of white society

Whit·gift (hwítgift, wítgift), John (c. 1530-1604), English churchman. As archbishop of Canterbury (1583-1604) he attempted to carry out Elizabeth I's policy of establishing religious uniformity

whith·er (hwíðər, wíðər) **1.** *adv.* (*rhet.*) to what place, where ‖ (*rhet.*) to what condition, result etc. **2.** *conj.* to what place [O.E. *hwider*]

whith·er·so·ev·er (hwiðərsouévər, wiðərsoévər) *adv.* (*archaic*) to whatever place

whit·ing (hwáitiŋ, wáitiŋ) *n.* a finely powdered chalk (calcium carbonate), used in whitewash, putty, paint, polish etc.

whiting *n. Merlangus merlangus,* fam. *Gadidae,* an edible European marine fish ‖ *Merluccius bilinearis,* a common North American hake, important as a food fish ‖ any of various members of *Menticirrhus,* fam. *Sciaenidae,* a genus of North American marine food fishes

whit·ish (hwáitiʃ, wáitiʃ) *adj.* somewhat white

Whitlam (hwítləm, wítləm) (Edward) Gough (1916-) Australian statesman, prime minister (1972-5). He joined the Australian Labor Party (ALP) in 1945, climbing the ranks to the leadership position in 1967. The ALP won the

CONCISE PRONUNCIATION KEY: **(a)** æ, *cat;* ɑ, *car;* ɔ *fawn;* ei, *snake.* **(e)** e, *hen;* i:, *sheep;* iə, *deer;* εə, *bear.* **(i)** i, *fish;* ai, *tiger;* ə:, *bird.* **(o)** o, *ox;* au, *cow;* ou, *goat;* u, *poor;* ɔi, *royal.* **(u)** ʌ, *duck;* u, *bull;* u:, *goose;* ə, *bacillus;* ju:, *cube.* x, *loch;* θ, *think;* ð, *bother;* z, *Zen;* ʒ, *corsage;* dʒ, *savage;* ŋ, *orangutang;* j, *yak;* ʃ, *fish;* tʃ, *fetch;* 'l, *rabble;* 'n, *redden.* Complete pronunciation key appears inside front cover.

election of 1972, putting Whitlam into the prime ministership. He attempted to make Australia independent of the larger world powers and fought for equal rights, but the failing worldwide economy intervened and his dismissal (1975) by the governor-general was endorsed by a subsequent election. He retired from leadership of the ALP in 1977

Whit·ley Council (hwítli:, wítli:) one of a number of joint boards of employers and workers, for negotiating wages and conditions of service, set up since 1917 in Great Britain in various industries, the civil service and local government [after J. H. *Whitley* (1866-1935), Br. politician]

Whit·lock (hwítlɒk, wítlɒk), Brand (1869-1934), U.S. diplomat and writer. As U.S. minister (1913-22, later ambassador) to Belgium during the German invasion, he saved many innocent Belgians from death at the hands of the German military

whit·low (hwítlou, wítlou) *n.* an infection of the pulp of the finger, esp. near the nail [M.E. *whitflaw, whitflow* perh.=white flaw]

Whit·man (hwítmən, wítmən), Walt (1819-92), American poet. His rhapsodic verse has virtually neither rhyme nor meter, but abounds in oratorical rhythms inspired esp. by Old Testament prophetic writings. His subject matter is his own expansive ego celebrating the democratic society and the wide horizons of developing America. There is an impressiveness in his invocations of America's multiplicity, and warm human feeling in his outgoing sympathy. 'Leaves of Grass' (1855, and several later editions) is his best-known collection

Whit·ney (hwítni:, wítni:), Eli (1765-1825), American inventor and manufacturer. He invented (1783) a mechanical cotton gin and developed the use of machine tools in producing small arms

Whitney, Josiah Dwight (1819-96), American geologist. He surveyed many parts of the U.S.A. and studied their mineral resources

Whitney, William Collins (1841-1904), U.S. lawyer, financier and (1885-9) secretary of the navy under President Grover Cleveland, providing the U.S.A. with an up-to-date naval force

Whitney, Mount the highest peak (14,495 ft) of the Sierra Nevada, California

Whit·sun (hwíts'n, wíts'n) **1.** *adj.* of or relating to Whitsuntide **2.** *n.* Whitsuntide

Whit·sun·day (hwítsʌ́ndi:, wítsʌ́ndi:, hwítsʌ́ndei, wítsʌ́ndei) *n.* the seventh Sunday after Easter Sunday, commemorating Pentecost [O.E. *Hwīta Sunnandæg,* White Sunday]

Whit·sun·tide (hwítsəntaid, wítsəntaid) *n.* the feast of Pentecost ‖ the holiday period at this time

Whit·ti·er (hwítiːər, wítiːər), John Greenleaf (1807-92), American Quaker poet and abolitionist. His most famous poem is 'Snow-Bound' (1866)

Whit·tle (hwít'l, wít'l), Sir Frank (1907-), British engineer. He invented the modern aircraft jet engine, the prototype of which made its first successful flight in 1941

whit·tle (hwít'l, wít'l) *pres. part.* **whit·tling** *past and past part.* **whit·tled** *v.t.* to slice pieces from (wood) with a knife ‖ to form (an object) by this method ‖ (*fig.*) to thin down, to reduce bit by bit ‖ *v.i.* to whittle wood **to whittle away** to take away by many small reductions **to whittle down** to reduce drastically by many small reductions [M.E. *thwitel* fr. O.E. *thwītan,* to cut, to pare]

whiz, whizz (hwiz, wiz) **1.** *v. pres. part.* **whiz·zing, whizz·ing** *past* and *past part.* **whizzed** *v.i.* (of objects moving through the air at great speed) to make a whirring or hissing sound ‖ *v.t.* to cause to move with such a sound **2.** *n.* this sound [imit.]

whiz·zer (hwízə:r) *n.* (*wrestling*) arm lock trapping one's arm against the opponent's body from a position beside the opponent

whiz kid (*colloq.*) a youth of prodigious intelligence

who (hu:) *pron.* what or which person or persons, *who is that woman?* ‖ which person or persons, *I didn't see who it was* ‖ that, the or a person or persons, *he likes women who dress well* [O.E. *hwā*]

whoa (hwou, wou) *interj.* a command to a horse to stop

who·dun·it (hu:dʌ́nit) *n.* (*pop.*) a detective story, or a play or film based on a detective story [coined from the jocular ungrammatical phrase 'who done it?']

who·ev·er (hu:évər) *pron.* whatever person, *whoever said that is a liar* ‖ (expressing surprise or puzzlement) who, *whoever said a thing like that?*

whole (houl) **1.** *adj.* not lacking any part, with no part excepted, *the whole truth* ‖ entire, undivided, *the snake swallowed the rat whole* ‖ containing all its natural components, *whole meal* ‖ not diseased or injured ‖ not broken or damaged ‖ having both parents in common, *whole sister* **2.** *n.* something which lacks none of its parts ‖ all that there is of something, *throughout the whole of history* **as a whole** taken altogether, *as a whole the piece isn't bad* **on the whole** everything being considered, *on the whole I agree with him* [O.E. *hāl*]

whole-bod·y scanner (houlbɒ́di:) (*med.*) device that X-rays the internal tissue of the body and records electronically on a cathode-ray image or prints out instead of on X-ray film. *Cf* CAT SCAN

whole gale a wind having a speed 55–63 m.p.h.

whole-heart·ed (hóulhártid) *adj.* with complete willingness and sincerity

whole meal meal or flour made from the whole grain of wheat

whole milk milk with none of its constituents taken away

whole note (*mus., Am.* =*Br.* semibreve) a note (symbol 𝅝) equal in duration to two half notes

whole number any number that is not a fraction

whole plate (*Br.*) a photographic plate or film of the size 6 ½ x 8 ½ ins

whole·sale (hóulseil) **1.** *n.* the sale of goods in relatively large quantities to be retailed by others (opp. RETAIL) **2.** *adj.* of or engaged in buying or selling in this way ‖ sold in this way ‖ on a large scale, indiscriminate, *wholesale slaughter* **3.** *adv.* in a wholesale manner **4.** *v. pres. part.* **whole·sal·ing** *past* and *past part.* **whole·saled** *v.i.* to be engaged in wholesale selling ‖ to be sold wholesale ‖ *v.t.* to sell (goods) wholesale

whole·some (hóulsəm) *adj.* good for the health, *wholesome food* ‖ healthy, *a wholesome climate* ‖ morally sound, *wholesome advice* [O.E. *hālsum*]

whole step a whole tone

whole tone (*mus.*) an interval consisting of two semitones

whole-tone scale a scale progressing only in whole tones, and hence outside the major and minor systems of ordinary diatonic notation. There are two such scales, one starting on C, the other on C♯

whole wheat *adj.* made of the pure meat of wheat, the whole grain being ground

whol·ly (hóulli:, hóuli:) *adv.* entirely, totally ‖ solely, exclusively [M.E. *holliche, iholliche*]

whom (hu:m) *pron.* the objective case of WHO

whoop (hu:p, hwu:p, wu:p) **1.** *n.* a loud cry of joy or excitement ‖ the loud gasping breath taken after a fit of coughing (esp. in whooping cough) ‖ the hoot of an owl ‖ a war cry **2.** *v.i.* to utter a loud cry of joy or excitement ‖ to gasp loudly in catching one's breath after a fit of coughing (esp. in whooping cough) ‖ (of an owl) to hoot ‖ *v.t.* to utter with a whoop ‖ (*pop.*) to increase, raise, *to whoop prices* [imit.]

whooping cough, *Br.* also **hooping cough** an infectious bacterial disease esp. prevalent among children, characterized by frequent coughs which are followed by a loud, convulsive intake of breath and often by vomiting

whooping crane *Grus americana,* a North American crane, now almost extinct, known for its mournful whooping cry

whop (hwɒp, wɒp) **1.** *n.* (*pop.*) a heavy thud ‖ (*pop.*) a heavy blow **2.** *v.t. pres. part.* **whop·ping** *past* and *past part.* **whopped** (*pop.*) to strike with a heavy blow **whóp·per** *n.* (*pop.*) anything uncommonly large of its kind ‖ (*pop.*) a shamelessly blatant big lie **whóp·ping** *adj.* (*pop.*) huge [origin unknown]

whore (hɔr, hour) **1.** *n.* a woman who engages in promiscuous sexual intercourse for money **2.** *v.i. pres. part.* **whor·ing** *past* and *past part.* **whored** (*rhet.*) to be a whore ‖ (*rhet.*) to fornicate with whores [O.E. *hōre*]

Whorf·i·an hypothesis (hwɔ́rfiːən) (*linguistics*) theory that language determines perception of the world; by Benjamin Lee Whorf, American anthropologist (1941–)

whorl (hwərl, wərl, hwə:rl, wə:rl) *n.* one of the spiral turns of a univalve shell ‖ a decorative motive resembling this ‖ a circle of flowers or parts of a flower (calyx, corolla etc.) or leaves arising from a node ‖ a small pulley on a spindle in spinning or weaving machinery **whorled** *adj.* [M.E. *wharwyl, whorwhil* prob. variants of WHIRL]

whor·tle·ber·ry (hwə́:rt'lberi:, wə́:rt'lberi:) *pl.* **whor·tle·ber·ries** *n.* a bilberry or blueberry ‖ a huckleberry

whose (hu:z) *pron.* the possessive case of WHO and, usually, of WHICH (used before a noun as a possessive adjective or absolutely as an interrogative) [M.E. *hwās* fr. O.E. *hwæs*]

who·so (hú:sou) *pron.* (*archaic*) whoever [M.E. *hwa swa*]

who·so·ev·er (hu:souévər) *pron.* (esp. in legal documents and formal declarations) whoever [M.E. fr. WHOSO+EVER]

why (hwai, wai) **1.** *adv.* for what reason, *why were you late?* ‖ with what intention, *why bother?* ‖ on account of which, for which, *I see no reason why you should despair* **2.** *n.* the reason, the explanation **3.** *interj.* an exclamation expressing surprise, protest, reflection etc. [O.E. *hwī, hwȳ* instrumental case of *hwæt,* what]

whydah *WHIDAH

wic·ca (wíkə) *n.* witchcraft —**wiccan** *adj.*

Wich·i·ta (wítʃitɔ) the chief city (pop. 279,835) of Kansas, a rail center and market on the Arkansas river: meat packing, oil refining, aircraft, food processing

wick (wik) *n.* a piece or bundle of twisted fiber, cord or tape that by capillary action supplies a lamp or candle flame with oil or melted grease ‖ (*med.*) a strip of gauze placed in a wound to drain away fluids [O.E. *wēoce, wēoc*]

wick·ed (wíkid) *adj.* not good morally, violating the rules of morality ‖ malicious, *a wicked tongue* ‖ (*pop.*) trying, unpleasant, troublesome etc., *a wicked winter, a wicked smell, a wicked blight on the tomatoes* ‖ (esp. of a horse) vicious ‖ mischievous, roguish, *a wicked grin* [M.E. fr. *wikke,* evil]

wick·er (wíkər) **1.** *n.* twigs or osiers plaited to make baskets, chairs, mats etc. **2.** *adj.* consisting of, or made of, wicker [of Scand. origin]

wick·er·work (wíkərwə:rk) *n.* objects made of wicker ‖ the craft of making such objects

wick·et (wíkit) *n.* a small door or gate, esp. one close beside or contained in a larger one ‖ a small window or opening, e.g. at a ticket office ‖ a small gate used to regulate a flow of water (e.g. in a waterwheel), or for emptying the chamber of a canal lock ‖ (*croquet*) one of a series of small metal arches through which the ball is hit ‖ (*cricket*) either of two sets of three stumps crowned by two bails (one set at either end of the pitch) ‖ (*cricket*) the playing space between these two sets, esp. as regards its condition, *a fast wicket* ‖ (*cricket*) an inning of one batsman, *a match won by 10 wickets* ‖ (*cricket*) a period during which a pair stay together batting, *a first-wicket stand* **to keep wicket** (*cricket*) to be wicketkeeper [A.F. *wiket,* etym. doubtful]

wick·et·keep·er (wíkitki:pər) *n.* (*cricket*) the padded and gloved player who fields immediately behind the batsman's wicket, primarily to prevent byes and to catch or stump the batsman

wick·ing (wíkiŋ) *n.* the loosely woven cotton cord or tape used in a lamp or candle wick

wick·i·up (wíki:ʌp) *n.* a cone-shaped hut covered with reeds, grass etc. and used by nomadic Indians in dry regions of the west and southwest U.S.A. [fr. Algonquian]

Wick·low (wíklou) an eastern county (area 782 sq. miles, pop. 87,209) of Leinster province, Irish Republic. County seat: Wicklow (pop. 3,200)

Wicklow Mountains a range in Leinster, S.E. Irish Republic: Lugnaquilla, 3,039 ft

wid·der·shins (wídərʃinz) *adv.* in a counterclockwise direction, esp. thus regarded as unlucky, *to walk widdershins around a billiard table* [fr. M.L.G. *weddersinnes* fr. M.H.G. *wider,* against + *sin,* direction]

wide (waid) **1.** *adj.* of relatively large extent from side to side, not narrow, *a wide road, a wide river* ‖ reaching over a vast area, *the wide world* ‖ relatively far apart, *at wide intervals* ‖ of a specified extent from side to side, *a table 2 feet wide* ‖ great in extent, *wide publicity, wide reading* ‖ roomy, loose, *wide sleeves* ‖ fully open, *wide eyes* ‖ (*fig.*, with 'of') far removed from, *wide of the truth* ‖ (*agric.*) containing a relatively small amount of protein compared with

CONCISE PRONUNCIATION KEY: (a) æ, *cat;* ɑ, *car;* ɔ *fawn;* ei, *snake.* (e) e, *hen;* i:, *sheep;* iə, *deer;* ɛə, *bear.* (i) i, *fish;* ai, *tiger;* ə:, *bird.* (o) ɒ, *ox;* au, *cow;* ou, *goat;* u, *poor;* ɔi, *royal.* (u) ʌ, *duck;* u, *bull;* u:, *goose;* ə, *bacillus;* ju:, *cube.* x, *loch;* θ, *think;* ð, *bother;* z, *Zen;* ʒ, *corsage;* dʒ, *savage;* ŋ, *orangutang;* j, *yak;* ʃ, *fish;* tʃ, *fetch;* 'l, *rabble;* 'n, *redden.* Complete pronunciation key appears inside front cover.

fats and carbohydrates, *a wide feed ration* ‖ (*finance,* of prices) fluctuating greatly between the highest and lowest levels ‖ (*phon.*) lax ‖ of considerable scope, *a wide selection of goods* ‖ (*Br., pop.*) sharp-witted but dishonest, *a wide boy* **wide of the mark** far from the point, purpose or truth, *a solution wide of the mark* **2.** *adv.* fully, as much as possible, *the door is wide open* ‖ far from the mark, aim, truth etc., *the remark went wide* **3.** *n.* (*cricket*) a wide ball [O.E. *wīd*]

wide-an·gle (wáidæŋg'l) *adj.* (of a camera lens) having or covering a wider field of view than an ordinary lens

Wide Area Telecommunications Service a Bell System service that lets contracting customers make or receive calls or transmit data within selected service areas at a fixed monthly rate, in lieu of individual call billing. (*acronym*) WATS

wide-a·wake (wáidəwéik) *adj.* fully awake, with one's eyes wide open ‖ alert, keen

wide ball (*cricket*) a ball judged by the umpire to be beyond the batsman's reach and counting one run to the batting side

wid·en (wáid'n) *v.t.* to make wide or wider ‖ *v.i.* to become wide or wider

wide-o·pen (wáidóupən) *adj.* lax in regulating or prohibiting the sale of alcoholic drinks, tolerating or allowing gambling, vice etc. ‖ open wide ‖ offering unlimited opportunity

wide receiver (*football*) pass receiver stationed at one side of the field

wide·spread (wáidspréd) *adj.* extended over a wide area, *widespread snowstorms* ‖ widely circulated, *widespread rumors*

widg·eon, wig·eon (wídʒən) *n.* any of numerous members of *Mareca,* a genus of freshwater ducks, esp. *M. penelope,* an Old World duck, *M. americana,* the American widgeon and *M. sibilatrix,* of southern South America [etym. doubtful]

Wi·dor (vi:dɔr), Charles Marie Jean Albert (1844-1937), French composer and organist. He was esp. famous for the organ compositions which he called symphonies

wid·ow (wídou) **1.** *n.* a woman who has not married again after her husband's death **2.** *v.t.* to make into a widow [O.E. *widewe, widuwe, wuduwe*]

widow bird any of numerous African weaverbirds, often kept as cage birds. During the breeding season, the males develop drooping tail feathers up to 1 ft in length

wid·ow·er (wídouər) *n.* a man who has not married again after his wife's death

wid·ow·hood (wídouhud) *n.* the state or period of time of being a widow

widow's peak a point formed by the roots of the hair in the center of the forehead

widow's weeds the heavy black mourning apparel, esp. the black veils, worn in many countries by a widow for a certain period [M.E. *wede* fr. O.E. *wǣd,* a garment]

width (widθ) *n.* measurement, distance or extent from side to side, *three feet in width* ‖ a piece of cloth etc. measured and cut, *a width of chintz* [17th-c. coinage]

Wie·de·mann-Franz law (ví:dəmɑnfrɑ́nts) (*phys.*) a law stating that the ratio of the electrical and thermal conductivities of a metal is proportional to the absolute temperature [after G. H. *Wiedemann* (1826–99) and K. *Franz* (1827–1902), G. physicists]

Wie·land (ví:lɑnt), Christoph Martin (1733-1831), German poet and author. His masterpiece 'Oberon' (1780), a romantic epic, exerted a powerful influence on German literature

wield (wi:ld) *v.t.* to use, exert (power, influence, authority etc.) ‖ to hold and use with the hands, *to wield a sledgehammer* **wield·y** *adj.* nicely balanced for handling, although weighty [fr. O.E. *wealdan* and *wyldan*]

Wie·licz·ka (vjelí:tʃkɑ) a town (pop. 12,000) in Poland near Krakow: salt mining (since the 11th c.)

wie·ner (wí:nər) *n.* (*pop.*) a frankfurter [fr. G. *wienerwurst,* sausage of Vienna]

wie·ner schnit·zel (ví:nərʃnítsəl) *n.* a breaded veal cutlet [G.=Vienna cutlet]

Wies·ba·den (ví:sbɑd'n) the capital (pop. 272,600) of Hesse, West Germany, a commercial center and spa at the foot of the Taunus Mtns: film making, publishing, chemical and pharmaceutical works. It was the capital (1806-66) of the duchy of Nassau

wife (waif) *pl.* **wives** (waivz) *n.* the female partner in a marriage [O.E. *wīf*]

wife·ly (wáifli:) *adj.* of, like or befitting a wife [O.E. *wīflīc*]

wig (wig) *n.* an artificial head covering of hair, worn e.g. as part of the official costume of a liveried servant or for ornamentation or for disguise [shortened fr. PERIWIG]

wig·an (wígən) *n.* a coarse canvaslike fabric used as a stiffening in tailoring [after *Wigan,* Lancashire]

wigeon *WIDGEON

wigged (wigd) *adj.* wearing a wig

wig·ging (wigiŋ) *n.* (esp. *Br., pop.*) a severe reprimand or scolding [fr. older *wig,* a wigging]

wig·gle (wíg'l) **1.** *v. pres. part.* **wig·gling** *past* and *past part.* **wig·gled** *v.t.* to cause to move in a small, rapid, to-and-fro, side-to-side or up-and-down movement ‖ *v.i.* to move in this way **2.** *n.* a wiggling movement [rel. to or fr. L.G. or M.L.G. *wiggelen*]

Wig·gles·worth (wig'lzwə:rθ), Michael (1631-1705), American colonial Calvinistic clergyman, physician and poet. His best known work is 'The Day of Doom; or a Poetical Description of the Great and Last Judgment' (1662), which was used as a catechism for children

Wight, Isle of (wait) (*abbr.* I.O.W.) an island (area 147 sq. miles, pop. 95,000) in the English Channel, forming part of Hamsphire. Administrative center: Newport (pop. 19,000). Chief port: Cowes. Industries: agriculture (wheat, fruit and vegetables, sheep), cement, tourism

wig·let (wíglət) *n.* a woman's hairpiece used to shape, lengthen, heighten, or frame a hairstyle

Wig·town (wígtən) a former county (area 485 sq. miles) of S.W. Scotland

wig·wag (wígwæg) **1.** *v. pres. part.* **wig·wag·ging** *past* and *past part.* **wig·wagged** *v.t.* to cause to move to and fro with considerable displacement ‖ *v.i.* to move in this way ‖ to signal by waving flags **2.** *n.* the act or art of wigwagging ‖ a wigwagged message

wig·wam (wígwɒm) *n.* a rounded or oval cabin or hut having a framework of poles, covered with hides, bark etc., used as a dwelling by North American Indians in the area of the Great Lakes and eastward [fr. Algonquian]

Wil·ber·force (wílbərfɔrs), William (1759-1833), British politician and evangelical, social reformer whose efforts resulted in the abolition of the slave trade (1807) and of slavery (1833) in the British Empire

Wil·bye (wílbi:), John (1574-1638), English composer noted esp. for his madrigals

wild (waild) **1.** *adj.* (of plants) propagated and growing without man's intervention ‖ (of animals) uncontrolled by man (opp. TAME, DOMESTICATED) ‖ (of a region) uninhabited and uncultivated by man ‖ uncivilized ‖ unrestrained by caution or convention ‖ fantastic, *wild fancies* ‖ (of the eyes or looks) suggesting near-madness ‖ out of control, *wild laughter* ‖ completely undisciplined, *a wild gang of boys* ‖ (of dress or appearance) peculiar in a fantastic way, *wild garb* ‖ (*pop.*) very angry ‖ (*pop.*) very enthusiastic ‖ irrational, *a wild guess* ‖ (*cards*) of a card which can be substituted for whatever card its player chooses **2.** *adv.* in a wild way **to run wild** to be uncontrolled **3.** *n.* **the wild** nature unspoiled by man **the wilds** great tracts of wild country [O.E. *wilde*]

wild and woolly disorderly and lacking in discipline or polish

wild boar *Sus scrofa,* *BOAR

wild·cat (wáildkæt) **1.** *n. Felis sylvestris,* a European cat larger than the domesticated cat, and with a shorter tail. It was notorious for its fierceness, but is now largely extinct ‖ *Felis ocreata* or *F. caffra,* an undomesticated cat of Africa and S.W. Asia ‖ (*pl.* **wildcat**) any of several other species of small undomesticated cat, e.g. lynx, ocelot ‖ a wildcat petroleum or gas well **2.** *adj.* risky, not to be relied upon, *a wildcat scheme* ‖ (of a petroleum or gas well) drilled in an area where there is no clear evidence that oil exists **3.** *v.i. pres. part.* **wild·cat·ting** *past* and *past part.* **wild·cat·ted** to drill a wildcat well

wildcat bank a bank which, before the National Bank Act of 1863–4, issued notes in excess of its assets

wildcat strike a strike in which the strikers act without the authority of their trade union

Wilde (waild), Oscar (1856-1900), Irish writer, playwright and wit. His fame now rests on the witty nonsense of the plays, esp. 'The Importance of Being Earnest' (1895). He also wrote in an aesthetic, mannered style, e.g. the novel 'The Picture of Dorian Grey,' (1884). He wrote a long poem, 'The Ballad of Reading Gaol' (1898), out of the experience of being imprisoned

wil·de·beest (wíldəbi:st) *n.* the gnu [Afrik.]

Wil·der (wáildər), Thornton (1897-1975), American writer. His works include the novel 'The Bridge of San Luis Rey' (1927) and the plays 'Our Town' (1938) and 'The Skin of Our Teeth' (1942) and 'Theophilus North' (1973)

wil·der·ness (wíldərnis) *n.* an uninhabited and uncultivated region ‖ a part of a large garden made to look as if it were independent of the gardener's mind or work [fr. O.E. *wildēor, wildedēor,* wild deer or *wildēoren,* wild]

wild·fire (wáildfaiər) *n.* (*hist.*) a highly combustible material hurled onto the deck of an enemy vessel in naval warfare **to spread like wildfire** (of rumor, plague etc.) to spread exceedingly fast

wild·fowl (wáildfaul) *pl.* **wild·fowl, wild·fowls** *n.* a game bird, esp. a game waterfowl **wild·fowl·ing** *n.* the sport of hunting such birds

wild goose any species of undomesticated goose, usually migratory from and to the Arctic

wild-goose chase a futile search, esp. one deliberately instigated

wild·ing (wáildiŋ) *n.* a plant sown by natural agencies, esp. a fruit tree ‖ the fruit of such a tree

wild·life (wáildlaif) *n.* animals living in the wild state

wild oat any of several noncultivated members of *Avena,* fam. *Gramineae,* esp. *A. fatua* of Europe **to sow one's wild oats** to indulge in pleasures and escapades (esp. amorous) in one's youth

wild rice *Zizania aquatica,* an aquatic perennial grass of North America, yielding edible grain ‖ *Z. latifolia,* a similar grass of Asia

wild-track (wáildtræk) *adj.* in filming, of an off-track sound, music, or commentary not connected with the story line

wild·wa·ter (wáildwɔtər) *n.* (*envir.*) a stream or river with strong turbulence or current; white water

Wild West the western states of the U.S.A. in the early days of their settlement, when there was no rule of law

wile (wail) **1.** *n.* an artful method of persuasion ‖ a trick using guile so as to deceive or snare **2.** *v.t. pres. part.* **wil·ing** *past* and *past part.* **wiled** to subject to blandishments or to guile **to wile away** to while away [M.E. *wīl,* prob. of Scand. origin]

Wil·frid (wílfrid), St (634–c. 709), Anglo-Saxon Benedictine monk, bishop of York. He was influential in winning the victory for the Roman usage in the English Church (*WHITBY, SYNOD OF). Feast: Oct. 12

wilful *WILLFUL

Wil·helm I (vílhelm, wílhelm) (1797-1888), king of Prussia (1861-88), emperor of Germany (1871-88), second son of Frederick William III of Prussia. His plan to reorganize the army, in collaboration with van Roon, roused parliamentary opposition, and led to the appointment (1861) of Bismarck as prime minister. Wilhelm was proclaimed (1871) first Emperor of the Reich, and his reign saw the rise of Germany as a world power. Although often in disagreement with Bismarck, Wilhelm usually followed the latter's policy. Two attempts on Wilhelm's life (1878) were used by Bismarck as an excuse for antisocialist legislation

Wilhelm II (the 'Kaiser') (1859-1941), German emperor and king of Prussia (1888-1918), grandson of Wilhelm I of Germany. He succeeded his father Frederick III (1888) and forced Bismarck to resign (1890). He was the dominating force in the government from then on, trying to forestall socialism in Germany, and to pursue a weltpolitik abroad. His naval, commercial and colonial aspirations (*BAGHDAD RAILWAY) drove Great Britain into the Entente Cordiale with France. His impetuousness, and the alliances he created, contributed largely to the 1st world war. After the war, naval mutiny and civilian revolt led to his flight to Holland (Nov. 10, 1918), where he died in exile

Wil·hel·mi·na (wilhelmí:nə, wiləmí:nə) (1880-1962), queen of the Netherlands (1890-1948). She abdicated in favor of her daughter, Juliana

Wilhelmina a mountain range rising to 4,200 ft in central Surinam

CONCISE PRONUNCIATION KEY: **(a)** æ, *cat*; ɑ, *car*; ɔ *fawn*; ei, *snake*. **(e)** e, *hen*; i:, *sheep*; iə, *deer*; ɛə, *bear*. **(i)** i, *fish*; ai, *tiger*; ə:, *bird*. **(o)** o, *ox*; au, *cow*; ou, *goat*; u, *poor*; ɔi, *royal*. **(u)** ʌ, *duck*; u, *bull*; u:, *goose*; ə, *bacillus*; ju:, *cube*. x, *loch*; θ, *think*; ð, *bother*; z, *Zen*; ʒ, *corsage*; dʒ, *savage*; ŋ, *orangutang*; j, *yak*; ʃ, *fish*; tʃ, *fetch*; 'l, *rabble*; 'n, *redden*. Complete pronunciation key appears inside front cover.

Wil·helms·ha·ven (vílhelmshɑfən) a port, resort and naval base (pop. 101,000) in N. Lower Saxony, West Germany: shipbuilding, textiles, engineering

wil·i·ly (wáilili:) adv. in a wily way

wil·i·ness (wáili:nis) n. the quality of being wily

Wilkes (wilks), Charles (1798-1877), American naval officer and explorer. He commanded (1838-42) a scientific and exploratory expedition to the South Seas which visited New South Wales, Samoa, Fiji and Hawaii. He crossed the Antarctic Circle to sail along the ice front between 150° and 70° S. and established that Antarctica is a continent

Wilkes, John (1727-97), British radical politician. Outlawed for his scurrilous attacks on the government, he was repeatedly elected to parliament despite ministerial attempts to exclude him. He became a popular champion of parliamentary reform and of the cause of the American colonies in the Revolutionary War

Wil·kins (wílkinz), Sir George Hubert (1888-1958), Australian explorer. He made many expeditions to the Arctic as well as to Antarctica, and carried out pioneer flights in these regions to further exploration

Wil·kin·son (wílkinsən), James (1757-1825), U.S. general. As governor (1805-6) of the Louisiana Territory, he became involved in the schemes of Aaron Burr. Fearing public exposure, he informed President Thomas Jefferson of Burr's plot to disrupt the Union and served as the chief prosecution witness at Burr's trial. He was cleared (1811) of complicity

Wilkinson, John (1728-1808), English ironmaster who built and managed ironworks for large-scale production. The accuracy of his machine for boring cylinders (1774) contributed to the success of Watt's steam engine

will (wil) **1.** n. the faculty of determining one's actions ‖ the act or action of willing ‖ something willed, an intention, command or request ‖ moral strength or energy ‖ determination, *the will to win* ‖ disposition towards others, *ill will* ‖ (*law*) a written statement of how one wishes one's property to be dealt with after one's death ‖ the legal document containing this statement **against one's will** contrary to one's own wish **at will** as and when one pleases ‖ (of property) held during the owner's good pleasure ‖ (**of a** tenant) who may be turned out at any time **of one's own free will, of one's own will** voluntarily, completely without coercion **with a will** heartily, energetically **2.** v.t. to dispose of (property) by a will ‖ to ordain by the force of authority, law etc. ‖ to determine by choice, *the separation was willed, not forced* ‖ to dominate so as to control the actions of (someone), e.g. by hypnotic suggestion ‖ v.i. to exercise the will [O.E. *willa*]

will past **would** (wud) auxiliary v. used to express futurity, usually implying determination, volition, necessity, obligation or acquiescence ‖ used to express habit, *she will cry for hours at a time* ‖ used to express ability or sufficiency, *this will be a suitable gift* ‖ used to express probability, *this will be his reasoning* ‖ used to express command, *everyone will meet here* ‖ v.i. to wish, *try as they will they don't succeed* ‖ v.t. to wish, choose, *do what you will* (cf. SHALL, cf. SHOULD, cf. WOULD) [O.E. *wyllan*]

Wil·laert (vílɑrt), Adrian (c. 1480-1562), Flemish composer, working chiefly at St Mark's, Venice. He wrote great double choir motets for antiphonal singing, Masses and madrigals

wil·let (wílit) n. *Catoptrophorus semipalmatus*, a large North American sandpiper, allied to the snipe [imit. of its call]

will·ful, wil·ful (wílfəl) adj. by intention, not accidental, *willful damage* ‖ acting according to one's own desire, regardless of the dictates of others or of reason **will·ful·ly** adv.

William emperors of Germany *WILHELM

Wil·liam I (wíljəm) 'the Conqueror' (c. 1027-87), king of England (1066-87), son of Robert I of Normandy. As duke of Normandy (1035-87), he defeated (1054 and 1058) Henri I of France, and conquered Maine (1063). Claiming that Edward the Confessor had promised him (1051) the English throne, and that the promise had been renewed (1064) by Harold of Wessex, he invaded England (1066), defeating and killing Harold at Hastings. He imposed his rule on England by ravaging wide areas and distributing estates to his followers. He appointed (1070) Lanfranc archbishop of Canterbury and ordered Domesday Book to be drawn up (1086).

He dealt firmly with risings (1070-1, 1075 and 1082) and spent the end of his reign fighting in France

William II 'Rufus' (c. 1056-1100), king of England (1087-1100), son of William I. Sporadically at war with his elder brother Robert, duke of Normandy, he resorted to financial extortion. He appointed Anselm archbishop of Canterbury (1093) and their quarrel (1095-7) began the rift between Church and State. William was killed by an arrow while hunting in the New Forest

William III (1650-1702), king of England, Scotland and Ireland (1689-1702), son of William II of Orange. As stadtholder of the Netherlands (1672-1702) he emerged as the leader of European resistance to Louis XIV's aggression, defending the Netherlands against French invasions (1672-8), and marrying (1677) Mary, the Protestant daughter of the future James II of England. Invited by a group of political leaders to intervene in England (1688), he invaded and, after James II had fled to France, was proclaimed (1689) joint sovereign with his wife, Mary II. He brought England into the Grand Alliance (1689) against Louis XIV, defeated an invasion of Ireland by James II in a decisive victory at the Boyne (1690), gained favorable terms at Ryswick (1697), and renewed the anti-French alliance in the War of the Spanish Succession (1701-14)

William IV (1765-1837), king of Great Britain (1830-7), son of George III. His threat to create sufficient Whig peers to secure the passage of the Reform Bill of 1832 persuaded the Lords to agree to the measure

William I 'the Silent' (1533-84), prince of Orange, stadtholder of Holland, Zeeland and Utrecht (1555-84). He led the struggle of the northern provinces of the Netherlands for independence from Spanish rule. He was assassinated

William II (1626-50), prince of Orange, stadtholder of the Netherlands (1647-50). In the hope of extending his territory to the whole of the Low Countries he tried to renew the struggle with Spain after the Treaties of Westphalia

William III prince of Orange *WILLIAM III, king of England

William I (1772-1843), first king of the Netherlands and grand duke of Luxembourg (1815-40). The Congress of Vienna (1815) gave him the throne of what is now Belgium, the Netherlands and Luxembourg, but his autocratic attempts to impose Dutch supremacy caused Belgium to break away (1830). In the face of growing discontent he abdicated

William I 'the Lion' (1143-1214), king of Scotland (1165-1214). He formed an alliance with France (1168) but was captured by Henry II of England and forced to recognize English overlordship (1174). He bought political independence from Richard I of England (1189)

William and Mary, College of a state liberal arts university at Williamsburg, Va., founded by James Blair and chartered (1693) by King William and Queen Mary. The second oldest university in the U.S.A., it was the first to establish a law school

William Augustus *CUMBERLAND

William of Malmes·bur·y (mámzbəri:) (d. c. 1143), English monk and historian. His 'Gesta regum Anglorum' and 'Historia novella' are authorities for Anglo-Norman history

William of Oc·cam (ókəm) (c. 1285–c. 1349), English nominalist philosopher. He was a Franciscan of independent thought, critical of Scholasticism and of the temporal power of the papacy. He opened the way for the Reformation by distinguishing between faith and reason. He was one of the first Christian thinkers to advocate the separation of Church and State

William of Tyre (c. 1130–c. 1185), archbishop of Tyre (1175–c. 1185), and historian of the Crusades to 1184

William of Wyke·ham (wíkəm) (1324-1404), English bishop and statesman. He was lord chancellor (1367-71 and 1389-91). He founded New College, Oxford (1379) and Winchester College at Winchester (1382)

Wil·liams (wíljəmz), Eric (1911-81), Trinidadian politician, leader of the People's National Movement, and prime minister (1962-81) of Trinidad and Tobago. He led his nation to independence (1962) from Britain and thereafter pursued a moderate policy opposed (1970) by black militants

Williams, Sir George (1821-1905), British philanthropist and founder (1844) of the Young Men's Christian Association (Y.M.C.A.)

Williams, Roger (c. 1603-83), colonial American clergyman who founded (1636) Providence (Rhode Island), which served as a refuge from religious persecution. He secured (1644) for his colony a grant from Parliament of absolute liberty of conscience, confirmed (1663) by royal charter

Williams, Tennessee (1914-83), American playwright, whose works convey the sexual tensions and suppressed violence of his characters, often in the idiom of his native South. His prodigious output of plays includes 'The Glass Menagerie' (1945), 'A Streetcar Named Desire' (1947), 'Cat on a Hot Tin Roof' (1955) 'Sweet Bird of Youth' (1959; film, 1961), and 'The Night of the Iguana' (1961; film, 1964). He also wrote film scripts, short stories, verse and novels, notably 'The Roman Spring of Mrs. Stone' (1950; film, 1961)

Williams, William Carlos (1883-1963), American poet. His long poem 'Paterson' appeared in five volumes (1946-1958)

Wil·li·brord (wílibrɔrd), St (658-739), Northumbrian missionary. He evangelized Friesland. Feast: Nov. 7

wil·lies, the (wíli:z) pl. n. (*pop.*) a mood of being jumpy, nervous and ill-at-ease

will·ing (wíliŋ) adj. working, helping etc. readily ‖ done, given etc. readily ‖ favorably disposed (to do something) ‖ of the power of the will

Will·kie (wílki:), Wendell Lewis (1892-1944), U.S. industrialist and political leader. He ran as the Republican candidate against President Franklin D. Roosevelt in the 1940 presidential race, supporting Roosevelt's foreign policy program but vigorously attacking his New Deal. He was defeated, but polled the largest popular vote (22 million) ever received by a defeated candidate up to that time

will-o'-the-wisp (wíləðəwisp) n. a small volume of marsh gas emitted by the rotting vegetable matter in a marsh and oxidizing rapidly enough to emit light as it moves above the marsh ‖ an objective which is beyond attainment or in some way illusory [older *Will with the wisp* (wisp=torch of burning hay or straw)]

Wil·lough·by (wíləbi:), Sir Hugh (d. 1554), English explorer. He died in an attempt to discover the Northeast Passage

wil·low (wílou) **1.** n. a member of *Salix*, fam. *Salicaceae*, a genus of trees or shrubs, comprising 300 species, mainly of north temperate and arctic regions, usually growing near surface water. They bear catkins and have tough, pliable shoots and branches (*OSIER) ‖ the wood of such a tree ‖ (*Br., rhet.*) a cricket bat made of this wood ‖ a machine used to beat, pick and cleanse raw wool etc. **2.** v.t. to deal with (raw wool etc.) using this machine [O.E. *welig*]

willow herb a member of *Epilobium*, fam. *Onagraceae*, esp. *E. angustifolium*, a perennial plant with a purple racemose inflorescence, common on burnt and waste ground, esp. in temperate regions

willow pattern a usually blue chinoiserie china design featuring a willow and a little bridge, originating in Nanking and introduced into England c. 1780

wil·low·y (wíloui:) adj. slender and graceful ‖ abounding in willows

will·pow·er (wílpauər) n. the power of controlling one's actions and emotions by an effort of the will

Will·stät·ter (vílʃtɛtər), Richard (1872-1942), German chemist, awarded the Nobel prize (1915) for his investigation of plant pigments

Wil·lugh·by (wíləbi:), Francis (1635-72), English naturalist. He worked on a systematic classification of birds and fishes, and traveled on the Continent with John Ray, collecting material for his 'Ornithologia' (1676)

wil·ly-nil·ly (wíli:níli:) adv. whatever the will of the person involved may be [fr. older *will I, nill I*, if I wish, if I do not wish]

Wil·ming·ton (wílmiŋtən) the largest city and port of entry (pop. 70,195) in Delaware: shipyards, tanneries, manufactures (rubber goods, iron and steel, textiles, leather, machinery, chemicals). It is the seat of DuPont Industries

Wil·mot Proviso (wílmət) an amendment initiated by U.S. Representative David Wilmot (1814-68) to a congressional bill, twice defeated (1846, 1847). It called for the prohibition of slavery and involuntary servitude in the terri-

CONCISE PRONUNCIATION KEY: **(a)** æ, c*a*t; ɑ, c*a*r; ɔ f*aw*n; ei, sn*a*ke. **(e)** e, h*e*n; i:, sh*ee*p; iə, d*ee*r; ɛə, b*ea*r. **(i)** i, f*i*sh; ai, t*i*ger; ə:, b*i*rd. **(o)** o, *o*x; au, c*ow*; ou, g*oa*t; u, p*oo*r; ɔi, r*oy*al. **(u)** ʌ, d*u*ck; u, b*u*ll; u:, g*oo*se, ə, b*a*cillus; ju:, c*u*be. x, lo*ch*; θ, *th*ink; ð, bo*th*er; z, *Z*en; ʒ, cor*s*age; dʒ, sava*g*e; ŋ, oranguta*ng*; j, *y*ak; ʃ, *fi*sh; tʃ, fe*tch*; 'l, rabb*le*; 'n, redd*en*.   Complete pronunciation key appears inside front cover.

tory newly acquired from Mexico. The Wilmot Proviso polarized the conflict between abolitionists and the advocates of slavery. This tension was relieved only by the Compromise of 1850

Wil·son (wílsən), Charles Thompson Rees (1869-1961), Scottish physicist. He invented the Wilson cloud chamber (*CLOUD CHAMBER). Nobel prize (1927)

Wilson, Edmund (1895-1972), American literary critic and writer. 'Axel's Castle' (1931), an analysis of symbolism, is the best known of his books of criticism. 'Memoirs of Hecate County' (1946) is a collection of satirical stories and sketches

Wilson, Henry Lane (1857-1932), U.S. ambassador to Mexico during the Mexican Revolution (1910-21). An opponent of President Francisco Madero's regime, he entered a claim for damages sustained by U.S. citizens as a result of the revolutionary turmoil and urged U.S. President William H. Taft to intervene against Madero's government. He gave active support to Victoriano Huerta's takeover, and was believed to have colluded in the assassination (1913) of Madero and Vice-president Pino Suárez. During the interim before the inauguration of U.S. President Woodrow Wilson, he resigned his ambassadorial post

Wilson, James (1742-98), U.S. jurist. He was largely responsible for writing into the Constitution the principle that sovereignty resides in the people. He was made (1790) the first professor of law at what became the University of Pennsylvania

Wilson, James Harold (1916-), British Labour statesman. He led the Labour party to victory in the 1964 general election, and was prime minister (1964-70, 1974-6). He was knighted (1976) upon his retirement as prime minister and Labour party leader

Wilson, Richard (1714-82), English painter. He painted actual English and Italian scenes and typical 18th-c. idealized landscapes. His feeling for the spirit of the countryside, its forms, colors and atmosphere, was important in the development of landscape art

Wilson, Thomas Woodrow (1856-1924), 28th president (1913-21) of the U.S.A., a Democrat. He served (1902-10) as the first nonclerical president of Princeton University. A division in Republican ranks helped to elect him president. His administration lowered tariffs, established (1913) the Federal Reserve System, created (1914) the Federal Trade Commission, and secured (1914) passage of the Clayton Anti-Trust Act. The 17th, 18th, and 19th amendments were implemented during his administration. The general disorder prevailing in Mexico during the Revolution induced him to send (1914) U.S. Marines to Veracruz and (1915) Gen. John Pershing across the border to pacify Pancho Villa. He dispatched U.S. marines to Haiti (1915), the Dominican Republic (1916), and Cuba (1917). He favored neutrality early in the 1st world war, but later led the U.S.A. to declare war (1917) on Germany. He proposed (1918) the Fourteen Points as a possible basis of peace, and attended (1919) the peace conference in Paris. The Treaty of Versailles failed to fulfill his hopes, and though he was instrumental in establishing the League of Nations, the U.S. Senate refused to ratify U.S. membership in it

Wilson cloud chamber *CLOUD CHAMBER

Wilson, Mount a mountain (5,710 ft) in S.W. California, site of an observatory (1904)

Wilson's disease (*med.*) an inherited abnormality in copper metabolism affecting the liver and nervous system; named for S. A. K. Wilson, U.S. neurosurgeon. *also* hepatolenticular degeneration

wilt (wilt) **1.** *v.i.* (of plants) to become limp due to a deficiency of water ‖ to lose strength or freshness ‖ *v.t.* to cause to wilt **2.** *n.* the act of wilting or state of being wilted ‖ (*bot.*) a disease characterized by the drying out of terminal shoots, branches etc., or this drying-out condition [perh. alt. of older *welk*, to fade]

Wil·ton (wíltən) *n.* a carpet with the loops cut to form a soft, elastic pile, commonly patterned with designs suggesting Oriental design [after *Wilton*, England, where it was originally made, and still is]

Wilt·shire (wíltʃiər) (*abbr.* Wilts.) a county (area 1,345 sq. miles, pop. 513,800) of S.W. England. County town: Salisbury. Administrative center: Trowbridge (pop. 15,000)

wil·y (wáili:) *comp.* **wil·i·er** *superl.* **wil·i·est** *adj.* full of wiles, cunning

wim·ble (wímb'l) **1.** *n.* a boring tool, e.g. a gimlet ‖ a tool for twisting rope **2.** *v.t. pres. part.* **wim·bling** *past* and *past part.* **wim·bled** to twist (rope) with a wimble [A.F. fr. M.L.G.]

wimp (wimp) *n.* (*colloq.*) one who is unimportant, overly solicitous, or out-of-touch

wim·ple (wímp'l) **1.** *n.* a covering for the head and neck and the sides of the face, worn by women in medieval times and still worn by many orders of nuns **2.** *v.t. pres. part.* **wim·pling** *past* and *past part.* **wim·pled** to clothe with a wimple ‖ to cause to ripple ‖ *v.i.* to fall in folds ‖ to ripple [O.E. *wimpel*]

win (win) **1.** *v. pres. part.* **win·ning** *past* and *past part.* **won** (wʌn) *v.i.* to come first in a contest ‖ to achieve a victory ‖ (sometimes with 'out') to triumph, prevail ‖ (with 'through' etc.) to succeed, after a struggle, in reaching a certain state or place ‖ *v.t.* to achieve victory in (a fight, argument, contest etc.) ‖ to obtain by effort, *to win recognition, to win land back from the sea* ‖ to gain (the affection, esteem etc.) of another or others ‖ (often with 'over') to persuade (another) to accept one's point of view, cause etc. ‖ (*mining*) to extract (a mineral) from the surrounding rocks ‖ to extract (a metal) from its ore **2.** *n.* a victory in a contest ‖ money etc. won, e.g. on a race [O.E. *winnan*]

wince (wins) **1.** *v.i. pres. part.* **winc·ing** *past* and *past part.* **winced** to draw suddenly back slightly and become more rigid, from pain or as if from pain **2.** *n.* a wincing [A.F.]

wince *n.* (*Br.*) a winch (reel over which a textile laps) [var. of WINCH]

winch (wintʃ) **1.** *n.* a large wheel turned by a handle or motor and having attached to its axle a cable or chain, by means of which a load may be raised or lowered ‖ the crank of a revolving part of a machine ‖ a reel over which a textile laps, enabling the textile to be dipped into either of two vats **2.** *v.t.* to haul with or as if with a winch [O.E. *wince*]

Win·ches·ter (wíntʃistər, wíntʃestər) a town (pop. 31,100) in Hampshire, England. Norman and Gothic cathedral (11th-14th cc.), boys' school (Winchester College, 1382)

Winchester *n.* an early type of breech-loading rifle, supplied automatically with fresh cartridges from a magazine [after O.F. *Winchester*, U.S. inventor]

Winck·el·mann (víŋkəlmɑn), Johann Joachim (1717-68), German archaeologist. His 'History of Ancient Art' (1764) marked the beginning of the academic study of classic art

wind (waind) **1.** *v. pres. part.* **wind·ing** *past* and *past part.* **wound** (waund) *v.i.* to go or move in a curved path, esp. in one which is sinuous or spiral ‖ to move in this way so as to encircle ‖ *v.t.* to cause to wind ‖ to make (one's or its way) in a winding course ‖ to cause to encircle, *he wound a bandage around his arm* ‖ to cause to assume an elliptical or round shape, or to coil ‖ (often with 'up') to tighten the spring of by turning the screw or handle of (a clock, watch etc.) ‖ (often with 'up') to hoist by means of a winch etc. **to wind up** to conclude, *he wound up with a quotation* ‖ to bring (some activity) to a stop and regulate its affairs, *to wind up a business* ‖ to come to an end, stop ‖ to arrive at a specified condition or place, *they'll wind up in jail* **2.** *n.* a winding or an instance of this ‖ a bend in a sinuous curve [O.E. *windan*]

wind (wind) **1.** *n.* a large body of air in rapid natural motion, its speed often being expressed (*BEAUFORT SCALE) in terms of the force it exerts on an obstacle to its motion. Its direction is that from which it comes, *a west wind* ‖ air set locally in motion, *he felt the wind it made as it rushed past him* ‖ air made to vibrate and thus produce sound, e.g. in the pipe or tube of a musical instrument ‖ (*mus., collect.*) the wind instruments (brass and woodwind) of an orchestra ‖ (*mus., pl.*) the players of such instruments ‖ breath, air drawn into or expelled from the lungs ‖ the ability to breathe air into the lungs ‖ (*boxing*) the solar plexus ‖ gas produced in the stomach and intestinal tract during digestion ‖ words spoken or written which have little significance **before the wind** (*naut.*) with the wind astern **close to** (or **near**) **the wind** (*naut.*) with the wind almost directly on the bow ‖ very close to indecency, or close to breaking the law **in the teeth of the wind, in the wind's eye** (*naut.*) with the wind directly on the bow of the boat **in the wind** in preparation or about to occur **off the wind** (*naut.*) with the wind on either quarter **on the wind** (*naut.*) with the wind on either bow **to break wind** to release intestinal gases **to cast** (or **fling** or **throw**) **to the wind** (or **winds**) to reject on sudden impulse, *to cast one's scruples to the winds* **to get** (or **have**) **the wind up** (*Br.*) to become (or be) frightened **to get wind of** to have scent or sound of (a hunter etc.) brought by a wind ‖ to receive information about (something secret) **to put the wind up someone** (*Br.*) to frighten someone **to see how the wind blows** to find out the state of affairs in order to judge what is likely to happen **to take the wind out of someone's sails** (*naut.*) to sail to the windward of a sailing vessel ‖ to frustrate someone, e.g. by saying what he was about to say, giving the reasons he was about to give etc. **2.** *v.t.* to cause to breathe with difficulty, either by exertion or by a blow to the diaphragm ‖ to receive the scent of ‖ to allow to recover breath by giving a rest to (a horse etc.) ‖ (waind, wind) *pres. part.* **wind·ing** *past* and *past part.* **wind·ed, wound** (waund) to sound (a horn or a note) [O.E.]

wind·age (wíndidʒ) *n.* the effect of the wind in deflecting a projectile, or the amount of this ‖ the allowance for this ‖ the difference in diameter between a bore of a firearm and the projectile ‖ the surface of e.g. a ship which is exposed to the wind

wind·bag (wíndbæg) *n.* a person who talks a great deal but who says nothing of importance ‖ a bag containing compressed air, e.g. in bagpipes

wind·blown (wíndblǫun) *adj.* blown or as if blown by the wind ‖ (of trees) having a permanently twisted shape because of strong prevailing winds

wind-borne (wíndbɔrn, windbǫurn) *adj.* carried along by the wind

wind·break (wíndbrẹik) *n.* a row of trees or other means of providing shelter from the wind

wind·break·er (wíndbrẹikər) *n.* (*Am.=Br.* windcheater) an outer garment of leather or other wind-resistant material, gathered at the wrists and waist ‖ a windbreak

wind-bro·ken (wíndbrǫukən) *adj.* (of a horse) having the heaves

wind·cheat·er (wíndtʃi:tər) *n.* (*Br.*) a windbreaker (outer garment)

wind·chill factor (wíndtʃil) **1.** the effect of wind velocity in raising or lowering discomfort caused by the temperature **2.** an estimate of the effect of temperature and wind on people. *Cf* COMFORT INDEX, THI

wind cone a wind sock

wind down *v.* to bring to an end gradually

wind·er (wáindər) *n.* a device for winding, esp. the stem of a watch ‖ one of the steps in a spiral staircase

Win·der·mere (wíndərmiər) the largest English lake (10 miles long, up to 1 mile wide), in Lancashire and Westmorland, in the Lake District

wind·fall (wíndfɔl) *n.* a fruit blown off a tree by the wind ‖ something of value received unexpectedly, without any effort of one's own to secure it ‖ a tree blown down by the wind, or a piece of ground where trees have been blown down

windfall *adj.* of unexpected income or profit, esp. as the result of new laws —**windfall** *adj.*

wind·flow·er (wíndflauər) *n.* the anemone

wind·gall (wíndgɔl) *n.* a soft tumor on a horse's fetlock **wind·galled** *adj.*

wind gap a narrow pass in a mountain ridge, without a river in it

wind gauge an anemometer ‖ an instrument for measuring the supply of wind in an organ bellows

Wind·hoek (vínthuk) the capital (pop. 36,051) of Namibia, in a pastoral and mining region

wind·hov·er (wíndhʌvər, wíndhɒvər) *n.* (esp. *Br.*) a kestrel

wind·i·ly (wíndili:) *adv.* in a windy manner

wind·i·ness (wíndi:nis) *n.* the state or quality of being windy

wind·ing (wáindiŋ) **1.** *n.* the act of someone or something that winds ‖ one complete turn of something which is wound ‖ the way in which something (e.g. a coil) is wound, *a shunt winding* ‖ the act of blowing a horn **2.** *adj.* which winds ‖ discursive, rambling

winding drum a power-driven cylinder around which hoisting tackle is wound

winding engine an engine used for hoisting

winding frame a machine which winds yarn or thread

CONCISE PRONUNCIATION KEY: **(a)** æ, *cat*; ɑ, *car*; ɔ *fawn*; ei, *snake*. **(e)** e, *hen*; i:, *sheep*; iə, *deer*; ɛə, *bear*. **(i)** i, *fish*; ai, *tiger*; ə:, *bird*. **(o)** o, *ox*; au, *cow*; ou, *goat*; u, *poor*; ɔi, *royal*. **(u)** ʌ, *duck*; u, *bull*; u:, *goose*; ə, *bacillus*; ju:, *cube*. x, *loch*; θ, *think*; ð, *bother*; z, *Zen*; ʒ, *corsage*; dʒ, *savage*; ŋ, *orangutang*; j, *yak*; ʃ, *fish*; tʃ, *fetch*; 'l, *rabble*; 'n, *redden*. Complete pronunciation key appears inside front cover.

winding sheet a shroud (long sheet)
wind instrument a musical instrument which produces sound by the vibration of air in a pipe or tube (the bassoon, clarinet, oboe, flute, saxophone etc. are woodwinds; the horn, trombone, trumpet, tuba etc. are brass winds)
Win·disch·gräts (víndiʃgrets), Alfred, Fürst zu (1787-1862), Austrian field marshal. He put down revolutions in Austria and Bohemia (1848)
wind·jam·mer (wínddʒæmər) *n.* (*hist.*) a large, fast merchant sailing vessel, esp. one fully rigged
wind·lass (wíndləs) *n.* a machine consisting of an axle around which a cable or chain is wound when a large wheel is turned, used for hauling and hoisting [altered after older *windle,* to wind, fr. M.E. *windas,* a windlass fr. O.N.]
wind loading provision for stress created by the wind on a high structure
wind·mill (wíndmil) *n.* a mill worked by sails turned by the wind, esp. to grind grain ‖ a pinwheel **to tilt at windmills** to expend energy in overcoming imaginary obstacles or opponents
win·dow (wíndou) *n.* an opening in the wall of a room, building etc. permitting light to enter, usually fitted with glass in a frame of wood or metal which may be partly slid, or turned on hinges, to permit air to pass ‖ a sash, casement etc. designed to fit such an opening ‖ the space directly behind such an opening used for displaying goods in a store etc. ‖ a window pane ‖ an opening resembling a window, e.g. that in a window envelope ‖ (*meteor.*) area on earth not closed to extraterrestrial observation by absorption of electromagnetic radiation of most wavelengths ‖ (*meteor.*) a time slot in cycles of celestial bodies when an atmospheric penetration is advantageous ‖ a period when an opening appears, e.g., when a nation's defenses are down ‖ (*mil.*) an area on enemy's defense through which a missile or spacecraft can pass advantageously ‖ (*electr.*) wavelength through which electromagnetic observation is advantageous [M.E. *windoge* fr. O.N.]
window box a box resting on or outside a window sill in which plants can be cultivated ‖ a hollow within the sides of a sash window frame containing a heavy weight on the end of a sash cord to balance the weight of the sash
window dressing the displaying of goods in a store window ‖ the presenting of facts in such a way that a more favorable judgment is made than they warrant
window envelope an envelope with an aperture through which the address written on the contents shows
win·dow·pane (wíndoupein) *n.* a sheet of glass forming part of a window
window screen a wooden frame fitted with fine wire mesh or cotton netting for use on open doors and windows to keep insects out
window seat a seat, often forming the lid of a chest, built into a window bay
win·dow-shop (wíndouʃɒp) *pres. part.* **win·dow-shop·ping** *past* and *past part.* **win·dow-shopped** *v.i.* to look at goods displayed in store windows without going inside to buy
win·dow·sill (wíndousil) *n.* the sill of a window
wind·pipe (wíndpaip) *n.* the trachea
wind-pol·li·nat·ed (wíndpɒlineitid) *adj.* (*bot.*) fertilized by pollen carried on the wind
wind pump a pump activated by the force of the wind turning a vaned propeller wheel
wind rose (*meteor.*) diagram designed to show distribution of wind directions at a specified time and place, sometimes with speed groupings
wind·row (wíndrou) **1.** *n.* a row of cut grass, wheat etc. raked up to dry in the wind ‖ a line of dust, leaves etc. piled up by the wind ‖ a trench in which sugar canes are laid to root **2.** *v.t.* to arrange in a windrow
wind·sail (wíndseil) *n.* a canvas funnel or tube for ventilating the lower decks of a ship
wind scale a numerical scale measuring the velocity of wind (*BEAUFORT SCALE)
wind·screen (wíndskri:n) *n.* (*Br.*) a windshield
wind·shield (wíndʃi:ld, wínʃi:ld) *n.* (*Am.=Br.* windscreen) a sheet of glass in the front of a car or other vehicle to protect the driver and other occupants from wind, dust etc.
wind sleeve a wind sock
wind sock a fabric bag, with the shape of a cone and open at both ends, erected on a tall pole to indicate wind direction. It is distended by the wind pressure through it, and is used esp. on airfields
Wind·sor (wínzər) the name adopted (1917) by the British royal house. Elizabeth II announced (1960) that her descendants, except those entitled to the title of prince or princess, will take the surname Mountbatten-Windsor
Windsor a town (pop. 27,000) in Berkshire, England, on the Thames, site of Windsor Castle (14th c., much restored, a royal residence, with a celebrated collection of paintings and drawings) and of Eton College
Windsor a port (pop. 192,083) in Ontario, Canada, across the Detroit River from Detroit: automobiles, chemical industries, metalworking
Windsor chair a plain wooden chair with or without arms, having a hoop-shaped back filled in with upright spindles. It has turned legs which are slightly raked, and a saddle seat
Windsor, duke of the title conferred (1936) on Edward VIII of Great Britain and Northern Ireland after his abdication
wind·storm (wíndstɔrm) *n.* a storm characterized by violent winds and occasionally accompanied by rain
wind·surf·ing (wíndsə:rfiŋ) *n.* (*surfing*) employment of a specially designed surfboard with an independently swiveling mast, using the body as a stabilizing force
wind·swept (wíndswept) *adj.* frequently raked by strong winds
wind tunnel a tunnel-like structure through which air can be forced at any required speed in order to test its effect on scale models of aircraft
wind·up (wáindʌp) *n.* the act of winding up or ending ‖ the last item bringing an entertainment or activity to a close ‖ (*baseball*) a swing of the arm before pitching
wind·ward (wíndwərd) **1.** *n.* the direction from which a wind blows (opp. LEEWARD) **2.** *adj.* in this direction ‖ of that side of a vessel etc. on which the wind blows **3.** *adv.* towards the source of the wind
Windward Islands the name of two island groups, one in the West Indies, the other (Iles du Vent) in French Polynesia (*SOCIETY ISLANDS). The West Indian group forms the southern chain of the Lesser Antilles. It consists of Barbados, Dominica, Grenada, the Grenadines, St Lucia and St Vincent, and the French island of Martinique
wind·y (wíndi:) *comp.* **wind·i·er** *superl.* **wind·i·est** *adj.* exposed to frequent winds, *a windy corner* ‖ accompanied or characterized by wind, *one windy night* ‖ afflicted with stomach or intestinal gas ‖ wordy and without much significance, *a windy speech* ‖ (*Br., pop.*) frightened
wine (wain) **1.** *n.* a drink made of the fermented juice of grapes ‖ a beverage prepared from fermented plant or fruit juice, *rhubarb wine* ‖ (*med.*) a solution of a drug in wine, *quinine wine* ‖ the dark, reddish-purple color of red wine **2.** *v.t. pres. part.* **win·ing** *past* and *past part.* **wined** to entertain with wine, *to wine and dine someone* [O.E. *wīn* fr. L.]
—Red wine derives its color from the skins of dark-skinned grapes, which are left in the juice for some days while it ferments before the fruit is put through the press. White wine (often pale yellow) is made from the juice of light-skinned grapes, the fruit being put through the press as soon as it is picked. The alcoholic content of wine varies according to the kind of grape and the conditions of ripening etc. The flavor (*BOUQUET) is due to the esters and ethers present. Fermentation is largely completed in vats or casks, though for some white wines it may continue after bottling, giving a sparkling wine
wine cellar a cellar for storing wine
wine gallon *GALLON
wine·glass (wáinglæs, wáinglɒs) *n.* a small glass, usually with a slender stem and a foot, used for drinking wine, different shapes and sizes being customarily used for different types of wine
wine·grow·er (wáingrouər) *n.* someone who grows grapes for making wine
wine gum (*Br.*) a gumdrop
wine palm any of various palms whose sap is used to make palm wine
wine·press (wáinpres) *n.* a vat or machine in which the juice is extracted from grapes for wine making
wine·skin (wáinskin) *n.* a skin, usually of a goat, sewed into a bag in which wine can be carried
wing (wiŋ) **1.** *n.* one of the specialized appendages used by a bird, bat, insect etc. in flying ‖ such an appendage in a flightless bird, e.g. the ostrich ‖ one of the structures, on either side of the fuselage of an aircraft, which support the machine in the air ‖ a section of a building projecting from the central section ‖ a division of an army or a fleet to the right or left of the central division ‖ a faction within an organization or political party ‖ (*soccer, hockey* etc.) a position in the forward line furthest from the center, or the player occupying it ‖ something resembling a wing in form, function or position, e.g. a lateral expansion on many fruits and seeds which serves in wind dispersal, or the cartilage of the nose forming the nostrils etc. ‖ (*Br.*) a fender of a motor vehicle ‖ a subunit of an air force ‖ a sidepiece fitting into the back of an easy chair as a head support or draft excluder ‖ (*theater, pl.*) the area just offstage right or left ‖ (*theater*) a piece of stage scenery, esp. a flat, which masks this area ‖ (*pl.*) insignia of proficiency worn by air force personnel ‖ one of the two lateral petals of a papilionaceous flower **on the wing** in flight **to clip someone's wings** to restrict someone's freedom of action **to lend wings to** (*rhet.*) to increase the speed of, *fear lent wings to his flight* **to take under one's wing** to assume a measure of protection for (someone), esp. by promoting his interests **to take wing** to fly away **under the wing of** in the state of having one's interests looked after by **2.** *v.i.* to fly ‖ *v.t.* to equip with wings ‖ to wound in the wing [M.E. *wenge, wengen, wenges* fr. O. N.]
Win·gate (wíŋgit, wíngeit), Orde Charles (1903-44), British army officer. As commander of the British and Chindit forces in Burma (1942-4) he developed the art of jungle guerrilla warfare
wing back formation (*football*) an attacking formation in which a back is immediately behind the end
wing case an elytron in insects
wing chair an easy chair the back of which has projecting sidepieces providing shelter from drafts and also a head support
wing commander an officer in the Royal Air Force ranking below a group captain and above a squadron leader
wing covert one of the small feathers lying over the flight feathers of a bird's wing
winged (wiŋd, esp. *rhet.* wíŋid) *adj.* having wings ‖ wounded in the wing
wing nut a butterfly nut
wing·spread (wíŋspred) *n.* the distance between the tips of the fully spread wings of a bird ‖ the distance from wing tip to wing tip of an aircraft
wink (wiŋk) **1.** *v.i.* to close an eye and then at once open it, esp. as a gesture or signal conveying a message or suggesting mutual understanding ‖ to blink ‖ (of a source of light) to shine momentarily or intermittently ‖ *v.t.* to cause (an eye or eyelid) to wink ‖ to cause (a source of light) to wink, esp. as a signal **to wink at** to communicate with by winking ‖ to tolerate (what ought strictly not to be) and pretend not to have seen or known **2.** *n.* an act of winking ‖ an instant of sleep, *forty winks* ‖ the message conveyed by a wink ‖ a short or intermittent gleam ‖ a very short time **not to sleep a wink** to get no sleep at all **to tip someone the wink** (esp. *Br.*) to give a hint or useful warning to someone [O.E. *wincian*]
win·kle (wíŋk'l) **1.** *n.* periwinkle **2.** *v.t. pres. part.* **win·kling** *past* and *past part.* **win·kled** (with 'out') to extract (something or someone) from a hiding place or strong defensive position [shortened fr. PERIWINKLE]
win·ner (wínər) *n.* someone who or something that wins ‖ (*pop.*) something extremely well done, made, thought out etc. ‖ (*pop.*) someone of first-rate ability
win·ning (wíniŋ) **1.** *adj.* securing victory or gaining a contest ‖ attractive, *a winning smile* **2.** *n.* a securing of victory ‖ (*pl.*) money won from gambling, contests etc.
winning gallery (*court tennis*) the netted opening below the side penthouse and furthest from the dedans
winning opening (*court tennis*) the dedans, the grille, or the winning gallery
Win·ni·peg (wínəpeg) the capital (pop. 564,473) of Manitoba, Canada, the country's largest grain market. Main industries: flour milling,

CONCISE PRONUNCIATION KEY: (a) æ, cat; ɑ, car; ɔ fawn; ei, snake. (e) e, hen; i:, sheep; iə, deer; εə, bear. (i) i, fish; ai, tiger; ə:, bird. (o) ɒ, ox; au, cow; ou, goat; u, poor; ɔi, royal. (u) ʌ, duck; u, bull; u:, goose; ə, bacillus; ju:, cube. x, loch; θ, think; ð, bother; z, Zen; ʒ, corsage; dʒ, savage; ŋ, orangutang; j, yak; ʃ, fish; tʃ, fetch; 'l, rabble; 'n, redden. Complete pronunciation key appears inside front cover.

meat packing, textiles and clothing. University of Manitoba (1877)

Winnipeg a lake (area 9,460 sq. miles) in Manitoba, Canada: fisheries

Win·ni·peg·o·sis (wɪnəpegóusis) a lake (area 2,086 sq. miles) in Manitoba and Saskatchewan, Canada

win·now (wínou) *v.t.* to blow (grain) free of chaff ‖ to blow away (chaff) from grain ‖ to treat as though separating chaff from grain, *they winnowed the candidates down from 60 to 10* [O.E. *windwian* fr. *wind* n., wind]

win·some (wínsəm) *adj.* charming, attractive, winning in manner [O.E. *wynsum*, pleasant]

Win·ston-Sa·lem (wínstənséiləm) a tobacco-industry center (pop. 131,885) in North Carolina

win·ter (wíntər) **1.** *n.* the season of the year in latitudes outside the Tropics when the warmth due to the sun's radiation is least (due to the inclination of the earth's axis as it moves in its orbit around the sun), i.e. the months of December, January and February in northern temperate latitudes, and of June, July and August in southern temperate latitudes **2.** *adj.* of, for or adapted to the winter ‖ sown in winter (not in spring), *winter oats* **3.** *v.i.* to live during the months of winter ‖ *v.t.* to maintain during the winter, *they winter the cattle in the lower valley* [O.E.]

winter aconite *Eranthis hyemalis*, fam. *Ranunculaceae*, a poisonous perennial herb of S.E. Europe and Asia with small yellow flowers appearing early in spring

winter book (*wagering*) handicapper's appraisal of odds for the following season

winter bud a dormant bud of a woody plant, protected by hard scales during the winter

winter cherry *Physalis alkekengi*, fam. *Solanaceae*, an Old World plant ‖ its small orange ornamental fruit

winter garden a conservatory, often built on to and accessible from a house, suitable for half-hardy plants

win·ter·green (wíntərgri:n) *n.* a member of *Pyrola*, fam. *Pyrolaceae*, esp. *P. minor*, a genus of evergreen, low-growing shrubs of north temperate and arctic regions ‖ a member of *Gaultheria*, fam. *Ericaceae*, esp. *G. procumbens*, a North American plant from which an oil, used as an embrocation and in ointments and as a flavoring, is distilled ‖ this oil ‖ its flavor

Win·ter·hal·ter (vínterhɑltər), Franz Xaver (1805-73), German portrait painter. He was Queen Victoria's court painter of portraits

win·ter·ize (wíntəraiz) *pres. part.* **win·ter·iz·ing** *past* and *past part.* **win·ter·ized** *v.t.* to prepare (a house, automobile etc.) for the freezing conditions of winter

win·ter·kill (wíntərkil) *v.t.* to kill (plants) by exposure to winter ‖ *v.i.* (of plants) to die by exposure to winter

winter quarters accommodation for the winter, e.g. for traveling circuses, geographical expeditions or (*hist.*) campaigning troops

winter solstice the time when the sun reaches the December solstice for the northern hemisphere or the June solstice for the southern hemisphere

Win·ter·thur (víntərtu:r) an industrial center (pop. 87,900) in Zurich canton, Switzerland, manufacturing rolling stock and locomotives

win·ter·time (wíntərtaim) *n.* the winter season

Win·throp (wínθrəp), John (1588-1649), Colonial governor (1630-4, 1637-40, 1642-4, 1646-9) of Massachusetts and founder (1630) of the settlement that became Boston. As governor he ruled autocratically, and he established the Puritan ethic in Massachusetts social life

win·tri·ly (wíntrili:) *adv.* in a wintry manner

win·tri·ness (wíntri:nis) *n.* the state or quality of being wintry

win·try (wíntri:) *comp.* **win·tri·er** *superl.* **win·tri·est** *adj.* of or like winter ‖ quite unfriendly, chilling

winze (wínz) *n.* (*mining*) a shaft connecting different levels in a mine, used either for ventilation or communication [etym. doubtful]

wipe (waip) **1.** *v. pres. part.* **wip·ing** *past* and *past part.* **wiped** *v.t.* to rub with a cloth etc. so as to free from surface moisture, dust etc. ‖ to clean by rubbing, *wipe your boots on the mat* ‖ to move one's hand over (a surface, e.g. one's brow) as if rubbing or cleaning ‖ (*plumbing*) to cover (a joint) smoothly with solder or soft lead ‖ *v.i.* to dry dishes etc. **to wipe away** (or **off**) to remove by wiping **to wipe out** to pay off (a debt) ‖ to destroy (e.g. a pocket of troops) ‖ to clean out or remove by wiping **to wipe the floor with** (*pop.*) to defeat overwhelmingly and easily **to wipe up** to dry the dishes etc. **2.** *n.* a wiping ‖ (*mach.*) a wiper **wíp·er** *n.* someone who or something that wipes, esp. a device for sweeping rain from the windshield of an automobile etc. ‖ (*mach.*) a cam ‖ (*cinematography*) a technique in which one scene appears to push another off the screen [O.E. *wīpian*]

wipe-out (wáipaut) *n.* **1.** (*colloq.*) a complete destruction **2.** (*surfing*) an accidental fall —**wipe out** *v.*

wire (wáiər) **1.** *n.* metal drawn out into a threadlike form of uniform diameter ‖ a length of this ‖ fencing or netting made of this ‖ a suspended length of this on which acrobats perform, or one strung high between the winning posts of a race track ‖ barbed wire ‖ a telegram ‖ the telegraphic system, *send flowers by wire* ‖ (*papermaking*) the mesh on which wet paper is drained ‖ a snare for rabbits ‖ (*pl.*) the lines by which a puppet is controlled **to pull wires** to use influence to secure some favor or advantage **under the wire** just ahead of the deadline, at the last possible moment **2.** *v. pres. part.* **wir·ing** *past* and *past part.* **wired** *v.t.* to furnish with a wire or wires ‖ to bind or fasten with wire ‖ to provide with an electric circuit, *to wire a house* ‖ to snare (an animal) using a noose of wire ‖ to telegraph ‖ (*croquet*) to place (a ball) behind a wicket in a way which prevents a successful shot ‖ *v.i.* to send a telegram [O.E. *wīr*]

wire cloth fabric woven from wire used e.g. for filters

wire cutter a tool with a very strong cutting edge, operated like scissors, used to cut wire

wire·draw (wáiərdrɔ) *pres. part.* **wire·draw·ing** *past* **wire·drew** (wáiərdru:) *past part.* **wire·drawn** (wáiərdrɔn) *v.t.* to draw (metal) into wire

wire gauge a gauge for measuring the diameter of wire or the thickness of sheet metal ‖ a system by which wire or sheet metal is graded according to size, or a size within such a system

wire gauze fine wire woven to make an open gauzy material, for strainers etc.

wire·hair (wáiərhɛər) *n.* a fox terrier with a short, stiff, curly coat

wire·haired (wáiərhɛərd) *adj.* (of a terrier) having short, stiff, curly hair

wire house (*securities*) a commission house with branch offices connected by electronic communications

wire·less (wáiərlis) **1.** *adj.* (esp. *Br.*) of or relating to radiotelephony, radiotelegraphy, or radio **2.** *n.* a method of communication by electromagnetic waves (often beamed) ‖ (esp. *Br.*) radio **3.** *v.t.* and *i.* (esp. *Br.*) to radio

wire netting openwork material, made of woven wire, used for caging, fencing etc.

wire·pull·ing (wáiərpuliŋ) *n.* the using of influence to secure favors etc.

wire recorder a magnetic recorder using a magnetized wire

wire rope a rope made by twisting a number of lengths of wire together

wire service a news agency which distributes copy to its subscribers by teletype

wire·sonde (wáiərsɒnd) *n.* (*meteor.*) device for gathering meteorological data, transmitted from a balloon to ground

wire·tap (wáiərtæp) **1.** *v. pres. part.* **wire·tap·ping** *past* and *past part.* **wire·tapped** *v.i.* to listen clandestinely to telephone conversations by secretly making a connection with the telephone wire in use ‖ *v.t.* to listen to in this way ‖ to obtain (information etc.) in this way **2.** *n.* this technique or an instance of it

wire·work (wáiərwə:rk) *n.* netting, gauze etc. constructed of wire

wire·worm (wáiərwə:rm) *n.* the larva of any of several insects destructive to the roots of plants, esp. the larva of click beetles, which may live for several years in the soil before metamorphosing into the imago ‖ a millepede

wire-wrap construction (wáiəræp) (*computer*) a method of constructing integrated circuits in which wires are used to connect two points with junctions and terminals; created by wrapping wire around those stakes without wiring

wir·i·ness (wáiəri:nis) *n.* the state or quality of being wiry

wir·ing (wáiəriŋ) *n.* the arrangement of electric circuits in a building, a machine, electrical equipment etc.

wir·y (wáiəri:) *comp.* **wir·i·er** *superl.* **wir·i·est** *adj.* made of wire ‖ strong and flexible ‖ (of persons) lean and sinewy ‖ (of hair) stiff

Wis. Wisconsin

Wisc. Wisconsin

Wis·con·sin (wiskɒ́nsin) (*abbr.* Wis., Wisc.) a state (area 56,164 sq. miles, pop. 4,765,000) in the N. Central U.S.A., on the Great Lakes. Capital: Madison. Chief city: Milwaukee. It is an undulating plain, with an upland region in the north and west. Agriculture: dairy products (first state producer of milk and butter), hay, corn and fodder crops, vegetables, fruit. Resources: iron ore, building materials. Industries: machinery, metal products, paper, food processing. State university (1849) at Madison. Wisconsin was explored by the French (late 17th c.), was ceded to Britain (1763), became part of the Northwest Territory (1783) and became (1848) the 30th state of the U.S.A.

Wisconsin, University of a U.S. coeducational institution chartered (1848) at Madison, Wis. with undergraduate and graduate curricula at campuses in Madison and other cities

Wis·dom (wízdəm) a book included in the Roman Catholic canon but placed in the Apocrypha in the King James Version, containing sayings traditionally attributed to Solomon

wis·dom (wízdəm) *n.* the quality of being wise ‖ intelligence drawing on experience and governed by prudence ‖ a store of knowledge ‖ such knowledge converted into teaching, *the wisdom of the East* [O.E. *wīsdōm*]

wisdom tooth the back tooth on either side of both jaws in man, usually developing at 18–20 years of age

Wise (waiz), Henry Alexander (1806-76), U.S. politician and Confederate general in the Civil War. As governor of Virginia (1856-60), he signed the death warrant of John Brown

Wise, Isaac Mayer (1819-1900), U.S. rabbi, founder of Reform Judaism in the U.S.A.

Wise, John (1652-1725), American colonial clergyman of Massachusetts. Opposing Increase Mather and Cotton Mather, he championed church democracy in his influential 'The Churches Quarrel Espoused' (1710) and 'A Vindication of the Government of New England Churches' (1717)

wise (waiz) *adj.* having the ability to make a right decision or judgment by applying intelligent thought to a wide range of experience and knowledge, with prudence ‖ (of a decision, judgment or action) resulting from the use of this ability, *a wise choice* ‖ possessing great knowledge and intelligence ‖ (*pop.*) crafty, cunning ‖ (*pop.*) cocky, self-important **to be** (or **get**) **wise to** to be (or become) fully aware of **to put someone wise to** to inform someone about [O.E. *wīs*]

wise *n.* (*rhet.*, except as a suffix) way, manner **in no wise** (*rhet.*) not at all [O.E. *wīse*]

-wise *suffix* denoting manner, position, direction as in 'lengthwise' ‖ (*pop.*) with regard to, as in 'salarywise he has no complaints'

wise·a·cre (wáizeikər) *n.* a man who foolishly pretends to great knowledge [fr. Du. *wijsseggher* fr. O.H.G. *wizago*, a prophet]

wise·crack (wáizkræk) **1.** *n.* a smart or flippant remark **2.** *v.i.* to make such remarks

Wise·man (wáizmən), Nicholas Patrick Stephen (1802-65), British cardinal. He was the first Roman Catholic archbishop of Westminster (1850-65)

wi·sent (wízənt) *n.* *Bison bonasus*, fam. *Bovidae*, a European bison thought to be the ancestor of the American bison or buffalo [fr. G. fr. O.H.G. *wisunt*]

wish (wíʃ) **1.** *v.t.* to have a feeling of unfulfilled satisfaction with respect to something or someone, *I wish I had a new car, I wish I knew more about him* ‖ to feel or express good or ill will or a specified wish, greeting or invocation (to or for someone), *I wish him no harm, he wished them every happiness* ‖ to require, *I wish you to do it* ‖ to foist off, *he wished the job on me* ‖ *v.i.* (with 'for') to hope, long to make a silent wish **2.** *n.* a desire felt or expressed ‖ something wished for ‖ a request ‖ (*pl.*) greetings, *best wishes* [O.E. *wȳscan*]

Wish·art (wíʃɑrt, wíʃərt), George (c. 1513-46), Scottish religious reformer. His Protestant teaching (1544-6) converted Knox. He was burned as a heretic

wish·bone (wíʃboun) *n.* the forked bone between the neck and breast in birds. (A dried wishbone is pulled by two people, who silently wish while pulling, until it snaps. A popular superstition holds that the person pulling the longer piece will have his wish fulfilled) ‖ (*football*) a variation of the T formation in which fullbacks are close to the scrimmage line and the halfbacks farther back

wish·ful (wíʃfəl) *adj.* having or manifesting a wish

wishful thinking thinking founded on desire and not on the facts

wish·y-wash·y (wíʃi:wɔʃi:, wíʃi:wɒʃi:) *adj.* weak, thin, watery ‖ (of a person) feeble and indecisive in character

Wis·la (ví:slə) *VISTULA

wisp (wisp) *n.* a small bunch, *a wisp of hair* ‖ a small amount or mere trace of something, *a wisp of smoke* **wísp·y** *comp.* **wisp·i·er** *superl.* **wisp·i·est** *adj.* [origin unknown]

wist *past* and *past part.* of archaic WIT

Wis·ter (wístər), Owen (1860-1938), U.S. writer, best known for his 'The Virginian' (1902), a novel dealing with Wyoming cowboys

wis·ter·i·a, wis·tar·i·a (wistέəri:ə) *n.* a member of *Wisteria (Wistaria)*, fam. *Papilionaceae*, a genus of chiefly Asiatic climbing shrubs cultivated for their sweet-scented pendulous racemes of white, blue, mauve or pink flowers [after Casper *Wistar*, U.S. physician]

wist·ful (wístfəl) *adj.* desiring a little sadly what it is not possible or easy to obtain, or revealing this state, *a wistful look* ‖ in a vague mood of unformulated melancholy or frustrated desire [prob. fr. older *wistly* adv., intently]

wit (wit) *n.* the association of apparently unrelated ideas in an unexpected, clever way, esp. with an effect of brilliance provoking laughter ‖ the ability to make such association ‖ a person with this ability ‖ intelligence, *shrewd native wit* ‖ (*pl.*) mental balance, *he must have lost his wits* **at one's wits' end** mentally in despair, baffled **out of one's wits** distracted, not thinking intelligently **to have** (or **keep**) **one's wits about one** to be mentally alert **to live by one's wits** to pick up a living as best one can, sometimes by trading on other people [O.E. *witt*, knowledge]

wit *pres. part.* **wit·ing, wit·ting** *past* **wist, wiste** (wist) *past part.* **wist** *v.t.* and *i.* (*archaic*) to know **to wit** (*rhet.*) namely [O.E. *witan*]

wit·an (wít'n) *pl. n.* (hist.) the members of the witenagemot [O.E. *pl.* of *Wita*, councilor, wise man]

witch (witʃ) **1.** *n.* a woman practicing sorcery usually with the aid, or through the medium, of an evil spirit ‖ (*pop.*) an ugly old woman **2.** *v.t.* (*rhet.*) to cast a spell on ‖ to bewitch [O.E. *wicce*]

witch ball (*hist.*) a hollow glass ball hung up in houses in the 18th c. to keep witches away

witch·craft (wítʃkræft, wítʃkrɑft) *n.* sorcery as practiced by a witch or witches [O.E. *wiececræft*]

—In medieval times witches were believed to be in league with Satan, from whom they received supernatural powers, to be guilty of the most hideous vices, including sexual intercourse with demons, and to be responsible for plagues, diseases of men and cattle, infanticide and the murder of their enemies. Persecution was authorized by Church and State, the most important ecclesiastical directive being Pope Innocent VII's bull 'Summis desiderantes' (1484). The use of torture to extract confessions provided what was taken to be convincing evidence of guilt, and these confessions confirmed the superstitions of the ignorant. At times witch-hunting became a mania and the climax came in England and Scotland, and in America, in the 17th c. Great numbers of people were cruelly put to death, commonly by burning. The next century brought a more skeptical attitude

witch doctor a medicine man among primitive peoples

witch elm *WYCH ELM

witch·er·y (wítʃəri:) *pl.* **witch·er·ies** *n.* witchcraft ‖ fascination

witches' sabbath a midnight assembly of witches, at which the powers of evil are supposed to be present, when black rites are celebrated and orgies held (*WALPURGIS NIGHT)

witch hazel, wych hazel a member of *Hamamelis*, fam. *Hamamelidaceae*, a genus of trees or shrubs which flower in late autumn after the leaves have fallen, esp. *H. virginiana*, native to North America ‖ an alcoholic solution of a substance extracted from the bark of *H. virginiana* and used as a medicinal lotion

witch-hunt (wítʃhʌnt) *n.* (*hist.*) a pursuing and persecution of people accused of witchcraft ‖ a persecution of individuals belonging to an organization or community whose views are repugnant to those in authority **wítch-hunt·ing** *n.*

wit·e·na·ge·mot, wit·e·na·ge·mote (wịt'nəgəmóut, wịt'nægəmóut) *n.* (*hist.*) an assembly of nobles, ecclesiastics and officials in Anglo-Saxon England, meeting irregularly to advise the king [O.E. fr. *witena*, gen. pl. of *wita*, wise man+*gemōt*, a gathering]

with (wið, wiθ) *prep.* used to indicate that two or more persons or things are together, near each other, in agreement, harmony etc., *red with blue* ‖ in the company of, *stay with your parents* ‖ accompanied by ‖ used to indicate someone spoken to, *he had a word with John* ‖ used to indicate the object of attention, sentiment etc., *she is pleased with her new dress* ‖ by means of, *to pay with a check* ‖ used to indicate the presence of, *crowded with people* ‖ among, *he lives with pygmies* ‖ possessing, characterized by, *a man with a wooden leg* ‖ by reason of having, because of, *in bed with a fever* ‖ having, *don't eat with your mouth open* ‖ in regard to, concerning, *what do you want with me?* ‖ used to indicate the object of a command, *off with his head!* ‖ in opposition to, *he fought with his friends* ‖ in the functioning of, *what's the matter with the television?* ‖ in the care or possession of, *leave the keys with the caretaker* ‖ at the same time as, *he gets up with the sun* ‖ at the time of, *with the ebbing tide his hopes dwindled* ‖ in the same direction as, *sail with the wind* ‖ in proportion to, *his avarice increased with his wealth* ‖ used to indicate the object of a comparison, *he is not on a level with the other competitors* ‖ used to indicate manner, *he walked with difficulty* ‖ plus, *these chairs, with the ones at the table, will be enough* ‖ including, *it's $20 with tax* ‖ as competently as, *he can swear with any of them* ‖ so as to be separated from, *he dispensed with their services* ‖ in spite of, *with all his faults he is a good man* ‖ used to indicate understanding or agreement, *are you with me?* ‖ used to indicate the object of a charge, threat etc., *menaced with eviction* **with this (with that)** thereupon, after this (after that) [O.E.]

with·al (wiðɔ́l, wiθɔ́l) *adv.* (*rhet.*) moreover, besides ‖ (*rhet.*) nevertheless

with·draw (wiðdrɔ́, wiθdrɔ́) *pres. part.* **with·draw·ing,** *past* **with·drew** (wiðdrú:, wiθdrú:) *past part.* **with·drawn** (wiðdrɔ́n, wiθdrɔ́n) *v.t.* to take away, remove, *to withdraw an application* ‖ to take back, to retract, *to withdraw an offer* ‖ to draw back, *to withdraw one's hand* ‖ *v.i.* to leave, retire, *they withdrew to an inner room* **with·dráw·al** *n.* a withdrawing **with·dráwn** *adj.* reserved, shy [fr. O.E. *with-*, away, back+ DRAW]

withe (wiθ) *n.* a tough flexible thin branch, esp. of willow or osier, used as a band for tying up bundles, e.g. of firewood [O.E. *withthe*]

with·er (wíðər) *v.i.* (of plants) to dry up and die for lack of moisture or because of extreme cold or heat, generally losing color ‖ to become lean and wrinkled ‖ (often with 'away') to lose vigor, *the opposition withered away* ‖ *v.t.* to cause to wither ‖ to reduce to silence, *she withered him with her sarcastic remarks* [prob. var. of WEATHER v.]

with·er·ite (wíðərait) *n.* (*mineral.*) a native barium carbonate, $BaCO_3$, found in white or gray crystals, also in columnar or granular masses [after W. *Withering*, English physician]

with·ers (wíðərz) *pl. n.* the ridge between the shoulder blades of a horse (and some other animals) [etym. doubtful]

with·er·shins (wíðərʃinz) *adv.* widdershins

With·er·spoon (wíðərspu:n), John (1723-94), Scottish-American Presbyterian minister, signer of the Declaration of Independence. His 'Ecclesiastical Characteristics' (1753) upheld dogmatic orthodoxy against the ministers who espoused humanism. He was appointed (1768) president of what became Princeton University

with·hold (wiðhóuld, wiθhóuld) *pres. part.* **with·hold·ing** *past* and *past part.* **with·held** (wiðhéld, wiθhéld) *v.t.* to hold back, refuse to give, *to withhold consent* [fr. O.E. *with-*, away, back+HOLD]

withholding tax the percentage of someone's income deducted at source by the employer and paid to the government in part payment of income tax

with·in (wiðín, wiθín) **1.** *prep.* not beyond the limits of, *within sight* ‖ in the scope of, *within his capacity* ‖ inside, *safe within walls* ‖ (in expressions of time) in the course of, *within his lifetime* **2.** *adv.* inside, indoors, *inquire within, seen from within* ‖ in the mind or conscience, *look within and consider your motives* [Late O.E. *withinnan*]

with·out (wiðáut, wiθáut) **1.** *prep.* not having, *he came without any money* ‖ free from, *without worry* ‖ (followed by the pres. part.) refraining from, avoiding, *without making any noise* ‖ in need of, *without a job* ‖ devoid of, *without initiative* **it goes without saying** it is self-evident **2.** *adv.* outside, outdoors, *seen from without* **to do** (or **go**) **without** to accept (or endure) a lack or deprivation (of some understood thing) [Late O.E. *withūtan*]

without prejudice (*law*) a caveat denoting that what is said or written must not impair an understood preexistent right or claim

with·stand (wiðstǽnd, wiθstǽnd) *pres. part.* **with·stand·ing** *past* and *past part.* **with·stood** (wiðstúd, wiθstúd) *v.t.* to stand up against, to resist, *to withstand a siege, to withstand criticism* [O.E. *withstandan*]

with·y (wíði:, wíθi:) *pl.* **with·ies** *n.* a withe

wit·less (wítlis) *adj.* foolish

wit·ness (wítnis) **1.** *n.* a person who has observed a certain event, *the unwilling witness of a quarrel* ‖ a person who testifies to this observation, esp. in a court of law, and esp. under oath ‖ a person who testifies to the genuineness of a signature on a document by signing his own name to the document ‖ an authentication of a fact, testimony ‖ public affirmation of the truths of a religious faith ‖ something taken as evidence, *the embers were a witness of recent occupation* **to bear witness** to declare, on the strength of personal observation, that something is true ‖ to affirm the truths of a religious faith **Witness** a Jehovah's Witness **2.** *v.t.* to observe (an event) ‖ to sign as a witness ‖ *v.i.* (esp. with 'to') to give as evidence, *this gift witnesses to his generosity* ‖ to bear witness [O.E. *witnes*, knowledge, testimony]

wit·ness-box (wítnisbɒks) *n.* (*Br.*) a witness stand

witness stand (*Am.*=*Br.* witness-box) an enclosure set aside for witnesses in a court of law

Wit·te (vítə), Count Sergei Yulievich (1849-1915), Russian statesman. As minister of finance, commerce and industry (1892-1903) he introduced the gold standard. He opened up Siberia by the Trans-Siberian Railroad. He was prime minister (1905-6)

wit·ted (wítid) *adj.* (in compounds) having wits of a specified quality, *slow-witted, dull-witted*

Wit·tels·bach (vítəlsbɑx) a German princely house which ruled in Bavaria and the Rhine Palatinate from the 12th c. to 1918

Wit·ten·berg (vítənberk) a town (pop. 52,500) in Halle, East Germany, on the middle Elbe. Luther nailed up (Oct. 31, 1517) his 95 theses here

Wit·te·veen Facility (vítəvi:n) an International Monetary Fund emergency pool of $10 billion. It was authorized in 1977 to be used for loans to countries with serious debts

Witt·gen·stein (vítgənʃtạin), Ludwig Joseph Johann (1889-1951), Austrian philosopher, author of 'Tractatus Logico-Philosophicus' (1921). His researches bore on the philosophy of psychology and mathematics, and were very influential in logical positivism

wit·ti·cism (wítisịzəm) *n.* a witty remark

wit·ti·ly (wítili:) *adv.* in a witty way

wit·ti·ness (wíti:nis) *n.* the quality of being witty

wit·ting (wítiŋ) *adj.* deliberate, intentional, *witting deception* ‖ conscious, *a witting accomplice* **wít·ting·ly** *adv.*

wit·ty (wíti:) *comp.* **wit·ti·er** *superl.* **wit·ti·est** *adj.* possessing or manifesting wit [O.E. *witig, wittig*]

Wit·wa·ters·rand (witwɔ́tərzrænd, witwɔ́tərzrænd) a district of gold-bearing hills, the main world source of gold, in the Transvaal, South Africa. Chief town: Johannesburg. University (1921)

Witz (vits), Konrad (15th c.) Swabian painter. His masterpiece was the Heilspiegel altar (1435), surviving in fragments. He painted in a very realistic style, and shows strong Flemish influence

wivern *WYVERN

wives *pl.* of WIFE

wiz·ard (wízərd) *n.* a sorcerer, magician ‖ a person who seems to perform magic, *a financial*

wizard **wiz·ard·ry** *n.* [M.E. *wysard* fr. *wys, wis,* wise]
wiz·ened (wízənd) *adj.* having a dried-up or shriveled appearance [fr. older *wizen* fr. O.E. *wisnian,* to become dry]
Wla·dy·slaw (vladíslaf) kings of Poland *LADISLAUS
woad (woud) *n. Isatis tinctoria,* fam. *Cruciferae,* a European biennial plant which yields a dark blue dye ‖ this dye, esp. as used by the ancient Britons as a body coloring [O.E. *wād*]
wob·ble (wɒ́b'l) **1.** *v. pres. part.* **wob·bling** *past* and *past part.* **wob·bled** *v.i.* to be unsteady on its or one's legs ‖ (of a top etc.) to move unsteadily from side to side while revolving ‖ to change repeatedly from one opinion or intention to another ‖ (of jelly etc.) to shake ‖ (of the voice or a sound) to quaver ‖ *v.t.* to cause to wobble **2.** *n.* a wobbling movement or gait ‖ an instance of indecision or vacillation ‖ (of the voice or a sound) a quaver **wób·bly** *comp.* **wob·bli·er** *superl.* **wob·bl·i·est** *adj.* [of Gmc origin]
wob·bu·la·tor (wɒ́bjuleitər) *n.* an instrument for testing radios, consisting of a device varying the carrier frequency rapidly [WOBBLE+MODULATOR]
Wo·dan, Wo·den (wóud'n) *(Anglo-Saxon mythol.)* the chief god, associated with Odin
Wode·house (wúdhaus), Pelham Grenville (1881-1975), English novelist, creator of a hilarious, coherent world. Among his best-known works are 'Leave it to Psmith' (1923), 'The Inimitable Jeeves' (1924), and 'Bertie Wooster Sees It Through' (1955)
Woden *WODAN
woe (wou) **1.** *n.* (*rhet.*) sorrow, grief ‖ (*pl., rhet.*) troubles, afflictions, calamities **2.** *interj.* (*rhet.*) alas [O.E. *wā, wǣ* interj., a cry of pain]
woe·be·gone (wóubigɒn, wóubigɒn) *adj.* sorrowful in appearance, dismal [WOE+older *begone* (past part.), beset]
woe·ful (wóufəl) *adj.* (*rhet.*) full of woe ‖ deplorable, *a woeful lack of tact*
wok (wɒk) *n.* bowllike traditional Chinese cooking pot
woke alt. *past* of WAKE
woken alt. *past part.* of WAKE
wold (would) *n.* (*Br.*) a tract of open, uncultivated country ‖ (*Br.*) an open, rolling hilly region including cultivated land [O.E. *wald, weald,* forest]
Wolf (vɔlf), Hugo (1860-1903), Austrian composer. He composed nearly 300 songs and brought the tradition of the German lied to the greatest pitch of refinement
wolf (wulf) **1.** *pl.* **wolves** (wulvz) *n.* a member of *Canis,* a genus of large (about 27 ins. from shoulder to ground), fierce, doglike, carnivorous mammals, of Europe, Asia and North America, which hunt in small groups and prey on deer, caribou etc., though they subsist mainly on rabbits, rodents etc. *C. lupus,* the gray or timber wolf, having coarse yellowish or brown fur, a straight bushy tail and erect pointed ears, was formerly very common throughout the northern hemisphere, but has been exterminated in most inhabited areas ‖ (*pop.*) a man who tries to pick up women and seduce them ‖ (*mus.*) a discordant sound sometimes heard in certain keys on organs tuned in meantone temperament ‖ (*mus.*) harshness due to unintended vibrations in some bowed instruments **a wolf in sheep's clothing** a person whose evil intentions are masked by a friendly manner **to cry wolf** to raise false alarms **to keep the wolf from the door** to avert hunger or poverty **2.** *v.t.* to eat greedily and quickly, *to wolf one's dinner* [O.E. *wulf*]
wolf call whistled approval by a man of a girl's appearance as she passes in the street, as a sign of sexual attraction
wolf cub (*Br.*) a cub scout
Wolfe (wulf), James (1727-59), British general. He commanded the British attack (1759) on the French positions at Quebec during the French and Indian War and won the decisive victory of the Heights of Abraham, but was killed in the battle
Wolfe, Thomas Clayton (1900-38), American author. 'Look Homeward, Angel' (1929) and its sequel 'Of Time and the River' (1935) are largely autobiographical
Wolff·i·an body (wúlfiːən) the mesonephros
wolf·hound (wúlfhaund) *n.* a very large dog used originally for hunting wolves (*BORZOI, *IRISH WOLFHOUND)
wolf·ish (wúlfiʃ) *adj.* of or like a wolf
wolf·ram (wúlfrəm) *n.* tungsten wolframite [G., etym. doubtful]
wolf·ram·ite (wúlfrəmait) *n.* ferrous tungstate, $(Fe, Mn)WO_4$, usually brownish or grayish-black, found in monoclinic crystals and granular or columnar masses [G. *wolframit*]
Wolf·ram von E·schen·bach (vɔ́lfrɑmfənéʃənbɑx) (c. 1170–c. 1220), German minnesinger. He is known esp. for 'Parzival', his only complete work
wolfs·bane (wúlfsbein) *n. Aconitum lycoctonum,* a variety of aconite ‖ winter aconite
wolf whistle a wolf call made by whistling. Traditionally it is a two-part sound, the second repeating the first and then sliding to a lower note
Wol·las·ton (wúləstən), William Hyde (1766-1828), English physicist and chemist. He devised the camera lucida, a goniometer for use in crystallography, and the collimator, and was the first to draw platinum wire
Wo·lof (wóulɒf) *n.* a people of the western Sudan near the mouth of the Senegal and Gambia Rivers ‖ a member of this people ‖ their language
Wols (vɔls), (Alfred Otto Wolfgang Schülze, 1913-51), German painter, living in France from 1932. Working in a manner parallel to that of abstract expressionism, and inspired by Klee, he painted small, nonobjective works of somber mood in a delicate, calligraphic style
Wolse·ley (wúlzliː), Garnet Joseph, lst Viscount Wolseley (1833-1913), British field marshal. His most noted campaigns were in Ashanti (1814) and in Egypt (1882 and 1884-5). As commander in chief he began to modernize the British army (1895-1900)
Wol·sey (wúlziː), Thomas (c. 1475-1530), English cardinal and statesman, archbishop of York (1514-30), lord chancellor of England (1515-29). He gained rapid promotion after the accession (1509) of Henry VIII and dominated the young king's foreign and domestic policy. He negotiated (1514) peace with France and a marriage between Henry's sister and Louis XII but, on the accession (1520) of the Emperor Charles V, Wolsey aligned England with the Empire against France. His policy ruined the royal finances, and his failure to obtain papal consent to Henry's divorce from Catherine of Aragon led to his arrest for treason (1530). He died on the way to stand trial
wolverene *WOLVERINE
Wol·ver·hamp·ton (wúlvərhæmptən) a county borough (pop. 150,000) in Staffordshire, England, in the Black Country: metalworking, chemical industries
wol·ver·ine, wol·ver·ene (wúlvəriːn) *n. Gulo luscus,* fam. *Mustelidae,* a carnivorous North American mammal about 3 ft. in length, having thick blackish fur and a pale forehead ‖ *Gulo gulo,* the glutton of N. Asian and European forests [dim. of WOLF]
wolves *pl.* of WOLF
wom·an (wúmən) **1.** *pl.* **wom·en** (wímən) *n.* an adult female human being ‖ (without article) the female sex, women in general ‖ (with 'old') a rather fussy and effeminate man **the woman** womanly feeling, womanliness, *the woman in her was roused* **2.** *adj.* female, *a woman doctor* [O.F. *wifmann* fr. *wif,* a female+*mann,* human being]
wom·an·hood (wúmənhud) *n.* the condition of being a woman ‖ women in general
wom·an·ish (wúməniʃ) *adj.* characteristic of a woman ‖ (of boys or men) not showing proper manly characteristics
wom·an·kind (wúmənkaind) *n.* women in general, the female sex
wom·an·li·ness (wúmənliːnis) *n.* the quality of being womanly
wom·an·ly (wúmənliː) *adj.* having the characteristics or qualities proper to a woman
womb (wuːm) *n.* the mammalian uterus ‖ (*fig.*) a place of origin and early development, *the womb of prehistory* [O.E. *wamb, womb*]
wom·bat (wɒ́mbæt) *n.* a member of *Phascolomys,* fam. *Vombatidae,* a genus of burrowing, nocturnal marsupial mammals native to Australia and Tasmania. They are about 3 ft. long, with coarse, bristly grayish fur ‖ the fur of the wombat [indigenous Australian name]
women *pl.* of WOMAN
wom·en·folk (wímənfouk) *n.* (*old-fash.*) the women of a family, village etc.
Women's Institute an organization founded in Canada (1897) and in Britain (1915) to enable women in rural areas to meet and work together in craft and cultural activities. It is now worldwide
Women's Lib *WOMEN'S LIBERATION
Women's Liberation (*abbr.* Women's Lib) the name given to the aggregate of organizations committed to redressing the inferior status of women. The movement has been effective esp. since 1970
women's liberation (sometimes initial capitals) feminist movement for equality of the sexes, including the elimination of formal and informal social and business restraints on women —**women's liberationist** *n.*
women's rights the position of political and economic legal equality with men claimed for women
won (wɒn) *n.* the basic monetary unit of North Korea ‖ a unit of currency of South Korea ‖ a coin or note of the value of one won [Korean]
won *past* and *past part.* of WIN
won·der (wʌ́ndər) *n.* (without article) a state of astonished admiration, *lost in wonder at the display* ‖ a fact or circumstance causing surprise, *it was a wonder she came at all* ‖ (*pl.*) wonderfully good things, *the holiday did wonders for us all* ‖ a person whose skill or efficiency compels great admiration ‖ *SEVEN WONDERS OF THE WORLD **it is no** (or **small**) **wonder that, no** (or **small**) **wonder...** it is not surprising that [O.E. *wundor*]
wonder *v.i.* to feel wonder ‖ to ask oneself questions ‖ *v.t.* to feel curiosity about, *he wondered what she would do next* ‖ to be in a state of perplexity about, *I wonder whether it is true* [O.E. *wundrian*]
won·der·ful (wʌ́ndərfəl) *adj.* arousing wonder ‖ unusually good, *wonderful weather* [O.E. *wunderfull*]
won·der·land (wʌ́ndərlænd) *n.* fairyland, an imaginary realm of magic and marvels
won·der·ment (wʌ́ndərmənt) *n.* the feeling of wonder
won·der-struck (wʌ́ndərstrʌk) *adj.* overcome with surprise, admiration or amazement
won·drous (wʌ́ndrəs) *adj.* (*rhet.*) wonderful [alteration of older *wonders* adj.]
won·ky (wɒ́ŋkiː) *comp.* **won·ki·er** *superl.* **won·ki·est** *adj.* (*Br., pop.*) loose, unsteady, wobbly ‖ (*Br., pop.*) amiss [etym. doubtful]
Won·san (wə́ːnsɑ́n) an ice-free port and rail center (pop. 275,000) in North Korea on the Sea of Japan: rolling stock, shipbuilding, oil refining
wont (wount) **1.** *adj.* (*rhet.*, used predicatively, with 'to') accustomed, *as he was wont to say* **2.** *n.* (*rhet.*) custom, habit, *as is his wont* [O.E. *gewunod* past. part. of *gewunian,* to dwell, be accustomed]
won't (wount) *contr.* of WILL NOT
wont·ed (wóuntid, wɔ́ntid) *attrib. adj.* (*rhet.*) customary, usual, *with her wonted charm*
woo (wuː) *v.t.* (*old-fash.*, of a man) to court, seek in marriage ‖ to be assiduously attentive in seeking to win (something or someone), *to woo someone's favor* ‖ *v.i.* (*old-fash.*) to court a woman [O.E. *wōgian*]
Wood (wud), Christopher (1901-30), British painter. His work, including many Cornish and Breton scenes and landscapes, shows a refined color sense
Wood, Grant (1891-1942), U.S. painter. His 'American scene' canvases show the people and landscapes of the rural Midwest in a stern, stylized fashion, notably his 'American Gothic' and 'Daughters of Revolution'
Wood, Leonard (1860-1927), U.S. general, commander of the Rough Riders in Cuba during the U.S. occupation (1899-1902). As military governor of Cuba, he helped to eradicate yellow fever from the island
wood (wud) **1.** *n.* the hard fibrous substance comprising the largest part of the stems and branches of trees and shrubs. It is predominantly xylem and phloem, intersected in many species with vascular rays (*LIGNOCELLULOSE, *HARDWOOD, *SOFTWOOD) ‖ this prepared for use in construction ‖ (also *pl.*) a collection of growing trees, larger than a thicket but smaller than a forest ‖ one of the large wooden balls used in the game of bowls ‖ (*golf*) a club with a wooden head ‖ (*mus.*) woodwind ‖ firewood **out of the woods** (*Am.=Br.* out of the wood) out of danger or difficulty **the wood** a keg, barrel etc. as distinguished from a bottle, *matured in the wood* **2.** *adj.* made of wood ‖ used for working on or holding wood ‖ living or growing in the woods [O.E. *widu, wiodu, wudu*]
wood alcohol, wood spirit methanol

wood anemone *Anemone nemorosa,* the wild anemone of Europe ‖ *Anemone quinquefolia,* the wild anemone of North America
wood·bin (wúdbin) *n.* a box or bin for holding firewood
wood·bind (wúdbaind) *n.* woodbine
wood·bine (wúdbain) *n. Lonicera periclymenum,* the wild honeysuckle of Europe ‖ Virginia creeper [O.E. *wudubinde*]
wood block a solid block of wood, used e.g. for paving ‖ a relief die for printing from, cut esp. in boxwood
wood·chat (wúdtʃæt) *n.* any of several Asiatic birds of fam. *Turdidae.* The males are mostly blue with vivid red markings ‖ a S. European bird of fam. *Laniidae* [etym. doubtful]
wood·chuck (wúdtʃʌk) *n. Marmota monax,* fam. *Sciuridae,* a thickset North American marmot [fr. a North American Indian name]
wood·cock (wúdkɒk) *pl.* **wood·cocks, wood·cock** *n. Scolopax rusticola,* a small brown game bird of Europe and Asia ‖ *Philohela minor,* a related bird of North America [O.E. *wuducoc, wudecoc*]
wood·craft (wúdkræft, wúdkrɑft) *n.* skill in hunting and trapping and in maintaining oneself in woods and forests
wood·cut (wúdkʌt) *n.* a design cut on wood, usually along the grain (cf. WOOD ENGRAVING), to be printed from by letterpress ‖ a print from such a block ‖ the art or technique of cutting such designs
wood·cut·ter (wúdkʌtər) *n.* a person who fells trees or cuts the lumber on the site where the trees grew
wood·ed (wúdid) *adj.* covered with growing trees
wood·en (wúd'n) *adj.* made of wood ‖ as if made of wood, lifeless, expressionless, *a wooden stare* ‖ stiff, clumsy, *wooden gestures*
wood engraving a design engraved on wood, esp. across the grain (cf. WOODCUT), to be printed from by letterpress ‖ a print from such a block ‖ the art or technique of cutting such designs
wood·en-head·ed (wúd'nhedid) *adj.* stupid, obtuse
Wood·hull (wúdhʌl), Victoria (née Claflin, 1838-1927), U.S. journalist and lecturer. She founded (1870) with her sister Tennessee Claflin (1845-1923) a sensational weekly which championed the cause of women's suffrage. In 1872 she was nominated by the radical People's party as U.S. presidential candidate
wood hyacinth *Scilla nonscripta,* a European plant bearing a raceme of nodding, blue, bell-shaped flowers
wood·land (wúdlənd) **1.** *n.* land largely given over to woods **2.** *adj.* living or growing in woodland
wood lark *Lullula arborea,* a European species of lark
wood louse *pl.* **wood lice** a terrestrial isopod crustacean of suborder *Oniscoidea,* found under stones or bark, in damp moss etc.
wood·man (wúdmən) *pl.* **wood·men** (wúdmən) *n.* (esp. *Br.*) a woodsman
wood nymph (*Gk mythol.*) a dryad ‖ (*Gk mythol.*) a hamadryad ‖ a member of *Euthisanotia,* a genus of brilliantly colored moths ‖ a member of *Thalurania,* a genus of South American hummingbirds
wood·peck·er (wúdpekər) *n.* a member of any of several genera (e.g. *Picus, Dendrolopus*) of fam. *Picidae,* almost universally distributed. They are chisel-billed, wood-boring birds, strong in flight and having remarkably long tongues, and short stiff tails. These act as props when the birds are climbing tree trunks, which they drill into with their very hard bills in search of insects. They nest in holes in trees
wood pigeon the European ringdove ‖ *Columba fasciata,* the band-tailed pigeon of western North America
wood·pile (wúdpail) *n.* a pile of wood, esp. firewood
wood pulp the fiber of wood pulped to make paper, rayon etc.
wood·ruff (wúdrəf) *n.* a member of *Asperula,* fam. *Rubiaceae,* a genus of low-growing European woodland plants. The dried leaves of *A. odorata* were formerly used for scenting clothes and as a moth deterrent. *A. tinctoria* yields a dye from its roots usable in place of madder
wood·shed (wúdʃed) *n.* a shed used esp. for preparing and storing firewood
woods·man (wúdzmən) *pl.* **woods·men** (wúdzmən) *n.* a woodcutter or forester ‖ someone who has great knowledge of woodland life
wood sorrel *Oxalis acetosella,* fam. *Oxalidaceae,* a low-growing perennial woodland plant of Europe, Asia and North America with creeping rhizomes, trifoliate leaves, and acid sap in its leaves
woods·y (wúdzi:) *comp.* **woods·i·er** *superl.* **woods·i·est** *adj.* (esp. of smells) of or suggesting the woods
wood tar tar obtained from distilled wood
wood thrush *Hylocichla mustelina,* a North American thrush with a brown head and back and a white breast marked with large spots. It has a loud, clear song
wood tick a member of *Ixodoidea,* a tick whose young cling to bushes and fasten onto the bodies of passing animals
wood turning the art or process of shaping wood on a lathe
wood·wax·en (wúdwæksən) *n. Genista tinctoria,* fam. *Fabaceae,* a yellow-flowered Eurasian shrub, originally the source of a yellow dye [O.E. *wuduweaxe*]
wood·wind (wúdwind) *n.* the section of the orchestra comprising instruments made originally (and still generally) of wood and either blown directly (e.g. the flute) or with a reed (e.g. the oboe). The saxophone, though metal, is classed as woodwind since it is played like a woodwind and not like a brass instrument ‖ an instrument of this group
wood·work (wúdwə:rk) *n.* objects made of wood, esp. parts of a building or interior fittings made of wood
wood·work·ing (wúdwə:rkiŋ) **1.** *n.* the art or activity of working wood **2.** *adj.* of, pertaining to or used for working wood
wood·worm (wúdwə:rm) *n.* the larva of *Anobium punctatum,* fam. *Anobiidae,* the common furniture beetle, which lays its small, oval, white eggs in cracks in wood. The larvae burrow into and through the wood. They molt at intervals, pupate, and the adult beetle emerges in spring, leaving clearly visible exit holes. The life cycle may take one year or several years to complete
wood·y (wúdi:) *comp.* **wood·i·er** *superl.* **wood·i·est** *adj.* abounding in woods, well-wooded ‖ consisting of or like wood ‖ (of a plant) making woody stems etc.
woof (wuf, wu:f) *n.* the weft [O.E. ōwef]
wool (wul) *n.* the fibrous, usually crisped, growth on the skin of certain animals, esp. the sheep. When shorn off, cleansed and spun into yarn, it is used for knitting or weaving a soft, warm fabric ‖ this yarn ‖ (*biol.*) any fibrous growth resembling wool **to pull the wool over someone's eyes** to deceive someone as to the true facts [O.E. *wull*]
—The fibers of wool are made of keratin, a scleroprotein, and have rough, scaly cuticles, which hook into one another when the fibers are spun into yarn. The yarn is full of air cells, making woolen textiles bad conductors of heat and thus suitable for wear in cold seasons or latitudes. The yarn made from fibers of long staple is called worsted
wool clip the annual crop of wool
wooled (wúld) *adj.* (in hyphenated compounds) having wool of a specified length or quality, *fine-wooled*
wool·en, esp. *Br.* **wool·len** (wúlən) **1.** *adj.* made of wool **2.** *n.* a fabric made of wool ‖ (*pl.*) woolen goods [O.E. *wullen*]
Woolf (wulf), Virginia (1882-1941), English novelist and critic. Her novels include 'Mrs. Dalloway' (1925), 'To the Lighthouse' (1927) and 'The Waves' (1931). Influenced by Proust and Joyce, she experimented in ways of making the novel seem more true to life by discarding plot and by allowing a character to emerge from the vision he forms out of his impressions of the life around him, with all its complexity and incoherence. She uses the interior monologue in the attempt to render sensitivity directly (*STREAM OF CONSCIOUSNESS). She was extremely eloquent, and her genius lies perhaps even more in her heightened language and arresting phrases than in her experiments with technique. In her criticism she justly rescued many minor figures from oblivion
wool fat wool grease
wool·gath·er·ing (wúlgæðəriŋ) **1.** *n.* the pursuit of stray thoughts when one should be concentrating **2.** *adj.* indulging in such stray thoughts [fr. wandering about gathering wool left by sheep on wire, hedges etc.]
wool grease a fatlike, wax coating on the surface of the fibers of sheep's wool, used in dressing leathers and furs, in making printing inks, and as a source of lanolin
wool·grow·er (wúlgrouər) *n.* (*Br.*) someone who breeds sheep to produce wool
wooliness *WOOLLINESS
woollen *WOOLEN
Wool·ley (wúli:), Sir Charles Leonard (1880-1960), British archaeologist who excavated Ur (1927)
wool·li·ness, wool·i·ness (wúli:nis) *n.* the quality of being woolly
wool·ly, wool·y (wúli:) **1.** *comp.* **wool·li·er, wool·i·er** *superl.* **wool·li·est, wool·i·est** *adj.* of or like wool ‖ covered with wool ‖ lacking clearness of definition ‖ (*pop.*) not thinking clearly ‖ showing lack of mental clarity **2.** *pl.* **wool·lies, wool·ies** n. a woolen undergarment, esp. a long one
woolly bear any of the hairy larvae of the moths of fam. *Arctiidae*
Wool·man (wúlmən), John (1720-72), American Quaker leader, one of the first spokesmen for the abolition of slavery
wool·pack (wúlpæk) *n.* a cover into which fleeces are packed for transport ‖ a bale of wool ‖ a fleecy-looking cumulus cloud rising from a flat base [M.E.]
wool·sack (wúlsæk) *n.* (*Br.*) a large square cushion stuffed with wool on which the lord chancellor sits in the House of Lords **the woolsack** (*Br.*) the office of lord chancellor [M.E.]
wool stapler a dealer in wool, esp. one who sorts by staple before selling to manufacturers
Wool·worth (wúlwə:rθ), Frank Winfield (1852-1919), U.S. merchant. He established (1879) at Lancaster, Pa., his first successful five-and-ten-cent store, and incorporated (1911) the F.W. Woolworth Company. He had the Woolworth Building in New York City built (1913). It was then the highest building (792 ft) in the world. At the time of his death he owned more than 1,000 stores
wooly *WOOLLY
Woo·mer·a (wú:mərə) a site, in central South Australia, of a weapons testing range (established 1947)
wooz·y (wú:zi:, wúzi:) *comp.* **wooz·i·er** *superl.* **wooz·i·est** *adj.* (*pop.*) confused or muddled as the result of a blow, too much alcohol etc. ‖ (*pop.*) physically weak, *to feel woozy after an operation*
Worces·ter (wústər) the county town (pop. 74,247) of Worcestershire, England, on the Severn, famous for its fine porcelain. Gothic cathedral (mainly 13th-14th cc.)
Worcester a manufacturing town (pop. 372,940) in central Massachusetts: mechanical engineering, metalworking, textiles, printing
Worces·ter·shire (wústərʃiər) (*abbr.* Worcs.) a W. Midland county (area 699 sq. miles, pop. 569,000) of England. County town: Worcester
word (wə:rd) **1.** *n.* a speech sound or combination of sounds having meaning and used as a basic unit of language and human communication ‖ the written or printed symbol of one of these basic units of language ‖ (*pl.*) things said, *his words went unheeded* ‖ (*pl.,* used without an article) a dispute, *they had words on the matter* ‖ information, a message, *word came that he was still alive* ‖ a promise, an assurance, *he was as good as his word, you have my word for it* ‖ (*pl.*) promises of performance as opposed to actual performance (cf. DEED) ‖ a command, an order, *to give the word to attack* ‖ a password, watchword ‖ (*pl.*) the text (as distinct from the music) of a song, opera etc. ‖ (*pl.*) the text spoken by an actor **the Word** (*Christian theol.*) God incarnate in Jesus Christ ‖ (*Christian theol.*) the Bible as the revelation of God ‖ (*Christian theol.*) the gospel message **a good word** a recommendation, *he said a good word on your behalf* **a man (woman) of few words** a man (woman) apt to be silent rather than talkative **a word in season** a piece of well-timed advice **a word of advice** a piece of advice **a word to the wise** admonishment offered to someone intelligent enough to act on it **by word of mouth** orally rather than in writing **his (her) word is law** what he (she) says is obeyed without argument **in a** (or **one**) **word** to sum up briefly **in so many words** in a frank, blunt manner leaving no room for doubt **in words of one syllable** in simple, forthright language **the last word** the

CONCISE PRONUNCIATION KEY: **(a)** æ, *c*a*t*; ɑ, *c*a*r*; ɔ *f*aw*n*; ei, *sn*a*ke*. **(e)** e, *h*e*n*; i:, *sh*ee*p*; iə, *d*ee*r*; εə, *b*ea*r*. **(i)** i, *f*i*sh*; ai, *t*i*ger*; ə:, *b*i*rd*. **(o)** o, *o*x; au, *c*ow; ou, *g*oa*t*; u, *p*oo*r*; ɔi, *r*oy*al*. **(u)** ʌ, *d*u*ck*; u, *b*u*ll*; u:, *g*oo*se*; ə, *bac*i*llus*; ju:, *c*u*be*. x, *lo*ch; θ, *th*ink; ð, *bo*th*er*; z, *Z*en; ʒ, *corsa*ge; dʒ, *sava*ge; ŋ, *orangut*ang; j, *y*ak; ʃ, *f*ish; tʃ, *fe*tch; 'l, *rabb*le; 'n, *redd*en. Complete pronunciation key appears inside front cover.

final decision ‖ the last thing said, esp. in a dispute ‖ the most up-to-date model, example etc., *the last word in sports cars* **to have a word with someone** to have a short talk with someone, esp. about some business matter ‖ to admonish someone mildly, *he had a word with them about their continual lateness* **to put in a word** (or **a good word**) **for** to use one's influence in order to recommend someone or something) **to take someone at his word** to believe that someone means what he says, esp. when he makes some attractive offer **to take someone's word for it** to believe that what a person says is true without verifying it **2.** *v.t.* to phrase, put into words, *he worded the protest very strongly* [O.E.]

word blindness alexia

word for word in exactly the same words ‖ (of translating) done taking each word in turn instead of finding equivalents for wholes **wórd-for-wórd** *adj.*

word·i·ly (wə́:rdili:) *adv.* in a wordy way

word·i·ness (wə́:rdi:nis) *n.* the quality of being wordy

word·ing (wə́:rdiŋ) *n.* a putting into words ‖ the words used

word·less (wə́:rdlis) *adj.* not expressed or capable of being expressed in words ‖ having or able to find no words with which to express oneself

word of command (*Br.*) the exclamatory word or phrase giving an order, esp. to soldiers being drilled

word of honor, *Br.* **word of honour** an assurance staking one's honor that one is telling the truth

word order the arrangement of words in a phrase, clause or sentence

word-paint·ing (wə́:rdpȩintiŋ) *n.* vivid or picturesque description in words

word-per·fect (wə́:rdpə́:rfikt) *adj.* in the condition of having committed (a speech, part in a play, poem etc.) accurately to memory

word·play (wə́:rdplȩi) *n.* verbal wit, esp. punning ‖ an instance of this

word processing work-saving system of recording, storing, and retrieving typewritten data utilizing correctible magnetic tape or other storage facility, often with visual presentation on a screen —**word processor** *n.* the machine used

Words·worth (wə́:rdzwə̧:rθ), Dorothy (1771-1855), sister of William. She was a firm supporter and helpful critic of her brother. Her own place in literature is ensured by her 'Journals', published posthumously (1897)

Wordsworth, William (1770-1850), English poet. The 'Lyrical Ballads' (1798 and 1800), written jointly with Coleridge, are usually taken as the inauguration of English Romantic poetry. Wordsworth wrote most of the lyrics, 'Lines Written above Tintern Abbey' and other famous poems in this collection as well as the preface (1800 edition), in which he expounded his theories of poetry. In 1807 he published 'Poems in Two Volumes', containing 'The Happy Warrior', 'Ode to Duty' and the 'Immortality' ode. His later work could be said to be undistinguished (his long autobiographical poem 'The Prelude', published in 1850, was in fact a revision of a version written many years earlier), but his genius often shone in a sonnet or an unexpected couplet.

One important aspect of Wordsworth's poetry and of his whole intellectual position is that he linked literary changes to intellectual changes generally. His feeling for external nature, his reflections on his own mysterious apprehensions of the 'otherness' of the universe and on his relations with it (did he create what he saw, or did he receive admonitions from some kind of universal spirit?): these led him to question the whole nature of perception, and with Coleridge to move away from the 18th-c. intellectual traditions inspired by Locke. The theorizing found expression as immediate and troubling perceptions which touch the reader still.

He was important also for his personal history. He is the supreme example of that band of writers who welcomed the French Revolution as the great forward step toward social justice and human perfection. 'The Prelude' records (along with much else) the failure of his hopes, the despair to which it brought him, and his return to health and balance.

Wordsworth is the preeminent rather than the representative Romantic: at his best he relates in language of mysterious simplicity the traffic of the individual soul with the whole framework of nature, the lasting force of childhood experience and, in adult life, 'the heavy and the weary weight of all this unintelligible world'. The verse of his great period seems to offer a way to acceptance, belonging and celebration which is entirely his own

word·y (wə́:rdi:) *comp.* **word·i·er** *superl.* **word·i·est** *adj.* using many or too many words, *a wordy style* ‖ using words, *wordy exchange*

wore *past* of WEAR

work (wə:rk) *n.* physical or mental activity undertaken to achieve a purpose (cf. PLAY) and involving the expenditure of effort ‖ the end or purpose for which one expends such effort, *he made the abolition of slavery his life's work* ‖ what one can achieve by such effort in a specified amount of time, *checking the entries will be a week's work* ‖ (*pl.*) the output of a writer, artist, composer etc., *the works of Shakespeare* ‖ any one item of this output, *'Measure for Measure' is a hard work to understand* ‖ literary, artistic or musical output of a specified kind, *Goethe's scientific work* ‖ what one does in order to earn money, *his work takes him abroad a lot* ‖ all the activities proper to a specified person or kind of person, *a mother's work is never done* ‖ toil involved in activities which one undertakes to do or which have to be done, *her sick mother made a lot of extra work* ‖ the visible effect of natural happenings resulting in change, *the tree's bent form is the work of wind and rain* ‖ a large engineering structure, e.g. a bridge ‖ (*phys.*) a transference of energy measured by the product of a force and the component of the displacement of the point of application of the force parallel to the force. Work has the dimensions of energy ‖ (*pl.*) a factory or industrial plant, *the works will shut completely during August* ‖ (*pl.*) a fortified structure ‖ (*pl.*) the moving parts of a mechanical device ‖ the piece being cut, ground etc. in a machine tool etc. ‖ (*pl., theol.*) good deeds (as contrasted with faith) ‖ an example of the use of some skill or faculty, *thorough detective work* ‖ needlework, embroidery etc. done for pleasure, *after dinner she got out her work* **out of work** unemployed because one is sick or cannot find work **to have one's work** (or **all one's work**) **cut out** to have as much as one can possibly cope with (to do something) **to make short** (or **quick**) **work of** to deal with or dispose of very quickly and effortlessly **to make work** to invent unnecessary tasks to do ‖ to be the cause of extra work for someone **to set** (or **get**) **to work on** to begin (*a large task*) [O.E. *weorc*]

work *pres. part.* **work·ing** *past* and *past part.* **worked,** (*archaic* and *technical*) **wrought** (rɔt) *v.i.* to engage in activity designed to achieve a particular purpose (cf. PLAY) and requiring an expenditure of considerable effort, *he worked fast to move the furniture out in time* ‖ to earn one's living, *she's too young to work and is still in school* ‖ to be effective, have the desired or intended effect, *I'm afraid your plan won't work, did the medicine work?* ‖ to be an employee of a specified sort, *he works in the printing business* ‖ to get into a specified condition or position by movement, *the knot worked loose, his shirt worked up his back* ‖ (of yeast or a liquid) to ferment ‖ to show emotion, esp. distress, by muscular twitches or nervous movements of the limbs, *you could tell by the way his face worked that it was bad news, her hands were working in her lap as she talked* ‖ (of a ship's timbers) to strain, esp. in a heavy sea ‖ to move or sink very slowly, *the foundations show signs of working* ‖ to proceed or make progress in some action or task, *it would be easier to work backwards* ‖ to progress with difficulty, *he worked slowly along the ledge* ‖ to apply oneself with effort, esp. to one's studies, *to work at one's scales* ‖ (with 'on') to use wiles or persuasion, *work on your father until he agrees* ‖ (of an artist) to use specified materials or techniques, *she works in oils, he works in blank verse occasionally* ‖ (with 'out') to come to a satisfactory conclusion, *things will work out if you will just be patient* ‖ *v.t.* to cause to labor, *he works his men too hard* ‖ to bring about by labor or as if by labor, *to work a miracle* ‖ to extract a mineral from (a mine etc.) ‖ to cause (a specified material) to be transformed by one's efforts, *to work wood, work the clay into a cylinder,* esp. to manipulate (iron) by heating and hammering it ‖ to make (one's way) or cause (oneself) to advance by slow stages and with effort, *he worked his way along the ledge, he worked himself up to be head of the firm* ‖ (with 'up', 'into' or 'up into') to excite or stimulate the emotions of, *she worked herself into a panic* ‖ to sew or make by needlework, *to work a sampler* ‖ to pay for (one's passage) in a ship by providing some service of equivalent value to the fare ‖ to pay for (oneself or one's way) by doing a paid job or jobs or by some service, *to work one's way through college* ‖ (with 'off') to repay (a debt) over a period by payments or services to the creditor at intervals ‖ to solve (an equation) ‖ to have (a region etc.) as one's sphere of operations, *he works the East Coast* ‖ to cause to operate, *to work a pump* ‖ to bring (oneself or an object) into or out of a specified condition by slow and esp. laborious effort, *he worked himself out of his fetters* ‖ (with 'in' or 'into') to insert gradually by pressure or other careful manipulation, *to work a knife into a crack* ‖ (with 'in') to mix or blend, esp. by stirring, *work the oil into the mixture drop by drop* ‖ (with 'off') to get rid of by expending energy, *to work off surplus weight* ‖ (with 'off') to find an outlet for (rage, excess energy etc.), *to work off one's bad temper on someone* ‖ (with 'out') to find (a solution or compromise) or solve (a problem) by an effort of the mind or will, *you must work it out among yourselves* ‖ (*pop.*, with 'it') to contrive, *try to work it so that you get some extra leave* ‖ (with 'up') to perfect the performance of by practice, *she will have to work up the last movement before the concert* **to work one's fingers to the bone** to exhaust oneself, esp. in menial tasks, often without receiving any gratitude **to work to death** to overwork ‖ to use too often, *to work a phrase to death* **wórk·a·ble** *adj.* that can be worked or worked on ‖ that will work, practicable [O.E. *wyrcan, wircan*]

work·a·day (wə́:rkədȩi) *adj.* dull and commonplace [M.E. *werkeday* fr. O.N.]

work·a·hol·ic (wə̧:rkəhɔ́lək) *n.* **1.** one addicted to work **2.** by extension, one who works excessively —**workaholism** *n.*

work·bag (wə́:rkbæg) *n.* a bag for sewing materials

work·bas·ket (wə́:rkbæskit, wə́:rkbɑskit) *n.* a basket for sewing materials

work·bench (wə́:rkbȩntʃ) *n.* a strong table on which manual or machine work is done

work·book (wə́:rkbųk) *n.* a pupil's exercise book with printed problems etc. and space for answers ‖ a book of instructions for procedure and operation ‖ a book in which is recorded work accomplished or planned

work·box (wə́:rkbɒks) *n.* a box of materials or equipment, esp. for sewing

work·day (wə́:rkdȩi) *n.* a day on which work is carried on as usual, not a Sunday or holiday ‖ the period of work on such a day, esp. the number of hours making up an accepted day for which a worker is entitled to full pay, *an eight-hour workday*

worked up agitated, emotionally upset or tense

work·er (wə́:rkər) *n.* a person who works ‖ an employee ‖ a member of the working class ‖ a person who works hard ‖ a neuter individual or sexually undeveloped female of certain social insects (bee, ant etc.)

work ethic belief that productive physical or mental labor is a prime virtue

work·fare (wə́:rkfɛər) *n.* government program that requires welfare recipients able to work to accept training or suitable public service work

work·horse (wə́:rkhɔ̧rs) *n.* a horse used to perform hard work, e.g. plowing, hauling etc. ‖ a steady, hard-working person

work·house (wə́:rkhąus) *pl.* **work·hous·es** (wə́:rkhąuziz) *n.* (*Br. hist.*) a public institution to shelter homeless and poor people in return for work ‖ a place of correction for petty offenders, e.g. drunkards or vagrants

work-in (wə́:rkin) *n.* a protest demonstration in which employees (or students) report to work but refuse to carry on the work

work·ing (wə́:rkiŋ) **1.** *adj.* engaging in manual labor or production, *the working class* ‖ sufficient or adequate to allow work to be done or for a desired end to be achieved, *a working knowledge of German* ‖ accurate enough to work by, *a working rule* ‖ capable of being operated, *a working model* **2.** *n.* (*pl.*) excavations made in mining etc.

working assets (*accounting*) noncapital assets available for running a business

working capital funds which can be used in meeting expenses, as distinct from the fixed capital represented by buildings, site values etc. ‖ current assets less current liabilities

working class the social and economic class of people who work for wages, esp. the industrial workers

working day a workday

working drawing a scale drawing guiding builders, engineers etc. in their work

work·ing·man (wə́:rkiŋmæn) *pl.* **work·ing·men** (wə́:rkiŋmen) *n.* a man of the working class

working papers legal papers which a minor under some legally fixed age must have before he is allowed to work

working party (*Br.*) a committee appointed to investigate and report on a social or industrial problem ‖ (*mil.*) a body of men detailed for some special job

work·man (wə́:rkmən) *pl.* **work·men** (wə́:rkmən) *n.* a workingman ‖ a workingman with respect to the quality of his work ‖ a skilled laborer or craftsman **wórk·man·like** *adj.* befitting a skilled workman ‖ thoroughly practical or well made **wórk·man·ship** *n.* the skill shown in a finished craft product or work of art

workmen's compensation compensation for accident or disease arising out of a workman's employment, which in certain countries the employer must pay by law

work of art a production of an artist, esp. in painting, sculpture etc. ‖ (*loosely*) anything very well made or performed

work·out (wə́:rkaut) *n.* a training session for a boxer, athlete etc.

work·peo·ple (wə́:rkpi:p'l) *pl. n.* (*Br.*) working men and women

work·room (wə́:rkru:m, wə́:rkrum) *n.* a room set apart for esp. manual work

work-rule action (wə́:rkrú:l) job slowdown action by strict application of regulations; (*Br.*) work-to-rule action

works council a committee formed by the management among the employees of a factory or plant, to consider problems of industrial relations, production etc.

work sheet a prepared document recording work done or to be done in a plant ‖ an accountant's trial statement sheet

work·shop (wə́:rkʃɒp) *n.* a room or building in which productive work or manufacture on a small scale is carried out ‖ an intensive seminar in some subject of study

work-shy (wə́:rkʃai) *adj.* lazy

Works Progress Administration (*abbr.* WPA), an independent agency established (1935) by executive order of President Franklin D. Roosevelt to employ persons on relief on useful projects. Headed (1935-8) by Harry Hopkins, it sponsored a large-scale construction program and many cultural projects, notably the Federal Theater Project. It employed 8.5 million persons and appropriated almost $11 billion from the federal government. An unfavorable Senate committee report (1939), as well as increasing employment, resulted in the reduction of its appropriations and (1943) in its dissolution

work study (*management*) system techniques utilizing analysis of ways of performing tasks, time studies, and creating standards, formerly part of time and motion studies

work·ta·ble (wə́:rkteib'l) *n.* a table having a surface on which work can be done and usually having drawers, e.g. for sewing materials

work-to-rule (wə́:rktu:rú:l) *n.* (*Br.*) labor demonstration applying strict interpretation to work rules, thus hampering production; (*U.S.*) work-rule action

world (wə:rld) **1.** *n.* the planet earth ‖ the universe ‖ the earth together with its inhabitants ‖ a distinct part of the universe or of the earth, *the Old World* ‖ human society, *the world lives in fear of nuclear warfare* ‖ a recognized part or period of human society, *the business world, the ancient world* ‖ any domain of existence, activity etc., *the animal world* ‖ everything other than oneself ‖ the totality of things, events etc. of which one has personal experience, *his world is rather limited* ‖ a great amount, *there is a world of difference between them* ‖ life on this earth, *he has departed from this world* ‖ secular rather than religious affairs ‖ a star or planet **for all the world** exactly, *it sounded for all the world as if he meant it* ‖ **for the world** for any consideration whatever, *I wouldn't hurt him for the world* **in the world** an intensive used with 'how', 'when', 'where', 'who' or 'why', *how in the world can they get there on time?* **out of this world** superb **to bring into the world** to give birth to **to come into the world** to be born **world without end** (*rhet.* and *eccles.*) forever [O.E. *weorold, worold*]

World Alliance of Y.M.C.A's *YOUNG MEN'S CHRISTIAN ASSOCIATION

World Bank the International Bank for Reconstruction and Development founded at the Bretton Woods Conference (1944) by the Western powers and provided by them with assets (in bullion and currency), on the basis of which member nations and private firms if repayment is guaranteed by a member, may obtain credit for approved development and reconstruction enterprises without drawing upon national reserves. By the mid-1980s there were nearly 150 member nations. The World Bank is affiliated with the U.N. Headquarters: Washington

world-class (wə:rldklǽs) *adj.* of a caliber suitable for international recognition, e.g., world-class tennis player

World Council of Churches an organization of the majority of Protestant and Orthodox Churches, constituted in 1948, enabling practical cooperation and common study to take place among its members. It sprang from the International Missionary Council (founded 1921), the Life and Work Movement (founded 1925) and the Faith and Order Movement (founded 1927). Its activities have been watched by the Roman Catholic Church with sympathetic interest. Headquarters: Geneva

World Federation of Trade Unions an international body representing the trade unions of the world, constituted in 1945, but confined since 1949 to the trade union federations with communist sympathies. Headquarters: Prague

World Food Conference 1974 conference sponsored by the United Nations, held in Rome, creating a 36-nation World Food Council and another meeting establishing the International Fund for Agricultural Development

World Health Organization an international body set up in 1948 under the aegis of the United Nations, though constitutionally independent. Its function is to direct and correlate efforts to overcome disease by technical assistance, research and education: in particular to combat diseases endemic in primitive or underdeveloped countries. Headquarters: Geneva

world line (*astron.*) space-time paths of photons emitted by the stars

world·li·ness (wə́:rldli:nis) *n.* the state or quality of being worldly

world·ling (wə́:rldliŋ) *n.* (*rhet.*) someone who is worldly-minded

world·ly (wə́:rldli:) *comp.* **world·li·er** *superl.* **world·li·est** *adj.* pertaining to the material world or its existence ‖ devoted to this life and its practical concerns and enjoyments rather than to spiritual concerns

world·ly-mind·ed (wə́:rldli:máindid) *adj.* intent on worldly interests or material success

world·ly-wise (wə́:rldli:wáiz) *adj.* experienced in the ways of the world and therefore cautious or prudent

World Meteorological Organization (*abbr.* W.M.O.) an agency of the U.N., set up in 1951 to promote international cooperation in meteorology

world power a state having sufficient economic and esp. military power to influence world politics

World Series a series of autumn games between champions of the two major U.S. baseball leagues to decide the national championship

World war, 1st the war (1914-18) between the Allies and the Central Powers. Its basic causes lay in the political, economic and colonial rivalries of the great powers, stretching back into the late 19th c. The rise of Pan-Slavism, with Russian encouragement, presented a grave threat to the stability of Austria-Hungary. The Franco-Prussian War had left France aggrieved by the loss of Alsace-Lorraine. The imperialism of the late 19th c., backed by an armaments race based on the rapid growth of heavy industry, esp. in Germany, added to international tension. Finally, the spread of secret diplomacy and the formation of the Triple Alliance and the Triple Entente made it inevitable that when war began it would rapidly involve many countries. The Moroccan crises (1905, 1911) brought France and Germany to the brink of war, and Austria's annexation of Bosnia-Herzegovina (1908) created another international crisis. The Balkan Wars (1912-13) were a further manifestation of the unrest in S.E. Europe. The assassination (June 28, 1914) of Archduke Franz Ferdinand at Sarajevo precipitated the 1st world war.

Austria, under the guidance of Berchtold, issued an unacceptable ultimatum to Serbia and declared war (July 28, 1914). Russia mobilized in support of Serbia (July 29). Germany declared war on Russia (Aug. 1) and on France (Aug. 3). Germany, applying the Schlieffen plan, immediately invaded Belgium. This violation of Belgian neutrality led Britain to declare war on Germany (Aug. 4). Austria declared war on Russia (Aug. 6). Germany and Austria were joined by Turkey (Oct. 30, 1914) and Bulgaria (Oct. 5, 1915). The Allies were joined, among others, by Japan (Aug. 23, 1914), Italy (May 23, 1915) and the U.S.A. (Apr. 6, 1917).

The Germans advanced rapidly through Belgium and Luxembourg into N.E. France, forcing the French and a British expeditionary force to fall back toward Paris, with much hard fighting. The German failure to give sufficient weight to the right wing, as well as faults of communication between their armies and their high command, enabled Joffre to counterattack at the Marne (Sept. 6-13, 1914), driving the Germans back to the Aisne. Both sides, each trying to outflank the other, advanced toward the Channel ports, and the Allies stemmed the German advance at Ypres (Oct. 14-Nov. 13, 1914). Both sides dug in, and the line of battle became stabilized between Flanders and the Swiss border. It remained almost stationary here for the next three years, despite repeated attempts by each side to dislodge the other from its trenches and gain ground. The German use of poison gas at the 2nd Battle of Ypres (Apr. 22–May 2, 1915), the massive German onslaught at Verdun (Feb. 21–Dec. 15, 1916) and the British use of tanks at the Somme (July-Oct. 1916) all failed to break the stalemate in spite of over 2,000,000 casualties.

Meanwhile the Russian attack on E. Prussia was decisively crushed by the Germans at Tannenberg and the Masurian Lakes (Aug.26–Sept. 15,1914). By the end of 1915, the Germans had forced the Russians out of most of Poland. Repeated heavy defeats sapped Russian morale, the czar abdicated (Mar. 15, 1917), and the Bolshevik revolution was followed by armistice negotiations (Dec. 1917). By the time the Treaty of Brest-Litovsk was signed (Mar. 3, 1918), the Germans had overrun the Ukraine. In S. Europe, an Allied expedition to Gallipoli (Apr. 1915-Jan. 1916), with the aim of attacking Turkey and opening the Straits to help Russia, was a failure.

Italy, renouncing the Triple Alliance, remained neutral at the start of the war and then joined the Allies (May 1915). Italian and Austrian forces faced each other in stalemate in N. Italy until the Italians were routed (Oct. 24–Nov. 12, 1917). They counterattacked successfully, however, a year later. Serbia repulsed three Austrian attempts at invasion (Aug. 12–Dec. 15, 1914) but succumbed to a concerted German, Austrian and Bulgarian onslaught (Oct.-Nov. 1915). An Allied expedition to Salonica in support of Serbia was halted by the Bulgarians (Oct. 1915), but Bulgaria was forced to sue for an armistice (Sept. 1918). Russia attacked Turkey in the Caucasus (1914) and British troops advanced from the Persian Gulf north through Mesopotamia (1914-18). A Turkish attack on the Suez Canal was repulsed (Feb. 1915), and British, Australian and New Zealand troops defeated the Turks in Palestine and Iraq (1917-18). German colonies in Africa and the Pacific, and at Kiaochow, were captured by the Allies. Rumania was occupied (1917) by the Central Powers.

At sea, the main battle was fought at Jutland (May 31, 1916), after which the German surface fleet remained in harbor for the rest of the war. The German use of unrestricted submarine warfare, in an attempt to starve Britain, had the effect of bringing the U.S.A. into the war (Apr. 6, 1917).

The arrival of the U.S. troops in Europe counterbalanced the arrival of more German troops liberated by Russia's withdrawal from the war. The Allies, now with a unified command under Foch, were able to halt renewed German offensives in N.E. France (Mar. 21–July 17, 1918) and to push back the German line toward the Belgian frontier. After Bulgaria had fallen to the Allies (Sept. 29, 1918), followed by Turkey (Oct. 30, 1918) and Austria (Nov. 3, 1918), German morale collapsed. In the face of naval mutiny and republican revolts, Wilhelm II fled to Holland (Nov. 10, 1918) and an armistice was signed (Nov. 11, 1918) at Compiègne.

The war was ended by a series of treaties, including the Treaty of Versailles (June 28, 1919), the Treaty of St Germain (Sept. 10, 1919) and the Treaty of Lausanne (1923). The war had cost about 8,700,000 lives, including about 3,350,000 on the side of the Central Powers, and 1,390,000 French, 1,700,000 Russians, 780,000 British and 120,000 Americans. The 1st world war saw the development of trench warfare and submarine warfare, increased mechanization (esp. the use of tanks), and the use of aircraft, first for observation and later also for bombing. Out of the war settlement came the establishment of the League of Nations. But tensions were also created which were to give rise to the 2nd world war 20 years later

World war, 2nd the war (1939-45) between the Allies and the Axis. Its origins lay in German resentment at the terms of the Treaty of Versailles (1919), the economic crisis of 1929-30 which favored the rise to power of Fascist dictators, the failure of the League of Nations to gain international acceptance for disarmament, and the policy of colonial conquest adopted by Germany, Italy and Japan as a means of acquiring raw materials and markets. Germany, prepared for military conquest by Hitler, remilitarized the Rhineland (1936) in violation of the Locarno Pact. The League of Nations failed to react firmly either to this or to the conquest (1935-6) of Ethiopia by Italy under Mussolini. The Spanish Civil War (1936-9), in which German and Italian intervention assured the victory of Franco, served as a proving ground for new techniques of warfare. Britain and France, unprepared for war, remained passive when Germany annexed Austria (Mar. 1938), and they continued their policy of appeasement in the Munich Agreement (Sept. 1938), sacrificing the Sudetenland to Germany. The German seizure of the whole of Czechoslovakia (Mar. 1939) and the Italian seizure of Albania (Apr. 1939) put an end to appeasement. Germany signed a military alliance with Italy (May 1939) and a nonaggression pact with the U.S.S.R. (Aug. 1939). After manufacturing incidents over the status of Danzig and the Polish Corridor, Germany invaded Poland (Sept. 1, 1939). Britain and France declared war on Germany (Sept. 3, 1939).

Poland succumbed rapidly to the German 'Blitzkrieg' (lightning war), a technique of massive concerted ground and air attack. The U.S.S.R. joined with Germany in partitioning Poland and then crushed Finland (1939-40). The British and French armies remained immobile throughout the winter, relying on the Maginot line. Germany invaded Denmark (Apr. 9, 1940), which fell immediately, and Norway, which was conquered by June 9, 1940. The Netherlands were overrun (May 10-14, 1940), as well as Belgium (May 10-28, 1940) and Luxembourg (May 10, 1940). The Maginot line was turned by the Germans at Sedan (May 13, 1940). A rapid German advance through N.E. France trapped the Allied forces on the coast at Dunkerque, whence they were evacuated to Britain (May 26–June 4, 1940). Italy declared war in support of Germany (June 10, 1940). The French armies under Weygand were unable to stop the German advance on Paris (June 14, 1940). France signed an armistice (June 22, 1940) with Germany, providing for German occupation of the north of the country. The Vichy government under Pétain was set up, while de Gaulle continued the struggle from London.

Britain, under the leadership of Churchill, defeated the German attempt to bomb it into submission in the Battle of Britain (Aug. 15, 1940–May 1941) and escaped invasion. In N. Africa, Italy invaded British Somaliland (Aug. 1940) and attempted to invade Egypt from Libya (Sept. 1940), but was checked by British forces. The British and Italian navies fought for control of the Mediterranean (1940-1), while German submarines attempted to cut off Britain's Atlantic supply routes. Greece repelled an Italian invasion from Albania (Oct. 1940–Mar. 1941), but fell to a German and Bulgarian attack (Apr. 1941) which also crushed Yugoslavia (Apr. 1941) and Crete (May 1941). The Allies conquered Italian East Africa (Dec. 1940–May 1941), Iraq (May 1941) and Syria (July 1941). Germany, with Finnish, Hungarian and Rumanian support, attacked the U.S.S.R (June 22, 1941) on a wide front and conquered most of European Russia by the winter of 1941, but halted west of Moscow. The U.S.A., while remaining neutral, agreed (1941) to supply lend-lease aid to Britain and the U.S.S.R. Churchill and Roosevelt drafted the Atlantic Charter (Aug. 1941). The U.S.A. was brought into the war (Dec. 8, 1941) by the Japanese attack on Pearl Harbor (Dec. 7, 1941). The Japanese rapidly overran the Philippines, Hong Kong, Malaya, Singapore, Burma, Indonesia and many of the Pacific islands, and were not checked by Allied naval and air victories until June 1942.

The war began to turn in the Allies' favor when the Axis forces under Rommel, sweeping back across N. Africa to Egypt, were routed by Montgomery's forces at Alamein (Oct. 1942). The U.S.A. landed troops in Algeria (Nov. 8, 1942) and, with British and Free French support, drove the Axis out of N. Africa by May 12, 1943. The Allies conquered Sicily (July-Aug. 1943) and advanced north up the mainland of Italy, which surrendered (Sept. 8, 1943), though German forces continued fighting in Italy. Meanwhile, the Russians, having successfully withstood a massive German offensive against Stalingrad (Sept. 1942-Feb. 1943), launched a counteroffensive which drove the Germans out of the U.S.S.R. by Aug. 1944. Underground movements in many German-occupied countries carried on successful guerrilla warfare and sabotage of German installations. The Poles rose in Warsaw (Aug. 1944). Allied counteroffensives gathered strength in New Guinea, the Pacific Is and Burma (1943-4).

The Allies had conferred together at Casablanca (Jan. 14-26, 1943), Quebec (Aug. 11-24, 1943) and Tehran (Nov. 28–Dec. 2, 1943), and had drawn up plans for the liberation of France. Under the command of Eisenhower, they invaded Normandy (June 6, 1944) and Provence (Aug. 15, 1944), and after much hard fighting drove the Germans out of France, liberating Paris on Aug. 25, 1944. Meanwhile the Russian offensive forced the surrender of Bulgaria (Sept. 11, 1944), Rumania (Sept. 12, 1944) and Finland (Sept. 19, 1944). Germany, fighting a rearguard action on all fronts, began to use rockets against Britain. The British landed in Greece (Oct. 1944), Belgrade was liberated by the Russians and the forces of Tito (Oct. 20, 1944) and the Germans withdrew from the Balkans. The Russians advanced through Poland, took E. Prussia and Czechoslovakia (Jan. 1945) and Vienna (Apr. 12, 1945), and overran E. Germany. The Allies crossed the Rhine (Mar. 7, 1945) and met Russian forces in Saxony (Apr. 25, 1945). As the Russians took Berlin (May 2, 1945), Hitler's suicide was reported. A German government formed by Doenitz surrendered unconditionally (May 7, 1945).

Meanwhile the British drove the Japanese from Burma (Feb. 1944–July 1945) and reestablished a supply route to China, which, by early 1945, had regained most of the territory lost to the Japanese. The Americans gradually expelled the Japanese from the scattered Pacific Is, the Philippines (1944-5), Okinawa (Apr. 1945) and Borneo (Aug. 1945). The U.S.S.R., having promised its support against Japan at Yalta (Feb. 4-12, 1945), invaded Manchuria. The U.S.A. dropped the first atomic bomb on Hiroshima (Aug. 6, 1945) and another on Nagasaki (Aug. 9, 1945), and Japan surrendered (Aug. 14, 1945).

The war, which cost more than 36 million lives, was the most destructive and widespread in history. Germany lost about 6 million lives, the U.S.S.R. about 17 million, Poland about 5,800,000, Yugoslavia about 1,600,000, Japan about 2 million, Italy about 450,000, Rumania about 460,000, France 570,000, the U.S.A. 400,000, Britain 400,000, Hungary about 430,000 and the Netherlands about 210,000. Millions were left homeless. Nazi Germany had attempted racial extermination, esp. of the Jews (of whom 6 million died), and had practiced atrocities in its concentration camps on a vast scale. Both the Allies and the Axis had increased their destructive power, culminating in the atomic bomb. After the war there emerged a new balance of power between the U.S.S.R., whose influence now spread throughout Eastern Europe, and the U.S.A. Germany was divided into zones of occupation, leading to the deeper division between East and West Germany and preventing the signing of a full peace treaty with Germany. Europe as a whole slowly recovered from economic exhaustion. The United Nations organization was set up (1945).

Peace treaties were signed between the Allies and Italy, Rumania, Bulgaria, Hungary and Finland in Paris (Feb. 1947), between the Allies (except for the U.S.S.R.) and Japan in San Francisco (Sept. 1951) and between the U.S.S.R. and Japan (1956), and between the Allies and Austria (May 1955), establishing Austrian independence

world-wea·ry (wə́:rldwi̯əri:) *adj.* tired of the world and its activities, esp. as the result of pursuing one's own pleasure

world-wide (wə́:rldwáid) *adj.* pertaining or extending to all parts of the world

worm (wə:rm) **1.** *n.* an earthworm ‖ any of various elongated creeping animals with soft, often segmented bodies, e.g. the blindworm ‖ a similar creature parasitical on a mammal's tissues or intestines, e.g. a tapeworm ‖ (*loosely*) any of certain larvae resembling these ‖ (*pl.*) a disorder due to the presence of parasitic worms in the intestines etc. ‖ (*rhet.*) a mean, groveling or contemptible person ‖ the thread of a screw ‖ the shaft on which a spiral groove is cut ‖ a short revolving screw whose threads engage with a worm wheel ‖ something helical, e.g. a spiral pipe ‖ the spiral tube of a still in which vapor is cooled ‖ (*zool.*) the lytta **2.** *v.t.* to work (oneself or one's way) in a winding or insidious manner, *he wormed his way into her confidence* ‖ to elicit (information etc.) by devious ways, *to worm a secret out of someone* ‖ to cut the lytta of (a dog) ‖ to purge of intestinal worms ‖ (*naut.*) to wind fine rope or yarn around (a cable etc.) in order to fill in the spaces between the strands ‖ *v.i.* to move like a worm ‖ to look for worms for bait ‖ (with 'in' or 'into') to insinuate oneself by artful means [O.E. *wyrm*]

worm·cast (wə́:rmkæst, wə́:rmkɑst) *n.* a tube-shaped mass of earth voided by an earthworm and left on the surface of the ground

worm-eat·en (wə́:rmi:t'n) *adj.* eaten into by worms, full of wormholes ‖ old-fashioned, worn out, *worm-eaten notions*

worm gear a gear consisting of a worm wheel engaging with a worm (short revolving screw) ‖ a worm wheel

worm·hole (wə́:rmhoul) *n.* a hole made in soil by an earthworm ‖ a hole made in wood, fruit etc. by a worm or larva

Worms (vɔrms) a river port (pop. 74,200) in Rhineland-Palatinate, West Germany, on the Rhine. Romanesque cathedral (12th-13th cc.). Many Imperial diets were held here

Worms, Concordat of an agreement (1122) between Pope Calixtus II and Emperor Henry V, settling the Investiture Controversy. The Empire conceded to the papacy the exclusive right to invest bishops and abbots, but retained the right to prevent undesirable appointments

Worms, Diet of an assembly of the Holy Roman Empire at which Luther defended (1521) his doctrines before Charles V

worm wheel a toothed wheel that engages with the threads of a worm (short revolving screw)

worm·wood (wə́:rmwud) *n.* *Artemisia absinthium,* fam. *Compositae,* an aromatic perennial woody plant of Europe and Asia yielding an oil used in making absinthe ‖ any plant of genus *Artemisia* ‖ (*rhet.*) bitterness, esp. bitter mortification [O.E. *wermod*]

worm·y (wə́:rmi:) *comp.* **worm·i·er** *superl.* **worm·i·est** *adj.* full of worms ‖ burrowed by worms or larvae ‖ like a worm

worn *past part.* of WEAR

worn-out (wɔ́rnáut) *adj.* made useless by wear, *worn-out shoes* ‖ exhausted, tired out

worried *past* and *past part.* of WORRY

wor·ri·er (wə́:ri:ər, wʌ́ri:ər) *n.* someone given to worrying

wor·ri·ment (wə́:ri:mənt, wʌ́ri:mənt) *n.* (*rhet.*) anxiety, irritation ‖ (*rhet.*) a source of worry

wor·ri·some (wə́:ri:səm, wʌ́ri:səm) *adj.* causing worry ‖ easily and frequently worried

wor·ry (wə́:ri:) **1.** *v. pres. part.* **wor·ry·ing** *past* and *past part.* **wor·ried** *v.t.* (esp. of a dog or wild carnivorous animal) to seize with the teeth and shake in order to kill or injure ‖ (esp. of a dog) to harass or tease by chasing, snapping at etc. ‖ to cause to feel disturbed or depressed, esp. through fear regarding some event, outcome

CONCISE PRONUNCIATION KEY: **(a)** æ, *cat*; ɑ, *car*; ɔ *fawn*; ei, *snake*. **(e)** e, *hen*; i:, *sheep*; iə, *deer*; ɛə, *bear*. **(i)** i, *fish*; ai, *tiger*; ə:, *bird*. **(o)** o, *ox*; au, *cow*; ou, *goat*; u, *poor*; ɔi, *royal*. **(u)** ʌ, *duck*; u, *bull*; u:, *goose*; ə, *bacillus*; ju:, *cube*. x, *loch*; θ, *think*; ð, *bother*; z, *Zen*; ʒ, *corsage*; dʒ, *savage*; ŋ, *orangutang*; j, *yak*; ʃ, *fish*; tʃ, *fetch*; 'l, *rabble*; 'n, *redden*. Complete pronunciation key appears inside front cover.

etc. ‖ to give petty annoyance to, esp. by making continual demands upon the attention ‖ *v.i.* to feel a nagging fear about something, *to worry about one's health* ‖ (with 'along') to manage to meet one's day-to-day expenses by persistent effort ‖ (with 'through') to get to the end of a difficult piece of work or some hardship etc. by persistent effort **2.** *pl.* **wor·ries** *n.* a worrying or being worried ‖ an instance of this ‖ something that causes worry [O.E. *wyrgan*, to strangle]

worse (wə:rs) **1.** *adj.* bad in greater degree, *worse weather than usual* ‖ in a less good state of health, condition etc. **2.** *adv.* more badly, *he behaved even worse than usual* **3.** *n.* something worse or a worse state, *worse was to follow* **wórs·en** *v.t.* to make worse ‖ *v.i.* to become worse [O.E. *wiersa, wyrsa*]

wor·ship (wə́:rʃip) **1.** *n.* reverence, homage or honor paid to God ‖ ceremonies or services expressing such reverence, *public worship* ‖ an utterly devoted admiration for a person **Your (His) Worship** (esp. *Br.*) a courtesy title used to (or of) certain magistrates, officials etc. **2.** *v. pres. part.* **wor·ship·ing**, esp. *Br.* **wor·ship·ping** *past* and *past part.* **wor·shiped,** esp. *Br.* **wor·shipped** *v.t.* to pay religious devotion to, *to worship God* ‖ to idolize, adore, *he worships every hair on her head* ‖ *v.i.* to be full of adoration ‖ to take part in religious ceremonies **wór·ship·er,** esp. *Br.* **wór·ship·per** *n.* someone who worships **wór·ship·ful** *adj.* (esp. *Br.*, usually in formal titles) worthy, esteemed ‖ offering worship, adoring [O.E. *weorthscipe*]

worst (wə:rst) **1.** *adj.* most bad **2.** *adv.* most badly **3.** *n.* that which is worst, the worst part or state, *the worst of the journey is over* **at worst, at the worst** even on the least favorable reckoning **if worst comes to worst** (*Am.=Br.* **if the worst comes to the worst**) if the worst happens **to get the worst of it** to be defeated **4.** *v.t.* to defeat, esp. in argument [O.E. *wierresta, wyrresta, wyrsta, wersta*]

wor·sted (wústid, wə́:rstid) **1.** *n.* woolen yarn spun from long-fibered wool ‖ fabric made of such yarn **2.** *adj.* made of worsted fabric [after *Worsted,* former spelling of *Worstead* in Norfolk, England]

wort (wə:rt, wɔrt) *n.* (only in plant names) a plant, esp. a herbaceous one, e.g. glasswort [O.E. *wyrt,* root, plant]

wort *n.* a sweet infusion of malt or other grain unfermented or in process of fermentation [O.E. *wyrt,* herb, root]

worth (wə:rθ) **1.** *n.* the amount of money etc. to which something is regarded as being equivalent, i.e. its monetary or material value ‖ the degree of excellence, importance etc. of someone or something as an indication of the degree to which he or it should be regarded as admirable, important, useful etc., *do not underestimate his worth, her poems are of little worth compared with her novels* ‖ the amount of something that may be purchased for a specified sum, *ten cents worth of nails* ‖ a person's material wealth, *what would you estimate his worth at?* **2.** *prep.* of the material worth of, *it is worth a great deal of money* ‖ deserving, *not worth consideration* ‖ rich to the extent of, *he died worth thousands* **for all one is worth** with all the energy, power etc. one possesses **for what it is worth** without any guarantee as to accuracy, truthfulness etc. [O.E. *weorth*]

wor·thi·ly (wə́:rðili:) *adv.* in a worthy way

wor·thi·ness (wə́:rði:nis) *n.* the quality of being worthy

worth·less (wə́:rθlis) *adj.* of no worth

worth·while (wə́:rθhwáil, wə́:rθwáil) *adj.* meriting the time, effort etc. involved, *was the excursion worthwhile?*

wor·thy (wə́:rði:) **1.** *comp.* **wor·thi·er** *superl.* **wor·thi·est** *adj.* having worth, *a worthy cause* ‖ respectable, *a worthy couple* ‖ (with 'of') deserving, *behavior worthy of punishment* ‖ (often with 'of') of a worth regarded as adequate, *a worthy opponent, an opponent worthy of him* **2.** *pl.* **wor·thies** *n.* a person of worth or eminence [M.E. *wurthi, worthy*]

Wouk (wouk), Herman (1915-), U.S. novelist, author of 'The Caine Mutiny' (1951), 'Marjorie Morningstar' (1955), 'Youngblood Hawke' (1962), 'The Winds of War' (1971) and 'War and Remembrance' (1978)

would (wud) *past* of WILL ‖ *auxiliary v.* used to express condition, *she would go if you would* ‖ used to express the future in indirect speech, *he said he would come* ‖ used in polite request, *would you please get me my hat?* ‖ (*rhet.*) used to express a wish, *would she were here!* ‖ used to express doubt, *it would appear to be the case* (cf. WILL, cf. SHOULD) [M.E.]

would-be (wúdbi:) *adj.* desiring to be or self-styled, *a would-be orator*

would·n't (wúd'nt) *contr.* of WOULD NOT

wound (wu:nd) *n.* an injury to living tissues, esp. as the result of violence ‖ an injury to the feelings [O.E. *wund*]

wound *v.t.* to cause a wound or wounds in ‖ to hurt the feelings of ‖ *v.i.* to inflict a wound or wounds ‖ to hurt someone's feelings [O.E. *wundian*]

wound (waund) *past* and *past part.* of WIND, to go in a curved path ‖ alt. *past* and *past part.* of WIND, to sound (a horn etc.)

Wounded Knee Creek the site in South Dakota of an atrocity committed (1890) by the U.S. 7th Cavalry against a band of 350 men, women and children of the Minneconjon Sioux. More than half the Indians were massacred. The Plains Indians never again offered serious armed resistance to the white invaders

wound·wort (wú:ndwə:rt, wú:ndwɔrt) *n.* a member of *Stachys,* fam. *Labiatae,* a genus of widely distributed annual or perennial low-growing plants with a tubular calyx and lipped corolla, formerly used for healing ‖ any of certain other plants that have been so used

Wou·wer·man (váuvərmɑn), Philips (1619-68), Dutch painter. He specialized in battle scenes, hunting scenes and seascapes

wove *past* and alt. *past part.* of WEAVE

woven alt. *past part.* of WEAVE

wove paper paper with a uniform, unlined surface, given to it by manipulation with a woven wire screen (cf. LAID PAPER)

WP (*abbr.*) for 'withdrawn passing,' a grade given to a passing student who withdraws from a course. *Cf* WF

W particle (*particle phys.*) hypothetical elementary particle believed to be the quantum of the weak force in nuclear interactions. *also* intermediate boson

wrack (ræk) *n.* seaweed thrown on shore by the tide, used e.g. as manure [M.Du. *wrak* or M.L.G. *wrack, wrak,* wreck]

wrack *n.* (esp. in phrase) **wrack and ruin** disaster, destruction, *he let the property go to wrack and ruin* [O.E. *wræc,* retribution]

wraith (reiθ) *n.* an apparition of a person, seen just before or just after his death ‖ a specter [Scot., etym. doubtful]

wran·gle (rǽŋg'l) **1.** *v. pres. part.* **wran·gling** *past* and *past part.* **wran·gled** *v.i.* to quarrel noisily ‖ to argue ‖ *v.t.* (*western U.S.A.*) to herd or round up (horses or cattle) **2.** *n.* a noisy or angry quarrel or argument **wrán·gler** *n.* someone who wrangles ‖ (*Cambridge University*) a person winning first-class honors in the mathematical tripos [M.E. *wranglen* rel. to L.G. *wrangeln,* M.H.G. *rangelen*]

wrap (ræp) **1.** *v. pres. part.* **wrap·ping** *past* and *past part.* **wrapped** *v.t.* (often with 'up') to cover or enclose, *to wrap oneself up in a blanket, a landscape wrapped in mist* ‖ to conceal, *an affair wrapped in mystery* ‖ to arrange or fold as a covering, *wrap a scarf around your neck* ‖ (often with 'up') to make a parcel of ‖ *v.i.* (with 'around' etc.) to twine, *ivy wrapping round a tree trunk* ‖ to be arranged around something as a drapery, *a sari wraps several times around the waist* ‖ (with 'up') to put on extra clothes against the cold **wrapped up in** engrossed in ‖ very devoted to **2.** *n.* something, esp. a rug, shawl or extra garment, used to wrap oneself in **wráp·per** *n.* a paper wrapping enclosing a newspaper, periodical etc. for mailing ‖ a book jacket ‖ anything that wraps ‖ a person whose job is wrapping ‖ a dressing gown ‖ the tobacco leaf that covers a cigar **wráp·ping** *n.* anything with which something or someone is wrapped [etym. doubtful]

wrap·a·round (rǽpəraund) *adj.* **1.** allembracing **2.** a flexible material used to wrap around an object **3.** a note, bond, or sale that leaves existing debts, leases, and agreements intact, e.g., in the purchase or sale of a property **4.** a type of skirt that wraps around the hips and ties at the waist

wraparound annuity a variable annuity to which a volatile investment (e.g., stocks, money market) has been added

wrasse (ræs) *n.* a member of *Labridue,* a family of brilliantly colored marine fish with spiny fins and prominent thick lips, found in warm seas [Cornish *wrach*]

wrath (ræθ, rɑθ, *Br.* esp. rɔθ) *n.* intense anger or indignation [O.E. *wrǣththu*]

Wrath, Cape the northwestern tip of Scotland, in Sutherland

wrath·ful (rǽθfəl, rɑ́θfəl, *Br.* esp. rɔ́θfəl) *adj.* intensely angry ‖ arising from or characterized by wrath

wreak (ri:k) *v.t.* (*rhet.*) to give full play or effort to (one's anger etc.) ‖ (*rhet.*) to inflict (vengeance, harm etc.) [O.E. *wrecan*]

wreath (ri:θ) *pl.* wreaths (riðz, ri:θs) *n.* a circular band of flowers, leaves etc. for laying on a grave or memorial or used to decorate a door or window etc. or (*hist.*) to honor a victor ‖ something resembling this in shape, *a wreath of smoke* ‖ a representation in stone, metal or wood of a circular band of flowers, leaves etc. [O.E. *writha* fr. *writhan* v., to writhe]

wreathe (ri:ð) *pres. part.* **wreath·ing** *past* and *past part.* **wreathed** *v.t.* to form (flowers etc.) into a wreath ‖ to wind so as to form a wreath, *the snake wreathed itself around a branch* ‖ to encircle, *smoke wreathed the housetop* ‖ (with 'in', *passive*) to arrange the expression of, esp. so as to form smiles, *a face wreathed in smiles* ‖ *v.i.* to move in coils [fr. M.E. *wrethen* past part. of *writhen,* to writhe and fr. WREATH]

wreck (rek) **1.** *n.* the destruction or disablement esp. of a ship ‖ the ruins of a wrecked ship ‖ what is left of a building, vehicle etc., after destruction ‖ a person wasted by mental or physical sickness ‖ a spoiling or confounding, *the wreck of one's hopes* ‖ goods cast up by the sea from sunken ships **2.** *v.t.* to cause the wreck of, destroy, ruin ‖ *v.i.* to suffer wreck **wréck·age** *n.* the remains of a wrecked ship, vehicle, building etc. ‖ fragments of any wrecked structure **wréck·er** *n.* a person who wrecks or ruins ‖ a person who contrives the wreck of ships, e.g. by false signals, in order to plunder them ‖ (*Am.*= *Br.* housebreaker) someone whose business is demolishing buildings and disposing of the building materials ‖ a tow truck ‖ a person employed to recover wrecked ships or cargoes [A.F. *wrec, wrech*]

Wren (ren), Sir Christopher (1632-1723), English architect. He designed St Paul's Cathedral (1675-1711), over 50 other churches in London, and secular buildings such as the Sheldonian Theater at Oxford (1660s) and a wing of Hampton Court Palace (1690s). He had great mathematical and engineering skill, and used the classical orders with great imagination

wren (ren) *n.* any of many small singing birds of fam. *Troglodytidae* of tropical and temperate regions, e.g. *Troglodytes troglodytes,* a very small, dark-brown European bird with a short, erect tail, or *T. Troglodytes hiemalis,* its northern U.S. and Canadian representatative (the winter wren)

wrench (rentʃ) **1.** *v.t.* to pull or twist violently, *to wrench a door open* ‖ to injure or hurt by twisting violently, *to wrench one's arm* ‖ *v.i.* to twist or turn violently **2.** *n.* a violent twist, often combined with a sharp pull ‖ an injury caused by this ‖ an emotional pain, esp. from parting ‖ a tool with adjustable jaws for gripping and turning nuts or bolts etc. ‖ (*Am.=Br.* spanner) a tool for tightening nuts etc. (cf. MONKEY WRENCH) [O.E. *wrencan,* to twist]

wrest (rest) *v.t.* to obtain by using strength or violence or by great effort, *to wrest a living from the soil* ‖ to pull or force with a violent twist ‖ to arrive at (a meaning or interpretation) by distortion [O.E. *wrǣstan*]

wrest block the wooden plank in a piano in which the wrest pins are set

wres·tle (rés'l) **1.** *v. pres. part.* **wres·tling** *past* and *past part.* **wres·tled** *v.i.* to struggle with an opponent by grappling and trying to throw or trip him ‖ (of two opponents) to engage in such a struggle ‖ to struggle, *to wrestle with one's accounts* ‖ *v.t.* to struggle with (an opponent) by grappling with him and trying to throw or trip him ‖ (*western U.S.A.*) to throw (esp. a calf) for branding **2.** *n.* a wrestling bout ‖ a hard struggle **wrés·tler** *n.* **wrés·tling** *n.* a sport under any of various codes of rules, in which unarmed opponents grapple and try to throw each other [O.E. fr. *wrǣstan,* to wrest]

wrest pin one of the pins on a piano or harp around which are wound the ends of the strings, and by which the strings are tightened or slackened in tuning

wretch (retʃ) *n.* a person in great misfortune ‖ a contemptible or wicked person **wretch·ed** (rétʃid) *adj.* miserably sad ‖ of exceedingly poor quality, construction etc. ‖ contemptible ‖ causing or characterized by misery, *they live under wretched conditions* ‖ causing inconvenience,

CONCISE PRONUNCIATION KEY: **(a)** æ, *cat;* ɑ, *car;* ɔ *fawn;* ei, *snake.* **(e)** e, *hen;* i:, *sheep;* iə, *deer;* εə, *bear.* **(i)** i, *fish;* ai, *tiger;* ə:, *bird.* **(o)** o, *ox;* au, *cow;* ou, *goat;* u, *poor;* ɔi, *royal.* **(u)** ʌ, *duck;* u, *bull;* u:, *goose;* ə, *bacillus;* ju:, *cube.* x, *loch;* θ, *think;* ð, *bother;* z, *Zen;* ʒ, *corsage;* dʒ, *savage;* ŋ, *orangutang;* j, *yak;* ʃ, *fish;* tʃ, *fetch;* 'l, *rabble;* 'n, *redden.* Complete pronunciation key appears inside front cover.

discomfort, boredom etc. [O.E. *wrecca, wrœcca,* an outcast]

wrig·gle (ríg'l) **1.** *v. pres. part.* **wrig·gling** *past* and *past part.* **wrig·gled** *v.i.* to twist and turn with short abrupt movements like those of a worm ‖ to move along in this way ‖ to act in an evasive, shifty way ‖ *v.t.* to cause to twist and turn with short abrupt movements ‖ to bring into a specified position or condition by twisting and turning abruptly, *to wriggle oneself free* **2.** *n.* a wriggling movement [M.L.G. *wriggeln*]

Wright (rait), Frank Lloyd (1869-1959), American architect, creator of 'organic architecture', a mode of construction in which buildings are in close compositional relationship to their natural surroundings. His 'prairie style' houses, which he began constructing in 1902, are characterized by long, low horizontal lines and functional interiors: kitchen, living and dining areas forming an unbroken whole. His work includes the Guggenheim Museum, New York (1945-59)

Wright, Joseph (1734-97), English painter, known as Wright of Derby, famous for his candlelit pieces, e.g. 'The Air Pump' (1768) and 'The Alchymist' (1771), and lunar landscapes

Wright, Orville (1871-1948) and his brother Wilbur (1867-1912), American aircraft engineers. They built the first stable and controllable heavier-than-air machine, which made its first flight (852 ft) at Kitty Hawk, North Carolina, in 1903

Wright, Richard (1908-60), U.S. black novelist. His 'Uncle Tom's Children' (1938) and 'Native Son' (1940) depict injustice against the blacks in the U.S.A.

wring (riŋ) **1.** *v. pres. part.* **wring·ing** *past* and *past part.* **wrung** (rʌŋ) *v.t.* to squeeze and twist (wet clothes etc.), esp. so as to force out the moisture ‖ to force out (water etc.) by squeezing and twisting ‖ to twist forcibly ‖ to extort by mental or bodily coercion, *to wring a confession from someone* ‖ to squeeze, clasp or press, esp. with emotion, *to wring someone's hand* ‖ (*rhet.*) to pain, distress, *the sight wrung my heart* **2.** *n.* a squeezing or twisting **wríng·er** *n.* a machine for pressing water out of clothes **wríng·ing** *adj.* (*Br.*) wringing wet [O.E. *wringan*]

wringing wet so wet that water can be squeezed out

wrin·kle (ríŋk'l) **1.** *n.* a small furrow or ridge caused by a fold in a flexible surface, e.g. one formed in the skin as a mark of age, or one that disfigures cloth or a garment ‖ (*pop.*) a clever hint or suggestion about how to do something ‖ (*pop.*) a novel technique **2.** *v. pres. part.* **wrin·kling** *past* and *past part.* **wrin·kled** *v.t.* to produce wrinkles in, *to wrinkle one's forehead* ‖ *v.i.* to acquire wrinkles or a wrinkle **wrín·kled, wrín·kly** *adjs* [etym. doubtful]

wrist (rist) *n.* the joint between the hand and the arm ‖ the corresponding part in an animal ‖ the part of a garment covering the wrist [O.E.]

wrist·band (rístbænd) *n.* the part of the sleeve (esp. of a shirt) which covers the wrist

wrist·let (ríst|it) *n.* a band around the wrist, esp. one incorporated in a glove or sleeve etc. for warmth

wristlet watch (*Br.*) a wristwatch

wrist·lock (ríst|ɒk) *n.* a twisting grip on the wrist used in wrestling to throw an opponent or make him helpless

wrist pin (*mech.*) a metal pin linking a piston and connecting rod

wrist·watch (rístwɒtʃ) *n.* a small watch worn on a strap or bracelet around the wrist

wrist wrestling arm wrestling with opponents, interlocking thumbs as the pressure point

writ (rit) *n.* a written command issued in the name of a sovereign, state, court of law etc. ‖ (*Br.*) a document issued by the crown, summoning one of the lords spiritual or temporal to attend Parliament or instructing a sheriff to hold an election of a member or members of parliament [O.E.=something written]

writ of cer·ti·o·ra·ri (sə:rʃi:əréərai) a writ issuing from a superior court calling up the record of a proceeding in an inferior court for review [L. *certiorari,* to be informed or certified, pass. infin. of *certiorare,* to inform, from the use of *certiorari* in the L. original]

write (rait) *pres. part.* **writ·ing** *past* **wrote** (rout) *past part.* **writ·ten** (rít'n) *v.i.* to form letters, figures or other significant symbols, esp. on paper, using a pencil, pen, brush etc. ‖ to compose books or other literary matter ‖ to write a letter (personal communication), *to write to somebody* ‖ to produce the letters of the alphabet etc. on paper etc., *this pen writes well* ‖ *v.t.* to form (letters, figures, symbols etc.) on a surface ‖ to set down (language, information etc.) in letters, words or symbols, *write your name and address here* ‖ to cover or fill in with writing, *to write three pages, to write a check* ‖ to compose (a book, poem etc.) as an author ‖ to send a letter to, *he wrote them last week* ‖ to communicate or state in writing or in print, *he wrote them the latest news* ‖ to underwrite ‖ to draw up in legal form ‖ to show clearly, mark, stamp, *despair was written on every face* **to write down** to put in writing, record ‖ to describe, criticize or judge in a disparaging way, *she wrote him down as a nonentity* ‖ to reduce the nominal value of (stocks, goods etc.) **to write off** to compose rapidly and easily ‖ to record the cancellation of, *to write off a debt* ‖ to send away by mail, *to write off for a catalog* ‖ to dismiss from consideration **to write out** to write in full (esp. something public or official) ‖ to put in writing ‖ to exhaust (oneself) as a writer **to write up** to review or describe in writing, esp. favorably, in a newspaper etc. ‖ to record (an experiment etc.) in writing ‖ to expand (notes) into a piece of writing ‖ (*accounting*) to put down an excessive value for (an asset) **wrít·er** *n.* someone who writes, esp. a professional author of books ‖ someone who writes insurance ‖ (*Br.*) a clerk, esp. in the navy or a government office [O.E. *wrītan,* to scratch, score, cut]

writer's cramp a painful spasmodic cramp of the finger muscles caused by writing for too long a time

write-up (ráitʌp) *n.* (*pop.*) an article in the press, esp. a favorable critical notice ‖ an unjustified increase in the assets on the books of a corporation

writhe (raið) **1.** *v. pres. part.* **writh·ing** *past* and *past part.* **writhed** *v.i.* to twist, roll or turn about, esp. in pain ‖ to have a sensation of mental suffering, *to writhe with shame* ‖ *v.t.* to twist or contort (one's body or a part of it), esp. in pain or embarrassment **2.** *n.* a writhing [O.E. *wrīthan,* to twist]

writ·ing (ráitiŋ) *n.* the act of someone who writes ‖ handwriting ‖ anything written, e.g. a literary composition, book, article, inscription etc. ‖ the occupation of a writer or author ‖ written form, *evidence in writing* ‖ style in literary composition, *sloppy ideas and shoddy writing* **the writing on the wall** a warning of doom to come (Daniel v)

written *past part.* of WRITE

Wro·claw (vrɔ́tslɑf) (*G.* Breslau) a communications center (pop. 584,500) in Silesia, Poland, on the Oder. Industries: metalworking, chemical industries, textiles, heavy engineering. Gothic cathedral (14th c.), town hall and churches. University (1702)

wrong (rɔŋ) **1.** *adj.* not in accordance with moral standards, not morally right ‖ not correct or accurate, false, *the wrong answer* ‖ mistaken, *you are wrong in thinking him intelligent* ‖ not suitable or proper, *they chose the wrong time to drop in* ‖ amiss, out of order, *what is wrong with the pump?* ‖ being other than the one it was expected to be, identified as or intended to be etc., *to take the wrong road* ‖ (of one side of a fabric) designed to be placed or worn downward or inward so as not to be seen **2.** *n.* that which is morally wrong, *to choose between right and wrong* ‖ an act of injustice ‖ (*law*) an invading of the rights of someone **in the wrong** mistaken ‖ morally responsible for an offense **to put (someone) in the wrong** to make (someone) appear to be the offender, affix blame to (someone) **3.** *adv.* incorrectly **to get (someone) wrong** to misunderstand the meaning or motives of (someone) **to go wrong** to take the wrong direction, road etc. ‖ to start on a course of wrongdoing or immoral behavior ‖ (of a mechanism, plan etc.) to get out of order, break down **4.** *v.t.* to treat unfairly or judge unjustly ‖ (*old-fash.*) to seduce (a woman) [O.E. *wrang, wrong,* curved or crooked in form, direction etc.]

wrong·do·er (rɔ́ŋdú:ər) *n.* someone who acts in a way contrary to law or moral order

wrong·do·ing (rɔ́ŋdú:iŋ) *n.* crime ‖ sin

wrong·ful (rɔ́ŋfəl) *adj.* not fair, not just ‖ not lawful

wrong·head·ed (rɔ́ŋhédid) *adj.* obstinately and perversely clinging to something mistaken or inaccurate

wrote *past* of WRITE

wroth (rɔθ, rɒθ, *Br.* esp. rouθ) *adj.* (*rhet.*) angry, wrathful [O.E. *wrāth*]

wrought (rɔt) alt. *past* and *past part.* of WORK ‖ *adj.* worked, made, formed, fashioned ‖ (of metals) hammered and beaten into shape

wrought iron a very pure form of commercial iron, having a very small carbon content. It is tough, malleable, ductile and easily welded

wrought-up (rɔ́tʌ́p) *adj.* nervously excited, agitated

wrung *past* and *past part.* of WRING

wry (rai) *comp.* **wri·er** *superl.* **wri·est** *adj.* (of the neck or features) distorted, turned abnormally to one side ‖ (of features) distorted for a moment to express distaste, irony or bitterness ‖ (of a smile) made with such a distortion ‖ (of humor, remarks etc.) neatly turned, but bitter or ironic [O.E. *wrīgian* v., to turn]

wry·neck (ráineck) *n. Jynx torquilla,* a gray-brown European woodpecker which has a characteristic habit of stretching and twisting its neck ‖ any woodpecker of genus *Jynx* ‖ torticollis

Wu·chang (wú:tʃǽŋ) *WUHAN

Wu·han (wú:hán) the capital (pop. 2,226,000) of Hupei, China, the head of oceangoing shipping on the Yangtzekiang, at its confluence with the Han. It consists of the former cities of Hankow (the commercial center and former international city, with textile industries), Hanyang (the industrial center: iron and steel, mechanical engineering, chemicals) and Wuchang (the old walled capital). University (1905)

Wu·hsien (wú:ʃjén) (or Soochow) a port (pop. 700,000) in Kiangsu, China, on the Grand Canal, celebrated for its canals, bridges and medieval buildings. Industries: textiles, food processing, handicrafts (jade, lace)

Wu·hu (wú:hú:) a river port and rice market (pop. 250,000) on the Yangtzekiang in Anhwei, China: cotton textiles

Wul·fi·la (wúlfələ) (or Ulfilas, c. 311-83), Gothic bishop. He spread Arian Christianity among the Goths, and in his translation of the New Testament left the only surviving Gothic texts

Wundt (vunt), Wilhelm (1832-1920), German psychologist and philosopher, founder of experimental psychology, author of 'Elements of Physiological Psychology' (1873-4)

Wup·per·tal (vúpertɑl) an industrial center (pop. 401,609) in central North Rhine-Westphalia, West Germany: textiles, chemical industries, pharmaceuticals, mechanical engineering, paper

Württemberg *BADEN-WÜRTTEMBERG

Würz·burg (výrtsburk) a river port (pop. 112,500) and agricultural market in Bavaria, West Germany, on the Main, with engineering industries. Castle (13th-16th cc.), Romanesque-Gothic cathedral (12th c.), churches (8th-18th cc.), all damaged in the 2nd world war. University (1582)

Wu·sih (wú:ʃí:) a rail and industrial center (pop. 650,000) in Kiangsu, China: textiles, food processing, engineering, chemicals

Wu·tsin (wú:dʒín) (Changchow) a trading center (pop. 297,000) in S. Kiangsu, China on the Grand Canal

W. Va. West Virginia

WWW (*meteor. abbr.*) for World Weather Watch, a global weather service established by World Meteorological Organization in 1967

Wy·an·dotte (wáiəndɒt) *n.* a chicken of an American breed, usually white laced with black [after a North American Indian tribe]

Wy·att (wáiət), James (1746-1813), English architect, an early exponent of neo-Gothic

Wyatt, Sir Thomas (c. 1503-42), English poet and statesman. His sonnets, probably written in prison, were the first written in English. They were based on Petrarch so far as the form went, but used the rhythm of the speaking voice to counterpoint the 'correct' pattern. His voice was direct and frank in a courtly or mannered period

wych elm, witch elm (wítʃélm) *n. Ulmus glabra,* a Eurasian elm common in the British Isles ‖ the wood of this tree [var. of WITCH (as in 'witch hazel')]

Wych·er·ley (wítʃərli:), William (c. 1640-1716), English playwright. His work was typical of the Restoration drama in its cynical acceptance of an amoral society, its surprising verbal coarseness, and its fondness for plots based on amorous intrigues. Best known are 'The Country-Wife' (1675) and 'The Plain-Dealer' (1677)

wych hazel the wych elm ‖ *WITCH HAZEL

CONCISE PRONUNCIATION KEY: **(a)** æ, *cat*; ɑ, *car*; ɔ *fawn*; ei, *snake*. **(e)** e, *hen*; i:, *sheep*; iə, *deer*; ɛə, *bear*. **(i)** i, *fish*; ai, *tiger*; ə:, *bird*. **(o)** o, *ox*; au, *cow*; ou, *goat*; u, *poor*; ɔi, *royal*. **(u)** ʌ, *duck*; u, *bull*; u:, *goose*; ə, *bacillus*; ju:, *cube*. x, *loch*; θ, *think*; ð, *bother*; z, *Zen*; ʒ, *corsage*; dʒ, *savage*; ŋ, *orangutang*; j, *yak*; ʃ, *fish*; tʃ, *fetch*; 'l, *rabble*; 'n, *redden*. Complete pronunciation key appears inside front cover.

Wyc·lif, Wyc·liffe (wíklif), John (c. 1320-84), English religious reformer. He and his followers translated the entire Bible into English. With the protection of his patron, John of Gaunt, he attacked many ecclesiastical abuses and doctrines, proclaimed that salvation depends upon predestination and grace rather than on membership of a visible Church, and insisted on the right of all men to have access to the Scriptures in the vernacular. His denial of transubstantiation was condemned (1381) as heretical. His followers were known as Lollards

Wyc·liff·ite (wíklifait) n. a Lollard

Wy·eth (wáiəθ), Andrew Newell (1917-   ), U.S. realist painter. His subjects are from Maine and Pennsylvania

Wy·lie (wáili:), Elinor (née Hoyt, 1885-1928), U.S. poet and novelist. Her verse shows the influence of the 17th-c. metaphysicals and includes 'Nets to Catch the Wind' (1921), 'Black Amour' (1923) and 'Trivial Breath' (1928). Her novels include 'Jennifer Lorn' (1923), 'The Orphan Angel' (1926) and 'Mr. Hodge and Mr. Hazard' (1928)

Wyo. Wyoming

Wy·o·ming (waióumiŋ) (abbr. Wyo.) a state (area 97,914 sq. miles, pop. 502,000) in the W. central U.S.A. Capital: Cheyenne. The Rocky Mtns lie in the west and south, and the east is mainly semiarid high plain. The Yellowstone National Park is in the northwest. Agriculture: cattle, sheep, hay, winter wheat, sugar beets (with much dependence on irrigation). Resources: oil, coal, uranium. Industries: oil refining, food processing. State university (1886) at Laramie. Most of Wyoming passed to the U.S.A. in the Louisiana Purchase (1803). It became (1890) the 44th state of the U.S.A. It was the first state of the U.S.A. to enfranchise women

Wys·pian·ski (vispjánski:), Stanislaw (1869-1907), Polish playwright and painter. His plays include 'The Wedding' (1901), 'Deliverance' (1903) and 'November Night' (1904)

Wyss (vi:s), Johann David (1743-1818), Swiss writer, author of the juvenile classic 'Swiss Family Robinson' (published 1812-27)

Wythe (wiθ), George (1726-1806), U.S. jurist and leader in Virginia's ratification of the U.S. Constitution. As professor of law (1779-90) at the College of William and Mary, he exerted a profound influence on the great men of his time, notably John Marshall, Thomas Jefferson and James Monroe

wy·vern (wáivər:n) n. (heraldry) a two-legged dragon with outspread wings and barbed tail [M.E. wyver fr. O.F. wyvre, var. of vivre, serpent]

CONCISE PRONUNCIATION KEY: **(a)** æ, cat; ɑ, car; ɔ fawn; ei, snake. **(e)** e, hen; i:, sheep; iə, deer; ɛə, bear. **(i)** i, fish; ai, tiger; ə:, bird. **(o)** o, ox; au, cow; ou, goat; u, poor; ɔi, royal. **(u)** ʌ, duck; u, bull; u:, goose; ə, bacillus; ju:, cube. x, loch; θ, think; δ, bother; z, Zen; ʒ, corsage; dʒ, savage; ŋ, orangutang; j, yak; ʃ, fish; tʃ, fetch; 'l, rabble; 'n, redden. Complete pronunciation key appears inside front cover.

			CLASSICAL GREEK		EARLY LATIN	CLASSICAL LATIN
			X		X	X
CURSIVE MAJUSCULE (ROMAN)	CURSIVE MINUSCULE (ROMAN)	ANGLO-IRISH MAJUSCULE	CAROLINE MINUSCULE	VENETIAN MINUSCULE (ITALIC)	N. ITALIAN MINUSCULE (ROMAN)	
X	X	X	X	X	X	

A. C. SYLVESTER, CAMBRIDGE, ENGLAND

Development of the letter **X**, beginning with the classical Greek letter. Evolution of both the majuscule, or capital, letter X and the minuscule, or lowercase, letter x are shown.

X, x (eks) the 24th letter of the English alphabet (sounded as 'z' when an initial letter) ‖ something shaped like this ‖ (*math.*) an unknown quantity or the symbol for this ‖ any unknown factor or quantity or the symbol for this ‖ the Roman symbol for the number 10 ‖ **X** a symbol for Christ used in abbreviations, e.g. 'Xmas' for 'Christmas' [from the initial letter chi of Gk *Christos*, which looks like an English X]

X (eks) *adj.* motion picture rating for erotic films, admission to which persons under the age of 17 or 18 are not permitted. *Cf* G, PG, R

xan·thate (zǽnθeit) *n.* a salt or ester of a xanthic acid (ROCS·SH), esp. cellulose xanthate, used in the manufacture of viscose [fr. Gk *xanthos*, yellow]

xan·thic (zǽnθik) *adj.* (esp. *bot.*, of a flower) yellow [fr. Gk *xanthos*, yellow]

xan·thin (zǽnθin) *n.* (*chem.*) a yellow, non-water-soluble pigment found in yellow plants [fr. Gk *xanthos*, yellow]

xan·thine (zǽnθi:n) *n.* (*biochem.*) a crystalline compound, $C_5H_4N_4O_2$, found in blood, urine, muscle tissue and some plants [fr. Gk *xanthos*, yellow]

Xan·thip·pe (zæntípi:, zænθípi:) the wife of Socrates, a proverbial scold

xan·tho·ma (zænθóumə) *pl.* **xan·tho·mas, xan·tho·ma·ta** (zænθóumətə) *n.* a condition arising from a disorder of cholesterol metabolism, characterized by the forming of yellow patches on the skin [Mod. L. fr. Gk *xanthos*, yellow]

xan·tho·phyll (zǽnθəfil) *n.* $C_{40}H_{56}O_2$, the yellow pigment found in plastids and present in many plants **xan·tho·phýl·lic, xan·tho·phyll·ous** (zænθəfíləs, zænθəfáləs) *adjs* [fr. Gk *xanthos*, yellow+*phullon*, leaf]

xan·thous (zǽnθəs) *adj.* (of a people) having yellowish, brown or red hair ‖ (of a people) having yellowish skin ‖ colored yellow [fr. Gk *xanthos*, yellow]

Xavier, St Francis *FRANCIS XAVIER

X-ax·is (éksæksis) *n.* (*mil.*) a horizontal axis in a system of rectangular coordinates, the line on which distances to the right or left (east or west) of the reference line are marked, especially on a map, chart, or graph

X chromosome *SEX CHROMOSOME

xe·bec (zí:bek) *n.* a small three-masted Mediterranean boat with triangular and square sails [earlier *chebec* fr. F.]

Xe·na·kis (zenáki:s), Yannis (1922-), Greek composer. He has applied the notion of probability to composition through the use of a computer where this has seemed useful. He was a pupil of Messiaen

xe·ni·a (zí:ni:ə) *n.* the appearance in seed, fruit or maternal tissues of characters belonging to the fertilizing plant or male parent [Mod. L. fr. Gk *xenia*, hospitality]

xe·no·bi·ol·o·gy (zɛnoubaióilədʒi:) *n.* study of extraterrestrial living organisms. *syn.* exobiology

Xe·noc·ra·tes (zinókrəti:z) (396-314 B.C.), Greek philosopher, a disciple of Plato, whose doctrine he tried to reconcile with that of Pythagoras

xe·nog·a·mous (zinógəməs) *adj.* of, pertaining to or characterized by xenogamy

xe·nog·a·my (zinógəmi:) *n.* (*bot.*) cross-fertilization [fr. Gk *xenos*, foreign+*gamos*, marriage]

xe·no·gen·e·ic (zɛnoudʒəní:ik) *adj.* derived from another species —**xenogenesis** —

xen·o·gen·e·sis (zɛnoudʒénisis) *n.* the supposed production of offspring completely unlike either parent [fr. Gk *xenos*, foreign+*genesis*, origin]

xe·no·graft (zénəgræft) *n.* tissue graft from a donor of a different specie. *also* heterograph —**xenoplastic** *adj. Cf* ALLOGRAFT, HOMOGRAFT

xe·nol·o·gy (zenólədʒi:) *n.* (*biol.*) study of the relationship between host and parasite

xen·o·mor·phic (zɛnoumórfik) *adj.* allotriomorphic [fr. Gk *xenos*, foreign+*morphē*, form]

xe·non (zí:nɒn, zénɒn) *n.* an inert gaseous element (symbol Xe, at. no. 54, at. mass 131.30), used to fill arc lamps, flash bulbs and electronic counters [fr. Gk neut. of *xenos*, strange]

xe·no·narc lamp (zénounɑrk) high-intensity lighting device used in motion picture projection, eye surgery, etc.

xenon lamp high-intensity lamp used in projectors and testing textile fading

Xe·noph·a·nes (zinófəni:z) (6th c. B.C.), Greek philosopher and poet, known for his monotheism

xen·o·phobe (zénəfoub) *n.* a person who shows xenophobia **xen·o·phó·bic** *adj.* [fr. Gk *xenos*, stranger, foreign+*phobos*, fear]

xen·o·pho·bi·a (zɛnəfóubi:ə) *n.* fear or dislike of strangers or foreigners [fr. Gk *xenos*, stranger, foreigner+*phobos*, fear]

Xen·o·phon (zénəfən, zénəfɒn) (c. 430-c. 355 B.C.), Greek general and writer. He was a disciple of Socrates, about whom he wrote the 'Memorabilia' and 'Apology'. In the 'Anabasis' he describes his part in Cyrus the Younger's expedition (401 B.C.) against Artaxerxes II and his command of the 10,000 Greek mercenaries. Exiled for 20 years from Athens for his Spartan sympathies, he wrote the 'Hellenica' (a history of Greece 411-362 B.C.), the 'Cyropaedia' (an idealized life of Cyrus the Great), and works on sport and politics

xe·ra·sia (zi:réiʒə) *n.* (*med.*) hair disease marked by dry hair and cessation of hair growth

xe·ric (zíərik) *adj.* (*bot.*, of an environment) having a low or deficient supply of moisture for plant life (cf. HYDRIC) ‖ tolerating or adapted to arid conditions [fr. Gk *xēros*, dry]

xe·rog·ra·phy (zirógrəfi:) *n.* a dry printing process in which a black mineral powder is deposited on, and adheres permanently to, those parts of a paper surface which are rendered sensitive by a photoelectric beam **xerox** *adj.* —**xerox** *n.* the copy —**xerox** *v.* to copy by xerography —Xerox trademark of the copiers of the Xerox Corporation [fr. Gk *xēros*, dry+*graphos*, written]

xe·roph·i·lous (zirófələs) *adj.* (*biol.*) adapted to or characteristic of an environment having a very limited water supply [fr. Gk *xēros*, dry+ -*philos*, loving]

xe·roph·thal·mi·a (zjərɒfθǽlmi:ə) *n.* abnormal dryness of the eyeball due to a severe deficiency of vitamin A [fr. Gk *xēros*, dry+*ophthalmia*, eye disease]

xe·ro·phyte (zíərəfait) *n.* any plant growing in desert conditions or in an alkaline, acid, salt or dry soil **xe·ro·phyt·ic** (zjərəfítik) *adj.* [fr. Gk *xēros*, dry+*phuton*, plant]

xe·ro·ra·di·og·ra·phy (zíəroureidi:ógrəfi:) *n.* 1. a process in which an electrostatic image is formed on a photoconductive medium by X-rays or gamma rays 2. variation of mammography in which a Xerox plate is used instead of film to create an image —**xeroradiogram** *n.*

xe·rox (zíərɒks) *v.t.* to reproduce by xerography [fr. *Xerox*, a trademark]

Xerx·es I (zə́:rksi:z) 'the Great' (c. 519-c. 465 B.C.), king of Persia (c. 485 -c. 465 B.C.), son of Darius I. He invaded Greece, defeating the Spartans at Thermopylae (480 B.C.), but withdrew after the destruction of his fleet at Salamis (480 B.C.)

xi (zai, ksai, ksi) *n.* the 14th letter (Ξ, ξ=x) of the Greek alphabet

Xin·gú (zingú:, ʃingú:) a river (about 1,300 miles long) in Brazil rising in the N. Mato Grosso and flowing to the Amazon delta, navigable between rapids

xiph·i·ster·num (zjfistə́:rnəm) *pl.* **xiph·i·ster·na** (zjfistə́:rnə) *n.* (*anat., zool.*) the posterior segment of the sternum [fr. Gk *xiphos*, sword+STERNUM]

xiph·oid (zífɔid) 1. *adj.* (*anat.*) sword-shaped ‖ (*anat.*) of, relating to or being the xiphisternum 2. *n.* the xiphisternum [fr. Mod. L. *xiphoides* fr. Gk]

xiphoid process the xiphisternum

xiph·o·su·ran (zjfəsúərən) *adj.* (*zool.*) belonging to the arthropod order of *Xiphosura*, which comprises the king crabs [fr. Mod. L. fr. Gk *xiphos*, sword+*oura*, tail]

CONCISE PRONUNCIATION KEY: **(a)** æ, c*a*t; ɑ, c*a*r; ɔ f*aw*n; ei, sn*a*ke. **(e)** e, h*e*n; i:, sh*ee*p; iə, d*ee*r; ɛə, b*ea*r. **(i)** i, f*i*sh; ai, t*i*ger; ə:, b*i*rd. **(o)** o, *o*x; au, c*ow*; ou, g*oa*t; u, p*oo*r; ɔi, r*oy*al. **(u)** ʌ, d*u*ck; u, b*u*ll; u:, g*oo*se; ə, b*a*cillus; ju:, c*u*be. x, lo*ch*; θ, *th*ink; ð, *b*other; z, *Z*en; ʒ, corsa*ge*; dʒ, sava*g*e; ŋ, ora*n*guta*ng*; j, *y*ak; ʃ, *fi*sh; tʃ, fe*tch*; 'l, rabb*le*; 'n, redd*en*.   Complete pronunciation key appears inside front cover.

Xmas (krísməs) *n.* Christmas [fr. X (symbol for Christ)+-*mas* fr. CHRISTMAS]

XMGM-31A *PERSHING

XM-1 *n.* (*mil.*) Chrysler-built, 60-ton, turbine-engine tank replacing M-60

X ray an electromagnetic radiation in the wavelength range 0.1–100 Å produced when the inner satellite electrons of esp. heavy atoms that have been excited by collision with a stream of fast electrons (*X-RAY TUBE) return to their ground state, giving up, in the form of X rays, the energy previously imparted to them. X rays, being of high energy, have considerable ionizing and penetrating power, and are used for the internal examination of large cast-metal parts, visual diagnosis of many organic malfunctions, analysis of crystal structure (*X-RAY DIFFRACTION), treatment (*RADIOTHERAPY) of certain diseases etc. ‖ a photograph made by exposure to X rays [trans. of G. *X-strahl,* so named because its essential nature was not known]

X-ray (éksrei) **1.** *v.t.* to examine or treat with X rays **2.** *adj.* of or pertaining to X rays

X-ray astronomy the science of astronomy carried on by analysis of X-rays emitted by celestial bodies —**X-ray astronomer** *n.*

X-ray diffraction (*phys., chem.*) a method of determining crystal structure (i.e. symmetry, bond lengths and angles) based on the principle that X rays are diffracted by many crystals whose atomic dimensions are such as to allow them to act as natural diffraction gratings. If the wavelength of the X rays is known these dimensions may be determined

X-ray diffractometer device for measuring and recording X-ray diffraction patterns in powders or crystals to analyze their structure —**X-ray defraction** *n.*

X-ray nova (*meteor.*) an exploding star that emits X-rays

X-ray pulsar (*astron.*) a pulsar that emits X-rays

X-ray scanning process for scanning a solid material with X-rays to detect flaws

X-ray star or **X-ray source** (*meteor.*) a celestial body that emits X-rays

X-ray telescope (*meteor.*) a telescope mounted on a space vehicle or rocket, used in taking X-rays

X-ray tube (*phys.*) a vacuum tube in which a metal target emits X rays when bombarded by electrons from a thermionic cathode (the electron gun). The radiation emitted is characteristic of the potential drop across the tube, the temperature of the cathode and of the target material

xy·lan (záilən) *n.* a polysaccharide found in plant cell walls, esp. in wood, straw etc. [fr. Gk *xulon,* wood]

xy·lem (záiləm, záilem) *n.* a complex lignified plant tissue, comprising the woody portion of the vascular system in higher plants. It is a mixed tissue consisting of parenchymalike and fiberlike tracheids and vessels. Xylem acts as a support, conveys water and minerals, and often stores food (cf. PHLOEM, *WOOD) [fr. Gk *xulon,* wood]

xy·lene (záili:n) *n.* any of three isomeric, colorless, liquid hydrocarbons, $C_6H_4(CH_3)_2$, found in coal and wood tar and resembling toluene [fr. Gk *xulon,* wood]

xy·lo·graph (záiləgræf, záiləgraf) *n.* a wood engraving ‖ an impression from such an engraving [back-formation fr. XYLOGRAPHY]

xy·log·ra·phy (zailógrəfi:) *n.* the art of engraving in wood or of taking impressions from wood engravings [fr. F. *xylographie*]

xy·loph·a·gous (zailófəgəs) *adj.* (*biol.,* of certain mollusks, crustaceans and insects) boring into and feeding on wood [fr. Gk *xulon,* wood+*phagein,* to eat]

xy·lo·phone (záiləfoun) *n.* a percussion instrument consisting of a series of horizontal wooden bars arranged in graded length and tuned in a chromatic scale. It is played by striking the bars with small wooden hammers **xy·loph·on·ist** (zailófənist, záiləfounist) *n.* a person who plays the xylophone [fr. Gk *xulon,* wood+*phōnē,* voice, sound]

xy·lose (záilous) *n.* (*chem.*) a polysaccharide, $C_5H_{10}O_5$, found as a constituent of xylan [fr. Gk *xulon,* wood]

xy·lot·o·mous (zailótəməs) *adj.* (*zool.,* of certain insects) able to bore into or cut wood [fr. Gk *xulon,* wood+*-tomos* fr. *temnein,* to cut]

xyst (zist) *n.* a xystus

xys·tus (zístəs) *pl.* **xys·ti** (zístai) *n.* a long, roofed colonnade used for athletic training in ancient Greece in cold or wet weather [L. fr. Gk *xustos,* smooth]

XYY syndrome *n.* (*med.*) congenital male disorder (of an extra Y chromosome), hypothesized to be a factor in causing social inadequacy, aggressive behavior, and low intelligence

XYZ Affair a Franco-U.S. incident arising (1797) in Paris during negotiations to settle a dispute stemming from French depredations on U.S. commerce. The three U.S. agents, Charles C. Pinckney, Elbridge Gerry, and John Marshall, commissioned by President John Adams, were asked by the three agents acting on behalf of France, dubbed X, Y, and Z, to make a payment as a precondition of negotiations. The U.S. ministers refused, and the commission broke up. The affair, which roused feelings of outrage in the U.S.A. against France and brought the two countries to the brink of war until France climbed down, strengthened the Federalist position

CONCISE PRONUNCIATION KEY: **(a)** æ, c*a*t; ɑ, c*a*r; ɔ f*aw*n; ei, sn*a*ke. **(e)** e, h*e*n; i:, sh*ee*p; iə, d*ee*r; ɛə, b*ea*r. **(i)** i, f*i*sh; ai, t*i*ger; əː, b*i*rd. **(o)** o, *o*x; au, c*ow*; ou, g*oa*t; u, p*oo*r; ɔi, r*oy*al. **(u)** ʌ, d*u*ck; u, b*u*ll; uː, g*oo*se; ə, b*a*cillus; juː, c*u*be. x, lo*ch*; θ, *th*ink; ð, *b*other; z, *Z*en; ʒ, corsa*g*e; dʒ, sava*g*e; ŋ, ora*ng*utan*g*; j, *y*ak; ʃ, *fi*sh; tʃ, fe*tch*; ˈl, rabb*le*; ˈn, redd*en*. Complete pronunciation key appears inside front cover.

	EARLY NORTH SEMITIC	PHOENICIAN	EARLY HEBREW (GEZER)	EARLY GREEK	CLASSICAL GREEK	ETRUSCAN		EARLY LATIN	CLASSICAL LATIN
						Early	Classical		
	ʒ	⅄	ʒʒ	l	l	l	Ɩ	lY	l Y (i)
	CURSIVE MAJUSCULE (ROMAN)	CURSIVE MINUSCULE (ROMAN)				VENETIAN MINUSCULE (ITALIC)		MODERN ROMAN	
	५	կ				y		y	

A. C. SYLVESTER, CAMBRIDGE, ENGLAND

Development of the letter Y, beginning with the early North Semitic letter. Evolution of both the majuscule, or capital, letter Y and the minuscule, or lowercase, letter y are shown.

Y, y (wai) the 25th letter of the English alphabet ‖ something shaped like a Y ‖ (*algebra*) a second unknown quantity (x being the first), or the symbol for this

-y, -ey *suffix* denoting likeness, as in 'glassy', 'clayey' ‖ denoting characteristic quality, as in 'greeny', 'juicy'

-y *suffix* denoting state or quality, as in 'jealousy'

Ya·blo·noi (jáblənɔi) (Yablonovy) a range of mountains (1,000 miles long) in S.E. Siberia, U.S.S.R., forming the Arctic-Pacific watershed. Highest peak: 8,228 ft

yacht (jɒt) **1.** *n.* any of various light, fast sailing or power-driven vessels, often luxuriously fitted, used for pleasure cruises, racing etc. **2.** *v.i.* to race or cruise in a yacht **yácht·ing** *n.* the act or sport of racing or cruising in a yacht [fr. early Mod. Du. *jaghte* fr. *jaghtschip,* fast pirate ship]

yachts·man (jɒ́tsmən) *pl.* **yachts·men** (jɒ́tsmən) *n.* someone who owns or sails a yacht

YAG (*acronym*) for yttrium aluminum garnet, used in generating laser beams. *Cf* YIG

ya·hoo (jáhu:, jəhú:) *n.* a brutish lout [coined by SWIFT in 'Gulliver's Travels' (1726)]

Yah·weh, Yah·veh, Jah·weh, Jah·veh (jáwei, jávei) *n.* God, a transliteration of the Hebrew word which in the English Bible is written 'Jehovah'

yak (jæk) *n. Poephagus grunniens* (or *Bos grunniens),* a large, long-haired ruminant sharing some characteristics of both the bison and the ox, native to the mountainous region of central Asia and domesticated in Tibet and the foothills of the Himalayas. It has cylindrical horns curving outwards, and when wild may weigh up to 1,200 lbs [Tibetan *gyag*]

Ya·kut A.S.S.R. (jəkú:t) an autonomous republic (area 1,197,760 sq. miles, pop. 152,000) in the R.S.F.S.R., U.S.S.R. (N.E. Siberia). Capital: Yakutsk

Ya·kutsk (jəkú:tsk) the capital (pop. 82,000) of the Yakut A.S.S.R., U.S.S.R., a trading center on the Lena. University

ya·ku·za (jəku:zɑ) *n.* membership in Yamaguchi, an organized criminal group (approximately 11,000 members) in Japan

Yale (jeil) Linus (1821-68), U.S. inventor of a compact pin-tumbler cylinder lock and of various improvements in lock mechanisms

Yale University a private university in New Haven, Connecticut, named after Elihu Yale (1648-1721), an early patron, and chartered in 1701. It consists of Yale College and other undergraduate schools for men and women, plus several graduate schools for men and women

Yalow (jálou), Rosalyn Sussman (1921-   ) U.S. physicist, co-winner of the Nobel prize for physiology or medicine (1977). She developed, with Solomon Berson, the radioimmunoassay (RIA) test to measure hormone, enzyme and protein amounts

Yal·ta Conference (jɔ́ltə, jɑ́ltə) a meeting (Feb. 4-11, 1945) at Yalta in the Crimea, U.S.S.R., between F. D. Roosevelt, Churchill and Stalin, at which the final defeat of Germany was planned. Germany was to be demilitarized and divided into four zones of occupation. The decision was taken to set up the U.N. and the frontiers of Poland were settled. Russian zones of influence in central and eastern Europe were established and the U.S.S.R. agreed to enter the war against Japan

Ya·lu (jálu:) a river (491 miles long, navigable for 420) flowing from S. Kirin, China (Manchuria) to the Yellow Sea, forming the border with North Korea: hydroelectricity

yam (jæm) *n.* the edible, starchy, tuberous root of certain plants of genus *Dioscorea,* fam. *Dioscoreaceae,* used as a staple food in tropical lowlands ‖ any plant of genus *Dioscorea* ‖ the sweet potato [Port. *inhame* or Span. *igname*]

Ya·ma·ga·ta (jɑmɑgɑtɑ), Prince Aritomo (1838-1922), Japanese soldier and statesman. As chief of the general staff during the Russo-Japanese War and as prime minister (1889-91 and 1898-1900) he ensured the rise of militarism in Japan

yam bean *Pachyrhizus erosus,* fam. *Papilionaceae,* a tropical perennial twining plant, cultivated for its edible turnip-like roots

yam·mer (jǽmər) **1.** *v.i.* to utter plaintive wailing or whimpering sounds ‖ to grumble and complain in a repetitious way ‖ to talk persistently and loudly **2.** *n.* a yammering sound [alteration of M.E. *yomer* fr. O.E. *geōmrian* fr. *geōmor,* sorrowful]

Ya·na·on (jænæɔ̃, janáun) (or Yanam) a port (pop. 6,000) in the Godavari delta, India. The French held it 1763-1954

Yang *YIN AND YANG

Yang·chow (jáŋtʃou) *KIANGTU

Yang·ku (jáŋký) *TAIYUAN

Yang·tze-kiang (jæŋtsi:kjǽŋ) the longest river (3,340 miles long, draining 750,000 sq. miles) and central artery of China, flowing south through gorges as deep as 13,000 ft from central Tibet to Yunnan, then north and east through the Red Basin and gorges in W. Szechwan across the central plain to a delta (where silt extends the coast by 20 yards a year) on the Pacific. It is navigable by steamer to Wuhan and by small vessels (hauled upstream at points) for half its length

Yank (jæŋk) *n.* (*pop.*) a Yankee

yank (jæŋk) **1.** *v.t.* and *v.i.* (*pop.*) to pull with a jerk **2.** *n.* (*pop.*) a sharp pull, a hard jerk [origin unknown]

Yan·kee (jǽŋki:) **1.** *n.* an inhabitant of New England ‖ a native of any of the northern states of the U.S.A. ‖ a Union soldier in the American Civil War ‖ a citizen of the U.S.A. ‖ English as spoken by U.S. citizens, esp. in New England **2.** *adj.* of or pertaining to Yankees [origin unknown]

Ya·oun·dé (jæu:ndei) the capital (pop. 450,000) of Cameroun, linked by rail with Douala

yap (jæp) **1.** *v.i. pres. part.* **yap·ping** *past* and *past part.* **yapped** to bark snappishly ‖ (*pop.*) to talk in a scolding or complaining manner ‖ (*pop.*) to chatter **2.** *n.* a sharp, shrill bark [imit.]

ya·pock, ya·pok (jəpɔ́k, jǽpək) *n. Chironectes minimus,* a small water opossum found in Central and South America, with webbed hind feet [after *Oyapok,* a river between Guiana and Brazil]

yapp (jæp) *n.* (*Br.*) divinity circuit binding [after *Yapp,* London bookseller for whom the style was first made (c. 1860)]

yar·bor·ough (járbə̩rou, járbʌrou, *Br.* esp. járbrə) *n.* (*bridge*) a hand with no card above a nine [after Charles Anderson Worsley, 2nd Earl of *Yarborough* (d. 1897), who used to offer 1,000 to 1 against such a hand occurring]

yard (jɑrd) **1.** *n.* a small open space completely or partly enclosed and adjoining a building ‖ an enclosure where a business or manufacture is carried on, *lumber yard* ‖ a space containing a complex system of railroad tracks (usually near a station) for shunting, assembling trains and parking passenger or freight cars ‖ a clearing in a forest where deer etc. gather in winter for feeding and protection **the Yard** Scotland Yard **2.** *v.t.* to confine (cattle etc.) in a yard [O.E. *geard,* enclosure]

yard *n.* (*abbr.* yd) a unit of length equal to 3 ft (36 ins) and equivalent to .9144 m. ‖ (*naut.*) a cylindrical spar tapering at the ends, slung from a mast to support and spread a sail [O.E. *gyrd,* gird, twig, stick]

yard·age (járdidʒ) *n.* the use of a yard for keeping cattle etc. at a railroad station ‖ the charge for such use [fr. YARD (small open space)]

yardage *n.* length, area or volume measured in linear, square or cubic yards [fr. YARD (unit of length)]

yard·arm (járdɑrm) *n.* (*naut.*) either half of a yard on a square-rigged vessel

yard goods piece goods (textiles sold to length, cut from the bolt)

yard·man (járdmən) *pl.* **yard·men** (járdmən) *n.* a man employed in a railroad or other yard ‖ a day laborer who does general outdoor work ‖ a

CONCISE PRONUNCIATION KEY: **(a)** æ, c*a*t; ɑ, c*ar*; ɔ f*aw*n; ei, sn*a*ke. **(e)** e, h*e*n; i:, sh*ee*p; iə, d*ee*r; ɛə, b*ea*r. **(i)** i, f*i*sh; ai, t*i*ger; ə:, b*i*rd. **(o)** o, *o*x; au, c*ow*; ou, g*oa*t; u, p*oo*r; ɔi, r*oy*al. **(u)** ʌ, d*u*ck; u, b*u*ll; u:, g*oo*se; ə, b*a*cillus; ju:, c*u*be. x, lo*ch*; θ, *th*ink; ð, bo*th*er; z, *Z*en; ʒ, cor*s*age; dʒ, sava*g*e; ŋ, ora*n*gutan*g*; j, *y*ak; ʃ, *f*ish; tʃ, fe*tch*; 'l, rabb*le*; 'n, redd*en*. Complete pronunciation key appears inside front cover.

man responsible for the building materials in a lumber yard

yard·mas·ter (jɑ́rdmæstər, jɑ́rdmɑstər) *n.* (*rail.*) a yard manager

yard sale *GARAGE SALE

yard·stick (jɑ́rdstik) *n.* a measuring stick a yard long, graduated in inches and feet ‖ a test of evaluation, standard of comparison, criterion

Yar·kand (jɑrkǽnd) (or Soche) an ancient oasis trading center (pop. 80,000) in S.W. Sinkiang-Uighur, China, in the Takla Makan: silk and wool weaving

yarn (jɑrn) **1.** *n.* any spun thread (wool, flax, silk, cotton etc.) prepared for weaving, knitting, rope making etc. ‖ a long continuous strand of glass, paper, plastic, metal etc. ‖ a long, often exaggerated tale of adventure, esp. told by a seaman or traveler **to spin a yarn** to tell a long tale of untrue adventures ‖ to make up a long rambling excuse **2.** *v.i.* to tell a yarn [O.E. *gearn*]

Ya·ro·slavl (jɑrʌslɑ́v'l) a city (pop. 608,000) in the R.S.F.S.R., U.S.S.R., on the upper Volga. Industries: textiles, engineering, chemicals. Cathedral (1215). University

yar·row (jǽrou) *n. Achillea millefolium,* fam. *Compositae,* a strong-scented perennial plant of temperate regions, with a woody stem and terminal corymbs of close, white flowers [O.E. *gearwe*]

yash·mak (jɑʃmɑ́k, jǽʃmæk) *n.* a double veil covering the face so that only the eyes are exposed, worn by some Moslem women in public [Arab. *yashmaq*]

yat·a·ghan (jǽtəgæn, jǽtəgən) *n.* a short Moslem sword with a double curved blade and no cross guard [Tui *yātāghan*]

Yates (jeits), Richard (1815-73), Civil War governor (1861-5) of Illinois. He aided the Union cause with large levies of troops and by curbing the powerful pro-Southern group in his state

yaup *YAWP

yaw (jɔ) **1.** *v.i.* (of a ship or aircraft) to go off course **2.** *n.* (of a ship or aircraft) a temporary deviation from course ‖ (of a missile) a wobble in flight [etym. doubtful]

Ya·wa·ta (jɑwɑtɑ) a port (pop. 332,000) in N. Kyushu, Japan, part of the Kita-Kyushu conurbation

yawl (jɔl) *n.* a ship's jolly boat with four or six oars ‖ a two-masted, fore-and-aft-rigged sailboat, the mizzenmast (much smaller than the mainmast) being placed far aft ‖ a fishing boat with stem and stern alike and carrying one lugsail or more [fr. M.L.G. *jolle* or Du. *jol*]

yawn (jɔn) **1.** *v.i.* to breathe in deeply, letting the mouth open wide, through sleepiness, weariness or boredom ‖ (*rhet.*) to open wide or stand wide open, *a yawning chasm* ‖ *v.t.* to say or express with a yawn, *to yawn agreement* **2.** *n.* the act or an instance of yawning ‖ (*colloq.*) a bore [O.E. *ginian, geonian*]

yawp, yaup (jɔp) **1.** *v.i.* to utter a loud, raucous cry ‖ (*pop.*) to talk continually and noisily **2.** *n.* a loud, raucous cry [imit.]

yaws (jɔz) *n.* a contagious disease common in the Tropics, caused by a spirochete and usually acquired in childhood through bodily contact. Initially characterized by chronic raspberrylike skin ulcers, it may in later years cause severe bony or facial deformity [etym. doubtful]

Yazd (jezd) *YEZD

Y chromosome *SEX CHROMOSOME

ye (ji:) *pron.* (*archaic* and *rhet.*) you (originally nominative pl., later as sing., and still later as acc. sing. and pl.) [O.E. *ge*]

ye (ji:,ði:) *def. art.* (old method of printing) the [fr. confusion between O.E. letter þ and Roman y]

yea (jei) **1.** *adv.* (*archaic* and *rhet.*) yes ‖ (*archaic* and *rhet.*) indeed ‖ (*archaic* and *rhet.*) moreover **2.** *n.* (*archaic*) an expression of assent or agreement ‖ someone who votes in the affirmative [O.E. *gēa, gē*]

year (jiər) *n.* the period of time taken by the earth to complete one orbit around the sun, 365.2425 days ‖ a period of 12 lunar months ‖ a period of 365 days (366 in a leap year) forming the basic cycle of the Gregorian calendar ‖ one identifiable unit of such a calendar sequence, *it happened in the year 1752* ‖ a period regarded as the major time unit in some way, though not corresponding with a calendar year, *the academic year ends in June* ‖ the period necessary for a planet to make one orbit around the sun ‖ a solar year ‖ a sidereal year ‖ a lunar year ‖ (*pl.*) age, *he is tall for his years* **all year round** at all times during the year [O.E. *gēar, gēr*]

year·book (jíərbuk) *n.* a book published yearly giving information (esp. statistics) covering the past year's activities, events etc.

year·ling (jíərliŋ) **1.** *n.* an animal more than one year old and less than two ‖ (*racing*) a colt which is a year old, dating from Jan. 1 of the year of foaling **2.** *adj.* a year old

year·ly (jíərli:) **1.** *adj.* occurring every year or once a year **2.** *adv.* every year or once a year

yearn (jə:rn) *v.i.* (often with 'for') to be filled with longing ‖ (often with 'over') to feel tender compassion and affection **yéarn·ing** *n.* deep longing ‖ tender compassion and affection [O.E. *giorna, geornan, giernan,* to long for]

year of grace a year of the Christian era

year-round (jíərráund) *adj.* continuing throughout the year

yeast (ji:st) *n.* a substance found on the surface of fermenting sugary liquids containing ascomycetes of fam. *Saccharomycetaceae,* that multiply by budding and cause the fermentation of sugars, with the production of alcohol and carbon dioxide. Yeast is used esp. in brewing and in bread making ‖ any of various fungi that produce alcohol and carbon dioxide from sugar **yéast·y** *adj.* of or containing yeast ‖ exuberant, *a yeasty performance* ‖ foamy ‖ frivolous, trivial [O.E. *gist*]

Yeats (jeits), William Butler (1865-1939), Irish poet. His early poems (e.g. 'The Wind among the Reeds', 1899) sprang from late 19th-c. aestheticism, and were languorous and mannered. But they were distinguished from other verse of the period by their use of Irish mythology, and this sense of belonging to the culture of his native land remained with him and was always a strength. Two tendencies can be discovered in Yeats. The first was to elaborate a private mythology based on elements of spiritualism, classical lore, astrology and Eastern philosophy: this was mainly a source of symbols for his poetry, and produced the rich, oblique, rhetorical, sounding verse e.g. of 'Byzantium'. The second was a movement toward a naked direct utterance, sinewy yet musical, with the simplicity of folk poetry. In this mode he produced some of his most moving work, helped by his own sense of involvement in the Irish nationalist cause. Yeats was also a playwright, writing some fine verse plays on Irish mythological subjects for the Abbey Theater, Dublin.

yegg (jeg) *n.* (*pop.*) a burglar, esp. a safebreaker [perh. fr. a surname]

yell (jel) **1.** *v.i.* to utter a loud, inarticulate cry or shout, esp. in expression of emotion, pain or excitement ‖ *v.t.* to utter or express with such a cry or shout **2.** *n.* an instance of yelling ‖ (*sports*) a rhythmic shout of encouragement to a competing team, consisting of a rhyme, sequence of syllables etc. [O.E. *gellan, giellan*]

yel·low (jélou) **1.** *adj.* of the color sensation stimulated by the wavelengths of light in that portion of the spectrum between orange and green, being the color of e.g. ripe lemons ‖ (of members of the Mongolian race etc.) having a skin somewhat of this color ‖ (of paper, skin etc.) changed to this color, e.g. by old age or disease ‖ (*pop.*) cowardly ‖ (of a newspaper) full of sensationalism **2.** *n.* a yellow color, pigment, fabric etc. ‖ the yolk of an egg ‖ (*pl.*) jaundice ‖ (*pl.*) any of several plant diseases characterized by yellowing of the foliage **3.** *v.t.* to make yellow ‖ *v.i.* to become yellow [O.E. *geolo, geolu*]

yel·low·bird (jéloubə:rd) *n.* any of various North American goldfinches

yellow bunting the yellowhammer

yellow-dog contract an employment agreement by which a worker forgoes membership in a labor union during the period of his contract

yellow fever an acute infectious disease esp. of tropical areas, caused by a virus communicated to man by certain mosquitoes. It is characterized by fever, low pulse rate, black vomit and jaundice, and can be fatal

yel·low·ham·mer (jélouhæmər) *n. Emberiza citrinella,* a European finch. The male has a yellow head, neck and breast

yellow jack yellow fever ‖ a flag flown at the masthead to signal quarantine ‖ *Caranx bartholomaei,* fam. *Carangidae,* a golden and silvery edible fish of Florida and the West Indies

yellow jacket any of several varieties of bright yellow social wasps

Yel·low·knife (jélounaif) a gold-mining center (pop. 9,483) in the Northwest Territories, Canada, on Great Slave Lake

yellow ocher, *Br.* **yellow ochre** a pigment compounded of limonite with clay and silica ‖ an orange-yellow color

Yellow Pages the classified telephone directory

yellow pine any of several pines of North America, incl. *Pinus echinata, P. rigida* and the loblolly pine ‖ their wood

yellow rattle *Rhinanthus crista-galli,* fam. *Scrophulariaceae,* an annual plant of temperate regions. It is semiparasitic on grasses, bears yellow flowers, and has seed capsules in which winged seeds rattle when they are ripe

Yellow River *HWANG-HO

Yellow Sea (*Chin.* Hwang-hai) a gulf of the Pacific between China and Korea, so named because of the sediment brought to it by the Yangtze-kiang and Hwang-ho

yellow spot a yellowish area near the center of the retina, constituting the region where the vision is most perfect

Yel·low·stone (jéloustoun) a national park (area 3,458 sq. miles) in Wyoming, Montana and Idaho, in the Rockies, incl. peaks to 12,073 ft, and a celebrated volcanic region (geysers, hot springs)

Yellowstone a river (671 miles long) rising in Wyoming, flowing through Yellowstone National Park, crossing the Montana border and emptying into the Missouri River on the Montana-North Dakota boundary. Its valley is the spectacular Grand Canyon of the Yellowstone (2,000 ft wide, 1,200 ft deep)

yellow warbler *Dendroica petechia,* a small North American warbler. The male is bright yellow, streaked with brown underneath

yelp (jelp) **1.** *v.i.* (esp. of a dog in fear, pain or great excitement) to make a sharp, high-pitched cry, or a series of such cries ‖ *v.t.* to utter with such a cry **2.** *n.* such a cry [O.E. *gielpan,* to boast]

Yem·en (jémən) a republic (area 75,000 sq. miles, pop. 7,161,800) in S.W. Arabia. Capital: San'a. People: Arab, with Somali and other African admixture on the coast. Language: Arabic. Religion: Moslem. Behind the hot, humid coastal plain (Tihama) the land is mountainous, rising to a crest (highest point 12,336 ft) in the center, then sloping eastward to the Great Sandy Desert. The central plateau is the most fertile part of Arabia, supporting a large peasantry. Average temperatures (F.) in Jan. and July: coast 60° and 80°, central plateau 50° and 60°. Rainfall: coast under 5 ins, plateau 12 ins. Livestock: sheep, goats, cattle, mules, horses, donkeys, camels. Agricultural products: millet, wheat, other cereals, mocha coffee, qat, indigo, sesame, rice, cotton, grapes, dates, almonds, citrus and other fruit, tobacco. Mineral resources: salt. Exports: coffee, hides and skins, salt, qat. Chief port: Hodeida. Monetary unit: riyal. HISTORY. (For early history *ARABIA). Yemen was converted to Islam (628) and was part of the Ottoman Empire (mid-16th.– mid-17th cc. and 1849-1918). Despite a treaty (1934) to settle the frontier with Aden Protectorate, border disputes continued. Yemen joined the Arab League (1945) and the U.N. (1947) and united in a Federal Union with the United Arab Republic (1958-61). The imam was overthrown (1962) and a republic was proclaimed. Fighting continued between republican tribes supported by the United Arab Republic and royalist tribes supported by Saudi Arabia. In support of its claim to sovereignty over the whole of southern Arabia, Yemen continued to attack the Federation of South Arabia and to incite subversion within it (1960s). A military coup d'état took place (Nov. 1967). An end to hostilities was negotiated (1970), the imam remaining in exile, but the constitution promulgated that same year was abrogated (1974) after a successful military coup led by Ibrahim al-Hamdi. Hamdi was assassinated (1977), as was his successor, but the country remained under military rule. Members of the Arab League began negotiations (1979) toward the eventual unification of the country with Yemen (Aden)

Yemen, People's Democratic Republic of (formerly People's Republic of South Yemen) a republic (area c. 60,000 sq. miles, pop. 1,998,000, *ARABIA) of S. Arabia, composing the former states making up the Federation of S. Arabia until independence (Nov. 1967): Aden, Audhali, Fadhli, Lahej, Lower Aulagi, Lower

Yafa'i, Wahidi, Beihan, Dhala, Aqrabi, Upper Aulaqi, Dathina, Haushabi, Sha'ib, Maflahi, Alawi together with the nonfederated states that were included in Aden Protectorate: Upper Yafai, Mausatta, Dhubi, Maflahi, Hadhrami, Quteibi, Alawi, Upper Aulaqi Sheikhdom, Quaiti, Kathiri, Mahri Sultanate of Quishn and Socotra, Birati, Mukalla. It also includes Perim and Kamaran, and claims the Kuria Muria Is. Capital: Aden. Products: subsistence crops, cotton, hides, skins, fish. The Minaean (1200-650 B.C.), Sabaean (930-115 B.C.) and Himyarite (115 B.C.–525 A.D.) civilizations dominated the area, which converted to Mohammedanism (mid-7th c.). Its trading and strategic potentialities were disputed by various European powers (16th-18th cc.). Local rulers entered into treaty relations with Britain (1839-1914). The Federation of South Arabia of six states was formed (1959) and extended (1959-63). Independence was achieved in Nov. 1967, and the name People's Republic of South Yemen was adopted. In 1970 the name was changed to People's Democratic Republic of Yemen. A 20-year treaty of friendship was signed (1979) with the U.S.S.R. Efforts to unite the two Yemens resulted in the drafting of a constitution for a unified state (1980) but relations remained tense, albeit slightly improved, between them

Yem·en·ite (jémənait) **1.** *n.* a native of Yemen **2.** *adj.* relating to Yemen or its inhabitants

yen (jen) *n.* (*pop.*) a persistent desire, *a yen to visit the East* [Chin.=opium]

yen *n.* the principal monetary unit of Japan, subdivided into 100 sen ‖ a coin or note representing this value [Jap. fr. Chin. *yüan*, round, dollar]

Ye·nan (jénán) (or Fushih) a town (pop. 50,000) in N. Shensi, China. It was the de facto political and military Communist capital (1935-47)

Ye·nan·gyaung (jénándʒáuŋ) an oil-field center (pop. 11,000) on the Irawaddy in central Burma

yen bond (*securities*) a bond payable in Japanese yen

Ye·ni·sei (jeniséi) a river in central Siberia, U.S.S.R., rising near the Mongolian border and flowing 2,500 miles to the Arctic Ocean: hydroelectricity (Krasnoyarsk)

yen·ta (jéntə) *n.* (*Yiddish*) a gossiping busybody, esp. a woman

Yen·tai (jéntái) *CHEFOO

yeo·man (jóumən) *pl.* **yeo·men** (jóumən) *n.* a farmer who owns the freehold of his land ‖ (*hist.*) a freeholder of land above a certain value, entitled to serve on a jury and to rank next below an esquire when attached to a noble or royal family ‖ (*U.S. Navy*) a petty officer who does clerical work ‖ (*hist.*) a member of the yeomanry [M.E. *yeman, yoman* prob. shortened fr. *yongman*, young man]

yeoman of the guard (*Br.*) one of a bodyguard of 100 men, formed in 1485, allocated various duties attached to the sovereign

yeo·man·ry (jóumənri:) *n.* (*Br. hist.*) a volunteer mounted armed force, formed in 1761 for home defense and absorbed (1907) in the Territorial Force ‖ yeomen collectively

yeoman service effective hard work contributed just when wanted or steadily over a period

yer·ba ma·té (jérbəmátei, jə́:rbəmátei) *MATÉ

Yerevan *EREVAN

yes (jes) **1.** *adv.* used to express agreement, consent, affirmation (opp. NO) ‖ used to express interest and as an invitation to say more **2.** *pl.* **yes·es, yes·ses** *n.* an act or instance of expressing agreement, consent or affirmation, esp. by saying 'yes' ‖ an affirmative reply or vote [O.E. *gēse, gīse*]

ye·shi·va (jeʃí:və) *n.* a school for Talmudic study ‖ a Jewish day school which offers both secular and religious education [Heb.]

yes-man (jésmæn) *pl.* **yes-men** (jésmen) *n.* a subordinate who always agrees with his superior and expresses no opinions of his own, esp. as a method of self-advancement

yes·ter·day (jéstərdei, jéstərdi:) **1.** *n.* the day which preceded today ‖ (*rhet.*) recent time **2.** *adv.* on or during yesterday ‖ (*rhet.*) at or during a recent time [O.E. *geostrandæg* fr. *geostran*, yesterday+*dæg*, day]

yes·ter·year (jéstərjiər) *n.* (*rhet.*) last year ‖ (*rhet.*) time not long ago [coined by D. G. ROSSETTI]

yet (jet) **1.** *adv.* up to and including the present time, *I have not seen him yet* ‖ as early as now, *don't go yet* ‖ at that time, *he was not yet mayor* ‖ at some future time, *we shall see him elected yet* ‖ before a specified time, *no one had yet been there until that voyage* ‖ still at present, *we must push on while there is yet light* ‖ in addition, *some want to go, some are willing to go, yet others prefer to stay* ‖ (with comparatives or after 'nor') even, *yet more important, it will not be finished next week, nor yet next year* **2.** *conj.* nevertheless, *he is rich, yet he is content* [O.E. *gīet, gīeta*]

yet·i (jéti:) *n.* the abominable snowman [Tibetan]

yew (ju:) *n.* any of several evergreen, coniferous shrubs or trees of genus *Taxus*, fam. *Taxaceae*, of the north temperate zone, esp. *T. baccata* of Europe and Asia. It grows slowly and lives long, having a massive reddish-brown trunk, dark green lustrous needles and a scarlet aril enclosing the fruit. Yews are often a symbol of mourning ‖ the wood of a yew, used for making bows and for veneers [O.E. *īw, ēow*]

yé-yé (jéijéi:) *n.* the French mod style in music and fashion, prominent in the 1960s —**yé-yé** *adj.*

Yezd (jezd) (or Yazd) a commercial center (pop. 135,978) in central Iran. Industries: cotton spinning, handicrafts (silk, wool, copperwork). It is a holy city for Zoroastrians

Yez·i·di (jézidi:) *n.* a member of a religious sect of Iraq and Syria of unknown origin. The religion is syncretistic and postulates belief in a Satan who, though formerly the author of evil, is now good and is the chief of the angelic hosts [origin unknown]

Ygg·dra·sil, Ygg·dra·sill (ígdrəsil) (*Norse mythol.*) a great ash tree binding together earth, heaven and hell with its roots and branches [O.N. fr. *Yggr*, Odin+*drasill*, horse]

Yid·dish (jídiʃ) **1.** *n.* a language, with origins perhaps as early as the 9th c., developed from the Middle High German (c. A.D. 1200–1350) spoken by Jews in Germany. In this were incorporated Hebrew words for religious customs, duties etc. Yiddish is written in the Hebrew alphabet, and shows a strong Slavic influence. As Jews migrated east and west it became the normal Jewish vernacular in Europe and America and the medium for a rich literature, still vigorous **2.** *adj.* of or in this language [fr. G. *jüdisch*, Jewish]

yield (ji:ld) **1.** *v.t.* to have as a product or result, *these trees will yield good lumber* ‖ to bring in as profit, interest, income etc., *an investment yielding 10%* ‖ to surrender (something), give (something) up, *to yield ground to one's opponents* ‖ to relinquish (the floor) to another speaker in a legislative assembly ‖ *v.i.* to be fruitful or profitable, *these fruit trees yield well* ‖ to admit the superiority of another, or admit defeat ‖ to give way to entreaty, pressure, argument etc. **to yield to no one in** to have as much of (a quality) as anyone else **2.** *n.* a yielding ‖ the amount yielded **yíeld·ing** *adj.* giving in or giving way to superior force ‖ readily submitting to another ‖ flexible, not rigid [O.E. *gieldan, geldan*, to pay]

yield point the point at which a body loses its elasticity so that deformation continues even though the body is not subjected to additional stress

YIG (*acronym*) for yttrium iron garnet, a synthetic iron-oxide crystal used in laser modulation as a sonic wave tuning filter. *Cf* YAG

Yin and Yang (jin, jæŋ) two forces through whose essences, according to Taoist cosmology, the universe was produced and cosmic harmony is maintained. Yin is dark, female and negative, and Yang is light, male and positive

Yip·pie (jípi:) *n.* a politically active radical group of hippies, from a member of the Youth International Party, prominent at Democratic Party National Convention in 1968

ylang-ylang *ILANG-ILANG

Y.M.C.A. *YOUNG MEN'S CHRISTIAN ASSOCIATION

yo·del (jóud'l) **1.** *v. pres. part.* **yo·del·ing,** esp. *Br.* **yo·del·ling** *past* and *past part.* **yo·deled,** esp. *Br.* **yo·delled** *v.i.* and *t.* to call or sing with repeated transitions to the falsetto (a custom of Swiss and Tyrolese mountaineers) **2.** *n.* a yodeled call or musical phrase or song **yó·del·er,** esp. *Br.* **yó·del·ler** *n.* [G. *jodeln*]

yo·ga (jóugə) *n.* a system of discipline and meditation widely practiced within Hinduism. The classic exposition is associated with the Sankhya school of philosophy, which maintains that enmeshed within the human organism is an eternally existent soul, and that complete control of the body can render the soul free from physical interference. The use of yoga is also advocated by the monistic schools within Hinduism, as a means towards attaining enlightenment. The eight steps of yoga fall into three main groups (cf. the Noble Eightfold Path of Buddhism): (1) moral disciplines (against killing, lying, stealing, sexual impurity and possessiveness, and towards purity, contentment, austerity, study and God-centeredness) (2) physical disciplines (control over bodily posture, breathing and excitation of the senses) (3) stages of meditation (concentration, contemplation and ecstasy) [Hind., Skr.=union]

yogh (jouk, joux, joug) *n.* a Middle English symbol (ʒ) denoting a voiceless fricative or guttural, or a voiced palatal fricative [M.E., etym. doubtful]

yo·gi (jóugi:) *n.* someone who practices yoga [Hind. *yogī*]

yo·gurt, yo·ghurt, yo·ghourt (jóugərt) *n.* a milk product prepared by partial evaporation and then fermentation by the bacteria *Lactobacillus acidophilus* and *Streptococcus thermophilus* [Turk. *yoghurt*]

yoke (jouk) **1.** *n.* a wooden frame fitted across the necks of two oxen or other draft animals, for joining them together as they pull a plow or vehicle ‖ a pair of oxen so linked together ‖ a wooden bar shaped so that it rests across a person's shoulders for carrying balanced loads suspended at each end ‖ a crossbar, e.g. one from which a bell swings, or one by which a rudder is turned ‖ a coupling for pipes or for parts of a machine ‖ a shaped part of a garment at the shoulders or hips, to which gathered or pleated parts are sewn ‖ (*fig.*) a bond. esp. of marriage ‖ (*hist.*) an arch of spears under which the Romans made their beaten enemies pass in sign of submission **2.** *v.t. pres. part.* **yok·ing** *past* and *past part.* **yoked** to put under a yoke, join by a yoke ‖ to attach (e.g. an ox) to a cart etc. ‖ (*fig.*) to unite [O.E. *geoc*]

yo·kel (jóuk'l) *n.* a man from the country, esp. an old-fashioned one, as spoken of condescendingly by someone from a big city [etym. doubtful]

Yok·kai·chi (jɔkkaitʃi:) a port (pop. 200,000) in E. Honshu, Japan: textiles, rubber, porcelain

Yo·ko·ha·ma (joukəhámə) the chief seaport (pop. 2,694,600) of Japan, adjoining Tokyo. Industries: steel, automobiles, oil refining, chemicals, shipyards, mechanical engineering. Destroyed (1923) by earthquake, it was rebuilt in Western style

Yo·ko·su·ka (jɔkɔsuka, jəkɔ́skə, joukəsú:kə) a port and naval base (pop. 421,000) in Honshu, Japan, at the entrance to Tokyo Bay

yolk (jouk) *n.* the yellow central part of the egg of a bird or reptile, containing proteins and serving as food for the developing embryo ‖ the material in any animal ovum that supplies food to the embryo [O.E. *geolca*, yellow part]

yolk *n.* an oily secretion found in the fleece of sheep [supposed O.E. *eowoca*]

yolk gland a gland (well developed in reptiles and birds) in connection with the reproductive system by which the ovum is furnished with a supply of food material

yolk·y (jóuki:) *adj.* of, like or containing egg yolk

Yom Kip·pur (jɔmkípər) *n.* the annual day of fasting and repentance ordained in the Mosaic Law and observed by Jews on the 10th day of Tishri (cf. JEWISH CALENDAR) [Heb. *yōm kippūr* fr. *yōm*, day+*kippūr*, atonement]

Yom Kippur War war initiated against Israel on Yom Kippur, October 6, 1973, by Egypt and Syria, and ended by the United Nations on October 24, 1973

yon (jɒn) *adj.* (*archaic* and *rhet.*) yonder [O.E. *geon*]

yon·der (jɒ́ndər) **1.** *adj.* (*old-fash.*) at a distance but visible, *yonder church tower* ‖ (*old-fash.*) more distant (opp. HITHER) **2.** *adv.* (*old-fash.*) at a somewhat distant yet visible place [M.E. *yonder, yender* fr. *yon*, yonder]

yo·ni (jóuni:) *n.* a symbol of the female genitals, venerated in Hindu worship [Skr.]

Yon·kers (jɒ́ŋkərz) a city and residential suburb (pop. 195,351) of New York City in S.E. New York

Yonne (jɔn) a department (area 2,892 sq. miles, pop. 313,800) in N.E. central France (*BURGUNDY, *ORLÉANAIS). Chief town: Auxerre

yore (jɔr, jour) *n.* (only in the archaic phrase) **of yore** long ago, in former years [O.E. *geāra, geāre, geāro*]

CONCISE PRONUNCIATION KEY: **(a)** æ, *cat*; ɑ, *car*; ɔ *fawn*; ei, *snake*. **(e)** e, *hen*; i:, *sheep*; iə, *deer*; εə, *bear*. **(i)** i, *fish*; ai, *tiger*; ə:, *bird*. **(o)** o, *ox*; au, *cow*; ou, *goat*; u, *poor*; ɔi, *royal*. **(u)** ʌ, *duck*; u, *bull*; u:, *goose*; ə, *bacillus*; ju:, *cube*. x, *loch*; θ, *think*; ð, *bother*; z, *Zen*; ʒ, *corsage*; dʒ, *savage*; ŋ, *orangutang*; j, *yak*; ʃ, *fish*; tʃ, *fetch*; 'l, *rabble*; 'n, *redden*. Complete pronunciation key appears inside front cover.

Yo·ri·to·mo Mi·na·mo·to (jɔri:tɔmɔmi:nɑmɔtɔ) (c. 1147-99), Japanese soldier and the first shogun (1192-9). As a leader of the Minamoto clan, he defeated the rival Taira clan (1185) and established a centralized government at Kamakura

York (jɔrk), Edmund of Langley, duke of (1341-1402), son of Edward III of England. The title 'duke of York' was created to reward him for supporting Richard II against the Scots (1385)

York, Richard, duke of (1411-60), great-grandson of Edward III of England. He attempted unsuccessfully to claim the English throne during the Wars of the Roses, in the course of which he was killed. His son seized the throne as Edward IV

York the county town (pop. 100,000) of Yorkshire, England, a county borough. Industries: metalworking, railroad stock, chocolate. Gothic cathedral (12th-15th cc.), guildhall (15th c.), city walls (14th c.), castle (12th c.). University (1963). York was the military capital of Roman Britain, was the capital of Northumbria, and became the seat of an archbishop

York an English royal dynasty (1461-85) whose reigning members were Edward IV, Edward V and Richard III. Their rivalry with the house of Lancaster resulted in the Wars of the Roses (1455-85), and ended when the Lancastrian Henry VII united the two houses by marrying (1486) Elizabeth, daughter of Edward IV

york·er (jɔ́rkər) *n.* (*cricket*) a ball which pitches immediately in front of the batsman's bat [etym. doubtful]

York·ist (jɔ́rkist) *n.* (*hist.*) a descendant of Edmund of Langley, duke of York ‖ a member or adherent of the house of York in the Wars of the Roses

York·shire (jɔ́rkʃər) (*abbr.* Yorks.) former county (area 6,089 sq. miles) in N. England. It was divided (1974) into three counties: North, West and South Yorkshire

Yorkshire pudding a thin batter of plain flour, milk, water and salt, baked in an oven in meat dripping and eaten with roast beef

Yorkshire terrier a toy terrier of a shaggy variety, with long, silky, steel-blue or tan hair

York·town (jɔ́rktɑun) a village (pop. 400) in S.E. Virginia, center of a national historical park. It was the scene of the surrender (1781) of the British forces under Cornwallis at the end of the Revolutionary War

Yo·ru·ba (jɔ́rubə, jóurubə) *pl.* **Yo·ru·ba, Yo·ru·bas** *n.* a member of a people of S.W. Nigeria, S. Togo and S.E. Dahomey numbering 5 million. Their historic kingdom dominated W. Africa until the 18th c. ‖ this people ‖ their language

Yo·sem·i·te Valley (jousémiti:) a famous valley (6 miles long, height 3,000–4,000 ft, floor c. 4,000 ft above sea level) in central California, in Yosemite National Park (area 1,182 sq. miles). It has spectacular U-shaped canyons with imposing summits

Yo·shi·da (jóuʃi:dɑ), Shigeru (1878-1967), Japanese political leader and prime minister (1946-7, 1948-54)

you (ju:) *pron., 2nd person sing.* and *pl., nominative* and *objective cases* the person or persons to whom one is speaking, *you are my friends, I overheard you* ‖ (in generalizing) a person, one, *you never know what may happen* [O.E. *ēow*]

you'd (ju:d) *contr.* of YOU HAD, YOU WOULD

you'll (ju:l) *contr.* of YOU WILL, YOU SHALL

Young (jʌŋ), Arthur (1741-1820), British agricultural writer. His 'Travels in France during the years 1787-90' (1792) is a classic description of social and economic conditions in France on the eve of the French Revolution

Young, Brigham (1801-77), American Mormon leader. He led the westward migration of Mormons to Utah and founded Salt Lake City (1847)

Young, Edward (1683-1765), English poet. His 'Night Thoughts' ('The Complaint: or Night-thoughts', 1742-5) initiated the romantic taste for reflections on mortality

Young, Thomas (1773-1829), English physicist and doctor of medicine, whose experimental work on optical interference lent support to the wave theory of light. He put forward a theory of color vision, and independently of Champollion deciphered Egyptian hieroglyphics (*ROSETTA STONE)

Young, Whitney M., Jr. (1921-71) U.S. social worker, executive director (1961-71) of the National Urban League

young (jʌŋ) **1.** *adj.* in the early stages of development, *a young child, a young country* ‖ not far advanced, *the night is still young* ‖ less advanced in years than another, *young Mr. Brown* (distinguishing him from his father) ‖ having the vigor, resilience etc. associated with those who are young, *he is young for his years* **2.** *n.* offspring **the young** young people **with young** (of an animal) pregnant [O.E. *geong*]

young·ber·ry (jʌ́ŋberi:) *pl.* **young·ber·ries** *n.* a large, sweet, reddish-black berry which is the fruit of a hybrid between the blackberry and the dewberry, grown in the U.S.A. ‖ the bramble which yields it [after B. M. *Young,* U.S. fruit grower, who produced it (c. 1900)]

Young England *DISRAELI

young fustic the yellow dyewood of *Cotinus coggygria,* fam. *Anacardiaceae,* a European shrub yielding a substitute for fustic

Young Italy *MAZZINI

Young Men's Christian Association (Y.M.C.A.) an organization founded (1844) in London by Sir George Williams and others. Christian but nondoctrinal, nonsectarian and nonpolitical, it evolved (1855) into an international organization, the World Alliance of Y.M.C.A.s, with its headquarters at Geneva. The first Y.M.C.A. club in the Western Hemisphere was founded in Montreal, the second in Boston

Young Pretender *STUART, Charles Edward

Young's modulus (*phys.*) the constant ratio, for a given elastic substance, of the applied longitudinal stress to the change in length of unit length (symbol E)

young·ster (jʌ́ŋstər) *n.* a child or adolescent

Youngs·town (jʌ́ŋztɑun) an industrial center (pop. 115,436) in N.E. Ohio: iron and steel, chemical industries, rubber, bricks

Young Turk a member of a reform movement within the Ottoman Empire (early 20th c.). The movement organized the revolt (1908) which deposed Abdul Hamid II (1909)

Young Women's Christian Association (Y.W.C.A.) an organization originated (1855-77) in England by Emma Robarts and Lady Kinnaird as a response to the ill-effects of the Industrial Revolution on the lives of young women, esp. in cities

your (juər, jɔr, jour, *unstressed* jər) *poss. pronominal adj.* of or belonging to you, *your father* ‖ used preceding certain titles in addressing the holder of the title, *Your Majesty, Your Worship* [O.E. *ēower*]

you're (juər) *contr.* of YOU ARE

yours (juərz, jɔrz, jourz) *possessive pron.* that or those belonging to you, *this book is yours*

your·self (juərsélf, jɔrsélf, joursélf, jərsélf) *pl.* **your·selves** *pron.* refl. form of YOU, *you hurt yourself* ‖ emphatic form of YOU, *you do it yourself* [M.E. *your selfe, your selven*]

youth (ju:θ) *pl.* **youths** (ju:ðz, ju:θs) *n.* the state or quality of being young ‖ the period from childhood to maturity ‖ a young man ‖ young people of both sexes ‖ an early stage of development [O.E. *geoguth*]

youth culture contemporary norms and lifestyle (dress, language, music) of young people. *Cf* COUNTER CULTURE

youth·ful (jú:θfəl) *adj.* of, pertaining to or befitting youth, *youthful fashions* ‖ young ‖ (*geol.*) of a land surface which has not yet suffered much erosion

youth hostel a building providing cheap overnight accommodation and often food for young travelers

youth·quake (jú:θkweik) *n.* major change brought about by the action of young people, e.g., China's Cultural Revolution

you've (ju:v) *contr.* of YOU HAVE

yowl (jaul) **1.** *v.i.* (esp. of an animal) to utter a long, loud, sad cry **2.** *n.* this cry [M.E. *yoyele, youle*]

yo-yo (jóujou) *pl.* **yo-yos, yo-yoes** *n.* a toy consisting of a double wooden disk, deeply grooved, which can be made to rise and fall on a string attached to its center and running in the groove ‖ (*slang*) a foolish person [fr. *Yo-Yo,* trademark]

Y·pi·ran·ga (i:pi:rĕŋgə) a river in Brazil, in the state of São Paolo. On its banks the regent Pedro uttered (Sept. 7, 1822) the 'cry of Ypiranga', proclaiming the independence of Brazil from Portugal

Y·po·á, Lake (i:pɔ́ɑ) a lake (area c. 100 sq. miles) in S. Paraguay, navigable for small boats

Y·pres (i:pr) (*Flem.* Ieper) a town (pop. 34.400) in West Flanders, Belgium. Gothic cloth market (13th-14th cc.), cathedral (12th-15th cc.)

Ypres, Battle of a battle (Oct. 14–Nov. 13, 1914) of the lst world war, ending in stalemate between the Germans and the Allies ‖ a battle (Apr. 22–May 2, 1915) of the 1st world war, in which an Allied advance was halted by the Germans, who used poison gas for the first time ‖ a battle (June 7–Nov. 6, 1917), also known as the Battle of Passchendaele, during the 1st world war, in which a British advance was achieved at a cost of 400,000 lives

Yp·si·lan·ti (ipsəlǽnti:), Alexander (1792-1828), Greek soldier and patriot. His revolt (1821) against the Turks in Moldavia marked the beginning of the Greek War of Independence

Ypsilanti, Demetrios (1793-1832), Greek soldier and patriot. The brother of Alexander, he played a prominent part in the Greek War of Independence

Y·ri·goy·en (i:ri:gɔ́ien), Hipólito (1852-1933), Argentinian politician, leader of the Radicals (a reform group opposing conservative rule), and president of the Republic (1916-22, 1928-30). He was overthrown in a coup led by Gen. José F. Uriburu

yt·ter·bic (itɔ́:rbik) *adj.* of or containing ytterbium

yt·ter·bi·um (itɔ́:rbi:əm) *n.* a rare-earth element (symbol Yb, at. no. 70, at. mass 173.04) [Mod. L. after *Ytterby,* Sweden]

yt·tri·a (ítri:ə) *n.* yttrium oxide, Y_2O_3 [Mod. L. after *Ytterby,* Sweden]

yt·tri·um (ítri:əm) *n.* a metallic element usually classed with the rare-earth metals (symbol Y, at. no. 39, at. mass 88.905) [Mod. L. fr. YTTRIA]

Yu·an (jyɑn) a Mongolian dynasty founded by Kublai Khan, which ruled China 1279-1368

yu·an (jyɑn) *n.* the former monetary unit of China (1914–49) ‖ the basic monetary unit of Taiwan ‖ a coin or note representing either of these

Yüan Shih-kai (jyɑ́nʃí:kái) (1859-1916), Chinese soldier and statesman, president of the Chinese republic (1912-16). He tried unsuccessfully to have himself proclaimed emperor

Yu·ca·tán (ju:kətǽn, ju:kɑtɑ́n) a low-lying peninsula (area 55,400 sq. miles), covered with rain forest, separating the Gulf of Mexico from the Caribbean. It comprises parts of Mexico, British Honduras and Guatemala. The northern half is one of the most important henequen-raising regions in the world. The forests yield mahogany and other cabinet woods, vanilla, rubber, logwood and dyewood. The area was the center of Mayan civilization (100 B.C.–1200 A.D.) and of the Toltecs (1200-1450). Sites of magnificent ruins include Chichén Itzá

Yucatán a state (area 14,868 sq. miles, pop. 926,000) in Mexico, in the north of the Yucatán peninsula. Manufactures include rope, cordage, and coarse fabrics for sacking. Capital: Mérida (pop. 100,000), a commercial center and the center of the Yucatán henequen industry. It is also a tourist base for visiting many Mayan ruins

Yucatán Channel a strait (135 miles wide) between the west end of Cuba and the Yucatán peninsula, Mexico, connecting the Gulf of Mexico and the Caribbean Sea

yuc·ca (jʌ́kə) *n.* a member of *Yucca,* fam. *Liliaceae,* a genus of American plants with thin, rigid, lance-shaped leaves and a panicle of large white or violet flowers borne on an erect undivided stem. Fiber is extracted from the species grown in Mexico esp. from *Y. baccata* ‖ the flower of any of these plants [of Carib. origin]

Yu·go·sla·vi·a, Ju·go·sla·vi·a (ju:gouslɑ́vi:ə) a socialist federal republic (area 98,725 sq. miles, pop. 22,738,000) in S.E. Europe. Capital: Belgrade. Federated nationalities: Serbs (42%), Croats (23%), Slovenes (9%), Macedonians (5%), Montenegrins (3%). Other peoples: Albanians (4%), Magyars (3%), Turks (2%), small Bulgar, Czech, Slovak, Italian, Rumanian and other minorities. Language: Serbo-Croatian, Slovene and Macedonian dialects. Religion: 41% Orthodox, 32% Roman Catholic, 12% Moslem, 1% Protestant. The land is 33% arable, 26% pasture and 34% forest (esp. oak, fir, beech). Except for the fertile Danube-Sava basin in the northeast (Serbia), where population is concentrated, the country is rugged and mountainous. The Julian Alps (Triglav, 9,400 ft) and Karawanken Alps cross the north, the Dinaric Alps (5,900 ft north of Rijeka) run along the west coast. The mountains in the interior rise to 8,800 ft near Skopje. Average temperatures (F.) in Belgrade: Jan. 32°, July 71°. Rainfall: south coast and center 60-85 ins, north coast and east 20-40 ins. Livestock: cattle, horses, sheep, hogs, goats, donkeys. Agricultural products: corn, wheat, barley, rye, sugar beets, tobacco, hemp, hay, sunflowers, potatoes, dairy products, apples, plums, pears, grapes, olives, walnuts. Mineral resources: coal, iron ore, copper, lead, bauxite, petroleum, zinc, gold, chrome, antimony, lignite, mercury, salt, manganese, barite, natural gas, magnesite, silver. Industries: iron and steel, oil refining, aluminum, mechanical engineering, heavy machinery, textiles, fertilizers, sulfuric acid, cement, sugar, wine, tourism, fishing, hydroelectricity, ships, paper, pulp, leather, bricks, tiles, soap. Exports: bauxite, lumber, pulp, cement, cattle, meat, lead, zinc, vegetables, fruit, tobacco, wine. Imports: machinery, vehicles, metals, coal, wheat, oil, fertilizers, textiles, chemicals, iron and steel, foodstuffs. Chief ports: Rijeka, Split, Dubrovnik, and Zadar on the Adriatic, Novi Sad and Belgrade on the Danube. Universities: Belgrade, Ljubljana, Sarajevo, Skopje, Zagreb. Monetary unit: dinar (100 paras). HISTORY. Yugoslavia was the name given (1929) to the kingdom formed (1918) by the union of Serbia, Bosnia-Herzegovina, Croatia, Macedonia, Montenegro and Slovenia. Such a union had been urged in the late 19th c. by the supporters of Pan-Slavism, and became possible when AustriaHungary collapsed in the 1st world war. Alexander I, as regent (1918-21) and king (1921-34), failed to reconcile the various nationalities and was assassinated by Croat nationalists. The regency in the name of Peter II followed an increasingly pro-Axis policy until overthrown (1941) in a coup d'état. Yugoslavia was occupied 10 days later by the Germans. Among several guerrilla resistance groups, a Communist group led by Tito received Allied support and controlled most of the country by the end of the 2nd world war. Yugoslavia was proclaimed a federal people's republic (1945) with Tito as head of state, and all means of production and natural resources were nationalized. It was a leading member of the Cominform until 1948, when it broke off relations with the U.S.S.R. Yugoslavia thereafter adopted an independent communist policy. The government was decentralized and collectivization of industry and agriculture was reduced. Yugoslavia's dispute with Italy over Trieste was settled (1954). Normal relations with the U.S.S.R. were resumed after 1955. The country was proclaimed a socialist federal republic (1963). The presidency became (1971) a collective presidency, with Tito at its head. After Tito's death (1980) his policies of nonalignment and decentralized economic management were continued. An austerity program was begun to reduce inflation and the country's large foreign debt

Yu·go·slav, Ju·go·slav (ju:gousláv, ju:gouslǽv) **1.** *n.* a native or inhabitant of Yugoslavia **2.** *adj.* of Yugoslavia or its people

Yu·go·sla·vi·an, Ju·go·sla·vi·an (ju:gouslávi:ən) *n.* and *adj.* Yugoslav

Yu·go·sla·vic, Ju·go·sla·vic (ju:gouslávik, ju:gouslǽvik) *adj.* Yugoslav

Yu·ka·wa (ju:kɑwɑ), Hideki (1907-81), Japanese physicist. His theory of nuclear forces postulated (1935) the existence of mesons two years before they were first observed. Nobel prize (1949)

Yu·kon (jú:kɒn) a territory (area 207,076 sq. miles, pop. 21,600) in extreme N.W. Canada. Capital: Whitehorse (pop. 16,771). It is mountainous with a broad central plateau, mainly forest (unexploited) and grassland, with tundra in the north. Highest peak: Mt Logan (19,850 ft). Occupations: mining (silver, lead, zinc, gold), trapping. The Alaska Highway crosses the southwest. The Yukon became famous with the discovery (1896) of gold in the Klondike River area, and was constituted a Canadian territory (1898)

Yukon a river (2,000 miles long) flowing from the N.W. Yukon across Alaska to the Bering Sea

yule (ju:l) *n.* the festival or season of Christmas [O.E. *geól, geóla*]

yule log a large log burned traditionally on an open fire on Christmas Eve

yule·tide (jú:ltaid) *n.* the Christmas season

Yun·gay (ju:ngái) a department and town (pop. 50,000) of Nuble province in central Chile, site of the victory (1839) of the Chileans under Manuel Bulnes over a Peru-Bolivian invasion force under Gen. Santa Cruz

Yung·ki (júŋkí:) (*Jap.* Kirin) a town (pop. 568,000) in Kirin; N.E. China, on the Sungari: wood and chemical industries, paper

Yung·kia (júŋdʒiá) *WENCHOW

Yung·ning (júŋníŋ) *NANNING

Yün·ho (júnhóu) *GRAND CANAL

Yun·nan (júnán) a province (area 123,539 sq. miles, pop. 32,553,817, one-third hill tribes) in S.W. China bordering Burma, Laos and North Vietnam. Capital: Kunming

Yun·nan·fu (júnánfú:) *KUNMING

yup·pie (jʌpi:) *n.* a quasi-acronym for young urban professional, noted for devotion to upward economic mobility and for conspicuous consumption.

Yur·ev (jú:rjəf) *TARTU

Y·ve·lines (i:vli:n) a department (area 876 sq. miles, pop. 1,230,000) in N. central France, west of Paris (*ILE-DE-FRANCE). Chief town: Versailles

Y.W.C.A. *YOUNG WOMEN'S CHRISTIAN ASSOCIATION

	EARLY NORTH SEMITIC	PHOENICIAN	EARLY HEBREW (GEZER)			CLASSICAL LATIN
Z	I	I	I			Z
	CURSIVE MAJUSCULE (ROMAN)	CURSIVE MINUSCULE (ROMAN)			VENETIAN MINUSCULE (ITALIC)	MODERN ROMAN
	Z	z			Z	Z

A. C. SYLVESTER, CAMBRIDGE, ENGLAND

Development of the letter Z, beginning with the early North Semitic letter. Evolution of both the majuscule, or capital, letter Z and the minuscule, or lowercase, letter z are shown.

Z, z (zi:, *Br.* zed) the last letter of the English alphabet

Zab·rze (záb3e) (*G.* Hindenburg) the chief coal-mining center (pop. 204,000) in Upper Silesia, Poland: iron and steel, chemicals

Za·ca·te·cas (sukutékus) a central plateau state (area 28,973 sq. miles, pop. 1,133,000) of Mexico. Its agricultural production (cereals, sugar and maguey) depends greatly on irrigation. Its 16th-c. mines (silver, gold, mercury, copper) are among the most famous in Mexico. Industries include the extraction of rubber from guayule and the making of sugar, rum, mescal, and various fabrics. There are many baroque churches of the colonial period

Zach·a·ri·as (zækəráiəs), St, Jewish priest of Jerusalem, father of John the Baptist. Feast: Nov. 5

Za·dar (zádɑr) (formerly Zara) a port (pop. 60,000) on the central Dalmatian coast, Yugoslavia. Romanesque cathedral (13th c.). It was Venetian (1409-1747), Austrian until 1920, and Italian until 1947

Zad·kine (zædki:n), Ossip (1890-1967), French cubist sculptor, born in Russia. He used complex abstract means in representing the human figure, notably voids or concave surfaces which suggest form (*CUBISM)

zaf·fer, zaf·fre (zéfər) *n.* an impure cobalt oxide used in enameling and as a blue pigment for painting on porcelain or glass [fr. Ital. *zaffera*]

Zag·a·zig (zégəzig) an agricultural market (pop. 200,800) in E. Egypt in the Nile delta. Ruins of the ancient city of Bubastis, a religious center (10th-4th cc. B.C.), are nearby

Za·greb (zágreb) the capital (pop. 768,700) of Croatia, Yugoslavia, on the Sava. Industries: metalworking, railroad stock, food processing, wood, plastics. Cathedral (13th-18th cc.), palace (14th c.). University (1874)

Zag·ros (zégrəs) a mountain system running from Lake Van, E. Turkey, through W. Iran to the Strait of Hormuz: Zardeh Kuh (14,921 ft)

zai·bat·su (zaibɑtsu:) *n.* the powerful Japanese financial establishment, from the Japanese word for 'wealth'

Za·ïre (zɑi:r) (formerly the Democratic Republic of the Congo) a republic (area 904,990 sq. miles, pop. 29,897,000) in central Africa. Capital: Kinshasa. Official language: French. Native languages: Kiswahili or Kingwana in the east, Tshiluba or Kiluba in the south, Lingala in the Congo basin, and Kikongo in the lower Congo. The land is 42% forest, 21% arable, 1% permanent pasture, and the rest savanna. The Congo basin forms a low-lying part (1,200–1,500 ft) of the African plateau. It is covered with dense tropical forest and marshes. In the east the land

rises toward the Mitumba highlands (highest point 16,795 ft, on the Uganda border). In the southeast the plateau rises to 6,500 ft. The Congo basin has a hot, wet, equatorial climate. Average temperature: 78° F. (seasonal variation 4°). Rainfall: 60 ins in the north, 20 ins along the coast, 40 ins in the south. Livestock: goats, cattle. Agricultural products: coffee, cotton, rubber, tea, cocoa, palm oil, bananas. Mineral resources (Katanga): copper, diamonds, gold, silver, tin, cobalt, uranium, germanium, zinc, iron. Exports: copper, diamonds, palm oil, cobalt, cotton, rubber, coffee. Imports: machinery, manufactures, fuel oils, vehicles. Chief port: Matadi. Two pipelines link Matadi with Kinshasa. The Congo and its tributaries provide 8,500 miles of navigable waterway. Universities: Kinshasa (1954, Roman Catholic), Lubumbashi (1956, national). Monetary unit: zaïre (100 makuta). HISTORY. The Sudanic kingdom of Kongo was flourishing in the region of the Congo estuary when the Portuguese arrived (1482). Inhabited by the Bakongo, it was destroyed (late 17th c.) by contact with the Portuguese. Other Bantu peoples, the Balunda and the Baluba, founded (17th c.) a vast kingdom covering what is now S. Zaïre, W. Angola and Zambia. The Congo was explored by Stanley (1874-84). The Congo Free State was established under the personal rule of Leopold II of Belgium (1885), and was annexed to Belgium (1908). It was declared an independent republic (June 30, 1960) with Kasavubu as president. The U.N. intervened in subsequent civil strife which went on intermittently until the secessionist province of Katanga was reintegrated into the State (1963). Rebel activity continued after the U.N. withdrawal (June 1964), but Belgian paratroopers intervened (Nov. 1964) to prevent further civilian massacres. Civil war continued under Tshombe's provisional government (1964-5). A coup d'état (Nov. 1965) overthrew Kasavubu. Gen. Mobutu became president. White mercenaries backed by police of Katangese origin occupied Bukavu (July 1967) and a second group of mercenaries, from Angola, infiltrated Katanga. Both groups were repulsed. The name Zaïre was adopted (Oct. 1971). Mobutu survived several coup attempts and plots to overthrow him, but opposition to him grew, esp. after Zaïre's involvement in Angola's civil war and the disclosure (1975) of Zaïre's bankruptcy. His regime was further threatened by Angola-based rebels who invaded (1977, 8) and had to be repelled by foreign troops. After 1977, Mobutu reversed his nationalization policy and agreed to submit Zaïre's economy to directives of the International Monetary Fund

za·ïre (zɑi:r) *n.* the basic monetary unit of Zaïre, divided into 100 makuta

Zaire Republic formerly Democratic Republic of the Congo, earlier of the Belgium Congo — **Zairean** *n.* a native

Za·kyn·thos (zəkínθəs) (or Zante) a Greek island (area 156 sq. miles, pop. 35,000) in the Ionian Sea: vines, currants

Za·ma, Battle of (zéimə, záma) a battle (202 B.C.) in N. Africa, in which Scipio Africanus defeated Hannibal, at the end of the 2nd Punic War

Zam·be·zi (zæmbí:zi:) a river (2,200 miles long, navigable over 1,700 miles in stretches between rapids) flowing from N. Zambia, forming the Zambian-Rhodesian border and crossing Mozambique to the Indian Ocean

Zam·bi·a (zæmbi:ə) (formerly Northern Rhodesia) a republic (area 290,600 sq. miles, pop. 6,330,000) in central Africa. Capital: Lusaka. People: Bantu, 2% European, small Asian minority. Language: Bantu languages and English. Religion: mainly Animist, with large Christian and small Moslem minorities. The land is 5% cultivated. It is a plateau and is largely covered by savanna forest, with grassy plains and swamps around Lake Bangweulu and in the Kafue and Zambezi valleys. The copper belt, the chief source of wealth, lies along the Congo border. Average temperatures (F.): May-Sept. 60-80°, Sept.-Nov. 80°-90°, Nov.-Apr. 70°-80°. Rainfall: 20-30 ins in the Zambezi basin and Barotse plains, over 50 ins in the north and east. Livestock: cattle, sheep, goats. Agricultural products: corn, tobacco, kaffir corn, millet, cassava, peanuts, wheat, dairy produce, cotton, rice, pulses, coffee. Forest products: redwood (*Baikiaea plurifuga*), teak. Resources: copper, zinc, lead and vanadium, cobalt, manganese, gold, hydroelectricity. Industries: mining, fishing, food processing, metallurgy, copper smelting, furniture, cement. Exports: copper, tobacco, wood products, hides and skins. Imports: machinery, vehicles, food. There is railroad access to Lobito (Angola), Beira (Mozambique) and South Africa. University of Zambia (1966). Monetary unit: kwacha (100 ngwee). HISTORY. The country has yielded important evidence of prehistoric settlement. It is thought that an Iron Age people migrated to Zambia from E. Africa (1st millennium A.D.). The Bantu invaded from the 17th c. onwards, followed by Arabs from the north and Zulu and Basuto from the south (19th c.). After Portuguese expeditions across the country (late 18th and early 19th cc.), Livingstone traveled through Barotseland (1851) and discovered the Victoria Falls (1855). On the initiative of Rhodes, the British South Africa Company was chartered (1889) and by 1900 had extended its control over the whole country. The slave trade was stamped out. The country was unified (1911) as Northern Rhodesia and its administration assumed by the Crown (1924). It was a member of the Central African Federation (1953-63). Universal adult suffrage and internal self-government were introduced (1963). Kaunda was elected Northern Rhodesia's first prime minister (1964) and was its first president when it became an independent republic within the Commonwealth, under the name of Zambia (Oct. 24, 1964). Zambia joined the U.N. (1964). Relations with Southern Rhodesia were strained after the latter's white government unilaterally declared independence (1965) as Rhodesia, but improved from 1980 when black majority rule was achieved in the renamed Zimbabwe. A rail link from the Copperbelt through Tanzania to the sea was completed (1976) with China's help

Zam·bo·an·ga (sɑmbouɑ́ŋgɑ) a port (pop. 265,000) in S.W. Mindanao, Philippines

Za·men·hof (zéimənhɔf, zɑ́mənhɔf), Lazarus Ludovic (1859-1917), Polish linguist, an oculist by profession. He invented Esperanto

Za·mo·ra (zəmɔ́rə) a province (area 4,097 sq. miles, pop. 224,369) in N.W. Spain (*LEON) ‖ its capital (pop. 39,000)

Zan·jón, Peace of (sɑnhɔ́n) an agreement (1878) between Spain and Cuba which ended the Ten Year War, or Great War (1868-78)

zan·shin (zɑnʃin) *n.* (*Japanese martial arts*) complete awareness

Zan·te (zǽnti:) *ZAKYNTHOS

ZANU (*acronym*) for Zimbabwe African National Party

za·ny (zéini:) **1.** *pl.* **za·nies** *n.* (*hist.*) a stage buffoon who mimicked the clown ‖ a person who acts like a buffoon **2.** *comp.* **za·ni·er** *superl.* **za·ni·est** *adj.* ludicrous in a rather crazy way [F. *zani* fr. Ital. *zani, zanni,* a clown, orig. a familiar form of *Giovanni,* John]

Zan·zi·bar (zǽnzəbɑr) a coralline island (area 640 sq. miles) in the Indian Ocean, 22 miles off Tanganyika ‖ a republic (area 1,020 sq. miles, pop. 475,655) consisting of Zanzibar and Pemba islands, forming part of Tanzania. Capital and port: Zanzibar. People: 80% African, 14% Arab, 6% Indian. Language: Swahili and other Bantu languages, Arabic, Gujarati, English. Religion: mainly Moslem, with minorities practicing Christianity or local African religions. The land is 51% cultivated. Zanzibar island is flat in the east and hilly (rising to 390 ft) in the west. Average temperature (Zanzibar): 80°. Rainfall: Zanzibar 58 ins, Pemba 80 ins. Exports: cloves (*PEMBA), clove oil, coconuts, copra, coconut oil, coir. Other products: rice, cassava, sweet potatoes, chilies, tobacco, corn, tropical fruit, soap, fish, jewelry, ivory and ebony ornaments. Imports: rice and other cereals, flour, textiles, gasoline, vehicles, tobacco. Monetary unit: Tanzanian shilling (100 cents). HISTORY. Arabs and Persians settled in Zanzibar from the 7th c. It was seized by the Portuguese (1503) and by the Arabs of Muscat and Oman (1698). A thriving trade in slaves and ivory developed, and the clove was introduced (early 19th c.). Zanzibar became independent (1856) and a British protectorate (1890). It gained independence (Dec. 10, 1963) within the Commonwealth. The sultan's government was overthrown by a coup d'état, and Zanzibar was declared a republic (Jan. 1964). It united (Apr. 27, 1964) with Tanganyika to form a republic which later took the name Tanzania

zap (zæp) **1.** *n.* a sudden hit or other occurrence **2.** *v.* to destroy suddenly **3.** *v.* to apply electroshock therapy

Za·pa·ta (sɑpɑ́tɑ), Emiliano (c. 1883-1919), Mexican revolutionary leader. To the cry of 'Land and liberty' he led (1910) a revolt against President Porfirio Díaz which helped to install Francisco Madero in power. But he opposed Madero's agrarian program, and formulated his own agrarian proposals in the Plan of Ayala (1911). A champion of land redistribution, he continued his fight against Presidents Francisco Madero, Victoriano Huerta, and Venustiano Carranza. With Pancho Villa he occupied (1914-15) Mexico City three times. He was assassinated by an emissary of Carranza

za·pa·tis·mo (sɑpɑtí:smɔ) *n.* the Mexican agrarian reform movement of Emiliano Zapata. It become synonymous with agrarismo and later indianismo [Span.]

Za·po·lya (zɑ́pəljə), John *JOHN I ZAPOLYA

Za·po·ro·zhe (zɑpərɔ́ʒə) (formerly Alexandrovsk) a city (pop. 760,000) in the S.E. Ukraine, U.S.S.R., on the Dnieper: iron and steel, aluminum, chemicals, agricultural machinery, automobiles

Za·ra (zɑ́rə, dzɑ́rɑ) *ZADAR

Za·ra·go·za (sɑrɑgɔ́sɑ), Ignacio (1829-62), Mexican general and politician. He routed (May 1862) the invading French forces at Puebla

Za·ra·go·za (θɑrɑgɔ́θɑ) *SARAGOSSA

Zar·a·thus·tra (zærəθú:strə) the name of Zoroaster in the Avesta

zar·a·tite (zǽrətait) *n.* a hydrated carbonate of nickel, $NiCO_3 \cdot 2Ni(OH)_2 \cdot 4H_2O$, occurring in bright green aggregates [fr. Span. *zaratita,* after a Señor *Zarate*]

Za·ri·a (zɑ́ri:ə) a market and rail center (pop. 224,000) in N. Nigeria, formerly a Hausa state. University (1962)

zeal (zi:l) *n.* persistent fervent devotion to a cause [M.E. *zele* fr. L. *zelus* fr. Gk *zēlos*]

Zea·land (zí:lənd) (*Dan.* Sjælland) Denmark's largest island (area 2,709 sq. miles), on which Copenhagen lies

zeal·ot (zélət) *n.* someone who acts for a cause with excessive zeal **Zealot** (*hist.*) a member of a Jewish sect which revolted against the Roman forces of occupation in Judea from 6 A.D. until the destruction of Jerusalem (70 A.D.) **zéal·ot·ry** *n.* behavior etc. characteristic of a zealot [fr. eccles. L. *zelotes* fr. Gk]

zeal·ous (zéləs) *adj.* full of zeal, showing zeal [fr. M.L. *zelosus*]

ze·a·tin (zí:ətən) *n.* (*biochem.*) a substance with self-dividing properties that enables plants to grow, derived from sperm of maize

ze·bra (zí:brə) *n.* any of several swift-running equine mammals of S. and E. Africa, covered with alternating black (or brown) and white (or buff) stripes. They are rarely domesticated [Congolese]

zebra crossing (*Br.*) a broad band of alternate black and white stripes painted across a road, denoting that pedestrians have absolute priority over drivers

ze·bra·wood (zí:brəwud) *n.* *Connarus guianensis,* fam. *Connaraceae,* a tree of tropical America and E. Africa, the striped hardwood of which is used in cabinetmaking ‖ any of several other trees or shrubs yielding similar wood ‖ the wood of any of these trees

ze·bu (zí:bju:, zí:bu:) *n.* *Bos indicus,* a bovine mammal, domesticated in the Malagasy Republic, India and the Far East for use as a draft animal. Zebus have a hump of fat on the shoulders. They tolerate heat well. They are often crossed with European breeds of cattle [fr. F. *zébu*]

Zeb·u·lun (zébjulən) Hebrew patriarch, son of Jacob ‖ the Israelite tribe of which he was the ancestor

Zech·a·ri·ah (zekəráiə) a Minor Prophet (6th c. B.C.) of the Old Testament. Like Haggai, he urged the Jews to rebuild the Temple in Jerusalem ‖ the book of the Old Testament which contains his prophecies

zed (zed) *n.* (Br.) zee

zee (zi:) *n.* (*Am.=Br.* zed) the letter z

Zee·land (zí:lənd, zéilɑnt) the southwestern province (area 690 sq. miles, pop. 335,624) of the Netherlands. Capital: Middelburg

Zee·man effect (zéimɑn) (*phys.*) the splitting up of the lines in a line spectrum by a strong magnetic field, from which deductions can be made as to the atomic structure [after Pieter *Zeeman* (1865–1943), Du. physicist and Nobel prizewinner (1902) with LORENTZ]

ze·in (zí:in) *n.* a protein found in corn and used in the manufacture of textiles, plastics etc. [fr. *Zea,* the genus to which corn belongs]

Zeit·ge·ber (zaítgeibə:r) *n.* (*German,* usu. italics) a factor that affects the biological clock, e.g., light, temperature

zeit·geist (tsáitgɑist) *n.* the dominant moral and intellectual character of a particular period [G.]

zel·ko·va (zélkəvə) *n.* a Japanese tree similar to American elm, imported into the U.S.

zem·stvo (zémstvou) *pl.* **zem·stvos** *n.* (*Russ. hist.*) any of the provincial or district councils established (1864) by Alexander II. The zemstvos played an important part in the formation of a liberal intelligentsia. They were abolished (1917) by the Bolsheviks in favor of the soviets [Russ.]

Zen (zen) *n.* a school of Mahayana Buddhism traditionally founded in China (early 6th c.) by Bodhidharma and widespread in Japan since the 12th c. It teaches that enlightenment may be achieved by meditation and intuition, stimulated by the contemplation of beauty and simplicity [Jap.=religious meditation fr. Chin. *ch'an* fr. Pali *jhāna* fr. Skr. *dhyāna*]

ze·na·na (zenɑ́nə) *n.* that part of a house in India or Persia which is reserved for the women [Hind. *zenāna, zanāna* fr. Pers.]

Zen Buddhism Zen **Zen Buddhist** an adherent of Zen

Zend (zend) *n.* the ancient Iranian language, allied to Sanskrit, in which the Avesta was written ‖ the Middle Persian translation of the Zoroastrian Avesta and commentary on it [Pers.=interpretation]

Zend-Avesta the Avesta

ze·ner diode (zí:nə:r) (*electr.*) a silicon semiconductor that maintains fixed voltage in a circuit, for American physicist Clarence M. Zener

zener effect (*electr.*) the pronounced curvature in reverse voltage current characteristic of a diode

Zeng·er (zéŋər), John Peter (1697-1746), U.S. journalist. As publisher of the New York 'Weekly Journal', in which he attacked the colonial administration, he was imprisoned on libel charges. In a subsequent trial he was defended by Alexander Hamilton, who established that in cases of libel the truth was sufficient defense (and so advanced the cause of freedom of the press in America). Zenger was subsequently acquitted of all charges

ze·nith (zí:niθ, *Br.* esp. zéniθ) *n.* the point in the sky vertically above the observer (opp. NADIR) ‖ (*fig.*) the highest point, *at the zenith of his power* **zé·nith·al** *adj.* of, at or relating to the zenith ‖ (of a map) so drawn that the true directions from a central point are shown [O.F. *cenith, cenit* or M.L. *cenit,* fr. Arab.]

zenith distance (*astron.*) the angular distance of a heavenly body from the zenith

Zenj (zendʒ) a Moslem empire (10th-15th cc.), comprising various E. African coastal settlements. It was centered on Kilwa

Ze·no (zí:nou) (*d.* 491), Byzantine emperor (474-91). He was forced to recognize Odoacer's supremacy in Italy, but encouraged Theodoric to invade Italy and overthrow him. Zeno's reign was marked by frequent revolts

Zeno of Citium (c.334–c. 262 B.C.) Greek philosopher, founder of Stoicism, at Athens

Zeno of Elea (c. 490–c. 430 B.C.), Greek philosopher who supported the monism of his teacher Parmenides. He devised a number of arguments to prove the unreality of motion, the best known being the paradox of Achilles and the tortoise: Achilles can never overtake the tortoise, for when he reaches each successive starting point the tortoise is always further on

ze·o·lite (zí:əlait) *n.* one of a group of minerals with an open structure having channelways which can act as molecular sieves. They occur in certain volcanic rocks, and are hydrated aluminum silicates **ze·o·lit·ic** (zi:əlítik) *adj.* [fr. Swed. and G. *zeolit* fr. Gk *zein,* to boil]

Zeph·a·ni·ah zefənáiə) a Minor Prophet (late 7th c. B.C.) of the Old Testament. He prophesied the doom of Judah and other nations ‖ the book of the Old Testament which contains his prophecies

zeph·yr (zéfər) *n.* (*rhet.*) a gentle breeze ‖ any lightweight fabric or yarn, or an article of clothing made from this [O.E. *zefferus* fr. L. *zephyrus* fr. Gk *zephuros,* the west wind]

Zep·pe·lin (zépələn) *n.* (*hist.*) a rigid, cigar-shaped dirigible airship used for transatlantic voyages (from 1928) and, in the 1st world war, by the Germans for bombing raids [after Graf Ferdinand von *Zeppelin,* (1828–1917), G. aeronautical pioneer who designed and built such aircraft]

Zer·matt (tsermɑ́t) a resort (pop. 3,101) in Valais, Switzerland, below the Matterhorn at 5,315 ft

ze·ro (zíərou) **1.** *n. pl.* **ze·ros, ze·roes** the numerical symbol 0 denoting absence of value (*NUMBER TABLE) ‖ the beginning of a numerical scale (of distance, time, temperature etc.) ‖ the temperature of pure melting ice under standard atmospheric pressure on the Centigrade and Réaumur scales ‖ *ABSOLUTE ZERO ‖ (*gunnery*) a sight setting which allows for elevation and wind deflection ‖ (*fig.*) the lowest point ‖ a nonentity **2.** *v.t.* (with 'in') to adjust the sights of (a rifle) by calibrated firing under conditions of no wind ‖ to adjust (an instrument etc.) to a zero point, or to a point representing zero ‖ **to zero**

in on to adjust fire on (a target) ‖ to move in close to ‖ to concentrate on **3.** *adj.* having the value of zero ‖ (*meteor.*) *ZERO VISIBILITY

ze·ro-based budgeting (zíəroubeisd) (*economics*) system of creating a budget without regard to previous budgets or present expenditures, in which each item must be justified for itself

zero bracket on U.S. income tax returns after 1978, amount of income on which no federal income tax is payable

zero hour the time at which a military operation (or other project) is planned to begin

zero norm *NIL NORM

ze·ro-or·der release (zíərouɔ́rdər) a perfect sustained-release timing mechanism in an encapsulated drug

zero point (*mil.*) the location of the center of a nuclear explosion at the instant of detonation

zero population growth conditions or program in which births and deaths are equalized. *abbr.* ZPG.

ze·ro-sum (zíərousʌm) *adj.* meaningless

zero visibility (*meteor.*) visibility restricted to 50 ft vertically or 165 ft horizontally

zest (zest) *n.* a piquant, enhancing quality ‖ enthusiastic enjoyment, *to work with zest* ‖ a piece of lemon or orange peel added to a drink etc. to give flavor **zést·ful** *adj.* [F. *zeste,* a piece of orange or lemon peel]

ze·ta (zéitə, zí:tə) *n.* the sixth letter (Z, ζ=z) of the Greek alphabet

Zet·land (zétlənd) a county of Scotland (*SHETLAND ISLANDS)

zeu·glo·don (zú:glədɒn) *n.* a member of *Basilosaurus,* fam. *Basilosauridae,* a genus of Eocene or Miocene fossil cetacean mammals, related to the toothed whale and reaching 50–70 ft in length [Mod. L. fr. Gk *zeuglē,* loop of a yoke+*odous* (*odontos*), tooth]

zeug·ma (zú:gmə) *n.* a figure of speech in which one word is made to refer to two or more other words, but has to be differently understood in the different contexts, usually with a ludicrous effect, as in 'he took his time and the floor' [Gk=a yoke]

Zeus (zu:s) (*Gk mythol.*) the supreme god, identified with the Latin Jupiter. He was the son of Rhea and of Cronos, whom he overthrew. He symbolized nature and the elements and was regarded variously as the god of the earth and giver of fertility, the dispenser of good and evil, the giver of laws, the guardian of the hearth, property and liberty. His symbols were the eagle, the scepter and the thunderbolt, and his principal shrines were in Athens and Olympia

Zeux·is (zú:ksis) (5th-4th cc. B.C.), one of the most famous of ancient Greek painters

Zhda·nov (ʒdɑ́nəf) (formerly Mariupol), a port (pop. 467,000) in the Ukraine, U.S.S.R., on the Sea of Azov, serving the Donbas: iron and steel industries

Zhu·kov (ʒú:kəf), Georgi Konstantinovich (1896-1974), Russian marshal. He was victorious in the battles of Moscow (1941) and Leningrad (1943) and drove the Nazi armies back from the U.S.S.R. (1944-5). He was minister of defense (1955-7)

Zia ul-Haq (zí:əulhɒk), Muhammad (1924-) Pakistani statesman, president (1978-). He served as army chief of staff (1976-7) and chief martial law administrator (1977-8). He overthrew Pres. Zulfiqar Ali Bhutto (1977), who was later executed. As president Zia worked at Pakistani Islamicization and for better international relations, esp. with the U.S.A., China and India

zib·el·ine, zib·el·line (zíbəli:n, zíbəlain) *n.* sable fur ‖ a soft woolen fabric mixed with alpaca etc., having long silky hairs on the right side [fr. F. *zibeline* fr. Slav. *sobol,* sable]

zib·et, zib·eth (zíbit) *n. Viverra zibetha,* the Asiatic or Indian civet [fr. M.L. *zibethum* fr. Arab.]

Zieg·feld (zígfeld), Florenz (1869-1932), U.S. theatrical producer. He produced (1907) the 'Ziegfeld Follies', an annual revue noted for its spectacular staging, variety performances, and chorus of beautiful girls

zig·gu·rat (zígəræt) *n.* a lofty pyramidal tower of ancient Babylonia, with outside stairways and a shrine at the top [Assyrian *ziqquratu,* height, pinnacle]

zig·zag (zígzæg) **1.** *adj.* turning sharply left and right alternately as its course proceeds **2.** *n.* one of a series of sudden turns in a road, course etc. ‖ such a road or course ‖ a design etc. having a zigzag form **3.** *adv.* in a zigzag path **4.** *v. pres. part.* **zig·zag·ging** *past* and *past part.* **zig·zagged** *v.i.* to be or take a zigzag course ‖ *v.t.* to make (one's way or its way) in a zigzag course [fr. F., origin unknown]

zik·ku·rat, zik·u·rat (zíkəræt) *n.* a ziggurat

zilch (ziltʃ) *n.* (*slang*) emphatically nothing — **zilch** *adj.*

Zimbabwe (zimbɑ́bwei) (formerly Rhodesia) a republic (area 150,333 sq. miles, pop. 8,376,000) in central Africa. Capital: Harare (formerly Salisbury). People: 96% Africans (mainly Matabele and Mashona), 3% European stock, small Asiatic and Colored minorities. Language: English, Bantu languages. Religion: mainly local African religions, with a Christian minority. A broad central plateau (averaging 4,000 ft, rising to over 5,000 ft in the northeast), mainly savanna woodland, forms the Zambezi-Limpopo watershed. Lowlands on either side fall to 2,000 ft along the Zambezi and along the southern border (under 1,000 ft in the southeast). Towards the Mozambique frontier rise the steep Inyanga and Melsetter massifs, culminating in Mt Inyangeni (8,250 ft). Average temperatures (F.): 65° on the plateau, with a mean Oct. maximum of 85° for the whole country. Rainfall: average 28 ins (from under 15 ins on the Limpopo Valley to over 40 ins along the Mozambique border). Livestock: cattle, sheep, goats, hogs. The land is 5% arable, 64% forest. Agricultural products: corn and tobacco, kaffir corn, vegetables, citrus fruits, beans, peanuts, sugar, rice, wheat, cotton, tea, dairy products. Resources: asbestos, gold, chrome ore, coal, tin, lithium, copper, timber (teak and mahogany). Manufactures and industries: mining, foodstuffs, textiles, iron and steel, clothing, cigarettes, electricity, metal products, oil refining. Exports: tobacco, cigarettes, minerals, hides, meat. Imports: metals, machinery, vehicles, textiles, food, fuel oils, paints, leather, rubber, chemicals, wines and spirits. There is railroad access to the ports of Beira and Maputo. University of Zimbabwe (1970). Monetary unit: Zimbabwe dollar (100 cents). HISTORY. The area was probably peopled by Bantu about the beginning of the Christian era. The Zimbabwe ruins (11th-15th cc.) give evidence of a high degree of political organization. The Matabele overran much of the area (early 19th c.). European interest in the region was stimulated by the discoveries (1850s) of Livingstone. Rhodes obtained from the Matabele chief a monopoly of the minerals in his kingdom (1888), and a British company was chartered (1889) to develop the region. Tribal warfare between the Matabele and the Mashona ended when their territories were united (1898) to form Southern Rhodesia. This became a self-governing British colony (1923) and was a member of the Central African Federation (1953-63). The Rhodesian government, led by Ian Smith, made a unilateral declaration of independence (Nov. 11, 1965) on the basis of white minority rule. Britain countered by an economic blockade and a comprehensive sanctions resolution was adopted (May 29, 1968) by the Security Council. Rhodesia became (1970) a republic, but black nationalists continued to seek greater representation in the government through the 1970s, despite considerable government repression. Smith negotiated an 'internal settlement' with black leaders (1978) and in 1979 elections the principle of universal suffrage was accepted. The country became Zimbabwe Rhodesia with Bishop Abel Muzorewa its first black prime minister. Guerrilla attacks on the government continued, however, as various rebel factions allied against it. An agreement was reached (1979) on a new constitution reducing the number of white-held seats in the parliament, and new elections were scheduled for 1980. The country was under direct British rule (Dec. 1979-April 1980) when it became independent Zimbabwe. Conflict continued, however, between blacks and whites and among various black factions, despite efforts by Prime Minister Robert Mugabe at conciliation and to improve the economy. In 1985 Mugabe announced plans to declare Zimbabwe a one-party state ‖ a group of ruins in W. Zimbabwe, probably of 11th-15th-c. Bantu origin: acropolis, temple, walls of granite monoliths. They were discovered in 1868

Zim·mer·mann Note (tsímərmɑn) a secret coded telegram addressed (Jan. 16, 1917) to the German minister in Mexico by German Foreign Minister Arthur Zimmermann (1864-1940). With the object of reducing or nullifying U.S. intervention in Europe in the 1st world war by engaging U.S. strength in hostilities with Mexico and Japan, the Note offered Mexican President Venustiano Carranza an offensive and defensive alliance, and invited Mexico 'to reconquer her lost territory in Texas, New Mexico and Arizona' and to seek the immediate adherence of Japan. Intercepted and decoded by British Naval Intelligence, it was passed to President Woodrow Wilson who published it on Mar. 1, 1917. It convinced Americans of Germany's ill will toward them, and became one of the principal causes of the U.S. declaration of war against Germany five weeks later

zinc (ziŋk) **1.** *n.* a metallic element (symbol Zn, at. no. 30, at. mass 65.37), hard and resisting corrosion. It is used for coating sheet iron to prevent rust, in the manufacture of brass, in electric cells (because of its high solution-tension constant) and in making printing blocks **2.** *v.t. pres. part.* **zinc·ing, zinck·ing** *past* and *past part.* **zinced, zincked** to coat with zinc [fr. G. *zink*]

zinc blende naturally occurring zinc sulfide, ZnS

zinc carbonate a crystalline salt, $ZnCO_3$, occurring naturally as smithsonite, and known formerly (*Br.*) as hemimorphite

zinc·ic (zíŋkik) *adj.* of or containing zinc

zinckenite *ZINKENITE

zinck·y, zink·y, zinc·y (zíŋki:) *adj.* zincic

zin·co·graph (zíŋkəgræf, zíŋkəgrɑf) *n.* a printing block of zinc with an etched design ‖ a print taken from this [ZINCOGRAPHY]

zin·cog·ra·pher (ziŋkɒ́grəfər) *n.* someone who practices zincography

zin·co·graph·ic (ziŋkəgrǽfik) *n.* of or relating to zincography **zin·co·gráph·i·cal** *adj.*

zin·cog·ra·phy (ziŋkɒ́grəfi:) *n.* the art or process of engraving on zinc or taking prints from such engravings [fr. Mod. L. *zincum,* zinc+Gk *graphos,* written]

zinc ointment an ointment containing zinc oxide, used to treat skin diseases

zinc·ous (zíŋkəs) *adj.* zincic

zinc oxide ZnO, an oxide used as a pigment and filler, in ointments etc. (*CALAMINE)

zinc silicate any of several silicates of zinc, including the basic variety, hemimorphite. It was known formerly (*Br.*) as smithsonite

zinc white zinc oxide used as a white pigment, e.g. in paint

zincy *ZINCKY

Zin·der (zíndər) a trading center (pop. 13,000) in S.E. Niger, terminus of a trans-Sahara motor route

zing (ziŋ) **1.** *n.* (*pop.*) zest, energy ‖ (*pop.*) a high-pitched humming noise **2.** *v.i.* (*pop.*) to make a high-pitched humming noise [*imit.*]

zing·er (zíŋə:r) *n.* (*slang*) a sharp witticism

zin·jan·thro·pus (zindʒǽnθrəpəs) *n.* a fossil hominid native to eastern Africa, believed extant 2 million B.C.

zin·ken·ite, zinck·en·ite (zíŋkənait) *n.* a double sulfide of antimony and lead, $PbSb_2S_4$, with a luster like steel [fr. G. *zinkenit* after J. K. L. *Zincken* (19th c.), G. mineralogist]

zinky *ZINCKY

zin·ni·a (zíni:ə) *n.* a member of *Zinnia,* fam. *Compositae,* a genus of half hardy annual plants, native to Mexico but widely cultivated. They bear showy, rayed flower heads [Mod. L. after J. G. *Zinn* (1727–59), G. botanist]

Zin·zen·dorf (tsíntsendɔrf), Nikolaus Ludwig, Graf von (1700-60), German religious leader. He established (1727) the Moravian Church, a revival of a Hussite protestant sect, and evangelized in Europe and the U.S.A. on behalf of it

Zi·on (záiən) a hill in Jerusalem on which the palace of King David was built, and later the Temple, taken as the religious, national and cultural center of the ancient Jews ‖ the Jewish people ‖ paradise, heaven ‖ a name often given to a Nonconformist chapel **Zi·on·ism** *n.* a worldwide political movement among Jews, begun (1897) by Theodor Herzl, to secure the reestablishing of a Jewish national home in Palestine. It triumphed with the setting up of Israel (1948) **Zí·on·ist** *n.* and *adj.* [O.E. fr. eccles. L. *Sion* fr. Heb.]

zip (zip) **1.** *n.* a short, sharp sound like that made by a bullet traveling through the air ‖ (*pop.*) vigor, snap ‖ (*Br.*) a zipper **2.** *v. pres. part.* **zip·ping** *past* and *past part.* **zipped** *v.i.* to go

CONCISE PRONUNCIATION KEY: **(a)** æ, *cat;* ɑ, *car;* ɔ *fawn;* ei, *snake.* **(e)** e, *hen;* i:, *sheep;* iə, *deer;* ɛə, *bear.* **(i)** i, *fish;* ai, *tiger;* ə:, *bird.* **(o)** o, *ox;* au, *cow;* ou, *goat;* u, *poor;* ɔi, *royal.* **(u)** ʌ, *duck;* u, *bull;* u:, *goose;* ə, *bacillus;* ju:, *cube.* x, *loch;* θ, *think;* ð, *bother;* z, *Zen;* ʒ, *corsage;* dʒ, *savage;* ŋ, *orangutang;* j, *yak;* ʃ, *fish;* tʃ, *fetch;* 'l, *rabble;* 'n, *redden.* Complete pronunciation key appears inside front cover.

with the sound of a bullet flying through the air || (*pop.*) to go very fast || to be opened and closed with a zipper || *v.t.* to fasten or unfasten with a zipper [imit.]

ZIP code U.S. postal-delivery zone number code of five digits used in the addressing of mail [Zone Improvement Program]; (*Br.*) postcode — **zip-code** *v.*

zip fastener (*Br.*) a zipper

zip·per (zípər) **1.** *n.* (*Am.*=*Br.* zip, zip fastener) a strip of interlocking metal or plastic teeth on tapes, used to fasten openings in garments, bags etc. **2.** *v.t.* and *i.* to fasten by means of a zipper [fr. *Zipper*, trademark]

zip·py (zípi:) *comp.* **zip·pi·er** *superl.* **zip·pi·est** *adj.* full of vigor

ZIPRA (*acronym*) for Peoples African Revolutionary Army led by Joshua Nkomo

zip top a package top removable by pulling a strip from the cover. *Cf* POP-TOP, RING-PULL

zir·cal·loy (zə:rkǽlɔi) *n.* (*metallurgy*) an alloy of zirconium and other metals with heat- and corrosion-resistant properties; used in nuclear reactors

zir·con (zə́:rkɒn) *n.* zirconium silicate, $ZrSiO_4$, a mineral found as tetragonal crystals of various colors. Some varieties (e.g. hyacinth) are cut into gems [fr. F. *zircone* fr. Ital. *giargone*]

zir·co·ni·a (zər:kóuni:ə) *n.* zirconium dioxide, ZrO_2, a crystalline compound which has a very high melting point and is used as a refractory and in giving opacity to enamels [Mod. L.]

zir·co·ni·um (zə:rkóuni:əm) *n.* a metallic element (symbol Zr, at. no 40, at. mass 91.22). Zirconium compounds are used in the manufacture of ceramics and refractory materials, and the metal itself as a structural and container material in nuclear reactors [Mod. L.]

zith·er (zíθər) *n.* a musical instrument, esp. popular in Austria, consisting of 30 to 40 strings stretched over a flat sounding board, the strings being plucked with the fingers or with a plectrum. Some of the strings pass over a fret and are stopped with the left hand [G. fr. L. *cithara* fr. Gk *kithara*]

zi·zith (tsi:tsí:t, tsítsis) *pl. n.* the tassels at the corners of the tallith or of the outer garment worn by Orthodox Jewish males [Heb. *sīsith*]

Žiž·ka (ʒíʃkə), Jan (c. 1370-1424), Bohemian soldier. He led the Hussite revolt (1420-4) against the Emperor Sigismund, winning several victories by unconventional military tactics

Zlin (zli:n) *GOTTWALDOV

zlo·ty (zlɔ́ti:) *pl.* **zlo·tys, zlo·ty** *n.* the basic Polish monetary unit || a coin or note of the value of one zloty [Pol. *zloty*, golden]

zo·di·ac (zóudi:æk) *n.* an imaginary band on the celestial sphere of width 16°, bounded by two circles equidistant from the ecliptic, within which are contained the paths of the sun, principal planets and moon, and which is divided into 12 equal parts, each named after a constellation || a figure showing the 12 parts with their symbols and emblems [O.F. *zodiaque* fr. L. *zodiacus* fr. Gk *zōidiakos (kuklos)*, (circle) of signs]

zo·di·a·cal (zoudáiək'l) *adj.* pertaining to or within the zodiac [fr. L. *zodiacus*]

zodiacal light a triangular glow of light, seen in the Tropics, rising from the point of sunrise or sunset

Zof·fa·ny (zɔ́fəni:), Johann (1733-1810), British painter, of German parentage. He excelled in family groups and conversation pieces

Zog (zoug), (Ahmed Zogu, 1893-1961), president (1925-8) and king (1928-39) of Albania. He ruled despotically and was forced to flee when Italian forces invaded Albania (1939)

zois·ite (zɔ́isait) *n.* a double silicate of aluminum (or iron) and calcium [fr. G. *zoisit* after Baron *Zois* Von Edelstein (1747-1819), who discovered it]

Zo·la (zoulə), Émile (1840-1902), French novelist and leading exponent of naturalism. In his 20-volume 'Rougon-Macquart' series (1869-93) he traces the social and natural history of a family whose members are under the controlling power of heredity and environment. The best known of these novels are 'l'Assommoir' (1877), 'Germinal' (1885) and 'la Terre' (1887). A passionate social reformer, he played a courageous part in the defense of Dreyfus with his pamphlet 'J'accuse' (1898)

Zöll·ner illusion (tsǿ:lnər) the optical illusion produced by Zöllner's lines [after J. F. K. *Zöllner* (1834-82), G. physicist]

Zöllner's lines parallel lines, made by the series of short parallel lines ruled obliquely across them, to look as if they converge or diverge [after J. F. K. *Zöllner*]

Zoll·ver·ein (tsɔ́lfərain) a customs union of German states, formed (1834) under Prussian leadership. It encouraged German industrialization, and represented a political victory for Prussia over Austria, which was excluded from the union

Zom·ba (zɔ́mbə) the capital (pop. 15,705) of Malawi in the Shire Highlands. University of Malawi (1965)

zom·bi, zom·bie (zɔ́mbi:) *n.* a corpse revived by magic || the snake deity of voodoo rites in Haiti and python deity in those of W. Africa || (*pop.*) someone who looks macabre or who behaves as though half-dead **zóm·bi·ism** *n.* [of African origin]

zon·al (zóun'l) *adj.* of, resembling, constituting or consisting of a zone or zones [fr. Mod. L. *zonalis* fr. L. *zona*, zone]

zon·ate (zóuneit) *adj.* marked with zones || (*bot.*) ringed, marked with bands of color **zón·at·ed** *adj.*

zo·na·tion (zounéiʃən) *n.* a zonate formation or structure || the state of being zonal || (*envir.*) formation of layers in soils, water, mountains, vegetations, etc., e.g., tree rings [ZONE]

zone (zoun) **1.** *n.* the area of the surface of a sphere bounded by two parallel planes which intersect the sphere || one of the five climatic zones of the earth's surface (two polar circles, extending to 23°27′ from the poles, two temperate zones, north and south between latitudes 23°27′ and the polar circles, and the torrid zone, between latitudes 23°27′ N. and 23°27′ S.) || (*biol.*) a region of characteristic fauna or flora || (*biol.*) a belt or area to which species are limited || an area or region of the body || (*geol.*) a rock series of characteristic composition or fossils || (*computer*) the channel on a tape, or position on a card, that designates the significance of the data || an area within which a characteristic activity is carried on, *a fishing zone* or one set aside for a special purpose, *military zone* || an area subject to a specific influence, *rain zone* || an area within which one rate of postage is charged for parcels (parcel post zone), or a city district having its individual number (postal delivery zone) **2.** *v.t. pres. part.* **zon·ing** *past* and *past part.* **zoned** to mark off into zones || to plan (a town) so that different sections are devoted to different purposes (residential, industrial etc.) [fr. L. *zona* fr. Gk *zōnē*, girdle]

zone (*computer*) the channel on a tape, or position on a card, that designates the significance of the data

zone refining (*metallurgy*) technique for purifying metals by passing a heat source past a metal so that impurities are concentrated at both ends. *also* zone melting

zoo (zu:) *n.* a place where live animals are kept in captivity for the public to see [ZOOLOGICAL GARDEN]

zo·o·chlo·rel·la (zouəklɔrélə) *pl.* **zo·o·chlo·rel·lae** (zouəklɔréli:) *n.* any of various symbiotic green algae of genus *Chlorella*, fam. *Chlorellaceae*, living in various animals, e.g. in hydra [Mod. L. fr. Gk *zōon*, animal+*Chlorella*, generic name]

zo·o·ge·o·graph·ic (zouədʒi:əgrǽfik) *adj.* of or pertaining to zoogeography **zo·o·ge·o·gráph·i·cal** *adj.*

zo·o·ge·og·ra·phy (zououdʒi:ɒ́grəfi:) *n.* the scientific study of the geographical distribution of animals [fr. Gk *zōon*, animal+GEOGRAPHY]

zo·o·gle·a, zo·o·gloe·a (zouəglí:ə) *pl.* **zo·o·gle·as, zo·o·gloe·as, zo·o·gle·ae, zo·o·gloe·ae** (zouəglí:i:) *n.* a mass of bacteria embedded in a mucilaginous matrix formed when cell membranes absorb water and swell, frequently forming an iridescent film [fr. Gk *zōon*, animal+*gloios*, gummy substance]

zo·oid (zóuɔid) *n.* a largely independent member of a compound animal organism, e.g. an individual in a coelenterate or polyzoan colony **zo·oi·dal** (zouɔ́id'l) *adj.* [fr. Gk *zōon*, animal]

zo·o·log·ic (zouəlɒ́dʒik) *adj.* zoological

zo·o·log·i·cal (zouəlɒ́dʒik'l) *adj.* of or relating to zoology

zoological garden a zoo

zo·ol·o·gist (zouɒ́lədʒist) *n.* a specialist in zoology [fr. Mod. L. *zoologia*, zoology]

zo·ol·o·gy (zouɒ́lədʒi:) *n.* the branch of biology concerned with animal life and all its manifestations (cf. BOTANY) || the animal life of a given region [fr. Gk *zōon*, animal+*logos*, discourse]

zoom (zu:m) **1.** *v.i.* (*aeron.*) to climb at a steep angle || to make a loud humming or buzzing noise || (of a motion picture or television image) to seem to approach or recede from the viewer rapidly || *v.t.* to cause (an aircraft) to climb at a steep angle || to cause (a motion picture or television image) to seem to approach or recede from the viewer **2.** *n.* a steep climb by a plane || a loud, low hum or buzz || a process by which a television or motion picture image is made to become quickly larger or smaller in the field of view [imit.]

zoom back (*optics*) camera-lens operation that makes the viewer seem to move rapidly away from a subject first seen from a relatively close viewpoint

zoom·er (zú:mər) *n.* (*optics*) camera with a zoom lens

zoom in (*optics*) camera-lens operation that makes the viewer seem to move rapidly toward a subject first seen at a greater distance, while remaining in constant focus. *Cf* ZOOM BACK

zoom lens a lens system used in motion picture and television cameras, in which the distance to the object being photographed may be changed rapidly while keeping the object in focus

zo·o·mor·phic (zouəmɔ́rfik) *adj.* representing a deity etc. in the form of an animal || relating to or being a deity etc. represented in this way || (of writing, art etc.) characterized by the use of animal forms **zo·o·mór·phism** *n.* [fr. *zoomorph*, a zoomorphic design or figure fr. Gk *zōon*, animal+*morphē*, shape]

zo·on (zóuɒn) *pl.* **zo·a** (zóuə) *n.* the product of a single egg (cf. ZOOID), whether an individual or a colony [Mod. L. fr. Gk *zōon*, animal]

zo·o·nos·es (zouənóusi:z) *n.* (*med.*) diseases and infections that naturally transmitted from vertebrate animals to human beings

zo·o·phyte (zóuəfait) *n.* an animal resembling a plant in appearance and/or growth **zo·o·phyt·ic** (zouəfítik), **zo·o·phýt·i·cal** *adjs* [fr. Mod. L. *zoophyton* fr. Gk fr. *zōon*, animal+*phuton*, plant]

zo·o·spo·ran·gi·al (zouousparǽndʒi:əl) *adj.* of or relating to a zoosporangium

zo·o·spo·ran·gi·um (zouousparǽndʒi:əm) *pl.* **zo·o·spo·ran·gi·a** (zouousparǽndʒi:ə) *n.* (*bot.*) a sporangium in which zoospores develop [fr. Gk *zōon*, animal+SPORANGIUM]

zo·o·spore (zóuəspɔr, zóuəspour) *n.* a motile spore, e.g. a flagellated asexual spore of some fungi or an amoeboid or flagellated product of protozoan sexual or asexual reproduction [fr. Gk *zōon*, animal+SPORE]

Zo·que·an (sóukeiən) *pl.* **Zo·que·an, Zo·que·ans** *n.* a Mexican Indian people of E. Tabasco, Chiapas and Oaxaca || a member of this people || the Mixe-Zoque language stock

zo·ri (zouri:) *n.* a thonged Japanese sandal of any material

zor·il (zɔ́ril, zóril) *n.* the striped muishond || *Ictonyxfrenata*, a carnivorous mammal of N. Africa related to the striped muishond [fr. F. *zorille* fr. Span.]

zo·ril·la (zəríla) *n.* a zoril

Zo·ro·as·ter (zórouæstər, zóurouæstər, zourouǽstər, zourouǽstər) (c. 660 –c. 583 B.C.), a prophet of ancient Persia. After seeing heavenly visions, he converted the king and court of Bactria to his faith. His sayings are collected in the Avesta. He instituted the caste of magus and founded a religion based on the belief that good and evil are absolutes. They are represented by the gods Ormazd and Ahriman who are engaged in constant warfare. The followers of Ormazd must strive for purity in thought, word and deed, based on a strict code of ethics. Man can attain perfection by individual choice of good. Zoroastrianism was the national religion of Persia and influential in the Near East until the rise of Islam (7th c.). The Parsees of India adhere to a form of this faith

Zo·ro·as·tri·an (zourouǽstri:ən, zourouǽstri:ən) **1.** *adj.* of or pertaining to Zoroaster or the religion of Zoroaster **2.** *n.* an adherent of the religion of Zoroaster **Zo·ro·às·tri·an·ism** *n.* [fr. L. *Zoroastres* fr. Gk fr. Zend *Zarathustra*]

Zor·ri·lla de San Mar·tín (sɔrríjɑ:ðesánmɑrtí:n), Juan (1855-1931), Uruguayan romantic poet, lawyer, and diplomat. His works include the national poem of Uruguay 'Tabaré' (1888), about a mestizo torn between his Indian and his Spanish heritage

Zor·ri·lla y del Mo·ral (θɔrrí:jɑi:ðelmɔrál), José (1817-93), Spanish poet. His romantic dramas include 'El zapatero y el rey' (1840-1) and Don Juan Tenorio' (1844)

Zos·i·mus (zósəməs, zóusəməs) (5th c. A.D.), Greek historian. He wrote a history of the Roman Empire from the late 3rd c. to 410

zos·ter (zŏstər) n. (med.) shingles [L. fr. Gk zōstēr, girdle]

Zou·ave (zu:áv) n. a member of a French light infantry corps created (1831) in Algeria ‖ (hist.) a member of certain corps adopting the Zouave uniform, e.g. in the American Civil War, and in the Papal States (1860) [F. fr. Zouaoua, a Kabyle tribe of Algeria]

ZPG (abbr.) for 'zero population growth' (which see)

ZSU 57-2 n. (mil.) U.S.S.R. anti-aircraft missile carrier including two 57-mm guns

zuc·chet·to (zu:kétou) pl. **zuc·chet·tos** n. a skullcap worn by a Roman Catholic priest (black), bishop (purple), cardinal (red), or the pope (white) [fr. Ital. zucchetta fr. zucca, gourd, head]

zuc·chi·ni (zu:kí:ni:) pl. **zuc·chi·ni, zuc·chi·nis** n. a variety of summer squash with a dark green skin. It is like a cucumber in shape and is usually picked when less than 1 ft in length [Ital. pl. of zucchin, dim. of zucca, gourd]

Zug (tsu:x) a canton (area 93 sq. miles, pop. 75,930), German-speaking and mainly Catholic, in N. Switzerland ‖ its capital (pop. 20,000) on Lake Zug (area 15 sq. miles)

Zug·spit·ze (tsú:xʃpitsə) the highest peak (9,719 ft) in West Germany, in Bavaria on the Austrian frontier

Zui·der Zee (záidərzí:, záidərzéi) a former inlet (80 miles long) of the North Sea in the Netherlands. Part has been closed off by a dam and forms the IJsselmeer. Drainage has enabled nearly 550,000 acres to be reclaimed from the rest

Zu·lu (zú:lu:) 1. n. pl. **Zu·lu, Zu·lus** a member of an African nation living largely in N.E. Natal. The Zulus were a powerful military force in the early 19th c., esp. under their chief Dingaan, until defeated by the Boers (1838). Their kingdom was gradually divided and its components absorbed into the Transvaal (1888) and Natal (1897) ‖ the Bantu language of this people 2. adj. of the Zulus, their language or culture

zulu n. (angling) an artificial fly

Zu·lu·land (zú:lu:lænd) a region of native reserves (area 10,375 sq. miles) in N.E. Natal, South Africa, inhabited by the Zulus. Capital: Eshowe (pop. 3.000). Industries: cattle raising, cereals, mining (gold, coal, zircon)

zulu time (mil.) Greenwich mean time

Zu·már·ra·ga (θu:márraɡa), Juan de (c. 1468-1548), Spanish Franciscan monk, the first bishop (1528-46) and archbishop (1546-8) of Mexico. He built the cathedral in Mexico City, introduced the printing press to the New World, and founded the college of Santa Cruz de Tlatelolco for the education of the Indians

Zu·ñi (zú:nji:, zú:ni:) n. a member of a North American Indian tribe in New Mexico ‖ their language, which constitutes a linguistic family

Zu·ñi·an n. the Zuñi language family [Span fr. Am. Ind.]

Zup·pa in·gle·se (tsú:pɑ iŋléisi:) n. Italian sponge rum cake with custard cream and fruit

Zur·ba·rán (θu:rbɑrán), Francisco de (1598 – c. 1669), Spanish painter. His best works are characterized by clear, austere use of color and massive solid forms, in a splendid fusion of the mystical and the realistic

Zu·rich (zúərik) (G. Zürich) a German speaking, largely Protestant canton (area 665 sq. miles, pop. 1,122,839) in N. Switzerland, admitted to the Swiss Confederation in 1351 ‖ its capital, the largest town (pop. 379,600) in Switzerland, and the country's most important center of commerce, banking and industry (silk, cotton, machinery, paper, food), and a main cultural center of German Switzerland. It is on Lake Zurich (area 34 sq. miles). Churches in the old city include Grossmünster (11th-13th cc.), Fraumünster (12th c.) and St Peter's (13th c.). Town Hall (1698), university (1832), Federal Institute of Technology (1855)

Zwick·au (tsvíkau) an industrial center (pop. 123,475) in Saxony, East Germany: coal mining, mechanical engineering, textiles, chemicals

zwie·back (swí:bæk, zwí:bæk, swáibæk, zwáibæk) n. a rusk of toasted sweetened bread made with eggs [G. fr. zwie-, twice+backen, ω bake]

Zwing·li (zwíŋli:, tsvíŋli:), Ulrich or Huldreich (1484-1531), Swiss religious reformer who rejected the papacy and attacked the authority of the priesthood, taking the Bible as the only rule of faith, with the object of restoring to the Church its former simplicity. He differed with Luther on the question of the real presence, holding that the communion was the commemoration of Christ's death, and not the repetition of the sacrifice

Zwing·li·an (zwíŋli:ən) 1. adj. pertaining to the doctrine of Zwingli 2. n. an adherent of this belief **Zwíng·li·an·ism** n.

zwit·ter·i·on (tsvítərạiən) n. an ion that bears both a positive and a negative charge, at differ-

ent positions **zwit·ter·i·on·ic** (tsvítərɑiónik) adj. [G. fr. zwitter, hybrid+ion, ion]

Zwol·le (zwólə) the capital (pop. 78,585) of Overijssel province, Netherlands: 15th-c. church, town hall

zy·ga·poph·y·sis (zɑigəpófisis) pl. **zy·ga·poph·y·ses** (zɑigəpófisi:z) n. (anat., zool.) one of the processes of a vertebra by which it articulates with adjacent vertebrae [Mod. L. fr. Gk zugon, yoke+apophusis, apophysis]

zy·go·dac·tyl (zɑigoudǽktil) 1. adj. (of a bird) having two toes in the front of the foot and two behind 2. n. a bird (e.g. a parrot) having toes arranged in this way [fr. Gk zugon, yoke+DACTYL]

zy·go·ma (zɑigóumə) pl. **zy·go·ma·ta** (zɑigóumətə), **zy·go·mas** n. (anat., zool.) the bony arch of the cheek **zy·go·mat·ic** (zɑigəmǽtik) adj. [Gk zugoma fr. zugon, yoke]

zy·go·mor·phic (zɑigəmórfik) adj. (biol.) bilaterally symmetrical, divisible into similar parts in only one plane (cf. ACTINOMORPHIC) **zy·go·mór·phism** n. **zy·go·mór·phous** adj. [fr. Gk zugon, yoke+morphē, shape]

zy·go·sis (zɑigóusis) pl. **zy·go·ses** (zɑigóusi:z) n. (biol., esp. in compounds) a union of gametes, e.g. conjugation [Mod. L. fr. Gk zugōsis, a yoking]

zy·go·spore (zɑigəspɔr, zɑigəspour) n. a resting spore, formed by a conjugation of two similar reproductive cells, that eventually gives rise to a sporophyte generation (cf. OOSPORE) **zy·go·spor·ic** (zɑigəspórik, zɑigəspórik) adj. [fr. Gk zugon, yoke+SPORE]

zy·gote (zɑigout) n. a cell formed by the union of two gametes, e.g. the fertilized ovum **zy·got·ic** (zɑigótik) adj. [fr. Gk zugōtos, yoked]

zy·mase (zɑimeis) n. an enzyme system found in yeast and other microorganisms, which is responsible for the fermentation of carbohydrates [fr. F. zymase fr. Gk zumē, leaven]

zy·mo·gen (zɑimədʒən) n. a substance capable of being transformed into a ferment, the precursor of an enzyme **zy·mo·gen·ic** (zɑimədʒénik) adj. [fr. Gk zumē, leaven+-genēs, of a (specified) kind]

zy·mol·o·gy (zɑimólədʒi:) n. the scientific study of fermentation [fr. Gk zumē, leaven ‖ logos, discourse]

zy·mo·sis (zɑimóusis) pl. **zy·mo·ses** (zɑimóusi:z) n. fermentation [fr. Gk zumōsis]

zy·mo·tic (zɑimótik) adj. of, causing or caused by fermentation [fr. Gk zumōtikos]

zy·mur·gy (zɑimərdʒi:) n. the applied chemistry of fermentation processes [fr. Gk zumē, leaven + -ourgia, working]

ENCYCLOPEDIC
SUPPLEMENTS

© Enrico Feroelli, Wheeler, Inc.

THE PRESIDENCY

In the course of some 200 years, the presidency of the United States has become the most powerful office in the world. The duties and responsibilities of the office are immense. Unlike many of the democratic governments of Europe and elsewhere that have both a chief of state and a head of government, the U.S. system of government has only one chief executive, the president. The holder of that office serves not only as head of government but also in the primarily ceremonial post of chief of state. As chief of state, the president performs many of the public and ceremonial duties undertaken by the king or queen of the United Kingdom, other monarchs, and the governor-general of Canada and other Commonwealth nations. Although some of the duties the president performs as chief of state may seem trivial, the role helps the occupant of the office maintain contact with the overall populace. As head of government, the president is the chief executive of the nation, the director of the government. In addition the president serves as commander in chief of the armed forces of the United States and the voice of the American people.

According to presidential scholar Clinton Rossiter, the presidency is a one-person job. The person "who holds it can never escape making the final decisions in each of many areas in which the American people and their constitution hold "him or her responsible." A sign on the presidential desk of Harry S. Truman, the nation's chief executive from April 1945 to January 1953, said it perfectly: "The buck stops here." According to Rossiter, "that, in the end, is the essence of the presidency. It is the one office in all of the land whose occupant is forbidden to pass the buck." Recognizing the value of President Truman's words, a White House successor of entirely different political persuasion adopted the motto for his administration 28 years later.

George Washington took the presidential oath in New York on April 30, 1789. The 20th amendment set the inauguration date as January 20.

The Role and Duties of the President

The role of the president has expanded considerably beyond that envisaged by the Founding Fathers in the Constitution. During such crises as the Civil War, world wars I and II, and the depression of the 1930s, Congress and the nation both turned to the executive for leadership and guidance. Crisis powers given to the president were to a great extent retained afterward, thereby adding new stature to the office. Likewise, as foreign affairs increased in importance during the 20th century, the president's role as the voice of the nation added new prestige and responsibilities to the office. Governmental efforts to provide for the social and economic welfare of its citizens, initiated in the depression of 1929-33 and subsequently expanded, have contributed to the president's duties and powers in the economic and social spheres. Likewise, the necessity for an expanded bureaucracy serving the president has heightened his prestige and influence at the expense of the legislative branch.

Such figures as Thomas Jefferson, Andrew Jackson, Abraham Lincoln, Theodore Roosevelt, Woodrow Wilson, Franklin D. Roosevelt, and Harry S. Truman have shaped the presidency. Normally regarded as "strong presidents," these individuals, exercising their prerogatives as leaders of the nation, utilized their influence to initiate major changes in American society. In so doing they added to the magnitude of the office. Although the Vietnam war and the Watergate scandal of Richard Nixon's administration strained the presidency during the 1960s and early 1970s, President Gerald Ford and his successors worked hard, and successfully, to restore the office to its former status.

The President as Leader of the Nation. The president as leader of the nation is confronted with a multiplicity of problems and tasks. As the only executive official elected by the people at large (the vice-president is assigned a legislative post as president of the Senate), he represents the nation to the world. His responsibilities do not stop there, for he is the chief policymaker for domestic and foreign affairs. In this capacity, although he is acknowledged as the leader of one of the political parties, he must represent all the people.

John Marshall, who was to become chief justice of the United States, recognized, as secretary of state, the inherent responsibilities of the president in the domain of foreign affairs. "The president," he noted in 1799, "is the sole organ of the nation in its external relations, and its sole representative with foreign nations." In receiving the credentials of foreign delegates the president exercises the prerogative of recognizing or rejecting the credentials of other governments. Likewise, he has the power to withdraw such recognition. He alone may address foreign governments or be addressed by them. Diplomatic communications are generally carried out through the numerous ministers and envoys who represent the president and the United States in other countries.

The president, with the advice and consent of the Senate, consummates treaties in his capacity as leader of the nation. (He signs treaties as chief of state.) Should he ignore the Senate's role in treaty making, especially by disregarding the Senate in the making of a pact, the president may endanger his own position. Thus President Wilson, by ignoring the senators in the negotiations on the Treaty of Versailles and the League of Nations, created acrimonious feelings that later led to the rejection by the United States of the treaty and the league. In addition to this, the president must recognize the need for congressional appropriations for his foreign policy measures. Consequently he must cultivate congressional support for his programs.

As leader of the nation, the president must determine the course of foreign and domestic policy. The Constitution stipulates that the executive "shall from time to time give to the Congress Information of the State of the Union, and recommend to their Consideration such Measures as he shall judge necessary and expedient." In his messages to Congress, including those on the annual budget, the state of the union, and the economic condition of the nation, the president suggests the programs and measures for legislative enactment that he considers vital to the nation's welfare and betterment.

Elected by the people, the president, unlike members of Congress, represents the entire nation rather than a district or state. Hence he must be a national leader. This he accomplishes by diverse means. In addition to his messages to Congress, he utilizes television and radio, including the live televised address and press conference, to inform the people of his position concerning the issues and problems confronting the nation.

Although elected specifically as a member of one political party, the president must work with both parties in determining public policy. Nevertheless, as the nominee of a specific party, he must also work toward the realization of that party's programs and goals. To prevent a complete cleavage in society, however, the president, along with the leaders of his party and the opposition, often works out programs on crucial matters like foreign affairs and national defense that are generally acceptable to both parties. If the president's party holds a majority in Congress that is in accord with his views, the president is more likely to see his program enacted. However, if his party is in a minority, or if the members of his own party disagree with his specific programs, the president's legislative measures may be ignored or defeated by Congress.

Early in 1986, President Ronald Reagan urged a major U.S. arms sale to Saudi Arabia. The Republican-controlled Senate and the Democratic-controlled House of Representatives passed a resolution blocking the sale. The president then vetoed the resolution and began a major campaign to have his veto sustained. On the morning that the Senate was to vote on the measure, all 100 senators were invited to breakfast at the White House; many senators also received presidential telephone calls on the issue. Although the merits of the sale were considered during Senate debate, some supporters of the president's position simply pointed out that the "prestige of the presidency" was "at stake" with the vote. The veto was sustained in the Senate by one vote. Eight senators, who originally voted against the sale, voted to sustain the veto. The incident is a classical example of the political clout and power of the presidency.

The President as Commander in Chief. Article II, Section 2, of the Constitution states that the president is "Commander in Chief of the Army and Navy . . . and of the Militia of the several States, when called into the actual Service of the United States."

This provision assures civilian control of the military. Although this stipulation grants the executive broad powers, the chief executive is limited somewhat by those powers left solely to Congress. These powers include the right of Congress to declare war, to appropriate funds for the armed forces, and to conscript men for military service.

Nevertheless, the executive's powers are extensive. He selects the key figures in the military establishment, including the secretary of defense, the secretaries of the Army, Navy, and Air Force, and the military chiefs of staff. He recommends the defense budget to Congress and administers laws pertaining to the defense of the nation. He directs strategy in times of war, and is held responsible for the success or failure of the entire defense program. As noted previously, the president has often been delegated extraordinary wartime powers. These include the right to make decisions pertaining to the fundamental military strategy of the nation and, on the domestic scene, to initiate measures, including the invoking of martial law if necessary, designed to win a war. In fact, in the 175 years between the late 1790s and the early 1970s, U.S. troops had been sent into military hostilities some 200 times without a declaration of war. In the age of the Cold War and possible nuclear conflict, the case for congressional involvement in decisions involving military force seemed to be weaker than at any time in U.S. history. In the event of a nuclear attack against the United States, there very likely would not be time for a president to consult Congress.

The Vietnam war of the 1960s and early 1970s, which took some 57,000 American lives and cost the nation billions of dollars, marked a turning point. In 1964 the Congress, responding to an alleged attack on U.S. vessels in the Gulf of Tonkin off Vietnam, passed a resolution authorizing the president to take the steps needed, "including the use of armed force," to assist South Vietnam preserve its freedom. As the U.S. involvement in the conflict mounted, so did congressional discontent with the implications of the Tonkin Gulf Resolution. By the early 1970s, Congress was debating legislation to limit the president's war-making power. Finally in October 1973, the Senate and House of Representatives passed the War Powers Resolution. Although President Richard M. Nixon vetoed the measure, there was sufficient support in Congress to override the veto.

The purpose of the War Powers Resolution is stated in Section 2(a):

> to fulfill the intent of the framers of the Constitution of the United States and insure that the collective judgment of both the Congress and the president will apply to the introduction of United States armed forces into hostilities, or into situations where imminent involvement in hostilities is clearly indicated by the circumstances, and to the continued use of such forces in hostilities or in such situations.

The resolution requires the president to keep Congress informed both before and during any involvement by U.S. forces in hostilities. Under Section 4(a), the president is required to report to Congress within 48 hours when U.S. troops are introduced:

> (1) into hostilities or into situations where imminent involvement in hostilities is clearly indicated by the circumstances;
> (2) into the territory, airspace or waters of a foreign nation, while equipped for combat, except for deployments which relate solely to supply, replacement, repair, or training of such forces; or
> (3) in numbers which substantially enlarge United States armed forces equipped for combat already located in a foreign nation.

A written report must be submitted to the speaker of the House of Representatives and the president pro tempore of the Senate setting forth:

> a—the circumstances necessitating the introduction of the United States armed forces;
> b—the constitutional and legislative authority under which such introduction took place; and
> c—the estimated scope and duration of the hostilities or involvement

Only in the first circumstance (U.S. forces likely to be engaged in combat) is the length of the commitment limited by the resolution. In that event, Section 5(b) of the resolution requires the president to withdraw U.S. troops within 60 to 90 days unless the Congress authorizes their continued presence. The resolution also contains a provision, 5(c), permitting Congress, by concurrent resolution without approval by the president, to order the withdrawal of U.S. troops from hostilities abroad.

Since passage of the act, Presidents Gerald Ford, Jimmy Carter, and Reagan sought ways to avoid the trigger mechanism in Section 5(b). The three presidents reported to the Congress under the act's provisions but often without citing which precise provision in the act applied to their deployment of forces. In this way they have been able to avoid the 60- to 90-day clock. As a result, the role of Congress in the deployment of U.S. troops abroad has not been any greater after enactment of the resolution than before.

The Presidency in History

Origins of the Office. The presidency, and what is often termed the "presidential system of government," is of distinctly American origin. Political philosophers such as John Locke (1632-1704) and Baron de Montesquieu (1689-1755) had written earlier on the separation of legislative and executive functions, but the transition from theory to practice was left to the framers of the Constitution. The term "president" was not new, however, for it had been applied to the presiding officer of legislative bodies in the colonies and in the Continental Congress. Likewise the New York constitution of 1777 and the Massachusetts constitution of 1780 suggested an independent executive, whose powers were somewhat comparable to those later granted to the president of the United States.

Delegates to the Constitutional Convention in Philadelphia in 1787 faced a dilemma when they considered establishing a "national executive." The majority of the framers of the constitution wanted an executive power capable of reaching the remotest parts of the Union, "not only for the purpose of enforcing national laws but also . . . for the purpose of bringing assistance to the states in grave emergencies of domestic disorder." The framers also wanted to avoid stirring up popular fear of the monarchy.

George P. A. Healy's "The Peacemakers" shows President Lincoln meeting with his military advisers toward the end of the Civil War. The U.S. Constitution clearly states that the president is commander in chief.

At the convention, Roger Sherman of Connecticut favored the notion of subordinating the chief executive to a legislature. According to James Madison's *Notes,* Sherman "considered the executive magistracy as nothing more than an institution for carrying the will of the legislature into effect," and he "wished that the number [of executives] might not be fixed, but that the legislature should be at liberty to appoint one or more as experience might dictate." Delegate James Wilson of Pennsylvania took an opposite view and argued in favor of a single executive with broad powers. Wilson, as James Madison recorded in his diary of the convention's proceedings, "preferred a single magistrate, as giving most energy, dispatch, and responsibility to the office." The executive, Wilson argued, should be independent of the legislature, and to preserve this status should be vested with an absolute veto over legislative enactments. Otherwise, the legislature would "at any moment sink it [the executive] into nonexistence." Furthermore the president should be elected directly by the people. Wilson had to compromise on a number of points, including the last one, for the convention decided that the president should be elected indirectly by the people through a college of electors. However, the core of Wilson's ideas, supported especially by Madison and Gouverneur Morris, was incorporated into the final document.

Section 1 of Article II of the Constitution clearly spells out and defines the basis of and qualifications for the office of president. It states:

Terry Arthur, The White House

The duties of the president are many. As "the sole organ of the nation in its foreign relations," Ronald Reagan met with Soviet General Secretary Gorbachev in 1985. In accordance with the Constitution, Jimmy Carter, *below left,*

> The executive Power shall be vested in a President of the United States of America. He shall hold his Office during the Term of four Years. . . .
>
> No Person except a natural born Citizen, or a Citizen of the United States, at the time of the Adoption of this Constitution, shall be eligible to the Office of President; neither shall any person be eligible to that Office who shall not have attained the Age of thirty five Years, and been fourteen Years a Resident within the United States.
>
> In Case of the Removal of the President from Office, or of his Death, Resignation, or Inability to discharge the Powers and Duties of the said Office, the Same shall devolve on the Vice-President, and the Congress may by Law provide for the Case of Removal, Death, Resignation or Inability, both of the President and Vice-President, declaring what Officer shall then act as President, and such Officer shall act accordingly, until the Disability be removed, or a President shall be elected.
>
> The President shall, at stated Times, receive for his Services, a Compensation, which shall neither be encreased nor diminished during the Period for which he shall have been elected, and he shall not receive within that period any other Emolument from the United States, or any of them.
>
> Before he enter on the Execution of his Office, he shall take the following Oath or Affirmation: —"I do solemnly swear (or affirm) that I will faithfully execute the Office of President of the United States, and will to the best of my Ability, preserve, protect and defend the Constitution of the United States."

© Arthur Grace, Sygma

Four constitutional amendments, relating directly to the presidency, were approved subsequently. The 12th amendment, proclaimed on Sept. 25, 1804, clarified the election procedure and defined the office of vice-president. A confused 1800 election result encouraged passage of the 12th amendment. The 20th, or Lame Duck amendment, was proclaimed on Feb. 6, 1933, and reduced the period between the election and inauguration of a president. The inauguration date now would be January 20, not March 4 as previously, and the session of Congress that had been held in the interim period was eliminated.

Franklin D. Roosevelt, an extremely active chief executive who took full advantage of his power, was the first and only president to be elected to four terms. As a result, sentiment in favor of limiting a president's time in office arose, and the 22nd amendment, limiting the president to two terms, was proclaimed on March 1, 1951.

The crises caused by the illness of President Dwight D. Eisenhower and the 1963 assassination of President John F. Kennedy focused attention on the issue of presidential succession and the need to establish a procedure for filling the vice-presidency when that office becomes vacant. As a result, the 25th amendment was passed by Congress, ratified by the states and proclaimed on Feb. 24, 1967.

Section I of the 25th amendment states that in case of the removal of the president from office or of his death or resignation, the vice-president shall become president. Section II provides that "whenever there is a vacancy in the office of vice-president, the president shall nominate a vice-president who shall take the office upon confirmation by a majority vote of both houses of Congress." Prior to the 25th amendment, the vice-presidency had been vacant on 16 occasions. Gerald R. Ford and Nelson A. Rockefeller were appointed vice-president by Presidents Nixon and Ford, respectively, and took office in accordance with the terms of the 25th amendment.

The amendment also provides for a means of dealing with a much more difficult aspect of presidential power: namely, that of

outlined the "State of the Union" to Congress. John Kennedy used the televised news conference to outline his program and objectives. Before a large audience, Lyndon Johnson signed the Civil Rights Bill on July 2, 1964. GOP leader Reagan campaigned for his reelection and the election of other Republicans in 1984.

presidential disability or inability to perform the powers and duties of the office. It provides for the resolution of the presidential inability problem in three ways. First, the president may declare his own inability, whereupon his "powers and duties shall be discharged by the vice-president as acting president." In this instance, the president may reclaim the powers and duties of the office by stating his ability to perform. Second, in the event the president cannot declare his own inability, the vice-president and a majority of the Cabinet may declare that such an inability exists, whereupon the "vice-president shall immediately assume the powers and duties of the office as acting president." Third, in the event that the vice-president and a majority of the Cabinet conclude that the president is unable to perform the powers and duties of the office and the president disagrees with this conclusion, the matter will be decided by Congress. "If the Congress, within 21 days . . . determines by two-thirds vote of both Houses that the president is unable to discharge the powers and duties of his office, the vice-

president shall . . . discharge the same as acting president; otherwise, the president shall resume the powers and duties of his office."

At various times there have been calls for reform of the presidency. A single, six-year term as well as a parliamentary government system have been suggested. During the 1950s, Sen. John W. Bricker, a Republican from Ohio, proposed an amendment to limit the power of the president under executive agreements. Generally, such efforts to change the office have not met with much success.

As presidential scholar Thomas E. Cronin has noted, "the original job of presidency has grown and yet the Founding Fathers wrote a marvelously flexible job description that is almost as appropriate today as it was when the nation was a new republic. The flexibility plus the willingness of the American people to place confidence in effective presidents give a president an enormous opportunity to serve the nation."

George Washington

1st president, 1789-97   Federalist

1732. Born on February 22 in Westmoreland county, VA.
1752. Inherited Mount Vernon, an estate on the Potomac.
1755-58. Was commander in chief of Virginian troops for the balance of the French and Indian War.
1759. On January 6, married Martha Dandridge Custis, a widow with two children.
1759-74. Served in the Virginia House of Burgesses.
1774. Was a delegate to the First Continental Congress.
1775. Elected a delegate to the Second Continental Congress; named commander in chief of the Continental Army.
1776. Forced British troops to evacuate Boston; after a series of defeats in New York, crossed the Delaware River on December 25-26 to take 1,000 British prisoners.
1781. Defeated British forces at Yorktown. Lord Cornwallis surrendered to end the Revolutionary War.
1787. Served as president of the Constitutional Convention.
1789. Unanimously elected president of the United States.
1797. Retired to Mount Vernon after two terms as president.
1798. Named commander in chief of new U.S. Army.
1799. Died on December 14 at Mount Vernon.

Highlights of Presidency

1789. Judiciary Act established federal court system; first tax laws were adopted.
1791. Bank Act established a nationwide banking system. □ The Bill of Rights became law on December 15.
1792. Unanimously reelected to a second term. □ Coinage Act gave the government power to mint coins.
1793. On April 22, proclaimed U.S. neutrality in war between Britain and France.
1794. Federal troops suppressed the Whiskey Rebellion, armed resistance to excise tax.
1795. The Jay Treaty, under which Britain gave up its frontier forts and ensured continued trade with the United States, was ratified.
1796. Delivered Farewell Address, announcing his retirement and advocating a strong central government and neutrality in foreign affairs.

John Adams

2nd president, 1797-1801   Federalist

1735. Born on October 30 in Braintree (now Quincy), MA.
1755. Graduated from Harvard College.
1758. Began law practice in Braintree.
1764. Married Abigail Smith on October 25. Five children would be born to the couple.
1765. Wrote resolutions opposing the British Stamp Act.
1775. As a delegate to the Second Continental Congress, argued for independence and the formation of a Continental Army.
1776. Headed Continental Board of War and Ordnance; served on committee drafting Declaration of Independence.
1779. Drafted most of the Massachusetts state constitution.
1780. In France and the Netherlands, negotiated treaties and a $1,400,000 loan for the United States.
1782. Helped negotiate peace treaty with Britain (the Treaty of Paris, signed Sept. 3, 1783).
1785-1788. Was U.S. minister to Britain.
1789. Elected as the nation's first vice-president.
1792. Reelected vice-president.
1796. As the Federalist candidate, successfully opposed Thomas Jefferson, the Democratic-Republican candidate, in presidential election. Jefferson became vice-president.
1801. Retired to Braintree.
1826. Died on July 4 in Braintree.

Highlights of Presidency

1797. XYZ Affair, in which French agents demanded a bribe to conclude favorable treaty negotiations, brought the United States to the brink of war with France. (Peace was secured by the Convention of 1800.)
1798. Alien and Sedition Acts, giving the president power to imprison or banish foreigners and making criticism of the government a crime, were adopted. The laws, supported by the Federalists, were highly unpopular.
1800. U.S. capital moved from Philadelphia to Washington, D.C. □ In the presidential election, Adams and the Federalists were defeated by the Democratic-Republican candidates, Thomas Jefferson and Aaron Burr.

Thomas Jefferson

3rd president, 1801-09   Democratic-Republican

1743. Born on April 13 at Shadwell, VA.
1762. Graduated from the College of William and Mary.
1767. Admitted to the bar; began practicing law.
1769. Elected to the Virginia House of Burgesses.
1772. Married Martha Wayles Skelton on January 1. The couple would have a son and five daughters, but only two daughters would live to maturity.
1775. Elected a delegate to the First Continental Congress.
1776. As a delegate to the Second Continental Congress, chosen to write the Declaration of Independence.
1776-79. A member of the Virginia House of Delegates, supported proposals on land reform and religious freedom.
1779-81. Served as governor of Virginia.
1783-84. As delegate to Congress from Virginia, helped establish the nation's coinage system.
1785-89. Served as minister to France.
1790-93. Was secretary of state under George Washington.
1796. Accepted Democratic-Republican nomination for president but was narrowly defeated by John Adams and thus became vice-president.
1800. In the presidential election, defeated Adams but tied with his running mate, Aaron Burr. The election went to the House of Representatives, which chose Jefferson on Feb. 17, 1801.
1809. Retired to his Virginia estate, Monticello.
1819. Founded the University of Virginia.
1826. Died on July 4 at Monticello.

Highlights of Presidency

1803. Supreme Court ruling in *Marbury v. Madison* established the principle that the court could declare unconstitutional a law passed by Congress. □ The Louisiana Territory was purchased from France.
1804. Elected to a second term as president. □ Meriwether Lewis and William Clark began to explore the Northwest.
1805. A peace treaty was signed with Tripoli, ending a four-year war.
1808. The importation of African slaves into the United States became illegal.
1809. The 1807 Embargo Act, prohibiting exports and sailings to foreign ports, was replaced by a law banning trade with Britain and France.

James Madison

4th president, 1809-17   Democratic-Republican

1751. Born on March 16 at Port Conway, VA.
1771. Graduated from the College of New Jersey (now Princeton University).
1776. Served on the committee that drafted Virginia's constitution and declaration of rights.
1777. Elected to Virginia governor's council, where he served under Patrick Henry and Thomas Jefferson.
1780. Elected to Congress as a delegate from Virginia.
1784. Returned to Virginia, where he served in the legislature.
1787. As a delegate to the Constitutional Convention, argued for a strong central government and a system of checks and balances. Also contributed to *The Federalist* papers.
1788. Debated for and won Virginian ratification of the U.S. Constitution.
1789-97. Served in the House of Representatives.
1794. Married Dolley Payne Todd on September 15.
1798. Wrote the Virginia Resolutions, defending states' rights and opposing the Alien and Sedition Acts.
1801-09. Was secretary of state under Thomas Jefferson.
1808. Elected president over Federalist candidate C. C. Pinckney.
1817. Retired to his Virginia estate, Montpelier.
1826. Succeeded Jefferson as rector of the University of Virginia.
1836. Died on June 28 at Montpelier.

Highlights of Presidency

1810. Congress ended a ban on trade with Britain and France, who continued to be at war.
1811. Trade with Britain was ended again, after Britain continued to enforce its blockade of France by attacking U.S. ships. □ Indian forces allied under Chief Tecumseh were defeated in the Battle of Tippecanoe on November 7.
1812. Citing continued attacks on its ships, the United States declared war on Britain in June. □ Reelected to a second term.
1814. Treaty of Ghent, ending the War of 1812, was signed on December 24. British troops earlier had burned the White House.
1815. Began a wide-ranging domestic program that included reorganization of the National Bank and development of roads and canals.

James Monroe

5th president, 1817-25   Democratic-Republican

1758. Born on April 28 in Westmoreland county, VA.
1774. Entered the College of William and Mary.
1776. Left school to join the Virginia Militia, enrolling as a lieutenant. Fought at White Plains and Trenton.
1782. Elected to the Virginia House of Delegates.
1783. Elected to Congress of the Confederation.
1786. Married Elizabeth Kortright of New York City on Febraury 16, and returned to Virginia to practice law. The couple would have two daughters, Eliza and Maria, and a son who died in infancy.
1790. Elected to the U.S. Senate, where he opposed greater centralization of government.
1794. Named minister to France by President Washington. His pro-France sympathies led to his recall in 1796.
1799. Elected governor of Virginia.
1803. Sent by President Jefferson to France, to negotiate the Louisiana Purchase. Subsequently named minister to Britain.
1808. Defeated by James Madison in bid for the Democratic-Republican presidential nomination.
1811. Appointed secretary of state by President Madison. His attempts to avert war with Britain were unsuccessful.
1814. Replaced John Armstrong as secretary of war following the British burning of Washington.
1816. Elected president by a wide margin.
1825. Retired to Oak Hill, near Leesburg, VA.
1829. Presided over the Virginia Constitutional Convention.
1830. Moved to New York to live with his daughter.
1831. Died on July 4 in New York City.

Highlights of Presidency

1818. The Convention of 1818 fixed the boundary between the United States and British North America.
1819. Spain agreed to give Florida to the United States in exchange for the cancellation of $5 million in debts.
1820. Congress adopted the Missouri Compromise, temporarily quieting sectional disputes over the expansion of slavery. □ Won election to a second term in a nearly unanimous vote.
1822. Vetoed a plan for the federal government to improve internal roads.
1823. On December 2, proclaimed the Monroe Doctrine, warning European powers not to interfere in U.S. affairs.

John Quincy Adams

6th president, 1825-29   Democratic-Republican

1767. Born on July 11 in Braintree (now Quincy), MA, the second child and eldest son of John and Abigail Adams.
1787. Graduated from Harvard College.
1790. Began law practice in Boston.
1791. Wrote the first of three series of articles supporting President Washington's policy of neutrality.
1797. On July 26, married Louisa Catherine Johnson. The couple would have four children.
1797-1801. Served as U.S. minister to Prussia.
1803. Elected to the U.S. Senate as a Federalist; however, his independent policies led the party to replace him before the end of his term.
1809-14. Was minister to Russia.
1814. Served on commission negotiating the Treaty of Ghent, ending the War of 1812.
1815-17. Was minister to Britain.
1817. Appointed secretary of state under James Monroe.
1824. Ran for president, opposed by Henry Clay, William Crawford, and Andrew Jackson (all Democratic-Republicans). Jackson received the most votes, but as none of the four had a majority, the election went to the House of Representatives. In the House, Clay, who had won the fewest electoral votes and was thus out of the running, threw his support to Adams and ensured his election in Febraury 1825.
1829. Returned to Quincy after four years as president.
1830. Elected to the House of Representatives, where he would serve for 17 years. As a Congressman, argued for government's right to free slaves and against the annexation of Texas.
1848. Died on February 23 in the Capitol.

Highlights of Presidency

1825. Divisions in the Democratic-Republican Party increased when Adams appointed Henry Clay secretary of state, leading to charges that the two men had made a bargain in the election of 1824. □ Opposition in Congress prevented Adams from enacting most of his domestic program. □ Erie Canal, linking New York City and the Great Lakes, was completed.
1828. Congress imposed stiff duties on imported manufactured goods. □ Soundly defeated by Andrew Jackson in bid for reelection.

Andrew Jackson

7th president, 1829-37   Democrat

1767. Born on March 15 in Waxhaw settlement, SC.
1780. Joined South Carolina militia; captured by the British in 1781.
1787. Admitted to the bar, after reading law in North Carolina.
1791. In August, married Rachel Donelson Robards. The couple remarried on Jan. 17, 1794, on learning that Mrs. Jackson's divorce from her first husband was not final until 1793. They had no children.
1796. After being a member of the Tennessee constitutional convention, was elected to the House of Representatives.
1797. Won a U.S. Senate seat; resigned a year later.
1798-1804. Served on the superior court of Tennessee.
1806. Killed Charles Dickinson, a Nashville lawyer, in a duel sparked by remarks he made about Mrs. Jackson.
1812. Mobilized a force of 2,500 for the War of 1812.
1815. Defeated the British in the Battle of New Orleans.
1817. Successfully led an expedition into Florida, to stop Seminole raids on U.S. territory.
1821. Named provisional governor of Florida.
1823-25. Served in the U.S. Senate.
1824. Opposed John Quincy Adams, Henry Clay, and William Crawford in the presidential election. Although Jackson won the most votes, no candidate had a majority, and the House chose Adams.
1828. Won a sweeping victory in the presidential race.
1837. Retired to the Hermitage, his estate near Nashville.
1845. Died on June 8 at the Hermitage.

Highlights of Presidency

1829. Among his first acts as president were to place some 2,000 of his supporters in government jobs and establish a "kitchen cabinet" of informal advisers.
1832. Won a second term. □ On December 10, federal troops were sent to South Carolina over the state's attempt to nullify federal tariff laws.
1833. Removed government funds from the Bank of the United States after vetoing a new charter for the bank in 1832.
1835. Final installment of national debt was paid, making Jackson the only president to clear the debt.
1836. On July 11, issued the Specie Circular, ordering that federal lands be purchased only in gold and silver.

Martin Van Buren

8th president, 1837-41   Democrat

1782. Born on December 5 in Kinderhook, NY.
1800. Named a delegate to the New York congressional caucus.
1803. Began law practice in Kinderhook.
1807. Married Hannah Hoes on February 21. The couple would have four sons.
1813-20. Was a member of the New York state Senate; also served as state attorney general (1816-19).
1821-28. As a U.S. senator, opposed international alliances and the extension of the slave trade.
1828. Elected governor of New York but resigned after two months to become secretary of state under Andrew Jackson.
1829-31. As secretary of state, settled a dispute with Britain over West Indies trade and obtained an agreement whereby France would pay claims for U.S. ships damaged in the Napoleonic wars.
1831. Resigned as secretary of state, bringing about the resignation of the rest of the cabinet and allowing Jackson to reorganize it.
1832. Elected vice-president as Jackson's running mate.
1836. Elected president with a wide electoral majority.
1841. Returned to his farm near Kinderhook, which he named Lindenwald.
1848. Nominated for president by the antislavery Free Soil Party, which had split from the Democrats. The party split opened the way for the election of the Whig candidate, Zachary Taylor.
1862. Died on July 24 at Kinderhook.

Highlights of Presidency

1837. On May 10, banks closed in Philadelphia and New York City, marking the start of the Panic of 1837. The panic, touched off by inflation and land speculation, was followed by an economic depression that lasted the rest of Van Buren's term.
1839. A boundary dispute between Maine and New Brunswick brought the United States to the brink of war with Britain.
1840. At Van Buren's urging, Congress established an independent treasury to hold federal funds. An attempt to safeguard funds from private bank failures, the treasury was abolished in 1841 but reinstated in 1846. □ Defeated by William Henry Harrison in the November presidential election.

William Henry Harrison

9th president, 1841   Whig

1773. Born on February 8 in Charles City county, VA.
1790. Left college to study medicine.
1791. Abandoned his studies to enlist in the army, serving in the Northwest Territory.
1795. Married Anna Symmes in November. The couple subsequently had ten children, only four of whom survived their father.
1798. After resigning from the army, appointed secretary of the Northwest Territory in June. Was elected the first delegate to Congress from the Northwest Territory in 1799.
1800. Following the division of the Northwest Territories into Ohio and Indiana, appointed governor of Indiana.
1809. As governor, negotiated the Treaty of Fort Wayne, which secured approximately 3 million acres (1.2 million ha) of land from four Indian tribes.
1811. In the Battle of Tippecanoe on November 7, defeated a federation of Indian tribes under the Shawnee chief Tecumseh, that was protesting the Treaty of Fort Wayne.
1812. Placed in command of the Army of the Northwest during the War of 1812.
1813. In October, won a major victory over combined British and Indian forces in the Battle of the Thames, in southern Ontario.
1814. Resigned from the army.
1816. Elected to the U.S. House of Representatives.
1819. Elected to the Ohio state Senate.
1825. Elected to the U.S. Senate.
1828. Resigned his Senate seat to become minister to Colombia. However, his outspoken views on democracy offended President Simón Bolívar, and he was recalled a month after his arrival there.
1836. Defeated for the presidency by Martin Van Buren.
1840. With John Tyler as his running mate, campaigned successfully for the presidency on the slogan "Tippecanoe and Tyler too."

Highlights of Presidency

1841. Inaugurated on March 4 as 9th president, delivering the longest inaugural address on record, in which he promised not to run for a second term. Having contracted pneumonia in late March, died at the White House on April 4.

John Tyler

10th president, 1841-45   Whig

1790. Born on March 29 in Charles City county, VA.
1807. Graduated from William and Mary College.
1809. Admitted to the bar.
1811. Elected to the Virginia House of Delegates.
1813. Married Letitia Christian on March 29. The couple would have eight children.
1816-21. Served in the U.S. House of Representatives.
1823. Elected again to the Virginia House of Delegates.
1825. Elected governor of Virginia.
1827. Elected to the U.S. Senate. His stand in favor of states rights eventually led him to break with the Democrats and ally himself with the Whigs.
1836. Resigned his Senate seat rather than follow the instructions of the Virginia legislature to expunge a vote of censure against Andrew Jackson. As a Whig, lost bid for the vice-presidency to Richard M. Johnson.
1840. Elected vice-president.
1841. Succeeded to the presidency following the death of William Henry Harrison.
1844. Two years after the death of his first wife, married Julia Gardiner on June 22. The couple subsequently had seven children.
1845. Retired to Sherwood Forest, his estate near Charles City, after one term as president.
1861. In February, chaired a peace convention attempting to avert the Civil War. □ At a Virginia convention, voted in favor of secession.
1862. Died on January 18 in Richmond, VA, before taking his seat in the Confederate House.

Highlights of Presidency

1841. Vetoed banking bills supported by the Whigs, prompting the resignation of his cabinet. Tyler quickly named a new cabinet, but the Whig Party disowned him.
1842. Seminole War in Florida ended; boundary dispute between Maine and New Brunswick settled.
1843. In January, the Whigs introduced impeachment resolutions in the House, but the measures were defeated.
1844. A treaty with China opened the Far East to U.S. traders.
1845. Among his last acts in office, signed bills permitting Texas and Florida to be admitted to the Union.

James Knox Polk

11th president, 1845-49 Democrat

1795. Born on November 2 in Mecklenburg county, NC, the eldest of ten children.

1806. Moved with his family to the Duck River valley in central Tennessee.

1818. Graduated from the University of North Carolina.

1820. Admitted to the bar and began practicing law in Columbia, TN.

1821. Became chief clerk of the Tennessee Senate.

1823. Elected to the Tennessee House of Representatives.

1824. Married Sarah Childress on January 1. There were no children from the marriage.

1825. Elected to the first of seven consecutive terms in the U.S. House of Representatives, where he quickly became known as a strong supporter of Andrew Jackson.

1832. As chairman of the House Ways and Means Committee, supported President Jackson's efforts to abolish the national bank.

1835. Became speaker of the House.

1839. Resigned his House seat to run for governor of Tennessee, winning by a slim margin.

1840. Sought the Democratic vice-presidential nomination but was turned down at the party's national convention.

1841. Defeated for a second term as governor.

1843. Again defeated in a bid for the governorship.

1844. At the Democratic presidential convention, the party split between opponents and supporters of Martin Van Buren. Polk took the nomination on the ninth ballot, the first "dark horse" candidate. He won the election by a slim margin, campaigning on a platform of territorial expansion.

1849. Died in Nashville, TN, on June 15, a few months after leaving the presidency.

Highlights of Presidency

1846. Two key pieces of Polk's domestic program, bills setting new tariffs and reestablishing a federal treasury, were adopted. □ A treaty with Britain settled a dispute over Oregon, giving both nations part of the territory.

1848. A treaty with Mexico ended two-year war and gave the United States control of most of present-day Arizona, California, Colorado, Nevada, New Mexico, Utah, and Wyoming. □ Gold was discovered in California in December.

Zachary Taylor

12th president, 1849-50 Whig

1784. Born on November 24 near Barboursville, VA.

1785. Moved with his family to a plantation near Louisville, KY, where he grew up and was educated by tutors.

1808. Entered the U.S. Army as a first lieutenant.

1810. Married Margaret Mackall Smith on June 21. The couple subsequently had six children, two of whom died in infancy.

1812. As commander of a company under William Henry Harrison, successfully defended Fort Harrison from Indian attack; subsequently brevetted a major.

1814. Led U.S. troops against British and Indian forces at Credit Island in Illinois Territory; outnumbered, he was forced to withdraw after some initial successes.

1829-32. Was Indian superintendent in the Northwest, at Fort Snelling, MN.

1832. Promoted to colonel; fought in the Black Hawk War.

1837-40. Earned the nickname "Old Rough and Ready" while fighting the Seminole Indians in Florida.

1841. Named commander of the second department of the army's western division, with headquarters at Fort Smith, AR.

1846. Advanced with a small army to the Rio Grande, in anticipation of conflict with Mexico. After war began, defeated Mexican forces at two battles, at Palo Alto and Resaca de la Palma, forcing their retreat across the Rio Grande. Later launched an attack against Monterrey, capturing the city after a prolonged fight.

1847. Leading a force mostly of volunteers, defeated a much larger Mexican force under Santa Anna at the Battle of Buena Vista, February 22-23; the battle secured U.S. victory in the war and made Taylor a national hero.

1848. Elected president as the Whig Party candidate, defeating Lewis Cass of the Democratic Party and Martin Van Buren, who ran on the Free Soil ticket.

1850. Died in the White House on July 9.

Highlights of Presidency

1849. Sectional debates over the extension of slavery occupied Congress, with Taylor supporting the admission of California without conditions.

1850. The United States and Britain signed the Clayton-Bulwer Treaty guaranteeing the neutrality of a future canal across Central America.

Millard Fillmore

13th president, 1850-53   Whig

1800. Born on January 7 in Cayuga county, NY.
1814. Apprenticed to a firm of clothmakers.
1823. Began to practice law in East Aurora, NY.
1826. Married Abigail Powers, a teacher, on February 5. The couple would have two children.
1828. Elected to the New York state House of Representatives on an Anti-Masonic platform. Was reelected twice.
1830. Moved to Buffalo, and began a law practice.
1832. Elected to the House of Representatives, again on the Anti-Masonic ticket.
1836. Reelected to the House as a Whig. Kept House seat until 1843.
1840. Became chairman of the Ways and Means Committee. He used that position to guide new protectionist tariff laws through Congress.
1844. Lost bid for the governorship of New York.
1846. Became the first chancellor of the University of Buffalo.
1847. Elected New York state comptroller.
1848. Elected vice-president, on the Whig ticket with Zachary Taylor.
1850. Zachary Taylor died in office on July 9. Took presidential oath the following day.
1853. Resumed his law practice in Buffalo.
1856. Nominated for president by the Whig Party and the American (Know-Nothing) Party. Ran third in the election, which James Buchanan won.
1858. Five years after the death of his first wife, married Caroline Carmichael McIntosh on February 10.
1874. Died on March 8 in Buffalo.

Highlights of Presidency

1850. In September, Congress passed the Compromise of 1850, which delayed conflict over slavery by admitting California as a free state, organizing the territories of Utah and New Mexico without reference to slavery, abolishing slavery in the District of Columbia, and establishing a stronger fugitive slave law.
1852. Authorized a mission to Japan by Commodore Matthew C. Perry. □ Rejected in his bid for nomination for a full term by Northern antislavery Whigs, who favored Gen. Winfield Scott.

Franklin Pierce

14th president, 1853-57   Democrat

1804. Born on November 23 in Hillsborough Lower Village, NH.
1824. Graduated from Bowdoin College.
1827. Admitted to the New Hampshire bar.
1829. Elected to the New Hampshire state legislature.
1833. Elected to the U.S. House of Representatives, where he became known as a supporter of Andrew Jackson.
1834. Married Jane Means Appleton in November. The couple later had three sons, all of whom died young.
1837. Elected to the U.S. Senate.
1842. Resigned his Senate seat under pressure from his wife, a temperance advocate. Returned to Concord to practice law and conduct a temperance drive.
1845. Appointed federal district attorney for New Hampshire.
1847. After enlisting to serve in the Mexican War, promoted to colonel and then brigadier general. Led an army to join Winfield Scott in attacking Mexico City and was wounded at Churubusco.
1852. After being nominated by the Democrats on the 49th ballot, defeated Whig candidate Winfield Scott for the presidency.
1853. En route to Washington, the Pierces' only surviving child, Benjamin, was killed in a train accident.
1857. After leaving office, traveled widely.
1860. Settled permanently in Concord.
1869. Died on October 8 in Concord.

Highlights of Presidency

1853. The Gadsden Purchase settled boundary disputes with Mexico and gave the United States a southern railway route to the Pacific.
1854. The Kansas Nebraska Act, endorsed by Pierce despite misgivings, was adopted. The law touched off rivalry between pro- and anti-slavery settlers that eventually led to fighting. □ The Ostend Manifesto, a document detailing a plan to buy Cuba from Spain, caused a furor when it was leaked to the press.
1856. Ordered federal troops into Kansas in an effort to end the fighting there. □ The Democrats, concerned about Pierce's connection with the Kansas issue, nominated James Buchanan for the presidency.

James Buchanan

15th president, 1857-61   Democrat

1791. Born on April 23 near Mercersburg, PA.
1809. Graduated from Dickinson College in Carlisle, PA.
1813. Admitted to the Pennsylvania bar and founded a law practice.
1814. After brief service in the War of 1812, elected as a Federalist to the Pennsylvania state assembly.
1819. Became engaged to Ann Caroline Coleman, but the engagement was broken when her parents disapproved. She died a week later, and Buchanan never married.
1820. Elected to Congress, where he served five terms.
1831. Appointed minister to Russia.
1834. Elected to the Senate from Pennsylvania. Served there until 1845, chairing the Foreign Relations Committee.
1845. Named secretary of state by President Polk.
1852. Supporters of Buchanan and Stephen A. Douglas split the Democratic Party, giving the presidential nomination and the election to Franklin Pierce.
1853. Appointed by Pierce to be minister to Britain.
1856. Running on a ''Save the Union'' platform as the Democratic presidential candidate, defeated Republican John C. Frémont and Whig Millard Fillmore.
1861. Returned to Wheatland, his estate near Lancaster, PA, where he remained a supporter of the Union.
1866. Published an account of his administration.
1868. Died on June 1 at Wheatland.

Highlights of Presidency

1857. Endorsing the concept of popular sovereignty, recommended that Congress approve a pro-slavery Kansas constitution. (Kansas antislavery forces had boycotted a vote on the measure.) The constitution was rejected, and the debate on it cost Buchanan Northern support.
1858. Northern candidates opposing Buchanan won a majority in both houses of Congress.
1859. John Brown was seized at Harpers Ferry and hanged for his attempt to start a slave revolt.
1860. Did not run for reelection but supported his vice-president, John C. Breckinridge, who was defeated in the November election by Abraham Lincoln.
1861. Seven Southern states formed the Confederacy on February 4.

Abraham Lincoln

16th president, 1861-65   Republican

1809. Born on February 12 in a log cabin in Hardin county, KY.
1832. Living in New Salem, IL, worked odd jobs. Served 80 days in Illinois militia during Black Hawk War. Lost election to Illinois House of Representatives.
1834. Elected to first of four consecutive two-year terms to Illinois House; aligned with Whigs.
1837. Became partner in Springfield, IL, law practice.
1842. Married Mary Todd Lincoln on November 4. The couple would have four sons.
1847-49. Served one two-year term in the U.S. House of Representatives, then resumed law practice in Springfield.
1858. Running as a Republican, lost election to U.S. Senate. Debates with opponent Stephen A. Douglas gained national attention.
1860. Elected president on the Republican ticket.
1865. Shot by actor John Wilkes Booth at Ford's Theater in Washington, DC, on April 14. Died early the next morning.

Highlights of Presidency

1861. On April 12, Confederate forces attacked Fort Sumter in Charleston, SC, setting off the Civil War. Lincoln moved quickly to mobilize the Union by executive order.
1862. Five days after the Battle of Antietam, Lincoln announced on September 22 that all slaves in states still in rebellion would be freed in 100 days.
1863. On January 1, formally issued Emancipation Proclamation. ▢ In the Battle of Gettysburg in southern Pennsylvania in July, Union forces led by Gen. George C. Meade turned back Gen. Robert E. Lee and the Confederate army. Lee retreated to Virginia, marking a major turning point in the war. ▢ At the dedication of the Soldiers' National Cemetery, Lincoln delivered the Gettysburg Address on November 19.
1864. The advancing Union army of Gen. William T. Sherman captured Atlanta on September 2. Sherman continued his ''March to the Sea,'' taking Savannah in December. ▢ In November, Lincoln was elected to a second term, defeating Gen. George B. McClellan.
1865. On April 9, General Lee and Gen. Ulysses S. Grant signed terms of Confederate surrender at Appomattox, VA.

Andrew Johnson

17th president, 1865-69   Republican

1808. Born on December 29 in Raleigh, NC.
1827. Married Eliza McCardle on May 17. The Johnsons would have five children.
1835. Elected to the Tennessee state legislature for the first of three terms. Defeated in 1837 but elected in 1839 and 1841.
1843-53. Represented Tennessee's first district in the U.S. House of Representatives.
1853. Narrowly defeated the Whig candidate to become governor of Tennessee. Served two two-year terms.
1857-62. As a U.S. senator, he supported the Union.
1862-65. Was military governor of occupied Tennessee.
1864. Running with Abraham Lincoln on the National Union (Republican) ticket, the former Democrat was elected vice-president.
1865. Sworn in as president on April 15 following the assassination of President Lincoln.
1874. Five years after leaving the White House, and after several bids for office, elected again to U.S. Senate.
1875. Died on July 31 near Carter Station, TN.

Highlights of Presidency

1865. On March 29, issued Amnesty Proclamation, pardoning all Confederates except those with property in excess of $20,000 and certain Confederate leaders. □ The 13th amendment, abolishing slavery, was proclaimed.
1866. Was engaged in an ongoing dispute with Congress over Reconstruction and the power of the president in Southern states.
1867. Over Johnson's continual vetoes, Congress passed its own series of Reconstruction laws, enforcing Negro suffrage and making ratification of the 14th amendment (granting citizenship to all persons born or naturalized in the United States) a condition for readmission to the Union. □ On March 30, the United States signed a treaty with Russia for the purchase of Alaska for $7,200,000.
1868. Ignoring the 1867 Tenure of Office Act, Johnson ordered the removal of Edwin M. Stanton as secretary of war in March. He later became the only president ever to be impeached by the House, but was acquitted in the Senate on May 26 by a one-vote margin. □ The 14th amendment was proclaimed on July 28.

Ulysses Simpson Grant

18th president, 1869-77   Republican

1822. Born on April 27 in Point Pleasant, OH.
1843. Graduated from West Point.
1846-48. Fought in Mexican War under Generals Zachary Taylor and Winfield Scott. Distinguished himself for bravery and was promoted to 1st lieutenant.
1848. Married Julia Dent on August 22. The couple would become the parents of four children.
1854. Resigned army commission and took up farming in Missouri.
1861. After outbreak of Civil War, named colonel of 21st Illinois Volunteers, then brigadier general.
1862. Tooks Forts Henry and Donelson, the first major Union victories in the war. Defeated at Shiloh.
1863. Forced Confederate surrender at Vicksburg, another major Union victory. Also won Battle of Chattanooga.
1864. Appointed lieutenant general and given command of all U.S. armies.
1865. Accepted surrender of Gen. Robert E. Lee at Appomattox.
1868. Elected president on the Republican ticket.
1885. Shortly after completing his two-volume *Personal Memoirs,* died of cancer at Mount McGregor, NY, on July 23.

Highlights of Presidency

1869. The first transcontinental railroad was completed.
1870. Ratification of 15th amendment, granting citizens the right to vote regardless of race, was proclaimed on March 30.
1872. Amnesty Act, restoring civil rights to citizens of the South, was enacted. □ Despite charges of widespread corruption in his administration, Grant won reelection, defeating Horace Greeley.
1873. Widespread bank failures set off panic. Depression lasted five years.
1875. Signed Specie Resumption Act, a "hard money" measure designed to contract the amount of paper currency in circulation. □ Civil Rights Act, giving equal rights to blacks in public accommodations and jury duty, was passed.
1876. Hayes nominated for president by Republican Party, making Grant a "lame duck." □ Col. George Custer and his 7th Cavalry massacred at Little Big Horn, MT.

Rutherford Birchard Hayes

19th president, 1877-81   Republican

1822. Born on October 4 in Delaware, OH.

1842. Earned B.A. degree from Kenyon College in Gambier, OH.

1845. Graduated from Harvard Law School, admitted to the Ohio bar and began practice of law.

1852. Married Lucy Ware Webb on December 30. The couple would have seven sons and one daughter.

1856. Helped found Ohio Republican Party.

1858. Elected city solicitor of Cincinnati; served four years.

1861. At the outbreak of the Civil War, appointed major in 23rd Ohio Volunteer Infantry. Wounded several times in combat and eventually rose to major general.

1864. Still in service, nominated and elected to U.S. House of Representatives, representing Ohio's second district. Won reelection in 1866. Supported Radical Reconstruction and impeachment of President Andrew Johnson.

1867. Nominated for governor of Ohio, resigned from Congress, and won election. Reelected in 1869. As governor, worked for social reforms.

1872. Ran for Congress and lost. Returned to private life.

1875. At urging of Ohio Republicans, ran for governor on a "sound money" platform. Election victory made him a national figure.

1876. Won Republican presidential nomination on the seventh ballot. In the most controversial presidential election in U.S. history, appeared to lose to Samuel J. Tilden. The outcome was disputed, and a special electoral commission was appointed. On March 2, 1877, it declared Hayes the winner.

1893. Died at Spiegel Grove, the family estate in Fremont, OH, on January 17.

Highlights of Presidency

1877. Within two months of taking office, withdrew federal troops from the South—ending the era of Reconstruction—and appointed a former Confederate, David M. Key, to be postmaster general. □ Called out federal troops to quell violent, widespread railroad strikes.

1878. Favoring a "hard-money" policy (specie backing of paper currency), vetoed Bland-Allison Silver Purchase Bill; Congress overrode veto.

1880. Kept pledge to serve only one term.

James Abram Garfield

20th president, 1881   Republican

1831. Born on November 19 near Cleveland, OH.

1848. Struck out on own and worked on a canal boat. Six weeks later, returned home seriously ill. Decided to get an education.

1851. Entered Western Reserve Eclectic Institute (later Hiram College). Studied and taught for three years.

1856. Graduated from Williams College. Returned to Hiram College, where he taught ancient languages and literature for five years, served as principal, and became a lay preacher for the Disciples of Christ.

1858. Married Lucretia Rudolph on November 11. Seven children would be born to the Garfields.

1859. Admitted to the Ohio bar. □ Elected to the state Senate.

1861. Volunteered for Union army after outbreak of Civil War. Made colonel of 42nd Ohio Volunteer Infantry. Appointed major general for gallantry at Battle of Chickamauga.

1862. While still in the service, elected to U.S. House of Representatives as a radical Republican.

1863. Resigned military commission to take seat in Congress. A member of the House until 1880, he supported Lincoln policies and Radical Reconstruction. Favored specie payment as opposed to paper money. Served as Republican minority leader from 1876.

1876. Was a member of electoral commission for disputed Hayes-Tilden presidential election, voted consistently for Hayes on a strict party line.

1880. Elected to U.S. Senate in January. At the Republican National Convention in May, nominated for president as compromise choice on 36th ballot. Chester A. Arthur chosen as running mate to placate disgruntled "Stalwart" faction. Despite party split, won narrow victory over Democrat Winfield S. Hancock in November election.

1881. Died on September 19 at Elberon, NJ, eleven weeks after taking an assassin's bullet.

Highlights of Presidency

1881. Inaugurated on March 4 as 20th president of the United States, age 49. □ Shot on July 12 while entering a Washington railroad station by Charles J. Guiteau, a disappointed office-seeker in the new administration. Guiteau shouted: "I am a 'Stalwart' and Arthur is president now."

Chester Alan Arthur

21st president, 1881-85   Republican

1829. Born on October 5 in Fairfield, VT.
1848. Graduated from Union College in Schenectady, NY. Took up private law studies and teaching.
1854. Admitted to the bar after receiving training in a New York city law office.
1856. Formed law firm in New York City. Gradually became known as a leading New York attorney.
1859. Married Ellen Lewis Herndon on October 25. The Arthurs would become the parents of three children.
1861. After outbreak of Civil War, became inspector general and quartermaster of New York, responsible for furnishing supplies to large numbers of troops.
1863. Returned to private law practice.
1871. Appointed by President Ulysses Grant as collector for the Port of New York.
1878. After a year-long federal investigation of the New York Customs House for political patronage and mismanagement, Arthur was removed from the position of collector by President Rutherford B. Hayes. The action created a rift in the Republican Party.
1880. As a member of the party's "Stalwart" faction, supported Grant at Republican National Convention in May. When the convention settled on James Garfield as a compromise candidate, Arthur was nominated as vice-president to placate "Stalwarts." Garfield-Arthur ticket narrowly won November election.
1881. On September 20, took oath as 21st president, one day after the death of President Garfield.
1886. Died in New York City on November 18.

Highlights of Presidency

1882. Vetoed the Chinese Exclusion Bill as well as a "pork barrel" appropriation for river and harbor improvement. Was overridden by Congress on both measures.
1883. The Pendleton Civil Service Act, a major reform of federal civil service, was signed into law on January 16. Tariff reform legislation and the Edmunds Anti-Polygamy Bill, aimed at the Mormons in Utah, also passed.
1884. With major railroads reaching the Pacific Coast, westward settlement came into full swing. □ Defeated for Republican presidential nomination by James G. Blaine.

Grover Cleveland

22nd and 24th president, 1885-89, 1893-97   Democrat

1837. Born on March 18 in Caldwell, NJ.
1841. Family moved to Fayetteville, NY. Spent his boyhood there and in nearby Clinton.
1853. After father's death, moved to Buffalo, NY. Worked for an uncle and later as a law clerk.
1859. Admitted to the bar and entered law practice.
1863-65. Was assistant district attorney of Erie county, NY.
1871-73. Served as sheriff of Erie county.
1881. Elected mayor of Buffalo.
1882. Backed by reform Democrats, elected governor of New York.
1884. Nominated for president at Democratic National Convention. Narrowly defeated James G. Blaine in November.
1886. Married Frances Folsom in a White House ceremony on June 2. The couple would have five children.
1888. Lost election for second term to Benjamin Harrison, despite garnering a larger popular vote. After leaving office, practiced law in New York City.
1892. Elected a second time to the presidency, defeating Harrison.
1908. Died on July 24 in Princeton, NJ, where he had settled after leaving the White House.

Highlights of Presidency

1886. Dedicated the Statue of Liberty in New York Harbor on October 28.
1887. Interstate Commerce Act, the first major federal program to regulate railroads and private business, was adopted. □ Tenure of Office Act was repealed.
1893. Financial panic began, leading to a four-year depression. □ Sherman Silver Purchase Act of 1890 was repealed.
1894. Jacob S. Coxey led march on Washington of 500 unemployed Midwesterners. "Coxey's Army" demanded unemployment relief. □ In July, President Cleveland called out federal troops to quell Pullman strike rioting in Chicago. To keep U.S. mails moving, trains ran under military guard.
1895. In support of Monroe Doctrine, Cleveland received Congressional authorization to appoint commission to resolve border dispute between Venezuela and British Guiana.
1896. Lost Democratic presidential nomination to William Jennings Bryan.

Benjamin Harrison

23rd president, 1889-93   Republican

1833. Born on August 20 in North Bend, OH, the grandson of William Henry Harrison, 9th president of the United States.
1852. Graduated from Miami University in Oxford, OH.
1853. Married Caroline Lavinia Scott on October 20. The couple would have a son and a daughter.
1854. Admitted to the bar and established law practice in Indianapolis.
1857. Ran successfully for city attorney of Indianapolis.
1860. Elected reporter of Indiana supreme court; reelected twice.
1862. After the outbreak of the Civil War, raised the 70th Indiana Volunteer Regiment. By 1865, had risen to rank of brigadier general.
1876. Lost election for governorship of Indiana.
1877. Became Republican Party leader in Indiana.
1880. Elected to U.S. Senate.
1888. Defeated Grover Cleveland in November presidential race despite having fewer popular votes.
1896. Married Mary Lord Dimmick on April 6. A daughter, Elizabeth, was born in 1897. (The first Mrs. Harrison had died in 1892.)
1897. Published *This Country of Ours,* a series of essays on how the federal government works.
1899. Acted as senior counsel for Venezuela in dispute with Great Britain over boundary with British Guiana.
1901. Died on March 13 in Indianapolis.

Highlights of Presidency

1889. The first Pan American Conference, encouraging cooperation between the United States and Latin America, was held in Washington.
1890. Four major bills were signed into law: Sherman Antitrust Act, outlawing trusts and monopolies that hinder trade; Sherman Silver Purchase Act, increasing amount of silver that could be coined; McKinley Tariff Act, setting duties at record high levels; and Dependent Pension Act, benefiting Civil War veterans. □ Battle of Wounded Knee, last major conflict between Indians and U.S. troops, was fought on December 29.
1892. Defeated for reelection by Grover Cleveland. Did not campaign because of wife's illness.

William McKinley

25th president, 1897-1901   Republican

1843. Born on January 29 in Niles, OH.
1860. Studies at Allegheny College in Meadville, PA, cut short by illness. Taught school briefly.
1861. At outset of Civil War, enlisted as private in 23rd Ohio Regiment, under Rutherford B. Hayes. Saw considerable action and left the Army a brevet major.
1865-67. Studied law in an Ohio law office and at Albany (NY) Law School. Admitted to bar and opened practice in Canton, OH.
1869. Elected prosecuting attorney of Stark county, OH.
1871. Married Ida Saxton on January 25. Two daughters would be born to the couple; both died very young.
1877. Entered U.S. Congress as representative of Ohio's seventeenth district. Served until 1891, except for 1884-85.
1891. Elected governor of Ohio. Served two terms.
1892. Had backing for Republican presidential nomination, but supported incumbent Benjamin Harrison.
1896. Defeated William Jennings Bryan in November presidential election.
1901. Died on September 14 in Buffalo, NY, eight days after being shot at Pan-American Exposition.

Highlights of Presidency

1897. Dingley Tariff passed, raising average duty to a record 57%.
1898. On February 15, the U.S. battleship *Maine* was blown up in Havana harbor. On April 25, the United States declared war on Spain. In Battle of Manila Bay on May 1, Adm. George Dewey led major U.S. victory over Spain.
1899. Treaty of Paris, ending the war, was approved by the U.S. Senate on February 6. Spain ceded Philippines, Puerto Rico, and Guam and agreed to independence for Cuba. □ In May, U.S. troops captured Emilio Aguinaldo, ending revolt in the Philippines. □ In September, U.S. Secretary of State John Hay sent notes to major European nations calling for Open Door trade policy toward China.
1900. U.S. troops joined international force in putting down Boxer Rebellion in China. □ Gold Standard Act passed, making the gold dollar the sole standard of currency.
1901. With Theodore Roosevelt as running-mate, reelected for a second term.

Theodore Roosevelt

26th president, 1901-09   Republican

1858. Born on October 27 in New York City.
1880. Graduated from Harvard University. Married Alice Hathaway Lee on October 27.
1881-84. Served in New York state legislature.
1884. Wife died following birth of daughter, Alice. Mother died the same day. Dropped out of politics and became cattle rancher in Dakota Territory; also wrote history.
1886. Married Edith Kermit Carow on December 2. Four sons and a daughter would be born to the couple.
1887-89. Lived as sportsman and gentleman-scholar at Sagamore Hill, estate at Oyster Bay, NY. Continued career as historian. Most important work, *The Winning of the West,* was published in four volumes, 1889-96. He would write a total of some 40 books.
1889. Appointed to U.S. Civil Service Commission.
1895. Became police commissioner of New York City.
1897. Appointed assistant secretary of the Navy by President William McKinley.
1898. After outbreak of Spanish-American War, organized First U.S. Volunteer Cavalry (Rough Riders). As colonel, led charge up Kettle Hill in battle of San Juan. □ In November, elected governor of New York; as such, sponsored tax reform and fought spoils system.
1900. Elected vice-president.
1901. On September 14, sworn in as 26th president after the assassination of President McKinley.
1912. Left GOP and ran for the presidency on his new Progressive (''Bull Moose'') ticket. Shot during campaign, but recovered. Lost election to Democrat Woodrow Wilson.
1919. Died on January 6 at Sagamore Hill.

Highlights of Presidency

1903. Panama signed treaty for a canal under U.S. sovereignty. □ Department of Commerce and Labor was created.
1904. Won election to full term.
1906. Awarded Nobel Peace Prize for arbitrating end of Russo-Japanese War. □ Hepburn Act, authorizing Interstate Commerce Commission to regulate railroad rates, and the Pure Food and Drug Act were enacted.
1907. Financial panic and depression started.
1908. Supported William Howard Taft for the presidency.

William Howard Taft

27th president, 1909-13   Republican

1857. Born on September 15 in Cincinnati, OH.
1878. Graduated from Yale University.
1880. Graduated from Cincinnati Law School and admitted to the Ohio bar.
1881. Became assistant prosecuting attorney of Hamilton county; served two years.
1886. Married Helen Herron on June 19. The Tafts would have three children.
1887. Appointed judge on the Ohio superior court. Elected to his own term the following year.
1890. Named U.S. solicitor-general.
1892. Chosen U.S. Circuit Court judge for the 6th district by President Benjamin Harrison.
1900. Named by President McKinley to head the commission charged with terminating U.S. military rule in Philippines.
1901. Became first civil governor of the Philippines.
1904. Appointed secretary of war by President Roosevelt.
1908. Won race for the presidency.
1913-21. Served as professor of law at Yale University. During World War I, was also joint chairman of the National War Labor Board.
1921. Appointed chief justice of the U.S. Supreme Court by President Warren Harding. Served until Feb. 3, 1930.
1930. Died on March 8 in Washington, DC.

Highlights of Presidency

1909. Payne-Aldrich Act passed, lowering tariffs.
1911. Standard Oil Co. dissolved by Supreme Court under Sherman Antitrust Act. Administration also effected dissolution of tobacco trusts and proceeded with scores of other antitrust suits.
1912. New Mexico and Arizona admitted to the union, the last of the 48 contiguous states. □ President Taft won renomination by Republican Party but lost election to Democrat Woodrow Wilson. ''Bull Moose'' candidacy of Theodore Roosevelt split the Republican vote.
1913. The 16th amendment, authorizing income taxes, was proclaimed on February 25. The 17th amendment, calling for direct popular election of U.S. senators, went into effect two months after Taft left office. □ Department of Commerce and Labor divided into separate departments.

(Thomas) Woodrow Wilson

28th president, 1913-21   Democrat

1856. Born on December 28 in Staunton, VA.
1879. Earned a A.B. from the College of New Jersey (now Princeton University).
1882. Admitted to the bar, but did not prosper as a lawyer.
1885. Married Ellen Louise Axson in Rome, GA on June 24. Three daughters would be born to the couple.
1886. Awarded a doctor's degree from Johns Hopkins University. His first book, *Congressional Government* (1885), analyzing the U.S. government, was his dissertation.
1890-1902. After teaching at Bryn Mawr College and Wesleyan University, served as a professor at Princeton University.
1902-10. Was president of Princeton University.
1911-13. Served as governor of New Jersey.
1912. Elected president.
1915. Married Edith Bolling Galt on December 18. (The first Mrs. Wilson died on Aug. 6, 1914.)
1919. Suffered a paralytic stroke in Washington, DC.
1924. Died on February 3 in Washington.

Highlights of Presidency

1913. The Federal Reserve Bill became law.
1914. The Clayton Antitrust Bill and the Federal Trade Bill were enacted. □ In April, Wilson ordered the U.S. Navy to occupy Veracruz, Mexico, during a dispute with President Victoriano Huerta. U.S.-Mexican relations remained troubled during Wilson era. □ In August, the president proclaimed neutrality as war broke out in Europe.
1915. More than 100 Americans were killed as a German submarine torpedoed the British liner *Lusitania* on May 7.
1916. Narrowly reelected.
1917. The United States purchased the Virgin Islands from Denmark. □ On April 6, Congress declared war on Germany.
1918. In a speech to Congress on January 8, outlined Fourteen Points as a basis for a peace settlement. □ On November 11, an armistice ending World War I was signed.
1920. For a second time, the U.S. Senate refused to ratify the 1919 Treaty of Versailles with Germany. □ Wilson was awarded the Nobel Peace Prize for 1919 for advocating the establishment of a League of Nations. □ The 19th amendment, giving woman the right to vote, was ratified. The 18th or Prohibition amendment had been proclaimed Jan. 29, 1919.

Warren Gamaliel Harding

29th president, 1921-23   Republican

1865. Born on November 2 in Blooming Grove, OH.
1882. Graduated from Ohio Central College in Iberin.
1884. Bought the Marion *Star,* a small, struggling weekly, and devoted himself to it wholly for some 15 years. The *Star* eventually became one of the most successful small-town newspapers in the state.
1891. Married Florence Kling DeWolfe on July 8.
1898. Elected to the Ohio state Senate; reelected in 1900. Served as floor leader during second term.
1902. Elected lieutenant governor of Ohio.
1910. Ran unsuccessfully for governor.
1912. Delivered nominating address for President Taft at GOP convention. Political fortunes began to rise.
1914. Elected to U.S. Senate.
1920. Won Republican nomination for president and campaigned on "Return to Normalcy" slogan. Easily defeated James M. Cox in November election.
1923. Returning from a trip to Alaska, died in San Francisco on August 2.

Highlights of Presidency

1921. In May, Congress set up a national quota system for immigration. □ In June, the Budget and Accounting Act was signed into law; the Bureau of the Budget was created. □ On July 2, the president signed joint congressional resolution of peace with Germany, Austria, and Hungary. Treaties were signed in August. □ On November 12, the International Conference on Limitation of Armaments opened in Washington. It lasted until Feb. 6, 1922. Major powers agreed to limit naval construction.
1921-22. Ordered federal troops into West Virginia during coal strike of 1921. Sweeping federal injunction issued against Railway Shopmen's Strike of 1922.
1922. Fordney-McCumber Act, raising tariffs on manufactured goods to highest level to date, signed into law.
1923. In June, the president set out on transcontinental "Voyage of Understanding" to promote U.S. participation in the World Court. Took ill on his way back. For months, evidence of corruption in his administration had been coming to light. After his death, several high officials were linked to Teapot Dome and other scandals.

Calvin Coolidge

30th president, 1923-29   Republican

1872. Born on July 4 in Plymouth Notch, VT.
1895. Graduated from Amherst College.
1897. Admitted to the Massachusetts bar.
1898. Elected city councilman of Northampton, MA.
1905. Married Grace Anna Goodhue on October 4. They would become the parents of two sons.
1906. Elected to the Massachusetts House of Representatives. Served two one-year terms.
1909. Elected mayor of Northampton. Reelected in 1910.
1911. Entered state Senate. Won reelection twice. In third term, elected president of Senate.
1915. Ran successfully for lieutenant governor of Massachusetts. Served three years.
1918. Elected governor of Massachusetts. Gained prominence in 1919 by calling out the National Guard in the Boston police strike, declaring, "There is no right to strike against the public safety by anybody, anywhere, anytime."
1920. Lost Republican presidential nomination to Warren G. Harding; selected as vice-presidential candidate.
1923. On August 3, sworn in as 30th president after the death of President Harding.
1929. Published *The Autobiography of Calvin Coolidge*.
1933. Died on January 5 in Northampton.

Highlights of Presidency

1924. Pressed for investigations and prosecutions relating to scandals involving members of the Harding administration. □ Was elected president in his own right.
1925. U.S. Marines sent to Nicaragua after outbreak of civil war. In 1927, the president sent Henry Stimson to work out compromise, but Gen. Augusto César Sandino launched guerrilla war that lasted until withdrawal of U.S. troops in 1933.
1926. Vetoed the McNary-Haugen farm bill, which called for dumping of agricultural surpluses. Vetoed the relief measure again in 1928.
1927. Despite strong party support, announced on August 2: "I do not choose to run for president in 1928."
1928. Kellogg-Briand Pact, an agreement "to renounce war as an instrument of national policy," was signed in Paris by 15 nations on August 24.

Herbert Clark Hoover

31st president, 1929-33   Republican

1874. Born on August 10 in West Branch, IA.
1895. Graduated from Stanford University.
1897. Began his career as a mining engineer.
1899. Married Lou Henry on February 10. The couple would become the parents of two sons.
1912. Appointed a trustee of Stanford University.
1914-15. Directed the American Relief Committee, organized to aid Americans stranded in Europe as World War I began.
1915-19. Directed the Commission for Relief in Belgium.
1917-19. Served as U.S. food administrator.
1921-28. Was U.S. secretary of commerce.
1928. Defeated New York Gov. Alfred E. Smith in the presidential race.
1942. *The Problems of Lasting Peace,* written by Hoover with Hugh Gibson, was published.
1951-52. Published his memoirs in three volumes.
1955. On June 30, retired after serving as chairman of two Commissions on Organization of the Executive Branch of Government.
1959-61. *An American Epic,* a three-volume study of his experience in international relief work, appeared.
1964. Died on October 20 in New York City.

Highlights of Presidency

1929. After taking oath of office on March 4, the new president called Congress into special session in April. Two months later the Agricultural Marketing Act, designed to assist farmers suffering from low incomes during an era of prosperity, was enacted. □ The New York Stock Market crashed on October 29, beginning a severe economic depression that dominated the Hoover presidency.
1930. The London Naval Conference limited the number of small vessels, battleships, and cruisers various nations could construct. □ On February 3, the president named Charles Evans Hughes chief justice of the Supreme Court.
1932. On January 7, Secretary of State Henry L. Stimson announced the Stimson Doctrine, declaring that the United States would not recognize territorial conquest. □ Also in January, Congress established the Reconstruction Finance Corporation. □ In November, Hoover was defeated in bid for reelection by Franklin D. Roosevelt.

Franklin Delano Roosevelt

32nd president, 1933-45   Democrat

1882. Born on January 30 in Hyde Park, NY.
1904. Earned B.A. degree from Harvard University.
1905. On March 17, married Anna Eleanor Roosevelt, a fifth cousin and a niece of President Theodore Roosevelt. A daughter and five sons would be born to the Roosevelts.
1907. Passed New York State Bar examination, withdrew from Columbia Law School, hired by Wall Street law firm.
1911-13. Was a New York state senator.
1913-20. Served as assistant secretary of the Navy.
1920. Ran unsuccessfully for vice-president on Democratic ticket with James M. Cox. Returned to law practice.
1921. Stricken with polio while vacationing in Campobello, ME. He would never regain the use of his legs.
1928. Elected to first of two terms as governor of New York.
1932. Elected president over incumbent Republican Herbert Hoover.
1945. Died on April 12 at Warm Springs, GA.

Highlights of Presidency

1933. During first 100 days as president, launched New Deal relief measures. Revived the banking industry; delivered the first of 28 "Fireside Chats." ☐ In December, the 21st amendment, ending Prohibition, was ratified.
1934. Became the first president to visit Latin America.
1935. Social Security Act passed; Works Progress Administration (WPA) was established; Wagner Act, creating National Labor Relations Board (NLRB), was enacted.
1936. Amid economic improvement, reelected in a landslide over Alfred M. Landon. Also reelected in 1940 and 1944.
1937. President's plan to "reform" the Supreme Court was criticized as a "court-packing scheme" and rejected.
1939. Hitler overran Poland, and war was declared in Europe.
1941. Congress enacted Lend-Lease, giving the president power to supply military equipment to U.S. allies. ☐ On December 7, Japanese launched surprise attack on Pearl Harbor. Congress declared war the next day.
1944. June 6, D-Day: Allied forces landed on the Normandy coast of France.
1945. Yalta Conference held in the Crimea in February. Roosevelt, Britain's Winston Churchill, and USSR's Joseph Stalin discussed the terms of peace and the postwar world.

Harry S. Truman

33d president, 1945-53   Democrat

1884. Born on May 8 in Lamar, MO.
1901. Graduated from high school. Studied at the Kansas City Law School (1923-25).
1906-17. Worked on family farm in Grandview, MO.
1917-18. Served with the American Expeditionary Force.
1919. On June 28, married Elizabeth (Bess) Wallace. A daughter, (Mary) Margaret would be born in 1924.
1922. Failed to succeed in clothing business. Elected judge of the Jackson county court. Lost reelection in 1924.
1926-34. Was presiding judge of the Jackson county court.
1934. Won first of two terms to the U.S. Senate.
1941-44. Served as chairman of a special Senate committee on defense.
1944. Running with F. D. Roosevelt, elected vice-president.
1945. On April 12, sworn in as president following the sudden death of President Roosevelt.
1953. Began retirement during which he traveled widely, wrote memoirs, and remained politically active.
1972. Died in Kansas City on December 26.

Highlights of Presidency

1945. On May 7, Germany surrendered ending World War II in Europe. ☐ On June 26, the UN Charter was signed. ☐ From July 17 to August 2, Truman attended the Potsdam Conference. ☐ After atomic bombs were dropped on Hiroshima and Nagasaki, Japan surrendered in September.
1946. Ordered the seizure of nation's railroads in face of a strike threat.
1947. On March 12, outlined the Truman Doctrine—U.S. aid to Greece, Turkey, and other nations "threatened by armed minorities and outside pressure." ☐ In June, the Marshall Plan (economic and technical assistance for Europe) was announced, and Congress overrode presidential veto of Taft Hartley labor bill.
1948. In a "political upset," won full term.
1949. In January, granted recognition to new state of Israel. ☐ The North Atlantic Treaty Organization was set up.
1950. U.S. forces entered combat in Korea.
1951. Relieved Gen. Douglas MacArthur of his command in the Far East.
1952. Declined to seek reelection.

Dwight David Eisenhower

34th president, 1953-61   Republican

1890. Born on October 14 in Denison, TX.
1915. Graduated from the U.S. Military Academy.
1916. Married Mary (Mamie) Geneva Doud on July 1. The couple would have two sons; one died in childhood.
1918. Took command of a tank training center in Gettysburg, PA.
1929-33. Served under the assistant secretary of war.
1935-39. Was a senior assistant to Gen. Douglas MacArthur in the Philippines.
1942. With United States fighting in World War II, became commander of the European Theater of Operations.
1943. Appointed supreme commander of the Allied Expeditionary Force.
1944. Directed the landing of allied forces in Normandy.
1945. Succeeded George Marshall as Army chief of staff.
1948. Installed as president of Columbia University.
1950. Became supreme commander of the forces of the North Atlantic Treaty Organization.
1952. Retired from the Army; elected president.
1955. Suffered a heart attack.
1961. Restored to the rank of general of the Army.
1965. The second and final volume of his memoirs was published.
1969. Died on March 28 in Washington.

Highlights of Presidency

1953. The Department of Health, Education, and Welfare was established. □ The Korean War ended. □ Eisenhower nominated Earl Warren as chief justice of the Supreme Court.
1956. After Egypt nationalized the Suez Canal, the president refused to join Britain, France, and Israel in an invasion of Egypt. □ Denounced the USSR for crushing Hungarian uprising. □ Reelected to a second term.
1957. Signed the Eisenhower Doctrine, promising that the United States would resist Communist aggression in the Middle East. □ Sent federal troops to Little Rock, AK, to ensure the integration of Central High School.
1959. The National Aeronautics and Space Administration was formed.
1960. After Soviets downed a U.S. reconnaissance flight, summit conference with Premier Nikita Khrushchev collapsed.

John Fitzgerald Kennedy

35th president, 1961-63   Democrat

1917. Born on May 29 in Brookline, MA.
1935. Studied at the London School of Economics.
1940. Graduated from Harvard University.
1941. Commissioned an ensign in the U.S. Navy.
1944. Received the Navy and Marine Corps Medal for his conduct while commander of a PT boat that was sunk by the Japanese in the Solomon Islands in 1943.
1945. Worked as a newspaper correspondent.
1947-53. Represented Massachusetts' 11th district in the U.S. House of Representatives.
1952. Elected to the U.S. Senate, defeating the Republican incumbent, Henry Cabot Lodge, by more than 70,000 votes.
1953. Married Jacqueline Bouvier on September 12 in Newport, RI. A daughter and a son would be born to the Kennedys. A second son died two days after birth in August 1963.
1956. Defeated in an open contest for the Democratic vice-presidential nomination.
1957. Won a Pulitzer Prize for *Profiles in Courage*.
1958. Reelected to the U.S. Senate.
1960. Defeated Richard M. Nixon for the presidency.
1963. Assassinated on November 22 in Dallas, TX.

Highlights of Presidency

1961. Established the Peace Corps. □ In April, a force of anti-Castro Cubans, trained by the Central Intelligence Agency, staged an unsuccessful attempt to establish a beachhead at the Bay of Pigs, Cuba. □ In August, East Germany constructed a wall separating East and West Berlin.
1962. On February 20, Lt. Col. John H. Glenn, Jr., became the first American to orbit the earth. □ After U.S. aerial reconnaissance revealed that Soviet offensive missiles were being installed in Cuba, the United States established a naval "quarantine" around Cuba in October. The Soviets then withdrew their missiles.
1963. On August 5, the United States, Britain, and the USSR signed a nuclear test-ban agreement, prohibiting atmospheric testing of nuclear weapons. □ On August 28, more than 200,000 persons staged a march in Washington, dramatizing the demands of blacks for equal rights. □ South Vietnam President Ngo Dinh Diem was overthrown on November 1.

Lyndon Baines Johnson

36th president, 1963-69   Democrat

1908. Born on August 27 near Johnson City, TX.
1930. After graduating from Southwest Texas State Teachers College in San Marcos, TX, taught school in Houston.
1931. Became secretary to U.S. Rep. Richard M. Kleberg.
1934. Married Claudia Alta ("Lady Bird") Taylor on November 17. The Johnsons would become the parents of two daughters.
1935-37. Headed the National Youth Administration in Texas.
1937-49. Served in the U.S. House of Representatives.
1941. Defeated in a special election for the U.S. Senate.
1942. After President Roosevelt ordered all congressmen on active military duty to return to Washington, concluded a brief tour of duty with the U.S. Navy.
1948. Elected to the U.S. Senate. Won reelection in 1954.
1955. In January, elected Senate majority leader. □ In July, suffered a major heart attack.
1960. After losing the Democratic presidential nomination to John F. Kennedy, ran successfully in the vice-presidential spot.
1963. Sworn in as 36th president following the assassination of President Kennedy.
1971. The president's memoirs, *The Vantage Point: Perspectives of the Presidency, 1963-1969*, were published.
1973. Died on January 22 near Johnson City, TX.

Highlights of Presidency

1964. Signed an $11.5 billion tax-reduction bill and a major civil-rights bill. □ Proclaimed a war on poverty. □ Elected to a full presidential term.
1965. On February 7, ordered the bombing of targets in North Vietnam and began escalating U.S. troop strength in Indochina. □ In April, ordered U.S. troops into the Dominican Republic to end a rebellion. □ Signed legislation setting up Medicare and the Department of Housing and Urban Development.
1966. The Department of Transportation was formed.
1967. Nominated Thurgood Marshall, a black, as an associate justice of the Supreme Court. □ Met with Soviet Premier Aleksei Kosygin in Glassboro, NJ.
1968. Withdrew from the 1968 presidential race and ordered a reduction in the bombing of North Vietnam.

Richard Milhous Nixon

37th president, 1969-74   Republican

1913. Born on January 9 in Yorba Linda, CA.
1934. Graduated from Whittier College.
1937. Received a law degree from Duke University Law School.
1940. Married Thelma Catherine ("Pat") Ryan on June 21. Two daughters would be born to the Nixons.
1942-45. Served in the U.S. Navy.
1947-51. Was a member of the U.S. House of Representatives.
1948. Participated in the House Committee of Un-American Activities investigation of Algier Hiss.
1950. Won election to the U.S. Senate.
1952. Nominated as Dwight D. Eisenhower's running mate on the Republican presidential ticket. Elected easily.
1955. Performed various presidential duties as President Eisenhower recuperated from a heart attack.
1956. The Eisenhower-Nixon ticket was reelected.
1960. Lost close presidential race to John F. Kennedy.
1962. His first book, *Six Crises*, was published. □ Lost California's gubernatorial contest to the Democratic incumbent, Edmund G. ("Pat") Brown.
1968. Elected president.

Highlights of Presidency

1969. On July 20, Neil A. Armstrong became the first man to walk on the moon.
1970. On April 30, announced that U.S. combat troops were being sent into Cambodia to destroy enemy sanctuaries.
1972. Visited China in February. □ Meeting in Moscow with Soviet General Secretary Leonid Brezhnev in May, signed agreements limiting antiballistic missile (ABM) systems and offensive missile launchers. □ In June, five men were arrested for breaking into the headquarters of the Democratic National Committee. The subsequent investigation of the "Watergate affair" led to the downfall of the Nixon presidency. □ Overwhelmingly reelected.
1973. The Vietnam cease-fire agreement was signed in January. □ On October 10, Spiro T. Agnew resigned as vice-president and pleaded no contest to one count of income tax evasion. The president named Gerald R. Ford as his successor.
1974. Toured Middle East in June. □ Resigned as president, effective at noon on August 9.

Gerald Rudolph Ford

38th president, 1974-77   Republican

1913. Born on July 14 in Omaha, NE.

1935. Graduated from the University of Michigan, where he starred on the football team.

1941. After graduating from Yale Law School, returned to Grand Rapids to practice law. While at Yale, served as assistant football coach and boxing coach.

1942-46. During 47 months in the U.S. Navy, was awarded ten battle stars for service in the South Pacific.

1948. Elected to the U.S. House of Representatives from Michigan's fifth district. Won reelection 12 times. □ Married Elizabeth Bloomer on October 15. Three sons and a daughter were born to the couple.

1963. Elected chairman of the House GOP Conference. □ Named by President Johnson to serve on the Warren Commission, the official investigation into the assassination of President Kennedy.

1965. Successfully challenged Charles A. Halleck for the post of House minority leader.

1973. Under the terms of the 25th amendment, took the oath as vice-president on December 6.

1974. Following the resignation of President Nixon, inaugurated as the 38th chief executive on August 9.

1980. An attempt by Ronald Reagan to persuade the former president to join him as the vice-presidential candidate on the GOP ticket failed.

Highlights of Presidency

1974. Nominated Nelson A. Rockefeller as vice-president. □ Granted Richard M. Nixon an "absolute" pardon for all federal crimes he may have "committed or taken part in" while president. □ In Vladivostok, USSR, joined Soviet General Secretary Brezhnev in signing a tentative agreement listing the number of offensive strategic nuclear weapons and delivery vehicles through 1985.

1975. In April, South Vietnam surrendered to the Communists, ending the war in Southeast Asia. U.S. evacuation airlift from the nation was completed. □ In May, U.S. forces rescued 39 crewmen of the U.S. merchant ship *Mayaguez*, seized by Cambodia.

1976. Led the nation in marking its 200th birthday. □ Defeated by Jimmy Carter in his bid to win a full term.

James Earl ("Jimmy") Carter, Jr.

39th president, 1977-81   Democrat

1924. Born on October 1 in Plains, GA.

1935. Baptized into the First Baptist Church of Plains.

1946. Graduated from the U.S. Naval Academy. Married Rosalynn Smith on July 7. The couple would become the parents of three sons and a daughter.

1946-53. Served in the U.S. Navy. Duty included work under Hyman Rickover.

1953. Following the death of his father, resigned from the Navy and returned to Plains to run the family farm.

1963-67. Served two terms in the Georgia Senate.

1966. Ran third in Georgia's Democratic primary for the gubernatorial nomination.

1971-75. Served as governor of Georgia.

1975. Published his first book, *Why Not the Best?*

1976. Defeated Gerald R. Ford for the presidency.

1982. Named a distinguished professor at Emory University. □ His memoirs, *Keeping Faith: Memoirs of a President,* were published.

Highlights of Presidency

1977. In September, signed treaties providing for U.S. operation of the Panama Canal to the end of 1999 and for the permanent neutralization of the canal.

1978. With Israeli Prime Minister Menahem Begin and Egypt's President Anwar el-Sadat, signed the "Framework of Peace in the Middle East" and the "Framework for the Conclusion of a Peace Treaty Between Egypt and Israel." The agreements followed 11 days of U.S.-sponsored talks at Camp David. □ In December, China and the United States agreed to establish diplomatic relations.

1979. Signed a bill creating the U.S. Department of Education; a Department of Energy was established in 1977. □ Reached Strategic Arms Limitation Agreement with Soviet President Brezhnev. □ Protesting U.S. support of the Shah, radical Iranian students seized a group of American diplomats and embassy officials in Teheran in November. The "hostage crisis" clouded the remaining months of the Carter presidency.

1980. After defeating Sen. Edward M. Kennedy for the Democratic presidential nomination, lost election to Ronald Reagan by a wide margin.

Ronald Wilson Reagan

40th president, 1981-   Republican

1911. Born on February 6 in Tampico, IL.

1932. After graduating from Eureka (IL) College, worked as a sports announcer for radio stations in Davenport and Des Moines, IA.

1937. Made film debut in *Love Is on the Air*. Appeared in more than 50 movies during a 27-year career as an actor.

1940. Married Jane Wyman on January 25. The couple would become the parents of a daughter and an adopted son, and be divorced in 1948.

1942-45. Served in the U.S. Army Air Forces.

1947-52; 1959. Was president of the Screen Actors Guild.

1952. Married actress Nancy Davis on March 4. The couple would have a daughter and a son.

1952-62. Served as a spokesperson for General Electric.

1962. Officially joined the Republican Party, after being a liberal Democrat during his younger years.

1967-75. Was governor of California.

1976. Failed to capture the GOP presidential nomination from the incumbent Gerald Ford.

1980. Elected president in a landslide win over Jimmy Carter and third party candidate John Anderson.

Highlights of Presidency

1981. On January 20, inaugurated as the 40th president. Moments later, 52 Americans, who had been held hostage in Iran since November 1979, were released. □ In July, nominated Sandra Day O'Connor as an associate justice of the U.S. Supreme Court. □ On August 13, signed into law the Economic Recovery Tax Bill and Omnibus Budget Reconciliation Bill.

1983. With U.S. forces participating in a multinational peacekeeping force in Lebanon, 241 U.S. servicemen are killed in terrorist attack in October. □ That same month, U.S.

troops invade the Caribbean island of Grenada in an "effort to restore order and democracy."

1984. Reelected in a landslide.

1985. In November, met with Soviet General Secretary Mikhail Gorbachev in Geneva.

1986. American warplanes bombed "terrorist-related targets" in Tripoli and Benghazi, Libya, in April.

Ronald Reagan, the 40th chief executive, welcomed his three predecessors to the White House in October 1981.

The White House

PRESIDENTIAL ELECTIONS 1789-1984

		PARTIES	POPULAR VOTE	ELECTORAL VOTE
1789[1]	George Washington			69
	John Adams			34
	John Jay			9
	R. H. Harrison			6
	John Rutledge			6
	John Hancock			4
	George Clinton			3
	Samuel Huntington			2
	John Milton			2
	James Armstrong			1
	Benjamin Lincoln			1
	Edward Telfair			1
	(Not voted)			12
1792[1]	George Washington	Federalist		132
	John Adams	Federalist		77
	George Clinton	Dem.-Rep.		50
	Thomas Jefferson	Dem.-Rep.		4
	Aaron Burr			1
1796[1]	John Adams	Federalist		71
	Thomas Jefferson	Dem.-Rep.		68
	Thomas Pinckney	Federalist		59
	Aaron Burr	Anti-Federalist		30
	Samuel Adams	Dem.-Rep.		15
	Oliver Ellsworth	Federalist		11
	George Clinton	Dem.-Rep.		7
	John Jay	Ind.-Fed.		5
	James Iredell	Federalist		3
	George Washington	Federalist		2
	John Henry	Independent		2
	S. Johnston	Ind.-Fed.		2
	C. C. Pinckney	Ind.-Fed.		1
1800[1]	Thomas Jefferson	Dem.-Rep.		73
	Aaron Burr	Dem.-Rep.		73
	John Adams	Federalist		65
	C. C. Pinckney	Federalist		64
	John Jay	Federalist		1
1804	Thomas Jefferson	Dem.-Rep.		162
	C. C. Pinckney	Federalist		14
1808	James Madison	Dem.-Rep.		122
	C. C. Pinckney	Federalist		47
	George Clinton	Ind.-Rep.		6
	(Not voted)			1
1812	James Madison	Dem.-Rep.		128
	DeWitt Clinton	Fusion		89
	(Not voted)			1
1816	James Monroe	Dem.-Rep.		183
	Rufus King	Federalist		34
	(Not voted)			4
1820	James Monroe	Dem.-Rep.		231
	John Q. Adams	Ind.-Rep.		1
	(Not voted)			3
1824	John Q. Adams	No distinct	108,740	84[2]
	Andrew Jackson	party	153,544	99[2]
	Henry Clay	designations	47,136	37
	W. H. Crawford		46,618	41
1828	Andrew Jackson	Democratic	647,286	178
	John Q. Adams	Nat.-Rep.	508,064	83
1832	Andrew Jackson	Democratic	687,502	219
	Henry Clay	Nat. Rep.	530,189	49
	William Wirt	Anti-Masonic	—	7
	John Floyd	Nullifiers	—	11
	(Not voted)			2
1836	Martin Van Buren	Democratic	765,483	170
	William H. Harrison	Whig		73
	Hugh L. White	Whig	739,795[3]	26
	Daniel Webster	Whig		14
	W. P. Mangum	Anti-Jackson		11
1840	William H. Harrison	Whig	1,274,624	234
	Martin Van Buren	Democratic	1,127,781	60
1844	James K. Polk	Democratic	1,338,464	170
	Henry Clay	Whig	1,300,097	105
	James G. Birney	Liberty	62,300	—
1848	Zachary Taylor	Whig	1,360,967	163
	Lewis Cass	Democratic	1,222,342	127
	Martin Van Buren	Free Soil	291,263	—
1852	Franklin Pierce	Democratic	1,601,117	254
	Winfield Scott	Whig	1,385,453	42
	John P. Hale	Free Soil	155,825	—
1856	James Buchanan	Democratic	1,832,955	174
	John C. Fremont	Republican	1,339,932	114
	Millard Fillmore	American	871,731	8
1860	Abraham Lincoln	Republican	1,865,593	180
	J. C. Breckinridge	Democratic (S)	848,356	72
	Stephen A. Douglas	Democratic	1,382,713	12
	John Bell	Con. Union	592,906	39
1864	Abraham Lincoln	Republican	2,206,938	212
	George B. McClellan	Democratic	1,803,787	21
	(Not voted)		—	81
1868	Ulysses S. Grant	Republican	3,013,421	214
	Horatio Seymour	Democratic	2,706,829	80
	(Not voted)		—	23
1872	Ulysses S. Grant	Republican	3,596,745	286
	Horace Greeley	Democratic	2,843,446	[4]
	Charles O'Connor	Straight Dem.	29,489	—
	Thomas A. Hendricks	Ind.-Dem.	—	42
	B. Gratz Brown	Democratic	—	18
	Charles J. Jenkins	Democratic	—	2
	David Davis	Democratic	—	1
	(Not voted)		—	17
1876	Rutherford B. Hayes	Republican	4,036,572	185
	Samuel J. Tilden	Democratic	4,284,020	184
	Peter Cooper	Greenback	81,737	—
1880	James A. Garfield	Republican	4,453,295	214
	Winfield S. Hancock	Democratic	4,414,082	155
	James B. Weaver	Green.-Labor	308,578	—
	Neal Dow	Prohibition	10,305	—
1884	Grover Cleveland	Democratic	4,879,507	219
	James G. Blaine	Republican	4,850,293	182
	Benjamin F. Butler	Green.-Labor	175,370	—
	John P. St. John	Prohibition	150,369	—
1888	Benjamin Harrison	Republican	5,447,129	233
	Grover Cleveland	Democratic	5,537,857	168
	Clinton B. Fisk	Prohibition	249,506	—
	Anson J. Streeter	Union Labor	146,935	—
1892	Grover Cleveland	Democratic	5,555,426	277
	Benjamin Harrison	Republican	5,182,690	145
	James B. Weaver	People's	1,029,846	22
	John Bidwell	Prohibition	264,133	—
	Simon Wing	Soc. Labor	21,164	—
1896	William McKinley	Republican	7,102,246	271
	William J. Bryan	Democratic[5]	6,492,559	176
	John M. Palmer	Nat. Dem.	133,148	—
	Joshua Levering	Prohibition	132,007	—
	Charles H. Matchett	Soc. Labor	36,274	—
	Charles E. Bentley	Nationalist	13,969	—
1900	William McKinley	Republican	7,218,491	292
	William J. Bryan	Democratic[5]	6,356,734	155
	John C. Wooley	Prohibition	208,914	—
	Eugene V. Debs	Socialist	87,814	—
	Wharton Barker	People's	50,373	—
	Jos. F. Malloney	Soc. Labor	39,739	—

Year	Candidate	Party	Popular Vote	Electoral Vote
1904	Theodore Roosevelt	Republican	7,628,461	336
	Alton B. Parker	Democratic	5,084,223	140
	Eugene V. Debs	Socialist	402,283	—
	Silas C. Swallow	Prohibition	258,536	—
	Thomas E. Watson	People's	117,183	—
	Charles H. Corregan	Soc. Labor	31,249	—
1908	William H. Taft	Republican	7,675,320	321
	William J. Bryan	Democratic	6,412,294	162
	Eugene V. Debs	Socialist	420,793	—
	Eugene W. Chafin	Prohibition	253,840	—
	Thomas L. Hisgen	Independence	82,872	—
	Thomas E. Watson	People's	29,100	—
	August Gillhaus	Soc. Labor	14,021	—
1912	Woodrow Wilson	Democratic	6,296,547	435
	Theodore Roosevelt	Progressive	4,118,571	88
	William H. Taft	Republican	3,486,720	8
	Eugene V. Debs	Socialist	900,672	—
	Eugene W. Chafin	Prohibition	206,275	—
	Arthur E. Reimer	Soc. Labor	28,750	—
1916	Woodrow Wilson	Democratic	9,127,695	277
	Charles E. Hughes	Republican	8,533,507	254
	A. L. Benson	Socialist	585,113	—
	J. Frank Hanly	Prohibition	220,506	—
	Arthur E. Reimer	Soc. Labor	13,403	—
1920	Warren G. Harding	Republican	16,143,407	404
	James M. Cox	Democratic	9,130,328	127
	Eugene V. Debs	Socialist	919,799	—
	P. P. Christensen	Farmer-Labor	265,411	—
	Aaron S. Watkins	Prohibition	189,408	—
	James E. Ferguson	American	48,000	—
	W. W. Cox	Soc. Labor	31,715	—
1924	Calvin Coolidge	Republican	15,718,211	382
	John W. Davis	Democratic	8,385,283	136
	Robert M. LaFollette	Progressive	4,831,289	13
	Herman P. Faris	Prohibition	57,520	—
	Frank T. Johns	Soc. Labor	36,428	—
	William Z. Foster	Workers	36,386	—
	Gilbert O. Nations	American	23,967	—
1928	Herbert C. Hoover	Republican	21,391,993	444
	Alfred E. Smith	Democratic	15,016,169	87
	Norman Thomas	Socialist	267,835	—
	Verne L. Reynolds	Soc. Labor	21,603	—
	William Z. Foster	Workers	21,181	—
	William F. Varney	Prohibition	20,106	—
1932	Franklin D. Roosevelt	Democratic	22,809,638	472
	Herbert C. Hoover	Republican	15,758,901	59
	Norman Thomas	Socialist	881,951	—
	William Z. Foster	Communist	102,785	—
	William D. Upshaw	Prohibition	81,869	—
	Verne L. Reynolds	Soc. Labor	33,276	—
	William H. Harvey	Liberty	53,425	—
1936	Franklin D. Roosevelt	Democratic	27,752,869	523
	Alfred M. Landon	Republican	16,674,665	8
	William Lemke	Union	882,479	—
	Norman Thomas	Socialist	187,720	—
	Earl Browder	Communist	80,159	—
	D. Leigh Colvin	Prohibition	37,847	—
	John W. Aiken	Soc. Labor	12,777	—
1940	Franklin D. Roosevelt	Democratic	27,307,819	449
	Wendell L. Willkie	Republican	22,321,018	82
	Norman Thomas	Socialist	99,557	—
	Roger Q. Babson	Prohibition	57,812	—
	Earl Browder	Communist	46,251	—
	John W. Aiken	Soc. Labor	14,892	—
1944	Franklin D. Roosevelt	Democratic	25,606,585	432
	Thomas E. Dewey	Republican	22,014,745	99
	Norman Thomas	Socialist	80,518	—
	Claude A. Watson	Prohibition	74,758	—
	Edward A. Teichert	Soc. Labor	45,336	—
1948	Harry S. Truman	Democratic	24,179,345	303
	Thomas E. Dewey	Republican	21,991,291	189
	Strom Thurmond	States' Rights	1,176,125	39
	Henry Wallace	Progressive	1,157,326	—
	Norman Thomas	Socialist	139,572	—
	Claude A. Watson	Prohibition	103,900	—
	Edward A. Teichert	Soc. Labor	29,241	—
	Farrell Dobbs	Soc. Workers	13,614	—
1952	Dwight D. Eisenhower	Republican	33,936,234	442
	Adlai E. Stevenson	Democratic	27,314,992	89
	Vincent Hallinan	Progressive	140,023	—
	Stuart Hamblen	Prohibition	72,949	—
	Eric Hass	Soc. Labor	30,267	—
	Darlington Hoopes	Socialist	20,203	—
	Douglas A. MacArthur	Constitution	17,205	—
	Farrell Dobbs	Soc. Workers	10,312	—
1956	Dwight D. Eisenhower	Republican	35,590,472	457
	Adlai E. Stevenson	Democratic	26,022,752	73[6]
	T. Coleman Andrews	States' Rights	111,178	—
	Eric Hass	Soc. Labor	44,450	—
	Enoch A. Holtwick	Prohibition	41,937	—
1960	John F. Kennedy	Democratic	34,226,731	303[7]
	Richard M. Nixon	Republican	34,108,157	219
	Eric Hass	Soc. Labor	47,522	—
	Rutherford L. Decker	Prohibition	46,203	—
	Orval E. Faubus	Nat. S. Rights	44,977	—
	Farrell Dobbs	Soc. Workers	40,165	—
	Charles L. Sullivan	Constitution	18,162	—
1964	Lyndon B. Johnson	Democratic	43,129,566	486
	Barry M. Goldwater	Republican	27,178,188	52
	Eric Hass	Soc. Labor	45,219	—
	Clifton DeBerry	Soc. Workers	32,720	—
	E. Harold Munn	Prohibition	23,267	—
1968	Richard M. Nixon	Republican	31,785,480	301
	Hubert H. Humphrey	Democratic	31,275,166	191
	George C. Wallace	Amer. Ind.	9,906,473	46
	Henning A. Blomen	Soc. Labor	52,588	—
	Dick Gregory		47,133[8]	—
	Fred Halstead	Soc. Workers	41,388	—
	Eldridge Cleaver	Peace-Freedom	36,563	—
	Eugene J. McCarthy		25,552[9]	—
	E. Harold Munn	Prohibition	15,123	—
1972	Richard M. Nixon	Republican	41,170,000	520[10]
	George McGovern	Democratic	29,170,000	17
	John Schmitz	American	1,099,482	—
	Benjamin Spock	People's	78,756	—
1976	Jimmy Carter	Democratic	40,831,000	297
	Gerald Ford	Republican	39,148,000	240[11]
	Eugene McCarthy	Independent	756,691	—
	Roger MacBride	Libertarian	173,011	—
1980	Ronald Reagan	Republican	43,904,000	489
	Jimmy Carter	Democratic	35,484,000	49
	John Anderson	Independent	5,720,060	—
	Ed Clark	Libertarian	921,299	—
1984	Ronald Reagan	Republican	54,455,000	525
	Walter Mondale	Democratic	37,577,000	13
	David Bergland	Libertarian	228,314	—
	Lyndon H. LaRouche	Independent	78,807	—

—Represents Zero

[1] Prior to the election of 1804, each elector voted for 2 candidates for president; the one receiving the highest number of votes, if a majority, was declared elected president, the next highest, vice-president. This provision was modified by adoption of the 12th amendment, which was declared ratified by the legislatures of three fourths of the states in a proclamation of the secretary of state, Sept. 25, 1804. [2] No candidate having a majority in the electoral college, the election was decided in the House of Representatives. [3] Whig tickets were pledged to various candidates in various states. [4] Greeley died shortly after the election and presidential electors supporting him cast their votes as indicated, including 3 for Greeley, which were not counted. [5] Includes a variety of joint tickets with People's Party electors committed to Bryan. [6] 1 Democratic elector in Alabama voted for Walter Jones. [7] 6 Democratic electors in Alabama, all 8 unpledged Democratic electors in Mississippi, and 1 Republican elector in Oklahoma voted for Sen. Harry F. Byrd. [8] Total vote for Gregory includes write-in votes as well as votes for the Freedom and Peace Party, the Peace Freedom Alternative, the Peace and Freedom Party, and the New Party. [9] Total vote for McCarthy includes write-in votes as well as votes for the Alternative in November Party, and the New Party. [10] John Hospers of California received one vote from an elector of Virginia. [11] An elector from the state of Washington voted for Ronald Reagan.

Party Abbreviations: Dem.-Rep. (Democratic-Republican); Ind.-Fed. (Independent-Federalist); Ind.-Rep. (Independent-Republican); Nat. Rep. (National Republican); Con. Union (Constitution Union); Ind.-Dem. (Independent-Democratic); Green.-Labor (Greenback-Labor); Soc. Labor (Socialist Labor); Nat. Dem. (National Democratic); Soc. Workers (Socialist Workers); Nat. S. Rights (National States Rights); Amer. Inc. (American Independent).

THE VICE-PRESIDENTS

1. JOHN ADAMS (1735-1826). Federalist. Served under George Washington, 1789-97; home state: MA; profession: lawyer.

2. THOMAS JEFFERSON (1743-1826). Democratic-Republican. Served under John Adams, 1797-1801; home state: VA; profession: lawyer, planter, public official.

3. AARON BURR (1756-1836). Democratic-Republican. Served under Thomas Jefferson, 1801-05; home state: NY; profession: public official.

4. GEORGE CLINTON (1739-1812). Democratic-Republican. Served under Thomas Jefferson, 1805-09, James Madison, 1809-12; home state: NY; profession: public official.

5. ELBRIDGE GERRY (1744-1814). Democratic-Republican. Served under James Madison, 1813-14; home state: MA; profession: public official.

6. DANIEL D. TOMPKINS (1774-1825). Democratic-Republican. Served under James Monroe, 1817-25; home state: NY; profession: lawyer and public official.

7. JOHN C. CALHOUN (1782-1850). Served as Democratic-Republican under John Quincy Adams, 1825-29; as Democrat under Andrew Jackson, 1829-32; home state: SC; profession: lawyer and public official.

8. MARTIN VAN BUREN (1782-1862). Democrat. Served under Andrew Jackson, 1833-37; home state: NY; profession: lawyer and public official.

9. RICHARD M. JOHNSON (1780-1850). Democrat. Served under Martin Van Buren, 1837-41; home state: KY; profession: public official.

10. JOHN TYLER (1790-1862). Whig. Served under William H. Harrison, March 4-April 4, 1841; home state: VA; profession: lawyer and public official.

11. GEORGE M. DALLAS (1792-1864). Democrat. Served under James K. Polk, 1845-49; home state: PA; profession: public official and diplomat.

12. MILLARD FILLMORE (1800-1874). Whig. Served under Zachary Taylor, 1849-50; home state: NY; profession: teacher, lawyer, public official.

13. WILLIAM R. D. KING (1786-1853). Democrat. Served under Franklin Pierce, March 4-April 18, 1853; home state: AL; profession: lawyer, public official, diplomat.

14. JOHN C. BRECKINRIDGE (1821-75). Democrat. Served under James Buchanan, 1857-61; home state: KY; profession: lawyer and public official.

15. HANNIBAL HAMLIN (1809-1891). Republican. Served under Abraham Lincoln, 1861-65; home state: ME; profession: lawyer and public official.

16. ANDREW JOHNSON (1808-1875). National Union (Republican). Served under Abraham Lincoln, March 4-April 15, 1865; home state: TN; profession: tailor and public official.

17. SCHUYLER COLFAX (1823-1885). Republican. Served under Ulysses S. Grant, 1869-73; home state: IN; profession: newspaperman and public official.

18. HENRY WILSON (1812-1875). Republican. Served under Ulysses S. Grant, 1873-75; home state: MA; profession: factory owner and public official.

19. WILLIAM A. WHEELER (1819-1887). Republican. Served under Rutherford B. Hayes, 1877-81; home state: NY; profession: businessman and public official.

20. CHESTER A. ARTHUR (1829-1886). Republican. Served under James A. Garfield, March 4-Sept. 20, 1881; home state: NY; profession: lawyer.

21. THOMAS A. HENDRICKS (1819-1885). Democrat. Served under Grover Cleveland, March 4-Nov. 25, 1885; home state: IN; profession: lawyer and public official.

22. LEVI P. MORTON (1824-1920). Republican. Served under Benjamin Harrison, 1889-93; home state: NY; profession: banker and public official.

23. ADLAI E. STEVENSON (1835-1914). Democrat. Served under G. Cleveland, 1893-97; home state: IL; profession: public official.

24. GARRET A. HOBART (1844-1899). Republican. Served under William McKinley, 1897-99; home state: NJ; profession: lawyer and public official.

25. THEODORE ROOSEVELT (1858-1919). Republican. Served under William McKinley, March 4-Sept. 14, 1901; home state: NY; profession: historian and public official.

26. CHARLES W. FAIRBANKS (1852-1918). Republican. Served under Theodore Roosevelt, 1905-09; home state: IN; profession: financier and public official.

27. JAMES S. SHERMAN (1855-1912). Republican. Served under William Howard Taft, 1909-12; home state: NY; profession: public official.

28. THOMAS R. MARSHALL (1854-1925). Democrat. Served under Woodrow Wilson, 1913-21; home state: IN; profession: lawyer and public official.

29. CALVIN COOLIDGE (1872-1933). Republican. Served under Warren G. Harding, 1921-23; home state: MA; profession: lawyer and public official.

30. CHARLES G. DAWES (1865-1951). Republican. Served under Calvin Coolidge, 1925-29; home state: IL; profession: financier and diplomat.

31. CHARLES CURTIS (1860-1936). Republican. Served under Herbert Hoover, 1929-33; home state: KS; profession: lawyer and public official.

32. JOHN N. GARNER (1868-1967). Democrat. Served under Franklin D. Roosevelt, 1933-41; home state: TX; profession: public official.

33. HENRY A. WALLACE (1888-1965). Democrat. Served under Franklin D. Roosevelt, 1941-45; home state: IA; profession: editor and agribusinessman.

34. HARRY S. TRUMAN (1884-1972). Democrat. Served under Franklin D. Roosevelt, Jan. 20-April 12, 1945; home state: MO; profession: public official.

35. ALBEN W. BARKLEY (1877-1956). Democrat. Served under Harry S. Truman, 1949-53; home state: KY; profession: public official.

36. RICHARD M. NIXON (1913-   ). Republican. Served under Dwight D. Eisenhower, 1953-61; home state: CA; profession: public official.

37. LYNDON B. JOHNSON (1908-1973). Democrat. Served under John F. Kennedy, Jan. 20, 1961-Nov. 22, 1963; home state: TX; profession: public official.

38. HUBERT H. HUMPHREY (1911-1978). Democrat. Served under L. B. Johnson, 1965-69; home state: MN; profession: public official.

39. SPIRO T. AGNEW (1918-   ). Republican. Served under R. M. Nixon, Jan. 20, 1969-Oct. 10, 1973; home state: MD; profession: public official.

40. GERALD R. FORD (1913-   ). Republican. Served under R. M. Nixon, Dec. 6, 1973-Aug. 9, 1974; home state: MI; profession: public official.

41. NELSON A. ROCKEFELLER (1908-1979). Republican. Served under Gerald R. Ford, Dec. 19, 1974-Jan. 20, 1977; home state: NY; profession: public official.

42. WALTER F. MONDALE (1928-   ). Democrat. Served under Jimmy Carter, 1977-81; home state: MN; profession: public official.

43. GEORGE BUSH (1924-   ). Republican. Served under Ronald Reagan, 1981-   ; home state: TX; profession: oilman and public official.

THE WHITE HOUSE

The White House, located at 1600 Pennsylvania Avenue, N.W., in Washington DC, has been the home of every U.S. president since John Adams. The presidential mansion is situated on some 18 acres (7.3 hectares) of land amid a parklike setting. The building's main section measures 170 feet (52 meters) long and 85 feet (26 meters) deep. Its 2½ stories are mounted on an English basement, which, because of the slope of the land, becomes a ground floor on the south side. Two wings flank the original structure. The West Wing was constructed in 1902, following a Congressional appropriation of $65,196. It contains the Oval (presidential) Office, the Roosevelt or staff meeting room, a reception room, and the Cabinet Room. French doors within the president's office open onto the Rose Garden, which continues to follow the plan of an 18th century flower garden. The president regularly receives official visitors in the Rose Garden. The East Wing was built in 1942 and contains offices for presidential aides. The Jacqueline Kennedy Garden, so named by Mrs. Lyndon B. Johnson in honor of her predecessor, is off the East Wing and is used by the First Lady as a reception area.

Prior to 1902, the ground floor served as the president's work area. This floor now features the Library, which was completely reorganized in 1962; the Vermeil or Gold Room, which serves as a display room as well as a ladies' sitting room; the China or "Presidential Collection Room," which includes a wide exhibit of White House China; the Diplomatic Reception Room, formerly a boiler room; and the Map Room, from which President Franklin D. Roosevelt monitored the events of World War II.

Although the rooms of the first (state) floor have been refurbished many times over the years, the floor has not changed architecturally since the White House was designed by John Hoban in 1792. The East Room, three reception rooms (the Green Room, Blue Room, and Red Room), the State Dining Room, and the Family Dining Room comprise the first floor. With the exception of the Family Dining Room, these rooms are open to the public. The East Room, called the "Public Audience Room" by Hoban, retains its classical style of the early 19th century. It has been the scene of many White House dances, concerts, weddings, funerals, and bill-signing ceremonies. Gerald R. Ford took the oath of office in the East Room when he succeeded Richard M. Nixon as chief executive. The State Dining Room was originally much smaller and functioned as a drawing room, office, and cabinet room. The dining hall now can seat as many as 140 guests. The second floor includes the Queen's Suite, formerly the Rose Guest Room and now a sitting room and bedroom; the Lincoln Bedroom, which was the office and the cabinet room of the 16th chief executive; the adjoining Lincoln Sitting Room; and a former Cabinet Room, which was designated the Treaty Room during the John Kennedy administration to reflect the many important decisions made in it. The private quarters of the president and his family are located on the west end of the second floor.

History. Construction of the White House was begun in 1792 after an architectural competition won by James Hoban, an Irish-born architect who had immigrated to America some years earlier. After many delays and financial problems the building was habitable (but not completed) in 1800, when President John Adams and his wife, Abigail, moved in. Hoban's original drawing of the north façade, which has survived, reflects the English-Palladian architecture of the mid-18th century.

Thomas Jefferson, the second president to occupy the White House, employed the gifted architect Benjamin H. Latrobe in 1806 to help design the east and west pavilions. The latter has survived in its nearly original state. Latrobe also made designs for the north and south porticoes which were executed in a modified form at a later date.

In 1814 during the War of 1812, British forces burned all of the public buildings in Washington. The White House was not spared. With the exception of a Gilbert Stuart portrait of George Washington, now in the East Room, all of the furnishings from the Adams, Jefferson, and Madison administrations were destroyed. Under James Hoban's supervision the White House was rebuilt and was ready for occupancy in 1817, refurnished in the Empire Style with items imported from France by President James Monroe. However, in the architecture of the building, and particularly in the interior, Hoban returned to his earlier Palladian style and did not repeat the neoclassic innovations made by Latrobe. The scorched exterior walls were painted white. There is misconception that this is why the building was called the White House. Actually it had borne that name since it was first built.

Throughout the 19th century the interior of the White House went through each successive decorative style, but the exterior appearance of the building remained the same. Gas lighting was introduced in 1849 and central heating in 1853. The first bathroom was installed in 1877. In 1833 pipes bringing water from a nearby spring replaced the pump formerly used. After 1853 water was piped in from the city's water system. Electricity came to the White House during the residency of Benjamin Harrison.

In 1902, during the administration of President Theodore Roosevelt, the White House underwent its first major renovation, under the direction of the architectural firm of McKim, Mead, and White. The rooms of the first floor were stripped of their Victorian

The White House: The large North Entrance Hall, *top left,* was part of James Hoban's original architectural plan for the mansion. Prior to completion of the West Wing in the early 1900s, the hall was a reception area. The oval Blue Room, *bottom left,* includes French Empire style furnishings from the James Monroe administration. Although each president can alter the design and decor of the Oval Office, tradition dictates the correct positions of the U.S. and presidential flags. The Lincoln Bedroom, *right,* which was used by the 16th chief executive as an office and cabinet room, was decorated with bedroom furniture from the Lincoln era during the Truman years. George P.A. Healy's portrait of Lincoln hangs over the mantel in the State Dining Room. As many as 140 guests can dine in the gold- and white-dominated room. The Cabinet Room, overlooking the Rose Garden, was added to the West Wing in 1909.

overlay and returned to their early-19th-century appearance. The grand staircase was moved into the entrance hall to permit the creation of the State Dining Room at the southwest corner of the building.

In 1949, during the administration of President Harry S. Truman, the White House was found unsafe for occupancy. The exterior walls were retained while the interior fabric of the building was removed and rebuilt on a steel and concrete frame. Great care was taken to preserve the original woodwork, marble mantlepieces, and decorative plasterwork. The original floor plan was followed faithfully. A balcony, now known as the Truman Balcony, was built on the second-floor level of the South portico. It has become a favorite spot of presidential families.

Under the guidance of Mrs. John F. Kennedy, the restoration of the interior of the White House to its original late-18th and early-19th-century appearance was begun. A Fine Arts Committee, composed of museum specialists and others, was formed to direct the work of restoration. This committee was further strenghtened by a special Advisory Committee and a Paintings Committee. Prior to this there had been little attempt to preserve or to use historic White House furnishings, and the rooms of the first floor were largely furnished with reproductions. Many important objects were recovered from White House storage areas. Other outstanding examples of American cabinetmaking and the decorative arts were supplied by generous donors. Mrs. Kennedy felt strongly that "everything in the White House must have a reason for being there." Subsequently, the Committee for the Preservation of the White House and the permanent office of curator were established by President Johnson. Additional pieces of valuable furniture and American paintings were acquired for the White House during the Nixon administration, and the principal rooms of the first and ground floors were redecorated during the Nixon years. After moving to the executive mansion in January 1981, Mrs. Ronald Reagan oversaw the remodeling of the first and second floor rooms and several preservation projects.

For the American public, the executive mansion has become a national palace as well as a home for the chief executive. For, in the words of President Dwight D. Eisenhower, the "White House has been and should always remain a place to be venerated by its occupants as well as by all Americans."

The Lyndon Baines Johnson Library

On the University of Texas campus in Austin, the Lyndon Baines Johnson Library, *above,* houses the papers of the 36th president's career in public service. The "Kennedy rocker," his desk, and other memorabilia are displayed at the John Fitzgerald Kennedy Library in Boston.

The John Fitzgerald Kennedy Library

U. S. PRESIDENTIAL LIBRARIES

At various times in American history, Congress has appropriated funds to maintain the papers of former presidents. These collections, extending from the administration of George Washington to the era of Calvin Coolidge and including some 2 million manuscripts, are located in the Library of Congress. The first separate presidential library, the Franklin D. Roosevelt Library in Hyde Park, was established by a joint resolution of Congress in 1939 and was dedicated on July 4, 1940. The other presidential libraries are:

Herbert Hoover Presidential Library; located in West Branch, IA; dedicated on Aug. 10, 1962.

Harry S. Truman Presidential Library; located in Independence, MO; dedicated on July 6, 1957.

Dwight D. Eisenhower Presidential Library; located in Abilene, KS; dedicated on May 1, 1962.

John F. Kennedy Presidential Library; located in Boston, MA; dedicated on Oct. 20, 1979.

Lyndon B. Johnson Presidential Library; located in Austin, TX; dedicated on May 22, 1971.

Gerald R. Ford Presidential Library; located in Ann Arbor, MI; dedicated on April 27, 1981.

Jimmy Carter Presidential Library; located in Atlanta, GA; scheduled for dedication in late 1986.

They were built with private monies, donated to the federal government, and are administrated by the National Archives.

DICTIONARY OF SYNONYMS AND ANTONYMS

A

abandon, abdicate, discontinue, relinguish, resign, surrender, vacate, desert, forsake, leave, quit. ANT.—defend, maintain, occupy, stay, support.

abase, degrade, disgrace, mock, shame. ANT.—dignify, elevate, honor, praise.

abate, assuage, decrease, diminish, lessen, lower, mitigate, moderate, reduce, suppress. ANT.—enlarge, increase, intensify, prolong, revive.

abbreviate, abridge, condense, contract, curtail, lessen, limit, reduce, shorten. ANT.—enlarge, expand, extend, lengthen.

abbreviation, abridgement, contraction, curtailment, reduction, shortening. ANT.—enlargement, expansion, extension.

abdicate, abandon, relinquish, renounce, resign, surrender, vacate; desert, forsake, leave, quit. ANT.—defend, maintain, retain, stay.

aberrant, abnormal, deviate, eccentric, peculiar, unnatural, unusual, variable. ANT.—normal, ordinary, regular, usual.

abet, aid, assist, encourage, help, incite, stimulate. ANT.—deter, discourage, hinder, oppose, resist.

abeyance, adjournment, inaction, reservation, suspension. ANT.—action, enforcement, renewal, revival.

abhor, despise, detest, dislike, execrate, hate, loathe. ANT.—admire, desire, esteem, like, relish.

ability, aptitude, aptness, capability, capacity, dexterity, efficiency, faculty, knowledge, power, skill, talent. ANT.—incapacity, incompetency, stupidity.

abnormal, aberrant, erratic, irregular, odd, unnatural, unusual. ANT.—normal, usual, standard.

abode, domicile, dwelling, habitation, house, home, quarters, residence.

abolish, end, eradicate, throw out; abrogate, annul, cancel, invalidate, nullify, revoke. ANT.—confirm, continue, establish, institute, legalize, restore.

abominable, detestable, foul, hateful, horrible, loathsome, odious, repugnant, revolting, vile. ANT.—agreeable, enjoyable, delightful, pleasant.

abominate, abhor, despise, detest, dislike, hate, loathe. ANT.—admire, approve, cherish, like, love.

abrupt, hasty, impetuous, precipitate, quick, sudden; blunt, brusque, curt, rude, short; craggy, precipitous, rugged, sharp, steep. ANT.—anticipated, expected; courteous, gradual, smooth.

absent, away, departed, missing; absent-minded, abstracted, distracted, preoccupied. ANT.—attending, here, present; attentive.

absolute, complete, entire, infinite, perfect, pure, total, ultimate, unconditional; arbitrary, autocratic, despotic, supreme, tyrannous, unrestricted. ANT.—accountable, conditional, contingent, dependent, limited.

absolve, acquit, clear, discharge, exonerate, pardon, release. ANT.—accuse, bind, blame, charge, convict, incriminate.

absorb, assimilate, consume, engulf, imbibe, incorporate, merge, swallow; engage, engross. ANT.—discharge, dispense, eject, emit, exude.

abstinence, abstention, continence, fasting, moderation, self-denial, self-restraint, sobriety, temperance. ANT.—excess, glutonny, greed, intemperance, self-indulgence.

abstract, detach, excerpt, remove, select, separate; appropriate, steal; abridge, summarize. ANT.—add, combine, insert, replace, return, unite.

abstracted, appropriated, drawn from, parted, removed, separated, stolen; abridged, summarized. ANT.—added, combined, replaced, returned, united.

absurd, foolish, inconsistent, irrational, ludicrous, nonsensical, preposterous, ridiculous, self-contradictory, senseless, unreasonable. ANT.—logical, rational, reasonable, sensible, sound.

abundant, bountiful, copious, lavish, opulent, plentiful, profuse, rich. ANT.—insufficient, rare, scant, scarce.

abuse, damage, desecrate, dishonor, disparage, insult, maltreat, molest, oppress, persecute, revile, upbraid. ANT.—approve, commend, laud, protect, respect, shield.

abuse, asperse, defame, disparage, harm, ill-use, malign, persecute, vilify; misuse. ANT.—cherish, favor, honor, praise, protect, respect, sustain.

academic, bookish, erudite, formal, learned, literary, pedantic, scholarly, theoretical. ANT.—common-sense, ignorant, practical, simple.

accede, agree, assent, consent. ANT.—dissent, protest, refuse.

accelerate, dispatch, expedite, facilitate, forward, hasten, hurry, push, quicken, rush, speed up. ANT.—block, hinder, impede, obstruct, resist, retard, slow.

accident, calamity, casualty, chance, diaster, happening, misfortune, mishap. ANT.—calculation, design, intention, plan, purpose.

accentuate, emphasize, exaggerate, heighten, intensify, stress, underline. ANT.—minimize, moderate, subdue.

acclaim, applaud, cheer, extol, honor, glorify, laud. ANT.—berate, dishonor, jear, revile.

accommodate, adapt, adjust, arrange, conform, harmonize, oblige, serve, supply. ANT.—embarass, disarrange, obstruct, prevent.

accompany, attend, chaperon, conduct, convoy, escort, follow, join. ANT.—desert, leave.

accomplice, abettor, accessory, ally, assistant, associate, confederate. ANT.—adversary, enemy, opponent, rival.

accomplish, achieve, attain, complete, consummate, do, effect, execute, finish, fulfill, manage, perform. ANT.—block, defeat, fail, frustrate, spoil.

accord, agree, allow, assent, concede, grant, permit; agreement, acquiesment, harmony, reconciliation, unison. ANT.—contend, disallow, dispute, question; dissension, opposition, strife.

accost, address, approach, greet, solicit, speak to. ANT.—avoid, evade, pass by.

account, chronicle, description, detail, history, narrative, recital, computation, reckoning, record, statement.

accrue, accumulate, amass, collect, gather, grow, increase, store. ANT.—diminish, disperse, dissipate.

accumulate, accrue, amass, assemble, collect, gather, hoard, increase, pile, store. ANT.—diminish, disperse, dissipate, spend, waste.

accuse, blame, censure, charge, denounce, incriminate, indict. ANT.—absolve, acquit, exonerate, vindicate.

achieve, accomplish, do, effect, execute, fulfill, gain, realize, win. ANT.—abandon, fail, lose, miss.

achievement, deed, exploit, feat, performance; accomplishment, attainment, execution, realization. ANT.—neglect, omission; defeat, failure, misfortune.

acquaintance, cognizance, companionship, experience, familiarity, friendship, intimacy, knowledge. ANT.—ignorance, inexperience, unfamiliarity.

acquire, attain, collect, earn, get, obtain, procure, reach, secure, win. ANT.—fail, forego, lose, miss, surrender.

act, accomplishment, action, deed, do, doing, enact, execute, feat, operation, perform, transaction; decree, edict, law, statute. ANT.—abstain, cease, discontinue, stop.

action, achievement, activity, battle, deed, exploit, motion, movement, performance. ANT.—idleness, inactivity, inertia, repose.

active, operative, working; busy, industrious; agile, alert, brisk, energetic, lively, mobile, nimble, quick, sprightly. ANT.—dormant, inactive; idle, indolent, passive.

activity, action, agility, alertness, briskness, energy, enterprise, exercise, intensity, liveliness, motion, progress, quickness, rapidity. ANT.—dullness, idleness, inactivity, inertia.

actuality, certainty, fact, reality, truth; act, circumstance, deed, event, factual, incident, occurrence, sure. ANT.—delusion, fiction, supposition, theory, unreal.

adapt, accommodate, adjust, conform, modify, fit. ANT.—derange, misapply, misfit.

add, adjoin, affix, annex, append, attach, augment, increase. ANT.—deduct, detach, reduce, remove, subtract, withdraw.

address, accost, approach, greet, hail, salute, speak to. ANT.—avoid, ignore, pass by.

adequate, ample, capable, commensurate, enough, fitting, qualified, satisfactory, sufficient, suitable. ANT.—deficient, insufficient, lacking, scant.

adhere, attach, clasp, cleave, cling, fasten, grasp, grip; have, hold, keep, maintain, occupy, possess, retain, support; check, confine, accommodate, carry, contain. ANT.—leave, loosen, unfasten.

adjacent, abuting, adjoining, beside, bordering, close, near, next, neighboring. ANT.—away from, beyond, distant, disconnected, separate.

admire, appreciate, approve, esteem, praise, respect, venerate. ANT.—abhor, despise, detest, dislike, hate.

admissible, acceptable, allowable, justifiable, permissible, tolerable, suitable, warranted. ANT.—inadmissible, irrelevant, unacceptable, unsuitable.

admit, accept, acknowledge, agree, allow, assent, concede, confess, grant, open, permit, sanction. ANT.—debar, deny, dismiss, refuse, reject.

advance, accelerate, elevate, forward, further, improve, move, proceed, promote; allege, bring forward, offer, propose, propound; proceed, suggest. ANT.—halt, oppose, retard, return, retreat, withdraw.

advantage, gain, mastery, superiority, victory; benefit, help, profit. ANT.—detriment, handicap, harm, hindrance, restriction.

adverse, antagonistic, contrary, hostile, opposed, opposite; unfavorable. ANT.—favor, cooperate, assist, approve.

advice, admonish, counsel, instruct, recommend, suggest; inform, notify. ANT.—deceive, misdirect, misinform.

affect, alter, change, influence, modify, concern, interest, regard; impress, melt, move, soften, subdue, touch; adopt, assume, feign, pretend.

affection, attachment, friendliness, fondness, goodwill, kindness, love, tenderness. ANT.—animosity, antipathy, aversion, dislike, indifference, repugnance.

affirm, assert, aver, declare, maintain, state, swear, warrent. ANT.—contradict, demur, deny, dispute, oppose, nullify.

afraid, alarmed, cowardly, fearful, frightened, scared, timid, timorous. ANT.—assured, bold, brave, composed, courageous, valorous.

aggravate, heighten, increase, intensify, magnify, worsen; annoy, embitter, exasperate, irritate, provoke. ANT.—appease, improve, mitigate, soften, soothe.

aggregate, amount, collection, conglomeration, entirety, mass, sum, total, whole. ANT.—element, part, particular, unit.

agility, activity, briskness, energy, enterprise, intensity, liveliness, movement, quickness, rapidity, vigor. ANT.—dullness, idleness, inactivity, inertia.

agitate, arouse, disturb, excite, perturb, provoke, rouse, ruffle, shake, stir, trouble. ANT.—calm, ease, placate, soothe, quiet.

agony, ache, anguish, distress, misery, pain, suffering, trial, torment, torture, woe. ANT.—comfort, ease, happiness, health, mitigation, relief.

agree, accede, acquiesce, approve, assent, comply, concur, conform, consent. ANT.—contradict, differ, disagree, dispute, dissent.

agreeable, acceptable, amiable, gratifying, pleasant, pleasing, suitable, welcome, willing. ANT.—disagreeable, obnoxious, offensive, unpleasant.

aim, aspiration, design, end, endeavor, goal, intention, purpose. ANT.—aimlessness, carelessness, lack of purpose.

alarm, affright, apprehension, consternation, dismay, fear, signal, terror, warning. ANT.—assurance, calm, composure, peace, quiet, security, tranquility.

alien, adverse, contrasted, foreign, hostile, irrelevant, remote, strange, unlike. ANT.—akin, germane, relevant.

allege, affirm, aver, cite, claim, declare, maintain. ANT.—contradict, deny, dissent, refute, repudiate.

alleviate, abate, allay, diminish, extenuate, lighten, mitigate, relieve, soften, soothe. ANT.—aggravate, agitate, augment, increase, intensify, irritate.

alliance, association, coalition, combination, confederacy, federation, partnership, union; compact, marriage, treaty. ANT.—divorce, schism, secession, separation.

allot, apportion, dispense, distribute, divide, mete; allocate, assign, give, grant, measure. ANT.—confiscate, deny, keep, refuse, retain, withhold.

allow, empower, permit, sanction, tolerate; authorize, give, grant, yield; acknowledge, admit, concede. ANT.—deny, forbid, protest, refuse, resist.

allude, hint, imply, insinuate, intimate, refer, suggest. ANT.—declare, specify, state.

allure, attract, bewitch, captivate, charm, coax, entice, invite, seduce, tempt. ANT.—dissuade, discourage, repel, threaten.

ally, accessory, accomplice, assistant, associate, confederate. ANT.—adversary, enemy, opponent.

alone, deserted, desolate, isolated, lonely, secluded; unaccompanied, unaided; lone, only, single, solitary. ANT.—accompanied, attended, together.

also, besides, furthermore, in addition, likewise, moreover.

alternative, choice, elective, option, preference. ANT.—no choice, obligation, required.

always, ceaselessly, constantly, continually, eternally, ever, forever, perpetually. ANT.—never, occasionally, rarely, sometimes.

amalgamate, blend, coalesce, combine, consolidate, fuse, mingle, merge, unite. ANT.—separate, divide.

amateur, apprentice, beginner, learner, neophyte, nonprofessional, novice. ANT.—authority, expert, master, professional.

ambiguous, dubious, equivocal, indefinite, obscure, vague. ANT.—clear; explicit, lucid, unequivocal.

ambition, aspiration, desire, eagerness, end, goal, incentive. ANT.—contentment, indifference, laziness, resignation, satisfaction.

amend, better, change, correct, improve, reform, repair. ANT.—blemish, corrupt, debase, spoil.

amiable, agreeable, engaging, friendly, good-natured, gracious, pleasant. ANT.—disagreeable, hateful, ill-natured.

among, amid, amidst, between, interspersed, mingle, mixed. ANT.—apart, alone, separate.

amount, aggregate, collection, mass, number, quantity, sum, total, whole. ANT.—individual, part, particular.

ample, broad, extensive, great, large, spacious, wide; abundant, bountiful, complete, copious, full, generous, plentiful, profuse, rich, sufficient. ANT.—limited, small; insufficient, lacking, meager, sparse.

amplification, accrual, augmentation, dilation, enhancement, enlargement, expansion, extension, growth, heighten, increase, intensification, magnification, multiplication, raising. ANT.—contraction, condensation, curtailment, decrease, diminishing, reduction.

analogous, akin, alike, allied, comparable, correlative, correspondent, like, parallel, resemblance, similar. ANT.—different, dissimilar, divergent, incongruous.

anger, animosity, displeasure, exasperation, fury, indignation, ire, irritation, passion, petulance, rage, resentment, temper, vexation, wrath. ANT.—calmness, conciliation, forbearance, patience, peace, pleasantness, self-control.

angry, enraged, exasperated, furious, incensed, indignant, irate, irritated, maddened, provoked, wrathful. ANT.—calm, happy, placid, pleased, satisfied.

anguish, agony, affliction, distress, grief, misery, pain, sorrow, suffering, torment, torture. ANT.—comfort, joy, relief, solace.

animate, activate, encourage, enliven, inspire, rouse, quicken, vitalize. ANT.—deactivate, discourage, kill.

animosity, bitterness, dislike, enmity, grudge, hatred, hostility, malevolence, malice, rancor, spite. ANT.—esteem, friendliness, goodwill, love.

annihilate, abolish, annul, destroy, eliminate, eradicate, extinguish, nullify, obliterate. ANT.—activate, preserve, save.

announce, advertise, broadcast, declare, expound, make known, notify, proclaim, promulgate, publish, report, reveal, tell. ANT.—bury, conceal, refrain, stifle, suppress, withhold.

annoy, bother, chafe, disturb, harass, harry, irk, irritate, molest, pester, plague, tease, trouble, vex. ANT.—accommodate, aid, console, gratify, please, soothe.

answer, acknowledge, confute, defend, rebut, rejoin, reply, respond, retort. ANT.—argue, ask, inquire, question.

anticipation, apprehension, contemplation, expectation, foresight, foretaste, forethought, hope, preconception, presentiment. ANT.—doubt, dread, fear, surprise, wonder, worry.

antipathy, abhorrence, antagonism, aversion, detest, dislike, hatred, opposition, repugnance, repulsion. ANT.—admiration, approval, liking, regard, respect.

anxiety, anguish, apprehension, care, concern, disquiet, dread, fear, misgiving, solicitude, trouble, worry. ANT.—assurance, confidence, contentment, equanimity, nonchalance, peace.

apology, alibi, acknowledgement, confession, defense, excuse, explanation, justification, plea. ANT.—accusation, censure, complaint, denial, dissimulation.

appalling, alarming, awful, dire, dreadful, frightful, ghastly, hideous, horrible, horrid, repulsive, terrible. ANT.—assuring, beautiful, calming, enchanting, enjoyable, fascinating.

apparent, clear, evident, manifest, obvious, plain, self-evident, transport, unambiguous, unmistakable, visible. ANT.—ambiguous, dubious, hidden, indistinct, uncertain, unclear.

appeal, apply, ask, beg, beseech, call, entreat, plead, pray, request, supplicate. ANT.—deny, disclaim, refuse, recall, renounce.

appear, arise, arrive, emanate, emerge, issue, look, seem. ANT.—be, exist; disappear, vanish, withdraw.

appearance, advent, arrival, coming, air, aspect, demeanor, form, look, manner, mien; fashion, guise, pretense, semblance. ANT.—absence, departure, disappearance, leaving.

appease, allay, alleviate, assuage, calm, compose, conciliate, lull, mollify, pacify, placate, quell, quiet, relieve, satisfy, soothe. ANT.—aggravate, arouse, excite, incense, inflame, provoke.

appetite, hunger, relish, stomach, thirst, zest; craving, desire, inclination, liking, longing, passion, zest. ANT.—aversion, dislike, distaste, renunciation, repugnance, satiety.

appoint, assign, choose, command, designate, direct, name, ordain, select. ANT.—cancel, dismiss, remove, withdraw.

appreciate, admire, cherish, enjoy, esteem, prize, regard, value; apprehend, comprehend, realize, understand; improve, rise. ANT.—belittle, depreciate, disparage, misapprehend, misunderstand.

approach, accost, address, arrive, come near, greet, hail, speak to. ANT.—avoid, leave, depart.

appropriate, applicable, apt, becoming, fitting, particular, proper, suitable; assume, embezzle, loot, pilfer, plagiarize, plunder, purloin, steal. ANT.—contrary, improper, inappropriate; bestow, give, restore, return.

approval, approbation, assent, commendation, consent, endorsement, praise, sanction, support. ANT.—censure, reprimand, rejection, reproach.

approve, accept, appreicate, commend, like, praise; authorize, confirm, countenance, endorse, ratify, sanction, validate. ANT.—criticize, disapprove, disparage; condemn, nullify, reject.

aptness, ability, aptitude, capability, capacity, dexterity, knowledge, power, qualification, skill, talent. ANT.—inability, incapacity, incompetencey.

ardent, eager, enthusiastic, earnest, enthusiastic, fervent, fervid, glowing, impassioned, intense, keen, passionate, vehement, warm, zealous. ANT.—apathetic, indifferent.

ardor, devotion, eagerness, enthusiasm, fervor, passion, rapture, spirit. ANT.—apathy, disinterest, indifference, unconcern.

argue, debate, differ, discuss, dispute, plead, reason, wrangle; imply, indicate, prove, show. ANT.—agree, ignore, overlook, reject.

arraign, accuse, censure, charge, cite, incriminate, indict. ANT.—absolve, acquit, discharge, exonerate, release.

arraignment, accusation, charge, incrimination, indictment. ANT.—exculpation, exoneration, pardon.

arrange, adjust, array, assort, classify, dispose, group, organize, place; devise, organize, plan, prepare. ANT.—confuse, disarrange, disorder, disturb, scatter.

arrest, apprehend, check, delay, detain, halt, hinder, interrupt, obsruct, restrain, seize, stop, withhold. ANT.—activate, discharge, free, liberate, release.

arrive, appear, attain, come, emerge, land, reach, visit. ANT.—disappear, depart, exit, go, leave.

arrogant, disdainful, haughty, insolent, overbearing, proud. ANT.—humble, meek, servile.

artificial, affected, assumed, bogus, counterfeit, ersatz, fake, fictitious, sham, spurious, synthetic, unreal. ANT.—genuine, natural, real, true.

ascend, advance, climb, mount, progress, rise, scale, soar, tower. ANT.—decline, descend, fall, sink.

ask, appeal, beg, claim, entreat, invite, petition, request, solicit; inquire, interrogate, query, question. ANT.—answer, command, demand, dictate, insist, order, refuse, reply.

aspersion, abuse, defamation, desecration, dishonor, disparagement, insult, invective, outrage, profanation, reproach, reviling, upbraiding. ANT.—approval, commendation, plaudit, respect.

aspiration, aim, ambition, craving, desire, goal, hope, longing, objective. ANT.—contentment, indifference, laziness.

assault, assail, attack, bombard, charge, invade, onslaught, pound, rape, storm, strike. ANT.—defend, oppose, protect, surrender.

assemble, collect, combine, congregate, convene, gather, join, meet, muster, unite. ANT.—disperse, scatter.

assent, accept, acquiesce, agree, allow, approve, concede, concur, consent, ratify, recognize. ANT.—disapprove, reject.

assert, affirm, allege, claim, declare, express, insist, maintain, state. ANT.—contradict, deny, refute, reject.

assist, abet, aid, further, help, promote, serve, support, sustain. ANT.—hamper, hinder, impede, prevent.

assistant, abettor, accessory, accomplice, accessory, accomplice, ally, associate, confederate. ANT.—adversary, opponent, rival.

associate, affiliate, ally, attach, combine, confederate, conjoin, connect, couple, join, link, unite. ANT.—disrupt, divide, disassociate, estrange, part, separate.

assume, appropriate, arrogate, take, usurp; adopt, affect, pretend, simulate, wear; presume, suppose. ANT.—relinquish, concede, grant, surrender; doff, remove; demonstrate, prove.

assurance, arrogance, assuredness, boldness, certainty, confidence, conviction, courage, firmness, security, self-reliance; pledge, promise; assertion, declaration, statement. ANT.—humility, modesty, shyness, timidity, trepedation.

astonish, amaze, astound, frighten, perplex, startle, surprise. ANT.—bore, calm.

attach, adjoin, affix, annex, append, connect, fasten, join, stick, unite. ANT.—detach, disengage, remove, separate, sever, unfasten.

attachment, adherence, affection, affinity, bond, devotion, esteem, friendship, liking, regard. ANT.—alienation, aversion, enmity, estrangement, separation.

attack, aggression, assail, assault, criticism, denunciation, invade, offense, onslaught; convulsion, fit, paroxysm. ANT.—aid, defend, oppose, protect, resistance, surrender.

attain, accomplish, achieve, acquire, arrive, earn, effect, gain, get, master, obtain, procure, reach, secure, win. ANT.—abandon, desert, discard, fail, relinquish.

attempt, attack, effort, endeavor, essay, experiment, trial, undertaking. ANT.—inaction, laziness, neglect.

attend, accompany, care for, escort, follow, guard, protect, serve, tend, watch; be present, frequent. ANT.—abandon, absent, desert.

attention, alertness, circumspection, concentration, consideration, diligence, mindfulness, notice, observation, watchfulness; application, contemplation, reflection, study. ANT.—disregard, indifference, negligence.

attraction, affinity, allure, captivation, charm, fascination, magnation, pull. ANT.—rejection, repulsion.

attitude, disposition, standpoint, viewpoint; aspect, pose, position, stance; stand.

attractive, alluring, captivating, charming, enchanting, engaging, enticing, inviting, magnetic, pleasing, seductive, winning. ANT.—forbidding, obnoxious, repellent, repulsive.

audacity, arrogance, boldness, effrontery, fearlessness, impudence, rashness, temerity. ANT.—circumspection, humility.

austere, cruel, harsh, exacting, rigid, severe, sharp, stern, unrelenting. ANT.—gentle, kind, meek, mild, gentility, humility, meekness, restraint.

authentic, genuine, pure, legitimate, true, verifiable; accurate, authortative, certain, correct, reliable, trustworthy. ANT.—counterfeit, disputed, erroneous, false, spurious.

authority, command, control, domination, dominion, force, justification, power, right, supremacy; authorization, license, permission, rule, sanction; importance, influence, prestige, weight. ANT.—impotence, incapacity, weakness; denial, prohibition.

auxiliary, aid, ally, ancillary, assisting, conducive, confederate, furthering, helping, instrumental, subsidiary. ANT.—competitive, obstructive, opposing, retarding.

available, accessible, obtainable, on hand, prepared, present, ready, usable. ANT.—inaccessible, unavailable.

average, fair, intermediate, mean, median, mediocre, medium, moderate, normal, ordinary, usual. ANT.—exceptional, extraordinary, outstanding, unusual.

aversion, abhorrence, antipathy, disgust, disinclination, dislike, distaste, dread, hatred, loathing, opposition, repugnance, repulsion, reluctance. ANT.—affection, attachment, devotion, enthusiasm, liking.

avoid, avert, dodge, escape, eschew, elude, evade, forbear, forestall, shun. ANT.—confront, encounter, meet, oppose, seek.

award, adjudge, allot, allow, bestow, honor, recognize, reward. ANT.—ignore, reject, withhold, withdraw.

aware, alert, apprised, cognizant, conscious, informed, mindful, observant, perceptive, ANT.—ignorant, oblivious, unaware.

away, abroad, absent, aside, departed, gone, distant. ANT.—close, here, present.

awful, appalling, dire, dreadful, frightful, gruesome, horrie, terrible; awe-inspiring, imposing, impressive, majestic, solemn. ANT.—attractive, pleasant, commonplace, lowly, vulgar.

awkward, bungling, clumsy, gauche, inept, maladroit, rough, ungraceful, unskillful. ANT.—adroit, graceful, skillful.

axiom, adage, aphorism, apothegn, byword, fundamental, maxim, principle, proposition, proverb, rule, saying, theorem, truism. ANT.—absurdity, paradox, sophism.

B

backward, regressive, retrogressive, retrograde, revisionary; dull, sluggish, stupid; disinclined, indisposed, loath, reluctant. ANT.—advanced, civilized, intelligent, progressive.

bad, base, deleterious, evil, immoral, noxious, pernicious, rotten, sinful, unsound, spurious, vile, villainous, wicked. ANT.—excellent, good, honorable, moral, right, virtuous.

balance, composure, equilibrium, harmony, poise, stability, steadiness, proportion, symmetry; excess, remainder, remains, residue. ANT.—fall, imbalance, instability, unsteadiness.

baleful, bad, base, deleterious, evil, harmful, immoral, noxious, pernicious, wicked. ANT.—excellent, good, honorable, moral.

banal, commonplace, fatuous, hackneyed, inane, insipid, ordinary, trite, vapid. ANT.—exciting, fresh, novel, original, striking.

banish, debar, deport, dismiss, eject, exclude, exile, expatriate, expel, ostracize, oust. ANT.—accept, admit, forgive, receive, repatriate.

barbarous, atrocious, barbaric, brutal, crude, cruel, inhuman, merciless, ruthless, savage, uncivilized, uncultured, uncouth. ANT.—civilized, cultured, humane, kind, polite, refined.

barren, desolate, empty, sterile, unproductive. ANT.—fecund, fertile, productive.

barrier, bar, blockade, bulwark, obstacle, obstruction, rampart. ANT.—admittance, entrance, opening, passage.

base, abject, contemptible, degraded, despicable, ignominious, inferior, low, mean, shamcful, sordid, vile, vulgar. ANT.—esteemed, exalted, lofty, moral, noble, righteous, superior.

bashful, abashed, coy, diffident, embarrassed, modest, sheepish, shy, timid, timorous. ANT.—adventurous, daring, fearless, gregarious.

basic, essential, fundamental, indispensable, primary, principal, vital. ANT.—additional, extra, secondary.

batter, beat, belabor, bruise, demolish, dent, disfigure, mar, pound, pummel, smash, thrash. ANT.—cover, protect, secure, treat gently.

battle, combat, conflict, contest, fight, fray, skirmish, strife, struggle. ANT.—accord, agree, peace, truce.

bear, support, sustain, uphold; allow, endure, maintain, permit, suffer, tolerate; carry, convey, transport; produce, spawn, yield. ANT.—avoid, cast aside, dodge, evade, refuse, shun.

beat, batter, belabor, buffet, castigate, flog, hit, knock, pound, pummel, punch, strike, thrash; conquer, defeat, overpower, overthrow, rout, subdue, vanquish, whip; palpitate, pulsate, pulse, throb. ANT.—assist, help, defend, shield; fail, relinquish, surrender.

beautiful, attractive, beauteous, charming, comely, elegant, graceful, handsome, lovely, pretty. ANT.—foul, hideous, homely, repulsive, unsightly.

becoming, befitting, comely, decorous, decent, fitting, pleasing, proper, seemly, suitable, worthy. ANT.—unbecoming, displeasing, unseemly, unsuitable.

before, ahead, earlier, forward, prior, sooner. ANT.—after, afterward, behind, later.

beg, adjure, ask, beseech, crave, entreat, implore, importune, petition, pray, request, solicit, supplicate. ANT.—assist, bestow, cede, favor, give, grant.

begin, commence, enter, inaugurate, initiate, institute, open, originate, start. ANT.—complete, conclude, end, finish, terminate.

beginning, commencement, inauguration, inception, opening, origin, outset, source, start. ANT.—close, completion, conclusion, consummation, end, finish, termination.

behavior, action, attitude, bearing, breeding, carriage, conduct, deed, demeanor, deportment, disposition, manner, strategy, tactics.

belief, certitude, confidence, conviction, credence, faith, opinion, persuasion, reliance, trust. ANT.—denial, doubt, heresy, incredulity.

beloved, dear, esteemed, precious, valued; costly, expensive, valuable. ANT.—despised, unwanted; cheap.

below, beneath, lower, under, underneath. ANT.—above, aloft, over, overhead.

bend, bow, contract, crook, curve, deflect, divert, flex, incline, lean, stoop, turn, twist; influence, mold; submit, yield. ANT.—break, resist, stiffen, straighten.

beneficial, advantageous, good, helpful, profitable, salutary, useful, wholesome. ANT.—destructive, detrimental, harmful, injurious.

benefit, advantage, avail, behalf, blessing, favor, gain, good, interest, profit, service. ANT.—distress, handicap, injury, trouble.

benevolence, altruism, beneficence, charity, generosity, goodwill, humanity, kindness, liberality, magnanimity, munificience, philanthropy. ANT.—cruelty, ill-will, malevolence, selfishness, unkindness.

beyond, above, distant, far, farther, more, over superior, yonder. ANT.—close by, here, near.

bias, bent, disposition, inclination, leaning, partiality, penchant, predilection, predisposition, prejudice, proneness, propensity, slant, tendency. ANT.—equity, fairness, impartiality, justice.

big, bulky, colossal, enormous, extensive, giant, great, huge, hulking, immense, large, majestic, massive, monstrous, vast. ANT.—little, petite, slight, small, tiny.

bigoted, dogmatic, fanatical, hidebound, illiberal, intolerant, narrow-minded, opinionated, prejudiced. ANT.—liberal, open-minded, progressive, tolerant.

bind, attach, connect, engage, fasten, fetter, join, link, obligate, restrain, restrict, secure, tie. ANT.—free, loose, release, unfasten, untie.

bitter, acrid, biting, distasteful, pungent, sharp, sour, tart; galling, grievous, painful, poignant; cruel, fierce; acrimonious, caustic, harsh, sardonic, severe. ANT.—agreeable, pleasant, sweet.

blame, accuse, censure, condemn, implicate, rebuke, reprehend, reproach, reprove, upbraid. ANT.—absolve, acquit, exonerate; praise.

blank, bare, barren, empty, vacant, void. ANT.—filled, occupied.

bleak, bare, chilly, cold, desolate, dreamy, dismal, dull, gloomy. ANT.—cheerful, pleasant, warm, serene.

blemish, blot, mark, speck, stain; defect, disfigurement, disgrace, dishonor, fault, flaw, imperfection. ANT.—adornment, decoration, embellishment, perfection, purity.

blend, adjoin, amalgamate, coalesce, combine, commingle, conjoin, consolidate, fuse, merge, mingle, mix, unite. ANT.—decompose, disintegrate, separate.

blind, ignorant, oblivious, sightless, undiscerning, unmindful, unseeing; careless, headlong, heedless, obtuse, rash; stupid. ANT.—aware, calculated, discerning, farsighted, perceiving, sensible.

bliss, blessedness, blissfulness, ecstasy, gladness, happiness, joy, rapture. ANT.—grief, misery, pain, sadness, wretchedness.

block, bar, barricade, clog, close, stop; impede, hinder, obstruct. ANT.—clear, open; aid, assist, further, promote.

bluff, abrupt, blunt, bold, brusque, brazen, coarse, discourteous, frank, outspoken, uncivil. ANT.—civil, courteous, pleasant.

blunt, dull, edgeless, obtuse, pointless, stolid, thick-witted, unsharpened; abrupt, bluff, brusque, direct, impolite, outspoken, harsh, forthright, rough, unceremonious. ANT.—polished, polite, suave, subtle, tactful.

boast, bluster, brag, crow, exult, flaunt, flourish, glory, vaunt. ANT.—apologize, deprecate, minimize.

body, carcass, corpse, remains; form, frame, torso; bulk, mass; aggregate, association, company, group, society.

bold, adventurous, audacious, brave, courageous, daring, determined, fearless, intrepid; brazen, forward, impudent, insolent, rude; abrupt, conspicuous, prominent, striking. ANT.—bashful, cowardly, timid, retiring, shy.

bondage, captivity, confinement, imprisonment, serfdom, servitude, slavery. ANT.—freedom, liberation.

book, booklet, brochure, compendium, handbook, manual, pamphlet, textbook, tract, treatise, volume, work.

border, boundry, brink, edge, extremity, fringe, frontier, limit, margin, outskirts, rim, termination, trimming, verge. ANT.—center, core, inside, interior, mainland, region.

boredom, doldrums, dullness, ennui, lack of interest, tedium, weariness. ANT.—activity, excitement, motive, stimulus.

bother, annoy, disturb, harass, haunt, inconvenience, molest, perplex, pester, plague, tease, trouble, upset, worry. ANT.—gratify, please, relieve, soothe.

bottom, base, basis, foot, foundation, groundwork, lowest part. ANT.—apex, peak, summit, top, upper part.

bound, hop, jump, leap, ski; spring, vault; circumscribe, confine, curb, define, limit. ANT.—crawl, walk; enlarge extend.

bountiful, abundant, ample, copious, opulent, overflowing, plenteous, plentiful, profuse, rich. ANT.—deficient, insufficient, scant, scarce.

brag, bluster, boast, flaunt, flourish, vaunt. ANT.—debase, degrade, demean, denigrate.

brave, adventurous, bold, courageous, daring, fearless, hardy, heroic, intrepid, undaunted, valiant, valorous, venturesome. ANT.—cowardly, cringing, fearful, timid, weak.

break, burst, crack, crush, demolish, destroy, fracture, infringe, pound, rack, rend, rupture, sever, shatter, shiver, smash, split, squeeze; disobey, infringe, transgress, violate. ANT.—join, mend, repair, restore, unite.

breed, bear, beget, conceive, engender, generate, procreate, propagate, start; foster, nurture, raise, rear. ANT.—abort, kill, murder.

brief, concise, curt, laconic, pithy, short, succinct, terse; fleeting, momentary, passing, short-lived, transient. ANT.—extended, lengthy, long, prolonged, protracted.

bright, brilliant, clear, gleaming, lucid, luminous, lustrous, radiant, scintillating, shining, sunny, translucent; clever, intelligent, smart, witty. ANT.—dark, dull, gloomy, stupid.

bring, adduce, attract, bear, carry, cause, conduct, convey, draw, fetch, impart, induce, produce, transfer, transport, transmit. ANT.—abandon, leave, relinquish.

brisk, cool, fresh, refreshing, stimulating.

briskness, action, activity, agility, energy, enterprise, intensity, liveliness, quickness, rapidity, vigor. ANT.—dullness, idleness, inactivity.

brittle, breakable, crisp, crumbling, delicate, fragile, frail, tenuous. ANT.—durable, enduring, tough, strong, unbreakable.

broad, ample, comprehensive, extensive, large, sweeping, vast, wide; liberal, tolerant. ANT.—confined, conservative, narrow, restricted.

broken, crushed, destroyed, fractured, interrupted, reduced, ruptured, separated, shattered, smashed, wrecked. ANT.—repaired, united, whole.

brotherhood, brotherliness, fellowship, kindness, solidarity, unity; association, clan, fraternity, society. ANT.—acrimony, discord, opposition, strife.

brusque, hasty, precipitate, sudden, unannounced, unexpected; abrupt, blunt, curt, rude; harsh, precipitous, rough, rugged, steep. ANT.—anticipated, expected; courteous, gradual.

brutal, barbarous, bestial, brutish, carnal, coarse, cruel, ferocious, gross, inhuman, merciless, rough, rude, ruthless, savage. ANT.—civilized, courteous gentle, humane, kind.

build, construct, erect, establish, found, make, manufacture, put up, raise, rear. ANT.—demolish, destroy.

buoyant, effervescent, light, resilient; animated, blithe, cheerful, elated, lively, spirited, vivacious. ANT.—dejected, depressed, despondent, sullen.

burden, afflict, encumber, load, oppress, overload, trouble. ANT.—alleviate, console, ease, mitigate.

burn, blaze, char, consume, cremate, incinerate, ignite, scald, scorch, sear, singe. ANT.—extinguish, stifle, subdue, quench.

bury, conceal, cover, entomb, hide, immure, inhume, inter. ANT.—display, exhume, expose, reveal.

business, art, commerce, concern, duty, employment, engagement, enterprise, job, occupation, profession, pursuit, trade, vocation, work. ANT.—avocation, hobby.

busy, active, assiduous, diligent, hard-working, industrious, perseverant. ANT.—apathetic, indifferent, lethargic.

but, and, barely, besides, except, further, furthermore, however, just, moreover, nevertheless, notwithstanding, provided, save, still, though, unless, yet.

buy, acquire, bribe, get, negotiate, obtain, procure, purchase, secure. ANT.—market, sell, transfer, vend.

by, beside, near, next to; by means of, through, with; according to; from.

C

calamity, adversity, casualty, catastrophe, disaster, misfortune, mishap, ruin. ANT.—advantage, benefit, blessing, fortune.

calculate, calculation, compute, consider, count, enumerate, estimate, figure, reckon, value, weigh. ANT.—assume, conjecture, guess, miscalculate.

call, address, assemble, clamour, command, convoke, cry, demand, designate, exclaim, ejaculate, invite, name, phone, proclaim, rally, roar, scream, shout, shriek, summon, utter, yell.

callous, hard, impenitent, indifferent, indurate, insensible, insensitive, obdurate, tough, unfeeling, unsusceptible. ANT.—compassionate, sensitive, soft, tender.

calm, alleviate, appease, assuage, lull, pacify, placate, quell, quiet, relieve, satisy, soothe, tranquilize. ANT.—agitate, anger, arouse, incite, incense, inflame.

calm, collected, composed, cool, dispassionate, peaceful, placid, quiet, sedate, self-possessed, serene, still, tranquil, undisturbed, unperturbed. ANT.—agitated, angry, excited, violent.

calumny, aspersion, detraction, defamation, libel, lying, scandal, slander, vilification. ANT.—charity, commendation, defense, flattery, kindness, praise.

cancel, abolish, annul, delete, eliminate, erase, expunge, invalidate, nullify, obliterate, quash, repeal, rescind, revoke. ANT.—approve, confirm, enforce, ratify.

candid, frank, free, honest, ingenous, open, sincere, straightforward, truthful; fair, impartial, just, unbiased. ANT.—artful, insincere, scheming, sly.

candor, fairness, frankness, impartiality, openness, rectitude, responsibility, sincerity, truthfulness, uprightness. ANT.—artifice, cheating, deceit, dishonesty, fraud, guile, stratagem.

capability, ability, aptitude, aptness, capacity, dexterity, efficiency, faculty, qualification, skill, talent. ANT.—incapacity, incompetency, unreadiness.

capable, able, clever, competent, efficient, fitted, qualified, skillful, suitable. ANT.—inadequate, incapable, incompetent, unable, unfit.

capacity, ability, aptness, capability, power, skill, talent; content, expanse, magnitude, size, volume. ANT.—impotence, inability, incapacity.

capital, chief, excellent, essential, fine, first, important, leading, major, principal, paramount; assets, collateral, money, property. ANT.—secondary, unimportant; impecunious, poor, poverty.

capitulate, abandon, acquiesce, relinquish, renounce, submit, surrender, yield. ANT.—conquer, overcome, rout.

capricious, changeable, fickle, idiosyncratic, inconstant, unstable, variable, vacillating. ANT.—constant, dependable, stable, steady.

captivity, bondage, confinement, imprisonment, servitude, slavery, subjection. ANT.—freedom, independence, liberty.

capture, apprehend, arrest, catch, grasp, take, seize, snare, take, trap. ANT.—free, liberate, lose, release.

care, concern, trouble, solicitude, worry; attention, caution, regard, precaution, vigilance, wariness, watchfulness; charge, custody, guardianship, ward. ANT.—disregard, indifference, neglect.

career, avocation, business, calling, course, experience, line, occupation, profession, pursuit, sphere, vocation. ANT.—idleness, retirement.

careful, attentive, meticulous, prudent, scrupulous, thoughtful; cautious, circumspect, discreet, guarded, vigilant, wary, watchful. ANT.—careless, improvident, indifferent, lax, negligent.

careless, inattentive, indiscrete, reckless, thoughtless, unconcerned. ANT.—accurate, careful, meticulous.

caress, cuddle, embrace, fondle, hug, kiss, pamper, pet. ANT.—annoy, buffet, neglect, spurn, tease, vex.

caricature, burlesque, exaggeration, farce, imitation, mimicry, parody, ridicule. ANT.—accuracy, exactitude, reality, truth.

carnal, base, concupisent, corporeal, lascivious, lustful, sensual, voluptuous, worldly. ANT.—chaste, ethereal, intellectual, spiritual.

carping, captious, caviling, disparaging, faultfinding, hypercritical, pedantic. ANT.—appreciative, approving, commendatory, encouraging.

carriage, bearing, behavior, demeanor, deportment, disposition, manner, mien.

carry, bring, convey, move, remove, support, sustain, transmit, transport. ANT.—abandon, drop, leave.

cartel, combination, monopoly, pool, trust.

case, circumstance, condition, contingency, event, example, occurrence, situation.

caste, ancestry, blood, category, class, descent, grade, kind, lineage, order, race, rank.

casual, careless, chance, cursoary, haphazard, incidental, informal, nonchalant, offhand, random, relaxed, unconcerned, unpremediated. ANT.—expected, formal, intended, planned.

casualty, accident, adversity, calamity, disaster, misfortune, mishap. ANT.—design, intention, prosperity, purpose.

catastrophe, adversity, affliction, blow, calamity, casualty, cataclysm, disaster, mishap, misery, ruin. ANT.—benefit, blessing, happiness.

catch, apprehend, arrest, capture, clasp, grasp, grip, overtake, seize, snare, trap. ANT.—cast aside, liberate, lose, release, miss.

catching, communicable, contagious, infectious, pestilential, virulent. ANT.—healthful, hygienic, noncommunicable.

category, caste, class, denomination, division, genre, heading, kind; grade, order, rank, set.

catharsis, cleansing, purge, purification.

cause, agent, antecedent, determinant, inducement, motive, origin, originator, principle, reason, source; create, effect, evoke, incite, induce, occasion, originate, prompt. ANT.—consequence, development, effect, end, result.

caustic, acrid, bitter, biting, distasteful, pungent, sour, tart; acrimonious, harsh, sardonic, severe. ANT.—mellow, pleasant, sweet.

caution, care, heed, prudence, vigilance, wariness, watchfulness; admonish, counsel, injunction, warning. ANT.—abandon, carelessness, recklessness.

cautious, attentive, heedful, prudent, scrupulous, thoughtful; careful, circumspect, discreet, careless, vigilant, wary. ANT.—hasty, heedless, impetuous.

cease, abandon, desist, conclude, desist, discontinue, stop, terminate; relinquish, resign, surrender. ANT.—continue, initiate, persist, stay.

cede, assign, convey, delivery, grant, relinquish, surrender, transfer, yield. ANT.—gain, receive, win.

celebrate, commemorate, honor, keep, observe, solemnize; commend, extol, honor, laud, praise. ANT.—disregard, ignore, neglect, disgrace, dishonor, profane.

celebrated, distinguished, eminent, famous, glorious, illustrious, noted, renowned. ANT.—ignominious, unknown.

celebration, commemoration, festivity, glorification, observance.

celerity, alacrity, haste, quickness, rapidity, speed, swiftness. ANT.—slowness, sluggishness.

celestial, divine, ethereal, godlike, heavenly, holy, supernatural, transcendant. ANT.—earthly, infernal, mortal.

censure, blame, condemn, criticize, denounce, reproach, reprimand, rebuke, reproach, reprove, upbraid. ANT.—approve, commend, endorse, praise.

center, core, focus, heart, hug, middle, midpoint, midst, nucleus. ANT.—border, periphery, rim.

ceremony, form, formality, observance, parade, pomp, protocol, rite, ritual, solemnity.

certain, assured, definite, fixed, incontrovertible, indubitable, inevitable, positive, reliable, secure, sure, true, undeniable, unquestionable. ANT.—doubtful, false, probable, questionable.

certainty, assuredness, confidence, conviction, firmness, self-reliance, surety, statement.

certify, assure, attest, aver, declare, demonstrate, inform, prove, state, testify. ANT.—deny, disown, repudiate.

chagrin, confusion, dismay, humiliation, mortification, shame, vexation.

chain, course, progression, sequence, series, set, string, succession.

challenge, defiance, demand, invitation, question; obstacle, opportunity, trial.

chance, accident, calamity, casualty, contingency, disaster, fate, fortune, happen, luck, misfortune, mishap, occur, random, transpire. ANT.—aim, design, intention, purpose.

change, alteration, alternation, innovation, modification, mutation, revolution, substitution, transition, variation. ANT.—permanence, stability, uniformity.

change, exchange, substitute; alter, convert, modify, shift, transform, vary, veer. ANT.—retain; continue, preserve, stabilize.

changeable, fickle, inconstant, shifting, unstable, vacillating, variable, wavering. ANT.—constant, stable, steady.

chaos, anarchy, confusion, disorder, disorganization, jumble, muddle, shambles, snarl. ANT.—order, organization, system.

character, class, description, disposition, individuality, kind, nature, personality, reputation, repute, standing, temperament; mark, sign, symbol, type.

characteristic, attribute, feature, idiosyncrasy, individuality, mark, peculiarity, property, singularity, quality, trait.

charge, accuse, arraign, ascribe, assess, attack, censure, exhort, incriminate, indict; tax. ANT.—absolve, acquit, exonerate.

charity, alms, altruism, benefaction, benevolence, bounty, generosity, humanity, kindness, liberality, magnanimity, philanthropy, tenderness. ANT.—inhumanity, malevolence, selfishness.

charlatan, cheat, faker, fraud, humbug, impostor, mountebank, pretender, quack.

charming, alluring, attractive, bewitching, captivating, delightful, enchanting, engaging, fascinating, irresistible, ravishing, winning. ANT.—offensive, repulsive, revolting.

chase, follow, hunt, persist, pursue, seek, stalk, track, trail. ANT.—avoid, elude, escape, flee, lose.

chaste, clean, clear, genuine, immaculate, pure, unadulterated, uncontaminated; guiltless, innocent, sincere, uncorrupted, undefiled, virgin, virtuous. ANT.—foul, polluted, tainted; corrupt, defiled, lewd, wanton.

chasten, afflict, correct, discipline, humble, humiliate, subdue. ANT.—assist, cheer, comfort, encourage.

chastise, castigate, correct, discipline, punish, reprove, reprimend, strike, whip. ANT.—comfort, forgive, pardon.

cheap, inexpensive, low-priced, poor; beggarly, common, inferior, mean, petty, shabby, contemptible, despicable. ANT.—costly, dear, expensive, valuable, dignified, noble, worthy.

cheat, beguile, bilk, deceive, defraud, dupe, fool, hoax, hoodwink, outwit, swindle, trick, victimize.

check, analyze, audit, curb, examine, hinder, impede, inquire, interrogate, question, quiz, repress, restrain, review, scan, scrutinize, survey, view, watch. ANT.—disregard, hasten, neglect, omit.

cheer, comfort, console, encourage, gladden, solace, soothe, sympathize. ANT.—antagonize, depress, dishearten.

cheerful, buoyant, gay, happy, joyous, lighthearted, merry, sprightly. ANT.—dejected, gloomy, morose, sad, sullen.

cherish, appreciate, hold dear, prize, treasure, value; foster, nurture, protect, shelter. ANT.—abandon, dislike, disregard, neglect.

chicanery, deception, duplicity, fraud, intrigue, machination, subterfuge, trickery. ANT.—fair dealing, honesty.

chief, captain, chieftain, commander, head, leader, master, principal, ruler. ANT.—attendant, servant, subordinate.

chief, cardinal, essential, first, leading, main, paramount, predominant, pre-eminent, prime, supreme. ANT.—minor, secondary.

chivalrous, brave, courageous, courteous, gallant, generous, heroic, knightly, spirited, valiant, valorous. ANT.—cowardly, rude, unmannerly, timerous.

choice, alternative, determination, election, option, preference, selection, volition; excellent.

choose, cull, elect, opt, pick, select. ANT.—refuse, reject.

chronic, confirmed, constant, established, inveterate, rooted, settled. ANT.—occasional, temporary.

chronicle, account, description, history, narration, narrative, recital, record.

circuitous, crooked, devious, distorted, erratic, indirect, roundabout, swerving, tortuous, wandering, winding. ANT.—direct, straight.

circular, bulbous, chubby, curved, cylindrical, globular, plump, rotund, round, spherical.

circumspection, anxiety, care, concern, solicitude, worry; attention, caution, discreetness, heed, regard, vigilance, wariness. ANT.—audaciousness, disregard, indifference, negligence.

circumstance, condition, detail, event, fact, happening, incident, item, occurrence, particular, point, position, situation.

circumvent, balk, check, foil, forestall, frustrate, outwit, prevent, thwart. ANT.—aid, help.

cite, advance, affirm, allege, assign, claim, declare, maintain, mention, name, quote, summon. ANT.—deny, disprove, neglect, refute.

civil, affable, considerate, courteous, cultivated, gracious, polite, refined, urbane, well-mannered. ANT.—boorish, ill-mannered, rude.

civilization, breeding, cultivation, culture, education, enlightenment, illumination, polish, refinement. ANT.—ignorance, illiteracy, vulgarity.

claim, advance, affirm, allege, assert, aver, contend, declare, demand, express, maintain, state; defend, support, uphold. ANT.—contradict, deny, refute.

clamor, blare, cry, din, hubbub, hullabaloo, noise, outcry, racket, row, sound, tumult, uproar. ANT.—quiet, silence, stillness.

clandestine, concealed, covert, furtive, hidden, private, secret, stealthy, surreptitious. ANT.—conspicuous, exposed, known, open.

clarify, decipher, educate, explain, illustrate, interpret, make clear, purify, refine, resolve, unravel. ANT.—confuse, muddy, obscure.

clasp, adhere, clutch, grasp, grip, hold, have, keep, maintain, occupy, possess, retain, support.

class, caste, category, denomination, division, genus, group, kind; degree, grade, order, rank, set, standing; elegance, excellence.

classic, antique, clean-cut, elegant, first-rate, model, neat, pure, refined, simple, trim; Greek or Roman. ANT.—barbaric, baroque, mixed, modern.

clean, unadulterated, cleanse, mop, purify, scrub, spotless, stainless, sweep, wash. ANT.—dirty, soiled, stained.

clear, cloudless, fair, sunny; limpid, transparent; apparent, distinct, evident, intelligible, lucid, manifest, obvious, plain, perspicuous, unmistakable, vivid; open, unobstructed. ANT.—cloudy, overcast; ambiguous, obscure, vague.

clemency, charity, compassion, forgiveness, leniency, mercy, mildness, pity. ANT.—punishment, vengeance.

clever, able, adroit, dexterous, keen, quick, quick-witted, skillfull, talented, witty; bright, expert, ingenious, intelligent, sharp, smart. ANT.—awkward, clumsy, slow, unskilled; foolish, ignorant, stupid.

cleverness, comprehension, intellect, intelligence, perspicacity, sagacity, sense, understanding; fun, humor, irony, pleasantry, satire, wit.

climax, acme, apex, cosummation, culmination, height, peak, summit, vertex, zenith. ANT.—anticlimax, depth, floor.

climb, ascend, mount, rise, scale, soar. ANT.—descend, fall.

cloak, clothe, conceal, cover, disguise, hide, mask, protect, screen, shield, shroud, veil. ANT.—bare, expose, reveal, unveil.

clog, see close.

cloister, abbey, convent, hermitage, monastery, nunnery, priory; isolation, meditation, retirement, seclusion, solitude.

close, abutting, adjacent, adjoining, contiguous, immediate, impending, near, nearby, neighboring; confidential, devoted, intimate. ANT.—away, distant, faraway, removed.

close, bar, enclose, fence in, occlude, seal, shut; clog, obstruct, plug, stop; cease, complete, conclude, end, finish, terminate. ANT.—open, unlock; begin, commence, start.

clothes, apparel, array, attire, clothing, dress, garb, garments, raiment. ANT.—nakedness, nudity.

cloudy, dark, dim, indistinct, murky, obscure, shadowy. ANT.—bright, clear, distinct, sunny.

clumsy, awkward, cumbersome, inept, maladroit, ponderous, unwieldly. ANT.—adroit, dexterous, skillful.

clutch; cling to, embrace, grapple, grasp, grip, seize. ANT.—free, release.

coalition, alliance, association, combination, confederacy, federation, league, partnership, union.

coarse, crude, harsh, impure, rough, unrefined; bawdy, gross, immodest, indelicate, inelegant, rude, unpolished, vulgar. ANT.—fine, refined, smooth; cultivated, cultured, dainty.

coax, cajole, entice, inveigle, invite, persuade, wheedle.

coerce, compel, constrain, drive, enforce, force, impel, oblige. ANT.—allure, convince, induce, persuade, prevent.

coercion, compulsion, constraint, force, pressure, violence. ANT.—persuasion.

cogent, convincing, effective, forcible, persuasive, potent, powerful, sound, strong, urgent. ANT.—ineffective, unconvincing, weak.

cognizance, acquaintance, awareness, information, knowing, knowledge, learning, perception, scholarship, understanding, wisdom. ANT.—ignorance.

cohesion, cementing, coagulation, coherence, concretion, consolidation, integration.

coincide, accord, agree, collude, concur, correspond, equal, harmonize, match, square, syncronize, tally. ANT.—differ, disagree, diverge.

cold, arctic, bleak, chilly, cool, freezing, frigid, frosty, frozen, icy, wintry; indifferent, passionless, reserved, stoical, unconcerned, unfeeling. ANT.—heated, hot, torrid; affectionate, passionate.

collapse, cave in, decline, decrease, diminish, drop, fail, faint, fall, fall down, sink, subside; stumble, topple, tumble.

colleague, ally, associate, collaborator, companion, comrade, confederate, consort, friend, mate, partner. ANT.—adversary, opponent, stranger.

collect, accumulate, amass, assemble, concentrate, congregate, consolidate, gather, gain, hoard, obtain, pile; reap, receive. ANT.—disperse, distribute, scatter.

collected, calm, composed, cool, placid, quiet, sedate, tranquil; unperturbed. ANT.—agitated, excited, perturbed.

collision, clash, conflict, encounter, fight, impact, meeting, shock, struggle; contention, controversy, discord, clashing, interference, opposition, variance. ANT.—agreement, concord, harmony.

colloquial, conversational, dialectal, familiar, informal.

collusion, cabal, combination, complicity, conspiracy, deceit, intrigue, machination, plot, treachery, treason.

color, complexion, dye, hue, paint, pigment, shade, stain, tincture, tinge, tint; blush, flush, redden.

colossal, elephantine, enormous, gargantuan, gigantic, huge, immense, large, mammoth, prodigious, tremendous. ANT.—little, small, tiny.

comatose, drowsy, faint, lethargic, stuporous, torpid, unconscious.

combat, battle, brawl, conflict, contest, duel, encounter, fight, skirmish, struggle; controversy, discord, opposition. ANT.—accord, peace, truce.

combination, alliance, association, coalition; confederacy, entente, federation, league, partnership, union; blend, mixture.

combine, accompany, adjoin, associate, attach, conjoin, connect, couple, join, link, unite; mix, blend.

combustion, burning, oxidation; disturbance, rioting, violence.

comely, beautiful, charming, elegant, fair, fine, graceful, handsome, lovely, pleasing, pretty. ANT.—homely, unattractive, unsightly.

comfort, aid, allay, alleviate, assist, cheer, console, encourage, gladden, relieve, solace, soothe, support, succor, sympathize. ANT.—antagonize, depress, dishearten, trouble.

comfortable, acceptable, agreeable, commodious, contented, cozy, gratifying, warm, pleasurable, protected, relaxed, restful, well-off. ANT.—miserable, wretched.

comical, amusing, diverting, droll, farcical, funny, humorous, laughable, ludicrous, ridiculous, witty. ANT.—serious, sober, solemn.

command, bidding, decree, dictate, direct, direction, injunction, instruction, mandate, order, requirement. ANT.—requisition; authority, control, govern, power, rule.

command, point, train; conduct, govern, guide, manage, regulate, rule; bid, direct, instruct, order. ANT.—countermand, distract, misdirect, misguide.

commemorate, celebrate, honor, memorialize, observe; solemnize. ANT.—disdain, dishonor, neglect.

commensurate, celebrate, honor, solemnize; commend, extol, glorify, praise. ANT.—overlook; disgrace, dishonor, profane.

commence, arise, begin, enter, establish, found, inaugurate, initiate, institute, introduce, open, originate, start. ANT.—cease, complete, finish, terminate.

commencement, beginning, inception, opening, outset, start. ANT.—completion, consummation, end, termination.

commend, appreciate, approve, praise; authorize, confirm, endorse, praise, ratify, sanction. ANT.—censure, criticize, condemn, rebuke.

comment, annotation, note, observation, remark, statement.

commerce, business, enterprise, industry, intercourse, trade, work.

commiseration, compassion, condolence, empathy. ANT.—coldness, indifference.

commission, appointment, authority, board, committee, delegation, duty, errand, function, power, warrant.

commit, perform, perpetrate; commend, consign, entrust, trust; bind, obligate, pledge. ANT.—fail, neglect, release, renounce; free, loose.

commodious, accommodating, appropriate, comfortable, convenient, expedient, favorable, roomy, timely, useful, suitable. ANT.—confined, inconvenient, troublesome, uncomfortable.

commodity, articles, assets, goods, materials, possessions, property, stock, wares.

common, habitual, frequent, mutual, ordinary, prevalent, public, usual; low, mean, vulgar. ANT.—aristocratic, extraordinary, scarce; noble, refined.

commotion, agitation, chaos, confusion, disarray, disorder, disturbance, ferment, tumult, turmoil. ANT.—calmness, order, peace, tranquility.

communicate, convey, disclose, divulge, impart, inform, promulgate, reveal, tell, transmit. ANT.—conceal, suppress, withhold.

communion, association, concord, fellowship, intercourse, sacrament, union. ANT.—alienation; contention, discord.

community, area, district, locality, neighborhood, region, section.

commute, exchange, interchange, reduce, substitute, travel.

compact, close, condensed, constricted, contracted, dense, firm, narrow, pressed, snug, stretched, tense, tight. ANT.—diffuse, loose, relaxed, slack.

compact, accordance, concord, concurrence, understanding, unison; agreement, bargain, contract, covenant, pact. ANT.—disagreement, dissension, variance.

companion, associate, colleague, comrade, consort, crony, fellow, friend, mate, partner. ANT.—adversary, enemy, stranger.

company, assembly, band, conclave, convention, party, throng, troop; association, fellowship, society, corporation. ANT.—dispersion, loneliness, seclusion, solitude.

comparable, akin, alike, allied, analogous, correlative, corresponding, like, parallel, similar. ANT.—dissimilar, divergent, incongruous, opposed.

compare, contrast, differentiate, discriminate, distinguish.

compassion, commiseration, kindness, mercy, pity, sympathy. ANT.—cruelty, inhumanity, ruthlessness, severity, tyranny.

compatible, accordant, agreeable, congruous, consonant, correspondent, harmonious. ANT.—

contradictory, incompatible, incongruous, inconsistent.

compel, coerce, constrain, drive, enforce, force, impel, oblige. ANT.—deter, hamper, impede, obstruct.

compensation, earnings, payment, recompense, return, reward, salary, stipend, wages. ANT.—forfeiture, loss, penalty.

competent, capable, efficient, fitted, proficient, qualified, skillful. ANT.—inadequate, incapable, incompetent, inept.

complain, deplore, grouch, grumble, lament, protest, remonstrate, repine, whine. ANT.—applaud, approve, praise, sanction.

complete, accomplish, achieve, conclude, consummate, end, finish, perfect, terminate; thorough, total, unbroken, undivided. ANT.—abandon, neglect, withdraw; deficient, lacking, unfinished.

complex, complicated, compound, intricate, involved, obscure. ANT.—apparent, plain, simple.

complexion, color, hue, pigment, shade, tincture, tinge, tint. ANT.—paleness, transparency.

compliant, humble, meek, modest, submissive, unassuming, unpretentious. ANT.—arrogant, boastful, haughty, ostentatious, proud, vain.

compliment, adulation, commendation, endorse, flattery, praise, tribute. ANT.—censure, criticism, denounce, reprehend.

comply, accede, acquiesce, agree, assent, consent; coincide, concur, conform, submit. ANT.—disagree, dissent, disobey, oppose.

comport, act, bear, behave, carry, conduct, operate.

compose, construct, create, fashion, formulate, forge, produce, shape; constitute, form; arrange, combine, organize; devise, frame, invent. ANT.—agitate, destroy, disfigure, dismantle.

composed, calm, collected, comfortable, imperturbable, peaceful, placid, quiet, sedate, tranquil. ANT.—agitated, excited, perturbed.

composer, author, creator, inventor, maker, originator.

composure, balance, calmness, equilibrium, poise, self-possession. ANT.—agitation, excitement, rage, turbulence.

compound, alloy, amalgamate, blend, combine, complex, complicated, composite, fraternize, join. ANT.—elemental, simple, single, unmixed.

comprehend, apprehend, conceive, discern, embrace, grasp, know, learn, perceive, realize, see, understand. ANT.—exclude, misapprehend, misinterpret, mistake, misunderstand.

comprehension, cognizance, discernment, insight, understanding. ANT.—ignorance, insensibility, misconception.

compress, condense, consolidate, constrict, crowd, reduce, squeeze. ANT.—expand, extend, increase, rarify, stretch, swell.

comprise, consist, contain, embody, embrace, encompass, hold, include, involve. ANT.—except, fall short, lack, reject.

compromise, accommodation, adjustment, agreement, arbitration, concession, conciliation. ANT.—controversy, disagreement, dispute, dissention.

compulsion, might, potency, power, strength, vigor; coercion, constraint, force, urgency. ANT.—feebleness, frailty, impotence, weakness; persuasion.

compute, calculate, count, enumerate, estimate, figure, reckon. ANT.—conjecture, guess, surmise.

comrade, associate, colleague, companion, consort, friend, partner. ANT.—adversary, stranger.

conceal, bury, camouflage, cover, disguise, hide, mask, screen, secrete, veil. ANT.—disclose, divulge, expose, lay bare, reveal, uncover.

concede, assent, acquiesce, permit, sanction, surrender; authorize, give, grant, relinquish yield; acknowledge, admit, allow. ANT.—object, protest, refuse, reject.

conceit, egotism, pride, self-glorification, vanity. ANT.—diffidence, humility, meekness, modesty.

conceive, become pregnant, concoct, design, devise, frame, imagine, visualize.

concentrated, close, compact, compressed, condensed, crowded, dense, thick. ANT.—diluted, dispersed, dissipated, sparse.

concept, conception, idea, notion, thought. ANT.—entity, matter, substance.

concern, affair, business; anxiety, care, solicitude, worry. ANT.—apathy, inconsequence, indifference, unconcern.

concise, brief, compact, condensed, crisp, incisive, pithy, succinct, terse. ANT.—lengthy, redundant, repetitive, verbose, wordy.

conclusion, close, completion, consummation, determination, termination; decision, deduction, inference, resolution, result. ANT.—beginning, commencement, inception, introduction, preamble, prelude, start.

concord, accordance, agreement, harmony, peace. ANT.—difference, disagreement, discord, dissension, variance.

concrete, actual, definite, firm, hard, material, particular, specific, solidified, tangible. ANT.—abstract, immaterial, intangible.

concur, agree, approve, assent, certify, comply, consent; coincide, conform, endorse. ANT.—argue, contradict, differ, disapprove, dispute, dissent, oppose, reject.

condemn, blame, censure, denounce, doom, reprehend, reproach, reprobate, reprove, upbraid; convict, sentence. ANT.—approve, commend, condone, forgive, praise; absolve, acquit, exonerate, pardon, set free.

condition, case, circumstance, situation, state; provision, requirement, specification, stipulation, term; make ready for work or use.

conditional, contingent, dependent, relying, subject, subordinate. ANT.—absolute, autonomous, independent.

condone, absolve, allow, disregard, excuse, forgive, overlook, pardon, remit. ANT.—condemn, forbid, punish.

conduct, action, attitude, bearing, behavior, carriage, demeanor, deportment, disposition, manner.

conduct, direct, govern, guide, lead, steer; manage, regulate, supervise.

confederate, abettor, accessory, accomplice, ally, assistant, associate, colleague, supporter. ANT.—adversary, enemy, opponent, opposition.

confederation, alliance, coalition, confederacy, entente, federation, league, union; compact, treaty. ANT.—schism, separation.

confer, converse, consult, deliberate, discuss, talk; bestow, donate, give, grant.

confess, acknowledge, admit, allow, avow, concede, disclose, divulge, own, reveal. ANT.—conceal, deny, disclaim, disguise, disown, repudiate, veil.

confidence, assurance, assuredness, boldness, certitude, conviction, self-possession, surety. ANT.—apprehension, diffidence.

confine, bind, bound, circumscribe, enclose, encompass, envelop, fence, imprison, limit, restrict. ANT.—develop, enlarge, expand, free, release, unfetter.

confirm, corroborate, substantiate, verify; assure, establish, settle; approve, fix, ratify, sanction; strengthen, validate. ANT.—annul, abrogate, cancel, destroy, shatter, void.

confiscate, appropriate, capture, commandeer, take; grip, seize. ANT.—give back, restore, return.

conflict, battle, combat, duel, encounter, fight, struggle; contention, discord, dissention, opposition, strife, variance, war. ANT.—concord, harmony, peace, repose, tranquility.

conform, adapt, adjust; assent, comply, submit. ANT.—dissent.

confront, combat, encounter, meet squarely, oppose. ANT.—agree, submit, support.

confuse, bewilder, complicate, confound, derange, disconcert, obscure, perplex, puzzle. ANT.—clarify, illumine, organize.

confusion, agitation, chaos, clutter, commotion, disarrangement, disarray, discomposure, disorder, ferment, jumble, pendemonium, stir, tumult, turmoil. ANT.—method, order, sense, system.

confute, confound, confuse, defect, dismay, disprove, refute. ANT.—affirm, confirm, endorse, prove, verify.

congruous, accordant, agreeing, compatible, consonant, correspondent, in harmony. ANT.—contradictory, discrepant, incongruous.

conjecture, guess, hypothesis, presumption, speculation, supposition, theory. ANT.—certainty, fact, proof, truth.

connect, adjoin, affiliate, affix, annex, append, attach, join, link, unite. ANT.—detach, disconnect, disengage, separate.

conquer, beat, checkmate, crush, defeat, humble, master, overcome, overthrow, prevail, quell, rout, subdue, subjugate, surmount, vanquish. ANT.—cede, forfeit, lose, retreat, succumb, surrender.

conquest, subjugation, triumph, victory. ANT.—defeat, failure.

conscientious, careful, exacting, honest, incorruptible, just, scrupulous, trusty, upright. ANT.—corrupt, dishonest, unjust.

conscious, apprised, aware, certain, cognizant, informed, mindful, percipient, sensible. ANT.—ignorant, insensible, oblivious, senseless, unaware.

consecrate, dedicate, exalt, extol, glorify, hallow, honor, revere, sanctify, venerate. ANT.—debase, degrade, dishonor.

consent, accede, acquiesce, agree, allow, assent, comply, concede, concur, conform, yield. ANT.—demur, disagree, dissent, prevent, protest, refuse.

consequence, effect, end, fruit, issue, outcome, product, sequel. ANT.—beginning, cause, commencement, origin, start.

conserve, maintain, preserve, save; retain; keep, guard, protect. ANT.—discard, reject; relinquish; neglect.

consider, contemplate, deliberate, examine, meditate, ponder, reflect, weigh; regard. ANT.—abandon, dismiss, forget, ignore, neglect, overlook.

considerate, cautious, charitable, kind, prudent; meditative, solicitous, sympathetic, unselfish. ANT.—harsh, impervious, inconsiderate, rash, repressive, scornful, thoughtless.

consideration, attention, care, mindfulness, watchfulness, reflection; pay, recompense, value. ANT.—disregard, failure, indifference, negligence, omission, oversight.

consign, commit, condemn, delegate, deliver, devote, send, ship. ANT.—hold, receive, retain.

consistent, accordant, agreeing, compatible, conforming, consonant, constant, equable, harmonious, regular, undeviating, uniform. ANT.—contradictory, discrepant, incongruous, inconsistent, varying.

console, cheer, comfort, ease, freshen, gladden, invigorate, soothe, support. ANT.—depress, grieve, wound.

consolidate, affiliate, amalgamate, blend, coalesce, combine, compact, compress, condense, conjoin, fuse, merge, solidify, unite. ANT.—disjoin, disperse, separate, sever, thin(out).

conspicuous, celebrated, clear, commanding, distinguished, manifest, noticeable, obvious, outstanding, plain, prominent, visible. ANT.—concealed, covered, hidden, obscure, unknown, unseen, secret.

conspiracy, cabal, collusion, combination, intrigue, plot, treachery.

constancy, faithfulness, fealty, fidelity, firmness, fixedness, loyalty, permanence, reliability, resolution, stability, steadiness. ANT.—capriciousness, disloyalty, faithlessness, fickleness, fluctuation, instability, vacillation.

constantly, always, continually, eternally, ever, evermore, forever, incessantly, perpetually, unceasingly. ANT—fitfully, never, occasionally, rarely, sometimes.

consternation, alarm, amazement, astonishment, dismay, fear, horror, panic, surprise, terror, wander. ANT.—calm, peacefulness, quietness, repose, tranquility.

constrain, compel, confine, drive, force, oblige, press, prevent, repress, restrain, urge. ANT.—ask, implore, plead, supplicate.

constrict, bind, compress, cramp, hamper, limit, shrink, squeeze, tighten. ANT.—expand, free, loosen, release, untie.

construct, build, compose, erect, fabricate, form, frame, make, produce. ANT.—demolish, destroy, dismantle, raze.

consult, confer, discuss, seek advisement.

consume, absorb, annihilate, assimilate, destroy, devour, engulf, exhaust, imbibe, squander, swallow, waste. ANT.—accumulate, collect, gather, hoard, store.

consummate, accomplish, achieve, close, complete, conclude, end, execute, finish, fulfill, perfect, terminate; absolute, best, excellent, supreme. ANT.—incomplete, second rate, unfinished.

contagious, catching, communicable, pestilential, spreading, virulent. ANT.—incommunicable.

contaminate, befoul, corrupt, debase, defile, deprave, infect, poison, pollute, soil, stain, taint, vitiate. ANT.—disinfect, purify.

contemplate, conceive, picture, meditate, muse, ponder, reflect, consider, study; intend, view. ANT.—discard, disregard, neglect, reject.

contemporary, coequal, coeval, coincident, contemporaneous, current, modern, new, simultaneous. ANT.—ancient, antiquated, bygone, old.

contempt, derision, detestation, disdain, disregard, disrespect, disparagement, mockery, scorn, slight, slur. ANT.—approbation, awe, endorsement, esteem, regard, respect.

contemptible, depraved, degenerate, despicable, low, mean, scurrilous, sordid, vile. ANT.—admirable, dignified, exalted, gracious, pleasing, respectable, worthy.

contend, battle, combat, compete, contest, cope, dispute, engage, fight, grapple, maintain, oppose, strain, struggle, vie. ANT.—cease, cede, desert, halt, stop, quit.

contention, altercation, animosity, battle, combat, conflict, duel, enmity, feud, fight, struggle; controversy, discord, opposition, quarrel, strife; variance. ANT.—amity, benevolence, concord, goodwill, harmony, kindness, regard, respect, sympathy.

contentment, acceptance, delight, ease, gladness, happiness, joy, satisfaction, serenity. ANT.—despair, discomfort, dissent, grief, misery, regret, sadness, sorrow.

contest, argue, contend, debate, dispute, fight, object, oppose; altercation, battle, conflict, engagement, feud, match, race. ANT.—agree, assent, relinquish; calm, repose, tranquility.

contingent, conditional, dependent, depending, relying, subject, subordinate. ANT.—autonomous, independent.

continual, ceaseless, constant, continuous, endless, incessant, invariable, perpetual, persistent, steady, unbroken, unceasing, uninterrupted, unremitting, unvarying. ANT.—checked, concluded, intermittent, interrupted, stopped.

continuance, continuation, duration, existence, extension, production, prolongation. ANT.—arrest, finish, hindrance, impediment, stoppage.

continue, advance, extend, maintain, proceed, persevere, persist, sustain. ANT.—arrest, check, complete, desist, end, finish, interrupt.

contract, abbreviate, abridge, condense, diminish, lessen, narrow, reduce, restrict, shorten, shrink; agreement, cartel, covenant, pledge, promise. ANT.—elongate, enlarge, expand, extend, lengthen.

contradict, correct, contravene, demur, disclaim, dispute, oppose, recall, recant, rectify, refute. ANT.—acquiesce, accept, approve, agree, confirm, sanction, seal, sign, verify, vouch.

contrary, adverse, antagonistic, opposed, opposite, conflicting, contradictory, counteractive, dissimilar, unlike. ANT.—agreeing, alike, correspondent, homogeneous, similar.

contrast, differentiate, discriminate, distinguish; antithesis, disparity, dissimilarity, divergence, incongruity, variation.

contravene, annul, contradict, defeat, hinder, interpose, nullify, obstruct, oppose, thwart, void. ANT.—agree, approve, assent, assist, concur, consent.

contribute, add(to), aid, assist, befriend, benefit, cooperate, donate, favor, furnish, help, share, subscribe, supply. ANT.—counteract, disapprove, harm, ignore, neglect, oppose, shun, withhold.

contrite, penitent, regretful, remorseful, repentant, sorrowful. ANT.—impenitent, obdurate, remorseless.

contrivance, apparatus, appliance, construction, design, device, invention, mechanism; plan, plot, ruse, scheme, trick.

contrive, arrange, design, devise, execute, form, frame, invent, make, plan, plot, project, scheme. ANT.—abolish demolish, disrupt, ruin, smash.

control, coerce, command, direct, dominate, guide, govern, hold, manage, regulate, rule, superintend; check, curb, prevent, repress, restrain. ANT.—abandon, forsake, ignore, relinquish, renounce, resign.

controversy, altercation, argument, bickering, contention, debate, disagreement, dispute, quarrel, squabble, wrangling. ANT.—agreement, concord, forbearance, harmony, peace, restraint.

convalesce, improve, rally, recover, recuperate, revive. ANT.—die, fail, falter, regress.

convene, assemble, collect, congregate, convoke, gather, meet, muster. ANT.—adjourn, disperse, scatter.

convenient, accessible, adapted, appropriate, available, commodious, favorable, fitting, handy, opportune, suitable. ANT.—inaccessible, inconvenient, inexpedient, troublesome, unsuitable.

conventional, accepted, customary, formal, ordinary, orthodox, prevalent, social, stipulated, usual. ANT.—extraordinary, foreign, informal, irregular, strange, unconventional, unusual.

convergence, approach, assemblage, concourse, confluence, conjunction, focal point, meeting. ANT.—disjunction, divergence, division.

conversation, chat, colloquy, communication, communion, conference, dialogue, discourse, discussion, intercourse, interview, palaver, parley, talk.

converse, chat, communicate with, discuss, speak with; communion, conversation, discussion, intercourse, parley.

convert, adapt, alter, change, metamorphose, modify, resolve, shift, transfigure, transform, transmute, turn(from), veer. ANT.—retain; continue, keep, maintain, persist, preserve.

convey, bring, carry, communicate, impart, inform, transmit, transport. ANT.—hold, keep, preserve, retain.

convict, criminal, culprit, felon, malefactor, offender, transgressor; censure, condemn, doom, sentence. ANT.—absolve, acquit, exonerate, pardon.

convince, affect, clarify, coax, exhort, induce, influence, persuade, prevail upon, satisfy, sway, touch, win over. ANT.—deprecate, dissuade, warn.

convivial, cordial, festive, hospitable, jolly, merry, sociable. ANT.—dismal, severe, solemn, staid.

convoke, assemble, call, collect, convene, gather, muster, summon. ANT.—adjourn, disband, discharge, dismiss, disperse, dissolve, separate.

convolution, circumvolution, coil, curl, involution, sinuosity, twist, wave, winding line. ANT.—level surface, straight line, uncurved.

convoy, accompany, attend, chaperone, escort, go with, protect, support, watch over. ANT.—abandon, avoid, desert, ignore, leave, neglect, quit.

cool, apathetic, calm, distant, fresh, frigid, frosty, gelid, indifferent, shivery, unfeeling, unresponsive, wintry; freeze, harden, refrigerate. ANT.—feeling, glowing, responsive, sultry, sunny, warm-hearted.

cooperate, aid, approve, assist, combine, connive, encourage, endorse, forward, fraternize, help, perform, plan, promote, relieve, second, support. ANT.—delay, disturb, encumber, handicap, hinder, impede, prevent.

copious, abundant, ample, bountiful, exuberant, overflowing, plenteous, plentiful, profuse, rich, teeming. ANT.—deficient, meager, scant, scarce, sparse.

cordial, amicable, earnest, friendly, genial, gracious, hearty, kindly, pleasant, sincere, sociable, warm. ANT.—aloof, cool, hostile, indifferent, inhospitable, taciturn, unfriendly.

corporal, bodily, carnal, corporeal, in the flesh, physical, somatic; material. ANT.—immaterial, incorporeal, spiritual.

corpulent, beefy, fat, fleshy, obese, paunchy, plump, portly, rotund, stocky, stout, thickset. ANT.—gaunt, lean, slender, thin.

correct, accurate, exact, faultless, impeccable, precise, proper, right, true. ANT.—erroneous, inaccurate, incorrect, false, faulty, untrue, wrong.

correct, amend, mend, improve, rectify, reform, remedy, repair; chastise, discipline, punish, reprove. ANT.—aggravate, ignore, spoil; coddle, condone, pamper.

correlation, correspondence, likeness, reciprocation, similarity. ANT.—difference, disparagement, divergence, unlikeness.

corroborate, affirm, approve, assure, back, certify, confirm, endorse, sanction, support. ANT.—contradict, deny, disallow, disclaim, disprove, oppose, refute.

corrupt, base, contaminated, contemptible, corrupted, crooked, debased, demoralized, depraved, dishonest, impure, infected, lewd, low, perverted, profligate, putrid, rotten, spoiled, tainted, unprincipled, unscrupulous, unsound, venal, vitiated. ANT.—clean, decent, honorable, noble, pure, wholesome.

corruption, baseness, criminality, decay, degradation, depravity, graft, guiltiness, infamy, perversion, putrefaction, rottenness, swindling, vice, wickedness. ANT.—honesty, integrity, morality, soundness, uprightness.

counsel, acquaint, admonish, advise, apprise, guide, inform, instruct, recommend, suggest, warn. ANT.—conceal, misinform, mislead, withhold.

count, calculate, compute, enumerate, figure, number, reckon, score, total. ANT.—conjecture, estimate, guess, miscalculate.

counterfeit, artificial, bogus, dishonest, ersatz, fake, false, feigned, fictitious, forged, fraudulent, phony, sham, spurious, synthetic, unreal. ANT.—genuine, honest, natural, real, true.

couple, adjoin, attach, combine, conjoin, connect, copulate, join, link, unite; brace, pair, two. ANT.—detach, disconnect, disjoin, separate.

courage, boldness, bravery, chivalry, daring, dauntlessness, fearlessness, fortitude, gallantry, hardihood, heroism, intrepidity, mettle, prowess, spirit, valor. ANT.—cowardice, fear, pusillanimity, timidity, weakness.

courteous, affable, agreeable, civil, considerate, cultivated, genteel, mannerly, obliging, polished, polite, refined, suave, urbane, well-bred, well-mannered. ANT.—boorish, dictatorial, discourteous, impertinent, rude, uncivil, uncouth.

covenant, agreement, alliance, concord, understanding; bargain, compact, concordat, contract, pact, stipulation. ANT.—difference, disagreement, variance.

cover, cloak, clothe, conceal, curtain, disguise, envelop, guard, hide, mask, overlay, overspread, protect, screen, shield, veil; comprise, embody, embrace. ANT.—bare, divulge, expose, reveal, uncover, unveil.

covert, clandestine, concealed, disguised, furtive, hidden, secret, sly, underhand, unseen. ANT.—candid, conspicuous, evident, explicit, frank, open, overt, unconcealed, visible.

covetousness, avarice, craving, cupidity, desire, envy, greed, jealousy. ANT.—benevolence, generosity, liberality, munificence.

cowardly, afraid, chicken-hearted, effeminate, faint-hearted, not courageous, shy, sissy, spiritless, timid, timorous. ANT.—bold, brave, courageous, daring, dauntless.

crafty, calculating, cunning, deceitful, foxy, furtive, guileful, plotting, scheming, shrewd, stealthy, surreptitious, sly, tricky, underhand, wily. ANT.—candid, frank, ingenuous, open, sincere, undesigning.

crass, brutish, coarse, crude, insensitive, raw, rough, uncouth, unfinished, unpolished, unrefined. ANT.—finished, cultivated, polished, refined.

craving, appetite, desire, longing, passion, yearning. ANT.—disgust, distaste, repugnance.

crazy, crazed, delirious, demented, deranged, idiotic, imbecilic, insane, lunatic, mad, maniacal. ANT.—rational, reasonable, sane, sensible.

create, bring about, cause, design, engender, fashion, form, formulate, generate, invent, make,

originate, produce; appoint, ordain. ANT.—annihilate, destroy; disband, terminate.

credible, believable, plausible, probable, reasonable, reliable, trustworthy. ANT.—improbable, incredible, unbelievable.

crest, acme, crown, head, peak, pinnacle, summit, top, plume, tuft; decoration, insignia. ANT.—base, bottom.

crime, atrocity, depravity, felony, immorality, infringement, injustice, misdeed, misdemeanor, offense, outrage, transgression, vice, wickedness, wrong. ANT.—benevolence, benignity, honor, innocence, morality, uprightness, virtue.

criminal, convict, culprit, delinquent, felon, malefactor, offender, transgressor; abominable, blamable, culpable, felonious, iniquitous, sinful, vicious, vile, wrong. ANT.—faultless, good, honest, innocent, just, legal, sinless, virtuous.

crisis, critical juncture, crucial point, emergency, exigency, strait, turning point. ANT.—calm, equilibrium, normality.

crisp, breakable, brittle, crumbling, fragile, frail, splintery; brisk, bracing, fresh, lively, sharp. ANT.—flexible, tough, unbreakable.

criterion, fact, gauge, law, measure, model, norm, opinion, principle, proof, rule, standard, test, touchstone. ANT.—chance, conjecture, guess, possibility, probability, supposition.

critical, discerning, discriminating, exact, fastidious, particular; captious, carping, caviling, censorious, disapproving, faultfinding; acute, crucial, decisive, momentous, pressing, urgent. ANT.—cursory, superficial; approving, commendatory, encouraging; insignificant, unimportant.

crooked, abased, adulterated, corrupt, criminal, deceitful, defiled, degraded, depraved, dishonest, fraudulent, lawbreaking, vitiated; angular, bent, bowed, curved, deformed, winding, wry, zig-zag. ANT.—honest, law-abiding, mortal, respectable, direct, regular, straight.

crowd, assembly, horde, masses, mob, multitude, populace, throng; compress, cramp, jostle, press, shove, squeeze, swarm.

crown, apex, chief, crest, head, peak, pinnacle, ridge, summit, top, vertex, vortex, zenith; coronet, tiara; decorate, glorify, honor. ANT.—base, bottom, foot, foundation.

cruel, barbarous, brutal, cold-blooded, ferocious, harsh, inhuman, merciless, pitiless, ruthless, savage, sadistic. ANT.—benevolent, charitable, passionate, considerate, gentle, humane, kind, merciful.

cull, choose, pick out, select, separate. ANT.—refuse, reject.

culmination, acme, apex, climax, conclusion, consummation, crown, end, height, peak, summit, termination, zenith. ANT.—base, beginning, inception.

culprit, criminal, delinquent, felon, malefactor, offender, sinner, transgressor, wrongdoer.

cultivate, civilize, develop, educate, farm, foster, grow, promote, pursue, raise, refine, tend, train, work. ANT.—depress, deteriorate.

culture, breeding, civilization, cultivation, development, education, enlightenment, knowledge, learning, propagation, refinement, scholarship. ANT.—boorishness, ignorance, illiteracy, pretension, stupidity, vulgarity.

cultured, cultivated, educated, enlightened, polished, refined, well-bred. ANT.—crude, ignorant, simple, uncouth.

cunning, calculating, crafty, devious, plotting, scheming, sly; artful, clever, skillful, tricky. ANT.—direct, honest; clumsy, dull, inept, stupid.

curb, bridle, check, constrain, control, hinder, hold back, inhibit, limit, repress, restrain, stop, suppress. ANT.—aid, encourage.

cure, antidote, healing, remedy, restorative.

curious, examining, inquiring, inquisitive, interesting, interrogative, meddling, prying, searching; odd, peculiar, queer, strange, unusual. ANT.—disinterested, dull, incurious, indifferent, unconcerned; common, ordinary.

cursory, careless, desultory, flimsy, frivolous, imperfect, shallow, slight, superficial. ANT.—complete, deep, meticulous, painstaking, perfect, profound, thorough.

curt, abrupt, unexpected, hasty, precipitate, sudden; blunt, brusque, rude; harsh, rough, sharp. ANT.—gradual, smooth; courteous.

curtail, abbreviate, abridge, condense, contract, diminish, lessen, limit, reduce, restrict, retrench, shorten. ANT.—elongate, enlarge, extend, lengthen, prolong.

custom, convention, fashion, habit, manner, mores, practice, precedent, rule, usage, wont. ANT.—departure, deviation, difference, divergence, irregularity.

cynical, contemptuous, distrustful, doubtful, pessimistic, petulant, satirical, testy. ANT.—believing, calm, good-natured, pleasant.

D

dainty, choice, delicate, elegant, exquisite, fastidious, fine, particular, pleasant, pleasing, pretty, pure, rare, refined, soft, sweet, tender. ANT.—coarse, harsh, inferior, repellent, unpleasant, vulgar.

dally, caress, coquet, dawdle, delay, flirt, fondle, idle, linger, philander, prolong, toy. ANT.—be attentive, hurry.

dam, bar, block, choke, clog, hamper, hinder, impede, obstruct, stop, suppress. ANT.—open, release, unblock.

damage, deface, harm, hurt, impair, injure, mar, spoil, wound; detriment, disadvantage, evil, injury, loss, misfortune, spoilation, wrong. ANT.—enhance, improve, mend, perfect, repair; advantage, award, benefit, favor, recompense, reward.

damn, anathematize, ban, banish, condemn, denounce, execrate, punish. ANT.—benefit, bless, exalt, favor, praise, promote.

danger, defenseless, exposure, hazard, insecurity, jeopardy, menace, peril, precariousness, risk. ANT.—carefulness, certainty, confidence, preservation, security, sureness.

daring, adventurous, audacious, bold, brave, chivalrous, courageous, defiant, enterprising, fearless, impudent, intrepid, obtrusive, stouthearted. ANT.—cautious, chicken-hearted, cowardly, diffident, hesitating, modest, retiring, shy, timid.

dark, black, clouded, dim, gloomy, murky, obscure, opaque, overcast, shadowy; dusky; dismal, gloomy, mournful, somber, sorrowful; evil, sinister, sullen, wicked; hidden, mysterious, mystic, occult, secret. ANT.—bright, clear, distinct, illumined, brilliant, pleasant; apparent, transparent, visible.

daunt, appall, discourage, dishearten, dismay, frighten, intimidate, scare, terrify. ANT.—aid, animate, assist, embolden, encourage, help, stimulate, succor.

dazzle, amaze, astonish, astound, bewilder, blind, confound, daze, impress, overpower. ANT.—befog, dampen, darken.

dead, deceased, defunct, departed, extinct, gone, inanimate, lifeless, obsolete, perished, spiritless. ANT.—alive, animate, being, continuing, enduring, existent, existing, living.

deadly, destructful, destructive, mortal, noxious, poisonous, virulent. ANT.—animating, energizing, invigorating, preservative, stimulating, strengthening, wholesome.

deal, affair, agreement, conspiracy, racket, transaction; allocate, allot, aportion, barter, distribute, give, mete, share. ANT.—hold, keep, receive, retain.

dear, beloved, esteemed, precious, valued; costly, exorbitant, expensive, high-priced, scarce, valuable. ANT.—despised, unwanted, valueless, worthless; cheap, common, inexpensive, low-priced.

debase, abase, adulterate, contaminate, corrupt, defile, degrade, deprave, dishonor, humiliate, impair, lower, pervert, shame, taint, vitiate. ANT.—elevate, enhance, improve, lift, raise, vitalize.

debate, argue, contend, discuss; dispute, reason.

debauch, adulterate, contaminate, corrupt, debase, defile, degrade, pervert, pollute, seduce.

debris, detritus, litter, remains, rubbish, rubble, ruins, sediment, trash, wreckage.

debt, arrears, charge, debit, deficit, liability, obligation. ANT.—asset, excess, overage.

decay, decline, decompose, degenerate, dwindle, ebb, molder, putrefy, rot, spoil, wane, waste. ANT.—bloom, flourish, grow, increase, luxuriate, rise.

deceit, artifice, beguilement, cheat, chicanery, cunning, deceitfulness, deception, delusion, duplicity, falseness, fraud, guile, sham, treachery, trickery, wiliness. ANT.—authenticity, candor, honesty, openness, sincerity, truthfulness, uprightness.

deceive, be dishonest with, beguile, cheat, circumvent, defraud, delude, dupe, entrap, lie to, mislead, outwit, trick. ANT.—advise, aid, assure, be candid, be frank, be truthful, counsel, help, succor.

decent, adequate, becoming, befitting, decorous, fit, proper, respectable, seemly, suitable; chaste, modest. ANT.—inadequate, reprehensible, unsuitable; coarse, improper, indecent, lewd, obscene, vulgar.

deception, beguilement, chicanery, craft, cunning, deceit, deceitfulness, delusion, dishonesty, duplicity, equivocation, fabrication, falsehood, fraud, guile, prevarication, trickery, sham, wiliness. ANT.—candor, frankness, honesty, openness, simplicity, square-dealing, sincerity, truthfulness, veracity.

decide, adjudicate, conclude, determine, end, judge, resolve, settle, terminate. ANT.—defer, delay, postpone, procrastinate, suspend, vacillate, wait, waver.

decision, conclusion, determination, finding, judgment, outcome, resolution, result, verdict. ANT.—deferment, delay, indefiniteness, indetermination, postponement, procrastination.

declaration, affirmation, allegation, announcement, assertion, avowal, proclamation, profession, statement, utterance. ANT.—denial, retraction, silence.

decline, descent, slant, slope; decay, decrease, degenerate, depreciate, deteriorate, diminish, dwindle, ebb, fail, lessen, retrogress, sink, wane, weaken; refuse, reject. ANT.—incline; improve, increase; accept.

decompose, crumble, decay, disintegrate, disperse, grow, improve, increase, multiply.

decorate, adorn, beautify, bedeck, embellish, enrich, garnish, ornament, trim. ANT.—strip, uncover.

decorum, dignity, etiquette, form, propriety, sedateness, seemliness. ANT.—impropriety, indecency, license.

decoy, beguile, entice, entrap, lure, mislead, tempt. ANT.—guide, lead, reveal, show.

decrease, abate, contract, curtail, decline, deduct, diminish, dwindle, lessen, minimize, narrow, reduce, shorten, shrink, subtract, wane. ANT.—add, develop, dilate, enlarge, expand, extend, grow, increase, widen.

decree, adjudicate, arbitrate, command, decide, determine, dictate, direct, judge, ordain, prescribe, sentence; edict, judgment, law, order, ordinance, statute.

decry, belittle, censure, condemn, criticize, depreciate, derogate, discredit, disparage, lower, minimize. ANT.—acclaim, aggrandize, approve, commend, exalt, extol, magnify, praise.

dedicate, apportion, bless, consecrate, devote, enshrine, give, hallow, offer, set apart. ANT.—alienate, desecrate, misapply, misconvert, misuse.

deduce, assume, believe, conclude, deem, derive, infer, judge, presume, reason, suppose, think.

deed, accomplishment, achievement, act, action, commission, exploit, feat, performance, perpetration, transaction. ANT.—failure, omission.

deface, blemish, damage, deform, disfigure, harm, hurt, impair, mar, spoil. ANT.—enhance, mend, repair.

defeat, beat, checkmate, conquer, crush, foil, frustrate, humble, master, overcome, quell, rout, subdue, subjugate, surmount, triumph, vanquish, whip, win. ANT.—capitulate, cede, lose, retreat, surrender, yield.

defect, blemish, deficiency, drawback, error, failure, fault, flaw, impediment, imperfection, incompleteness. ANT.—advantage, completeness, excellence, faultlessness, perfection.

defend, cover, fortify, guard, insure, plead, protect, safeguard, save, screen, secure, shelter, shield; advocate, espouse, justify, maintain, uphold, vindicate. ANT.—abandon, abdicate, attack, desert, forsake, oppose, relinquish, renounce, resign, surrender.

defense, apology, bulwark, excuse, fortress, guard, justification, protection, refuge, safeguard, shelter, shield, vindication. ANT.—abandonment, betrayal, capitulation, desertion, surrender.

defer, adjourn, break up, delay, dissolve, hinder, postpone, procrastinate, prolong, protract, put off, restrain, retard, suspend. ANT.—accelerate, advance, expedite, forward, further, hasten, quicken, stimulated.

deficient, defective, imperfect, inadequate, incomplete, insufficient, lacking, scanty, scarce, short, wanting. ANT.—adequate, ample, perfect, satisfactory, sufficient.

defile, befoul, contaminate, corrupt, debauch, infect, seduce, soil, spoil, stain, sully, taint. ANT.—clean, cleanse, disinfect, glorify, purify, sanctify, wash.

define, ascertain, decide, describe, determine, elucidate, explain, fix, interpret, limit. ANT.—confuse, derange, distort, mix, tangle, twist.

definite, bounded, certain, circumscribed, clear, definitive, determined, exact, explicit, fixed, limited, positive, precise, specific. ANT.—confused, equivocal, indefinite, indistinct, unbounded, vague.

definition, commentary, description, determination, elucidation, explanation, exposition, interpretation, meaning, rendering, restriction, significance, specification, translation. ANT.—absurdity, confusion, nonsense, vagueness.

deflate, empty, exhaust, reduce; humble. ANT.—blow up, fill, inflate, raise; flatter, praise.

deflect, avert, deviate, diverge, divert, swerve, turn, twist. ANT.—hit, strike.

deform, contort, cripple, deface, disfigure, distort, impair, injure, spoil. ANT.—beautify, improve, perfect, repair.

deformed, crippled, disfigured, disjointed, distorted, malformed, misshapen, twisted, unseemly, unsightly. ANT.—graceful, shapely, symmetrical, regular, well-built, well-formed.

defraud, beguile, cheat, deceive, delude, deprive, dupe, fool, gull, hoodwink, inveigle, overreach, rob, swindle, trick. ANT.—assist, befriend, contribute, help, remunerate, requite, support.

defray, adjust, bear, clear, discharge, liquidate, meet, pay, satisfy, settle. ANT.—abjure, deny, disclaim, disown, embezzle, refuse, repudiate.

deft, adept, adroit, agile, assured, clever, dexterous, expert, handy, nimble, skillful. ANT.—awkward, clumsy, inept, maladroit, ungainly.

defy, attack, brave, challenge, dare, disobey, flout, obstruct, oppose, provoke, resist, slight, spurn, thwart. ANT.—accept, cooperate, obey, relent, yield.

degenerate, corrupt, debase, debauch, decay, decline, demoralize, depreciate, deteriorate, diminish, dwindle, sink, weaken, worsen. ANT.—ameliorate, ascend, improve, increase.

degradation, abasement, baseness, debasement, decline, degeneracy, disgrace, dishonor, dismissal, humiliation, meanness, removal, vice. ANT.—admiration, ascendancy, elevation, exaltation, honor, reward, superiority.

degrade, abase, abash, break, corrupt, crush, debase, demote, discredit, humble, humiliate, mortify, shame, subdue, vitiate. ANT.—elevate, exalt, honor, praise.

degree, class, distinction, division, extent, grade, honor, interval, mark, measure, order, qualification, quality, rank, space, stage, station, step, testimony. ANT.—size, space, mass, numbers.

dejection, depression, despair, despondency, discontent, gloom, heaviness, melancholy, pensiveness, sadness, sorrow. ANT.—cheer, delight, exhilaration, gaiety, hilarity, joy, merriment.

delay, defer, postpone, procrastinate; arrest, detain, hinder, impede, prolong, protract, retard, stay; dally, dawdle, linger, loiter, tarry. ANT.—dispatch, expedite, facilitate, hasten, precipitate, quicken.

delectable, agreeable, delightful, delicious, gratifying, luscious, palatable, pleasant, savory, sweet, tasty, toothsome. ANT.—acrid, distasteful, loathsome, nauseating, repulsive, unpalatable, unsavory.

deleterious, bad, baleful, base, damaging, deadly, destructive, evil, harmful, hurtful, immoral, iniquitous, noxious, pernicious, poisonous, sinful, unsound, unwholesome, villainous, wicked. ANT.—advantageous, healthful, helpful, honorable, moral, reputable, salutary.

deliberate, careful, cautious, considered, contemplated, designed, intentional, judged, pondered, prudent, reasoned, slow, studied, thoughtful, unhurried, weighed; consider, consult, contemplate, estimate, examine, heed, meditate, ponder, regard, reflect, study, weigh. ANT.—careless, hasty, imprudent, unintentional; discard, neglect, reject, spurn.

delicate, compassionate, dainty, fastidious, feeble, fine, fragile, frail, gentle, nice, refined, sensitive, sickly, slender, slight, soft, tender,

weak. ANT.—boisterous, coarse, depraved, indelicate, robust, rude, vulgar.

delicious, appetizing, choice, dainty, delectable, delightful, exquisite, gratifying, luscious, luxurious, palatable, pleasing, savory, sweet, tasteful. ANT.—acrid, coarse, disagreeable, distasteful, nauseous, unpalatable, unsavory.

delightful, agreeable, alluring, charming, enjoyable, glad, gratifying, inspiring, merry, pleasant, pleasing, pleasurable, satisfactory. ANT.—depressing, mournful, offensive, painful, wearisome.

delirium, aberration, dementia, frenzy, hallucination, insanity, lunacy, madness, mania, raving, wandering. ANT.—normality, reason, saneness, sanity, steadiness.

deliver, convey, give, hand over, impart, surrender, transfer, yield; announce, communicate, impart, proclaim, pronounce; discharge, emancipate, free, liberate, redeem, release, rescue, save. ANT.—confine, withhold; betray, capture, imprison, restrain, restrict.

delusion, chimera, deception, error, fallacy, fantasy, hallucination, illusion, mirage, misconception, phantom. ANT.—actuality, certainty, fact, materiality, reality, substance, truth.

demand, ask, beg, beseech, charge, crave, exact, implore, inquire, levy, order, request, require, seek, solicit, supplicate. ANT.—give, offer, present, reply, tender.

demeanor, air, appearance, attitude, bearing, behavior, conduct, manner. ANT.—misbehavior, unmannerliness.

demented, crazy, frenzied, insane, irrational, lunatic, maniacal. ANT.—lucid, normal, rational, reasonable, sane.

demise, alienation, conveyance, death, decease, end, transfer. ANT.—birth, non-alienation.

demolish, annihilate, destroy, devastate, dismantle, eradicate, exterminate, extinguish, level, obliterate, overturn, ravage, raze, ruin, wreck. ANT.—construct, embellish, improve, mend, restore, uphold.

demonstration, certainty, conclusion, consequence, corroboration, deduction, evidence, exhibition, explanation, exposition, induction, manifestation, presentation, proof, show, substantiation, verification. ANT.—concealment, confusion, distortion, falsification, misrepresentation.

demoralize, confuse, corrupt, disconcert, discourage, disorganize, incapacitate, pervert, undermine. ANT.—encourage, exalt, hearten, inspire, invigorate, organize.

demur, balk, delay, disapprove, dissent, falter, hesitate, object, pause, scruple, vacillate, waver. ANT.—accept, agree, assent, consent, decide, persevere, proceed.

demure, coy, decorous, diffident, modest, prim, prudish, sedate, shy, sober, staid. ANT.—impudent, indecorous, shameless, wanton.

denote, connote, express, imply, indicate, intend, mark, mean, signify, specify.

denounce, accuse, arraign, blame, censure, charge, condemn, curse, decry, indict, reprehend, reprimand, reproach, reprove, scold, upbraid. ANT.—applaud, commend, praise.

dense, close, compact, compressed, concentrated, crowded, impenetrable, thick; dull, obtuse, slow, solid, stupid, substantial. ANT.—dispersed, open, rare, scattered, sparse, thin; clever, quick.

deny, contradict, contravene, gainsay, oppose, refute; abjure, disavow, disclaim, disown, forbid, renounce; refuse, repudiate, withhold. ANT.—admit, affirm, agree, assert, concede, confirm.

depart, abandon, decamp, decease, desert, deviate, die, forsake, go, leave, quit, retire, set

out, vanish, vary, withdraw. ANT.—abide, dwell, linger, remain, stay, tarry.

dependable, certain, reliable, sure, trustworthy, trusty. ANT.—questionable, uncertain, unreliable, untrustworthy.

dependent, collateral, conditional, consequent, contingent, relative, reliant, relying, subject. ANT.—absolute, autonomous, categorical, independent, unconditional.

depict, characterize, delineate, describe, draw, illustrate, paint, picture, portray, sketch. ANT.—caricature, confound, confuse, distort.

deplete, diminish, drain, empty, exhaust, lessen, weaken. ANT.—augment, enlarge, fill, increase, strengthen.

deplore, be sorry (for), complain, cry (for), deprecate, fret, grieve, lament, mourn, wail, weep. ANT.—boast, cheer, delight, rejoice, revel.

deportment, air, bearing, behavior, carriage, comportment, conduct, demeanor, form, manner, mien, style.

deposit, hoard, lay down, leave, pledge, place, save, store; precipitate; sediment.

depravity, corruption, degeneracy, depravation, deterioration, immorality, sinfulness, wickedness. ANT.—honor, integrity, justice, morality, purity, virtue.

deprecate, condemn, deplore, disapprove, protest, regret. ANT.—approve, commend, endorse.

depreciate, decline, decrease, degenerate, deteriorate, diminish, dwindle, weaken; decry, denounce, despise, detract, disparage, underrate, undervalue. ANT.—increase, magnify, raise; approve, commend, extol, praise.

depress, abase, debase, degrade, deject, discourage, disgrace, dispirit, humble, humiliate, lower, sink. ANT.—cheer, comfort, encourage, praise, stimulate.

depression, despair, despondency, gloom, hopelessness, melancholy, misery, pessimism. ANT.—business boom; contentment, elation, hope, lightheartedness, optimism.

deprive, abridge, bereave, debar, depose, despoil, dispossess, divest, rob, separate, strip, take. ANT.—assist, confer, endow, enrich, repay, restore.

derelict, abandoned, neglected, wrecked; delinquent, negligent; bum, outcast, tramp, vagrant.

derision, contempt, disdain, disregard, disrespect, insult, irony, jeering, mockery, raillery, ridicule, sarcasm, scorn, slight, slur, sneering. ANT.—adulation, flattery, regard, respect, reference.

derivation, beginning, birth, cause, commencement, cradle, foundation, fountain, inception, nucleus, origin, rise, root, source, spring. ANT.—consequence, end, harvest, issue, outgrowth, termination.

derogatory, belittling, defamatory, deprecatory, disparaging, lessening. ANT.—favoring, helping, lauding, praising.

descent, debasement, degradation, decline; declivity, fall, slant, slope; ancestry, genesis, lineage, origin, pedigree. ANT.—ascension, ascent, climb, elevation, mountain, rise.

describe, characterize, define, delineate, depict, explain, express, illustrate, narrate, picture, portray, recite, recount, relate, represent. ANT.—caricature, confuse, deceive, distort, exaggerate, misrepresent.

desecrate, abuse, debase, defile, misuse, pervert, pollute, profane, secularize. ANT.—cleanse, consecrate, hallow, purify, sanctify.

desert, abandon, abdicate, abjure, forsake, leave, quit, relinquish, secede; surrender, vacate; wasteland, wilderness; due, merit, reward.

ANT.—continue, remain; garden, oasis, pasture; penalty, retribution.

deserve, be worthy of, earn, have right to, merit, win. ANT.—undeserving, unworthy of.

design, decoration, delineation, diagram, draft, drawing, object, outline, pattern, picture, plan, project, sketch; artfulness, contrivance, cunning, end, intention, purpose, scheme. ANT.—accident, chance; candor, sincerity.

designate, appoint, characterize, choose, denominate, denote, indicate, manifest, name, reveal, select, show, signify, specify. ANT.—conceal, divert, falsify.

designing, astute, crafty, cunning, scheming, sly, tricky, underhanded, unscrupulous. ANT.—candid, frank, honest, naïve, open.

desire, affection, ambition, appetite, ardor, aspiration, concupiscence, coveting, craving, eagerness, hungering, inclination, longing, wish, yearning, zeal. ANT.—abhorrence, aversion, detestation, distaste, repulsion.

desirable, acceptable, advisable, beneficial, delightful, enviable, judicious, pleasing, profitable, proper, valuable, wanted, worthy. ANT.—baneful, detrimental, harmful, injurious, noxious.

desist, abstain, arrest, bar, cease, check, discontinue, drop, end, halt, impede, obstruct, quit, relinquish, seal, stop, terminate. ANT.—continue, endure, proceed, retain, wait.

desolate, abandoned, alone, bare, bereaved, bleak, dejected, deserted, dismal, dreary, forgotten, forlorn, forsaken, inhospitable, lonely, miserable, secluded, solitary, uninhabited, unpeopled, waste, wild. ANT.—cultivated, enjoyable, fertile, inhabited, pleasant, teeming.

despair, dejection, depression, desperation, despondency, discouragement, gloom, hopelessness, pessimism, sadness. ANT.—anticipation, confidence, elation, faith, optimism.

desperate, audacious, bold, careless, critical, despondent, determined, extreme, foolhardy, frantic, furious, hopeless, irretrievable, mad, reckless, wild. ANT.—cautious, composed, confident, hopeful, peaceful, satisfied.

despicable, abject, base, contemptible, corrupt, cowardly, depraved, low, lying, malicious, nasty, pitiful, mean, scurrilous, shameless, sordid, vile, vulgar, worthless. ANT.—exalted, honorable, noble, praiseworthy, respectable.

despise, abhor, abominate, condemn, denounce, deride, detest, disdain, dislike, hold in contempt, loathe, scorn, spurn. ANT.—admire, applaud, cherish, commend, love.

despondent, dejected, depressed, despairing, disconsolate, disheartened, dispirited, doleful, low, melancholy, sad. ANT.—buoyant, ebullient, elated, happy, joyous.

despotic, absolute, arbitrary, arrogant, autocratic, cruel, tyrannical, tyrannous. ANT.—conditional, constitutional, limited.

destination, bourn, design, doom, end, fate, goal, intention, location, objective, point, port, purpose, terminus.

destiny, chance, conclusion, condition, decree, doom, end, fate, finality, fortune, judgment, lot, necessity, outcome, portion, predestination, predetermination. ANT.—choice, freedom, volition, will.

destitution, beggary, distress, indigence, lack, need, pauperism, penury, poverty, privation, want. ANT.—abundance, affluence, opulence, prosperity, security.

destroy, annihilate, consume, demolish, devastate, dismantle, dispel, eradicate, exterminate, extirpate, kill, obliterate, overthrow, ravage, raze, ruin, slaughter, terminate. ANT.—construct, fabricate, invigorate, renew, strengthen.

destruction, abolishment, annihilation, cataclysm, demolition, desolation, devastation, downfall, eradication, extermination, extinction, extirpation, fall, havoc, obliteration, overthrow, subversion. ANT.—recovery, renewal, restitution, restoration, revival.

desultory, abnormal, cursory, discursive, erratic, flighty, irregular, loose, rambling, superficial, unsettled, wandering. ANT.—constant, firm, methodical, stable, unalterable.

detach, disconnect, disengage, disjoin, disunite, loosen, part, remove, separate, sever, unfasten, untie, withdraw. ANT.—adhere, bind, coalesce, link, merge.

detail, appoint, assign, describe, itemize, narrate, particularize, relate, report, tell; account, article, description, item, minutia, narrative, particular, portion, recital, specification, trifle. ANT.—conceal, reserve, stifle, suppress; entirety, whole.

detain, arrest, bar, check, confine, curb, delay, hinder, impede, keep, limit, prevent, repress, restrain, retain, retard, stay, stop, withhold. ANT.—free, hasten, liberate, release, precipitate.

detect, apprehend, ascertain, catch, determine, disclose, discover, espy, expose, ferret out, find, identify, perceive, uncover, unearth, unmask. ANT.—blunder, miss, omit, overlook, pass by.

deter, discourage, disincline, dissuade, frighten, hinder, prevent, stop, warn. ANT.—encourage, foster, promote, stimulate, urge.

deteriorate, atrophy, collapse, corrode, decay, decline, decompose, discolor, disintegrate, ebb, erode, mold, oxidize, recede, retrogress, rot, rust, wane, wear. ANT.—improve, refurbish, renew.

determine, affect, ascertain, bound, conclude, decide, define, end, find out, fix, influence, limit, resolve, restrict, settle, specify. ANT.—doubt, falter, hesitate, vacillate, waver.

determined, decided, firm, fixed, immovable, resolute, stable, stubborn, unalterable, unwavering, willful. ANT.—irresolute, fluctuating, uncertain, undecided, wavering.

detest, abhor, abominate, despise, dislike, execrate, hate, loathe. ANT.—admire, appreciate, cherish, love, respect.

detour, by-pass, deviation, digression, side road. ANT.—direct route, highway.

detraction, aspersion, backbiting, calumny, defamation, depreciation, derogation, diminution, disparagement, libel, slander, vilification. ANT.—admiration, commendation, praise, recommendation, respect.

detriment, bane, damage, deterioration, disadvantage, evil, harm, hurt, impairment, inconvenience, infliction, injury, loss, misfortune, wrong. ANT.—advantage, assistance, benefit, favor, gain, profit.

devastate, demolish, desolate, despoil, pillage, ruin, sack, strip, waste, wreck. ANT.—benefit, cultivate, enrich, preserve, restore.

develop, amplify, cultivate, disclose, disentangle, enlarge, evolve, exhibit, expand, extend, grow, mature, uncover, unfold, unravel. ANT.—compress, conceal, contract, hide, restrict.

development, disclosure, expansion, evolution, growth, improvement, maturing, progress, project, subdivision, unfolding. ANT.—compression, curtailment, decline, degeneration.

deviate, bend, deflect, depart from, digress, diverge, divert, shift, shunt, sidetrack, stray, swerve, wander. ANT.—continue, direct, persevere, persist, remain.

device, agent, channel, instrument, means, medium, vehicle; apparatus, artifice, contrivance, design, gadget, invention, machine; plan, ruse, scheme, stratagem. ANT.— hindrance, impediment, obstruction.

devious, circuitous, crooked, indirect, mazy, roundabout, swerving, tortuous, wandering, winding; crooked, cunning, tricky. ANT.—direct, straight; honest, straightforward.

devise, arrange, bequeath, concoct, contrive, invent, make, plan, prepare, will. ANT.—disarrange, fumble, muddle.

devoid, bare, destitute, empty, lacking, unendowed, unprovided, void, wanting, without. ANT.—abundant, complete, full, possessing, replete.

devolve, alienate, authorize, be handed down, commission, consign, depute, deliver, fall (upon).

devote, allot, apply, apportion, appropriate, assign, attend, consign, dedicate, study. ANT.—misappropriate, misuse, pervert, squander, waste.

devotion, adherence, ardor, consecration, dedication, devoutness, earnestness, fidelity, intensity, observance, piety, religiousness, sincerity, zeal. ANT.—alienation, apathy, aversion, indifference, neglect, unfaithfulness.

devour, bolt, consume, destroy, eat greedily, gobble, gorge, prey upon, swallow (up), waste. ANT.—disgorge, vomit.

devout, devotional, earnest, fervent, godly, holy, moral, pietistic, pious, religious, reverent, righteous, sacred, sincere, spiritual. ANT.—atheistic, impious, profane, secular, worldly.

dexterity, ability, adroitness, aptitude, aptness, art, capability, cleverness, deftness, facility, handiness, skill. ANT.—awkwardness, blundering, clumsiness, ineptitude.

diagram, blueprint, chart, drawing, map, outline, plan, sketch.

dialect, accent, idiom, jargon, patois, provincialism, vernacular. ANT.—official language, standard speech.

dictate, command, decree, direct, order, prescribe. ANT.—ask, beg, follow, obey, plead.

dictatorial, arbitrary, arrogant, dogmatic, domineering, haughty, imperious, overbearing, tyrannical. ANT.—acquiescent, docile, obsequious, submissive, subservient, passive.

diction, choice of words, enunciation, phraseology, pronunciation, vocal expression.

die, cease, decay, decease, decline, depart, expire, fade, languish, pass away, perish, recede, sink, vanish, wane, wither; mold, stamp. ANT.—begin, endure, flourish, grow, live, survive.

difference, deviation, discrepancy, disparity, dissimilarity, distinction, divergence, inequality, separation, variation, variety; disagreement, discord, dissension, estrangement. ANT.—congruity, similarity, uniformity; agreement, harmony.

different, contrary, differing, discordant, dissimilar, distinct, distinctive, divers, diverse, heterogeneous, incongruous, unlike, variant, various. ANT.—alike, congruous, harmonious, homogeneous, same.

differentiate, contrast, discriminate, distinguish, isolate, particularize, separate. ANT.—confound, confuse, group, mingle.

difficult, arduous, complex, complicated, demanding, enigmatical, hard, intricate, involved, laborious, obscure, perplexing, puzzling, rigid, toilsome, troublesome, trying, unmanageable, unyielding. ANT.—easy, facile, pleasant, simple, tranquil.

difficulty, annoyance, anxiety, argument, complication, contention, dilemma, discouragement, dispute, distress, embarrassment, entanglement, impediment, intricacy, obstacle, obstruction, oppression, perplexity, problem, trouble, worry. ANT.—comfort, facility, felicity, flexibility, pleasure, satisfaction.

diffident, bashful, hesitant, modest, shrinking, shy, timid. ANT.—bold, brash, brazen.

diffuse, copious, discursive, repetitive, tedious, tiresome, wordy. ANT.—abbreviated, brief, restricted.

diffusion, broadcasting, circulation, distribution, dispersion, spreading. ANT.—collection, restriction, suppression.

dignify, adorn, advance, award, decorate, elevate, ennoble, exalt, extol, glorify, honor, magnify, prefer, proclaim, promote, revere. ANT.—belittle, degrade, demean, humiliate, slander.

dignity, decency, decorum, eminence, grace, greatness, propriety, stateliness, station, worth. ANT.—degradation, lowliness.

digress, bend, deflect, depart, deviate, diverge, divert, ramble, sidetrack, stray, turn aside, wander. ANT.—continue, persevere, persist, preserve.

dilapidated, crumbling, decayed, depreciating, deteriorating, sagging. ANT.—rebuilt, renewed, restored.

dilate, broaden, distend, enlarge, expand, extend, increase, magnify, open, spread, stretch, swell, widen. ANT.—abridge, compress, contract, diminish, reduce.

dilemma, difficulty, fix, perplexity, plight, predicament, problem, quandary. ANT.—advantage, freedom, solution.

diligence, alertness, application, assiduity, attention, care, carefulness, earnestness, heed, industry, intensity, keenness, perseverance, quickness. ANT.—ennui, indolence, laziness, lethargy, slowness.

dilute, reduced, thin, watery, weak. ANT.—concentrated, rich, strong, thick.

dim, blurred, clouded, dull, faint, gloomy, indefinite, indistinct, misty, mysterious, obscure, shaded, shadowy. ANT.—bright, brilliant, clear, distinct.

dimension, amplitude, area, bulk, capacity, extent, magnitude, measurement, size.

diminish, abate, abridge, assuage, compress, contract, curtail, decrease, degrade, dwindle, impair, lessen, lower, minimize, moderate, reduce, shorten, shrink. ANT.—amplify, enlarge, increase, intensify, magnify.

din, clamor, clangor, clash, clatter, hubbub, noise, racket, row, tumult, uproar. ANT.—quiet, silence, stillness.

diplomatic, adroit, artful, courteous, discreet, judicious, politic, tactful. ANT.—blunt, gruff, rude, tactless.

direct, aim, point, train; conduct, control, demonstrate, explain, govern, guide, head, inform, instruct, lead, manage, order, regulate, supervise, teach, usher. ANT.—deceive, delude, misdirect, misguide.

direction, address, aim, course, end, goal, inclination, line, tendency, way; administration, government, leadership, management, superintendence; command, control, guidance, instruction, order.

dirty, dingy, discolored, filthy, foul, grimy, muddy, soiled, squalid; indecent, obscene, sordid; base, contemptible, despicable, low, mean, shabby. ANT.—clean, immaculate, spotless; pure, wholesome.

disability, decrepitude, defect, disqualification, feebleness, forfeiture, handicap, impotence, inability, inadequacy, incompetence, infirmity, powerlessness, unfitness, weakness. ANT.—ability, capability, capacity, power, strength.

disadvantage, block, check, detriment, difficulty, drawback, evil, harm, hindrance, hurt, prejudice, stumbling, block. ANT.—advantage, assistance, benefit, profit, utility.

disaffect, alienate, disdain, dislike, disorder, estrange.

disagree, argue, clash, combat, contend, differ, dispute, dissent, fight, oppose, quarrel, vary. ANT.—agree, coincide, concur, harmonize.

disappear, cease, depart, dissolve, evaporate, fade, melt, vanish, withdraw. ANT.—appear, materialize.

disappoint, baffle, betray, deceive, delude, fail, foil, frustrate, thwart, vex. ANT.—assist, befriend, please, support, relieve.

disapproval, blame, censure, condemnation, depreciation, disapprobation, dislike, disparagement, odium. ANT.—approval, sanction.

disaster, adversity, calamity, casualty, cataclysm, catastrophe, evil, misadventure, mischance, misfortune, mishap, tragedy. ANT.—advantage, fortune, privilege, prosperity.

disband, break up, demobilize, disperse, dissolve. ANT.—assemble, mobilize, unite.

disburse, expend, distribute, pay, settle, spend. ANT.—collect, deposit, receive, retain, save.

discard, abandon, cancel, discharge, dismiss, divorce, eliminate, reject, repudiate, scrap, shed. ANT.—adopt, embrace, keep, retain.

discern, descry, detect, discover, discriminate, distinguish, espy, know, observe, perceive, recognize, see, understand. ANT.—disregard, neglect, omit, overlook, slight.

discerning, acute, critical, discriminating, exacting, fastidious, particular, sharp sighted, shrewd. ANT.—cursory, shallow, superficial, uncritical.

discernment, acumen, discrimination, insight, judgment, penetration, perspicuity. ANT.—obtuseness.

discharge, acquit, clear, dismiss, eject, emit, exile, expel, fire, free, oust, pay, perform, project, release, retire, settle, shoot. ANT.—load, hire, imprison, retain.

disciple, adherent, devotee, follower, votary.

discipline, control, order, regulation, restraint; drill, instruction, method, rule, training; chastisement, correction, punishment. ANT.—chaos, confusion, disorder, mutiny, turbulence.

disclaim, abandon, deny, disallow, disavow, disown, reject, renounce, repudiate, retract. ANT.—acknowledge, claim, own, recognize.

disclose, acknowledge, betray, concede, declare, discover, divulge, expose, grant, inform, reveal, show, tell, uncover, unfold, unmask, unveil, utter. ANT.—cloak, conceal, cover, deceive, withhold.

disconsolate, broken-hearted, cheerless, dejected, depressed, despondent, dismal, doleful, gloomy, inconsolable, lugubrious, melancholy, mournful, sad, sorrowful. ANT.—cheerful, glad, happy, joyous, merry.

discontent, disappointment, disillusionment, dissatisfaction, frustration, uneasiness, vexation. ANT.—content, peace, satisfaction.

discord, animosity, clash, confusion, contention, difference, disagreement, disharmony, dissension, dissonance, disturbance, harshness, quarreling, variance, wrangling. ANT.—agreement, amity, concord, harmony, peace.

discount, allowance, deduction, drawback, loss, rebate, reduction, refund. ANT.—increase, increment, premium, rise.

discourage, block, check, dampen, depress, deter, dishearten, dispirit, dissuade, hamper, hinder, impede, obstruct, oppose, prevent, resist, restrain, retard, thwart. ANT.—assist, encourage, expedite, facilitate, promote.

discourteous, abusive, blunt, boorish, disrespectful, forward, gruff, ill-mannered, impolite, impudent, insolent, rough, rude, surly, uncivil, ungracious, unmannerly, unpolished, vulgar. ANT.—civil, courteous, genteel, polished, polite.

discover, ascertain, contrive, descry, detect, discern, disclose, elicit, expose, find, find out, invent, learn, manifest, realize, reveal, uncover, unearth. ANT.—cover, hide, mask, screen, suppress.

discreet, attentive, careful, cautious, circumspect, considerate, discerning, discriminating, judicious, prudent, sensible, serious, thoughtful, watchful, wise. ANT.—indiscreet, injudicious, rash, thoughtless.

discrepancy, contrariety, difference, disagreement, inconsistency, variance. ANT.—accordance, agreement, concurrence, harmony.

discretion, carefulness, caution, circumspection, finesse, foresight, judgment, prudence, sagacity, thoughtfulness. ANT.—foolishness, imprudence, rashness, recklessness, thoughtlessness.

discrimination, acumen, acuteness, care, caution, circumspection, differentiation, discernment, distinction, foresight, forethought, heed, perception, perspicacity, prudence, sagacity, vigilance, wisdom. ANT.—carelessness, imprudence, negligence, rashness, senselessness.

discuss, analyze, argue, confer, consult, controvert, converse, debate, deliberate, dispute, examine, explain.

disdain, arrogance, contempt, contumely, derision, detestation, haughtiness, pride, scorn, scornfulness, superciliousness. ANT.—admiration, esteem, regard, respect, reverence.

disease, affliction, ailment, complaint, disorder, distemper, illness, infirmity, malady, plague, pestilence, sickness, unhealthiness, unsoundness. ANT.—health, healthiness, soundness, sturdiness, vigor.

disengage, clear, detach, disentangle, extricate, free, liberate, loose, loosen, release, separate, unravel, withdraw. ANT.—attach, bind, fasten, tighten, unite.

disfigure, blemish, damage, deface, deform, distort, injure, mar, mutilate, spoil. ANT.—adorn, decorate, repair, restore.

disgrace, abasement, baseness, disfavor, dishonor, disrepute, humiliation, infamy, ignominy, mortification, odium, opprobrium, reproach, scandal, shame. ANT.—dignity, exaltation, glory, honor, renown, respect.

disguise, camouflage, change, cloak, conceal, cover, dissemble, feign, hide, mask, masquerade, pretend, screen, secrete, shroud, suppress, veil, withhold. ANT.—bare, disclose, divulge, expose, reveal, uncover.

disgust, abhorrence, abomination, aversion, detestation, dislike, distaste, hatred, loathing, nausea, repugnance, resentment, revulsion. ANT.—admiration, approbation, esteem, respect, reverence.

dishonest, cheating, corrupt, corruptible, crooked, debased, deceitful, false, fraudulent, lying, perfidious, unsound, unscrupulous, untrue, untrustworthy, venal, vitiated. ANT.—honest, scrupulous, trustworthy.

dislike, abhorrence, antipathy, aversion, disaffection, disapproval, disinclination, distaste, hatred, loathing, repugnance, repulsion. ANT.—affection, attachment, devotion.

disloyal, apostate, disaffected, faithless, false, perfidious, subversive, traitorous, treacherous, treasonable, unfaithful, unpatriotic. ANT.—faithful, loyal, true, worthy.

dismal, bleak, cheerless, dark, depressing, dingy, direful, doleful, dolorous, dreadful, dreary, dull, funereal, gloomy, horrible, horrid, melancholy, sad, somber, sorrowful, unhappy. ANT.—bright, cheerful, joyous, pleasant.

dismantle, demolish, raze, strip, take apart, take down. ANT.—assemble, build, construct, raise.

dismay, alarm, anxiety, apprehension, awe, consternation, discouragement, dread, fear, fright, horror, misgiving, trepidation. ANT.—assurance, confidence, courage, intrepidity.

dismiss, banish, bounce, decline, depose, discard, discharge, exile, expel, fire, oust, remove, repel, repudiate, suspend. ANT.—accept, recall, retain.

disobey, defy, disregard, ignore, infringe, invade, rebel, resist, transgress, violate. ANT.—accept, obey, submit.

disorder, anarchy, bustle, chaos, confusion, disarrangement, disorganization, disturbance, illness, indisposition, irregularity, jumble, muddle, riot, sickness, tumult. ANT.—order, organization, system, vigor.

disorderly, chaotic, confused, disheveled, irregular, lawless, tumultuous, unrestrained, unruly. ANT.—calm, disciplined, law-abiding, neat, orderly.

disparage, asperse, belittle, decry, defame, deprecate, depreciate, derogate, discredit, dishonor, lower, minimize, traduce, underestimate, underrate, undervalue. ANT.—aggrandize, commend, exalt, magnify, praise, sanction.

dispatch, accelerate, conclude, expedite, hasten, kill, perform, send, speed, transmit. ANT.—hold, retain, slow.

dispel, banish, diffuse, dismiss, disperse, disseminate, dissipate, dissolve, rout, scatter, spread, strew. ANT.—accumulate, amass, assemble, collect, gather, increase.

dispense, administer, allocate, allot, apply, apportion, appropriate, assign, carry out, distribute, dole out, execute, mete, sell; excuse, exempt, release. ANT.—absorb, keep, retain, withhold.

disperse, diffuse, dispel, disseminate, dissipate, dissolve, distribute, fade, scatter, separate, sow, strew. ANT.—amass, assemble, collect, concentrate, gather.

displace, confuse, crowd out, depose, derange, disarrange, discharge, dislodge, dismiss, displant, dispossess, disturb, eject, jumble, mislay, misplace, mix, remove, shift, unseat, unsettle, uproot. ANT.—arrange, classify, group, sort.

display, exhibit expose, flaunt, open, parade, reveal, show, unfold; evince, manifest; array, demonstration, exhibition, flourish, layout, manifestation, ostentation, show. ANT.—conceal, cover, disguise, hide, suppress.

displease, anger, annoy, antagonize, bother, chagrin, disappoint, disgruntle, disgust, dissatisfy, disturb, exasperate, gall, harass, irritate, mortify, pester, pique, plague, provoke, tantalize, taunt, tease, trouble, vex, worry. ANT.—delight, gratify, pacify, propitiate, satisfy.

dispose, adapt, adjust, arrange, bestow, classify, conform, give, locate, order, place, regulate, settle. ANT.—conceal, disarrange, disorder, displace, retain.

disposition, bent, bias, character, inclination, leaning, make-up, nature, personality, proclivity, temper, temperament, tendency; adjustment, arrangement, control, disposal.

dispute, altercation, argument, contention, contest, controversy, debate, denial, difference, disagreement, discord, discussion, dissension, estrangement, feud, quarrel, questioning, squabble, variance. ANT.—agreement, concord, harmony, unison.

disqualify, bar, disable, disenfranchise, incapacitate, prohibit, remove from contention. ANT.—accept, fit, quality.

disregard, contemn, disobey, ignore, neglect, omit, overlook, skip, slight. ANT.—include, notice, regard.

disrespectful, contemptuous, derisive, discourteous, disparaging, flippant, impertinent, impious, impolite, insolent, insulting, irreverent, uncivil. ANT.—courteous, respectful.

dissatisfaction, disappointment, disapproval, discomfort, discontent, disgruntlement, dislike, displeasure, distaste, malcontentment, uneasiness. ANT.—contentment, gratification, happiness, recompense, satisfaction.

dissect, analyze, anatomize, cut up, examine. ANT.—assemble, synthesize.

dissent, censure, condemn, conflict, contend, differ, disagree, disapprove, disclaim, dispute, except, oppose, vary. ANT.—agree, commend, concur, endorse, sanction.

dissertation, commentary, composition, discourse, essay, homily, lecture, sermon, study, theme, thesis, tract.

dissipate, debauch, diffuse, disperse, lavish, scatter, spread, squander, waste. ANT.—absorb, accumulate, conserve, preserve, save.

dissolve, destroy, disappear, disintegrate, disorganize, divide, evanesce, evaporate, fade, render, thaw, vanish. ANT.—assemble, concentrate, unite.

distant, afar, apart, faint, far, indistinct, remove, removed, separated; aloof, cold, cool, haughty, indifferent, reserved, shy, stiff, unfriendly. ANT.—close, near, nigh, cordial, friendly, sympathetic, warm.

distasteful, disagreeable, disgusting, displeasing, loathsome, nauseating, objectionable, obnoxious, offensive, repellent, repugnant, repulsive, unpalatable, unsavory. ANT.—agreeable, delectable, pleasing, savory, welcome.

distend, blow up, dilate, expand, grow, inflate, stretch, swell, tumefy. ANT.—constrict, contract, narrow, shrink.

distinct, apparent, clear, definite, evident, exact, lucid, manifest, obvious, plain, precise, unmistakable, visible. ANT.—ambiguous, indefinite, obscure, unclear, vague.

distinction, attribute, characteristic, feature, peculiarity, property, quality, trait; acumen, acuteness, clearness, discernment, discrimination, elevation, eminence, judgment, note, rank, superiority. ANT.—amalgamation, combination; inferiority, mediocrity, sameness.

distinguished, brilliant, celebrated, conspicuous, eminent, extraordinary, famous, glorious, great, illustrious, noble, noted, prominent, renowned, well-known. ANT.—common, obscure, ordinary, unknown, unobtrusive.

distort, bend, contort, deface, deform, disfigure, falsify, gnarl, impair, mangle, misconstrue, misshape, pervert, slant. ANT.—align, balance, explain, straighten.

distract, bewilder, confound, confuse, daze, derange, disorder, embarrass, mislead, mystify, perplex. ANT.—allay, assure, mitigate, pacify, reassure.

distress, adversity, agony, anguish, calamity, catastrophe, danger, grief, hardship, misadventure, misery, misfortune, need, pain, perplexity, sorrow, suffering, torment, trouble, unhappiness, wretchedness. ANT.—comfort, joy, relief, satisfaction.

distribution, allotment, apportionment, arrangement, classification, deal, dispensation, disposal, division, dole, partition. ANT.—collection, hoard, maintenance, retention, storage.

distrust, disbelief, doubt, misgiving, mistrust, skepticism, suspicion, uncertainty. ANT.—belief, certainty, conviction, faith, trust.

disturb, agitate, annoy, arouse, bother, confuse, derange, disarrange, discompose, disconcert, disorder, displace, distress, interrupt, perplex, perturb, rouse, trouble, unbalance, unsettle, vex, worry. ANT.—compose, pacify, quiet, settle, soothe.

divergent, branching, contrary, deviating, differing, disagreeing, diverse, separating, varying. ANT.—convergent, identical, parallel, similar.

divest, bare, denude, deprive, disrobe, peel, strip, unclothe, uncover, undress. ANT.—clothe, cover, invest, restore (property).

diverse, contrary, different, dissimilar, distinct, divergent, diversified, heterogeneous, unlike, variant; divers, miscellaneous, numerous, several, sundry, various. ANT.—alike, identical, same, selfsame, similar.

divide, detach, disconnect, disengage, disjoin, dissolve, disunite, partition, separate, sever, split, sunder; allot, apportion, assign, dispense, distribute. ANT.—combine, convene, fasten, join, unite.

divine, celestial, consecrated, godlike, heavenly, holy, sacred, sanctified, spiritual, superhuman, supernatural, transcendent, venerable. ANT.—blasphemous, diabolical, impious, profane, wicked.

division, allotment, compartment, department, detachment, difference, discord, disunion, partition, portion, share. ANT.—concord, indivisibility, oneness, union, unity.

divulge, betray, communicate, describe, disclose, discover, expose, impart, inform, relate, reveal, show, tell, uncover, unveil. ANT.—cloak, conceal, disguise, hide, obscure.

do, accomplish, achieve, complete, conclude, consummate, effect, enact, execute, finish, fulfill, perform, terminate; carry on, conduct, discharge, transact; make, produce, work; commit, perpetrate. ANT.—evade, shirk.

docile, amenable, compliant, gentle, manageable, meek, mild, obedient, pliable, pliant, submissive, tame, tractable, yielding. ANT.—determined, mulish, obstinate, stubborn, unyielding.

doctrine, belief, conviction, creed, cult, dogma, faith, gospel, opinion, persuasion, precept, principle, propaganda, proposition, religion, rule, teaching, tenet, theory.

document, account, archive, certificate, chronicle, deed, manuscript, notation, paper, record, script, statement, writing.

dodge, avoid, elude, equivocate, escape, evade, quibble, side-step. ANT.—approach, confront, encounter, face, meet.

dogmatic, arrogant, authoritarian, dictatorial, doctrinaire, domineering, imperious, immovable, magisterial, opinionated, overbearing, peremptory, positive, unchangeable; authoritative, doctrinal. ANT.—fluctuating, indecisive, questioning, skeptical, vacillating.

dole, allot, apportion, dispense, distribute; allotment, alms, apportionment, benefit, distribution, division, gratuity, pittance, portion, share.

domestic, domesticated, gentle, household, internal, native, tame. ANT.—foreign, savage, untamed, wild.

domicile, abode, accommodations, apartment, dwelling, habitation, home, lodging, residence, quarters.

dominant, aggressive, authoritative, commanding, controlling, domineering, governing, imperative, imperious, lordly, predominant, prevailing, ruling. ANT.—humble, non-aggressive, obscure, retiring, subordinate.

dominion, ascendancy, authority, control, government, jurisdiction, sway; commonwealth, country, district, empire, region, territory. ANT.—bondage, dependency, inferiority, subjection, submission.

donation, benefaction, benefit, bequest, boon, bounty, charity, contribution, endowment, favor, gift, grant, gratuity, largess, present, provision, subscription. ANT.—deprivation, loss.

done, achieved, completed, concluded, consummated, ended, executed, finished, over, performed, solved. ANT.—inchoate, incomplete, partial, raw, unfinished.

dormant, inactive, inert, quiescent, sleeping, unconscious, unoccupied. ANT.—active, awake, industrious, occupied, working.

double, counterpart, duplicate, stand-in, twin, understudy; duplicate, enlarge, repeat; bipartite, coupled, dual, duplex, paired, twin, twofold. ANT.—lone, single, unique.

doubt, agnosticism, concern, disbelief, distrust, dubiousness, hesitancy, hesitation, incredulity, indecision, irresolution, misgiving, mistrust, perplexity, qualm, quandary, question, scruple, skepticism, suspense, suspicion, unbelief, uncertainty. ANT.—assurance, belief, certainty, conviction, faith.

doubt, hesitate, question, waver; distrust, mistrust, suspect. ANT.—believe, confide, rely upon, trust.

draft, delineate, draw, sketch; call up, conscript, impress; bill of exchange, check, letter of credit, money order; breeze, wind.

draw, drag, haul, pull, tow, tug; extract, remove, take out; unsheathe; allure, attract, entice, induce, lure; delineate, depict, sketch, trace; compose, draft, formulate, write; conclude, deduce, derive, infer; extend, lengthen, prolong, protract, stretch. ANT.—alienate, rebuff, reject, repel, repulse.

drawback, allowance, defect, detriment, discount, flaw, hindrance, injury, rebate. ANT.—advantage, benefit, extra, premium.

dread, alarm, anxiety, apprehension, awe, consternation, dismay, fear, fright, horror, misgiving, panic, terror, trepidation. ANT.—boldness, bravery, confidence, courage.

dreadful, appalling, awful, dire, fearful, formidable, frightful, ghastly, horrible, terrible. ANT.—beautiful, enchanting, enjoyable, lovely.

dream, chimera, conceit, deception, delusion, fallacy, fancy, fantasy, hallucination, illusion, imagination, nightmare, reverie. ANT.—actuality, materiality, reality, solidity, verity.

dreary, bleak, cheerless, dark, depressing, discouraging, disheartening, dismal, doleful, dull, funereal, gloomy, lonesome, melancholy, sad, somber, wearisome. ANT.—cheerful, joyous, lively, pleasant.

dress, apparel, appearance, array, attire, clothing, costume, drapery, frock, garb, garments, gown, habiliments, habit, raiment, robes, uniform, vestments, vesture. ANT.—bareness, disarray, nakedness, nudity.

drift, end, inference, intent, meaning, objective, purpose, result, scope, tendency, tenor; bearing, course, direction; advance, be carried, deviate (from course), float, heap up, move, wander.

drill, condition, discipline, exercise, instruction, lesson, practice, repetition, study, training; boring tool; bore, perforate, puncture. ANT.—idleness, repose, rest.

drive, coerce, compel, force, hammer, hurl, impel, incite, propel, push, thrust; actuate, conduct, control, direct, guide, move, steer, ride. ANT.—drag, tow, tug; discourage, hinder, repress.

drop, collapse, decline, decrease, descend, diminish, fall, plunge, sink, subside; stumble, topple, tumble, droop, extend downward, faint, hang; dribble, drip, trickle, percolate; abandon, dismiss, give up, relinquish; cease, stop, terminate. ANT.—rise, soar; flow, splash; continue, pursue.

drown, deluge, engulf, immerse, inundate, muffle, overflow, overpower, overwhelm, perish, plunge, sink, submerge, suffocate, swamp. ANT.—extricate, preserve, recover.

drug, anesthetic, biological compound, dope, extract, medicine, narcotic, pharmaceutical; anesthetize, desensitize, knock out, narcotize, sedate.

dry, arid, dehydrated, desiccated, drained, juiceless, moistless, parched, thirsty, watertight; barren, dull, jejune, prosy, stale, tedious, tiresome, uninteresting, vapid. ANT.—damp, moist; fresh, interesting, lively.

dubious, doubtful, equivocal, hesitant, problematical, questionable, reluctant, uncertain, unclear, unreliable, unsettled, unsure. ANT.—certain, definite, positive, sure.

dull, dense, doltish, half-witted, insipid, obtuse, senseless, slow, stolid, stupid, vapid, witless; blunt, obtuse; boring, commonplace, dismal, dreary, gloomy, monotonous, prosy, sad, tedious, uninteresting; insensate, unfeeling; dry, lifeless; dark, dim. ANT.—animated, intelligent, sharp; clear, interesting.

dumb, brainless, dense, dull, foolish, obtuse, senseless, stupid, witless; aphonic, mute, speechless, voiceless. ANT.—alert, bright, clever, discerning, intelligent; articulate, fluent, talkative, voluble.

duplicate, copy, counterpart, exemplar, facsimile, likeness, replica, reproduction, tracing, transcript, twin; copy, redo, repeat, reproduce, trace. ANT.—original, prototype.

duplicity, artifice, deceit, dishonesty, fraud, guile, hypocrisy, perfidy. ANT.—guilelessness, honesty, openness, simplicity.

durable, abiding, changeless, constant, continuing, enduring, fixed, hard, indestructible, lasting, permanent, remaining, strong, unchangeable. ANT.—ephemeral, temporary, transient, transitory, unstable.

duress, captivity, coercion, compulsion, confinement, constraint.

duty, accountability, allegiance, business, calling, charge, employment, function, obligation, office, province, responsibility, service, task. ANT.—betrayal, disloyalty, falsehood, inconstancy, irresponsibility.

dwelling, abode, accommodations, apartment, domicile, flat, habitat, habitation, hearth, home, house, quarters, residence, seat.

dwindle, abridge, contract, curtail, decline, decrease, diminish, drop, fade, fall, lessen, melt, narrow, reduce, shorten, shrink, wane. ANT.—augment, enlarge, expand, multiply, widen.

dye, color, imbue, infuse, pigment, stain, tinge, tint. ANT.—bleach, fade.

E

eager, ablaze, ambitious, anxious, ardent, athirst, avid, burning, desirous, earnest, enthusiastic, fervent, glowing, hot, impassioned, impatient, impetuous, importunate, intense, intent, keen, longing, solicitous, vehement, yearning, zealous. ANT.—apathetic, indifferent, phlegmatic, uninterested.

earn, achieve, acquire, attain, deserve, gain, get, make, merit, obtain, secure, win. ANT.—forfeit, lose.

earnest, ardent, candid, eager, fervent, frank, genuine, heartfelt, honest, open, resolute, serious, sincere, straightforward, true, truthful, unfeigned, upright, warm, zealous. ANT.—affected, capricious, dishonest, insincere, untruthful.

earnings, allowance, commission, emolument, income, interest, profits, remuneration, reward, salary, stipend, wages. ANT.—costs, expenses, losses.

earthly, base, carnal, earthy, global, material, mundane, profane, sordid, temporal, worldly. ANT.—heavenly, immaterial, incorporeal, spiritual.

ease, allay, alleviate, assuage, comfort, facilitate, lighten, mitigate, pacify, relieve, soothe; comfort, contentment, peace, quietude, repose, security, solace, tranquility; easiness, expertise, facility. ANT.—annoyance, discomfort, disquiet, turmoil, vexation; difficulty.

easy, comfortable, effortless, elementary, facile, light, relaxed, simple, unanxious, uncomplicated; flexible, manageable, pliant, smooth. ANT.—arduous, demanding, difficult, hard, laborious.

ebb, abate, decay, decline, dwindle, fall, lessen, recede, retire, retreat, sink, wane. ANT.—flow, improve, increase, revive, wax.

eccentric, aberrant, bizarre, curious, deviating, erratic, odd, outlandish, peculiar, quaint, queer, singular, strange, unusual, wayward. ANT.—common, conventional, familiar, normal, regular.

economical, circumspect, frugal, moderate, penurious, provident, reasonable, saving, sparing, thrifty, watchful. ANT.—extravagant, improvident, lavish, munificent, wasteful.

ecstasy, bliss, delight, ebullience, elation, exaltation, glee, glorification, joy, rapture, ravishment, transport. ANT.—depression, despair, doldrums, melancholy, pessimism.

eddy, reverse, spin, swirl, whirl; maelstrom, vortex, whirlpool. ANT.—calm, still.

edge, border, boundary, brim, brink, butt, circumference, extremity, fringe, margin, periphery, rim, ring, side, tip, verge; intensity, keenness, sharpness, sting. ANT.—center, extension, interior; bluntness, dullness.

edict, announcement, command, decree, law, mandate, manifesto, order, ordinance, proclamation, public notice, statute, writ.

edifice, building, establishment, house, skyscraper, structure.

edit, adapt, arrange, change, compile, compose, correct, rectify, reduce, revise, select, trim.

education, background, cultivation, culture, development, discipline, edification, enlightenment, instruction, knowledge, learning, scholarship, schooling, study, training. ANT.—ignorance, illiteracy.

eerie, curious, fantastic, grotesque, odd, peculiar, strange, supernatural, uncanny, weird. ANT.—natural, normal, usual.

efface, annul, blot, cancel, destroy, erase, expunge, obliterate, wipe. ANT.—confirm, keep, renew, retain, strengthen.

effect, achieve, accomplish, attain, complete, conclude, consummate, do, execute, finish, fulfill, perform, realize; completion, conclusion, consequence, consummation, issue, outcome, result. ANT.—abandon, defeat, fail, neglect, omit; beginning, cause, commencement, origin, source.

effective, adept, capable, competent, conducive, effectual, efficacious, efficient, fruitful, potent, productive, proficient, serviceable, talented, trenchant, useful. ANT.—fruitless, incompetent, ineffectual, inefficient, nonproductive.

effeminate, feminine, unmanly, unvirile, womanish. ANT.—manly, masculine, robust, virile.

effervescent, bubbling, buoyant, frothy, gay, gleeful, volatile. ANT.—flat, sedate, sober, staid.

efficiency, ability, adaptability, capability, capacity, competency, effectiveness, fitness, power, proficiency, suitability, thoroughness. ANT.—impotence, inability, inadequacy, incompetency, weakness.

effort, application, attempt, endeavor, energy, essay, exertion, trial, work; labor, pains, strain, strife, struggle, toil, trouble. ANT.—ease, failure, neglect.

egotistic, boastful, bombastic, conceited, egocentric, inflated, narcissistic, ostentatious, pretentious, pompous, self-centered, self-important, showy, vain. ANT.—deferent, humble, modest, reserved, unobtrusive.

eject, banish, cast out, discard, discharge, dislodge, dismiss, exile, expel, evict, oust, propel, remove. ANT.—accept, appoint, establish, settle, retain.

elaborate, gaudy, ostentatious, showy; complex, complicated, detailed, intricate, perfected, polished, refined. ANT.—common, ordinary, simple, unrefined, usual.

elapse, expire, glide, go away, intervene, lapse, pass, vanish. ANT.—remain, stand still, stay.

elastic, adaptable, compliant, ductile, extensible, flexible, limber, lithe, pliable, pliant, resilient, rubbery, springy, stretchable, supple, tractable. ANT.—brittle, rigid, stiff, tense, unbending.

elated, animated, delighted, ecstatic, exhilarated, exultant, gleeful, high-spirited. ANT.—depressed, downhearted, gloomy, low.

elect, call, choose, cull, decide on, judge, opt, ordain, pick, prefer, select. ANT.—cancel, recall, refuse, reject.

elegant, beautiful, courtly, elaborate, fair, fine, handsome, lovely, luxurious, opulent, polished, pretty, refined, rich, sophisticated, sumptuous. ANT.—common, repulsive, rustic, unrefined, vulgar.

elementary, basic, constituent, easy, elemental, fundamental, initial, primary, rudimentary; pure, simple, uncompounded, unmixed. ANT.—abstruse, advanced, complex, intricate; compounded, mixed.

elevate, advance, buoy, dignify, erect, exalt, glorify, heighten, hoist, honor, improve, lift, promote, raise, revere, uplift. ANT.—abase, condemn, deprecate, depreciate, depress.

elicit, bring forth, draw, educe, evoke, extort, extract, prompt, wrest. ANT.—repress, suppress.

eliminate, abolish, abrogate, banish, cancel, delete, discharge, dislodge, efface, eject, eradicate, erase, excise, exclude, expel, expunge,

expurgate, exterminate, extirpate, liquidate, obliterate, oust, proscribe, pluck, remove. ANT.—accept, admit, include, maintain, preserve.

elongate, extend, lengthen, prolong, protract, stretch. ANT.—contract, shrink, slacken, shorten.

elucidate, clarify, decipher, explain, expound, illuminate, illustrate, interpret. ANT.—becloud, confuse, darken, distract, obscure.

elude, avert, avoid, baffle, dodge, escape, eschew, evade, foil, frustrate, parry. ANT.—attract, confront, encounter, meet, solicit.

emanate, arise, come, emerge, flow, issue, originate, proceed, radiate, stem. ANT.—return, sink, withdraw.

emancipate, free, let go, liberate, release, set free. ANT.—confine, imprison, subjugate.

embarrass, abash, annoy, bewilder, bother, complicate, confound, confuse, discomfit, disconcert, distress, encumber, entangle, fluster, hamper, hinder, mortify, obstruct, perplex, plague, rattle, trouble, vex. ANT.—cheer, encourage, help, inspire, relieve.

embellish, adorn, beautify, deck, decorate, enrich, garnish, ornament, trim; exaggerate. ANT.—debase, defame, strip, obliterate; simplify.

embezzle, appropriate, cheat, defalcate, defraud, falsify, filch, forge, misapply, misappropriate, misuse, pilfer, plunder, purloin, rob, swindle. ANT.—balance, recompense, reimburse, return, satisfy.

emblem, brand, figure, image, representation, sign, symbol, token, trademark.

embody, codify, comprise, concentrate, contain, embrace, hold, include, incorporate, integrate, systematize. ANT.—discharge, disperse, disintegrate, exclude.

embrace, caress, clasp, encircle, hug; accept, adopt, espouse, receive, subscribe to, welcome; comprehend, comprise, contain, embody, include, incorporate. ANT.—exclude, reject, renounce, scorn, spurn.

emergency, casualty, crisis, dilemma, distress, exigency, juncture, pressure, quandary, strait, urgency. ANT.—conventionality, regularity, routine, stability, solution.

emigrate, abandon, depart, egress, escape, leave, migrate, move, part, quit. ANT.—dwell, remain, reside, stay.

eminent, celebrated, conspicuous, distinguished, elevated, exalted, famous, foremost, glorious, illustrious, noted, prominent, renowned, superior, supreme, well-known. ANT.—common, humble, insignificant, obscure, ordinary.

emit, breathe forth, discharge, eject, emanate, exhale, expel, express, hurl, issue, open, publish, report, shoot, spurt, utter, vent. ANT.—contain, retain, stop, suppress.

emotion, affection, feeling, impression, inspiration, mood, passion, presentiment, sensation, sensibility, sentiment. ANT.—apathy, dispassion, impassivity, indifference, insensibility.

empathy, affinity, appreciation, commiseration, compassion, insight, sensitivity, understanding. ANT.—insensitivity, unfeelingness.

emphatic, affecting, determined, effective, energetic, forceful, forcible, insistent, pointed, potent. ANT.—bashful, bland, modest, reserved, weak.

employment, business, calling, career, craft, engagement, job, occupation, profession, pursuit, service, vocation, work. ANT.—ennui, idleness, inactivity, laziness, leisure.

empty, bare, barren, destitute, devoid, foolish, hollow, hungry, meaningless, senseless, stupid,

unfilled, unfurnished, unoccupied, vacant, vacuous, void, worthless. ANT.—erudite, full, inhabited, occupied, replete.

enable, allow, authorize, empower, let, permit, sanction. ANT.—disallow, oppose, prevent.

enchant, bewitch, captivate, charm, enrapture, enthrall, entice, fascinate, ravish. ANT.—disenchant, disgust, offend, repel.

encompass, beset, circumscribe, encircle, enclose, enfold, envelop, environ, gird, hem in, invest, span, surround. ANT.—free, release, unwrap.

encounter, assailment, assault, attack, battle, clash, collision, combat, conflict, engagement, fight, invasion, meeting, onslaught, skirmish, struggle. ANT.—amity, avoidance, concord, consonance, harmony, retreat, union.

encourage, advise, animate, cheer, comfort, embolden, enliven, exhilarate, favor, hearten, impel, incite, inspire, inspirit, urge; foster, promote, sanction, stimulate, spur, support. ANT.—deject, deter, discourage, dispirit, dissuade.

encroach, attack, infract, infringe, intrude, invade, poach, transgress, trespass, violate. ANT.—abandon, avoid, evacuate, relinquish, shun.

encumbrance, burden, clog, drag, difficulty, drawback, hindrance, impediment, lien, load, mortgage, obstacle, weight. ANT.—advantage, assistance, incentive, stimulant.

end, aim, ambition, cessation, close, completion, conclusion, consequence, expiration, extremity, finish, goal, issue, limit, object, purpose, result, termination, terminus; cease, close, conclude, stop, terminate. ANT.—beginning, commencement, inception, introduction; inaugurate, institute, establish, start.

endanger, expose, hazard, imperil, jeopardize, peril, risk. ANT.—guard, protect, secure.

endeavor, aim, aspire, attempt, contend, contest, essay, exert, strive, try, undertake; labor, pains, strain, strife, struggle, toil.

endless, boundless, ceaseless, constant, continuous, eternal, everlasting, illimitable, immeasurable, imperishable, incessant, infinite, interminable, perpetual, unbounded, uninterrupted, unlimited. ANT.—bounded, finite, limited, transient, transitory.

endorse (also spelled indorse), assist, attest, authorize, back, confirm, corroborate, guarantee, ratify, recommend, sanction, secure, sign, subscribe, support, warrant. ANT.—admonish, censure, denounce, oppose, reject.

endowment, ability, attainment, benefaction, benefit, bequest, bounty, capacity, donation, empowerment, genius, gift, grant, gratuity, mentality, natural gift, provision, qualification, talent. ANT.—drawback, harm, injury, loss.

endurance, allowance, continuance, courage, diligence, firmness, forbearance, fortitude, long-suffering, patience, perseverance, persistence, resignation, resistance, stamina, strength, submission, tolerance. ANT.—faltering, succumbing, surrender, weakness.

enemy, adversary, antagonist, attacker, calumniator, competitor, defamer, defiler, falsifier, foe, opponent, predator, rival, slanderer, traducer, vilifier. ANT.—accomplice, ally, comrade, confederate, friend.

energetic, active, aggressive, animated, brisk, cogent, determined, diligent, dynamic, enterprising, forcible, industrious, lively, mighty, potent, powerful, spirited, strong, vigorous. ANT.—idle, lazy, listless, spiritless, vacillating.

energy, effectiveness, efficiency, force, might, potency, power, puissance, robustness, strength,

vigor, vim, vitality, zeal. ANT.—apathy, frailty, impotence, indolence, weakness.

enervate, attenuate, daze, debilitate, enfeeble, impair, injure, paralyze, reduce, sap, soften, weaken, weary. ANT.—animate, buoy, energize, invigorate, strengthen.

enforce, coerce, compel, constrain, drive, exact, execute, exert, force, impel, necessitate, oblige, persuade, press, require, strain, urge. ANT.—dismiss, disregard, give up, leave, omit.

enfranchise, emancipate, empower, enable, free, license, release, right, qualify. ANT.—disenfranchise, disqualify, revoke (license).

engage, busy, employ, engross, enlist, hire; bind, commit, pledge; mesh (with gears). ANT.—dismiss, release; decline, refuse; disengage.

engagement, appointment; battle, combat, encounter; betrothal, bond, commitment, compact, consenting, espousal, pledge, plighting.

engender, breed, cause, create, excite, fashion, form, formulate, generate, incite, make, originate, procreate, produce, reproduce. ANT.—annihilate, demolish, destroy.

engross, absorb, assimilate, bewitch, captivate, consume, engulf, fascinate, monopolize, swallow up; busy, engage, occupy. ANT.—dissatisfy, neglect, repel.

engulf, absorb, assimilate, bury, consume, deluge, drown, entomb, fill up, inundate, overcome, overflow, overwhelm, sink, swallow up. ANT.—discharge, dispense, emit, expel.

enhance, advance, augment, elevate, heighten, increase, intensify, magnify, raise, swell. ANT.—assuage, degrade, diminish, reduce.

enigmatic, baffling, cryptic, inscrutable, mysterious, puzzling, vague. ANT.—clear, explicit, obvious, open, plain.

enjoyment, bliss, comfort, delight, ecstasy, exultation, gladness, gratification, happiness, hedonism, indulgence, joy, liking, pleasure, rapture, satisfaction. ANT.—dejection, discomfort, misery, sorrow, unhappiness.

enlarge, add, amplify, augment, broaden, dilate, distend, expand, extend, grow, heighten, increase, lengthen, magnify, protuberate, spread, swell, widen. ANT.—abbreviate, abridge, condense, contract, diminish.

enlighten, brighten, clarify, communicate, disclose, edify, educate, elucidate, illuminate, illumine, illustrate, inculcate, indoctrinate, irradiate. ANT.—confound, confuse, darken, obfuscate, obscure.

enlist, attract, engage, employ, enroll, enter, get, hire, incorporate, induce, interest, join, obtain, procure, register, reserve, retain. ANT.—check, constrain, demobilize, deter, hold back.

enliven, animate, arouse, brighten, cheer, encourage, excite, exhilarate, gladden, quicken, refresh, rouse, stimulate, vivify. ANT.—dampen, debilitate, exhaust, sadden, stultify.

enmity, abhorrence, acrimony, animosity, antagonism, antipathy, aversion, detestation, disgust, hatred, hostility, illwill, invidiousness, malevolence, malice, malignity, rancor, repugnance, spitefulness. ANT.—affection, cordiality, friendliness, good will, love.

ennui, boredom, languor, listlessness, surfeit, tedium. ANT.—buoyancy, enthusiasm, energy, vigor.

enough, adequate, ample, full, plenty, satisfactory, sufficient. ANT.—deficient, inadequate, lacking, scant.

enrage, anger, chafe, craze, exasperate, goad, incense, inflame, infuriate, irk, madden. ANT.—appease, conciliate, soften, soothe, pacify.

enrich, adorn, beautify, embellish; cultivate, fertilize, improve; endow. ANT.—deplete, impoverish, reduce, rob, take from.

enroll, enlist, enter, inscribe, join, list, record, register, subscribe. ANT.—cancel, deactivate, discard, reject.

ensue, follow; succeed, come next; result. ANT.—forsake; precede; cause.

enter, penetrate, pierce, perforate; enlist in, enroll, join, register; encroach, intrude; begin, introduce, start. ANT.—depart, exit, vacate, withdraw.

enterprise, achievement, activity, adventure, business, commerce, endeavor, engagement, project, undertaking, venture, work. ANT.—inaction, indolence, passivity, sloth.

entertainment, amusement, diversion, enjoyment, fun, game, merriment, party, pastime, play, pleasure, recreation, social event, sport. ANT.—boredom, ennui, labor, toil, work.

enthusiasm, ardor, devotion, eagerness, earnestness, excitement, fervency, fervor, inspiration, intensity, optimism, passion, vehemence, vigor, warmth, zeal. ANT.—apathy, calmness, ennui, indifference, lethargy, pessimism.

entice, allure, attract, beguile, captivate, charm, draw, enchant, ensnare, fascinate, inveigle, lure, prevail upon, seduce, tempt, wheedle. ANT.—alienate, disgust, reject, repel, repulse.

entire, all, complete, intact, integral, perfect, total, unabridged, unbroken, undivided, unimpaired, unscathed, whole. ANT.—defective, deficient, incomplete, partial.

entrance, door, doorway, entry, gate, gateway, ingress, inlet, opening, portal; admission, beginning, commencement, initiation. ANT.—egress, exit, outlet; departure, exclusion, rejection, withdrawal.

entreat, ask, beg, beseech, implore, importune, petition, plead, request, solicit, supplicate. ANT.—command, compel, demand, force, take.

envelop, blanket, conceal, cover, embrace, enclose, encompass, enfold, hide, surround, wrap. ANT.—open, reveal, uncover, unwrap.

envious, cautious, covetous, displeased, invidious, jealous, malicious, odious, resentful, suspicious. ANT.—benevolent, charitable, helpful, laudatory, pleased, well-disposed.

environment, background, conditions, location, neighborhood, setting, surroundings, vicinity.

envoy, agent, ambassador, commissioner, delegate, diplomat, messenger, nuncio, plenipotentiary, representative.

epicurean, fastidious, gastronomic, luxurious, particular, sensual, sybaritic, voluptuous. ANT.—ascetic, austere, puritanical, self-denying.

episode, affair, circumstance, event, happening, incident, issue, occurrence.

epistle, communication, dispatch, lesson, letter, message, missive, note, writing.

epitome, abridgment, abstract, compendium, condensation, digest, summary, syllabus, synopsis, synthesis; embodiment, essence, ideal example of. ANT.—augmentation, development, expansion, extension, increment.

equable, calm, constant, equal, even, regular, serene, steady, unchanging, uniform, unruffled. ANT.—changeable, fluctuating, spasmodic, variable.

equal, adequate, alike, commensurate, equable, equitable, equivalent, even, fair, identical, invariable, just, like, same, uniform, unvarying; compeer, match, parallel, peer, rival, tie. ANT.—different, disparate, disproportionate, dissimilar, unjust; inferior, subordinate.

equanimity, balance, calmness, composure, evenness, poise, serenity, self-control. ANT.—agitation, anxiety, disturbance, excitation, perturbation.

equipment, accouterments, apparatus, array, furnishings, gear, material, outfit, paraphernalia.

equitable, fair, honest, impartial, just, objective, reasonable, unbiased, unprejudiced. ANT.—biased, dishonorable, fraudulent, inequitable, partial.

equivalent, alike, commensurate, equal, identical, indistinguishable, interchangeable, like, reciprocal, same, synonomous, tantamount. ANT.—contrary, disparate, dissimilar, opposed, unequal.

eradicate, abolish, annihilate, destroy, eliminate, erase, expel, exterminate, extinguish, extirpate, kill, nullify, oust, remove, uproot. ANT.—establish, fortify, foster, propagate, secure.

erase, cancel, cross out, delete, efface, eliminate, expunge, obliterate, rub out; abolish, abrogate, annul, invalidate, nullify, quash, repeal, rescind, revoke. ANT.—confirm, enact, perpetuate.

erect, unbent, upright, straight, vertical; build, construct, raise. ANT.—bent, cringing, crooked, horizontal, recumbent; raze.

erode, abrade, corrode, destroy, deteriorate, eat, gnaw, rub, wear, weather.

erotic, carnal, concupiscent, erogenous, libidinous, lustful, passionate, sensual, sexual. ANT.—celibate, passionless, spiritual.

erratic, aberrant, capricious, changeable, desultory, flighty, fluctuating, odd, peculiar, strange, uncertain, unreliable, unruly, wandering. ANT.—dependable, methodical, regular, reliable, steady.

erroneous, fallacious, false, faulty, inaccurate, incorrect, mistaken, unprecise, untrue, wrong. ANT.—correct, right, true.

error, blunder, deviation, fall, fallacy, fault, inaccuracy, indiscretion, misapprehension, misconception, omission, oversight, slip, transgression. ANT.—accuracy, certitude, correction, precision, truth.

erudite, cultured, educated, enlightened, knowing, learned, scholarly. ANT.—ignorant, illiterate, uneducated, unlettered.

eruption, commotion, discharge, efflorescence, explosion, outbreak, outburst; rash.

escape, abscond, break, decamp, defect, flee, fly; avert, avoid, elude, evade, shun. ANT.—confront, face, invite, meet.

escort, accompany, attend, chaperon, conduct, convoy, guard, guide, lead, protect, safeguard, serve, tend, squire, usher, watch.

especially, chiefly, definitely, mainly, particularly, primarily, principally, specially, specifically.

essay, article, composition, disquisition, dissertation, thesis; attempt, effort, trial.

essential, basic, characteristic, fundamental, indispensable, inherent, intrinsic, key, necessary, requisite, vital. ANT.—auxiliary, expendable, extrinsic, optional, peripheral.

establish, authorize, form, found, institute, organize, raise, set up; confirm, fix, ordain, sanction, settle, strengthen; confirm, demonstrate, prove, substantiate, verify. ANT.—abolish, demolish, overthrow, unsettle, upset; controvert, disprove, scorn.

estate, belongings, commodities, domain, effects, goods, holdings, inheritance, land, merchandise, possessions, property, stock, wares, wealth. ANT.—destitution, poverty, privation, want.

esteem, admiration, appreciation, approbation, approval, commendation, deference, favor, honor, praise, regard, reverence, sanction, value, veneration; estimate, rate, reckon.

estimate, appraise, assess, assign, calculate, compute, count, evaluate, measure, rate, reckon, value, weigh. ANT.—disregard, guess.

estrangement, alienation, disaffection, removal, separation, withdrawal. ANT.—affinity, alliance, bond, coalition, union.

eternal, boundless, ceaseless, deathless, endless, enduring, immortal, imperishable, infinite, never-ending, perpetual, timeless, undying, unending. ANT.—ephemeral, finite, mortal, mutable, temporal, transient.

ethical, decent, good, honest, honorable, just, moral, principled, righteous, scrupulous, virtuous. ANT.—amoral, corrupt, dishonest, licentious, unethical.

eulogize, applaud, celebrate, commend, compliment, extol, laud, praise. ANT.—condemn, degrade, demean, scorn.

evacuate, abandon, clear, desert, emit, empty, expel, leave, purge, quit, relinquish, retreat, vacate. ANT.—charge, enter, fill, occupy, take over.

evade, avoid, shun; dodge, equivocate, quibble; conceal, deceive, trick. ANT.—confront, face; confess, declare, verify.

evaporate, disappear, disperse, dissolve, dry, evanesce, fade, vanish, vaporize. ANT.—appear, consolidate, crystallize.

evaluate, appraise, assess, calculate, estimate, judge, rate, value, weigh. ANT.—guess, hazard.

even, flat, flush, level, plane, smooth; equal, unbroken, uniform, unvarying; calm, peaceful. ANT.—jagged, rough; broken, irregular; agitated, troubled.

event, affair, circumstance, episode, happening, incident, issue, milestone, occurrence; consequence, end, outcome, result. ANT.—antecedent, cause, origin, start.

everlasting, ceaseless, deathless, endless, eternal, immortal, imperishable, incessant, infinite, interminable, perpetual, timeless, unceasing, undying. ANT.—ephemeral, finite, mortal, temporal, transient.

evict, debar, deprive, discard, dispossess, eject, exclude, expel, oust. ANT.—accept, admit, receive, welcome.

evidence, confirmation, corroboration, data, demonstration, documentation, facts, grounds, indication, premises, proof, testimony, verification. ANT.—contradiction, disproof, fallacy, invalidity, refutation.

evident, apparent, clear, conspicuous, discernible, distinct, incontrovertible, indisputable, indubitable, manifest, obvious, open, overt, patent, perceptible, plain, unmistakable, visible. ANT.—concealed, covert, hidden, obscure, questionable.

evil, baseness, calamity, contamination, corruption, crime, depravity, disaster, harm, ill, immorality, iniquity, malignity, mischief, misfortune, offense, profligacy, sin, transgression, ungodliness, vice, viciousness, wickedness, wrong; base, deleterious, immoral, noxious, pernicious, sinful, vicious, wicked. ANT.—goodness, innocence, purity, virtue; honorable, moral, reputable.

evince, demonstrate, disclose, display, evidence, exhibit, indicate, manifest, prove, show. ANT.—conceal, hide, repress, suppress.

evoke, arouse, educe, elicit, excite, provoke, rouse, stimulate, summon, waken. ANT.—quiet, repress, silence, squelch, stifle.

exact, accurate, correct, definite, distinct, literal, methodical, particular, precise, punctual, rigorous, scrupulous, specific, strict, true, undeviating, unequivocal; demand, extort, wrest.

ANT.—approximate, careless, erroneous, inaccurate, vague, variable; request.

exaggerate, amplify, embellish, embroider, enlarge, expand, heighten, magnify, overdo, overstate, stretch. ANT.—depreciate, lessen, minimize, reduce, understate.

exalt, advance, aggrandize, applaud, commend, consecrate, dignify, elevate, ennoble, erect, extol, glorify, hallow, honor, laud, magnify, praise, raise. ANT.—degrade, dishonor, humble, humiliate, scorn.

examination, analysis, audit, check-up, exploration, inquiry, inquisition, inspection, interrogation, investigation, probing, query, quest, questioning, quiz, research, scrutiny, search, test, trial, review. ANT.—disregard, inattention, negligence.

example, archetype, exemplification, ideal, illustration, instance, model, pattern, precedent, prototype, representation, sample, specimen, symbol, typical case.

exasperate, aggravate, annoy, chafe, enrage, exacerbate, frustrate, incense, inflame, infuriate, irritate, nettle, provoke, vex. ANT.—appease, calm, mitigate, palliate, soften.

exceed, eclipse, excel, outdo, outstrip, surmount, surpass, top, transcend. ANT.—fail, fall behind, lag, tarry.

excellent, admirable, commendable, eminent, estimable, exemplary, expert, favorable, honorable, meritorious, peerless, prime, proficient, superior, surpassing, valuable, worthy. ANT.—inferior, lesser, negligible, poor.

except, barring, but, excepting, excluding, exempting, omitting, rejecting, saving. ANT.—admitting, embracing, including.

exceptional, infrequent, occasional, unusual; choice, extraordinary, incomparable, marvelous, novel, precious, rare, remarkable, scarce, singular, uncommon, unique, unparalleled, unprecedented, wonderful. ANT.—customary, frequent, ordinary, usual; abundant, commonplace, numerous, worthless.

excerpt, abbreviation, citing, clipping, culling, extract, quote, selection.

excess, extravagance, immoderation, intemperance, lavishness, luxuriance, plenty, profusion, redundance, redundancy, superabundance, superfluity, surplus, waste. ANT.—dearth, deficiency, lack, paucity, want.

exchange, barter, change, convert, reciprocate, substitute, swap, switch, trade, transfer. ANT.—preserve, retain.

excite, activate, aggravate, agitate, arouse, awaken, disconcert, disquiet, disturb, goad, incense, incite, induce, inflame, irritate, kindle, perturb, provoke, rouse, stimulate, stir up, taunt, unsettle. ANT.—allay, calm, pacify, quiet, tranquilize.

exclaim, call out, clamor, cry, cry out, ejaculate, proclaim, shout, vociferate. ANT.—murmur, mutter, whisper.

exclude, ban, bar, blackball, boycott, debar, except, expel, obviate, omit, ostracize, prevent, prohibit, reject, shut out, veto. ANT.—accept, admit, include, incorporate, welcome.

excruciating, acute, agonizing, extreme, grueling, intense, overwhelming, painful, racking, rending, severe, tormenting. ANT.—comforting, mild, pleasing, soothing.

excursion, digression, divergence, episode, expedition, jaunt, journey, outing, travel, trip, tour, voyage.

excuse, absolve, acquit, exculpate, exempt, exonerate, forgive, free, pardon, release, remit; alibi, apology, defense, explanation, plea, pretext, vindication. ANT.—convict, prosecute, punish; accusation.

execrate, abhor, berate, condemn, curse, damn, objurgate, reprehend, revile. ANT.—applaud, commend, extol, laud, praise.

execute, accomplish, achieve, administer, attain, carry out, complete, consummate, do, effect, finish, fulfill, obtain, perfect, perform, realize; behead, electrocute, guillotine, hang. ANT.—abandon, fail, neglect, omit, shelve.

exempt, absolved, clear, excluded, excused, free, freed, liberated, privileged, released, unbound, unchecked, uncontrolled, undrafted, unrestricted. ANT.—answerable, bound, compelled, nonexempt, obliged.

exercise, act, action, activity, application, drill, employment, exertion, lesson, operation, performance, practice, task, training, use; calisthenics, gymnastics. ANT.—idleness, indolence, relaxation, repose, rest.

exertion, attempt, effort, endeavor, grind, labor, strain, struggle, toil, travail, trial. ANT.—idleness, inaction, laziness, lethargy.

exhausted, consumed, depleted, drained, empty, faint, fatigued, jaded, spent, tired, wasted, wearied, weary, worn. ANT.—fresh, hearty, invigorated, rested, restored.

exhibit, demonstrate, disclose, display, evince, expose, flaunt, manifest, parade, present, reveal, show. ANT.—conceal, cover, disguise, hide.

exhilarate, elate, enliven, inspirit, invigorate, rejoice, stimulate, thrill. ANT.—deject, depress, discourage, repress, sadden.

exigency, crisis, demand, difficulty, distress, emergency, need, strait, urgency, want. ANT.—normality, regularity.

exile, banishment, deportation, expatriation, expulsion, extradition, ostracism, proscription. ANT.—admittance, welcome.

existence, animation, being, life, liveliness, reality, spirit, vigor, vitality, vivacity. ANT.—death, demise, languor, lethargy.

exonerate, absolve, acquit, clear, discharge, except, exempt, free, justify, release, relieve, restore, vindicate. ANT.—accuse, blame, censure, condemn, indict.

exorbitant, excessive, extravagant, extreme, inordinate, over-priced, unreasonable. ANT.—below cost, fair, inexpensive, moderate, reasonable.

expand, advance, amplify, augment, develop, dilate, distend, enlarge, extend, grow, increase, magnify, mature, spread, stretch, swell, widen. ANT.—abbreviate, atrophy, contract, diminish, shrink, wane.

expansion, development, dilation, distention, elaboration, enlargement, unfolding, unraveling; evolution, growth, maturing, progress. ANT.—abbreviation, compression, curtailment.

expect, anticipate, await, contemplate, envision, foresee, hope, look for. ANT.—despair of, doubt, fear.

expedite, accelerate, advance, dispatch, facilitate, forward, hasten, hurry, push, quicken, rush, speed, urge. ANT.—hinder, impede, obstruct, retard, slow.

expedition, campaign, cruise, excursion, journey, mission, passage, pilgrimage, quest, safari, tour, travel, trek, trip, undertaking, voyage; alacrity, speed.

expel, banish, discharge, dismiss, evict, excommunicate, exile, ostracize, oust, proscribe, remove; dislodge, eject, eliminate, excrete, void. ANT.—accept, admit, include, invite; absorb, take in.

expense, charge, cost, disbursement, expenditure, outgo, outlay, payment, price, upkeep, value. ANT.—gain, income, profits, receipts, revenue.

expensive, costly, dear, high-priced. ANT.—cheap, inexpensive, worthless.

experience, adventure, encounter, episode, happening, incident, meeting, occurrence; feeling, sensation; background, knowledge, practice, sagacity, seasoning, testing, wisdom. ANT.—ignorance, inexperience, lack of knowledge.

experiment, assay, attempt, endeavor, examination, exercise, practice, research, test, trial, undertaking.

expert, able, accomplished, adept, adroit, apt, clever, competent, ingenious, masterful, practiced, proficient, skilled, skillful. ANT.—awkward, bungling, incompetent, inexpert, maladroit, unskillful.

expire, cease, decease, depart, die, disappear, end, pass away, perish, sink, vanish. ANT.—commence, live, survive.

explain, clarify, decipher, elucidate, expound, illustrate, interpret, manifest, resolve, solve, teach, unfold, unravel. ANT.—baffle, cloud, confuse, mystify, obscure.

explanation, clarification, deduction, defense, elucidation, explication, exposition, excuse, interpretation, justification, key, solution.

explicit, clear, comprehensible, definitive, determinate, distinct, evident, exact, express, intelligible, lucid, manifest, obvious, plain, positive, precise, specific. ANT.—ambiguous, equivocal, hazy, obscure, vague.

exploit, adventure, bold act, deed, feat; accomplishment, achievement, attainment, performance, realization; manipulate, take advantage of, use unfairly. ANT.—neglect, omission; defeat, failure.

exposed, agape, ajar, open, unclosed, uncovered, unlocked, unmasked, unveiled; clear, passable, unobstructed; accessible, public, unrestricted. ANT.—concealed, hidden, suppressed.

expound, analyze, clarify, construe, elucidate, explain, express, illuminate, illustrate, interpret, lecture, present, state, teach. ANT.—baffle, confuse, darken, obscure.

express, clear, definitive, explicit, lucid, manifest, positive, specific, unmistakable; fast, quick, rapid, speedy; affirm, assert, avow, claim, communicate, declare, denote, designate, dispatch, explain, forward, propound, recite, represent, say, send, signify, specify, state, tell, utter. ANT.—ambiguous, equivocal, implied, obscure, vague; slow; conceal, restrain, retain, suppress, withhold.

exquisite, appealing, attractive, charming, choice, dainty, delicate, elegant, excellent, fine, matchless, perfect, precious, rare, refined, select, splendid, superb, vintage; beautiful, debonair, handsome, pretty; acute, intense, sharp. ANT.—common, ordinary, unrefined, worthless; ugly; dull, mild.

extant, contemporary, enduring, existent, existing, lasting, surviving, undestroyed. ANT.—departed, destroyed, extinct, gone.

extemporaneous, ad lib, extempory, informal, impromptu, improvised, informal, offhand, unplanned, unpremeditated, unprepared, unstudied. ANT.—designed, planned, premeditated, prepared, studied.

extend, add, amplify, augment, dilate, distend, enlarge, elongate, expand, lengthen, protract, spread, stretch; give, grant. ANT.—contract, decrease, loosen, reduce, shrink, slacken; take.

extensive, broad, expanded, sweeping, vast, wide. ANT.—confined, narrow, restricted.

extent, amount, compass, degree, expanse, length, magnitude, measure, range, reach, scope, size, stretch, volume.

exterior, cover, face, front, outside, shell, skin, surface. ANT.—core, inside, interior, internal (part).

exterminate, abolish, annihilate, banish, decimate, destroy, eradicate, expel, extirpate, kill, overthrow, uproot. ANT.—cherish, guard, maintain, preserve, protect.

external, exterior, extrinsic, foreign, outer, outside, superficial. ANT.—domestic, inside, internal, intrinsic, within.

extinguish, abate, abolish, annihilate, choke, destroy, eradicate, exterminate, extirpate, obscure, quench, suppress. ANT.—animate, ignite, kindle, light.

extol, celebrate, commend, eulogize, exalt, glorify, honor, laud, praise. ANT.—decry, disgrace, dishonor, profane.

extract, derive, distill, draw, educe, elicit, eradicate, evoke, extirpate, extort, obtain, pull, remove. ANT.—insert, instill, introduce.

extraneous, foreign, irrelevant, remote, strange, unconnected. ANT.—akin, germane, relevant.

extraordinary, egregious, exceptional, inordinate, marvelous, peculiar, phenomenal, rare, remarkable, singular, special, uncommon, unusual, unwonted, wonderful. ANT.—common, customary, ordinary, standard, usual.

extravagant, abundant, copious, excessive, extreme, exuberant, immoderate, improvident, inordinate, lavish, liberal, luxuriant, overflowing, plentiful, prodigal, profuse, wasteful. ANT.—economical, meager, parsimonious, penurious, sparse.

extreme, farthest, greatest, maximum, outermost, utmost; final, last, terminal, ultimate; extravagant, immoderate, intensive; fanatical, radical. ANT.—adjacent, near; calm, dispassionate; moderate.

extricate, affranchise, deliver, disengage, disentangle, free, let go, liberate, loose, ransom, release, rescue, unbind, unchain, unfasten, untie. ANT.—bind, chain, confine, incarcerate, restrain.

exuberant, abundant, copious, energetic, lavish, luxuriant, overflowing, profuse, prolific, rank, vigorous, wanton. ANT.—austere, barren, depleted, needy, sterile.

F

fabric, cloth, dry goods, material, organization, structure, stuff, substance, textile.

fabricate, arrange, build, compose, construct, counterfeit, devise, erect, fake, feign, forge, form, frame, invent, plan, prevaricate, produce, put together. ANT.—demolish, disrupt, ruin, shatter, wreck.

fabulous, amazing, astounding, exaggerated, extraordinary, false, feigned, fictitious, incredible, legendary, mythical, ridiculous, untrue. ANT.—common, credible, proven, usual, true.

facade, affectation, appearance, cover-up, false front, front, ornamentation, veneer. ANT.—base, character, sincerity.

face, appearance, countenance, features, mien, physiognomy, visage; assurance, audacity, boldness, confidence, effrontery, impertinence, impudence; brave, challenge, confront, dare, defy, meet, oppose, resist, venture; cover, exterior, front, outside, surface. ANT.—humility, timidity; shrink, retreat, withdraw; interior, rear.

facile, able, adroit, agreeable, apt, artful, clever, dexterous, easy, expert, flexible, proficient, skillful, smooth, tactful. ANT.—awkward, difficult, disagreeable, rude, tedious.

facilitate, allay, alleviate, assuage, ease, lighten, mitigate, relieve, soothe. ANT.—confound, distress, disturb.

facility, ability, adroitness, civility, cleverness, courtesy, dexterity, ease, expertness, proficiency, readiness, skillfulness. ANT.—awkwardness, difficulty, discourtesy, ineptitude.

facsimile, copy, duplicate, pattern, photograph, picture, replica, reproduction, transcript. ANT.—distinction, opposite, variation.

fact, actuality, certainty, evidence, reality, truth; act, circumstance, deed, detail, event, incident, item, occurrence, point. ANT.—fiction, supposition, theory, delusion, falsehood.

faction, block, cabal, circle, clique, combination, coterie, denomination, division, party, sect, wing. ANT.—conformity, entirety, homogeneity, unity.

factious, contentious, dissident, insubordinate, rebellious, recalcitrant, seditious. ANT.—cooperative, helpful, united.

factitious, artificial, bogus, counterfeit, fabricated, forced, phony, sham, spurious, synthetic, unnatural. ANT.—authentic, bona fide, genuine, natural, real.

factor, actor, agent, attorney, bailiff, commissioner, delegate, deputy, manager, proxy, representative, steward, vicar; constituent, element, part.

faculty, ability, aptitude, bent, capability, capacity, function, gift, knack, power, skill, talent. ANT.—impotence, inability, incapacity, incompetence, ineptness.

fade, bleach, blur, deteriorate, dim, disappear, dwindle, ebb, evanesce, pale, taper off, vanish, wane, wither. ANT.—darken, enhance, improve, recover, strengthen.

fail, abandon, abort, collapse, decline, default, defeat, desert, disappoint, drop, fade, flounder, leave, miscarry, neglect, omit, quit, wither. ANT.—accomplish, achieve, capture, deliver, recover.

faint, dim, faded, faltering, fatigued, feeble, inaudible, indistinct, irresolute, languid, listless, pale, powerless, thin, timid, weak, wearied, worn. ANT.—distinct, forceful, intrepid, strong, vigorous.

fair, bright, clear, dry, light, mild, pleasant, sunny; attractive, blond, comely, lovely; candid, decent, equitable, frank, honest, impartial, just, open, reasonable, unbiased; average, mediocre, passable. ANT.—foul, tempestuous, ugly, unattractive; devious, dishonorable, fraudulent, partial; excellent, first-rate, worst.

faith, assurance, conviction, credence, reliance, trust; belief, creed, doctrine, dogma, tenet; constancy, fidelity, loyalty, promise, word. ANT.—doubt, incredulity, mistrust, skepticism; infidelity.

faithful, attached, constant, dependable, devoted, firm, honorable, incorruptible, loyal, staunch, steadfast, true, unswerving, unwavering; accurate, reliable, trusty. ANT.—disloyal, false, fickle, treacherous, untrustworthy.

fall, abate, collapse, decline, decrease, descend, diminish, drop, ebb, lessen, plunge, sink, subside, weaken; stumble, topple, totter, tumble; droop, extend downward, hang. ANT.—arise, ascend, climb, reach, scale, soar.

fallacy, casuistry, delusion, equivocation, error, fantasy, illusion, misconception, mistake, sophistry, subterfuge, untruth. ANT.—certainty, fact, reality, truth, verity.

false, bogus, counterfeit, deceptive, dishonest, erroneous, fabricated, fallacious, illusory, incorrect, lying, mendacious, misleading, mock, pretended, sham, spurious, unreal, untrue.

ANT.—accurate, confirmed, substantiated, true, valid.

falter, delay, demur, doubt, flinch, fluctuate, hesitate, hobble, pause, reel, shrink, slip, stammer, stutter, totter, tremble, vacillate, weaken. ANT.— continue, endure, persevere, persist.

familiar, acquainted, cognizant, conversant, informed, intimate, knowing, versed, well-known; accessible, affable, amicable, approachable, casual, close, comfortable, courteous, easy, friendly, informal, sociable, unconstrained, unreserved; common, customary, usual; disrespectful, impudent. ANT.—constrained, distant, formal, reserved, unfamiliar.

famous, celebrated, distinguished, eminent, glorious, honorable, illustrious, noted, renowned, well-known. ANT.—ignominious, infamous, obscure, undistinguished, unknown.

fanatical, biased, bigoted, dogmatic, extreme, illiberal, intolerant, narrow-minded, obsessed, prejudiced, rabid, radical, unreasonable, zealous. ANT.—dispassionate, liberal, reasonable, tolerant.

fancy, conceit, conception, idea, imagination, notion; caprice, fantasy, vagary, whim; fondness, inclination; elaborate, ornamental, ornate. ANT.—actuality, reality; precision, stability; aversion; plain, unadorned.

fantastic, capricious, fanciful, far-fetched, imaginary, visionary, whimsical; bizarre, eccentric, odd, peculiar, quaint, strange, vague; amazing, wonderful. ANT.—fixed, precise, steady; common, ordinary, usual.

far, away, distant, remote, removed. ANT.—close, convenient, handy, near.

farcical, absurd, comic, droll, foolish, funny, hilarious, ludicrous, ridiculous. ANT.—sober, tragic.

far-sighted, clairvoyant, clear-sighted, foresighted, judicious, level-headed, prepared, prudent. ANT.—impractical, imprudent, injudicious, rash, unprepared.

fascinate, allure, beguile, bewitch, captivate, delight, enamor, enchant, enrapture, enthrall, entrance, ravish. ANT.—agitate, anger, disgust, repel, weary.

fashion, appearance, fashion, manner, mode, vague; cast, contrive, create, design, fabricate, form, make, manufacture, mold, sculpture, style.

fast, accelerated, brisk, expeditious, fleet, lively, quick, rapid, speedy, swift; constant, firm, inflexible, lasting, permanent, secure, solid, stable, steadfast, steady, tight, unswerving, unyielding; dissipated, dissolute, reckless, wild. ANT.—slow, sluggish; insecure, loose, unstable, unsteady; exemplary, upright, virtuous.

fasten, affix, anchor, attach, bind, connect, link, lock, secure, tie. ANT.—detach, loosen, open, release, untie.

fastidious, choosy, critical, finicky, fussy, meticulous, particular, squeamish. ANT.—gross, indifferent, tasteless, uncritical.

fat, beefy, corpulent, fleshy, obese, portly, rotund, stout, swollen, thickset, unctuous, unwieldy; luxuriant, rich, wealthy, well-to-do. ANT.—gaunt, lean, slender, slim, thin; indigent, penniless, poor.

fatal, deadly, lethal, mortal, murderous, pernicious. ANT.—animating, enlivening, invigorating, nourishing, vital.

fate, chance, consequence, fortune; destiny, doom, issue, lot, outcome, result; predestination, predetermination.

fatigue, debilitation, enervation, exhaustion, languor, lassitude, tiredness, weakness, weariness. ANT.—liveliness, rejuvenation, restoration, vigor, vivacity.

fault, blemish, defect, detriment, drawback, error, failure, flaw, foible, imperfection, misdeed, misdemeanor, mistake, omission, shortcoming, slip, weakness. ANT.—correctness, merit, perfection.

favorable, advantageous, assisting, auspicious, beneficial, conducive, helpful, propitious, salutary, useful. ANT.—detrimental, disadvantageous, harmful, hindering, opposed.

fear, alarm, apprehension, anxiety, cowardice, dismay, disquietude, dread, fright, horror, panic, phobia, scare, terror, timidity, trepidation; awe, reverence. ANT.—assurance, boldness, bravery, courage, fearlessness; nonchalance, unconcern.

feasible, achievable, attainable, practicable, practical, workable. ANT.—impractical, inconceivable, unrealistic, visionary.

feat, accomplishment, achievement, act, action, attainment, deed, execution, exercise, exploit, maneuver, operation, performance. ANT.—failure, inactivity, laziness, passivity, stagnation.

fee, account, bill, charge, compensation, cost, emolument, pay, payment, remuneration.

feeble, debilitated, decrepit, delicate, enervated, exhausted, faint, forceless, frail, impaired, infirm, languid, puny, sickly, weak. ANT.—forceful, hearty, lusty, stout, strong, vigorous.

feeling, consciousness, sensation, sense, sensitivity; affection, emotion, passion, sensibility, sentiment, sympathy, tenderness; conviction, impression, opinion. ANT.—anesthesia, unconsciousness; coldness, imperturbability, insensibility, stoicism; fact.

felicitate, compliment, congratulate, greet. ANT.—discourage, dismay, reject.

felonious, corrupt, criminal, depraved, evil, heinous, injurious, malicious, noxious, perfidious, perverse, vicious. ANT.—commendable, decent, honorable, meritorious, praiseworthy.

feminine, female, ladylike, maidenly, womanish, womanlike, womanly; delicate, soft, tender. ANT.—male, manly, mannish, masculine; hardy, strong, virile.

ferment, agitate, boil, bubble, concoct, embroil, excite, fret, heat, leaven, raise, roil, seethe, stir. ANT.—calm, cool, dampen, quiet, soothe.

ferocious, barbarous, brutal, brutish, cruel, fearsome, fierce, murderous, ravenous, vehement, violent, wild. ANT.—docile, gentle, harmless, manageable, tame.

fertile, abundant, bountiful, copious, exuberant, fecund, fruitful, luxuriant, plenteous, plentiful, productive, prolific, rich, teeming. ANT.—barren, childless, fruitless, sterile, unproductive.

fervent, animated, ardent, eager, enthusiastic, intense, passionate, zealous. ANT.—cool, grudging, hesitant, impassive, phlegmatic.

fetid, foul-smelling, malodorous, noisome, putrid, rank, repulsive, stinking. ANT.—aromatic, fragrant, perfumed, sweet-smelling.

feudal, dependent, downtrodden, enslaved, peasant, servile, subject, vassal. ANT.—aristocratic, free, independent.

fever, ardor, delirium, excitement, frenzy, heat, mania, temperature. ANT.—calmness, coolness.

fiasco, catastrophe, debacle, failure, miscarriage. ANT.—achievement, success, triumph, victory.

fickle, capricious, changeable, fanciful, fitful, inconstant, irresolute, restless, shifting, unreliable, unstable, variable, volatile, wavering, wayward. ANT.—constant, reliable, stable, steady, trustworthy.

fiction, allegory, creation, epic, fable, fabrication, falsehood, fancy, figment, imagination, invention, legend, myth, narrative, novel, parable, romance, story, tale. ANT.—fact, history, reality, truth, verity.

fidelity, adherence, allegiance, constancy, devotion, faithfulness, fealty, integrity, loyalty, obedience, steadfastness, support, zeal; accuracy, exactness, precision, truth. ANT.—disloyalty, faithlessness, inconstancy, perfidy, treachery.

fiendish, atrocious, cruel, demoniac, devilish, diabolical, infernal, inhuman, malicious, malignant. ANT.—angelic, benign, kindly.

fierce, angry, barbarous, brutal, dangerous, enraged, ferocious, fiery, passionate, savage, truculent, violent, wild. ANT.—docile, kind, peaceful, placid, tender.

fight, battle, box, brawl, combat, conflict, contend, contest, dispute, quarrel, scuffle, skirmish, squabble, strive, struggle, wrangle.

figment, fabrication, falsehood, fantasy, fiction, imagination, invention. ANT.—fact, reality, truth.

figure, allegory, amount, appearance, character, construction, design, emblem, form, metaphor, numeral, outline, picture, representation, shape, sum, symbol, type.

fill, fill up, occupy, pack, pervade; distend, feed, glut, gorge, load, permeate, sate, satiate, satisfy, saturate, stuff, swell. ANT.—deplete, drain, empty, exhaust, void.

filter, clarify, infiltrate, purify, refine, screen, separate, settle, strain.

final, concluding, conclusive, decisive, definitive, ending, extreme, last, terminal, ultimate. ANT.—first, inaugural, original, rudimentary, unending.

fine, admirable, attractive, choice, clarified, dainty, delicate, elegant, excellent, exquisite, keen, minute, nice, polished, pure, refined, sensitive, smooth, splendid, small, thin; ground, pulverized; amercement, charge, cost, forfeiture, penalty. ANT.—blunt, coarse, rough, unpolished, thick; amends, compensation, reward.

finish, accomplish, achieve, close, complete, conclude, consummate, end, execute, fulfill, get done, perfect, terminate; close, completion, end, termination, terminus. ANT.—begin, initiate, start; initiation, origin, source.

finite, bounded, circumscribed, determinate, limited, measurable, restricted, terminate. ANT.—endless, eternal, infinite, unbounded.

firm, constant, enduring, fixed, resolute, rugged, solid, stable, steadfast, steady, strong, tenacious, unfaltering, unyielding. ANT.—defective, disjointed, irresolute, wavering, weak.

first, beginning, chief, earliest, initial, leading, original, premier, primary, prime, primeval, primitive, pristine; chief, foremost. ANT.—hindmost, last, latest, least, subordinate.

fit, accommodate, adapt, adjust, conform, equip, prepare, suit; adapted, appropriate, becoming, befitting, competent, congruous, pertinent, prepared, proper, qualified, seemly. ANT.—disturb, misapply, misfit; awkward, inadequate, incongruous, unfit.

fitful, capricious, changeable, convulsive, desultory, fickle, inconstant, intermittent, restless, spasmodic, unstable, variable, whimsical. ANT.—constant, reliable, stable, steady, trustworthy, uniform.

fix, affix, attach, bind, fasten, link, place, plant, root, secure, set, stick, tie; define, determine, establish, limit, locate, prepare, set, settle; adjust, correct, mend, rectify, regulate, repair, restore. ANT.—displace, remove, unfasten; alter, change, disturb, modify; damage, mistreat.

flaccid, drooping, flabby, lax, limber, loose, soft, weak, yielding. ANT.—firm, strong, sturdy, tenacious, unyielding.

flagrant, atrocious, glaring, gross, infamous, monstrous, outrageous, rank, wicked. ANT.—mild, unrestrained.

flame, blaze, burn, flare, ignite, light. ANT.—extinguish, quench.

flashy, flamboyant, gaudy, garish, jazzy, meretricious, pretentious, showy. ANT.—simple, sober, subdued.

flat, even, flush, horizontal, level, plane; dull, insipid, stale, tasteless, vapid; dejected, depressed, heavy, low, spiritless. ANT.—hilly, irregular, mountainous, sloping; bubbling, exciting, frothy, savory; keen, spirited.

flatter, blandish, blarney, cajole, coax, court, entice, exalt, extol, fawn, laud, praise, soften, wheedle. ANT.—denounce, insult, mock, ridicule, spurn.

flaunt, blazon, brandish, expose, flash, flourish, parade, vaunt. ANT.—cloak, conceal, disguise, hide, retire.

flavor, essence, gusto, quality, relish, savor, soul, spirit, tang, taste, zest.

flawless, exact, immaculate, impeccable, perfect, pure, spotless, unblemished, unmarred, whole. ANT.—damaged, defective, flawed, imperfect, tainted.

fleeting, brief, ephemeral, evanescent, flitting, fugitive, momentary, passing, short, temporary, transient, transitory, vanishing. ANT.—constant, enduring, eternal, long-lived, perpetual.

flexible, bending, compliant, docile, ductile, elastic, limber, lithe, plastic, pliable, pliant, supple, tractable, yielding. ANT.—brittle, obstinate, rigid, stiff, unbending.

flicker, flare, fluctuate, flutter, glint, quiver, shimmer, waver. ANT.—glow, shine steadily.

flinch, cower, cringe, falter, recoil, retreat, run, shrink, wince, withdraw. ANT.—confront, face, hold out, sustain.

fling, cast, chuck, heave, pitch, throw, toss. ANT.—catch.

float, drift, fly, glide, hover, sail, skim, wave.

flourish, brandish, conquer, grow, increase, prosper, thrive, triumph, vaunt, wave, win. ANT.—collapse, decay, diminish, fade, weaken.

flow, circulate, course, float, glide, gush, move, pass, roll, run, spout, spurt, stream; emanate, issue, originate, proceed, progress, result; abound, be copious. ANT.—cease, cork, retard, stagnate, stop.

fluctuate, change, deflect, detour, deviate, digress, hesitate, oscillate, sway, swerve, teeter, totter, undulate, vacillate, vary, veer, vibrate, wander, waver. ANT.—adhere, decide, persist, remain, stick.

fluent, copious, easy, expert, flowing, liquid, moving, smooth, voluble. ANT.—hesitant, motionless, slow, sluggish, stammering.

flux, activity, change, discharge, flow, fluctuation, motion, mutation, transition. ANT.—constancy, fixity, inactivity, stability.

fly, ascend, flit, float, flutter, glide, hover, mount, rise, sail, skim, soar, wing; dart, rush, shoot, spring; abscond, decamp, escape, flee, run away. ANT.—descend, fall, plummet, sink; remain, stay.

focus, center, centrum, concentration, cynosure, limelight.

foe, adversary, antagonist, enemy, opponent, rival, vilifier. ANT.—assistant, comrade, friend, helper.

follow, come next, succeed; comply, conform, heed, obey, observe, practice; adopt, copy, imitate, mimic; accompany, attend; chase, pursue, trace, track, trail; ensue, result. ANT.—precede; guide, lead; avoid, elude, flee; cause.

follower, adherent, attendant, devotee, disciple, henchman, partisan, pupil, protege, pursuer, servant, successor, supporter, votary. ANT.—chief, head, leader, master; adversary, antagonist, objector, oppressor, scorner.

folly, absurdity, fatuity, foolishness, imbecility, imprudence, indiscretion, madness, misconduct, shallowness, silliness, simplicity, weakmindedness, weakness. ANT.—cunning, discernment, judgment, prudence, reasonableness, wisdom.

fondle, caress, cuddle, indulge, neck, nuzzle, pet, stroke, toy. ANT.—disdain, reject.

fool, cheat, con, deceive, delude, dupe, hoodwink, trick; buffoon, clown, harlequin, jester; blockhead, dolt, dunce, idiot, imbecile, nincompoop, numbskull, oaf, simpleton. ANT.—genius, philosopher, sage, scholar.

foolish, absurd, asinine, brainless, crazy, fatuous, idiotic, imbecile, irrational, nonsensical, preposterous, ridiculous, senseless, silly, simple, witless. ANT.—astute, judicious, prudent, sagacious, wise.

forbearance, abstention, abstinence, fortitude, leniency, patience, self-denial, tolerance. ANT.—excess, haste, impatience, intolerance, self-indulgence, strictness.

force, energy, intensity, might, potency, power, strength, vigor; coercion, compulsion, constraint, duress, violence; aggregation, armament, army, battalion, body, company, division, navy, number, organization, regiment, troops; coerce, compel, constrain, drive, impel, incite, instigate, push, rush. ANT.—feebleness, frailty, impotence, weakness; persuasion; hamper, retard, suppress, thwart.

forego, see FORGO.

foreign, alien, distant, extraneous, far, remote, strange, unaccustomed, unknown, unnatural. ANT.—accustomed, familiar, indigenous, known.

forever, always, continually, endlessly, eternally, everlastingly, immortally, unremittingly. ANT.—briefly, fleetingly, shortly, temporarily.

forget, disregard, ignore, lose, neglect, omit, overlook, slight. ANT.—recall, recollect, remember, reminisce.

forgo (forego), abandon, abstain, desist, leave, quit, relinquish, renounce, resign, waive. ANT.—accomplish, execute, fulfill, perform, yield.

form, assemble, build, construct, create, design, erect, fashion, forge, make, mold, produce, shape; compose, constitute, make up; arrange, combine, organize, plan; devise, frame, invent; conformation, figure, formation, structure; ceremony, ritual, image, likeness. ANT.—destroy, disfigure, dismantle, misshape, wreck; amorphism, distortion, irregularity, shapelessness.

formal, ceremonial, ceremonious, decorous, exact, functional, methodical, orderly, precise, proper, punctilious, regular, ritualistic, solemn, stiff, systematic. ANT.—casual, easy, natural, unconstrained, unconventional.

former, antecedent, anterior, before, foregoing, preceding, previous, prior. ANT.—after, ensuing, latter, succeeding, subsequent.

formulate, devise, concoct, express, fabricate, frame. ANT.—fumble, guess, hazard.

forte, feature, genius, knack, skill, strong point, talent. ANT.—clumsiness, impotence, incompetence.

fortuitous, accidental, casual, chance, contingent, felicitous, fortunate, happy, incidental, lucky, propitious, random. ANT.—arranged, calculated, deliberate, plotted, unlucky.

fortunate, advantageous, auspicious, benign, encouraging, favored, felicitous, fortuitous, fortunate, happy, lucky, propitious, prosperous, satisfied, successful. ANT.—cheerless, condemned, crushed, ill-fated, persecuted.

fortune, accident, chance, destiny, end, fate, goal, luck; determination, judgment; inheritance, possession, property, riches, wealth. ANT.—catastrophe, downfall, hardship, misfortune, poverty.

forward, advance, aggrandize, bring forward, cultivate, elevate, encourage, expedite, favor, further, help, promote. ANT.—hinder, oppose, retard, retreat, withhold.

foul, dirty, fetid, filthy, grimy, muddy, polluted, putrid, soiled, squalid, tainted; indecent, nasty, obscene, offensive, vulgar; base, contemptible, corrupt, despicable, low, mean, pitiful, shabby. ANT.—clean, immaculate, neat, presentable; pure, unblemished, wholesome.

foundation, base, basis, bottom, endowment, establishment, footing, ground, groundwork, institution, origin, root, substructure, support, underpinning, understructure. ANT.—arch, crown, peak, superstructure, top.

fraction, bit, division, part, percentage, piece, portion, section, segment. ANT.—all, entirety, total, whole.

fracture, breach, break, crack, rent, rift, rupture, split. ANT.—conjugation, juncture, union.

fragile, breakable, brittle, delicate, feeble, frail, infirm, weak. ANT.—durable, enduring, hardy, strong, sturdy, tough.

frank, aboveboard, candid, direct, easy, familiar, free, honest, ingenuous, plain, sincere, straightforward. ANT.—cunning, deceptive, dishonest, hypocritical, insincere.

fraud, artifice, cheat, chicanery, deceit, deception, dishonesty, duplicity, forgery, guile, hoax, imposition, imposture, swindle, treachery, trick. ANT.—fairness, honesty, integrity, sincerity, truth.

free, autonomous, emancipated, exempt, freed, independent, liberated, unconfined, unconstrained, unencumbered, unfettered, unobstructed, unrestricted; clear, loose, open, unfastened, unobstructed; immune; careless, candid, easy, familiar, frank, open, unreserved; artless, bounteous, bountiful, generous, liberal, munificent; costless, gratis. ANT.—confined, restrained, restricted; blocked, clogged, impeded; subject; illiberal, parsimonious, stingy; costly, expensive, priceless.

freedom, deliverance, emancipation, exemption, familiarity, franchise, frankness, immunity, independence, liberation, liberty, license, openness, prerogative, privilege, right, unrestraint. ANT.—bondage, coercion, compulsion, constraint, servitude.

freight, burden, cargo, lading, load, shipment, transportation.

frenzy, agitation, delirium, derangement, excitement, fury, madness, mania, rage, wildness. ANT.—calmness, delight, sanity.

frequent, common, general, habitual, many, numerous, often, persistent, recurrent, recurring, regular, repeated, usual. ANT.—exceptional, infrequent, rare, scanty, sporadic.

fresh, modern, new, novel, recent, unused; additional, further; brisk, cool, hardy, healthy, natural, refreshing, vigorous, young; artless, green, inexperienced, natural, raw; bold, cheeky, flippant, impertinent. ANT.—decayed, faded, hackneyed, musty, stagnant; courteous, deferential, respectful.

fret, agitate, anger, annoy, chafe, corrode, disturb, fidget, gall, gnaw, worry. ANT.—calm, placate, please, soften, soothe.

friction, abrasion, attrition, erosion, frication, grating, rubbing, traction; conflict, disagreement, discord, disharmony. ANT.—lubrication, smoothness; accord, agreement, harmony, unity.

friend, companion, comrade, confidant, crony, intimate, pal; adherent, advocate, defender, patron, supporter; ally, associate, colleague. ANT.—adversary, enemy, stranger.

friendly, affable, affectionate, amicable, brotherly, companionable, cordial, genial, intimate, kindly, neighborly, propitious, sociable, solicitous, sympathetic. ANT.—antagonistic, cool, distant, hostile, reserved.

frighten, abash, affright, alarm, appall, astound, browbeat, daunt, discourage, dishearten, dismay, dispirit, hector, horrify, intimidate, scare, startle, terrify, terrorize, threaten. ANT.—embolden, gladden, inspire, reassure, soothe.

frigid, arctic, chilling, cool, ice-cold; dull, formal, inhibited, lifeless, passionless, reserved, rigid. ANT.—temperate, warm; amorous, fervid, responsive, uninhibited.

fringe, border, boundary, edge, edging, flounce, outskirts, perimeter, tassel, trimming. ANT.—center, core, heart, inside, interior.

front, anterior, facade, face, forepart, prow, van; bearing, brow, forehead, manner, mien. ANT.—astern, back, posterior, rear.

frown, disapprove, glare, glower, lower, scowl, sulk. ANT.—approve, beam, shine, smile.

frugal, conservative, economical, miserly, moderate, parsimonious, penurious, provident, saving, sparing, stingy, temperate, thrifty. ANT.—extravagant, intemperate, self-indulgent, wasteful.

fruitful, abundant, ample, bountiful, copious, exuberant, fecund, fertile, luxuriant, plenteous, productive, prolific, rich, teeming, yielding. ANT.—barren, fruitless, impotent, sterile, unproductive.

frustrate, baffle, balk, bar, circumvent, confound, counteract, defeat, disappoint, disconcert, foil, hinder, nullify, prevent, stop, thwart. ANT.—accomplish, facilitate, fulfill, further, promote.

fulfill, accomplish, complete, consummate, finish, realize, terminate; discharge, perform; comply, fill, meet, satisfy. ANT.—abandon, disappoint, fail, neglect, withdraw.

full, crammed, filled, glutted, gorged, packed, replete, sated, satiated, soaked, stocked, surfeited, swollen; ample, complete, copious, extensive, plentiful, sufficient, whole; baggy, flowing, loose, voluminous; circumstantial, detailed, exhaustive. ANT.—depleted, devoid, empty, vacant; insufficient, lacking, partial.

function, bailiwick, business, duty, job, office, position, role, task; do, moderate, officiate, operate, perform, preside, serve, work. ANT.—idleness, unemployment; ignore, malfunction, mismanage.

fundamental, basic, chief, elemental, essential, indispensable, intrinsic, primary, principal, radical. ANT.—auxiliary, dispensable, secondary, subordinate, superficial.

funny, absurd, amusing, bizarre, comical, diverting, droll, farcical, humorous, laughable, ludicrous, ridiculous, witty; curious, odd, queer. ANT.—melancholy, sad, serious, sober, solemn.

furious, angry, ferocious, fierce, frenzied, fuming, inflamed, infuriated, raging, turbulent, violent, wild. ANT.—calm, composed, peaceful, self-possessed, tranquil.

furnish, appoint, cater, endow, equip, fit, outfit, provide, purvey, supply; afford, give, produce, yield. ANT.—denude, despoil, divest, strip, withhold.

further, advance, aid, assist, expedite, promote, support. ANT.—check, delay, frustrate, hinder, impede.

furtive, clandestine, covert, secret, sly, stealthy, surreptitious. ANT.—aboveboard, forthright, open, overt.

futile, abortive, empty, fruitless, idle, ineffective, ineffectual, resultless, unsatisfying, useless, vain, valueless. ANT.—beneficial, conducive, efficient, profitable, useful.

G

gain, accretion, acquisition, advantage, behalf, benefit, emolument, favor, good, increase, increment, interest, net, profit; accomplish, achieve acquire, attain, benefit, consummate, earn, effect, get, obtain, procure, profit, reach, realize, reap, secure, win. ANT.—decrease, handicap, loss; forfeit, lose, surrender.

galaxy, array, assemblage, bevy, cluster, collection, company, constellation, group.

gamble, bet, chance, hazard, play, risk, speculate, stake, wager. ANT.—insure, invest, plan, safeguard.

game, adventure, amusement, contest, diversion, entertainment, festivity, frolic, fun, gaiety, gambol, lark, match, merriment, merrymaking, pastime, play, recreation, sport; courageous, daring, disposed, favorable, sporting, valiant, willing. ANT.—business.

gamut, compass, extent, range, register, scope.

gap, abyss, aperture, breach, cavity, chasm, chink, cleft, crack, crevice, fissure, gulf, hiatus, hole, hollow, interstice, lacuna, opening, orifice, passage, space, vacancy, vacuity, void.

garble, corrupt, deface, distort, falsify, misquote, misrepresent, misstate, mix, muddle, mutilate, pervert, scramble. ANT.—clarify, communicate, correct, edit, unscramble.

garment, apparel, array, attire, clothes, clothing, drapery, dress, garb, habiliment, raiment, robe, vestment, vesture, wrap. ANT.—nakedness, nudity.

garner, accumulate, collect, deposit, harvest, hoard, husband, reserve, save, store.

garnish, adorn, array, beautify, bedeck, deck, decorate, embellish, enhance, enrich, furnish, grace, ornament, strew, trim. ANT.—debase, defame, expose, strip, uncover.

garrulous, babbling, bumptious, chattering, chatty, loquacious, prattling, prolix, talkative, verbose, wordy. ANT.—laconic, reticent, silent, taciturn, uncommunicative.

gather, accumulate, acquire, amass, assemble, collect, congregate, convene, convoke, group, meet, muster; compress, contract; cull, garner, glean, harvest, heap, pick, pile, reap; conclude, deduce, infer, judge. ANT.—disband, disperse, distribute, scatter, separate.

gaudy, cheap, flamboyant, flashy, garish, glaring, tasteless, tawdry, vulgar. ANT.—pale, refined, solemn, somber, tasteful.

gauge, calculation, caliber, criterion, diameter, evaluation, measure, norm, standard, template, thickness. ANT.—estimate, guess, hazard.

gaunt, attenuated, bony, emaciated, empty, flimsy, haggard, hollow, hungry, lank, lean, meager, scanty, scraggy, scrawny, shriveled, shrunken, skinny, slender, slight, slim, spare, thin, withered. ANT.—broad, bulky, fat, obese, portly.

gay, blithe, buoyant, cheerful, colorful, convivial, festive, frolicsome, glad, happy, hilarious, jolly, jovial, joyful, lighthearted, lively, merry, sprightly, vivacious, waggish. ANT.—depressed, glum, mournful, sad, sullen.

gaze, behold, discern, eye, gape, gawk, glance, look, peer, stare, survey, view, watch; examine, inspect, observe, regard. ANT.—avert, ignore, miss, overlook.

genealogy, ancestry, descent, lineage, parentage, pedigree, progeniture, stock.

general, all-embracing, common, commonplace, comprehensive, conventional, customary, everyday, extensive, familiar, frequent, generic, habitual, inclusive, indefinite, normal, ordinary, popular, prevailing, prevalent, regular, universal, usual, whole, widespread; indefinite, inexact, vague. ANT.—exceptional, rare, singular; definite, particular, specific.

generally, chiefly, commonly, mainly, ordinarily, principally, usually. ANT.—especially, occasionally, particularly, rarely, seldom.

generation, age, breed, creation, engendering, family, formation, procreation, production, reproduction; epoch, era, period, span, time. ANT.—breakdown, dissolution, obliteration, wreckage.

generic, characteristic, comprehensive, general, ideal, representative, typical. ANT.—individual, particular, peculiar, special.

generosity, altruism, beneficence, benevolence, bounty, bountifulness, charity, humanity, kindness, lavishness, liberality, magnanimity, munificence, nobleness, philanthropy. ANT.—cruelty, inhumanity, malevolence, selfishness, unkindness.

generous, beneficent, bountiful, forgiving, giving, high-minded, honorable, liberal, magnanimous, munificent, openhanded, open-hearted, unselfish, wholehearted. ANT.—covetous, greedy, miserly, selfish, stingy.

genial, affable, animated, brotherly, cheerful, congenial, convivial, cordial, fraternal, hospitable, pleasant, pleasing, warm-hearted, well-disposed. ANT.—doleful, inhospitable, moody, petulant, sullen.

genius, ability, acumen, aptitude, brains, brilliance, capacity, creativity, endowment, faculty, gift, inspiration, intellect, knack, leaning, perspicacity, propensity, sagacity, talent; intellectual, master, prodigy, wizard. ANT.—ineptitude, obtuseness, shallowness, stupidity; dolt, dullard, moron.

gentle, benign, calm, compliant, docile, genteel, meek, mild, moderate, pacific, peaceful, placid, relaxed, serene, soft, soothing, tame, temperate, tender, tractable. ANT.—fierce, harsh, rough, savage, violent.

genuine, actual, authentic, bona fide, exact, frank, honest, legitimate, natural, proven, real, sincere, tested, true, unadulterated, unaffected, unalloyed, unmixed, unquestionable, valid, veritable. ANT.—artificial, bogus, counterfeit, false, sham.

germ, beginning, first principal, origin, rudiment, source; bud, embryo, seed; spore; microbe, microorganism, pathogen. ANT.—conclusion, end, fruit, issue, outgrowth.

germane, allied, appropriate, apropos, cognate, fitting, pertinent, related, relevant. ANT.—inapplicable, irrelevant, unfitting, unrelated.

germinate, bud, develop, effloresce, evolve, grow, shoot, sprout, swell, vegetate. ANT.—die.

gesture, indication, motion, movement, portent, sign, signal, symbol.

get, achieve, acquire, arrive, attain, capture, comprehend, earn, gain, generate, grasp, learn, obtain, procure, propagate, reach, receive, secure, seize. ANT.—abnegate, forfeit, leave, renounce, surrender.

ghastly, ashen, cadaverous, dreadful, frightful, ghostly, grisly, hideous, horrible, pallid, revolting, shocking, terrifying. ANT.—attractive, captivating, healthy, pleasant, rosy.

ghost, apparition, banshee, fairy, goblin, haunt, image, phantom, shade, shadow, specter, spirit, sprite, spook, wraith. ANT.—essence, existence, fact, reality, substance.

giant, colossal, enormous, gigantic, huge, immense, monstrous, super, titanic, vast, whopping. ANT.—dwarf, infinitesimal, minute, stunted, tiny.

gift, alms, benefaction, bequest, bestowal, boon, bounty, charity, donation, endowment, favor, grant, gratuity, largess, legacy, munificence, present; provision, support; aptitude, faculty, genius, knack, talent. ANT.—deprivation, forfeiture, indemnity, loss; incapacity, ineptitude, stupidity.

gigantic, amazing, colossal, elephantine, enormous, extensive, gargantuan, great, huge, immense, mammoth, massive, monstrous, prodigious, stupendous, titanic, vast. ANT.—diminutive, insignificant, little, minute, tiny.

gimmick, adjunct, angle, contrivance, device, fraud, gadget, swindle, trick.

gird, arm, bind, clothe, encircle, endow, equip, fortify, furnish, girdle, invest, support, surround. ANT.—divest, loosen, release, strip, untie.

girth, boundary, cinch, circumference, corpulence, dimensions, measure, outline, perimeter.

gist, core, crux, drift, essence, import, meaning, pith, point, purpose, sense, significance, signification, substance, tenor, upshot.

give, bestow, bequeath, confer, contribute, convey, deliver, donate, furnish, grant, impart, present, provide, supply, yield. ANT.—deprive, keep, retain, seize, withdraw.

glad, blithesome, cheerful, cheering, content, delighted, exulting, gay, gratified, happy, jolly, joyful, joyous, lighthearted, merry, pleased, pleasing, vivacious. ANT.—dejected, depressed, dispirited, melancholy, sad.

glamour, allure, aura, bewitchment, charm, enchantment, fascination, magic, spell. ANT.—blandness, dullness, lackluster, obscurity.

glance, eye, gaze, look, scan, see; view, watch. ANT.—avert, hide, miss, overlook.

glare, beam, dazzle, flash, gleam, glimmer, glisten, glow, radiate, scintillate, sparkle, twinkle; frown, glower, scowl, stare.

glassy, bright, crystalline, glossy, lustrous, polished, silken, smooth, transparent, vitreous; dull-eyed, expressionless, limpid. ANT.—dim, lusterless, obscure, opaque, tarnished.

gleam, beam, blaze, flash, flicker, glare, glimmer, glance, glint, glisten, glitter, glow, radiate, ray, scintillate, shimmer, shine, sparkle, twinkle.

glib, articulate, diplomatic, facile, fluent, oily, polished, sleek; smooth, suave, urbane, vocal, voluble. ANT.—harsh, inarticulate, rough, rugged, stammering.

gloat, brag, boast, crow, exult, flaunt, rejoice, revel, triumph. ANT.—condole, commiserate, sympathize.

gloomy, cheerless, crestfallen, dejected, depressed, depressing, despondent, disconsolate, discontented, discouraged, dismal, dispirited, doleful, downcast, down-hearted, dull, funereal, glum, heavy, melancholy, miserable, moody, morose, oppressive, pessimistic, sad, somber, sorrowful, sullen, unhappy; clouded, dark, dim, dusky, shady. ANT.—cheerful, happy, joyous, merry, optimistic.

glorify, adore, applaud, bless, celebrate, consecrate, dignify, elevate, enshrine, enthrone, esteem, exaggerate, exalt, extol, hallow, honor, idolize, laud, magnify, prize, revere, sanctify, value, venerate. ANT.—abase, debase, degrade, dishonor, mock.

glorious, brilliant, celebrated, elevated, exalted, grand, high, lofty, magnificent, majestic, marvelous, noble, raised, resplendent, shining, splendid, sublime, supreme, wondrous. ANT.—atrocious, base, contemptible, ignoble, ridiculous.

glossy, elegant, glazed, lustrous, polished, refined, reflecting, shining, sleek, velvety; deceptive, showy, specious, superficial. ANT.—lusterless, rough, unpolished; genuine, honest, uncouth, unrefined.

glow, beam, blaze, burn, flame, flare, flash, flicker, glare, gleam, glimmer, glisten, glitter, light, radiate, scintillate, shimmer, shine, sparkle, twinkle. ANT.—die, fade.

glum, blue, dejected, dismal, dispirited, dour, gloomy, low, moody, morose, sulky, sullen. ANT.—amiable, buoyant, cheerful, joyous, merry.

glut, overfeed, overstock, oversupply; cloy, cram, deluge, flood, gorge, overeat, sate, satiate, satisfy, stuff, surfeit. ANT.—abstain, curb, deplete, empty, void.

glutinous, adhesive, cohesive, gluey, gummy, sticky, viscid, viscous. ANT.—clean, dry, glueless, powdery.

gnarled, contorted, knotted, knotty, rugged, twisted. ANT.—direct, plain, smooth, straight.

go, abandon, abscond, budge, decamp, depart, desert, disappear, exit, fade, flee, leave, move, pass, proceed, quit, recede, relinquish, retire, retreat, run, step, stir, travel, vanish, walk, withdraw. ANT.—arrive, come, enter, stay, stop.

goad, impel, pressure, prod, prompt, provoke, push, spur, urge. ANT.—deter, discourage, dissuade, restrain.

goal, aim, ambition, aspiration, desire, destination, end, hope, intention, object, objective; basket, end zone, finish line, target.

godly, consecrated, devotional, devout, divine, godlike, hallowed, immaculate, incorrupt, inviolate, pious, pure, religious, reverent, sacred, saintly, sinless, stainless. ANT.—corrupt, profane, sacrilegious, ungodly, wicked.

good, chaste, conscientious, exemplary, honest, incorrupt, moral, pure, reliable, reputable, righteous, sinless, upright, virtuous, worthy; admirable, commendable, excellent, genuine, precious, real, sound, valid; benevolent, gracious, humane, kind; agreeable, cheerful, friendly, genial, gratifying, health-giving, invigorating, pleasant; fair, honorable, immaculate, stainless, unspotted, untainted; auspicious, beneficial, favorable, profitable, propitious, serviceable, suitable, useful, valuable; able, capable, efficient, expert, proficient, skillful; adequate, ample, satisfactory, sufficient. ANT.—contemptible, evil, injurious, odious, vile.

goods, belongings, chattels, commodities, effects, freight, material, merchandise, property, stock, wares.

gorge, bolt, cram, fill, glut, gobble, sate, satiate, surfeit. ANT.—diet, fast, starve.

gorgeous, dazzling, glorious, grand, magnificent, majestic, resplendent, splendid, superb, surpassing. ANT.—common, homely, modest, plain, unpretentious.

govern, administer, command, conduct, control, curb, dictate, direct, dominate, guide, influence, lead, manage, mold, order, oversee, regulate, reign, restrain, rule, superintend, supervise. ANT.—acquiesce, assent, obey, submit, surrender.

graceful, beautiful, becoming, comely, congruous, dignified, easy, elegant, flowing, fluid, harmonious, lithe, nimble, pleasing, refined, smooth, supple, symmetrical, tasteful, trim, unaffected. ANT.—awkward, clumsy, gawky, ungainly, unrefined.

gracious, agreeable, amiable, beneficent, benevolent, compassionate, congenial, courteous, engaging, friendly, good-natured, hospitable, kind, merciful, mild, munificent, pleasing, tender. ANT.—acrimonious, churlish, disagreeable, ill-natured, surly.

grade, brand, category, denomination, genre, kind; order, rank, set, stage, step; hill, incline, slope. ANT.—sameness, uniformity; level, plane.

gradual, creeping, dawdling, delaying, deliberate, dull, inching, laggard, leisurely, progressive, sluggish, slow, step-by-step, tired, unintermittent. ANT.—abrupt, hasty, quick, rapid, swift.

graduate, end, finish, qualify; adapt, adjust, calibrate, measure, proportion, regulate.

graft, bud, scion, shoot, transplant; booty, bribe, corruption, favoritism, kickback, loot.

grandeur, augustness, dignity, greatness, loftiness, magnificence, majesty, pomp, splendor, stateliness. ANT.—humility, lowliness, simplicity.

grant, allocate, allot, apportion, appropriate, assign, bestow, confer, deal, dispense, distribute, divide, furnish, give, measure, mete, present, transfer; accede, agree, allow, comply, concede, concur, permit, yield; benefaction, endowment, gift, present, privilege, reward. ANT.—confiscate, damage, refuse, retain, withhold; oppose, reject, renounce; charge, decrement, deduction, forfeiture, loss.

graphic, clear, definite, detailed, distinct, explicit, forcible, illustrative, pictorial, powerful, striking, telling, vivid. ANT.—abstract, ambiguous, obscure, weak.

grapple, clasp, clinch, clutch, contend, hook, seize, struggle, wrestle; comprehend, understand, unite. ANT.—abandon, ignore, loose, release, surrender.

grasp, apprehend, arrest, capture, catch, clasp, clutch, grapple, grip, lay hold of, retain, seize, snare, trap; comprehend, discern, perceive, recognize, understand. ANT.—extricate, liberate, lose, release; misconstrue, misunderstand.

grate, abrade, creak, grind, pulverize, rasp, scrape, scratch; annoy, irritate, jar, vex. ANT.—comfort, placate, please, soothe.

grateful, appreciative, beholden, gratified, indebted, obliged, thankful; acceptable, agreeable, pleasing. ANT.—thankless, unappreciative; abusive, careless, rude.

gratification, comfort, consolation, contentment, delight, ease, enjoyment, fulfillment, happiness, indulgence, pleasure, relief, reward, satisfaction, self-indulgence, solace, succor. ANT.—affliction, discomfort, misery, sacrifice, submission, suffering.

gratis, free, freely, gratuitous. ANT.—costly.

gratuitous, free, groundless, spontaneous, unfounded, unprovoked, voluntary, wanton. ANT.—deserved, earned, merited, warranted.

grave, consequential, critical, heavy, important, momentous, serious, weighty; demure, dignified, earnest, intense, ponderous, sedate, sober, solemn, staid, thoughtful. ANT.—insignificant, trifling, trivial; airy, buoyant, frivolous, merry.

great, big, enormous, gigantic, huge, immense, large, vast; numerous, countless; celebrated, eminent, famed, famous, illustrious, prominent, renowned; critical, important, momentous, serious, vital, weighty; august, dignified, elevated, exalted, glorious, grand, honorable, majestic, noble; excellent, fine, magnificent, splendid; brave, chivalrous, courageous, daring, fearless, heroic, intrepid, valiant. ANT.—diminutive, little, minute, small; common, obscure, ordinary, unknown; menial, paltry, servile, shameful.

greedy, acquisitive, avaricious, covetous, grasping, grudging, illiberal, mercenary, miserly, parsimonious, rapacious, selfish; devouring, gluttonous, ravenous, stingy, voracious. ANT.—charitable, generous, munificent, philanthropic, sharing, full, satisfied.

greet, accost, address, approach, hail, receive, salute, speak to, welcome. ANT.—avoid, ignore, pass by.

gregarious, affable, amicable, companionable, convivial, friendly, hospitable, neighborly, outgoing, sociable. ANT.—antisocial, disagreeable, hermitic, inhospitable, unsociable.

grief, adversity, affliction, anguish, bereavement, calamity, catastrophe, distress, heartache, lamentation, misery, mourning, pain, sadness, sorrow, trial, tribulation, woe. ANT.—comfort, exhilaration, gladness, happiness, joy.

grievance, affliction, burden, complaint, damage, detriment, grief, hardship, harm, injury, injustice, sorrow, trial, tribulation, wrong. ANT.—benefit, happiness, justice, right, victory.

grieve, bemoan, bewail, deplore, lament, mourn, regret, rue, sorrow, suffer, weep; afflict, distress, pain, try, wound. ANT.—celebrate, rejoice, revel; console, heal.

grim, austere, dour, forbidding, gloomy, glum, inflexible, morose, severe, sinister, stern, sullen, terrifying, threatening. ANT.—blithe, enlivening, pleasant, serene, wining.

grip, capture, clasp, clutch, grab, grasp, hold, seize, snare, trap. ANT.—drop, loosen, relax, release.

grit, courage, decision, endurance, fortitude, mettle, nerve, pluck, spirit; abrasive, gravel, sand. ANT.—cowardice, fear, timidity.

groan, complain, cry, growl, grumble, lament, moan, sigh, sob, wail. ANT.—applaud, cheer, laugh, rejoice, sing.

grope, attempt, finger, fumble, grapple, hesitate, search, try. ANT.—comprehend, perceive.

gross, aggregate, entire, total, whole; brutal, enormous, glaring, grievous, manifest, plain; coarse, crass, earthy, indelicate, lewd, obscene, repulsive; rough, rude, vulgar; big, bulky, corpulent, fat, fleshy, great, large, monstrous, obese, thick. ANT.—proper, refined; moral, purified, spiritual; appealing, comely, delicate.

grotesque, absurd, bizarre, fantastic, incongruous, misshapen, monstrous, odd, strange, unnatural. ANT.—average, customary, normal, typical, usual.

grouch, complain, grumble, lament, murmur, mutter, mope, protest, remonstrate, repine, sulk, whine. ANT.—applaud, approve, praise, rejoice.

ground, base, basis, bottom, foundation, groundwork, support, underpinning; assumption, postulate, premise, presumption, presupposition, principle; land, locality, property, region, territory; base, establish, fix, set, settle; educate, instruct, train. ANT.—derivative, superstructure, trimming; demolish, unsettle.

group, aggregation, assemblage, assembly, audience, band, brood, bunch, class, clique, cluster, collection, company, crowd, flock, herd,

horde, lot, meeting, mob, order, pack, party, set, swarm, throng, troupe.

groveling, abject, begging, contemptible, debased, crawling, cringing, cowering, crouching, despicable, dishonorable, fawning, ignoble, ignominious, low, lowly, mean, menial, servile, sneaking, snivelling, sordid, vile, vulgar. ANT.—commanding, controlling, esteemed, exalted, righteous.

grow, advance, accumulate, amplify, augment, bud, burgeon, develop, dilate, distend, enlarge, expand, extend, germinate, increase, inflate, mature, puff, stretch, swell, thicken, tumefy; breed, cultivate, farm, nurture, plant, raise, sow. ANT.—atrophy, contract, decay, diminish, shrink, stagnate; destroy, kill.

growl, bemoan, complain, groan, grumble, howl, mumble, murmur, mutter, snarl. ANT.—hum, purr, sing.

growth, accretion, advancement, development, elaboration, expansion, extension, increase, unfolding, unraveling; evolution, maturing, multiplication, progress, proliferation. ANT.—abbreviation, compression, curtailment, decline, failure.

grudge, animosity, aversion, detestation, enmity, grievance, hatred, hostility, ill will, malevolence, malice, malignity, rancor, resentment, resistance, spite. ANT.—affection, kindness, love, sympathy, toleration.

gruff, abrupt, acrimonious, blunt, brusque, churlish, coarse, cross, curt, harsh, morose, rough, rude, short, snappish, snarling, sour, stern, surly, unceremonious, uncivil, unpolished. ANT.—affable, complaisant, gracious, polished, serene.

guarantee, security, surety, warranty; affirm, allege, assert, attest, certify, declare, endorse, insure, guard, support, testify, verify, vouch, warrant. ANT.—deny, disown, ignore, reject, renounce.

guard, conceal, cover, curtain, defend, disguise, envelop, fortify, hide, mask, preserve, protect, safeguard, screen, secure, shield, shroud, treasure, veil. ANT.—disregard, divulge, expose, neglect, reveal.

guess, assume, believe, conjecture, estimate, fancy, imagine, opine, reckon, speculate, suppose, surmise. ANT.—ascertain, calculate, know, measure.

guide, conduct, control, direct, govern, lead, manage, pilot, regulate, shepherd, steer, supervise. ANT.—abandon, misguide, mislead, neglect.

guile, artifice, beguilement, cheat, chicanery, cunning, deceit, deception, dishonesty, double-dealing, duplicity, fraud, hypocrisy, imposture, sham, slyness, subtlety, trick, wiliness. ANT.—candor, honesty, integrity, openness, sincerity, truthfulness.

guilty, blameworthy, censurable, corrupt, criminal, culpable, faulty, immoral, liable, sinful, stained, tarnished, wicked. ANT.—blameless, faultless, innocent, innocuous, spotless.

guise, air, appearance, aspect, behavior, clothing, custom, demeanor, dress, garb, look, manner, mien, pose, posture, practice, role, semblance.

gush, burst, flood, flow, issue, pour, rave, spout, spurt. ANT.—fade, stop, trickle, wane.

H

habit, addiction, continuation, custom, fashion, manner, method, mode, observance, practice, prevalence, routine, style, use, way, wont; clothes, dress, garb, raiment.

habitual, accustomed, common, customary, established, frequent, general, often, perpetual, persistent, recurrent, regular, usual. ANT.—

exceptional, infrequent, rare, uncommon, unique.

hack, botch, break, chip, chop, cut, drudge, lacerate, mangle, mutilate, split, tear, toil.

haggard, careworn, debilitated, emaciated, exhausted, fretted, gaunt, hollow-eyed, wasted, weak, weary. ANT.—exuberant, forcible, powerful, robust, vigorous.

haggle, bargain, cavil, deal, dicker, patter, quibble, stickle, wrangle.

hail, acclaim, accost, address, applaud, approach, cheer, greet, herald, honor, salute, summon, welcome. ANT.—avoid, disregard, ignore, scorn, shun.

hale, chipper, healthy, hearty, lusty, robust, salubrious, salutary, sound, strong, vigorous, well, wholesome. ANT.—delicate, diseased, feeble, frail, infirm.

half-hearted, cool, dull, indifferent, perfunctory, unenthusiastic, uninterested. ANT.—ardent, enthusiastic, warm, wholehearted, zealous.

hall, atrium, auditorium, building, corridor, dormitory, edifice, entrance, headquarters; house, manor, mansion, passage, residence, vestibule.

hallow, aggrandize, bless, consecrate, dignify, elevate, ennoble, erect, exalt, extol, glorify, raise, reverse, sanctify, venerate. ANT.—debase, degrade, curse, dishonor, humble.

hallucination, aberration, chimera, delusion, fantasy, illusion, mirage, phantasm, vision. ANT.—existence, reality, truth.

halt, arrest, bar, cease, check, close, cork, desist, discontinue, doubt, end, falter, hesitate, hinder, impede, intermit, interrupt, linger, obstruct, pause, stop, suspend, terminate. ANT.—advance, persevere, proceed, promote, speed.

hamper, encumber, hinder, impede, obstruct, perplex, prevent, restrain, restrict, retard, shackle, thwart. ANT.—assist, ease, facilitate, promote, relieve.

handicap, burden, defect, disadvantage, drag, encumbrance, impediment, limitation, obstruction, penalty; allowance, odds. ANT.—advantage, asset, benefit, remuneration, reward.

handle, direct, feel, finger, manage, manipulate, negotiate, operate, ply, wield; cope.

handsome, attractive, beauteous, beautiful, charming, comely, elegant, fair, fine, good-looking, graceful, lovely, pretty, shapely; ample, generous, large, liberal. ANT.—foul, hideous, homely, repulsive; insignificant, mean, poor, small.

handy, able, accessible, adapted, adept, adroit, advantageous, appropriate, available, clever, commodious, convenient, dexterous, favorable, fitting, helpful, ready, resourceful, skilled, skillful, suitable, timely, useful. ANT.—awkward, inconvenient, inopportune, troublesome, unskilled.

hang, attach, dangle, depend, drape, droop, hover, lean, suspend, swing; execute, gibbet, lynch.

happen, accrue, arrive, bechance, befall, betide, chance, come, ensue, eventuate, follow, occur, result, supervene, take place, transpire.

happiness, beatitude, blessedness, bliss, contentment, delight, ecstasy, exultation, felicity, gladness, merriment, mirth, peace, pleasure, rapture, satisfaction, wellbeing. ANT.—adversity, catastrophe, despair, grief, misery.

happy, blessed, blissful, blithe, bright, buoyant, cheerful, contented, delighted, delightful, ecstatic, elated, exhilarated, favorable, fortunate, gay, glad, gratified, jocund, jovial, joyful, joyous, merry, mirthful, opportune, pleasing, propitious, prosperous, rapturous, spirited, successful, thrilled, vivacious. ANT.—depressed, distressed, gloomy, heartsick, morose.

harass, aggravate, agitate, anger, annoy, badger, bother, calumniate, chafe, deride, disturb, enrage, exasperate, harry, incense, inflame, infuriate, irritate, molest, nag, nettle, pester, plague, provoke, rouse, ruffle, tantalize, taunt, tease, torment, traduce, twit, vex, vilify, worry. ANT.—comfort, delight, encourage, gratify, soothe.

harbor, cherish, contain, cover, foster, guard, house, nurture, protect, shield. ANT.—banish, eject, exile, expel.

hard, compact, concrete, durable, firm, impenetrable, impervious, rigid, solid, stable, steady, strong; arduous, burdensome, difficult, laborious, onerous, toilsome, tough, troublesome; intricate, perplexing, puzzling; austere, cruel, demanding, exacting, grinding, harsh, pitiless, rigorous, severe, stern, strict, unfeeling, unforgiving, unrelenting. ANT.—elastic, flabby, fluid, plastic, pliable, soft; easy, effortless, facile; compassionate, gentle, tender.

harden, anneal, cool, ossify, petrify, solidify, stiffen, toughen; accustom, brace, confirm, discipline, fortify, habituate, inure, season, steel, train. ANT.—melt, soften, warm; coddle, indulge, pamper, spoil.

hardship, adversity, affliction, burden, calamity, catastrophe, disaster, distress, injustice, misery, misfortune, oppression, ordeal, privation, suffering, trial, tribulation, trouble. ANT.—alleviation, assistance, blessing, consolation, profit.

hardy, brave, courageous, enduring, fearless, intrepid, resistant, robust, tenacious, undaunted, unyielding, vigorous. ANT.—delicate, feeble, infirm, puny, weak.

harm, abuse, damage, deprivation, deterioration, detriment, evil, hurt, ill, impairment, infliction, injury, loss, mischief, misfortune, mishap, wrong. ANT.—advancement, benefit, boon, favor.

harmful, baneful, damaging, deleterious, detrimental, hurtful, injurious, mischievous, noxious, pernicious, prejudicial, ruinous. ANT.—advantageous, beneficial, healing, helpful, profitable.

harmless, blameless, dependable, faultless, incorrupt, innocuous, inoffensive, protected, pure, reliable, safe, secure, trustworthy, undefiled. ANT.—dangerous, hazardous, injurious, perilous, unsafe.

harmony, agreement, alliance, coincidence, concord, concurrence, consonance, unanimity, understanding, unison; adaptation, concordance, congruity, consistency; amity, agreeableness, compatibility, suitableness. ANT.—conflict, disagreement, discord, dissension, variance.

harsh, abusive, acrimonious, austere, bitter, blunt, brutal, caustic, coarse, cutting, exacting, grating, gruff, hard, harsh, heartless, jarring, overbearing, rigorous, rough, rugged, severe, stern, strict, stringent, uncivil, unfeeling. ANT.—courteous, gentle, melodious, mild, soft.

harvest, crop, fruit, proceeds, produce, product, reaping, result, return, store, yield; consequence, effect, outcome, result; acquire, gain, garner, gather, glean, reap. ANT.—lose, plant, sow, squander.

hassle, argument, brawl, controversy, disagreement, dispute, fight, melee, quarrel, scrap, wrangle. ANT.—agreement, harmony.

haste, acceleration, briskness, celerity, dispatch, expedition, fleetness, flurry, hurry, quickness, rapidity, rush, speed, swiftness, urgency, velocity; accelerate, expedite, hurry, precipitate,

press, quicken, urge. ANT.—delay, lingering, slowness, tarrying; decelerate, delay, procrastinate, retard.

hasten, accelerate, expedite, hurry, hustle, precipitate, quicken, race, run, rush, speed, spur. ANT.—delay, detain, prolong, retard, tarry.

hasty, brisk, cursory, fast, hurried, lively, precipitate, quick, rapid, rushing, speedy, swift; careless; excitable, foolhardy, impatient, imprudent, impulsive, indiscreet, irascible, rash, reckless, sharp, testy. ANT.—slow, sluggish; cautious, judicious, patient, thoughtful.

hate, abhor, abominate, despise, detest, dislike, execrate, loathe. ANT.—admire, cherish, like, love, revere.

hatred, abhorrence, acrimony, animosity, antipathy, aversion, bitterness, detestation, dislike, enmity, grudge, hostility, ill will, loathing, malevolence, malice, malignity, odium, rancor, repugnance. ANT.—admiration, affection, friendship, love, reverence.

haughty, arrogant, cavalier, contemptuous, disdainful, egotistical, overbearing, proud, supercilious, swaggering, vain. ANT.—ashamed, humble, lowly, meek, unpretentious.

haul, deliver, drag, draw, lug, pull, tow, trail, tug. ANT.—drive, impel, shove, thrust.

haunt, attend, frequent, return (to); visit; disturb, frighten, obsess, persecute, terrorize; follow, importune, resort.

hauteur, arrogance, contempt, disdain, haughtiness, loftiness, pomp, pride, sauciness, scorn, superciliousness. ANT.—condescension, humility, lowliness, plainness.

have, carry, control, get, hold, obtain, occupy, maintain, own, possess, seize, take. ANT.—abandon, lack, lose, need, surrender.

haven, anchorage, asylum, harbor, port, refuge, retreat, shelter.

hazard, casualty, chance, contingency, danger, gamble, jeopardy, peril, risk, uncertainty, venture. ANT.—certainty, immunity, protection, safety, security.

hazardous, critical, dangerous, fearful, insecure, menacing, perilous, precarious, risky, threatening, uncertain, unsafe. ANT.—assured, firm, protected, safe, secure.

hazy, ambiguous, cloudy, dim, foggy, gauzy, indefinite, indistinct, murky, nebulous, obscure, uncertain, unclear, undetermined, unsettled, vague, wavering. ANT.—clear, explicit, lucid, precise, specific.

head, boss, chief, commander, director, foreman, leader, manager, master, principal, ruler; acme, apex, crest, crown, culmination, peak, pinnacle, summit, top; crisis, culmination; capacity, instinct, mind, understanding. ANT.—follower, subordinate; base, bottom, foot; incapacity, incompetence.

heal, cure, fix, harmonize, knit, mend, reconcile, remedy, repair, restore, soothe. ANT.—break, damage, harm, injure.

healthy, bracing, hale, hearty, invigorating, lusty, robust, sound, strong, vigorous, virile, well; beneficial, harmless, healing, hygienic, nutritious, salubrious, salutary, sanitary, wholesome. ANT.—delicate, frail, infirm; injurious, insalubrious, noxious.

heap, accrue, accumulate, add, aggregate, amass, augment, bank, collect, enlarge, expand, gather, hoard, increase, load, stock, store, swell; bestow, cast, give. ANT.—diminish, disperse, dissipate, minimize, scatter.

hear, attend, audit, consider, harken, heed, judge, learn, listen, monitor, note, regard.

heart, center, core, essence, focus, kernel, middle, midpoint, midst, nub, nucleus, pith. ANT.—

border, exterior, outside, outskirts, periphery, rim.

heartache, affliction, anguish, distress, grief, heartbreak, lamentation, misery, misfortune, mourning, sadness, sorrow, trial, tribulation, woe. ANT.—blitheness, comfort, happiness, joy, solace.

heartbroken, abject, comfortless, desolate, disconsolate, discouraged, disheartened, distressed, forlorn, miserable, pitiable, wretched. ANT.—consoled, contented, fortunate, happy, joyful.

hearty, ardent, cheerful, cordial, enthusiastic, friendly, genial, glowing, gracious, sincere, sociable, warm; healthy, robust, sturdy, vigorous; earnest, genuine. ANT.—aloof, cool, reserved, taciturn; feeble, weak; deceptive, hypocritical, insincere.

heat, caloric, warmth, torridity; ardor, enthusiasm, excitement, fervency, fervor, fever, fire, impetuosity, intensity, passion, vehemence, zeal. ANT.—cold, frigidity, gelidity; apathy, lethargy, stoicism.

heathen, godless, heathenish, infidel, irreligious, pagan, paganic, unbelieving, unconverted. ANT.—believer, Christian, Jewish, Moslem.

heave, billow, bulge, elevate, hoist, lift, raise, rise, surge, swell, throw, toss, vomit. ANT.—ebb, lower, recede.

heavy, bulky, massive, ponderous, unwieldy, weighty; burdensome, cumbersome, grievous, onerous, oppressive, severe, troublesome, trying, vexatious; depressed, dull, gloomy, grave, sad, serious, sluggish. ANT.—inconsiderable, light; animated, brisk.

hectic, agitated, excited, feverish, flustered, nervous, restless, unsettling. ANT.—calm, cool, serene, unhurried.

heed, alertness, attachment, attention, care, caution, circumspection, consideration, devotion, mindfulness, notice, observance, vigilance, watchfulness; application, concentration, contemplation, reflection, study; attend, consider, contemplate, deliberate, examine, meditate, mind, notice, ponder, reflect, study, weigh; esteem, regard, respect. ANT.—apathy, indifference, omission; ignore, neglect, overlook.

height, acme, apex, culmination, peak, summit, zenith; altitude, loftiness; elevation; eminence, prominence, stature. ANT.—base, depth, floor, lowliness.

heighten, advance, amplify, augment, enhance, improve, increase, intensify, magnify, strengthen. ANT.—decrease, diminish, lessen, reduce, traduce.

heir, beneficiary, inheritor, legatee, scion, successor.

help, abet, aid, assist, benefit, cooperate, encourage, foster, nourish, succor, support, sustain, uphold; facilitate, further, improve, promote; alleviate, ameliorate, mitigate, relieve, remedy. ANT.—discourage, impede, thwart; arrest, counteract, hinder; afflict, injure.

herald, announce, declare, foretell, inform, introduce, precede, proclaim, publish. ANT.—silence, stifle, suppress.

herd, assemblage, drove, clock, gathering, group, horde, mob, multitude, school, throng.

hereditary, ancestral, congenital, constitutional, genetic, inherent, inherited, innate, patrimonial, transmitted. ANT.—acquired, bought, earned, won.

heretic, apostate, dissenter, nonconformist, nonjuror, renegade, schismatic, sectarian, sectary, secularist, separatist, traitor, unbeliever. ANT.—believer, loyalist.

hermetic, air-tight, sealed; cabalistic, emblematic, mysterious, occult. ANT.—clear, obvious, open, plain.

heroic, audacious, bold, brave, chivalrous, courageous, daring, dauntless, fearless, gallant, intrepid, majestic, noble, undaunted, valiant, valorous. ANT.—cowardly, cringing, fearful, spiritless, timid.

hesitate, defer, delay, demur, doubt, falter, fear, fluctuate, pause, question, scruple, stall, stammer, stutter, vacillate, wait, waver. ANT.—continue, decide, persevere, proceed, resolve, tackle.

heterogeneous, conglomerate, contrary, contrasted, different, discordant, dissimilar, mingled, mixed, nonhomogeneous, unlike, variant. ANT.—homogeneous, identical, same, uniform, unvarying.

hidden, abstruse, concealed, covert, esoteric, latent, masked, quiescent, recondite, secret, undeveloped, unrevealed, unseen. ANT.—conspicuous, evident, explicit, exposed, manifest, visible.

hide, bury, camouflage, cloak, conceal, cover, curtain, disguise, dissemble, mask, screen, secrete, sequester, shade, shield, shroud, suppress, veil, withhold. ANT.—disclose, divulge, exhibit, expose, reveal.

hideous, abhorrent, abominable, awful, disgusting, dreadful, frightful, ghastly, grim, grisly, horrible, loathsome, monstrous, nauseating, putrid, repellent, repulsive, revolting, shocking, terrifying, ugly. ANT.—alluring, captivating, delightful, soothing, splendid.

high, elevated, lofty, raised, tall, towering; eminent, exalted, noble; arrogant, boastful, bumptious, conceited, haughty, ostentatious, proud; costly, expensive; acute, intense, shrill, strident, strong; happy, intoxicated, merry. ANT.—short, stunted, tiny; base, low, mean; humble, meek; cheap, inexpensive; mild, weak; sober.

hilarious, blithe, gay, gleeful, jocund, jolly, joyful, lighthearted, merry, mirthful. ANT.—glum, morose, sad, somber.

hinder, block, check, encumber, hamper, impede, inhibit, interrupt, obstruct, postpone, prevent, resist, restrain, retard, stop, thwart. ANT.—assist, expedite, facilitate, hasten, promote.

hint, allusion, implication, intimation, inkling, innuendo, insinuation, reminder; allude (to), imply, insinuate, intimate, refer (to), suggest. ANT.—affirmation, declaration, statement; conceal, suppress, withhold.

hire, employ, engage, use; contract (for), lease, let, rent. ANT.—discard, discharge, reject; buy, purchase.

history, account, annals, archives, autobiography, biography, chronicle, description, detail, events, facts, log, lore, memoir, memorial, muniments, narration, narrative, recital, record, relation, report, saga, story; past. ANT.—fable, fiction, legend, myth, romance.

hit, batter, beat, knock, pound, pummel, punch, rap, slap, smite, strike; achieve, attain, contact, find, gain, reach, win.

hoard, accrue, accumulate, amass, collect, garner, gather, heap, increase, pile, save, stock, store, treasure. ANT.—diminish, disperse, dissipate, scatter, waste.

hoax, antic, artifice, canard, cheat, deception, delusion, device, fakery, fraud, guile, humbug, imposture, joke, ploy, ruse, spoof, stunt, subterfuge, swindle, trick, wile. ANT.—candor, honesty, openness, sincerity.

hobble, falter, limp, stagger, totter; bind, fetter, handicap, hold, impede, limit, restrain, shackle. ANT.—progress, speed, travel; aid, expedite, help, release.

hobby, amusement, avocation, diversion, enjoyment, fad, game, interest, pastime, recreation.

hold, adhere, clasp, clutch, grasp, grip; have, keep, maintain, occupy, own, possess, retain, support; check, confine, control, curb, detain, restrain; accommodate, carry, contain, receive, stow; affirm, attest, consider, judge, regard, think. ANT.—abandon, relinquish, renounce, surrender, vacate.

hole, abyss, aperture, cavity, chasm, excavation, fissure, gap, gulf, perforation, pit, rent; cave, den, holt, lair; opening, pore, void. ANT.—closure, imperforation.

hollow, empty, unfilled, vacant, void; artificial, faithless, false, hypocritical, insincere, superficial, transparent, vain; cavernous, concave, depressed, sunken. ANT.—full, solid, sound; genuine, sincere; convex, raised.

holy, angelic, blessed, consecrated, dedicated, devoted, devotional, devout, divine, godly, hallowed, immaculate, incorrupt, pious, pure, religious, reverent, righteous, sacred, saintly, spiritual, uncorrupt, virtuous. ANT.—diabolical, profane, sacrilegious, secular.

home, abode, domicile, dwelling, habitat, hearth, hearthstone, quarters, residence, seat; asylum, haven, refuge, retreat, sanctuary; birthplace, country, native land; heaven; family.

homely, common, ordinary, plain, unadorned, unattractive, uncomely; coarse, inelegant, rough, rude. ANT.—attractive, beautiful, fair, handsome, pretty; charming, dignified, polished, suave.

homogeneous, alike, consonant, harmonious, identical, same, similar, uniform. ANT.—heterogeneous, miscellaneous, mixed, unharmonious, variegated.

hone, file, grind, sharpen, strengthen, strop, whet. ANT.—make dull, roughen.

honest, candid, conscientious, fair, frank, genuine, honorable, ingenuous, just, principled, reliable, reputable, scrupulous, sincere, trustworthy, truthful, upright, unadulterated, unmixed. ANT.—deceitful, dishonest, fraudulent, lying, tricky; adulterated.

honesty, candor, fairness, faithfulness, frankness, honor, integrity, justice, openness, probity, rectitude, responsibility, self-respect, sincerity, trustworthiness, uprightness, veracity. ANT.—cheating, deceit, dishonesty, fraud, perfidy.

honor, admiration, adoration, adulation, commendation, deference, dignity, esteem, fame, glory, homage, praise, renown, respect, reverence, worship; confidence, faith, reliance, trust; admire, consider, esteem, heed, respect, revere, reverence, value, venerate; dignify, elevate, esteem. ANT.—contempt, derision, disgrace, reproach; abuse, despise, disdain, neglect, scorn.

honorary, commemorative, emeritus, gratuitous, titular. ANT.—complete, full, true.

hope, anticipation, aspiration, assurance, belief, desire, expectancy, expectation; confidence, faith, optimism, prospect, trust. ANT.—despair, despondency, fear, gloom, pessimism.

hopeless, abandoned, brokenhearted, condemned, dejected, despairing, futile, immitigable, inconsolable, incurable, irredeemable, irreparable, irretrievable, irrevocable, rash, reckless, ruined, useless. ANT.—cheering, encouraging, promising, reassuring, stimulating.

horde, army, assemblage, band, bevy, crew, crowd, crush, gang, host, masses, mob, multitude, pack, populace, press, rabble, swarm, throng, troop.

horizontal, even, flat, level, linear, parallel, plane, straight; prone, supine. ANT.—hilly, inclined, sloping; erect, upright, vertical.

horrible, appalling, atrocious, awful, dire, dreadful, fearful, frightful, ghastly, grim, heinous, hideous, horrid, repulsive, shocking, terrible. ANT.—beautiful, enchanting, enjoyable, fascinating, lovely.

horror, alarm, antipathy, apprehension, aversion, awe, consternation, disgust, dismay, dread, fear, foreboding, loathing, terror. ANT.—assurance, comfort, confidence, consolation, delight.

hospitable, companionable, convivial, cordial, friendly, kind, neighborly, receptive, sociable. ANT.—grudging, inhospitable, reserved, solitary, unsociable.

host, entertainer; innkeeper, landlord; army, legion; horde, multitude, throng. ANT.—boarder, caller, guest, patron, visitor.

hostile, adverse, antagonistic, antipathetic, belligerent, bitter, contrary, inimical, malevolent, opposed, rancorous, repugnant, unfriendly, warlike. ANT.—amicable, cordial, favorable, neutral, uncommitted.

hot, blazing, burning, flaming, heated, scalding, scorching, searing, torrid, warm; ardent, eager, excited, fervent, fervid, fiery, hot-blooded, impetuous, intense, passionate; peppery, pungent, spicy. ANT.—cold, cool, freezing; apathetic, frigid, impassive, indifferent, passionless, phlegmatic; bland, sweet.

however, albeit, although, but, nevertheless, notwithstanding, still, though, yet; whatever, whatsoever.

hug, caress, clasp, coddle, cuddle, embrace, enfold, fondle, hold, press, squeeze. ANT.—annoy, buffet, spurn.

huge, capacious, colossal, enormous, extensive, giant, gigantic, great, immense, monstrous, tremendous, vast. ANT.—diminutive, little, miniature, small, tiny.

humane, benevolent, benign, benignant, charitable, civilized, clement, compassionate, forbearing, forgiving, gracious, human, kind, lenient, merciful, sympathetic, tender, tolerant. ANT.—brutal, cruel, merciless, pitiless, unfeeling.

humble, compliant, lowly, meek, modest, plain, poor, simple, submissive, unassuming, unobtrusive, unostentatious, unpretentious; abase, abash, break, crush, debase, degrade, humiliate, mortify, shame, subdue. ANT.—arrogant, boastful, haughty, proud, vain; dignify, elevate, exalt, honor, praise.

humbug, cheat, counterfeit, deception, dodge, fake, falseness, feint, fraud, hoax, hypocrisy, imposition, pretense, sham, trick. ANT.—honesty, reality, truth, validity.

humdrum, boring, commonplace, dull, everyday, monotonous, ordinary, prosaic, routine, tedious, tiresome, usual. ANT.—exciting, lively, stimulating.

humiliation, abashment, chagrin, mortification; abasement, disgrace, dishonor, disrepute, ignominy, odium, opprobrium, scandal, shame; humbleness, meekness. ANT.—dignity, glory, honor, praise, renown.

humor, caprice, chaff, comicality, drollery, facetiousness, fancy, jesting, jocosity, jocularity, joke, waggery, whimsicality, wit; disposition, mood, temper; favor, indulge, pamper, pet, placate, please, satisfy, spoil. ANT.—depression, gloom, gravity, melancholy, sorrow; affront, enrage, exasperate, irritate, provoke.

hunch, feeling, impression, intuition, omen, premonition, presentiment, suspicion; hump, protuberance; chunk, lump.

hunger, appetite, craving, desire, eagerness, inclination, longing, passion, relish; starvation.

ANT.—disgust, distaste, renunciation, repugnance; satiety.

hungry, avid, covetous, famished, greedy, ravenous, starving, thirsting, voracious. ANT.—replete, sated, satisfied.

hunt, examination, exploration, inquiry, investigation, pursuit, quest, search; chase, ferret, investigate, probe, pursue, search, seek, stalk. ANT.—abandonment, cession, resignation; desert, forsake, quit, relinquish, surrender.

hurl, cast, dart, expel, explode, fling, impel, pitch, project, propel, release, shoot, spring, throw, thrust, toss. ANT.—draw, haul, hold, pull, retain.

hurry, accelerate, drive, expedite, force, hasten, impel, precipitate, press, quicken, rush, scurry, speed. ANT.—dawdle, delay, detain, hinder, impede, procrastinate, retard, stall, tarry.

hurt, abuse, affront, damage, deteriorate, disfigure, harm, impair, injure, insult, maltreat, mar, outrage, pain, spoil, victimize, wound, wrong. ANT.—ameliorate, benefit, compliment, help, preserve.

hush, calm, muffle, quiet, relieve, silence, stifle, still. ANT.—amplify, encourage, excite, incite.

hustle, accelerate, bustle, dash, drive, expedite, hasten, hurry, jostle, push, run, rush, scurry, spur. ANT.—dawdle, delay, procrastinate, slow, stall.

hybrid, crossbred, half-blooded, half-bred, mixed, mongrel, mutant. ANT.—pedigreed, purebred, thoroughbred, unmixed.

hygienic, healthy, salubrious, salutary, sanitary, sterile, uncontaminated, wholesome. ANT.—contagious, contaminated, diseased, foul, infectious, noxious, unsanitary.

hypnotic, influential, impelling, irresistible, lethargic, magnetic, mesmeric, narcotic, quieting, soporific. ANT.—disturbing, exciting, reviving, stimulating.

hypocritical, canting, deceiving, deceptive, deluding, dishonest, dishonorable, dissembling, dissimulating, double-dealing, false, feigning, pharisaical, pretending, pretentious, sanctimonious, specious, unctuous, unprincipled. ANT.—candid, honest, ingenuous, principled, sincere.

hypothesis, assumption, conjecture, inference, postulate, presumption, proposal, supposition, theory, thesis. ANT.—certainty, confirmation, demonstration, fact, proof.

I

icy, chilled, chilling, cold, frigid, frosty, frozen, polar; cool, distant, forbidding, unemotional. ANT.—fiery, hot, torrid, tropical; ardent, fervent, passionate.

idea, abstraction, belief, concept, conception, fancy, image, impression, notion, opinion, principle, scheme, theory, thought. ANT.—actuality, entity, matter, reality, substance.

ideal, fancied, illusory, imaginary, impractical, intellectual, metaphysical, psychical, psychological, spiritual, unreal, utopian, visionary; complete, exemplary, faultless, perfect, supreme. ANT.—actual, material, real; faulty, imperfect.

identical, alike, coalescent, coincident, duplicate, equal, equivalent, indistinguishable, same, synonymous, uniform. ANT.—contrary, disparate, dissimilar, distinct, opposite.

identify, analyze, catalog, characterize, classify, determine, distinguish, name, note, point out, recognize; brand, label, mark, tag. ANT.—confuse, misinterpret, misname, mistake, mix up.

idiomatic, colloquial, dialectal, peculiar, regional, special, standard, stylized, vernacular. ANT.—classic, cultured, standard.

idle, aimless, barren, dormant, futile, inactive, indolent, inert, lazy, pointless, shiftless, slothful, unemployed, unimportant, unoccupied, unprofitable, unused, useless, vain. ANT.—active, employed, fruitful, industrious, occupied.

idolize, adore, deify, glorify, revere, venerate, worship. ANT.—abase, defile, desecrate, hate, profane.

ignoble, abject, base, coarse, contemptible, debased, degenerate, degraded, depraved, despicable, dishonorable, groveling, ignominious, low, lowly, mean, menial, scandalous, scurrilous, servile, shameful, sordid, vile, vulgar, worthless; humble, low-born, plebeian, poor, untitled. ANT.—esteemed, exalted, honored, lofty, noble, righteous.

ignorant, dense, illiterate, obtuse, shallow, superficial, unacquainted, uncultivated, uneducated, uninformed, uninstructed, unknowing, unlearned, unlettered, untaught. ANT.—cultured, educated, erudite, literate, wise.

ignore, disregard, forget, neglect, omit, overlook, reject, shun, skip, slight, snub. ANT.—acknowledge, heed, notice, recognize, regard.

ill, afflicted, ailing, diseased, distempered, feeble, impaired, indisposed, infirm, morbid, sick, sickly, unhealthy, unwell; calamity, danger, distress, evil, hardship, misery, pain, sorrow, trouble, vexation. ANT.—healthy, robust, vigorous, well; favor, fortune, prosperity, welfare.

illegal, banned, contraband, criminal, dishonest, illegitimate, illicit, interdicted, outlawed, prohibited, proscribed, unauthorized, unlawful, unlicensed. ANT.—authorized, honest, judicial, lawful, legal, permissible.

illogical, fallacious, incoherent, inconsistent, specious, spurious, unreasoned, unsound, untenable. ANT.—logical, reasoned, sensible, sound.

illuminate, brighten, clarify, demonstrate, elucidate, enlighten, explain, illumine, illustrate, irradiate, lighten, reveal. ANT.—complicate, confuse, darken, obfuscate, obscure, puzzle.

illusion, apparition, chimera, deception, delusion, dream, fallacy, fancy, fantasy, hallucination, mirage, phantom, vision; fairy, ghost, ghoul, poltergeist, specter, spirit, sprite. ANT.—actuality, certainty, happening, reality, substance.

illustration, drawing, engraving, etching, image, likeness, painting, panorama, photograph, picture, portrait, portrayal, print, representation, scene, sketch, view; case, comparison, example, instance, specimen.

illustrious, acclaimed, celebrated, distinguished, eminent, famed, famous, great, prominent, renowned; critical, important, momentous, serious, vital, weighty; august, dignified, elevated, grand, majestic, noble; brilliant, excellent, fine, magnificent, superior, superlative. ANT.—diminutive, little, minute, small; common, humble, obscure, ordinary, unknown; menial, paltry.

imagination, conceit, concept, conception, creation, fancy, fantasy, idea, impression, mental image, notion. ANT.—actuality, existence, materiality, realism, substance.

imaginative, artistic, clever, creative, fanciful, inventive, mystical, original, poetical, talented, visionary. ANT.—dull, factual, literal, methodical, prosaic.

imagine, conceive, dream, envision, fancy, picture, pretend, visualize; apprehend, assume, believe, conjecture, guess, opine, presume, suppose, surmise, think.

imbecile, blockhead, buffoon, cretin, dolt, dunce, fool, halfwit, idiot, ignoramus, moron, nincompoop, numbskull, oaf, simpleton, witling. ANT.—genius, intellectual, philosopher, sage, scholar.

imbue, animate, color, impregnate, infuse, inspire, instill, penetrate, permeate, pervade, saturate, suffuse.

imitate, ape, caricature, copy, counterfeit, duplicate, falsify, follow, impersonate, mimic, mirror, mock, personate, parody, represent, reproduce, simulate, transcribe. ANT.—alter, distort, diverge, oppose, vary.

immanent, inborn, inherent, innate, internal, intrinsic, natural, subjective; universal (as God). ANT.—acquired, external, extrinsic, objective.

immaterial, inessential, insignificant, irrelevant, trifling, trivial, unimportant; disembodied, impalpable, impertinent, incorporeal, spiritual, unsubstantial. ANT.—essential, important, relevant; corporeal, material, substantial.

immature, callow, childish, crude, embryonic, green, juvenile, premature, raw, undeveloped, unready, unripe, untimely. ANT.—adult, aged, grown, mature, ripe.

immeasurable, abysmal, boundless, endless, eternal, illimitable, immense, infinite, interminable, measureless, unbounded, unfathomable, unlimited, vast. ANT.—bounded, circumscribed, finite, limited, measurable.

immediately, abruptly, at once, directly, forthwith, instantaneously, instantly, now, presently, promptly, right away, speedily, straightaway. ANT.—after a while, by and by, distantly, hereafter, later.

immemorial, ancient, dateless, early, immemorable, old, prehistoric, timeless. ANT.—memorable, new, recent, young.

immense, colossal, elephantine, enormous, gargantuan, gigantic, great, huge, large, mighty, monstrous, prodigious, stupendous, titanic, tremendous, vast. ANT.—diminutive, dwarfish, microscopic, minute, tiny.

immerse, bathe, dip, douse, dunk, engulf, flood, inundate, plunge, sink, submerge; absorb, engage, engross, involve, overwhelm. ANT.—elevate, recover, retrieve, uncover, uplift.

imminent, abeyant, approaching, brewing, coming, destined, impending, inevitable, menacing, near, nigh, ominous, overhanging, pressing, threatening. ANT.—afar, distant, improbable, remote, retreating.

immoderation, excess, exorbitance, extravagance, extremism, inordinateness, intemperance, profusion, superabundance, superfluity, surplus. ANT.—dearth, deficiency, moderation, paucity, restraint.

immoral, bad, corrupt, depraved, dissolute, evil, indecent, lecherous, licentious, loose, profligate, unprincipled, vicious, wicked. ANT.—chaste, high-minded, noble, pure, virtuous.

immortal, abiding, ceaseless, deathless, endless, eternal, everlasting, imperishable, infinite, permanent, perpetual, timeless, undying. ANT.—ephemeral, finite, mortal, temporal, transitory.

immovable, anchored, cemented, constant, firm, fixed, fused, immobile, obdurate, rooted, stable, steadfast. ANT.—mobile, movable, plastic, wavering, yielding.

immune, excused, exempt, free, freed, hardened to, not liable, resistant, unaffected by, unsusceptible; clear, loose, open, unfastened, unobstructed. ANT.—subject.

immunity, acquittal, clearance, discharge, dispensation, exculpation, exemption, exoneration, freedom, license, privilege, protection, release, respite. ANT.—condemnation, conviction, indictment, interdiction, sequestration.

immutable, abiding, ceaseless, constant, continual, enduring, faithful, fixed, invariant, permanent, perpetual, persistent, stable, unalterable, unchanging, unwavering. ANT.—fluctuating, mutable, vacillating, variable, wavering.

impair, adulterate, blemish, blight, corrode, corrupt, cripple, damage, deface, degrade, deteriorate, harm, hurt, injure, mar, spoil, taint, weaken. ANT.—ameliorate, benefit, enhance, mend, repair.

impart, bestow, communicate, confer, convey, disclose, divulge, enlighten, give, grant, inform, instruct, notify, relate, reveal, tell, transmit. ANT.—conceal, hide, puzzle, suppress, withhold.

impartial, disinterested, equitable, fair, honest, indifferent, just, neutral, nonpartisan, nonsectarian, reasonable, unbiased, unconcerned, unprejudiced. ANT.—biased, dishonorable, fraudulent, involved, partial.

impasse, bar, deadlock, end, limit, obstacle. ANT.—clearance, gain, opening, solution.

impatient, abrupt, brusque, eager, fidgety, fretful, fussy, impetuous, nervous, restless. ANT.—calm, controlled, forbearing, patient, tolerant.

impeccable, faultless, immaculate, incorrupt, innocent, perfect, spotless. ANT.—defective, imperfect, messy, stained, sullied.

impede, arrest, bar, block, check, clog, counteract, delay, encumber, frustrate, hamper, hinder, interrupt, obstruct, offset, oppose, prevent, repress, restrain, retard, stop, thwart. ANT.—advance, assist, further, help, promote.

impediment, barrier, block, difficulty, disability, encumbrance, hindrance, inhibition, obstacle, obstruction, restriction, wall, weakness. ANT.—aid, assistance, collaboration, help, support.

impel, actuate, coerce, compel, constrain, drive, force, goad, induce, influence, instigate, move, oblige, prod, push, stimulate, urge. ANT.—delay, prevent, repress, repulse, suppress.

impenetrable, compact, dense, firm, hard, impervious, rigid, solid; arduous, burdensome, difficult, onerous, tough; abstruse, esoteric, intricate, perplexing, puzzling; adamant, cruel, harsh, obtuse, rigorous, severe, stern, stolid, strict, unfeeling. ANT.—brittle, elastic, flabby, fluid, penetrable, plastic, soft; easy, effortless, facile, simple; clear, comprehensible, intelligible; gentle, lenient, tender.

imperative, absolute, commanding, compelling, compulsory, critical, essential, exigent, impelling, important, importunate, inescapable, inexorable, insistent, mandatory, necessary, obligatory, peremptory, pressing, required, requisite, unavoidable, urgent, vital. ANT.—insignificant, optional, petty, trivial, unimportant.

imperceptible, inappreciable, inconspicuous, indistinct, indistinguishable, insignificant, invisible, negligible, undiscernible, unseen. ANT.—apparent, evident, perceptible, striking, visible.

imperfection, blemish, defect, deficiency, drawback, error, failure, fault, flaw, frailty, inadequacy, infirmity, mistake, shortcoming, stain, transgression, wrong. ANT.—completeness, correctness, faultlessness, perfection, purity.

imperil, endanger, expose, hazard, jeopardize, risk, threaten, uncover. ANT.—defend, guard, safeguard, secure, shield.

impersonate, ape, copy, duplicate, feign, imitate, mimic, mock, personify, portray, represent, simulate. ANT.—alter, distort, diverge, invent.

impertinent, abusive, arrogant, audacious, bold, brazen, contemptuous, impudent, insolent, insulting, intrusive, meddling, offensive, officious, rude; absurd, inane, inapplicable,

irrelevant, trivial. ANT.—considerate, courteous, polite, respectful; important, momentous, pertinent, serious, significant.

impetuous, careless, fiery, hasty, heedless, impulsive, incautious, intractable, passionate, quick, rash, reckless, ungovernable, unruly. ANT.—cautious, composed, reasoning, retiring, tranquil.

impetus, force, impulse, incentive, momentum, motive, pressure, stimulus.

impinge, clash, collide, encroach, infringe, hit, strike, trespass, touch, violate. ANT.—avoid, defer, miss, pass, respect.

implant, embed, engraft, fix, graft, inculcate, infuse, insert, instill, plant, set in, sow. ANT.—eliminate, excise, remove, uproot.

implement, accomplish, achieve, do, effect, effectuate, execute, expedite, fulfill, perform, realize. ANT.—cancel, defer, hinder, restrict.

implicate, accuse, blame, censure, challenge, charge, cite, embroil, enfold, entangle, imply, impute, incriminate, inculpate, involve, link, rebuke, reproach, trap, upbraid. ANT.—absolve, acquit, defend, exonerate, support.

implicit, accepted, implied, inferred, known, presupposed, recognized, tacit, understood, unspoken. ANT.—declared, explicit, expressed, specific.

imply, connote, hint, infer, insinuate, involve, mean, signify, suggest. ANT.—assert, define, describe, express, state.

import, emphasis, importance, influence, significance, stress, value, weight; bring in, convey, imply, introduce, purport, signify, transport. ANT.—insignificance, triviality; export, send out, ship out.

important, appreciable, authoritative, consequential, critical, decisive, essential, grave, great, imposing, influential, leading, material, momentous, paramount, powerful, pressing, principal, prominent, relevant, serious, significant, substantial, urgent, weighty. ANT.—insignificant, irrelevant, petty, picayune, trivial.

imposing, arresting, august, commanding, eminent, grand, grandiose, high, illustrious, imperial, impressive, lofty, magnificent, majestic, noble, stately, striking, sublime, towering. ANT.—common, humble, insignificant, ordinary, undignified.

impractical, impracticable, inexpedient, unachievable, unattainable, unfeasible, unrealistic, unworkable, visionary. ANT.—feasible, possible, practical, reasonable, workable.

impressive, absorbing, affecting, arresting, awesome, commanding, considerable, deep, exciting, forcible, imposing, majestic, momentous, moving, notable, penetrating, profound, prominent, remarkable, stirring, striking, thrilling, touching, vital. ANT.—commonplace, ordinary, shallow, trivial, unimpressive.

imprison, cage, confine, constrain, detain, enclose, hold, impound, incarcerate, limit, lock up, restrain. ANT.—acquit, discharge, extricate, free, release.

impromptu, ad lib, extemporaneous, improvised, impulsive, offhand, spontaneous, unplanned, unrehearsed. ANT.—deliberate, planned, premeditated, prepared, rehearsed.

improper, discourteous, immodest, incorrect, indecent, indelicate, lewd, offensive, unbecoming, unsuitable, wrong. ANT.—considerate, correct, fitting, proper, seemly.

improve, advance, ameliorate, amend, better, correct, help, mend, purify, rectify, refine, reform, revise; gain, get better, progress. ANT.—corrupt, damage, debase, impair, vitiate; decline, worsen.

imprudent, careless, heedless, incautious, indiscreet, reckless, thoughtless, unforeseeing, unwise. ANT.—careful, cautious, circumspect, meticulous, prudent.

impudence, arrogance, audacity, boldness, crudity, discourtesy, disrespect, effrontery, impertinence, incivility, insolence, presumption, rudeness, sauciness. ANT.—courtesy, diffidence, gentility, politeness, respect.

impulsive, careless, excitable, fiery, foolhardy, forcible, hasty, headstrong, heedless, impatient, impetuous, imprudent, incautious, indiscreet, quick, rash, reckless, uninhibited. ANT.—cautious, heedful, prudent, reasoning, restrained.

impure, adulterated, contaminated, corrupt, corrupted, debased, defiled, depraved, foul, indecent, mingled, mixed, obscene, polluted, profligate, putrid, spoiled, smutty, tainted, unsound, venal, vitiated. ANT.—clean, immaculate, impeccable, pure, spotless.

impute, allege, ascribe, assign, attribute, blame, brand, charge, implicate, inculpate, indict, trace (to). ANT.—defend, endorse, exculpate, exonerate, vindicate.

inactive, dormant, idle, inanimate, indolent, inert, latent, lazy, motionless, passive, quiescent, resting, sedentary, torpid, unemployed, unoccupied. ANT.—active, dynamic, industrious, occupied, working.

inadequate, defective, deficient, incompetent, incomplete, insufficient, lacking, partial, scanty, short, unfit, wanting. ANT.—adequate, ample, enough, satisfactory, sufficient.

inadvertent, accidental, careless, chance, heedless, negligent, thoughtless, unconscious, unintentional, unobservant. ANT.—attentive, careful, intentional, planned.

inane, absurd, banal, foolish, frivolous, insipid, pointless, silly, trite, vapid. ANT.—expressive, important, meaningful, salient, significant.

inappropriate, discordant, improper, inapt, incongruous, infelicitous, tasteless, unfitted, unsuitable. ANT.—appropriate, apt, becoming, fitting, proper.

inaugurate, arise, begin, commence, found, initiate, install, institute, introduce, open, originate, start. ANT.—adjourn, close, complete, finish, terminate.

incentive, enticement, incitement, inducement, lure, motive, provocation, spur, stimulus.

inception, beginning, birth, commencement, founding, inauguration, initiation, opening, origin, onset, source, start. ANT.—close, completion, consummation, end, termination.

incessant, ceaseless, constant, continual, continuous, endless, everlasting, interminable, perennial, perpetual, persistent, unceasing, uninterrupted, unremitting. ANT.—interrupted, occasional, periodic, rare, sporadic.

incident, chance, episode, event, happening, occasion, occurrence, situation.

incidental, accidental, accessory, associated, casual, collateral, concomitant, contingent, fortuitous, minor, nonessential, occasional, secondary, subordinate, undesigned, unintended. ANT.—cardinal, elementary, essential, fundamental, vital.

incisive, brief, compact, concise, condensed, crisp, decisive, direct, pithy, succinct, summary, terse. ANT.—lengthy, prolix, verbose, wordy.

incite, actuate, animate, arouse, cause, encourage, enrage, excite, fire, foment, goad, impel, induce, inflame, instigate, prompt, provoke, rouse, stimulate, stir up, urge. ANT.—deter, pacify, quiet, restrain, soothe.

inclination, bending, gradient, incline, leaning, slope; affection, allurement, attachment, attraction, bent, bias, desire, disposition, fancy, liking, partiality, penchant, predilection, preference, prejudice, proneness, propensity, tendency. ANT.—apathy, aversion, distaste, nonchalance, repugnance.

include, accommodate, comprise, consist of, contain, embody, embrace, encompass, hold, incorporate, involve, surround, take in. ANT.—eliminate, exclude, omit, preclude, reject.

income, annuity, dividends, earnings, emolument, gain, interest, proceeds, profits, receipts, rents, revenue, salary, stipend, wages, winnings. ANT.—charge, cost, expense, loss, outgo.

incompetent, bungling, clumsy, floundering, heavy-handed, inadequate, incapable, ineffectual, inefficient, inept, inexpert, maladroit, stumbling, unable, unfit, unqualified, unskilled, unsuitable, untalented. ANT.—competent, deft, expert, proficient, skillful.

incongruous, conflicting, contradictory, contrary, disagreeing, discordant, discrepant, disparate, divergent, illogical, incompatible, inconsistent, inharmonious, irreconcilable, mismatched, paradoxical. ANT.—compatible, congruous, consistent, correspondent, harmonious, homologous.

inconsiderate, careless, selfish, tasteless, thoughtless, undiscerning, unfeeling, unsympathetic. ANT.—considerate, helpful, sensitive, sympathetic, thoughtful.

inconsistent, changeable, contrary, fluctuating, incompatible, inconsonant, inconstant, shifting, unstable, unsteady, unsuitable, vacillating, variable, varying, wavering. ANT.—constant, stable, steady, unchanging, uniform.

incorporate, amalgamate, blend, consolidate, embody, establish, form, merge, mix, unite. ANT.—disperse, dissolve, divide, remove, separate.

increase, accelerate, accrue, advance, amplify, augment, develop, dilate, distend, enhance, enlarge, expand, extend, grow, heighten, inflate, intensify, magnify, multiply, raise, spread, swell, wax. ANT.—atrophy, contract, decrease, diminish, reduce.

incredible, astonishing, fantastic, far-fetched, implausible, suspicious, unbelievable. ANT.—believable, credible, creditable, plausible, realistic.

increment, addition, enlargement, increase, raise. ANT.—decline, decrease, diminution, loss.

incriminate, accuse, arraign, blame, censure, charge, implicate, impute, indict, involve, link. ANT.—absolve, acquit, exonerate, release, vindicate.

inculcate, discipline, drill (into), imbue, impart, implant, impress, indoctrinate, instill, instruct, teach.

incumbent, binding, coercive, imperative, inescapable, necessary, peremptory, pressing, stringent, urgent; occupant, officeholder. ANT.—absolved, exempt, free, liberated, released.

indebted, appreciative, beholden, grateful, thankful; bound, liable, obligated, owing, unpaid. ANT.—thankless, unappreciative; cleared (up), settled (accounts), squared (with) paid.

indecent, coarse, dirty, disgusting, filthy, gross, immodest, immoral, improper, impure, indelicate, lewd, obscene, offensive, pornographic, shameless, smutty, unbecoming. ANT.—decent, modest, pure, refined, virtuous.

indefinite, ambiguous, confused, dim, equivocal, hazy, inconclusive, indeterminate, inexact, lax, loose, obscure, uncertain, unclear, undefined, unfixed, unlimited, unsettled. ANT.—absolute, certain, evident, positive, unquestionable.

independent, alone, autonomous, exempt, free, liberated, self-governing, self-reliant, self-sufficient, separate, single, sovereign, unallied, unconfined, uncontrolled, unrestrained, unrestricted; affluent, rich, wealthy; exclusive, irrespective. ANT.—contingent, dependent, enslaved, restricted, subordinate; poor; inclusive.

indicate, connote, denote, designate, differentiate, disclose, evidence, hint, imply, intimate, manifest, mark, point out, register, reveal, show, signal, signify, specify, testify. ANT.—conceal, distract, divert, falsify, mislead.

indication, designation, emblem, evidence, gesture, hint, implication, manifestation, mark, note, omen, portent, proof, sign, signal, suggestion, symbol, symptom, token.

indict, accuse, arraign, blame, censure, charge, impeach, incriminate. ANT.—absolve, acquit, exonerate, release, vindicate.

indifference, apathy, callousness, carelessness, coldness, detachment, disinterest, disinterestedness, impartiality, impassivity, inattention, insensibility, insouciance, insusceptibility, neutrality, nonchalance, supineness, unconcern. ANT.—affection, ardor, fervor, passion, vivacity.

indigence, dearth, destitution, distress, famine, hunger, insufficiency, misery, necessity, need, pauperism, penury, poverty, privation, starvation, tenuity, want. ANT.—abundance, affluence, plenty, riches, wealth.

indigenous, aboriginal, domestic, endemic, inborn, inherent, innate, native, natural. ANT.—alien, foreign, imported, introduced, naturalized.

indignation, acrimony, agitation, anger, animosity, annoyance, exasperation, fury, huff, irascibility, ire, passion, petulance, pique, rage, resentment, scorn, temper, virulence, wrath. ANT.—forbearance, equanimity, patience, self-control, tranquility.

indignity, abuse, affront, discourtesy, dishonor, disparagement, disrespect, embarrassment, humiliation, ignominy, insult, irreverence, mockery, offense, opprobrium, outrage, scurrility, slight, taunt, vituperation. ANT.—courtesy, dignity, homage, praise, reverence.

indirect, circuitous, crooked, distorted, erratic, implied, inferred, oblique, roundabout, swerving, tortuous, wandering, winding; crooked, cunning, devious, tricky. ANT.—direct, straight, unswerving; blunt, candid, explicit, straightforward.

indiscreet, foolhardy, foolish, heedless, imprudent, rash, reckless, thoughtless, unwise. ANT.—careful, discreet, prudent, sensible, wise.

indiscriminate, heterogeneous, mixed, promiscuous, uncritical, unwise. ANT.—chosen, critical, homogeneous, selective.

indispensable, basic, essential, expedient, fundamental, imperative, intrinsic, necessary, needed, prerequisite, required, requisite, vital. ANT.—dispensable, extrinsic, optional, peripheral, superfluous.

indistinct, abstruse, ambiguous, blurred, cloudy, confused, cryptic, darkened, dim, dusky, faint, hazy, indefinite, imperceptible, inaudible, indistinguishable, misty, mysterious, nebulous, obscure, shadowy, uncertain, unintelligible, vague. ANT.—clear, distinct, lucid, obvious, perceptible.

individual, characteristic, different, distinct, distinctive, idiosyncratic, marked, original, particular, peculiar, personal, separate, singular, special, specific, unique. ANT.—common, conventional, general, ordinary, universal.

indoctrinate, discipline, drill, imbue, initiate, instruct, teach, train. ANT.—confuse, misguide, mislead, neglect.

indolent, drowsy, dull, idle, inactive, ineffectual, inert, lackadaisical, languid, lazy, lethargic, listless, remiss, slack, slothful, sluggish, somnolent, soporific, supine, torpid. ANT.—active, alert, assiduous, diligent, industrious.

indomitable, firm, impregnable, insurmountable, invincible, invulnerable, unassailable, unconquerable, untameable, unyielding. ANT.—feeble, powerless, vulnerable, weak, yielding.

induce, actuate, bring about, cause, create, effect, encourage, evoke, impel, incite, influence, instigate, motivate, move, originate, persuade, prompt, spur, stimulate, urge. ANT.—discourage, dissuade, hamper, repel, repress.

induct, initiate, install, introduce, invest, lead into; conclude, generalized, infer. ANT.—expel, lead away, reject; end, withdraw.

industrious, active, assiduous, busy, diligent, hard-working, indefatigable, perseverant, persistent, sedulous, zealous. ANT.—inactive, indolent, lackadaisical, laggard, lethargic.

inebriated, drunk, drunken, high, intoxicated, tight, tipsy; exhilarated, heartened, refreshed, stimulated. ANT.—abstinent, sober, temperate; calm, unmoved.

ineffective, assailable, feeble, frail, futile, idle, impotent, inadequate, ineffectual, inefficacious, unavailing, unfruitful, unproductive, useless, vain, vulnerable, weak. ANT.—effective, efficacious, potent, powerful, successful.

inept, awkward, clumsy, foolish, fumbling, inappropriate, incapable, maladroit, unfit, unhandy, unproductive, unskillful. ANT.—able, adroit, apt, competent, skillful.

inert, dead, dilatory, dormant, idle, impassive, impotent, inactive, indolent, lazy, lifeless, phlegmatic, powerless, quiescent, slothful, sluggish, stolid, supine, torpid. ANT.—active, industrious, moving, operational, working.

inevitable, assured, avoidless, certain, definite, fated, imminent, indefeasible, indubitable, ineluctable, inescapable, necessary, positive, predestined, sure, unavoidable, undeniable, unquestionable. ANT.—avoidable, doubtful, indeterminate, questionable, uncertain.

inexhaustible, illimitable, indefatigable, infinite, limitless, never-ending, untiring, unwearied. ANT.—ending, finite, limited, short-lived, wearying.

inexpensive, cheap, low-priced, reasonable (in price); beggarly, common, inferior, mean, shabby. ANT.—costly, dear, expensive, high-priced; valuable.

infantile, babyish, childish, immature, juvenile, naïve, puerile, young. ANT.—adult, grown up, mature, of age.

infatuated, beguiled, captivated, charmed, deluded, enamored, enthralled, fascinated, foolish. ANT.—disgusted, disillusioned, fancy-free, prudent, sensible.

infection, communicability, contagion, contamination, disease, epidemic, germs, impurity, poison, pollution, vitiation.

infectious, catching, communicable, contagious, contaminating, defiling, epidemic, noxious, pestiferous, pestilential, polluting, sickening, virulent, vitiating. ANT.—antiseptic, harmless, healthful, hygienic, sanitary.

inference, answer, conclusion, consequence, corollary, deduction, derivation, illation, judgment, result, solution. ANT.—assumption, foreboding, foresight, preconception, presupposition.

inferior, deficient, inadequate, lesser, lower, minor, poorer, secondary, shoddy, subordinate, substandard. ANT.—better, first-class, foremost, prime, superior.

infinite, boundless, continual, continuing, countless, endless, eternal, everlasting, illimitable, immeasurable, incalculable, incomprehensible, inexhaustible, innumerable, interminable, perpetual, termless, timeless, unbounded, unlimited. ANT.—bounded, circumscribed, finite, limited, restricted.

infirm, ailing, debilitated, decrepit, doddering, drooping, enervated, enfeebled, exhausted, faint, feeble, forceless, frail, impaired, invalid, languid, powerless, sickly, spent, unhealthy, weak, worn. ANT.—forceful, hale, robust, sturdy, vigorous.

inflate, bloat, blow up, dilate, distend, elate, enlarge, exaggerate, expand, fill, pad, stuff. ANT.—compress, condense, deflate, shrink, trim.

inflexible, determined, dogged, firm, headstrong, immovable, inexorable, intractable, obdurate, obstinate, rigid, stiff, strict, stubborn, tenacious, uncompromising, unyielding. ANT.—compliant, elastic, flexible, pliable, yielding.

influence, absolutism, ascendancy, attraction, authority, character, command, control, credit, despotism, domination, effect, importance, leadership, magnetism, mastery, patronage, power, predominance, prerogative, pressure, prominence, reputation, rule, superiority, supremacy, sway, weight; actuate, act upon, affect, bias, carry weight, compel, control, counteract, direct, dominate, draw, drive, modify, move, outweigh, predominate, prejudice, pull, regulate, restrain, rouse, rule, spur. ANT.—impotence, inferiority, subjection, subserviency, weakness.

inform, acquaint, advise, apprise, edify, educate, enlighten, explain, impart, instruct, notify, relate, teach, tell, warn. ANT.—conceal, delude, distract, mislead.

informal, conventional, customary, easy, familiar, natural, offhand, regular, simple, unceremonious, unconstrained, unconventional, unofficial. ANT.—ceremonious, formal, official, perfunctory, rigid.

information, data, fact, instruction, intelligence, knowledge, learning, lore, news. ANT.—conjecture, guesswork, ignorance, rumor.

infrequent, irregular, isolated, occasional, odd, rare, scarce, sporadic, strange, unusual. ANT.—customary, frequent, ordinary, scheduled, usual.

infuse, animate, imbue, implant, inoculate, inspire, instill, permeate, steep.

ingenious, able, adroit, apt, bright, brilliant, capable, clever, competent, creative, deft, dexterous, endowed, expert, fertile, fresh, gifted, handy, imaginative, inventive, novel, original, productive, proficient, qualified, quick-witted, ready, resourceful, sagacious, sharp, skillful, talented. ANT.—bungling, clumsiness, fumbling, ineptitude, unqualified.

ingenuous, aboveboard, artless, candid, direct, fair, frank, free, guileless, honest, literal, natural, open, outspoken, plain, simple, sincere, straightforward, truthful, unaffected, undisguised, unsophisticated, unworldly. ANT.—artificial, cunning, deceptive, designing, scheming.

ingratitude, lack of response, thanklessness, unappreciation, unconcern, ungratefulness. ANT.—appreciation, gratefulness, gratitude, responsiveness, thankfulness.

ingredient, component, constituent, element, factor, material, part, substance.

inhabit, abide, dwell, establish residence, fill, live in, lodge, make home at, nestle, occupy, remain, rent, reside, room, settle, sojourn, stay, tenant. ANT.—abandon, exit, retreat, vacate, withdraw.

inherent, congenital, connatal, genetic, inborn, inbred, ingrained, inherent, inherited, innate, intrinsic, native, natural, real. ANT.—acquired, external, extraneous, extrinsic, supplemental.

inheritance, bequest, birthright, heritage, legacy, patrimony.

inhibit, arrest, bar, block, bridle, check, constrain, cramp, curb, disallow, discourage, hinder, hold back, impede, interdict, limit, obstruct, obtrude, oppose, prevent, prohibit, proscribe, repress, restrain, restrict, stop, sublimate, suppress, suspend, thwart. ANT.—aid, encourage, free, incite, liberate.

inhuman, barbarous, bestial, bloodthirsty, brutal, cold-blooded, cruel, diabolical, ferocious, fiendish, harsh, hateful, hellish, infernal, malevolent, malignant, pitiless, rancorous, remorseless, ruthless, savage, truculent, unfeeling, venomous. ANT.—benevolent, charitable, compassionate, humane, merciful.

iniquitous, baleful, base, criminal, degrading, deleterious, diabolical, dissolute, evil, fiendish, foul, immoral, infamous, infernal, lawless, nefarious, noxious, profligate, reprobate, shameful, sinful, transgressing, unjust, unprincipled, unrighteous, unsound, villainous, wicked. ANT.—exemplary, good, honorable, moral, reputable.

initial, antecedent, basic, beginning, earliest, elementary, first, fundamental, original, primary, prime, primeval, primitive, pristine, rudimentary; chief, foremost. ANT.—hindmost, last, latest; least, subordinate.

initiate, arise, begin, commence, enter, establish, inaugurate, indoctrinate, institute, introduce, invest, open, originate, start. ANT.—close, complete, finish, raze, terminate.

initiative, acceleration, action, drive, energy, enterprise, leadership, responsibility. ANT.—cowardice, lethargy, shyness, timidity.

injunction, bidding, canon, command, directive, law, mandate, order (of a judge), ordinance, regulation, rule.

injurious, damaging, defamatory, deleterious, destructive, detrimental, disadvantageous, harmful, hurtful, libelous, mischievous, pernicious, prejudicial, wrongful. ANT.—advantageous, beneficial, helpful, profitable, salutory.

injury, blemish, damage, detriment, disadvantage, grievance, harm, hurt, impairment, injustice, loss, mischief, prejudice, wound, wrong. ANT.—benefit, blessing, emolument, relief, remedy.

injustice, bias, encroachment, favoritism, grievance, illegality, inequality, inequity, infringement, injury, unfairness, violation, wrong. ANT.—equity, fairness, justice, lawfulness, righteousness.

inkling, clue, hint, idea, impression, indication, inference, innuendo, notice, suggestion, suspicion, tip.

innocent, artless, blameless, clean, exemplary, faultless, harmless, guiltless, impeccable, innocuous, irreproachable, lawful, pure, righteous, sinless, spotless, stainless, uninvolved, upright, virginal, virtuous. ANT.—corrupt, culpable, guilty, lascivious, sinful.

innocuous, gentle, harmless, inoffensive, insipid, mild, pallid, safe, undetrimental, uninjurious. ANT.—blighting, destructive, detrimental, injurious, pestilential.

innovation, addition, alteration, change, introduction, invention, modification, newness, novelty, remodeling, variation. ANT.—custom, habit, old (way), rut, tradition.

inquest, audit, examination, inquiry, inquisition, inspection, interrogation, investigation, probe, research, scrutiny.

inquire, examine, explore, hunt, interrogate, meddle, probe, pry, pursue, query, question, reconnoiter, research, scan, scout, scrutinize, search, seek, sift; ask, beg, claim, demand, entreat, invite, request, solicit. ANT.—abandon, neglect, shelve; answer, contradict, reply.

inquisitive, curious, inquiring, interrogative, intruding, intrusive, meddlesome, meddling, nosy, peeping, peering, prying, scrutinizing, searching, sniffing, snoopy. ANT.—apathetic, indifferent, lackadaisical, negligent, unconcerned.

insane, aberrant, crazy, daft, delirious, demented, deranged, fanatical, foolish, frenetic, frenzied, idiotic, imbecilic, incoherent, irrational, lunatic, mad, maniacal, manic, mentally ill, paranoiac, psychopathic, psychotic, rabid, raging, unbalanced, unsound. ANT.—lucid, rational, reasonable, sane, stable.

insecure, dangerous, endangered, exposed, hazardous, ill-protected, imperiled, precarious, rickety, risky, shaky, unguarded, unsafe, unstable; anxious, apprehensive, concerned, fearful, troubled, uncertain, worried. ANT.—safe, secure, fortified, strong; assured, certain, confident, serene.

insensitive, callous, cold, dull, hard, impenitent, indurate, insensible, obdurate, obtuse, phlegmatic, remote, thick-skinned, tough, unaffected, unemotional, unfeeling, unimpressionable, unresponsive. ANT.—compassionate, empathetic, responsive, sensitive, tender.

insertion, implantation, infusion, injection, inlay, inoculation, installation, interpolation, introduction. ANT.—extraction, removal, transfer, withdrawal.

insolent, abusive, arrogant, blustering, brazen, bumptious, contemptuous, contumelious, defiant, disdainful, disrespectful, domineering, haughty, imperious, impertinent, impudent, insulting, offensive, overbearing, presumptuous, rude, supercilious, swaggering, threatening, unmannerly. ANT.—considerate, courteous, humble, polite, respectful; abased, cowardly, groveling, parasitic, sniveling.

inspection, audit, checking, comparison, critique, examination, inquest, inquiry, inquisition, investigation, measuring, observation, overseeing, probing, review, scanning, scrutiny, study, supervision, survey.

inspiration, animation, arousal, enthusiasm, exaltation, fire, incitement, predilection, revelation, stimulation; fancy, hunch, impulse, notion, whim; incentive, influence, spur, stimulus; inhalation. ANT.—apathy, habitude, lethargy; aversion; exhalation.

insight, acumen, comprehension, discernment, intuition, introspection, judgment, keenness, penetration, perception, perspicacity, perspicuity, shrewdness, understanding. ANT.—confusion, ignorance, obtuseness, perplexity, shallowness.

insignificant, cheap, frivolous, inconsequential, meaningless, minute, paltry, petty, small, trifling, trivial, unimportant, valueless, worthless. ANT.—important, momentous, significant, valuable, weighty.

insinuate, connote, hint, imply, indicate, infer, ingratiate, intimate, involve, mean, purport, signify, suggest. ANT.—assert, express, state; conceal, disguise, suppress, veil.

insipid, bland, characterless, dull, flat, flavorless, inanimate, lifeless, mawkish, stale, tasteless, unimaginative, uninteresting, unsavory, vapid. ANT.—appetizing, exhilarating, racy, savory, tasty.

insistent, aggressive, clamorous, demanding, exigent, imperative, importunate, pressing, urgent. ANT.—acquiescent, agreeable, indifferent, lenient, tolerant.

instance, application, case, elucidation, example, exemplification, illustration, lesson, object, occurrence, point, sample, specimen, type.

instantaneous, abrupt, at once, direct, hasty, immediate, prompt, rapid, sudden, unexpected. ANT.—anticipated, delayed, gradual, late, slow.

instantly, abruptly, directly, forthwith, immediately, instantaneously, now, presently, promptly, straightaway, suddenly, urgently, without delay. ANT.—distantly, hereafter, in a while, later, sometime.

instinctive, accustomed, automatic, congenital, constitutional, fundamental, habitual, impulsive, inborn, ingrained, inherent, innate, intrinsic, involuntary, mechanical, natural, offhand, reflexive, regular, spontaneous, typical, usual. ANT.—acquired, deliberate, learned, meditated, voluntary, willed.

institute, begin, build, enact, erect, establish, fix, form, found, initiate, introduce, invent, invest, ordain, order, organize, originate, plan, raise, sanction, settle, start. ANT.—abolish, demolish, raze, terminate, unsettle.

instruct, admonish, advise, coach, command, convey, counsel, direct, discipline, drill, edify, educate, enlighten, exhort, expound, guide, impart, inculcate, indoctrinate, inform, instill, prime, promulgate, school, teach, train, tutor. ANT.—delude, falsify, misguide, misinform, misinterpret.

instrumental, accessory, assisting, auxiliary, conducive, contributory, expeditious, helpful, promoting, serviceable, serving, subsidiary. ANT.—detrimental, hindering, impeding, injurious, obstructive.

insubordination, contrariness, contumacy, defiance, disobedience, intractability, mutiny, perversity, rebellion, refractoriness, revolt, stubbornness. ANT.—loyalty, obedience, submission, tractability.

insufficient, bare, deficient, drained, imperfect, inadequate, incompetent, incomplete, lacking, limited, meager, rare, scant, scarce, short, slack, sparse ANT.— abundant, ample, copious, rich, sufficient.

insulate, alienate, cover, detach, disconnect, disengage, isolate, part, protect, quarantine, retire, seclude, segregate, separate, sequester, sunder, withdraw, wrap. ANT.—associate, connect, integrate, mingle, unite.

insult, abuse, acerbity, affront, derision, discourtesy, disrespect, gall, impudence, incivility, indignity, insolence, libel, mockery, offense, rudeness, scurrility, slight, slur, snub; abuse, affront, dishonor, injure, mock, offend, outrage, wrong. ANT.—apology, courtesy, homage, salutation; defer, praise, respect, revere.

integral, centralized, complete, consummate, constituent, definite, entire, one, perfect, uncut, unitary, whole. ANT.—divisional, fractional, indefinite, partial, segmental.

integration, alliance, amalgamation, blending, combination, consolidation, fusion, joining, merger, mingling, mixture, unification, union. ANT.—isolation, seclusion, segregation, separation.

integrity, candor, constancy, fairness, faithfulness, fidelity, frankness, honesty, honor, incorruptness, justice, loyalty, morality, openness, probity, purity, rectitude, responsibility, righteousness, sincerity, trustworthiness, uprightness, virtue; completeness, entirety, soundness, value, wholeness, worth. ANT.—deceit, fraud, infidelity, treason, turpitude; fragmentation, imperfection, loss, worthlessness.

intelligence, acumen, aptitude, astuteness, comprehension, discernment, grasp, insight, intellect, knowledge, mental ability, mind, penetration, perspicacity, reason, sense, understanding, wit; inside facts, secret information, secret report. ANT.—emotion, feeling, passion.

intelligent, alert, apt, astute, bright, brilliant, capable, clever, discerning, exceptional, keen, knowing, perceptive, quick, sensible, sharp, smart; enlightened, intellectual, knowledgeable, well-informed. ANT.—dull, insipid, obtuse, shallow, stupid.

intend, aim, contemplate, delineate, design, desire, destine, devise, hope, mean, outline, plan, plot, prepare, project, propose, purpose, scheme, sketch, try, want, wish.

intensity, acuteness, ardor, concentration, depth, eagerness, earnestness, emphasis, fervor, force, magnitude, might, potency, power, pressure, strain, strength, tension, toughness, vehemence, vigor. ANT.—feebleness, lassitude, lethargy, passivity, weakness.

intentional, aimed at, calculated, contemplated, deliberate, designed, determined, intended, meant, planned, premeditated, projected, purposed, studied, voluntary, willful. ANT.—accidental, fortuitous, haphazard, random, unforeseen.

intercept, ambush, appropriate, arrest, avert, block, catch, check, cut off, hinder, interpose, interrupt, obstruct, prevent, stop, take away, waylay. ANT.—aid, boost, forward, succor, uphold.

interest, advantage, appeal, attention, behalf, benefit, charm, claim, concern, curiosity, fascination, gain, inquisitiveness, portion, premium, profit, right, share, stake, title; absorb, amuse, appeal to, beguile, cheer, concern, delight, divert, enliven, entertain, enthrall, fascinate, gratify, hold attention, intrigue, occupy, please. ANT.—apathy, indifference, insolvency, loss; bore, displease, stupefy, tire, vex.

interfere, bar, block, clash, collide, conflict, delay, frustrate, hamper, hinder, impede, inconvenience, interpose, interrupt, intrude, meddle, mediate, obstruct, obtrude, oppose, stall, tamper, thwart. ANT.—abet, aid, clear, help, stand aside.

interior, heart, inmost, inner, inside, internal, inward, middle; bowels, core, enclosure, hinterlands, inland. ANT.—boundary, coast, exterior, external, periphery.

interminable, boundless, continuous, endless, eternal, everlasting, illimitable, immeasurable, incessant, infinite, limitless, permanent, tedious, unbounded, unlimited, vast. ANT.—bounded, confined, finite, intermittent, periodic.

intermittent, alternate, broken, cyclic, discontinuous, fitful, flickering, fluttering, infrequent, interrupted, occasional, periodic, recurrent, remittent, spasmodic. ANT.—constant, continual, incessant, perpetual, regular.

internal, domestic, enclosed, esoteric, ingrained, inherent, innate, inner, inside, interior, intrinsic, inward. ANT.—alien, external, foreign, outer, superficial.

interpose, inject, insert, intercalate, interject, interpolate, introduce; arbitrate, intercede, intercept, interfere, interrupt, intersperse, intervene,

intrude, meddle, mediate, negotiate, obtrude, sandwich, tamper. ANT.—extract, omit, withdraw; avoid, overlook, shun.

interpret, clarify, construe, decipher, decode, define, describe, disentangle, elucidate, explain, explicate, expound, illuminate, manifest, paraphrase, render, reveal, solve, translate, unfold, unravel. ANT.—confuse, distort, misconstrue, misinterpret, mystify.

interrogation, examination, inquiry, inquisition, interpellation, investigation, probe, query, test. ANT.—acknowledgement, answer, rejoinder, reply, response.

interrupt, arrest, adjourn, break, check, cut, defer, delay, disconnect, discontinue, disturb, divide, hinder, interfere, obstruct, postpone, sever, stay, stop, suspend. ANT.—continue, maintain, persist, prolong, sustain.

intervene, arbitrate, intercede, interpose, mediate, negotiate, step in; inject, insert, interfere, interject, interlope, introduce, intrude, meddle; divide, part, sever; befall, happen, occur. ANT.—ignore, stand aside; assist, help; assemble, convene.

intimate, affectionate, close, confidential, familiar, friendly, internal, loving, near, personal, private, secret, special, trusted. ANT.—ceremonious, cool, distant, formal, remote.

intimate, v. see insinuate.

intolerable, detestable, impossible, insufferable, insupportable, offensive, painful, unbearable, unendurable. ANT.—bearable, endurable, passable, satisfying, tolerable.

intolerant, biased, bigoted, discriminatory, dogmatic, fanatical, illiberal, narrow-minded, prejudiced, unfair, unyielding. ANT.—impartial, lenient, nondiscriminatory, open-minded, unbiased.

intrepid, adventurous, audacious, bold, brave, courageous, daring, dauntless, fearless, lionhearted, mighty, nervy, plucky, powerful, strong, unafraid, unflinching, unshrinking, valiant, valorous. ANT.—cowardly, cringing, fainthearted, flinching, timid, trembling.

intricate, complex, complicated, compound, confused, convoluted, difficult, disarranged, inextricable, involved, irregular, knotted, labyrinthine, mixed, perplexing, raveled, tangled. ANT.—arranged, clear, plain, simple, uncompounded.

intrigue, cabal, chicanery, collusion, complication, connivance, conspiracy, craft, cunning, design, double-dealing, duplicity, machination, maneuvering, plan, plot, scheme, secret, stratagem, trickery, wire-pulling.

intrinsic, congenital, essential, fundamental, genuine, honest, inborn, inbred, indigenous, ingrained, inherent, innate, native, natural, real, subjective, true. ANT.—external, extraneous, extrinsic, incidental, objective.

introduction, beginning, commencement, foreword, inception, initiation, interjection, interpolation, meeting, overture, preamble, preface, prelude, presentation, prologue, start. ANT.—conclusion, end, epilogue, finale, postlude.

intrusive, encroaching, infringing, inquisitive, interfering, invading, meddlesome, obtrusive, snooping, trespassing. ANT.—unintrusive, unobtrusive, retiring.

intuitive, emotional, guessing, heedless, impulsive, instinctive, involuntary, unreasoning, unreflective; discerning, insightful, knowing, perceptive. ANT.—calculated, meditated, planned, reasoned; obtuse.

invalidate, abolish, abrogate, annul, cancel, counteract, negate, neutralize, null, nullify, quash, recall, revoke, stop, void. ANT.—endorse, establish, promote, sustain, validate.

invaluable, dear, expensive, inestimable, precious, priceless, valuable. ANT.—cheap, nugatory, useless, worthless.

invasion, aggression, assault, attack, entrance, foray, incursion, ingress, ingression, inroad, intrusion, irruption, onslaught, outbreak, raid, take-over. ANT.—defense, evacuation, fortification, protection, safeguard.

invective, abuse, aspersion, blasphemy, censure, condemnation, contumely, defamation, denouncement, denunciation, deprecation, disapprobation, disapproval, disparagement, insult, obloquy, opprobrium, raillery, reprimand, reprehension, reproach, sarcasm, scurrility, upbraiding, vituperation. ANT.—approval, commendation, laudation, plaudit, sanction.

invent, coin, conceive, concoct, conjure, contrive, design, devise, draft, fabricate, fashion, form, frame, imagine, improvise, manufacture, originate, outline, plan, project, sketch, visualize; deceive, equivocate, fake, falsify, lie, misrepresent, misstate. ANT.—copy, imitate, reproduce; disabuse, disillusionize.

inventory, catalog, itemization, list, record, register, roll, roster, schedule, table; contents, stock, store, supply; examination, inspection, investigation.

investigation, catechism, discussion, examination, exploitation, exploration, inquiry, inquisition, interrogation, pursuit, query, quest, question, research, review, search, scrutiny. ANT.—disregard, inactivity, inattention, neglect, overlooking.

invincible, formidable, impregnable, incontestable, indomitable, inseparable, insuperable, insurmountable, invulnerable, irresistible, mighty, overpowering, resistless, sovereign, unassailable, unconquerable, unvanquishable, unyielding. ANT.—impotent, powerless, puny, vulnerable, weak.

invisible, evanescent, gaseous, imperceptible, indistinguishable, intangible, microscopic, occult, undiscernible, undisclosed, unreal, unseen, vaporous. ANT.—evident, perceptible, real, substantial, visible.

involve, comprehend, compromise, contain, cover, denote, embarrass, embroil, entail, entangle, envelop, enwrap, implicate, imply, include, incriminate, overwhelm, signify. ANT.—disconnect, disengage, extricate, separate, unravel.

irate, angry, enraged, ferocious, fierce, fuming, furious, incensed, infuriated, irritated, mad, nettled, piqued, provoked, rabid, raging, stormy, wrathful. ANT.—appeased, calm, pleased, quiet, restrained.

irk, annoy, bother, chafe, discompose, disturb, fret, inconvenience, irritate, perturb, pester, tease, trouble, upset, vex. ANT.—console, delight, gladden, please, soothe.

irony, banter, criticism, derision, mockery, paradox, quip, raillery, reproach, ridicule, sarcasm, satire, twist. ANT.—approval, courtesy, deference, esteem, respect.

irrational, absurd, crazed, crazy, daft, demented, fatuous, feeble-minded, foolish, inconsistent, injudicious, illogical, nonsensical, odd, preposterous, queer, ridiculous, self-contradictory, silly, strange, stupid, unreasonable, unsound, vacuous, weak-minded. ANT.—logical, lucid, rational, reasonable, sound.

irreconcilable, divergent, implacable, incompatible, incongruous, inconsequent, inexorable, quarrelsome, unappeasable. ANT.—appeasable, compatible, congruous, reconcilable, solvable.

irregularity, aberration, abnormality, anomaly, asymmetry, caprice, deviation, disorderliness, eccentricity, fitfulness, inordinateness, inconstancy, intermittency, tardiness, unruliness, variation. ANT.—method, order, regularity, stability, system.

irrelevant, alien, extraneous, foreign, immaterial, inapplicable, inapposite, inappropriate, inconsequent, remote, strange, unconnected, unessential, unrelated. ANT.—apt, fitting, germane, pertinent, relevant.

irremediable, beyond help, hopeless, incurable, irrecoverable, irreparable, irretrievable, irrevocable, useless. ANT.—curable, recoverable, reparable.

irresolute, doubting, drifting, fickle, fluctuating, half-hearted, hesitant, hesitating, ineffective, irresponsible, lukewarm, pliable, shaky, uncertain, undecided, undetermined, unsettled, unstable, unsteady, vacillating, volatile, wavering, wobbling; bending, fragile, frail, yielding. ANT.—enduring, potent, powerful, relentless, tenacious.

irresponsible, arbitrary, capricious, careless, faltering, flighty, fluctuating, foolish, giddy, heedless, immature, irresolute, purposeless, rash, reckless, thoughtless, unaccountable, unanswerable, unreliable, unstable, unsteady, wobbly. ANT.—accountable, dependable, reliable, steady, trustworthy.

irritable, cantankerous, captious, choleric, excitable, fidgety, fiery, fractious, fretful, hasty, hot, ill-tempered, irascible, peevish, petulant, querulous, sensitive, snappy, susceptible, testy, thin-skinned, touchy. ANT.—agreeable, calm, composed, serene, tranquil.

irritate, aggravate, agitate, anger, annoy, bother, chafe, disturb, enrage, exacerbate, exasperate, fluster, foment, harass, inconvenience, inflame, infuriate, irk, madden, pester, pique, provoke, ruffle, sting, taunt, tease, trouble, vex. ANT.—accommodate, console, gratify, moderate, pacify.

isolate, alienate, disconnect, dissociate, exclude, insulate, quarantine, retire, seclude, segregate, separate, sequester, withdraw. ANT.—associate, integrate, join, mingle, unite.

issue, aftermath, conclusion, consequence, culmination, denouement, effect, emanation, eventuality, finish, fruits, offspring, product, progeny, result, termination; event, incident; point, question, subject, topic; arise, emanate, emerge, emit, ensue, eventuate, exude, flow, originate, proceed, result, spew, spread, spring, start; publish; circulate money; abound, be copious. ANT.—contain, repress, retain, suppress.

itinerary, circuit, course, flight, guidebook, log, map, path, plan, record, route, travel plans, trip.

J

jam, block, bruise, cram, crowd, crush, force, impede, improvise (music), interfere, mass, pack, press, push, squeeze, tamp, wedge. ANT.—expand, free, diffuse, disperse, separate.

jargon, argot, babble, bosh, cant, dialect, gibberish, idiom, jive, lingo, patois, phraseology, shop talk, slang, trade talk, vernacular.

jealous, covetous, distrustful, doubtful, doubting, dubious, envious, invidious, jaundiced, mistrustful, resentful, suspicious; solicitous, vigilant, watchful. ANT.—content, indifferent, lenient, serene, trusting.

jeer, deride, fleer, flout, gibe, hoot, mock, ridicule, scoff, sneer, taunt. ANT.—compliment, flatter, honor, laud, praise.

jeopardize, chance, compromise, conjecture, dare, endanger, expose, hazard, imperil, menace, peril, risk, threaten, venture. ANT.—determine, guard, insure, protect, shield.

jest, banter, humor, joke, prank, quip, wisecrack, witticism.

jocular, comical, droll, facetious, funny, humorous, joking, merry, pleasant, sportive, waggish, witty. ANT.—dull, grave, morose, serious.

join, accompany, add, adjoin, affiliate, associate, attach, bind, cement, combine, conjoin, connect, consolidate, couple, enter, knit, link, marry, tie, unify, unite. ANT.—detach, disconnect, leave, sever, sunder.

joint, articulation, collaboration, combination, connection, cooperation, junction, juncture, link, meeting, union; dove-tail, dowel, hinge, mitre, mortise, pivot, seam, welding; associated, combined, shared, united. ANT.—separate, single.

jolly, blithe, cheerful, congenial, convivial, frolicsome, gay, happy, humorous, jocose, jocular, jocund, jovial, joyous, merry, playful, sprightly, vivacious, witty. ANT.—depressed, glum, melancholy, mournful, sullen.

journal, account, chart, daily register, daybook, diary, gazette, log, magazine, newspaper, periodical, publication, record, register.

journey, course, cruise, excursion, expedition, jaunt, passage, peregrination, pilgrimage, safari, tour, travel, trek, trip, voyage. ANT.—stay, stop.

joy, bliss, cheer, delight, ecstasy, elation, exultation, felicity, gaiety, gladness, glee, happiness, merriment, mirth, pleasure, rapture, transport. ANT.—affliction, depression, despair, grief, wretchedness.

judge, adjudicator, arbiter, arbitrator, censor, connoisseur, critic, custodian, guardian, interpreter, judiciary, magistrate, protector, referee, reviewer, umpire; decide, decree, determine; adjudicate, arbitrate, condemn, try, umpire; appreciate, consider, estimate, evaluate, measure, think.

judgment, award, decision, discernment, decree, discrimination, injunction, intellectuality, perspicacity, ruling, sagacity, sentence, understanding, wisdom. ANT.—arbitrariness, senselessness, stupidity, thoughtlessness, vacuity.

jumble, confuse, disarrange, mess, mingle, mix up, muddle, shuffle; agitation, chaos, commotion, confusion, disarrangement, disarray, disorder, ferment, stir, tumult, turmoil. ANT.—arrange, classify, file, rectify, systematize; certainty, order, peace, tranquility.

jump, bounce, bound, caper, hop, jerk, leap, pounce, skip, spring, start, twitch, vault.

just, blameless, candid, conscientious, earned, equitable, fair, honest, honorable, impartial, innocent, judicious, lawful, legal, legitimate, merited, precise, rightful, scrupulous, sincere, true, unbiased, upright. ANT.—corrupt, deceitful, dishonest, fraudulent, lying, villainous.

justice, equity, fairness, fair play, impartiality, justness, lawfulness, legality, propriety, reasonableness, rectitude, right, righteousness, uprightness. ANT.—corruption, dishonor, favoritism, inequity, unlawfulness.

justify, absolve, acquit, advocate, clear, defend, excuse, exonerate, extenuate, forgive, free, maintain, support, uphold, vindicate. ANT.—accuse, blame, convict, indict, stigmatize.

K

keen, acrid, acute, ardent, bitter, caustic, clever, cunning, cutting, discerning, fervid, incisive, intense, lively, penetrating, perspicacious, piercing, pointed, quick, sagacious, severe, sharp, shrewd, stinging, vivid, wily, witty, zealous. ANT.—apathetic, blunt, dull, lethargic, sluggish.

keep, conserve, continue, defend, guard, maintain, preserve, protect, save, secure, support, sustain, tend, uphold; confine, detail, hold, imprison, reserve, restrain, retain, suppress, withhold; adhere, execute, obey; celebrate, commemorate, honor, observe. ANT.—destroy, discard, reject; dismiss, release, relinquish; disobey, ignore; abandon, forsake.

kill, assassinate, annul, butcher, choke, decimate, delete, destroy, extinguish, immolate, massacre, murder, obliterate, slaughter, slay, smother, strangle, veto. ANT.—animate, protect, resuscitate, safeguard, vivify.

kin, clan, family, kindred, kinsfolk, kinsmen, kith, relatives, siblings, tribe.

kind, accommodating, affable, affectionate, amiable, beneficent, benevolent, benign, caring, charitable, compassionate, considerate, cordial, forbearing, gentle, good, gracious, humane, indulgent, kind-hearted, kindly, loving, merciful, obliging, sympathetic, tender, thoughtful; brand, breed, category, character, class, family, genus, ilk, offspring, order, progeny, race, relation, sort, species, stock, strain, type, variety. ANT.—cruel, inhuman, merciless, ruthless, vicious.

kindred, affinity, consanguinity, family, kin, kinsfolk, kinsmen, relations, relationship, relatives; allied, analogous, congenial, corresponding, empathetic, like, parallel, related, similar, sympathetic. ANT.—disconnection, foreigners, strangers; dissimilar, foreign, heterogeneous, unlike, unrelated.

kingdom, country, domain, dominion, empire, monarchy, nation, realm, rule, sovereignty.

kiss, buss, caress, cuddle, embrace, fondle, osculation, pax (kiss of peace), touch of the lips.

knack, ability, adeptness, adroitness, aptitude, cleverness, deftness, dexterity, expertness, facility, faculty, ingenuity, proficiency, readiness, skill, skillfulness, talent; device, trick. ANT.—awkwardness, clumsiness, incompetence, ineptitude.

knit, affiliate, bind, connect, crochet, interlace, intermingle, intertwine, join, link, loop, net, spin, tie, unite, weave, web. ANT.—divide, separate, unravel, untie.

knot, assemblage, bond, bunch, cluster, collection, complication, connection, difficulty, entanglement, gathering, intricacy, ligature, perplexity, protuberance, snarl, tangle, tie, tuft.

know, appreciate, apprehend, ascertain, cognize, comprehend, conceive, discern, distinguish, fathom, hold, interpret, perceive, recognize, remember, think, understand. ANT.—dispute, doubt, forget, misapprehend, misconstrue.

knowledge, acquaintance, apperception, apprehension, cognition, cognizance, comprehension, education, enlightenment, erudition, experience, familiarity, information, learning, light, lore, perception, recognition, scholarship, science, understanding, wisdom. ANT.—blindness, enigma, ignorance, illiteracy, stupidity.

L

labor, drudgery, effort, endeavor, exertion, industry, pains, painstaking, plodding, striving, struggle, task, toil, travail, work; childbirth. ANT.—idleness, inertia, lethargy, relaxation, sloth.

lack, dearth, deficiency, demerit, depletion, distress, failing, fault, inadequacy, insufficiency, neediness, privation, poverty, scantiness, scarcity, shortage; need, want. ANT.—abundance, excess, profusion, sufficiency, surplus.

lag, dally, dawdle, delay, fall behind, falter, idle, linger, loiter, plod, retard, saunter, slacken, stagger, tarry, trudge. ANT.—accelerate, bound, dash, hasten, hustle.

lame, crippled, defective, deformed, disabled, faltering, halt, hesitating, hobbling, impotent, limping, maimed; feeble, ineffective, unconvincing, unsatisfactory, weak. ANT.—agile, robust, vigorous; convincing, effective, forceful.

lament, anguish, bemoan, bewail, commiserate, cry, deplore, fret, grieve, mourn, regret, repine, rue, wail, weep, worry. ANT.—celebrate, cheer, delight in, exult, rejoice.

language, brogue, cant, dialect, diction, expression, idiom, jargon, lingo, linguistics, literature, patois, philology, phraseology, slang, speech, terminology, tongue, utterance, vernacular, vocabulary, voice, words.

languid, apathetic, debilitated, drooping, drowsy, dull, faint, feeble, flagging, heartless, irresolute, laggard, languorous, leisurely, lethargic, listless, pensive, pining, sickly, slack, slow, sluggish, torpid, weak, wearied. ANT.—animated, brisk, enthusiastic, spirited, vigorous.

lanky, bony, gangling, gaunt, lank, lean, narrow, overgrown, raw-boned, slim, spare, wiry. ANT.—brawny, burly, husky, portly, sturdy.

lapse, backsliding, blunder, boner, delay, error, fault, flaw, fumble, gap, indiscretion, misstep, mistake, omission, oversight, passing, sin, slip.

larceny, appropriation, burglary, embezzlement, peculation, pilfering, pillage, plunder, purloinment, robbery, shoplifting, theft. ANT.—compensation, recoupment, repayment, restoration, return.

large, abundant, ample, big, broad, bulky, capacious, colossal, commodious, copious, corpulent, enormous, extensive, gigantic, grand, great, huge, immense, magnificent, massive, mighty, monstrous, long, obese, plentiful, roomy, sizeable, towering, vast, wide. ANT.—infinitesimal, microscopic, minute, paltry, puny.

lash, abuse, beat, castigate, drive, flagellate, flail, goad, impel, press, pummel, scourge, spank, spur, strike, urge, whip; satirize, scold, rate.

last, closing, concluding, conclusive, crowning, extreme, final, finishing, hindmost, latest, least, supreme, terminal, ultimate, utmost. ANT.—commencing, first, foremost, leading, primary.

late, delayed, dilatory, lagging, overdue, slow, tardy; deceased, demised, departed; bygone, defunct, extinct, gone, lapsed; advanced, new, recent. ANT.—early, prompt, punctual, ready; alive, animated, living; aged, ancient, antique, old.

latent, allusive, concealed, dormant, hidden, implicit, implied, inactive, inherent, invisible, involved, lurking, passive, potential, quiescent, recondite, secret, undeveloped, unknown, unobserved, unperceived, unseen, vestigial. ANT.—apparent, conspicuous, known, prominent, unmistakable, visible.

latitude, breadth, compass, distance, extent, freedom, leeway, length, range, reach, room, scope, space, sweep, width; laxity.

laudable, admirable, commendable, creditable, deserving, dutiful, estimable, excellent, exemplary, honorable, ideal; meritorious, model, praiseworthy, righteous, worthy. ANT.—corrupt, damnable, degraded, iniquitous, odious.

laughable, absurd, amusing, asinine, bizarre, comic, comical, droll, eccentric, facetious, farcical, foolish, funny, jocose, ludicrous, quaint, ridiculous, waggish, whimsical. ANT.—depressive, funereal, melancholy, morbid, painful.

launch, begin, cast, commence, dart, dispatch, enlarge, expatiate, float, hurl, inaugurate, initiate, open, project, start, throw. ANT.—close, end, finish, land, splash down.

lavish, abundant, costly, dear, excessive, exhaustive, exorbitant, exuberant, generous, inordinate, liberal, luxuriant, prodigal, profligate, profuse, replete, superabundant, unrestrained, unstinted, wasteful; bestow, deluge, dissipate, expend, flood, glut, gorge, indulge, inundate, load, misuse, overload, overrun, scatter, spend, squander, waste, wear out. ANT.—deficient, inadequate, jejune, meager, scanty; conserve, curtail, economize, skimp, treasure.

law, act, canon, code, command, commandment, constitution, covenant, decree, edict, enactment, equity, formula, jurisprudence, justice, legality, legislation, mandate, order, ordinance, precept, principle, regulation, rule, statute. ANT.—felony, illegality, lawlessness, outlawry, transgression.

lawful, admitted, allowable, approved, authorized, canonical, conceded, constitutional, granted, judicial, legal, legislative, legitimate, licit, official, permissible, recognized, right, rightful, sanctioned, warranted. ANT.—arbitrary, criminal, illegal, prohibited, unauthorized.

lax, careless, depraved, derelict, desultory, flaccid, immoral, inaccurate, lawless, limp, neglectful, negligent, relaxed, remiss, unconscientious, undutiful, unobservant, unprincipled, vague, weak. ANT.—determined, faithful, honorable, meticulous, rigid, rigorous.

lay, common, earthly, mundane, noncleric, nonecclesiastical, nonprofessional, popular, profane, secular, temporal, worldly; arrange, deposit, dispose, place, put, set. ANT.—professional, spiritual, unworldly; disarrange, disturb, misplace, remove.

lazy, idle, inactive, indolent, inert, lackadaisical, laggard, lethargic, negligent, shiftless, sleepy, slothful, sluggish, supine, torpid, weak, worn. ANT.—active, assiduous, diligent, industrious, persevering.

lead, conduct, direct, escort, guide, pilot, shepherd, steer; command, control, govern, manage, regulate, superintend, supervise; begin, open, pioneer, precede, start. ANT.—perform; acquiesce, comply, obey, submit; follow.

leader, captain, chief, chieftain, commander, conductor, director, guide, head, master, principal, ruler, superior, vanguard. ANT.—adherent, devotee, disciple, follower, henchman.

league, alliance, association, cartel, club, coalition, combination, confederacy, confederation, entente, federation, fraternity, partnership, pool, society, union.

leak, dribble, drip, escape, exude, filter, ooze, overflow, pass, percolate, seep, spill, trickle.

lean, bend, cant, careen, crook, decline, deflect, deviate, dip, hang, heel, incline, list, sag, shelve, sidle, slant, slope, tend, tip; depend, rely, trust. ANT.—erect, raise, rise, straighten.

leap, bound, caper, dance, frisk, frolic, gambol, hop, jerk, jump, romp, skip, spring, start, trip, vault.

learn, acquire, ascertain, determine, discern, discover, gain, gather, hear, imbibe, master, memorize, read, receive, study, unearth.

learned, academic, accomplished, deep, discerning, educated, enlightened, erudite, informed, intelligent, knowing, lettered, literate, pedantic, penetrating, philosophic, profound, sagacious, scholarly, solid, sound, well-informed, wise. ANT.—dull, ignorant, illiterate, shallow, uncultured.

leave, absence, allowance, concession, consent, freedom, furlough, holiday, liberty, license, permission, vacation, withdrawal; abandon, allow, decamp, depart, desert, forsake, give up, go, let, permit, quit, relinquish, renounce, retire, vacate, withdraw. ANT.—confinement, hindrance, prohibition, restriction, taboo; abide, endure, persist, remain, tarry.

lecture, address, discourse, dissertation, homily, lesson, prelection, sermon, speech, talk; scold, upbraid.

legal, admitted, allowable, allowed, authorized, constitutional, correct, equitable, fair, lawful, legitimate, permissible, rightful, sanctioned, valid, warranted. ANT.—criminal, illegal, illicit, prohibited, unconstitutional.

legendary, fabulous, fanciful, fictitious, mythical, romantic, traditional. ANT.—actual, factual, historical, real, true.

legitimate, correct, genuine, justifiable, lawful, legal, logical, real, sanctioned, true, valid, warranted. ANT.—illegal, illegitimate, invalid.

leisure, calm, ease, peace, quiet, relaxation, repose, rest, tranquility; cessation, freedom, idleness, intermission, leave, liberty, pause, retirement, respite, sparetime, vacation. ANT.—agitation, commotion, disturbance, tumult; drudgery, duty, toil, travail, work.

lengthen, dilate, draw out, elongate, extend, increase, prolong, protract, stretch. ANT.—abbreviate, curtail, cut, shorten, speed.

lenient, assuaging, charitable, clement, compassionate, easy-going, forbearing, forgiving, gentle, humane, indulgent, kind, merciful, moderate, reasonable, tender, tolerant. ANT.—brutal, cruel, pitiless, tyrannical, unfeeling.

lessen, abate, abridge, contract, curtail, decrease, deduct, diminish, narrow, pare, reduce, shrink, shorten, subtract, trim. ANT.—amplify, enlarge, expand, increase, strengthen.

let, allow, authorize, bear, concede, empower, grant, permit, sanction, suffer, tolerate, warrant, yield; lease, rent. ANT.—defeat, halt, inhibit, obstruct, prevent.

lethargy, apathy, drowsiness, insensibility, languor, lassitude, listlessness, numbness, passivity, stupefaction, stupor, torpor. ANT.—activity, alertness, energy, liveliness, vitality.

level, balanced, equal, even, flat, flush, horizontal, plane, smooth, uniform; genuine, honest. ANT.—hilly, irregular, learning, lumpy, rugged; dishonest.

lewd, coarse, dirty, disgusting, filthy, gross, impure, indecent, lecherous, lustful, obscene, offensive, pornographic, prurient, smutty. ANT.—chaste, decent, modest, pure, refined.

liable, accountable, amenable, answerable, apt, bound, chargeable, exposed to, likely, responsible, subject to, susceptible. ANT.—absolved, exempt, free, immune, unlikely.

libel, asperse, damage, defame, detract, injure, lampoon, satirize, slander, vilify; aspersion, backbiting, calumny, defamation, slander, vilification. ANT.—defend, elevate, help, justify; applause, commendation, defense, flattery, praise.

liberal, ample, bountiful, broad-minded, extensive, extravagant, free, generous, large, lavish, leftist, lenient, magnanimous, munificent, noble-minded, prodigal, profuse, tolerant, unselfish. ANT.—confined, conservative, greedy, penurious, narrow, restricted.

liberate, absolve, acquit, clear, deliver, discharge, dismiss, emancipate, extricate, free, loose, pardon, ransom, redeem, release, rescue, save, set free, unchain, unshackle, untie. ANT.—confine, imprison, oppress, prohibit, restrict.

liberty, autonomy, emancipation, freedom, independence, liberation, self-government; allowance, dismissal, exemption, furlough, immunity, leisure, license, opportunity, permission, privilege, right. ANT.—bondage, captivity, imprisonment, oppression, slavery; confinement, constraint, detention, duress, obligation.

license, allow, approve, authorize, commission, endorse, permit, sanction, warrant; exemption, familiarity, freedom, immunity, independence, liberty, privilege. ANT.—ban, check, forbid, limit, withhold; bondage, compulsion, necessity, servitude.

lie, deceive, deviate, distort, equivocate, evade, exaggerate, falsify, fib, misinform, misrepresent, stretch; lie (down), recline, remain, repose, rest, stay. ANT.—be honest, declare (truth); arise, be upright, rise, sit, stand.

life, animation, being, buoyancy, essence, existence, liveliness, principle, spirit, vigor, vitality, vivacity; origin, source; duration, longevity, survival. ANT.—cessation, death, demise, inaction, languor.

lifeless, dead, deceased, defunct, demised, departed, dull, extinct, flat, gone, inactive, inanimate, insensible, spiritless, stagnant, unconscious. ANT.—alive, animate, brisk, living, vigorous, vital.

lift, boost, elevate, erect, exalt, heave, heighten, hoist, intensify, lift, raise, uplift; purloin, steal, take. ANT.—abase, depreciate, depress, destroy, lower; repay, return.

light, beam, blaze, brightness, brilliancy, dawn, flame, gleam, glow, illumination, incandescence, lamp, luminosity, lustre, radiance, scintillation, shimmer, sparkle, shine; comprehension, enlightenment, insight, knowledge, understanding; airy, buoyant, effervescent; ethereal, resilient, volatile; animated, blithe, capricious, cheerful, elated, hopeful, jocund, lively, sparkling, spirited, vivacious. ANT.—darkness, gloom, ignorance, obscurity, shadow; burdensome, heavy, weighty; depressed, gloomy, morose, sullen, weary.

likable, agreeable, amiable, companionable, enjoyable, friendly, good-natured, pleasant. ANT.—disagreeable, offensive, unattractive, unlikable, unpleasant.

like, akin, allied, analogous, cognate, coincident, comparable, equal, equivalent, identical, indistinguishable, parallel, related, resembling, same, similar. ANT.—contrary, disparate, dissimilar, distinct, opposed.

likeness, analogy, correspondence, counterpart, equivalence, parity, resemblance, similarity, similitude; copy, facsimile, illustration, photograph, portrait, representation. ANT.—difference, distinction, variation.

limit, border, boundary, brink, confine, edge, end, extent, extreme, frontier, limitation, line, restraint, restriction, rim, terminus. ANT.—boundlessness, endlessness, extension, infinity.

limpid, bright, clear, crystal, crystalline, glassy, lucid, pellucid, pure, translucent, transparent. ANT.—cloudy, dark, muddy, opaque, turbid.

lineage, ancestry, birth, breed, children, clan, descent, extraction, family, folk, forefathers, genealogy, nation, people, progeny, race, stock, strain, succession, tribe.

linger, abide, bide, dawdle, delay, falter, hesitate, lag, loiter, lumber, remain, rest, stay, tarry, wait. ANT.—bustle, dash, dart, hurry, speed.

link, associate, attach, bind, bond, conjoin, connect, couple, fasten, go with, join, pin, tie, unite. ANT.—cut, detach, divide, separate, sever.

liquid, dissolved, flowing, fluent, fluid, juicy, liquefied, melted, molten, sappy, serous, solvent, succulent, watery. ANT.—congealed, dense, gaseous, solid, undissolved.

listen, attend to, audit, hear, hearken, heed, list, monitor, overhear; follow, grant, obey, observe. ANT.—disregard, ignore, reject, scorn.

little, condensed, diminutive, dwarfish, elfin, infinitesimal, insignificant, meager, miniature, minute, petite, petty, puny, scanty, slight, small, tiny, trifling, trivial, wee; mean, petty, selfish. ANT.—colossal, enormous, huge, immense, mighty, titanic.

lively, active, animated, blithe, brisk bustling, ebullient, energetic, exhilarated, frolicsome, intense, rapid, spirited, sprightly, supple, vigorous, vivacious; bright, clear, fresh, glowing, sparkling, vivid. ANT.—dull, insipid, listless, stale, vapid.

load, afflict, burden, encumber, oppress, overlook, pressure, tax, trouble, weigh. ANT.—alleviate, console, ease, lighten, mitigate.

loathe, abhor, abominate, condemn, denounce, despise, detest, dislike, hate, imprecate, oppose. ANT.—admire, approve, cherish, love, respect.

location, area, locale, locality, neighborhood, place, position, post, region, site, situation, spot, station, vicinity.

lock, attachment, bar, barrier, bolt, catch, clasp, connection, fastening, grapple, hasp, hook, latch, link, padlock; curl, ringlet, tress, tuft.

lofty, dignified, elevated, exalted, grand, grandiose, high, imposing, magnificent, majestic, noble, pompous, proud, stately, sublime; arrogant, conceited, haughty, pretentious, vain. ANT.—common, humble, lowly, modest, ordinary, plebian.

logical, cogent, coherent, convincing, dialectical, discriminating, effective, efficacious, rational, reasonable, sound, strong, telling, valid, weighty. ANT.—crazy, foolish, incoherent, incongruous, weak.

lone, deserted, desolate, isolated, lonely, lonesome, secluded, unaided, unattached; alone, only, single, sole, solitary, unique. ANT.—accompanied, attended, joined, surrounded, together.

lonely, alone, cheerless, desolate, dreary, forlorn, forsaken, isolated, lonesome, secluded, sequestered, solitary. ANT.—befriended, cheerful.

long, drawn out, elongated, enduring, extended, interminable, lasting, lengthy, lingering, prolix, prolonged, protracted, tedious, wordy; distant, far-away, far-off, remote. ANT.—abridged, brief, concise, short, terse; accessible, adjacent, close, neighboring.

look, behold, contemplate, discern, distinguish, eye, gaze, glance, glimpse, perceive, scan, see, stare, survey, view, watch, witness; appear, seem; examine, inspect, investigate, observe; air, appearance, aspect, bearing, behavior, carriage, conduct, condition, department, expression, face, front, manner, mien. ANT.—avert, hide, ignore, miss, overlook.

loose, disengaged, flowing, free, indefinite, lax, limp, relaxed, separate, slack, unbound, unconfined, unfastened, untied, vague; careless, dissolute, heedless, immoral, licentious, unrestrained, wanton. ANT.—fast, taut, tied, tight; inhibited, moral, restrained.

lose, blunder, botch, drop, fail, falter, flounder, flunk, fold, forfeit, fumble, miscarry, mislay, miss, squander, stumble, waste. ANT.—accomplish, improve, master, overcome, regain.

loss, casualty, damage, death, decline, deficiency, deprivation, deterioration, detriment, disadvantage, failure, impairment, lack, retardation, want. ANT.—achievement, acquisition, advancement, gain, improvement.

lot, doom, fate, fortune, portion; award, destiny, issue, outcome, result; chance, luck; assemblage, batch, gathering, group; land parcel.

loud, blaring, blatant, clamorous, crashing, deafening, noisy, piercing, resonant, resounding, shrill, sonorous, stentorian, vociferous; coarse, ill-bred, vulgar; bright, gaudy. ANT.—dulcet, faint, inaudible, quiet, soft, subdued; tasteful.

love, adoration, affection, ardor, attachment, charity, devotion, endearment, fervor, fondness, intimacy, liking, passion, regard, respect, sentiment, warmth, worship, yearning. ANT.—aversion, dislike, enmity, hatred, indifference, scorn.

lovely, adorable, attractive, beauteous, beautiful, captivating, charming, comely, delightful, elegant, enchanting, enticing, fair, fine, graceful, handsome, inviting, lovable, pretty, satisfying, sweet, winsome. ANT.—foul, hideous, homely, repulsive, repugnant.

low, abject, contemptible, debased, degraded, despicable, disgraceful, dishonorable, groveling, ignoble, ignominious, lowly, mean, menial, servile, shameless, sordid, vile, vulgar; feeble, ill, sick, weak; cheap, inexpensive, moderate; short, small; faint, hushed, muffled, soft; blue, dejected, moody; below, beneath, deep, depressed, flat, inferior, nether, prone, prostrate, squat, sunken, supine. ANT.—esteemed, exalted, honored, lofty, noble; healthy, strong, vigorous; costly, expensive; tall, towering; blatant, clamorous, deafening, loud, thunderous; elated, exhilarated; inflated, superior.

lower, inferior, minor, poorer, secondary, subordinate; abase, adulterate, corrupt, debase, defile, degrade, deprave, depress, humiliate, impair, pervert, vitiate. ANT.—better, greater, higher, superior; enhance, improve, raise, restore, vitalize.

loyal, constant, dedicated, devoted, earnest, faithful, patriotic, steadfast, true, trustworthy, unfailing, unswerving. ANT.—disloyal, faithless, false, seditious, treacherous.

lubricate, anoint, cream, grease, lather, oil, salve, wax.

lucid, bright, clear, diaphanous, glossy, limpid, luminous, radiant, serene, transparent; sane, sound, rational; distinct, evident, explicit, intelligible, manifest, obvious, plain, understandable, unmistakable, visible. ANT.—dark, gloomy, murky, nebulous, obscure; demented, deranged; confused, cryptic, enigmatic, puzzling, unintelligible.

lucky, advantageous, auspicious, benign, conquering, favored, felicitous, flourishing, fortuitous, fortunate, happy, propitious, prosperous, successful, thriving, triumphant, victorious. ANT.—cheerless, defeated, downtrodden, ill-fated, persecuted.

lucrative, advantageous, gainful, profitable, remunerative, self-sustaining, worthwhile. ANT.—costly, failing, losing, troublesome, wasteful.

ludicrous, absurd, bizarre, comical, farcical, funny, incongruous, laughable, outlandish, ridiculous, /logical, normal, reasonable, serious, solemn.

luminous, bright, brilliant, clear, gleaming, glowing, incandescent, lucid, lustrous, radiant, shining. ANT.—dim, dull, murky, obscure, unclear.

lunacy, aberration, craziness, delirium, delusion, dementia, derangement, frenzy, hallucination, imbalance, insanity, madness, mania, psychosis. ANT.—balance, normality, rationality, sanity, stability.

lure, allure, attract, bait, bewitch, charm, coax, decoy, ensnare, entangle, entice, entrap, fascinate, induce, inveigle, lead astray, mesmerize, persuade, seduce, tempt, trick, wheedle. ANT.—alienate, antagonize, discourage, repel, revolt.

lust, appetite, avarice, carnality, concupiscence, craving, cupidity, desire, greed, hankering, hungering, longing, urge, wantonness, yearning. ANT.—chastity, purity, restraint; abomination, aversion, distaste, loathing.

luster, brightness, brilliance, brilliancy, effulgence, glossiness, luminosity, radiance, sheen, shimmer, splendor; distinction, fame, renown, repute. ANT.—cloudiness, darkness, drabness, murkiness, shade; baseness, dishonor, disrepute, reproach, shame.

luxurious, epicurean, opulent, ornate, pampered, rich, self-indulgent, sensuous, splendid, sumptuous, voluptuous, wanton. ANT.—ascetic, bare, drab, monastic, spartan.

M

machine, apparatus, appliance, automatism, contrivance, engine, implement, instrument, mechanism, motor, tool, utensil; agent, cabal, organization, system.

mad, angry, enraged, exasperated, furious, incensed, provoked, raging, upset, wrathful; crazy, daft, delirious, demented, deranged, insane, lunatic, maniacal, paranoid, psychotic, scatterbrained, unbalanced, unhinged, unsettled. ANT.—calm, cool, serene; balanced, rational, reasonable, sane, sensible.

magic, black art, charm, conjuring, demonology, divination, enchantment, hexing, hocus-pocus, illusion, jugglery, legerdemain, necromancy, occultism, omen, prediction, rune, sorcery, trickery, voodoo, witchcraft, wizardry.

magnanimous, beneficent, bountiful, charitable, chivalrous, forgiving, generous, giving, greathearted, heroic, liberal, munificent, openhanded, unselfish. ANT.—covetous, egotistical, greedy, miserly, selfish.

magnificent, elegant, excellent, glorious, gorgeous, grand, kingly, majestic, overwhelming, radiant, rich, spectacular, splendid, stately, sublime, sumptuous, superb. ANT.—common, humble, modest, ordinary, plebeian.

magnify, aggrandize, amplify, augment, embroider, enhance, enlarge, exaggerate, expand, heighten, hyperbolize, increase, overstate, romanticize, stretch. ANT.—decrease, depreciate, diminish, minimize, understate.

magnitude, amplitude, bigness, brightness, bulk, dimensions, expanse, extension, extent, girth, greatness, highness, importance, intensity, largeness, loudness, mass, power, proportions, quantity, range, size, vastness, volume. ANT.—dimness, insignificance, paucity, mediocrity, quietness.

main, cardinal, central, chief, essential, first, foremost, highest, leading, necessary, paramount, predominant, prime, principal, supreme.

ANT.—auxiliary, inessential, minor, secondary, subordinate.

maintain, continue, keep, preserve, retain, support, sustain, uphold; affirm, allege, assert, claim, confirm, contend, declare, defend, hold, justify, prove, vindicate. ANT.—abandon, discontinue, desert, forsake, quit; condemn, deny, oppose, reject, resist.

majestic, august, dignified, distinguished, eminent, exalted, grand, grandiose, high, illustrious, imperial, imposing, impressive, inspiring, lofty, magnificent, noble, pompous, prominent, splendid, stately, sublime, towering. ANT.—humble, insignificant, low, ordinary, shabby.

make, accomplish, achieve, assemble, build, carve, cause, compel, complete, compose, construct, create, do, drive, establish, execute, fabricate, fashion, force, forge, form, frame, gain, generate, invent, manufacture, mold, perfect, produce, shape. ANT.—annihilate, break, demolish, destroy, mutilate.

makeshift, alternative, expedient, momentary, provisional, short-term, stopgap, substitute, temporary. ANT.—abiding, fixed, permanent.

malady, affliction, ailment, disease, disorder, illness, indisposition, infirmity, sickness. ANT.—health, soundness, vigor, well-being.

malevolence, animosity, enmity, evil, grudge, hate, hostility, ill will, malice, malignancy, malignity, rancor, recrimination, spite, treachery. ANT.—affection, charity, love, sympathy, toleration.

malice, see **malevolence.**

malign, abuse, asperse, besmirch, calumniate, defame, detract, discredit, disparage, libel, revile, scandalize, slander, traduce, vilify; misapply, misemploy, misuse. ANT.—acclaim, celebrate, extol, praise, respect.

malignant, bitter, deadly, evil, fatal, hostile, malevolent, malign, mischievous, pernicious, spiteful, virulent. ANT.—benign, good, helpful, peaceful.

malleable, changeable, ductile, flexible, impressionable, moldable, plastic, pliant, shapeable, supple, yielding. ANT.—fixed, indomitable, resolute, rigid, unyielding.

manage, administer, command, conduct, control, direct, dominate, govern, guide, head, officiate, oversee, regulate, rule, run, steer, superintendent, supervise, watch; bridle, check, curb, repress, restrain. ANT.—abandon, bungle, mismanage, muff, spoil.

mandate, behest, charge, command, commission, decree, edict, fiat, injunction, law, order, ordinance, requirement, requisite, rule, statute, ukase.

maneuver, action, artifice, design, enterprise, execution, feint, movement, operation, performance, plan, plot, procedure, proceeding, ruse, scheme, stratagem, tactic, wile. ANT.—cessation, inaction, inactivity, rest.

mangle, cripple, crush, disfigure, dismember, fracture, hack, lacerate, maim, mutilate, rend, slash.

manifest, clear, cloudless, fair, sunny; limpid, transparent; apparent, conspicuous, defined, definite, distinct, evident, explicit, intelligible, lucid, obvious, patent, plain, unmistakable, unveiled, visible; open, unobstructed; disclose, exhibit, indicate, reveal, show. ANT.—cloudy, foul, overcast; ambiguous, complex, obscure, unclear, vague; buried, concealed, covered, hidden; conceal, distract, divert, falsify, mislead.

manipulate, bribe, compel, control, direct, feel, finger, guide, handle, lead, operate, rule, threaten.

manner, approach, custom, fashion, form, habit, method, mode, practice, style, way; air, bearing, behavior, carriage, conduct, demeanor, deportment, guise, mien.

many, countless, diverse, manifold, multifarious, multitudinous, myriad, numerous, several, sundry, various. ANT.—few, infrequent, meager, scanty, scarce, uniform.

mar, botch, bungle, damage, deface, deform, distort, harm, hurt, impair, injure, mutilate, scar, spoil, stain, twist, warp, waste. ANT.—adorn, beautify, benefit, enhance, vivify.

margin, bank, border, brim, brink, boundary, confines, fence, fringe, leeway, limit, lip, rim, shore, strand, wall. ANT.—center, extension, heart, interior, surface.

marine, aquatic, hydrographic, maritime, natatorial, nautical, naval, ocean, oceanic, oceanographic, pelagic, seafaring, seagoing. ANT. alluvial, ashore, earthly, geodetic, terrestrial.

mark, brand, engraving, impression, imprint, scar, stamp, stigma, trace, vestige; badge, emblem, label, sign, symbol, token; characteristic, feature, indication, representation, symptom, trait; goal, target; attend to, behold, notice, observe, perceive, recognize, regard, see. ANT.—disregard, ignore, overlook, skip.

marriage, conjugality, espousal, matrimony, nuptials, oath, union, wedding, wedlock. ANT.—celibacy, divorce, separation, singleness, virginity.

marvelous, amazing, astonishing, awesome, exceptional, extraordinary, fabulous, incredible, indescribable, ineffable, miraculous, mysterious, peculiar, phenomenal, rare, remarkable, singular, superb, uncommon, unexpected, unusual, wonderful, wondrous. ANT.—commonplace, ordinary, plain, unremarkable, worthless.

masculine, aggressive, bold, brave, daring, hardy, husky, lusty, male, manly, mannish, robust, strong, vigorous, virile. ANT.—effeminate, emasculated, feminine, timorous, womanish.

mask, camouflage, cloak, conceal, cover, disguise, dissemble, falsify, hide, hoodwink, hush, muffle, mystify, screen, secrete, shield, suppress, veil, withhold. ANT.—bare, disclose, expose, reveal, unveil.

mass, body, carcass, corpse, remains; form, frame, torso; bigness, bulk, dimensions, magnitude, size; accumulation, aggregate, aggregation, assemblage, association, collection, company, heap, lump, society, sum, total, totality, whole; agglomeration, conglomeration. ANT.—mind, soul, spirit; individual, factor, part, portion.

massacre, annihilation, bloodshed, butchery, carnage, decimation, execution, extermination, genocide, killing, murder, pogrom, slaughter, slaying. ANT.—animation, preservation, protection, resuscitation.

massive, colossal, dense, heavy, huge, large, majestic, ponderous, weighty; burdensome, cumbersome, cumbrous, grievous, trying, unwieldy; gloomy, grave, serious, sluggish. ANT.—airy, delicate, light, small; flexible, pliant; animated, brisk, buoyant.

master, captain, champion, chief, commander, conqueror, director, employer, governor, head, leader, lord, manager, mentor, overseer, potentate, principal, ruler, superior, teacher, victor; holder, owner, proprietor; adept, expert. ANT.—apprentice, dependent, follower, pupil, servitor; amateur, beginner, greenhorn, neophyte, novice.

masterpiece, chef-d'oeuvre, forte, greatest accomplishment, magnum opus, masterstroke, masterwork, monument, paragon, peak.

mastery, advantage, ascendancy, command, conquest, control, domination, dominion, expertise, exultation, predominance, rule, skill, sovereignty, superiority, supremacy, sway, transcendence, triumph, victory. ANT.—defeat, failure, impotence, inferiority, subjugation.

mate, assistant, associate, attendant, chum, colleague, companion, comrade, consort, crony, friend, intimate, pal, partner, spouse; ship's officer; match, marry.

material, body, cloth, fabric, gear, matter, staple, stuff, substance; affair, cause, concern, occasion, subject, theme, thing, topic; consequence, essence, importance, moment; bodily, concrete, corporeal, palpable, physical, ponderable, sensible, solid, somatic, substantial, tangible, temporal. ANT.— nothingness; airy, bodiless, ethereal, intangible, spiritual.

matrimony, see **marriage**.

matter, see **material**.

mature, adult, aged, complete, consummate, developed, experienced, fertile, finished, full-grown, hardened, matronly, matured, mellow, prime, pubescent, ready, ripe, seasoned, virile; age, develop, perfect, ripen, season. ANT.—deficient, immature, juvenile, premature, raw, undeveloped.

mean, average, mediocre, medium, middle, model, normal; abject, base, contemptible, debased, degraded, despicable, ignoble, low, obscure, plebeian, sordid, vile, vulgar; bad-tempered, malicious, nasty, offensive; mercenary, miserly, parsimonious, penurious, selfish, stingy; contemplate, design, imply, indicate, intend, ordain, purpose, say, signify, state, suggest. ANT.—admirable, distinguished, extraordinary, high, superior; benevolent, charitable, kind; generous, indulgent, liberal, philanthropic, profuse.

meaning, acceptation, connotation, drift, explanation, gist, implication, import, intent, interpretation, purport, purpose, sense, significance, signification.

means, agent, apparatus, channel, device, expedient, factor, instrument, materials, measure, medium, method, tool, utensil, vehicle; capital, income, property, resources, riches, stock, wealth.

measure, criterion, gauge, law, principle, proof, rule, scale, standard, test, touchstone; amplitude, capacity, degree, extent, magnitude, limit, range, scope, size; amount, quantity; allotment, proportion, share; bill, design, draft, outline, plan, plot, project, proposal, proposition, scheme, sketch, suggestion.

mechanical, automated, automatic, autonomic, contrived, controlled, impulsive, instinctive, involuntary, machinelike, perfunctory, rote, routine, unreasoned.

meddle, annoy, impede, interfere, interpose, interrupt, intervene, intrude, mix, monkey, obtrude, pester, pry, tamper. ANT.—aid, avoid, encourage, shun, support.

mediocre, average, commonplace, fair, intermediate, mean, median, medium, middling, moderate, ordinary, passable. ANT.—exceptional, extraordinary, outstanding, superior, unusual.

meditate, cogitate, consider, contemplate, deliberate, muse, ponder, reason, reflect, speculate, study, think; conceive, imagine, picture, recall, recollect, remember; devise, intend, mean, plan, project, purpose, resolve. ANT.—dismiss, disregard, divert, neglect, overlook.

meek, calm, compliant, demure, docile, domestic, gentle, humble, mild, modest, obedient, pacific, patient, peaceable, subdued, submissive, tame, tolerant, unpretentious, yielding; dull, flat, insipid, tedious. ANT.—arrogant, fierce, obstinate, pompous, savage; animated, exciting, lively, spirited.

meet, collide, confront, connect, converge, cross, encounter, engage, find, greet, intersect, join, touch; answer, fulfill, gratify, satisfy; experience, suffer, undergo. ANT.—avoid, cleave, disperse, miss, separate.

melancholy, dejected, depressed, despondent, disconsolate, dismal, dispirited, doleful, forlorn, funereal, gloomy, glum, grim, joyless, moody, mournful, sad, sorrowful, sulky, wistful; grave, pensive, somber. ANT.—cheerful, happy, jubilant, spirited, vivacious.

mellow, aged, full-flavored, mature, perfected, ripe, sweet; delicate, pleasing, refined, relaxed, subdued, sweet-sounding. ANT.—dull, hard, immature, sour, stale; callous, crude, harsh, stubborn.

melody, air, aria, chant, concord, descant, euphony, harmony, lyric, mellifluence, monophony, strain, theme, tune.

member, allotment, apportionment, division, fragment, moiety, piece, portion, scrap, section, segment, share; component, constituent, element, ingredient; limb, organ, part.

memorial, commemoration, commemorative, inscription, memento, monument, remembrance, souvenir; chair, professorship, scholarship.

memory, mental trace, recollection, remembrance, reminiscence, retention, retrospection; fame, renown, reputation. ANT.—amnesia, effacement, forgetfulness, oblivion, unconsciousness.

mend, fix, patch, repair, restore, sew, touch up; ameliorate, better, correct, enhance, improve, rectify, refine, reform, refresh, remedy, renew, revive; get well, heal, recover. ANT.—damage, deform, impair, mar, wound; deteriorate, fall ill, wane, weaken.

mendicant, beggar, pauper, ragamuffin, scrub, solicitor, starveling, tatterdemalion, vagabond, wretch. ANT.—benefactor, contributor, donor, giver.

menial, abject, base, degrading, humble, ignoble, lowly, mean, servile, unimportant, unskilled. ANT.—elevated, expert, noble, professional, uplifting.

mentality, brain, capacity, comprehension, consciousness, faculties, intellect, intelligence, judgment, mind, perception, psyche, reason, reasoning, thought, understanding, wisdom; disposition, inclination, intention, purpose, will, wish. ANT.—corporeality, materiality, matter.

mentor, advisor, counselor, guide, instructor, leader, monitor, teacher. ANT.—disciple, follower, pupil, student.

mercenary, avaricious, corrupt, grasping, greedy, selfish, sordid, venal. ANT.—generous, honorable, liberal, unselfish.

merciful, beneficent, benignant, clement, compassionate, feeling, forbearing, forgiving, gracious, humane, kind, lenient, philanthropic, pitying, soft-hearted, sympathetic, tender, tolerant. ANT.—barbarous, cruel, pitiless, ruthless, tyrannical.

mercy, benevolence, benignity, charity, clemency, compassion, forbearance, forgiveness, grace, humanity, kindness, leniency, mildness, pardon, pity, tolerance. ANT.—banishment, inhumanity, oppression, punishment, vengeance.

merge, amalgamate, blend, coalesce, combine, commingle, conjoin, consolidate, fuse, integrate, join, mingle, mix, unify, unite. ANT.—decompose, divest, divide, separate.

merit, effectiveness, efficacy, force, power, strength; excellence, goodness, regard, value, virtue, worth, worthiness; reward; achieve, attain, deserve, earn, gain, obtain, win. ANT.—corruption, dishonor, evil, weakness, unworthiness; forfeit, lose, spend, waste.

merry, animated, blithe, buoyant, cheerful, ebullient, elated, exhilarated, exuberant, festive, gay, gleeful, hilarious, jocular, jolly, jovial, joyous, jubilant, light-hearted, lively, mirthful, rollicking, spirited, sprightly, vivacious. ANT.—gloomy, melancholy, morose, pessimistic, wretched.

mess, allowance, portion, ration; difficulty, dilemma, plight, predicament, problem; confusion, conglomeration, disorder, disorganization, hodgepodge, jumble, litter, medley, mélange, mixture, potpourri. ANT.—arrangement, method, order, system, tidiness.

message, indication, mark, sign, signal, symbol, token; annotation, comment, communication, dispatch, letter, memorandum, news, note, observation, remark, report, word.

method, arrangement, custom, design, fashion, form, manner, mode, order, plan, procedure, process, rule, scheme, style, system, technique, vogue, way. ANT.—chaos, confusion, disarrangement, disorder, irregularity, muddle.

meticulous, exacting, fastidious, finical, fussy, painstaking, particular, precise, punctilious, scrupulous, tidy. ANT.—careless, cursory, disheveled, sloppy, unkempt.

methodical, accurate, correct, definite, distinct, exact, formal, orderly, precise, regular, rigid, strict, systematic, unequivocal, well-regulated. ANT.—careless, informal, loose, rough, vague.

microscopic, diminutive, fine, infinitesimal, minimal, minute, tiny; detailed, exact, particular, precise. ANT.—enormous, huge, large; general.

middle, axis, center, core, focus, heart, marrow, mean, midpoint, midst, nucleus, pivot; average, axial, central, equidistant, halfway, interjacent, intermediate, mediocre, pivotal. ANT.—border, boundary, outskirts, periphery, rim; beginning, end; extreme, high, low.

might, ability, brawn, energy, force, potency, power, puissance, strength, sturdiness, sway, tenacity, vigor, vitality. ANT.—frailty, impotence, inability, vulnerability, weakness.

mighty, able, bold, concentrated, doughty, enduring, firm, forceful, great, hale, hardy, heavy, husky, immense, impregnable, indomitable, invincible, large, lusty, majestic, manful, momentous, muscular, overpowering, potent, powerful, puissant, resistless, robust, sinewy, stalwart, strapping, strong, stupendous, sturdy, tough, vigorous. ANT.—delicate, enervated, feeble, flaccid, weak.

mild, calm, genial, gentle, humane, kind, meek, mellow, moderate, pacific, patient, peaceful, placid, quiet, smooth, soft, soothing, temperate, tender, tepid, tranquil; bland, savory, sweet. ANT.—bitter, fierce, harsh, irritating, uncouth; acid, biting, bitter, sour, stringent.

militant, active, aggressive, armed, belligerent, combative, contentious, fighting, hostile, pugnacious, pushing, warring. ANT.—acquiescent, amenable, compliant, peaceful, submissive.

mimic, ape, burlesque, caricature, copy, counterfeit, duplicate, echo, feign, forge, imitate, impersonate, mock, parody, parrot, repeat, reproduce, simulate. ANT.—distort, diverge, invent.

mind, see **mentality**.

mingle, amalgamate, associate, blend, combine, commingle, compound, concoct, confound, conjoin, consort, fraternize, fuse, intermingle, intermix, join, jumble, merge, mix, participate, unite. ANT.—disjoin, distinguish, separate, sort.

miniature, abridged, bantam, diminutive, little, minuscule, minute, reduced, small, tiny. ANT.—full-size, large, normal, regular.

minimize, belittle, curtail, deduct, degrade, depreciate, derogate, detract, diminish, disparage, fault, lessen, reduce, shorten, subtract. ANT.—amplify, enlarge, exalt, expand, magnify, praise.

minister, ambassador, churchman, clergyman, cleric, consul, curate, delegate, diplomat, divine, ecclesiastic, envoy, official, padre, parson, pastor, preacher, priest, rector, representative, reverend, vicar; aid, assist, help, nourish, nurture, serve, support, sustain. ANT.—apostate, disciple, follower, layman, renegade; encumber, hinder, impede, obstruct, oppose.

minor, inconsiderable, inferior, junior, lesser, lower, petty, poorer, secondary, smaller, subordinate, unimportant, younger; adolescent, child. ANT.—first, greater, important, major; adult, of age.

minute, accurate, atomic, critical, detailed, diminutive, exact, exiguous, fine, inconsiderable, infinitesimal, insignificant, little, microscopic, miniature, minuscule, molecular, petty, precise, puny, small, tiny. ANT.—colossal, comprehensive, enormous, extensive, magnificent.

miraculous, astonishing, awesome, extraordinary, incredible, inexplicable, marvelous, metaphysical, preternatural, spectacular, spiritual, stupefying, superhuman, supernatural, unearthly. ANT.—commonplace, customary, insignificant, natural, ordinary.

mirage, apparition, delusion, dream, fantasy, figment, hallucination, illusion, phantasm, vision. ANT.—actuality, reality, substance.

miscarriage, defeat, failure, fiasco, frustration, malfunction; spontaneous abortion. ANT.—achievement, success, victory; pregnancy.

miscellaneous, assorted, dissimilar, diverse, diversified, heterogeneous, indiscriminate, mingled, mixed, motley, promiscuous, sundry, variant, varied, various. ANT.—classified, homogeneous, ordered, same, sorted.

mischief, affront, annoyance, damage, detriment, deviltry, disservice, evil, grievance, harm, hurt, ill, infliction, injury, misfortune, mishap, outrage, prank, roguery, wrong. ANT.—betterment, favor, kindness, support, vindication.

miserable, afflicted, ailing, comfortless, crushed, disconsolate, discontented, dismal, distressed, forlorn, heartbroken, pained, pitiable, sickly, sorrowful, suffering, wretched; abject, contemptible, despicable, lamentable, low, mean; insufficient, meager, paltry, poor, scanty, small, stingy. ANT.—contented, happy, lively, rejoicing; noble, respectable; fortunate, prosperous, significant.

miserly, avaricious, close, covetous, greedy, niggardly, parsimonious, penurious, rapacious, selfish, stingy, tight, tight-fisted. ANT.—altruistic, bountiful, extravagant, generous, liberal, munificent.

misery, agony, anguish, anxiety, desolation, despair, despondency, distress, grief, heartache, mortification, pain, sorrow, suffering, torment, trial, tribulation, woe, wretchedness; affliction, calamity, disaster, evil, misfortune, ordeal, trouble; illness, sickness. ANT.—bliss, delight, ecstasy, elation, joy; comfort, contentment, fortune, peace; health, salubrity, vigor.

misfortune, accident, adversity, affliction, bereavement, calamity, casualty, catastrophe, chastening, disaster, distress, hardship, harm, hurt, ill fortune, infliction, injury, loss, misadventure, mishap, privation, ruin, set-back, tribulation. ANT.—advantage, blessing, contentment, prosperity, success, well-being.

misgiving, distrust, doubt, hesitation, mistrust, suspicion, uncertainty. ANT.—certainty, security, sureness, trust.

mishap, accident, calamity, casualty, contretemps, disaster, misadventure, mischance, misfortune, reverse. ANT.—good fortune, luck.

misinterpret, distort, falsify, misconceive, misconstrue, misunderstand, pervert. ANT.—comprehend, perceive, understand.

misleading, deceitful, deceptive, delusive, delusory, fallacious, false, furtive, illusive, specious. ANT.—authentic, direct, forthright, genuine, straightforward, truthful.

misrepresent, belie, caricature, dissemble, distort, exaggerate, falsify, mislead, misstate, pervert, simulate. ANT.—delineate, depict, represent.

miss, fail, default, lack, lose, miscarry, omit, overlook, skip; crave, desire, want, yearn; drop, fumble, muff, snatch at; blunder, mishap, slip. ANT.—achieve, attain, have, succeed; detest, shun; catch, grab, hold; accomplishment, advancement, gain.

mission, activity, affair, attack, business, commission, delegation, errand, purpose; calling, duty, task, work.

mistake, aberration, blunder, downfall, error, failure, fallacy, fault, flaw, illusion, inaccuracy, lapse, misapprehension, misconception, mishap, omission, oversight, slip. ANT.—accuracy, correctness, perfection, precision, truth, veracity.

misunderstanding, confusion, difference, disagreement, discord, dissension, error, misapprehension, misconception, misinterpretation, mistake, quarrel, variance. ANT.—agreement, concord, understanding.

misuse, abuse, asperse, defame, desecrate, disparage, harm, ill-use, injure, malign, maltreat, maul, mishandle, pervert, revile, scandalize, traduce, vilify, wrong; consume, dissipate, scatter, spend, squander, waste. ANT.—cherish, honor, protect, respect, succor; accumulate, conserve, economize, preserve, retain.

mitigate, abate, allay, alleviate, ameliorate, appease, assuage, calm, decrease, dilute, diminish, extenuate, lessen, lighten, moderate, modify, mollify, relieve, soften, solace, soothe, subdue, temper, weaken. ANT.—aggravate, deepen, increase, inflate, intensify, provoke.

mix, adulterate, alloy, blend, combine, commingle, commix, compound, concoct, crossbreed, homogenize, incorporate, intermingle, intermix, fuse, join, mingle, shuffle, stir; coalesce, integrate; confound, confuse, jumble, mix up, tangle; associate, consort, fraternize, join, unite. ANT.—detach, disperse, divide, separate, sort; segregate; clarify, enlighten, unravel, untangle; abandon, desert, dissociate, divide.

mixture, assortment, change, difference, dissimilarity, diversity, heterogeneity, hodgepodge, jumble, medley, mélange, miscellany, multifariousness, olio, potpourri, variety; alloy, amalgam, blend, composite, compound, fusion; breed, strain, subspecies. ANT.—homogeneity, likeness, sameness, uniformity; isolation, purity, separation; simplicity; pedigree, purebred.

mob, assemblage, bevy, crowd, crush, drove, flock, gang, gathering, herd, horde, host, masses, multitude, populace, press, rabble, riffraff, swarm, throng.

mobilize, adapt, assemble, call up, command, gather, increase, marshal, order, organize, prepare, transport, unify, unite. ANT.—demobilize, disperse, end, scatter, separate.

mock, ape, defy, deride, fleer, flout, gibe, insult, jeer, mimic, ridicule, satirize, scoff, sneer at, taunt. ANT.—compliment, flatter, honor, praise, support.

mode, condition, course, custom, design, fashion, habit, kind, manner, method, order, plan, practice, procedure, rule, scheme, state, system, usage, vogue, way. ANT.—confusion, disorder.

model, archetype, copy, criterion, design, duplicate, example, facsimile, form, gauge, image, mold, original, paragon, pattern, prototype, replica, representation, specimen, standard, tracing, type.

moderate, abate, allay, assuage, check, curb, deaden, decrease, diminish, lessen, lower, palliate, quell, reduce, subdue, suppress, temper, weaken; abstemious, cool, dispassionate, fair, judicious, measured, mild, regulated, sparing, steady, temperate, tolerant. ANT.—agitate, anger, excite, inflame, stimulate; excessive, extravagant, liberal, outrageous, radical.

modern, contemporary, current, fashionable, fresh, latest, new, novel, present, recent, renovated. ANT.—ancient, antiquated, bygone, primitive, obsolete, outmoded.

modest, bashful, constrained, demure, diffident, humble, meek, reserved, retiring, shy, timid, unassuming, unpretentious; inconsiderable, insignificant, minute, small; chaste, pure, undefiled, virtuous. ANT.—arrogant, bold, conceited, egotistical, ostentatious; excessive, grand, huge, magnificent; immodest, indelicate, obscene, prurient, unchaste.

modification, adaptation, alteration, alternation, change, limitation, modulation, mutation, qualification, substitution, transformation, variation, variety, vicissitude. ANT.—monotony, stability, uniformity.

modify, adapt, alter, change, convert, exchange, expand, limit, lower, moderate, qualify, shape, reform, restrict, shift, soften, substitute, temper, transfigure, transform, vary, veer. ANT.—preserve, retain, stabilize.

moist, aqueous, damp, dank, dewy, dripping, fresh, humid, infiltrated, juicy, muggy, saturated, sloppy, soaked, sodden, soppy, swampy, vaporous, watery. ANT.—arid, barren, dehydrated, dry, parched, waterless.

mold, alter, carve, cast, create, fashion, forge, form, frame, influence, make, model, modify, produce, sculpt, shape. ANT.—destroy, dismantle, mutilate, wreck.

molest, aggrieve, annoy, assail, attack, bother, chafe, damage, disturb, harass, hurt, inconvenience, injure, irk, irritate, maltreat, misuse, oppress, persecute, pester, plague, tease, trouble, vex, worry. ANT.—aid, comfort, defend, encourage, protect, soothe.

moment, flash, instant, jiffy, minute, second, twinkling, wink; consequence, gravity, importance, significance, weight.

momentous, consequential, critical, crucial, decisive, far-reaching, grave, important, influential, material, memorable, pressing, prominent, relevant, salient, serious, significant, solemn, vital, weighty. ANT.—boring, commonplace, immaterial, insignificant, trivial.

monastery, abbey, cloister, convent, hermitage, lamasery, nunnery, priory.

money, assets, bills, bullion, cash, change, checks, coin, currency, finances, gold, legal tender, lucre, notes, pelf, resources, revenue, silver, specie, sterling, wherewithal; capital, funds,

opulence, property, riches, stock, wealth; payment, salary, wages.

monopolize, absorb, control, corner, direct, engross, own, possess.

monotonous, boring, burdensome, depressive, dilatory, dreary, dry, dull, flat, heavy, humdrum, irksome, prosy, repetitious, slow, sluggish, tardy, tedious, tiresome, undiversified, uninteresting, unvaried, wearisome. ANT.—appealing, entertaining, exciting, refreshing, varied, versatile.

monument, commemoration, memento, memorial, remembrance, souvenir, testimonial; gravestone, headstone, mausoleum, plaque, pyramid, shrine, statue, tomb, tombstone.

mood, behavior, conduct, disposition, frame of mind, humor, manner, nature, spirit, temper, temperament; inclination, propensity, tendency.

moral, chaste, decent, ethical, good, honest, honorable, just, noble, pure, right, righteous, scrupulous, upright, virtuous. ANT.—amoral, dishonorable, evil, immoral, unethical.

morose, acrimonious, cantankerous, churlish, crabbed, depressed, dour, fretful, gloomy, glum, grouchy, gruff, moody, morbid, petulant, splenetic, sulky, sullen, surly, unamiable. ANT.—buoyant, cheerful, exhilarated, good-natured, pleasant.

mortal, deadly, destructive, fatal, final, lethal, poisonous; extreme, serious; ephemeral, human, passing, temporal, transient. ANT.—curative, life-giving, reviving, strengthening, vivifying; trifling, trivial; external, everlasting, immortal, perpetual.

mortification, abasement, annoyance, chagrin, dissatisfaction, embarrassment, humiliation, shame, vexation; gangrene, necrosis. ANT.—elevation, happiness, praise, satisfaction, success.

motion, action, activity, change, gesture, mobility, move, movement, passage, revolution, transit, transition; proposal, proposition, recommendation, suggestion. ANT.—halt, immobility, inaction, repose, stillness.

motive, cause, determinant, encouragement, ground, impulse, incentive, incitement, inducement, influence, instigation, motivation, principle, prompting, purpose, reason, spur, stimulus, urge; mobile, motile, movable.

motley, assorted, composite, disparate, diverse, heterogeneous, incongruous, indiscriminate, miscellaneous, mixed, mottled, speckled, sundry, varied. ANT.—homogeneous, like, pure, similar, unvaried.

motto, adage, aphorism, apothegm, axiom, byword, epigram, maxim, proverb, saw, saying, sentiment, slogan.

mount, arise, ascend, aspire, climb, grow, increase, rise, scale, scramble, soar, surge, swell, tower. ANT.—collapse, decline, descend, diminish, drop, slump.

mourn, agonize, anguish, bemoan, bewail, cry, deplore, droop, fret, grieve, groan, languish, lament, miss, pray, regret, repine, rue, sigh, sing, sorrow, suffer, wail, weep (over), whimper, yearn. ANT.—celebrate, exult, laugh, rejoice, revel.

move, actuate, advance, agitate, arouse, convey, drive, excite, impel, incite, induce, influence, instigate, operate, persuade, proceed, propel, propose, push, rouse, run, shift, start, stimulate, stir, transfer, transport, travel, urge. ANT.—cease, deter, dissuade, halt, pacify, rest, suppress.

movement, see **motion**.

muddled, addled, befuddled, bewildered, chaotic, confounded, confused, deranged, disarrayed,

disconcerted, disordered, disorganized, indistinct, jumbled, messy, mixed, obscured, perplexed, puzzled, snarled, stupid. ANT.—distinguished, lucid, obvious, ordered, organized.

multiply, augment, enlarge, generate, grow, increase, propagate, reproduce. ANT.—divide, lessen, reduce, shrink, waste.

multitude, aggregation, army, assemblage, congregation, crowd, galaxy, gathering, horde, host, legion, mob, populace, swarm, throng. ANT.—fraction, handful, nobody, paucity, scarcity.

mundane, carnal, earthly, laic, lay, mortal, profane, secular, temporal, terrestrial, worldly; everyday, normal, ordinary. ANT.—celestial, eternal, heavenly, paradisaic, spiritual, unearthly; extraordinary, special, unique.

munificent, altruistic, beneficent, benevolent, charitable, generous, hospitable, liberal, philanthropic, princely, unselfish. ANT.—avaricious, covetous, grasping, miserly, selfish.

murder, annihilate, assassinate, butcher, choke, destroy, execute, exterminate, immolate, kill, massacre, poison, shoot, slaughter, slay, stab, victimize. ANT.—animate, propagate, nurse, refresh, restore, vitalize.

murmur, babble, complain, grouse, grumble, hum, mumble, mutter, protest, remonstrate, repine, ripple, rustle, whisper. ANT.—applaud, approve, honor, praise, recommend.

muscular, athletic, brawny, forceful, husky, powerful, sinewy, stalwart, strong, sturdy, vigorous. ANT.—feeble, flabby, infirm, puny, weak.

musical, agreeable, assonant, choral, euphonic, euphonious, harmonious, lyrical, mellow, melodic, melodious, pleasing, symphonic, tonal, tuneful, unisonant, vocal. ANT.—clashing, discordant, dissonant, grating, harsh.

muster, accumulate, amass, arrange, assemble, call, collect, congregate, convene, convoke, gather; marshal, organize, summon; cull, garner, harvest, pick, reap. ANT.—disjoin, disperse, divert, scatter, separate.

mute, calm, dumb, gagged, hushed, inarticulate, inaudible, noiseless, peaceful, quiet, silent, soundless, speechless, still, taciturn, tranquil, voiceless. ANT.—articulate, garrulous, loquacious, loud, raucous, talkative, vocal.

mutiny, anarchy, coup, insubordination, insurrection, outbreak, overthrow, rebellion, resistance, revolt, revolution, riot, upheaval, uprising.

mutter, complain, grouse, grumble, groan, grunt, maunder, moan, mumble, murmur, rumble, sputter, whisper.

mutual, analogous, common, convertible, correlative, correspondent, equivalent, identical, interchangeable, joint, like, reciprocal, self-same, shared, similar. ANT.—dissociated, divergent, separate, unlike, unshared.

mysterious, abstruse, ambiguous, baffling, cabalistic, covert, cryptic, dark, dim, enigmatical, hidden, impenetrable, incomprehensible, inconceivable, incredible, inexplicable, inscrutable, mystical, mystifying, obscure, occult, secret, surreptitious, unaccountable, unfathomable, unintelligible. ANT.—apparent, distinct, explicit, lucid, obvious.

mystery, conundrum, enigma, obscurity, perplexity, problem, puzzle, riddle, secret. ANT.—answer, key, solution.

mystical, see **mysterious**.

myth, allegory, chronicle, fable, fiction, folk ballad, folk tale, legend, lore, parable, saga, tale. ANT.—fact, history.

mythical, allegorical, apocryphal, fabricated, fabulous, fanciful, fantastic, fictitious, imaginary, invented, legendary, visionary. ANT.—actual, factual, historical, real, true.

N

nag, aggravate, annoy, badger, bother, browbeat, discompose, disturb, goad, harass, harry, heckle, irritate, molest, pester, plague, provoke, scold, tantalize, taunt, tease, torment, vex, worry. ANT.—comfort, delight, mollify, please, soothe.

naive, artless, guileless, inexperienced, ingenuous, innocent, natural, open, plain, provincial, simple, unaffected, unsophisticated. ANT.—crafty, cunning, experienced, sophisticated, wise.

naked, bare, exposed, nude, stripped, threadbare, unclad, unclothed, uncovered, undressed; bald, barren, unfurnished; definite, distinct, evident, exact, explicit, literal, mere, obvious, plain, simple, uncolored; defenseless, open, unprotected. ANT.—attired, clothed, dressed; furnished; artful, complex, concealed, secret; protected, shielded.

name, appellation, cognomen, denomination, designation, epithet, surname, title; character, reputation, repute; distinction, eminence, fame, renown; autograph, signature; nom de plume, pseudonym; appoint, call, characterize, christen, define, denominate, denote, designate, elect, entitle, identify, list, mark, mention, proclaim, signify, specify, term, title. ANT.—anonymity, namelessness.

narcotic, anaesthetic, anodyne, dope, drug, opiate, sedative, soporific, tranquilizer; anesthetizing, doping, drugging, nepenthic, stupefying, tranquilizing.

narrate, declaim, deliver, describe, detail, disclose, enumerate, mention, paint, picture, portray, proclaim, recite, recapitulate, recount, rehearse, relate, repeat, report, reveal, state, tell, unfold. ANT.—conceal, disguise, repress, stifle, withhold.

narrow, bigoted, dogmatic, fanatical, illiberal, intolerant, narrow-minded, prejudiced; miserly, parsimonious; close, confined, contracted, cramped, limited, restricted; scrawny, slender, spindling, thread-like. ANT.—liberal, progressive, radical, tolerant; bountiful, charitable, generous; broad, expanded, extended, wide; corpulent, fat, fleshy, stout.

nasty, dirty, foul, polluted, squalid; gross, indecent, lewd, obscene, smutty; disgusting, nauseating, offensive, repulsive, selfish; inclement, rainy, sleeting, stormy. ANT.—clean, spotless, unsullied; decent, pure; attractive, delightful, pleasant, sweet; clear, sunny.

nation, colony, commonwealth, community, country, empire, kingdom, nationality, people, principality, realm, republic, state, territory; clan, community, folk, people, populace, population, public, race, society.

native, aboriginal, congenital, domestic, endemic, inborn, indigenous, inherent, innate, local, natal, natural, original, pristine, regional, vernacular. ANT.—acquired, alien, artificial, extrinsic, foreign, imported, unnatural.

natural, characteristic, essential, fundamental, genetic, inherent, innate, intrinsic, native, original; normal, regular; artless, genuine, ingenuous, legitimate, real, simple, spontaneous, unaffected, unsophisticated. ANT.—contingent, external, extrinsic, objective; abnormal, artificial, irregular; beautified, embellished, forced, formal, unnatural.

nature, bent, character, constitution, disposition, essence, humor, individuality, kind, mood, reputation, repute, sort, temperament; creation, universe.

nauseous, abhorrent, abominable, despicable, detestable, disgusting, loathsome, nasty, offensive, repulsive, revolting, sickening, unpalatable. ANT.—ambrosial, delectable, delicious, desirable, savory.

naval, marine, maritime, nautical, navigating, ocean, oceanic, sailing, seafaring, seagoing, seaworthy.

near, abutting, adjacent, adjoining, bordering, close, contiguous, neighboring, proximate; approaching, coming, expected, imminent, impending, looming, next, prospective; dear, familiar, intimate. ANT.—far, remote; deferred, expired, postponed, stopped; distant, remote.

neat, adroit, clear, compact, correct, exact, finished, orderly, precise, proportioned, shapely, spotless, spruce, suitable, symmetrical, tidy, trim, well-done, well-ordered. ANT.—awkward, disordered, irregular, lax, slipshod, slovenly.

necessary, binding, compulsory, essential, expedient, imperative, indispensable, inevitable, inexorable, irrevocable, needed, obligatory, pressing, required, requisite, unavoidable, undeniable, urgent. ANT.—extravagant, optional, superfluous, unnecessary, worthless.

need, destitution, indigence, penury, pennilessness, poverty; distress, inadequacy, insufficiency, lack, misery, privation, shortage; emergency, necessity, obligation, requirement, urgency; lack, require, want, wish. ANT.—property, wealth; comfort, luxury, plenty; independence; competence, fullness.

neglect, apathy, carelessness, default, deferment, dereliction, disregard, disrespect, evasion, failure, heedlessness, indifference, negligence, nonchalance, omission, oversight, procrastination, recklessness, scorn, slight, thoughtlessness; defer, dismiss, disregard, fail, forget, ignore, omit, overlook, skip, slight, spurn, suspend, underestimate, undervalue. ANT.—attention, care, diligence, surveillance; accomplish, complete, perform, preserve, safeguard, work.

negotiate, accomplish, achieve, agree, arrange, bargain, compromise, confer, consult, contract, deal, debate, dicker, overcome, reflect, sell, transact.

neighborhood, community, district, environs, locality, region; adjacency, nearness, proximity, vicinity.

nerve, audacity, courage, determination, fortitude, hardihood, intrepidity, pluck, resolution, strength, vigor, vitality.

neutral, disinterested, impartial, indeterminate, indifferent, nonpartisan, unallied, unconcerned. ANT.—biased, decided, involved, positive, predisposed.

new, fresh, late, modern, novel, original, recent, strange, unaccustomed, unfamiliar, untried, up-to-date. ANT.—ancient, archaic, familiar, obsolete, outmoded.

news, advice, bulletin, communication, copy, information, intelligence, message, report, tidings.

nimble, active, agile, alert, brisk, bustling, coordinated, fast, flexible, lively, prompt, quick, rapid, speedy, sprightly, spry, supple, swift. ANT.—clumsy, dull, inert, lumbering, slow.

noble, aristocratic, august, dignified, distinguished, elevated, eminent, exalted, genteel, grand, honorable, illustrious, imperial, lofty, lordly, loyal, majestic, princely, regal, royal, stately, sublime, superior. ANT.—abject, base, ignoble, low, plebeian, servile.

noise, babel, blare, clamor, clangor, clatter, cry, din, hubbub, outcry, pandemonium, racket, row, sound, tumult, uproar. ANT.—calm, hush, quiet, silence, tranquility.

nonchalant, careless, inconsiderate, indifferent, negligent, unconcerned; casual, composed, cool, imperturbable, unruffled. ANT.—attentive, careful, considerate, concerned, vigilant; active, agitated, eager, enthusiastic, excitable, fervid, zealous.

nonsense, absurdity, babble, drivel, foolishness, gibberish, imbecility, inanity, inconsistency, jargon, jest, joke, rigamarole, senselessness, shallowness, silliness. ANT.—accuracy, clarify, common sense, substance, wisdom.

normal, average, common, conventional, customary, general, natural, ordinary, rational, reasonable, regular, sane, standard, steady, typical, uniform, unvaried, usual. ANT.—abnormal, exceptional, irregular, peculiar, strange.

nosy, curious, inquiring, inquisitive, interrogative, intrusive, meddling, peeping, prying, searching, snoopy. ANT.—decorous, incurious, indifferent, polite, restrained, unconcerned.

note, commentary, indication, explanation, mark, sign, symbol, token; acknowledgment, annotation, comment, dispatch, epistle, letter, memorandum, message, missive, notation, notice, observation, remark; distinction, fame, renown, reputation; contemplate, discern, notice, observe, perceive, remark, see, view.

noted, celebrated, distinguished, eminent, exalted, exceptional, extraordinary, famous, glorious, illustrious, imposing, memorable, outstanding, prominent, remarkable, renowned, significant, striking, uncommon, well-known. ANT.—common, insignificant, obscure, trivial, unknown.

notice, attend to, behold, detect, discern, discover, distinguish, examine, heed, mark, note, observe, perceive, recognize, regard, remark, see, warn; announcement, attention, bulletin, civility, cognizance, comment, consideration, heed, mention, note, observation, placard, poster, recognition, regard, respect, warning. ANT.—avoid, disregard, ignore, overlook, shun; evasion, forgetfulness, laxity, omission.

notify, acquaint, advise, alert, apprise, call, communicate, convey, disclose, divulge, enlighten, express, impart, indicate, inform, instruct, intimate, signify, specify, spread, teach, tell, warn. ANT.—conceal, deceive, delude, mystify, suppress.

notion, abstraction, belief, caprice, concept, conception, conviction, fancy, idea, image, imagination, impression, inclination, inkling, knowledge, opinion, perception, presumption, sentiment, theory, thought, understanding, view, viewpoint, whim.

novel, fiction, narrative, romance, story, tale; fresh, modern, new, original, unique, unprecedented, untried. ANT.—fact, history, reality, truth, verity; ancient, common, customary, familiar, primitive.

novice, amateur, apprentice, beginner, dabbler, dilettante, greenhorn, intern, learner, neophyte, newcomer, postulant, probationer, recruit, tenderfoot, tyro. ANT.—authority, expert, master, mentor, professional.

nude, see **naked.**

nullify, cancel, countermand, cross out, delete, destroy, discard, dispel, eliminate, erase, expunge, negate, obliterate, suppress, upset, void; abolish, abrogate, annul, invalidate, quash, repeal, rescind, revoke. ANT.—confirm, enact, enforce, execute, ratify, support.

number, aggregate, amount, quantity, sum, volume; calculate, compute, count, enumerate, figure, list, score. ANT.—nothing, nothingness, zero; estimate, guess.

numerous, see **many.**

nurture, cherish, hold dear, prize, treasure, uphold, value; feed, foster, nourish, nurse, rear, support, sustain, tend. ANT.—dislike, disregard, ignore, neglect; abandon, deprive, reject.

nutriment, aliment, diet, edibles, fare, feed, food, meal, nourishment, nutrition, provision, rations, repast, sustenance, viands, victuals. ANT.—hunger, starvation, want.

O

obdurate, adamant, callous, dogged, hard, headstrong, impenitent, indurate, inflexible, insensible, insensitive, mulish, obstinate, stubborn, tenacious, tough, unbending, unfeeling, unyielding. ANT.—amenable, compassionate, sensitive, submissive, tractable.

obedient, acquiescent, compliant, conformable, deferential, dutiful, faithful, law-abiding, loyal, submissive, surrendering, tractable, yielding. ANT.—defiant, insubordinate, intractable, lawless, obstinate, rebellious.

obese, adipose, corpulent, fat, fleshy, portly, rotund, stout, swollen, thickset, unwieldy. ANT.—emaciated, gaunt, lean, skeletal, slender, thin.

object, article, particular, thing; aim, design, end, goal, intention, mark, objective, purpose; balk, disapprove, oppose, protest, resist. ANT.—acquiesce, approve, comply, concur, sanction, welcome.

objection, argument, censure, criticism, disagreement, disapproval, dissent, opposition, protest, rejection, remonstrance, variance. ANT.—acceptance, accord, agreement, approval, compliance.

objective, aim, ambition, aspiration, design, desire, destination, end, goal, hope, intention, longing, mark, motive, object, purpose, scheme, target; dispassionate, equitable, fair, impartial, impersonal, unbiased. ANT.—biased, emotional, partial, personal, subjective.

obligation, accountability, bond, contract, duty, engagement, indebtedness, liability, pledge, promise, requirement, responsibility, stipulation. ANT.—choice, exemption, freedom.

oblige, bind, coerce, command, compel, constrain, drive, enforce, force, hinder, impel, insist, necessitate, restrain; accommodate, benefit, favor, gratify, help, please. ANT.—absolve, discharge, exempt, free, release, spare, unshackle.

obliterate, annihilate, cancel, delete, demolish, destroy, devastate, efface, eradicate, erase, exterminate, extinguish, nullify, ravage, raze, ruin, wreck.

obscene, coarse, corrupt, defiled, dirty, disgusting, filthy, foul, gross, impure, indecent, lascivious, lewd, licentious, offensive, polluted, pornographic, smutty, vulgar, wanton. ANT.—immaculate, innocent, modest, pure, virtuous.

obscure, abstruse, ambiguous, blurred, cloudy, complex, complicated, concealed, cryptic, dark, dim, dusky, enigmatic, hazy, incomprehensible, indistinct, mysterious, nebulous, shadowy, unintelligible, unknown, vague, veiled. ANT.—apparent, clear, explicit, lucid, visible.

observant, alert, attentive, aware, careful, considerate, heedful, mindful, perceptive, wary, watchful; obedient, submissive. ANT.—careless, inattentive, indifferent, lax, nonobservant; disobedient, disrespectful.

observe, behold, comprehend, detect, discover, examine, eye, heed, inspect, mark, note, perceive, regard, see, view, watch; celebrate, commemorate, keep; express, mention, remark, utter. ANT.—avoid, disobey, disregard, ignore, neglect, overlook.

obsolete, ancient, antiquated, antique, archaic, disused, extinct, forgotten, obsolescent, old, old-fashioned, outdated, outmoded, out-of-date, outworn, primitive, rejected, timeworn. ANT.—current, modern, new, novel, recent, up-to-date.

obstacle, bar, barrier, block, check, difficulty, hindrance, impediment, interruption, obstruction, snag, stumbling block. ANT.—aid, blessing, boost, clearance, encouragement, help.

obstinate, contumacious, determined, dogged, firm, fixed, headstrong, immovable, indomitable, inflexible, intractable, mulish, obdurate, persistent, pertinacious, recalcitrant, resolute, stubborn, unaffected, uncompromising, unflinching, unyielding, willful. ANT.—amenable, compliant, docile, pliable, submissive.

obstruct, bar, barricade, block, choke, clog, close, cramp, cripple, curb, dam, frustrate, hamper, hinder, impede, inhibit, interfere, oppose, prevent, restrain, retard, stop, thwart. ANT.—assist, facilitate, forward, promote, support; clear, open.

obtain, acquire, assimilate, attain, collect, earn, gain, gather, get, procure, recover, secure, win. ANT.—forfeit, forsake, lose, miss, sacrifice.

obtuse, blunt, dense, dull, heavy, impassive, insensitive, phlegmatic, slow, stolid, stupid, unintelligent. ANT.—acute, brilliant, imaginative, keen, quick, sharp.

obvious, apparent, clear, comprehensible, conclusive, definite, distinct, evident, explicit, intelligible, lurid, manifest, palpable, patent, plain, precise, self-evident, unmistakable, visible. ANT.—ambiguous, confused, esoteric, obscure, puzzling.

occupation, business, calling, commerce, craft, employment, enterprise, job, mission, position, profession, pursuit, trade, vocation, work.

occupy, absorb, busy, employ, engage, engross, entertain, fill, hold, keep, monopolize; capture, invade, seize; dwell, inhabit, own, possess, tenant, use. ANT.—relinquish, surrender; abandon, empty, leave, vacate.

occurrence, affair, circumstance, episode, event, eventuality, happening, incident, issue, occasion, proceeding, transaction.

odd, abnormal, bizarre, curious, eccentric, erratic, exceptional, extraordinary, mysterious, peculiar, quaint, queer, rare, singular, strange, unique, unnatural, unusual, weird; alone, lone, remaining, single, uneven, unmatched. ANT.—common, familiar, natural, normal, ordinary; even, matched.

odious, abhorrent, base, debased, depraved, detestable, disgusting, foul, hateful, hideous, horrible, loathsome, obnoxious, repellent, repugnant, repulsive, revolting, vicious, vile, wicked; abject, ignoble, low, mean, worthless, wretched. ANT.—delightful, inviting, lovable, pleasant, refreshing; honorable, upright, wholesome.

odor, aroma, essence, fetidness, fetor, fragrance, fume, incense, perfume, redolence, reek, scent, smell, stench, stink.

offense, affront, atrocity, indignity, injury, insult, outrage; aggression, assault, attack, crime, fault, felony, injustice, misdeed, misdemeanor, scandal, sin, transgression, trespass, vice, wrong. ANT.—compliment, defense, gentleness, support; justice, morality, right.

offer, overture, proposal, proposition, suggestion; advance, bid, exhibit, extend, move, present, proffer, propose, sacrifice, submit, suggest, tender, volunteer. ANT.—denial, rejection, withdrawal; refuse, reject, withdraw, withhold.

often, commonly, frequently, generally, ofttimes, recurrently, repeatedly. ANT.—infrequently, rarely, seldom, sporadically.

old, aged, ancient, antediluvian, antiquated, antique, archaic, elderly, experienced, faded, immemorial, obsolete, old-fashioned, patriarchal, prehistoric, remote, superannuated, venerable. ANT.—contemporary, current, fresh, inexperienced, modern.

omen, augury, auspice, emblem, foreboding, foreshadow, gesture, harbinger, indication, mark, note, portent, precursor, prediction, presage, proof, sign, signal, symbol, symptom, token, warning.

omit, bar, cancel, delete, discard, disregard, drop, eliminate, evade, except, exclude, forget, ignore, miss, neglect, overlook, preclude, reject, repudiate, skip, spare. ANT.—add, enroll, enter, include, insert, introduce, notice.

onerous, arduous, burdensome, difficult, hard, heavy, laborious, oppressive, tough; exacting, intricate, perplexing, ponderous, puzzling, troublesome. ANT.—easy, effortless, facile, trivial; clear, simple.

only, barely, but, entirely, exclusively, just, merely, particularly, simply, singly, solely, totally, uniquely, utterly, wholly.

opaque, cloudy, dark, dim, dull, dusky, filmy, gloomy, misty, murky, non-transparent, obfuscated, obscure, shadowy, shady, smoky, uniluminated. ANT.—crystalline, glassy, lustrous, pellucid, transparent.

open, agape, ajar, apart, gaping, unbarred, unclosed, uncovered, unlocked, unobstructed, unsealed; clear, passable, unobstructed; available, disengaged, free, unoccupied; accessible, exposed, public, undefended, unrestricted; artless, candid, explicit, frank, honest, overt, plain, sincere, unreserved; exhibit, expand, expose, rend, reveal, show, spread, start, unbar, unfasten, unfold, unlock, unseal. ANT.—blocked, closed, locked; impassable, obstructed; busy, engaged, occupied; concealed, hidden, private; covert, crafty, cunning, designing, hypocritical; block, conceal, exclude, hinder, secrete.

operate, act, behave, comport, conduct, demean, deport, direct, execute, function, interact, manage, manipulate, perform, react, run, transact, work.

operation, act, action, agency, effort, enterprise, execution, instrumentality, maneuver, manipulation, performance, procedure, proceeding, process, transaction, working. ANT.—cessation, inaction, inactivity, inefficiency, uselessness.

operative, acting, active, busy, efficacious, efficient, effective, effectual, industrious, moving, performing, working. ANT.—dormant, inactive, inefficient, quiet, still.

opinion, belief, conclusion, consensus, conviction, determination, feeling, idea, impression, judgment, notion, persuasion, sentiment, theory, thought, verdict, view. ANT.—fact, knowledge.

opponent, adversary, antagonist, assailant, challenger, competitor, contestant, disputant, encroacher, enemy, foe, infringer, intruder, rival, violator. ANT.—ally, colleague, comrade, consort, partner.

opportunity, advantage, chance, contingency, occasion, occurrence, opening, possibility, situation, timeliness. ANT.—blockage, deterrent, disadvantage, hindrance, obstacle.

oppose, antagonize, bar, check, combat, confront, contradict, contrast, contravene, counteract, cross, defy, deny, hinder, impede, interfere, obstruct, protest, rebuff, resist, restrain, retaliate, snub, thwart, withstand. ANT.—approve, collude, endorse, fraternize, sanction, support.

opposite, antithesis, antonymous, contradictory, contrary, inverse, reverse. ANT.—compatible, counterpart, identical, like, same.

oppress, afflict, annoy, badger, burden, crush, harass, harry, hound, maltreat, overbear, overwhelm, persecute, pester, plague, torment, torture, tyrannize, vex, worry. ANT.—aid, assist, comfort, relieve, support.

optimistic, assured, confident, encouraging, enthusiastic, expectant, heartening, hopeful, inspiriting, promising, trusting. ANT.—despairing, doubtful, gloomy, hopeless, pessimistic.

option, alternative, choice, discretion, election, preference, prerogative, right, selection.

opulent, abundant, affluent, luxurious, moneyed, plentiful, profuse, rich, sumptuous, wealthy. ANT.—destitute, indigent, limited, poor, scarce, squalid.

oral, articulate, mouthed, said, spoken, uttered, verbal, vocal. ANT.—printed, recorded, written.

ordain, appoint, assign, command, commission, constitute, create, decree, delegate, destine, enact, install, institute, invest, order, prescribe, select. ANT.—abolish, abrogate, cancel, depose, dismiss, invalidate.

ordeal, affliction, agony, assay, cross, hardship, judgment, misery, misfortune, pain, strain, suffering, test, trial, tribulation. ANT.—alleviation, comfort, joy, pleasure.

order, arrangement, class, method, plan, rank, regularity, sequence, series, succession, symmetry, system; bidding, canon, command, decree, dictate, directive, injunction, instruction, law, mandate, precept, prescription, regulation, requirement, rule; appoint, arrange, bid, conduct, demand, direct, govern, exact, impose, methodize, ordain, proclaim, regulate, rule, systematize. ANT.—chaos, confusion, disorder, irregularity, muddle, perplexity; allowance, consent, liberty, permission; confuse, disorganize, misdirect, misguide.

ordinary, accustomed, average, common, consistent, conventional, customary, familiar, habitual, medium, natural, normal, regular, typical, usual; inferior, low, plain, trite, vulgar. ANT.—bizarre, eccentric, irregular, strange, unconventional; exceptional, exclusive, extraordinary, wonderful.

organic, constitutional, essential, fundamental, inherent, innate, natural, radical, structural, systematic, vital. ANT.—external, extraneous, inorganic, nonessential.

organization, arrangement, association, constitution, construction, establishment institution, method, mode, order, plan, process, regularity, rule, scheme, system. ANT.—chaos, disarray, disorganization, irregularity, labyrinth, maze.

organize, adjust, arrange, assort, classify, constitute, co-ordinate, devise, dispose, establish, form, found, frame, institute, plan, prepare, regulate, shape, systematize. ANT.—destroy, disband, disorganize, disperse, divide, scatter.

origin, beginning, birth, cause, commencement, cradle, derivation, foundation, inception, outset, rise, root, source, spring, start. ANT.—conclusion, consequence, finality, harvest, result, termination.

original, aboriginal, archetypal, causal, etiological, first, formative, inceptive, initial, primary, rudimentary; creative, fresh, inventive, model, new, novel, unique. ANT.—consequential, derivative, emanating, evolved, terminal; banal, copied, imitated, plagiarized.

ornamental, adorning, beautifying, decorative, embellishing, garnishing, gilt, ornate.

oscillate, change, fluctuate, hesitate, swing, undulate, vacillate, vary, vibrate, waver. ANT.—halt, persist, remain, resolve, stay.

ostentation, boasting, bravado, display, exhibition, flourish, glitter, gloss, pageantry, parade, pomp, pomposity, pretension, show, tinsel, vanity, vaunting, veneer. ANT.—humility, modesty, reserve, restraint, timidity.

ostracize, banish, bar, blackball, deport, except, exclude, exile, expel, hinder, omit, prevent, prohibit, restrain. ANT.—accept, admit, embrace, include, welcome.

oust, banish, deport, depose, discharge, dislodge, dismiss, dispel, dispossess, eject, evict, exclude, exile, expatriate, expel, fire, ostracize, proscribe, reject, remove. ANT.—admit, appoint, empower, harbor, retain, shelter.

outcome, conclusion, consequence, destiny, effect, end, fate, fortune, issue, lot, outgrowth, portion, result, sequel, termination, upshot.

outline, alignment, boundary, brief, configuration, contour, delineation, draft, drawing, figure, form, framework, perimeter, plan, profile, representation, silhouette, skeleton, sketch, tracing.

outrage, abuse, affront, atrocity, grievance, indignity, injury, insult, maltreatment, mortification, offense, oppression, persecution, shock, transgression, trespass, vice, violation.

outrageous, abominable, abusive, atrocious, despicable, excessive, fierce, flagrant, furious, heinous, monstrous, nefarious, scandalous, villainous, violent, wanton, wicked. ANT.—calm, dispassionate, favorable, peaceable, soothing, tranquil.

outspoken, abrupt, bluff, blunt, brusque, candid, direct, forthright, frank, impolite, open, plain, rough, rude, unceremonious, unreserved. ANT.—cautious, circumspect, misleading, reserved, sincere, suave, taciturn.

outstanding, conspicuous, distinguished, dominant, eminent, exceptional, important, notable, noticeable, prominent, remarkable, salient, striking, superior; owing, unpaid, unsettled. ANT.—average, commonplace, inconspicuous, ordinary, usual; paid, settled.

overcome, beat, conquer, crush, defeat, humble, master, overpower, overthrow, quell, rout, subdue, subjugate, suppress, surmount, vanquish. ANT.—fail, lose, succumb, surrender, yield.

overflowing, abounding, abundant, ample, bountiful, copious, fruitful, plenteous, plentiful, profuse, sufficient, teeming, unlimited. ANT.—deficient, insufficient, poor, scanty, scarce.

overlook, disregard, drop, eliminate, exclude, forget, ignore, miss, neglect, omit, skip, slight; condone, excuse, forgive, pardon; dominate, examine, inspect, oversee, supervise. ANT.—note, observe, regard, see, watch; charge, indict, punish; acquiesce, serve, surrender.

oversee, administer, command, direct, engineer, execute, guide, maintain, manage, order, preside, superintend, supervise. ANT.—obey, follow, take orders.

oversight, aberration, blunder, error, failure, fault, inadvertence, inattention, lapse, mistake, neglect, omission, slip; charge, control, direction, guidance, inspection, management, regulation, superintendence, supervision, surveillance, watchfulness. ANT.—attention, care, diligence.

overt, apparent, candid, frank, honest, manifest, obvious, open, patent, plain, public, unconcealed, undisguised. ANT.—concealed, covert, hidden, latent, private, secret.

overthrow, abolish, conquer, crush, defeat, demolish, destroy, extirpate, obliterate, overcome, overpower, overturn, rout, ruin, subjugate, subvert, supplant, upset, vanquish. ANT.—assist, develop, maintain, preserve, restore, support.

overwhelm, see **overthrow.**

own, admit, allow, avow, concede, confess, control, disclose, hold, possess, recognize, retain, reveal. ANT.—deny, disavow, lack, lose, need, reject.

P

pacific, calm, composed, conciliatory, dispassionate, gentle, imperturbable, nonviolent, peaceful, placid, quiet, restful, serene, smooth, tranquil, undisturbed, unruffled, untroubled. ANT.—belligerent, combative, rough, stormy, tempestuous, turbulent.

pacify, allay, alleviate, ameliorate, appease, assuage, calm, compose, lull, mollify, placate, quell, quiet, reconcile, relieve, satisfy, soothe, still, subdue, quell, settle, tranquilize. ANT.—anger, antagonize, excite, incense, rile, roil.

pack, assemblage, amount, bag, band, bundle, collection, company, concourse, gathering, group, load, luggage, number, package, parcel, trunk, valise; arrange, bind, brace, collect, compress, condense, cram, gather, prepare, press, squeeze, stuff, tie. ANT.—allocate, distribute, dispose, loosen, scatter.

pact, agreement, alliance, arrangement, bargain, bond, cartel, compact, concord, contract, covenant, deal, league, stipulation, treaty, understanding, union.

pain, affliction, agony, anguish, discomfort, distress, grief, misery, suffering, torment, torture, woe, ache, pang, paroxysm, throe, twinge. ANT.—happiness, pleasure, well-being; comfort, ease, relief.

painful, agonizing, bitter, distressing, excruciating, galling, grievous, poignant, racking; arduous, difficult, toilsome. ANT.—delightful, enjoyable, pleasant, sweet; easy, effortless, facile.

paint, adorn, color, daub, decorate, delineate, describe, explain, express, ornament, picture, portray, reveal; pigment; cosmetic, rouge.

palpable, apparent, appreciable, clear, discernible, evident, explicit, manifest, obvious, patent, perceptible, plain, prominent, self-evident, sensible, unmistakable, visible; bodily, corporeal, material, physical, real, sensible, tangible. ANT.—concealed, doubtful, mysterious, obscure, questionable; incorporeal, mental, spiritual.

paltry, abject, contemptible, despicable, insignificant, low, mean, measly, miserable, petty, picayune, pitiful, poor, puny, worthless. ANT.—important, large, momentous, rich, significant.

panic, alarm, apprehension, consternation, dismay, dread, fear, fright, horror, perturbation, terror, trembling, tremor, trepidation. ANT.—calm, composure, placidity, repose, serenity.

parade, cavalcade, cortege, file, procession, retinue, sequence, succession, train; display, expose, flaunt, publish, show, vaunt; march, strut.

paradox, absurdity, ambiguity, contradiction, enigma, inconsistency, mystery, perplexity, puzzle.

parallel, akin, alike, allied, analogous, comparable, concentric, concurrent, congruent, congruous, correlative, correspondent, corresponding, like, regular, similar, uniform. ANT.—different, divergent, incongruous, opposed, unique.

paralyze, astound, benumb, cripple, daunt, daze, deaden, demoralize, disable, dumfound, incapacitate, petrify, prostrate, stun, unnerve. ANT.—excite, revive, stimulate, vitalize.

pardon, absolve, acquit, condone, efface, exculpate, excuse, exonerate, forgive, liberate, overlook, quash, release, remit; absolution, acquittal, amnesty, deliverance, discharge, forgiveness, freedom, parole, release, remission, respite. ANT.—banish, castigate, chastise, condemn, punish; chastisement, penalty, punishment, retaliation, vengeance.

parley, chat, colloquy, conference, conversation, dialogue, interview, talk; argue, confer, converse, debate, dispute, negotiate, palaver, talk.

parody, burlesque, caricature, imitation, joke, lampoon, mimicry, mockery, spoof, travesty.

parsimonious, acquisitive, avaricious, covetous, frugal, greedy, grudging, mercenary, miserly, penurious, scrimping, sparing, stingy, tight, ungenerous. ANT.—altruistic, generous, lavish, liberal, prodigal.

part, allotment, apportionment, bit, chip, chunk, division, fragment, lump, moiety, morsel, piece, portion, scrap, section, segment, share, slice, subdivision; component, element, ingredient, member; concern, constituent, faction, interest, party, side; character, lines, role; detach, disunite, dissever, dissociate, divide, separate, sever, sunder; allot, apportion, distribute, share. ANT.—aggregate, entirety, sum, whole; combine, gather, join, unite; keep, withhold.

partiality, bent, bias, bigotry, favoritism, fondness, inclination, leaning, liking, preconception, predisposition, preference, prejudice, tendency, unfairness. ANT.—equality, fairness, honor, impartiality, justice.

participate, associate, commune, cooperate, enjoy, join, mingle, partake, share, unite, use.

particle, atom, bit, corpuscle, crumb, element, grain, iota, jot, mite, molecule, scintilla, scrap, shred, smidgen, speck, whit. ANT.—aggregate, entirety, mass, total, whole.

particular, characteristic, distinctive, exclusive, individual, peculiar, singular, specific, unusual; detailed, exact, minute, precise; careful, discrete, fastidious, meticulous, painstaking, scrupulous, squeamish; circumstance, detail, item, minutia, part, portion, section. ANT.—comprehensive, general, universal, usual; fallacious, ordinary; negligent, nonchalant, slovenly, untidy; generality.

partisan, adherent, aide, ally, assistant, attendant, backer, champion, devotee, disciple, follower, henchman, successor, supporter, votary. ANT.—chief, director, leader, master.

partner, accomplice, ally, assistant, associate, colleague, companion, comrade, confederate, consort, co-worker, crony, mate, participant, spouse. ANT.—adversary, enemy, foe, opponent, stranger.

pass, course, crossing, opening, passageway, route; license, passport, permit, ticket; lunge, thrust; advance, approve, depart, die, disappear, disregard, expire, go, ignore, move, overcome, overlook, overstep, ratify, recede, sanction, skip, surpass, transcend, vanish.

passable, acceptable, adequate, admissible, allowable, average, endurable, fair, mediocre, middling, ordinary, so-so, tolerable; navigable,

penetrable, traversable. ANT.—excellent, inferior, intolerable, superior; impassable.

passage, aisle, arcade, avenue, channel, corridor, course, gateway, hall, pass, path, road, way.

passion, ardor, craving, desire, ecstasy, eroticism, excitement, fascination, fervor, frenzy, hunger, infatuation, intensity, lust, yearning. ANT.—calm, dispassion, frigidity, indifference, restraint, tranquility.

passionate, ardent, burning, excitable, extreme, fervent, fervid, feverish, fiery, glowing, hot, impetuous, intense, irascible, quickened, vehement, violent. ANT.—apathetic, calm, cool, dull, impassive, phlegmatic.

passive, cold, dull, idle, inactive, indifferent, inert, quiet, receptive, relaxed, resigned, stoical, submissive, supine, unresisting. ANT.—active, assertive, dynamic, operative, resistant.

patch, fix, mend, rebuild, renew, repair, restore, revamp, sew; ameliorate, better, correct, improve, rectify, remedy. ANT.—damage, destroy, impair, injure, ravage.

patent, apparent, clear, conspicuous, evident, manifest, obvious, open, overt, plain, unconcealed, unmistakable. ANT.—concealed, covered, covert, hidden, obscure.

path, access, avenue, channel, course, lane, passage, pathway, read, route, runway, sidewalk, street, thoroughfare, track, trail, walk, way.

pathetic, affecting, distressing, heart-rending, moving, piteous, pitiable, pitiful, plaintive, poignant, sad, touching. ANT.—cheering, comical, funny, happy, joyful.

patience, composure, constancy, endurance, forbearance, fortitude, imperturbability, moderation, perseverance, persistence, resignation, submission, sufferance, tolerance. ANT.—disquietude, excitability, impatience, petulance, perturbation, rage.

patient, assiduous, calm, composed, enduring, forbearing, gentle, imperturbable, indulgent, lenient, long-suffering, passive, placid, resigned, serene, stoical, submissive, tolerant, uncomplaining. ANT.—clamorous, high-strung, hysterical, irritable, turbulent, ungovernable.

pattern, archetype, blueprint, conformation, copy, exemplar, guide, ideal, model, mold, norm, original, outline, paradigm, paragon, plan, prototype, sample, standard.

pause, delay, demur, desist, doubt, falter, halt, hesitate, intermit, stop, vacillate, waver, wait; break, cessation, discontinuance, hesitation, intermission, interruption, lull, recess, suspension. ANT.—continue, persevere, proceed, resolve; continuance, continuity, extension, persistence, progression.

pay, allowance, compensation, earnings, fee, indemnity, payment, recompense, remuneration, reparation, retribution, reward, salary, settlement, stipend, wages; compensate, defray, discharge, expend, liquidate, offer, recompense, refund, reimburse, remunerate, reward, settle. ANT.—default, expenditure, expense, forfeiture, nonpayment, outlay, penalty; bilk, cheat, defraud, swindle, victimize.

peace, accord, agreement, amity, armistice, calm, conciliation, concord, harmony, hush, order, pacifism, quiescence, quiet, repose, serenity, silence, stillness, tranquility. ANT.—conflict, discord, disruption, fracas, uproar, warfare.

peaceful, calm, complacent, composed, gentle, mellow, mild, pacific, placid, quiet, serene, still, tranquil, undisturbed, unruffled. ANT.—agitated, noisy, perturbed, turbulent, upset, violent.

peak, acme, apex, climax, consummation, crest, culmination, height, high point, pinnacle, spire,

summit, top, zenith. ANT.—abyss, base, bottom, lowest point, nadir.

peculiar, abnormal, bizarre, eccentric, exceptional, extraordinary, idiosyncratic, odd, rare, singular, strange, striking, unusual; characteristic, distinctive, especial, individual, particular, special, specific. ANT.—common, normal, ordinary, regular, visual.

peculiarity, attribute, characteristic, eccentricity, feature, idiosyncrasy, irregularity, mark, oddity, property, quality, singularity, trait. ANT.—normality, regularity, uniformity.

pedantic, academic, bookish, erudite, formal, impractical, learned, precise, professorial, scholarly, scholastic, theoretical; affected, dry, dull, stilted, stuffy, tedious. ANT.—ignorant, practical, simple; interesting, lively, stimulating.

peer, colleague, companion, compeer, equal, fellow, match, mate; aristocrat, knight, lord, nobleman. ANT.—commoner, inferior, superior.

peevish, acrimonious, cantankerous, cross, faultfinding, fractious, fretful, grouchy, grumbling, ill-natured, ill-tempered, irritable, moody, petulant, snappish, sulky, testy, touchy, ungracious, waspish. ANT.—affable, genial, gracious, pleasant, soothing.

penalty, chastisement, damages, fine, forfeiture, punishment, retribution; disadvantage, handicap. ANT.—benefit, compensation, forgiveness, prize, remuneration, reward.

penetrating, abstruse, deep, profound, recondite, solemn; acute, astute, clever, discerning, discriminating, incisive, keen, piercing, sagacious, sharp, shrewd. ANT.—shallow, slight, superficial, trivial; dull, idiotic, muddled, obtuse, stupid.

penitent, contrite, regretful, remorseful, repentant, sorrowful, sorry. ANT.—impenitent, incontrite, obdurate, remorseless.

penniless, beggared, destitute, empty-handed, fortuneless, impecunious, indigent, needy, poor, poverty-stricken. ANT.—affluent, opulent, prosperous, rich, wealthy.

pensive, contemplative, dreamy, grave, introspective, meditative, musing, reflective, serious, solemn, speculative, thoughtful. ANT.—careless, extroverted, heedless, rash, thoughtless, unconcerned.

penurious, avaricious, cheap, covetous, grasping, greedy, mercenary, miserly, parsimonious, stingy, tight, ungenerous. ANT.—altruistic, bountiful, charitable, generous, liberal, philanthropic.

people, citizens, community, inhabitants, populace, population; family, kindred, relations, siblings; humanity, human race, mankind; nationality, race, tribe; crowd, folk, masses, mob, multitude, rabble.

perceive, conceive, discern, note, notice, observe, recognize, see, sense; apprehend, comprehend, realize, understand. ANT.—confuse, ignore, miss, overlook; misapprehend, misunderstand.

perceptible, apparent, appreciable, apprehensible, discernible, noticeable, palpable, sensible, tangible, visible. ANT.—absurd, impalpable, imperceptible, invisible, obscure.

perception, acumen, acuteness, apprehension, cognizance, comprehension, discernment, insight, keenness, recognition, sharpness, understanding.

perceptive, alert, apprised, aware, cognizant, incisive, keen, observant. ANT.—dense, ignorant, mindless, obtuse, unaware.

perfect, complete, consummate, entire, finished, whole; blameless, faultless, flawless, immaculate, impeccable, ideal, infallible, inviolate, irreproachable, supreme, unblemished, unqualified. ANT.—deficient, incomplete, lacking, unfinished; blemished, defective, flawed, imperfect, worthless.

perform, accomplish, achieve, act, conduct, do, effect, execute, fulfill, impersonate, play, pretend. ANT.—fail, loaf, neglect, refrain, rest.

performance, accomplishment, achievement, action, deed, demonstration, entertainment, exploit, feat, production, show, spectacle, stunt.

perhaps, conceivably, haply, maybe, mayhap, peradventure, perchance, possibly, reasonably. ANT.—certainly, definitely, impossibly.

peril, danger, exposure, hazard, insecurity, jeopardy, liability, menace, pitfall, risk, snare. ANT.—immunity, protection, safety, security.

perimeter, ambit, border, boundary, circuit, circumference, compass, edge, periphery. ANT.—center, core, heart, hub, middle.

period, age, circuit, cycle, date, duration, epoch, era, interim, interval, limit, season, span, spell, tempo, term, time.

perish, cease, decay, decease, depart, die, expire, pass away, succumb, vanish. ANT.—exist, flourish, live, survive, thrive.

permanent, abiding, changeless, constant, durable, enduring, established, everlasting, fixed, indelible, indestructible, invariant, lasting, perpetual, persistent, stable, unalterable, unchangeable, unchanging. ANT.—ephemeral, mutable, temporary, transitory, vacillating, variable.

permeate, drench, imbue, impregnate, infiltrate, infuse, ingrain, penetrate, pervade, saturate, soak, steep.

permission, allowance, approval, authority, authorization, confirmation, consent, dispensation, enfranchisement, grace, leave, liberty, license, permit, sanction, tolerance, toleration, verification. ANT.—denial, opposition, prohibition, refusal, veto.

permit, admit, allow, approve, authorize, empower, endorse, give, grant, let, recognize, sanction, suffer, tolerate, yield; charter, law, license, pass, passport, patent, permission, warrant. ANT.—bar, forbid, inhibit, oppose, restrain; ban, embargo, inhibition, injunction, restriction.

perpendicular, erect, plumb, straight, upright, upstanding, vertical. ANT.—horizontal, level, oblique, slanting.

perpetrate, accomplish, do, commit, enact, execute, inflict, perform. ANT.—fail, miscarry, ignore, neglect.

perpetual, ceaseless, continual, constant, deathless, endless, enduring, eternal, everlasting, immortal, incessant, infinite, interminable, lasting, permanent, timeless, unceasing, undying, uninterrupted. ANT.—ephemeral, evanescent, finite, fleeting, temporal.

perplex, annoy, baffle, bewilder, complicate, confound, confuse, disconcert, disorganize, dumfound, entangle, fluster, mislead, muddle, mystify, puzzle, snarl, trouble, worry. ANT.—clarify, explain, illumine, inform, instruct.

perplexing, bewildering, complex, complicated, compound, confusing, difficult, intricate, involved, mystifying, puzzling. ANT.—clear, lucid, manifest, obvious, plain, simple.

persecute, abuse, afflict, aggrieve, annoy, badger, bother, castigate, gall, harass, harry, hound, maltreat, oppress, pester, plague, punish, rile, scourge, tease, torment, torture, vex, victimize, worry. ANT.—aid, assist, comfort, gladden, nurture, support.

persevere, abide, continue, endure, last, persist, prevail, pursue, remain, survive, sustain.

ANT.—cease, desist, surrender, vacillate, waver.

perseverance, assiduity, constancy, determination, diligence, grit, industry, persistence, persistency, pertinacity, pluck, resolution, steadfastness, tenacity. ANT.—cessation, idleness, inertia, laziness, procrastination, sloth.

persist, see persevere.

persistence, see perseverance.

persistent, constant, determined, enduring, firm, fixed, immovable, indefatigable, lasting, persevering, resolute, steadfast, steady, tenacious; contumacious, dogged, headstrong, importunate, insistent, obstinate, pertinacious, perverse, stubborn. ANT.—dawdling, doubtful, hesitant, unsure, vacillating, wavering; humble, pliable, reasonable, submissive, yielding.

personality, being, character, disposition, identify, individuality, nature, oneself, self, style, temper, temperament; celebrity, cynosure, notable, star.

perspicuity, clarity, clearness, discrimination, distinctness, explicitness, intelligibility, lucidity, preciseness. ANT.—confusion, mystification, obscurity, perplexity, vagueness.

persuade, allure, arouse, cajole, coax, convince, entice, exhort, incite, induce, influence, lead, lure, move, prevail upon, prompt, provoke, urge, win over. ANT.—deter, dissuade, divert, hinder, repress, restrain.

persuasion, allegiance, belief, conviction, creed, faith, religion; enticement, incitement, inducement, influence, suasion.

pertain, appertain, apply, belong (to), concern, refer (to), relate (to).

pertinacious, constant, contumacious, determined, dogged, firm, headstrong, immovable, inflexible, intractable, obdurate, obstinate, persistent, resolute, stubborn, tenacious, unyielding. ANT.—compliant, docile, flexible, submissive, yielding.

pertinent, applicable, appropriate, apropos, apt, fit, fitting, germane, material, proper, relating, relevant, suited. ANT.—alien, extraneous, foreign, improper, irrelevant, unrelated.

perturb, agitate, aggravate, annoy, bother, discommode, disquiet, harass, heckle, irk, irritate, perplex, pester, plague, vex, worry. ANT.—assist, calm, delight, help, please.

pervade, diffuse, extend, fill, imbue, impregnate, infiltrate, overspread, penetrate, permeate, run through, saturate, spread.

perverse, cantankerous, contrary, contumacious, disobedient, dogged, forward, fractious, intractable, irascible, obstinate, peevish, petulant, resolute, splenetic, stubborn, ungovernable, unyielding; perverted, sinful, wayward, wicked. ANT.—agreeable, docile, manageable, obliging, tractable; angelic, saintly, virtuous.

perversion, abasement, abuse, corruption, debasement, degradation, depravity, desecration, falsification, humiliation, maltreatment, misuse, outrage, profanation, reviling, vitiation, wickedness. ANT.—elevation, enhancement, improvement, respect, veneration.

pessimistic, blue, cynical, depressed, desolate, despairing, despondent, doleful, downcast, foreboding, forlorn, gloomy, glum, hopeless, melancholy, misanthropic, rueful, spiritless. ANT.—bright, enthusiastic, hopeful, optimistic, trusting.

pester, annoy, badger, bait, bother, chafe, disturb, fret, harass, harry, heckle, inconvenience, irk, irritate, molest, plague, provoke, tease, torment, trouble, vex. ANT.—accommodate, comfort, delight, gratify, soothe, support.

petition, appeal, application, entreaty, invocation, plea, prayer, proposal, request, requisition, suit, solicitation, supplication.

petrify, calcify, deaden, fossilize, harden, lapidify, mineralize, ossify, solidify; amaze, astonish, benumb, frighten, paralyze, shock, stun, stupefy.

petty, childish, frivolous, insignificant, negligible, nugatory, paltry, puny, shallow, slight, small, trifling, trivial, unimportant, weak, worthless. ANT.—important, momentous, serious, significant, vital.

petulant, acrimonious, choleric, cranky, cross, crusty, fretful, ill-humored, ill-natured, ill-tempered, irascible, irritable, peevish, querulous, snappish, sullen, surly, testy, touchy, unamiable, waspish. ANT.—affable, congenial, good-natured, pleasant, temperate.

philanthropic, altruistic, beneficent, benevolent, charitable, compassionate, generous, gracious, humanitarian, liberal, magnanimous, munificent. ANT.—antisocial, cruel, egotistical, merciless, selfish.

phlegmatic, cold, dispassionate, impassive, inexcitable, passionless, stoical, stolid, unemotional, unfeeling. ANT.—ardent, demonstrative, enthusiastic, lively, passionate.

phobia, aversion, avoidance, disgust, dislike, distaste, fear, hatred, resentment. ANT.—attraction, endurance, liking, love, tolerance.

phraseology, diction, expression, idiom, language, locution, manner, phrasing, speech, style, usage, vocabulary, wording.

physical, anatomical, bodily, carnal, corporal, corporeal, material, mortal, natural, palpable, real, sensible, somatic, tangible, visible. ANT.—abstract, immaterial, incorporeal, spiritual, unreal.

pick, acquire, choose, cull, elect, gather, opt, prefer, select, single, take. ANT.—decline, refuse, reject.

picture, advertisement, appearance, blueprint, cartoon, cinema, design, draft, drawing, effigy, engraving, etching, facsimile, figure, film, illustration, image, landscape, likeness, lithograph, outline, pageant, painting, panorama, photo, photograph, portrait, portrayal, print, representation, scene, sketch, spectacle, tableau, tracing, view; delineate, depict, draw, represent, sketch.

piece, amount, bit, chunk, fraction, fragment, hunk, morsel, part, portion, scrap, section, segment, shred; combine, patch, repair, unite. ANT.—all, entirety, sum, total, whole.

pigment, brilliance, color, coloration, coloring, complexion, dye, hue, intensity, oil paint, paint, shade, stain, taint, tincture, tinge, tint, wash.

pinnacle, acme, apex, chief, climax, crest, crown, culmination, head, peak, summit, top, zenith. ANT.—base, bottom, depths, foot, foundation, nadir.

pious, blessed, consecrated, devotional, devout, divine, godly, hallowed, holy, prayerful, pure, religious, reverent, sacred, saintly, sanctified, seraphic, spiritual, unworldly. ANT—blasphemous, evil, irreverent, profane, sacrilegious, wicked.

pitch, cast, chuck, fling, heave, hurl, launch, propel, sling, throw, thrust, toss; decline, slant, slope. ANT.—catch, grab, receive.

pitiful, clement, compassionate, lenient, merciful, tender, tender-hearted, sympathetic; abject, contemptible, despicable, vile, wretched; cheerless, doleful, lamentable, miserable, mournful, piteous, sad, sorrowful, tearful. ANT.—dignified, exalted, grand, joyful, noble, sublime.

pity, charity, clemency, commiseration, compassion, condolence, empathy, kindness, mercy, philanthropy, sympathy, tenderness. ANT.—brutality, cruelty, inhumanity, ruthlessness, vengeance.

place, allocate, allot, arrange, assign, deposit, dispose, distribute, group, install, invest, locate, plant, put, set, store, stow; abode, dwelling, home, residence; area, locality, point, position, post, region, site, situation, spot, station. ANT.—disarrange, disturb, empty, remove, unsettle.

placid, calm, composed, dispassionate, equable, gentle, imperturbable, pacific, peaceful, quiet, serene, still, tranquil, undisturbed, unmoved, unruffled. ANT.—agitated, disturbed, excited, stormy, turbulent, wild.

plague, see persecute.

plain, even, flat, level, smooth; apparent, clear, distinct, evident, exposed, lucid, manifest, obvious, palpable, perceptible, recognizable, unmistakable, visible; candid, definite, explicit, frank, open, simple, sincere, unpretentious; absolute, unqualified. ANT.—broken, rough, uneven; abstruse, ambiguous, cloudy, enigmatical, obscure, puzzling; adorned, embellished, feigned, insincere, pretentious; qualified.

plan, chart, contrive, create, delineate, design, devise, invent, map, plot, prepare, scheme, shape; intent, mean, purpose; depict, draw, illustrate, outline, sketch; arrangement, blueprint, chart, contrivance, delineation, design, device, diagram, draft, drawing, map, method, model, outline, plot, policy, program, project, proposal, proposition, prospectus, sketch, view.

plant, complex, establishment, factory, foundry, mill, shop; bush, flower, herb, organism, shoot, shrub, sprout, vegetable; establish, locate, place, put, set, settle; bed, implant, pot, sow.

plastic, ductile, flexible, formable, formative, impressible, malleable, pliant, resilient; artificial, counterfeit, fabricated, false, simulated. ANT.—brittle, hard, rigid, stiff; authentic, genuine, real.

plausible, acceptable, believable, credible, defensible, feasible, justifiable, likely, possible, practical, probable, reasonable, specious. ANT.—implausible, impossible, incredible, unlikely, visionary.

play, amusement, diversion, enjoyment, entertainment, fun, game, pastime, pleasure, recreation, relaxation, sport; caper, frisk, frolic, gambol, revel, romp, skip, sport, stake, toy, wager; execute, perform, work; act, impersonate, personate, pretend; finger, pedal, pipe, sound, strum, thrum; dissemble, feign, imagine, pretend, simulate; drama piece, musical, theatrical; compete, engage, participate, rival.

plead, appeal, ask, beg, beseech, crave, entreat, implore, petition, press, request, solicit, supplicate, urge; advocate, argue, attest, claim, contend, declare, defend, indicate, maintain, proclaim, profess, pronounce, state, swear.

pleasant, acceptable, agreeable, amiable, attractive, charming, comforting, cordial, delightful, engaging, enjoyable, gratifying, honeyed, mellifluous, melodious, pleasing, pleasurable, suitable, welcome, winning. ANT.—disagreeable, hateful, obnoxious, offensive, painful, repellent, repulsive.

pleasing, see pleasant.

pleasure, amusement, bliss, comfort, contentment, delight, diversion, ease, ecstasy, enjoyment, entertainment, felicity, exhilaration, gladness, gratification, happiness, indulgence, light-heartedness, joy, rapture, satisfaction. ANT.—affliction, distress, grief, hopelessness, misery, suffering.

pledge, affirmation, agreement, assertion, assurance, commitment, contract, covenant, declaration, engagement, guarantee, oath, pact, promise, security, token, troth, vow, word; candidate; affirm, agree, bind, commit, declare, deposit, engage, guarantee, hypothecate, obligate, promise, swear, vouch, vow, wage. ANT.—break faith, deceive, deny, renounce.

plentiful, abundant, ample, bounteous, bountiful, copious, inexhaustible, lavish, liberal, luxurious, plenteous, profuse, replete, rich, teeming, unsparing. ANT.—deficient, drained, impoverished, scanty, scarce, stripped.

pliable, adaptable, adjustable, compliant, docile, ductile, elastic, flexible, limber, manageable, pliant, resilient, supple, tractable, wavering, yielding. ANT.—brittle, intractable, rigid, stiff, unyielding.

plot, artifice, cabal, conspiracy, design, development, intrigue, machination, plan, progress, scheme, stratagem, trick, unfolding; chart, diagram, draft, graph, outline, sketch; contrive, frame, plan, scheme; area, land, lot, parcel.

plump, buxom, chubby, corpulent, fleshy, paunchy, portly, pudgy, puffy, rotund, round, stout, swollen, thickset. ANT.—emaciated, gaunt, lean, slender, slim.

poignant, affecting, heart-rending, moving, pitiable, sad, tender, touching; acute, biting, penetrating, piercing, pungent, trenchant. ANT.—painless, pleasant; blunt, dull, insipid, numb, obtuse.

point, aim, designate, direct, indicate, level, punctuate, sharpen, show; acme, apex, characteristic, end, gist, goal, intent, juncture, location, meaning, object, peak, place, position, promontory, prong, purpose, significance, summit, trait.

pointed, acute, biting, caustic, cutting, keen, knifelike, penetrating, piercing, razor-edged, sarcastic, severe, sharp, spiked, stinging, trenchant. ANT.—bland, blunt, dull, gentle, unsharpened.

poise, balance, equilibrium, equipoise, gravity; class, composure, culture, dignity, self-possession, serenity, stateliness.

poisonous, corrupt, deadly, deleterious, destructive, evil, fatal, malignant, morbid, noisome, noxious, pestilential, toxic, venomous, virulent. ANT.—curative, harmless, healthful, invigorating, nourishing, wholesome.

policy, contract, course, handling, management, method, order, outline, plan, plank, platform, procedure, strategy, system, tactic.

polish, art, breeding, courtesy, culture, elegance, finish, glaze, gloss, glossiness, grace, luster, politeness, refinement, skill, smoothness, suavity, tact, training; brighten, burnish, civilize, discipline, refine, refinish, rub, shine, smooth, wax. ANT.—baseness, crudity, harshness, lowliness, roughness; debase, dull, mar, roughen, ruin.

polite, accomplished, attentive, civil, considerate, cordial, courteous, cultivated, decorous, diplomatic, genteel, mannerly, polished, refined, tactful, urbane, well-bred, well-mannered. ANT.—abusive, coarse, discourteous, impudent, offensive, rude.

pollute, adulterate, befoul, contaminate, corrupt, defile, demoralize, infect, pervert, poison, soil, sully, taint, vitiate. ANT.—clean, disinfect, purge, purify, sanitize.

pomp, boasting, display, flourish, glory, grandeur, magnificence, ostentation, pageantry, parade, show, splendor, vaunting. ANT.—humility, modesty, plainness, shabbiness, simplicity, tawdriness.

pompous, august, dignified, grand, high, imposing, lofty, magnificent, majestic, noble, spectacular, stately, sublime; arrogant, boastful, domineering, egotistical, flaunting, haughty, inflated, ostentatious, pretentious, swaggering. ANT.—banal, common, humble, lowly, ordinary; bashful, demure, modest, reserved, submissive.

ponder, calculate, cogitate, contemplate, deliberate, devise, examine, investigate, meditate, muse, reflect, ruminate, scrutinize, study, weigh. ANT.—forget, ignore, neglect, overlook.

ponderous, burdensome, cumbersome, heavy, massive, unwieldy, weighty; dull, gloomy, grave, spiritless; important, momentous, serious, significant. ANT.—airy, fluffy, light; animated, brisk, buoyant, volatile; insignificant, petty, trivial, unimportant.

poor, destitute, impecunious, impoverished, indigent, insolvent, needy, penniless, poverty-stricken, substandard, underprivileged; bad, defective, deficient, inferior, insignificant, mediocre, miserable, shabby, unfavorable. ANT.—affluent, opulent, rich, solvent, wealthy; ample, commendable, excellent, favorable, superior.

popular, common, current, familiar, general, lay, ordinary, plebeian, prevailing, prevalent, public, universal; admired, approved, desired, favorite, liked. ANT.—esoteric, exclusive, restricted; disliked, disreputable, shunned, unpopular.

pornographic, coarse, corrupt, debauched, depraved, dirty, disgusting, filthy, gross, immoral, indecent, lascivious, lecherous, lewd, obscene, prurient, smutty. ANT.—chaste, decent, modest, pure, refined.

port, anchorage, bay, berth, cove, dock, door, entrance, gateway, harbor, haven, inlet, portal, shelter; bearing, carriage, deportment, demeanor, manner, mien, presence.

portion, allotment, consignment, cutting, dividend, division, fraction, fragment, measure, morsel, parcel, part, piece, quota, ration, section, segment, share, slice, subdivision. ANT.—aggregation, entirety, mass, sum, total.

portray, act, characterize, copy, delineate, depict, describe, draw, figure, impersonate, paint, picture, represent, reproduce, reveal, show, sketch.

position, bearings, environment, ground, locality, location, place, post, seat, site, situation, spot, station; caste, condition, place, rank, standing, status; berth, employment, incumbency, job, occupation, office, post, profession, situation; attitude, belief, judgment, opinion, view; bearing, carriage, pose, posture.

positive, absolute, affirmative, assertive, assured, certain, concrete, decided, definite, dogmatic, emphatic, firm, fixed, incontrovertible, indubitable, inevitable, resolute, secure, sure, uncompromising, undeniable, unmistakable, unquestionable. ANT.—ambiguous, doubtful, dubious, hazy, questionable, uncertain.

possess, appropriate, control, dominate, have, hold, keep, obtain, occupy, own, reserve, retain, seize, take. ANT.—abandon, lack, lose, need, renounce, surrender.

possessions, assets, belongings, capital, commodities, effects, equity, estate, goods, holdings, investments, lands, legacy, merchandise, property, resources, stock, wares, wealth.

possibility, chance, contingency, event, feasibility, happening, hope, incident, occasion, occurrence, opening, opportunity, outside chance, plausibility, potentiality. ANT.—disadvantage, impossibility, hindrance, obstacle.

possible, achievable, attainable, conceivable, contingent, credible, feasible, liable, likely, obtainable, performable, plausible, potential, practical, probable. ANT.—foolish, impossible, inconceivable, unattainable, unreasonable.

postpone, adjourn, defer, delay, discontinue, interrupt, pigeonhole, procrastinate, protract, remand, retard, shelve, stall, stay, suspend, table, waive. ANT.—accelerate, continue, maintain, persevere, persist, proceed.

potent, capable, cogent, compelling, effective, efficacious, enduring, firm, forceful, forcible, great, hardy, influential, intense, irresistible, mighty, overpowering, powerful, puissant, robust, staunch, strong, sturdy, vigorous, virile. ANT.—delicate, enervated, fragile, impotent, weak.

pound, batter, beat, buffet, clout, club, crush, dash, drum, flail, hammer, hit, knock, pelt, pulverize, pummel, punch, smite, strike, thrash, thump, whack; palpitate, pulsate, pulse, throb.

poverty, dearth, deficiency, destitution, distress, exigency, inadequacy, indigence, necessity, need, pauperism, penury, privation, scarcity, want. ANT.—abundance, affluence, opulence, riches, wealth.

power, ability, capability, capacity, competence, efficacy, efficiency, endowment, potency, skill, talent; energy, force, might, stamina, strength, vigor; authority, command, control, dominion, government, influence, jurisdiction, mastery, predominance, preponderance, sway, sovereignty, superiority, supremacy. ANT.—impotence, inability, ineptitude; debility, infirmity, weakness; servitude, subjection, subservience.

powerful, see potent.

practical, balanced, down-to-earth, effective, feasible, functional, operative, pragmatic, rational, realistic, reasonable, sensible, sound, unromantic, useful, utilitarian, workable. ANT.—foolish, idealistic, imperceptible, impractical, outlandish, useless.

practice, application, custom, drill, exercise, fashion, habit, manner, method, mode, recitation, rehearsal, repetition, system, training, usage, use; clients, patients.

praise, acclaim, admire, applaud, approve, boost, commend, compliment, endorse, exalt, extol, flatter, glorify, laud, magnify, recommend, sanction. ANT.—admonish, berate, condemn, impugn, reproach, upbraid.

precarious, critical, dangerous, deadly, hazardous, insecure, menacing, perilous, risky, threatening, treacherous, unsafe, unstable; doubtful, dubious, unassured, uncertain. ANT.—protected, safe, secure, stable; assured, certain, unquestionable.

precept, adage, belief, canon, code, commandment, direction, creed, doctrine, dogma, injunction, instruction, law, mandate, maxim, regulation, rule, teaching, tenet.

precious, beloved, costly, darling, dear, esteemed, excellent, expensive, exquisite, high-priced, inestimable, invaluable, priceless, profitable, select, superior, superlative, unequaled, useful, valuable, worthy. ANT.—cheap, insignificant, trifling, valueless, worthless.

precipitate, accelerate, hasten, quicken, speed; abrupt, hasty, headlong, impetuous, rash, sudden. ANT.—check, delay, moderate, preclude, retard, slow; deliberate, intentional, reflective, thoughtful.

precise, accurate, correct, definite, distinct, exact, meticulous, punctilious, rigorous, scrupulous, strict, unequivocal; ceremonious, formal, prim, prudish, rigid, stiff. ANT.—ambiguous, fallacious, inexact, negligent, slipshod; casual, informal, loose, relaxed.

predicament, bind, corner, crisis, difficulty, dilemma, fix, mess, muddle, perplexity, pinch, plight, puzzle, quandary, scrape, situation, strait. ANT.—comfort, ease, security, solace, tranquility.

prediction, augury, divination, foreboding, forecast, foretelling, fortunetelling, horoscope, omen, presage, prognosis, prognostication, prophecy.

predominant, cardinal, chief, controlling, distinguished, dominant, essential, first, foremost, highest, leading, main, notable, paramount, preponderant, prevailing, prevalent, principal, reigning, ruling, sovereign, supreme. ANT.—insignificant, minor, obscure, subordinate, subsidiary.

preface, beginning, foreword, introduction, overture, preamble, prelude, prologue. ANT.—addendum, afterword, conclusion, ending, epilogue.

preference, alternative, choice, decision, election, favorite, option, pick, selection.

prejudice, animosity, antipathy, apartheid, aversion, bias, contempt, detriment, dislike, enmity, intolerance, objection, partiality, pique, preconception, predilection, prejudgment, prepossession, repugnance, revulsion, unfairness. ANT.—approval, benevolence, kindness, regard, respect, tolerance.

premature, anticipatory, early, green, hasty, immature, incomplete, precipitate, precocious, rash, raw, sudden, unanticipated, unexpected, unfinished, unprepared, unripe, unseasonable, untimely. ANT.—anticipated, completed, expected, fully developed, matured, tardy.

premeditated, calculated, contemplated, deliberate, designed, intended, intentional, planned, plotted, prearranged, predetermined, studied, voluntary. ANT.—accidental, casual, fortuitous, spontaneous, unforeseen.

premise, assumption, basis, criterion, evidence, foundation, groundwork, justification, postulate, presumption, presupposition, principle, proof, proposition, reason. ANT.—derivative, superstructure, trimming.

premium, appreciation, award, bonus, boon, bounty, enhancement, favor, gift, gratuity, present, prize, recompense, remuneration; best, choicest, highest quality, top grade. ANT.—inferior, low grade, poor, third rate.

preoccupied, absorbed, abstracted, distracted, engrossed, inattentive, musing, oblivious, unobservant. ANT.—attentive, watchful.

prepare, adjust, adapt, anticipate, arm, arrange, concoct, cook, develop, devise, equip, fit, fix, foresee, form, furnish, outfit, plan, predispose, prime, provide, qualify, ready, settle. ANT.—forget, ignore, neglect, overlook.

prerogative, authority, birthright, claim, grant, immunity, liberty, license, perquisite, privilege, right. ANT.—duty, injustice, limitation, obligation, violation.

present, advance, assign, award, bestow, confer, deliver, endow, exhibit, extend, give, grant, introduce, offer, proffer, propose, sacrifice, show, tender; boon, donation, gift, grant, gratuity; instant, now, today. ANT.—accept, receive, reject, spurn, take.

preserve, conserve, defend, guard, hold, keep, maintain, protect, rescue, safeguard, save, secure, shield, spare, support, sustain, uphold. ANT.—abandon, abolish, abrogate, destroy, forego, waste.

pressing, absorbing, compelling, constraining, critical, crucial, crying, distressing, exigent, impelling, imperative, important, importunate, insistent, necessary, serious, urgent, vital. ANT.—insignificant, meaningless, petty, superficial, trivial.

pressure, burden, compression, encumbrance, force, stress, tension, thrust, weight; affliction, coercion, compulsion, constraint, exigency, hurry, obligation, persuasion, stress, urgency. ANT.—relief, release; assistance, ease, encouragement, leniency, relaxation.

prestige, ascendancy, authority, credit, effect, fame, glory, honor, influence, power, rank, renown, repute, supremacy, weight. ANT.—impotence, insignificance, weakness, unimportance.

presume, assume, believe, conclude, conjecture, consider, guess, hypothesize, imagine, posit, presuppose, regard, speculate, suppose, surmise, theorize, think. ANT.—ascertain, confirm, demonstrate, manifest, prove.

pretense, affectation, affection, cloak, deceit, disguise, dissimulation, evasion, excuse, fabrication, falsification, garb, mask, pomposity, pretension, pretext, prevarication, ruse, semblance, sham, show, simulation, subterfuge, trickery, wile. ANT.—candor, frankness, honesty, sincerity, truth, veracity.

pretty, see handsome.

prevalent, accepted, catholic, common, comprehensive, controlling, familiar, frequent, general, ordinary, popular, predominant, prevailing, sweeping, ubiquitous, universal, usual, widespread, world-wide. ANT.—exceptional, extraordinary, infrequent, isolated, sporadic.

prevent, avert, block, check, foil, forestall, halt, hinder, impede, inhibit, interrupt, obstruct, obviate, preclude, prohibit, repress, stop, thwart. ANT.—allow, assist, expedite, further, promote, stimulate.

previous, aforesaid, antecedent, anterior, earlier, foregoing, former, preceding, prefatory, preliminary, preparatory, prior. ANT.—ensuing, latter, pursuant, subsequent, succeeding.

pride, arrogance, conceit, egoism, egotism, haughtiness, loftiness, pomposity, pretension, self-esteem; self-glorification, self-love, self-respect, superciliousness, vanity. ANT.—humility, meekness, modesty, reserve, self-effacement.

primary, basic, beginning, chief, earliest, elementary, first, fundamental, initial, leading, main, opening, original, prime, primeval, primitive, principal, pristine; chief, foremost. ANT.—following, hindmost, last, latest; inferior, least, secondary, subordinate.

primeval, first, initial, original, primary, primordial, pristine; creative, fresh, inventive, new, novel. ANT.—derivative, subsequent, terminal; banal, trite.

primitive, aboriginal, ancient, antiquated, archaic, early, old, primary, primeval, primordial, pristine; barbaric, crude, first, fundamental, rudimentary, simple, uncivilized, untaught. ANT.—civilized, complex, modern, polished, sophisticated.

primordial, see primeval.

principal, cardinal, chief, dominant, essential, first, foremost, greatest, highest, leading, main, paramount, predominant, preeminent, prime, supreme; chief, commander, director, executive, head, leader, master. ANT.—accessory, auxiliary, inferior, minor, negligible, unimportant; attendant, follower, pupil, subordinate.

principle, axiom, base, canon, doctrine, formula, foundation, ground, guide, law, maxim, method, order, policy, precept, reason, regulation, rule, statute, system, teaching, theorem; belief, conviction, faith; integrity, rectitude, uprightness.

prior, see previous.

private, clandestine, concealed, covert, hidden, latent, secluded, secret, sequestered, surreptitious, unknown, unrevealed; individual, personal. ANT.—disclosed, exposed, known, open, public.

privation, see poverty.

privilege, advantage, benefit, exemption, favor, franchise, freedom, immunity, liberty, license, perquisite, prerogative, right, sanction; chance, event, occasion, opportunity. ANT.—deprivation, disallowance, inhibition, limitation, prohibition, restriction.

prize, accolade, advantage, award, bonus, booty, bounty, citation, compensation, honor, inducement, laurel, possession, premium, privilege, recompense, remuneration, requital, reward, spoil. ANT.—charge, earnings, forfeiture, penalty, punishment.

problem, conundrum, difficulty, dilemma, enigma, intricacy, mystery, obstacle, perplexity, plight, puzzle, quandary, query, riddle. ANT.—answer, certainty, clarification, explanation, solution.

procedure, arrangement, course, custom, fashion, form, formula, habit, manner, method, mode, order, plan, practice, proceeding, process, routine, rule, style, system, technique, way.

proceed, advance, continue, forge ahead, improve, move, progress, rise, thrive. ANT.—recede, regress, retire, retreat, withdraw.

proceeds, crop, fruit, earnings, gain, gross, harvest, income, net, produce, product, profits, reaping, receipts, result, return, store, yield. ANT.—costs, expenses, outlay.

proclaim, advertise, affirm, announce, assert, aver, broadcast, circulate, declare, divulge, express, make known, profess, promulgate, protest, publish, reveal, state, tell, voice. ANT.—camouflage, conceal, mask, repress, suppress.

procrastinate, adjourn, dally, dawdle, defer, delay, extend, loiter, postpone, prolong, protract, retard, stall, suspend, tarry. ANT.—accelerate, hasten, hurry, persevere, quicken.

produce, aftermath, consequence, crop, effect, fruit, gain, goods, harvest, outcome, outgrowth, proceeds, product, profit, realization, reaping, result, return, store, yield; bear, breed, conceive, generate, hatch, procreate, propagate, sire, yield; fabricate, make, manufacture, supply; bring forward, exhibit, present, show; accomplish, author, cause, create, institute, issue, originate.

production, authoring, bearing, creation, erection, generation, harvest, making, origination, output, performance, procreation, product, project, rendering, work, yield.

profess, see proclaim.

proficient, able, accomplished, adept, adroit, agile, clever, competent, cunning, deft, dexterous, expert, gifted, ingenious, masterful, practiced, skilled, skillful, talented, versed. ANT.—bungling, incapable, incompetent, inept, maladroit, unskilled.

profit, advantage, benefit, earnings, emolument, gain, improvement, interest, proceeds, receipts, remuneration, return, returns, service, use. ANT.—destruction, detriment, failure, loss, ruin.

profligate, see corrupt.

profound, abstruse, abysmal, consummate, deep, erudite, heartfelt, heavy, intense, mysterious,

penetrating, recondite, scholarly, serious, solemn. ANT.—frivolous, shallow, superficial, trivial, unenlightened, unlearned.

profuse, abundant, copious, excessive, extravagant, exuberant, immoderate, improvident, lavish, liberal, luxuriant, overflowing, plentiful, prodigal, redundant, superfluous, wasteful. ANT.—barren, deficient, inadequate, meager, scanty.

progress, advance, advancement, attainment, betterment, development, growth, headway, improvement, increase, locomotion, movement, proficiency, progression; advance, improve, move onward, press on, proceed, rise, thrive. ANT.—deferment, delay, moratorium, regression, suspension; backtrack, regress, resign, retard, retreat.

prohibit, ban, block, check, circumscribe, debar, deny, exclude, forbid, hinder, inhibit, interdict, preclude, prevent, proscribe, refuse, restrain, restrict, taboo, veto, withhold. ANT.—allow, empower, endorse, license, permit, sanction.

project, contrivance, design, device, idea, outline, plan, plot, procedure, projection, scheme, undertaking, working draft.

prolific, bountiful, breeding, fecund, fertile, fruitful, luxuriant, plenteous, productive, propagating, rich, swarming, teeming. ANT.—barren, sterile, unfruitful, unproductive.

prolong, amplify, augment, continue, elongate, extend, increase, lengthen, protract, stretch, sustain. ANT.—condense, curtail, shorten, shrink.

prominent, celebrated, conspicuous, distinguished, eminent, famous, illustrious, influential, leading, noteworthy, outstanding, popular, remarkable, salient, renowned, well-known; convex, extended, jutting, projecting, protruding. ANT.—common, humble, obscure, ordinary, unknown; concave, depressed, flat, level, sunken.

promise, affirmation, agreement, assurance, bestowal, betrothal, commitment, consent, contract, covenant, engagement, fulfillment, guarantee, insurance, oath, obligation, pact, pledge, swearing, troth, undertaking, vow.

promote, advance, aggrandize, aid, assist, contribute, cultivate, dignify, elevate, encourage, endow, exalt, facilitate, forward, foster, further, help, push, raise, urge. ANT.—degrade, discourage, hinder, impair, impede, obstruct.

prompt, arouse, cause, evoke, incite, induce, inspire, make, occasion, originate, provoke; active, alert, direct, early, immediate, instant, keen, precise, punctual, quick, ready, swift, timely, vigilant. ANT.—dilatory, late, overdue, slow, tardy.

promulgate, see proclaim.

proof, affidavit, attestation, confirmation, corroboration, credentials, data, demonstration, evidence, facts, reasons, substantiation, test, testimony, verification, warrant, witness. ANT.—aberrancy, failure, fallacy, invalidity, misconception, untruth.

propagate, beget, breed, create, develop, diffuse, disseminate, engender, father, generate, grow, increase, multiply, originate, procreate, produce, publish, raise, reproduce, sire, spread, teach. ANT.—annihilate, destroy, exterminate, extinguish, kill, ravage.

propel, actuate, agitate, drive, force, impel, induce, instigate, move, persuade, push, start, thrust, urge. ANT.—delay, discourage, drag, halt, hinder, stop.

propensity, aim, aptitude, bent, bias, drift, flair, gift, inclination, knack, leaning, penchant, predilection, predisposition, prejudice, proclivity,

proneness, tendency, trend. ANT.—antipathy, aversion, deviation, disinclination, dislike.

proper, appropriate, befitting, conventional, correct, decent, fair, fit, formal, just, legitimate, meet, pertinent, respectable, right, seemly, suitable; individual, peculiar, special. ANT.—improper, inaccurate, objectionable, unfit, unsuitable.

property, assets, belongings, capital, commodities, effects, equity, estate, goods, holdings, lands, merchandise, plot, possessions, premises, resources, stock, wares, wealth; attribute, characteristic, peculiarity, quality, trait.

propitious, auspicious, encouraging, favorable, fortunate, kindly, hopeful, lucky, opportune, promising.

proportion, balance, composure, dimension, equilibrium, equivalence, poise, relationship, share, stability, steadiness, symmetry. ANT.—fall, imbalance, inequality, instability, unsteadiness.

proposal, offer, overture, presentation, proposition, recommendation, suggestion, tender; design, idea, intention, outline, plan, program, prospectus, scheme. ANT.—acceptance, refusal, rejection, withdrawal.

proposition, see proposal.

proprietor, heritor, holder, keeper, landlady, landlord, master, owner, possessor, proprietary, title holder. ANT.—leaseholder, renter, resident, servant, tenant.

propriety, appropriateness, aptness, conventionality, correctness, decency, decorum, dignity, fitness, righteousness. ANT.—impropriety, misconduct, unfitness, unseemliness.

prosper, achieve, advance, be fortunate, bloom, blossom, flourish, flower, gain, increase, prevail, rise, succeed, thrive, win. ANT.—fail, lose, miscarry, miss, perish.

prosperous, affluent, flourishing, luxurious, moneyed, opulent, rich, sumptuous, wealthy, well-off, well-to-do. ANT.—destitute, indigent, needy, poor, poverty-stricken.

protect, see preserve.

protection, bulwark, camouflage, covering, fence, refuge, safeguard, screen, shelter, shield; assurance, certainty, defense, guard, invulnerability, reassurance, security, stability, strength. ANT.—exposure, insecurity, fragility, frailty, weakness.

protest, challenge, clamor, demonstration, difference, disagreement, dissent, dissentience, mass meeting, moratorium, noncompliance, nonconformity, objection, opposition, recusancy, rejection, remonstrance, tumult, turmoil, variance. ANT.—acceptance, agreement, assent, compliance, peace, recognition.

protract, continue, defer, delay, distend, distort, elongate, expand, extend, lengthen, postpone, procrastinate, prolong, spread, strain, stretch. ANT.—abridge, condense, curtail, hasten, reduce, shorten.

proud, arrogant, dignified, disdainful, exalted, haughty, imperious, lofty, lordly, majestic, overbearing, stately, supercilious, vain. ANT.—ashamed, humble, lowly, meek, modest.

prove, confirm, corroborate, demonstrate, establish, justify, manifest, show, substantiate, test, try, verify. ANT.—contradict, deny, disprove, expose, refute.

proverb, adage, aphorism, apothegm, axiom, bromide, byword, dictum, epigram, maxim, moral, motto, platitude, precept, saying, teaching, tenet, theorem, truism.

provide, afford, arm, cater, contribute, endow, equip, fit, fit out, furnish, give, produce, purvey, replenish, stock, store, supply, yield. ANT.—denude, deprive, divest, remove, strip, withhold.

provident, careful, cautious, discreet, economical, foresighted, frugal, prudent, saving, sparing, thoughtful, thrifty, wise. ANT.—extravagant, lavish, prodigal, profuse, wasteful.

provision, accumulation, arrangement, emergency equipment, fund, hoard, outline, plan, preparation, procurement, reserve, stock, store, supply; prerequisite, requirement, stipulation, terms.

provoke, see disturb.

proximate, adjacent, adjoining, beside, bordering, close, contiguous, handy, near, neighboring, nigh; approaching, imminent, impending. ANT.—distant, far, remote, removed.

prudent, careful, cautious, circumspect, discerning, discreet, judicious, reasonable, sensible, sound, vigilant, wary, watchful, wise. ANT.—absurd, foolish, impetuous, rash, reckless, stupid, unaware.

prying, curious, inquisitive, interfering, meddling, nosy, peeping, peering, searching, seeking, snoopy, spying. ANT.—aloof, incurious, indifferent, nonchalant, uncaring, unconcerned.

pseudo, bogus, counterfeit, fake, false, imitation, mock, phony, quasi, sham, simulated, spurious. ANT.—genuine, honest, real, sound, true.

public, complimentary, free, gratis, known, open, unrestricted. ANT.—charged, costly, personal, private, restricted.

publish, announce, broadcast, circulate, communicate, declare, disclose, disseminate, divulge, impart, issue, post, print, proclaim, promulgate, publicize, reveal, utter.

pull, drag, draw, haul, lift, stretch, tow, tug; extract, pluck, remove, take out, unsheathe; allure, attract, entice, induce, lure, persuade.

pulse, beat, oscillation, palpitation, throb, vibration.

punctual, dependable, early, exact, meticulous, particular, precise, prompt, punctilious, ready, scrupulous, strict, timely. ANT.—careless, desultory, dilatory, late, tardy.

punish, afflict, castigate, chasten, chastise, correct, discipline, fine, flog, imprison, inflict, pummel, scold, strike. ANT.—acquit, exonerate, forgive, free, pardon, reward.

puny, decrepit, delicate, diminutive, dwarfish, enervated, exhausted, faint, feeble, frail, impaired, inferior, infirm, languid, powerless, small, stunted, undeveloped, weak. ANT.—mighty, robust, strong, sturdy, vigorous.

purchase, see obtain.

pure, clean, clear, genuine, immaculate, perfect, spotless, stainless, unadulterated, unblemished, unmixed, untainted; chaste, guiltless, holy, incorrupt, innocent, modest, undefiled, virginal, virtuous; absolute, bare, sheer. ANT.—adulterated, foul, polluted, rotten, tainted; corrupt, defiled, licentious, immodest, obscene.

purge, see eliminate.

purify, chasten, clarify, clean, cleanse, clear, correct, deodorize, disinfect, filter, fumigate, mop, purge, refine, revise, scrub, sweep, wash. ANT.—debase, dirty, pollute, stain, tarnish, vitiate.

purpose, aim, design, determination, end, goal, inclination, intent, intention, object, objective, resolve, view. ANT.—accident, chance, fate, hazard.

pursue, chase, follow, hound, hunt, persist, seek, shadow, track, trail. ANT.—abandon, elude, flee, ignore, stop.

push, butt, compel, crowd, drive, elbow, force, impel, jostle, nudge, press, propel, shove, thrust; hasten, expedite, promote, urge. ANT.—drag, halt, pull, retreat; discourage, ignore, oppose.

put, assign, deposit, establish, imbed, insert, install, lay, locate, lodge, place, plant, settle. ANT.—displace, misplace, oust, remove, transfer.

putrid, contaminated, corrupt, decayed, disgusting, polluted, purulent, rotten. ANT.—clean, fragrant, pure, wholesome, uncontaminated.

puzzle, complexity, conundrum, enigma, intricacy, labyrinth, maze, mystery, perplexity, problem, riddle; baffle, bewilder, confound, confuse, disconcert, entangle, mystify, perplex. ANT.—answer, key, solution; clarify, elucidate, explain, reveal, solve, unravel.

Q

quack, charlatan, cheat, counterfeiter, deceiver, faker, imposter, phony, pretender, swindler.

quaint, anomalous, antique, curious, droll, eccentric, fanciful, odd, old-fashioned, peculiar, queer, strange, unique, unusual, whimsical. ANT.—common, familiar, fashionable, regular, usual.

quake, flutter, quail, quiver, shake, shiver, shudder, totter, tremble, vibrate; earthquake, temblor.

qualified, able, adequate, capable, clever, competent, efficacious, efficient, eligible, experienced, fitted, skillful, tempered. ANT.—incapable, ineffectual, inept, unfit, unqualified.

quality, attribute, character, characteristic, condition, distinction, feature, nature, peculiarity, property, qualification, trait; caliber, grade, rank, status, value.

quantity, abundance, amount, bulk, capacity, extent, mass, measure, multitude, number, pile, portion, sum, volume.

quarrel, affray, altercation, argument, bickering, brawl, clash, contention, disagreement, dispute, dissension, feud, fray, fuse, row, spat, squabble, strife, tiff, wrangle. ANT.—agreement, armistice, harmony, peace, silence.

quaver, see quake.

queer, see quaint.

query, ask, challenge, dispute, doubt, examine, inquire, interrogate, probe, quest, question, quiz, search, seek. ANT.—answer, reply, respond, retort, state.

quest, adventure, crusade, enterprise, examination, expedition, exploration, inquiry, inspection, interrogation, investigation, journey, pursuit, research, scrutiny, search, seeking, survey, trek.

question, see query.

quick, brisk, expeditious, fast, fleet, hasty, immediate, instantaneous, lively, precipitate, prompt, rapid, speedy, swift; excitable, impatient, impetuous, irascible, mercurial, rash, sharp, testy, touchy; active, acute, alert, clever, discerning, keen, ready, sensitive, sharp, shrewd, vigorous. ANT.—slow, sluggish; apathetic, drowsy, languid, lazy, listless; dull, insipid, obtuse, vapid.

quicken, see hurry.

quiescent, abeyant, calm, dormant, hidden, inactive, latent, motionless, peaceful, placid, quiet, resting, secret, serene, smooth, still, tranquil, undeveloped, undisturbed, unruffled. ANT.—active, dynamic, manifest, spirited, stirring, vivacious.

quiet, hushed, motionless, muffled, mute, pacific, peaceful, placid, quiescent, secluded, serene, soundless, still, tranquil, undisturbed; calm, contented, gentle, meek, mild, passive, patient, silent; allay, alleviate, appease, assuage, calm, compose, cool, gratify, lull, moderate, pacify, placate, please, quell, relax, relieve, restrain, smooth, soothe, still, tranquilize. ANT.—loud,

noisy, strident; agitated, excited, impatient, perturbed; arouse, excite, incense, inflame, provoke.

quiet, abandon, cease, depart, desert, desist, discontinue, forsake, leave, stop; give up, relinquish, resign, surrender, withdraw, yield. ANT.—continue, endure, keep, persevere, remain, retain, stay.

quiver, see quake.

quiz, see query.

quotation, blurb, citation, citing, excerpt, extract, passage, quote, recitation, reference, repetition, selection; estimate, price, rate.

R

race, ancestry, breed, clan, cultural group, family, folk, lineage, mankind, nation, nationality, people, stock, strain, tribe.

racket, see noise.

radiant, beaming, bright, brilliant, dazzling, effulgent, glittering, glorious, glowing, grand, luminous, lustrous, magnificent, resplendent, shimmering, shining, sparkling, splendid. ANT.—cloudy, dark, dim, dull, obscure.

radiate, brighten, broadcast, circulate, diffuse, disperse, disseminate, emanate, emit, gleam, glitter, illumine, propagate, shed, shine, spread, transmit. ANT.—absorb, concentrate, converge, gather.

radical, complete, entire, total, thorough; basic, congenital, constitutional, essential, fundamental, inborn, ingrained, inherent, inherited, innate, intrinsic, native, natural, organic, original; communistic, excessive, extreme, fanatical, insurgent, leftist, liberal, militant, progressive, revolutionary, ultra, uncompromising, violent. ANT.—incomplete, partial; extraneous, extrinsic, nonessential, superficial; casual, conservative, moderate, stable, traditional.

rage, anger, animosity, choler, exasperation, explosion, frenzy, fury, hysterics, indignation, ire, irritation, outburst, passion, petulance, storm, tantrum, temper, uproar, vehemence, wrath; boil (over), foam, fume, rail at, rant, rave, roar, scold, scream, seethe, splutter, yell. ANT.—conciliation, forbearance, patience, peace, self-control, tranquility; appease, calm, lull, placate, quiet, soothe.

raise, elevate, erect, exalt, heave, heighten, hoist, honor, lift, uplift; breed, cultivate, grow, produce, rear; collect, gather, levy, muster; advance, aggrandize, amplify, augment, boost, increase, intensify, magnify. ANT.—abase, degrade, depreciate, destroy, lower, reduce.

ramble, deviate, digress, drift, meander, range, roam, rove, saunter, straggle, stray, stroll, traipse, wander.

rancor, see malice.

rank, column, file, line, order, range, row, series, string, tier; class, division, grade, order; degree, position, seniority, standing, station; dignity, distinction, eminence, reputation.

rapid, see quick.

rapture, bliss, delight, ecstasy, enchantment, exultation, felicity, gladness, happiness, joy, passion, transport. ANT.—depression, grief, melancholy, misery, pain, suffering.

rare, infrequent, occasional; odd, peculiar, strange, unusual; choice, exceptional, extraordinary, incomparable, precious, remarkable, scarce, singular, uncommon, unique, unparalleled, unprecedented. ANT.—frequent, habitual, incessant, recurring; common, normal, ordinary, regular, typical; cheap, worthless.

rash, see impetuous.

rate, appraise, assess, calculate, determine, estimate, evaluate, measure, price, rank, value; succeed, triumph; comparison, degree, fixed amount, measure, percentage, proportion, quota, ratio, relationship, standard.

ration, see portion.

rational, deductive, discriminating, intelligent, judicious, logical, prudent, reasonable, sagacious, sensible, wise; conscious, lucid, sane, sober, sound. ANT.—absurd, foolish, inconsistent, ridiculous, stupid; insane, irrational, unconscious.

ravage, see devastate.

ravenous, see hungry.

raw, callow, coarse, crude, green, harsh, ill-prepared, immature, inexperienced, rough, rude, undisciplined, unfinished, unpolished, unprepared, unrefined, unripe. ANT.—adult, courteous, mature, polished, ripe, seasoned, well-prepared.

raze, annihilate, demolish, destroy, devastate, dismantle, efface, eradicate, exterminate, extinguish, level, obliterate, overthrow, ravage, ruin, topple, wreck. ANT.—build, construct, erect, raise, repair, restore.

reach, extend to, span, stretch, touch; accomplish, achieve, arrive at, attain, earn, gain, get to, join, overtake. ANT.—bungle, fail, fall short, leave, miss.

react, act, answer, reciprocate, rejoin, reply, respond; be affected, be involved, be moved, feel. ANT.—disregard, ignore, overlook; be insensitive to.

read, apprehend, browse, comprehend, decipher, discern, glance over, grasp, interpret, learn, perceive, peruse, scan, skim, study, translate, understand, unravel.

ready, active, available, complete, consummate, disposed, equipped, finished, fit, mature, mellow, prepared, prompt, ripe, seasonable, suitable, willing; concoct, condition, equip, fit, furnish, make ready, order, predispose, prepare. ANT.—immature, unavailable, undeveloped, unready.

real, see genuine.

reality, actuality, authenticity, entity, existence, realness, substance, tangibility, truth, verity. ANT.—fantasy, fiction, imagination, nonentity.

realization, accomplishment, achievement, attainment, completion, performance; appreciation, awareness, comprehension, perception, understanding. ANT.—defeat, failure; blindness, disregard, ignorance.

realm, area, department, district, domain, estate, farm, kingdom, land, province, region, sphere, territory, vicinity.

reap, accumulate, acquire, collect, cut, earn, gain, garner, gather, glean, harvest, hoard, obtain, pick, win. ANT.—lose, plant, seed, sow.

rear, bring up, elevate, foster, lift, nurture, raise, support, train; build, erect.

reason, account, aim, argument, basis, cause, design, end, foundation, ground, motive, object, purpose, sake, view; intelligence, intuition, judgment, mind, rationality, sense, understanding; analyze, argue, conclude, contend, debate, deduce, deliberate, discuss, establish, infer, judge, question, reflect, speculate, study, trace. ANT.—bewilder, confuse, fabricate, guess.

reasonable, see rational.

rebellion, coup, disorder, disturbance, insurrection, mutiny, outbreak, overthrow, revolt, revolution, riot, sedition, tumult, upheaval, uprising. ANT.—conciliation, law, order, peace, submission.

rebellious, contumacious, defiant, disobedient, insubordinate, intractable, mutinous, pugnacious, recalcitrant, refractory, undutiful, unmanageable, unruly. ANT.—docile, dutiful, manageable, obedient, subservient, tractable.

rebuke, accuse, admonish, berate, censure, chide, condemn, criticize, implicate, punish, reprimand, reproach, reprove, scold, upbraid. ANT.—approve, exonerate, laud, praise, reward.

recall, recollect, remember, remind, reminisce, review, revive; annul, disqualify, revoke; reassemble, reconvene, summon. ANT.—forget, ignore, overlook; reestablish, restore; disperse, separate, terminate.

recede, abate, decline, ebb, fade, lessen, regress, retire, retreat, revert, shrink from, withdraw. ANT.—advance, approach, gain, increase, near, rise.

receive, accept, acquire, catch, gain, get, obtain, take, win; admit, shelter; entertain, welcome. ANT.—bequeath, donate, give, return; evict, expel, oust; deny, refuse, reject.

recent, contemporary, foregoing, fresh, late, latter, modern, new, newfangled, novel, original, preceding, retiring, streamlined, young. ANT.—ancient, antiquated, archaic, obsolete, old-fashioned.

recite, address, convey, declaim, delineate, deliver, describe, detail, discourse, enumerate, explain, impart, mention, narrate, quote, read, recapitulate, recount, rehearse, relate, repeat, report, state, tell.

reckless, careless, daring, foolhardy, heedless, impetuous, imprudent, precipitate, rash, wild. ANT.—cautious, circumspect, prudent, wary.

recognize, accede, accept, acknowledge, admit, apprehend, concede, confess, distinguish, identify, know, perceive, realize, recollect, remember. ANT.—forget, ignore, overlook, renounce, repudiate.

recommend, advise, allude, counsel, hint, imply, insinuate, intimate, offer, prescribe, propose, refer, suggest, urge; acclaim, advocate, applaud, approve, commend, endorse, extol, praise, sanction. ANT.—demand, dictate, insist; condemn, denigrate, disapprove.

reconcile, accommodate, adapt, adjust, arrange, conciliate, conform, correct, harmonize, mediate, mitigate, pacify, placate, rectify, regulate, reunite, settle. ANT.—alienate, annoy, bother, divide, irritate, separate.

record, account, archive, chronicle, docket, document, inventory, memorandum, note, register, registry, report, schedule; inscription, mark, memorial, trace, vestige; achievement, career, experience, history; catalogue, enroll, enter, file, list, note, register, report, tape.

recover, cure, heal, mend, rally, recuperate, revive; recapture, recoup, redeem, regain, renew, renovate, repossess, restore, retrieve, salvage. ANT.—perish, regress, relapse, wane, weaken; forfeit, lose, mislay.

recreation, amusement, diversion, entertainment, frolic, fun, game, pastime, play, refreshment, relaxation, relief, sport. ANT.—drudgery, labor, task, toil, work.

rectify, adjust, amend, correct, fix, improve, mend, purify, refine, reform, remedy, repair, revise, right. ANT.—adulterate, debase, falsify, ruin, spoil.

recuperate, see recover.

redeem, atone, deliver, emancipate, expiate, extricate, free, liberate, propitiate, ransom, recoup, recover, regain, repair, repurchase, rescue, retrieve, save. ANT.—abandon, forfeit, ignore, neglect, overlook, shun.

reduce, abate, abbreviate, abridge, assuage, condense, contract, curtail, decimate, decrease, degrade, diminish, impoverish, lessen, lower, moderate, modify, shorten, subdue, suppress, thin, weaken. ANT.—amplify, enlarge, increase, magnify, strengthen.

redundant, copious, diffuse, excessive, extra, profuse, prolix, repetitious, verbose, wordy. ANT.—concise, laconic, succinct, terse.

refer, advert, allude, appeal, apply, ascribe, attribute, belong, cite, commit, concern, connect, consign, consult, deliver, include, involve, pertain, point, quote, regard, relate, submit, suggest.

refinement, breeding, civilization, clarification, cultivation, culture, delicacy, education, elegance, enlightenment, finesse, poise, polish, purification, purity. ANT.—barbarism, coarseness, crudity, rusticity, vulgarity.

reflect, cogitate, concentrate, consider, contemplate, deliberate, meditate, muse, ponder, reason, ruminate, speculate, study, think, weigh; copy, echo, imitate, mirror, reproduce; rebound, revert.

reform, amend, better, correct, freshen, improve, mend, reconstruct, rectify, redress, renew, renovate, reorganize, repair, restore, revise, right, transmute. ANT.—aggravate, corrupt, damage, impair, ruin, vitiate.

refrain, abstain, avoid, check, curb, desist, forebear, restrain, withhold; burden, chorus, undersong. ANT.—continue, indulge, persevere, persist.

refresh, air, animate, brace, cheer, enliven, freshen, invigorate, renew, renovate, rest, restore, revive, stimulate. ANT.—bore, exhaust, fatigue, tire, weary.

refuge, asylum, fortress, harbor, haven, hideaway, protection, retreat, sanctuary, seclusion, shelter, stronghold. ANT.—danger, exposure, hazard, jeopardy, pitfall, risk.

refuse, decline, deny, disavow, disown, negate, protest, rebuff, reject, renounce, repel, repudiate, spurn, veto, withhold; dross, garbage, junk, litter, rubbish, rubble, scoria, sweepings, trash, waste. ANT.—accept, consent, grant, present, sanction, welcome; assets, resources, valuables.

refute, confound, confute, controvert, disprove, expose, falsify, invalidate, overthrow, parry, rebut, repel, stultify. ANT.—assist, defend, encourage, sanction, strengthen, uphold.

regal, courtly, dignified, imperial, kingly, lordly, magnificent, majestic, monarchial, noble, princely, queenly, royal, sovereign, splendid, stately, sublime. ANT.—common, ignoble, lowly, ordinary, plebeian, servile.

regard, attention, concern, consideration, notice, observation; reference, relation, respect; affection, esteem, estimation, liking; honor, value; contemplate, notice, observe, view, watch; believe, hold, imagine, reckon, suppose, think. ANT.—avoidance, neglect; antipathy, disgust; deride, insult, mock; forget, ignore, neglect, omit, overlook.

register, admit, chronicle, declare, enroll, enter, establish, express, fix, indicate, insert, list, note, record, save, table; annal, archive, catalogue, list, roll, roster, schedule.

region, area, belt, climate, district, domain, locale, locality, location, neighborhood, place, quarter, realm, sector, site, spot, station, territory, vicinity, zone.

regression, backsliding, deterioration, ebb, recession, recidivism, retrogression, return, reversion, withdrawal. ANT.—advancement, headway, progress, progression.

regret, bitterness, compunction, contrition, disappointment, grief, heartache, lamentation, penitence, qualm, remorse, repentance, repining, self-reproach, sorrow, vexation, worry; bewail, deplore, lament, repent, repine, rue, sorrow. ANT.—contentment, impenitence, induration, obduracy, satisfaction, tranquility; celebrate, cheer, enjoy, exult, rejoice.

regular, consistent, conventional, customary, homogeneous, homologous, invariable, methodical, natural, normal, orderly, ordinary, periodic, punctual, steady, symmetrical, systematic, uniform, unvaried, usual. ANT.—anomalous, erratic, inconsistent, infrequent, rare, strange, unusual.

regulate, adapt, adjust, allocate, arrange, classify, control, correct, direct, fix, govern, legislate, organize, readjust, reconcile, rectify, rule, systematize. ANT.—confuse, disarrange, disorganize, entangle, jumble, sunder.

rehabilitate, overhaul, reawaken, rebuild, reconstitute, reconstruct, recreate, reestablish, refinish, refresh, reinstate, reinvigorate, renew, renovate, repair, replenish, restore, revamp, revive.

reinforce, augment, buttress, energize, fortify, invigorate, pillar, strengthen, support. ANT.—detract, weaken.

reject, decline, deny, discard, dismiss, eject, eliminate, exclude, rebuff, refuse, renounce, repudiate, spurn, veto, withhold. ANT.—accept, admit, choose, select, welcome.

relate, describe, detail, narrate, recite, recount, rehearse, report, state, tell; apply, associate, compare, connect, correlate, link, parallel, pertain, refer.

relation, alliance, bearing, connection, correlation, correspondence, likeness, reference, relationship, relevancy, similarity; affinity, bond, family connection, filiation, kindred, kinship, link, sibling, tie, union.

relationship, see relation.

relative, appositive, cognate, comparative, conditional, contingent, definite, dependent, germane, particular, pertinent, referable, relevant, respecting, special; connection, kin, relation.

relaxation, abatement, amusement, comfort, diversion, ease, leisure, loosening, mitigation, peacefulness, reclining, recreation, relief, repose, respite, rest, slackening, tranquility. ANT.—drudgery, exertion, labor, striving, struggle, toil.

release, deliver, discharge, emancipate, free, liberate, set free; absolution, acquittal, deliverance, discharge, dispensation, emancipation, exoneration, freedom, liberation, relinquishment, surrender. ANT.—confine, imprison, oppress; restriction, subjugation.

relent, abdicate, accede, acquiesce, capitulate, cede, comply, defer, quit, relinquish, resign, submit, succumb, surrender; abate, bend, bow, relax, soften, subside, yield. ANT.—assert, persevere, persist, strive, struggle; harden, stiffen.

relentless, fierce, hard, implacable, inexorable, inflexible, obdurate, pitiless, rigid, rigorous, ruthless, strict, stringent, unyielding, vindictive. ANT.—compassionate, gentle, lenient, merciful.

relevant, see pertinent.

reliable, certain, conscientious, constant, definite, dependable, faithful, firm, positive, reputable, responsible, safe, secure, solid, stable, staunch, steadfast, sterling, strong, sure, tried, true, trustworthy, unimpeachable. ANT.—dangerous, dubious, insecure, questionable, undependable, unreliable.

relief, aid, alleviation, assistance, backing, comfort, ease, help, mitigation, palliation, succor, support. ANT.—aggravation, agitation, distress.

relieve, abate, aid, allay, alleviate, assist, assuage, calm, comfort, disburden, disentangle, ease, extricate, facilitate, free, lighten, mitigate, pacify, redress, remedy, solace, soothe. ANT.—disturb, irritate, trouble, vex.

religious, believing, canonical, devout, divine, ecclesiastical, ethical, god-fearing, godly, holy, ministerial, moral, pietistic, pious, reverent, sacred, sanctimonious, spiritual, theological; careful, methodical, scrupulous, thorough. ANT.—atheistic, free-thinking, immoral, impious, profane, secular; careless, indifferent, negligent, slovenly.

relinquish, abandon, abdicate, abjure, acquiesce, capitulate, cede, deny, desert, discard, dismiss, forego, forsake, quit, reject, renounce, resign, revoke, sacrifice, spare, submit, surrender, vacate, yield. ANT.—conquer, keep, perpetuate, persist, pursue, retain.

relish, appetizer, seasoning, spice; appreciation, enjoyment, gratification, gusto, inclination, partiality, preference, satisfaction, zest. ANT.—disfavor, distaste.

reluctant, averse, backward, demurring, disinclined, doubtful, hesitant, indisposed, loathe, opposed, slow, tardy, unready, unwilling. ANT.—amenable, disposed, eager, enthusiastic, ready, willing.

rely, bank, confide, count, depend, lean, trust. ANT.—distrust, doubt.

remain, abide, continue, dwell, endure, inhabit, last, reside, rest, stay, survive. ANT.—depart, dissipate, go, leave, terminate.

remainder, balance, dregs, excess, leavings, leftovers, remains, remnant, residue, residuum, rest, surplus.

remark, comment, mention, note, observation, point, saying, statement, utterance; assert, declare, express, maintain, mention, observe, relate, say, speak, talk, tell, utter.

remarkable, arresting, awesome, commanding, distinguished, exceptional, exciting, extraordinary, great, impressive, memorable, moving, notable, peculiar, prominent, rare, special, stirring, striking, wonderful, uncommon, unusual. ANT.—common, inconspicuous, normal, regular, unimpressive, usual.

remedy, antidote, bracer, cure, help, medicant, medication, nostrum, panacea, redress, relief, reparation, restorative; ameliorate, amend, better, correct, cure, fix, heal, improve, mend, rectify, redress, reform, relieve, renew, repair, restore. ANT.—burden, hindrance, impediment, ruination; aggravate, intensify, neglect, worsen.

remember, memorize, recall, recollect, remind, reminisce, retain, retrace, review. ANT.—disregard, forget, obliterate, overlook, repress, suppress.

remembrance, commemoration, keepsake, memento, memoir, memorial, memory, recollection, reminiscence, reminder, souvenir, token, trophy. ANT.—forgetfulness, nirvana, oblivion.

remit, absolve, alleviate, defer, discontinue, excuse, exempt, forgive, mitigate, moderate, overlook, pardon, postpone, relax, release, relinquish, restore, soften; compensate, make payment, pay, reimburse, remunerate. ANT.—avenge, bind, control, dominate, restrict, suppress; deceive, swindle, victimize.

remorse, see regret.

remorseless, see inhuman.

remote, alien, distant, far, faraway, foreign, inaccessible, indirect, removed, secluded, unconnected, unrelated. ANT.—adjacent, close, near, proximate, related.

remove, depart, dislodge, displace, evacuate, leave, migrate, move, separate, shift, transfer, transport, vacate; discharge, dismiss, eject, evict, oust, unseat; eliminate, extract, pull, uproot, wrench; destroy, kill. ANT.—dwell, place, remain; establish, maintain; imbed, plant, root; preserve.

renew, continue, reestablish, refresh, regenerate, reiterate, renovate, repeat, replace, replenish, restore, resume, resuscitate, revive. ANT.—deplete, diminish, enfeeble, exhaust.

renounce, abandon, abdicate, desert, drop, forego, forsake, quit, relinquish, resign, sacrifice, secede, surrender; deny, disavow, disclaim, disown, recant, reject, repudiate, retract, revoke. ANT.—maintain, persevere, persist, remain; acknowledge, assert, claim.

renovate, see rehabilitate.

renowned, see eminent.

repair, amend, correct, darn, fix, mend, patch, rectify, refit, remedy, remodel, renew, renovate, replace, restore. ANT.—damage, destroy, mar, neglect, ruin.

repeal, abolish, abrogate, annul, cancel, invalidate, nullify, quash, recall, rescind, revoke, veto. ANT.—continue, keep, maintain, renew, validate.

repeat, duplicate, echo, iterate, quote, recapitulate, recite, recur, rehearse, reiterate, relate, reproduce, tell.

repentance, compunction, contrition, penitence, regret, regretfulness, remorse, self-disgust, self-reproach, sorrow. ANT.—callousness, complacency, impenitence, recusancy, shamelessness.

replace, reconstitute, reconstruct, refund, rehabilitate, reinstate, repay, restore, return, substitute, succeed, supersede, supplant. ANT.—alter, change, diversify, modify, transform.

replicate, see duplicate.

reply, acknowledge, answer, counter, echo, react, rejoin, respond, retort; answer, rejoinder, repartee, response, retort. ANT.—ask, disregard, ignore, question; examination, inquiry, question, summoning.

report, advertise, announce, broadcast, chronicle, communicate, declare, describe, detail, disclose, herald, impart, inform, mention, notify, proclaim, promulgate, publish, recite, relate, specify, state, tell; account, announcement, chronicle, communication, description, dispatch, hearsay, intelligence, message, narration, narrative, news, publication, recital, record, statement, story, tidings. ANT.—conceal, delete, mask, screen, veil; concealment, evasion, deletion, reserve, secrecy, suppression.

repose, calm, calmness, comfort, ease, hush, leisure, peace, quiescence, quiet, quietude, relaxation, respite, rest, serenity, silence, stillness, tranquility. ANT.—activity, disturbance, noise, tumult, turmoil.

represent, delineate, depict, describe, draw, imitate, impersonate, paint, personate, picture, portray, show, sketch, symbolize, typify.

repress, bridle, check, choke, constrain, curb, dull, hinder, inhibit, overpower, quell, restrain, silence, smother, still, stop, subdue, suppress. ANT.—advance, assist, encourage, exhilarate, invigorate, stimulate.

reprimand, admonish, berate, blame, censure, chide, lecture, punish, rebuke, reprehend, reproach, reprove, revile, scold, upbraid, vilify, vituperate. ANT.—approve, commend, forgive, laud, praise, reward.

reproach, see blame.

reproduction, casting, copy, duplicate, exemplar, facsimile, imitation, print, replica, representation, tracing, transcript; generation, procreation, propagation. ANT.—archetype, original, pattern, prototype; infertility, sterility.

repugnant, abhorrent, adverse, antagonistic, contrary, disagreeable, disgusting, distasteful, hostile, invidious, obnoxious, offensive, opposed, refractory, repellent, revolting, unbearable. ANT.—agreeable, appealing, conciliatory, harmonious, pleasant.

repulsive, abhorrent, abominable, detestable, disgusting, gross, gruesome, hideous, homely, horrible, horrid, nauseating, obnoxious, odious, offensive, repellent, repugnant, revolting, ugly, uncomely. ANT.—alluring, captivating, enticing, inviting, pleasing.

reputation, acceptability, character, class, credit, dependability, description, esteem, honor, kind, name, nature, prestige, reliability, repute, respectability, sort, standing, trustworthiness; eminence, notoriety, prominence.

repute, see reputation.

request, appeal, apply, ask, beg, beseech, bid, entreat, implore, importune, invite, petition, plead, pray, seek, solicit, sue, summon, supplicate.

requirement, behest, bidding, call, charge, claim, command, decree, demand, essential, exigency, injunction, mandate, necessity, need, pinch, requisite, requisition, urgency, want.

requisite, basic, binding, compelling, compulsory, crucial, essential, expedient, fundamental, imperative, important, indispensable, intrinsic, mandatory, necessary, needed, obligatory, required, urgent, vital. ANT.—accidental, expendable, extrinsic, nonessential, optional.

rescue, deliver, disenthrall, extricate, free, liberate, preserve, ransom, recapture, reclaim, recover, redeem, release, retrieve, save. ANT.—abandon, bind, enslave, hinder, incarcerate.

research, analysis, examination, experimentation, exploration, inquiry, interrogation, investigation, observation, query, quest, question, scrutiny, study, testing.

resemblance, affinity, agreement, analogy, correspondence, facsimile, likeness, match, purity, semblance, similarity, simile, similitude. ANT.—contrast, deviation, dissimilarity, distinction, inconsistency, variance.

resentment, acerbity, anger, animosity, annoyance, bitterness, displeasure, exasperation, grudge, huff, indignation, ire, irritation, perturbation, pique, rancor, rankling, umbrage. ANT.—affection, concord, geniality, good humor, happiness, harmony.

reserved, aloof, bashful, cautious, demure, detached, diffident, distant, formal, modest, restrained, reticent, retiring, shy, taciturn, timorous, undemonstrative, wary; booked, preserved, saved. ANT.—affable, blatant, expansive, uninhibited; unreserved.

residue, see remainder.

resign, abandon, abdicate, abjure, cede, eschew, forego, quit, relinquish, renounce, retract, surrender, vacate, waive, withdraw, yield. ANT.—accept, receive, remain, retain, stay.

resilient, buoyant, elastic, flexible, spirited, springy, supple. ANT.—inflexible, stiff, tense, unbending.

resist, attack, check, confront, contest, counteract, defy, frustrate, hinder, impede, impugn, neutralize, obstruct, oppose, thwart, withstand. ANT.—acquiesce, assist, collaborate, comply, defer, submit, yield.

resolution, constancy, courage, decision, determination, devotion, firmness, fortitude, persistence, resolve, stamina, steadfastness, zeal. ANT.—caprice, hesitation, indecision, uncertainty, vacillation.

resolve, adjudicate, choose, close, conclude, decide, decree, determine, elect, end, fix, propose, purpose, settle, terminate. ANT.—hesitate, procrastinate, vacillate, waver.

respect, admiration, consideration, deference, esteem, fealty, honor, recognition, regard, reverence, veneration; admire, appreciate, consider, heed, honor, note, notice, prize, regard, revere, reverence, treasure, uphold, value, venerate. ANT.—contempt, disdain, irreverence, scorn; abuse, blame, censure, deride, despise.

respectable, adequate, becoming, comely, decent, decorous, estimable, honorable, mediocre, moderate, presentable, proper, seemly, suitable, tolerable, upright, virtuous, worthy. ANT.—dishonorable, improper, indecent, reprehensible, scandalous, unworthy.

resplendent, see radiant.

respond, see reply.

response, see reply.

responsible, accountable, amenable, answerable, liable, obligatory, subject; dependable, reliable, trustworthy. ANT.—arbitrary, exempt, free, immune, unbound; careless, irresponsible, lax, negligent, unreliable.

restful, calm, comfortable, cozy, easy, mild, peaceful, placid, quiet, relaxing, reposeful, serene, soothing, still, tranquil, untroubled. ANT.—alarming, annoying, disconcerting, disturbing, upsetting.

restless, agitated, anxious, changeable, disquieted, disturbed, fidgety, fitful, irresolute, nervous, sleepless, uneasy, unsettled, worried; active, moving, roving, transient, wandering. ANT.—calm, composed, placid, tranquil, unperturbed.

restore, see rehabilitate.

restrain, see repress.

restrict, bind, bridle, check, confine, constrain, curb, fence, hinder, impede, inhibit, limit, obstruct, repress, restrain, stop, suppress. ANT.—enlarge, expand, extend, free, release.

result, conclusion, consequence, determination, effect, end, eventuality, fruit, issue, outcome, product, resolution, resolve, termination, upshot; accrue, arise, come, eventuate, flow, follow, issue, originate, proceed, resolve, spring.

retain, detain, employ, engage, hire, hold, keep, maintain, preserve, reserve, secure, withhold. ANT.—discard, dismiss, jettison, relinquish, surrender.

retaliate, avenge, match, punish, reciprocate, repay, requite, retort, return, vindicate. ANT.—forget, forgive, ignore, pardon.

retard, arrest, check, clog, delay, detain, hamper, hinder, impede, interrupt, postpone, stay. ANT.—accelerate, advance, hasten, speed.

retire, see relinquish.

retort, see reply.

retract, abjure, abnegate, abrogate, annul, cancel, deny, disclaim, disown, nullify, recall, recant, renounce, reverse, revoke. ANT.—affirm, confirm, endorse, ratify, uphold.

retrogress, backslide, decline, degenerate, deteriorate, regress, relapse, retreat, retrograde, revert. ANT.—advance, develop, improve, proceed, progress.

return, reappear, recur, retreat, revert; reciprocate, repay, replace, reply, requite, restore. ANT.—appropriate, retain, take.

reveal, announce, betray, confess, disclose, divulge, explain, expose, express, impart, inform, open, publish, show, uncover, unfold, unmask, unveil. ANT.—conceal, deceive, disguise, mask, secrete.

revenge, avenging, implacability, malevolence, reprisal, requital, retaliation, retribution, vengeance, vindictiveness. ANT.—forgiveness, mercy, pardon, reconciliation, remission.

reverence, admiration, adoration, approbation, awe, deference, dignity, esteem, fame, glory, homage, honor, praise, regard, renown, respect, veneration, worship. ANT.—contempt, derision, execration, dishonor, irreverence, mockery.

reverse, alter, convert, invert, modify, shift, transpose, turn about; overthrow, overturn, subvert, upset; annul, cancel, countermand, invalidate, nullify, repeal, rescind, retract, revoke, undo.

revert, go back, recur, repeat, retreat, return, reverse. ANT.—advance, go forward, proceed.

review, consider, examine, inspect, reconsider, rehearse, retrace, survey; analyze, correct, criticize, edit, judge, revise; commentary, criticism, critique, examination, inspection, reconsideration, reflection, retrospection, revision, study, survey; digest, journal, periodical; abstract, outline, summary, synopsis.

revision, see review.

revive, animate, awaken, freshen, improve, invigorate, reanimate, recall, refresh, reinforce, renew, renovate, repair, reproduce, resuscitate, revivify, rouse. ANT.—decay, decline, fade, perish, waste, wither.

revoke, see repeal.

revolting, see repulsive.

revolution, anarchy, *coup d'état*, disorder, foment, insubordination, insurrection, mutiny, overthrow, rebellion, revolt, tumult, uprising; gyration, revolving, rotation, spin, swirl, twirl.

revolve, circle, circulate, eddy, gyrate, orbit, roll, rotate, spin, turn, twirl, wheel, whirl; brood over, consider, ponder, ruminate, study.

reward, acknowledgment, amends, award, bonus, bounty, compensation, gain, gratuity, indemnity, payment, premium, prize, recompense, recoupment, redress, remuneration, requital, retribution, return, satisfaction. ANT.—assessment, charge, deprivation, divestment, forfeiture, levy, seizure.

rhythm, accent, beat, cadence, lilt, measure, meter, periodicity, pulsation, regularity, swing, tempo.

rich, ample, bountiful, costly, elegant, exorbitant, expensive, generous, luscious, luxurious, opulent, resplendent, splendid, sumptuous, superb, valuable; abundant, exuberant, fecund, fertile, fruitful, lush, luxuriant, plentiful, profuse, prolific; intense, strong, vivid; affluent, moneyed, prosperous, wealthy, well-to-do. ANT.—drab, plain, unadorned; barren, sterile, unfruitful, unproductive; faint, powerless, unsubstantial, weak; destitute, impoverished, indigent, penniless, poor.

riddle, see mystery.

ridicule, banter, contempt, derision, disdain, disparagement, gibe, irony, jeering, mockery, persiflage, raillery, sarcasm, satire, scorn, sneering. ANT.—approval, commendation, honor, praise, respect.

ridiculous, absurd, bizarre, comic, droll, farcical, foolish, funny, hilarious, inconsistent, irrational, laughable, ludicrous, nonsensical, odd, preposterous, self-contradictory, silly, unreasonable. ANT.—conventional, rational, reasonable, sensible, wise.

right, ethical, fair, honest, just, lawful, legitimate, reasonable, rightful; accurate, correct, true, valid; appropriate, proper, suitable; direct, erect, straight, upright; authority, exemption, immunity, liberty, license, prerogative, privilege; equity, honesty, integrity, justice, morality, propriety, rectitude, uprightness, virtue. ANT.—dishonest, illegitimate, unethical, unreasonable; false, inaccurate, invalid; improper, inappropriate, unsuitable; crooked, devious, dishonest, twisted; encroachment, injustice, violation, wrong; dishonesty, immorality, inequity, injustice, vice.

righteous, chaste, commendable, conscientious, decent, equitable, ethical, good, honorable, just, pure, right, scrupulous, virtuous, worthy; devout, godly, pious, religious, saintly. ANT.—amoral, corrupt, immoral, licentious, unethical; impious, irreligious.

rigid, austere, exacting, harsh, precise, relentless, rigorous, scrupulous, severe, stern, stony, strict, stringent, unyielding; inelastic, inflexible, petrified, stiff, unbending. ANT.—compassionate, considerate, forbearing, indulgent, lenient, tolerant; elastic, flexible, limber, mobile, pliant.

rigorous, austere, blunt, coarse, cruel, exacting, grating, gruff, hard, harsh, inflexible, jarring, oppressive, rigid, rough, severe, stern, stiff, strict, stringent, uncompromising, unfeeling. ANT.—easy, easygoing, lax, lenient, mild, soft, tender.

rim, border, brim, brink, brow, curb, edge, fringe, hem, limit, lip, margin, outskirts, terminus, top, verge. ANT.—center, core, interior, middle.

ring, arena, band, chime, circle, clangor, clique, confederation, coterie, faction, gang, hoop, resonance, reverberation; chime, circle, clang, encircle, enclose, girdle, jingle, knell, peal, resound, surround, tinkle, toll.

riot, altercation, commotion, fray, insurgence, melee, pandemonium, protest, rebellion, row, strife, tumult, turmoil, uprising. ANT.—order, peace, quiet, regularity, tranquility.

rip, burst, cleave, cut, disunite, lacerate, rend, rive, separate, sever, shear, shred, slash, slit, split, sunder, tear. ANT.—join, mend, unite.

ripe, complete, consummate, developed, finished, full-grown, mature, matured, mellow, perfect, ready, ripened, seasonable, seasoned. ANT.—budding, green, immature, undeveloped, unfit, unseasoned.

rise, arise, ascend, begin, climb, commence, grow, increase, mount, originate, proceed, progress, prosper, scale, soar, spring, start, thrive, tower. ANT.—decline, descend, fall, recede, sink, tumble.

risk, danger, hazard, imperilment, jeopardy, peril; chance, gamble, opportunity, prospect, uncertainty, venture; endanger, expose, hazard, jeopardize, venture. ANT.—defense, immunity, protection, safety; certainty, guarantee; defend, insure, protect, secure, shield.

risky, chancy, critical, dangerous, hazardous, insecure, jeopardous, menacing, perilous, precarious, threatening, uncertain, unsafe. ANT.—certain, protected, safe, sure.

rite, ceremony, custom, duty, formality, liturgy, observance, ordinance, parade, pomp, protocol, ritual, sacrament, service, solemnity.

ritual, see rite.

rival, adversary, antagonist, combatant, competitor, contestant, disputant, emulator, enemy, foe, opponent; antagonize, attack, battle, challenge, combat, compete, conflict, confront, contend, contest, dispute, emulate, fight, oppose, struggle, wrestle. ANT.—advocate, ally, assistant,

helper, partner, patron, supporter; assist, champion, cooperate, encourage, support, uphold.

roam, deviate, digress, err, gallivant, hike, meander, prowl, ramble, range, rove, saunter, straggle, stray, stroll, traipse, traverse, wander. ANT.—halt, lodge, settle, stay.

rob, appropriate, burglarize, cheat, defraud, embezzle, fleece, forge, loot, pilfer, pillage, plunder, purloin, rifle, sack, steal, strip.

robber, bandit, burglar, despoiler, forager, forger, marauder, pillager, pirate, plunderer, poacher, raider, rustler, swindler, thief.

robust, brawny, hale, hardy, healthy, muscular, powerful, sound, strapping, strong, sturdy, tough, vigorous, well. ANT.—debilitated, feeble, flabby, frail, sickly, weak.

rock, boulder, cliff, crag, gravel, jewel, pebble, promontory, reef, slab, stone; defense, foundation, support; agitate, convulse, jiggle, jolt, oscillate, roll, shake, shove, sway, swing, tremble, vibrate.

role, acting, character, characterization, function, impersonation, part, performance, presentation, task.

roll, catalogue, document, inventory, list, register, rota, schedule, scroll; bind, enfold, flatten, fluctuate, level, press, resound, reverberate, revolve, rotate, rumble, smooth, swathe, tumble, turn, undulate, wallow, wheel, whirl.

romantic, charming, chimerical, chivalrous, courtly, dreamy, enchanting, extravagant, fanciful, fantastic, fictitious, ideal, idealistic, imaginary, imaginative, improbable, picturesque, poetic, sentimental. ANT.—definite, practical, pragmatic, realistic, solid.

roomy, ample, broad, capacious, commodious, extensive, grand, immense, large, spacious, vast, wide. ANT.—condensed, cramped, inconsiderable, little, small, tiny.

root, base, basis, bottom, foundation, groundwork, substructure, support, underpinning; cause, motive, reason; etymon, radical, radix, stem.

rot, corrode, decay, decline, decompose, decrease, degenerate, disintegrate, dwindle, ebb, fade, putrefy, spoil, wane, waste, weaken, wither. ANT.—bloom, flourish, grow, thrive.

rotate, circle, circulate, eddy, gyrate, invert, loop, revolve, roll, spin, swirl, swivel, turn, twirl, twist, wheel, whirl.

rough, bumpy, craggy, irregular, jagged, rugged, scabrous, scraggy, scratchy, serrated, uneven; approximate, coarse, cursory, imperfect, incomplete, unfinished, unpolished, unrefined; hard, harsh, severe, stormy, tempestuous, violent; austere, blunt, burly, crude, gruff, impolite, indecent, rude, uncivil. ANT.—even, level, sleek, smooth; complete, finished, polished, refined, thorough; gentle, mild, placid; courteous, cultivated, polite.

round, annular, circular, cylindrical, discoid, globular, orbed, orbicular, rotund, spherical; bulging, convex, protuberant; arched, bowed, coiled, curled, looped.

rouse, agitate, animate, arouse, awaken, excite, inflame, inspire, inspirit, motivate, provoke, raise, revive, stimulate, urge, whet. ANT.—calm, lull, pacify, tranquilize.

route, avenue, beat, channel, circuit, course, detour, digression, divergence, meandering, passage, path, rambling, road, rounds, street, thoroughfare, track, trail, walk, way.

routine, course, custom, cycle, fashion, habit, method, practice, round, system, usage, use; conventional, customary, habitual, methodical.

royal, august, courtly, dignified, elevated, grand, high, honorable, imperial, kingly, lofty, lordly,

majestic, monarchial, noble, princely, regal, reigning, resplendent, ruling, sovereign, stately, sublime, superior, supreme, worthy. ANT.—low, plebeian, proletarian, servile, unadorned.

rude, abusive, arrogant, blunt, boorish, brash, brazen, brusque, churlish, crass, crusty, discourteous, disrespectful, gross, gruff, impertinent, impolite, impudent, insolent, insulting, obstreperous, rough, saucy, surly, uncouth, ungracious, vulgar; barbarous, coarse, crude, ignorant, ill-bred, illiterate, inelegant, primitive, raw, rough, savage, uncivilized, uncouth, unpolished, unrefined, untaught; harsh, inclement, rough, stormy, turbulent, violent; approximate, guessed, unprecise. ANT.—affable, considerate, engaging, genial, tactful; chivalrous, civilized, courtly, cultured, genteel, refined; gentle, peaceful, placid, tranquil; exact, precise.

rugged, arduous, brawny, broken, corrugated, craggy, difficult, furrowed, harsh, husky, irregular, jagged, rough, scabrous, scratchy, uneven. ANT.—delicate, even, feeble, gentle, level, refined.

ruin, see destroy.

rule, axiom, canon, criterion, edict, formula, guide, law, maxim, method, norm, order, precept, prescript, principle, propriety, regulation, ruling, standard, statute, system; administration, authority, control, direction, domination, dominion, dynasty, empire, government, jurisdiction, mastery, regency, regime, reign, sovereignty, sway; command, control, dictate, direct, dominate, domineer, govern, influence, manage, prevail, regulate, restrain, superintend, sway. ANT.—accident, chance, hazard, irregularity; anarchy, chaos, disorder, disorganization, servility; abandon, follow, forsake, submit, yield.

rupture, break, burst, cleave, crack, crush, demolish, destroy, disjoin, fracture, gash, infringe, pound, puncture, rack, rend, rive, sever, shatter, slash, slice, smash, split, squeeze, sunder, tear. ANT.—join, mend, renew, repair, restore.

rural, agrarian, agrestic, agricultural, agronomic, backwoods, bucolic, country, countrified, farm, nonurban, pastoral, ranch, rustic, suburban. ANT.—commercial, industrial, urban, urbane.

rush, accelerate, bolt, bustle, dash, expedite, fly, gallop, hasten, hurry, precipitate, press, quicken, scurry, scuttle, speed, sprint, tear, zoom; activity, demand, haste, hurry. ANT.—delay, detain, hinder, procrastinate, tarry.

rustic, agrestic, agricultural, country, pastoral, rural; coarse, homely, inelegant, plain, simple; boorish, bucolic, countrified, rough, rude, uncouth, unpolished, unsophisticated; artless, unaffected. ANT.—commercial, industrial, urban; cultured, elegant, polished, refined, urbane; artificial, insincere, pretentious, unnatural.

rut, channel, crevice, furrow, groove, hollow, track, trench; course, custom, habit, practice, procedure, routine; rote, tedium.

ruthless, barbarous, bestial, brutal, brutish, coarse, cruel, ferocious, gross, harsh, implacable, inhuman, malevolent, merciless, pitiless, rancorous, relentless, remorseless, rough, rude, savage, tyrannical, unforgiving, unkind, vengeful, vindictive. ANT.—benevolent, charitable, compassionate, humane, merciful, sympathetic.

S

sack, demolish, despoil, devastate, loot, pillage, plunder, ravage, ruin, strip, waste; bag, pack, package, pocket.

sacred, blessed, consecrated, devout, divine, hallowed, holy, inviolable, pious, religious, sacrosanct, sanctified, saintly, spiritual, venerable. ANT.—blasphemous, evil, profane, sacrilegious, temporal, worldly.

sacrifice, abnegation, atonement, giving up, immolation, libation, loss, oblation, offering, self-denial, surrender, tribute; destroy, forfeit, forgo, give up, immolate, lose, offer, relinquish, renounce, surrender, yield.

sad, cheerless, dejected, depressed, despondent, disconsolate, dismal, doleful, downcast, funereal, gloomy, lugubrious, melancholy, mournful, pathetic, piteous, plaintive, somber, sorrowful, unhappy, woeful. ANT.—blithe, cheerful, elated, happy, joyful.

safe, certain, dependable, harmless, immune, impregnable, intact, invulnerable, protected, reliable, secure, snug, sure, trustworthy, unharmed, unscathed. ANT.—endangered, hazardous, insecure, perilous, unsafe.

safeguard, bulwark, fence, palladium, protection, refuge, shelter, shield; convoy, defense, escort, guard, guardian, security.

safety, asylum, custody, escape, harbor, haven, preservation, protection, refuge, sanctuary, security, shelter, surety; exemption, immunity. ANT.—danger, hazard, jeopardy, peril, risk.

sag, bend, crumple, decline, droop, incline, lean, list, settle, sink, slant, slope, stoop, strain, sway, tend, tilt, waver, weaken. ANT.—ascend, climb, mount, rise, straighten.

sage, intellectual, philosopher, professor, pundit, savant, scholar. ANT.—dolt, dunce, fool, idiot, lunatic.

salary, allowance, commission, compensation, earnings, fee, pay, payment, recompense, redress, reimbursement, remuneration, settlement, stipend, wages.

salient, clear, conspicuous, distinguished, impressive, manifest, marked, notable, noticeable, obvious, outstanding, prominent, significant, striking, visible. ANT.—hidden, inconspicuous, insignificant, minor, obscure, unimportant.

salubrious, see healthy.

same, alike, analogous, corresponding, duplicate, equal, equivalent, identical, indistinguishable, invariable, isomeric, like, matching, twin, uniform. ANT.—contrary, different, disparate, distinct, opposed.

sample, case, cutting, example, exemplification, illustration, instance, model, part, pattern, prototype, representation, slice, specimen; check, examine, experiment, inspect, judge, smell, taste, test, try.

sanction, allowance, approbation, approval, assent, authority, authorization, commendation, consent, endorsement, permission, permit, praise, privilege, ratification, support; allow, approve, authorize, confirm, endorse, favor, let, permit, promote, ratify, suffer, support, sustain, tolerate. ANT.—censure, denunciation, objection, prohibition, stricture; ban, exclude, forbid, prevent, refuse, veto.

sanctuary, see safety.

sane, healthy, lucid, normal, rational, reasonable, self-possessed, sensible, sober, sound, sound-minded, steady, wholesome. ANT.—delirious, demented, insane, irrational, maniacal.

sap, debilitate, deplete, drain, enervate, enfeeble, exhaust, impair, impoverish, mine, subvert, tunnel, undermine, unsettle, weaken.

sarcastic, acrimonious, biting, bitter, caustic, cutting, derisive, hostile, ironic, mocking, sardonic, satirical, scornful, sneering, taunting.

ANT.—affable, agreeable, amiable, courteous, gracious, respectful.

sate, cloy, content, fill, fill up, glut, gorge, gratify, pervade, please, quench, satiate, satisfy, saturate, slake, stuff. ANT.—deplete, drain, empty, exhaust, frustrate.

satire, abuse, banter, burlesque, derision, invective, irony, lampoon, mockery, parody, quip, raillery, ridicule, sarcasm, twist, wit.

satisfaction, comfort, content, contentment, delight, fulfillment, gladness, gratification, happiness, joy, pleasure, relief, serenity; amends, atonement; recompense, reimbursement, reparation. ANT.—despair, discontent, dissatisfaction, misery, sadness.

satisfactory, acceptable, adequate, ample, enough, fitting, gratifying, pleasing, satisfying, sufficient, suitable. ANT.—deficient, inadequate, insufficient, lacking, scanty.

satisfy, appease, cheer, comfort, compensate, content, gladden, gratify, please, remunerate, satiate; indemnify, repay; accomplish, complete, do, fill, fulfill, meet requirements, perform, qualify, suffice. ANT.—annoy, displease, fail to do, frustrate, neglect.

saturate, diffuse, drench, drown, fill, flood, immerse, impregnate, infiltrate, overfill, penetrate, permeate, pervade, run through, soak, steep, wet. ANT.—dehydrate, desiccate, dry, wipe.

savage, see ruthless.

save, accumulate, amass, collect, store; conserve, defend, deliver, economize, extricate, free, guard, hoard, keep, liberate, maintain, preserve, prevent, protect, redeem, rescue, reserve, safeguard, secure, shield, spare, uphold. ANT.—spend, waste; abandon, condemn, desert, impair, injure, leave.

savory, see delicious.

say, affirm, allege, articulate, assert, cite, declare, express, mention, pronounce, recite, rehearse, speak, state, talk, tell, utter.

saying, adage, affirmation, aphorism, apothegm, assertion, byword, citation, declaration, dictum, maxim, motto, pronunciation, proverb, quotation, remark, saw, statement, utterance.

scalding, blazing, blistering, burning, hot, red-hot, scorching, searing, torrid; ardent, fervent, fiery, flaming, passionate; peppery, pungent, spicy. ANT.—cold, freezing, frigid, frozen; apathetic, indifferent, phlegmatic, unconcerned; bland, dull, tasteless.

scan, audit, browse, consider, examine, inspect, investigate, regard, scrutinize, skim, survey, thumb over.

scandal, see disgrace.

scandalize, abuse, asperse, backbite, defame, detract, disgrace, disparage, libel, malign, offend, revile, shock, slander, traduce, vilify. ANT.—applaud, eulogize, honor, praise, respect.

scandalous, despicable, discreditable, disgraceful, disgusting, dishonorable, disreputable, flagrant, gross, hellish, ignominious, infamous, infernal, outrageous, shameful. ANT.—admirable, creditable, esteemed, honorable, respectable.

scanty, bare, few, inadequate, insufficient, lacking, limited, little, meager, narrow, pinched, ragged, scarce, scrimpy, skimpy, small, sparse, thin. ANT.—abundant, ample, plentiful, profuse, sufficient.

scarce, deficient, expensive, infrequent, isolated, limited, occasional, precious, rare, scanty, sparse, uncommon, unique, unplentiful. ANT.—cheap, customary, frequent, numerous, profuse.

scare, alarm, astound, cow, daunt, dismay, frighten, horrify, intimidate, petrify, shock,

startle, terrify, terrorize, threaten. ANT.—calm, compose, encourage, inspirit, pacify, soothe.

scared, afraid, alarmed, apprehensive, fainthearted, fearful, frightened, nervous, petrified, startled, timorous, trembling, upset, worried. ANT.—assured, bold, composed, confident, self-assured.

scatter, see disperse.

scene, display, exhibition, pageant, panorama, representation, scenery, setting, show, sight, spectacle, tableau, view.

scent, aroma, bouquet, essence, fragrance, fume, incense, odor, perfume, redolence, smell, stench, stink, sweetness.

scheme, arrangement, cabal, conspiracy, design, intrigue, machination, method, plan, plot, procedure, project, stratagem, system; chart, diagram, draft, graph, outline, sketch; conspire, contrive, delineate, design, devise, engineer, frame, intend, invent, map, outline, plan, plot, prepare, project, shape, sketch.

scholar, apprentice, disciple, learner, novice, pupil, student; intellectual, philomath, sage, savant. ANT.—dolt, dunce, fool, ignoramus, numskull, simpleton.

scholarly, see learned, pedantic.

scholarship, see knowledge.

scoff, deride, fleer, flout, gibe, jeer, mock, rail, ridicule, scorn, sneer, taunt, twit. ANT.—applaud, approve, commend, laud, praise.

scold, see reprimand.

scope, amount, area, compass, degree, expanse, extent, field, length, magnitude, measure, purview, range, reach, room, size, space, span, stretch, sweep, width.

scorch, blaze, brand, burn, char, incinerate, kindle, parch, roast, scald, sear, shrivel, singe. ANT.—douse, extinguish, quench, snuff out, stifle.

scorn, see contempt, disdain.

scrap, apportionment, bit, crumb, fragment, moiety, morsel, part, particle, piece, portion, section, segment, share; trash, waste material; brawl, fight, quarrel, squabble.

screen, camouflage, cloak, conceal, cover, defend, examine, guard, hide, inspect, protect, separate, shield, sift, sort, winnow.

scrub, clean, cleanse, purify, rub, scour, wash. ANT.—dirty, pollute, soil, stain, smirch.

scrupulous, see honest, just.

scrutinize, analyze, appraise, criticize, evaluate, examine, inspect, investigate, observe, probe, review, scan, search, stare, study, view. ANT.—disregard, ignore, neglect, overlook, slight.

search, examination, exploration, hunting, inquiry, investigation, pursuit, quest, research, seeking out; examine, explore, ferret out, hunt, investigate, look for, probe, ransack, rummage, scour, scrutinize, seek, shadow, track down, trail. ANT.—abandonment, cession, resignation, withdrawal; forgo, quit, relinquish, waive, vacate.

searching, see inquisitive.

season, age, complete, develop, mature, perfect, ripen; acclimate, accustom, harden, inure; flavor, spice.

seclusion, alienation, aloofness, apartness, concealment, insulation, isolation, loneliness, privacy, quarantine, quiet, refuge, remoteness, retirement, retreat, segregation, separation, sequestration, solitude, tranquility, withdrawal. ANT.—association, communion, connection, exposure, union.

secondary, see inferior.

secret, see clandestine.

secrete, see disguise, mask.

section, component, division, fragment, part, piece, portion, segment, share, slice, subdivision; country, district, division, domain, locality, province, realm, region, sector, territory, vicinity, zone.

secular, see lay, mundane.

secure, adjusted, assured, bound, certain, confident, definite, fastened, firm, fixed, immovable, indemnified, indubitable, inevitable, positive, safe, stable, sure, tight, undeniable, unharmed, unquestionable; accomplish, achieve, acquire, attain, earn, gain, get, grasp, obtain, possess, procure, realize, receive, win; assure, ensure, guarantee; defend, guard, protect, shield; adjust, bind, fasten, moor, settle, tighten. ANT.—doubtful, dubious, indefinite, questionable, uncertain; abandon, fail, forsake, relinquish; deny, disaffirm, disclaim, renounce; desert, leave, quit, relinquish, withdraw; detach, loosen, release, unfasten.

security, see refuge, safeguard.

sedate, calm, composed, demure, dignified, earnest, grave, imperturbable, proper, serene, serious, sober, solemn, staid. ANT.—excitable, flighty, frivolous, lively, mercurial.

see, behold, contemplate, descry, detect, discern, distinguish, espy, examine, gaze, grasp, heed, inspect, mark, mind, note, notice, observe, perceive, recognize, regard, scan, scrutinize, spy, stare, survey, understand, view, watch, witness; accompany, attend, escort; consult, discuss, interview, visit.

seek, see search.

seeming, apparent, external, ostensible, pretending, specious, superficial. ANT.—certain, definite, real, specific, true.

segment, allotment, apportionment, compartment, component, department, division, element, fraction, fragment, ingredient, moiety, parcel, part, piece, portion, scrap, section, share. ANT.—aggregate, entirety, sum, total, whole.

seize, see hinder, restrain.

select, adopt, appoint, choose, cull, decide, designate, elect, nominate, opt, pick, prefer, single out, specify. ANT.—eliminate, rebuff, refuse, reject.

selection, adoption, alternative, appropriation, choice, determination, election, favorite, option, pick, preference, reservation; assortment, collection.

self-contradictory, see irrational.

self-denial, see abstinence.

selfish, covetous, egoistic, egotistical, grasping, greedy, illiberal, mercenary, miserly, narrow, narrow-minded, parsimonious, rapacious, self-centered, self-indulgent, self-seeking, stingy, uncharitable, ungenerous. ANT.—altruistic, charitable, generous, liberal, magnanimous, philanthropic.

send, carry, cast, consign, convey, delegate, deliver, discharge, dispatch, drive, emit, fling, forward, hurl, impel, project, propel, ship, sling, throw, toss, transfer, transmit. ANT.—get, hold, keep, receive, retain.

senile, aged, ancient, decrepit, doddering, elderly, enfeebled, feeble, infirm, old, superannuated. ANT.—alert, strong, young, youthful, vigorous.

senior, advanced, chief, dean, elder, older, superior.

sensation, consciousness, excitement, feeling, passion, perception, response, sense, sensibility, sentiment. ANT.—apathy, insensibility, lethargy, narcosis, stupor.

sense, apprehension, connotation, consciousness, discernment, drift, explanation, feeling, gist, implication, import, insight, intent, interpretation, judgment, meaning, notion, opinion, purport, purpose, reason, sagacity, sensation, sensibility, sentiment, significance, signification, understanding, view, wisdom.

senseless, absurd, brainless, dense, dull, dumb, fatuous, foolish, idiotic, insensible, nonsensical, obtuse, ridiculous, silly, stupid, unconscious, unwise, witless. ANT.—alert, brilliant, clever, discerning, perceptive.

sensibility, awareness, consciousness, delicacy, discernment, emotion, feeling, impressibility, insight, sensation, sense, sensitiveness, subtlety, susceptibility, sympathetic response, sympathy, taste. ANT.—anesthesia, coldness, detachment, indifference, insensitivity, nonchalance.

sensible, apprehensible, perceptible; alive, attentive, awake, aware, cognizant, comprehending, conscious, informed, perceiving, sentient; capable, careful, discreet, intelligent, judicious, keen, prudent, rational, reasonable, sagacious, sage, sharp, shrewd, sober, sound, thoughtful, wise. ANT.—foolish, half-witted, inattentive, insensitive, unaware.

sensitive, alert, aware, conscious, delicate, impressionable, liable, painful, perceptive, predisposed, prone, responsive, sentient, subject, susceptible, sore, tender; irritable, high-strung, nervous, tense. ANT.—heartless, indifferent, obdurate, unconscious, unfeeling; calm, placid, relaxed, serene, tranquil.

sensual, arousing, carnal, debauched, dissolute, earthy, fleshly, intemperate, lascivious, lecherous, lewd, licentious, orgiastic, pleasure-loving, salacious, self-indulgent, sensory, sensuous, sybaritic, unspiritual, voluptuous, wanton. ANT.—ascetic, chaste, moderate, self-controlled, spiritual, temperate.

sentence, see condemn.

sentiment, sensation; affection, emotion, feeling, passion, sensibility, sympathy, tenderness; impression, judgment, notion, opinion, perception, remark, thought; maxim, saying, toast.

sentimental, dreamy, effusive, emotional, fanciful, gushing, idealistic, imaginative, languishing, maudlin, mushy, mawkish, overemotional, poetic, romantic, sappy, tender, unrealistic, visionary. ANT.—factual, literal, matter-of-fact, pragmatic, realistic.

separate, detach, disconnect, disjoin, dissociate, dissolve, disunite, divide, isolate, part, rend, segregate, sequester, sever, sunder, withdraw; alone, apart, disjoined, distinct, disunited, divergent, independent, parted, private, radial, unconnected, unique. ANT.—assemble, attach, combine, fuse, intertwine; associated, connected, joined, mixed, united.

separation, alienation, disconnection, disengagement, disjunction, dissolution, disunion, division, divorce, insulation, isolation, loneliness, partition, quarantine, retirement, rupture, seclusion, segregation, solitude, severance, withdrawal. ANT.—association, communion, connection, relationship, union.

sequence, arrangement, chain, following, graduation, order, progression, series, string, succession, train; consequence, result, sequel.

serene, see quiescent, quiet.

serenity, see peace, repose.

series, see sequence.

serious, great, important, momentous, weighty; austere, deep, earnest, grave, profound, sedate, sober, solemn, somber, staid, thoughtful; alarming, critical, dangerous, risky. ANT.—flippant, insignificant, small, trifling, trivial; informal, reassuring, relaxed, safe.

serve, advance, aid, answer, assist, attend, benefit, content, contribute, distribute, forward, give, help, promote, requite, satisfy, succor, suffice, supply, support, treat, uphold, wait on. ANT.—attack, combat, impede, oppose, rival.

service, advantage, assistance, avail, behalf, benefit, co-operation, favor, gain, good, help, interest, profit, use, utility; ceremony, ritual, rite, worship; business, duty, employment, function, labor, ministry, office.

serviceable, advantageous, applicable, beneficial, conducive, contributive, favorable, good, helpful, important, practical, profitable, salutary, usable, useful, valuable, wholesome. ANT.—deleterious, detrimental, impractical, ineffective, useless.

servile, see contemptible, ignoble.

set, adjust, anchor, appoint, arrange, deposit, dispose, establish, expose, fix, lay, locate, mount, place, plant, predetermine, put, regulate, settle, situate, stand, station; coagulate, congeal, harden, jell, solidify, thicken; established, firm, fixed, formal, immovable, located, placed, positive; arrangement, association, attitude, circle, class, club, cluster, collection, company, coterie, group, party, position, posture, series.

settle, adjudicate, close, conclude, confirm, decide, determine, dispose, end, reconcile, resolve, terminate; drop, fall, sink, subside; calm, pacify, quiet, tranquilize; colonize, domesticate, people; establish, fix, locate, place, put, set, station; adjust, arbitrate, regulate, stabilize, straighten. ANT.—doubt, hesitate, suspend, vacillate, waver; anger, antagonize, roil, stir; destroy, disestablish, raze, ruin, unsettle; confuse, disarrange, disorganize, disrupt, entangle.

settlement, close, completion, conclusion, end, finale, issue, termination; decision, deduction, inference, judgment; colonization, colony, community, establishment; adjustment, compensation, pay, recompense, reimbursement, remuneration, reward; agreement, arrangement, compact, contract, covenant, pledge, understanding.

sever, see divide, separate.

several, different, distinct, divers, diverse, manifold, many, numerous, quite a few, separate, sundry, unlike, various. ANT.—one, none.

severe, acute, arduous, austere, despotic, distressing, domineering, drastic, exacting, extreme, forbidding, grim, hard, harsh, inflexible, intense, obdurate, oppressive, relentless, rigid, rigorous, sharp, stern, stiff, strict, stringent, uncompromising, unmitigated, unrelenting, unyielding, violent; plain, simple, unadorned. ANT.—compassionate, courteous, gentle, lenient, placid; beautified, decorated, embellished.

sew, baste, bind, fasten, fix, mend, patch, piece, refit, repair, restore, seam, stitch, tack, tailor. ANT.—deface, destroy, hurt, rend, ruin.

shabby, see inferior, poor.

shade, brilliance, color, complexion, dye, hue, paint, pigment, saturation, stain, tincture, tinge, tint; shadow, umbrage; cloud, darken, dim, eclipse, obscure. ANT.—achromatism, paleness, transparency; brighten, illuminate, manifest, reveal.

shake, agitate, convulse, discourage, dishearten, dissuade, flutter, intimidate, jar, joggle, jolt, jounce, oscillate, quake, quiver, rock, shiver, shudder, sway, totter, tremble, trill, vibrate, wave, waver.

shallow, cursory, exterior, flimsy, frivolous, imperfect, inconsiderable, senseless, silly, simple, slight, stupid, superficial, trifling, trivial. ANT.—bottomless, complete, deep, intelligent, profound, thorough, unfathomable.

sham, affect, assume, dissimulate, feign, imitate, personate, pretend, simulate; counterfeit, deceit, delusion, dissimulation, fake, fakery, fraud, humbug, imitation, mockery, pretense, pretext, ruse, stratagem, trick, wile. ANT.—disclose, expose, reveal, unmask, unveil; actuality, fact, reality, substance, truth.

shame, abash, degrade, discomfit, discredit, dishonor, embarrass, humiliate, mortify; abashment, chagrin, discomfiture, embarrassment, humiliation, mortification, remorse; baseness, contempt, disfavor, disgrace, dishonor, disrepute, ignominy, infamy, odium, opprobrium, reproach, scandal. ANT.—encourage, glorify, honor, respect, uphold; contentment, impenitence, satisfaction, serenity, tranquility; dignity, glory, honor, praise, respect.

shameful, see scandalous.

shape, appearance, aspect, build, cast, configuration, conformation, construction, contour, cut, figure, form, frame, guise, image, mold, outline, pattern; arrange, cast, combine, compose, constitute, construct, create, develop, devise, direct, discipline, fashion, forge, form, frame, invent, make, make up, model, mold, organize, produce, regulate, sketch. ANT.—contortion, deformity, distortion, malformation, mutilation; destroy, disfigure, distort, injure, mar, wreck.

shapeless, amorphic, amorphous, deformed, disfigured, formless, irregular, misshapen, unshapely, unsymmetrical. ANT.—proportionate, proportioned, shapely, symmetrical, well-formed.

share, allotment, bit, contingent, dividend, division, dole, dose, fraction, fragment, helping, parcel, part, percentage, piece, portion, quota, ration, section, segment; administer, allot, apportion, appropriate, assign, deal, dispense, distribute, divide, experience, parcel, partake, participate in, partition, portion. ANT.—bulk, entirety, sum, totality, whole; aggregate, amass, combine, unite, withhold.

shared, see mutual.

sharp, acute, honed, keen, pointed, razor-edged, sharpened; acrid, barbed, biting, bitter, cutting, peppery, piquant, pungent, sour, spicy, stinging; excruciating, penetrating, piercing, severe, shrill; astute, brilliant, clever, cunning, discerning, incisive, intelligent, quick, sagacious, shrewd, wily, wise, witty; abrupt, harsh, precipitous, rough, rugged, steep. ANT.—blunt, dull, pointless, unsharpened; bland, tasteless, unsavory; delicate, faint, low, melodious, mild, soft; dull-witted, inept, insipid, stupid, vapid; even, flat, gradual, level, smooth.

shatter, see break.

shattered, broken, collapsed, crushed, demolished, destroyed, flattened, fractured, hurt, interrupted, mutilated, reduced, ruptured, separated, slivered, smashed, splintered, wrecked. ANT.—intact, integral, repaired, sound, united.

shelter, asylum, harbor, haven, refuge, retreat, sanctuary; cover, defense, lee, protection, safety, screen, security, shield; cloak, clothe, conceal, cover, curtain, defend, disguise, ensconce, envelop, guard, harbor, hide, house, mask, preserve, protect, safeguard, screen, secure, shield, shroud, veil. ANT.—danger, exposure, hazard, jeopardy, menace, threat; endanger, expose, ignore, neglect, uncover.

shield, avert, forbid, repel; also see shelter.

shift, displace, exchange, remove, substitute; adapt, adjust, alter, change, convert, moderate, modify, transfigure, transform, vary; move, stir, turn,

veer. ANT.—keep, retain; continue, establish, preserve, stabilize; cease, halt, rest, stop.

shifting, see fickle.

shine, beam, blaze, dazzle, flare, flash, glare, gleam, glimmer, glisten, glitter, glow, irradiate, radiate, scintillate, shimmer, sparkle, twinkle; excel, surpass; buff, burnish, polish, wax.

shining, see magnificent, radiant.

ship, consign, convey, dispatch, forward, remit, route, send, transmit, transport; deport, dismiss, send away.

shock, alarm, amaze, appall, astonish, astound, disconcert, dumfound, embarrass, flabbergast, frighten, horrify, offend, startle, stun, surprise, terrify, terrorize. ANT.—calm, console, mitigate, pacify, prepare, soothe.

shocking, see horrible.

shoot, cast, catapult, dart, discharge, eject, emit, expel, fire, hit, hurl, propel; kill, wound; bloom, bud, germinate, sprout; branch, channel, chute, offshoot, scion, sprout, sucker, trough, twig.

shore, bank, beach, border, brink, coast, margin, seacoast, seaside, strand; brace, buttress, prop, stabilize, support.

short, compact, diminutive, little, low, slight, small, tiny; abbreviated, abridged, abrupt, brief, compendious, compressed, concise, condensed, laconic, pithy, precise, succinct, summary, terse; deficient, inadequate, insufficient, lacking, limited, scanty; abrupt, curt, uncivil. ANT.—colossal, enormous, gigantic, titanic, towering; diffuse, jumbled, redundant, repetitive, wordy; abundant, adequate, excessive, profuse, sufficient; civil, courteous, gracious, patient, polite.

shortcoming, see defect, imperfection.

shorten, see contract, diminish.

shout, acclaim, bellow, call out, clamor, cry, cry out, ejaculate, exclaim, howl, roar, scream, screech, shriek, vociferate, yell, yelp. ANT.—intimate, murmur, mutter, suggest, whisper.

shove, butt, crowd, drive, elbow, force, impel, jostle, press, propel, push, ram, shoulder, thrust. ANT.—drag, halt, pull, stop.

show, array, demonstration, display, entertainment, exhibition, exposition, exposure, flourish, ostentation, pageantry, parade, performance, production, spectacle, splendor, splurge; appearance, semblance; pretense, puppetry, sham, simulation, speciousness; disclose, display, exhibit, expose, indicate, parade, present, reveal, unfold; demonstrate, evidence, explain, manifest, prove, verify; conduct, direct, guide, usher; inform, instruct, teach.

showy, affected, artificial, ceremonious, dramatic, flashy, gaudy, glaring, histrionic, melodramatic, ornate, pompous, theatrical, tinseled. ANT.—genuine, humble, modest, subdued, unaffected.

shred, bit, fragment, frazzle, jot, mite, particle, rag, scrap, smidgen, speck, strip, tatter; lacerate, rend, rip, slice, slit, split, strip, tear, wound. ANT.—aggregate, bulk, mass, quantity, volume; heal, join, mend, repair, restore, unite.

shrewd, artful, clandestine, covert, crafty, cunning, foxy, furtive, guileful, insidious, sly, stealthy, surreptitious, tricky, underhand, wily; acute, alert, astute, careful, circumspect, clever, discerning, ingenious, intelligent, knowing, mindful, observant, perspicacious, prudent, reflective, sagacious, sapient, sharp. ANT.—candid, frank, genuine, open, sincere; dense, frivolous, ignorant, impetuous, undiscerning.

shrill, see keen, severe.

shrink, balk, contract, cringe, decline, decrease, deflate, diminish, droop, dwindle, fail, flinch,

languish, lessen, quail, recoil, shrivel, waste, weaken, wilt, wince, withdraw, wither. ANT.—expand, grow, rejuvenate, renew, revive.

shun, see avoid, escape.

shut, close, lock, seal; debar, exclude, preclude, confine, immure, imprison, incarcerate; complete, conclude, end, finish, terminate. ANT.—open, unbar, unlock; clear, free, liberate, release; begin, commence, initiate, start.

shy, see modest, reserved.

sick, ailing, confined, diseased, ill, impaired, indisposed, infirm, invalid, morbid, sickly, unhealthy, unwell. ANT.—hale, hardy, healthy, robust, vigorous.

sift, analyze, discuss, evaluate, examine, investigate, probe, screen, scrutinize, separate, sort, winnow; bolt, colander, filter, grade, screen, size, sort, strain.

sign, augury, badge, emblem, gesture, identification, indication, manifestation, mark, note, notice, omen, portent, presage, proof, representation, signal, suggestion, symbol, symptom, token.

signal, alarm, cue, gesture, indicator, mark, message, sign, warning; conspicuous, famous, important, memorable, momentous, outstanding, prominent, remarkable, salient, striking.

significance, consequence, effect, force, implication, import, importance, meaning, point, purpose, relevance, substance, weight.

significant, critical, emphatic, expressive, grave, important, indicative, meaningful, momentous, notable, outstanding, prominent, remarkable, serious, suggestive, telling, vital, weighty, worthy. ANT.—inconsequential, insignificant, petty, shallow, trivial.

signify, denote, designate, disclose, express, imply, import, indicate, intimate, manifest, mean, purport, reveal, show, specify, suggest. ANT.—conceal, cover, hide, obscure, withhold.

silent, calm, hushed, mute, noiseless, peaceful, placid, quiescent, quiet, reserved, reticent, secretive, still, taciturn, tight-lipped, tranquil, uncommunicative. ANT.—clamorous, communicative, loquacious, noisy, raucous, voluble.

silhouette, configuration, conformation, contour, delineation, figure, form, outline, profile, shape.

silly, see irrational, preposterous, ridiculous.

similar, akin, alike, allied, analogous, comparable, correlative, correspondent, corresponding, facsimile, homogeneous, like, parallel, reciprocal, related, resembling. ANT.—alien, different, dissimilar, divergent, opposed, unlike.

similarity, affinity, analogy, association, comparison, concordance, conformity, correlation, correspondence, harmony, homogeneity, likeness, parallelism, parity, relation, resemblance, semblance, simile, similitude. ANT.—difference, disparity, distinction, divergence, variance.

simple, apparent, easy, effortless, elementary, facile, mere, obvious, pure, simplistic, single, unblended, uncompounded, unmixed; homely, humble, modest, plain, unadorned; artless, frank, naive, natural, open, unaffected, unpretentious, unsophisticated; asinine, credulous, foolish, gullible, ignorant, oafish, silly. ANT.—complicated, complex, difficult, intricate; decorated, embellished, opulent, ornate; contrived, deceptive, pretentious, sophisticated; discerning, intelligent, judicious, sagacious, wise.

simulate, see mimic.

simultaneous, accompanying, coeval, coincident, concomitant, concurrent, contemporaneous, synchronal, synchronous. ANT.—foregoing, following, preceding, prior, subsequent.

sin, see evil, offense.

sincere, candid, conscientious, direct, earnest, frank, genuine, guileless, heartfelt, honest, ingenuous, open, straightforward, true, trustworthy, truthful, unaffected, undisguised, unfeigned, unreserved, upright, veracious. ANT.—deceitful, deceptive, evasive, false, hypocritical, untrustworthy.

sincerity, see honesty.

sinewy, able-bodied, active, athletic, brawny, burly, energetic, firm, hardy, husky, manly, mighty, muscular, powerful, robust, stalwart, steely, strapping, strong, sturdy, tough, vigorous, virile, wiry. ANT.—delicate, emaciated, feeble, puny, weak.

sinful, see bad, corrupt, immoral.

sing, carol, chant, chirp, croon, hum, hymn, intone, lilt, trill, troll, vocalize, warble, yodel.

singe, see scorch.

single, celibate, distinctive, elemental, individual, isolated, marked, one, only, particular, pure, separate, simple, singular, sole, solitary, special, specific, unaccompanied, unique, unmixed, unwed. ANT.—associated, common, general, multiple, ordinary, universal.

singular, see eccentric, extraordinary, rare.

sinister, adverse, corrupt, deleterious, dire, disastrous, dishonest, evil, foreboding, harmful, hostile, malefic, mischievous, ominous, pernicious, perverse, threatening, unfavorable, unlucky. ANT.—auspicious, expedient, favorable, opportune, propitious.

sink, collapse, decline, decrease, descend, diminish, drop, fall, slump, subside; droop, extend downward, hang; be submerged, engulf, go down, immerse, touch bottom. ANT.—arise, ascend, climb, mount, surge; come up, float, rise, stay afloat, swim.

site, district, locality, locus, place, position, region, section, situation, spot, station.

situation, case, circumstance, condition, exigency, plight, predicament, state, status; employment, environment, job, location, place, position, post, setting, site, spot, station, surroundings, whereabouts.

size, amplitude, area, bigness, bulk, capacity, dimensions, enormity, expanse, extent, greatness, immensity, largeness, magnitude, measurement, mass, quantity, scope, space, vastness, volume.

skeleton, frame, shell, structure; also see outline.

skeptic, agnostic, apostate, cynic, deist, detractor, dissenter, doubter, free-thinker, idolator, infidel, nihilist, questioner, schismatic, unbeliever. ANT.—believer, devotee, disciple, evangelist, worshiper.

skepticism, agnosticism, cynicism, disbelief, distrust, doubt, doubting, hesitation, incredulity, infidelity, misgiving, mistrust, questioning, suspicion, wavering. ANT.—belief, certainty, conviction, faith, reliance, trust.

sketch, see outline.

skill, cunning, ingenuity, knack; also see dexterity, facility.

skillful, able, accomplished, adept, adroit, apt, capable, clever, competent, cunning, deft, dexterous, efficient, expert, handy, ingenious, masterful, practiced, proficient, ready, skilled, talented, trained, versed. ANT.—awkward, blundering, clumsy, inept, inexperienced.

skin, bark, coat, covering, cuticle, derma, dermis, epidermis, hide, husk, integument, lamina, lining, parchment, peel, pelt, plating, rind, surface, tegument, veneer.

skip, drop, miss, neglect; also see eliminate, exclude, ignore.

slack, disengaged, free, indefinite, lax, limp, loose, relaxed, slow, stagnant, unbound, unfastened,

untied, vague; backward, careless, dilatory, dissolute, heedless, indifferent, negligent, remiss, tardy, unrestrained, wanton. ANT.—drawn, engaged, fast, taut, tied; alert, careful, disciplined, dutiful, restrained.

slander, see libel, scandalize.

slant, bent, bias, disposition, inclination, leaning, partiality, penchant, predilection, predisposition, prejudice, proclivity, proneness, propensity, tendency, turn; acclivity, angle, declivity, divergence, grade, list, obliquity, slope, tilt; lean, slope, tilt, tip, slope.

slavery, serfdom, thralldom, vassalage; also see captivity.

slaughter, see kill, massacre.

sleazy, feeble, flabby, flaccid, flimsy, fragile, limp, poor, tenuous, thin, trashy, weak, worthless. ANT.—excellent, fine, firm, forceful, strong.

sleek, glossy, lustrous, oily, polished, satiny, shiny, silky, slick, smooth, velvety. ANT.—coarse, dry, dull, harsh, rough.

sleep, catnap, coma, doze, dozing, drowse, hibernation, lethargy, nap, nod, repose, rest, siesta, slumber, snooze, somnolism, stupor, trance.

slender, feeble, flimsy, gaunt, lank, lean, meager, narrow, rare, scrawny, skinny, slight, slim, spare, tenuous, thin, trivial. ANT.—broad, bulky, fat, strong, thick, wide.

slide, glide, skate, skid, skim, skip, slip, slither; chute, incline, ramp.

slight, disregard, ignore, neglect, omit, overlook, skip; also see slender.

sling, cast, dangle, hang, heave, hoist, hurl, impel, pitch, propel, shove, suspend, throw, toss.

slip, blunder, boner, error, fallacy, fault, fluff, inaccuracy, indiscretion, lapse, misstep, mistake. ANT.—accuracy, perfection, precision, truth.

slope, see slant.

slothful, see lazy.

slow, crawling, creeping, dawdling, deliberate, dull, gradual, laggard, languid, leisurely, lingering, loitering, moderate, slack, torpid, unready; apathetic, dilatory, idle, indolent, lazy, lethargic, negligent, phlegmatic, procrastinating, sleepy, sluggish, tired; belated, delayed, overdue. ANT.—quick, rapid, speedy, swift; conscientious, enthusiastic, industrious, lively, zealous; prompt, punctilious, punctual, timely.

sluggish, see slow.

slumber, see sleep.

sly, artful, astute, calculating, clandestine, covert, crafty, cunning, deceitful, designing, foxy, furtive, guileful, insidious, knowing, mischievous, nimble, scheming, shifty, shrewd, stealthy, subtle, surreptitious, traitorous, tricky, underhand, wary, wily. ANT.—artless, candid, frank, genuine, open, sincere.

small, diminutive, feeble, inconsiderable, insignificant, little, microscopic, miniature, minute, petty, puny, pygmy, scanty, slender, slight, tiny, trivial, ungenerous, weak, wee, young. ANT.—enormous, generous, huge, immense, powerful.

smart, adroit, apt, clever, dexterous, quick, quick-witted, skillful, talented, witty; acute, alert, bright, intelligent, keen, sharp, shrewd; chic, dapper, modish, stylish. ANT.—awkward, bungling, clumsy, slow; dense, dull, stupid, unintelligent; dowdy, frowzy, shabby.

smash, see rupture.

smell, see odor.

smooth, even, flat, flush, level, plane; glossy, polished, silky, sleek, slick; diplomatic, glib,

suave, unruffled, urbane; calm, mild, still, tranquil. ANT.—craggy, jagged, rocky, uneven; hairy, rough, rugged; blunt, rash, rude, tactless; agitated, inflamed, furious, stormy, violent.

snag, see obstacle.

snare, ambush, apprehend, arrest, capture, catch, clutch, grasp, grip, lure, net, seize, trap; artifice, deception, decoy, hoax, lure, pitfall, ruse, stratagem, trap, trick, wile. ANT.—free, liberate, release, unchain, unshackle; fact, fidelity, genuineness, honesty, truth.

sneer, fleer, scoff; also see mock.

snub, abash, crush, cut, discomfit, disdain, disregard, humble, humiliate, ignore, neglect, rebuke. ANT.—comfort, honor, love, regard, respect.

snug, compact, constricted, contracted, firm, narrow, neat, stretched, taut, tense, tight, trim; close, comfortable, cozy, warm. ANT.—lax, loose, open, relaxed, slack; cold, detached, distant, removed, uncomfortable.

soar, circle, dart, flit, float, flutter, fly, glide, hover, mount, remain aloft, sail, swoop, wing. ANT.—descend, fall, plummet, sink, topple.

sober, abstemious, austere, calm, dispassionate, earnest, grave, moderate, quiet, reasonable, sedate, serious, solemn, staid, steady, temperate, unintoxicated, unruffled. ANT.—boisterous, dissipated, drunk, excited, immoderate, joyful, overwrought.

social, affable, communicative, out-going; also see hospitable, pleasant.

soft, amenable, bland, compassionate, downy, elastic, flaccid, flexible, fluffy, gentle, impressible, indulgent, lenient, malleable, meek, mellow, merciful, mild, pliable, pliant, silky, smooth, spongy, subdued, supple, tender, tolerant, tractable, yielding. ANT.—brittle, cruel, domineering, insensible, self-possessed, unyielding.

soften, abate, allay, alleviate, diminish, dissolve, extenuate, lessen, melt, mitigate, moderate, relax, relieve, solace, soothe, tenderize, thaw, weaken. ANT.—aggravate, agitate, augment, increase, irritate, lengthen.

soil, continent, country, earth, field, ground, land, plain, region, tract; blemish, blight; also see defile.

solace, see console.

sole, alone, deserted, desolate, isolated, lonely, secluded, unaided; individual, lone, one, only, remaining, single, solitary. ANT.—accompanied, attended, surrounded; collective, multiple, public, social.

solemn, august, awe-inspiring, ceremonious, consequential, formal, imposing, impressive, majestic, momentous, precise, regular, reverential, ritualistic; austere, earnest, grave, grim, heavy, intense, reserved, sedate, serious, sober, somber, staid, stern, thoughtful. ANT.—informal, insignificant, ordinary, transitory, uneventful; animated, cheerful, frivolous, giddy, lively.

solid, compact, dense, firm, hard, rigid, sound, stable, substantial, unyielding. ANT.—liquid, porous, vaporous, vulnerable, weak.

solitary, see sole.

solitude, alienation, asylum, concealment, isolation, loneliness, privacy, quiet, refuge, retirement, retreat, seclusion, silence, stillness. ANT.—clamor, exposure, notoriety, publicity, tumult.

solve, decipher, discover, elucidate, explain, interpret, resolve, unfold, untangle. ANT.—complicate, involve, tangle.

somatic, bodily, carnal, corporal, corporeal, fleshly, human, material, natural, organic, physical, substantial, tangible, unspiritual. ANT.—ethereal, mental, spiritual.

somber, bleak, dull, funereal; also see dismal.

soon, beforehand, before long, early, quickly, shortly. ANT.—late, overdue, slow, tardy.

soothe, allay, alleviate, assuage, calm, cheer, comfort, compose, console, ease, encourage, gladden, lull, mollify, pacify, please, relieve, solace, sympathize, tranquilize. ANT.—afflict, annoy, antagonize, distress, vex.

soothing, docile, relaxed, soft; also see gentle, peaceful.

sophisticated, astute, blase, cultivated, cultured, experienced, knowledgeable, polished, refined, wise, worldly. ANT.—artless, crude, immature, ingenuous, naive.

sorcery, see magic.

sordid, base, debased, depraved, dirty, foul, loathsome, obscene, odious, revolting, squalid, vicious, vile, vulgar, wicked; abject, contemptible, degraded, despicable, ignoble, low, mean, worthless, wretched. ANT.—attractive, charming, decent, laudable; distinguished, eminent, honorable, noble, upright.

sorrow, affliction, anguish, contrition, distress, grief, heartache, lamentation, misery, misfortune, mourning, penitence, regret, remorse, sadness, trial, tribulation, woe. ANT.—comfort, delight, happiness, joy, solace.

sorrowful, see gloomy, melancholy.

sort, category, character, class, description, kind, nature, species, strain, type, variety.

sound, binding, cogent, durable, effective, efficacious, faithful, genuine, hale, healthy, intact, legal, logical, powerful, reliable, satisfactory, solvent, stable, strong, substantial, unimpaired, valid, vigorous, weighty; din, noise, note, tone. ANT.—counterfeit, defective, impaired, spurious, void; hush, quiet, stillness.

sour, acid, acrid, acrimonious, astringent, bitter, complaining, curdled, embittered, glum, grouchy, morose, peevish, querulous, rancid, sharp, spoiled, sullen, tart, vinegary. ANT.—amiable, cheerful, cordial, kindly, sugary, sweet.

source, agent, cause, determinant, incentive, inducement, motive, origin, principle, reason; beginning, birth, commencement, cradle, derivation, foundation, fountain, inception, incipience, origin, primogenitor, rise, root, spring, start, wellspring. ANT.—consequence, effect, result; harvest, issue, outcome, product, termination.

souvenir, see memorial.

spacious, see roomy.

spare, rescue, safeguard; also see preserve.

sparkle, see glare.

speak, announce, articulate, chatter, communicate, converse, debate, declaim, declare, discourse, discuss, express, proclaim, pronounce, report, say, talk, tell, utter, vocalize, voice.

special, choice, definite, determinate, distinctive, exceptional, exclusive, extraordinary, individual, particular, peculiar, proper, rare, restricted, singular, specific, uncommon, unique, unusual. ANT.—broad, commonplace, ecumenical, prevalent, universal.

specific, categorical, characteristic, concrete, definite, especial, exact, explicit, express, individual, limited, particular, peculiar, precise, special. ANT.—general, generic, indefinite, uncertain, vague.

specify, appoint, call, choose, denominate, designate, entitle, individualize, mention, name, particularize, select, single out, stipulate. ANT.—discard, generalize, hint, miscall, misname, reject.

specimen, instance, unit; see also example.

speck, crumb, smidgen; see also particle.

spectacle, parade, representation, scene, splurge; see also display.

speculate, apprehend, assume, believe, conjecture, consider, contemplate, deduce, guess, imagine, meditate, muse, ponder, presume, reflect, suppose, surmise, think, weigh. ANT.—ascertain, conclude, demonstrate, prove, substantiate.

speech, articulation, chatter, communication, diction, discourse, enunciation, lecture, locution, oration, pronunciation, report; see also conversation; language.

speed, facilitate, forward, further, promote, rush, urge; see also hasten.

spend, consume, deplete, disburse, dispense, dissipate, exhaust, expend, liquidate, pay, scatter, squander, use, waste. ANT.—cache, collect, conserve, hoard, pocket, retain.

sphere, ball, circle, compass, department, domain, globe, orb, province, realm, scope, spheroid.

spirit, apparition, ghost, phantom, specter, vision; animation, courage, energy, enthusiasm, fervor, fortitude, life, liveliness, verve, vigor, vitality, vivacity, zeal; intent, meaning; disposition, feeling, mood, nature, temper; essence, psyche, soul, substance.

spiritual, divine, ecclesiastical, ethereal, ghostly, holy, immaterial, incorporeal, pure, refined, religious, sacred, supernatural, unearthly, unworldly. ANT.—carnal, corporeal, material, physical, secular, worldly.

spite, see malice.

spiteful, antagonistic, disagreeable, hostile, ill-natured, malevolent, malicious, malign, mean, rancorous, surly, ugly, vengeful, venomous, vicious, vindictive. ANT.—forgiving, friendly, generous, helpful, merciful.

splendid, brilliant, bright, dazzling, effulgent, eminent, excellent, glorious, gorgeous, grand, illustrious, magnificent, radiant, refulgent, resplendent, shining, showy, sumptuous, superb. ANT.—drab, dull, humble, mediocre, unimpressive.

splendor, brilliance, radiance; see also luster.

split, rive, sever, shred, wound. see also rip; sever.

spoil, decay, decompose, disintegrate, putrefy, rot, waste; corrupt, damage, debase, destroy, disfigure, harm, impair, injure, mar, pervert, ruin, vitiate; booty, loot, plunder. ANT.—flourish, grow, increase, luxuriate, thrive; enhance, improve, mend, perfect, repair.

spoken, announced, expressed, oral, unwritten, uttered, verbal, vocal, voiced. ANT.—documentary, nonverbal, recorded, written.

sponsor, advertiser, advocate, backer, champion, helper, patron, protector, subscriber, supporter, surety; godparent.

spontaneous, automatic, casual, extemporaneous, impulsive, instinctive, involuntary, offhand, unbidden, unconscious, unforced, unintentional, unwilling. ANT.—deliberate, designed, intended, premeditated, rehearsed.

sport, contest, match, merriment; caper, frolic, gamble, play, revel, romp, stake, toy, wager, display, exhibit, wear; see also recreation.

spread, circulate, diffuse, dispense, disperse, disseminate, distribute, exhibit, expand, extend, open, promulgate, propagate, publish, radiate, scatter, sow, stretch, strew, unfold, unroll, unseal. ANT.—collect, conceal, condense, suppress, tighten.

sprightly, agile, animated, blithe, brisk, buoyant, cheerful, debonair, effervescent, elated, hopeful, jocund, lively, quick, spirited, sportive, vivacious. ANT.—dejected, depressed, despondent, gloomy, pessimistic.

spring, birth, cradle, derivation, foundation. see also beginning.

sprout, bud, burgeon, develop, germinate, grow, shoot. ANT.—decrease, shrink, wither.

spry, active, agile, alacritous, alert, blithe, brisk, flexible, frisky, lively, nimble, quick, spirited, sprightly, supple, vivacious. ANT.—feeble, inactive, lethargic, sluggish, torpid.

spur, cause, incitement, principle, purpose, reason; see also incentive.

squabble, see quarrel.

squalid, dirty, filthy, foul, grimy, muddy, soiled, sordid, unclean; base, contemptible, despicable, low, mean, miserable, pitiful, poor, shabby, unkempt, wretched. ANT.—clean, immaculate, pure, spotless; appealing, attractive, comfortable, inviting, presentable.

squander, abuse, consume, corrode, dissipate, drain, exhaust, expend, lavish, misspend, misuse, scatter, spend, splurge, waste. ANT.—economize, hoard, invest, preserve, retain.

squeamish, see particular.

stability, composure, steadiness; see also balance.

stable, balanced, constant, determined, durable, enduring, equable, established, firm, fixed, immovable, immutable, lasting, permanent, regular, resolute, secure, settled, solid, staunch, steadfast, steady, unwavering. ANT.—erratic, fluctuating, mercurial, mutable, vacillating.

staid, dignified, earnest, grave, reserved, sedate, serious, sober, solemn, steady, stuffy, unimaginative. ANT.—boisterous, flighty, frivolous, impulsive, volatile.

stain, befoul, blemish, blight, blot, defile, discolor, disgrace, dishonor, mark, soil, spot, sully, taint, tarnish; color, dye, tinge, tint. ANT.—cleanse, decorate, honor, purify; blanch, bleach, whiten.

stale, see insipid.

stand, abide, bear, continue, endure, hold, last, persist, prevail, remain, suffer, survive, sustain, tolerate; discontinue, halt, hold, pause, remain, rest, stay, stop. ANT.—falter, succumb, surrender, weaken, yield; advance, continue, develop, grow, progress, run.

standard, gauge, touchstone; see also criterion.

start, see commence; origin.

startle, alarm, amaze, astonish, astound, bewilder, confound, daze, disconcert, dumbfound, flabbergast, overwhelm, petrify, shock, stun, surprise, unsettle. ANT.—caution, forewarn, prepare, signal, warn.

starving, craving, dying, longing, weakening; see also hungry.

state, claim, explain, express, propound, recount, say, specify, utter; see also assert; recite; situation.

stately, courtly, lordly, monarchial, princely, regal, royal, ruling, sovereign, supreme; see also majestic.

statement, acknowledgment, affirmation, allegation, announcement, assertion, declaration, dictum, mention, profession, proposition, report, specification, thesis.

status, caste, circumstance, condition, distinction, footing, grade, place, position, rank, reputation, situation, standing, state, station.

statute, act, decree, edict, injunction, law, order, ordinance, regulation, ruling.

staunch, reliable, trusty. see also loyal.

stay, abide, delay, halt, linger, lodge, pause, persist, remain, sojourn, stand, tarry, visit, wait; arrest, check, hinder, impede, obstruct, restrain, retard. ANT.—dart, hasten, leave, progress, scurry; assist, encourage, facilitate, promote, sustain.

steady, inflexible, unswerving, unyielding; see also stable.

steal, pillage, plagiarize, snitch, swipe; see also embezzle; rob.

steep, abrupt, angular, craggy, hilly, perpendicular, precipitous, rugged, sharp, sheer, sudden, vertical. ANT.—flat, gradual, horizontal, level, smooth.

steer, control, escort, supervise; see also guide.

stench, fetidness, fetor, stink. see also odor.

sterile, arid, barren, childless, fallow, fruitless, impotent, infecund, infertile, unfruitful, unproductive, unprolific, worthless; antiseptic, decontaminated, pure, sanitary, sterilized. ANT.—fecund, fertile, fruitful, generative, prolific, proliferous; contaminated, infectious, noxious, unhygienic, unsanitary.

stern, see severe.

stiff, firm, hard, hardened, inflexible, petrified, rigid, solid, tense, unbending; see also severe.

stigma, brand, defect, disfigurement, imprint, mark, scar, stain, trace, vestige.

still, hushed, inaudible, inert, motionless, mum, mute, noiseless, quiet, quiescent, soundless, stagnant, stationary, undisturbed, unruffled; calm, gentle, meek, mild, passive, peaceful, patient, placid, silent, tranquil; besides, but, furthermore, however, yet. ANT.—clamorous, disturbed, loud, piercing, stirring, tumultuous; aggressive, dynamic, hostile, impassive, perturbed.

stilted, affected, bombastic, fustian, grandiose, grandiloquent, high-flown, high-sounding, magniloquent, pompous, pretentious, swelling, turgid. ANT.—candid, honest, humble, reserved, shy, simple.

stimulate, animate, arouse, awaken, disquiet, energize, excite, impel, incite, instigate, invigorate, irritate, kindle, pique, provoke, rouse, stir up, urge. ANT.—calm, deaden, pacify, quell, tranquilize.

stimulus, arousal, encouragement, goad, stimulant; see also incentive.

stingy, see greedy; miserly.

stir, beat, mix; impel, persuade; see also move.

stock, accumulation, fund, goods, hoard, inventory, merchandise, produce, provision, reserve, store, wares; calves, cattle, cows, herd, steers; fill, fill up, furnish, replenish, store, supply.

stoical, assiduous, forbearing, indulgent, uncomplaining; see also patient.

stone, boulder, crag, flint, gem, granite, gravel, jewel, marble, pebble, quartz, rock, rubble, shale.

stop, see cease; halt; hinder; interrupt.

store, see heap.

storm, agitation, commotion, cyclone, disturbance, fury, hurricane, outbreak, paroxysm, rage, tornado, tumult, turbulence, turmoil, upheaval, violence, whirlwind; assail, assault, attack, blow, boil, bombard, fume, hail, rage, rain, rant, snow, whirlwind. ANT.—calm, peace, placidity, repose, serenity, tranquility; assuage, ease, lull, pacify, soothe.

stormy, agitated, angry, blustery, excitable, frenzied, furious, gusty, inclement, passionate, raging, raving, roaring, rough, tempestuous, turbulent, violent, windy. ANT.—calm, clear, composed, gentle, peaceful, tranquil.

story, account, allegory, anecdote, apologue, burlesque, chronicle, epic, fable, fantasy, fiction, history, legend, memoir, myth, narration, narrative, novel, parable, report, romance, saga, satire, tale, yarn; canard, fabrication, falsehood.

stout, paunchy, pudgy, stocky, thickset; see also fat; obese.

straight, direct, erect, even, level, perpendicular, rectilinear, right, unbent, undeviating, unswerving, upright, vertical; candid, fair, honest,

honorable, just, regular, reliable, trustworthy, upright. ANT.—bent, circuitous, crooked, distorted, swerving, twisted; deceptive, devious, dishonest, fraudulent, unreliable.

strain, breed, extraction, lineage, pedigree, race, stock; kind, sort, variety; effort, endeavor, overexertion, struggle; melody, tune; manner, style; anxiety, burden, mental tension, pressure, stress.

strange, abnormal, alien, anomalous, bewildering, bizarre, curious, dissociated, eccentric, exotic, extraordinary, fantastic, foreign, grotesque, inapplicable, incredible, irregular, irrelevant, misplaced, mysterious, nondescript, odd, peculiar, remote, singular, stupefying, surprising, unaccustomed, uncommon, unfamiliar, unrelated, unusual. ANT.—conventional, familiar, ordinary, prevailing, regular, typical.

stranger, alien, drifter, foreigner, immigrant, interloper, intruder, newcomer, outsider, squatter, visitor. ANT.—acquaintance, associate, companion, friend, neighbor, peer.

stratagem, artifice, cabal, conspiracy, design, device, finesse, intrigue, logistics, machination, maneuver, plan, plot, ruse, scheme, strategy, tactics, trick.

stray, err, go astray, traipse, wander; see also deviate; ramble.

stream, spout, spurt; abound, be copious. see also emanate; flow.

strength, durability, fortitude, intensity, lustiness, stamina, sturdiness, toughness; see also power.

strengthen, confirm, corroborate, substantiate, sustain, verify; brace, buttress, fortify, harden, invigorate, reinforce, rejuvenate, steel; augment, enlarge, extend, heighten, intensify, sharpen.

stress, burden, compulsion, exigency, force, press, pressure, strain, tension, urgency; accent, emphasis, importance, significance, weight.

stretch, distort, spread, strain. see also distend; extend.

strict, accurate, exact, precise, stern, rough, rugged; see also severe.

strike, hurt, knock, pummel, smite. see also hit.

striking, affecting, august, grandiose, majestic, over-powering, splendid; see also impressive.

stripped, defenseless, unprotected; see also naked.

strive, see endeavor.

strong, athletic, concentrated, durable, enduring, forcible, fortified, hale, impregnable, resistant, resolute, solid, strenuous, tough; see also mighty; sinewy.

struggle, brawl, feud, fray, quarrel, row, scuffle, skirmish; see also combat; conflict.

stubborn, adamant, contumacious, determined, dogged, headstrong, immovable, inflexible, intractable, mulish, obdurate, obstinate, pertinacious, recalcitrant, refractory, uncompromising, ungovernable, unyielding. ANT.—amenable, compliant, reasonable, submissive, tractable, yielding.

student, apprentice, disciple, learner, novice, observer, pupil, scholar.

study, cogitate, examine, investigate, scrutinize, weigh; see also contemplate.

stumble, fall, pitch, slide, slip, sprawl, tilt, topple, trip, tumble. ANT.—arise, ascend, mount, soar.

stun, amaze, astonish, disconcert, dumbfound, flabbergast, surprise; see also shock.

stupid, asinine, brainless, crass, dense, dull, dumb, feeble-minded, foolish, inane, inept, moronic, obtuse, senseless, vapid, witless. ANT.—clever, discerning, perspicacious, saga, wise.

stupor, apathy, coma, daze, drowsiness, inertness, insensibility, languor, lethargy, narcosis,

numbness, stupefaction, torpor, unconsciousness. ANT.—activity, consciousness, liveliness, sensibility, vivacity.

sturdy, see mighty; sinewy; strong.

suave, adroit, affable, amiable, courteous, cultured, debonair, gallant, genteel, glib, gracious, pleasing, polished, polite, smooth, sophisticated, tactful, urbane, well-bred. ANT.—brusque, crude, displeasing, inept, rude.

subdue, beat, conquer, control, crush, defeat, humble, master, moderate, overcome, quell, restrain, rout, soften, subjugate, suppress, surmount, tame, temper, vanquish. ANT.—awaken, enrage, incite, rouse, stimulate.

subject, citizen, dependent, inferior, liegeman, subordinate, vassal; argument, case, material, matter, point, problem, question, substance, theme, thesis, thought, topic.

sublime, elevated, glorious, lofty, raised, supreme; see also majestic.

submerge, see immerse.

submit, abdicate, abide, accede, acquiesce, bear, bend, capitulate, cede, defer, obey, quit, relent, resign, succumb, suffer, surrender, yield; offer, present, propose, suggest. ANT.—defy, obstruct, resist, struggle, withstand; deny, refuse, reject, retain, withhold.

subordinate, ancillary, dependent, inferior, insignificant, junior, minor, paltry, secondary, subject, subservient, subsidiary, unimportant; control, subdue, subjugate. ANT.—chief, dominant, excellent, leading, superior; dignify, elevate, glorify, promote, revere.

subsequent, after, consequent, ensuing, following, later, next, posterior, succeeding, successive. ANT.—antecedent, anterior, earlier, preceding, prior.

subside, descend, drop, fall, sink; droop, extend downward, hang; see also collapse; decline.

substance, see material; moment.

substantiate, see confirm.

substitution, alternation, exchange, replacement, variety. see also change; modification.

subtract, deduct, remove, take away, withhold; see also decrease; lessen.

subvert, demolish, depress, destroy, extinguish, invert, overthrow, overturn, overwhelm, pervert, reverse, supplant, topple, upset. ANT.—conserve, establish, perpetuate, preserve, sustain.

succeed, achieve, accomplish, attain, conquer, defeat, flourish, gain, prevail, prosper, surmount, thrive, triumph, vanquish, win; ensue, follow, replace, supersede, supervene, supplant. ANT.—blunder, fail, lose, miscarry, miss; anticipate, herald, introduce, precede, preface.

succession, continuation, progression; see also sequence.

succinct, compendious, curt; see also concise.

sudden, abrupt, immediate, instantaneous, unexpected; see also hasty; rapid.

suffer, bear, endure, experience, feel, stand, sustain; admit, allow, indulge, let, permit, submit, tolerate; ache, agonize, undergo. ANT.—avoid, resist, surrender; deny, disallow, prohibit, refuse; heal, rally, overcome, recover, revive.

suffering, see distress; pain.

sufficient, abundant, adequate, ample, commensurate, enough, fitting, plenty, proper, satisfactory, satisfying, suitable. ANT.—deficient, inadequate, insufficient, lacking, scant.

suggest, advise, allude to, counsel, hint, imply, infer, insinuate, intimate, offer, propose, recommend, submit.

suggestion, admonition, advice, allusion, caution, counsel, exhortation, hint, idea, implication, indication, innuendo, insinuation, intimation,

proposal, recommendation, thought, warning; design, layout, outline, plan, project, scheme, strategy.

suit, accommodate, adapt, adjust, alter, conform, fit, revise; fill, gratify, please, satisfy. ANT.—misapply, misfit; annoy, disturb, vex.

suitable, acceptable, accordant, adapted, agreeable, applicable, appropriate, becoming, conformable, congruous, consonant, eligible, expedient, fitting, gratifying, just, meet, pertinent, proper, relevant. ANT.—disagreeable, improper, incongruous, irrelevant, obnoxious, reprehensible.

sullen, churlish, crabbed, cross, dismal, dour, fretful, gloomy, glum, moody, morose, sour, stubborn, sulky, surly. ANT.—amiable, cheerful, genial, jovial, sociable.

sum, aggregate, amount, bulk, collection, entirety, entity, everything, gross, lump, total, totality, unity, value, whole, worth. ANT.—fraction, ingredient, part, portion.

summary, abstract, analysis, condensation, core, digest, epitome, outline, recapitulation, reduction, report, resumé, survey, syllabus, synopsis.

summit, apex, cap, crest, crown, culmination, head, height, peak, pinnacle, tip, top, vertex, zenith. ANT.—base, bottom, foot, foundation, nadir.

sunny, bright, brilliant, clear, cloudless, dazzling, fair, gleaming, shining, shiny, splendid, sunlit. ANT.—cloudy, dark, dull, foul, overcast.

superficial, cursory, desultory, exterior, external, flimsy, frivolous, hasty, ignorant, imperfect, outward, shallow, short-sighted, slight, surface, unenlightened. ANT.—careful, deep, deliberate, learned, profound, thorough.

superfluous, abounding, exaggerated, excessive, exorbitant, extra, extravagant, extreme, inexhaustible, inordinate, lavish, lush, luxuriant, needless, overmuch, profuse, redundant, spare, superabundant, unnecessary, useless. ANT.—inadequate, insufficient, scanty, scarce.

superior, above, better, distinguished, excellent, finer, greater, higher, major, preferred, sovereign, supreme, unsurpassed, upper. ANT.—below, deficient, inferior, minor, substandard.

supernatural, ghostly, metaphysical, mysterious, mystic, spectral, spiritual, superhuman, unearthly; see also miraculous.

supervise, command, dominate, manage, superintend; see also regulate.

supple, see elastic.

supplicate, adjure, importune, request; see also beg.

supply, fund, reserve; endow, fit out, produce; see also hoard; furnish.

support, base, basis, bolster, brace, buttress, foundation, fulcrum, groundwork, prop, shore, stanchion, stay; advocacy, aid, assistance, backing, comfort, contribution, encouragement, favor, help, patronage, succor; livelihood, living, maintenance, subsistence, sustenance; confirmation, evidence; advance, advocate, aid, assist, back, bear, bolster, brace, carry, contribute, defend, encourage, expedite, foster, further, help, hold, keep, maintain, preserve, prop, shore, sustain, uphold, verify. ANT.—apex, cupola, peak, pinnacle, summit; blockage, discouragement, hindrance, impediment, injury, opposition; abandonment, betrayal, denial, desertion; delusion, fantasy, illusion; check, cripple, destroy, encumber, frustrate, obstruct, undermine.

supporter, advocate, defender, devotee, pillar, sustainer, upholder, votary; see also follower.

suppose, conjecture, deduce, speculate, surmise; see also imagine.

suppress, lower, moderate; see also lessen.

supremacy, domination, predominance, sovereignty, transcendence; see also mastery.

supreme, best, cardinal, chief, dominant, essential, final, first, foremost, greatest, highest, leading, main, paramount, peerless, predominant, principal, transcendent, ultimate. ANT.—auxiliary, inferior, subordinate, subsidiary, supplemental.

sure, assured, indubitable, inevitable, secure, undeniable, unquestionable; see also definite.

surplus, see excess.

surprise, curiosity, marvel, miracle, phenomenon, oddity, prodigy, rarity, sensation, spectacle; admiration, amazement, astonishment, awe, bewilderment, curiosity, incredulity, perplexity, shock, stupefaction, wonder, wonderment; alarm, amaze, astonish, astound, bewilder, confound, dazzle, disconcert, dumbfound, flabbergast, overwhelm, shock, startle, stun. ANT.—familiarity, habit, routine, triviality; anticipation, apathy, expectation, indifference, tranquility; admonish, caution, forewarn, prepare, warn.

surrender, acquiesce, capitulate, resign, sacrifice, submit; see also relinquish.

surround, bound, confine, enclose, fence, limit; see also encircle, encompass.

surveillance, charge, control, management, superintendence; see also inspection.

suspect, disbelieve, dispute, distrust, doubt, mistrust, query, question, waver; assume, guess, imagine, presume, speculate, suppose, theorize. ANT.—believe, confide in, rely on, trust; ascertain, discern, know.

suspend, adjourn, cease, defer, delay, desist, discontinue, interrupt, postpone, stay; append, balance, dangle, hang, hitch, poise, sling, swing. ANT.—accelerate, continue, expedite, persist, proceed, support.

suspicion, incredulity, scruple, skepticism, suspense, unbelief; see also distrust.

sustain, advocate, back, bear, brace, further; see also encourage, help, preserve.

swallow, absorb, accept, assimilate, bear, believe, bolt, consume, devour, endure, engulf, envelop, imbibe, stomach, tolerate; recant, retract, suppress, withdraw. ANT.—discharge, doubt, emit, expel, reject; affirm, confirm, uphold.

swarthy, brown, dark, dusky, sable, tawny. ANT.—bright, fair, light.

sway, impel, incite, stir; see also influence.

swear, affirm, declare, protest, state; see also maintain.

sweep, brush, clean, clear, graze, mop, rake, remove, touch, traverse, whisk; amplitude, bend, compass, contour, curve, extent, range, reach, scope, stretch, swing.

sweet, engaging, gentle, honeyed, mellifluous, melodious, saccharine, sugary, winning; see also luscious.

swell, amplify, bulge, dilate, distend, expand, heave, increase, inflate, intensify, protrude, puff, rise, tumefy; bulge, crescendo, curve, elevation, intensity, power, protuberance, swelling. ANT.—compress, contract, diminish, shrink, shrivel; decline, depression, flatness, reduction, shrinkage.

swift, see fast.

swindle, cheat, chicanery, guile, imposture; bilk, dupe, fool, gull, hoax, hoodwink, victimize; see also deceit; deceive.

symbol, character, figure, mark, representative, sign, token, type.

symmetry, agreement, arrangement, balance, centrality, conformity, equality, equilibrium, equivalence, evenness, finish, form, harmony, order, proportion, regularity, shapeliness. ANT.—disagreement, disparity, distortion, imbalance, irregularity.

sympathetic, forbearing, kindly, tender, thoughtful; see also humane.

sympathize, gladden, soothe; see also comfort.

sympathy, accord, affinity, agreement, alliance, concord, condolence, congeniality, consolation, empathy, harmony, warmth. see also compassion. ANT.—antipathy, harshness, indifference, insensitivity, malevolence.

symptom, characteristic, diagnostic, evidence, feature, indication, mark, property, token, trace, trait, vestige.

synthetic, artificial, ersatz, fake, feigned, fictitious, phony, unreal; see also counterfeit.

system, network, operation, organization, policy, program; see also method.

T

tact, adroitness, dexterity, diplomacy, discretion, discrimination, finesse, knack, perception, perspicacity, poise, savoir-faire, skill, subtlety.

tactful, discreet, discriminating, judicious, politic; see also diplomatic.

take, catch, clasp, clutch, grasp, grip, procure, seize; appropriate, arrogate, capture, confiscate, ensnare, steal, usurp; apprehend, deprehend; necessitate, need, require; adopt, assume, choose, select; bear, endure, stand, tolerate; attract, captivate, charm, delight, interest; accept, obtain, receive.

tale, account, anecdote, chronicle, history, narration, narrative, report, yarn; see also fiction.

talent, cleverness, endowment, genius; see also ability, faculty.

talented, bright, sharp, smart, quick, quick-witted, witty; see also skillful.

talk, chatter, gossip, lecture, report; blab, chat, comment, gossip, harangue, jabber, mutter, plead, prattle, preach, rant, speak, spout, tattle; see also conversation; discourse, speak.

talkative, chatty, communicative, glib, voluble; see also garrulous.

tall, see high.

tame, domestic, domesticated, gentle, obedient, subdued, timid; boring, dull, flat, insipid, tedious, vapid; see also docile.

tamper, alter, discommode, inconvenience, interrupt, intervene, mix in, monkey, trouble; see also interfere.

tangible, palpable, sensible; see also corporeal.

tangle, complicate, confuse, ensnare, entrap, hinder, interfere, intertwine, involve, jumble, muddle, snare, spoil; dilemma, disorder, embarrassment, muddle, perplexity, puzzle, quandary, snarl.

tardy, detained, lax, overdue, retarded, slack; see also late.

tarnish, befoul, besmirch, blemish, blight, blot, defame, defile, discolor, disgrace, dishonor, smudge, soil, spot, stain, sully, taint. ANT.—brighten, cleanse, defend, honor, restore.

tart, see bitter.

task, assignment, burden, business, charge, chore, duty, function, job, labor, mission, office, pursuit, stint, toil, work, undertaking.

taste, flavor, gusto, piquancy, relish, savor, tang, zest; acumen, appreciation, discernment, discrimination, disposition, inclination, judgment, liking, predilection, refinement, sensibility, susceptibility. ANT.—antipathy, disinclination, indelicacy, rudeness, vulgarity.

taut, bound up, constricted, firm, fixed, snug, stretched, tight, unbending, unyielding. ANT.—lax, loose, relaxed, shaky, slack.

tax, assessment, charge, custom, dues, duty, exaction, excise, fine, impost, levy, obligation, rate, tariff, toll, tribute; burden, demand, strain, task. ANT.—gift, grant, present, remuneration, reward; comfort, ease, relaxation, rest.

teach, advise, coach, direct, educate, enlighten, explain, expound, guide, imbue, inculcate, indoctrinate, inform, instill, instruct, interpret, lecture, nurture, prepare, school, train, tutor. ANT.—follow, imbibe, learn, misguide, misinform.

tear, cleave, disunite, rive, sever, shed, sunder, wound; see also rip.

tease, aggravate, badger, bother, disturb, harry, nag; see also harass.

tedious, boring, burdensome, dilatory, dreary, drowsy, dull, fatiguing, humdrum, irksome, monotonous, slow, sluggish, soporific, tardy, tiresome, uninteresting, wearisome. ANT.—animating, exhilarating, fascinating, inspiring, refreshing.

teeming, abounding, abundant, ample, bountiful, copious, overflowing, plenteous, plentiful, profuse, prolific, replete, rich, rife. ANT.—deficient, inadequate, meager, scant, scarce.

tell, describe, narrate, recite, recount, rehearse, relate, report; assert, communicate, declare, discuss, express, mention, publish, say, speak, state, utter; announce, betray, confess, disclose, divulge, reveal; discern, discover, distinguish, recognize; acquaint, apprise, explain, impart, inform, instruct, notify; direct, order, request.

temper, anger, animosity, choler, fury, indignation, ire, irritation, petulance, rage, resentment, wrath; composition, disposition, humor, mood, nature, quality, structure, type; anneal, assuage, change, moderate, modify, mollify, qualify, soften, soothe. ANT.—composure, conciliation, patience, peace, repose; agitate, harden, intensify, strengthen, toughen.

temperament, constitution, disposition, humor, makeup, mood, nature, personality, propensity, spirit, temper.

temperate, abstemious, abstinent, frugal, mild, moderate, reasonable, self-restrained, sober, unruffled. ANT.—excessive, immoderate, impetuous, tempestuous, uncontrolled.

temporal, earthly, ephemeral, fleeting, laic, lay, mundane, profane, secular, temporary, transient, transitory, worldly. ANT.—ecclesiastical, eternal, everlasting, religious, spiritual.

temporary, brief, changeable, cyclical, ephemeral, evanescent, fleeting, impermanent, momentary, passing, provisional, shifting, short, summary, transient, transitory. ANT.—abiding, durable, endless, permanent, perpetual, timeless.

tempt, allure, bait, captivate, charm, coax, court, decoy, entice, fascinate, incite, induce, inveigle, lure, rouse, seduce, test, try. ANT.—discourage, disenchant, nauseate, repel, repulse.

tend, accompany, attend, escort, guard, keep, manage, nurse, protect, serve, watch; gravitate, incline, lean, point, verge on.

tendency, aim, aptness, bent, bias, direction, disposition, drift, inclination, learning, mood, predisposition, proclivity, proneness, propensity, susceptibility, tone, trend, turn. ANT.—apathy, aversion, deviation, disinclination, opposition.

tender, benevolent, delicate, loving, merciful, responsive, sympathetic, warm; feeble, fragile, immature, weak, young; advance, extend, offer, present, proffer, propose, suggest, volunteer; see also mild.

tenet, belief, conviction, creed, doctrine, dogma, position, precept, principle, system, teaching, view.

tense, firm, rigid, stiff, strained, taut, tight; anxious, distraught, edgy, high-strung, nervous, overwrought, restless, troubled. ANT.—lax, limp, loose, slack; calm, placid, relaxed, tranquil, unruffled.

tentative, experimental, makeshift, probationary, provisional, temporary. ANT.—conclusive, decisive, definitive, final, permanent.

term, boundary, course, cycle, duration, interval, limit, period, phase, span, time; condition, stipulation; expression, name, nomenclature, phrase, terminology, word.

terminate, abolish, achieve, cease, close, complete, conclude, end, expire, finish, perfect, stop. ANT.—begin, commence, inaugurate, initiate, start.

terrible, alarming, appalling, awful, dire, dreadful, fearful, frightful, gruesome, hideous, horrible, horrid, severe, shocking, terrifying. ANT.—appealing, attractive, captivating, happy, pleasing.

terrify, see frighten.

territory, area, boundary, country, district, division, domain, dominion, land, place, province, quarter, region, section, township.

terror, see fear.

terse, brief, compact, compendious, concise, condensed, crisp, incisive, laconic, neat, pithy, sententious, short, succinct, summary, trenchant. ANT.—profuse, rambling, redundant, verbose, wordy.

test, assay, examine, experiment, inspect, prove, scrutinize, substantiate, try, verify; criterion, demonstration, essay, examination, proof, standard, trial.

testimony, affidavit, attestation, certification, confirmation, credentials, declaration, deposition, evidence, indication, proof, warrant, witness.

text, book, handbook, manual, manuscript, matter, passage, publication, quotation, sentence, stanza, subject, textbook, theme, topic, verse, volume, wording, writing.

texture, character, coarseness, composition, constitution, disposition, feel, fiber, firmness, flexibility, grain, makeup, nap, organization, rigidity, roughness, smoothness, structure, tissue.

thankful, appreciative, beholden, contented, grateful, gratified, pleased, satisfied. ANT.—critical, discontented, dissatisfied, faultfinding, thankless.

thaw, deliquesce, dissolve, flow, liquate, liquefy, melt, run. ANT.—chill, congeal, freeze, petrify, solidify.

theft, burglary, depredation, embezzlement, fraud, holdup, larceny, misappropriation, pillage, piracy, plagiarism, plunder, rapine, robbery, spoliation, swindle.

theme, composition, description, discourse, dissertation, essay, idea, motive, narrative, proposition, report, statement, subject, tenor, text, thesis, topic, trend, writing.

theoretical, analytical, formal, ideal, scholastic; see also learned.

theory, assumption, attribution, doctrine, guess, opinion, perception, plea, presupposition, speculation, surmise, thesis, viewpoint; see also hypothesis.

therefore, accordingly, consequently, for, hence, since, so, then, thence, wherefore.

thesis, affirmation, argument, composition, dictum, dissertation, doctrine, essay, position, proposition, report, study, theme.

thick, abundant, close, compact, compressed, condensed, crowded, dense, impenetrable, multitudinous, numerous, packed, populous, profuse, solid, swarming; coagulated, curdled, gelatinous, glutinous, gummy, heavy, miry, muddy, opaque, ropy, solidified, viscid, viscous; cloudy, dull, indistinct, turbid; doltish, dull, ignorant, obtuse, stolid, stupid; coarse, crass, gross; broad, chunky, dumpy, squat, thickset. ANT.—barren, inadequate, scattered, spacious, sparse; clear, diaphanous, gaseous, limpid, rarified, transparent; clear, distinct; acute, bright, intelligent, perceptive; genteel, polite, refined; fragile, frail, slender, thin.

thin, diaphanous, diluted, fine, gauzy, gossamer, rare, scanty, scrawny, skeletal, threadlike, wasted; see also gaunt, slender.

think, conceive, imagine, picture, recall, recollect, remember; cogitate, contemplate, deliberate, determine, examine, meditate, muse, ponder, reason, reflect, ruminate, speculate, study; apprehend, believe, conjecture, consider, deem, esteem, guess, hold, judge, opine, presume, reckon, regard, suppose, surmise; devise, intend, mean, plan, propose.

thorough, absolute, accurate, complete, concluded, consummate, ended, entire, exact, exhaustive, finished, full, painstaking, perfect, plenary, radical, scrupulous, sweeping, thoroughgoing, total, unbroken, undivided, unmitigated. ANT.—deficient, incomplete, perfunctory, sketchy, superficial.

thought, cerebration, cogitation, conception, consideration, contemplation, deliberation, fancy, idea, imagination, impression, judgment, lucubration, meditation, memory, notion, opinion, perception, recollection, reflection, regard, retrospection, sentiment, speculation, view. ANT.—emptiness, fatuity, inanity, vacancy, vacuity.

thoughtful, attentive, careful, cautious, charitable, concerned, considerate, empathic, heedful, kind, provident, prudent, sympathetic; cogitative, contemplative, engrossed, introspective, meditative, pensive, philosophic, rapt, reflective, speculative, studious. ANT.—careless, heedless, indifferent, negligent, thoughtless; fatuous, idiotic, inane, obtuse, vacuous.

thoughtless, desultory, heedless, imprudent, inaccurate, inattentive, neglectful, reckless, unconcerned. see also inconsiderate, lax.

threatening, see imminent.

thrift, conservation, economy, frugality, parsimony, providence, prudence, saving. ANT.—extravagance, prodigality, shiftlessness, waste.

thrill, excitement, flutter, sensation, shock, tingling, tremor; affect, agitate, electrify, inspire, move, penetrate, rouse, stimulate, stir, strike, tingle, touch, tremble, vibrate.

thrive, advance, bloom, flourish, grow, improve, increase, luxuriate, prosper, succeed. ANT.—decline, fail, fall, lose.

throb, beat, oscillate, palpitate, pulsate, pulse, vibrate; beating, palpitation, pulsation, vibration.

throng, aggregation, assemblage, assembly, bevy, concourse, crowd, crush, gang, horde, host, legion, masses, mob, multitude, populace, press, rabble, swarm.

throw, cast, chuck, drive, fling, hurl, impel, launch, pitch, project, propel, sling, thrust, toss. ANT.—catch, draw, haul, hold, retain.

thrust, cast, crowd, drive, extend, fling, force, impel, jostle, penetrate, pierce, press, propel, push, shove, stab, tilt; hasten, promote, urge; explosion, force, impact, pressure, propulsion, push. ANT.—drag, falter, halt, retreat; impede, obstruct, oppose; debility, powerlessness, weakness.

thwart, see frustrate.

tidy, clean, clear, methodical, neat, nice, orderly, precise, shipshape, snug, spruce, systematic, trim. ANT.—deranged, disheveled, littered, slovenly, unkempt.

tie, affinity, alliance, association, band, bond, brace, conjunction, connection, cord, coupling, ligament, ligature, link, relationship, rope, security, strap, string, tackle, union, yoke; attach, bind, confine, connect, constrain, engage, fasten, fetter, hitch, join, link, moor, obligate, restrain, restrict, secure, shackle, tether, unite. ANT. detachment, disunion, isolation, separation, sunderance; detach, free, loosen, unbind, separate.

tight, close, compact, contracted, narrow, tense; penny-pinching; see also taut; greedy, miserly.

time, age, course, cycle, date, duration, eon, epoch, era, interim, interval, measure, period, season, sequence, span, spell, stage, succession, tempo, term, while; adjust, measure, regulate, set.

timely, appropriate, convenient, exact, opportune, precise, prompt, proper, propitious, providential, punctual, ready, seasonable, suitable, well-timed. ANT.—dilatory, inexpedient, inopportune, tardy, untimely.

timid, abashed, afraid, bashful, coy, daunted, diffident, embarrassed, faltering, fearful, hesitant, humble, irresolute, modest, recoiling, scared, shamefaced, sheepish, shy, skulking, spiritless, terrified, timorous, unspirited, vacillating, wavering. ANT.—adventurous, courageous, dauntless, determined, gregarious, intrepid.

tiny, insignificant, trivial, wee; see also small.

tire, bore, drain, exhaust, fatigue, harass, irk, jade, overtax, overwork, pall, prostrate, strain, tucker, wear out, weary, worry. ANT.—amuse, energize, invigorate, refresh, restore.

tired, collapsing, drained, drooping, drowsy, exhausted, faint, fatigued, haggard, jaded, spent, wasted, weary, wearied, worn. ANT.—active, energetic, fresh, invigorated, lively.

title, appellation, caption, cognomen, denomination, designation, epithet, heading, inscription, name; birthright, claim, due, honor, ownership, possession, prerogative, privilege, right.

toil, achievement, business, drudgery, effort, employment, grind, labor, occupation, opus, pains, performance, production, task, travail, work. ANT.—leisure, recreation, relaxation, repose, rest.

token, badge, emblem, evidence, index, manifestation, mark, memorial, note, symbol, trait; see also souvenir.

tolerant, enduring, fair, forbearing, lenient, liberal, open-minded, patient, receptive, understanding. ANT.—bigoted, discriminatory, intolerant, prejudiced, unyielding.

tolerate, allow, authorize, concede, let, license, sanction, permit; abide, bear, brook, endure, persevere, prevail, stand, stomach, sustain, swallow, undergo. ANT.—bar, forbid, hinder, inhibit, veto; avoid, evade, falter, succumb, surrender, yield.

toll, see tax.

tongue, cant, lingo, slang; see also language.

too, additionally, also, as well, besides, further, furthermore, in addition, likewise, moreover, similarly.

tool, agent, apparatus, appliance, device, equipment, implement, instrument, means, mechanism, medium, utensil, vehicle. ANT.—hindrance, impediment, obstacle, obstruction.

top, acme, apex, chief, crest, crown, culmination, head, peak, pinnacle, summit, surface, tip, vertex, zenith. ANT.—base, bottom, foot, foundation, nadir.

topic, affair, argument, issue, material, matter, motion, point, problem, proposition, question, resolution, subject, text, theme, theorem, thesis.

torment, abuse, ache, agony, anguish, cruelty, distress, excruciation, malady, martyrdom, misery, pain, persecution, rack, suffering, throe, torture, woe, wretchedness; afflict, aggravate, annoy, badger, bait, bother, distress, disturb, grill, gull, harass, harry, hurt, irritate, mistrust, nag, oppress, pain, pester, plague, provoke, rack, tantalize, taunt, tease, torture, trouble, vex. ANT.—comfort, ease, mitigation, relief, solace; console, help, mollify, please, relieve, soothe.

torrid, hot-blooded, scalding, scorching, sweltering, warm; see also hot, passionate.

torture, see torment.

toss, see throw.

total, see sum; thorough.

touch, affect, allude, brush, concern, feel, finger, glance, graze, handle, hint, impress, melt, mollify, pat, regard, soften, strike, stroke, tap; dash, feeling, infusion, palpability, sensation, sprinkling, tangency, taste, tinge, trace.

touching, affecting, heart-rending, impressive, pitiable, sad; adjacent, adjunct, bordering, tangent; see also impressive; poignant; tender.

touchy, choleric, fiery, hasty, snappish; see also irritable.

tough, adhesive, coherent, fibrous, firm, hardened, hardy, seasoned, stalwart, strong, sturdy, tenacious, wiry; difficult, formidable, hard, intricate, laborious, puzzling, rigorous, troublesome, trying; boisterous, bullying, callous, fierce, incorrigible, intractable, obdurate, obstinate, raging, savage, stubborn, turbulent, unmanageable, unyielding, vicious. ANT.—defenseless, delicate, fragile, puny, vulnerable, weak; easy, effortless, elementary, facile, simple; amenable, compliant, deferential, docile, passive, tractable, yielding.

tour, see journey.

tow, see draw, pull.

towering, see lofty.

toy, caper, frisk, frolic, gamble, gambol, play, revel, romp, sport, wager; bauble, game, pastime, plaything, trinket; little, miniature, small.

trace, mark, scar, stain, stigma, tinge; characteristic, clue, evidence, feature, fragment, impression, indication, memorial, property, record, sign, symptom, trait, vestige. ANT.—deletion, effacement, extinction, nonexistence, obliteration.

track, see pursue.

tractable, acquiescent, adaptable, amenable, compliant, deferential, docile, dutiful, governable, manageable, obedient, pliant, submissive, willing, yielding. ANT.—insubordinate, intractable, obstinate, rebellious, stubborn.

trade, barter, business, calling, commerce, contract, dealing, employment, enterprise, exchange, job, livelihood, metier, occupation, position, profession, pursuit, sales, speculation, traffic, transaction, undertaking, vocation, work; art, craft, handicraft; bargain, barter, buy, deal, exchange, patronize, purchase, sell, shop, swap.

traffic, see business; trade.

trail, course, footprint, mark, path, scent, trace, track; chase, climb, crawl, creep, drag, draw,

follow, grow, hunt, persist, pull, straggle, track. ANT.—abandon, elude, escape, evade, withdraw.

train, chain, line, procession, retinue, sequel, sequence, series, staff, string, succession, suite; accustom, aim, bend, coach, direct, discipline, drill, educate, enlighten, exercise, guide, habituate, imbue, implant, inculcate, indoctrinate, inform, infuse, innure, instruct, lead, practice, prepare, prime, rear, school, teach.

training, background, coaching, cultivation, development, direction, discipline, drilling, education, exercise, foundation, groundwork, guidance, instruction, learning, nurture, practice, preparation, schooling, study, tutelage.

trait, attribute, characteristic, distinction, earmark, feature, habit, mannerism, mark, nature, peculiarity, property, quality, style, tone, trademark.

traitorous, apostate, disloyal, faithless, false, insidious, mutinous, perfidious, rebellious, recreant, renegade, seditious, treacherous, treasonable. ANT.—constant, devoted, faithful, loyal, steadfast.

tramp, beggar, bum, derelict, hobo, indigent, landloper, nomad, rover, vagabond, vagrant, wanderer; harlot, prostitute.

tranquil, dispassionate, dulcet, imperturbable, sedative, softened, solacing, stifled, unstirred, whispering; see also peaceful, placid, quiet.

tranquility, calmness, hush, quiescence, quietude, rest, serenity; see also peace.

transact, accomplish, achieve, buy, carry on, conclude, conduct, dispatch, enact, execute, exercise, manage, negotiate, operate, perform, perpetrate, sell, settle, treat, work.

transaction, act, action, activity, affair, business, deal, deed, disposal, doing, event, execution, matter, negotiation, occurrence, performance, proceeding, purchase, sale, step, undertaking.

transfer, carry, dispatch, relegate, send, shift, transmit, transplant, transport; assign, confer, convey, dispense, give, grant, impart, sell.

transform, shift, vary, veer; see also convert.

transgression, breach, crime, delinquency, encroachment, error, fault, infraction, infringement, iniquity, injustice, invasion, misbehavior, misdeed, misdemeanor, offense, sin, slip, trespass, vice, violation, wrong. ANT.—benevolence, goodness, honor, innocence, virtue.

transient, flitting, flying, fugitive, short-lived, temporal, vanishing, volatile; see also temporary.

translate, explicate, transform, transmute. see also interpret.

transmit, broadcast, communicate, confer, convey, disclose, dispatch, divulge, forward, impart, inform, notify, pass on, relate, relay, reveal, send, tell, transfer. ANT.—conceal, hide, mask, secrete, shroud, withhold.

transparent, crystalline, thin; guileless, manifest, open, patent; see also lucid.

transport, bring, cart, haul, relocate, transplant; see also convey.

trap, ambush, artifice, bait, blind, intrigue, lure, maneuver, net, noose, pit, pitfall, plot, ruse, snare, stratagem, trick, wile; ambush, deceive, decoy, dupe, ensnare, entrap, fool, lure, mislead, outwit, seduce, swindle, victimize.

trash, debris, dregs, dross, garbage, junk, leavings, litter, rags, refuse, riffraff, rubbish, rubble, scourings, slag, sweepings, trumpery, waste. ANT.—advantages, benefits, goods, perquisites, valuables.

travel, drive, fly, go, journey, move, ramble, roam, rove, sail, tour, walk, wander; circuit, course, cruise, excursion, exodus, expedition, journey, march, migration, peregrination, pilgrimage, ramble, ride, sojourn, tour, trip, wandering.

treacherous, base, deceitful, disloyal, evil, faithless, false, foul, ignominious, inglorious, malevolent, malicious, malign, perfidious, rancorous, recreant, traitorous, treasonable, unfaithful, unreliable, venomous, vile. ANT.—dependable, faithful, honest, reliable, trustworthy.

treason, betrayal, cabal, collusion, conspiracy, deception, dishonesty, disloyalty, intrigue, machination, plot, revolution, sedition, subversion, treachery.

treasure, appreciate, cherish, foster, guard, hold dear, love, nurture, prize, sustain, value. ANT.—abandon, detest, disregard, loathe, reject.

treat, arrange, employ, handle, manage, manipulate, operate, use, utilize; administer, assist, attend, care for, doctor, heal, minister to, nurse, prescribe; amuse, divert, entertain, indulge, satisfy; comment, criticize, discuss, explain, interpret, negotiate, review. ANT.—disarrange, disorder, mismanage, spoil, waste; ignore, neglect, overlook; annoy, bore, irritate, offend, vex; befuddle, cloud, confuse, mystify, perplex.

treaty, agreement, alliance, arrangement, bargain, compact, concordat, covenant, negotiation, pact, protocol, settlement.

tremble, agitate, flutter, jar, jolt, oscillate, pulsate, quail, quake, quaver, quiver, rock, shake, shiver, shudder, sway, teeter, totter, vibrate, waver, wobble.

tremendous, alarming, amazing, appalling, astounding, awesome, colossal, enormous, gigantic, great, huge, immense, monstrous, monumental, prodigious, startling, stupendous, vast. ANT.—insignificant, miniature, tiny, trivial, unimportant.

trespass, encroach, infringe, interfere, interlope, intrude, invade, meddle, penetrate, poach, transgress, violate. ANT.—abandon, evacuate, guard, protect, relinquish, vacate.

trial, analysis, examination, experiment, proof, test; attempt, effort, endeavor, exertion; adversity, affliction, difficulty, hardship, misery, misfortune, ordeal, suffering, tribulation, trouble; arraignment, case, cross-examination, hearing, lawsuit, litigation, prosecution.

tribulation, adversity, affliction, agony, anguish, distress, grief, hardship, misery, oppression, sorrow, suffering, trial, trouble, woe, wretchedness. ANT.—consolation, delight, elation, joy, peace.

trick, antic, artifice, caper, cheat, deceit, deception, device, fraud, guile, hoax, humbug, illusion, imposture, maneuver, ploy, ruse, stratagem, stunt, subterfuge, swindle, wile. ANT.—candor, honesty, justness, openness, sincerity.

tricky, foxy, guileful, insidious, stealthy, subtle; see also covert, shrewd.

trim, clean-cut, compact, harmonious, precise, streamlined, symmetrical; bedeck, embellish, gild; clip, cut, lop, prune, scissor, shave, shear, snip; see also spruce, tidy; embellish.

trip, see journey, travel.

trite, banal, bromidic, common, driveling, dull, hackneyed, humdrum, monotonous, obvious, ordinary, prosaic, shopworn, stale, stereotyped, tedious, uninspiring, uninteresting, wearisome. ANT.—bracing, effectual, novel, original, rousing.

triumph, achievement, ascendancy, celebration, conquest, exultation, gain, joy, jubilation, mastery, ovation, prize, routing, success, trophy, victory; celebrate, exult, flourish, glory, master, prevail, rejoice, succeed, surpass, thrive, win. ANT.—adversity, defeat, downfall, failure, subjugation; default, fail, flounder, lose, quit, succumb.

trivial, beggarly, diminutive, dribbling, frivolous, inappreciable, inconsiderable, insignificant, little, meager, minute, paltry, petty, scanty, small, trifling, unessential, unimportant, useless, valueless, worthless. ANT.—paramount, precious, significant, valuable, vital, weighty.

troop, army, band, company, crowd, group, herd, host, legion, multitude, party, squad, throng, unit.

trophy, award, citation, crown, cup, honor, laurel, loving cup, medal, memento, memorial, palm, prize, reward, token, wreath.

trouble, afflict, agitate, annoy, bother, concern, distract, distress, disturb, inconvenience, irk, irritate, molest, perturb, pester, plague, tease, upset, vex, worry; affliction, ailment, bind, crisis, difficulty, distress, effort, grief, hardship, illness, ordeal, pain, sorrow, woe; annoyance, bother, embarrassment, irritation, torment, worry; disorder, disturbance, hindrance, predicament, plight, problem; care, drudgery, effort, exertion, grind, labor, toil; altercation, argument, controversy, dispute, feud, fight, hostility, wrangle. ANT.—accommodate, console, gratify, please, soothe; delight, ecstasy, happiness, joy, pleasure; comfort, gratification, peace, quietude, repose, satisfaction, security, solace, tranquility.

troublesome, afflictive, annoying, bothersome, burdensome, damaging, difficult, distressing, disturbing, galling, harassing, irksome, tedious, trying, upsetting, wearisome. ANT.—comfortable, facile, gratifying, manageable, smooth.

true, absolute, accurate, actual, authentic, correct, definite, exact, factual, genuine, legal, legitimate, positive, precise, real, uncontradictable, valid, veracious, veritable; constant, dependable, faithful, honest, honorable, incorrupt, just, loyal, reliable, righteous, scrupulous, sincere, steadfast, straight, trustworthy, upright. ANT.—erroneous, false, fictional, imaginary, inaccurate, invalid, mythical; deceitful, disloyal, fickle, perfidious, treacherous.

trunk, body, bole, box, casing, chest, coffer, column, compartment, portmanteau, proboscis, shaft, snout, stalk, stem, stock, thorax, torso.

trust, assurance, belief, certainty, certitude, confidence, conviction, credence, credit, dependence, faith, reassurance, reliance, security; corporation, estate, holding, institution, monopoly; bank, believe, commit, confide, count on, credit, depend upon, entrust, esteem, expect, hope, intrust, presume, rely on. ANT.—disbelief, incredibility, misgiving, skepticism, suspicion; assail, disbelieve, discredit, impugn, suspect.

trustworthy, certain, constant, dependable, faithful, honest, honorable, loyal, reliable, safe, secure, sincere, steadfast, steady, sure, tried, true, truthful, upright, veracious. ANT.—deceitful, perfidious, sneaking, traitorous, underhand, unfaithful.

truth, accuracy, actuality, authenticity, candor, constancy, correctness, exactness, fact, fidelity, honesty, honor, ingenuousness, rectitude, rightness, sincerity, truthfulness, uprightness, veracity, verisimilitude, verity. ANT.—deception, duplicity, evasion, fabrication, falsehood, hypocrisy.

truthful, candid, frank, honest, just, open, reliable, sincere, true, trustworthy, veracious; accurate, correct, exact, factual, legitimate, verifiable. ANT.—deceitful, misleading, sly, venal; fictitious, inaccurate, incorrect, inexact.

try, aim, aspire, attempt, design, endeavor, essay, exert, intend, labor, mean, risk, seek, strive, struggle, tackle, undertake, venture; afflict, test, torment, trouble; adjudicate, adjudge, assay, decide, examine, hear, investigate, judge, probe. ANT.—abandon, decline, ignore, neglect, omit; comfort, console, ease, solace, support; cover, defer, hide, postpone, procrastinate.

trying, aggravating, annoying, bothersome, disquieting, distressing, disturbing, galling, irksome, irritating, perturbing, provoking, troublesome, upsetting, vexatious; arduous, backbreaking, burdensome, demanding, difficult, hard, laborious, painful, strenuous, tedious. ANT.—accommodating, encouraging, gratifying, pleasing, soothing; easy, facile, inconsiderable, manageable, paltry, simple.

tug, drag, draw, haul, labor, lug, pull, strive, struggle, tow, wrench, yank; effort, haul, jerk, pull, rending, strain, towboat, uprooting.

tumble, derange, disarrange, dishevel, disturb, fall, heave, pitch, plunge, roll, rumple, sprawl, stumble, topple, toss, trip, wallow.

tumult, disarray, hubbub, jumble, stir; see also chaos, commotion, disorder.

tune, accord, air, harmony, lyric, melody, song, strain, unison.

turbulent, agitated, blustery, brawling, disturbed, gusty, inclement, insurgent, obstreperous, restless, riotous, roaring, rough, stormy, tempestuous, tumultuous, violent, wild, windy. ANT.—calm, orderly, peaceful, placid, tranquil.

turmoil, disarray, hubbub, jumble, stir, tumult. see also chaos, commotion, disorder.

turn, circle, circulate, gyrate, invert, loop, oscillate, pivot, reel, revolve, rotate, spin, swing, swivel, twirl, twist, wheel, whirl; alter, change, convert, invert, transform, transmute, vary; avert, avoid, deflect, deviate, divert, dodge, sidetrack, swerve, veer; cycle, gyration, pirouette, revolution, rotation; bend, curve, hook, twist; climax, crisis, juncture, shift.

twist, bend, bow, coil, complicate, contort, convolve, crook, curve, deflect, distort, encircle, gnarl, incline, knot, lean, pervert, rotate, screw, squirm, turn, twine, wind, wreathe, wrench, wring, writhe.

type, emblem, figure, letter, mark, sign, symbol; assortment, breed, cast, category, character, class, description, genus, kind, nature, sort, species, stamp, variety; example, exemplar, form, model, mold, pattern, representation, sample.

typical, accustomed, average, common, conventional, customary, figurative, habitual, ideal, illustrative, indicative, middling, modal, model, normal, ordinary, plain, regular, representative, symbolic, usual. ANT.—aberrant, atypical, deviant, distinctive, rare.

tyrannous, authoritative, dictatorial, domineering, imperious, oppressive. see also despotic.

tyrant, autocrat, despot, dictator, inquisitor, martinet, oppressor, persecutor, slavedriver.

U

ugly, deformed, hideous, homely, horrible, offensive, repellent, repulsive, revolting, uncomely, unsightly; bullying, corrupt, disagreeable, disorderly, ill-natured, pugnacious, quarrelsome, rough, rude, spiteful, surly, threatening, tough, vicious, vile. ANT.—beautiful, captivating, dazzling, exquisite, magnificent; agreeable, charming, gentle, inviting, loving, pleasant.

ultimate, absolute, concluding, decisive, eventual, extreme, farthest, final, hindmost, last, latest, maximum, terminal, utmost. ANT.—beginning, first, initial, opening, preliminary, primary.

umpire, arbiter, arbitrator, assessor, censor, compromiser, inspector, judge, mediator, moderator, negotiator, peacemaker, propitiator, referee, settler.

unadulterated, see clean, clear, immaculate.

unanimity, accord, agreement, apposition, compatibility, concert, concord, concordance, conformity, congruence, correspondence, harmony, unity. ANT.—disagreement, discord, dissonance, division, variance.

unassuming, compliant, lowly, plain, simple, submissive; see also modest.

unbecoming, gauche, improper, inappropriate, indecent, indecorous, inept, maladroit, unbefitting, unfit, unseemly, unsuitable. ANT.—appropriate, becoming, fitting, proper, suitable.

unbeliever, see heretic.

unbiased, equitable, fair, honest, impartial, judicial, just, neutral, objective, reasonable, unimpassioned, unjaundiced, unprejudiced. ANT.—biased, partial, prejudiced, slanted, unfair.

uncertain, ambiguous, dim, doubtful, dubious, equivocal, hazy, indefinite, indistinct, insecure, irresolute, obscure, precarious, questionable, unclear, undecided, undetermined, unsettled, unstable, unsure, vacillating, vague. ANT.—certain, definite, explicit, lucid, precise, specific.

uncertainty, see distrust; doubt.

uncivilized, barbarian, crude, discourteous, heathenish, ignorant, low, remorseless, ruthless, uncultured, unenlightened, unrelenting. see also barbarous; cruel.

unclad, see naked.

unclean, abominable, beastly, dirty, fetid, filthy, foul, grimy, impure, nasty, obscene, offensive, repulsive, slimy, smutty, soiled, sooty, squalid, unwashed, vile. ANT.—chaste, clean, immaculate, impeccable, pure.

uncommon, different, exceptional, exotic, extraordinary, infrequent, noteworthy, occasional, odd, rare, remarkable, scarce, singular, strange, unconventional, unique, unusual, unwonted. ANT.—conventional, customary, expected, typical, usual.

uncompromising, confirmed, contumacious, determined, dogged, firm, fixed, headstrong, immovable, inflexible, intractable, intransigent, narrow, obdurate, obstinate, orthodox, pertinacious, rigid, stiff, strict, stubborn, tough, unyielding. ANT.—adaptable, amenable, compliant, flexible, submissive, yielding.

unconcern, see indifference.

unconditional, absolute, carte blanche, certain, complete, definite, entire, full, genuine, positive, thorough, unequivocal, unlimited, unqualified, unrestricted, whole. ANT.—conditional, contingent, limited, partial, qualified.

uncouth, awkward, clumsy, coarse, crass, crude, gawky, graceless, harsh, ill-prepared, raw, rough, rude, rustic, unfinished, ungainly, ungraceful, unpolished, unrefined, vulgar. ANT.—cultivated, elegant, graceful, refined, symmetrical.

uncover, betray, divulge, impart; see also open.

under, below, beneath, following, inferior, subject to, subordinate, underneath. ANT.—above, over, superior.

undergo, feel, encounter, experience, sustain; see also tolerate.

understand, accept, appreciate, experience, gather, hear, interpret, learn, realize, recognize; see also comprehend.

understanding, accordance, agreement, concord, concurrence, harmony, unison; bargain, compact, contract, covenant, pact, stipulation; comprehension, discernment, grasp, insight, intellect, intelligence, knowledge, perception, perspicacity, rationality, reason, reasoning, sapience, wisdom. ANT.—contention, disagreement, discord, dissension, variance, wrangling; fatuity, foolishness, imbecility, incapacity, stupidity.

undertaking, action, attempt, business, effort, endeavor, engagement, enterprise, essay, experiment, performance, project, task, trial, venture, work. ANT.—inertia, laziness, negligence, passivity, shiftlessness.

undisguised, genuine, open, real, true, unadulterated, uncovered; see also sincere.

undivided, intact, integral, unimpaired; see also complete.

undying, see eternal.

unearthly, metaphysical, spiritual, superhuman; see also miraculous.

uneasy, afraid, alarmed, anxious, apprehensive, disturbed, fearful, fidgety, fretful, frightened, harried, irritable, nervous, peevish, petulant, restless, shaky, troubled, uncomfortable, unquiet, wakeful, worried. ANT.—calm, content, peaceful, serene, undismayed.

uneducated, uninformed, unlettered, unschooled; see also ignorant.

unemployed, idle, inactive, inert, jobless, loafing, out of work, unoccupied. ANT.—active, busy, employed, industrious, occupied.

unequal, disparate, ill-matched, inequitable, irregular, lop-sided, odd, one-sided, unbalanced, uneven, unfair, unlike, unparallel. ANT.—balanced, coequal, even, matched, uniform.

uneven, intermittent, irregular, jagged, notched, rough, rugged, spasmodic, unequal, variable. ANT.—even, matched, regular, smooth.

unexpected, amazing, astonishing, immediate, instantaneous, rapid, surprising, unforeseen; see also hasty.

unfair, biased, dishonest, disingenuous, hypocritical, inequitable, one-sided, partial, prejudiced, slanted, unethical, unjust. ANT.—ethical, fair, honest, just, unbiased.

unfavorable, counteractive, disastrous, unlucky; see also hostile.

unfeeling, apathetic, callous, cold, cruel, hard, harsh, inconsiderate, insensate, insensible, merciless, numb, pitiless, rigorous, senseless, severe, stony, unkind, unsympathetic. ANT.—compassionate, empathic, merciful, responsive, sympathetic.

unfit, improper, inappropriate, incapable, incompetent, inexpert, objectionable, unconditioned, unhealthy, unqualified, unsuitable. ANT.—capable, competent, fit, skilled, suitable.

unfold, elaborate, evolve, mature; see also expand.

unfortunate, afflicted, burdened, calamitous, desolate, disastrous, doomed, ill-fated, ill-starred, inexpedient, inopportune, miserable, overwhelmed, ruined, troubled, unhappy, unlucky, unsuccessful, unpropitious, untimely, wretched. ANT.—advantageous, beneficial, fortunate, opportune, propitious.

unhappy, calamitous, dejected, despondent, disconsolate, dismal, distressed, dolorous, gloomy, grievous, heartsick, miserable, mournful, sad, sorrowful, troubled, unfortunate, woeful, wretched. ANT.—contented, delighted, exhilarated, gratified, peaceful, satisfied.

uniform, agreeable, agreeing, alike, comformable, consistent, constant, customary, equable, equal, even, harmonious, homogenous, homologous, methodical, natural, normal, orderly, ordinary, periodical, proportionate, regular, stable, steady, symmetrical, systematic, unchanging, undeviating, undiversified, unvaried, unvarying. ANT.—amorphous, disordered, distorted, diversified, erratic, irregular, unsystematic.

unify, ally, amalgamate, blend, combine, concentrate, conjoin, connect, consolidate, entwine, join, merge, mix, organize, rally, solidify, strengthen, unite. ANT.—disperse, disrupt, divide, separate, split.

unimportant, commonplace, immaterial, incidental, inconsequential, inferior, irrelevant, mediocre, nugatory, ordinary, picayune, poor, slight; see also trivial.

uninformed, see ignorant.

unintelligible, cloudy, dim, dusky, indistinct, vague; see also mysterious.

uninteresting, burdensome, dreary, sluggish; see also monotonous.

union, amalgamation, annexation, attachment, blending, combination, commixture, concurrence, conjunction, connection, consolidation, coupling, fusion, incorporation, joining, junction, meeting, merging, mingling, solidarity, symbiosis, unification, uniting; affinity, agreement, concord, cooperation, harmony, unanimity, unison, unity; alliance, association, coalition, concert, confederacy, federation, league, marriage, organization. ANT.—disconnection, dispersion, division, separation; clash, conflict, disagreement, discordance, rebellion; dissociation, divorce, segregation, schism.

unique, choice, different, distinctive, exceptional, individual, matchless, novel, one, only, original, peculiar, rare, remarkable, single, singular, sole, solitary, uncommon, unequaled, unlike, unmatched, unparalleled, unprecedented, unrivaled, unusual. ANT.—commonplace, conventional, familiar, ordinary, prevailing.

unite, affiliate, ally, amalgamate, annex, associate, attach, blend, coalesce, combine, concur, confederate, conjoin, connect, consolidate, cooperate, couple, embody, embrace, entwine, fuse, join, link, meet, merge, mingle, mix, solidify, strengthen, unify. ANT.—disconnect, divide, part, separate, sever.

unity, agreement, concert, concord, constancy, continuity, harmony, oneness, singleness, solidarity, unification, uniformity, union. ANT.—discord, dissimilarity, diversity, multiplicity, variety.

universal, all, all-embracing, boundless, catholic, complete, comprehensive, cosmic, cosmopolitan, ecumenical, entire, exhaustive, generic, pandemic, prevailing, sweeping, total, unlimited, whole, world-wide. ANT.—distinctive, individual, partial, singular, unique.

universe, cosmos, creation, earth, firmament, galaxy, heavens, macrocosm, nature, world.

unlawful, see illegal.

unlike, divergent, incongruous, miscellaneous, sundry, variant; see also contrary, different.

unlimited, limitless, unconfined, unconstrained, undefined, unrestrained, unrestricted; see also infinite.

unlocked, ajar, disengaged, exposed, open, unclosed, unlatched; accessible, clear, free, passable, unobstructed. ANT.—closed, locked, sealed, shut; barred, blocked, impassable, inaccessible, obstructed, unobtainable.

unmistakable, see obvious.

unpretentious, candid, frank, modest, open, plain, simple, sincere, unobtrusive, unostentatious, unpretending. ANT.—deceitful, false, hypocritical, ostentatious, pompous.

unqualified, absolute, certain, conclusive, downright, indisputable, outright, positive, unconditional, unquestionable, unrestricted, utter; inappropriate, incapable, incompetent, ineligible, inept, inexperienced, unfit, unprepared. ANT.—conditional, contingent, dependent, qualified, questionable, uncertain; capable, competent, eligible, experienced, qualified.

unreasonable, absurd, fatuous, foolish, illogical, implausible, inconsistent, irrational, ludicrous, mindless, nonsensical, preposterous, ridiculous, self-contradictory, senseless, silly, stupid, untenable. ANT.—consistent, judicious, rational, reasonable, sensible, wise.

unrestricted, accessible, accorded, allowable, available, clear, exposed, free, open, passable, permitted, public, sanctioned, unobstructed, welcoming. ANT.—denied, forbidden, private, prohibited, refused.

unruly, disobedient, fractious, headstrong, lawless, mutinous, obstreperous, rebellious, recalcitrant, refractory, stubborn, ungovernable, violent, wanton, willful. ANT.—docile, law-abiding, manageable, obedient, tractable.

unsafe, critical, dangerous, hazardous, imperiled, insecure, menacing, perilous, precarious, risky, threatening, treacherous, unreliable, unstable. ANT.—firm, harmless, protected, safe, secure.

unscrupulous, dishonorable, reckless, ruthless, unconscientious, unprincipled, unrestrained; see also dishonest.

unseemly, boorish, brutish, clownish, depraved, disgraceful, disorderly, dissolute, dowdy, gross, ill-advised, immoral, improper, imprudent, inappropriate, indecorous, inept, inexpedient, inopportune, objectionable, rowdy, slovenly, unbecoming, unfit, ungraceful, unkempt, unpolished, unsightly, unsuitable, vulgar, worthless. ANT.—commendable, cultivated, fitting, polished, proper, suave.

unselfish, see generous.

unsettled, adrift, apprehensive, changeable, fickle, inconstant, nervous, perturbed, restless, stirred, troubled, unhinged, unnerved, unstable, unsteady, vacillating, wavering; uninhabited, wild; outstanding, owing, unpaid; foul, muddy, roily, turbid. ANT.—calm, certain, constant, peaceful, secure; inhabited, settled; cleared, paid, solvent; clarified, immaculate, pure, sparkling, untainted.

unskilled, awkward, clumsy, ignorant, ill-qualified, incompetent, inept, inexperienced, maladroit, rusty, unfit, unpracticed. ANT.—accomplished, competent, efficient, expert, trained.

unsophisticated, artless, candid, frank, fresh, genuine, guileless, ignorant, ingenuous, innocent, naive, natural, open, pure, real, simple, true, unaffected, undesigning, unspoiled, unstudied, unvitiated. ANT.—experienced, guileful, hard, initiated, sophisticated, worldly.

unstable, see fickle.

unswerving, fast, inflexible, solid, unyielding; see also stable.

unusual, aberrant, abnormal, anomalous, atypical, awesome, capricious, curious, devious, distinguished, eccentric, exceptional, extraordinary, incredible, irregular, odd, rare, strange, uncommon, unique, unnatural, unparalleled, variable. ANT.—common, normal, ordinary, regular, usual.

unyielding, see unswerving.

upbraid, blame, lecture, reprehend, vituperate; see also rebuke.

uphold, see maintain.

upright, direct, right, undeviating, unswerving; erect, standing, straight, unbent, vertical; conscientious, ethical, fair, faithful, honest, honorable, incorruptible, just, moral, scrupulous, square, straightforward, true, trustworthy, virtuous. ANT.—deviating, indirect, swerving; bent, horizontal, prone; corruptible, crooked, dishonest, fraudulent, immoral, lax.

upset, disturb, haunt, inconvenience, perplex, worry; see also pester.

urbane, considerate, well-mannered; see also polite.

urge, appetite, aspiration, hungering, lust; induce, prevail upon, win over; see also desire; persuade.

urgency, importance, need, seriousness; see also emergency.

urgent, absorbing, breathless, chief, cogent, compelling, critical, crucial, demanded, essential, exigent, grave, impelling, imperative, important, importunate, insistent, instant, momentous, necessary, pressing, principal, required, salient, serious, vital, weighty. ANT.—common, insignificant, petty, trivial, unessential, uneventful.

use, apply, avail, employ, exploit, handle, manage, manipulate, operate, ply, utilize, wield; exercise, exert, practice, work; consume, exhaust, expend; accustom, familiarize, habituate, inure; application, employment, service, utilization; necessity, need; advantage, usefulness; method, technique, usage; see also habit.

useful, advantageous, applicable, beneficial, gainful, good, helpful, practical, pragmatic, profitable, remunerative, salutory, serviceable, suitable, utilitarian, valuable, wholesome. ANT.—deleterious, destructive, detrimental, harmful, noxious.

usefulness, adaptability, advantage, application, convenience, helpfulness, practicality, utility, versatility; see also merit.

useless, abortive, empty, fruitless, futile, idle, inadequate, ineffective, ineffectual, pointless, unavailing, unproductive, unserviceable, vain, valueless, vapid, worthless. ANT.—beneficial, effective, potent, profitable, valuable.

usual, accustomed, common, commonplace, conventional, current, customary, everyday, expected, familiar, frequent, general, habitual, normal, ordinary, prevailing, prevalent, prosaic, recognized, regular, stereotyped. ANT.—abnormal, exceptional, extraordinary, rare, unconventional.

utensil, apparatus, appliance, device, equipment, implement, instrument, medium, tool, vehicle, ware.

utility, adequacy, advantage, avail, benefit, convenience, efficacy, efficiency, expediency, favor, productiveness, profit, service, serviceableness, usefulness, utilitarianism, value, worth. ANT.—disadvantage, futility, inefficacy, uselessness, worthlessness.

utilize, adopt, apply, appropriate, avail, employ, exercise, exert, exploit, occupy, practice, use. ANT.—discard, discharge, expel, refuse, reject.

utmost, absolute, chief, extreme, farthest, greatest, highest, last, main, maximum, most, ultimate, unqualified, uttermost. ANT.—closest, least, merest, minimum, nearest.

utopian, chimerical, exemplary, fabulous, fancied, fantastic, faultless, ideal, illusory, imaginary, perfect, supreme, unreal, visionary. ANT.—actual, faulty, imperfect, substantial, tangible, visible.

utter, complete, entire, finished, full, perfect, thorough, total, whole; consummate, excellent, ideal, pure, superlative, supreme; absolute, downright, sheer, unconditional, unqualified, unrestricted, wholehearted; acclaim, air, announce, articulate, assert, claim, declare, disclose, divulge, emit, enunciate, express, inform, proclaim, pronounce, speak, talk, tell, vocalize, voice, whisper. ANT.—imperfect, incomplete, lacking, partial, unfinished; inferior, lesser, negligible, poor; conditional, limited, qualified, restricted; conceal, cover, hide, mask, withhold.

V

vacant, abandoned, bare, barren, blank, depleted, deserted, empty, hollow, idle, tenantless, unfilled, uninhabited, unoccupied, untenanted, unused, vacuous, void; dreaming, empty-headed, foolish, inane, silly, thoughtless. ANT.—filled, full, inhabited, occupied, overflowing; cogitative, contemplative, meditative, reflective, thoughtful, wise.

vacate, abandon, abdicate, abjure, depart, desert, empty, evacuate, forsake, leave, quit, relinquish, resign, surrender, waive. ANT.—assume, maintain, remain, stay, support.

vacillate, change, oscillate, undulate, vary; see also hesitate.

vacillation, changeableness, faltering, fluctuation, hesitation, inconstancy, indecision, irresolution, oscillation, reeling, rocking, swaying, uncertainty, unsteadiness, wavering. ANT.—certainty, constancy, dependability, firmness.

vagrant, beggar, bum, hobo, idler, loafer, rambler, rogue, rover, straggler, tramp, truant, vagabond, wanderer; changeable, digressive, discursive, divergent, erratic, fickle, fluctuating, homeless, idle, inconstant, irresolute, itinerant, nomadic, peripatetic, ranging, roaming, roving, straying, traveling, unsettled, unstable, unsteady, wandering. ANT.—gentleman, laborer, toiler, worker, workman; anchored, established, fixed, rooted, stable.

vague, cryptic, dark, doubtful, dubious, enigmatic, formless, imprecise, mysterious, nebulous, questionable, unsure, visionary; see also indefinite.

vain, abortive, bootless, delusive, empty, fleeting, frivolous, fruitless, futile, hollow, idle, ineffective, ineffectual, nugatory, pointless, shadowy, trifling, trivial, unavailing, unprofitable, unsatisfactory, useless, valueless, vapid, visionary, worthless; arrogant, conceited, egotistical, inflated, ostentatious, proud, showy, vainglorious. ANT.—advantageous, effective, potent, profitable, valuable; demure, genuine, humble, meek, modest, unpretentious.

valiant, adventurous, assertive, audacious, bold, brave, chivalrous, courageous, daring, dauntless, fearless, gallant, heroic, indomitable, intrepid, magnanimous, manly, plucky, puissant, spirited, strong-willed, unafraid, undismayed, unflinching, unshrinking, valorous, venturesome, vigorous. ANT.—cowardly, craven, fearful, timid, timorous, weak.

valid, accurate, actual, authentic, binding, cogent, conclusive, convincing, definite, effective, efficacious, efficient, factual, forceful, genuine, legal, legitimate, logical, operative, powerful, real, solid, sound, strong, substantial, sufficient, telling, tested, true, weighty. ANT.—counterfeit, erroneous, fallacious, invalid, spurious.

valor, chivalry, manliness, prowess, spiritedness; see also courage.

valuable, costly, expensive, high-priced, rare; dear, esteemed, precious, worthy; profitable, serviceable, useful. ANT.—cheap, common, unmarketable; abhorred, disliked, disrespectable, worthless; profitless, useless.

value, appreciate, cherish, esteem, hold dear, prize, treasure; appraise, assess, compute, estimate, figure, rate; advantage, appreciation, consideration, esteem, estimation, excellence, importance, merit, price, profit, quality, significance, usefulness, utility, valuation, virtue, worth, worthiness. ANT.—abandon, despise, ignore, neglect, overlook, reject; inexpedience, inutility, unfitness, uselessness, worthlessness.

vandalism, barbarism, burning, damage, destruction, looting, piracy, spoliation, wasting, wrecking. ANT.—care, preservation, protection, repair, replacement.

vanish, cease, depart, die, disappear, dissolve, evaporate, fade, go away, sink. ANT.—appear, emerge, reappear.

vanity, affectation, arrogance, conceit, conceitedness, display, egotism, ostentation, pretension, self-applause, self-glorification, selfishness, self-laudation, self-love, show, vainglory. ANT.—bashfulness, diffidence, humility, modesty, unobtrusiveness.

vanquish, beat, outwit, suppress; see also conquer.

vapid, banal, bland, commonplace, dry, dull, feeble, flat, hackneyed, inane, insipid, lifeless, prosaic, spiritless, tasteless, trite, uninteresting. ANT.—bright, fresh, original, pungent, stimulating, striking.

vapor, breath, cloud, condensation, effluvium, emanation, exhalation, fog, fume, gas, haze, mist, smoke, smog, spray, steam.

variable, see fickle.

variation, aberration, alteration, change, contrariety, contrast, departure, deviation, difference, disagreement, discord, discrepancy, disparity, dissent, dissidence, dissimilarity, dissimilitude, distinction, diversity, fluctuation, heterogeneity, incongruity, inconsistency, innovation, modification, mutation, noncomformity, oscillation, variety, vicissitude. ANT.—agreement, congruity, homogeneity, permanence, stability, uniformity.

variety, change, difference, dissimilarity, diversification, diversity, heterogeneity, medley, miscellany, mixture, multifariousness, variance; array, assortment, brand, breed, category, class, division, family, genus, grade, kind, race, rank, sort, species, stock, strain, subspecies, tribe, type. ANT.—homogeneity, likeness, monotony, sameness, uniformity, unity.

various, assorted, different, disparate, divergent, divers, diverse, manifold, many, miscellaneous, numerous, several, sundry. ANT.—alike, congruous, identical, same, uniform.

vary, exchange, substitute; shift, transfigure, veer; see also modify.

vast, ample, big, capacious, extensive, great, large; see also colossal.

vault, see jump.

vehement, ardent, burning, eager, enthusiastic, excitable, fervent, fervid, fiery, glowing, hot, impetuous, intense, irascible, passionate. ANT.—apathetic, calm, cool, indifferent, lukewarm.

veil, cloak, clothe, curtain, envelop, guard; see also conceal.

velocity, alacrity, celerity, impetus, pace, quickness, rapidity, speed, swiftness.

venerable, adored, aged, ancient, antiquated, antique, archaic, elderly, erudite, esteemed, honored, old, patriarchal, respected, revered, superannuated, time-worn, venerated, worshipped. ANT.—callow, immature, inexperienced, modern, new.

venerate, admire, adore, appreciate, approve, cherish, esteem, honor, regard, respect, revere, worship. ANT.—abhor, despise, dislike, loathe, scorn.

vengeance, reparation, reprisal, requital, spitefulness; see also revenge.

venom, acerbity, bitterness, contempt, enmity, gall, hate, malevolence, malice, malignity, poison, rancor, resentment, virulence. ANT.—benevolence, charity, fellowship, love, warmheartedness.

vent, belch, breathe, discharge, eject, emanate, emit, expel, explode, shoot, spurt, ventilate; airhole, crenel, emission, escape, hole, inlet, loophole, mouth, nostril, opening, orifice, outlet, overflow, passage, plug, spiracle, spout, tap, valve.

ventilate, aerate, air, circulate air, cool, explain, express, fan, freshen, open, oxygenate, purify, refresh, vent.

venture, adventure, attempt, business, chance, dare, enterprise, experiment, gamble, hazard, investment, peril, project, risk, speculation, stake, trial, undertaking, work; advance, assay, attempt, bet, brave, dare, experiment, gamble, grope, hazard, invest, risk, speculate, try, wager.

veracity, accuracy, candor, credibility, exactitude, fidelity, frankness, honesty, probity, reality, sincerity, truth, truthfulness. ANT.—chicanery, deception, duplicity, falsehood, misrepresentation.

verbal, announced, communicated, expressed, lingual, literal, nuncupative, oral, sounded, spoken, told, unwritten, uttered, vocal, voiced. ANT.—documentary, printed, unspoken, written.

verbose, chattering, chatty, fluent, garrulous, long-winded, loquacious, redundant, talkative, verbal, wordy. ANT.—concise, laconic, silent, stammering, taciturn, uncommunicative.

verdict, adjudication, arbitrament, conclusion, decision, decree, determination, finding, judgment, result.

verge, border, boundary, brim, brink, confine, edge, end, extreme, limit, lip, margin, rim, skirt. ANT.—body, bulk, center, inside.

verification, affirmation, attestation, authentication, confirmation, corroboration, demonstration, evidence, proof, recognition, support, testimony. ANT.—contradiction, denial, failure, fallacy, invalidity.

verify, acknowledge, affirm, approve, assure, attest, authenticate, certify, corroborate, confirm, determine, establish, fix, prove, ratify, sanction, settle, strengthen, substantiate, validate. ANT.—contradict, deny, disprove, invalidate, repudiate.

versed, acquainted, aware, cognizant, conversant, familiar, intimate, knowing, proficient, skilled. ANT.—unaware, unfamiliar, unknowing.

versatile, adaptable, apt, changeable, many-sided, movable, ready, variable. ANT.—awkward, limited, unadaptable, unchanging.

vertical, erect, perpendicular, plumb, standing, straight, upright. ANT.—flat, horizontal, inclined, oblique, prone, supine.

vestige, mark, remainder, remains, remnant, residue, scrap, sign, trace.

vex, aggravate, embitter, inflame; see also irritate.

vibrate, agitate, flicker, fluctuate, flutter, jar, jolt, oscillate, pulsate, quake, quaver, quiver, rock, shake, shiver, shudder, sway, swing, totter, tremble, undulate, wave, waver.

vice, blemish, blot, carnality, debauchery, defect, excess, fault, impropriety, impurity, iniquity, offense, perversity, sin, transgression, ungodliness; see also evil.

vicinity, district, domain, environment, environs, locality, neighborhood, realm, region, sector, territory; adjacency, nearness, proximity. ANT.—outskirts; distance, remoteness.

vicious, bad, base, corrupt, debased, degenerate, demoralized, depraved, destructive, evil, harmful, hurtful, malignant, obnoxious, pernicious, profligate, reprehensible, sinful, unruly, vile, virulent, wicked. ANT.—admirable, exemplary, honorable, noble, upright, virtuous.

victim, dupe, gull, martyr, prey, puppet, quarry, sacrifice, scapegoat, sufferer, wretch. ANT.—culprit, evil-doer, felon, swindler.

victor, champion, conqueror, hero, master, vanquisher, winner. ANT.—failure, loser, underdog, vanquished, victim.

victory, achievement, ascendancy, conquest, defeating, mastery, overcoming, subjugation, success, superiority, supremacy, triumph, win, winning. ANT.—collapse, defeat, failure, frustration, overthrow.

view, aim, belief, conception, examination, glance, glimpse, goal, impression, inspection, judgment, look, object, observation, opinion, outlook, panorama, perspective, picture, prospect, range, regard, scene, sight, survey, theory, vision, vista; behold, consider, discern, examine, eye, gaze, glance, inspect, look, observe, regard, scan, scrutinize, see, stare, survey, watch, witness. ANT.—avert, disregard, ignore, miss, overlook, sidetrack.

viewpoint, angle, aspect, attitude, disposition, light, outlook, perspective, pose, position, posture, slant, stand, standpoint.

vigilant, alert, attentive, careful, cautious, circumspect, guarded, heedful, observant, wakeful, wary, watchful, wide-awake. ANT.—careless, foolhardy, negligent, rash, reckless.

vigor, endurance, energy, force, fortitude, hardihood, health, liveliness, lustiness, spirit, strength, verge, virility, vitality, well-being, zeal. ANT.—exhaustion, languor, lassitude, listlessness.

vigorous, active, animated, blithe, brisk, energetic, flourishing, forceful, frolicsome, healthy, lively, lusty, powerful, robust, spirited, sprightly, strenuous, strong, virile, vital, vivacious. ANT.—debilitated, feeble, frail, inactive, lethargic.

vile, abject, base, brutish, cheap, contemptible, debased, depraved, despicable, disgusting, evil, foul, gross, ignoble, impure, iniquitous, loathsome, low, mean, obscene, odious, repulsive, revolting, sinful, sordid, ugly, vicious, vulgar, wicked, worthless, wretched. ANT.—attractive, decent, elevated, honorable, laudable, valuable.

vilify, abuse, asperse, ill-use, revile, scandalize; see also malign.

villainous, bad, base, evil, unsound, unwholesome; see also deleterious, iniquitous.

vindicate, advocate, assert, avenge, defend, excuse, maintain, support, uphold; see also exonerate.

vindictive, avenging, grudgeful, implacable, malevolent, malicious, rancorous, resentful, unforgiving, vengeful. ANT.—conciliatory, excusing, forgiving, placable.

violate, break, disobey, disregard, encroach, infringe, invade, transgress; debauch, defile, deflower, desecrate, dishonor, outrage, pollute, profane, rape, ravish.

violence, assault, fury, intensity, outrage, vehemence, violation, wildness; see also force.

violent, angry, convulsive, fierce, fiery, frantic, frenzied, fuming, furious, hysterical, obstreperous, passionate, raging, rampant, raving, riotous, savage, turbulent, ungovernable, uproarious, vehement, wild; acute, extreme, forceful, great, intense, mighty, potent, powerful, severe, strong. ANT.—composed, kind, pacific, peaceful, tranquil, unruffled; feeble, insignificant, mild, moderate, weak.

virgin, chaste, clean, immaculate, innocent, modest, pure, spotless, stainless, unadulterated, unblemished, undefiled, unsullied, untainted, virginal; first, fresh, genuine, natural, new, original, undisturbed, untamed, untouched. ANT.—corrupt, defiled, shameless; foul, poisoned, polluted, soiled.

virile, hardy, lusty, vigorous; see also masculine.

virtue, chastity, decency, goodness, honesty, honor, impeccability, innocence, integrity, morality, probity, prudence, purity, rectitude, sanctity, temperance, uprightness, virginity; effectiveness, efficacy, force, fortitude, power, strength; distinction, excellence, merit, superiority, value, worth. ANT.—corruption, depravity, dishonor, vileness, wickedness; debility, enervation, infirmity, weakness; deficiency, inferiority, inutility, uselessness, worthlessness.

virtuous, decent, honorable, just, right, scrupulous; see also chaste, ethical.

visible, see evident, fair, manifest.

vision, apparition, appearance, chimera, conception, daydream, discernment, dream, fancy, ghost, hallucination, hope, illusion, image, manifestation, mirage, perception, phantasm, phantom, prophecy, revelation, shadow, sight, specter. ANT.—actuality, blindness, corporality, fact, substantiality, verity.

visionary, chimerical, delusory, dreamy, fancied, fanciful, ideal, illusory, imaginary, imaginative, romantic, unreal, utopian. ANT.—actual, material, real, substantial.

vital, alive, animate, existing, living; basic, cardinal, essential, fundamental, important, indispensable, necessary, paramount, requisite, urgent. ANT.—dead, inanimate, lifeless; dispensable, excessive, insignificant, trivial, unimportant.

vitality, being, existence, life; animation, ardor, buoyancy, energy, intensity, liveliness, spirit, spunk, verve, vigor, vim, vivacity. ANT.—death, demise, extinction; apathy, lassitude, lethargy, passivity, torpor.

vitiate, abase, adulterate, alloy, annul, contaminate, corrupt, damage, debase, defile, degrade, deprave, depress, deteriorate, humiliate, impair, infect, injure, lower, nullify, pervert, poison, pollute, ruin, spoil, void. ANT.—clean, enhance, improve, purify, revive, vitalize.

vivid, animated, bright, brilliant, clear, expressive, fresh, graphic, intense, lifelike, lively, lucid, pictorial, picturesque, realistic, sprightly, striking, strong, telling, vibrant. ANT.—cloudy, dreary, dull, vague, weak.

vocal, announced, articulate, communicated, expressed, expressive, fluent, musical, oral, spoken, sung, uttered, verbal, vocalized, voiced, voluble. ANT.—printed, quiet, silent, unspoken, written.

vocation, art, business, calling, commerce, employment, engagement, enterprise, field, job, lifework, mission, occupation, office, position, profession, pursuit, role, situation, trade, trading, undertaking, work. ANT.—avocation, diversion, entertainment, hobby, pastime.

voice, accent, articulation, call, cry, enunciation, expression, intonation, noise, pronunciation, sound, speech, tongue, utterance, vocalization; choice, election, suffrage, vote; announce, assert, cry, declaim, declare, express, say, sound, speak, talk, tell, utter.

void, blank, lacking; see also empty.

volatile, airy, buoyant, changeable, effervescent, evaporable, fleeting, gaseous, inconstant, irresolute, light, resilient, vacillating, vaporous, vapory, wavering, weak; active, animated, blithe, cheerful, elated, jocund, lively, playful, vivacious. ANT.—durable, heavy, massive, soluble, weighty; dejected, despondent, hopeless, melancholy, sad.

volition, choice, decision, determination, election, intention, resolution, resolve, selection, will. ANT.—coercion, compulsion, force, persuasion, pressure.

volume, capability, power, talent; amount, extent, mass, size; book, edition, printed document, publication; see also capacity.

voluntary, deliberate, elective, free, intentional, self-determining, uncoerced, unforced, volitional, willful, willing. ANT.—compulsory, enforced, forced, instinctive, involuntary, mandatory, required.

volunteer, come forward, enlist, extend, sacrifice, submit oneself; see also offer.

vouch, affirm, assert, attest, avow, certify, confirm, declare, depose, guarantee, support, swear, testify, uphold, warrant. ANT.—abnegate, controvert, deny, disavow, repudiate.

vow, oath, pledge, promise; affirm, assert, certify, consecrate, dedicate, devote, pledge, promise, swear.

vulgar, abusive, base, brutish, cheap, coarse, common, crass, disgusting, general, gross, ignorant, ill-bred, indecent, inelegant, low, obscene, odious, offensive, plebeian, popular, profane, ribald, rough, rowdy, rude, tawdry, uncouth, uncultured, unpolished, unrefined. ANT.—aristocratic, charming, cultured, elegant, polished, refined.

vulnerable, assailable, defenseless, exposed, unprotected, unsafe; see also insecure.

W

wager, bet, chance, gage, gamble, hazard, play, punt, risk, sport, stake; betting, gambling, risk, speculation.

wages, compensation, earnings, fee, income, pay, payment, recompense, remuneration, salary, stipend. ANT.—donation, gift, gratuity.

wait, abide, bide, delay, linger, remain, rest, stay, tarry; await, expect, watch; attend, minister, serve. ANT.—act, depart, hasten, leave, proceed; disregard, neglect, reject; hamper, hinder, impede, oppose.

waive, see renounce.

wake, activate, animate, arouse, awake, awaken, call, enkindle, excite, kindle, prod, revive, rouse, stimulate, stir, wake.

wallow, flounder, grovel, immerse, revel, roll, toss, welter.

wander, deviate, digress, diverge, drift, err, journey, meander, peregrinate, ramble, range, roam, rove, saunter, straggle, stray, stroll, tour, traipse, travel, traverse. ANT.—halt, pause, remain, settle, stay.

want, aspire, covet, crave, desire, long for, wish; be destitute, lack, need, require, suffer privation; dearth, deficiency, depletion, destitution, exigency, inadequacy, indigence, insufficiency, lack, necessity, need, neediness, pauperism, penury, poverty, privation, scarcity, starvation. ANT.—abhor, detest, dislike; enjoy, have, own, possess; abundance, affluence, opulence, riches, wealth.

ward, care, charge, custody, dependent, guardianship, minor, protection; district, division, precinct, quarter, section; defend, guard, keep, parry, protect, safeguard, watch.

warfare, armed struggle, battle, combat, conflict, contest, fighting, hostilities, military operations, mobilization. ANT.—accord, armistice, harmony, peace, truce.

wariness, see heed.

warlike, see hostile.

warm, affable, affectionate, ardent, compassionate, cordial, earnest, empathic, enthusiastic, fervent, friendly, genial, gracious, heartfelt, hearty, loving, responsive, sincere, sociable, sympathetic, tender, warmhearted; feverish, flushed, heated, lukewarm, melting, mild, sunny, temperate, tepid; comfortable, cozy, secure, sheltered, snug; chafe, foment, heat, incite, melt, thaw. ANT.—aloof, cold, detached, diffident, taciturn; cold, cool, freezing, frosty, icy; disturbed, exposed, insecure, uncomfortable, uneasy; calm, chill, freeze, soothe, temper.

warn, admonish, caution, counsel, forebode, forewarn, signal, summon; see also notify.

warning, admonition, advice, alarm, augury, caution, indication, information, notice, omen, portent, prediction, premonition, sign, signal, summons, threat.

wary, attentive, alert, awake, aware, careful, cautious, circumspect, discreet, guarded, heedful, mindful, observant, provident, scrupulous, thoughtful, vigilant, watchful. ANT.—foolhardy, impulsive, negligent, precipitate, rash.

wash, bathe, clean, cleanse, douse, immerse, launder, lave, rinse, scour, scrub, soak, soap, wet, wipe. ANT.—dirty, foul, soil, stain.

waste, abandoned, bare, bleak, deserted, desolate, discarded, empty, forlorn, forsaken, futile, lonely, pointless, solitary, uninhabited, useless, wild, worthless; abuse, consume, dissipate, exhaust, lavish, misapply, misspend, misuse, scatter, spend, squander, wear out; decay, diminish, dwindle, pine, wither; corrode, damage, despoil, destroy, devastate, pillage, plunder, ravage, ruin, sack, strip. ANT.—attended, cultivated, fertile, inhabited, productive; hoard, preserve, redeem, retain, save; grow, prosper, thrive, triumph; defend, guard, harbor, protect, shield.

wasteful, careless, destructive, dissipated, extravagant, improvident, lavish, prodigal, profligate, profuse, reckless, ruinous, squandering, thriftless, unthrifty, wild. ANT.—conservative, economical, hoarding, mercenary, thrifty.

watch, attend, behold, contemplate, descry, discern, distinguish, espy, follow, glimpse, guard, inspect, mark, mind, notice, observe, perceive, regard, scan, scrutinize, see, view, wait, witness.

watchful, alert, attentive, careful, cautious, circumspect, guarded, heedful, observant, prudent, vigilant, wakeful, wary, watchful, wideawake. ANT.—careless, inattentive, lax, neglectful, oblivious.

water, bathe, deluge, dilute, douse, drench, flood, immerse, irrigate, moisten, soak, sprinkle, steep, wash, wet. ANT.—dehydrate, drain, dry, parch, sear.

wave, billow, breaker, ripple, roller, surge, swell, undulation; beckon, flap, flutter, oscillate, shake, signal, stir, sway, swing.

waver, boggle, deliberate, dillydally, equivocate, falter, flicker, fluctuate, flutter, hesitate, oscillate, quiver, reel, shake, totter, tremble, twitch, vacillate, vibrate.

wavering, see fickle.

way, allay, approach, artery, avenue, channel, course, driveway, entrance, gateway, highway, lane, pass, passage, path, pathway, road, roadway, route, street, thoroughfare, track, trail, walk; design, fashion, form, habit, manner, means, method, mode, plan, practice, procedure, process, style, system.

weak, bending, delicate, faint, fragile, frail, pliant, soft, tender, yielding; debilitated, decrepit, enervated, exhausted, feeble, flaccid, impotent, infirm, nervous, shaky, wasted, worn; illogical, inadequate, ineffective, ineffectual, lame, poor, vague; assailable, defenseless, exposed, helpless, powerless, unguarded, unsubstantial, vulnerable. ANT.—rigid, strong, unyielding; animated, healthy, robust, vigorous; cogent, effective, efficacious, persuasive, potent; defended, protected, safe, secure, unthreatened.

weaken, attenuate, cramp, cripple, debilitate, devitalize, dilute, diminish, enervate, enfeeble, exhaust, impair, incapacitate, reduce, relax, sap, thin, undermine. ANT.—brace, energize, fortify, invigorate, strengthen.

weakness, see disability.

wealth, abundance, affluence, assets, capital, fortune, luxury, means, money, opulence, plenty, possessions, prosperity, riches, resources, securities, stock, substance, treasure. ANT.—indigence, need, poverty, privation, want.

wear, abrade, bear, carry, consume, diminish, display, endure, erode, impair, use, waste; service, use, utilization.

weariness, annoyance, disgust, ennui, exhaustion, faintness, fatigue, languor, lassitude, lethargy, prostration, tedium, tiredness. ANT.—alertness, amusement, energy, strength, vim.

weary, bored, exhausted, faint, fatigued, jaded, spent, tired, wearied, worn; anger, annoy, bore, bother, deject, depress, discourage, disgust, dishearten, dispirit, displease, distress, enfeeble, exhaust, fatigue, grieve, irk, irritate, jade, overburden, overtax, pain, prostrate, sadden, strain, tire, vex. ANT.—animated, fresh, invigorated, refreshed, rested; arouse, brace, energize, enliven, revive, strengthen.

weather, bear, bleach, discolor, disintegrate, dry, endure, expand, fade, overcome, resist, rot, shrink, split, stand, sustain, tan, toughen.

weave, braid, compose, construct, crochet, design, fabricate, form, imagine, intertwine, knit, lace, mat, twist.

wedding, see marriage.

weigh, consider, examine, heed, study; see also ponder.

weight, ballast, burden, contents, density, gravity, heaviness, load, mass, tonnage; pressure; authority, consequence, domination, emphasis, import, importance, influence, moment, power, seriousness, significance, stress, sway, value. ANT.—airiness, buoyancy, levity, lightness; insignificance, pettiness, smallness, triviality, worthlessness.

weird, curious, eerie, ghostly, mysterious, odd, peculiar, spooky, strange, supernatural, uncanny, unearthly, wild. ANT.—common, normal, ordinary, regular, usual.

welcome, accept, address, admit, embrace, entertain, greet, hail, hug, receive, recognize, salute, shelter, take in. ANT.—discharge, ignore, reject, snub, turn away.

well, adequately, admirably, competently, expertly, extremely, favorably, satisfactorily, strongly, suitably; see also healthy.

well-being, contentment, delight, felicity, fortune, gladness, happiness, health, pleasure, prosperity, satisfaction, serenity, welfare, wholeness.

ANT.—depression, distress, illness, suffering, trouble.

well-bred, see polite.

well-known, see distinguished.

wheel, bicycle, circle, disk, roller; eddy, gyrate, pirouette, revolve, roll, rotate, spin, swirl, transport, turn, twist, veer, whirl, wind.

whim, caprice, dream, fancy, fantasy, humor, idea, impulse, inclination, notion, quirk, tendency, vagary, vision, whimsy.

whimsical, curious, droll, peculiar, quaint; see also eccentric.

whole, absolute, all, complete, entire, full, inclusive, intact integral, inviolate, perfect, plenary, total, unabridged, unbroken, undivided, unimpaired; hale, healed, healthy, sound, well. ANT.—defective, fragmentary, imperfect, incomplete, partial; diseased, feeble, impaired, infirm, sickly.

wholesome, beneficial, nourishing, nutritive; hearty, robust, strong; see also healthy; whole.

wicked, atrocious, base, corrupt, criminal, deleterious, disorderly, disreputable, dissolute, erring, evil, fiendish, foul, gross, hellish, immoral, impure, infamous, iniquitous, irreligious, malevolent, murderous, nefarious, noxious, pernicious, scandalous, shameful, sinful, unrighteous, unsound, vicious, vile, villainous, wayward, wrong. ANT.—admirable, commendable, honorable, moral, noble, praiseworthy, virtuous.

wide, all-inclusive, blanket, broad, comprehensive, expanded, extensive, general, large, sweeping, universal, vast. ANT.—confined, hampered, limited, narrow, restricted.

wild, undomesticated, untamed; rough, uncultivated; impetuous, irregular, turbulent, wayward; extravagant, foolish, giddy; boisterous. see also barbarous, fierce; desolate; reckless; stormy.

will, choice, conviction, decision, desire, determination, inclination, intent, intention, mind, preference, purpose, resolution, volition, willingness, wish. ANT.—coercion, compulsion, doubt, indecision, wavering.

willful, see intentional.

win, see gain, succeed.

wind, air, blast, breeze, current, cyclone, draft, flurry, flutter, gale, gust, hurricane, squall, storm, tempest, typhoon, zephyr; coil, fold, twine, twist, wreathe; bend, crook, curve, deviate, meander, sinuate, snake, zigzag.

winding, bending, coiling, crooked, curving, devious, involuted, meandering, sinuous, turning, twining, twisting, writhing. ANT.—direct, plain, straight.

wisdom, acumen, astuteness, comprehension, depth, discernment, discretion, discrimination, enlightenment, erudition, farsightedness, foresight, insight, intelligence, judgment, knowledge, learning, perspicacity, prudence, reason, reasoning, sagacity, sense, understanding. ANT.—absurdity, fatuity, foolishness, ignorance, imprudence, misjudgment.

wise, advisable, alert, astute, calculating, deep, discerning, discreet, enlightened, erudite, foresighted, informed, intelligent, judicious, penetrating, profound, prudent, rational, sagacious, sage, sane, sensible, shrewd, smart, sound.

wish, appetite, aspiration, bid, craving, desire, hungering, longing, lust, need, petition, plea, request, urge, yearning; covet, crave, desire, hanker, hope, hunger, long, pine, thirst, want, yearn.

wit, comprehension, intellect, intelligence, mind, perception, perspicacity, reason, sagacity, sense, understanding; banter, burlesque, cleverness,

drollery, facetiousness, fun, humor, irony, jest, jocularity, playfulness, raillery, sarcasm, satire, witticism; comedian, humorist, joker, wag. ANT.—dullness, stupidity; gloom, gravity, melancholy, pessimism, solemnity; cynic, misanthrope, pessimist.

witchcraft, bewitchment, black art, black magic, charm, conjuration, conjuring, demonology, divination, enchantment, incantation, legerdemain, magic, necromancy, sorcery, spell, voodooism, witchery, wizardry.

withdraw, abandon, abjure, abstract, deduct, depart, desert, dissociate, disengage, draw, forsake, give up, go, leave, part, quit, recall, recant, relinquish, remove, renounce, retire, retract, retreat, revoke, secede, separate, sequester, shrink, vacate, wean. ANT.—abide, introduce, remain, return, stay, tarry.

wither, decay, decline, deteriorate, droop, dry up, fail, languish, shrink, shrivel, sink, waste, weaken, wilt, wizen, wrinkle. ANT.—bloom, invigorate, refresh, rejuvenate, revive.

withhold, abstain, check, conceal, deny, desist, detain, forbear, hide, hinder, keep, refrain, refuse, reserve, restrain, retain, suppress. ANT.—accord, concede, grant, indulge, persist, yield.

withstand, bar, combat, confront, contradict, counteract, defy, endure, face, hinder, hold out, obstruct, resist, thwart. ANT.—acquiesce, consent, submit, succumb, yield.

witness, attestation, confirmation, declaration, evidence, proof, testimony; attestor, beholder, bystander, corroborator, deponent, eyewitness, observer, onlooker, spectator, testifier, watcher; attest, bear witness, confirm, corroborate, mark, note, observe, see, testify, vouch, watch.

witty, droll, facetious, funny; see also clever.

wizardry, see witchcraft.

woe, see disaster; misery.

womanly, compassionate, gentle, ladylike, maidenly, modest, protective. see also feminine.

wonder, curiosity, marvel, miracle, oddity, phenomenon, portent, prodigy, rarity, sight, sign, spectacle; admiration, amazement, astonishment, awe, bewilderment, confusion, curiosity, fascination, perplexity, stupefaction, surprise, wonderment; admire, doubt, gape, marvel, ponder, query, stare. ANT.—commonness, familiarity, triviality; anticipation, apathy, expectation, indifference, stolidity; abhor, disregard, ignore, ridicule, scorn.

wordy, diffuse, digressive, long-winded, loquacious, prolix, rambling, redundant, talkative, verbose, voluble. ANT.—brief, concise, succinct, summary, terse.

work, accomplishment, achievement, action, business, calling, deed, drudgery, duty, effort, employment, exertion, function, job, labor, occupation, office, opus, performance, production, profession, pursuit, task, toil, travail; accomplish, achieve, act, control, do, form, function, labor, manage, operate, make, mold, react, serve, slave, strive, struggle, sweat, toil. ANT.—ease, idleness, leisure, recreation, relaxation; abandon, ignore, malfunction, mismanage, quit, rest.

working, see industrious; operative.

worldly, carnal, corporeal, earthly, irreligious, materialistic, mundane, opportunistic, practical, secular, sensual, temporal, terrestrial, ungodly. ANT.—exalted, incorporeal, intellectual, refined, spiritual.

worn, exhausted, faint, fatigued, jaded, shabby, spent, threadbare, tired, used, wasted, wearied, weary. ANT.—fresh, invigorated, new, rested, unused.

worry, agitation, anxiety, apprehension, care, concern, disquiet, doubt, fear, trouble, uneasiness; annoy, bother, disturb, gall, gnaw, harass, harry, haze, irritate, pain, persecute, pester, plague, tease, torment, torture, trouble, vex; fret, fume, fuss, grieve. ANT.—contentment, ease, peace, satisfaction, serenity; aid, comfort, please, soothe, support; enjoy, rejoice, relax, rest, unbend.

worship, honor, respect; see also idolize; reverence.

worth, advantage, benefit, estimation, price, usefulness, utility; see also merit.

worthless, barren, bootless, inane, insignificant, meritless, pointless, poor, profitless, unimportant, unproductive; see also futile.

worthy, charitable, creditable, decent, dependable, deserving, dutiful, exemplary, fit, good, honorable, incorrupt, incorruptible, meritorious, model, moral, noble, pure, reliable, reputable, righteous, suitable, trustworthy, virtuous, worthy. ANT.—corrupt, dishonorable, iniquitous, reprehensible, vicious, villainous.

wound, affront, dishonor, insult; disfigure, gash, scrape; see also abuse; hurt.

wrangle, affray, bickering, spat, squabble; see also dispute.

wrap, bundle, cloak, clothe, conceal, cover, curtain, disguise, enclose, enfold, envelop, furl, guard, hide, lap, mask, muffle, package, protect, roll, screen, shield, shroud, swathe, veil, wind; blanket, cape, cloak, coat, coverlet, overcoat, shawl. ANT.—bare, divulge, expose, open, reveal, unfold.

wrath, choler, irritation, petulance, provocation, tantrum; see also indignation.

wreck, annihilate, break, damage, demolish, destroy, devastate, eradicate, exterminate, extinguish, injure, obliterate, ravage, raze, ruin, shatter, smash; accident, crash, desolation, destruction, junk, litter, loss, perdition, shreds, smash, wreckage. ANT.—conserve, construct, establish, preserve, repair; gain, improvement, recovery, renewal, restoration.

wretched, see miserable.

write, compose, correspond, draft, draw, formulate, inscribe, pen, record, scrawl, scribble, sign, transcribe.

writer, author, biographer, calligrapher, composer, contributor, correspondent, creator, editor, essayist, father, inventor, journalist, maker, novelist, originator, playwright, poet, reporter, scribe, stenographer.

writing, calligraphy, composition, document, handwriting, inscription, manuscript, penmanship.

wrong, amiss, askew, awry, erroneous, fallacious, false, faulty, imprecise, inaccurate, incorrect, inexact, mistaken, untrue; improper, inappropriate, unsuitable; aberrant, abusive, bad, base, corrupt, criminal, cruel, evil, hurtful, immoral, indecent, iniquitous, injurious, malevolent, reprehensible, sinful, wicked. ANT.—accurate, correct, exact, precise, right; appropriate, becoming, fitting, proper, suitable; blameless, decent, ethical, honest, noble, virtuous.

X

xanthic, dusky, fulvous, saffron, swarthy, tawny, yellow, yellowish.

xerox, copy, ditto, duplicate, recreate, reproduce.

x-ray, radiant energy, radiation, radioactivity, radiograph, radium emanation, Roentgen ray.

xylography, woodcutting, woodengraving.

Y

yard, backyard, corral, court, courtyard, enclosure, garden, playground, terrace.

yardstick, criterion, gauge, measure, rule, ruler, standard, test, touchstone.

yearning, see wish.

yell, bawl, bellow, cry, howl, roar, scream, screech, shout, shriek, shrill, squall, squeal, vociferate, whoop, yelp.

yet, additionally, although, besides, but, despite, further, furthermore, hitherto, however, nevertheless, notwithstanding, now, still, though.

yield, crop, fruit, harvest, proceeds, produce, product, reaping, result, store; bear, breed, generate, impart, produce, supply; allow, bestow, concede, confer, grant, permit, sanction, tolerate; abdicate, accede, acquiesce, capitulate, cede, defer, quit, relent, relinquish, resign, submit, succumb, surrender, waive. ANT.—deny, forbid, oppose, prevent, refuse; assert, master, overcome, overpower, strive, struggle.

young, active, adolescent, blooming, budding, childish, childlike, fresh, green, growing, immature, inexperienced, juvenile, pubescent, puerile, strong, vibrant, vigorous, youthful. ANT.—aged, ancient, elderly, experienced, mature, withered.

youthful, see young.

Z

zeal, activity, ardor, courage, dedication, determination, devotion, eagerness, energy, enthusiasm, excitement, fanaticism, fervency, fervor, inclination, industry, inspiration, intensity, intentness, involvement, passion, perseverance, vehemence, vigilance, warmth, willingness. ANT.—apathy, detachment, ennui, indifference, nonchalance.

zealot, adherent, bigot, devotee, dogmatist, dreamer, enthusiast, fanatic, martyr, opinionist, partisan, patriot, visionary. ANT.—dawdler, idler, shirker, slacker.

zealous, alert, animated, assiduous, brisk, bustling, diligent, fervid, fiery, hustling, indefatigable, passionate, resolute, sedulous, steadfast, vivacious. see also eager.

zenith, acme, apex, apogee, cap, climax, consummation, crest, crown, culmination, eminence, height, maximum, peak, pinnacle, pitch, summit, top. ANT.—base, bottom, floor, foundation, nadir.

zero, blank, cipher, naught, nil, nobody, nonentity, nothing, nullity, unreality, unsubstantiality. ANT.—corporeality, existence, matter, object, substance.

zest, ardor, delight, desire, energy, enhancement, enjoyment, enthusiasm, exhilaration, gusto, passion, pleasure, relish, spirit; flavor, piquancy, pungency, savor, savoriness, sharpness, tang, taste.

zigzag, askew, awry, bent, crinkled, crooked, curved, devious, diagonal, erratic, fluctuating, forked, inclined, indirect, jagged, meandering, oblique, oscillating, rambling, serrated, sinuous, sloping, spiral, straggling, transverse, twisted, undulatory, vibratory, waggling, wry. ANT.—direct, even, rectilinear, straight, unbent.

zone, area, band, belt, circuit, climate, commune, district, dominion, enclosure, ground, latitude, locality, location, locus, meridian, precinct, quarter, region, section, sector, segment, site, terrain, territory, tract, ward.

World in Summary

Country	Capital	Monetary Unit	Major languages	IDD code	Telex code
Algeria	Algiers	Algerian dinar (AD) = 100 centimes	Arabic, French, Berber	213	408
Argentina	Buenos Aires	Argentine peso (Arg$) = 100 centavos	Spanish, Italian, German	—	33
Australia	Canberra	Australian dollar (A$) = 100 cents	English	61	71
Austria	Vienna	Schilling (Sch) = 100 groschen	German	43	47
Bangladesh	Dacca	Taka (TK) = 100 poisha	Bengali, English	—	780
Belgium	Brussels	Belgian franc (BFr) = 100 centimes	Flemish, French, English	32	46
Bolivia	LaPaz	Bolivian peso (B$) = 100 centavos	Spanish, Quochua, Aymara	—	309
Brazil	Brasilia	Cruzeiro (Cr) = 100 centavos	Portuguese, Italian, German, Spanish	55	38
Brunei	Bandar Seri Begawan	Brunei dollar (Br$) = 100 cents	Malay, English	673	809
Bulgaria	Sofia	Lev (Lv) = 100 Stotinki	Bulgarian, Turkish, Greek		67
Burma	Rangoon	Kyat (Kt) = 100 pyas	Burmese, Karen, Shan, English	—	83
Canada	Ottawa	Canadian dollar (C$) = 100 cents	English, French	1	21/26
Chile	Santiago	Chilean peso (Ch$) = 100 centavos	Spanish, German, Araucanian	56	34
China	Beijing	Yuan (Y) = 10 chiao 100 fen	Mandarin	—	85
Colombia	Bogota	Colombian peso (Col$) = 100 centavos	Spanish, Arawak, Carib	57	35
Czechoslovakia	Prague	Koruna or Crown (KCS) = 100 haler	Czech, Slovak, Hungarian	42	66
Denmark	Copenhagen	Danish Krone (DKr) = 100 ore	Danish, English	45	55
Egypt	Cairo	Egyptian pound (E£) = 100 piastres	Arabic	20	91
Finland	Helsinki	Markka (FMk) = 100 penni	Finnish, Swedish	358	57
France	Paris	Franc (Fr) = 100 centimes	French	33	42
Germany (GFR) West	Bonn	Deutsche mark (DM) = 100 pfenning	German	49	41
Germany (GDR) East	Berlin (East)	Mark (M) = 100 pfenning	German	37	69
Ghana	Accra	Cedi (C) = 100 pesewas	English, Twi, Fonti, Ewe	—	—
Greece	Athens	Drachma (Dr) = 100 lepta	Greek, Turkish	30	601
Guatemala	Guatemala	Quetzal (Q) = 100 centavos	Spanish, Mayan	502	372
Hong Kong	Victoria	Hongkong Dollar (HK$) = 100 cents	English, Chinese	852	802
Hungary	Budapest	Forint (Ft) = 100 filler	Hungarian	36	61
India	New Delhi	Indian rupee (IR) = 100 paise	Hindi, Urdu, Bengali, Telugu, Tamil	—	81
Indonesia	Jakarta	Rupiah (Rp) = 100 sen	Indonesian, Sudanese, Javanese	62	73
Iran	Teheran	Rial (Rl) = 100 dinars	Persian, Kurdish, Azkerbaijani	98	88
Iraq	Baghdad	Iraqi dinar (ID) = 20 dirhams	Arabic, Kurdish	964	491
Ireland	Dublin	Punt (1£) = 100 pighne	English, Irish	353	500
Israel	Jerusalem	She Kel (SK) = 100 new agorot	Hebrew, Arabic, English	972	606
Italy	Rome	Lira (L) = 100 centesimi	Italian, French	39	43
Ivory Coast	Abidjan	CFA fance (CFAFr) = 100 centimes	French, Dyula, Senulu, Agni, Baule	225	983
Japan	Tokyo	Yen (Y) = 100 sen	Japanese	81	72
Jordan	Amman	Jordan dinar (JD) = 1000 fils	Arabic	—	493
Kenya	Nairobi	Kenya Shilling (KSh) = 100 cents	Swahili, English, Bantu	254	987
Korea North	Pyongyang	N. Korean Won (SKW) = 100 chon	Korean	—	899
Korea South	Seoul	S. Korean Won (NKW) = 100 chon	Korean	82	801

Country	Capital	Monetary Unit	Major languages	IDD code	Telex code
Kuwait	Kuwait City	Kuwaiti dinar (KD) = 10 dirhams	Arabic	965	496
Lebanon	Beirut	Lebanese pound (L£) = 100 piastres	Arabic, French	—	494
Libya	Tripoli	Libyan dinar (LD) = 1000 dirhams	Arabic	—	901
Malaysia	Kuala Lumpur	Ringgit (Ma$) = 100 sen	Malay, Chinese, English, Tamil	—	84
Mexico	Mexico City	Mexican peso (Mex$) = 100 cntavos	Spanish, Nahuati, Maya	52	22
Mongolia	Ultan Bator	Tugrik (Tug) = 100 mongo	Mongolian	—	800
Morrocco	Rabat	Dirham (Dh) = 100 centimes	Arabic, French, Berber, Spanish	—	407
Netherlands	Amsterdam	Guilder (Gld) = 100 cents	Dutch	31	44
New Zealand	Wellington	New Zealand dollar (NZ$) = 100 cents	English, Maori	64	74
Niger	Niamey	CFA franc (CFA Fr) = 100 centimes	French, local African	227	
Nigeria	Lagos	Naira (#) = 100 koko	English, Hausa, Yoruha, Ibo, Fulani	234	905
Norway	Oslo	Norwegian Krone (NKr) = 100 ore	Norwegian	47	56
Pakistan	Islamabad	Pakistan rupee (PR) = 100 paisa	Urdu, Punjabi, English	—	82
Panama	Panama City	Balboa (BA) = 100 centesimos	Spanish, English	—	377
Papua New Guinea	Port Moresby	Kina (Ka) = 100 toea	Pidgin English, Police Motu	675	703
Peru	Lima	Sol (S) = 100 centavos	Spanish, Quechua	—	36
Philippines	Metro Manila	Pilippine peso (PP) = 100 centavos	Philipino (Tagalog), English, Spanish	63	75
Poland	Warsaw	Zloty (zl) = 100 groszy	Polish	48	63
Portugal	Lisbon	Escudo (Esc) = 100 centavos	Portuguese	351	404
Rumania	Bucharest	Leu = 100 bani	Rumanian, Hungarian	40	65
Saudi Arabia	Riyadh	Saudi riyal (SAR) = 100 hallalas	Arabic	966	495
Singapore	Singapore	Singapore dollar (S$) = 100 cents	English, Chinese, Malay, Tamil	65	87
South Africa	Pretoria	Rand (R) = 100 cents	Afrikaans, English	27	95
Spain	Madrid	Peseta (Pa) = 100 centimos	Spanish	34	52
Sri Lanka	Colombo	Sri Lanka rupee (SLR) = 100 cents	Singhalese, Tamil, English	94	803
Sudan	Khartoum	Sudanese pound (S£) = 100 piastres	Arabic, French, Kurdish	—	984
Sweden	Stockholm	Swedish krona (SKr) = 100 ore	Swedish	46	54
Switzerland	Berne	Swiss franc (SFr) = 100 centimes	Swiss, German, French, Italian	41	45
Syria	Damascus	Syrian pound (Sy£) = 100 piastres	Arabic, French, Kurdish	963	492
Tanzania	Dares Salaam	Tanzanian Shilling (TSh) = 100 cents	Swahili, English	255	989
Thailand	Bangkok	Baht (Bt) = 100 satang	Thai, English, Chinese	66	86
Tunisia	Tunis	Tunisian dinar (TD) = 100 millimes	Arabic, French	216	409
Turkey	Ankara	Turkish Lira (TL) = 100 Kurus	Turkish, Kurdish	90	607
United Kingdom	London	Pound (£) = 100 new pence	English	44	51
U.S.A.	Washington	Dollar ($) = 100 cents	English	1	23/230
Uruguay	Montevideo	Uruguayan new peso (Urug N$) = 100 centesimos	Spanish	—	—
Venezuela	Caracas	Bolivar (B) = 100 centimos	Spanish, Arawak, Carib	—	31
Yugoslavia	Belgrade	Dinar (D) = 100 paras	Serbo-Croatian	38	62
Zaire	Kinshasa	Zaire (Z) = 100 makuta	French, Kongo, Kingwara, Luba	—	
Zambia	Lusaka	Kwacha (K) = 100 ngwee	English, Bemba, Tonga, Nyanja	260	902
Zimbabwe	Harare	Zimbabwe dollar (Z$) = 100 cents	English African	—	907

COMMON ABBREVIATIONS

ABBREVIATIONS, ə-brē-vē-ā′shənz, are letter symbols or contractions used as shortened forms of words and phrases to facilitate writing and to save space. The practice of abbreviating goes back to antiquity; early examples of abbreviation have survived on coins and inscriptions, where lack of space made the shortening of words necessary. With the development of papyrus and, later, of parchment, writing increased and abbreviations were adopted by copyists to save labor.

In modern times the rapid growth of the sciences, technology, and business, and the increase of governmental agencies have produced a vastly increased vocabulary of abbreviations for use in some fields, symbols other than letters are employed, as in physics and mathematics. The following list of abbreviations often used in printing or writing includes only letter symbols or contractions, in the Roman alphabet.

A

A.—absolute (temperature)
A., Å., A—angstrom unit
a.—about; acre(s)
AA—Alcoholics Anonymous
A.A.—Associate in Arts
AAA—Agricultural Adjustment Administration; Amateur Athletic Association; American Automobile Association; antiaircraft artillery
AAAL—American Academy of Arts and Letters
AAAS—American Association for the Advancement of Science
AAU—Amateur Athletic Union
AAUP—American Association of University Professors
A.B.—Artium Baccalaureus (Lat.), Bachelor of Arts
A.B., a.b.—able-bodied (seaman); airborne
ABA—American Bar Association
abbr., abbrev.—abbreviation; abbreviated
ABC—American Broadcasting Company
abp.—archbishop
abr.—abridged; abridgment
ABS—American Bible Society
AC—Air Corps; Army Corps; Athletic Club
AC, A.C., a.c., a-c—alternating current
A/C, a/c, ac.—account
Ac—actinium
ac—acre(s)
acad.—academic; academy
accel.—accelerando (It.), more quickly (music)
acct.—account; accountant
ACDA—Arms Control and Disarmament Agency
ACLS—American Council of Learned Societies
ACLU—American Civil Liberties Union
ACP—American College of Physicians
ACS—American Chemical Society; American College of Surgeons
ACTH—adrenocorticotropic hormone
A.D.—anno Domini (Lat.), in the year of our Lord
ADA—American Dental Association; Americans for Democratic Action
adag.—adagio (It.), slowly (music)
ADC, a.d.c.—aide-de-camp
add.—addenda; addendum; addition; additional; address
adj.—adjacent; adjective; adjourned; adjustment; adjutant
ad lib., ad libit.—ad libitum (Lat.), at one's pleasure

adm.—administration; administrative; admiral
adv.—adverb; adversus; advertisement; advocate
ad val.—ad valorem (Lat.), according to the value
ae., aet., adtat.—aetatis (Lat.), of age, aged
AEC—Atomic Energy Commission
AEF—American Expeditionary Force
aero.—aeronautics
AF—Air Force; audio frequency
AFAM—Ancient Free and Accepted Masons
AFB—Air Force Base
AFC—automatic frequency control
AFL-CIO—American Federation of Labor-Congress of Industrial Organizations
AFTRA—American Federation of Television and Radio Artists
Ag—argentum (Lat.), silver
agr., agri., agric.—agricultural; agriculture
agt.—agent
A.H.—anno Hegirae (Lat.), in the year of Hegira (Mohammedan era)
AHA—American Historical Association
AIA—American Institute of Architects
A.I.Ch.E.—American Institute of Chemical Engineers
AID—Agency for International Development
AIEE—American Institute of Electrical Engineers
AKC—American Kennel Club
Al—aluminum
ALA—American Library Association
Ala.—Alabama
Alas.—Alaska
Alba.—Alberta
alg.—algebra
alt.—alternate; alternating; altitude; alto
Alta.—Alberta
AM—amplitude modulation
A.M., A.M., a.m.—ante meridiem (Lat.), before midday
A.M.—Artium Magister (Lat.), Master of Arts
Am—americium
AMA—American Medical Association
amb.—ambassador
A.M.E.—African Methodist Episcopal
amp.—amperage; ampere
AMS—Agricultural Marketing Service
amt.—amount
AMVETS—American Veterans (of World War II and Korea)
AN, AN.—Anglo-Norman

ANA—American Nurses Association
anal.—analogy, analysis; analytic
ANC—Army Nurse Corps
and.—andante (It.), slowly (music)
anon.—anonymous
ant.—antenna; antonym
anthrop., anthropol.—anthropological; anthropologist; anthropology
antiq.—antiquarian; antiquary
ANZAC—Australian and New Zealand Army Corps
AOH—Ancient Order of Hiberians
AP—Associated Press
APA—American Philological Association
APO—Army Post Office
app.—apparent; appended; appendix; appointed; apprentice
approx.—approximately
Apr., Apr—April
apt.—apartment
AQ—accomplishment quotient; achievement quotient
aq.—aqua; aqueous
Ar—argon
Ar.—Arabian; Arabic; Aramaic
ARA—Agricultural Research Administration; American Railway Association
A.R.A.—Associate of the Royal Academy
Arab.—Arabian; Arabic
ARC—American Red Cross
arch.—archaic; archbishop; archery; archipelago; architect; architecture
archaeol.—archaeological; archaeology
archd.—archduke
arith.—arithmetic
Ariz.—Arizona
Ark.—Arkansas
ARS—Agricultural Research Service
AS, AS.—Anglo-Saxon
As—arsenic
ASCAP—American Society of Composers, Authors and Publishers
ASCE—American Society of Civil Engineers
ASME—American Society of Mechanical Engineers
ASPCA—American Society for the Prevention of Cruelty to Animals
assn., assoc.—association
ASSR—Autonomous Soviet Socialist Republic
asst.—assistant
ASTM—American Society for Testing Materials
ASTP—Army Secialized Training Program
astrol.—astrologer; astrological; astrology

TWO-LETTER GEOGRAPHICAL ABBREVIATIONS RECOMMENDED BY THE UNITED STATES POSTAL SERVICE									
ALABAMA	AL	GEORGIA	GA	MARYLAND	MD	NEW MEXICO	NM	SOUTH DAKOTA	SD
ALASKA	AK	GUAM	GU	MASSACHUSETTS	MA	NEW YORK	NY	TENNESSEE	TN
ARIZONA	AZ	HAWAII	HI	MICHIGAN	MI	NORTH CAROLINA	NC	TEXAS	TX
ARKANSAS	AR	IDAHO	ID	MINNESOTA	MN	NORTH DAKOTA	ND	UTAH	UT
CALIFORNIA	CA	ILLINOIS	IL	MISSISSIPPI	MS	OHIO	OH	VERMONT	VT
CANAL ZONE	CZ	INDIANA	IN	MISSOURI	MO	OKLAHOMA	OK	VIRGINIA	VA
COLORADO	CO	IOWA	IA	MONTANA	MT	OREGON	OR	VIRGIN ISLANDS	VI
CONNECTICUT	CT	KANSAS	KS	NEBRASKA	NE	PENNSYLVANIA	PA	WASHINGTON	WA
DELAWARE	DE	KENTUCKY	KY	NEVADA	NV	PUERTO RICO	PR	WEST VIRGINIA	WV
D. OF C.	DC	LOUISIANA	LA	NEW HAMPSHIRE	NH	RHODE ISLAND	RI	WISCONSIN	WI
FLORIDA	FL	MAINE	ME	NEW JERSEY	NJ	SOUTH CAROLINA	SC	WYOMING	WY

astron.—astronomer; astronomical; astronomy
ASV—American Standard Version
ATC—Air Transport Command
at. no.—atomic number
ATP—adenosine triphosphate
ATS—Army Transport Service
attn.—attention
atty.—attorney
atty. gen.—attorney general
at. wt.—atomic weight
A.U., A.U., a.u., a.u.—angstrom unit
Au—aurum (Lat.), gold
Aug., Aug—August
AUS—Army of the United States
aux.—auxiliary
A.V.—Authorized Version (Bible)
av.—avenue; average; avoirdupois
AVC—American Veterans Committee; automatic volume control
advp.—avoirdupois
ave.—avenue
avoir—avoirdupois
AWOL—absent without leave

B

B—bishop (chess); boron
b.—base; bass; bat; battery; bay; book; born; brother
B.A.—Baccalaureus Artium (Lat.), Bachelor of Arts; British Association (for the Advancement of Science); Buenos Aires
Ba—barium
bact.—bacteria; bacteriology
Bap., Bapt.—Baptist
bap.—baptized
B.Ar., B. Arch.—Bachelor of Architecture
Bart.—Baronet
B.B.A.—Bachelor of Business Administration
BBB—Better Business Bureau
BBC—British Broadcasting Corporation
bbl—barrel, barrels
B.C.—before Christ; British Columbia
B.C.E.—Bachelor of Civil Engineering
B.Ch.E.—Bahelor of Chemical Engineering
B.C.L.—Bachelor of Civil Law
B.D.—Bachelor of Divinity
BSDA—Business and Defense Services Administration
B.E.—Bachelor of Engineering; Bachelor of Education
Be—beryllium
Bé.—Baumé
B.Ed.—Bachelor of Education
BEF—British Expeditionary Force(s)
B.E.M.—British Empire Medal
BEV, bev—billion electron volts
bf.—boldface
Bi—bismuth
bib.—Bible; biblical
bibliog.—bibliography
biochem.—biochemistry
biog.—biographer; biographical; biography
biol.—biology
B.I.S.—Bank for International Settlements; British Information Service
Bk—berkelium
bk.—bank; block; book
bkg.—banking
B.L.—Baccalaureus Legum (Lat.), Bachelor of Laws
bldg.—building
B.Lit(t).—Baccalaureus Lit(t)erarum (Lat.), Bachelor of Literature (or Letters)
BLS—Bureau of Labor Statistics
B.L.S.—Bachelor of Library Science
blvd.—boulevard
BM—basal metabolism
B.M.—Baccalaureus Medicinae (Lat.), Bachelor of Medicine; British Museum
B.Mus.—Baccalaureus Musicae (Lat.), Bachelor of Music
BOAC—British Overseas Airways Corporation
bor.—borough

bot.—botanical, botany
bp.—bishop
b.p.—boiling point
BPOE—Benevolent and Protective Order of Elks
Br—bromine
brig.—brigade; brigadier
brig. gen.—brigadier general
bro.—brother
B.S.—Bachelor of Science
BSA—Boy Scouts of America
B.S.A.—Bachelor of Science in Agriculture
B.Sc.—Baccalaureus Scientiae (Lat.), Bachelor of Science
B.T., B.Th.—Baccalaureus Theologiae (Lat.), Bachelor of Theology
B.T.U., Btu, b.t.u., btu—British thermal unit
bu—bushel
bur.—bureau
B.V.M.—Blessed Virgin Mary

C

C—carbon
C., c.—candle; capacitance; cape; carat; cathode; cent; center; century; chapter; circa (Lat.), about; cirrus (meteor.); copyright; cubic; cup; current; cycle
C., C, c., c—centigrade; centimeter
CA—chronological age; Coast Artillery
Ca—calcium
c.a.—chartered accountant; chief accountant; commercial agent; consular agent; controller of accounts
CAA—Civil Aeronautics Administration (or Authority)
CAB—Civil Aeronautics Board; Consumers' Advisory Board
Cal.—California; large calorie
cal.—calendar; caliber; small calorie
Calif.—California
Cant.—Canticles
CAP—Civil Air Patrol
cap.—capital; capitalize
capt.—captain
CAR—Civil Air Regulations
CARE—Cooperative for American Remittances to Everywhere
Cath.—Catholic
cath.—cathedral
CAVU—ceiling and visibility unlimited
C.B.—Chirurgiae Baccalaureus (Lat.), Bachelor of Surgery; Companion of the Bath
Cb—columbium
CBC—Canadian Broadcasting Corporation
C.B.E.—Commander (of the Order) of the British Empire
CBS—Columbia Broadcasting System
cc, cc., c.c.—cubic centimeters
CCC—Commodity Credit Corporation
CCS—Combined Chiefs of Staff
Cd—cadmium
CE—Chemical Engineer; Chief Engineer; Civil Engineer; Church of England; Christian Endeavor
Ce—cerium
CEA—Council of Economic Advisers
CED—Committee for Economic Development
CEF—Canadian Expeditionary Force(s)
Celt.—Celtic
CEMA—Council for Mutual Economic Assistance
cent.—centigrade; centimeter; central; century
CENTO—Central Treaty Organization
Cf—californium
cf.—confer (Lat.), compare
CG—center of gravity; Coast Guard; commanding general; consul general
cg, cgm—centigram
cgs—centimeter-gram-second
CGT—Confédération Générale du Travail (Fr.), General Confederation of Labor

CH—clearing house; courthouse; customhouse
C.H.—Companion of Honor
ch.—chaplain; chapter; check (chess); chief; child; children; chirurgia (Lat.), surgery; church
chan.—channel
chap.—chaplain; chapter
Ch.E.—Chemical Engineer
chem.—chemical; chemist; chemistry
chm.—chairman; checkmate
Chr.—Christ; Christian
Chron.—Chronicles
chron.—chronology
CIA—Central Intelligence Agency
C.I.E.—Companion (of the Order) of the Indian Empire
CIF—cost, insurance, freight
C. in C.—Commander in Chief
CIO—Congress of (formerly Committee for) Industrial Organizations
cir., circ.—circular; circa (Lat.), about
cit.—citation; cited; citizen
civ.—civil; civilian
Cl—chlorine
clk.—clerk
C.M.—Chirurgiae Magister (Lat.), Master in Surgery
Cm—curium
cm, cm.—centimeter(s)
C.M.G.—Companion (of the Order) of St. Michael and St. George
CO—Commanding Officer; conscientious objector
Co—cobalt
co.—company; county
c.o., c/o—care of; carried over
COD, c.o.d.—cash on delivery; collect on delivery
C. of C.—Chamber of Commerce
C. of S.—Chief of Staff
Col.—Colorado; Colossians
col.—collected; collector; college; colonel; colonial; colony; column
colloq.—colloquial; colloquialism
Colo.—Colorado
Coloss.—Colossians
com.—comedy; command; commandant; commerce; commercial; commission(er); committee; commodore; common; communication; community
comdr.—commander
COMECON—Council for Mutual Economic Assistance
comr.—commissioner
con.—concerto; consolidated; consul
conf.—conference
confed.—confederate
Cong.—Congregational
cong.—congress
conj.—conjugation; conjunction
Conn.—Connecticut
consol.—consolidated
constr.—construction
cont.—containing; contents; continent; continental; continue(d)
Cor.—Corinthians
CORE—Congress of Racial Equality
corp.—corporal; corporation
cos—cosine
CP—candlepower; chemically pure; command post; Communist Party
cp.—candlepower; compare
CPA—Certified Public Accountant
cpl.—corporal
CPO—chief petty officer
Cr—chromium
cr.—credit; creditor; creek
cres., cresc.—crescendo (It.), increasingly loud (music)
crit.—criticism
CS—civil service
C.S.—Christian Science
Cs—cesium
CSA—Confederate States of America
C.S.B.—Bachelor of Christian Science
CSC—Civil Service Commission

C.S.I.—Companion of (the Order of) the Star of India
CST—Central Standard Time
ct.—carat; cent; court
Cu—cuprum (Lat.), copper
cu—cubic
CWA—Civil Works Administration
cwt—hundredweight
CYO—Catholic Youth Organization

D

D—deuterium
D., d.—dam (in pedigrees); date; daughter; day(s); dead; democrat; density; diameter; died
d.—pence, penny
D.A.—delayed action; district attorney
DAB—Dictionary of American Biography
Dan., Danl.—Daniel
DAR—Daughters of the American Revolution
DAV—Disabled American Veterans
D.B.E.—Dame Commander (of the Order of the) British Empire
D. Bib.—Douay Bible
DC, D.C., d.c., d-c—direct current
D.C.—da capo (Lat.), repeat (music); District of Columbia; Doctor of Chiropractic
D.C.L.—Doctor of Civil Law
D.C.M.—Distinguished Conduct Medal (Brit. Army)
D.C.T.—Doctor of Christian Theology
D.D.—Divinitatis Doctor (Lat.), Doctor of Divinity
D.D.S.—Doctor of Dental Surgery
Dec., Dec—December
dec.—deceased; declaration; declension; declination; decrease; decrescendo (It.), decreasing in loudness (music)
deg.—degree(s)
Del.—Delaware
Dem.—Democrat; Democratic
D.Eng.—Doctor of Engineering
dep.—department; departure; deposit; depot; deputy
dept.—department; deputy
der., deriv.—derivation; derivative
dermatol.—dermatology
Deut.—Deuteronomy
DEW—distant early warning
DFC—Distinguished Flying Cross
diag.—diagram
dial.—dialect
dict.—dictionary
dim.—diminuendo (It.), diminishing in loudness (music)
dipl.—diplomat; diplomatic
dir.—director
disc.—discount; discovered
dist.—distinguished; district
div.—dividend; division; divorced
D.Lit., D.Litt.—Doctor Lit(t)erarum (Lat.), Doctor of Literature (or, Letters)
D.L.S.—Doctor of Library Science
dm, dm.—decameter; decimeter
D.M.D.—Doctor of Medical Dentistry
D.Mus.—Doctor of Music
DNA—deoxyribonucleic acid
DNB—Dictionary of National Biography (Brit.)
D.O.—Doctor of Optometry; Doctor of Osteopathy
do.—ditto (It.), the same
DOA—dead on arrival
doc.—document
doz.—dozen
DP—degree of polymerization; diametrical pitch; displaced person
dpt.—department
D.R., D/R, d.r.—dead reckoning; deposit receipt
Dr.—doctor
dr.—debit; debtor; drachma; dram
D.S., D.Sc.—Doctor of Science
DSC—Distinguished Service Cross

DSM—Distinguished Service Medal
DSO—Distinguished Service Order
DST—Daylight Saving Time
d.t.—delirium tremens; double time
dup., dupl.—duplicate
D.V.—Deo volente (Lat.), God willing; Douay Version
D.V.M.—Doctor of Veterinary Medicine
dwt—pennyweight
Dy—dysprosium

E

E, E., e.—east, eastern
e., e—erg: errors (baseball)
ea.—each
ECA—Economic Cooperation Administration
eccl., eccles.—ecclesiastical
Eccles., Eccl.—Ecclesiastes
Ecclus.—Ecclesiasticus
ECG—electrocardiogram
ecol.—ecology
econ.—economic; economics; economy
ECSC—European Coal and Steel Community
ed.—edited; editor; edition
EDC—European Defense Community
Ed.D.—Doctor of Education
EDT—Eastern Daylight Time
EEC—European Economic Community
EEG—electroencephalogram
EFTA—European Free Trade Association
e.g.—exempli gratia (Lat.), for example
Egyptol.—Egyptology
EHF, e.h.f.—extremely high frequency
EIB—Export-Import Bank
EKG—electrocardiogram
elec., elect.—electric(al); electrician; electricity
elev.—elevation
Eliz.—Elizabeth; Elizabethan
E.M.—Engineer of Mines
EMF, e.m.f., emf.—electromotive force
emp.—emperor; empire; empress
e.m.u.—electromagnetic unit
enc.—enclosed
ency., encyc., encycl.—encyclopedia
eng.—engineer; engineering; engraved
ens.—ensign
entom., entomol.—entomologist; entomology
Eph., Ephes.—Ephesians
Epis., Episc.—Episcopal
Er—erbium
ERA—Emergency Relief Administration
ERP—European Recovery Program
Es—einsteinium
ESB—Economic Stabilization Board
ESC—Economic and Social Council (United Nations)
Esk.—Eskimo
ESP—extrasensory perception
Esq., Esqr.—Esquire
EST—Eastern Standard Time
est.,—established; estimate
Esth.—Esther
et al.—et alibi (Lat.), and elsewhere; et alii (Lat.), and others
etc.—et cetera (Lat.), and so forth
ETO—European Theater of Operations
et seq.—et sequens (Lat.), and the following; et sequentes or seqentia (Lat.), and those that follow
Eu—europium
Ex.—Exodus
ex.—examined; example
exch.—exchange; exchequer
exec.—executive; executor
ex lib.—ex libris (Lat.), from the books of
Exod.—Exodus
Ez., Ezr.—Ezra
Ezek.—Ezekiel

F

F—Fahrenheit; farad; fathom; fluorine; function (math.)

F.—Fahrenheit; Fellow; Friday
f.—forte (It.), loud (music)
f.—farad; father; farthing; fathom; feminine; fluid (ounce); folio; following; franc; frequency
FAA—Federal Aviation Agency
fac.—facsimile
Fahr.—Fahrenheit
FAO—Food and Agricultural Organization of the United Nations
FBI—Federal Bureau of Investigation
FCA—Farm Credit Administration
FCC—Federal Communications Commission
FCIC—Federal Crop Insurance Corporation
FDA—Food and Drug Administration
FDIC—Federal Deposit Insurance Corporation
Fe—ferrum (Lat.), iron
Feb., Feb—February
fec.—fecit (Lat.), he (she) did, *or* made, it
fed.—federal; federated; federation
fem.—female; feminine
FEPC—Fair Employment Practice Committee
ff—fortissimo (It.), very loud (music)
ff.—folios; following
FFA—Future Farmers of America
FHA—Farmers Home Administration; Federal Housing Administration; Future Homemakers of America
FICA—Federal Insurance Contributions Act
fig.—figure
fin.—finance
fl.—florin; flourished; fluid
Fla., Flor.—Florida
F.L.S.—Fellow of the Linnaean Society
FM—frequency modulation
Fm—fermium
FMB—Federal Maritime Board
FMCS—Federal Mediation and Conciliation Service
fn.—footnote
FOB, f.o.b.—free on board
FOE—Fraternal Order of Eagles
fol.—folio; following
F.P., f.p.—foot pound; freezing point
FPC—Federal Power Commission
FPHA—Federal Public Housing Authority
FPO—Fleet Post Office
fps—feet per second
Fr.—francium
Fr.—Father (eccl.); Frater (Lat.), brother; Friar; Friday
fr.—fragment; franc; from
F.R.A.S.—Fellow of the Royal Astronomical Society
F.R.C.P.—Fellow of the Royal College of Physicians
F.R.C.S.—Fellow of the Royal College of Surgeons
F.R.G.S.—Fellow of the Royal Geographical Society
F.R.Hist.S.—Fellow of the Royal Historical Society
Fri.—Friday
F.R.I.B.A.—Fellow of the Royal Institution of British Architects
front.—frontispiece
FRS—Federal Reserve System
F.R.S.—Fellow of the Royal Society
F.R.S.C.—Fellow of the Royal Society of Canada
F.R.S.E.—Fellow of the Royal Society, Edinburgh
F.R.S.L.—Fellow of the Royal Society of Literature; Fellow of the Royal Society, London
FSA—Farm Security Administration; Federal Security Agency
F.S.A.—Fellow of the Society of Antiquaries, or Arts
FSCC—Federal Surplus Commodities Corporation
FSH—follicle-stimulating hormone

F.S.A.—Fellow of the Society of Antiquaries, or Arts
FSCC—Federal Surplus Commodities Corporation
FSH—follicle-stimulating hormone
F.S.S.—Fellow of the (Royal) Statistical Society
ft—feet; foot
ft.—fort
FTC—Federal Trade Commission
F.Z.S.—Fellow of the Zoological Society

G

G., g.—conductance; gauge; grain; gravity; guinea; gulf
g., g—gram
GA—general agent; General Assembly
Ga—gallium
Ga.—Gallic; Georgia
Gael.—Gaelic
Gal.—Galatians; Galen
gal, gall. gallon
GAO—General Accounting Office
GAR—Grand Army of the Republic
GATT—General Agreement on Tariffs and Trade
gaz.—gazette; gazetteer
G.B.E.—Grand (Cross, Order) of the British Empire
GCA—ground-controlled approach
G.C.B.—(Knight) Grand Cross of the Bath
GCI—ground-controlled interceptor
G.C.I.E.—(Knight) Grand Commander (of the Order) of the Indian Empire
G.C.L.H.—Grand Cross of the Legion of Honor
G.C.M.G.—(Knight of the) Grand Cross (of the Order) of St. Michael and St. George
G.C.S.I.—(Knight) Grand Commander (of the Order) of the Star of India
GCT—Greenwich civil time
G.C.V.O.—(Knight) Grand Cross of the (Royal) Victorian Order
Gd—gadolinium
Ge—germanium
Gen.—Genesis
gen.—gender; genera; general; genus
geod.—geodesy; geodetic
geog.—geographer; geographical; geography
geol.—geologic; geologist; geology
geom.—geometric; geometry
ger.—gerund
GHA—Greenwich hour angle
GHQ—General Headquarters
GI—general issue, or government issue (U.S. Army)
GI, g.i.—gastrointestinal
gloss.—glossary
GM—General Manager; George Medal (Brit.); Grand Master; guided missiles
gm—gram
GMT—Greenwich mean time
GNP—gross national product
GOP—Grand Old Party (Republican)
Goth.—Gothic
gov.—governor
govt.—government
GP—general practitioner
GPO—General Post Office; Government Printing Office
gr—grain(s); gram(s)
gram.—grammar; grammarian
GS—General Staff
GSA—General Services Administration; Girl Scouts of America
GSC—General Staff Corps

H

H—henry (elec.); hydrogen; intensity of magnetic field
h.—hard; hardness; high; hits (baseball); husband
Hab.—Habakkuk
hab. corp.—habeas corpus (Lat.), that you have the body

Hag.—Haggai
Hal.—halogen
Haw.—Hawaii
Hb—hemoglobin
H.B.M.—His (Her) Britannic Majesty
H.C.—House of Commons
H.C.M.—His (Her) Catholic Majesty
H.E.—His Eminence; His Excellency
He—helium
Heb., Hebr.—Hebrew(s)
her.—heraldry
HF—high frequency
Hf—hafnium
Hg—hydrargyrum (Lat.), mercury
H.H.—His (Her) Highness; His Holiness (the Pope)
HHFA—Housing and Home Finance Agency
HIFI—high fidelity
H.I.H.—His (Her) Imperial Highness
hist.—historical; historian; history
H.J.S.—hic jacet sepultus (Lat.), here lies buried
H.L.—House of Lords
H.M.—His (Her) Majesty
H.M.S.—His Majesty's Service, Ship, or Steamer
Ho—holmium
Hon.—Honorable
hort.—horticultural; horticulture
Hos.—Hosea
H.P., HP, h.p., hp—high pressure; horsepower
HQ, H.Q., hq, h.q.—headquarters
H.R.—Home Rule; House of Representatives
hr—hour(s)
H.R.H.—His (Her) Royal Highness
H.R.I.P.—hic requiescit in pace (Lat.), here rests in peace
H.S.H.—His (Her) Serene Highness
ht.—height

I

I—iodine
I.—Island; Isle
Ia.—Iowa (not official)
IADB—Inter-American Defense Board
ib., ibid.—ibidem (Lat.), in the same place
IBRD—International Bank for Reconstruction and Development
ICAO—International Civil Aviation Organization
ICBM—intercontinental ballistic missile
ICC—Interstate Commerce Commission; Indian Claims Commission
ichth.—ichthyology
ICJ—International Court of Justice
Id.—Idaho (not official)
id.—idem (Lat.), the same
i.e.—id est (Lat.), that is
IFC—International Finance Corporation
IGY—International Geophysical Year
IHS—the first three letters of the Greek word for Jesus
ILA—International Longshoremen's Association
ILGWU—International Ladies' Garment Workers' Union
Ill.—Illinois
ILO—International Labor Organization
I.L.P.—Independent Labour Party
IMF—International Monetary Fund
imp.—imperative; imperial; imports; imprimatur (Lat.), let it be printed
In—indium
in.—inch; inches
inc.—including; income; incorporated
Ind.—Indian; Indiana
Inf.—infantry
in loc. cit.—in loco citato (Lat.), in the place cited
INRI—Iesus Nazarenus, Rex Iudaeorum (Lat.), Jesus of Nazareth, King of the Jews
INS—International News Service

ins.—inches; insurance
inst.—instant, the present month; institute
introd.—introduction
IOF—Independent Order of Foresters
IOOF—Independent Order of Odd Fellows
IOU—I owe you
IQ—intelligence quotient
Ir—iridium
IRA—Irish Republican Army
IRO—International Refugee Organization
IRS—Internal Revenue Service
Is., is.—island(s); isle
Isa.—Isaiah
ITO—International Trade Organization
ITU—International Telecommunications Union
IU—international unit
IWW—Industrial Workers of the World

J

J—joule
J.—Justice; Judge
JA—Judge Advocate
Jan., Jan—January
Jas.—James
JCC—Junior Chamber of Commerce
J.C.D.—Juris Civilis Doctor (Lat.), Doctor of Civil Law
J.D.—Juris Doctor (Lat.), Doctor of Law
Jer.—Jeremiah
j.g.—junior grade
Jno.—John
Josh.—Joshua
jour.—journal
J.P.—Justice of the Peace
Jr., jr.—junior
J.U.D.—Juris Utriusque Doctor (Lat.), doctor of both laws (canon and civil)
jud.—judicial
Judg.—Judges (Bible)

K

K—kalium (Lat.), potassium; king (chess)
K, k.—kilogram; king
K.—Kelvin
k.—kilo, thousand
ka—kathode or cathode
Kan., Kans., Kas.—Kansas
KB—king's bishop (chess)
K.B.—King's Bench; Knight Bachelor; Knight of the Bath
K.B.E.—Knight (Commander of the Order) of the British Empire
KBP—king's bishop's pawn (chess)
K.C.—King's Counsel; Knights of Columbus
kc—kilocycle
K.C.B.—Knight Commander of the Bath
K.C.I.E.—Knight Commander (of the Order) of the Indian Empire
K.C.M.G.—Knight Commander of St. Michael and St. George
K.C.S.I.—Knight Commander of the Star of India
K.C.V.O.—Knight Commander of the Victorian Order
KEV, Kev—thousand electron volts
K.G.—Knight of the Garter
kg—kilogram
Ki.—Kings (Bible)
kilo.—kilogram; kilometer
KKK—Ku Klux Klan
K Kt—king's knight (chess)
K Kt P—king's knight's pawn (chess)
KLM—Royal Dutch Airlines
km—kilometer
KO—knockout
K. of P.—Knights of Pythias
KP—king's pawn (chess); kitchen police, assistants to cooks
K.P.—Knight of St. Patrick; Knights of Pythias
KR—king's rook (chess)
Kr—krypton
KRP—king's rook's pawn (chess)

K.T.—Knight of the Thistle; Knight Templar
Kt.—Knight
kt.—carat
kv.—kilovolt
kw—kilowatt
K.W.H., kw-h, kw-hr—kilowatt-hour
Ky.—Kentucky

L

£, L, l.—libra (Lat.), pound
L., l.—lake; left; length; liber (Lat.), book; lira
l., l—liter
l., ll.—line; lines
La—lanthanum
La.—Louisiana
Lab.—Labrador
lab.—laboratory
Lam.—Lamentations
lang.—language
Lat.—Latin
lat.—latitude
lb—libra (Lat.), pound
LC—landing craft (following letter specifies type, for example, LCI Landing Craft Infantry)
L.C.—Library of Congress
l.c.—loco citato (Lat.), in the place cited; lower case (print.)
LD—lethal dose; Low Dutch
leg.—legal; legend; legato (It.), in a smooth manner (music); legislative; legislature
legis.—legislation; legislative; legislature
Lev.—Leviticus
LG—Low German
LH—luteinizing hormone
L.H.D.—lit(t)erarum Humaniorum Doctor, or In Litteris Humanioribus Doctor (Lat.), Doctor of Humanities
L.I.—Long Island
Li—lithium
lib.—liberal; librarian; library
lieut.—lieutenant
ling.—linguistics
Linn.—Linnaeus; Linnaean
liq.—liquid; liquidation; liquor
lit.—literally; literary; literature
Lit.B., Litt.B.—Lit(t)erarum Baccalaurcus (Lat), Bachelor of Letters or Literature
Lit.D., Litt.D.—Lit(t)erarum Doctor (Lat.); Doctor of Literature
LL—Late Latin; Low Latin
LL.B.—Legum Baccalaureus (Lat.), Bachelor of Laws
LL.D.—Legum Doctor (Lat.), Doctor of Laws
LL.M.—Legum Magister (Lat.), Master of Laws
loc. cit.—lococitato (Lat.), in the place cited
log.—logarithm
Lon., Lond.—London
lon., long.—longitude
LOOM—Loyal Order of Moose
loq.—loquitur (Lat.), he, or she, speaks
L.R.A.M.—Licentiate of the Royal Academy of Music
L.R.C.P.—Licentiate of the Royal College of Physicians
L.R.C.S.—Licentiate of the Royal College of Surgeons
LS—landing ship (following letter specifies type, for example, LST, Landing Ship Tank)
l.s.—locus sigilli (Lat.), place of the seal
L.S.A.—Licentiate of the Society of Apothecaries
LSD—lysergic acid diethylamide
L.S.D., l.s.d., l.s.d.—librae, solidi, denarii (Lat.), pounds, shillings, and pence
lt.—lieutenant
Ltd., ltd.—limited
Lu—lutetium
Luth.—Lutheran
Lw—lawrencium

M

M—magnitude; thousand
M.—Majesty; Monsieur (Fr.), miter
m.—male; mark (German money); married; meridian; meridies (Lat.), noon; meter; mile; minute; month
MA—Maritime Administration; mental age
M.A.—Magister Artium (Lat.), Master of Arts
ma, ma., mA—milliampere
Mac., Macc.—Maccabees
Maced.—Macedonia(n)
mach.—machine; machinist
maj.—major
Mal.—Malachi
Man.—Manitoba
MAP—Military Assistance Program
Mar., Mar—March
mas., masc.—masculine
Mass.—Massachusetts
math.—mathematician; mathematics
MATS—Military Air Transport Service
Matt.—Matthew
M.B.—Medicinae Baccalaureus (Lat.), Bachelor of Medicine
M.B.A.—Master of Business Administration
MBS—Mutual Broadcasting System
M.C.—Medical Corps; Master of Ceremonies; Member of Congress
mc—megacycle
M.D.—Medicinae Doctor (Lat.), Doctor of Medicine; Medical Department
Md—mendelevium
Md.—Maryland
M.D.S.—Master of Dental Surgery
mdse.—merchandise
ME, ME., M.E.—Middle English
M.E.—Methodist Episcopal; mining or mechanical, engineer
Me.—Maine
mech.—mechanical; mechanics
med.—medical; medicine; medieval
Medit.—Mediterranean
M.E.E.—Master of Electrical Engineering
mem.—memento (Lat.), remember, memorandum
mep—mean effective pressure
Messrs.—Messieurs (Fr.), gentlemen
metal.—metallurgy
meteorol.—meteorology
Meth.—Methodist
MEV, Mev—million electron volts
mf—mezzo forte (It.), moderately loud (music); millifarad
mf, mfd—microfarad
M.F.A.—Master of Fine Arts
mfg.—manufacturing
mfr.—manufacture; manufacturer
MG—Military Government
Mg—magnesium
mg, mg., mgm—milligram
MGB—Ministerstvo Gosudarstvennoi Bezopasnosti (from the Russian), the Soviet Ministry of State Security
mgr.—manager; monsignor
MHG, M.H.G.—Middle High German
M.I.—Military intelligence
mi—mile; mill
Mic.—Micah
Mich.—Michigan
M.I.E.E.—Member of the Institution of Electrical Engineers
mil., milit.—militia; military
M.I.Mech.E.—Member of the Institution of Mechanical Engineers
M.I.Min.E., M.I.M.E.—Member of the Institution of Mining Engineers
min—Minute(s)
min.—mineralogy; minimum; mining
Minn.—Minnesota
M.Inst.C.E.—Member of the Institution of Civil Engineers
misc.—miscellaneous
Miss.—Mississippi

M.I.T.—Massachusetts Institute of Technology
ML, M.L.—Medieval, or Middle, Latin
M.L.—Magister Legum (Lat.), Master of Laws; Medieval, or Middle, Latin
ml, ml.—milliliter
MLA—Modern Language Association
MLG, M.L.G.—Middle Low German
M. Lit(t).—Magister Lit(t)erarum (Lat.), Master of Letters
Mlle.—Mademoiselle (Fr.), Miss
MM—Messieurs (Fr.), gentlemen; (Their) Majesties
mm—millimeter(s); millia (Lat.), thousands
M.M.E.—Master of Mining, or Mechanical, Engineering
Mme.—Madame (Fr.), Madam
Mn—manganese
MO, m.o.—medical officer; money order
Mo—molybdenum
Mo.—Missouri
mo.—month(s)
mod.—moderate
Moham.—Mohammedan
Mon.—Monday; Monsignor
Mont.—Montana
MOS—military occupational specialty (duty classification by serial number)
MP—military police
M.P.—Member of Parliament
mp—mezzo piano (It.), moderately soft (music)
MPH, mph—miles per hour
Mr., Mr—Mister
MRA—Moral Re-Armament
MRP—Mouvement Républicain Populaire (Fr.), Popular Republican Movement
Mrs.—Mistress
MS, Ms, ms.—manuscript
M.S., M.Sc.—Master of Science
msgr.—monsignor
m.s.l.—mean sea level
MSS, MSS., mss, mss.—manuscripts
MST—Mountain Standard Time
M.S.W.—Master of Social Work
mt.—mount; mountain
MTO—Mediterranean Theater of Operations
Mt. Rev.—Most Reverend
mts.—mountains
mu—micron
mus.—museum; music; musician
Mus.B., Mus.Bac.—Musicae Baccalaureus (Lat.), Bachelor of Music
Mus. D.—Musicae Doctor (Lat.), Doctor of Music
MVA—Missouri Valley Authority
MVD—Ministerstvo Vnutrennikh Del (from the Russian), the Soviet Ministry of Internal Affairs
M.V.O.—Member of the (Royal) Victorian Order
myth., mythol.—mythology

N

N—nitrogen
N, N., n—north, northern
N., n.—navy; noon; normal (solution)
n.—natus (Lat.), born; neuter; note; noun
Na—natrium (Lat.), sodium
NAACP—National Association for the Advancement of Colored People
NAB—National Association of Broadcasters
NAD—National Academy of Design
Nah.—Nahum
NAM—National Association of Manufacturers
NAS—National Academy of Sciences
NASA—National Aeronautics and Space Administration
nat.—national; native; natural
natl.—National
NATO—North Atlantic Treaty Organization
NATS—Naval Air Transport Service

naut.—nautical
nav.—naval; navigation
N.B.—New Brunswick
N.B., n.b.—nota bene (Lat.), mark well, take notice
Nb—niobium
NBA—National Basketball Association; National Boxing Association
NBC—National Broadcasting Company
NBS—National Bureau of Standards
NC—Nurse Corps
N.C.—North Carolina
NCAA—National Collegiate Athletic Association
NCCJ—National Conference of Christians and Jews
NCO, n.c.o.—noncommissioned officer
N.D.—North Dakota
N.D., n.d.—no date
Nd—neodymium
N.Dak.—North Dakota
N.E.—New England
Ne—neon
NEA—National Education Association
Neb., Nebr.—Nebraska
NED—New English Dictionary (the Oxford English Dictionary)
neg.—negative
Neh.—Nehemiah
neur., neurol.—neurology
Nev.—Nevada
Newf.—Newfoundland
New M.—New Mexico
New Test.—New Testament
N.F.—Newfoundland; Norman French
NFL—National Football League
Nfld.—Newfoundland
NG—National Guard
N.G., n.g.—No good
N.H.—New Hampshire
NHA—National Housing Administration
NHG, NHG., H.H.G.—New High German
Ni—nickel
NIH—National Institutes of Health
NIRA—National Industrial Recovery Administration
N.J.—New Jersey
NKVD—from the Russian for People's Commissariat for Internal Affairs, the secret police succeeding OGPU
NL, N.L.—New Latin
n.l.—new line (print.); non licet (Lat.), it is not permitted or it is not lawful; non liquet (Lat.), it is not clear
NLRB—National Labor Relations Board
N.M., N.Mex.—New Mexico
NMU—National Maritime Union
No—nobelium
No.—north; northern
No., no.—numero (Lat.), number
noncom.—noncommissioned officer
non obst.—non obstante (Lat.), notwithstanding
non pros.—non prosequitur (Lat.), he does not prosecute
non seq.—non sequitur (Lat.), it does not follow
Nor.—Norman; North
NORAD—North American Air Defense Command
Nov., Nov—November
N.P.—nisi prius (Lat.), no protest (banking); Notary Public
Np—neptunium
n.p. or d.—no place or date
NRA—National Recovery Administration
NRAB—National Railroad Adjustment Board
N.S.—New Style (calendar); Nova Scotia
NSC—National Security Council
NSF—National Science Foundation
NSPCA—National Society for the Prevention of Cruelty to Animals
NSPCC—National Society for the Prevention of Cruelty to Children
NT., N.T.—New Testament
Num., Numb.—Numbers (Bible)
NWLB—National War Labor Board

N.W.T.—Northwest Territories
N.Y.—New York
NYA—National Youth Administration
N.Y.C.—New York City

O

O—oxygen
o—ohm
o.—ocean; order
OAS—Organization of American States
Obad.—Obadiah
O.B.E.—Officer (of the Order) of the British Empire
obit.—obituary
obj.—object, objective
obs.—observation; obsolete
OCD—Office of Civilian Defense
OCDM—Office of Civil and Defense Mobilization
OCS—Officer Candidate School
Oct., Oct—October
oct., 8vo.—octavo (print.)
O.D.—Officer of the Day; ordinary seaman; overdraft or overdrawn
ODT—Office of Defense Transportation
OE, O.E.—Old English
OECD—Organization for Economic Co-operation and Development
OED—Oxford English Dictionary
OEO—Office of Economic Opportunity
OES—Office of Economic Stabilization
O.E.S.—Order of the Eastern Star
OF, O.F.—Old French
O.F.M.—Order of Friars Minor
OHG, O.H.G.—Old High German
O.H.M.S.—On His (Her) Majesty's Service
O.K., OK—correct or approved
Okla.—Oklahoma
Old Test.—Old Testament
O.M.—Order of Merit
ON, O.N.—Old Norse
Ont.—Ontario
O.P.—Order of Preachers (Dominicans)
op. cit.—opere citato (Lat.), in the work cited
Ore., Oreg.—Oregon
orig.—original; originally
ornith.—ornithology
OS, O.S.—Old Saxon
O.S.—Old Style (calendar)
Os—osmium
O.S.A.—Order of St. Augustine
O.S.B.—Order of St. Benedict
O.S.F.—Order of St. Francis (Franciscan, or Capuchin, Order)
OSRD—Office of Scientific Research and Development
OSS—Office of Strategic Services
O.T.—Old Testament
OTS, O.T.S.—Officers' Training School
oz.—ounce (It. abbrev. of onza)

P

P—phosphorus
P., p.—pater (Lat.), father; pawn (chess); père (Fr.) father; post (Lat.), after; president; priest; prince
p—piano (It.), softly (music)
p,—page; part; participle; penny; per (Lat.), by
PA—public address (system); power of attorney
Pa—protactinium
Pa.—Pennsylvania
PAC—Political Action Committee
Pac., Pacif.—Pacific
PAL—Police Athletic League
paleon.—paleontology
par.—paragraph; parallel
parl.—parliamentary
pat., patd.—patent; patented
Pat. Off.—Patent Office
path., pathol.—pathology
PAU—Pan American Union
Pb—plumbum (Lat.), lead
PBS—Public Buildings Service

PBX—private branch exchange
PC—Preparatory Commission
P.C.—Police Constable; Privy Council; Privy Councilor
PCA—Progressive Citizens of America
pct.—percent
P.D.—Police Department
Pd—palladium
Pd.—paid
p.d.—per diem (Lat.), by the day
P.E.N.—Poets, Playwrights, Editors, Essayists and Novelists (International Association of)
pen.—peninsula
Penn., Penna.—Pennsylvania
per an.—per annum (Lat.), by the year
pers.—person; personal
Pet.—Peter
pfc, pfc.—private first class
PGA—Professional Golfers Association
*p*H—(not an abbrev.) a symbol indicating the negative logarithm of the hydrogen ion concentration.
Ph—phenyl
PHA—Public Housing Administration
phar., pharm.—pharmaceutical; pharmacology; pharmacopoeia; pharmacy
Ph.B.—Philosophiae Baccalaureus (Lat.), Bachelor of Philosophy
Ph.C.—Pharmaceutical Chemist
Ph.D.—Philosophiae Doctor (Lat.), Doctor of Philosophy
Phil.—Philemon
Phila.—Philadelphia
Philem.—Philemon
philol.—philologist; philology
philos.—philosopher; philosophy
phon.—phonetics
PHS—Public Health Service
phys.—physical; physician; physicist; physics
pizz.—pizzicato (It.), plucked (music)
pl.—plural
P.M.—Past Master; Police Magistrate; Postmaster
P.M., P.M., p.m.—post meridiem (Lat.), after noon
Pm—promethium
P.M.G.—Paymaster General; Postmaster General
Po—polonium
po.—putouts (baseball)
p.o.—petty officer; postal order; post office
POE—Port of Embarkation
pop.—population
POW, P.O.W., POWs, P.O.W.'s—prisoner(s) of war
P.P., p.p.—parcel post; parish priest; postpaid
pp—pianissimo (It.), very soft (music)
pp.—pages
P.P.C.—pour prendre congé (Fr.), to take leave
ppd.—postpaid; prepaid
P.Q.—Province of Quebec
p.q.—previous question
P.R.—Puerto Rico; proportional representation
Pr—praseodymium
PRA—Public Roads Administration
prep.—preparation; preparatory; preposition
pres.—president
Presb.—Presbyterian
prin.—principal; principle
PRO—public relations officer
proc.—proceedings; process
prod.—production
Prof., prof.—professor
prom.—promontory
pron.—pronoun; pronunciation
Prot.—Protestant
pro tem.—pro tempore (Lat.), for the time being
Prov.—Provençal; Proverbs
prov.—province; provisional; provost
prox.—proximo mense (Lat.), next month
Prus.—Prussia(n)

P.S.—Privy Seal; Public School
P.S., p.s.—post scriptum (Lat.), postscript
Ps.—Psalm(s)
pseud.—pseudonym
psi—pounds per square inch
PST—Pacific Standard Time
psychol., psych.—psychological; psychologist; psychology
Pt—platinum
pt—pint
pt.—part; payment; point; port
PTA—Parent-Teacher Association
PT boat—patrol torpedo boat
P.T.O.—please turn over
Pu—plutonium
pub.—public; published; publisher; publication
pvt.—private
PW—Prisoner of War
PWA—Public Works Administration
PWD—Public Works Department
pwt—pennyweight
PX—Post Exchange

Q

Q—Queen (chess)
Q—quasi (Lat.), as it were, almost; Quebec; queen; query; question
q.—quarto; question
QB—queen's bishop (chess)
Q.B.—Queen's Bench
QBP—queen's bishop's pawn (chess)
Q.C.—Quartermaster Corps; Queen's Counsel
Q.E.D.—quod erat demonstrandum (Lat.), which was to be proved
Q.E.F.—quod erat faciendum (Lat.), which was to be done
QKT—queen's knight (chess)
QM, Q.M.—quartermaster
QMG—quartermaster-general
QP—queen's pawn (chess)
Q.P., q.pl.—quantum placet (Lat.), as much as you please
qq.v.—quae vide (Lat.), which see (plural)
QR—queen's rook (chess)
qr.—quarter
QRP—queen's rook's pawn (chess)
qs—quantum sufficit (Lat.), as much as may suffice
qt—quart
q.t.—quiet (slang)
Que.—Quebec
ques.—question
quot.—quotation
q.v.—quod vide (Lat.), which, *or* whom, see

R

R—radical (hydrocarbon radical, chem.); radius; rates (math.); rook (chess)
R, r—resistance (elec.); royal; ruble
R.—Reaumur
R., r.—rabbi; rector; regina; river; road; royal; rupee
r.—radius; reigned; runs (baseball)
R.A.—Rear Admiral; Royal Academy, *or* Academician: Royal Artillery
Ra—radium
RAAF—Royal Australian Air Force
RAF—Royal Air Force
R.A.M.—Royal Academy of Music; Royal Arch Mason
Rb—rubidium
RBC—red blood cells; red blood count
r.b.i., rbi, RBI—run(s) batted in (baseball)
R.C.—Red Cross; Reserve Corps; Roman Catholic
RCAF—Royal Canadian Air Force
RCMP—Royal Canadian Mounted Police
R.D.—Rural Delivery
Rd., rd.—road
R.E.—real estate; Reformed Episcopal; Right Excellent; Royal Engineers
Re—rhenium
REA—Rural Electrification Administration
rec.—receipt; recipe; record; recorded

rect.—receipt; rector
ref.—referee; reference; reformed
Ref. Ch.—Reformed Church
reg.—regent; regiment; region; register; registrar; regular; regulation
Rep., Repub.—Republic; Republican
Rev.—Revelation (Bible); Reverend
Rev. Ver.—Revised Version (Bible)
RF—radio frequency
RFC—Reconstruction Finance Corporation
R.F.D.—Rural Free Delivery
Rh—rhodium
Rh factor—Rhesus factor (agglutinogen often present in human blood, biochem.)
R.I.—Rhode Island
RIBA—Royal Institute of British Architects
R.I.P.—requiescat in pace (Lat.), let him, *or* her, rest in peace
rit., ritard.—ritardando (It.), more slowly (music)
riv.—river
R.M.S.—Railway Mail Service
R.N.—Registered Nurse; Royal Navy
Rn—radon
RNA—ribonucleic acid
R.N.R.—Royal Naval Reserve
R.N.V.R.—Royal Naval Volunteer Reserve
Rom.—Roman; Romans (Bible)
ROTC—Reserve Officers Training Corps
R.P.—Regius Professor (Lat.), Royal Professor; Reformed Presbyterian
RPF—Rassemblement du Peuple Français (Fr.), Reunion of the French People
rpm—revolutions per minute
rps—revolutions per second
R.R.—Railroad; Right Reverend
RRB—Railroad Retirement Board
R.S.A.—Royal Society for Antiquarians; Royal Scottish Academy
RSFSR—Russian Socialist Federated Soviet Republic
RSV—Revised Standard Version (Bible)
R.S.V.P., r.s.v.p.—répondez s'il vous plait (Fr.), answer if you please
Rt. Hon.—Right Honorable
Rt. Rev.—Right Reverend
Ru—ruthenium
R.V.—Revised Version (Bible)
Ry.—Railway

S

S—sulfur
S, S., s.—south
S.—Sabbath; Samuel (Bible); Saturday; Saxon; Seaman; September; Signor; Sunday
S., s.—saint, soprano; southern
s.—second; semi-; shilling; silver; sire; solo; son
S.A.—Salvation Army
SAC—Strategic Air Command
Sam., Saml.—Samuel
Sans., Sansk.—Sanskrit
SAR—Sons of the American Revolution
S.A.S.—Societatis Antiquariorum Socius (Lat.), Fellow of the Society of Antiquaries
Sask.—Saskatchewan
Sat.—Saturday; Saturn
S.B.—Scientiae Baccalaureus (Lat.), Bachelor of Science
Sb—stibium (Lat.), antimony
SBA—Small Business Administration
SC—Security Council (United Nations)
S.S.—Sanitary Corps; Signal Corps; South Carolina; Supreme Court
Sc—scandium
Sc.—science; Scotch; Scots; Scottish
sc.—scale; scene; science; screw
s.c.—small capitals (print.)
Scan., Scand.—Scandinavia(n)
SCAP—Supreme Commander Allied Powers
Sc.B.—Scientiae Baccalaureus (Lat.), Bachelor of Science

Sc.D.—Scientiae Doctor (Lat.), Doctor of Science
sch.—school
sci.—science; scientific; scientist
Sc.M.—Scientiae Magister (Lat.), Master of Science
Scot.—Scotch; Scotland; Scottish
scr.—scruple (pharm.)
Script.—Scripture
sculp., sculp.—sculptor; sculptural; sculpture
S.C.V.—Sons of Confederate Veterans
s.d.—sine die (Lat.), without day *or* without appointing a day
S.Dak.—South Dakota
Se—selenium
SEATO—Southeast Asia Treaty Organization
SEC—Securities and Exchange Commission
sec—secant; second(s)
sec.—secretary
sect.—section
secy.—secretary
sen.—senate; senator
Sep.—Septuagint
Sept., Sept—September
seq., seqq.—sequentia (Lat.), following
serg., sergt.—sergeant
sf., sfz.—sforzando (It.), sudden strong accent (music)
SFSR—Soviet Federated Socialist Republic
sg, s.g.—senior grade
s.g.—specific gravity
sgt.—sergeant
SHAEF—Supreme Headquarters, Allied Expeditionary Forces
SHAPE—Supreme Headquarters Allied Powers (Europe)
Si—silicon
Sig., sig.—signature; signor (It.), mister
sin—sine
sing.—singular
S.J.—Society of Jesus
S.J.D.—Scientiae Juridicae Doctor (Lat.), Doctor of Juridical Science
Slav.—Slavic; Slavonian; Slavonic
S.M.—Scientiae Magister (Lat.), Master of Science; Sergeant Major; Soldier's Medal; State Militia
Sm—samarium
Sn—stannum (Lat.), tin
So.—South; Southern
soc.—society
S. of Sol.—Song of Solomon
sol.—solicitor
sop.—soprano
SOS—Service of Supply; the signal of distress is not an abbreviation but a prescribed code
SP—shore patrol or shore police (U.S. Navy)
sp.—special; species; specific; specimen; spelling; spirit
s.p.—sine prole (Lat.), without issue
SPARS—Women's Coast Guard Reserves (from the Coast Guard motto, "Semper Paratus—Always Ready")
SPCA—Society for the Prevention of Cruelty to Animals
spec.—special
sp gr—specific gravity
sp ht—specific heat
SPR—Society for Psychical Research
Sq.—Squadron
sq.—square; sequence
SR—Sons of the Revolution
Sr—strontium
Sr.—Senior; Señor; Sir
SRO—standing room only
SS, S.S.—Schutzstaffel (Ger.), protective force (a military unit of the Nazis)
SS, S.S., S/S—Steamship
SS.—Saints
S.S.—Sunday School
SSA—Social Security Administration

SSR—Soviet Socialist Republic
SSS—Selective Service System
St.—saint; strait; street
stacc.—staccato (It.), detached (music)
S.T.B.—Sacrae Theologiae Baccalaureus (Lat.), Bachelor of Sacred Theology
S.T.B.—Sacrae Theologiae Doctor (Lat.), Doctor of Sacred Theology
Ste.—Sainte (Fr., fem. of saint)
ster., stg.—sterling
St. Ex.—Stock Exchange
sub.—submarine; substitute; suburb
subj.—subject; subjective; subjunctive
Sun., Sund.—Sunday
sup.—superior; supplement; supply; supra (Lat.), above; supreme
supp., suppl.—supplement
supt.—superintendent
surg.—surgeon; surgery
sym.—symbol; symphony
syn.—synonym; synonymous

T

T—tantalum; temperature (absolute scale); (surface) tension; tritium
T.—Testament; Tuesday
t.—temperature; tempo; tempore (Lat.), in the time of; tenor; tense (gram.); territory; time; ton(s); town; transitive; troy (wt.)
Ta—tantalum
TAC—tactical air command
tan—tangent
TASS—Telegraphnoye Argentstvo Sovyetskovo Soyuza (Russ.), the Soviet News Agency
T.B., Tb., Tb, t.b.—tubercle bacillus; tuberculosis
Tb—terbium
tbs., tbsp.—tablespoon
TC—Trusteeship Council (United Nations); teachers college
Tc—technetium
Te—tellurium
tech.—technical; technology
tel.—telegram; telephone; telegraph
temp.—temperature; temporary
ten.—tenor; tenuto
Tenn.—Tennessee
terr., terr.—territory
Test.—Testament
Teut.—Teuton(ic)
Tex.—Texas
TF—Task Force
Th—thorium
Th.D.—Theologiae Doctor (Lat.), Doctor of Theology
theol.—theologian; theological; theology
Thess.—Thessalonians
Thur., Thurs.—Thursday
Ti—titanium
Tim.—Timothy
Tit.—Titus
TKO—technical knockout
Tl—thallium
Tm—thulium
TNT, T.N.T.—trinotrotoluene; trinitrotoluol
Tob.—Tobias
topog.—topography; topographical
tox.—toxicology
tr.—transitive; translated; translation; translator; transpose
trag.—tragedy; tragic
trans.—transaction; translation; translator; transportation
treas.—treasurer; treasury
trem.—tremolo, wavering, trembling (music)
trig., trigon.—trigonometric; trigonometry
tsp.—teaspoon
Tu., Tues.—Tuesday
TV—television; terminal velocity
TVA—Tennessee Valley Authority
TWA—Trans World Airlines
twp.—township

TWU—Transport Workers Union
typ.—typographer; typographical; typical

U

U—uranium
UAR—United Arab Republic
UAW—United Automobile Workers
U.B.—United Brethren
UDC—United Daughters of the Confederacy
UFO—unidentified flying objects
UHF—ultrahigh frequency
UK—United Kingdom
ult.—ultimate
UMT—Universal Military Training
UMW—United Mine Workers
UN, U.N.—United Nations
UNESCO—United Nations Educational, Scientific and Cultural Organization
UNICEF—United Nations Children's Fund
Unit.—Unitarian
Univ.—Universalists
univ.—universal; university
UNRRA—United Nations Relief and Rehabilitation Administration
UPI—United Press International
UPU—Universal Postal Union
U.S., US—United States
U.S.A., USA—United States Army; United States of America
USAF—United States Air Force
USCG—United States Coast Guard
USDA—United States Department of Agriculture
USES—United States Employment Service
USIA—United States Information Agency
USM—United States Mail; United States Mint
USMA—United States Military Academy
USMC—United States Marine Corps; United States Maritime Commission
USN—United States Navy
USNA—United States Naval Academy
USNG—United States National Guard
USNR—United States Naval Reserve
USO—United Service Organizations
USP—United States Pharmacopoeia
USPHS—United States Public Health Service
USS—United States Ship or Steamer
USSR—Union of Soviet Socialist Republics
U.S.W.A.—United Steel Workers of America
U.S.W.V.—United Spanish War Veterans
Ut.—Utah (not official)
U.T.W.A.—United Textile Workers of America
uv—ultraviolet

V

V—vanadium; vector (math.); velocity; victory
v.—verb; verse; versus; vide (Lat.), see; voltage; von (in German names)
VA—Veterans Administration
Va.—Virginia
VAR—visual-aural range
Vat.—Vatican
V.C.—Veterinary Corps; Vice-Chancellor; Victoria Cross
VD—venereal disease
ven.—venerable
vet.—veteran; veterinary
VFW—Veterans of Foreign Wars
V.G.—Vicar General
VHF—very high frequency
vid.—vide (Lat.), see
VIP—very important person
VISTA—Volunteers in Service to America
viz.—videlicet (Lat.), namely
V.M.D.—Veterinariae Medicinae Doctor (Lat.), Doctor of Veterinary Medicine
VNA—Visiting Nurse Association
vol.—volcano; volume
VOR—very high frequency omnirange

vox pop.—vox populi (Lat.), voice of the people
v.p.—vice president
V.R.—Victoria Regina (Lat.), Queen Victoria
V. Rev.—Very Reverend
V.S.—Veterinary Surgeon
vs.—versus (Lat.), against
vs., vss.—verse, verses
v.s.—vide supra (Lat.), see above
VSS—versions
Vt.—Vermont
VTOL—vertical take off and landing
Vulg., Vul.—Vulgate (Bible)

W

W—wolfram (Ger.), tungsten
W, W., w—watt; west
W.—Wales; Wednesday; Welsh
W., w.—width; work (physics)
WAAF—Women's Auxiliary Air Force (Brit.)
WAAS—Women's Auxiliary Army Service (Brit.)
WAC—Women's Army Corps (U.S.)
WAF—Women in the Air Force (U.S.)
Wash.—Washington
WASP—Women's Air Force Service Pilots
WAVES—Women Accepted for Volunteer Emergency Service (U.S. Navy)
WBC—white blood cells; white blood count
WCTU—Women's Christian Temperance Union
WD, W.D.—War Department
Wed.—Wednesday
w.f.—wrong font (print.)
WFU—World Federation of Trade Unions
WHO—World Health Organization (United Nations)
Wis., Wisc.—Wisconsin
WMO—World Meteorological Organization (United Nations)
WO—warrant officer
WPA—Works Projects Administration
wpm—words per minute
WRENS, W.R.N.S.—Women's Royal Naval Service (Brit.)
wt—weight
W.Va.—West Virginia
WVS—Women's Voluntary Service (Brit.)
WW—world war
Wyo., Wy.—Wyoming

X

X—Christ; Christian
x—an abscissa (math.); an unknown quantity
Xe—xenon
Xmas—Christmas

Y

Y—yttrium
Y.—Young Men's (Women's) Christian Association
y—an ordinate (math.); an unknown quantity
Yb—ytterbium
yd—yards(s)
YMCA—Young Men's Christian Association
YMHA—Young Men's Hebrew Association
yrbk.—yearbook
yr—year(s)
YWCA—Young Women's Christian Association
YWHA—Young Women's Hebrew Association

Z

Z—atomic number; zenith distance
z—an unknown quantity
Zech.—Zechariah
zn—zinc
Z.O.A.—zoological; zoology
Zr—zirconium

MUSICAL TERMS

Term	Origin	Meaning	Term	Origin	Meaning
Accelerando	(It.)	Becoming quicker	Lento	(It.)	Slow
Adagietto	(It.)	Somewhat faster than *adagio*	Lo stesso tempo	(It.)	The same speed
Adagio	(It.)	Slow	Lourd	(F.)	Heavy
Ad libitum	(Lat.)	At the performer's discretion	Lusingando	(It.)	Flattering, coaxing
Affettuoso	(It.)	Tenderly	Lustig	(G.)	Merry, cheerful
Agitato	(It.)	Agitated	Maestoso	(It.)	Majestic
Al fine	(It.)	To the end. Usually with *da capo* or *dal segno*	Marcando, marcato	(It.)	Marked
			Meno	(It.)	Less
Alla brev	(It.)	Double the tempo (with half note as the beat)	Mesto	(It.)	Mournful
			Mezza voce	(It.)	Half voice; in instrumental music, half volume
Allargando	(It.)	Getting slower			
Allegretto	(It.)	Less movement than *allegro*	Mezzo	(It.)	Half
Allegro	(It.)	Fast	Moderato	(It.)	Moderate tempor
Andante	(It.)	In moderate walking speed	Molto	(It.)	Very
Andantino	(It.)	Modification of *andante,* whether faster or slower is not always clear	Obbligato	(It.)	Indispensable part; opposite of *ad libitum*
			Parlando, Parlante	(It.)	Speechlike
Arco	(It.)	With the bow. Cancels *pizzicato*	Piacevole	(It.)	Agreeable
			Piano	(It.)	Soft (*p*)
Assai	(It.)	Very; sometimes, rather	Pianissimo	(It.)	Very soft (*pp*)
A tempo	(It.)	Resume earlier tempo	Più	(It.)	More
Attacca	(It.)	Continue without pause	Pizzicato	(It.)	Plucked instead of bowed (*pizz.*)
Ausdrucksvoll	(G.)	With expression			
Bewegt	(G.)	With motion	Poco	(It.)	Little
Breit	(G.)	*Largo.* Also, broad	Quasi	(It.)	As if, or nearly
Brio, con	(It.)	With spirit or vigor	Rallentando	(It.)	Gradually slowing (*rall.*)
Calando	(It.)	Getting weaker and slower	Rasch	(G.)	Quick
Cantabile	(It.)	Singing, songlike	Ritardando	(It.)	Gradually slowing (*rit.*)
Cédez	(F.)	Slow down	Ritenuto	(It.)	Immediately slower
Col legno	(It.)	With the wood (of the bow)	Rubato	(It.)	Flexible melody against an inflexible accompaniment
Comodo	(It.)	Leisurely			
Crescendo	(It.)	Gradually getting louder (< or *cresc.*)	Ruhig	(G.)	Peaceful
			Scherzando	(It.)	Playfully
Da capó	(It.)	Repeat from the beginning (D.C.)	Schleppend, nicht	(G.)	Not dragging
			Schnell	(G.)	Fast
Dal segno	(It.)	Repeat from the sign: (D.S.)	Segue	(It.)	Continue without a break
Decrescendo	(It.)	Gradually getting softer (> or *decr.*)	Semplice	(It.)	Simple
			Senza	(It.)	Without
Détaché	(F.)	Broad, separate bow strokes	Sforzando	(It.)	Sudden accent (*sf.*)
Diminuendo	(It.)	Gradually getting softer (> or *dim.*)	Slentando	(It.)	Slowing down
			Soave	(It.)	Gentle
Dolce	(It.)	Sweetly	Solo	(It.)	Alone; one player
Dolente	(It.)	Sorrowful	Sordino, con	(It.)	With the mute
Doucement	(F.)	Gently, sweetly	Sospirando	(It.)	Sighing
Empfindung, mit	(G.)	With feeling	Sostenuto	(It.)	Sustained; smoothly
Ernst	(G.)	Serious	Sotto voce	(It.)	In an undertone
Espressivo	(It.)	Expressively (*espr.*)	Spiritoso	(It.)	Spirited
Feierlich	(G.)	Solemn, exalted	Staccato	(It.)	Disconnected; opposite of legato
Festivo	(It.)	Festive			
Fine	(It.)	End	Staff	(E.)	5 parallel lines used in musical notation
Flüssig	(G.)	Flowing			
Forte	(It.)	Loud (*f*)	Tace	(It.)	Silent
Fortissimo	(It.)	Very loud (*ff*)	Tempo		Rate of Speed
Fuoco, con	(It.)	With fire	Tempo giusto	(It.)	Strict time; fitting speed
Giocoso	(It.)	Playful	Tenuto	(It.)	Held, legato
Gioioso	(It.)	Joyous	Tremolo	(It.)	Rapid reiteration of a single pitch
Glissando	(mock It.)	sliding			
Grandezza, con	(It.)	With dignity, grandeur	Trill		Rapid alternation of notes
Grave	(It.)	Solemn, serious	Troppo, non	(It.)	Not too much
Gusto, con	(It.)	With style, taste	Tutti	(It.)	All (players)
Lacrimoso	(It.)	Tearful	Una corda	(It.)	Use of soft pedal on piano to achieve muting
Langsam	(G.)	Slow			
Largamente	(It.)	Broadly	Veloce	(It.)	Fast
Largo	(It.)	Slow, dignified tempo	Vif	(F.)	Lively
Legato	(It.)	Smooth, connected	Vivace	(It.)	Quick, vivacious
Leggiero	(It.)	Light	Volti subito	(It.)	Turn (the page) quickly (*v.s.*)

Purpose of This Book

The purpose of this *Handbook* is to provide a quick, easy-to-use guide to grammar, correct usage, and punctuation. It is intended for use in the business office, in the home, and in school. Secretaries, writers, teachers, and students, will find it especially useful.

The *Handbook* is divided into 25 sections or chapters each covering an important aspect or problem in English. The book is designed so that it may be used as a step-by-step complete self-study English review. But, in addition, it is a complete reference handbook for day-to-day use whenever a question arises concerning English usage or punctuation.

Special Features

Complete Table of Contents

Starting on page 1, is a detailed table of contents for use in finding subtopics within each chapter.

Clear Explanations and Examples

Throughout the book, each explanation is followed by one or more specific examples. The examples clarify the principles and rules of good English usage.

TABLE OF CONTENTS

1. THE PARTS OF SPEECH—I

When we speak and write, we use words to express our thoughts and ideas. The English language has thousands of words, but all of them fall into eight groups or classes known as the *parts of speech*. The following names have been given to the *parts of speech*:

Nouns   Pronouns   Verbs

Adjectives   Adverbs   Prepositions

Conjunctions   Interjections

Each group has its special work to do. *Nouns* are the names of persons, places, and things. *Pronouns* take the place of nouns. *Adjectives* and *adverbs* help express the ideas that give color and more definite meanings to nouns, verbs, and other words. *Conjunctions* are joining or connecting words.

Words, then, are the tools of communication. Like any other tool, a word may be used for different purposes at different times. For example, a word might be used as a noun in one sentence and as a verb in another sentence. Another word might be used as a preposition in one sentence and as an adverb in another sentence. All words do not have more than one use, but many words do.

The most important fact concerning any word is its *function* or use in a particular sentence. If you keep this fact in mind, you will have no difficulty in understanding the simple principles that govern the relationship of words in sentences.

NOUNS
WORDS USED AS NAMES

A **noun** is one of the most important words that you use when either speaking or writing. It is the word that tells what you are talking about. *A noun is a word that names something.* There are names for *persons, animals, places,* and *objects* that can be pointed out and recognized. There are also names for *substances, qualities, actions,* and *measures* of time or quantity. The following list includes examples of different kinds of nouns.

Persons:	soldier—Jane—friend
Animals:	elephant—mouse—zebra
Places:	home—Chicago—camp
Objects:	desk—picture—computer
Substances:	iron—air—water—food
Qualities:	kindness—heroism—beauty
Actions:	climbing—cooking—reading
Measures:	year—pound—inch—day

Nouns Used in Sentences

The words in *italics* in the following sentences are nouns.

The *soldier* is wearing his new *uniform*.

Chicago is a great industrial *city*.

Iron is a useful *metal*.

PRONOUNS
SUBSTITUTES FOR NOUNS

You will often find it necessary to refer to a *name* a number of times in a single sentence. This repetition usually results in a sentence that is very awkward or monotonous. You can readily see what might happen from the following illustration:

Jack went to *Jack's* closet and took out *Jack's* new suit because *Jack* was going to a dance given by *Jack's* company.

In this sentence the word *Jack* is stated five times. This awkward repetition of the word *Jack* and *Jack's* could be avoided by substituting another part of speech for these words.

Jack went to *his* closet and took out *his* new suit because *he* was going to a dance given by *his* company.

The words *his* and *he* used in the revision of the sentence are called **pronouns.** They are substitutes for the noun *Jack*. The prefix **pro** in the word pronoun means *for*. The word **pronoun** simply means *for a noun, or in place of a noun*.

In the following sentences, the pronouns and the nouns to which they refer are underlined.

Mary said she was going.

The men forgot their tickets.

The officer blew his whistle.

Commonly Used Pronouns

You should be familiar with the pronouns in common use. For that reason a list of pronouns is a handy reference guide. Whenever you are not certain whether a word is a pronoun, refer to the following list. In a short time you will be familiar with most of them.

I	she	this	several
my	her	that	other
mine	hers	these	another
me	it	those	anybody
we	its	all	everybody
our	they	any	nobody
ours	their	both	somebody
us	theirs	each	no one
you	them	either	someone
yours	which	neither	everyone
your	what	few	one
he	who	many	whoever
his	whose	none	whosoever
him	whom	some	anyone

VERBS
ACTION AND LINKING VERBS

The **verb** is the most important part of speech. *It is the only part of speech that can make a statement about the subject.* The subject is the part of a sentence that names the person, place, or thing that is talked about. If you wanted to write or say something about a *hunter,* you could not complete your statement without the use of a verb. You must have a verb in every sentence. The following illustration will make this clear.

The hunter *shot* the deer.
(The verb is the word *shot.*)

If you take the verb *shot* out of the sentence, you have left the words, *the hunter, the deer,* but you do not have a complete thought. You need a verb to state what the hunter did to the deer. When you supply a verb, you have a complete statement.

Most of the verbs in common use express **action.** The action is not always physical action like the action expressed in the sentence, *The hunter shot the deer.* In the sentence, *I solved the problem,* the meaning of the verb *solved* implies both mental and physical activity.

In the sentence, *The engineer built a bridge,* all the types of activity that went on until the bridge was completed are implied in the verb *built.* The same would be true of the verb *made* in the sentence, *The chef made a cake.* All the verbs in the following sentences express action of some kind:

The painter *decorated* the hall.
I *pricked* my finger.
The manager *wrote* a letter.
The president *called* a meeting.

A small, but very important group of verbs, *do not* express action. The verb **to be** is the most important verb in this group. The most common forms of the verb *to be* include *is, are, was* and *were.* Since the verb *to be* does not express action, it must have another function in the sentence. With the help of some other word or words, it makes a statement about the *condition* of the subject, or the person, place, or thing that is talked about.

In the sentence, *Henry is ill,* the verb *is* does not express action of any kind, but it serves two purposes in the sentence. With the help of the word *ill* it makes a statement about the subject, *Henry.* It also serves to connect the word *ill* with *Henry.* The sentence really means *ill Henry,* but you need the verb *is* to make the statement a complete sentence. Because the verb has this connecting function, it is called a **linking verb.**

From the following illustrations, you will see that the verb *to be* with the help of some other word describes or explains the condition of the subject in some way. The verb *is* is a form of the verb *to be.*

My uncle *is* a famous surgeon.
   (classifies uncle as surgeon)
Mother *is* very happy.
   (describes the condition of mother)
Her dress *is* beautiful.
   (describes dress)

VERB PHRASES
PRINCIPAL AND AUXILIARY VERBS

A *verb* is not always a single word. *When the verb is composed of two or more words, it is called a* **verb phrase.** The verb form at the end of the verb phrase is always the *principal verb*. It is the verb form that indicates the nature of the action, if the verb expresses action. The other verb forms in the verb phrase are called *auxiliary verbs* or *helping verbs*.

The men *work* in the fields.
The men *are working* in the fields.
The men *have been working*.
The men *must have been working*.

In the first sentence the verb consists of one word, the verb *work*. The verb *work* tells the kind of action that is going on. The verb in the second sentence consists of two words. The principal verb is *working*. The auxiliary, or helping verb is *are*. The verb phrase is *are working*. The verb phrase in the third sentence is *have been working*. The principal verb is *working*, and the two helping verbs are *have been*. The verb phrase in the fourth senpence is *must have been working*. The principal verb is *working* and the three helping verbs are *must have been*.

One of the first things you should learn to do in your study of grammar is to be able to identify the verb or the verb phrase in any sentence. Some persons have trouble in deciding what words belong in the verb phrase. You will never encounter this difficulty if you become familiar with the commonly used auxiliary verbs. A list of these auxiliary verbs follows. You should refer to this list constantly until you become familiar with the verbs that help make verb phrases.

Commonly Used Auxiliary Verbs

am	have been	could
is	had been	would
are	has been	should
was	shall	must
were	will	should have
will be	do	would have
shall be	did	must have
could be	does	should have been
have	may	could have been
has	can	must have been
had	might	

Verb Phrases Used in Sentences

In the following sentences, the words in *italics* are verb phrases.

You *will receive* the money.

He *was talking* with the manager.

The building *was destroyed* by fire.

2. THE PARTS OF SPEECH—II

Chapter One explained how *nouns, pronouns, verbs*, and *verb phrases* function in English. With these three parts of speech you can build the framework of any sentence. But it is only a framework. The sentence that contains only a noun or a pronoun and a verb is not a very interesting sentence. It does not give very specific information, or present a very interesting picture. Such sentences become very monotonous if repeated often, as you will readily see from the following illustrations:

Birds fly.	Dogs bark.
Men work.	She knits.
He swims.	They sing.

ADJECTIVES-Modifiers

You will generally find it necessary to add other parts of speech to a skeleton sentence to make the meaning clearer and more exact. You can add words to nouns and pronouns that tell *what kind, what color, which one*, etc. If you wanted to tell about the hat a woman was wearing, you would describe the hat in some way. You might say that it was a *large* hat, an *atrocious* hat, or a *red* hat, depending upon the meaning which you intended to convey.

When you add one or more of these *describing words* to hat, you give a clearer picture of what the hat is like. *Words which add new ideas to nouns and pronouns are called* **adjectives.**

The adjective not only describes by telling what kind or what color, but it may limit the meaning by telling *which* hat, *whose* hat, or the *number* of hats. For example, you might limit the meaning by saying *that* hat, *Fred's* hat, *two* hats, or *several* hats.

In grammar, we say that the adjective *modifies* the meaning of the noun or pronoun.

The word **modify** means *to change the meaning slightly* by *describing* or *limiting* the meaning to a certain kind or to a certain number.

When we speak of a hat as an *attractive* hat, we are limiting the meaning because we are leaving out all the hats that are not attractive. If a word describes, limits, or restricts the meaning in any way, it is called a **modifier.** This is an important term that is frequently used in grammar.

The words *a, an*, and *the* are adjectives although in grammar they are called **articles.** The word *the* is called the *definite* article. The words *a* and *an* are called the *indefinite articles*. When we say, *the* book on the table, we are pointing out a particular book on a particular table. When we say, *I have a book*, no specific or particular book is indicated.

Adjectives Modifying Nouns

The following examples show how adjectives modify nouns and how their use makes the meaning clearer or more explicit.

long road	*good* friend	*rainy* day
rusty nail	*worthy* cause	*rapid* typist
old piano	*steep* hill	*essential* parts

ADVERBS—Modifiers

Another interesting group of words that serve as modifiers are **adverbs.** The prefix *ad* in the word adverb means *to, toward*, or *in addition to*. An adverb is a word that you *add to a verb to modify or expand the meaning of the verb*. Adverbs may also modify adjectives or other adverbs. In this unit we shall consider the adverb as a modifier of the verb. A later unit will give you the other uses of an adverb.

Adverbs are easy to identify because they usually answer the questions *when, where, how, in what manner*, or *to what extent or degree*. The following illustrations will make this clear:

You must set up the copy *now*.
  (*Now* tells when to set it up.)
We put the desk *there*.
  (*There* tells where it was put.)
Mary walks *gracefully*.
  (*Gracefully* tells how she walks.)

When we say, *The paper is issued weekly*, the adverb *weekly* introduces an additional idea of *time*. The adverb *weekly* makes the meaning explicit because we know *how often* or *when* the paper is issued. When we say, *Dandelions grow everywhere*, we have introduced the idea of *place*, or we tell *where* the dandelions grow. In the sentence, *We walked farther into the forest*, we have added the idea of *extent* or the *degree to which*. The adverbs in the preceding sentences are called adverbs of *time, place, manner*, or *degree*.

POSITION OF THE ADVERB

Although an adverb often modifies the verb in the sentence, it is not always placed directly after the verb. Sometimes the adverb introduces the sentence. In this position it gives more emphasis. At times the adverb is placed between the parts of the verb phrase. Study the following sentences carefully. Note the position of the adverb.

Sometimes I take a walk in the woods.
Jack *usually* leaves the house at seven.
We added a room to our house *recently*.
I have *always* admired him.

PREPOSITIONS
Words That Show a Relationship

Another important part of speech is the **preposition.** A preposition is not a modifier. The only parts of speech that are modifiers are adjectives and adverbs. The preposition has a different function to perform in the sentence. *A preposition shows the relationship that exists between certain words in a sentence.*

The word *preposition* comes from two Latin words which mean *placed before*. A preposition is a word that is *placed before some noun or pronoun*. It shows the relationship that exists between that noun or pronoun and some other word in the sentence. When we say "a bag *for* the mail," the word *for* is a preposition. It shows a relationship between *bag* and *mail*. The word *mail* which follows the preposition is called the **object** of the *preposition*.

In the sentence, *The accident occurred on the bridge*, the word *on* is a preposition. The preposition *on* is followed by the word *bridge* which is called its object. The entire group of words, *on the bridge*, is called a **prepositional phrase.** The preposition *on* shows the relation between the noun *bridge* and the verb *occurred*. The entire phrase *on the bridge* tells where the accident occurred.

We might use a number of prepositions to show the relationship between the noun *bridge* and the verb *occurred*. Each preposition would show a slightly different type of relationship, as you will readily see from the following illustrations:

The accident occurred *under* the bridge.
The accident occurred *near* the bridge.
The accident occurred *above* the bridge.
The accident occurred *behind* the bridge.
The accident occurred *beneath* the bridge.

You should become acquainted with the words that are commonly used as prepositions. A list of these prepositions is given here for your reference. Refer to this list repeatedly until you are able to identify the prepositions that are in common use.

A List of Commonly Used Prepositions

above	behind	for	since
about	below	from	to
across	beneath	in	toward
after	beside	inside	through
against	between	into	under
along	beyond	like	until
among	by	near	up
around	down	of	upon
at	during	off	with
before	except	on	within

CONJUNCTIONS—Connecting Words

In many sentences you need words that serve to join words or groups of words. In grammar, words that have this connecting function are called **conjunctions.**

The word *conjunction* comes from two Latin words which mean to *join with* or to *join together.* In the sentence, *Jane and Alice are secretaries,* the word *and* connects the two nouns, *Jane* and *Alice.* The word *and* in this sentence is a conjunction. In the sentence, *The manager or his secretary will see you,* the word *or* connects the words *manager* and *secretary.* The word *or* in this sentence is a conjunction. In the sentence, *Her small but attractive apartment is for rent,* the word *but* joins the words *small* and *attractive.*

The conjunctions that were used in the preceding illustrations were *and, but,* and *or.* These conjunctions always connect words or groups of words of equal rank. For the present, we shall limit our discussion to the use of these three conjunctions. In the following sentences, the underlined words are the words joined by the conjunction.

Mark drives too fast *and* too recklessly.
  (joins two adverbs)

He *or* I will audit the account.
  (joins two pronouns)

I fell *and* broke my arm.
  (joins two verbs)

He gave it to Mary *or* Jane.
  (joins two nouns)

It is a large *but* attractive home.
  (joins two adjectives)

INTERJECTIONS—Exclamatory Words

In English we have a number of words that are used to express strong feeling or sudden emotion. Words that serve this purpose are called **interjections.** The word *interjection* comes from two Latin words which mean to *throw between.* Interjections are really thrown into the sentence to express some type of emotion such as disgust, joy, excitement, enthusiasm, etc.

Interjections have no grammatical relation to any word or group of words in the sentence. In grammar we call words of this type *independent elements.* Sometimes words which are independent elements stand for an entire sentence. The following illustrations show the kinds of words that are commonly used as interjections. The interjections are in *italics.*

Alas! This is the end!

Hey! Where are you going?

Bah! I can't believe that.

Pshaw! Why did I do that?

The words classified as interjections in the preceding illustrations *are always interjections.* In addition to such words, nouns, pronouns, adjectives, and other parts of speech *are often used* as interjections.

Heavens! I cut my finger.

Good! I'm glad to hear that.

Horrors! Look at that hat!

Well! When are you going?

FUNCTION OF WORDS

One of the most important things to learn about the English language is the fact that *the same words are often used as different parts of speech.* A word may perform a certain function in one sentence and an entirely different function in another sentence.

Adjectives are commonly used as nouns, and nouns are frequently used as adjectives. The same word may function both as an adverb and as a preposition. Almost any type of word may be used as an interjection. The following sentences show how words function as different parts of speech:

The *light* in my study is poor.
  (*Light* is a noun.)

Please *light* the candles.
  (*Light* is a verb.)

Her hat is a *light* shade of blue.
  (*Light* is an adjective.)

Father is a *fast* driver.
  (*Fast* is an adjective.)

Father drives too *fast.*
  (*Fast* is an adverb.)

I *fast* one day every week.
  (*Fast* is a verb.)

3. THE SENTENCE

When a number of words (parts of speech) are put together in such a way that they express a **complete thought,** you have a *sentence.* The sentence may consist of one word, or it may consist of as many as three hundred words. The tendency in modern writing is to use short, effective sentences. Twenty words is about the average length in present-day writing.

Often those who are beginning the study of language find it difficult to understand what is meant by a *complete thought.* Some students punctuate parts of sentences as if they were sentences because they do not realize that some essential element is missing. None of the following groups of words are sentences, although they are punctuated as if they were complete.

The officers of our company.
Enjoyed the banquet.
On the top of the hill.

These groups of words are not sentences because they lack something that is necessary in order to express a complete thought. When you examine the first group of words, you will readily see that you know what the writer is talking about. However, the writer did not complete the sentence by telling you what the officers did. The second group of words tells you that somebody enjoyed a banquet. But the author neglected to tell you who it was. The third group of words tells you very little. You

have no way of knowing what the writer is talking about.

SUBJECT AND PREDICATE

In order to express a complete thought, a sentence must have both a *subject* and a *predicate.* These are two important grammatical terms used to describe the essential elements of a sentence.

The **subject** is the word or group of words that tells us *what or whom the speaker or writer is talking about.* The **predicate** is the part of the sentence *that makes a statement about the subject.* The *predicate* usually tells what the subject is doing, or what is happening to the subject.

Study the following sentences carefully. Note that the subjects have been separated from the predicates so that you will be able to see the relationship between the two parts more easily.

Subject	Predicates
My friend	lives in New York.
The letter	contains exciting news.
Both men	are experienced salesmen.

In the first sentence, I am talking about *my friend.* Therefore, *my friend* is the subject of the sentence. I complete the sentence by making a statement about my friend. I say that my friend *lives in New York.* The predicate is *lives in New York.* This group of words, *My friend lives in New York,* is a sentence because it expresses a complete thought. It has both a subject and a predicate. The other two sentences also have a subject and predicate.

COMPLETE SUBJECT AND COMPLETE PREDICATE

In many sentences the subject or the predicate is only a single word. But more often, the subject consists of two or more words. In grammar, we call the entire subject, regardless of the number of words, the **complete subject.** We call the entire predicate the **complete predicate.**

If the subject of a sentence is a single word, that word is the *complete subject.* If the predicate of the sentence is a single word, that word is the *complete predicate.* In the sentence, *Birds fly,* the word *birds* is the complete subject, and the word *fly* is the complete predicate.

SIMPLE SUBJECT AND SIMPLE PREDICATE

After you have learned how to identify the complete subject and the complete predicate, you can easily find the **simple subject** and the **simple predicate.**

Somewhere in the complete subject you will find the *particular word* about which something is said. That word is the *simple subject.* It is usually either a noun or a pronoun.

Somewhere in the predicate you will find a word that serves as the *key* to the predicate. That word is the *verb,* the most important word in any sentence. If the verb consists of more than one word, it is called a *verb phrase.* In the following examples the simple subjects and predicates are underlined:

The ambassador attended a conference.
The hero of the story had many adventures.
My friend in Boston bought a new car.

Sometimes you will find only one word in the subject or one word in the predicate. In that case, the single word in the subject is the simple subject. It is also the complete subject.

The single word in the predicate is the simple predicate and also the complete predicate.

Pronouns are often used as the simple subject and the complete subject. In the sentence, *We are buying a new home,* the pronoun *we* is the simple subject. It is also the complete subject since there are no other words in the subject.

In the sentence, *The building collapsed,* the verb *collapsed* is the simple predicate. It is also the complete predicate since it is the only word in the predicate.

In the following illustrations, the simple subjects and simple predicates are underlined.

Fast driving is often dangerous.
The detectives on the case found the jewels.
Children play.

COMPOUND SUBJECT AND COMPOUND PREDICATE

A sentence may have two or more simple subjects and two or more simple predicates. In the sentence, *Harry and Fred joined a lodge,* there are two simple subjects, *Harry* and *Fred.* The connecting word is *and.* In grammar we say that the sentence has a **compound subject.**

In the sentence, *The stenographer wrote the letter and mailed it,* there are two predicate verbs, *wrote* and *mailed.* The connecting word is *and.* This sentence has a **compound predicate.**

Some sentences have a compound subject and a compound predicate. In the sentence, *Alice and Jane washed the curtains and ironed them,* there are two simple subjects and two simple predicates. The subject nouns are *Alice* and *Jane.* The two predicate verbs are *washed* and *ironed.* In both cases, the connecting word is *and.*

The following sentences contain either a compound subject, a compound predicate, or both.

Corn and beans are grown in the valley.
(*compound subject*)
I attended the lecture and took notes.
(*compound predicate*)
The boys and girls sang and danced at the club.
(*compound subject and compound predicate*)

SENTENCE FRAGMENTS

If you have studies this unit carefully, you will have a thorough understanding of the essential elements of a sentence. But even persons who have this knowledge often punctuate groups of words as sentences when one or both of the essential elements are missing.

Any incomplete group of words punctuated as if it were a sentence is called a *sentence fragment* or a *fragmentary sentence.* As you know, a fragment is only a piece or a part of the whole. A fragment always refers to something that is incomplete.

A fragmentary sentence always lacks one or both of the essential elements of a sentence. That is, either the subject or the predicate, or both the subject and predicate are missing. Whenever you are in doubt about a particular sentence, apply this test: Does the group of words contain both a subject and a predicate? Does it express a complete thought?

Very often the subject of the sentence is missing. The following group of words is *not* a sentence because it does not tell who it is that the writer is talking about:

Interviewed the candidate.
(This is not a sentence.)
The president interviewed the candidate.
(This is a complete sentence.)

The sentence was completed by supplying a subject, *The president.*

Sometimes the predicate is missing. The following group of words is *not* a sentence because the entire predicate is missing:

The sound of footsteps.
(This is not a sentence.)
The sound of footsteps *alarmed us.*
(This is a complete sentence.)

The use of fragmentary or incomplete sentences is an unsatisfactory way of communicating your ideas. Surprising as it may seem, sentence fragments similar to the following examples can be found repeatedly in letters sent out by reputable business firms. Check the letters of your company. You may be amazed at what you find. Be sure you do not use fragments in your own personal writing.

Received your letter this morning.
(*Subject* is missing.)
Will send order at onec.
(*Subject* is missing.)
Have shipped your order.
(*Subject* is missing.)
Hoping this meets with your approval.
(*No subject or predicate.*)

4. SENTENCE PATTERNS

In Chapter Three it was explained that a sentence must express a complete thought. It must also have both a subject and a predicate. This unit shows how it is possible to express a complete thought in a variety of ways. You should become familiar with the different ways of arranging words in sentences and the different sentence patterns that are the result of these arrangements.

KINDS OF SENTENCES

Sentences fall into four groups according to the purpose the sentence serves and the manner in which the thought is expressed. Some sentences simply *make statements.* Some sentences *ask questions.* Another type of sentence *gives a command* or *makes a request.* The last group is the kind of sentence that *expresses strong feeling* or *sudden emotion.*

In grammar, the sentence that makes a statement is called a **declarative sentence.** The sentence that asks a question is called an **interrogative sentence.** The sentence that gives a command or makes a request is called an **imperative sentence,** and the sentence that expresses strong feeling is called an **exclamatory sentence.** Following are examples of the four types of sentences:

My friend is a business executive.
(*declarative sentence*)

Have you entered the contest?
(*interrogative sentence*)

Clear the road at once!
(*imperative sentence*—command)

Please shut the door.
(*imperative sentence*—request)

What a tragedy this is!
(*exclamatory sentence*)

If you examine the preceding illustrations carefully, you will notice that the *declarative sentence* ends with a *period.* The *interrogative sentence ends with a question mark* (?). Sometimes the *imperative sentence* ends with an *exclamation mark* (!) and sometimes it ends with a *period.* If the command is given in a very emphatic or decisive manner, an exclamation mark is placed at the end. A mild request always ends with a period. An *exclamatory sentence* usually ends with an *exclamation mark.* Briefly summarized, then:

A **declarative** sentence *makes a statement.*

An **interrogative** sentence *asks a question.*

An **imperative** sentence *gives a command* or makes a *request.*

An **exclamatory** sentence expresses *strong feeling* or *sudden emotion.*

INVERTED ORDER

You have probably observed that the four types of sentences follow certain patterns of word arrangement. These patterns will now be discussed in more detail.

Every sentence has a basic structure or framework. This is true of all four types of sentences—*declarative, interrogative, imperative,* and *exclamatory.* This framework, as you already know, consists of the subject noun or pronoun and the predicate verb.

There are a number of ways of introducing the subject in a declarative sentence. The **normal order,** or the grammatical order, is *subject first,* followed by the predicate. If you always followed this pattern, your sentences would soon become monotonous and uninteresting. The following illustration will make this clear. The sentences in this paragraph sound very much like the sentences in a primer or in a first reader.

I like this book. It is a book about Mexico. My friend sent this book to me. My friend lives in New York. She speaks Spanish.

In this short paragraph, all the sentences follow the same pattern—subject first, followed by the predicate. You can give more variety to your sentence patterns by placing words in unusual positions.

You can put the subject after the verb or place it at the very end of the sentence. Varying the position of the subject gives you an opportunity to place other words at the beginning of the sentence to give them more emphasis. This also makes our sentences more interesting.

On my desk I found an interesting book about Mexico.

In this sentence, the subject is placed after the group of words, or the phrase, *on my desk.* This arrangement throws the phrase to the front of the sentence and gives it more emphasis.

When the subject of the sentence does not appear in its normal position, we say that the order of the sentence is inverted, or turned around. Always remember that *normal* or grammatical order *means subject first,* followed by the predicate. Examine the following sentences carefully. Note the position of the subject in the two sentences.

The *band* marched down the street.
Down the street marched the *band.*

The first sentence is in normal, or grammatical order. The subject noun *band* appears at the beginning of the sentence. The verb *marched* follows the subject.

The second sentence is the same sentence in **inverted order.** The subject noun *band* now appears at the end of the sentence. The verb *marched* comes before the subject. A phrase, *Down the street,* appears at the beginning of the sentence.

An adverb often introduces a sentence. The following sentence begins with an adverb, and not with the subject.

Suddenly the train stopped. (*inverted order*)
The train stopped *suddenly*. (*normal order*)

Some persons find it difficult to determine the true subject when a sentence is not in grammatical order. This difficulty can be avoided by *transposing* the sentence and putting it back in normal order. The only purpose in transposing a sentence is to see the grammatical relations more clearly.

Sometimes when you put a sentence back in grammatical order by transposing it, you will find that the transposed sentence is not so smooth as the original sentence. However, the following sentence is just as effective in either order.

Along the road we passed a number of army trucks.
We passed a number of army trucks *along the road.*

Whenever you are dealing with a sentence in inverted order, you should transpose it before you attempt to analyze the sentence from the grammatical point of view.

INTERROGATIVE SENTENCE PATTERNS

In asking a question, you seldon start with the subject first, as you do in a declarative sentence. For that reason, *the interrogative sentence is generally in inverted order.* Sometimes the interrogative sentence starts with the *verb.* Often it begins with an *adverb,* which is used to ask the question.

Did you bring your camera?
    (introduced by the *verb*)
Where did you buy your watch?
    (introduced by an *adverb*)

In order to see the grammatical constructions in an interrogative sentence that is inverted, you must transpose the sentence and put it in normal order. Sometimes the interrogative sentence becomes a statement when it is transposed.

You did bring your camera?
You did buy your watch where?

IMPERATIVE AND EXCLAMATORY SENTENCE PATTERNS

The imperative sentence presents a different problem. The *subject* of the sentence that gives a command or makes a request *is seldom expressed.* If the subject is not expressed, it is the word *you* understood.

Sound the alarm at once!
    (Subject is not expressed.)
(You) Sound the alarm at once!
    (Subject *you* is understood.)
Please read the announcement.
    (Subject is not expressed.)
(You) Please read the announcement.
    (Subject *you* is understood.)

Sometimes an imperative sentence begins with a noun that indicates the name of the person to whom the command or the request is given. An interrogative sentence may also begin in this way. The point to keep in mind is that such a noun *is not the subject* of the sentence. In fact, it has no grammatical connection with the rest of the sentence. It is an independent element. For that reason, it is separated from the rest of the sentence by a comma. Study the following illustrations carefully:

Imperative Sentence

Fred, please close the door.
    (*Fred* is the person addressed.)
Fred, (you) please close the door.
    (Subject is *you* understood.)

Interrogative Sentence

Alice, did you lock the door?
    (*Alice* is a noun in direct address.)
Alice, you did lock the door?
    (Subject is *you* expressed.)

In the first sentence, the word *Fred* is a noun in **direct address** because it names the person spoken to directly. It is not the subject of the sentence. The subject of an imperative sentence is *you* understood. The word *Fred* is set off from the rest of the sentence by a comma to show that it is used *independently.*

In the second sentence, the word *Alice* is a noun in direct address because it names the person spoken to directly. Since this is an interrogative sentence, the subject is expressed. When the sentence is placed in normal order, you can easily see that the subject is *you,* and not Alice.

A noun in *direct address* may appear at the beginning or at the end of the sentence. It may even appear within the sentence.

Fred, please close the door.
    (beginning of the sentence)
Please close the door, *Fred.*
    (end of the sentence)
Come here, *Fred,* and look at this book.
    (within the sentence)

The exclamatory sentence is often expressed in inverted order. In the sentence, *What a feast she spread!,* the subject and the verb appear at the end of the sentence. When the sentence is transposed, the subject appears at the beginning of the sentence and is followed by the verb.

What a feast she spread! (*inverted order*)
She spread what a feast! (*normal order*)

How beautiful the sunset is tonight! (*inverted order*)
The sunset is how beautiful tonight! (*normal order*)

What a tragedy that would be! (*inverted order*)
That would be what a tragedy! (*normal order*)

SENTENCES THAT BEGIN WITH "THERE"

Another sentence pattern that we use frequently is the sentence that begins with the word *there.* We have a very good reason for beginning some of our sentences in this way.

When the word *there* is used to introduce the sentence, it is possible to place the subject after the verb. In many cases this results in a much smoother sentence, as you will see from the following illustration:

A heavy frost was last night.
There was a heavy frost last night.

Although the first sentence is in grammatical order, it is a very awkward sentence. The second arrangement results in a much smoother style, but it presents a grammatical problem. In dealing with a sentence that begins with *there,* you must always remember that the word *there* is neither the subject of the sentence, nor an adverbial modifier. It is merely an introductory word which has a special function, that of introducing the sentence.

When the word *there* functions in this way, it is called an **expletive.** The word **expletive** comes from the Latin and means "*added merely to fill up.*" This is a very suitable term because it explains exactly what takes place.

The word *there* merely "fills up" the place normally occupied by the subject. It has no other function in the sentence. Like the noun in direct address, it is an independent construction. When the sentence is transposed, and placed in grammatical order, you should enclose the word *there* in parentheses to show that it is used independently.

There are twelve candidates for the position.
(There) twelve candidates are for the position.

It is important to transpose the sentence beginning with *there* in order to determine the true subject of the sentence. It is also important to determine whether the word *there* is used as an introductory word or whether it is used as an adverb.

There they are. (*There* is an adverb of place.)
They are *there.* (*There,* is an adverb of place.)

There were ten men in the band. (*there*—expletive)
(*There*) ten men were in the band. (*there*—expletive)

The coach stood *there* watching the game. (*there*—adverb of place)
There is a telephone directory on the table. (*there*—expletive)
We met *there* last year. (*there*—adverb of place)
There will be some objection to the plan. (*there*—expletive)

The word *it* is also used as an expletive in certain sentence patterns. The use of *it* as an expletive will be discussed in later units.

5. NOUNS
KINDS OF NOUNS

Chapter One explained that a noun is a word used as a name. You also learned that some nouns begin with capital letters, and others begin with small letters. The subject of *capitalization* is very important because it is closely concerned sith the division of nouns into groups or classes.

In English, nouns are divided into two main classes called **common nouns** and **proper nouns.** A *common noun* names any one of a class of persons, places, or things. We have a name for all the chairs in the world when we use the common noun *chair.* We have a name for all the lakes in the world when we use the common noun *lake.*

But when we want to name a particular lake, we must give it a special name. The name of a particular lake might be *Lake Louise, Lake George,* or *Lake Michigan.* These particular names are called proper nouns. *A proper noun always begins with a capital letter.*

We have particular names for persons, such as *John Adams, General Eisenhower, Queen Elizabeth,* and *Governor Stevenson.* We also have particular names for certain objects, such as buildings, hotels, theaters, and clubs: *Conway Building, Congress Hotel, Harris Theater,* and *Union League Club.*

Sometimes a common noun names a collection of objects or a group of persons. When we use the word *band* in music, we include under one name all the musicians who play the different instruments. When we use the word *jury,* we include all the members who make up the jury. Nouns that name a group of persons or a collection of objects are called *collective nouns.*

A **common noun** is the name of *any one* of a class of *persons, places,* or *things.*

aviator	ocean	tiger	meat
city	book	lily	desk

A **proper noun** is the name of a *particular person, place,* or *thing.*

Pacific Ocean	Thomas Edison
Chicago	Amazon River
England	Wrigley Building
State Street	Bay of Fundy

A **collective noun** is a common noun whose singular form names a *group* of persons, objects, or acts.

herd	company	team	crowd
army	corps	audience	faculty

Some nouns are *common nouns* in one sentence and *proper nouns* in another sentence.

Common Nouns

Roy is studying to be a doctor.
John's uncle is an engineer.
I went to the theater with May.
We spent the summer at the lake.

Proper Nouns

The family called in Dr. Allen.
Uncle John is a colonel in the army.
The play was given at the Grand Theater.
Did you ever cross Lake Erie?

CAPITALIZATION OF PROPER NOUNS

A student of language should be familiar with the accepted rules regarding the capitalization of *proper nouns* and *proper adjectives.* **Proper adjectives** *are adjectives derived from proper nouns.*

Proper Nouns	Proper Adjectives
America	an *American* soldier
Spain	a *Spanish* house
China	a *Chinese* vase

The following list of rules for the capitalization of proper nouns follows accepted, present-day usage:

1. Capitalize names of *particular persons* and *places.*

Mr. Smith	Yankee Stadium
Helen Hayes	Radio City
Senator Clark	Ellis Island

2. Capitalize *geographic names:* continents, countries, states, cities, rivers, mountains, lakes, falls, harbors, valleys, bays, etc.

Africa	Gulf of Mexico
Montana	Rocky Moutains
Pikes Peak	New York Harbor
Cleveland	Long Island

3. Capitalize names of *definite regions, localities,* and *political divisions.*

the Orient	Third Precinct
the Bad Lands	Wheeling Township
the Arctic Circle	French Republic

4. Capitalize names of *bridges, buildings, monuments, parks, ships, automobiles, hotels, forts, dams, railroads, streets,* etc.

Brooklyn Bridge	Michigan Avenue
Fine Arts Building	Plaza Hotel
Statue of Liberty	Eiffel Tower
Central Park	Boulder Dam

5. Capitalize names of *historical events, historical periods,* and *historical documents.*

the Middle Ages	Battle of Gettysburg
World War II	Louisiana Purchase
the Crusades	Fourteenth Amendment
Magna Charta	the Civil War (American)

6. Capitalize names of *governmental bodies* and *departments.*

Bureau of Mines	Civil Service Commission
the Federal Government	Federal Trade Commission
United States Senate	the President's Cabinet
Federal Courts	Supreme Court of the United States

7. Capitalize names of *political parties, business* and *fraternal organizations, clubs* and *societies, companies,* and *institutions.*

Republicans	County Hospital
Democratic Party (or party)	John Crerar Library
	a Shriner
Chapman Chemical Company	the Elks
	Ford Motor Company
Volunteers of America	Rutgers University

8. Capitalize *titles of rank* when they are joined to a person's name.

President Lincoln	Professor Thomas
Senator Lodge	Doctor Hayden
Dr. Allen Reed	Dean Mary Allison
Chancellor Harris	Cardinal Wolsey
Secretary Henderson	His Honor the Mayor

9. Capitalize *days* of the *week, months* of the *year, holidays,* and *days* of *special observance,* such as feast and fast days.

Monday	Feast of the Passover
September	Mothers's Day
Labor Day	Good Friday
Easter Sunday	Memorial Day

10. You should not capitalize names of the seasons unless they are personified. When something is personified it is represented or considered as if it were a person. Personification is frequently used in poetry.

spring	winter
Spring's warn touch	Winter's icy breath

11. The words *north, east, south,* and *west* are capitalized when they refer to *sections* of the country. They are not capitalized when they refer to *directions.*

Sections of Countries

the Midwest
the Far West
the Near East

Directions

I travel north on my way home.
The sun rises in the east.
The southern part of Idaho is beautiful.

12. The *special names* given to planets and stars are capitalized. The words *sun, moon, star,* and *planet* are not capitalized.

Jupiter	The *sun* rose at six that morning.
Venus	The *moon* is a heavenly body.
Mars	A *planet* shines by reflected light.
Milky Way	A *constellation* is a group of stars.

SPECIAL USES OF CAPITAL LETTERS

1. Words derived from proper nouns are usually capitalized. If the word has acquired a special meaning, it is not capitalized.

Capitalized	Not Capitalized
Mongolian race	navy blue
Venetian blinds	china cabinet
Swiss cheese	morocco leather
English tweeds	chinaware
Turkish bath	turkish towel or Turkish towel

2. The principal words in *titles of books, magazines, pictures, songs, articles,* etc., are capitalized. Prepositions, conjunctions, and the articles *a, an,* and *the* are not capitalized unless the title begins with one of these words.

The Last of the Mohicans (book)
The Saturday Evening Post (magazine)
"Outside Our World" (article)
Battle Hymn of the Republic (song)
"Meet the Press" (television program)

3. The definite article *the* is not capitalized unless it is the first word of a title. Many titles do not begin with *the.* If the word *the* is within the title, it is written with a small letter. The only way to be sure about the correct form of a title is to check the official form, or the form adopted by the company, publication, etc.

The Christian Science Monitor
The John C. Harris Company
National Geographic Magazine
Pinnacle Oil Company

4. All words referring to the Deity, the Bible, books of the Bible, and other *sacred books* are capitalized.

God, the Father	the Koran
Savior	Genesis
the Trinity	Supreme Being
Talmud	Bible
Book of Job	New Testament

5. The pronoun *I* and the interjection *O* are capitalized. The word *oh* is not capitalized unless it is the first word of a sentence.

"O say! can you see, by the dawn's early light, ..."
" 'Tis the Star Spangled Banner, oh, long may it wave. . ."

6. Names of school subjects are not capitalized unless they are names of the languages. Subjects listed in school catalogs as names of special courses are capitalized.

mathematics	History 101
French	Advanced Chemistry II
economics	Economics 345
English	Physics II

7. Capitalize words which show family relationships when they are used with a person's name. The words *father* and *mother* are not capitalized when they are preceded by a pronoun. When used without a pronoun, they are usually capitalized.

Aunt Martha	her cousin
Cousin John	their uncle
Uncle Jack	my father

8. Capitalize the first word in a *compound word that is used as a proper noun.* If the second word in the compound word is a proper noun, it should also be capitalized. Capitalize both parts of *compound titles of distinction.*

Forty-third Street	un-American activities
Army-Navy game	ex-President Eisenhower
The Honorable	Rear Admiral Simpson
John Willis	

9. The names of special departments of business firms may be written with small or with capital letters. In business writing, it is considered good practice to capitalize titles such as *president, secretary, office manager, general superintendent,* etc. They may also be written with small letters.

claim department *or* Claim Department
The Company will reimburse you. (or company)
Our President will see you. (or president)

PLURAL FORMS OF NOUNS

When a noun refers to one person or thing, it is singular in number. When a noun refers to more than one person or thing, it is plural in number. Nouns have special forms to show these distinctions, as you will see from the following illustrations:

Singular   Plural

boy	boys
box	boxes
leaf	leaves
tomato	tomatoes

The plurals of nouns are formed in a number of different ways. Since there are exceptions to almost every one of these methods, you should consult a reliable dictionary whenever you are in doubt regarding a correct plural form. You should also be familiar with the following methods of forming the plurals of nouns:

1. Most nouns add the letter *s* to the singular to form the plural.

lamp	lamps	college	colleges
dance	dances	manager	managers
chief	chiefs	dynamo	dynamos

2. Nouns ending in *s, sh, ch, x,* or *z* form the plural by adding *es.* The plural adds another syllable in the pronunciation.

dress	dresses	couch	couches
match	matches	waltz	waltzes
tax	taxes	loss	losses

3. Nouns ending in *o* preceded by a vowel add *s.* Musical terms ending in *o* add *s.*

Vowel Preceding "o"   Musical Terms

patio	patios	piano	pianos
rodeo	rodeos	alto	altos

Some nouns ending in o preceded by a consonant add *s.* Others add *es.* Some form the plural either way.

Add "s"   Add "es"

kimono	kimonos	Negro	Negroes
zero	zeros	hero	heroes

Add "s" or "es"

cargo	cargos	cargoes
motto	mottos	mottoes

4. Nouns ending in *y* preceded by a consonant, change the *y* to *i* and add *es.*

party	parties	country	countries
city	cities	enemy	enemies
lady	ladies	berry	berries

5. Nouns ending in *y* preceded by a vowel, usually add *s.* In many cases the vowel before the final *y* is *e.*

alley	alleys	journey	journeys
boy	boys	valley	valleys
key	keys	day	days

6. Some nouns ending in *f* or *fe* change the *f* or the *fe* to *v* and add *es.* Some nouns ending in *f* have two plurals, one in *s* and one in *ves.* Some simply add *s.*

Change to "ves"		Add "s" or Change to "ves"	
wife	wifes	scarf	scarfs scarves
thief	thieves	wharf	wharfs wharves
half	halves	hoof	hoofs hooves

7. Some nouns form the plural by a change in the vowel.

man	men	mouse	mice
foot	feet	goose	geese
tooth	teeth	louse	lice

8. Some nouns have the same form for both singular and plural.

Singular and Plural

fish	fish	species	species
sheep	sheep	series	series
Chinese	Chinese	salmon	salmon

9. The plurals of compound nouns are generally formed by adding *s* to the *principal word* in the compound.

mother-in-law	*mothers*-in-law
board of education	*boards* of education
attorney general	*attorneys* general or attorney *generals*
court-martial	*courts*-martial

Sometimes *both parts* of the compound are made plural.

manservant	menservants
woman doctor	women doctors

Sometimes an *s* or *es* is added to the end of the compound. In that case, there is no important word in the compound.

forget-me-not	forget-me-nots
toothbrush	toothbrushes

Compounds ending in *ful* are made plural by adding *s* to the end of the compound. This rule applies when the same container is filled a number of times.

spoonful	spoonfuls	handful	handfuls
bucketful	bucketfuls	cupful	cupfuls

10. The plurals of proper names are formed by adding *s* or *es.*

There are three *Ruths* in this class.
The two *Burnses* left the hall.
The *Joneses* and the *Smiths* attended.

The spelling of proper names must not be changed. If we followed the rule for words ending in *y* in the case of *Mary,* we would change the *y* to *i* and add *es.* The name would then be changed to *Marie,* for the plural would be *Maries.* The correct plural of *Mary* is *Marys.*

11. Titles are made plural in several ways. The plural of *Miss* is *Misses;* the plural of *Mr.* is *Messrs. Mrs.* has no plural. The plural of

Madam is *Mesdames,* which is sometimes used for the plural of *Mrs. Misses* should not be followed by a period. It is not an abbreviation. In the first column of the following examples, the title is made plural. In the second column the name is made plural. Either form is correct.

the *Misses* Thomas   *or*   the Miss *Thomases*
the *Messrs.* Churchill   *or*   the Mr. *Churchills*

Foreign Plurals

Words taken from foreign languages usually retain their foreign plurals. Some of these words are used so commonly that they have acquired an English plural which is formed in the regular way; that is, by adding *s* or *es* to the singular.

The following list gives the foreign and English plurals for some commonly used foreign words. If no English plural is given, the foreign plural is used.

Foreign Word	Foreign Plural	English Plural
alumna (*feminine*)	alumnae	_____
alumnus (*masculine*)	alumni	_____
analysis	analyses	_____
appendix	appendices	appendixes
bacterium	bacteria	_____
basis	bases	_____
cactus	cacti	cactuses
crisis	crises	_____
criterion	criteria	criterions
curriculum	curricula	curriculums
datum	data	_____
formula	formulae	formulas
gymnasium	gymnasia	gymnasiums
hypothesis	hypotheses	_____
index	indices	indexes
madam	mesdames	_____
medium	media	mediums
memorandum	memoranda	memorandums
parenthesis	parentheses	_____
phenomenon	phenomena	_____
radius	radii	radiuses

12. The plural of numbers, letters, signs, and symbols is formed by adding the apostrophe and *s.*

Your *2's* look like your *3's.*
You use too many *ands* in your writing. (correct)
or
You use too many *and's* in your writing. (correct)
You must always cross your *t's.*
He received three *A's* and two *B's* last semester.

13. The following nouns are used only in the plural. You may find some of them used in the singular, but the general practice is to regard them as plural. When you are in doubt, consult the dictionary.

trousers	shears	contents
pants	pliers	riches
scissors	scales (weighing)	alms
billiards	nuptials	remains
clothes	gallows	victuals

6. PRONOUNS

In Chapter One you learned that a *pronoun* is a word used in place of a noun. Because pronouns can be used in place of nouns, they avoid the monotonous repetition of nouns. The following illustration shows what happens when we repeat the same noun too often in a sentence:

Alice went to **Alice's** room to dress because **Alice** was going to a reception given by **Alice's** club in **Alice's** honor.

This sentence is very awkward and monotonous because of the tiresome repetition of *Alice* and *Alice's*. When we rewrite the sentence and substitute pronouns for *Alice* and *Alice's*, we have a much better sentence.

Alice went to **her** room to dress because **she** was going to a reception given by **her** club in **her** honor.

You should not only learn how to use pronouns effectively, but you should also learn how to use them correctly. Many of the language errors that are commonly made are errors in the use of pronouns. These mistakes occur because some of the pronouns that we use constantly have a number of different forms.

As a student of English you should know how and when to use the different forms of pronouns. In order to do this, you must be familiar with the changes in form that certain pronouns undergo. To illustrate: The pronoun **I** is used as the subject of a sentence. When this same pronoun is used as the object of a preposition, the form changes to *me*. It is incorrect to say, "between *you* and **I**." The correct form to use in this phrase is *me*.

Illustrations of Changes in the Forms of Pronouns

I saw the accident. (The pronoun **I** is the subject.)

Jane saw **me** at the game. (The pronoun **me** is the object of *saw*.)

He *won* the first prize. (The pronoun *he* is the subject).

We met **him** in the lobby. (The pronoun *him* is the object of *met*.)

In the first sentence, the pronoun *I* is used as the **subject** of the sentence. When this same pronoun is used as the **object of a verb,** the form changes to *me*. In the third sentence, the pronoun *he* is the subject of the sentence. When this same pronoun is used as the object of the verb *met*, the form changes to *him*.

KINDS OF PRONOUNS

There are five groups or classes of pronouns in English: **personal** pronouns, **interrogative** pronouns, **demonstrative** pronouns, **indefinite** pronouns, and **relative** pronouns. The personal pronouns include the *compound personal* pronouns, and the relative pronouns include the *compound relative* pronouns.

PERSONAL PRONOUNS

The personal pronouns are the most important group of pronouns. They are also the pronouns that will give you the most trouble unless you are familiar with the various forms that belong to each pronoun.

A **personal pronoun** is a pronoun that shows by its form whether it refers to the *person speaking*, the *person spoken to*, or the *person or thing spoken of*. All the personal pronouns, with the exception of the pronoun *it*, refer to persons. The following sentences show the use of personal pronouns in the first, second, and third person:

I shall spend the winter in Texas. (*I* is the *person speaking.*)

You are working too hard. (*You* is the *person spoken to.*)

He bought a new Ford. (*He* is the *person spoken about.*)

We built the garage. (*We* refers to the *persons speaking.*)

They operate two farms. (*They* refers to the *persons spoken about.*)

Ted has a new radio. **It** is a Zenith. (*It* refers to the *thing spoken about.*)

Jan has two fur coats. **They** are both mink. (*They* refers to the *things spoken about.*)

The pronoun of the **first person** is the pronoun **I** with its plural form *we*. The pronoun of the **second person** is *you*. The plural form is also *you*. The pronouns of the **third person** are *he, she,* and *it* with the common plural *they* for all three persons.

The personal pronouns also have different forms to indicate case. You will learn more about the case of pronouns in Chapter Nine. For the present, you should be familiar with all the forms of the personal pronouns and the pronoun *who* so that you will be able to identify them.

Forms of the Personal Pronouns

1. **First person**—personal pronouns referring to the *speaker*:

   I, my, mine, me (singular)
   we, our, ours, us (plural)

2. **Second person**—personal pronouns referring to the *person spoken to*:

   you, your, yours (same forms in both singular and plural)

3. **Third person**—personal pronouns referring to the *persons* or *things spoken about*:

   he, his, him, she, her, hers, it, its (singular)
   they, their, theirs, them (plural)

4. Forms of the pronoun **who**:

   who, whose, whom

COMPOUND PERSONAL PRONOUNS

Sometimes the word *self* or *selves* is added to certain forms of the personal pronouns. Pronouns formed in this way are called **compound personal pronouns.**

List of Compound Personal Pronouns

myself	herself
yourself	ourselves
himself	yourselves
itself	themselves

Compound personal pronouns are used in two ways: (1) as *reflexive pronouns* and (2) as *intensive pronouns.* A compound personal pronoun is used *reflexively* when the pronoun is the object of the verb. It tells *who* or *what* received *the* action expressed by the verb. In this case the pronoun *always refers back* to the same person or thing as the subject. The following illustration will help to make this clear.

The chef burned himself yesterday.

In this sentence the word *himself* is a compound personal pronoun used as the object of the verb *burned. Himself* refers to the same person as the subject, which is the word *chef.* In other words, *chef* and *himself* are the same person. This is called the **reflexive** use of the compound personal pronoun. It means that the pronoun *refers* or *reflects back* to the subject.

Sometimes the compound personal pronoun is used to give added emphasis to a noun or pronoun in the sentence. This is called the **emphatic** or **intensive** use of the compound personal pronoun.

When a compound personal pronoun is used in this way, it must give emphasis to some noun or pronoun that is already in the sentence. Observe the following sentences carefully. In each sentence you will find that there is a *noun* or a *pronoun* to which the compound personal pronoun refers.

I made the dress myself. (*Myself* intensifies the pronoun I.)

John himself built the canoe. (*Himself* intensifies the noun *John.*)

Incorrect Use of Compound Personal Pronouns

One of the mistakes commonly made in English is to use the compound personal pronoun when there is no word in the sentence to which it refers. These pronouns should never be used as a substitute for a personal pronoun. They should never be used as the subject of the sentence.

My wife and *myself* appreciate your courtesy. (incorrect)

My wife and **I** appreciate your courtesy. (correct)

The manager and *myself* checked the accounts. (incorrect)

The manager and **I** checked the accounts. (correct)

He sent the book to John and *myself.* (incorrect)

He sent the book to John and **me.** (correct)

The first sentence is incorrect because there is no noun or pronoun in the sentence which the pronoun *myself* refers to or gives emphasis to. The second sentence is correct because a *personal pronoun* is used.

Whenever you use a compound personal pronoun in a sentence, always remember that such a pronoun must have an *antecedent*, or a word in the sentence which refers to the same person or thing as the pronoun does. In other words, it must have its own antecedent in the sentence. Do not make mistakes like the following:

Alice and *yourself* were appointed on the committee. (incorrect)

Alice and **you** were appointed on the committee. (correct)

The owner gave Tom and *myself* his old lawn mower. (incorrect)

The owner gave Tom and **me** his old lawn mower. (correct)

Everyone in the club has a car as well as *myself.* (incorrect)

Everyone in the club has a car as well as **I.** (correct)

They sent an invitation to the Smiths and *ourselves.* (incorrect)

They sent an invitation to the Smiths and **us.** (correct)

INTERROGATIVE PRONOUNS

Interrogative pronouns are pronouns that are used in asking questions. The interrogative pronouns are *who (whose, whom), which,* and *what.* An interrogative pronoun also has another function to perform in the sentence, just as any other pronoun has. It may be the *subject* of the sentence, or it may be the *object* of the verb or of a preposition.

Who is the director of the band?

For **whom** are you waiting?

What did they say about his speech?

Which is your car?

Whose car did you borrow?

DEMONSTRATIVE PRONOUNS

Demonstrative pronouns are pronouns that point out definite persons, places, or things. There are only two demonstrative pronouns: *this* with its plural *these*, and *that* with its plural *those*.

This is my hat. (A definite hat is pointed out.)

That is your book. (A definite book is pointed out.)

These are the theater tickets. (Definite tickets are pointed out.)

Those are John's shoes. (Definite shoes are pointed out.)

INDEFINITE PRONOUNS

A large group of pronouns are called **indefinite pronouns** because they do not point out particular places, persons, or things.

Somebody took my coat. (*Somebody* is an indefinite pronoun.)

A **few** left the hall early. (*Few* is an indefinite pronoun.)

The following list contains the commonly used indefinite pronouns. Refer to this list, and to the other lists in this unit, whenever you are not sure of the classification of a pronoun.

Commonly Used Indefinite Pronouns

all	everybody	one
any	everyone	one another
anybody	everything	ones
anyone	few	other
anything	many	others
both	neither	several
each	nobody	some
each one	none	somebody
each other	no one	someone
either	nothing	something

RELATIVE PRONOUNS

A **relative pronoun** is a pronoun that joins the clause which it introduces to its own antecedent. The *antecedent* of a pronoun is the noun or pronoun to which it refers. (Clauses will be explained in later chapters.)

The relative pronouns are *who, which, that,* and *what*. The pronoun *who* has two other forms, *whose* and *whom*. When the relative pronoun is combined with *ever* or *soever*, it is called a **compound relative pronoun**.

List of Compound Relative Pronouns

whoever	whosoever	whichsoever
whomever	whatsoever	whomsoever
whatever	whosesoever	whichever

The *relative pronoun* is always found in a clause which it introduces. For that reason, we shall postpone further study of relative pronouns until we take up the study of subordinate clauses.

Use of Relative Pronouns

The following distinctions are generally observed in the use of relative pronouns. A careful writer or speaker always observes these distinctions:

Who is used when the antecedent is a *person*.

That is used to refer to either *persons* or *things*.

Which is used to refer to anything *except persons*.

She is the girl **who** won the award. (*Who* refers only to persons.)

This is the dog **that** (or **which**) was lost. (*That* or *which* refers to things.)

She is the girl **that** won the award. (*That* may refer to persons.)

PRONOUNS USED AS ADJECTIVES

The *possessive forms* of the personal pronouns are often used with nouns in much the same way as adjectives are used to modify nouns. Although they function as adjectives when they are placed before the noun, they still retain the idea of possession. For that reason, they are sometimes called **possessive adjectives** to distinguish them from other types of adjectives.

In the sentence, *Herbert forgot his coat*, the possessive form of the pronoun *he*, which is *his*, is used as an adjective modifying the noun *coat*. It also shows that the coat belongs to Herbert. Therefore, it is called a possessive adjective. All the adjectives in the following sentences show possession. They are called possessive adjectives.

Possessive Forms of Personal Pronouns Used as Adjectives

These are **her** gloves. (modifies *gloves*)
I bought **their** home. (modifies *home*)
Did you bring **your** violin? (modifies *violin*)
The dog lost **its** collar. (modifies *collar*)
We like **our** new radio. (modifies *radio*)
Do you like **my** new coat? (modifies *coat*)
The manager has **his** report. (modifies *report*)

Demonstrative and *indefinite pronouns* are also used as adjectives. Demonstrative pronouns that function as adjectives are often called **demonstrative adjectives** because they have not lost their pointing out function. In the following sentences the demonstrative pronouns are used as adjectives:

This camera belongs to Jane. (modifies *camera*)
Those apples are delicious. (modifies *apples*)
That man is an army officer. (modifies *man*)
These cards are Easter cards. (modifies *cards*)

Indefinite pronouns used as adjectives are generally regarded as pure adjectives, although they may be called **indefinite adjectives.** They have no special function. The following examples illustrate their use as adjectives:

Each girl carried a flag. (modifies *girl*)
Both men received a promotion. (modifies *men*)
Neither answer is correct. (modifies *answer*)
Many soldiers were on that ship. (modifies *soldiers*)
Any mechanic could do that job. (modifies *mechanic*)
Several tables were ruined. (modifies *tables*)

Interrogative pronouns are also often used as adjectives. Since the adjective is the word that asks the question, these adjectives are called **interrogative adjectives.** In the sentence, *Which house did you buy?* the word *which* asks the question. It is also an adjective modifying the noun *house*. Note how the pronouns are used to ask questions in the following sentences:

What newspapers does he read? (modifies *newspapers*)
Whose name did he call? (modifies *name*)
Which play do you like best? (modifies *play*)

POSSESSIVE FORMS OF PRONOUNS

The possessive forms of the *personal pronouns* and the possessive form of the pronoun *who* are never written with an apostrophe. These pronouns have a special form to show possession and do not require an apostrophe. The correct forms to use in order to show possession are the following: *my, mine, yours, his, hers, its, ours, theirs, whose*. Do not place an apostrophe either before or after the **s** in any of these words.

The word *it's* is a contraction of *it is*. It is not a form of the pronoun, and should never be used to show possession. The word *who's* is a contraction of *who is* or *who has,* and should not be confused with the possessive form *whose*.

Contractions

It's on my desk. (*It is* on my desk.)
Who's speaking tonight? (*Who is* speaking tonight?)
Who's finished the test? (*Who has* finished the test?)

Indefinite pronouns do not have special forms to show possession. Therefore, it is necessary to use the apostrophe to show the possessive forms of these pronouns. Since most of these pronouns are used only in the singular, the possessive is formed by adding the *apostrophe* and **s** (**'s**). The plural of the indefinite pronoun *other* is *others*. In the case of this plural form, the apostrophe is placed after the **s**. Study these forms carefully:

Possessive Forms of Indefinite Pronouns

everybody's job	*anyone's* opinions
somebody's hat	*someone's* car
one's relatives	*each one's* duty
another's problems	*others'* affairs (plural)

When *else* is added to an indefinite pronoun, it is regarded as part of the pronoun. In this case, the apostrophe and **s** are added to *else* to form the possessive.

I came home with *somebody else's* coat.
Someone else's book was substituted for mine.

7. AGREEMENT OF PRONOUN WITH ANTECEDENT

You have already learned that a pronoun usually refers to a noun or pronoun which precedes it in the sentence. The word to which the pronoun refers is called its antecedent. The word *antecedent* comes from two Latin words which mean "*going before*." The antecedent of a pronoun is the word which "*goes before*" the pronoun. It is the word to which the pronoun refers.

In the sentence, *Robert lost his fishing tackle,* the pronoun *his* refers to *Robert*. The word *Robert* precedes the pronoun *his* or "goes before" it. *Robert* is the antecedent of *his*. It is the word to which the pronoun *his* refers.

Antecedents of Pronouns

Margaret attended her class reunion. (*Margaret*—antecedent of *her*)

Every day brings its duties. (*day*—antecedent of *its*)

The men brought their golf clubs. (*men*—antecedent of *their*)

Only a few brought their equipment. (*few*—antecedent of *their*)

The professor himself did not know the answer. (*professor*—antecedent of *himself*)

AGREEMENT OF PRONOUN AND ANTECEDENT IN GENDER

Since a pronoun stands for, or replaces a noun, it must agree with that noun in person, number, and gender. We have already considered the problems of number and person in Chapters Five and Six. In this unit we shall take up the problem of gender, and show its connection with the agreement of pronoun and antecedent.

In grammar **gender** means the classification of nouns and pronouns according to distinctions in sex. There are four genders: *masculine gender, feminine gender, common gender,* and *neuter gender.*

Masculine gender denotes the male sex. **Feminine gender** denotes the female sex. **Common gender** denotes either sex. **Neuter gender** denotes absence of sex. The following are examples of nouns and pronouns in the four genders:

Masculine gender—he, him, father, kind
Feminine gender—sister, she, her, princess
Common gender—child, adult, cousin, neighbor
Neuter gender—table, book, dress, radio, it

Some nouns and a few pronouns have special forms to show gender. The following list shows the changes that occur in some words to indicate a change in the gender. Some of the distinctions formerly used to show gender are passing out of use. The words *authoress* and *poetess,* for example, are seldom used.

SPECIAL FORMS TO SHOW GENDER

Masculine	Feminine	Masculine	Feminine
uncle	aunt	god	goddess
bull	cow	aviator	aviatrix
waiter	waitress	hero	heroine
alumnus	alumna	count (title)	countess
emperor	empress	gander	goose
host	hostess	sir	madam
peacock	peahen	ram	ewe
male	female	lion	lioness
monk	nun	duke	duchess
actor	actress	nephew	niece
bachelor	spinster	prince	princess
executor	executrix	fiance	fiancee
baron	baroness	stallion	mare
he	she	father	mother
lad	lass	him	her
man	woman	boy	girl
rooster	hen	husband	wife
master	mistress	buck(stag)	doe
brother	sister	landlord	landlady
drake	duck	son	daughter

GENDER AND NUMBER OF INDEFINITE PRONOUNS

Indefinite pronouns present a problem in gender. These pronouns often refer to both sexes, masculine and feminine. When we say, *Everybody went to the game,* the indefinite pronoun *everybody* includes individuals of both genders, masculine and feminine.

The problem arises when the indefinite pronoun is the antecedent of another pronoun. In that case, the accepted practice is to *use the masculine gender for the pronoun that is used in place of the indefinite pronoun.*

In the sentence, *Everyone received his income tax form,* the indefinite pronoun *everyone* is the antecedent of the pronoun *his.* It is the word to which the pronoun *his* refers. Although *everyone* includes persons of both genders, the masculine pronoun *his* is used instead of saying *his or her* income tax form.

If the sentence shows clearly that the indefinite pronoun refers to members of only one sex, the pronoun that refers to that sex should be used.

Everyone attending the meeting of the Women's Athletic Club presented **her** membership card.

In this sentence the members are women, and the pronoun *her* is used correctly. In cases where it is not clear whether the antecedent is masculine or feminine, use the pronoun *his.*

Anyone may have **his** money refunded.
Somebody left **his** pen on my desk.

Indefinite pronouns also present a problem in number. Some of them are always singular. Some are always plural, and some may be either singular or plural.

Pronouns That Are Always Singular

The following pronouns are always singular. A pronoun that is used in place of one of these indefinite pronouns must also be singular.

anybody	everybody	neither
anyone	everyone	one
another	many a one	other
each	nobody	someone
either	no one	somebody

Study the following illustrations carefully. These sentences show the proper agreement between pronoun and antecedent when the antecedent is singular.

Neither of the men had **his** tools. (not *their*)
If **anyone** wants a pen, **he** can obtain one here. (not *they*)
One likes to do what **he** can do well. (not *they*)
Someone left **his** coat in **his** locker. (not *their*)

Pronouns That Are Always Plural

The following pronouns are always plural. A pronoun that is used in place of one of them must also be plural.

many	both	few	several	others

Notice that *many a one* is included in the list of pronouns that are always singular, whereas *many* is included in this plural list. When singular expressions, such as *a man, a one, a person,* etc., are added to *many,* the *pronoun* is singular, not plural.

Several found **their** cars unlocked. (*Several*—plural)
Only a **few** would sacrifice **their** savings. (*few*—plural)
Many brought **their** lunches with them. (*Many*—plural)
Others found **their** friends in the balcony. (*Others*—plural)

Pronouns That May Be Either Singular or Plural

The pronouns *all, any, some,* and *none* are singular or plural according to the meaning of the sentence. When these pronouns refer to **number,** they are generally regarded as plural.

When they refer to **quantity** or to a **mass,** they are regarded as singular.

The pronoun *none* is singular when it clearly means *no one,* or *not one.* It is often difficult to determine the number of this pronoun since there are sentences in which it carries a plural idea. If you want to express the singular idea use *no one,* or *not one.*

Some found **their** children in the park. (*Some* is plural.)
Some of the candy has lost **its** flavor. (*Some* is singular.)
All were waiting for **their** salary checks. (*All* is plural.)
There is no candy in the box. **All** of **it** has been eaten. (*All* is singular.)
Did **any** of the men have **their** membership cards? (*Any* is plural.)
None have arrived. (*None*—plural in use)
None of these is a typical example. (*None*—singular in use)

AGREEMENT OF THE PRONOUN WITH A COMPOUND ANTECEDENT

Sometimes the pronoun refers to two antecedents connected by *and.* If both of these antecedents are singular and refer to *different persons or things,* the antecedent is plural. The pronoun that refers to these antecedents must also be plural.

The president and the manager have outlined their plans.

If the antecedent refers to *one* person who fulfills *two* functions, the pronoun that takes the place of the antecedent is singular. In the following sentence *cook* and *housekeeper* are the same person.

The cook and housekeeper did not like her duties.

If the housekeeper were another individual, the word *the* would be placed before the word *housekeeper.*

The cook and the housekeeper did not like their duties.

When the connectives, *either—or* and *neither—nor* join singular nouns, the antecedent is singular. When they join plural nouns, the antecedent is plural. When they join nouns that differ in number, the pronoun should agree with the antecedent that is nearer to it.

Either *Jane* or *Alice* left **her** book on **her** desk.
(Nouns are singular—pronoun is singular)

Either the *boys* or the *girls* left **their** books on the table.
(Both nouns are plural—pronoun is plural)

Neither *Harvey* nor his *cousins* wore **their** dress suits.
(Pronoun is plural—agrees with cousins)

Neither the *men* nor the *boy* could find **his** place in the line.
(Pronoun agrees with *boy* which is nearer to it.)

In sentences like the last one, it is better to place the plural noun nearer to the pronoun. By doing so, you make the antecedent plural, and the sentence sounds better.

AGREEMENT OF PRONOUN WITH COLLECTIVE NOUNS

Collective nouns are singular when they designate a group *acting as a unit.* They are plural when the members who make up the group are *acting independently.* The pronoun that takes the place of the collective noun must agree with it in number. If the collective noun expresses a singular idea, the pronoun is singular. If the collective noun expresses a plural idea, the pronoun is plural.

The band played its fifth concert. (*acting as a unit*)

The band were tuning up their instruments. (*as individuals*)

You can readily see that the second sentence could not refer to the band as a unit. That would mean that the members of the band were all working on the same instrument.

AGREEMENT OF PRONOUN AND ANTECEDENT IN PERSON

A pronoun must agree with its antecedent in **person.** If the antecedent of the pronoun is in the *third person,* the pronoun that refers to it must also be in the *third person.* If the antecedent is in the *second person,* the pronoun should be in the *second person.*

One of the most common mistakes in English is to start the sentence in the *third person* and then put the pronoun that refers to the antecedent in the *second person.* Study the following examples carefully:

If anybody wants an education, you can get it. (*incorrect*)

If anybody wants an education, he can get it. (*correct*)

When one pays attention, you learn better. (*incorrect*)

When one pays attention, he (or *one*) learns better. (*correct*)

VAGUE ANTECEDENTS

A pronoun should not have two possible antecedents in the same sentence. If it is not clear which of two nouns a pronoun refers to, there will be two possible interpretations of the sentence. Observe the two possible interpretations in the following illustration:

James told his friend that **he** had been elected president.

In this sentence, does the pronoun *he* refer to *James* or to *friend?* If the antecedent of the pronoun *he* is *friend,* the sentence means that *James told his friend that he* (the friend) *had been elected president.* If the antecedent of the pronoun *he* is *James,* the sentence means that *James told his friend that he* (*James*) *had been elected president.*

The sentence might be rewritten in either of the two following ways, since we do not know which meaning the author intended:

James said to his friend, "You have been elected president."

James said to his friend, "I have been elected president."

Many of the errors that are made in the use of pronouns are caused by a lack of agreement between pronoun and antecedent. The pronoun should refer definitely to the noun which it represents. In the following sentence, to what does the pronoun *it* refer?

Your letter and your check arrived promptly, but we cannot ship **it** at present.

There is no antecedent for the pronoun *it* in the sentence. Neither the word *letter* nor the word *check* could be the antecedent. *It* probably refers to an order for goods which was included in the letter. If the word *it* refers

to an order for goods, the sentence might be written as follows:

Your letter and your check arrived promptly, but at present we cannot ship the goods ordered.

ADJECTIVE—PRONOUN AGREEMENT

Demonstrative adjectives should agree in *number* with the nouns they modify. The adjectives *this, that, these,* and *those* sometimes cause agreement trouble when they modify such nouns as *kind, sort, type,* and *variety.*

Keep in mind that the demonstrative adjectives *this* and *that* are singular and should be used only with singular nouns. *These* and *those* are plural and should be used only with the plural nouns.

these kind of apples (**incorrect**)
this kind of apples (or apple) (**correct**)
or **these kinds** of apples (plural)

those sort of roses (**incorrect**)
that sort of roses (or rose) (**correct**)
or **those sorts** of roses (plural)

these variety of fruits (**incorrect**)
this variety of fruits or fruit (**correct**)
or **these varieties** of fruits (plural)

The forms in italic are incorrect because the adjective does not agree with the noun in number.The forms in bold face are correct because the adjective agrees with the noun in number.

8. COMPLEMENTS OF VERBS
THE DIRECT OBJECT

Every sentence must have a basic structure in order to express a complete thought. This basic structure may consist of only two parts, a subject noun or pronoun and a predicate verb or verb phrase. Many sentences require a third part or an additional word in order to express a complete thought. This additional word or group of words is necessary to complete the idea expressed by the verb.

The group of words, *The men lifted,* contains a subject noun *men* and a predicate verb *lifted.* Still it does not express a complete thought. A word is needed to tell **what** the men lifted. The sentence might be completed by adding the word *beam.* The completed sentence, *The men lifted the beam,* expresses a complete thought.

The word *beam* completes the meaning expressed by the verb *lifted.* For that reason it is called a **complement** or a completing word. The three essential parts of this sentence are the **subject,** the **verb,** and the **complement.** The complement is *beam.*

A complement completes the meaning expressed by a verb. The *complement* of a verb that expresses *action* is called the **direct object** of the verb. A direct object usually answers the questions *what?* or *whom?* In the preceding sentence the verb *lifted* expresses action. The complement *beam* tells *what* the men lifted. Notice how the underlined complements in the following sentences complete the meaning of the verb.

I saw Evelyn at the convention.
(*Evelyn* tells whom I saw.)
The engineer stopped the train.
(*Train* tells what he stopped.)

The sailors saluted the captain.
(tells *whom* they saluted)
She refused the invitation.
(tells *what* she refused)

Some verbs that express action are complete without the addition of a complement. When such verbs are used in sentences, only two parts are essential—the *subject* and the *verb.* Study the following illustrations. You will readily see that the thought is complete without the addition of a complement.

Jane is singing.
We have been studying.
The boys are playing.

Although the verbs in the preceding sentences do not require a complement or a completing word, a complement might be added to some of them to make the meaning more explicit. The underlined words are complements and are called *direct objects.*

Jane is singing a ballad.
(tells *what* Jane is singing)
We have been studying Spanish.
(tells *what* we have been studying)
The boys are playing games.
(tells *what* the boys are playing)

The **direct object** of a verb names the *receiver* of the action. It completes the meaning of the verb. A direct object is usually a noun or a pronoun. Adjectives and adverbs are never used as direct objects. Adjectives and adverbs are always used as modifiers. If you have any difficulty in deciding which word is the direct object, apply this test: Find the word that answers the question *what?* or *whom?* Apply the test in the following sentences:

The farmer planted the **seeds** in rows.

What did the farmer plant? The answer is, "He planted the *seeds."* The word *seeds* is the direct object of the verb planted. It tells **what** he planted.

I met *Uncle Henry* in the bank.

Whom did I meet? The answer is, "I met Uncle Henry." The direct object is *Uncle Henry.* It tells **whom** I met.

A verb may take two or more direct objects. In this case, the verb or verb phrase has a compound object.

He grows *orchids* and *lilies* in his garden.

I met *Jerry* and *Jane* at the stadium.

TRANSITIVE AND INTRANSITIVE VERBS

When an action verb takes a direct object, it is called a **transitive verb.** The word *transitive* comes from two Latin words which mean *"passing across."* When the verb is transitive, the action passes across from a **doer** (the subject) to a **receiver** of the action (the direct object). When we say that a verb is *transitive,* it is the same as saying that it has a *direct object.*

Any verb that does not take a direct object is **intransitive.** That is, the verb does *not* express action that passes over to a receiver.

A verb may be transitive in one sentence and intransitive in another sentence. The verb may express action, but the action may not pass over to a receiver. In that case the verb is intransitive. When the verb is transitive, it always takes a direct object—the receiver of the action.

The following sentences show the same verb used as a *transitive* verb with a direct object (underlined) in the first sentence and as an *intransitive* verb with no object in the second sentence:

The sexton rang the bell.
The bell rang loudly. (*no object*)

The ship sailed the seas.
The ship sails at noon. (*no object*)

I met my friend at the airport.
The delegates met yesterday. (*no object*)

THE INDIRECT OBJECT

Some verbs that express action take two objects, a direct object and an indirect object. The **indirect object** tells *to whom* the action is directed or *for whom* the action is performed.

The indirect object is used after certain verbs: *get, give, lend, offer, read, tell, buy, send, show, make, pay,* etc.

In the sentence, *Mother bought Ellen a coat,* there are two objects, a direct object and an indirect object. The word *coat* is the direct object. It tells *what* Mother bought. The word *Ellen* is the indirect object. It tells *for whom* Mother bought a coat. The indirect object *always* precedes or comes before the direct object. In the following sentences the indirect object and the direct object are underlined.

The librarian read the children a story.
Give him five dollars for his services.
The tailor made Edward a brown suit.

There are two tests that you can apply in order to identify an indirect object. One test is to determine the position of the object. *The indirect object always precedes the direct object.* The other test is to determine whether the indirect object seems to be the object of the preposition *to* or *for* understood. The following sentences illustrate this point:

The librarian read **(to)** the children a story.
Give **(to)** him five dollars for his services.
The tailor made **(for)** Edward a brown suit.

The words *to* and *for* are never expressed when a word functions as an indirect object. If we change the order of the sentence and supply the preposition, our sentence would read as follows: *The librarian read a story to the children.* In this sentence the word *children* is no longer the indirect object but is the object of the preposition *to.*

LINKING VERBS

Most verbs describe or express action. However, there are a small group that do not. The verb **to be** is the most important verb in this group. Since it is the most irregular verb in our language, you should be familiar with its various forms. The following verbs and verb phrases are forms of the verb *to be:*

Forms of the Verb "To Be"

am	will be	shall have been
are	shall be	will have been
is	have been	could have been
was	has been	would have been
were	had been	might have been

Although the verb *to be*, as well as the other verbs belonging in this group, does not express action, it has another function in the sentence. The chief purpose of this verb is to

serve as a link which joins the subject to some word in the predicate that gives the meaning to the sentence. For that reason, it is called a **linking verb.**

Linking verbs have very little meaning of their own. With the help of another word, they express various ideas in regard to the subject. In the sentence, *Mary is ill,* the verb *is* (a form of *to be*) is used with the adjective *ill* to describe the condition of the subject, *Mary.* The sentence really means *ill Mary,* but you need a verb in order to make a complete statement.

In the sentence, *The young man was an aviator,* the verb *was* is a linking verb. With the help of the noun *aviator,* it identifies of classifies the young man. The noun *aviator* means the same as the subject. In the sentence, *The actress is very beautiful,* the verb *is,* with the help of the adjective *beautiful,* describes the appearance of the actress.

The verbs *become* and *seem,* like the verb *to be,* are almost always used as linking verbs. The following verbs are used both as linking verbs and as action verbs. The meaning of the sentence will show to which classification they belong:

Linking and Action Verbs

grow	look	smell	remain
turn	feel	taste	keep
prove	sound	appear	stay

This group of words is important because a great many mistakes in English are made when a speaker of writer does not understand their linking function.

When these words have a linking function, they have practically the same meaning as the verb *to be* would have in the same sentence. By supplying the the verb *to be* mentally after one of these verbs, you can readily tell whether the verb has a linking function or whether it is used as an action verb. Every one of the verbs in the following sentences is a linking verb. The verb *to be* has been supplied to show you how to interpret the sentence when the verbs have a linking function.

The cookies **are** wonderful.
(wonderful cookies)
The cookies **look** (to be) delicious.
(delicious cookies)
The cookies **smell** (to be) good.
(good cookies)
The cookies **taste** (to be) sweet.
(sweet cookies)
The cookies **seem** (to be) brittle.
(brittle cookies)
The cookies **became** (to be) stale.
(stale cookies)
The cookies **proved** (to be) sweet.
(sweet cookies)
The cookies **feel** (to be) hard.
(hard cookies)
The cookies **stayed** (to be) fresh.
(fresh cookies)
The cookies **appear** (to be) tempting.
(tempting cookies)
The cookies **remained** (to be) soft.
(soft cookies)
The cookies **kept** (to be) fresh.
(fresh cookies)

Some of the same verbs that were used in the preceding illustrations may also be used to express action. Note the differences in meaning when these verbs function as action verbs and not as linking verbs.

John **appeared** promptly.
(made his appearance)

The horticulturist **grows** orchids.
(produces by cultivation)
I **turned** the key in the lock.
We **proved** a theorem in geometry.
The doctor **felt** the broken bone.
The warden **sounded** the gong.
The chef **tasted** the sauce.
We **kept** a record of our journey.
The dog **smelled** the meat.
The judge **will stay** the trial. (postpone)
The committee **looked** at the pictures.

COMPLEMENTS OF LINKING VERBS

A *linking verb* cannot make a complete predicate. It always requires a *complement.* The group of words, *My friend is,* does not make a complete statement. The verb *is* requires some additional word to complete the meaning of the sentence. That word may be a noun, a pronoun, or an adjective.

My friend is an executive.
My friend is very ambitious.
That is he.

The noun that completes the meaning of a linking verb is called a *predicate noun* because it is found in the predicate. A **predicate noun** completes the verb and renames or explains the subject. In the preceding illustration, *executive* is a predicate noun. It renames the subject *friend* and classifies *friend* as an *executive.* The noun *friend* and the noun *executive* refer to the same person.

A pronoun that follows a linking verb functions in the same way as the noun. It completes the verb and means the same person or thing as the subject. It is called a **predicate pronoun.**

An adjective that follows a linking verb is called a **predicate adjective** because it is found in the predicate. A predicate adjective always modifies the subject.

The following sentences illustrate the use of the predicate noun, predicate pronoun, and predicate adjective:

Our manager was a former army colonel.
(*manager* and *colonel*—same person)
Our manager is very efficient.
(*efficient* modifies *manager*)
The candidate for the position is he.
(*he* and *candidate*—same person)

In the first sentence, *colonel* is a **predicate noun.** It completes the meaning of the verb *was* and refers to the same person as the subject. In the second sentence *efficient* is a **predicate adjective.** it modifies the subject noun *manager.* In the third sentence, *he* is a **predicate pronoun.** It means the same person as the subject *candidate.*

9. CASE OF NOUNS AND PRONOUNS

Nouns and pronouns have certain relationships to other words in a sentence. We call attention to these relationships by indicating the case of the noun or pronoun. The word **case** is used in grammar to indicate the *relationship* a noun or a pronoun has to other words in the sentence. The case of a noun or a pronoun is determined by the particular use of that noun or pronoun in the sentence.

There are only three cases in English: the *nominative case*, the *objective case*, and the *possessive case*. The **nominative case** is the case of the *subject*. The **objective case** is the case of the *object*. The **possessive case** is the case that shows *ownership*.

CASE OF NOUNS

Nouns present very few problems in case because the same form is used for the nominative case and the objective case. The only way to determine whether a noun is in the nominative case or in the objective case is to determine its relationship to other words in the sentence. If the noun is used as the *subject* of the sentence, it is in the *nominative case*. If the noun is used as the *object* of a verb or a preposition, it is in the *objective case*.

The **door** is open.
(*nominative case*—subject)
I closed the **door**.
(*objective case*—direct object)

In the first sentence, the noun *door* is used as the subject of the sentence. It is in the nominative case. In the second sentence, the same form *door* is used as the direct object of the verb *closed*. *Door* is in the objective case in this sentence.

Like nouns, *indefinite pronouns* have the same form for the nominative case and the objective case.

Everyone contributed five dollars.
(*nominative case*—subject)
I saw **everyone** at the game.
(*objective case*—direct object)

NOMINATIVE CASE

The word *nominative* comes from a Latin word which means *name*. The **nominative case** names the case of the subject of the sentence. It also names the case of a predicate noun. A predicate noun is in the nominative case. For this reason, it is often called a **predicate nominative**.

A *predicate noun* must agree in case with the *subject* because it refers to the same person or thing as the subject. It also follows a verb which cannot take an object. Nouns used after linking verbs are called predicate nouns. In the following sentences the subjects and the predicate nouns are underlined.

My friend is a naval officer.
The leading lady was Mary Harris.

In the first sentence, *officer* is a predicate noun. It is used after the linking verb *is* and refers to the same person as the subject. It is in the nominative case to agree with the case of the subject *friend*.

In the second sentence, *Mary Harris* is a predicate noun. It is in the nominative case to agree with the subject *lady*. *Mary Harris* and *lady* refer to the same person.

OBJECTIVE CASE

The **objective case** is the case of the *subject*. The *direct object* of a verb, the *indirect object*, and the *object* of a *preposition* are in the objective case.

Lester writes **articles** for the paper.
(*articles*—direct object)
Arthur sent the **manager** a detailed report.
(*manager*—indirect object)

In the first sentence, *articles* is the direct object of the verb *writes*. It tells **what** Lester writes. *Articles* is in the objective case. In the second sentence, *manager* is the indirect object. It tells **to whom** Arthur sent his report. *Manager* is in the objective case.

In Chapter Two you learned that a preposition is always followed by some noun or pronoun which is called the *object* of the *preposition*. The object of a preposition is always in the objective case.

Edward met his lawyer at the **bank**.
(object of preposition **at**)
We met Marvin in the **lobby**.
(object of preposition **in**)

In the first sentence, the preposition *at* is followed by the noun *bank*. The object of the preposition is *bank*, which is in the objective case. In the second sentence, *lobby* is the object of the preposition *in*. *Lobby* is in the objective case.

It is easy to remember that direct objects of verbs, indirect objects of verbs, and objects of prepositions are in the objective case because they are all called **objects** of some type. The fact that they are objects indicates that they are in the **objective case**.

CASE OF PRONOUNS

Nouns do not present any problems in case because the form of the noun is the same for the nominative case and the objective case. Pronouns do present problems in case. The *personal pronouns* and the pronoun *who* have different forms to indicate the different cases.

There are only *six pronouns* in English that have these special forms to show *case*, but the changes that occur to indicate case are very important. They are responsible for many of the errors that frequently occur in the use of pronouns. You should become familiar with the different forms of these pronouns, and you should learn how to use them correctly. The six pronouns are *I, you, he, she, it, who*. The following table gives the nominative case forms and the objective case forms of each of the six pronouns:

Nominative Case		Objective Case	
Singular	Plural	Singular	Plural
I	we	me	us
you	you	you	you
he	they	him	them
she	they	her	them
it	they	it	them
who	who	whom	whom

The pronouns *he, she,* and *it* all have the same plural form. *They* is the pronoun used in the nominative case in the plural for each of the three pronouns. *Them* is the pronoun used in the objective case in the plural for each of the three pronouns.

NOMINATIVE CASE OF PRONOUNS

Like nouns, pronouns are in the nominative case when they are used as the subjects of sentences, or as predicate pronouns after one of the linking verbs. Mistakes are seldom made in selecting the correct form of the pronoun to use as the subject of the sentence. Mistakes are frequently made, however, when a pronoun is used as a *predicate nominative*. The following sentences illustrate the correct use of the six pronouns in the nominative case:

Subject of the Sentence	Predicate Pronoun
I saw the accident.	It is **I**.
You have been elected.	It is **you**.
He attended the lecture.	It might be **he**.
She gave me her note book.	It could be **she**.
It is my overcoat.	Could this be **it**?

We are great friends. (plural)	It is **we**.
They arrived early. (Plural)	It was **they**. (plural)
Who came in?	**Who** was it? (It was **who**?)

The pronoun *you* does not present any problem in the plural, because the forms for the plural are the same as the forms for the singular. The form of the pronoun *you* is also the same for the nominative case and the objective case.

Interrogative sentences should always be transposed and put in normal order. When this is done, it is easy to determine the case of the pronoun.

OBJECTIVE CASE OF PRONOUNS

Pronouns are in the objective case when they are used as direct objects of verbs, or as objects of prepositions. The correct forms to use in the objective case are *me, you, him, her, it,* and *whom* in the singular, and *us, you them, whom* in the plural. The following sentences illustrate the correct use of these pronouns in the objective case:

Object of the Verb

Mother called **me**.
Jack saw **him** yesterday.
I met **you** in Paris.
The firm sent **her** to Texas.
My friend invited **us** to the game.
Sue drove **them** to the station.
Whom did you call?

Indirect Object of the Verb

Ethel gave **me** her pen.
I sent **him** a notice.
David sent **you** a ticket.
Jack offered **her** a seat.
The tailor made **us** new uniforms.
The teacher read **them** a story.

Object of a Preposition

The telegram was sent to **me**. (object of the preposition *to*)
The manager created the position for **him**. (object of *for*)
The author wrote an article about **us**. (object of *about*)
The waiter placed their table near **us**. (object of *near*)
We distributed the gifts among **them**. (object of *among*)

THE POSSESSIVE CASE OF NOUNS

The **possessive case** shows *ownership* or *possession*. The use of the possessive case does not present much of a problem in speaking, but it does present a problem in writing and spelling. Although the rule for forming the possessive case of nouns is very simple, many persons have considerable difficulty in spelling and writing the forms correctly.

One simple rule applies to all cases: If the singular form of the noun does not end in **s**, add the *apostrophe* and **s** (**'s**). If the singular ends in **s**, add the *apostrophe* (**'**). Study the following examples carefully and try to apply the rule:

Singular		Plural	
boy	boy's	boys	boys'
lady	lady's	ladies	ladies'
hero	hero's	heroes	heroes'
man	man's	men	men's
Charles	Charles'	Charleses	Charleses'
child	child's	children	children's

There is one fact that you must always keep in mind in order to form the possessive case correctly; that is, the sign of the possessive is something that is *added* to the word. It is not something that is inserted within the word. You must be absolutely sure of the correct form for the singular and the correct form for the plural before you add the sign of the possessive.

Take the proper name, *Dickens*, for example. This is a proper noun in the singular which ends in **s**. The sign of the possessive must be added to the complete word and not inserted within the word. The possessive form is often incorrectly written as *Dicken's*. That would be the possessive form of the name *Dicken*, and not the possessive form of the name *Dickens*. The singular possessive form of *Dickens* is *Dickens'* as shown below:

Oliver Twist is one of **Dicken's** novels. (incorrect)
Oliver Twist is one of **Dickens'** novels. (correct)

The possessive forms of proper nouns are formed according to the rule. If the singular form of the name does not end in **s**, add the *apostrophe* and **s**. If the singular ends in **s**, add the *apostrophe*. The same rule applies to the plural.

Singular		Plural	
Mary	Mary's	Marys	Marys'
Jones	Jones'	Joneses	Joneses'
Henry	Henry's	Henrys	Henrys'
Burns	Burns'	Burnses	Burnses'

There is one slight modification of the rule which may be followed in the case of the possessive singular of nouns that end in **s**. If you want the sound of the additional **s**, the *apostrophe* and **s** may be added

This is **Charles'** fishing rod. (correct)
This is **Charles's** fishing rod. (correct)
I saw **Doris'** picture at the studio. (correct)
I saw **Doris's** picture at the studio. (correct)

In modern practice, the first form (*Charles' fishing rod*) is the form that is generally used. It follows the rule given, and is the simpler form to use in writing and in pronunciation. This rule also applies to nouns ending in **x** and **z**.

I bought a jar of **Heinz'** pickles. (correct)
She has always worn **Knox'** hats. (correct)
I bought a jar of **Heinz's** pickles. (correct)
She has always worn **Knox's** hats. (correct)

USE OF THE POSSESSIVE —SPECIAL FORMS

As a rule, it is better practice not to use the possessive forms for inanimate objects. Inanimate objects cannot possess anything in the sense that animate objects can. Avoid expressions such as *the table's top, the book's ending, the lake's shore,* and *the shop's window*. It is much better to use the phrase with *of* in such cases.

the top **of the table**	the shore **of the lake**
the ending **of the book**	the window **of the shop**

There are certain exceptions to this rule. Usage has established authority for using expressions such as the following:

the earth's surface	the sun's rays
the world's progress	today's edition
the law's delay	time's flight
the season's greetings	the water's edge

Certain expressions relating to *time, distance,* and *value* are also written with the sign of the possessive case. The apostrophe is generally used in expressions like the following:

a moment's delay	a stone's throw
two weeks' salary	a week's journey
a month's vacation	ten cents' worth
a few minutes' quiet	thirty days' notice

The singular possessive and the plural possessive of compound nouns are formed by adding the sign of the possessive to the end of the compound word.

Singular	Plural
sister-in-law's	sisters-in-law's
editor-in-chief's	editors-in-chief's
maid of honor's	maids of honor's

Joint ownership is shown by making the last word in the series possessive. Individual ownership is shown by making both parts possessive.

Baker and Johnson's factory. (joint ownership)
Baker's and Johnson's factories. (individual ownership)
Asia and China's problems. (common to both)
Asia's and China's problems. (separate problems)

Some trade names and names of organizations and institutions are written with the sign of the possessive case, and some are not. In writing letters, one should follow the form established by the organization.

When the apostrophe and **s** (**'s**) are not used, the word which would ordinarily be written as a possessive is regarded as an adjective modifier. In the name of an institution, such as *Teachers College*, the apostrophe is not used. The word *Teachers* is regarded as an adjective modifying *College*. It tells the type of college. It does not mean that the teachers possess the college.

The following illustrations show the methods used in writing place names, institutional names, and titles of publications:

With the Apostrophe	Without the Apostrophe
Harper's Magazine	Womens Athletic Club
Hansen's Pharmacy	Bricklayers Union
Queen's College (Oxford)	Executives Club
Charles Scribner's Sons	Pikes Peak
Young Men's Christian Association	Downers Grove
Working Girl's Club	Harris Brothers Company
Illinois Chirldren's Home and Aid Society	Citizens League
Nowak's Optical Service	American Bankers Association
Ladies' Home Journal	Buzzards Bay
Martha's Vineyard Island	Peoples Finance Company

THE POSSESSIVE CASE OF PRONOUNS

The indefinite pronouns do not have special forms to show case. The possessive case of indefinite pronouns is formed in the same way as the possessive case of nouns. Indefinite pronouns are seldom used in the plural. Two of the indefinite pronouns, *one* and *other*, have the plural forms *ones* and *others*. The following are illustrations of the possessive case form of indefinite pronouns:

everyone's opinion	*one's* relatives (singular)
someone's hat	*somebody's* car
anybody's guess	*another's* choice

The *personal pronouns* and the pronoun *who* have special forms to show the possessive case: *my, mine, our, ours, your, yours, her, hers, his, its, their, theirs,* and *whose*. These forms are never written with an apostrophe. To add an apostrophe would be adding a possessive sign to a word that is already possessive.

Whose report did you check? (not *Who's*)
The automobile was **theirs**. (not *their's*)
I did not know that book was **yours**. (not *your's*)
The ship lost **its** anchor in the storm. (not *it's*)
That ranch type house is **ours**. (not *our's*)

PERSONAL PRONOUNS

Singular and Plural
First Person

Nominative	I
	we
Possessive	my, mine
	our, ours
Objective	me
	us

Second Person

Nominative	you
	you
Possessive	your, yours
	your, yours
Objective	you
	you

Third Person

Nominative	he she it
	they
Possessive	his her, hers its
	their, theirs
Objective	you
	you

RELATIVE AND INTERROGATIVE PRONOUN "WHO"

Singular and Plural

Nominative	who
Possessive	whose
Objective	whom

10. MODIFIERS: ADJECTIVES

Adjectives give life and color to language. They also help us give more exact pictures of what we are telling about, if we know how to select them carefully. As you improve your skill in using these words, your language will become more interesting and more explicit.

Let us assume that you were telling someone about a man whom you had seen. You might start out with a sentence like this: "I met a man walking down the street." This sentence does not give us an interesting description or very accurate information. It tells very little about the man, his manner of walking, or the street down which he walked.

Someone who has skill in selecting words that would give a more definite and colorful description might change the sentence into something like this:

I met a **weary** and **disheartened old** man hobbling down the **narrow, winding** street.

This sentence has been made more colorful and more accurate by the use of the adjectives *weary, disheartened,* and *old* to describe the man, and by the use of the adjectives *narrow* and *winding* to describe the street.

In order to use adjectives effectively, you must know the exact shade of meaning that you wish to convey. Then you must be able to select the adjective or adjectives that express that shade of meaning.

You might want to use an adjective to describe a certain type of individual, and you are not sure whether to use the adjective *sly* or the adjective *cunning.* Whenever you are in doubt, consult a reliable, up-to-date dictionary. In most dictionaries these differences in meaning are pointed out.

The adjective *sly* always implies that the individual is working or acting secretly, or is using underhand methods. The adjective *cunning* implies the use of intelligence, skill, or ingenuity. The two words do not mean *exactly* the same thing.

The following exercise will give you excellent practice in learning how to select the adjective that expresses the exact meaning you would like to convey. The adjectives listed below are divided into groups of three. Each adjective in a group of three expresses a different shade of meaning. Try to write sentences using these words. Be sure that your sentences show the differences in meaning. The dictionary will be a great help.

1. small—diminutive—little
2. funny—strange—queer
3. strong—robust—sturdy
4. beautiful—handsome—lovely
5. bright—shining—brilliant

"OVERWORKED" ADJECTIVES

There is a tendency on the part of many people to use the same adjective to apply to a number of different situations. When a person does this, the assumption is that he has a very limited vocabulary. As a result, he is not able to express his meaning precisely. For example, he may use the word *lovely* to describe many different things. In certain cases, the adjective *lovely* is appropriate. In other cases, it is not the most appropriate or the most precise word to use. Study the following illustrations.

a *lovely* time	a *lovely* view
a *lovely* dress	a *lovely* voice
a *lovely* picnic	a *lovely* program
a *lovely* picture	a *lovely* day
a *lovely* street	a *lovely* necktie

If you wanted to describe a dress, instead of using the word *lovely,* you might use any one of the following adjectives: *becoming, stylish, fashionable, smart, colorful, modish, dashing, beautiful,* etc. The careful speaker or writer would choose the one that expressed the most exact shade of meaning he wished to convey. This requires careful analysis, but it is worth the effort.

Adjectives that are applied in many different types of situations are often called "overworked" or "shopworn" adjectives. The following adjectives belong in this list:

fine	lovely	swell
grand	nice	adorable
funny	terrible	keen
awful	crazy	sweet

KINDS OF ADJECTIVES

There are two kinds of adjectives: *descriptive* adjectives and *limiting* adjectives. **Descriptive adjectives,** as the name implies, give color and vividness to the persons, places, or things we talk or write about. **Limiting adjectives** indicate number or quantity.

Descriptive adjectives tell *what kind, what color, what size, what shape,* etc. Limiting adjectives tell *how many, how much, which one, whose,* etc.

three checks (limiting)	**brilliant** speaker (descriptive)
high mountain (descriptive)	**one** airplane (limiting)
a **new** car (descriptive)	a **few** children (limiting)
two branches (limiting)	a **sympathetic** listener (descriptive)

Adjectives derived from proper nouns are called **proper adjectives.** They are usually written with a capital letter. They are usually descriptive adjectives.

Canadian bacon	**Turkish** tobacco
American industries	**Norwegian** sardines
Mexican pottery	**Danish** silver
United States flag	**Swedish** crystal
English wool	**Indian** summer

PREDICATE ADJECTIVES

Adjectives that complete the meaning of the verb and modify the subject are called **predicate adjectives.** If an adjective is found in the predicate and modifies a noun in the predicate, it is not a predicate adjective. The adjective must follow a linking verb and modify the subject in order to be classified as a predicate adjective. The predicate adjective usually *describes* the subject noun or pronoun.

The list of linking verbs which was given in Chapter Eight is repeated here for reference. You should become familiar with this important list of verbs. It will help you identify the predicate adjectives that are used after linking verbs.

Linking Verbs

is	grow	look	smell	remain
become	turn	feel	taste	keep
seem	prove	sound	appear	stay

Illustrations

The predicate adjectives are underlined in the following sentences.

The cookies are delicious. (*delicious* cookies)

Corn is plentiful in Illinois. (*plentiful* corn)

The street has become very muddy. (*muddy* street)

Position of the Adjective

An adjective is usually placed directly before the noun it modifies. Sometimes the adjective follows the word it modifies. The predicate adjective is always found in the predicate after the verb it completes.

1. Adjectives placed before the noun.
   An **old, gnarled** tree lay across the stream.
2. Adjectives placed after the noun.
   A tree, **old** and **gnarled,** lay across the stream.
3. Predicate adjectives, placed after the verb.
   The tree was **old** and **gnarled.**

NOUNS USED AS ADJECTIVES

The use of pronouns as adjectives was explained in Chapter Six. Nouns are also frequently *used as adjectives.* The nouns in the following expressions are used as adjectives:

college credits (modifies *credits*)
dress accessories (modifies *accessories*)
window sash (modifies *sash*)
Fourth of July speech (modifies *speech*)
summer clothes (modifies *clothes*)
table lamp (modifies *lamp*)

A noun in the *possessive case* is often placed before another noun which it modifies. In such cases, the noun in the possessive case is used as an adjective although it has not lost the function of showing ownership or possession. Nouns used in this way are sometimes called **possessive adjectives.** Sometimes they are described as nouns in the possessive case used as adjectives. Observe how nouns in the possessive case are used in the following sentences:

John's car was wrecked in the crash. (*John's* modifies *car.*)

I like to shop in **Macy's** store. (*Macy's* modifies *store.*)

I am wearing my **sister's** coat. (*sister's* modifies *coat.*)

COMPARISON OF ADJECTIVES

The form of an adjective is often changed to show the extent or degree to which a certain quality is present. In grammar, this change in form to show a difference in degree is called *comparison.*

There are three degrees of comparison in English: the *positive degree,* the *comparative degree,* and the *superlative degree.*

The **positive degree** is really not a degree of comparison because no comparison is indicated when the positive degree is used. The positive degree is the simple form of the adjective. It shows that the quality is present, but it does not show a comparison with anything else. The adjectives in the following sentences are all positive degree:

That is a **beautiful** rose.
It is a very **cold** day.
Peter is very **energetic.**
Jane is **studious.**
The **old** house was sold.
it was a very **warm** day.

In the preceding illustrations, the adjective simply shows that the quality is present. No comparison is made with any other person or thing.

The **comparative degree** of the adjective is used when a comparison *is* made between **two** persons or things. The comparative degree shows that the quality expressed by the adjective exists to a *greater* or to a *lesser* degree in one of the two persons or things that are being compared.

The comparative degree of almost all adjectives of *one* syllable is formed by adding **er** to the positive degree, or to the simple form of the adjective; for example, *colder, smoother, longer, greater, stronger, firmer, thicker,* etc.

John is **stronger** than Michael. (*two persons* compared)

This table is **larger** than that table. (*two objects* compared)

In the first sentence, *two persons* are compared as to strength. According to the sentence, John possesses this quality of strength to a greater degree than Michael. The comparative degree of the adjective is used because a comparison is made between *two* persons.

In the second sentence, *two tables* are being compared as to size. The comparative degree of the adjective *large* is used because a comparison is made between *two objects*.

The **superlative degree** of the adjective is used when **more than two** persons or things are compared. The superlative degree indicates that the quality (expressed by the adjective) is possessed to the *greatest* or to the *least* degree by one of the persons or things included in the comparison.

Our house is the **largest** house in the block. (More than two are compared.)
Louis is the **smallest** boy in his class. (More than two are compared.)

In the first sentence, *more than two* houses are being compared. The superlative degree of the adjective *large* is used to show this fact. The house that possesses the quality expressed by the adjective *large* to the greatest degree is *our* house. It is the *largest* house in a block which contains more than two houses.

In the second sentence, more than two boys are being compared as to size. Louis possesses this quality to the *least* degree. The superlative degree of the adjective *small* is used to show this fact.

DEGREES OF COMPARISON

Adjectives of One Syllable

Positive	Comparative	Superlative
neat	neater	neatest
sharp	sharper	sharpest
dark	darker	darkest
keen	keener	keenest
long	longer	longest

Adjectives of *two or more syllables* are usually compared by prefixing the words *more* and *most* to the simple form of the adjective. *More* is used to indicate the comparison between two persons or things. *Most* is used to indicate the comparison between more than two persons or things. *Less* and *least* are used in a similar way.

Positive	Comparative	Superlative
fragrant	*more* fragrant	*most* fragrant
famous	*less* famous	*least* famous
precious	*more* precious	*most* precious
difficult	*less* difficult	*least* difficult

Sometimes adjectives of *one syllable* are compared by prefixing *more* and *most*. Sometimes adjectives of *more than one syllable* are compared by adding **er** and **est**. There is no rule to follow for making these exceptions. It is usually a matter of sound. If one form of comparison sounds better than the other, that is the form of comparison to use. It sounds better to say *crisp, more crisp, most crisp*, than to say *crisp, crisper, crispest*. Therefore, the comparison with *more* and *most* is preferred.

Adjectives of more than one syllable that end in **y** are usually compared by adding **er** and **est**. Notice the change in spelling in the comparative and in the superlative degrees. The **y** changes to **i** before the addition of **er** or **est**.

Positive	Comparative	Superlative
silly	sillier	silliest
dainty	daintier	daintiest
clumsy	clumsier	clumsiest
handy	handier	handiest
noisy	noisier	noisiest

IRREGULAR COMPARISON OF ADJECTIVES

Some adjectives are compared *irregularly*. The forms for the comparative degree and for the superlative degree usually show a marked

change in the form of the word; for example, *many, more, most*. You should be familiar with these changes in order to use the correct forms for the comparative and superlative degrees.

Adjectives Compared Irregularly

Positive	Comparative	Superlative
bad, evil, ill	worse	worst
far	further	furthest
far	farther	farthest
good, well	better	best
little	less	least
many	more	most
much	more	most
out	outer	outmost or outermost

Farther refers to *distance* or remoteness in space. **Further** refers to remoteness in *time*, to *degree, extent*, or *quantity*. It is also used to express the idea of something *more* or *additional*.

The garage is **farther** than I thought. (distance in space)
I shall give you **further** instructions tomorrow. (*additional* instructions)

The distinctions between *farther* and *further* are passing out of use. These words are now used interchangeably. There is also a tendency to use *further* to express all the meanings discussed. (See latest dictionaries.)

ADJECTIVES NOT COMPARED

There are a number of adjectives that should not be compared because the **simple** form of the adjective expresses the quality to the highest possible degree. For example, if an answer to a problem is *correct*, another answer could not possibly be *more correct*. If a circle is absolutely *round*, another circle could not be *more round*. If a bottle is *empty*, another bottle could not be *more empty*.

The following are some of the adjectives that are not compared for the reasons given:

perfect	unique	square	universal
single	supreme	fatal	empty
vertical	full	alone	dead
final	mortal	round	deadly
straight	blind	everlasting	wrong

The expression, *more nearly round*, is often used when comparing two things, one of which is *more nearly round* than the other. In this case, however, neither of the things compared is round. A line could be *more nearly straight* than another line if neither of the lines was absolutely straight.

Sometimes an adjective such as the word *honest* is used in the comparative and superlative degrees. In such cases, we have no standard of absolute honesty. What the writer or speaker means is that one person approaches the absolute state of honesty to a greater or to a lesser degree than another person. The adjective *perfect* is often used in the same way.

11. MODIFIERS: ADVERBS

Chapter Two explained the uses of the adverb as a modifier of the verb, telling *how, when, where*, and *to what degree* the action is performed. This unit presents other uses of the adverb, and the relation of adverbs to adjectives and to other adverbs.

FORMS OF ADVERBS

Some people have the idea that all adverbs end in **ly**. There are a great many adverbs that do end in **ly**, but there are probably just as many that do not end in **ly**. Many adverbs are formed by adding **ly** to the adjective form:

Adjective	Adverb	Adjective	Adverb
strange	strangely	awkward	awkwardly
sudden	suddenly	necessary	necessarily
calm	calmly	strict	strictly
sure	surely	forcible	forcibly
usual	usually	extreme	extremely
swift	swiftly	similar	similarly
rapid	rapidly	slight	slightly

The following are some of the adverbs that do not end in **ly**:

seldom	little	why	fast
again	here	now	twice
soon	there	then	too
very	rather	since	much
almost	often	well	quite
late	when	near	yonder
hard	where	far	how

Many adjectives end in **ly**. They should not be confused with adverbs that end in **ly**. The following words ending in **ly** are commonly used as adjectives. Some of them might also be used as adverbs:

stately	lovely	saintly	manly
lonely	womanly	lively	courtly

Some adjectives have the same form as the adverb. In such cases, the only way you can tell whether the word is an *adjective* or an *adverb*, is to determine its use in a particular sentence. Study the following illustrations carefully:

That was a **hard** task. (*hard* adjective, modifies *task*)
Our janitor works **hard**. (*hard* adverb, modifies *works*)
We arrived at the airport **early**. (*early* adverb, modifies *arrived*)
We had to make an **early** start. (*early* adjective, modifies *start*)
That was a **cowardly** act. (*cowardly* adjective, modifies *act*)
He acted **cowardly** in that situation. (*cowardly* adverb, modifies *acted*)

INTERROGATIVE ADVERBS

An adverb is often used at the beginning of a sentence to ask a question. When an adverb is used in this way, it is called an **interrogative adverb**. An *interrogative adverb* also modifies some word in the sentence.

When did you arrive? (*When* interrogative adverb)
Where did you put my hat? (*Where* interrogative adverb)
How many books have you read? (*How* interrogative adverb)

In the first sentence, the adverb *When* asks the question. It also modifies the verb *did arrive*. (You *did arrive* when?) In the second sentence, the adverb *Where* asks the question and modifies the verb *did put*. (You *did put* my hat where?) In the third sentence, the adverb *How* asks the question and modifies the adjective *many*. (You have read how *many* books?)

YES, NO, AND NOT

The affirmative adverb *yes* and the negative adverb *no* are used independently. They are usually set off by commas. *Not* is an adverb. It is never used as part of the verb, although it often comes between the parts of a verb phrase. The adverb *not* makes the verb express an idea which is the exact opposite of the regular meaning of the verb.

Yes, I shall take the course.
I did *not* give him the plans. (No plans were given.)
No, we are *not* going to Florida this winter.

ADVERBS OF DEGREE

Adverbs of degree tell *how large, how small, how long, how much, to what extent*, etc. They answer the questions *"How much?" "To what extent?" "In what degree?"* Adverbs of degree usually modify adjective: or other adverbs. In the following illustrations the adverbs of degree modify *adjectives*:

This apple is very sour. (*very* modifies the adjective *sour*)
The play was rather dull. (*rather* modifies the adjective *dull*)
The price is too high. (*too* modifies the adjective *high*)

In the first sentence, the adverb of degree *very* modifies the predicate adjective *sour*. It tells to what degree the apple is sour, or how sour it is. In the second sentence, the adverb *rather* modifies the predicate adjective *dull*. It tells the extent to which the play was *dull*. In the third sentence, the adverb *too* modifies the predicate adjective *high*. It tells the extent to which the price is *high*. The adverbs *very, too,* and *rather* are commonly used as adverbs of degree.

In the following sentences, the adverbs of degree modify other *adverbs*:

The old man moved too slowly. (*too* modifies the adverb *slowly*)
John swims much faster than Ned. (*much* modifies the adverb *faster*)
Don't talk so loud. (*so* modifies the adverb *loud*)

In the first sentence, the adverb of degree *too* modifies the adverb *slowly*. It tells the extent to which the old man moved *slowly*. In the second sentence, the adverb of degree *much* modifies the adverb *faster*. The adverb of degree tells that John swims fast to a greater degree than Ned. In the third sentence, the adverb of degree *so* modifies the adverb *loud*. The sentence means that you should not talk loud to the extent expressed by the adverb *so*. In this sentence, the short form of the adverb (*loud*) is used instead of the longer form, *loudly*.

NOUNS USED AS ADVERBS

Nouns that express *time, size, place, measurement, degree,* or *number* are often used as adverbs. We identify these nouns by calling them *nouns used as adverbs*. Such nouns are not only used as adverbs, but they retain an important characteristic of nouns; namely, they may take an *adjective modifier*.

I am going *home*. (*home* noun used as an adverb)
Horace will arrive *Monday*. (*Monday* noun used as an adverb)
We worked all *day*. (*day* noun used as an adverb)
The fish weighed five *pounds*. (*pounds* noun used as an adverb)

In the first sentence, the noun *home* tells **where** I am going. It performs the same function as an **adverb of place.** In the second sentence, the noun *Monday* tells **when** Horace will arrive. It performs the same function as an **adverb of time.** In the third sentence, the noun *day* tells **how long** we worked, or the extent to which we worked. In the last sentence, the noun *pounds* tells the amount, or **how much** the fish weighed.

The noun *pounds* in the last sentence is modified by the adjective *five*. Although the noun *pounds* functions as an adverb, it may take an adjective modifier. It still retains that particular characteristic of a noun. It functions as two parts of speech at the same time both as a **noun** and as an **adverb.**

Some persons have difficulty in understanding the use of a noun as an adverb. A noun used as an adverb is really the equivalent of a phrase. The following illustrations will help make this clear:

I am going home. This sentence really means that I am going to *my home*. The noun *home* is the equivalent of the phrase, *to my home.*

Horace will arrive Monday. This sentence means that Horace will arrive *on Monday*. The noun *Monday* is the equivalent of the phrase, *on Monday.*

We worked all day. This sentence means that we worked for the period or to *the extent of a day.*

The fish weighed five pounds. This sentence means that the fish weighed to the extent or *to the amount of five pounds.*

COMPARISON OF ADVERBS

Adverbs are compared in exactly the same way as adjectives are compared. They have the same three degrees of comparison: the *positive degree*, the *comparative degree*, and the *superlative degree.*

A few adverbs form the comparative degree by adding **er** to the positive degree. They form the superlative degree by adding **est** to the positive degree.

Positive	Comparative	Superlative
late	later	latest
hard	harder	hardest
soon	sooner	soonest
fast	faster	fastest
near	nearer	nearest
quick (*short form*)	quicker	quickest
slow (*short form*)	slower	slowest

Most adverbs are compared by placing *more* (for the comparative degree) and *most* (for the superlative degree) before the positive forms. *Less* and *least* are used in the same way as *more* and *most.*

Positive	Comparative	Superlative
carefully	more carefully	most carefully
discreetly	more discreetly	most discreetly
abruptly	more abruptly	most abruptly
gratefully	more gratefully	most gratefully
efficiently	more efficiently	most efficiently
awkwardly	less awkwardly	least awkwardly
favorably	less favorably	least favorably
gracefully	less gracefully	least gracefully

IRREGULAR COMPARISON OF ADVERBS

A few adverbs are compared *irregularly*. In the following list you will find some words that were also in the list of adjectives that compared irregularly. Such words are used both as *adjectives* and as *adverbs*.

Positive	Comparative	Superlative
far	farther	farthest
far	further	furthest
badly	worse	worst
little	less	least
much	more	most
well	better	best

Some adverbs are not compared. The following adverbs can not be used in the comparative or in the superlative degrees:

before	never	now	there	very	by
ever	no	so	thus	past	back
here	not	then	too	yes	whenever

The comparative degree of adverbs is used when comparing two things. The superlative degree is used when comparing more than two.

We drove *more slowly* than our guide. (Comparative)
Of the three speakers, the senator spoke *most convincingly*. (Superlative)

12. PRINCIPAL PARTS OF VERBS

Studies have shown that more than half of the errors made in English are errors in the use of verbs. Most of this trouble occurs because of confusion in the use of the principal parts.

Every verb has *three basic forms* which are called the *principal parts* of the verb. These three forms are the **present tense**, the **past tense**, and the **past participle**. They are called the principal parts of the verb because (with a few exceptions) the six tenses of the verb can be built from them.

Tense is a property that belongs to verbs. In grammar, *tense* means *time*. Every verb has certain forms which show the *time* of the *action* or the *time* of the *state of condition*. When we want to indicate that a certain action is going on now, or that a certain state of condition exists at the present time, we use the **present tense.**

Present Tense
I **drive.** (Action occurs at the *present time*.)
He **sings.** (Action occurs at the *present time*.)
Florence **is** ill. (state of condition exists at the *present time*.)

When we want to indicate that the action occurred yesterday, or in some past time, we use the **past tense** of the verb. With a few exceptions, the past tense of the verb is not the same form as the present tense of the verb.

Past Tense
I **drove.** (The action occurred in the *past*.)
He **sang** at the concert. (The action occurred in the *past*.)
Florence **was** ill yesterday. (State of condition existed in the *past*.)

In the preceding illustrations, the forms, *drive* and *sings*, are used to show that action is going on at the present time. The forms, *drove* and *sang*, are used to show that action occurred at some time in the past. The forms *drive* and *sings* are the present tense of the verbs *drive* and *sing*. The forms *drove* and *sang* are the past tense of the verbs *drive* and *sing*.

The **past participle** of the verb is a verb form that is used with *have*, *has*, or *had* to form the perfect tenses. The past participle cannot function as the predicate verb. It is always combined with an auxiliary, such as *have*, *has*, or *had*. It is a part of the verb phrase.

Past Participles

I have **called** her every day this week. (*called* past participle)

We have **driven** there often. (*driven* participle)

The three forms, the *present tense*, *past tense*, and the *past participle*, constitute the **principal parts** of a verb. Become familiar with the principal parts of certain verbs so that you will be able to use them correctly. The verbs that cause most of our verb troubles are the verbs that form the principal part irregularly. We shall make a special study of these verbs.

REGULAR AND IRREGULAR VERBS

Verbs are divided into two classes on the basis of the way in which the past tense and the past participle are formed. Some are called *regular* or weak verbs, and others are called *irregular* or strong verbs.

A **regular verb** is a verb that forms the past tense and the past participle by adding **ed** or **d** to the form of the present tense. Sometimes the **ed** or **d** changes to **t**: *build*, *built*, *built*.

Verb	Past Tense	Past Participle
call	called	called
bake	baked	baked
build	built	built

The past tense and the past participle of the verb *call* are formed by adding **ed** to the form of the present tense: *call***ed**. The past tense and the past participle of the verb *bake* are formed by simply adding **d** to the form of the present tense: *bake***d**. The past tense and the past participle of the verb *build* are formed by changing the **d** to **t**. The old form of the verb build was *builded* in the past tense. That form is no longer used. The simpler form *built* has taken its place.

An **irregular verb** is a verb that does *not* form the past tense and the past participle in the regular way; that is, by adding **d** or **ed** to the form of the present tense. The past tense and the past participle of irregular verbs are formed in various ways. The most common way is by a change in the vowel; for example, *sing*, *sang*, *sung*. In the case of a few verbs, the same form is used for the present tense, the past tense and the past participle: *hurt*, *hurt*, *hurt*.

Verb	Past Tense	Past Participle
sing	sang	sung
drive	drove	driven
begin	began	begun
go	went	gone
burst	burst	burst

The past tense and the past participle of the verb *sing* are formed by a change in vowel. The **i** in *sing* changes to **a** in the past tense (*sang*) and to **u** in the past participle (*sung*). The verb *begin* follows a similar change in the vowel. The verb *go* has a different form for the past tense and for the past participle: *go*, *went*, *gone*. The verb *burst* has the same form for the present tense, the past tense, and the past participle.

VERBS ADDED TO THE LANGUAGE

New verbs are added to the English language as the need arises. Practically all of new verbs form the past tense and the past participle by adding **ed** or **d**; that is, they follow the pattern of the regular verbs. To form the past tense or the past participle of these verbs add **ed** or **d**.

Verb	Past Tense	Past Participle
activate	activated	activated
radio	radioed	radioed
camouflage	camouflaged	camouflaged
audition	auditioned	auditioned
laminate	laminated	laminated

THE TROUBLESOME VERBS

The *regular verbs* cause very little trouble in speaking and writing because the past tense and the past participle usually follow the rule of forming the past tense and the past participle by adding **d** or **ed.** It is the *irregular verbs* that are responsible for most of the verb errors.

Errors are frequently made in using the *past tense* and the *perfect tense* forms of irregular verbs. This is due to the fact that these verbs form the past tense and the perfect tenses irregularly. In order to use these verbs correctly, it is highly important for you to become familiar with the principal parts of the irregular verbs that are in common use. You will learn these forms by checking constantly until you are familiar with the correct forms for the past tense and the past participle.

Mistakes are commonly made in using the wrong form for the **past tense:** *done* for *did*; *seen* for *saw*; *come* for *came*; *swum* for *swan*; *dove* for *dived*; *run* for *ran*; *drunk* for *drank*. Mistakes are also made in using the wrong form for the **past participle:** *went* for *gone*; *did* for *done*; *swam* for *swum*; *tore* for *torn*; *began* for *begun*; *came* for *come*. The past participle is used in forming the perfect tenses.

Correct Forms for the Past Tense

I *did* the work assigned to me. (not *done*)
We *saw* the parade yesterday. (not *seen*)
He *came* from Ireland two years ago. (not *come*)
She *swam* across the English Channel last summer. (not *swum*)
The swimming teacher *dived* off the pier. (not *dove*)
The boy *ran* through the traffic. (not *run*)
We *drank* all the milk in the pitcher. (not *drunk*)

Correct Forms for the Past Participle

The delegates **have gone** home. (not *have went*)
He **has done** the work well. (not *has did*)
She **has swum** the channel several times. (not *has swam*)
The actress **has torn** her dress. (not *has tore*)
They **have begun** to check the accounts. (not *have began*)
Has the mail **come**? (not *has came*)

In the first sentence, the past participle is *gone*. It is combined with the auxiliary *have* to form the verb phrase *have gone*. The form *went* should never be used with *have*, *has* or *had*.

In the second sentence, the past participle is *done*. It is the correct form of the verb to combine with *has*. In the third sentence, the past participle is *swum*. It is correctly used

with *has*. *Tore* should never be used with *have*, *has*, or *had* The correct form is *have*, *has*, or *had torn*.

Began is the correct form for the past tense. It should not be used for the past participle. The correct form for the past participle is *begun*. Never use the forms *have began*, *had began*, or *has began*. The correct forms are *have begun*, *had begun*, and *has begun*.

The following table gives the principal parts of the irregular verbs that cause most of the verb errors. You should become familiar with the principal parts of these verbs. Consult this list whenever you are in doubt about the correct form to use. If the verb you want is not in this list, consult a reliable, up-to-date dictionary. The principal parts of verbs are given in most dictionaries.

PRINCIPAL PARTS OF TROUBLESOME VERBS

Present Tense (present time)	Past Tense (past time)	Past Participles (*used with have, has, had*)
awake	awaked awoke	awaked awoke
be (am)	was	been
beat	beat	beaten
become	became	become
begin	began	begun
bid (offer)	bid	bid
bid (command)	bade	bidden, bid
blow	blew	blown
break	broke	broken
bring	brought	brought
broadcast	broadcast broadcasted	broadcast broadcasted
burst	burst	burst
catch	caught	caught
choose	chose	chosen
climb	climbed	climbed
come	came	come
cut	cut	cut
dive	dived	dived
do	did	done
drag	dragged	dragged
draw	drew	drawn
drink	drank	drunk
drive	drove	driven
drown	drowned	drowned
eat	ate	eaten
fall	fell	fallen
flow	flowed	flowed
fly	flew	flown
forget	forgot	forgotten, forgot
freeze	froze	frozen
get	got	got, gotten
give	gave	given
go	went	gone
hang (a picture)	hung	hung
hang (a criminal)	hanged	hanged
know	knew	known
lay (to place, to put)	laid	laid
lead	led	led
leave	left	left
lend	lent	lent
let	let	let
lie (recline)	lay (not laid)	lain (not laid)
lie (false)	lied	lied
lose	lost	lost
prove	proved	proved

ride	rode	ridden
ring	rang	rung
rise	rose	risen (not rose)
run	ran	run
say	said	said
see	saw	seen
send	sent	sent
set	set	set
shake	shook	shaken
shine (light)	shone	shone
shine (polish)	shined	shined
show	showed	shown, showed
shrink	shrank	shrunk
sing	sang	sung
sink	sank	sunk
sit	sat	sat
spring	sprang, sprung	sprung
steal	stole	stolen
swear	swore	sworn
swim	swam	swum
swing	swung	swung
take	took	taken
teach	taught	taught
tear	tore	torn
tell	told	told
think	thought	thought
throw	threw	thrown
try	tried	tried
understand	understood	understood
wake	waked, woke	waked
wear	wore	worn
weave	wove	woven
weep	wept	wept
wind	wound	wound
wring	wrung	wrung
write	wrote	written

SIX CONFUSING VERBS

Six of the irregular verbs require special attention and study because they are so frequently confused. As a result, they are used incorrectly more often than any of the other irregular verbs. These forms of the verbs in each pair are somewhat similar, but the meanings are quite different. We shall make a special study of these verbs so that you will be able to use them correctly.

LIE AND LAY

There are two different verbs that are spelled alike (*lie*). One means to tell a falsehood. This is a regular verb and causes no difficulty, either in speaking or in writing. The verb that is confused with *lay* is the verb *lie*, which means *to recline, to rest,* or *to remain in a reclining position.* This verb is an irregular verb. The principal parts are *lie, lay,* and (*have, has, had*) *lain.* The present participle, the form that ends in *ing,* is *lying.*

There are two important facts regarding the verb *lie* (to recline) that you should always keep in mind: (1) There is no form ending in **d** that belongs to the verb *lie,* meaning *to recline.* The form *laid* should never be used when you mean *to recline, rest,* or *remain in a reclining position.* (2) The verb *lie* never takes an object.

Mother **lies** down every afternoon. (*rests, reclines*)

Mother **lay** on the couch all afternoon. (not *laid*)

Mother **is lying** on the couch. (not *laying*)

Mother **has lain** on that couch often. (not *has laid*)

The verb *lie* is also the verb to use when we speak about inanimate objects that are in a reclining or in a *lying down* position.

The pen **lies** on my desk. (not *lays*)
The pen **lay** on my desk all day. (not *laid*)
The pen **is lying** on my desk. (not *is laying*)
The pen **has lain** on my desk all week. (not *has laid*)

The verb **lay**, that is so often confused with *lie*, means *to put something down, to place something somewhere.* The principal parts of this verb are *lay, laid,* (*have, has,* or *had*) *laid.* The present participle is *laying.* The verb *lay* always takes an object.

John **lays** carpets for Macey's store. (*carpets* object of *lays*)

John **laid** carpets all week. (*carpets* object of *laid*)

John **has laid** carpets for many years. (*carpets* object of *has laid*)

In the first sentence, the verb *lays* is the present tense of the verb *lay,* which means to put something down. The word *carpets* is the direct object of the verb *lays.* It tells what John put down. In the second sentence, the verb *laid* is the past tense of the verb *lay.*

When we use the form *laid,* we must supply an object telling what we *laid,* or *what we put down.* Carpets is the direct object of the verb *laid.* It tells what John *laid.* In the last sentence, *laid* is the correct form of the verb *lay* to combine with *has.* It helps form the verb phrase *has laid.*

SIT AND SET

The verb *sit* means to *assume a sitting position* or *to occupy a seat.* The principal parts of the verb *sit* are *sit, sat,* (*have, has, had*) *sat.* The present participle is *sitting.* The verb *sit* never takes an object. The form *set* does not belong to this verb.

Joe **sat** very still, watching the game.
The children **were sitting** on the floor.
I always **sit** near the fireplace when I read.
My aunt likes **to sit** in a rocking chair.
She **has sat** in the same chair for many years.

The verb *set* means *to place, to put something in position, to make rigid, solid,* or *stiff.* The principal parts of the verb *set* are *set, set,* (*have, has, had*) *set.* The present participle is *setting.* The verb *set* usually takes an object. There are a few idiomatic uses of the verb in which it does *not* take an object. The verb *set* takes an object in the following sentences:

Esther **set** the basket on the table. (*basket* direct object)

We **set** the clock back yesterday. (*clock* direct object)

The operator **set** her hair beautifully. (*hair* direct object)

The buyer **has set** the price too low. (*price* direct object)

Idiomatic Uses

The verb *set* is used *without an object* in the following sentences. Study the types of situations in which the verb *set* is used without an object. These are idiomatic uses of the verb *set.*

The sun **was setting** when we left the lodge.
The cement **will set** in two hours.
We **set** out on a long journey.
The men **set** to work at once.
Jelly **sets** as it cools.

RISE AND RAISE

The verb *rise* means to *ascend, to go up, to extend upward, to swell up,* as bread dough in fermentation, *to increase in value, force* or *intensity.* The principal parts of the verb *rise* are *rise, rose,* and (*have, has, had*) *risen.* The present participle is *rising.* The verb *rise* expresses action, but it does not take an object.

The building **rises** to a height of eighty feet.
This river **rises** in the north.
The tide **was rising.**
Dan **has risen** in his profession.
The plane **rose** steadily.
The sun **will rise** at six o'clock tomorrow.
The cliffs **rise** far above the sea.

The verb *raise* means *to lift up something* or cause it *to go up, to increase the amount or price, to collect a number of things,* etc. The verb *raise* always takes an object. You can't raise without raising something. The verb *raise* is a regular verb. The principal parts are *raise, raised, raised.* The present participle is *raising.*

I **raised** my arm. (to lift up)
Don't **raise** so much dust! (to cause to rise)
The leader **raised** an army. (collected)
We **shall raise** the flag at sunrise. (to cause to go up)
The farmer **raises** wheat. (to cause to grow)
The landlord **raised** the rent. (increased)
Do not **raise** your voice. (to make louder)

13. THE TENSES OF VERBS

THE SIX TENSES

A verb is the most important word in any sentence because more constructions depend upon the verb than upon any other part of speech. Verbs have a number of properties which other parts of speech do not have. One of the properties that belongs exclusively to verbs and verb forms is tense.

Chapter 12 explained that in grammar *tense* means *time.* Verbs have **six tenses** which show differences in the time of *action* or the time of the *state of being* or *condition* (linking verbs).

I *see* a robin on the fence. (**present** time)
I *saw* a robin on the fence yesterday. (**past time**)
I *shall see* a number of birds when I go to the woods. (**future** time)

These sentences do not mean the same thing. The meaning depends to a large extent upon the verb form that is used; that is, the verb form that is used to show the *time* of the action.

The first sentence means that the action expressed by the verb *see* is going on now. The second sentence means that the action expressed by the verb *saw* happened at some time in the past (yesterday). The third sentence means that the action expressed by the verb *shall see* will occur at some future time.

The verbs used in the three sentences are forms of the verb *see.* The verb *see* in the first sentence is the form used in the present tense. It expresses or denotes *present time.* The verb *saw* in the second sentence is the form used to express *past time.* The verb *shall see* is the form used to express *future time.*

Remember, there are six tenses in English. The three tenses which you have just studied are called the **simple tenses.** The other three tenses are called the **perfect tenses.** The only difference between the simple tenses and the perfect tenses is that the perfect tenses include the idea of completion. In grammar, the word *perfect* refers to an action or state of being that is completed at the time of speaking or writing.

Simple Tenses	Perfect Tenses
present tense	*present perfect* tense
past tense	*past perfect* tense
future tense	*future perfect* tense

THE SIMPLE TENSES

The present tense denotes *present time*. It is also used to express *habitual action*, or to express an idea that is *generally accepted as true*.

I *hear* the bell. (present time)
Oscar *works* in an airplane factory. (habitual action)
"Honesty *is* the best policy.' (generally accepted truth)

The present tense is often used to express *future time*. Examine the following sentences carefully. In all of them the present tense expresses a future idea:

If it *rains*, we shall not go to the woods.
If the bill *passes*, the tax will be removed.
Our lease on the factory *expires* tomorrow.

The past tense denotes *past time*. The past tense of **regular verbs** is formed by adding *d* or *ed* to the present tense form: call, call*ed*; dive, div*ed*. Sometimes the *d* at the end of the present tense form changes to *t* in the past tense: build, buil*t*.

I *mailed* the letter yesterday. (addition of *ed*)
We *dived* into the pool. (addition of *d*)
The hunter *built* a cabin in the woods. (change of *d* to *t*)

The past tense of **irregular verbs** is formed in various ways. Sometimes there is a change in the vowel: sing, sang; swim, swam; begin, began; drive, drove; break, broke. Sometimes the same form is used in the past tense and in the present tense: bid, bid; hurt, hurt; cut, cut; slit, slit.

The future tense denotes *future time*. The future tense is formed by combining the auxiliary *shall* or *will* with the present tense form of the verb. Use *shall* with the pronouns **I** and *we*. Use *will* with the pronouns *you, he, she, it, they*.

I *shall see* you tomorrow. (*shall* first person)
I am sure that you *will be* late. (*will* second person)
The speaker *will arrive* at seven. (*will* third person)

To express future time, use *shall* in the first person and *will* in the second and third persons.

THE PERFECT TENSES

You can remember the *perfect tenses* easily, if you remember that the work **perfect** is always used in identifying them. The three perfect tenses are the *present perfect tense*, the *past perfect tense*, and the *future perfect tense*.

The present perfect tense denotes *action that is completed* at the time of speaking or writing. It may also indicate action that is *continuing into the present*.

The present perfect tense is formed by combining the auxiliary *have* or *has* with the past participle of the principal verb. The auxiliary *has* is always used in the third person singular: He *has spoken* to the manager.

I *have seen* three of Shaw's plays. (*have seen* first person)
You *have earned* a promotion. (*have earned* second person)
John *has washed* the car. (*has washed* third person)

In the first sentence, the verb phrase is *have seen*. It is in the present perfect tense. The verb phrase is made up of the auxiliary *have* and the past participle of the verb *see*, which is *seen* (*have seen*). In the third sentence, the auxiliary *has* is used instead of *have* (*has washed*).

The past perfect tense denotes *action that was completed* before some definite time in the past. The past perfect tense is formed by combining the auxiliary *had* with the past participle of the principal verb: *had walked, had known, had given, had drunk, had become, had been*, etc.

In the following sentences, verbs in the past tense are underlined once. Verbs in the past perfect tense are underlined twice.

By the time the officer <u>arrived</u>, the thief <u>had</u> <u>disappeared</u>.
I <u>liked</u> the speaker better after I <u>had heard</u> him the second time.
The agent <u>had sold</u> all the tickets before I <u>applied</u> for mine.

The future perfect tense denotes *action that will be completed* at some definite time in the future. The future perfect tense is seldom used in informal speaking or writing.

The future perfect tense is formed by combining the auxiliaries *shall have* or *will have* with the past participle of the principal verb. *Shall have* is used in the first person, and *will have* in the second and third persons. The *italicized* words are in the future perfect tense.

My friend *will have sailed* before I reach the pier.
By January, the committee *will have completed* the investigation.
I *shall have crossed* the river three times before noon.

Many verb errors are made because the writer or speaker is not familiar with the forms for the past tense and the past participle. Whenever you are not sure of one of these forms, consult the tables in Chapter 12. If the verb you are interested in is not listed, consult a reliable, up-to-date dictionary. You will find these forms listed after the verb.

You can also avoid verb errors if you know the auxiliaries that indicate the tense:

shall and *will* for the future tense
have and *has* for the present perfect tense
had for the past perfect tense
shall have or *will have* for the future perfect tense

THE VERB "TO BE"

Every person should be thoroughly familiar with the forms of the verb **to be**. It is the most irregular, and also the most important verb in the English language. The verb *to be* is used as an independent verb, and is also used as an auxiliary verb. The entire passive voice and all the progressive forms of other verbs are formed by using the verb *to be* as an auxiliary or helping verb. You should become familiar with the forms for the six tenses of this important verb.

On the following pages you will find reference tables for the tenses of three verbs: the verb *to be*, the regular verb *call*, and the irregular verb *ring*. Study these tables carefully.

REFERENCE TABLE

SIX TENSES OF THE VERB "TO BE"

Singular and Plural

PRESENT TENSE

First person:	I am
	we are
Second person:	you are
	you are
Third person:	he, she, it is
	they are

PAST TENSE

First person:	I was
	we were
Second person:	you were
	you were
Third person:	he, she, it was
	they were

FUTURE TENSE

First person:	I *shall* be
	we *shall* be
Second person:	you *will* be
	you *will* be
Third person:	he, she, it *will* be
	they *will* be.

Singular and Plural

PRESENT PERFECT TENSE

First person:	I *have* been
	we *have* been
Second person:	you *have* been
	you *have* been
Third person:	he, she, it *has* been
	they *have* been

PAST PERFECT TENSE

First person:	I *had* been
	we *had* been
Second person:	you *had* been
	you *had* been
Third person:	he, she, it *had* been
	they *had* been

FUTURE PERFECT TENSE

First person:	I *shall have* been
	we *shall have* been
Second person:	you *will have* been
	you *will have* been
Third person:	he, she, it *will have* been
	they *will have* been

THE SIX TENSES OF A REGULAR VERB

VERB "CALL" ACTIVE VOICE

PRESENT TENSE

Singular and Plural

First person:	I call
	we call
Second person:	you call
	you call
Third person:	he, she, it *calls*
	they call

VERB "CALL" ACTIVE VOICE (Cont'd)
Singular and Plural

PAST TENSE

First person:	I called we called
Second person:	you called you called
Third person:	he, she, it called they called

FUTURE TENSE

First person:	I *shall* call we *shall* call
Second person:	you *will* call you *will* call
Third person:	he, she, it *will* call they *will* call

PRESENT PERFECT TENSE

First person:	I *have* called we *have* called
Second person:	you *have* called you *have* called
Third person:	he, she, it *has* called they *have* called

PAST PERFECT TENSE

First person:	I *had* called we *had* called
Second person:	you *had* called you *had* called
Third person:	he, she, it *had* called they *had* called

FUTURE PERFECT TENSE

First person:	I *shall have* called we *shall have* called
Second person:	you *will have* called you *will have* called
Third person:	he, she, it *will have* called they *will have* called

SIX TENSES OF AN IRREGULAR VERB
VERB "RING" ACTIVE VOICE
Singular and Plural

PRESENT TENSE

First person:	I ring we ring
Second person:	you ring you ring
Third person:	he, she, it *rings* they ring

PAST TENSE

First person:	I *rang* we *rang*
Second person:	you *rang* you *rang*
Third person:	he, she, it *rang* they *rang*

FUTURE TENSE

First person:	I *shall* ring we *shall* ring
Second person:	you *will* ring you *will* ring
Third person:	he, she, it *will* ring they *will* ring

PRESENT PERFECT TENSE

First person:	I have *rung* we have *rung*
Second person:	you have *rung* you have *rung*
Third person:	he, she, it has *rung* they have *rung*

PAST PERFECT TENSE

First person:	I had *rung* we had *rung*
Second person:	you had *rung* you had *rung*
Third person:	he, she, it had *rung* they had *rung*

FUTURE PERFECT TENSE

First person:	I shall have *rung* we shall have *rung*
Second person:	you will have *rung* you will have *rung*
Third person:	he, she, it will have *rung* they will have *rung*

PROGRESSIVE FORMS OF VERBS

In addition to the forms which have already been given to show tense, a verb has special forms to show that the *action is continuing*. These forms are called the **progressive forms** of a verb. The *progressive forms* are used to show that an action is *continuing* or *progressing* at the time indicated by a particular tense.

I *am studying* English. (The action is continuing.)

He *is planning* a trip to Mexico. (The action is continuing.)

The progressive form of a verb is made up by using some form of the verb *to be* with the *ing* form of the principal verb. The form of a verb that ends in *ing* is called the **present participle.**

In the first sentence, the progressive form of the verb is *am studying*. It is made up of a form of the verb *to be*, which is *am*, and the present participle of the principal verb, which is *studying*. In the second sentence, the progressive form of the verb, *is planning*, is made up in a similar way.

The following are the progressive forms of the verb *call* for the six tenses (first person, singular).

I *am calling* you. (present progressive)
I *was calling* you. (past progressive)
I *shall be calling* you. (future progressive)
I *have been calling* you. (present perfect progressive)
I *had been calling* you. (past perfect progressive)
I *shall have been calling* you. (future perfect progressive)

The present tense, progressive form often expresses a future idea. The verb *to go* is commonly used in this way:

I *am going* to New York next week. (in the future)

He *is going* to buy a new home in the suburbs. (in the future)

VERB "CALL"
PROGRESSIVE FORMS ACTIVE VOICE
Singular and Plural

PRESENT TENSE

First Person:	I *am* calling we *are* calling
Second person:	you *are* calling you *are* calling
Third person:	he, she, it *is* calling they *are* calling

PAST TENSE

First person:	I *was* calling we *were* calling
Second person:	you *were* calling you *were* calling
Third person:	he, she, it *was* calling they *were* calling

FUTURE TENSE

First person:	I *shall be* calling we *shall be* calling
Second person:	you *will be* calling you *will be* calling
Third person:	he, she, it *will be* calling they *will be* calling

PRESENT PERFECT TENSE

First person:	I *have been* calling we *have been* calling
Second person:	you *have been* calling you *have been* calling
Third person:	he, she, it *has been* calling they *have been* calling

PAST PERFECT TENSE

First person:	I *had been* calling we *had been* calling
Second person:	you *had been* calling you *had been* calling
Third person:	he, she, it *had been* calling they *had been* calling

FUTURE PERFECT TENSE

First person:	I *shall have been* calling we *shall have been* calling
Second person:	you *will have been* calling you *will have been* calling
Third person:	he, she, it *will have been* calling they *will have been* calling

EMPHATIC FORMS OF THE VERB

The **emphatic forms** of a verb are often used to give greater emphasis to the idea expressed by the verb. The auxiliaries *do, does,* and *did* are used to give this additional emphasis. The emphatic forms are used in only two tenses, the *present tense* and the *past tense.*

I *do agree* with you. (present tense)
Jane *did send* the letter. (past tense)
The editor *does need* to know the facts. (present tense)

EMPHATIC FORMS —*PRESENT TENSE*

Singular and Plural

First person: I *do* call
we *do* call

Second person: you *do* call
you *do* call

Third person: he *does* call
they *do* call

EMPHATIC FORMS—*PAST TENSE*

First person: I *did* call
we *did* call

Second person: you *did* call
you *did* call

Third person: he *did* call
they *did* call

When *do, does,* and *did* are used in questions, the form is not used for emphasis. The use of *do, does,* and *did* in questions is an idiomatic way of asking question in English. In the following questions *do, does,* and *did* are not the emphatic form of the verb:

Did he buy that hat last week?
Do you know her?
Does he want to pay the bill?

Also, when *do, does,* and *did* are used to mean *accomplish, carry out,* etc., the form is not used for emphasis in these cases. This sentence is an example:

We *did* our homework quickly.

THE USE OF SHALL AND WILL

Many of the precise distinctions concerning the use of *shall* and *will* are rapidly passing out of informal speaking and writing. Careful writers, however, still observe some of these distinctions. The following are some of the distinctions that are most generally observed:

Simple Futurity

Use *shall* in the first person and *will* in the second and third persons to express **simple futurity.** Simple futurity means anticipation or expectation of what is likely to happen, or what one is likely to do. It follows the regular forms of the future tense:

First person: I *shall* go
we *shall* go

Second person: you *will* go
you *will* go

Third person: he *will* go
they *will* go

Determination, Threat, Promise

If you want to express determination, compulsion, threat, or promise (willingness to do something), reverse the order of *shall* and *will.* Use *will* in the first person, and *shall* in the second and third persons.

First person: I *will* go
we *will* go

Second person: you *shall* go
you *shall* go

Third person: he *shall* go
they *shall* go

Special Cases

When *shall* and *will* are followed by such expressions as *be glad, be sorry, be happy, be delighted, be pleased,* etc., use *shall* in the first person, and *will* in the second and third persons. If *will* is used in the first person, it would mean that you are determined *to be glad, sorry, delighted,* etc. If *shall* is used in the second and third persons, it would mean that you are compelling someone *to be glad, sorry,* etc. The following are the accepted ways of using such expressions:

I shall be glad to see you. (not *will*)
We shall be delighted to help you. (not *will*)
You will be sorry to learn of his misfortune. (not *shall*)
He will be pleased to see you at four. (not *shall*)

In giving courteous commands, you should use *will* in the second and third persons instead of *shall.* This is the form that is generally followed in giving military orders and instructions:

Corporal Smith will report to Captain Allen. (not *shall report*)
You will hand in your report on Wednesday. (not *shall*)
The meeting will come to order. (not *shall*)
Mr. Ames, you will meet with the committee today. (not *shall*)

SHOULD AND WOULD

Should is the past tense of *shall* and in general, follows the same rules that apply to the use of *shall. Would* is the past tense of *will* and follows the same rules that apply to the use of *will.*

Both *should* and *would* have special uses. *Would* is used in all three persons to express *habitual* or *customary* action. *Should* is often used in all three persons to express *obligation. Ought* and *should* both express obligation and are used interchangeable.

Every evening we would play cards for hours. (*habitual action*)
You should read something worth while every day. (*obligation*)
You ought to read something worth while every day. (*obligation*)

Study the following sentences carefully. Note especially the explanations given in parentheses. This will help you understand the distinctions which have been made in the preceding discussion:

I shall go to the theater this evening. (*simple futurity expectation*)
I will not *see* him today. (*determination* on the part of the speaker)
You will enjoy meeting him. (*simple futurity* or *expectation*)
He will enter Harvard in September. (*simple futurity*)
I will accompany you to the clinic. (*promise willingness*)
He shall report to the judge every month. (*I am determined* that he shall.)
You shall have any assistance that you may need. (*I am determined* that you shall.)

We shall be pleased to grant you an interview. (*simple futurity*)
You would drown if you ventured out in deep water. (*simple futurity*)
He would drown if he ventured out in deep water. (*simple futurity*)
We should be very happy if *you would call* for us. (*simple futurity*)
I should be the first one to volunteer. (*obligation*)
You should read good books. (*obligation*)
They should offer their services to the committee. (*obligation*)

MIXED TENSES

Unless there is a good reason for making a change, the tenses of the verbs in a sentence or in a paragraph should agree. If you start out with a verb in the *past tense,* you should not change to another verb in the *present tense.* If you start with a verb in the *present tense,* you should not change to the *past tense.*

Tense means *time,* and when you change the tense, you also change the time. Tenses must be consistent; that is, there must be a logical sequence of time. It is illogical to shift from one tense to another tense. Study the following illustrations carefully:

Dr. Smith *examined* the patient and *calls* the nurse. (*incorrect*)

In this sentence, the verb *examined* is in the past tense. It is followed by the verb *calls* which is in the present tense. There is a shift from the past tense to the present tense. Both verbs should be in the past tense or both verbs should be in the present tense.

Dr. Smith *examines* the patient and *calls* the nurse. (*correct*)
or
Dr. Smith *examined* the patient and *called* the nurse. (*correct*)

I *went* into the hall and there I *see* a strange man. (*incorrect*)
I *went* into the hall and there I *saw* a strange man. (*correct*)

The officer *stopped* the car and *speaks* to the driver. (*incorrect*)
The officer *stopped* the car and *spoke* to the driver. (*correct*)

THE "OF" ERROR

Careless speakers and writers often use the preposition *of* in place of the auxiliary verb *have.* The word *of* is a preposition and should never be used as part of a verb phrase.

The "*of*" error is generally caused by the use of contractions or by careless enunciation on the part of a speaker. The mistake is commonly made after the words *could, might, ought to, should,* and *would.* When *have* is used following any of these words, and the two words are contracted, the resulting combination sounds as if *of* were being used rather than *have: could've* sounds like *could of, should've* sounds like *should of,* etc.

Since in speech the contracted form of *have* cannot readily be distinguished from *of,* many persons have the mistaken belief that *of* is the word being said and that it is the correct word to use. As a result they carry over the mistake from their speech into their writing, and never know they are in error. To avoid making the "*of*" error when you are speaking, never contract *have* to *'ve.*

Study the following examples. The presposition *of* should never be used in place of *have* as part of a verb phrase.

We should *of* been more careful. (*incorrect*)
We shoud *have* been more careful. (*correct*)

He must *of* taken it. (*incorrect*)
He must *have* taken it. (*correct*)

They might *of* notified us. (*incorrect*)
They might *have* notified us. (*correct*)

I should *of* prepared the report. (*incorrect*)
I should *have* prepared the report. (*correct*)

14. VERBS: VOICE AND MOOD

ACTIVE AND PASSIVE VOICE

A verb not only undergoes certain changes to show *tense*, or the time of the action, but it changes in form to show *voice*. **Voice** is a grammatical term which is used to *tell whether the subject of the sentence is acting or is receiving the action expressed by the verb.*

When the subject is acting, we say that the subject is the *doer*. When the subject is receiving the action, we say that the subject is the *receiver*. If you keep these two terms, *doer* and *receiver*, in mind, you will have no difficulty in understanding what *voice* means in grammar.

Study the following sentences carefully. Note the changes that occur in the form of the verb. Note the change that occurs in the subject of the sentence:

Ned washed the car. (*Ned* is the *doer* of the action.)

The car was washed by Ned. (*Car* is the *receiver* of the action.)

In the first sentence, the subject is *Ned*. He is the *doer*, the one who is performing the action expressed by the verb *washed*. The *car* is receiving the action. In grammar we say that the verb in this sentence is in the **active voice** because the subject is the *doer*, or is doing the washing. The car is the *receiver* of the action.

The second sentence is written in the reverse order. The subject is now the receiver of the action instead of the doer. In order to express this idea, it was necessary to use another verb form, *was washed*. What happened to *Ned*, the doer? *Ned* is still in the sentence but is now in a phrase introduced by the preposition *by*.

The verb *was washed* is in the **passive voice** because it represents the subject of the sentence as the receiver of the action. In other words, the subject is not acting, but is *passive*. The doer, or the actor, appears in a phrase introduced by the preposition *by*.

A verb in the passive voice is *never* a simple verb. It is always a verb phrase. In the sentence, *Our car was stolen yesterday*, the verb *was stolen* is in the *passive voice*. The subject is the receiver of the action. Since the doer is unknown, the "*by* phrase" is omitted. But we know that it was stolen by someone. If we discover who stole the car, the doer might be added to the sentence:

Our car was stolen yesterday by two strangers.

If a verb is in the **active voice**, *the subject is the doer of the action*. If a verb is in the **passive voice,** *the subject is the receiver of the action*. When a verb is in the passive voice, the doer is often omitted. Sometimes the doer is unknown, and sometimes the doer is so evident that it is not necessary to include the "*by* phrase."

HOW THE PASSIVE VOICE IS FORMED

You cannot express an idea in the passive voice without using an auxiliary or helping verb. The verb *to be* is the auxiliary verb that is used to help form the six tenses of the passive voice. If you are familiar with the conjugation of the verb *to be*, you will have no difficulty in forming the passive voice of any verb that takes an object.

The passive voice is formed by combining the verb *to be* with the **past participle** of the principal verb. The principal verb is the verb that names the action.

The verb *was washed* in the sentence, *The car was washed by Ned*, is made up of the auxiliary verb *was*, which is a form of the verb *to be*. The *past participle* of the principal verb is added to the auxiliary *was*. The past participle of the verb *wash* is *washed*. The verb phrase is *was washed*. It is a verb phrase in the passive voice.

The verb phrases in the following sentences are in the *passive voice*. They are formed by combining some form of the verb *to be* with the past participle of the principal verb, or the verb that names the action.

The plans will be made by the general.

Trees have been planted in the park by the commissioners.

The verb in the first sentence is *will be made*. It is made up of the auxiliary *will be*, which is a form of the verb *to be* and the past participle of the verb *make*, which is *made* (*will be made*).

The verb in the second sentence is *have been planted*. It is made up of the auxiliary verb *have been*, which is a form of the verb *to be* and the past participle of the verb *plant* (*planted*).

The six tenses of the verb *call* were given in Chapter Thirteen for the *active voice*. The forms for the *passive voice* follow. If you examine these forms carefully, you will see that the tenses follow the regular conjugation of the verb *to be*. The past participle of the verb *call* (*called*) is added to the forms of the verb *to be*.

SIX TENSES OF THE VERB "CALL"

PASSIVE VOICE
Singular and Plural
PRESENT TENSE

First person:	I *am* called we *are* called
Second person:	you *are* called you *are* called
Third person:	he *is* called they *are* called

PAST TENSE

First person:	I *was* called we *were* called
Second person:	you *were* called you *were* called
Third person:	he *was* called they *were* called

FUTURE TENSE

First person:	I *shall* be called we *shall* be called
Second person:	you *will* be called you *will* be called
Third person:	he *will* be called they *will* be called

PRESENT PERFECT TENSE
Singular and Plural

First person:	I *have been* called we *have been* called
Second person:	you *have been* called you *have been* called
Third person:	he *has been* called they *have been* called

PAST PERFECT TENSE

First person:	I *had been* called we *had been* called
Second person:	you *had been* called you *had been* called
Third person:	he *had been* called they *had been* called

FUTURE PERFECT TENSE

First person:	I *shall have been* called we *shall have been* called
Second person:	you *will have been* called you *will have been* called
Third person:	he *will have been* called they *will have been* called

SIX TENSES OF THE IRREGULAR VERB "KNOW"

PASSIVE VOICE

Singular and Plural
PRESENT TENSE

First person:	I *am* known we *are* known
Second person:	you *are* known you *are* known
Third person:	he *is* known they *are* known

PAST TENSE

First person:	I *was* known we *were* known
Second person:	you *were* known you *were* known
Third person:	he *was* known they *were* known

FUTURE TENSE

First person:	I *shall* be known we *shall* be known
Second person:	you *will* be known you *will* be known
Third person:	he *will* be known they *will* be known

PRESENT PERFECT TENSE

First person:	I *have been* known we *have been* known
Second person:	you *have been* known you *have been* known
Third person:	he *has been* known they *have been* known

PAST PERFECT TENSE

First person:	I *had been* known we *had been* known
Second person:	you *had been* known you *had been* known
Third person:	he *had been* known they *had been* known

SIX TENSES OF THE IRREGULAR VERB "KNOW" (Cont'd)

FUTURE PERFECT TENSE

First person: I *shall* have been known
                we *shall* have been known

Second person: you *will* have been known
                you *will* have been known

Third person: he *will* have been known
                they *will* have been known

WHEN TO USE THE PASSIVE VOICE

Since you may show that the subject is either the doer or the receiver of the action, the question naturally arises. "Which form is better?" The use of the passive voice often results in a roundabout, awkward method of expression.

In the large majority of cases the *active voice is the better form to use.* Never use the passive voice, either in speaking or writing, when the active voice would be more natural or more direct. The following illustrations show clearly that the active voice would be more natural and more direct than the passive voice.

The concert was enjoyed by us. (*passive voice*)
We enjoyed the concert. (*active voice*)

Your order was sent by us by express today. (*passive voice*)
We sent your order by express today. (*active voice*)

The stranger was barked at by a dog. (*passive voice*)
A dog barked at the stranger. (*active voice*)

As a rule, the active voice is preferred for business writing, and for and other form of writing that requires the direct approach. The use of the *active voice increases vividness.* The passive voice expresses reversed action, since the receiver comes before the doer. Active verbs are often used in newspaper headlines because they are more vivid and take less space. The following headlines are all in the active voice:

"Lion Gets Out of Cage"

"White Sox Capture First Title"

"Urges France to Begin Defense Plan"

"Governor Advises Aid for Workers"

The passive voice is generally used when the subject of the sentence is *indefinite, general,* or *unimportant.* In the sentence, *They mine coal in Pennsylvania,* the subject is so indefinite that it is not clear what is meant by *they.* It might mean the miners, the people, or the companies. This sentence, and sentences like it, are improved by putting the verb in the passive voice.

They *mine* coal in Pennsylvania. (*poor*)
Coal *is mined* in Pennsylvania. (*better*)

They *grow* wheat in many of our states. (*poor*)
Wheat *is grown* in many of our states. (*better*)

They *use* tractors on most farms. (*poor*)
Tractors *are used* on most farms. (*better*)

The passive voice is also used when *what was done.* is more important than the doer of the action. Study the following sentences:

The play, "Man and Superman," *was written* by Shaw. (*passive*)
Shaw *wrote* the play "Man and Superman." (*active*)

America *was discovered* by Columbus. (*passive*)
Columbus *discovered* America. (*active*)

In the first sentence, if you wish to emphasize the play more than the author, put the verb in the passive voice. In the third sentence, if you wish to emphasize the discovery more than the discoverer, put the verb in the passive voice.

The use of the passive voice is generally used when you want to emphasize the *receiver* rather than the *doer.* However, in the great majority of cases the active voice is more effective than the passive voice.

MOOD OF VERBS

In addition to tense and voice, verbs have another property which is called **mood** (or *mode*). The word *mood* comes from a Latin word which means *manner.* When we apply the term mood to verbs, we mean *the manner in which the verb expresses the action or state of being.*

There are three moods in English, the *indicative mood,* the *imperative mood,* and the *subjunctive mood.* The *indicative mood* is used *to make statements* and *to ask questions.* Most of the verbs that you commonly use are in the indicative mood.

The stenographer *wrote* the letter. (*statement of fact*)
Did you hear the President's address? (*question*)

The imperative mood is used to *express a command* or *a request.* The imperative mood is found only in the present tense, second person. The subject is always the pronoun *you,* which is seldom expressed.

Come here at once! (*command*)
Close the door, Jane. (*request*)

The subjunctive mood is used to *express a wish* or *a condition which is contrary to fact.* By contrary to fact we mean something which is not true. A contrary to fact condition is usually introduced by the word *if* or *as if.*

If *he were* here, I would give him the keys. (*He is not here.*)
I wish *I were* in Florida. (*expresses a wish*)

The indicative and the imperative moods do not present any problems in English. The verb has the same form to express a statement or to ask a question. You can identify the imperative mood easily because the subject is *you,* which is usually understood. The imperative mood always expresses a command or a request.

Although most of the forms for the subjunctive have disappeared from our language, there are a few forms left that you should be able to recognize and to use. The verb *to be* still retains more of the subjunctive forms than any other verb. In the following, the subjunctive forms of the verb *to be* are given.

Reference Table

SUBJUNCTIVE FORMS OF VERB "TO BE"

PRESENT TENSE——SINGULAR AND PLURAL
First person: (If) I *be*
                 (If) we *be*
Second person: (If) you *be*
                 (If) you *be*

Third person: (If) he *be*
                 (If) they *be*

PAST TENSE——SINGULAR
First person: (If) I *were*
Second person: (If) you *were*
Third person: (If) he *were*

PRESENT PERFECT TENSE——SINGULAR
First person: (If) I *have* been
Second person: (If) you *have* been
Third person: (If) he *have* been

The subjunctive with *be* (present tense) is almost never used in informal speaking and writing. The subjunctive form *have been* instead of *has been* is also passing out of use.

In the preceding table, the forms for the subjunctive that are different from the indicative are printed in *italics;* that is, *be* in the present tense; *were* in the past tense, first person, singular, and third person, singular; *have* in the present tense, third person, singular.

There is only one change that occurs in the subjunctive in the case of other verbs. In the present tense, third person, singular, the *s* is dropped in the subjunctive.

The verb *have* has only one form in the subjunctive that is different from the indicative. In the present tense, third person, singular, *have* is used in place of *has:*

If he *have* the time, he will meet with you. (subjunctive)
He *has* the time, he will meet with you. (indicative)

If he fail—— (not *fails*)
If he have—— (not *has*)
If he call—— (not *calls*

The word *if* is not a part of the subjunctive. The forms for the subjunctive are usually given with the word *if* because the group of words in which the subjunctive is used is very frequently introduced by the word *if.*

Although the subjunctive mood is rapidly passing out of use in informal speaking and writing, there are certain uses that are still observed by discriminating writers and speakers. The subjunctive expressing a *wish* and the subjunctive in a *contrary to fact condition* are two of these uses.

USES OF THE SUBJUNCTIVE MOOD

You have just learned that careful writers and speakers use the subjunctive to express a wish, a condition that is contrary to fact (not true), and a condition of uncertainty (it may be true or not true). Sometimes careful writers and speakers also use the subjunctive *in making a suggestion, in making a demand, or in expressing a need.*

I wish I *were* a millionaire. (wish)
If I *were* you, I should give up the contest. (contrary to fact)
If this plan *fail,* we shall give up the project. (condition of uncertainty)
I suggest that he *work* full time in the future. (suggestion)
The supervisor insists that the bookkeeper *prove* his report. (a demand)
It is imperative that the play *begin* at once. (a necessity)

The subjunctive is used in certain parliamentary expressions, such as the following:

I move that the nominations *be closed.*
He moved that the report of the committee *be accepted.*

She moved that the minutes *be adopted* as read.
I move that the meeting *be adjourned*.

The *two most important* uses of the subjunctive are the subjunctive expressing a wish and the subjunctive in a contrary to fact, condition after *if, as if,* and *as though*.

15. AGREEMENT OF SUBJECT AND VERB

One of the common errors made both in speaking and writing is the lack of agreement between the subject noun or pronoun and the predicate verb. In order to have harmonious relations between the parts of the sentence, you must have this agreement.

AGREEMENT IN PERSON AND NUMBER

The grammatical principle upon which agreement of subject and verb depends is very simple: *The verb must agree with its subject in person and number.* If the subject of the sentence is singular, the verb must also be in the singular. If the subject is plural, the verb must also be plural. If the subject is in the first person, the verb must also be in the first person. If the subject is in the second or third persons, the verb must agree.

He *doesn't* know the answer. (correct——subject and verb are in third person)
He *don't* know the answer. (incorrect——lack of agreement)
You *were invited* to the meeting. (correct——subject and verb are in second person)
You *was invited* to the meeting. (incorrect——lack of agreement)

In the first sentence the subject and verb agree. The subject *He* is in the third person, singular. The verb *doesn't* is also in the third person, singular. In the second sentence, *He don't* is incorrect. The incorrect form for third person, singular is *doesn't* not *don't*.

Although the rule is very simple, there are a number of problems involved in agreement of subject and verb. These problems are responsible for the errors that are commonly made. Sometimes the speaker or writer does not know whether the subject should be regarded as singular or plural. Sometimes he is not sure about the form of the verb for the singular and for the plural. Sometimes he does not know which word is the real subject of the sentence.

In this unit you will consider some of the problems that are responsible for the errors that occur in making the subject and the verb agree. Your first problem will be the one that occurs when you have a sentence with a compound subject.

AGREEMENT OF VERB WITH COMPOUND SUBJECT

The parts of a compound subject are usually connected by *and, or, nor, either-or,* and *neither-nor*. Usually, when two or more subjects are connected by *and,* the subject is plural and requires a plural verb. The following examples have compound subjects:

Mary and Jane are taking Spanish.
The president and the vice-president speak at every meeting.

In the first sentence, the two parts of the compound subject are connected by *and.* The subject is plural and takes a plural verb, *are.* In the second sentence, the two parts of the compound subject are also connected by *and.* The subject takes the plural form of the verb which is *speak.*

There is one exception to the "and" rule. Sometimes the two subjects connected by *and* form a unit. In this case, *the subject is regarded as singular and takes a singular verb.*

Bacon and eggs is a popular combination. (*Verb is singular.*)
The Stars and Stripes flies overhead. (*Verb is singular.*)

When two subjects connected by *and* refer to the same person or thing, the subject is singular.

His companion and friend is very devoted to him. (*same person*)
The secretary and treasurer was present at the meeting. (*same person*)

If the subjects in the preceding sentences referred to *two individuals,* the verbs would be plural. The sentences would read as follows:

His companion and his friend are very devoted to him.
The secretary and the treasurer were present at the meeting.

By placing the word *his* before friend and the word *the* before treasurer, you clearly indicate that there are two individuals.

Subjects Connected by 'Or' or 'Nor'

When two singular subjects are connected by the word *or,* the subject is singular. The sentence means *either the one or the other.* It does not mean *both.* The same rule applies when *nor* is used to join two singular subjects. *Either or* and *neither nor* follow the same rule.

Mary or Jane is going to the fashion show. (*the one or the other*)
Neither the man nor the boy was responsible. (*neither the one nor the other*)

When one of the subjects connected by *or, nor, either or, neither nor* is singular and the other is plural, the verb agrees with the subject that is *nearer to* it. If both subjects are plural, the verb is also plural.

Neither the boy nor the men were responsible. (*Verb is plural.*)
Neither the men nor the boy was responsible. (*Verb is singular.*)
Neither the men nor the boys were responsible. (*Verb is plural.*)

In the first sentence, the plural subject is nearer to the verb. In the second sentence, the singular subject is nearer to the verb. In the third sentence, both subjects are plural. When one of the subjects is singular and the other is plural, you should put the plural subject nearer to the verb. It makes the verb plural and sounds better.

Either I or they are responsible for the small attendance.

This sentence would sound better if it were written as follows:

Either I am responsible for the small attendance, or they are.

AGREEMENT OF VERB WITH COLLECTIVE NOUNS

A **collective noun** is a noun that represents a group or a collection of objects usually considered as a unit. Words like *crowd, troop, herd, people, flock,* and *jury* are collective nouns.

A collective noun that is singular in meaning requires a singular verb. A collective noun that is plural in meaning requires a plural verb.

If the collective noun in a particular sentence represents the individuals acting as a unit, the noun is singular. If the sentence indicates clearly that the individuals are acting separately, the noun is plural. The following examples will help you see this distinction:

The *committee is opposed* to the plan. (*acting as a unit*)
The *board of directors is* in session. (*as a unit*)
The *jury returned its* verdict. (*as a unit*)
The *jury have returned* to their homes. (*as individuals*)
The *family have given* their contributions. (*as individuals*)

In most cases where the individuals composing a group are acting separately, it is better to use such expressions as *the members of the jury, the members of the family,* etc. These expressions sound better and clearly indicate that the individuals are acting separately.

The members of the jury have returned to their homes.
The people in the audience were waving their hands.

INTERVENING PHRASES

Sometimes the subject is followed by prepositional phrases or such expressions as *accompanied by, in accordance with, together with, as well as, including,* etc. The subject of the sentence is not affected in any way by the introduction of such phrases. You will never find the subject of the sentence in a prepositional phrase or in any one of the expressions listed in the following sentences:

A *package* (of books) *was delivered* today.
Materials (for the building) *have been shipped.*
Important *papers,* as well as his will, *were found* in his desk.
The *checks,* including a statement, *were mailed* today.

In the first sentence, the subject is the word *package.* Since package is singular, the verb must be singular. In the second sentence, the subject is the word *Materials.* Since the subject is plural, the verb must be plural. The prepositional phrases, of *books,* and *for the building,* do not affect the number of the subject.

The subject of the third sentence is *papers,* which is plural. The verb must be plural to agree with the subject. The group of words, *as well as his will,* does not affect the number of the subject. In the fourth sentence, the expression, *including a statement,* does not affect the number of the subject. The subject is *checks,* which is plural. The verb must also be plural, to agree with the subject.

AGREEMENT OF SUBJECT WITH CONTRACTIONS

Contractions are verbs that have been shortened by the omission of one or more letters. The omission of the letters is indicated by the use of an apostrophe. Many persons make mistakes in agreement of subject and verb when they use contractions. The use of the contractions *don't* and *ain't* are responsible for a great many of these errors.

Although the word *ain't* is frequently heard in informal conversation. most educated persons consider its use incorrect and unacceptable.

Do not use *ain't* for *am not, are not,* or *isn't.* The contraction *aren't* should be used for *are not.* There is no contraction for the words *am not.*

I *am not* interested in the position. (not *ain't*)
We *are not* going to the theater. (not *ain't*)
We *aren't* going to the meeting. (not *ain't*)
Isn't this a beautiful day! (not *ain't*)

Another error commonly made is the use of **don't** for **doesn't. Don't** is a contraction for *do not.* It should not be used in the third person, singular. The expressions, *it don't, he don't* and *she don't* are incorrect. Do no misuse them for *it doesn't, he doesn't,* and *she doesn't.*

It *don't* make any difference. (incorrect)
It *doesn't* make any difference. (correct)

He *don't belong to our union. (incorrect)*
He *doesn't* belong to our union. (correct)

AGREEMENT OF VERB WITH INDEFINITE PRONOUNS

The indefinite pronouns *one, no one, anyone, everyone, someone, anybody, nobody, everybody, somebody, each, either,* and *neither* are always singular. Since these pronouns are singular, they take a singular verb.

Only *one* of the candidates is eligible. (*singular verb*)
Each of these bags has been examined. (*singular verb*)
Neither has lost his ticket. (*singular verb*)
Somebody is responsible for the accident. (*singular verb*)
Anyone has the right to offer criticism. (*singular verb*)
Nobody has access to the vault. (*singular verb*)

When *many a, each,* and *every* are used to introduce a sentence and function as adjectives, the *subject* is singular.

Many a *man* wishes that he had gone to college.
Each *window* and *door* was locked securely.
Every *man, woman,* and *child* is expected to report.

The indefinite pronouns *several, few, both* and *many* are always plural.

Several were called to the platform. (*plural verb*)
A *few* were opposed to the bill. (*plural verb*)
Both were anxious to receive the award. (*plural verb*)
Many in the audience objected to his speech. (*plural verb*)

The indefinite pronouns *some, none, any,* and *all* are singular or plural according to the meaning of the sentence. When these words refer to a *quantity* or a *mass* taken as a whole, they are generally considered as singular. When they refer to a *number,* they are regarded as plural in meaning.

Some are going by plane. (*more than one*——plural)
Some of the ice cream *is* left. (*mass or quantity*——singular)
Are any of the men going by plane? (*more than one*——plural)

Is there *any* gasoline in the tank? (*mass or quantity*——singular)
None of these apples *are* ripe. (*more than one*——plural)
We needed a ball but *none was* available. (*not one*——singular)
All of the gasoline *has* been sold. (*mass or quantity*——singular)
All of the women *have brought* gifts. (*more than one*——plural)

Some nouns are plural in form, but singular in meaning. Examples of nouns that take a singular verb are *mumps, measles, news, summons, physics, mathematics.*

Physics is a very interesting subject. *Verb is singular.*)

The news this week is startling. (*Verb is singular.*)

Measles is a contagious disease. (*Verb is singular.*)

Mathematics was his favorite study. (*Verb is singular.*)

SPECIAL CASES OF AGREEMENT

1. Words like *pants, trousers, pliers, scissors, shears,* and *tongs* are plural and take a plural verb. When the word *pair* is used as the subject, the subject is regarded as singular and takes a singular verb.

The *scissors* are very sharp. (*plural*)
A *pair* of scissors was left on the desk. (*singular*)

2. A plural noun which shows *weight, extent,* or *quantity* is singular, and takes a singular verb. Ten miles is a long distance to walk. (*singular*)

Five dollars is the price of the hat. (*singular*)

Twelve inches is the proper length. (*singular*)

3. The words *half* and *part* are singular or plural according to the meaning of the sentence. When these words refer to a *mass* or a *section,* they are singular. When they refer to a *number* of individuals or things, they are plural.

Half of the boys are in camp. (*number*——plural)

Half of the pie is left. (*mass or section*——singular)

Part of the roof was destroyed. (*mass or section*——singular)

Part of the guests have arrived. (*number*——plural)

4. When the word *number* is preceded by the article *a,* it takes a plural verb. When it is immediately preceded by the article *the,* it takes a singular verb.

A *number* of men *were working* on the project. (*plural*)
The *number* of men present *was* small. (*singular*)

5. The name of a firm is often regarded as singular even when there is a plural form in the title. If the entire name carries a plural idea, the name is regarded as plural.

Harrison Brothers are having a sale on furs. (*plural*)

The Lexicon Company publishes books. (*singular*)
Tractors *are* uGeneral Motors Company has declared a dividend. (*singular*)

6. Sometimes a sentence begins with the word *there* or *here.* Neither of these words could be the subject of the sentence. The word *there* is used either as an expletive or as an adverb. The word *here* is an adverb. When a sentence begins with *here* or *there,* you should transpose it so that the true subject will appear at the beginning of the sentence. Then it will be possible for you to determine whether the subject is singular or plural.

There are six men on the committee.

Six men are on the committee. (*plural subject*——*plural verb*)

Here comes the general with his staff.

The general comes here with his staff. (*singular subject and verb*)

Sometimes a sentence beginning with the introductory *there* or *here* has a *compound subject,* which requires a plural verb. Mistakes in the number of the verb are frequently made because the speaker or the writer does not realize that the subject is *compound.* When the sentence is transposed, it is easy to determine whether the subject is simple or compound. The following sentences have compound subjects:

There goes the boy and his mother. (incorrect)
There go the boy and his mother. (correct)
The boy and his mother go there. (*compound subject*——*plural verb*)

Here comes John and Mary. (incorrect)
Here come John and Mary. (correct)

John and Mary come here. (*compound subject*——*plural verb*)

16. PREPOSITIONAL PHRASES

Chapter Two explained that a preposition is a word that shows the relation between its object and some other word in the sentence. In this unit you will study the function of the phrase which the preposition introduces.

A *prepositional phrase consists of the preposition and its object.* Sometimes the noun which serves as the object of the preposition has modifiers, but the important words in the phrase are the two words–the *preposition* and the *object.* The prepositions and their objects are underlined.

I walked down the winding street.

The girl with red hair is an artist.

In the first sentence, the preposition is the word *down.* The object is *street.* The entire phrase is *down the winding street.* The two important words in the phrase are the preposition *down* and the object *street.*

In the second sentence, the preposition is *with* and the object is *hair.* The prepositional phrase is the group of words, *with red hair.*

In grammar, a **phrase** is a group of words, *without a subject and predicate,* that functions as *a single part of speech.* A prepositional phrase is a phrase that functions as an *adjective* or an *adverb.* Since adjectives and adverbs are modifiers, the prepositional phrase is also a modifier.

ADJECTIVE PHRASES

An *adjective phrase* is a prepositional phrase that modifies a *noun* or a *pronoun*. An adjective phrase is often the equivalent of an adjective, as you will readily see from the following illustrations:

The man *at the gate* sold us the tickets.
We followed the path *near the river*.

In the first sentence, the prepositional phrase is *at the gate*. It is an adjective phrase because it modifies the noun *man*. The phrase, *at the gate*, is the equivalent of an adjective because it means the *gate* man.

In the second sentence, the prepositional phrase is *near the river*. This is also an adjective phrase because it modifies the noun *path*. The sentence means that we followed the *river* path. The phrase *near the river* is the equivalent of an adjective.

Like the adjective, the adjective phrase *describes* or *limits* the noun or pronoun which it modifies.

She wore a hat *with blue trimming*. (describes the hat)
He lives in the house *to your right*. (limited to a particular house)

An adjective phrase may follow the noun which it modifies, or it may be used in the predicate after a linking verb.

The accident *on the bridge* was not serious. (follows the noun)
The injured man seemed *in a daze*. (follows a linking verb)

You will not acquire skill in recognizing prepositional phrases unless you become familiar with the words that are commonly used as prepositions. This list appeared in Chapter Two, and it is repeated here for reference. Refer to this list until you are able to identify the prepositions that are in common use.

Commonly Used Prepositions

above	at	by	into	toward
about	before	down	like	through
across	behind	during	near	under
after	below	except	of	until
against	beneath	for	off	up
among	between	in	since	with
around	but	inside	to	within
	(except)			

The fact that a word appears in this list does not mean that it is always used as a preposition. Many of the words that are commonly used as prepositions are also used as adverbs.

Planes were flying *above the city*. (*Above* is a preposition.)
Planes were flying *above*. (*Above* is an adverb.)

ADVERBIAL PHRASES

An *adverbial phrase* is a prepositional phrase that modifies a *verb*, an *adjective*, or an *adverb*. Like the adverb, the adverbial phrase answers the questions: *when? where? how?* and *to what extent?* Adverbial phrases express *time, place, manner,* and *degree.*

I shall return *at noon*. (Phrase expresses *time*.)
The sailor was working *on the deck*. (Phrase expresses *place*.)
Tell the story *in your own words*. (Phrase expresses *manner*.)

In the first sentence, the adverbial phrase is *at noon*. The phrase tells *when* or at what time I shall return. It modifies the verb *shall return*.

The adverbial phrase in the second sentence is *on the deck*. This phrase tells *where* or *at what place* the sailor was working. It modifies the verb *was working*. The adverbial phrase in the third sentence is *in your own words*. It tells *how* or *in what manner* you should tell the story. The phrase modifies the verb *tell*.

Adverbial phrases that modify verbs are very easy to identify. Those that modify adjectives and adverbs are not always easy to identify. The adverbial phrase that modifies an adjective usually follows that adjective. Study the following illustration carefully:

The child seemed afraid *of the noise*. (modifies *afraid*)

In this sentence, the adverbial phrase *of the noise* modifies the predicate adjective *afraid*. Adverbial phrases that modify adjectives usually follow this pattern.

COMPOUND OR PHRASAL PREPOSITIONS

A preposition is not always a single word. There are a number of prepositions in common use that are made up of a group of two or more words. Such prepositions are called **compound prepositions** or **phrasal prepositions**.

Although the *compound preposition* consists of two or more words, it is regarded as a unit, or as a single preposition. The following list includes the compound prepositions that are in common use:

according to	in consideration of
along side of	in apposition with
along with	in front of
because of	in regard to
by means of	in respect to
by reason of	in spite of
by way of	instead of
contrary to	on account of
for the sake of	out of
in addition to	with reference to
in accordance with	with regard to
in case of	with respect to

Compound Prepositions in Sentences

In compliance with his request, we closed the account.
According to our schedule, the job will be completed tomorrow.
The president resigned *on account of illness*.

PRONOUNS USED AS OBJECT OF PREPOSITIONS

You have already learned that the object of a preposition is always in the **objective case**. When nouns are used as objects of prepositions, they do not present a problem because nouns do not have different forms for the objective case.

Pronouns do present a problem in case because some of the *personal pronouns* and the pronoun *who* have one form for the nominative case and another form for the objective case. When a pronoun is used as the object of a preposition, the form for the objective case must be used.

It is incorrect to use the forms *I, he, she, we, they,* or *who* as objects of prepositions. They are **nominative case** forms. The correct forms to use are *me, him, her, us, them,* and *whom*. In the following sentences, all the pronouns that are used as objects of prepositions are in the **objective case:**

The speaker spoke to **me** after the meeting. (*me*——objective case)
I went to the Art Institute with **her**. (*her*——objective case)
We looked at **him** while he was dancing. (*him*——objective case)
The women prepared a dinner for **them**. (*them*——objective case)
The librarian found the books for **us**. (*us*——objective case)
For **whom** are you working now? (*whom*——objective case)

Watch the two words, *but* and *like*, carefully when they are followed by pronouns. The word *but* is a preposition when it means *except*. When the word *but* is used as a preposition, it must be followed by the objective case. Similarly, when the word *like* is used as a preposition, it must be followed by the objective case of the pronoun. As a preposition, *like* means *similar to*, or *in a manner similar to*. (Other uses of the word *like* will be found in Chapter 19.)

No one knew the answer **but** me. (*but*—— preposition)
His son looks **like** him. (*like*——preposition)

THE CORRECT USE OF PREPOSITIONS

Many of the common prepositions are often used incorrectly. Since a preposition expresses a relationship between the object and some other word in the sentence, the preposition that you use must be selected with care. Very often the speaker or writer is not aware of the distinctions in meaning that careful writers and speakers observe in using prepositions. The following are some of the prepositions that you should use with discrimination.

Differences in Meaning

1. **Around, about.** *Around* means encircling. *About* often means approximately. Do not use *around* when you mean approximately.

The fish weighed *around* three pounds. (incorrect)
The fish weighed *about* two pounds. (correct)
She tied a ribbon *about* her head. (incorrect)
She tied a ribbon *around* her head. (correct)

2. **Agree to, agree with.** One *agrees to* a proposal, but *agrees with* a person.

The members *agreed with* the president. (correct——*person*)
I *agree to* your plan for saving money. (correct——*proposal*)

3. **Beside, besides.** *Beside* means by the side of. *Besides* means in addition to.

Margaret sat *beside* her father. (*by the side of*)
There were three *besides* Jerry in the boat. (*in addition to*)

4. **Between, among.** *Between* is used when referring to two. *Among* is used when referring to more than two.

Frank and Harry divided the money *between* them. (*two persons*)
The money was divided *among* the five heirs. (*more than two*)

5. **Differ with, differ from.** One differs *with* a person in the matter of opinion. A person or thing *differs from* another in certain respects; that is, the person or thing is *unlike* another in certain respects.

I *differ with* you about his qualifications. (*matter of opinion*)

Maine *differs from* Florida in many ways. (*in certain respects*)

6. Different from, different than. *Different from* is correct. Do not use *different than*, which is incorrect.

The motion picture is *different from* the book. (correct)

The motion picture is *different than* the book. (incorrect)

7. In, into. The preposition *in* indicates location or motion within a place. *Into* indicates motion *toward the inside* of a place from the outside.

The tea was held *in* the garden. (*within a place*)

The swimmer jumped *into* the pool. (*from the outside*)

He swam *in* the pool. (*motion within a place*)

8. In back of, behind. *In back of* should never be used for *behind*.

The car is *in back* of the house. (incorrect)
The car is *behind* the house. (correct)

9. Over, more than. *Over* expresses the idea of *place*. *More than* expresses the idea of *quantity*.

The actress has *over* a hundred dresses. (incorrect)

The actress has *more than* a hundred dresses. (correct)

She wore a cape *over* her shoulders. (correct——*place*)

10. Outside of, except. Do not use *outside of* when you mean *except*.

No one went *outside of* James. (incorrect)
No one went *except* James. (correct)

11. To, too. The preposition *to* should not be confused with the adverb *too*.

I am going *to* the Dunes. (preposition *to*)
Will you go, *too*? (adverb, meaning *also*)

12. Within, inside of. Do not use *inside of* to express time. Use *within*.

He will leave *inside of* a week. (incorrect)
He will leave *within* a week. (correct)

13. In regard to, with regard to. Do not say *in regards to* or *with regards to*. The correct expressions are *in regard to* and *with regard to*.

In regards to your order (incorrect)
In regard to your order (correct)

14. Unnecessary prepositions. Do not use *off of* for *off*. The *of* should not be added. Always omit the unnecessary prepositions in sentences like the following:

He jumped *off of* the pier. (*of* is superfluous)
He jumped *off* the pier. (correct)
Where is he *at*? (incorrect)
Where is he? (correct)
Where is he going *to*? (incorrect)
Where is he going? (correct)
Is the rain over *with*? (incorrect)
Is the rain over? (correct)

POSITION OF THE PREPOSITION

Many persons believe that it is incorrect to end a sentence with a preposition. Very often it is more natural and more emphatic to place the preposition at the end of the sentence. In many questions, the preposition comes naturally at the end. But a preposition should not be used at the end of a sentence if it sounds awkward or changes the meaning of the sentence. The following sentences end with a preposition. The prepositions fall naturally and correctly at the end.

Whom are you looking *for*?
What kind of plane is he traveling *in*?
They sold the car you were looking *at*.

Ordinarily, the preposition should not be placed at the end of the sentence. However, many of our best writers and speakers occasionally end sentences in this way.

17. THE COMPOUND SENTENCE

Chapter Four explained that there are four types of sentences: *declarative, interrogative, imperative,* and *exclamatory sentences.* A particular sentence falls into one of these groups according to the purpose which it serves.

When you make a statement, you use a declarative sentence, but when you ask a question, you use an interrogative sentence. If your purpose is to issue a command or make a request, you use the imperative sentence. When you want to express strong feeling or sudden emotion, you use an exclamatory sentence.

KINDS OF CLAUSES

There is still another way of classifying sentences. This classification is based upon the internal structure of the sentence or the way in which it is built up. Thus far, we have been dealing with the sentence that has the simplest form of internal structure——the *simple sentence.* We have been dealing with the simple sentence because our chief problem has been the relationships that words have to each other.

In this unit you will begin a study of the more complicated sentence patterns. You will learn how to build up sentences in a number of different ways. This knowledge will enable you to express your ideas in a variety of ways and will give you more power over language.

The type of classification of sentences which you will study is based upon the *number* and *kinds* of **clauses** which a sentence contains. According to this classification, sentences are divided into four groups: *simple, compound, complex,* and *compound complex.* In this unit we shall limit our study to the simple sentence and the compound sentence.

Before you can understand the difference between a simple sentence and a compound sentence, you must have a very clear idea of what is meant by a clause in grammar.

A **clause** is a group of words that has a *subject* and a *predicate.* There are two kinds of clauses: *independent* or *main* clauses and *dependent* or *subordinate* clauses.

INDEPENDENT CLAUSES

An **independent clause** is a group of words that has a subject and a predicate. An independent clause does not depend upon anything else for its meaning. It expresses a complete thought. An independent clause is a simple sentence when it stands alone.

The officer blew his whistle and the cars stopped.

In this sentence, there are two independent clauses. The first independent clause is *The officer blew his whistle.* The second independent clause is *the cars stopped.* These clauses could be written as two simple sentences by omitting the conjunction *and.* The conjunction *and* does not belong to either of the independent clauses. It simple brings the two independent clauses together in one sentence.

The officer blew his whistle. The cars stopped.

SUBORDINATE CLAUSES

A **subordinate clause** is a group of words that has a subject and a predicate, *but the clause cannot stand alone.* A subordinate clause does not express a complete thought. It depends upon the main clause for its meaning. The connective, or the word that introduces the subordinate clause, plays an important part in making it a dependent clause. In the following sentence the subordinate clause is underlined.

The cars stopped when the officer blew his whistle.

In this sentence, the group of words, *when the officer blew his whistle*, is a subordinate clause. It cannot stand alone although it has both a subject and a predicate. The word *when*, which introduces the clause, makes the words which follow it dependent upon the main clause for the meaning. That is the reason why the clause, *when the officer blew his whistle*, is called a dependent or a subordinate clause.

The group of words, *the cars stopped*, is an independent clause. It could stand alone. It is the main clause in the sentence because it states the main idea in the sentence.

THE SIMPLE SENTENCE

A **simple sentence** is a sentence having *one* subject and *one* predicate, either or both of which may be *compound.* A simple sentence consists of one and only one independent clause. All of the following sentences are simple sentences, but some have compound subjects or predicates. The last sentence has both a compound subject and a compound predicate.

John joined the Navy. (simple subject and predicate)

John and Fred joined the Marines. (compound subject)

Mary sang and played at the concert. (compound predicate)

Mary and Jane sang and played at the concert. (compound subject and predicate)

Note that a compound subject does not mean two subjects. It means the *one* subject is made up of two or more nouns or pronouns. A *compound predicate* does not mean two predicates. It means that *one* predicate is made up of two or more verbs or verb phrases.

THE COMPOUND SENTENCE

A **compound sentence** is a sentence that *contains two or more independent clauses.* The independent clauses of a compound sentence must be joined in some way to indicate that the independent clauses form one sentence.

When you put two independent clauses or two simple sentences together to form one longer sentence, you have a compound sentence:

John joined the Navy. (simple sentence)
Harry joined the Marines. (simple sentence)

If you join these two simple sentences in order to make a compound sentence, you have the problem of punctuation and the problem of using a conjunction. The following sentences show the ways in which two simple sentences might be joined to form one compound sentence:

John joined the Navy, **but** Harry joined the Marines. (*comma* and *conjunction*)
John joined the Navy; Harry joined the Marines. (*semicolon*)
John joined the Navy **but** Harry joined the Marines. (*conjunction only*)

From these illustrations you can see that the independent clauses of a compound sentence may be connected in one of three ways:

1. By using a comma before a conjunction
2. By using a semicolon without a conjunction
3. By using a conjunction without a comma

All three methods of writing a compound sentence are correct. However, you will use the first method, a comma before a conjunction, much more frequently than the other two methods. You will learn more about each method of punctuation as you progress in this unit.

IDENTIFYING THE COMPOUND SENTENCE

Some persons have difficulty in distinguishing between a simple sentence with a compound subject or predicate, and a compound sentence. The point to keep in mind is that the compound sentence must be the equivalent of at least *two complete simple sentences*. Examine the following illustration carefully:

The Indian squaw cooks, sews, and builds the wigwam.

This is not a compound sentence. It is a simple sentence with a compound predicate. You could not possibly make two independent clauses out of the sentence as it is written. In order to turn it into a compound sentence, you would have to supply another subject and write the sentence as two independent clauses:

The Indian squaw cooks and sews, **and** she builds the wigwam.

COORDINATE CONJUNCTIONS

The independent clauses of a compound sentence are often connected by a coordinate conjunction. **Coordinate** means of the *same rank* or *of equal rank*. **Coordinate conjunctions** are used to connect words, phrases, and clauses of equal rank. The independent clauses of a compound sentence are of the same rank; therefore, we use a coordinate conjunction to connect them. The coordinate conjunctions that are commonly used for this purpose are *for, and, but, or, not,* and *while* when it means the same as *but*.

Use of the Comma and Coordinate Conjunction

When a coordinate conjunction is used in a compound sentence, it is usually preceded by a comma. The comma should not be omitted unless the independent clauses are very short and the thought is closely connected. Observe the use of the comma and the coordinate conjunction in each of the following compound sentences. The independent clauses are underlined.

Arthur washed our new car, **and** Ned polished it.
I may consider your plan, **or** I may disregard it.
I did not seek the position, **nor** do I want it.
Michael likes tennis, **but** he prefers to play golf.
Their team was untrained, **while** ours was highly trained.
Jack went to bed early, **for** he was very tired.

In modern writing, the comma is often omitted before the conjunctions *and* and *or*. Careful writers, however, usually place a comma before the conjunctions *but* and *for*. If a comma is not placed before the word *for* when it is used as a coordinate conjunction, *for* might be mistaken for a preposition.

USE OF THE SEMICOLON IN THE COMPOUND SENTENCE

You have learned that a comma and a coordinate conjunction are often used to separate the clauses of a compound sentence. Sometimes the ideas combined in a compound sentence are so closely related that it is not necessary to use a conjunction. In that case, a semicolon is used to separate the two clauses. The following are two important uses of the semicolon in the compound sentence:

1. A semicolon should be used between the independent clauses of a compound sentence *when they are not joined by a coordinate conjunction*. In the following sentence, there is no conjunction between the two independent clauses; therefore, a semicolon is used.

The doctor came in late; he did not stop to read the telegram.

2. When the independent clauses of a compound sentence are very long, or have *internal punctuation*, a semicolon is generally used before the coordinate conjunction. **Internal punctuation** means that there are commas within one or both of the independent clauses.

Shakespeare, a great dramatist, wrote a great many plays; and he also wrote a number of sonnets.

Temperamental and lazy, John managed to get along without working; but he was never contented or happy.

Both of these sentences have one or more commas in the first independent clause; that is, the first clause has *internal punctuation*. A semicolon is used between the two independent clauses even though a coordinate conjunction is used.

THE "COMMA FAULT"

You have just learned that two independent clauses may be joined by a semicolon when no conjunction is used. You have also learned that two independent clauses are often joined by a coordinate conjunction and a comma. The point to keep in mind is that two independent clauses should not be joined by a comma unless a coordinate conjunction is used. When a writer uses a comma between the independent clauses of a compound sentence, he makes an error known as the "comma fault." The following sentence illustrates the "comma fault."

The author wrote many stories for children, she also wrote a number of historical novels. (*comma fault*)

In this sentence, two independent clauses are joined by means of a comma. This is known as the "comma fault" because the comma is the sole connection between two independent clauses. This error may be eliminated by punctuating the sentence in any one of the three ways that have been given in this unit:

1. Use a coordinate conjunction after the comma:

The author wrote many stories for children, and she also wrote a number of historical novels. (*correct*)

2. Use a semicolon between the two independent clauses:

The author wrote many stories for children; she also wrote a number of historical novels. (*correct*)

3. Punctuate the two independent clauses as two simple sentences:

The author wrote many stories for children. She also wrote a number of historical novels. (*correct*)

A skillful writer sometimes puts commas between the independent clauses of a compound sentence. This is done deliberately for the purpose of producing a certain effect. The clauses are usually very short and similar in length and structure. The following sentence is a famous example:

"I came, I saw, I conquered.'

THE RUN ON SENTENCE

The **run on sentence error** is very similar to the "*comma fault.*" The only difference is that the run on sentence consists of two or more independent statements that are run together without any mark of punctuation, or without any connecting word. The following sentence is an illustration of the run on sentence:

Money provided by stockholders has helped the company purchase equipment and supplies it has also enabled the company to expand its production.

In this sentence, two independent statements have been run together without any punctuation or without any connecting word or words. The sentence might be correctly written by following any of the suggestions given for removing the "*comma fault.*"

Since the run on sentence error is commonly made, you should check your writing carefully. Be sure that you do not run sentences together without punctuation or proper connectives.

TRANSITIONAL WORDS

There is another type of connecting word that you may use between the independent clauses of a compound sentence. The words that belong in this group are not coordinate conjunctions. They are sometimes called **transitional words** because they are not pure conjunctions.

Some of these words have a slight connecting force. Others have some adverbial force. But they all belong to the independent clause which they introduce or in which they are found. Connectives that belong to this group *are always preceded by a semicolon*.

Since many of these words are regarded as independent elements, they are usually set off by commas. Words like *moreover, however, therefore,* and *nevertheless* are usually set off. Words like *then, still, yet,* and *so* are seldom set off by commas when they retain their adverbial force.

Sometimes the connection is made by a group of words. Expressions like the following are transitional words and are regarded as a single connecting word: *in fact, on the other hand, that is,* etc. Study the following illustrations carefully:

The road was unpaved; **nevertheless,** we drove on in the rain.

I missed the first boat; **however,** I arrived on time.

The president introduced the speaker; **then** he sat down.

Ethel was sick; **in fact,** she had one of her usual colds.

We arrived early; **as a result,** we had time to visit with our friends.

We cannot get materials; **consequently,** we cannot finish the job.

I became tired of doing his work; **moreover,** I had my own work to do.

I did not dislike the play; **on the contrary,** I enjoyed it immensely.

Commonly Used Transitional Words

Following is a list of transitional words which are used frequently. Become familiar with them.

accordingly	indeed	as a result
afterwards	likewise	at last
again	meanwhile	at the same time
anyhow	moreover	for example
besides	namely	for instance
consequently	nevertheless	for this reason
doubtless	next	in any case
eventually	otherwise	in fact
evidently	perhaps	in like manner
finally	possibly	in short
furthermore	still	on the contrary
hence	then	on the other hand
however	therefore	that is
yet	thus	in addition

18. THE COMPLEX SENTENCE

Chapter 17 explained how to form a compound sentence by combining two or more simple sentences into one longer sentence. It also explained how to punctuate the compound sentence when a coordinate conjunction is used, when transitional words are used, and when no conjunction is used.

The compound sentence is an important type of sentence because it enables us to combine two or more related ideas. However, it is just as ineffective to use a number of compound sentences strung along with *ands* and *buts* as it is to use a number of short, choppy sentences.

In this unit you will learn how to use a type of sentence that will enable you to put less important ideas in subordinate positions in the sentence. This type of sentence is called the *complex sentence.*

A **complex sentence** is a sentence that consists of one *independent clause* and *one or more subordinate clauses. Subordinate* means lower in rank, power, or importance. A subordinate clause is less important than an independent clause because it depends upon the independent clause for its meaning. The independent clause is also called the *main* or the *principal* clause. An independent clause is

a group of words that has a subject and a predicate, and does not depend upon anything else for its meaning. It expresses a complete thought, and can stand alone.

A **subordinate clause** is a group of words that has a subject and a predicate, but *cannot stand alone.* A subordinate clause does not express a complete thought. It should never be punctuated as if it were a complete sentence.

A subordinate clause is usually introduced by some type of *subordinate conjunction* or by a *relative pronoun.* These connecting words make it clear that the clause expresses an idea that is subordinate to the main clause. They also join the subordinate clause to some word in the independent clause. In the following sentences, the independent clauses and the subordinate clauses are underlined.

Complex Sentences

I shall be at the station when you arrive.

I shall not go to the park if it rains.

She wore a beautiful dress which her grandmother had worn.

In the first sentence, the subordinate clause is *when you arrive.* The clause is introduced by the **subordinate conjunction** *when.* The group of words, *when you arrive,* has a subject and a predicate, but it cannot stand alone. That is the reason why the clause is called a *subordinate clause.* It depends upon the main clause for its meaning.

The subordinate clause in the second sentence is *if it rains.* This group of words cannot stand alone. The clause is introduced by the subordinate conjunction *if.* This conjunction helps the subordinate clause express the idea that there is a condition upon which *my going* depends.

The subordinate clause in the third sentence is *which her grandmother had worn.* This clause is introduced by the relative pronoun *which.* The word *which* refers to the word *dress* in the independent clause. It also introduces the subordinate clause. A **relative pronoun** always joins a clause to the *antecedent* of the pronoun. In this sentence, the antecedent of the relative pronoun is *dress. Dress* is the word to which the pronoun refers.

The relative pronoun also has an important function in the subordinate clause. It might be the subject of the clause, the object of the verb in the clause, the object of a preposition, or a predicate pronoun after a linking verb.

KINDS OF SUBORDINATE CLAUSES

There are three kinds of subordinate clauses: *adverbial clauses, adjective clauses,* and *noun clauses.* Each of these different types is used as a part of speech. That is why subordinate clauses are called adverbial clauses, adjective clauses, and noun clauses.

The **adverbial clause** functions as an adverb. The **adjective clause** functions as an adjective, and the **noun clause** functions as a noun.

Adverbs modify verbs, adjectives, and other adverbs. Adverbial clauses also modify verbs, adjectives, and adverbs. Adjectives modify nouns and pronouns. Adjective clauses also modify nouns and pronouns. Nouns are used as subjects of sentences, as objects of verbs, and as objects of prepositions. Noun clauses are used in the same ways.

Subordinate Clauses

The man who received the medal was my uncle. (adjective clause)

We always stop working when the bell rings. (adverbial clause)

I believe that the bookkeeper is honest. (noun clause)

In the first sentence, the subordinate clause is the group of words, *who received the medal.* The subordinate clause is an **adjective clause** and modifies the word *man.* In the second sentence, the subordinate clause is *when the bell rings.* It is an **adverbial clause** and modifies the verb *stop.* This clause expresses *time* just as an adverb expresses *time.* The subordinate clause in the third sentence is the group of words, *that the bookkeeper is honest.* This subordinate clause is a **noun clause** and is used as the object of the verb *believe.*

ADJECTIVE CLAUSES

An **adjective clause** *is a subordinate clause that functions as an adjective.* Adjectives are used to describe or limit nouns or pronouns. An adjective clause is also used to describe or limit a noun or a pronoun.

An adjective clause is usually introduced by a relative pronoun. A **relative pronoun** *is a pronoun that joins an adjective clause to some word in the independent or main clause.* The word to which it joins the clause is the *antecedent* of the relative pronoun. The relative pronouns used in this way are *who* (*whom*), *which,* and *that.*

Adjective Clauses Introduced by Relative Pronouns

John brought the books that you ordered. (*that* —— relative pronoun)

I favored the plan which the senator proposed. (*which* ——relative pronoun)

Men who are thinkers look for facts. (*who* —— relative pronoun)

I saw the salesman whom I met at the office. (*whom* ——relative pronoun)

The subordinate clause in the first sentence is *that you ordered.* It is an adjective clause and modifies the noun *books.* This clause is introduced by the relative pronoun *that.* The antecedent of the relative pronoun *that* is the word *books.* The pronoun *that* joins its clause to the word *books* in the main clause.

The subordinate clause in the second sentence is *which the senator proposed.* It is an adjective clause and modifies the noun *plan.* The antecedent of the relative pronoun *which* is the word *plan.* The adjective clause limits the meaning to the *plan which the senator proposed.*

The subordinate clause in the third sentence is *who are thinkers.* The main clause is *Men look for facts.* In this sentence the subordinate clause comes between the subject and the predicate of the main clause. The subordinate clause is introduced by the relative pronoun *who.* The antecedent of *who* is *men.*

The adjective clause in the fourth sentence is *whom I met at the office.* This clause is introduced by the relative pronoun *whom.* The antecedent of the pronoun is the word *salesman.*

Relative Adjectives

Sometimes an adjective clause is introduced by the word *whose,* which is the possessive form of the pronoun *who.* In such cases the word *whose* modifies a noun which follows it. When the word *whose* is used in an adjective clause, it is called a **relative adjective.** The word *relative* is used to show that the word *whose* refers to its antecedent in the main clause.

That is the *man* **whose** car was stolen. (*man*——antecedent)

In this sentence the word *whose* is a relative adjective, modifying the word *car*. The antecedent of *whose* is the word *man* in the main clause. The word *whose* connects the clause *whose car was stolen* to the word *man*.

Adjective Clauses Introduced by Relative Adverbs

Adjective clauses are often introduced by the relative adverbs *where, when,* and *why*. When these adverbs introduce adjective clauses they relate to some word in the main clause in much the same way as a relative pronoun docs. A relative adverb always has an antecedent and joins its clause to that antecedent. In addition, a relative adverb performs the function of an adverb in its own clause. It is called a *relative adverb* because it relates to an antecedent.

I found the house where the poet lived. (*where*——relative adverb)

The doctor selected a time when I was not working. (*when*——relative adverb)

I discovered the reason why he is leaving. (*why*——relative adverb)

In the first sentence, the relative adverb is *where*. It introduces the clause, *where the poet lived*. It also refers to its antecedent, *house*. As an adverb, it modifies the verb *lived* in the subordinate clause.

The relative adverb in the second sentence is *when*. Its antecedent is *time*. The relative adverb *when* joins the clause, *when I was not working*, to its antecedent *time*. It also functions as an adverb, modifying the verb *was working*.

The relative adverb in the third sentence is *why*. Its antecedent is *reason*. It modifies the verb *is leaving* in its own clause.

The only difference between a relative adverb and a simple adverb is the fact that the relative adverb is found in an adjective clause and refers to its antecedent in the main clause. Both relative adverbs and simple adverbs modify verbs.

"WHO" AND "WHOM" IN SUBORDINATE CLAUSES

It is often difficult to determine whether to use "who" or "whom" when one of these words is used to introduce a subordinate clause. Always keep in mind that *who* is the correct form for the nominative case, and *whom* is the correct form for the objective case.

When a relative pronoun introduces a clause, it has a double function. It joins the clause to its antecedent which is in the main clause, and in addition it performs one of the following three functions in the subordinate clause:

1. The pronoun may be the *subject* of the subordinate clause.
2. The pronoun may be used as a *predicate pronoun* after a linking verb.
3. The pronoun may be used as the *object* of the verb or a preposition.

In order to determine how the pronoun is used, it is often necessary to put the subordinate clause in grammatical order, or to transpose it.

Allen was the one *who published the report*. (*who*——subject)

In this sentence, it is clear that *who* is the subject of the subordinate clause. The form *who* is correct because the subject is in the nominative case.

The president is a man *whom everyone admires*. (*whom*——direct object)

In this sentence, the word *whom* is the direct object of the verb *admires*. By transposing the clause, you will be able to see this clearly: *everyone admires whom*. The subject of the clause is *everyone*, not *whom*.

Jack is the boy *to whom they gave the camera*. (*whom*——object of preposition)

In this sentence, the pronoun *whom* is the object of the preposition *to*. Whcn thc subordinate clause is transposed, the use of *whom* becomes clear: *they gave the camera to whom. They* is the subject of the clause, not *whom*.

RESTRICTIVE AND NONRESTRICTIVE CLAUSES

Adjective clauses present a problem in meaning and in punctuation. Sometimes the adjective clause is set off by commas. Sometimes the adjective clause is not set off by commas. The following sentences are illustrations of adjective clauses that are *not* set off by commas:

I spoke to the woman *who was giving the demonstration*.
This is the man *who discovered the leak in the pipe*.
I dislike driving in a town *where there are no stop signals*.

In the first sentence, the adjective clause is *who was giving the demonstration*. If you leave the clause out, the meaning of the sentence is changed. The sentence now gives no indication of *who* the woman was. Since the clause identifies that woman, it is essential to the meaning of the sentence.

In the second sentence, the clause is *who discovered the leak in the pipe*. This clause identifies the man and is essential to the meaning of the sentence. The clause restricts the meaning of the sentence to the man *who discovered the leak in the pipe*. Therefore, it is essential to the meaning of the sentence.

The third sentence does not mean that *I dislike driving in a town*. The meaning is restricted to driving in a certain type of town; that is, in a town *where there are no stop signals*.

Clauses that are necessary to the meaning of the sentence are called *restrictive clauses*. A restrictive clause is not set off by commas. A **restrictive clause** identifies the word it modifies.

Some adjective clauses are not essential to the meaning of the sentence. They give added information, but the essential meaning of the sentence would not be changed if such clauses were omitted. Study the following sentences carefully:

Mr. Miller, *who lived next door*, moved to Canada.
Will James, *who was once a cowboy*, wrote many stories.
Father, *who was working in the garden*, missed the broadcast.

The speaker, *who was accompanied by his wife*, left early.

In the first sentence, the clause, *who lived next door*, gives additional information about Mr. Miller, but the meaning of the sentence is not changed if you leave the clause out. The clause does not place any restrictions on the meaning. Therefore it is called a *nonrestrictive clause*. Nonrestrictive clauses are set off by commas.

A **nonrestrictive clause** is a clause that is *not* essential to the meaning of the sentence. All the clauses in the preceding illustrations are nonrestrictive clauses. They are set off by commas. They are not needed in the sentence to identify the person who is mentioned in the main clause.

A nonrestrictive clause functions more like an appositive or a parenthetical expression. You might call it a thrown in remark. That is the reason why the nonrestrictive clause is set off by commas.

19. ADVERBIAL CLAUSES

Chapter Eighteen explained that an adjective clause functions in the same way as an adjective functions. Adjectives modify nouns and pronouns. Adjective clauses also modify nouns and pronouns.

An *adverbial clause* functions in the same way as an adverb functions. Adverbs tell *how, when, where,* and *to what extent* the action is performed. Adverbial clauses answer the same questions and, in addition, express several other ideas which the simple adverb does not express.

Adverbs modify verbs, adjectives, and other adverbs. Adverbial clauses also modify verbs, adjectives, and adverbs. The adverbial clause modifies a verb more often than it modifies an adjective or an adverb.

SUBORDINATE CONJUNCTIONS

An adverbial clause is usually introduced by a *subordinate conjunction*. This connecting word is called a subordinate conjunction because it makes the idea expressed by its clause *subordinate to the main idea in the sentence*. The subordinate conjunction also shows the relation between the subordinate clause and the word in the main clause which the subordinate clause modifies.

The **subordinate conjunction** is used to show that the clause which it introduces is a subordinate clause, and not a main clause. The subordinate conjunction also indicates the exact type of relationship that the subordinate clause has to the main clause.

The following illustrations will make clear the function of the *subordinate conjunction* in a subordinate clause:

We listened to the radio because we wanted to hear the news. (adverbial clause—modifies listened)
She will find the telegram on her desk when she returns. (adverbial clause—modifies will find)

In the first sentence, the subordinate clause is *because we wanted to hear the news*. It is an adverbial clause and modifies the verb *listened* in the main clause. The subordinate conjunction is the word *because*.

If you leave out the word *because*, the words that follow no longer express a subordinate idea. They express a complete thought. It is the word *because* that makes the group of words, *we wanted to hear the news*, subordinate to the main clause. The **subordinate conjunction** is the key to the adverbial clause.

You should become familiar with the subordinate conjunctions that are commonly used to introduce *adverbial clauses*. The subordinate conjunction will help you identify the adverbial clause. It will also help you determine the **kind** of adverbial clause which it introduces.

WORDS USED AS SUBORDINATE CONJUNCTIONS

after	even though,	till
although	except	though
as	if	unless
as—as	in order that	until
as if	provided	when
as long as	provided that	whenever
as soon as	since	where
as though	so—as	wherever
because	so that	whether
before	than	while
even if	that	

KINDS OF ADVERBIAL CLAUSES

Adverbial clauses are used to express a number of different ideas. The following are the ten important ideas which are expressed by adverbial clauses: *time, place, manner, degree, comparison, purpose, result, condition, concession, cause (reason)*.

Since the subordinate conjunction helps the adverbial clause express the idea intended, you should become familiar with the conjunctions that are used to express certain ideas, such as *time, place,* etc. The following is a list of the subordinate conjunctions commonly used in adverbial clauses of the various types:

Time: after, before, when, whenever, since, until, as soon as, while
Place: where, wherever
Manner: as, as if, as though
Degree: that, as—as, not so—as, than
Comparison: as, than, so—as, as—as
Purpose: that, so that, in order that
Result: that, so that
Condition: if, provided, provided that, unless
Concession: although, though, even if
Cause: as, because, since

Ideas Expressed by Adverbial Clauses

Time: I watched the crowd while I was waiting for you.

Place: Put the notice where it can be seen.

Manner: The soldier walks as if he were lame.

Degree: Marvin is not so industrious as his brother (is industrious).

Comparison: The train was later than it usually is.

Purpose: Ted practiced every day so that he might win the contest.

Result: The salesman was so persuasive that I finally bought the car.

Condition: I shall attend the meeting if I have the time.

Concession: Frances will sing at the concert although she has a cold.

Cause or Reason: Gerald read the book because I recommended it.

CLAUSES OF DEGREE

An *adverbial clause of degree* that is introduced by the subordinate conjunction *that* usually expresses a **result** idea as well as the idea of **degree**. The degree idea is expressed by words like *such, such a,* and *so* which precede the subordinate clause.

Jane practiced so long that she became very tired.

Harold made such a poor sales record that he lost his position.

In both these sentences, the adverbial clauses introduced by *that* express a *degree idea* and a *result idea*.

An adverbial clause of degree usually modifies an adjective or an adverb in the main clause.

He talked so loud that he annoyed the speaker.

In this sentence, the adverbial clause *that he annoyed the speaker* is introduced by the subordinate conjunction *that*. The adverbial clause modifies the adverb *so* in the main clause.

THE POSITION OF THE ADVERBIAL CLAUSE

In all of the preceding illustrations, the adverbial clause follows the main clause. An adverbial clause is often placed at the beginning of the sentence for emphasis, or for variety in sentence patterns. When the subordinate clause precedes the main clause, it is usually set off by a comma.

He went to the office when it was convenient. (follows main clause)

When it was convenient, he went to the office. (precedes main clause)

The men work overtime whenever it is necessary. (follows main clause)

Whenever it is necessary, the men work overtime. (precedes main clause)

In the first sentence, the adverbial clause *follows* the main clause. In the second sentence, the same adverbial clause *precedes* the main clause. The adverbial clause is placed at the beginning of the sentence for emphasis. Since the adverbial clause is in inverted or transposed order, it is set off by a comma.

The adverbial clause in the third sentence *follows* the main clause. In the fourth sentence, this same clause is placed at the beginning of the sentence for emphasis. The adverbial clause is set off by a comma because it is in transposed order.

Sometimes it is necessary to change the position of a noun and a pronoun when the adverbial clause is placed at the beginning of a sentence:

I shall visit **Margaret** in Texas if she sends me her address.

If Margaret sends me her address, I shall visit **her** in Texas.

CLAUSES OF COMPARISON

In both speaking and writing, words are often omitted that are necessary to the grammatical completeness of the sentence. Certain words are sometimes omitted because the meaning of the sentence is perfectly clear without them. Sometimes they are omitted in order to avoid using a sentence that is awkward or monotonous.

Certain words are usually omitted in an *adverbial clause of comparison* for the reasons just given. The verb is often omitted because it can be readily supplied. It is important to realize that the verb has been omitted in order to decide upon the correct form of the pronoun that should be used as the subject of the verb. We often hear sentences like the following, which are incorrect:

I am younger than **him**. (incorrect)
John can run as fast as **us**. (incorrect)

In both sentences the *incorrect form* of the pronoun is used in the adverbial clause of comparison. If the speaker had finished the clause, he would have used the correct form of the pronoun. When the clause is finished, it becomes evident that the pronoun is the *subject* of the clause. A pronoun used as the subject should be in the *nominative case*.

I am younger than **he** (is young). (*he*—subject)
John can run as fast as **we** (can run). (*we*—subject)

In the unfinished clause of comparison the word *than* is a conjunction, and not a preposition. The word *than* introduces a clause which must be finished grammatically. When we supply the words that are necessary to complete the clause, we realize that the form of the pronoun should be *he* and not *him*. *He* is the correct form to use for the subject. The subject requires the *nominative case*.

Study the following illustrations carefully. Pay special attention to the form of the pronoun used in the *adverbial clause of comparison*.

You have lived longer than *I* (have lived). (not *me*)
Martha sews as well as *she* (sews). (not *her*)
Some of the men worked harder than *we* (worked). (not *us*)
I speak as correctly as *he* (does). (not *him*)

"As—As" and "Not So—As" In Comparisons

The connectives *as—as* and *not so—as* are often used in sentences that contain adverbial clauses of comparison. Careful writers and speakers make a distinction in the use of these combinations. They use *as—as* when the comparison is **positive,** and *not so—as* when the comparison is **negative.**

The comparison is said to be positive when the two things compared are approximately the same or equal. The comparison is said to be negative when there is an inequality between the two things compared. An illustration will help make this clear.

John is **as** tall **as** his brother. (positive comparison)
John is **not so** tall **as** his father. (negative comparison)

In the first sentence, the comparison is *positive*. The two persons compared are approximately *equal* in height. The combination *as—as* is used to indicate this type of comparison. In the second sentence, the combination *not so—as* is used to show an *inequality* in height, or a *negative* comparison.

In speaking and in informal writing *as—as* is commonly used to show both types of comparison—positive and negative. However, in formal writing it is advisable to observe the distinctions that discriminating writers make.

Use of "Like" in Clauses

The word *like* is commonly used as a preposition. When the word *like* is used as a preposition, it should be followed by an object.

If the object is a pronoun, the pronoun should be in the *objective case*. This usage was explained in Chapter 16.

Many careful speakers and writers feel that *like* should not be used as a conjunction to introduce a subordinate clause of manner or comparison. The words *as, as if,* and *as though* should be used to introduce this type of clause.

I shall write the letter *like* you advised me. (colloquial)
I shall write the letter *as* you advised me. (preferred)

You look *like* you were tired. (colloquial)
You look *as if* you were tired. (preferred)

It looks *like* it might snow. (colloquial)
It looks *as if* it might snow. (preferred)

In the last few years, the colloquial use of *like* as a conjunction has increased. This use sometimes appears in print. We often hear the word *like* used as a conjunction in popular television programs. However, in general, it has not been accepted as standard English for written use.

When *like* is used as a preposition, it means *similar to,* or *in a similar manner to.*

Mary's hat is *like* the one I bought in Paris. (*like*—preposition)
John is *like* his father in temperament. (*like*—preposition)

20. NOUN CLAUSES

Chapters Eighteen and Nineteen explained the form and function of two types of subordinate clause—the *adjective clause* and the *adverbial clause*. In this unit you will study the form and function of another type of subordinate clause—the *noun clause.*

You have learned that adjective clauses and adverbial clauses are used as *modifiers* in the same way that adjectives and adverbs are used as modifiers. Noun clauses are not used as modifiers. They perform tha same functions that a *noun* performs.

FUNCTION OF THE NOUN CLAUSE

Noun Clause — Subject of a Sentence

A noun is commonly used as the *subject* of a sentence. A *noun clause* may also be used as the **subject** of a sentence. The following illustrations show how the noun clause is used as the subject of a sentence. The whole clause is the subject.

What the chairman proposed was not practical.
How you manage on your income is a puzzle to me.
That their house is for sale is a well-known fact.
Where we could find an apartment was our problem.

The subject of a sentence usually tells what we are talking about. The noun clause in the first sentence tells *what* was not practical; namely, *What the chairman proposed.* In the second sentence, the subject, or the noun clause, tells *what* it is that is a puzzle to me; namely, *How you manage on your income.* In the third sentence, the noun clause tells *what* is a well-known fact; namely, *That their house is for sale.* The noun clause in the last sentence tells *what our problem was.*

If you examine the preceding illustrations, you will see that the following words introduce the noun clauses: *what, how, that,* and *where.* These same words are often used to introduce adjective or adverbial clauses. The only way to be sure that you are dealing with a *noun clause* is to determine how the clause is used in the sentence. If it functions in the way that a noun functions, it is a noun clause.

Noun Clause — Direct Object of a Verb

A *noun clause* is frequently used as the **direct object** of a verb. A noun used as an object completes the meaning of the verb and answers the question *What?* A noun clause used as the direct object of a verb completes the verb and in almost all cases answers the question *What?* Study the following illustrations. They show how noun clauses are used as objects of verbs:

I hope (*what?*) that you will be promoted. (object of *hope*)
We knew (*what?*) where we could park the car. (object of *knew*)
Tell the manager (*what?*) why you are leaving. (object of *tell*)
I believe (*what?*) that it is going to rain. (object of *believe*)
He understood (*what?*) what we were trying to do. (object of *understood*)

The noun clause in the first sentence tells *what I hope.* It is used as the object of the verb *hope.* The noun clause in the second sentence tells *what we knew.* It is the object of the verb *knew.* The noun clause in the third sentence tells *what you should tell the manager.* It is the object of the verb *tell.* The noun clause in the fourth sentence tells *what I believe.* The noun clause in the last sentence tells *what he understood.*

Noun Clause — Predicate Noun

A *noun clause* may be used as a **predicate noun** after one of the linking verbs. Like the predicate noun, a noun clause used after a linking verb means the same as the subject. It is also used to complete the verb. The noun clauses in the following sentences are used as *predicate nouns* after linking verbs:

The rumor was that he had left the city. (means the same as *rumor*)
That is what we agreed to do. (means the same as *that*)
My first impression was that I had seen him before. (means the same as *impression*)
The report was that he was drowned. (means the same as *report*)

The noun clause in the first sentence is *that he had left the city.* It completes the verb *was* and means the same as the subject *rumor.* The noun clause in the second sentence is *what we agreed to do.* It completes the linking verb *is* and means the same as the subject *that.* The noun clause in the third sentence is *that I had seen him before.* It completes the linking verb *was* and means the same as the subject *impression.* The noun clause in the last sentence means the same as *report* and completes the linking verb *was.*

Noun Clause — Object of a Preposition

Like the noun, a *noun clause* is sometimes used as the **object of a preposition.** You may often find it difficult to determine whether the noun clause is the object of the preposition or

whether some word in the clause is the object of the preposition. If you study the following illustrations carefully, you will see why an entire *clause* is the object of the preposition.

Give the message to whoever is in the office. (noun clause—object of the preposition *to*)
We did not agree about what the doctor ordered. (noun clause—object of the preposition *about*)
Do the job in whatever way you wish. (noun clause—object of *in*)

In the first sentence, the noun clause *whoever is in the office* is the object of the preposition *to. Whoever* could not be the object of the preposition because it is the subject of the clause. In addition, the sentence does not mean that you should give the message to *whoever.* It means that you should give the message to *whoever is in the office.* The entire clause is the object of the preposition *to.*

In the second sentence, the noun clause *what the doctor ordered* is the object of the preposition *about.* The sentence does not mean that we did not agree about *what.* It means that we did not agree about *what the doctor ordered.* The word *what* could not be the object of the preposition because it has another function to perform in the clause. It is the object of the verb *ordered.*

The noun clause in the third sentence must be the object of the preposition. The word *way* could not be the object of the preposition because that is not the meaning intended. The sentence does not mean that you should do the job in *whatever way,* but it means that you should do the job in *whatever way you wish.* The entire clause is the object of the preposition *in.*

OMISSION OF THE CONNECTING WORD

Sometimes the word that introduces a subordinate clause is omitted. The reason for this omission is to bring the main idea and the subordinate idea closer together. Although the best writers and speakers often omit the connecting word, you should supply it whenever there is any doubt about the construction of the clause.

I believe that you will be promoted. (*that*—subordinate conjunction)
I believe you will be promoted. (subordinate conjunction omitted)

NOUN CLAUSE USED AS AN APPOSITIVE

A noun is often used *in apposition* with another noun. The word **apposition** comes from two Latin words which mean "placed by" or "put near to." A word in *apposition* is placed near another word to explain it or to identify it in some way. We often speak of a person and then add something to explain who the person is, or to identify him in some way.

Mike, our *janitor,* is very accommodating.
We called on Dr. Allen, a famous *scientist.*
Paris, a *city* in France, is famous as a fashion center.

In the first sentence, the noun *janitor* is in apposition with the noun *Mike.* It explains who Mike was. In the second sentence, *scientist* is in apposition with *Dr. Allen.* It identifies him as a scientist. In the third sentence, *city* is in apposition with *Paris.*

In all three sentences the nouns that are in apposition with other nouns are set off by commas. Sometimes the appositive is so closely connected with the noun that no commas are required. It is not good practice to set off the appositive by commas in sentences like the following:

My brother Andrew is in London.
The poet Whittier wrote "Snowbound."

Like the noun, a *noun clause* is often used in **apposition** with a word or a group of words. When the noun clause is used in apposition, it usually explains such words as *idea, fact, belief, report, rumor*, etc. Noun clauses used in apposition are not set off by commas.

The rumor that John would be elected spread rapidly.
The fact that the contract was signed was important.
The announcement that the strike was over was received with cheers.
We entertained the hope that the crew had survived.

NOUN CLAUSE AND THE INTRODUCTORY "IT"

Sometimes a sentence begins with the introductory word *it*. In sentences of this type the word *it* is not the real subject of the sentence. The grammatical or real subject appears later. The real subject is often a *noun clause*. Sentences are arranged in this way either for emphasis or for smoothness.

It is obvious that you do not have the money.
(It) That you do not have the money is obvious.
 (*transposed order*)

This sentence begins with the introductory word *it*. The real or grammatical subject appears later in the sentence. The subject is the noun clause, *that you do not have the money*. When the sentence was transposed, the word *it*, which has no grammatical connection with any part of the sentence, was dropped, and the real subject was put in its proper place.

The word *it* has only one purpose in sentences of this type. It fills in the place normally occupied by the subject. Its function is similar to that of the introductory word *there*, which was explained in Chapter Four. When the word *it* is used in this way, it is called an **expletive.**

Sentences that begin with *it* as an expletive, or "filling in" word, are easily recognized because they always follow the same pattern:

It is important that you see him at once.
(It) That you see him at once is important.
 (*transposed order*)

WORDS THAT INTRODUCE NOUN CLAUSES

A *noun clause* may be introduced by a **subordinate conjunction.** The subordinate conjunctions commonly used in this way are *that, whether*, and *whether or*. The sole duty of the subordinate conjunction is to connect the noun clause to the main clause.

I wonder *whether* they will recognize me.
John knows *that* he will be nominated for an office.

Whether (not *if*) should be used to introduce noun clauses used as the direct object of the verbs *say, learn, understand, know, doubt, ask, tell, discover, wonder*, etc.

Ask John *if* he has washed the car. (incorrect)
Ask John *whether* he has washed the car. (correct)

I did not know *if* he would leave or stay. (incorrect)
I did not know *whether* he would leave or stay. (correct)

A noun clause is often introduced by a **relative pronoun:** *who, what, whatever, whoever, whomever, whichever. Whoever* and *whomever* are seldom used in informal writing and speaking.

The agent does not know *what* he should do about repairs.
Give to the fund *whatever* you can afford.
A copy of the speech was given to *whoever* wanted it.

The relative pronoun that introduces a noun clause is sometimes called an **indefinite relative pronoun** because it does not have an antecedent expressed in the sentence.

Sometimes the relative pronoun is used as an *adjective* in the noun clause. A pronoun used in this way is called a **relative adjective,** or an **indefinite relative adjective** because it has no antecedent.

I shall accept *whatever salary* is offered me. (*whatever*—adjective modifies *salary*)
The manager always knows *what course* he should follow. (*what*—adjective modifies *course*)

Noun clauses are also introduced by the adverbs *how, when, why*, and *where*. The introductory adverb also modifies the verb in the noun clause. The noun clause is underlined in the following sentences.

How we should invest the money is the question. (*how*—adverb)
He asked where the president lived. (*where*—adverb)
I do not know when the speaker will arrive. (*when*—adverb)

21. PARTICIPLES

THE NATURE OF VERBALS

There are three verb forms in English that are known as **verbals:** *participles, gerunds*, and *infinitives*. Participles are discussed in this unit, gerunds in Chapter 22, and infinitives in Chapter 23. These verb forms are called *verbals* because they are derived from verbs and retain many of the characteristics of the verb.

A **verbal** may take any kind of modifier or any kind of complement that a verb might take. In addition to this verb function, a verbal has a special function of its own. A verbal usually performs the work of two parts of speech at the same time.

There is one function that a *verbal* cannot perform. It cannot function as the predicate verb in a sentence because it is an incomplete form of the verb. A verbal cannot make a statement or ask a question.

A **participle** is a verbal (verb form) which is *used as an adjective*. Since a participle is a verb form and partakes of the nature of a verb, it may take modifiers and complements.

Participles do not always take modifiers or complements. Very often they are used as **pure**

adjectives and are placed directly before the nouns which they modify. Sometimes they are used as **predicate adjectives** after linking verbs. The following illustrations show the participle used as a simple adjective:

He conducts a *flourishing* business. (*flourishing* —— modifies *business*)
The reports were *discouraging*. (*discouraging*—modifies *reports*)
We are reading an *interesting* book. (*interesting*—modifies *book*)

The participle that is most commonly used as an adjective is the participle that ends in *ing*. This is called the **present participle.** In the following illustrations the *present participles* are placed directly before the nouns which they modify. When used in this way, they are generally regarded as pure adjectives.

running water	*singing* brook
shaking knees	*rustling* leaves
murmuring pines	*dangling* modifiers
coming events	*whistling* boy
soaring prices	*sleeping* child

The participles found in the preceding illustrations are *running, shaking, murmuring, coming, soaring, singing, rustling, dangling, whistling*, and *sleeping*. All these forms derived from verbs.

Many participles are used as pure adjectives. When the participle is used as a pure adjective, it is usually placed directly before the noun which it modifies. When the participle is used as a **predicate adjective,** it is found in the predicate and modifies the subject.

The game was *exciting*. (*exciting*——used as a predicate adjective)
The book is *interesting*. (*interesting*——predicate adjective)
The rumors were *startling*. (*startling*——used as a predicate adjective)

In the first sentence, the participle *exciting* is used as a predicate adjective, modifying the noun *game*. The participle *interesting*, in the second sentence modifies the noun *book*. In the third sentence, the participle *startling* is used as a predicate adjective, modifying the subject noun *rumors*. The participles *exciting, interesting*, and *startling* are forms of verbs.

FORMS OF THE PARTICIPLE

There are three participles that are commonly used as adjectives: the *present participle* (active voice); the *past participle* (passive voice); and the *perfect participle* (active voice). There is no active past participle in English.

These participles are easily recognized. The **present participle** always ends in *ing*; the **past participle** usually ends in *ed, d, t, n*, or *en*. The past participles of some of the irregular verbs do not have distinctive endings: *swum, drunk, gone, sung*, etc. The **perfect participle** is always formed by prefixing the word *having* to the past participle: *having sung, having called, having driven, having seen*, etc.

Regular Verbs		
Present Participle	Past Participle	Perfect Participle
(*active*)	(*passive*)	(*active*)
calling	called	having called
watching	watched	having watched
Irregular Verbs		
singing	sung	having sung
driving	driven	having driven
going	gone	having gone

PAST PARTICIPLES AND PERFECT PARTICIPLES

The past participle ending in *ed* is commonly used as an adjective. The following illustrations show how *past participles* function as *adjectives*:

A doctor, **called** to the scene, examined the injured man.
The **neglected** and **forgotten** child was picked up by an officer.
The army, **surprised** by the attack, fled into the woods.
The street was littered with paper, **thrown** from the windows.

In the first sentence, the past participle, *called* is used as an adjective to modify *doctor*. The participle is modified by the adverbial phrase, *to the scene*. There are two past participles in the second sentence, *neglected* and *forgotten*. One ends in *ed* and the other ends in *en*. These participles modify the noun *child*. In this sentence, the participles are placed directly before the noun *child*, which they modify.

The past participle *surprised* in the third sentence modifies *army*. The participle is modified by the adverbial phrase *by the attack*. The past participle *thrown* in the last sentence is modified by the adverbial phrase *from the windows*. The participle *thrown* modifies the noun *paper*.

The following sentences show the adjective use of the *perfect participle*:

Having finished the dress, Mary packed it carefully in a box.
Having completed the job, the men left early.
Having accomplished his mission, the ambassador returned home.
Having recovered completely, Ted left the hospital.

The perfect participles in the preceding illustrations are *having finished, having completed, having accomplished,* and *having recovered*. The first three take direct objects——*dress, job,* and *mission*. The last one, *having recovered*, is modified by the adverb *completely*. They are all in the active voice.

The perfect participle, *having finished,* modifies the noun *Mary. Having completed* modifies the noun *men; having accomplished* modifies *ambassador,* and *having recovered* modifies *Ted*. These participles are used as adjectives.

THE PARTICIPIAL PHRASE

Since the participle is derived from a verb, it retains many of the characteristics of a verb. Like the verb, a participle may take **modifiers** and **complements**. The participle with its *modifiers* or *complements,* or with both complements and modifiers is called a **participial phrase.**

MODIFIERS OF PARTICIPLES

A participle is often modified by an adverb or an adverbial phrase:

Looking up suddenly, Robert saw a rainbow in the sky.
Coming close to the rock, we saw a strange sight.

In the first sentence, the participle *looking* modifies the noun *Robert*. The participle *looking* is modified by the adverb *up* and the adverb *suddenly. Looking up suddenly* is a **participial phrase.**

In the second sentence, the participle *coming* modifies the pronoun *we*. The participle *coming* is modified by the adverb *close* and the adverbial phrase *to the rock. Coming close to the rock* is a **participial phrase.**

The participles in the following sentences also take *adverbial modifiers*:

Trembling with excitement, Sara waited for her friends.

(Participial phrase modifies the noun *Sara*.)
The house, remodeled recently, is very attractive.

(Participial phrase modifies the noun *house*.)
We saw an old man lying on the road.
(Participial phrase modifies the noun *man*.)

In the first sentence, the participial phrase consists of the participle *trembling* and its modifier, the adverbial phrase *with excitement*. The phrase, taken as a whole, modifies the noun *Sara*. The participial phrase *trembling with excitement* is used as an adjective, modifying *Sara*.

In the second sentence, the participial phrase consists of the participle *remodeled* and the adverbial modifier, the adverb *recently*. The entire phrase, *remodeled recently*, is used as an adjective, modifying the noun *house*.

In the third sentence, the participial phrase is *lying on the road*. It consists of the participle *lying* and the adverbial phrase *on the road*. The entire phrase, *lying on the road*, modifies the noun *man*.

COMPLEMENTS OF PARTICIPLES

1. Like the verb, a participle may take a direct object if the verb expresses action.

Carrying a suitcase, the porter entered the train.
Realizing the danger, the captain ordered a retreat.

In the first sentence, the noun *suitcase* is the direct object of the participle *Carrying*. The entire expression, *Carrying a suitcase*, is a participial phrase. The participial phrase modifies the noun *porter*.

In the second sentence, the noun *danger* is the direct object of the participle *realizing*. The entire expression, *Realizing the danger*, is a participial phrase. The participial phrase modifies the noun *captain*.

2. Like the verb, a participle may be followed by a predicate noun or a predicate adjective.

Participles that take predicate nouns or predicate adjectives as complements are forms of *linking verbs*.

Being an invalid, he could not climb the steep hill.
Becoming weary, the traveler sat down to rest.

In the first sentence, the participle *being* is followed by the predicate noun *invalid*. The noun *invalid* refers to the same person as the subject *he*. The entire expression, *being an invalid*, is a participial phrase. The participial phrase modifies the subject pronoun *he. Being* is a form of the linking verb *to be*.

In the second sentence, the participle *becoming* is followed by the predicate adjective *weary*. The entire expression, *becoming weary*, is a participial phrase, modifying the noun *traveler. Becoming* is a form of the linking verb *to become*.

PARTICIPLES USED IN INDEPENDENT CONSTRUCTIONS

Sometimes a participle is used with a noun in an independent construction; that is, the participle and the noun which it modifies are not related grammatically to any other part of the sentence. Such a construction is called the **nominative absolute construction.**

The term *absolute* is used because the entire expression is an *independent construction*. It forms part of a sentence, but is not connected with the rest of the sentence grammatically. The term *nominative* is used because the noun which the participle modifies is in the *nominative case*. The following illustrations will make this use of the participle clear. The independent constructions are underlined.

The sun having set, we decided to return home.
The train being late, the soldiers missed the boat.

In the first sentence, the expression, *The sun having set,* consists of the perfect participle *having set* and the noun *sun* with its modifier *The*. The entire expression, *The sun having set,* is used *absolutely* or independently. It has no grammatical connection with the rest of the sentence. The noun *sun* is in the nominative case.

The expression, *The train being late,* in the second sentence is also a *nominative absolute construction;* that is, it has no grammatical relation to the rest of the sentence. The noun *train* is in the nominative case. It is modified by the expression *being late,* which consists of the participle *being* and the predicate adjective *late*.

DANGLING PARTICIPLES

Participles are often used incorrectly in speaking and writing. One of the most common mistakes in English is to use what is commonly referred to as the **dangling participle.** Anything that dangles is said *to hang loosely,* without secure attachment. A participle "dangles' when there is no word in the sentence which it could properly modify, or when it seems to be related to a word which does not convey the meaning intended.

It is easy to detect these loose participial modifiers. Sometimes the use of a *dangling modifier* gives a ridiculous or a humorous slant to the meaning of the sentence. You can avoid this error if you think through your sentences carefully and relate the participle to the proper word.

When the participial phrase is placed at the beginning of a sentence, it should refer to the subject. When it could not possibly modify the subject from the standpoint of meaning, the sentence must be rewritten and a suitable subject supplied which it could logically modify.

Walking through the tunnel, a wallet was picked up.
Entering the harbor, the Statue of Liberty came into view.
Taking the test, the teacher gave me a passing grade.

In the first sentence, the participial phrase *walking through the tunnel* modifies the subject of the sentence, which is *wallet*. A participle used at the beginning of a sentence modifies the subject. It is evident that the wallet was not walking through the tunnel; however, that is the meaning conveyed by the sentence as it is written. Very often the best way to get rid of a dangling participle is to substitute a clause for it.

While we were walking through the tunnel, we picked up a wallet.

In the second sentence, the participial phrase modifies *Statue of Liberty*. But it was not the *Statue of Liberty* that was entering the harbor. The phrase seems to be related to a word which it could not modify. The word which the participial phrase really modifies is not in the sentence. The sentence might be revised as follows:

As we entered the harbour, the Statue of Liberty came into view.

In the last sentence, the participial phrase modifies the word *teacher*. If you read the sentence carefully, you will readily see that it was not the teacher who took the test. The sentence would be correctly written if a clause were substituted for the dangling phrase.

After I took the test, the teacher gave me a passing grade.

MISPLACED MODIFIERS

Sometimes there is a word in the sentence which the participial phrase properly modifies, but the participle is not placed correctly. As a result, the meaning is confused. This error is commonly referred to as a **misplaced modifier.**

Jumping into the water, the children were rescued by the life guard.

Several soldiers passed by in their uniforms recently drafted.

If you read the first sentence carefully, you will see that the word which the participle modifies is in the sentence. It is the word *lifeguard*. It was the *lifeguard* who jumped into the water. It was not the *children*. The trouble with the sentence is that the participial phrase should modify the subject. As the sentence is written, the subject is *children*. The subject should be the word *lifeguard*. The sentence might be rewritten as follows:

Jumping into the water, the lifeguard rescued the children.

In the second sentence, a participial modifier is also misplaced. As the sentence is written, the participial phrase modifies the word *uniforms*. But it was not the *uniforms* that were recently drafted, it was the *soldiers*. The sentence might be rewritten as follows:

Several recently drafted soldiers passed by in their uniforms.

PARTICIPLES USED IN VERB PHRASES

Participles are not always used as adjectives. One of their most important uses is to help form a *verb phrase*. When the participle forms part of a verb phrase, it is not considered as a separate word, but as part of the verb phrase.

A participle is never used alone as the predicate verb in a sentence because it is an incomplete form of the verb. It is used as part of a verb phrase. The following illustrations show how the participle is used as part of a verb phrase:

The janitor is washing the windows. (*washing*——part of verb phrase)

The gardener has planted the shrubs. (*planted*——part of verb phrase)

In the first sentence, the verb phrase *is washing* is made up of the auxiliary verb *is* and the present participle of the verb *wash*, or the *ing* participle, *washing*. In the second sentence, the verb phrase *has planted* is made up of the auxiliary *has* and the past participle of the verb *plant*, which is *planted*.

Sometimes it is difficult to determine whether the participle is part of the verb phrase, or whether it is used as an adjective modifying the subject. This is often true when a participle follows a linking verb. The meaning of the sentence will help you determine which use is intended by the speaker or writer. Study the following sentences carefully:

The talk was *inspiring*. (participle, used as an *adjective*)

We *were inspired* by his talk. (participle, part of *verb phrase*)

In the first sentence, the verb is *was*, not *was inspiring*. The verb *was* is a linking verb and requires a complement. In this sentence the complement is *inspiring*, which is used as a predicate adjective modifying the noun *talk*. The sentence means *inspiring talk. Inspiring* is a participle used as an adjective.

In the second sentence, the verb is *were inspired*. In this sentence, the past participle *inspired* is part of the verb phrase, *were inspired*. Study the following sentences carefully. Try to determine whether the participle is used as an adjective or is part of the verb phrase:

Robert was elected secretary at our last meeting. (*elected*——part of the verb phrase)

The old man looked neglected. (*neglected*——participle used as adjective)

The milk seems frozen. (*frozen*——participle used as adjective)

The house was furnished by an interior decorator. (*furnished*——part of verb phrase)

I have been sitting here for an hour. (*sitting*——part of verb phrase)

22. GERUNDS

Nature of the Gerund

If you understand the dual nature of the participle, you will have little difficulty in understanding the dual nature of the **gerund.** You have already learned that the participle is both *verb* and *adjective*. The gerund is both *verb* and *noun*.

Gerunds are like participles in many respects. Gerunds and participles are verbals; that is, they are *forms derived from verbs.* Both participles and gerunds have the same "ing' forms. Both take the same kinds of complements and modifiers that verbs take.

Gerunds differ from participles in one fundamental respect. **Gerunds** are *verb forms used as nouns.* Participles are verb forms used as adjectives. Because a gerund functions as a noun, it can take certain modifiers that a participle cannot take. Like the noun, a gerund is often modified by an *adjective* or by an *adjective phrase*. Participles cannot take adjective modifiers.

Since the gerund functions as a noun, it may be used as the *subject* of a sentence, the *direct object* of a verb, the *object of a preposition*, or

as a *predicate noun* after one of the linking verbs. Gerunds are often called *verbal nouns* because they are derived from verbs.

Painting is Martha's hobby. (gerund used as *subject*).

Martha enjoys painting. (gerund used as *direct object*)

Martha earns a living by painting. (gerund used as *object of a preposition*)

Martha's hobby is painting. (gerund used as a *predicate noun*)

In the first sentence, the word *painting* is a gerund. It is a verb form that is used as a noun. *Painting* is the subject of the sentence. In the second sentence the same verb form *painting* is used as the direct object of the verb *enjoys.* . In the third sentence *painting* is used as the object of the preposition *by*, and in the fourth sentence it is used as a predicate noun after the linking verb *is*.

The Gerund Phrase

Like the participle, the gerund retains many of the characteristics of a verb. Because the gerund is a verb form, it may take any of the complements or any of the modifiers that a verb might take. The gerund with its complements and modifiers is called a **gerund phrase.**

COMPLEMENTS OF GERUNDS

Like the verb, a *gerund* may take a **direct object.** Study the following sentence carefully. You will readily see that although the gerund is used as a noun, it retains the characteristics of a verb because it takes a *direct object.*

Sweeping the floor was one of Jack's duties.

In this sentence the *sweeping* is a gerund. It is used as the *subject* of the sentence. This is its noun function. Since the gerund is a verb form, it retains some of the characteristics of a verb. The verb *sweep* is an action verb and may take a *direct object*. The gerund *sweeping* may also take a direct object. In this sentence the direct object of the gerund *sweeping* is the noun *floor.*

Some verbs take both a direct and an indirect object. Gerunds formed from such verbs may also take a **direct** and an **indirect object.**

Giving the girls a holiday will please them.

In this sentence, *giving* is a gerund used as the subject of the sentence. This is its use as a **noun.** As a **verb form,** it takes the direct object *holiday* and the indirect object *girls*. The entire expression, *giving the girls a holiday* is a gerund phrase.

If the gerund is a form of a linking verb, it may take a **predicate noun** or a **predicate adjective** as a *complement*. Study the following sentences carefully. In both sentences the gerund requires a complement to complete its meaning. The gerunds are forms of linking verbs.

His becoming a captain involved certain responsibilities.

I had not heard of Jane's being ill.

In the first sentence, the gerund *becoming* takes the predicate noun *captain* as a complement. In the second sentence, the gerund *being* takes the predicate adjective *ill* as a complement.

ADVERBIAL MODIFIERS OF GERUNDS

The gerund, like the participle, may be modified by an **adverb** or an **adverbial**

phrase. You should have no trouble in identifying the adverbial modifiers of the gerunds in the following sentences:

Sitting on a park bench was his favorite pastime.
Driving a truck in the city is difficult.

I do not advise your seeing him now.

The gerund *sitting* in the first sentence is modified by the adverbial phrase *on a park bench*. The gerund *driving* in the second sentence is modified by the adverbial phrase *in the city*. The gerund *seeing* in the third sentence is modified by the adverb *now*.

ADJECTIVE MODIFIERS OF GERUNDS

Because the gerund functions as a noun, it may be modified by an *adjective*, or by a *noun* or a *pronoun* used as an *adjective*.

The slow driving in the mountains irritated Max.
(*slow*—adjective, modifying the gerund *driving*)
The dog's barking saved the child's life.
(*dog's*—noun used as an adjective, modifying *barking*)
The critics praised her wonderful dancing.
(*her*—pronoun used as an adjective, modifying *dancing*)
(*wonderful*—adjective, modifying *dancing*)

In the first sentence, the gerund *driving* is modified by the adjective *slow*. In the second sentence, the gerund *barking* is modified by the word *dog's*, which is a noun in the possessive case used as an adjective. In the third sentence, the gerund *dancing* is modified by the possessive adjective *her* (pronoun used as an adjective) and the adjective *wonderful*.

Like the noun, a gerund is often modified by an *adjective phrase*. In the following sentences, the gerunds take adjective phrases as modifiers:

We heard the rustling of the leaves.
The villagers listened to the tolling of the bell.

In the first sentence, the gerund *rustling* is modified by the adjective phrase *of the leaves*. You can readily see that the adjective phrase modifies *rustling* because the sentence means that we heard the *leaves' rustling*. The second sentence means that the villagers listened to the *bell's tolling*.

THE POSSESSIVE CASE BEFORE THE GERUND

The gerund is frequently modified by a noun or a pronoun in the *possessive case*. A mistake commonly made is to forget to put the noun or pronoun in the possessive case to show that it is a modifier. The important word in such sentences is the *gerund*, and not the modifier. The following illustration will help to make this clear:

The men objected to me playing on the team. (*incorrect*)
The men objected to my playing on the team. (*correct*)

The first sentence is incorrect because it conveys the wrong meaning. The sentence does not mean that the men objected to *me*. The word *me* is not the object of the preposition *to*. The object of the preposition *to* is the gerund *playing*. The sentence means that the men objected to the *playing*. The use of the form *me* before the gerund is incorrect. The possessive form *my* should be used.

The following sentences are incorrect because the wrong form of the noun or pronoun is used before the gerund:

I am interested in William advancing in his profession (*incorrect*)

Mother did not like me taking part in the contest. (*incorrect*)

The first sentence does not mean that I am interested in *William* primarily. but that I am interested in *Williams's advancing*. The object of the preposition *in* is the gerund *advancing*, and not the proper noun *William*. Since the noun is a modifier of the gerund, it must be put in the possessive case (*William's* advancing).

The second sentence does not mean that Mother did not like *me*. It means that she *did* not like the *taking part in the contest*. The correct form of the pronoun before the gerund is *my* (*my* taking part).

THE DANGLING GERUND

Gerunds are often found in prepositional phrases which are placed at the beginning of the sentence. The gerund or the gerund phrase is the *object of the preposition*. The entire prepositional phrase should modify some work in the main part of the sentence. If there is no such word, the phrase "*dangles*" in the sentence; that is, the phrase is an unattached modifier.

The gerund almost always expresses action. There must be some word in the sentence to indicate the *doer* of this action. That word would logically be the subject of the sentence. Examine the following sentence carefully:

Upon receiving the telegram, the trip was cancelled.

This sentence begins with a prepositional phrase. The object of the preposition *upon* is the gerund phrase, *receiving the telegram*. The gerund *receiving* implies that someone received the telegram. The way the sentence is written, the *trip received the telegram*. The trouble with the sentence is that the subject has no logical relation to the gerund. The subject of the sentence should indicate *who* is doing the *receiving*. The following sentences are written correctly:

Upon receiving the telegram, *we* cancelled the trip.
or
After we had received the telegram, we cancelled the trip.

This error might be corrected in one of two ways as shown in the preceding illustration:

1. By supplying the word which the prepositional phrase logically refers to.
2. By substituting a subordinate clause for the gerund phrase.

When the gerund phrase at the beginning of a sentence does not have a logical relation to the subject of the sentence, the result is often humorous. The careful study of a sentence like the following will help you understand the error and the reason for the correction:

By pressing a button, the table comes out of the wall. (*incorrect*) (*pressing* dangling gerund)

This sentence clearly indicates that *someone must press a button* before *the table* will come out of the wall. According to the way in which the sentence is written, *the table* performs that function. Such an interpretation would be absurd.

The trouble with the sentence is that the *subject* has no logical relation to the *gerund*. The subject of the sentence should be a word that would indicate the *doer* of the action expressed by the gerund. That word does not

appear in the sentence as it is written. The sentence would be correctly written in either one of the following ways:

By pressing a button, you will release the table from the wall.

If you press a button, the table will come out of the wall.

23. INFINITIVES

Nature of the Infinitive

Participles, gerunds, and *infinitives* are called **verbals** because they are derived from verbs and function like verbs in many respects. They are unlike verbs because they cannot function as the predicate verb in a sentence. They are incomplete forms that cannot be used to make statements, ask questions, or give commands or requests. This is an important fact regarding verbals that you should always keep in mind.

You have learned how to recognize a participle or a gerund by its form. The infinitive is very easy to identify because it carries a definite sign which indicates that it is an infinitive. An infinitive is usually preceded by the word **to,** which is commonly called the *sign of the infinitive*.

When the word *to* is used with a verb form to complete the infinitive, it is *not a preposition*. It is merely the *sign* of the infinitive. The way to be sure that the expression is an infinitive, and not a prepositional phrase, is to look at the word which follows *to*. If this word is a verb form, the expression is an infinitive, and not a prepositional phrase.

Like the gerund, the infinitive is *used as a noun*. It may also function as an *adjective* or as an *adverb*. An infinitive may take any complement or any modifier that a verb might take.

The sign of the infinitive (*to*) is usually omitted after certain verbs in order to avoid awkward or stilted expressions. The *to* is usually omitted after the following verbs: *bear, feel, watch, let, dare, help, see, make, please, bid, need,* etc.

USES OF THE INFINITIVE

You have already studied the two sided character of the participle and the gerund. The participle functions as an adjective and retains some of the characteristics of a verb. The gerund functions as a noun and also retains some of the characteristics of a verb. The **infinitive** retains its verb nature, and in addition may function as a *noun*, an *adjective*, or an *adverb*.

The noun function of an infinitive is very similar to the noun function of a gerund. An infinitive may be the *subject* of a sentence, the *direct object* of a verb, the *object of a preposition*, or a *predicate noun* after a linking verb.

To write was his ambition. (*subject*)
His ambition was to write. (*predicate noun*)
He did nothing except (to) write. (*object of preposition*)
He likes to write. (*direct object*)

In the first sentence, the infinitive *To write* is the subject of the sentence. In the second sentence, the infinitive *to write* is used as a predicate noun after the linking verb *was*. In the third sentence, the infinitive *to write* is used as the object of the preposition *except*. In this sentence, the sign of the infinitive is omitted. In the fourth sentence, the infinitive *to write* is used as the direct object of the verb *likes*.

INFINITIVES USED AS ADJECTIVES

The infinitive is often used as an *adjective* or an *adverb*. When the infinitive is used as an adjective, it usually modifies a noun which precedes it. It is easy to identify the adjective use of the infinitive because an adjective could be readily substituted for the infinitive. Study the following illustrations carefully:

The desire **to win** was apparent. (*the winning desire*)
They asked permission **to leave.** (*leaving permission*)
He obtained a permit **to build.** (*building permit*)
We had fresh water **to drink.** (*drinking water*)

In the first sentence, the infinitive *to win* is used as an adjective. It modifies the noun *desire*. In the second sentence, the infinitive *to leave* modifies the noun *permission*. In the third sentence, the infinitive *to build* modifies the noun *permit*. In the last sentence, the infinitive *to drink* modifies water.

INFINITIVES USED AS ADVERBS

The infinitive is often used as an *adverb* to modify a verb, an adjective, or an adverb. When the infinitive is used as an adverb, it usually expresses *purpose* or *degree*.

It is easy to identify an infinitive used as an adverb when it modifies a verb. In almost every case, the infinitive expresses *purpose*. It tells why, or for what purpose the action is performed. When an infinitive is used in this way, it is often called the *infinitive of purpose*. The infinitives in the following illustrations express purpose and modify the verb:

The traveler stopped **to rest.** (*to rest*— expresses purpose)
The composer came **to listen.** (*to listen*— expresses purpose)
The officer returned **to help.** (*to help*— expresses purpose)

In the first sentence, the infinitive *to rest* modifies the verb *stopped*. The infinitive expresses purpose; that is, it tells why the traveler stopped. The infinitive *to listen* modifies the verb *came*. The infinitive also expresses purpose. It tells why the composer came. The infinitive in the third sentence tells why the officer returned. It modifies the verb and expresses purpose.

An infinitive used as an adverb frequently modifies an *adjective*. This use of the infinitive is also easy to identify. In most cases, the infinitive modifies an adjective which follows a linking verb. Examine the following illustrations carefully:

The cake was ready **to bake.** (*to bake* modifies the adjective *ready*)
The men were anxious **to work.** (*to work* modifies the adjective *anxious*)
We are sorry **to leave.** (*to leave* modifies the adjective *sorry*)
I shall be glad **to help.** (*to help* modifies the adjective *glad*)

In the first sentence, the linking verb *was* is followed by the predicate adjective *ready*. The adjective *ready* is modified by the infinitive *to bake* which is used as an adverb. As you have learned, only adverbs can modify adjectives. The sentence means that the cake was ready *for baking*. The infinitive *to bake* could readily be turned into an adverbial phrase. This should make its adverbial function clear.

In the second sentence, the linking verb *were* is followed by the predicate adjective *anxious*. The adjective *anxious* is modified by the infinitive *to work*. In the third sentence, the predicate adjective *sorry* is modified by the infinitive *to leave*. In the last sentence, the predicate adjective *glad* is modified by the infinitive *to help*.

In all of the preceding illustrations a linking verb is followed by a predicate adjective. The predicate adjective is modified by an infinitive which is used as an adverb.

COMPLEMENTS OF INFINITIVES

Like the gerund and the participle, the infinitive may take any kind of complement a verb might take. Sometimes the infinitive takes a *direct object*. Sometimes it takes both a *direct* and an *indirect object*. If the infinitive is a form of a linking verb, it may take a *predicate noun* or a *predicate adjective* as a complement.

Arlene wanted to buy a fur coat. (*coat* object of *to buy*)
The tailor promised to make me a suit. (*me* indirect object) (*suit* direct object)
John would like to be an aviator. (*aviator* predicate noun)
His ambition is to become rich. (*rich* predicate adjective)

In the first sentence, the infinitive *to buy* takes the direct object *coat*. In the second sentence, the infinitive *to make* takes both an indirect object and a direct object. *Me* is the indirect object and *suit* is the direct object. In the third sentence, the infinitive *to be* takes the predicate noun *aviator* as a complement. In the last sentence, the infinitive *to become* takes the predicate adjective *rich* as a complement.

MODIFIERS OF INFINITIVES

1. Like the verb, an infinitive may be modified by an *adverb* or by an *adverbial phrase*.

The boys like to swim fast. (*fast* adverb, modifies *to swim*)
The boys like to swim in Lake Michigan. (adverbial phrase modifies *to swim*)
To write well is an accomplishment. (*well* adverb modifies *To write*)
To fish in that stream is a pleasure. (adverbial phrase modifies *To fish*)

2. Sometimes the infinitive has both a complement and a modifier.

To do the job properly would require a month's time.

In this sentence the infinitive *To do* takes the direct object *job*. The infinitive is also modified by the adverb *properly*.

THE INFINITIVE PHRASE

In the preceding illustration, the entire phrase, *To do the job properly*, regarded as a whole, is the **complete subject** of the sentence. This group of words is called an **infinitive phrase.** An *infinitive phrase* consists of an infinitive with its complements or its modifiers, or both if it takes both.

Ted's aim was to please others. (infinitive with a *direct object*)
We did not want to travel by plane. (infinitive with an *adverbial phrase* as a modifier)
The men would like to begin the project now. (infinitive with a *direct object* and an *adverb* as modifier)

The infinitive phrase in the first sentence is *to please others.* The phrase consists of the infinitive *to please* and its object *others*. The infinitive phrase in the second sentence is *to travel by plane*. It consists of the infinitive *to travel* and the adverbial phrase *by plane*, which modifies the infinitive. The infinitive phrase in the last sentence is *to begin the project now.* The infinitive takes the direct object *project* and the adverbial modifier *now.*

THE OMISSION OF THE SIGN 'TO'

You have learned that the sign of the infinitive (*to*) is omitted when the infinitive is used after certain verbs. The sign is not used because the sentence would sound awkward or stilted with the sign placed before the verb form. You should become familiar with the verbs that are followed by the infinitive without the sign "*to*."

The sign of the infinitive is usually omitted when the infinitive is used after the following verbs: *hear, feel let, watch, dare, help, see, make, please, bid, need, do,* etc. Tthe following sentences illustrate the use of the infinitive without the sign. The *to* is enclosed in parentheses to show you that you should supply it mentally in order to recognize the infinitive construction.

1. I felt the floor (to) shake under me.
2. We heard him (to) sing some old ballads.
3. I saw her (to) enter the theater.
4. They bid us (to) leave immediately.
5. They dare not (to) create a disturbance.
6. Help me (to) carry the luggage.
7. Let his friend (to) help him.
8. They made him (to) wait for an hour.

24. PROBLEMS IN THE USE OF INFINITIVES

THE INFINITIVE CLAUSE

Sometimes the infinitive has its own *subject.* With this subject, the infinitive is used in a construction which is commonly called the **infinitive clause.** *The infinitive clause is not a true clause* because the infinitive cannot function as a predicate verb. An infinitive cannot function as the predicate verb in a clause because it is an incomplete verb form. The following illustrations will help make this clear:

The officers want the men to sing at the Rotary Club.
We believed him to be capable.

In the first sentence, the group of words, *the men to sing at the Rotary Club,* is called an **infinitive clause.** This expression is called a clause because the infinitive has a subject, and the entire group of words functions in the same way as a **noun clause** would function. The *infinitive clause* is used as the direct object of the verb *want*.

In the second sentence, the group of words *him to be capable* is an infinitive clause. The subject of the infinitive is the pronoun *him*. The entire expression *him to be capable* is used as the direct object of the verb *believed*, but it is not a true clause. The infinitive *to be* is not a predicate verb.

Jean asked me to go with her. (*me* subject of the infinitive *to go*)

Father advised <u>him to buy the bonds</u>. (*him* subject of the infinitive *to buy*)

He believed <u>her to be honest</u>. (*her* subject of the infinitive *to be*)

We want <u>them to build a house</u>. (*them* subject of the infinitive *to build*)

The underlined expression in each of the preceding sentences is the **object** of the preceding verb. In the first sentence, *me to go with her* is the object of the verb *asked*. The sentence does not mean that she asked *me*. It means that she asked *me to go with her*. The entire expression, *me to go with her*, is the object of the verb *asked*.

The group of words, *me to go with her*, is called an "infinitive clause." It consists of the subject *me* and the infinitive *to go* with the modifier of the infinitive, the adverbial phrase *with her*. You can readily see that this is not a true clause because the infinitive *to go* is an incomplete verb form and cannot function as the predicate verb.

The important fact to keep in mind about this construction is that the *subject* of the infinitive is always in the **objective case**. This is an *exception* to the rule that subjects of sentences and subjects of clauses are always in the nominative case.

Examine the preceding illustrations again. In the second sentence, *him* is the subject of the infinitive clause, *him to buy the bonds*. *Him* is in the objective case. In the third sentence, *her* is the subject of the infinitive clause, *her to be honest*. *Her* is in the objective case. In the last sentence, *them* is the subject of the infinitive clause *them to build a house*. *Them* is in the objective case.

You will not have any difficulty with the **case** of the subject of the infinitive. No one would think of saying, "Jean asked *I* to go with her," or "Father advised *he* to buy the bonds." It is natural to use the *objective case* as the subject of the infinitive. However, it is important to keep the following rule in mind. It will help you understand some of the other problems connected with the use of infinitives.

Sometimes the sign of the infinitive is omitted in the "infinitive clause." You must learn how to recognize such "clauses" even if the sign is omitted.

The manager made <u>Mary copy the report again</u>.

The manager made <u>Mary (to) copy the report again</u>.

I saw <u>her dance at the carnival</u>.

I saw <u>her (to) dance at the carnival</u>.

In the first sentence, the infinitive clause, *Mary (to copy the report again*, is the direct object of the verb *made*. The sign of the infinitive *(to)* is omitted in this sentence. In the second sentence, the infinitive clause *her (to) dance at the carnival* is the object of the verb *saw*. The sign of the infinitive is omitted before *dance*.

VERB 'TO BE' IN AN INFINITIVE CLAUSE

When we use the infinitive *to be* in an "infinitive clause," we have a problem in agreement of subject and complement which is often confusing. You have just learned that the subject of an infinitive is always in the objective case. This rule applies in the case of *action verbs* and *linking verbs*.

The problem arises when the infinitive is a form of a linking verb. You learned in your previous study that the noun or pronoun used after a linking verb is in the *nominative case* to agree with the subject of the sentence. Up to this point, every word used as the subject of a sentence or of a clause has been in the nominative case. In the case of the "infinitive clause" we are dealing with a subject that is in the **objective case**.

The verb *to be*, as well as other linking verbs, always takes the same case after it as it takes before it. If the case before it is the *objective case*, the *objective case* must follow it. A noun or pronoun following a linking verb must be in the same case as the subject. Since the noun or pronoun that follows a linking verb means the same person or thing as the subject, it must agree with the subject in case. Therefore, the noun or pronoun that follows the verb *to be* in an infinitive clause is in the objective case to agree with the *subject*, which is in the objective case. This is the logical agreement of *subject* and *complement* after a linking verb functioning as an infinitive in an infinitive clause.

A few illustrations will make this clear. Notice the form of the pronoun after the linking verbs in the "infinitive clauses."

I should like <u>the chairman to be him</u>. (*chairman* objective case, *him* objective case)

Many of the guests thought <u>us to be them</u>. (*us* objective case, *them* objective case)

In the first sentence, the subject of the infinitive clause is *chairman*, which is in the objective case. The infinitive *to be* is followed by the predicate pronoun *him*. The pronoun used as the complement of a linking verb must agree in case with the subject. Since the subject is in the objective case, the pronoun must be in the objective case to agree with the subject.

In the second sentence, the pronoun *us* is the subject of the infinitive clause. *Us* is in the objective case. The pronoun that follows the infinitive *to be* must be in the same case as the subject. *Them* is in the object case to agree with the case of the subject, *us*.

THE SPLIT INFINITIVE

The parts of an infinitive (*to* with a verb form) are regarded as a unit. They should not be separated unless there is a good reason for doing so. The usual method of separating the parts of the infinitive is to place an adverb between the *to* and the *verb form*. When the parts of the infinitive are separated in this way, we refer to the infinitive as a **"split infinitive."** The adverbial modifier "splits" the infinitive.

As a rule, the infinitive should *not* be split by a modifier. Sometimes it is both desirable and effective to split the infinitive, as many authorities in grammar are pointing out. Ordinarily, it is not the best practice, as you will readily see from the following illustrations:

I asked you **to immediately return** my camera.

The judge was <u>determined</u> **to** <u>intently</u> and <u>carefully</u> **examine** the evidence.

In the first sentence, the infinitive is *to return*. The adverbial modifier, *immediately,* is placed between the sign of the infinitive and the verb form. In this particular sentence there is no justifiable reason for splitting the infinitive. The sentence would sound much better if it were written as follows:

I asked you **to return** my camera immediately.

In the second sentence, two adverbial modifiers connected by *and* are placed between the parts of the infinitive. This sentence would sound better if the infinitive were not split in this matter.

The judge was determined **to examine** the evidence intently and carefully.

Many authorities in English call our attention to the fact that some of the best writers split infinitives. When writers do this, they have a good reason for the "split." They also know how to do it so that the sentence will not sound awkward or stilted. When a writer splits an infinitive, his purpose is to throw the emphasis in a certain direction. The following are examples of split infinitives found in good writing:

1. "I feel like inviting them to <u>first</u> consider."

2. "I desire to <u>so</u> arrange my affairs"

3. "his ability to <u>effectually</u> carry on"

4. "to enable him to <u>properly</u> perform his work"

5. "to <u>better</u> acquaint myself with the problems"

6. "Our object is to <u>further</u> cement trade relations."

7. "He worked silently and swiftly, hoping to <u>speedily</u> end his patient's discomfort."

Although there is plenty of evidence that good writers sometimes split the infinitive, ordinarily it is better practice to keep the parts of the infinitive together. A writer or speaker should certainly avoid using such awkward sentences as the following:

Edwin was eager for me to <u>especially</u> see the art exhibit. *to se* infinitive)

Eugene promised to <u>never</u> <u>again</u> be late to work. *to be* infinitive)

The committee wanted to)<u>beautifully</u> decorate the hall. *to decorate* infinitive

I want to <u>next year</u> go to Europe. (*to go* infinitive)

In the first sentence, the infinitive *to see* is "split" by placing the adverb *especially* between the sign of the infinitive *to* and the verb form *see*. In the second sentence, two adverbial modifiers "split" the infinitive. In the third sentence, the adverb *beautifully* "splits" the infinitive. In the fourth sentence, the adverbial modifier *year* is placed between the sign *to* and the verb form, *go*. *Year* is a noun used as an adverb.

SPECIAL USES OF THE INFINITIVE

The infinitive is often used in **apposition** with a noun to explain or identify that noun. This is a very useful construction, for it enables us to explain the noun in a very few words. The infinitive used as an *appositive* is usually set off by commas. Sometimes a dash is used.

His first proposal, <u>to borrow money</u>, was rejected.

We were given our orders <u>to finish the job before ten</u>.

In the first sentence, the infinitive phrase, *to borrow money*, is in apposition with the word *proposal*. It explains the nature of the proposal or tells what the proposal was. In the second sentence, the infinitive phrase, *to finish the job before ten,* is in apposition with the word *orders*. It explains what our orders were.

The infinitive is also used as the **delayed subject** in a sentence that begins with the introductory word *it.* In this case *it* is an **expletive.**

It always pays to tell the truth.
(It) To tell the truth always pays.

It is your duty to protect your interests.
(It) To protect your interests is your duty. Sentences that begin with the pronoun *it* used as an expletive should always be transposed in order to see the grammatical relations more clearly.

THE THREE SIDED CHARACTER OF THE INFINITIVE
NOUN USES OF THE INFINITIVE

1. **Subject** of the sentence
2. **Direct object** of a verb
3. **Object** of a *preposition*
4. **Predicate noun** after a *linking verb*
5. **Appositive**
6. **Delayed subject** after an expletive
7. May take an *adjective modifier*

The Infinitive As A Modifier

1. May function as an **adjective,** modifying a noun
2. May function as an **adrerb** expressing purpose or degree

Verb Characteristics Of The Infinitive

1. Expresses *action* or *state of being,* but *cannot* function as the predicate verb in a sentence
2. May take a complement: *direct object, indirect object, predicate noun,* or *predicate adjective*
3. May take modifier: *adverbs* and *adverbial phrases*
4. May form part of an infinitive clause.

25. PUNCTUATION REVIEW

All punctuation marks are "signals" from the writer to the reader. A period shows that a sentence has been ended or that an abbreviation has been used. A comma may show a slight break in thought, separate the two parts of a compound sentence, or be used in one of several other ways.

Keep in mind that *some sentences may be punctuated in more than one way* and that, in some instances, a punctuation mark may or may not be used at the writer's discretion.

Remember, also, that *some professions and businesses have their own style of punctuation.* A journalist, for example, may omit some punctuation marks which normally are included in a business letter. A lawyer, on the other hand, uses many more punctuation marks when preparing a legal form than are essential for most types of business writing.

OPEN AND CLOSED PUNCTUATION

The terms *open* and *closed* punctuation apply only to the business letter and only to the heading and inside address of the letter. They do not apply to the salutation and complimentary close. If your company uses *open* punctuation, as most firms do, *omit all commas and periods at the ends of lines in the heading and inside address* unless the line ends in an abbreviation. If your firm uses *closed* punctua-

tion, *include commas and periods at the ends of the lines in the heading and in the inside address.* The following examples illustrate the two styles of punctuation. Remember that most firms prefer open punctuation.

Open Punctuation	Closed Punctuation
Acme Rug Cleaners	Acme Rug Cleaners.
1823 Timber Avenue	1823 Timber Avenue.
New York, New York	Mahwah, New Jersey.
10016	07430

The salutation and complimentary close of a business letter are usually punctuated by a colon after the salutation and a comma following the complimentary close, regardless of open or closed punctuation.

USE OF THE PERIOD

1. The period (.) is used after a declarative or an imperative sentence.

She went to the office. (declarative)
Close the car door. (imperative)

Exception: If you wish to give a declarative or an imperative sentence the force of an exclamatory sentence, use an exclamation point rather than a period.

I was so shocked that I was speechless! (declarative)
Bring the Pulmotor quickly! (imperative)

2. After requests, use a period rather than a question mark.

May I send you a copy of our latest bulletin. (request)
Will you send me any further information which you have available. (request)

3. The period is used after abbreviations and initials.

Dr.	Mrs.	A.M.	Jan.
Sr.	Sat.	C. I. Jones	Inc.
B.S.	Ph.D.	U.S.A.	Gen.

Note: When a sentence ends with an abbreviation, one period is sufficient for both the abbreviation and the sentence.

Mail the package to Conley and Green, Inc.

4. The period is used to indicate the omission of words in quoted passages.

(a) Use three periods (. . .) to indicate the omission of words within a quoted passage.

"ı pledge allegiance to the flag of the United States. . . one nation, indivisible, with liberty and justice for all."

(b) Use four periods (. . . .) to indicate the omission of words at the end of a quoted passage.

"Fame is the spur . . . ." John Milton

USE OF THE COMMA

1. The comma (,) is used after an adverbial dependent clause when the dependent clause precedes the main clause. When the dependent clause does not begin the sentence, the comma is usually unnecessary. (See Chapter 19 for a detailed discussion of adverbial clauses.)

After the director had read the minutes of the meeting, he called for the financial report. (comma)

The director called for the financial report after he had read the minutes of the meeting. (no comma)

2. The comma is used after a participial phrase or an absolute phrase at the beginning of a sentence. (See Chapter 21 for a detailed discussion of participial phrases and absolute constructions.)

Seeing the address across the street, he wrote a note in his little book.
The rain having stopped, we went to lunch.

3. The comma is used after an introductory infinitive phrase.

To be successful, you must read widely.

Note: When the subject of the sentence is an infinitive, do not separate the subject from the rest of the sentence.

To be successful was his goal.

4. The comma is used to set off parenthetical expressions, whether words, phrases, or clauses.

(a) Transitional words such as *however, therefore, moreover, besides, consequently* should be set off by commas.

Consequently, I did not receive an answer to his letter.

Exception: The word *also* is not set off by commas unless the writer wishes *also* to be emphasized strongly. In such a case, *also* is generally placed in an unusual position in the sentence.

We also noticed that the salaries declined after the first of thc year. (no emphasis).
Also, we noticed that the salaries declined after the first of the year (emphasis intended)

(b) Phrases such as *so to speak, in short, as a result, of course* should be set off by commas.

We found, in short, many errors ın his work.
Of course, there are many ways to tackle the problem.

(c) Clauses such as *I think, we suppose, he says* should be set off by commas.

Someone, I suppose, should check the report.

(d) Explanatory expressions, such as *and I agree with him, so far as he is concerned,* etc., which break the logical sequence of words should be set off by commas.

The president disliked the policy, and I agreed with him, of letting all employees name their vacation time.

5. The comma is used after introductory expressions such as *yes, indeed, surely* (when it means *yes), well.*

Well, the next thing we knew he had shot the deer.
Yes, I will attend to the matter.

6. The comma is used to set off a nonrestrictive clause. A nonrestrictive clause is set off because *it is not essential to complete the meaning of a sentence.* A nonrestrictive clause is similar to a parenthetical expression in that it gives added information about the word it modifies.

Restrictive clauses are never set off by commas. *A restrictive clause is a clause that is necessary to complete the meaning of the sentence* because the clause identifies the word it modifies. A restrictive clause *cannot* be left out of a sentence, whereas a nonrestrictive clause can be. (See Chapter 18 for further information on restrictive and nonrestrictive clauses.)

The girl who lives next door came to work in our office. (The clause *who lives next door* is restrictive because it is needed to identify the word *girl*. The clause is not set off by commas.)

Mary Jones, who lives next door, came to work in our office. (The clause *who lives next door* is nonrestrictive because it is not needed to identify the name *Mary Jones*. The name *Mary Jones* clearly identifies the person being talked about, and the clause merely gives added information about the person *Mary Jones*.)

7. The comma is used to set off words in apposition. An appositive is a word or phrase that defines or identifies another word. An appositive means the same as the word it defines.

Jones, our office manager, is ill.
Reverend Brown, our minister, is an intelligent man.

Note 1: An appositive at the end of a sentence should be preceded by a comma.

I sent the memorandum to Jones, our office manager.

Note 2: Very closely related appositives do not require a comma.

my cousin Mary	Louis the Fourth
his friend Bill	Mary Queen of Scots

8. The comma is used to set off words used in direct address.

We regret, Mr. Thomas, that your order was unsatisfactorily filled.
Henry, bring me the December file.

9. The comma is used to separate a series of three or more words, phrases, or clauses.

Alice planned to have steak, potatoes, beans, lettuce, and ice cream for dinner.
He stalked off the stage, turned around, came back, and glared at the audience.
At the meeting it was decided to (1) give two weeks' vacation with pay, (2) give pensions at age sixty five, (3) establish a profit sharing-plan.

Note 1: A comma should always be placed before the conjunction joining the last two members of a series.

She asked for paper, pencils, and a ruler.

Note 2: A comma should separate pairs of words in a series. A comma should not be placed before a conjunction joining words of a series that are considered as one unit.

Typing and shorthand, spelling and vocabulary, grammar and punctuation are the most popular courses. (pairs of words in a series)
For breakfast she ordered orange juice, toast, coffee, and ham and eggs. (*Ham and eggs* is considered to be one unit.)

10. The comma is used to separate coordinate adjectives which modify the same noun. Adjectives are coordinate adjectives which modify the same noun. Adjectives are coordinate if the word *and* can be used between them.

The efficient, business-like secretary received an advance in pay. (Comma—the efficient *and* business-like secretary. Both adjectives modify *secretary*.)
The five silver spoons were very expensive. (No comma—you would not say *five and silver spoons*.)

11. The comma is used in a compound sentence to separate independent clauses joined by one of the coordinate conjunctions *and, but, for, or, nor,* and *while* when it means the same as *but*. See Chapter Seventeen for a detailed discussion of compound sentences.)

I dictated the letter as you ordered, but she did not transcribe it correctly.
Minneapolis is a large industrial center, and it has many cultural attractions.

(a) If the clauses of a compound sentence are very short and closely connected, the comma may be omitted.

He looked but he did not see her.

(b) Do not use a comma between two independent clauses unless a coordinate conjunction is used. The use of a comma without a coordinate conjunction between two independent clauses is called the *comma fault*. The following sentence illustrates the comma fault:

The men in the shipping department will not follow instructions, they repeatedly make serious errors. (Incorrect—comma should not be used without a coordinate conjunction.)

Note 1: The comma fault may be eliminated by punctuating the sentence in one of the three following ways:

(a) Use a coordinate conjunction after the comma:

The men in the shipping department will not follow instructions, and they repeatedly make serious errors. (correct)

(b) Use a semicolon between the two independent clauses:

The men in the shipping department will not follow instructions; they repeatedly make serious errors. (correct—see Rule 1 under semicolons.)

(c) Punctuate the two independent clauses as two simple sentences:

The men in the shipping department will not follow instructions. They repeatedly make serious errors. (correct)

Note 2: When the independent clauses of a compound sentence are very long or have *internal punctuation,* a semicolon is generally used before the coordinate conjunction. Internal punctuation means that there are commas within one or both of the independent clauses.
Copyboy, take this folder to Alan Toms, the fellow in brown over there; and be sure to come back.
Quietly efficient, Joan continued in her position; but she never got the raise.

Both of these sentences have one or more commas in the first independent clause. Since the first clause has internal punctuation, a semicolon is used between the two independent clauses even though a coordinate conjunction is used. (See Rule 3 under semicolons.)

12. The comma is used to set off words or phrases expressing contrast.

I asked you to file the contract, not destroy it.
You may be excused from the conference this time, but never again.
Children should be seen, not heard.

13. The comma is used to set off a definite place, month, or year.

Cleveland, Ohio   July 12, 1986
Cook County, Illinois in December, 1985

Or, in sentence form, the comma is used in the following manner:

The president was born April 8, 1872, at 1224 Elm Street, Cleveland, Ohio.

14. The comma is used to set off a direct quotation.

The director asked, "How many of you are in favor of this change in policy?"

15. The comma is used as a substitute for an exclamation point after a mild interjection.

Well, I'm glad that's over.
My, it's really raining.

16. The comma is used after inverted names

Thackeray, William M.
Whittier, John Greenleaf

17. The comma is used to indicate the omission of a word.

Fishing forms a quiet man; hunting, an eager man; racing, a greedy man.

18. The comma is used to set off a proper name when followed by an academic degree or honorary title. the comma is used to separate two or more degrees or titles.

Philip F. Adams, A.B., M.A., Ph.D., lecturer in English.

19. The comma is used to point off the thousands in figures of four digits or more.

1,117   20,718   1,817,000

Note: Do not use the comma in street addresses, page and policy numbers, or in years.

the year 1985	Policy No. 903451
page 2348	1117 Pensacola Ave.

20. The comma is used to separate two sets of figures or two identical words.

John told you, you should apply immediately.
Send me 10, No. 1234 and 7, No. 138.
Since 1986, 12,000 new machines have been sold.

21. The comma is used to separate a declarative clause and an interrogative clause which immediately follows.

The plane will arrive on time, will it not?
Jack is to get a promotion, isn't he?

22. The comma is used to separate a phrase from the rest of the sentence when the phrase is inverted or out of its natural order.

Like you, I think the policy is a worthwhile one.
For me, it will mean extra work and less pay.
In spite of his promise, he was late to work again.

USE OF THE SEMICOLON

The semicolon (;) is used to show a stronger separation between the parts of a sentence than does a comma. In practical writing, however, avoid using the semicolon because it is generally too stiff and formal. If you use a great many semicolons, the chances are that you are either using them incorrectly, or you are writing sentences which are too long. Semicolons produce rather involved sentence patterns. Use them sparingly.

1. The semicolon is used to separate independent coordinate clauses closely connected in meaning when no coordinate conjunction is used.

The sales staff meets every other Tuesday; the production staff meets only once a month.

He would not approve the art layout as presented; he suggested several drastic changes.

Note: An example of this rule, as used to avoid the comma fault, was given in Rule 11 under commas.

2. The semicolon is used between coordinate clauses of a compound sentence when they are joined by transitional words and phrases. The following is a list of commonly used transitional words and phrases:

accordingly	indeed	as a result
afterwards	likewise	at last
again	meanwhile	at the same time
anyhow	moreover	for example
besides	namely	for instance
consequently	nevertheless	for this reason
doubtless	next	in any case
eventually	otherwise	in fact
evidently	perhaps	in like manner
finally	possibly	in short
furthermore	still	on the contrary
hence	then	on the other hand
however	therefore	that is
yet	thus	in addition

For a further discussion of transitional words, see chapter 17.

Note: You have already learned that transitional words are usually set off by commas. When you use a semicolon in place of a comma before the transitional word, you usually put a comma after the transitional word. However, when the transitional word retains its adverbial force and is not regarded as an independent element, it is seldom set off with a comma.

The members of the board of directors approved the change in distribution; consequently, you should appeal to them.

The weather was cold and icy; therefore we didn't go.

3. The semicolon is used before a coordinate conjunction (*and, but, for, or, nor*) between two independent clauses when either one or both have internal punctuation.

The president, a well-read man, predicted a cost of living increase for the first of the year; but his prediction, which spread throughout the plant, proved to be wrong.

The staff housekeeper ordered carpets, divans, lamps, tables, and chairs; but her order was incorrectly filled.

4. The semicolon is used before such words as *for example, for instance, that is,* and *namely* that introduce an example, enumeration, or a list in a sentence. A comma is placed after such words.

These special artist's pencils are available in three colors; namely, red, green, and blue.

Many of our policies will be changed this year; for example, salesmen will be paid a commission instead of a salary.

5. The semicolon is used in lists where a comma is insufficient to separate the members clearly.

Guests at the convention were Mr. Leonard Key, the past president of the corporation; Mrs. F. K. Small, the wife of the founder; and Mr. Paul Wells, the speaker of the evening.

USE OF THE COLON

The colon (:) indicates the strongest possible break within a sentence.

1. The colon is used before a list of items or details.
Please send out the following items: No. 378, No. 315, No. 519, and No. 570.
His actions were as follows: He went to the drugstore, purchased a hypodermic needle, got into his car, and drove away.

Note 1: Capitalize the first letter of each item in a list when the list is in column form.

You should know how to use the following office machines:
   1. Typewriter
   2. Duplicator
   3. Copy Machine
   4. Calculator

Note 2: Do not capitalize the first letter of each item in a list when the items are included in a sentence.

You should know how to use the following office machines: typewriter, duplicator, copy machine, and calculator.

2. The colon is used before an appositive phrase or clause.

Our company has always had this motto: The customer is always right.
These are your duties: Sort the mail, open all that is not personal, throw away the envelopes, and bring the letters to me.

Note: Capitalize the first letter of the word which follows the colon when that word introduces a complete sentence, as in the above exaiples.

3. The colon is used after the salutation of a business letter.

Dear Mr. Roe: Gentlemen: My Dear Madam:
Note: Never use a semicolon after a salutation. A comma may be used after the salutation of a friendly or informal letter.

Dear Jane,   Dear Father,   Dear Jones,

4. The colon is used to divide the parts of references, titles, formulas, and numerals.

The time was 9:15 p.m.
He assigned Chapter XII: Section 19.
Grammar Unit Eight: Complements of Verbs

USE OF PARENTHESES

1. Parentheses ( ) are used to set off words, phrases, clauses, or sentences which are used by way of explanation, translation, or comment, but which are independent constructions:

Hilda (my sister's roommate at college) is coming to visit us.
The motto read as follows: *'De gustibus non disputandum est.'* (In matters of taste there is no dispute.)

2. Parentheses are used to enclose a number, letter, or symbol when used as an appositive.

She ordered twelve (12) night stands for the hotel.
The bookkeeper ornamented his letterhead with the percent symbol (%).

Note 1: When using parentheses with other punctuation marks, punctuate the main part of the sentence as if the parenthetical portion was not there. A punctuation mark comes after the second parenthesis if the punctuation mark

applies to the whole sentence and not just to the parenthetical portion.

He analyzed and presented standards of evaluation (business and technical), but his conditions proved nothing.

Note 2: Place the punctuation mark inside the second parenthesis if the punctuation mark applies only to material within the parenthetical portion.

A simplified fire-fighting plan will help you. (See the back cover of this brochure.)

USE OF THE DASH

The dash (—) is used to indicate an abrupt change of ideas, but should be used sparingly. Excessive use of the dash usually indicates that the writer does not know what punctuation mark to use.

There are times you may want to use the dash for visual effect or emphasis. A glance at advertisements in a newspaper shows that copy writers make frequent use of the dash. However, in business writing, such as letters, reports, minutes, and in social correspondence, use the dash with caution.

1. The dash may be used to indicate a sudden change of thought in a sentence.

I was certain that the manager—indeed, all of the office force—wanted John to receive the promotion.

2. The dash may be used to indicate a summarizing thought or an afterthought added to the end of the sentence.

I shall make out an estimate, draw up a contract, send out a man to interpret it for you—give you every help I can.

3. The dash may be used to set off a word or phrase repeated for emphasis.

We invited them for one meeting—one meeting only—not for the entire convention!

4. The dash may be used between numbers or dates to indicate *to* and *and.*

His chapter covered from 1860—1868.
My appointment was scheduled from 12:15—1:15.

Note on the punctuation of parenthetical matter: Close study of the rules on commas, parentheses, and dashes will show you that any one of the three punctuation marks may be used to set off parenthetical words, phrases, or clauses. When should you use the commas, dash, or parentheses? No strict rule can be stated. In general, follow this practice: In punctuating parenthetical matter, use dashes mainly for visual effect; use commas if the material is short; and use parentheses if the material is long.

USE OF BRACKETS

1. Brackets [ ] are used to enclose material added by someone other than the writer; for example, editorial additions or comments.

The investigation [from June 1, 1985 to April 8, 1986] caused considerable speculation.

The poet [Robert Browning] did not approve of the excessive adulation during the meeting.

2. Brackets are used to enclose parenthetical matter within parenthetical matter.

Your order (including items No. 391, No. 394, and No. 286 [No. 288 was out of stock])was filled last week.

Note: Brackets are rarely used in business and social writing. Generally they are found only in printed material of a scholarly or technical nature.

USE OF THE QUESTION MARK

1. The question mark (**?**) is used after all interrogative sentences that ask direct questions.

Where are the current files?
Are you going to the next meeting of the club?

Note: After requests, use a period instead of a question mark. (See Rule 2 under periods.)

2. The question mark may be used after each separate part of a sentence containing more than one question.

Can we be sure of his willingness? his capability? his honesty?

Note: If the question is not complete until the end of the sentence, place a question mark at the end only.

Will delivery be made today, tomorrow, or Friday?

3. The question mark is used in several ways when only part of the sentence is a question. In such sentences the question is generally introduced by a comma or colon; a semicolon or dash may also be used.

May I ask, what is his purpose?
This is our problem: What should be done to prevent further damage?
Our questions are, what date will you arrive? where will you stay? and, do you desire us to furnish transportation?

USE OF THE EXCLAMATION MARK

1. The exclamation mark (**!**) is used after all exclamatory sentences—sentences that express surprise, emotion, or deep feeling.

Look out for that train!
Headlines read, "Peace Treaty Signed!"
Your answer was hard to believe!

2. The exclamation mark is used after an interjection or a word used as an interjection. At times, the sentence following the interjection may be exclamatory.

Hurry! The train will pull out in three minutes!
Oh! I haven't heard that before.

3. The exclamation mark is used after statements which are commands or which imply need for immediate action.

Return the card today! Don't delay!
Hurry! Send your order now!

4. The exclamation point is used after an interrogative sentence that is exclamatory in form or intended to be exclamatory.

Oh, how could he say that!
But can he be trusted!

5. The exclamation point is sometimes used to add emphasis.

Realize what this means!
This offer absolutely expires April 6!

USE OF QUOTATION MARKS

1. Quotation marks (" ") are used to enclose a direct quotation. Each part of an interrupted quotation begins and ends with quotation marks.

The inspector said, "Well, your case is not hopeless."
"Where," he asked, "are you going to keep it?"
"What will we do?" he asked. "Where can we raise the money?"

Note: Capitalize the first word of a direct quotation. Do not capitalize the first word in the second part of an interrupted quotation unless the second part begins a new sentence. Do not use quotation marks or capital letters in an indirect quotation.

The inspector said that your case is not hopeless. (Many indirect quotations are introduced by the word *that.*)
He asked where we would keep it.

2. Quotation marks are used to enclose the titles of magazine articles, chapters of books, names of songs, titles of poems, and other titles.

The New Yorker includes a section entitled "The Talk of the Town."

She asked Ellen to sing "Because" at her wedding.
"Rabbi Ben Ezra" is one of my favorite poems.
Note: In typing or writing, underline the titles of books, magazines, operas, and any other works of art long enough to appear in book form. Underlining signifies italics for printing. The words, "The New Yorker" in the first sentence above are printed in italic type.

The anthology, Toward Liberal Education, includes A. E. Housman's "Introductory Lecture" and S. I. Hayakawa's "Poetry and Advertising."
The soprano sang "If Madam Should Call You" from Mozart's Marriage of Figaro.

3. Quotation marks are used to set off words, phrases, or sentences referred to within a sentence.

The word "proceed" is frequently mispronounced.
The phrase "on the other hand" is sometimes used as a transitional phrase.
The sentence "Now is the time for all good men to come to the aid of their party" is an excellent typing exercise.

4. Quotation marks are used to set off slang words or expressions.

She said that the office party was held at a "swank" hotel.

5. If several paragraphs are quoted, use quotation marks at the beginning of each paragraph but at the end of the last paragraph only. Long quotations are usually introduced by a colon instead of a comma. Quotations of three or more lines are usually indented and set apart from the body of the text.

USE OF QUOTATION MARKS WITH OTHER PUNCTUATION

(a) The period and comma are always placed before ending quotation marks.

He said, "They are not here."
"They are not here," he said.

(b) The question mark and exclamation point are placed before quotation marks when they refer only to the quoted material.

She asked, "When are you going to be promoted?"

(c) The question mark and exclamation point follow ending quotation marks when they refer to the entire sentence.

Did she say, "You are to be promoted next month"?

(d) The semicolon and colon follow ending quotation marks unless they are part of the quoted matter.

She said, "You are to be promoted next month"; consequently, I expected to be promoted.

USE OF SINGLE QUOTATION MARKS

1. Single quotation marks are used to set off a quotation within a quotation.

"Jane," I asked, "did you tell me how to spell the word 'pathologically'?"

The irate mother said, "You must get all of this 'junk' out of the living room at once."

Note: Other punctuation marks are used with single quotation marks in the same way as with double quotation marks.

USE OF THE APOSTROPHE

1. The apostrophe (**'**) is used in nouns to show possession.

Note: Keep in mind that the sign of the possessive case is always added to a word. It is not something that is inserted within a word.

(a) If the singular form of the noun does not end in **s** or an **s** sound, add the apostrophe and **s** (**'s**).

Singular	Singular Possessive
boy	boy's
girl	girl's
lady	lady's

(b) If the singular ends in **s** or an **s** sound, add the apostrophe (**'**) or the apostrophe and **s** (**'s**) if the additional **s** sound is desired.

Singular	Singular Possessive
boss	boss' or boss's
dress	dress' or dress's
box	box' or box's

(c) If the plural form of the noun does not end in **s,** add the apostrophe and **s** (**s'**)

Plural	Plural Possessive
men	men's
children	children's
mice	mice's
teeth	teeth's
geese	geese's

(d) If the plural form of the noun ends in **s,** add the apostrophe (**'**)

Plural	Plural Possessive
boys	boys'
girls	girls'
ladies	ladies'

(e) The possessives of proper nouns are formed in the same way as the possessives of common nouns. If the singular form of the name does not end in **s**, add the apostrophe and **s**. If the singular ends in **s** or an **s** sound, add the apostrophe (**'**) or the apostrophe and **s** (**'s**). The plural possessive is always formed by adding the apostrophe to the plural form.

Proper Noun	Singular Possessive	Plural	Plural Possessive
John	John's	Johns	Johns'
Phyllis	Phyllis' or Phyllis's	Phyllises	Phyllises'
Jane	Jane's	Janes	Janes'

(f) Certain expressions relating to *time, distance,* and *value* are also written with an apostrophe.

the day's task	five cents's worth
a year's time	six miles' distance
a minute's notice	three weeks' vacation

(g) The singular possessive and the plural possessive of compound nouns are formed by adding the apostrophe to the end of the compound word.

Singular	**Plural**
brother-in-law's	brothers-in-law's
father-in-law's	fathers-in-law's

(h) Joint ownership is shown by making the last word in the series possessive. Individual ownership is shown by making both parts possessive.

Alice and Jack's apartment. (joint ownership)
Alice's and Jack's apartments. (individual ownership)

2. The apostrophe is used in indefinite pronouns to show possession. The possessive case of indefinite pronouns is formed in the same way as the possessive case of nouns.

everybody's duty	others' positions
one's coat	someone's hat

3. The apostrophe is used with **s** to form the plural of numbers, letters, signs, and symbols.

Your "r's" look like "n's."
He used twelve "r's" to decorate his paper.

4. The apostrophe is used to indicate the omission of a word, letters, or numerals.

don't	let's	o'clock
hadn't	it's	she's
isn't	'tis	wouldn't

The accident happened in '86.

SPELLING DICTIONARY

A

aard·vark
ab·a·cus
abaft
ab·a·lo·ne
aban·don
  aban·doned
  aban·don·ment
abase
  abased
  abas·ing
  abase·ment
abate
  abat·ed
  abat·ing
  abate·ment
ab·at·toir
ab·axial
ab·bey
ab·bot
  ab·bess
a·bre·vi·ate
  ab·bre·vi·at·ed
  ab·bre·vi·at·ing
  ab·bre·vi·a·tion
ab·di·cate
  ab·di·cat·ed
  ab·di·cat·ing
ab·di·ca·tion
ab·do·men
  ab·dom·i·nal
ab·duct
  ab·duc·tion
  ab·duc·tor
ab·er·rant
  ab·er·ra·tion
  ab·er·rance
  ab·er·ran·cy
abet
  abet·ted
  abet·ting
  abet·ment
abey·ance
ab·hor
  ab·horred
  ab·hor·ring
  ab·hor·rence
  ab·hor·rent
abide
  abode
  abi·ded
  abid·ing
abil·i·ty
  abil·i·ties
ab·ject
  ab·ject·ly
  ab·ject·ness
ab·jure
  ab·jured
  ab·jur·ing
  ab·ju·ra·tion
ab·late
  ab·lat·ed
  ab·lat·ing
ab·la·tion
  ab·la·tive
able
  ably
able-bod·ied
ab·lu·tion
ab·ne·gate

ab·ne·gat·ed
ab·ne·gat·ing
ab·nor·mal
  ab·nor·mal·i·ty
  ab·nor·mal·i·ties
abol·ish
  abol·ish·a·ble
  abol·ish·ment
ab·o·li·tion
  ab·o·li·tion·ism
  ab·o·li·tion·ist
A-bomb
abom·i·nate
  abom·i·nat·ed
  abom·i·nat·ing
  abom·i·na·tion
abom·i·na·ble
  abom·i·na·bly
ab·o·rig·i·ne
  ab·o·rig·i·nal
abort
  abor·tion
  abor·tion·ist
  abor·tive
above·board
ab·ra·ca·dab·ra
abrade
  abrad·ed
  abrad·ing
  abra·sion
  abra·sive
abreast
abridge
  abridged
  abridg·ing
abroad
ab·rogate
  ab·ro·gat·ed
  ab·ro·gat·ing
  ab·ro·ga·tion
ab·rupt
ab·scess
  ab·scessed
ab·scis·sa
ab·scis·sion
ab·scond
ab·sence
ab·sent
  ab·sen·tee
  ab·sent-mind·ed
ab·sinthe
ab·so·lute
  ab·so·lute·ly
ab·so·lu·tion
ab·solve
  ab·solved
  ab·solv·ing
  ab·sol·vent
ab·sorb
  ab·sorb·ent
  ab·sorp·tion
  ab·sorp·tive
  ab·sorb·a·ble
  ab·sorb·en·cy
ab·stain
  ab·sten·tion
  ab·sti·nence
  ab·sti·nent
  ab·ste·mi·ous
ab·stract
  ab·strac·tion
  ab·stract·ed
ab·struce

ab·surd
  ab·surd·i·ty
  ab·surd·ness
abund·dant
abun·dance
abuse
  abused
  abus·ing
  abus·er
abu·sive
  abu·sive·ly
  abu·sive·ness
abut
  abut·ted
  abut·ting
  abut·ment
abys·mal
abyss
ac·a·dem·ic
  ac·a·dem·i·cal
  acad·e·mi·cian
acad·e·my
  acad·e·mies
ac·cede
  ac·ced·ed
  ac·ced·ing
ac·ce·le·ran·do
ac·cel·er·ate
  ac·cel·er·at·ed
  ac·cel·er·at·ing
  ac·cel·er·ant
  ac·cel·er·a·tion
  ac·cel·er·a·tor
ac·cent
ac·cen·tu·ate
  ac·cen·tu·at·ed
  ac·cen·tu·at·ing
  ac·cen·tu·a·tion
ac·cept
  ac·cept·ed
  ac·cept·ance
  ac·cept·a·ble
  ac·cept·a·bil·i·ty
ac·cess
  ac·ces·si·ble
  ac·ces·si·bil·i·ty
ac·ces·sion
ac·ces·so·ry
ac·ci·dence
ac·ci·dent
  ac·ci·den·tal
ac·claim
  ac·cla·ma·tion
ac·cli·mate
  ac·cli·mat·ed
  ac·cli·mat·ing
  ac·cli·ma·tion
ac·cli·ma·tize
  ac·cli·ma·tized
  ac·cli·ma·tiz·ing
  ac·cli·ma·ti·za·tion
ac·cliv·i·ty
  ac·cliv·i·ties
ac·co·lade
ac·com·mo·date
  ac·com·mo·dat·ed
  ac·com·mo·dat·ing
  ac·com·mo·da·tive
  ac·com·mo·da·tion
ac·com·pa·ny
  ac·com·pa·nied
  ac·com·pa·ny·ing
  ac·com·pa·ni·ment

ac·com·pa·nist
ac·com·plice
ac·com·plish
  ac·com·plished
  ac·com·plish·ing
  ac·com·plish·ment
ac·cord
  ac·cord·ing
  ac·cord·ance
ac·cor·di·on
ac·cost
ac·couche·ment
ac·count
  ac·count·a·ble
  ac·count·a·bil·i·ty
ac·count·ant
ac·count·ing
ac·cred·it
  ac·cred·i·ta·tion
ac·cre·tion
ac·cre·tive
ac·cru·al
ac·crue
  ac·crued
  ac·cru·ing
ac·cum·u·late
  ac·cum·u·lat·ed
  ac·cum·u·lat·ing
  ac·cum·u·la·tion
  ac·cu·mu·la·tive
ac·cu·rate
  ac·cu·ra·cy
  ac·cu·rate·ly
  ac·cu·rate·ness
ac·curs·ed
ac·curst
ac·cu·sa·tive
ac·cuse
  ac·cused
  ac·cus·ing
  ac·cu·sa·tion
  ac·cu·sa·to·ry
ac·cus·tom
  ac·cus·tomed
acer·bi·ty
ace·tate
ace·tic
acet·i·fy
ac·e·tone
acet·y·lene
ache
  ached
  ach·ing
achieve
  achieved
  achiev·ing
  achiev·a·ble
  achieve·ment
ach·ro·mat·ic
ac·id
  acid·ic
  acid·i·fy
  acid·i·ty
ac·i·do·sis
acid·u·late
  acid·u·la·tion
acid·u·lous
ac·knowl·edge
  ac·knowl·edged
  ac·knowl·edg·ing
  ac·knowl·edge·a·ble
  ac·knowl·edg·ment
ac·me

ac·ne
ac·o·lyte
ac·o·nite
acous·tic
  acous·tics
  acous·ti·cal
ac·quaint
  ac·quaint·ance
ac·qui·esce
  ac·qui·esced
  ac·qui·esc·ing
  ac·qui·es·cence
  ac·qui·es·cent
ac·quire
  ac·quired
  ac·quir·ing
  ac·quire·ment
  ac·qui·si·tion
ac·quit
  ac·quit·ted
  ac·quit·ting
  ac·quit·tal
  ac·quit·tance
acre
  acre·age
ac·rid
  acrid·i·ty
ac·ri·mo·ny
  ac·ri·mo·ni·ous
ac·ro·bat
  ac·ro·bat·ic
ac·ro·nym
ac·ro·pho·bia
across
acryl·ic
act·ing
ac·tion
  ac·tion·a·ble
  ac·tion·a·bly
ac·ti·vate
  ac·ti·vat·ed
  ac·ti·vat·ing
  ac·ti·va·tion
  ac·ti·va·tor
ac·tive
  ac·tive·ly
  ac·tive·ness
ac·tiv·ism
ac·tiv·ist
ac·tiv·i·ty
  ac·tiv·i·ties
ac·tor
ac·tress
ac·tu·al
  ac·tu·al·ly
  ac·tu·al·i·ty
ac·tu·al·ize
  ac·tu·al·i·za·tion
ac·tu·ary
  ac·tu·ar·ies
  ac·tu·ar·i·al
ac·tu·ate
  ac·tu·at·ed
  ac·tu·at·ing
  ac·tu·a·tion
  ac·tu·a·tor
acu·i·ty
acu·men
ac·u·punc·ture
acute
  acute·ly
  acute·ness
ad·age

ada·gio
ad·a·mant
ad·a·man·tine
adapt
  adapt·a·ble
  adapt·a·bil·i·ty
  ad·ap·ta·tion
  adap·tive
ad·dend
ad·den·dum
  ad·den·da
ad·dict
  ad·dict·ed
  ad·dic·tive
  ad·dic·tion
ad·di·tion
  ad·di·tion·al
ad·di·tive
ad·dle
ad·dress
ad·dress·ee
ad·duce
ad·e·noid
  ad·e·noi·dal
adept
  adept·ly
ad·e·quate
  ad·e·qua·cy
  ad·e·quate·ly
ad·here
  ad·hered
  ad·her·ing
  ad·her·ence
  ad·her·ent
ad·he·sion
ad·he·sive
  ad·he·sive·ness
ad·hib·it
adi·a·bat·ic
a·dieu
ad in·fi·ni·tum
adi·os
ad·i·pose
  ad·i·pose·ness
ad·ja·cent
  ad·ja·cent·ly
  ad·ja·cen·cy
  ad·ja·cen·cies
ad·jec·tive
ad·join
  ad·join·ing
ad·journ
  ad·journ·ment
ad·judge
  ad·judged
  ad·judg·ing
ad·ju·di·cate
  ad·ju·di·cat·ed
  ad·ju·di·cat·ing
  ad·ju·di·ca·tion
ad·junct
  ad·junc·tive
ad·jure
  ad·jured
  ad·jur·ing
  ad·ju·ra·tion
ad·just
  ad·just·a·ble
  ad·just·er
  ad·just·ment
ad·ju·tant
ad·lib
  ad·libbed
  ad·lib·bing
ad·min·is·ter
ad·min·is·trate
ad·min·is·tra·tion
  ad·min·is·tra·tive

ad·min·is·tra·tor
ad·mi·ral
ad·mi·ral·ty
ad·mire
  ad·mired
  ad·mir·ing
  ad·mi·ra·ble
  ad·mi·ra·bly
  ad·mi·ra·tion
  ad·mir·er
  ad·mir·ing·ly
ad·mis·si·ble
  ad·mis·si·bil·i·ty
ad·mis·sion
ad·mit
  ad·mit·ted
  ad·mit·ting
  ad·mit·tance
ad·mix·ture
ad·mon·ish
  ad·mo·ni·tion
  ad·mon·i·to·ry
ado·be
ad·o·les·cence
ad·o·les·cent
adopt
  adopt·a·ble
  adopt·er
  adop·tion
  adop·tive
adore
  adored
  ador·ing
  ador·a·ble
  ad·o·ra·tion
adorn
  adorn·ment
ad·re·nal
adren·a·line
adrift
adroit
  adroit·ly
  adroit·ness
ad·sorb
  ad·sor·bent
  ad·sorp·tion
ad·u·late
  ad·u·lat·ing
  ad·u·la·tion
  ad·u·la·to·ry
adult
  adult·hood
adul·ter·ate
  adul·ter·at·ed
  adul·ter·at·ing
  adul·ter·ant
  adul·ter·a·tion
adul·tery
  adul·ter·er
  adul·ter·ess
  adul·ter·ous
ad va·lo·rem
ad·vance
  ad·vanc·ing
  ad·vance·ment
ad·van·tage
  ad·van·tag·ing
  ad·van·ta·geous
ad·vent
ad·ven·ti·tious
ad·ven·ture
  ad·ven·tur·ing
  ad·ven·tur·er
  ad·ven·ture·some
  ad·ven·tur·ous
ad·verb
  ad·ver·bi·al·ly
ad·ver·sary

ad·ver·sar·ies
ad·verse
  ad·verse·ly
  ad·verse·ness
ad·ver·si·ty
  ad·ver·si·ties
ad·vert
  ad·vert·ence
  ad·vert·ent
ad·ver·tise
  ad·ver·tised
  ad·ver·tis·ing
  ad·ver·tis·er
  ad·ver·tise·ment
ad·vice
ad·vise
  ad·vis·ing
  ad·vis·a·bil·i·ty
  ad·vis·a·ble
  ad·vis·a·bly
  ad·vis·er
  ad·vis·ed·ly
  ad·vise·ment
  ad·vi·so·ry
ad·vo·cate
  ad·vo·cat·ed
  ad·vo·cat·ing
  ad·vo·ca·cy
  ad·vo·ca·tion
ae·on
  ae·o·ni·an
aer·ate
  aer·at·ed
  aer·at·ing
  aer·a·tion
  aer·a·tor
aer·i·al
  aer·i·al·ist
aero·dy·nam·ics
aer·o·log·i·cal
  aer·ol·o·gist
aer·o·naut·ics
  aer·o·nau·ti·cal
aer·o·sol
aero·space
aes·thete
aes·thet·ic
  aes·thet·i·cal·ly
af·fa·ble
  af·fa·bil·i·ty
  af·fa·bly
af·fair
af·fect
  af·fect·ing
af·fec·tive
af·fec·ta·tion
af·fect·ed
  af·fect·ed·ly
  af·fect·ed·ness
af·fec·tion
  af·fec·tion·ate
af·fi·ance
af·fi·da·vit
af·fil·i·ate
  af·fil·i·at·ed
  af·fil·i·a·tion
af·fin·i·ty
af·firm
  af·fir·ma·tion
  af·firm·a·tive
af·flict
  af·flic·tion
af·flu·ence
  af·flu·ent
af·ford
af·fray
af·fright
af·front

af·ghan
afore·men·tioned
afore·said
afore·thought
afraid
Af·ri·can
Af·ri·kan·der
af·ter·birth
af·ter·burn·er
af·ter·ef·fect
af·ter·glow
af·ter·math
af·ter·most
af·ter·noon
af·ter·thought
af·ter·ward
again
against
agape
ag·ate
aga·ve
age
  aged
  ag·ing
  age·ing
age·less
agen·cy
  agen·cies
agen·da
agent
ag·glom·er·ate
  ag·glom·er·at·ing
  ag·glom·er·a·tion
ag·glu·ti·nate
  ag·glu·ti·nat·ing
  ag·glu·ti·na·tion
  ag·glu·ti·na·tive
ag·gran·dize
  ag·gran·dized
  ag·gran·diz·ing
  ag·gran·dize·ment
ag·gra·vate
  ag·gra·vat·ed
  ag·gra·vat·ing
  ag·gra·va·tion
ag·gre·gate
  ag·gre·gat·ed
  ag·gre·gat·ing
  ag·gre·ga·tion
  ag·gre·ga·tive
ag·gress
  ag·gress·ive
  ag·gress·or
  ag·gres·sion
ag·grieve
  ag·grieved
  ag·griev·ing
aghast
ag·ile
  ag·ile·ly
  agil·i·ty
ag·i·tate
  ag·i·tat·ed
  ag·i·tat·ing
  ag·i·ta·tion
  ag·i·ta·tor
agleam
ag·nos·tic
  ag·nos·ti·cism
ag·o·nize
  ag·o·niz·ing
ag·o·ny
  ag·o·nies
ag·o·ra·pho·bia
agrar·i·an
agree
  agreed
  agree·ing

agree·ment
agree·a·ble
agree·a·bil·i·ty
agree·a·bly
ag·ri·cul·ture
  ag·ri·cul·tur·al
  ag·ri·cul·tur·ist
agron·o·my
  ag·ro·nom·ic
  ag·ro·nom·i·cal
  agron·o·mist
aground
ague
aide-de-camp
ai·grette
ail·ing
  ail·ment
ai·ler·on
aim·less
air·less
air·borne
air·brush
air-con·di·tion
  air-con·di·tioned
  air con·di·tion·ing
  air con·di·tion·er
air·craft
air·drop
  air·dropped
  air·drop·ping
Aire·dale
air·field
air·foil
air·plane
air·port
air pres·sure
air·sick·ness
air·space
air·tight
air·wave
air·worthy
airy
  air·i·er
  air·i·est
  air·i·ness
  air·i·ly
aisle
ajar
akin
al·a·bas·ter
a la carte
alac·ri·ty
alarm
  alarm·ing
al·ba·core
al·ba·tross
al·be·it
al·bi·no
  al·bi·nos
  al·bi·nism
al·bum
al·bu·men
al·bu·min
  al·bu·mi·nous
al·che·my
  al·che·mist
al·co·hol
  al·co·hol·ic
  al·co·hol·ism
al·cove
al·der·man
alert
  alert·ness
al·fal·fa
al·fres·co
al·ga
  al·gae
  al·ge·bra

al·ge·bra·ic
al·ge·bra·ic·al
al·go·ri·thm
ali·as
ali·as·es
al·i·bi
al·ien
al·ien·a·ble
al·ien·ate
al·ien·at·ed
al·ien·at·ing
al·ien·ist
al·ien·ism
alight
alight·ed
alit
alight·ing
align
align·ment
aline·ment
alike
al·i·ment
al·i·men·tal
al·i·men·ta·ry
al·i·mo·ny
al·ka·li
al·ka·lies
al·ka·line
al·ka·lin·i·ty
al·ka·lize
al·ka·lized
al·ka·liz·ing
al·ka·li·za·tion
al·ka·loid
al·ka·loi·dal
all-Amer·i·can
all-around
al·lay
al·layed
al·lay·ing
al·lege
al·leged
al·leg·ing
al·le·ga·tion
al·lege·a·ble
al·le·giance
al·le·go·ry
al·le·go·ries
al·le·gor·ic
al·le·gor·i·cal
al·le·gret·to
al·le·gro
al·ler·gen
al·ler·gy
al·ler·gies
al·ler·gic
al·ler·gist
al·le·vi·ate
al·le·vi·at·ed
al·le·vi·at·ing
al·le·vi·a·tion
al·le·vi·a·tive
al·le·vi·a·to·ry
al·ley
al·leys
al·li·ance
al·lied
al·li·ga·tor
al·lit·er·ate
al·lit·er·at·ed
al·lit·er·at·ing
al·lit·er·a·tive
al·lit·er·a·tion
al·lo·cate
al·lo·cat·ed
al·lo·cat·ing
al·lo·ca·tion
al·lop·a·thy

al·lo·path·ic
al·lot
al·lot·ted
al·lot·ting
al·lot·ment
al·lot·ta·ble
al·low
al·low·ing
al·low·a·ble
al·low·ed·ly
al·low·ance
al·loy
all·spice
al·lude
al·lud·ed
al·lud·ing
al·lure
al·lured
al·lur·ing
al·lure·ment
al·lu·sion
al·lu·sive
al·lu·sive·ly
al·lu·vi·al
al·lu·vi·um
al·ly
al·lies
al·lied
al·ly·ing
al·li·ance
al·ma ma·ter
al·ma·nac
al·mighty
almond
almost
al·oe
aloft
alo·ha
alone
alone·ness
along
along·side
aloof
aloof·ness
al·pha
al·pha·bet
al·pha·bet·ic
al·pha·bet·i·cal
al·pha·bet·ize
al·pha·nu·mer·ic
al·ready
al·so
al·tar
al·ter
al·ter·a·bil·i·ty
al·ter·a·ble
al·ter·ant
al·ter·a·tion
al·ter·a·tive
al·ter·cate
al·ter·ca·tion
al·ter e·go
al·ter·nate
al·ter·nat·ed
al·ter·nat·ing
al·ter·nate·ly
al·ter·na·tion
al·ter·na·tor
al·ter·na·tive
al·though
al·tim·e·ter
al·ti·tude
al·to
al·to·gether
al·tru·ism
al·tru·ist
al·tru·is·tic
al·um

a·lu·min·na
alu·mi·num
alum·na
alum·nae
alum·nus
alum·ni
al·ve·o·lar
al·ways
amal·gam
amal·gam·ate
amal·gam·a·tion
am·a·ryl·lis
amass
amass·ment
am·a·teur
am·a·teur·ism
am·a·teur·ish
am·a·to·ry
amaze
amazed
amaz·ing
amaze·ment
Am·a·zon
am·bas·sa·dor
am·bas·sa·dress
am·bas·sa·do·ri·al
am·ber
am·ber·gris
am·bi·dex·trous
am·bi·dex·ter·i·ty
am·bi·ance
am·bi·ence
am·bi·ent
am·big·u·ous
am·big·u·ous·ly
am·bi·gu·i·ty
am·bi·tion
am·bi·tious
am·bi·tious·ly
am·bi·tious·ness
am·biv·a·lence
am·biv·a·lent
am·ble
am·bled
am·bling
am·bro·sia
am·bro·sial
am·bu·lance
am·bu·la·to·ry
am·bu·lant
am·bu·late
am·bu·lat·ed
am·bu·lat·ing
am·bus·cade
am·bush
am·bush·ment
ame·ba
amel·io·rate
amel·io·rat·ed
amel·io·rat·ing
amel·io·ra·ble
amel·io·ra·tion
amel·ior·a·tive
amel·io·ra·tor
ame·na·ble
ame·na·bil·i·ty
ame·na·ble·ness
ame·na·bly
amend
amend·a·ble
amend·ment
amen·i·ty
amerce
amerce·ment
Amer·i·ca
Amer·i·can
Amer·i·cana
Amer·i·can·ism

Amer·i·can·i·za·tion
am·e·thyst
ami·a·ble
ami·a·bil·i·ty
ami·a·bly
am·i·ca·ble
am·i·ca·bil·i·ty
am·i·ca·bly
amid
amidst
ami·go
am·i·ty
am·me·ter
am·mo·nia
am·mo·ni·um
am·mu·ni·tion
am·ne·sia
am·ne·sic
am·nes·ty
am·ni·on
amoe·ba
amoe·bae
amoe·bas
amoe·bic
amoe·boid
amok
among
amongst
amor·al
am·o·rous
am·o·rous·ly
am·o·rous·ness
amor·phous
am·or·tize
am·or·tized
am·or·tiz·ing
am·or·ti·za·tion
amount
amour
am·pere
am·per·age
am·per·sand
am·phet·a·mine
am·phib·i·an
am·phib·i·ous
am·phi·the·a·ter
am·ple
am·ple·ness
am·ply
am·pli·fy
am·pli·fied
am·pli·fy·ing
am·pli·fi·ca·tion
am·pli·fi·er
am·pli·tude
am·poule
am·pule
am·pu·tate
am·pu·tat·ed
am·pu·tat·ing
am·pu·ta·tion
am·pu·tee
amuck
am·u·let
amuse
amused
amus·ing
amuse·ment
anach·ro·nism
anach·ro·nis·tic
anach·ro·nous
an·a·con·da
an·aes·the·sia
an·aes·thet·ic
an·aes·the·tize
an·a·gram
an·a·gram·mat·ic
an·a·gram·mat·i·cal

anal
anus
an·al·ge·sia
an·al·ge·sic
an·a·logue
an·a·log
an·a·log·i·cal
anal·o·gize
anal·o·gy
anal·o·gies
anal·o·gous
anal·y·sis
anal·y·ses
an·a·lyst
an·a·lyt·ic
an·a·lyze
an·a·lyzed
an·a·lyz·ing
an·a·ly·za·tion
an·a·pest
an·ar·chist
an·ar·chism
an·ar·chis·tic
an·ar·chy
an·ar·chic
an·ar·chi·cal
anath·e·ma
anath·e·ma·tize
anat·o·mize
anat·o·mized
anat·o·mizing
anat·o·mi·za·tion
anat·o·my
anat·o·mies
an·a·tom·i·cal
anat·o·mist
an·ces·tor
an·ces·tral
an·ces·tress
an·ces·try
an·chor
an·chor·age
an·cho·rite
an·chor·man
an·chovy
an·cient
an·cient·ness
an·cil·lary
an·dan·te
an·dan·ti·no
and·i·ron
an·dro·gen
an·drog·y·nous
an·drog·y·ny
an·ec·dote
an·ec·do·tal
an·ec·dot·ti·cal
ane·mia
ane·mic
an·e·mom·e·ter
anem·o·ne
an·er·oid
an·es·the·sia
an·es·thet·ic
an·es·the·tist
an·es·the·si·ol·ogist
an·es·the·tize
an·es·the·tiz·ing
an·eu·rysm
an·eu·rism
an·gel
an·gel·ic
an·gel·i·cal·ly
an·ger
an·gerily
an·gi·na pec·to·ris
an·gle
an·gling

angler
An·gli·can
An·gli·can·ism
An·gli·cism
An·gli·cize
An·gli·ci·za·tion
An·glo-Amer·i·can
An·glo-Sax·on
an·go·ra
an·gos·tu·ra
an·gry
an·gri·ly
an·gri·ness
ang·strom unit
an·guish
an·guished
an·gu·lar
an·gu·lar·i·ty
an·gu·la·tion
an·hy·dride
an·hy·drous
an·i·mad·vert
an·i·mad·ver·sion
an·i·mal
an·i·mal·ism
an·i·mal·i·ty
an·i·mal·ize
an·i·mate
an·i·mat·ed
an·i·mat·ing
an·i·ma·tion
an·i·mism
an·i·mis·tic
an·i·mos·i·ty
an·i·mus
an·ise
an·i·sette
an·kle
an·klet
an·ky·lose
an·ky·lo·sis
an·nals
an·nal·ist
an·nal·is·tic
An·nap·o·lis
an·neal
an·ne·lid
an·nex
an·nex·a·tion
an·ni·hi·late
an·ni·hi·lat·ed
an·ni·hi·lat·ing
an·ni·hi·la·tion
an·ni·hi·la·tor
an·ni·ver·sa·ry
an·ni·ver·sa·ries
an·no Do·mi·ni
an·no·tate
an·no·tat·ed
an·no·tat·ing
an·no·ta·tion
an·no·ta·tor
an·nounce
an·nounced
an·nounc·ing
an·nounce·ment
an·nounc·er
an·noy
an·noy·ance
an·nu·al
an·nu·i·ty
an·nu·i·tant
an·nul
an·nulled
an·nul·ling
an·nul·ment
an·nu·lar
an·nun·ci·ate

an·nun·ci·at·ing
an·nun·ci·a·tion
an·nun·ci·a·tor
an·ode
an·od·ize
an·o·dyne
anoint
anoint·ment
anom·a·ly
anom·a·lism
anom·a·lous
anon·y·mous
an·o·nym·i·ty
anon·y·mous·ly
an·oth·er
an·swer
an·swer·a·ble
ant·ac·id
an·tag·o·nist
an·tag·o·nism
an·tag·o·nis·tic
an·tag·o·nize
an·tag·o·niz·ing
ant·arc·tic
Ant·arc·ti·ca
an·te
ant·eat·er
an·te-bel·lum
an·te·cede
an·te·ced·ed
an·te·ced·ing
an·te·ced·ence
an·te·ced·ent
an·te·cham·ber
an·te·date
an·te·di·lu·vi·an
an·te·lope
an·te me·ri·di·em
an·ten·na
an·ten·nae
an·ten·nas
an·te·pe·nult
an·te·ri·or
an·te·room
an·them
an·thol·o·gy
an·thol·o·gies
an·thol·o·gist
an·thra·cite
an·thrax
an·thro·po·cen·tric
an·thro·poid
an·thro·pol·o·gy
an·thro·po·log·ic
an·thro·po·log·i·cal
an·thro·pol·o·gist
an·thro·pom·e·try
an·thro·po·mor·phic
an·ti·air·craft
an·ti·bac·te·ri·al
an·ti·bal·lis·tic
an·ti·bi·ot·ic
an·ti·body
an·ti·bod·ies
an·tic
An·ti·christ
an·tic·i·pate
an·tic·i·pat·ed
an·tic·i·pat·ing
an·tic·i·pa·tion
an·tic·i·pa·tive
an·tic·i·pa·to·ry
an·ti·cler·i·cal
an·ti·cli·max
an·ti·cli·mac·tic
an·ti·dote
an·ti·dot·al
an·ti·freeze

an·ti·gen
an·ti·his·ta·mine
an·ti·log·a·rithm
an·ti·ma·cas·sar
an·ti·mis·sile
an·ti·mo·ny
an·ti·pas·to
an·tip·a·thy
an·ti·pa·thet·ic
an·ti·pode
an·ti·quar·i·an
an·ti·quary
an·ti·quar·ies
an·ti·quate
an·ti·quat·ed
an·ti·quat·ing
an·tique
an·tiqued
an·tiq·uing
an·tique·ness
an·tiq·ui·ty
an·ti-Sem·i·tism
an·ti·sep·sis
an·ti·sep·tic
an·ti·sep·ti·cal·ly
an·ti·se·rum
an·ti·slav·ery
an·ti·so·cial
an·tith·e·sis
an·tith·e·ses
an·ti·thet·i·cal
an·ti·tox·in
an·ti·tox·ic
an·ti·trust
ant·ler
ant·lered
an·to·nym
anus
an·vil
anx·i·e·ty
anx·i·e·ties
anx·ious
anx·ious·ness
any·body
any·bod·ies
any·how
any·more
any·one
any·place
any·thing
any·way
any·where
any·wise
aor·ta
aor·tal
aor·tic
apace
apart
apart·heid
apart·ment
ap·a·thy
ap·a·thet·ic
ap·a·thet·i·cal·ly
aper·ri·tif
ap·er·ture
apex
apex·es
api·ces
api·cal
apha·sia
aphid
aph·o·rism
aph·o·rist
aph·o·ris·tic
aph·ro·dis·i·ac
api·ar·i·an
api·a·rist
api·ary

an·ti·gen
api·ar·ies
api·cul·ture
api·cul·tur·al
api·cul·tur·ist
apiece
ap·ish
aplomb
apoc·a·lypse
apoc·a·lyp·tic
apoc·o·pe
apoc·ry·pha
ap·o·dic·tic
ap·o·gee
apol·o·get·ics
apol·o·gist
apol·o·gize
apol·o·gized
apol·o·giz·ing
apol·o·gy
apol·o·gies
apol·o·get·ic
apol·o·get·i·cal
ap·o·plec·tic
ap·o·plex·y
apos·ta·sy
apos·tate
apos·ta·tize
a pos·te·ri·o·ri
apos·tle
apos·to·late
ap·os·tol·ic
ap·os·tol·i·cal
apos·trophe
apoth·e·cary
apoth·e·car·ies
ap·o·thegm
apoth·e·o·sis
apoth·e·o·size
Ap·pa·la·chi·an
ap·pall
ap·palled
ap·pal·ling
ap·pa·rat·us
ap·pa·rat·us
ap·pa·rat·us·es
ap·par·el
ap·par·ent
ap·pa·ri·tion
ap·peal
ap·peal·a·ble
ap·peal·ing·ly
ap·pear
ap·pear·ance
ap·pease
ap·peased
ap·peasing
ap·pease·ment
ap·peas·er
ap·pel·late
ap·pel·lant
ap·pel·la·tion
ap·pel·la·tive
ap·pend
ad·pen·dage
ap·pend·ant
ap·pen·di·ci·tis
ap·pen·dec·to·my
ap·pen·dix
ap·pen·dix·es
ap·pen·di·ces
ap·per·cep·tion
ap·per·tain
ap·pe·tite
ap·pe·tiz·er
ap·pe·tiz·ing
ap·plaud
ap·plause
ap·ple

ap·pli·ance
ap·pli·ca·ble
ap·pli·ca·bil·i·ty
ap·pli·cant
ap·pli·ca·tion
ap·pli·ca·to·ry
ap·pli·ca·tor
ap·pli·que
ap·ply
ap·plied
ap·ply·ing
ap·point
ap·point·ee
ap·poin·tive
ap·point·ment
ap·por·tion
ap·por·tion·ment
ap·pose
ap·posed
ap·pos·ing
ap·po·site
ap·po·si·tion
ap·pos·i·tive
ap·praise
ap·praised
ap·prais·ing
ap·prais·er
ap·prais·al
ap·pre·ci·a·ble
ap·pre·ci·a·bly
ap·pre·ci·ate
ap·pre·ci·at·ing
ap·pre·ci·a·tion
ap·pre·ci·a·tive
ap·pre·hend
ap·pre·hen·si·ble
ap·pre·hen·sion
ap·pre·hen·sive
ap·pren·tice
ap·prise
ap·prised
ap·pris·ing
ap·proach
ap·proach·a·ble
ap·pro·ba·tion
ap·pro·ba·to·ry
ap·pro·pri·ate
ap·pro·pri·at·ed
ap·pro·pri·at·ing
ap·pro·pri·ate·ness
ap·pro·pri·a·tion
ap·prov·al
ap·prove
ap·proved
ap·prov·ing
ap·prox·i·mate
ap·prox·i·mate·ly
ap·prox·i·ma·tion
ap·pur·te·nance
ap·pur·te·nant
ap·ri·cot
a pri·o·ri
apron
ap·ro·pos
apt
apt·ly
apt·ness
ap·ti·tude
aq·ua
aqua·cul·ture
aqua·lung
aq·ua·ma·rine
aq·ua·naut
aq·ua·plane
aquar·i·um
aquat·ic
aq·ue·duct
aque·ous

aq·ui·line
ar·a·besque
Ara·bi·an
Ara·bic
ar·a·ble
arach·nid
ar·ba·lest
ar·bi·ter
ar·bi·trary
arbi·trari·ly
ar·bit·ra·ment
ar·bi·trate
ar·bi·trat·ed
ar·bi·trat·ing
ar·bi·tra·tor
ar·bi·tra·tion
ar·bor
ar·bo·re·al
ar·bo·re·tum
arc
arced
arc·ing
ar·cade
ar·chae·ol·o·gy
ar·che·ol·o·gy
ar·chae·o·log·i·cal
ar·che·o·log·i·cal
ar·chae·ol·o·gist
ar·che·ol·o·gist
ar·cha·ic
ar·cha·ism
arch·an·gel
arch·bish·op
arch·dea·con
arch·di·o·cese
arch·di·oc·e·san
arch·du·cal
arch·duke
arch·duch·ess
arch·er
ar·chery
ar·che·type
arch·fiend
ar·chi·e·pis·co·pal
ar·chi·pel·a·go
ar·chi·tect
ar·chi·tec·ton·ic
ar·chi·tec·ture
ar·chi·tec·tur·al
ar·chive
ar·chi·val
ar·chi·vist
arc·tic
ar·cu·ate
ar·dent
ar·dor
ar·du·ous
ar·ea
are·na
ar·go·sy
ar·got
ar·gue
ar·gued
ar·gu·ing
ar·gu·a·ble
ar·gu·ment
ar·gu·men·ta·tion
ar·gu·men·ta·tive
ar·gu·men·tive
ar·gyle
aria
ar·id
arid·i·ty
arise
arose
aris·en
aris·ing
aris·to·crat

aris·to·crat·ic
aris·toc·ra·cy
aris·toc·ra·cies
arith·me·tic
ar·ith·met·i·cal
arith·me·ti·cian
arm
armed
arm·ing
ar·ma·da
ar·ma·dil·lo
Ar·ma·ged·don
ar·ma·ment
ar·ma·ture
ar·mi·stice
ar·moire
ar·mor
ar·mored
ar·mory
ar·mor·ies
ar·my
ar·mies
aro·ma
ar·o·mat·ic
ar·o·mat·i·cal
around
arouse
aroused
arous·ing
arous·al
ar·peg·gio
ar·raign
ar·raign·ment
ar·range
ar·ranged
ar·rang·ing
ar·range·ment
ar·rant
ar·ray
ar·ray·al
ar·rear
ar·rear·age
ar·rest
ar·rest·er
ar·rive
ar·rived
ar·riv·ing
ar·ri·val
ar·ro·gant
ar·ro·gance
ar·ro·gant·ly
ar·ro·gate
ar·ro·gat·ed
ar·ro·ga·tion
ar·row
ar·row·head
ar·royo
ar·se·nal
ar·se·nic
ar·son
ar·son·ist
ar·te·ri·al
ar·te·ri·o·scle·ro·sis
ar·tery
ar·ter·ies
ar·te·sian
art·ful
art·ful·ly
ar·thri·tis
ar·thrit·ic
ar·thro·pod
ar·ti·choke
ar·ti·cle
ar·tic·u·lar
ar·tic·u·late
ar·tic·u·lat·ed
ar·tic·u·lat·ing
ar·tic·u·late·ly

ar·tic·u·late·ness
ar·tic·u·la·tor
ar·tic·u·la·tion
ar·ti·fact
ar·te·fact
ar·ti·fice
ar·ti·fi·cial
ar·ti·fi·ci·al·i·ty
ar·ti·fi·cial·ly
ar·til·lery
ar·ti·san
art·ist
ar·tiste
ar·tis·tic
ar·tis·ti·cal·ly
art·ist·ry
art·less
arty
ar·ti·ness
as·bes·tos
as·bes·tus
as·cend
as·cend·ance
as·cend·ence
as·cend·an·cy
as·cend·en·cy
as·cend·ant
as·cend·ent
as·cent
as·cen·sion
as·cer·tain
as·cer·tain·a·ble
as·cer·tain·ment
as·cet·ic
as·cet·i·cism
as·cot
as·cribe
as·cribed
as·crib·ing
as·crib·a·ble
as·crip·tion
asep·sis
asep·tic
asex·u·al
asex·u·al·i·ty
ashamed
asham·ed·ly
ash
ash·en
ash·es
ashy
Asi·at·ic
as·i·nine
as·i·nin·i·ty
askance
askew
asleep
aso·cial
as·par·a·gus
as·pect
as·pen
as·per·i·ty
as·perse
as·persed
as·pers·ing
as·per·sion
as·phalt
as·phyx·ia
as·phyx·i·ate
as·phyx·i·at·ed
as·phyx·i·at·ing
as·phyx·i·a·tion
as·pic
as·pir·ant
as·pir·rate
as·pir·rat·ed
as·pir·rat·ing
as·pi·ra·tion

as·pi·ra·tor
as·pire
as·pir·ing
as·pi·rin
as·sail
as·sail·a·ble
as·sail·ant
as·sas·sin
as·sas·si·nate
as·sas·si·nat·ed
as·sas·si·nat·ing
as·sas·si·na·tion
as·sas·si·na·tor
as·sault
as·say
as·say·er
as·sem·blage
as·sem·ble
as·sem·bled
as·sem·bling
as·sem·bler
as·sem·bly
as·sem·blies
as·sem·bly·man
as·sent
as·sen·ta·tion
as·sert
as·ser·tion
as·ser·tive
as·ser·tive·ness
as·sess
as·sess·a·ble
as·sess·ment
as·sess·or
as·set
as·sev·er·ate
as·sev·er·at·ed
as·sev·er·at·ing
as·sev·er·a·tion
as·si·du·i·ty
as·sid·u·ous
as·sign
as·sign·a·ble
as·sign·a·bly
as·sign·ment
as·sig·na·tion
as·sim·i·late
as·sim·i·lat·ed
as·sim·i·lat·ing
as·sim·i·la·ble
as·sim·i·la·tion
as·sist
as·sist·ance
as·sis·tant
as·size
as·so·ci·ate
as·so·ci·at·ed
as·so·ci·at·ing
as·so·ci·a·tion
as·so·ci·a·tive
as·so·nance
as·so·nant
as·sort
as·sort·ed
as·sort·ment
as·suage
as·suaged
as·suag·ing
as·suage·ment
as·sua·sive
as·sume
as·sumed
as·sum·ing
as·sump·tion
as·sure
as·sured
as·sur·ing
as·sur·ance

as·sur·ed·ly
as·sur·ed·ness
as·ter·isk
as·ter·oid
asth·ma
asth·mat·ic
astig·ma·tism
as·tig·mat·ic
as·ton·ish
as·ton·ish·ing
as·ton·ish·ment
as·tound
astrad·dle
as·tra·khan
as·tral
astray
astride
as·trin·gent
as·trin·gen·cy
as·tro·dome
as·tro·labe
as·trol·o·gy
as·trol·o·ger
as·tro·log·ic
as·tro·log·i·cal
as·tro·naut
as·tro·nau·tics
as·tro·nau·ti·cal
as·tro·nom·ic
as·tro·nom·i·cal·ly
as·tron·o·my
as·tron·o·mer
as·tro·phys·ics
as·tro·phys·i·cist
as·tute
as·tute·ly
as·tu·cious
asun·der
asy·lum
asym·me·try
asym·met·ric
asym·met·ri·cal
at·a·vism
at·a·vis·tic
at·el·ier
athe·ism
athe·ist
athe·is·tic
athe·is·ti·cal
ath·er·o·scle·ro·sis
ath·lete
ath·let·ic
ath·let·ics
ath·let·i·cal·ly
athwart
at·las
at·las·es
at·mos·phere
at·mos·pher·ic
at·mos·pher·i·cal
at·oll
at·om
atom·ic
atom·i·cal
at·om·ism
at·om·ize
at·om·ized
at·om·iz·ing
at·om·iz·er
atonal
ato·nal·i·ty
atone
atoned
aton·ing
atone·ment
atri·um
atro·cious
atroc·i·ty

atroc·i·ties
at·ro·phy
  at·ro·phies
  at·ro·phied
  at·ro·phy·ing
  atroph·ic
at·tach
  at·tach·ment
at·ta·che
at·tack
at·tain
  at·tain·a·ble
  at·tain·ment
at·tain·der
at·taint
at·tar
at·tempt
at·tend
  at·tend·ance
  at·tend·ant
at·ten·tion
  at·ten·tive
at·ten·u·ate
  at·ten·u·at·ed
  at·ten·u·at·ing
  at·ten·u·a·tion
at·test
  at·test·ta·tion
at·tic
at·tire
  at·tired
  at·tir·ing
  at·tire·ment
at·ti·tude
at·ti·tu·di·nize
at·tor·ney
  at·tor·neys
at·tract
at·trac·tive
at·trac·tion
at·tri·bute
  at·tri·but·ed
  at·tri·but·ing
  at·tri·but·a·ble
  at·tri·bu·tion
  at·trib·u·tive
at·tri·tion
  at·trite
at·tune
  at·tuned
  at·tun·ing
atyp·i·cal
au·burn
auc·tion
  auc·tion·eer
au·da·cious
  au·dac·i·ty
au·di·ble
  au·di·bil·i·ty
  au·di·bly
au·di·ence
au·dio
au·dio·phile*
au·di·o·vis·u·al
au·dit
au·di·tion
au·dit·or
au·di·to·ri·um
au·di·to·ry
aught
aug·ment
aug·men·ta·tion
au grat·in
au·gust
  au·gust·ly
auld·lang syne
au·ral
  au·ral·ly

au·re·ate
au·re·ole
au·re·o·my·cin
au re·voir
au·ri·cle
au·ric·u·lar
au·ro·ra
au·ro·ra aus·tra·lis
au·ro·ra bor·e·al·is
aus·pice
aus·pic·es
aus·pi·cious
aus·tere
aus·ter·i·ty
au·then·tic
au·then·ti·cate
  au·then·ti·cat·ed
  au·then·ti·cat·ing
  au·then·ti·ca·tion
  au·then·tic·i·ty
au·thor
  au·thor·ess
  au·thor·ship
au·thor·i·tar·i·an
au·thor·i·ta·tive
au·thor·i·ty
  au·thor·i·ties
au·thor·ize
  au·thor·ized
  au·thor·iz·ing
  au·thor·i·za·tion
au·to·bi·og·ra·phy
  au·to·bi·og·ra·phies
  au·to·bi·og·ra·pher
  au·to·bi·o·graph·ic
  au·to·bi·o·graph·i·cal
au·toc·ra·cy
  au·toc·ra·cies
au·to·crat
  au·to·crat·ic
  au·to·crat·i·cal·ly
au·to·graph
au·to·mate
  au·to·mat·ed
  au·to·mat·ing
au·to·mat·ic
  au·to·mat·i·cal
au·to·ma·tion
au·tom·a·tism
au·tom·a·ton
au·to·mo·bile
au·to·mo·tive
au·ton·o·mous
au·to·nom·ic
au·ton·o·my
  au·ton·o·mies
au·top·sy
au·tumn
  au·tum·nal
aux·il·ia·ry
  aux·il·ia·ries
avail
avail·a·ble
  avail·a·bil·i·ty
av·a·lanche
  av·a·lanch·ing
avant·garde
av·a·rice
  av·a·ri·cious
Ave Ma·ria
avenge
  avenged
  aveng·ing
  aveng·er
av·e·nue
aver
  averred
  aver·ring

aver·ment
av·er·age
  av·er·aged
  av·er·ag·ing
averse
  averse·ly
aver·sion
avert
  avert·a·ble
avi·ary
  avi·ar·ies
avi·a·tion
avi·a·tor
avi·a·trix
av·id
  avid·i·ty
  av·id·ly
av·o·ca·do
av·o·ca·tion
avoid
  avoid·a·ble
  avoid·ance
av·oir·du·pois
avow
  avow·al
  avowed
avun·cu·lar
await
awake
  awoke
  awaked
  awak·ing
  awak·en
award
aware
  aware·ness
away
awe
  awed
  aw·ing
aweigh
awe·some
awe·strick·en
  awe·struck
aw·ful
  aw·ful·ly
  aw·ful·ness
awhile
awhirl
awk·ward
  awk·ward·ness
awn·ing
awry
ax
  ax·es
ax·i·om
  ax·i·o·mat·ic
  ax·i·o·mat·i·cal
ax·is
  ax·es
  ax·i·al
ax·le
azal·ea
az·i·muth
az·ure

B

bab·bitt
bab·ble
  bab·bled
  bab·bling
ba·boon
ba·bush·ka
ba·by
  ba·bics
  ba·bied

ba·by·ing
ba·by·sit
  ba·by·sit·ting
  ba·by·sit·ter
bac·ca·lau·re·ate
bac·ca·rat
bac·cha·nal
  bac·cha·na·li·an
bach·e·lor
ba·cil·lus
  ba·cil·li
back·ache
back·bite
back·board
back·bone
back·drop
back·field
back·fire
back·gam·mon
back·ground
back·hand
back·hand·ed
back·ing
back·lash
back·log
back·side
back·slide
  back·slid·den
  back·slid·er
back·spin
back·stage
back·stairs
back·stop
back·talk
back·ward
  back·ward·ness
back·wash
ba·con
bac·te·ria
  bac·te·ri·um
  bac·te·ri·al
bac·te·ri·cide
  bac·te·ri·ci·dal
bac·te·ri·ol·o·gy
  bac·te·ri·ol·o·gist
  bac·te·ri·o·log·i·cal
bad
  worse
  worst
badge
badg·er
bad·i·nage
bad·land
bad·ly
bad·min·ton
baf·fle
  baf·fled
  baf·fling
bag
  bagged
  bag·ging
bag·a·telle
ba·gel
bag·gage
bag·gy
  bag·gi·er
  bag·ging
ba·gnio
bag·pipe
ba·guette
bail·a·ble
bail·iff
bail·i·wick
bails·man
baize
bake
  baked
  bak·ing

bak·er
bak·er·y
  bak·er·ies
bak·sheesh
bal·a·lai·ka
bal·ance
  bal·anced
  bal·anc·ing
  bal·anc·er
bal·co·ny
  bal·co·nies
bald
  bald·ness
bal·der·dash
bald·head
bale
  baled
  bal·ing
bale·ful
balk
balky
  balk·i·est
bal·lad
bal·last
bal·le·ri·na
bal·let
bal·lis·tic
  bal·lis·tics
  bal·lis·ti·cian
bal·loon
bal·lot
  bal·lot·ed
  bal·lot·ing
ball·room
bal·ly·hoo
balmy
  balm·i·er
ba·lo·ney
bal·sa
bal·sam
bal·us·ter
  bal·us·trade
bam·bi·no
bam·boo
bam·boo·zle
  bam·boo·zled
  bam·boo·zling
ban
  banned
  ban·ning
ba·nal
  ba·nal·i·ty
ba·nana
band·age
  band·aged
  band·ag·ing
ban·dana
  ban·dan·na
ban·deau
ban·de·role
ban·dit
  ban·dit·ry
ban·do·leer
  ban·do·lier
band·stand
band·wag·on
ban·dy
  ban·died
  ban·dy·ing
bane·ful
ban·gle
ban·ish
  ban·ish·ment
ban·is·ter
  ban·nis·ter
ban·jo
bank·book
bank·er

bank·ing
bank·rupt
bank·rupt·cy
bank·rupt·cies
ban·ner
banquet
ban·quette
ban·shee
ban·tam
ban·ter
ban·ter·ing·ly
ban·yan
ban·zai
bap·tism
bap·tis·mal
Bap·tist
bap·tis·tery
bap·tize
bap·tized
bap·tiz·ing
bar
barred
bar·ring
bar·bar·ic
bar·bar·i·an
bar·ba·rism
bar·ba·rous
bar·bar·i·ty
bar·bar·i·ties
bar·be·cue
bar·be·cued
bar·be·cu·ing
bar·ber
bar·bi·can
bar·bi·tal
bar·bi·tu·rate
bar·ca·role
bare
bare·ness
bare·back
bare·faced
bare·foot
bare·ly
bar·gain
barge
barged
barg·ing
bar·i·tone
bar·i·um
bar·ley
bar mitz·vah
bar·na·cle
bar·o·graph
ba·rom·et·er
bar·o·met·ric
bar·on
bar·on·ess
ba·ro·ni·al
bar·on·et
ba·roque
bar·rack
bar·ra·cu·da
bar·rage
bar·rel
bar·reled
bar·rel·ing
bar·ren
bar·ren·ness
bar·rette
bar·ri·cade
bar·ri·cad·ed
bar·ri·cad·ing
bar·ri·er
bar·row
bar·ten·der
bar·ter
bar·ter·er
ba·sal

bas·al·ly
ba·salt
base
based
bas·ing
base·ball
base·less
base·ment
bash·ful
bash·ful·ly
ba·sic
ba·si·cal·ly
ba·sil
ba·sil·i·ca
bas·i·lisk
ba·sin
ba·sis
ba·ses
bas·ket·ball
bas·ket·ry
bas-re·lief
bas·si·net
bas·so
bas·sos
bas·soon
bas·tard
bas·tard·ize
bas·tard·ly
baste
bast·ed
bast·ing
bat
bat·ted
bat·ting
bat·ter
bate
bat·ed
bat·ing
bathe
bathed
bath·ing
bath·y·sphere
ba·tiste
bat·on
bat·tal·ion
bat·ten
bat·ter
bat·tery
bat·tle
bat·tled
bat·tling
bat·tle·field
bat·tle·ment
bau·ble
baux·ite
bawdy
bay·o·net
bay·ou
ba·zaar
ba·zoo·ka
beach·comb·er
beach·head
bea·con
bead·ed
bead·like
beak·er
beamed
bear
bore
borne
bear·ing
bear·a·ble
bear·a·bly
beard·ed
beard·less
bear·ish
beast
beast·li·ness

beast·ly
beat
beat·en
beat·ing
be·a·tif·ic
be·at·i·fy
be·at·i·fied
be·at·i·fy·ing
be·at·i·fi·ca·tion
be·at·i·tude
beat·nik
beau
beaus
beaux
beau geste
beau·te·ous
beau·ti·cian
beau·ti·fy
beau·ti·fied
beau·ti·fi·ca·tion
beauty
beau·ti·ful
beaux-arts
bea·ver
be·calm
be·cause
beck·on
be·cloud
be·come
be·came
be·com·ing
bed
bcd·dcd
bed·ding
be·daz·zle
be·daz·zlcd
be·daz·zling
be·daz·zle·ment
be·dev·il
be·dev·iled
be·dev·il·ing
be·dev·il·ment
be·dim
be·dimmed
be·dim·ming
bed·lam
bed·drag·gle
be·drag·gling
bed·rid·den
bed·room
beech-nut
beef
beeves
beef·eat·er
beef·steak
bccfy
beef·i·er
bee·hive
bee·line
Bee·tho·ven
bee·tle
be·fall
be·fell
be·fall·en
be·fall·ing
be·fit
be·fit·ted
be·fit·ting
be·fog
be·fogged
be·fog·ging
be·fore
be·friend
be·fud·dle
be·fud·dled
be·fud·dling
beg
begged

beg·ging
be·get
be·got
be·got·ten
beg·gar
beg·gar·ly
be·gin
be·gan
be·gun
be·gin·ning
be·gin·ner
be·gone
be·go·nia
be·got·ten
be·grime
be·grudge
be·grudged
be·grudg·ing
be·guile
be·guiled
be·guil·ing
be·half
be·have
be·haved
be·hav·ing
be·hav·ior
be·hav·ior·ism
be·hav·ior·ist
be·head
be·he·moth
be·hest
be·hind
be·hold
be·held
he·hold·ing
be·hold·en
be·hoove
beige
be·ing
be·la·bor
be·lat·ed
be·lat·ed·ly
be·lay
be·layed
be·lay·ing
belch
be·lea·guer
bel·fry
bel·fries
be·lie
be·lied
be·ly·ing
be·lief
be·lieve
be·lieved
be·liev·ing
be·liev·a·ble
be·liev·er
be·lit·tle
be·lit·tled
be·lit·tling
bel·la·don·na
belles let·tres
bel·li·cose
bel·li·cos·i·ty
bel·lig·er·ence
bel·lig·er·en·cy
bel·lig·er·ent
bel·lig·er·ent·ly
bel·low
bel·ly
bel·lies
bel·lied
bel·ly·ing
bel·ly·ache
bel·ly·ach·ing
be·long
be·long·ings

be·loved
be·low
belt·ed
be·mire
be·mired
be·mir·ing
be·moan
be·muse
be·mused
be·mus·ing
bend
bent
bend·ing
be·neath
ben·e·dict
ben·e·dic·tion
ben·e·dic·to·ry
ben·e·fac·tion
ben·e·fac·tor
ben·e·fac·tress
ben·e·fice
ben·e·ficed
ben·e·fic·ing
be·nef·i·cent
be·nef·i·cence
ben·e·fi·cial
ben·e·fi·ci·a·ry
ben·e·fi·ci·a·ries
ben·e·fit
ben·e·fit·ed
ben·e·fit·ing
be·nev·o·lence
be·nev·o·lent
be·night·ed
be·nign
be·nign·ly
be·nig·nant
be·nig·nan·cy
be·numb
ben·zene
ben·zine
be·queath
be·quest
be·rate
be·rat·ed
be·rat·ing
be·reave
be·reaved
be·reft
be·reav·ing
be·ret
ber·ga·mot
ber·i·beri
ber·ke·li·um
ber·ret·ta
bir·ret·ta
berry
ber·ries
ber·serk
berth
ber·yl
be·ryl·li·um
be·seech
be·sought
be·seeched
be·seech·ing
be·set
be·set·ting
be·side
be·siege
be·sieged
be·sieg·ing
be·sieg·er
be·smear
be·smirch
be·sot·ted
be·speak
be·spoke

be·spok·en
be·speak·ing
bes·tial
bes·tial·ly
bes·ti·al·i·ty
be·stir
be·stirred
be·stir·ring
be·stow
be·stow·al
be·stride
be·strode
be·strid·den
be·strid·ing
bet
bet·ted
bet·ting
bet·tor
be·take
be·took
be·tak·en
be·tak·ing
be·ta·tron
be·tel
beth·el
be·tide
be·tid·ed
be·tid·ing
be·to·ken
be·tray
be·tray·al
be·tray·er
be·troth
be·troth·al
be·trothed
bet·ter
bet·ter·ment
bet·tor
be·tween
be·twixt
bev·el
bev·eled
bev·el·ing
bev·er·age
bevy
bev·ies
be·wail
be·ware
be·wil·der
be·wil·der·ing·ly
be·wil·der·ment
be·witch
be·witch·ing
be·witch·ment
be·yond
bi·an·nu·al
bi·as
bi·ased
bi·as·ing
bi·ax·i·al
bi·be·lot
Bi·ble
Bib·li·cal
bib·li·og·ra·phy
bib·li·og·ra·phies
bib·li·og·ra·pher
bib·li·o·graph·ic
bib·li·o·ma·nia
bib·li·o·ma·ni·ac
bib·li·o·phile
bib·u·lous
bi·cam·er·al
bi·car·bo·nate
bi·cen·ten·ni·al
bi·cen·te·nary
bi·ceps
bi·chlo·ride
bick·er

bi·cus·pid
bi·cy·cle
bi·cy·cled
bi·cy·cling
bi·cy·cler
bi·cy·clist
bid
bade
bid·den
bid·ding
bid·da·ble
bid·der
bide
bode
bid·ed
bid·ing
bi·en·ni·al
bi·en·ni·al·ly
bi·en·ni·um
bier
bi·fo·cals
bi·fur·cate
bi·fur·ca·tion
big
big·ger
big·gest
big·a·my
big·a·mist
big·a·mous
big-heart·ed
big·ot
big·ot·ed
big·ot·ry
bi·jou
bi·ki·ni
bi·la·bi·al
bi·lat·er·al
bilge
bi·lin·gual
bil·ious
billed
bill·ing
bil·let
bil·let-doux
bil·liards
bil·lion
bil·lionth
bil·lion·aire
bil·low
bil·low·y
bi·met·al·lism
bi·month·ly
bi·na·ry
bind
bound
bind·ing
bind·er
bind·ery
binge
bin·go
bin·na·cle
bi·noc·u·lar
bi·no·mi·al
bi·o·chem·is·try
bi·o·chem·i·cal
bi·o·chem·ist
bio·de·grad·able
bi·o·e·col·o·gy
bi·o·en·gi·neer·ing
bi·o·gen·e·sis
bi·og·ra·phy
bi·og·ra·pher
bi·o·graph·ic
bi·o·graph·i·cal
bi·ol·o·gy
bi·o·log·i·cal
bi·ol·o·gist
bi·om·e·try

bi·o·met·rics
bi·on·ics
bi·o·nom·ics
bi·o·phys·ics
bi·op·sy
bi·op·sies
bi·par·ti·san
bi·par·tite
bi·ped
bi·plane
bi·po·lar
bi·ra·cial
birch
bird·brained
bird·ie
bird's-eye
bi·ret·ta
be·ret·ta
birth·day
birth·mark
birth·place
birth·stone
bis·cuit
bi·sect
bi·sec·tion
bi·sec·tor
bi·sex·u·al
bish·op
bish·op·ric
bis·muth
bi·son
bisque
bis·tro
bitch
bit·chy
bite
bit
bit·ten
bit·ing
bit·ter
bit·ter·ly
bit·ter·ness
bit·tern
bi·tu·men
bi·tu·mi·nous
bi·va·lent
bi·va·lence
bi·valve
bi·val·vu·lar
biv·ou·ac
biv·ou·acked
biv·ou·ack·ing
bi·week·ly
bi·zarre
bi·zarre·ness
blab
blabbed
blab·bing
black·ball
black·ber·ry
black·bird
black·board
black·en
black·eyed
black·guard
black·head
black·jack
black·ly
black·mail
black·out
black·top
blad·der
blade
blad·ed
blame
blamed
blam·ing
blam·a·ble

blame·less
blame·wor·thy
blanch
blanc·mange
bland
bland·ly
bland·ness
blan·dish
blan·dish·ment
blank
blank·ly
blan·ket
blare
blared
blar·ing
blar·ney
bla·se
blas·pheme
blas·phemed
blas·phem·ing
blas·phem·er
blas·phem·ous
blas·phe·my
blas·phem·ies
blast·ed
bla·tant
bla·tan·cy
bla·tant·ly
blaze
blazed
blaz·ing
bleach·er
bleak
bleak·ly
bleary
blear·i·ness
bleed
bled
bleed·ing
blem·ish
blend·er
bless·ed
blest
bles·sing
blind
blind·ing
blind·ness
blind·er
blink·er
bliss·ful
blis·ter
blithe·ly
blitz·krieg
bliz·zard
block·ade
block·ad·ed
block·ad·ing
block·bus·ter
blond·ness
blood·curd·ling
blood·hound
blood·less
blood·shed
blood·shot
blood·stained
blood·suck·er
blood·thirsty
bloody
blood·i·est
blood·ied
blood·y·ing
bloom
bloom·ing
bloop·er
blos·som
blot
blot·ted
blot·ting

blotch
blotchy
blot·ter
blow
blew
blown
blow·ing
blow·er
blow·torch
blub·ber
bludg·eon
blue
blu·est
blu·ing
blue·ness
blue·bell
blue·ber·ry
blue·bird
blue·blood·ed
blue-col·lar
blue·print
blun·der
blun·der·ing
blun·der·buss
blunt·ly
blunt·ness
blur
blurred
blur·ring
blur·ry
blush
blushed
blush·ing
blus·ter
blus·ter·ing·ly
blus·ter·ous
blus·tery
boar
board·er
board·walk
boast
boast·fulness
boast·ing·ly
boat·house
boat·swain
bob
bobbed
bob·bing
bob·bin
bob·ble
bob·bled
bob·bling
bob·o·link
bob·sled
bob·white
bode
bod·ed
bod·ing
bod·ice
bod·kin
bod·y
bod·ies
bod·i·ly
bod·y·guard
bog
bog·gy
bo·gey
bog·gle
bog·gled
bog·gling
bo·gus
bogy
bo·he·mi·an
boil·er
bois·ter·ous
bois·ter·ous·ness
bold
bold·ly

bold·face	bor·dered	boy·hood	bread·win·ner	brought
bo·le·ro	bor·der·land	boy·ish	break	bring·ing
boll·worm	bor·der·line	boy·cott	broke	brink
bo·lo	bore	boy·friend	bro·ken	bri·quette
bo·lo·gna	bored	boy·sen·ber·ry	break·ing	briquet
bo·lo·ney	bor·ing	brace	break·a·ble	brisk
Bol·she·vik	bor·er	braced	break·age	brisk·ly
Bol·she·vism	bore·dom	brac·ing	break·down	brisk·ness
bol·ster	bor·ough	brace·let	break·er	bris·ket
bol·ster·er	bor·row	brac·er	break·fast	bris·tle
bolt	bor·row·er	bra·ces	break·neck	bris·tled
bolt·ed	borsch	brack·et	break·out	Brit·ain
bom·bard	borscht	brack·ish	break·through	Bri·tan·nia
bom·bard·ment	bos·om	brad	break·wa·ter	Brit·ish
bom·bar·dier	bossy	brad·ded	breast·bone	Brit·on
bom·bast	boss·i·est	brad·ding	breath	Brit·ta·ny
bom·bas·tic	boss·i·ness	brag	breathe	britch·es
bom·bas·ti·cal·ly	bo·sun	bragged	breathed	brit·tle
bomb·er	bot·a·ny	brag·ging	breath·ing	broach
bomb·proof	bo·tan·i·cal	brag·ga·do·cio	breath·less	broached
bomb·shell	bot·a·nist	brag·gart	breath·tak·ing	broach·ing
bomb·sight	bot·a·nize	Brah·ma	breathy	broad·cast
bo·na fide	botch	Brah·min	breech·es	broad·cast·ed
bo·nan·za	botchy	Brah·man	breech·load·er	broad·cast·ing
bon·bon	botch·i·est	braid	breed	broad·cloth
bond·age	both·er	braid·ing	bred	broad·mind·ed
bond·ed	both·er·some	braille	breed·ing	broad·side
bond·man	bot·tle	brain·child	breeze	bro·cade
bone	bot·tled	brain·less	breezy	bro·cad·ed
boned	bot·tling	brain·pow·er	breez·i·ness	bro·cad·ing
bon·ing	bot·tle·ful	brain·storm	breth·ren	broc·co·li
bone·head	bot·tle·neck	brain·wash·ing	bre·vct	bro·chure
bon·fire	bot·tom	brainy	bre·vet·ted	broque
bon·go	bot·tom·less	brain·i·er	bre·vet·ting	broil·er
bon·ho·mie	bot·u·lism	brain·i·est	bre·vi·a·ry	bro·ken
bon·net	bou·doir	braise	bre·vi·a·ries	bro·ken-heart·ed
bon·ny	bouf·fant	braised	brev·i·ty	bro·ker
bo·nus	bough	brais·ing	brew·ery	bro·ker·age
bo·nus·es	bought	brake	brew·er·ies	bro·mide
bon voy·age	bouil·lon	brak·ing	bri·ar	bron·chi
bony	boul·der	bram·ble	bribe	bron·chi·al
bon·i·er	boul·e·vard	bram·bly	bribed	bron·chi·tis
boo·by	bounce	branch	brib·ing	bron·co
boo·bies	bounced	branch·ed	brib·a·ble	bron·to·sau·rus
boo·by trap	bounc·ing	brand	brib·ery	bronze
boo·dle	bound	brand·er	brib·er·ies	bronzed
book·bind·er	bound·a·ry	bran·dish	bric·a·brac	bronz·ing
book·case	bound·a·ries	bran·dy	brick·lay·er	brooch
book·end	bound·less	bran·dies	brick·yard	brood
book·ie	boun·te·ous	bran·died	bride	brood·ing
book·ish	boun·ti·ful	bra·sier	brid·al	broth·el
book·keep·ing	boun·ty	bras·siere	bride·groom	broth·er
book·keep·er	boun·ties	brassy	brides·maid	broth·er·hood
book·let	bou·quet	brass·i·er	bridge	broth·er-in-law
book·mark	bour·bon	brat	bridge·work	broth·er·ly
book·mo·bile	bour·geois	brat·tish	bri·dle	broth·er·li·ness
book·plate	bour·geoi·sie	brat·ty	bri·dled	brow·beat
book·sell·er	bou·tique	bra·va·do	bri·dling	brow·beat·en
book·shelf	bou·ton·niere	brave	brief	brown
book·worm	bo·vine	braved	brief·ly	brown·ie
boom·er·ang	bow·el	brav·ing	brief·ing	browse
boon·dog·gle	bow·er	brave·ness	bri·er	browsed
boor	bow·ery	brav·ery	bri·gade	brows·ing
boor·ish	bow·ie	brav·er·ies	brig·a·dier	bru·in
boost	bow·ing	bra·vo	brig·and	bruise
boost·er	bow·knot	bra·vu·ra	brig·an·tine	bruised
booth	bowl	brawl	bright	bruis·ing
boot·leg	bow·leg	brawl·er	bright·ness	bruis·er
boot·legged	bow·leg·ged	brawn	bright·en	bru·net
boot·leg·ging	bowl·er	brawny	bril·liance	brush-off
boot·leg·ger	bow·line	brawn·i·er	bril·lian·cy	brusque
boot·ty	bowl·ing	brawn·i·ness	bril·liant	brusk
booze	bow·string	braze	brim·ful	bru·tal
booz·er	box·car	bra·zen	brim·ming	bru·tal·i·ty
boozy	box·er	bra·zier	brim·stone	bru·tal·ize
bo·rax	box·ful	breach	brine	bru·tal·ized
Bor·deaux	box·ing	bread	briny	bru·tal·iz·ing
bor·der	boy	bread·ed	bring	bru·tal·i·za·tion

brut·ish
bub·ble
  bub·bled
  bub·bling
bu·bon·ic
buc·ca·neer
buck·a·roo
buck·board
buck·et·ful
buck·le
buck·ram
buck·skin
buck·tooth
buck·wheat
bu·col·ic
bud
  bud·ded
  bud·ding
Bud·dha
  Bud·dhism
  Bud·dhist
bud·dy
budge
budg·et
buf·fa·lo
buf·fa·loed
buff·er
buf·fet
buf·foon
  buf·foon·ery
bug
  bugged
  bug·ging
bug·a·boo
bug·gy
bu·gle
  bu·gling
  bu·gler
build
  built
  build·ing
bulb
  bul·bous
bulge
  bulged
  bulg·ing
  bulgy
bulk·head
bulky
  bulk·i·er
  bulk·i·ness
bull·doze
  bull·dozed
  bull·doz·ing
  bull·doz·er
bul·let
bul·le·tin
bul·let·proof
bull·fight
bull·frog
bull·head·ed
bul·lion
bull·ock
bull's-eye
bul·ly
  bul·lies
  bul·lied
  bul·ly·ing
bul·rush
bul·wark
bum
  bummed
  bum·ming
bum·ble·bee
bump·er
bump·kin
bump·tious
bumpy

bump·i·est
bump·i·ness
bunch
  bunchy
bun·co
bun·dle
  bun·dled
  bun·dling
bun·ga·low
bun·gle
  bun·gled
  bun·gling
bun·ion
bunk·er
bun·ny
  bun·nies
Bun·sen burner
bun·ting
bu·oy
buoy·ant
  buoy·an·cy
bur·den
  bur·den·some
bu·reau
  bu·reaus
  bu·reaux
bu·reauc·ra·cy
  bu·reauc·ra·cies
  bu·reau·crat
  bu·reau·crat·ic
bur·geon
bur·gess
bur·gher
bur·glar
  bur·glar·ize
  bur·glar·ized
  bur·glar·iz·ing
  bur·gla·ry
  bur·gla·ries
bur·gle
  bur·gled
  bur·gling
Bur·gun·dy
bur·i·al
bur·lap
bur·lesque
  bur·lesqued
  bur·les·quing
bur·ly
  bur·li·ness
burn
  burned
  burnt
  burn·ing
burn·er
bur·nish
bur·noose
burr
  burred
  bur·ring
bur·ro
bur·row
bur·sa
bur·sar
bur·sa·ry
bur·si·tis
burst
  burst·ing
bury
  bur·ied
  bur·y·ing
bus
  bus·es
bush·el
Bu·shi·do
bush·ing
bush·man
bush·mas·ter

bush·whack
bushy
bus·i·ly
busi·ness
busi·ness·like
busi·ness·man
bus·tle
  bus·tled
  bus·tling
busy
  bus·ied
  bus·y·ing
  bus·i·ly
  bus·i·er
bu·tane
butch·er
butch·ery
but·ler
butt
butte
but·ter
but·ter·fin·gered
but·ter·fly
  but·ter·flies
but·ter·scotch
but·tery
but·tock
but·ton·hole
  but·ton·hol·ing
but·tress
bux·om
buy
  bought
  buy·ing
buy·er
buz·zard
buzz·er
by·law
by·line
by·pass
by·play
by·prod·uct
by·stand·er
byte
by·way
by·word
Byz·an·tine

C

ca·bal
  ca·ball·ed
  ca·ball·ing
ca·bal·le·ro
ca·ba·na
cab·a·ret
cab·bage
cab·in
cab·i·net
ca·ble
  ca·bled
  ca·bling
ca·ble·gram
ca·boose
cab·ri·o·let
ca·cao
cache
  cached
  cach·ing
ca·chet
cack·le
  cack·led
  cack·ling
ca·coph·o·ny
  ca·coph·o·nous
cac·tus
  cac·ti

cad
  cad·dish
ca·dav·er
  ca·dav·er·ous
cad·die
  cad·died
  cad·dy·ing
cad·dy
ca·dence
ca·den·za
ca·det
cadge
  cadged
  cadg·ing
cad·mi·um
ca·dre
ca·du·ce·us
Cae·sar
cae·sar·e·an
  ces·ar·ean
ca·fe au lait
caf·e·te·ria
caf·feine
caf·tan
cage
  caged
  cag·ing
cagey
  ca·gi·ly
cai·man
cais·son
ca·jole
  ca·joled
  ca·jol·ing
Ca·jun
cake
  caked
  cak·ing
cal·a·bash
cal·a·boose
cal·a·mine
ca·lam·i·ty
  ca·lam·i·ties
  ca·lam·i·tous
cal·ci·fy
  cal·ci·fied
  cal·ci·fy·ing
  cal·ci·fi·ca·tion
cal·ci·mine
cal·ci·um
cal·cu·la·ble
  cal·cu·la·bil·i·ty
cal·cu·late
  cal·cu·lat·ed
  cal·cu·lat·ing
  cal·cu·la·tion
  cal·cu·la·tor
cal·cu·lus
cal·dron
cal·en·dar
calf
  calves
cal·i·ber
cal·i·brate
  cal·i·brat·ed
  cal·i·brat·ing
  cal·i·bra·tion
cal·i·co
  cal·i·coes
cal·i·per
ca·liph
cal·is·then·ics
cal·lig·ra·phy
  cal·lig·ra·pher
call·ing
cal·li·o·pe
cal·lous
  cal·loused

cal·low
cal·lus
calm·ly
ca·lor·ic
cal·o·rie
  cal·o·ries
cal·um·ny
  cal·um·nies
cal·lum·ni·ate
  ca·lum·ni·at·ed
  ca·lum·ni·at·ing
  ca·lum·ni·a·tion
Cal·va·ry
calve
  calved
  calv·ing
ca·lyp·so
ca·ma·ra·de·rie
cam·ber
cam·bric
cam·el
ca·mel·lia
Cam·em·bert
cam·eo
cam·era
cam·i·sole
cam·ou·flage
  cam·ou·flaged
  cam·ou·flag·ing
cam·paign
camp·er
cam·phor
cam·pus
  cam·pus·es
cam·shaft
can
  canned
  can·ning
Can·a·da
  Ca·na·di·an
ca·nal
can·a·pe
ca·nary
ca·nas·ta
can·can
can·cel
  can·celed
  can·cel·ing
  can·cel·la·tion
can·cer
can·de·la·brum
  can·de·la·bra
can·des·cent
  can·des·cence
can·did
can·di·da·cy
  can·di·da·cies
can·di·date
can·died
can·dle
  can·dled
  can·dling
can·dor
can·dy
  can·dies
  can·died
cane
  caned
  can·ing
ca·nine
can·is·ter
can·ker
canned
can·nery
  can·ner·ies
can·ni·bal
  can·ni·bal·ism
  can·ni·bal·ize

can·ni·bal·iz·ing
can·non
can·ny
can·ni·ly
can·ni·ness
ca·noe
ca·noed
ca·noe·ing
ca·noe·ist
can·on
can·on·ize
can·on·iz·ing
can·on·i·za·tion
can·o·py
can·o·pies
can·o·pied
can·o·py·ing
can·ta·loupe
can·ta·lope
can·tan·ker·ous
can·ta·ta
can·teen
can·ter
can·ti·lev·er
can·to
can·tor
can·vas
can·vass
can·yon
cap
capped
cap·ping
ca·pa·bil·i·ty
ca·pa·bil·i·ties
ca·pa·ble
ca·pa·bly
ca·pa·cious
ca·pac·i·tate
ca·pac·i·tat·ed
ca·pac·i·tat·ing
ca·pac·i·ty
ca·pac·i·ties
ca·per
cap·il·lar·i·ty
cap·il·lary
cap·il·lar·ies
cap·i·tal
cap·i·tal·ism
cap·i·tal·is·tic
cap·i·tal·ist
cap·i·tal·ize
cap·i·tal·i·za·tion
cap·i·tal·ly
cap·i·ta·tion
ca·pit·u·late
ca·pit·u·lat·ed
ca·pit·u·lat·ing
ca·pit·u·la·tion
ca·pon
ca·pric·cio
ca·price
ca·pri·cious
cap·ri·ole
cap·ri·oled
cap·ri·ol·ing
cap·size
cap·siz·ing
cap·stan
cap·sule
cap·su·lar
cap·tain
cap·tain·cy
cap·tion
cap·tious
cap·ti·vate
cap·ti·vat·ed
cap·ti·vat·ing
cap·ti·va·tion

cap·tive
cap·tiv·i·ty
cap·tor
cap·ture
cap·tured
cap·tur·ing
car·a·cole
car·a·cul
ca·rafe
car·a·mel
car·at
car·a·van
car·a·way
car·bide
car·bine
car·bohy·drate
car·bol·ic
car·bon
car·bo·na·ceous
car·bo·na·tion
car·bon di·ox·ide
car·bon·ize
car·bon·ized
car·bon·iz·ing
car·bon·i·za·tion
car·bon mon·ox·ide
car·bo·run·dum
car·boy
car·buncle
car·bu·re·tor
car·cass
car·cin·o·gen
car·cin·o·gen·ic
car·ci·no·ma
car·da·mom
card·board
car·di·ac
car·di·gan
car·di·nal
car·di·o·graph
car·di·og·ra·phy
car·dio·vas·cu·lar
card·sharp
care
cared
caring
ca·reen
ca·reer
care·free
care·ful
care·ful·ly
care·less
care·less·ness
ca·ress
ca·ress·ing·ly
car·et
care·tak·er
car·go
Car·ib·be·an
car·i·bou
car·i·ca·ture
car·i·ca·tured
car·i·ca·tur·ing
car·i·ca·tur·ist
car·il·lon
car·mine
car·nage
car·nal
car·nal·i·ty
car·nal·ly
car·na·tion
car·nel·ian
car·ni·val
car·ni·vore
car·niv·o·rous
car·ol
car·oled
car·ol·ing

car·om
ca·rouse
ca·roused
ca·rous·ing
ca·rous·al
car·ou·sel
car·pen·ter
car·pen·try
car·pet
car·pet·bag·ger
car·pet·ing
car·rel
car·riage
car·ri·er
car·ri·on
car·rot
car·roty
car·ry
car·ried
car·ry·ing
cart·age
carte blanche
car·tel
car·te·lize
car·ti·lage
car·ti·lag·i·nous
car·tog·ra·phy
car·tog·ra·pher
car·to·graph·ic
car·ton
car·toon
car·tridge
carve
carved
carv·ing
car·y·at·id
ca·sa·ba
cas·cade
cas·cad·ed
cas·cad·ing
case
cased
cas·ing
case·ment
ca·se·ous
cash·ew
cash·ier
cash·mere
ca·si·no
cas·ket
cas·sa·ba
cas·se·role
cas·sette
cas·sock
cast
cast·ing
cas·ta·net
cast·a·way
caste
cast·er
cast·ing
cas·ti·gate
cas·ti·gat·ed
cas·ti·gat·ing
cas·ti·ga·tion
cast i·ron
cas·tle
cas·tor
cas·trate
cas·trat·ed
cas·trat·ing
cas·tra·tion
cas·u·al
cas·u·al·ness
cas·u·al·ty
cas·u·al·ties
cas·u·ist
cas·u·is·tic

cas·u·ist·ry
cat·a·clysm
cat·a·clys·mal
cat·a·clys·mic
cat·a·comb
cat·a·falque
cat·a·lep·sy
cat·a·lep·tic
cat·a·log
cat·a·logue
cat·a·loged
cat·a·log·ing
ca·tal·y·sis
cat·a·lyt·ic
cat·a·lyst
cat·a·lyze
cat·a·lyz·ing
cat·a·ma·ran
cat·a·pult
cat·a·ract
ca·tarrh
ca·tas·tro·phe
cat·as·troph·ic
Ca·taw·ba
catch
caught
catch·ing
catch·er
catchy
catch·i·er
cat·e·chism
cat·e·chize
cat·e·chized
cat·e·chiz·ing
cat·e·chi·za·tion
cat·e·chist
cat·e·gor·i·cal
cat·e·go·ry
cat·e·go·ries
cat·e·gor·ize
cat·e·gor·iz·ing
ca·ter
ca·ter·er
cat·er·pil·lar
cat·er·waul
cat·fish
ca·thar·sis
ca·thar·tic
ca·the·dral
cath·e·ter
cath·ode
cath·o·lic
cath·o·lic·i·ty
ca·thol·i·cize
Cath·o·lic
Ca·thol·i·cism
cat·nap
cat·nap·ping
cat·nip
cat·tle
cat·tle·man
cat·ty
cat·ti·ness
Cau·ca·sian
cau·cus
cau·cus·es
cau·cus·ing
caul·dron
cau·li·flow·er
caulk
caus·al
cau·sal·i·ty
cause
caused
caus·ing
cau·sa·tion
cause·less
cause·way

caus·tic
cau·ter·ize
cau·ter·ized
cau·ter·iz·ing
cau·ter·i·za·tion
cau·tery
cau·tion
cau·tion·ary
cau·tious
cav·al·cade
cav·a·lier
cav·al·ry
cave
caved
cav·ing
ca·ve·at
cav·ern
cav·ern·ous
cav·i·ar
cav·il
cav·iled
cav·il·ing
cav·i·ty
cav·i·ties
ca·vort
cay·enne
cay·man
cay·use
cease
ceased
ceas·ing
cease·less
cease·fire
ce·dar
cede
ced·ed
ced·ing
ceil·ing
cel·e·brate
cel·e·brat·ing
cel·e·bra·tion
cel·e·brant
cel·e·bra·tor
ce·leb·ri·ty
ce·leb·ri·ties
ce·ler·i·ty
cel·ery
ce·les·tial
cel·i·ba·cy
cel·i·bate
cel·lar
cel·lo
cel·list
cel·lo·phane
cel·lu·lar
cel·lu·lose
ce·ment
cem·e·tery
cem·e·ter·ies
cen·o·taph
cen·ser
cen·sor
cen·so·ri·al
cen·sor·ship
cen·so·ri·ous
cen·sure
cen·sured
cen·sur·ing
cen·sur·er
cen·sur·a·ble
cen·sus
cen·sus·ing
cen·taur
cen·te·nar·i·an
cen·te·na·ry
cen·te·na·ries
cen·ten·ni·al
cen·tes·i·mal

cen·ter·board
cen·ter·piece
cen·ti·grade
cen·ti·gram
cen·ti·li·ter
cen·ti·me·ter
central
cen·tral·ize
  cen·tral·ized
  cen·tral·iz·ing
cen·tri·fuge
  cen·trif·u·gal
cen·trip·e·tal
cen·tro·bar·ic
cen·tu·ri·on
cen·tu·ry
  cen·tu·ries
ce·ram·ic
  ce·ram·ics
ce·re·al
cer·e·bral
  cer·e·bel·lum
cer·e·bric
  cer·e·brum
cer·e·mo·ny
  cer·e·mo·nies
  cer·e·mo·ni·al
  cer·e·mo·ni·ous
ce·rise
cer·tain
  cer·tain·ly
cer·tain·ty
  cer·tain·ties
cer·tif·i·cate
  cer·ti·fi·ca·tion
cer·ti·fy
  cer·ti·fied
  cer·ti·fy·ing
cer·ti·fi·a·ble
  cer·ti·fi·er
cer·ti·tude
ce·ru·le·an
cer·vix
  cer·vi·cal
ce·sar·ean
  cae·sar·ean
ces·sa·tion
ce·ta·cean
Cha·blis
chafe
  chafed
  chaf·ing
chaff
cha·grin
  cha·grined
  cha·grin·ing
chain
chair·man
  chair·per·son
  chair·wom·an
chaise longue
chal·et
chal·ice
chalk
  chalky
chal·lenge
  chal·lenged
  chal·leng·ing
cham·ber
cham·bray
cha·me·le·on
cham·ois
cham·pagne
cham·pi·on
  cham·pi·on·ship
chance
  chanced
  chanc·ing

chancy
chan·cel·lor
chan·de·lier
change
  changed
  chang·ing
  change·a·ble
  change·ful
  change·less
chan·nel
  chan·nel·ing
chan·teuse
chan·tey
chan·ti·cleer
cha·os
  cha·ot·ic
chap
  chapped
  chap·ping
chap·ar·ral
cha·peau
chap·el
chap·e·ron
chap·lain
chap·ter
char
  charred
  char·ring
char·ac·ter
  char·ac·ter·is·tic
char·ac·ter·ize
  char·ac·ter·ized
  char·ac·ter·iz·ing
  char·ac·ter·i·za·tion
cha·rade
char·coal
charge
  charged
  char·ging
charge d'af·faires
charg·er
char·i·ot
  char·i·ot·eer
cha·ris·ma
char·i·ta·ble
  char·i·ta·bly
char·i·ty
  char·i·ties
char·la·tan
charm
  charm·er
  charm·ing
char·ter
char·treuse
chary
  char·i·er
  char·i·est
chase
  chased
  chas·ing
chasm
chas·sis
chaste
  chaste·ness
  chas·ti·ty
chas·ten
  chas·tise
  chas·tis·ing
  chas·tise·ment
chat
  chat·ted
  chat·ting
cha·teau
chat·tel
chat·ter
chat·ty
  chat·ti·ly
  chat·ti·ness

chauf·feur
chau·vin·ist
  chau·vin·ism
  chau·vin·is·tic
cheap
  cheap·ness
  cheap·en
cheap·skate
cheat
  cheat·er
check·book
check·er·board
check·list
check·mate
check·point
check·room
ched·dar
cheek·bone
cheeky
  cheek·i·ness
cheer·ful
  cheer·ful·ness
  cheer·less
cheery
  cheer·i·er
  cheer·i·ness
cheese
  cheesy
chee·tah
chef
chem·i·cal
  chem·i·cal·ly
che·mise
chem·ist
  chem·is·try
chem·o·ther·a·py
che·nille
cher·ish
cher·ry
  cher·ries
cher·ub
  cher·ubs
  che·ru·bic
chess·man
chest·nut
chesty
  chest·i·er
chev·ron
chew
  chew·er
  chewy
Chi·an·ti
chi·a·ro·scu·ro
chi·can·ery
chi·chi
chick·a·dee
chic·ken
chic·le
chic·o·ry
chide
  chid·ed
  chid·ing
chief
  chief·ly
chief·tain
chif·fon
chif·fo·nier
chig·ger
chi·gnon
Chi·hua·hua
chil·blain
chil·dren
child·bear·ing
child·birth
child·hood
child·ish
child·like
chili

chill
  chill·ing
chilly
  chill·i·er
  chill·i·ness
chime
  chim·ing
chim·ney
chim·pan·zee
chin
  chinned
  chin·ning
chi·na
Chi·na
  Chi·nese
chin·chil·la
chintz
chintzy
chip
  chipped
  chip·ping
chip·munk
Chip·pen·dale
chip·per
chi·rog·ra·phy
  chi·rog·ra·pher
chi·rop·o·dist
chi·ro·prac·tic
  chi·ro·prac·tor
chis·el
  chis·eled
  chis·el·ing
  chis·el·er
chit·chat
chit·ter·ling
chiv·al·ry
  chiv·al·ric
  chiv·al·rous
chlo·rine
chlo·ro·form
chlo·ro·phyll
chock·full
choc·o·late
choice
  choice·ness
choir·boy
choke
  choked
  chok·ing
chok·er
chol·er
chol·era
cho·les·te·rol
choose
  chose
  cho·sen
  choos·ing
choosy
  choos·i·est
chop
  chopped
  chop·ping
chop·per
chop·py
  chop·pi·ness
chop su·ey
cho·ral
  cho·ral·ly
cho·rale
chord
chore
cho·reo·graph
  cho·re·og·ra·phy
  cho·re·og·ra·pher
  cho·re·o·graph·ic
chor·tle
  chor·tled
  chor·tling

cho·rus
cho·rus·es
chor·is·ter
cho·rus·ing
chos·en
chow·der
chow mein
Christ
chris·ten
  chris·ten·ing
Chris·ten·dom
Chris·tian
  Chris·ti·an·i·ty
  Chris·tian·ize
  Chris·tian·ized
Christ·like
Christ·mas
chro·mat·ic
  chro·mat·i·cal·ly
  chro·mat·ics
chrome
  chro·mi·um
chro·mo·lith·o·graph
chron·ic
  chron·i·cal·ly
chron·i·cle
  chron·i·cled
  chron·i·cling
chron·o·log·i·cal
chro·nol·o·gy
  chro·nol·o·gies
chro·nom·e·ter
chrys·a·lis
chry·san·the·mum
chub·by
  chub·bi·ness
chuck·full
chuck·le
  chuck·ling
chuck·ker
chum·my
chunk
  chunky
  chunk·i·est
church
  church·li·ness
church·go·er
church·man
church·war·den
church·yard
churl·ish
  churl·ish·ness
churn·ing
chut·ney
chutz·pah
ci·ca·da
cic·e·ro·ne
ci·der
ci·gar
cig·a·rette
cil·ia
  cil·i·ar·y
cinc·ture
cin·der
cin·e·ma
cin·e·mat·o·graph
  cin·e·ma·tog·ra·pher
cin·e·rar·i·um
cin·na·bar
cin·na·mon
ci·pher
cir·ca
cir·cle
  cir·cled
  cir·cling
cir·clet
cir·cuit
cir·cu·i·tous

cir·cu·lar
cir·cu·lar·ize
  cir·cu·lar·iz·ing
  cir·cu·lar·i·za·tion
cir·cu·la·tion
  cir·cu·late
  cir·cu·lat·ed
  cir·cu·lat·ing
  cir·cu·la·tive
  cir·cu·la·to·ry
cir·cum·am·bi·ent
cir·cum·cise
  circum·cised
  cir·cum·cis·ing
  cir·cum·ci·sion
cir·cum·fer·ence
cir·cum·flex
cir·cum·flu·ent
cir·cum·fuse
cir·cum·lo·cu·tion
  cir·cum·lo·cu·to·ry
cir·cum·nav·i·gate
  cir·cum·nav·i·ga·tion
cir·cum·scribe
  cir·cum·scrip·tion
cir·cum·spect
cir·cum·stance
cir·cum·stan·tial
  cir·cum·stan·ti·ate
  cir·cum·stan·ti·a·tion
cir·cum·vent
  cir·cum·ven·tion
cir·cus
  circus·es
cir·rho·sis
cir·rus
cis·soid
cis·tern
cit·a·del
cite
  cit·ed
  cit·ing
  cit·ta·tion
cit·i·zen
  cit·i·zen·ship
cit·i·zen·ry
  cit·i·zen·ries
cit·re·ous
cit·ron
cit·ron·el·la
cit·rus
city
  cit·ies
civ·ic
civ·ics
civ·il
civ·il·ly
ci·vil·ian
ci·vil·i·ty
  ci·vil·i·ties
civ·i·li·za·tion
civ·i·lize
  civ·i·lized
  civ·i·liz·ing
civ·et
claim
  claim·a·ble
  claim·ant
clair·voy·ance
  clair·voy·ant
clam
  clammed
  clam·ming
clam·my
  clam·mi·ness
clam·or
  clam·or·ous
clamp·er

clan
  clan·nish
clan·des·tine
clang·or
  clang·or·ous
clans·man
clap
  clapped
  clap·ping
clap·board
clap·per
claque
clar·et
clar·i·fy
  clar·i·fied
  clar·i·fy·ing
  clar·i·fi·ca·tion
clar·i·net
  clar·i·net·ist
clar·i·on
clar·i·ty
clas·sic
clas·si·cal
clas·si·cism
  clas·si·cist
clas·si·fy
  clas·si·fied
  clas·si·fy·ing
  clas·si·fi·ca·tion
classy
  class·i·er
clat·ter
clause
  claus·al
claus·tro·pho·bia
clav·i·chord
clav·i·cle
clay·ey
clean·cut
clean·er
clean·ly
  clean·li·ness
cleanse
  cleansed
  cleans·ing
  cleans·er
clear
  clear·ly
  clear·ness
clear·ance
clear·cut
clear·ing
clear·sight·ed
cleav·age
cleave
  cleaved
  cleav·ing
cleav·er
clef
cleft
clem·en·cy
  clem·ent
cler·gy
  cler·gies
cler·gy·man
cler·ic
  cler·i·cal
cler·i·cal·ism
clev·er
  clev·er·ness
clev·is
clew
cli·ché
cli·ent
cli·en·tele
cli·mac·ter·ic
cli·mate
  cli·mat·ic

cli·mat·i·cal
cli·max
  cli·mac·tic
climb
  climb·er
clinch·er
cling
  clung
  cling·ing
clin·ic
  clin·i·cal
clink·er
clin·quant
clip
  clipped
  clip·ping
clip·per
clique
  cliqu·ish
clit·o·ris
clo·a·ca
clob·ber
clock·wise
clod
  clod·dish
clog
  clogged
  clog·ging
cloi·son·ne
clois·ter
  clois·tral
close
  closed
  clos·ing
  clos·est
  close·ly
  close·ness
clos·et
  clos·et·ed
  clos·et·ing
close·up
clo·sure
clot
  clot·ted
  clot·ting
clothe
  clothed
  cloth·ing
cloth·ier
cloth·ing
clo·ture
cloud·burst
cloudy
  cloud·i·ness
clo·ven
clo·ver
clown
  clown·ish
cloy
  cloy·ing·ly
club
  clubbed
  club·bing
club·foot
club·house
clue
clump
clum·sy
  clum·si·ly
  clum·si·ness
clus·ter
clut·ter
coach·man
co·ag·u·late
  co·ag·u·lat·ed
  co·ag·u·lat·ing
  co·ag·u·la·tion
co·a·lesce

co·a·lesced
co·a·les·cing
co·a·les·cence
co·a·les·cent
co·a·li·tion
coarse
  coars·en
  coarse·ness
coast·er
coast·guard
coast·line
coat·ing
co·au·thor
coax
  coax·ing·ly
co·balt
cob·ble
  cob·bler
cob·ble·stone
co·bra
cob·web
co·ca
co·caine
coc·cyx
cock·ade
cock·a·too
cock·er·al
cock·le
  cock·le·bur
cock·le·shell
cock·ney
cock·roach
cock·tail
cocky
  cock·i·ly
  cock·i·ness
co·coa
co·co·nut
co·coon
cod·dle
  cod·dled
  cod·dling
code
  cod·ed
  cod·ing
co·deine
codg·er
cod·i·cil
cod·i·fy
  cod·i·fied
  cod·i·fy·ing
  cod·i·fi·ca·tion
co·ed
co·ed·u·ca·tion
co·ef·fi·cient
co·e·qual
co·erce
  co·erced
  co·erc·ing
  co·er·cion
  co·er·cive
co·ex·ist
  co·ex·ist·ence
co·ex·tend
cof·fee
cof·fer
cof·fin
co·gent
  co·gen·cy
  co·gent·ly
cog·i·tate
  cog·i·tat·ed
  cog·i·tat·ing
  cog·i·ta·tive
cog·nac
cog·nate
  cog·nat·tion
cog·ni·tion

cog·ni·tive
cog·ni·zance
cog·ni·zant
co·hab·it
  co·hab·i·ta·tion
co·here
  co·hered
  co·her·ing
  co·her·ent
  co·her·ence
  co·her·en·cy
  co·her·ent·ly
co·he·sion
  co·he·sive
  co·he·sive·ness
co·hort
coif
coif·feur
coif·fure
coin·age
co·in·cide
  co·in·cid·ed
  co·in·cid·ing
  co·in·ci·dence
  co·in·ci·dent
  co·in·ci·den·tal
co·i·tion
  co·i·tus
col·an·der
cold
  cold·ly
  cold·ness
cold·blood·ed
cole·slaw
col·ic
  col·icky
col·i·se·um
co·li·tis
col·lab·o·rate
  col·lab·o·rat·ed
  col·lab·o·rat·ing
  col·lab·o·ra·tion
  col·lab·o·ra·tor
col·lage
col·lapse
  col·lapsed
  col·laps·ing
  col·lap·si·ble
col·lar
col·late
  col·lat·ed
  col·lat·ing
  col·la·tion
col·lat·er·al
col·league
col·lect
  col·lect·ed
  col·lect·i·ble
  col·lect·or
  col·lec·tion
col·lec·tive
  col·lec·tiv·i·ty
  col·lec·tiv·ism
  col·lec·tiv·ize
  col·lec·tiv·i·za·tion
col·lege
col·le·gian
col·le·giate
col·lide
  col·lid·ed
  col·lid·ing
  col·li·sion
col·lie
col·li·mate
col·lin·e·ar
col·lo·cate
col·loid
col·lo·qui·al

col·lo·qui·al·ly
col·lo·qui·al·ism
col·lo·quy
col·lu·sion
col·lu·sive
col·logne
co·lon
colo·nel
co·lo·ni·al
co·lo·ni·al·ism
co·lo·ni·al·ist
col·on·nade
col·o·ny
col·o·nist
col·o·nies
col·o·nize
col·o·niz·ing
col·o·ni·za·tion
col·or
col·or·ful
col·or·ing
col·or·a·tion
col·or·blind
col·or·less
co·los·sal
Col·os·se·um
co·los·sus
Co·lum·bia
col·um·bine
col·umn
co·lum·nar
col·um·nist
co·ma
co·ma·tose
com·bat
com·bat·ed
com·bat·ing
com·bat·ant
com·bat·ive
comb·er
com·bi·na·tion
com·bi·na·tive
com·bine
com·bined
com·bin·ing
com·bus·ti·ble
com·bus·tion
com·bus·tive
come
came
come
coming
co·me·di·an
co·me·di·enne
com·e·dy
com·e·dies
come·ly
come·li·ness
com·et
come·up·pance
com·fort
com·fort·a·ble
com·fort·er
com·ic
com·i·cal
com·ma
com·mand
com·man·dant
com·man·deer
com·mand·er
com·mand·ment
com·man·do
com·mem·o·rate
com·mem·o·rat·ed
com·mem·o·rat·ing
com·mem·o·ra·tion
com·mem·o·ra·tive
com·mence

com·menc·ing
com·mence·ment
com·mend
com·mend·a·ble
com·men·da·tion
com·men·su·rate
com·men·su·ra·tion
com·ment
com·men·tary
com·men·ta·ries
com·men·ta·tor
com·merce
com·mer·cial
com·mer·cial·ism
com·mer·cial·ize
com·mer·cial·i·za·tion
com·mis·er·ate
com·mis·er·at·ed
com·mis·er·at·ing
com·mis·er·a·tion
com·mis·sar
com·mis·sary
com·mis·sa·ries
com·mis·sion
com·mis·sioned
com·mis·sion·er
com·mit
com·mit·ted
com·mit·ting
com·mit·ment
com·mit·tee
com·mode
com·mo·di·ous
com·mod·i·ty
com·mod·i·ties
com·mo·dore
com·mon
com·mon·al·ty
com·mon·place
com·mons
com·mon·weal
com·mon·wealth
com·mo·tion
com·mu·nal
com·mune
com·muned
com·mun·ing
com·mu·ni·cant
com·mu·ni·cate
com·mu·ni·cat·ed
com·mu·ni·cat·ing
com·mu·ni·ca·ble
com·mu·ni·ca·tive
com·mu·ni·ca·tion
com·mun·ion
com·mu·ni·qué
com·mu·nism
com·mu·nist
com·mu·nis·tic
com·mu·ni·ty
com·mu·ni·ties
com·mu·nize
com·mu·niz·ing
com·mu·ta·tion
com·mute
com·mut·ed
com·mut·ing
com·mut·a·ble
com·mut·er
com·pact
com·pac·tor
com·pan·ion
com·pan·ion·a·ble
com·pan·ion·ship
com·pa·ny
com·pa·nies
com·pa·ra·ble
com·pa·ra·bil·i·ty

com·par·a·tive
com·pare
com·pared
com·par·ing
com·par·i·son
com·part·ment
com·part·ment·ed
com·part·men·tal·ize
com·pass
com·pas·sion
com·pas·sion·ate
com·pat·i·ble
com·pat·i·bly
com·pat·i·bil·i·ty
com·pa·tri·ot
com·peer
com·pel
com·pelled
com·pel·ling
com·pen·di·um
com·pen·sate
com·pen·sat·ing
com·pen·sa·tive
com·pen·sa·to·ry
com·pen·sa·tion
com·pete
com·pet·ed
com·pet·ing
com·pet·i·tor
com·pe·ti·tion
com·pet·i·tive
com·pe·tent
com·pe·tence
com·pe·ten·cy
com·pile
com·piled
com·pil·ing
com·pi·la·tion
com·pla·cent
com·pla·cence
com·pla·cen·cy
com·plain
com·plain·ant
com·plaint
com·plai·sance
com·plai·sant
com·plect·ed
com·ple·ment
com·ple·men·ta·ry
com·plete
com·plet·ed
com·plet·ing
com·ple·tion
com·plex
com·plex·i·ty
com·plex·ion
com·pli·ance
com·pli·an·cy
com·pli·ant
com·pli·cate
com·pli·cat·ed
com·pli·cat·ing
com·pli·ca·tion
com·plic·i·ty
com·plic·i·ties
com·pli·ment
com·pli·men·ta·ry
com·pli·men·ta·ri·ly
com·ply
com·plied
com·ply·ing
com·po·nent
com·port
com·port·ment
com·pose
com·posed
com·pos·ing
com·pos·er

com·pos·ite
com·po·si·tion
com·post
com·po·sure
com·pote
com·pound
com·pre·hend
com·pre·hen·si·ble
com·pre·hen·si·bil·i·ty
com·pre·hen·sion
com·pre·hen·sive
com·press
com·press·ing
com·press·i·ble
com·pres·sion
com·pres·sor
com·prise
com·prised
com·pris·ing
com·pro·mise
com·pro·mised
com·pro·mis·ing
comp·trol·ler
com·pul·sion
com·pul·sive
com·pul·so·ry
com·punc·tion
com·pute
com·put·ed
com·put·ing
com·pu·ta·tion
com·put·er
com·put·er·ize
com·put·er·iz·ing
com·put·er·i·za·tion
com·rade
con
conned
con·ning
con·cave
con·cav·i·ty
con·ceal
con·ceal·ment
con·cede
con·ced·ed
con·ced·ing
con·ceit
con·ceit·ed
con·ceive
con·ceived
con·ceiv·ing
con·ceiv·a·ble
con·ceiv·a·bly
con·cen·trate
con·cen·trat·ed
con·cen·trat·ing
con·cen·tra·tion
con·cen·tric
con·cen·tri·cal
con·cept
con·cep·tu·al
con·cep·tion
con·cep·tu·al·ize
con·cep·tu·al·i·za·tion
con·cern
con·cerned
con·cern·ment
con·cert
con·cert·ed
con·cer·ti·na
con·cer·to
con·ces·sion
con·ces·sion·aire
conch
con·cierge
con·cil·i·ate
con·cil·i·at·ed
con·cil·i·at·ing

con·cil·i·a·tion
con·cil·i·a·to·ry
con·cise
con·cise·ness
con·cise·ly
con·clave
con·clude
con·clud·ed
con·clud·ing
con·clu·sion
con·clu·sive
con·coct
con·coc·tion
con·com·i·tant
con·cord
con·cord·ance
con·cord·ant
con·course
con·crete
con·cret·ed
con·cret·ing
con·cre·tion
con·cu·bine
con·cu·pis·cent
con·cur
con·curred
con·cur·ring
con·cur·rence
con·cur·rent
con·cus·sion
con·cus·sive
con·demn
con·dem·na·ble
con·dem·na·tion
con·dense
con·densed
con·dens·ing
con·den·sa·tion
con·dens·er
con·de·scend
con·de·scend·ing
con·de·scen·sion
con·di·ment
con·di·tion
con·di·tion·al
con·di·tion·er
con·di·tioned
con·dole
con·doled
con·dol·ing
con·do·lence
con·do·min·i·um
con·done
con·doned
con·don·ing
con·do·na·tion
con·dor
con·duce
con·duced
con·duc·ing
con·du·cive
con·duct
con·duct·ance
con·duc·tion
con·duc·tor
con·duit
con·fer·ence
con·fess
con·fess·ed
con·fes·sion
con·fes·sion·al
con·fes·sor
con·fet·ti
con·fi·dant
con·fi·dante
con·fide
con·fid·ed
con·fid·ing

con·fi·dence
con·fi·dent
con·fi·den·tial
con·fig·u·ra·tion
con·fine
con·fined
con·fin·ing
con·fine·ment
con·firm
con·firmed
con·fir·ma·tion
con·firm·a·tive
con·firm·a·to·ry
con·fis·cate
con·fis·cat·ed
con·fis·cat·ing
con·fis·ca·tion
con·fis·ca·tor
con·fis·ca·to·ry
con·fla·gra·tion
con·flict
con·flict·ing
con·flic·tion
con·flu·ence
con·flu·ent
con·flux
con·form
con·form·ist
con·form·a·ble
con·form·ance
con·for·ma·tion
con·form·i·ty
con·found
con·found·ed
con·front
con·fron·ta·tion
Con·fu·cius
con·fuse
con·fused
con·fus·ing
con·fu·sion
con·fute
con·fut·ed
con·fut·ing
con·fu·ta·tion
con·ga
con·geal
con·geal·ment
con·gen·ial
con·ge·ni·al·i·ty
con·gen·ial·ly
con·gen·i·tal
con·gest
con·ges·tion
con·ges·tive
con·glom·er·ate
con·glom·er·at·ed
con·glom·er·at·ing
con·glom·er·a·tion
con·grat·u·late
con·grat·u·lat·ed
con·grat·u·lat·ing
con·grat·u·la·to·ry
con·grat·u·la·tion
con·gre·gate
con·gre·gat·ed
con·gre·gat·ing
con·gre·ga·tion
con·gre·ga·tion·al
con·gress
con·gres·sion·al
con·gress·man
con·gress·wom·an
con·gru·ent
con·gru·ent·ly
con·gru·ence
con·gru·en·cy
con·gru·ous

con·gru·ous·ly
con·gru·ous·ness
con·gru·i·ty
cone
con·ic
con·i·cal
co·ni·fer
con·jec·ture
con·jec·tured
con·jec·tur·ing
con·jec·tur·al
con·join
con·joint
con·ju·gal
con·ju·gal·ly
con·ju·gate
con·ju·gat·ed
con·ju·gat·ing
con·ju·ga·tion
con·ju·ga·tive
con·junc·tion
con·junc·tive
con·jure
con·jured
con·jur·ing
con·jur·a·tion
con·nect
con·nec·tor
con·nec·tion
con·nec·tive
con·nip·tion
con·nive
con·nived
con·niv·ing
con·niv·ance
con·nois·seur
con·note
con·not·ed
con·not·ing
con·no·ta·tion
con·no·ta·tive
con·nu·bi·al
con·quer
con·quer·a·ble
con·quer·or
con·quest
con·quis·ta·dor
con·san·guin·e·ous
con·san·guin·i·ty
con·science
con·sci·en·tious
con·scion·able
con·scious
con·scious·ly
con·scious·ness
con·script
con·scrip·tion
con·se·crate
con·se·crat·ed
con·se·crat·ing
con·se·cra·tor
con·se·cra·tion
con·sec·u·tive
con·sen·sus
con·sent
con·se·quence
con·se·quent
con·se·quent·ly
con·se·quen·tial
con·ser·va·tion
con·ser·va·tion·ist
con·serv·a·tive
con·serv·a·tism
con·serv·a·tive·ly
con·serv·a·to·ry
con·serv·a·to·ries
con·serve
con·served

con·serv·ing
con·sid·er
con·sid·er·ing
con·sid·er·able
con·sid·er·ably
con·sid·er·ate
con·sid·er·a·tion
con·sign
con·sign·er
con·sign·or
con·sign·ment
con·sist
con·sist·en·cy
con·sist·en·cies
con·sist·ence
con·sist·ent
con·sis·to·ry
con·so·la·tion
con·sol·a·to·ry
con·sole
con·soled
con·sol·ing
con·sol·a·ble
con·sol·i·date
con·sol·i·dat·ed
con·sol·i·dat·ing
con·sol·i·da·tion
con·som·mé
con·so·nant
con·sort
con·sor·ti·um
con·spic·u·ous
con·spic·u·ous·ness
con·spire
con·spired
con·spir·ing
con·spir·a·cy
con·spir·a·cies
con·spir·a·tor
con·spir·a·to·ri·al
con·spir·er
con·sta·ble
con·stab·u·lary
con·stant
con·stan·cy
con·stel·la·tion
con·ster·na·tion
con·sti·pa·tion
con·sti·pate
con·stit·u·en·cy
con·stit·u·en·cies
con·stit·u·ent
con·sti·tute
con·sti·tu·tion
con·sti·tu·tion·al
con·sti·tu·tion·al·i·ty
con·sti·tu·tion·al·ly
con·strain
con·strained
con·straint
con·strict
con·stric·tive
con·stric·tion
con·stric·tor
con·struct
con·struc·tor
con·struc·tion
con·struc·tive
con·strue
con·strued
con·stru·ing
con·stru·a·ble
con·sul
con·su·lar
con·sul·ship
con·su·late
con·sult
con·sul·ta·tion

con·sult·ant
con·sume
con·sumed
con·sum·ing
con·sum·a·ble
con·sum·er
con·sum·er·ism
con·sum·mate
con·sum·mat·ed
con·sum·mat·ing
con·sum·ma·tion
con·sump·tion
con·sump·tive
con·tact
con·ta·gion
con·ta·gious
con·ta·gious·ness
con·tain
con·tain·er
con·tain·ment
con·tam·i·nate
con·tam·i·nat·ed
con·tam·i·nat·ing
con·tam·i·nant
con·tam·i·na·tion
con·tem·plate
con·tem·plat·ed
con·tem·plat·ing
con·tem·pla·tion
con·tem·pla·tive
con·tem·po·ra·ne·ous
con·tem·po·rary
con·tem·po·rar·ies
con·tempt
con·tempt·i·ble
con·tempt·i·bly
con·temp·tu·ous
con·tend
con·tend·er
con·tent
con·tent·ment
con·tent·ed
con·tent·ed·ness
con·ten·tion
con·ten·tious
con·ter·mi·nous
con·test
con·test·a·ble
con·test·ant
con·text
con·tex·tu·al
con·tex·ture
con·tig·u·ous
con·ti·gu·i·ty
con·ti·gu·i·ties
con·tig·u·ous·ly
con·ti·nent
con·ti·nence
con·ti·nen·cy
con·ti·nent
con·ti·nen·tal
con·tin·gent
con·tin·gen·cy
con·tin·gen·cies
con·tin·u·al
con·tin·u·al·ly
con·tin·ue
con·tin·ued
con·tin·u·ing
con·tin·u·a·tion
con·tin·u·ance
con·ti·nu·i·ty
con·tin·u·ous
con·tin·u·um
con·tort
con·tor·tion
con·tor·tion·ist
con·tour

con·tra·band
con·tra·cep·tive
con·tra·cep·tion
con·tract
con·tract·ed
con·trac·tu·al
con·trac·tion
con·trac·tive
con·trac·tile
con·trac·tor
con·tra·dict
con·tra·dic·tion
con·tra·dic·to·ry
con·tra·dis·tinc·tion
con·tral·to
con·trap·tion
con·tra·pun·tal
con·tra·ri·wise
con·tra·ry
con·tra·ri·ly
con·tra·ri·ness
con·trast
con·trast·ing·ly
con·tra·vene
con·tra·ven·ing
con·trib·ute
con·trib·ut·ed
con·trib·ut·ing
con·trib·ut·a·ble
con·trib·u·tor
con·trib·u·tory
con·tri·bu·tion
con·trite
con·trite·ness
con·tri·tion
con·trive
con·trived
con·triv·ing
con·triv·ance
con·trol
con·trolled
con·trol·ling
con·trol·la·ble
con·trol·ler
con·tro·ver·sy
con·tro·ver·sies
con·tro·ver·sial
con·tro·vert
con·tu·ma·cy
con·tu·me·ly
con·tuse
con·tused
con·tus·ing
con·tu·sion
co·nun·drum
con·va·lesce
con·va·lesced
con·va·les·cence
con·va·les·cent
con·vec·tion
con·vene
con·vened
con·ven·ing
con·ven·ience
con·ven·ient
con·vent
con·ven·tion
con·ven·tion·al
con·ven·tion·al·ism
con·ven·tion·al·ize
con·verge
con·verg·ing
con·ver·gence
con·ver·gent
con·ver·sant
con·verse
con·versed
con·vers·ing

con·verse·ly
con·ver·sion
con·vert
con·vert·er
con·vert·i·ble
con·vex
con·vex·i·ty
con·vey
con·vey·a·ble
con·vey·ance
con·vey·er
con·vey·or
con·vict
con·vic·tion
con·vince
con·vinced
con·vinc·ing
con·vinc·i·ble
con·viv·i·al
con·viv·i·al·ity
con·voke
con·voked
con·vok·ing
con·vo·cation
con·vo·lute
con·vo·lut·ed
con·vo·lut·ing
con·vo·lute·ly
con·vo·lu·tion
con·voy
con·vulse
con·vulsed
con·vuls·ing
con·vul·sion
con·vul·sive
cook·e·ry
cook·ie
cool
cool·ish
cool·ly
cool·ness
cool·ant
coo·lie
coop·er·age
co·op·er·ate
co·op·er·at·ed
co·op·er·at·ing
co·op·er·a·tion
co·op·er·a·tive
co·or·di·nate
co·or·di·nat·ed
co·or·di·nat·ing
co·or·di·na·tor
co·or·di·na·tion
co·part·ner
cope
coped
cop·ing
cop·i·er
co·pi·lot
co·pi·ous
co·pi·ous·ly
cop·per
cop·pery
cop·pice
copse
cop·ra
cop·u·la
cop·u·late
cop·u·lat·ed
cop·u·lat·ing
cop·u·la·tion
cop·u·la·tive
copy
cop·ies
cop·ied
copy·ing
copy·right

co·quet
co·quet·ry
co·quette
cor·al
cord·age
cor·dial
cor·dial·i·ty
cor·dial·ly
cord·ite
cor·don
cor·do·van
cor·du·roy
core
cored
cor·ing
cor·nea
cor·ner
cor·net
cor·nice
cor·nu·co·pia
corny
corn·i·er
corn·i·est
co·rol·la
co·rol·lary
co·ro·na
cor·o·nary
cor·o·na·tion
cor·o·ner
cor·o·net
cor·po·ral
cor·po·rate
cor·po·rate·ly
cor·po·ra·tive
cor·po·ra·tion
cor·po·re·al
corps
corps·man
corpse
cor·pu·lent
cor·pu·lence
cor·pus
cor·pus·cle
cor·pus·cu·lar
cor·ral
cor·ralled
cor·ral·ling
cor·rect
cor·rect·a·ble
cor·rect·ness
cor·rec·tion
cor·rec·tion·al
cor·rec·tive
cor·re·late
cor·re·lat·ed
cor·re·lat·ing
cor·re·la·tion
cor·rel·a·tive
cor·re·spond
cor·re·spond·ing
cor·re·spond·ence
cor·re·spond·ent
cor·ri·dor
cor·ri·gi·ble
cor·ri·gi·bil·i·ty
cor·rob·o·rate
cor·rob·o·rat·ed
cor·rob·o·rat·ing
cor·rob·o·rat·tion
cor·rob·o·ra·to·ry
cor·rode
cor·rod·ed
cor·rod·ing
cor·ro·sion
cor·ro·sive
cor·ru·gate
cor·ru·gat·ed
cor·ru·gat·ing

cor·ru·ga·tion
cor·rupt
cor·rup·ti·ble
cor·rup·ti·bil·i·ty
cor·rupt·ly
cor·rupt·ness
cor·rup·tion
cor·sage
cor·sair
cor·set
cor·tege
cor·tex
cor·ti·cal
cor·ti·sone
co·run·dum
cor·us·cate
cor·vette
co·sig·na·to·ry
cos·met·ic
cos·me·tol·o·gist
cos·mic
cos·mi·cal·ly
cos·mog·o·ny
cos·mog·o·nist
cos·mog·ra·phy
cos·mog·ra·pher
cos·mol·o·gy
cos·mol·o·gist
cos·mo·naut
cos·mo·pol·i·tan
cos·mop·o·lite
cos·mos
cos·mo·tron
cost·ly
cost·li·er
cos·tume
cos·tumed
cos·tum·ing
cos·tum·er
co·sy
co·si·er
co·tan·gent
co·te·rie
co·til·lion
cot·tage
cot·ter
cot·ton
cot·tony
couch
couch·ant
cough
coun·cil
coun·cil·or
coun·cil·man
coun·sel
coun·seled
coun·sel·ing
coun·se·lor
count
count·a·ble
count·down
coun·te·nance
coun·te·nanced
coun·te·nanc·ing
count·er
coun·ter·act
coun·ter·ac·tive
coun·ter·at·tack
coun·ter·charge
coun·ter·claim
coun·ter·claim·ant
coun·ter·clock·wise
coun·ter·cul·ture
coun·ter·es·pi·o·nage
coun·ter·feit
coun·ter·feit·er
coun·ter·in·tel·li·gence
coun·ter·mand

coun·ter·meas·ure
coun·ter·of·fen·sive
coun·ter·pane
coun·ter·part
coun·ter·point
coun·ter·poise
coun·ter·rev·o·lu·tion
coun·ter·sign
coun·ter·sig·na·ture
coun·ter·sink
coun·ter·spy
coun·ter·weight
coun·tess
count·less
coun·tri·fied
coun·try
coun·tries
coun·ty
coun·ties
coup de grace
coup d'e·tat
cou·pé
coup·le
coup·ling
coup·ler
coup·let
cou·pon
cour·age
cou·ra·geous
cour·i·er
course
coursed
cours·ing
cours·er
cour·te·ous
cour·te·son
cour·te·sy
cour·te·sies
court·house
cour·ti·er
court·ly
court·li·ness
court·mar·tial
courts·mar·tial
court·room
court·ship
cous·in
cou·tu·rier
cov·e·nant
cov·er
cov·ered
cov·er·ing
cov·er·ess
cov·er·age
cov·er·all
cov·er·let
cov·ert
cov·ert·ly
cov·er·up
cov·et
cov·et·ous
cov·ey
cow·ard
cow·ard·li·ness
cow·ard·ice
cow·er
cow·er·ing
cowl
co·worker
cow·ry
cow·rie
cox·swain
coy
coy·ness
coy·o·te
coz·en
coz·en·er
co·zy

co·zi·ly
co·zi·ness
crab
crabbed
crab·bing
crab·by
crack·down
crack·er
crack·ing
crack·le
crack·led
crack·ling
crack·up
cra·dle
cra·dled
cra·dling
crafts·man
crafty
craft·i·ly
crag
crag·ged
crag·gy
crag·gi·ness
cram
crammed
cram·ming
cran·ber·ry
crane
craned
cran·ing
cra·ni·um
cranky
crank·i·ly
crank·i·ness
cran·ny
cran·nies
cran·nied
crap·shooter
crass
crass·ly
crate
crat·ed
crat·ing
cra·ter
cra·tered
cra·vat
crave
craved
crav·ing
cra·ven
craw·fish
crawl
cray·fish
cray·on
craze
crazed
craz·ing
cra·zy
cra·zi·er
cra·zi·ness
creak
creak·i·ly
creaky
cream
cream·i·ness
creamy
crease
creased
creas·ing
creasy
cre·ate
cre·at·ed
cre·at·ing
cre·a·tion
cre·a·tive
cre·a·tiv·i·ty
cre·a·tor
crea·ture

crèche
cre·dence
cre·den·tial
cre·den·za
cred·i·ble
  cred·i·bil·i·ty
  cred·i·bly
cred·it
  cred·it·a·ble
  cred·it·a·bil·i·ty
  cred·it·a·bly
cred·i·tor
cre·do
cred·u·lous
cre·du·li·ty
creek
creel
creep
  crept
  creep·ing
creepy
  creep·i·ness
creep·er
cre·mate
  cre·mat·ed
  cre·mat·ing
  cre·ma·tion
cre·ma·to·ry
  cre·ma·to·ri·um
cren·el·ate
  cren·el·la·tion
Cre·ole
cre·o·sote
crepe de Chine
crepe su·zette
cre·pus·cu·lar
cres·cen·do
cres·cent
crest
  crest·ed
  crest·less
crest·fall·en
cre·ta·ceous
cre·tonne
cre·vasse
crev·ice
crew·ed
crib
  cribbed
  crib·bing
crib·bage
crick·et
crim·i·nal
  crim·i·nal·i·ty
  crim·i·nal·ly
crim·i·nol·o·gy
  crim·i·nol·o·gist
crim·son
cringe
  cringed
  cring·ing
crin·kle
  crin·kled
  crin·kling
  crin·o·line
crip·ple
  crip·pled
  crip·pling
cri·sis
  cri·ses
crisp
  crisp·ness
  crispy
  crisp·i·er
criss·cross
cri·te·ri·on
  cri·te·ria
crit·ic

crit·i·cal
  crit·i·cal·ly
crit·i·cism
crit·i·cize
  crit·i·cized
  crit·i·cizing
  crit·i·ciz·a·ble
cri·tique
croaky
cro·chet
  cro·cheted
  cro·chet·ing
crock·ery
croc·o·dile
cro·cus
crois·sant
cro·ny
  cro·nies
crook·ed
croon·er
crop
  cropped
  crop·ping
cro·quet
cro·quette
cross·bar
cross·breed
cross·coun·try
cross·ex·am·ine
  cross·ex·am·i·na·tion
  cross·fer·ti·li·za·tion
cross·ing
cross·pol·li·na·tion
  cross·pol·li·nate
cross·ref·er·ence
crotch·ety
  crotch·et·i·ness
crouch
croup
crou·pi·er
crou·ton
cru·cial
  cru·ci·al·i·ty
cru·ci·ble
cru·ci·fix
cru·ci·fix·ion
cru·ci·form
cru·ci·fy
  cru·ci·fied
  cru·ci·fy·ing
crude
  crud·est
  crude·ness
  cru·di·ty
cru·el
  cru·el·ly
  cru·el·ness
  cru·el·ty
cru·et
cruise
  cruised
  cruis·ing
cruis·er
crul·ler
crum·ble
  crum·bling
crum·my
  crum·mi·est
crum·pet
crum·ple
  crum·pled
  crum·pling
crunchy
  crunch·i·er
cru·sade
  cru·sad·er
crush·er
  crush·ing

crus·ta·cean
crusty
  crust·i·ly
crutch
crux
cry
  cried
  cry·ing
cry·o·gen·ics
crypt
cryp·to·gram
  cryp·to·graph
crys·tal
  crys·tal·line
  crys·tal·lize
  crys·tal·li·za·tion
cube
  cubed
  cub·ing
cu·bic
  cu·bi·cal
cu·bi·cle
cub·ism
cuck·old
cuck·oo
cu·cum·ber
cud·dle
  cud·dled
  cud·dling
  cud·dle·some
cudg·el
  cudg·eled
  cudg·el·ing
cue
  cued
  cu·ing
cui·sine
cul-de-sac
cu·li·nary
cul·mi·nate
  cul·mi·nat·ed
  cul·mi·nat·ing
  cul·mi·na·tion
cu·lottes
cul·pa·ble
  cul·pa·bil·i·ty
  cul·pa·bly
cul·prit
cult
  cul·tist
cul·ti·vate
  cul·ti·vat·ed
  cul·ti·vat·ing
  cul·ti·va·tion
  cul·ti·va·tor
cul·tur·al
cul·ture
  cul·tured
  cul·tur·ing
cul·vert
cum·ber
  cum·ber·some
  cum·brance
cum lau·de
cum·mer·bund
cu·mu·late
cu·mu·la·tion
cu·mu·la·tive
cu·mu·lo·nim·bus
cu·mu·lus
  cu·mu·lous
cu·ne·i·form
cun·ning
  cun·ning·ly
  cun·ning·ness
cup
  cupped
  cup·ping

cup·board
cup·ful
cu·pid·i·ty
cu·po·la
cur·a·ble
  cur·a·bil·i·ty
cu·rate
cu·ra·tive
cu·ra·tor
curb·ing
curb·stone
cur·dle
  cur·dled
  cur·dling
cure
  cured
  cur·ing
cur·few
cu·rio
cu·ri·o·sa
cu·ri·os·i·ty
  cu·ri·os·i·ties
cu·ri·ous
  cu·ri·ous·ness
curl·i·cue
curl·ing
curly
  curl·i·ness
cur·rant
cur·ren·cy
  cur·ren·cies
current
cur·ric·u·lum
  cur·ric·u·la
  cur·ric·u·lar
cur·rish
cur·ry
  cur·ried
curse
  curs·ing
  curs·ed·ness
cur·sive
cur·so·ry
  cur·so·ri·ly
curt
  curt·ly
  curt·ness
cur·tail
  cur·tail·ment
cur·tain
curt·sy
  curt·sied
  curt·sy·ing
cur·va·ceous
cur·va·ture
curve
  curved
  curv·ing
cur·vi·lin·e·ar
cush·ion
cushy
  cush·i·est
cus·pid
cus·pi·dor
cuss·ed
  cuss·ed·ness
cus·tard
cus·to·di·an
cus·to·dy
  cus·to·di·al
cus·tom
cus·tom·ary
  cus·tom·ar·i·ly
cus·tom·er
cus·tom·ize
  cus·tom·ized
  cus·tom·iz·ing
cut

cut·ting
cur·ta·ne·ous
cute
  cut·est
  cute·ness
cu·ti·cle
cut·lass
cut·lery
cut·let
cut·throat
cut·tle·fish
cy·a·nide
cy·ber·net·ics
cyc·la·men
cy·cle
  cy·cled
  cy·cling
  cy·clist
cy·clic
  cy·cli·cal
cy·clone
cy·clo·pe·di·a
cy·clo·rama
  cy·clo·ram·ic
cy·clo·tron
cyg·net
cyl·in·der
  cy·lin·dric
  cy·lin·dri·cal
cym·bal
cyn·ic
  cyn·i·cism
  cyn·i·cal
cy·no·sure
cy·pher
cy·press
cyst
czar

D

dab
  dabbed
  dab·bing
dab·ble
  dab·bled
  dab·bling
  dab·bler
dachs·hund
dac·tyl
  dac·tyl·ic
daf·fo·dil
daf·fy
dag·ger
da·guerre·o·type
dahl·ia
dai·ly
  dai·lies
dain·ty
  dain·ti·est
  dain·ti·ly
  dain·ti·ness
dai·qui·ri
dairy
  dair·ies
da·is
dai·sy
  dai·sies
dal·ly
  dal·lied
  dal·ly·ing
  da·li·ance
Dal·ma·tian
dam
  dammed
  dam·ming
dam·age

dam·aged
dam·ag·ing
dam·ask
damn
  dam·na·ble
  dam·na·bly
  dam·na·tion
  damned
damp·en
damp·er
damp·ness
dam·sel
dam·son
dance
  danced
  danc·ing
dan·de·li·on
dan·der
dan·dle
  dan·dled
  dan·dling
dan·druff
dan·dy
  dan·dies
  dan·dy·ism
dan·ger
dan·ger·ous
dan·gle
  dan·gled
  dan·gling
dank
  dank·ness
dan·seuse
dap·per
dap·ple
  dap·pled
  dap·pling
dare
  dared
  dar·ing
dare·dev·il
dark
  dark·ish
  dark·ly
  dark·ness
dark·en
dark·room
dar·ling
  dar·ling·ness
Dar·win·ism
dash·board
dash·ing
das·tard
  das·tard·li·ness
  das·tard·ly
da·ta
date
  dat·ed
  dat·ing
  dat·a·ble
date·less
  date·line
da·tive
da·tum
  da·ta
daub
daugh·ter
daugh·ter-in-law
daunt·less
dau·phin
dav·en·port
dav·it
daw·dle
  daw·dled
  daw·dling
  daw·dler
dawn
  dawn·ing

day·break
day·dream
day·light
day·time
daze
  dazed
  daz·ing
  daz·ed·ly
daz·zle
  daz·zled
  daz·zling
dea·con
dea·con·ess
de·ac·ti·vate
  de·ac·ti·va·tion
dead·beat
dead·en
dead·end
dead·line
dead·lock
dead·ly
  dead·li·ness
deaf
  deaf·ness
deaf·en
  deaf·en·ing·ly
deaf·mute
deal
  dealt
  deal·ing
dean·ship
dear
  dear·ness
dearth
death
  death·less
  death·ly
death·blow
death's·head
death·watch
de·ba·cle
de·bar
  de·barred
  de·bar·ring
  de·bar·ment
de·bark
  de·bar·ka·tion
de·base
  de·based
  de·bas·ing
  de·base·ment
de·bate
  de·bat·ing
  de·bat·a·ble
  de·bat·er
de·bauch
  de·bauch·er
  de·bauch·ment
  de·bauch·ery
deb·au·chee
de·ben·ture
de·bil·i·tate
  de·bil·i·tat·ed
  de·bil·i·tat·ing
  de·bil·i·ta·tion
de·bil·i·ty
  de·bil·i·ties
deb·it
deb·o·nair
de·brief
de·bris
debt·or
de·bunk
de·but
deb·u·tante
de·cade
dec·a·dent
  dec·a·dence

dec·a·dent·ly
dec·a·gon
dec·a·gram
dec·a·he·dron
de·cal
Dec·a·logue
de·camp
  de·camp·ment
de·cant
  de·cant·er
de·cap·i·tate
  de·cap·i·tat·ed
  de·cap·i·tat·ing
  de·cap·i·ta·tion
dec·a·pod
de·cath·lon
de·cay
de·cease
  de·ceased
  de·ce·dent
de·ceit
  de·ceit·ful
  de·ceit·ful·ness
de·ceive
  de·ceived
  de·ceiv·ing
  de·ceiv·er
de·cel·er·ate
  de·cel·er·at·ed
  de·cel·er·at·ing
  de·cel·er·a·tion
de·cen·cy
  de·cen·cies
de·cen·ni·al
de·cent
  de·cent·ly
de·cen·tral·ize
  de·cen·tral·ized
  de·cen·tral·iz·ing
  de·cen·tral·i·za·tion
de·cep·tion
de·cep·tive
dec·i·bel
de·cide
  de·cid·ed
  de·cid·ing
  de·cid·ed·ly
de·cid·u·ous
dec·i·mal
dec·i·mate
  dec·i·mat·ed
  dec·i·mat·ing
  dec·i·ma·tion
de·ci·pher
  de·ci·pher·a·ble
de·ci·sion
de·ci·sive
de·claim
  dec·la·ma·tion
  de·clam·a·tory
de·clare
  de·clared
  de·clar·ing
  de·clar·a·tive
  de·clar·a·to·ry
  dec·la·ra·tion
de·clas·si·fy
  de·clas·si·fied
  de·clas·si·fy·ing
de·clen·sion
dec·li·na·tion
de·cline
  de·clined
  de·clin·ing
  de·clin·a·ble
de·cliv·i·ty
  de·cliv·i·ties
de·code

de·cod·ed
de·cod·ing
de·cod·er
de·colle·tage
de·com·mis·sion
de·com·pose
  de·com·posed
  de·com·pos·ing
  de·com·po·si·tion
de·com·press
  de·com·pres·sion
de·con·tam·i·nate
  de·con·tam·i·nat·ed
  de·con·tam·i·nat·ing
  de·con·tam·i·na·tion
de·con·trol
  de·con·trolled
  de·con·trol·ling
de·cor
dec·o·rate
  dec·o·rat·ed
  dec·o·rat·ing
  dec·o·ra·tion
  dec·o·ra·tive
  dec·o·ra·tor
de·co·rous
de·co·rum
de·coy
de·crease
  de·creased
  de·creas·ing
de·cree
  de·creed
  de·cree·ing
de·cre·ment
de·crep·it
  de·crep·i·tude
  de·crep·it·ly
de·cre·scen·do
de·cry
  de·cried
  de·cry·ing
de·cri·al
ded·i·cate
  ded·i·cat·ed
  ded·i·cat·ing
  ded·i·ca·to·ry
  ded·i·ca·tion
de·duce
  de·duc·i·ble
de·duct
  de·duct·i·ble
  de·duc·tion
  de·duc·tive
deep
  deep·ness
  deep·en
deep·root·ed
deep·seat·ed
de·es·ca·late
  de·es·ca·lat·ed
  de·es·ca·lat·ing
  de·es·ca·la·tion
de·face
  de·faced
  de·fac·ing
  de·face·ment
de fac·to
de·fal·cate
  de·fal·ca·tion
de·fame
  de·famed
  de·fam·ing
  def·a·ma·tion
  de·fam·a·to·ry
de·fault
de·feat
  de·feat·ism

de·feat·ist
def·e·cate
  def·e·cat·ed
  def·e·cat·ing
  def·e·ca·tion
de·fect
de·fec·tion
de·fec·tor
de·fec·tive
de·fend
  de·fend·er
  de·fend·ant
de·fense
  de·fense·less
  de·fen·si·ble
  de·fen·si·bil·i·ty
  de·fen·sive
de·fer
  de·ferred
  de·fer·ring
  de·fer·ment
def·er·ence
  def·er·en·tial
de·fi·ance
  de·fi·ant
de·fi·cient
  de·fi·cien·cy
  de·fi·cien·cies
def·i·cit
de·file
  de·filed
  de·fil·ing
  de·file·ment
de·fine
  de·fined
  de·fin·ing
  de·fin·a·ble
def·i·nite
  def·i·nite·ly
def·i·ni·tion
  de·fin·i·tive
de·flate
  de·flat·ed
  de·flat·ing
  de·fla·tion
  de·fla·tion·ary
de·flect
  de·flec·tion
  de·flec·tive
  de·flec·tor
de·flow·er
de·fo·li·ate
  de·fo·li·at·ed
  de·fo·li·at·ing
  de·fo·li·a·tion
de·for·est
  de·for·est·a·tion
de·form
  de·for·ma·tion
  de·formed
  de·form·i·ty
  de·form·i·ties
de·fraud
de·fray
  de·fray·al
  de·fray·ment
de·frost
deft
  deft·ness
de·funct
de·fy
  de·fied
  de·fy·ing
de·gen·er·ate
  de·gen·er·at·ed
  de·gen·er·at·ing
  de·gen·er·ate·ly
  de·gen·er·a·cy

de·gen·er·a·tion
de·grade
  de·grad·ed
  de·grad·ing
  de·grad·able
  deg·ra·da·tion
de·gree
de·his·cence
  de·his·cent
de·hu·mid·i·fy
de·hy·drate
  de·hy·drat·ed
  de·hy·drat·ing
  de·hy·dra·tion
de·i·fy
  de·i·fied
  de·i·fy·ing
  de·i·fi·ca·tion
deign
de·ist
  de·ism
  de·is·tic
  de·is·ti·cal
de·i·ty
  de·i·ties
de·ject·ed
  de·jec·ted·ly
  de·jec·tion
de ju·re
de·lay
de·lec·ta·ble
  de·lec·ta·bly
  de·lec·ta·tion
del·e·gate
  del·e·gat·ed
  del·e·gat·ing
  del·e·ga·tion
de·lete
  de·let·ed
  de·let·ing
  de·le·tion
del·e·te·ri·ous
delft·ware
de·lib·er·ate
  de·lib·er·at·ed
  de·lib·er·at·ing
  de·lib·er·ate·ly
  de·lib·er·a·tion
del·i·ca·cy
  del·i·ca·cies
del·i·cate
  del·i·cate·ly
del·i·ca·tes·sen
de·li·cious
  de·li·cious·ness
de·light
  de·light·ed
  de·light·ed·ly
  de·light·ful
  de·light·ful·ly
de·lim·it
  de·lim·i·ta·tion
de·lin·e·ate
  de·lin·e·at·ed
  de·lin·e·at·ing
  de·lin·e·a·tion
  de·lin·e·a·tor
de·lin·quent
  de·lin·quen·cy
  de·lin·quen·cies
del·i·quesce
de·lir·i·um
  de·lir·i·ous
de·liv·er
  de·liv·er·er
  de·liv·er·ance
de·liv·ery
  de·liv·er·ies

de·louse
  de·loused
  de·lous·ing
del·phin·i·um
del·ta
del·toid
de·lude
  de·lud·ed
  de·lud·ing
del·uge
  del·uged
  del·ug·ing
de·lu·sion
  de·lu·sive
  de·lu·so·ry
  de·lu·sive·ly
de·luxe
delve
  delv·ing
de·mag·ne·tize
dem·a·gogue
  dem·a·gogu·ery
  dem·a·gog·ic
  dem·a·gog·i·cal
de·mand
de·mar·cate
  de·mar·ca·tion
de·mean
  de·mean·or
de·ment·ed
de·men·tia
de·mer·it
de·mesne
dem·i·god
dem·i·john
de·mil·i·ta·rize
  de·mil·l·tar·i·za·tion
de·mise
  de·mised
  de·mis·ing
dem·i·tasse
de·mo·bi·lize
  de·mo·bi·lized
  de·mo·bi·liz·ing
  de·mo·bi·li·za·tion
de·moc·ra·cy
  de·moc·ra·cies
dem·o·crat
dem·o·crat·ic
  dem·o·crat·i·cal·ly
de·moc·ra·tize
  de·moc·ra·tized
  de·moc·ra·tiz·ing
  de·moc·ra·ti·za·tion
de·mog·ra·phy
  de·mog·ra·pher
  dem·o·graph·ic
de·mol·ish
de·plor·a·bly
de·plore
  de·plored
  de·plor·ing
de·ploy
  de·ploy·ment
de·pol·ar·ize
de·pop·u·late
  de·pop·u·lat·ed
  de·pop·u·lat·ing
  de·pop·u·la·tion
de·port
  de·por·ta·tion
  de·port·ment
de·pose
  de·posed
  de·pos·ing
  de·pos·a·ble
de·pos·it
  de·pos·i·tor

dep·o·si·tion
de·pos·i·to·ry
de·pot
de·prave
  de·praved
  de·prav·ing
  de·prav·i·ty
  de·pra·va·tion
dep·re·cate
  dep·re·cat·ed
  dep·re·cat·ing
  dep·re·ca·tion
  dep·re·ca·to·ry
de·pre·ci·ate
  de·pre·ci·at·ed
  de·pre·ci·at·ing
  de·pre·ci·a·tion
  de·pre·ci·a·to·ry
dep·re·diate
dep·re·dat·ed
dep·re·dat·ing
dep·re·da·tion
de·press
  de·pres·sant
  de·pressed
  de·pres·sion
de·prive
  de·prived
  de·priv·ing
  dep·ri·va·tion
depth
dep·u·rate
dep·u·ta·tion
de·pute
  de·put·ed
  de·put·ing
dep·u·tize
  dep·u·tized
  dep·u·tiz·ing
dep·u·ty
  dep·u·ties
de·raign
  de·raign·ment
de·rail
  de·rail·ment
de·range
  de·ranged
  de·rang·ing
  de·range·ment
der·by
der·e·lict
  der·e·lic·tion
de·ride
  de·rid·ing
de·ri·gueur
de·ri·sion
  de·ri·sive
  de·ri·so·ry
der·i·va·tion
de·riv·a·tive
de·rive
  de·riv·ing
  de·riv·a·ble
der·ma·ti·tis
der·ma·tol·o·gy
  der·ma·to·log·i·cal
  der·ma·tol·o·gist
der·mis
der·o·gate
  der·o·gat·ed
  der·o·gat·ing
  der·o·ga·tion
de·rog·a·to·ry
  de·rog·a·to·ri·ly
der·rick
der·rin·ger
der·vish
de·sal·i·nate

des·cant
de·scend
  de·scend·ed
  de·scend·ing
  de·scend·ant
  de·scend·ent
  de·scent
de·scribe
  de·scribed
  de·scrib·ing
  de·scrib·a·ble
de·scrip·tion
  de·scrip·tive
de·scry
  de·scried
  de·scry·ing
des·e·crate
  des·e·crat·ed
  des·e·crat·ing
  des·e·cra·tion
de·seg·re·gate
  de·seg·re·gat·ed
  de·seg·re·gat·ing
  de·seg·re·ga·tion
  de·sen·si·tize
des·ert
de·sert
  de·sert·ed
  de·sert·er
  de·ser·tion
de·serve
  de·served
  de·serv·ing
  de·serv·ed·ly
des·ha·bille
des·ic·cate
  des·ic·cated
  des·ic·cat·ing
  des·ic·ca·tion
de·sid·er·a·tum
de·sign
  de·signed
  de·sign·ing
  de·sign·ed·ly
  de·signer
des·ig·nate
  des·ig·nat·ed
  des·ig·nat·ing
  des·ig·na·tion
de·sire
  de·sired
  de·sir·ing
  de·sir·a·ble
  de·sir·a·bil·i·ty
  de·sir·ous
de·sist
des·o·late
  des·o·lat·ed
  des·o·lat·ing
  des·o·la·tion
de·spair
  de·spair·ing
des·per·a·do
des·per·ate
  des·per·ate·ly
  des·per·a·tion
des·pi·ca·ble
  des·pi·ca·bly
de·spise
  de·spised
  de·spis·ing
de·spite
de·spoil
  de·spoil·ment
  de·spo·li·a·tion
de·spond
  de·spond·en·cy
  de·spond·ence

de·spond·ent
des·pot
  des·pot·ic
  des·pot·i·cal·ly
  des·pot·ism
des·sert
des·ti·na·tion
des·tine
  des·tined
  des·tin·ing
des·ti·ny
  des·ti·nies
des·ti·tute
  des·ti·tu·tion
de·stroy
  de·stroy·er
de·struc·tion
  de·struct·i·ble
  de·struct·i·bil·i·ty
  de·struc·tive
  de·struc·tive·ness
des·ue·tude
des·ul·to·ry
  des·ul·to·ri·ly
de·tach
  de·tached
  de·tach·a·ble
  de·tach·ment
de·tail
de·tain
  de·tain·ment
  de·tain·er
  de·ten·tion
de·tect
  dc·tcct·a·ble
  de·tec·tion
  de·tec·tor
  de·tec·tive
dé·tente
de·ten·tion
de·ter
  de·terred
  de·ter·ring
de·ter·gent
de·te·ri·o·rate
  de·te·ri·o·rat·ed
  de·te·ri·o·rat·ing
  de·te·ri·o·ra·tion
de·ter·mine
  de·ter·mined
  de·ter·min·ing
  de·ter·mi·na·ble
  de·ter·mi·nant
  de·ter·mi·nate
  de·ter·mi·na·tion
  de·ter·mined·ly
de·ter·min·ism
de·ter·rent
  de·ter·rence
de·test
  de·test·a·ble
  de·tes·ta·tion
de·throne
  de·throne·ment
det·o·nate
  det·o·nat·ed
  det·o·nat·ing
  det·o·na·tion
  det·o·na·tor
de·tour
de·tract
  de·trac·tion
  de·trac·tor
det·ri·ment
  det·ri·men·tal
de·tri·tus
deuce
de·value

de·val·u·ate
de·val·u·at·ed
de·val·u·at·ing
de·val·u·a·tion
dev·as·tate
dev·as·tat·ed
dev·as·tat·ing
dev·as·ta·tion
de·vel·op
de·vel·op·ment
de·vel·op·er
de·vi·ate
de·vi·at·ed
de·vi·at·ing
de·vi·ant
de·vi·a·tion
de·vice
dev·il
dev·il·ment
dev·il·try
dev·il·tries
dev·il·ry
dev·il·ish
de·vi·ous
de·vi·ous·ness
de·vise
de·vised
de·vis·ing
de·vis·a·ble
de·vis·al
de·vi·see
de·vi·sor
de·void
de·volve
de·volved
de·volv·ing
dev·o·lu·tion
de·vote
de·vot·ed
de·vot·ing
de·vote·ment
dev·o·tee
de·vo·tion
de·vo·tion·al
de·vour
de·vour·ing
de·vout
de·vout·ly
de·vout·ness
dewy
dew·i·ness
dew·y·eyed
dex·ter·ous
dex·ter·i·ty
dex·ter·ous·ly
dex·trose
di·a·be·tes
di·a·bet·ic
di·a·bol·ic
di·a·bol·i·cal
di·a·crit·ic
di·a·crit·i·cal
di·a·dem
di·ag·nose
di·ag·nosed
di·ag·nos·ing
di·ag·no·sis
di·ag·nos·tic
di·ag·nos·ti·cian
di·ag·o·nal
di·a·gram
di·a·gramed
di·a·gram·ing
di·a·gram·matic
di·a·gram·mat·i·cal
di·al
di·aled
di·al·ing

di·a·lect
di·a·lec·tal
di·a·lec·tic
di·a·lec·ti·cal
di·a·lec·ti·cian
di·a·logue
di·am·e·ter
di·a·met·ric
dia·mond
di·a·pa·son
dia·per
di·aph·a·nous
di·a·phragm
di·ar·rhea
di·a·ry
di·a·ries
di·as·to·le
di·as·tol·ic
di·as·tro·phism
di·a·ther·my
di·a·ton·ic
di·a·tribe
dice
diced
dic·ing
di·chot·o·my
di·chot·o·mies
di·chot·o·mous
di·cho·tom·ic
dick·ey
dic·tate
dic·tat·ed
dic·tat·ing
dic·ta·tion
dic·ta·tor
dic·ta·tor·ship
dic·ta·to·ri·al
dic·ta·to·ri·al·ly
dic·tion
dic·tion·ary
dic·tion·ar·ies
dic·tum
di·dac·tic
di·dac·ti·cal
di·dac·ti·cism
die
died
dy·ing
die·sel
di·et
di·e·tary
di·e·tet·ic
di·e·tet·ics
di·e·ti·cian
dif·fer
dif·fer·ence
dif·fer·ent
dif·fer·en·tial
dif·fer·en·ti·ate
dif·fer·en·ti·a·tion
dif·fi·cult
dif·fi·cul·ty
dif·fi·cul·ties
dif·fi·dent
dif·fi·dence
dif·fuse
dif·fused
dif·fus·ing
dif·fuse·ly
dif·fuse·ness
dif·fu·sion
dig
dug
dig·ging
di·gest
di·gest·i·ble
di·gest·i·bil·i·ty
di·ges·tion

di·ges·tive
dig·ger
dig·gings
dig·it
dig·it·al
dig·i·tal·is
dig·ni·fy
dig·ni·fied
dig·ni·fy·ing
dig·ni·tary
dig·ni·tar·ies
dig·ni·ty
dig·ni·ties
di·gress
di·gres·sion
di·gres·sive
di·he·dral
di·lap·i·date
di·lap·i·dat·ed
di·lap·i·dat·ing
di·lap·i·da·tion
dil·a·ta·tion
di·late
di·lat·ed
di·lat·ing
di·la·tion
dil·a·to·ry
dil·a·to·ri·ly
di·lem·ma
dil·et·tan·te
dil·i·gence
dil·i·gent
dil·ly·dal·ly
dil·ly·dal·lied
dil·ute
di·lut·ed
di·lut·ing
di·lu·tion
di·lu·vi·al
dim
dim·mer
dimmed
dim·ming
dim·ly
dim·ness
di·men·sion
di·men·sion·al
di·min·ish
di·min·ish·ing
di·min·u·en·do
dim·i·nu·tion
di·min·u·tive
dim·ple
dim·wit·ted
din
dinned
din·ning
dine
dined
din·ing
din·er
di·nette
din·ghy
din·ghies
din·gy
din·gi·ness
din·ner
di·no·saur
di·o·cese
di·oc·e·san
di·o·rama
di·ox·ide
dip
dipped
dip·ping
diph·the·ria
diph·thong
di·plo·ma

di·plo·ma·cy
di·plo·ma·cies
dip·lo·mat
dip·lo·mat·ic
dip·lo·mat·i·cal·ly
dip·so·ma·nia
dip·so·ma·ni·ac
dire
dire·ness
di·rect
di·rect·ness
di·rec·tion
di·rec·tive
di·rect·ly
di·rec·tor
di·rec·to·ri·al
di·rec·to·rate
di·rec·to·ry
di·rec·to·ries
dirge
di·ri·gi·ble
dirndl
dirty
dirt·i·ness
dis·a·ble
dis·a·bled
dis·a·bling
dis·a·bil·i·ty
dis·a·ble·ment
dis·a·buse
dis·a·bused
dis·a·bus·ing
dis·ad·van·tage
dis·ad·van·taged
dis·ad·van·tag·ing
dis·ad·van·ta·geous
dis·af·fect
dis·af·fec·tion
dis·af·fect·ed
dis·a·gree
dis·a·greed
dis·a·gree·ing
dis·a·gree·a·ble
dis·a·gree·ment
dis·al·low
dis·al·low·ance
dis·ap·pear
dis·ap·pear·ance
dis·ap·point
dis·ap·point·ment
dis·ap·prove
dis·ap·proved
dis·ap·prov·ing
dis·ap·prov·al
dis·ap·pro·ba·tion
dis·arm
dis·ar·ma·ment
dis·ar·range
dis·ar·ranged
dis·ar·rang·ing
dis·ar·range·ment
dis·ar·ray
dis·as·sem·ble
dis·as·so·ci·ate
dis·as·ter
dis·as·trous
dis·a·vow
dis·a·vow·al
dis·band
dis·band·ment
dis·bar
dis·barred
dis·bar·ring
dis·bar·ment
dis·be·lieve
dis·be·lieved
dis·be·liev·ing
dis·be·lief

dis·be·liev·er
dis·burse
dis·bursed
dis·burs·ing
dis·burse·ment
dis·burs·er
disc
disk
dis·card
dis·cern
dis·cern·ing
dis·cern·i·ble
dis·cern·i·bly
dis·cern·ment
dis·charge
dis·charged
dis·charg·ing
dis·charg·er
dis·ci·ple
dis·ci·pline
dis·ci·plined
dis·ci·plin·ing
dis·ci·pli·nary
dis·ci·pli·nar·i·an
dis·claim
dis·claim·er
dis·close
dis·closed
dis·clos·ing
dis·clo·sure
dis·coid
dis·col·or
dis·col·or·a·tion
dis·com·fit
dis·com·fi·ture
dis·com·fort
dis·com·mode
dis·com·mod·ed
dis·com·mod·ing
dis·com·pose
dis·com·posed
dis·com·pos·ing
dis·com·po·sure
dis·con·cert
dis·con·cert·ing
dis·con·cert·ed
dis·con·nect
dis·con·nec·tion
dis·con·nect·ed
dis·con·so·late
dis·con·so·late·ly
dis·con·tent
dis·con·tent·ment
dis·con·tent·ed
dis·con·tin·ue
dis·con·tin·ued
dis·con·tin·u·ing
dis·con·tin·u·ance
dis·con·tin·u·a·tion
dis·con·tin·u·ous
dis·cord
dis·cord·ance
dis·cord·an·cy
dis·cord·ant·ly
dis·co·théque
dis·count
dis·cour·age
dis·cour·ag·ing
dis·cour·age·ment
dis·course
dis·coursed
dis·cours·ing
dis·cour·te·ous
dis·cour·te·ous·ly
dis·cour·te·sy
dis·cour·te·sies
dis·cov·er
dis·cov·er·a·ble

dis·cov·er·er
dis·cov·er·y
dis·cov·er·ies
dis·cred·it
dis·cred·it·a·ble
dis·creet
dis·creet·ly
dis·crep·ant
dis·crep·an·cy
dis·crep·an·cies
dis·crete
dis·cre·tion
dis·cre·tion·ary
dis·crim·i·nate
dis·crim·i·nat·ed
dis·crim·i·nat·ing
dis·crim·i·nate·ly
dis·crim·i·na·tion
dis·crim·i·na·to·ry
dis·cur·sive
dis·cur·sive·ness
dis·cus
dis·cuss
dis·cus·sion
dis·dain
dis·dain·ful
dis·ease
dis·eased
dis·eas·ing
dis·em·bark
dis·em·bar·ka·tion
dis·em·bark·ment
dis·em·body
dis·em·bod·ied
dis·em·bod·y·ing
dis·em·bod·i·ment
dis·em·bow·el
dis·em·bow·eled
dis·em·bow·el·ing
dis·em·bow·el·ment
dis·en·chant
dis·en·chant·ment
dis·en·cum·ber
dis·en·fran·chise
dis·en·fran·chised
dis·en·fran·chis·ing
dis·en·gage
dis·en·gaged
dis·en·gag·ing
dis·en·gage·ment
dis·en·tan·gle
dis·en·tan·gled
dis·en·tan·gling
dis·en·tan·gle·ment
dis·es·tab·lish
dis·es·tab·lish·ment
dis·fa·vor
dis·fig·ure
dis·fig·ured
dis·fig·ur·ing
dis·fig·ure·ment
dis·fran·chise
dis·fran·chised
dis·fran·chis·ing
dis·fran·chise·ment
dis·gorge
dis·gorged
dis·gorg·ing
dis·grace
dis·graced
dis·grac·ing
dis·grace·ful
dis·grun·tle
dis·grun·tled
dis·grun·tling
dis·guise
dis·guised
dis·guis·ing

dis·gust
dis·gust·ed
dis·gust·ing
dis·ha·bille
dis·har·mo·ny
dis·har·mo·nies
dis·heart·en
dis·heart·en·ing
di·shev·eled
dis·hon·est
dis·hon·est·ly
dis·hon·es·ty
dis·hon·es·ties
dis·hon·or
dis·hon·or·a·ble
dis·hon·or·a·bly
dis·il·lu·sion
dis·il·lu·sion·ment
dis·in·cline
dis·in·clined
dis·in·clin·ing
dis·in·cli·na·tion
dis·in·fect
dis·in·fect·ant
dis·in·fec·tion
dis·in·gen·u·ous
dis·in·her·it
dis·in·her·i·tance
dis·in·te·grate
dis·in·te·grat·ed
dis·in·te·grat·ing
dis·in·te·gra·tion
dis·in·ter
dis·in·terred
dis·in·ter·ring
dis·in·ter·ment
dis·in·ter·est
dis·in·ter·es·ted
dis·join
dis·joint
dis·joint·ed
dis·junc·tion
disk
disc
dis·like
dis·liked
dis·lik·ing
dis·lik·a·ble
dis·lo·cate
dis·lo·cat·ing
dis·lo·ca·tion
dis·lodge
dis·lodged
dis·lodg·ing
dis·lodg·ment
dis·loy·al
dis·loy·al·ly
dis·loy·al·ty
dis·mal
dis·mal·ly
dis·man·tle
dis·man·tled
dis·man·tling
dis·may
dis·mem·ber
dis·mem·ber·ment
dis·miss
dis·mis·sal
dis·mount
dis·o·bey
dis·o·be·di·ence
dis·o·be·di·ent
dis·or·der
dis·or·dered
dis·or·der·ly
dis·or·der·li·ness
dis·or·gan·ize
dis·or·gan·ized

dis·or·gan·i·za·tion
dis·o·ri·ent
dis·o·ri·en·ta·tion
dis·own
dis·par·age
dis·par·aged
dis·par·ag·ing
dis·par·age·ment
dis·pa·rate
dis·pa·rate·ly
dis·par·i·ty
dis·par·i·ties
dis·pas·sion
dis·pas·sion·ate
dis·patch
dis·patch·er
dis·pel
dis·pelled
dis·pel·ling
dis·pen·sa·ble
dis·pen·sa·bil·i·ty
dis·pen·sa·ry
dis·pen·sa·ries
dis·pense
dis·pensed
dis·pens·ing
dis·pen·sa·tion
dis·perse
dis·persed
dis·pers·ing
dis·per·sion
dis·place
dis·placed
dis·plac·ing
dis·place·ment
dis·play
dis·please
dis·pleas·ing
dis·pleas·ure
dis·port
dis·pose
dis·pos·ing
dis·pos·a·ble
dis·po·si·tion
dis·pos·sess
dis·pos·ses·sion
dis·pro·por·tion
dis·pro·por·tion·ate
dis·prove
dis·prov·ing
dis·pute
dis·put·ed
dis·put·ing
dis·put·a·ble
dis·pu·tant
dis·pu·ta·tious
dis·qual·i·fy
dis·qual·i·fied
dis·qual·i·fy·ing
dis·qual·i·fi·ca·tion
dis·qui·et
dis·qui·etude
dis·qui·si·tion
dis·re·gard
dis·re·pair
dis·re·pute
dis·rep·u·ta·ble
dis·re·spect
dis·re·spect·ful
dis·robe
dis·robed
dis·rob·ing
dis·rupt
dis·rup·tion
dis·rup·tive
dis·rupt·er
dis·sat·is·fy
dis·sat·is·fac·tion

dis·sat·is·fac·to·ry
dis·sat·is·fied
dis·sat·is·fy·ing
dis·sect
dis·sect·ed
dis·sec·tion
dis·sem·ble
dis·sem·blance
dis·sem·bled
dis·sem·bling
dis·sem·i·nate
dis·sem·i·nat·ed
dis·sem·i·nat·ing
dis·sem·i·na·tion
dis·sent
dis·sent·ing
dis·sen·sion
dis·sen·tious
dis·sent·er
dis·sen·tient
dis·ser·tate
dis·ser·ta·ted
dis·ser·ta·ting
dis·ser·ta·tion
dis·serve
dis·served
dis·serv·ing
dis·serv·ice
dis·si·dence
dis·si·dent
dis·sim·i·lar
dis·sim·i·lar·i·ty
dis·sim·i·late
dis·sim·i·lat·ed
dis·sim·i·lat·ing
dis·sim·i·la·tion
dis·si·mil·i·tude
dis·sim·u·late
dis·sim·u·lat·ed
dis·sim·u·lat·ing
dis·sim·u·la·tion
dis·si·pate
dis·si·pat·ed
dis·si·pat·ing
dis·si·pa·tion
dis·so·ci·ate
dis·so·ci·at·ed
dis·so·ci·at·ing
dis·so·ci·a·tion
dis·sol·u·ble
dis·so·lute
dis·so·lu·tion
dis·solve
dis·solv·ing
dis·solv·a·ble
dis·so·nance
dis·so·nant
dis·suade
dis·suad·ed
dis·suad·ing
dis·sua·sion
dis·taff
dis·tance
dis·tant
dis·taste
dis·taste·ful
dis·tem·per
dis·tend
dis·ten·sion
dis·ten·tion
dis·till
dis·tilled
dis·till·ing
dis·til·la·tion
dis·til·late
dis·till·er
dis·till·er·y
dis·till·er·ies

dis·tinct
dis·tinc·tion
dis·tinc·tive
dis·tin·guish
dis·tin·guished
dis·tort
dis·tort·ed
dis·tor·tion
dis·tract
dis·tract·ing
dis·trac·tion
dis·trait
dis·traught
dis·tress
dis·tress·ing
dis·tress·ful
dis·tress·ing
dis·trib·ute
dis·trib·ut·ed
dis·trib·ut·ing
dis·tri·bu·tion
dis·trib·u·tor
dis·trict
dis·trict at·tor·ney
dis·trust
dis·trust·ful
dis·turb
dis·turb·ance
dis·turbed
dis·u·nite
dis·u·nit·ed
dis·u·nit·ing
dis·u·ni·ty
dis·un·ion
dis·use
dis·used
dis·us·ing
ditch
dith·er
dit·to
dit·to·ing
dit·ty
di·u·ret·ic
di·ur·nal
di·va
di·va·gate
di·va·ga·tion
di·van
dive
dived
dove
div·ing
di·verge
di·verged
di·verg·ing
di·ver·gence
di·ver·gent
di·verse
di·ver·si·fi·ca·tion
di·ver·si·fy
di·ver·si·fied
di·ver·si·ty
di·ver·si·ties
di·ver·sion
di·ver·sion·ary
di·vert
di·vide
di·vid·ed
di·vid·ing
di·vis·i·ble
di·vi·sion
di·vi·sive
di·vi·sor
div·i·dend
di·vine
di·vin·i·ty
di·vin·i·ties
di·vorce

di·vorc·ing
di·vor·cee
di·vulge
di·vulged
di·vulg·ing
di·vul·gence
diz·zy
diz·zi·est
diz·zied
diz·zy·ing
diz·zi·ly
diz·zi·ness
do
did
done
do·ing
does
Do·ber·man pin·scher
doc·ile
doc·tor
doc·tor·al
doc·tor·ate
doc·trine
doc·tri·nal
doc·tri·naire
doc·u·ment
doc·u·men·ta·tion
doc·u·men·tary
dod·der
dodge
dodg·ing
doesn't
dog
dogged
dog·ging
dog·eared
dog·ged
dog·ged·ly
dog·ger·el
dog·ma
dog·mas
dog·mat·ic
dog·mat·i·cal
dog·ma·tism
dog·ma·tist
doi·ly
doi·lies
dol·drums
dole
doled
dol·ing
dole·ful
dol·lar
dol·or·ous
dol·phin
dolt
dolt·ish
do·main
dome
domed
dom·ing
do·mes·tic
do·mes·ti·cal·ly
do·mes·ti·cate
do·mes·ti·cat·ed
do·mes·ti·cat·ing
do·mes·ti·ca·tion
do·mes·tic·i·ty
do·mes·tic·i·ties
dom·i·cile
dom·i·ciled
dom·i·cil·ing
dom·i·nant
dom·i·nance
dom·i·nancy
dom·i·nate
dom·i·nat·ing
dom·i·na·tion

dom·i·neer
dom·i·neer·ing
do·min·ion
dom·i·no
dom·i·noes
don
donned
don·ning
do·nate
do·nat·ed
do·nat·ing
do·na·tor
do·na·tion
do·nor
don·key
doo·dle
dooms·day
dope
doped
dop·ing
dop·ey
dop·i·ness
dor·mant
dor·man·cy
dor·mer
dor·mered
dor·mi·to·ry
dor·mi·to·ries
dor·sal
dose
dosed
dos·ing
dos·age
dos·si·er
dot
dot·ted
dot·ting
dot·age
dote
dot·ed
dot·ing
dou·ble
dou·bled
dou·bling
doub·ly
dou·ble·breast·ed
dou·ble·cross
dou·ble·deck·er
dou·ble·faced
dou·ble·head·er
dou·ble·joint·ed
dou·ble·time
doubt
doubt·ful
doubt·ful·ly
doubt·less
douche
douched
douch·ing
dough
dough·ty
dough·ti·ness
dour
dour·ness
douse
doused
dous·ing
dove·cote
dove·tail
dow·a·ger
dow·dy
dowd·i·ly
dow·di·ness
dow·el
dow·eled
dow·el·ing
dow·er
down

down·i·ness
downy
down·grade
down·grad·ed
down·grad·ing
down·heart·ed
down·stream
down·town
down·trod·den
dow·ry
dow·ries
dox·ol·o·gy
doze
dozed
dozing
doz·en
doz·enth
drab
drab·ness
dra·co·ni·an
draft
draft·ee
drafts·man
drafty
draft·i·er
drag
dragged
drag·ging
drag·net
drain
drain·age
drake
dra·ma
dra·ma·tic
dra·mat·ics
dram·a·tist
dram·a·tize
dram·a·ti·za·tion
drape
draped
draping
dra·pery
dra·per·ies
dras·tic
drast·i·cal·ly
draught
draw
drew
drawn
draw·ing
draw·bridge
draw·er
drawl
dread
dread·ful
dream
dreamed
dreamt
dream·ing
dream·er
dream·i·ly
dreamy
dream·i·est
dreary
drear·i·er
drear·i·ly
drear·i·ness
dredge
dredged
dredg·ing
dredg·er
dreg
dreg·gy
drench
dress
dressed
dres·sing
dress·er

dressy
dress·i·est
drib·ble
drib·bled
drib·bling
dri·er
drift
drift·age
drift·er
drill·ing
dri·ly
drink
drank
drunk
drink·ing
drink·a·ble
drink·er
drip
dripped
drip·ping
drip·py
drive
drove
driv·en
driv·ing
driv·el
driv·eled
driv·el·ing
driz·zle
driz·zled
driz·zling
driz·zly
droll
drol·ly
droll·ery
drom·e·dary
drom·e·dar·ies
drone
droned
dron·ing
drool
droop
droop·ing·ly
droop·y
drop
dropped
drop·ping
drop·let
drop·per
drop·sy
dross
drought
drought·y
drought·i·est
drove
drowned
drowse
drows·ing
drow·sy
drow·si·ness
drub
drubbed
drub·bing
drudge
drudg·ing
drudg·ery
drug
drugged
drug·ging
drug·gist
dru·id
drum
drummed
drum·ming
drum·mer
drunk·ard
drunk·en
drunk·en·ly

drunk·en·ness
dry
dry·ing
dri·er
dried
dry·ad
du·al
du·al·i·ty
du·al·ism
du·al·is·tic
dub
dubbed
dub·bing
du·bi·ous
du·bi·e·ty
du·bi·ous·ly
du·cal
du·cat
duch·ess
duchy
duck·ling
ducky
duck·i·est
duct·less
duc·tile
dudg·eon
du·el
du·eled
du·el·ing
du·el·ist
du·en·na
du·et
duf·fel
duff·er
dug·out
duke·dom
dul·cet
dul·ci·mer
dull
dull·ard
dull·ness
du·ly
dumb
dumb·ness
dum·dum
dum·found
dum·my
dum·mies
dump·ling
dumpy
dump·i·er
dump·i·ness
dun
dunned
dun·ning
dunce
dun·der·head
dune
dung·hill
dun·ga·ree
dun·geon
dun·nage
du·o·dec·i·mal
du·o·de·nal
du·o·de·num
dupe
duped
dup·ing
du·plex
du·pli·cate
du·pli·cat·ed
du·pli·cat·ing
du·pli·ca·tion
du·pli·ca·tor
du·plic·i·ty
du·plic·i·ties
du·ra·ble
du·ra·bil·i·ty

dur·ance
du·ra·tion
du·ress
dur·ing
dusk
  dusk·i·ness
  dusky
dust·er
dust·less
dusty
  dust·i·er
  dust·i·ness
du·ti·a·ble
du·ti·ful
  du·ti·ful·ly
du·ty
  du·ties
dwarf
  dwarf·ish
dwell
  dwelt
  dwelled
  dwell·ing
dwindle
  dwin·dled
  dwin·dling
dye
  dyed
  dye·ing
dy·ing
dy·nam·ic
  dy·nam·i·cal·ly
  dy·na·mism
dy·nam·ics
dy·na·mite
  dy·na·mit·er
dy·na·mo
dy·na·mo·tor
dy·nas·ty
  dy·nas·ties
dy·na·tron
dys·en·tery
dys·func·tion
dys·pep·sia
  dys·pep·tic
dys·tro·phy
  dys·tro·phic·

E

ea·ger
  ea·ger·ness
ea·gle
ea·gle-eyed
ca·glet
ear·ache
ear·drum
earl·dom
ear·ly
  ear·li·est
  ear·li·ness
ear·lobe
ear·mark
earn
earn·ings
ear·nest
  ear·nest·ness
ear·ring
ear·shot
ear·split·ting
earth·bound
earth·en
earth·en·ware
earth·ly
earth·quake
earth·shaking
earth·work

earth·worm
earthy
  earth·i·ness
ease
  eased
  eas·ing
ea·sel
ease·ment
eas·i·ly
  eas·i·ness
east·er·ly
east·ern
East·ern·er
east·ward
easy
  eas·i·er
  eas·i·est
eas·y·go·ing
eat
  ate
  eat·en
  eat·ing
eau de co·logne
eaves·drop
  eaves·dropped
  eaves·drop·ping
  eaves·drop·per
ebb
  ebb·ing
eb·ony
ebul·lience
  ebul·lient
  eb·ul·li·tion
ec·cen·tric
  ec·cen·tric·i·ty
ec·cle·si·as·tic
  ec·cle·si·as·ti·cal
ech·e·lon
echo
  ech·oes
  ech·oed
  ech·o·ing
eclair
ec·lec·tic
  ec·lec·ti·cal·ly
  ec·lec·ti·cism
eclipse
  eclipsed
  eclips·ing
eclip·tic
ecol·o·gy
  ec·o·log·ic
  ec·o·log·i·cal
  ecol·o·gist
eco·nom·ic
eco·nomi·cal
eco·nom·ics
econ·o·mist
econ·o·mize
  econ·o·miz·ing
econ·o·my
  econ·o·mies
ec·ru
ec·sta·sy
  ec·sta·sies
ec·stat·ic
  ec·stat·i·cal
ec·u·men·ic
  ec·u·men·i·cal
  ec·u·men·ism
ec·ze·ma
  ec·zem·a·tous
e·da·cious
ed·dy
  ed·dies
  ed·died
  ed·dy·ing
edel·weiss

ede·ma
edge
  edged
  edg·ing
edgy
  edg·i·ness
ed·i·ble
  ed·i·bil·i·ty
edict
ed·i·fice
ed·i·fy
  ed·i·fied
  ed·i·fy·ing
  ed·i·fi·ca·tion
ed·it
edi·tion
ed·i·tor
ed·i·to·ri·al
  ed·i·to·ri·al·ly
  ed·i·to·ri·al·ize
  ed·i·to·ri·al·iz·ing
ed·u·cate
  ed·u·cat·ed
  ed·u·cat·ing
  ed·u·ca·ble
  ed·u·ca·tive
  ed·u·ca·tion
  ed·u·ca·tion·al
  ed·u·ca·tor
educe
  educed
  educ·ing
  educ·i·ble
  educ·tion
eel
  eely
ee·rie
  ee·ri·ly
  ee·ri·ness
ef·face
  ef·faced
  ef·fac·ing
  ef·face·ment
ef·fect
ef·fec·tive
  ef·fec·tive·ness
  ef·fec·tive·ly
ef·fec·tu·al
ef·fec·tu·ate
  ef·fec·tu·at·ed
  ef·fec·tu·at·ing
ef·fem·i·nate
  ef·fem·i·na·cy
  ef·fem·i·nate·ly
ef·fer·vesce
  ef·fer·vesc·ing
  ef·fer·ves·cence
  ef·fer·ves·cent
ef·fete
ef·fi·ca·cy
  ef·fi·ca·cies
  ef·fi·ca·cious
ef·fi·cient
  ef·fi·cient·ly
ef·fi·gy
  ef·fi·gies
ef·flo·resce
  ef·flo·resced
  ef·flo·resc·ing
  ef·flo·res·cence
  ef·flo·res·cent
ef·flu·ent
  ef·flu·ence
ef·flu·vi·um
  ef·flu·vi·al
ef·fort
  ef·fort·less
ef·fron·tery

ef·fron·ter·ies
ef·ful·gent
  ef·ful·gence
ef·fuse
  ef·fused
  ef·fus·ing
  ef·fu·sion
  ef·fu·sive
egal·i·tar·i·an
  egal·i·tar·i·an·ism
ego·cen·tric
ego·ism
  ego·ist
  ego·is·tic
ego·tism
  ego·tist
  ego·tis·tic
  ego·tis·ti·cal
egre·gious
egress
  e·gre·sion
egret
eight
  eighth
eight·een
  eight·eenth
eight·fold
eighty
  eight·ies
  eight·i·eth
ei·ther
ejac·u·late
  ejac·u·lat·ed
  ejac·u·lat·ing
  ejac·u·la·tion
  cjac·u·la·to·ry
eject
  ejec·tion
  eject·ment
  ejec·tor
eke
  eked
  ek·ing
elab·o·rate
  elab·o·rat·ed
  elab·o·rat·ing
  elab·o·rate·ness
  elab·o·ra·tion
elapse
  elapsed
  elaps·ing
elas·tic
  elas·ti·cal
  elas·tic·i·ty
elate
  elat·ed
  elat·ing
  ela·tion
el·bow
eld·er
  el·er·ly
  eld·er·li·ness
  eld·est
elect
  elec·tion
  elec·tion·eer
  elec·tive
  elec·tor
  elec·tor·al
  elec·tor·ate
elec·tric
  elec·tri·cal
  elec·tri·cian
  elec·tric·i·ty
elec·tri·fy
  elec·tri·fied
  elec·tri·fy·ing
  elec·tri·fi·ca·tion

elec·tro·car·di·o·gram
elec·tro·cute
  elec·tro·cut·ed
  elec·tro·cut·ing
  elec·tro·cu·tion
elec·trode
elec·tro·dy·nam·ics
elec·tro·en·ceph·a·lo·gram
elec·trol·y·sis
  elec·tro·lyze
  elec·tro·lyzed
  elec·tro·lyz·ing
  elec·tro·lyte
  elec·tro·lyt·ic
elec·tro·mag·net
  elec·tro·mag·net·ism
  elec·tro·mag·net·ic
elec·tron
elec·tron·ic
  elec·tron·ics
  elec·tron·i·cal·ly
elec·tro·plate
  elec·tro·plat·ed
  elec·tro·plat·ing
elec·tro·ther·a·py
el·ee·mos·y·nary
el·e·gant
  el·e·gance
  el·e·gan·cy
  el·e·gant·ly
el·e·gy
  el·e·gies
  el·e·gize
  el·e·giz·ing
el·e·ment
el·e·men·tal
el·e·men·ta·ry
  el·e·men·ta·ri·ly
ele·phant
  el·e·phan·ti·a·sis
  el·e·phan·tine
el·e·vate
  el·e·vat·ed
  el·e·vat·ing
  el·e·va·tion
  el·e·va·tor
elev·en
  elev·enth
elf
  elves
  elf·in
elic·it
el·i·gi·ble
  el·i·gi·bil·i·ty
elim·i·nate
  elim·i·nat·ed
  elim·i·nat·ing
  elim·i·na·tion
elite
  elit·ism
  elit·ist
elix·ir
Eliz·a·beth·an
el·lipse
el·lip·sis
el·lip·ti·cal
  el·lip·tic
el·o·cu·tion
  el·o·cu·tion·ary
  el·o·cu·tion·ist
elon·gate
  elon·gat·ed
  elon·gat·ing
  elon·ga·tion
elope
  eloped
  elop·ing
  elope·ment

el·o·quence
el·o·quent
elu·ci·date
  elu·ci·dat·ed
  elu·ci·dat·ing
  elu·ci·da·tion
elude
  elud·ed
  elud·ing
  elu·sion
elu·sive
  elu·so·ry
  elu·sive·ness
ema·ci·ate
  ema·ci·at·ed
  ema·ci·at·ed
  ema·ci·a·tion
em·a·nate
  em·a·nat·ed
  em·a·nat·ing
  em·a·na·tion
eman·ci·pate
  eman·ci·pat·ed
  eman·ci·pat·ing
  eman·ci·pa·tor
emas·cu·late
  emas·cu·lat·ed
  emas·cu·lating
  emas·cu·la·tion
em·balm
  em·balm·ment
em·bank·ment
em·bar·go
  em·bar·goes
  em·bar·go·ing
em·bark
  em·bar·ka·tion
  em·bark·ment
em·bar·rass
  em·bar·rass·ed
  em·bar·rass·ing
  em·bar·rass·ment
em·bas·sy
  em·bas·sies
em·bat·tle
  em·bat·tled
  em·bat·tling
  em·bat·tle·ment
em·bed
  em·bed·ded
  em·bed·ding
em·bel·lish
  em·bel·lish·ment
em·ber
em·bez·zle
  em·bez·zled
  em·bez·zling
  em·bez·zle·ment
  em·bez·zler
em·bit·ter
  em·bit·ter·ment
em·bla·zon
  em·blaz·on·ment
em·blem
  em·blem·at·ic
  em·blem·at·i·cal
em·bod·y
  em·bod·ied
  em·bod·y·ing
  em·bod·i·ment
em·bold·en
em·bo·lism
em·bo·lus
em·boss
  em·boss·ment
em·bou·chure
em·brace
  em·brac·ing

em·bra·sure
em·bro·cate
em·broi·der
  em·broi·dery
em·broil
  em·broil·ment
em·bryo
  em·bry·os
  em·bry·on·ic
  em·bry·ol·o·gy
em·cee
  em·ceed
  em·cee·ing
emend
  emen·da·ble
  emen·da·tion
em·er·ald
emerge
  emerged
  emerg·ing
  emer·gence
  emer·gent
  emer·gen·cy
  emer·gen·cies
emer·i·tus
em·ery
emet·ic
em·i·grant
em·i·grate
  em·i·grat·ing
  em·i·gra·tion
émi·gré
em·i·nence
  em·i·nent
  em·i·nent do·main
em·is·sary
  em·is·sar·ies
emis·sion
  emis·sive
emit
  emit·ted
  emit·ting
emol·lient
emol·u·ment
emote
  emot·ed
  emot·ing
  emo·tive
  emo·tion
  emo·tion·al·ly
  emo·tion·al·ism
em·pan·el
em·pa·thize
  em·pa·thized
  em·pa·thiz·ing
em·pa·thy
  em·pa·thet·ic
  em·path·ic
em·per·or
em·pha·sis
  em·pha·ses
em·pha·size
  em·pha·sized
  em·pha·siz·ing
em·phat·ic
  em·phat·i·cal·ly
em·phy·se·ma
em·pire
em·pir·i·cal
em·pir·i·cism
em·place·ment
em·ploy
  em·ploy·a·ble
  em·ploy·ee
  em·ploy·er
  em·ploy·ment
em·po·ri·um
em·pow·er

em·press
emp·ty
  emp·tied
  emp·ty·ing
  emp·ti·ness
em·u·late
  em·u·lat·ing
  em·u·la·tion
emul·si·fy
  emul·si·fied
  emul·si·fy·ing
  emul·si·fi·ca·tion
  emul·si·fi·er
emul·sion
  emul·sive
en·a·ble
  en·a·bled
  en·a·bling
en·act
  en·act·ment
enam·el
  enam·eled
  enam·el·ing
  enam·el·ware
en·am·or
  en·am·ored
en·camp
  en·camp·ment
en·cap·su·late
  en·cap·sul·lat·ed
  en·cap·su·lat·ing
  en·cap·sule
en·case
  en·cased
  en·cas·ing
en·ceinte
en·ceph·a·li·tis
en·chant
  en·chant·ing
  en·chant·ment
  en·chant·ress
en·chi·la·da
en·cir·cle
  en·cir·cled
  en·cir·cling
  en·cir·cle·ment
en·clave
en·close
  en·closed
  en·clos·ing
  en·clo·sure
en·code
  en·cod·ed
  en·cod·ing
en·com·pass
en·core
en·coun·ter
en·cour·age
  en·cour·aged
  en·cour·ag·ing
  en·cour·age·ment
en·croach
  en·croach·ment
en·crust
  en·crus·ta·tion
en·cum·ber
  en·cum·brance
en·cy·clo·pe·dia
en·cy·clo·pe·dic
en·dan·ger
  en·dan·ger·ment
en·dear
  en·dear·ment
en·deav·or
en·dem·ic
  en·dem·i·cal
en·dive
end·ing

end·less
en·do·crine
en·do·cri·nol·o·gy
en·dog·a·mous
en·dorse
  en·dors·ing
  en·dor·see
  en·dor·ser
  en·dorse·ment
en·do·scope
endow
  en·dow·ment
en·due
  en·dued
  en·du·ing
en·dure
  en·dur·ing
  en·dur·a·ble
  en·dur·ance
  en·dur·ing·ness
en·e·ma
en·e·my
  en·e·mies
en·er·get·ic
  en·er·get·i·cal·ly
en·er·gize
  en·er·gized
  en·er·giz·ing
  en·er·gi·zer
en·er·gy
  en·er·gies
en·er·vate
  en·er·vat·ed
  en·er·vat·ing
  en·er·va·tion
en·fee·ble
  en·fee·bled
  en·fee·bling
  en·fee·ble·ment
en·fold
en·force
  en·forced
  en·forc·ing
  en·force·ment
en·fran·chise
  en·fran·chised
  en·fran·chis·ing
  en·fran·chise·ment
en·gage
  en·gaged
  en·gag·ing
  en·gage·ment
en·gen·der
en·gine
en·gi·neer
En·gland
En·glish
en·gorge
  en·gorged
  en·gorg·ing
  en·gorge·ment
en·grave
  en·graved
  en·grav·ing
  en·grav·er
en·gross
  en·grossed
  en·gross·ing
  en·gross·ment
en·gulf
  en·gulf·ment
en·hance
  en·hanced
  en·hanc·ing
  en·hance·ment
enig·ma
  en·ig·mat·ic
  en·ig·mat·i·cal

en·join
  en·join·ment
en·joy
  en·joy·a·ble
  en·joy·ment
en·large
  en·larged
  en·larg·ing
  en·larg·er
  en·large·ment
en·light·en
  en·light·en·ment
en·list
  en·list·ed
  en·list·ment
en·liv·en
en·masse
en·mesh
cn·mi·ty
en·mi·ties
en·no·ble
  en·no·bled
  en·no·bling
  en·no·ble·ment
en·nui
enor·mi·ty
  enor·mi·ties
enor·mous
enough
en·plane
  en·planed
  en·plan·ing
en·quire
  en·quiry
en·rage
  en·raged
  en·rag·ing
en·rap·ture
  en·rap·tured
  en·rap·tur·ing
  en·rapt
en·rich
  en·rich·ment
en·roll
  en·roll·ment
en route
en·sconce
  en·sconced
  en·sconc·ing
en·semble
en·shrine
  en·shrined
  en·shrin·ing
en·shroud
en·sign
en·si·lage
  en·si·laged
  en·si·lag·ing
en·slave
  en·slaved
  en·slav·ing
  en·slave·ment
en·snare
  en·snared
  en·snar·ing
  en·snare·ment
en·sue
  en·sued
  en·su·ing
en·sure
  en·sured
  en·sur·ing
en·tail
  en·tail·ment
en·tan·gle
  en·tan·gled
  en·tan·gling
  en·tan·gle·ment

en·tente
en·ter
  en·ter·ing
en·ter·prise
  en·ter·pris·ing
en·ter·tain
  en·ter·tain·ing
  en·ter·tain·er
  en·ter·tain·ment
en·thrall
  en·thralled
  en·thrall·ing
  en·thrall·ment
en·throne
  en·throned
  en·thron·ing
  en·throne·ment
en·thuse
  en·thused
  en·thus·ing
en·thu·si·asm
en·thu·si·ast
en·thu·si·as·tic
en·thu·si·as·ti·cal·ly
en·tice
  en·ticed
  en·tic·ing
  en·tice·ment
en·tire
  en·tire·ly
  en·tire·ness
  en·tire·ty
en·ti·tle
  en·ti·tled
  en·ti·tling
  en·ti·tle·ment
en·ti·ty
  en·ti·ties
en·tomb
  en·tomb·ment
en·to·mol·o·gy
en·tou·rage
en·trails
en·train
en·trance
en·trant
en·trap
  en·trapped
  en·trap·ping
  en·trap·ment
en·treat
  en·treat·ment
  en·treaty
en·tree
en·trench
  en·trench·ment
en·tre·pre·neur
en·trust
  en·trust·ment
en·try
  en·tries
en·twine
  en·twined
  en·twin·ing
enu·mer·ate
  enu·mer·at·ed
  enu·mer·at·ing
  enu·mer·a·tion
  enu·mer·a·tor
enun·ci·ate
  enun·ci·at·ed
  enun·ci·at·ing
  enun·ci·a·tion
en·vel·op
  en·vel·op·ing
en·ve·lope
en·vi·a·ble
en·vi·ous

en·vi·ous·ness
en·vi·ron
  en·vi·ron·ment
en·vis·age
  en·vis·ag·ing
en·vi·sion
en·voy
en·vy
  en·vies
  en·vied
  en·vy·ing
  en·vi·a·ble
  en·vi·ous
en·zyme
  en·zy·mat·ic
en·vi·ron·ment
  en·vi·ron·men·tal
ep·au·let
epergne
ephed·rine
ephem·er·al
ep·ic
  ep·i·cal
ep·i·cen·ter
ep·i·cure
  epi·cu·re·an
ep·i·dem·ic
ep·i·der·mis
  ep·i·der·mal
  ep·i·der·mic
ep·i·glot·tis
ep·i·gram
  ep·i·gram·mat·ic
ep·i·graph
ep·i·lep·sy
  ep·i·lep·tic
ep·i·logue
epis·co·pal
  epis·co·pa·cy
  epis·co·pate
  Epis·co·pa·lian
ep·i·sode
  ep·i·sod·ic
  ep·i·sod·i·cal
epis·te·mol·o·gy
epis·tle
ep·i·taph
ep·i·thet
epit·o·me
  epit·o·mize
ep·och
  ep·och·al
ep·oxy
equ·a·ble
  eq·ua·bil·i·ty
  eq·ua·ble·ness
  eq·ua·bly
equal
  equaled
  equal·ling
  equal·ly
  equal·ness
equal·i·tar·i·an
equal·i·ty
  equal·i·ties
equal·ize
  equal·ized
  equal·iz·ing
  equal·i·za·tion
equa·nim·i·ty
equate
  equat·ed
  equat·ing
equa·tion
  equa·tion·al
equa·tor
  equa·to·ri·al
eques·tri·an

eques·tri·enne
equi·dis·tant
  equi·dis·tance
equil·lat·er·al
equi·li·brate
  equi·li·brat·ed
  equi·li·brat·ing
  equi·li·bra·tion
  equi·lib·ri·um
equine
equi·nox
  equi·noc·tial
equip
  equipped
  equip·ping
  equip·ment
equi·page
equi·poise
eq·ui·ty
  eq·ui·ties
  eq·ui·ta·ble
  eq·ui·ta·bly
equiv·a·lent
  equiv·a·lence
equiv·o·cal
equiv·o·cate
  equiv·o·cat·ed
  equiv·o·cat·ing
  equiv·o·ca·tion
erad·i·cate
  erad·i·cat·ed
  erad·i·cat·ing
  erad·i·ca·ble
  erad·i·ca·tion
  erad·i·ca·tor
erase
  erased
  eras·ing
  eras·a·ble
  eras·ure
erect
  erect·a·ble
  erec·tive
  erect·ly
  erect·ness
  erec·tor
erec·tile
  erec·tion
er·mine
erode
  erod·ed
  erod·ing
ero·sion
ero·sive
erot·ic
  erot·i·cal·ly
  erot·i·cism
err
  err·ing·ly
er·rand
er·rant
er·rat·ic
  er·rat·i·cal·ly
er·ra·tum
  er·ra·ta
er·ro·ne·ous
er·ror
  er·ror·less
er·satz
er·st·while
er·u·dite
  er·u·dite·ness
  er·u·di·tion
erupt
  erup·tion
  erup·tive
es·ca·lade
es·ca·late

es·ca·lat·ed
es·ca·lat·ing
es·ca·la·tion
es·ca·la·tor
es·cal·lop
es·ca·pade
es·cape
  es·caped
  es·cap·ing
  es·ca·pee
  es·cap·ist
  es·cap·ism
es·ca·role
es·carp·ment
es·chew
  es·chew·al
es·cort
es·crow
es·cutch·eon
Es·ki·mo
esoph·a·gus
es·o·ter·ic
  es·o·ter·i·cal
es·pal·ier
es·pe·cial
  es·pe·cial·ly
Es·pe·ran·to
es·pi·o·nage
es·pla·nade
es·pouse
  es·poused
  es·pous·ing
  es·pous·al
es·prit de corps
es·py
  es·pied
  es·py·ing
es·quire
es·say
  es·say·ist
es·sence
es·sen·tial
  es·sen·tial·ly
es·tab·lish
  es·tab·lish·ment
es·tate
es·teem
es·thet·ic
es·ti·ma·ble
  es·ti·ma·bly
es·ti·mate
  es·ti·mat·ed
  es·ti·mat·ing
  es·ti·ma·tor
  es·ti·ma·tion
es·trange
  es·tranged
  es·trang·ing
  es·trange·ment
es·tro·gen
es·tu·ary
  es·tu·ar·ies
et cet·era
etch
  etch·ing
eter·nal
  eter·nal·ly
  eter·ni·ty
  eter·nize
  eter·ni·za·tion
eth·a·nol
ether
ethe·re·al
  ethe·re·al·ly
  ethe·re·al·ize
  ethe·re·al·i·za·tion
eth·ic
  eth·i·cal

eth·ics
eth·nic
  eth·ni·cal
eth·nog·ra·phy
eth·nol·o·gy
eth·yl
eti·ol·o·gy
  eti·o·log·i·cal
et·i·quette
etude
et·y·mol·o·gy
  et·y·mo·log·i·cal
eu·ca·lyp·tus
Eu·cha·rist
  Eu·cha·ris·tic
  Eu·cha·ris·ti·cal
eu·chre
eu·gen·ic
  eu·gen·i·cal·ly
eu·lo·gize
  eu·lo·gized
  eu·lo·giz·ing
eu·lo·gy
  eu·lo·gies
  eu·lo·gis·tic
eu·nuch
eu·phe·mism
  eu·phe·mist
  eu·phe·mis·tic
  eu·phe·mis·ti·cal
eu·phe·mize
  eu·phe·mized
  eu·phe·miz·ing
eu·pho·ny
  eu·phon·ic
  eu·phon·i·cal
  eu·pho·ni·ous
eu·pho·ria
  eu·phor·ic
Eu·rope
  Eu·ro·pe·an
eu·tha·na·sia
evac·u·ate
  evac·u·at·ed
  evac·u·at·ing
  evac·u·a·tion
  evac·u·ee
evade
  evad·ed
  evad·ing
eval·u·ate
  eval·u·at·ed
  eval·u·at·ing
  eval·u·a·tion
  eval·u·a·tor
ev·a·nesce
  ev·a·nesced
  ev·a·nesc·ing
  ev·a·nes·cent
evan·gel·i·cal
  evan·gel·ic
  evan·gel·i·cal·ism
  evan·gel·i·cal·ly
evan·ge·lism
  evan·ge·lis·tic
  evan·ge·lis·ti·cal·ly
  evan·ge·list
evan·ge·lize
  evan·ge·lized
  evan·ge·liz·ing
  evan·ge·li·za·tion
evap·o·rate
  evap·o·rat·ed
  evap·o·rat·ing
  evap·o·ra·tion
  evap·o·ra·tor
eva·sion
  eva·sive

eva·sive·ness
even
  even·ly
eve·ning
event·ful
  event·ful·ly
even·tu·al
  even·tu·al·ly
  even·tu·al·i·ty
even·tu·ate
  even·tu·at·ed
  even·tu·at·ing
ev·er·green
ev·er·last·ing
evert
  ever·sion
ev·ery·body
ev·ery·day
cv·cry·one
ev·ery·thing
ev·ery·where
evict
  evic·tion
  evic·tor
ev·i·dence
  ev·i·denced
  ev·i·denc·ing
ev·i·dent
  ev·i·dent·ly
ev·i·den·tial
evil
  evil·do·er
  evil·ly
  evil·ness
  evil·mind·ed
evince
  evinced
  evinc·ing
  evin·ci·ble
evis·cer·ate
  evis·cer·at·ed
  evis·cer·at·ing
  evis·cer·a·tion
evoke
  evoked
  evok·ing
  ev·o·ca·tion
ev·o·lu·tion
  ev·o·lu·tion·al
  ev·o·lu·tion·ary
  ev·o·lu·tion·ism
  ev·o·lu·tion·ist
evolve
  evolved
  evolv·ing
  evolve·ment
ew·er
ex·ac·er·bate
  ex·ac·er·bat·ed
  ex·ac·er·bat·ing
  ex·ac·er·ba·tion
ex·act
  ex·act·a·ble
ex·act·ing
  ex·act·ing·ly
ex·act·i·tude
ex·act·ly
ex·ag·ger·ate
  ex·ag·ger·at·ed
  ex·ag·ger·at·ing
  ex·ag·ger·a·tion
ex·alt
  ex·al·ta·tion
  ex·alt·ed
ex·am·ine
  ex·am·ined
  ex·am·in·ing
  ex·am·in·er

ex·am·i·na·tion
ex·am·ple
  ex·am·pled
  ex·am·pling
ex·as·per·ate
  ex·as·per·at·ed
  ex·as·per·at·ing
  ex·as·per·a·tion
ex·ca·vate
  ex·ca·vat·ed
  ex·ca·vat·ing
  ex·ca·va·tion
  ex·ca·va·tor
ex·ceed
  ex·ceed·ed
  ex·ceed·ing
ex·cel
  ex·celled
  ex·cel·ling
ex·cel·lent
  ex·cel·lence
  ex·cel·len·cy
ex·cel·si·or
ex·cept
  ex·cept·ing
  ex·cep·tion
  ex·cep·tion·al
ex·cerpt
  ex·cerp·tion
ex·cess
  ex·ces·sive
ex·change
  ex·changed
  ex·chang·ing
  ex·change·a·bil·i·ty
  ex·change·a·ble
ex·cheq·uer
ex·cise
  ex·cised
  ex·cis·ing
  ex·cis·a·ble
  ex·ci·sion
ex·cit·a·ble
  ex·cit·a·bil·i·ty
ex·cite
  ex·cit·ed
  ex·cit·ing
  ex·ci·ta·tion
  ex·cit·ed·ly
  ex·cite·ment
ex·claim
  ex·cla·ma·tion
  ex·clam·a·to·ry
ex·clude
  ex·clud·ed
  ex·clud·ing
  ex·clud·a·ble
  ex·clu·sion
ex·clu·sive
  ex·clu·sive·ness
  ex·clu·siv·i·ty
ex·com·mu·ni·cate
  ex·com·mu·ni·cat·ed
  ex·com·mu·ni·cat·ing
  ex·com·mu·ni·cant
  ex·com·mu·ni·ca·ble
  ex·com·mu·ni·ca·tion
ex·co·ri·ate
  ex·co·ri·at·ed
  ex·co·ri·at·ing
  ex·co·ri·a·tion
ex·cre·ment
  ex·cre·men·tal
ex·cres·cent
  ex·cres·cense
ex·cre·ta
  ex·cre·tal
ex·crete

ex·cret·ed
ex·cret·ing
ex·cre·tion
ex·cru·ci·ate
  ex·cru·ci·at·ing
  ex·cru·ci·a·tion
ex·cul·pate
  ex·cul·pat·ed
  ex·cul·pat·ing
  ex·cul·pa·tion
  ex·cul·pa·to·ry
ex·cur·sion
  ex·cur·sion·al
  ex·cur·sion·ary
ex·cur·sive
ex·cuse
  ex·cused
  ex·cus·ing
  ex·cus·a·ble
  ex·cus·a·bly
  ex·cus·a·to·ry
ex·e·cra·ble
  ex·e·cra·bly
ex·e·crate
  ex·e·crat·ed
  ex·e·crat·ing
  ex·e·cra·tive
  ex·e·cra·tor
  ex·e·cra·tion
ex·e·cute
  ex·e·cut·ed
  ex·e·cut·ing
  ex·e·cut·er
  ex·e·cu·tion
  ex·e·cu·tion·er
ex·ec·u·tive
ex·ec·u·tor
  ex·ec·u·trix
ex·e·ge·sis
  ex·e·ge·ses
ex·em·plar
  ex·em·pla·ry
  ex·em·pla·ri·ly
ex·em·pli·fy
  ex·em·pli·fied
  ex·em·pli·fy·ing
  ex·em·pli·fi·ca·tion
ex·empt
  ex·emp·tion
ex·er·cise
  ex·er·cised
  ex·er·cis·ing
  ex·er·cis·er
ex·ert
  ex·er·tion
ex·fo·li·ate
  ex·fo·li·at·ed
  ex·fo·li·at·ing
  ex·fo·li·a·tion
ex·hale
  ex·haled
  ex·hal·ing
  ex·ha·la·tion
ex·haust
  ex·haust·ed
  ex·haust·ing
  ex·haus·tion
  ex·haus·tive
ex·hib·it
  ex·hib·i·tor
  ex·hi·bi·tion
  ex·hi·bi·tion·ism
  ex·hi·bi·tion·ist
ex·hil·a·rate
  ex·hil·a·rat·ed
  ex·hil·a·rat·ing
  ex·hil·a·ra·tion
  ex·hil·a·ra·tive

ex·hort
  ex·hor·ta·tive
  ex·hor·ta·tion
  ex·hor·ta·to·ry
  ex·hort·ing·ly
ex·hume
  ex·humed
  ex·hum·ing
  ex·hu·ma·tion
ex·i·gen·cy
  ex·i·gen·cies
ex·i·gent
  ex·i·gent·ly
ex·ig·u·ous
ex·ile
  ex·iled
  ex·il·ing
ex·ist
  ex·ist·ence
  ex·ist·ent
ex·is·ten·tial
  ex·is·ten·tial·ism
ex li·bris
ex·o·dus
ex of·fi·cio
ex·og·a·my
  ex·og·a·mous
ex·og·e·nous
ex·on·er·ate
  ex·on·er·at·ed
  ex·on·er·at·ing
  ex·on·er·a·tion
  ex·on·er·a·tive
ex·or·bi·tant
  ex·or·bi·tance
  ex·or·bi·tant·ly
ex·or·cise
  ex·or·cised
  ex·or·cis·ing
  ex·or·cism
  ex·or·cist
ex·o·tic
  ex·ot·i·cal·ly
  ex·ot·i·cism
ex·pand
  ex·pand·er
  ex·pand·able
ex·panse
ex·pan·si·ble
  ex·pan·si·bil·i·ty
ex·pan·sion
  ex·pan·sion·ism
  ex·pan·sion·ist
ex·pan·sive
  ex·pan·sive·ly
  ex·pan·sive·ness
ex·pa·ti·ate
  ex·pa·ti·at·ed
  ex·pa·ti·at·ing
  ex·pa·ti·a·tion
ex·pa·tri·ate
  ex·pa·tri·at·ed
  ex·pa·tri·at·ing
  ex·pa·tri·a·tion
ex·pect
  ex·pect·a·ble
  ex·pect·a·bly
  ex·pect·ing·ly
  ex·pect·an·cy
  ex·pect·ant
  ex·pec·ta·tion
ex·pec·to·rate
  ex·pec·to·rat·ed
  ex·pec·to·rat·ing
  ex·pec·to·ra·tion
ex·pe·di·ent
  ex·pe·di·en·cy
ex·pe·dite

ex·pe·dit·ed
ex·pe·dit·ing
ex·pe·dit·er
ex·pe·di·tious
ex·pe·di·tion
ex·pel
  ex·pelled
  ex·pel·ling
ex·pend
  ex·pend·a·ble
  ex·pend·a·bil·i·ty
ex·pend·i·ture
ex·pense
  ex·pen·sive
ex·pe·ri·ence
  ex·pe·ri·enced
  ex·pe·ri·enc·ing
  ex·pe·ri·en·tial
ex·per·i·ment
  ex·per·i·men·tal
  ex·per·i·men·ta·tion
ex·pert
  ex·pert·ly
  ex·pert·ness
ex·per·tise
ex·pi·ate
  ex·pi·at·ed
  ex·pi·at·ing
  ex·pi·a·tion
  ex·pi·a·to·ry
ex·pire
  ex·pired
  ex·pir·ing
  ex·pi·ra·tion
  ex·pi·ra·to·ry
ex·plain
  ex·plain·a·ble
  ex·pla·na·tion
  ex·plan·a·to·ry
ex·ple·tive
ex·pli·cate
  ex·pli·cat·ed
  ex·pli·cat·ing
  ex·pli·ca·ble
  ex·pli·ca·tion
  ex·pli·ca·tive
ex·plic·it
  ex·plic·it·ly
  ex·plic·it·ness
ex·plode
  ex·plod·ed
  ex·plod·ing
ex·plo·sion
  ex·plo·sive
ex·ploit
  ex·ploit·a·ble
  ex·ploi·ta·tion
  ex·ploit·er
  ex·ploit·ive
ex·plore
  ex·plo·ra·tion
  ex·plor·a·to·ry
ex·po·nent
  ex·po·nen·tial
ex·port
  ex·port·a·ble
  ex·por·ta·tion
  ex·port·er
ex·pose
  ex·posed
  ex·pos·ing
  ex·pos·er
  ex·po·sure
ex·po·se
ex·po·si·tion
  ex·pos·i·tor
  ex·pos·i·to·ry
ex·pos·tu·late

ex·pos·tu·lat·ed
ex·pos·tu·lat·ing
ex·pos·tu·la·tion
ex·pos·tu·la·to·ry
ex·po·sure
ex·pound
ex·press
ex·press·i·ble
ex·pres·sion
ex·pres·sive
ex·press·ly
ex·pres·sion·ism
ex·pres·sion·ist
ex·pro·pri·ate
ex·pro·pri·at·ed
ex·pro·pri·at·ing
ex·pro·pri·a·tion
ex·pul·sion
ex·pul·sive
ex·punge
ex·punged
ex·pung·ing
ex·pur·gate
ex·pur·gat·ed
ex·pur·gat·ing
ex·pur·ga·tion
ex·pur·ga·to·ry
ex·qui·site
ex·qui·site·ly
ex·qui·site·ness
ex·tant
ex·tem·po·re
ex·tem·po·rize
ex·tem·po·rized
ex·tem·po·riz·ing
ex·tem·po·ri·za·tion
ex·tem·po·ra·ne·ous
ex·tend
ex·tend·ed
ex·tend·i·ble
ex·ten·si·ble
ex·ten·sion
ex·ten·sive
ex·tent
ex·ten·u·ate
ex·ten·u·at·ed
ex·ten·u·at·ing
ex·ten·u·a·tion
ex·te·ri·or
ex·ter·mi·nate
ex·ter·mi·nat·ed
ex·ter·mi·nat·ing
ex·ter·mi·na·tion
ex·ter·nal
ex·ter·nal·ly
ex·ter·ri·to·ri·al
ex·tinct
ex·tinc·tion
ex·tin·guish
ex·tin·guish·a·ble
ex·tin·guish·er
ex·tin·guish·ment
ex·tir·pate
ex·tir·pat·ed
ex·tir·pat·ing
ex·tir·pa·tion
ex·tol
ex·tolled
ex·tol·ling
ex·tol·ment
ex·tort
ex·tor·ter
ex·tor·tive
ex·tor·tion
ex·tor·tion·ary
ex·tor·tion·ate
ex·tor·tion·er
ex·tor·tion·ist

ex·tra
ex·tract
ex·trac·tive
ex·trac·tor
ex·trac·tion
ex·tra·cur·ric·u·lar
ex·tra·dite
ex·tra·dit·ed
ex·tra·dit·ing
ex·tra·dit·a·ble
ex·tra·di·tion
ex·tra·ne·ous
ex·traor·di·nary
ex·trap·o·late
ex·trap·o·la·tion
ex·tra·sen·so·ry
ex·tra·ter·res·tri·al
ex·tra·ter·ri·to·ri·al
ex·trav·a·gant
ex·trav·a·gance
ex·trav·a·gan·cy
ex·trav·a·gan·za
ex·treme
ex·treme·ly
ex·trem·ist
ex·trem·ism
ex·trem·i·ty
ex·trem·i·ties
ex·tri·cate
ex·tri·cat·ed
ex·tri·cat·ing
ex·tri·ca·tion
ex·trin·sic
ex·tro·vert
ex·tro·ver·sion
ex·trude
ex·trud·ed
ex·trud·ing
ex·tru·sion
ex·u·ber·ant
ex·u·ber·ance
ex·ude
ex·ud·ed
ex·ud·ing
ex·u·da·tion
ex·ult
ex·ult·ant
ex·ul·ta·tion
ex·ult·ing·ly
ex·ur·bia
ex·ur·ban·ite
eye
eyed
eyeing
eye·ball
eye·glass·es
eye·o·pen·er
eye·wit·ness

F

fa·ble
fa·bled
fab·ric
fab·ri·cate
fab·ri·cat·ed
fab·ri·cat·ing
fab·ri·ca·tion
fab·ri·ca·tor
fab·u·lous
fa·cade
face
faced
fac·ing
fac·et
fa·ce·tious
fa·cial

fa·cial·ly
fac·ile
fac·ile·ly
fa·cil·i·tate
fa·cil·i·tat·ed
fa·cil·i·tat·ing
fa·cil·i·ty
fa·cil·i·ties
fac·sim·i·le
fac·tion
fac·tion·al
fac·tion·al·ism
fac·ti·tious
fac·tor
fac·to·ry
fac·to·ries
fac·to·tum
fac·tu·al
fac·tu·al·ly
fac·ul·ty
fad·dist
fade
fad·ed
fad·ing
fade·less
fag·
fagged
fag·ging
fag·got
Fahr·en·heit
fa·ience
fail·ing
fail·ure
faint·ly
faint·ness
faint·heart·ed
fair·ly
fair·mind·ed
fair·ness
fairy
fair·ies
faith·ful
faith·less
fake
faked
fak·ing
fak·er
fa·kir
fal·con
fall
fell
fall·en
fall·ing
fal·la·cious
fal·la·cy
fal·li·ble
fal·li·bil·i·ty
Fal·lo·pi·an
fal·low
false
false·ly
false·ness
false·hood
fal·si·fy
fal·si·fied
fal·si·fy·ing
fal·si·fi·ca·tion
fal·si·ty
fal·ter
fal·ter·ing
famed
fa·mil·ial
fa·mil·iar
fa·mil·i·ar·i·ty
fa·mil·iar·ize
fa·mil·iar·ized
fa·mil·iar·iz·ing
fa·mil·iar·i·za·tion

fam·i·ly
fam·i·lies
fa·mil·ial
fa·mil·iar
fam·ine
fam·ish
fam·ished
fa·mous
fan
fanned
fan·ning
fa·nat·ic
fa·nat·i·cal
fa·nat·i·cism
fa·nat·i·cize
fan·ci·ful
fan·ci·ful·ly
fan·cy
fan·cies
fan·ci·er
fan·ci·est
fan·cied
fan·cy·ing
fan·ci·ly
fan·ci·ness
fan·dan·go
fang
fanged
fan·ta·sia
fan·tas·tic
fan·tas·ti·cal
fan·tas·ti·cal·ly
fan·tas·ti·cal·ness
fan·ta·sy
fan·ta·sies
far
farther
farthest
far·ther·most
far·a·way
farce
farced
farc·ing
farc·i·cal
fare
fared
far·ing
fa·ri·na
farm·er
farm·ing
far·reach·ing
far·see·ing
far·sight·ed
far·sight·ed·ness
far·ther·most
fas·cia
fas·ci·cle
fas·ci·cled
fas·ci·nate
fas·ci·nat·ed
fas·ci·nat·ing
fas·ci·na·tion
fas·cism
fas·cist
fas·scis·tic
fash·ion
fash·ion·a·ble
fash·ion·a·ble·ness
fash·ion·a·bly
fas·ten
fas·ten·er
fas·ten·ing
fas·tid·i·ous
fat
fat·ter
fat·test
fat·ted
fat·ten
fat·ting

fat·ty
fat·ti·ness
fat·ness
fa·tal
fa·tal·ly
fa·tal·i·ty
fa·tal·i·ties
fa·tal·ism
fa·tal·ist
fa·tal·is·tic
fate
fat·ed
fat·ing
fate·ful
fa·ther
fa·ther·hood
fa·ther·li·ness
fa·ther·ly
fa·ther·land
fa·ther-in-law
fa·thers-in-law
fath·om
fath·om·a·ble
fath·om·less
fa·tigue
fa·tigued
fa·tig·u·ing
fat·i·ga·ble
fat·i·ga·bil·i·ty
fa·tu·i·ty
fa·tu·i·ties
fat·u·ous
fat·u·ous·ly
fau·cet
fault
fault·find·ing
fault·less·ly
faulty
fault·i·er
fault·i·ly
fault·i·ness
fau·na
fau·nas
fau·nae
faux pas
fa·vor
fa·vored
fa·vor·ing
fa·vor·a·ble
fa·vor·a·ble·ness
fa·vor·a·bly
fa·vored·ness
fa·vor·ite
fa·vor·it·ism
fawn
faze
fazed
faz·ing
fe·al·ty
fear·ful
fear·ful·ness
fear·less
fear·less·ness
fear·some
fear·some·ness
fea·si·ble
fea·si·bil·i·ty
fea·si·ble·ness
fea·si·bly
feath·er
feath·ered
feath·er·bed·ding
fea·ture
fea·tured
fea·tur·ing
fea·ture·less
fe·brile
Feb·ru·ary

Feb·ru·ar·ies
fe·ces
fe·cal
fe·cund
fe·cun·di·ty
fe·cun·date
fe·cun·dat·ed
fe·cun·dat·ing
fe·cun·da·tion
fed·er·al
fed·er·al·ism
fed·er·al·ist
fed·er·al·ly
fed·er·al·ize
fed·er·al·ized
fed·er·al·iz·ing
fed·er·al·i·za·tion
fed·er·ate
fed·er·at·ed
fed·er·at·ing
fe·do·ra
fee·ble
fee·bler
fee·bly
fee·ble·mind·ed
feed
fed
feed·ing
feed·er
feel
felt
feel·ing
feel·er
feign
feigned
feign·ing
feign·er
feint
feisty
feist·i·est
fe·lic·i·tate
fe·lic·i·tat·ed
fe·lic·i·tat·ing
fe·lic·i·ta·tion
fe·lic·i·tous
fe·lic·i·ty
fe·lic·i·ties
fe·line
fe·lin·i·ty
fel·la·tio
fel·low·ship
fel·on
fel·o·ny
fel·o·nies
fe·lo·ni·ous
fe·male
fem·i·nine
fem·i·nine·ness
fem·i·nin·i·ty
fem·i·nism
fem·i·nist
fem·i·nis·tic
fem·i·nize
fem·i·nized
fem·i·niz·ing
fem·i·ni·za·tion
fe·mur
fence
fenced
fenc·ing
fenc·er
fen·der
fe·ra·cious
fe·ral
fer·ment
fer·men·ta·tion
fe·ro·cious
fe·ro·cious·ness

fe·ro·cious·ly
fe·ro·ci·ty
fer·ret
Fer·ris wheel
fer·ro·con·crete
fer·ro·mag·net·ic
fer·ru·gi·nous
fer·rule
fer·ry
fer·ries
fer·tile
fer·tile·ness
fer·til·i·ty
fer·ti·lize
fer·ti·lized
fer·ti·liz·ing
fer·ti·liz·er
fer·ti·li·za·tion
fer·ule
fer·vent
fer·ven·cy
fer·vent·ly
fer·vid
fer·vid·ness
fer·vor
fes·ter
fes·ti·val
fes·tive
fes·tive·ness
fes·tiv·i·ty
fes·toon
fe·tal
fetch
fetch·ing
fete
fet·id
fet·id·ness
fet·ish
fet·ish·ism
fet·ish·ist
fet·lock
fet·ter
fet·tle
fe·tus
feud
feud·ist
feu·dal
feu·dal·ism
feu·dal·is·tic
feu·dal·i·za·tion
feu·dal·ize
fe·ver
fe·ver·ish
fe·ver·ish·ness
fe·ver·ous
fez·zes
fi·an·ce
fi·an·cee
fi·as·co
fi·at
fib
fibbed
fib·ber
fi·ber
fi·bered
fi·bril
fi·broid
fi·brous
fib·u·la
fick·le
fick·le·ness
fic·tion
fic·tion·al
fic·ti·tious
fic·ti·tious·ness
fid·dle
fid·dler
fid·dled

fid·dling
fi·del·i·ty
fidg·et
fidg·ety
fi·du·ci·ary
fief
field·er
fiend
fiend·ish
fierce
fierce·ness
fiery
fier·i·est
fier·i·ly
fier·i·ness
fif·teen
fif·teenth
fif·ty
fif·ti·eth
fight
fought
fight·ing
fight·er
fig·ment
fig·ur·ate
fig·u·ra·tion
fig·u·ra·tive
fig·ure
fig·ured
fig·ur·ing
fig·ure·less
fig·ur·ine
fil·a·ment
fil·a·men·ta·ry
fil·a·ment·ed
fil·a·men·tous
file
filed
fil·ing
fi·let
fi·let mi·gnon
fil·i·al
fil·i·al·ly
fil·i·bus·ter
fil·i·gree
fil·i·greed
fil·i·gree·ing
Fil·i·pi·no
fill·er
fil·let
fill·ing
fil·lip
fil·ly
fil·lies
filmy
film·i·est
film·i·ness
fil·ter
fil·ter·able
fil·tra·tion
filth
filth·i·ness
filthy
filth·i·est
fin
finned
fin·ning
fin·less
fi·na·gle
fi·na·gled
fi·na·gling
fi·na·gler
fi·nal
fi·na·le
fi·nal·ist
fi·nal·i·ty
fi·nal·ly
fi·nal·i·ties
fi·nal·ize

fi·nal·ized
fi·nal·iz·ing
fi·nal·ly
fi·nance
fi·nanced
fi·nanc·ing
fi·nan·cial
fi·nan·cial·ly
fin·an·cier
finch
find
found
find·ing
fine
fin·er
fin·est
fine·ness
fin·ery
fin·er·ies
fi·nesse
fi·nessed
fi·nes·sing
fin·ger
fin·ger·ing
fin·ger·print
fin·i·cal
fin·icky
fin·is
fin·ish
fin·ished
fin·ish·er
fi·nite
fi·nite·ly
fi·nite·ness
Fin·land
Finn·ish
fire
fired
fir·ing
fire·arm
fire·crack·er
fire·fight·er
fire·fly
fire·flies
fire·man
fire·place
fire·pow·er
fire·proof
fire·trap
firm
firm·ly
fir·ma·ment
first·born
first·hand
first·rate
first·string
fis·cal
fis·cal·ly
fish·er·man
fish·er·men
fish·ery
fish·er·ies
fish·ing
fishy
fis·sion
fis·sion·able
fis·sure
fis·sured
fis·sur·ing
fist·i·cuffs
fit
fit·ter
fit·test
fit·ted
fit·ting
fit·ly
fit·ness
fit·ful

fit·ful·ness
fit·ting
fit·ting·ly
five·fold
five-and-ten
fix
fix·a·ble
fixed
fix·ed·ly
fix·er
fix·a·tion
fix·a·tive
fix·ings
fix·i·ty
fix·ture
fiz·zle
fiz·zled
fiz·zling
fiz·zy
fjord
flab·ber·gast
flab·by
flab·bi·er
flab·bi·est
flab·bi·ly
flab·bi·ness
flac·cid
fla·con
flag
flagged
flag·ging
flag·el·lant
flag·el·late
flag·el·lat·ed
flag·el·lat·ing
flag·el·la·tion
fla·gi·tious
flag·on
fla·grant
fla·grant·ly
flail
flair
flake
flaked
flak·ing
flaky
flak·i·est
flak·i·ness
flam·boy·ant
flam·boy·ance
flam·boy·an·cy
flam·boy·ant·ly
flame
flamed
flam·ing
flam·ing·ly
flam·ma·ble
fla·men·co
fla·min·go
flange
flank
flank·er
flan·nel·ette
flap
flapped
flap·ping
flap·per
flare
flared
flar·ing
flare-up
flash·back
flash·light
flashy
flash·i·est
flash·i·ness
flask
flat

flat·ly
flat·ted
flat·ting
flat·ness
flat·ten
flat·foot·ed
flat·ter
flat·ter·er
flat·ter·ing·ly
flat·tery
flat·ter·ies
flat·u·lent
flat·u·lence
flat·u·len·cy
fla·tus
flat·ware
flaunt
flaunt·ed
flaunt·ing·ly
flaunty
fla·vor
fla·vored
fla·vor·less
fla·vor·ing
flawed
flaw·less
flax·en
flea·bit·ten
flec·tion
fledge
fledged
fledg·ing
fledg·ling
flee
fled
flee·ing
fleece
fleeced
fleec·ing
fleecy
fleec·i·ness
fleet
fleet·ly
fleet·ness
fleet·ing
flesh·ly
flesh·li·est
fleshy
flesh·i·ness
fleur·de·lis
flex·i·ble
flex·i·bil·i·ty
flex·i·bly
flex·ure
flib·ber·ti·gib·bet
flick·er
flick·er·ing
fli·er
flight
flight·less
flighty
flight·i·est
flight·i·ly
flight·i·ness
flim·flam
flim·flammed
flim·flam·ming
flim·sy
flim·si·est
flim·si·ly
flim·si·ness
flinch
flinch·ing
fling
flung
fling·ing
flinty
flint·i·ness

flip
flipped
flip·ping
flip·flop
flip·pant
flip·pan·cy
flip·pant·ly
flip·per
flir·ta·tion
flir·ta·tious
flit
flit·ted
flit·ting
flit·ter
float·a·ble
float·a·tion
float·er
float·ing
floc·cu·lent
floc·cu·lence
flocked
floe
flog
flogged
flog·ging
flog·ger
flood·light
flood·light·ed
flood·lit
flood·light·ing
floor·ing
floo·zy
floo·zies
flop
flopped
flop·ping
flop·per
flop·house
flop·py
flop·pi·est
flop·pi·ness
flo·ra
flo·rae
flo·ral
flo·res·cence
flo·res·cent
flo·ret
flo·ri·cul·ture
flo·ri·cul·tur·ist
flor·id
flor·id·i·ty
flor·id·ness
flo·rist
floss
flossy
flo·ta·tion
flo·til·la
flot·sam
flounce
flounced
flounc·ing
floun·der
floury
flour·ish
flour·ish·ing
flout·er
flow
flow·er
flow·ered
flow·er·ing
flow·ery
flub
flubbed
flub·bing
fluc·tu·ate
fluc·tu·at·ed
fluc·tu·at·ing
fluc·tu·a·tion

flue
flu·ent
flu·en·cy
flu·ent·ly
fluff
fluff·i·ness
fluffy
flu·id
flu·id·i·ty
flu·id·ness
fluke
fluky
flun·ky
flun·kies
flu·o·resce
flu·o·resced
flu·o·resc·ing
flu·o·res·cence
flu·o·res·cent
fluor·i·date
fluor·i·da·tion
fluor·i·dat·ed
fluor·i·dat·ing
fluor·o·scope
flur·ry
flur·ries
flur·ried
flur·ry·ing
flus·ter
flute
flut·ed
flut·ing
flut·ist
flut·ter
flut·ter·ing
flut·tery
flux·ion
fly
flew
flown
flying
fly-by-night
fly·er
fly·leaf
fly·pa·per
fly·wheel
foal
foam
foam·i·ness
foamy
fo·cal
fo·cal·ly
fo·cal·ize
fo·cal·ized
fo·cal·iz·ing
fo·cus
fo·cus·es
fo·cused
fo·cus·ing
fod·der
foe·tus
foe·tal
fog
fogged
fog·ging
fog·gy
fog·gi·ly
fog·gi·ness
fo·gy
fo·gies
fo·gy·ish
foi·ble
fold·er
fol·de·rol
fo·li·a·ceous
fo·li·age
fo·li·ate
fo·li·at·ed

fo·li·at·ing
fo·li·a·tion
fo·lio
folk·lore
folk·sy
folk·si·ness
fol·li·cle
fol·lic·u·lar
fol·low
fol·low·er
fol·low·ing
fol·ly
fol·lies
fo·ment
fo·men·ta·tion
fo·ment·er
fon·dant
fon·dle
fon·dled
fon·dling
fond·ly
fond·ness
fon·due
food·stuff
fool·ery
fool·er·ies
fool·har·dy
fool·har·di·ness
fool·ish
fool·ish·ly
fool·proof
foot·age
foot·ball
foot·can·dle
foot·hold
foot·lights
foot·note
foot·path
foot·print
foot·step
fop
fop·pery
fop·pish
for·age
for·aged
for·ag·ing
for·ay
for·bear
for·bore
for·borne
for·bear·ing
for·bear·ance
for·bid
for·bade
for·bid·den
for·bid·ding
for·bid·dance
force
forced
forc·ing
force·a·ble
force·less
force·ful
force·ful·ly
for·ceps
for·ci·ble
for·ci·bly
ford·a·ble
fore·bode
fore·bod·ed
fore·bod·ing
fore·castle
fore·cast
fore·cast·ed
fore·cast·ing
fore·cast·er
fore·close
fore·closed

fore·clos·ing
fore·clo·sure
fore·fa·ther
fore·fin·ger
fore·gath·er
fore·go
fore·went
fore·gone
fore·go·ing
fore·ground
fore·hand·ed
for·eign
for·eign·er
fore·know
fore·knew
fore·known
fore·know·ing
fore·knowl·edge
fore·man
fore·most
fore·name
fore·noon
fo·ren·sic
fore·or·dain
fore·or·di·na·tion
fore·quar·ter
fore·run·ner
fore·see
fore·saw
fore·seen
fore·see·ing
fore·see·a·ble
fore·shad·ow
fore·short·en
fore·sight
fore·skin
for·est
for·est·a·tion
for·es·ter
for·est·ry
fore·stall
fore·taste
fore·tell
fore·told
fore·tell·ing
fore·tell·er
fore·thought
for·ev·er
for·ev·er·more
fore·warn
fore·woman
fore·word
for·feit
for·fei·ture
for·gath·er
forge
forged
forg·ing
forg·er
for·gery
for·ger·ies
for·get
for·got
for·got·ten
for·get·ting
for·get·ta·ble
for·get·ful
for·give
for·gave
for·giv·en
for·giv·ing
for·giv·a·ble
for·give·ness
for·go
for·went
for·gone
for·go·ing
forked

fork·lift
for·lorn
  for·lorn·ly
for·mal
  for·mal·ly
for·mal·ism
for·mal·i·ty
  for·mal·i·ties
for·mal·ize
  for·mal·ized
  for·mal·iz·ing
  for·mal·i·za·tion
for·mat
for·ma·tion
form·a·tive
for·mer
  for·mer·ly
form·fit·ting
for·mi·da·ble
  for·mi·da·bly
form·less
  form·less·ness
for·mu·la
  for·mu·las
for·mu·lary
  for·mu·lar·ies
for·mu·late
  for·mu·lat·ed
  for·mu·lat·ing
  for·mu·la·tion
  for·mu·la·tor
for·ni·cate
  for·ni·cat·ed
  for·ni·cat·ing
  for·ni·cat·or
  for·ni·ca·tion
for·sake
  for·sook
  for·sak·en
  for·sak·ing
  for·sak·en
for·swear
  for·swore
  for·sworn
  for·swear·ing
fort
  for·ti·fi·ca·tion
  for·ti·fy
  for·ti·fied
  for·ti·fy·ing
forte
for·te
forth·com·ing
forth·right
forth·with
for·tis·si·mo
for·ti·tude
fort·night
for·tress
for·tu·i·tous
  for·tu·i·tous·ness
for·tu·nate
  for·tu·nate·ly
for·tune
for·tune·tell·er
for·ty
  for·ties
fo·rum
  fo·rums
for·ward
  for·ward·ness
fos·sil
  fos·sil·ized
  fos·sil·iz·ing
  fos·sil·i·za·tion
fos·ter
  fos·tered
  fos·ter·ing

fought
fou·lard
found
foun·da·tion
  foun·da·tion·al
found·er
found·ling
found·ry
  found·ries
foun·tain
four·flush·er
four·fold
four·post·er
four·score
four·some
four·teen
  four·teenth
fourth
  fourth·ly
foxy
  fox·i·ly
  fox·i·ness
foy·er
fra·cas
frac·tion
  frac·tion·al
frac·tious
frac·ture
  frac·tured
  frac·tur·ing
frag·ile
  fra·gil·i·ty
frag·ment
  frag·men·tal
  frag·men·tary
  frag·men·ta·tion
  frag·ment·ize
fra·grance
fra·grant
  fra·grant·ly
frail
  frail·ty
  frail·ness
frame
  framed
  fram·ing
frame·work
franc
France
fran·chise
  fran·chised
  fran·chis·ing
  fran·chise·ment
Fran·cis·can
fran·gi·ble
fran·gi·pan·i
frank
  frank·ly
  frank·ness
frank·furt·er
frank·in·cense
fran·tic
  fran·ti·cal·ly
frap·pe
fra·ter·nal
  fra·ter·nal·ly
fra·ter·ni·ty
  fra·ter·ni·ties
frat·er·nize
  frat·er·nized
  frat·er·niz·ing
  frat·er·ni·za·tion
frat·ri·cide
  frat·ri·cid·al
fraud·u·lent
  fraud·u·lence
  fraud·u·lent·ly
fraught

fräz·zle
  fraz·zled
freak
  freak·ish
freaky
  freak·i·est
freck·le
  freck·led
  freck·ling
  freck·led
free
  fre·er
  fre·est
  free·ly
free·bie
free·boot·er
free·dom
free·lance
  free·lanced
  free·lanc·ing
Free·ma·son
free·stand·ing
free·spo·ken
free·think·er
freeze
  froze
  fro·zen
  freez·ing
freeze·dry
freez·er
freight·age
freight·er
fre·net·ic
  fre·net·i·cal·ly
fren·zy
  fren·zies
  fren·zied
  fren·zy·ing
fre·quen·cy
  fre·quen·cies
fre·quent
  fre·quent·ly
fres·co
  fres·coes
  fres·coed
  fres·co·ing
fresh
  fresh·en
  fresh·ness
fresh·man
fret
  fret·ted
  fret·ting
  fret·ful
  fret·ful·ly
Freud·i·an
fri·a·ble
fri·ar
fric·as·see
  fric·as·seed
  fric·as·see·ing
fric·tion
  fric·tion·al
  fric·tion·less
friend
  friend·less
  friend·ship
friend·ly
  friend·li·est
  friend·li·ness
frieze
fright·en
  fright·en·ing
  fright·ful
frig·id
  fri·gid·i·ty
  frig·id·ness
frilly

frill·i·est
fringe
  fringed
  fring·ing
frip·pery
frisky
  frisk·i·ness
frit·ter
friv·o·lous
  fri·vol·i·ty
  fri·vol·i·ties
  friv·o·lous·ly
frizz
  friz·zi·ness
  friz·zy
friz·zle
frog
  frogged
  frog·ging
trol·ic
  frol·icked
  frol·ick·ing
  frol·ic·some
front·age
fron·tal
fron·tier
  fron·tiers·man
fron·tis·piece
frost
  frost·ed
  frost·bite
  frost·bit
  frost·bit·ten
  frost·bit·ing
  frost·ing
frosty
  frost·i·ly
  frost·i·ness
froth
  froth·i·ness
  frothy
frou·frou
fro·ward
frown
frow·zy
fro·zen
  fro·zen·ness
fruc·ti·fy
  fruc·ti·fi·ca·tion
fruc·tose
fru·gal
  fru·gal·i·ty
  fru·gal·i·ties
  fru·gal·ly
fruit·ful
  fruit·ful·ly
  fruit·ful·ness
fru·i·tion
fruit·less
frump
  frump·ish
  frumpy
frus·trate
  frus·trat·ed
  frus·trat·ing
  frus·tra·tion
fry
  fried
  fry·ing
fuch·sia
fud·dle
fud·dy-dud·dy
fudge
  fudged
  fudg·ing
fu·el
  fu·eled
  fu·el·ing

fu·gi·tive
fugue
ful·crum
ful·fill
  ful·filled
  ful·fil·ling
  ful·fill·ment
full
  full·ness
  ful·ly
full·fledged
ful·mi·nate
  ful·mi·nat·ed
  ful·mi·nat·ing
  ful·mi·na·tion
ful·some
fum·ble
  fum·bled
  fum·bling
  fum·bler
fume
  fumed
  fum·ing
  fum·ing·ly
fu·mi·gate
  fu·mi·gat·ed
  fu·mi·gat·ing
  fu·mi·ga·tion
  fu·mi·ga·tor
func·tion
  func·tion·al
  func·tion·less
  func·tion·ary
  func·tion·ar·ies
fun·da·men·tal
  fun·da·men·tal·ly
  fun·da·men·tal·ism
  fun·da·men·tal·ist
fu·ner·al
  fu·ne·re·al
fun·gi·cide
  fun·gi·cid·al
fun·gus
fun·gi
fu·nic·u·lar
fun·nel
  fun·neled
  fun·nel·ing
fun·ny
  fun·ni·er
  fun·ni·est
  fun·nies
  fun·ni·ness
fur
  furred
  fur·ring
fur·be·low
fur·bish
fu·ri·ous
  fu·ri·ous·ly
fur·long
fur·lough
fur·nace
fur·nish
  fur·nish·ings
fur·ni·ture
fu·ror
fu·rore
fur·ri·er
fur·row
fur·ry
fur·ther
  fur·ther·ance
  fur·ther·more
  fur·ther·most
  fur·thest
fur·tive
  fur·tive·ly

fu·ry
  fu·ries
fuse
  fused
  fus·ing
fu·se·lage
fu·si·ble
  fu·si·bil·i·ty
fu·sil·lade
  fu·sil·lad·ed
  fu·sil·lad·ing
fu·sion
fussy
  fuss·i·ness
fus·tian
fu·tile
fu·til·i·ty
  fu·til·i·ties
fu·ture
  fu·tu·ri·ty
  fu·tu·ri·ties
fu·tur·ism
  fu·tur·is·tic
fuzzy
  fuzz·i·ness

G

gab
  gabbed
  gab·bing
gab·ar·dine
gab·ble
gab·by
ga·ble
  ga·bled
  ga·bling
gad
gad·ded
  gad·ding
gad·a·bout
gad·fly
gad·get
  gad·get·ry
gag
  gagged
  gag·ging
gai·e·ty
  gai·e·ties
gai·ly
gain·er
gain·ful
gain·say
  gain·said
gait
ga·la
gal·axy
  gal·ax·ies
  ga·lac·tic
gal·lant
  gal·lant·ry
  gal·lant·ries
gal·lery
  gal·ler·ies
gal·ley
gal·li·mau·fry
gall·ing
gal·li·vant
gal·lon
gal·lop
gal·lows
gall·stone
ga·lore
ga·losh·es
gal·van·ic
gal·va·nize
  gal·va·nized

gal·va·niz·ing
gal·va·nom·e·ter
gam·bit
gam·ble
  gam·bled
  gam·bling
  gam·bler
gam·bol
game
  gam·ing
games·man·ship
gam·in
gam·ma
gam·ma glob·u·lin
gam·ut
gamy
  gam·i·ly
  gam·i·ness
gan·der
gang·land
gan·gling
gan·gly
gan·grene
  gan·gre·nous
gang·ster
gant·let
gan·try
gaol
gap
  gapped
  gap·ping
ga·rage
  ga·raged
  ga·rag·ing
gar·bage
gar·ble
  gar·bled
  gar·bling
gar·den
gar·gan·tu·an
gar·gle
  gar·gled
  gar·gling
gar·goyle
gar·ish
gar·land
gar·ment
gar·ner
gar·net
gar·nish
gar·nish·ee
  gar·nish·eed
  gar·nish·ee·ing
gar·nish·ment
gar·ni·ture
gar·ret
gar·ri·son
gar·rote
  gar·rot·ed
  gar·rot·ing
gar·ru·lous
gar·ter
gas
  gassed
  gas·sing
  gas·e·ous
gas·i·fy
  gas·i·fied
  gas·i·fy·ing
  gas·i·fi·ca·tion
gas·ket
gas·light
gas·o·line
gas·sy
  gas·si·ness
gas·tric
gas·tri·tis
gas·tro·en·ter·ol·o·gy

gas·tro·in·tes·ti·nal
gas·tron·o·my
  gas·tro·nom·ic
gath·er
  gath·er·ing
gauche
gau·che·rie
gau·cho
gaudy
  gaud·i·ly
  gaud·i·ness
gauge
  gauged
  gaug·ing
gaunt
  gaunt·let
gauze
  gauz·i·ness
  gauzy
gav·el
ga·votte
gawky
  gawk·i·ly
  gawk·i·ness
gay·e·ty
gay·ly
gaze
  gazed
  gaz·ing
ga·ze·bo
ga·zelle
ga·zette
gaz·et·teer
gear·shift
gear·wheel
Gei·ger count·er
gei·sha
gel
  gelled
  gel·ling
gel·a·tin
  ge·la·ti·nize
  ge·lat·i·nous
ge·la·tion
geld
  geld·ed
  gelt
  geld·ing
gel·id
  ge·lid·i·ty
gem
  gemmed
  gem·ming
gem·i·nate
  gem·i·nat·ed
  gem·i·nat·ing
  gem·i·nate·ly
  gem·i·na·tion
Gem·i·ni
gem·ol·o·gy
  gem·o·log·i·cal
  gem·ol·o·gist
gen·darme
gen·der
gene
ge·ne·al·o·gy
  ge·ne·a·log·i·cal
  ge·ne·al·o·gist
gen·er·al
  gen·er·al·is·si·mo
gen·er·al·ist
gen·er·al·i·ty
  gen·er·al·i·ties
gen·er·al·ize
  gen·er·al·ized
  gen·er·al·iz·ing
  gen·er·al·i·za·tion
gen·er·ate

gen·er·at·ed
gen·er·at·ing
gen·er·a·tive
gen·er·a·tion
gen·er·a·tor
ge·ner·ic
  ge·ner·i·cal
gen·er·ous
  gen·er·os·i·ty
  gen·er·os·i·ties
gen·e·sis
  gen·e·ses
ge·net·ic
  ge·net·i·cal·ly
ge·net·ics
  ge·net·i·cist
gen·ial
  ge·ni·al·i·ty
ge·nie
gen·i·tal
  gen·i·ta·lia
  gen·i·tals
gen·i·tive
ge·nius
  gen·ius·es
gen·o·cide
  gen·o·ci·dal
gen·re
gen·teel
gen·tian
gen·tile
gen·til·i·ty
gen·tle
  gen·tlest
  gen·tly
gen·tle·man
gen·tle·wom·an
gen·try
gen·u·flect
  gen·u·flec·tion
gen·u·ine
  gen·u·ine·ness
ge·nus
ge·o·cen·tric
  ge·o·cen·tri·cal·ly
ge·o·chem·is·try
  ge·o·chem·i·cal
  ge·o·chem·ist
ge·ode
ge·o·des·ic
ge·od·e·sy
geo·og·ra·phy
  ge·o·gra·phies
  ge·o·gra·pher
  ge·o·graph·ic
  ge·o·graph·i·cal
ge·ol·o·gy
  ge·o·ol·o·gies
  ge·o·log·ic
  ge·o·log·i·cal
  ge·o·log·i·cal·ly
  ge·ol·o·gist
ge·o·mag·net·ic
  geo·o·mag·ne·tism
ge·o·met·ric
ge·om·e·try
  ge·om·e·tries
ge·o·phys·ics
  ge·o·phys·i·cal
  ge·o·phys·i·cist
ge·o·pol·i·tics
  ge·o·pol·i·tic
  ge·o·po·lit·i·cal
  ge·o·po·lit·i·cal·ly
ge·o·ther·mal
ge·ra·ni·um
ger·bil
geri·at·rics

ger·i·at·ric
ger·i·a·tri·cian
ger·i·at·rist
ger·mane
Ger·ma·ny
ger·mi·cide
  ger·mi·cid·al
ger·mi·nate
  ger·mi·nat·ed
  ger·mi·nat·ing
  ger·mi·na·tion
ger·on·tol·o·gy
  ger·on·tol·o·gist
ger·ry·man·der
ger·und
Ge·stalt
ge·sta·po
ges·tate
  ges·tat·ed
  ges·tat·ing
  ges·ta·tion
ges·tic·u·late
  ges·tic·u·lat·ed
  ges·tic·u·lat·ing
  ges·tic·u·la·tion
  ges·tic·u·la·to·ry
ges·ture
  ges·tured
  ges·tur·ing
ge·sund·heit
Geth·sem·a·ne
gew·gaw
gey·ser
ghast·ly
  ghast·li·er
  ghast·li·est
  ghast·li·ness
gher·kin
ghet·to
ghost·ly
  ghost·li·est
  ghost·li·ness
ghost·write
  ghost·writ·ten
ghoul
gi·ant
gib·ber·ish
gib·bon
gib·bous
gibe
  gib·ing·ly
gib·let
gid·dy
  gid·di·ly
  gid·di·ness
gift·ed
gi·gan·tic
  gi·gan·tism
gig·gle
  gig·gled
  gig·gling
  gig·gly
gig·o·lo
gild·ed
gilt·edged
gim·let
gim·mick
  gim·mick·y
gin·ger·bread
gin·ger·ly
  gin·ger·li·ness
ging·ham
gip·sy
  gip·sies
gi·raffe
gird·er
gir·dle
  gir·dled

girdling
girl·hood
girl·ish
girth
gist
give
gave
giv·en
giv·ing
giz·zard
gla·cial
gla·cier
glad
glad·der
glad·dest
glad·ly
glad·ness
glad·den
glad·i·a·tor
glad·i·a·to·ri·al
glad·i·o·lus
glad·i·o·lus·es
glad·i·o·la
glam·or·ize
glam·or·ized
glam·or·iz·ing
glam·or·i·za·tion
glam·or·ous
glam·or·ous·ness
glam·our
glance
glanced
glanc·ing
glan·du·lar
glare
glared
glar·ing
glar·i·ness
glary
glass·blow·ing
glass·ful
glass·ware
glassy
glass·i·er
glass·i·est
glass·i·ly
glass·i·ness
glau·co·ma
glaze
glazed
glaz·ing
gla·zier
gleam
gleam·ing
gleamy
glean
glean·er
glean·ing
glee
glee·ful
gleee·ful·ly
glee·ful·ness
glib
glib·best
glib·ly
glib·ness
glide
glid·ed
glid·ing
glim·mer
glimpse
glimpsed
glimps·ing
glis·san·do
glis·ten
glit·ter
glit·tery
gloam·ing

gloat
gloat·er
gloat·ing
glob·al
glob·al·ly
globe·trot·ter
globe·trot·ting
glob·u·lar
glob·ule
glock·en·spiel
gloomy
gloom·i·er
gloom·i·ly
gloom·i·ness
glo·ri·fy
glo·ri·fied
glo·ri·fy·ing
glo·ri·fi·ca·tion
glo·ri·ous
glo·ri·ous·ly
glo·ry
glo·ries
glo·ried
glo·ry·ing
glos·sa·ry
glossy
gloss·i·er
gloss·i·ly
gloss·i·ness
glot·tis
glove
glow
glow·er
glow·ing
glu·cose
glue
glued
glu·ing
glum
glum·mer
glum·mest
glut
glut·ted
glut·ting
glu·ten
glu·ten·ous
glu·ti·nous
glut·ton
glut·ton·ous
glut·tony
glyc·er·in
glyc·er·ine
gnarl
gnarled
gnash
gnat
gnaw
gnawed
gnaw·ing
gnome
gnu
go
went
gone
go·ing
goad·ed
goal·ie
goat·ee
goat·skin
gob·ble
gob·bled
gob·bling
gob·ble·dy·gook
gob·bler
gob·let
gob·lin
god·child
god·daugh·ter

god·son
god·dess
god·fa·ther
god·head
god·less
god·less·ness
god·ly
god·li·ness
god·moth·er
god·send
go·get·ter
gog·gle
gog·gled
gog·gling
go·ing
goi·ter
gold·en·rod
go·nad
gon·do·la
gon·do·lier
gon·or·rhea
good
better
best
good-by
good-bye
good-heart·ed
good·ish
good-look·ing
good·ly
good-na·tured
good·ness
good-tem·pered
goofy
goof·i·er
goof·i·est
goof·i·ness
goose·ber·ry
go·pher
gore
gored
gor·ing
gorge
gorged
gorg·ing
gor·geous
gor·geous·ness
gory
gor·i·er
gor·i·est
gos·ling
gos·pel
gos·sa·mer
gos·sip
gos·sip·ing
gos·sipy
Goth·ic
gouge
gouged
goug·ing
gou·lash
gourd
gour·mand
gour·met
gout
gouty
gov·ern
gov·ern·a·ble
gov·ern·ess
gov·ern·ment
gov·ern·men·tal
gov·er·nor
gowned
grab
grabbed
grab·bing
grab·ber
grace

graced
grac·ing
grace·ful
grace·ful·ly
grace·less
gra·cious
grack·le
gra·da·tion
grade
grad·ed
grad·ing
gra·di·ent
grad·u·al
grad·u·al·ly
grad·u·al·ness
grad·u·ate
grad·u·at·ed
grad·u·at·ing
grad·u·a·tion
graf·fi·ti
graft
graft·age
graft·er
graft·ing
gra·ham
grain
grainy
gran·i·ness
gram
gram·mar
gram·mar·i·an
gram·mat·i·cal
gra·na·ry
grand
grand·ly
grand·child
gran·dee
gran·deur
gran·dil·o·quence
gran·dil·o·quent
gran·di·ose
gran·di·ose·ly
grange
gran·ite
gran·ny
gran·u·lar
gran·u·lar·i·ty
gran·u·late
gran·u·lat·ed
gran·u·lat·ing
gran·u·la·tion
gran·ule
grape·fruit
graph·ic
graph·i·cal
graph·ite
graph·ol·o·gy
graph·ol·o·gist
grap·nel
grap·ple
grap·pled
grap·pling
grap·pler
grasp·ing
grass
grassy
grass·i·est
grass·hop·per
grass·land
grate
grat·ed
grat·ing
grate·ful
grat·i·fy
grat·i·fied
grat·i·fy·ing
grat·i·fi·ca·tion
grat·ing

gra·tis
grat·i·tude
gra·tu·i·tous
gra·tu·i·ty
gra·tu·i·ties
grave
graved
grav·en
grav·ing
grav·er
grave·ly
grave·ness
grav·el
grav·eled
grav·el·ing
grav·el·ly
grav·i·tate
grav·i·tat·ed
grav·i·tat·ing
grav·i·ta·tion
grav·i·ty
gra·vy
gray·ness
gray·ling
graze
grazed
graz·ing
grease
greased
greas·ing
greasy
greas·i·ness
great
great·ness
Great Brit·ain
Gre·cian
Greece
greedy
greed·i·er
greed·i·est
greed·i·ly
greed·i·ness
green·house
green·ing
green·ish
greet
greet·ing
gre·gar·i·ous
gre·gar·i·ous·ly
gre·gar·i·ous·ness
grem·lin
gre·nade
gren·a·dier
gren·a·dine
grey·ness
grid·dle
grid·i·ron
grief
griev·ance
grieve
grieved
griev·ing
griev·ous
grill
gril·lage
grille
grim
grim·ly
grim·ness
grim·ace
grim·aced
grim·ac·ing
grime
grimy
grim·i·ness
grin
grinncd
grin·ning

grind
  ground
  grind·ing
grin·go
grip
  gripped
  grip·ping
gripe
  griped
  grip·ing
  grip·er
grippe
gris·ly
  gris·li·ness
gris·tle
  gris·tly
grit
  grit·ted
  grit·ting
grit·ty
  grit·ti·ness
griz·zled
griz·zly
groan
gro·cer
gro·cery
  gro·cer·ies
grog·gy
  grog·gi·ly
  grog·gi·ness
groin
grom·met
groom
groove
  grooved
  groov·ing
  groov·er
grope
  groped
  grop·ing
gros·grain
gross
  gross·ly
  gross·ness
gro·tesque
  gro·tesque·ly
  gro·tesque·ness
grot·to
grouch
  grouchy
  grouch·i·ness
  grouch·i·ly
ground·less
ground·work
group
  group·ing
grouse
  groused
  grous·ing
grov·el
  grov·eled
  grov·el·ing
grow
  grew
  grown
  grow·ing
growl
  growl·er
  growl·ing
grown·up
growth
grub
  grubbed
  grub·bing
grub·by
  grub·bi·ness
grub·stake
grudge

grudged
grudg·ing
gru·el
gru·el·ing
grue·some
gruff
  gruff·ly
  gruff·ness
grum·ble
  grum·bled
  grum·bling
grumpy
  grump·i·ly
  grump·i·ness
grunt
  grunt·ed
  grunt·ing
gua·no
guar·an·tee
  guar·an·teed
  guar·an·tee·ing
guar·an·tor
guar·an·ty
  guar·an·ties
  guar·an·tied
  guar·an·ty·ing
guard·ed
  guard·ed·ly
guard·house
guard·i·an
guards·man
gua·va
gu·ber·na·to·ri·al
gudg·eon
guern·sey
guer·ril·la
guess
  guess·ing
guess·work
guest
guf·faw
guid·ance
guide
  guid·ed
  guid·ing
gui·don
guild
guile
  guile·ful
  guile·less
guil·lo·tine
guilt
  guilt·less
guilty
  guilt·i·er
  guilt·i·ly
  guilt·i·ness
guin·ea
guise
gui·tar
  gui·tar·ist
gul·let
gul·li·ble
  gul·li·bil·i·ty
  gul·li·bly
gul·ly
  gul·lies
gum
  gummed
  gum·ming
  gum·my
  gum·mi·ness
gum·bo
gump·tion
gun
  gunned
  gun·ning
gun·ner

gun·nery
gun·ny
gun·wale
gup·py
  gup·pies
gur·gle
  gur·gled
  gur·gling
gu·ru
gush·er
gush·ing
gushy
  gush·i·er
  gush·i·est
  gush·i·ness
gus·set
gus·ta·to·ry
gus·to
gusty
  gust·i·er
  gust·i·est
  gust·i·ly
  gust·i·ness
gut
  gut·ted
  gut·ting
gut·less
gut·ter
gut·tur·al
  gut·tur·al·ly
guz·zle
  guz·zled
  guz·zling
gym·na·si·um
  gym·na·si·ums
gym·nast
gym·nas·tic
gy·ne·col·o·gy
  gy·ne·co·log·i·cal
  gy·ne·col·o·gist
gyp
  gypped
  gyp·ping
gyp·sum
gyp·sy
  gyp·sies
gy·rate
  gy·rat·ed
  gy·rat·ing
  gy·ra·tion
  gy·ra·tor
gy·ro·com·pass
gy·rom·e·ter
gy·ro·plane
gy·ro·scope
gy·rose
gy·ro·sta·bi·liz·er
gy·ro·sta·tics

H

ha·be·as· cor·pus
hab·er·dash·ery
ha·bil·i·ment
hab·it
hab·it·a·ble
hab·i·tat
hab·i·ta·tion
ha·bit·u·al
  ha·bit·u·al·ly
  ha·bit·u·al·ness
ha·bit·u·ate
  ha·bit·u·at·ed
  ha·bit·u·at·ing
  ha·bit·u·a·tion
ha·bit·ue
ha·ci·en·da

hack·le
hack·led
hack·ling
hack·ney
hack·neyed
hack·saw
had·dock
Ha·des
had·n't
hag·gard
  hag·gard·ness
hag·gis
hag·gle
  hag·gled
  hag·gling
  hag·gler
ha·gi·og·ra·phy
hag·i·ol·o·gy
hail·storm
hair·breadth
hair·dress·er
hair·rais·ing
hairy
  hair·i·er
  hair·i·est
hale
  haled
  hal·ing
half
  halves
half·heart·ed
half·wit·ted
hal·i·but
hal·i·to·sis
hal·le·lu·jah
hall·mark
hal·lo
hal·low
  hal·lowed
Hal·low·een
hal·lu·ci·nate
  hal·lu·ci·nat·ed
  hal·lu·ci·nat·ing
  hal·lu·ci·na·tion
ha·lo
halt
  halt·ing
hal·ter
halve
  halved
  halv·ing
halves
hal·yard
ham·burg·er
ham·let
ham·mer
ham·mock
ham·per
ham·ster
ham·string
  ham·strung
hand·ed
hand·ful
hand·i·cap
  hand·i·capped
  hand·i·cap·ping
  hand·i·cap·per
hand·i·craft
hand·i·ly
  hand·i·ness
hand·i·work
hand·ker·chief
han·dle
  han·dled
  han·dling
hand·made
hand·picked
hand·some

hand·som·est
hand·some·ness
hand·writ·ing
handy
  hand·i·er
  hand·y·man
hang
  hung
  hanged
  hang·ing
hang·ar
hang·er
hang·o·ver
hank·er
han·som
Ha·nuk·kah
hap·haz·ard
  hap·haz·ard·ly
hap·less
hap·pen
  hap·pen·ing
  hap·pen·stance
hap·py
  hap·pi·ly
  hap·pi·ness
ha·ra·ki·ri
ha·rangue
  ha·rangued
  ha·rang·uing
har·ass
  har·ass·ment
har·bin·ger
har·bor
hard·bit·ten
hard·boiled
hard·en
  hard·en·er
har·di·hood
har·di·ness
hard·ly
hard·ware
hard·wood
har·dy
  har·di·er
  har·di·est
  har·di·ly
hare·brained
hare·lip
har·em
har·ken
har·le·quin
har·lot
  har·lot·ry
harm·ful
  harm·ful·ly
  harm·ful·ness
harm·less
  harm·less·ly
  harm·less·ness
har·mon·ic
  har·mon·i·cal·ly
  har·mon·i·ca
har·mon·ics
har·mo·ni·ous
har·mo·nize
  har·mo·nized
  har·mo·niz·ing
har·mo·ny
  har·mo·nies
har·ness
harp·ist
har·poon
harp·si·chord
har·ri·dan
har·row
har·ry
  har·ried
  har·ry·ing

harsh
  harsh·ly
  harsh·ness
har·um-scar·um
har·vest
har·ves·ter
hash·ish
  hash·eesh
has·n't
has·sle
  has·sled
  has·sling
has·sock
haste
has·ten
hast·y
  hast·i·ly
  hast·i·ness
hatch·ery
hatch·et
hate
  hat·ed
  hat·ing
hate·ful
  hate·ful·ly
  hate·ful·ness
ha·tred
haugh·ty
  haugh·ti·ly
  haugh·ti·ness
haul
  haul·age
haunch
  haunch·es
haunt·ed
haunt·ing
hau·teur
have
  had
  hav·ing
  has
ha·ven
have·n't
hav·er·sack
hav·oc
Ha·waii
hawk
  hawk·ish
haw·ser
haz·ard
  haz·ard·ous
  haz·ard·ous·ness
haze
  hazed
  haz·ing
ha·zel·nut
ha·zy
  ha·zi·ly
  ha·zi·ness
head·ache
head·dress
head·first
  head·fore·most
head·hunt·er
head·ing
head·line
  head·lined
  head·lin·ing
head·long
head·quar·ters
heady
  head·i·ly
  head·i·ness
heal·er
health·ful
  health·ful·ly
hcalthy
  health·i·er

health·i·est
health·i·ly
health·i·ness
heaped
hear
  heard
  hear·ing
heark·en
hear·say
hearse
heart·ache
heart·break
  heart·brok·en
heart·burn
heart·en
hearth·stone
heart·less
  heart·less·ly
  heart·less·ness
heart·rend·ing
heart·sick
hearty
  heart·i·ly
  heart·i·ness
heat·ed
heat·er
heath
hea·then
heath·er
heave
  heaved
  heav·ing
heav·en
  heav·en·ly
  heav·en·ward
heavy
  heav·i·ness
heav·y-hand·ed
heav·y-heart·ed
heav·y·weight
He·brew
  He·bra·ic
heck·le
  heck·led
  heck·ling
  heck·ler
hec·tare
hec·tic
  hec·ti·cal·ly
hec·to·gram
hec·to·li·ter
hec·to·me·ter
hedge
  hedged
  hedg·ing
  hedg·er
he·don·ism
  he·don·ist
  he·do·nis·tic
heed·ful
heed·less
hefty
  heft·i·er
he·gem·o·ny
heif·er
height·en
hei·nous
  hei·nous·ness
heir·ess
heir·loom
heist
hel·i·cop·ter
he·li·um
he·lix
  he·lix·es
he·li·cal
hel·lion
hell·ish

hell·ish·ness
hel·lo
helm
  helm·less
hel·met
  hel·met·ed
helms·man
help·er
help·ful
  help·ful·ly
  help·ful·ness
help·ing
help·less
  help·less·ness
hel·ter-skel·ter
hem
  hemmed
  hem·ming
he·ma·tol·o·gy
hem·i·sphere
  hem·i·spher·i·cal
hem·lock
he·mo·glo·bin
he·mo·phil·ia
hem·or·rhage
  hem·or·rhag·ing
hem·or·rhoid
hem·stitch
hence·forth
hench·man
hen·na
hep·a·ti·tis
her·ald
  he·ral·dic
her·ald·ry
herb
  her·ba·ceous
her·bi·cide
her·biv·o·rous
her·cu·le·an
he·red·i·ty
  he·red·i·tary
  he·red·i·tar·i·ly
her·e·sy
  her·e·sies
her·e·tic
  he·ret·i·cal
her·it·a·ble
  her·it·a·bil·i·ty
her·it·age
her·maph·ro·dite
  her·maph·ro·dit·ism
her·met·ic
  her·met·i·cal·ly
her·mit
her·nia
  her·ni·al
he·ro
  he·roes
  her·o·ine
  her·o·ism
he·ro·ic
  he·ro·i·cal·ly
her·o·in
her·on
her·pes
her·pe·tol·o·gy
her·ring·bone
her·self
hes·i·tant
  hes·i·tan·cy
  hes·i·tance
  hes·i·tant·ly
hes·i·tate
  hes·i·tat·ed
  hes·i·tat·ing
  hes·i·ta·tion
het·er·o·dox

het·er·o·doxy
het·er·o·ge·ne·ous
het·er·o·ge·ne·i·ty
het·er·o·ge·ne·ous·ness
het·er·o·sex·u·al
het·er·o·sex·u·al·i·ty
hew
  hewed
  hewn
  hew·ing
hex·a·gon
  hex·ag·o·nal
hexa·gram
hi·a·tus
hi·ba·chi
hi·ber·nate
  hi·ber·nat·ed
  hi·ber·nat·ing
  hi·ber·na·tion
hi·bis·cus
hic·cup
  hic·cuped
  hic·cup·ing
hick·o·ry
hid·den
hide
  hid
  hid·den
  hid·ing
hide·bound
hid·e·ous
  hid·e·ous·ness
hi·er·ar·chy
  hi·er·ar·chal
  hi·er·ar·chic
  hi·er·ar·chi·cal·ly
hi·er·o·glyph
hi·er·o·glyph·ic
high·grade
high·hand·ed
high·mind·ed
high·ness
high-pres·sure
  high-pres·sured
  high-pres·sur·ing
high-spir·it·ed
high-ten·sion
high-toned
high·way
hi·jack
  hi·jack·er
  hi·jack·ing
hike
  hiked
  hik·ing
hi·lar·i·ous
  hi·lar·i·ous·ly
  hi·lar·i·ous·ness
  hi·lar·i·ty
hill·bil·ly
  hill·bil·lies
hill·ock
hilly
  hill·i·er
  hill·i·est
him·self
hin·der
  hind·er·er
hind·most
hind·quar·ter
hin·drance
hind·sight
Hin·du·ism
hinge
  hinged
  hing·ing
hin·ter·land
hipped

Hip·poc·ra·tes
Hip·po·crat·ic
hip·po·dróme
hip·po·pot·a·mus
hire·ling
hir·sute
His·pan·ic
his·ta·mine
his·to·ri·an
his·tor·ic
his·tor·i·cal
  his·tor·i·cal·ly
  his·tor·i·cal·ness
his·to·ry
  his·to·ries
his·tri·on·ic
  his·tri·on·i·cal·ly
  his·tri·on·ics
hit
  hit·ting
hitch·hike
  hitch·hiked
  hitch·hik·ing
  hitch·hik·er
hith·er
hith·er·to
hit·ter
hoard
  hoard·er
  hoard·ing
hoar·frost
hoarse
  hoarse·ly
  hoarse·ness
hoary
  hoar·i·ness
hoax
  hoax·er
hob·ble
  hob·bled
  hob·bling
hob·by
  hob·bies
  hob·by·ist
hob·gob·lin
hob·nail
hob·nob
  hob·nobbed
  hob·nob·bing
ho·bo
  ho·boes
hock·ey
ho·cus·-po·cus
hodge·podge
hoe
  hoed
  hoe·ing
hoe·down
hog
  hogged
  hog·ging
  hog·gish
hogs·head
hog·tie
hoi·poi·loi
hoist·ing
ho·kum
hold
  held
  hold·ing
hole
  holed
  hol·ing
  holey
hol·i·day
ho·li·ness
Hol·land
hol·low

hol·low·ness
hol·ly
hol·ly·hock
hol·o·caust
hol·o·graph
Hol·stein
hol·ster
ho·ly
  ho·li·er
  ho·li·est
  ho·li·ness
hom·age
hom·bre
home·com·ing
home·less
home·ly
  home·li·ness
ho·me·op·a·thy
home·spun
home·stead
home·ward
homey
  hom·i·ness
hom·i·cide
  ho·mi·cid·al
hom·i·let·ics
hom·i·ly
hom·i·ny
ho·mo·ge·ne·ous
  ho·mo·ge·ne·i·ty
ho·mog·e·nize
  ho·mog·e·nized
  ho·mog·e·niz·ing
hom·o·graph
hom·o·nym
hom·o·phone
Ho·mo sa·pi·ens
ho·mo·sex·u·al
  ho·mo·sex·u·al·i·ty
hone
  honed
  hon·ing
hon·est
  hon·est·ly
hon·es·ty
  hon·es·ties
hon·ey
hon·ey·moon·er
hon·ey·suck·le
honk·y·tonk
hon·or
hon·or·a·ble
  hon·or·a·bly
hon·o·rar·i·um
hon·or·ary
hon·or·if·ic
hood·ed
hood·lum
hoo·doo
hood·wink
hoof
  hoofs
  hooves
  hoofed
hooked
hook·er
hoo·li·gan
hoop
  hooped
hop
  hopped
  hop·ping
hope
  hoped
  hop·ing
hope·ful
  hope·ful·ness
hope·less

hope·less·ness
hop·head
hop·per
hop·scotch
horde
  hord·ed
  hord·ing
ho·ri·zon
hor·i·zon·tal
  hor·i·zon·tal·ly
hor·mone
horn
  horned
  horny
hor·net
horn·swog·gle
ho·rol·o·gy
  ho·rol·o·gist
hor·o·scope
hor·ren·dous
hor·ri·ble
  hor·ri·bly
hor·rid
  hor·rid·ly
  hor·rid·ness
hor·ri·fy
  hor·ri·fied
  hor·ri·fy·ing
  hor·ri·fi·ca·tion
nor·ror
hors d'oeu·vre
horse
  hors·cs
  horsed
  hors·ing
horse·back
horse·man
horse op·era
horse·play
horse·pow·er
horse·rad·ish
horse·whipped
hors·ey
hor·ta·to·ry
hor·ti·cul·ture
  hor·ti·cul·tur·al
  hor·ti·cul·tur·ist
ho·san·na
hose
ho·siery
hos·pice
hos·pi·ta·ble
  hos·pi·ta·bly
hos·pi·tal
hos·pi·tal·i·ty
hos·pi·tal·i·tics
hos·pi·tal·i·za·tion
hos·pi·tal·ize
  hos·pi·tal·ized
  hos·pi·tal·iz·ing
hos·tage
hos·tel
  hos·tel·ry
host·ess
hos·tile
  hos·tile·ly
hos·til·i·ty
  hos·til·i·ties
hot
  hot·ter
  hot·test
  hot·ly
hot-blood·ed
ho·tel
hot·head·ed
hound
hour·glass
hour·ly

house
  hous·es
  housed
  hous·ing
house·bro·ken
house·hold
house·keep·er
house·warm·ing
house·wife
  house·wives
hov·el
hov·er
  hov·er·ing
how·ev·er
how·itz·er
howl·er
hoy·den
  hoy·den·ish
hub·bub
huck·le·ber·ry
huck·ster
hud·dle
  hud·dled
  hud·dling
huffy
  huff·i·ness
hug
  hugged
  hug·ging
  hug·ger
huge
  huge·ness
hulk·ing
hum
  hummed
  hum·ming
  hum·mer
hu·man
hu·mane
hu·man·ism
hu·man·i·tar·i·an
hu·man·i·ty
hu·man·ize
hum·blc
  hum·bled
  hum·bling
  hum·ble·ness
  hum·bly
hum·bug
hum·drum
hu·mer·us
hu·mid
hu·midi·fy
  hu·mid·i·fied
  hu·mid·i·fy·ing
  hu·mid·i·fi·er
hu·mid·i·ty
hu·mi·dor
hu·mil·i·ate
  hu·mil·i·at·ed
  hu·mil·i·at·ing
  hu·mil·i·a·tion
hu·mil·i·ty
hum·ming·bird
hum·mock
hu·mor
hu·mor·ist
hu·mor·ous
  hu·mor·ous·ness
hump
  humped
  humpy
hump·back
hu·mus
hunch·back
hun·dred
hun·dredth
hun·dred·weight

hun·ger
hun·gry
  hun·gri·ly
  hun·gri·ness
hunt
  hunt·er
  hunt·ing
  hunts·man
hur·dle
  hur·dled
  hur·dling
  hur·dler
hur·dy-gur·dy
hurl·er
hur·rah
hur·ri·cane
hur·ry
  hur·ried
  hur·ry·ing
hurt·ful
hurt·ing
hur·tle
  hur·tled
  hur·tling
hus·band
hus·band·ry
husk·er
husky
  husk·i·ly
  husk·i·ness
hus·sy
hus·tings
hus·tle
  hus·tled
  hus·tling
  hus·tler
hutch
huz·zah
hy·a·cinth
hy·brid
  hy·brid·ize
  hy·brid·ized
  hy·brid·iz·ing
  hy·brid·i·za·tion
hy·dran·gea
hy·drant
hy·drate
  hy·dra·ted
  hy·dra·ting
  hy·dra·tion
hy·drau·lic
  hy·drau·li·cal·ly
  hy·drau·lics
hy·dro·car·bon
hy·dro·chlo·ric ac·id
hy·dro·dy·nam·ics
  hy·dro·dy·nam·ic
hy·dro·e·lec·tric
hy·dro·gen
  hy·drog·e·nous
hy·drol·y·sis
hy·drom·e·ter
hy·dro·pho·bia
hy·dro·plane
hy·dro·pon·ics
hy·dro·ther·a·py
  hy·dro·ther·a·pist
hy·drous
hy·drox·ide
hy·e·na
hy·giene
  hy·gi·en·ic
  hy·gi·en·i·cal·ly
  hy·gien·ist
hy·grom·e·ter
hy·men
hy·me·ne·al
  hy·me·ne·al·ly

hymn
  hym·nal
hy·per·bo·la
hy·per·bo·le
  hy·per·bo·lize
  hy·per·bo·lized
  hy·per·bo·liz·ing
  hy·per·bol·ic
hy·per·crit·i·cal
hy·per·sen·si·tive
  hy·per·sen·si·tiv·i·ty
hy·per·ten·sion
hy·per·thy·roid·ism
hy·phen
hy·phen·ate
  hy·phen·at·ed
  hy·phen·at·ing
hyp·no·sis
hyp·not·ic
hyp·no·tism
  hyp·no·tist
hyp·no·tize
  hyp·no·tized
  hyp·no·tiz·ing
hy·po·chon·dria
  hy·po·chon·dri·ac
hy·poc·ri·sy
  hy·poc·ri·sies
hyp·o·crite
hy·po·der·mic
hy·po·gly·ce·mia
hy·po·sen·si·tize
hy·po·ten·sion
hy·pot·e·nuse
hy·poth·e·cate
  hy·poth·e·cat·ed
  hy·poth·e·cat·ing
  hy·poth·e·ca·tion
hy·poth·e·sis
  hy·poth·e·ses
  hy·poth·e·size
  hy·poth·e·sized
  hy·poth·e·siz·ing
hy·po·thet·i·cal
hys·ter·ec·to·my
hys·ter·e·sis
hys·te·ria
  hys·ter·ic
  hys·ter·i·cal
  hys·ter·i·cal·ly
hys·ter·ics

I

iamb
  iam·bic
ibid
ibi·dem
ice
  iced
  ic·ing
  icy
  ici·ness
ice cream
ice-skate
  ice-skat·ed
  ice-skat·ing
ich·thy·ol·o·gy
  ich·thy·o·log·i·cal
  ich·thy·ol·o·gist
ici·cle
ici·ly
icon
icon·o·clast
  icon·o·clasm
  icon·o·clas·tic
idea

ide·al
  ide·al·ly
ide·al·ism
  ide·al·ist
  ide·al·is·tic
ide·al·ize
  ide·al·ized
  ide·al·iz·ing
  ide·al·i·za·tion
ide·ate
  ide·a·tion
iden·ti·cal
  iden·ti·cal·ly
  iden·ti·cal·ness
iden·ti·fi·a·ble
  iden·ti·fi·a·bly
iden·ti·fy
  iden·ti·fied
  iden·ti·fy·ing
  iden·ti·fi·ca·tion
iden·ti·ty
  iden·ti·ties
ide·ol·o·gist
ide·ol·o·gy
  ide·ol·o·gies
ides
id·i·o·cy
  id·i·o·cies
id·i·om
  id·i·o·mat·ic
  id·i·o·mat·i·cal·ly
id·i·o·syn·cra·sy
  id·i·o·syn·cra·sies
  id·i·o·syn·crat·ic
id·i·ot
  id·i·ot·ic
  id·i·ot·i·cal·ly
idle
  idler
  idlest
  idled
  idling
  idle·ness
  idly
idol
idol·a·try
  idol·a·tries
  idol·a·ter
  idol·a·trous
idol·ize
  idol·ized
  idol·iz·ing
  idol·i·za·tion
idyll
  idyl·lic
  idyl·lic·al·ly
ig·loo
ig·ne·ous
ig·nite
  ig·nit·ed
  ig·nit·ing
  ig·nit·er
  ig·nit·a·ble
  ig·nit·a·bil·i·ty
  ig·ni·tion
ig·no·ble
  ig·no·bil·i·ty
  ig·no·ble·ness
  ig·no·bly
ig·no·miny
  ig·no·min·ies
  ig·no·min·i·ous
ig·no·ra·mus
ig·no·rant
  ig·no·rance
  ig·no·rant·ly
ig·nore
  ig·nored

ig·nor·ing
i·gua·na
ikon
ill
  worse
  worst
ill-ad·vised
ill-bred
il·le·gal
  il·le·gal·i·ty
  il·le·gal·ly
il·leg·i·ble
  il·leg·i·bil·i·ty
  il·leg·i·ble·ness
  il·leg·i·bly
il·le·git·i·mate
  il·le·git·i·ma·cy
  il·le·git·i·ma·cies
  il·le·git·i·mate·ly
ill-fat·ed
ill-fa·vored
ill-got·ten
il·lib·er·al
il·lic·it
il·lim·it·a·ble
il·lit·er·ate
  il·lit·er·a·cy
ill·ness
il·log·i·cal
ill-tempered
ill-timed
il·lu·mi·nate
  il·lu·mi·nat·ed
  il·lu·mi·nat·ing
  il·lu·mi·na·tor
  il·lu·mi·na·tion
il·lu·mine
  il·lu·mined
  il·lu·min·ing
ill-us·age
il·lu·sion
il·lu·sive
  il·lu·sive·ness
il·lu·so·ry
  il·lu·so·ri·ness
il·lus·trate
  il·lus·trat·ed
  il·lus·trat·ing
  il·lus·tra·tion
  il·lus·tra·tive
  il·lus·tra·tor
  il·lus·tri·ous
  il·lus·tri·ous·ness
im·age
  im·aged
  im·ag·ing
im·age·ry
  im·age·ries
  im·a·ge·ri·al
im·ag·ine
  im·ag·ined
  im·ag·in·ing
  im·ag·i·na·ble
  imag·i·na·bly
  im·ag·i·nary
  imag·i·nar·i·ly
  im·ag·i·na·tion
  im·ag·i·na·tive
im·bal·ance
im·be·cile
  im·be·cil·ic
  im·be·cil·i·ty
im·bed
  im·bed·ded
  im·bed·ding
im·bibe
  im·bibed
  im·bib·ing

im·bro·glio
im·bue
  im·bued
  im·bu·ing
im·i·tate
  im·i·tat·ed
  im·i·tat·ing
  im·i·ta·tor
  im·i·ta·tion
  im·i·ta·tive
im·mac·u·late
  im·mac·u·la·cy
  im·mac·u·late·ness
  im·mac·u·late·ly
im·ma·nent
  im·ma·nence
  im·ma·nen·cy
  im·ma·nent·ly
im·ma·te·ri·al
  im·ma·te·ri·al·ness
  im·ma·te·ri·al·i·ty
im·ma·ture
  im·ma·ture·ly
  im·ma·ture·ness
  im·ma·tu·ri·ty
im·meas·ur·a·ble
  im·meas·ur·a·bly
im·me·di·a·cy
  im·me·di·a·cies
im·me·di·ate
  im·me·di·ate·ly
im·me·mo·ri·al
im·mense
  im·mense·ness
  im·men·si·ty
im·merge
  im·merged
  im·merg·ing
  im·mer·gence
im·merse
  im·mersed
  im·mers·ing
  im·mer·sion
im·mi·grate
  im·mi·grat·ed
  im·mi·grat·ing
  im·mi·gra·tion
im·mi·grant
  im·mi·gra·tor
im·mi·nent
  im·mi·nence
im·mo·bile
  im·mo·bil·i·ty
  im·mo·bi·lize
  im·mo·bi·lized
  im·mo·bi·liz·ing
im·mod·er·ate
  im·mod·er·ate·ly
im·mod·est
  im·mod·est·ly
  im·mod·es·ty
im·mo·late
  im·mo·lat·ed
  im·mo·lat·ing
  im·mo·la·tion
  im·mo·la·tor
im·mor·al
  im·mo·ral·i·ty
  im·mo·ral·i·ties
  im·mor·al·ly
im·mor·tal
  im·mor·tal·i·ty
  im·mor·tal·ize
  im·mor·tal·ized
  im·mor·tal·iz·ing
  im·mor·tal·ly
im·mov·a·ble
  im·mov·a·bil·i·ty

im·mov·a·bly
im·mune
  im·mu·ni·ty
  im·mu·nize
  im·mu·nized
  im·mu·niz·ing
  im·mu·ni·za·tion
im·mu·nol·o·gy
im·mure
  im·mured
  im·mur·ing
im·mu·ta·ble
  im·mu·ta·bil·i·ty
  im·mu·ta·ble·ness
  im·mu·ta·bly
im·pact
  im·pac·tion
  im·pact·ed
im·pair
  im·pair·ment
impala
im·pale
  im·paled
  im·pal·ing
  im·pale·ment
im·pal·pa·ble
  im·pal·pa·bil·i·ty
im·pan·el
  im·pan·eled
  im·pan·el·ing
im·part
im·par·tial
  im·par·ti·al·i·ty
  im·par·tial·ness
  im·par·tial·ly
im·pass·a·ble
  im·pass·a·bil·i·ty
  im·pass·a·ble·ness
  im·pass·a·bly
im·passe
im·pas·si·ble
  im·pas·si·bil·i·ty
  im·pas·si·ble·ness
im·pas·sion
  im·pas·sioned
  im·pas·sioned·ness
im·pas·sive
  im·pas·sive·ly
  im·pas·sive·ness
  im·pas·siv·i·ty
im·pa·tient
  im·pa·tience
  im·pa·tient·ly
im·peach
  im·peach·a·ble
  im·peach·ment
im·pec·ca·ble
  im·pec·ca·bil·i·ty
  im·pec·ca·bly
im·pe·cu·ni·ous
  im·pe·cu·ni·ous·ness
im·pede
  im·ped·ed
  im·ped·ing
  im·ped·i·ment
im·pel
  im·pelled
  im·pel·ling
im·pend
  im·pend·ing
im·pen·e·tra·ble
  im·pen·e·tra·bil·i·ty
im·pen·i·tent
  im·pen·i·tence
im·per·a·tive
  im·per·a·tive·ness
im·per·cep·ti·ble
  im·per·cep·ti·bil·i·ty

im·per·cep·ti·bly
  im·per·cep·tive
im·per·fect
  im·per·fect·ly
  im·per·fect·ness
  im·per·fec·tion
im·pe·ri·al
  im·pe·ri·al·ly
  im·pe·ri·al·ism
  im·pe·ri·al·ist
  im·pe·ri·al·is·tic
  im·pe·ri·al·is·ti·cal·ly
im·per·il
  im·per·iled
  im·per·il·ing
  im·per·il·ment
im·pe·ri·ous
  im·pe·ri·ous·ly
  im·pe·ri·ous·ness
im·per·ish·a·ble
  im·per·ish·a·bil·i·ty
im·per·ma·nent
  im·per·ma·nence
  im·per·ma·nen·cy
  im·per·ma·nent·ly
im·per·me·a·ble
  im·per·me·a·bil·i·ty
  im·per·me·a·ble·ness
im·per·son·al
  im·per·son·al·ly
im·per·son·ate
  im·per·son·at·ed
  im·per·son·at·ing
  im·per·son·a·tion
  im·per·son·a·tor
im·per·ti·nent
  im·per·ti·nence
  im·per·ti·nent·ly
im·per·turb·a·ble
  im·per·turb·a·bly
im·per·vi·ous
  im·per·vi·ous·ly
  im·per·vi·ous·ness
im·pe·ti·go
im·pet·u·ous
  im·pet·u·os·i·ty
  im·pet·u·ous·ly
  im·pet·u·ous·ness
im·pe·tus
im·pi·e·ty
  im·pi·e·ties
im·pinge
  im·pinged
  im·ping·ing
  im·pinge·ment
im·pi·ous
  im·pi·ous·ly
  im·pi·ous·ness
im·plac·a·ble
  im·plac·a·bil·i·ty
  im·plac·a·ble·ness
  im·plac·a·bly
im·plant
  im·plan·ta·tion
im·plau·si·ble
  im·plau·si·bly
  im·plau·si·bil·i·ty
im·ple·ment
  im·ple·men·tal
  im·ple·men·ta·tion
im·pli·cate
  im·pli·cat·ed
  im·pli·cat·ing
  im·pli·ca·tion
im·plic·it
  im·plic·it·ly
  im·plic·it·ness
im·plode

im·plod·ed
im·plod·ing
im·plo·sion
im·plo·sive
im·plore
im·plored
im·plor·ing
im·plo·ra·tion
im·ply
im·plied
im·ply·ing
im·po·lite
im·po·lite·ly
im·po·lite·ness
im·pol·i·tic
im·pol·i·tic·ly
im·pon·der·a·ble
im·pon·der·a·bil·i·ty
im·pon·der·a·ble·ness
im·port
im·port·a·ble
im·port·er
im·por·ta·tion
im·por·tance
im·por·tant
im·por·tant·ly
im·por·tu·nate
im·por·tune
im·por·tuned
im·por·tun·ing
im·pose
im·posed
im·pos·ing
im·po·si·tion
im·pos·si·ble
im·pos·si·bil·i·ty
im·pos·si·bil·i·ties
im·pos·si·bly
im·pos·tor
im·pos·ture
im·po·tent
im·po·tence
im·po·ten·cy
im·po·tent·ly
im·pound
im·pound·age
im·pov·er·ish
im·pov·er·ish·ment
im·prac·ti·cal
im·prac·ti·ca·ble
im·prac·ti·ca·bil·i·ty
im·prac·ti·ca·ble·ness
im·pre·cate
im·pre·cat·ed
im·pre·cat·ing
im·pre·ca·tion
im·preg·na·ble
im·preg·na·bil·i·ty
im·preg·na·ble·ness
im·preg·nate
im·preg·nat·ed
im·preg·nat·ing
im·preg·na·tion
im·preg·na·tor
im·pre·sa·rio
im·pre·sa·ri·os
im·press
im·press·i·ble
im·press·ment
im·pres·sion
im·pres·sion·ist
im·pres·sion·a·ble
im·pres·sion·a·bly
im·pres·sion·ism
im·pres·sion·ist
im·pres·sion·is·tic
im·pres·sive
im·pres·sive·ly

im·pres·sive·ness
im·pri·ma·tur
im·print
im·prin·ter
im·pris·on
im·pris·on·ment
im·prob·a·ble
im·prob·a·bil·i·ty
im·prob·a·ble·ness
im·prob·a·bly
im·promp·tu
im·prop·er
im·prop·er·ly
im·prop·er·ness
im·pro·pri·e·ty
im·pro·pri·e·ties
im·prove
im·proved
im·prov·ing
im·prov·a·bil·i·ty
im·prov·a·ble
im·prove·ment
im·prov·i·dent
im·prov·i·dence
im·prov·i·dent·ly
im·prov·i·sa·tion
im·prov·i·sa·tion·al
im·pro·vise
im·pro·vised
im·pro·vis·ing
im·pru·dent
im·pru·dence
im·pru·dent·ly
im·pu·dent
im·pu·dence
im·pugn
im·pugn·er
im·pug·na·tion
im·pulse
im·pul·sion
im·pul·sive
im·pu·ni·ty
im·pure
im·pure·ness
im·pu·ri·ty
im·pu·ri·ties
im·pute
im·put·ed
im·put·ing
im·pu·ta·tion
in·a·bil·i·ty
in ab·sen·tia
in·ac·ces·si·ble
in·ac·ces·si·bil·i·ty
in·ac·ces·si·bly
in·ac·cu·rate
in·ac·cu·ra·cy
in·ac·cu·ra·cies
in·ac·tion
in·ac·ti·vate
in·ac·ti·va·tion
in·ac·tive
in·ac·tive·ly
in·ac·tiv·i·ty
in·ad·e·quate
in·ad·e·qua·cy
in·ad·e·qua·cies
in·ad·mis·si·ble
in·ad·mis·si·bly
in·ad·ver·tent
in·ad·ver·tence
in·ad·ver·ten·cy
in·al·ien·a·ble
in·al·ien·a·bil·i·ty
in·al·ien·a·bly
in·al·ter·a·ble
in·ane
in·ane·ness

in·an·i·ty
in·an·i·mate
in·ap·pli·ca·ble
in·ap·pre·cia·bly
in·ap·pro·pri·ate
in·ap·pro·pri·ate·ly
in·apt
in·ap·ti·tude
in·apt·ly
in·ar·tic·u·late
in·as·much as
in·at·ten·tion
in·at·ten·tive
in·au·di·ble
in·au·di·bly
in·au·gu·ral
in·au·gu·rate
in·au·gu·rat·ed
in·au·gu·rat·ing
in·au·gu·ra·tion
in·aus·pi·cious
in·bred
in·breed
in·breed·ing
in·cal·cu·la·ble
in·cal·cu·la·bil·i·ty
in·can·des·cent
in·can·des·cence
in·can·ta·tion
in·ca·pa·ble
in·ca·pa·bly
in·ca·pac·i·tate
in·ca·pac·i·tat·ed
in·ca·pac·i·tat·ing
in·ca·pac·i·ty
in·ca·pac·i·ties
in·ca·pac·i·ta·tion
in·car·cer·ate
in·car·cer·at·ed
in·car·cer·at·ing
in·car·cer·a·tion
in·car·nate
in·car·nat·ed
in·car·nat·ing
in·car·na·tion
in·cen·di·a·ry
in·cense
in·censed
in·cens·ing
in·cen·tive
in·cep·tion
in·cer·ti·tude
in·ces·sant
in·cest
in·ces·tu·ous
in·cho·ate
in·ci·dence
in·ci·dent
in·ci·den·tal
in·cin·er·ate
in·cin·er·at·ed
in·cin·er·at·ing
in·cin·er·a·tion
in·cin·er·a·tor
in·cip·i·ent
in·cise
in·cised
in·cis·ing
in·ci·sion
in·ci·sive
in·ci·sor
in·cite
in·cit·ed
in·cit·ing
in·cite·ment
in·ci·ta·tion
in·ci·vil·i·ty
in·clem·ent

in·clem·en·cy
in·cline
in·clined
in·clin·ing
in·cli·na·tion
in·clude
in·clud·ed
in·clud·ing
in·clu·sion
in·clu·sive
in·cog·ni·to
in·cog·ni·zant
in·co·her·ent
in·co·her·ence
in·com·bus·ti·ble
in·come
in·com·ing
in·com·men·su·rate
in·com·men·su·ra·ble
in·com·mode
in·com·mo·di·ous
in·com·mu·ni·ca·ble
in·com·mu·ni·ca·do
in·com·pa·ra·ble
in·com·pa·ra·bly
in·com·pat·i·ble
in·com·pat·i·bil·i·ty
in·com·pe·tent
in·com·pe·tence
in·com·pe·ten·cy
in·com·plctc
in·com·ple·tion
in·com·pre·hen·si·ble
in·com·pre·hen·sion
in·con·ceiv·a·ble
in·con·ceiv·a·bly
in·con·clu·sive
in·con·gru·ous
in·con·gru·i·ty
in·con·se·quen·tial
in·con·sid·er·a·ble
in·con·sid·er·ate
in·con·sis·tent
in·con·sis·ten·cy
in·con·sol·a·ble
in·con·spic·u·ous
in·con·stant
in·con·stan·cy
in·con·test·a·ble
in·con·test·abil·i·ty
in·con·ti·nent
in·con·ti·nence
in·con·ti·nen·cy
in·con·trol·la·ble
in·con·ven·ient
in·con·ven·ience
in·con·ven·ienced
in·con·ven·ienc·ing
in·cor·po·rate
in·cor·po·rat·ed
in·cor·po·rat·ing
in·cor·po·ra·tion
in·cor·po·re·al
in·cor·rect
in·cor·ri·gi·ble
in·cor·ri·gi·bil·i·ty
in·cor·ri·gi·ble·ness
in·cor·rupt·i·ble
in·cor·rupt·i·bil·i·ty
in·cor·rupt·i·bly
in·crease
in·creased
in·creas·ing
in·creas·a·ble
in·cred·i·ble
in·cred·i·bil·i·ty
in·cred·i·bly
in·cred·u·lous

in·cre·du·li·ty
in·cre·ment
in·cre·men·tal
in·crim·i·nate
in·crim·i·nat·ed
in·crim·i·nat·ing
in·crim·i·na·tion
in·crust
in·crus·ta·tion
in·cu·bate
in·cu·bat·ed
in·cu·bat·ing
in·cu·ba·tion
in·cu·ba·tor
in·cul·cate
in·cul·cat·ed
in·cul·cat·ing
in·cul·ca·tion
in·cul·pate
in·cul·pat·ed
in·cul·pat·ing
in·cul·pa·tion
in·cum·bent
in·cum·ben·cy
in·cur
in·curred
in·cur·ring
in·cur·a·ble
in·cur·a·bly
in·cu·ri·ous
in·cur·sion
in·cur·sive
in·debt·ed
in·de·cent
in·de·cen·cy
in·de·ci·sion
in·de·ci·sive
in·de·co·rous
in·de·co·rum
in·deed
in·de·fat·i·ga·ble
in·de·fat·i·ga·bil·i·ty
in·de·fat·i·ga·bly
in·de·fea·si·ble
in·de·fen·si·ble
in·de·fen·si·bil·i·ty
in·de·fen·si·bly
in·de·fin·a·ble
in·def·i·nite
in·def·i·nite·ly
in·del·i·ble
in·del·i·bly
in·del·i·cate
in·del·i·ca·cy
in·dem·ni·fy
in·dem·ni·fied
in·dem·ni·fy·ing
in·dem·ni·fi·ca·tion
in·dem·ni·ty
in·dent
in·den·ta·tion
in·dent·ed
in·den·ture
in·den·tur·ing
in·de·pend·ent
in·de·pend·ence
in·de·pend·en·cy
in·de·scrib·a·ble
in·de·scrib·a·bil·i·ty
in·de·struct·i·ble
in·de·struct·i·bil·i·ty
in·de·ter·mi·nate
in·de·ter·mi·na·cy
in·de·ter·mi·na·tion
in·dex
in·di·cate
in·di·cat·ed
in·di·cat·ing

in·di·ca·tion
in·dic·a·tive
in·di·ca·tor
in·dict
in·dict·a·ble
in·dict·ment
in·dif·fer·ent
in·dif·fer·ence
in·dif·fer·ent·ly
in·dig·e·nous
in·di·gent
in·di·gence
in·di·ges·tion
in·di·gest·i·ble
in·di·gest·i·bil·i·ty
in·di·gest·i·ble·ness
in·dig·nant
in·dig·nant·ly
in·dig·na·tion
in·dig·ni·ty
in·di·go
in·di·rect
in·di·rec·tion
in·dis·creet
in·dis·cre·tion
in·dis·crete
in·dis·crim·i·nate
in·dis·crim·i·nat·ing
in·dis·crim·i·na·tion
in·dis·pen·sa·ble
in·dis·pen·sa·bil·i·ty
in·dis·pen·sa·ble·ness
in·dis·posed
in·dis·po·si·tion
in·dis·put·a·ble
in·dis·sol·u·ble
in·dis·sol·u·bil·i·ty
in·dis·tinct
in·dis·tin·guish·a·ble
in·di·vid·u·al
in·di·vid·u·al·ly
in·di·vid·u·al·is·tic
in·di·vid·u·al·i·ty
in·di·vid·u·al·ize
in·di·vis·i·ble
in·doc·tri·nate
in·doc·tri·nat·ed
in·doc·tri·nat·ing
in·doc·tri·na·tion
in·do·lent
in·do·lence
in·dom·i·ta·ble
in·dom·i·ta·bil·i·ty
in·dom·i·ta·bly
in·du·bi·ta·ble
in·du·bi·ta·bil·i·ty
in·du·bi·ta·bly
in·duce
in·duced
in·duc·ing
in·duce·ment
in·duct
in·duct·ee
in·duc·tion
in·duct·ance
in·duc·tive
in·dulge
in·dulged
in·dulg·ing
in·dul·gence
in·dul·gent
in·dus·try
in·dus·tries
in·dus·tri·al
in·dus·tri·al·ize
in·dus·tri·al·i·za·tion
in·dus·tri·al·ist
in·dus·tri·ous

in·e·bri·ate
in·e·bri·at·ed
in·e·bri·at·ing
in·e·bri·a·tion
in·ed·i·ble
in·ef·fa·ble
in·ef·fa·bil·i·ty
in·ef·fa·bly
in·ef·fec·tive
in·ef·fec·tu·al
in·ef·fi·ca·cy
in·ef·fi·cient
in·ef·fi·cien·cy
in·el·e·gant
in·el·i·gi·ble
in·el·i·gi·bil·i·ty
in·ept
in·ept·i·tude
in·e·qual·i·ty
in·e·rad·i·ca·ble
in·er·rant
in·ert
in·er·tia
in·er·tial
in·es·cap·a·ble
in·es·sen·tial
in·es·ti·ma·ble
in·es·ti·ma·bly
in·ev·i·ta·ble
in·ev·i·ta·bil·i·ty
in·ev·i·ta·bly
in·ex·act
in·ex·cus·a·ble
in·ex·haust·i·ble
in·ex·haust·i·bil·i·ty
in·ex·o·ra·ble
in·ex·o·ra·bil·i·ty
in·ex·o·ra·bly
in·ex·pe·ri·ence
in·ex·pe·ri·enced
in·ex·pert
in·ex·pi·a·ble
in·ex·pi·a·bly
in·ex·pli·ca·ble
in·ex·pli·ca·bil·i·ty
in·ex·pli·ca·bly
in·ex·press·i·ble
in·ex·press·i·bil·i·ty
in·ex·press·i·bly
in·ex·pres·sive
in·ex·tin·guish·a·ble
in·ex·tri·ca·ble
in·ex·tri·ca·bil·i·ty
in·ex·tri·ca·bly
in·fal·li·ble
in·fal·li·bil·i·ty
in·fal·li·bly
in·fa·mous
in·fa·my
in·fa·mies
in·fan·cy
in·fan·cies
in·fant
in·fant·hood
in·fan·ti·cide
in·fan·tile
in·fan·tine
in·fan·try
in·fan·tries
in·fat·u·ate
in·fat·u·at·ed
in·fat·u·at·ing
in·fat·u·a·tion
in·fect
in·fec·tion
in·fec·tious
in·fec·tive
in·fe·lic·i·ty

in·fer
in·ferred
in·fer·ring
in·fer·a·ble
in·fer·ence
in·fer·en·tial
in·fe·ri·or
in·fe·ri·or·i·ty
in·fer·nal
in·fer·no
in·fer·nos
in·fest
in·fes·ta·tion
in·fi·del
in·fi·del·i·ty
in·fi·del·i·ties
in·field
in·field·er
in·fight·ing
in·fight·er
in·fil·trate
in·fil·trat·ed
in·fil·trat·ing
in·fil·tra·tion
in·fil·tra·tor
in·fi·nite
in·fi·nite·ness
in·fin·i·tes·i·mal
in·fin·i·tive
in·fin·i·tive·ly
in·fin·i·ty
in·fin·i·ties
in·firm
in·fir·ma·ry
in·fir·ma·ries
in·fir·mi·ty
in·fir·mi·ties
in·flame
in·flamed
in·flam·ing
in·flam·ma·ble
in·flam·ma·bil·i·ty
in·flam·ma·ble·ness
in·flam·ma·tion
in·flam·ma·to·ry
in·flate
in·flat·ed
in·flat·ing
in·flat·a·ble
in·fla·tion
in·fla·tion·ary
in·flect
in·flec·tion
in·flec·tion·less
in·flec·tive
in·flex·i·ble
in·flex·i·bil·i·ty
in·flex·i·bly
in·flict
in·flict·a·ble
in·flic·tion
in·flo·res·cence
in·flu·ence
in·flu·enced
in·flu·enc·ing
in·flu·en·tial
in·flu·en·za
in·flux
in·form
in·formed
in·for·mer
in·for·mal
in·for·mal·i·ty
in·for·mal·ly
in·form·ant
in·for·ma·tion
in·for·ma·tion·al
in·for·ma·tive

in·for·ma·to·ry
in·frac·tion
in·fran·gi·ble
in·fran·gi·bil·i·ty
in·fran·gi·bly
in·fra·red
in·fra·son·ic
in·fra·struc·ture
in·fre·quent
in·fre·quen·cy
in·fringe
in·fringed
in·fring·ing
in·fringe·ment
in·fu·ri·ate
in·fu·ri·at·ed
in·fu·ri·at·ing
in·fu·ri·a·tion
in·fuse
in·fused
in·fus·ing
in·fus·i·ble
in·fu·sion
in·gen·ious
in·gé·nue
in·ge·nu·i·ty
in·gen·u·ous
in·gest
in·ges·tion
in·glo·ri·ous
in·got
in·grain
in·grate
in·gra·ti·ate
in·gra·ti·at·ed
in·gra·ti·at·ing
in·gra·ti·a·tion
in·grat·i·tude
in·gre·di·ent
in·gress
in·grow·ing
in·grown
in·hab·it
in·hab·it·a·ble
in·hab·i·ta·tion
in·hab·it·ed
in·hab·it·ant
in·hal·ant
in·ha·la·tion
in·ha·la·tor
in·hale
in·haled
in·hal·ing
in·har·mo·ny
in·har·mon·ic
in·here
in·hered
in·her·ing
in·her·ence
in·her·ent
in·her·it
in·her·i·tor
in·her·i·tance
in·hib·it
in·hib·i·tive
in·hib·i·to·ry
in·hib·i·ter
in·hi·bi·tion
in·hos·pi·ta·ble
in·hos·pi·tal·i·ty
in·hu·man
in·hu·man·i·ty
in·hu·mane
in·hu·ma·tion
in·im·i·cal
in·im·i·ta·ble
in·im·i·ta·bly
in·iq·ui·ty

in·iq·ui·ties
in·iq·ui·tous
in·i·tial
in·i·tialed
in·i·tial·ing
in·i·tial·ly
in·i·ti·ate
in·i·ti·at·ed
in·i·ti·at·ing
in·i·ti·a·tion
in·i·ti·a·tor
in·i·ti·a·tive
in·ject
in·jec·tion
in·jec·tor
in·ju·di·cious
in·junc·tion
in·jure
in·jured
in·jur·ing
in·ju·ri·ous
in·ju·ry
in·ju·ries
in·jus·tice
ink·blot
ink·ling
inky
ink·i·er
in·law
in·lay
in·laid
in·lay·ing
in·let
in·mate
in me·mo·ri·am
in·most
in·nards
in·nate
in·ner
in·ner·most
in·ner·sole
in·ner·vate
in·ner·vat·ed
in·ner·vat·ing
in·ner·va·tion
in·ning
inn·keep·er
in·no·cent
in·no·cence
in·noc·u·ous
in·no·vate
in·no·vat·ed
in·no·vat·ing
in·no·va·tion
in·no·va·tive
in·no·va·tor
in·nu·en·do
in·nu·en·dos
in·nu·en·does
in·nu·mer·a·ble
in·nu·mer·ous
in·nu·mer·a·bly
in·nu·tri·tion
in·ob·serv·ance
in·ob·serv·ant
in·oc·u·late
in·oc·u·lat·ed
in·oc·u·lat·ing
in·oc·u·lant
in·oc·u·la·tion
in·of·fen·sive
in·op·er·a·ble
in·op·er·a·tive
in·op·por·tune
in·op·por·tu·ni·ty
in·or·di·nate
in·or·gan·ic
in·pa·tient

in·pour
in·put
in·quest
in·qui·e·tude
in·quire
  in·quired
  in·quir·ing
  in·quir·er
in·quiry
  in·quir·ies
in·qui·si·tion
in·quis·i·tive
in·quis·i·tor
in·road
in·sa·lu·bri·ous
in·sane
  in·san·i·ty
  in·san·i·ties
in·san·i·tary
in·sa·ti·ate
  in·sa·tia·ble
  in·sa·tia·bil·i·ty
  in·sa·tia·bly
in·scribe
  in·scribed
  in·scrib·ing
  in·scrip·tion
  in·scrip·tive
in·scru·ta·ble
  in·scru·ta·bil·i·ty
  in·scru·ta·bly
in·seam
in·sect
in·sec·ti·cide
  in·sec·ti·cid·al
in·se·cure
  in·se·cu·ri·ty
in·sem·i·nate
  in·sem·i·nat·ed
  in·sem·i·nat·ing
  in·sem·i·na·tion
in·sen·sate
in·sen·si·ble
  in·sen·si·bil·i·ty
in·sen·si·tive
  in·sen·si·tiv·i·ty
in·sen·ti·ent
in·sep·a·ra·ble
  in·sep·a·ra·bil·i·ty
  in·sep·a·ra·bly
in·sert
  in·sert·er
  in·ser·tion
in·set
  in·set·ting
in·shore
in·side
in·sid·er
in·sid·i·ous
in·sight
in·sig·nia
in·sig·nif·i·cant
  in·sig·nif·i·cance
in·sin·cere
  in·sin·cer·i·ty
  in·sin·cer·i·ties
in·sin·u·ate
  in·sin·u·at·ed
  in·sin·u·at·ing
  in·sin·u·a·tor
  in·sin·u·a·tion
in·sip·id
  in·si·pid·i·ty
  in·sip·id·ness
in·sist
  in·sist·ence
  in·sist·ent
in·so·bri·e·ty

in·so·cia·ble
in·so·cia·bil·i·ty
in·so·cia·bly
in·so·far
in·so·lent
  in·so·lence
in·sol·u·ble
  in·sol·u·bil·i·ty
  in·sol·u·bly
in·solv·a·ble
in·sol·vent
  in·sol·ven·cy
in·som·nia
  in·som·ni·ac
in·so·much
in·sou·ci·ant
  in·sou·ci·ance
in·spect
  in·spec·tion
  in·spec·tor
in·spire
  in·spired
  in·spir·ing
  in·spi·ra·tion
in·spir·it
in·sta·ble
  in·sta·bil·i·ty
in·stall
  in·stalled
  in·stall·ing
  in·stal·la·tion
in·stall·ment
in·stance
in·stant
in·stan·ta·ne·ous
in·state
  in·stat·ed
  in·stat·ing
  in·state·ment
in·stead
in·step
in·sti·gate
  in·sti·gat·ed
  in·sti·gat·ing
  in·sti·ga·tion
  in·sti·ga·tor
in·still
  in·stilled
  in·stil·ling
  in·stil·la·tion
in·stinct
  in·stinc·tive
  in·stinc·tu·al
in·sti·tute
  in·sti·tut·ed
  in·sti·tut·ing
in·sti·tu·tion
  in·sti·tu·tion·al
  in·sti·tu·tion·al·ism
  in·sti·tu·tion·al·ize
  in·sti·tu·tion·al·ized
  in·sti·tu·tion·al·iz·ing
in·struct
  in·struc·tion
  in·struc·tive
  in·struc·tor
in·stru·ment
  in·stru·men·tal
  in·stru·men·ta·list
  in·stru·men·ta·tion
in·sub·or·di·nate
  in·sub·or·di·na·tion
in·sub·stan·tial
  in·sub·stan·ti·al·i·ty
in·suf·fer·a·ble
  in·suf·fer·a·bly
in·suf·fi·cient
  in·suf·fi·cience

in·suf·fi·cien·cy
in·su·lar
  in·su·lar·i·ty
in·su·late
  in·su·lat·ed
  in·su·lat·ing
  in·su·la·tion
  in·su·la·tor
in·su·lin
in·sult
in·sup·port·a·ble
in·sup·press·i·ble
in·sure
  in·sured
  in·sur·ing
  in·sur·a·ble
  in·sur·a·bil·i·ty
  in·sur·ance
in·sur·gent
  in·sur·gence
  in·sur·gen·cy
in·sur·mount·a·ble
in·sur·rec·tion
in·sus·cep·ti·ble
in·tact
in·ta·glio
in·take
in·tan·gi·ble
  in·tan·gi·bil·i·ty
  in·tan·gi·ble·ness
  in·tan·gi·bly
in·te·ger
in·te·gral
in·te·grate
  in·te·grat·ed
  in·te·grat·ing
  in·te·grant
  in·te·gra·tion
in·teg·ri·ty
in·tel·lect
in·tel·lec·tu·al
  in·tel·lec·tu·al·ism
  in·tel·lec·tu·al·ize
  in·tel·lec·tu·al·ly
in·tel·li·gent
  in·tel·li·gence
  in·tel·li·gent·sia
in·tel·li·gi·ble
  in·tel·li·gi·bil·i·ty
  in·tel·li·gi·bly
in·tem·per·ate
  in·tem·per·ance
in·tend
  in·tend·ant
in·tense
  in·tense·ness
in·ten·si·fy
  in·ten·si·fied
  in·ten·si·fy·ing
  in·ten·si·fi·ca·tion
  in·ten·sion
  in·ten·si·ty
  in·ten·si·ties
  in·ten·sive
in·tent
  in·ten·tion
  in·ten·tion·al·ly
in·ter
  in·terred
  in·ter·ring
  in·ter·ment
in·ter·act
  in·ter·ac·tion
  in·ter·ac·tive
in·ter·breed
  in·ter·bred
  in·ter·breed·ing
in·ter·ca·late

in·ter·cede
  in·terced·ed
  in·terced·ing
in·ter·cept
  in·ter·cept·or
  in·ter·cep·tion
in·ter·ces·sion
  in·ter·ces·sor
in·ter·change
  in·ter·changed
  in·ter·chang·ing
  in·ter·change·a·ble
  in·ter·change·a·bil·i·ty
in·ter·col·le·gi·ate
in·ter·com
in·ter·com·mu·ni·cate
  in·ter·com·mu·ni·cat·ed
  in·ter·com·mu·ni·cat·ing
  in·ter·com·mu·ni·ca·tion
in·ter·con·nect
  in·ter·con·nec·tion
in·ter·con·ti·nen·tal
in·ter·course
in·ter·cul·tur·al
in·ter·de·nom·i·na·tion·al
in·ter·de·part·men·tal
in·ter·de·pend·ent
  in·ter·de·pend·ence
in·ter·dict
  in·ter·dic·tion
in·ter·dis·ci·pli·nary
in·ter·est
  in·ter·est·ed
  in·ter·est·ing
in·ter·face
in·ter·faith
in·ter·fere
  in·ter·fered
  in·ter·fer·ing
  in·ter·fer·ence
in·ter·fer·on
in·ter·ga·lac·tic
in·ter·im
in·te·ri·or
in·ter·ject
  in·ter·jec·tion
  in·ter·jec·to·ry
in·ter·lay·er
in·ter·leaf
  in·ter·leave
in·ter·line
in·ter·link
in·ter·lock
in·ter·lo·cu·tion
  in·ter·loc·u·tor
  in·ter·loc·u·to·ry
in·ter·lope
  in·ter·loped
  in·ter·lop·ing
  in·ter·lop·er
in·ter·lude
in·ter·lu·nar
  in·ter·lu·na·ry
in·ter·marry
  in·ter·mar·riage
in·ter·me·di·ate
  in·ter·me·di·at·ing
  in·ter·me·di·a·tion
  in·ter·me·di·ary
  in·ter·me·di·a·tor
in·ter·mi·na·ble
in·ter·min·gle
  in·ter·min·gled
  in·ter·min·gling
in·ter·mis·sion
in·ter·mit
  in·ter·mit·ted
  in·ter·mit·ting

in·ter·mit·tence
in·ter·mit·ten·cy
in·ter·mit·tent
in·ter·mix
in·ter·mix·ture
in·tern
in·terne
in·ter·nal
  in·ter·nal·ize
  in·ter·nal·i·za·tion
in·ter·na·tion·al
  in·ter·na·tion·al·i·ty
  in·ter·na·tion·al·ly
  in·ter·na·tion·al·ize
  in·ter·na·tion·al·ized
  in·ter·na·tion·al·iz·ing
  in·ter·na·tion·al·i·za·tion
  in·ter·na·tion·al·ism
in·tern·ee
in·tern·ist
in·tern·ment
in·ter·nun·cio
in·ter·of·fice
in·ter·pen·e·trate
  in·ter·pen·e·tra·tion
in·ter·plan·e·tary
in·ter·play
in·ter·po·late
  in·ter·po·la·tion
  in·ter·po·la·tor
in·ter·pose
  in·ter·posed
  in·ter·pos·ing
  in·ter·po·si·tion
in·ter·pret
  in·ter·pret·er
  in·ter·pre·tive
  in·ter·pre·ta·tion
in·ter·ra·cial
in·ter·re·late
  in·ter·re·lat·ed
  in·ter·re·lat·ing
in·ter·ro·gate
  in·ter·ro·gat·ed
  in·ter·ro·gat·ing
  in·ter·ro·ga·tion
  in·ter·rog·a·tive
in·ter·rupt
  in·ter·rup·tion
in·ter·scho·las·tic
in·ter·sect
  in·ter·sec·tion
in·ter·space
in·ter·sperse
  in·ter·spersed
  in·ter·spers·ing
  in·ter·sper·sion
in·ter·state
in·ter·stel·lar
in·ter·tid·al
in·ter·twine
in·ter·ur·ban
in·ter·val
in·ter·vene
  in·ter·vened
  in·ter·ven·ing
  in·ter·ven·tion
in·ter·view
in·ter·weave
  in·ter·wove
  in·ter·weav·ing
  in·ter·wo·ven
in·tes·tate
in·tes·tine
  in·tes·ti·nal
in·ti·mate
  in·ti·mat·ed
  in·ti·mat·ing

in·ti·ma·tion
in·ti·mate
in·ti·mate·ness
in·ti·mate·ly
in·tim·i·date
in·tim·i·dat·ed
in·tim·i·dat·ing
in·tim·i·da·tion
in·to
in·tol·er·ant
in·tol·er·able
in·tol·er·ance
in·tomb
in·to·nate
in·to·nat·ed
in·to·nat·ing
in·to·na·tion
in·tone
in·toned
in·ton·ing
in·tox·i·cate
in·tox·i·cat·ed
in·tox·i·cat·ing
in·tox·i·ca·tion
in·trac·ta·ble
in·trac·ta·bil·i·ty
in·tra·mu·ral
in·tra·mu·ral·ly
in·tran·si·gent
in·tran·si·gence
in·tran·si·gen·cy
in·tran·si·tive
in·tra·state
in·tra·u·ter·ine
in·tra·ve·nous
in·trench
in·trep·id
in·tre·pid·i·ty
in·tri·cate
in·tri·ca·cy
in·tri·ca·cies
in·trigue
in·trigued
in·tri·guing
in·trin·sic
in·trin·si·cal·ly
in·tro·duce
in·tro·duced
in·tro·duc·ing
in·tro·duc·tion
in·tro·duc·to·ry
in·tro·spect
in·tro·spec·tion
in·tro·spec·tive
in·tro·ver·sion
in·tro·vert
in·trude
in·trud·ed
in·trud·ing
in·trud·er
in·tru·sion
in·tu·i·tion
in·tu·i·tive
in·tu·mes·cent
in·tu·mes·cence
in·un·date
in·un·dat·ed
in·un·dat·ing
in·un·da·tion
in·ure
in·ured
in·ur·ing
in·vade
in·vad·ed
in·vad·ing
in·vad·er
in·va·lid
in·va·lid·ism

in·val·id
in·val·u·able
in·var·i·a·ble
in·var·i·a·bil·i·ty
in·var·i·ant
in·va·sion
in·vec·tive
in·veigh
in·vei·gle
in·vent
in·ven·tion
in·ven·tive
in·ven·tor
in·ven·to·ry
in·ven·to·ries
in·ven·to·ried
in·ven·to·ry·ing
in·verse
in·ver·sion
in·vert·ed
in·vert
in·ver·te·brate
in·vest
in·ves·tor
in·ves·ti·gate
in·ves·ti·gat·ed
in·ves·ti·gat·ing
in·ves·ti·ga·tion
in·ves·ti·ture
in·vest·ment
in·vet·er·ate
in·vid·i·ous
in·vig·or·ate
in·vig·or·at·ed
in·vig·or·at·ing
in·vig·or·a·tion
in·vin·ci·ble
in·vin·ci·bil·i·ty
in·vin·ci·bly
in·vi·o·la·ble
in·vi·o·la·bil·i·ty
in·vi·o·la·bly
in·vi·o·late
in·vis·i·ble
in·vis·i·bil·i·ty
in·vite
in·vit·ed
in·vit·ing
in·vi·ta·tion
in·vo·ca·tion
in·voice
in·voke
in·voked
in·vok·ing
in·vol·un·tary
in·vol·un·tar·i·ly
in·vo·lute
in·vo·lu·tion
in·volve
in·volved
in·volv·ing
in·volve·ment
in·vul·ner·a·ble
in·vul·ner·a·bil·i·ty
in·ward
in·ward·ly
in·weave
in·wove
in·weaved
in·wov·en
in·weav·ing
in·wrought
io·dine
ion
ion·ic
ion·ize
ion·i·za·tion
ion·o·sphere

io·ta
ip·so fac·to
iras·ci·ble
iras·ci·bil·i·ty
irate
Ire·land
ir·i·des·cent
ir·i·des·cence
iris
iris·es
Irish·man
irk·some
iron
iron·er
iron·clad
iron·hand·ed
iron·heart·ed
iron·ic
iron·i·cal
iron·stone
iron·ware
iron·work
ir·ra·di·ate
ir·ra·di·at·ed
ir·ra·di·at·ing
ir·ra·di·a·tion
ir·rad·i·ca·ble
ir·ra·tion·al
ir·ra·tion·al·i·ty
ir·re·claim·a·ble
ir·rec·on·cil·a·ble
ir·rec·on·cil·a·bil·i·ty
ir·re·cov·er·a·ble
ir·re·deem·a·ble
ir·re·duc·i·ble
ir·ref·u·ta·ble
ir·reg·u·lar
ir·reg·u·lar·i·ty
ir·rel·e·vant
ir·rel·e·vance
ir·rel·e·van·cy
ir·re·li·gious
ir·re·me·di·a·ble
ir·re·mis·si·ble
ir·re·mov·a·ble
ir·rep·a·ra·ble
ir·re·place·a·ble
ir·re·press·i·ble
ir·re·proach·a·ble
ir·re·sist·i·ble
ir·re·sist·i·bil·i·ty
ir·res·o·lute
ir·res·o·lu·tion
ir·re·spec·tive
ir·re·spon·si·ble
ir·re·spon·si·bil·i·ty
ir·re·spon·sive
ir·re·triev·a·ble
ir·re·triev·a·bil·i·ty
ir·rev·er·ence
ir·rev·er·ent
ir·re·vers·i·ble
ir·re·vers·i·bil·i·ty
ir·rev·o·ca·ble
ir·rev·o·ca·bil·i·ty
ir·ri·gate
ir·ri·gat·ed
ir·ri·gat·ing
ir·ri·ga·tion
ir·ri·ta·ble
ir·ri·ta·bil·i·ty
ir·ri·tant
ir·ri·tate
ir·ri·tat·ed
ir·ri·tat·ing
ir·ri·ta·tion
ir·rupt
Is·lam

Is·lam·ic
Is·lam·ism
is·land
isle
is·let
iso·bar
iso·late
iso·lat·ed
iso·lat·ing
iso·la·tion
iso·la·tion·ist
iso·met·ric
iso·met·ri·cal
isos·ce·les
iso·therm
iso·ther·mal
iso·ton·ic
iso·tope
iso·top·ic
Is·ra·el
Is·rae·li
is·sue
is·sued
is·su·ing
is·su·ance
isth·mus
Ital·ian
ital·ic
ital·i·cize
ital·i·cized
ital·i·ciz·ing
ital·i·ci·za·tion
It·a·ly
itch
itch·i·ness
itchy
item
item·ize
item·ized
item·iz·ing
it·er·ate
it·er·a·tion
itin·er·ant
itin·er·ate
itin·er·a·tion
itin·er·ary
itin·er·ar·ies
ivo·ry
ivy
ivied
ivies

J

jab
jabbed
jab·bing
jab·ber
jack·al
jack·ass
jack·et
jack·et·ed
jack·ham·mer
jack-in-the-box
jack·knife
jack-of-all-trades
jack-o'-lan·tern
jack rab·bit
jade
jad·ed
jad·ing
jag
jagged
jag·ging
jag·uar
jail·bird
jail·break

ja·lopy
ja·lop·ies
jal·ou·sie
jam
jammed
jam·ming
jam·mer
jamb
jam·bo·ree
jan·gle
jan·gled
jan·gling
jan·i·tor
jan·i·to·ri·al
Jan·u·ary
Ja·pan
Jap·a·nese
jar
jarred
jar·ring
jar·ful
jar·di·niere
jar·gon
jas·mine
jaun·dice
jaun·diced
jaunt
jaun·ty
jaun·ti·ly
jaun·ti·ness
jave·lin
jaw·bone
jaw·break·er
jay·walk
jazz
jazzy
jazz·i·ly
jazz·i·ness
jeal·ous
jeal·ousy
jeal·ous·ies
jeer·er
Jef·fer·son
Je·ho·vah
Jek·yll
jel·li·fy
jel·ly
jel·ly·fish
jen·ny
jeop·ardy
jeop·ar·dize
jeop·ar·dized
jeop·ar·diz·ing
jerk
jerk·i·ly
jerk·i·ness
jerky
jer·kin
jer·ry·build
jer·ry·built
jer·sey
Je·ru·sa·lem
jes·sa·mine
jest·er
Jes·u·it
Je·sus
jet
jet·ted
jet·ting
jet·lin·er
jet-pro·pelled
jet·sam
jet·ti·son
jet·ty
jew·el
jew·el·er
jew·el·ry
Jew·ish

Jew·ry
jew's-harp
Jez·e·bel
jibe
jif·fy
jig
jigged
jig·ging
jig·gle
jig·gled
jig·gling
jig·gly
jilt·er
Jim Crow-ism
jim-dan·dy
jim·my
jim·mied
jim·my·ing
jin·gle
jin·gled
jin·gling
jin·go·ism
jin·rik·i·sha
jinx
jit·ney
jit·ter
jit·ters
jit·tery
jit·ter·bug
jit·ter·bug·ging
job
jobbed
job·bing
job·ber
job·hold·er
jock·ey
jock·ey·ing
jock·strap
jo·cose
jo·cos·i·ty
joc·u·lar
joc·u·lar·i·ty
joc·und
jo·cun·di·ty
jodh·pur
jog
jogged
jog·ging
jog·ger
jog·gle
jog·gled
jog·gling
join·er
joint
joint·ed
joint·ly
joist
joke
joked
jok·ing
joke·ster
jol·ly
jolt
jolt·ing·ly
jolty
jon·quil
jos·tle
jos·tled
jos·tling
jot
jot·ted
jot·ting
joule
jour·nal·ism
jour·nal·ist
jour·nal·is·tic
jour·ney
joust

jo·vi·al
jo·vi·al·i·ty
jowl
joy·ful
joy·less
joy·ous
joy·ride
ju·bi·lant
ju·bi·lance
ju·bi·la·tion
ju·bi·lee
Ju·da·ism
Ju·da·ic
Ju·da·i·cal
judge
judged
judg·ing
judg·ment
ju·di·cial
ju·di·ci·ary
ju·di·cious
ju·do
jug·ger·naut
jug·gle
jug·gled
jug·gling
jug·gler
jug·u·lar
juice
juic·er
juicy
juic·i·er
juic·i·ness
ju·jit·su
ju·jube
juke·box
ju·lep
ju·li·enne
jum·ble
jum·bled
jum·bling
jum·bo
jump
jump·ing
jump·i·ness
jumpy
junc·tion
junc·ture
jun·gle
jun·ior
ju·ni·per
junk
junky
jun·ket
junk·ie
jun·ta
Ju·pi·ter
ju·ris·dic·tion
ju·ris·dic·tion·al
ju·ris·pru·dence
ju·ris·pru·dent
ju·ris·pru·den·tial
ju·rist
ju·ror
ju·ry
ju·ries
just
just·ness
jus·tice
jus·tice·less
jus·ti·fy
jus·ti·fied
jus·ti·fy·ing
jus·ti·fi·a·ble
jus·ti·fi·ca·to·ry
jus·ti·fi·ca·tion
jut
jut·ted

jut·ting
jute
ju·ve·nes·cent
ju·ve·nile
ju·ve·nil·i·ty
jux·ta·pose
jux·ta·posed
jux·ta·pos·ing
jux·ta·po·si·tion

K

ka·bob
kai·ser
ka·lei·do·scope
ka·lei·do·scop·ic
ka·mi·ka·ze
kan·ga·roo
ka·o·lin
ka·o·line
ka·pok
ka·put
kar·a·kul
kar·at
ka·ra·te
kar·ma
ka·ty·did
kay·ak
kayo
kedge
kedged
kedg·ing
keel·haul
keel·son
keen·ly
keen·ness
keep
kept
keep·ing
keep·sake
keg·ler
kelp
ken·nel
ken·neled
ke·no
ker·a·tin
ker·chief
ker·nel
ker·o·sene
kes·trel
ketch·up
ke·tone
ket·tle·drum
key
keyed
key·board
key·hole
key·note
key·not·ing
key·stone
kha·ki
kha·lif
khan
kib·butz
kib·but·zim
kib·itz·er
kick·back
kick·off
kid
kid·dish
kid·dish·ness
kid·ded
kid·ding
kid·nap
kid·naped
kid·napped
kid·nap·ing

kid·nap·ping
kid·nap·er
kid·nap·per
kid·ney
kill·deer
kill·ing
kill·joy
kiln
kilo
kil·o·cy·cle
kil·o·gram
kil·o·li·ter
kil·o·me·ter
kil·o·volt
kil·o·watt
kilt
kilt·er
ki·mo·no
kin·der·gar·ten
kind·heart·ed
kin·dle
kin·dled
kin·dling
kind·ly
kind·li·est
kind·li·ness
kin·dred
kin·e·mat·ics
kin·e·mat·ic
kin·e·mat·i·cal
kin·e·scope
ki·net·ic
ki·net·ics
kin·folk
king·bolt
king·dom
king·fish·er
king·ly
king·li·ness
king·pin
king-size
king-sized
kinky
kink·i·est
kins·folk
kin·ship
kins·man
kins·wom·an
ki·osk
kip·per
kis·met
kiss·a·ble
kitch·en
kitch·en·ette
kitch·en·ware
kite
kit·ed
kit·ing
kit·ten
kit·ten·ish
kit·ty
kit·ties
kit·ty-cor·ner
ki·wi
klatch
klep·to·ma·nia
klep·to·ma·ni·ac
knack
knap·sack
knave
knav·ish
knead
knee
kneed
knee·ing
knee·cap
knee·deep
kneel

knelt
kneeled
kneel·ing
knell
knick·ers
knick·er·bock·ers
knick·knack
knife
knives
knifed
knif·ing
knight
knight·hood
knight·ly
knight-er·rant
knit
knit·ted
knit·ting
knob
knobbed
knob·by
knob·bi·er
knock
knock·down
knock·er
knock-kneed
knock·out
knoll
knot
knot·ted
knot·ting
knot·less
knot·ty
knot·hole
knout
know
knew
known
know·ing
know·a·ble
know·ing·ly
know-how
knowl·edge
knowl·edge·a·ble
know-noth·ing
knuck·le
knuck·led
knuck·ling
knurl
knurled
knurly
ko·a·la
kohl·ra·bi
ko·la
ko·lin·sky
kook
kooky
kook·i·er
kook·a·bur·ra
Ko·ran
Ko·rea
ko·sher
Krem·lin
krim·mer
Krish·na
kryp·ton
Ku·blai Khan
ku·dos
ku·miss
küm·mel
kum·mer·bund
kum·quat

L

la·bel
la·beled

la·bel·ing
la·bel·er
la·bi·al
la·bi·ate
la·bile
la·bi·o·den·tal
la·bi·um
la·bor
la·bor·er
lab·o·ra·to·ry
la·bored
la·bo·ri·ous
la·bo·ri·ous·ly
la·bor-sav·ing
la·bur·num
lab·y·rinth
lab·y·rin·thine
lab·y·rin·thi·an
lace
laced
lac·ing
lacy
lac·i·est
lac·er·ate
lac·er·at·ed
lac·er·at·ing
lac·er·a·tion
lach·ry·mal
lach·ry·mose
lach·ry·mose·ly
lack·a·dai·si·cal
lack·ey
lack·lus·ter
la·con·ic
la·con·i·cal·ly
lac·quer
la·crosse
lac·tate
lac·tat·ed
lac·tat·ing
lac·ta·tion
lac·te·al
lac·tic
lac·tose
la·cu·na
la·cus·trine
lad·der
lad·die
lade
lad·ed
lad·en
lad·ing
la·dle
la·dled
la·dling
la·dy·bug
la·dy·fin·ger
la·dy-in-wait·ing
la·dy-kil·ler
la·dy's-slip·per
lag
lagged
lag·ging
lag·gard
la·ger
la·gniappe
la·goon
La Guar·dia
lair
lais·sez faire
la·i·ty
lake·side
lal·la·tion
lam
lammed
lam·ming
la·ma
la·ma·sery

La·ma·ism
La·ma·ist
lam·baste
lam·bast·ed
lam·bast·ing
lam·bent
lam·bent·ly
lam·bre·quin
lamb·skin
lame
lamed
lam·ing
lame·ness
la·mé
la·ment
lam·en·ta·ble
lam·en·ta·bly
lam·en·ta·tion
lam·i·nate
lam·i·nat·ed
lam·i·nat·ing
lam·i·na·tion
lamp·black
lam·poon
lam·prey
lance
lanced
lanc·ing
lan·ce·o·late
lan·cet
lan·dau
land·ed
land·fall
land·hold·er
land·ing
land·la·dy
land·locked
land·lord
land·lub·ber
land·mark
land·own·er
land·scape
land·scap·ing
land·scap·er
land·slide
land·ward
lang·syne
lan·guage
lan·guid
lan·guish
lan·guish·ing
lan·guor
lan·guor·ous
lank·ness
lanky
lank·i·ness
lan·o·lin
lan·tern
lan·yard
lap
lapped
lap·ping
la·pel
lap·ful
lap·i·dary
lap·in
lap·is laz·u·li
lap·pet
lapse
lapsed
laps·ing
lar·board
lar·ce·ny
lar·ce·nous
larch
lar·der
large
larg·er

larg·est
large·ness
large·ly
large-scale
lar·gess
lar·ghet·to
lar·go
lar·i·at
lark·spur
lar·va
lar·ynx
la·ryn·ge·al
la·ryn·gi·tis
las·civ·i·ous
las·civ·i·ous·ly
la·ser
lash
lash·ing
las·si·tude
las·so
last·ing
last·ly
latch·key
late
lat·er
lat·est
late·ness
late·ly
la·teen
la·tent
la·ten·cy
la·tent·ly
lat·er·al
lat·er·al·ly
la·tex
lath
lath·ing
lathe
lath·er
lath·ery
Lat·in-A·mer·i·can
lat·i·tude
lat·i·tu·di·nal
lat·i·tu·di·nar·i·an
la·trine
lat·ter
Lat·ter-day Saint
lat·tice
lat·ticed
lat·tic·ing
lat·tice·work
laud·a·ble
laud·a·bly
lau·da·num
laud·a·to·ry
laud·a·tive
laugh
laugh·ing
laugh·a·ble
laugh·a·bly
laugh·ter
launch
launch·er
laun·der
laun·dress
Laun·dro·mat
laun·dry
lau·re·ate
lau·rel
la·va
lav·a·liere
lav·a·to·ry
lav·a·to·ries
lav·en·der
lav·ish
lav·ish·ness
law-a·bid·ing
law·break·er

law·ful
law·ful·ly
law·ful·ness
law·less
law·less·ness
law·mak·er
law·mak·ing
lawn
law·suit
law·yer
lax
lax·i·ty
lax·ness
lax·a·tive
lay
laid
laying
lay·er
lay·ette
lay·man
lay·off
lay·out
lay·o·ver
la·zy
la·zi·est
la·zi·ly
la·zi·ness
leach
lead
led
lead·ing
lead·en
lead·er
lead·er·ship
leaf·age
leaf·less
leaf·let
leaf·stalk
leafy
leaf·i·ness
league
leak
leak·age
leak·i·ness
leaky
lean
lean·ness
lean·ing
lean-to
leap
leaped
leapt
leap·ing
learn
learned
learnt
learn·ing
learn·er
lease
leased
leas·ing
leash
least·wise
least·ways
leath·er
leath·er·neck
leath·ery
leave
left
leav·ing
leav·en
leaves
leave-tak·ing
Leb·a·nese
Leb·a·non
lech·er
lech·er·ous
lech·ery

lec·tern
lec·ture
lec·tured
lec·tur·ing
lec·tur·er
ledge
ledg·er
leech
leek
leer·ing·ly
leery
lee·ward
lee·way
left-hand·ed
left·ist
left·o·ver
left-wing
leg
legged
leg·ging
leg·a·cy
leg·a·cies
le·gal
le·gal·ly
le·gal·ism
le·gal·ist
le·gal·is·tic
le·gal·i·ty
le·gal·i·ties
le·gal·ize
le·gal·ized
le·gal·iz·ing
le·gal·i·za·tion
leg·ate
leg·a·tee
le·ga·tion
le·ga·to
leg·end
leg·end·ary
leg·er·de·main
leg·gy
leg·horn
leg·i·ble
leg·i·bil·i·ty
leg·i·bly
le·gion
le·gion·ary
le·gion·naire
leg·is·late
leg·is·lat·ed
leg·is·lat·ing
leg·is·la·tive
leg·is·la·tor
leg·is·la·tion
leg·is·la·ture
le·git·i·mate
le·git·i·mat·ed
le·git·i·mat·ing
le·git·i·ma·cy
le·git·i·mate·ly
le·git·i·mize
le·git·i·mized
le·git·i·miz·ing
leg·ume
le·gu·mi·nous
lei
leis
lei·sure
lei·sure·ly
lei·sure·li·ness
leit·mo·tif
lem·ming
lem·on
lem·on·ade
le·mur
lend
lent
lend·ing

length
  length·en
length·wise
lengthy
  length·i·ly
  length·i·ness
le·ni·ent
  le·ni·ence
  le·ni·en·cy
len·i·tive
len·i·ty
lens
Lent·en
len·til
le·o·nine
leop·ard
le·o·tard
lep·er
  lep·ro·sy
  lep·rous
lep·re·chaun
les·bi·an
  les·bi·an·ism
le·sion
les·see
less·en
less·er
les·son
les·sor
least
let
  let·ting
le·thal
  le·thal·ly
leth·ar·gy
  le·thar·gic
  le·thar·gi·cal
let·ter
  let·ter·er
let·tered
let·ter·head
let·ter·ing
let·ter-per·fect
let·ter·press
let·tuce
leu·ke·mia
leu·ko·cyte
lev·ee
lev·el
  lev·eled
  lev·el·ing
  lev·el·ness
lev·el-head·ed
lev·er
  lev·er·age
le·vi·a·than
lev·i·tate
  lev·i·tat·ed
  lev·i·tat·ing
  lev·i·ta·tion
lev·i·ty
levy
  lev·ies
lewd
  lewd·ly
  lewd·ness
lex·i·cog·ra·phy
  lex·i·cog·ra·pher
  lex·i·co·graph·ic
lex·i·con
li·a·bil·i·ty
  li·a·bil·i·ties
li·a·ble
li·ai·son
li·ar
li·ba·tion
li·bel
  li·beled

li·bel·ing
li·bel·er
li·bel·ous
lib·er·al
  lib·er·al·ly
  lib·er·al·i·ty
  lib·er·al·ism
  lib·er·al·ize
  lib·er·al·ized
  lib·er·al·iz·ing
  lib·er·al·i·za·tion
lib·er·ate
  lb·er·at·ed
  lib·er·at·ing
  lib·er·a·tion
  lib·er·a·tor
lib·er·tine
  lib·er·tin·ism
lib·er·ty
  lib·er·ties
li·bid·i·nous
  li·bid·i·nous·ness
li·bi·do
  li·bid·in·al
li·brary
  li·brar·ies
  li·brar·i·an
li·bret·to
lice
  louse
li·cense
  li·censed
  li·cens·ing
  li·cen·see
  li·cens·er
li·cen·ti·ate
  li·cen·tious·ness
li·chen
lic·it
lick·e·ty-split
lic·o·rice
lid·ded
lie
  lay
  lain
  lay·ing
lie
  lied
  ly·ing
Lieb·frau·milch
Lie·der·kranz
lien
lieu
lieu·ten·ant
  lieu·ten·an·cy
life·blood
life·boat
life·guard
life·less
life·like
life·line
life·sav·er
life-size
life·style
life·time
life·work
lift-off
lig·a·ment
lig·a·ture
light·en
light·er
light-fin·gered
light·foot·ed
light-head·ed
light-heart·ed
light·house
light·ing
light·ly

light-mind·ed
light·ning
light·weight
light-year
lig·nite
like
  liked
  lik·ing
  like·a·ble
like·li·hood
like·ly
  like·li·est
lik·en
like·ness
like·wise
li·lac
lilt·ing
lily
limb
lim·ber
lim·bo
Lim·burg·er
lime
  limed
  lim·ing
  limy
lime·light
lim·er·ick
lime·stone
lim·it
  lim·it·a·ble
  lim·i·ta·tive
  lim·i·ta·tion
  lim·it·ed
  lim·it·less
lim·ou·sine
limp
  limp·ing·ly
  limp·ly
lim·pet
lim·pid
  lim·pid·ness
Lin·coln
lin·den
line
  lined
  lin·ing
lin·age
lin·er
lin·e·age
lin·e·al
lin·e·a·ment
lin·e·ar
line·back·er
line·man
lin·en
lin·ger
  lin·ger·ing·ly
lin·ge·rie
lin·go
lin·gua fran·ca
lin·gual
lin·guist
lin·guis·tics
lin·guis·tic
lin·i·ment
link
  linked
  link·er
link·age
lin·net
li·no·le·um
lin·seed
lint
  linty
  lint·i·er
lin·tel
li·on

li·on·ess
li·on·heart·ed
li·on·ize
  li·on·ized
  li·on·iz·ing
  li·on·i·za·tion
lip·py
lip·stick
liq·ue·fy
  liq·ue·fied
  liq·ue·fy·ing
  liq·ue·fac·tion
  liq·ue·fi·a·ble
li·queur
liq·uid
  li·quid·i·ty
  liq·uid·ness
liq·ui·date
  liq·ui·dat·ed
  liq·ui·dat·ing
  liq·ui·da·tion
  liq·ui·da·tor
liq·uor
lisle
lisp
lis·some
  lis·some·ness
list
  list·ing
lis·ten
  lis·ten·er
list·less
lit·a·ny
  lit·a·nies
li·tchi
li·ter
lit·er·al
  lit·er·al·i·ty
  lit·er·al·ly
  lit·er·al·ism
lit·er·ary
  lit·er·ar·i·ness
lit·er·ate
  lit·er·a·cy
lit·e·ra·ti
lit·er·a·ture
lithe
  lithe·some
li·thog·ra·phy
  li·thog·ra·pher
  lith·o·graph·ic
lit·i·gate
  lit·i·gat·ed
  lit·i·gat·ing
  lit·i·ga·tion
lit·mus
lit·ter
lit·ter·bug
lit·tle
lit·to·ral
lit·ur·gy
  lit·ur·gist
  li·tur·gic
  li·tur·gi·cal
liv·a·ble
  live·a·ble
live·li·hood
live·ly
  live·li·est
  live·li·ness
liv·en
liv·er
liv·er·wurst
liv·ery
  liv·er·ied
live·stock
liv·id
  li·vid·i·ty

liv·id·ly
liv·ing
liz·ard
lla·ma
lla·no
load
  load·ed
loaf
  loaves
loamy
loath
loathe
  loathed
  loath·ing
  loath·some
lob
  lobbed
  lob·bing
lob·by
  lob·bies
  lob·by·ist
lobe
  lo·bar
  lobed
lob·ster
lo·cal
  lo·cal·ly
lo·cale
  lo·cal·i·ty
  lo·cal·i·ties
lo·cal·ize
  lo·cal·ized
  lo·cal·iz·ing
  lo·cal·i·za·tion
lo·cate
  lo·cat·ed
  lo·cat·ing
  lo·ca·tion
  lo·ca·tor
lock·a·ble
lock·er
lock·et
lock·jaw
lock·out
lock·smith
lock·up
lo·co·mo·tion
lo·co·mo·tive
lo·cus
lo·ci
lo·cust
lo·cu·tion
lode·star
lode·stone
lodge
  lodged
  lodg·ing
  lodg·er
  lodg·ment
lofty
  loft·i·est
  loft·i·ly
  loft·i·ness
lo·gan·ber·ry
log·a·rithm
  log·a·rith·mic
loge
log·ger
log·ger·head
log·ic
  lo·gi·cian
log·i·cal
  log·i·cal·ly
  log·i·cal·ness
lo·gis·tics
  lo·gis·tic
  lo·gis·ti·cal
log·roll·ing

lo·gy
loin·cloth
loi·ter
  loi·ter·er
lone·ly
lone·li·ness
  lone·some
lon·er
lon·gev·i·ty
long·hair
long·hand
long·ing
lon·gi·tude
  lon·gi·tu·di·nal
long·lived
long·play·ing
long·range
long·shore·man
long·suf·fer·ing
long·term
long·wind·ed
look·out
loony
  loon·ies
  loon·i·est
  loon·i·ness
loop·hole
loose
  loosed
  loos·ing
  loos·er
  loos·est
  loose·ness
  loos·en
loot·er
lop
  lopped
  lop·ping
lope
  loped
  lop·ing
  lop·er
lop·sid·ed
lo·qua·cious
  lo·qua·cious·ness
  lo·quac·i·ty
lord·ly
  lord·li·est
  lord·li·ness
lor·gnette
lor·ry
lose
  lost
  los·ing
  los·a·ble
  los·er
lot
  lot·ted
  lot·ting
lo·tion
lot·tery
lo·tus
loud
  loud·ness
loud·mouthed
loud·speak·er
lounge
  lounged
  loung·ing
lousy
  lous·i·ness
lout
  lout·ish·ness
lou·ver
love
  loved
  lov·ing
  lov·a·ble

lov·a·bil·i·ty
lov·a·ble·ness
lov·a·bly
love·less
love·ly
  love·li·er
  love·li·est
lov·er
lov·ing
  lov·ing·ness
low·born
low·boy
low·brow
low·down
low·er
low·er·case
low·er·ing
low·keyed
low·land
low·lev·el
low·ly
  low·li·est
  low·li·ness
low·mind·ed
low·pres·sure
low·ten·sion
loy·al
  loy·al·ist
  loy·al·ly
  loy·al·ty
  loy·al·ties
loz·enge
lu·au
lub·ber
lu·bri·cate
  lu·bri·cat·ed
  lu·bri·cat·ing
  lu·bri·cant
  lu·bri·ca·tion
  lu·bri·ca·tor
lu·bri·cious
lu·cid
  lu·cid·i·ty
  lu·cid·ness
luck
  luck·i·est
  luck·i·ly
  luck·i·ness
  lucky
lu·cra·tive
  lu·cra·tive·ness
lu·cre
lu·cu·brate
  lu·cu·bra·tion
lu·di·crous
  lu·di·crous·ness
lug
  lugged
  lug·ging
lug·gage
lug·ger
lu·gu·bri·ous
luke·warm
lull·a·by
  lull·a·bies
lum·ba·go
lum·bar
lum·ber
lum·ber·ing
lum·ber·jack
lu·men
lu·mi·nary
  lu·mi·nar·ies
lu·mi·nous
  lu·mi·nous·ness
lu·mi·nes·cence
lu·mi·nes·cent
lum·mox

lumpy
  lump·i·est
  lump·i·ness
lu·nar
lu·nate
lu·na·tic
lu·na·cy
  lu·na·cies
lunch
  lunch·eon
lunge
  lunged
  lung·ing
lunk·head
lu·pine
lurch
lure
  lured
  lur·ing
lu·rid
  lu·rid·ly
  lu·rid·ness
lurk
  lurk·er
lus·cious
  lus·cious·ly
  lus·cious·ness
lush
  lush·ness
lust
  lust·ful·ness
lus·ter
  lus·ter·less
  lus·trous
lusty
  lust·i·ly
  lust·i·ness
Lu·ther·an
lux·u·ri·ate
  lux·u·ri·at·ed
  lux·u·ri·at·ing
  lux·u·ri·a·tion
lux·u·ry
  lux·u·ries
  lux·u·ri·ous
  lux·u·ri·ant
  lux·u·ri·ance
ly·ce·um
ly·ing
lymph
  lym·phat·ic
lynch
  lynch·ing
lynx
lyre
ly·ric
  lyr·i·cal
  lyr·i·cism
  lyr·i·cist

M

ma·ca·bre
mac·ad·am
  mac·ad·am·ize
ma·caque
mac·a·ro·ni
mac·a·roon
ma·caw
mace
  maced
  mac·ing
mac·er·ate
  mac·er·at·ed
  mac·er·at·ing
  mac·er·a·tion
Mach

ma·chete
Mach·i·a·vel·li·an
mach·i·nate
  mach·i·nat·ed
  mach·i·nat·ing
  mach·i·na·tion
ma·chine
  ma·chined
  ma·chin·ing
  ma·chin·ery
  ma·chin·ist
mack·er·el
mack·i·naw
mack·in·tosh
mac·ra·mé
mac·ro·cosm
ma·cron
mac·ro·scop·ic
mad
  mad·den
  mad·dest
  mad·ly
  mad·ness
mad·am
  mad·ame
  mes·dames
Ma·dei·ra
mad·e·moi·selle
Ma·don·na
mad·ras
mad·ri·gal
mael·strom
maes·tro
Ma·fia
mag·a·zine
ma·gen·ta
mag·got
  mag·goty
mag·ic
  mag·i·cal
  ma·gi·cian
mag·is·trate
mag·is·te·ri·al
mag·is·tra·cy
mag·is·tra·cies
mag·ma
Mag·na Car·ta
mag·nan·i·mous
  mag·na·nim·i·ty
mag·nate
mag·ne·sia
mag·ne·si·um
mag·net
  mag·net·ic
  mag·net·i·cal·ly
  mag·net·ism
mag·net·ize
  mag·net·ized
  mag·net·iz·ing
mag·ne·to
mag·ne·tom·e·ter
mag·nif·i·cent
  mag·nif·i·cence
  mag·nif·i·cent·ly
mag·ni·fy
  mag·ni·fied
  mag·ni·fy·ing
  mag·ni·fi·ca·tion
  mag·ni·fi·er
mag·nil·o·quent
mag·ni·tude
mag·no·lia
mag·num
mag·pie
ma·ha·ra·jah
  ma·ha·ra·ni
ma·hat·ma
mah·jongg

ma·hog·a·ny
ma·hout
maid·en
  maid·en·hair
  maid·en·head
mail·a·ble
mail·box
mail·man
maim
main·land
main·ly
main·mast
main·sail
main·spring
main·stream
main·tain
  main·tain·a·ble
  main·te·nance
maî·tre d'hô·tel
maize
ma·jes·tic
  ma·jes·ti·cal
maj·es·ty
ma·jol·i·ca
ma·jor
ma·jor-do·mo
  ma·jor-do·mos
ma·jor·i·ty
  ma·jor·i·ties
make
  mak·a·ble
  ma·ker
  mak·ing
make-be·lieve
make·shift
make-up
mal·a·dapt·ed
  mal·ad·ap·ta·tion
mal·ad·just·ment
mal·ad·just·ed
mal·ad·min·is·ter
  mal·ad·min·is·tra·tion
mal·a·droit
  mal·a·droit·ness
mal·a·dy
  mal·a·dies
ma·laise
mal·a·prop
  mal·a·prop·ism
ma·lar·ia
ma·lar·i·al
ma·lar·key
mal·con·tent
mal de mer
mal·e·dic·tion
  mal·e·dic·to·ry
mal·e·fac·tion
  mal·e·fac·tor
ma·lef·ic
  ma·lef·i·cent
ma·lev·o·lent
  ma·lev·o·lence
  ma·lev·o·lent·ly
mal·fea·sance
  mal·fea·sant
mal·for·ma·tion
  mal·formed
mal·func·tion
mal·ice
  ma·li·cious
  ma·li·cious·ly
ma·lign
  ma·lign·ly
ma·lig·nant
  ma·lig·nan·cy
  ma·lig·nan·cies
  ma·lig·nant·ly
ma·lin·ger

ma·lin·ger·er
mal·lard
mal·le·a·ble
 mal·le·a·bil·i·ty
 mal·le·a·ble·ness
mal·let
mal·low
mal·nour·ished
mal·nu·tri·tion
mal·oc·clu·sion
mal·o·dor
 mal·o·dor·ous
mal·prac·tice
 mal·prac·ti·tion·er
malt
 malty
mal·tose
mal·treat
 mal·treat·ment
mam·bo
mam·ma
 ma·ma
mam·mal
 mam·ma·li·an
mam·ma·ry
 mam·ma·ries
mam·mon
mam·moth
mam·my
man
 manned
 man·ning
man·a·cle
 man·a·cled
 man·a·cling
man·age
 man·aged
 man·ag·ing
 man·age·a·ble
 man·age·a·bil·i·ty
 man·age·a·ble·ness
 man·age·a·bly
 man·age·ment
man·ag·er
 man·ag·er·ship
 man·a·ge·ri·al
ma·ña·na
man·a·tee
man·da·mus
man·da·rin
man·date
 man·dat·ed
 man·dat·ing
 man·da·to·ry
 man·da·to·ri·ly
man·di·ble
man·do·lin
man·drake
man·drel
man·drill
man-eat·er
 man-eat·ing
ma·nege
ma·neu·ver
 ma·neu·ver·a·bil·i·ty
 ma·neu·ver·a·ble
man·ful
 man·ful·ly
man·ga·nese
mange
 man·gy
 man·gi·ness
man·ger
man·gle
 man·gled
 man·gling
man·go
man·grove

man·han·dle
Man·hat·tan
man·hole
man·hood
man-hour
man·hunt
ma·nia
 man·ic
ma·ni·ac
 ma·ni·a·cal
man·ic-de·pres·sive
man·i·cure
 man·i·cured
 man·i·cur·ing
 man·i·cur·ist
man·i·fest
 man·i·fest·ly
man·i·fes·ta·tion
man·i·fes·to
man·i·fold
man·i·kin
 man·a·kin
 man·ni·kin
ma·nil·la
ma·nip·u·late
 ma·nip·u·lat·ed
 ma·nip·u·lat·ing
 ma·nip·u·la·ble
 ma·nip·u·la·tion
 ma·nip·u·la·tive
 ma·nip·u·la·tor
 ma·nip·u·la·to·ry
man·kind
man·like
man·ly
 man·li·er
 man·li·ness
man-made
man·na
 manned
man·ne·quin
man·ner
 man·nered
 man·ner·ism
 man·ner·ly
man·nish
man-of-war
 men-of-war
ma·nom·e·ter
man·or
 ma·no·ri·al
man·pow·er
man·sard
man·sion
man-sized
man·slaugh·ter
man·slay·er
man·tel
 man·tle
man·til·la
man·tis
man·tle
man·u·al
 man·u·al·ly
man·u·fac·ture
 man·u·fac·tured
 man·u·fac·tur·ing
 man·u·fac·tur·er
man·u·mis·sion
ma·nure
man·u·script
many
 more
 most
man·y-sid·ed
map
 mapped
 map·ping

ma·ple
mar
 marred
 mar·ring
ma·ra·ca
mar·a·schi·no
mar·a·thon
ma·raud
 ma·raud·er
mar·ble
 mar·bled
 mar·bling
 mar·ble·ize
mar·cel
 mar·celled
 mar·cel·ling
march·er
mar·chion·ess
mar·ga·rine
mar·ga·ri·ta
mar·gin
mar·gi·nal
 mar·gin·al·ly
mar·gue·rite
mar·i·gold
ma·ri·jua·na
ma·rim·ba
ma·ri·na
mar·i·nade
mar·i·nate
 mar·i·nat·ing
ma·rine
mar·i·ncr
mar·i·on·ette
mar·i·tal
mar·i·time
mar·jo·ram
marked
 mark·ed·ly
mark·er
mar·ket
 mar·ket·a·ble
 mar·ket·a·bil·i·ty
 mar·ket·ing
 mar·ket·place
mark·ing
marks·man
 marks·man·ship
mar·lin
 mar·line
mar·ma·lade
mar·mo·set
mar·mot
ma·roon
mar·que·try
mar·quis
 mar·quess
 mar·quise
mar·qui·sette
mar·riage
 mar·riage·a·ble
mar·row
 mar·rowy
mar·row·bone
mar·ry
 mar·ried
 mar·ry·ing
mar·shal
 mar·shaled
 mar·shal·ing
marsh·mal·low
marshy
 marsh·i·ness
mar·su·pi·al
mar·tial
Mar·tian
mar·ten
mar·tin

mar·ti·ni
mar·tyr
 mar·tyr·dom
mar·vel
 mar·veled
 mar·vel·ing
 mar·vel·ous
Marx·ism
 Marx·ist
mar·zi·pan
mas·cara
mas·cot
mas·cu·line
 mas·cu·lin·i·ty
 mas·cu·lin·ize
mask
 masked
mas·och·ism
 mas·och·ist
 mas·och·is·tic
ma·son
 ma·son·ic
ma·son·ry
masque
mas·quer·ade
 mas·quer·ad·ing
Mas·sa·chu·setts
mas·sa·cre
 mas·sa·cred
 mas·sa·cring
mas·sage
 mas·saged
 mas·sag·ing
mas·seur
 mas·seuse
mas·sive
mass-pro·duce
 mass-pro·duc·tion
mas·tec·to·my
mas·ter
 mas·ter·ful
 mas·ter·mind
 mas·ter·piece
 mas·tery
mast·head
mas·ti·cate
 mas·ti·ca·ting
 mas·ti·ca·tion
mas·tiff
mas·to·don
mas·toid
mas·tur·bate
 mas·tur·ba·tion
mat
 mat·ted
 mat·ting
mat·a·dor
match·mak·ing
mate
 mat·ed
 mat·ing
ma·te·ri·al
 ma·te·ri·al·ly
 ma·te·ri·al·ism
 ma·te·ri·al·ist
 ma·te·ri·al·is·tic
 ma·te·ri·al·is·ti·cal·ly
 ma·te·ri·al·ize
 ma·te·ri·al·ized
 ma·te·ri·al·iz·ing
 ma·te·ri·al·iza·tion
ma·te·ri·el
ma·ter·nal
 ma·ter·nal·is·tic
 ma·ter·nal·ly
ma·ter·ni·ty
math·e·mat·ics
math·e·mat·i·cal

math·e·ma·ti·cian
mat·i·nee
ma·tri·arch
 ma·tri·ar·chal·ism
ma·tri·ar·chy
mat·ri·cide
ma·tric·u·late
 ma·tric·u·lat·ed
 ma·tric·u·lat·ing
 ma·tric·u·lant
 ma·tric·u·la·tion
ma·tri·lin·e·al
mat·ri·mo·ny
 mat·ri·mo·ni·al
ma·trix
 ma·tri·ces
ma·tron
 ma·tron·ly
mat·ter
mat·ter-of-course
mat·ter-of-fact
mat·ting
mat·tress
ma·ture
mat·u·rate
 mat·u·rat·ing
 mat·u·ra·tion
 ma·tu·ri·ty
mat·zo
maud·lin
maul
mau·so·le·um
mauve
mav·er·ick
mawk·ish
max·im
max·i·mal
max·i·mize
 max·i·mized
 max·i·miz·ing
max·i·mum
may·be
may·flow·er
may·hem
may·on·naise
may·or
 may·or·al
 may·or·al·ty
maze
 mazed
 maz·ing
ma·zy
mead·ow
mead·ow·lark
mea·ger
 mea·ger·ness
mealy
 meal·i·ness
meal·y-mouthed
mean
 meant
 mean·ing
 mean·ing·ful
 mean·ing·ful·ly
 mean·ing·less
mean·ly
 mean·ness
me·an·der
mean·time
mean·while
mea·sles
mea·sly
 mea·sli·est
meas·ur·a·ble
 meas·ur·a·bil·i·ty
 meas·ur·a·bly
meas·ure
 meas·ur·er

meas·ured
meas·ure·ment
meat
  meaty
  meat·i·ness
mec·ca
me·chan·ic
me·chan·i·cal
me·chan·ics
mech·a·nism
mech·a·nis·tic
mech·a·nize
  mech·a·nized
  mech·a·niz·ing
  mech·a·ni·za·tion
med·al
  med·aled
  med·al·ist
me·dal·lion
med·dle
  med·dled
  med·dling
  med·dler
med·dle·some
me·dia
me·di·al
me·di·an
me·di·ate
  me·di·at·ed
  me·di·at·ing
  me·di·a·tion
  me·di·a·to·ry
  me·di·a·tor
med·ic
med·i·ca·ble
Med·i·caid
med·i·cal
  med·i·cal·ly
Med·i·care
med·i·cate
  med·i·cat·ed
  med·i·cat·ing
med·i·ca·tion
me·dic·i·nal
med·i·cine
me·di·e·val
  me·di·e·val·ism
me·di·o·cre
  me·di·oc·ri·ty
med·i·tate
  med·i·tat·ed
  med·i·tat·ing
  med·i·ta·tor
  med·i·ta·tion
  med·i·ta·tive
Med·i·ter·ra·ne·an
me·di·um
  me·dia
  me·di·ums
med·ley
meet
  met
  meet·ing
meet·ing·house
meg·a·cy·cle
meg·a·lo·ma·nia
  meg·a·lo·ma·ni·ac
meg·a·lop·o·lis
meg·a·phone
meg·a·ton
meg·a·watt
mel·an·choly
  mel·an·cho·lia
  mel·an·chol·ic
  mel·an·chol·i·ness
mé·lange
mel·a·no·ma
me·lee

mel·io·rate
  mel·io·rat·ed
  mel·io·rat·ing
  mel·io·ra·ble
  mel·io·ra·tion
  mel·io·ra·tor
mel·lif·lu·ous
  mel·lif·lu·ent
mel·low
me·lo·de·on
mel·o·dra·ma
  mel·o·dra·mat·ic
  mel·o·dra·mat·i·cal·ly
mel·o·dy
  mel·o·dies
  me·lod·ic
  me·lod·i·cal·ly
  me·lo·di·ous
  me·lo·di·ous·ness
mel·on
melt
  melt·ed or mol·ten
  melt·ing
  melt·a·ble
mem·ber
  mem·ber·less
  mem·ber·ship
mem·brane
  mem·bra·nous
me·men·to
memo
mem·oir
mem·o·ra·bil·ia
mem·o·ra·ble
mem·o·ra·bly
mem·o·ran·dum
me·mo·ri·al
  me·mo·ri·al·ly
me·mo·ri·al·ize
  me·mo·ri·al·ized
  me·mo·ri·al·iz·ing
  me·mo·ri·al·i·za·tion
  me·mo·ri·al·ly
mem·o·rize
  mem·o·rized
  mem·o·riz·ing
  mem·o·ri·za·tion
mem·o·ry
  mem·o·ries
men·ace
  men·aced
  men·ac·ing
mé·nage
me·nag·er·ie
mend
  mend·a·ble
men·da·cious
  men·dac·i·ty
men·di·cant
me·ni·al
  me·ni·al·ly
men·in·gi·tis
me·nis·cus
Men·no·nite
men·o·pause
  men·o·pau·sal
men·sal
men·ses
men·stru·al
men·stru·a·tion
  men·stru·ate
  men·stru·at·ed
  men·stru·at·ing
men·su·ra·ble
men·su·ra·tion
men·tal
  men·tal·ly
  men·tal·i·ty

men·tal·i·ties
men·thol
  men·tho·lat·ed
men·tion
  men·tion·a·ble
men·tor
menu
me·phit·ic
mer·can·tile
mer·can·til·ism
mer·ce·nary
  mer·ce·nar·ies
mer·cer·ize
  mer·cer·ized
mer·chan·dise
  mer·chan·dised
  mer·chan·dis·ing
  mer·chan·dis·er
mer·chant
mer·cu·ri·al
mer·cu·ro·chrome
mer·cu·ry
mer·cy
  mer·cies
  mer·ci·ful
  mer·ci·ful·ly
  mer·ci·less
mere·ly
mer·e·tri·cious
  mer·e·tri·cious·ness
merge
  merged
  merg·ing
  mer·gence
merg·er
me·rid·i·an
me·ringue
mer·it
  mer·it·ed
  mer·it·ed·ly
  mer·it·less
  mer·i·to·ri·ous
mer·maid
mer·ry
  mer·ri·est
  mer·ri·ness
  mer·ri·ment
merry-go-round
mer·ry·mak·er
mer·ry·mak·ing
me·sa
mes·cal
mes·dames
mes·de·moi·selles
mesh·work
mes·mer·ism
  mes·mer·ic
  mes·mer·i·cal·ly
mes·mer·ize
  mes·mer·ized
  mes·mer·iz·ing
  mes·mer·i·za·tion
Me·so·zo·ic
mes·quite
mess
  mess·i·ly
  mess·i·ness
  messy
mes·sage
mes·sen·ger
Mes·si·ah
  Mes·si·an·ic
mes·sieurs
mes·ti·zo
me·tab·o·lism
  met·a·bol·ic
  met·a·bol·i·cal
me·tab·o·lize

me·tab·o·lized
me·tab·o·liz·ing
met·al
  met·aled
  met·al·ing
met·al·ize
  met·al·ized
  met·al·iz·ing
me·tal·lic
met·al·loid
met·al·lur·gy
  met·al·lur·gic
  met·al·lur·gi·cal
  met·al·lur·gist
met·al·work
met·a·mor·phism
  met·a·mor·phic
met·a·mor·phose
  met·a·mor·phosed
  met·a·mor·phos·ing
  met·a·mor·pho·sis
met·a·phor
  met·a·phor·ic
  met·a·phor·i·cal
met·a·phys·ic
  met·a·phys·ics
  met·a·phys·i·cal
met·a·tar·sus
Met·a·zo·a
mete
  met·ed
  met·ing
me·te·or
  me·te·or·ic
  me·te·or·ite
  me·te·or·oid
me·te·or·ol·o·gy
  me·te·or·o·log·i·cal
  me·te·or·ol·o·gist
me·ter
  me·tre
me·ter-kil·o·gram-sec·ond
meth·a·done
meth·ane
meth·a·nol
meth·od
  me·thod·i·cal
Meth·od·ist
meth·od·ize
meth·od·ol·o·gy
  meth·od·o·log·i·cal
  meth·od·ol·o·gist
me·tic·u·lous
  me·tic·u·los·i·ty
  me·tic·u·lous·ly
mé·tier
met·ric
met·ri·cal
  met·ri·cal·ly
met·ro
met·ro·nome
  met·ro·nom·ic
me·trop·o·lis
met·ro·pol·i·tan
met·tle
met·tle·some
Mex·i·can
Mex·i·co
mez·za·nine
mez·zo
mi·as·ma
mi·ca
Mi·chel·an·ge·lo
mi·cro·a·nal·y·sis
mi·crobe
  mi·cro·bi·al
  mi·cro·bi·ol·o·gy
mi·cro·copy

mi·cro·cosm
mi·cro·fiche
mi·cro·film
mi·cro·gram
mi·cro·groove
mi·crom·e·ter
mi·cro·mi·cron
mi·cro·mil·li·me·ter
mi·cron
mi·cro·or·gan·ism
mi·cro·phone
mi·cro·pho·to·graph
mi·cro·read·er
mi·cro·scope
mi·cro·scop·ic
  mi·cro·scop·i·cal·ly
mi·cros·co·py
mi·cro·sec·ond
mi·cro·wave
mid·day
mid·dle
mid·dle-aged
mid·dle·man
mid·dle·weight
mid·dling
mid·dy
  mid·dies
midg·et
mid·land
mid·most
mid·night
mid·point
mid·riff
mid·sec·tion
mid·ship·man
midst
mid·sum·mer
mid·term
mid·way
mid·wife
mid·year
mien
mighty
  might·i·er
  might·i·est
  might·i·ly
  might·i·ness
mi·graine
mi·grant
mi·grate
  mi·grat·ed
  mi·grat·ing
  mi·gra·tion
  mi·gra·tor
  mi·gra·to·ry
mi·ka·do
mi·la·dy
  mi·la·dies
mild
  mild·ly
  mild·ness
mil·dew
  mil·dewy
mile·age
mil·er
mile·stone
mi·lieu
mil·i·tant
  mil·i·tan·cy
  mil·i·tant·ness
mil·i·ta·rism
  mil·i·ta·ris·tic
  mil·i·ta·ris·ti·cal·ly
  mil·i·ta·rize
  mil·i·ta·ri·za·tion
mil·i·tary
  mil·i·tar·i·ly
mi·li·tia

milk
milk·er
milky
milk·i·ness
milk·maid
milk·man
milk·weed
mil·len·ni·um
mil·len·nia
mil·len·ni·al
mill·er
mil·let
mil·li·gram
mil·li·li·ter
mil·li·me·ter
mil·li·ner
mil·li·nery
mill·ing
mil·lion
mil·lionth
mil·lion·aire
mil·li·sec·ond
mill·pond
mime
mimed
mim·ing
mim·er
mim·ic
mim·icked
mim·ick·ing
mim·i·cal
mim·ick·er
mim·ic·ry
mim·ic·ries
mi·mo·sa
min·a·ret
mi·na·to·ry
mince
minced
minc·ing
minc·er
minc·ing·ly
mince·meat
mind·ed
mind·less
min·er
mine·field
min·er·al
min·er·al·ize
min·er·al·ized
min·er·al·iz·ing
min·er·al·i·za·tion
min·er·al·o·gy
min·er·al·og·i·cal
min·er·al·o·gist
min·e·stro·ne
mine·sweep·er
min·gle
min·gled
min·gling
min·i·a·ture
min·i·a·tur·ize
min·i·a·tur·ized
min·i·a·tur·iz·ing
min·i·a·tur·i·za·tion
min·im
min·i·mal
min·i·mal·ly
min·i·mize
min·i·mized
min·i·miz·ing
min·i·mi·za·tion
min·i·mum
min·ing
min·ion
min·is·cule
min·is·ter
min·is·te·ri·al

min·is·trant
min·is·tra·tion
min·is·try
min·is·tries
min·now
mi·nor
mi·nor·i·ty
mi·nor·i·ties
min·strel
mint·age
min·u·end
mi·nus
mi·nus·cule
min·ute
mi·nute
mi·nut·est
min·ute·man
mi·nu·tia
minx
mir·a·cle
mi·rac·u·lous
mi·rage
mire
mired
mir·ing
miry
mir·ror
mirth
mirth·ful·ly
mirth·ful·ness
mirth·less
mis·ad·ven·ture
mis·ad·vise
mis·al·li·ance
mis·an·thrope
mis·an·throp·ic
mis·an·thro·py
mis·ap·ply
mis·ap·plied
mis·ap·ply·ing
mis·ap·pli·ca·tion
mis·ap·pre·hend
mis·ap·pre·hen·sion
mis·ap·pro·pri·ate
mis·ap·pro·pri·at·ed
mis·ap·pro·pri·at·ing
mis·ap·pro·pri·a·tion
mis·be·have
mis·be·haved
mis·be·hav·ing
mis·be·ha·vior
mis·belief
mis·believ·er
mis·cal·cu·late
mis·cal·cu·lat·ed
mis·cal·cu·lat·ing
mis·cal·cu·la·tion
mis·cal·cu·la·tor
mis·call
mis·car·ry
mis·car·ried
mis·car·ry·ing
mis·car·rige
mis·ce·ge·na·tion
mis·cel·la·ne·ous
mis·cel·la·ny
mis·chance
mis·chief
mis·chie·vous
mis·ci·ble
mis·ci·bil·i·ty
mis·con·ceive
mis·con·ceived
mis·con·ceiv·ing
mis·con·cep·tion
mis·con·duct
mis·con·strue
mis·con·strued

mis·con·stru·ing
mis·con·struc·tion
mis·count
mis·cre·ant
mis·cue
mis·cued
mis·cu·ing
mis·deal
mis·dealt
mis·deal·ing
mis·deed
mis·de·mean·or
mis·di·rect
mis·di·rec·tion
mis·do
mis·did
mis·done
mis·do·ing
mis·em·ploy
mis·em·ploy·ment
mi·ser
mi·ser·li·ness
mi·ser·ly
mis·er·a·ble
mis·er·a·ble·ness
mis·er·a·bly
mis·ery
mis·er·ies
mis·es·ti·mate
mis·fea·sance
mis·fire
mis·fired
mis·fit
mis·fit·ted
mis·fit·ting
mis·for·tune
mis·giv·ing
mis·gov·ern
mis·gov·ern·ment
mis·guide
mis·guid·ed
mis·guid·ing
mis·guid·ance
mis·han·dle
mis·han·dled
mis·han·dling
mis·hap
mish·mash
mis·in·form
mis·in·orm·ant
mis·in·form·er
mis·in·for·ma·tion
mis·in·ter·pret
mis·in·ter·pre·ta·tion
mis·in·ter·pret·er
mis·judge
mis·judged
mis·judg·ing
mis·judg·ment
mis·lay
mis·laid
mis·lay·ing
mis·lead
mis·lead·ing
mis·lead·er
mis·man·age
mis·man·aged
mis·man·ag·ing
mis·man·age·ment
mis·match
mis·mate
mis·mat·ed
mis·mat·ing
mis·name
mis·named
mis·nam·ing
mis·no·mer
mi·sog·a·my

mi·sog·y·ny
mi·sog·y·nist
mi·sog·y·nous
mis·place
mis·placed
mis·plac·ing
mis·place·ment
mis·play
mis·print
mis·pri·sion
mis·prize
mis·pro·nounce
mis·pro·nounced
mis·pro·nounc·ing
mis·pro·nun·ci·a·tion
mis·quote
mis·quot·ed
mis·quot·ing
mis·quo·ta·tion
mis·read
mis·read·ing
mis·rep·re·sent
mis·rep·re·sen·ta·tion
mis·rep·re·sen·ta·tive
mis·rule
mis·ruled
mis·rul·ing
mis·sal
mis·shape
mis·shaped
mis·shap·ing
mis·shap·en
mis·sile
miss·ing
mis·sion
mis·sion·ary
mis·sion·ar·ies
mis·sive
mis·spell
mis·spelled
mis·spelt
mis·spel·ling
mis·spend
mis·spent
mis·spend·ing
mis·state
mis·stat·ed
mis·stat·ing
mis·state·ment
mis·step
mist
mist·i·ly
mist·i·ness
mis·tak·a·ble
mis·take
mis·took
mis·tak·en
mis·tak·ing
mis·tak·en·ly
mis·tak·en·ness
Mis·ter
mis·tle·toe
mis·treat
mis·treat·ment
mis·tress
mis·tri·al
mis·trust
mis·trust·ful
mis·trust·ful·ly
mis·trust·ing·ly
misty
mist·i·er
mist·i·ness
mis·un·der·stand
mis·un·der·stood
mis·un·der·stand·ing
mis·use
mis·used

mis·us·ing
mis·us·age
mis·val·ue
mi·ter
mi·tre
mit·i·gate
mit·i·gat·ing
mit·i·ga·tion
mit·i·ga·tive
mit·i·ga·tor
mit·i·ga·to·ry
mi·to·sis
mitt
mit·ten
mix
mixed
mix·ing
mix·er
mix·ture
miz·zen
mne·mon·ic
mne·mon·ics
mob
mobbed
mob·bing
mob·bish
mo·bile
mo·bil·i·ty
mo·bi·lize
mo·bi·lized
mo·bi·liz·ing
mo·bi·li·za·tion
mob·ster
moc·ca·sin
mo·cha
mock
mock·er
mock·ing·ly
mock·ery
mock·ing·bird
mock-up
mod·al
mo·dal·i·ty
mod·al·ly
mod·el
mod·eled
mod·el·ing
mod·er·ate
mod·er·at·ed
mod·er·at·ing
mod·er·ate·ness
mod·er·a·tion
mod·er·a·tor
mod·ern
mod·ern·ism
mod·ern·ist
mod·ern·is·tic
mod·ern·ize
mod·ern·ized
mod·ern·iz·ing
mod·ern·i·za·tion
mod·est
mod·est·ly
mod·es·ty
mod·i·cum
mod·i·fi·ca·tion
mod·i·fy
mod·i·fied
mod·i·fy·ing
mod·i·fi·a·ble
mod·i·fi·er
mod·ish
mod·ish·ly
mod·ish·ness
mo·diste
mod·u·late
mod·u·lat·ed

mod·u·lat·ing
mod·u·la·tion
mod·u·la·to·ry
mod·ule
mod·u·lar
mo·dus o·pe·ran·di
mo·dus vi·ven·di
mo·gul
mo·hair
Mo·ham·med
moi·e·ty
moi·ré
mois·ten
moist·en·er
mois·ture
mois·tur·ize
mois·tur·ized
mois·tur·iz·ing
mois·tur·iz·er
mo·lar
mo·las·ses
mold
mold·a·ble
mold·er
mold·ing
moldy
mold·i·er
mold·i·ness
mol·e·cule
mo·lec·u·lar
mole·skin
mo·lest
mo·les·ta·tion
mo·lest·er
mol·li·fy
mol·li·fied
mol·li·fy·ing
mol·li·fi·ca·tion
mol·li·fi·er
mol·lusk
mol·ly·cod·dle
molt
molt·er
mol·ten
mo·lyb·de·num
mo·ment
mo·men·tary
mo·men·tar·i·ly
mo·men·tous
mo·men·tous·ness
mo·men·tum
mon·ad
mo·nad·ic
mo·nad·i·cal
mon·arch
mo·nar·chal
mo·nar·chic
mo·nar·chi·cal·ly
mon·ar·chism
mon·ar·chist
mon·ar·chy
mon·ar·chies
mon·as·tery
mon·as·te·ri·al
mo·nas·tic
mo·nas·ti·cal
mo·nas·ti·cism
mon·au·ral
mon·au·ral·ly
mon·e·tary
mon·e·tar·i·ly
mon·e·tize
mon·e·tized
mon·e·tiz·ing
mon·e·ti·za·tion
mon·ey
mon·eyed
mon·ied

mon·ger
Mon·gol·ism
mon·gol·oid
mon·goose
mon·grel
mon·i·ker
mon·ism
mo·nis·tic
mo·nis·ti·cal·ly
mo·ni·tion
mon·i·tor
mon·i·to·ri·al
monk
monk·ish
mon·key
mon·keys
mon·keyed
mon·key·ing
mon·key·shines
mon·o·chro·mat·ic
mon·o·chro·mat·i·cal·ly
mon·o·chrome
mon·o·chro·mic
mon·o·chro·mi·cal
mon·o·chro·mi·cal·ly
mon·o·cle
mon·o·dist
mon·o·dy
mo·nod·ic
mo·nog·a·my
mo·nog·a·mist
mo·nog·a·mous
mon·o·gram
mon·o·grammed
mon·o·gram·ming
mon·o·gram·mat·ic
mon·o·graph
mo·nog·ra·pher
mon·o·graph·ic
mon·o·lith
mon·o·logue
mon·o·log
mon·o·logu·ist
mon·o·log·ist
mon·o·ma·nia
mon·o·ma·ni·ac
mon·o·met·al·lism
mon·o·me·tal·lic
mo·no·mi·al
mon·o·nu·cle·o·sis
mon·o·plane
mo·nop·o·lize
mo·nop·o·lized
mo·nop·o·liz·ing
mo·nop·o·li·za·tion
mo·nop·o·liz·er
mo·nop·o·ly
mo·nop·o·lies
mon·o·rail
mon·o·so·di·um glu·ta·mate
mon·o·syl·lab·ic
mon·o·the·ism
mon·o·the·ist
mon·o·the·is·tic
mon·o·tone
mo·not·o·ny
mo·not·o·nous
mon·o·type
mon·ox·ide
mon·sei·gneur
mon·sieur
mes·sieurs
Mon·si·gnor
mon·soon
mon·ster
mon·stros·i·ty
mon·strous
mon·tage

Mon·tes·so·ri
month·ly
month·lies
mon·u·ment
mon·u·men·tal
mon·u·men·tal·ly
mooch
mooch·er
moody
mood·i·er
mood·i·ly
mood·i·ness
moon·beam
moon·light·ing
moon·scape
moon·shine
moor·ing
moot·ness
mop
mopped
mop·ping
mope
moped
mop·ing
mop·pet
mo·raine
mor·al
mor·al·ly
mo·rale
mor·al·ist
mor·al·is·tic
mo·ral·i·ty
mor·al·ize
mor·al·ized
mor·al·iz·ing
mor·al·i·za·tion
mor·al·iz·er
mo·rass
mor·a·to·ri·um
mo·ray
mor·bid
mor·bid·ly
mor·bid·i·ty
mor·bid·ness
mor·dant
mor·dan·cy
more·o·ver
mo·res
mor·ga·nat·ic
morgue
mor·i·bund
Mor·mon·ism
morn·ing
morn·ing-glo·ry
mo·roc·co
mo·ron
mo·ron·ic
mo·ron·i·cal·ly
mo·rose
mo·rose·ly
mo·rose·ness
mor·pheme
mor·phine
mor·phol·o·gy
mor·pho·log·ic
mor·pho·log·i·cal
mor·phol·o·gist
mor·row
mor·sel
mor·tal
mor·tal·ly
mor·tal·i·ty
mor·tal·i·ties
mor·tar
mor·tar·board
mort·gage
mort·gaged
mort·gag·ing

mort·ga·gee
mort·ga·ger
mor·ti·cian
mor·ti·fy
mor·ti·fied
mor·ti·fy·ing
mor·ti·fi·ca·tion
mor·tise
mor·tised
mor·tis·ing
mor·tu·ary
mor·tu·ar·ies
mo·sa·ic
mo·sey
mo·seyed
mo·sey·ing
Mos·lem
mosque
mos·qui·to
mos·qui·toes
mos·qui·tos
moss
moss·like
mossy
moss·i·er
moss·back
most·ly
mo·tel
mo·tet
moth·ball
moth-eat·en
moth·er
moth·er·less
moth·er·hood
moth·er·ly
moth·er·li·ness
moth·er-in-law
moth·ers-in-law
moth·er·land
moth·er-of-pearl
mo·tif
mo·tile
mo·til·i·ty
mo·tion
mo·tion·less·ness
mo·ti·vate
mo·ti·vat·ed
mo·ti·vat·ing
mo·ti·va·tion
mo·ti·va·tion·al
mo·tive
mot·ley
mo·tor
mo·tor·bike
mo·tor·boat
mo·tor·bus
mo·tor·cade
mo·tor·car
mo·tor court
mo·tor·cy·cle
mo·tor·cy·cled
mo·tor·cy·cling
mo·tor·cy·clist
mo·tor·ist
mo·tor·ize
mo·tor·ized
mo·tor·iz·ing
mo·tor·i·za·tion
mo·tor·man
mot·tle
mot·tled
mot·tling
mound
mount
mount·a·ble
moun·tain
moun·tain·eer
moun·tain·ous

moun·te·bank
mount·ing
mourn
mourn·er
mourn·ful
mourn·ful·ly
mourn·ing
mouse
mous·er
mousse
mous·tache
mousy
mous·i·er
mouth
mouthed
mouth·ful
mouth·piece
mouthy
mouth·i·ness
mou·ton
mov·a·ble
mov·a·bil·i·ty
mov·a·bly
move
moved
mov·ing
move·ment
mov·ie
mow
mowed or mown
mow·ing
mow·er
mox·ie
mu·ci·lage
mu·ci·lag·i·nous
muck
mucky
muck·rake
muck·raked
muck·rak·ing
muck·rak·er
mu·cous
mu·cos·i·ty
mu·cus
mud
mud·ded
mud·ding
mud·dle
mud·dled
mud·dling
mud·dler
mud·dy
mud·di·er
mud·di·ness
mu·ez·zin
muf·fin
muf·fle
muf·fled
muf·fling
muf·fler
muf·ti
mug
mugged
mug·ging
mug·ger
mug·gy
mug·gi·ness
mu·lat·to
mu·lat·toes
mul·ber·ry
mulch
mulct
mu·le·teer
mul·ish
mul·ish·ness
mul·let
mul·li·gan
mul·li·ga·taw·ny

mul·lion
  mul·lioned
mul·ti·col·ored
mul·ti·far·i·ous
  mul·ti·far·i·ous·ness
mul·ti·lat·er·al
mul·ti·lev·el
mul·ti·mil·lion·aire
mul·ti·par·tite
mul·ti·ple
mul·ti·ple-choice
mul·ti·ple scle·ro·sis
mul·ti·pli·cand
mul·ti·pli·ca·tion
mul·ti·plic·i·ty
mul·ti·pli·er
mul·ti·ply
  mul·ti·plied
  mul·ti·ply·ing
  mul·ti·pli·a·ble
mul·ti·tude
  mul·ti·tu·di·nous
mum·ble
  mum·bled
  mum·bling
  mum·bler
mum·bo jum·bo
mum·mer
mum·mi·fy
  mum·mi·fied
  mum·mi·fy·ing
  mum·mi·fi·ca·tion
mum·my
  mum·mies
munch
mun·dane
mu·nic·i·pal
  mu·nic·i·pal·ly
  mu·nic·i·pal·i·ty
mu·nif·i·cent
  mu·nif·i·cence
  mu·nif·i·cent·ly
mu·ni·tion
mu·ral
  mu·ral·ist
mur·der
  mur·der·er
  mur·der·ess
  mur·der·ous
  mur·der·ous·ly
mu·ri·at·ic ac·id
murky
  murk·i·er
  murk·i·ness
mur·mur
  mur·mur·er
  mur·mur·ing
mur·rain
mus·cat
  mus·ca·tel
mus·cle
  mus·cled
  mus·cling
mus·cle-bound
mus·cu·lar
  mus·cu·lar·i·ty
mus·cu·lar dys·tro·phy
mus·cu·la·ture
muse
  mused
  mus·ing
mu·se·um
mush
  mushy
  mush·i·ness
mush·room
mu·sic
mu·si·cal

mu·si·cal·ly
mu·si·cal·ness
mu·si·cale
mu·si·cian
musk
musky
musk·i·ness
mus·kel·lunge
mus·ket
mus·ket·eer
mus·ket·ry
musk·mel·on
musk·rat
Mus·lim
mus·lin
muss
  mussy
mus·sel
mus·tache
mus·tang
mus·tard
mus·ter
mus·ty
  mus·ti·ly
  mus·ti·ness
mu·ta·ble
  mu·ta·bil·i·ty
  mu·ta·ble·ness
  mu·ta·bly
mu·tant
mu·ta·tion
mu·tate
  mu·tat·ed
  mu·tat·ing
  mu·ta·tion·al
mute
  mut·ed
  mut·ing
  mute·ly
  mute·ness
mu·ti·late
  mu·ti·lat·ed
  mu·ti·lat·ing
  mu·ti·la·tion
  mu·ti·la·tor
mu·ti·neer
mu·ti·ny
  mu·ti·nied
  mu·ti·ny·ing
  mu·ti·nous
mut·ter
  mut·tered
  mut·ter·ing
mut·ton
mu·tu·al
  mu·tu·al·i·ty
  mu·tu·al·ly
muu·muu
muz·zle
  muz·zled
  muz·zling
my·col·o·gy
  my·col·o·gist
my·na
my·o·pia
my·op·ic
myr·i·ad
myrrh
myr·tle
my·self
mys·te·ri·ous
  mys·te·ri·ous·ly
mys·tery
  mys·ter·ies
mys·tic
mys·ti·cal
  mys·ti·cal·ly
mys·ti·cism

mys·ti·fy
  mys·ti·fied
  mys·ti·fy·ing
  mys·ti·fi·ca·tion
mys·tique
myth
  myth·i·cal
  myth·i·cal·ly
my·thol·o·gy
  myth·o·log·ic
  myth·o·log·i·cal
  my·thol·o·gist

N

nab
  nabbed
  nab·bing
na·bob
na·celle
na·cre
  na·cre·ous
na·dir
nag
  nagged
  nag·ging
  nag·ger
nain·sook
na·ive
  na·ive·ly
  na·ive·ness
na·ive·te
na·ked
na·ked·ness
nam·by-pam·by
name
  named
  nam·ing
  name·less
name·ly
name·sake
nan·keen
nan·ny
nap
  napped
  nap·ping
na·palm
nape
naph·tha
naph·tha·lene
nap·kin
Na·po·leon
nar·cis·sism
  nar·cism
  nar·cis·sist
  nar·cis·sis·tic
nar·cis·sus
nar·co·sis
nar·cot·ic
  nar·co·tize
  nar·co·tized
  nar·co·tiz·ing
  nar·cot·ism
nar·rate
  nar·ra·ted
  nar·ra·ting
  nar·ra·tor
  nar·ra·tion
  nar·ra·tive
nar·row
  nar·row·ly
nar·row-mind·ed
na·sal
  na·sal·i·ty
  na·sal·ize
  na·sal·ized
  na·sal·iz·ing

na·sal·ly
nas·cent
  nas·cence
  nas·cen·cy
na·stur·tium
nas·ty
  nas·ti·er
  nas·ti·ly
  nas·ti·ness
na·tal
  na·tal·i·ty
na·tant
  na·ta·to·ri·al
  na·ta·to·ri·um
na·tion
  na·tion·hood
na·tion·al
  na·tion·al·ly
  na·tion·al·ism
  na·tion·al·ist
  na·tion·al·is·tic
  na·tion·al·i·ty
  na·tion·al·i·ties
  na·tion·al·ize
  na·tion·al·ized
  na·tion·al·iz·ing
  na·tion·al·i·za·tion
na·tion-wide
na·tive
  na·tive·ly
  na·tive·ness
na·tiv·ism
  na·tiv·ist
na·tiv·i·ty
  na·tiv·i·ties
nat·ty
  nat·ti·ly
  nat·ti·ness
nat·u·ral
  nat·u·ral·ly
  nat·u·ral·ness
nat·u·ral·ism
  nat·u·ral·ist
  nat·u·ral·is·tic
nat·u·ral·ize
  nat·u·ral·ized
  nat·u·ral·iz·ing
  nat·u·ral·i·za·tion
na·ture
naught
naugh·ty
  naugh·ti·est
  naugh·ti·ly
  naugh·ti·ness
nau·sea
nau·se·ate
  nau·se·at·ed
  nau·se·at·ing
nau·seous
  nau·seous·ness
nau·ti·cal
  nau·ti·cal·ly
nau·ti·lus
  nau·ti·lus·es
Nav·a·ho
na·vel
nav·i·ga·ble
  nav·i·ga·bil·i·ty
  nav·i·ga·ble·ness
nav·i·gate
  nav·i·gat·ed
  nav·i·gat·ing
  nav·i·ga·tion
  nav·i·ga·tor
na·vy
  na·vies
na·val
Naz·a·reth

Na·zi
  Na·zism
  Na·si·ism
Ne·an·der·thal
near
  near·ly
  near·ness
near·by
near-sight·ed
neat
  neat·ly
  neat·ness
Neb·u·chad·nez·zar
neb·u·la
  neb·u·lae
neb·u·lous
  neb·u·lar
  neb·u·lous·ness
  neb·u·los·i·ty
nec·es·sary
  nec·es·sar·ies
  nec·es·sar·i·ly
ne·ces·si·tate
  ne·ces·si·ta·ted
  ne·ces·si·ta·ting
ne·ces·si·ty
  ne·ces·si·ites
neck·er·chief
neck·lace
neck·tie
ne·crol·o·gy
  ne·crol·o·gies
nec·ro·man·cy
  nec·ro·man·cer
ne·crop·o·lis
nec·tar
nec·tar·ine
need·ful
  need·ful·ly
nee·dle
nee·dled
  nee·dling
  nee·dle·point
need·less
  need·less·ly
nee·dle·work
needy
  need·i·est
  need·i·ness
ne'er-do-well
ne·far·i·ous
  ne·far·i·ous·ness
ne·gate
  ne·ga·ted
  ne·ga·ting
  ne·ga·tion
neg·a·tive
  neg·a·tive·ness
  neg·a·tiv·i·ty
  neg·a·tiv·ism
ne·glect
  ne·glect·ful
  ne·glect·ful·ly
neg·li·gee
neg·li·gent
  neg·li·gence
  neg·li·gent·ly
neg·li·gi·ble
  neg·li·gi·bly
  neg·li·gi·bil·i·ty
ne·go·ti·a·ble
  ne·go·ti·a·bil·i·ty
ne·go·ti·ate
  ne·go·ti·at·ed
  ne·go·ti·at·ing
  ne·go·ti·a·tion
  ne·go·ti·a·tor
Ne·gro

Ne·groes
Ne·groid
neigh
neigh·bor
neigh·bor·ing
neigh·bor·ly
neigh·bor·li·ness
neigh·bor·hood
nei·ther
nem·a·tode
nem·e·sis
ne·o·clas·sic
ne·o·clas·si·cal
ne·o·clas·si·cism
ne·o·lith·ic
ne·ol·o·gism
ne·ol·o·gy
ne·on
ne·o·phyte
neo·prene
neph·ew
ne·phri·tis
nep·o·tism
nep·o·tist
nerve
nerve·less
nerve·rack·ing
nerve·wrack·ing
nerv·ous
nerv·ous·ness
nervy
nerv·i·ness
nes·tle
nes·tled
nes·tling
net
net·ted
net·ting
neth·er
Neth·er·lands
neth·er·most
net·tle
net·tled
net·tling
net·tle·some
net·work
neu·ral
neu·ral·gia
neu·ras·the·nia
neu·ri·tis
neu·riti·c
neu·rol·o·gy
neu·ro·log·i·cal
neu·rol·o·gist
neu·ron
neu·ro·sis
neu·ro·ses
neu·rot·ic
neu·rot·i·cal·ly
neu·ter
neu·tral
neu·tral·i·ty
neu·tral·ly
neu·tral·ism
neu·tral·ist
neu·tral·ize
neu·tral·ized
neu·tral·iz·ing
neu·tral·i·za·tion
neu·tral·iz·er
neu·tron
nev·er
nev·er·more
nev·er·the·less
new
new·ish
new·ness
new·born

new·com·er
new·el
new·fan·gled
new·ly·wed
news·cast·er
news·pa·per
news·print
news·reel
news·stand
New Test·a·ment
New Zea·land
nex·us
ni·a·cin
Ni·ag·a·ra
nib·ble
nib·bled
nib·bling
Nic·a·ra·gua
nice
nice·ly
nice·ness
ni·ce·ty
ni·ce·ties
niche
nick·el·o·de·on
nick·name
nic·o·tine
nic·o·tin·ic
niece
nif·ty
nif·ti·est
Ni·ge·ria
nig·gard
nig·gard·li·ness
nig·gard·ly
nig·gling
night·fall
night·gown
night·in·gale
night·ly
night·mare
night·mar·ish
night·time
ni·hil·ism
ni·hil·ist
ni·hil·is·tic
nim·ble
nim·ble·ness
nim·bly
nim·bus
nim·rod
nin·comp·poop
nine·teen
nine·teenth
nine·ty
nine·ties
nine·ti·eth
nin·ny
ninth
nip
nipped
nip·ping
nip·per
nip·ple
Nip·pon
nip·py
nir·va·na
Ni·sei
nit·pick
ni·trate
ni·tra·tion
ni·tric
ni·tro·gen
ni·trog·e·nous
ni·tro·glyc·er·in
nit·ty-grit·ty
nit·wit
no·bil·i·ty

no·ble
no·bler
no·blest
no·ble·man
no·ble·ness
no·bly
no·blesse oblige
no·body
noc·tur·nal
noc·turne
nod
nod·ded
nod·ding
node
nod·al
nod·ule
nod·u·lar
no·el
nog·gin
noise
noised
nois·ing
noise·less
noi·some
noisy
nois·i·ly
nois·i·ness
no·lo con·ten·de·re
no·mad
no·mad·ic
no·mad·i·cal·ly
no·mad·ism
nom de plume
no·men·cla·ture
nom·i·nal
nom·i·nal·ly
nom·i·nate
nom·i·nat·ed
nom·i·nat·ing
nom·i·na·tion
nom·i·na·tive
nom·i·nee
non·age
non·align·ment
non·cha·lant
non·cha·lance
non·cha·lant·ly
non·com
non·com·bat·ant
non·com·mis·sioned
non·com·mit·tal
non·con·duc·tor
non·con·form·ist
non·con·form·i·ty
non·de·script
non·en·ti·ty
none·the·less
non·in·ter·ven·tion
non·met·al
non·me·tal·lic
non·pa·reil
non·par·ti·san
non·plus
non·plused
non·plus·ing
non·prof·it
non·res·i·dent
non·res·i·dence
non·res·i·den·cy
non·re·sis·tance
non·re·stric·tive
non·sched·uled
non·sec·tar·i·an
non·sense
non·sen·si·cal
non·sen·si·cal·ly
non se·qui·tur
non·stop

non·sup·port
non·un·ion
non·vi·o·lence
non·vi·o·lent·ly
noo·dle
noon
noon·day
noon·time
noose
nor·mal
nor·mal·cy
nor·mal·i·ty
nor·mal·ly
nor·mal·ize
nor·mal·ized
nor·mal·iz·ing
nor·mal·i·za·tion
Norse·man
North Amer·i·ca
north·east
north·east·ern
north·east·ern
north·east·er
north·east·er·ly
north·east·ward
north·er
nor·ther·ly
north·er·li·ness
north·ern
north·ern·most
north·ern·er
north·ward
north·wards
north·ward·ly
north·west
north·west·ern
north·west·ward
Nor·we·gian
nose
nosed
nos·ing
nose·gay
nos·tal·gia
nos·tal·gic
nos·tril
nos·trum
nosy
nos·i·ly
nos·i·ness
no·ta·ble
no·ta·ble·ness
no·ta·bil·i·ty
no·ta·bly
no·ta·rize
no·ta·rized
no·ta·riz·ing
no·ta·ri·za·tion
no·ta·ry
no·ta·tion
no·ta·tion·al
notch
notched
note
not·ed
not·ing
not·ed
not·ed·ness
note·wor·thy
note·wor·thi·ness
noth·ing
noth·ing·ness
no·tice
no·ticed
no·tic·ing
no·tice·a·ble
no·tice·a·bly
no·ti·fy
no·ti·fied

no·ti·fy·ing
no·ti·fi·ca·tion
no·tion
no·to·ri·ous
no·to·ri·ous·ness
no·to·ri·e·ty
no-trump
nought
nour·ish
nour·ish·ing
nour·ish·ment
no·va
No·va Sco·tia
nov·el
nov·el·ist
nov·el·is·tic
nov·el·ette
nov·el·ty
nov·el·ties
no·ve·na
nov·ice
no·vi·ti·ate
no·vo·cain
now·a·days
no·where
no·wise
nox·ious
noz·zle
nu·ance
nub·bin
nu·bile
nu·cle·ar
nu·cle·ate
nu·cle·on
nu·cle·onics
nu·cle·us
nu·clei
nude
nude·ness
nu·di·ty
nud·ism
nud·ist
nudge
nudged
nudg·ing
nu·ga·to·ry
nug·get
nui·sance
null
nul·li·ty
nul·li·fy
nul·li·fied
nul·li·fy·ing
nul·li·fi·ca·tion
nul·li·fi·er
numb
numb·ly
numb·ness
num·ber
num·ber·less
nu·mer·al
num·er·al·ly
nu·mer·a·ble
nu·mer·ate
nu·mer·at·ed
nu·mer·at·ing
nu·mer·a·tion
nu·mer·a·tor
nu·mer·i·cal
nu·mer·ous
nu·mis·mat·ics
nu·mis·mat·ic
nu·mis·ma·tist
num·skull
numb·skull
nun·cio
nun·nery
nun·ner·ies

nup·tial
  nup·tial·ly
nurse
  nursed
  nurs·ing
nurse·maid
nurs·ery
  nurs·er·ies
nur·ture
  nur·tured
  nur·tur·ing
nut
  nut·ty
nut·crack·er
nut·hatch
nut·meg
nu·tri·ent
  nu·tri·ment
nu·tri·tion
  nu·tri·tion·al
  nu·tri·tion·al·ly
  nu·tri·tion·ist
nu·tri·tious
nu·tri·tive
nut·shell
nut·ty
nuz·zle
  nuz·zled
  nuz·zling
ny·lon
nymph
nym·pho·ma·nia
  nym·pho·ma·ni·ac

O

oaf
  oaf·ish
oak·en
oa·kum
oar·lock
oars·man
oa·sis
oath
oat·meal
ob·bli·ga·to
ob·du·rate
  ob·du·ra·cy
  ob·du·rate·ness
obe·di·ence
  obe·di·ent
obei·sance
  obei·sant
ob·e·lisk
obese
obese·ness
  obes·i·ty
obey
ob·fus·cate
  ob·fus·cat·ed
  ob·fus·cat·ing
  ob·fus·ca·tion
obit·u·ary
  obit·u·ar·ies
ob·ject
  ob·ject·less
  ob·ject·or
ob·jec·tion
  ob·jec·tion·a·ble
  ob·jec·tion·a·bly
ob·jec·tive
  ob·jec·tive·ly
  ob·jec·tive·ness
  ob·jec·tiv·i·ty
ob·jet d'art
ob·jur·gate
  ob·jur·gat·ed

ob·jur·gat·ing
ob·jur·ga·tion
ob·jur·ga·to·ry
ob·late
  ob·la·tion
ob·li·gate
  ob·li·gat·ed
  ob·li·gat·ing
  ob·li·ga·tion
  ob·lig·a·to·ry
oblige
  obliged
  oblig·ing
ob·lique
  ob·lique·ly
  ob·liq·ui·ty
ob·lit·er·ate
  ob·lit·er·at·ed
  ob·lit·er·at·ing
  ob·lit·er·a·tion
  ob·lit·er·a·tive
ob·liv·i·on
  ob·liv·i·ous
ob·long
ob·lo·quy
ob·nox·ious
oboe
  obo·ist
ob·scene
  ob·scene·ly
  ob·scene·ness
  ob·scen·i·ty
ob·scure
  ob·scured
  ob·scur·ing
  ob·scure·ness
  ob·scu·ri·ty
ob·se·qui·ous
ob·se·quy
ob·ser·va·to·ry
ob·serve
  ob·served
  ob·serv·ing
  ob·serv·er
  ob·serv·a·ble
  ob·serv·a·bly
  ob·ser·vance
  ob·ser·vant
  ob·ser·va·tion
ob·sess
  ob·ses·sive
  ob·ses·sion
ob·sid·i·an
ob·so·les·cent
  ob·so·les·cence
ob·so·lete
  ob·so·lete·ness
ob·sta·cle
ob·stet·rics
  ob·stet·ric
  ob·stet·ri·cal
  ob·ste·tri·cian
ob·sti·nate
  ob·sti·na·cy
  ob·sti·nate·ly
  ob·sti·nate·ness
ob·strep·er·ous
  ob·strep·er·ous·ness
ob·struct
  ob·struc·tive
  ob·struc·tor
  ob·struc·tion
  ob·struc·tion·ism
  ob·struc·tion·ist
ob·tain
  ob·tain·a·ble
  ob·tain·ment
ob·trude

ob·trud·ed
ob·trud·ing
ob·tru·sion
ob·tru·sive
ob·tuse
  ob·tuse·ness
ob·verse
  ob·verse·ly
ob·vert
ob·vi·ate
  ob·vi·at·ed
  ob·vi·at·ing
  ob·vi·a·tion
ob·vi·ous
  ob·vi·ous·ness
ob·vo·lute
oc·a·ri·na
oc·ca·sion
oc·ca·sion·al
  oc·ca·sion·al·ly
oc·ci·dent
  oc·ci·den·tal
oc·clude
  oc·clud·ed
  oc·clud·ing
  oc·clu·sive
  oc·clu·sion
oc·cult
  oc·cult·ism
  oc·cult·ist
oc·cu·pa·tion
  oc·cu·pa·tion·al
  oc·cu·pa·tion·al·ly
oc·cu·py
  oc·cu·pied
  oc·cu·py·ing
  oc·cu·pi·er
  oc·cu·pan·cy
  oc·cu·pant
oc·cur
  oc·curred
  oc·cur·ring
  oc·cur·rence
  oc·cur·rent
ocean
  oce·an·ic
oce·a·nog·ra·phy
  oce·a·nog·ra·pher
  oce·a·no·graph·ic
  oce·a·no·graph·i·cal
oce·lot
ocher
  ochery
o'clock
oc·ta·gon
  oc·tag·o·nal·ly
oc·ta·he·dron
  oc·ta·he·dra
  oc·ta·he·dral
oc·tane
oc·tave
oc·ta·vo
oc·tet
oc·to·ge·nar·i·an
oc·to·pus
oc·to·roon
oc·u·lar
oc·u·list
odd
  odd·ness
odd·ball
odd·i·ty
  odd·i·ties
odi·ous
  odi·ous·ness
odi·um
odom·e·ter
odor

odored
odor·less
odor·ous
odor·if·er·ous
od·ys·sey
Oed·i·pus
of·fal
off·beat
off·col·or
of·fend
  of·fend·er
of·fense
  of·fense·less
of·fen·sive
  of·fen·sive·ly
of·fer
of·fer·er
of·fer·ing
of·fer·to·ry
  of·fer·to·ries
  of·fer·to·ri·al
off·hand
  off·hand·ed·ness
of·fice
of·fice·hold·er
of·fic·er
of·fi·cial
  of·fi·cial·ly
  of·fi·cial·dom
of·fi·ci·ate
  of·fi·ci·at·ed
  of·fi·ci·at·ing
  of·fi·ci·a·tion
  of·fi·ci·a·tor
of·fi·cious
  of·fi·cious·ly
off·ing
off·set
  off·set·ting
off·shoot
off·shore
off·side
off·spring
off·stage
off-the-record
of·ten
of·ten·times
ogle
  ogled
  ogling
  ogler
ogre
  ogre·ish
ohm
  ohm·age
  ohm·ic
ohm·me·ter
oil·cloth
oil·skin
oily
  oil·i·ness
oint·ment
okra
old
old·er
  old·est
  old·en
  old·ish
  old·ness
old-fash·ioned
old·ster
Old Test·a·ment
old-tim·er
old-world
ole·ag·i·nous
ole·o·mar·ga·rine
ol·fac·tion
  ol·fac·to·ry

ol·i·gar·chy
ol·i·gar·chic
oli·gar·chi·cal
ol·i·garch
ol·i·gop·o·ly
ol·ive
Olym·pi·an
O·lym·pic
om·buds·man
ome·ga
om·e·let
omen
om·i·nous
  om·i·nous·ly
omis·sion
omit
  omit·ted
  omit·ting
om·ni·bus
om·nip·o·tence
  om·nip·o·tent·ly
om·ni·pres·ent
  om·ni·pres·ence
om·nis·cience
  om·nis·cient
om·niv·or·ous
on·com·ing
on·er·ous
one·self
one-sid·ed
one-up·man·ship
one-way
on·go·ing
on·ion
  on·iony
on·look·er
on·ly
on·o·mat·o·poe·ia
  on·o·mat·o·poe·ic
  on·o·mat·o·poe·i·cal·ly
on·rush·ing
on·set
on·shore
on·slaught
on·to
onus
on·ward
on·yx
oo·dles
ooze
  oozed
  ooz·ing
  oo·zi·ness
  oo·zy
opac·i·ty
opal
opal·es·cence
  opal·es·cent
opaque
  opaque·ly
open
  open·ly
  open·ness
open-hand·ed
open house
open·ing
open-mind·ed
open-mouthed
open ses·a·me
open·work
opera
op·er·at·ic
op·er·a·ble
  op·er·a·bil·i·ty
  op·er·a·bly
op·er·ate
  op·er·at·ed
  op·er·at·ing

op·er·a·tion
op·er·a·tive
op·er·a·tor
op·er·et·ta
oph·thal·mic
oph·thal·mol·o·gist
oph·thal·mol·o·gy
opi·ate
opin·ion
opin·ion·at·ed
opi·um
opos·sum
op·po·nent
op·por·tune
op·por·tune·ly
op·por·tun·ism
op·por·tun·ist
op·por·tun·is·tic
op·por·tu·ni·ty
op·por·tu·ni·ties
op·pose
op·posed
op·pos·ing
op·pos·er
op·po·site
op·po·site·ness
op·po·si·tion
op·press
op·pres·sor
op·pres·sion
op·pres·sive
op·pro·bri·um
op·pro·bri·ous
op·tic
op·ti·cal
op·ti·cal
op·ti·cian
op·tics
op·ti·mal
op·ti·mism
op·ti·mist
op·ti·mis·tic
op·ti·mis·ti·cal·ly
op·ti·mize
op·ti·mized
op·ti·miz·ing
op·ti·mi·za·tion
op·ti·mum
op·tion
op·tion·al
op·tom·e·try
op·to·met·ric
op·tom·e·trist
op·u·lent
op·u·lence
op·u·lent·ly
opus
opus·es
or·a·cle
orac·u·lar
oral
oral·ly
or·ange
orang·u·tan
orate
orat·ed
orat·ing
ora·tion
or·a·tor
or·a·tor·i·cal
or·a·to·ry
or·a·to·rio
or·bic·u·lar
orbit
or·bit·al
or·chard
or·ches·tra
or·ches·tral

or·ches·trate
or·ches·trat·ed
or·ches·trat·ing
or·ches·tra·tion
or·chid
or·dain
or·dain·er
or·dain·ment
or·deal
or·der
or·dered
or·der·ly
or·der·li·ness
or·di·nal
or·di·nance
or·di·nar·i·ly
or·di·nary
or·di·nar·i·ness
or·di·na·tion
ord·nance
oreg·a·no
or·gan
or·gan·dy
or·gan·ic
or·gan·i·cal·ly
or·gan·ism
or·gan·ist
or·gan·i·za·tion
or·gan·i·za·tion·al
or·gan·ize
or·gan·ized
or·gan·iz·ing
or·gan·iz·a·ble
or·gan·iz·er
or·gasm
or·gas·mic
or·gi·as·tic
or·gi·as·ti·cal·ly
or·gy
or·gies
ori·ent
Ori·en·tal
ori·en·tate
ori·en·tat·ed
ori·en·tat·ing
ori·en·ta·tion
or·i·fice
orig·i·nal
orig·i·nal·i·ty
orig·i·nal·ly
orig·i·nate
orig·i·nat·ed
orig·i·nat·ing
orig·i·na·tion
orig·i·na·tor
orig·i·na·tive
or·i·son
or·mo·lu
or·na·ment
or·na·men·tal
or·na·men·ta·tion
or·nate
or·nate·ness
or·nery
or·ner·i·ness
or·ni·thol·o·gy
or·ni·tho·log·ic
or·ni·thol·o·gist
oro·tund
oro·tun·di·ty
or·phan
or·phan·age
or·tho·don·tics
or·tho·don·tic
or·tho·don·tist
or·tho·dox
or·tho·dox·ly
or·tho·dox·ness

or·tho·doxy
or·thog·o·nal
or·thog·ra·phy
or·tho·graph·ic
or·tho·pe·dics
or·tho·pe·dic
or·tho·pe·dist
os·cil·late
os·cil·lat·ed
os·cil·lat·ing
os·cil·la·tion
os·cil·la·tor
os·cil·la·to·ry
os·cil·lo·scope
os·cu·late
os·cu·la·tion
os·mo·sis
os·mot·ic
os·prey
os·si·fy
os·si·fied
os·si·fy·ing
os·si·fi·ca·tion
os·ten·sive
os·ten·si·ble
os·ten·si·bly
os·ten·sive·ly
os·ten·ta·tion
os·ten·ta·tious
os·te·op·a·thy
os·te·o·path
os·te·o·path·ic
os·tra·cize
os·tra·cized
os·tra·ciz·ing
os·tra·cism
os·trich
oth·er
oth·er·ness
oth·er·wise
oti·ose
ot·ter
ot·to·man
ought
ounce
our·self
our·selves
oust·er
out·bid
out·bid·ding
out·board
out·bound
out·brave
out·break
out·build·ing
out·burst
out·cast
out·come
out·cry
out·cries
out·dat·ed
out·dis·tance
out·do
out·door
out·er
out·er·most
out·er space
out·face
out·field
out·flank
out·grow
out·growth
out·land·ish
out·last
out·law
out·let
out·ly·ing
out·mod·ed

out·num·ber
out-of-date
out·post
out·rage
out·ra·geous
out·range
out·rank
out·right
out·sid·er
out·skirts
out·spo·ken
out·stand·ing
out·strip
out·ward
out·wear
out·weigh
ova
oval
oval·ness
ova·ry
ova·ries
ovar·i·an
ovate
ova·tion
ov·en
over
over·act
over·age
over·bear·ing
over·board
over·charge
over·charged
over·charg·ing
over·come
over·com·pen·sa·tion
over·con·fi·dence
over·dose
over·drawn
over·em·pha·sis
over·es·ti·mate
over·flow·ing
over·gen·er·ous
over·growth
over·hand
over·hang·ing
over·haul·ing
over·in·dul·gence
over·joyed
over·much
over·night
over·pass
over·pow·er
over·rat·ed
over·reach
over·ride
over·rule
over·sexed
over·shad·ow
over·shoot
over·sight
over·sim·pli·fy
over·state·ment
over·stepped
overt
overt·ly
over·take
over-the-coun·ter
over·throw
over·time
over·ture
over·weight
over·whelm
over·worked
ovip·a·rous
ovoid
ovu·late
ovu·la·tion
ovum

ova
owe
owed
ow·ing
owl·ish
own·er
ox·en
ox·ford
ox·i·da·tion
ox·ide
ox·i·dize
ox·i·dized
ox·i·diz·ing
ox·y·acet·y·lene
ox·y·gen
ox·y·gen·ate
ox·y·gen·at·ed
ox·y·gen·at·ing
ox·y·gen·a·tion
oys·ter
ozone

P

pab·u·lum
pace
paced
pac·ing
pac·er
pace·mak·er
pachy·derm
pa·cif·ic
pa·cif·i·ca·tion
pa·cif·i·ca·tor
pa·cif·i·ca·to·ry
pac·i·fi·er
pac·i·fism
pac·i·fist
pac·i·fy
pac·i·fied
pac·i·fy·ing
pack·age
pack·ag·er
pack·er
pack·et
pack·ing
pack·sad·dle
pad
pad·ded
pad·ding
pad·dle
pad·dled
pad·dling
pad·dock
pad·dy
pad·lock
pa·dre
pae·an
pa·gan
pa·gan·ism
page
paged
pag·ing
pag·eant
pag·eant·ry
pag·i·nate
pag·i·na·tion
pa·go·da
pail·ful
pain
pain·ful·ly
pain·less
pains·tak·ing
paint·er
paint·ing
pais·ley
pa·jam·as

pal·ace
pa·lan·quin
pal·at·a·ble
   pal·at·a·bil·i·ty
   pal·at·a·bly
pal·ate
pa·la·tial
   pa·la·tial·ly
pal·a·tine
pa·lav·er
pale
   paled
   pal·ing
   pale·ly
   pale·ness
pa·le·og·ra·phy
Pa·le·o·lith·ic
pa·le·on·tol·o·gy
   pa·le·on·tol·o·gist
Pa·le·o·zo·ic
pal·ette
pal·ing
pal·i·sade
   pal·i·sad·ed
   pal·i·sad·ing
pal·la·di·um
pall·bear·er
pal·let
pal·li·ate
   pal·li·at·ed
   pal·li·at·ing
   pal·li·a·tion
   pal·lia·tive
pal·lid
pal·lor
palm
pal·mate
pal·met·to
palm·is·try
   palm·ist
pal·o·mi·no
pal·pa·ble
   pal·pa·bil·i·ty
   pal·pa·bly
pal·pate
   pal·pat·ed
   pal·pat·ing
   pal·pa·tion
pal·pi·tate
   pal·pi·tat·ed
   pal·pi·tat·ing
   pal·pi·ta·tion
pal·sy
   pal·sied
pal·try
   pal·tri·ness
pam·pas
pam·per
pam·phlet
   pam·phle·teer
pan
   panned
   pan·ning
pan·a·ce·a
pa·nache
Pan-Amer·i·can
pan·cake
   pan·caked
   pan·cak·ing
pan·chro·mat·ic
pan·cre·as
   pan·cre·at·ic
pan·da
pan·dem·ic
pan·de·mo·ni·um
pan·der
   pan·der·er
pan·el

pan·eled
pan·el·ing
pan·el·ist
pang
pan·han·dler
pan·ic
   pan·icked
   pan·ick·ing
pan·nier
pan·o·ply
pan·o·rama
   pan·o·ram·ic
   pan·o·ram·i·cal·ly
pan·sy
   pan·sies
pan·ta·loon
pan·the·ism
   pan·the·ist
   pan·the·is·tic
pan·the·on
pan·ther
pan·tie
pan·ty
pan·to·mime
   pan·to·mimed
   pan·to·mim·ing
   pan·to·mim·ic
   pan·to·mim·ist
pan·try
   pan·tries
pant·y·hose
pa·pa
pa·pa·cy
pa·pal
pa·pau
pa·pa·ya
pa·per
   pa·per·er
   pa·pery
pa·per·back
pa·per·weight
pa·per·work
pa·pier·ma·che
pa·pil·la
pa·poose
pap·ri·ka
pa·py·rus
par·a·ble
par·ab·o·la
par·a·chute
   par·a·chut·ed
   par·a·chut·ing
   par·a·chut·ist
pa·rade
   pa·rad·ed
   pa·rad·ing
par·a·digm
par·a·dise
   par·a·di·si·a·cal
par·a·dox
   par·a·dox·i·cal
par·a·dox
   par·a·dox·i·cal
par·af·fin
par·a·gon
par·a·graph
Par·a·guay
par·a·keet
par·al·lax
   par·al·lac·tic
par·al·lel
   par·al·leled
   par·a·lel·ing
par·al·lel·o·gram
pa·ral·y·sis
   par·a·lyt·ic
par·a·lyze
   par·a·lyzed

par·a·lyz·ing
   par·a·ly·za·tion
par·a·med·ic
pa·ram·e·ter
par·a·mount
   par·a·mount·cy
par·a·mour
par·a·noia
   para·noi·ac
   para·noid
par·a·pet
par·a·pher·nal·ia
par·a·phrase
   par·a·phrased
   par·a·phras·ing
par·a·ple·gia
   par·a·ple·gic
par·a·psy·chol·o·gy
par·a·site
   par·a·sit·ic
   par·a·sit·i·cal·ly
   par·a·sit·ism
par·a·sol
par·a·troop·er
par·boil
par·cel
   par·celed
   par·cel·ling
parch·ment
par·don
   par·don·a·ble
   par·don·a·bly
pare
   pared
   par·ing
pare·gor·ic
parent
   pa·ren·tal
   par·ent·age
pa·ren·the·sis
   pa·ren·the·ses
   par·en·thet·ic
   par·en·thet·i·cal
pa·re·sis
par·fait
pa·ri·ah
par·i·mu·tu·el
par·ish
   pa·rish·ion·er
par·i·ty
par·ka
par·lance
par·lay
   par·layed
   par·lay·ing
par·ley
   par·leyed
   par·ley·ing
par·lia·ment
   par·lia·men·tar·i·an
   par·lia·men·ta·ry
par·lor
pa·ro·chi·al
par·o·dy
   par·o·died
   par·o·dy·ing
   par·o·dist
pa·role
   pa·roled
   pa·rol·ing
   pa·rol·ee
par·ox·ysm
   par·ox·ys·mal
par·quet
   par·queted
   par·quet·ing
   par·quet·ry
par·ra·keet

par·ri·cide
par·ry
   par·ried
   par·ry·ing
parse
par·si·mo·ny
   par·si·mo·ni·ous
   par·si·mo·ni·ous·ness
par·sley
pars·nip
par·son
   par·son·age
par·take
   par·took
   par·tak·en
   par·tak·ing
   par·tak·er
part·ed
par·the·no·gen·e·sis
par·tial
   par·tial·ly
   par·ti·al·i·ty
par·tic·i·pate
   par·tic·i·pat·ed
   par·tic·i·pat·ing
   par·tic·i·pant
   par·tic·i·pa·tion
   par·tic·i·pa·tive
   par·tic·i·pa·tor
par·ti·ci·ple
   par·ti·cip·i·al
par·ti·cle
par·ti·col·ored
par·tic·u·lar
   par·tic·u·lar·i·ty
   par·tic·u·lar·ize
   par·tic·u·late
part·ing
par·ti·san
   par·ti·san·ship
par·tite
   par·ti·tion
   par·ti·tive
part·ly
part·ner
   part·ner·ship
par·tridge
par·tu·ri·ent
par·tu·ri·tion
par·ty
   par·ties
par·ve·nu
pas·chal
pa·sha
pass·a·ble
   pass·a·bly
pass·sage
   pas·sage·way
pas·se
pas·sen·ger
pass·er·by
pass·ing
pas·sion
   pas·sion·less
pas·sion·ate
   pas·sion·ate·ly
   pas·sion·ate·ness
pas·sive
   pas·siv·i·ty
Pass·over
pass·word
pas·ta
paste
   pas·ted
   pas·ting
paste·board
pas·tel
pas·teur·ize

pas·teur·ized
pas·teur·iz·ing
pas·teur·i·za·tion
pas·tille
pas·time
pas·tor
pas·tor·ate
pas·to·ral
pas·tra·mi
pas·try
   pas·tries
pas·ture
   pas·tured
   pas·tur·ing
   pas·tur·age
pasty
   past·i·ness
pat
   pat·ted
   pat·ting
patchy
   patch·i·est
pâ·té
pat·ent
   pa·ten·cy
   pat·ent·ly
   pat·ent·ee
pat·er·nal
   pat·ter·nal·ly
   pa·ter·nal·ism
   pa·ter·nal·is·tic
   pa·ter·ni·ty
pa·ter·noster
pa·thet·ic
   pa·thet·i·cal·ly
patho·gen·ic
pa·thol·o·gy
   path·o·log·ic
   path·o·log·i·cal
   pa·thol·o·gist
pa·thos
pa·tient
   pa·tience
   pa·tient·ly
pat·i·na
pa·tio
pat·ois
pa·tri·arch
   pa·tri·archy
   pa·tri·ar·chal
pa·tri·cian
pat·ri·cide
pat·ri·mo·ny
pa·tri·ot
   pa·tri·ot·ic
   pa·tri·ot·i·cal·ly
   pa·tri·ot·ism
pa·trol
   pa·trolled
   pa·trol·ling
   pa·trol·ler
   pa·trol·man
pa·tron
   pa·tron·ess
   pa·tron·age
   pa·tron·ize
   pa·tron·ized
   pa·tron·iz·ing
pat·ro·nym·ic
pat·sy
   pat·sies
pat·ter
pat·tern
   pat·terned
pat·ty
   pat·ties
pau·ci·ty
paunch

paunch·i·ness
paunchy
pau·per
  pau·per·ism
  pau·per·ize
pause
  paused
  paus·ing
pave
  paved
  pav·ing
pave·ment
pa·vil·ion
Pav·lov
pawn
  pawn·bro·ker
pay
  paid
  pay·ing
  pay·ee
  pay·ment
  pay·a·ble
peace
  peace·a·ble
  peace·a·bly
  peace·ful
  peace·ful·ly
peach
pea·cock
peak·ed
peal
pea·nut
pearl
  pearly
peas·ant
  peas·ant·ry
peaty
peb·ble
  peb·bled
  peb·bling
  peb·bly
pe·can
pec·ca·dil·lo
pec·tin
pec·to·ral
pec·u·late
  pec·u·la·tion
pe·cu·liar
  pe·cu·liar·ly
  pe·cu·li·ar·i·ty
  pe·cu·li·ar·i·ties
pe·cu·ni·ary
ped·a·gogue
  ped·a·gog·ic
  ped·a·gog·i·cal
  ped·a·go·gy
ped·al
  ped·aled
  ped·al·ing
ped·ant
  pe·dan·tic
  pe·dan·ti·cal·ly
  ped·ant·ry
ped·dle
  ped·dler
ped·es·tal
pe·des·tri·an
pe·di·at·rics
  pe·di·at·ric
  pe·di·a·tri·cian
  pe·di·a·trist
ped·i·cure
  ped·i·cur·ist
ped·i·gree
  ped·i·greed
ped·i·ment
pe·dol·o·gy
pe·dom·e·ter

peel·ing
peer
peer·age
  peer·ess
peer·less
peeve
  peeved
  peev·ing
  peev·ish
peg
  pegged
  peg·ging
pei·gnoir
pe·jo·ra·tive
Pe·king·ese
pe·koe
pel·age
pe·lag·ic
pel·i·can
pel·la·gra
pel·let
pell-mell
pel·vis
  pel·vic
pem·mi·can
pen
  penned
  pen·ning
pe·nal
pe·nal·ize
  pe·nal·ized
  pe·nal·iz·ing
  pe·nal·i·za·tion
pen·al·ty
  pen·al·ties
pen·ance
pen·chant
pen·cil
  pen·ciled
  pen·cil·ing
pend·ant
pend·ent
  pend·en·cy
  pend·ent·ly
pend·ing
pen·du·lous
pen·e·trate
  pen·e·trat·ed
  pen·e·trat·ing
  pen·e·tra·tive
  pen·e·tra·ble
  pen·e·tra·bil·i·ty
  pen·e·tra·ble·ness
  pen·e·tra·bly
  pen·e·tra·tion
pen·guin
pen·i·cil·lin
pen·in·su·la
  pen·in·su·lar
pe·nis
pen·i·tent
  pen·i·tence
  pen·i·ten·tial
  pen·i·tent·ly
pen·i·ten·tia·ry
  pen·i·ten·tia·ries
pen·knife
pen·man·ship
pen·nant
Penn·syl·va·nia
pen·ny
  pen·nies
  pen·ni·less
  pen·ny an·te
  pen·ny pinch·er
pe·nol·o·gy
  pe·no·log·i·cal
  pen·nol·o·gist

pen·sion
  pen·sion·a·ble
  pen·sion·er
pen·sive
  pen·sive·ness
pen·ta·cle
pen·ta·gon
  pen·tag·o·nal
pen·tam·e·ter
pen·tath·lon
Pen·te·cost
  Pen·te·cos·tal
pent·house
pen·tom·ic
pe·nult
pe·num·bra
pe·nu·ri·ous
pen·u·ry
pe·on
  pe·on·age
pe·o·ny
peo·ple
  peo·pled
  peo·pling
pep
  pepped
  pep·ping
pep·lum
pep·per
pep·per·corn
pep·per·mint
pep·pery
  pep·per·i·ness
pep·py
  pep·pi·er
  pep·pi·ness
pep·sin
pep·tic
per·am·bu·late
  per·am·bu·lat·ed
  per·am·bu·lat·ing
  per·am·bu·la·tion
  per·am·bu·la·to·ry
per an·num
per·cale
per cap·i·ta
per·ceive
  per·ceived
  per·ceiv·ing
  per·ceiv·a·ble
  per·ceiv·a·bly
per·cent
  per·cent·age
  per·cen·tile
per·cept
  per·cep·ti·ble
  per·cep·ti·bil·i·ty
  per·cep·ti·bly
  per·cep·tion
  per·cep·tive
  per·cep·tu·al
per·chance
Per·che·ron
per·cip·i·ent
  per·cip·i·ence
per·co·late
  per·co·lat·ed
  per·co·lat·ing
  per·co·la·tion
  per·co·la·tor
per·cus·sion
  per·cus·sive
per di·em
per·di·tion
per·du·ra·ble
per·e·grine
  per·e·gri·na·tion
per·emp·to·ry

per·emp·to·ri·ly
per·emp·to·ri·ness
per·en·ni·al
  per·en·ni·al·ly
per·fect
  per·fect·er
  per·fect·ness
  per·fect·i·ble
  per·fect·i·bil·i·ty
  per·fec·tive
  per·fec·tion
  per·fect·ly
per·fi·dy
  per·fid·i·ous
per·fo·rate
  per·fo·rat·ed
  per·fo·rat·ing
  per·fo·ra·tor
  per·fo·ra·tion
per·force
per·form
  per·form·a·ble
  per·form·er
  per·for·mance
per·fume
  per·fumed
  per·fum·ing
  per·fum·ery
per·func·to·ry
  per·func·to·ri·ly
  per·func·to·ri·ness
per·haps
per·go·la
per·i·gee
per·il
  per·iled
  per·il·ing
  per·il·ous
  per·il·ous·ly
pe·rim·e·ter
  per·i·met·ric
  per·i·met·ri·cal
pe·ri·od
  pe·ri·od·ic
  pe·ri·o·dic·i·ty
  pe·ri·od·i·cal
  pe·ri·od·i·cal·ly
per·i·pa·tet·ic
pe·riph·ery
  pe·riph·er·al
  pe·riph·er·al·ly
per·i·phrase
per·i·scope
  per·i·scopic
per·ish
  per·ish·a·ble
  per·ish·a·bil·i·ty
  per·ish·a·ble·ness
  per·ish·a·bly
per·i·stal·sis
  per·i·stal·tic
per·i·style
per·i·to·ni·tis
per·i·win·kle
per·jure
  per·jured
  per·jur·ing
  per·jur·er
  per·ju·ri·ous
  per·ju·ry
perky
  perk·i·est
perma·frost
per·ma·nent
  per·ma·nen·cy
per·me·ate
  per·me·at·ed
  per·me·at·ing

per·me·a·ble
per·me·a·bil·i·ty
per·me·a·bly
per·me·a·tion
per·me·a·tive
per·mis·si·ble
per·mis·si·bil·i·ty
per·mis·si·bly
per·mis·sion
per·mis·sive
per·mit
  per·mit·ted
  per·mit·ting
per·mute
  per·mu·ta·tion
per·ni·cious
per·o·rate
  per·o·ra·tion
per·ox·ide
per·pen·dic·u·lar
per·pe·trate
  per·pe·trat·ed
  per·pe·trat·ing
  per·pe·tra·tion
  per·pe·tra·tor
per·pet·u·al
  per·pet·u·al·ly
per·pet·u·ate
  per·pet·u·at·ed
  per·pet·u·at·ing
  per·pet·u·a·tor
per·pe·tu·i·ty
per·plex
  per·plexed
  per·plex·ing
  per·plex·i·ty
per·qui·site
per se
per·se·cute
  per·se·cut·ed
  per·se·cut·ing
  per·se·cu·tive
  per·se·cu·tor
  per·se·cu·tion
per·se·vere
  per·se·vered
  per·se·ver·ing
  per·se·ver·ance
per·si·flage
per·sim·mon
per·sist
  per·sist·ence
  per·sis·ten·cy
  per·sist·ent
per·snick·ety
per·son
  per·son·a·ble
  per·son·age
  per·son·al
  per·son·al·i·ty
  per·son·al·ize
    per·son·al·ized
    per·son·al·iz·ing
  per·son·al·ly
  per·so·na non gra·ta
  per·son·ate
    per·son·at·ed
    per·son·at·ing
    per·son·a·tion
    per·son·a·tor
  per·son·i·fy
    per·son·i·fied
    per·son·i·fy·ing
    per·son·i·fi·ca·tion
  per·son·nel
per·spec·tive
per·spi·ca·cious
  per·spi·cac·i·ty

per·spi·cu·i·ty
  per·spic·u·ous
per·spire
  per·spired
  per·spir·ing
  per·spi·ra·tion
per·suade
  per·suad·ed
  per·suad·ing
  per·suad·a·ble
  per·sua·sion
  per·sua·sive
pert
  pert·ly
  pert·ness
per·tain
per·ti·na·cious
  per·ti·nac·i·ty
per·ti·nent
  per·ti·nence
  per·ti·nent·ly
per·turb
  per·turb·a·ble
  per·tur·ba·tion
pe·ruse
  pe·rused
  pe·rus·ing
  pe·rus·al
per·vade
  per·vad·ed
  per·vad·ing
  per·vad·er
  per·va·sion
  per·va·sive
per·verse
  per·verse·ness
  per·ver·si·ty
  per·ver·sion
per·vert
  per·vert·ed
per·vi·ous
pes·ky
  pesk·i·ness
pes·si·mism
  pes·si·mist
  pes·si·mis·tic
  pes·si·mis·ti·cal·ly
pes·ter
pest·i·cide
pes·tif·er·ous
pes·ti·lent
  pes·ti·lence
  pes·ti·len·tial
pes·tle
pet
  pet·ted
  pet·ting
pet·al
  pet·aled
pet·i·ole
pe·tite
  pe·tite·ness
pet·it four
pe·ti·tion
  pe·ti·tion·ary
  pe·ti·tion·er
pet·rel
pet·ri·fy
  pet·ri·fied
  pet·ri·fy·ing
  pet·ri·fac·tion
pe·tro·chem·is·try
pe·trog·ra·phy
pet·rol
pe·tro·le·um
pe·trol·o·gy
pet·ti·coat
pet·ti·fog

pet·ti·fogged
pet·ti·fog·ging
pet·tish
  pet·tish·ness
pet·ty
  pet·ti·ly
  pet·ti·ness
pet·u·lant
  pet·u·lance
  pet·u·lan·cy
pe·tu·nia
pew·ter
pe·yo·te
pha·e·ton
pha·lanx
phal·lus
  phal·lic
phan·tasm
  phan·tas·mal
  phan·tas·ma·go·ria
  phan·tas·ma·gor·ic
phan·ta·sy
  phan·ta·sies
phan·tom
phar·aoh
phar·ma·ceu·ti·cal
  phar·ma·ceu·tic
  phar·ma·ceu·tics
phar·ma·cist
phar·ma·col·o·gy
  phar·ma·col·o·gist
phar·ma·co·poe·ia
  phar·ma·co·poe·ial
phar·ma·cy
phar·ynx
phase
  phased
  phas·ing
pheas·ant
phe·no·bar·bi·tal
phe·nom·e·non
  phe·nom·e·na
  phe·nom·e·nal
phi·al
phi·lan·der
  phi·lan·der·er
phi·lan·thro·py
  phi·lan·thro·pies
  phil·an·throp·ic
  phil·an·throp·i·cal
  phi·lan·thro·pist
phi·lat·e·ly
  phil·a·tel·ic
  phi·lat·e·list
phil·har·mon·ic
Phil·ip·pine
phi·lo·den·dron
phi·lol·o·gy
  phi·lol·o·gist
  phil·o·lo·gian
  phil·o·log·i·cal
phi·los·o·phy
  phi·los·o·pher
  phil·o·soph·i·cal
  phil·o·soph·ic
  phi·los·o·phize
phil·ter
phle·bi·tis
phle·bot·o·my
phlegm
phleg·mat·ic
  phleg·mat·i·cal
phlox
pho·bia
  pho·bic
phoe·be
phoe·nix
phone

phoned
phon·ing
pho·neme
  pho·ne·mic
pho·net·ics
  pho·net·ic
  pho·net·i·cal·ly
phon·ic
  phon·ics
pho·no·graph
pho·nol·o·gy
  pho·no·log·ic
pho·ny
  pho·ni·ness
phos·phate
phos·pho·resce
  phos·pho·res·cence
  phos·pho·resced
  phos·pho·resc·ing
  phos·pho·res·cent
phos·pho·rus
pho·to·copy
  pho·to·cop·ies
  pho·to·cop·ied
  pho·to·cop·y·ing
pho·to·en·grave
  pho·to·en·grav·ing
pho·to·gen·ic
pho·to·graph
  pho·tog·ra·pher
  pho·tog·ra·phy
  pho·to·graph·ic
pho·to·gra·vure
pho·to·stat
pho·to·syn·the·sis
phrase
  phrased
  phras·ing
phra·se·ol·o·gy
phre·net·ic
phre·nol·o·gy
  phre·nol·o·gist
phy·lac·tery
phy·log·e·ny
phy·lum
phys·ic
  phys·ick·ing
phys·i·cal
  phys·i·cal·ly
phy·si·cian
phys·ics
  phys·i·cist
phys·i·og·no·my
  phys·i·og·nom·i·cal
  phys·i·og·no·mist
phys·i·og·ra·phy
  phys·i·o·graph·ic
phys·i·ol·o·gy
  phys·i·o·log·i·cal
  phys·i·ol·o·gist
phys·i·o·ther·a·py
phy·sique
pi·a·nis·si·mo
pi·ano
pi·an·o·for·te
pi·az·za
pi·ca
pic·a·dor
pic·a·resque
pic·a·yune
  pic·a·yun·ish
pic·ca·lil·li
pic·co·lo
picked
pick·er·el
pick·et
  pick·et·er
pick·ing

pick·le
  pick·led
  pick·ling
pick·pock·et
picky
  pick·i·est
pic·nic
  pic·nick·ing
  pic·nick·er
pic·to·ri·al
pic·ture
  pic·tured
  pic·tur·ing
pic·tur·esque
pid·dle
  pid·dled
  pid·dling
pidg·in
piece·meal
piece·work
pierce
  pierced
  pierc·ing
pi·e·ty
pi·geon·hole
pi·geon-toed
pig·gish
pig·gy·back
pig·head·ed
pig·ment
  pig·men·ta·tion
pik·er
pi·las·tcr
pile
  piled
  pil·ing
pil·fer
  pil·fer·age
  pil·fer·er
pil·grim
  pil·grim·age
pil·lage
  pil·laged
  pil·lag·ing
  pil·lag·er
pil·lar
pil·lion
pil·lo·ry
  pil·lo·ried
pil·low
pi·lot
  pi·lot·age
  pi·lot·less
pi·men·to
pim·ple
  pim·plcd
  pim·ply
pin
  pinned
  pin·ning
pin·a·fore
pince-nez
pin·cers
pinch
  pinch·er
pin·cush·ion
pine
  piney
  pined
  pin·ing
pine·ap·ple
pin·feath·er
ping·pong
pin·ion
pin·na·cle
pin·nate
pi·noch·le
pin·to

pin·wheel
pi·o·neer
pi·ous
  pi·ous·ness
pipe·line
pip·er
pi·pette
pip·ing
pip-squeak
pi·quant
  pi·quan·cy
  pi·quant·ness
pique
  piqued
  pi·quing
pi·ra·nha
pi·rate
  pi·rat·ed
  pi·rat·ing
  pi·rat·i·cal
  pi·ra·cy
pi·rogue
pir·ou·ette
  pir·ou·et·ted
  pir·ou·et·ting
pis·ca·to·ri·al
pis·ta·chio
pis·til
  pis·til·late
pis·tol
  pis·toled
  pis·tol·ing
pis·ton
pit
  pit·ted
  pit·ting
pitch·black
pitch·blende
pitch·er
pitch·fork
pitchy
pith
  pithy
  pith·i·ness
pit·man
pi·ton
pit·tance
pi·tu·i·tar·y
pity
  pit·ied
  pit·y·ing
  pit·e·ous
  pit·i·a·ble
  pit·i·ful
  pit·i·less
piv·ot
  piv·ot·al·ly
pixy
  pix·ie
  pix·ie·ish
piz·za
  piz·ze·ri·a
piz·zi·ca·to
plac·a·ble
  plac·a·bil·i·ty
  plac·a·bly
plac·ard
pla·cate
  pla·cat·ed
  pla·cat·ing
  pla·ca·tion
  pla·ca·tive
place
  plac·ed
  plac·ing
  pla·ce·bo
place·ment
pla·cen·ta

pla·cen·tal
plac·er
plac·id
  pla·cid·i·ty
  plac·id·ness
  plac·id·ly
plack·et
pla·gia·rize
  pla·gia·rized
  pla·gia·riz·ing
  pla·gia·riz·er
  pla·gia·rism
  pla·gia·rist
  pla·gia·ris·tic
  pla·gia·ry
plague
  plagued
  pla·guing
plaid
plain
  plain·ness
plain-clothes man
plain-spo·ken
plain·tiff
plain·tive
  plain·tive·ly
plait
  plait·ing
plan
  planned
  plan·ning
  plan·less
plane
  planed
  plan·ing
plan·et
plan·e·tar·i·um
plan·e·tary
plan·e·toid
plan·ish
plank·ing
plank·ton
plant
plant·a·ble
  plant·er
plan·tain
plan·ta·tion
plaque
plas·ma
plas·ter
  plas·tered
  plas·ter·ing
  plas·ter·er
  plas·ter·work
plas·ter·board
plas·tic
  plas·ti·cal·ly
  plas·tic·i·ty
plat
  plat·ted
  plat·ting
plate
  plat·ed
  plat·ing
pla·teau
plate·ful
plate·let
plat·en
plat·form
plat·i·num
plat·i·tude
  plat·i·tu·di·nal
  plat·i·tu·di·nous
  plat·i·tu·di·nize
pla·ton·ic
  pla·ton·i·cal·ly
pla·toon
plat·ter

plat·y·pus
plau·dit
plau·si·ble
  plau·si·bil·i·ty
  plau·si·ble·ness
  plau·si·bly
play·act·ing
play·back
play·boy
play·ful
  play·ful·ly
play·ground
play·house
play·mate
play·wright
pla·za
plea
plead
  plead·ed
  plead·ing
  plead·a·ble
pleas·ant
  pleas·ant·ly
  pleas·ant·ry
please
  pleased
  pleas·ing
  pleas·ing·ly
pleas·ure
  pleas·ur·a·ble
  pleas·ur·a·bly
pleat
  pleat·ed
plebe
ple·be·ian
pleb·i·scite
plec·trum
pledge
  pledged
  pledg·ing
  pledg·ee
Pleis·to·cene
ple·na·ry
ple·nip·o·tent
  plen·i·po·ten·ti·ar·y
plen·ty
  plen·i·tude
  plen·te·ous
  plen·ti·ful
  plen·ti·ful·ly
pleth·o·ra
pleu·ri·sy
plex·us
pli·a·ble
  pli·a·bil·i·ty
  pli·a·ble·ness
  pli·a·bly
pli·ant
  pli·an·cy
  pli·ant·ness
  pli·ant·ly
pli·ers
plight
plod
  plod·ded
  plod·ding
  plod·der
plop
  plopped
  plop·ping
plot
  plot·ted
  plot·ting
  plot·ter
plov·er
plow
  plow·a·ble
  plow·er

plow·share
pluck
plucky
  pluck·i·ly
  pluck·i·ness
plug
  plugged
  plug·ging
plum·age
plumb·er
plumb·ing
plume
  plumed
  plum·ing
plum·met
plump
  plump·ish
  plump·ly
  plump·ness
plun·der
  plun·der·er
plunge
  plunged
  plung·ing
plung·er
plu·ral
  plu·ral·ly
  plu·ral·ize
  plu·ral·iza·tion
plu·ral·ism
  plu·ral·ist
  plu·ral·is·tic
plu·ral·i·ty
  plu·ral·i·ties
plush
  plush·i·ness
  plushy
  plush·i·est
plu·toc·ra·cy
  plu·to·crat
  plu·to·crat·ic
plu·to·ni·um
plu·vi·al
ply
  plied
  ply·ing
ply·wood
pneu·mat·ic
  pneu·mat·i·cal·ly
pneu·mo·nia
poach
  poach·er
pock·et·book
pock·et·ful
pock·et·knife
pock·mark
pod
  pod·ded
  pod·ding
  pod·like
po·di·a·try
  po·di·a·trist
po·di·um
po·em
  po·et·ic
  po·et·i·cal
  po·et·i·cal·ly
po·e·sy
  po·e·sies
po·et
  po·et·ess
  po·et·ize
  po·et·lau·re·ate
  po·et·ry
po·grom
poign·ant
  poign·an·cy
  poig·nant·ly

poin·ci·ana
poin·set·tia
point
  point·ed
  point·ed·ly
  point·er
  point·less
poin·til·lism
poise
  poised
  pois·ing
poi·son
  poi·son·er
  poi·son·ing
  poi·son·ous
poke
  poked
  pok·ing
pok·er
poky
po·lar
Po·lar·is
po·lar·i·ty
  po·lar·i·za·tion
  po·lar·ize
  po·lar·ized
  po·lar·iz·ing
pole
  poled
  pol·ing
  pole·less
po·lem·ic
  po·lem·i·cal
  po·lem·i·cist
po·lice
  po·liced
  po·lic·ing
pol·i·cy
  pol·i·cies
pol·i·cy·hold·er
po·lio
pol·i·o·my·e·li·tis
pol·ish
po·lite
  po·lite·ly
  po·lite·ness
pol·i·tic
pol·i·tics
  po·lit·i·cal
  po·lit·i·cal·ly
  pol·i·ti·cian
  po·lit·i·cize
  po·lit·i·cized
  po·lit·i·ciz·ing
pol·i·ty
pol·ka
  pol·kaed
  pol·ka·ing
poll
  poll·ee
  poll·er
  poll·ster
pol·len
pol·li·nate
  pol·li·nat·ed
  pol·li·nat·ing
  pol·li·na·tion
  pol·li·na·tor
pol·li·wog
pol·lute
  pol·lut·ed
  pol·lut·ing
  pol·lu·tant
  pol·lu·ter
  pol·lu·tion
po·lo
  po·lo·ist
pol·o·naise

pol·ter·geist
pol·y·an·dry
  pol·y·an·drous
pol·y·chro·mat·ic
pol·y·chrome
  pol·y·chro·mat·ic
pol·y·es·ter
pol·y·eth·yl·ene
po·lyg·a·my
  po·lyg·a·mous
  po·lyg·a·mist
pol·y·glot
pol·y·gon
  po·lyg·o·nal
pol·y·graph
po·lyg·y·ny
  po·lyg·y·nous
pol·y·he·dron
pol·y·mer
  pol·y·mer·ize
  po·lym·er·i·za·tion
pol·y·mor·phism
Poly·ne·sia
pol·y·no·mi·al
pol·yp
pol·y·phon·ic
  po·lyph·o·ny
pol·y·sty·rene
pol·y·syl·lab·ic
  pol·y·syl·la·ble
pol·y·tech·nic
pol·y·the·ism
  pol·y·the·ist
  pol·y·the·is·tic
pol·y·un·sat·u·rat·ed
po·made
pome·gran·ate
pom·mel
  pom·meled
  pom·mel·ing
pom·pa·dour
pom·pa·no
pom·pon
pomp·ous
  pom·pos·i·ty
pon·cho
pon·der
  pon·der·a·ble
  pon·der·ous
pon·gee
pon·iard
pon·tiff
pon·tif·i·cal
  pon·tif·i·cal·ly
pon·tif·i·cate
  pon·tif·i·cat·ed
  pon·tif·i·cat·ing
pon·toon
po·ny
  po·nies
poo·dle
poor
  poor·ish
  poor·ly
pop·ery
  pop·ish
pop·eyed
pop·in·jay
pop·lar
pop·lin
pop·per
pop·py
  pop·pies
  pop·py·cock
pop·u·lace
pop·u·lar
  pop·u·lar·ly
  pop·u·lar·i·ty

pop·u·lar·ize
  pop·u·lar·ized
  pop·u·lar·iz·ing
  pop·u·lar·i·za·tion
pop·u·late
  pop·u·lat·ed
  pop·u·lat·ing
  pop·u·la·tion
  pop·u·lous
por·ce·lain
por·cine
por·cu·pine
pore
  pored
  por·ing
pork·er
por·nog·ra·phy
  por·nog·ra·pher
  por·no·graph·ic
  por·no·graph·i·cal·ly
po·rous
  po·ros·i·ty
  po·rous·ness
por·poise
por·ridge
port·a·ble
  port·a·bil·i·ty
  port·a·bly
por·tage
  por·taged
  por·tag·ing
por·tal
por·tend
por·tent
  por·ten·tous
por·ter
port·fo·lio
port·hole
por·ti·co
por·tion
port·ly
  port·li·er
  port·li·ness
por·trait
  por·trait·ist
por·trai·ture
por·tray
  por·tray·er
  por·tray·al
Por·tu·gal
Por·tu·guese
pose
  posed
  pos·ing
pos·er
pos·seur
pos·it
po·si·tion
pos·i·tive
  pos·i·tive·ly
  pos·i·tive·ness
pos·i·tiv·ism
pos·i·tron
pos·se
pos·sess
  pos·ses·sor
pos·sessed
pos·ses·sion
pos·ses·sive
pos·si·bil·i·ty
pos·si·ble
pos·si·bly
pos·sum
post·age
post·date
  post·dat·ed
  post·dat·ing
post·er

pos·te·ri·or
  pos·te·ri·or·i·ty
pos·ter·i·ty
post·grad·u·ate
post·haste
post·hu·mous
pos·til·ion
post·lude
post·man
post·mark
post·mas·ter
  post·mis·tress
post me·rid·i·em
post mor·tem
post·na·sal
post·na·tal
post·paid
post·par·tum
post·pone
  post·poned
  post·pon·ing
  post·pon·a·ble
  post·pone·ment
post·script
pos·tu·lant
pos·tu·late
  pos·tu·lat·ed
  pos·tu·lat·ing
  pos·tu·la·tion
  pos·tu·la·tor
pos·ture
  pos·tured
  pos·tur·ing
post·war
po·sy
  po·sies
pot
  pot·ted
  pot·ting
po·ta·ble
pot·ash
po·tas·si·um
po·ta·to
  po·ta·toes
pot·bel·ly
  pot·bel·lied
po·tent
  po·ten·cy
  po·tent·ly
po·ten·tate
po·ten·tial
  po·ten·ti·al·i·ty
  po·ten·tial·ly
pot·hole
po·tion
pot·luck
pot·pour·ri
pot·tage
pot·ter
pot·tery
pouch
  pouched
  pouchy
poul·tice
poul·try
pounce
  pounced
  pounc·ing
pound·age
pound-fool·ish
pour
  pour·a·ble
pout
pov·er·ty
pov·er·ty-strick·en
pow·der
  pow·dery
pow·er

pow·er·ful
  pow·er·ful·ly
  pow·er·ful·ness
pow·er·less
pow·wow
prac·ti·ca·ble
  prac·ti·ca·bil·i·ty
  prac·ti·ca·ble·ness
  prac·ti·ca·bly
prac·ti·cal
  prac·ti·cal·i·ty
  prac·ti·cal·ly
prac·tice
prac·ticed
prac·ti·tion·er
prae·di·al
prae·to·ri·an
prag·mat·ic
  prag·mat·i·cal
  prag·mat·i·cal·ly
prag·ma·tism
  prag·ma·tist
  prag·ma·tis·tic
prai·rie
praise
  praised
  prais·ing
praise·wor·thy
pra·line
prance
  pranced
  pranc·ing
prank
  prank·ish
  prank·ster
prate
  prat·ed
  prat·ing
prat·fall
prat·tle
  prat·tled
  prat·tling
prawn
  prawn·er
prayer
  prayer·ful
preach
  preach·er
preach·ment
preachy
pre·ad·o·les·cence
  pre·ad·o·les·cent
pre·am·ble
pre·ar·range
  pre·ar·ranged
  pre·ar·rang·ing
  pre·ar·range·ment
pre·as·signed
pre·can·cel
pre·car·i·ous
  pre·car·i·ous·ness
pre·cau·tion
  pre·cau·tion·ary
pre·cede
  pre·ced·ed
  pre·ced·ing
prec·e·dence
prec·e·dent
pre·cept
  pre·cep·tive
  pre·cep·tor
  pre·cep·to·ri·al
pre·ces·sion
pre·cinct
pre·cious
  pre·ci·os·i·ty
  pre·cious·ness
prec·i·pice

pre·cip·i·tous
pre·cip·i·tant
pre·cip·i·tate
  pre·cip·i·tat·ed
  pre·cip·i·tat·ing
  pre·cip·i·ta·tive
  pre·cip·i·ta·tor
  pre·cip·i·ta·tion
  pre·cip·i·tous
pre·cis
pre·cise
  pre·cise·ness
pre·ci·sion
  pre·ci·sion·ist
pre·clude
  pre·clud·ed
  pre·clud·ing
  pre·clu·sion
  pre·clu·sive
pre·co·cious
  pre·co·cious·ness
  pre·coc·i·ty
pre·cog·ni·tion
  pre·cog·ni·tive
pre·con·ceive
  pre·con·ceiv·ing
  pre·con·cep·tion
pre·con·di·tion
pre·cook
pre·cur·sor
  pre·cur·so·ry
pre·date
pred·a·tor
  pred·a·to·ry
pre·de·cease
pred·e·ces·sor
pre·des·ti·nate
  pre·des·ti·nat·ed
  pre·des·ti·nat·ing
  pre·des·ti·na·tion
pre·des·tine
  pre·des·tined
pre·de·ter·mine
  pre·de·ter·mined
  pre·de·ter·min·ing
  pre·de·ter·mi·na·tion
pred·i·ca·ble
  pred·i·ca·bil·i·ty
pre·dic·a·ment
pred·i·cate
  pred·i·ca·tion
  pred·i·ca·tive
pre·dict
  pre·dict·a·ble
  pre·dict·a·bly
  pre·dict·a·bil·i·ty
  pre·dic·tion
  pre·dic·tive
  pre·di·lec·tion
pre·dis·pose
  pre·dis·posed
  pre·dis·pos·ing
  pre·dis·po·si·tion
pre·dom·i·nant
  pre·dom·i·nance
  pre·dom·i·nan·cy
pre·dom·i·nate
  pre·dom·i·nat·ed
  pre·dom·i·nat·ing
  pre·dom·i·na·tion
pre·em·i·nent
  pre·em·i·nence
pre·empt
  pre·emp·tor
  pre·emp·tion
  pre·emp·tive
pre·ex·ist
  pre·ex·ist·ence

pre·ex·ist·ent
pre·fab·ri·cate
  pre·fab·ri·cat·ed
  pre·fab·ri·cat·ing
  pre·fab·ri·ca·tion
pref·ace
  pref·aced
  pref·ac·ing
  pref·a·to·ry
pre·fer
  pre·ferred
  pre·fer·ring
pref·er·a·ble
  pref·er·a·ble·ness
  pref·er·a·bil·i·ty
  pref·er·a·bly
pref·er·ence
pref·er·en·tial
pre·fer·ment
pre·fix
pre·flight
pre·form
preg·nant
  preg·nan·cy
  preg·na·bil·i·ty
pre·heat
pre·hen·sile
pre·his·tor·ic
pre·judge
  pre·judged
  pre·judg·ing
  pre·judg·ment
prej·u·dice
  prej·u·diced
  prej·u·dic·ing
  prej·u·di·cial
prel·ate
pre·lim·i·nary
  pre·lim·i·nar·ies
  pre·lim·i·nar·i·ly
prel·ude
  prel·ud·ing
pre·ma·ture
  pre·ma·ture·ness
  pre·ma·tu·ri·ty
pre·med·i·cal
pre·med·i·tate
  pre·med·i·tat·ed
  pre·med·i·tat·ing
  pre·med·i·ta·tive
  pre·med·i·ta·tion
pre·men·stru·al
pre·mier
pre·miere
prem·ise
  prem·ised
  prem·is·ing
pre·mi·um
pre·mo·ni·tion
  pre·mon·i·to·ry
  pre·mon·i·to·ri·ly
pre·na·tal
  pre·na·tal·ly
pre·oc·cu·py
  pre·oc·cu·pied
  pre·oc·cu·py·ing
  pre·oc·cu·pa·tion
pre·op·er·a·tive
pre·or·dain
pre·pare
  pre·pared
  pre·par·ing
  prep·a·ra·tion
  pre·par·a·to·ry
  pre·par·a·to·ri·ly
  pre·pared·ness
pre·pay
  pre·paid

pre·pay·ing
pre·pay·ment
pre·plan
pre·planned
pre·plan·ning
pre·pon·der·ant
pre·pon·der·ance
pre·pon·der·an·cy
pre·pon·der·ant·ly
pre·pon·der·ate
pre·pon·der·at·ed
pre·pon·der·at·ing
pre·pon·der·at·ing·ly
pre·pon·der·a·tion
prep·o·si·tion
pre·pos·sess
pre·pos·sess·ing
pre·pos·ses·sion
pre·pos·ter·ous
pre·puce
pre·re·cord
pre·req·ui·site
pre·rog·a·tive
pres·age
pres·aged
pres·ag·ing
Pres·by·te·ri·an
pres·by·tery
pre·school
pre·scind
pre·sci·ence
pre·sci·ent
pre·scribe
pre·scribed
pre·scrib·ing
pre·script
pre·scrip·tion
pre·scrip·tive
pre·sea·son
pres·ence
pre·sent
pre·sent·er
pres·ent
pre·sent·a·ble
pre·sent·a·bil·i·ty
pre·sent·a·ble·ness
pre·sent·a·bly
pres·en·ta·tion
pres·ent·ly
pre·serve
pre·served
pre·serv·ing
pre·serv·a·ble
pres·er·va·tion
pre·serv·a·tive
pre·side
pre·sid·ed
pre·sid·ing
pres·i·dent
pres·i·den·tial
pres·i·den·cy
pre·sid·i·um
pre·sig·ni·fy
press·ing
pres·sure
pres·sured
pres·sur·ing
pres·sur·ize
pres·sur·ized
pres·sur·iz·er
pres·sur·i·za·tion
press·work
pres·ti·dig·i·ta·tion
pres·it·dig·i·ta·tor
pres·tige
pres·tig·ious
pres·tis·si·mo
pres·to

pre·sum·a·ble
pre·sum·a·bly
pre·sume
pre·sumed
pre·sum·ing
pre·sump·tion
pre·sump·tive
pre·sump·tu·ous
pre·sup·pose
pre·sup·posed
pre·sup·pos·ing
pre·sup·po·si·tion
pre·tend
pre·tend·ed
pre·tend·er
pre·tense
pre·ten·sion
pre·ten·tious
pret·er·it
pret·er·i·tion
pre·ter·nat·u·ral
pre·test
pre·text
pret·ti·fy
preti·ti·fi·ca·tion
pret·ty
pret·ti·ly
pret·ti·ness
pret·zel
pre·vail
pre·vail·ing
prev·a·lent
prev·a·lence
pre·vent
pre·vent·a·ble
pre·vent·a·bil·i·ty
pre·ven·ta·tive
pre·ven·tion
pre·ven·tive
pre·view
pre·vi·ous
pre·vi·sion
pre·war
prey
prey·er
price·less
prick·le
prick·ly
prick·li·ness
pride
prid·ed
prid·ing
pride·ful·ly
prie-dieu
priest
priest·ess
priest·hood
priest·ly
priest·li·ness
prig
prig·gish
prim
primmed
prim·ming
prim·ness
pri·ma·cy
pri·ma don·na
pri·ma fa·cie
pri·mal
pri·ma·ri·ly
pri·ma·ry
pri·mar·ies
pri·mate
prime
primed
prim·ing
prime me·rid·i·an
prim·er

pri·me·val
prim·i·tive
pri·mo·gen·i·tor
pri·mo·gen·i·ture
pri·mor·di·al
prim·rose
prince·ly
prince·li·ness
prin·cess
prin·ci·pal
prin·ci·pal·ly
prin·ci·pal·i·ty
prin·ci·pal·i·ties
prin·ci·ple
prin·ci·pled
print·a·ble
print·ing
print·out
pri·or
pri·or·ess
pri·or·i·ty
pri·or·i·ties
pri·ory
prism
pris·mat·ic
pris·on
pris·on·er
pris·sy
pris·si·ness
pris·tine
pri·va·cy
pri·vate
pri·vate·ly
pri·va·tion
priv·et
priv·i·lege
priv·i·leged
priv·i·leg·ing
privy
priv·ies
prize
prized
priz·ing
prize·fight·er
prob·a·ble
prob·a·bly
prob·a·bil·i·ty
prob·a·bil·i·ties
pro·bate
pro·bat·ed
pro·bat·ing
pro·ba·tion
pro·ba·tion·al
pro·ba·tion·ary
pro·ba·tion·al·ly
pro·ba·tion·er
pro·ba·tive
pro·ba·to·ry
probe
probed
prob·ing
prob·lem
prob·lem·at·ic
pro·lem·at·i·cal
pro·bos·cis
pro·ce·dure
pro·ce·dur·al
pro·ce·dur·al·ly
pro·ceed
pro·ceed·ing
pro·ceeds
proc·ess
pro·ces·sion
pro·ces·sion·al
pro·claim
proc·la·ma·tion
pro·cliv·i·ty
pro·cliv·i·ties

pro·con·sul
pro·cras·ti·nate
pro·cras·ti·nat·ed
pro·cras·ti·nat·ing
pro·cras·ti·na·tion
pro·cras·ti·na·tor
pro·cre·ate
pro·cre·at·ed
pro·cre·at·ing
pro·cre·a·tion
pro·cre·a·tive
pro·cre·a·tor
pro·cre·ant
proc·tor
proc·to·ri·al
pro·cure
pro·cured
pro·cur·ing
pro·cur·a·ble
pro·cur·ance
pro·cure·ment
pro·cur·er
prod
prod·ded
prod·ding
prod·der
prod·i·gal
prod·i·gal·i·ty
prod·i·gal·ly
pro·di·gious
pro·di·gious·ness
prod·i·gy
pro·duce
pro·duced
pro·duc·ing
pro·duc·er
prod·uct
pro·duc·tion
pro·duc·tive
pro·duc·tiv·i·ty
pro·fane
pro·faned
pro·fan·ing
pro·fan·a·to·ry
pro·fane·ness
pro·fan·er
pro·fan·i·ty
pro·fess
pro·fessed
pro·fess·ed·ly
pro·fes·sion
pro·fes·sion·al
pro·fes·sion·al·ism
pro·fes·sion·al·ize
pro·fes·sion·al·ized
pro·fes·sion·al·iz·ing
pro·fes·sor
pro·fes·so·ri·al
pro·fes·so·ri·al·ly
pro·fes·sor·ship
prof·fer
pro·fi·cient
pro·fi·cien·cy
pro·file
pro·filed
pro·fil·ing
prof·it
prof·it·less
prof·it·a·ble
prof·it·a·bil·i·ty
prof·it·a·ble·ness
prof·it·a·bly
prof·it·eer
prof·li·gate
prof·li·ga·cy
pro·found
pro·fun·di·ty
pro·fuse

pro·fuse·ly
pro·fu·sion
pro·gen·i·tor
prog·e·ny
prog·no·sis
prog·nos·tic
prog·nos·ti·cate
prog·nos·ti·cat·ed
prog·nos·ti·cat·ing
prog·nos·ti·ca·tion
prog·nos·ti·ca·tive
prog·nos·ti·ca·tor
pro·gram
pro·grammed
pro·gram·ming
pro·gramed
pro·gram·ing
pro·gram·mer
pro·gram·er
prog·ress
pro·gres·sion
pro·gres·sive
pro·hib·it
pro·hi·bi·tion
pro·hi·bi·tion·ist
pro·hib·i·tive
pro·hib·i·to·ry
pro·ject
pro·jec·tile
pro·jec·tion
pro·jec·tion·ist
pro·jec·tive
pro·jec·tive·ly
pro·jec·tiv·i·ty
pro·jec·tor
pro·le·tar·i·at
pro·le·tar·i·an
pro·lif·er·ate
pro·lif·er·at·ed
pro·lif·er·at·ing
pro·lif·er·a·tion
pro·lif·er·a·tive
pro·lif·ic
pro·lif·i·ca·cy
pro·lif·ic·ness
pro·lif·i·cal·ly
pro·lix
pro·lix·i·ty
pro·loc·u·tor
pro·logue
pro·long
pro·lon·ga·tion
prom·e·nade
prom·e·nad·ed
prom·e·nad·ing
prom·e·nad·er
prom·i·nence
prom·i·nent
prom·i·nent·ly
pro·mis·cu·ous
pro·mis·cu·ous·ly
pro·mis·cu·ous·ness
pro·mis·cu·i·ty
prom·ise
prom·ised
prom·is·ing
prom·ise·ful
prom·is·so·ry
prom·on·to·ry
pro·mote
pro·mot·ed
pro·mot·ing
pro·mot·a·ble
pro·mot·er
pro·mo·tion
pro·mo·tive
prompt
prompt·er

prompt·ly
prompt·ness
promp·ti·tude
prom·ul·gate
prom·ul·gat·ed
prom·ul·gat·ing
prom·ul·ga·tion
prone
prone·ness
prong
pro·noun
pro·nounce
pro·nounced
pro·nounc·ing
pro·nounce·a·ble
pro·nun·ci·a·tion
pro·nounce·ment
pron·to
proof
proof·read·er
prop
propped
prop·ping
prop·a·gan·da
prop·a·gan·dist
prop·a·gan·dis·tic
prop·a·gan·dis·ti·cal·ly
prop·a·gan·dism
prop·a·gan·dize
prop·a·gan·dized
prop·a·gan·diz·ing
prop·a·gate
prop·a·gat·ed
prop·a·gat·ing
prop·a·ga·tive
prop·a·ga·tor
prop·a·ga·tion
prop·a·ga·tion·al
pro·pane
pro·pel
pro·pelled
pro·pel·ling
pro·pel·lant
pro·pel·ler
pro·pen·si·ty
pro·pen·si·ties
prop·er
prop·er·ly
prop·er·ty
prop·er·ties
prop·er·tied
proph·e·cy
proph·e·cies
proph·e·sy
proph·e·sied
proph·e·sy·ing
proph·et
pro·phet·ic
pro·phet·i·cal·ly
pro·phy·lac·tic
pro·phy·lax·is
pro·pin·qui·ty
pro·pi·ti·ate
pro·pi·ti·at·ed
pro·pi·ti·at·ing
pro·pi·ti·a·tion
pro·pi·ti·a·to·ry
pro·pi·tious
pro·pi·tious·ly
pro·po·nent
pro·por·tion
pro·por·tion·a·ble
pro·por·tion·a·bly
pro·por·tion·al
pro·por·tion·al·i·ty
pro·por·tion·ate
pro·pose
pro·posed

pro·pos·ing
pro·pos·al
pro·pos·er
prop·o·si·tion
pro·pound
pro·pri·e·tary
pro·pri·e·tor
pro·pri·etress
pro·pri·e·ty
pro·pri·e·ties
pro·pul·sion
pro·pul·sive
pro·rata
pro·rate
pro·rat·ed
pro·rat·ing
pro·ra·tion
pro·sa·ic
pro·sa·i·cal·ly
pro·sa·ic·ness
pro·scribe
pro·scribed
pro·scrib·ing
pro·scrib·er
pro·scrip·tion
pro·scrip·tive
pros·e·cute
pros·e·cut·a·ble
pros·e·cu·tion
pros·e·cu·tor
pros·e·lyte
pros·e·ly·tism
pros·e·ly·tize
pros·pect
pros·pec·tor
pro·spec·tive
pro·spec·tus
pros·per
pros·per·i·ty
pros·per·ous
pros·tate
pros·the·sis
pros·thet·ic
pros·tho·don·tics
pros·tho·don·tist
pros·ti·tute
pros·ti·tut·ed
pros·ti·tut·ing
pros·ti·tu·tion
pros·ti·tu·tor
pros·trate
pros·trat·ed
pros·trat·ing
pros·tra·tion
pro·tag·o·nist
pro·te·an
pro·tect
pro·tect·ing
pro·tec·tive
pro·tec·tive·ness
pro·tec·tor
pro·tec·tion
pro·tec·tion·ism
pro·tec·tion·ist
pro·tec·tor·ate
pro·te·ge
pro·tein
Prot·er·o·zo·ic
pro·test
prot·es·ta·tion
Prot·es·tant
Prot·es·tant·ism
pro·to·col
pro·ton
pro·to·plasm
pro·to·type
pro·to·zo·an
pro·tract

pro·trac·tion
pro·trac·tive
pro·trac·tile
pro·trac·tor
pro·trud·ed
pro·trud·ing
pro·trud·ent
pro·tru·sion
pro·tru·sive
pro·tu·ber·ance
pro·tu·ber·ant
proud
proud·ly
prove
proved
prov·en
prov·ing
prov·a·ble
prov·a·bly
prov·erb
pro·ver·bi·al
pro·vide
pro·vid·ed
pro·vid·ing
pro·vid·a·ble
pro·vid·er
prov·i·dence
prov·i·den·tial
prov·i·dent
prov·ince
pro·vin·cial
pro·vin·ci·al·i·ty
pro·vin·cial·ly
pro·vin·cial·ist
pro·vin·cial·ize
pro·vin·cial·ized
pro·vin·cial·iz·ing
pro·vin·cial·ism
pro·vi·sion
pro·vi·sion·al
pro·vi·sion·al·ly
pro·vi·sion·ary
pro·vi·so·ry
pro·vi·so
pro·voke
pro·voked
pro·vok·ing
pro·vok·ing·ly
prov·o·ca·tion
pro·voc·a·tive
prov·ost
prow·ess
prowl
prowl·er
prox·i·mal
prox·i·mate
prox·im·i·ty
proxy
prox·ies
prude
prud·ery
prud·ish
pru·dence
pru·dent
pru·den·tial
prune
pruned
prun·ing
pru·ri·ent
pru·ri·ence
pru·ri·en·cy
pry
pried
pry·ing
psalm·book
psalm·ist
Psal·ter

pseu·do
pseu·do·nym
pseu·don·y·mous
pseu·do·sci·ence
pseu·do·sci·en·tif·ic
pshaw
pso·ri·a·sis
psy·che
psych·e·del·ic
psy·chi·a·try
psy·chi·at·ric
psy·chi·at·ri·cal·ly
psy·chi·a·trist
psy·chic
psy·chi·cal
psy·chi·cal·ly
psy·cho·a·nal·y·sis
psy·cho·an·a·lyt·ic
psy·cho·an·a·lyt·i·cal
psy·cho·an·a·lyze
psy·cho·an·a·lyzed
psy·cho·an·a·lyz·ing
psy·cho·an·a·lyst
psy·cho·bi·ol·o·gy
psy·cho·dra·ma
psy·cho·dy·nam·ic
psy·cho·dy·nam·i·cal·ly
psy·cho·gen·e·sis
psy·cho·ge·net·ic
psy·cho·gen·ic
psy·cho·gen·i·cal·ly
psy·cho·log·i·cal
psy·cho·log·ic
psy·cho·log·i·cal·ly
psy·chol·o·gy
psy·chol·o·gist
psy·cho·met·ric
psy·cho·met·ri·cal·ly
psy·cho·mo·tor
psy·cho·neu·ro·sis
psy·cho·neu·ro·ses
psy·cho·neu·rot·ic
psy·cho·path
psy·cho·pa·thol·o·gy
psy·cho·pa·thol·o·gist
psy·cho·path·o·log·ic
psy·cho·path·o·log·i·cal
psy·chop·a·thy
psy·cho·path·ic
psy·cho·path·i·cal·ly
psy·cho·sis
psy·cho·ses
psy·chot·ic
psy·chot·i·cal·ly
psy·cho·so·mat·ic
psy·cho·so·mat·i·cal·ly
psy·cho·ther·a·py
psy·cho·ther·a·peu·tics
psy·cho·ther·a·peu·tic
psy·cho·ther·a·peu·ti·cal·ly
psy·cho·ther·a·pist
pto·maine
pu·ber·ty
pu·bes·cence
pu·bes·cen·cy
pu·bes·cent
pu·bic
pub·lic
pub·lic·ly
pub·lic·ness
pub·li·cist
pub·li·ci·ty
pub·li·cize
pub·li·cized
pub·li·ciz·ing
pub·lish
pub·lish·er
pub·li·ca·tion

puck·er
pud·ding
pud·dle
pud·dled
pud·dling
pudgy
pudg·i·ness
pueb·lo
pu·er·ile
pu·er·il·i·ty
pu·er·per·al
Puer·to Ri·co
puff
puff·i·ness
puffy
pu·gil·ism
pu·gil·ist
pu·gil·is·tic
pug·na·cious
pug·na·cious·ness
pug·nac·i·ty
puke
puked
puk·ing
pul·let
pul·ley
pul·mo·nary
pul·mo·tor
pulp
pulp·i·ness
pulpy
pul·pit
pul·sar
pul·sate
pul·sat·ed
pul·sat·ing
pul·sa·tion
pul·sa·tor
pulse
pulsed
puls·ing
pul·ver·ize
pul·ver·ized
pul·ver·iz·ing
pul·ver·iz·a·ble
pul·ver·i·za·tion
pul·ver·iz·er
pu·ma
pum·ice
pum·mel
pum·meled
pum·melled
pum·mel·ing
pum·mel·ling
pump
pump·a·ble
pump·er
pum·per·nick·el
pump·kin
pun
punned
pun·ning
punch
punch-drunk
punc·til·io
punc·til·i·ous
punc·tu·al
punc·tu·al·i·ty
punc·tu·al·ly
punc·tu·al·ness
punc·tu·ate
punc·tu·at·ed
punc·tu·at·ing
punc·tu·a·tion
punc·ture
punc·tured
punc·tur·ing
punc·tur·a·ble

pun·dit
pun·gent
　pun·gen·cy
　pun·gent·ly
pun·ish
　pun·ish·a·ble
　pun·ish·ment
pu·ni·tive
pun·ster
pu·ny
　pu·ni·er
　pu·ni·est
　pu·ni·ness
pu·pa
pu·pil
pup·pet
　pup·pet·eer
　pup·pet·ry
pup·py
　pup·pies
　pup·py·ish
pur·chase
　pur·chased
　pur·chas·ing
　pur·chas·a·ble
　pur·chas·er
pure
　pure·ly
　pure·ness
　pu·ri·fy
　pu·ri·ty
pu·ree
pur·ga·tive
　pur·ga·tion
pur·ga·to·ry
　pur·ga·to·ri·al
purge
　purged
　purg·ing
pu·ri·fy
　pu·ri·fied
　pu·ri·fy·ing
　pu·ri·fi·ca·tion
　pu·ri·fi·er
pur·ism
　pur·ist
　pu·ris·tic
pu·ri·tan
　pu·ri·tan·i·cal
　pu·ri·tan·i·cal·ly
pu·ri·ty
purl
pur·loin
　pur·loin·er
pur·ple
　pur·plish
pur·port
　pur·port·ed·ly
pur·pose
　pur·pose·ful·ly
　pur·pose·ly
　pur·pos·ive
purse
　pursed
　purs·ing
purs·er
pur·su·ant
　pur·su·ance
pur·sue
　pur·sued
　pur·su·ing
　pur·su·er
　pur·suit
pu·ru·lent
　pu·ru·lence
　pu·ru·len·cy
　pu·ru·lent·ly
pur·vey

pur·vey·or
pur·vey·ance
pur·view
pushy
　push·i·ly
　push·i·ness
push·cart
push·o·ver
pu·sil·lan·i·mous
　pu·sil·la·nim·i·ty
　pu·sil·lan·i·mous·ly
puss·y·foot
puss·y·wil·low
pus·tule
put
　put
　put·ting
pu·ta·tive
pu·tre·fy
　pu·tre·fied
　pu·tre·fy·ing
　pu·tre·fac·tion
pu·trid
　pu·trid·ness
putt
　putt·ed
　putt·ing
put·ter
put·ty
puz·zle
　puz·zled
　puz·zling
　puz·zler
　puz·zle·ment
pyg·my
py·lon
py·or·rhea
pyr·a·mid
　py·ram·i·dal
pyre
py·ro·ma·nia
　py·ro·ma·ni·ac
　py·ro·ma·ni·a·cal
py·rom·e·ter
py·ro·tech·nics
py·thon

Q

quack·ery
quad·ran·gle
　quad·ran·gu·lar
quad·rant
　quad·ran·tal
quad·rate
　quad·rat·ed
　quad·rat·ing
quad·rat·ic
　quad·rat·ics
quad·ra·ture
qua·dren·ni·al
quad·ri·lat·er·al
qua·drille
quad·ril·lion
　quad·ril·lionth
quad·roon
quad·ru·ped
quad·ru·ple
　quad·ru·pled
　quad·ru·pling
quad·ru·plet
quad·ru·pli·cate
quaff
quag·mire
quail
quaint·ly
quake

quaked
quak·ing
Quak·er
qual·i·fy
　qual·i·fied
　qual·i·fy·ing
　qual·i·fi·a·ble
　qual·i·fi·ca·tion
qual·i·ta·tive
qual·i·ty
　qual·i·ties
qualm
　qualm·ish
quan·da·ry
quan·ti·fy
　quan·ti·fied
　quan·ti·fy·ing
　quan·ti·fi·a·ble
　quan·ti·fi·ca·tion
quan·ti·ta·tive
quan·ti·ty
　quan·ti·ties
quan·tum
quar·an·tine
　quar·an·tin·a·ble
quar·rel
　quar·reled
　quar·rel·ing
　quar·rel·some
quar·ry
　quar·ries
　quar·ried
　quar·ry·ing
quart
quar·ter
　quar·ter·back
　quar·ter·ing
　quar·ter·ly
　quar·ter·mas·ter
quar·tet
qua·sar
quash
qua·si
qua·si·ju·di·cial
qua·ter·nary
quat·rain
qua·ver
　quav·er·ing·ly
quay
quea·sy
　quea·si·ly
　quea·si·ness
queen
　queen·li·ness
　queen·ly
queer
　queer·ness
quell
quench
　quench·a·ble
quer·u·lous
que·ry
　que·ried
　que·ry·ing
quest
　quest·ing·ly
ques·tion
　ques·tion·er
ques·tion·a·ble
　ques·tion·a·ble·ness
　ques·tion·a·bil·i·ty
　ques·tion·a·bly
　ques·tion·naire
queue
　queued
　queu·ing
quib·ble
　quib·bled

quib·bling
quick
　quick·en
　quick·ness
　quick·freeze
　quick·sand
　quick·sil·ver
　quick-tem·pered
　quick-wit·ted
qui·es·cent
　qui·es·cence
qui·et
　qui·et·ly
　qui·et·ness
qui·e·tude
quill
quilt
　quilt·ing
quince
qui·nine
quin·quen·ni·al
quin·tes·sence
　quin·tes·sen·tial
quin·tet
quin·til·lion
　quin·til·lion·th
quin·tu·ple
　quin·tu·pled
　quin·tu·pling
quin·tu·plet
quip
　quipped
　quip·ping
　quip·ster
quirk
　quirk·i·ness
　quirky
quis·ling
quit
　quit·ted
　quit·ting
quit·claim
quit·tance
quite
quit·ter
quiv·er
quix·ot·ic
　quix·ot·i·cal·ly
quiz
　quiz·zes
　quizzed
　quiz·zing
　quiz·zi·cal
quoit
quon·dam
Quon·set
quo·rum
quo·ta
　quo·ta·tion
quote
　quot·ed
　quot·ing
　quot·able
quo·tid·i·an
quo·tient

R

rab·bet
　rab·bet·ed
　rab·bet·ing
rab·bi
　rab·bis
rab·bin·i·cal
　rab·bin·i·cal·ly
rab·bit
rab·ble

rab·id
　rab·id·ly
ra·bies
race
　raced
　rac·ing
race·horse
rac·er
race·track
ra·cial
　ra·cial·ly
rac·ism
　ra·cial·ism
rac·ist
rack·et
rack·et·eer
rac·on·teur
racy
　rac·i·ly
　rac·i·ness
ra·dar
ra·di·al
　ra·di·al·ly
ra·di·ate
　ra·di·at·ed
　ra·di·at·ing
　ra·di·ance
　ra·di·an·cy
　ra·di·ant
　ra·di·a·tion
　ra·di·a·tor
rad·i·cal
　rad·i·cal·ly
　rad·i·cal·ism
ra·dio
　ra·di·oed
　ra·di·o·ing
　ra·di·o·ac·tive
　ra·di·o·ac·tiv·i·ty
　ra·di·o·fre·quen·cy
　ra·di·o·gram
　ra·di·o·graph
　ra·dio·iso·tope
　ra·di·ol·o·gy
　ra·di·ol·o·gist
　ra·di·os·co·py
rad·ish
ra·di·um
ra·di·us
ra·don
raf·fia
raf·fish
raft·er
rag
　ragged
rag·a·muf·fin
rage
　raged
　rag·ing
rag·ged
　rag·ged·ness
rag·time
rag·weed
raid·er
rail·ing
rail·lery
rail·road
rail·way
rai·ment
rain·bow
rain·coat
rain·fall
rainy
　rain·i·er
　rain·i·ly
　rain·i·ness
　rainy
raise

raised
rais·ing
rai·sin
rake
  raked
  rak·ing
rak·ish
  rak·ish·ness
ral·ly
  ral·lied
  ral·ly·ing
ram
  rammed
  ram·ming
ram·ble
  ram·bled
  ram·bling
ram·bler
ram·bunc·tious
ram·i·fy
  ram·i·fied
  ram·i·fy·ing
  ram·i·fi·ca·tion
ram·page
  ram·paged
  ram·pag·ing
ramp·ant
  ram·pan·cy
  ram·pant·ly
ram·part
ram·rod
ram·shack·le
ran·cid
  ran·cid·i·ty
  ran·cid·ness
ran·cor
  ran·cor·ous
ran·dom
  ran·dom·ly
  ran·dom·ness
  ran·dom·ize
range
  ranged
  rang·ing
rangy
  rang·i·ness
ran·kle
  ran·kled
  ran·kling
ran·sack
ran·som
rant·er
rap
  rapped
  rap·ping
ra·pa·cious
  ra·pa·cious·ly
  ra·pac·i·ty
rape
  rap·ist
rap·id
  ra·pid·i·ty
  rap·id·ly
  rap·id·ness
rap·id·fire
ra·pi·er
rap·ine
rap·port
rap·proche·ment
rap·scal·lion
rapt
  rapt·ly
rap·ture
  rap·tur·ous
  rap·tur·ous·ly
rare
  rar·er
  rar·est

rare·bit
rar·e·fy
  rar·e·fied
  rar·e·fy·ing
  rar·e·fac·tion
  rar·e·fied
rare·ly
rar·i·ty
  rar·i·ties
ras·cal
  ras·cal·i·ty
  ras·cal·ly
rash
  rash·ly
  rash·ness
rasp
  rasp·ing·ly
  raspy
rasp·ber·ry
rat
  rat·ted
  rat·ting
rat·a·ble
  rate·a·ble
ratch·et
rate
  rat·ed
  rat·ing
rath·er
rat·i·fy
  rat·i·fied
  rat·i·fy·ing
  rat·i·fi·ca·tion
  rat·i·fi·er
ra·tio
  ra·tios
ra·ti·oc·i·na·tion
ra·tion
ra·tion·al
  ra·tion·al·i·ty
  ra·tion·al·ly
  ra·tion·ale
  ra·tion·al·ism
  ra·tion·al·ist
  ra·tion·al·is·tic
  ra·tion·al·is·ti·cal·ly
  ra·tion·al·ize
  ra·tion·al·ized
  ra·tion·al·iz·ing
  ra·tion·al·i·za·tion
  ra·tion·al·iz·er
rat·tan
rat·tle
  rat·tled
  rat·tling
rat·tle·brain
rat·tler
rat·tle·snake
rat·ty
  rat·ti·est
rau·cous
  rau·cous·ly
raun·chy
  raun·chi·er
rav·age
  rav·aged
  rav·ag·ing
  rav·ag·er
rave
  raved
  rav·ing
rav·el
  rav·eled
  rav·el·ing
ra·ven
rav·en·ous
ra·vine
ra·vi·o·li

rav·ish
  rav·ish·ment
  rav·ish·ing
raw
  raw·ness
ray·on
raze
  razed
  raz·ing
ra·zor
raz·zle-daz·zle
reach·able
re·act
  re·ac·tive
  re·ac·tion
  re·ac·tion·ary
  re·ac·ti·vate
  re·ac·ti·vat·ed
  re·ac·ti·vat·ing
  re·ac·tor
read·a·ble
  read·a·bil·i·ty
  read·a·ble·ness
re·ad·just
  re·ad·just·ment
ready
  read·ied
  read·y·ing
  read·i·ly
  read·i·ness
read·y·made
re·a·gent
re·al
re·al·ism
  re·al·ist
  re·al·is·tic
  re·al·is·ti·cal·ly
re·al·i·ty
  re·al·i·ties
re·al·ize
  re·al·ized
  re·al·iz·ing
  re·al·iz·a·ble
  re·al·i·za·tion
re·al·ly
realm
re·al·tor
re·al·ty
ream·er
re·an·i·mate
  re·an·i·mat·ed
  re·an·i·mat·ing
  re·an·i·ma·tion
reap·er
re·ap·pear
  re·ap·pear·ance
re·ap·por·tion
  re·ap·por·tion·ment
rear ad·mi·ral
re·arm
  re·ar·ma·ment
re·ar·range
  re·ar·ranged
  re·ar·rang·ing
  re·ar·range·ment
rea·son
  rea·son·er
rea·son·a·ble
  rea·son·a·bil·i·ty
  rea·son·a·ble·ness
  rea·son·a·bly
rea·son·ing
re·as·sem·ble
  re·as·sem·bled
  re·as·sem·bling
  re·as·sem·bly
re·as·sume
  re·as·sump·tion

re·as·sure
  re·as·sured
  re·as·sur·ing
  re·as·sur·ance
re·bate
  re·bat·ed
  re·bat·ing
reb·el
re·bel
  re·belled
  re·bel·ling
  re·bel·lion
  re·bel·lious
  re·bel·lious·ness
re·birth
re·born
re·bound
re·buff
re·build
  re·built
  re·build·ing
re·buke
  re·buked
  re·buk·ing
re·but
  re·but·ted
  re·but·ting
  re·but·ter
  re·but·tal
re·cal·ci·trant
  re·cal·ci·trance
  re·cal·ci·tran·cy
re·call
re·cant
  re·can·ta·tion
re·cap
  re·capped
  re·cap·ping
  re·cap·pable
re·ca·pit·u·late
  re·ca·pit·u·lat·ed
  re·ca·pit·u·lat·ing
  re·ca·pit·u·la·tion
re·cap·ture
  re·cap·tured
  re·cap·tur·ing
re·cast
re·cede
  re·ced·ed
  re·ced·ing
re·ceipt
re·ceiv·a·ble
re·ceive
  re·ceived
  re·ceiv·ing
re·ceiv·er
re·ceiv·er·ship
re·cent
  re·cent·ly
  re·cen·cy
  re·cent·ness
re·cep·ta·cle
re·cep·tion
  re·cep·tion·ist
re·cep·tive
  re·cep·tive·ly
  re·cep·tive·ness
  re·cep·tiv·i·ty
re·cess
re·ces·sion
  re·ces·sion·ary
  re·ces·sion·al
  re·ces·sive
re·charge
  re·charged
  re·charg·ing
re·cid·i·vism
  re·cid·i·vist

rec·i·pe
re·cip·i·ent
  re·cip·i·ence
  re·cip·i·en·cy
re·cip·ro·cal
  re·cip·ro·cal·ly
re·cip·ro·cate
  re·cip·ro·cat·ed
  re·cip·ro·cat·ing
  re·cip·ro·ca·tion
  re·cip·ro·ca·tive
rec·i·proc·i·ty
re·ci·sion
re·cit·al
re·cite
  re·cit·ed
  re·cit·ing
  rec·i·ta·tion
  rec·i·ta·tive
reck·less
  reck·less·ness
reck·on
  reck·on·ing
re·claim
  re·claim·able
  rec·la·ma·tion
re·cline
  re·clined
  re·clin·ing
  re·clin·er
rec·luse
  re·clu·sion
  re·clu·sive
rec·og·nize
  rec·og·nized
  rec·og·niz·ing
  rec·og·niz·a·ble
  rec·og·niz·a·bly
  rec·og·ni·tion
  re·cog·ni·zance
re·coil
  re·coil·less
re·col·lect
rec·ol·lect
  rec·ol·lec·tion
rec·om·mend
  rec·om·mend·a·ble
  rec·om·mend·er
  rec·om·men·da·tion
re·com·mit
  re·com·mit·tal
rec·om·pense
  rec·om·pensed
  rec·om·pens·ing
rec·on·cile
  rec·on·ciled
  rec·on·cil·ing
  rec·on·cil·a·ble
  rec·on·cil·a·bly
  rec·on·cil·er
  rec·on·cil·i·a·tion
  rec·on·cile·ment
rec·on·dite
re·con·di·tion
re·con·firm
  re·con·fir·ma·tion
re·con·noi·ter
  re·con·noi·tered
  re·con·noi·ter·ing
  re·con·nais·sance
re·con·sid·er
  re·con·sid·er·a·tion
re·con·sti·tute
re·con·struct
  re·con·struc·tion
re·cord
rec·ord
  re·cord·er

re·cord·ing
re·count
re·coup
re·course
re·cov·er
  re·cov·ery
  re·cov·er·able
rec·re·ant
re·cre·ate
  re·cre·at·ed
  re·cre·at·ing
  re·cre·a·tion
rec·re·a·tion
  rec·re·a·tion·al
  rec·re·a·tive
re·crim·i·nate
  re·crim·i·nat·ed
  re·crim·i·nat·ing
  re·crim·i·na·tion
  re·crim·i·na·tive
  re·crim·i·na·to·ry
re·cruit
  re·cruit·er
  re·cruit·ment
rec·tal
rec·tan·gle
  rec·tan·gu·lar
  rec·ti·fy
  rec·ti·fied
  rec·ti·fy·ing
  rec·ti·fi·a·ble
  rec·ti·fi·ca·tion
  rec·ti·fi·er
rec·ti·lin·e·ar
rec·ti·tude
rec·tor
rec·to·ry
rec·tum
re·cum·bent
  re·cum·ben·cy
  re·cum·bent·ly
re·cu·per·ate
  re·cu·per·at·ed
  re·cu·per·at·ing
  re·cu·per·a·tion
  re·cu·per·a·tive
re·cur
  re·curred
  re·cur·ring
  re·cur·rence
  re·cur·rent
re·cy·cle
red
  red·der
  red·ness
  red·den
  red·dish
red-blood·ed
re·dec·o·rate
  re·dec·o·rat·ed
  re·dec·o·rat·ing
  re·dec·o·ra·tion
re·ded·i·cate
  re·ded·i·cat·ed
  re·ded·i·cat·ing
  re·ded·i·ca·tion
re·deem
  re·deem·a·ble
  re·deem·er
  re·demp·tion
  re·demp·tive
  re·demp·to·ry
red-hand·ed
re·di·rect
  re·di·rec·tion
re·dis·trib·ute
  re·dis·tri·bu·tion
re·dis·trict

red-let·ter
re·do
  re·did
  re·done
  re·do·ing
red·o·lent
  red·o·lence
  red·o·len·cy
re·dou·ble
  re·dou·bled
  re·dou·bling
  re·doubt·a·ble
  re·doubt·a·bly
re·dress
re·duce
  re·duced
  re·duc·ing
  re·duc·er
  re·duc·i·ble
  re·duc·tion
re·dun·dant
  re·dun·dance
  re·dun·dan·cy
  re·dun·dan·cies
  re·dun·dant·ly
re·du·pli·cate
  re·du·pli·cat·ed
  re·du·pli·cat·ing
  re·du·pli·ca·tion
re·echo
  re·ech·o·ing
  re·ech·oes
re·ed·u·cate
  re·ed·u·ca·tion
reedy
  reed·i·ness
re·e·lect
  re·e·lec·tion
re·em·pha·size
  re·em·pha·sized
  re·em·pha·siz·ing
re·em·ploy
re·en·act
re·en·force
  re·en·forced
  re·en·forc·ing
  re·en·force·ment
re·en·list
  re·en·list·ment
re·en·ter
  re·en·trance
  re·en·try
re·es·tab·lish
  re·es·tab·lish·ment
re·ex·am·ine
  re·ex·am·ined
  re·ex·am·in·ing
  re·ex·am·i·na·tion
re·fer
  re·ferred
  re·fer·ring
  re·fer·a·ble
  re·fer·ral
ref·er·ee
  ref·er·eed
  ref·er·ee·ing
ref·er·ence
  ref·er·enced
  ref·er·enc·ing
ref·er·en·dum
ref·er·ent
  ref·er·en·tial
re·fer·ral
re·fill
  re·fill·a·ble
re·fi·nance
re·fine
  re·fined

re·fin·ing
re·fine·ment
re·fin·ery
re·fin·ish
re·fit
  re·fit·ted
  re·fit·ting
re·flect
  re·flec·tion
  re·flec·tive
  re·flec·tive·ly
re·flec·tor
re·flex
  re·flex·ive
re·for·est
  re·for·est·a·tion
re·form
  re·formed
  re·form·er
  re·form·ist
ref·or·ma·tion
re·form·a·to·ry
  re·form·a·tive
re·fract
  re·frac·tive
  re·frac·tion
re·frac·to·ry
  re·frac·to·ri·ness
re·frain
  re·fran·gi·ble
re·fresh
  re·fresh·ing
  re·fresh·ment
re·frig·er·ate
  re·frig·er·at·ed
  re·frig·er·at·ing
  re·frig·er·ant
  re·frig·er·a·tion
  re·frig·er·a·tor
ref·uge
ref·u·gee
re·ful·gent
  re·ful·gence
re·fund
re·fur·bish
re·fuse
  re·fused
  re·fus·ing
  re·fus·al
ref·use
re·fute
  re·fut·ed
  re·fut·ing
  re·fut·a·ble
ref·u·ta·tion
re·gain
re·gal
  re·gal·ly
re·gale
  re·galed
  re·gal·ing
re·ga·lia
re·gard
  re·gard·ful
  re·gard·ing
  re·gard·less
re·gat·ta
re·gen·cy
re·gen·er·ate
  re·gen·er·at·ed
  re·gen·er·at·ing
  re·gen·er·a·cy
  re·gen·er·a·tion
  re·gen·er·a·tive
re·gent
re·gime
reg·i·men
reg·i·ment

reg·i·men·tal
reg·i·men·ta·tion
re·gion
  re·gion·al
  re·gion·al·ly
reg·is·ter
  reg·is·tered
  reg·is·trant
  reg·is·trar
  reg·is·tra·tion
  reg·is·try
re·gress
  re·gres·sion
  re·gres·sive
re·gret
  re·gret·ted
  re·gret·ting
  re·gret·ta·ble
  re·gret·ta·bly
  re·gret·ful·ly
  re·gret·ful·ness
reg·u·lar
  reg·u·lar·i·ty
reg·u·late
  reg·u·lat·ed
  reg·u·lat·ing
  reg·u·la·tive
  reg·u·la·tor
  reg·u·la·to·ry
  reg·u·la·tion
re·gur·gi·tate
  re·gur·gi·tat·ed
  re·gur·gi·tat·ing
  re·gur·gi·ta·tion
re·ha·bil·i·tate
  re·ha·bil·i·tat·ed
  re·ha·bil·i·tat·ing
  re·ha·bil·i·ta·tion
  re·ha·bil·i·ta·tive
re·hash
re·hears·al
re·hearse
  re·hearsed
  re·hears·ing
reign
re·im·burse
  re·im·bursed
  re·im·burs·ing
  re·im·burse·ment
rein
re·in·car·nate
  re·in·car·na·tion
rein·deer
re·in·fec·tion
re·in·force
  re·in·forced
  re·in·forc·ing
  re·in·force·ment
re·in·state
  re·in·stat·ed
  re·in·stat·ing
  re·in·state·ment
re·in·sur·ance
re·in·ter·pre·ta·tion
re·is·sue
re·it·er·ate
  re·it·er·at·ed
  re·it·er·at·ing
  re·it·er·a·tion
re·ject
  re·jec·tion
re·joice
  re·joiced
  re·joic·ing
re·join
  re·join·der
re·ju·ve·nate
  re·ju·ve·nat·ed

re·ju·ve·nat·ing
re·ju·ve·na·tion
re·kin·dle
  re·kin·dled
  re·kin·dling
re·lapse
  re·lapsed
  re·laps·ing
re·late
  re·lat·ed
  re·lat·ing
re·la·tion
  re·la·tion·al
  re·la·tion·ship
rel·a·tive
  rel·a·tive·ly
  rel·a·tiv·i·ty
re·lax
  re·lax·a·tion
re·lay
  re·laid
  re·lay·ing
re·lay
  re·layed
  re·lay·ing
re·lease
  re·leased
  re·leas·ing
rel·e·gate
  rel·e·gat·ed
  rel·e·gat·ing
  rel·e·ga·tion
re·lent
  re·lent·less
rel·e·vant
  rel·e·vance
  rel·e·van·cy
re·li·a·ble
  re·li·a·bil·i·ty
  re·li·a·ble·ness
  re·li·a·bly
re·li·ant
  re·li·ance
rel·ic
re·lief
re·lieve
  re·lieved
  re·liev·ing
  re·liev·a·ble
re·li·gion
  re·li·gi·os·i·ty
  re·li·gious
re·lin·quish
rel·ish
re·live
  re·lived
  re·liv·ing
re·lo·cate
  re·lo·cat·ed
  re·lo·cat·ing
  re·lo·ca·tion
re·luc·tant
  re·luc·tance
re·ly
  re·lied
  re·ly·ing
re·main
  re·main·der
re·mand
re·mark
  re·mark·a·ble
  re·mark·a·ble·ness
  re·mark·a·bly
re·me·di·al
  re·me·di·a·ble
rem·e·dy
  rem·e·dies
  rem·e·died

rem·e·dy·ing
re·mem·ber
re·mem·brance
re·mind
re·mind·er
rem·i·nisce
rem·i·nisced
rem·i·nisc·ing
rem·i·nis·cence
rem·i·nis·cent
re·miss
re·mis·sion
re·mit
re·mit·ted
re·mit·ting
re·mit·tance
rem·nant
re·mod·el
re·mon·strate
re·mon·strat·ed
re·mon·strat·ing
re·mon·strance
re·morse
re·morse·ful·ly
re·morse·less
re·mote
re·mote·ly
re·mote·ness
re·mount
re·move
re·moved
re·mov·ing
re·mov·a·ble
re·mov·al
re·mu·ner·ate
re·mu·ner·at·ed
re·mu·ner·at·ing
re·mu·ner·a·tion
re·mu·ner·a·tive
ren·ais·sance
re·nas·cence
re·nas·cent
rend
rend·ed
rend·ing
ren·der
ren·di·tion
ren·dez·vous
ren·dez·voused
ren·dez·vous·ing
ren·e·gade
re·nege
re·neged
re·neg·ing
re·new
re·new·al
re·nom·i·nate
re·nounce
re·nounced
re·nounc·ing
ren·o·vate
ren·o·vat·ed
ren·o·vat·ing
ren·o·va·tion
re·nown
re·nowned
rent·al
re·nun·ci·a·tion
re·or·gan·ize
re·or·gan·ized
re·or·gan·iz·ing
re·or·gan·i·za·tion
re·pair
rep·a·ra·ble
rep·a·ra·tion
rep·ar·tee
re·past
re·pa·tri·ate

re·pa·tri·at·ed
re·pa·tri·at·ing
re·pa·tri·a·tion
re·pay
re·paid
re·pay·ing
re·pay·ment
re·peal
re·peat
re·peat·a·ble
re·peat·ed
re·peat·er
re·pel
re·pelled
re·pel·ling
re·pel·lent
re·pent
re·pent·ance
re·pent·ant
re·per·cus·sion
rep·er·toire
rep·er·to·ry
rep·e·ti·tion
rep·e·ti·tious
re·pet·i·tive
re·place
re·placed
re·plac·ing
re·place·a·ble
re·place·ment
re·plen·ish
re·plete
re·ple·tion
rep·li·ca
re·ply
re·plied
re·ply·ing
re·plies
re·port
re·port·able
re·port·ed·ly
re·port·er
rep·or·to·ri·al
re·pose
re·posed
re·pos·ing
re·pos·i·tory
re·pos·sess
re·pos·ses·sion
rep·re·hend
rep·re·hen·si·ble
rep·re·hen·sion
rep·re·sent
rep·re·sen·ta·tion
rep·re·sent·a·tive
re·press
re·pres·sion
re·prieve
re·prieved
re·priev·ing
re·pri·mand
re·pris·al
re·proach
re·proach·ful·ly
rep·ro·bate
rep·ro·ba·tion
re·pro·duce
re·pro·duced
re·pro·duc·ing
re·pro·duc·tion
re·pro·duc·tive
re·proof
re·prove
re·proved
re·prov·ing
rep·tile
rep·til·i·an
re·pub·lic

re·pub·li·can
re·pu·di·ate
re·pu·di·at·ed
re·pu·di·at·ing
re·pu·di·a·tion
re·pug·nant
re·pug·nance
re·pug·nan·cy
re·pulse
re·plused
re·puls·ing
re·pul·sion
re·pul·sive
rep·u·ta·ble
rep·u·ta·bly
rep·u·ta·bil·i·ty
rep·u·ta·tion
re·pute
re·put·ed
re·put·ing
re·quest
req·ui·em
re·quire
re·quired
re·quir·ing
re·quire·ment
req·ui·site
req·ui·si·tion
re·quit·al
re·quite
re·run
re·run·ning
re·scind
re·scis·sion
res·cue
res·cued
res·cu·ing
re·search
re·search·er
re·sem·ble
re·sem·bled
re·sem·bling
re·sem·blance
re·sent
re·sent·ful
re·sent·ment
re·serve
re·served
re·serv·ing
res·er·va·tion
re·serv·ist
res·er·voir
re·set
re·set·ting
re·side
re·sid·ed
re·sid·ing
res·i·dence
res·i·den·cy
res·i·dent
res·i·den·tial
res·i·due
re·sid·u·al
re·sign
res·ig·na·tion
re·signed
re·sil·ient
re·sil·ience
re·sil·ien·cy
res·in
res·in·ous
re·sist
re·sist·er
re·sist·i·ble
re·sist·ance
re·sist·ant
re·sis·tor
res·o·lute

res·o·lu·tion
re·solve
re·solved
re·solv·ing
res·o·nant
res·o·nance
res·o·nate
res·o·nat·ed
res·o·nat·ing
res·o·na·tor
re·sort
re·sound
re·source
re·spect
re·spect·ful·ly
re·spect·ful·ness
re·spect·a·ble
re·spect·a·bil·i·ty
re·spect·ing
re·spec·tive
res·pi·ra·tion
res·pi·ra·to·ry
res·pi·ra·tor
re·spire
re·spired
re·spir·ing
re·spite
re·splend·ent
re·splend·ence
re·spond
re·spond·ent
re·sponse
re·spon·sive
re·spon·si·ble
re·spon·si·bil·i·ty
re·spon·si·bil·i·ties
res·tau·rant
res·tau·ra·teur
rest·ful·ly
res·ti·tu·tion
res·tive
re·store
re·stored
re·stor·ing
res·to·ra·tion
re·stor·a·tive
re·strained
re·straint
re·strict
re·strict·ed
re·stric·tion
re·stric·tive
re·sult
re·sult·ant
re·sume
re·sumed
re·sum·ing
re·sump·tion
re·su·me
re·sur·gent
re·sur·gence
res·ur·rect
res·ur·rec·tion
re·sus·ci·tate
re·sus·ci·tat·ed
re·sus·ci·tat·ing
re·sus·ci·ta·tion
re·sus·ci·ta·tor
re·tail·er
re·tain·er
re·take
re·took
re·tak·en
re·tak·ing
re·tal·i·ate
re·tal·i·at·ed
re·tal·i·at·ing
re·tal·i·a·tion

re·tal·i·a·to·ry
re·tard
re·tard·ant
re·tar·da·tion
re·tard·ed
retch
re·tell
re·told
re·tell·ing
re·ten·tion
re·ten·tive
re·ten·tiv·i·ty
ret·i·cent
ret·i·cence
re·tic·u·lar
ret·i·na
ret·i·nue
re·tire
re·tired
re·tir·ing
re·tire·ment
re·tort
re·touch
re·trace
re·traced
re·trac·ing
re·tract
re·trac·tion
re·trac·tor
re·trac·tile
re·tread
re·treat
re·trench
re·trench·ment
re·tri·al
ret·ri·bu·tion
re·trieve
re·trieved
re·triev·ing
re·triev·er
ret·ro·ac·tive
ret·ro·fire
ret·ro·grade
ret·ro·gress
ret·ro·gres·sion
ret·ro·gres·sive
ret·ro·rock·et
ret·ro·spect
ret·ro·spec·tion
ret·ro·spec·tive
re·turn
re·turn·a·ble
re·turn·ee
re·un·ion
re·u·nite
re·u·nit·ed
re·u·nit·ing
rev
revved
rev·ving
re·value
re·val·u·ate
re·val·u·a·tion
re·vamp
re·veal
rev·e·la·tion
rev·eil·le
rev·el
rev·el·ry
re·venge
re·venged
re·veng·ing
re·venge·ful
rev·e·nue
re·ven·u·er
re·ver·ber·ate
re·ver·ber·at·ed
re·ver·ber·at·ing

re·ver·ber·a·tion
re·vere
re·vered
re·ver·ing
rev·er·ence
rev·er·enced
rev·er·enc·ing
rev·er·end
rev·er·ent
rev·er·en·tial
rev·er·ie
re·ver·sal
re·verse
re·versed
re·vers·ing
re·vers·i·ble
re·ver·sion
re·vert
re·view
re·vile
re·viled
re·vil·ing
re·vise
re·vised
re·vis·ing
re·vi·sion
re·vi·sion·ist
re·vi·tal·ize
re·vi·tal·iza·tion
re·viv·al
re·viv·al·ist
re·vive
re·vived
re·viv·ing
re·viv·i·fy
rev·o·ca·tion
re·voke
re·voked
re·vok·ing
rev·o·ca·ble
rev·o·ca·tion
re·volt
rev·o·lu·tion
rev·o·lu·tion·ary
rev·o·lu·tion·aries
rev·o·lu·tion·ist
rev·o·lu·tion·ize
re·volve
re·volved
re·volv·ing
re·volv·er
re·vue
re·vul·sion
re·wak·en
re·ward
re·wind
re·wound
re·wind·ing
re·write
re·wrote
re·writ·ten
re·writ·ing
rhap·sod·ic
rhap·sod·i·cal·ly
rhap·so·dize
rhap·so·dized
rhap·so·diz·ing
rhap·so·dy
rhap·so·dies
rhap·so·dist
rhe·o·stat
rhe·sus
rhet·o·ric
rhe·tor·i·cal·ly
rhet·o·ri·cian
rheu·mat·ic
rheu·ma·tism
rheu·ma·toid

rhine·stone
rhi·noc·er·os
rhi·zome
rho·do·den·dron
rhom·boid
rhom·bus
rhu·barb
rhyme
rhymed
rhym·ing
rhythm
rhyth·mic
rhyth·mi·cal
rhyth·mi·cal·ly
rib
ribbed
rib·bing
rib·ald
rib·ald·ry
rib·bon
ri·bo·fla·vin
rib·bo·nu·cle·ic
rich·es
rich·ness
rick·ets
rick·ety
rick·et·i·ness
rick·shaw
ric·o·chet
ric·o·cheted
ric·o·chet·ing
rid
rid·ded
rid·ding
rid·dance
rid·dle
rid·dled
rid·dling
ride
rode
rid·den
rid·ing
rid·er
ridge
ridged
ridg·ing
rid·i·cule
rid·i·culed
rid·i·cul·ing
ri·dic·u·lous
rif·fle
rif·fled
rif·fling
ri·fle
ri·fled
ri·fling
rig
rigged
rig·ging
rig·ger
right·eous
right·ful·ly
right·hand·ed
right-of-way
right·wing·er
rig·id
ri·gid·i·ty
rig·ma·role
rig·or
rig·or·ous
ri·gor mor·tis
rile
riled
ril·ing
rim
rimmed
rim·ming
ring

ringed
ring·ing
ring
rang
rung
ring·ing
ring·lead·er
ring·mas·ter
rinse
rinsed
rins·ing
Rio de Ja·nei·ro
ri·ot·er
ri·ot·ous
rip
ripped
rip·ping
ri·par·i·an
rip·en
ripe·ness
rip·ple
rip·pled
rip·pling
rise
rose
ris·en
ris·ing
ris·i·ble
ris·i·bil·i·ty
risky
risk·i·er
risk·i·ness
ris·que
rite
rit·u·al
rit·u·al·ism
rit·u·al·ist
rit·u·al·is·tic
ritzy
ritz·i·er
ri·val
ri·val·ry
ri·val·ries
riv·er·side
riv·et·er
riv·i·er·a
riv·u·let
roach·es
road·bed
road·block
road·run·ner
roast·er
rob
robbed
rob·bing
rob·ber
rob·bery
rob·ber·ies
robe
robed
rob·ing
rob·in
ro·bot
ro·bot·ics
ro·bust
rock-bound
rock·er
rock·et
rock·et·ry
rock-ribbed
rocky
rock·i·ness
ro·co·co
ro·dent
ro·deo
roent·gen
rogue
ro·guish

ro·guery
roist·er
roll·er bear·ing
roll·er coast·er
roll·er-skate
rol·lick
rol·lick·ing
roll·ing mill
ro·ly-po·ly
ro·maine
ro·mance
ro·manced
ro·manc·ing
ro·man·tic
ro·man·ti·cism
ro·man·ti·cist
ro·man·ti·cize
ro·man·ti·cized
ro·man·ti·ciz·ing
romp·er
roof·ing
rook·ery
rook·ie
room·mate
roomy
room·i·er
room·i·ness
roost·er
rope
roped
rop·ing
ropy
ro·sa·ry
ro·sa·ries
ro·se·ate
ro·sette
Rosh Ha·sha·nah
ros·in
ros·ter
ros·trum
rosy
ros·i·ness
rot
rot·ted
rot·ting
rot·ten
ro·tate
ro·tat·ed
ro·tat·ing
ro·ta·ry
ro·ta·tion
ro·tis·ser·ie
ro·tund
ro·tun·di·ty
ro·tun·da
rou·e
rouge
rouged
roug·ing
rough·age
rough-and-tum·ble
rough·en
rough-hewed
rough·house
rough·neck
rough·rid·er
rough·shod
rou·lette
round·a·bout
round·ed
round·er
round-shoul·dered
rouse
roused
rous·ing
roust·a·bout
rout
route

rout·ed
rout·ing
rou·tine
rou·tin·ize
rou·tin·ized
rou·tin·iz·ing
rove
roved
rov·ing
row·dy
row·dies
row·di·ly
row·di·ness
roy·al
roy·al·ly
roy·al·ist
roy·al·ty
roy·al·ties
rub
rubbed
rub·bing
rub·ber
rub·bery
rub·ber·ize
rub·ber·ized
rub·ber·iz·ing
rub·bish
rub·ble
ru·bel·la
ru·bi·cund
ru·bric
ru·by
ru·bies
ruck·sack
ruck·us
rud·der
rud·dy
rud·di·ness
rude
rude·ly
rude·ness
ru·di·ment
ru·di·men·tal
ru·di·men·ta·ry
rue
rued
ru·ing
rue·ful·ly
rue·ful·ness
ruf·fi·an
ruf·fle
ruf·fled
ruf·fling
rug·ged
rug·ged·ness
ru·in
ru·in·a·tion
ru·in·ous
rule
ruled
rul·ing
rum·ba
rum·ble
rum·bled
rum·bling
ru·mi·nant
ru·mi·nate
ru·mi·nat·ing
ru·mi·na·tion
rum·mage
rum·mag·ing
rum·my
ru·mor
ru·mor·mon·ger
rum·ple
rum·pled
rum·pling
rum·pus

run
  ran
  run
  run·ning
run·a·way
run·ner-up
run·ny
runt
  runty
  runt·i·est
run·way
rup·ture
  rup·tured
  rup·tur·ing
ru·ral
  ru·ral·ly
  ru·ral·ized
  ru·ral·i·za·tion
rus·set
Rus·sia
Rus·sian
rus·tic
rus·ti·cate
  rus·ti·cat·ed
  rus·ti·cat·ing
  rus·ti·ca·tion
  rus·tic·i·ty
rus·tle
  rus·tled
  rus·tling
rus·tler
rusty
  rust·i·ness
rut
  rut·ted
  rut·ting
ru·ta·ba·ga
ruth·less
  ruth·less·ness
rut·ty
  rut·ti·est

S

Sab·a·oth
Sab·bath
sab·bat·i·cal
sa·ber
sa·ble
sab·o·tage
  sab·o·taged
  sab·o·tag·ing
  sab·o·teur
sac·cha·rin
sac·cha·rine
sac·er·do·tal
sa·chet
sack·ful
sack·ing
sac·ra·ment
sa·cred
  sa·cred·ly
  sa·cred·ness
sac·ri·fice
  sac·ri·ficed
  sac·ri·fic·ing
  sac·ri·fi·cial
sac·ri·lege
  sac·ri·le·gious
sac·ris·ty
sac·ro·il·i·ac
sac·ro·sanct
  sac·ro·sanc·ti·ty
sad
  sad·der
  sad·ly
  sad·ness

sad·den
sad·dle
  sad·dled
  sad·dling
sad·ism
sad·ist
sa·dis·tic
  sa·dis·ti·cal·ly
sa·fa·ri
safe
  saf·er
  saf·est
safe-con·duct
safe-de·pos·it
safe-keep·ing
safe·ty
saf·flow·er
saf·fron
sag
  sagged
  sag·ging
sa·ga
sa·ga·cious
  sa·gac·i·ty
sage
  sage·ness
Sag·it·ta·ri·us
sail·ing
sail·or
saint·hood
saint·ed
saint·ly
  saint·li·ness
sa·ke
sa·laam
sale·a·ble
  sal·a·bil·i·ty
sa·la·cious
sal·ad
sal·a·man·der
sa·la·mi
sal·a·ry
  sal·a·ries
sales·man
sales·per·son
sales·wom·an
sa·li·ent
  sa·li·ence
  sa·li·en·cy
  sa·li·ent·ly
  sa·li·ent·ness
sa·line
  sa·lin·i·ty
sa·li·va
  sal·i·vary
sal·i·vate
  sal·i·vat·ed
  sal·i·vat·ing
  sal·i·va·tion
sal·low
sal·ly
  sal·lied
salm·on
sal·mo·nel·la
sa·lon
sa·loon
salt·cel·lar
salt·ed
sal·tine
salt·shak·er
salt-wa·ter
salty
  salt·i·ness
sa·lu·bri·ous
sal·u·tary
sal·u·ta·tion
sa·lu·ta·to·ry
sa·lute

sa·lut·ed
sa·lut·ing
sal·vage
  sal·vaged
  sal·vag·ing
  sal·vage·a·ble
sal·va·tion
salve
  salved
  salv·ing
sal·vo
sam·ba
same·ness
sam·o·var
sam·ple
  sam·pled
  sam·pling
sam·pler
san·a·to·ri·um
sanc·ti·fy
  sanc·ti·fied
  sanc·ti·fy·ing
  sanc·ti·fi·ca·tion
sanc·ti·mo·ny
  sanc·ti·mo·ni·ous
sanc·tion
  sanc·tion·a·ble
sanc·ti·ty
sanc·tu·ary
sanc·tum
san·dal
sand·bag
  sand·bagged
  sand·bag·ging
sand-cast
  sand-cast·ed
  sand-cast·ing
sand·pa·per
sand·pi·per
sand·wich
sandy
  sand·i·ness
sane
  sane·ly
  sane·ness
sang-froid
san·gria
san·gui·nary
san·guine
san·i·tar·i·um
san·i·tary
  san·i·tar·i·ly
  san·i·ta·tion
san·i·tize
  san·i·tized
  san·i·tiz·ing
san·i·ty
San·ta Claus
sap
  sapped
  sap·ping
sa·pi·ent
  sa·pi·ence
  sa·pi·en·cy
  sa·pi·en·tial
sap·ling
sap·phire
sap·py
sap·suck·er
sa·ran
sar·casm
sar·cas·tic
  sar·cas·ti·cal·ly
sar·co·ma
sar·coph·a·gus
sar·dine
sar·don·ic
  sar·don·i·cal·ly

sa·ri
sa·rong
sar·sa·pa·ril·la
sar·to·ri·al
sa·shay
Sas·katch·e·wan
sas·sa·fras
sas·sy
  sas·si·ness
sa·tan·ic
  sa·tan·i·cal
satch·el
sate
  sat·ed
  sat·ing
sa·teen
sat·el·lite
sa·ti·a·ble
  sa·ti·a·bly
  sa·ti·a·bil·i·ty
  sa·ti·a·ble·ness
sa·ti·ate
  sa·ti·at·ed
  sa·ti·at·ing
  sa·ti·a·tion
sa·ti·e·ty
sat·in
  sat·iny
sat·ire
  sa·tir·i·cal·ly
  sat·i·rist
  sat·i·rize
  sat·i·rized
  sat·i·riz·ing
sat·is·fac·tion
sat·is·fac·to·ry
  sat·is·fac·to·ri·ly
sat·is·fy
  sat·is·fied
  sat·is·fy·ing
  sat·is·fi·a·ble
sat·u·rate
  sat·u·rat·ed
  sat·u·rat·ing
  sat·u·ra·ble
  sat·u·ra·tion
sat·ur·nine
sa·tyr
  sa·tyr·ic
sauce
sau·cer
sau·cy
  sau·ci·ness
Sau·di Ara·bia
sau·er·bra·tne
sau·er·kraut
sau·na
saun·ter
sau·sage
sau·te
  sau·teed
  sau·tee·ing
sau·terne
sav·age
  sav·age·ness
  sav·age·ry
sa·van·na
sa·vant
save
  saved
  sav·ing
sav·ior
sa·vior-faire
sa·vor
sa·vory
  sa·vor·i·ly
  sa·vor·i·ness
sav·vy

sax·o·phone
sax·o·phon·ist
say
  said
  say·ing
scab
  scabbed
  scab·bing
scab·bard
scab·by
  scab·bi·ness
sca·bies
scaf·fold
  scaf·fold·ing
scal·a·wag
scald
  scald·ing
scale
  scaled
  scal·ing
  scal·i·ness
scal·lion
scal·lop
scalp
  scalp·er
scal·pel
scaly
  scal·i·ness
scamp·er
scan
  scanned
  scan·ning
  scan·ner
scan·dal
scan·dal·ize
  scan·dal·ized
  scan·dal·iz·ing
  scan·dal·i·za·tion
scan·dal·mon·ger
scan·dal·ous
Scan·di·na·via
scant
  scant·ness
scanty
  scant·i·ness
scape·goat
scap·u·la
scar
  scarred
  scar·ring
scar·ab
scarce
  scarce·ness
  scar·ci·ty
scare
  scared
  scar·ing
scarf
  scarfs
  scarves
scar·i·fy
  scar·i·fied
  scar·i·fy·ing
  scar·i·fi·ca·tion
scar·let
scarp
scary
  scar·i·er
  scar·i·est
scat
  scat·ted
  scat·ting
scathe
  scathed
  scath·ing
scat·ter
scat·ter-brained
scav·enge

scav·enged
scav·eng·ing
scav·en·ger
sce·nar·io
sce·nar·ist
scen·ery
sce·nic
sce·ni·cal
scent
scep·ter
sched·ule
sched·uled
sched·ul·ing
sche·ma
sche·mat·i·cal·ly
sche·ma·tize
sche·ma·tized
sche·ma·tiz·ing
scheme
schem·er
schem·ing
scher·zo
schism
schis·mat·ic
schis·mat·i·cal
schiz·oid
schiz·o·phre·nia
schiz·o·phren·ic
schol·ar
schol·ar·ly
schol·ar·li·ness
schol·ar·ship
scho·las·tic
scho·las·ti·cal
scho·las·ti·cism
school board
school·ing
school·teach·er
schoon·er
sci·at·ic
sci·at·i·ca
sci·ence
sci·en·tif·ic
sci·en·tif·i·cal·ly
sci·en·tist
scim·i·tar
scin·til·la
scin·til·lant
scin·til·late
scin·til·lat·ed
scin·til·lat·ing
scin·til·la·tion
sci·on
scis·sors
scle·ro·sis
scoff·er
scoff·ing·ly
scoff·law
scold·ing
scol·lop
sconce
scone
scoop·er
scoop·ful
scoot·er
scope
scorch
scorched
scorch·ing
score
scored
scor·ing
score·less
scor·er
score·keep·er
scorn
scorn·er
scorn·ful·ness

scor·pi·on
scot-free
scot·tie
scoun·drel
scoun·drel·ly
scour
scour·er
scourge
scourged
scourg·ing
scout·ing
scout·mas·ter
scowl
scrab·ble
scrab·bled
scrab·bling
scrag
scragged
scrag·ging
scrag·gly
scrag·gy
scram
scrammed
scram·ming
scram·ble
scram·bled
scram·bling
scrap
scrapped
scrap·ping
scrape
scraped
scrap·ing
scrap·per
scrap·py
scrap·pi·ness
scratch
scratchy
scratch·i·ness
scrawl
scrawny
scrawn·i·ness
scream·er
scream·ing
screech
screen
screen·er
screen·ing
screw·driv·er
screwy
scrib·ble
scrib·bled
scrib·bling
scrib·bler
scribe
scribed
scrib·ing
scrim·mage
scrim·maged
scrim·mag·ing
scrim·mag·er
scrimpy
scrimp·i·ness
scrim·shaw
script
scrip·ture
scrip·tur·al
script·writ·er
scriv·en·er
scroll-work
scrooge
scro·tum
scrounge
scroung·er
scroung·ing
scrub
scrubbed
scrub·bing

scrub·by
scruffy
scruff·i·ness
scrump·tious
scru·ple
scru·pu·lous
scru·pu·los·i·ty
scru·pu·lous·ness
scru·pu·lous·ly
scru·ta·ble
scru·ti·nize
scru·ti·nized
scru·ti·niz·er
scru·ti·niz·ing·ly
scru·ti·ny
scu·ba
scuf·fle
scuf·fled
scuf·fling
scul·lery
sculp·tor
sculp·tress
sculp·ture
sculp·tured
sculp·tur·ing
sculp·tur·al
scum
scum·my
scup·per
scur·ri·lous
scur·ril·i·ty
scur·ry
scur·ried
scur·ry·ing
scur·vy
scur·vi·ness
scut·tle
scut·tled
scut·tling
scut·tle·butt
scythe
scythed
scyth·ing
sea·far·ing
sea·far·er
sea·go·ing
seal·ant
sea lam·prey
seal·skin
sea·man·ship
seam·stress
seamy
seam·i·ness
se·ance
search
search·er
search·ing
search·light
sea·scape
sea·shell
sea·shore
sea·sick·ness
sea·side
sea·son
sea·son·er
sea·son·ing
sea·son·a·ble
sea·son·al
sea·son·al·ly
seat·ing
sea·wor·thy
sea·wor·thi·ness
se·ba·ceous
se·cant
se·cede
se·ced·ed
se·ced·ing
se·ces·sion

se·ces·sion·ist
se·clude
se·clud·ed
se·clud·ing
se·clud·ed·ness
se·clu·sion
se·clu·sive
sec·ond
sec·ond·ary
sec·ond·ar·i·ly
sec·ond-best
sec·ond-class
sec·ond-guess
sec·ond·hand
sec·ond-rate
se·cret
se·cre·cy
sec·re·tar·i·at
sec·re·tary
sec·re·tar·ies
sec·re·tar·i·al
se·crete
se·cret·ed
se·cret·ing
se·cre·tion
se·cre·tive
se·cre·to·ry
sec·tar·i·an
sec·tar·i·an·ism
sec·tion
sec·tion·al
sec·tor
sec·to·ri·al
sec·u·lar
sec·u·lar·ism
sec·u·lar·ize
sec·u·lar·ized
sec·u·lar·iz·ing
sec·u·lar·i·za·tion
se·cure
se·cured
se·cur·ing
se·cur·a·ble
se·cure·ness
se·cu·ri·ty
se·cu·ri·ties
se·dan
se·date
se·date·ness
se·da·tion
se·dat·ed
se·dat·ing
sed·a·tive
sed·en·tary
sed·en·tar·i·ness
sed·i·ment
sed·i·men·ta·ry
sed·i·men·ta·tion
se·di·tion
se·di·tion·ary
se·di·tious
se·duce
se·duced
se·duc·ing
se·duc·er
se·duc·i·ble
se·duce·a·ble
se·duc·tion
se·duce·ment
se·duc·tive
sed·u·lous
se·du·li·ty
sed·u·lous·ness
see
saw
seen
see·ing
seed·ling

seedy
seed·i·er
seed·i·est
seed·i·ly
seed·i·ness
seek
sought
seek·ing
seem·ing
seem·ly
seem·li·est
seem·li·ness
seep
seepy
seep·age
se·er
seer·ess
seer·suck·er
see·saw
seethe
seethed
seeth·ing
seg·ment
seg·men·tal
seg·men·tary
seg·men·ta·tion
seg·re·gate
seg·re·gat·ed
seg·re·gat·ing
seg·re·ga·tion
seg·re·ga·tion·ist
seine
seined
sein·ing
seis·mic
seis·mo·graph
seis·mog·ra·phy
seis·mol·o·gy
seis·mol·o·gist
seize
seized
seiz·ing
sei·zure
sel·dom
se·lect
se·lect·ed
se·lec·tor
se·lec·tion
se·lec·tive
se·lec·tiv·i·ty
self
selves
self-a·base·ment
self-ab·ne·ga·tion
self-a·buse
self-ad·dressed
self-ad·just·ing
self-ag·gran·dize·ment
self-ag·gran·diz·ing
self-as·sur·ance
self-as·sured
self-cen·tered
self-col·lect·ed
self-com·posed
self-con·fessed
self-con·fi·dence
self-con·fi·dent
self-con·scious
self-con·scious·ness
self-con·tained
self-con·trol
self-con·trolled
self-cor·rect·ing
self-crit·i·cism
self-de·cep·tion
self-de·cep·tive
self-de·feat·ing
self-de·fense

self-de·ni·al
self-de·ter·mi·na·tion
self-dis·ci·pline
self-ed·u·cat·ed
self-ef·fac·ing
self-em·ployed
self-es·teem
self-ev·i·dent
self-ex·plan·a·to·ry
self-ex·pres·sion
self-ful·fill·ment
self-gov·ern·ment
   self-gov·ern·ing
self-im·age
self-im·por·tance
self-im·posed
self-im·prove·ment
self-in·crim·i·na·tion
self-in·duced
self-in·dul·gence
self-in·flict·ed
self-in·ter·est
self·ish
   self·ish·ness
self·less
   self·less·ness
self-liq·ui·dat·ing
self-made
self-op·er·at·ing
self-per·pet·u·at·ing
self-pity
self-pol·li·na·tion
self-pos·sessed
self-pres·er·va·tion
self-pro·pelled
self-pro·tec·tion
self-re·al·i·za·tion
self-re·li·ance
self-re·spect
self-re·straint
self-right·eous
self-sac·ri·fice
self-sat·is·fied
   self-sat·is·fac·tion
   self-sat·is·fy·ing
self-serv·ice
self-serv·ing
self-suf·fi·cient
   self-suf·fi·cien·cy
self-sup·port
self-taught
sell
   sold
   sell·ing
sell·er
sell·out
sel·vage
selves
se·man·tics
   se·man·tic
   se·man·ti·cal
sem·a·phore
sem·blance
se·men
se·mes·ter
sem·i·an·nu·al
   sem·i·an·nu·al·ly
sem·i·ar·id
sem·i·au·to·mat·ic
sem·i·cir·cle
   sem·i·cir·cu·lar
sem·i·clas·si·cal
   sem·i·clas·sic
sem·i·co·lon
sem·i·con·duc·tor
   sem·i·con·duct·ing·
sem·i·con·scious
sem·i·de·tached

sem·i·fi·nal
sem·i·fi·nal·ist
sem·i·flu·id
sem·i·for·mal
sem·i·liq·uid
sem·i·month·ly
sem·i·nal
sem·i·nar
sem·i·nary
   sem·i·nar·i·an
sem·i·of·fi·cial
se·mi·ot·ic
sem·i·per·ma·nent
sem·i·per·me·able
sem·i·pre·cious
sem·i·pri·vate
sem·i·pro·fes·sion·al
sem·i·pub·lic
sem·i·skilled
sem·i·sol·id
Sem·ite
Se·mit·ic
Sem·i·tism
sem·i·trail·er
sem·i·trop·ics
   sem·i·trop·i·cal
sem·i·week·ly
sem·i·year·ly
sen·a·ry
sen·ate
sen·a·tor
   sen·a·to·ri·al
send
   sent
   send·ing
se·nes·cent
se·nes·cence
se·nile
se·nil·i·ty
sen·ior
sen·ior·i·ty
se·nor
   se·nors
se·no·ra
se·no·ri·ta
sen·sate
sen·sa·tion
sen·sa·tion·al
   sen·sa·tion·al·ly
   sen·sa·tion·al·ism
sense
   sensed
   sens·ing
sense·less
   sense·less·ness
sen·si·bil·i·ty
   sen·si·bil·i·ties
sen·si·ble
   sen·si·ble·ness
   sen·si·bly
sen·si·tive
   sen·si·tiv·i·ty
sen·si·tize
   sen·si·tized
   sen·si·tiz·ing
   sen·si·ti·za·tion
   sen·si·tiz·er
sen·sor
sen·so·ry
   sen·so·ri·al
sen·su·al
   sen·su·al·i·ty
   sen·su·al·ly
   sen·su·al·ism
   sen·su·al·ize
   sen·su·al·ized
   sen·su·al·iz·ing
   sen·su·al·i·za·tion

sen·su·ous
sen·tence
   sen·tenced
   sen·tenc·ing
sen·tient
sen·ti·ment
sen·ti·men·tal
   sen·ti·men·tal·ly
   sen·ti·men·tal·i·ty
   sen·ti·men·tal·i·ties
   sen·ti·men·tal·ize
   sen·ti·men·tal·ized
   sen·ti·men·tal·iz·ing
   sen·ti·men·ta·li·za·tion
sen·ti·nel
sen·try
   sen·tries
sep·a·ra·ble
   sep·a·ra·bil·i·ty
   sep·a·ra·bly
sep·a·rate
   sep·a·rat·ed
   sep·a·rat·ing
   sep·a·rate·ness
   sep·a·ra·tion
   sep·a·ra·tist
   sep·a·ra·tism
   sep·a·ra·tive
   sep·a·ra·tor
se·pia
sep·sis
sep·ten·ni·al
sep·tet
sep·tic
   sep·ti·cal·ly
   sep·tic·i·ty
sep·tu·a·ge·nar·i·an
sep·tu·ple
sep·ul·cher
   se·pul·chral
se·quel
se·quence
se·quen·tial
   se·quen·tial·ly
se·ques·ter
   se·ques·tered
   se·ques·tra·ble
   se·ques·tra·tion
se·quin
se·quoia
se·ra·pe
ser·aph
   ser·aphs
   ser·a·phim
   se·raph·ic
ser·e·nade
   ser·e·nad·ed
   ser·e·nad·ing
ser·en·dip·i·ty
se·rene
   se·ren·i·ty
serf·dom
serge
ser·geant
se·ri·al
   se·ri·al·ly
   se·ri·al·i·za·tion
   se·ri·al·ize
   se·ri·al·ized
   se·ri·al·iz·ing
se·ries
se·ri·ous
   se·ri·ous·ly
   se·ri·ous·ness
   se·ri·ous-mind·ed
ser·mon
   ser·mon·ize
   ser·mon·ized

ser·mon·iz·ing
   ser·mon·iz·er
se·rous
ser·pent
ser·pen·tine
ser·rate
   ser·rat·ed
   ser·rat·ing
   ser·ra·tion
se·rum
serv·ant
serve
   served
   serv·ing
ser·vice
   serv·iced
   serv·ic·ing
serv·ice·a·ble
   serv·ice·a·bil·i·ty
   serv·ice·a·ble·ness
   serv·ice·a·bly
ser·vile
   ser·vil·i·ty
   ser·vile·ness
ser·vi·tude
ser·vo·mech·an·ism
ses·ame
ses·qui·cen·ten·ni·al
ses·sion
set
   set
   set·ting
set·tee
set·ter
set·tle
   set·tled
   set·tling
set·tle·ment
set·tler
sev·en
   sev·enth
sev·en·teen
   sev·en·teenth
sev·en·ty
   sev·en·ti·eth
sev·er
   sev·er·a·bil·i·ty
   sev·er·a·ble
   sev·er·ance
sev·er·al
   sev·er·al·ly
se·vere
   se·ver·est
   se·vere·ness
   se·ver·i·ty
sew·age
sew·er
sew·er·age
sew·ing   ma·chine
sex·less
sex·tant
sex·tet
sex·ton
sex·tu·ple
sex·tu·plet
sex·u·al
   sex·u·al·ly
   sex·u·al·i·ty
sexy
   sex·i·er
   sex·i·est
   sex·i·ness
shab·by
   shab·bi·er
   shab·bi·ly
   shab·bi·ness
shack·le
   shack·led

shack·ling
shade
   shad·ed
   shad·ing
shad·ow
   shad·owy
shady
   shad·i·er
   shad·i·ly
   shad·i·ness
shaft·ing
shag
   shagged
   shag·ging
   shag·ged
shag·gy
   shag·gi·er
   shag·gi·ly
   shag·gi·ness
shake
   shook
   shak·en
   shak·ing
   shak·er
Shake·spear·e·an
shaky
   shak·i·ly
   shak·i·ness
shal·lot
shal·low
   shal·low·ness
sham
   shammed
   sham·ming
sha·man
sham·bles
shame
   shamed
   sham·ing
shame·faced
shame·ful
   shame·ful·ly
shame·less
   shame·less·ly
   shame·less·ness
sham·mer
sham·poo
   sham·pooed
   sham·poo·ing
sham·rock
shang·hai
   shang·haied
   shang·hai·ing
shan·tung
shan·ty
   shan·ties
shape
   shaped
   shap·ing
   shap·a·ble
   shap·er
shape·less
shape·ly
   shape·li·est
   shape·li·ness
share
   shared
   shar·ing
   shar·er
share·crop
   share·crop·per
   share·cropped
   share·crop·ping
share·hold·er
shark·skin
sharp·en
   sharp·en·er
sharp-eyed

sharp·ie
sharp·shoot·er
sharp-tongued
sharp-wit·ted
shat·ter
shat·ter·proof
shave
    shaved
    shav·en
    shav·ing
shawl
sheaf
    sheaves
shear
    sheared
    shear·ing
sheath
sheathe
    sheathed
    sheath·ing
    sheath·er
she·bang
shed
    shed·ding
sheen
    sheeny
sheep·herd·er
sheep·ish
sheep·skin
sheer
    sheer·ness
sheet·ing
sheik
shelf
    shelves
shell
    shelled
    shel·ly
shel·lac
    shel·lacked
    shel·lack·ing
shel·ter
shelve
    shelved
    shelv·ing
she·nan·i·gan
shep·herd
    shep·herd·ess
sher·bet
sher·iff
sher·ry
shib·bo·leth
shield
shift
    shift·ing·ness
shift·less
shifty
    shift·i·er
    shift·i·ly
    shift·i·ness
shil·le·lagh
shil·ling
shi·ly·shal·ly
shim·mer
    shim·mery
shim·my
    shim·mied
shin
    shinned
    shin·ning
shin·dig
shine
    shined
    shone
    shin·ing
shin·er
shin·gle
    shin·gled

shin·gling
shin·gles
shin·ing
shiny
    shin·i·ness
ship
    shipped
    ship·ping
    ship·pa·ble
ship·build·ing
ship·mate
ship·ment
shirk
    shirk·er
shish ke·bab
shiv·er
    shiv·ery
shoal
shock·er
shock·ing
shod·dy
    shod·di·ly
    shod·di·ness
shoe·mak·er
shoe·string
shoot
    shot
    shoot·ing
shop
    shopped
    shop·ping
shop·lift·er
    shop·lift·ing
shop·per
shore·line
short
    short·ly
    short·ness
short·age
short-change
    short-changed
    short-chang·ing
short-cir·cuit
short-com·ing
short-cut
    short-cut·ting
short·en
short·en·ing
short·hand
short-hand·ed
short-lived
short-sight·ed
short-tem·pered
short-wind·ed
shot·gun
    shot·gunned
    shot·gun·ning
should
shoul·der
shout·ing
shove
    shoved
    shov·ing
shov·el
    shov·eled
    shov·el·ing
show
    showed
    shown
    show·ing
show·case
    show·cased
    show·cas·ing
show·er
    show·ery
show·man·ship
showy
    show·i·ly

show·i·ness
shrap·nel
shred
    shred·ded
    shred·ding
    shred·der
shrew
    shrew·ish
shrewd
    shrewd·ly
    shrewd·ness
shriek
shrill
    shril·ly
    shrill·ness
shrimp
shrine
shrink
    shrunk·en
    shrink·a·ble
shrink·age
shrive
shriv·el
    shriv·eled
    shriv·el·ing
shroud
shrub·bery
shrug
    shrugged
    shrug·ging
shud·der
shuf·fle
    shuf·fled
    shuf·fling
shuf·fle·board
shun
    shunned
    shun·ning
    shun·ner
shunt
shut·ter
shut·tle
    shut·tled
    shut·tling
shy
    shied
    shy·ing
    shy·ly
    shy·ness
shy·ster
Si·a·mese
sib·i·lant
    sib·i·lance
sib·ling
sick·en
    sick·en·ing
sick·le
sick·ly
    sick·li·ness
sick·ness
sid·ed
side·line
    side·lined
    side·lin·ing
si·de·re·al
side·split·ting
side·step
    side·stepped
    side·step·ping
side·swipe
    side·swiped
    side·swip·ing
sid·ing
si·dle
    si·dled
    si·dling
siege
si·er·ra

si·es·ta
sieve
sift·er
sift·ings
sigh·ing
sight·ed
sight·less
sight·ly
sight-read·ing
sight·see·ing
    sight·see·er
sig·nal
    sig·naled
    sig·nal·ing
sig·na·to·ry
sig·na·ture
sig·net
sig·nif·i·cance
    sig·nif·i·cant
    sig·ni·fi·ca·tion
sig·ni·fy
    sig·ni·fied
    sig·ni·fy·ing
si·lage
si·lence
    si·lenced
    si·lenc·ing
si·lenc·er
si·lent
sil·hou·ette
    sil·hou·et·ted
    sil·hou·et·ting
sil·i·ca
sil·i·co·sis
sil·i·cone
silk·en
silky
    silk·i·est
    silk·i·ly
    silk·i·ness
sil·ly
    sil·li·er
    sil·li·est
    sil·li·ly
    sil·li·ness
si·lo
    si·los
    si·loed
    si·lo·ing
silt
    sil·ta·tion
    silty
sil·ver
sil·ver·fish
sil·ver-tongued
sil·ver·ware
sil·very
    sil·ver·i·ness
sim·i·an
sim·i·lar
    sim·i·lar·i·ty
    sim·i·lar·i·ties
sim·i·le
si·mil·i·tude
sim·mer
si·mon·ize
    si·mon·ized
    si·mon·iz·ing
sim·per
    sim·per·ing·ly
sim·ple
    sim·pler
    sim·plest
    sim·ple·ness
sim·ple-mind·ed
sim·ple·ton
sim·plex
sim·plic·i·ty

sim·pli·fy
    sim·pli·fied
    sim·pli·fy·ing
    sim·pli·fi·ca·tion
sim·plis·tic
    sim·plis·ti·cal·ly
sim·ply
sim·u·late
    sim·u·lat·ed
    sim·u·lat·ing
    sim·u·la·tion
    sim·u·la·tive
    sim·u·la·tor
si·mul·cast
si·mul·ta·ne·ous
    si·mul·ta·ne·ous·ness
    si·mul·ta·ne·i·ty
sin
    sinned
    sin·ning
    sin·ner
Si·nai
sin·cere
    sin·cer·i·ty
si·ne·cure
sin·ew
    sin·ewy
sin·ful
    sin·ful·ly
    sin·ful·ness
sing
    sang
    sung
    sing·ing
singe
    singed
    singe·ing
sing·er
sin·gle
    sin·gled
    sin·gling
    sin·gle·ness
sin·gle-breast·ed
sin·gle-hand·ed
sin·gle-mind·ed
sin·gle-space
    sin·gle-spaced
    sin·gle-spac·ing
sin·gle·ton
sin·gle-track
sin·gly
sing·song
sin·gu·lar
    sin·gu·lar·i·ty
    sin·gu·lar·i·ties
sin·is·ter
sink
    sank
    sunk
    sink·ing
sink·a·ble
sink·er
sink·hole
sin·less
sin·ner
sin·u·ate
    sin·u·at·ed
    sin·u·at·ing
sin·u·ous
    sin·u·os·i·ty
    sin·u·ous·ness
si·nus
    si·nus·i·tis
sip
    sipped
    sip·ping
si·phon
sire

sired
sir·ing
si·ren
sir·loin
si·roc·co
sis·sy
sis·ter
sis·ter·li·ness
sis·ter·ly
sis·ter-in-law
sit
sat
sit·ting
sit·ter
sit·ting
sit·u·ate
sit·u·at·ed
sit·u·at·ing
sit·u·a·tion
six-shoot·er
six·teen
six·teenth
sixth
six·ty
six·ti·eth
siz·a·ble
siz·a·ble·ness
siz·a·bly
size
sized
siz·ing
siz·zle
siz·zled
siz·zling
skate
skat·ed
skat·ing
skein
skel·e·ton
skel·e·tal
skep·tic
skep·ti·cal
skep·ti·cism
sketch
sketchy
sketch·i·ly
sketch·i·ness
skew·er
ski
skied
ski·ing
ski·er
skid
skid·ded
skid·ding
skiff
skilled
skil·let
skill·ful·ly
skim
skimmed
skim·ming
skimp
skimp·i·ly
skimp·i·ness
skimp·y
skin
skinned
skin·ning
skin-dive
skin-dived
skin-diving
skin·ny
skin·ni·er
skin·ni·est
skip
skipped
skip·ping

skip·per
skir·mish
skit·ter
skit·tish
skoal
skul·dug·ger·y
skulk·er
skunk
sky·div·ing
sky·jack·er
sky·rock·et
sky·scrap·er
sky·writ·ing
slab
slabbed
slab·bing
slack
slack·ness
slack·en
slack·er
slake
slaked
slak·ing
sla·lom
slam
slammed
slam·ming
slan·der
slan·der·er
slan·der·ous
slang
slang·i·ness
slangy
slant
slant·ways
slant·wise
slap
slapped
slap·ping
slap·hap·py
slap·stick
slasher
slash·ing
slat
slat·ted
slat·ting
slate
slat·ed
slat·ing
slat·tern
slat·tern·li·ness
slat·tern·ly
slaugh·ter
slave
slaved
slav·ing
slav·ery
slav·ish
sla·vish·ly
slay
slew
slain
slay·ing
slea·zy
slea·zi·ly
slea·zi·ness
sled
sled·ded
sled·ding
sledge
sleek
sleek·ness
sleep·less·ness
sleep·walk·ing
sleepy
sleep·i·ly
sleep·i·ness
sleet

sleety
sleet·i·ness
sleeve
sleeved
sleev·ing
sleeve·less
sleigh
sleight
slen·der
slen·der·ize
sleuth
slice
sliced
slic·ing
slick·er
slick·ness
slide
slid
slid·ing
slight
slim
slimmed
slim·ming
slim·mest
slim·ness
slime
slimy
slim·i·ness
sling
slung
sling·ing
slink
slunk
slink·ing
slinky
slip
slipped
slip·ping
slip·page
slip·per
slip·pery
slip·per·i·er
slip·per·i·est
slip·per·i·ness
slip·shod
slip·stream
slit
slit·ting
slith·er
slith·ery
sliv·er
slob·ber
sloe-eyed
slog
slogged
slog·ging
slo·gan
slo·gan·eer
sloop
slop
slopped
slop·ping
slope
sloped
slop·ing
slop·py
slop·pi·ly
slop·pi·ness
sloshy
slot
slot·ted
slot·ting
sloth
sloth·ful·ly
slouch
slouch·i·ly
slouchy
slough

sloughy
slov·en
slov·en·ly
slov·en·li·ness
slow·down
slow-mo·tion
sludge
sludgy
slug
slugged
slug·ging
slug·gard
slug·gard·li·ness
slug·gish
sluice
sluiced
sluic·ing
slum
slummed
slum·ming
slum·ber
slum·ber·er
slum·ber·ous
slump
slumped
slur
slurred
slur·ring
slush
slush·i·ness
slushy
slut
slut·tish
sly
sly·ly
sly·ness
smack·ing
small·pox
smart
smart·ness
smart al·eck
smash·ing
smat·ter·ing
smear
smeary
smear·i·ness
smell
smelled
smel·ling
smelly
smelt
smelt·er
smid·gen
smile
smil·ling·ly
smirch
smirk
smirk·ing·ly
smite
smote
smit·ten
smit·ting
smith·er·eens
Smith·so·ni·an
smock·ing
smog·gy
smoke
smoked
smok·ing
smok·er
smoke·house
smoke·stack
smoky
smok·i·ness
smol·der
smooth
smooth·ness
smooth·en

smor·gas·bord
smoth·er
smudge
smudged
smudg·ing
smudg·i·ness
smudgy
smug
smug·gest
smug·ly
smug·ness
smug·gle
smug·gled
smug·gling
smug·gler
smut
smut·ty
smut·ti·ness
snaf·fle
sna·fu
sna·fued
snag
snagged
snag·ging
snag·gy
snail
snake
snaked
snak·ing
snak·i·ly
snaky
snak·i·ness
snap
snapped
snap·ping
snap·drag·on
snap·py
snap·pish
snare
snared
snar·ing
snarl
snarly
snatch
snatchy
snaz·zy
snaz·zi·est
sneak·er
sneak·ing
sneaky
sneak·i·ly
sneak·i·ness
sneer
sneer·ing·ly
sneeze
sneezed
sneez·ing
sneezy
snick·er
snif·fle
snif·fled
snif·fling
snif·fy
snif·fi·ly
snif·ter
snig·ger
snip
snipped
snip·ping
snipe
sniped
snip·ing
snip·py
snip·pi·ness
snitch·er
sniv·el
sniv·eled
sniv·el·ing

snob
  snob·bery
  snob·bish·ness
snoop
  snoopy
  snoop·er
snooty
  snoot·i·ness
snooze
  snoozed
  snooz·ing
snore
  snored
  snor·ing
snor·kel
snort
  snort·ed
snot·ty
  snot·ti·ness
snout
snow·blow·er
snow·man
snow·mo·bile
snowy
  snow·i·er
  snow·i·ness
snub
  snubbed
  snub·bing
snuf·fle
  snuf·fled
  snuf·fling
snuffy
  snuff·i·ness
snug
  snugged
  snug·ging
  snug·ness
snug·gle
  snug·gled
  snug·gling
soak·ing
soap
  soapy
  soap·i·ness
soar
  soaring
sob
  sobbed
  sob·bing
so·ber
  so·ber·ness
so·bri·e·ty
so·bri·quet
soc·cer
so·cia·ble
  so·cia·bil·i·ty
  so·cia·ble·ness
  so·cia·bly
so·cial
  so·ci·al·i·ty
  so·cial·ly
so·cial·ism
  so·cial·ist
  so·cial·is·tic
so·cial·ite
so·cial·ize
  so·cial·ized
  so·cial·iz·ing
  so·cial·i·za·tion
so·ci·e·ty
  so·ci·e·ties
  so·ci·e·tal
so·ci·o·ec·o·nom·ic
so·ci·ol·o·gy
  so·ci·o·log·i·cal
  so·ci·ol·o·gist
so·ci·o·po·lit·i·cal

sock·et
sod
  sod·ded
  sod·ding
so·da
so·dal·i·ty
sod·den
  sod·den·ness
so·di·um
sod·omy
so·fa
soft
  soft·ness
  sof·ten
soft-heart·ed
soft-ped·al
  soft-ped·aled
  soft-ped·al·ing
soft-spo·ken
sog·gy
  sog·gi·ness
soi·ree
so·journ
sol·ace
  sol·aced
  sol·ac·ing
so·lar
so·lar·i·um
so·lar·ize
  so·lar·ized
  so·lar·iz·ing
  so·lar·i·za·tion
so·lar plex·us
sol·der
sol·dier
sol·e·cism
sole·ly
sol·emn
  sol·emn·ly
  sol·emn·ness
so·lem·ni·ty
sol·em·nize
  sol·em·nized
  sol·em·niz·ing
  sol·em·ni·za·tion
sole·ness
so·le·noid
so·lic·it
  so·lic·i·ta·tion
  so·lic·i·tor
  so·lic·i·tous
  so·lic·i·tude
sol·id
  so·lid·i·ty
  sol·id·ness
sol·i·dar·i·ty
so·lid·i·fy
  so·lid·i·fied
  so·lid·i·fy·ing
  so·lid·i·fi·ca·tion
sol·id·state
so·lil·o·quize
  so·lil·o·quized
  so·lil·o·quiz·ing
so·lil·o·quy
  so·lil·o·quies
sol·i·taire
sol·i·tary
  sol·i·tar·i·ness
sol·i·tude
so·lo
  so·loed
  so·lo·ing
  so·lo·ist
sol·stice
sol·u·ble
  sol·u·bil·i·ty
  sol·u·ble·ness

sol·u·bly
sol·ute
so·lu·tion
solve
  solved
  solv·ing
  solv·a·ble
  solv·a·bil·i·ty
  solv·a·ble·ness
sol·vent
  sol·ven·cy
so·mat·ic
som·ber
  som·ber·ness
som·bre·ro
some·body
som·er·sault
some·thing
some·where
som·nam·bu·late
  som·nam·bu·lat·ed
  som·nam·bu·lat·ing
  som·nam·bu·lant
  som·nam·bu·la·tion
  som·nam·bu·lism
  som·nam·bu·list
som·no·lent
  som·no·lence
  som·no·len·cy
so·nant
so·nar
so·na·ta
song·ster
  song·stress
son·ic
son-in-law
son·net
son·ny
  son·nies
so·no·rous
  so·nor·i·ty
  so·no·rous·ness
soothe
  soothed
  sooth·ing
sooth·say·er
sooty
  soot·i·ness
sop
  sopped
  sop·ping
soph·ist
  soph·ism
  so·phis·tic
  so·phis·ti·cal
so·phis·ti·cate
  so·phis·ti·cat·ed
  so·phis·ti·cat·ing
  so·phis·ti·ca·tion
soph·ist·ry
soph·o·more
soph·o·mor·ic
sop·o·rif·ic
sop·py
so·pra·no
Sor·bonne
sor·cer·er
  sor·cer·ess
  sor·cery
  sor·cer·ous
sor·did
  sor·did·ness
sore
  sor·est
  sore·ly
  sore·ness
sor·ghum
so·ror·i·ty

so·ror·i·ties
sor·rel
sor·row
  sor·row·ful·ly
sor·ry
  sor·ri·ly
  sor·ri·ness
sort·a·ble
sor·tie
sot
  sot·ted
  sot·tish·ness
sot·to vo·ce
sou·bri·quet
souf·fle
  souf·fleed
sought
soul·ful
  soul·ful·ly
soul·search·ing
sound
  sound·a·ble
  sound·ly
  sound·ness
sound·ing
sound·less·ly
soupy
  soup·i·er
sour
  sour·ish
  sour·ness
source
souse
  soused
  sous·ing
south·east·er·ly
south·east·ern
south·er·ly
south·ern
  south·ern·er
south·west·er·ly
south·west·ern
sou·ve·nir
sov·er·eign·
  sov·er·eign·ty
so·vi·et
  so·vi·et·ism
sow
  sowed
  sown
  sow·ing
soy·bean
space
  spaced
  spac·ing
space·craft
space·ship
spa·cious
  spa·cious·ness
spack·le
  spack·led
  spack·ling
spade
  spad·ed
  spad·ing
  spade·ful
spa·ghet·ti
span
  spanned
  span·ning
span·gle
  span·gled
  span·gling
Spain
  Span·iard
  Span·ish
span·iel
spank·ing

spar
  sparred
  spar·ring
spare
  spared
  spar·ing
  spare·ness
  spar·ing·ness
spar·kle
  spar·kled
  spar·kling
spar·kler
spar·row
sparse
  sparse·ness
spasm
spas·mod·ic
  spas·mod·i·cal·ly
spas·tic
  spas·ti·cal·ly
spat
  spat·ted
  spat·ting
spa·tial
  spa·cial
  spa·ti·al·i·ty
  spa·tial·ly
spat·ter
spat·u·la
spav·in
spawn
speak
  spok·en
  speak·ing
speak-easy
speak·er
spear·head
spear·mint
spe·cial
  spe·cial·ly
  spe·cial·ist
  spe·cial·ize
  spe·cial·ized
  spe·cial·iz·ing
  spe·cial·i·za·tion
  spe·cial·ty
  spe·cial·ties
spe·cie
spe·cif·ic
  spec·i·fi·able
  spe·cif·i·cal·ly
  spec·i·fic·i·ty
spec·i·fy
  spec·i·fied
  spec·i·fy·ing
  spec·i·fi·ca·tion
spec·i·men
spe·cious
  spe·ci·os·i·ty
  spe·cious·ness
speck·le
  speck·led
  speck·ling
spec·ta·cle
  spec·tac·u·lar
spec·ta·tor
spec·ter
spec·tral
spec·tro·scope
  spec·tros·co·py
spec·trum
spec·u·late
  spec·u·lat·ed
  spec·u·lat·ing
  spec·u·la·tion
  spec·u·la·tor
  spec·u·la·tive
speech·i·fy

speech·less
speed
  speed·ed
  sped
  speed·ing
speed·om·e·ter
speedy
  speed·i·ly
  speed·i·ness
spe·le·ol·o·gy
  spe·le·ol·o·gist
spell
  spelled
  spell·ing
spell·bound
  spell·bind·ing
spe·lun·ker
spend
  spent
  spend·ing
  spend·a·ble
spend·thrift
sper·ma·ceti
sper·mat·ic
sper·ma·to·zo·on
  sper·ma·to·zo·a
  sper·ma·to·zo·ic
spew·er
sphag·num
sphere
  sphered
  spher·ing
  spher·ic
  sphe·ric·i·ty
spher·i·cal
sphe·roid
  sphe·roi·dal
sphinc·ter
sphinx
spice
  spiced
  spic·ing
spi·cule
spicy
  spic·i·er
  spic·i·est
  spic·i·ly
  spic·i·ness
spi·der
spi·dery
spiel
spiffy
  spiff·i·ness
spig·ot
spike
  spiked
  spiky
spill
  spilled
  spill·ing
spil·lage
spin
  spun
  spin·ning
spin·ach
spi·nal
spin·dle
  spin·dled
  spin·dling
spin·dly
spine·less
spin·et
spin·na·ker
spin·ner
spin·ning
spin·ster
spiny
  spin·i·ness

spi·ra·cle
spi·ral
  spi·raled
  spi·ral·ing
  spi·ral·ly
spire
  spired
  spir·ing
spir·it
  spir·it·ed
  spir·it·less·ness
spir·i·tous
spir·it·u·al
  spir·it·u·al·ism
  spir·it·u·al·ist
  spir·it·u·al·i·ty
  spir·it·u·al·ize
  spir·it·u·al·ized
  spir·it·u·al·iz·ing
  spir·it·u·al·i·za·tion
spir·it·u·ous
  spir·it·u·os·i·ty
spi·ro·chete
spit
  spat
  spit·ting
spite
  spit·ing
  spite·ful
spit·tle
spit·toon
splash
  splashy
  splash·i·ness
splat·ter
splay·foot
spleen
  spleen·ful
  sple·net·ic
splen·did
  splen·dif·er·ous
splen·dor
splice
  spliced
  splic·ing
splin·ter
split
  split·ting
split·lev·el
split·sec·ond
splotch
  splotchy
splurge
  splurged
  splurg·ing
splut·ter
spoil
  spoiled
  spoil·ing
spoil·age
spoil·er
spoke
  spo·ken
spokes·man
  spokes·wom·an
spo·li·a·tion
sponge
  sponged
  spong·ing
spong·er
spon·gy
  spon·gi·ness
spon·sor
spon·ta·ne·i·ty
spon·ta·ne·ous
  spon·ta·ne·ous·ness
spook
  spooky

spook·i·ness
spoon·er·ism
spoon-feed
  spoon-fed
spoon·fuls
spo·rad·ic
  spo·rad·i·cal·ly
spo·ran·gi·um
spore
sport
  sport·ful·ly
  sport·ing
  spor·tive
sports·cast·er
sports·man
sports·man·ship
sporty
  sport·i·ness
spot
  spot·ted
  spot·ting
spot·less·ness
spot·ty
  spot·ti·ly
  spot·ti·ness
spouse
sprained
sprawl
spray·er
spread
  spread·ing
  spread-ea·gle
spread·er
sprig
spright·ly
  spright·li·ness
spring
  sprang
  sprung
  spring·ing
spring-clean·ing
spring·time
springy
  spring·i·ness
sprin·kle
  sprin·kled
  sprin·kling
  sprink·ler
sprint
  sprint·er
sprock·et
spruce
  spruced
  spruc·ing
  spruce·ly
spry
  spry·ness
spume
  spumed
  spum·ing
  spum·ous
spunky
  spunk·i·ness
spur
  spurred
  spur·ring
spu·ri·ous
  spu·ri·ous·ness
spurner
spurt
  spur·tive
sput·nik
sput·ter
spu·tum
spy
  spies
  spied
  spy·ing

squab·ble
  squab·bled
  squab·bling
squad·ron
squal·id
  squal·id·ness
squall
  squally
squal·or
squan·der
square
  squared
  squar·ing
  square·ness
  squar·ish
square-danc·ing
squash
  squashy
  squash·i·ness
squat
  squat·ted
  squat·ting
  squat·ness
squat·ter
squat·ty
squawk
  squawky
squeak
  squeak·er
  squeak·ing·ly
  squeaky
squeal
  squeal·er
squeam·ish
  squeam·ish·ness
squee·gee
squeeze
  squeezed
  squeez·ing
  squeez·er
squelch
squib
squid
squig·gle
  squig·gled
  squig·gling
squint
  squint·er
  squint·ing·ly
  squinty
squire
squirm
  squirmy
squir·rel
squirt
squish
  squishy
stab
  stabbed
  stab·bing
  stab·ber
sta·bile
sta·bil·i·ty
  sta·bil·i·ties
sta·bi·lize
  sta·bi·lized
  sta·bi·liz·ing
  sta·bi·li·za·tion
  sta·bi·liz·er
sta·ble
  sta·bled
  sta·bling
stac·ca·to
sta·di·um
staff
stag
  stagged
  stag·ging

stage
  staged
  stag·ing
  stagy
stag·ger
  stag·ger·ing
stag·nant
  stag·nan·cy
stag·nate
  stag·nat·ed
  stag·nat·ing
  stag·na·tion
staid·ness
stain
  stained
  stain·less
stake
  staked
  stak·ing
stake·hold·er
sta·lac·tite
sta·lag·mite
stale
  stale·ness
stale·mate
  stale·mat·ed
  stale·mat·ing
stalk
  stalked
  stalky
stalled
stal·lion
stal·wart
sta·men
stam·i·na
stam·mer
  stam·mer·ing·ly
stam·pede
  stam·ped·ed
  stam·ped·ing
stance
stand
  stand·ing
stand·ard
stand·ard·ize
  stand·ard·ized
  stand·ard·iz·ing
  stand·ard·i·za·tion
stand·point
stan·za
staph·y·lo·coc·cus
sta·ple
  sta·pled
  sta·pling
  sta·pler
star
  starred
  star·ring
starchy
  starch·i·ness
star·dom
stare
  stared
  star·ing
star·gaze
  star·gazed
  star·gaz·ing
stark·ly
star·let
star·ling
star·ry
  star·ri·ness
star·ry-eyed
star-span·gled
start·er
star·tle
  star·tled
  star·tling

star·va·tion
starve
  starved
  starv·ing
starve·ling
sta·sis
state
  stat·ed
  stat·ing
  state·ment
state·craft
state·hood
state·less
state·ly
  state·li·er
  state·li·ness
states·man
  states·man·ship
stat·ic
  stat·i·cal·ly
sta·tion
sta·tion·ary
sta·tion·er
sta·tion·ery
stat·ism
  stat·ist
sta·tis·tic
  sta·tis·ti·cal
  sta·tis·ti·cal·ly
  stat·is·ti·cian
  sta·tis·tics
sta·tor
stat·u·ary
stat·ue
stat·u·esque
stat·u·ette
stat·ure
sta·tus
sta·tus quo
stat·ute
  stat·u·to·ry
staunch
stave
  staved
  stav·ing
stay
  stayed
  stay·ing
stead·fast
  stead·fast·ness
steady
  stead·ied
  stead·y·ing
  stead·i·ly
  stead·i·ness
steal
  stol·en
  steal·ing
stealth
  stealthy
  stealth·i·ly
  stealth·i·ness
steam·er
steam·fit·ter
steam·roll·er
steam·ship
steamy
  steam·i·ness
sted·fast
steel·work·er
steely
  steel·i·ness
steep
  steep·ly
  steep·ness
steep·en
stee·ple
stee·ple·chase

steer
  steer·a·ble
steer·age
stein
stel·lar
stem
  stemmed
  stem·ming
  stem·less
stem·wind·ing
stench
sten·cil
  sten·ciled
  sten·cil·ing
ste·nog·ra·pher
ste·nog·ra·phy
sten·o·graph·ic
sten·o·graph·i·cal·ly
sten·to·ri·an
step
  stepped
  step·ping
step·broth·er
step·child·ren
step·daugh·ter
step·fa·ther
step·lad·der
step·moth·er
steppe
step·ping·stone
ster·eo
ster·e·o·phon·ic
  ster·e·o·phon·i·cal·ly
  ster·e·o·scope
  ster·e·o·scop·ic
ster·e·o·type
  ster·e·o·typed
  ster·e·o·typ·ing
ster·ile
ste·ril·i·ty
ster·i·lize
  ster·i·lized
  ster·i·liz·ing
  ster·i·li·za·tion
  ster·i·liz·er
ster·ling
stern
  stern·ly
  stern·ness
ster·num
ster·oid
steth·o·scope
ste·ve·dore
stew·ard
  stew·ard·ess
stick
  stuck
  stick·ing
stick·er
stick·ler
stick-to-it·ive·ness
sticky
  stick·i·ness
stiff
  stiff·ness
  stiff·en
sti·fle
  sti·fled
  sti·fling
stig·ma
  stig·ma·tic
  stig·mat·i·cal·ly
  stig·ma·tize
  stig·ma·tized
  stig·ma·tiz·ing
  stig·ma·ti·za·tion
stile
sti·let·to

still·born
still·ness
stilt·ed
stim·u·late
  stim·u·lat·ed
  stim·u·lat·ing
  stim·u·lant
  stim·u·la·tion
  stim·u·la·tive
  stim·u·lus
  stim·u·li
sting
  stung
  sting·ing
stin·gy
  stin·gi·ness
stink
  stank
  stunk
  stink·ing
  stinky
stint·ing
sti·pend
stip·ple
  stip·pled
  stip·pling
stip·u·late
  stip·u·lat·ed
  stip·u·lat·ing
  stip·u·la·tion
  stip·u·la·to·ry
stir
  stirred
  stir·ring
stir-rup
stitch
stock·ade
stock·brok·er
stock·hold·er
stock·ing
stock·pile
  stock·piled
  stock·pil·ing
stocky
  stock·i·ness
stodgy
  stodg·i·ness
sto·ic
  sto·i·cal
stoke
  stoked
  stok·ing
stol·id
  sto·lid·i·ty
  stol·id·ly
stom·ach
stom·ach·ache
stone
  stoned
  ston·ing
stone·ma·son
stony
  ston·i·er
  ston·i·ness
stop
  stopped
  stop·ping
stop·page
stop·per
stor·age
store
  stored
  stor·ing
sto·ried
stormy
  storm·i·ness
story
  sto·ries

sto·ry·tell·er
stout
  stout·ly
  stout·ness
stout-heart·ed
stove
  stoved
  stov·ing
stow·age
stow·a·way
strad·dle
  strad·dled
  strad·dling
strafe
  strafed
  straf·ing
strag·gle
  strag·gled
  strag·gling
  strag·gler
  strag·gly
straight·a·way
straight-edge
straight·en
straight·for·ward
straight·way
strain·er
strait·en
strait·jack·et
strait-laced
strange
  strang·er
  strang·est
  strange·ly
  strange·ness
stran·ger
stran·gle
  stran·gled
  stran·gling
  stran·gler
stran·gu·la·tion
  stran·gu·late
  stran·gu·lat·ed
  stran·gu·lat·ing
strap
  strapped
  strap·ping
  strap·less
strat·a·gem
stra·te·gic
  stra·te·gi·cal·ly
strat·e·gy
  strat·e·gies
  strat·e·gist
strat·i·fy
  strat·i·fied
  strat·i·fy·ing
  strat·i·fi·ca·tion
stra·to·cu·mu·lus
strat·o·sphere
  strat·o·spher·ic
stra·tum
stra·tus
straw·ber·ry
  straw·ber·ries
stray·ing
streak
  streaky
stream·er
stream·line
  stream·lined
  stream·lin·ing
street·walk·er
strength·en
stren·u·ous
  stren·u·os·i·ty
  stren·u·ous·ly
strep·to·coc·cus

strep·to·my·cin
stress
  stress·ful·ly
stretch
  stretch·a·bil·i·ty
  stretch·a·ble
  stretch·er
strew
  strewed
  strew·ing
stri·ate
  stri·at·ed
  stri·at·ing
  stri·a·tion
strick·en
strict
  strict·ly
  strict·ness
stric·ture
stride
  strode
  strid·den
  strid·ing
stri·dent
  stri·den·cy
strid·u·late
  strid·u·la·tion
  strid·u·lous
strife
  strife·less
strike
  struck
  strick·en
  strik·ing
strike·break·er
string
  strung
  string·ing
strin·gent
  strin·gen·cy
  strin·gent·ly
stringy
  string·i·ness
strip
  stripped
  strip·ping
strip·crop·ping
stripe
  striped
  strip·ing
strip·ling
strip·per
strip·tease
strive
  strove
  striv·en
  striv·ing
stro·bo·scope
  stro·bo·scop·ic
stroke
  stroked
  strok·ing
stroll·er
strong
  strong·ly
  strong·ness
strong-mind·ed
strop
  stropped
  strop·ping
struc·tural
  struc·tur·al·ly
struc·ture
  struc·tured
  struc·tur·ing
strug·gle
  strug·gled
  strug·gling

strug·gler
strum
strummed
strum·ming
strum·pet
strut
strut·ted
strut·ting
strych·nine
stub
stubbed
stub·bing
stub·by
stub·ble
stub·bled
stub·bly
stub·born
stub·born·ly
stub·born·ness
stuc·co
stuc·coed
stuc·co·ing
stud
stud·ded
stud·ding
stu·dent
stud·ied
stud·ied·ness
stu·dio
stu·di·ous
stu·di·ous·ly
stu·di·ous·ness
study
stud·ies
stud·ied
stud·y·ing
stuff·er
stuff·ing
stuffy
stuff·i·ness
stul·ti·fy
stul·ti·fied
stul·ti·fy·ing
stul·ti·fi·ca·tion
stum·ble
stum·bled
stum·bling
stump
stumpy
stun
stunned
stun·ning
stunt
stunt·ed
stunt·ed·ness
stu·pe·fy
stu·pe·fied
stu·pe·fy·ing
stu·pe·fac·tion
stu·pen·dous
stu·pen·dous·ly
stu·pen·dous·ness
stu·pid
stu·pid·i·ty
stu·pid·ly
stu·pid·ness
stu·por
stu·por·ous
stur·dy
stur·di·est
stur·geon
stut·ter
stut·ter·ing·ly
style
styled
styl·ing
styl·ish
styl·ish·ness

styl·ist
sty·lis·tic
sty·lis·ti·cal
sty·lis·ti·cal·ly
styl·ize
styl·ized
styl·iz·ing
styl·i·za·tion
sty·lus
sty·mie
sty·mied
sty·mie·ing
styp·tic
sty·rene
suave
suave·ly
suave·ness
suav·i·ty
sub
subbed
sub·bing
sub·al·tern
sub·arc·tic
sub·as·sem·bly
sub·as·sem·bler
sub·atom·ic
sub·base·ment
sub·chas·er
sub·com·mit·tee
sub·con·scious
sub·con·scious·ness
sub·con·ti·nent
sub·con·trac·tor
sub·cul·ture
sub·cu·ta·ne·ous
sub·di·vide
sub·di·vid·ed
sub·di·vid·ing
sub·di·vi·sion
sub·due
sub·dued
sub·du·ing
sub·en·try
sub·en·tries
sub·freez·ing
sub·group
sub·hu·man
sub·ject
sub·jec·tion
sub·jec·tive
sub·jec·tive·ly
sub·jec·tive·ness
sub·jec·tiv·i·ty
sub·join
sub·ju·gate
sub·ju·gat·ed
sub·ju·gat·ing
sub·ju·ga·tion
sub·junc·tive
sub·lease
sub·leased
sub·leas·ing
sub·let
sub·let·ting
sub·li·mate
sub·li·mat·ed
sub·li·mat·ing
sub·li·ma·tion
sub·lime
sub·lim·est
sub·lime·ly
sub·lime·ness
sub·lim·i·ty
sub·lim·i·nal
sub·lim·i·nal·ly
sub·ma·chine
sub·mar·gin·al
sub·ma·rine

sub·merge
sub·merged
sub·merg·ing
sub·mer·gence
sub·mer·gi·ble
sub·merse
sub·mersed
sub·mers·ing
sub·mers·i·ble
sub·mer·sion
sub·mi·cro·scop·ic
sub·mis·sion
sub·mis·sive
sub·miss·ive·ly
sub·miss·ive·ness
sub·mit
sub·mit·ted
sub·mit·ting
sub·nor·mal
sub·nor·mal·i·ty
sub·or·bit·al
sub·or·di·nate
sub·or·di·nat·ed
sub·or·di·nat·ing
sub·or·di·nate·ly
sub·or·di·nate·ness
sub·or·di·na·tion
sub·or·di·na·tive
sub·orn
sub·or·na·tion
sub·poe·na
sub·poe·naed
sub·poe·na·ing
sub·re·gion
sub·rosa
sub·scribe
sub·scribed
sub·scrib·ing
sub·scrib·er
sub·scrip·tion
sub·se·quent
sub·se·quence
sub·se·quent·ly
sub·se·quent·ness
sub·ser·vi·ent
sub·ser·vi·ence
sub·ser·vi·en·cy
sub·ser·vi·ent·ly
sub·side
sub·sid·ed
sub·sid·ing
sub·sid·ence
sub·sid·i·ary
sub·sid·i·ar·ies
sub·si·dize
sub·si·dized
sub·si·diz·ing
sub·si·di·za·tion
sub·si·dy
sub·si·dies
sub·sist
sub·sist·ence
sub·soil
sub·son·ic
sub·spe·cies
sub·stance
sub·stand·ard
sub·stan·tial
sub·stan·ti·al·i·ty
sub·stan·tial·ly
sub·stan·tial·ness
sub·stan·ti·ate
sub·stan·ti·at·ed
sub·stan·ti·at·ing
sub·stan·ti·a·tion
sub·stan·ti·a·tive
sub·stan·tive
sub·stan·ti·val

sub·stan·ti·val·ly
sub·stan·tive·ly
sub·stan·tive·ness
sub·sta·tion
sub·sti·tute
sub·sti·tut·ed
sub·sti·tut·ing
sub·sti·tut·able
sub·sti·tu·tion
sub·sti·tu·tion·al
sub·stra·tum
sub·stra·ta
sub·struc·ture
sub·sume
sub·sumed
sub·sum·ing
sub·sum·a·ble
sub·sump·tive
sub·sump·tion
sub·teen
sub·tend
sub·ter·fuge
sub·ter·ra·ne·an
sub·ter·ra·ne·ous
sub·ti·tle
sub·tle
sub·tle·ness
sub·tle·ty
sub·tle·ties
sub·tly
sub·tly
sub·tract
sub·tract·er
sub·trac·ion
sub·trac·tive
sub·tra·hend
sub·trop·i·cal
sub·trop·ic
sub·urb
sub·ur·ban
sub·ur·ban·ite
sub·ur·bia
sub·vene
sub·ven·tion
sub·version
sub·version·ary
sub·versive
sub·versive·ly
sub·versive·ness
sub·vert
sub·vert·er
sub·way
suc·ceed
suc·ceed·ing
suc·cess
suc·cess·ful·ly
suc·cess·ful·ness
suc·ces·sion
suc·ces·sion·al
suc·ces·sive
suc·ces·sive·ly
suc·ces·sive·ness
suc·ces·sor
suc·cinct
suc·cinct·ly
suc·cinct·ness
suc·cor
suc·cor·er
suc·co·tash
suc·cu·lent
suc·cu·lence
suc·cu·len·cy
suc·cu·lent·ly
suc·cumb
suck·er
suck·le
suck·led
suck·ling

su·crose
suc·tion
sud·den
sud·den·ly
sud·den·ness
sudsy
suds·i·er
sue
sued
su·ing
su·er
suede
su·et
suf·fer
suf·fer·a·ble
suf·fer·a·bly
suf·fer·er
suf·fer·ing
suf·fer·ance
suf·fice
suf·ficed
suf·fic·ing
suf·fi·cien·cy
suf·fi·cien·cies
suf·fi·cient
suf·fi·cient·ly
suf·fix
suf·fo·cate
suf·fo·cat·ed
suf·fo·cat·ing
suf·fo·ca·tion
suf·fo·ca·tive
suf·ra·gan
suf·frage
suf·fra·gette
suf·frag·ist
suf·fuse
suf·fused
suf·fus·ing
suf·fu·sion
suf·fu·sive
sug·ar
sug·ary
sug·ar·coat
sug·gest
sug·gest·i·ble
sug·gest·i·bil·i·ty
sug·ges·tion
sug·ges·tive
sug·ges·tive·ly
sug·ges·tive·ness
su·i·cide
su·i·cid·al
suit·a·ble
suit·a·bil·i·ty
suit·a·ble·ness
suit·a·bly
suite
suit·ing
suit·or
sul·fa·nil·a·mide
sul·fate
sul·fide
sul·fur
sul·fu·ric
sul·fur·ous
sulky
sulk·i·ly
sulk·i·ness
sul·len
sul·len·ly
sul·len·ness
sul·ly
sul·lied
sul·ly·ing
sul·tan
sul·tana
sul·tan·ate

sul·try
sul·tri·ly
sul·tri·ness
sum
summed
sum·ming
su·mac
sum·ma·rize
sum·ma·rized
sum·ma·riz·ing
sum·ma·ri·za·tion
sum·ma·ry
sum·ma·ries
sum·mar·i·ly
sum·mar·i·ness
sum·ma·tion
sum·ma·tion·al
sum·mer
sum·mit
sum·mon
sum·mons
sump·tu·ary
sump·tu·ous
sump·tu·ous·ly
sump·tu·ous·ness
sun
sunned
sun·ning
sun·bathe
sun·bathed
sun·bath·ing
sun·bath·er
sun·burn
sun·burned
sun·burnt
sun·burn·ing
sun·dae
sun·der
sun·der·ance
sun·di·al
sun·dry
sun·dries
sun·flow·er
sun·glass·es
sunk·en
sun·ny
sun·ni·er
sun·ni·ness
sun·shine
sun·spot
sun·stroke
sup
supped
sup·ping
su·per·a·bun·dant
su·per·a·bun·dance
su·per·a·bun·dant·ly
su·per·an·nu·ate
su·per·an·nu·at·ed
su·per·an·nu·at·ing
su·per·an·nu·a·tion
su·perb
su·perb·ly
su·perb·ness
su·per·car·go
su·per·charge
su·per·charged
su·per·charg·ing
su·per·charg·er
su·per·cil·i·ous
su·per·cil·i·ous·ly
su·per·cil·i·ous·ness
su·per·e·go
su·per·e·rog·a·to·ry
su·per·fi·cial
su·per·fi·ci·al·i·ty
su·per·fi·ci·al·i·ties
su·per·fi·cial·ly

su·per·fi·cial·ness
su·per·fine
su·per·flu·ous
su·per·flu·i·ty
su·per·flu·ous·ly
su·per·flu·ous·ness
su·per·high·way
su·per·hu·man
su·per·im·pose
su·per·im·posed
su·per·im·pos·ing
su·per·im·po·si·tion
super·in·duce
super·in·tend
su·per·in·tend·ence
su·per·in·tend·en·cy
su·per·in·tend·ent
su·pe·ri·or
su·pe·ri·or·i·ty
su·pe·ri·or·ly
su·per·la·tive
su·per·la·tive·ly
su·per·la·tive·ness
su·per·man
su·per·mar·ket
su·per·nal
su·per·nat·u·ral
su·per·nat·u·ral·ism
su·per·nat·u·ral·ly
su·per·nat·u·ral·ness
su·per·nu·mer·ary
su·per·pow·er
su·per·scribe
su·per·scrip·tion
su·per·script
su·per·sede
su·per·sed·ed
su·per·sed·ing
su·per·son·ic
su·per·son·i·cal·ly
su·per·sti·tion
su·per·sti·tious
su·per·sti·tious·ly
su·per·sti·tious·ness
su·per·struc·ture
su·per·tank·er
su·per·vene
su·per·vened
su·per·ven·ing
super·ven·tion
su·per·vise
su·per·vised
su·per·vis·ing
su·per·vi·sion
su·per·vi·sor
su·per·vi·so·ry
su·pine
su·pine·ness
sup·per
sup·plant
sup·plan·ta·tion
sup·ple
sup·plest
sup·ple·ness
sup·ple·ment
sup·ple·men·tal
sup·ple·men·ta·ry
sup·ple·men·ta·tion
sup·pli·ant
sup·pli·cate
sup·pli·cat·ed
sup·pli·cat·ing
sup·pli·cant
sup·pli·ca·tion
sup·pli·ca·to·ry
sup·ply
sup·plied
sup·ply·ing

sup·plies
sup·pli·er
sup·port
sup·port·a·ble
sup·port·a·bly
sup·port·er
sup·port·ive
sup·pose
sup·posed
sup·pos·ing
sup·pos·a·ble
sup·pos·a·bly
sup·pos·ed·ly
sup·po·si·tion
sup·po·si·tion·al·ly
sup·pos·i·to·ry
sup·press
sup·press·i·ble
sup·pres·sion
sup·pres·sor
sup·pu·rate
sup·pu·rat·ed
sup·pu·rat·ing
sup·pu·ra·tion
su·prem·a·cy
su·prem·a·cist
su·preme
su·preme·ly
su·preme·ness
sur·cease
sur·charge
sur·charged
sur·charg·ing
sur·cin·gle
sure
sur·er
sur·est
sure·ly
sure·ness
sure-foot·ed
sure·ty
surf
surf·board
surf·ing
sur·face
sur·faced
sur·fac·ing
sur·feit
surge
surged
surg·ing
sur·geon
sur·gery
sur·gi·cal
sur·gi·cal·ly
sur·ly
sur·li·ly
sur·li·ness
sur·mise
sur·mised
sur·mis·ing
sur·mount
sur·mount·a·ble
sur·name
sur·pass
sur·pass·a·ble
sur·pass·ing
sur·plice
sur·plus
sur·plus·age
sur·prise
sur·prised
sur·pris·ing
sur·pris·al
sur·re·al·ism
sur·re·al·ist
sur·re·al·is·tic
sur·re·al·is·ti·cal·ly

sur·ren·der
sur·rep·ti·tious
sur·rep·ti·tious·ly
sur·rep·ti·tious·ness
sur·rey
sur·ro·gate
sur·ro·gat·ed
sur·ro·gat·ing
sur·round
sur·round·ings
sur·tax
sur·veil·lance
sur·veil·lant
sur·vey
sur·vey·ing
sur·vey·or
sur·vive
sur·vived
sur·viv·ing
sur·viv·al
sur·vi·vor
sus·cep·ti·ble
sus·cep·ti·bil·i·ty
sus·cep·ti·ble·ness
sus·cep·ti·bly
sus·pect
sus·pend
sus·pend·er
sus·pense
sus·pen·sion
sus·pi·cion
sus·pi·cious
sus·pi·cious·ly
sus·pi·cious·ness
sus·tain
sus·tain·a·ble
sus·tain·er
sus·tain·ment
sus·te·nance
su·ture
su·tured
su·tur·ing
su·ze·rain
svelte
svelte·ly
svelte·ness
swab
swabbed
swab·bing
swad·dle
swad·dled
swad·dling
swag·ger
swag·ger·ing
swal·low
swa·mi
swamp
swampy
swamp·i·ness
swank
swank·i·ly
swank·i·ness
swanky
swan dive
swap
swapped
swap·ping
sward
swarthy
swarth·i·er
swarth·i·ness
swash·buck·ling
swas·ti·ka
swat
swat·ted
swat·ting
swat·ter
swathe

swathed
swath·ing
sway
sway·a·ble
sway·backed
swear
swore
sworn
swear·ing
swear·er
sweat
sweat·ing
sweat·i·ly
sweat·i·ness
sweaty
sweat·er
Swe·den
Swed·ish
sweep
swept
sweep·ing
sweep·ing·ness
sweep·stakes
sweet
sweet·ish
sweet·ly
sweet·ness
sweet·en
swell
swelled
swoll·en
swell·ing
swel·ter
swel·ter·ing
swerve
swerved
swerv·ing
swift
swift·ly
swift·ness
swig
swigged
swig·ging
swill
swim
swam
swum
swim·ming
swim·mer
swin·dle
swin·dled
swin·dling
swin·dler
swine
swin·ish
swing
swung
swing·ing
swing·a·ble
swing·er
swipe
swip·ed
swip·ing
swirl
swirl·ing·ly
swirly
swish
swishy
switch
switch·blade
switch·board
switch-hit·ter
Switz·er·land
swiv·el
swiv·eled
swiv·el·ing
swiz·zle
swoon

swoon·ed
swoon·ing·ly
swoop
swop
swopped
swop·ping
sword
swords·man
syc·a·more
syc·o·phant
syc·o·phan·cy
syc·o·phan·tic
syc·o·phan·ti·cal
syl·lab·ic
syl·lab·i·cate
syl·lab·i·ca·tion
syl·lab·i·fy
syl·lab·i·fi·ca·tion
syl·la·ble
syl·la·bus
syl·lo·gism
syl·lo·gis·tic
sylph·like
syl·van
sym·bi·o·sis
sym·bol
sym·bol·ic
sym·bol·i·cal
sym·bol·ism
sym·bol·ize
sym·bol·ized
sym·bol·iz·ing
sym·bol·i·za·tion
sym·me·try
sym·met·ric
sym·met·ri·cal
sym·pa·thet·ic
sym·pa·thet·i·cal·ly
sym·pa·thize
sym·pa·thized
sym·pa·thiz·ing
sym·pa·thiz·er
sym·pa·thiz·ing·ly
sym·pa·thy
sym·pa·thies
sym·pho·ny
sym·pho·nies
sym·phon·ic
sym·po·si·um
sym·po·sia
symp·tom
symp·to·mat·ic
symp·to·mat·i·cal
symp·to·mat·i·cal·ly
syn·a·gogue
syn·a·gog·al
syn·a·gog·i·cal
syn·chro·nism
syn·chro·nis·tic
syn·chro·nis·ti·cal
syn·chro·nis·ti·cal·ly
syn·chro·nize
syn·chro·nized
syn·chro·niz·ing
syn·chro·ni·za·tion
syn·chro·niz·er
syn·chro·nous
syn·chro·nous·ly
syn·chro·nous·ness
syn·chro·tron
syn·co·pate
syn·co·pat·ed
syn·co·pat·ing
syn·co·pa·tion
syn·co·pa·tor
syn·cre·tism
syn·cre·tic
syn·di·cate

syn·di·cat·ed
syn·di·cat·ing
syn·di·ca·tion
syn·di·ca·tor
syn·drome
syn·ec·do·che
syn·ecol·o·gy
syn·er·gism
syn·od
syn·od·al
syn·on·ym
syn·on·y·mous
syn·on·y·my
syn·op·sis
syn·op·tic
syn·tax
syn·tac·tic
syn·tac·ti·cal
syn·the·sis
syn·the·sist
syn·the·size
syn·the·sized
syn·the·siz·ing
syn·thet·ic
syn·thet·i·cal
syn·thet·i·cal·ly
syph·i·lis
syph·i·lit·ic
sy·ringe
syr·up
syr·upy
system
sys·tem·at·ic
sys·tem·at·i·cal
sys·tem·at·i·cal·ly
sys·tem·at·ic·ness
sys·tem·a·tize
sys·tem·a·tized
sys·tem·a·tiz·ing
sys·tem·a·ti·za·tion
sys·tem·a·tiz·er
sys·tem·ic
sys·tem·i·cal·ly
sys·to·le
sys·tol·ic

T

tab
tabbed
tab·bing
Ta·bas·co
tab·by
tab·er·na·cle
tab·er·nac·u·lar
ta·ble
ta·bled
ta·bling
tab·leau
tab·le d'hote
ta·ble·spoon·fuls
tab·let
tab·loid
ta·boo
ta·booed
ta·boo·ing
ta·bor
tab·o·ret
tab·u·lar
tab·u·lar·ly
tab·u·late
tab·u·lat·ed
tab·u·lat·ing
tab·u·la·tion
tab·u·la·tor
ta·chom·e·ter
tac·it

tac·it·ly
tac·it·ness
tac·i·turn
tac·i·tur·ni·ty
tack
tacked
tack·ing
tack·le
tack·led
tack·ling
tack·ler
tacky
tack·i·ness
ta·cos
tact
tact·ful·ly
tact·ful·ness
tact·less
tac·tics
tac·ti·cal
tac·ti·cian
tac·tile
tac·til·i·ty
tad·pole
taf·fe·ta
taf·fy
tag
tagged
tag·ging
tail
tailed
tail·less
tail·gate
tail·gat·ed
tail·gat·ing
tai·lor
tai·lored
tai·lor·ing
taint
taint·ed
take
took
tak·en
tak·ing
take·off
tal·cum
tale·bear·ing
tal·ent
tal·ent·ed
tal·is·man
talk·a·tive
talk·a·tive·ly
talk·a·tive·ness
talky
talk·i·er
talk·i·est
tal·low
tal·lowy
tal·ly
tal·lies
tal·lied
tal·ly·ing
tal·ly·ho
Tal·mud
Tal·mud·ic
Tal·mud·i·cal
tal·on
tal·oned
ta·ma·le
tam·a·rack
tam·a·rind
tam·bour
tam·bou·rine
tame
tamed
tam·ing
tam·a·ble
tame·ly

tame·ness
tam·o'·shan·ter
tam·per
tam·pon
tan
tanned
tan·ning
tan·nish
tan·a·ger
tan·bark
tan·dem
tang
tangy
tang·i·er
tan·ge·lo
tan·gent
tan·gen·cy
tan·gen·tial
tan·ge·rine
tan·gi·ble
tan·gi·bil·i·ty
tan·gi·ble·ness
tan·gi·bly
tan·gle
tan·gled
tan·gling
tan·gle·ment
tan·go
tan·goed
tan·go·ing
tank·age
tank·ard
tank·er
tan·nery
tan·nin
tan·ta·lize
tan·ta·lized
tan·ta·liz·ing
tan·ta·mount
tan·trum
tap
tapped
tap·ping
tape
taped
tap·ing
ta·per
ta·per·ing·ly
tap·es·try
tap·es·tries
tap·es·tried
tap·es·try·ing
tap·i·o·ca
ta·pir
tar
tarred
tar·ring
tar·ry
tar·an·tel·la
ta·ran·tu·la
ta·ran·tu·las
ta·ran·tu·lae
tar·dy
tar·di·ly
tar·di·ness
tar·get
tar·iff
tar·nish
tar·nish·a·ble
ta·ro
tar·pau·lin
tar·pon
tar·ra·gon
tar·ry
tar·ried
tar·ry·ing
tart
tart·ness

tar·tan
tar·tar
tar·tar·ic
tar·tar·ous
tas·sel
tas·seled
tas·sel·ing
taste
tast·ed
tast·ing
taste·ful
taste·ful·ly
taste·ful·ness
taste·less
taste·less·ness
tasty
tast·i·ness
tat
tat·ted
tat·ting
tat·ter·de·ma·lion
tat·tered
tat·tle
tat·tled
tat·tling
tat·tle·tale
tat·too
tat·tooed
tat·too·ing
taught
taunt
taunt·ing·ly
taut
taut·ly
taut·ness
tau·tol·o·gy
tau·to·log·i·cal
tau·to·log·i·cal·ly
tav·ern
taw·dry
taw·dri·ly
taw·dri·ness
taw·ny
taw·ni·ness
tax
tax·a·bil·i·ty
tax·a·ble
tax·a·tion
tax·ex·empt
taxi
tax·i·cab
tax·i·der·my
tax·i·der·mic
tax·i·der·mist
tax·on·o·my
tax·o·nom·i·cal
tax·o·nom·i·cal·ly
tax·on·o·mist
tax·pay·er
teach
taught
teach·ing
teach·a·ble
teach·a·ble·ness
teach·a·bil·i·ty
teach·er
teak·wood
tea·ket·tle
team·mate
team·ster
tear
tore
torn
tear·ing
tear·ful
tear·ful·ly
tear·ful·ness
teary

tease
teased
teas·ing
tea·sel
tea·seled
tea·sel·ing
tea·spoon·fuls
teat
tech·ni·cal
tech·ni·cal·ly
tech·ni·cal·ness
tech·ni·cal·i·ty
tech·ni·cian
tech·nique
tech·noc·ra·cy
tech·no·crat
tech·no·crat·ic
tech·nol·o·gy
tech·no·log·i·cal
tech·no·log·ic
tech·nol·o·gist
tec·ton·ic
te·di·ous
te·di·ous·ly
te·di·ous·ness
te·di·um
tee
teed
tee·ing
teem
teem·ing
teen·ag·er
tee·pee
tee·ter
teethe
teethed
teeth·ing
tee·to·tal
tee·to·tal·er
tee·to·tal·ist
tee·to·tal·ism
tee·to·tal·ly
teg·u·ment
tel·e·cast
tel·e·cast·ing
tel·e·cast·er
tel·e·com·mu·ni·ca·tion
tel·e·gram
tel·e·graph
tel·e·graph·ic
te·leg·ra·phy
tele·ki·ne·sis
tele·me·ter
te·le·ol·o·gy
te·lep·a·thy
tel·e·path·ic
tel·e·path·i·cal·ly
tel·lep·a·thist
tel·e·phone
tel·e·phoned
tel·e·phon·ing
tle·e·phon·ic
tel·e·pho·to
tel·e·pho·tog·ra·phy
tel·e·pho·to·graph·ic
Tel·e·promp·ter
tel·e·ran
tel·e·scope
tel·e·scoped
tel·e·scop·ing
tel·e·scop·ic
tel·e·scop·i·cal
tel·e·thon
Tel·e·type
tel·e·vise
tel·e·vised
tel·e·vis·ing
tel·e·vi·sion

tell
told
tell·ing
tell·er
tem·blor
te·mer·i·ty
tem·per
tem·per·a·bil·i·ty
tem·per·a·ble
tem·pered
tem·per·er
tem·pera
tem·per·a·ment
tem·per·a·men·tal
tem·per·ance
tem·per·ate
tem·per·ate·ly
tem·per·ate·ness
tem·per·a·ture
tem·pest
tem·pes·tu·ous
tem·pes·tu·ous·ly
tem·pes·tu·ous·ness
tem·plate
tem·ple
tem·po
tem·po·ral
tem·por·al·i·ty
tem·por·ral·ly
tem·por·ral·ness
tem·po·rary
tem·po·rar·i·ty
tem·po·rar·i·ness
tem·po·rize
tem·po·ri·za·tion
tem·po·riz·er
tem·po·riz·ing·ly
tempt
tempt·a·ble
temp·ta·tion
tempt·ing
ten·a·ble
ten·a·bil·i·ty
ten·a·ble·ness
ten·a·bly
te·na·cious
te·na·cious·ly
te·na·cious·ness
te·nac·i·ty
ten·ant
ten·an·cy
ten·an·cies
ten·ant·a·ble
ten·den·cy
ten·den·cies
ten·den·tious
ten·den·tious·ly
ten·den·tious·ness
ten·der
ten·der·ly
ten·der·ness
ten·der·foot
ten·der·ize
ten·der·ized
ten·der·iz·ing
ten·der·iz·er
ten·der·loin
ten·don
ten·dril
te·neb·ri·ous
ten·e·ment
ten·et
ten·nis
ten·on
ten·or
tcnsc
tensed
tens·ing

tense·ly
tense·ness
ten·si·ty
ten·sile
ten·sil·i·ty
ten·sion
ten·sion·al
ten·sion·less
ten·sive
ten·ta·cle
ten·ta·cled
ten·tac·u·lar
ten·ta·tive
ten·ta·tive·ly
ten·ta·tive·ness
tenth
te·nu·i·ty
ten·u·ous
ten·u·ous·ly
ten·u·ous·ness
ten·ure
ten·ured
ten·u·ri·al
ten·u·ri·al·ly
te·pee
tep·id
te·pid·i·ty
tep·id·ness
te·qui·la
ter·cen·te·nary
ter·cen·ten·ni·al
ter·gi·ver·sate
ter·i·ya·ki
ter·ma·gant
ter·mi·nal
ter·mi·nal·ly
ter·mi·nate
ter·mi·nat·ed
ter·mi·nat·ing
ter·mi·na·ble
ter·mi·na·tion
ter·mi·na·tive
ter·mi·na·tor
ter·mi·nol·o·gy
ter·mi·nol·o·gies
ter·mi·no·log·i·cal
ter·mi·no·log·i·cal·ly
ter·mi·nus
ter·mite
ter·na·ry
terp·sich·o·re·an
ter·race
ter·raced
ter·rac·ing
ter·ra-cot·ta
ter·ra fir·ma
ter·rain
Ter·ra·my·cin
ter·ra·pin
ter·rar·i·um
ter·raz·zo
ter·res·tri·al
ter·res·tri·al·ly
ter·ri·ble
ter·ri·ble·ness
ter·ri·bly
ter·ri·er
ter·rif·ic
ter·rif·i·cal·ly
ter·ri·fy
ter·ri·fied
ter·ri·fy·ing
ter·ri·to·ry
ter·ri·to·ri·al
ter·ri·to·ri·al·i·ty
ter·ror
ter·ror·less
ter·ror·ism

ter·ror·ist
ter·ror·is·tic
ter·ror·less
ter·ror·ize
ter·ror·ized
ter·ror·iz·ing
ter·ror·i·za·tion
ter·ror·iz·er
ter·ry
terse
ters·er
terse·ly
terse·ness
ter·ti·ary
tes·sel·late
tes·sel·lat·ed
tes·sel·lat·ing
tes·sel·la·tion
tes·ta·ment
tes·ta·men·ta·ry
tes·tate
tes·ta·tor
tes·ta·trix
tes·ti·cle
tes·tic·u·lar
tes·ti·fy
tes·ti·fied
tes·ti·fy·ing
tes·ti·mo·ni·al
tes·ti·mo·ny
tes·ti·mo·nies
tes·tis
tes·tes
tes·tos·ter·one
tes·ty
tes·ti·ly
tes·ti·ness
tet·a·nus
tete-a-tete
teth·er
tet·ra·eth·yl
tet·ra·he·dron
tex·tile
tex·tu·al
tex·ture
tex·tur·al
tex·tur·al·ly
tex·tured
thank
thank·ful·ly
thank·ful·ness
thank·less
thank·less·ly
thank·less·ness
thanks·giv·ing
thatch
thatch·ing
thaw
the·a·ter
the·a·tre
the·at·ri·cal
the·at·ri·cal·ism
the·at·ri·cal·i·ty
the·at·ri·cal·ly
the·ism
the·ist
the·is·tic
theme
the·mat·ic
the·mat·i·cal·ly
them·selves
thence·forth
the·oc·ra·cy
the·oc·ra·cies
the·o·crat
the·o·crat·ic
the·o·crat·i·cal
the·o·cart·i·cal·ly

the·ol·o·gy
the·ol·o·gies
the·o·lo·gian
the·o·log·ic
the·o·log·i·cal
the·o·log·i·cal·ly
the·o·rem
the·o·re·mat·ic
the·o·ret·i·cal
the·o·ret·ic
the·o·ret·i·cal·ly
the·o·rize
the·o·rized
the·o·riz·ing
the·o·re·ti·cian
the·o·rist
the·o·ri·za·tion
the·o·riz·er
the·o·ry
the·o·ries
the·os·o·phy
the·o·soph·ic
the·o·soph·i·cal
the·o·soph·i·cal·ly
the·os·o·phist
ther·a·peu·tic
ther·a·peu·ti·cal
ther·a·peu·ti·cal·ly
ther·a·peu·tics
ther·a·peu·tist
ther·a·py
ther·a·pist
there·fore
ther·mal
ther·mal·ly
ther·mo·dy·nam·ics
ther·mo·dy·nam·ic
ther·mo·dy·nam·i·cal
ther·mo·e·lec·tric
ther·mom·e·ter
ther·mo·met·ric
ther·mo·nu·cle·ar
ther·mo·plas·tic
ther·mos
ther·mo·stat
ther·mo·stat·ic
the·sau·rus
the·sis
the·ses
thes·pi·an
thi·a·mine
thick
thick·ish
thick·ly
thick·ness
thick·en
thick·et
thick·et·ed
thick-head·ed
thief
thieves
thieve
thieved
thiev·ing
thiev·ish
thiev·ish·ness
thiev·ery
thiev·er·ies
thim·ble
thin
thin·ner
thin·nest
thinned
thin·ning
thin·ly
thin·ness
thine
thing

think
  thought
  think·ing
third·ly
thirsty
  thirst·i·er
  thirst·i·est
  thirst·i·ly
  thirst·i·ness
thir·teen
  thir·teenth
thir·ti·eth
thirty
  thir·ties
this·tle
thith·er
thong
tho·rax
tho·ri·um
thorn
  thorny
  thorn·i·ness
thor·ough
  thor·ough·ly
  thor·ough·ness
thor·ough·bred
thor·ough·fare
thor·ough·go·ing
though
thought·ful
  thought·ful·ly
  thought·ful·ness
thought·less
thou·sand
  thou·santh
thrall
  thrall·dom
thrash·er
thrash·ing
thread
thread·bare
thready
  thread·i·ness
threat·en
  threat·en·ing·ly
three-deck·er
three-di·men·sion·al
three·fold
three-quar·ter
three·score
three·some
thren·o·dy
thresh·er
thresh·old
thrice
thrift·less
thrifty
  thrift·i·ly
  thrift·i·ness
thrill
  thrill·ing
thrive
  throve
  thrived
  thriven
  thriv·ing
throat
throaty
  throat·i·ly
  throat·i·ness
throb
  throbbed
  throb·bing
throe
throm·bo·sis
throne
throng
throt·tle

throt·tled
throt·tling
through
through·out
through·way
  thru·way
throw
  threw
  thrown
  throw·ing
  throw·a·way
  throw·back
thrum
  thrummed
  thrum·ming
thrust
  thrust·ing
thud
  thud·ded
  thud·ding
thug
  thug·gery
  thug·gish
thumb
  thumb·nail
  thumb·screw
  thumb·tack
thump·ing
thun·der
  thun·der·ous
  thun·der·bolt
  thun·der·cloud
  thun·der·head
  thun·der·show·er
  thun·der·storm
  thun·der·struck
thwack
thwart
thyme
thy·mus
thy·roid
ti·ara
tib·ia
tic
tick
tick·er
tick·et
tick·ing
tick·le
  tick·led
  tick·ling
tick·lish
  tick·lish·ness
tick-tack-toe
ti·dal
tid·bit
tid·dly·winks
tide
tide·land
tide·water
ti·dings
ti·dy
  ti·di·ly
  ti·di·ness
tie
  tied
  ty·ing
tier
ti·ger
  ti·gress
  ti·ger·ish
tight
  tight·ly
  tight·ness
tight·en
tight-fist·ed
tight-lipped
tight·rope

tight·wad
til·de
tile
  tiled
  til·ing
till
  till·a·ble
till·age
tilt
  tilt·ed
tim·bal
tim·ber
  tim·bered
tim·ber·line
tim·bre
tim·brel
time
  timed
  tim·ing
time-con·sum·ing
time-hon·ored
time·keep·er
time·less·ness
time·out
time-shar·ing
time·ta·ble
tim·id
  tim·id·ly
  tim·id·i·ty
  tim·id·ness
tim·or·ous
  tim·or·ous·ly
  tim·or·ous·ness
tim·o·thy
tim·pa·ni
  tim·pa·nist
tin
  tinned
  tin·ning
tinc·ture
  tinc·tur·ing
tin·der
tinge
  tinged
  tinge·ing
tin·gle
  tin·gled
  tin·gling
  tin·gly
tink·er
tin·kle
  tin·kled
  tin·kling
tin·ny
  tin·ni·ly
  tin·ni·ness
tin·sel
  tin·seled
  tin·sel·ing
tint
  tint·er
  tint·ing
tin·tin·nab·u·la·tion
ti·ny
  ti·ni·er
  ti·ni·ness
tip
  tipped
  tip·ping
tip·ple
  tip·pled
  tip·pling
  tip·pler
tip·sy
  tip·si·ly
  tip·si·ness
tip·toe
  tip·toed

tip·to·ing
tip·top
ti·rade
tire
  tired
  tir·ing
  tire·less
tire·some
  tire·some·ness
tis·sue
ti·tan
ti·tan·ic
tithe
  tithed
  tith·ing
ti·tian
tit·il·late
  tit·il·lat·ed
  tit·il·lat·ing
  tit·il·la·tion
ti·tle
  ti·tled
tit·mouse
tit·ter
  tit·ter·ing
tit·u·lar
tiz·zy
toady
  toad·y·ing
  toad·y·ism
toast·er
toast·mas·ter
  toast·mis·tress
to·bac·co
to·bog·gan
toc·sin
to·day
tod·dle
  tod·dled
  tod·dling
  tod·dler
tod·dy
toe
  toed
  toe·ing
toe·nail
tof·fee
tog
  togged
  tog·ging
to·ga
to·geth·er
  to·geth·er·ness
tog·gle
  tog·gled
  tog·gling
toil·er
toi·let
toi·let·ry
toil·some
to·ken·ism
To·kyo
tol·er·a·ble
  tol·er·a·ble·ness
  tol·er·a·bil·i·ty
  tol·er·a·bly
tol·er·ant
  tol·er·ance
tol·er·ate
  tol·er·at·ed
  tol·er·at·ing
  tol·er·a·tion
  tol·er·a·tive
toll·booth
tom·a·hawk
to·ma·to
tom·boy
  tom·boy·ish

tomb·stone
tom·cat
tom·fool·ery
to·mor·row
tom·tit
tom-tom
tone
  ton·al
  to·nal·i·ty
  ton·al·ly
  tone·less
tongue
tongue-lash
tongue-tied
ton·ic
to·night
ton·nage
ton·neau
ton·sil
ton·sil·lec·to·my
ton·sil·li·tis
ton·so·ri·al
ton·sure
  ton·sured
  ton·sur·ing
ton·tine
tool·mak·er
tooth
  teeth
tooth·ache
tooth·brush
tooth·less
tooth·paste
tooth·pick
tooth·some
toothy
  tooth·i·ness
top
  topped
  top·ping
to·paz
tope
  toped
  top·ing
  top·er
to·pi·ary
top·ic
top·i·cal
top·i·cal·i·ty
to·pog·ra·phy
  to·pog·ra·pher
  top·o·graph·i·cal
  top·o·graph·i·cal·ly
to·pol·o·gy
  top·o·log·i·cal
top·ping
top·ple
  top·pled
  top·pling
top-se·cret
top·sy-tur·vy
toque
To·rah
torch·bear·er
torch·light
tor·e·a·dor
to·re·ro
tor·ment
  tor·ment·ing
  tor·men·tor
tor·na·do
  tor·na·dos
  tor·nad·ic
tor·pe·do
  tor·pe·doed
  tor·pe·do·ing
tor·pid
  tor·pid·i·ty

tor·pid·ly
tor·por
torque
tor·rent
tor·ren·tial
tor·rid
tor·rid·i·ty
tor·rid·ness
tor·rid·ly
tor·sion
tor·sion·al
tor·so
tort
torte
tor·til·la
tor·toise
tor·to·ni
tor·tu·ous
tor·tu·ous·ly
tor·tu·ous·ness
tor·ture
tor·tured
tor·tur·ing
tor·tur·er
tor·ture·some
tossing
to·tal
to·taled
to·tal·ing
to·tal·i·tar·i·an
to·tal·i·tar·i·an·ism
to·tal·i·ty
to·tal·i·za·tor
to·tal·ly
tote
tot·ed
tot·ing
to·tem
to·tem·ic
to·tem·ism
to·tem·ist
to·tem·is·tic
tot·ter
tot·ter·ing
tou·can
touch
touched
touch·ing
touch·a·ble
touchy
touch·i·ness
touch·down
tou·ché
tough
tough·ness
tough·en
tou·pee
tour de force
tour·ism
tour·ist
tour·ma·line
tour·na·ment
tour·ney
tour·ni·quet
tou·sle
tou·sled
tout·er
tow·age
to·ward
tow·boat
tow·el
tow·eled
tow·el·ing
tow·er
tow·ered
tow·er·ing
tow-head·ed
town·ship

tox·e·mia
tox·ic
tox·ic·i·ty
tox·i·col·o·gy
tox·i·co·log·i·cal
tox·i·co·log·i·cal·ly
tox·i·col·o·gist
tox·in
tox·oid
trace
traced
trac·ing
trace·a·ble
trace·a·bly
trac·ery
tra·chea
tra·che·ot·o·my
tra·cho·ma
track·age
track·er
tract
trac·ta·ble
trac·ta·bil·i·ty
trac·ta·ble·ness
trac·ta·bly
trac·tion
trac·tion·al
trac·tive
trac·tor
trade
trad·ed
trad·ing
trade·mark
trades·man
tra·di·tion
tra·di·tion·al
tra·di·tion·al·ism
tra·di·tion·al·ist
tra·di·tion·al·ly
tra·duce
tra·duced
tra·duc·ing
tra·duce·ment
traf·fic
traf·ficked
traf·fick·ing
traf·fick·er
tra·ge·di·an
tra·ge·di·enne
trag·e·dy
trag·e·dies
trag·ic
trag·i·cal
trag·i·cal·ly
trag·i·cal·ness
tragi·com·e·dy
trail·blaz·er
trail·blaz·ing
trail·er
train
train·a·ble
train·er
train·ing
traipse
traipsed
traips·ing
trait
trai·tor
trai·tor·ous
trai·tor·ous·ly
tra·jec·to·ry
tra·jec·to·ries
tram·mel
tram·meled
tram·mel·ing
tramp·ing
tram·ple
tram·pled

tram·pling
tram·po·line
tram·po·lin·ist
trance
tran·quil
tran·quil·li·ty
tran·quil·ly
tran·quil·ness
tran·quil·ize
tran·quil·ized
tran·quil·iz·ing
tran·quil·iz·er
trans·act
trans·ac·tor
trans·ac·tion
trans·ac·tion·al
trans·at·lan·tic
trans·ceiv·er
tran·scend
tran·scend·ent
tran·scen·den·tal
tran·scen·den·tal·ly
tran·scen·den·tal·ism
trans·con·ti·nen·tal
tran·scribe
tran·scribed
tran·scrib·ing
tran·scrib·er
tran·script
tran·scrip·tion
tran·scrip·tion·al
tran·scrip·tive
tran·sect
trans·sec·tion
tran·sept
tran·sep·tal
tran·sep·tal·ly
trans·fer
trans·ferred
trans·fer·ring
trans·fer·al
trans·fer·a·ble
trans·fer·ence
trans·fig·ure
trans·fig·ured
trans·fig·ur·ing
trans·fig·ure·ment
trans·fig·u·ra·tion
trans·fix
trans·fixed
trans·fix·ing
trans·fix·ion
trans·form
trans·form·a·ble
trans·for·ma·tion
trans·for·ma·tive
trans·form·er
trans·fuse
trans·fused
trans·fus·ing
trans·fus·a·ble
trans·fu·sion
trans·gress
trans·gres·sive
trans·gres·sor
trans·gres·sion
tran·sient
tran·sience
tran·sis·tor
tran·sis·tor·ize
tran·sis·tor·ized
tran·sis·tor·iz·ing
trans·it
tran·si·tion
tran·si·tion·al
tran·si·tion·al·ly
tran·si·tive
tran·si·tive·ly

tran·si·tive·ness
tran·si·tiv·i·ty
tran·si·to·ry
tran·si·to·ri·ly
tran·si·to·ri·ness
trans·late
trans·lat·ed
trans·lat·ing
trans·lat·a·bil·i·ty
trans·lat·a·ble
trans·lat·or
trans·la·tion
trans·la·tion·al
trans·la·tive
trans·lit·er·ate
trans·lit·er·at·ed
trans·lit·er·at·ing
trans·lit·er·a·tion
trans·lu·cent
trans·lu·cence
trans·lu·cen·cy
trans·lu·cent·ly
trans·me·rid·i·o·nal
trans·mi·grate
trans·mi·grat·ed
trans·mi·grat·ing
trans·mi·gra·tion
trans·mi·gra·tor
trans·mi·gra·to·ry
trans·mis·sion
trans·mis·si·bil·i·ty
trans·mis·siv·i·ty
trans·mis·si·ble
trans·mis·sive
trans·mit
trans·mit·ted
trans·mit·ting
trans·mit·ta·ble
trans·mit·tal
trans·mit·ter
trans·mute
trans·mut·ed
trans·mut·ing
trans·mut·er
trans·mut·a·ble·ness
trans·mut·a·bil·i·ty
trans·mut·a·bly
trans·mu·ta·tion
trans·mut·a·ble
trans·o·ce·an·ic
tran·som
tran·son·ic
trans·pa·cif·ic
trans·par·ent
trans·par·en·cy
trans·par·en·cies
trans·par·ent·ly
trans·par·ent·ness
tran·spire
tran·spired
tran·spir·ing
tran·spi·ra·tion
trans·plant
trans·plant·a·ble
trans·plan·ta·tion
trans·port
trans·port·a·bil·i·ty
trans·port·a·ble
trans·port·er
trans·por·ta·tion
trans·pose
trans·posed
trans·pos·ing
trans·pos·a·ble
trans·po·si·tion
trans·ship
trans·shipped
trans·ship·ping

trans·ship·ment
trans·verse
trans·verse·ly
trans·ves·tism
trans·ves·tite
trap
trapped
trap·ping
tra·peze
tra·pe·zi·um
trap·e·zoid
trap·per
trap·pings
trap·shoot·ing
trash
trash·i·est
trash·i·ness
trashy
trau·ma
trau·mat·ic
trau·mat·i·cal·ly
trau·ma·tize
tra·vail
tra·vel
tra·vel·ed
tra·vel·ing
trav·e·logue
trav·e·log
trav·erse
trav·ersed
trav·ers·ing
tra·vers·a·ble
tra·vers·al
trav·es·ty
trawl·er
treach·er·ous
treach·er·ous·ly
treach·er·ous·ness
treach·ery
treach·er·ies
tread
trod
trod·den
tread·ing
trea·dle
trea·son
trea·son·a·ble
trea·son·ous
trea·son·a·bly
treas·ure
treas·ured
treas·ur·ing
treas·ur·a·ble
treas·ur·er
treas·ury
treas·ur·ies
treat
treat·a·ble
treat·ment
trea·tise
trea·ty
trea·ties
tre·ble
tre·bled
tre·bling
tre·bly
tre·foil
trek
trekked
trek·king
trel·lis
trem·ble
trem·bled
trem·bling
trem·bly
tre·men·dous
tre·men·dous·ly
tre·men·dous·ness

trem·o·lo
trem·or
  trem·or·ous
trem·u·lous
  trem·u·lous·ly
  trem·u·lous·ness
trench·ant
  trench·an·cy
  trench·ant·ly
trench·er
trend
  trendy
tre·pan
  tre·panned
  tre·pan·ning
  trep·an·a·tion
tre·phine
trep·i·da·tion
tres·pass
  tres·pass·er
tres·tle
tri·ad
  tri·ad·ic
tri·al
tri·an·gle
  tri·an·gu·lar
  tri·an·gu·lar·i·ty
  tri·an·gu·lar·ly
  tri·an·gu·late
  tri·an·gu·lat·ed
  tri·an·gu·lat·ing
  tri·an·gu·la·tion
tribe
  trib·al
  tribes·men
trib·u·la·tion
tri·bu·nal
trib·une
trib·u·tary
  trib·u·tar·ies
  trib·u·tar·i·ly
trib·ute
trice
tri·ceps
trich·i·no·sis
tri·chot·o·my
trick·ery
trick·le
  trick·led
  trick·ling
trick·ster
tricky
  trick·i·er
  trick·i·ly
  trick·i·ness
tri·col·or
tri·cus·pid
tri·cy·cle
tri·dent
  tri·den·tate
tri·di·men·sion·al
tri·en·ni·al
tri·en·ni·um
tri·fle
  tri·fled
  tri·fling
  trif·ler
  tri·fling·ness
tri·fo·cals
trig·ger
trig·o·nom·e·try
  trig·o·no·met·ric
  trig·o·no·met·ri·cal
  trig·o·no·met·ri·cal·ly
tri·lin·gual
tril·lion
  tril·lionth
tril·o·gy

trim
  trimmed
  trim·ming
  trim·mer
  trim·mest
  trim·ly
  trim·ness
tri·mes·ter
tri·mes·tral
tri·mes·tri·al
tri·month·ly
Trin·i·tar·i·an
Trin·i·ty
trin·ket
trio
trip
  tripped
  trip·ping
tri·par·tite
trip·ham·mer
tri·ple
  tri·pled
  tri·pling
  tri·ply
  tri·plet
trip·li·cate
  trip·li·cat·ed
  trip·li·cat·ing
  trip·li·ca·tion
tri·pod
trip·tych
tri·sect
  tri·sec·tion
  tri·sec·tor
trite
  trite·ly
  trite·ness
trit·u·rate
tri·umph
  tri·um·phal
  tri·um·phal·ly
  tri·um·phant
  tri·um·phant·ly
tri·um·vi·rate
triv·et
triv·ia
triv·i·al
  triv·i·al·i·ty
  triv·i·al·i·ties
  triv·i·al·i·za·tion
  triv·i·al·ly
tri·week·ly
tro·che
trog·lo·dyte
troi·ka
troll
trol·ley
trol·lop
trom·bone
  trom·bon·ist
troop·er
tro·phy
  tro·phies
trop·ic
  trop·i·cal
trop·o·sphere
trot
  trot·ted
  trot·ting
trot·ter
trou·ba·dour
trou·ble
  trou·bled
  trou·bling
  trou·ble·mak·er
  trou·ble·shoot·er
  trou·ble·some
trough

trounce
  trounced
  trounc·ing
troupe
  trouped
  troup·ing
troup·er
trou·sers
trous·seau
trow·el
tru·ant
  tru·an·cy
  tru·an·cies
  tru·ant·ry
truck·age
truck·er
truck·ing
truc·u·lent
  truc·u·lence
  truc·u·lent·ly
trudge
  trudged
  trudg·ing
true
  tru·er
  tru·est
  true·ness
truf·fle
tru·ism
  tru·is·tic
tru·ly
trump
  trump·er·y
trum·pet
  trum·pet·er
trun·cate
  trun·cat·ed
  trun·cat·ing
  trun·ca·tion
trun·cheon
trun·dle
  trun·dled
  trun·dling
truss
  truss·ing
trust
trus·tee
  trus·teed
  trus·tee·ing
  trus·tee·ship
trust·ful
  trust·ful·ly
trust·wor·thy
  trust·wor·thi·ly
  trust·wor·thi·ness
trusty
  trust·i·est
  trust·i·ness
truth·ful
  truth·ful·ly
  truth·ful·ness
try
  tried
  try·ing
tryst
tsu·na·mi
tu·ba
tu·bal
tub·by
  tub·bi·ness
tube
  tubed
  tub·ing
tu·ber
tu·ber·cle
tu·ber·cu·lo·sis
tu·ber·cu·lar
tu·ber·ous

tu·bu·lar
tu·bule
tuck-point
tuft·ed
tu·i·tion
tu·la·re·mia
tu·lip
tulle
tum·ble
  tum·bled
  tum·bling
tum·ble-down
tum·bler
tum·ble·weed
tu·mes·cent
tu·mid
  tu·mid·i·ty
tu·mor
  tu·mor·ous
tu·mult
  tu·mul·tu·ous
  tu·mul·tu·ous·ly
  tu·mul·tu·ous·ness
tu·na
tun·dra
tune
  tuned
  tun·ing
  tun·a·ble
tune·ful
tung·sten
tu·nic
tun·nel
  tun·neled
  tun·nel·ing
tuque
tur·ban
tur·bid
  tur·bid·i·ty
  tur·bid·ness
tur·bine
tur·bo
tur·bo·fan
tur·bo·jet
tur·bo·prop
tur·bot
tur·bu·lent
  tur·bu·lence
  tru·bu·len·cy
tu·reen
turf
tur·gid
  tur·gid·i·ty
  tur·gid·ness
tur·key
tur·mer·ic
tur·moil
turn·coat
turn·ing
tur·nip
turn·key
turn·pike
turn·ta·ble
tur·pen·tine
tur·pi·tude
tur·quoise
tur·ret
tur·tle
tur·tle·dove
tur·tle·neck
tusk
  tusked
tus·sle
  tus·sled
  tus·sling
tu·te·lage
tu·tor
  tu·tor·age

tu·to·ri·al
tu·ti-fru·ti
tu·tu
tux·e·do
twad·dle
twain
twang
  twangy
tweak
tweed
  tweedy
  tweed·i·ness
tweet·er
tweez·ers
tweeze
  tweezed
  tweez·ing
twelve
  twelfth
twen·ty
  twen·ties
  twen·ti·eth
twid·dle
  twid·dled
  twid·dling
twig
  twig·gy
twi·light
twilled
twin
  twinned
  twin·ning
twine
  twined
  twin·ing
twinge
  twinged
  twing·ing
twin·kle
  twin·kled
  twin·kling
twirl
  twirl·er
  twirly
twist·er
twit
  twit·ted
  twit·ting
twitch
twit·ter
  twit·tery
two-di·men·sion·al
two-faced
two-fist·ed
two-sid·ed
two·some
two-time
ty·coon
tym·pan·ic
type
  typed
  typ·ing
  typ·ist
type·face
type·set·ter
  type·set
type·write
  type·writ·ten
  type·writ·ing
type·writ·er
ty·phoid
ty·phoon
ty·phus
typ·i·cal
  typ·i·cal·ly
  typ·i·cal·ness
  typ·i·cal·i·ty
typ·i·fy

typ·i·fied
typ·i·fy·ing
typ·i·fi·ca·tion
ty·pog·ra·phy
ty·pog·ra·pher
ty·po·graph·ic
ty·po·graph·i·cal
ty·po·graph·i·cal·ly
ty·pol·o·gy
ty·ran·ni·cal
ty·ran·nic
ty·ran·ni·cal·ly
ty·ran·nous
tyr·an·nize
tyr·an·nized
tyr·an·niz·ing
tyr·an·niz·er
tyr·an·ny
ty·rant
ty·ro

U

ubiq·ui·ty
ubiq·ui·tous
ubiq·ui·tary
ubiq·ui·tous·ly
ubiq·ui·tous·ness
ud·der
ug·ly
ug·li·er
ug·li·est
ug·li·ly
ug·li·ness
uku·le·le
ul·cer
ul·cer·ous
ul·cer·ate
ul·cer·at·ed
ul·cer·at·ing
ul·cer·a·tion
ul·ster
ul·te·ri·or
ul·te·ri·or·ly
ul·ti·mate
ul·ti·mate·ly
ul·ti·mate·ness
ul·ti·ma·tum
ul·tra
ul·tra·con·serv·a·tive
ul·tra·fash·ion·a·ble
ul·tra·lib·er·al
ul·tra·ma·rine
ul·tra·mod·ern
ul·tra·re·li·gious
ul·tra·son·ic
ul·tra·vi·o·let
ul·u·late
ul·u·la·tion
um·bel
um·ber
um·bil·i·cal
um·bra
um·brage
um·bra·geous
um·bra·geous·ly
um·bra·geous·ness
um·brel·la
u·mi·ak
um·laut
um·pire
um·pired
um·pir·ing
un·a·bashed
un·a·ble
un·a·bridged
un·ac·cep·ta·ble

un·ac·com·pa·nied
un·ac·count·ed
un·ac·count·a·ble
un·ac·count·a·bly
un·ac·cus·tomed
un·ac·quaint·ed
un·a·dorned
un·a·dul·ter·at·ed
un·ad·vised
un·ad·vis·ed·ly
un·ad·vis·ed·ness
un·af·fect·ed
un·af·fect·ed·ly
un·af·fect·ed·ness
un·a·fraid
un·aligned
un-A·mer·i·can
unan·i·mous
una·nim·i·ty
unan·i·mous·ly
unan·i·mous·ness
un·an·swer·a·ble
un·an·swered
un·ap·peal·a·ble
un·ap·peal·ing
un·ap·pe·tiz·ing
un·ap·pre·ci·at·ed
un·ap·pre·ci·a·tive
un·ap·pro·pri·at·ed
un·ap·proach·a·ble
un·ap·proach·a·ble·ness
un·armed
un·a·shamed
un·asked
un·a·spir·ing
un·as·sail·a·ble
un·as·sailed
un·as·sum·ing
un·at·tached
un·at·tain·a·ble
un·at·tained
un·at·tended
un·au·thor·ized
un·a·vail·a·ble
un·a·vail·a·bil·i·ty
un·a·vail·a·bly
un·a·void·a·ble
un·a·void·a·bil·i·ty
un·a·void·a·bly
un·a·ware
un·a·ware·ness
un·a·wares
un·backed
un·bal·anced
un·bar
un·barred
un·bar·ring
un·bear·a·ble
un·bear·a·ble·ness
un·bear·a·bly
un·beat·en
un·beat·a·ble
un·be·com·ing
un·be·com·ing·ness
un·be·known
un·be·lief
un·be·liev·a·ble
un·be·liev·a·bly
un·be·liev·er
un·be·liev·ing
un·bend
un·bend·ed
un·bend·ing
un·bend·ing·ness
un·be·seem·ing
un·bi·ased
un·bid·den
un·bind

un·blem·ished
un·blush·ing
un·blot
un·born
un·bos·om
un·bound
un·bound·ed
un·bound·ed·ness
un·bowed
un·bred
un·break·a·ble
un·bri·dled
un·bro·ken
un·buck·le
un·bur·den
un·but·ton
un·called-for
un·can·ny
un·can·ni·ly
un·can·ni·ness
un·cap
un·capped
un·cap·ping
un·ceas·ing
un·ceas·ing·ly
un·ceas·ing·ness
un·cere·mo·ni·ous
un·cere·mo·ni·ous·ly
un·cere·mo·ni·ous·ness
un·certain
un·cer·tain·ly
un·cer·tain·ness
un·cer·tain·ty
un·chal·lenged
un·change·a·ble
un·changed
un·chang·ing
un·char·i·ta·ble
un·char·i·ta·ble·ness
un·char·i·ta·bly
un·chart·ed
un·chris·tian
un·cir·cum·cised
un·civ·il
un·civ·il·ly
un·civ·i·lized
un·clad
un·class·i·fi·a·ble
un·clas·si·fied
un·cle
un·clear
un·clean·ly
un·clean·li·ness
un·clothe
un·clothed
un·clut·tered
un·com·fort·a·ble
un·com·fort·a·ble·ness
un·com·fort·a·bly
un·com·mit·ted
un·com·mon
un·com·mon·ly
un·com·mon·ness
un·com·mu·ni·ca·tive
un·com·mu·ni·ca·tive·ness
un·com·pre·hend·ing
un·com·pro·mis·ing
un·com·pro·mised
un·com·pro·mis·ing·ly
un·com·pro·mis·ing·ness
un·con·cerned
un·con·cern·ed·ly
un·con·cern·ed·ness
un·con·di·tion·al
un·con·di·tion·al·ly
un·con·firmed
un·con·for·mi·ty
un·con·nect·ed

un·con·nect·ed·ness
un·con·quer·a·ble
un·con·quered
un·con·scion·a·ble
un·con·scion·a·ble·ness
un·con·scion·a·bly
un·con·scious
un·con·scious·ly
un·con·scious·ness
un·con·sti·tu·tion·al
un·con·sti·tu·tion·al·i·ty
un·con·sti·tu·tion·al·ly
un·con·strained
un·con·test·ed
un·con·trol·la·ble
un·con·trolled
un·con·ven·tion·al
un·con·ven·tion·al·i·ty
un·con·ven·tion·al·ly
un·count·ed
un·cou·ple
un·cour·te·ous
un·couth
un·couth·ly
un·couth·ness
un·cov·er
un·cov·ered
un·crit·i·cal
unc·tion
unc·tu·ous
un·daunt·ed
un·daunt·ed·ly
un·daunt·ed·ness
un·de·ceived
un·de·ceiv·ing
un·de·cid·ed
un·de·cid·ed·ness
un·de·fined
un·de·fin·a·ble
un·de·mon·stra·tive
un·de·mon·stra·tive·ly
un·de·mon·stra·tive·ness
un·de·nied
un·de·ni·a·ble
un·de·ni·a·ble·ness
un·de·ni·a·bly
un·de·pend·a·ble
un·de·pend·a·bil·i·ty
un·de·pend·a·ble·ness
un·der·a·chiev·er
un·der·a·chiev·ment
un·der·act
un·der·age
un·der·armed
un·der·bid
un·der·brush
un·der·car·riage
un·der·charge
un·der·class·man
un·der·clothes
un·der·coat·ing
un·der·cov·er
un·der·cur·rent
un·der·cut
un·der·cut·ting
un·der·de·vel·oped
un·der·de·vel·op·ing
un·der·dog
un·der·es·ti·mate
un·der·es·ti·mat·ed
un·der·es·ti·ma·tion
un·der·ex·pose
un·der·go
un·der·went
un·der·gone
un·der·go·ing
un·der·grad·u·ate
un·der·ground

un·der·growth
un·der·hand·
un·der·hand·ed
un·der·hand·ed·ness
un·der·lie
un·der·lay
un·der·lain
un·der·ly·ing
un·der·line
un·der·lined
un·der·lin·ing
un·der·ling
un·der·mine
un·der·mined
un·der·min·ing
un·der·most
un·der·neath
un·der·nour·ished
un·der·paid
un·der·pass
un·der·pin·ning
un·der·play
un·der·priv·i·leged
un·der·rate
un·der·rat·ed
un·der·score
un·der·scored
un·der·scor·ing
un·der·sea
un·der·sec·re·tary
un·der·sec·re·tar·ies
un·der·sell
un·der·sold
un·der·shirt
un·der·shoot
un·der·side
un·der·signed
un·der·sized
un·der·slung
un·der·stand
un·der·stood
un·der·stand·ing
un·der·stand·a·bil·i·ty
un·der·stand·a·ble
un·der·stand·a·bly
un·der·state
un·der·stat·ed
un·der·stat·ing
un·der·state·ment
un·der·study
un·der·stud·ied
un·der·stud·y·ing
un·der·take
un·der·took
un·der·tak·en
un·der·tak·ing
un·der·tak·er
un·der-the-coun·ter
un·der·tone
un·der·tow
un·der·val·ue
un·der·wa·ter
un·der·wear
un·der·weight
un·der·world
un·der·write
un·der·wrote
un·der·writ·ten
un·der·writ·ing
un·der·writ·er
un·de·sign·ing
un·de·sir·a·ble
un·de·sir·a·bil·i·ty
un·de·sir·a·ble·ness
un·de·sir·a·bly
un·de·ter·minded
un·de·vel·oped
un·di·gest·i·ble

un·dip·lo·mat·ic
  un·dip·lo·mat·i·cal·ly
un·di·rect·ed
un·dis·ci·plined
un·dis·closed
un·dis·posed
un·dis·tin·guished
un·di·vid·ed
un·do
  un·did
  un·done
  un·do·ing
un·doubt·ed
  un·doubt·ed·ly
  un·doubt·ing
un·dress
  un·dressed
  un·dress·ing
un·due
un·du·lant
un·du·late
  un·du·lat·ed
  un·du·lat·ing
  un·du·la·tion
  un·du·la·tory
un·du·ly
un·dy·ing
un·earned
un·earth
un·earth·ly
  un·earth·li·ness
un·easy
  un·ease
  un·eas·i·ly
  un·eas·i·ness
un·ed·u·cat·ed
un·em·ployed
  un·em·ploy·ment
  un·em·ploy·a·ble
un·end·ing
un·e·qual
  un·e·qual·ly
  un·e·qualed
un·e·quiv·o·cal
  un·e·quiv·o·cal·ly
un·err·ing
  un·err·ing·ly
un·es·sen·tial
un·eth·i·cal
  un·eth·i·cal·ly
un·e·ven
  un·e·ven·ly
  un·e·ven·ness
un·event·ful
un·ex·am·pled
un·ex·cep·tion·al
  un·ex·cep·tion·a·ble
un·ex·pect·ed
  un·ex·pect·ed·ly
  un·ex·pect·ed·ness
un·ex·pres·sive
un·fail·ing
  un·fail·ing·ly
un·fair·ness
un·faith·ful
  un·faith·ful·ly
  un·faith·ful·ness
un·fa·mil·iar
  un·fa·mil·i·ar·i·ty
un·fast·en
un·fath·om·a·ble
un·fa·vor·a·ble
  un·fa·vor·a·ble·ness
  un·fa·vor·a·bly
un·feel·ing
  un·feel·ing·ly
  un·feel·ing·ness
un·feigned

un·fet·ter
un·fet·tered
un·fin·ished
un·fit
  un·fit·ness
  un·fit·ting
un·flat·ter·ing
un·flinch·ing
un·fold
un·for·get·ta·ble
  un·for·get·ta·bly
un·for·giv·a·ble
un·formed
un·for·tu·nate
  un·for·tu·nate·ly
  un·for·tu·nate·ness
un·found·ed
un·fre·quent·ed
un·friend·ly
  un·friend·li·ness
un·fruit·ful
un·gain·ly
  un·gain·li·ness
un·gen·er·ous
un·god·ly
  un·god·li·ness
un·gov·ern·a·ble
un·grace·ful
un·gra·cious
  un·gra·cious·ly
  un·gra·cious·ness
un·gram·mat·i·cal
un·grate·ful
  un·grate·ful·ly
  un·grate·ful·ness
un·grudg·ing
un·guard·ed
un·guent
un·ham·pered
un·handy
un·hap·py
  un·hap·pi·ly
  un·hap·pi·ness
un·harmed
un·healthy
  un·health·i·ness
un·heard
un·heed·ed
un·heed·ful
un·heed·ing
un·hinge
un·ho·ly
  un·ho·li·ly
  un·ho·li·ness
un·hook
un·hur·ried
uni·cel·lu·lar
uni·corn
uni·cy·cle
uni·form
  uni·formed
  uni·form·i·ty
  uni·form·ly
  uni·form·ness
uni·fy
  uni·fied
  uni·fy·ing
  uni·fi·ca·tion
uni·lat·er·al
  uni·lat·er·al·ly
un·im·ag·i·na·ble
un·im·paired
un·im·peach·a·ble
  un·im·peach·a·bly
un·im·por·tance
un·im·por·tant
un·im·proved
un·in·hib·it·ed

un·in·tel·li·gent
  un·in·tel·li·gi·ble
un·in·ten·tion·al
un·in·ter·est·ed
  un·in·ter·est·ing
un·in·ter·rupt·ed
un·ion
un·ion·ism
  un·ion·ist
un·ion·ize
  un·ion·ized
  un·ion·iz·ing
  un·ion·i·za·tion
unique
  unique·ly
  unique·ness
uni·sex
uni·son
unit
Uni·tar·i·an
unite
  unit·ed
  unit·ing
Unit·ed Ar·ab Emir·ates
Unit·ed King·dom
Unit·ed Na·tions
Unit·ed States
uni·ty
uni·valve
uni·ver·sal
  uni·ver·sal·i·ty
  uni·ver·sal·ly
  uni·ver·sal·ness
uni·verse
uni·ver·si·ty
  uni·ver·si·ties
un·just
  un·just·ly
  un·just·ness
un·kempt
un·kind
  un·kind·ly
  un·kind·ness
  un·kind·li·ness
un·know·ing
un·known
un·law·ful
  un·law·ful·ly
  un·law·ful·ness
un·learn
  un·learned
un·learn·ed
un·leash
un·less
un·let·tered
un·like
  un·like·ness
un·like·ly
  un·like·li·hood
  un·like·li·ness
un·lim·ber
un·lim·it·ed
un·list·ed
un·load
un·lock
un·looked-for
un·loose
  un·loos·en
un·lucky
  un·luck·i·est
  un·luck·i·ly
  un·luck·i·ness
un·make
  un·made
  un·mak·ing
  un·mak·er
un·man·ly
un·manned

un·man·ner·ly
un·mask
un·mean·ing
  un·mean·ing·ly
un·men·tion·a·ble
un·mer·ci·ful
  un·mer·ci·ful·ly
un·mind·ful
un·mis·tak·a·ble
  un·mis·tak·a·bly
un·mit·i·gat·ed
un·nat·u·ral
  un·nat·u·ral·ly
  un·nat·u·ral·ness
un·nec·es·sary
  un·nec·es·sar·i·ly
un·nerve
  un·nerved
  un·nerv·ing
un·num·bered
un·ob·jec·tion·a·ble
un·ob·tru·sive
un·oc·cu·pied
un·or·gan·ized
un·or·tho·dox
un·pack
un·par·al·leled
un·par·don·a·ble
un·pleas·ant
  un·pleas·ant·ly
  un·pleas·ant·ness
un·plumbed
un·pop·u·lar
  un·pop·u·lar·i·ty
un·prec·e·dent·ed
un·pre·dict·a·ble
un·prej·u·diced
un·pre·ten·tious
un·prin·ci·pled
un·print·a·ble
un·pro·fes·sion·al
un·prof·it·a·ble
un·prom·is·ing
un·qual·i·fied
  un·qual·i·fied·ly
un·ques·tion·a·ble
  un·ques·tion·a·bly
un·ques·tioned
un·rav·el
  un·rav·eled
  un·rav·el·ing
un·ready
  un·read·i·ness
un·re·al
un·re·al·is·tic
un·re·al·i·ty
un·rea·son·a·ble
  un·rea·son·a·ble·ness
  un·rea·son·a·bly
un·rea·son·ing
un·re·con·struct·ed
un·re·fined
un·re·gen·er·ate
un·re·lat·ed
un·re·lent·ing
un·re·mit·ting
un·re·serve
  un·re·serv·ed·ly
un·rest
un·re·strained
un·ri·valed
un·ruf·fled
un·ru·ly
  un·ru·li·ness
un·sad·dle
un·said
un·sat·u·rat·ed
un·sa·vory

un·scathed
un·schooled
un·sci·en·tif·ic
un·scram·ble
un·screw
un·scru·pu·lous
  un·scru·pu·lous·ness
un·seal
un·sea·son·a·ble
  un·sea·son·a·bly
un·seat
un·seem·ly
  un·seem·li·ness
un·seg·re·gat·ed
un·self·ish
un·set·tle
  un·set·tled
  un·set·tling
un·sheathe
un·shod
un·sight·ly
  un·sight·li·ness
un·skilled
un·skill·ful
un·snap
  un·snapped
  un·snap·ping
un·snarl
un·so·phis·ti·cat·ed
  un·so·phis·ti·ca·tion
un·sought
un·sound
  un·sound·ness
un·spar·ing
un·speak·a·ble
un·spot·ted
un·sta·ble
  un·sta·ble·ness
un·steady
  un·stead·i·ly
un·stop
  un·stopped
  un·stop·ping
un·stressed
un·strung
un·stud·ied
un·suc·cess·ful
un·suit·a·ble
un·sung
un·tan·gle
un·taught
un·think·a·ble
un·think·ing
un·ti·dy
  un·ti·di·ness
un·tie
  un·tied
  un·ty·ing
un·til
un·time·ly
  un·time·li·ness
un·to
un·told
un·touch·a·ble
un·to·ward
un·truth·ful
un·tu·tored
un·used
un·u·su·al
  un·u·su·al·ness
un·ut·ter·a·ble
un·var·nished
un·veil
un·war·rant·ed
un·wary
  un·war·i·ness
un·well
un·whole·some

un·wieldy
  un·wield·i·ness
un·will·ing
  un·will·ing·ness
un·wind
  un·wound
  un·wind·ing
un·wise
un·wit·ting
  un·wit·ting·ly
un·wont·ed
un·world·li·ness
un·wor·thy
  un·wor·thi·ly
  un·wor·thi·ness
un·wrap
  un·wrapped
  un·wrap·ping
un·writ·ten
un·yield·ing
up-and-com·ing
up-and-down
up·beat
up·braid
up·bring·ing
up·com·ing
up·coun·try
up·date
  up·dat·ed
  up·dat·ing
up·grade
  up·grad·ed
  up·grad·ing
up·heav·al
up·heave
up·hold
  up·held
  up·hold·ing
up·hol·ster
up·hol·stery
up·keep
up·land
up·most
up·on
up·per·class
up·per·cut
up·per·most
up·pish·ness
up·pi·ty
up·raise
  up·raised
  up·rais·ing
up·rear
up·right
  up·right·ness
up·ris·ing
up·roar
up·roar·i·ous
up·root
up·set·ting
up·shot
up·stage
  up·staged
  up·stag·ing
up·stairs
up·stand·ing
up·start
up·state
up·stream
up·swing
up·take
up-to-date
up·town
up·trend
up·turn
up·ward
ura·ni·um
Ura·nus

ur·ban
ur·bane
  ur·bane·ness
  ur·ban·i·ty
ur·ban·ize
  ur·ban·ized
  ur·ban·iz·ing
  ur·ban·i·za·tion
ur·chin
ure·mia
ure·ter
ure·thra
urge
  urged
  urg·ing
ur·gent
  ur·gen·cy
  ur·gent·ly
uri·nal
uri·nal·y·sis
uri·nary
uri·nate
  uri·na·tion
urine
urol·o·gy
uro·log·ic
Uru·guay
us·a·ble
  us·a·ble·ness
  us·a·bil·i·ty
us·age
use
  used
  us·ing
use·ful
  use·ful·ly
  use·ful·ness
use·less·ness
ush·er
usu·al
  usu·al·ly
usurp
  usur·pa·tion
  usurp·er
usu·ry
  usu·ri·ous
uten·sil
uter·us
util·i·tar·ian
util·i·ty
  util·i·ties
uti·lize
  uti·lized
  uti·liz·ing
  uti·li·za·tion
ut·most
Uto·pia
  Uto·pi·an
ut·ter
  ut·ter·a·ble
  ut·ter·ance
  ut·ter·most
uvu·la
ux·o·ri·ous

V

va·can·cy
  va·can·cies
va·cant
va·cate
  va·cat·ed
  va·cat·ing
va·ca·tion
vac·ci·nate
  vac·ci·nat·ed
  vac·ci·nat·ing

vac·ci·na·tion
vac·cine
vac·il·late
  vac·il·lat·ed
  vac·il·lat·ing
  vac·il·la·tion
  vac·il·la·tor
va·cu·i·ty
vac·u·ous
  vac·u·ous·ness
vac·u·um
vag·a·bond
  vag·a·bond·age
va·gary
va·gar·i·ous
va·gi·na
vag·i·nal
va·grant
  va·gran·cy
vague
  vague·ness
vain
  vain·ly
  vain·ness
vain·glo·ry
  vain·glo·ri·ous
  vain·glo·ri·ous·ness
val·ance
  val·anced
val·e·dic·tion
  val·e·dic·to·ri·an
  val·e·dic·to·ry
va·lence
  va·len·cy
val·en·tine
val·et
val·iant
  val·iant·ly
  val·iant·ness
val·id
  val·id·ly
  val·id·ness
val·i·date
  val·i·dat·ed
  val·i·dat·ing
  val·i·da·tion
va·lid·i·ty
va·lise
val·ley
  val·leys
val·or
  val·or·ous
  val·or·ous·ly
  val·or·ous·ness
val·or·ize
  val·or·i·za·tion
val·u·a·ble
  val·u·a·ble·ness
  val·u·a·bly
val·u·a·tion
  val·u·a·tion·al
val·ue
  val·ued
  val·u·ing
  val·ue·less
valve
  valve·less
  val·vu·lar
va·moose
vam·pire
vam·pir·ic
van·dal
van·dal·ism
van·dal·ize
  van·dal·ized
  van·dal·iz·ing
vane
vaned

vane·less
van·guard
va·nil·la
van·ish
van·i·ty
  van·i·ties
van·quish
  van·quish·a·ble
  van·quish·er
van·tage
vap·id
  va·pid·i·ty
  vap·id·ness
  vap·id·ly
va·por
  va·por·er
  va·por·ish
  va·por·ish·ness
va·por·es·cence
va·por·ize
  va·por·ized
  va·por·iz·ing
  va·por·i·za·tion
  va·por·iz·er
va·por·ous
  va·por·ous·ly
va·que·ro
var·i·a·ble
  var·i·a·bil·i·ty
  var·i·a·ble·ness
  var·i·a·bly
var·i·ance
var·i·ant
var·i·a·tion
  var·i·a·tion·al
  var·i·a·tion·al·ly
var·i·col·ored
var·i·cose
var·i·cos·i·ty
var·ied
  var·ied·ness
var·i·e·gate
  var·i·e·gat·ed
  var·i·e·gat·ing
  var·i·e·ga·tion
va·ri·e·tal
  va·ri·e·tal·ly
va·ri·e·ty
  va·ri·e·ties
var·i·o·rum
var·i·ous
  var·i·ous·ly
  var·i·ous·ness
var·mint
var·nish
var·si·ty
  var·si·ties
vary
  var·ied
  var·y·ing
  var·y·ing·ly
vas·cu·lar
  vas·cu·lar·i·ty
vas·ec·to·my
Vas·e·line
vas·o·mo·tor
vas·sal
  vas·sal·age
vast·ness
vas·ti·tude
vat
  vat·ted
  vat·ting
Vat·i·can
vaude·ville
  vaude·vil·lian
vault
  vault·ed

vault·er
vault·ing
vaunt
  vaunt·er
  vaunt·ing·ly
vec·tor
  vec·to·ri·al
veer·ing
veg·e·ta·ble
veg·e·tal
veg·e·tar·i·an
  veg·e·tar·i·an·ism
veg·e·tate
  veg·e·tat·ed
  veg·e·tat·ing
veg·e·ta·tion
  veg·e·ta·tion·al
  veg·e·ta·tion·less
veg·e·ta·tive
ve·he·ment
  ve·he·mence
  ve·he·men·cy
ve·hi·cle
  ve·hic·u·lar
veil
veiled
veil·ing
vein
veiny
vein·ing
vel·lum
ve·loc·i·ty
  ve·loc·i·ties
ve·lour
ve·lum
vel·vet
  vel·vet·ed
  vel·vety
  vel·vet·een
ve·nal
  ve·nal·i·ty
  ve·nal·ly
ve·na·tion
  ve·na·tion·al
vend·er
  vend·or
ven·det·ta
vend·i·ble
  vend·i·bil·i·ty
ve·neer
  ve·neer·ing
ven·er·a·ble
  ven·er·a·bil·i·ty
  ven·er·a·ble·ness
  ven·er·a·bly
ven·er·ate
  ven·er·a·tion
  ven·er·a·tor
ve·ne·re·al
venge·ance
venge·ful
  venge·ful·ness
ve·ni·al
  ve·ni·al·i·ty
  ve·ni·al·ness
  ve·ni·al·ly
ven·i·son
ven·om
  ven·om·ous
  ven·om·ous·ness
ve·nous
  ve·nous·ly
  ve·nous·ness
vent
  vent·ed
  vent·ing
ven·ti·late
  ven·ti·lat·ed

ven·ti·lat·ing
ven·ti·la·tion
ven·ti·la·tor
ven·tral
ven·tri·cle
ven·tril·o·quism
ven·tri·lo·qui·al
ven·tril·o·quist
ven·tril·o·quize
ven·tril·o·quized
ven·tril·o·quiz·ing
ven·ture
ven·ture·some
ven·tur·ous
ven·tur·ous·ness
ven·ue
ve·ra·cious
ve·ra·cious·ness
ve·rac·i·ty
ve·rac·i·ties
ve·ran·da
ver·bal
ver·bal·ly
ver·bal·ize
ver·bal·ized
ver·bal·iz·ing
ver·bal·i·za·tion
ver·ba·tim
ver·be·na
ver·bi·age
ver·bose
ver·bose·ness
ver·bos·i·ty
ver·bo·ten
ver·dant
ver·dan·cy
ver·dict
ver·di·gris
ver·dure
ver·dured
ver·dur·ous
verge
verged
verg·ing
verify
ver·i·fied
ver·i·fy·ing
ver·i·fi·a·bil·i·ty
ver·i·fi·a·ble·ness
ver·i·fi·a·ble
ver·i·fi·ca·tion
ver·i·fi·er
ver·i·si·mil·i·tude
ver·i·ta·ble
ver·i·ta·ble·ness
ver·i·ta·bly
ver·i·ty
ver·i·ties
ver·meil
ver·mi·cel·li
ver·mic·u·lar
ver·mic·u·late
ver·mi·fuge
ver·mil·ion
ver·min
ver·min·ous
ver·mouth
ver·nac·u·lar
ver·nac·u·lar·ism
ver·nal
ver·nal·ly
ver·ni·er
Ver·sailles
ver·sa·tile
ver·sa·tile·ness
ver·sa·til·i·ty
versed
ver·si·fy

ver·si·fi·ca·tion
ver·sion
ver·sion·al
ver·sus
ver·te·bra
ver·te·brae
ver·te·bral
ver·te·brate
ver·tex
ver·tex·es
ver·ti·cal
ver·ti·cal·i·ty
ver·ti·cal·ness
ver·ti·cal·ly
ver·ti·go
ver·tig·i·nous
verve
ves·i·cant
vas·pers
ves·sel
ves·tal
vest·ed
ves·ti·bule
ves·tige
ves·tig·i·al
ves·tig·i·al·ly
vest·ment
vest-pock·et
ves·try
ves·tries
vet·er·an
vet·er·i·nar·i·an
vet·er·i·nary
ve·to
ve·toed
vc·to·ing
ve·to·er
vex
vexed
vex·ing
vex·a·tion
vex·a·tious
vi·a·ble
vi·a·bil·i·ty
vi·a·bly
vi·a·duct
vi·al
vi·and
vi·brant
vi·bran·cy
vi·brate
vi·brat·ed
vi·brat·ing
vi·bra·tion
vi·bra·to
vi·bra·tor
vi·bra·to·ry
vi·bur·num
vic·ar
vic·ar·age
vi·car·i·ous
vi·car·i·ous·ly
vi·car·i·ous·ness
vice-ad·mi·ral
vice-chan·cel·lor
vice-con·sul
vice-con·su·lar
vice-con·su·late
vice-con·sul·ship
vice-pres·i·dent
vice-pres·i·den·cy
vice-pres·i·den·cies
vice-pres·i·den·tial
vice·roy
vice   ver·sa
vi·chys·soise
vi·cin·i·ty
vi·cin·i·ties

vi·cious
vi·cious·ly
vi·cious·ness
vi·cis·si·tude
vic·tim
vic·tim·ize
vic·tim·ized
vic·tim·iz·ing
vic·tim·i·za·tion
vic·tor
Vic·to·ri·an
vic·to·ri·ous
vic·to·ri·ous·ly
vic·to·ri·ous·ness
vic·to·ry
vic·to·ries
vict·ual
vi·cu·na
vid·eo
vid·e·o·tape
vid·e·o·taped
vid·e·o·tap·ing
vie
vied
vy·ing
vi·er
Vi·et·nam·ese
view·er
view·point
vig·il
vig·i·lance
vig·i·lant
vig·i·lan·tc
vig·i·lan·tism
vi·gnette
vig·or
vig·or·ous
vig·or·ous·ly
Vi·king
vile
vil·er
vil·est
vile·ly
vil·i·fy
vil·i·fied
vil·i·fy·ing
vil·i·fi·ca·tion
vil·la
vil·lage
vil·lain
vil·lain·ous
vil·lain·ous·ly
vil·lain·ous·ness
vil·lainy
vil·lain·ies
vil·lcin
vil·lous
vin·ai·grette
vin·ci·ble
vin·ci·bil·i·ty
vin·di·cate
vin·di·cat·ed
vin·di·cat·ing
vin·di·ca·tion
vin·di·ca·tor
vin·dic·tive
vin·dic·tive·ly
vin·dic·tive·ness
vin·e·gar
vin·e·gary
vine·yard
vi·ni·cul·ture
vi·nous
vin·tage
vint·ner
vi·nyl
vi·ol
vi·o·la

vi·o·list
vi·o·la·ble
vi·o·la·bil·i·ty
vi·o·late
vi·o·lat·ed
vi·o·lat·ing
vi·o·la·tor
vi·o·la·tion
vi·o·lence
vi·o·lent
vi·o·let
vi·o·lin
vi·o·lin·ist
vi·o·list
vi·o·lon·cel·lo
vi·o·lon·cel·list
vi·per
vi·ra·go
vi·ral
vi·reo
vir·gin
vir·gin·al
vir·gin·al·ly
vir·gin·i·ty
vir·gule
vir·ile
vi·ril·i·ty
vi·rol·o·gy
vi·rol·o·gist
vir·tu·al
vir·tu·al·ly
vir·tue
vir·tu·os·i·ty
vir·tu·o·so
vir·tu·ous
vir·tu·ous·ly
vir·tu·ous·ness
vir·u·lent
vir·u·lence
vir·u·len·cy
vi·rus
vi·rus·es
vi·sa
vis·age
vis-a-vis
vis·cera
vis·cer·al
vis·cid
vis·cid·i·ty
vis·cid·ly
vis·cid·ness
vis·cos·i·ty
vis·cos·i·ties
vis·count
vis·count·ess
vis·cous
vis·i·bil·i·ty
vis·i·ble
vi·sion
vi·sion·ary
vis·it
vis·i·tant
vis·i·ta·tion
vis·it·ing
vis·i·tor
vi·sor
vis·ta
vis·u·al
vis·u·al·ly
vis·u·al·ize
vis·u·al·ized
vis·u·al·iz·ing
vis·u·al·i·za·tion
vi·tal
vi·tal·ly
vi·tal·i·ty
vi·tal·ize
vi·tal·ized

vi·tal·iz·ing
vi·tal·i·za·tion
vi·tals
vi·ta·min
vi·ti·ate
vi·ti·at·ed
vi·ti·at·ing
vi·ti·a·tion
vit·re·ous
vit·re·os·i·ty
vit·ri·fy
vit·ri·fied
vit·ri·fy·ing
vit·ri·fi·a·ble
vit·ri·fi·ca·tion
vit·ri·ol
vit·ri·ol·ic
vit·tles
vi·tu·per·ate
vi·tu·per·at·ed
vi·tu·per·at·ing
vi·tu·per·a·tion
vi·va
vi·va·cious
vi·vac·i·ty
vi·var·i·um
vi·va vo·ce
viv·id
viv·i·fy
viv·i·fied
viv·i·fy·ing
viv·i·fi·ca·tion
vi·vip·ar·ous
vivi·sect
viv·i·sec·tion
vix·en
vi·zier
vi·zor
vo·cab·u·lary
vo·cab·u·lar·ies
vo·cal
vo·cal·ic
vo·cal·ist
vo·cal·ize
vo·cal·ized
vo·cal·iz·ing
vo·cal·i·za·tion
vo·ca·tion
vo·ca·tion·al
vo·cif·er·ate
vo·cif·er·ous
vod·ka
vogue
vogu·ish
voice
voiced
voic·ing
voice·print
void·a·ble
voile
vol·a·tile
vol·a·til·i·ty
vol·can·ic
vol·can·i·cal·ly
vol·ca·no
vol·ca·noes
vol·ca·nos
vo·li·tion
vol·ley
vol·leys
vol·leyed
vol·ley·ing
vol·ley·ball
volt·age
vol·ta·ic
vol·u·ble
vol·u·bly
vol·u·bil·i·ty

vol·ume
vo·lu·mi·nous
vo·lu·mi·nous·ly
vo·lu·mi·nous·ness
vol·un·tary
vol·un·tar·i·ly
vol·un·teer
vo·lup·tu·ary
vo·lup·tu·ous
vo·lute
vom·it
voo·doo
voo·doo·ism
voo·doo·ist
voo·doo·is·tic
vo·ra·cious
vo·rac·i·ty
vor·tex
vor·tex·es
vor·ti·ces
vo·ta·ry
vo·ta·ries
vote
vot·ed
vot·ing
vot·er
vo·tive
vouch·er
vouch·safe
vouch·safed
vouch·saf·ing
vow·el
vox po·pu·li
voy·age
voy·aged
voy·ag·ing
voy·ag·er
vo·yeur
vo·yeur·ism
voy·eur·is·tic
vul·can·ize
vul·can·ized
vul·can·iz·ing
vul·can·i·za·tion
vul·gar
vul·gar·ism
vul·gar·i·ty
vul·gar·ize
vul·gar·ized
vul·gar·iz·ing
vul·gar·i·za·tion
Vul·gate
vul·ner·a·ble
vul·ner·a·bil·i·ty
vul·ner·a·bly
vul·ture
vul·tur·ous
vul·va

W

wab·ble
wab·bled
wab·bling
wacky
wack·i·er
wack·i·est
wack·i·ly
wack·i·ness
wad
wad·ded
wad·ding
wad·dle
wad·dled
wad·dling
wad·dler
wad·dly

wade
wad·ed
wad·ing
wa·fer
waf·fle
waft
wag
wagged
wag·ging
wage
waged
wag·ing
wa·ger
wag·gery
wag·gish
wag·gle
wag·gled
wag·gling
wag·on
wa·hi·ne
Wai·ki·ki
wain·scot
wain·scot·ing
wain·wright
waist·band
waist·coat
waist·line
wait·er
wait·ress
wait·ing
waive
waived
waiv·ing
waiv·er
wake
waked
wok·en
wak·ing
wake·ful
wake·ful·ly
wake·ful·ness
wak·en
wale
waled
wal·ing
walk·a·way
walk·er
walk·ie-talk·ie
walk·out
walk·o·ver
walk-up
walk·way
wal·la·by
wal·la·bies
wall·board
wal·let
wall·flow·er
wal·lop
wall·pa·per
wall-to-wall
wal·nut
wal·rus
waltz
wam·pum
wan
wan·ner
wan·ness
wan·der
wan·der·lust
wane
waned
wan·ing
wan·gle
wan·gled
wan·gling
want·ing
wan·ton
war

warred
war·ring
war·ble
war·bled
war·bling
war·bler
war·den
ward·er
ward·robe
ware·house
war·fare
war·head
warm
warm·er
warm·est
warm-blood·ed
warm-heart·ed
war·mong·er
warmth
warn·ing
war·path
war·rant
war·ran·ty
war·ren
war·ri·or
war·ship
war·time
wary
war·i·er
war·i·est
war·i·ly
war·i·ness
wash·a·ble
wash·ba·sin
wash·bowl
wash·cloth
wash·er
wash·ing
Wash·ing·ton
wash·out
wash·room
wash·tub
wasp·ish
wasp·ish·ness
was·sail
wast·age
waste
wast·ed
wast·ing
waste·ful
waste·bas·ket
waste·land
waste·pa·per
wast·rel
watch·dog
watch·ful
watch·man
watch·tow·er
watch·word
wa·ter·borne
wa·ter·col·or
wa·ter·course
wa·ter·cress
wa·ter·fall
wa·ter·fowl
wa·ter·front
wa·ter·less
wa·ter lev·el
wa·ter lily
wa·ter line
wa·ter·logged
wa·ter main
wa·ter·mark
wa·ter·mel·on
wa·ter moc·ca·sin
wa·ter·pow·er
wa·ter·proof
wa·ter-re·pel·lent

wa·ter·side
wa·ter-ski
wa·ter-skied
wa·ter-ski·ing
wa·ter·spout
wa·ter·tight
wa·ter·works
wa·tery
wa·ter·i·ness
watt·age
watt-hour
wat·tle
wat·tled
wat·tling
wave
waved
wav·ing
wave·length
wave·let
wa·ver
wav·y
wav·i·ly
wav·i·ness
wax
waxed
wax·ing
wax·en
wax·wing
wax·work
waxy
wax·i·er
wax·i·ness
way·far·er
way·far·ing
way·lay
way·laid
way·lay·ing
way·side
way·ward
weak·en
weak-kneed
weak·ling
weak·ly
weak·li·er
weak·li·ness
weak-mind·ed
weak·ness
wealthy
wealth·i·er
wealth·i·est
wealth·i·ness
wean
weap·on
weap·on·ry
wear
wore
worn
wear·ing
wea·ri·some
wea·ry
wea·ried
wea·ry·ing
wea·ri·ly
wea·ri·ness
wea·sel
weath·er
weath·er·a·bil·i·ty
weath·er-beat·en
weath·er·cock
weath·er·glass
weath·er·ing
weath·er·man
weath·er·proof
weath·er·vane
weave
wove
weaved
wov·en

weav·ing
web
webbed
web·bing
web-foot·ed
wed·ding
wedge
wedged
wedg·ing
wed·lock
weedy
weed·i·er
weed·i·ness
week·day
week·end
week·ly
weep
wept
weep·ing
wee·vil
weigh
weight
weighty
weight·i·er
weight·i·est
weight·i·ness
weird
weird·er
weird·est
wel·come
wel·comed
wel·com·ing
wel·fare
well-ad·vised
well-be·ing
well·born
well-bred
well-dis·posed
well-done
well-found·ed
well-groomed
well-ground·ed
well-known
well-mean·ing
well-off
well-read
well-spo·ken
well·spring
well-timed
well-to-do
well-wish·er
well-worn
wel·ter
wel·ter·weight
were·wolf
west·er·ly
west·ern
West·ern·er
west·ern·ize
west·ern·ized
west·ern·iz·ing
west·ern·i·za·tion
west·ern·most
west·ward
wet
wet·ter
wet·test
wet·ting
wet·back
whale
whaled
whal·ing
whale·boat
whale·bone
whal·er
wharf
wharves
wharf·age

what·ev·er
what·not
what·so·ev·er
wheal
wheat
whee·dle
   whee·dled
   whee·dling
wheel·bar·row
wheel·chair
wheeled
wheel·house
wheeze
   wheezed
   wheez·ing
wheezy
   wheez·i·ness
whelm
whelp
whence·so·ev·er
when·ev·er
where·a·bouts
where·as
where·by
where·fore
where·in
where·on
where·so·ev·er
where·to
where·up·on
wher·ev·er
where·with
where·with·al
wher·ry
whet
   whet·ted
   whet·ting
wheth·er
whet·stone
which·ev·er
while
whim·per
whim·sy
   whim·si·cal
whine
   whin·ed
   whin·ing
whin·ny
   whin·nied
   whin·ny·ing
whip
   whipped
   whip·ping
whip·lash
whip·per·snap·per
whip·pet
whip·poor·will
whir
   whirred
   whir·ring
whirl·i·gig
whirl·pool
whirl·wind
whisk·er
whis·key
whis·ky
whis·per
whist
whis·tle
   whis·tled
   whis·tling
whis·tler
white
   whit·er
   whit·ish
white·col·lar
white·faced
whit·en

white·wash
whith·er
whit·tle
   whit·tled
   whit·tling
whiz
   whizzed
   whiz·zing
   whiz·zes
whoa
who·ev·er
whole·heart·ed
whole·sale
   whole·sal·ing
   whole·sal·er
whole·some
whol·ly
whom·ev·er
whom·so·ev·er
whoop·ing
whop·per
whop·ping
whore
whorled
whose·so·ev·er
who·so·ev·er
wick·ed
wick·er·work
wick·et
wide
   wid·er
   wid·est
wide-a·wake
wide-eyed
wid·en
wide·spread
widg·eon
wid·ow
wid·ow·er
width
wield·er
wieldy
wie·ner
wife·ly
   wife·li·ness
wig·gle
   wig·gled
   wig·gling
   wig·gly
   wig·gli·est
wig·wag
   wig·wagged
   wig·wag·ging
wig·wam
wild·cat
   wild·cat·ted
   wild·cat·ting
wil·der·ness
wild-eyed
wild·fire
wild·fowl
wild·life
wild·wood
wile
   wil·i·ly
   wil·i·ness
wily
willed
will·ful·ly
will·ing
will-o'-the-wisp
wil·low
wil·lowy
wil·ly-nil·ly
win
   won
   win·ning
wince

winc·ing
wind
   wound
   wind·ing
wind·break
wind·ed
wind·fall
wind·jam·mer
wind·lass
wind·mill
win·dow
win·dow·pane
win·dow-shop
   win·dow·shop·ping
wind·pipe
wind·shield
wind·storm
wind·up
wind·ward
windy
   wind·i·er
   wind·i·ness
wine
   wined
   win·ing
win·ery
winged
wing·span
wing·spread
win·na·ble
win·ner
win·ning
win·now
win·some
win·ter
win·ter·green
win·ter·ize
   win·ter·ized
   win·ter·iz·ing
   win·ter·i·za·tion
win·try
   win·ter·y
   win·tri·ness
wipe
   wiped
   wip·ing
wire-haired
wire·less
wire·tap
   wire·tapped
   wire·tap·ping
   wire·tap·per
wir·ing
wiry
   wir·i·er
   wir·i·ness
wis·dom
wise
   wis·er
   wis·est
   wise·ly
wise·crack
wish·bone
wish·ful·ly
wish·y-washy
wisp
   wispy
   wisp·i·er
wis·te·ria
wist·ful·ly
witch·craft
witch·ery
witch·ing
with·al
with·draw
   with·drew
   with·drawn
   with·draw·ing

with·draw·al
with·er
with·hold
   with·held
   with·hold·ing
with·in
with·out
with·stand
   with·stood
   with·stand·ing
wit·less
wit·ness
wit·ti·cism
wit·ting
   wit·ting·ly
wit·ty
   wit·ti·est
   wit·ti·ly
   wit·ti·ness
wiz·ard
   wiz·ard·ry
wiz·en
   wiz·ened
wob·ble
   wob·bled
   wob·bling
   wob·bly
woe·be·gone
woe·ful·ly
wolf·hound
wolf·ram
wol·ver·ine
wom·an
   wom·en
wom·an·ly
   wom·an·li·ness
wom·an·hood
wom·an·ish
wom·an·kind
womb
won·der·ful
won·der·land
won·der·ment
won·drous
wont·ed
wood·bine
wood·chuck
wood·cock
wood·craft
wood·ed
wood·en
wood·land
wood·peck·er
wood·pile
woods·man
woodsy
wood·wind
wood·work
woody
woo·er
woof·er
wool·en
wool·gath·er·ing
wool·ly
   wool·li·ness
   wool·ly-head·ed
woozy
   wooz·i·ly
   wooz·i·ness
word·ing
word·less
wordy
   word·i·est
   word·i·ly
   word·i·ness
work·a·ble
work·a·bil·i·ty
work·a·day

work·bench
worked-up
work·er
work·horse
work·ing
work·ing·man
work·man
work·man·like
work·man·ship
work·out
work·room
work·shop
work·ta·ble
world·ly
   world·li·er
   world·li·est
   world·li·ness
   world·ly-wise
world-wea·ry
world-wide
worm-eat·en
wormy
worn-out
wor·ri·some
wor·ry
   wor·ried
   wor·ry·ing
   wor·ries
   wor·ri·er
wor·ry·wart
wors·en
worship
   wor·ship·ful
wor·sted
worth·less
worth·while
worthy
   wor·thi·er
   wor·thi·est
   wor·thi·ly
   wor·thi·ness
would-be
wound·ed
wrack
wraith
wran·gle
   wran·gled
   wran·gling
wran·gler
wrap
   wrapped
   wrap·ping
wrap·per
wrath·ful
wreak
wreath
wreathe
   wreathed
   wreath·ing
wreck·age
wrench
wres·tle
   wres·tled
   wres·tling
wretch
wretch·ed
wrig·gle
   wrig·gled
   wrig·gling
   wrig·gly
   wrig·gler
wring
   wrung
   wring·ing
wring·er
wrin·kle
   wrin·kled
   wrin·kling

wrin·kly
write
  wrote
  writ·ten
  writ·ing
  writ·er
writhe
  writhed
  writh·ing
wrong·do·er
  wrong·do·ing
wronged
wrong·ful·ly
wrong-head·ed
wrought
wry
  wri·er
  wri·est
  wry·ly

X

xan·thous
xe·bec
xe·non
xen·o·phobe
  xen·o·pho·bia
X-ray
  x·ray
xy·lem
xy·lo·graph
  xy·log·ra·phy
xy·loid
xy·lo·phone
  xy·lo·phon·ist

Y

yacht
yacht·ing
yachts·man
ya·hoo
yak
yam
yam·mer
yank
Yan·kee
yap
  yapped
  yap·ping
yard·age
yard·arm
yard·mas·ter
yard·stick
yarn
yar·row
yawl
yawn
year·book
year·ling
year·long
year·ly
yearn
  yearn·ing
year-round
yeast
  yeasty
yel·low
  yel·low·ish
yel·low·bird
yel·low fe·ver
yel·low·ham·mer

yel·low jack·et
yelp
yen
  yenned
  yen·ning

yeo·man
  yeo·men
ye·shi·va
yes·ter·day
yes·ter·year
yew
Yid·dish
yield
  yield·ing
yip
  yipped
  yip·ping
yo·del
  yo·deled
  yo·del·ing
  yo·del·er
yo·ga
yo·gi
yo·gurt
yoke
  yoked
  yok·ing
yo·kel
yolk
Yom Kip·pur
yon·der
yore
young
  young·er
  young·ish
young·ling

young·ster
your·self
  your·selves
youth·ful
  youth·ful·ly
yowl
yuc·ca
yule·tide

Z

za·ny
  za·nies
  za·ni·er
  za·ni·est
  za·ni·ly
  za·ni·ness
zeal
  zeal·ot
  zeal·ous
ze·bra
ze·bu
ze·nith
zeph·yr
zep·pe·lin
ze·ro
  ze·ros
  ze·roes
zest
  zesty
  zest·i·er
  zest·ful
  zest·ful·ly
zig·zag
  zig·zagged
  zig·zag·ging

zinc
  zinced
  zinc·ing
zing
zin·nia
Zi·on
Zi·on·ism
  Zi·on·ist
zip
  zipped
  zip·ping
zip·per
zip·py
  zip·pi·er
  zip·pi·est
zir·con
zir·co·ni·um
zith·er
zo·di·ac
  zo·di·a·cal
zom·bie
zon·al
  zon·al·ly
zone
  zoned
  zon·ing
zoo
  zoos
zoo·ge·og·ra·phy
zo·ol·o·gy
  zo·o·log·i·cal
  zo·o·log·i·cal·ly
  zo·ol·o·gist
zuc·chet·to
zuc·chi·ni
zwie·back
zy·gote

Metric Measurement

JOULE (J) = the work done when the point of application of a force of 1 newton is displaced through a distance of 1 metre in the direction of the force.

erg = 1 dyn acting through a distance of 1 centimetre = 100^7J

watt (W) = the power which in 1 second gives rise to energy of 1 joule.

metric horsepower (ch or CV or cv or PS or pk) = the power which raises 75 kilograms against the force of gravity through a distance of 1 metre per second = 75 × 9.806 65 joules per second = 735.498 75 watts.

coulomb (C) = the quantity of electricity carried in 1 second by a current of 1 ampere.

volt (V) = the difference of electric potential between two points of a conducting wire carrying a constant current of 1 ampere, when the power dissipated between these points is equal to 1 watt.

ohm (Ω) = the electric resistance between two points of a conductor when a constant potential difference of 1 volt, applied to these points, produces in the conductor a current of 1 ampere, the conductor not being the seat of any electromotive force.

siemens (S) = 1 ampere per volt, being the unit of electric conductance; this unit has also been known as the reciprocal ohm (ohm^{-1}) or 'mho'.

farad (F) the capacitance of a capacitor between the plates of which there appears a difference of electric potential of 1 volt when it is charged by a quantity of electricity of 1 coulomb.

weber (Wb) = the magnetic flux which, linking a circuit of 1 turn, would produce in it an electromotive force of 1 volt if it were reduced to zero at a uniform rate in 1 second.

henry (H) = the inductance of a closed circuit in which an electromotive force of 1 volt is produced when the electric current in the circuit varies uniformly at the rate of 1 ampere per second.

tesla (T) = the flux density in vacuum produced by a magnetic field of strength 1 ampere per metre; this is the unit of magnetic flux density and equals 1 weber per square metre.

lumen (lm) = the luminous flux emitted within unit solid angle of 1 steradian by a point source having a uniform luminous intensity of 1 candela. lux (lx) = an illuminance of 1 lumen per square metre.

LENGTH

1000 picometres	= 1 nanometre
1000 nanometres	= 1 micrometre
1000 micrometres	= 1 millimetre
10 millimetres	= 1 centimetre
100 millimetres	= 1 decimetre
10 centimetres	= 1 decimetre
1000 millimetres	= 1 metre
100 centimetres	= 1 metre
10 decimetres	= 1 metre
100 metres	= 1 hectometre
1000 metres	= 1 kilometre
10 hectometres	= 1 kilometre
1000 kilometres	= 1 megametre
1852 nautical metres	= 1 international nautical mile

AREA

100 sq millimetres	= 1 sq centimetre
100 sq centimetres	= 1 sq decimetre
10 000 sq centimetres	= 1 sq metre
100 sq decimetres	= 1 sq metre
100 sq metres	= 1 are
10 ares	= 1 dekare
10 000 sq metres	= 1 sq hectometre
	= 1 hectare
100 ares	= 1 hectare
10 dekares	= 1 hectare
100 sq hectometres	= 1 sq kilometre
100 hectares	= 1 sq kilometre

MASS

1000 nanograms	= 1 microgram
1000 micrograms	= 1 milligram
200 milligrams	= 1 metric carat
1000 milligrams	= 1 gram
5 metric carats	= 1 gram
25 grams	= 1 metric ounce
100 grams	= 1 hectogram
1000 grams	= 1 kilogram
100 kilograms	= 1 quintal
1000 kilograms	= 1 megagram
10 quintals	= 1 megagram
	= 1 tonne

ENERGY (WORK & HEAT)

10 000 ergs	= 1 millijoule
1000 millijoules	= 1 joule
1000 joules	= 1 kilojoule
1000 kilojoules	= 1 megajoule
3.6 megajoules	= 1 kilowatt hour
1000 megajoules	= 1 gigajoule
1000 gigajoules	= 1 terajoule

POWER

1000 microwatts	= 1 milliwatt
1000 milliwatts	= 1 watt
1000 watts	= 1 kilowatt
1000 kilowatts	= 1 megawatt
1000 megawatts	= 1 gigawatt
1000 gigawatts	= 1 terawatt

VOLUME & CAPACITY

1000 cu millimetres	= 1 cu centimetre
1000 cu centimetres	= 1 cu decimetre
1000 cu decimetres	= 1 cu metre
1000 cu metres	= 1 dekametre
1000 cu dekametres	= 1 cu hectometre
1000 cu hectometres	= 1 cu kilometre
1000 microlitres	= 1 millilitre
	= 1 cu centimetre
10 millilitre	= 1 centilitre
10 centilitres	= 1 decilitre
1000 millilitres	= 1 litre
100 centilitres	= 1 litre
100 litres	= 1 hectolitre
1000 litres	= 1 kilolitre
	= 1 cu metre
10 hectolitres	= 1 kilolitre

PRESSURE AND STRESS

1000 micropascals	= 1 millipascal
100 millipascals	= 1 microbar
1000 millipascals	= 1 pascal
10 microbars	= 1 pascal
1000 microbars	= 1 millibar
100 pascals	= 1 millibar
1000 pascals	= 1 kilopascal
10 millibars	= 1 kilopascal
	= 1 pieze
1000 millibars	= 1 bar
	= 1 hectopieze
1000 kilopascals	= 1 megapascal
100 bars	= 1 hectobar
1000 bars	= 1 kilobar
1000 megapascals	= 1 gigapascal

ELECTRICITY & MAGNETISM

1000 picoamperes	= 1 nanoampere
1000 nanoamperes	= 1 microampere
1000 microamperes	= 1 milliampere
1000 milliamperes	= 1 ampere
1000 amperes	= 1 kiloampere
1000 millicoulombs	= 1 coulomb
1000 coulombs	= 1 kilocoulomb
1000 microvolts	= 1 millivolt
1000 millivolts	= 1 volts
1000 volts	= 1 kilovolt
1000 kilovolts	= 1 megavolt
1000 microhm	= 1 milliohm
1000 milliohm	= 1 ohm

1000 ohms	= 1 kilohm	**FORCE**		1000 kilograms per	= 1 tonne per
1000 kilohms	= 1 megohm	10 micronewtons	= 1 dyne	cu metre	cu metre
1000 megohms	= 1 gigohm	1000 micronewtons	= 1 millinewton		= 1 kilogram per
1000 millisiemens	= 1 siemens	10 millinewtons	= 1 centinewton		cu decimetre
1000 millihenrys	= 1 henry	1000 millinewtons	= 1 newton		
1000 milliteslas	= 1 tesla	1000 newtons	= 1 kilonewton	**TIME**	
		1000 kilonewtons	= 1 meganewton	1000 nanoseconds	= 1 microsecond
FREQUENCY				1000 microseconds	= 1 millisecond
1000 hertz	= 1 kilohertz	**DENSITY & CONCENTRATION**		1000 milliseconds	= 1 second
1000 kilohertz	= 1 megahertz	1 gram per cubic	= 1 milligram per	1000 seconds	= 1 kilosecond
1000 megahertz	= 1 gigahertz	metre	cu decimetre		
1000 gigahertz	= 1 terahertz	1000 milligrams per	= 1 gram per	3.6 kilometres	= 1 metre per
1000 terahertz	= 1 petahertz	cu decimetre	cu decimetre	per hour	second
1000 petahertz	= 1 exahertz		= 1 kilogram per	3 600 kilometres	= 1 kilometre per
			cu metre	per hour	second

Metric Conversions

CONVERSION FORMULAE
Non-metric to metric

LENGTH

To convert   *Multiply by*

milli-inches into micrometres 25.4
inches into millimetres 25.4
inches into centimetres 2.54
inches into metres 0.0254
feet into millimetres 304.8
feet into centimetres 30.48
feet into metres 0.3048
yards into metres 0.9144
fathoms into metres 1.8288
chains into metres 20.1168
furlongs into metres 201.168
miles, statute into kilometres ...1.609344
miles, nautical into kilometres 1.852

VOLUME & CAPACITY

To convert   *Multiply by*

cubic inches into cubic
    centimetres 16.387064
cubic inches into litres 0.016387
cubic feet into cubic metres ...0.0283168
cubic feet into litres 28.316847
pints into litres 0.5682613
quarts into litres 1.1365225
cubic yards into cubic metres .0.7645549
gallons into litres 4.54609
fluid ounces into cubic
    centimetres 28.413063

AREA

To convert   *Multiply by*

square inches into square
    millimetres 645.16
square inches into square
    centimetres 6.4516
square feet into square
    centimetres 929.0304
square feet into square metres ..0.092903

square yards into square metres 0.836123
square yards into ares 0.0083613
acres into square metres 4046.8564
acres into ares 40.468564
acres into hectares 0.4046856
square miles into hectares 258.9988
square miles into square
    kilometres 2.589988

MASS

To convert   *Multiply by*

grains into milligrams 64.79891
grains into metric carats 0.323995
grains into grams 0.064799
pennyweights into grams 1.555174
drams into grams 1.77185
ounces into grams 28.349523
ounces troy into metric carats ..155.5174
ounces into kilograms 0.0283495
pounds into kilograms 0.4535924
stones into kilograms 6.3502932
hundred weights into
    kilograms 50.802345
tons into kilograms 1016.0469
tons into metric tonnes 1.01604
tahils into grams 37.799
kati into kilograms 0.60479

POWER

To convert   *Multiply by*

foot pounds-force per second into
    watts 1.35582
horsepower into watts 745.7
foot pounds-force per second into
    kilowatts 0.001356
horsepower into kilowatts 0.7457
horsepower into metric
    horsepower 1.01387

Metric to non-metric

VOLUME & CAPACITY

To convert   *Multiply by*

cu.centimetres into cu.inches 0.06102
cu.metres into cu.feet 35.3147
cu.metres into cu.yards 1.30795
litres into cu.inches 61.03
litres into pints 1.7598
litres into quarts 0.8799
litres into U.K. gallons 0.219976
litres into U.S. gallons 0.264178

MASS

To convert   *Multiply by*

grams into ounces 0.03527
grams into grains 15.4324
grams into tahil 0.02646
kilograms into pounds 2.2046
kilograms into tons 0.0009842
kilograms into katis 1.653
kilograms into stones 0.1575
kilograms into hundredweights ..0.01968

VELOCITY

To convert   *Multiply by*

centimetres per second into
    feet per second 0.03281
metres per second into
    feet per minute 196.9
metres per second into
    feet per second 3.281
kilometres per hour into
    miles per hour 0.6214

POWER

To convert	Multiply by
kilowatts into horsepower	1.341
metric horsepower into horsepower	0.98632
metric horsepower into foot pounds—force per second	542.48

FORCE

To convert	Multiply by
newtons into pounds force	0.2248
newtons into pounds	7.2330

LINEAR

To convert	Multiply by
millimetres into feet	3.281×10
millimetres into inches	0.03937
centimetres into inches	0.3937
metres into yards	1.09361
metres into feet	3.281
kilometres into yards	1093.61
kilometres into miles	0.62137

AREA

To convert	Multiply by
sq.millimetres into sq.inches	1.550×10^{-3}
sq.centimetres into sq.inches	0.1550
sq.metres into sq.feet	10.7639
sq.metres into sq.yards	1.19599
sq.metres into acres	2.47105×10^{-4}
sq.kilometres into sq.miles	0.3861
sq.kilometres into acres	247.105
hectares into acres	2.47105

LENGTH

Inches			Millimetres
0.03937	.	1 .	25.40
0.07874	.	2 .	50.80
0.11811	.	3 .	76.20
0.15748	.	4 .	101.60
0.19685	.	5 .	127.00
0.23622	.	6 .	152.40
0.27559	.	7 .	177.80
0.31396	.	8 .	203.20
0.35433	.	9 .	228.60

inches			Centimetres
.393700	.	1 .	2.540
.787402	.	2 .	5.080
1.181102	.	3 .	7.620
1.574803	.	4 .	10.160
1.968504	.	5 .	12.700
2.362205	.	6 .	15.240
2.755906	.	7 .	17.780
3.149606	.	8 .	20.320
3.543307	.	9 .	22.860

Feet			Metres
3.280840	.	1 .	.3048
6.561680	.	2 .	.6096
9.842520	.	3 .	.9144
13.123359	.	4 .	1.2192
16.404199	.	5 .	1.5240
19.685038	.	6 .	1.8288
22.965878	.	7 .	2.1336
26.246718	.	8 .	2.4384
29.527558	.	9 .	2.7432

Yards			Metres
1.093613	.	1 .	0.91440
2.187226	.	2 .	1.82880
3.280839	.	3 .	2.74320
4.374452	.	4 .	3.65760
5.468065	.	5 .	4.57200
6.561678	.	6 .	5.48640
7.655291	.	7 .	6.40080
8.748904	.	8 .	7.31520
0.842517	.	9 .	8.22960

Miles			Kilometres
.621371	.	1 .	1.60934
1.242742	.	2 .	3.21869
1.864113	.	3 .	4.82803
2.485484	.	4 .	6.43738
3.106855	.	5 .	8.04672
3.728226	.	6 .	9.65606
4.349597	.	7 .	11.26541
4.970968	.	8 .	12.87475
5.592339	.	9 .	14.48410

VOLUME & CAPACITY

Cu. Inches			Cu. Centimetres
.061024	.	1 .	16.38706
.122048	.	2 .	32.77413
.183072	.	3 .	49.16119
.244096	.	4 .	65.54826
.305120	.	5 .	81.93532
.366144	.	6 .	98.32238
.427168	.	7 .	114.70945
.488192	.	8 .	131.09651
.549216	.	9 .	147.48358

Metric Conversions

009VOLUME & CAPACITY

Fluid ounces		Cu. Centimetres	Quarts		Litres	Cwt.		Kiloframs
0.03520	. 1 .	28,4131	.87988	. 1 .	1.13652	0.19684	. 1 .	50.80234
0.07039	. 2 .	56.8261	1.75976	. 2 .	2.27304	.039368	. 2 .	101.60469
0.10009	. 3 .	85.2392	2.63964	. 3 .	3.40956	.059052	. 3 .	152.40704
0.14078	. 4 .	113.6522	3.51952	. 4 .	4.54608	.078736	. 4 .	203.20938
0.17598	. 5 .	142.0653	4.39940	. 5 .	5.68260	.098420	. 5 .	254.01173
0.21117	. 6 .	170.4784	5.27928	. 6 .	6.81912	.118104	. 6 .	304.81408
0.24637	. 7 .	198.8914	6.15916	. 7 .	7.95564	.137788	. 7 .	355.61642
0.28156	. 8 .	227.3045	7.03904	. 8 .	9.09216	.157472	. 8 .	406.41977
0.31676	. 9 .	255.7176	7.91892	. 9 .	10.22868	.177156	. 9 .	457.22112

VOLUME & CAPACITY

Cu. Feet		Litres	Gallons		Litres	Tons		Kilograms
						.000984	. 1 .	1016.0469
0.035315	. 1 .	28.3168				.001968	. 2 .	2032.0938
0.070630	. 2 .	56.6337	.21997	. 1 .	4.54609	.002952	. 3 .	3048.1407
0.105940	. 3 .	84.9505	.43994	. 2 .	9.09218	.003936	. 4 .	4064.1876
0.140588	. 4 .	113.2674	.65991	. 3 .	13.63827	.004920	. 5 .	5080.2345
0.176574	. 5 .	141.5842	.87988	. 4 .	18.18436	.005904	. 6 .	6096.2814
0.211888	. 6 .	169.9011	1.09985	. 5 .	22.73045	.006888	. 7 .	7112.3283
0.247203	. 7 .	198.2179	1.31982	. 6 .	27.27654	.007872	. 8 .	8128.3752
0.282518	. 8 .	226.5348	1.53979	. 7 .	31.82263	.008856	. 9 .	9144.4221
0.317832	. 9 .	254.8516	1.75976	. 8 .	36.36872			
			1.97973	. 9 .	40.91481			

MASS / POWER

Cu. Feet		Cu. Metres	Ounces		Grams	Horsepower		Kilowatts
35.31467	. 1 .	0.02832				1.341022	. 1 .	.7457
70.62934	. 2 .	0.05664	.035274	. 1 .	28.34952	2.682044	. 2 .	1.4914
105.94401	. 3 .	0.08496	.070548	. 2 .	56.69905	4.023066	. 3 .	2.2371
141.25868	. 4 .	0.11328	.105812	. 3 .	85.04857	5.364088	. 4 .	2.9828
176.57335	. 5 .	0.14160	.141096	. 4 .	113.39809	6.705110	. 5 .	3.7285
211.88802	. 6 .	0.16992	.176370	. 5 .	141.74762	8.046132	. 6 .	4.4742
247.20269	. 7 .	0.19824	.211644	. 6 .	170.09714	9.387154	. 7 .	5.2199
282.51736	. 8 .	0.22656	.246918	. 7 .	198.44666	10.728176	. 8 .	5.9656
317.83203	. 9 .	0.25488	.282192	. 8 .	226.79618	12.069198	. 9 .	6.7113
			.317466	. 9 .	255.14571			

AREA

Cu. Yards		Cu. Metres	Grains		Grams	Sq. Inches		Sq. Centimetr
1.30795	. 1 .	.76455	15.4324	. 1 .	0.06480	.15500	. 1 .	6.45160
2.61590	. 2 .	1.52910	30.8648	. 2 .	0.12960	.31000	. 2 .	12.90320
3.92385	. 3 .	2.29365	46.2972	. 3 .	0.19440	.46500	. 3 .	19.35480
5.23180	. 4 .	3.05820	61.7296	. 4 .	0.25920	.62000	. 4 .	25.80640
6.53975	. 5 .	3.82275	77.1620	. 5 .	0.32400	.77500	. 5 .	32.25800
7.84770	. 6 .	4.58730	92.5944	. 6 .	0.38880	.93000	. 6 .	38.70960
9.15565	. 7 .	5.35185	108.0268	. 7 .	0.45360	1.08500	. 7 .	45.16120
10.46360	. 8 .	6.11640	123.4592	. 8 .	0.51840	1.24000	. 8 .	51.61280
11.77155	. 9 .	6.88095	138.8916	. 9 .	0.58320	1.39500	. 9 .	58.06440

Pints		Litres	Pounds		Kilograms	Sq. Feet		Sq. Metres
1.75976	. 1 .	.56826	2.204622	. 1 .	.453592	10.76391	. 1 .	0.09290
3.51952	. 2 .	1.13652	4.409244	. 2 .	.907184	21.52782	. 2 .	0.18580
5.27928	. 3 .	1.70478	6.613866	. 3 .	1.360776	32.29173	. 3 .	0.27870
7.03904	. 4 .	2.27305	8.818488	. 4 .	1.814368	43.05564	. 4 .	0.37160
8.79880	. 5 .	2.84131	11.023110	. 5 .	2.267960	53.81955	. 5 .	0.46450
10.55856	. 6 .	3.40957	13.227732	. 6 .	2.721552	64.58346	. 6 .	0.55740
12.31832	. 7 .	3.97783	15.432354	. 7 .	3.175144	75.34737	. 7 .	0.65030
14.07808	. 8 .	4.54609	17.636976	. 8 .	3.628736	86.11128	. 8 .	0.74320
15.83784	. 9 .	5.11435	19.841598	. 9 .	4.082328	96.87519	. 9 .	0.83610

Sq. Yards			Sq. Metres	Acres				Hectaares	Sq. Miles				Sq. Kilometres
1.19599	.	1	.	0.83613	2.47105	.	1	.	.40469	.38610	.	1	.	2.58999
2.39198	.	2	.	1.67226	4.94210	.	2	.	.80938	.77220	.	2	.	5.17998
3.58797	.	3	.	2.50839	7.41315	.	3	.	1.21407	1.15830	.	3	.	7.76997
4.78396	.	4	.	3.34453	9.88420	.	4	.	1.61876	1.54440	.	4	.	10.35996
5.97995	.	5	.	4.18065	12.35525	.	5	.	2.02345	1.93050	.	5	.	12.94995
7.17594	.	6	.	5.01678	14.82630	.	6	.	2.42814	2.31660	.	6	.	15.53994
8.37193	.	7	.	5.85291	17.29735	.	7	.	2.83283	2.70270	.	7	.	18.12993
9.56792	.	8	.	6.68904	19.76840	.	8	.	3.23752	3.08880	.	8	.	20.71992
10.76391	.	9	.	7.52517	22.23945	.	9	.	3.64221	3.47490	.	9	.	23.30991

Metric System

Multiples and Submultiples

The multiples and submultiples of the base and other units are formed by applying established prefixes, which are the same whichever unit is used. Examples are: milligram (mg), millimetre (mm), kilowatt (kW).

Only one multiplying prefix is applied at one time to a given unit. Thus one thousandth of a milligram is not referred to as a millimilligram but as a microgram (g). There are a few cases where, in attaching a prefix to the name of a unit, a contraction of the prefix name is made for convenience in pronunciation; for example megohm, microhm and hectare. Unit names take a plural 's' when associated with numbers greater than 1, eg 1.5 metres; the names hertz, lux and siemens are, however, the same in the plural. Symbols are not altered in the plural form; eg 1.5 m.

The names and values of prefixes in use are given below; also indicated are the equivalent powers to base 10 of the multiplying factors which can be used to relate any multiple or submultiple to the main unit: for example 1 mm = 10^{-3}m and 1 MN = 10^6 N. The general use of prefixes representing 10 raised to a power which is multiple of ± 3 is recommended in SI; for example, milimetre (10^{-3} m), metre (m) and kilometre (10^3 m). Other prefixes, notably centi, deci, deka and hecto can be used where others are inconvenient. Myria, as a prefix symbol, is not an SI multiple, but is included for reference.

Prefix name	Prefix symbol	Factor by which the unit is multiplied			Description
atto	a	10^{-18}	=	0 000 000 000 000 000 001	one million million millionth
femto	f	10^{-15}	=	0 000 000 000 000 001	one thousand million millionth
pico	p	10^{-12}	=	0 000 000 000 001	one million millionth
nano	n	10^{-9}	=	0 000 000 001	one thousand millionth
micro	m	10^{-6}	=	0 000 001	one millionth
milli	m	10^{-3}	=	0 001	one thousandth
centi	c	10^{-2}	=	0 01	one hundredth
deci	d	10^{-1}	=	0 1	one tenth
deca (or deka)	da	10^1	=	1 0	ten
hecto	h	10^2	=	100 0	one hundred
kilo	k	10^3	=	1 00 0	one thousand
myria	my	10^4	=	10 00 0	ten thousand
mega	M	10^6	=	1 000 00 0	one million
giga	G	10^9	=	1 000 000 00 0	one thousand million
tera	T	10^{12}	=	1 000 000 000 00 0	one million million
peta	P	10^{15}	=	1 000 000 000 000 00 0	one thousand million million
exa	E	10^{18}	=	1 000 000 000 000 000 00 0	one million million million

METRIC STANDARD ABBREVIATIONS

A	= ampere	cP	= centipoise	EHz	= exahertz	hm^2	= square hectometre
a	= are	cSt	= centistokes	F	= farad	hm^3	= cubic hectometre
bar	= bar	daa	= dekare	g	= gram	hpz	= hectopièze
C	= coulomb	dag	= dekagram	GHz	= gigahertz	Hz	= hertz
°C	= Celsius	dal	= dekalitre	GJ	= gigajoule	J	= joule
cc	= cubic centimetre	dam	= dekametre	GΩ	= gigohm	kA	= kiloampere
cg	= centigram	dam^2	= square dekametre	GPa	= gigapascal	kbar	= kilobar
cl	= centilitre	dam^3	= cubic dekametre	GW	= gigawatt	kC	= kilocoulomb
cm	= centimetre	dB	= decibel	h	= hour	kg	= kilogram
cm^2	= square centimetre	dg	= decigram	H	= henry	kgf	= kilogram-force
cm²⁄s	= square centimetre per second	dl	= decilitre	ha	= hectare	kgf m	= kilogram-force metre
cm^3	= cubic centimetre	dm	= decimetre	hbar	= hectobar	kHz	= kilohetz
		dm^2	= square decimetre	hg	= hectogram		
CM	= metric carat	dm^3	= cubic decimetre	hl	= hectolitre	kJ	= kilojoule
cN	= centinewton	dyn	= dyne	hm	= hectometre	kl	= kilolitre

km	= kilimetre	mg	= milligram	mW	= milliwatt	Ω	= ohm
km²	= square kilometre	Mg	= megagram	MW	= megawatt	p	= pond
km³	= cubic kilometre	mH	= millihenry	μA	= microampere	P	= poise
km/h	kilometre per hour	MHz	= megahertz	μbar	= microbar	pA	= picoampere
km/s	= kilometre per second	mJ	= millijoule	μC	= microcoulomb	Pa	= pascal
		MJ	= megajoule	μF	= microfarad	Pa s	= pascal second
kN	= kilonewton	ml	= millilitre	μg	= microgram	pC	= picocoulomb
kΩ	= kilohm	Mm	= megametre	μH	= microhenry	pF	= picofarad
kp	= kilopond	mm	= millimetre	μl	= microlitre	pH	= picohenry
kPa	= kilopascal	mm²	= square millimetre	μm	= micrometre	PHz	= petahertz
ks	= kilosecond	mm²/s	= square millimetre per second	μN	= micronewton	pm	= picometre
kS	= kilosiemens			μΩ	= microhm	pz	= pièze
kV	= kilovolt	mm³	= cubic millimetre	μPa	= micropascal	q	= quintal
kW	= kilowatt	mN	= millinewton	μS	= microsecond	s	= second
kWh	= kilowatt hour	MN	= meganewton	μS	= microsiemens	S	= siemens
l or L	= litre	mΩ	= milliohm	μT	= microtesia	sn	= sthène
m	= metre	MΩ	= megohm	μV	= microvolt	St	= stokes
m/s	= metre per second	mPa	= millipascal	μW	= microwatt	t	= tonne
m²	= square metre	MPa	= megapascal	N	= Newton	T	= tesla
m²/s	= square metre per second	mPa s	= millipascal second	nA	= nanoampere	THz	= terahertz
		ms	= millisecond	nC	= nanocoulomb	TJ	= terajoule
m³	= cubic metre	m/s	= metre per second	ng	= nanogram	TW	= terawatt
mA	= milliampere	mS	= millisicmens	nH	= nanohenry	V	= volt
mbar	= millibar	mT	= millitesia	nm	= nanometre	W	= watt
mC	= millicoulomb	mV	= millivolt	ns	= nanosecond		
MC	= megacoulomb	MV	= megavolt	nT	= nanotesia		

ANNUAL PERCENTAGE RATE TABLE FOR MONTHLY PAYMENT PLANS

ANNUAL PERCENTAGE RATE

(FINANCE CHARGE PER $100 OF AMOUNT FINANCED)

NUMBER OF PAYMENTS	10.00%	10.50%	11.00%	11.50%	12.00%	12.50%	13.00%	13.50%	14.00%	14.50%	15.00%	15.50%	16.00%	16.50%	17.00%	17.50%	18.00%
1	0.83	0.87	0.92	0.96	1.00	1.04	1.08	1.12	1.17	1.21	1.25	1.29	1.33	1.37	1.42	1.46	1.50
2	1.25	1.31	1.38	1.44	1.50	1.57	1.63	1.69	1.75	1.82	1.88	1.94	2.00	2.07	2.13	2.19	2.26
3	1.67	1.76	1.84	1.92	2.01	2.09	2.17	2.26	2.34	2.43	2.51	2.59	2.68	2.76	2.85	2.93	3.01
4	2.09	2.20	2.30	2.41	2.51	2.62	2.72	2.83	2.93	3.04	3.14	3.25	3.36	3.46	3.57	3.67	3.78
5	2.51	2.64	2.77	2.89	3.02	3.15	3.27	3.40	3.53	3.65	3.78	3.91	4.04	4.16	4.29	4.42	4.54
6	2.94	3.08	3.23	3.38	3.53	3.68	3.83	3.97	4.12	4.27	4.42	4.57	4.72	4.87	5.02	5.17	5.32
7	3.36	3.53	3.70	3.87	4.04	4.21	4.38	4.55	4.72	4.89	5.06	5.23	5.40	5.58	5.75	5.92	6.09
8	3.79	3.98	4.17	4.36	4.55	4.74	4.94	5.13	5.32	5.51	5.71	5.90	6.09	6.29	6.48	6.67	6.87
9	4.21	4.43	4.64	4.85	5.07	5.28	5.49	5.71	5.92	6.14	6.35	6.57	6.78	7.00	7.22	7.43	7.65
10	4.64	4.88	5.11	5.35	5.58	5.82	6.05	6.29	6.53	6.77	7.00	7.24	7.48	7.72	7.96	8.19	8.43
11	5.07	5.33	5.58	5.84	6.10	6.36	6.62	6.88	7.14	7.40	7.66	7.92	8.18	8.44	8.70	8.96	9.22
12	5.50	5.78	6.06	6.34	6.62	6.90	7.18	7.46	7.74	8.03	8.31	8.59	8.88	9.16	9.45	9.73	10.02
18	8.10	8.52	8.93	9.35	9.77	10.19	10.61	11.03	11.45	11.87	12.29	12.72	13.14	13.57	13.99	14.42	14.85
24	10.75	11.30	11.86	12.42	12.98	13.54	14.10	14.66	15.23	15.80	16.37	16.94	17.51	18.09	18.66	19.24	19.82
30	13.43	14.13	14.83	15.54	16.24	16.95	17.66	18.38	19.10	19.81	20.54	21.26	21.99	22.72	23.45	24.18	24.92
36	16.16	17.01	17.86	18.71	19.57	20.43	21.30	22.17	23.04	23.92	24.80	25.68	26.57	27.46	28.35	29.25	30.15
42	18.93	19.93	20.93	21.94	22.96	23.98	25.00	26.03	27.06	28.10	29.15	30.19	31.25	32.31	33.37	34.44	35.51
48	21.74	22.90	24.06	25.23	26.40	27.58	28.77	29.97	31.17	32.37	33.59	34.81	36.03	37.27	38.50	39.75	41.00
54	24.59	25.91	27.23	28.56	29.91	31.25	32.61	33.98	35.35	36.73	38.12	39.52	40.92	42.33	43.75	45.18	46.62
60	27.48	28.96	30.45	31.96	33.47	34.99	36.52	38.06	39.61	41.17	42.74	44.32	45.91	47.51	49.12	50.73	52.36
66	30.41	32.06	33.73	35.40	37.09	38.78	40.49	42.21	43.95	45.69	47.45	49.22	51.00	52.79	54.59	56.40	58.23
72	33.39	35.21	37.05	38.90	40.76	42.64	44.53	46.44	48.36	50.30	52.24	54.21	56.18	58.17	60.17	62.19	64.22
78	36.40	38.40	40.41	42.45	44.49	46.56	48.64	50.74	52.85	54.98	57.13	59.29	61.46	63.66	65.86	68.09	70.32
84	39.45	41.63	43.83	46.05	48.28	50.54	52.81	55.11	57.42	59.75	62.09	64.46	66.84	69.24	71.66	74.10	76.55
90	42.54	44.91	47.29	49.70	52.13	54.58	57.05	59.54	62.05	64.59	67.14	69.72	72.31	74.93	77.56	80.22	82.89
96	45.67	48.22	50.80	53.40	56.03	58.68	61.35	64.05	66.77	69.51	72.28	75.06	77.88	80.71	83.57	86.44	89.34
102	48.84	51.59	54.36	57.16	59.98	62.83	65.71	68.62	71.55	74.51	77.49	80.50	83.53	86.59	89.67	92.78	95.91
108	52.05	54.99	57.96	60.96	63.99	67.05	70.14	73.26	76.40	79.58	82.78	86.01	89.27	92.56	95.87	99.21	102.57
114	55.30	58.43	61.61	64.81	68.05	71.32	74.63	77.96	81.33	84.73	88.15	91.61	95.10	98.62	102.17	105.74	109.35
120	58.58	61.92	65.30	68.71	72.17	75.65	79.17	82.73	86.32	89.94	93.60	97.29	101.02	104.77	108.56	112.37	116.22
180	93.43	98.97	104.59	110.27	116.03	121.85	127.74	133.70	139.71	145.79	151.93	158.12	164.37	170.67	177.02	183.42	189.88
240	131.61	139.61	147.73	155.94	164.32	172.67	181.18	189.77	198.44	207.20	216.03	224.93	233.90	242.94	252.03	261.19	270.39
300	172.61	183.25	194.03	204.94	215.97	227.11	238.35	249.69	261.13	272.65	284.25	295.92	307.67	319.47	331.34	343.26	355.23
360	215.93	229.31	242.84	256.50	270.30	284.21	298.23	312.35	326.55	340.84	355.20	369.63	384.11	398.65	413.24	427.88	442.55

DAILY COMPOUNDING INTEREST TABLE

ANNUAL PERCENTAGE RATE

(WHAT A $1 DEPOSIT WILL GROW TO IN THE FUTURE)

NUMBER OF YEARS	5.00%	5.25%	5.50%	5.75%	6.00%	6.50%	7.00%	7.50%	8.00%	8.50%	9.00%	9.50%	10.00%
1	1.0520	1.0547	1.0573	1.0600	1.0627	1.0681	1.0735	1.0790	1.0845	1.0900	1.0955	1.1011	1.1067
2	1.1067	1.1123	1.1180	1.1237	1.1294	1.1409	1.1525	1.1642	1.1761	1.1881	1.2002	1.2124	1.2248
3	1.1642	1.1731	1.1821	1.1911	1.2002	1.2186	1.2373	1.2562	1.2755	1.2950	1.3148	1.3350	1.3554
4	1.2248	1.2373	1.2499	1.2626	1.2755	1.3016	1.3282	1.3555	1.3832	1.4115	1.4404	1.4699	1.5001
5	1.2885	1.3049	1.3215	1.3384	1.3555	1.3903	1.4259	1.4625	1.5001	1.5386	1.5781	1.6186	1.6601
6	1.3555	1.3762	1.3973	1.4187	1.4405	1.4850	1.5308	1.5781	1.6268	1.6770	1.7288	1.7822	1.8372
7	1.4259	1.4515	1.4774	1.5039	1.5308	1.5861	1.6434	1.7027	1.7642	1.8279	1.8940	1.9624	2.0332
8	1.5001	1.5308	1.5622	1.5942	1.6268	1.6941	1.7642	1.8373	1.9133	1.9924	2.0749	2.1607	2.2502
9	1.5781	1.6145	1.6518	1.6899	1.7288	1.8095	1.8940	1.9824	2.0749	2.1718	2.2731	2.3792	2.4902
10	1.6602	1.7028	1.7465	1.7913	1.8373	1.9328	2.0333	2.1390	2.2502	2.3672	2.4903	2.6197	2.7559
15	2.1391	2.2219	2.3080	2.3975	2.4904	2.6871	2.8993	3.1284	3.3755	3.6421	3.9298	4.2402	4.5751
20	2.7561	2.8994	3.0502	3.2087	3.3756	3.7357	4.1343	4.5753	5.0634	5.6036	6.2014	6.8629	7.5950
25	3.5512	3.7834	4.0309	4.2946	4.5755	5.1936	5.8952	6.6915	7.5955	8.6215	9.7861	11.1080	12.6085
30	4.5756	4.9370	5.3270	5.7478	6.2019	7.2204	8.4061	9.7866	11.3937	13.2648	15.4430	17.9790	20.9313

ANNUAL PERCENTAGE RATE

(WHAT A $1 DEPOSIT WILL GROW TO IN THE FUTURE)

NUMBER OF YEARS	10.50%	11.00%	11.50%	12.00%	12.50%	13.00%	13.50%	14.00%	14.50%	15.00%	15.50%	16.00%	16.50%
1	1.1123	1.1180	1.1236	1.1294	1.1351	1.1409	1.1467	1.1525	1.1583	1.1642	1.1701	1.1761	1.1821
2	1.2372	1.2498	1.2626	1.2754	1.2884	1.3016	1.3148	1.3282	1.3417	1.3554	1.3692	1.3832	1.3973
3	1.3762	1.3973	1.4187	1.4404	1.4625	1.4849	1.5076	1.5307	1.5542	1.5780	1.6022	1.6267	1.6516
4	1.5308	1.5621	1.5941	1.6268	1.6601	1.6941	1.7287	1.7641	1.8003	1.8371	1.8748	1.9131	1.9523
5	1.7027	1.7464	1.7912	1.8372	1.8843	1.9327	1.9823	2.0331	2.0853	2.1388	2.1937	2.2500	2.3077
6	1.8939	1.9524	2.0127	2.0748	2.1389	2.2049	2.2730	2.3432	2.4155	2.4901	2.5669	2.6462	2.7279
7	2.1067	2.1827	2.2615	2.3432	2.4278	2.5155	2.6063	2.7004	2.7980	2.8990	3.0037	3.1121	3.2245
8	2.3433	2.4402	2.5412	2.6463	2.7558	2.8698	2.9886	3.1122	3.2410	3.3751	3.5147	3.6601	3.8115
9	2.6064	2.7281	2.8554	2.9886	3.1281	3.2741	3.4269	3.5868	3.7541	3.9293	4.1127	4.3046	4.5054
10	2.8992	3.0499	3.2084	3.3752	3.5507	3.7353	3.9294	4.1337	4.3486	4.5746	4.8124	5.0625	5.3256
15	4.9364	5.3263	5.7470	6.2009	6.6907	7.2191	7.7892	8.4044	9.0681	9.7843	10.5570	11.3907	12.2902
20	8.4053	9.3019	10.2941	11.3922	12.6074	13.9522	15.4404	17.0873	18.9099	20.9269	23.1589	25.6290	28.3625
25	14.3116	16.2447	18.4390	20.9295	23.7564	26.9651	30.6072	34.7410	39.4332	44.7590	50.8040	57.6653	65.4531
30	24.3683	28.3697	33.0281	38.4513	44.7649	52.1150	60.6719	70.6336	82.2307	95.7318	111.4493	129.7470	151.0484

COMPOUND INTEREST TABLE

ANNUAL PERCENTAGE RATE

(FUTURE VALUE OF $1—PRINCIPAL PLUS ACCUMULATED INTEREST)

NUMBER OF PERIODS	1.00%	1.50%	2.00%	2.50%	3.00%	3.50%	4.00%	4.50%	5.00%	6.00%	7.00%	8.00%	9.00%	10.00%	12.00%	14.00%	16.00%	18.00%
1	1.010	1.015	1.020	1.025	1.030	1.035	1.040	1.045	1.050	1.060	1.070	1.080	1.090	1.100	1.120	1.140	1.160	1.180
2	1.020	1.030	1.040	1.051	1.061	1.071	1.082	1.092	1.103	1.124	1.145	1.166	1.188	1.210	1.254	1.300	1.346	1.392
3	1.030	1.046	1.061	1.077	1.093	1.109	1.125	1.141	1.158	1.191	1.225	1.260	1.295	1.331	1.405	1.482	1.561	1.643
4	1.041	1.061	1.082	1.104	1.126	1.148	1.170	1.193	1.216	1.262	1.311	1.360	1.412	1.464	1.574	1.689	1.811	1.939
5	1.051	1.077	1.104	1.131	1.159	1.188	1.217	1.246	1.276	1.338	1.403	1.469	1.539	1.611	1.762	1.925	2.100	2.288
6	1.062	1.093	1.126	1.160	1.194	1.229	1.265	1.302	1.340	1.419	1.501	1.587	1.677	1.772	1.974	2.195	2.436	2.700
7	1.072	1.110	1.149	1.189	1.230	1.272	1.316	1.361	1.407	1.504	1.606	1.714	1.828	1.949	2.211	2.502	2.826	3.185
8	1.083	1.126	1.172	1.218	1.267	1.317	1.369	1.422	1.477	1.594	1.718	1.851	1.993	2.144	2.476	2.853	3.278	3.759
9	1.094	1.143	1.195	1.249	1.305	1.363	1.423	1.486	1.551	1.689	1.838	1.999	2.172	2.358	2.773	3.252	3.803	4.435
10	1.105	1.161	1.219	1.280	1.344	1.411	1.480	1.553	1.629	1.791	1.967	2.159	2.367	2.594	3.106	3.707	4.411	5.234
11	1.116	1.178	1.243	1.312	1.384	1.460	1.539	1.623	1.710	1.898	2.105	2.332	2.580	2.853	3.479	4.226	5.117	6.176
12	1.127	1.196	1.268	1.345	1.426	1.511	1.601	1.696	1.796	2.012	2.252	2.518	2.813	3.138	3.896	4.818	5.936	7.288
14	1.149	1.232	1.319	1.413	1.513	1.619	1.732	1.852	1.980	2.261	2.579	2.937	3.342	3.797	4.887	6.261	7.988	10.147
16	1.173	1.269	1.373	1.485	1.605	1.734	1.873	2.022	2.183	2.540	2.952	3.426	3.970	4.595	6.130	8.137	10.748	14.129
18	1.196	1.307	1.428	1.560	1.702	1.857	2.026	2.208	2.407	2.854	3.380	3.996	4.717	5.560	7.690	10.575	14.463	19.673
20	1.220	1.347	1.486	1.639	1.806	1.990	2.191	2.412	2.653	3.207	3.870	4.661	5.604	6.727	9.646	13.743	19.461	27.393
22	1.245	1.388	1.546	1.722	1.916	2.132	2.370	2.634	2.925	3.604	4.430	5.437	6.659	8.140	12.100	17.861	26.186	38.142
24	1.270	1.430	1.608	1.809	2.033	2.283	2.563	2.876	3.225	4.049	5.072	6.341	7.911	9.850	15.179	23.212	35.236	53.109
26	1.295	1.473	1.673	1.900	2.157	2.446	2.772	3.141	3.556	4.549	5.807	7.396	9.399	11.918	19.040	30.167	47.414	73.949
28	1.321	1.517	1.741	1.996	2.288	2.620	2.999	3.430	3.920	5.112	6.649	8.627	11.167	14.421	23.884	39.204	63.800	102.967
30	1.348	1.563	1.811	2.098	2.427	2.807	3.243	3.745	4.322	5.743	7.612	10.063	13.268	17.449	29.960	50.950	85.850	143.371
32	1.375	1.610	1.884	2.204	2.575	3.007	3.508	4.090	4.765	6.453	8.715	11.737	15.763	21.114	37.582	66.215	115.520	199.629
34	1.403	1.659	1.961	2.315	2.732	3.221	3.794	4.466	5.253	7.251	9.978	13.690	18.728	25.548	47.143	86.053	155.443	277.964
36	1.431	1.709	2.040	2.433	2.898	3.450	4.104	4.877	5.792	8.147	11.424	15.968	22.251	30.913	59.136	111.834	209.164	387.037
38	1.460	1.761	2.122	2.556	3.075	3.696	4.439	5.326	6.385	9.154	13.079	18.625	26.437	37.404	74.180	145.340	281.452	538.910
40	1.489	1.814	2.208	2.685	3.262	3.959	4.801	5.816	7.040	10.286	14.974	21.725	31.409	45.259	93.051	188.884	378.721	750.378
42	1.519	1.869	2.297	2.821	3.461	4.241	5.193	6.352	7.762	11.557	17.144	25.339	37.318	54.764	116.723	245.473	509.607	1044.827
44	1.549	1.925	2.390	2.964	3.671	4.543	5.617	6.936	8.557	12.985	19.628	29.556	44.337	66.264	146.418	319.017	685.727	1454.817
46	1.580	1.984	2.487	3.114	3.895	4.867	6.075	7.574	9.434	14.590	22.473	34.474	52.677	80.180	183.666	414.594	922.715	2025.687
48	1.612	2.043	2.587	3.271	4.132	5.214	6.571	8.271	10.401	16.394	25.729	40.211	62.585	97.017	230.391	538.807	1241.605	2820.567
50	1.645	2.105	2.692	3.437	4.384	5.585	7.107	9.033	11.467	18.420	29.457	46.902	74.357	117.391	289.002	700.233	1670.704	3927.357
52	1.678	2.169	2.800	3.611	4.651	5.983	7.687	9.864	12.643	20.697	33.725	54.706	88.344	142.043	362.524	910.023	2248.099	5468.452
54	1.711	2.234	2.913	3.794	4.934	6.409	8.314	10.771	13.939	23.255	38.612	63.809	104.962	171.872	454.751	1182.666	3025.042	7614.272
56	1.746	2.302	3.031	3.986	5.235	6.865	8.992	11.763	15.367	26.129	44.207	74.427	124.705	207.965	570.439	1536.992	4070.497	10602.113
58	1.781	2.372	3.154	4.188	5.553	7.354	9.726	12.845	16.943	29.359	50.613	86.812	148.162	251.638	715.559	1997.475	5477.260	14762.381
60	1.817	2.443	3.281	4.400	5.892	7.878	10.520	14.027	18.679	32.988	57.946	101.257	176.031	304.482	897.597	2595.919	7370.201	20555.140

MONTHLY SALARY TABLE

MONTHLY RATE	ANNUAL	QUARTERLY	WEEKLY	DAILY	HOURLY	¼ HOURLY
$ 300	$ 3,600	$ 900	$ 69.23	$13.85	$1.73	$0.43
325	3,900	975	75.00	15.00	1.87	0.47
350	4,200	1,050	80.77	16.15	2.02	0.51
375	4,500	1,125	86.54	17.31	2.16	0.54
400	4,800	1,200	92.31	18.46	2.31	0.58
425	5,100	1,275	98.08	19.62	2.45	0.61
450	5,400	1,350	103.84	20.77	2.60	0.65
475	5,700	1,425	109.61	21.92	2.74	0.69
500	6,000	1,500	115.38	23.08	2.88	0.72
550	6,600	1,650	126.92	25.38	3.17	0.79
600	7,200	1,800	138.46	27.69	3.46	0.87
650	7,800	1,950	150.00	30.00	3.75	0.94
700	8,400	2,100	161.54	32.31	4.04	1.01
750	9,000	2,250	173.08	34.62	4.33	1.08
800	9,600	2,400	184.61	36.92	4.62	1.16
850	10,200	2,550	196.15	39.23	4.91	1.23
900	10,800	2,700	207.69	41.54	5.19	1.30
950	11,400	2,850	219.23	43.85	5.48	1.37
1,000	12,000	3,000	230.77	46.15	5.77	1.44
1,100	13,200	3,300	253.85	50.77	6.35	1.58
1,200	14,400	3,600	276.93	55.38	6.93	1.73
1,300	15,600	3,900	300.00	60.00	7.50	1.88
1,400	16,800	4,200	323.08	64.61	8.08	2.02
1,500	18,000	4,500	346.15	69.23	8.65	2.16

40 Hours a Week—5 Days of 8 Hours

ANNUAL SALARY TABLE

ANNUAL RATE	QUARTERLY	MONTHLY	WEEKLY	DAILY	HOURLY	¼ HOURLY
$ 5,000	$1,250	$ 416.67	$ 96.15	$19.23	$2.40	$0.60
5,500	1,375	458.33	105.77	21.15	2.64	0.66
6,000	1,500	500.00	115.38	23.08	2.88	0.72
6,500	1,625	541.67	125.00	25.00	3.13	0.78
7,000	1,750	583.33	134.62	26.92	3.37	0.84
7,500	1,875	625.00	144.23	28.85	3.60	0.90
8,000	2,000	666.67	153.85	30.76	3.84	0.96
8,500	2,125	708.33	163.47	32.72	4.09	1.02
9,000	2,250	750.00	173.08	34.62	4.33	1.08
9,500	2,375	791.67	182.70	36.54	4.57	1.14
10,000	2,500	833.33	192.31	38.46	4.81	1.20
11,000	2,750	916.67	211.54	42.31	5.29	1.32
12,000	3,000	1,000.00	230.77	46.15	5.77	1.44
13,000	3,250	1,083.33	250.00	50.00	6.25	1.56
14,000	3,500	1,166.67	269.23	53.84	6.73	1.68
15,000	3,750	1,250.00	288.46	57.69	7.21	1.80
16,000	4,000	1,333.33	307.69	61.53	7.69	1.92
17,000	4,250	1,416.67	326.92	65.38	8.17	2.04
18,000	4,500	1,500.00	346.15	69.23	8.65	2.16
19,000	4,750	1,583.33	365.38	73.07	9.13	2.28
20,000	5,000	1,666.67	384.61	76.92	9.61	2.40

40 Hours a Week—5 Days of 8 Hours

MULTIPLICATION TABLE

To multiply two numbers find one of the numbers along the side of the table and follow this row to the column headed at the top by the other number. Thus 12 × 17 = 204

	1	2	3	4	5	6	7	8	9	10	11	12	13	14	15	16	17	18	19	20	21	22	23	24	25	26	27	28	29	30
2	2	4	6	8	10	12	14	16	18	20	22	24	26	28	30	32	34	36	38	40	42	44	46	48	50	52	54	56	58	60
3	3	6	9	12	15	18	21	24	27	30	33	36	39	42	45	48	51	54	57	60	63	66	69	72	75	78	81	84	87	90
4	4	8	12	16	20	24	28	32	36	40	44	48	52	56	60	64	68	72	76	80	84	88	92	96	100	104	108	112	116	120
5	5	10	15	20	25	30	35	40	45	50	55	60	65	70	75	80	85	90	95	100	105	110	115	120	125	130	135	140	145	150
6	6	12	18	24	30	36	42	48	54	60	66	72	78	84	90	96	102	108	114	120	126	132	138	144	150	156	162	168	174	180
7	7	14	21	28	35	42	49	56	63	70	77	84	91	98	105	112	119	126	133	140	147	154	161	168	175	182	189	196	203	210
8	8	16	24	32	40	48	56	64	72	80	88	96	104	112	120	128	136	144	152	160	168	176	184	192	200	208	216	224	232	240
9	9	18	27	36	45	54	63	72	81	90	99	108	117	126	135	144	153	162	171	180	189	198	207	216	225	234	243	252	261	270
10	10	20	30	40	50	60	70	80	90	100	110	120	130	140	150	160	170	180	190	200	210	220	230	240	250	260	270	280	290	300
11	11	22	33	44	55	66	77	88	99	110	121	132	143	154	165	176	187	198	209	220	231	242	253	264	275	286	297	308	319	330
12	12	24	36	48	60	72	84	96	108	120	132	144	156	168	180	192	204	216	228	240	252	264	276	288	300	312	324	336	348	360
13	13	26	39	52	65	78	91	104	117	130	143	156	169	182	195	208	221	234	247	260	273	286	299	312	325	338	351	364	377	390
14	14	28	42	56	70	84	98	112	126	140	154	168	182	196	210	224	238	252	266	280	294	308	322	336	350	364	378	392	406	420
15	15	30	45	60	75	90	105	120	135	150	165	180	195	210	225	240	255	270	285	300	315	330	345	360	375	390	405	420	435	450
16	16	32	48	64	80	96	112	128	144	160	176	192	208	224	240	256	272	288	304	320	336	352	368	384	400	416	432	448	464	480
17	17	34	51	68	85	102	119	136	153	170	187	204	221	238	255	272	289	306	323	340	357	374	391	408	425	442	459	476	493	510
18	18	36	54	72	90	108	126	144	162	180	198	216	234	252	270	288	306	324	342	360	378	396	414	432	450	468	486	504	522	540
19	19	38	57	76	95	114	133	152	171	190	209	228	247	266	285	304	323	342	361	380	399	418	437	456	475	494	513	532	551	570
20	20	40	60	80	100	120	140	160	180	200	220	240	260	280	300	320	340	360	380	400	420	440	460	480	500	520	540	560	580	600
21	21	42	63	84	105	126	147	168	189	210	231	252	273	294	315	336	357	378	399	420	441	462	483	504	525	546	567	588	609	630
22	22	44	66	88	110	132	154	176	198	220	242	264	286	308	330	352	374	396	418	440	462	484	506	528	550	572	594	616	638	660
23	23	46	69	92	115	138	161	184	207	230	253	276	299	322	345	368	391	414	437	460	483	506	529	552	575	598	621	644	667	690
24	24	48	72	96	120	144	168	192	216	240	264	288	312	336	360	384	408	432	456	480	504	528	552	576	600	624	648	672	696	720
25	25	50	75	100	125	150	175	200	225	250	275	300	325	350	375	400	425	450	475	500	525	550	575	600	625	650	675	700	725	750
26	26	52	78	104	130	156	182	208	234	260	286	312	338	364	390	416	442	468	494	520	546	572	598	624	650	676	702	728	754	780
27	27	54	81	108	135	162	189	216	243	270	297	324	351	378	405	432	459	486	513	540	567	594	621	648	675	702	729	756	783	810
28	28	56	84	112	140	168	196	224	252	280	308	336	364	392	420	448	476	504	532	560	588	616	644	672	700	728	756	784	812	840
29	29	58	87	116	145	174	203	232	261	290	319	348	377	406	435	464	493	522	551	580	609	638	667	696	725	754	783	812	841	870
30	30	60	90	120	150	180	210	240	270	300	330	360	390	420	450	480	510	540	570	600	630	660	690	720	750	780	810	840	870	900

TABLE OF SQUARES, CUBES, SQUARE ROOTS, AND CUBE ROOTS

No.	Square	Cube	Square Root	Cube Root	No.	Square	Cube	Square Root	Cube Root
1	1	1	1.000	1.000	51	2,601	132,651	7.141	3.708
2	4	8	1.414	1.260	52	2,704	140,608	7.211	3.732
3	9	27	1.732	1.442	53	2,809	148,877	7.280	3.756
4	16	64	2.000	1.587	54	2,916	157,464	7.348	3.780
5	25	125	2.236	1.710	55	3,025	166,375	7.416	3.803
6	36	216	2.449	1.817	56	3,136	175,616	7.483	3.826
7	49	343	2.646	1.913	57	3,249	185,193	7.550	3.848
8	64	512	2.828	2.000	58	3,364	195,112	7.616	3.871
9	81	729	3.000	2.080	59	3,481	205,379	7.681	3.893
10	100	1,000	3.162	2.154	60	3,600	216,000	7.746	3.915
11	121	1,331	3.317	2.224	61	3,721	226,981	7.810	3.936
12	144	1,728	3.464	2.289	62	3,844	238,328	7.874	3.958
13	169	2,197	3.606	2.351	63	3,969	250,047	7.937	3.979
14	196	2,744	3.742	2.410	64	4,096	262,144	8.000	4.000
15	225	3,375	3.873	2.466	65	4,225	274,625	8.062	4.021
16	256	4,096	4.000	2.520	66	4,356	287,496	8.124	4.041
17	289	4,913	4.123	2.571	67	4,489	300,763	8.185	4.061
18	324	5,832	4.243	2.621	68	4,624	314,432	8.246	4.082
19	361	6,859	4.359	2.668	69	4,761	328,509	8.307	4.101
20	400	8,000	4.472	2.714	70	4,900	343,000	8.367	4.121
21	441	9,261	4.583	2.759	71	5,041	357,911	8.426	4.141
22	484	10,648	4.690	2.802	72	5,184	373,248	8.485	4.160
23	529	12,167	4.796	2.844	73	5,329	389,017	8.544	4.179
24	576	13,824	4.899	2.884	74	5,476	405,224	8.602	4.198
25	625	15,625	5.000	2.924	75	5,625	421,875	8.660	4.217
26	676	17,576	5.099	2.962	76	5,776	438,976	8.718	4.236
27	729	19,683	5.196	3.000	77	5,929	456,533	8.775	4.254
28	784	21,952	5.292	3.037	78	6,084	474,552	8.832	4.273
29	841	24,389	5.385	3.072	79	6,241	493,039	8.888	4.291
30	900	27,000	5.477	3.107	80	6,400	512,000	8.944	4.309
31	961	29,791	5.568	3.141	81	6,561	531,441	9.000	4.327
32	1,024	32,768	5.657	3.175	82	6,724	551,368	9.055	4.344
33	1,089	35,937	5.745	3.208	83	6,889	571,787	9.110	4.362
34	1,156	39,304	5.831	3.240	84	7,056	592,704	9.165	4.379
35	1,225	42,875	5.916	3.271	85	7,225	614,125	9.219	4.397
36	1,296	46,656	6.000	3.302	86	7,396	636,056	9.274	4.414
37	1,369	50,653	6.083	3.332	87	7,569	658,503	9.327	4.431
38	1,444	54,872	6.164	3.362	88	7,744	681,472	9.381	4.448
39	1,521	59,319	6.245	3.391	89	7,921	704,969	9.434	4.465
40	1,600	64,000	6.325	3.420	90	8,100	729,000	9.487	4.481
41	1,681	68,921	6.403	3.448	91	8,281	753,571	9.539	4.498
42	1,764	74,088	6.481	3.476	92	8,464	778,688	9.592	4.514
43	1,849	79,507	6.557	3.503	93	8,649	804,357	9.644	4.531
44	1,936	85,184	6.633	3.530	94	8,836	830,584	9.695	4.547
45	2,025	91,125	6.708	3.557	95	9,025	857,375	9.747	4.563
46	2,116	97,336	6.782	3.583	96	9,216	884,736	9.798	4.579
47	2,209	103,823	6.856	3.609	97	9,409	912,673	9.849	4.595
48	2,304	110,592	6.928	3.634	98	9,604	941,192	9.899	4.610
49	2,401	117,649	7.000	3.659	99	9,801	970,299	9.950	4.626
50	2,500	125,000	7.071	3.684	100	10,000	1,000,000	10,000	4.642

SPACE EXPLORATION

NASA

Expanding Our Horizons

"That's one small step for a man, one giant leap for mankind." These memorable words were spoken by Neil A. Armstrong on July 20, 1969, as he became the first person to step onto the moon. Armstrong's words aptly describe not only the mission that landed people on the moon but space exploration in general. For as President Lyndon B. Johnson had pointed out, "the moon trip is just one of the many goals" of space exploration.

Some of the goals, such as landing people on the moon and sending unmanned craft to other planets, have been achieved. But with each accomplishment new goals are set, new plans made for the future. By the late 1980s, scientists were looking toward the time when people would visit Mars, when permanent manufacturing facilities would operate in space, when contact would be made with life on other worlds.

The knowledge gained from space exploration has been immense. Instruments aboard spacecraft discovered the Van Allen belt (a zone of radiation encircling Earth) and previously unknown moons circling around Jupiter, Saturn, and Uranus. They have provided much data on such phenomena as solar flares, planetary rings, exploding galaxies, and binary stars. They have yielded valuable information about natural processes occurring on Earth, and about people and how they function in strange environments.

There also have been many practical rewards from the space program. Space-based sensors identify areas that are likely to have petroleum or other mineral deposits. They help forecast harvests and find new fishing grounds in remote waters. They monitor the movement of storms, air pollutants, and volcanic debris. They aid in search-and-rescue missions for lost ships, monitor temperatures to warn farmers of an approaching freeze, enable the evacuation of people from the paths of hurricanes. Thanks to communication satellites, previously isolated communities receive radio and television service.

The transfer of space technology to everyday life has been enormous: new systems for purifying and treating water and wastes . . . the rapid development and miniaturization of computers . . . new food preservation methods . . . .

Epoxy graphite materials that are light yet strong and rigid were developed for use in spacecraft, and now are also used to make ski poles and fishing rods. High-intensity flashlights developed to mimic the effects of sunlight on spacecraft are now used by campers and search-and-rescue teams. And in 1985 the first commercial products actually made in space became available: tiny latex spheres all exactly the same size. These spheres are used for instrument calibration in medical and industrial work, and they cannot be produced on Earth because of the adverse effects of gravity.

Finally, space exploration has changed forever the way we view our planet. Color photographs taken from outer space show how very beautiful Earth is—and how very different from the barren surfaces of other planets. No other planet in the solar system has the lush greenery, the sparkling oceans, the oxygen-filled atmosphere that form our most precious heritage.

A CHRONOLOGY

The following chronological review of the highlights of space exploration is divided into three broad groups: earth satellites, planetary and lunar missions, and manned space missions.

Earth Satellites

Earth-orbiting satellites are the oldest type of spacecraft—the first one, Sputnik 1, was launched on Oct. 4, 1957. Since then thousands more have been launched; these vehicles have become the workhorses of communications, navigation, weather forecasting, and intelligence gathering. (The date at the beginning of each entry is the craft's launch date.)

1957

Oct. 4: Sputnik 1 (USSR). The first successful artificial satellite.
Nov. 3: Sputnik 2 (USSR). The second satellite and the first to carry a living organism—a dog named Laika—into space.

1958

Jan. 31: Explorer 1 (U.S.). The first American satellite. Discovered the inner (Van Allen) radiation belt.
March 17: Vanguard 1 (U.S.). Contained two transmitters, one operating on solar power supply.
May 15: Sputnik 3 (USSR). A geophysical laboratory.
Dec. 18: Score (U.S.). A military communications relay satellite. On Dec. 19, transmitted a prerecorded tape of President Eisenhower's Christmas message to the nation.

Sputnik 1, the first artificial satellite, was a metal ball 23 inches (58 centimeters) in diameter. It circled Earth for 1 hour 36.2 minutes.

Tass/Sovfoto

1959

Aug. 7: Explorer 6 (U.S.). Gathered radiation, magnetic field, and micrometeorite data. Took the first TV photographs of Earth as seen from space.

1960

April 1: Tiros—Television and Infrared Observation Satellite (U.S.). The first weather satellite. During a period of 2½ months it sent back 22,952 photographs of global cloud conditions.
May 24: Midas 2 (U.S.). The first missile launch detection satellite. It was equipped with infrared sensors capable of picking up the exhaust heat from a ballistic missile as it left the ground.
Aug. 10: Discoverer 13 (U.S.). Ejected a 300-lb (136-kg) reentry capsule recovered from the Pacific Ocean—the first object recovered from space.
Aug. 12: Echo 1 (U.S.). The first passive communication satellite. Reflected communications between the U.S. and the United Kingdom (U.K.).

1961

Feb. 16: Explorer 9 (U.S.). The first satellite launching by an all-solid-propellant rocket vehicle.
June 29: Transit 4A, Injun 1, and **Solrad 3** (U.S.). The first triple launch. The first nuclear power supply in space.
Dec. 12: Oscar—Orbiting Satellite Carrying Amateur Radio (U.S.). The first privately built satellite, constructed by radio hams. It transmitted for 18 days.

1962

March 7: OSO 1—Orbiting Solar Observatory (U.S.). Carried out the first comprehensive study of the sun from a satellite.
April 26: Ariel 1 (U.S.-U.K.; launched by U.S.). The first international satellite. Conducted atmospheric studies.
July 10: Telstar 1 (U.S.). The first commercially financed communications satellite and the first satellite to transmit live TV and telephone conversations across the Atlantic, between the U.S., U.K., and France.
Sept. 28: Alouette 1 (Canada; launched by U.S.). The first satellite to be wholly designed and built by a nation other than the U.S. or USSR. Conducted ionospheric measurements.
Oct. 31: Anna 1-B (U.S.). The first in a series of geodetic satellites.

1963

July 26: Syncom 2 (U.S.). The first synchronous communications satellite.
Sept. 28: Transit 5-B (U.S.). The first satellite to be completely powered by a nuclear isotope generator.
Oct. 16: Vela 1 and **Vela 2** (U.S.). Designed to detect nuclear explosions.

Nov. 1: Polyot 1 (USSR). The first satellite capable of maneuvering in all directions and able to change its orbit.

1964

Jan. 30: Electron 1 and **Electron 2** (USSR). The first Soviet dual launch. The craft measured Earth's radiation belt.
March 27: Ariel 2 (U.K.; launched by U.S.). Britain's second satellite.
Aug. 28: Nimbus 1 (U.S.). The first of a new type of weather satellite. Unlike Tiros, its cameras moved to keep Earth's surface in view at all times.
Sept. 4: OGO 1—Orbiting Geophysical Observatory (U.S.). Carried 20 coordinated geophysical experiments.
Dec. 15: San Marco 1 (Italy; launched in U.S.). Launched by an Italian crew.

1965

Feb. 16: Pegasus 1 (U.S.). The first in a series of satellites designed to evaluate the danger of a puncture of a spacecraft by micrometeorites and dust in the vicinity of Earth.
April 6: Intelsat 1 (U.S.). Also known as Early Bird. The first commercial communications satellite in synchronous orbit.
April 23: Molniya 1A (USSR). The first Soviet communications satellite.
April 3: Snapshot (U.S.). Tested the performance of the SNAP 10-A (Systems Nuclear Auxiliary Power) system under space conditions. The first known launch of a nuclear-fission reactor into Earth orbit.
Nov. 26: A-1 (France). France thereby became the third nation to launch satellites by its own means.
Dec. 6: FR-1 (France; launched jointly by France and U.S.).

1966

Feb. 3: ESSA 1 (U.S.). An Environmental Sciences Services Administration satellite. Together with ESSA 2, launched Feb. 28, marked the beginning of regular operational use by the U.S. Weather Bureau of information gained from cloud-covered observations. The two satellites were placed into nearly polar orbits, enabling them to survey Earth's entire surface every day.
Feb. 22: Cosmos 110 (USSR). Carrying two dogs, orbited Earth for 22 days. Helped determine the effects of radiation and long periods of weightlessness.
Dec. 6: ATS 1—Applications Technology Satellite (U.S.). Proved the possibility of two-way communications between ground stations and aircraft in flight.

1967

Apr. 26: San Marco 2 (Italy). Italy thereby became the fourth nation to launch satellites by its own means.
Sept. 7: Biosatellite 2 (U.S.). Aboard were plants, insects, amoebas, frog eggs, and other specimens. Tested the effects of weightlessness and radiation.
Nov. 28: WRESAT 1 (Australia). Australia became the fifth nation to launch satellites by its own means.

1968

April 14-15: Cosmos 212 and **Cosmos 213** (USSR). Docked and undocked automatically in space.
May 17: ESRO 2B—European Space Research Organization. (A ten-nation international group; launched by U.S.). The satellite studied space physics and Earth's environment.
July 4: Explorer 38 (U.S.). The first of a series of radio astronomy satellites.

1969

April 14: Nimbus 3 (U.S.). The first weather satellite to provide radiometric data for determining vertical temperature and water-vapor profiles (needed for numerical weather prediction).

COMSTAT

Intelsat V, launched in late 1980, is part of a global communications system established by the International Telecommunications Satellite Consortium.

Nov. 8: Azur (West Germany; launched by U.S.). The first West German satellite. Studied Earth's atmosphere and radiation belt.

1970

Feb. 11: Ohsumi (Japan). The first satellite launched by Japan.
April 24: China 1 (China). The first satellite launched by China. It transmitted music and telemetric signals.
Nov. 9: OFO—Orbiting Frog Otolith (U.S.). Two frogs with microelectrodes implanted in their inner ears were monitored to study the effects of weightlessness and simulated gravity conditions.

1971

Oct. 28: Prospero (U.K.; launched in Australia). Britain's first technology satellite.
Dec. 27: Aureole (USSR). The first satellite launched by the USSR with French assistance. It studied the upper atmosphere in high latitudes and the polar lights.

1972

July 23: ERTS 1—Earth Resources Technology Satellite (U.S.). Carried remote sensing devices to gather data on Earth's resources. Later renamed Landsat 1.
Aug. 21: OAD 3—Orbiting Astronomical Observatory; also named Copernicus (U.S.). Studied stellar ultraviolet radiation. Operated until Dec. 30, 1980.
Nov. 10: Anik 1 (Canada). Canada's first domestic communications satellite.

1973

Oct. 31: Cosmos 605 (USSR). An animal flight test of manned spaceflight systems.

1974

May 17: SMS-1 (U.S.). The first meteorological satellite placed in a synchronous orbit.

1975

April 19: Aryabhata (India; launched by USSR). India's first satellite.

1976

Feb. 19: Marisat 1 (U.S.). The first of a new class of maritime satellites designed to enable merchant ships to transmit voice, data, facsimile, and telex messages to U.S. shore stations interconnected with domestic terrestrial networks.
May 4: Lageos—Laser Geodynamics Satellite (U.S.). Conducted long-term geodetic studies.
July 8: Palapa 1 (Indonesia; launched by U.S.). Provided transmission of television, voice, and data throughout Indonesia.

1977

Aug. 12: HEAO 1—High Energy Astronomy Observatory (U.S.). Surveyed and mapped X-ray sources.
Sept. 18: Cosmos 954 (USSR). Ocean surveillance craft with a nuclear reactor. In Jan. 1978, disintegrated and fell over northern Canada; no known injuries.
Nov. 22: Meteosat 1 (ESA; launched by U.S.). The first of a series of five global weather satellites sponsored by a total of 145 nations.
Dec. 15: Sakura (Japan; launched by U.S.). An experimental communications satellite that tested the relay of various communication signals among the Japanese islands.

1978

April 26: HCMM—Heat-Capacity-Mapping Mission (U.S.). Measured day and night temperature differences on Earth's surface.
Aug. 12: ISEE—International Sun Earth Explorer-C (U.S.). Monitored sun spots, solar flares, and the solar wind. In Dec. 1983, was renamed International Cometary Explorer (ICE) and redirected to intercept comet Giacobini-Zinner. On Sept. 11, 1985, passed through the tail of Giacobini-Zinner—the first spacecraft to probe a comet.
Oct. 24: Nimbus 7 (U.S.). The first pollution monitoring satellite.
Nov. 13: HEAO 2 (U.S.). Also known as the Einstein Observatory. Studied pulsars, quasars, black holes, and exploding galaxies.

1979

June 27: NOAA-6 (U.S.). Weather and earth-resources satellite orbited for the National Oceanic and Atmospheric Administration. It and Tiros-N (launched Oct. 13, 1978) provided round-the-clock scanning of Earth's surface and atmosphere and monitored solar radiation levels above the atmosphere.
Sept. 20: HEAO 3 (U.S.). Measured cosmic and gamma radiation.
Oct. 30: MAGSAT—Magnetic Field Satellite (U.S.). Provided a complete survey of Earth's magnetic field for use in updating maps. Assisted in the search for mineral resources on Earth.

1980

Feb. 14: Solar Maximum Mission or Solar Max (U.S.). Examined the physics of solar flares and their effects on Earth.
Sept. 9: GOES-4—Geostationary Operational Environmental Satellite (U.S.). The first in a series of weather satellites placed into synchronous orbits to provide high-resolution images over large areas of North and South America and surrounding oceans at least every 30 minutes. Part of the Global Weather Watch project.

Satellites have proven invaluable. Communications craft (*top:* AUSSAT) provide radio, TV, and telephone services. Weather craft (*above:* Tiros) monitor storms. Surveying craft (*facing page, left:* ERTS) map natural resources. Astronomical craft (*facing page, right:* IRAS) study heavenly bodies.

1981

June 19: Meteostat 2, a European Space Agency (ESA) weather satellite, and Apple, a communications satellite for India. The first satellite launched by ESA.
Aug. 3: Dynamics Explorers 1 and 2 (U.S.). Studied space around Earth from the limits of the upper atmosphere to distances far out in Earth's magnetic field.
Oct. 6: Solar Mesosphere Explorer (U.S.). Studied reactions between sunlight and molecules in the atmosphere.
Dec. 20: MARECS-1—Maritime Communications Satellite (ESA). Part of a global communications system designed to provide voice, data, and teleprinter services between ship and land stations.

1982

May 17: Iskra 2 (USSR). An amateur radio satellite placed into orbit by cosmonauts aboard Salyut 7—believed to be the first launch of a satellite from an orbiting space station.
Nov. 11: SBS 3—Satellite Business System (U.S.). and Anik C (Canada). The first satellite deployed from a space shuttle.

1983

Jan. 25: IRAS—Infrared Astronomical Satellite (U.S.). Provided first direct evidence of the possible existence of other planetary systems.

Photos, NASA

April 5: TDRS—Tracking and Data Relay Satellite (U.S.). Designed to provide a communication link between space shuttles and ground stations. Launched by Mission STS 6.

1984

Jan. 23: Yuri 2A (Japan). The first high-power direct TV broadcast satellite, designed for transmission to remote areas and urban areas inhibited by high buildings.

Aug. 16: AMPTE—Active Magnetospheric Particle Tracer Explorers (U.S.). Three satellites from West Germany, the U.K., and the U.S. launched simultaneously to study the interaction of the solar wind with Earth's magnetosphere. On Dec. 27, the German satellite released two containers of barium, which discharged their contents to form a dense cloud—the first artificial comet.

1985

Feb. 8: Arabsat-1 (Arab League; launched by Arianespace). The first of a series of satellites designed to provide the 22-member states of the Arab League with various TV and communications services.

July 10: Cosmos 1667 Biosatellite (USSR). Carried two rhesus monkeys, one of which was equipped with sensors provided by the U.S. On July 17, returned to Earth; flight data provided to American investigators for analysis.

1986

Feb. 21: SPOT (France). A commercial remote-sensing satellite that provides extremely detailed photographs of Earth's surface.

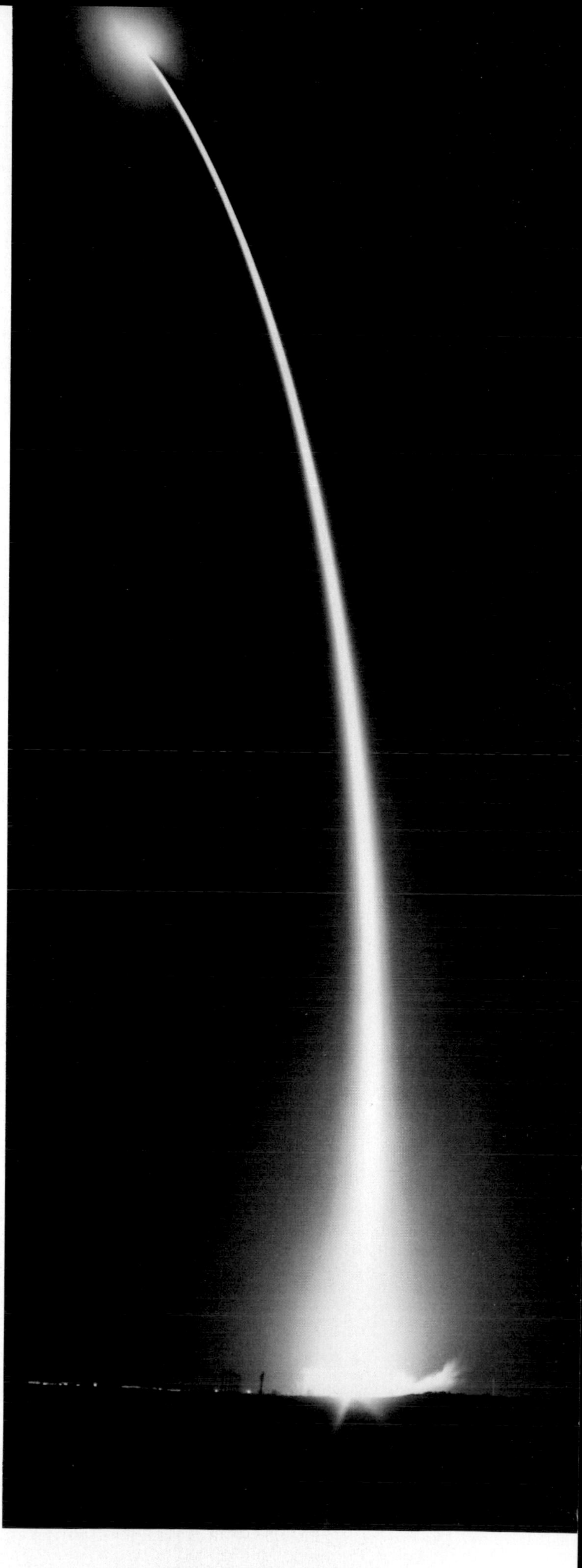

NASA

An artist's rendition of an unmanned Surveyor craft on the moon's surface, with Earth on the horizon, some 240,000 miles (386,000 kilometers) distant.

Planetary and Lunar Missions

Unmanned space probes are the pioneers of the solar system and, indeed, of the universe itself. Such planetary and lunar missions were the first to visit the moon, to orbit the sun, to visit other planets. One such probe has left the solar system. (The date at the beginning of each entry is the craft's launch date.)

1959

Jan. 2: Luna 1 (USSR). The first successful lunar probe. Passed within 3,728 mi (6,000 km) of the moon.

March 3: Pioneer 4 (U.S.). The first successful U.S. lunar probe. Passed within 37,300 mi (60,000 km) of the moon.

Sept. 12: Luna 2 (USSR) moon probe. The first spacecraft to hit the moon's surface. Obtained magnetic field, cosmic and solar radiation, micrometeoroid, and gas composition data.

Oct. 4: Luna 3 (USSR) moon probe. Took the first photographs of the moon's far side.

1960

March 11: Pioneer 5 (U.S.) solar satellite. Radioed back data on the interplanetary magnetic field and the interaction of Earth's magnetic field with the solar wind.

1962

March 7: OSO 1 (U.S.) solar satellite. Obtained data on solar flares.

April 23: Ranger 4 (U.S.) lunar probe. An apparent electronics failure caused it to impact on the moon—the first U.S. spacecraft to make contact with the moon's surface. No scientific data obtained.

Aug. 27: Mariner 2 (U.S.) launched toward Venus. On Dec. 14, passed within 22,000 mi (35,400 km) of Venus—the first spacecraft to visit another planet. Radioed back information on Venus' atmosphere, surface temperatures, and cloud cover.

1964

July 28: Ranger 7 (U.S.) moon probe. Transmitted more than 4,300 photographs of the lunar surface before impact.

Nov. 28: Mariner 4 (U.S.) Mars probe. On July 14, 1965, passed within 6,200 mi (9,980 km) of Mars—the first spacecraft to visit the planet. During the 25-minute encounter it took 21 photographs of the Martian surface.

1965

Feb. 17: Ranger 8 (U.S.) lunar probe. Impacted on the moon Feb. 20. Transmitted more than 7,100 photographs of the lunar surface.

March 21: Ranger 9 (U.S.) lunar probe. Impacted on the moon March 24. Transmitted more than 5,800 photographs.

July 18: Zond 3 (USSR) lunar probe. On July 20, flew past the far side of the moon, photographing the surface.

Nov. 16: Venera 3 (USSR) launched toward Venus. On March 1, 1966, hit Venus—the first spacecraft to impact another planet. Failed to return planetary data.

Dec. 16: Pioneer 6 (U.S.) solar satellite. Obtained a wealth of data on the sun.

1966

Jan. 31: Luna 9 (USSR) lunar probe. On Feb. 3, became first spacecraft to soft-land on the moon. For three days it transmitted photographs of the lunar surface.

March 31: Luna 10 (USSR) lunar probe. On April 3, became the first probe to enter a lunar orbit.

May 30: Surveyor 1 (U.S.) moon probe. On June 2, became the first U.S. probe to soft-land on the moon. Transmitted 11,150 photographs of itself and the lunar surface before ceasing transmission on July 14.

Aug. 10: Lunar Orbiter 1 (U.S.) moon satellite. First U.S. lunar orbiting probe. Photographed the lunar surface for studies of possible Apollo landing sites.

Aug. 17: Pioneer 7 (U.S.) solar satellite. Investigated phenomena of interplanetary space.

Aug. 24: Luna 11 (USSR). Launched into an orbit around the moon.

Oct. 22: Luna 12 (USSR). Launched into an orbit around the moon. Transmitted photographs and scientific data.

Nov. 6: Lunar Orbiter 2 (U.S.) moon probe. Provided photographs and data that helped in selecting locations for a manned lunar landing.

Dec. 21: Luna 13 (USSR) lunar probe. Landed on the moon Dec. 24. Returned photographs and soil density data.

1967

April 17: Surveyor 3 (U.S.). Landed on the moon April 20. Took photographs and soil samples.

June 12: Venera 4 (USSR) Venus probe. On Oct. 18, the main body of the probe crashed into the planet's surface. As it approached, it ejected a capsule that parachuted to the surface. Instruments in the capsule returned data on the Venusian atmosphere during the descent.

June 14: Mariner 5 (U.S.) Venus probe. On Oct. 19, passed within 25,000 mi (40,230 km) of Venus.

July 19: Explorer 35 (U.S.). Placed into a lunar orbit. Measured Earth's magnetic tail every 29.5 days.

August 1: Lunar Orbiter 5 (U.S.). Last in a series of moon probes. On Aug. 5, entered a lunar polar orbit. Photographed areas not previously covered.

Sept. 8: Surveyor 5 (U.S.). Landed on the moon Sept. 11. Transmitted soil analysis data and 19,000 photographs.

Nov. 7: Surveyor 6 (U.S.) moon probe. On Nov. 10, landed on the moon. On Nov. 24, its three engines were fired to lift it slightly off the lunar surface and move sideways about 8 ft (2.4 m)—the first lateral movement on the moon's surface. It then photographed the spot where it originally stood.

Dec. 13: Pioneer 8 (U.S.) solar satellite. Studied solar phenomena.

1968

Jan. 7: Surveyor 7 (U.S.) moon probe. Landed on the moon Jan. 10—the only Surveyor to land in lunar highlands and in the debris of a relatively young crater. Relayed 21,000 photographs and soil-analysis data. The last of the Surveyor series.

April 7: Luna 14 (USSR) moon probe. On April 10, entered a lunar orbit. Provided data on Earth-Moon mass relationship and the moon's gravitational field.

Sept. 15: Zond 5 (USSR) moon probe. First unmanned round-trip flight to moon. On Sept. 21, returned to Earth.

Nov. 8: Pioneer 9 (U.S.) launched into a solar orbit. Provided data on solar radiation and the space environment between Mars and Venus.

Nov. 10: Zond 6 (U.S.) moon probe. Unmanned circumlunar flight. On Nov. 17, returned to Earth.

1969

Jan. 5: Venera 5 (USSR) Venus probe. On May 16, descent capsule entered Venusian atmosphere and returned 53 minutes of data as it parachuted toward the planet's surface.

Jan. 10: Venera 6 (USSR) Venus probe. On May 17, descent capsule entered Venusian atmosphere but did not transmit data.

Feb. 24: Mariner 6 (U.S.) Mars probe. On July 31, passed Mars at a distance of 2,200 mi (3,540 km). Transmitted photographs of the Martian surface.

March 27: Mariner 7 (U.S.) Mars probe. On Aug. 5, flew over the south pole of Mars. Transmitted 126 photographs.

July 13: Luna 15 (USSR) moon probe. Orbited the moon 52 times before crashing onto the surface on July 21.

Aug. 8: Zond 7 (USSR). Unmanned circumlunar flight. Returned to Earth Aug. 14.

1970

Aug. 17: Venera 7 (USSR) Venus probe. On Dec. 15, reached Venus and released an instrumented capsule that parachuted down to the surface. The capsule transmitted data for 23 minutes—the first time that data was received on Earth from the surface of another planet.

Sept. 12: Luna 16 (USSR) moon probe. On Sept. 20, landed on the Sea of Fertility. Drilled 14 in (35 cm) into the surface and extracted a 3.5-oz (109-g) core, which was placed into Luna's upper stage. On Sept. 24, the upper stage returned to Earth.

Oct. 20: Zond 8 (USSR) moon probe. Unmanned circumlunar flight. On Oct. 27, returned to Earth.

Nov. 10: Luna 17 (USSR) moon probe. On Nov. 17, landed on the Sea of Rains. Released Lunokhod 1, the first automated moon-roving vehicle, which moved over the lunar surface making observations and telemetering data back to Earth.

1971

May 19: Mars 2 (USSR) Mars probe. First Soviet craft to land on Mars.

May 22: Kosmos 422 (USSR) launched into an orbit around Mars.

May 28: Mars 3 (USSR) Mars probe.

May 30: Mariner 9 (USSR) Mars probe. On Nov. 13, entered into an orbit around Mars. Transmitted photographs and data.

Sept. 2: Luna 18 (USSR) moon probe. Completed 54 orbits of the moon. On Sept. 11, impacted on the lunar surface.

Sept. 28: Luna 19 (USSR) moon probe. Entered an orbit around the moon. Photographed the lunar surface.

1972

Feb. 14: Luna 20 (USSR) moon probe. On Feb. 21, landed on the Sea of Fertility. Collected lunar rock and soil samples. On Feb. 25, returned to Earth.

March 2: Pioneer 10 (U.S.) launched toward Jupiter and outer space. On Dec. 3, 1973, passed within 81,000 mi (130,000 km) of Jupiter—the first spacecraft to visit the planet. Transmitted photographs of Jupiter and several of its moons, and sent back data on the planet's atmosphere and magnetic field. On June 13, 1983, crossed the orbit of Neptune, the most distant planet, becoming the first man-made object to go beyond the solar system.

March 27: Venera 8 (USSR) launched toward Venus. On July 22, reached Venus and released a descent capsule that landed on the planet's sunlit side—the first daylight landing on Venus. Capsule instruments transmitted data on the atmosphere and the landing site.

1973

Jan. 8: Luna 21 (USSR) moon probe. On Jan. 16, landed on the moon; unloaded Lunokhod 2 vehicle, which traveled 23 mi (37 km) on the lunar surface during next four months, transmitting pictures and data.

April 5: Pioneer 11 (U.S.). The second probe to the outer planets. On Dec. 2, 1974, flew within 26,600 mi (42,800 km) of Jupiter; transmitted many photographs, including the first pictures of planet's polar regions. On Sept. 1, 1979, made closest approach to Saturn—the first spacecraft to visit the planet; returned photographs and data. Continued on path to escape solar system.

June 10: Explorer 49 (U.S.). Placed in a lunar orbit. Measured galactic and solar radio noise.

July 25: Mars 5 (USSR) Mars probe. Orbited the planet and returned high-resolution photographs.

Nov. 3: Mariner 10 (U.S.) Venus and Mercury probe—the first spacecraft to explore two planets in the course of a mission and the first to reconnoiter with Mercury. On Feb. 5, 1974, flew past Venus at distance of about 3,600 mi (5,800 km); photographed the planet's thick cloud cover. On March 29, 1974, came with 460 mi (740 km) of Mercury; sent back about 2,000 photographs of the innermost planet. On Sept. 21, 1974, and March 16, 1975, made two additional flybys of Mercury.

Photographs of Jupiter taken by Pioneer 10 in 1973 revealed that the Great Red Spot, the planet's most prominent feature, has a "pinwheel" structure.

NASA

Detailed studies of Mars began with the Viking 1 and 2 probes. Here, two television cameras aboard the Viking 1 orbiter scan the planet's surface.

1974

May 29: Luna 22 (USSR) moon probe. In orbit around moon.
Oct. 28: Luna 23 (USSR). Placed in a lunar orbit. Relayed limited data.
Dec. 10: Helios 1 (West Germany; launched by U.S.) solar probe. Obtained data on interplanetary space in the region near the sun.

1975

June 8: Venera 9 (USSR) Venus probe. On Oct. 22, entered an orbit around Venus and landed an instrument-laden capsule on the planet, which during its 53-minute operational life returned data and the first photographs of the planet's surface.
June 14: Venera 10 (USSR) Venus probe. On Oct. 25, entered an orbit around Venus and landed a capsule, which during its 65-minute operational life returned data and photographs.
Aug. 20: Viking 1 (U.S.) Mars orbiter-lander. On July 20, 1976, the lander made a soft landing on Mars. It sent back the first photographs from the planet's surface and much data. On Aug. 7, 1980, the orbiter, which had mapped the Martian surface, was shut off by radio command.
Sept. 9: Viking 2 (U.S.) Mars orbiter-lander. On Sept 3, 1976, the lander made a soft landing on the Martian surface. Mission objectives similar to those for Viking 1.

1976

Jan 15: Helios 2 (West Germany; launched by U.S.). Solar probe. Three of the ten experiments on board were built by the United States and seven by West Germany. These instruments measured solar wind, magnetic fields, solar and galactic cosmic rays, as well as electromagnetic waves.
Aug. 9: Luna 24 (USSR) lunar probe. Landed on the Sea of Crises and collected a core of lunar soil about 6 ft (1.8 m) long. Returned to Earth Aug. 22.

1977

Aug. 20: Voyager 2 (U.S.) probe to the outer planets. On July 9, 1979, reached Jupiter; transmitted photographs and data. On Aug. 25, 1981, flew past Saturn; transmitted more than 18,000 images of Saturn's rings and satellites. On Jan. 24, 1986, flew within 51,000 mi (82,000 km) of Uranus—the first spacecraft to visit the planet; returned photographs and a wealth of new data. The probe was scheduled to visit Neptune in 1989.
Sept. 5: Voyager 1 (U.S.) probe of outer planets. On March 5, 1979, made closest approach to Jupiter; transmitted photographs of the planet and its moons. On Nov. 12, 1980, made closest approach to Saturn; returned photographs and data; discovered unknown rings and moons.

1978

May 20: Pioneer Venus 1 (U.S.) Venus probe. On Dec. 4, placed in orbit around Venus. Returned data on the atmosphere and weather of Venus.
Aug. 8: Pioneer Venus 2 (U.S.) Venus probe. On Dec. 9, entered an orbit around Venus; five payloads entered the planet's atmosphere to measure temperature, chemical composition, and weather conditions.
Sept. 9: Venera 11 (USSR) Venus orbiter. On Dec. 25, deployed a probe that landed on Venus and transmitted data for 95 minutes.
Sept. 14: Venera 12 (USSR) Venus orbiter. On Dec. 21, deployed a probe that descended to the planet's surface transmitting data for 110 minutes.

1981

Oct. 30: Venera 13 (USSR) Venus probe. On March 1, 1982, parachute-landed on the planet's surface. Survived 127 minutes before the planet's intense heat put it out of commission. Radioed back eight photographs and information on water vapor content of the atmosphere. Inert gases of neon, krypton, and possibly xenon also were discovered in an atmosphere that is composed principally of carbon dioxide.
Nov. 4: Venera 14 (USSR) Venus probe. On March 5, 1982, parachute-landed on the planet. Operated for about an hour. Provided spectra obtained from Venusian soil samples.

1983

June 2: Venera 15 (USSR) Venus probe. On Oct. 10, 1983, arrived at Venus. Conducted high-resolution radar-mapping of the planet's surface.
June 7: Venera 16 (USSR) Venus probe. On Oct. 14, 1983, arrived at Venus. Conducted high-resolution radar mapping of the planet's surface.

1984

Dec. 15: Vega 1 (USSR). On June 11, 1985: flew past Venus, deploying a descent module containing a balloon probe and a lander, which gathered data on the planet's atmosphere and soil composition. On March 6, 1986, flew within 5,500 mi (8,850 km) of Comet Halley's core, transmitting the first views of the comet's nucleus.
Dec. 21: Vega 2 (USSR). On June 15, 1985: flew past Venus, deploying a descent module containing a balloon probe and a lander, which gathered data on the planet's atmosphere and soil composition. On March 9, 1986, flew within 5,200 mi (8,360 km) of Comet Halley's nucleus, sending data to Earth on the comet's structure.

1985

Jan 8: Sakigake (Japan) launched toward an encounter with Comet Halley. It flew within 4.3 million mi (6.9 million km) of the comet on March 11, 1986, for an examination of solar winds and magnetic fields.
July 2: Giotto (ESA) probe launched toward an encounter with Comet Halley. On March 14, 1986, came within 335 mi (539 km) of the comet's nucleus, sending back the closest pictures ever taken of the object.
Aug. 19: Suisei (Japan) probe launched toward an encounter with Comet Halley. On March 8, 1986, passed within 94,000 mi (151,000 km) of the comet, transmitting data on the interaction between the solar wind and the comet's enveloping gases.

Space probes have sent back to Earth a great deal of information about other planets. Venera probes revealed that Venus (*top*), hidden beneath thick clouds that telescopes on Earth cannot penetrate, has a crated surface. Voyagers 1 and 2 discovered previously unknown moons circling Saturn (*middle*) and revealed that this planet has more than 100 rings. Voyager 2 detected unknown moons and a tenth ring around Uranus (*bottom*), and determined that Uranus has a magnetic field that is only about a third the strength of Earth's.

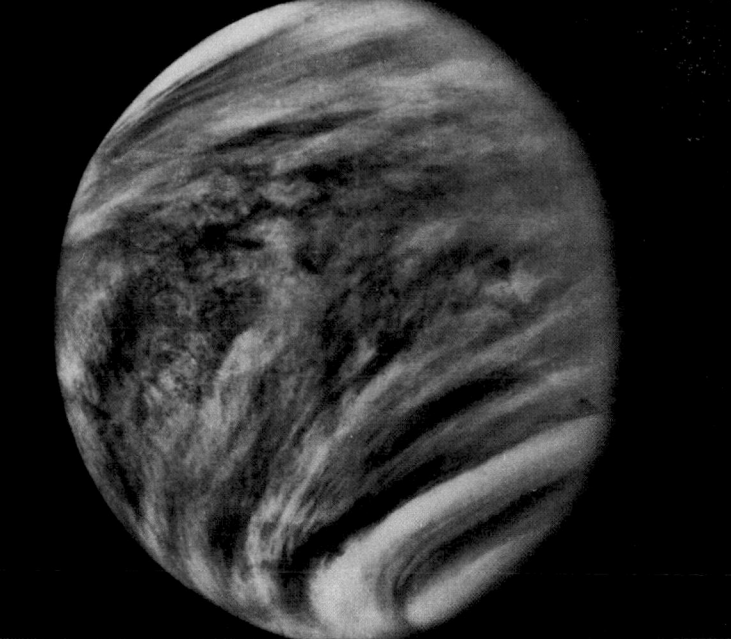

NASA, Hansen Planetarium

NASA

JPL

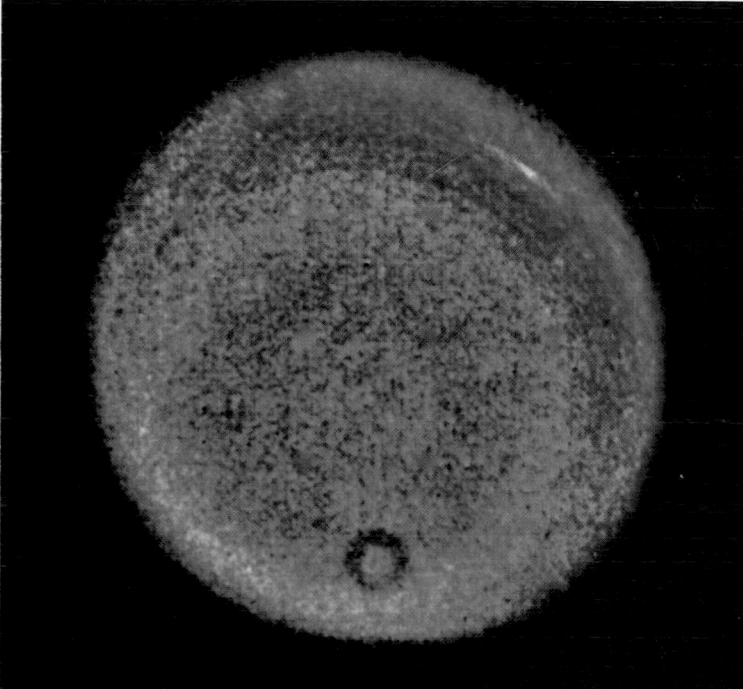

Manned Space Missions

Of all the space missions, the manned one have most captured people's imaginations. Such missions began after unmanned vehicles had helped perfect the necessary technologies and studies had been conducted to determine how to overcome the hazards of weightlessness, radiation, and other perils faced by people in a space environment. (A single date at the beginning of an entry denotes a one-day mission or the date of launch. A combined date, e.g. Dec. 10-March 16, 1968, is the date of the flight. It was launched on Dec. 10, 1967, and concluded on March 16, 1968.)

1961

April 12: Vostok 1 (USSR). Crew: Yuri A. Gagarin—the first person in space. Completed one orbit of Earth. The flight lasted 1 hour 48 minutes.

May 5: Freedom7 (U.S.). Crew: Alan B. Shepard, Jr.—the first American in space. A suborbital flight, lasting 15 minutes.

July 21: Liberty Bell 7 (U.S.). Crew: Virgil I. Grissom. A suborbital flight, lasting 16 minutes.

Aug. 6-7: Vostok 2 (USSR). Crew: Gherman S. Titov. The flight lasted 25 hours 18 minutes and completed 17 orbits of Earth.

1962

Feb. 20: Friendship 7 (U.S.). Crew: John H. Glenn, Jr. The first U.S. manned orbital mission. The flight lasted 4 hours 56 minutes and completed three orbits of Earth.

May 24: Aurora 7 (U.S.). Crew: M. Scott Carpenter. Completed three orbits of Earth.

Aug. 11-15: Vostok 3 (USSR). Crew: Andrian G. Nikolayev.

Aug. 12-15: Vostok 4 (USSR). Crew: Pavel R. Popovich. Together with Vostok 3, the first Soviet "group flight." At their closest approach the two craft were about 3 mi (4.8 km) apart.

Oct. 3: Sigma 7 (U.S.). Crew: Walter M. Schirra, Jr. Completed six orbits of Earth.

1963

May 15-16: Faith 7 (U.S.). Crew: L. Gordon Cooper, Jr. The last flight of the Mercury program.

June 14-19: Vostok 5 (USSR). Crew: Valery F. Bykovsky.

June 16-19: Vostok 6 (USSR). Crew: Valentina Tereshkova—the first woman in space. Together with Vostok 5, the second Soviet "group flight." The two craft came within 3 mi (4.8 km) of each other.

1964

Oct. 12-13: Voskhod 1 (USSR). Crew: Vladimir M. Komarov, Konstantin P. Feoktistov, and Boris B. Yegorov. The first craft to carry more than one person into space.

1965

March 18-19: Voskhod 2 (USSR). Crew: Pavel I. Belyayev and Aleksei A. Leonov. Leonov spent ten minutes outside the spacecraft—the first walk in space.

March 23: Gemini 3 (U.S.). Crew: Virgil I. Grissom and John W. Young. The first U.S. two-member crew in space.

June 3-7: Gemini 4 (U.S.). Crew: James A. McDivitt and Edward H. White 2d. Secured by umbilical and tether lines, White spent 21 minutes outside the spacecraft—the first American to walk in space.

Aug. 21-29: Gemini 5 (U.S.). Crew: L. Gordon Cooper, Jr., and Charles Conrad, Jr. The first use of fuel cells instead of conventional batteries for electric power. Carried out rendezvous maneuvers with a hypothetical target.

Dec. 4-18: Gemini 7 (U.S.). Crew: Frank Borman and James A. Lovell, Jr.

Dec. 15-16: Gemini 6 (U.S.). Crew: Walter M. Schirra, Jr., and Thomas P. Stafford. Rendezvoused within 1 ft. (0.3 m) of Gemini 7.

1966

March 16: Gemini 8 (U.S.). Crew: David R. Scott and Neil A. Armstrong. Docked with an unmanned Agena—the first docking in space with a previously launched target vehicle.

June 3-6: Gemini 9 (U.S.). Crew: Thomas P. Stafford and Eugene A. Cernan. Rendezvoused with an orbiting Agena. Cernan spent 2 hours 5 minutes outside the spacecraft.

July 18-21: Gemini 10 (U.S.). Crew: Michael Collins and John W. Young. Docked with an orbiting Agena. During extravehicular activity (EVA), Collins retrieved a test package from Agena—the first retrieval of a space object.

Sept. 12-15: Gemini 11 (U.S.). Crew: Charles Conrad, Jr., and Richard F. Gordon, Jr. Docked with an Agena target vehicle. Gordon made a brief space walk.

Nov. 11-15: Gemini 12 (U.S.). Crew: James A. Lovell, Jr., and Edwin E. Aldrin, Jr. Docked with an Agena target vehicle. Aldrin spent more than five hours outside the spacecraft.

1967

Jan. 27: Apollo (U.S.). During a check of the ship on the launch pad, a fire destroyed the module and killed the three astronauts on board: Virgil I. Grissom, Edward H. White 2d, and Roger B. Chaffee.

April 23-24: Soyuz 1 (USSR). Crew: Vladimir M. Komarov. Cosmonaut killed in reentry accident—the first actual space fatality.

1968

Oct. 11-22: Apollo 7 (U.S.). Crew: Walter M. Schirra, Jr., Donn F. Eisele, and R. Walter Cunningham. The first flight of the three-person Apollo command module.

Oct. 25-28: Soyuz 2 (USSR). Unmanned.

Oct. 26-30: Soyuz 3 (USSR). Crew: Georgi T. Beregovoi. The cosmonaut maneuvered Soyuz 3 to within 650 ft (198 m) of Soyuz 2. Returned to Earth after 64 orbits.

Dec. 21-27: Apollo (U.S.). Crew: Frank Borman, James A. Lovell, Jr., and William A. Anders. The first manned flight around the moon. Completed ten orbits of the moon.

1969

Jan. 14-17: Soyuz 4 (USSR). Crew: Vladimir A. Shatalov.

Jan. 15-18: Soyuz 5 (USSR). Crew: Boris V. Volynov, Aleksei S. Yeliseyev, and Yevgeny V. Khrunov. Docked with Soyuz 4. Yeliseyev and Khrunov transferred to Soyuz 4 and landed with it.

March 3-13: Apollo 9 (U.S.). Crew: James A. McDivitt, David R. Scott, and Russell L. Schweikart. Tested the lunar module.

May 18-26: Apollo 10 (U.S.). Crew: Thomas P. Stafford, Eugene A. Cernan, and John W. Young. Completed 31 orbits of the moon. Descended in the lunar module to within 9 mi (14.5 km) of the moon's surface.

July 16-24: Apollo 11 (U.S.). Crew: Neil A. Armstrong, Edwin E. Aldrin, Jr., and Michael Collins. First manned landing on the moon. Armstrong and Aldrin landed on *Mare Tranquillitatis* and on July 20 became the first people to walk on the lunar surface.

Oct. 11-16: Soyuz 6 (USSR). Crew: Georgy Shonin and Valery Kubasov. Conducted the first welding experiments in space.

Oct. 12-17: Soyuz 7 (USSR). Crew: Anatoly Filipchenko, Vladislav Volkov, and Viktor Gorbatko.

Using a Manned Maneuvering Unit and a life-support system on his back, an astronaut has left the space shuttle to make an untethered spacewalk.
Photo: NASA

Pioneers in the exploration of space. *Above:* Yuri Gagarin, who on April 12, 1961, became the first human being to travel in space when he completed one orbit of Earth aboard Vostok 1. *Top right:* John Glenn, who on Feb. 20, 1962, became the first American to orbit the Earth, piloting Friendship 7. *Bottom right:* Valentina Tereshkova, who on June 16, 1963, became the first woman to fly in space, piloting Vostok 6 for 48 orbits of Earth.

Tass/Sovfoto

NASA from FPG International

Tass/Sovfoto

Oct. 13-18: Soyuz 8 (USSR). Crew: V. Shatalov and A. Yeliseyev. Part of a group flight with Soyuz 6 and 7, although the three craft did not dock with one another. Each conducted experiments plus observations of Earth and stars.

Nov. 14-24: Apollo 12 (U.S.). Crew: Charles Conrad, Jr., Richard F. Gordon, Jr., and Alan L. Bean. The second manned lunar landing. Conrad and Bean landed on *Oceanus Procellarum*. They spent a total of 7 hours 39 minutes outside the lunar module, exploring the moon's surface and visiting the Surveyor 3 probe, which landed on the moon April 20, 1967.

1970

April 11-17: Apollo 13 (U.S.). Crew: James A. Lovell, Jr., Fred W. Haise, Jr., and John L. Swigert, Jr. The planned lunar landing was aborted after the oxygen tank in the service module ruptured.

June 2-19: Soyuz 9 (USSR). Crew: Andrian G. Nikolayev and Vitaly I. Sevastyanov. The cosmonauts performed space navigation experiments and made Earth and celestial observations. The flight tested people's reactions to long periods of weightlessness.

1971

Jan. 31–Feb. 9: Apollo 14 (U.S.). Crew: Alan B. Shepard, Jr., Stuart A. Roosa, and Edgar D. Mitchell. The third manned lunar landing, Shepard and Mitchell landed on the *Fra Mauro* highlands. They spent two periods outside their craft, for a total of 9 hours 19 minutes.

April 19: Salyut 1 (USSR). The first space station, launched unmanned into an orbit around Earth.

April 23-25: Soyuz 10 (USSR). Crew: Vladimir A. Shatalov, Aleksei S. Yeliseyev, and Nikolai N. Rukavishnikov. Docked with Salyut 1 but did not board the space station.

June 6-30: Soyuz 11 (USSR). Crew: Georgi T. Dobrovolsky, Vladislav N. Volkov, and Viktor I. Patsayev. Docked with Salyut 1 and occupied the space station for 22 days. The crew died as they returned to Earth, when a faulty valve caused cabin decompression.

July 26–Aug. 7: Apollo 15 (U.S.). Crew: David R. Scott, James B. Irwin, and Alfred M. Worden. The fourth manned lunar landing. Scott and Irwin landed on Hadley Rill. They made three exploratory trips, spending a total of 18 hours 37 minutes outside their craft. They made the first use of the lunar roving vehicle.

1972

April 16-27: Apollo 16 (U.S.). Crew: John W. Young, Charles M. Duke, Jr., and Thomas K. Mattingly, II. The fifth manned lunar landing. Young and Duke landed in Descartes crater. They made three lunar excursions, spending a total of 20 hours 14 minutes outside their craft. They used the lunar roving vehicle and launched a lunar orbiter.

Dec. 7-19: Apollo 17 (U.S.). Crew: Eugene A. Cernan, Harrison Schmitt, and Ronald E. Evans. The sixth and last U.S. manned lunar landing. Cernan and Schmitt landed in Taurus-Littrow Valley. They made three lunar excursions, spending a total of 22 hours 5 minutes outside their craft.

1973

April 3: Salyut 2 (USSR) space station launched, unmanned. Not visited by any crews.

May 14: Skylab (U.S.). The first U.S. space station, launched unmanned and placed into Earth orbit at an altitude of 271 mi (436 km). On July 11, 1979, entered Earth's atmosphere and broke up over Australia, without causing any injury or damage.

May 25–June 22: Skylab 1 (U.S.). Crew: Charles Conrad, Jr., Joseph P. Kerwin, and Paul J. Weitz. Launched aboard an

Apollo spacecraft and docked with Skylab. Conducted studies of space, sun, and Earth. Tested people's ability to endure long periods in space.

July 28–Sept. 26: Skylab 2 (U.S.). Crew: Alan L. Bean, Jack R. Lousma, and Owen K. Garriott. Launched aboard an Apollo spacecraft and docked with Skylab. Conducted photographic surveys of Earth's surface. During a 6 hour 31 minute space walk, Lousma and Garriott erected a sunshade on Skylab and loaded new film in the solar telescope cameras.

Sept. 27-29: Soyuz 12 (USSR). Crew: Vasily Lazarev and Oleg Makarov. Test of an improved Soyuz craft, in which chemical batteries replaced solar cell arrays found on earlier models.

Nov. 16–Feb. 8, 1974: Skylab 3 (U.S.). Crew: Gerald P. Carr, Edward G. Gibson, and William R. Pogue. Launched in an Apollo spacecraft and docked with Skylab. Conducted extensive studies of Earth and sun. Photographed comet Kohoutek.

Dec. 18-26: Soyuz 13 (USSR). Crew: Pyotr Klimuk and Valentin Lebedev. Tested experiments related to the Salyut program.

1974

June 24: Salyut 3 (USSR) space station launched, unmanned.

July 3-19: Soyuz 14 (USSR). Crew: Pavel Popovich and Yuri Artyukhin. Docked with Salyut 3. Performed wide range of experiments.

Aug. 26-28: Soyuz 15 (USSR). Crew: Gennady Sarafanov and Lev Demin. Attempt to dock with Salyut 3 failed because of fault in automatic control system.

Dec. 2-8: Soyuz 16 (USSR). Crew: Anatoly V. Filipchenko and Nikolai N. Rukavishnikov. Tested docking system of Soyuz and reduction of cabin pressure as required for future joint docking experiment with Apollo.

Dec. 26: Salyut 4 (USSR) space station launched, unmanned.

1975

Jan. 11–Feb. 9: Soyuz 17 (USSR). Crew: Aleksei Gubarev and Georgi Grechko. Docked with Salyut 4. Conducted medical tests and observations of Earth's atmosphere and surface, as well as research into space.

May 24–July 26: Soyuz 18 (USSR). Crew: Pyotr Klimuk and Vitaly Sevastyanov. Docked with Salyut 4. Conducted various astronomical studies, surveyed the USSR, and tended a small space greenhouse.

July 15-24: Apollo (U.S.). Crew: Thomas P. Stafford, Donald K. Slayton, and Vance D. Brand. Together with Soyuz 19, launched on the same date, the first cooperative international space flight. The craft linked up for two days, during which the crews visited one another and conducted a series of experiments. (The last Apollo mission and last U.S. manned mission until April 1981.)

July 15-21: Soyuz 19 (USSR). Crew: Aleksei A. Leonov and Valery N. Kubasov. Two-day linkup with Apollo launched on same date.

Nov. 17–Feb. 19, 1976: Soyuz 20 (USSR). Unmanned mission. Docked with Salyut 4. Test of a resupply and rescue system needed for the development of permanent space stations.

1976

June 22: Salyut 5 (USSR) space station launched, unmanned, into orbit.

July 6–Aug. 24: Soyuz 21 (USSR). Crew: Boris Volynov and Vitaly Zholobov. Conducted geographical and meteorological studies and various scientific experiments.

Sept. 15-23: Soyuz 22 (USSR). Crew: Valery F. Bykovsky and Vladimir Aksenov. Carried out a photographic survey of Earth.

In 1969 humans first walked on the moon. During their 2½-hour walk on the surface, Edwin Aldrin (*below*) and Neil Armstrong (photographer) collected rocks and soil samples and set up a series of instruments to relay scientific data to Earth.

NASA

Oct. 14-16: Soyuz 23 (USSR). Crew: Vyacheslav Zudov and Valery Rozhdestvensky. A malfunction prevented the craft from docking with Salyut 5. An emergency landing was made.

1977

Feb. 7-25: Soyuz 24 (USSR). Crew: Viktor Gorbatko and Yuri Glazkov. Docked with Salyut 5. Conducted research on the effects of weightlessness. Carried out extensive photographic studies of Earth.

Sept. 29: Salyut 6 (USSR). space station launched, unmanned, into orbit. During its nearly five years in orbit, 17 manned craft docked with Salyut 6.

Oct. 9-11: Soyuz 25 (USSR). Crew: Vladimir Kovalenok and Valery Ryumin. Attempt to dock with Salyut 6 failed.

Dec. 10–March 16, 1978: Soyuz 26 (USSR). Crew: Yuri Romanenko and Georgi M. Grechko. First ship to dock with Salyut 6. Conducted numerous experiments. Hosted two groups of visiting cosmonauts; employed the first resupply of a space station by an unmanned tanker/transport spacecraft, Progress 1. Crew returned to Earth in Soyuz 27.

1978

Jan. 10-16: Soyuz 27 (USSR). Crew: Vladimir Dzhanibekov and Oleg Makarov. Docked with Salyut 6/Soyuz 26 complex—the first time that two spacecraft were simultaneously docked with a space station. Crew returned to Earth in Soyuz 26.

Each Apollo mission ended with an ocean landing of the command module. Large parachutes slowed the module's speed for a gentle "splashdown."

March 2-10: Soyuz 28 (USSR). Crew: Aleksei A. Gubarev and Vladimir Remek (Czechoslovakia). Docked with Salyut 6/Soyuz 27 complex.

June 15–Nov. 2: Soyuz 29 (USSR). Vladimir Kovalenok and Alexandr Ivanchenkov. Docked with Salyut 6. Performed experiments in biology, physics, and technology. Hosted two visiting pairs of cosmonauts. Resupplied by three Progress tanker/transport vehicles.

June 27–July 5: Soyuz 30 (USSR). Crew: Pyotr Klimuk and Miroslaw Hermaszewski (Poland). Docked with Salyut 6/Soyuz 29 complex.

Aug. 26–Sept. 3: Soyuz 31 (USSR). Crew: Valery Bykovsky and Sigmund Jaehn (East Germany). Docked with Salyut 6/Soyuz 29 complex.

1979

Feb. 26–Aug. 19: Soyuz 32 (USSR). Crew: Vladimir Lyakhov and Valery Ryumin. Docked with Salyut 6. Performed scientific research. Resupplied by Progress 5, 6, and 7. Progress 5 also boosted the Salyut 6/Soyuz 32 complex into a higher orbit. Crew returned aboard Soyuz 34, launched unmanned on June 6.

April 10-12: Soyuz 33 (USSR). Crew: Nikolai Rukavishnikov and Georgi Ivanov (Bulgaria). The craft's docking mechanism failed and it returned to Earth rather than link up with Salyut 6.

Dec. 16: Soyuz T-1 (USSR). Unmanned. Test flight of new generation of manned spacecraft. Docked with Salyut 6.

1980

April 9–Oct. 11:Soyuz 35 (USSR). Crew: Valery Ryumin and Leonid Popov. Docked with Salyut 6. Hosted four visiting pairs of cosmonauts. Crew returned aboard Soyuz 37.

May 26–June 3: Soyuz 36 (USSR). Crew: Valery Kubasov and Bertalan Farkas (Hungary). Docked with Salyut 6/Soyuz 35 complex. Crew returned aboard Soyuz 35.

June 5-9: Soyuz T-2 (USSR). The first manned flight of a new generation of manned space ship. Crew: Yuri Malyshev and Vladimir Aksenov. Docked with Salyut 6/Soyuz 36 complex.

July 23-31: Soyuz 37 (USSR). Crew: Viktor Gorbatko and Pham Tuan (Vietnam). Docked with Salyut 6/Soyuz 36 complex. Crew returned in Soyuz 36.

Sept. 18-26: Soyuz 38 (USSR). Crew: Yuri Romanenko and Arnaldo Tamayo Mendez (Cuba). Docked with Salyut 6.

Nov. 27–Dec. 10: Soyuz T-3 (USSR). Crew: Leonid Kizim, Oleg Makarov, and Gennady Strekalov. Docked with Salyut 6. Made repairs to Salyut 6 to extend its life.

1981

March 12–May 26: Soyuz T-4 (USSR). Crew: Vladimir Kovalenok and Viktor Savinykh. Docked with Salyut 6. Conducted a wide range of experiments and did repair work. Hosted two visiting groups of cosmonauts.

March 22-30: Soyuz 39 (USSR). Crew: Vladimir Dzhanibekov and Jugderdemidiyn Gurragcha (Mongolia). Docked with Salyut 6/Soyuz T-4 complex.

April 12-14, Space Transportation System 1 (STS-1): *Columbia* (U.S.). The first test flight of the first reusable space shuttle. Crew: John W. Young and Robert L. Crippen. Like all succeeding shuttle missions, *Columbia* lifted off from a launchpad but landed on a runway like a conventional airplane.

May 14-22: Soyuz 40 (USSR). Crew: Leonid Popov and Dumitru Prunariu (Rumania). Docked with Salyut 6/Soyuz T-4 complex.

Nov. 12-14, STS-2: *Columbia* (U.S.). Crew: Joe H. Engle and Richard H. Truly. Conducted tests of the shuttle's mechanical arm, which would be used to launch and retrieve satellites.

1982

March 22-30, STS-3: *Columbia* (U.S.). Crew: Jack R. Lousma and C. Gordon Fullerton. Tested the vehicle's ability to withstand the extreme temperatures of space.

April 19: Salyut 7 (USSR) space station launched, unmanned, to an altitude of 186 mi (300 km).

May 13–Dec. 10: Soyuz T-5 (USSR). Crew: Anatoly Berezovoy and Valentin Lebedev. Docked with Salyut 7. Conducted a variety of experiments. Hosted two groups of visiting cosmonauts. Crew returned aboard Soyuz T-7.

June 27–July 4, STS-4: *Columbia* (U.S.). Crew: Thomas K. Mattingly II and Henry Hartsfield, Jr. The final test flight of the shuttle. Carried a secret military payload. Landed at Edwards Air Force Base, California, the first shuttle landing on a hard-surface runway.

June 24–July 2: Soyuz T-6 (USSR). Crew: Vladimir Dzhanibekov, Aleksandr Ivanchenkov, and Jean-Loup Chrétien (France). Docked with Salyut 7/Soyuz T-5 complex.

Aug. 19-27: Soyuz T-7 (USSR). Crew: Leonid Popov, Aleksandr Serebrov, and Svetlana Savitskaya (the second woman in space). Docked with Salyut 7/Soyuz T-5 complex. Crew returned aboard Soyuz T-5.

Nov. 11-16, STS-5: *Columbia* (U.S.). Crew: Vance Brand, Robert Overmyer, William Lenoir, and Joseph Allen. Launched two communications satellites—the first deployment of satellites by the shuttle.

1983

April 4-9, STS-6: *Challenger* (U.S.). Maiden flight of the second American space shuttle. Crew: Paul Weitz, Karol Bobko, Story Musgrave, and Donald Peterson. Two crew members took a space walk, the first U.S. extravehicular activity since 1972.

April 21: Soyuz T-8 (USSR). Crew: Vladimir Titov, Aleksandr Serebrov, and Gennady Strekalov. The mission was aborted when the ship's rendezvous radar failed to deploy, preventing docking with Salyut 7.

June 18-24, STS-7: *Challenger* (U.S.). Crew: Robert L. Crippen, John M. Fabian, Frederick H. Hauck, Norman E. Thagard, and Sally K. Ride (the first American woman in space). Launched two communications satellites and tested the shuttle's 50-ft. (15-m) robotic arm.

June 27–Nov. 23: Soyuz T-9 (USSR). Crew: Vladimir Lyakhov and Aleksandr Aleksandrov. Docked with Salyut 7. Conducted a series of scientific and technical experiments, including materials processing, Earth observations, and medical and biological studies.

Aug. 30–Sept. 5, STS-8: *Challenger* (U.S.). Crew: Daniel C. Brandenstein, Dale A. Gardner, William E. Thornton, Richard H. Truly, and Guion S. Bluford, Jr. Launched a weather and communications satellite. Conducted further tests of the shuttle's robotic arm.

Sept. 27: Soyuz (USSR). Crew: Vladimir Titov and Gennady Strekalov. The crew was saved by an emergency escape system seconds before the SL-4 booster rocket exploded on the launchpad.

Nov. 28–Dec. 8, STS-9: *Columbia* (U.S.). Crew: Owen K. Garriott, Byron K. Lichtenberg, Robert A. Parker, Brewster H. Shaw, John W. Young, and Ulf Merbold (West Germany). The first use of Spacelab, a research facility developed by ESA.

1984

Feb. 3-11, STS-10: *Challenger* (U.S.). Crew: Vance D. Brand, Robert L. Gibson, Bruce McCandless II, Ronald E. McNair, and Robert L. Stewart. The first use of jet-propelled backpacks known as Manned Maneuvering Units, which allow astronauts to make untethered spacewalks.

Feb. 9–Oct. 2: Soyuz T-10 (USSR). Crew: Leonid Kizim, Oleg Atkov, Vladimir Solovyov. Docked with Salyut 7. Performed five extravehicular activities to repair the Salyut propulsion system. Hosted two groups of visiting cosmonauts. Crew returned to Earth aboard Soyuz T-11.

The space shuttle can be launched into Earth orbit, then fly back to a conventional landing on a runway. It has three main parts: two solid-fuel rocket boosters, a large external fuel tank, and a piloted delta-wing orbiter.

Tass/Sovfoto

Space stations, such as Mir (seen prior to launch in the assembly and testing shop), enable people to work in space for weeks or months at a time.

April 3-11: Soyuz T-11 (USSR). Crew: Gennady Strekalov, Yuri Malyshev, Rakesh Sharma (India). Docked with Salyut 7/Soyuz T-10 complex. Crew returned to Earth aboard Soyuz T-10.

April 6-13, STS-11: *Challenger* (U.S.). Crew: Robert L. Crippen, Terry J. Hart, George D. Nelson, Francis R. Scobee, James D. van Hoften. Retrieved and repaired Solar Max, a satellite launched in Feb. 1980 to study the sun's outer surface. Deployed the Long Duration Exposure Facility, a satellite carrying 57 materials-processing experiments.

July 17-29: Soyuz T-12 (USSR). Crew: Vladimir Dzhanibekov, Igor Volk, and Svetlana Savitskaya. Docked with Salyut 7/Soyuz T-11 comples. Savitskaya performed the first spacewalk by a woman.

Aug. 30–Sept. 5, STS-12: *Discovery* (U.S.). Maiden flight of the third American space shuttle. Crew: Henry W. Hartsfield, Jr., Michael L. Coats, Steven A. Hawley, Richard M. Mullane, Judith A. Resnik, and Charles D. Walker. Launched three communications satellites.

Oct. 5-13, STS-13: *Challenger* (U.S.). Crew: Robert L. Crippen, David C. Leestma, Jon A. McBride, Sally K. Ride, Paul Scully-Power, Kathryn D. Sullivan, and Mark Garneau (Canada). Sullivan became the first American woman to walk in space.

Nov. 8-16, STS-14: *Discovery* (U.S.). Crew: Frederick H. Hauck, Joseph P. Allen, Dale A. Gardner, David M. Walker, and Anna L. Fisher. Retrieved and brought back to Earth two communications satellites that had misfired into useless orbits after their launch by STS-10.

1985

Jan. 24-27, STS-15: *Discovery* (U.S.). Crew: James F. Buchli, Thomas K. Mattingly II, Ellison S. Onizuka, Gary E. Payton, and Loren J. Shriver. The first shuttle mission devoted exclusively to secret military objectives. It was believed to have included the deployment of an intelligence-gathering satellite.

April 12-19, STS-16: *Discovery* (U.S.). Crew: Karol J. Bobko, S. David Griggs, Jeffrey A. Hoffman, M. Rhea Seddon, Charles D. Walker, Donald E. Williams, and Sen. Jake Garn of Utah, the first member of Congress to participate in a space mission. Two communications satellites were deployed. One, Leasat-3, failed to activate and efforts to repair it were unsuccessful.

April 29-May 6, STS-17: *Challenger* (U.S.). Crew: Frederick D. Gregory, Donald L. Lind, Robert F. Overmyer, Norman Thagard, William Thornton, Lodewijk van den Berg, and

Taylor G. Wang. Conducted investigations in crystal growth, materials and fluid processing, and weightlessness.

June 7-Sept. 26: Soyuz T-13 (USSR). Crew: Vladimir Dzhanibekov and Viktor Savinykh. Manually docked with Salyut 7, which had lost all its electrical power by the beginning of 1985. The men spent ten days repairing and reactivating the space station. On August 2, using equipment carried up by an unmanned Progress 24 on June 21, the men installed additional solar panels on Salyut 7.

June 17-24, STS-18: *Discovery* (U.S.). Crew: Daniel C. Brandenstein, John O. Creighton, John M. Fabian, Shannon W. Lucid, Steven R. Nagel, Patrick Baudry (France), and Sultan Salman al-Saud (Saudi Arabia). Three communications satellites and the Spartan payload carrier for studies of galactic X-ray emissions were deployed; the latter was subsequently retrieved and carried back to Earth.

July 29–Aug. 6, STS-19: *Challenger* (U.S.). Crew: Loren W. Acton, John-David F. Bartoe, Roy D. Bridges, Jr., Anthony W. England, C. Gordon Fullerton, Karl G. Henize, and F. Story Musgrave. Conducted a series of astronomical observations using Spacelab's experiment mounting structure to carry several large telescopes.

Aug. 27–Sept. 3, STS-20: *Discovery* (U.S.). Crew: Richard O. Covey, Joe H. Engle, William F. Fisher, John M. Lounge, and James D. van Hoften. Three communications satellites were deployed. The mission's primary accomplishment was the capture, repair, and redeployment of Leasat-3, a communications satellite that failed to activate when launched by STS-16.

Sept. 17–Nov. 21: Soyuz T-14 (USSR). Crew: Georgi Grechko, Vladimir Vasyutin, and Alexander Volkov. Docked with Salyut 7/Soyuz T-13 complex. On Sept. 26, Grechko and Dzhanibekov returned to Earth aboard Soyuz T-13—the first in-flight rotation of space crews. On Sept. 27, a new unmanned module docked to Salyut 7, nearly doubling the station's size. On Nov. 21, Vasyutin became ill and the three cosmonauts returned to Earth in Soyuz T-14.

Oct. 3-7, STS-21: *Atlantis* (U.S.). Maiden flight of the fourth American space shuttle. Crew: Karol J. Bobko, Ronald J. Grabe, David C. Hilmers, William A. Pailes, and Robert C. Stewart. A secret mission, it was believed to have deployed two Department of Defense communications satellites.

Oct. 30–Nov. 6, STS-22: *Challenger* (U.S.). Crew: Guion S. Bluford, Jr., James F. Buchli, Bonnie J. Dunbar, Henry W. Hartsfield, Jr., Steven R. Nagel, Reinhard Furrer (W. Germany), Ernst Messerschmid (W. Germany), and Wubbo Ockels (Netherlands). A scientific mission directed by West Germany—the first shuttle mission paid for and dedicated to a payload provided by another nation. Investigations focused on microgravity research, communications, and navigation.

Nov. 26–Dec. 3, STS-23: *Atlantis* (U.S.). Crew: Mary L. Cleave, Bryan D. O'Connor, Jerry L. Ross, Brewster H. Shaw, Jr., Sherwood C. Spring, Charles D. Walker, and Rodolfo Neri (Mexico). Three communications satellites were launched and construction methods designed to be used in building a space station were tested.

1986

Jan. 12-18, STS-24: *Columbia* (U.S.). Crew: Robert L. Gibson, Steven A. Hawley, Robert J. Cenker, Charles F. Bolden Jr., George D. Nelson, Franklin R. Chang-Diaz, and Rep. Bill Nelson of Florida. A communications satellite was launched and various scientific experiments were performed.

Jan. 28: *Challenger* (U.S.). Exploded seconds after liftoff, killing the crew: Francis R. Scobee, Michael J. Smith, Judith Resnik, Ellison S. Onizuka, Ronald E. McNair, Gregory B. Jarvis, and Christa McAuliffe, a Concord, NH, high-school teacher. Subsequent investigation indicated the accident was caused by the rupture of seals on the booster rockets.

Feb. 20: Mir (USSR). space station launched, unmanned, into a slightly elliptical orbit at an altitude of 210 mi (338 km).

March 13–July 16: Soyuz T-15 (USSR). Crew: Leonid Kizim and Vladimir Solovyov. Docked with Mir. On May 5, the cosmonauts flew to Salyut 7 in Soyuz T-15, the first transfer of crew from one space station to another. Various activities of the crew were televised live during the mission.

INVESTMENT AND MONETARY GLOSSARY

ADR American Depository Receipt. This receipt is issued by various American banks for shares of a stock in a foreign company. The stock certificates are deposited by the bank and the **ADR's** are traded in their place.

ANNUITY A contract with an insurance company to pay you a fixed amount periodically (monthly, yearly, etc.) over a given period of time or for life.

ARBITRAGE The purchase of an asset in one market accompanied by a simultaneous sale of the same (or a similar asset in a different market, to take advantage of differences in price. The arbitrage principle can be applied to simultaneous buying and selling of related currencies, commodities, or securities, the same commodity with different delivery dates, etc.

BALANCE OF PAYMENTS A nation's exports less its imports.

BANKNOTE A unit of currency in paper form, as opposed to a bank deposit.

BANKNOTE A unit of currency in paper form, as opposed to a bank deposit.

BARTER The trading of one commodity for another; in modern usage, any exchange that doesn't involve the use of money or money substitutes.

BID PRICE The price at which a dealer or trader offers to buy.

BLACK MARKET A free market operating without the government's legal sanction.

BULLION Refined bars of gold or silver.

BULL MARKET OR BULLISH When prices are going up in value, or are expected to.

CALL OPTION The right to buy a given asset at a fixed price any time to a specified date.

CARRYING CHARGES In futures trading, the difference between the spot price and a future price—usually equal to the cost of interest and storage for the period of time involved.

CASH:(1)Money substitutes in paper form. (2) The absence of credit.

CENTRAL BANK An agency created by a government to issue its currency and to supervise the nation's banking system.

CERTIFICATE OF DEPOSIT A deposit with a fixed time period and a fixed rate of interest.

COIN Real money (gold or silver) transformed into a recognizable shape and weight in order to facilitate exchange.

CONSERVATIVE Involving a minimum of risk.

CONTENT The metal in a coin or token.

CONVERTIBILITY The metal in a coin or token.

CONVERTIBILITY The ability to receive gold in exchange for currency, at a stated rate of exchange, from the agency that issued the currency.

CURRENCY Correctly, receipts for real money in storage; in modern practice, any money substitues in use—even if not backed by real money (synonymous with *paper money*).

CURRENT ACCOUNT A bank deposit that can be withdrawn by the depositor at any time.

DEFLATION A decrease in the amount of money substitutes that have been issued in excess of the real money in storage. (The opposite of *inflation*).

DEMAND DEPOSIT A bank deposit that can be withdrawn by the depositor at any time.

DEPOSIT ACCOUNT A bank deposit in which interest is earned and withrawals are limited.

DEPRESSION A period during which most people are no longer able to maintain their previous standards of living. It is caused by the General Market's attempts to cleanse itself of the misguided uses of resources that have been encouraged by government intervention to productive activity more desired by consumers.

DEVALUATION Repudiation of the government's promise to redeem its money substitutes at the stated rate of exchange, causing a new rate for convertibility.

DIRTY FLOAT A period during which the government intervenes in the foreign exchange market while claiming that it isn't. (See also *floating exchanges rates* and *fixed exchange rates*.)

DOWNSIDE RISK The possible depth to which the price of an investment can drop.

ECONOMICS The study that seeks to allocate limited resources in ways that will provide maximum happiness (whether on a personal, commercial, national, or international scale); the art of making decisions.

ENTREPRENEUR An individual who forecasts future demand for a product or service and arranges a business enterprise to respond to that demand.

EQUITY The value of an investment after deduction of all claims against it— loan amount, interest, commissions, and any other fees.

EUROCURRENCY Currency that is circulating outside the nation where it was issued.

EXCHANGE CONTROLS Governmental regulations limiting or prohibiting the exporting or importing of currencies.

EXCHANGE RATE The price of a currency as expressed in units of another currency. (Synonymous with *foreign exchange rate*.)

FACE VALUE The legal tender value of a coin, toke, or banknote. On bonds, the amount that will be paid to the holder at maturity.

FIAT MONEY The extent to which bullion is pure gold or silver to back it with.

FINESS The extent to which bullion is pure gold or silver, expressed as a decimal of the total gross weight involved. For example, gold bullion of .995 fineness means that 99.5% of the total weight is pure gold.

FIXED DEPOSIT ACCOUNT A bank deposit for a fixed period of time.

FIXED EXCHANGE RATES Currency exchange rates that are prevented from fluctuating by governmental purchases and sales of the currencies involved.

FLOATING EXCHANGE RATES Currency exchange rates that fluctuate freely because governments are *not* stabilizing the rates through purchases and sales. (See *dirty float* and *fixed exchange rates*.)

FLUCTUATION A change in price—upward or downward.

FOREIGN EXCHANGE RATE The price of a currency as expressed in units of another currency. (Synonymous with *exchange rate*.)

FRACTIONAL RESERVE BANKING A banking system in which money that is payable upon demand to depositors is lent to others by the bank; in other words, a system in which the bank doesn't maintain 100% reserves against demand deposits.

FREE MARKET A market free of governmental intervention.

FUTURES CONTRACT a contract for delivery of a commodity or currency in the future at a price determined in the present.

GAP A condition created on a price graph when the prices for one day's trading do not overlap the previous day's range.

GOVERNMENT The institution of greatest economic, political, and police power in a given area.

GRAM Used in gold weights; there are 31.1042 grams to a troy ounce; one gram = 03215 troy ounces. A kilogram in 1,000 grams; there are 1,000 milligrams to a gram.

HARD MONEY Silver and gold.

INCOME (INVESTMENT) Dividends or interest received from an investment.

INCONVERTIBILITY The inability to receive gold in exchange for currency from the agency that issued the currency.

INFLATION An increase in money substitutes above the stored stock of real money; the conterfeiting of money receipts.

INFLATIONARY DEPRESSION A depression within a period of inflation.

LEGAL TENDER A form of money that an individual is legally required to accept in payment of debts.

LEVERAGE In investments, the ability to purchase more than a monetary investment could purchase on a cash basis.

LIQUIDATION: Normally, the sale of an investment. With regard to depressions, *liquidation* refers to the acceptance of losses and the closing of businesses that existed only because of the miscalculations caused by inflation.

LIQUIDITY The availability of spending money.

LONG The expectation that a price will go up; buying before selling. (See also *short*).

LOT In gold coins, the basic unit of trading. A lot contains 100 British sovereigns, 30 Mexican 50-peso pieces, or 20 U.S. double eagles.

MARGIN In a margin account, the amount of one's equity expressed as a percentage of the total current market value of the investment; also, it can refer to the amount of cash equity.

MARGIN ACCOUNT An investment account in which the investment purchase is increased by borrowing money and using the investment as collateral.

MARGIN CALL In a margin account, a request by the lender for the borrower to make a payment on his loan.

MARGIN SALE A sale forced by margin call conditions.

MARKET (1) A group of transactions integrated by geography or items traded. (2) An opportunity to exchange.

MARKET-MAKER A *dealer* who continually offers to buy and sell a given investment.

MARKETABLE Salable in liquid market. (See also *Liquidity*.)

MATURITY The date on which a contractual obligation such as repayment of a bond) falls due.

MONETARY INFLATION An increase in the *money supply*.

MONEY An asset that is generally accepted in exchange with the intention of trading it for something else; normally, usage is confined to gold, bank notes, bank deposits, coins, or tokens.

MONEY MARKET FUND A *mutual fund* that invests only in short-term interest-earning securities.

MONEY MARKET PAPER Easily marketable short-term notes and bills carrying little risk of default.

MONEY SUPPLY Currency held outside of the commercial marketplace.

OPTION The privilege to buy or sell something at a specific price within a specified time.

OUT OF THE MONEY For an *option* (or a *warrant*), the condition that exists when the price of the *underlying investment* is lower than the striking price of the option.

PAR (1) See *Par value.* (2) Equal in value.

PAR VALUE The nominal or face value of a security or currency. (A currency is often referred to as being at par value when it is trading at the price announced as official by the government.)

PERMANENT PORTFOLIO An assortment of ivestments that remains unchanged from year to year.

PORTFOLIO An assortment of investments held by an individual or company.

POWER OF ATTORNEY *Signature authority.*

PREMIUM (1) The amount by which a security is priced above its *face value, book value,* or inherent value. (2) The amount by which the *forward price* exceeds the *spot price.*

PRIME RATE The interest rate charged by commercial banks to their best customers.

PUBLIC MARKET An investment market in which most relevant information is publicly available.

PUBLICLY TRADED INVESTMENT FUND A *closed-end investment company.*

PURCHASING POWER The value of a unit of money or other asset, measured by the quantity of goods and services it will purchase.

PURCHASING POWER PARITY The exchange rate at which a country's price level is equivalent to price levels in other countries.

PURCHASING POWER PARITY THEORY The system of currency forecasting that maintains that exchange rates will gravitate toward their *purchasing power parities.*

PUT OPTION The right to sell a given asset at a fixed price any time prior to a specified date.

RATIO SCALE On a graph drawn to a ratio scale, a given percentage change in value will cover the same vertical distance, no matter at what level it occurs—so that the significance of the change is graphically illustrated. On a *linear scale,* a given absolute change will cover the same vertical distance, no matter at what level it occurs.

REDEMPTION The repurchase of a security by by its issuer.

RESERVE An allocation of capital for possbile losses or to meet a statutory requirement.

RESISTANCE LEVEL An investment price level at which an unusually large volume of selling is expected.

RESTRIKE A coin that was minted after the date marked, but is otherwise genuine.

RUNAWAY INFLATION A period of intense inflation in which vast "paper money" increases cause all retail prices to zoom upward. During this inflationary period prices can increase daily. As bad as inflation is today (1981), we are not yet in a true state of runaway inflation.

SHORT The expectation that a price will drop; the sale of a commodity the seller doesn't own, with the exception of buying the commodity at a lower price later. (See also *long.*)

SPECIAL DRAWING RIGHTS (SDRs) A currency issued by the International Monetary Fund, used only by governments in place of gold as a monetary reserve.

SPECIE Gold or silver.

SPECULATIVE Involving more than a minimum of risk.

SPOT PRICE The price charged in a sale made for delivery today—as opposed to a price quoted for future delivery.

SUBSIDY Payment to an individual or a company by other than a customer or investor; or a purchase at a price higher than the market price; or a loan that doesn't carry a rate of interest commensurate with normal marketplace interest for the risk involved.

SWAPS An arrangement by which one government borrows another government's currency in order to buy its own currency in the marketplace—in order to keep its own currency from sinking in price.

TAX Property coercively taken from its owner by a government.

TAX HAVEN A country where government offers tax advantages to foreigners. Usually in the hopes that wealthy foreigners will come and help boost the economy.

TECHNICAL ANALYSIS A system, usually related to the stock market, in which supply and demand factors are considered.

TECHNOLOGY The increase of productive output from a given unit of human effort—through the use of machines or improved skills.

TERM INSURSANCE Insurance in which the benefits are payable only upon the death of the insured.

TIME DEPOSIT A bank deposit that isn't payable on demand.

TOKEN A money substitute in metallic form (includes gold and silver if the legal tender face value of the token is considerably above the market value of the gold or silver content).

TON, METRIC See *Gram.*

TRADE BALANCE A nation's product exports less its product imports. (See also *Balance of payments* and *Current account.*)

TRADING Buying and/or selling.

TREND A persistent movement in one direction.

TROY OUNCE The unit of weight used to measure gold and silver. One troy ounce equals 1.097 avoirdupois ounces.

TRUST ACCOUNT A **Discretionary account.**

UNDERLYING INVESTMENT For an *option* (or a *warrant* or other *convertible security*), the investment for which the option provides the right of purchase or sale.

UNEARNED INCOME Interest, dividends, rents, and royalties, when measuring taxable income.

UPSIDE POTENTIAL The probability of an increase in price, and its potential extent.

UPVALUATION (Colloquial) The opposite of a *devaluation;* a *revaluation*.

VALUE DATE The date on which payment is considered to have been made, and from which interest charges will be computed.

VARIABLE PORTFOLIO An assortment of investments that is altered as investment prospects change.

WARRANT An option to purchase a share of stock at a fixed price until a specified date. (A warrant differs from a *call option* in that a warrant is issued by the company whose stock is involved.)

WEAK HANDS Investors holding a given investment who are prone to be easily influenced in their trading by short-term trends or events.

WEALTH Resources that can be used or sold.

THE
NEW WEBSTER'S
Handbook
of
Practical
Information

Donald O. Bolander, M.A., Litt. D.

LEXICON PUBLICATIONS, INC.

Chapter 1

EFFECTIVE LETTER WRITING

In commerce and industry, there are three kinds of contacts between business firms and their customers, suppliers, and others — *personal contacts, telephone calls,* and *letters.* By far the majority of business contacts are made by letter!

But good letter writing is equally important for those in education, government, fund-raising and other private organizations, clubs, church groups, and many others.

In the pages that follow you will be given a solid working knowledge of good letter writing. You will easily and quickly be able to understand the principles and techniques presented. However, you must then put them into practice in your own work or activities.

EVERY LETTER A SELLING LETTER

First of all, remember that your letters represent you, your company, or your organization to the recipient or reader. If the person has not met or talked with you, his or her opinion of you or your organization depends on the way they react to your letter.

If the reaction is favorable, you have sold yourself to the person. If the reaction is negative, you have not sold the reader your idea.

The fundamental principle of good letter writing, then, is this: **Every letter is a selling letter.** The aim of every letter is to sell one or more ideas. The one idea that should be included and sold in every letter is *good will.* Additional ideas included in the letter will depend upon the writer's purpose.

Of course, certain business letters are specifically called sales letters. They are designed to get an order or to aid in getting an order for some product or service. In the average business organization, sales letters are considered the most important of all. But consider the selling problem of the writer who must refuse an adjustment, refuse credit, or demand payment, but who still wants to retain the good will of the customer. He, indeed, has a difficult problem.

But letters other than business letters must sell, too. Fund-raising letters must convince the reader to send in a contribution. Letters from a club or other organization may be to sell the member on attending the next meeting or perhaps just to convey information. But even so, the letters are selling the value of the organization, its benefits, the pride the member can feel in the group.

Keep in mind, then, that all letters should have the aim of being silent salesmen of good will, but in addition a letter will usually include other ideas. How does a successful letter sell its ideas? It does so in two ways: first by its *appearance*, and second by its *contents*.

APPEARANCE OF THE LETTER

Letters, like salesmen and window displays, depend upon their appearance for a favorable first impression. If a letter is slovenly, carelessly written, or unattractive, it gives the same impression as a salesman with unshined shoes and unpressed clothes. If the appearance is not attractive, the potential customer may reject the messenger — whether by salesman or letter — before he hears or reads the message.

Based on the principle that every letter is a selling letter, the first rule of effective letter writing is that *the letter must be pleasing in appearance and correct in form.*

The appearance of your letter depends upon many things. The color and quality of stationery, the way the letter is set on the page, its form, the perfection of the typing — all these create the fleeting, but important, first impression.

So that you may recognize the main features of good mechanical layout of a letter, they are discussed briefly here. This discussion applies to all correspondence as well as business letters.

Page Arrangement:

1. A letter should be framed within its margins, with narrow margins for a long letter and wide margins for a short letter.

2. There should be a little more space at the bottom than at the top of a typed letter to balance it properly, since the optical center of a page is slightly higher than the actual center.

3. The date should be placed close to the body of the letter rather than near the letterhead, either four or six spaces above the inside address, depending upon the length of the letter.

4. If a letter is more than one page, the heading of each subsequent page should show the name of the recipient, the page number, and the date as follows:

Mr. H. J. James   Page 2   June 30, 19___

5. Single spacing between lines is normally used rather than double spacing because single spacing is more economical and more attractive. When single spacing is used, two spaces are left between paragraphs.

Letter Styles:

As mentioned, a part of the success of any letter is its appearance. On the pages which follow, types of letter layout or format are shown. The *full-block* and *modified-block* are the most widely used. However, the *simplified* form is often used particularly when the letter is not addressed to a specific person.

Note: In business, a company may have a standard format which they want all typists to use. If so, follow company instructions.

Full Block Format

```
_____(Date)

_____
_____(Inside Address)
_____
_____: (Salutation)

_____
_____
_____(Body)_____
_____
_____(Body con't)___
_____, (Complimentary Close)

_____(Signature)

____(Typist's initials)
____(Enclosure or cc: line)
```

The *full-block format* starts all writing at the left-hand margin. This makes it unnecessary to set tab stops for indenting the date line and the complimentary close. A colon is placed after the salutation and a comma is placed after the complimentary close.

Note: The above sample layout illustrates the typed portion only. This typed portion, of course, would be on a letterhead with white margins left, right, and bottom.

Modified Block Format

```
              (Date) _____

_____
_____(Inside Address)
_____

_____: (Salutation)

_____
_____
_____(Body)_____
_____
_____(Body con't)___
(Complimentary Close) _____

        (Signature) _____

____(Typist's Initials)
____(Enclosure or cc: line)
```

In the *modified-block format*, the date line and complimentary close and signature line are indented to the right. All other lines start flush left.

Note: Some writers also indent the first line of each paragraph five spaces. This is called *mixed style.*

Simplified Format

```
_____(Date)

_____
_____(Inside Address)
_____

_____(Subject  or  Attention
          Line)

_____
_____
_____(Body)_____
_____
_____(Body con't)_____
_____

_____(Signature Line-underline)
_____(Typed Name and Title)

_____(Typist's Initials)
_____(Enclosure or cc: line)
```

The *simplified format* is similar to the full-block format in that all items begin at the left margin. The salutation is replaced by a subject line or an attention line; e.g., Attention: Accounts Receivable Department.

OTHER LETTER ELEMENTS

Punctuation — The most widely-accepted style of punctuation uses no end punctuation for the date and address but retains the colon after the salutation and the comma after the complimentary close. Use this punctuation unless your company specifies otherwise. For complete punctuation rules, see the *Punctuation Rules* section of this handbook.

Postscripts — If you want to add a friendly personal comment or reminder as a handwritten postscript to a typed letter, by all means do so. Typewritten postscripts, although they should not be overused, are permissible and actually are very effective when used judiciously. Start the postscript at the bottom of the letter, three or four spaces below the signature line. Place it even with the left-hand margin or indent to conform with the other paragraphs.

Abbreviations — Good form forbids the use of abbreviations in the date line (Sept. 26, 19—) or in the address (St., W., Co.). Even though it takes a little more time to write out Street, West, and Company, the appearance of your letter is important enough to merit the extra effort. There is one exception to this no-abbreviation rule. If the corporate name of the company you are addressing contains the abbreviation *Co.* or *Inc.*, use it. Always use such widely accepted abbreviations as *Mr., Mrs., Jr., Sr., Dr., D.C.*, and *St.* as in *St. Louis*. For more information, see the *Rules for Abbreviations* sections of this handbook.

Spelling — Be extremely careful to spell correctly the name of either a company or an individual to whom a letter is addressed. Verify spellings, if you have the slightest doubt.

Note: Elsewhere in this book you will find a complete presentation of *Spelling Rules*, a listing of commonly *Misspelled Words*, plus a special listing of *Words Confused and Misused.*

Spelling includes the correct division of words at the end of lines. The pronounciation of words governs their division or syllabication. Your reader might well be bewildered by such incorrect division as *daug-hter, cynical, progr-ess.*

Note: See the section on *Word Division* in this book.

Readability — Does your letter look inviting and easy to read? It won't, if it is composed of long, solid, difficult-looking paragraphs. Vary the length of your paragraphs. Usually they should not exceed ten lines. Don't be afraid of a one-sentence or two-line paragraph, especially if you want an important idea to stand out. Your sentences, too, should be short enough to read easily.

CONTENTS OF THE LETTER

The appearance of your letter is important because from it your reader gets his first impression of you and your message. But the contents are even more important in making sure that every letter is a selling letter.

Fundamentally, your letters will sell *only if they are written from the other person's point of view* rather than from your own. Much has been said and written — and properly so — about the "you" attitude in business letters, and it is equally important in social correspondence. There are still far too many letters which begin almost every paragraph with *I* or *we* because the writer is thinking of himself rather than the reader.

BE COURTEOUS AND CONSIDERATE

The "you" attitude is not merely an appeal to vanity or pride. If it were, it would be insincere and ineffective. The real "you" attitude is the ability to put yourself in the other person's place and to govern your actions — or write your letters — accordingly. This assures the sincerity that is essential to the effectiveness of any letter.

To accomplish your aim of making every letter a selling letter, therefore, your second rule is: *Be courteous and considerate.*

Certain words or phrases should never appear in a courteous, considerate letter. They invariably cause resentment and hostility by connotation, if not by denotation. Consider the words *you claim* or *your claim, you state* or *your assertion.* If you use these words, you might as well add, *but we don't believe you,* for that is the impression you will give.

Obviously is another word to shun as you would poison ivy, for it almost always has a bad effect on the reader. Here is an example from an adjustment letter which lost a valuable customer for a retail store: "Obviously you did not read our last letter carefully or you would have understood that the credit would be shown on next month's bill."

It didn't matter to the customer that her complaint was unjustified and that the adjustment had been made. She had been insulted by a discourteous correspondent who, in effect, had said, "If you're so stupid that you can't understand what we write, we'll just have to point out that *obviously* the credit will appear next month." The customer retaliated by sending back her credit card. Since her account had averaged more than $100 a month, this was truly an expensive letter.

How much better it would have been to say, "Our last letter evidently was not clearly expressed. We are glad to assure you that the credit will be shown on next month's bill. Thank you for writing us."

Evidently, apparently, and *manifestly* are other adverbs which should be used with care. Although you can safely say, *we evidently* or *we apparently*, don't say, *you evidently* or *you apparently.* Keep the other person's viewpoint in mind, and your letters will be courteous and considerate.

"Thank you" is one phrase that never becomes trite. You may say thank you in nine letters out of ten, and yet never sound stale to your reader. It is one positive way of putting the you before the I in your letters. How many letters do you receive or write which begin, "We have your letter . . . ." or "In response to your letter of . . . ." or even "On receipt of your letter . . . ."? If it is necessary to acknowledge the receipt of a letter — and in business it is sometimes helpful in keeping files in proper order — why not simply say, "Thank you for your letter of . . . ." or "Thank you for writing us about . . . ."?

This simple, natural way of expressing friendly appreciation illustrates the third rule in making every letter a selling letter: *Be informal and natural.*

BE INFORMAL AND NATURAL

There are varying degrees of formality in both written and spoken communication. Conversation is the most informal kind of spoken communication, and letters should be the most informal written communication. Personal letters are even more informal than business letters.

Conversation does not require the same degree of organization as the letter, and it has the added advantage of immediate give-and-take. The letter is documentary in nature (although it should never read like a legal document) and must await a reply. Although you cannot say everything in a letter that you would in conversation (the "Hi ya, Joe, whadda yu know" type conversation), you might safely follow this rule: If you wouldn't say it, don't write it — but don't write everything you'd say. Don't let the idea of writing become too high a hurdle. What you are really doing is *talking* to the other person — on paper.

TRITE WORDS AND PHRASES

To be natural and informal, watch your letters carefully until you have eliminated all the cliches — hackneyed, trite, old-fashioned words and phrases — which make a letter sound stilted and formal. You would never dream of using such a vocabulary if you were talking to the other person.

Would you in talking, for instance, use such obsequious language as *your kind favor, your esteemed favor, your obedient servant,* or *I beg to state?* These are hangovers from the nineteenth century. Many a modern, progressive business fails to sell its ideas by letter because of antiquated phraseology. In social correspondence as well, the artificially exaggerated expressions of courtesy have given way to friendly informality.

Approach all your correspondence with an analytical mind. If a word or phrase jars you, question its importance and meaningfulness. Ask yourself if you would use it in talking with the other person. If you would not, the word probably would not be effective in a letter, Apply the "Would I say it?" test with judgment, of course, remembering that you do not want your letters — except the most personal — to be chatty or intimate. You merely want them to be friendly and informal.

BE CLEAR AND CONCISE

Have your facts clearly in mind before starting to write. Otherwise, your reader may misunderstand, necessitating additional, expensive correspondence. The second letter is always more difficult to write, for it is harder to explain a misunderstanding which has arisen because of confused information than it is to say it right the first time.

The fourth general rule, then, to make every letter a selling letter is: *Be clear and concise.*

Take time to analyze the situation before you begin. Ask yourself, "What do I have to say?" Then marshal your facts, mentally or by penciled notation, and put your ideas in logical order. Finally, express what you have to say clearly and simply. When you read your mail, you may find it helpful to put small dots or question marks or even brief penciled notes in the margin opposite the sentences you want to answer. Then, when you are ready to reply, you will not need to reread the letter word for word.

If you are explaining or questioning several different items on a bill, or a number of insurance policies, or various steps in assembling a piece of machinery, use one paragraph for each item or each stem.

Test the clarity of your letter by reading it from the other person's viewpoint before you mail it. Does it answer every question? Does it anticipate those which might result from this correspondence? Is the information given in simple, clear, concise language?

Concise does not mean abrupt or curt. By definition, it means to express much in a few words. It means, therefore, that you should express your thoughts completely but briefly. Do not be disturbed if you find that a letter must be long to cover the information completely. A letter is not ineffective merely because it is long. It is ineffective if it is incomplete. Short letters are manifestly more economical than long ones, but don't make a letter short at the expense of courtesy or completeness.

For conciseness, try to eliminate from your letter the "cluttering" words — words which do not advance an idea. If you are doubtful of a word or phrase, ask yourself, "Does it advance the idea or hinder its advancement?" If it does not advance the idea, drop it! You will find that your ideas are more clearly expressed and your letters more interesting and effective.

INTRODUCTIONS AND CONCLUSIONS

An important aspect of letter writing is how to open and close your letter. Frequently you hear letter writers exclaim, "If I could just get started, I'd be all right" or "I wish I knew how to end this thing." It is true that a lame beginning or ending will detract from the effectiveness of a letter. A poor beginning fails to capture attention — the first essential of a good letter as well as a good speech. A weak ending will leave the other person feeling let down instead of stimulated to action as he should be.

TYPES OF OPENING SENTENCES

Here are some suggestions that will aid you in writing effective openings:

"Thank You" Opening — Like the salesman, you want to make your first words count. The beginning of a letter is the most important place to express the "you" attitude, and there is no better "you" than a "thank you." For example, *Thank you for your letter asking for information about our computer software programs.*

Positive Opening — Shun negative ideas in your openings, and minimize them as much as possible throughout your letter. Don't open a letter with *We are sorry to learn* or *It was most unfortunate.* For every negative there is a positive, and if you have made a mistake, the other person will be glad to know it has been corrected. Instead of apologizing, make positive statements such as *You will be glad to know* or *Fortunately, we were able to.*

Summary Opening — Try the journalistic approach. Summarize the facts or give the main idea in your opening sentence as is done in this example: *The adjustment you requested in your letter of October 10 has been made, and the credit will appear on your November bill.*

Question Opening — Don't be afraid to open with a question if it is natural and sensible to do so. For example, *Have you had an opportunity to consider the proposition we outlined in our letter of April 10?*

"Please" Opening — Use a "please" opening occasionally when it is important that you have immediate action. *Please give us the dates of the bills which are past due.* Or, *Please tell us when you returned the merchandise referred to in your letter of March 5 so that we can check our records.*

"If" Opening — Does an "if" opening seem unusual? Because it is different, it is frequently effective in arousing attention and stimulating action. Watch for opportunities to use the "if" opening, as shown in these examples: *If you will give us the name of the salesman you wrote us about last week, we will check the order with him.* Or, *If you can come in to our office next week, we shall be glad to talk with you about the proposition you suggested in your letter.*

Remember that every sentence in your letter is important, but none is more important than the first sentence. It is there that you gain or lose the reader's interest.

TYPES OF CLOSING SENTENCES

Of only secondary importance to the opening is the closing sentence. Here is where salesmen apply what is known as the "hook," a slang term meaning *stimulus to action.* Like a firecracker which fails to explode, a letter which fizzles out is a "dud." Don't spoil the effectiveness of a letter with an ending that fizzles.

Use definite, to-the-point statements that are not high pressure but emphatic enough to induce action. Here is the place where the word *we* can be used to advantage. *As soon as we hear from you, we will,* or *If we can answer any questions, we shall be glad to do so.*

Avoid long, vague generalizations and negatives. Be sure to leave a clear idea of what you expect. You can do this by calling attention to some idea previously expressed, or by summarizing the main purpose of the letter, or by saving your most important idea for the last, as a climax to your letter.

Use questions. A question may formulate a courteous request such as, *Will you please give us this information before the end of the week?* Or, *Will you please handle this promptly?* Other questions might be, *Can you arrange to handle this shipment?* or *What is your opinion?* You can change the courteous request to a courteous demand by changing from the interrogative to the imperative mood. *Please give us this information* or *Please handle this.*

Avoid connections. The last sentence of your letter should never be connected with the complimentary close. Do not say, *Awaiting your reply, we are — Yours very truly.* It is also incorrect to say, *With best wishes, we are,* or *With kindest regards, we are.*

Because *Please accept my best wishes* sounds stilted, try to find some other friendly closing idea. Occasionally, when letter writers are close friends, just the words *best wishes* or *best regards* may be used as a breezy, personal closing. Such phrases should never take the place of the complimentary close in a business letter. They should be placed as a separate, final paragraph.

ANALYZING LETTERS

Now that you have considered the general principles of letter writing, you are ready to analyze and evaluate specific types of correspondence, both business and social. The most effective method of analysis is to ask questions that will train you to detect the good and bad points of any letter.

The following check list gives a series of questions that you should ask yourself about the specific letter which you are analyzing. This list is called the Four-A Check List since, when you are writing, you are concerned with the *aim, appearance, accuracy,* and *attitude* of a letter.

FOUR-A CHECK LIST
For Business and Social Letters

Aim

    a. What are the specific purposes of the letter?

    b. Does it accomplish these purposes?

Appearance

    c. Is the letter pleasing in appearance?

    d. Is it correct and consistent in mechanics according to the style used?

Accuracy

    e. Is the letter grammatical?

    f. Are spelling, syllabication, capitalization, punctuation, and abbreviations correct?

    g. Are the sentences and paragraphs varied in length?

    h. Are the ideas presented in logical order?

    i. Is the letter clear and concise? Does it include any irrelevant ideas or use any unnecessary words?

    j. Is the choice of words fully effective?

Attitude

    k. Does the letter have the ''you'' attitude — not merely through the use of the pronoun ''you'' but through ideas expressed from the other person's viewpoint?

    l. Does the letter have words that are negative or words that will have a bad effect on the reader?

    m. Does it include, whenever necessary, courteous expressions of thanks, appreciation, etc?

    n. Are trite or old-fashioned words and phrases avoided?

    o. Is the letter informal and natural in tone?

    p. Is abrupt or curt wording avoided?

    q. Does the closing thought leave the reader with the desired idea?

Using the Check List

You will find that the questions in the Four-A Check List are easy to apply to any letter. When you begin to analyze your letters, have the check list open in front of you and check your letter carefully against each question in the list. You will soon be able to detect faults almost automatically and will need to refer to the list only occasionally.

LETTER PARTS

As discussed earlier in this section, the appearance of your letter creates either a favorable or unfavorable impression. Here is a brief explanation of the specific parts of a letter so that your letters conform to generally accepted usages.

Sender's Address: If you are writing on printed stationary, your name and address or the name of your company or organization is given on the letterhead. However, if you are writing a personal letter on plain paper, place your address immediately above the date line.

    670 Walnut Street
    Little Falls, NJ 07424
    June 27, 19—

Date Line: Do not abbreviate dates. Spell out the month and do not use ordinals (*nd, rd, st, th*). Do not use the military version except in military correspondence.

    No: 9/21/87
    No: Sept. 21st, 1987
    No: 21 September 87 (military)
    Yes: September 21, 1987

Receiver's Address: Use the proper complimentary title (*Mr., Mrs., Ms., Dr.*) with the person's name, his or her position if known, and the name of the company or organization followed by the complete address.

    Mr. Robert Costantini
    Director of Publications
    Hexagon Publishers, Inc.
    1000 Lexington Avenue
    New York, NY 10018

Apartment or suite numbers may be placed either on the same line with the address or if the address is too long, on a separate line immediately above it.

Note 1: For titles of educational, governmental, military, and religious dignitaries, see the *Forms of Address* section of this book.

Note 2: If writing to an individual at a home address, only the name and address would be given.

Salutations: The salutation should follow two spaces after the inside address. It is generally followed by a colon, but some writers omit the colon. The choice of the salutation depends on the relationship with the reader. Unless you know the reader quite well, use a moderately dignified salutation.

Recommended Salutations
Dear Mr. Henderson:
Dear Mrs. Chambers:
Dear Ms. Risner:

Salutations To Be Avoided
Dear Sir: Dear Madam:
Gentlemen: Mesdames:

If you are not writing to a specific person, use a *subject* line or *attention* line as explained for the simplified letter format.

Instead of a salutation some modern writers recommend an opening *attention getting phrase* which is generally part of the first sentence as follows:

    It was great seeing you again, Tom . . .
    . . . at the annual convention.

    Thank you for the time . . .
    . . . you gave me yesterday, Mr. Henderson, to review my qualifications.

    It's true, Mrs. Jordan,
    — It was our error. Your account has not been credited.

Body of the Letter: Begin the body of the letter two spaces below the salutation or subject line. Unless the letter is very brief, it should be single-spaced with a double space between paragraphs. If double spacing is used, the first line of each paragraph should be indented.

Complimentary Close: Complimentary closes should be followed by commas, capitalizing only the first word. Here are some accepted closes.

    Sincerely,   Cordially,
    Sincerely yours,   Best regards,
    Very truly yours,   Regards,

The close *Respectfully yours* may be used for a top business executive, government official, or church dignitary. Other complimentary closes are given in the *Forms of Address* section of this book.

Signature and Writers Identification: Type the writer's name and title immediately below the complimentary close. Leave three to five spaces for the signature.

    Sincerely yours,

    Henry K. Peters
    Director of Public Relations

Typist's Initials: The initials should be placed two spaces below the writer's title or name and flush left with the margin. The writer's initials need not be shown.

No: HKP: dob   *Yes*: dob

Enclosure Line: Use an enclosure line when other items are included in the letter. If there is more than one enclosure indicate the number. Place the enclosure line two spaces below the typist's initials.

Enclosure   Enclosures (3)

Carbon Copy Notation: If copies of the letter are being sent to other people note their names one or two spaces (depending on letter length) below the typist's initials or enclosure line. If necessary, give the person's title so the addressee knows his identity.

cc: Mr. Harry Rigio   cc: Walter Brown
      Ms. Jane Friedlan   Sales Coordinator

Chapter 2

FORMS OF ADDRESS

The following are preferred forms and correct use of titles:

Business Names and Titles

1. All titles in a business address should be capitalized. The "Zip" code should be placed two spaces after the state name without separating punctuation. Do not abbreviate *Company* or *Incorporated* unless the firm uses the abbreviations on its official letterhead.

> Mr. John Rae, President
> Graphic Products, Inc.
> Monroe, Michigan 48048

> Mr. Richard Greene
> Chairman of the Board
> General Dynamics Company
> Quincy, Maine 02169

2. An educational or business title may be used with a personal title or degree for the same person.

> Dr. Jay Howard
> Director of Research
> Dexter Electronics, Inc.

> Thruman Hardwick, Ph.D.
> Professor of History
> Cornell University

3. A position title may be placed either on the same line, or on a separate line, based on length and convenience.

> Mr. James Gordon, Superintendent
> Riverdale Public Schools
> Riverdale, Illinois

> Mr. James Gordon
> Superintendent of Schools
> Riverdale, Illinois

4. The salutation *Gentlemen* may be used if the letter is not addressed to a specific person within the company, even though the letter is marked for the attention of that person.

> Gould Incorporated
> Chicago, Illinois
>   Attention: Mr. Andrew Williams
> Gentlemen:

Titles for Addressing Men

1. The title *Mr.* always precedes the name when addressing letters to a man, if he has no professional title.

> Mr. Gary Jones
> *or*
> Mr. Gary Jones, Manager

> *Salutation:*   Dear Sir:
> *or*
> Dear Mr. Jones:

2. For two or more men who have no professional title, *Mr.* should precede each name.

> Mr. James North
> Mr. Leo James

> *Salutation:*   Dear Sirs:
> *or*
> Gentlemen:

3. The proper title for a boy under 12 is *Master*. From ages 12 to 18 usually no title is used. *Mr.* becomes the correct title at age 18.

> Master Tommy Burns
> Masters Tommy and Jim Burns

> *Salutation:* Dear Tommy and Jim:

4. Designations such as Sr., Jr., III, etc., should be capitalized and usually are separated from the name by commas.

> Mr. R.J. Hooker, Sr.
> Peter Brady, Jr., Ph.D.
> Dr. Arnold Smith, III
> Mr. Raymond Gallo, Sr., President

Titles for Professional Men and Women

1. The title *Doctor* is designated for persons who have attained that degree.

> Martin Gould, Ph.D.
> *or*
> Dr. Martin Gould

> Martha Merk, M.D.
> *or*
> Dr. Martha Merk

> *Salutation:*   Dear Dr. Merk:

2. *Dr.* and *Mr.* should not be used with the same name.

> Martin Gould, Ph.D.
> *not*
> Dr. Martin Gould, Ph.D.

3. College or university teachers who hold professional rank are called *Professor* or *Prof.*

> Professor Lenore Klein
> *not*
> Professor Mrs. Klein

> Professor Donald Boone
> *not*
> Prof. Boone

4. A professional man and his wife are addressed as:

> Dr. and Mrs. Richard Warner
> Professor and Mrs. James Donalson

5. The title *Messrs.* (*Messieurs*) precedes

the name of two or more professional men jointly engaged in practice.

> Messrs. Carl Bunker and Robert Black
> Attorneys at Law

Titles for Addressing Women

1. The title *Miss* is used when addressing an unmarried woman. Authorities prefer the use of the title *Ms* for a woman whose marital status is unknown.

> Miss Jean Peterson
> Secretary to the President
>
> Ms Shelly Streeter, Office Manager
> Turner Supply Company

Misses is recommened when addressing two or more unmarried women.

> The Misses Baker and Frederickson
> The Misses Lena and Sarah Bronson

2. To address a married woman you should use *Mrs.* In business correspondence, the woman's personal first name is preferred. In social correspondence, her husband's name should be used.

> Mrs. Linda Reisman
> (business)
> Mrs. John Reisman
> (social)

For two or more married women *Mesdames* is used (or if one is married and one is single, *Mesdames* is also suggested).

> Mesdames Elyse Brown
> and Cynthia Birch
>
> Dear Ladies:
> Mesdames:
> Ladies:

3. The wife of a doctor or professor should not be addressed as Mrs. Dr. John Toomey or Mrs. Prof. B.T. Brown. The correct form is Mrs. B. T. Brown.

4. A divorced woman may use either her married name or her maiden name, and *Ms, Miss* or *Mrs.* are all correct. The preferred usage by the divorced woman should be followed.

Military Titles

1. Military personnel should be addressed with the rank or grade held. If the military title contains a prefix as in Brigadier, the prefix may be omitted in the salutation. Military personnel may be greeted with Dear Sir: for example.

> Brigadier General Mark Reis, U.S.A.
> Address
> Dear General Reis:
> *or*
> Dear Sir:

2. Naval commissioned officers below the rank of *Commander* may be addressed either with their rank or addressed as *Mr.* in the salutation.

> Lieutenant Fred Buckner, U.S.N.
> Address
> Dear Lieutenant Buckner:
> *or*
> Dear Mr. Buckner:

The Complimentary Close

1. There are various complimentary closes which are acceptable for business correspondence. The preferred close is largely determined by the writer and the degree of friendliness he has with the person being written to. The first word of the close is always capitalized.

Sincerely,	Yours very truly,
Sincerely yours,	Respectfully,
Yours truly,	Respectfully yours,
Very truly yours,	Cordially,

2. Any of the following may be used for government officials:

Respectfully yours,	Very truly yours,
Respectfully,	Yours very truly,
Yours respectfully,	Sincerely yours,

3. For dignitaries of the church, any of the following may be used:

Faithfully yours	Yours in Christ
Respectfully yours,	Sincerely yours in Christ,
Respectfully,	Sincerely yours,

Chapter 3

TABLES OF ADDRESSES AND SALUTATIONS FOR GOVERNMENT, SCHOOL, AND CHURCH DIGNITARIES

Admiral (Four Star)
Adm. Robert Stone, USN
Address

Dear Admiral Stone:

Ambassador, American
The Honorable John Adams
The American Ambassador
Address

Sir:
Dear Mr. Ambassador:

Ambassador, Foreign

His Excellency Ronald Scala
The Ambassador of Italy
Address

Sir:
Excellency:
Dear Mr. Ambassador:

Archbishop (Catholic)
Most Rev. Robert Carson
Archbishop of (Ecclesiastical
Province)
Address

Dear Archbishop Carson:

The Most Reverend Archbishop
of (Ecclesiastical Province)
Address

Most Reverend Sir:
Your Excellency:
Your Grace:

Archdeacon (Episcopal)
The Venerable Alexander Roth
Archdeacon of (Diocese)
Address

Venerable Sir:

The Venerable Archdeacon
of (Diocese)
Address

Venerable Sir:

Attorney General
Hon. Charles Scott
Attorney General of the State
of (State Name)
Address

Dear Mr. Scott

The Attorney General of the State
of (State Name)
Address

Subject Line

Attorney
Ms. Nancy T. Bell
Attorney-at-Law
Address

Dear Ms. Bell:

Bishop (Catholic)
Most Rev. Stephen Lewis
Bishop of (Diocese)
Address

Dear Bishop Lewis
Your Excellency:
Most Reverend Sir:

Bishop (Episcopal)
Right Rev. Gerald Berg
Bishop of (Diocese)
Address

Dear Bishop Berg:
Your Excellency:
Right Reverend Sir:

Bishop, Other Denominations
Rev. Thomas Birch
Bishop of (Diocese)
Address

Dear Bishop Birch:

The Reverend Bishop Birch
Bishop of Memphis
Address

Reverend Sir:
Dear Bishop:
Dear Sir:

Brother
Brother James Dunne,*
LaSalle University
Address
*Add abbreviation of order

Dear Brother:

Dear Brother Dunne:

Cabinet Officer (Federal or State)
The Honorable Samuel Stern
Secretary of _____(State, etc.)
Address

Sir:
Dear Sir:
Dear Mr. Secretary:

Cardinal
His Eminence Martin,
Cardinal _____
Address

Your Eminence:

Chancellor
Dr. Patrick Bacon
Chancellor of Pace University
Address

Dear Dr. Bacon:

The Chancellor
Pace University
Address

Subject Line:

Chaplin
Chaplain Donald Folley
Captain, U.S. Army
Address

Dear Chaplain:
Dear Chaplain Folley:

City Council
The City Council
City of Toledo
Address

Honorable Sirs:
Honorable Gentlemen:

Clerk of the Court
Sally T. Brown, Esq.
Clerk of the Court of Illinois
Address

Dear Ms. Brown:

The Clerk of the Court of Illinois
State Capital, State Zip

Subject Line:

Colonel
Col. Terrence Black, USA (or USAF
or USMC)
Address

Dear Colonel Black:

Commodore
Com. Robert James, USCG (or USN)
Address

Dear Commodore James:

Congressman or State Representative
The Honorable Dean Shelly
The House of Representatives
Address

Sir:
Dear Mr. Shelly:
Dear Congressman Shelly:
(United States only)

Consul, American
The American Consul

(or: Gerald Dole, Esquire)
American Consul
Address

Sir:
Dear Sir:
Dear Mr. Consul:

Consul, Foreign
The Spanish Consul
Address

Sir:
Dear Sir:
Dear Mr. Consul:

Dean (Church)
The Very Reverend Timothy Bello
St. Patrick's Church
Address

Very Reverend Sir:
Dear Dean:

Dean (College)
Dean Gina Hawes,*
LaFayette University
Address
*Add abbreviation of degree.

Dear Dean (Dr.) Hawes:
Dear Madam: (or Sir)
Dear Dean:

General (Four Star)
Gen. Richard Cornwall, USA
(or USAF or USMC)
Address

Dear General Cornwall:

Governor
The Honorable William Mason
Governor, State of New Jersey
Address

Dear Sir:
Dear Governor:

Judge
The Honorable Daniel Galton
Judge of the Circuit Court
Address

Dear Sir:
Dear Judge:

Judge, Federal
Hon. Nancy Bell
Judge of the U.S. District
Court of (District)
Address

Dear Judge Bell:

Mayor
The Honorable Robert Benson
Mayor, City of Richmond
Address

Sir:
Dear Mr. Mayor:
Dear Mayor:

Minister, American
Hon. Donald Brown
American Minister
Foreign City, Country

Dear Mr. Brown:

Minister, Foreign
Hon. Mary Marquette
Minister of (Country)
Washington, DC Zip

Dear Ms. Marquette:

Minister (Protestant)
The Reverend Jessie Burke
First Methodist Church
Address

Dear Sir:
Dear Doctor: (if D.D.)
Dear Mr. Burke:

Monsignor
The Right Reverend
Monsignor Ben Stacey
Name of Church
Address

Right Reverend Sir:
Dear Monsignor:
Right Reverend and
Dear Monsignor:

The Pope
His Holiness, Pope —————
The Vatican
Vatican City, Italy

Your Holiness:
Most Heavenly Father:

Postmaster General
Hon. Victor Johns
The Postmaster General
Washington, DC 20540

Dear Mr. Johns:

The Postmaster General
Washington, DC 20540

Subject Line:

President (College or University)
William Buchner,*
President, Indiana University
Address
*Add abbreviation of highest degree.

Dear Sir:
Dear Mr. President:

President of the United States
The President
The White House
Washington, D.C.

Sir:
Dear Mr. President:

Priest
The Reverend Stephen Wilson,*
University of Minnesota
Address
*Add abbreviation of order.

Reverend Father:
Dear Reverend Father:
Dear Father:

Principal
Dr. (Ms.) Martha Truman
Principal of Paterson High School
Address

Dear Dr. (Ms.) Truman

Rabbi
Rabbi Nathan Greene
(or: The Reverend Nathan Greene)
Sinai Congregation
Address

Dear Rabbi Greene:

(With Doctor's Degree)
Rabbi Nathan Greene, D.D.
(Name of Synagogue)
Address

Dear Rabbi (or Dr.) Greene:

Rear Admiral
Rear Admiral Dean Thelander, USCG
(or USN)
Address

Dear Admiral Thelander:

Rector
The Very Reverend Timothy Hart
Name of Church
Address

Dear Father Hart:
Very Reverend Sir:
Dear Reverend Hart:

Secretary of State (Treasurer
or Commissioner)
Hon. Mark Andrews
Secretary of State of (State)
Address

Dear Mr. Andrews:

Senator (U.S. or State)
The Honorable Charles Nutley
United States Senate
(or: The State Senate)
Address

Sir:
Dear Senator:
Dear Senator Nutley:

Sister
Sister Catherine Mary,*
St. Elizabeth's Convent
Address
*Add abbreviation of order.

Dear Sister:
Dear Sister Mary:

Superintendent of Schools
Dr. (Mr.) Raymond McArdle
Superintendent of Glencoe City
School System
Address

Dear Dr. (Mr.) McArdle:

Superior of Sister Order
Mother Teresa Mullens,*
Mother General
Address
*Add abbreviation of order.

Reverend Mother:
Dear Mother General:
Dear Sister Superior:

Supreme Court: Chief Justice
Hon. Joseph Tiernan
Chief Justice of the Supreme Court
of (State)
Address

Dear Mr. Chief Justice:

Vice-President
The Honorable Justine Smith
The Vice-President of the
United States
Washington, D.C. 20025

Sir:
Mr. Vice-President:
Dear Mr. Vice-President:

Chapter 4

IMPROVING YOUR SPELLING

To write a letter, report, or article that contains misspelled words is an almost unforgivable error. Frequent misspellings in business writing may prevent a person from being promoted to a position for which he or she is otherwise qualified. In high school or college a lower grade may be given to papers or reports that contain several misspelled words. Misspellings in social correspondence or in minutes, reports, etc. for club or church groups often affect a person's social or personal standing because errors create an impression of a lack of education or cultural background.

Suggestions for Improvement

Learning to spell well is not difficult, particularly if you set up a spelling improvement program for yourself. The program is simple and consists of the following steps:

1. **Learn the six basic spelling rules.** The rules are given on the following pages. The rules for forming plurals are also given.

2. **Keep a notebook of words you misspell.** Go over the words frequently until you are sure you know their correct spelling. You will be surprised how effective this notebook system will be and how little of your time it will take. Continue keeping the notebook until you have learned to spell correctly the majority of words you regularly use in your writing.

3. **Don't guess about the spelling of a word.** Look up any word you are not sure of in a spelling dictionary or regular dictionary. If you find you have misspelled a word, add it to your spelling notebook. Looking up words in a dictionary takes a little time, but it prevents embarrassing mistakes.

In addition, immediately following this section you will find a list of 400 words which are frequently misspelled. Go over this list just as you do your notebook to help eliminate any errors you may now make. You will be pleased with how rapidly your spelling will improve.

SIX BASIC SPELLING RULES

Following are six basic spelling rules which will guide you in your program of spelling improvement. Each rule is illustrated by examples, and exceptions (if any) are noted.

Note: In another section of this handbook, a list of word roots, prefixes, and suffixes is given.

Rule 1. Words ending with a silent e usually drop the e when a suffix beginning with a vowel is added.

Root Word	Suffix		Complete Word
survive	+ al	=	survival
divide	+ ing	=	dividing
fortune	+ ate	=	fortunate
abuse	+ ive	=	abusive

Exceptions to the rule:

a. Words containing the soft sounds of **g** or **c** retain the **e** before the suffixes **able** or **ous**. *Examples*: Courageous, advantageous, peaceable, noticeable, changeable, manageable, serviceable.

b. Retain the **e** in words that might be mistaken for another word if the rule were applied. *Examples*: singe, singeing; dye, dyeing; shoe, shoeing; canoe, canoeing.

c. Words ending in **ie** drop the e and change the **i** to **y** when the suffix **ing** is added. This is done to prevent two **i**'s from coming together. Examples: die, dying; tie, tying; lie, lying.

d. In the words *mileage, acreage, lineage*, the **e** is not dropped before the suffix **age**.

Rule 2. Words ending with a silent e usually retain the **e** before a suffix beginning with a consonant.

Word	Suffix		Complete Word
arrange	+ ment	=	arrangement
awe	+ some	=	awesome
forgive	+ ness	=	forgiveness
safe	+ ty	=	safety
shame	+ less	=	shameless

Exceptions to the rule: judge, judgment; acknowledge, acknowledgment; argue, argument; true, truly; nine, ninth; pursue, pursuant; value, valuation; wise, wisdom; whole, wholly; awe, awful.

Rule 3. Words ending in a single consonant preceded by a single vowel, usually double the final consonant before a suffix beginning with a vowel.

run	+ ing	=	running
big	+ est	=	biggest
hot	+ er	=	hotter
plan	+ ing	=	planning
bag	+ age	=	baggage

If the word ends with two or more consonants, or if the final consonant is preceded by two vowels instead of one, the rule does not apply.

Two Consonants

debt	+ or	=	debtor
calm	+ est	=	calmest

Two Vowels

frail	+ est	=	frailest
swear	+ ing	=	swearing
sweet	+ er	=	sweeter

Rule 4. Words of two or more syllables, that are accented on the final syllable and end in a single consonant preceded by a single vowel, double the final consonant before a suffix beginning with a vowel. If the accent is not on the last syllable, the final consonant is not doubled.

Accent on Last Syllable

refer	+ ing	=	referring
regret	+ able	=	regrettable
occur	+ ence	=	occurrence

Accent Not on Last Syllable

benefit	+ ed	=	benefited
differ	+ ence	=	difference
travel	+ er	=	traveler

If the word ends in two consonants, if the final consonant is preceded by two vowels, or if the accent shifts to the first syllable when the suffix is added, the rule does not apply.

perform + ance = performance	(two consonants)
repeal + ing = repealing	(two vowels)
refer + ence = reference	(accent shifts)

Rule 5. Use of "ei" and "ie." Use **i** before **e** except when the two letters follow **c** and have a long **e** sound, or when the two vowels are pronounced long **a**.

Long e after c	Long a sound	After letters other than c
conceit	vein	shield
deceive	weight	believe
ceiling	veil	grieve
receipt	freight	niece
perceive	neighbor	mischievous

Exceptions to the rule:

weird	foreign	seize	leisure
either	forfeit	height	ancient
neither	sleight	surfeit	sovereign

Words that end in **ie** change the ie to **y** when the suffix **ing** is added.

lie - lying   die - dying   vie - vying

Rule 6. Words ending in **y** preceded by a consonant usually change the **y** to **i** before any suffix except one beginning with an **i**.

beauty + ful = beautiful
lady + es = ladies
lovely + ness = loveliness
ratify + es = ratifies
accompany + ment = accompaniment
accompany + ing = accompanying

Exceptions to the rule:

shy + ness = shyness
baby + hood = babyhood
plenty + ous = plenteous
lady + like = ladylike
beauty + ous = beauteous
wry + ly = wryly

If the final **y** is preceded by a vowel, the rule does not apply.

journey + s = journeys
buy + s = buys
essay + s = essays
obey + ing = obeying
repay + ing = repaying
attorney + s = attorneys

Note: This rule will be referred to later in the section on forming plurals.

FORMING PLURALS OF NOUNS

If a word is incorrectly pluralized, it is, of course, misspelled. There are thirteen rules on forming plurals listed here, together with examples and exceptions to the rules.

1. Plurals of most nouns are formed by adding **s** to the singular word.

Singular	Plural	Singular	Plural
bell	bells	pencil	pencils
college	colleges	tablet	tablets

2. When nouns end in **y** preceded by a consonant, the plural is formed by changing the **y** to **i** and adding **es**.

Final y preceded by a consonant:		Final y preceded by a vowel:	
Singular	**Plural**	**Singular**	**Plural**
baby	babies	valley	valleys
century	centuries	donkey	donkeys
lady	ladies	turkey	turkeys

Note: See Rule 6 under Basic Spelling Rules in this unit.

3. When nouns end in **ch, sh, ss, s, x,** or **z**, add **es** to form the plural.

Singular	Plural	Singular	Plural
dress	dresses	church	churches
fox	foxes	dish	dishes

4. The plurals of nouns ending in **f, ff,** or **fe** are formed by adding **s** to the singular. However, some nouns with these endings change the **f** or **fe** to **v** and add **es**.

Add s for plural		Change f to v and add es	
Singular	**Plural**	**Singular**	**Plural**
cliff	cliffs	wife	wives
handkerchief	hankerchiefs	leaf	leaves
safe	safes	self	selves

5. (a) The plurals of nouns ending in **o** preceded by a vowel usually are formed by adding **s** to the singular. Musical terms ending in **o** add **s** although the final **o** is not always preceded by a vowel.

Singular	Plural	Singular	Plural
studio	studios	piano	pianos
ratio	ratios	trio	trios
portfolio	portfolios	soprano	sopranos

(b) Nouns ending in **o** preceded by a consonant usually add **es** to form the plural.

Singular	Plural	Singular	Plural
motto	mottoes	hero	heroes
tomato	tomatoes	echo	echoes
potato	potatoes	Negro	Negroes

(c) Some nouns ending in **o** have two plural forms. In the following examples, the preferred plural form is given first:

Singular	Plural
memento	mementos or mementoes
cargo	cargos or cargoes
zero	zeros or zeroes

6. (a) Plurals of compound nouns are formed by adding **s** to the important word or most essential part of the compound.

Singular	Plural
sister-in-law	sisters-in-law
passer-by	passers-by
editor-in-chief	editors-in-chief
co-editor	co-editors

(b) Sometimes both parts of a compound are made plural.

manservant	menservants

(c) Compounds ending in **ful** form the plural by adding **s** to the ending of the compound.

Singular	Plural	Singular	Plural
cupful	cupfuls	handful	handfuls
spoonful	spoonfuls	tubful	tubfuls

(d) If there is no important word in the compound, or if both words are equal in importance, make the last part of the compound plural.

Singular	Plural
clothesbrush	clothesbrushes
scrubwoman	scrubwomen
washcloth	washcloths

7. Plurals of some nouns are formed either by a change in the vowel or by a complete change of spelling.

Singular	Plural	Singular	Plural
man	men	foot	feet
child	children	woman	women
mouse	mice	goose	geese
ox	oxen	tooth	teeth

8. Some nouns have the same form in both the singular and plural.

Examples: athletics, corps, deer, fish, moose, sheep, species

9. Some nouns are plural in form but are almost always considered to be singular in usage.

Examples: economics, ethics, news, mathematics, politics

10. Some nouns are rarely or never used in the singular.

Examples: cattle, cosmetics, scissors, statistics, trousers

11. Some words derived from a foreign language retain their foreign plurals.

Singular	Plural	Singular	Plural
datum	data	analysis	analyses
alumnus	alumni (masc.)	alumna	alumnae (fem.)
stratum	strata	synopsis	synopses

Sometimes, however, the English plurals are used instead of the foreign plurals.

Singular	Plural
referendum	referendums or referenda
curriculum	curriculums or curricula
trousseau	trousseaux or trousseaus

12. The plurals of proper nouns are formed by adding **s** if the name does not end in **s**, or by adding **es** if the name ends in **s**.

There are two **Marys** in our family.
Three **Besses** answered the roll call.
The **Adamses** have a new automobile.
The **Joneses** and the **Halls** are old college friends.

13. Plurals of letters, symbols, and numbers are formed by adding an apostrophe and **s ('s)**.

Examples: A's x's 2's ?'s
+'s if's $'s 100's

FORMING POSSESSIVES

The apostrophe (') is a mark to show that a noun (or indefinite pronoun) is possessive, or to indicate a contraction. Just as a word is misspelled if it is pluralized incorrectly, so is it misspelled if the apostrophe is omitted or inserted in the wrong place in a word that shows possession.

1. If the singular form of the noun does not end in **s**, add the apostrophe and **s** (**'s**). If the singular ends in **s**, add the apostrophe (**'**).

Note: In the possessive singular of nouns that end in **s**, if you want the sound of an additional **s**, the apostrophe and **s** (**'s**) may be added.

Singular	Possessive	Singular	Possessive
boy	boy's	Harold	Harold's
child	child's	woman	woman's
Ross	Ross'	Davis	Davis'
	(or Ross's)		(or Davis's)

2. If the plural does not end in **s**, add the apostrophe and **s** (**'s**). If the plural ends in **s**, add the apostrophe (**'**).

Helpful hint: Make the word plural first; then make it possessive.

Plural	Possessive	Plural	Possessive
calves	calves'	bosses	bosses'
boys	boys'	children	children's
men	men's	sheep	sheep's
weeks	weeks'	Joneses	Joneses'

Caution: Be sure that you always add the apostrophe to the end of a word and that you do not insert it within the word. For example, take the proper name Jones. If you insert the apostrophe before the **s** (Jone's), it would mean that the proper name was Jone.

3. Possessive personal pronouns do not require an apostrophe.

my, mine	you, your
he, his	we, ours
she, hers	they, theirs
it, its	who, whose

Note: *It's* is a contraction of *it is* not the possessive of *it*.

4. Possessives of indefinite pronouns are formed by adding an apostrophe and **s**(**'s**).

else's	someone's	everybody's
somebody's	everyone's	one's

5. Possession of a compound word is shown at the end of the word, regardless of which part of the compound may be pluralized.

Singular	Singular Possessive
tradesman	tradesman's
editor-in-chief	editor-in-chief's
secretary-treasurer	secretary-treasurer's

Plural	Plural Possessive
brothers-in-law	brothers-in-law's
menservants	menservants'
freshmen	freshmen's

FORMING CONTRACTIONS

The second use of the apostrophe is to show the omission of one or more letters in words that are contracted.

it's (it is)	wouldn't (would not)
can't (cannot)	haven't (have not)
don't (do not)	hadn't (had not)
I've (I have)	isn't (is not)
I'm (I am)	you're (you are)
doesn't (does not)	won't (will not)
couldn't (could not)	who's (who is)

Chapter 5

440 WORDS
FREQUENTLY MISSPELLED

In business letters and reports and in reports or papers prepared by students in high school and college, there are certain words which are misspelled more often than others. Following is a list of words which are frequently misspelled. Refer to the list if you are unsure of the spelling of a word. If the word you are seeking is not in the list and you still are not sure, refer to a spelling dictionary or a regular dictionary.

abeyance	advantageous	ascertain	bureau	commodities	convincing
absence	advisable	assessment	business	comparatively	correlation
abundance	aggravate	assistant	calendar	competent	correspondence
accelerate	aggressive	association	cancel	competition	courteous
acceptable	allege	attendance	canceled	concede	criticism
acceptance	allowance	attorney	cancellation	conceivable	criticize
accessible	amendment	automatically	candidate	conferred	crucial
accidentally	among	auxiliary	capital	confidence	debtor
accommodate	analysis	available	capitol	confidentially	deceive
accompanying	analyze	bankruptcy	career	consummation	deductible
accomplish	announce	bargain	catalog	controlled	defendant
accumulate	annoyance	beginning	category	conscience	deferred
accurate	apologize	belief	certain	conscientious	deficiency
accustom	apparatus	believe	changeable	conscious	deficit
achievement	apparent	believing	chargeable	consistent	definite
acknowledgment	appealing	belligerent	collateral	conspicuous	dependent
acknowledging	appearance	beneficial	collectible	continuously	description
acquaintance	appreciate	beneficiary	column	controlling	desirable
acquisition	approach	benefited	commission	controversial	despair
acquitted	appropriate	bookkeeping	commitment	counterfeit	detrimental
across	argument	budget	committed	convenient	develop
actually	arrangement	bulletin	committee	conversant	difference

disappearance	forfeit	liability	particularly	receive	surely
disappoint	forty	license	pastime	recipient	surprise
disastrous	forward	likable	patient	recognize	susceptible
disbursement	foresee	likely	patronize	recommend	symmetrical
discipline	fourth	liquidate	perceive	recruit	sympathize
discussion	freight	lucrative	permanent	refer	technique
dissatisfaction	fulfill	lying	permissible	reference	temperament
distribute	generally	maintenance	perseverance	referred	temperature
divide	government	manageable	personnel	regrettable	temporarily
efficiency	grammar	management	persuade	relevant	tendency
efficient	grateful	maneuver	pertain	relieve	therefore
eighth	guidance	manual	pertinent	repetition	thorough
either	handling	manufacturer	physically	representative	through
elaborate	happiness	meant	plausible	requirement	totaled
eligible	harass	mileage	pleasant	rescind	toward
eliminate	height	millionaire	policies	research	transferred
embarrass	hierarchy	miniature	possession	resistance	transferring
eminently	hindrance	minute	possible	responsibility	transient
emphatically	hurriedly	miscellaneous	possibly	restaurant	tremendous
encouraging	hygiene	misspelled	practical	rhythm	typical
endeavor	image	monotonous	practically	ridiculous	unanimous
enforceable	immediately	moral	precede	sacrifice	undoubtedly
enthusiastic	immensely	morale	predictable	safety	unnecessary
entirely	imminent	mortgage	predominant	salable	unusual
environment	impossible	movable	prejudice	salient	unwieldy
equipment	incidentally	necessary	prefer	schedule	usage
equipped	incredible	negligible	preferable	secretary	useful
equivalent	independent	negotiate	preference	seize	usually
erroneous	indispensable	neither	preferred	separate	vacillate
especially	inevitable	ninety	preparation	severely	vacuum
exaggerate	influence	ninth	prerogative	signature	valuable
exceed	install	noticeable	presumptuous	significant	variable
excellent	insistence	oblige	prevalent	similar	various
exhaustible	integrity	obstacle	principal	simultaneous	vegetable
exhibition	intelligence	occasionally	principle	sincerely	vengeance
existence	intelligent	occupant	privilege	sizeable	vice versa
existent	intentionally	occur	probably	skillful	victim
exorbitant	interfere	occurred	procedure	source	voluntary
expense	interrupt	occurrence	proceed	specialized	warehouse
experience	irrelevant	offered	programmed	specifically	warrant
explanation	itinerary	omission	programmer	strenuous	Wednesday
extension	judgment	omitted	propaganda	subtle	weather
extraordinary	judiciary	oneself	proportion	subtlety	weight
facilities	knowledge	operate	psychology	succeed	whether
familiar	knowledgeable	opinion	pursue	success	wholly
feasible	labeled	opportunity	quality	suffered	write
February	laboratory	ordinance	quantity	sufficient	writing
finally	laissez-faire	originally	questionnaire	summarize	written
financially	legible	paid	realize	superintendent	yield
financier	legitimate	pamphlet	recede	supersede	
forbade	leisure	parallel	receipt	supplies	
foreign	liable	partially	receivables	suppress	

Chapter 6

WORDS OFTEN CONFUSED
AND MISUSED

Many words, for whatever reason, are often confused with another word and therefore misused. Sometimes the words look or sound somewhat alike, or they may have a somewhat similar meaning but have different accepted usages. Following are words often confused and misused. Examples of the correct use of the words is given following the definitions.

accept -- except:
Accept means to receive or to agree to something.
He did not *accept* the position.
Except means to exclude or leave out.
Everyone *except* John is here.

adapt -- adept -- adopt:
Adapt means to adjust to or to modify.
She did not *adapt* to her new job.
Adept means skillful.
She is an *adept* typist.
Adopt means to embrace or accept.
We will *adopt* a child.
They *adopted* the plan.

advice -- advise:
Advice is a noun meaning a recommendation that is given.
He gave me his *advice.*
Advise is a verb meaning an act of guidance.
Advise her what she should do.

affect -- effect:
Affect is a verb meaning to influence.
His attitude will *affect* his chances.
Effect is a noun indicating result or outcome.

What *effect* will the new plan have?
Effect is occasionally used as an action verb meaning to bring about.
We did *effect* your instructions.

aggravate -- irritate:
Aggravate means to make worse (a situation or condition).
His actions *aggravated* the situation.
The rubbing *aggravated* the wound.
Irritate means to annoy or to make sore.
The loud noise *irritated* me.
My skin is quite *irritated.*

allusion -- delusion -- illusion:
Allusion is an indirect reference to something.
She made an *allusion* to the mistake.
Delusion is a false or irrational belief.
He had a *delusion* that he would be made president.
He had *delusions* that he was being persecuted.

Illusion is a wrong idea or concept, or an optical misconception (In some usages, illusion and delusion mean about the same).
He had the *illusion* that he was to become president.
The mirage was strictly an *illusion.*

all ready -- already:
All ready means all prepared, i.e., a state of readiness.
The students were *all ready* to go.
Already is an adverb meaning previously.
The students had *already* gone.

all together -- altogether:
All together means a group as a whole.
The tools were *all together* on the bench.
Altogether means completely.
The two plans were *altogether* different.

among -- between:
Among is used when more than two persons or things are involved.
The supplies were divided *among* the group.
Between is used when only two persons or things are involved.
Jim and Ed divided the supplies *between* them.

amount -- number:
Amount, except for money, is used when mentioning something that cannot be counted.
The bill *amounted* to $64.50.
She had a large *amount* of cash.
He has a great *amount* of courage.
Number is used for things that can be counted.
A *number* of dogs were in the kennel.
A great *number* voted ''no''.

anxious -- eager:
Anxious means to have a degree of anxiety or fear.
I am *anxious* to hear the results of the operation.
Eager means pleasant anticipation.
I am *eager* to meet her.

any one -- anyone:
Any one is used to refer to one of several things or persons.
I do not like *any one* of the plans.
Any one who wishes may go.
Anyone is a pronoun meaning any person.
Has *anyone* arrived yet?

avenge -- revenge:
Avenge is used when there is a moral intention to right a wrong.

I will try to *avenge* the injustice done to him.
Revenge is a desire to inflict a punishment for an insult or injury.
He is so angry that he is going to seek *revenge.*

bad -- badly:
Bad is an adjective meaning disagreeable, offensive, defective.
Mother feels *bad* this morning.
The sales results were very *bad.*
There is a *bad* odor in the room.
Badly is an adverb meaning in a bad manner.
He behaved *badly* at the meeting.

best -- better:
Best is used when comparing more than two persons or things.
His plan was the *best* of those submitted.
Better is used when comparing two people or things.
His plan is the *better* of the two.

borrow -- lend:
Borrow means that the person is taking or wishes to take.
May I *borrow* your car?
Lend means to give or to let use.
I am going to *lend* him my car.

can -- may:
Can means to be able or capable of doing something.
He *can* operate the machine. (is able to)
Can he operate the machine? (does he know how?)
May means to seek or give permission.
He *may* operate the machine. (giving permission)
May he operate the machine? (seeking permission)

capital -- capitol:
Capital refers to a city where a national, state, or province government is located; also to monetary possessions, including money.
Washington, D.C. is the *capital* of the United States.
He invested most of his *capital* (money) in the new company.
Capitol refers to the main government building.
His office is in the *capitol.* (building)

complement -- compliment:
Complement refers to people or things that go well or work well together.
The advertising program *complemented*

the increased sales effort.

Compliment means to praise.

They *complimented* us on the increased sales.

counsel -- council -- counsul:

Counsel as a verb means to give advice; as a noun it means a lawyer or other person who gives advice.

He *counseled* us on the strategy we should use.

He is our company legal *counsel*.

Council is a group of people who discuss and/or take action on various matters.

The city *council* is meeting today.

Counsul is a government official appointed to represent citizens of his country in a foreign country.

The new *counsul* is leaving for Mexico tomorrow.

continual -- continuous:

Continual refers to something that occurs regularly, but with interruption.

His *continual* complaints are irritating.

Continuous means something that occurs without pause.

The *continous* noise in the shop is irritating.

emigrate -- immigrate:

Emigrate means to leave one's country to settle in another.

To avoid political persecution, he *emigrated* from Russia.

Immigrate means to enter a new country to settle there.

Because of political persecution, he *immigrated* to the United States.

eminent -- imminent:

Eminent means prominent or distinguished.

He is an *eminent* author.

Imminent means about to occur or threatening to occur.

A strike appeared to be *imminent*.

fewer -- less:

Fewer is used for things that can be counted.

We have had *fewer* plant accidents this year.

Less is used for things or ideas that cannot be counted.

He is *less* qualified than she is.

farther -- further:

Farther pertains to distance.

How much *farther* do we have to go?

Further refers to degree or extent but not to distance.

She can go no *further* in that type of work.

good -- well:

Good is an adjective that describes something positive.

She has a *good* educational background.

Well is an adjective meaning skillful, satisfactory, or thorough. It is also used to describe a state of health.

He is doing *well* in his new job.

The office manager does not look *well* today.

imply -- infer:

Imply means a hint or indirect suggestion.

He *implied* that he was going to quit.

Infer means to draw a conclusion from or interpret the meaning.

From what he said, I *infer* he may quit.

in -- into:

In indicates that something is already at a place or location.

The computers are *in* the next room.

Into indicates that someone or something is moving from the outside to the inside of a place.

He went *into* the computer room.

lay -- lie:

Lay means to put something down, to place something somewhere.

The principal parts are *lay, laid, (have, has, or had) laid.*

The present participle form is *laying*. The verb *lay* always takes an object.

He *lays* tile for the Regal store.

He *laid* tile for the Petersons.

He *has laid* tile for our neighbors.

He is *laying* tile today.

(Tile is the object of all the above sentences.)

Lie means to recline, to rest, or to remain in a reclining position.

The principal parts are *lie, lay, (have, has had) lain.*

The present participle form is *lying*.

He *lies* down every afternoon.

He *lay* on the couch all afternoon.

He *has lain* on the couch at times.

He *is lying* on the couch.

The verb *lie* is also the verb to use when speaking of inanimate objects that are in a reclining or in a *lying-down* position.

The report *lies* on my desk.

The report *lay* on my desk for a week.

The report *has lain* on my desk for weeks.

The report *is lying* on my desk.

There is another verb *lie* which means falsehood. It causes no special problems. Its principal parts are *lie, lied, lying.*

learn -- teach:

Learn indicates that knowledge or behavior is being acquired.

He should *learn* from that experience.

He *learned* Spanish in college.

Teach indicates that knowledge is being provided.

That experience should *teach* him a lesson.

He was *taught* conversational Spanish in college.

liable -- likely:

Liable is used either to indicate legal responsibility or the likelihood of an undesirable possibility.

If you injure someone, you are *liable* for damages.

If you don't change your ways, you are *liable* to be fired.

Likely indicates the probability of something.

She is *likely* to be the next one promoted.

It is *likely* you will be fired if you don't change your ways.

precede -- proceed:

Precede means to come or go before someone or something.

The band will *precede* the float.

Careful investigation should *precede* any action.

Proceed means to go on, usually after an interruption.

We can now *proceed* with the plan.

principal -- principle:

Principal means 1) something that is most important, 2) the amount of money owed or invested, 3) the head officer of a school, 4) the employer of a person to act in his behalf.

The *principal* purpose of the plan is to reduce expenses.

The *principal* amounts to $100,000.

She is *principal* of the Bergen Grade School.

The lawyer did his best to protect the interests of his *principal*.

Principle is used to indicate a law, basic truth, rule of conduct, or guidance.

Democracies are based on the *principle* of self-government.

The *principles* of his religion govern his action.

quite -- quiet:

Quite is an adverb meaning completely or very.

The new plan is not *quite* ready.

I am *quite* sure he will agree.

Quiet means still, calm, motionless, silent.

After hearing the announcement, the audience remained *quiet*.

raise -- rise:

Raise means to lift or raise. It requires an object.

Those who agree, *raise* your hand.

We will have to *raise* our prices.

Rise means to get up or go up. It requires no direct object.

Please *rise* when the President enters.

The audience *rose* (stood up) when the President arrived.

Our taxes seem to *rise* every year.

set -- sit:

Set means to put something down or in a certain place, or to bring to a specified state or condition.

He *set* the books on the president's desk.
The trees were *set* on fire.
She has *set* her heart on going.
Sit means to be seated.
Please do not *sit* on the desk.

stationary, stationery:
Stationary means inmovable, not moving, or unchanging.

Once the machine is installed, it will be *stationary*.
The troops stood *stationary* until the flag was past.
Stationery refers to writing paper, envelopes, and other office supplies.
Our new *stationery* order has just arrived.

whose -- who's:
Whose is an adjective showing possession.
He is the one *whose* car was stolen.
Who's is a contraction of *who* and *is*. In writing, its use should be avoided.
Who's going to be at the meeting?

Chapter 7

WORD PREFIXES, SUFFIXES, AND ROOTS

Following arc some of the important word prefixes used in English. The prefix is indicated in boldface type followed by the basic meaning of the prefix. Examples of the prefixes used in words are given in italic type.

ab-, a-, abs-, away from, *abduct, avert, abstain*

a-, an-, not, less, without, *agnostic, atheist, anarchy*

ad-, a-, ac-, af-, to, toward, *adhere, ascribe, accord, affirm*

ag-, al-, an-, *aggressor, allude, annex*

ap-, ar-, as-, at-, to, toward, *associate, attend*

ante-, before, *antedate, antecedent*

anti-, ant-, against, *antiseptic, antipathy, antacid*

ana-, up, through, throughout, *analysis, anatomy*

be-, by or near, *below, beside*

bene-, good, well, *benevolent, beneficial*

bi-, two, twice, *bicycle, biennial*

circum-, around, all round, *circumstance, circumvent*

com-, con-, col-, together, *combine, confound, collate*

contra-, against, *contradict, contravene*

de-, from, down away, *depart, descend, denude*

dis-, di-, apart, apart from, *distract, divert*

ex-, ef-, e-, out, out of, *export, effect, emit*

hypo-, under, beneath, *hypodermic, hypothesis*

in-, in, into, *intrude, inside, include, insight*

in-, im-, il-, ir-, un-, not, *inactive, impress, illicit, irrestible, unreal*

inter-, between, *intermingle, interstate*

intra-, intro-, within, *intramural, introduction*

mal-, bad, *malcontent, malnourished*

mis-, wrong, *misdeed, mislead*

non-, not, *nonentity, nonconformist*

ob-, against, *object, objective*

par-, para-, beside, beyond, *paradox, parallel*

per-, through, throughout, *persist, pervade*

peri-, around, *periscope, perimeter*

post-, after, *postpone, postscript*

pre-, before, *prefer, predict*

pro-, before, forward, *prologue, promote, pronoun*

re-, back, again, *refer, report, review*

retro-, backward, *retroactive, retrogress*

se-, apart, *seduce, sedate*

semi-, half, *semicircle, semiconscious*

sub-, under, *submit, subordinate*

super-, supra-, above, over, *supernatural, suprarational*

syn-, sym-, with, *synopsis, symphony, synonym*

trans-, tra-, across, *transfer, traverse*

un-, not, reversal of action, *uncovered, untie*

uni-, single, *unity, universal*

vice-, instead of, *vice-president, vice-consul*

with-, against, back, *withdraw, withhold*

Word Suffixes

Following are some of the important word suffixes used in English. The suffix is indicated in boldface type followed by the basic meaning of the suffix. Examples of the suffixes used in words are given in italic type.

-able, -ible, -ble, capable of being, as *bearable, reversible, voluble*

-ac, -ic, pertaining to, as *cardiac, angelic*

-ac, -ic, condition or quality of, as *maniac, mechanic*

-acious, characterized by, as *pugnacious, tenacious*

-acity, quality of, as *tenacity, veracity*

-acy, having the quality of, as *accuracy, fallacy*

-age, collection of, state of being, as *garbage, marriage, storage*

-al, -el, -le, pertaining to, as *fanatical, novel, single*

-an, -ian, belonging to, one who, as *American, physician, historian*

-ance, relating to, as *reliance, distance*

-ancy, -ency, denoting state or quality, as *occupancy, dependency*

-ant, -ent, one who, as *tenant, correspondent*

-ar, -ary, ory, relating to, as *popular, dictionary, mandatory*

-ate, act, as *mandate, confiscate*

-ation, action, as *elation, separation*

-cle, -ule, -ling, diminutive, as *article, globule, suckling*

-cracy, rule, as *democracy, autocracy*

-cy, quality, as *idiocy, ascendency*

-dom, state of being, as *freedom, kingdom*

-ee, one who is acted upon, as *employee, trustee*

-ence, relating to, as *confidence, abstinence*

-er, -or, -ar, one who, as *butler, actor, scholar*

-ful, abounding in, as *grateful, sinful*

-fy, -efy, -ify, to make, as *deify, liquefy, solidify*

-hood, condition, as *fatherhood, falsehood*

-ic, pertaining to, as *historic, democratic*

-ice, act of, as *justice, police, practice*

-il, -ile, pertaining to, capable of being, as *civil, juvenile, mobile*

-ity, -ty, state or condition, as *sanity, acidity, safety*

-ious, full of, as *laborious, rebellious*

-ist, one who, as *pianist, machinist*

-ity, ty, state or condition, as *sanity, acidity, safety*

-ize, -yze, to make like, as *sympathize, analyze*

-less, without, as *careless, needless, hopeless*

-ly, manner, like, as *bodily, truthfully*

-ment, result, as *management, fragment*

-meter, measurement, as *thermometer, hydrometer*

-ness, state of being, as *sickness, happiness*

-nomy, pertaining to laws or government, distribution, arrangement, as *economy, harmony, astronomy*

-ory, place where, as *directory, rectory*

-ous, -ious, -eous, -uous, full of, as *dangerous, melodious, beauteous, strenuous*

-ose, full of, as *morose, verbose*

-ship, state or quality, as *friendship, worship*

-some, like, full of, as *gruesome, tiresome*

-ster, one who, person doing something, as *gangster, songster*

-sion, -tion, act or state of being, as *conception, perception*

-tude, condition, as *fortitude, magnitude*

-ty, ity, condition, as *clarity, peculiarity, sanity*

-ule, little, as *globule, granule*

-ure, act of, as *departure, manufacture*

-ward, direction of course, as *backward, forward, downward*

-y, full of, characterized by, as *filthy, icy, soapy*

Latin and Greek Word Roots

Following are Latin and Greek word roots which are used in English words. Word roots give the word its basic meaning, whereas prefixes or suffixes modify or change the root word. The root word is given in bold face type followed by the meaning of the root. Examples of the roots are printed in italic type. Many word roots are generally used only as prefixes or suffixes. However, as you examine the examples, you will note that many appear at the beginning, in the middle, or at the end of the English word.

aero, air, as *aerodynamics, aerospace*

ag, ac, to do, as *agenda, action*

agr, agri, agro, farm, as *agriculture, agronomy*

anthropo, man, as *anthropology, anthropoid, misanthrope*

aqua, water, as *aqueous, aquatic*

arch, rule, principle, chief, as *archbishop, archenemy, anarchy*

astra, astro, star, as *astronomy, astral, astronomical*

aud, audi, audio, hearing, as *audience, auditor, audiovisual*

auto, self, oneself, as *automatic, autograph*

biblio, bib, book, as *bibliophile, Bible*

bio, life, as *biology, biosphere*

cad, cas, fall, as *cadence, cascade, casual*

cant, sing, as *cantata, chant*

cap, cep, take, as *captive, accept*

capit, head, as *capital, capitate*

cat, cath, down, through, as *cataract, catheter*

ced, cess, go, yield, as *procedure, cession, antecedent*

cide, cis, kill, cut, as *suicide, excise, incision*

clud, clus, close, as *include, inclusion, preclude*

cred, believe, as *creditor, creditable, creed*

dec, ten, as *decimal*

dem, people, as *democracy, demagogue*

dent, tooth, as *indent, dental*

derm, skin, as *dermatology, taxidermist*

dic, dict, say, speak, as *diction, dictate, predicate*

duc, lead, as *induce, ductile*

equ, equal, as *equivalent, equitable, equality*

fac, fec, make, do, as *manufacture, infection*

fring, break as *infringement*

fract break as *fracture, fractious*

frater, brother, as *fraternal, fraternize*

fund, fus, pour as *refund, confuse*

gam, gamos marriage as *monogamous, bigamist, polygamous*

gen, produce as *generate, generation*

geo, earth as *geology, geometry, geography*

gastro, gast, stomach as *gastronomy, gastritis*

greg, group as *gregarious*

gress, grad walking, moving as *progress, degrade, retrograde*

gyn, woman as *gynecologist*

hemo, blood, as *hemorrhage, hemorroid*

homo, man, same as *homocide, homogeneous*

hydr, water as *dehydrate, hydralic*

idio, own, private, as *idiocy, idiosyncrasy*

iso, equal as *isothermal, isomorph*

ject, throw as *reject, project*

jud, jur, right as *judge, jury*

logy, study of as *psychology, biology*

loqu, speak as *loquacious, eloquent*

mand, order as *remand, command, demand*

manu, hand as *manuscript, manual*

mater, mother as *maternal, matricide*

meter, measure, as *thermometer, barometric*

micro, small as *microscopic, microbe*

mit, mis send as *permit, commission*

mono, mon, single, one as *monotony, monogram, monarch*

mort, death as *mortician, mortal*

nom, law as *economy, astronomy*

onym, name as *synonym, pseudonym*

pathos, feeling as *pathology, pathos*

philo, love as *philosophy, philosophical*

phobia, fear as *claustrophobia, hydrophobia*

porto, carry as *portable, export, report, transport*

pseudo, false as *pseudonym, pseudo*

psych, mind as *psychiatry, psychic, psychology*

scope, see as *telescope, microscope*

scrib, write as *inscription, description*

sec, cut as *dissect, bisect, resection*

sens, feel as *sensuous, sensitive*

sequ, follow as *sequence, inconsequent*

spec, spect, look as *specimen, inspect, spectacular*

spir, breath as *inspire, respiratory*

state, stand as *status, statutory*

ten, hold as *retention, detention*

term, end as *terminal, interminable*

typ, print as *typography, typewriter*

ven, vent, come as *prevent, convene, adventure*

vert, vers, turn as *divert, subversion, controversy*

vict, conquer as *evict, victim*

vid, vis, see as *video, visual, revise*

voc, call as *vocal, vocation*

Chapter 8

GUIDE FOR COMPOUNDING WORDS AND USE OF HYPHENS

A compound is two or more words joined together either with a hyphen or without a hyphen. Many words have become compound words through custom or usage because they are regularly used in succession or because the meaning is somewhat more clear or precise when the words are combined. The hyphen, when used in a compound word, is a mark of punctuation. Its purpose is to join the parts of a compound but also to separate the parts for better readability and clearer understanding. When in doubt about the compounding or hyphenation of a word, always consult your dictionary.

1. General Rule. Two or more words are not compounded unless the compounding aids understanding or readability. If the first word is principally an adjective describing the second word the words usually are not joined.

real estate	martial law	machine shop
book value	marble cake	fish hawk
tail wind	sun parlor	roller bearing

2. Nouns. Many nouns are formed by two other nouns (including gerunds) and are written as one word either by repeated usage or because as one word they better express a single thought or idea.

redhead	northeast	eggplant
locksmith	raindrop	doorman
eyewitness	laughingstock	bathroom

3. Verb and Adverb Compounds. Verbs and adverbs are often joined together or with nouns to express a literal or nonliteral figurative thought.

viewpoint	striptease	outwork
upgrade	rearmost	pushover
troublesome	pennywise	breakdown

4. Compound Personal Pronouns. Write compound personal pronouns as one word.

myself	himself	ourself
yourself	herself	themselves

5. Any, Every, Some, No. When these words are combined with *body, thing* or *where*, they should be written as one word. When *one* is the second element, and the meaning is a single or particular person, group, or thing, write as two words. *No one* is always two words.

anybody	everywhere	nowhere
anything	somebody	nothing
everyone	something	no one

Everyone came. *but*: Every one of the boys came.

6. Compound Modifiers (Adjectives). When words or numerals are combined to modify a noun, they should be hyphenated when they precede the word modified. However, see the rules which follow.

long-term lease	two-time candidate
short-wave radio	reddish-brown color
2-volume set	single-engine plane

(a) Certain types of unit modifiers should not be hyphenated. A precise rule can not be given. However, in general the two modifying words are words that are regularly used together in other contexts, the first word is a modifier of the second word, and then the two words together serve to identify or describe the third word.

life insurance policy	high school student
special delivery mail	civil rights law
income tax return	real estate tax
atomic energy plant	social security law

(b) Omit the hyphen in a unit modifier when it follows the word modified.

The area is middle class.
but: It is a middle-class area.
The company is well financed.
but: It is a well-financed company.

(c) Omit the hyphen in a unit modifier if the first word is a comparative or superlative.

lower priced stock	low-priced stock
best developed plan	well-developed plan
highest salaried group	high-salary group

(d) Descriptive words are not hyphenated when one of the words is an adverb.

happily awaited event	suprisingly long time
socially accepted custom	lovely young girl

(e) If a series of two or more compounds has the same basic word and this word is omitted except as the last term, retain all the hyphens.

first-, second-, and third-class mail
part- or full-time work
4-, 5-, and 6-foot lumber

(f) Omit the hyphen in foreign phrases used as modifiers.

prima facie evidence	bona fide signature
per diem payment	ex officio chairman

7. Miscellaneous Rules.

(a) Compound words containing proper nouns and beginning with the prefixes *anti-, ex, pro,* and *un,* as well as those ending with the suffix *elect,* are hyphenated.

ex-President Carter	Senator-elect Harris
pro-British	un-American

(b) Use hyphens to connect capital letters to words forming adjectives or nouns.

an A-line skirt	a V-line blouse
an S-curve	a T-square

(c) Compound numbers over twenty and less than one hundred are hyphenated.

twenty-one	one hundred eighty-six
sixty-three	six hundred forty-two

(d) Two-word fractions are hyphenated only when they are used as adjectives. They are not hyphenated when functioning as nouns.

A two-thirds majority voted in favor, (an adjective)
Two thirds of the members voted in favor. (a noun)

(e) A range in numbers or in the alphabet is indicated by a hyphen.

10-31 (meaning 10 through 31)
M-S (meaning M through S)

(f) Compound nouns and adjectives with the prefix *self* are hyphenated.

self-restraint (n)	self-induced (a)
self-interest (n)	self-service (a)

Chapter 9

RULES FOR WORD DIVISION

1. Avoid dividing a word at the end of a line unless necessary to maintain good margins. Do not divide the last word in a paragraph or the last word on a page.

2. If it is necessary to divide, divide a word only between syllables; but even then, apply the following rules:

3. Do not separate a single letter syllable from the rest of the word.

Right: emo-tion	Wrong: e-motion
Right: abu-sive	Wrong: a-busive

4. Avoid dividing a word before or after a two letter syllable.

Avoid: el-evate	Better: ele-vate
Avoid: cavi-ty	Better: cav-ity

5. Do not divide words of five or fewer letters even if the word has more than one syllable.

Wrong: In-dia, Indi-a	Correct: India
Wrong: i-deal, ide-al	Correct: ideal

6. Where the final consonant is doubled before a suffix, the added consonant goes with the suffix. However, if the root word ends with a double letter, divide after the double letter.

Right: assess-ing	Wrong: asses-sing
Right: allot-ted	Wrong: allotted

7. Words of one syllable should never be divided. Examples: whom, mend, passed, scrubbed.

Chapter 10

PUNCTUATION RULES

When you are writing, punctuation marks are signals from you to your reader. A period indicates that you have ended a sentence or that an abbreviation has been used. A comma may mean that there is a slight break in thought, indicate two separate parts of a compound sentence; or it may be used in one of several other ways.

Some sentences may be punctuated in more than one way; and, in some instances, a punctuation mark is a matter of choice by the writer. To help you punctuate expertly, the following rules and examples are given.

THE PERIOD (.)

1. Use a period at the end of a declarative or imperative sentence. (Also see Rule 5 under quotations.)

> The letter arrived this morning. (declarative)
> Ship our order immediately. (imperative)

2. Use a period rather than a question mark after an indirect question or courteous request.
> He asked if you had received it yet. (indirect question)
> Will you please ship it today. (courteous request)

3. Use a period after abbreviations, initials, and contractions. Abbreviations do not have internal spacing.

Mr.   qt.   P.M.   etc.   U.S.A.

4. At the end of a sentence, a period is sufficient for both an abbreviation and the sentence.

> Send it to McDonald and Son, Inc.

5. Use three periods (ellipsis marks) to indicate the omission of words from a quotation.

> "Democracy is the government of the people . . . for the people." --Abraham Lincoln

6. Use four periods when the omission comes at the end of a quoted passage.

> "Get your facts first, and then you can distort them . . . ." --Mark Twain

Note: Do not use a period at the end of a title of a book, magazine article, poem, etc. unless the title ends a sentence. In typed material, there should be two spaces between a period ending a sentence and the beginning of the next sentence.

THE QUESTION MARK (?)

1. Use the question mark after all direct questions.

> Did you receive the report?
> Have you shipped our order yet?

2. In a sentence containing more than one question each separate query may use a question mark.

> Are you certain of the place? the time? the date?

But if a question is not complete until the final word of the sentence, the question mark should be at the end only.

> Do you want to meet me at two p.m., three p.m., or four p.m.?

3. The question mark may also be used when only part of the sentence is a question, and in such sentences, the question is often introduced by a comma or colon; a semicolon or dash is sometimes used.

> Please tell me, why are you going?
> We must analyze the problem: Have you any suggestions?
> I have explained the problem: Have you any suggestions?

Note: In typed material, leave two spaces after the question mark and the beginning of the next sentence.

THE EXCLAMATION MARK (!)

1. Use the exclamation mark after all exclamatory sentences which convey surprise, strong emotion, or deep feeling.

> I can't believe you failed to complete the job!
> What a lovely thing to do!

2. Use the exclamation mark after interjections or after statements which emphasize commands or which suggest immediate action.

> Please! Ship our order immediately.
> Act now! Don't wait!

3. Use the exclamation mark after an interrogative sentence that is intended to be exclamatory.

> Oh no, how can you tell him that!
> Isn't she too young to understand!

4. The exclamation mark is also used to add emphasis.

> Your deadline is midnight!
> This is your last chance!

Note: In typed material, use two spaces after an exclamation mark and before the beginning of the next sentence.

THE COMMA (,)

1. When a dependent clause precedes the main clause, use the comma to separate the introductory clause. However, the comma is usually unnecessary when the dependent clause does not begin the sentence.

> When he completed his assignment, he went to see the dean. (comma)
> The chairman asked for the voting to begin after everyone was in the room. (no comma)

2. Use the comma after an absolute phrase or a participial phrase at the beginning of a sentence.

> The snow storm having begun, we decided to stay at home.
> Having completed the test in less than an hour, she left the room.

3. Use the comma after an introductory infinitive phrase. But do not separate the subject from the rest of the sentence when it is an infinitive.

> To be helpful, you must know when to offer help.
> To be helpful was her wish.

4. Use the comma to set off parenthetical elements in a sentence, such as words, phrases, clauses, or expressions. (Also see Rule 1 under parenthesis and Rule 1 under the dash.)

(a) Transitional words should be followed by commas (*besides, consequently, however, moreover, therefore*).

> However, I did not feel it was necessary.

Phrases, such as *in short, as a result, of course*, or *so to speak*, should be set off by commas.

> As I wrote before, there is, of course, a way out.
> As a result, our losses will be less than expected.

Use the comma to set off clauses (*I think, he says, we suppose*).

> The president, I think, will be concerned.

Expressions should be set off by commas when the logical progression of words is interrupted (*so far as she is concerned, and I respect his view*).

> The chairman did not object, and I respect his view, to staggering vacation time over a two-month period.

5. Introductory expressions are set off by commas (*indeed, yes, surely*, meaning *yes, well*).

Yes, I am going to attend.

Well, I would not have accepted the report.

6. A nonrestrictive clause is set off by a comma because it gives added information about the word it modifys, but it is not needed to complete sentence meaning.

A restrictive clause is needed to complete the meaning of a sentence, and, therefore, is never set off by commas.

The new manager, who is thirty-three, certainly is doing a good job. (The non-restrictive clause *who is thirty-three* gives added information but is not needed to complete the meaning of the sentence.)

The new manager who came from sales is now in charge. (The restrictive clause *who came from sales* is necessary to identify the word *manager*. Therefore, no commas are used.)

7. Use a comma to separate a word in opposition that defines or identifies another word with a noun.

Mary, my secretary, is very efficient.

My secretary, Mary, is very efficient.

8. Use a comma to separate words that indicate direct address.

Scott, please read the enclosed report.

9. Use a comma to separate a series of words, phrases, or clauses.

The recipe calls for, eggs, cream, and sugar.

She ran down the street, into a driveway, back to the curb, and sat down crying.

If we accept the proposal, it means that: (1) we will have three weeks vacation, (2) we will be paid for overtime, (3) we will have maternity leave.

10. Use the comma to separate coordinate adjectives which modify the same noun if the word *and* can be substituted for the comma.

The new, efficient machine will increase our production. (The new *and* efficient machine.)

The present operating plan will be changed. (No comma. You would not say present *and* operating.)

11. Use a comma before the conjunctions *and, but, for, or, nor,* and *yet* when they join the independent clauses of a compound sentence.

I sent the letter as you requested, and we should have a reply soon.

She asked for him on the telephone, but no one was there by that name.

(a) The comma may be omitted between most short clauses and between some long clauses when the meaing is clear.

He searched but did not find the report.

(b) When the comma is used without a coordinate conjunction between two independent clauses it is called the *comma fault*.

The children going to school do not cross at the intersection, they repeatedly jay-walk. (Incorrect -- a coordinate conjunction should be used after the comma.)

To eliminate the comma fault, the sentence may be punctuated in any one of the three following ways:

The children going to school do not cross at the intersection, and they repeatedly jay-walk. (using a coordinate conjunction)

The children going to school do not cross at the intersection; they repeatedly jay-walk. (using a semicolon)

The children going to school do not cross at the intersection. They repeatedly jay-walk. (using two simple sentences)

Use a semicolon before the coordinate conjunction when the independent clauses of a compound sentence are very long or contain internal punctuation.

The children going to school do not cross at the intersection; and, as a result, they repeatedly jay-walk.

12. Use the comma to separate words or phrases that express contrast.

The supervisor, not the foreman, offered to help.

13. Use the comma to set off a month, year or definite place.

He was born December 3, 1954, at 1612 Fardale Road, Jenkintown, Pennsylvania.

14. Use the comma to set off a direct short quotation. (See rule 4 under Quotations.)

The employer asked, ''Where do you expect to be in the next five years?''

15. Use the comma to separate a declarative clause and an interrogative clause which follows it.

Terry will receive the award, will she not?

16. Use the comma to set off a sentence element when it is out of its natural order or when it separates inverted names, or phrases.

That she could accept the suggestion, none of us seriously doubted.

Buckley, William S.

Like you, I feel the time is not right.

17. Use a comma to indicate the omission of a word.

Mark is extremely sensitive to the feelings of others; Scott, totally indifferent. (The word *is* has been omitted.)

18. Use the comma to separate a proper name from an academic degree or honorary title. Also use a comma between two or more degrees or titles.

Mary Jones, B.S.N., M.S., F.A.A.N., Director of Nursing.

19. Use a comma to separate the thousands in figures of four digits or more.

1,200   22,200   3,000,000

20. Use a comma to separate two sets of figures or two identical words.

Bring me 5, No. 1040, and 10, No. 1140.

Where he is, is not known.

Note: In typed material, use one space after a comma.

THE SEMICOLON (;)

The semicolon (;) indicates a more complete separation between sentence elements than does the comma. Overuse of the semicolon should be avoided.

1. Use the semicolon to separate independent coordinate clauses that are related in meaning when no coordinate conjunction is used. (Rule 11 under Comma.)

The staff members desired a change in direction; they were eager to offer suggestions.

2. Use the semicolon between coordinate clauses of a compound sentence when they are united by transitional words.

The freeholders approved the building plans; as a result, construction will resume next spring.

Commonly used transitional words:

accordingly	furthermore	nevertheless
as a result	however	otherwise
besides	in addition	that is
consequently	indeed	therefore
finally	in fact	thus
for example	moreover	yet
for this reason	namely	

3. Use the semicolon before a coordinate conjunction (*and, but, for, or, nor*) to separate two independent clauses with internal punctuation. (Rule 11 under Commas.)

The meeting, which ran overtime, was boring; but some decisions were made in spite of weak presentations.

4. Use the semicolon before words such as *for example, for instance, namely,* or *that is* which introduce an example, enumeration, or items in a series.

The committee was represented by four officers; namely, the president, vice-president, secretary, and treasurer.

5. Use the semicolon in clarifying listings where a comma is insufficient to separate the items clearly.

Committee members who attended were James Farley, president; Timothy Sullivan, vice-president; and Jean Shelley, secretary.

Note: In typed material use one space after a semi-colon.

THE COLON (:)

1. Use the colon before a list of items or enumerations.

See if we have the following merchandise in stock: No. 42, No. 63, and No. 67.

My itinerary included: going on a bus trip, visiting several museums, and shopping for jewelery.

(a) When the list of items is in a column, capitalize the first letter.

You must hire someone who has technical skills in the following areas:
1. Computer programming
2. Audio/Video camera
3. Software production

(b) When the items are presented in a sentence it is not necessary to capitalize the first letter.

You must hire someone who has technical skills in the following areas: computer programming, audio/visual camera, and software production.

2. Use the colon before an appositive phrase.

The jury rules were simply stated: no radio, no television, no visitors.

3. Use the colon following the salutation of a business letter.

Dear Mr. Greene: Gentlemen:

Do not use a semicolon after a salutation. However, a comma may be used after the salutation of an informal letter.

Dear Kathy,   Dear Mother,

4. Use the colon to divide the parts of formulas, numbers, references, or titles.

The conferences will begin at 10:30 A.M.

The pastor quoted from Chapter VI: Page 10.

PARENTHESES ( )

1. Use parentheses to separate words, phrases, clauses, or sentences which enclose material that explains, translates or comments. (Rule 4 under commas. Rule 1 under the dash.)

She swam 1500 meters (somewhat less than a mile).

He stated, "E pluribus unum." (One out of many.)

2. Use parentheses to enclose letters, numbers, or symbols when referring to an appositive.

We made reservations for fifteen (15) days.

(a) Use parentheses with other punctuation marks. If the punctuation mark is connected to the entire sentence and not just to the parenthetical part, the punctuation mark follows the second parenthesis.

They carefully analyzed and evaluated the standards (legal and moral), but could not reach a decision.

(b) The punctuation mark should be placed within the second parenthesis if it applies only to material concerning the parenthetical section.

You may save a life by giving first-aid to someone who is choking. (See the back cover of this pamphlet.)

- THE DASH (—)

The dash should be used to indicate a sudden change of ideas, but should be used sparingly. The dash may be used for emphasis or for visual effect.

1. Use the dash to indicate an abrupt change of thought in a sentence or strong parenthetical expressions.

She feels — how can I say that? — like an outcast.

I was annoyed — no, shocked to be more specific — by his behavior.

2. Use the dash to set off a summary or an afterthought that is added to a sentence.

The educational team will make an evaluation and draw up a plan — in fact, they will provide a complete special program for the child.

3. Use the dash to emphasize a word or phrase that is repeated.

The president stated that we had one week — one week only — to make a decision.

4. Use a dash to mark limits between dates, numbers, places, and times.

The admissions office is open 9:00 — 4:30 daily.

Read pages 22-40.

THE QUOTATION MARK (" ")

1. Use quotation marks to enclose all direct quotations.

"Yes," she said, "I did help to raise funds."

The teacher asked, "Did I give you the date for the test?"

Rules governing the use of quotation marks: Capitalize the first word of a direct quotation. The first word in the second section of an interrupted quotation is not capitalized unless it begins a new sentence. Quotation marks or capital letters are not used in an indirect quotation.

The teacher asked if she gave you the date for the test.

2. Use quotation marks to enclose the chapters of a book, names of songs, titles of magazine articles or poems, and other similar titles. In typing or writing, underline titles of books, magazines, operas, and any other work long enough to appear in book form. Underlining of titles signifies italics for printing.

The National Geographic includes a section called "Members Forum."

"The Owl and the Pussy Cat" is a child's favorite poem.

3. Use quotation marks to set off words, phrases, or sentences referred to within a sentence or to emphasize a word. (Italics may also be used in such cases.)

The sentence "you can't take it with you" has deep meaning for some people.

The word "judgement" is often misspelled.

What was the real "meaning" of his asking?

4. Use quotation marks at the beginning of each paragraph if several paragraphs are quoted, and at the end of the last paragraph. Very long quotations are frequently introduced by a colon instead of a comma. (Rule 14 under commas.) Usually indent quotations of three or more lines from the body.

5. Using quotation marks with other punctuation:

(a) Place a period or comma before ending quotation marks.

She said, "No one is home."

"No one is home," she said.

(b) Place the question mark before quotation marks when they refer to the quoted content, or after when they refer to the complete sentence.

He said, "Why do you want to see her"?

Did he say, "Why do you want to see her?"

(c) Place the semicolon and colon after ending quotation marks unless they are part of the quoted material.

He said, "You are to be our next president"; therefore, I hope you you will consider me for your present job.

Chapter 11

RULES OF CAPITALIZATION

1. Capitalize the first word of a sentence.

Your order has been shipped.

2. Capitalize the first word of a line of poetry.

''Poems are made by fools like me....''

3. Capitalize the first word of a direct quotation.

He asked, ''Where are the parts?''

4. Capitalize *proper nouns* (names of specific persons, places, or things).

New York City	Henry Jones	Wall Street
Lake Michigan	Brazil	Holiday Inn

5. Capitalize *proper adjectives* (adjectives formed from proper nouns).

American	Spanish	Southern
Communistic	Chinese	Russian

6. Capitalize names of *specific organizations* or *institutions*.

Northwestern University	Republican Party
American Red Cross	Ford Motor Company

7. Capitalize *days of the week, months of the year, holidays,* and *days of special observance.*

Sunday	August	Yom Kippur
Mother's Day	Easter	Christmas
Feast of the Passover	St. Valentines Day	

8. Capitalize *names of the seasons* only if they are personified.

Personified	*Season*
Springs warm touch	spring breezes
Winter's icy breath	winter's snow

9. Always capitalize *languages* but not other school subjects unless they are names of specific courses.

English	Chemistry 101	but: chemistry
French	Economics 102	economics
Spanish	Composition 200	composition

10. Capitalize *races, religions,* and *ethnic groups.*

Negro	Catholic	Moslem
Eurasian	Presbyterian	Japanese

11. Capitalize references to the *Diety* and to the *titles of holy books.*

God, the Father	the Trinity	the Koran
Supreme Being	Genesis	Talmud

12. Capitalize *titles of people* when they are followed by a name.

President Henderson	Senator Hutchins
Cardinal Wilson	Professor Stark
Doctor Allison	Reverend Harmon

13. Capitalize sections of a *country,* but do not capitalize directions.

Sections	*Directions*
the Midwest	I traveled west.
the Near East	The sun rose in the east.
the South	They went south.

14. Capitalize titles of *works of literature, art,* and *music.* However, in such titles do not capitalize short prepositions, articles, and conjunctions unless they are the first word.

War and Peace	Battle Hymn of the Republic
The Angelus	Beethoven's Fifth Symphony
Book of Job	The Last of the Mohicans

15. Capitalize *names of governmental bodies* and *departments.*

President's Cabinet	Civil Service Commission
Supreme Court	Bureau of the Census
United States Senate	the Federal Government

16. Capitalize *words which show family relationships* when they are used with a person's name or when they stand unmodified as a substitute for a person's name.

Aunt Alyce	my aunt
Grandfather Scott	his grandfather

I sent a package to Mother. (but: My mother will be there.)

17. Capitalize names of *definite regions, localities,* and *political divisions.*

the Orient	Fourth Precinct
the Artic Circle	First Ward (of a city)
French Republic	Bergen County

18. Capitalize names of *historical events, historical periods* and *historical documents.*

the Middle Ages	Magna Carta
World War II	the Crusades
Bill of Rights	Third Amendment

19. The names of separate departments of a business may be written with either capital or small letters. Business titles such as president, office manager, superintendent, etc. may be written either way.

The Company will pay your expenses.
(or company)
Our President will see you June 6.
(or president)
Research Department *or* research department.

20. The pronoun *I* should always be capitalized.

It is I who will go.

Chapter 12

POST OFFICE INFORMATION

Air Mail: The post office now moves all first-class mail within distant cities in the United States by air. Do not waste money by sending letters within the United States via airmail. However, much time can be saved by sending letters and packages to foreign countries (including Canada and Mexico) by air. To overseas countries, regular mail by sea may take one to three months for delivery. By airmail, delivery will usually take place in one to three weeks. If time is important, it may pay to send even some bulky materials by airmail. Air-freight companies or export brokers can give you information about shipping materials and supplies by air using their services.

Bulk Rate: See Third-class Mail.

Bulk Mail: If your company, club, etc. makes simultaneous mailings of fifty or more items with any frequency, you can secure a bulk mail permit. Items that carry a permit or are meter stamped and presorted by postal zones may be mailed at a special reduced rate. Larger mailings receive still lower rates. Since rates change from time to time, check with your postoffice for specific rates and requirements.

Business Reply Permits: If your company is making large mailings to secure orders or to seek a reply, you generally can increase response by paying the return postage. Rather than apply postage to each return envelope or card (which is costly since many envelopes will not be returned), businesses or individuals can secure business reply permits by paying an annual fee. The envelopes must carry certain insignia and facing identification marks (series of horizontal and vertical bars) printed from negatives that are available free at the post office. Upon return of envelopes or cards the regular postage is paid plus an extra fee which almost doubles the total postage. However, postage is paid only for items actually returned.

C.O.D. Mail: First-, third-, and fourth-class mail may be sent *collect on delivery*. The post office carrier collects the amount due from the receiver at the time of delivery. The sender must prepay the postage and a collection fee. However, the mailer may include the charges in the amount to be collected from the addressee.

Insurance is included in the fee, and a return receipt may be requested. The addressee (receiver) is not allowed to inspect the contents before paying for the item.

Certified Mail: First-class mailings in the U.S. of items having no insurance value but for which assured delivery is desired may be sent *certified mail*. Delivery may be restricted to the addressee (only the addressee may sign for it) by writing the words *Restricted Delivery* above the address. A return receipt showing the addressee's signature and date of delivery may also be requested. There is an extra fee for these services.

Electronic-mail System: The U.S. Post Office provides a system whereby businesses may send communications through government computers. E-COM (Electronic-Computer Originated Mail) accepts material up to two pages in length for mailing to multiple addresses. Messages are routed to an E-Com center where they are placed in local mail for the next scheduled delivery. There is an annual subscriber fee plus a per page charge. A somewhat similar service is available through Western Union where the same letter can be sent to multiple addressees with next day delivery by mail.

Express Mail: Any item from a letter to a 70-pound package may be mailed from a designated post office (ask the post office for a list) before 5:00 p.m. with delivery guaranteed by 3:00 p.m. the next day (except Sunday). Or, if addressed to someone in care of a post office, the addressee may pick up the item at any time after 10:00 a.m. Postage is determined by weight and distance and the cost is relatively high. However, the post office refunds the full amount if delivery is made later than promised. Special labels and envelopes for this service are available at your post office. Private air-express companies also offer the same service.

First-class mail: Letters, bills, checks, receipts, orders, etc. as well as post cards must be mailed first-class mail. Postage on the first ounce is the price of a regular first-class stamp with slightly lower rates for additional ounces. Inter-city mail of any distance is sent by air without extra charge. The weight limit is 70 pounds with a size limitation from 2 by $4^1/_4$ inches to a maximum of 100 inches in combined length and girth (the measurement around the package).

Stamp all large envelopes and packages *first-class* so that post office employees will not mistake them as being third-class. First-class mail, such as letters, may be included in second-, third-, or fourth-class mail provided you note on the outside of the package *letter enclosed*, etc. and affix the additional first-class postage to the package. Or you may attach a stamped envelope containing a letter, etc. to the outside of the package. Any item weighing more than 12 ounces is classified as *priority mail*, described later in this section.

Fourth-class Mail (Parcel Post): Items weighing 16 ounces or more and not shipped first-, second-, or third-class mail are designated *Parcel Post*. Postage is based on weight and distance. Weight cannot exceed 70 pounds and size cannot exceed 108 inces of combined length and girth (distance around the package).

Special delivery is available for fourth-class mail. However, sending a package by priority mail (first-class mail) is oftentimes better and less costly then fourth-class, special delivery.

Special fourth-class rates are available for books, educational materials, manuscripts, catalogs, films, records, etc. Check with your post office for details.

General Delivery: For persons not permanently located in a city, mail may be sent to the destination post office in that person's name. Write *General Delivery* above the person's name and then the post office (or a specific branch) address (city, state, and zip code). The person addressed will have to call at the post office and provide identification to secure his mail.

Insured Mail: Insured mail is available for only third- and fourth class mail. In the event of loss, the post office will pay only the cost value of the item sent.

International Mail: First-class mail, air mail, and parcel post service are available to other countries. However, the rates and mailing rules vary from country to country. Check with your post office for the specific rates, etc. for the country to which you are mailing. A copy of *International Postage Rates and Fees* may also be secured from the U.S. Postal Service without charge.

Metered Mail: Small businesses may buy or rent manual meters. However, larger businesses usually have electically powered meter machines that automatically feed, seal, meter-stamp, and count the mail. The sealed meter box is taken to the post office to replenish the postage.

Money Order: A *postal money order* for up to $500 may be purchased or cashed at any U.S. post office.

National Zip Code Directory: A large directory listing zip codes by state, city, and street may be secured at any post office for a nominal fee.

Parcel Post: See fourth-class mail.

Post Cards: Cards ranging in size from $3^1/_2$ by 5 inches to $4^1/_4$ by 6 inches may be mailed at rates lower than first-class envelope mail. A post card carrying first-class prepaid postage may be purchased at your local post office.

Post Office Box: Boxes or bins may be rented at any post office. A box enables a business or individual to pick up mail at anytime that post office lobbies are open. Many larger businesses may rent several boxes so that their mail is automatically presorted by box number (such as for payments, new orders, sales reports, etc.).

Priority Mail (Air Parcel Post): All first-class mail weighing from 13 ounces to 70 pounds is classified as *Priority Mail*. Priority mail receives air service the same as other first-class mail.

Registered Mail: First-class mail that is registered is kept locked and separate from other mail. It is the safest way for mailing valuable documents or other papers that are uninsurable. All items that are irreplaceable or difficult to replace should be registered (such as money, stock certificates, manuscripts, signed documents, jewelry of unusual value, etc.).

At the time of mailing, the sender receives a numbered receipt and the post office maintains a record of the number. As proof of delivery a return receipt may be requested.

In addition, to first-class postage and return receipt fee, the sender must pay a registration fee based on the declared value (up to $10,000) of the item.

Second-class Mail: This mail class provides special rates for publishers who have permits to mail magazines or newspapers, for publications of certain non-profit organizations, or for individuals mailing complete publications. The wrapper must be marked *second-class* and no other communication may be included without making all the items subject to first-class postage.

Special Delivery: A special delivery fee may be paid for all classes of mail. For this fee, in addition to regular postage, delivery is assured immediately after arrival at the destination post office.

Third-class Mail: This class mail may be used for individual or bulk mailings of advertising material such as booklets, circulars, and catalogs, and for merchandise, seeds, bulbs, and plants that weigh less than 16 ounces apiece. Items weighing more than 16 ounces are classified as fourth-class (parcel post). Third-class mail must be left unsealed for postal inspection, or if sealed, marked *bulk mail* or *third-class mail*. it must not include written messages or directions on the outside. Check with your post office for the specific requirements for the type of item you are mailing.

Chapter 13

TIME CHANGE

Business today in many industries is done on a worldwide basis. Government and military personnel, too, often must communicate with others in many foreign countries. There is often a need, then, for knowing the time in other locations or other travel itineraries. The listings on the pages which follow will enable you to quickly determine the time in other locations.

In the listing, if all of a country is in one time zone, only the name of the country is given. Where there is more than one zone, the principal cities of the country are given with their time zone.

The *Eastern Standard Time* Zone in the United States is used as a base. If you are in that zone, you only need to add or subtract the number of hours indicated after the name of the country or city whose time you are determining.

For example, if you are in New York or New Jersey or any other Eastern Time Zone area, and wish to know the time in Rome, Italy, look up *Italy*. You will find it has only one time zone indicated as +6. Simply add 6 hours to your time. In other words, if it is 12 o'clock where you are, it is 6 p.m. in Rome.

If you are not in the Eastern Standard Time Zone, follow these steps:

1. In the list, find the name of the country or city *where you are* or near.
2. Reverse the sign given for your location; e.g. change a +3 to a −3. Then add or subtract that number from the actual time where you are.
3. Find the name of the country whose time you wish to know and add or subtract the figure you arrived at in step 2 above.

For example, if you are in San Francisco and wish to know the time in Hong Kong when your time is 2 p.m.:

1. Locate San Francisco in the list.
2. Change the −3 to +3 and then add that amount to your actual time. Your time 2 p.m. plus 3 = 5 p.m.
3. Look up Hong Kong which shows + 13. Add that amount to the time from step 2 above: 5 p.m. + 13 = 18 or, in other words, it would be 11 a.m. in Hong Kong when the time is 2 p.m. in San Francisco.

Note: If Daylight Savings Time is in effect in your time zone, *subtract* one hour from the result you found by following the steps above. In the example above, you would subtract one hour from 6 a.m. making it 5 a.m. You would then not want to call until after 5 p.m. San Francisco time to reach someone in Hong Kong after 8 a.m.

Afghanistan $+9\frac{1}{2}$	Bolivia $+1$	Canada	Czechoslovakia $+6$	Ghana $+5$	Semarang $+13$
Algeria $+6$	Botswana $+7$	Montreal 0	Dahomey $+6$	Greece $+7$	Surabaya $+12$
Angola $+6$	Brazil	Ottawa 0	Denmark $+6$	Greenland $+2$	Iran $+8\frac{1}{2}$
Argentina $+1$	Belo Horizonte $+2$	Toronto 0	Dominican Rep. 0	Guatemala -1	Iraq $+8$
Australia	Brasilia $+2$	Vancouver -3	Ecuador 0	Guinea $+5$	Ireland $+6$
Adelaide $+14\frac{1}{2}$	Campo Grande $+1$	Winnipeg -1	Egypt $+7$	Guyana $+2$	Italy $+6$
Brisbane $+15$	Recife $+2$	Central Africa	El Salvador -1	Haiti 0	Ivory Coast $+5$
Canberra $+15$	Pôrto Velho $+1$	Republic $+6$	Equatorial	Honduras -1	Jamaica 0
Darwin $+14\frac{1}{2}$	Rio de Janeiro $+2$	Chad $+6$	Guinea $+6$	Hong Kong $+13$	Japan $+14$
Melbourne $+15$	Sao Luis $+2$	Chile $+1$	Ethiopia $+8$	Hungary $+6$	Jordan $+7$
Perth $+13$	Sao Paulo $+2$	China $+13$	Finland $+7$	Iceland $+4$	Kenya $+8$
Sydney $+15$	Bulgaria $+7$	Columbia 0	France $+6$	India $+10\frac{1}{2}$	Korea $+14$
Austria $+6$	Burma $+11\frac{1}{2}$	Congo, Rep. of $+6$	Gabon $+6$	Indonesia	Kuwait $+8$
Bangladesh $+11$	Burundi $+7$	Costa Rica -1	Gambia $+5$	Bandung $+12$	Laos $+12$
Barbados $+1$	Cambodia $+12$	Cuba 0	Germany, East $+6$	Djakarta $+12$	Lebanon $+7$
Belgium $+6$	Cameroon $+6$	Cyprus $+6$	Germany, West $+6$	Irian Jaya $+14$	Lesotho $+7$

Liberia + 5³/₄	Newfoundland +1¹/₂	South Africa +7	Kharkov +8	Boston 0	Oklahoma City −1
Libya +7	New Zealand +17	Spain +6	Kiev +8	Buffalo 0	Phoenix −2
Luxembourg +6	Nicaragua −1	Sri Lanka +10¹/₂	Kuybyshev +9	Chicago −1	Pittsburgh 0
Malagasy Rep. +8	Niger + 6	Sudan +7	Leningrad +8	Cincinnati 0	Philadelphia 0
Malawi +7	Nigeria +6	Sweden +6	Minsk +8	Cleveland 0	St. Louis −1
Malasia + 12¹/₂	Nova Scotia +1	Switzerland +6	Moscow +8	Columbus 0	San Antonio −1
Maldive Is. +10	Pakistan +10	Syria +7	Novosibirsk +12	Dallas −1	San Francisco −3
Mali +5	Panama 0	Taiwan +13	Odessa +8	Denver −2	Seattle −3
Malta +6	Paraguay +1	Tanzania +8	Omsk +12	Detroit 0	Washington 0
Mauritania +5	Peru 0	Thailand +12	Perm +12	Ft. Worth −1	Upper Volta +5
Mauritius +9	Philippines +13	Togo Rep. +5	Rija +8	Honolulu −5	Uruguay +2
Mexico	Poland +6	Trinidad and	Rostov +9	Houston −1	Venezuela +1
Guadalajara −1	Portugal +6	Tobago +1	Tashkent +11	Indianapolis −1	Vietnam +13
Mexico City −1	Rhodesia +7	Tunisia +6	Vladivostok +15	Kansas City −1	Yemen +8
Monterey −1	Rumania +7	Turkey +7	Volgograd +9	Memphis −1	Yugoslavia +6
Mazatlán −2	Samoa, W. −6	Uganda +8	United Kingdom +6	Minneapolis −1	Zaire
Mongolian Rep. +13	Saudia Arabia +9	USSR	United States	New York 0	Kinshasa +6
Morocco +5	Senegal +5	Alma-Ata +11	Anchorage −5	Los Angeles −3	Lumbumbashi +7
Nepal +10¹/₂	Singapore + 12¹/₂	Baku +9	Atlanta 0	Milwaukee −1	Zambia +7
Netherlands +6	Somalia +8	Gorki +9	Baltimore 0	New Orleans −1	

Chapter 14

ROMAN NUMERALS

Roman numerals are not widely used, but used often enough so you should be able to read or interpret them. Following is a table of Arabic numerals and their equivalent Roman Numerals.

Table of Roman Numerals

Arabic Numeral	Roman Numeral	Arabic Numeral	Roman Numeral
1	I	50	L
2	II	60	LX
3	III	70	LXX
4	IV	80	LXXX
5	V	90	XC
6	VI	100	C
7	VII	200	CC
8	VIII	300	CCC
9	IX	400	CD
10	X	500	D
11	XI	600	DC
12	XII	700	DCC
13	XIII	800	DCCC
14	XIV	900	CM
15	XV	1,000	M
16	XVI	4,000	$M\overline{V}$
17	XVII	5,000	$\overline{V}$
18	XVII	10,000	$\overline{X}$
19	XIX	15,000	$\overline{XV}$
20	XX	20,000	$\overline{XX}$
30	XXX	100,000	$\overline{C}$
40	XL	1,000,000	$\overline{M}$

The following examples illustrate the use and meaning of Roman Numerals.

1. A Roman Numeral or letter preceding *a letter of greater value* subtracts from it:

V = 5	IV = 4
L = 50	XL = 40
C = 100	XC = 90

2. A letter preceding *a letter of equal or lesser value* adds to it.

V = 5	VI = 6
L = 50	LX = 60
C = 100	CXI = 111

3. You will quickly, of course, be able to remember and recognize smaller numbers.

XVI = 16
   X (10) + VI (6) = 16
XLIV = 44
   XL (40) + IV (4) = 44
XCI = 91
   XC (90) + I (1) = 91

For larger numbers simply examine the numbers and break it down into its elements and you will readily interpret the number. You will be able to recognize the elements or parts by applying rules 1 and 2 given above or by looking at the table of Roman Numerals.

CDXCIII = 493
   CD (400) + XC (90) + III (3) = 493
DCXCIX = 699
   DC (600) + XC (90) + IX (9) = 699
MDCLXXV = 1,675
   M (1,000) + DC (600) + LXX (70)
   + V (5) = 1,675

4. A bar over a Roman Numeral multiplies it by 1,000.

$M\overline{V}$ = 4,000	$\overline{V}$ = 5,000
$\overline{XV}$ = 15,000	$\overline{XX}$ = 20,000

Chapter 15

PERPETUAL CALENDAR

The use of this perpetual calendar will enable you to determine the day of the week on which any date fell or will fall during the two centuries from 1901 to 2100. To locate a date and day of the week, first locate the year in which you are interested in the list below. Following the year is a letter to tell you which calendar to use on the pages which follow. In addition, if you are planning schedules, etc. for the next year or two and do not yet have copies of those calendars, simply look up the year and the calendar letter, and you will then have a calendar for the entire year in question.

Year		Year		Year		Year		Year		Year		Year		Year		Year		Year		Year		Year	
1901	C	1918	C	1935	C	1952	J	1969	D	1986	D	2003	D	2020	K	2037	E	2054	E	2071	E	2088	L
1902	D	1919	D	1936	K	1953	E	1970	E	1987	E	2004	L	2021	F	2038	F	2055	F	2072	M	2089	G
1903	E	1920	L	1937	F	1954	F	1971	F	1988	M	2005	G	2022	G	2039	G	2056	N	2073	A	2090	A
1904	M	1921	G	1938	G	1955	G	1972	N	1989	A	2006	A	2023	A	2040	H	2057	B	2074	B	2091	B
1905	A	1922	A	1939	A	1956	H	1973	B	1990	B	2007	B	2024	I	2041	C	2058	C	2075	C	2092	J
1906	B	1923	B	1940	I	1957	C	1974	C	1991	C	2008	J	2025	D	2042	D	2059	D	2076	K	2093	E
1907	C	1924	J	1941	D	1958	D	1975	D	1992	K	2009	E	2026	E	2043	E	2060	L	2077	F	2094	F
1908	K	1925	E	1942	E	1959	E	1976	L	1993	F	2010	F	2027	F	2044	M	2061	G	2078	G	2095	G
1909	F	1926	F	1943	F	1960	M	1977	G	1994	G	2011	G	2028	N	2045	A	2062	A	2079	A	2096	H
1910	G	1927	G	1944	N	1961	A	1978	A	1995	A	2012	H	2029	B	2046	B	2063	B	2080	I	2097	C
1911	A	1928	H	1945	B	1962	B	1979	B	1996	I	2013	C	2030	C	2047	C	2064	J	2081	D	2098	D
1912	I	1929	C	1946	C	1963	C	1980	J	1997	D	2014	D	2031	D	2048	K	2065	E	2082	E	2099	E
1913	D	1930	D	1947	D	1964	K	1981	E	1998	E	2015	E	2032	L	2049	F	2066	F	2083	F	2100	F
1914	E	1931	E	1948	L	1965	F	1982	F	1999	F	2016	M	2033	G	2050	G	2067	G	2084	N		
1915	F	1932	M	1949	G	1966	G	1983	G	2000	N	2017	A	2034	A	2051	A	2068	H	2085	B		
1916	N	1933	A	1950	A	1967	A	1984	H	2001	B	2018	B	2035	B	2052	I	2069	C	2086	C		
1917	B	1934	B	1951	B	1968	I	1985	C	2002	C	2019	C	2036	J	2053	D	2070	D	2087	D		

Calendar charts **A** through **H**, each showing the twelve months (January, February, March, April, May, June, July, August, September, October, November, December) with day-of-week columns S M T W T F S.

I

```
       JANUARY                  MAY                 SEPTEMBER
 S  M  T  W  T  F  S     S  M  T  W  T  F  S     S  M  T  W  T  F  S
    1  2  3  4  5  6              1  2  3  4      1  2  3  4  5  6  7
 7  8  9 10 11 12 13     5  6  7  8  9 10 11      8  9 10 11 12 13 14
14 15 16 17 18 19 20    12 13 14 15 16 17 18     15 16 17 18 19 20 21
21 22 23 24 25 26 27    19 20 21 22 23 24 25     22 23 24 25 26 27 28
28 29 30 31             26 27 28 29 30 31        29 30

       FEBRUARY                 JUNE                  OCTOBER
 S  M  T  W  T  F  S     S  M  T  W  T  F  S     S  M  T  W  T  F  S
             1  2  3                       1           1  2  3  4  5
 4  5  6  7  8  9 10     2  3  4  5  6  7  8      6  7  8  9 10 11 12
11 12 13 14 15 16 17     9 10 11 12 13 14 15     13 14 15 16 17 18 19
18 19 20 21 22 23 24    16 17 18 19 20 21 22     20 21 22 23 24 25 26
25 26 27 28 29          23 24 25 26 27 28 29     27 28 29 30 31
                        30

       MARCH                    JULY                  NOVEMBER
 S  M  T  W  T  F  S     S  M  T  W  T  F  S     S  M  T  W  T  F  S
                1  2        1  2  3  4  5  6                    1  2
 3  4  5  6  7  8  9     7  8  9 10 11 12 13      3  4  5  6  7  8  9
10 11 12 13 14 15 16    14 15 16 17 18 19 20     10 11 12 13 14 15 16
17 18 19 20 21 22 23    21 22 23 24 25 26 27     17 18 19 20 21 22 23
24 25 26 27 28 29 30    28 29 30 31              24 25 26 27 28 29 30
31

       APRIL                    AUGUST                DECEMBER
 S  M  T  W  T  F  S     S  M  T  W  T  F  S     S  M  T  W  T  F  S
    1  2  3  4  5  6              1  2  3      1  2  3  4  5  6  7
 7  8  9 10 11 12 13     4  5  6  7  8  9 10      8  9 10 11 12 13 14
14 15 16 17 18 19 20    11 12 13 14 15 16 17     15 16 17 18 19 20 21
21 22 23 24 25 26 27    18 19 20 21 22 23 24     22 23 24 25 26 27 28
28 29 30                25 26 27 28 29 30 31     29 30 31
```

K

```
       JANUARY                  MAY                 SEPTEMBER
 S  M  T  W  T  F  S     S  M  T  W  T  F  S     S  M  T  W  T  F  S
          1  2  3  4                 1  2  3           1  2  3  4  5
 5  6  7  8  9 10 11     4  5  6  7  8  9 10      6  7  8  9 10 11 12
12 13 14 15 16 17 18    11 12 13 14 15 16 17     13 14 15 16 17 18 19
19 20 21 22 23 24 25    18 19 20 21 22 23 24     20 21 22 23 24 25 26
26 27 28 29 30 31       25 26 27 28 29 30 31     27 28 29 30

       FEBRUARY                 JUNE                  OCTOBER
 S  M  T  W  T  F  S     S  M  T  W  T  F  S     S  M  T  W  T  F  S
                   1        1  2  3  4  5  6                 1  2  3
 2  3  4  5  6  7  8     7  8  9 10 11 12 13      4  5  6  7  8  9 10
 9 10 11 12 13 14 15    14 15 16 17 18 19 20     11 12 13 14 15 16 17
16 17 18 19 20 21 22    21 22 23 24 25 26 27     18 19 20 21 22 23 24
23 24 25 26 27 28 29    28 29 30                 25 26 27 28 29 30 31

       MARCH                    JULY                  NOVEMBER
 S  M  T  W  T  F  S     S  M  T  W  T  F  S     S  M  T  W  T  F  S
 1  2  3  4  5  6  7              1  2  3  4      1  2  3  4  5  6  7
 8  9 10 11 12 13 14     5  6  7  8  9 10 11      8  9 10 11 12 13 14
15 16 17 18 19 20 21    12 13 14 15 16 17 18     15 16 17 18 19 20 21
22 23 24 25 26 27 28    19 20 21 22 23 24 25     22 23 24 25 26 27 28
29 30 31                26 27 28 29 30 31        29 30

       APRIL                    AUGUST                DECEMBER
 S  M  T  W  T  F  S     S  M  T  W  T  F  S     S  M  T  W  T  F  S
          1  2  3  4                       1           1  2  3  4  5
 5  6  7  8  9 10 11     2  3  4  5  6  7  8      6  7  8  9 10 11 12
12 13 14 15 16 17 18     9 10 11 12 13 14 15     13 14 15 16 17 18 19
19 20 21 22 23 24 25    16 17 18 19 20 21 22     20 21 22 23 24 25 26
26 27 28 29 30          23 24 25 26 27 28 29     27 28 29 30 31
                        30 31
```

M

```
       JANUARY                  MAY                 SEPTEMBER
 S  M  T  W  T  F  S     S  M  T  W  T  F  S     S  M  T  W  T  F  S
                1  2     1  2  3  4  5  6  7              1  2  3
 3  4  5  6  7  8  9     8  9 10 11 12 13 14      4  5  6  7  8  9 10
10 11 12 13 14 15 16    15 16 17 18 19 20 21     11 12 13 14 15 16 17
17 18 19 20 21 22 23    22 23 24 25 26 27 28     18 19 20 21 22 23 24
24 25 26 27 28 29 30    29 30 31                 25 26 27 28 29 30
31

       FEBRUARY                 JUNE                  OCTOBER
 S  M  T  W  T  F  S     S  M  T  W  T  F  S     S  M  T  W  T  F  S
    1  2  3  4  5  6              1  2  3  4                       1
 7  8  9 10 11 12 13     5  6  7  8  9 10 11      2  3  4  5  6  7  8
14 15 16 17 18 19 20    12 13 14 15 16 17 18      9 10 11 12 13 14 15
21 22 23 24 25 26 27    19 20 21 22 23 24 25     16 17 18 19 20 21 22
28 29                   26 27 28 29 30           23 24 25 26 27 28 29
                                                 30 31

       MARCH                    JULY                  NOVEMBER
 S  M  T  W  T  F  S     S  M  T  W  T  F  S     S  M  T  W  T  F  S
          1  2  3  4  5              1  2                 1  2  3  4  5
 6  7  8  9 10 11 12     3  4  5  6  7  8  9      6  7  8  9 10 11 12
13 14 15 16 17 18 19    10 11 12 13 14 15 16     13 14 15 16 17 18 19
20 21 22 23 24 25 26    17 18 19 20 21 22 23     20 21 22 23 24 25 26
27 28 29 30 31          24 25 26 27 28 29 30     27 28 29 30
                        31

       APRIL                    AUGUST                DECEMBER
 S  M  T  W  T  F  S     S  M  T  W  T  F  S     S  M  T  W  T  F  S
                1  2              1  2  3  4                 1  2  3
 3  4  5  6  7  8  9     7  8  9 10 11 12 13      4  5  6  7  8  9 10
10 11 12 13 14 15 16    14 15 16 17 18 19 20     11 12 13 14 15 16 17
17 18 19 20 21 22 23    21 22 23 24 25 26 27     18 19 20 21 22 23 24
24 25 26 27 28 29 30    28 29 30 31              25 26 27 28 29 30 31
```

J

```
       JANUARY                  MAY                 SEPTEMBER
 S  M  T  W  T  F  S     S  M  T  W  T  F  S     S  M  T  W  T  F  S
          1  2  3  4  5              1  2  3         1  2  3  4  5  6
 6  7  8  9 10 11 12     4  5  6  7  8  9 10      7  8  9 10 11 12 13
13 14 15 16 17 18 19    11 12 13 14 15 16 17     14 15 16 17 18 19 20
20 21 22 23 24 25 26    18 19 20 21 22 23 24     21 22 23 24 25 26 27
27 28 29 30 31          25 26 27 28 29 30 31     28 29 30

       FEBRUARY                 JUNE                  OCTOBER
 S  M  T  W  T  F  S     S  M  T  W  T  F  S     S  M  T  W  T  F  S
                1  2     1  2  3  4  5  6  7              1  2  3  4
 3  4  5  6  7  8  9     8  9 10 11 12 13 14      5  6  7  8  9 10 11
10 11 12 13 14 15 16    15 16 17 18 19 20 21     12 13 14 15 16 17 18
17 18 19 20 21 22 23    22 23 24 25 26 27 28     19 20 21 22 23 24 25
24 25 26 27 28 29       29 30                    26 27 28 29 30 31

       MARCH                    JULY                  NOVEMBER
 S  M  T  W  T  F  S     S  M  T  W  T  F  S     S  M  T  W  T  F  S
                   1           1  2  3  4  5                       1
 2  3  4  5  6  7  8     6  7  8  9 10 11 12      2  3  4  5  6  7  8
 9 10 11 12 13 14 15    13 14 15 16 17 18 19      9 10 11 12 13 14 15
16 17 18 19 20 21 22    20 21 22 23 24 25 26     16 17 18 19 20 21 22
23 24 25 26 27 28 29    27 28 29 30 31           23 24 25 26 27 28 29
30 31                                            30

       APRIL                    AUGUST                DECEMBER
 S  M  T  W  T  F  S     S  M  T  W  T  F  S     S  M  T  W  T  F  S
          1  2  3  4  5                 1  2              1  2  3  4  5  6
 6  7  8  9 10 11 12     3  4  5  6  7  8  9      7  8  9 10 11 12 13
13 14 15 16 17 18 19    10 11 12 13 14 15 16     14 15 16 17 18 19 20
20 21 22 23 24 25 26    17 18 19 20 21 22 23     21 22 23 24 25 26 27
27 28 29 30             24 25 26 27 28 29 30     28 29 30 31
                        31
```

L

```
       JANUARY                  MAY                 SEPTEMBER
 S  M  T  W  T  F  S     S  M  T  W  T  F  S     S  M  T  W  T  F  S
             1  2  3                       1              1  2  3  4
 4  5  6  7  8  9 10     2  3  4  5  6  7  8      5  6  7  8  9 10 11
11 12 13 14 15 16 17     9 10 11 12 13 14 15     12 13 14 15 16 17 18
18 19 20 21 22 23 24    16 17 18 19 20 21 22     19 20 21 22 23 24 25
25 26 27 28 29 30 31    23 24 25 26 27 28 29     26 27 28 29 30
                        30 31

       FEBRUARY                 JUNE                  OCTOBER
 S  M  T  W  T  F  S     S  M  T  W  T  F  S     S  M  T  W  T  F  S
 1  2  3  4  5  6  7              1  2  3  4  5                 1  2
 8  9 10 11 12 13 14     6  7  8  9 10 11 12      3  4  5  6  7  8  9
15 16 17 18 19 20 21    13 14 15 16 17 18 19     10 11 12 13 14 15 16
22 23 24 25 26 27 28    20 21 22 23 24 25 26     17 18 19 20 21 22 23
29                      27 28 29 30              24 25 26 27 28 29 30
                                                 31

       MARCH                    JULY                  NOVEMBER
 S  M  T  W  T  F  S     S  M  T  W  T  F  S     S  M  T  W  T  F  S
    1  2  3  4  5  6              1  2  3              1  2  3  4  5  6
 7  8  9 10 11 12 13     4  5  6  7  8  9 10      7  8  9 10 11 12 13
14 15 16 17 18 19 20    11 12 13 14 15 16 17     14 15 16 17 18 19 20
21 22 23 24 25 26 27    18 19 20 21 22 23 24     21 22 23 24 25 26 27
28 29 30 31             25 26 27 28 29 30 31     28 29 30

       APRIL                    AUGUST                DECEMBER
 S  M  T  W  T  F  S     S  M  T  W  T  F  S     S  M  T  W  T  F  S
             1  2  3     1  2  3  4  5  6  7              1  2  3  4
 4  5  6  7  8  9 10     8  9 10 11 12 13 14      5  6  7  8  9 10 11
11 12 13 14 15 16 17    15 16 17 18 19 20 21     12 13 14 15 16 17 18
18 19 20 21 22 23 24    22 23 24 25 26 27 28     19 20 21 22 23 24 25
25 26 27 28 29 30       29 30 31                 26 27 28 29 30 31
```

N

```
       JANUARY                  MAY                 SEPTEMBER
 S  M  T  W  T  F  S     S  M  T  W  T  F  S     S  M  T  W  T  F  S
                   1        1  2  3  4  5  6                 1  2
 2  3  4  5  6  7  8     7  8  9 10 11 12 13      3  4  5  6  7  8  9
 9 10 11 12 13 14 15    14 15 16 17 18 19 20     10 11 12 13 14 15 16
16 17 18 19 20 21 22    21 22 23 24 25 26 27     17 18 19 20 21 22 23
23 24 25 26 27 28 29    28 29 30 31              24 25 26 27 28 29 30
30 31

       FEBRUARY                 JUNE                  OCTOBER
 S  M  T  W  T  F  S     S  M  T  W  T  F  S     S  M  T  W  T  F  S
          1  2  3  4  5              1  2  3      1  2  3  4  5  6  7
 6  7  8  9 10 11 12     4  5  6  7  8  9 10      8  9 10 11 12 13 14
13 14 15 16 17 18 19    11 12 13 14 15 16 17     15 16 17 18 19 20 21
20 21 22 23 24 25 26    18 19 20 21 22 23 24     22 23 24 25 26 27 28
27 28 29                25 26 27 28 29 30        29 30 31

       MARCH                    JULY                  NOVEMBER
 S  M  T  W  T  F  S     S  M  T  W  T  F  S     S  M  T  W  T  F  S
          1  2  3  4                       1              1  2  3  4
 5  6  7  8  9 10 11     2  3  4  5  6  7  8      5  6  7  8  9 10 11
12 13 14 15 16 17 18     9 10 11 12 13 14 15     12 13 14 15 16 17 18
19 20 21 22 23 24 25    16 17 18 19 20 21 22     19 20 21 22 23 24 25
26 27 28 29 30 31       23 24 25 26 27 28 29     26 27 28 29 30
                        30 31

       APRIL                    AUGUST                DECEMBER
 S  M  T  W  T  F  S     S  M  T  W  T  F  S     S  M  T  W  T  F  S
                   1           1  2  3  4  5                 1  2
 2  3  4  5  6  7  8     6  7  8  9 10 11 12      3  4  5  6  7  8  9
 9 10 11 12 13 14 15    13 14 15 16 17 18 19     10 11 12 13 14 15 16
16 17 18 19 20 21 22    20 21 22 23 24 25 26     17 18 19 20 21 22 23
23 24 25 26 27 28 29    27 28 29 30 31           24 25 26 27 28 29 30
30                                               31
```

FLAGS FROM WORLD HISTORY

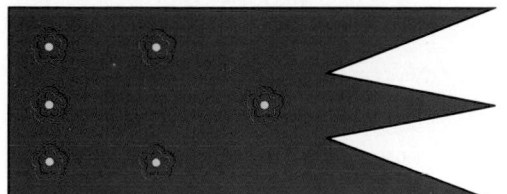

CHARLEMAGNE

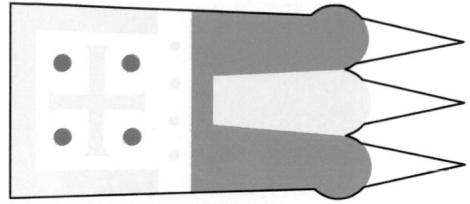

WILLIAM I (THE CONQUEROR) OF ENGLAND

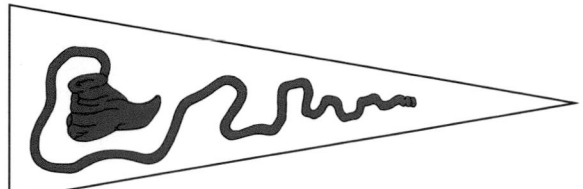

PEASANTS' WAR (16TH-CENTURY GERMANY)

PETER I (THE GREAT) OF RUSSIA

HUDSON'S BAY COMPANY

JOSÉ DE SAN MARTIN

CHINA UNDER THE CH'ING DYNASTY (19TH-CENTURY)

FLAG PROPOSED BY CECIL RHODES FOR BRITISH AFRICA

FLAGS FROM AMERICAN HISTORY

VIKINGS

CHRISTOPHER COLUMBUS

HENRY HUDSON

BRITISH EXPLORERS AND SETTLERS (FIRST UNION JACK)

FRENCH EXPLORERS AND SETTLERS (17TH AND 18TH CENTURIES)

CONTINENTAL COLORS (1776)

FIRST STARS AND STRIPES (1777-95)

ESEK HOPKINS, FIRST COMMANDER IN CHIEF OF THE CONTINENTAL NAVY

FIRST STAR-SPANGLED BANNER (1795-1818)

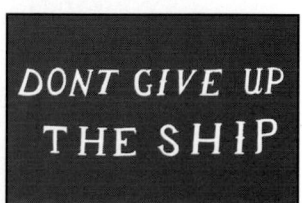

OLIVER HAZARD PERRY (WAR OF 1812)

BEAR FLAG REPUBLIC (1846)

STARS AND BARS OF THE CONFEDERACY (1861-63)

FORT SUMTER FLAG (1861)

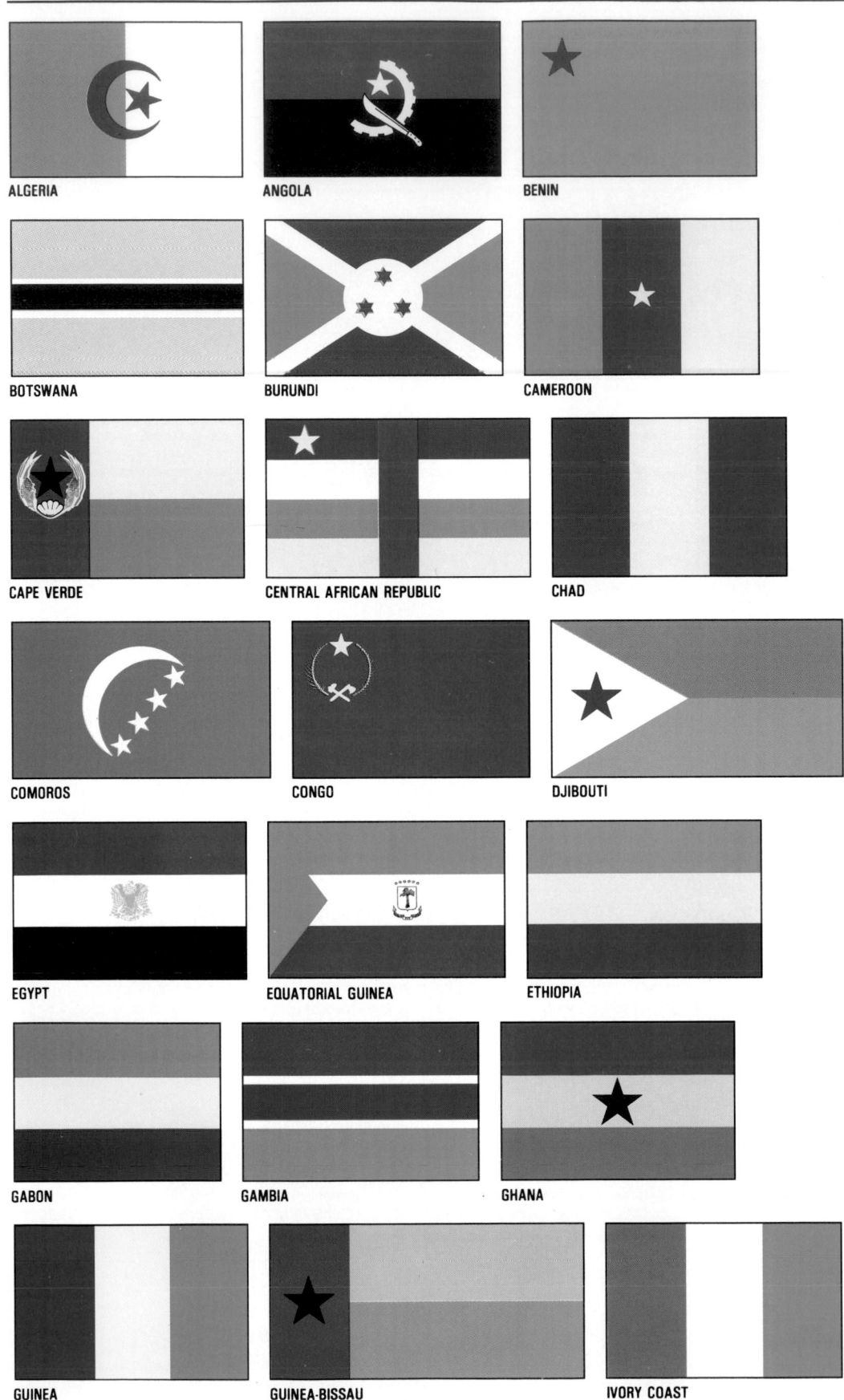

ALGERIA

ANGOLA

BENIN

BOTSWANA

BURUNDI

CAMEROON

CAPE VERDE

CENTRAL AFRICAN REPUBLIC

CHAD

COMOROS

CONGO

DJIBOUTI

EGYPT

EQUATORIAL GUINEA

ETHIOPIA

GABON

GAMBIA

GHANA

GUINEA

GUINEA-BISSAU

IVORY COAST

FLAGS OF AFRICA (continued)

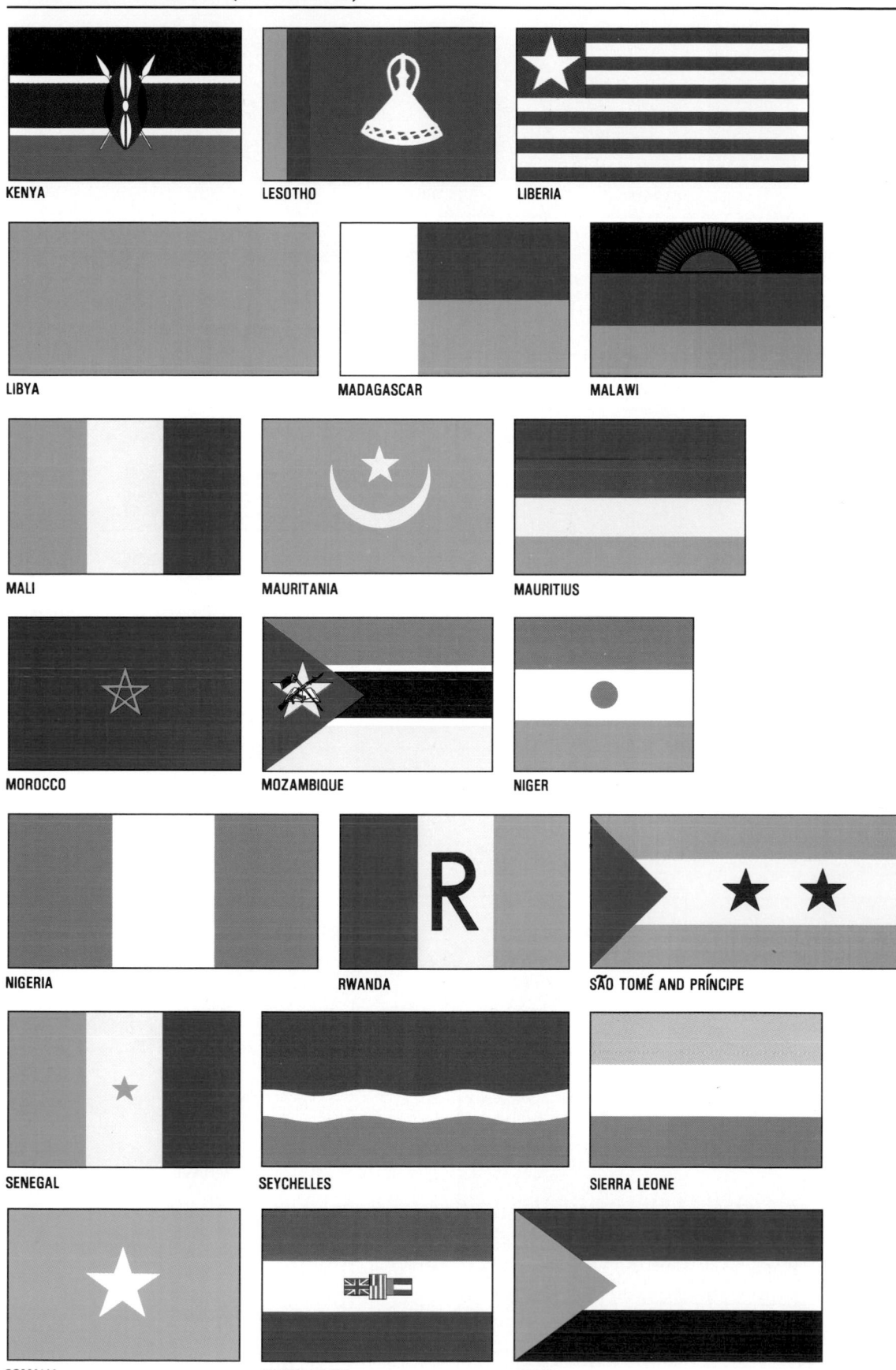

KENYA

LESOTHO

LIBERIA

LIBYA

MADAGASCAR

MALAWI

MALI

MAURITANIA

MAURITIUS

MOROCCO

MOZAMBIQUE

NIGER

NIGERIA

RWANDA

SÃO TOMÉ AND PRÍNCIPE

SENEGAL

SEYCHELLES

SIERRA LEONE

SOMALIA

SOUTH AFRICA

SUDAN

FLAGS OF AFRICA (continued)

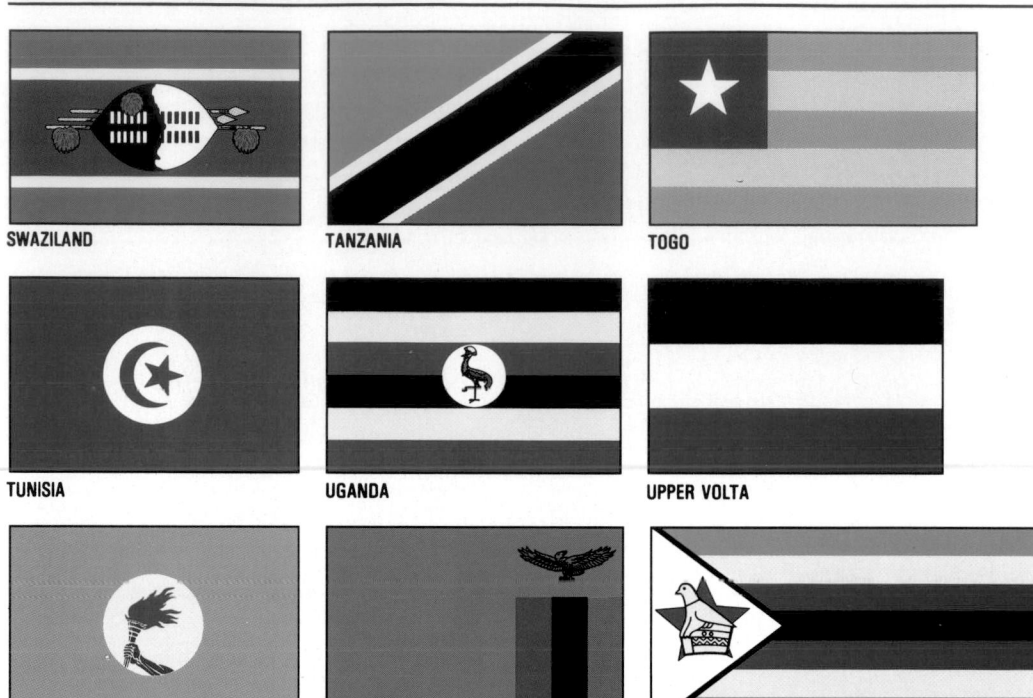

SWAZILAND

TANZANIA

TOGO

TUNISIA

UGANDA

UPPER VOLTA

ZAIRE

ZAMBIA

ZIMBABWE

FLAGS OF ASIA

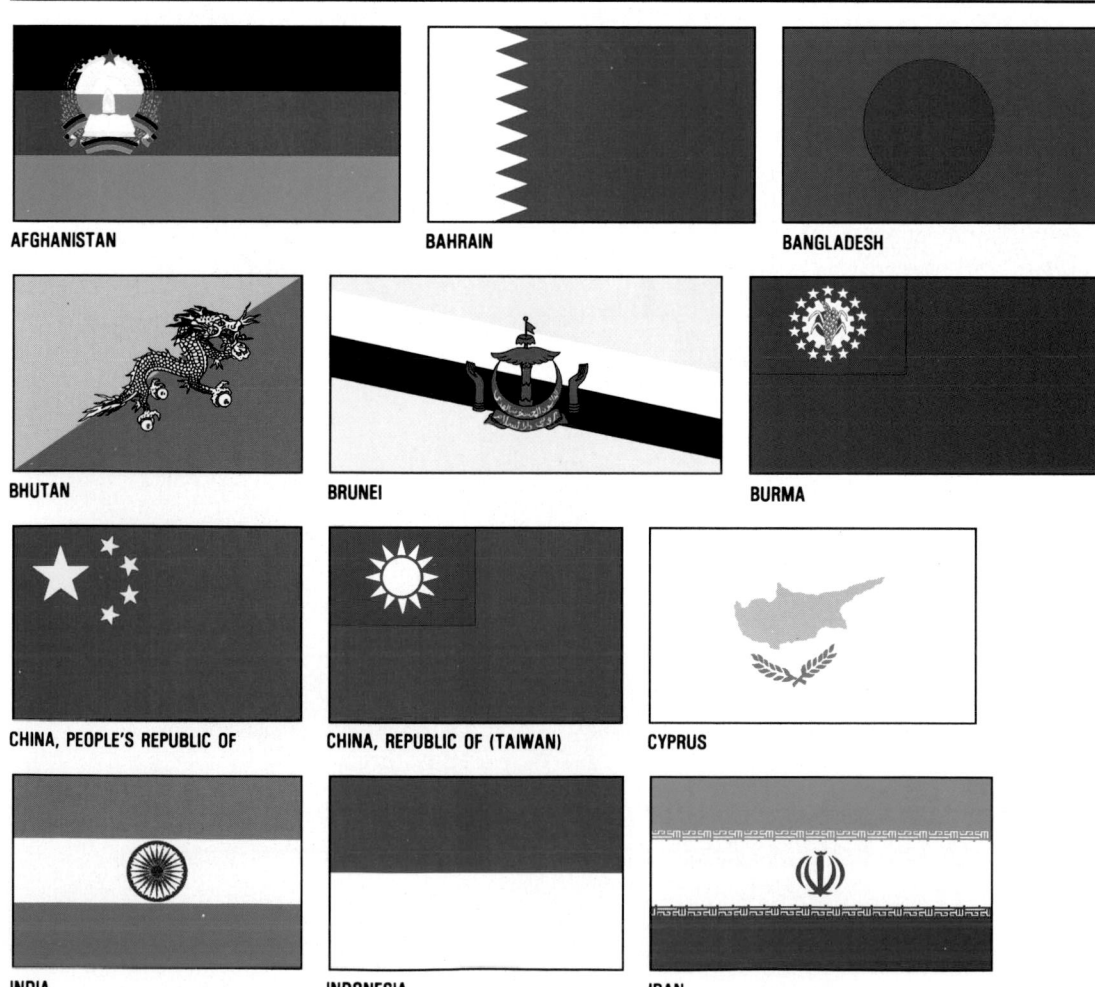

AFGHANISTAN

BAHRAIN

BANGLADESH

BHUTAN

BRUNEI

BURMA

CHINA, PEOPLE'S REPUBLIC OF

CHINA, REPUBLIC OF (TAIWAN)

CYPRUS

INDIA

INDONESIA

IRAN

FLAGS OF ASIA (continued)

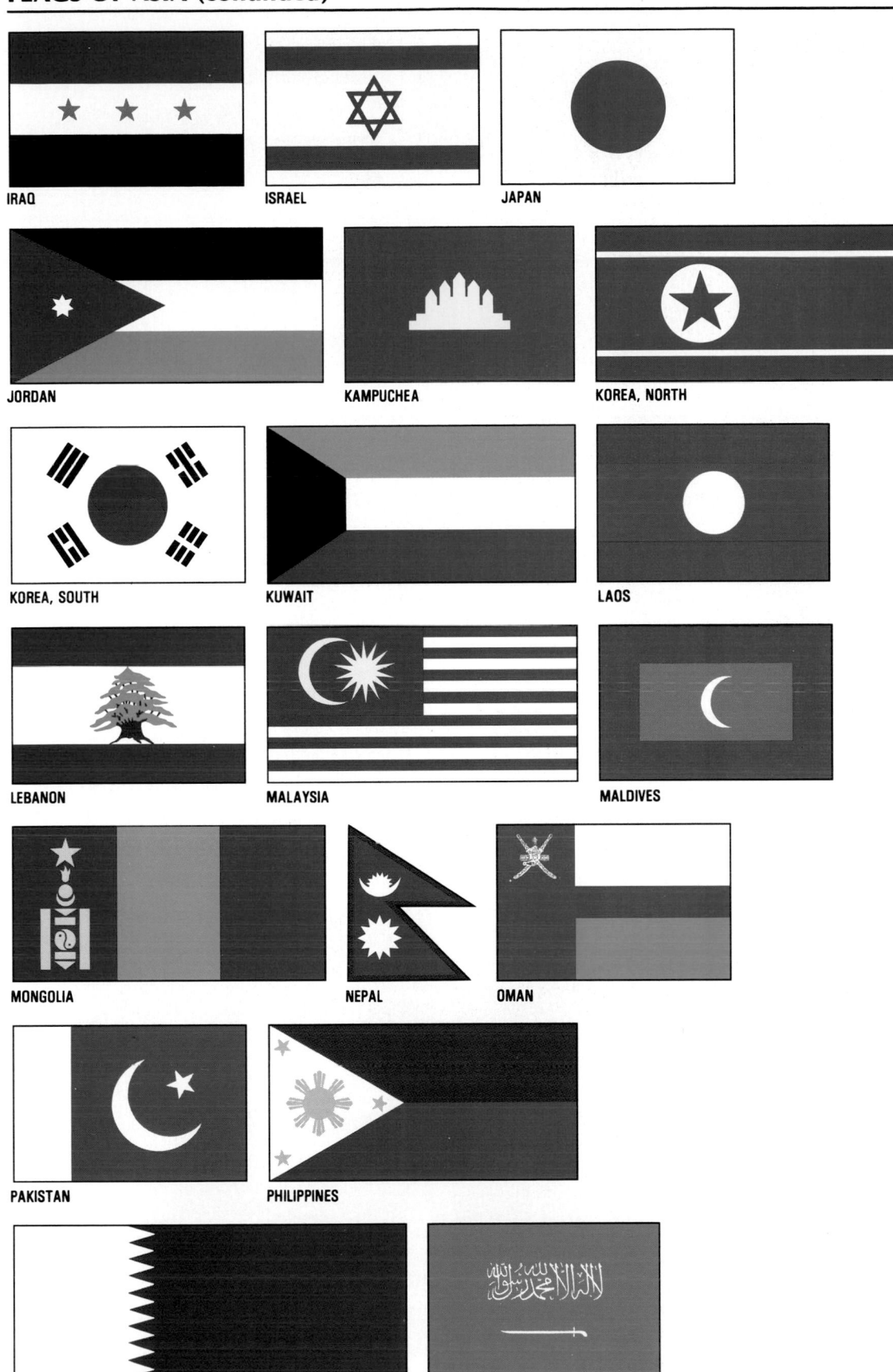

IRAQ

ISRAEL

JAPAN

JORDAN

KAMPUCHEA

KOREA, NORTH

KOREA, SOUTH

KUWAIT

LAOS

LEBANON

MALAYSIA

MALDIVES

MONGOLIA

NEPAL

OMAN

PAKISTAN

PHILIPPINES

QATAR

SAUDI ARABIA

FLAGS OF ASIA (continued)

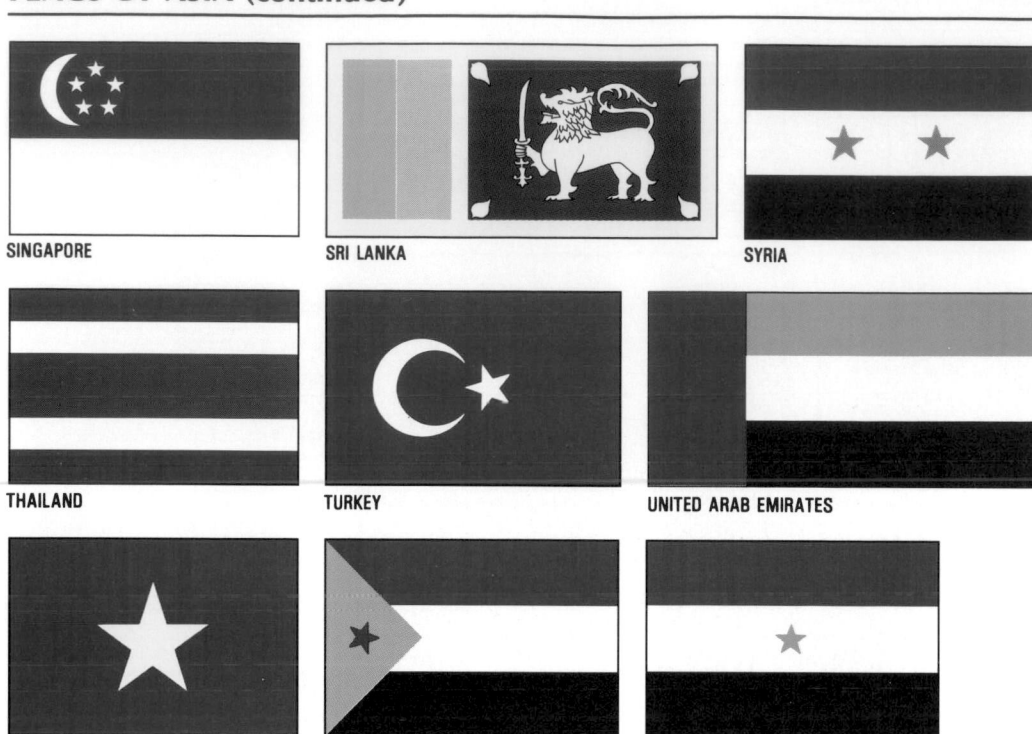

SINGAPORE

SRI LANKA

SYRIA

THAILAND

TURKEY

UNITED ARAB EMIRATES

VIETNAM

YEMEN (ADEN)

YEMEN (SANA)

FLAGS OF EUROPE

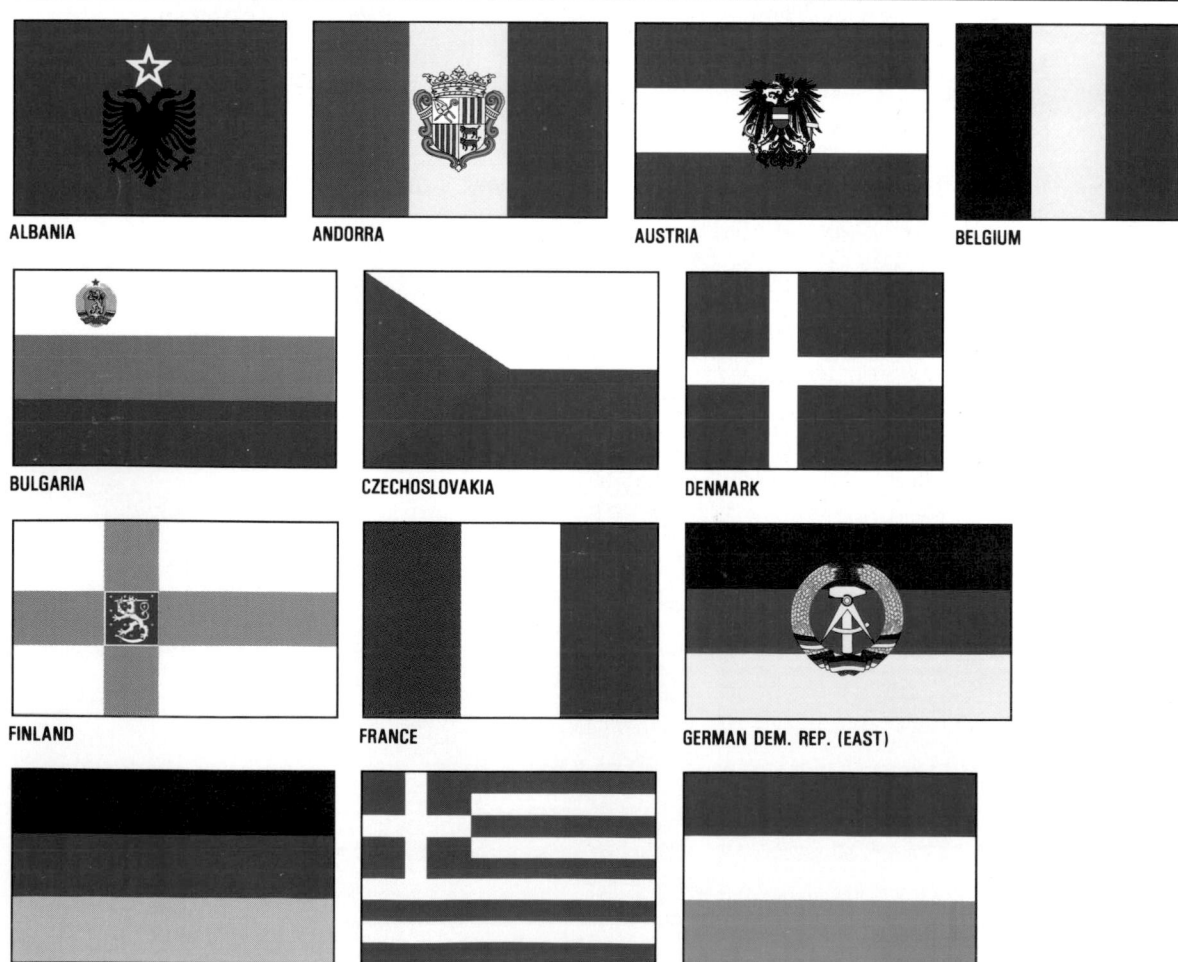

ALBANIA

ANDORRA

AUSTRIA

BELGIUM

BULGARIA

CZECHOSLOVAKIA

DENMARK

FINLAND

FRANCE

GERMAN DEM. REP. (EAST)

GERMANY, FED. REP. OF (WEST)

GREECE

HUNGARY

FLAGS OF EUROPE (continued)

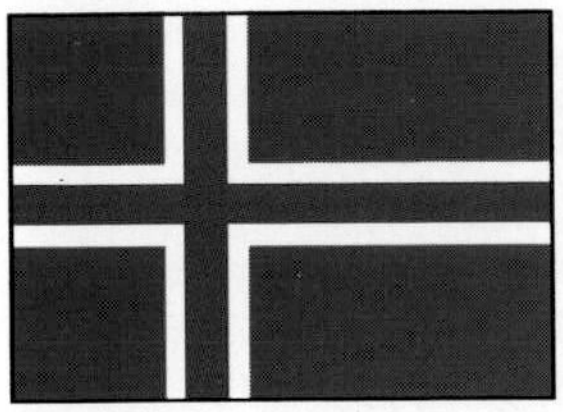

ICELAND

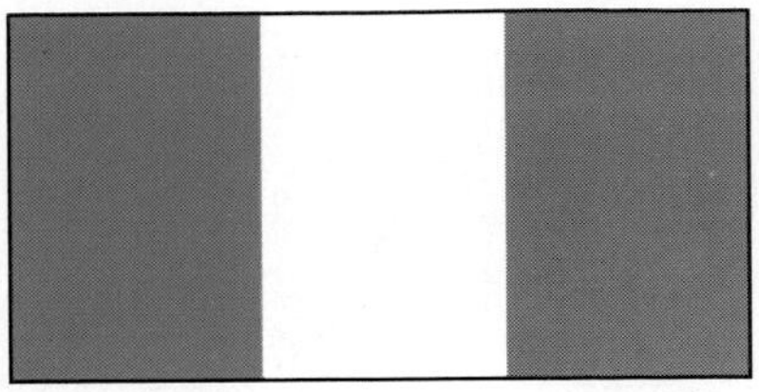

IRELAND

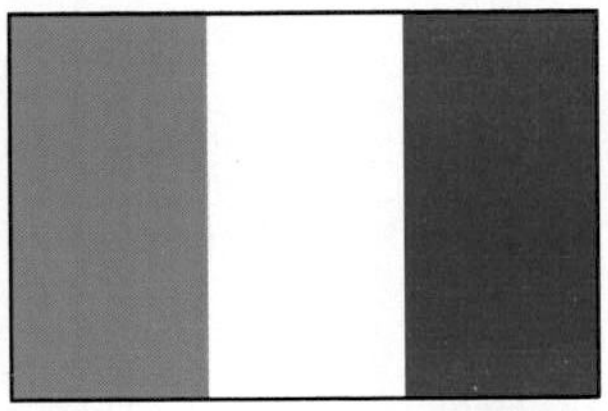

ITALY

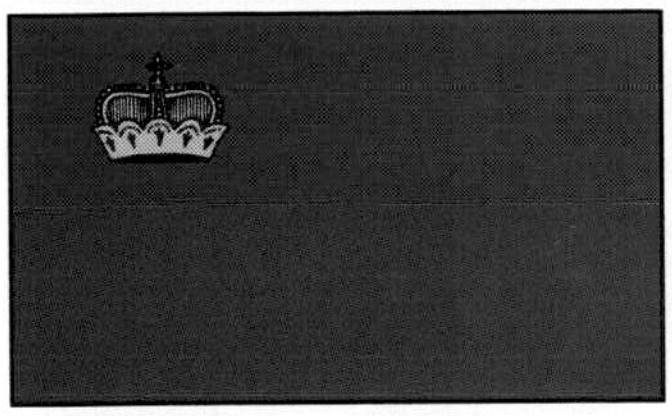

LIECHTENSTEIN

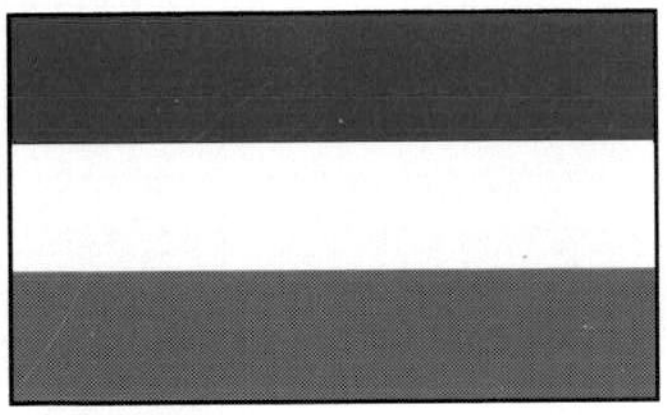

LUXEMBOURG

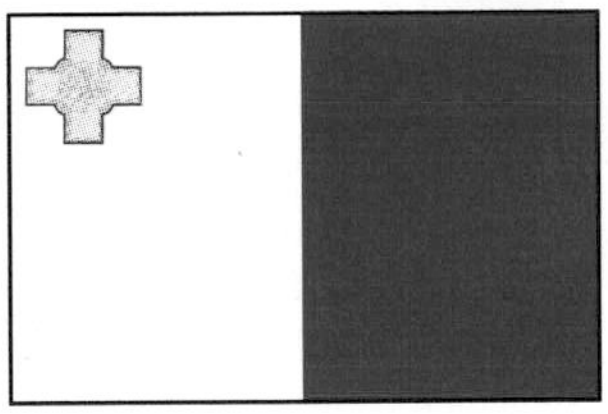

MALTA

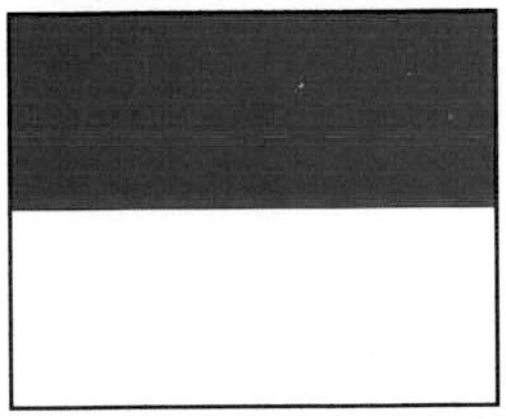

MONACO

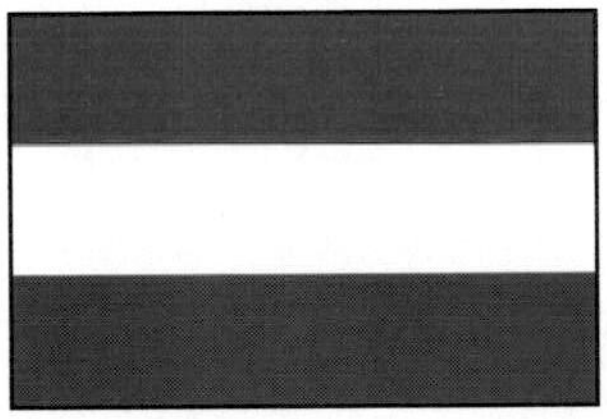

NETHERLANDS

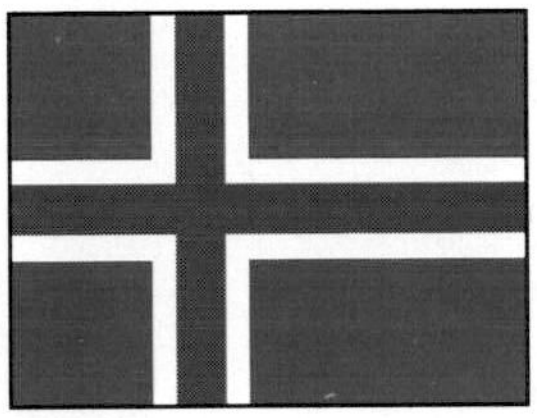

NORWAY

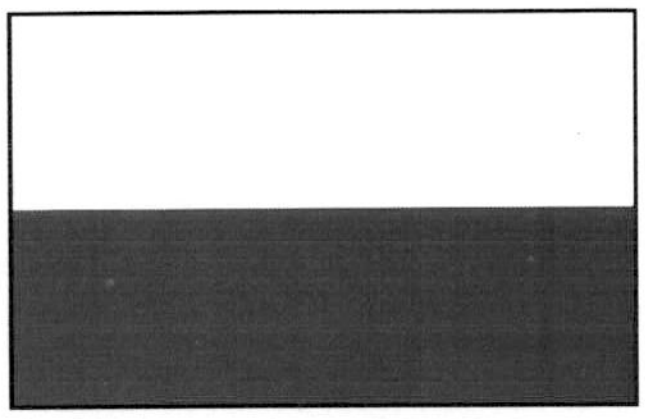

POLAND

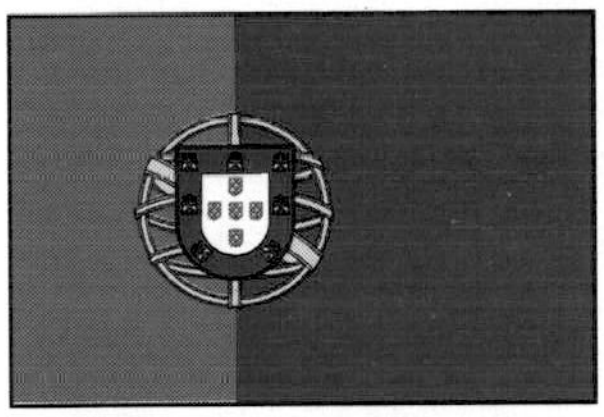

PORTUGAL

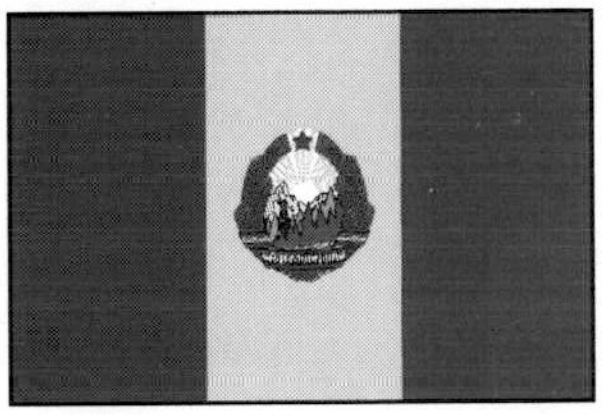

ROMANIA

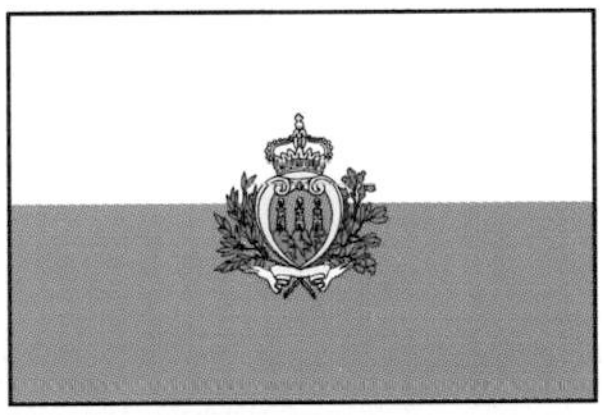

SAN MARINO

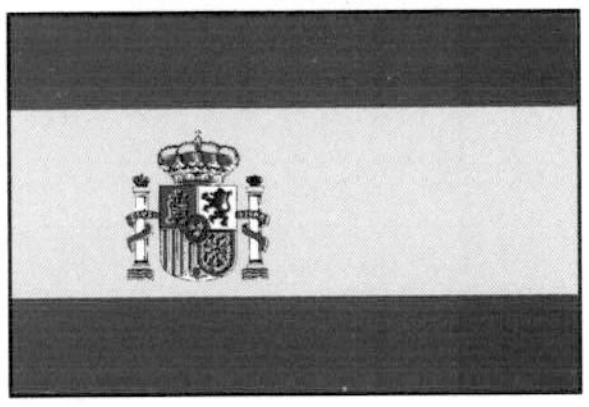

SPAIN

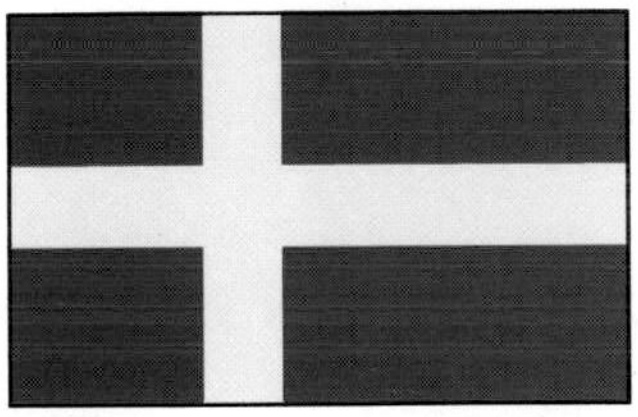

SWEDEN

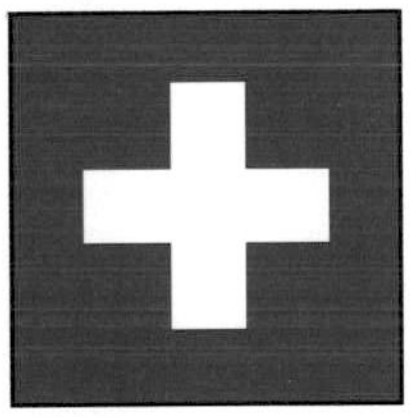

SWITZERLAND

UNION OF SOVIET SOCIALIST REPUBLICS

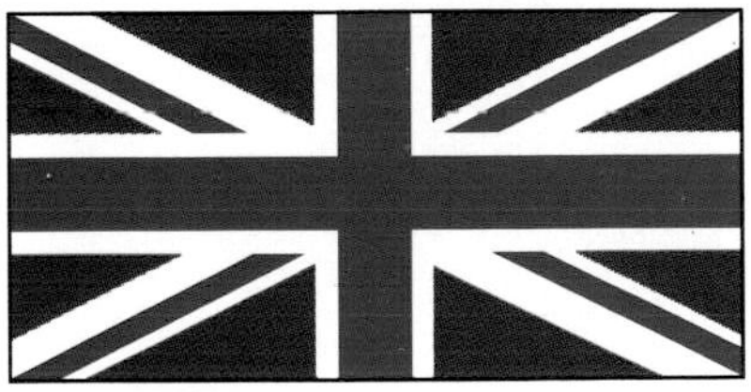

UNITED KINGDOM

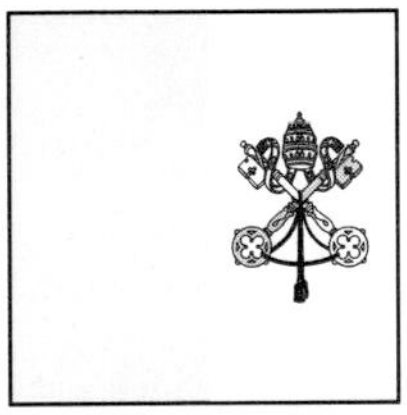

VATICAN CITY

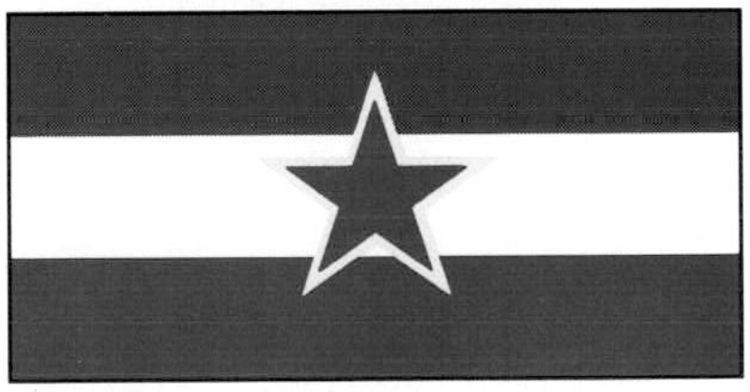

YUGOSLAVIA

FLAGS OF NORTH AMERICA

CANADA

MEXICO

UNITED STATES

FLAGS OF THE CARIBBEAN

ANTIGUA AND BARBUDA

BAHAMAS

BARBADOS

CUBA

DOMINICA

DOMINICAN REPUBLIC

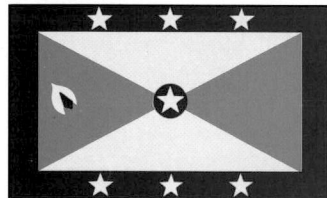

GRENADA

HAITI

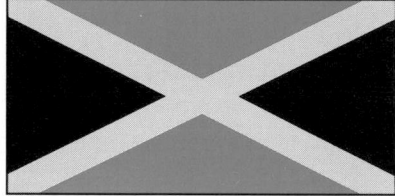

JAMAICA

ITTS-NEVIS

SAINT LUCIA

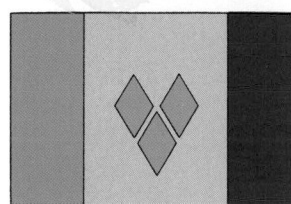

SAINT VINCENT AND THE GRENADINES

TRINIDAD AND TOBAGO

FLAGS OF CENTRAL AMERICA

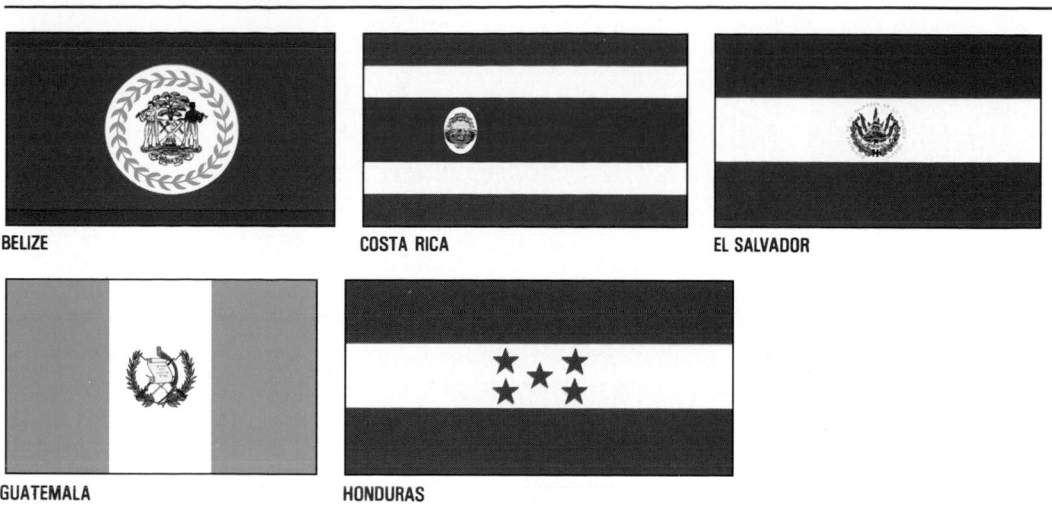

BELIZE

COSTA RICA

EL SALVADOR

GUATEMALA

HONDURAS

NICARAGUA

PANAMA

FLAGS OF SOUTH AMERICA

ARGENTINA

BOLIVIA

BRAZIL

CHILE

COLOMBIA

ECUADOR

GUYANA

PARAGUAY

PERU

SURINAME

URUGUAY

VENEZUELA

FLAGS OF OCEANIA

AUSTRALIA

FIJI

KIRIBATI

NAURU

NEW ZEALAND

PAPUA NEW GUINEA

SOLOMON ISLANDS

TONGA

TUVALU

VANUATU

WESTERN SAMOA

FLAGS OF AUSTRALIA

NEW SOUTH WALES

NORFOLK ISLAND

NORTHERN TERRITORY

QUEENSLAND

SOUTH AUSTRALIA

TASMANIA

VICTORIA

WESTERN AUSTRALIA

FLAGS OF CANADA

ALBERTA

BRITISH COLUMBIA

MANITOBA

NEW BRUNSWICK

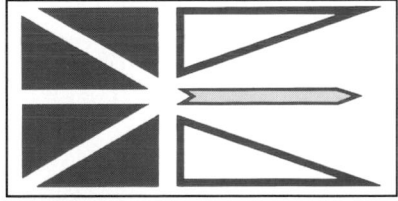
NEWFOUNDLAND

NORTHWEST TERRITORIES

NOVA SCOTIA

ONTARIO

PRINCE EDWARD ISLAND

QUEBEC

SASKATCHEWAN

YUKON TERRITORY

FLAGS OF THE UNITED STATES

ALABAMA

ALASKA

ARIZONA

ARKANSAS

CALIFORNIA

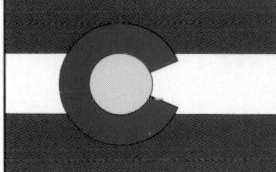

COLORADO

CONNECTICUT

DELAWARE

DISTRICT OF COLUMBIA

FLORIDA

GEORGIA

HAWAII

IDAHO

ILLINOIS

INDIANA

IOWA

KANSAS

KENTUCKY

LOUISIANA

MAINE

MARYLAND

MASSACHUSETTS

MICHIGAN

MINNESOTA

MISSISSIPPI

MISSOURI

MONTANA

FLAGS OF THE UNITED STATES (continued)

NEBRASKA

NEVADA

NEW HAMPSHIRE

NEW JERSEY

NEW MEXICO

NEW YORK

NORTH CAROLINA

NORTH DAKOTA

OHIO-

OKLAHOMA

OREGON

PENNSYLVANIA

RHODE ISLAND

SOUTH CAROLINA

SOUTH DAKOTA

TENNESSEE

TEXAS

UTAH

VERMONT

VIRGINIA

WASHINGTON

WEST VIRGINIA

WISCONSIN

WYOMING

FLAGS OF THE U.S. GOVERNMENT

PRESIDENT

VICE-PRESIDENT

SECRETARY OF STATE

DEPT. OF THE TREASURY

SECRETARY OF DEFENSE

ATTORNEY GENERAL

DEPT. OF THE INTERIOR

DEPT. OF AGRICULTURE

SECRETARY OF COMMERCE

DEPT. OF LABOR

DEPT. OF TRANSPORTATION

DEPT. OF HEALTH AND
HUMAN SERVICES

DEPT. OF HOUSING AND
URBAN DEVELOPMENT

DEPT. OF ENERGY

DEPT. OF EDUCATION

U.S. ARMY

U.S. MARINE CORPS

U.S. NAVY

U.S. AIR FORCE

U.S. COAST GUARD

JACK OF U.S. WARSHIPS

FLAGS OF UNITED STATES TERRITORIES

AMERICAN SAMOA

PALAU (BELAU)

GUAM

NORTHERN MARIANAS

MARSHALL ISLANDS

FEDERATED STATES OF MICRONESIA

PUERTO RICO

U.S. VIRGIN ISLANDS

FLAGS OF INTERNATIONAL ORGANIZATIONS

UNITED NATIONS

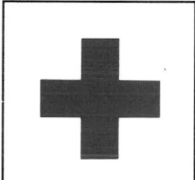

RED CROSS

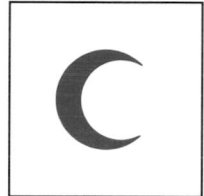

RED CRESCENT

RED MAGEN DAVID

OLYMPICS

NATO

ORG. OF AMERICAN STATES

COMECON

ORG. OF AFRICAN UNITY

ARAB LEAGUE

INTERNATIONAL CODE FLAGS

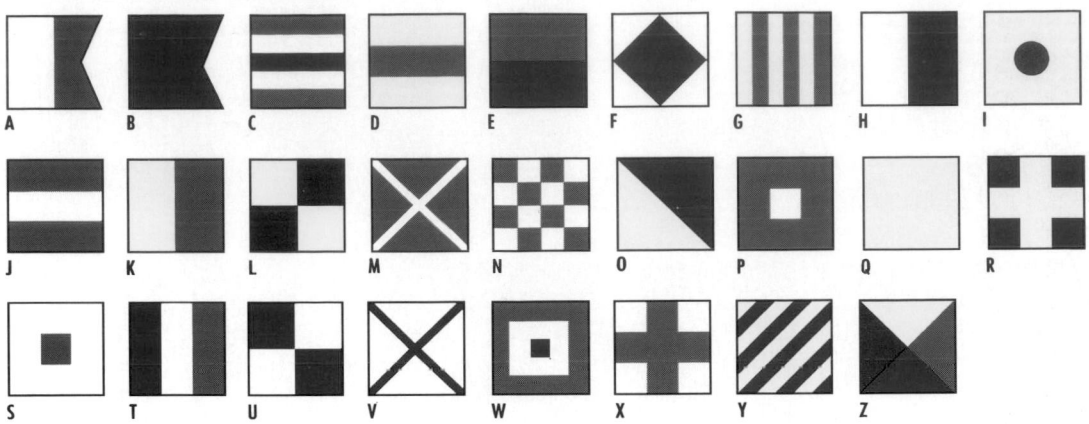

INTERNATIONAL CODE PENNANTS

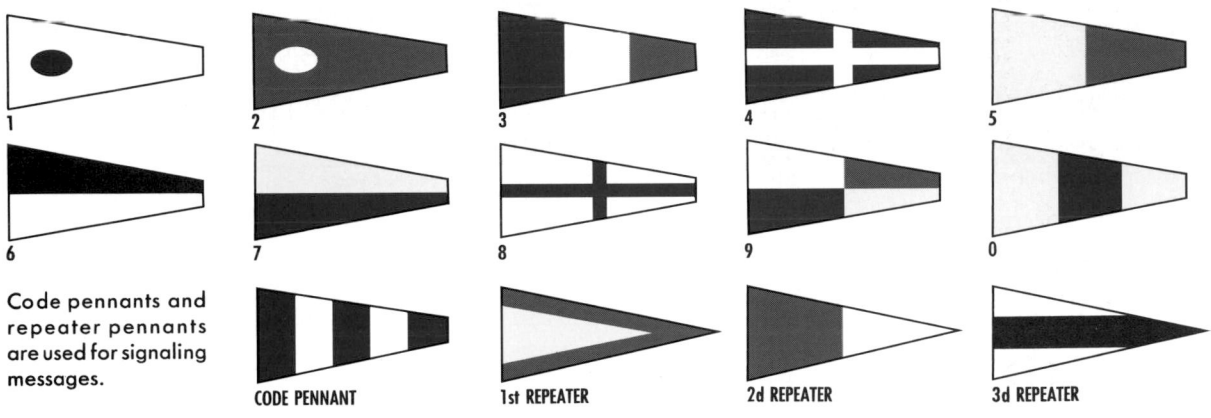

Code pennants and repeater pennants are used for signaling messages.

WEATHER BUREAU FLAGS

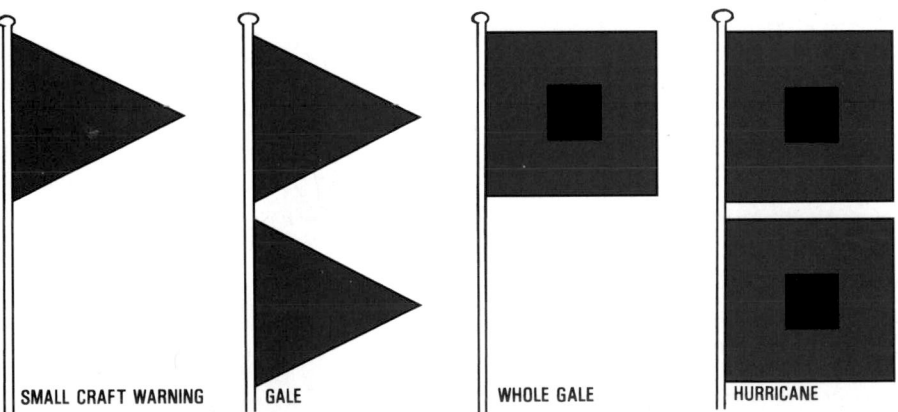

MONOCHROMATIC MESSAGE FLAGS

DEATH DANGER QUARANTINE PROCEED TRUCE DISTRESS